Langenscheidt's Compact German Dictionary

German-English
English-German

by

Heinz Messinger, Gisela Türck
and
Helmut Willmann

LANGENSCHEIDT

NEW YORK · BERLIN · MUNICH
VIENNA · ZURICH

*Copyright 1993 by Langenscheidt KG, Berlin and Munich
Printed in Germany*

Preface

All Langenscheidt dictionaries are regularly revised. The present Compact German Dictionary has been specifically prepared for the English-speaking user; it provides the pronunciation and stress of the German entry, states the genitive and plural of nouns and, in the case of verbs, indicates whether they are conjugated with "haben" or "sein". All irregular forms are also given.

The introduction of new typefaces has made the dictionary even clearer and thus more user-friendly. The headwords now appear in sans serif letters, which makes them easier to find. Phrases – example sentences, idioms, collocations – are emphasized by a new boldface type, which, as it is an italic face, cannot be confused with the boldface of the headwords.

Another feature that adds to the clarity of presentation is the restructuring of the individual entries making more use of Roman and Arabic numerals to separate the main meanings from subsidiary meanings, and more economical use of the tilde to represent the headword.

As part of the updating process, every entry of the previous edition has been carefully examined and any obsolescent vocabulary "rooted out", thus guaranteeing that the present revised edition truly reflects the language of today.

One of the Compact German Dictionary's strengths has always been its large number of new words. Great care has therefore again been taken to ensure that alongside general vocabulary and modern technical terms, a particularly large number of new colloquialisms and young people's jargon should be taken up.

The editors responsible for the present German-English/English-German Compact Dictionary, Helmut Willmann, Heinz Messinger and Gisela Türck, also compiled "Langenscheidts Kleiner Muret-Sanders" (1982, 1985). Thus we have been able to draw on their long experience as lexicographers.

The result is a dictionary ultimately suitable for today's user.

Langenscheidt Publishers

Herausgegeben von der Langenscheidt-Redaktion

Table of Contents

First Part

Second Part

First Part

German-English

by

Heinz Messinger
and
Gisela Türck

Guide for the User

1. Alphabetical order has been maintained throughout the dictionary. Note that the umlaut forms ä, ö and ü are treated as a, o and u. Thus "Müll" will be found directly after "Mull" and before "Müsli". ß is treated as ss.

2. The **tilde** or **swung dash** (~, ~) is used for economy of space. The boldface tilde (~) stands for the entire headword or, in the case of compounds, for the part of the word preceding the vertical bar (|). In the example phrases and the explanations in *italics*, the tilde (~, ~) stands for the boldfaced word immediately preceding, which itself may have been formed with the aid of the boldfaced tilde.

When the initial letter of a headword changes from a capital to a small letter, or vice versa, this is indicated by a circle placed above the tilde: ♀ or ♀, e.g.

Abflug *m* ... takeoff, ... **♀bereit** *adj* ready for takeoff. **~halle** *f* ...

3. Arrangement of the entries. Entries are generally divided up by means of

a) Roman numerals to distinguish parts of speech (noun, adjective, adverb; transitive, intransitive or reflexive verb, etc).

b) Arabic numerals (running consecutively within the article and independent of Roman numerals) to differentiate between meanings,

c) small letters for further differentiation of meaning.

Examples:

a) **gehen** ['geːən] (ging, gegangen, sn) **I** *v/i* **1.** (*zu Fuß ~*) walk, ... **II** *v/impers* **17.** *fig.* **es geht** a) it works, ... **III** *v/t* **20.** walk (*distance etc*), ...

b) **böse** ['bøːzə] **I** *adj* **1.** bad, evil, ... **II** *adv* **6.** badly ...

c) **machen** ... **13.** do: *laß ihn nur ~!* a) let him (do as he pleases)!, b) just leave it to him!

4. Semantic differences are indicated by symbols and abbreviations preceding the translation (see list on page 8).

5. Untranslatable German words are defined in *italics*:

Assessor ... *civil servant (lawyer, teacher, etc) who has completed his/her second state examination.*

6. Spelling. Differences in British and American spelling are indicated as follows:

colo(u)r
defen/ce (*Am.* -se)
program(me *Br.*)
sulphonamide (*Am.* -f-)

The abbreviations *esp. Am.* and *esp. Br.* indicate that the spelling or translation referred to also occurs in British and American English respectively, though far less frequently.

8

7. Pronunciation. As a general rule either full or partial pronunciation is given for every simple entry word. The symbols used are those laid down by the International Phonetic Association. All the phonetic symbols used in the dictionary are explained in the Key to Pronunciation on page 10ff.

Every headword that does not consist of words listed and phonetically transcribed elsewhere in the dictionary is followed by its pronunciation in square brackets: **Blüte** ['bly:tə] ...

Compound and derivative entries formed with elements listed and phonetically transcribed elsewhere in the dictionary are provided with a stress mark ['] in front of the stressed syllable: **'Blütenhonig** ...

Derivatives after a simple entry are often only provided with accents and part of the pronunciation. That part of the word which is not transcribed phonetically has, except for differences in stress, a pronunciation identical with that of the corresponding part of the preceding entry:

Kondensat [kɔndɛn'za:t] *n* ... **Kondensation** [-za'tsɪoːn] *f* ... **Kondensator** [-'za:tɔr] *m* ... **kondensieren** [-'zi:rən] ...

A number of the more common initial and final elements occurring in derivatives and compounds have not been transcribed phonetically after every derivative entry. They have been collected, together with their phonetic transcription, in a comprehensive list on page 12.

8. Symbols

⌀ }	*see Guide for the User, paragraph 2, on page 7 and paragraph 1.4 on page 722*	🚊	*railway*
		✈	*aviation*
F	*familiar, colloquial language*	📯	*postal affairs*
V	*vulgar*	♪	*musical term*
†	*obsolete*	⌂	*architecture*
🔟	*technical term*	⚡	*electrical engineering, electronics*
♣	*botany*	⚖	*legal term*
⊙	*technology*	A̶	*mathematics*
✕	*mining*	✓	*agriculture*
✕	*military term*	🜍	*chemistry*
⚓	*nautical term*	🜔	*medicine*
✝	*economic term*	→	*see*

9. Abbreviations

a.	*also*	*antiq.*	*antiquity, Antike*
abbr.	*abbreviation*	*art*	*article*
acc	*accusative (case)*	*astr.*	*astronomy*
adj	*adjective*	*attr*	*attributively*
adm.	*administrative*	*bibl.*	*biblical*
adv	*adverb*	*biol.*	*biology*
allg.	allgemein, *generally*	*Br.*	*in British usage only*
Am.	*(originally or chiefly) American English*	*b.s.*	*bad sense*
		coll	*collective noun*
amer.	*American*, amerikanisch	*comp*	*comparative*
anat.	*anatomy*		

conj	conjunction	j-n, *j-n*	jemanden, *somebody*
contp.	contemptuously	j-s, *j-s*	jemandes, *of somebody*
cpds.	compound words	k-e, *k-e*	keine
dat	dative *(case)*	k-m, *k-m*	keinem
d-e, d-e	deine, *your*	k-n, *k-n*	keinen
dem	demonstrative	k-r, *k-r*	keiner
dial.	dialectal	k-s, *k-s*	keines
d-m, d-m	deinem, *to your*	*ling.*	linguistics
d-n, d-n	deinen, *your*	*lit.*	literary
d-r, d-r	deiner, *of your, to your*	*m*	masculine
d-s, d-s	deines, *of your*	m-e, *m-e*	meine, *my*
eccl.	ecclesiastical	*metall.*	metallurgy
e-e, e-e	eine, *a, an*	*meteor.*	meteorology
e-m, e-m	einem, *to a(n)*	*min.*	mineralogy
e-n, e-n	einen, *a, an*	m-m, *m-m*	meinem, *to my*
engS.	in engerem Sinne, *more strictly*	m-n, *m-n*	meinen, *my*
	taken	*mot.*	motoring
e-r, e-r	einer, *of a(n), to a(n)*	*mount.*	mountaineering
e-s, e-s	eines, *of a(n)*	m-r, *m-r*	meiner, *of my, to my*
esp.	especially	m-s, *m-s*	meines, *of my*
et., et.	etwas, *something*	*mst*	mostly
etc	et cetera, and others, and so forth	*myth.*	mythology
euphem.	euphemistic	*n*	neuter
f	feminine	*neg*	negative
fenc.	fencing	*nom*	nominative *(case)*
fig.	figurative	*npr*	proper name
fr.	French	*n.s.*	in the narrower sense
gastr.	gastronomical	*nucl.*	nuclear physics
GB	Great Britain	*obs.*	obsolete
gen	genitive *(case)*	*od.*	oder, *or*
geogr.	geography	*opt.*	optics
geol.	geology	*orn.*	ornithology
ger	gerund	*o.s.*	oneself
Ggs.	Gegensatz, *antonym*	*paint.*	painting
gym.	gymnastics	*parl.*	parliamentary term
hist.	history	*part*	particle
humor.	humorously	*ped.*	pedagogics
hunt.	hunting	*pers*	personal
ichth.	ichthyology	*pharm.*	pharmacy
imp	imperative *(mood)*	*philos.*	philosophy
impers	impersonal	*phot.*	photography
ind	indicative *(mood)*	*phys.*	physics
indef	indefinite	*physiol.*	physiology
inf	infinitive *(mood)*	*pl*	plural
insep	inseparable	*poet.*	poetry
int	interjection	*pol.*	politics
interrog	interrogative	*pos*	possessive
invar	invariable	*pp*	past participle
ir.	Irish	*pred*	predicative
iro.	ironically	*prep*	preposition
irr.	irregular	*pres*	present
Jh.	Jahrhundert, *century*	*pres p*	present participle
j-d	jemand, *someone*	*pret*	preterite
j-m, j-m	jemandem, *to somebody*	*print.*	printing

pron	pronoun	*surv.*	surveying
psych.	psychology	*tel.*	telegraphy
reflex	reflexive	*teleph.*	telephone
rel	relative	*textil.*	textiles
rhet.	rhetoric	*thea.*	theatre
s	substantive	*(TM)*	Trademark
s-e, s-e	seine, *his, one's*	*TV*	television
schott.	schottisch, *Scottish*	*univ.*	university
sep	separable	*USA*	United States
sg	singular	*usu.*	usually
sl.	slang	*v/aux*	auxiliary verb
s-m, s-m	seinem, *to his, to one's*	*vet.*	veterinary medicine
s-n, s-n	seinen, *his, one's*	*v/i*	intransitive verb
s.o., s.o.	someone	*v/impers*	impersonal verb
sociol.	sociology	*v/t*	transitive verb
s-r, s-r	seiner, *of his*	*w.s./weitS.*	more widely taken
s-s, s-s	seines, *of his, of one's*	*z. B.*	zum Beispiel, *for instance*
s.th., s.th.	something	*zo.*	zoology
su	substantive	*zs.-, Zs.-*	zusammen, *together*
subj	subjunctive (mood)	*Zssg(n)*	Zusammensetzung(en),
sup	superlative		compound word(s)

10. Key to Pronunciation. The phonetic alphabet used in this German-English dictionary is that of the Association Phonétique Internationale (A.P.I. or I.P.A. = International Phonetic Association). A long vowel is indicated by [ː] following the vowel symbol, the stress by ['] preceding the stressed syllable. [̆] placed over a vowel indicates that the vowel in question is nonsyllabic. A glottal stop [ʔ] is the forced stop between one word or syllable and the following one beginning with a stressed vowel, as in "beobachten" [bə'ʔoːbaxtən].

Sym-bol	Examples	Nearest English Equivalents	Remarks
		A. Vowels	
a	Mann [man]		short a as in French "ca**rt**e" or in British English "c**a**st" said quickly
aː	Wagen ['vaːgən]	f**a**ther	long a
e	egal [e'gaːl]	b**e**d	
eː	Weg [veːk]		unlike any English sound, though it has a resemblance to the sound in "d**ay**"
ə	Bitte ['bɪtə]	**a**go	a short sound, that of unaccented e
ɛ	Männer ['mɛnər] Geld [gɛlt]	f**ai**r	There is no *-er* sound at the end. It is one pure short vowel-sound.
ɛː	prägen ['prɛːgən]		same sound, but long
ɪ	Wind [vɪnt]	**i**t	
iː	hier [hiːr]	m**ee**t	
ɔ	Ort [ɔrt]	l**o**ng	
o	Modell [mo'dɛl]	m**o**lest	
oː	Boot [boːt]		[oː] resembles the English sound in g**o** [gəʊ] but without the [ʊ]

Sym-bol	Examples	Nearest English Equivalents	Remarks
ø:	schön [ʃøːn]		as in French "**feu**". The sound may be acquired by saying [e] through closely rounded lips.
ø	Ödem [øˈdeːm]		same sound, but short
œ	öffnen [ˈœfnən]		as in French "**neuf**". The sound has a resemblance to the English vowel in "h**er**". Lips, however, must be well rounded as for ɔ.
ʊ	Mutter [ˈmʊtər]	b**oo**k	
u:	Uhr [uːr]	b**oo**t	
Y	Glück [glʏk]		almost like the French u as in s**ur**. It may be acquired by saying [i] through fairly closely rounded lips.
y:	führen [ˈfyːrən]		same sound, but long

B. Diphthongs

aɪ	Mai [maɪ]	l**i**ke	
aʊ	Maus [maʊs]	m**ou**se	
ɔY	Beute [ˈbɔYtə]	b**oy**	
	Läufer [ˈlɔYfər]		

C. Consonants

b	besser [ˈbɛsər]	**b**etter	
d	du [duː]	**d**ance	
f	finden [ˈfɪndən]	**f**ind	
	Vater [ˈfaːtər]		
	Photo [ˈfoːto]		
g	Gold [gɔlt]	**g**old	
	Geld [gɛlt]		
ʒ	Genie [ʒeˈniː]	mea**s**ure	
h	Haus [haʊs]	**h**ouse	
ç	Licht [lɪçt]		An approximation to this sound may be produced by assuming the mouth configuration for [i] and emitting a strong current of breath.
	manch [manç]		
	traurig [ˈtraʊrɪç]		
x	Loch [lɔx]	Scotch: lo**ch**	Whereas [ç] is pronounced at the front of the mouth, x is pronounced in the throat.
j	ja [jaː]	**y**ear	
k	keck [kɛk]	**k**ick	
	Tag [taːk]		
	Chronist [kroˈnɪst]		
	Café [kaˈfeː]		
l	lassen [ˈlasən]	**l**ump	pronounced like English initial "clear l"
m	Maus [maʊs]	**m**ouse	

Symbol	Examples	Nearest English Equivalents	Remarks
n	nein [naın]	**n**ot	
ŋ	klingen ['klıŋən]	si**ng**	
	sinken ['zıŋkən]	dri**nk**	
p	Paß [pas]	**p**ass	
	Weib [vaıp]		
	obgleich [ɔp'glaıç]		
r	rot [ro:t]	**r**ot	There are two pronunciations: the frontal or lingual r and the uvular r (the latter unknown in England).
s	Glas [gla:s]	mi**ss**	unvoiced when final, doubled, or next to a voiceless consonant
	Masse ['masə]		
	Mast [mast]		
	naß [nas]		
z	Sohn [zo:n]	**z**e-	voiced when at the beginning of a word or a syllable
	Rose ['ro:zə]	ro	
ʃ	Schiff [ʃıf]		
	Charme [ʃarm]	**sh**op	
	Spiel [ʃpi:l]		
	Stein [ʃtaın]		
t	Tee [te:]	**t**ea	
	Thron [tro:n]		
	Stadt [ʃtat]		
	Bad [ba:t]		
	Findling ['fıntlıŋ]		
	Wind [vınt]		
v	Vase ['va:zə]	**v**ast	
	Winter ['vıntər]		

ã, ɛ̃, ɔ̃ are nasalized vowels. Examples: Engagement [ãgaʒə'mã:], Terrain [tɛ'rɛ̃:], Feuilleton [fœjə'tɔ̃:].

11. List of Initial and Final Elements normally given without Phonetic Transcription

Initial elements

be- [bə]	ent- [ɛnt]	miß- [mıs]	ver- [fɛr]
er- [ɛr]	ge- [gə]	un- [ʊn]	zer- [tsɛr]

Final elements

-bar [ba:r]	-fach [fax]	-kunft [kʊnft]	-schaft [ʃaft]
-chen [çən]	-haft [haft]	-lein [laın]	-st [st]
-d [t]	-halber [halbər]	-lich [lıç]	-ste [stə]
-e [ə]	-haltig [haltıç]	-los [lo:s]	-stel [stəl]
-ei [aı]	-heit [haıt]	-n [n]	-t [t]
-el [əl]	-ig [ıç]	-nis [nıs]	-te [tə]
-en [ən]	-in [ın]	-s [s]	-tät [tɛ:t]
-end [ənt]	-isch [ıʃ]	-sal [za:l]	-tum [tu:m]
-er [ər]	-keit [kaıt]	-sam [za:m]	-ung [ʊŋ]
			-wärts [vɛrts]

12. Grammatical References. Parts of speech (adjective, verb, etc.) have been indicated throughout. Entries have been subdivided by Roman numerals to distinguish the various parts of speech.

Nouns. The inflectional forms (genitive singular/nominative plural) follow immediately after the indication of gender. No forms are given for compounds if the parts appear as separate headwords. The horizontal stroke replaces that part of the word which remains unchanged in the inflexion:

Affe *m* (-n; -n): des Affen, die Affen   **Affäre** *f* (-; -n): der Affäre, die Affären

The sign ⁓ indicates that an umlaut appears in the inflected form in question:

Blatt *n* (-[e]s; ⁓er): des Blatt(e)s, die Blätter

Verbs

a) The past participle is generally formed by prefixing ge- and adding -(e)t to the stem of the verb: **bändigen** – gebändigt, **heiraten** – geheiratet.

Verbs ending with -ieren or -eien do not use the prefix ge-: **reagieren** – reagiert, **prophezeien** – prophezeit.

Verbs with the inseparable prefixes be-, em-, ent-, er-, ge-, ver- and zer- simply add -(e)t to the stem: **begrüßen** – begrüßt, **entbehren** – entbehrt, etc.

In all the above cases the entries indicate only whether the perfect tense is formed with "haben" or "sein": **bändigen** ... *v/t* (h) ..., **klettern** ... *v/i* (sn) ...

b) The preterite and past participle of an irregular verb are given under the headword: **gehen** ... (ging, gegangen, sn) **I** *v/i* **1.** ...: the perfect tense of this verb is formed by means of the auxiliary verb "sein": er ging, er ist gegangen.

c) Separable verbs form the past participle by placing -ge- between the prefix and the stem: **hinausgehen** *v/i* (*irr, sep*, -ge-, sn, → **gehen**): The reference *irr* indicates that the compound verb "hinausgehen" is conjugated like the root verb "gehen", the → refers the user to the entry "gehen" for the preterite and past participle. *sep* indicates that the verb is separated: er geht/ging hinaus, er ist hinausgegangen.

d) Homographic verbs like "über'treten", "'übertreten" are differentiated as follows:

'übertreten (*irr, sep*, -ge-, sn, → **treten**): er trat über, er ist übergetreten

über'treten (*irr, insep, no* -ge-, h, → **treten**): er übertrat, er hat übertreten

Prepositions. Prepositions governing a headword are given in both languages. The grammatical construction following a German preposition is indicated only if the preposition governs two different cases. If a German preposition applies to all translations, it is given only with the first, whereas its English equivalents are given after each translation:

schützen ... (*gegen, vor dat*) protect (from, against), defend (against), shelter (from) ...

A

A, a [aː] *n* (-; -) A, a (*a.* ♪): *fig.* **das A und O** the be-all and end-all, the essence; **von A bis Z** from beginning to end; **wer A sagt, muß auch B sagen** in for a penny, in for a pound.

à [a] *prep* ✝ (at) ... each.

Aal [aːl] *m* (-[e]s, -e) eel: *fig.* **sich winden wie ein ~** wriggle like an eel.

aalen ['aːlən] **sich ~** (h) F laze; **sich in der Sonne ~** bask in the sun.

'aal'glatt *adj fig.* slippery as an eel.

Aas [aːs] *n* (-) **1.** *no pl* carrion. **2.** V *pl* **Äser** beast, (*woman*) *a.* bitch: **kein ~** not a blessed soul.

'Aasgeier *m* (-s; -) F *fig.* vulture.

ab [ap] **I** *adv* **1.** off, away, *thea.* exit, *pl* (*beide or alle ~*) exeunt: **links ~** (to the) left; **weit ~** far off; F **~** (*durch die Mitte*)*!* off with you! **2.** F **der Knopf** *etc* **ist ~** the button *etc* is (or has come) off; → **Hut¹** 1. **3.** from: 🚂 **Berlin ~ 16:30** dep. (= departure from) Berlin 16:30; F **von** ... **~** → 6. **4. ~ und zu** now and then. **II** *prep* **5.** from: **~ Seite 17** from page 17; ✝ **~ Berlin** (**Fabrik**) ex Berlin (factory). **6.** from ... (on): **~ heute** from (*adm.* as of) today. **7. ~ 18 Jahren** *persons* from (the age of) 18 up(wards); **~ 30 DM** shoes *etc* from DM 30 up. **8.** ✝ less, deducting. **III** *adj pred* **9.** F **sie war ganz ~** she was dead beat (or bushed).

'ab|ändern *v/t* (*sep*, -ge-, h) alter, change, modify, *parl.* amend, ⚖ commute.

Ab'änderung *f* (-; -en) alteration, modification, *parl.* amendment, ⚖ commutation. **Ab'änderungsantrag** *m parl.* **e-n ~ einbringen** move an amendment.

'abarbeiten: sich ~ (*sep*, -ge-, h) slave (away): → **abgearbeitet**.

Abart ['apˀart] *f* (-; -en) *biol.* variety.

abartig ['apˀartɪç] *adj* abnormal, *sexually: a.* perverse.

'Abbau *m* (-[e]s; *no pl*) **1.** ⚙ dismantling. **2.** ⛏ working, exploitation (*of a mine*), mining (*of coal*): **~ unter Tage** underground working. **3.** 🧪 decomposition, disintegration, *physiol.* breakdown (of blood alcohol *etc*). **4.** *fig.* decline (*of physical or mental powers*). **5.** *fig.* a) reduction, cutback (*of expenditures etc*), b) dismissal (*of employee*), retrenchment (*of personnel*). **6.** *fig.* (gradual) overcoming (*of prejudices etc*).

'abbauen (*sep*, -ge-, h) **I** *v/t* **1.** ⚙ dismantle, take down. **2.** ⛏ work (*a mine*), mine (*coal etc*). **3.** 🧪 (*a. sich ~*) decompose, *a. physiol.* break down: **sich ~** be broken down. **4.** *fig.* reduce, cut back (*expenditures etc*), dismiss (*employee*). **5.** *fig.* (gradually) overcome (*prejudices etc*). **II** *v/i* **6.** → **nachlassen** 2.

'abbeißen *v/t* (*irr*, *sep*, -ge-, h, → **beißen**) bite off.

'abbeizen *v/t* (*sep*, -ge-, h) remove with corrosives. **'Abbeizmittel** *n* remover.

'abbekommen *v/t* (*irr*, *sep*, h, → **bekommen**) **1.** get *s.th.* off. **2.** get: **et. ~** a) *a.* **sein Teil ~** get one's share, b) get hurt, c) be damaged.

'abberufen *v/t* (*irr*, *sep*, h, → **berufen**) recall (*ambassador etc*): **j-n von e-m Amt ~** relieve s.o. from office.

'abbestellen *v/t* (*sep*, h) cancel (one's order for), discontinue (*newspaper*). **'Abbestellung** *f* (-; -en) cancel(l)ation.

'abbetteln *v/t* (*sep*, -ge-, h) **j-m et. ~** wheedle s.th. out of s.o.

'abbiegen (*irr*, *sep*, -ge-, → **biegen**) **I** *v/i* (sn) turn (off): (*nach*) **links ~** turn off left. **II** *v/t* (h) F *fig.* head off, avoid.

'Abbiegespur *f* (-; -en) turning lane.

'Abbild *n* (-[e]s, -er) **1.** copy. **2.** a) picture, b) image, likeness. **3.** *fig.* reflection. **'abbilden** *v/t* (*sep*, -ge-, h) **1.** copy. **2.** portray, depict: **wie oben abgebildet** as shown above. **'Abbildung** *f* (-; -en) picture, illustration.

'abbinden (*irr*, *sep*, -ge-, h, → **binden**) **I** *v/t* **1.** untie, undo, take off (*necktie etc*). **2.** tie off, 💊 ligate. **II** *v/i* **3.** *cement:* set.

'Abbitte *f* (-; -n) apology: **j-m ~ leisten** apologize to s.o. (**wegen** for).

'**abbitten** v/t (irr, sep, -ge-, h, → **bitten**)
j-m et. ~ ask s.o.'s pardon for s.th.

'**abblasen** v/t (irr, sep, -ge-, h, → **blasen**) **1.** ◎ blow off (steam etc). **2.** F fig.
call off, cancel (meeting etc).

'**abblättern** v/i (sep, -ge-, sn) **1.** shed its
leaves (or petals). **2.** paint etc: flake
off.

'**abblenden** (sep, -ge-, h) **I** v/t **1.** dim
(light etc), mot. dip (Am. dim) (the
headlights). **II** v/i **2.** mot. dip (Am. dim)
the headlights. **3.** phot. stop down.

'**Abblendlicht** n mot. dipped (Am.
dimmed) headlights, low beam.

'**abblitzen** v/i (sep, -ge-, sn) F (**bei j-m**) ~
meet with a rebuff (from s.o.); **j-n** ~
lassen send s.o. packing.

abblocken ['apblɔkən] v/t (sep, -ge-, h)
a. fig. block.

'**abbrechen** (irr, sep, -ge-, → **brechen**) **I**
v/t (h) **1.** break off: F **sich e-n** ~ nearly
kill o.s. (**bei** doing s.th.). **2.** demolish,
pull down (house etc), take down (scaf-
folding etc), strike (tent): **das Lager** ~
break camp. **3.** fig. stop (fight, match,
etc), break off (relations), call off (a
strike), abandon (studies, test, etc),
raise (a siege). **II** v/i **4.** (sn) break off. **5.**
(h) fig. break off, stop.

'**abbremsen** v/t, v/i (sep, -ge-, h) slow
down, brake.

'**abbrennen** (irr, sep, -ge-, → **brennen**) **I**
v/t (h) burn down, let off (fireworks). **II**
v/i (sn) burn down: → **abgebrannt**.

'**abbringen** v/t (irr, sep, -ge-, h, → **bringen**) **j-n** ~ **von** dissuade s.o. from; **j-n**
davon ~, **et. zu tun** stop s.o. doing s.th.,
talk s.o. out of doing s.th.

'**abbröckeln** v/i (sep, -ge-, sn) crumble
(away), fig. prices etc: crumble.

'**Abbruch** m (-[e]s; no pl) **1.** demolition.
2. fig. breaking off (of diplomatic relations etc), esp. sports: break-off,
stop(ping). **3.** ~ **tun** (dat) detract from,
be detrimental to; **das tut der Sache
k-n** ~! that makes no difference!

'**abbruchreif** adj due for demolition,
adm. condemned.

'**abbuchen** v/t (sep, -ge-, h) **1.** e-e Summe von j-s Konto ~ debit a sum to s.o.'s
account. **2.** → **abschreiben 2.**

'**Abbuchung** f (-; -en) **1.** debit entry. **2.**
payment by standing order.

'**Abbuchungsauftrag** m debit order.

ABC-Waffen [a:be:'tse:-] pl NBC-weap-
ons.

'**Abdampf** m (-[e]s; ⸚e) ◎ exhaust steam.

'**abdampfen** v/i (sep, -ge-, sn) **1.** F clear
(or push) off. **2.** ◎ (a. v/t) evaporate.

'**abdanken** v/i (sep, -ge-, h) resign, ruler:
abdicate. '**Abdankung** f (-; -en) resignation, abdication.

'**abdecken** v/t (sep, -ge-, h) **1.** take off,
uncover; untile (roof), unroof (house),
clear (the table), turn down (the bed). **2.**
cover (up), phot. blank out. **3.** ✝ cover,
meet (debts).

'**abdichten** v/t (sep, -ge-, h) ◎ seal, pack,
ca(u)lk, make s.th. watertight.

'**abdrängen** v/t (sep, -ge-, h) push (or
force) s.o., s.th. aside.

'**abdrehen** (sep, -ge-, h) **I** v/t **1.** ◎ twist
off. **2.** turn off (gas, water), ⚡ a. switch
off. **3.** finish (shooting) (a film). **II** v/i **4.**
a. (sn) ⚓, ⚓ turn away, sheer off.

'**abdriften** v/i (sep, -ge-, sn) drift off.

'**Abdruck¹** m (-[e]s; ⸚e) **1.** (im)print,
mark. **2.** in wax etc: impression.

'**Abdruck²** m (-[e]s) **1.** no pl printing. **2.**
(pl -e) copy.

'**abdrucken** v/t (sep, -ge-, h) print.

'**abdrücken** (sep, -ge-, h) **I** v/t **1.** fire (off)
(gun) (**auf** acc at). **2.** make an impression of s.th.: **sich** ~ leave an imprint. **3.**
F j-n ~ hug s.o., squeeze s.o. **II** v/i **4.** pull
the trigger: **auf j-n** ~ fire at s.o.

'**abdüsen** v/i (sep, -ge-, sn) F zoom off.

'**abebben** v/i (sep, -ge-, sn) ebb away,
anger, noise, etc: a. die down, subside.

Abend ['a:bənt] m (-s; -e) evening, night
(both a. performance): **am** (**späten**) ~
(late) in the evening, (late) at night;
heute 2 this evening, tonight; **morgen**
(**gestern**) 2 tomorrow (last) night;
Sonntag 2 Sunday evening; **guten** ~**!**
good evening!; **zu** ~ **essen** have supper
(or dinner); **es wird** ~ it's getting dark;
man soll den Tag nicht vor dem ~
loben don't count your chickens before they are hatched; **es ist noch nicht
aller Tage** ~ things may take a turn yet.

'**Abend|andacht** f evening prayer(s).
~**blatt** n evening paper. ~**dämmerung** f
dusk. ~**essen** n evening meal, dinner,
supper. **2füllend** adj full-length (film).
~**kasse** f box office. ~**kleid** n evening
dress (Am. gown). ~**kurs** m, ~**kursus** m
evening class(es).

abfaulen

'**Abendland** n (-[e]s; no pl) the Occident.
abendländisch ['a:bəntlɛndɪʃ] adj occidental, Western.
'**abendlich** adj of (or in) the evening.
'**Abendmahl** n (-[e]s; no pl) eccl. the Holy Communion, the Lord's (paint. the Last) Supper: **das ~ nehmen** take Communion.
abends ['a:bənts] adv in the evening(s): **bis ~** till evening; **um 7 Uhr ~** at 7 p.m.
'**Abend**|**schule** f night school. **~sonne** f setting sun. **~stern** m evening star. **~vorstellung** f thea. evening performance. **~zeitung** f → **Abendblatt.**
Abenteuer ['a:bəntɔyər] n (-s; -) adventure (a. in cpds film, novel, playground, etc). '**abenteuerlich** adj adventurous, fig. risky, wild (idea, plan, etc), eccentric, odd (getup etc). '**Abenteuerlust** f (-; no pl) love of adventure.
'**Abenteurer** m (-s; -) adventurer.
'**Abenteurerin** f (-; -nen) adventuress.
aber ['a:bər] **I** conj but: **~ dennoch** yet, (but) still; **oder ~** otherwise, or else. **II** interj **~, ~!** come, come!; **~ ja!, ~ sicher!** (but) of course!; **~ nein!** oh no!, of course not!; **das ist ~ nett von dir** that's really nice of you. **III** adv **hundert und ~ hundert** hundreds and hundreds.
'**Aber** n (-s; -) but: **die Sache hat ein ~** there's just one catch to it; → **Wenn.**
'**Aberglaube** m (-ns; no pl) superstition.
abergläubisch ['a:bərglɔybɪʃ] adj superstitious.
'**aberkennen** v/t (irr, sep, h, → **erkennen**) esp. ⚖ **j-m et. ~** deprive s.o. of.
'**Aberkennung** f (-; -en) deprivation.
abermalig ['a:bərma:lıç] adj renewed, repeated. **abermals** ['a:bərma:ls] adv again, once more.
'**aberwitzig** adj crazy, mad.
'**abfackeln** v/t (h) burn off (gas).
'**abfahren** (irr, sep, -ge-, → **fahren**) **I** v/i (sn) **1.** (nach for) leave, depart, start, ⚓ sail: F **j-n ~ lassen** send s.o. packing. **2.** skiing: run (n.s. start) downhill. **3.** F **auf j-n** (et.) (**voll**) **~** be wild about s.o. (s.th.), dig s.o. (s.th.) (the big way). **II** v/t (h) **4.** cart off, remove. **5.** a) cover, travel (a distance), b) patrol. **6.** wear down (a tyre). **7.** start, run (film, tape). **8.** use up (a ticket). **9. ihm wurde ein**

Bein etc **abgefahren** he was run over and lost a leg etc.
'**Abfahrt** f (-; -en) **1.** (nach for) start, departure. **2.** exit (of a motorway). **3.** skiing: a) downhill (run), b) slope.
'**abfahrtbereit** adj ready to leave.
'**Abfahrtslauf** m skiing: downhill (run).
'**Abfahrtsläufer(in** f) m downhiller.
'**Abfahrtszeit** f time of departure.
'**Abfall¹** m (-[e]s; ⸗e) pl a) waste (a. ⊙), refuse, rubbish, Am. garbage, b) offal, c) litter.
'**Abfall²** m (-[e]s; no pl) **1.** decrease (a. ⚡, a. fig.), drop. **2.** pol. defection: **~ von e-r Partei** desertion from a party. **3.** eccl. apostasy.
'**Abfallbeseitigung** f waste disposal.
'**Abfalleimer** m rubbish (or litter) bin, Am. garbage can.
'**abfallen** v/i (irr, sep, -ge-, sn, → **fallen**) **1.** fall off, drop off: fig. **von j-m ~** fear etc: fall away from s.o., leave s.o. **2.** terrain: fall away, slope: **steil ~** drop steeply. **3.** fig. fall (off), drop, decrease, runner etc: drop back: **~ gegen** compare badly with. **4.** be left (over). **5.** F be gained (**bei** by): **was fällt für mich dabei ab?** what's in it for me? **6. von e-r Partei ~** break away (or defect) from a party. **7.** eccl. apostatize (**von** from).
'**abfallend** adj sloping (terrain etc): **steil ~** steep, precipitous.
'**abfällig** adj disparaging (remark), adverse (criticism), unfavo(u)rable (opinion etc): **~ sprechen über** (acc) speak disparagingly of.
'**Abfallpro,dukt** n **1.** waste product. **2.** spin-off, by-product. '**Abfallverwertung** f waste recovery, recycling.
'**abfangen** v/t (irr, sep, -ge-, h, → **fangen**) **1.** catch. **2.** intercept (message, letter, etc). **3.** check (attack). **4.** sports: parry (blow), catch up with (a runner). **5.** get a car etc under control, ✈ pull out. **6.** △ prop up. **7.** ⊙ absorb, cushion (shocks).
'**Abfangjäger** m interceptor (plane).
'**abfärben** v/i (sep, -ge-, h) run: **~ auf** (acc) a) run into, b) fig. rub off on.
'**abfassen** v/t (sep, -ge-, h) write, draft, esp. adm. draw up, formulate, word.
'**Abfassung** f (-; -en) composition, drafting, wording.
'**abfaulen** v/i (sep, -ge-, sn) rot off.

'**abfedern** v/t (sep, -ge-, h) ⊚ absorb (shocks), cushion (a. fig.), spring.
'**abfeilen** v/t (sep, -ge-, h) ⊚ file off.
'**abfertigen** v/t (sep, -ge-, h) **1.** a. ✔, 🚚, ✈ dispatch, clear, b) check in (passengers): **e-n Zug** ~ start a train. **2.** attend to, serve, deal with (customers): F **j-n kurz** ~ give s.o. short shrift. **3.** F sports: dispose of, beat.
'**Abfertigung** f (-; -en) **1.** dispatch (a. ✔, 🚚), (customs) clearance. **2.** ✈ attendance (gen to customers, an order). **3.** → '**Abfertigungsschalter** m dispatch counter, ✔ check-in counter.
'**abfeuern** v/t (sep, -ge-, h) fire (off) (gun etc), sports: let go with (a shot).
'**abfinden** (irr, sep, -ge-, h) **I** v/t a) pay (off), satisfy (creditors), buy out (a partner), b) pay s.o. compensation. **II sich ~ mit** come to terms with, resign o.s. to, put up with, accept; **damit kann ich mich nicht ~!** I just can't accept it!
'**Abfindung** f (-; -en) a) satisfaction, paying off, b) of employees: severance pay, c) compensation.
'**abflachen** v/t (sep, -ge-, h) (a. **sich ~**) flatten (out).
'**abflauen** v/i (sep, -ge-, h) wind etc: drop, a. fig. die down, abate, crisis, traffic, etc: ease off, ✈ business etc: slacken (off), interest etc: flag.
'**abfliegen** (irr, sep, -ge-, → **fliegen**) **I** v/i (sn) ✔ start, take off, passenger: fly. **II** v/t (h) patrol (by plane).
'**abfließen** v/i (irr, sep, -ge-, sn, → **fließen**) flow off (a. capital).
'**Abflug** m (-[e]s; ~e) takeoff, departure. **2bereit** adj ready for takeoff. **~halle** f departure lounge. **~zeit** f (time of) departure.
'**Abfluß** m (-sses; ~sse) **1.** flowing off, discharge, outflow (of capital). **2.** ⊚ outlet. '**Abflußrohr** n ⊚ drainpipe.
'**abfordern** v/t (sep, -ge-, h) **j-m et.** ~ a. fig. demand s.th. of s.o.
'**abfragen** v/t (sep, -ge-, h) **1. j-n (et.)** ~ test (Am. quiz) s.o. (on s.th.). **2.** computer: interrogate.
'**abfressen** v/t (irr, sep, -ge-, h, → **fressen**) crop, eat bare.
'**abfrieren** v/i (irr, sep, -ge-, sn, → **frieren**) **ihm sind drei Zehen** etc **abgefroren** he lost three toes etc through frostbite; F **sich e-n** ~ be freezing to death.

'**Abfuhr** ['apfuːr] f (-; -en) **1.** removal. **2.** a) fig. rebuff, F brush-off, b) sports: defeat, beating: **sich e-e** ~ **holen** get a beating, fig. meet with a rebuff.
'**abführen** (sep, -ge-, h) **I** v/t **1.** lead s.o. away, forcibly: march s.o. off, take prisoner into custody: **j-n ~ lassen** have s.o. taken away. **2.** fig. ~ **von** lead away from (a subject). **3.** ~ **an** (acc) pay money, taxes (over) to. **4.** ⊚ drain off (water), carry off (heat). **II** v/i **5.** ✈ a) act as a laxative, b) move the bowels.
'**abführend** adj, '**Abführmittel** n (-s; -) ✈ laxative.
'**Abfüllanlage** f bottling plant.
'**abfüllen** v/t (sep, -ge-, h) draw off, fill, rack (off) (wine etc): **in Beutel** ~ bag; **in** (or **auf**) **Flaschen** ~ bottle.
'**abfüttern** v/t (sep, -ge-, h) a. F fig. feed.
'**Abgabe** f (-; -n pl) a) delivery, handing over, b) depositing (luggage), Am. checking (baggage), c) making (an offer, a comment, etc), giving (an opinion etc), d) emission (of heat, steam, etc), release (of energy), ⚡ output, e) ✈ sale, f) firing (of a shot). **2.** a) tax, duty, b) rate, Am. local tax, c) (social) contribution. **3.** sports: pass.
'**abgabenfrei** adj a) tax-free, b) duty--free. '**abgabenpflichtig** adj person: liable to payment of taxes (etc), goods: dutiable, income: taxable.
'**Abgang** m (-[e]s; ~e) **1.** no pl leaving, departure, a. thea. exit, retirement (aus from an office): **nach dem ~ von der Schule** after leaving school; fig. **sich e-n guten ~ verschaffen** make a graceful exit. **2.** no pl a) ✈ dispatch, b) 🚚 etc departure, c) ⚓ sailing, c) ✈ discharge (of blood, pus), passage (of stones). **3.** gym. dismount. **4.** ✈ a) → **Absatz** 3, b) loss, c) banking: items disposed of.
'**Abgangszeugnis** n (school-)leaving certificate, Am. diploma.
'**Abgas** n (-es; -e) waste gas, mot. exhaust fumes. **2arm** adj low-emission. **~entgiftung** f waste gas detoxification. **2frei** adj emission-free. **~test** m mot. fume emission test.
'**abgearbeitet I** pp of **abarbeiten**. **II** adj worn(-)out.
'**abgeben** (irr, sep, -ge-, h, → **geben**) **I** v/t **1.** (**bei**) a) hand in (or over) (to), deliver (to), b) deposit (luggage etc)

(at), *Am.* check (*baggage etc*) (at). **2.** (*an acc* to) a) give away, b) transfer (*employee*): **j-m et. ~ von** a. share s.th. with s.o. **3.** ✝ sell (*an acc* to). **4.** *sports*: (*an acc* to) pass (*the ball*), lose (*game, set*), concede (*a point*). **5.** make (*a statement*), give (*one's opinion*), cast (*one's vote*). **6.** give off, emit (*heat, steam, etc*), release (*energy*). **7.** **e-n Schuß ~** fire (*sports*: a. deliver) a shot, shoot. **8.** F be, act as (*referee etc*), provide, serve as (*background etc*): **er würde e-n guten Lehrer** *etc* **~** he would make a good teacher *etc*. II *v/i sports*: pass (the ball). III **sich ~ mit** concern o.s. with; F **sich mit j-m ~** have dealings with s.o., associate with s.o.; **damit kann ich mich nicht ~!** I can't be bothered with that!

'**abgebrannt I** *pp of* **abbrennen. II** *adj* F *fig.* broke.

'**abgebrüht** *adj* F *fig.* hardened.

'**abgedroschen** *adj* F trite, hackneyed.

'**abgefahren I** *pp of* **abfahren. II** *adj* bald (*tyre*).

'**abgegriffen** *adj* **1.** a) (well-)worn, b) well-thumbed (*book*). **2.** → **abgedroschen.**

'**abgehackt I** *pp of* **abhacken. II** *adj* chopped (*speech*), disjointed (*sentences*).

'**abgehangen I** *pp of* **abhängen². II** *adj* hung (*meat*).

'**abgehärtet I** *pp of* **abhärten. II** *adj* tough, (*gegen*) inured (to), a. *fig.* hardened (against).

'**abgehen** (*irr, sep, -ge-, sn,* → **gehen**) I *v/i* **1.** leave, ✔, 🚋 a. depart, ⚓ a. sail (*all*: **nach** for), *letter, parcel, etc*: go off, be dispatched: **von der Schule ~** leave school. **2.** *thea.,* a. *fig.* make one's exit: **... geht (gehen) ab** exit (exeunt) ... **3.** *button, paint, etc*: come off. **4.** 🦵 *fetus*: be aborted, *stones etc*: be discharged, pass. **5.** *road etc*: branch off. **6.** → **weggehen** 2. **7.** *amount etc*: be deducted (**von** from): **hiervon gehen 7% ab** 7 per cent to be deducted (from this amount). **8.** *fig.* **von e-r Regel** *etc* **~** deviate (*totally*: depart) from a rule *etc*; **davon gehe ich nicht ab!** nothing can change my mind about that!; **davon kann ich nicht ~!** I must insist on that! **9.** F *fig.* **was ihm abgeht, ist Mut** what he lacks is courage; **ihm geht jeder Humor ab** he has no sense of humo(u)r at all; **ihr geht nichts ab** she doesn't go short of anything. **10.** **gut** (*glatt etc*) **~** go well (smoothly *etc*); **schlecht ~** turn out badly; **es kann nicht gut ~** there's sure to be trouble; **es ging nicht ohne Streit ab** there was a quarrel after all. II *v/t* **11.** a) go (*or* walk) along, b) patrol.

'**abgehend** *adj* 🚋, 📮 outgoing.

'**abgehetzt I** *pp of* **abhetzen. II** *adj* **1.** breathless, *pred* out of breath. **2.** worn(-)out, exhausted.

'**abgekämpft** *adj* exhausted, spent.

'**abgekartet** *adj* F **~es Spiel** put-up job.

'**abgeklärt I** *pp of* **abklären. II** *adj* balanced (*opinion etc*), mellow (*person*).

'**abgelagert I** *pp of* **ablagern. II** *adj* seasoned (*wood etc*), matured (*wine*).

'**abgelegen** *adj* remote, secluded.

'**abgelten** *v/t* (*irr, sep, -ge-,* h, → **gelten**) satisfy (*claims*).

'**abgemagert I** *pp of* **abmagern. II** *adj* emaciated.

'**abgeneigt** *adj* **nicht ~ sein, et. zu tun** be quite prepared to do s.th.

'**abgenutzt I** *pp of* **abnutzen. II** *adj* a. *fig.* worn(-out).

Abgeordnete ['apgəʔɔrdnətə] *m, f* (-n; -n) a) delegate, representative, b) Member of Parliament, *Am.* Congressman (Congresswoman).

'**Abgeordnetenhaus** *n* chamber of deputies, *Am.* House of Representatives.

'**abgepackt I** *pp of* **abpacken. II** *adj* ✝ prepacked, packaged.

'**abgerissen I** *pp of* **abreißen. II** *adj* **1.** ragged, *person*: a. seedy. **2.** incoherent, disjointed (*sentences etc*).

'**abgerundet I** *pp of* **abrunden. II** *adj* round(ed) (*sum etc*), *fig.* (well-)rounded. III *adv* in round figures.

'**Abgesandte** *m, f* (-n; -n) envoy, *pol.* a. emissary.

'**abgeschieden** *adj* secluded.

'**Abgeschiedenheit** *f* (-; *no pl*) seclusion.

'**abgeschlafft** *adj* F whacked, dead beat.

'**abgeschlossen I** *pp of* **abschließen. II** *adj* **1.** completed. **2.** ⊚ self-contained.

'**abgeschmackt** *adj fig.* a) tasteless, *pred* in bad taste, b) fatuous.

'**abgesehen** *adv* **~ von** apart (*esp. Am.* aside) from, except for; **vom Wetter ganz ~** to say nothing of the weather.

'**abgespannt** *adj* worn(-)out, exhausted.

'Abgespanntheit f (-; no pl) exhaustion.
'abgestanden adj a. fig. stale.
'abgestorben I pp of absterben. **II** adj dead, numb.
'abgestumpft I pp of abstumpfen. **II** adj fig. deadened, dull(ed), person: insensitive (**gegen** to).
'abgetakelt adj F down(-)at(-)heel.
'abgetragen I pp of abtragen. **II** adj worn, shabby, worn-down (shoes).
'abgewinnen v/t (irr, sep, h, → gewinnen) j-m et. ~ win s.th. from s.o.; e-r Sache Geschmack ~ acquire a taste for s.th.
'abgewirtschaftet adj run(-)down.
'abgewöhnen v/t (sep, h) j-m et. ~ cure (or break) s.o. of s.th.; j-m das Rauchen ~ make s.o. stop smoking; sich das Rauchen ~ give up smoking.
'abgezehrt adj emaciated.
'abgießen v/t (irr, sep, -ge-, h, → gießen) **1.** a) pour off, b) strain (vegetables etc). **2.** ⊙ cast.
'Abglanz m (fig. schwacher ~ pale) reflection.
'abgleichen v/t (irr, sep, -ge-, h, → gleichen) ⊙ equalize, ⚡ align.
'abgleiten v/i (irr, sep, -ge-, sn, → gleiten) slip (off): fig. Kritik etc gleitet von ihm ab he is deaf to criticism etc.
abgöttisch ['apgœtɪʃ] adj idolatrous: ~ lieben idolize, adore.
'abgrasen v/t (sep, -ge-, h) **1.** graze. **2.** F fig. (nach for) scour, comb.
'abgrenzen v/t (sep, -ge-, h) **1.** a. fig. mark off, demarcate (**gegen** from). **2.** fig. a) differentiate, b) define.
'Abgrenzung f (-; -en) **1.** demarcation. **2.** fig. a) differentiation, b) definition.
'Abgrund m (-[e]s; ⁓e) abyss (a. fig.), chasm, precipice: fig. die Abgründe der Seele etc the depths of the soul etc; am Rande des ⁓s on the brink of ruin (or disaster). **abgründig** ['apgryndɪç] adj **1.** cryptic. **2.** → **'abgrundtief** adj abysmal (a. fig.), fig. deadly (hate etc).
'abgucken v/t (sep, -ge-, h) F j-m et. ~ learn (or copy) s.th. from s.o.
'Abguß m (-sses; ⁓sse) ⊙ cast.
'abhaben v/t (irr, sep, -ge-, h, → haben) F er kann et. ~ he can have some (of it).
'abhacken v/t (sep, -ge-, h) chop off, cut off: → abgehackt.
'abhaken v/t (sep, -ge-, h) **1.** unhook. **2.**

tick (Am. check) off: fig. et. ~ cross s.th. off one's list.
'abhalftern v/t (sep, -ge-, h) F fig. sack.
'abhalten v/t (irr, sep, -ge-, h, → halten) **1.** hold s.th. away (von sich from o.s.). **2.** keep away (or off), ward off. **3.** deter, discourage: j-n ~ von stop (or keep, prevent) s.o. from doing; lassen Sie sich (durch mich) nicht ~! don't let me disturb you! **4.** hold (conference, exam, election, etc), give (lesson, lecture): abgehalten werden be held, take place. **5.** ein Kind ~ hold a child over the pot. **6.** ♣ (a. v/i) bear off.
'abhandeln v/t (sep, -ge-, h) **1.** j-m et. ~ buy s.th. from s.o.; j-m 10 Mark (vom Preis) ~ beat s.o. down by ten marks. **2.** deal with, treat (a subject etc).
abhanden [ap'handən] adv ~ kommen get lost; mir ist mein Bleistift ~ gekommen I have lost my pencil.
'Abhandlung f (-; -en) (über acc on) treatise, paper.
'Abhang m (-[e]s; ⁓e) slope, precipice.
'abhängen¹ I v/t (h) **1.** take down, unhook, ☎ etc uncouple. **2.** fig. shake off, give s.o. the slip. **II** v/i teleph. hang up.
'abhängen² v/i (irr, sep, -ge-, h, → hängen¹) **1.** hang: → abgehangen **II. 2.** ~ von depend on, financially: be dependent on; letztlich ~ von hinge on; es hängt von ihm ab it's for him to decide.
abhängig ['apheŋɪç] adj (von) dependent (on), 🐟, psych. addicted to: ling. ~e Rede indirect speech; ~er Satz subordinate clause; ~ sein von → abhängen² 2; ~ machen von make s.th. conditional on. **'Abhängigkeit** f (-; -en) (von) dependence (on), 🐟, psych. dependency (on), addiction (to): gegenseitige ~ interdependence.
'abhärmen: sich ~ (sep, -ge-, h) pine away; sich ~ um grieve over.
'abhärten v/t (sep, -ge-, h) (gegen to, against) toughen, a. fig. harden (sich o.s.). **'Abhärtung** f (-; no pl) hardening.
'abhauen (irr, sep, -ge-, → hauen) **I** v/t (h) cut off, chop off. **II** v/i (sn) F beat it: hau ab! beat it!, get lost!
'abheben (irr, sep, -ge-, h, → heben) **I** v/t **1.** lift off, take off, teleph. pick up. **2.** cut (cards). **3.** slip (meshes). **4.** withdraw (money). **II** v/i **5.** ✈ take off. **6.** F fig. flip. **7.** answer the (tele)phone. **8.**

21   **Abkürzung**

cards: cut. **9.** *esp. adm.* **~ *auf*** (*acc*) refer
to. **III sich ~** (*gegen, von*) contrast
(with), stand out (against).
'**abheften** *v/t* (*sep*, -ge-, h) file (away).
'**abheilen** *v/i* (*sep*, -ge-, sn) heal (up).
'**abhelfen** *v/i* (*irr, sep*, -ge-, h, → *helfen*)
e-r Sache **~** remedy s.th.
'**abhetzen**: *sich* **~** (*sep*, -ge-, h) rush, *w.s.*
wear (*or* tire) o.s. out.
Abhilfe *f* (-; *no pl*) remedy: **~ *schaffen***
remedy things.
'**abhobeln** *v/t* (*sep*, -ge-, h) ✪ plane off.
'**abholen** *v/t* (*sep*, -ge-, h) call for, come
for, pick up, collect: **~ *lassen*** send for;
j-n von der Bahn ~ go to meet s.o. at
the station.
'**abholzen** *v/t* (*sep*, -ge-, h) cut down
(*trees*), deforest (*area*).
'**Abhöranlage** *f* bugging system.
'**abhorchen** *v/t* (*sep*, -ge-, h) ✚ sound,
auscultate.
'**abhören** *v/t* (*sep*, -ge-, h) **1.** → *abfragen*
1. **2.** → *abhorchen*. **3.** intercept (*radio
message etc*), listen in on, monitor, F
bug (*phone calls*), tap (*telephone*). **4.**
play back (*tape recording*).
Abi ['abi] *n* (-s; *no pl*) F → *Abitur*.
'**abirren** *v/i* (*sep*, -ge-, sn) *a. fig.* stray
(*von* from).
Abitur [abi'tu:r] *n* (-s; *no pl*) school-leaving (*Am.* final) examination.
Abiturient [abitu'rient] *m* (-en; -en) a)
candidate for the school-leaving examination, b) school-leaver with the
Abitur.
Abi'turzeugnis *n* Abitur certificate, *Br.*
GCE A-levels, *Am.* (Senior High
School) graduation diploma.
'**abjagen** *v/t* (*sep*, -ge-, h) *j-m et.* **~** snatch
s.th. away from s.o.
'**abkanzeln** *v/t* (*sep*, -ge-, h) F *j-n* **~** give
s.o. a dressing-down.
'**abkapseln**: *sich* **~** (*sep*, -ge-, h) shut (*or*
cut) o.s. off.
'**abkarten** *v/t* (*sep*, -ge-, h) F fix, rig: →
abgekartet.
'**abkas,sieren** *v/i* (*sep*, h) F *fig.* cash
in.
'**abkaufen** *v/t* (*sep*, -ge-, h) buy (*dat*
from): F *fig.* **das kaufe ich dir** *etc* **nicht
ab!** I won't buy that!
Abkehr *f* (-; *no pl*) break (*von*
with). '**abkehren** *v/t* (*sep*, -ge-, h) (*a.
sich* **~**) turn away (*von* from). *fig. sich*

~ von *a.* turn one's back on (*a person*),
abandon (*a policy etc*).
'**abklappern** *v/t* (*sep*, -ge-, h) F scour
(*shops*) (*nach* for), do (*museums etc*).
'**abklären** *v/t* (*sep*, -ge-, h) clear: → *abgeklärt*.
Abklatsch *m* (-[e]s; -e) *fig.* imitation.
'**abklemmen** *v/t* (*sep*, -ge-, h) pinch off,
✚ clamp, ⚡ disconnect.
'**abklingen** *v/i* (*irr, sep*, -ge-, sn, → *klingen*) *noise etc*: abate, *pain*: ease, *fever,
swelling*: go down, *effect*: wear off, *excitement, storm, etc*: subside, die down.
'**abklopfen** (*sep*, -ge-, h) **I** *v/t* **1.** brush off
(*dust etc*). **2.** *esp.* ✚ tap, percuss. **3.** F
fig. scrutinize (*auf acc* for). **II** *v/i* **4.** ♪
stop the orchestra.
'**abknallen** *v/t* (*sep*, -ge-, h) F bump s.o.
off.
'**abknicken** *v/t* (*sep*, -ge-, h), *v/i* (sn) snap
(off): **~de Vorfahrt** left-hand (*or
right-hand) turn of a main road at a
road junction.
'**abknöpfen** *v/t* (*sep*, -ge-, h) **1.** unbutton.
2. F *j-m et.* **~** wangle s.th. out of s.o.
'**abknutschen** *v/t* (*sep*, -ge-, h) F kiss and
cuddle: *sich* **~** snog, smooch.
'**abkochen** *v/t* (*sep*, -ge-, h) boil, scald.
'**abkommandieren** *v/t* (*sep*, h) a) detail,
b) second (*officer*) (*nach, zu* to).
'**abkommen** *v/i* (*irr, sep*, -ge-, sn, →
kommen) **1.** get away (*a. sports*): **vom
Kurs ~** deviate (from one's course);
mot. von der Straße **~** get (*or* skid) off
the road; **vom Thema ~** stray from the
point; **vom Wege ~** lose one's way, *fig.*
go astray. **2. ~ von** give up, drop (*idea,
plan, etc*); **von e-r Ansicht ~** change
one's views about s.th.
'**Abkommen** *n* (-s; -) *esp. pol.* agreement.
abkömmlich ['apkœmlıç] *adj* available:
er ist nicht ~ he cannot get away.
'**Abkömmling** *m* (-s; -e) ⚛ derivative.
'**abkoppeln** *v/t* (*sep*, -ge-, h) uncouple.
'**abkratzen** (*sep*, -ge-) **I** *v/t* (h) scrape off.
II *v/i* (sn) F kick the bucket.
'**abkühlen** *v/t, v/i and sich* **~** (*sep*, -ge-, h)
a. fig. cool off.
'**Abkühlung** *f* (-; *no pl*) cooling.
'**abkürzen** (*sep*, -ge-, h) **I** *v/t* shorten,
abridge, abbreviate (*word*): (*den Weg*)
~ take a short cut. **II** *v/i* take (*road etc*:
be) a short cut. '**Abkürzung** *f* (-; -en) **1.**
abbreviation, abridg(e)ment. **2.** *a. fig.*

short cut. **'Abkürzungsverzeichnis** n list of abbreviations.

'abküssen v/t (sep, -ge-, h) **j-n ~** smother s.o. with kisses.

'abladen v/t (irr, sep, -ge-, h, → **laden**) **1.** a) unload, b) dump. **2.** fig. off-load: **s-n Ärger ~ bei** vent one's anger on.

'Abladeplatz m a) unloading point, b) dump.

'Ablage f (-; -n) **1.** no pl filing. **2.** a) place to put s.th., b) file.

'ablagern v/t (sep, -ge-, h) **1.** (a. **sich ~**) 🍂, geol., 🐟 deposit. **2.** (a. v/i) season (wood etc), mature (wine).

'Ablagerung f (-; -en) 🍂, geol., 🐟 a) deposition, b) deposit, sediment.

Ablaß ['aplas] m (-sses; ⸚sse) eccl. indulgence.

'ablassen (irr, sep, -ge-, h, → **lassen**) **I** v/t **1.** let s.th. off (or out), drain off (water etc), drain (tank etc), blow off (steam): **die Luft ~ aus** deflate. **2.** 🛒 sell (dat to), b) et. (**vom Preis**) **~** knock s.th. off the price. **II** v/i **3. ~ von** a) stop doing, give s.th. up, b) leave s.o. alone.

Ablativ ['ablati:f; -ap-] m (-s; -e) ling. ablative.

'Ablauf m (-[-e]s; ⸚e) **1.** ⚙ a) discharge, b) outlet, drain. **2.** course, run, of program(me): order of events: **der ~ der Ereignisse** the course of events. **3.** no pl end, 🛒, ✝ expiration (of contract etc), maturity (of bill of exchange): **nach ~** upon expiration (gen of): **nach ~ von zwei Wochen** after two weeks.

'ablaufen (irr, sep, -ge-, → **laufen**) **I** v/i (sn) **1.** (a. **~ lassen**) water etc: run off, drain off: fig. **an ihm läuft alles ab** everything runs off him like water off a duck's back. **2.** fig. go: **alles ist gut abgelaufen** everything went off well. **3.** end, run out, expire. **4.** unwind, film, tape: run, watch: run down: fig. **s-e Uhr ist abgelaufen** his hour is come. **II** v/t (h) **5.** walk the length of. **6.** (nach for) scour, comb (shops). **7.** wear out, wear down (heels): → **Rang** 1.

'Ableben n (-s; no pl) death, decease.

'ablecken v/t (sep, -ge-, h) lick off.

'ablegen (sep, -ge-, h) **I** v/t **1.** a) take off (one's coat etc), b) discard (old clothes): **abgelegte Kleider** cast-offs. **2.** put down (load). **3.** file (papers), discard (playing cards). **4.** zo. deposit (eggs). **5.**

give up, drop (habit). **6.** take (oath etc): **e-e Prüfung ~** take (or pass) an examination; → **Gelübde, Geständnis, Rechenschaft** etc. **II** v/t **7.** take off one's things (or coat, hat, etc): **bitte, legen Sie ab!** take off your coat, please! **8.** ⚓ cast off, space shuttle: separate.

'Ableger m (-s; -) ⚘ layer, scion.

'ablehnen (sep, -ge-, h) **I** v/t **1.** refuse, turn down, reject (a. parl.), decline, ⚖ challenge (witness). **2.** disapprove of, condemn. **II** v/i **3.** refuse, decline.

'ablehnend adj negative, disapproving.

'Ablehnung f (-; -en) refusal, rejection (a. parl.), disapproval (gen of).

'ableisten v/t (sep, -ge-, h) serve: → **Wehrdienst.**

'ableiten (sep, -ge-, h) **1.** ⚙ divert, drain off (water), carry off (steam). **2.** 🍂, 🖋, ling., a. fig. derive (aus from): **sich ~** a. be derived: **s-e Herkunft ~ von** trace one's origin back to.

'Ableitung f (-; -en) **1.** ⚙ diversion, draining off (etc, → **ableiten** 1). **2.** 🖋, ling. etc a) derivation, b) derivative.

'ablenken (sep, -ge-, h) **I** v/t **1.** a) divert, b) deflect (ball, light rays, etc). **2.** fig. divert, distract: **den Verdacht von sich ~** divert suspicion from o.s.; **j-n (von s-n Sorgen) ~** take s.o.'s mind off his worries. **II** v/i **3.** change the subject. **4.** be a diversion: **das lenkt ab** that takes one's mind off things. **'Ablenkung** f (-; -en) **1.** deviation, deflection. **2.** diversion, distraction. **'Ablenkungsma‚növer** n diversion, fig. a. red herring.

'ablesen[1] v/t (sep, -ge-, h, → **lesen**) pick off. **'ablesen**[2] v/t (irr, sep, -ge-, h, → **lesen**) **1.** read a speech (from notes). **2.** ⚙ read: **Strom (Gas) ~** read the gas (electricity) meter. **3.** fig. see (an dat from): **j-m et. vom Gesicht ~** read s.th. in s.o.'s face; **j-m e-n Wunsch von den Augen ~** anticipate s.o.'s wish.

'Ablesung f (-; -en) ⚙ reading.

'abliefern v/t (sep, -ge-, h) deliver (**bei** to, at).

'ablösbar adj ✝ redeemable.

Ablöse ['aplø:zə] f (-; -n) F sports: transfer fee.

'ablösen v/t (sep, -ge-, h) **1.** remove, detach. **2.** relieve (guards etc), take over from, replace (a colleague): **j-n ~** a. relieve s.o. of his duties; **sich (or einan-**

der) ~ take turns (*bei* at). **3.** *fig.* follow. **4.** redeem (*mortgage*), pay off (*debt*).

'**Ablösesumme** *f sports:* transfer fee.

'**Ablösung** *f* (-; -en) **1.** removal. **2.** relief. **3.** ✝ redemption, repayment.

'**Abluft** *f* (-; *no pl*) ⊙ waste air.

'**ablutschen** *v/t* (*sep*, -ge-, h) lick (off).

'**abmachen** *v/t* (*sep*, -ge-, h) **1.** remove, take off. **2.** arrange, agree on, settle on: *abgemacht!* agreed!, it's a deal!, o.k.! '**Abmachung** *f* (-; -en) arrangement, agreement.

'**abmagern** *v/i* (*sep*, -ge-, sn) grow thin, lose weight: → *abgemagert.*

'**Abmagerungskur** *f* (-; -en) (*e-e ~ machen* go [*or* be] on a) slimming diet.

'**abmalen** *v/t* (*sep*, -ge-, h) paint, copy.

'**Abmarsch** *m* (-[e]s, ⸚e) marching off.

'**abmar,schieren** *v/i* (*sep*, sn) march off.

'**abmelden** (*sep*, -ge-, h) **I** *v/t* cancel: *sein Auto* ~ take one's car off the road; *sein Telefon* ~ have one's telephone disconnected; *j-n* ~ a) give notice of s.o.'s change of address (*to the police*), b) cancel s.o.'s membership (*of a club etc*); F *bei mir ist er abgemeldet!* I'm through with him! **II** *sich* ~ a) give notice of one's change of address (*to the police*), b) cancel one's membership (*of a club etc*); *sich bei j-m* (*vom Dienst etc*) ~ report to s.o. that one is leaving. '**Abmeldung** *f* (-; -en) **1.** cancel(l)ation. **2.** notice of change of address.

'**abmessen** *v/t* (*irr, sep*, -ge-, h, → *messen*) measure. '**Abmessung** *f* (-; -en) measurement: ~*en a.* dimensions.

'**abmon,tieren** *v/t* (*sep*, h) ⊙ take off, dismount, remove.

'**abmühen: sich** ~ (*sep*, -ge-, h) try hard (*to do s.th.*); *sich* ~ *mit* struggle with.

'**abmurksen** *v/t* (*sep*, -ge-, h) F do s.o. in.

'**abmustern** *v/t* (*sep*, -ge-, h) ♣ pay off.

'**abnabeln** *v/t* (*sep*, -ge-, h) cut a *baby's* umbilical cord; *fig. sich* ~ cut the cord.

'**abnagen** *v/t* (*sep*, -ge-, h) gnaw off: *e-n Knochen* ~ gnaw (*person:* pick) a bone.

'**abnähen** *v/t* (*sep*, -ge-, h) take in, tuck.

'**Abnäher** *m* (-s; -) tuck.

'**Abnahme** *f* (-; *no pl*) **1.** taking off (*or* down), removal, ✂ amputation. **2.** ✝ (*bei* ~ on) purchase (*von* of). **3.** ⊙ a) acceptance, b) inspection (test). **4.** ~ *e-r Parade* review (of the troops). **5.** *fig.*

decrease, decline, drop (*all: gen* in), loss (*gen* in, of *speed, weight*), flagging (*of interest*), waning (*of the moon*).

'**abnehmbar** *adj* removable.

'**abnehmen** (*irr, sep*, -ge-, h, → *nehmen*) **I** *v/t* **1.** take off, ⊙ *a.* remove, ✂ *a.* amputate, take down (*picture etc*), shave off (*beard*), gather (*fruit*), pick up (*the receiver*): *j-m Blut* ~ take a blood sample from s.o.; *j-m Fingerabdrücke* ~ take s.o.'s fingerprints. **2.** *j-m et.* ~ a) relieve s.o. of s.th., save s.o. (*trouble, an errand, etc*), b) take s.th. (away) from s.o., c) charge s.o. s.th.; *j-m zuviel* ~ overcharge s.o. **3.** (*dat* from) buy, purchase: F *das nimmt ihm keiner ab!* nobody will buy that! **4.** ⊙ a) accept, b) inspect, test. **5.** *die Parade* ~ review the troops. **6.** hold (*an examination*): → *Beichte, Eid etc.* **7.** decrease (*meshes*). **8.** lose, get rid of (*pounds, weight*). **II** *v/i* **9.** decrease, diminish, drop off, *strength etc:* decline, *vision etc:* fail, *interest:* flag, *speed:* slacken (off), slow down, *storm:* abate, *moon:* (be on the) wane, *days:* grow shorter. **10.** a) lose weight, b) be slimming. '**Abnehmer** *m* (-s; -) ✝ a) buyer, b) customer, c) consumer: *keine* ~ *finden* find no market.

'**Abneigung** *f* (-; -en) (*gegen*) dislike (of, for), aversion (to).

abnorm [ap'nɔrm] *adj* abnormal, *w.s.* exceptional, unusual.

Abnormität [apnɔrmi'tɛ:t] *f* (-; -en) **1.** abnormality. **2.** monstrosity.

'**abnötigen** *v/t* (*sep*, -ge-, h) *j-m Respekt* ~ command s.o.'s respect.

'**abnutzen** *v/t* (*sep*, -ge-, h) (*a. sich* ~) wear out. '**Abnutzung** *f* (-; *no pl*) wear and tear. '**Abnutzungserscheinung** *f* sign of wear, ✂ sign of degeneration.

Abonnement [abɔnə'mã:] *n* (-s; -s) subscription (*auf acc* to), *thea. a.* season ticket (*bei* for). **Abonnent** [abo'nɛnt] *m* (-en; -en) subscriber (*gen* to), *thea.* season-ticket holder.

abonnieren [abo'ni:rən] *v/t* (h) subscribe to: *abonniert sein auf* (*acc*) have a subscription to, take (*a paper*).

'**abordnen** *v/t* (*sep*, -ge-, h) delegate. '**Abordnung** *f* (-; -en) delegation.

'**abpacken** *v/t* (*sep*, -ge-, h) ✝ pack(age).

'**abpassen** *v/t* (*sep*, -ge-, h) wait for.

'**abpausen** *v/t* (*sep*, -ge-, h) trace.

'**abpfeifen** v/t, v/i (irr, sep, -ge-, h, →
pfeifen) (**das Spiel**) ~ stop the game.
'**Abpfiff** m (-[e]s; -e] sports: final whistle.
'**abprallen** v/i (sep, -ge-, sn) rebound,
bounce off, bullet: ricochet: fig. **an j-m**
~ make no impression on s.o.
'**Abpraller** m (-s; -) sports: rebound.
'**abputzen** v/t (sep, -ge-, h) clean, wipe:
sich die Schuhe ~ wipe one's feet.
'**abquälen: sich** ~ (sep, -ge-, h) 1. worry
(o.s.), fret. 2. slave (away). 3. → **abmühen**.
'**abqualifi,zieren** v/t (sep, h) dismiss.
'**abrackern: sich** ~ (sep, -ge-, h) F slave
(away).
'**abraten** v/i (irr, sep, -ge-, h, → **raten**)
j-m ~ **von** advise (or warn) s.o. against
(doing).
'**abräumen** v/t (sep, -ge-, h) clear away,
remove: **den Tisch** ~ clear the table.
'**abrea,gieren** (sep, h) **I** v/t (**an** dat on)
abreact, work off. **II sich** ~ get rid of
one's aggressions, F let off steam.
'**abrechnen** (sep, -ge-, h) **I** v/t deduct,
account for (expenses etc). **II** v/i settle
accounts: **mit j-m** ~ settle up with s.o.,
fig. a. get even with s.o.
'**Abrechnung** f (-; -en) **1.** a) settlement
(of accounts), b) statement. **2.** fig. re-
quital: **Tag der** ~ day of reckoning.
'**abreiben** v/t (irr, sep, -ge-, h, → **reiben**)
1. a) rub off, b) rub down (body). **2.**
wipe s.th. clean, polish. **3.** grate (lemon
etc). '**Abreibung** f (-; -en) **1.** ~
rub-down, sponge-down. **2.** F beating.
'**Abreise** f (-; -n) (**bei** m-r etc ~ on
my etc) departure (**nach** for).
'**abreisen** v/i (sep, -ge-, sn) (**nach** for)
depart, leave.
'**Abreiß...** tear-off (pad, calendar, etc).
'**abreißen** (irr, sep, -ge-, → **reißen**) **I** v/t
(h) a) tear (or pull, rip) off, b) pull
down, demolish (building). **II** v/i (sn)
come off, thread etc: snap, fig. break
off: **die Arbeit reißt nicht ab** there's no
end of work.
'**abrichten** v/t (sep, -ge-, h) train (animal), break in (horse).
'**abriegeln** v/t (sep, -ge-, h) **1.** bolt, bar.
2. block (off), cordon off, ✕ seal off.
'**abringen** v/t (irr, sep, -ge-, h, → **ringen**)
j-m et. ~ wrest s.th. from s.o.; **sich ein
Lächeln** ~ force a smile.
'**Abriß** m (-sses, -sse) **1.** a) summary,

outline, b) survey, c) compendium. **2.**
demolition.
'**abrollen** (sep, -ge-) **I** v/t (h) unroll, unwind, unreel. **II** v/i (sn) fig. unfold.
'**abrücken** (sep, -ge-) **I** v/t (h) move
away. **II** v/i (sn) march off, move off:
fig. **von j-m** ~ disassociate o.s. from s.o.
'**Abruf** m (-[e]s; no pl) **1.** recall: **sich auf** ~
bereithalten stand by. **2.** ✝ **auf** ~ on
call. '**abrufbereit** adj on call.
'**abrufen** v/t (irr, sep, -ge-, h, → **rufen**)
1. call s.o. away, recall. **2.** ✝ call (for)
(goods). **3.** computer: call in (data).
'**abrunden** v/t (sep, -ge-, h) round off:
nach oben (**unten**) ~ round up (down);
→ **abgerundet**.
abrupt [ap'rʊpt] adj abrupt, sudden.
'**abrüsten** v/i (sep, -ge-, h) disarm.
'**Abrüstung** f (-; no pl) disarmament.
'**abrutschen** v/i (sep, -ge-, sn) **1.** slip
off, slip down, knife: slip. **2.** fig. go
down.
'**absacken** v/i (sep, -ge-, sn) F **1.** sag, a.
⚓ sink, ✈ pancake. **2.** fig. go down.
'**Absage** f (-; -n) **1.** cancel(l)ation. **2.**
refusal, fig. rejection (**an** acc of).
'**absagen** (sep, -ge-, h) **I** v/t cancel, call
off. **II** v/i beg off, cry off: **j-m** ~ tell s.o.
that one can't come.
'**absägen** v/t (sep, -ge-, h) **1.** saw off. **2.**
fig. ax(e), fire.
'**absahnen** v/t (sep, -ge-, h) F cream off.
'**absatteln** v/t (sep, -ge-, h) unsaddle.
'**Absatz** m (-[e]s; ⁓e) **1.** heel: **Schuhe mit
hohen Absätzen** high-heeled shoes. **2.**
🖋, print. paragraph: **neuer** ~ new line.
3. ✝ sale(s): **guten** (**reißenden**) ~ **finden** find a ready market (F sell like hot
cakes). **4.** (staircase) landing.
'**Absatz|gebiet** n ✝ market(ing area).
~**markt** m, ~**möglichkeit** f ✝ market,
outlet. ~**steigerung** f ✝ sales increase.
~**stockung** f ✝ stagnation of trade.
'**Absatztrick** m soccer: backheel trick.
'**absaufen** v/i (irr, sep, -ge-, sn, → **saufen**) F 🌊, mot. be flooded, ⚓ go down,
person: drown.
'**absaugen** v/t (sep, -ge-, h) **1.** suck off, a.
🖋 aspirate. **2.** vacuum (carpet).
'**abschaben** v/t (sep, -ge-, h) scrape off.
'**abschaffen** v/t (sep, -ge-, h) **1.** abolish.
2. get rid of, give up.
'**Abschaffung** f (-; no pl) abolition.
'**abschalten** (sep, -ge-, h) **I** v/t switch off,

turn off, ⚡ cut off, disconnect. **II** v/i F fig. switch off, relax.

'**abschätzen** v/t (sep, -ge-, h) estimate, a. fig. assess, F fig. size s.o., s.th. up.

'**abschätzend** adj assessing, speculative.

abschätzig ['apʃɛtsɪç] adj contemptuous, disparaging.

'**Abschaum** m (-[e]s; no pl) scum: fig. ~ der Menschheit scum of the earth.

'**Abscheu** m (-s; no pl) (vor dat, gegen) disgust (at, for), loathing (for): e-n ~ haben vor (dat) detest, loathe.

'**abscheuern** v/t (sep, -ge-, h) **1.** scrub (off). **2.** rub off, scrape. **3.** (a. sich ~) wear thin.

ab'scheulich adj dreadful, abominable, heinous, atrocious (a. crime etc).

'**abschicken** v/t (sep, -ge-, h) → **absenden.**

'**abschieben** (irr, sep, -ge-, → **schieben**) **I** v/t (h) **1.** push away (von from). **2.** deport. **3.** F get rid of. **II** v/i (sn) **4.** F push off. '**Abschiebung** f (-; -en) ⚖ deportation. '**Abschiebungshaft** f (j-n in ~ nehmen put s.o. on) remand pending deportation.

Abschied ['apʃiːt] m (-[e]s; no pl) **1.** farewell, parting, departure: ~ nehmen (von) take leave (of), say goodbye (to); beim ~, zum ~ on parting. **2.** dismissal, ✗ discharge, resignation.

'**Abschieds...** farewell (letter, visit, etc). ~kuß m goodby(e) kiss: j-m e-n ~ geben kiss s.o. goodby(e). ~schmerz m (-es; no pl) wrench. ~stunde f hour of parting. ~worte pl words of farewell.

'**abschießen** v/t (irr, sep, -ge-, h, → **schießen**) **1.** fire (gun), shoot (bullet, arrow, etc), launch (rocket). **2.** shoot, kill, shoot (or bring) down (plane): F fig. j-n ~ put the skids under s.o.; → **Vogel 1.**

'**abschirmen** v/t (sep, -ge-, h) (gegen) shield (from), protect (against).

'**Abschirmung** f (-; -en) protection.

'**abschlachten** v/t (sep, -ge-, h) a. fig. slaughter.

'**abschlaffen** v/i (sep, -ge-, sn) F wilt: → **abgeschlafft.**

'**Abschlag** m (-[e]s; ⸚e) **1.** soccer: goal kick, golf: tee(-off). **2.** † a) drop (in prices), b) reduction, c) part payment: auf ~ on account. '**abschlagen** v/t (irr, sep, -ge-, h, → **schlagen**) **1.** knock off

(or down), cut off. **2.** (a. v/i) soccer: kick off, golf: tee off. **3.** beat off (attack). **4.** fig. refuse, turn down.

abschlägig ['apʃlɛːgɪç] adj negative: adm. j-n (j-s Bitte) ~ bescheiden reject s.o. (s.o.'s request).

'**Abschlagszahlung** f part payment.

'**abschleifen** v/t (irr, sep, -ge-, h, → **schleifen**) ⊙ grind off, a. fig. polish: sich ~ a. fig. wear off.

'**Abschleppdienst** m breakdown (Am. wrecking) service. '**abschleppen** v/t (sep, -ge-, h) ⚙, mot. tow off.

'**Abschleppwagen** m breakdown lorry, Am. wrecker (truck).

'**abschließbar** adj lockable.

'**abschließen** (irr, sep, -ge-, h, → **schließen**) **I** v/t **1.** lock (up). **2.** shut off, ⊙ a. seal (off): → **abgeschlossen** 2. **3.** a) end, close, finish, b) complete: → **abgeschlossen** 1. **4.** † conclude, sign (contract), settle (accounts), close, balance (books), effect (sale): e-n Handel ~ strike a bargain, close a deal; e-e Versicherung ~ take out a policy; → **Wette. II** v/i **5.** end, close (a. †), finish: mit dem Leben abgeschlossen haben have done with life.

'**abschließend I** adj concluding, closing, final. **II** adv in conclusion, finally.

'**Abschluß** m (-sses; ⸚sse) **1.** no pl conclusion, † closing (of books etc), settlement (of accounts): zum ~ → **abschließend** II; et. zum ~ bringen bring s.th. to a close. **2.** † deal, sale. **3.** F ped., univ. final examination. ~prüfung f **1.** final examination, finals, Am. a. graduation: s-e ~ machen (an dat) graduate (at, Am. from). **2.** † audit (of books). ~zeugnis n (school-)leaving certificate, Am. (high-school) diploma.

'**abschmecken** v/t (sep, -ge-, h) season.

'**abschmieren** v/t (sep, -ge-, h) ⊙ grease.

'**abschminken** v/t (sep, -ge-, h) (a. sich ~) take off (or remove) s.o.'s (one's) make-up: F fig. das kannst du dir ~! forget it!

'**abschnallen** v/t (sep, -ge-, h) undo, take off: sich ~ unfasten one's seat belt.

'**abschneiden** (irr, sep, -ge-, h, → **schneiden**) **I** v/t **1.** cut off (a. fig. supplies etc): j-m den Weg ~ bar s.o.'s way; j-m das Wort ~ cut s.o. short. **II** v/i **2.** (den Weg) ~ take a short cut. **3.** gut

(*schlecht*) ~ do (*or* come off) well (badly). '**Abschneiden** *n* (-s) performance.
'**Abschnitt** *m* (-[e]s; -e) **1.** section, paragraph (*of a book etc*). **2.** *biol.*, *A* segment. **3.** *a.* X sector. **4.** period, phase, stage (*a. of a trip*). **5.** 🕆 counterfoil, stub (*of ticket etc*), coupon.
'**abschnüren** *v/t* (*sep*, -ge-, h) **1.** → *abbinden* 2. **2.** *esp.* X cut off. **3.** *j m die Luft* ~ choke s.o.
'**abschöpfen** *v/t* (*sep*, -ge-, h) skim off (*a.* 🕆 *profits*), 🕆 absorb (*excessive buying power*): *a. fig. den Rahm* ~ take the cream off.
'**abschotten:** *sich* ~ (*sep*, -ge-, h) *fig.* batten down the hatches, seal o.s. off.
'**abschrägen** *v/t* (*sep*, -ge-, h) bevel.
'**abschrauben** *v/t* (*sep*, -ge-, h) screw off.
'**abschrecken** *v/t* (*sep*, -ge-, h) **1.** deter, put *s.o.* off. **2.** ⊙ quench. **3.** *gastr.* rinse with cold water. '**abschreckend** *adj* deterrent: *~es Beispiel* warning; *~e Strafe* exemplary punishment; *~ wirken* act as a deterrent.
'**Abschreckung** *f* (-; -en) deterrence: *zur ~ dienen* act as a deterrent.
'**Abschreckungs|poli,tik** *f* policy of deterrence. *~waffe f* deterrent (weapon).
'**abschreiben** (*irr*, *sep*, -ge-, h, → *schreiben*) **I** *v/t* **1.** copy (out), *ped.* crib. **2.** 🕆 depreciate, write down (*equipment*), *totally:* write off (*a. F fig. s.o.*, *s.th.*), deduct (*amount*). **II** *v/i* **3.** *ped.* crib. '**Abschreibung** *f* (-; -en) 🕆 depreciation, write-off.
'**Abschrift** *f* (-; -en) copy: → *beglaubigt*.
'**abschürfen** *v/t* (*sep*, -ge-, h) 💉 graze.
'**Abschürfung** *f* (-; -en) 💉 graze.
'**Abschuß** *m* (-sses; -üsse) **1.** discharge (*of gun*). **2.** launching (*of rocket*).
abschüssig ['apʃʏsɪç] *adj* steep.
'**Abschußliste** *f* F hit list: *j-n auf die ~ setzen* put the skids under s.o.; *auf der ~ stehen* be a marked man.
'**Abschußrampe** *f* launching pad.
'**abschütteln** *v/t* (*sep*, -ge-, h) *a. fig.* shake off.
'**abschwächen** (*sep*, -ge-, h) **I** *v/t* weaken, soften (*a. impact*), tone down (*a. remark etc*). **II** *sich* ~ weaken, *noise*, *storm, etc*: subside.
'**abschweifen** *v/i* (*sep*, -ge-, sn) *fig.* deviate, stray, *thoughts etc*: wander: *vom Thema* ~ digress (from one's subject).

'**abschwellen** *v/i* (*irr*, *sep*, -ge-, sn, → *schwellen*) **1.** 💉 go down. **2.** *noise*: die down.
'**abschwirren** *v/i* (*sep*, -ge-, sn) F buzz off.
'**abschwören** *v/i* (*irr*, *sep*, -ge-, h, → *schwören*) *s-m Glauben* ~ renounce one's faith.
'**absegnen** *v/t* (*sep*, -ge-, h) F *humor.* give one's blessing to.
'**absehbar** *adj in ~er Zeit* in the foreseeable future. '**absehen** (*irr*, *sep*, -ge-, h, → *sehen*) **I** *v/t* **1.** foresee: *es ist kein Ende abzusehen* there's no end in sight. **2.** *es abgesehen haben auf* (*acc*) a) be out to get, have an eye on, b) *j-n* F have it in for s.o. **3.** → *abgucken*. **II** *v/i* **4.** ~ *von* a) refrain from, b) disregard: → *abgesehen*.
'**abseifen** *v/t* (*sep*, -ge-, h) soap down.
'**abseilen** (*sep*, -ge-, h) *v/t* (*a. sich ~*) rope down: F *fig. sich* ~ make off.
'**absein** *v/i* (*irr*, *sep*, -ge-, sn) → *ab* 2, 9.
abseits ['apzaɪts] **I** *prep* (*gen*) off *the road etc*. **II** *adv* ~ *stehen* stand aside, *sports*: be offside; ~ *liegen* be out of the way; *fig. sich* ~ *halten* keep aloof. '**Abseits** *n* (-; -) *sports*: (*im* ~ *stehen* be) offside; *fig. sich ins* ~ *manövrieren*, *ins* ~ *geraten* get (o.s.) isolated. *~falle f sports*: offside trap. *~tor n sports*: goal scored from an offside position.
'**absenden** *v/t* (*irr*, *sep*, -ge-, h, → *senden*) send (off), dispatch, forward, post, *Am.* mail. '**Absender** *m* (-s; -) **1.** sender. **2.** sender's address.
'**absetzbar** *adj* **1.** 🕆 sal(e)able. **2.** (*steuerlich ~*) deductible (for taxation). **3.** *official etc*: removable.
'**absetzen** (*sep*, -ge-, h) **I** *v/t* **1.** set down (*load*), take off (*hat, glasses, etc*), lift (*violin bow*). **2.** set down (*passengers*), drop (*a. parachutist*). **3.** remove *official* (from office), depose (*ruler*). **4.** cancel (*meeting etc*), remove (*item on the agenda*), take off (*film etc*). **5.** 🕆 a) deduct, b) sell: *steuerlich* ~ deduct from tax. **6.** 💉 stop taking (*a medicament*), go off (*a drug*), break off (*treatment*). **7.** *print.* set (up) in type: *e-e Zeile* ~ begin a new paragraph. **8.** 🐎 *etc* deposit. **II** *v/i* **9.** stop, break off: *ohne abzusetzen* in one go, *drink* in one gulp. **III** *sich* ~ **10.** X retreat, *sports*: *runner etc*: break

abstecken

27

away, F *fig.* make off. **'Absetzung** f (-; -en) **1.** removal (from office), deposition (*of a ruler*). **2.** cancel(l)ation (*of a meeting etc*), withdrawal (*of a film etc*).

'absichern (*sep*, -ge-, h) **I** v/t ~ **sichern**. **II sich** ~ cover o.s.

'Absicht f (-; -en) intention, a. ⚖ intent, aim, object: **in der** ~ **zu** inf with the intention of ger; **ich habe die** ~ **zu kommen** I intend (*or* I'm planning) to come; **mit e-r bestimmten** ~ for a purpose; **mit** ~ on purpose. **'absichtlich I** adj intentional, deliberate, esp. ⚖ wil(l)ful. **II** adv intentionally etc, on purpose. **'Absichtserklärung** f (-; -en) declaration of intent.

'absitzen (*irr, sep*, -ge-, → **sitzen**) **I** v/i (sn) rider: dismount. **II** v/t (h) F sit out (*time*), serve (*a sentence*).

absolut [apzo'lu:t] adj absolute, total, complete: ~ **nicht** by no means.

Absolution [apzolu'tsjo:n] f (-; -en) eccl. absolution.

Absolutismus [apzolu'tɪsmʊs] m (-; no pl) pol. absolutism.

Absolvent [apzɔl'vɛnt] m (-en; -en), **Absol'ventin** f (-; -nen) school-leaver, Am. graduate. **absolvieren** [apzɔl'vi:-rən] v/t (h) **1.** ped. finish, Am. graduate from. **2.** attend, complete (*a course*). **3.** pass (*an exam*). **4.** F do, get through.

ab'sonderlich adj odd, peculiar.

'absondern (*sep*, -ge-, h) **I** v/t **1.** separate, ~ isolate. **2.** biol. secrete. **II sich** ~ fig. cut o.s. off (**von** from).

'Absonderung f (-; -en) **1.** separation, ~ isolation. **2.** biol. secretion.

absorbieren [apzɔr'bi:rən] v/t (h) a. fig. absorb.

'abspalten v/t (*irr, sep*, -ge-, h, → **spalten**) (a. **sich** ~) split off.

'Abspann m (-[e]s, -e) film, TV end titles (and credits).

'Abspannung f (-; no pl) exhaustion.

'absparen v/t (*sep*, -ge-, h) **sich et. (vom Munde)** ~ pinch and scrape for s.th.

'abspecken (*sep*, -ge-, h) F → **abnehmen** 8, 10.

'abspeisen v/t (*sep*, -ge-, h) F feed; fig. **j-n** ~ **mit** fob s.o. off with.

abspenstig ['apʃpɛnstɪç] ~ **machen** lure away (*dat* from); **j-m die Freundin** ~ **machen** steal s.o.'s girl(friend).

'absperren v/t (*sep*, -ge-, h) **1.** block off

(*road*), police: cordon off. **2.** turn (*adm.* cut) off (*gas etc*). **3.** dial. lock (up). **'Absperrhahn** m ⊙ stopcock. **'Absperrung** f (-; -en) **1.** barrier, cordon. **2.** blocking off (*etc*, → **absperren**)

'abspielen (*sep*, -ge-, h) **I** v/t **1.** play (*record, tape, etc*). **2.** pass (*the ball*). **II sich** ~ a) happen, take place, b) be going on: F **da spielt sich nichts ab!** nothing doing!

'absplittern v/i (*sep*, -ge-, sn) and v/t (h) (a. **sich** ~ fig. group) splinter off.

'Absprache f (-; -n) arrangement: **laut** ~ → **'absprachegemäß** adv as agreed.

'absprechen (*irr, sep*, -ge-, h, → **sprechen**) **I** v/t **1.** **j-m et.** ~ dispute (*or* deny) s.o.'s talent etc; ⚖ **j-m ein Recht** ~ deprive s.o. of a right. **2.** agree (up)on, arrange. **II sich mit j-m** ~ agree with s.o. (**über** acc about).

'abspringen v/i (*irr, sep*, -ge-, sn, → **springen**) **1.** jump off, sports: a. take off, ✈ jump, bail out, varnish etc: come off, ball etc: bounce off. **2.** F fig. quit, get (*or* back) out (**von** of).

'abspritzen v/t (*sep*, -ge-, h) hose down. **'Absprung** m (-[e]s, ⁛e) jump, sports: take-off. **~balken** m take-off board.

'abspulen v/t (*sep*, -ge-, h) unreel.

'abspülen v/t (*sep*, -ge-, h) rinse (off).

'abstammen v/i (*sep*, no pp) (**von** from) be descended, ling. be derived.

'Abstammung f (-; no pl) **1.** descent, origin: **deutscher** ~ of German extraction. **2.** ling. derivation. **'Abstammungslehre** f theory of evolution.

'Abstand m (-[e]s; ⁛e) **1.** distance (a. fig.), space, a. time: interval, fig. gap, difference: **mit** ~ a) **besser** far better, b) **gewinnen** win by a wide margin; **in regelmäßigen Abständen** at regular intervals; fig. ~ **halten** (*or* **wahren**) keep one's distance; **von et.** ~ **nehmen** refrain from (doing) s.th. **2.** → **'Abstandssumme** f indemnity.

abstatten ['apʃtatən] v/t (*sep*, -ge-, h) **j-m e-n Besuch** ~ pay s.o. a visit; → **Dank.**

'abstauben (*sep*, -ge-, h) **I** v/t **1.** dust. **2.** F swipe. **II** v/i **3.** soccer: tap the ball in.

'abstechen (*irr, sep*, -ge-, h, → **stechen**) **I** v/t stick (*pigs*). **II** v/i **von** stand out against (fig. from).

'Abstecher m (-s; -) a. fig. excursion.

'abstecken v/t (*sep*, -ge-, h) **1.** fit (*dress*

etc). **2.** mark out (*area, course, etc*), stake out, mark (*borders etc*). **3.** *fig.* define (*positions*).

'**abstehen** *v/i* (*irr, sep, -ge-,* h, → **stehen**) stick out.

Absteige ['apʃtaɪɡə] *f* (-; -n) F *contp.* dosshouse, *Am.* flophouse. '**absteigen** *v/i* (*irr, sep, -ge-,* sn, → **steigen**) **1.** climb down, get off (*a bike, horse*). **2.** (*in dat* at) stay, put up. **3.** *sports:* go down, be relegated. '**Absteiger** *m* (-s; -) *sports:* relegated team (*or* club).

'**abstellen** *v/t* (*sep, -ge-,* h) **1.** put down. **2.** leave (*bei* with), *mot.* park. **3.** turn (*adm.* cut) off (*gas etc*), stop (*machine*), switch off (*radio, engine, etc*). **4.** *fig.* remedy, stop (*grievances*). **5.** *fig.* (*auf acc*) gear (to), aim (at). **6.** → **abkommandieren**.

'**Abstell|fläche** *f mot.* parking space. **~gleis** *n* ⚐ siding: *fig.* **j-n aufs ~ schieben** shelve s.o. **~raum** *m* storeroom.

'**abstempeln** *v/t* (*sep, -ge-,* h) stamp (*a. fig.*), postmark.

'**absterben** *v/i* (*irr, sep, -ge-,* sn, → **sterben**) **1.** die (*a. fig.*), *toes etc:* go numb. **2.** F *mot.* stall.

Abstieg ['apʃtiːk] *m* (-[e]s; -e) **1.** descent, way down. **2.** *fig.* decline, comedown. **3.** *sports:* relegation.

'**abstillen** *v/t* (*sep, -ge-,* h) wean (*baby*).

'**abstimmen** (*sep, -ge-,* h) **I** *v/i* **1.** vote (*über acc* on): **über et. ~ lassen** put s.th. to the vote. **II** *v/t* **2.** (*auf acc*) tune (to), *a.* match *colo(u)rs* (with), *fig.* coordinate *interests* (with): **aufeinander ~** synchronize. **3.** ♪ balance (*accounts*). **III** *sich ~* come to an agreement (*mit* with). '**Abstimmung** *f* (-; -en) **1.** voting, vote (*über acc* on), poll: **die ~ ist geheim** voting is by ballot; **e-e ~ vornehmen** take a vote. **2.** tuning (*etc,* → **abstimmen** II).

abstinent [apstiˈnɛnt] *adj* abstinent, abstemious. **Abstinenz** [apstiˈnɛnts] *f* (-; *no pl*) abstinence.

Absti'nenzler *m* (-s; -) teetotal(l)er.

'**Abstoß** *m* (-[e]s; ⸗e) *soccer:* goal kick.

'**abstoßen** (*sep, -ge-,* h, → **stoßen**) **I** *v/t* **1.** (*a. v/i*) push off (*boat etc*). **2.** knock, batter (*furniture*), scuff (*shoes*). **3.** shed (*skin, antlers*): → **Horn** 1. **4.** 🗡 reject (*tissue etc*). **5.** *phys.* repel. **6.** *fig.* get rid of. **7.** ♣ a) sell off, b) get out of

(*debt*). **8.** *fig.* repel, disgust. **II** *v/i* **9.** *soccer:* take a goal kick. '**abstoßend** *adj fig.* repulsive (*a. phys.*), repellent, revolting. '**Abstoßung** *f* (-; *no pl*) **1.** *phys., a. fig.* repulsion. **2.** 🗡 rejection.

'**abstottern** *v/t* (*sep, -ge-,* h) F *et.* **~** pay for s.th. in instal(l)ments.

abstrahieren [apstraˈhiːrən] *v/t, v/i* (h) abstract. **abstrakt** [apˈstrakt] *adj* abstract. **Abstraktion** [apstrakˈtsi̯oːn] *f* (-; -en) abstraction. **Abstraktum** [apˈstraktʊm] *n* (-s; -ta) abstract noun.

'**abstreifen** *v/t* (*sep, -ge-,* h) **1.** slip off. **2.** wipe (*shoes*). **3.** search, scour.

'**abstreiten** *v/t* (*irr, sep, -ge-,* h, → **streiten**) **1.** deny. **2.** → **absprechen** 1.

'**Abstrich** *m* (-[e]s; -e) **1.** (*an dat* in) cut, curtailment: *fig.* **~e machen müssen** have to lower one's sights. **2.** 🗡 (*e-n ~ machen* take a) smear (*from tonsils:* swab). **3.** downstroke, ♪ down-bow.

abstrus [apˈstruːs] *adj* abstruse.

'**abstufen** *v/t* (*sep, -ge-,* h) **1.** terrace. **2.** shade off. **3.** *fig.* grade, graduate. '**Abstufung** *f* (-; -en) **1.** shade. **2.** *fig.* gradation.

'**abstumpfen** (*sep, -ge-*) **I** *v/t* (h) *a. fig.* blunt, dull: *j-n* **~** make s.o. insensible. **II** *v/i* (sn) become blunt (*fig.* dulled, *person:* insensible); → **abgestumpft**.

Absturz *m* (-[e]s; ⸗e) **1.** plunge, ✈ crash. **2.** *fig.* downfall. '**abstürzen** *v/i* (*sep, -ge-,* sn) plunge (down), ✈ crash.

'**abstützen** *v/t* (*sep, -ge-,* h) ⟁ prop.

'**absuchen** *v/t* (*sep, -ge-,* h) (*nach* for) search all over, scour, comb (*area*), sweep, scan (*horizon, sky*).

absurd [apˈzʊrt] *adj* absurd. **Absurdität** [apzʊrdiˈtɛːt] *f* (-; -en) absurdity.

Abszeß [apsˈtsɛs] *m* (-sses; -sse) abscess.

Abszisse [apsˈtsɪsə] *f* (-; -n) ♣ abscissa.

Abt [apt] *m* (-[e]s; ⸗e) *eccl.* abbot.

'**abtasten** *v/t* (*sep, -ge-,* h) **1.** feel (*nach* for), 🗡 palpate: *fig.* **j-n** feel s.o. out, size s.o. up. **2.** 🗲, *TV* scan.

'**abtauchen** *v/i* (*sep, -ge-,* sn) **1.** dive under. **2.** F *fig.* go to earth.

'**abtauen** (*sep, -ge-*) **I** *v/t* (h) thaw (*ice*), defrost (*refrigerator*). **II** *v/i* (sn) thaw.

Abtei [apˈtaɪ] *f* (-; -en) *eccl.* abbey.

Abteil [apˈtaɪl] *n* (-[e]s; -e) compartment.

'**abteilen** *v/t* (*sep, -ge-,* h) divide, partition off. '**Abteilung** *f* (-; -en) division, partitioning.

Ab'teilung² f (-; -en) **1.** department, ✗ ward. **2.** ✗ detachment. **3.** sports: section, squad.

Ab'teilungsleiter(in f) m a) head of a department, b) floor manager(ess).

'abtippen v/t (sep, -ge-, h) F type (out).

Äbtissin [ɛp'tɪsɪn] f (-; -nen) abbess.

'abtöten v/t (sep, -ge-, h) kill, deaden.

'abtragen v/t (irr, sep, -ge-, h, → tragen) **1.** clear away, pull down (house), level (hill). **2.** (a. sich ~) wear out. **3.** pay off.

abträglich ['aptrɛ:klɪç] adj detrimental (dat to).

'abtrai,nieren v/t (sep, h) work off.

'Abtrans,port m (-[e]s; -e) transportation. **'abtranspor,tieren** v/t (sep, h) take away.

'abtreiben (irr, sep, -ge-, → treiben) I v/t (h) **1.** ✗ abort. II v/i **2.** (h) ✗ have an abortion. **3.** (sn) drift off (course).

'Abtreibung f (-; -en) ✗ (e-e ~ vornehmen lassen have an) abortion.

'abtrennen v/t (sep, -ge-, h) **1.** separate. **2.** detach. **3.** take off (sleeve etc). **4.** sever (limb).

'abtreten (irr, sep, -ge-, → treten) I v/t (h) **1.** (dat, an acc to) give up, ⚖ cede: j-m et. ~ a. let s.o. have s.th. **2.** wear (out) (carpet etc), wear down (heels etc). **3.** wipe off (mud, snow): F (sich) die Füße ~ wipe one's shoes. II v/i (sn) **4.** go off, thea. (make one's) exit (a. F fig.), government etc: resign. **5.** ✗ ~! dismiss! **'Abtretung** f (-; -en) (an acc to) ⚖ transfer, cession.

'abtrocknen v/t, v/i (sep, -ge-, h) dry: (Geschirr) ~ dry up.

'abtupfen v/t (sep, -ge-, h) dab.

'abverlangen v/t (sep, h) → abfordern.

'abwägen v/t (irr, sep, -ge-, h, → wägen) fig. weigh.

'abwählen v/t (sep, -ge-, h) **1.** j-n ~ vote s.o. out of office. **2.** ped. drop (subject).

'abwälzen v/t (sep, -ge-, h) (auf acc on[to]) shuffle off, offload: die Verantwortung auf j-n ~ shift the responsibility (F pass the buck) to s.o.

'abwandeln v/t (sep, -ge-, h) modify.

'abwandern v/i (sep, -ge-, sn) **1.** move (away), migrate, sports: leave (the club). **2.** † capital: be drained off.

'Abwanderung f (-; -en) migration, a. † exodus, of scientists: brain drain.

'Abwärme f (-; no pl) waste heat.

'abwarten (sep, -ge-, h) I v/t wait for: das bleibt abzuwarten that remains to be seen. II v/i wait (and see): F ~ (und Tee trinken)! (let's) wait and see!

abwärts ['apvɛrts] adv down, downward(s). **'abwärtsgehen** v/impers (irr, sep, -ge-, sn, → gehen) es geht abwärts mit s.o., s.th. is going downhill.

Abwärtstrend m downward trend.

'Abwasch m (-[e]s; no pl) **1.** washing-up: F das ist ein ~! that can be done in one go! **2.** dirty dishes. **'abwaschbar** adj washable. **'abwaschen** (irr, sep, -ge-, h, → waschen) I v/t wash off, wash up. II v/i do the dishes, do the washing-up.

'Abwaschwasser n dishwater.

'Abwasser n (-s; ⁻) waste water, sewage.

'Abwasserleitung f sewerage.

'abwechseln v/i (sep, -ge-, h) alternate, persons: (a. sich ~) a. take turns (bei in), rotate. **'abwechselnd** I adj alternating. II adv alternately, by turns.

'Abwechslung f (-; -en) change, diversion: ~ brauchen need a change; ~ bringen in (acc) vary, liven up; zur ~ for a change. **'abwechslungsreich** adj varied, life: eventful.

'Abweg m (-[e]s; -e) fig. auf ~e geraten go astray. **abwegig** ['apve:gɪç] adj **1.** wrong. **2.** absurd.

'Abwehr f (-; no pl) **1.** warding off, repulse (of attack etc). **2.** sports: a) defen/ce (Am. -se), b) goalkeeper: save. **3.** fig. refusal. **4.** (auf ~ stoßen meet with) resistance. **5.** F ✗ counterintelligence. **'abwehren** (sep, -ge-, h) I v/t **1.** a) beat back, repulse (attack), b) sports: block (shot, punch), c) fig. ward of (danger etc). **2.** fig. refuse (thanks). II v/i **3.** fig. refuse. **4.** sports: block, goalkeeper: save, soccer: clear.

'Abwehr|haltung f psych. defensiveness. **~kräfte** pl ✗ resistance. **~mecha,nismus** m defen/ce (Am. -se) mechanism. **~reakti,on** f defensive reaction (gegen to). **~spieler(in** f) m sports: defender, *pl* defen/ce (*Am.* -se). **~stoffe** *pl* 🐾 antibodies.

'**abweichen** *v/i* (*irr, sep,* -ge-, sn, → **weichen**) deviate (**vom Kurs** from the course), depart (**von der Regel** from the rule): (**voneinander**) ~ differ, vary; **vom Thema** ~ digress from the subject.

'**abweichend** *adj* divergent: (**voneinander**) ~ differing, varying.

'**Abweichler** *m* (-s; -) *pol.* deviationist.

'**Abweichung** *f* (-; -en) **1.** difference. **2.** (**von** from) deviation, digression, departure.

'**abweiden** *v/t* (*sep,* -ge-, h) crop.

'**abweisen** *v/t* (*irr, sep,* -ge-, h, → **weisen**) **1.** turn *s.o.* away, refuse to see: **schroff** ~ rebuff. **2.** reject, refuse, 🏛 dismiss. **3.** ✕ repulse. '**abweisend** *adj* unfriendly, cool. '**Abweisung** *f* (-; -en) rejection, refusal, 🏛 *etc* dismissal.

'**abwenden** *v/t* (*irr, sep,* -ge-, h, → **wenden**) turn away (*a.* **sich** ~), *a. fig.* avert, ward off: **sich** (**innerlich**) ~ **von** turn one's back on.

'**abwerben** *v/t* (*irr, sep,* -ge-, h, → **werben**) entice away.

'**abwerfen** *v/t* (*irr, sep,* -ge-, h, → **werfen**) **1.** throw off (*coat etc*). **2.** drop (*bombs*). **3.** throw (*rider*). **4.** shed (*skin, leaves, etc*). **5.** discard (*playing card*). **6.** *fig.* yield (*profit*), bear (*interest*).

'**abwerten** *v/t* (*sep,* -ge-, h) 🏛 devalue.

'**abwertend** *adj fig.* depreciative.

'**Abwertung** *f* (-; -en) **1.** 🏛 devaluation. **2.** *fig.* depreciation.

'**abwesend** *adj* **1.** absent, *pred* away, out, not in. **2.** *fig.* absent-minded, faraway (*look*). '**Abwesende** *m, f* (-n; -n) absentee: **die ~n** those absent.

'**Abwesenheit** *f* (-; *no pl*) **1.** (**durch** ~ **glänzen** be conspicuous by one's) absence. **2.** *fig.* absent-mindedness.

'**abwetzen** *v/t* (*sep,* -ge-, h) wear out.

'**abwickeln** *v/t* (*sep,* -ge-, h) **1.** unwind. **2.** 🏛 deal with, handle (*orders*), transact, settle (*business*), carry out (*or* through), conduct, 🏛 wind up.

'**Abwicklung** *f* (-; -en) 🏛 handling, settlement, 🏛 winding-up, *Am.* wind-up.

'**abwiegen** *v/t* (*sep,* -ge-, h, → **wiegen**) weigh out.

'**abwimmeln** *v/t* (*sep,* -ge-, h) F brush *s.o.* off.

'**abwinkeln** *v/t* (*sep,* -ge-, h) bend.

'**abwinken** (*sep,* -ge-, h) **I** *v/t mot. racing*: flag down. **II** *v/i* give a sign of refusal.

'**abwischen** *v/t* (*sep,* -ge-, h) a) wipe *s.th.* (clean), b) wipe *s.th.* off.

abwracken ['apvrakən] *v/t* (*sep,* -ge-, h) break up, scrap.

'**abwürgen** *v/t* (*sep,* -ge-, h) **1.** stall, kill (*engine*). **2.** *fig.* choke off (*discussion*).

'**abzahlen** *v/t* (*sep,* -ge-, h) a) pay off, b) pay by instal(l)ments.

'**abzählen** *v/t* (*sep,* -ge-, h) a) count, b) count out: F **das kann man sich an den Fingern** ~ that's not hard to guess.

'**Abzahlung** *f* (-; -en) a) payment by (*Am.* on) instal(l)ments, b) payment (in full), c) instal(l)ment: **auf** ~ on hire purchase, on the instal(l)ment plan.

'**abzapfen** *v/t* (*sep,* -ge-, h) tap, draw.

abzäunen ['aptsɔynən] *v/t* (*sep,* -ge-, h) fence off (*or* in).

'**Abzeichen** *n* (-s; -) badge, ✕ *a.* insignia, ✔ marking.

'**abzeichnen** (*sep,* -ge-, h) **I** *v/t* **1.** (**von** from) copy, draw. **2.** initial, sign. **II sich** ~ **3.** stand out (**gegen** against), show. **4.** *fig.* be emerging, be in the offing, *danger etc*: loom.

'**abziehen** (*irr, sep,* -ge-, → **ziehen**) **I** *v/t* (h) **1.** take off, pull off (*ring etc*). **2.** strip off (*skin, bedsheets*), strip (*bed*), skin (*rabbit, tomato, etc*). **3.** take out (*key*). **4.** (**von** from) **A** subtract, 🏛 deduct. **5.** make a copy (*or* copies) of, *phot.* print. **6.** whet, sharpen (*knife*), surface (*parquet*). **7.** ✕ withdraw. **8.** draw off, tap. **9.** F give, throw (*a party*): → **Schau** 2. **II** *v/i* (sn) **10.** move off, F *a.* go off, clear out (*or* off), *esp.* ✕ *a.* withdraw. **11.** *smoke*: escape. **12.** *storm*: pass.

'**abzielen** *v/i* (*sep,* -ge-, h) ~ **auf** (*acc*) aim at, be aimed at.

'**Abzug** *m* (-[e]s; ⸚e) **1.** *no pl esp.* ✕ withdrawal. **2.** ⚙ outlet, escape. **3.** copy, *phot.* print, *print.* proof. **4.** 🏛 a) deduction, b) discount: **nach** ~ **aller Kosten** all charges deducted; **vor** (**nach**) ~ **der Steuern** before (after) taxation. **5.** trigger (*of gun*). **abzüglich** ['aptsy:klıç] *prep* (*gen*) less, deducting.

'**abzugsfähig** *adj* deductible.

'**Abzugshaube** *f* cooker hood.

'**Abzugsrohr** *n* ⚙ offlet.

'**Abzweigdose** *f* 🔌 conduit box.

'**abzweigen** (*sep*, -ge-) **I** *v/i* (sn) branch off. **II** *v/t* (h) set aside.
'**Abzweigung** *f* (-; -en) turn-off.
Accessoires [aksɛ'sõaːr(s)] *pl* accessories.
Acetat [atse'taːt] *n* (-s; -e) 🜩 acetate.
ach [ax] *int* oh!: ~ *je!* oh dear!; ~ *komm!* come on!; ~ *nein?* you don't say so?; ~ *so!* oh, I see!; ~ *was!*, ~ *wo!* of course not!; ~ *und weh schreien* wail. **Ach:** F *mit* ~ *und Krach* by the skin of one's teeth; *mit* ~ *und Krach durch e-e Prüfung kommen* scrape through an exam.
Achat [a'xaːt] *m* (-[e]s; -e) *min.* agate.
Achillesferse [a'xɪles-] *f* (-; *no pl*) *fig.* Achilles' heel. **A'chillessehne** *f* *anat.* Achilles' tendon.
Achse ['aksə] *f* (-; -n) axis, *pl* axes, ⚙ axle: F *auf (der)* ~ *sein* be on the move.
Achsel ['aksəl] *f* (-; -n) shoulder: *die* ~ (*or mit den* ~*n*) *zucken* shrug one's shoulders. ~*höhle f* armpit. ~*zucken n* (-s) shrug (of one's shoulders).
'**Achsschenkel** *m* (-s; -) *mot.* stub axle, *Am.* steering knuckle.
'**Achsschenkelbolzen** *m* *mot.* kingpin.
acht [axt] *adj* eight: *in* ~ *Tagen* in a week('s time); *heute in* ~ *Tagen* today week; *vor* ~ *Tagen* a week ago; *alle* ~ *Tage* once a week.
Acht[1] *f* (-; -en) eight.
Acht[2] *f* (-; *no pl*) *hist.* outlawry.
Acht[3]: *außer* ♀ *lassen* disregard; *et. in* ♀ *nehmen* take care of s.th., watch s.th; *sich in* ♀ *nehmen vor* (*dat*) beware of.
'**achte** *adj* eighth: *am* ~*n Mai* on the eighth of May, on May the eighth.
'**Achteck** *n* (-[e]s; -e) A octagon.
Achtel ['axtəl] *n* (-s; -) eighth (part). ~*note f* ♪ quaver. ~*takt m* ♪ quaver time.
achten ['axtən] (h) *v/t* **1.** respect. **2.** observe (*laws*). **II** *v/i* ~ *auf* (*acc*) a) pay attention to, b) keep an eye on, c) be careful with, d) attach importance to; ~ *Sie darauf, daß ...* see to it that ...
ächten ['ɛçtən] *v/t* (h) *hist.* outlaw, *fig.* ostracize.
achtens ['axtəns] *adv* eighthly.
'**Achter** *m* (-s; -) *rowing:* eight. ~*bahn f* roller coaster. ~*deck n* ⚓ quarterdeck.
'**achtfach** *adj and adv* eightfold.
'**achtgeben** (*v/i* (*irr*, *sep*, -ge-, h, → *geben*) ~ *auf* (*acc*) → *achten* II a-c; *gib acht!* look out!, be careful!

'**acht'hundert** *adj* eight hundred.
achtjährig ['axtjɛːrɪç] *adj* **1.** eight-year-old. **2.** *period etc* of eight years.
'**achtlos** *adj* careless, thoughtless.
'**Achtlosigkeit** *f* (-; *no pl*) carelessness.
'**achtmal** *adv* eight times.
Acht'stundentag *m* eight-hour day.
'**achtstündig** [-ʃtʏndɪç] *adj* eight-hour.
'**achttägig** [-tɛːgɪç] *adj* lasting a week, a week's *trip etc*.
'**Achtung** *f* (-; *no pl*) **1.** (*vor* for) respect, esteem: *große* ~ *genießen* be highly regarded; *in j-s* ~ *steigen* rise in s.o.'s esteem; *sich* ~ *verschaffen* make o.s. respected; F *alle* ~*!* hats off! **2.** ~*!* look out!, *esp. adm. and* ✕ attention!, *on signboards:* danger!, caution!
'**Ächtung** *f* (-; -en) *hist.* outlawing, *fig.* ostracism.
'**Achtungserfolg** *m* succès d'estime.
'**achtungsvoll** *adj* respectful.
'**achtzehn** *adj* eighteen.
achtzig ['axtsɪç] *adj* eighty: F *auf* ~ *sein* be hopping mad. '**Achtzig** *f* (-; *no pl*) eighty: *er ist Mitte* (*der*) ~ he is in his mid-eighties. **achtziger** ['axttsɪgər] *adj* *die* ~ *Jahre* the eighties. '**Achtziger** *m* (-s; -), '**Achtzigerin** *f* (-; -nen) octogenarian, man (woman) in his (her) eighties. '**achtzigst** *adj* eightieth.
ächzen ['ɛçtsən] *v/i* (h) groan (*vor* with).
Acker ['akər] *m* (-s; ⸗) field, farmland. ~*bau m* (-[e]s; *no pl*) agriculture, farming. ~*land n* (-[e]s; *no pl*) farmland.
ackern ['akərn] *v/i* (h) **1.** plough, *Am.* plow. **2.** F slog away.
Acrylfarbe [a'kryːl-] *f* acrylic paint.
ad absurdum [at ap'zʊrdʊm] *et.* ~ *führen* reduce s.th. to absurdity.
ad acta [at 'akta] *fig. et.* ~ *legen* consider s.th. closed.
Adam ['aːdam] *m* (-s; *no pl*) *Bibl. and fig.* Adam: F *seit* ~*s Zeiten* from the beginning of time. '**Adam 'Riese:** F *humor.* *nach* ~ according to Cocker.
'**Adamsapfel** *m* *anat.* Adam's apple.
'**Adamsko̱stüm** *n* F *humor.* *im* ~ in one's birthday suit.
Adapter [a'daptər] *m* (-s; -) ⚡ adapter.
adäquat [adɛ'kvaːt] *adj* adequate.
addieren [a'diːrən] *v/t* (h) add (up).
Ad'dierma,schine *f* adding machine.
Addition [adi'tsi̯oːn] *f* (-; -en) addition.

ade [a'de:] *int* goodbye(e) (*a. fig.*).
Adel [a'da:l] *m* (-s; *no pl*) a) aristocracy, b) title: **von ~ sein** be of noble birth. **ad(e)lig** ['a:d(ə)lɪç] *adj* noble (*a. fig.*), titled. **Ad(e)lige** ['a:d(ə)lɪgə] *m, f* (-n; -n) aristocrat, nobleman (noblewoman): **die ~n** the nobility. **adeln** ['a:dəln] *v/t* (h) make *s.o.* a peer, *a. fig.* ennoble.
'Adelskrone *f* coronet.
'Adelsstand *m* (-[e]s; *no pl*) nobility: **in den ~ erheben** raise to the peerage.
Ader ['a:dər] *f* (-; -n) vein, *fig. a.* bent: **er hat e-e humoristische ~** he has a streak of humo(u)r.
'Aderlaß *m* (-sses; ·sse) 🩸, *a. fig.* bloodletting, bleeding.
ädern ['ɛ:dərn] *v/t* (h) vein.
Adjektiv ['atjɛkti:f] *n* (-s; -e) adjective. **adjektivisch** ['atjɛkti:vɪʃ] *adj* adjectival.
Adjutant [atju'tant *m* (-en; -en) ✕ adjutant.
Adler ['a:dlər] *m* (-s; -) eagle. **'Adlerauge** *n* eagle eye: *fig.* **~n haben** be eagle-eyed. **'Adlernase** *f* aquiline nose.
Admiral [atmi'ra:l] *m* (-s; -e) admiral. **Admiralität** [atmirali'tɛ:t] *f* (-; -en) admiralty. **Admi'ralstab** *m* naval staff.
adoptieren [adɔp'ti:rən] *v/t* (h) adopt. **Adoption** [adɔp'tsi̯o:n] *f* (-; -en) adoption. **Adop'tiveltern** *pl* adoptive parents. **Adop'tivkind** *n* adopted child.
Adrenalin [adrena'li:n] *n* (-s; *no pl*) 🔬, 💉 adrenalin(e).
Adreßbuch [a'drɛsbu:x] *n* directory.
Adresse [a'drɛsə] *f* (-; -n) address: 📮 **erste ~** first-class borrower; F *fig.* **bei j-m an die falsche ~ geraten** come to the wrong person.
A'dressenverzeichnis *n* mailing list.
adressieren [adrɛ'si:rən] *v/t* (h) (*an acc* to) address, direct: *falsch ~* misdirect.
adrett [a'drɛt] *adj* neat.
adsorbieren [atzɔr'bi:rən] *v/t* (h) 🔬 adsorb. **Adsorption** [atzɔrp'tsi̯o:n] *f* (-; -en) 🔬 adsorption.
Advent [at'vɛnt] *m* (-[e]s; *no pl*) Advent.
Ad'vents... Advent (*wreath, season, etc.*).
Adverb [at'vɛrp] *n* (-s; -bien [-bi̯ən]) adverb. **adverbial** [-'bi̯a:l] *adj* adverbial.
Aerobic [ɛ'ro:bɪk] *n* (-s; *no pl*) aerobics.
aerodynamisch [aerody'na:mɪʃ] *adj* aerodynamic.
Affäre [a'fɛ:rə] *f* (-; -n) affair: F *sich aus der ~ ziehen* get out of it.

Affe ['afə] *m* (-n; -n) monkey, ape: F (*blöder*) ~ twit; *eingebildeter* ~ conceited ass.
Affekt [a'fɛkt] *m* (-[e]s; -e) emotion: *im ~* in the heat of passion. **~handlung** *f* 🏛 act committed in the heat of passion.
affektiert [afɛk'ti:rt] *adj* affected.
Affek'tiertheit *f* (; *no pl*) affectation.
'affenartig *adj* apelike, simian.
'Affen|brotbaum *m* baobab. **~liebe** *f* F doting love. **~schande** *f* F crying shame. **~the‚ater** *n* F hell of a fuss. **~zahn** *m* F (*e-n ~ draufhaben* go at) breakneck speed.
affig ['afɪç] *adj* F silly, affected.
Äffin ['ɛfɪn] *f* (-; -nen) she-ape, she-monkey.
Afghane [af'ga:nə] *m* (-n; -n), **Af'ghanin** *f* (-; -nen), **af'ghanisch** *adj* Afghan. **Afghanistan** [af'ga:nɪsta:n] *n* (-s) Afghanistan.
Afrika ['a:frika] *n* (-s) Africa. **Afrikaner** [afri'ka:nər] *m* (-s; -), **Afri'kanerin** *f* (-; -nen), **afri'kanisch** *adj* African.
Afro-Look ['afrolʊk] *m* (-s; *no pl*) (*im ~* with an) Afro hairstyle.
After ['aftər] *m* (-s; -) *anat.* anus.
Agent [a'gɛnt] *m* (-en; -en), **A'gentin** *f* (-; -nen) agent.
Agentur [agɛn'tu:r] *f* (-; -en) agency.
Aggregat [agre'ga:t] *n* (-[e]s; -e) aggregate, ⚙ unit. **Aggre'gatzustand** *m* *phys.* aggregate (state).
Aggression [agrɛ'si̯o:n] *f* (-; -en) aggression. **aggressiv** [agrɛ'si:f] *adj* aggressive. **Aggressivität** [agrɛsivi'tɛ:t] *f* (-; *no pl*) aggressiveness. **Aggressor** [a'grɛsɔr] *m* (-s; -en [agrɛ'so:rən]) aggressor.
agieren [a'gi:rən] *v/i* (h) act.
Agitation [agita'tsi̯o:n] *f* (-; -en) political agitation. **Agitator** [agi'ta:tɔr] *m* (-s; -en [-ta'to:rən]) (political) agitator. **agitatorisch** [agita'to:rɪʃ] *adj* rabble-rousing. **agitieren** [agi'ti:rən] *v/i* (h) agitate.
Agonie [ago'ni:] *f* (-; -n) death throes.
Agrar... [a'gra:r-] agrarian, agricultural. **~erzeugnisse** *pl* agricultural produce. **~markt** *m* agricultural commodities market. **~poli‚tik** *f* agricultural policy.
Ägypten [ɛ'gʏptən] *n* (-s) Egypt.
Ägypter [ɛ'gʏptər] *m* (-s; -), **Ä'gypterin** *f* (-; -nen), **ä'gyptisch** *adj* Egyptian.

ah [a:] *int* oh!, ah! **äh** [ɛ:] *int* **1.** ugh! **2.** er!

aha [a'ha:] *int* aha!, I see!

A'ha-Erlebnis *n* aha-experience.

Ahle ['a:lə] *f* (-; -n) awl, pricker.

Ahn [a:n] *m* (-[e]s, -en; -en) ancestor.

ahnden ['a:ndən] *v/t* (h) punish.

ähneln ['ɛ:nəln] *v/i* (h) (*dat*) be (*or* look) like, resemble, take after *one's father*: **sich** (*or* **einander**) ~ be (*or* look) alike.

ahnen ['a:nən] *v/t* (h) **1.** foresee, have a presentiment (*or* foreboding) of. **2.** suspect, guess: **ohne zu ~, daß ...** without dreaming that ...; **wie konnte ich ~, daß ...** how was I to know that ...; **ich habe es geahnt!** I knew it!

'Ahnentafel *f* genealogical table.

ähnlich ['ɛ:nlɪç] *adj* similar (*dat* to): ~ **sein → ähneln**; F **das sieht ihm ~!** that's just like him!; **so et. Ähnliches** s.th. like that. **'Ähnlichkeit** *f* (-; -en) (*mit* to) likeness, resemblance, similarity: ~ **haben mit → ähneln.**

'Ahnung *f* (-; -en) presentiment, foreboding, misgiving, suspicion, F hunch: F **k-e ~!** no idea!; **er hat k-e (blasse) ~ davon** he doesn't know the first thing about it, he hasn't got a clue.

'ahnungslos *adj* **1.** unsuspecting. **2.** ignorant.

'ahnungsvoll *adj* full of misgivings.

Ahorn ['a:hɔrn] *m* (-s; -e) maple.

Ähre ['ɛ:rə] *f* (-; -n) ear: ~**n lesen** glean.

A-is ['a:ɪs] *n* (-; -) ♪ A sharp.

Akademie [akade'mi:] *f* (-; -n) academy.

Akademiker [aka'de:mikər] *m* (-s; -), **Aka'demikerin** *f* (-; -nen) university man (woman).

akademisch [aka'de:mɪʃ] *adj* academic: ~**e Bildung** university education.

Akazie [a'ka:tsiə] *f* (-; -n) acacia.

akklimatisieren [aklimati'zi:rən] *v/t* (h) (*a.* **sich ~**) *a. fig.* acclimatize. **Akklimati'sierung** *f* (-; -en) acclimatization.

Akkord¹ [a'kɔrt] *m* (-[e]s; -e) ♪ chord.

Ak'kord² *m* (*im ~ arbeiten* do) piecework. ~**arbeit** *f* → **Akkord²**. ~**arbeiter(in** *f*) *m* pieceworker.

Akkordeon [a'kɔrdeɔn] *n* (-s; -s) ♪ accordion.

Ak'kordlohn *m* piece wages.

akkreditieren [akredi'ti:rən] *v/t* (h) **1.** *pol.* accredit (*bei* to). **2.** ✝ open a credit for. **Akkreditiv** [akredi'ti:f] *n* (-s; -e) **1.**

pol. credentials. **2.** ✝ letter of credit (*abbr. L/C*): **j-m ein ~ eröffnen** open a credit in favo(u)r of s.o.

Akku ['aku] *m* (-s; -s) F, **Akkumulator** [akumu'la:tɔr] *m* (-s; -en [-la'to:rən]) accumulator.

Akkusativ ['akuzati:f] *m* (-s; -e) accusative (case). ~**ob,jekt** *n* direct object.

Akne ['aknə] *f* (-; -n) ♂ acne.

Akquisiteur [akvizi'tø:r] *m* (-s; -e) ✝ canvasser, agent.

Akribie [akri'bi:] *f* (-; *no pl*) meticulousness.

Akrobat [akro'ba:t] *m* (-en; -en), **Akro'batin** *f* (-; -nen) acrobat.

akro'batisch *adj* acrobatic.

Akt [akt] *m* (-[e]s; -e) **1.** *a. thea.* act. **2.** (sexual) act. **3.** *paint., phot.* nude.

Akte ['aktə] *f* (-; -n) *usu. pl* file, record: **e-e ~ anlegen** open a file (*über acc* on); **zu den ~n legen** file, *fig.* shelve.

'Akten|deckel *m* folder. ~**koffer** *m* attaché case. ⊇**kundig** *adj* on record. ~**mappe** *f* **1.** folder. **2.** → **Aktentasche.** ~**no,tiz** *f* note, memorandum, F memo. ~**ordner** *m* file. ~**schrank** *m* filing cabinet. ~**tasche** *f* briefcase. ~**wolf** *m* (paper) shredder. ~**zeichen** *n* file (*letter:* reference) number.

Akteur [ak'tø:r] *m* (-s; -e) *a. fig.* actor.

'Aktfoto *n* nude (photograph).

Aktie ['aktsiə] *f* (-; -n) share, *Am.* stock: ~**n besitzen** hold shares (*Am.* stock) (*gen in,* of); F **wie stehen die ~n?** how are things?

'Aktien|gesellschaft *f* joint-stock company, *Am.* (stock) corporation. ~**kapi-,tal** *n* share capital, (joint) stock. ~**mehrheit** *f* majority of stock: **die ~ besitzen** hold the controlling interest. ~**pa,ket** *n* block of shares.

Aktion [ak'tsio:n] *f* (-; -en) action, measure(s), ✝ campaign, drive: ~**en** activities; **in ~ treten** act.

Aktionär [aktsio'nɛ:r] *m* (-s; -e), **Aktio'närin** *f* (-; -nen) ✝ shareholder, *Am.* stockholder.

Akti'onsradius *m* range (of action).

aktiv [ak'ti:f] *adj* active, ✝ favo(u)rable (*balance*), ✗ regular: ~**es Wahlrecht** right to vote; ~**er Wortschatz** *a.* using vocabulary. **'Aktiv** *n* (-s; *rare* -e) *ling.* active voice. **Aktiva** [ak'ti:va] *pl* ✝ assets: ~ **und Passiva** assets and liabilities. **aktivieren** [akti'vi:rən] *v/t* (h) *a. fig.* activate.

Ak'tivposten *m* ✝, *a. fig.* asset.

Ak'tivurlaub *m* activity holiday.

'Aktmo,dell *n* nude model.

aktualisieren [aktŏali'zi:rən] *v/t* (h) make topical. **aktuell** [ak'tŏɛl] *adj* a) topical, current, present-day, b) modern, up(-)to(-)date: **~es Problem** acute (*or* immediate) problem; **~e Sendung** current-affairs program(me *Br.*).

Akupunkteur [akupʊŋk'tø:r] *m* (-s; -e) acupuncturist. **Akupunktur** [akupʊŋk'tu:r] *f* (-; -en) acupuncture.

Akustik [a'kʊstɪk] *f* (-; *no pl*) acoustics.

a'kustisch *adj* acoustic.

akut [a'ku:t] *adj* ♂ acute, *fig. a.* urgent.

Akzent [ak'tsɛnt] *m* (-[e]s; -e) accent: *fig.* **besonderen ~ legen auf** (*acc*) stress. **ak'zentfrei** *adj and adv* without an accent. **akzentuieren** [aktsɛntu'i:rən] *v/t* (h) accent, *esp. fig.* accentuate, stress.

Akzept [ak'tsɛpt] *n* (-[e]s; -e) acceptance.

akzeptabel [aktsɛp'ta:bəl] *adj* acceptable (**für** to). **Akzeptanz** [-'tants] *f* (-; *no pl*) *fig.* acceptance. **akzeptieren** [-'ti:rən] *v/t* (h) accept (*a.* ✝), agree to.

Alarm [a'larm] *m* (-[e]s; -e) (**blinder ~** false) alarm: *a. fig.* **~ schlagen** sound the alarm. **~anlage** *f* alarm (system).

A'larmbereitschaft *f* (**in ~** on the) alert.

alarmieren [alar'mi:rən] *v/t* (h) alarm (*a. fig.*), alert, call (*police*).

A'larm|si,gnal *n* alarm signal. **~stufe** *f* alert phase. **~zustand** *m* (-[e]s; *no pl*) (**in den ~ versetzen** put on the) alert.

Albanien [al'ba:nĭən] *n* (-s) Albania. **Al'baner** *m* (-s; -), **Al'banerin** *f* (-; -nen), **al'banisch** *adj* Albanian.

albern ['albərn] **I** *adj* silly. **II** *v/i* (h) fool around. **'Albernheit** *f* (-; -en) **1.** *no pl* silliness. **2.** silly remark.

Album ['albʊm] *n* (-s; Alben) album.

Alchimie [alçi'mi:] *f* (-; *no pl*) alchemy.

Alge ['algə] *f* (-; -n) alga, *pl* algae.

Algebra ['algəbra] *f* (-; *no pl*) algebra.

alge'braisch [-'bra:ɪʃ] *adj* algebraic(al).

Algerien [al'ge:rĭən] *n* (-s) Algeria. **Al'gerier** *m* (-s; -), **Al'gerierin** *f* (-; -nen), **al'gerisch** *adj* Algerian.

Alibi [a'li:bi] *n* (-s; -s) alibi.

'Alibifrau *f* token woman.

'Alibifunkti,on *f* cover-up function.

Alimente [ali'mɛntə] *pl* maintenance.

alkalisch [al'ka:lɪʃ] *adj* 🜔 alkaline.

Alkohol ['alkoho:l] *m* (-[e]s; -e) alcohol, liquor, drink. **~einfluß** *m* **unter ~** under the influence of alcohol. **2frei** *adj* non-alcoholic, soft *drink*. **~gehalt** *m* alcoholic content. **~genuß** *m* consumption of alcohol.

Alkoholiker [alko'ho:likər] *m* (-s;), **Alko'holikerin** *f* (-; -nen), **alko'holisch** *adj* alcoholic. **alkoholisieren** [alkoholi'zi:rən] *v/t* (h) alcoholize: **alkoholisiert** drunk. **Alkoholismus** [alkoho'lɪsmʊs] *m* (-; *no pl*) alcoholism.

'Alkohol|mißbrauch *m* excessive drinking. **~nachweis** *m* mot. alcohol test. **~schmuggel** *m* bootlegging. **~spiegel** *m* blood alcohol concentration. **2süchtig** *adj* addicted to alcohol. **~sünder(in** *f)* *m* F mot. drunken driver. **~vergiftung** *f* alcoholic poisoning.

all [al] *indef pron* a) all, b) every: **~e beide** both (of them); **wir ~e** all of us; **fast ~e** almost everyone; **~(e) und jeder** all and sundry; **~e Welt** all the world; **ohne ~en Zweifel** without any doubt; → **alle, alles, Fall** 2.

All *n* (-s; *no pl*) **1.** universe. **2.** (outer) space.

alle ['alə] *adj pred* F **1.** all gone, finished, *money:* all spent: **~ machen** finish. **2.** dead beat, bushed.

Allee [a'le:] *f* (-; -n) avenue.

Allegorie [alego'ri:] *f* (-; -n) allegory.

allein [a'laɪn] **I** *adj pred and adv* a) alone, *a.* by oneself, on one's own, *a.* in private, b) only: **ganz ~** all alone; **~ stehen** be unattached, be single; **einzig und ~** (simply and) solely; **du ~ bist schuld!** it's all your fault!; **(schon) ~ der Gedanke** the very (*or* mere) thought. **II** *conj* but, however.

Al'lein|erbe *m* sole heir. **~erbin** *f* sole heiress. **~erziehende** *m, f* (-n; -n) single parent (*or* father, mother). **~gang** *m* solo: **im ~** sports: solo, *fig. a.* single-handed. **~herrschaft** *f* autocracy. **~herrscher(in** *f)* *m* autocrat.

al'leinig *adj* only, sole, exclusive.

Al'lein|inhaber(in *f)* *m* sole owner. **2reisend** *adj* **~e Kinder** unaccompanied minors. **~schuld** *f* (-; *no pl*) sole responsibility. **~sein** *n* (-s; *no pl*) loneliness: **Angst vor dem ~** fear of being alone. **2stehend** *adj* single, *w.s.* unattached.

~stehende m, f (-n; -n) single. ~unterhalter(in f) m thea. solo entertainer. ~verdiener(in f) m sole earner. ~vertretung f (-; no pl) sole agency. ~vertrieb m (-s; no pl) den ~ haben für be the sole distributors of.

'alle'mal adv 1. always, every time: ein für ~ once and for all. 2. F easily.

'allen'falls adv 1. if need be. 2. possibly, perhaps. 3. at (the) most, at best.

'allent'halben adv everywhere.

aller... ['alər-] with sup very best, highest, etc, best, highest, etc of all.

'aller'dings [-'dɪŋs] adv 1. but, though, however. 2. F indeed, certainly.

'aller'erst adv zu ~ first of all.

Allergen [alɛr'ge:n] n (-s; -e) allergenic.

Allergie [alɛr'gi:] f (-; -n) allergy.

al'lergisch ['-] adj allergic (gegen to).

'aller'hand adj F quite a lot, a good deal: das ist ja ~! a) not bad!, b) that's a bit thick!

'Aller'heiligen n (-) All Saints' Day.

'aller'höchstens adv at the very most.

allerlei ['alər'lai] adj all kinds of.

'Aller'lei n (-s; no pl) medley.

'aller'letzt adj very latest.

'aller'liebst adj (very) lovely, sweet.

'Aller'seelen n (-) All Souls' Day.

'aller'seits adv F guten Morgen ~! good morning everybody!

'Aller'welts... ordinary, common.

'Aller'werteste m (-n; -n) F posterior.

'alles indef pron 1. all, everything, the lot: ~ in allem (taken) all in all; vor allem above all; er kann ~ he can do anything; auf ~ gefaßt sein be prepared for the worst; j-n über ~ lieben love s.o. more than anything; F um ~ in der Welt! for heaven's sake!; → Mädchen 2. 2. F everybody: ~ aussteigen! get out everybody, please!

'alle'samt adv F all (of them or us etc).

'all'gegenwärtig adj omnipresent.

'allge'mein I adj general: von ~em Interesse of general interest; auf ~en Wunsch by popular request; unter ~er Zustimmung by common consent; ~es Wahlrecht universal suffrage; ~e Wehrpflicht compulsory military service; im ~en → II adv generally, in general, on the whole: es ist ~ bekannt, daß it is a well-known fact that; ~ beliebt popular with everyone; ~ gespro-

chen generally speaking; es ist ~ üblich it is common usage.

'Allge'mein|befinden n general state of health. ~bildung f general education.

'allge'meingültig adj universally valid.

'Allge'meinheit f (-; no pl) (general) public.

'Allge'meinmedi‚zin f general medicine: Arzt für ~ general practitioner.

'allge'meinverständlich adj (easily) intelligible.

'Allge'mein|wissen n general knowledge. ~wohl n public welfare.

All'heilmittel n a. fig. cure-all.

Allianz [a'liants] f (-; -en) alliance.

Alligator [ali'ga:tɔr] m (-s; -en [-ga'to:rən]) alligator.

alliiert [ali'i:rt] adj allied: hist. die Alliierten the Allies.

'all'jährlich adj annual(ly adv), yearly, adv a. every year.

'Allmacht f (-; no pl) omnipotence.

all'mächtig adj omnipotent, almighty.

allmählich [al'mɛ:lɪç] adj gradual(ly adv), adv a. by degrees, slowly.

Allopathie [alopa'ti:] f (-; no pl) 🡒 allopathy.

'Allpar'teien... all-party ...

'Allrad... all-wheel (drive etc).

allseitig ['alzaitɪç] adj general, universal, allround: zur ~en Zufriedenheit to the satisfaction of everybody.

'allseits adv on (or from) all sides.

'Alltag m (-[e]s; no pl) everyday life: (grauer) ~ daily routine. all'täglich adj everyday, usual, ordinary, banal.

'alltags adv on workdays.

'Alltags... everyday (clothes etc).

Allüren [a'ly:rən] pl contp. affectation, airs (and graces).

'all'wissend adj omniscient.

'all'wöchentlich adj and adv weekly.

'allzu adv far too: nicht ~ spät not too late. ~'gut adv only too well. ~'sehr adv all too much. ~'viel adv too much: ~ ist ungesund enough is as good as a feast.

'Allzweck... all-purpose ...

Alm [alm] f (-; -en) alpine pasture, alp.

Almosen ['almo:zən] n (-s; -) alms, fig. contp. pittance, Am. handout.

'Almosenempfänger(in f) m pauper.

Alpen ['alpən] pl Alps. ~rose f Alpine rose. ~veilchen n cyclamen. ~vorland n (-[e]s; no pl) foothills of the Alps.

Alphabet [alfa'be:t] *n* (-[e]s; -e) alphabet. **alpha'betisch** *adj* alphabetical: ~ *ordnen* → **alphabetisieren** [-beti'zi:rən] *v/t* (h) arrange in alphabetical order.

alphanu'merisch *adj* alphanumeric.

alpin [al'pi:n] *adj* Alpine: → *Kombination* 5. **Alpinismus** [alpi'nɪsmʊs] *m* (-; *no pl*) alpinism. **Alpinist** [-'nɪst] *m* (-en; -en), **Alpi'nistin** *f* (-; -nen) alpinist.

'**Alptraum** *m a. fig.* nightmare.

als [als] *conj* **1.** a) as, *after comp:* than: *sobald ~ möglich* as soon as possible; *mehr ~ genug* more than enough, b) *negation:* but: *alles andere ~ hübsch* anything but pretty. **2.** as, in one's capacity of: ~ *Entschuldigung* as (or by way of) excuse; *er starb ~ Bettler* he died (as) a beggar; ~ *Mädchen hatte sie k-e Chance* being a girl she had no chance. **3.** ~ *ob* as if, as though. **4.** a) when, as, b) while: *damals, ~* at the time when; *gerade ~* just as.

also ['alzo] *conj* **1.** so, therefore. **2.** F then: ~ *gut!* very well (then)!; *na ~!* there you are!; *du kommst ~ nicht?* you're not coming then?

alt [alt] *adj* **1.** old, aged: ~ *werden* → *altern;* ~ *bist du?* how old are you?; *er ist zehn Jahre* ~ he is ten (years old); *ein zehn Jahre ~er Junge* a ten-year-old boy; *er ist (doppelt) so ~ wie ich* he is (twice) my age; *auf m-e ~en Tage* in my old age; *fig. das ~e Lied* the same old story; *humor. hier werde ich nicht ~* I won't be here much longer; → *älter, Hase.* **2.** old, ancient: *das ~e Rom* ancient Rome; *die ~en Sprachen* the classical languages. **3.** old, long-standing (*friendship etc*). **4.** old, former (*pupil etc*): *in ~en Zeiten* in former times; *es bleibt alles beim ~en* everything remains as it was (before). **5.** old, stale (*bread etc*), used, second--hand: → *Eisen.*

Alt *m* (-s; -e) *J* alto.

Altar [al'ta:r] *m* (-[e]s; ¨e) altar. ~**bild** *n,* ~**blatt** *n,* ~**gemälde** *n* altarpiece.

'**altbacken** *adj* **1.** stale. **2.** F *fig.* antiquated.

'**Altbau** *m* (-[e]s; -ten) old building.

'**Altbausa,nierung** *f* rehabilitation of old housing. '**Altbauwohnung** *f* flat (*Am.* apartment) in an old building.

'**altbe'kannt** *adj* well-known.

'**altbe'währt** *adj* well-tried.

'**altdeutsch** *adj* old German.

Alte[1] ['altə] *m* (-n; -n) old man: *die ~n* old people; F *der ~* a) (*father, husband*) the old man, b) the boss; *er ist wieder ganz der* ⚥ he is quite himself again.

'**Alte**[2] *f* (-n; -n) **1.** old woman: F *die ~* a) (*mother, wife*) the old lady, b) the boss. **2.** *zo.* mother.

'**alt'ehrwürdig** *adj* time-hono(u)red.

'**alt'eingesessen** *adj* old-established.

'**Alteisen** *n* scrap iron.

'**Altenheim** *n* old people's home. '**Altenpfleger(in** *f*) *m* geriatric nurse. '**Altenteil** *n sich aufs ~ zurückziehen* retire.

Alter ['altər] *n* (-s; *no pl*) **1.** a) age, b) (old) age: *im ~ von 20 Jahren* at the age of 20; *er ist in m-m ~* he is my age; *mittleren ~s* middle-aged. **2.** old people.

älter ['ɛltər] *adj* **1.** older, elder: *mein ~er Bruder* my elder brother; *er ist (3 Jahre) ~ als ich* he is my senior (by three years); *er sieht (10 Jahre) ~ aus als er ist* he looks (10 years) more than his age. **2.** elderly. **3.** 🎵 *♭♭* prior.

altern ['altərn] *v/i* (sn) grow old, age.

alternativ [altɛrna'ti:f] *adj,* **Alternative** [-'ti:və] *f* (-; -n) alternative.

'**Alterserscheinung** *f* sign of old age. ~**genosse** *m,* ~**genossin** *f* contemporary. ~**grenze** *f* age-limit: *flexible ~* flexible retirement age. ~**gründe** *pl aus ~n* for reasons of age. ~**gruppe** *f* age group. ~**heim** *n* old people's home. ~**klasse** *f esp. sports:* age group. ~**pyra,mide** *f sociol.* age pyramid. ~**rente** *f* old-age pension. ⚥**schwach** *adj* infirm, *a.* F *fig.* decrepit, rickety. ~**schwäche** *f* (-; *no pl*) infirmity (of old age): *an ~ sterben* die of old age. ~**unterschied** *m* age difference. ~**versorgung** *f* old-age pension (scheme).

'**Altertum** *n* (-[e]s; *no pl*) antiquity.

altertümlich ['altərty:mlɪç] *adj* **1.** ancient. **2.** antiquated.

ältest ['ɛltəst] *adj* **1.** oldest. **2.** eldest (*son etc*). '**Älteste** *m, f* (-n; -n) oldest, eldest: *mein ~r* my eldest son.

'**Altglas** *n* ⚙ used glass.

'**Altgriechisch** *n* Old Greek.

'**alt'hergebracht** *adj* traditional.

'**Althochdeutsch** *n* Old High German.

Altist [al'tɪst] *m* (-en; -en), **Al'tistin** *f* (-; -nen) *♪* alto(-singer).

'**altjüngferlich** adj old-maidish.
'**altklug** adj precocious.
'**Altlasten** pl old neglected deposits of toxic waste.
ältlich ['ɛltlɪç] adj elderly, oldish.
'**Altmateri,al** n ⊙ salvage.
'**Altmeister** m 1. sports: ex-champion. 2. fig. past master.
'**Altme,tall** n scrap metal.
'**altmodisch** adj old-fashioned.
'**Altöl** n ⊙ waste oil, used oil.
'**Altpa,pier** n ⊙ waste (or used) paper.
'**Altphilo,loge** m classical philologist.
altruistisch [altru'ɪstɪʃ] adj altruistic.
'**altsprachlich** adj classical.
'**Altstadt** f old town.
'**Altstimme** f ♪ alto (voice).
'**Altwarenhändler(in** f) m second-hand dealer.
Alt'weibersommer m Indian summer.
Alufolie ['a:lu-] f alumin(i)um foil.
Aluminium [alu'mi:niʊm] n (-s; no pl) aluminium, Am. aluminum.
am [am] (= an dem) prep 1. at the, on the, time: a. in the: ~ Fenster at the window; ~ Ufer on the shore; ~ 1. Mai (on) May 1st, (on) the first of May; ~ Anfang at the beginning; ~ Himmel in the sky; ~ Leben alive; ~ Morgen in the morning; ~ Wege by the wayside. 2. before sup er war ~ tapfersten he was (the) bravest; ~ besten best.
Amalgam [amal'ga:m] n (-s; -e) 🔧 amalgam. **amalgamieren** [amalga'mi:rən] v/t (h) a. fig. amalgamate.
Amateur [ama'tø:r] m (-s; -e) amateur (a. in cpds. boxer, sport, etc).
Amazone [ama'tso:nə] f (-; -n) Amazon.
Ambiente [am'biɛntə] n (-s; no pl) ambience.
Ambition [ambi'tsio:n] f (-; -en) ambition.
ambivalent [ambiva'lɛnt] adj ambivalent.
Amboß ['ambɔs] m (-sses; -sse) anvil.
ambulant [ambu'lant] adj 1. ambulant, (a. ~ behandelter Patient) outpatient: ~ behandelt werden receive outpatient treatment. 2. itinerant (trade etc).
Ambulanz [ambu'lants] f (-; -en) a) mot. ambulance, b) outpatients' department, c) first-aid room.
Ameise ['a:maizə] f (-; -n) ant.
'**Ameisen,bär** m anteater. **~haufen** m anthill. **~säure** f 🔧 formic acid.

amen ['a:mɛn] int amen: zu allem ja und ~ sagen agree (meekly) to everything.
Amerika [a'me:rika] n (-s) America. **Amerikaner** [ameri'ka:nər] m (-s; -), **Ameri'kanerin** f (-; -nen), **ameri'kanisch** adj American. **amerikanisieren** [amerikani'zi:rən] v/t (h) Americanize. **Amerikanismus** [amerika'nɪsmʊs] m (-; -men) ling. Americanism.
Amethyst [ame'tyst] m (-en; -en) min. amethyst.
Ami ['ami] m (-[s]; -[s]) F Yank.
Aminosäure [a'mi:no-] f 🔧 amino acid.
Amme ['amə] f (-; -n) (wet) nurse. '**Ammenmärchen** n contp. old wives' tale.
Ammer ['amər] f (-; -n) zo. bunting.
Ammoniak [amo'niak] n (-s; no pl) 🔧 ammonia.
Amnesie [amne'zi:] f (-; -n) 🔧 amnesia.
Amnestie [amnɛs'ti:] f (-; -n), **amne'stieren** [-'ti:rən] v/t (h) 🔧 amnesty.
Amöbe [a'mø:bə] f (-; -n) am(o)eba.
Amok ['a:mɔk]: ~ laufen (fahren) run (drive) amok. '**Amokfahrer** m mad driver. '**Amokläufer** m person running amok. '**Amokschütze** m mad gunman.
Amor ['a:mɔr] m (-s; no pl) Cupid.
amorph [a'mɔrf] adj amorphous.
Amortisation [amɔrtiza'tsio:n] f (-; -en) 🕆 amortization. **amortisieren** [amɔrti'zi:rən] v/t (h) amortize.
Ampel ['ampəl] f (-; -n) 1. hanging lamp. 2. traffic light(s).
Amperemeter [ampɛr'me:tər] n (-s; -) ⚡ ammeter. **Amperestunde** [am'pɛ:r-] f ⚡ ampere-hour.
Amphibien... [am'fi:biən-] amphibian.
Amphitheater [am'fi:teatər] n (-s; -) amphitheat/re (Am. -er).
Ampulle [am'pʊlə] f (-; -n) ampoule.
Amputation [amputa'tsio:n] f (-; -en) 🩺 amputation. **amputieren** [ampu'ti:rən] v/t (h) 🩺 amputate.
Ampu'tierte m, f (-n; -n) 🩺 amputee.
Amsel ['amzəl] f (-; -n) zo. blackbird.
Amt [amt] n (-[e]s; ⸚er) 1. a) post, office, b) (official) duty, function, c) task: von ~s wegen ex officio, officially; → antreten 1 etc. 2. office, agency, department. 3. teleph. exchange. **amtieren** [am'ti:rən] v/i (h) hold office: ~ als act (or officiate) as. **am'tierend** adj a) acting (mayor etc), b) reigning (champion etc). '**amtlich** adj official.

'**Amts|antritt** *m bei s-m etc* ~ upon his *etc* assuming office. **~arzt** *m* public-health officer. **~bereich** *m* competence. **~blatt** *n* official gazette. **~eid** *m* **den ~ ablegen** take the oath of office, be sworn in. **~enthebung** *f* removal from office, dismissal. **~führung** *f* administration (of [an] office). **~geheimnis** *n* a) official secret, b) official secrecy. **~gericht** *n lower district court.* **~geschäfte** *pl* official duties. **~gewalt** *f* (official) authority. **~handlung** *f* official act. **~mißbrauch** *m* abuse of (official) authority. **2müde** *adj* weary of one's office. **~peri,ode** *f* term (of office). **~schimmel** *m humor.* red tape. **~stunden** *pl* office hours. **~träger(in***f***)** *m* office holder. **~vorgänger(in** *f*) *m* predecessor (in office). **~vormund** *m* public guardian. **~zeichen** *n teleph.* dial(ling) tone. **~zeit** *f* term (of office).

Amulett [amu'let] *n* (-[e]s; -e) charm.

amüsant [amy'zant] *adj* amusing.

amüsieren [amy'zi:rən] (h) **I** *v/t* amuse, entertain. **II sich ~** a) amuse o.s., have a good time, b) (*über acc*) laugh (at), make fun (of).

an [an] **I** *prep* (*dat*) **1.** *time:* on: ~ **e-m kalten Tag** on a cold day. **2.** *place:* on, at, by, near, next to: ~ *der Themse* on the Thames; ~ *der Wand* on the wall; ~ *der Kreuzung* at the crossing; *alles ist ~ s-m Platz* everything is in its place; *Tür ~ Tür wohnen* live door to door; *fig. Kopf ~ Kopf* neck and neck; *er hat so et. ~ sich* there is s.th. about him; *es ist ~ ihm zu reden* it is up to him to speak; ~ *s-r Stelle* in his place. **3.** *by:* *j-n ~ der Hand führen* lead s.o. by the hand; *j-n ~ der Stimme erkennen* recognize s.o. from (*or* by) his voice. **4.** ~ (*und für*) *sich* in itself, as such. **II** *prep* (*acc*) **5.** to, for: *ein Brief ~ mich* a letter for me. **6.** at, against: ~ *die Tür klopfen* knock at the door. **III** *adv* **7.** *von ... ~* from ... (on *or* onward); *von heute ~* from today (on); *von nun ~* from now on, henceforth. **8.** F ~ - *aus* on - off; *das Licht ist ~* the light is on; *er hatte noch s-n Mantel ~* he still had his coat on. **9.** F ~ *die 100 Mark* about 100 marks.

Anabolikum [ana'bo:likʊm] *n* (-s; -ka) *♣* anabolic drug.

Anachronismus [anakro'nɪzmʊs] *m* (-; -men) anachronism.

anal [a'na:l] *adj ♣, psych.* anal.

Analgetikum [anal'ge:tikʊm] *n ♣* analgesic.

analog [ana'lo:k] *adj* analogous (*zu* to).

Ana'logrechner *m* analogue computer.

Analpabet [analfa'be:t] *m* (-en; -en), **Analpha'betin** *f* (-; -nen) illiterate (person). **Analpha'betentum** *n* (-s; *no pl*) illiteracy.

Analyse [ana'ly:zə] *f* (-; -n) analysis. **analysieren** [analy'zi:rən] *v/t* (h) analy/se (*Am.* -ze). **Analysis** [a'na:lyzɪs] *f* (-; *no pl*) analysis. **Analytiker** [ana'ly:tɪkər] *m* (-s; -), **Ana'lytikerin** *f* (-; -nen) *psych.* analyst. **ana'lytisch** *adj* analytic(al).

Anämie [anɛ'mi:] *f* (-; -n) *♣* an(a)emia. **Ananas** ['ananas] *f* (-; -[se]) pineapple.

Anarchie [anar'çi:] *f* (-; -n) anarchy.

Anarchismus [anar'çɪsmʊs] *m* (-; *no pl*) anarchism. **Anarchist** [-'çɪst] *m* (-en; -en), **Anar'chistin** *f* (-; -nen) anarchist. **anar'chistisch** *adj* anarchic(al).

Anästhesie [anɛste'zi:] *f* (-; -n) *♣* an(a)esthesia. **anästhesieren** [anɛste'zi:rən] *v/t* (h) *♣* an(a)esthetize. **Anästhe'sist** [-'zɪst] *m* (-en; -en), **Anästhe'sistin** *f* (-; -nen) *♣* an(a)esthetist.

Anatomie [anato'mi:] *f* (-; -n) **1.** anatomy. **2.** institute of anatomy. **anatomisch** [ana'to:mɪʃ] *adj* anatomical.

'**anbahnen** (*sep*, -ge-, h) **I** *v/t* a) pave the way for, b) open, begin (*talks etc*). **II sich ~** be developing.

anbändeln ['anbɛndəln] *v/i* (*sep*, -ge-, h) F *mit j-m ~* a) make up to s.o., b) pick a quarrel with s.o.

'**Anbau¹** *m* (-[e]s; *no pl*) *♫* cultivation.

'**Anbau²** *m* (-[e]s; -ten) Δ annex, extension. '**anbauen** *v/t* (*sep*, -ge-, h) **1.** cultivate, grow. **2.** (*an acc*) to build, add.

'**Anbau|fläche** *f ♫* a) arable land, b) area under cultivation. **~küche** *f* unit kitchen. **~möbel** *pl* sectional (*or* unit) furniture. **~schrank** *m* cupboard unit. **~wand** *f* wall unit.

'**anbehalten** *v/t* (*irr, sep,* h, → *behalten*) keep on (*coat etc*).

an'bei *adv* † enclosed: ~ *schicke ich Ihnen ...* I am enclosing ...

'**anbeißen** (*irr, sep,* -ge-, h, → *beißen*) **I**

v/t bite into. **II** *v/i* bite, *a. fig.* take the bait.

'**anbellen** *v/t* (*sep*, -ge-, h) *a. fig.* bark at.

anberaumen ['anbərauman] *v/t* (*sep*, h) fix, appoint.

'**anbeten** *v/t* (*sep*, -ge-, h) *a. fig.* worship, adore. '**Anbeter** *m* (-s; -) **1.** worship(p)er. **2.** admirer (*of a woman*).

'**Anbetracht**: *in ~* (*gen*) considering.

'**anbetteln** *v/t* (*sep*, -ge-, h) *j-n ~* beg s.o. (*um* for).

'**Anbetung** *f* (-; *no pl*) *a. fig.* worship, adoration.

anbiedern ['anbi:dərn] *sich ~* (*sep*, -ge-, h) *contp.* ingratiate o.s. (*bei* with).

'**anbieten** (*irr*, *sep*, -ge-, h, → **bieten**) **I** *v/t* offer. **II** *sich ~ person:* offer one's services, *opportunity:* present itself.

'**Anbieter** *m* (-s; -) ♯ (potential) seller.

'**anbinden** *v/t* (*irr*, *sep*, -ge-, h, → **binden**) (*an dat or acc* to) tie (up), bind, ♫ moor, *fig.* link: → **angebunden.**

'**Anblick** *m* (-[e]s; -e) sight.

'**anblicken** *v/t* (*sep*, -ge-, h) look at, glance at: *j-n finster ~* scowl at s.o.

'**anblinken** *v/t* (*sep*, -ge-, h) flash one's headlights at.

'**anbrechen** (*irr*, *sep*, -ge-, → **brechen**) **I** *v/t* (h) break into (*supplies*), start (on) (*can*, *pack*), open (*bottle*). **II** *v/i* (sn) begin, *a. fig.* dawn.

'**anbrennen** *v/i* (*irr*, *sep*, -ge-, sn, → **brennen**) (*a. ~ lassen*) burn: F *fig.* **er läßt nichts ~** he doesn't miss a trick.

'**anbringen** *v/t* (*irr*, *sep*, -ge-, h, → **bringen**) **1.** a) put up (*curtain*, *sign*, *etc*), b) (*an dat* to) fix, fasten. **2.** F bring (along). **3.** make (*a request*, *improvements*, *etc*), get in (*a remark etc*), display (*knowledge*), land (*a blow*): *Kritik ~* criticize; → **angebracht.**

'**Anbruch** *m* (-[e]s; *no pl*) beginning.

'**anbrüllen** *v/t* (*sep*, -ge-, h) bawl at.

Andacht ['andaxt] *f* (-; -en) *eccl.* a) devotion, b) prayers, c) (short) service.

andächtig ['andɛçtiç] *adj* **1.** devout, pious. **2.** a) rapt, attentive, b) solemn: *~ zuhören* listen with rapt attention.

'**andauern** *v/i* (*sep*, -ge-, h) continue, last, go on. '**andauernd** *adj* constant, continual, incessant: *er störte uns ~* he kept interrupting us.

'**Andenken** *n* (-s; -) **1.** *no pl* memory: *zum ~ an* (*acc*) in memory of. **2.** a) keepsake, b) souvenir (*an acc* of).

ander ['andər] **I** *adj* **1.** a) other, b) different: *ein ~es Buch* another book; *am ~en Tag* (on) the next day; *das ~e Geschlecht* the opposite sex; *er ist ein ganz ~er Mensch* he is a changed man; → **Ansicht** 1. **II** *indef pron* **2.** *ein ~er*, *e-e ~e* someone else; *die ~en* the others; *der eine oder ~e* someone or other; *kein ~er als* a) no one else (*or* none) but, b) no less than. **3.** *~es, andres* other things; *alles ~e* everything else; *alles ~e als* anything but, far from; *unter ~em* among other things; *eins nach dem ~en* one thing after the other; *das ist et. ganz ~es* that's a different thing altogether.

'**anderen falls** *adv* otherwise.

'**anderer seits** *adv* on the other hand.

andermal *adv* *ein ~* some other time.

ändern ['ɛndərn] **I** *v/t* (h) change, alter, vary: *sein Testament ~* alter one's will; *es läßt sich nicht ~* it can't be helped; *ich kann es nicht ~* I cannot help it; *das ändert nichts an der Tatsache, daß ...* that doesn't alter the fact that ... **II** *sich ~* alter, change; *die Zeiten ~ sich* times are changing.

'**anders** *adv* **1.** differently (*als* from): *~ werden* change; *~ als s-e Freunde* unlike his friends; *~ gesagt* in other words. **2.** *with pron* else: *jemand ~* somebody (*or* anybody) else; *niemand ~ als* nobody but he; *wer ~?* who else? '**andersartig** *adj* different. '**andersdenkend** *adj* thinking differently, *pol. a.* dissident. '**andersgläubig** *adj* of a different faith, heterodox. '**andersher um I** *adv* the other way round. **II** *adj* F gay, queer. '**anderswo** *adv*, '**anderswo hin** *adv* F elsewhere, somewhere else.

andert halb ['andərt-] *adj* one and a half: *~ Pfund* a pound and a half.

'**Änderung** *f* (-; -en) change, alteration.

'**Änderungsantrag** *m pol.* amendment.

'**ander weitig** [-'vaitiç] **I** *adj* **1.** other, further. **II** *adv* **2.** otherwise: *~ vergeben s.th.* to s.o. else. **3.** elsewhere.

'**andeuten** (*sep*, -ge-, h) **I** *v/t* **1.** a) hint at, suggest, intimate, b) indicate, mention *s.th.* briefly. *2. a. fig.* outline. **II** *sich ~* be in the offing. '**Andeutung** *f* (-; -en) hint, suggestion, insinuation.

'**andeutungsweise** *adv* ~ **zu verstehen geben** → **andeuten** 1 a.

'**Andrang** *m* (-[e]s; *no pl*) a) crush, press, b) rush, ♦ run (**auf** *acc* on).

'**andrehen** *v/t* (*sep*, -ge-, h) **1.** turn on, switch on (*light etc*). **2.** F *fig.* **j-m et.** ~ fob s.th. off on s.o.

'**androhen** *v/t* (*sep*, -ge-, h) **j-m et.** ~ threaten s.o with s.th.

'**Androhung** *f* (-; -en) threat.

'**anecken** *v/i* (*sep*, -ge-, sn) F **bei j-m** ~ give offen/ce (*Am.* -se) to s.o.

'**aneignen** *v/t* (*sep*, -ge-, h) **sich** ~ **1.** a) appropriate *s.th.* to o.s., take possession of, b) misappropriate, usurp. **2.** acquire (*knowledge*), adopt (*view etc*).

'**Aneignung** *f* (-; *no pl*) **1.** appropriation. **2.** acquisition.

anein'ander *adv* (to, of, *etc*) each other: ~ **denken** think of each other. ~**geraten** *v/i* (*irr*, *sep*, sn, → **geraten**) (*mit* with) a) clash, b) come to blows. ~**grenzen** *v/i* (*sep*, -ge-, h) border on each other. ~**reihen** *v/t* (*sep*, -ge-, h) line up, *fig.* string *words etc* together.

Anekdote [anɛk'do:tə] *f* (-; -n) anecdote.

'**anekeln** *v/t* (*sep*, -ge-, h) disgust, sicken: **es ekelt mich an** it makes me sick.

Anemone [ane'mo:nə] *f* (-; -n) anemone.

'**Anerbieten** *n* (-s; -) offer.

'**anerkannt** *adj* recognized, accepted.

'**anerkennen** *v/t* (*irr*, *sep*, h, → **erkennen**) a) acknowledge, recognize, b) appreciate, c) approve: *sports*: (**nicht**) ~ (dis)allow; ~**de Worte** appreciative words. '**anerkennenswert** *adj* commendable. '**Anerkennung** *f* (-; *no pl*) a) acknowledgement, recognition (*a. pol.*), b) appreciation, c) approval, ♦ acceptance (*of bill*): **in** ~ (*gen*) in recognition of; ~ **verdienen** deserve credit.

'**anerziehen** *v/t* (*irr*, *sep*, h, → **erziehen**) **j-m et.** ~ instil(l) s.th. into s.o.

'**anerzogen** *adj* acquired.

'**anfachen** *v/t* (*sep*, -ge-, h) **1.** fan. **2.** *fig.* kindle, stir up.

'**anfahren** (*irr*, *sep*, -ge-, → **fahren**) **I** *v/i* (sn) **1.** start (up). **II** *v/t* (h) **2.** deliver. **3.** ram, run into, hit. **4.** stop (♣ call) at. **5.** ⚙ start. **6.** F **j-n** ~ snap at s.o.

'**Anfahrt** *f* (-; -en) **1.** journey, ride. **2.** approach, drive(way). **3.** delivery.

'**Anfall** *m* (-[e]s; ⸚e) **1.** ⚕ attack, fit (*a. fig.*): *humor.* **in e-m** ~ **von Großzügig-**

keit in a fit (*or* burst) of generosity. **2.** ♦, ⚖ accrual (*of a dividend etc*).

'**anfallen** (*irr*, *sep*, -ge-, → **fallen**) **I** *v/t* (h) attack. **II** *v/i* (sn) result, *work etc*: come up, *costs etc*: arise, *profit etc*: accrue. '**anfällig** *adj* ~ **für** *a. fig.* susceptible (*or* prone) to. '**Anfälligkeit** *f* (-; *no pl*) proneness (**für** to), *w.s* delicacy.

'**Anfang** *m* (-[e]s; ⸚e) beginning, start: **am** ~, **im** ~, **zu** ~ ~ **anfangs**; **von** ~ **an** (right) from the beginning (*or* start); ~ **Mai** early in May; **den** ~ **machen** begin, lead off; **ein** ~ **ist gemacht** a start has been made; **noch in den Anfängen stecken** be still in its infancy.

'**anfangen** (*irr*, *sep*, -ge-, h, → **fangen**) **I** *v/t* a) begin, start, b) do: **ein neues Leben** ~ turn over a new leaf; **was soll ich bloß** ~? what on earth am I to do?; **er hat wieder angefangen zu rudern** he has taken up rowing again; **et. schlau** ~ set about s.th. cleverly; **mit ihm ist nichts anzufangen** he's hopeless. **II** *v/i* begin, start: **mit der Arbeit** ~ begin (*or* start) (to) work; **bei e-r Firma** ~ start work(ing) with a firm; **ich weiß nichts damit anzufangen** I don't know what to do with (*fig.* make of) it; **das fängt ja gut an!** that's a fine start; **du hast angefangen!** you started it!; **fängst du schon wieder an?** are you at it again? '**Anfänger** *m* (-s; -), '**Anfängerin** *f* (-; -nen) beginner.

'**Anfängerkurs(us)** *m* beginners' course.

anfänglich ['anfɛŋlɪç] **I** *adj* initial, original. **II** *adv* → '**anfangs** *adv* at first, at (*or* in) the beginning.

'**Anfangs|buchstabe** *m* initial letter: **großer** (**kleiner**) ~ capital (small) letter. ~**gehalt** *n* starting (*or* initial) salary. ~**gründe** *pl* rudiments. ~**kapi‚tal** *n* opening capital. ~**stadium** *n* initial stage. ~**zeit** *f* starting time.

'**anfassen** (*sep*, -ge-, h) **I** *v/t* **1.** seize, grab (**an** *dat* by), touch: **j-n** ~ take s.o. by the hand; *fig.* **zum** ♀ *politician etc* of the people, popular. **2.** *fig.* treat, handle, tackle (*problem etc*). **II** *v/i* (**mit**) ~ lend a hand, help.

'**anfauchen** *v/t* (*sep*, -ge-, h) *cat*: spit at: *fig.* **j-n** ~ snap at s.o.

anfechtbar ['anfɛçtba:r] *adj a.* ⚖ contestable. '**anfechten** *v/t* (*irr*, *sep*, -ge-, h, → **fechten**) contest (*a.* ⚖), appeal

from (*sentence*). '**Anfechtung** *f* (-; -en)
1. contesting, ⚖ appeal (*gen* from). **2.**
temptation.

anfeinden ['anfaɪndən] *v/t* (*sep*, -ge-, h)
be hostile to: *angefeindet werden*
meet with hostility. '**Anfeindung** *f* (-;
-en) hostility (*gen* to).

'**anfertigen** *v/t* (*sep*, -ge-, h) make, do,
✝, ⚙ manufacture, *pharm.* prepare:
ein Gutachten ~ deliver an expert
opinion (*über acc* on). '**Anfertigung** *f*
(-; -en) making *etc*, manufacture.

anfeuern *v/t* (*sep*, -ge-, h) a) encourage,
b) cheer (on), *Am.* F root for.

'**anflehen** *v/t* (*sep*, -ge-, h) implore.

'**anfliegen** (*irr, sep*, -ge-, → *fliegen*) I *v/t*
(h) a) fly to, b) land at. II *v/i* (sn)
approach: *angeflogen kommen* come
flying (along). '**Anflug** *m* (-[e]s; ⸚e) **1.** ✈
approach: *im ~ sein auf* (*acc*) be approaching. **2.** *fig.* touch, trace, hint.
'**Anflugschneise** *f* ✈ approach lane.

'**anfordern** *v/t* (*sep*, -ge-, h) ask for, demand, request. '**Anforderung** *f* (-; -en)
1. (*gen* for) demand, request: *auf ~* on
request. **2.** *pl* demands, standard: *allen
~en genügen* meet all requirements,
fill the bill; *den ~en nicht genügen* not
to be up to standard; *hohe ~en stellen*
make high demands (*an acc* on), *task
etc*: *a.* be very exacting.

'**Anfrage** *f* (-; -n) inquiry, *a. parl.* question. '**anfragen** *v/i* (*sep*, -ge-, h) inquire
(*bei j-m wegen et.* of s.o. about s.th.).

anfreunden ['anfrɔʏndən] *sich ~* (*sep*,
-ge-, h) become friends; *sich mit j-m ~*
make friends with s.o.; *sich mit e-m
Gedanken etc ~* get to like the idea *etc*.

'**anfügen** *v/t* (*sep*, -ge-, h) **1.** add. **2.** enclose. **3.** ⚙ join, attach.

'**anfühlen** *v/t* (*sep*, -ge-, h) (*a. sich ~*) feel.

'**anführen** *v/t* (*sep*, -ge-, h) **1.** lead, be at
the head of, ✗ command. **2.** state,
mention, specify, give (*facts, reasons*),
produce (*evidence*), quote (*example,
book*): *zur Entschuldigung ~* plead as
an excuse). **3.** F dupe. '**Anführer** *m* (-s;
-), '**Anführerin** *f* (-; -nen) leader.
'**Anführungs|striche**, **~zeichen** *pl* quo-
tation marks, inverted commas.

'**Angabe** *f* (-; -n) **1.** statement, declaration, specification: *~n* information; *~n
zur Person* personal data; *nähere ~n
machen* give (further) details; *ohne ~*

von Gründen without giving reasons.
2. F showing-off. **3.** *tennis etc*: service.

'**angeben** (*irr, sep*, -ge-, h, → *geben*) I
v/t **1.** give, state, specify, fix (*deadline*),
name (*witness etc*). **2.** declare (*value
etc*), quote (*prices*). **3.** indicate (*direction etc*), set (*the pace*). II *v/i* **4.** F (*mit*)
show off ([with] *s.o., s.th.*), brag (about,
of). **5.** *cards*: deal first. **6.** *tennis etc*:
serve. '**Angeber** *m* (-s; -), '**Angeberin** *f*
(-; -nen) F show-off. **Angebe'rei** *f* (-;
-en) F showing-off. '**angeberisch** *adj* F
bragging.

angeblich ['angeːplɪç] *adj* alleged, *contp.*
would-be: *~ ist er ...* he is said to be ...

'**angeboren** *adj* innate, inborn (*both:
dat* in), ⚕ congenital, hereditary.

'**Angebot** *n* (-[e]s; -e) offer, *auction*: bid,
supply (*of goods*), ✝ tender, *Am.* bid: *~
und Nachfrage* supply and demand.

'**angebracht** I *pp of* **anbringen.** II *adj* a)
advisable, b) proper, appropriate: *es
für ~ halten zu gehen etc* see fit to go
etc; *nicht ~* inappropriate.

'**angebunden** I *pp of* **anbinden.** II *adj
fig. kurz ~* curt, short.

'**angegossen** *adj* F *wie ~ passen* (*or
sitzen*) fit like a glove.

'**angegriffen** I *pp of* **angreifen.** II *adj*
exhausted, weakened, poor (*health*),
affected (*organ*), strained (*nerves*).

'**angehaucht** I *pp of* **anhauchen.** II *adj fig.
er ist kommunistisch ~* he has
Communist leanings.

'**angeheiratet** *adj* (related) by marriage:
~er Vetter cousin by marriage.

'**angeheitert** *adj* (a bit) tipsy, merry.

'**angehen** (*irr, sep*, -ge-, → *gehen*) I *v/i*
(sn) **1.** F begin, start. **2.** *light etc*: go on,
fire etc: (begin to) burn. **3.** *plant etc*:
take root. **4.** *~ gegen* fight against. II
v/t **5.** (h) attack, *fig.* tackle (*problem*). **6.**
(sn) *fig.* concern: *das geht dich nichts
an!* that's none of your business!; *was
geht mich das an?* what's that got to
do with me? **7.** (sn) F *j-n um et. ~* ask
s.o. for s.th. III *v/impers* (sn) **8.** *es geht
an* it's passable; *es kann nicht ~, daß ...*
it can't be true that ...

'**angehend** *adj* future, budding.

'**angehören** *v/i* (*sep*, h) (*dat*) belong (to)
(*a. fig.*), be a member (of).

'**Angehörige** *m, f* (-n; -n) **1.** relative,

dependant: *die nächsten ~n* the next of kin; *m-e ~n* my family. **2.** member.

Angeklagte ['angəkla:ktə] *m*, *f* (-n; -n) 🗲🗲 defendant.

Angel[1] ['aŋəl] *f* (-; -n) hinge: *a. fig. aus den ~n heben* unhinge; *zwischen Tür und ~* a) in passing, b) in a hurry.

Angel[2] *f* (-; -n) fishing rod.

Angelegenheit *f* (-; -en) affair, matter: *das ist m-e ~* that's my business; *kümmere dich um d-e ~en!* mind your own business!

angelehnt ['angəle:nt] *adj* ajar.

angelernt I *pp of* **anlernen. II** *adj* semi-skilled (*worker*).

Angelgerät *n* fishing tackle.

Angelhaken *m* fish(ing) hook.

angeln ['aŋəln] **I** *v/i* (h) (*nach* for) fish, angle. **II** *v/t* (h) (*a.* F *fig. sich ~*) hook.

Angelpunkt *m fig.* pivot, central issue.

Angelrute *f* fishing rod.

Angelsachse *m*, **Angelsächsin** *f*, **angelsächsisch** *adj* Anglo-Saxon.

Angelschein *m* fishing permit.

Angelschnur *f* fishing line.

angemessen *adj* suitable, adequate (*both: dat* to), reasonable, fair (*price*).

angenehm *adj* (*dat* to) pleasant, agreeable: → *verbinden* 2.

angenommen I *pp of* **annehmen. II** *adj* adopted, *a.* assumed (*name*). **III** *conj* suppose, supposing.

angepaßt I *pp of* **anpassen. II** *adj psych.* adjusted.

angeregt I *pp of* **anregen. II** *adj* lively.

angeschlagen I *pp of* **anschlagen. II** *adj* **1.** chipped. **2.** *boxing:* groggy. **3.** shaken, shaky, weakened (*health etc*).

angeschlossen I *pp of* **anschließen. II** *adj* 🗲 linked-up, connected.

angeschmutzt *adj* soiled.

angesehen I *pp of* **ansehen. II** *adj* respected, reputable.

Angesicht *n* (-[e]s; -er) face: *von ~ by* sight; *von ~ zu ~* face to face; *im ~ (gen)* → *angesichts* 2. **'angesichts** *prep* (*gen*) **1.** at the sight of. **2.** *fig.* in view of.

angespannt I *pp of* **anspannen. II** *adj fig.* tense, strained (*nerves etc*).

Angestellte ['angəʃtɛltə] *m*, *f* (-n; -n) (salaried) employee: *die ~n a.* the staff. **'Angestelltenversicherung** *f* employees' insurance.

angestrengt ['angəʃtrɛŋt] **I** *pp of* **an-**strengen. **II** *adj* **1.** strained. **2.** close (*attention etc*): *~ nachdenken* think hard.

angetan I *pp of* **antun. II** *adj ~ sein von* be taken with.

angetrunken I *pp of* **antrinken. II** *adj* slightly drunk.

angewandt I *pp of* **anwenden. II** *adj* applied (*arts etc*).

angewiesen I *pp of* **anweisen. II** *adj ~ sein auf* (*acc*) depend on.

angewöhnen *v/t* (*sep*, h) *j-m et. ~* get s.o. used to s.th.; *sich et. ~* get into the habit of, take to *smoking etc*. **'Angewohnheit** *f* (-; -en) habit.

angewurzelt *adj wie ~ dastehen* stand rooted to the spot.

Angina [aŋ'gi:na] *f* (-; -nen) 🗲 tonsil(l)itis: *~ pectoris* angina (pectoris).

angleichen *v/t* (*irr*, *sep*, -ge-, h, → *gleichen*) (*a. sich ~*) (*dat*, *an acc* to) adapt, adjust. **'Angleichung** *f* (-; -en) (*an acc* to) adaptation, adjustment.

Angler ['aŋlər] *m* (-s; -) angler.

angliedern *v/t* (*sep*, -ge-, h) (*an acc* to) affiliate, *pol.* annex. **'Angliederung** *f* (-; -en) affiliation, *pol.* annexation.

Anglikaner [aŋli'ka:nər] *m* (-s; -), **Angli'kanerin** *f* (-; -nen), **angli'ka-nisch** *adj* Anglican.

Anglist [aŋ'glɪst] *m* (-en; -en), **An'glistin** *f* (-; -nen) professor (*or* student) of English. **Anglistik** [aŋ'glɪstɪk] *f* (-; *no pl*) English language and literature, *Am.* English philology. **Anglizismus** [aŋgli'tsɪsmʊs] *m* (-; -men) Anglicism.

Anglo... [aŋglo-] Anglo-...

anglotzen *v/t* (*sep*, -ge-, h) F stare at.

Angorawolle [aŋ'go:ra-] *f* angora wool.

angreifbar *adj* open to attack, *fig. a.* vulnerable. **'angreifen** (*irr*, *sep*, -ge-, h, → *greifen*) **I** *v/t* **1.** attack, 🗲 corrode: → *angegriffen* **II. 3.** break into (*supplies*). **4.** → *anpacken* **2. II** *v/i* attack. **'Angreifer** *m* (-s; -) attacker, *pol.* aggressor.

angrenzen *v/i* (*sep*, -ge-, h) *~ an* (*acc*) border on. **'angrenzend** *adj* adjacent, adjoining, *fig.* related (*subjects etc*).

Angriff *m* (-[e]s; -e) attack: 🗲🗲 *tätlicher ~* assault (and battery); *zum ~ übergehen* take the offensive; *fig. et. in ~ nehmen* tackle s.th.

'**Angriffs|fläche** f fig. point of attack: **e-e ~ bieten** be vulnerable to attack; **j-m e-e ~ bieten** give s.o. a handle. **~krieg** m war of aggression. **♀lustig** adj aggressive. **~spiel** n sports: attacking play. **~waffe** f offensive weapon.

'**angrinsen** v/t (sep, -ge-, h) grin at.

Angst [aŋst] f (-; ⸚e) fear, dread, terror (all: **vor** dat of), a. psych. anxiety (**um** about): (**nur**) **k-e ~!** don't be afraid!; **aus ~ lügen** lie out of fear; **aus ~, bestraft zu werden** for fear of being punished; **~ haben** be afraid (**vor** dat of); **um j-n ~ haben** be worried about s.o.; **j-n in ~ (und Schrecken) versetzen** frighten s.o. (to death); **es mit der ~ (zu tun) bekommen** get the wind up; **mir ist ♀ und bange** I'm scared stiff.

'**Angstgegner** m sports: bogy team.

'**Angsthase** m F scaredy-cat.

ängstigen ['ɛŋstɪɡən] v/t (h) a) frighten, alarm, b) worry: **sich ~** be afraid (**vor** dat of), be worried (**um** about).

'**Angstkäufe** [-kɔʏfə] pl panic buying.

ängstlich ['ɛŋstlɪç] adj timid, nervous, anxious: **~ gehütet** jealously guarded; **~ bemüht** anxious (**zu** to). '**Ängstlichkeit** f (-; no pl) nervousness, anxiety.

'**Angstneu,rose** f anxiety neurosis.

'**Angstschrei** m cry of fear.

'**Angstschweiß** m cold sweat.

'**angstvoll** adj anxious, fearful.

'**angucken** v/t (sep, -ge-, h) F look at.

'**anhaben** v/t (irr, sep, -ge-, h, → **haben**) **1.** F wear, have on. **2.** **j-m nichts ~ können** be unable to get at s.o.

'**anhaften** v/i (sep, -ge-, h) **1.** (dat to) stick, cling. **2.** fig. be inherent (dat in).

'**anhalten** (irr, sep, -ge-, h, → **halten**) **I** v/t **1.** stop: **den Atem ~** hold one's breath; **mit angehaltenem Atem** with bated breath. **2.** **j-n zu Fleiß** etc **~** urge s.o. to be diligent etc. **II** v/i **3.** stop, pull up. **4.** last, continue, go on, weather: hold. '**anhaltend** adj constant, persistent, sustained. '**Anhalter** m (-s; -), '**Anhalterin** f (-; -nen) F hitchhiker: **per Anhalter fahren** hitchhike.

'**Anhaltspunkt** m clue: **k-e ~e haben** have nothing to go by.

Anhang ['anhaŋ] m (-[e]s; ⸚e) **1.** a) appendix, b) supplement, c) annex. **2.** dependants, family. **3.** followers.

'**anhängen**[1] (sep, -ge-, h) **I** v/t **1.** hang

up. **2.** (an acc to) mot., 🚗 couple, fig. add. **3.** F **j-m et. ~** → **andrehen** 2; **j-m e-n Mord** etc **~** pin a murder etc on s.o. **II sich ~** (an acc to) hold on, cling; F fig. **sich ~ an** (acc) in a race etc: follow.

'**anhängen**[2] v/i (irr, sep, -ge-, h, → **hängen**[1]) follow (a fashion etc), believe in (an idea etc): **j-m ~ reputation** etc: cling to s.o. **Anhänger** ['anhɛŋər] m (-s; -) **1.** follower, supporter, disciple, fan. **2.** pendant. **3.** mot. trailer. **4.** tag, label. '**Anhängerin** f (-; -nen) → **Anhänger** 1. '**Anhängerschaft** f (-; no pl) followers, following, fans. **anhängig** ['anhɛŋɪç] adj esp. ⚖ pending: **e-e Klage ~ machen** institute legal proceedings (**gegen** against). **anhänglich** ['anhɛŋlɪç] adj **1.** devoted. **2.** affectionate. **Anhängsel** ['anhɛŋzəl] n (-s; -) a. fig. appendage.

'**anhauchen** v/t (sep, -ge-, h) **1.** breathe on. **2.** → **angehaucht** II.

'**anhauen** v/t (sep, -ge-, h) F **j-n ~** touch s.o. (**um** for).

'**anhäufen** v/t (sep, -ge-, h) (a. **sich ~**) accumulate, pile up. '**Anhäufung** f (-; -en) accumulation.

'**anheben** v/t (irr, sep, -ge-, h, → **heben**) lift (up), a. fig. raise.

'**anheften** v/t (sep, -ge-, h) (an acc to) a) fasten, b) tack, c) pin.

anheimelnd ['anhaiməlnd] adj hom(e)y, cosy, familiar.

anheimstellen [an'haim-] v/t (sep, -ge-, h) **es j-m ~** leave it to s.o.('s discretion).

'**anheizen** v/t (sep, -ge-, h) **1.** fire. **2.** F fig. fuel (strife), heat up (♣ boom): **die Stimmung ~** whip up emotions.

'**anheuern** v/t, v/i (sep, -ge-, h) sign on.

'**Anhieb:** F **auf ~ a)** at the first go, b) right off, off the cuff.

'**anhimmeln** v/t (sep, -ge-, h) F idolize.

'**Anhöhe** f (-; -n) rise, hill, elevation.

'**anhören** (sep, -ge-, h) **I** v/t listen to (a. **sich ~**), hear (witness etc): **mit ~** overhear; **j-n bis zu Ende ~** hear s.o. out; **das hört man ihm an!** you can tell by the way he talks! **II sich ~** sound; ⊢ **das hört sich gut an!** that sounds good!

'**Anhörung** f (-; -en) ⚖, parl. hearing.

Anilinfarbe [ani'li:n-] f anilin(e) dye.

animalisch [ani'ma:lɪʃ] adj animal.

Animateur [anima'tø:r] m (-s; -e) animator, entertainer.

Animierdame [ani'miːr-] *f* hostess.

animieren [ani'miːrən] *v/t* (h) **1.** encourage. **2.** *film*: animate.

Animosität [animozi'tɛːt] *f* (-; -en) animosity.

Anis [a'niːs] *m* (-[es]; -e) **1.** ♀ anise. **2.** aniseed. **3.** aniseed brandy.

'**ankämpfen** *v/i* (*sep*, -ge-, h) ~ *gegen* fight (*or* struggle) against.

'**Ankauf** *m* (-[e]s; ⁓e) buying, purchase.

'**ankaufen** *v/t* (*sep*, -ge-, h) purchase, buy.

Anker ['aŋkər] *m* (-s; -) ♣ anchor: *vor* ~ *gehen* drop anchor; *den* ~ *lichten* weigh anchor; *vor* ~ *liegen* ride at anchor. **2.** ⚡ armature. ~**kette** *f* cable.

ankern ['aŋkərn] *v/i* (h *a.*) (cast) anchor, b) ride at anchor.

'**Ankerplatz** *m* anchorage.

'**Ankerwinde** *f* windlass.

'**anketten** *v/t* (*sep*, -ge-, h) chain (*an acc* to).

'**Anklage** *f* (-; -n) accusation, charge, ⚖ *a.* indictment (*wegen* for): ~ *erheben* bring (*or* prefer) a charge (*wegen* of); *unter* ~ *stehen* (*wegen*) a) be accused (of), b) be on trial (for). '**Anklagebank** *f* (-; ⁓e) ⚖ (*auf der* ~ in the) dock.

'**anklagen** *v/t* (*sep*, -ge-, h) (*gen or wegen*) accuse (of), charge (with). '**anklagend** *adj* accusing. '**Ankläger** *m* (-s; -) ⚖ accuser: *öffentlicher* ~ Public Prosecutor. '**Anklageschrift** *f* (bill of) indictment. '**Anklagevertreter** *m* counsel for the prosecution.

'**anklammern** (*sep*, -ge-, h) (*an acc* to) **I** *v/t* peg (on), ◎ cramp. **II** *sich* ~ cling.

'**Anklang** *m* (-[e]s; ⁓e) **1.** reminiscence (*an acc* of). **2.** ~ *finden* (*bei*) be well received (by), go down well (with); *k-n* ~ *finden* fall flat.

'**ankleben** *v/t* (*sep*, -ge-, h) stick on (*an acc* to).

'**Ankleideka,bine** *f* cubicle. '**ankleiden** *v/t* (*sep*, -ge-, h) (*a. sich* ~) dress.

'**Ankleideraum** *m* dressing room.

'**anklopfen** *v/i* (*sep*, -ge-, h) knock (*an acc or dat* at).

'**anknabbern** *v/t* (*sep*, -ge-, h) nibble at.

'**anknipsen** *v/t* (*sep*, -ge-, h) F switch on.

'**anknüpfen** (*sep*, -ge-, h) **I** *v/t* **1.** (*an acc* to) tie, knot. **2.** *fig.* begin, start (*conversation etc*), establish (*contacts*). **II** *v/i* **3.** *fig.* ~ *an* (*acc or dat*) a) go on from, b)

go back to (*s.o.'s words etc*), c) pick up the thread of (*a story etc*), d) continue (*a tradition*). '**Anknüpfungspunkt** *m* *fig.* starting point.

'**ankommen** (*irr, sep*, -ge-, sn, → **kommen**) **I** *v/i* **1.** arrive (*in dat* at, in): ~ *in* (*dat*) *a.* reach; ~ *um train etc*: arrive at, be due at. **2.** F ~ (*bei* with) a) get a job, b) go down well, *a. person*: be a success; *nicht* ~ *a.* be a flop; *damit kommt er bei mir nicht an* that cuts no ice with me. **3.** ~ *gegen* cope (*or* deal) with, *j-n a.* get the better of s.o.; *nicht* ~ *gegen a.* be powerless against. **II** *v/impers* **4.** ~ *auf* (*acc*) depend on; *es kommt (ganz) darauf an* it (all) depends. **5.** ~ *auf* (*acc*) matter; *worauf es (ihm) ankommt, ist zu gewinnen* the important thing (to him) is to win; *darauf kommt es an* that's the point. **6.** *es auf et.* ~ *lassen* risk s.th.; *ich lasse es darauf* ~ I'll risk it, I'll take a chance. **7.** *es kommt mich hart an* I find it hard.

Ankömmling ['ankœmlɪŋ] *m* (-s; -e) arrival.

'**ankoppeln** *v/t* (*sep*, -ge-, h) (*an acc*) couple (to), dock *spacecraft* (with).

'**ankotzen** *v/t* (*sep*, -ge-, h) V *es kotzt e-n an* it makes you sick.

'**ankreiden** *v/t* (*sep*, -ge-, h) F *j-m et.* ~ blame s.o. for s.th.

'**ankreuzen** *v/t* (*sep*, -ge-, h) mark *s.th.* with a cross.

'**ankündigen** (*sep*, -ge-, h) **I** *v/t* announce, bill, advertise, *fig.* herald. **II** *sich* ~ announce one's visit (*fig.* itself).

'**Ankündigung** *f* (-; -en) announcement (*a. fig.*), advertisement.

Ankunft ['ankʊnft] *f* (-; *no pl*) arrival.

'**Ankunfts...** arrival (*airport, lounge, etc*).

'**Ankunftszeit** *f* time of arrival.

'**ankurbeln** *v/t* (*sep*, -ge-, h) *fig.* step up, boost.

'**anlächeln** *v/t* (*sep*, -ge-, h) smile at.

'**anlachen** *v/t* (*sep*, -ge-, h) smile (*or* laugh) at: F *sich j-n* ~ pick s.o. up.

'**Anlage** *f* (-; -n) **1.** *no pl* a) laying out, b) construction, c) arrangement, layout. **2.** installation, facility, (manufacturing) plant, work(s): *sanitäre* ~*n* sanitary facilities. **3.** a) (public) garden(s) (*or* park), grounds, b) sports facilities. **4.** F (hi-fi) set. **5.** draft, structure, design. **6.** (*zu* for) talent, gift. **7.** (*zu*) (natural) tendency (of), *a.* 🌶 disposition (to). **8.** ✝ investment: **~n** assets. **9.** enclosure: *in der* (*or als*) *~ sende ich Ihnen* enclosed please find.

'**anlagebedingt** *adj* inherent.

'**Anlage|berater(in** *f*) *m* investment consultant. **~kapi₁tal** *n* invested capital. **~pa₁piere** *pl* investment securities. **~vermögen** *n* fixed assets.

Anlaß ['anlas] *m* (-sses; -sse) **1.** occasion: *aus* ~ (*gen*) → *anläßlich.* **2.** cause, reason: ~ *geben zu* give rise to; *j-m ~ zur Klage geben* give s.o. cause to complain; *beim geringsten ~* at the slightest provocation; *ohne jeden ~* for no reason at all; *ich sehe k-n ~ zu gehen* I see no reason to go; *et. zum ~ nehmen* take occasion (*zu* to).

'**anlassen** (*irr*, *sep*, -ge-, h, → *lassen*) I *v/t* **1.** F → *anbehalten.* **2.** leave *the light*, *radio*, *etc* on. **3.** start (up) (*engine etc*). II *sich gut ~* shape up well, *business etc:* promise well; *wie läßt er sich an?* how is he making out?

Anlasser ['anlasər] *m* (-s; -) *mot.* starter.

anläßlich ['anlɛslɪç] *prep* (*gen*) on the occasion of.

'**anlasten** *v/t* (*sep*, -ge-, h) *j-m et. ~* blame s.o. for s.th.

'**Anlauf** *m* (-[e]s; ⁻e) **1.** *sports:* run-up, *ski jumping:* approach: (*e-n*) ~ *nehmen* take a run. *fig.* (*beim ersten ~* at the first) attempt: *e-n neuen ~ nehmen* have another go. **3.** *a.* ✪ start.

'**anlaufen** (*irr*, *sep*, -ge-, → *laufen*) I *v/i* (sn) **1.** *sports:* run up (for the jump). **2.** *angelaufen kommen* come running along. **3.** ~ *gegen* → *anrennen* 1. **4.** (*a.* ~ *lassen*) start (up). **5.** *fig.* start, get under way, *film:* be shown. **6.** *costs etc:* mount up, *interest etc:* accrue. **7.** *glass:* fog, *metal:* tarnish: *blau ~* go blue. II *v/t* (h) **8.** call at (*a port etc*).

'**Anlauf|schwierigkeiten** *pl* initial problems. **~stelle** *f* address (*or* office) to turn to. **~zeit** *f* initial period.

'**Anlaut** *m* (-[e]s; -e) *ling.* initial sound.

'**anlauten** *v/i* (*sep*, -ge-, h) *ling.* begin.

'**Anlegebrücke** *f* landing stage.

'**anlegen** (*sep*, -ge-, h) I *v/t* **1.** put on (*jewellery etc*). **2.** (*an acc*) put up *a ladder etc* (against); line up *a ruler etc* (against), lay down *a card etc* (next to): *e-n strengen Maßstab ~* apply a strict

standard; → *Hand.* **3.** lay out (*garden*), plan, design, construct, set up, instal(l). **4.** start (*a file*). **5.** get in (*supplies*). **6.** invest (*capital*), spend *a sum* (*für* on). **7.** *e-n Säugling ~* give a baby the breast. **8.** *die Ohren ~ dog etc:* set back its ears. **9.** put on (*coals etc*). **10.** apply (*bandage*). **11.** *es ~ auf* (*acc*) have set for (*or* to *inf*); *darauf angelegt sein zu inf* be designed to *inf.* II *v/i* **12.** land: *im Hafen* (*or am Kai*) ~ dock. **13.** (take) aim (*auf acc* at). III *sich mit j-m ~* tangle with s.o.

Anleger ['anle:gər] *m* (-s; -) ✝ investor.

'**Anlegestelle** *f* ⚓ landing place.

'**anlehnen** (*sep*, -ge-, h) I *v/t* **1.** lean (*an acc* against). **2.** leave ajar. II *sich ~ an* (*acc*) **3.** lean against. **4.** *fig.* be model(l)ed on.

'**Anlehnung** *f* (-; -en) dependence (*an acc* on): *in ~ an* (*acc*) following.

Anleihe ['anlaɪə] *f* (-; -n) ✝ loan: *e-e ~ bei j-m machen* borrow money from s.o., *fig.* borrow from s.o.

'**anleiten** *v/t* (*sep*, -ge-, h) **1.** guide, instruct. **2.** → *anhalten* 2.

'**Anleitung** *f* (-; -en) **1.** guidance, direction. **2.** directions, instructions.

'**anlernen** *v/t* (*sep*, -ge-, h) teach, train: → *angelernt* II.

Anlernling ['anlɛrnlɪŋ] *m* (-s; -e) trainee.

'**anliegen** *v/i* (*irr*, *sep*, -ge-, h, → *liegen*) **1.** *eng* ~ fit tightly, cling (*an dat* to). **2.** F *was liegt an?* what's on the agenda?

'**Anliegen** *n* (-s; -) **1.** request. **2.** matter, concern: *ein nationales ~* a matter of national concern.

'**anliegend** *adj* **1.** *eng* ~ tight(-fitting), clinging. **2.** adjacent. **3.** ✝ enclosed (*senden wir Ihnen* please find).

Anlieger ['anli:gər] *m* (-s; -) *mot.* resident: ~ *frei!* residents only! **~staat** *m* neighbo(u)ring (*on waters:* riparian) state. **~verkehr** *m* resident traffic.

'**anlocken** *v/t* (*sep*, -ge-, h) *fig.* attract.

'**anlügen** *v/t* (*irr*, *sep*, -ge-, h, → *lügen*) *j-n ~* lie to s.o.

'**anmachen** *v/t* (*sep*, -ge-, h) F **1.** fasten (*an dat* to). **2.** switch on (*light*), light (*fire*). **3.** *gastr.* prepare, dress. **4.** *j-n ~* a) give s.o. the come-on, b) snap at s.o., c) turn s.o. on.

'**anmalen** *v/t* (*sep*, -ge-, h) paint: F *sich ~* paint one's face.

'**Anmarsch** m (-[e]s; no pl) ✕ im ~ sein be advancing (auf acc towards).

anmaßen ['anma:sən] v/t (sep, -ge-, h) sich et. ~ arrogate s.th. to o.s., usurp s.th.; sich ~ zu inf presume to inf.

'**anmaßend** adj arrogant, overbearing. '**Anmaßung** f (-; -en) arrogance.

'**Anmeldeformu,lar** n application form. '**anmelden** (sep, -ge-, h) **I** v/t **1.** announce (visitor etc). **2.** j-n in der Schule (zu e-m Kursus etc) ~ enrol(l) s.o. at school (for a course etc); j-n beim Arzt ~ make an appointment for s.o. with the doctor; j-n polizeilich ~ register s.o. (with the police). **3.** teleph. book, Am. place: den Fernseher (das Radio) ~ get a television (radio) licen/ce (Am. -se). **4.** put forward (claims etc), raise (doubts etc): → Patent 1. **II** sich ~ **5.** announce o.s. **6.** enrol(l) (zu for, in dat at): sich beim Arzt etc ~ make an appointment with the doctor etc; sich polizeilich ~ register (with the police).

'**Anmeldung** f (-; -en) **1.** announcement. **2.** enrol(l)ment: (polizeiliche) ~ registration (with the police); nur nach vorheriger ~ by appointment only. **3.** reception (desk).

'**anmerken** v/t (sep, -ge-, h) **1.** a) mark, b) make s-e a note of. **2.** remark, observe. **3.** j-m s-e Verlegenheit etc ~ notice s.o.'s embarrassment etc; sich nichts ~ lassen not to show one's feelings; man merkte ihr sofort an, daß ... you only had to look at her to see that ...; laß dir nichts ~! don't let on!

'**Anmerkung** f (-; -en) (über acc on) remark, comment, (foot)note, annotation: mit ~en versehen annotate.

Anmut ['anmu:t] f (-; no pl) grace(fulness), charm, sweetness.

'**anmuten** v/t (sep, -ge-, h) j-n seltsam etc ~ strike s.o. as (being) odd etc.

'**anmutig** adj graceful, charming.

'**annageln** v/t (sep, -ge-, h) nail on (an acc to).

'**annähen** v/t (sep, -ge-, h) sew on (an acc to).

'**annähernd** **I** adj approximate. **II** adv (nicht ~ not) nearly. '**Annäherung** f (-; -en) approximation (a. fig.), pol. rapprochement. '**Annäherungsversuche** pl approaches, (amorous) advances.

Annahme ['ana:mə] f (-; -n) **1.** accept-

ance. **2.** adoption (of a child, motion, etc), passing (of a law). **3.** (in der ~ on the) assumption (daß that): ich habe Grund zu der ~, daß ... I have reasons to believe that ...; gehe ich recht in der ~, daß ...? am I right in thinking that ...? **4.** → ~stelle f receiving office. ~verweigerung f nonacceptance.

Annalen [a'na:lən] pl annals.

annehmbar ['ane:mba:r] adj a) acceptable (für by), a. reasonable, fair (price etc), b) passable. '**annehmen** (irr, sep, -ge-, h, → nehmen) **I** v/t **1.** accept (gift, letter, etc). **2.** adopt (child, name, title). **3.** parl. carry (a motion), pass (a bill). **4.** admit (students). **5.** assume (shape etc), take (on) (colo[u]r, smell, etc), acquire (habit etc). **6.** assume, suppose, guess: das ist nicht anzunehmen that's unlikely; ich nehme es an I suppose so; nehmen wir an (or angenommen), er stirbt suppose he dies. **II** sich j-s (e-r Sache) ~ take care of s.o. (s.th.).

'**Annehmlichkeit** f (-; -en) amenity: ~en des Lebens a. comforts of life.

annektieren [anɛk'ti:rən] v/t pol. annex.

Annonce [a'nõ:sə] f (-; -n) advertisement, F ad. **annoncieren** [anõ'si:rən] v/t, v/i (h) advertise.

annullieren [anʊ'li:rən] v/t (h) annul, ✝ cancel (order), sports: disallow (goal).

Anode [a'no:də] f (-; -n) ∮ anode, plate.

anöden ['anø:dən] v/t (sep, -ge-, h) F j-n ~ bore s.o. stiff.

anomal [ano'ma:l] adj anomalous.

Anomalie [anoma'li:] f (-; -n) anomaly.

anonym [ano'ny:m] adj anonymous.

Anonymität [anonymi'tɛ:t] f (-; no pl) anonymity.

Anorak ['anorak] m (-s; -s) anorak.

'**anordnen** v/t (sep, -ge-, h) **1.** arrange. **2.** order, direct.

'**Anordnung** f (-; -en) **1.** arrangement. **2.** order, direction: auf ~ von (or gen) by order of; ~en treffen give orders.

Anorexie [anorɛ'ksi:] f (-; no pl) ✻ anorexia (nervosa).

'**anor,ganisch** adj inorganic.

'**anormal** adj abnormal.

'**anpacken** (sep, -ge-, h) **I** v/t **1.** → packen 2. **2.** F fig. treat, tackle. **II** v/i ~ anfassen II.

'**anpassen** (sep, -ge-, h) **I** v/t **1.** fit (on). **2.** (dat or an acc) adapt (to), a. ✝, ⊙

47   **anschaffen**

adjust (to), *in colo[u]r:* match (with). **II sich ~** (*dat or an acc* to) adapt (o.s.), adjust (o.s.): → **angepaßt.**
'Anpassung *f* (-; -en) (*an acc* to) adaptation, adjustment. **'anpassungsfähig** *adj* adaptable (*an acc* to). **'Anpassungsfähigkeit** *f* (-; *no pl*) adaptability. **'Anpassungsschwierigkeiten** *pl* difficulties in adapting.
'anpeilen *v/t* (*sep*, -ge-, h) **1.** ✈, ⚓ take a bearing of. **2.** *fig.* aim at.
'anpfeifen *v/t* (*irr, sep*, -ge-, h, → *pfeifen*) **1.** *sports:* **ein Spiel ~** give the starting whistle. **2.** F *j-n ~* blow s.o. up.
'Anpfiff *m* (-[e]s; -e) **1.** *sports:* (starting) whistle. **2.** F *e-n ~ kriegen* get ticked off.
'anpflanzen *v/t* (*sep*, -ge-, h) **1.** plant. **2.** cultivate, grow.
'anpöbeln *v/t* (*sep*, -ge-, h) molest, mob.
'Anprall *m* (-[e]s; *no pl*) impact (*gegen* [up]on).
anprangern ['anpraŋərn] *v/t* (*sep*, -ge-, h) denounce.
'anpreisen *v/t* (*irr, sep*, -ge-, h, → *preisen*) praise, F plug.
'Anprobe *f* (-; -n) (*zur ~* for a) fitting.
'anpro,bieren *v/t, v/i* (h) try on, fit on.
'anpumpen *v/t* (*sep*, -ge-, h) F *j-n ~* touch s.o. (*um* for).
'Anraten *n:* **auf ~ des Arztes** *etc* on the doctor's *etc* advice.
'anrechnen *v/t* (*sep*, -ge-, h) a) charge, b) credit, allow, c) take into account, d) deduct: *ped. et. als Fehler ~* count s.th. as a mistake; *fig. j-m et. als Verdienst ~* give s.o. credit for s.th.; *j-m et. hoch ~* think highly of s.o. for s.th.
'Anrecht *n* (-[e]s; -e) (*auf acc* to) right, claim.
'Anrede *f* (-; -n) address. **'anreden** *v/t* (*sep*, -ge-, h) *j-n ~* address s.o.
'anregen *v/t* (*sep*, -ge-, h) **1.** stimulate (*a. v/i*), whet (*appetite*), *fig. a.* encourage: *j-n zum Nachdenken ~* give s.o. food for thought. **2.** suggest. **'anregend** *adj* stimulating: **~ wirken** have a stimulating effect. **'Anregung** *f* (-; -en) **1.** *no pl* stimulation, *fig. a.* encouragement. **2.** suggestion: *auf ~ von* (*or gen*) at the suggestion of.
'anreichern (*sep*, -ge-, h) **I** *v/t* 🏭, ⚙ enrich. **II sich ~** accumulate.
'Anreise *f* (-; -n) **1.** journey there (*or*

here). **2.** arrival. **'anreisen** *v/i* (*sep*, -ge-, sn) **1.** travel. **2.** arrive.
'anreißen *v/t* (*irr, sep*, -ge-, h, → *reißen*) **1.** F → **anbrechen** I. **2.** *fig.* raise.
'Anreiz *m* (-es; -e) incentive.
'anrennen *v/i* (*irr, sep*, -ge-, sn, → *rennen*) **1.** **~ gegen** run against, ✗ attack. **2.** *angerannt kommen* come running (up).
'Anrichte *f* (-; -n) sideboard.
'anrichten *v/t* (*sep*, -ge-, h) **1.** *gastr.* prepare, dress: **es ist angerichtet!** dinner *etc* is served! **2.** *fig.* cause (*disaster etc*), do (*damage*).
anrüchig ['anrʏçɪç] *adj* disreputable, dubious, F shady.
'anrücken *v/i* (*sep*, -ge-, sn) approach, ✗ advance, F turn up, come.
'Anruf *m* (-[e]s; -e) call. **Anrufbeantworter** *m* (telephone) answering machine.
'anrufen (*irr, sep*, -ge-, h, → *rufen*) **I** *v/t j-n ~* a) call s.o., b) *teleph.* call (*or* ring) s.o. (up), c) *fig.* appeal to s.o. (*um Hilfe etc* for help *etc*); **ein Gericht ~** appeal to a court. **II** *v/i* make a (phone)call: *bei j-m ~* → **I** b.
'anrühren *v/t* (*sep*, -ge-, h) **1.** touch (*a. fig.*). **2.** mix.
ans = *an das:* → *Herz, Licht etc.*
Ansage ['anzaːgə] *f* **1.** *radio, TV* announcement. **2.** *cards:* bid(ding).
'ansagen *v/t, v/i* (*sep*, -ge-, h) **1.** announce, *cards:* bid: **Trumpf ~** declare trumps; F **Sparen ist angesagt!** saving is the word!; → *Kampf* 1. **'Ansager** *m* (-s; -), **'Ansagerin** *f* (-; -nen) announcer.
'ansammeln *v/t* (*sep*, -ge-, h) a) (*a. sich ~*) collect, gather, assemble, b) accumulate, amass. **'Ansammlung** *f* (-; -en) **1.** accumulation. **2.** gathering, crowd.
ansässig ['anzɛsɪç] *adj* resident (*in dat* at, in): **~ werden** take up (one's) residence, settle.
'Ansatz *m* (-es; ⁀e) **1.** ⚙ deposit, crust. **2.** *anat.* base: → *Haaransatz.* **3.** *fig.* a) first sign(s), b) attempt, c) approach: *im ~ richtig* basically right; *gute (gewisse) Ansätze zeigen* show good (some) promise; *in den Ansätzen stekkenbleiben* get stuck at the beginning. **4.** ⚮ statement. **5.** ♱ estimate.
'Ansatzpunkt *m fig.* point of departure.
'ansaugen *v/t* (*sep*, -ge-, h) suck in.
'anschaffen *v/t* (*sep*, -ge-, h) buy: F *sich*

Kinder ~ have children. **'Anschaffung** *f* (-; -en) **1.** buying, purchase. **2.** acquisition. **'Anschaffungskosten** *pl* purchase cost.

'anschalten *v/t* (*sep*, -ge-, h) switch on.

'anschauen *v/t* (*sep*, -ge-, h) → **ansehen. anschaulich** ['anʃaʊlɪç] *adj* clear, vivid, graphic. **'Anschauung** *f* (-, -en) view, opinion, idea.

'Anschauungs|materi,al *n* illustrative material, *n.s.* audiovisual aids. **~unterricht** *m* **1.** object-teaching, visual instruction. **2.** *fig.* object-lesson.

'Anschein *m* (-[e]s; *no pl*) appearance: *allem ~ nach* to all appearances; *den ~ erwecken* give the impression; *sich den ~ geben* pretend, make believe; *es hat den ~, als ob* it looks as if.

'anscheinend *adj* apparent: *er ist ~ krank* he seems to be ill.

'anschicken: sich ~ (*sep*, -ge-, h) get ready (*or* be going) (**zu** to).

'anschieben *v/t* (*irr*, *sep*, -ge-, h, → **schieben**) *mot.* push-start.

'anschirren *v/t* (*sep*, -ge-, h) harness.

'Anschlag *m* (-[e]s; ⸚e) **1.** a) poster, bill, b) notice. **2.** attack (*auf acc* on): *~ auf j-n* (*j-s Leben*) attempt on s.o.'s life; *e-m ~ zum Opfer fallen* be assassinated. **3.** a) ♪ touch, b) *on typewriter*: stroke: *sie schreibt 400 Anschläge in der Minute* she types 400 strokes per minute. **4.** ♰ estimate. **5.** ⚙ (limit) stop. **6.** *das Gewehr im ~ halten* point the gun (*auf acc* at). **7.** impact, *swimming*: touch. **'Anschlagbrett** *n* notice (*Am.* bulletin) board.

'anschlagen (*irr*, *sep*, -ge-, → **schlagen**) **I** *v/t* (h) **1.** a) fasten (*an acc* to), b) stick up, put up (*notice etc*). **2.** strike, hit (*key*, *note*), ring (*bell*): *fig. e-n anderen Ton ~* change one's tune; *ein schnelleres Tempo ~* quicken one's pace. **3.** a) strike, hit, knock, b) chip. **II** *v/i* **4.** (sn) hit (*waves*: break) (*an acc* against): *mit dem Kopf an die Wand ~* hit one's head against the wall. **5.** (h) (begin to) ring, *dog*: bark. **6.** (h) *swimming*: touch. **7.** (h) (*bei* on) take effect, F *food*: show.

'anschleppen *v/t* (*sep*, -ge-, h) (*a. angeschleppt bringen*) drag along.

'anschließen (*irr*, *sep*, -ge-, h, → **schließen**) **I** *v/t* **1.** (*an acc* to) lock, chain. **2.** (*an acc*) ⚡, ⚙ connect (to, with), link

up (with), ⚡ *a.* plug in: → **angeschlossen. 3.** add (*dat* to). **II** *sich* ~ **4.** (*an acc*) adjoin (*s.th.*), border (on). **5.** *fig.* follow: *an den Vortrag schloß sich e-e Diskussion an* the lecture was followed by a discussion. **6.** *sich j-m ~* follow s.o., join s.o., *fig.* take s.o.'s side; *sich j-s Meinung ~* agree with s.o.; *ich schließe mich an!* a) I agree, b) I'll join you! **7.** *sich an j-n ~* befriend s.o.; *er schließt sich leicht an* he makes friends easily. **III** *v/i* **8.** fit closely.

'anschließend I *adj* **1.** adjacent, next. **2.** following. **3.** close-fitting. **II** *adv* **4.** afterward(s): *~ an die Vorstellung* following the performance.

'Anschluß *m* (-sses; ⸚sse) **1.** ⚡, 🕾, ⚙ *etc* a) connection, telephone (connection), b) line: *teleph. k-n ~ bekommen* not to get through; 🕾 *~ haben* have a connection (*nach* to); *s-n ~ verpassen* miss one's connection; *fig. den ~ verpassen* miss the boat; *den ~ finden an* (*acc*) catch up with. **2.** affiliation (*an acc* with *a party etc*), *pol.* union. **3.** *im ~ an* (*acc*) after, following. **4.** F contact, acquaintance: *~ finden* make contact (*or* friends) (*bei* with); *~ suchen* look for company. **~dose** *f* ⚡ wall socket. **~flug** *m* connecting flight. **~schnur** *f* ⚡ flex. **~treffer** *m* goal that leaves one more to level the score. **~zug** *m* connecting train.

'anschmiegen: sich ~ (*sep*, -ge-, h) (*an acc*) nestle (against), dress *etc*: cling (to). **'anschmiegsam** *adj* affectionate.

'anschmieren *v/t* (*sep*, -ge-, h) F cheat.

'anschnallen (*sep*, -ge-, h) **I** *v/t* a) buckle on, b) put on (*skis*). **II** *sich* ~ ✈, *mot.* fasten one's seat belt.

'Anschnallgurt *m* seat belt.

'anschnauzen *v/t* (*sep*, -ge-, h) F *j-n ~* blow s.o. up.

'anschneiden *v/t* (*irr*, *sep*, -ge-, h, → **schneiden**) **1.** cut into (*bread etc*). **2.** cut (*ball etc*). **3.** *fig.* broach: *ein anderes Thema ~* change the subject.

'Anschnitt *m* (-[e]s; -e) first slice.

'anschreiben (*irr*, *sep*, -ge-, h, → **schreiben**) **I** *v/t* **1.** write down: *j-m et. ~* charge s.o. with s.th.; *et. ~ lassen* buy s.th. on credit; *bei j-m gut* (*schlecht*) *angeschrieben sein* be in s.o.'s good (bad) books. **2.** *j-n ~* write to s.o.

'**Anschreiben** *n* (-s; -) covering letter.

'**anschreien** *v/t* (*irr, sep*, -ge-, h, → **schreien**) shout at, scream at.

'**Anschrift** *f* (-; -en) address.

Anschuldigung ['anʃʊldɪɡʊŋ] *f* (-; -en) accusation.

'**anschwärzen** *v/t* (*sep*, -ge-, h) F a) run *s.o.* down, b) denounce (*bei* to).

'**anschwellen** *v/i* (*irr, sep*, -ge-, sn, → **schwellen**) swell, *fig.* increase, rise.

'**anschwemmen** *v/t* (*sep*, -ge-, h) a) wash ashore, b) *geol.* deposit.

'**ansehen** (*irr, sep*, -ge-, h, → **sehen**) *v/t* look at: **sich** *et.* ~ take a look at, examine, watch; **sich e-n Film** (**e-e Fernsehsendung**) ~ go and see a film (watch a program[me]); **sich** *et.* **genau** ~ have a close look at s.th.; **man sieht es ihr an, daß** ... you can tell by her face that ...; **man sieht ihm sein Alter nicht an** he doesn't look his age; **ich sehe es für** (or **als**) **m-e Pflicht an zu** *inf* I consider it my duty to *inf*; *et.* **mit** ~ watch (or witness) s.th.; **ich kann es nicht länger mit** ~! I can't stand it any longer!; **F sieh mal einer an!** fancy that!; → **finster** 2, **schief** 3.

'**Ansehen** *n* (-s) 1. reputation, prestige: **von hohem** ~ of high standing; **großes** ~ **genießen** be highly esteemed; **an** ~ **verlieren** lose credit. 2. *fig.* **ohne** ~ **der Person** without respect of persons.

ansehnlich ['anzeːnlɪç] *adj* handsome, considerable.

'**anseilen** *v/t* (*sep*, -ge-, h) (*a.* **sich** ~) rope (up).

'**ansetzen** (*sep*, -ge-, h) **I** *v/t* 1. (**an** *acc*) put (on, to), apply *drill etc* (to), put *flute, glass, etc* to one's lips. 2. (**an** *acc* to) a) add, join, b) sew on. 3. fix, set (*date etc*), assess (*costs*), quote (*price*). 4. ⚡ set up (*equation*). 5. develop, ⚕ a. put forth (*buds*), put on (*rust*): **Fett** ~ put on weight. 6. *gastr.* prepare (*a.* 🍲), make, mix. 7. bring in: **j-n** ~ **auf** (*acc*) put s.o. onto; **e-n Hund** (**auf e-e Spur**) ~ set a dog on the trail. **II** *v/i* 8. begin, (make a) start: *a. fig.* **zum Endspurt** ~ set o.s. for the final spurt; **zur Landung** ~ come in (to land); **zum Sprechen** ~ start to speak; **zum Sprung** ~ get ready for the jump. 9. *fig.* criticism, reform, *etc*: set in. **III sich** ~ accumulate.

'**Ansicht** *f* (-; -en) 1. (**über** *acc*) opinion

(on), view (of): **m-r** ~ **nach** in my opinion, as I see it; **der** ~ **sein** (or **die** ~ **vertreten**), **daß** ... take the view that ...; **anderer** ~ **sein** take a different view, *w.s.* disagree; **die** ~**en sind geteilt** opinion differs; **zu der** ~ **gelangen** (or **kommen**), **daß** ... decide that ... 2. view (*a.* 📷). 3. ✝ **zur** ~ on approval.

'**Ansichts(post)karte** *f* picture postcard.

'**Ansichtssache**: **das ist** ~ that's a matter of opinion.

'**ansiedeln** *v/t* (*sep*, -ge-, h) 1. settle (*a.* **sich** ~), ✝ base, site: **in London angesiedelt** London-based. 2. *fig.* place.

'**Ansiedler(in** *f*) *m* settler.

'**Ansiedlung** *f* (-; -en) settlement.

'**Ansinnen** *n* (-s; -) request, demand.

'**anspannen** *v/t* (*sep*, -ge-, h) 1. harness (**an** *acc* to). 2. tighten, stretch (*rope etc*). 3. flex (*muscles*). 4. *fig.* strain: **alle Kräfte** ~ strain every nerve.

'**Anspannung** *f* (-; -en) *fig.* strain.

'**anspielen** (*sep*, -ge-, h) **I** *v/i* 1. *cards*: (have the) lead. 2. *sports*: lead off, *soccer*: kick off. 3. *fig.* ~ **auf** (*acc*) allude to, insinuate (*s.th.*). **II** *v/t* 4. lead (*card*). 5. *sports*: **j-n** ~ pass to s.o.

'**Anspielung** *f* (-; -en) (**auf** *acc*) allusion (to), insinuation (about).

'**anspinnen**: **sich** ~ (*irr, sep*, -ge-, h, → **spinnen**) *fig.* develop.

'**anspitzen** *v/t* (*sep*, -ge-, h) point.

'**Ansporn** *m* (-[e]s; *no pl*) incentive (**für** to). '**anspornen** *v/t* (*sep*, -ge-, h) *a. fig.* spur (on).

'**Ansprache** *f* (-; -n) 1. (**e-e** ~ **halten** deliver an) address (**an** *acc* to). 2. F **k-e** ~ **haben** have no one to talk to.

ansprechbar ['anʃpreçbaːr] *adj* 1. ✧ responsive. 2. F **er war nicht** ~ you couldn't talk to him. '**ansprechen** (*irr, sep*, -ge-, h, → **sprechen**) **I** *v/t* 1. speak to, address, appeal to *s.o.* (**wegen** for). 2. please, appeal to. 3. touch (up)on (*problem etc*). **II** *v/i* 4. *a.* ✧ respond (**auf** *acc* to). 5. appeal (to the public).

'**ansprechend** *adj* pleasing, attractive.

'**Ansprechpartner** *m* person to turn to.

'**anspringen** (*irr, sep*, -ge-, → **springen**) **I** *v/i* (sn) start (up). **II** *v/t* (h) jump at.

'**Anspruch** *m* (-[e]s; ⸚e) (**auf** *acc* to) *a.* ⚖ claim, right, *contp.* pretension: **hohe Ansprüche stellen** be very demanding, **an j-n** make heavy demands on s.o.; ~

haben auf (*acc*) be entitled to; *in ~ nehmen* a) *a. ~ erheben auf* (*acc*) lay claim to, b) call on (*s.o.'s time etc*); take up (*s.o.'s time etc*); *j-n in ~ nehmen* keep s.o. busy; *j-n ganz in ~ nehmen* claim s.o.'s full attention.

'**anspruchslos** *adj* **1.** undemanding (*a. fig. book, music, etc*), b) easily satisfied. **2.** plain, simple. '**Anspruchslosigkeit** *f* (*-; no pl*) undemandingness, modesty. '**anspruchsvoll** *adj* demanding (*a. fig.*), particular.

'**anspucken** *v/t* (*sep, -ge-, h*) spit at.

'**anstacheln** *v/t* (*sep, -ge-, h*) goad on.

Anstalt ['anʃtalt] *f* (*-; -en*) **1.** establishment, institution, *ped.* institute, school. **2.** a) sanatorium, *Am.* sanitarium, b) F mental home: *j-n in e-e ~ einweisen* institutionalize s.o. **3.** *~en treffen zu* make arrangements for; *~en machen zu gehen etc* get ready to go *etc*.

Anstand ['anʃtant] *m* (*-[e]s; no pl*) **1.** (sense of) decency. **2.** (good) manners. **anständig** ['anʃtɛndɪç] *adj* **1.** proper, decent, respectable: *benimm dich ~!* behave yourself! **2.** F fair (*price etc*): *ein ~es Essen* a decent meal; *e-e ~e Arbeit* a good job. '**Anstandsbesuch** *m* formal call. '**Anstandsdame** *f* chaperon. '**anstandshalber** *adv* for decency's sake. '**anstandslos** *adv* **1.** unhesitatingly. **2.** freely.

'**anstarren** *v/t* (*sep, -ge-, h*) stare at.

an'statt I *prep* (*gen*) instead of. **II** *conj ~ zu arbeiten etc* instead of working *etc*.

'**anstauen** (*sep, -ge-, h*) **I** *v/t* dam up. **II** *sich ~* accumulate, *fig. rage etc*: build up; *angestaute Wut* pent-up rage.

'**anstechen** *v/t* (*irr, sep, -ge-, h, → stechen*) prick, tap (*barrel*).

'**anstecken** (*sep, -ge-, h*) **I** *v/t* **1.** pin on, put on, slip on. **2.** set *house* on fire, light (*cigar, candle*). **3.** *,* *a. fig.* infect (*mit* with): *er hat mich* (*mit s-m Schnupfen*) *angesteckt* he has given me his cold. **II** *v/i* **4.** *,* *a. fig.* be infectious. **III** *sich ~* **5.** *ich habe mich bei ihm* (*mit Grippe*) *angesteckt* I have caught the flu from him. '**ansteckend** *adj* *,* *a. fig.* infectious. '**Anstecknadel** *f* a) pin, b) badge. **Ansteckung** ['anʃtɛkʊŋ] *f* (*-; -en*) *,* infection. '**Ansteckungsgefahr** *f* danger of infection.

'**anstehen** *v/i* (*irr, sep, -ge-, h, → ste-*

hen) **1.** queue (*Am.* line) up (*nach* for). **2.** *†, ♻* be up (*zur Entscheidung* for decision), be on the agenda.

'**ansteigen** *v/i* (*irr, sep, -ge-, sn, → steigen*) rise.

an'stelle *prep ~ von* (*or gen*) instead of.

'**anstellen** (*sep, -ge-, h*) **I** *v/t* **1.** (*an acc* against) put, lean. **2.** start (*machine*), turn on (*heating etc*), switch on (*radio etc*). **3.** employ, *Am.* hire, engage: *angestellt sein bei* work for; F *j-n zu et. ~* have s.o. do s.th. **4.** a) make, carry out, b) F do, manage: *Nachforschungen ~* make inquiries; F *was haben sie mit dir angestellt?* what have they done to you?; *Dummheiten ~, et.* (*Dummes*) *~* get up to mischief; *was hast du* (*da*) *wieder angestellt?* what have you been up to (again)?; *wie hast du das angestellt?* how did you manage that?; → *Überlegung*. **II** *sich ~* **5.** queue (*Am.* line) up (*nach* for). **6.** F act, make (*als ob* as if): *sich bei et. ungeschickt ~* go about s.th. clumsily; *stell dich nicht so an!* don't make such a fuss!; *stell dich nicht so dumm an!* don't act stupid!

'**anstellig** ['anʃtɛlɪç] *adj* handy, clever.

'**Anstellung** *f* (*-; -en*) place, employment, job.

'**ansteuern** *v/t* (*sep, -ge-, h*) head for.

Anstieg ['anʃtiːk] *m* (*-[e]s; -e*) **1.** ascent. **2.** *fig.* (*gen*) rise (in), increase (of).

'**anstiften** *v/t* (*sep, -ge-, h*) (*zu* to) incite, instigate: *j-n zu et.* put s.o. up to. '**Anstifter** *m* (*-s; -*), '**Anstifterin** *f* (*-; -nen*) instigator. '**Anstiftung** *f* (*-; -en*) (*auf ~ gen* at the) instigation (of).

'**anstimmen** *v/t* (*sep, -ge-, h*) ♪ strike up: *ein Lied ~* break into a song.

Anstoß *m* (*-es; ⁓e*) **1.** *soccer:* kickoff. **2.** impulse: *den ~ geben zu* start off, initiate. **3.** F *bei j-m ~ erregen* scandalize s.o., give offen/ce (*Am. -se*) to s.o.; *~ nehmen an* (*dat*) take exception to.

'**anstoßen** (*irr, sep, -ge-, → stoßen*) **I** *v/t* (*h*) **1.** knock (*or* bump) against: *sich den Kopf ~* bump one's head (*an dat* against); *j-n* (*mit dem Ellbogen*) *~* nudge s.o. (with the elbow). **II** *v/i* **2.** (*h*) clink glasses: *~ auf* (*acc*) drink to. **3.** (*sn*) (*an dat*) knock (against), bump (into): *mit dem Kopf ~* → **1. 4.** (*h*) *mit der Zunge ~* lisp. **5.** (*h*) *soccer:* kick off.

anstößig ['anʃtøːsɪç] *adj* a) offensive, scandalous, b) indecent.

'**anstrahlen** *v/t* (*sep*, -ge-, h) illuminate: *mit Scheinwerfern* ~ floodlight; F *fig. j-n* ~ beam at s.o.

'**anstreben** *v/t* (*sep*, -ge-, h) aim at, strive for.

'**anstreichen** *v/t* (*irr, sep*, -ge-, h, → *streichen*) 1. paint. 2. mark (*rot etc* in red *etc*). '**Anstreicher** *m* (-s; -) painter.

anstrengen ['anʃtrɛŋən] (*sep*, -ge-, h) **I** *v/t* 1. strain, be a strain on, exhaust: → *angestrengt* 1. 2. → *Prozeß* 2. **II** *v/i* 3. be exhausting, be a strain. **III** *sich* ~ make an effort, try (hard), exert o.s.; *streng dich mal an!* you could try a bit harder! '**anstrengend** *adj* strenuous, trying (*für* to). '**Anstrengung** *f* (-; -en) 1. (*mit äußerster* ~ with a supreme) effort. 2. strain, exertion.

'**Anstrich** *m* (-[e]s; -e) 1. a) painting, b) paint, c) coat. 2. *no pl* air, semblance.

'**Ansturm** *m* (-[e]s; ⁓e) onrush (*a. fig.*), ✕ assault, *a. sports*: attack, ✝ (*auf acc*) run (on), rush (for). '**anstürmen** *v/i* (*sep*, -ge-, sn) ~ *gegen a. fig.* attack.

Antagonismus [antago'nɪsmʊs] *m* (-; -men) antagonism.

antarktisch [ant'arktɪʃ] *adj* Antarctic.

'**antasten** *v/t* (*sep*, -ge-, h) infringe on (*rights etc*), touch (*capital*), break into (*supplies*).

'**Anteil** *m* (-[e]s; -e) 1. (*an dat*) share (of, in), ✝ *a.* interest (in), participation (of): *fig.* **er hatte k-n** ~ **am Erfolg** he had no part in the success. 2. *no pl* a) interest, b) sympathy: ~ *nehmen an* (*dat*) take an interest (in), *j-s Unglück* sympathize with s.o. in his misfortune, *j-s Freude* share in s.o.'s joy. **anteilig** ['antaɪlɪç], '**anteilmäßig** *adj and adv* proportionate(ly). '**Anteilnahme** *f* (-; *no pl*) sympathy (*an dat* with).

'**Anteilschein** *m* (-[e]s; -e) → *Aktie*.

'**Anteilseigner(in** *f*) *m* → *Aktionär(in)*.

Antenne [an'tɛnə] *f* (-; -n) aerial, *Am.* antenna (*a. fig.*).

Anthologie [antolo'giː] *f* (-; -n) anthology.

Anthrazit [antra'tsiːt] *m* (-s; -e) *min.* anthracite.

Anti..., **anti...** [anti-] anti...

Antialko'holiker(in *f*) *m* teetotal(l)er.

Anti'babypille *f* F the pill.

Antibiotikum [antibi'oːtikʊm] *n* (-s; -ka), **antibi'otisch** [-tɪʃ] *adj* antibiotic.

Antibloc'kiersystem *n mot.* (*abbr. ABS*) antilocking system.

Antidepressivum [antideprɛ'siːvʊm] *n* (-s; -va) antidepressant.

Antifa'schismus *m* antifascism.

Antifa'schist(in *f*) *m*, **antifa'schistisch** *adj* antifascist.

Antigen [anti'geːn] *n* (-s; -e) ♂ antigen.

Anti'haftbeschichtung: mit ~ nonstick.

antik [an'tiːk] *adj* 1. classical, ancient. 2. antique, period (*furniture etc*).

An'tike¹ *f* (-; *no pl*) (classical) antiquity.

An'tike² *f* (-; -n) *usu. pl* antique.

'**Antikörper** *m* ♂ antibody.

Antilope [anti'loːpə] *f* (-; -n) antelope.

Antipathie [antipa'tiː] *f* (-; -n) (*gegen* antipathy (to, against), dislike (of, for).

Antipode [anti'poːdə] *m* (-n; -n) antipode.

Antiqua [an'tiːkva] *f* (-; *no pl*) *print.* Roman (type).

Antiquar [anti'kvaːr] *m* (-s; -e), **Anti'quarin** *f* (-; -nen) 1. second-hand bookseller. 2. antique dealer.

Antiquariat [antikva'riaːt] *n* (-[e]s; -e) second-hand bookshop. **antiquarisch** [-'kvaːrɪʃ] *adj and adv* second-hand.

antiquiert [anti'kviːrt] *adj* antiquated.

Antiquität [antikvi'tɛːt] *f* (-; -en) *usu. pl* antique. **Antiqui'täten|händler(in** *f*) *m* antique dealer. **~laden** *m* antique shop.

Antise'mit(in *f*) *m* anti-Semite.

antise'mitisch *adj* anti-Semitic.

Antisemi'tismus *m* anti-Semitism.

anti'septisch *adj* antiseptic.

anti'statisch *adj* antistatic.

Antrag ['antraːk] *m* (-[e]s; ⁓e) 1. application (*auf acc* for), ⚖ petition, *parl.* motion, bill: **e-n** ~ **stellen auf** (*acc*) apply (⚖ petition, *parl.* move) for; *auf* ~ *von* (*or gen*) on the application *etc* of. 2. **er machte ihr e-n** ~ he proposed to her. 3. → '**Antragsformu,lar** *n* application form. '**Antragsteller** *m* (-s; -), '**Antragstellerin** *f* (-; -nen) applicant, *parl.* mover.

'**antreffen** *v/t* (*irr, sep*, -ge-, h, → *treffen*) find, come across.

'**antreiben** *v/t* (*irr, sep*, -ge-, h, → *treiben*) 1. *a. fig.* drive (on), urge (on). 2. ⚙ drive. 3. *a. v/i* drift ashore.

'**antreten** (*irr, sep*, -ge-, → *treten*) **I** *v/t*

(h) **1.** *ein Amt* ~ take up an office; *die Arbeit* (*den Dienst*) ~ report for work (duty); *e-e Reise* ~ start off on a journey; *e-e Strafe* ~ begin to serve a sentence; → *Erbschaft.* **2.** kick (*bike*). **II** *v/i* (sn) **3.** line up. **4.** report (*bei* to). **5.** *sports:* enter (*bei, zu* for): ~ *gegen* compete against.

'**Antrieb** *m* (-[e]s; e) **1.** *fig.* a) impulse, urge, b) motive, c) incentive: *aus eigenem* ~ of one's own accord; *neuen* ~ *geben* a) *e-r Sache* give a fresh impetus to s.th., b) *j-m* give s.o. a new interest. **2.** ⚙ drive.

'**Antriebs|aggre,gat** *n* ⚙ drive assembly. ~**kraft** *f* driving power. ~**schwäche** *f* (-; *no pl*) *psych.* lack of drive.

'**antriebsstark** *adj psych.* full of drive.

'**Antriebswelle** *f mot.* axle-drive shaft.

'**antrinken** *v/t* (*irr, sep,* -ge-, h, → *trinken*) F *sich e-n* ~ get drunk; *sich Mut* ~ give o.s. Dutch courage.

'**Antritt** *m* (-[e]s; *no pl*) *bei* ~ a) s-r *Reise* upon setting out on his journey, b) *s-s Amtes* on entering upon his office, c) *der Macht* on coming into power, d) *e-r Erbschaft* upon accession to an inheritance. '**Antrittsbesuch** *m* first call. '**Antrittsrede** *f* inaugural speech, *parl.* maiden speech.

'**antun** *v/t* (*irr, sep,* -ge-, h, → *tun*) **1.** *j-m et.* ~ do s.th. to s.o; *j-m et. Gutes* ~ do s.o. a good turn; *sich et.* ~ lay hands upon o.s. **2.** *es j-m* ~ take s.o.'s fancy; → *angetan.*

Antwort ['antvɔrt] *f* (-; -en) (*auf acc* to) answer, *fig.* response. '**antworten** *v/i, v/t* (h) answer, reply, *fig.* respond: *auf e-e Frage* ~ answer a question; *j-m* ~ answer s.o., reply to s.o.

'**Antwortschein** *m* (international) reply coupon.

'**anvertrauen** (*sep,* h) **I** *v/t j-m et.* ~ a) entrust s.o. with s.th., b) confide s.th. to s.o. **II** *sich j-m* ~ a) confide in s.o., b) entrust o.s. to s.o.

'**anwachsen** *v/i* (*irr, sep,* -ge-, sn, → *wachsen*[1]) **1.** grow on (*an acc* to), take root. **2.** *fig.* increase (*auf acc* to). '**Anwachsen** *n* (-s) *fig.* increase, growth.

Anwalt ['anvalt] *m* (-[e]s; ⸚e), **Anwältin** ['anvɛltɪn] *f* (-; -nen) **1.** ⚖ a) lawyer, *Am.* attorney(-at-law), b) solicitor, barrister, *Am.* counselor-at-law, coun-

sel (*des Angeklagten* for the defence). **2.** *fig.* advocate.

'**Anwaltschaft** *f* (-; -en) *the* Bar.

'**Anwalts|hono,rar** *n* lawyer's fee. ~**kammer** *f* Bar Council (*Am.* Association). ~**kosten** *pl* lawyer's fees.

'**Anwandlung** *f* (-; -en) (*aus e-r* ~ *heraus* on an) impulse.

'**anwärmen** *v/t* (*sep,* -ge-, h) warm (up).

'**Anwärter(in** *f*) *m* (*auf acc*) candidate (for), aspirant (to).

Anwartschaft ['anvartʃaft] *f* (-; -en) (*auf acc*) candidacy (for), qualification (for), ⚖ expectancy (of).

'**anweisen** *v/t* (*irr, sep,* -ge-, h, → *weisen*) **1.** a) instruct, direct, b) guide, train. **2.** assign (*dat* to): *j-m e-n Platz* ~ show s.o. to his seat. **3.** (*dat* to) remit (*sum*), order the payment of (*fee etc*).

'**Anweisung** *f* (-; -en) **1.** instruction, direction. **2.** assignment. **3.** remittance.

anwendbar ['anvɛntba:r] *adj* applicable (*auf acc* to). '**anwenden** *v/t* (*irr, sep,* -ge-, h, → *wenden*) use, make use of, *a.* ⚖, ✿ apply (*auf acc* to): *falsch* ~ misapply; *nutzbringend* ~ make good use of; → *äußerlich, Gewalt* 1.

'**Anwender** *m* (-s; -) *computer*: user.

'**Anwendung** *f* (-; -en) **1.** use, application (*auf acc* to): *unter* ~ *von Zwang* by (using) force. **2.** ✿ (hydrotherapeutic) treatment.

'**Anwendungs|beispiel** *n* example of use. ~**pro,gramm** *n computer*: application program. ~**vorschrift** *f* directions for use.

'**anwerben** *v/t* (*irr, sep,* -ge-, h, → *werben*) recruit, ⚔ *a.* enlist.

'**Anwerbung** *f* (-; -en) recruitment.

'**Anwesen** *n* (-s; -) property, estate.

anwesend ['anve:zənt] *adj* present (*bei* at): *nicht* ~ *sein* be absent. '**Anwesende** *m, f* (-n; -n) person present: ~ *ausgenommen* present company excepted. '**Anwesenheit** *f* (-; *no pl*) presence: *in* ~ *von* (*or gen*) in the presence of. '**Anwesenheitsliste** *f* attendance list.

'**anwidern** *v/t* (*sep,* -ge-, h) → *anekeln.*

Anwohner ['anvo:nər] *m* (-s; -), '**Anwohnerin** *f* (-; -nen) resident.

'**Anzahl** *f* (-; *no pl*) number.

'**anzahlen** *v/t* (*sep,* -ge-, h) (pay a sum as a) deposit, make a down payment (on).

'**Anzahlung** f (-; -en) deposit, down payment.

'**anzapfen** v/t (sep, -ge-, h) tap (a. F fig.).

'**Anzeichen** n (-s; -) (**für** of) sign, a. 🕈 symptom: **alle ~ sprechen dafür, daß ...** there is every indication that ...

'**Anzeige** ['antsaɪɡə] f (-; -n) **1.** announcement, notice, esp. 🕈 advice. **2.** advertisement, F ad(vert): **e-e ~ aufgeben** a. advertise. **3.** notification, 🏛 information: (**bei der Polizei**) **~ erstatten →** **anzeigen** 3. '**anzeigen** v/t (sep, -ge-, h) **1.** j-m et. ~ notify s.o. of s.th. **2.** indicate, ⊙ a. register. **3.** denounce: **j-n (bei der Polizei) ~** report s.o. to the police. **4.** fig. indicate: **es erscheint angezeigt zu** inf it seems advisable to inf.

'**Anzeigen|blatt** n advertising paper. **~teil** m newspaper: advertisements.

'**Anzeiger** m (-s; -) **1.** gazette. **2.** ⊙ indicator.

'**Anzeigetafel** f sports: scoreboard.

'**anzetteln** v/t (sep, -ge-, h) instigate.

'**anziehen** (irr, sep, -ge-, h, → **ziehen**) **I** v/t **1.** put on (clothes): **j-n ~** dress s.o. **2.** phys. attract (a. fig.), absorb (humidity etc). **3.** fig. draw (people). **4.** tighten (screw, rope), apply (brake), draw in (reins). **5.** draw up (legs). **II** v/i **6.** horse etc: pull away. **7.** fig. prices etc: go up. **III** sich ~ dress (o.s.), get dressed.

'**anziehend** adj fig. attractive, charming: **~ wirken auf** (acc) attract.

'**Anziehung** f (-; no pl) a. fig. attraction.

'**Anziehungskraft** f **1.** phys. a) attraction, b) gravitational pull. **2.** no pl (**auf** acc) attraction (for), appeal (to).

'**Anziehungspunkt** m fig. cent/re (Am. -er) of attraction.

'**Anzug** m (-[e]s; ⁺e) **1.** suit. **2.** im ~ **sein** be approaching, storm: be coming up.

anzüglich ['antsy:klɪç] adj personal (remark), suggestive (joke): **~ werden** get personal. '**Anzüglichkeit** f (-; -en) usu. pl personal remark.

'**anzünden** v/t (sep, -ge-, h) light (cigar etc), strike (match), set house on fire.

'**Anzünder** m (-s; -) lighter.

'**anzweifeln** v/t (sep, -ge-, h) question, doubt.

Aorta [a'ɔrta] f (-; -ten) anat. aorta.

apart [a'part] adj striking, unusual.

Apartheid [a'parthaɪt] f (-; no pl) apartheid. **~poli,tik** f apartheid policy.

Apartment [a'partmənt] n (-s; -s) flatlet, Am. apartment. **~haus** n block of flatlets, Am. apartment building.

Apathie [apa'ti:] f (-; -n) apathy.

apathisch [a'pa:tɪʃ] adj apathetic.

Aperitif [aperi'ti:f] m (-s; -s, -e) aperitif.

Apfel ['apfəl] m (-s; ⁺) apple: → **sauer** 1.

'**Apfel|baum** m apple tree. **~kuchen** m **gedeckter ~** apple pie. **~mus** n apple sauce. **~saft** m apple juice.

Apfelsine [apfəl'zi:nə] f (-; -n) orange.

'**Apfelstrudel** m gastr. apfelstrudel.

'**Apfelwein** m cider.

Aphorismus [afo'rɪsmʊs] m (-; -men) aphorism.

Apokalypse [apoka'lʏpsə] f (-; -n) apocalypse.

Apostel [a'pɔstəl] m (-s; -) a. fig. apostle. **A'postelgeschichte** f bibl. the Acts (of the Apostles). **apostolisch** [apos'to:lɪʃ] adj apostolic.

Apostroph [apos'tro:f] m (-s; -e) apostrophe.

Apotheke [apo'te:kə] f (-; -n) chemist's shop, pharmacy. **apo'thekenpflichtig** adj obtainable in a pharmacy only.

Apotheker [apo'te:kər] m (-s; -), **Apo'thekerin** f (-; -nen) pharmacist, (dispensing) chemist.

Apparat [apa'ra:t] m (-[e]s; -e) **1.** a) apparatus (a. fig.), fig. a. machinery, b) instrument, c) device. **2.** camera. **3.** a) radio, b) (TV) set. **4.** F phone: **am ~!** speaking!; **am ~ bleiben** hold the line.

Apparatur [apara'tu:r] f (-; -en) equipment.

Appartement [apartə'mã:] n (-s; -s) **1.** → **Apartment. 2.** (hotel) suite.

Appell [a'pɛl] m (-s; -e) ⚔ roll call: fig. **e-n ~ richten an** (acc) → **appellieren**

appellieren [apɛ'li:rən] v/i (h) **an** (acc) (make an) appeal to.

Appetit [ape'ti:t] m (-[e]s; -e) (**j-m ~ machen** give s.o. an) appetite (**auf** acc for); **ich habe ~ auf ...** I feel like ... **appe'titanregend** adj, **appe'titlich** adj a. fig. appetizing. **Appe'titlosigkeit** f (-; no pl) loss of appetite. **Appe'titzügler** m (-s; -) appetite suppressant.

applaudieren [aplaʊ'di:rən] v/i (h) (dat) applaud, cheer. **Applaus** [a'plaʊs] m (-es; no pl) applause.

apportieren [apɔr'ti:rən] v/t (h) retrieve.

appretieren [aprɛˈtiːrən] v/t (h), **Appretur** [apreˈtuːr] f (-; -en) ⊙ finish.
approbiert [aproˈbiːrt] adj qualified.
Aprikose [apriˈkoːzə] f (-; -n) apricot.
April [aˈprɪl] m (-[s]; -e) April: **j-n in den ~ schicken** make an April fool of s.o.; **~, ~!** April fool! **~scherz** m April-fool joke. **~wetter** n April weather.
Aquaplaning [akvaˈplaːnɪŋ] n (-[s]; no pl) mot. aquaplaning.
Aquarell [akvaˈrɛl] n (-s; -e), **Aqua'rellfarbe** f water colo(u)r. **Aqua'rellmaler(in** f) m water colo(u)rist.
Aquarium [aˈkvaːriʊm] n (-s; -rien) aquarium.
Äquator [ɛˈkvaːtɔr] m (-s; no pl) equator. **~taufe** f crossing-the-line ceremony.
äquivalent [ɛkvivaˈlɛnt] adj equivalent. **Äquiva'lent** n (-[e]s; -e) equivalent.
Ära [ˈɛːra] f (-; rare Ären) era.
Araber [ˈarabər] m (-s; -) Arab (a. horse).
'Araberin f (-; -nen) Arab (woman).
Arabien [aˈraːbiən] n (-s) Arabia.
a'rabisch [-bɪʃ] adj Arab states etc, Arabian nights etc, Arabic language etc.
Arbeit [ˈarbaɪt] f (-; -en) **1.** a) work (a. phys.), b) hard work, labo(u)r, c) task, job: **Tag der ~** May Day, Am. Labor Day; **geistige ~** brainwork; **an** (or **bei) der ~** at work; **an die ~ gehen** start work; **zur** (F **auf) ~ gehen** go to work; **et. in ~ haben** be working on s.th. **2.** **(j-m viel) ~ machen** give s.o. a lot (of) trouble. **3.** work, employment, job: **~ suchen** look for a job; **~ haben** be in work, have a job; **k-e ~ haben** be out of work, be without a job. **4.** a) (piece of) work, b) workmanship: **künstlerische ~** work of art. **5.** ped., univ. paper: **wissenschaftliche ~** treatise.
'arbeiten (h) **I** v/i work, ⊙ function, run, a. ✝ operate: **~ an** (dat) be working on; **~ bei** work for; **(geschäftlich) ~ mit** deal with, do business with; **mit Verlust ~** operate at a loss; **sein Geld ~ lassen** invest one's money. **II** v/t make. **III sich ~ durch** work one's way through.
'Arbeiter m (-s; -) a) worker, workman, b) labo(u)rer: **die ~ → Arbeiterschaft**; **~ und Unternehmer** labo(u)r and management.
'Arbeiter... workers' ..., working-class (family, area, etc). **~gewerkschaft** f trade (Am. labor) union.

'Arbeiterin f (-; -nen) **1.** (female) worker. **2.** zo. worker (bee or ant).
'Arbeiterklasse f working class(es).
'Arbeiterpar,tei f workers' party.
'Arbeiterschaft f (-; no pl) working class(es), a. pol. Labo(u)r.
'Arbeitgeber m (-s; -) employer. **~anteil** m employer's contribution. **~verband** m employers' association.
'Arbeitnehmer m (-s; -) employee. **~anteil** m employee's contribution.
'Arbeitsablauf m work routine.
'arbeitsam adj industrious, diligent.
'Arbeits|amt n employment exchange, Br. job centre. **~bedingungen** pl working (⊙ operating) conditions. **~be,schaffungspro,gramm** n job creation scheme. **~bescheinigung** f certificate of employment. **~bogen** m ped. work folder. **~eifer** m zeal. **~einkommen** n earned income. **~einstellung** f a) stoppage of work, b) shutdown, c) strike. **~erlaubnis** f work permit. **~essen** n working lunch (or dinner). **~fähig** adj fit for work: pol. **~e Mehrheit** working majority. **~fläche** f in kitchen: worktop. **~frieden** m industrial peace. **~gang** m ⊙ working cycle: **in einem ~** in a single pass. **~gebiet** n sphere of work. **~gemeinschaft** f working pool, ped. etc study group. **~gericht** n industrial tribunal. **~grundlage** f work(ing) basis. ⎱**inten,siv** adj labo(u)r-intensive. **~kampf** m labo(u)r dispute. **~kleidung** f work clothes. **~klima** n work climate. **~kraft** f **1.** capacity for work. **2.** worker, pl manpower. **~kräftemangel** m manpower shortage. **~leistung** f efficiency, ⊙ a. output. **~lohn** m wages, pay.
'arbeitslos adj unemployed, jobless: **~ sein** a. be out of work. **'Arbeitslose** m, f (-n; -n) unemployed person: **die ~n** the unemployed, the jobless.
'Arbeitslosen|geld n unemployment benefit: **~ beziehen** F be on the dole. **~hilfe** f unemployment relief. **~zahl** f unemployment figures.
'Arbeitslosigkeit f (-; no pl) unemployment.
'Arbeits|markt m labo(u)r (or job) market: **die Lage auf dem ~** the job situation. **~mi,nister** m employment (Am. labor) minister. **~mo,ral** f (working)

morale. **∼nachweis** *m* employment agency. **∼niederlegung** *f* (-; -en) walkout, strike.

'**arbeitsparend** *adj* labo(u)r-saving.

'**Arbeitspensum** *n* workload.

'**Arbeitsplatz** *m* **1.** job: *freie Arbeitsplätze* vacancies; *Schaffung von Arbeitsplätzen* job creation. **2.** working place. **∼beschreibung** *f* job description. **∼sicherung** *f* job security. **∼vernichter** *m* job killer.

'**Arbeits|pro,zeß** *m* *j-n wieder in den ∼ eingliedern* put s.o. back to work. **∼raum** *m* workroom. **∼recht** *n* industrial law. **⊈reich** *adj* busy. **⊈scheu** *adj* work-shy. **∼schluß** *m* end of work: *∼ ist um ...* work finishes at ...; *nach ∼* after work. **∼schutz** *m* industrial safety. **∼speicher** *m computer:* main memory. **∼stunde** *f* manhour, *pl* working hours. **⊈süchtig** *adj ∼ sein* be a workaholic. **∼tag** *m* working day, workday. **∼teilung** *f* division of labo(u)r. **∼tier** *n* F demon for work.

'**Arbeitsuche** *f* (-; *no pl*) (*auf ∼ sein* be) job-hunting. '**Arbeitsuchende** *m, f* (-n; -n) job seeker, job hunter.

'**arbeitsunfähig** *adj* a) unfit for work, b) permanently disabled.

'**Arbeits|unfall** *m* industrial accident. **∼vermittlung** *f* employment agency. **∼vertrag** *m* employment contract. **∼vorbereitung** *f* ☻ operations scheduling. **∼weise** *f* (working) method, ☻ *a.* procedure. **∼willige** *m, f* (-n; -n) person willing to work, *n.s.* nonstriker. **∼zeit** *f* (*gleitende ∼* flexible) working hours. **∼zeitverkürzung** *f* reduction in working hours. **∼zimmer** *n* study.

Archäologe [arçɛoˈloːgə] *m* (-n; -n) arch(a)eologist. **Archäologie** [-loˈgiː] *f* (-; *no pl*) arch(a)eology. **archäologisch** [-ˈloːgɪʃ] *adj* arch(a)eological.

Arche [ˈarçə] *f* (-; -n) ark: *die ∼ Noah* Noah's ark.

Archipel [arçiˈpeːl] *m* (-s; -e) *geogr.* archipelago.

Architekt [arçiˈtɛkt] *m* (-en; -en), **Archi'tektin** *f* (-; -nen) architect.

architektonisch [arçitɛkˈtoːnɪʃ] *adj* architectural. **Architektur** [arçitɛkˈtuːr] *f* (-; -en) architecture.

Archiv [arˈçiːf] *n* (-s; -e) archives. **Ar'chivbild** *n* library picture.

Areal [areˈaːl] *n* (-s; -e) area.

Arena [aˈreːna] *f* (-; -nen) arena.

arg [ark] **I** *adj* bad: *mein ärgster Feind* my worst enemy; *im ∼en liegen* be in a bad way. **II** *adv* badly, F *a.* awfully.

Argentinien [argɛnˈtiːniən] *n* (-s) Argentina, *the* Argentine. **Argen'tinier** *m* (-s; -), **Argen'tinierin** *f* (-; -nen), **argen'tinisch** *adj* Argentine.

Ärger [ˈɛrgər] *m* (-s; *no pl*) **1.** (*über acc* at, about *s.th.*, *with s.o.*) annoyance, irritation, anger: *zu m-m ∼* to my annoyance. **2.** (*j-m ∼ machen* cause s.o.) trouble: *das gibt ∼* there will be trouble. '**ärgerlich** *adj* **1.** (*über acc* at, about *s.th.*, *with s.o.*) annoyed, angry, F cross. **2.** annoying: *wie ∼! a.* what a nuisance! '**ärgern** (h) **I** *v/t* annoy, make *s.o.* angry. **II sich ∼** (*über acc* at, about *s.th.*, *with s.o.*) be angry, be (*or* get) annoyed: *ärgere dich nicht!* take it easy! '**Ärgernis** *n* (-ses; -se) annoyance: *∼ erregen* give offen/ce (*Am.* -se); *sts öffentliches ∼* public nuisance.

'**arglistig** *adj* malicious, *sts* fraudulent: *∼e Täuschung* wilful deceit.

'**arglos** *adj* a) innocent, b) unsuspecting.

'**Arglosigkeit** *f* (-; *no pl*) innocence.

Argument [arguˈmɛnt] *n* (-[e]s; -e) argument. **Argumentation** [argumɛntaˈtsioːn] *f* (-; -en) argumentation.

argumen'tieren *v/i* (h) argue, reason.

Argwohn [ˈarkvoːn] *m* (-[e]s; *no pl*) suspicion (*gegen* of). **argwöhnisch** [ˈarkvøːnɪʃ] *adj* suspicious (*gegen* of).

Arie [ˈaːriə] *f* (-; -n) ♪ aria.

Arier [ˈaːriər] *m* (-s; -), '**Arierin** *f* (-; -nen), '**arisch** *adj* Aryan.

Aristokrat [arıstoˈkraːt] *m* (-en; -en), **Aristo'kratin** *f* (-; -nen) aristocrat. **Aristokratie** [arıstokraˈtiː] *f* (-; -n) aristocracy. **aristokratisch** [arıstoˈkraːtɪʃ] *adj* aristocratic.

Arithmetik [arɪtˈmeːtɪk] *f* (-; *no pl*) arithmetic.

Arktis [ˈarktɪs] *f* (-; *no pl*) *the* Arctic (regions). '**arktisch** *adj a. fig.* arctic.

arm [arm] *adj* poor (*an dat* in).

Arm *m* (-[e]s; -e) arm: *in die ∼e nehmen* embrace, hug; *j-n auf den ∼ nehmen* a) pick s.o. up, b) F *fig.* pull s.o.'s leg; *j-m in die ∼e laufen* bump into s.o.; *j-m unter die ∼e greifen* (*mit*) help s.o. (out with).

Armatur [arma'tu:r] *f* (-; -en) armature, *pl* fittings.

Arma'turenbrett *n* dashboard.

'Armband *n* (-[e]s, ⇸er) bracelet.

'Armbanduhr *f* wrist watch.

'Armbrüste *f* **1.** armlet. **2.** ⚓ sling.

'Arme *m, f* (-n; -n) poor man (woman): **die ~n** the poor; **ich ~(r)!** poor me!

Armee [ar'me:] *f* (-; -n) army.

Ar'meekorps *n* army corps.

Ärmel ['ɛrməl] *m* (-s; -) sleeve: **ohne ~** sleeveless; **F et. aus dem ~ schütteln** a) pull s.th. out of a hat, b) do s.th. off the cuff. **'Ärmelaufschlag** *m* cuff.

'ärmellos *adj* sleeveless.

armieren [ar'mi:rən] *v/t* (h) **1.** armo(u)r (*cable*). **2.** reinforce (*concrete*).

...armig ...-armed, ...-branched.

'Armlehne *f* arm. **'Armleuchter** *m* (-s; -) **1.** chandelier. **2.** F *contp.* idiot, twerp.

ärmlich ['ɛrmlıç] *adj* poor, *w.s.* a. shabby: **in ~en Verhältnissen leben** be poorly off; **aus ~en Verhältnissen stammen** come from a poor family.

'Armreif(en) *m* bangle.

armselig ['armze:lıç] *adj* wretched, *a. fig.* miserable.

'Armsessel *m*, **'Armstuhl** *m* armchair.

Armut ['armu:t] *f* (-; *no pl*) poverty (*a. fig. an dat* in, of).

'Armuts|grenze *f* **an** (**unter**) **der ~ liegen** be on (under) the poverty line. **~zeugnis** *n* **j-m** (**sich**) **ein ~ ausstellen** show s.o.'s (one's own) incompetence.

Aroma [a'ro:ma] *n* (-s; -men) a) aroma, b) flavo(u)r. **aromatisch** [aro'ma:tıʃ] *adj* aromatic. **aromatisieren** [aromati'zi:rən] *v/t* (h) flavo(u)r.

arrangieren [arã'ʒi:rən] (h) **I** *v/t* arrange. **II sich ~** come to an arrangement (*or* agreement) (*mit* with).

Arrest [a'rɛst] *m* (-[e]s; -e) detention.

arretieren [are'ti:rən] *v/t* (h) ⊕ arrest, stop.

arriviert [ari'vi:rt] *adj* successful.

arrogant [aro'gant] *adj* arrogant.

Arsch [arʃ] *m* (-[e]s; ⇸e) V **1.** arse, *Am. a.* ass: **leck mich am ~!** fuck you!; **er (es) ist im ~** he (it) has had it; **j-m in den ~ kriechen** suck up to s.o. **2.** → **Arschloch. Arschkriecher** *m* V arse licker.

'Arschloch *n* V arsehole, *Am. a.* asshole, (*person*) a. (stupid) bastard, shit.

Arsen [ar'ze:n] *n* (-s; *no pl*) 🜍 arsenic.

Arsenal [arze'na:l] *n* (-s; -e) arsenal.

Art [art] *f* (-; -en) **1.** nature, kind: **sie hat e-e nette ~ mit Kindern** she has a way with children; **es ist nicht s-e ~ zu** *inf* he's not the sort to *inf*; **das entspricht nicht ihrer ~** it's not like her; **Fragen allgemeiner ~** questions of general interest. **2.** *a.* **~ und Weise** way, manner, method; **auf diese ~** in this way; **s-e ~ zu sprechen** the way he talks; *gastr.* **nach ~ des Hauses** à la maison. **3.** F behavio(u)r, manners. **4.** kind, sort, type, *biol.* species: **... aller ~** all sorts of ...; *iro.* **e-e ~ Dichter** a poet of sorts; *fig.* **aus der ~ schlagen** go one's own way.

Arterie [ar'te:riə] *f* (-; -n) artery.

Arteriosklerose [arterioskle'ro:zə] *f* (-; -n) ✚ arteriosclerosis.

'artfremd *adj biol.*, ✚ alien, foreign.

artig ['artıç] *adj* well-behaved: **sei ~!** be good!, be a good boy (girl)!

Artikel [ar'ti:kəl] *m* (-s; -) article.

artikulieren [artiku'li:rən] (h) **I** *v/t* articulate. **II sich ~** express o.s.

Artillerie [artılə'ri:] *f* (-; -n) artillery.

Artischocke [arti'ʃɔkə] *f* (-; -n) 🌿 artichoke. **Arti'schockenboden** *m gastr.* artichoke heart.

Artist [ar'tıst] *m* (-en; -en), **Ar'tistin** *f* (-; -nen) (variety) artist.

ar'tistisch *adj* artistic, acrobatic.

Arznei [arts'naɪ] *f* (-; -en) (*gegen* for) medicine, medicament, drug. **Arz'neikunde** *f* (-; *no pl*) pharmaceutics. **Arz'neimittel** *n* → **Arznei. ~abhängigkeit** *f* drug dependence. **~mißbrauch** *m* drug abuse.

Arz'neipflanze *f* medicinal plant.

Arz'neischrank *m* medicine cabinet.

Arzt [a:rtst] *m* (-es; ⇸e) doctor, physician: **zum ~ gehen** (go to) see the doctor.

'Arztberuf *m* medical profession.

Ärztekammer ['ɛrtstə-] *f* medical association. **'Ärztemuster** *n* drug sample. **'Ärzteschaft** *f* (-; *no pl*) medical profession. **'Arzthelferin** *f* doctor's receptionist (*or* assistant). **Ärztin** ['ɛrtstın] *f* (-; -nen) lady doctor (*or* physician). **ärztlich** ['ɛrtstlıç] *adj* medical: **~es Attest** medical (*or* doctor's) certificate; **~ behandeln** attend; **~ verordnet** prescribed by a doctor.

as [as], **As¹** *n* (-; -) ♪ A flat.

As² [as] *n* (-ses; -se) ace (*a.* F *person*).

Asbest [as'bɛst] *m* (-[e]s; -e) asbestos.

Asche ['aʃə] *f* (-; ◑ -n) ashes (*a. fig.*), (*cigarette etc*) ash: **glühende ~** embers.

'**Aschen|bahn** *f sports:* cinder (*mot.* dirt) track. **~becher** *m* ashtray. **~brödel** [-brɔːdəl] *n* (-s; -), **~puttel** [-putəl] *n* (-s; -) *fig.* Cinderella.

Ascher'mittwoch *m* Ash Wednesday.

'**aschfahl** *adj* ashen.

'**aschgrau** *adj* ash-grey, *Am.* ash-gray.

Ascorbinsäure [askɔr'biːn-] *f* ascorbic acid.

äsen ['ɛːzən] *v/i* (h) graze, browse.

aseptisch [a'zɛptɪʃ] *adj* aseptic.

Asiat [a'zǐaːt] *m* (-en; -en), **Asi'atin** *f* (-; -nen), **asi'atisch** *adj* Asian. **Asien** ['aːzǐən] *n* (-s) Asia.

Askese [as'keːzə] *f* (-; *no pl*) asceticism.

Asket [as'keːt] *m* (-en; -en), **As'ketin** *f* (-; -nen), **as'ketisch** *adj* ascetic.

asozial ['azotsǐaːl] *adj* antisocial.

Aspekt [as'pɛkt] *m* (-s; ◑ -e) aspect.

Asphalt [as'falt] *m* (-s; ◑ -e), **asphaltieren** [asfal'tiːrən] *v/t* (h) asphalt.

aß [aːs] *pret of* **essen**.

Assessor [a'sɛsɔr] *m* (-s; -en), **Assessorin** [asɛ'soːrɪn] *f* (-; -nen) *civil servant* (*lawyer, teacher, etc*) *who has completed his/her second state examination.*

Assistent [asɪs'tɛnt] *m* (-en; -en), **Assi'stentin** *f* (-; -nen) assistant.

Assi'stenzarzt *m* assistant doctor.

assistieren [asɪs'tiːrən] *v/i* (h) assist (*bei* in).

Assoziation [asotsǐa'tsǐoːn] *f* (-; -en) association. **assoziieren** [asotsi'iːrən] *v/t* (h) associate.

Ast [ast] *m* (-[e]s; ⁓e) branch, *in wood:* knot: F **auf dem absteigenden ~ sein** be going downhill.

Aster ['astər] *f* (-; -n) ⚘ aster.

Ästhet [ɛs'teːt] *m* (-en; -en), **Äs'thetin** *f* (-; -nen) (a)esthete.

äs'thetisch *adj* (a)esthetical.

Asthma ['astma] *n* (-s; *no pl*) ⚕ asthma.

Asthmatiker [ast'maːtɪkər] *m* (-s; -), **asth'matisch** [-tɪʃ] *adj* asthmatic.

Astrologe [astro'loːgə] *m* (-n; -n) astrologer. **Astrologie** [-lo'giː] *f* (-; *no pl*) astrology. **Astronaut** [-'naʊt] *m* (-en; -en) astronaut. **Astronomie** [-no'miː] *f* (-; *no pl*) astronomy. **astronomisch** [-'noːmɪʃ] *adj a.* F *fig.* astronomical. **Astrophy'sik** *f* astrophysics.

Asyl [a'zyːl] *n* (-s; *no pl*) (**um politisches ~ bitten** ask for political) asylum.

Asylant [azy'lant] *m* (-en; -en), **Asy'lantin** *f* (-; -nen) person seeking (*or* having been granted) (political) asylum.

A'sylrecht *n* right of asylum.

'**asymmetrisch** *adj* asymmetric(al).

'**asynchron** *adj* asynchronous.

Atelier [ate'lǐeː] *n* (-s; -s) studio.

Atem ['aːtəm] *m* (-s; *no pl*) breath: **außer ~ (kommen** get) out of breath; **~ holen** take a breath; *fig.* **mir stockte der ~** my heart stood still; **das verschlug mir den ~** that took my breath away; **j-n in ~ halten** keep s.o. on the jump (*or* in suspense); → **anhalten** 1. '**atemberaubend** *adj fig.* breathtaking. '**Atembeschwerden** *pl* difficulty in breathing. '**Atemgerät** *n* breathing apparatus, ⚕ respirator. '**atemlos** *adj a. fig.* breathless. '**Atempause** *f* F breather. '**Atemwege** *pl* respiratory tract. '**Atemzug** *m* breath: **im gleichen ~** in one breath.

Atheismus [ate'ɪsmʊs] *m* (-; *no pl*) atheism. **Atheist** [ate'ɪst] *m* (-en; -en) atheist. **athe'istisch** *adj* atheistic(al).

Äther ['ɛːtər] *m* (-s; *no pl*) ⚗ ether.

ätherisch [ɛ'teːrɪʃ] *adj* ethereal, etheric: **~es Öl** essential (*or* volatile) oil.

Äthiopien [ɛ'tǐoːpǐən] *n* (-s) Ethiopia. **Äthi'opier** *m* (-s; -), **Äthi'opierin** *f* (-; -nen), **äthi'opisch** *adj* Ethiopian.

Athlet [at'leːt] *m* (-en; -en), **Ath'letin** *f* (-; -nen) athlete. **ath'letisch** *adj* athletic.

Äthyl [ɛ'tyːl] *n* (-s; *no pl*) ethyl.

Äthylen [ɛty'leːn] *n* (-s; *no pl*) ethylene.

atlantisch [at'lantɪʃ] *adj* Atlantic: **der ≎e Ozean** the Atlantic (Ocean).

Atlas ['atlas] *m* (-[ses]; -se) atlas.

atmen ['aːtmən] *v/i, v/t* (h) breathe: **tief ~** breathe deep. '**Atmen** *n* (-s) breathing.

Atmosphäre [atmo'sfɛːrə] *f* (-; -n) *a. fig.* atmosphere. **atmo'sphärisch** *adj* atmospheric. **⚡ ~e Störungen** statics, atmospherics.

'**Atmung** *f* (-; *no pl*) breathing, respiration: **künstliche ~** artificial respiration.

Atom [a'toːm] *n* (-s; -e) atom.

atomar [ato'maːr] *adj* atomic, nuclear.

A'tom|bombe *f* atom(ic) (*or* nuclear) bomb, A-bomb. **~bunker** *m* nuclear shelter. **~ener|gie** *f* atomic energy. **~explosi|on** *f* atomic explosion. **~forschung** *f* atomic research. ⚛**getrieben**

adj nuclear-powered. **~gewicht** *n* atomic weight. **~hülle** *f* atomic shell.
atomisieren [atomi'zi:rən] *v/t* (h) *a. fig.* atomize.

A'tom|kern *m* atomic nucleus. **~kraft** *f* (-; *no pl*) nuclear power. **~kraftwerk** *n* nuclear power station. **~krieg** *m* atomic (*or* nuclear) war(fare). **~macht** *f pol.* nuclear power. **~mo‚dell** *n* atomic model. **~müll** *m* radioactive waste. **~phy‚sik** *f* atomic physics. **~pilz** *m fig.* mushroom cloud. **~re‚aktor** *m* atom reactor. **~spaltung** *f* atom splitting. **~sperrvertrag** *m pol.* nonproliferation treaty. **~sprengkopf** *m* nuclear warhead. **~test** *m* nuclear test. **~teststopp(abkommen** *n*) *m* test ban (treaty). **~tod** *m* nuclear death. **~U-Boot** *n* nuclear(-powered) submarine.

A'tomwaffen *pl* atomic (*or* nuclear) weapons. **2frei** *adj* nuclear-free *zone*. **~gegner(in** *f*) *m* anti-nuclear protester.
A'tomzahl *f* atomic number.
A'tomzeitalter *n* atomic age.
atonal ['atona:l] *adj* ♪ atonal.
Atrophie [atro'fi:] *f* (-; -en) ♪ atrophy.
ätsch [ε:tʃ] *int* there!, serves you right!
Attaché [ata'ʃe:] *m* (-s; -s) attaché.
Attacke [a'takə] *f* (-; -n), **attackieren** [ata'ki:rən] *v/t, v/i* (h) attack.
Attentat [atɛn'ta:t] *n* (-[e]s; -e) a) (**ein ~ auf j-n verüben** make an) attempt on s.o.'s life, b) assassination.
Atten'täter(in *f*) *m* assassin.
Attest [a'tɛst] *n* (-[e]s; -e) certificate.
Attraktion [atrak'tsio:n] *f* (-; -en) attraction. **attraktiv** [-'ti:f] *adj* attractive.
Attrappe [a'trapə] *f* (-; -n) dummy.
Attribut [atri'bu:t] *n* (-[e]s; -e) attribute. **attributiv** [atribu'ti:f] *adj* attributive.
ätzen ['ɛtsən] *v/t* (h) **1.** ♠ corrode, eat into. **2.** ♪ cauterize. **3.** *arts:* etch.
'ätzend *adj* corrosive, *a. fig.* caustic.
au [aʊ] *int* **1.** ouch! **2. ~ ja!** oh yes!
Aubergine [obɛr'ʒi:nə] *f* (-; -n) ♣ aubergine, eggplant.
auch [aʊx] *adv* **1.** also, too, as well: **ich habe Hunger - ich ~** I am hungry - so am I (F me too); **ich glaube es - ich ~** I believe it - so do I; **ich kann es nicht - ich ~ nicht** I can't do it - nor (*or* neither) can I. **2.** even: **ohne ~ nur zu fragen** without so much as asking. **3. wenn ~** even if, although; **so sehr ich es ~**

bedauere however much I regret it. **4. wann ~** (*immer*) whenever; **wer es ~** (*immer*) *sei* whoever it may be; **was er ~** (*immer*) *sagt* whatever he may say; **so schwierig es ~ sein mag** difficult as it may be. **5. wirst du es ~ tun?** are you really going to do it?; **so schlimm ist es ~ wieder nicht!** it's not all that bad!
Audienz [aʊ'diɛnts] *f* (-; -en) audience (**bei** with).
audiovisu'ell [aʊdĭo-] *adj* audiovisual.
Auditorium [aʊdi'to:rĭʊm] *n* (-s; -rien) **1.** *univ.* (**~ maximum** main) lecture hall. **2.** audience.
auf [aʊf] **I** *prep* (*dat*) **1.** *space:* on, in, at: **~ dem Tisch** on the table; **~ der Straße** in (*Am.* on) the street, on the road; **~ See** at sea; **~ der Post** at the post office; **~ der Welt** in the world; **~ dem Land** in the country; **er ist ~ s-m Zimmer** he is in his room. **2.** at, during, on: **~ dem Ball** at the ball; **~ s-r Reise** during (*or* on) his journey; **~ Urlaub** on vacation, *esp. Br.* on holiday. **II** *prep* (*acc*) **3.** *place:* a) (down) on, onto, into, b) up, c) to, toward(s): **er setzte sich ~ e-n Stuhl** he sat down on a chair; **~ die Erde fallen** fall (on)to the ground; **er ging ~ die Straße** he went (out) into the street; **ich ging ~ die Post** I went to the post office; **geh ~ dein Zimmer!** go to your room!; **sie zogen ~ das Land** they moved (in)to the country; *fig.* **~ Besuch kommen** come for a visit; **~ e-e Reise gehen** go on a journey. **4.** *time:* a) for: **~ ein paar Tage** for a few days; **~ Jahre hinaus** for years to come; **es geht ~ 9 (Uhr)** it's getting on for nine (o'clock); F **~ e-e Tasse Kaffee** for a cup of coffee, b) after: **Stunde ~ Stunde verging** hour after hour went by, c) until: **~ morgen verschieben** postpone until tomorrow; F **~ bald!** see you soon! **5. ~ diese Weise** (in) this way; **~ deutsch** in German; **~ s-n Befehl** by (*or* at) his order; **~ m-e Bitte** (**hin**) on my request. **6.** *quantities:* **von 80 Tonnen ~ 100 erhöhen** increase from 80 tons to 100; **~ jeden entfallen ...** there is/are ... (for) each; **~ die Sekunde** to the second; **~ 100 m** *see, hear, etc* at (*or* from) a hundred metres, *come etc* as close as 100 metres. **III** *adv* **7.** F a) open: **Augen ~!** watch out!, b) awake,

c) up (and going): *ich war die ganze Nacht ~* I was up all night. **8. ~ und ab gehen** walk up and down (*or* to and fro); F *~ und davon gehen* run away. **IV** *int ~!* a) (get) up!, b) F *a. ~ geht's!* let's go!, c) come on!

Auf: *das ~ und Ab des Lebens* the ups and downs of life; *das ~ und Ab der Preise* the rise and fall of prices.

'**aufarbeiten** *v/t* (*sep*, -ge-, h) **1.** work (*or* clear) off, catch up on. **2.** furbish up, do up. **3.** *fig.* a) work *s.th.* up, b) digest.

'**aufatmen** *v/i* (*sep*, -ge-, h) draw a deep breath, *fig.* breathe again (*or* freely).

'**aufbahren** *v/t* (*sep*, -ge-, h) put *coffin* on the bier, lay *body* out (in state).

'**Aufbau** *m* (-[e]s; -ten) **1.** *no pl* building, erection, construction, ⚙ assembly: *fig. im ~ (begriffen) sein* be in its initial stages. **2.** *no pl fig.* structure. **3.** *mot.* car body. **4.** *no pl computer:* format.

'**aufbauen** (*sep*, -ge-, h) **I** *v/t* **1.** build, erect, construct: *wieder ~* rebuild, reconstruct. **2.** *fig.* a) build up (*business, attack*, F *politician etc*) b) organize, set up: *sich e-e Existenz ~* build o.s. an existence; *e-e Theorie etc ~ auf* (*dat*) base (*or* found) a theory *etc* on. **3.** ⚙ a) assemble, b) set up, c) arrange. **II** *v/i* **4.** (*a. sich*) *~ auf* (*dat*) be based (*or* founded) on. **III** *sich ~* **5.** be composed (*aus* of). **6.** *sich ~ vor* (*dat*) plant o.s. (*or* line up) in front of.

'**aufbäumen:** *sich ~* (*sep*, -ge-, h) *horse:* rear; *fig. sich ~ gegen* rebel against.

'**aufbauschen** *v/t* (*sep*, -ge-, h) *fig.* exaggerate.

'**Aufbauten** *pl of Aufbau* ⇩ superstructure.

'**aufbegehren** *v/i* (*sep*, h) rebel.

'**aufbehalten** *v/t* (*irr*, *sep*, h, → *behalten*) F *den Hut ~* keep one's hat on.

'**aufbekommen** *v/t* (*irr*, *sep*, h, → *bekommen*) F **1.** get *the door* open, get a *knot* undone. **2.** be given *a task* (to do).

'**aufbereiten** *v/t* (*sep*, -ge-, h) prepare, process, ⚙ *a.* treat, *computer:* edit, *fig.* work *s.th.* up.

'**aufbessern** *v/t* (*sep*, -ge-, h) **1.** improve. **2.** raise (*salary*).

'**aufbewahren** *v/t* (*sep*, h) preserve, keep, store (up). '**Aufbewahrung** *f* (-; *no pl*) (*sichere ~*) safekeeping: *j-m et. zur ~ geben* leave s.th. with s.o.

'**aufbieten** *v/t* (*irr*, *sep*, -ge-, h, → *bieten*) **1.** muster, summon (up) (*courage*), use (*one's influence*). **2.** ✕ mobilize.

'**Aufbietung** *f* (-; *no pl*) *unter ~ aller Kräfte* by (a) supreme effort.

'**aufbinden** *v/t* (*irr*, *sep*, -ge-, h, → *binden*) undo, untie: → *Bär.*

'**aufblähen** (*sep*, -ge-, h) **I** *v/t* **1.** (*a. sich ~*) blow out, swell. **2.** ✝, 🏥 inflate. **II** *sich ~* F *contp.* puff o.s. up.

'**aufblasbar** *adj* inflatable. '**aufblasen** (*irr*, *sep*, -ge-, h, → *blasen*) **I** *v/t* blow up, inflate. **II** *sich ~* F puff o.s. up.

'**aufbleiben** *v/i* (*irr*, *sep*, -ge-, sn, → *bleiben*) **1.** sit up, stay up. **2.** remain open.

'**aufblenden** *v/i* (*sep*, -ge-, h) **1.** *mot.* turn on the headlights full beam. **2.** *phot.* open the diaphragm.

'**aufblicken** *v/i* (*sep*, -ge-, h) look up: *zu j-m ~* look up at s.o. (*esp. fig.* to s.o.).

'**aufblitzen** *v/i* (*sep*, -ge-, sn) flash (up).

'**aufblühen** *v/i* (*sep*, -ge-, sn) **1.** (begin to) bloom. **2.** *fig. girl:* blossom (out), *town, economy, etc:* (begin to) flourish.

'**aufbocken** *v/t* (*sep*, -ge-, h) jack up.

'**aufbohren** *v/t* (*sep*, -ge-, h) a) bore open, b) rebore (*engine*), c) drill (*tooth*).

'**aufbrauchen** *v/t* (*sep*, -ge-, h) use up.

'**aufbrausen** *v/i* (*sep*, -ge-, sn) flare up.

'**aufbrausend** *adj fig.* quick-tempered.

'**aufbrechen** (*irr*, *sep*, -ge-, → *brechen*) **I** *v/t* (h) **1.** a) break (*or* prize) open, b) break up. **II** *v/i* (sn) **2.** bud, boil, *etc:* (burst) open, *ice:* break up. **3.** (*nach* for) start, set out.

'**aufbringen** *v/t* (*irr*, *sep*, -ge-, h, → *bringen*) **1.** → *aufbekommen* **1. 2.** muster, summon (up) (*courage*). **3.** raise (*money*). **4.** start (*rumo[u]r, fashion*). **5.** anger: *j-n gegen sich ~* get s.o.'s back up; → *aufgebracht.* **6.** ⇩ capture.

'**Aufbruch** *m* (-[e]s; ⸚e) (*nach, zu* for) departure, start: *das Zeichen zum ~ geben* give the sign to leave.

'**aufbrühen** *v/t* (*sep*, -ge-, h) make (*coffee, tea*).

'**aufbügeln** *v/t* (*sep*, -ge-, h) **1.** transfer *pattern* (*auf acc* on). **2.** iron, press.

'**aufbürden** *v/t* (*sep*, -ge-, h) *fig. j-m et. ~* saddle s.o. with s.th.

'**aufdecken** (*sep*, -ge-, h) **I** *v/t* **1.** uncover, *fig. a.* reveal, expose. **2.** *das Bett ~* turn down the bed. **II** *v/i* **3.** lay the table.

'**aufdrängen** (*sep*, -ge-, h) **I** *v/t j-m et. ~*

force s.th. on s.o. **II sich ~** a) (dat on) intrude, impose o.s., b) suggest itself.

'**aufdrehen** (sep, -ge-, h) **I** v/t **1.** turn on (gas etc). **2.** untwist (rope). **3.** F turn up (radio). **4.** put up one's hair in curlers. **II** v/i **5.** F mot. step on the gas. **6.** F fig. person: get going: → **aufgedreht**.

'**aufdringlich** adj obtrusive, a. importunate, pushing (person), a. loud (colo[u]r), noisy (music), overpowering (smell). '**Aufdringlichkeit** f (-; no pl) obtrusiveness.

'**Aufdruck** m (-[e]s; -e) imprint, philat. overprint. '**aufdrucken** v/t (sep, -ge-, h) print (**auf** acc on).

'**aufdrücken** v/t (sep, -ge-, h) **1.** push (or press) open. **2.** F squeeze boil open. **3.** impress stamp etc (dat or **auf** acc on).

aufein'ander adv **1.** one on top of another (or the other). **2.** one another, each other: **~ angewiesen sein** depend on each other; **~ abgestimmte Farben** matching colo(u)rs. **3.** one after the other. **~folgen** v/i (sep, -ge-, sn) succeed (one another). **~folgend** adj successive, consecutive: **an drei ~en Tagen** three days running. **~prallen** v/i (sep, -ge-, sn), **~stoßen** v/i (irr, sep, -ge-, sn, → **stoßen**) collide, fig. a. clash. **~treffen** v/i (irr, sep, -ge-, sn, → **treffen**) meet (one another).

Aufenthalt ['aʊfɛnthalt] m (-[e]s; -e) **1.** stay. **2.** 🚋 etc (fünf Minuten ~ five minutes') stop: **ohne ~** nonstop; **wir hatten zwei Stunden ~ in ...** we stopped in ... for two hours.

'**Aufenthalts|erlaubnis** f residence permit. **~ort** m a) whereabouts, b) residence. **~raum** m a) hotel etc: lounge, b) school etc: common room.

'**auferlegen** v/t (sep, h) impose (dat on): **sich k-n Zwang ~** be free and easy.

'**auferstehen** v/i (irr, sep, sn, → **erstehen**) eccl. rise (from the dead).

'**Auferstehung** f (-; no pl) resurrection.

'**aufessen** v/t (irr, sep, -ge-, h, → **essen**) eat up, finish.

auffädeln ['aʊffɛːdəln] v/t (sep, -ge-, h) thread, string.

'**auffahren** (irr, sep, -ge-, → **fahren**) **I** v/i (sn) **1.** ~ **auf** (acc) mot. crash into, ⚓ run on; mot. zu dicht ~ tailgate. **2.** fig. a) (give a) start, b) flare up. **II** v/t (h) **3.** F bring on (food etc). '**Auffahrt** f (-; -en)

1. driving up. **2.** a) approach, b) slip road, c) drive(way Am.).

'**Auffahrunfall** m rear-end collision.

'**auffallen** v/i (irr, sep, -ge-, sn, → **fallen**) be conspicuous, attract attention: **j-m ~** strike s.o.; **das fällt nicht auf** nobody will notice; **unangenehm ~** make a bad impression. '**auffallend** adj a) noticeable, b) striking (beauty, resemblance, etc). '**auffällig** adj **1.** → **auffallend**. **2.** a) conspicuous, b) odd, strange, c) loud, F flashy (clothes etc).

'**auffangen** v/t (irr, sep, -ge-, h, → **fangen**) **1.** catch (a. fig. words etc). **2.** pick up, intercept (message). **3.** cushion (fall etc), parry, block (blow), stop (attack), absorb (price increases etc). **4.** collect. **5.** receive (refugees).

'**Auffanglager** n reception camp.

'**auffassen** v/t (sep, -ge-, h) **1.** understand, grasp. **2.** interpret: **et. als Scherz ~** take s.th. as a joke; **falsch ~** misunderstand, misinterpret.

'**Auffassung** f (-; -en) **1.** view, opinion: **nach m-r ~** in my view, as I see it. **2.** interpretation. **3.** no pl → '**Auffassungsgabe** f (-; no pl) intellectual grasp, intelligence.

auffindbar ['aʊffɪntbaːr] adj **nicht ~** not to be found. '**auffinden** v/t (irr, sep, -ge-, h, → **finden**) find, discover.

'**auffischen** v/t (sep, -ge-, h) F **1.** fish out (of the water). **2.** → **aufgabeln**.

'**aufflackern** v/i (sep, -ge-, sn) flicker up.

'**aufflammen** v/i (sep, -ge-, sn) a. fig. flare up.

'**auffliegen** v/i (irr, sep, -ge-, sn, → **fliegen**) **1.** fly up. **2.** door etc: fly open. **3.** F plan etc: blow up: **~ lassen** expose (s.o.), bust (gang), break up (meeting).

'**auffordern** v/t (sep, -ge-, h) **1.** j-n ~ (, et. zu tun) ask (or order, ⚖ summon) s.o. (to do s.th.): **j-n dringend ~** urge s.o. **2.** invite: **e-e Dame (zum Tanz) ~** ask a lady to dance.

'**Aufforderung** f (-; -en) **1.** request, call. **2.** order, ⚖ summons. **3.** invitation.

'**aufforsten** v/t (sep, -ge-, h) reafforest.

'**auffressen** v/t (irr, sep, -ge-, h, → **fressen**) eat up, devour: F fig. **die Arbeit frißt mich auf** I'm drowning in work.

'**auffrischen** (sep, -ge-, h) **I** v/t **1.** freshen up, refresh (a. fig. memory). **2.** replenish (supplies). **3.** fig. brush up (knowl-

edge), revive (*friendship etc*). **II** *v/i* **4.** *wind*: freshen.

'Auffrischungskurs *m* refresher course.

'aufführen (*sep*, *-ge-*, *h*) **I** *v/t* **1.** ♪, *thea. etc* perform, present, *a.* show (*film*). **2.** state, show, list: *namentlich* ~ name; *einzeln* ~ specify, itemize. **II** *sich* ~ behave: *sich schlecht* ~ *a.* misbehave.

'Aufführung *f* (-; -en) *thea. etc* performance, showing, show. **'Aufführungsrechte** *pl* performing rights.

'auffüllen *v/t* (*sep*, *-ge-*, *h*) fill up, top up (*glass etc*), replenish (*stocks*).

'Aufgabe *f* (-; -n) **1.** *no pl* posting, *Am.* mailing (*of letter*), sending (*of telegram[me]*). **2.** *no pl* registering, *Am.* checking (*of luggage*). **3.** *no pl* insertion (*of an ad*), giving, placing (*of orders*). **4.** *no pl* giving up (*a. sports*), ♱ closing down (*of business etc*), resignation (*gen from an office*). **5.** a) task, assignment, job, b) duty, c) purpose, function: *es ist nicht m-e* ~ *zu inf* it's not my job to *inf*; *es sich zur* ~ *machen zu inf* make it one's business to *inf*. **6.** ♱ problem, *ped.* homework, lesson, exercise. **7.** *sports*: service.

'aufgeben (*irr*, *sep*, *-ge-*, *h*, → *geben*) **I** *v/t* **1.** post, *Am.* mail (*letter*), send (*telegram[me]*). **2.** register, *Am.* check (*luggage*). **3.** insert (*ad*), give, place (*orders*). **4.** give up (*job*, *business*, *hope*, *patient*, *etc*), retire from (*office etc*), abandon (*plan etc*), stop (*contest*): *das Rauchen* ~ give up (*or* stop) smoking; F *gib's auf!* give (it) up! **5.** ask (*riddle*), *ped.* set, give (*task*). **6.** *sports*: serve. **II** *v/i* **7.** give up.

'aufgeblasen I *pp* of *aufblasen*. **II** *adj fig.* arrogant, bumptious.

'Aufgebot *n* (-[e]s, -e) **1.** *das* ~ *bestellen* give notice of an intended marriage, ask the banns. **2.** *no pl* array, crowd, (*police*) force, *sports*: a) team, b) squad, pool of players: *mit starkem* ~ *erscheinen* turn out (*or* up) in full force.

'aufgebracht I *pp* of *aufbringen*. **II** *adj* (*gegen* with, *über acc* at, about) angry, furious.

'aufgedonnert *adj* F dolled-up.

'aufgedreht I *pp* of *aufdrehen*. **II** *adj* F *fig.* in high spirits.

'aufgehen *v/i* (*irr*, *sep*, *-ge-*, *sn*, → *gehen*) **1.** *sun etc*, *a. dough*: rise, *curtain*: *a.* go up. **2.** *seed etc*: come up. **3.** open, *knot etc*: *a.* come undone, *seam*: come open, *boil etc*: burst. **4.** ♱ come out even: *die Aufgabe geht nicht auf* the sum doesn't work out; → *Rechnung* 1. **5.** ~ *in* (*dat*) be (all) wrapped up in *one's work etc*. **6.** *j-m* ~ dawn on s.o.; *jetzt geht mir die Bedeutung s-r Worte auf* now I realize what he meant; → *Licht* 2. **7.** *in Flammen* ~ go up in flames.

'aufgehoben I *pp* of *aufheben*. **II** *adj gut* ~ *sein* be in good hands (*bei* with).

'aufgeilen (*sep*, *-ge-*, *h*) V **I** *v/t* turn *s.o.* on. **II** *sich* ~ *an* (*dat*) get turned on by.

'aufgeklärt I *pp* of *aufklären*. **II** *adj* enlightened: ~ *sein* know the facts of life.

'aufgeknöpft I *pp* of *aufknöpfen*. **II** *adj* F *fig.* chatty.

'aufgekratzt I *pp* of *aufkratzen*. **II** *adj* F *fig.* chirpy.

'aufgelegt I *pp* of *auflegen*. **II** *adj zu et.* ~ *sein* be in the mood for s.th., feel like (doing) s.th.; *gut* (*schlecht*) ~ *sein* be in a good (bad) mood.

'aufgelöst I *pp* of *auflösen*. **II** *adj fig.* **1.** distraught. **2.** all in.

'aufgeräumt I *pp* of *aufräumen*. **II** *adj fig.* cheerful.

'aufgeregt I *pp* of *aufregen*. **II** *adj* upset, excited, nervous.

'aufgeschlossen I *pp* of *aufschließen*. **II** *adj fig.* open (*für* to), open-minded. **'Aufgeschlossenheit** *f* (-; *no pl*) open-mindedness.

'aufgeschmissen *adj* F ~ *sein* be stuck. **'aufgeschossen** *adj hoch* ~ lanky. **'aufgesetzt I** *pp* of *aufsetzen*. **II** *adj fig.* artificial.

'aufgesprungen I *pp* of *aufspringen*. **II** *adj* chapped (*lips etc*).

'aufgestaut I *pp* of *aufstauen*. **II** *adj* pent-up (*rage etc*).

'aufgeweckt I *pp* of *aufwecken*. **II** *adj fig.* bright, clever.

'aufgießen *v/t* (*irr*, *sep*, *-ge-*, *h*, → *gießen*) **1.** make (*tea etc*). **2.** add, pour on.

'aufgliedern *v/t* (*sep*, *-ge-*, *h*) a) (sub)divide, b) classify, c) break down (*nach* by), d) analyze (*sentence*).

'aufgraben v/t (irr, sep, -ge-, h, → **graben**) dig up.

'aufgreifen v/t (irr, sep, -ge-, h, → **greifen**) **1.** pick up, seize. **2.** take up (idea).

auf'grund → **Grund** 3.

'Aufguß m (-sses; ⸚sse) **1.** infusion. **2.** fig. rehash.

'aufhaben (irr, sep, -ge-, h, → **haben**) F **I** v/t **1.** have a hat etc on. **2.** have door etc open. **3.** ped. have to do: **wir haben heute nichts auf** we have no homework today. **II** v/i **4.** shop etc: be open.

'aufhacken v/t (sep, -ge-, h) pick up.

'aufhaken v/t (sep, -ge-, h) unhook.

aufhalsen ['aʊfhalzən] v/t (sep, -ge-, h) F **j-m et. ~** land s.o. with s.th.

'aufhalten (irr, sep, -ge-, h, → **halten**) v/t **1.** keep open. **2.** stop, hold up, check, stay, delay: **ich wurde durch den Regen aufgehalten** I was delayed by the rain; **ich will Sie nicht länger ~** don't let me keep you. **II sich ~ 3.** stay (im Ausland abroad, bei Freunden with friends). **4.** sich ~ mit spend (contp. waste) one's time on.

'aufhängen v/t (sep, -ge-, h, → **hängen**) **I** v/t **1.** (an dat) hang (up) (on), ⊚ suspend (from): **j-n ~** hang s.o. **2.** F → **aufbürden**. **II sich ~** hang o.s.

'Aufhänger m (-s; -) **1.** tab. **2.** F fig. ~ (für e-n Artikel etc) peg (on which to hang a story etc).

'Aufhängung f (-; -en) ⊚ suspension.

'aufhäufen v/t (sep, -ge-, h) (a. sich ~) pile up, heap up, accumulate.

'aufheben v/t (irr, sep, -ge-, h, → **heben**) **1.** pick up, lift (up), raise: **j-n ~** help s.o. up. **2.** keep (für später for later): → **aufgehoben**. **3.** close (meeting), raise (siege), call off (boycott etc). **4.** abolish (law), cancel (contract), annul (marriage etc), quash (sentence): **ein Verbot ~** lift a ban. **5.** compensate, cancel, neutralize: **sich** (or **einander**) **~** cancel each other out (a. ⚛), neutralize each other. **'Aufheben** n (-s; no pl) fuss, ado: **viel ~(s) machen** make a big fuss (von about). **'Aufhebung** f (-; -en) **1.** abolition (der Todesstrafe of capital punishment), abrogation (of a law), cancel(l)ation (of contract), annulment (of marriage etc), calling-off (of strike etc). **3.** neutralization.

aufheitern ['aʊfhaɪtərn] (sep, -ge-, h) **I**

v/t **j-n ~** cheer s.o. up. **II sich ~** weather: clear (up), a. fig. brighten (up). **'Aufheiterungen** pl meteor. sunny spells.

aufhellen ['aʊfhɛlən] (sep, -ge-, h) **I** v/t **1.** lighten (a. phot.). **2.** fig. shed light on. **II sich ~** → **aufheitern** II.

'aufhetzen v/t (sep, -ge-, h) **j-n ~** incite s.o. (zu et. to [do] s.th.); **j-n ~ gegen** set s.o. against. **'Aufhetzung** f (-; -en) instigation, pol. agitation.

'aufheulen v/i (sep, -ge-, h) (give a) howl, mot. roar.

'aufholen (sep, -ge-, h) **I** v/t catch up on: **e-n Rückstand** (or **Zeitverlust**) **~** make up leeway. **II** v/i (**gegenüber**) catch up (with, on), gain (on).

'aufhorchen v/i (sep, -ge-, h) prick up one's ears, fig. sit up (and take notice).

'aufhören v/i (sep, -ge-, h) stop (a. ~ mit), (come to an) end: **sie hörte nicht auf zu reden** she didn't stop talking; **wo haben wir aufgehört?** where did we leave off?; **hör auf (damit)!** stop it!; **~ zu arbeiten** F knock off (work); **ohne aufzuhören** without letup.

'aufkaufen v/t (sep, -ge-, h) buy up.

'Aufkäufer m (-s; -) (wholesale) buyer.

'aufklappen (sep, -ge-) v/t (h), v/i (sn) open.

'aufklaren v/i (sep, -ge-, h) meteor. clear.

'aufklären (sep, -ge-, h) **I** v/t **1.** clear up (mystery etc), solve (crime), correct (mistake). **2.** enlighten, inform (**über** acc of): **j-n ~** explain the facts of life to s.o. **3.** ✕ reconnoit/re (Am. -er). **II sich ~ 4.** be cleared up, be solved. **5.** → **aufklaren**. **'Aufklärung** f (-; -en) **1.** clearing up, solution: **~ verlangen** demand an explanation. **2.** enlightenment, education, information. **3.** no pl (sexuelle) **~** sex education. **4.** ✕ reconnaissance. **5.** no pl philos. hist. Enlightenment.

'Aufklärungs|film m sex education film. **~flugzeug** n reconnaissance (or scout) plane. **~quote** f clear-up rate.

'aufkleben v/t (sep, -ge-, h) stick on (auf acc to), phot. mount.

'Aufkleber m (-s; -) sticker.

'aufknöpfen v/t (sep, -ge-, h) unbutton, undo.

'aufkochen v/t (sep, -ge-, h) (a. **~lassen**) bring s.th. to the boil.

'aufkommen v/i (irr, sep, -ge-, sn, →

kommen) **1.** arise (*a. suspicion etc*): *Zweifel ~ lassen* give rise to doubt; *nicht ~ lassen* suppress. **2.** *wind*: spring up, *fog etc*: come up. **3.** *rumo(u)r etc*: start. **4.** *miniskirts etc*: come into fashion. **5.** *~ für* a) answer for, be responsible for, b) pay; *für den Schaden ~* compensate for the damage. **6.** *~ gegen* prevail against; *er kommt gegen sie nicht auf* he is no match for her; *niemanden neben sich ~ lassen* suffer no rival. **7.** → *aufholen* II.

'**Aufkommen** *n* (-s) **1.** rise. **2.** † yield.
'**aufkratzen** *v/t* (*sep*, -ge-, h) scratch open: *sich ~* scratch o.s. sore.
'**aufkreuzen** *v/i* (*sep*, -ge-, sn) F turn up.
'**aufladen** (*irr, sep*, -ge-, h, → *laden*) **I** *v/t* **1.** load (*auf acc* onto): F *fig. j-m* (*sich*) *et. ~* saddle s.o. (o.s.) with s.th. **2.** supercharge, boost (*engine*), charge (*battery*). **II** *sich ~* ⚡ become charged.
'**Auflader** *m* (-s; -) *mot.* supercharger.
'**Auflage** *f* (-; -n) **1.** edition (*of book*), circulation (*of newspaper*). **2.** ([*j-m*] *et. zur ~ machen* make s.th. a. condition (for s.o.). **3.** ⊙ a) rest, support, b) layer, c) coating, lining. '**Auflagenhöhe** *f* a) number of copies, b) circulation.
'**auflassen** *v/t* (*irr, sep*, -ge-, h, → *lassen*) **1.** F leave *door etc* open. **2.** F keep *hat etc* on. **3.** ⚖ convey (*property*).
'**auflauern** *v/i* (*sep*, -ge-, h) *j-m ~* waylay s.o., lie in wait for s.o.
'**Auflauf** *m* (-[e]s; ⁓e) **1.** crowd. **2.** riot. **3.** *gastr.* soufflé. '**auflaufen** *v/i* (*irr, sep*, -ge-, sn, → *laufen*) **1.** ⚓ run aground: *auf e-e Mine ~* hit a mine. **2.** run (or bump) (*auf acc* into): *j-n ~ lassen* a) *sports*: obstruct s.o. unfairly, b) *fig.* give s.o. what for. **3.** *money etc*: accumulate, run up, *interest*: a. accrue.
'**Auflaufform** *f* ovenproof dish.
'**aufleben** *v/i* (*sep*, -ge-, sn) (*wieder*) *~ a. fig.* revive; *er lebte förmlich auf* he really livened up.
'**auflegen** (*sep*, -ge-, h) **I** *v/t* **1.** put on (*coal, disc, make-up, etc*), lay (*tablecloth etc*): *den* (*Telefon*)*Hörer ~* → **4**; → *Gedeck* **1. 2.** publish, print. **3.** † issue (*shares*). **II** *v/i* **4.** *teleph.* replace the receiver, hang up.
'**auflehnen**: *sich ~* (*gegen*) oppose (*s.o., s.th.*), rebel (against). '**Auflehnung** *f* (-; -cn) rcbellion (*gegen* against)

'**auflesen** *v/t* (*irr, sep*, -ge-, h, → *lesen*) pick up (*a.* F *fig. s.o.*).
'**aufleuchten** *v/i* (*sep*, -ge-, h) light up.
'**aufliegen** (*irr, sep*, -ge-, h, → *liegen*) **I** *v/i* lie (*or* rest, lean) (*auf dat* on). **II** *sich ~* F 🌶 get bedsore(s).
'**auflisten** *v/t* (*sep*, -ge-, h) list, make a list of.
'**auflockern** *v/t* (*sep*, -ge-, h) **1.** loosen (*the soil*). **2.** *fig.* a) liven up, b) relax.
'**auflodern** *v/i* (*sep*, -ge-, sn) flare up.
'**auflösen** (*sep*, -ge-, h) **I** *v/t* **1.** a) dissolve, b) break off (*engagement*), c) ⚔ disband (*unit*): ([*sich*] *in s-e Bestandteile*) *~* disintegrate. **2.** ⚕ resolve (*equation, a. riddle*), remove (*brackets*). **3.** a) cancel, annul, b) † liquidate, wind up. **II** *sich ~* **4.** dissolve, *meeting etc*: a. break up, ⚔ *unit*: disband: *sich in nichts ~* vanish (into thin air), *hope etc*: go up in smoke. '**Auflösung** *f* (-; -en) **1.** disintegration (*a. fig.*), dissolution, a. breakup (*of meeting*). **2.** † a) liquidation, b) annulment. **3.** ⚔ disbandment. **4.** ♩, ♪, *phot.* resolution.
'**Auflösungszeichen** *n* ♩ natural.
'**aufmachen** (*sep*, -ge-, h) **I** *v/t* F **1.** open: *mach di-e Augen auf!* watch out! **2.** make up, get up, design: *et. in der Presse groß ~* splash s.th.; *e-e Rechnung ~* write out (*fig.* present) a bill. **II** *v/i* F open, answer the door: *j-m ~* let s.o. in. **III** *sich ~* set out (*nach* for). '**Aufmacher** *m* (-s; -) F lead, *n.s.* feature story (*or* photo). '**Aufmachung** *f* (-; -en) **1.** presentation, getup, *print.* layout: *et. in großer ~ herausbringen* feature s.th. prominently. **2.** F outfit, getup.
'**Aufmarsch** *m* (-[e]s; ⁓e) marching up, ⚔ a. deployment. '**aufmar,schieren** *v/i* (sn) a. fig. march up.
aufmerksam ['aʊfmɛrkzaːm] *adj* a) attentive, b) watchful, c) obliging: *j-n ~ machen auf* (*acc*) call (*or* draw) s.o.'s attention to; *~ werden auf* (*acc*) notice, become aware of; *~ zuhören* listen attentively; *et. ~ verfolgen* follow s.th. closely. '**Aufmerksamkeit** *f* (-; -en) **1.** *no pl* attention, attentiveness: *~ erregen* attract attention, (*dat*) *~ schenken* pay attention (to). **2.** small gift.
'**aufmöbeln** *v/t* (*sep*, -ge-, h) F jazz up.
'**aufmuntern** *v/t* (*sep*, -ge-, h) **1.** → *er-*

muntern 1. 2. *j-n* ~ cheer (F pep) s.o. up: ~*de Worte* pep talk.

'**Aufmunterung** *f* (-; -en) cheering up.

aufmüpfig ['aʊfmʏpfɪç] *adj* F rebellious.

'**aufnähen** *v/t* (*sep*, -ge-, h) sew on (*auf acc* to).

Aufnahme ['aʊfnaːmə] *f* (-; -n) 1. *no pl* a) taking up (*of activity etc*), establishing (*relations*), b) intake (*of food*), c) *fig.* absorption (*of knowledge, a. fig.*), taking in (*impressions*). 2. *no pl* (*in acc*) a) integration (within), b) inclusion (into), c) admission (in[to]), d) registration: ~ *finden* be admitted (*bei* [in]to). 3. *no pl* (*a. fig. e-e kühle etc* ~ *finden* meet with a cool *etc*) reception (*bei* from). 4. *no pl* a) accommodation, ⚕ admission (*in acc* to), b) reception (office). 5. *no pl* ✚ a) raising (*funds*), b) assessment (*of damage*). 6. a) *film etc*: taking, shooting, b) photo(graph), shot, c) (sound) recording, pickup: *e-e ~ machen* (*von* of) take a picture, make a (tape-)recording; *Achtung ~!* Action!, Camera! '**aufnahmefähig** *adj* receptive (*für* to). '**Aufnahmefähigkeit** *f* (-; *no pl*) receptivity.

'**Aufnahme|gebühr** *f* admission fee. ~*leiter* *m film*: production (*radio*: recording) manager. ~*prüfung* *f* entrance examination. ~*raum* *m film etc*: studio. ~*wagen* *m* recording van (*Am.* truck).

'**aufnehmen** *v/t* (*irr, sep*, -ge-, h, → *nehmen*) 1. pick up (*load, fig. trail etc*), take up (*meshes*). 2. receive (*a. fig. news*), accommodate, admit (*in acc* to a club, hospital, etc), enter (*in acc* into a list *etc*), include (*in acc* into): *j-n bei sich* ~ put s.o. up; *fig. et. übel* ~ take s.th. amiss. 3. hold (*audience, cargo*), seat (*passengers etc*). 4. take in (*impressions*), (*a. in sich* ~) grasp, absorb (*knowledge*). 5. a) ✿, *phys.* absorb, b) take in (*food*). 6. take up (*activity etc*), enter into (*relations etc*), open (*traffic*): *wieder* ~ resume; *fig. den Kampf mit j-m* ~ take s.o. on; *ich kann es mit ihm nicht* ~ I'm no match for him; → *Kontakt.* 7. a) record, draw up, b) make an inventory of, c) assess (*damage*). 8. record, tape(-record). 9. take (down) (*dictation etc*), take (*order, picture, telegram*[*me*]), shoot (*film*): *j-n* ~ take s.o.'s

picture. 10. ✚ borrow (*money*), raise *mortgage* (*auf acc* on).

'**aufopfern** *v/t* (*sep*, -ge-, h) sacrifice (*sich* ~ o.s.): ~*d* self-sacrificing.

'**aufpäppeln** *v/t* (*sep*, -ge-, h) F feed s.o. up.

'**aufpassen** *v/i* (*sep*, -ge-, h) 1. pay attention: *paß(t) auf!* watch out!; F *paß(t) mal auf!* listen! 2. ~ *auf* (*acc*) a) look after, take care of, b) watch (over); F *paß gut auf dich auf!* take care of yourself)! '**Aufpasser** *m* (-s; -), '**Aufpasserin** *f* (-; -nen) *contp.* watchdog.

'**aufpeitschen** *v/t* (*sep*, -ge-, h) *a. fig.* whip up: *sich* ~ whip o.s. up.

'**aufpflanzen** *v/t* (*sep*, -ge-, h) plant: *fig. sich* ~ plant o.s. (*vor dat* before).

'**aufplustern: sich** ~ (*sep*, -ge-, h) a) *bird:* ruffle its feathers, b) F *fig.* puff o.s. up.

'**aufpo,lieren** *v/t* (*sep*, -ge-, h) polish up.

'**Aufprall** *m* (-[e]s; *no pl*) impact.

'**aufprallen** *v/i* (*sep*, -ge-, sn) ~ *auf* (*acc*) hit, *car etc*: *a.* crash into.

'**Aufpreis** *m* (-es; -e) ✚ extra charge.

'**aufpumpen** *v/t* (*sep*, -ge-, h) pump up.

'**aufputschen** *v/t* (*sep*, -ge-, h) 1. → *aufhetzen.* 2. a) *with drugs etc:* F pep up (*sich* o.s.), b) *fig.* hype up, psych up. '**Aufputschmittel** *n* stimulant, F pep pill, *sl.* upper.

'**aufraffen** (*sep*, -ge-, h) **I** *v/t* snatch up. **II** *sich* ~ *fig.* pull o.s. together; *sich* ~, *et. zu tun* bring o.s. to do s.th.

'**aufragen** *v/i* (*sep*, -ge-, h) loom (up).

'**aufräumen** *v/t, v/i* (*sep*, -ge-, h) tidy (up): ~ *mit* do away with (*abuses etc*).

'**aufrechnen** *v/t* (*sep*, -ge-, h) *et.* ~ set s.th. off (*gegen* against).

'**aufrecht** *adj* upright (*a. fig.*), erect: ~ *sitzen* sit up. ~*erhalten* *v/t* (*irr, sep*, -ge-, h, → *erhalten*) 1. maintain. 2. adhere to. ℒ*erhaltung* *f* (-; *no pl*) maintenance.

'**aufregen** (*sep*, -ge-, h) **I** *v/t* a) excite, b) worry, upset, c) annoy. **II** *sich* ~ (*über acc* about) get excited, be upset. '**aufregend** *adj* a) exciting, b) upsetting. '**Aufregung** *f* (-; -en) excitement: *nur k-e ~!* don't panic!

'**aufreiben** (*irr, sep*, -ge-, h, → *reiben*) *v/t* 1. *fig.* wear down. 2. ✗ wipe out. **II** *sich* ~ *fig.* wear o.s. out. '**aufreibend** *adj* exhausting, trying, stressful.

'**aufreihen** *v/t* (*sep*, -ge-, h) (*a. sich* ~) line up, put *books etc* in a row.

'**aufreißen** (*irr, sep,* -ge-, → *reißen*) **I** *v/t* (h) **1.** tear open (*package etc*), tear up (*road*). **2.** fling *door etc* open, F open *eyes, mouth* wide. **3.** F a) *j-n* ~ pick s.o. up, b) land (*a job etc*). **II** *v/i* (sn) burst, split, break up.

'**aufreizend** *adj* provocative.

'**aufrichten** (*sep,* -ge-, h) **I** *v/t* **1.** → **errichten. 2.** a) set *s.th.* upright, b) straighten up, c) raise (*s.o. in bed*), d) help *s.o.* up. **3.** *fig.* a) comfort, b) encourage. **II sich** ~ **4.** a) straighten o.s. (up), b) sit up (*in bed*). **5.** *fig.* take heart (**an** *dat* from).

'**aufrichtig** *adj* sincere, heartfelt, honest: **es tut mir** ~ **leid** I really am sorry.

'**Aufrichtigkeit** *f* (-; *no pl*) sincerity.

'**aufriegeln** *v/t* (*sep,* -ge-, h) unbolt.

'**Aufriß** *m* (-sses; -sse) △, ℞ elevation.

'**aufrollen** *v/t* (*sep,* -ge-, h) **1.** roll up, furl. **2.** unroll, unfurl. **3.** *fig.* (*wieder*) ~ bring *a subject etc* up (again), reopen (*a case etc*).

'**aufrücken** *v/i* (*sep,* -ge-, sn) **1.** move up (**zu** to, with). **2.** be promoted, rise. **3.** ✕ close the ranks.

'**Aufruf** *m* (-[e]s; -e) call, appeal (**an** *acc* to). '**aufrufen** *v/t* (*irr, sep,* -ge-, h, → *rufen*) *j-n* ~ call (out) s.o.'s name; *j-n* ~, *et. zu tun* call (up)on s.o. to do s.th.; **zum Streik** ~ call a strike.

Aufruhr ['aʊfruːr] *m* (-[e]s; -e) a) turmoil (*a. fig.*), b) uprising, revolt, c) riot (*a. ㅻ*). '**aufrühren** *v/t* (*sep,* -ge-, h) *fig.* **1.** a) rouse (*feelings etc*), b) rake up (*old scandals etc*). **2.** → *aufwühlen* 2.

Aufrührer ['aʊfryːrər] *m* (-s; -), '**Aufrührerin** *f* (-; -nen) rebel, *pol.* agitator.

'**aufrührerisch** *adj* rebellious, seditious.

'**aufrunden** *v/t* (*sep,* -ge-, h) round up (**auf** *acc* to).

'**aufrüsten** *v/t, v/i* (*sep,* -ge-, h) ✕ arm: **wieder** ~ rearm.

'**Aufrüstung** *f* (-; -en) armament.

aufs [aʊfs] = **auf das.**

'**aufsagen** *v/t* (*sep,* -ge-, h) recite.

aufsässig ['aʊfzɛsɪç] *adj* rebellious.

'**Aufsatz** *m* (-es; ⸚e) **1.** essay, *ped. a.* composition, *univ.* paper, (*newspaper*) article. **2.** ✿ top, cap.

'**aufsaugen** *v/t* (*sep,* -ge-, h) absorb.

'**aufscheuchen** *v/t* (*sep,* -ge-, h) *a. fig.* startle.

'**aufschichten** *v/t* (*sep,* -ge-, h) stack up.

'**aufschieben** *v/t* (*irr, sep,* -ge-, h, → *schieben*) **1.** push open. **2.** *fig.* (**auf** *acc, bis* till) put off, postpone.

'**Aufschlag** *m* (-[e]s; ⸚e) **1.** impact (**auf** *acc or dat* on): **dumpfer** ~ thud. **2.** a) cuff, b) turnup, c) lapel. **3.** ♰ extra charge. **4.** *tennis:* service: *j-m den* ~ **abnehmen** break s.o.'s serve; ~ **haben** serve. ~**ball** *m tennis:* service (ball).

'**aufschlagen** (*irr, sep,* -ge-, → *schlagen*) **I** *v/i* **1.** (sn) hit: **auf den** (*or* **dem**) **Boden** ~ hit the ground; **dumpf** ~ thud. **2.** (h) *tennis:* serve. **II** *v/t* (h) **3.** open (*a book, one's eyes*), turn down (*the bed*): **Seite 10** ~ open at page 10. **5.** roll up (*sleeve*). **6. sich das Knie** *etc* ~ bruise one's knee *etc*. **7.** mount (*scaffold etc*), pitch (*tent*): **s-n Wohnsitz in X** ~ take up residence in X. **8.** add 5% *etc* (**auf** *acc* to).

'**Aufschläger** *m* (-s; -) *tennis etc:* server.

'**aufschließen** (*irr, sep,* -ge-, h, → *schließen*) **I** *v/t* **1.** unlock, open. **2.** *biol.,* ㅻ break down (*or* up). **3.** develop (*land, resources*). **II** *v/i* **4.** open the door *etc* (*j-m* for s.o.). **5.** ✕ close (the) ranks, *sports:* move up: ~ **zu** catch up with.

'**aufschlitzen** *v/t* (*sep,* -ge-, h) slit open, slash.

'**Aufschluß** *m* (-sses; ⸚sse) ~ **geben** (*über acc*) give information (on), explain (*s.th.*), *j-m* inform s.o. (about). '**aufschlüsseln** *v/t* (*sep,* -ge-, h) allocate, *statistically:* break down. '**aufschlußreich** *adj* informative, *w.s.* revealing.

'**aufschnallen** *v/t* (*sep,* -ge-, h) **1.** unbuckle. **2.** strap *s.th.* on (**auf** *acc* to).

'**aufschnappen** *v/t* (*sep,* -ge-, h) F *fig.* pick up.

'**aufschneiden** (*irr, sep,* -ge-, h, → *schneiden*) **I** *v/t* cut open, slice (*bread etc*), carve (*meat*), ✂ open, lance (*boil*). **II** *v/i* F brag, boast, show off.

'**Aufschneider** *m* (-s; -) F show-off.

'**Aufschnitt** *m* (-[e]s; *no pl*) cold cuts.

'**aufschnüren** *v/t* (*sep,* -ge-, h) untie, undo, unlace.

'**aufschrauben** *v/t* (*sep,* -ge-, h) **1.** unscrew. **2.** screw *s.th.* on (**auf** *acc* to).

'**aufschrecken** (*sep,* -ge-) **I** *v/t* startle: *j-n* ~ *aus* rouse s.o. from. **II** *v/i* (sn) (give a) start: **aus dem Schlaf** ~ wake with a start.

'**Aufschrei** *m* ([e]s; -e) cry, *fig.* outcry.

'**aufschreiben** v/t (irr, sep, -ge-, h, →
schreiben) write down, take a note of:
F **j-n ~** book s.o.

'**aufschreien** v/i (irr, sep, -ge-, h, →
schreien) cry out (vor with).

'**Aufschrift** f (-; -en) inscription.

'**Aufschub** m (-[e]s; ⸚e) postponement,
delay, ✝ respite, 🏛 a. fig. reprieve: **k-n
~ dulden** bear no delay.

'**aufschürfen** v/t (sep, -ge-, h) graze: **sich
das Knie ~** bark one's knee.

'**aufschütteln** v/t (sep, -ge-, h) plump up.

'**aufschütten** v/t (sep, -ge-, h) heap up.

'**aufschwatzen** v/t (sep, -ge-, h) F **j-m et.
~** talk s.o. into buying s.th.

'**aufschweißen** v/t (sep, -ge-, h) weld
open.

'**aufschwemmen** v/t (sep, -ge-, h) bloat.

'**aufschwingen**: **sich ~** v/i (irr, sep, -ge-, h,
→ **schwingen**) soar (up).

'**Aufschwung** m (-[e]s; ⸚e) **1.** gym. swing-
-up. **2.** no pl fig. (fresh) impetus, ✝
upswing, recovery, boom.

'**aufsehen** v/i (irr, sep, -ge-, h, → **sehen**)
→ **aufblicken. Aufsehen** n (-s) **-erre-
gen** attract attention, w.s. cause a stir
(or sensation); **um ~ zu vermeiden** to
avoid notice. '**aufsehenerregend** adj
sensational. '**Aufseher** m (-s; -), '**Auf-
seherin** f (-; -nen) **1.** attendant. **2.**
(prison) warder, Am. guard.

'**aufsein** v/i (irr, sep, -ge-, sn, → **sein**)
F **1.** door etc: be open. **2.** person: be
up.

'**aufsetzen** (sep, -ge-, h) **I** v/t **1.** a. fig. put
on: **aufgesetzte Tasche** patch pocket.
2. draft (speech etc). **3.** a. v/i ✈ land:
weich ~ make a soft landing. **II** **sich ~**
sit up (**im Bett** in bed). '**Aufsetzer** m
(-s; -) soccer etc: bounce shot.

'**Aufsicht** f (-; -en) **1.** no pl supervision,
🏛 custody: **die ~ haben** (or **führen**) be
in charge (**über** acc of), invigilate (an
exam); **unter ärztlicher ~** under medical supervision; **ohne ~** unattended
(children). **2.** supervisor, person in
charge. '**aufsichtführend** adj supervisory, teacher etc in charge.

'**Aufsichts|beamte** m **1.** supervisor. **2.**
(prison) warder, Am. guard. **-behörde**
f supervisory board. **-rat** m ✝ supervisory board.

'**aufsitzen** v/i (irr, sep, -ge-, sn, → **sitzen**)
1. get on, mount (horse etc). **2.** fig. be

taken in (dat by). **3.** F **j-n ~ lassen** let
s.o. down.

'**aufspannen** v/t (sep, -ge-, h) spread
out, put up (umbrella etc).

'**aufsparen** v/t (sep, -ge-, h) save (up).

'**aufsperren** v/t (sep, -ge-, h) open wide:
F **Mund und Nase ~** gape.

'**aufspielen** (sep, -ge-, h) **I** v/t, v/i play. **II**
sich ~ F give o.s. airs; **sich als Held** etc
~ play the hero etc.

'**aufspießen** v/t (sep, -ge-, h) a) spear,
impale, b) a. fig. skewer.

'**aufspringen** v/i (irr, sep, -ge-, sn, →
springen) **1.** jump up, leap up, ball:
bounce: **~ auf** (acc) jump on to (a train
etc). **2.** buds, door: burst open. **3.** skin:
chap, lips: crack.

'**aufspulen** v/t (sep, -ge-, h) wind (up).

'**aufspüren** v/t (sep, -ge-, h) track down.

'**aufstampfen** v/i (sep, -ge-, h) (**mit dem
Fuß**) **~** stamp one's foot.

'**Aufstand** m (-[e]s; ⸚e) **1.** rebellion, revolt. **2.** F fig. (big) fuss. '**Aufständi-
sche** m, f (-n; -n) rebel, insurgent.

'**aufstauen** v/t (sep, -ge-, h) dam up.

'**aufstechen** v/t (irr, sep, -ge-, h, → **stechen**) puncture, 🗡 lance.

'**aufstecken** v/t (sep, -ge-, h) **1.** put up,
pin up (one's hair). **2.** put on (candles):
→ **Licht** 2. **3.** a. v/i F give up.

'**aufstehen** v/i (irr, sep, -ge-, sn, → **stehen**) **1.** rise, get up (**vom Tisch** from the
table): **~ dürfen** patient: be allowed (to
get) up. **2.** fig. rise (in arms), rebel.

'**aufsteigen** v/i (irr, sep, -ge-, sn, → **steigen**) **1.** rise, bird: a. soar (up), ✈ take
off, mount. go up. **2.** fig. be promoted
(a. sports), rise. **3.** **~ auf** (acc) get on,
mount (vehicle, horse). **4.** fig. feeling
etc: rise, well up: **ein Verdacht stieg in
mir auf** I had a suspicion (**daß** that).

'**Aufsteiger** m (-s; -) **1.** F a) social climber, b) (professional) success, F whiz kid.
2. sports: (newly-)promoted team.

'**aufstellen** (sep, -ge-, h) **I** v/t **1.** a) set up,
put up, raise (ladder), pitch (tent), b)
arrange, c) line up, place, post (guard
etc), d) erect (monument), e) install (machine), f) set (trap): **die Ohren ~** animal:
prick its ears. **2.** nominate (candidate,
player), compose (team), ⚔ activate
(troops): pol. **sich als Kandidaten ~**
lassen stand (Am. run) for election etc.
3. make (up), prepare (list). **4.** advance

(*theory*), lay down, state (*rules etc*), a form (*equation*): **e-n Rekord ~** set (up) (*or establish*) a record. **II sich ~** place o.s. (**vor** *dat* before), ✕ form up; **sich hintereinander ~** line up.

'**Aufstellung** *f* (-; -en) **1.** *no pl* setting up (*etc*, → **aufstellen** 1), installation. **2.** *no pl* nomination (*of candidate, player*), line-up (*of team*). **3.** list, table, survey, ✝ statement: **~ e-r Bilanz** preparation of a balance sheet.

'**aufstemmen** *v/t* (*sep*, -ge-, h) prize open.

'**Aufstieg** ['aʊfʃtiːk] *m* (-[e]s; -e) **1.** ascent (*a.* ✈), way up. **2.** *fig.* rise, promotion (*a. sports*): **im ~ begriffen sein** be on the rise, be rising; *sports*: **den ~ schaffen** be promoted.

'**Aufstiegs|chancen** *pl* promotion prospects. **~spiel** *n sports*: promotion tie.

'**aufstöbern** *v/t* (*sep*, -ge-, h) track down.

'**aufstocken** *v/t* (*sep*, -ge-, h) **1.** △ raise. **2.** increase (*one's capital*).

'**aufstöhnen** *v/i* (*sep*, -ge-, h) (give a loud) groan.

'**aufstoßen** (*irr, sep*, -ge-, h, → **stoßen**) **I** *v/t* push open. **II** *v/i* burp, belch: **j-m ~** repeat on s.o., **F** *fig.* strike s.o.

'**aufstrebend** *adj fig.* a) up-and-coming, rising, b) emergent (*nation*).

'**Aufstrich** *m* (-[e]s; -e) spread.

'**aufstützen** (*sep*, -ge-, h) **I** *v/t* prop up (**auf** *dat, acc* on). **II sich ~ auf** (*dat, acc*) lean (up)on.

'**aufsuchen** *v/t* (*sep*, -ge-, h) a) visit, (go and) see (*a doctor etc*), b) go to.

'**auftakeln** (*sep*, -ge-, h) **I** *v/t* ⚓ rig out. **II sich ~ F** get dolled up.

'**Auftakt** *m* (-[e]s; -e) **1.** ♪ upbeat. **2.** *fig.* (**den ~ bilden** be a) prelude (**zu** to).

'**auftanken** *v/t, v/i* (*sep*, -ge-, h) fill up, refuel.

'**auftauchen** *v/i* (*sep*, -ge-, sn) come up (*a. fig. problem etc*), emerge, *submarine*: surface, *fig.* turn up, *doubts etc*: arise.

'**auftauen** (*sep*, -ge-) **I** *v/t* (h) a) thaw, b) defrost. **II** *v/i* (sn) *a. fig.* thaw.

'**aufteilen** *v/t* (*sep*, -ge-, h) **1.** distribute, share (out). **2.** divide (**in** *acc* into).

auftischen ['aʊftɪʃən] *v/t* (*sep*, -ge-, h) *a. fig.* dish up.

Auftrag ['aʊftraːk] *m* (-[e]s; ⸚e) **1.** ✝ order, commission: **et. in ~ geben** order

(*or* commission) s.th. (**bei j-m** from s.o.); **im ~ und auf Rechnung von** by order and for account of. **2.** order(s) (*a.* ✕), instructions, (*a.* ✕ combat) mission: **im ~ von** (*or gen*) by order of, **handeln** act on behalf of.

'**auftragen** (*irr, sep*, -ge-, h, → **tragen**) **I** *v/t* **1.** serve (up) (*food*). **2.** apply, put on (*make-up, paint, etc*). **3.** *j-m et.* **~**, *j-m* **~**, *et.* **zu tun** instruct (*or* tell) s.o. to do s.th. **4.** wear out (*clothes*). **II** *v/i* **5.** *pullover etc*: make s.o. look fat(ter); **F** *fig.* **dick ~** lay it on thick.

'**Auftraggeber(in** *f*) *m* client, customer.

'**Auftrags|bestätigung** *f* ✝ confirmation (*by supplier*: acknowledg[e]ment) of (an) order. **~buch** *n* ✝ order book. **~dienst** *m* telephone answering service. **≈gemäß** *adv* according to instructions, ✝ as per order. **~lage** *f* ✝ orders situation. **~polster** *n* ✝ filled order books. **~werk** *n* commissioned work.

'**auftreffen** *v/i* (*irr, sep*, -ge-, sn, → **treffen**) hit (**auf** *dat, acc* on).

'**auftreiben** *v/t* (*irr, sep*, -ge-, h, → **treiben**) **F** get hold of, find.

'**auftrennen** *v/t* (*sep*, -ge-, h) undo (*a seam*), unravel (*knitting*).

'**auftreten** *v/i* (*irr, sep*, -ge-, sn, → **treten**) **1.** *leise* **~** tread softly; **er kann mit dem verletzten Fuß nicht ~** he can't walk on his injured foot. **2.** *thea.* a) make one's entrance, b) appear (on stage) (**als** as), *a. musician*: perform: **Hamlet tritt auf** enter Hamlet; **zum ersten Mal ~** make one's debut. **3.** a) appear (**öffentlich** in public, **als Zeuge** as a witness, **vor Gericht** in court), b) present o.s. (**als** as), c) behave: **als Vermittler ~** act as go-between. **4.** *fig. problem, doubts, etc*: arise, *epidemic etc*: occur. '**Auftreten** *n* (-s) **1.** appearance, *thea.* performance. **2.** occurrence, arising. **3.** behavio(u)r.

'**Auftrieb** *m* (-[e]s; *no pl*) **1.** *phys.* buoyancy, ✈ a. lift. **2.** *fig.* (fresh) impetus, ✝ upswing: (**neuen**) **~ verleihen** give a (fresh) impetus (*dat* to).

'**Auftritt** *m* (-[e]s; -e) **1.** *thea.* a) entrance, b) scene. **2.** *fig.* scene, **F** row.

'**auftrumpfen** *v/i* (*sep*, -ge-, h) *fig.* come it strong: **~ gegen** make a strong showing against; **mit e-m Rekord etc ~** come up with a record *etc*.

'**auftun: sich ~** (*irr, sep,* -ge-, h, → **tun**) *a. fig.* open

'**auftürmen** (*sep,* -ge-, h) *v/t* pile up.

'**aufwachen** *v/i* (*sep,* -ge-, sn) wake up: **aus der Narkose ~** come round.

'**aufwachsen** *v/i* (*irr, sep,* -ge-, sn, → **wachsen**) grow up.

'**aufwallen** *v/i* (*sep,* -ge-, sn) **1.** boil (up). **2.** *fig.* surge, well up.

'**Aufwand** ['aʊfvant] *m* (-[e]s; *no pl*) **1.** expenditure (**an** *dat of*), cost, expense: **e-n großen ~ an Energie** *etc* **erfordern** require a great deal of energy *etc*; **der ganze ~ war umsonst** it was a waste of time (energy, money, *etc*). **2.** luxury, extravagance: **e-n großen ~ treiben** be very extravagant. '**Aufwandsentschädigung** *f* expense allowance.

'**aufwärmen** (*sep,* -ge-, h) **I** *v/t* **1.** warm up, heat up. **2.** *fig.* rehash. **II sich ~** warm o.s., *sports:* limber up.

aufwärts ['aʊfverts] *adv* up, upward(s). '**Aufwärtsentwicklung** *f* upward trend. '**aufwärtsgehen** *v/impers* (*irr, sep,* -ge-, sn, → **gehen**) **es geht aufwärts** (**mit ihm**) things are looking up (with him); **mit dem Geschäft geht es aufwärts** business is improving.

'**Aufwärtshaken** *m boxing:* uppercut.

'**Aufwasch** *m* (-[e]s; *no pl*) → **Abwasch**.

'**aufwaschen** *v/t* (*irr, sep,* -ge-, h) → **abwaschen**.

'**aufwecken** *v/t* (*sep,* -ge-, h) wake (up).

'**aufweichen** (*sep,* -ge-) **I** *v/t* (h) **1.** a) soak, b) make soggy. **2.** *fig.* undermine. **II** *v/i* (sn) become soggy, *a. fig.* soften.

'**aufweisen** *v/t* (*irr, sep,* -ge-, h, → **weisen**) **et. ~, et. aufzuweisen haben** have (or show) s.th.; **große Mängel ~** have many defects.

'**aufwenden** *v/t* (*irr, sep,* -ge-, h, → **wenden**) a) use, apply, b) spend (**für** on): **(viel) Mühe ~** take (great) pains. '**aufwendig** *adj* **1.** large-scale. **2.** expensive. '**Aufwendungen** *pl* expenditure.

'**aufwerfen** (*irr, sep,* -ge-, h, → **werfen**) **I** *v/t* **1.** throw up (*dam etc*). **2.** *fig.* raise (*question etc*). **II sich ~** set o.s. up (**zum Richter** *etc* as judge *etc*).

'**aufwerten** *v/t* (*sep,* -ge-, h) ✝ revalue (upward), *a. fig.* upvalue.

'**Aufwertung** *f* (-; -en) ✝ revaluation (upward), *fig.* upgrading.

'**aufwickeln** *v/t* (*sep,* -ge-, h) **1.** (*a. sich ~*)

roll (*or* coil) up. **2.** F put *one's hair* up in curlers. **3.** → **auswickeln**.

aufwiegeln ['aʊfviːɡəln] *v/t* (*sep,* -ge-, h) → **aufhetzen**.

'**aufwiegen** *v/t* (*irr, sep,* -ge-, h, → **wiegen**) *fig.* offset, make up for.

'**Aufwind** *m* (-[e]s; -e) **1.** ✈ upwind. **2.** → **Auftrieb 2**, **3**, ✝ **im ~** on the upswing.

'**aufwirbeln** *v/t* (*sep,* -ge-, h) whirl up (*a. v/i,* sn), raise (*dust*): *fig.* (**viel**) **Staub ~** cause quite a stir.

'**aufwischen** *v/t* (*sep,* -ge-, h) a) mop up, b) wipe, mop.

'**aufwühlen** *v/t* (*sep,* -ge-, h) **1.** turn up (*ground*), churn up (*sea*). **2.** *fig. j-n ~* stir s.o. deeply; **~d** stirring.

'**aufzählen** *v/t* (*sep,* -ge-, h) enumerate. '**Aufzählung** *f* (-; -en) enumeration.

'**aufzäumen** *v/t* (*sep,* -ge-, h) bridle: → **Pferd 1**.

'**aufzehren** *v/t* (*sep,* -ge-, h) *fig.* use up.

'**aufzeichnen** *v/t* (*sep,* -ge-, h) **1.** a) record, write down, b) tape(-record), *TV* (video-)tape. **2.** draw (**auf** *acc* on), sketch, ⊙ trace. '**Aufzeichnung** *f* (-; -en) **1.** *a.* ⊙, *TV* recording. **2.** *pl* notes, record, *w.s.* papers: **sich ~en machen** make notes (**über** *acc* of).

'**aufzeigen** *v/t* (*sep,* -ge-, h) show, demonstrate, point out.

'**aufziehen** (*irr, sep,* -ge-, → **ziehen**) **I** *v/t* (h) **1.** wind up: **Spielzeug zum ♁ Aufziehen** clockwork toys. **2.** draw up, pull up, hoist (*flag etc*), *thea.* raise (*the curtain*). **3.** (pull) open (*drawer*), open, draw (*curtains*), undo (*knot*). **4.** mount (*tyre*), put on (*strings*), mount *picture* (on cardboard): *fig.* **andere Saiten ~** change one's tune. **5.** raise, bring up, rear. **6.** F organize, mount, set up (*business etc*). **7.** F *j-n ~* tease s.o., pull s.o.'s leg. **8.** ⚕ fill (*syringe*). **II** *v/i* (sn) **9.** *clouds:* gather, *storm: a.* be brewing (*a. fig.*). **10.** ✕ march up.

'**Aufzucht** *f* (-; -en) breeding, raising.

'**Aufzug** *m* (-[e]s; -¨e) **1.** procession, parade. **2.** lift, *Am.* elevator. **3.** F *contp.* getup. **4.** *thea.* act. **5.** *gym.* pull-up.

'**aufzwingen** *v/t* (*irr, sep,* -ge-, h, → **zwingen**) *j-m et.* **~** force s.th. (up)on s.o., impose *one's will* on s.o.

'**Augapfel** *m anat.* eyeball: *fig.* **et. wie s-n ~ hüten** guard s.th. like gold.

Auge ['aʊɡə] *n* (-s; -n) **1.** *anat.* eye: **gute**

(**schlechte**) **⁓n haben** have good (bad) eyesight (*or* eyes); **vor aller ⁓n** openly, in full view; **unter vier ⁓n** in private; **nur fürs ⁓** just for show; **⁓ um ⁓!** an eye for an eye!; F *fig.* **blaues ⁓** black eye; **mit e-m blauen ⁓ davonkommen** get off cheaply; **mit bloßem ⁓** with the naked eye; **vor m-m geistigen ⁓** in my mind's eye; *a. fig.* **mit verbundenen ⁓n** blindfold; **das ⁓ des Gesetzes** the law; **im ⁓ behalten** keep an eye on, *fig.* keep *s.th.* in mind; **ins ⁓ fallen** catch the eye; **ins ⁓ fallend** a) striking, b) obvious; **ins ⁓ fassen** consider; **j-m et. vor ⁓n führen** make *s.th.* clear to *s.o.*; F **das kann leicht ins ⁓ gehen** that can easily go wrong; **das hätte leicht ins ⁓ gehen können!** that was close!; **et. im ⁓ haben** have *s.th.* in mind; **ein ⁓ haben auf** (*acc*) have an eye on *s.o.*, *s.th.*; **⁓ überall haben** see everything; **sich et. vor ⁓n halten** bear *s.th.* in mind; **nicht aus den ⁓n lassen** keep one's eyes on; **große ⁓n machen** gape; F **er wird ⁓n machen!** he's in for a surprise!; **sie hat** (**vielleicht**) **⁓n gemacht!** you should have seen her face!; **j-m** (**schöne**) **⁓n machen** make eyes at *s.o.*; *fig.* **j-m die ⁓n öffnen** open *s.o.*'s eyes; **soweit das ⁓ reicht** as far as the eye can see; F **ein ⁓ riskieren** risk a glance; **dem Tod** *etc* **ins ⁓ sehen** look death *etc* in the eye, face death *etc*; **j-m in die ⁓n sehen** look *s.o.* full in the face; *fig.* **in die ⁓n springen** leap to the eye, be obvious; **das stach mir ins ⁓** it caught my fancy; **ich traute m-n ⁓n kaum** I could hardly believe my eyes; **aus den ⁓n verlieren** lose sight of; **die ⁓n verschließen vor** close one's eyes to; F **ein ⁓ zudrücken** turn a blind eye; **ich habe kein ⁓ zugetan** I didn't sleep a wink. **2.** *on dice, card*: pip. **3.** ♣ eye. **4.** globule of fat.

äugen ['ɔʏgən] *v/i* (h) *esp. hunt.* look.

'**Augen|arzt** *m* eye specialist, ophthalmologist. **⁓bank** *f* (-; -en) 🩸 eye bank.

'**Augenblick** *m* (-[e]s; -e) moment: **e-n ⁓ bitte!** just a moment, please!; **im ⁓ at** the moment; **im ersten ⁓** for a moment; **im letzten ⁓** at the (very) last moment; **alle ⁓e** every (*or* any) moment. '**augenblicklich** I *adj* **1.** immediate. **2.** present, current. **3.** momenta-

ry. **II** *adv* **4.** immediately. **5.** at the moment, (just) now.

'**Augen|braue** *f* eyebrow. **⁓brauenstift** *m* eyebrow pencil. **⁓fältchen** *pl* crow's-feet. **⁓farbe** *f* colo(u)r of eyes. **⁓heilkunde** *f* ophthalmology. **⁓höhe** *f* (**in ⁓** at) eye level. **⁓höhle** *f anat.* eye socket, orbit. **⁓innendruck** *m* 🩸 intra-ocular pressure. **⁓klappe** *f* eye patch. **⁓klinik** *f* eye clinic. **⁓leiden** *n* eye disease. **⁓licht** *n* (-[e]s; *no pl*) (eye)sight. **⁓lid** *n* eyelid. **⁓maß** *n* (-es; *no pl*) **1.** *ein gutes ⁓ haben* have a sure eye. **2.** *fig.* (good) *political etc* judg(e)ment.

'**Augenmerk** *n* **sein ⁓ richten auf** (*acc*) direct one's attention to.

'**Augen|muskel** *m* eye muscle. **⁓nerv** *m* optic nerve. **⁓operati,on** *f* eye operation. **⁓salbe** *f* eye ointment.

'**Augenschein** *m* (-[e]s; *no pl*) appearance(s): **dem ⁓ nach** to all appearances; **in ⁓ nehmen** inspect closely. '**augenscheinlich** *adj* evident, apparent, obvious.

'**Augen|spiegel** *m* 🩸 ophthalmoscope. **⁓tropfen** *pl* 🩸 eyedrops. **⁓weide** *f fig.* feast for the eyes. **⁓wimper** *f* eyelash. **⁓wischerei** [-vɪʃə'raɪ] *f* (-; -en) F eyewash. **⁓zahn** *m* eyetooth. **⁓zeuge** *m* eyewitness. **⁓zeugenbericht** *m* eyewitness report. **⁓zwinkern** *n* (-s) (**mit e-m ⁓** with a) wink.

August [aʊ'gʊst] *m* (-[e]s, -; -e) (**im ⁓ in**) August.

Auktion [aʊk'tsɪ̯oːn] *f* (-; -en) 🔨 auction (sale), public sale. **Auktionator** [aʊktsɪ̯o'naːtɔr] *m* (-s; -en [-na'toːrən]) auctioneer. **Aukti'onshaus** *n* auctioneers.

Aula ['aʊla] *f* (-; -s, Aulen) *ped.*, *univ.* assembly hall.

Au-pair-Mädchen [o'pɛːr-] *n* au pair (girl).

aus [aʊs] **I** *prep* (*dat*) **1.** out of, from: **⁓ dem Fenster sehen** look out of (*Am.* out) the window; **⁓ dem Haus gehen** leave the house; 🚂 **⁓ Berlin** from Berlin; **⁓ unserer Mitte** from among us; **⁓ der Flasche** drink from the bottle. **2.** (*origin*) from, (*time*) *a.* of: **er ist ⁓ Berlin** he comes from Berlin; **⁓ ganz Spanien** from all over Spain; **⁓ dem 19. Jh.** of the 19th century; **er liest ⁓ s-m Roman** he reads from his novel; **⁓ dem Deutschen** *translated* from (the) Ger-

man. **3.** (made) of, from: *fig.* ~ *ihm wurde ein guter Arzt* he became a good doctor. **4.** ~ *Mitleid* (*Neugier etc*) out of pity (curiosity *etc*); ~ *Liebe* from love; ~ *Liebe zu* for the love of; ~ *Prinzip* on principle; ~ *Spaß* for fun; ~ *Versehen* by mistake. **II** *adv* **5.** *von ... ~* from; *von hier* ~ from here; *fig. von Natur* ~ by nature; *von mir ~ kann er gehen* he may go, for all I care; F *von mir* ~! I don't care!; *von sich* ~ of one's own accord. **6.** F a) (*switched*) off, out: *ein - aus* on - off, b) over, out; *die Schule ist* ~ school is over; *damit ist es* (*jetzt*) ~! that's all over now!; *mit ihm ist es* ~ he has had it; ~ *der Mode* out of fashion. **7.** ~ *und ein* in and out; *fig. bei j-m ein und* ~ *gehen* be a frequent visitor at s.o.'s house; *ich weiß nicht mehr ein noch* ~ I'm at my wits' end.
Aus *n* (-; *no pl*) *sports: im* (*ins*) ~ out; *a. fig. das bedeutete das* ~ *für ihn* with that he was out (of the game).

'**ausarbeiten** *v/t* (*sep*, -ge-, h) work out, elaborate, develop, draw up. '**Ausarbeitung** *f* (-; -en) **1.** working out, elaboration, development. **2.** draft.

'**ausarten** *v/i* (*sep*, -ge-, sn) degenerate (*in acc, zu* into), *game, party, etc*: get out of hand.

'**ausatmen** *v/i, v/t* (*sep*, -ge-, h) breathe out, exhale.

'**ausbaden** *v/t* (*sep*, -ge-, h) F *et.* ~ *müssen* have to carry the can.

'**ausbaggern** *v/t* (*sep*, -ge-, h) excavate, dredge.

'**ausbalan,cieren** *v/t* (*sep*, h) *a. fig.* balance out.

'**Ausbau** *m* (-[e]s; *no pl*) **1.** ⚙ disassembly, removal. **2.** △ a) extension, b) interior works. **3.** *a. fig.* expansion, development. **4.** *fig.* consolidation.

'**ausbauen** *v/t* (*sep*, -ge-, h) **1.** ⚙ dismantle, remove. **2.** △ extend: *das Dach* ~ build rooms into the attic. **3.** *a. fig.* extend, expand, develop: *sports: s-n Vorsprung* ~ increase one's lead. **4.** strengthen, consolidate. '**ausbaufähig** *adj* capable of development: ~*e Stellung* position with good prospects.

'**ausbedingen** *v/t* (*irr, sep*, h, → *bedingen*) *sich et.* ~ reserve (*o.s.*) s.th.; *sich* ~, *daß ...* make it a condition that ...

'**ausbessern** *v/t* (*sep*, -ge-, h) mend, re-

pair. '**Ausbesserung** *f* (-; -en) repair(s).

'**ausbeulen** *v/t* (*sep*, -ge-, h) **1.** ⚙ beat out. **2.** make *trousers etc* baggy.

'**Ausbeute** *f* (-; *no pl*) profit, *a.* ⚔, ⚙ yield, output, *fig.* result(s). '**ausbeuten** *v/t* (*sep*, -ge-, h) exploit (*a. b.s.*), ⚔ *a.* work. '**Ausbeuter** *m* (-s; -) *b.s.* exploiter. '**ausbeuterisch** *adj b.s.* exploitative. '**Ausbeutung** *f* (-; *no pl*) *a. b.s.* exploitation.

'**ausbilden** (*sep*, -ge-, h) **I** *v/t* **1.** a) train, instruct, educate, b) develop: *j-n zum Sänger* ~ train s.o. to be a singer. **2.** *biol.* form, develop. **II** *sich* ~ (*lassen*) *zu* train (*or* be trained, study) to be: ~ *ausgebildet.* '**Ausbilder** *m* (-s; -) *a.* ⚔ instructor. '**Ausbildung** *f* (-; -en) training, *ped., univ.* education: *in der* ~ *stehen* be undergoing training.

'**Ausbildungs|beihilfe** *f* grant. ~*gang m* training. ~*platz m* training post. ~*zeit f* period of training.

'**ausbitten** *v/t* (*irr, sep*, -ge-, h, → *bitten*) *sich et.* ~ ask for s.th.

'**ausblasen** *v/t* (*irr, sep*, -ge-, h, → *blasen*) blow out.

'**ausbleiben** *v/i* (*irr, sep*, -ge-, sn, → *bleiben*) a) fail to come, b) stay away, c) stop: ⚕ *ihre Periode blieb aus* she missed her period; *fig. es konnte nicht* ~, *daß* it was inevitable that; (*nicht*) *lange* ~ (not to) be long in coming.

'**Ausbleiben** *n* (-s) absence.

'**ausbleichen** *v/i* (*irr, sep*, -ge-, sn) bleach (*a. v/t*, h), fade.

'**ausblenden** *v/t* (*sep*, -ge-, h) *film, radio*: fade out.

'**Ausblick** *m* (-[e]s; -e) view (*auf acc* of): *Zimmer mit* ~ *auf den See* room(s) overlooking the lake.

'**ausbomben** *v/t* (*sep*, -ge-, h) bomb out.

'**ausbooten** *v/t* (*sep*, -ge-, h) ⚓ disembark. **2.** F *fig.* oust, get rid of s.o.

'**ausbrechen** (*irr, sep*, -ge-, → *brechen*) **I** *v/t* (h) **1.** break out (*or* off). **2.** → *erbrechen* 2. **II** *v/i* (sn) **3.** ~ *aus* (*dat*) break out of, escape from, *fig.* break away from (*a. sports*): F *aus der Gesellschaft* ~ drop out of society. **4.** *fire, war, epidemic, etc*: break out, *volcano*: erupt. **5.** *in Tränen* ~ burst into tears; *ihm brach der Schweiß aus* he broke into a sweat; *in Gelächter* ~ burst out

laughing; *in Beifall* ~ break into applause. **6.** *mot.* swerve out of line.
'**Ausbrecher** *m* (-s; -) escaped prisoner.
'**ausbreiten** (*sep*, -ge-, h) **I** *v/t* **1.** spread (out). **2.** *fig.* extend, expand (*power etc*), display (*knowledge*). **II** *sich* ~ **3.** *fire, epidemic, etc*: spread. **4.** *terrain*: spread (out), stretch (out), *panorama*: open up (*vor j-m* before s.o.). **5.** F spread (o.s.) out. '**Ausbreitung** *f* (-; *no pl*) spread(ing), extension, expansion.
'**ausbrennen** (*irr, sep*, -ge-, → **brennen**) **I** *v/t* (h) burn out, 🔥 cauterize: → *ausgebrannt*. **II** *v/i* (sn) burn out.
'**Ausbruch** *m* (-[e]s; ⸚e) **1.** escape: ~ *aus dem Gefängnis* jailbreak, breakout. **2.** *fig.* outbreak (*of war, epidemic, etc*), eruption (*of volcano*): *zum* ~ *kommen* break out. **3.** *fig.* outburst.
'**ausbrüten** *v/t* (*sep*, -ge-, h) *a. fig.* hatch, F be sickening for (*a disease*).
'**ausbuchen** *v/t* (*sep*, -ge-, h) **1.** ✝ cancel. **2.** → *ausgebucht*.
'**ausbuchten**: *sich* ~ (*sep*, -ge-, h) bulge (*or* curve) out(wards).
'**ausbuddeln** *v/t* (*sep*, -ge-, h) F dig up.
'**ausbügeln** *v/t* (*sep*, -ge-, h) *a. F fig.* iron out.
'**ausbürgern** *v/t* (*sep*, -ge-, h) denaturalize.
'**ausbürsten** *v/t* (*sep*, -ge-, h) brush down.
'**Ausdauer** *f* (-; *no pl*) perseverance, *a.* ⊚ endurance, tenacity, *esp. sports*: staying power, stamina. '**ausdauernd** *adj* **1.** persevering, tireless. **2.** 🌱 perennial.
'**ausdehnen** *v/t* (*sep*, -ge-, h) (*a. sich* ~) *a. phys.*) ⊚ stretch, expand, extend (*auf acc* to): → *ausgedehnt*. '**Ausdehnung** *f* (-; en) **1.** *no pl* extension (*auf acc* to), expansion, spread(ing). **2.** extent, size.
'**ausdenken** *v/t* (*irr, sep*, -ge-, h, → **denken**) *sich et.* ~ **a.**) think *s.th.* up, F come up with, **b.**) imagine, **c.**) invent, devise; *nicht auszudenken sein* be inconceivable; *die Folgen sind nicht auszudenken* the consequences could be disastrous.
'**ausdiskutieren** *v/t* (*sep*, -ge-, h) thresh out.
'**ausdörren** *v/t* (*sep*, -ge-, h) dry up, parch: → *ausgedörrt*.
'**ausdrehen** *v/t* (*sep*, -ge-, h) F turn off.
'**Ausdruck**[1] *m* (-[e]s; ⸚e) expression (*a.* 🇦 *etc*), word, term, phrase: *idiomati*-

scher ~ idiom; *juristischer* ~ legal term; *zum* ~ *bringen* express; *zum* ~ *kommen* be expressed; F *das ist gar kein* ~*!* that's putting it mildly!
'**Ausdruck**[2] *m* (-[e]s; -e) *computer*: printout. '**ausdrucken** *v/t* (*sep*, -ge-, h) print *s.th.* in full, *computer*: print out.
'**ausdrücken** (*sep*, -ge-, h) **I** *v/t* **1.** stub out (*cigarette*). **2.** squeeze (out). **3.** *fig.* **a.**) express, put into words, **b.**) show, reveal: *ich weiß nicht, wie ich es* ~ *soll* I don't know how to put it; *anders ausgedrückt* in other words. **II** *sich* ~ **4.** express o.s. **5.** be revealed.
'**ausdrücklich I** *adj* express; ~*er Befehl* strict order. **II** *adv* expressly, specially.
'**Ausdruckskraft** *f* (-; *no pl*) expressiveness. '**ausdruckslos** *adj* blank, expressionless. '**ausdrucksvoll** *adj* expressive. '**Ausdrucksweise** *f* style, diction.
'**ausdünsten** *v/t* (*sep*, -ge-, h) give off.
'**Ausdünstung** *f* (-; -en) odo(u)r.
ausein'ander *adv* apart, separated, F *marriage*: on the rocks: *... schreibt man* ~ ... is written in two words; *die Kinder sind zwei Jahre* ~ the children are two years apart in age. ~**brechen** *v/t* (*irr, sep*, -ge-, h, → **brechen**) *and v/i* (sn) break asunder. ~**bringen** *v/t* (*irr, sep*, -ge-, h, → **bringen**) separate. ~**fallen** *v/i* (*irr, sep*, -ge-, sn, → **fallen**) fall apart, *fig. a.* break up. ~**gehen** *v/i* (*irr, sep*, -ge-, sn, → **gehen**) **1.** separate, part, *crowd*: disperse. **2.** *fig. opinions etc*: be divided (*über acc* on): ~*d* differing, divergent. **3.** F come apart, *fig. relationship etc*: break off, *engagement*: be broken off, *marriage*: go on the rocks. **4.** F grow fat. ~**halten** *v/t* (*irr, sep*, -ge-, h, → **halten**) tell apart, distinguish between. ~**leben**: *sich* ~ (*sep*, -ge-, h) drift apart. ~**nehmen** *v/t* (*irr, sep*, -ge-, h, → **nehmen**) **1.** take apart, ⊚ *a.* dismantle. **2.** F *sports*: clobber. ~**reißen** *v/t* (*irr, sep*, -ge-, h, → **reißen**) tear apart, *fig. a.* separate.
ausein'andersetzen (*sep*, -ge-, h) **I** *v/t j-m et.* ~ explain s.th. to s.o. **II** *sich* ~ *mit* deal with, tackle (*a problem etc*). **Ausein'andersetzung** *f* (-; -en) **1.** dealing (*mit* with). **2.** argument: *esp. pol. kriegerische* ~ armed conflict.
'**ausfahren** (*irr, sep*, -ge-, → **fahren**) **I** *v/t* (h) **1. a.**) 🔧 extend, **b.**) lower (*landing*

gear). **2.** *mot.* run *the engine* at top speed, round (*curve*). **3.** take *s.o.* out for a drive. **4.** deliver (*goods*). **5.** wear out, rut: → *ausgefahren* II. **II** *v/i* (sn) **6.** go for a drive. **'Ausfahrt** *f* (-; -en) **1.** drive. **2.** a) gateway, b) exit (*of motorway*), c) mouth (*of port*): *mot.* ~ *freihalten!* keep exit clear!

'Ausfall *m* (-[e]s; ⁓e) **1.** ◎ failure, breakdown. **2.** *no pl* a) loss, b) absence, c) cancel(l)ation (*of lesson etc*). **3.** *sports:* ein glatter ~ (*player*) F a dead loss. **4.** *fenc.* lunge. **5.** *fig.* attack (*gegen* on).

'ausfallen *v/i* (*irr, sep, -ge-, sn,* → *fallen*) **1.** ◎ fail, break down. **2.** *hair etc:* fall out. **3.** not to take place: ~ *lassen* call off, cancel (*lecture etc*); *morgen fällt die Schule aus* there is no school tomorrow. **4.** *person:* be absent, be unavailable. **5.** *gut* (*schlecht*) ~ turn out well (badly); *der Sieg fiel knapp aus* it was a close victory.

'ausfällen *v/t* (*sep, -ge-, h*) precipitate.

'ausfallend → **'ausfällig** *adj* (er wurde ~ he became) abusive.

'Ausfall|muster *n* ⊤ production (or proof) sample. **~(s)erscheinung** *f* 𝄪 deficiency (*in addicts:* withdrawal) symptom. **~straße** *f* arterial road.

'ausfasern *v/i* (*sep, -ge-, sn*) fray (out).

'ausfechten *v/t* (*irr, sep, -ge-, h,* → *fechten*) *fig.* fight out.

'ausfertigen *v/t* (*sep, -ge-, h*) draw up, execute (*document*), *adm.* issue (*passport etc*). **'Ausfertigung** *f* (-; -en) **1.** drawing up, 𝄪𝄪 execution. **2.** (𝄪𝄪 certified) copy: → *doppelt* II, *dreifach*.

'ausfindig *adv* ~ *machen* find, discover.

'ausfliegen *v/i* (*irr, sep, -ge-, sn,* → *fliegen*) fly out (*a. v/t* ✕, h), *birds:* leave the nest.

'ausfließen *v/i* (*irr, sep, -ge-, sn,* → *fließen*) flow out.

'ausflippen *v/i* (*sep, -ge-, sn*) F a) freak out, b) flip one's lid.

'Ausflucht *f* (-; ⁓e) *usu. pl* excuse.

'Ausflug *m* (-[e]s; ⁓e) (e-n ~ *machen* (make an) excursion, (go on a) trip, (go for an) outing. **'Ausflügler** [-fly:glər] *m* (-s; -) day tripper, excursionist.

'Ausfluß *m* (-sses; ⁓sse) **1.** ◎ a) outflow, b) outlet. **2.** 𝄪 discharge.

'ausfragen *v/t* (*sep, -ge-, h*) (*über acc* about) question, quiz, *contp.* pump.

'ausfransen *v/i* (*sep, -ge-, h*) fray (out).

'ausfressen *v/t* (*irr, sep, -ge-, h,* → *fressen*) F *fig.* was hat er *etc* ausgefressen? what has he *etc* been up to?

'Ausfuhr *f* (-; -en) **1.** *no pl* export. **2.** exports. **'ausführbar** *adj* **1.** practicable. **2.** ⊤ exportable. **'ausführen** *v/t* (*sep, -ge, h*) **1.** ⊤ export. **2.** carry out, execute: *Reparaturen* ~ make repairs. **3.** explain, argue. **4.** take *s.o.* out, take a *dog* for a walk.

'Ausführende *m, f* (-n; -n) ♪ performer.

'Ausfuhr|genehmigung *f* ⊤ export licen/ce (*Am.* -se). **~handel** *m* export trade. **~land** *n* exporting country.

ausführlich ['aʊsfy:rlɪç] **I** *adj* detailed, full. **II** *adv* in detail: *sehr* ~ at great length; ~ *beschreiben* give a detailed description (or account) of.

'Ausfuhrprämie *f* export bounty.

'Ausfuhrquote *f* export quota.

'Ausfuhrsperre *f* embargo on exports.

'Ausführung *f* (-; -en) **1.** *no pl* carrying out, execution, *w.s.* completion. **2.** a) quality, b) type, model, c) design. **3.** *pl* remarks, comments.

'Ausfuhrzoll *m* export duty.

'ausfüllen *v/t* (*sep, -ge-, h*) **1.** fill, *fig.* a. occupy: *ihre Arbeit füllt sie nicht aus* she is not satisfied by her work. **2.** fill in, *Am.* fill out, complete (*form*).

'Ausgabe *f* (-; -n) **1.** *no pl* a) handing out, distribution, b) issue (*of order, material, etc,* ⊤ *of shares*), emission (*of banknotes*). **2.** a) edition, copy (*of a book*), b) issue, number (*of a periodical*). **3.** *pl* expenditure, expense(s). **4.** *computer:* output. **~kurs** *m* ⊤ issue price. **~stelle** *f* issuing office.

'Ausgang *m* (-[e]s; ⁓e) **1.** way out, exit: *am* ~ *des Dorfes* at the end of the village. **2.** *no pl* a) end, close, b) result, outcome: *Unfall mit tödlichem* ~ fatal accident. **3.** *no pl* beginning: *s-n* ~ *nehmen von* start from. **4.** outing: ~ *haben* have the day *etc* off, ✕ have a pass.

'Ausgangspunkt *m a. fig.* starting point.

'Ausgangssperre *f* → *Ausgehverbot.*

'Ausgangssprache *f* source language.

'ausgeben (*irr, sep, -ge-, h,* → *geben*) **I** *v/t* **1.** hand out, distribute, deal (*cards*), ⊤ issue (*shares etc*), spend (*money*), *computer:* output: F e-n (*or e-e Runde*) ~ stand a round (of drinks). **2.** ~ *für,* *als* pass *s.o.*, *s.th.* off as. II *sich* ~ 3. pose (*für*, *als* as). 4. → *verausgaben* 2.

'**ausgebeult** I *pp of ausbeulen.* II *adj* baggy (*pants etc*).

'**ausgebildet** I *pp of ausbilden.* II *adj* trained.

'**ausgebombt** I *pp of ausbomben.* II *adj* ~ *sein* be bombed(-)out.

'**ausgebrannt** I *pp of ausbrennen.* II *adj* gutted (by fire), *a. fig.* burnt(-)out.

'**ausgebucht** I *pp of ausbuchen.* II *adj* booked(-)up.

'**ausgedehnt** I *pp of ausdehnen.* II *adj* a) *a. fig.* extensive, b) long (*period etc*).

'**ausgedient** *adj* useless, discarded.

'**ausgefahren** I *pp of ausfahren.* II *adj* worn(-)out, rutty: → *Gleis.*

'**ausgefallen** I *pp of ausfallen.* II *adj fig.* unusual, F off-beat.

'**ausgefeilt** *adj fig.* polished.

'**ausgeglichen** I *pp of ausgleichen.* II *adj fig.* (well-)balanced.

'**ausgehen** *v/i (irr, sep, -ge-, sn,* → *gehen)* 1. go out: *er ist ausgegangen a.* he is not in. 2. end: *gut* ~ *a.* turn out well; *ling.*: *auf e-n Vokal* ~ end in a vowel; *sports*: *unentschieden* ~ end in a draw. 3. *light, cigar, etc*: go out. 4. *fig. money, supplies, etc*: run out: *mir ging das Geld aus* I ran out of money; *ihr ging die Geduld aus* she lost all patience; F *ihm ging die Puste aus* he ran out of steam. 5. → *ausfallen* 2. 6. ~ *von fig.* a) *idea etc*: come from, b) proceed from, assume; *wenn wir davon* ~, *daß* proceeding on the assumption that; *man kann (ruhig) davon* ~, *daß* ... it is safe to assume that ...; *ich gehe davon aus, daß* ... I would think (that) ... 7. ~ *auf (acc)* be bent on; *auf Abenteuer* ~ seek adventure; *auf Betrug* ~ be out to cheat. 8. *leer* ~ come away empty-handed, *w.s.* a. be left out in the cold; (*straf*)*frei* ~ get off scot-free.

'**ausgehend** *adj das* ~*e Mittelalter* the late Middle Ages; *im* ~*en 19. Jh.* toward(s) the end of the 19th century.

'**ausgehungert** I *pp of aushungern.* II *adj* starved (*fig. nach* for).

'**Ausgehverbot** *n* curfew: ✕ ~ *bekommen (haben)* be confined to barracks.

'**ausgeklügelt** [-kly:gəlt] *adj* ingenious.

'**ausgekocht** I *pp of auskochen.* II *adj* F *fig.* shrewd, crafty.

'**ausgelassen** I *pp of auslassen.* II *adj* gay, exuberant, boisterous: ~ *sein* be in high spirits.

'**ausgelastet** I *pp of auslasten.* II *adj a.* *voll* ~ ✝, ⚙ working to capacity, *person*: fully stretched.

'**ausgelaugt** *adj* F ~ *sein* be washed out.

'**ausgemacht** I *pp of ausmachen.* II *adj* 1. settled: *e-e* ~*e Sache* a foregone conclusion. 2. utter, perfect (*fool etc*).

'**ausgemergelt** [-mɛrgəlt] *adj* emaciated.

'**ausgenommen** I *pp of ausnehmen.* II *conj* (*a.* ~, *wenn*) unless *it rains etc*: ~, *daß* except that. III *prep* except(ing), with the exception of: → *Anwesende.*

'**ausgeprägt** *adj* marked, pronounced: ~*es Pflichtgefühl* strongly developed sense of duty.

'**ausgepumpt** I *pp of auspumpen.* II *adj* F *fig.* bushed, *Am.* pooped.

'**ausgerechnet** I *pp of ausrechnen.* II *adv* F *fig.* ~ *er* he of all people; ~ *Bananen* bananas of all things; ~ *heute* to-day of all days; ~ *jetzt* just now.

'**ausgereift** *adj* a) mature(d) (*a. fig.*), b) perfected (*design etc*).

'**ausgeschlossen** I *pp of ausschließen.* II *adj* 1. *sich* ~ *fühlen* feel left out of things. 2. impossible: *das ist* ~*!* that's out of the question!; *jeder Zweifel ist* ~ there is no doubt about it.

'**ausgeschnitten** I *pp of ausschneiden.* II *adj* (*tief*) ~ low-necked.

'**ausgesprochen** I *pp of aussprechen.* II *adj fig.* pronounced, marked: *das war* ~*es Pech* that really was bad luck; *es ist* ~ *falsch* it is positively wrong.

'**ausgestorben** I *pp of aussterben.* II *adj* extinct: *wie* ~ completely deserted.

'**ausgesucht** I *pp of aussuchen.* II *adj fig.* select, exquisite: ~*e Qualität* choice quality.

'**ausgewachsen** I *pp of auswachsen.* II *adj* 1. full(y)-grown. 2. F *fig.* full-blown (*scandal etc*).

Ausgewiesene ['aʊsɡəvi:zənə] *m, f* (-n; -n) expellee.

'**ausgewogen** I *pp of auswiegen.* II *adj fig.* (well-)balanced.

'**ausgezeichnet** I *pp of auszeichnen.* II *adj* excellent: *das paßt mir* ~ that suits me fine.

'**ausgiebig** [-gi:bɪç] I *adj* ~*en Gebrauch*

machen von make full use of. **II** *adv* ~
duschen have a good long shower.

'**ausgießen** *v/t* (*irr, sep,* -ge-, h, → *gie-*
ßen) pour out, empty.

'**Ausgleich** *m* (-[e]s; -e) **1.** a) balance (*für*
to), b) settlement (*of account, bill*), c)
compensation: *als ~ für* by way of compensation for; *zum ~* (*gen*) in settlement of. **2.** *sports.* equalizer. *den ~*
erzielen → ausgleichen 3. '**ausglei-**
chen (*irr, sep,* -ge-, h, → *gleichen*) **I** *v/t*
1. compensate (for), offset: *~de Ge-*
rechtigkeit poetic justice. **2.** ✝ a) balance, settle (*accounts etc*), b) cover (*loss*
etc). **II** *v/i* **3.** *sports:* equalize.

'**Ausgleichs|getriebe** *n* mot. differen-
tial (gear). *~sport* *m ich jogge als ~* I
do jogging to keep fit. *~tor* *n*, *~treffer*
m equalizer.

'**ausgleiten** *v/i* (*irr, sep,* -ge-, sn, →
gleiten) a. *fig.* slip.

'**ausgraben** *v/t* (*irr, sep,* -ge-, h, → *gra-*
ben) a. *fig.* dig up. '**Ausgrabung** *f* (-;
-en) excavation, F dig.

'**ausgrenzen** *v/t* (*sep,* -ge-, h) exclude.

'**Ausguck** *m* (-[e]s; -e) ⚓, ✕ lookout.

'**Ausguß** *m* (-sses; ⸗sse) sink, ⊚ outlet.

'**aushaken** (*sep,* -ge-, h) **I** *v/t* unhook. **II**
v/impers F *es hakte bei ihm aus* a) he
lost the thread, b) he lost his cool, c) he
flipped; *da hakt's bei mir aus!* I just
don't get it!

'**aushalten** (*irr, sep,* -ge-, h, → *halten*) **I**
v/t **1.** a) bear, stand (*pain etc*), b) sustain: *es ist nicht auszuhalten* (or *zum*
☻) it is unbearable. **2.** F keep (*a woman*).
3. ♪ hold. **II** *v/i* **4.** hold out: *er hält* (es)
nirgends lange aus he never lasts long
in any place (or job).

'**aushandeln** *v/t* (*sep,* -ge-, h) negotiate.

aushändigen ['aʊshɛndɪɡən] *v/t* (*sep,*
-ge-, h) hand over.

'**Aushang** *m* (-[e]s; ⸗e) notice, bulletin.

'**aushängen** *v/t* (*sep,* -ge-, h) **1.** take *door*
etc off its hinges. **2.** put up (*notice etc*),
show (*paintings*). '**Aushängeschild** *n*
1. sign. **2.** *fig.* figurehead.

'**ausharren** *v/i* (*sep,* -ge-, h) hold out.

'**ausheben** *v/t* (*irr, sep,* -ge-, h, →
heben) **1.** dig. **2.** → *aushängen* 1. **3.**
fig. round up (*gang*).

'**aushecken** *v/t* (*sep,* -ge-, h) F cook up.

'**ausheilen** *v/i* (*sep,* -ge-, sn) be (completely) cured, *wound*: heal up.

'**aushelfen** *v/i* (*irr, sep,* -ge-, h, → *hel-*
fen) *j-m ~* help s.o. out (*mit* with).

'**Aushilfe** *f* (-; -n) **1.** temporary help: *zur*
~ als j-m arbeiten help s.o. out. **2.** →
'**Aushilfskraft** *f* temporary worker.

'**aushilfsweise** *adv* temporarily.

'**aushöhlen** *v/t* (*sep,* -ge-, h) hollow out,
geol., a. fig. erode, undermine.

'**ausholen** *v/i* (*sep,* -ge-, h) (*weit*) ~ a)
swing back (*to strike*), b) *fig. narrator:*
go far back; *mit der Axt* (*zum Schlag*)
~ raise the axe (to strike).

'**aushorchen** *v/t* (*sep,* -ge-, h) *j-n ~* sound
s.o. out (*über acc* on).

'**aushungern** *v/t* (*sep,* -ge-, h) starve
(out): → *ausgehungert*.

'**auskennen: sich ~** (*irr, sep,* -ge-, h, →
kennen) **1. sich ~ in** (*dat*) know (one's
way around) *a place.* **2.** *fig. sich ~ in*
(*dat*), *sich ~ mit* know all about *s.th.*

'**ausklammern** *v/t* (*sep,* -ge-, h) *fig.* leave
s.th. out of consideration, ignore.

'**Ausklang** *m* (-[e]s; *no pl*) a. *fig.* finale.

'**auskleiden** *v/t* (*sep,* -ge-, h) ⊚ line.

'**ausklingen** *v/i* (*irr, sep,* -ge-, sn, → *klin-*
gen) *fig.* end (*in dat* with).

'**ausklinken** *v/t* (*sep,* -ge-, h) ⊚ release.

'**ausknipsen** *v/t* (*sep,* -ge-, h) F switch
off.

'**ausknobeln** *v/t* (*sep,* -ge-, h) F *fig. et.*
figure *s.th.* out.

'**auskochen** *v/t* (*sep,* -ge-, h) boil, ⚕
sterilize (by boiling); → *ausgekocht* II.

'**auskommen** *v/i* (*irr, sep,* -ge-, sn, →
kommen) **1. ~ mit** make do (*or* manage)
with; *mit s-m Geld ~* make both ends
meet; *~ ohne* manage (*or* do) without.
2. *mit j-m ~* get on (*or* along) with s.o.

'**Auskommen** *n* (-s) **1.** livelihood: *sein ~*
haben make a (decent) living. **2.** *mit ihr*
ist kein ~ you can't get on with her.

'**auskosten** *v/t* (*sep,* -ge-, h) *fig.* enjoy to
the full.

'**auskratzen** *v/t* (*sep,* -ge-, h) **1.** scrape
out. **2.** ⚕ curette.

'**auskühlen** (*sep,* -ge-) **I** *v/t* (h) chill *body*
through. **II** *v/i* (sn) cool (off).

'**auskundschaften** *v/t* (*sep,* -ge-, h) spy
out.

Auskunft ['aʊskʊnft] *f* (-; ⸗e) **1.** information (*über acc* on, about): *nähere ~*
further particulars; *Auskünfte einho-*
len make inquiries. **2.** information office (*or* desk), *a. teleph.* Inquiries.

Auskunftei [aʊskʊnfˈtaɪ] f (-; -en) ✝ inquiry office.

'**Auskunftsbeamte** m inquiry clerk.

'**Auskunftsbü̱ro** n inquiry office.

'**auskuppeln** v/i (sep, -ge-, h) mot. declutch.

'**auslachen** v/t (sep, -ge-, h) laugh at.

'**ausladen** v/t (irr, sep, -ge-, h, → **laden**) 1. unload, ⚓ disembark. 2. F disinvite: **j-n ~** ask s.o. not to come.

'**ausladend** adj 1. projecting, jutting out. 2. fig. sweeping (gesture).

'**Auslage** f (-; -n) 1. a) (window) display, b) shop-window. 2. pl (j-m s-e ~n ersetzen refund s.o.'s) expenses.

'**Ausland** n (-[e]s; no pl) foreign countries: **im** (**ins**) ~ abroad; **aus dem** ~ from abroad; **die Reaktion des** ~**s** reactions abroad. **Ausländer** ['aʊslɛndər] m (-s; -), '**Ausländerin** f (-; -nen) foreigner. '**ausländerfeindlich** adj hostile to foreigners. '**Ausländerfeindlichkeit** f anti-alien feeling.

'**ausländisch** adj foreign: ~**e Besucher** a. visitors from abroad.

'**Auslands...** foreign (department etc). ~**aufenthalt** m stay abroad. ~**flug** m international flight. ~**gespräch** n teleph. international call. ~**reise** f journey (or trip) abroad. ~**schutzbrief** m mot. (certificate of) international travel cover. ~**tour̠nee** f tour abroad. ~**verschuldung** f ✝ foreign debts.

'**auslassen** (irr, sep, -ge-, h, → **lassen**) **I** v/t 1. leave out, omit (word etc), skip (page etc), miss (opportunity). 2. vent one's anger etc (**an** dat on): **s-n Ärger an j-n ~** a. take it out on s.o. 3. melt (butter etc). 4. let out (seam). **II sich ~** talk (at length) (**über** acc about).

'**Auslassung** f (-; -en) omission.

'**auslasten** v/t (sep, -ge-, h) ⚙ use to capacity: → **ausgelastet**.

'**Auslauf** m (-[e]s; ⸚e) 1. sports: run-out. 2. (chicken etc) run: **die Kinder haben k-n ~** the children have nowhere to play. '**auslaufen** v/i (irr, sep, -ge-, sn, → **laufen**) 1. liquid, tank etc: run out. 2. ⚓ sail. 3. end, contract etc: run out: ✝ ~ **lassen** phase out, discontinue (model). 4. colo(u)r: run, bleed.

'**Ausläufer** pl 1. foothills. 2. outskirts.

'**Auslaufmo̱dell** n ✝ phase-out model.

'**Auslaut** m (-[e]s; -e) ling. final sound.

'**ausleben: sich ~** (sep, -ge-, h) live it up.

'**auslecken** v/t (sep, -ge-, h) lick out.

'**auslegen** v/t (sep, -ge-, h) 1. lay out, display (goods). 2. a) cover, b) inlay: **mit Teppich ~** a. carpet; **mit Papier ~** line with paper. 3. advance (sum). 4. interpret: **falsch ~** misinterpret. 5. ⚙ design (auf acc for).

'**Ausleger** m (-s; -) 1. jib, boom. 2. a. '**Auslegerboot** n outrigger.

'**Auslegeware** f (-; no pl) floor coverings, a. wall-to-wall carpeting.

'**Auslegung** f (-; -en) interpretation.

'**ausleiern** v/t (sep, -ge-, h) (a. **sich ~**) wear out.

'**ausleihen** v/t (irr, sep, -ge-, h, → **leihen**) 1. lend (out), loan. 2. **sich et. ~ von** borrow s.th. from.

'**auslernen** v/i (sep, -ge-, h) complete one's training: **man lernt nie aus** (we) live and learn.

'**Auslese** f (-; -n) 1. choice, selection: biol. **natürliche ~** natural selection. 2. fig. élite, flower. 3. wine made from selected grapes.

'**auslesen**[1] v/t (irr, sep, -ge-, h, → **lesen**) select, ⚙ sort. '**auslesen**[2] v/t (irr, sep, -ge-, h, → **lesen**) finish (reading).

'**ausleuchten** v/t (sep, -ge-, h) a. fig. illuminate.

'**ausliefern** v/t (sep, -ge-, h) 1. hand over (dat to), ✝ deliver: fig. **j-m ausgeliefert sein** be at s.o.'s mercy. 2. pol. extradite. '**Auslieferung** f (-; -en) 1. ✝ delivery. 2. pol. extradition. **Auslieferungsvertrag** m ⚖, pol. extradition treaty.

'**ausliegen** v/i (irr, sep, -ge-, h, → **liegen**) be on display, newspapers: be available.

'**auslöffeln** v/t (sep, -ge-, h) spoon up: → **Suppe**.

'**auslöschen** v/t (sep, -ge-, h) 1. → **löschen** 1. 2. fig. wipe out.

'**auslosen** v/t (sep, -ge-, h) draw (lots) for.

'**auslösen** v/t (sep, -ge-, h) 1. phot., ⚙ release, a. fig. trigger (off). 2. fig. produce (effect), cause (panic etc), arouse (enthusiasm etc). 3. redeem (pawned object). '**Auslöser** m (-s; -) release, a. fig. trigger. '**Auslösung** f (-; -en) 1. releasing, triggering (etc, → **auslösen**). 2. ✝ compensation.

'**Auslosung** f (-; -en) draw.

'**ausloten** v/t (sep, -ge-, h) a. fig. sound.
'**ausmachen** v/t (sep, -ge-, h) **1.** F → a) **löschen** 1, b) **ausschalten** 1. **2.** make out, spot, locate. **3.** → **abmachen** 2. **4.** amount to. **5.** fig. make up, form (part of): **das macht den Reiz s-r Bilder aus** this is what makes his pictures so attractive. **6. das macht nichts (viel) aus** that doesn't matter (it matters a great deal); **wenn es Ihnen nichts ausmacht** if you don't mind; **macht es Ihnen et. aus, wenn ich rauche?** do you mind my smoking?; **die Kälte macht mir nichts aus** I don't mind the cold.
'**ausmalen** v/t (sep, -ge-, h) **1.** a) paint, b) colo(u)r (picture). **2.** fig. depict (dat to): **sich et. ~** picture s.th. (to o.s.).
'**Ausmaß** n (-es; -e) dimensions, a. fig. extent: **das ~ des Schadens** the extent of the damage; **gewaltige ~e annehmen** assume horrendous proportions.
'**ausmerzen** v/t (sep, -ge-, h) eliminate.
'**ausmessen** v/t (irr, sep, -ge-, h, → **messen**) measure.
'**ausmisten** v/t (sep, -ge-, h) **1.** muck out.
'**ausmustern** v/t (sep, -ge-, h) **1.** sort out, discard. **2.** ✕ reject (as unfit).
Ausnahme ['aʊsnaːmə] f (-; -n) exception: **mit ~ von** (or gen) with the exception of, except (for); **e-e ~ bilden** a. be exceptional; **bei j-m e-e ~ machen** make an exception in s.o.'s case.
'**Ausnahme...** exceptional (athlete, case, etc). '**Ausnahmezustand** m (den ~ **verhängen** declare a) state of emergency (**über** acc in).
'**ausnahmslos** adv and adj without exception. '**ausnahmsweise** adv a) by way of exception, b) for once.
'**ausnehmen** v/t (irr, sep, -ge-, h, → **nehmen**) **1.** gut (fish etc), draw (goose etc). **2.** F j-n ~ fleece s.o. **3.** exclude, except.
'**ausnüchtern** v/t (sep, -ge-, h) sober up.
'**ausnutzen** v/t (sep, -ge-, h) a. b.s. use, exploit, b.s. take advantage of. '**Ausnutzung** f (-; no pl) a. b.s. exploitation.
'**auspacken** (sep, -ge-, h) **I** v/t unpack, unwrap. **II** v/i F fig. spill the beans.
'**auspfeifen** v/t (irr, sep, -ge-, h, → **pfeifen**) boo.
'**ausplaudern** v/t (sep, -ge-, h) blab out.
'**auspo,saunen** v/t (sep, h) F broadcast.
'**auspressen** v/t (sep, -ge-, h) squeeze (out).

'**auspro,bieren** v/t (sep, h) try (out).
'**Auspuff** m (-[e]s; -e) mot. exhaust.
'**Auspufftopf** m silencer, Am. muffler.
'**auspumpen** v/t (sep, -ge-, h) pump out.
'**ausquar,tieren** v/t (sep, h) lodge s.o. elsewhere.
'**ausquetschen** v/t (sep, -ge-, h) F fig. j-n ~ grill s.o.
'**ausra,dieren** v/t (sep, h) **1.** erase. **2.** fig. wipe out, wipe town etc off the map.
'**ausran,gieren** v/t (sep, h) throw out.
'**ausrasten** v/i (sep, -ge-, sn) **1.** ⚙ be released. **2.** F fig. flip.
'**ausrauben** v/t (sep, -ge-, h) rob.
'**ausräuchern** v/t (sep, -ge-, h) fumigate, hunt., a. fig. smoke out.
'**ausräumen** v/t (sep, -ge-, h) **1.** clear (room etc), remove furniture (**aus** dat from). **2.** fig. clear up (misunderstanding etc), dispel (doubts).
'**ausrechnen** v/t (sep, -ge-, h) (fig. **sich**) **et. ~** work s.th. out (for o.s.); F **er ist leicht auszurechnen** he is quite predictable; → **ausgerechnet.**
'**Ausrede** f (-; -n) (**faule ~** lame) excuse.
'**ausreden** (sep, -ge-, h) **I** v/i finish (speaking): **j-n ~ lassen** hear s.o. out; **j-n nicht ~ lassen** cut s.o. short. **II** v/t **j-m et. ~** talk s.o. out of s.th.
'**ausreichen** v/i (sep, -ge-, h) be enough: **~ für** last (a week etc). '**ausreichend** adj **1.** sufficient, enough. **2.** ped. D.
'**Ausreise** f (-; -n) departure: **bei der ~** on leaving the country; **j-m die ~ verweigern** refuse s.o. permission to leave the country. **~visum** n exit visa.
'**ausreißen** (irr, sep, -ge-, → **reißen**) **I** v/t (h) pull out, tear out. **II** v/i (sn) F run away (**vor** j-m before s.o., **von zu Hause** from home). '**Ausreißer** m (-s; -), '**Ausreißerin** f (-; -nen) F runaway.
'**ausreiten** v/i (irr, sep, -ge-, sn, → **reiten**) ride out.
'**ausrenken** v/t (sep, -ge-, h) **sich den Arm** etc ~ dislocate one's arm etc.
'**ausrichten** v/t (sep, -ge-, h) **1.** a) straighten, b) align, c) adjust (a. fig., **nach** to): **sich ~** line up; fig. **sich** (or **sein Verhalten**) ~ **nach** orientate o.s. to; **ausgerichtet auf** (acc) aimed at. **2.** achieve: **er wird (bei ihr) nichts ~ (können)** he won't get anywhere (with her). **3.** tell: **kann ich et. ~?** can I take a message?; **bitte richten Sie ihm Grüße**

von mir aus please give him my (kind) regards. **4.** organize, arrange.
'**Ausrichter** *m* (-s; -) organizer.
'**ausrollen** (*sep*, -ge-, h) **I** *v/t* roll (out) (*dough*). **II** *v/i mot.* coast (✔ *taxi*) to a standstill.
'**ausrotten** *v/t* (*sep*, -ge-, h) exterminate.
'**Ausrottung** *f* (-; -en) extermination.
'**ausrücken** (*sep*, -ge-) **I** *v/i* (sn) **1.** *fire brigade etc*: turn out, ✗ march out. **2.** F → *ausreißen* II. **II** *v/t* (h) **3.** *print.* move out.
'**Ausruf** *m* (-[e]s; -e) cry, exclamation.
'**ausrufen** *v/t* (*irr*, *sep*, -ge-, h, → *rufen*) **1.** call out (*name etc*): **j-n ~ lassen** page s.o. **2.** call (*strike*), *pol.* proclaim: **j-n zum König ~** proclaim s.o. king. '**Ausrufungszeichen** *n* exclamation mark.
'**ausruhen** *v/i* (*sep*, -ge-, h) (*a.* **sich ~**) rest.
'**ausrüsten** *v/t* (*sep*, -ge-, h) *a. fig.* equip (**mit** with). '**Ausrüstung** *f* (-; -en) **1.** equipment, gear. **2.** accessories.
'**ausrutschen** *v/i* (*sep*, -ge-, sn) slip (**auf** *dat* on). '**Ausrutscher** *m* (-s; -) F *fig.* slip, gaffel.
'**Aussaat** *f* (-; -en) a) sowing, b) seed.
'**Aussage** *f* (-; -n) statement, *a. author's etc* message, 🏛 *a.* testimony: **🏛 die ~ verweigern** refuse to give evidence; **hier steht ~ gegen ~** it's his word against hers *etc*. '**aussagen** (*sep*, -ge-, h) **I** *v/i* 🏛 testify, give evidence. **II** *v/t* state, say, *esp. fig.* express.
'**Aussagesatz** *m* clause of statement.
'**Aussatz** *m* (-es; *no pl*) 🏥 leprosy.
'**Aussätzige** *m*, *f* (-n; -n) *a. fig.* leper.
'**aussaugen** *v/t* (*sep*, -ge-, h) suck: *fig.* **j-n** (**bis aufs Blut**) **~** bleed s.o. (white).
'**ausschaben** *v/t* (*sep*, -ge-, h) 🏥 curette.
'**Ausschabung** *f* (-; -en) 🏥 curettage.
'**ausschachten** *v/t* (*sep*, -ge-, h) dig.
'**ausschalten** *v/t* (*sep*, -ge-, h) **1.** switch off (*light, radio, etc*), cut out (*current*), stop, cut (*engine*). **2.** *fig.* eliminate, *esp. sports*: neutralize. '**Ausschaltung** *f* (-; -en) *fig.* elimination.
'**Ausschau:** **~ halten** → '**ausschauen** *v/i* (*sep*, -ge-, h) look out (**nach** for).
'**ausscheiden** (*irr*, *sep*, -ge-, → *scheiden*) **I** *v/t* (h) **1.** eliminate, exclude, sort out, remove. **2.** *physiol.* excrete. **II** *v/i* (sn) **3.** be ruled out, *person*: be not

eligible. **4.** **~ aus** (*dat*) a) retire from (*an office*), leave (*a firm*), b) *sports*: be eliminated from (*contest*), drop out of (*a race*). '**Ausscheidung** *f* (-; -en) **1.** elimination. **2.** *physiol.* excretion, excrements. **3.** → '**Ausscheidungskampf** *m sports*: qualifying contest.
'**ausschenken** *v/t* (*sep*, -ge-, h) **1.** pour (out). **2.** sell.
'**ausscheren** *v/i* (*sep*, -ge-, sn) **1.** *mot.* swing out. **2.** *fig.* deviate (**aus** from).
'**ausschiffen** *v/t* (*sep*, -ge-, h) (*a.* **sich ~**) disembark.
'**ausschlachten** *v/t* (*sep*, -ge-, h) **1.** cut up. **2.** F *fig.* a) cannibalize (*car etc*), b) *contp.* exploit, capitalize on.
'**ausschlafen** (*irr*, *sep*, -ge-, h, → *schlafen*) **I** *v/t* sleep off. **II** *v/i* (*a.* **sich ~**) a) get a good night's sleep, b) sleep late.
'**Ausschlag** *m* (-[e]s; ⸚e) **1.** 🏥 (**e-n ~ bekommen** break out into a) rash. **2.** *fig.* **den ~ geben für** be decisive of; **das gab den ~ that** (decided or settled) it. **3.** *phys.* a) swing (*of pendulum*), deflection (*of pointer*), b) amplitude. '**ausschlagen** (*irr*, *sep*, -ge-, h, → *schlagen*) **I** *v/i* **1.** *horse*: kick out. **2.** *pendulum etc*: swing, *pointer etc*: deflect. **3.** 🌱 sprout, *tree*: come into leaf. **II** *v/t* **4.** knock out (*tooth*): → *Faß.* **5.** line. **6.** refuse, turn *s.th.* down. '**ausschlaggebend** *adj* (*a.* **von ~er Bedeutung**) decisive (**für** of).
'**ausschließen** (*irr*, *sep*, -ge-, h, → *schließen*) **I** *v/t* **1.** → *aussperren.* **2.** (**aus** from) exclude, expel (*from the party etc*), bar, *sports*: disqualify: **zeitweilig ~ suspend**; **🏛 die Öffentlichkeit ~** exclude the public. **3.** a) rule out (*mistake etc*), b) exclude, → *ausgeschlossen.* **II sich ~** exclude o.s. (**von** from).
'**ausschließlich** *adj* exclusive.
'**Ausschluß** *m* (-sses; ⸚sse) (**aus** from) a) exclusion, expulsion, b) *sports*: disqualification: **zeitweiliger ~** suspension; **🏛 unter ~ der Öffentlichkeit** in closed session.
'**ausschmücken** *v/t* (*sep*, -ge-, h) **1.** decorate. **2.** *fig.* embroider (*story etc*).
'**ausschneiden** *v/t* (*irr*, *sep*, -ge-, h, → *schneiden*) **1.** cut out: → *ausgeschnitten.* **2.** ✂ prune (*trees etc*).
'**Ausschnitt** *m* (-[e]s; -e) **1.** neck(line): **mit tiefem ~** décolleté, low-necked. **2.** (*newspaper*) cutting, *Am.* clipping. **3.**

phot. etc detail, *sports, TV* scene. **4.** *fig.* (*aus*) part (of), extract (from).

'**ausschöpfen** *v/t* (*sep*, -ge-, h) **1.** bail out. **2.** *fig.* exhaust (*subject*).

'**ausschreiben** *v/t* (*irr, sep*, -ge-, h, → **schreiben**) **1.** a) write out, b) write *figure* out (in words). **2.** → **ausstellen** 2. **3.** a) announce, b) advertise (*post*), c) ✝ invite tenders (for): **e-n Wettbewerb** ~ invite entries (✝ tenders) for a competition; **Wahlen** ~ go to the country.

'**Ausschreibung** *f* (-; -en) ✝ invitation to bid (*sports*: to a competition).

'**Ausschreitung** *f* (-; -en) *usu. pl* riot.

'**Ausschuß** *m* (-sses; ꞏsse) **1.** (*in e-m ~ sein* be *or* sit on a) committee. **2.** ✝ rejects, ⊘ waste, scrap. '**Ausschußmitglied** *n* committee member. '**Ausschußsitzung** *f* committee meeting.

'**ausschütteln** *v/t* (*sep*, -ge-, h) shake out.

'**ausschütten** (*sep*, -ge-, h) **I** *v/t* **1.** a) pour out, empty (*bucket etc*), b) spill: *fig. j-m sein Herz* ~ unburden o.s. to s.o. **2.** ✝ pay (*dividend*). **II** *v/i* (*vor Lachen*) ~ split one's sides laughing.

'**ausschweifend** *adj* unbridled (*imagination*), dissolute (*life*).

'**Ausschweifungen** *pl* excesses.

'**ausschweigen**: *sich* ~ (*irr, sep*, -ge-, h, → **schweigen**) remain silent (*über acc* about).

'**ausschwitzen** *v/t* (*sep*, -ge-, h) exude.

'**aussehen** (*irr, sep*, -ge-, h, → **sehen**) **I** *v/i* look: *gut* ~ a) be good-looking, b) look well; *schlecht* ~ look bad (*or* ill); *wie sieht er aus?* what does he look like?; F *sie sah vielleicht aus!* she did look a sight!; *so siehst du aus!* nothing doing! **II** *v/impers* F *es sieht nach Regen aus* it looks like rain; *damit es nass et. aussieht* to make it look impressive.

'**Aussehen** *n* (-s) looks, appearance.

'**aussein** *v/i* (*irr, sep*, -ge-, sn, → **sein**) F **1.** be over: *fig. mit ihm ist es aus* he is finished. **2.** light, radio, *etc*: be off, *fire etc*: be out. **3.** *wir waren gestern abend aus* we were out last night. **4.** *sports*: be out. **5.** ~ *auf* (*acc*) be out for (*or* to get); *sie ist auf sein Geld aus* she is after his money.

außen ['aʊsən] *adv* outside: *von* ~ from (the) outside; *nach* ~ outward(s), *fig.*

outwardly (*calm etc*); F *er bleibt* ~ *vor* he's (left) out of it.

'**Außen|aufnahmen** *pl film*: location shooting. ~**bezirke** *pl* outskirts.

'**Außenbordmotor** *m* outboard motor.

'**aussenden** *v/t* (*irr, sep*, -ge-, h, → **senden**) send out.

'**Außendienst** *m* field work: *Im* ~ in the field. ~**mitarbeiter(in** *f*) *m* field worker, ✝ *a.* sales representative.

'**Außen|handel** *m* foreign trade. ~**kante** *f* outer edge. ~**mi nister** *m* Foreign Minister (*Br.* Secretary), *Am.* Secretary of State. ~**mini sterium** *n* Foreign Ministry (*Br.* Office), *Am.* State Department. ~**poli tik** *f* foreign politics (*or* policy). 2**po litisch** *adj* foreign: ~**e Debatte** debate on foreign affairs.

'**Außenseite** *f* outside. **Außenseiter** ['aʊsənzaɪtɐ] *m* (-s; -) outsider.

'**Außenspiegel** *m mot.* outside rear--view mirror.

Außenstände ['aʊsənʃtɛndə] *pl* ✝ outstanding debts.

'**Außen|stelle** *f* branch (office). ~**stürmer** *m sports*: winger, outside. ~**wand** *f* outer wall. ~**welt** *f* outside world.

außer ['aʊsɐ] **I** *prep* (*dat*) **1.** out of: → **Atem, Betrieb** 2, **Dienst** 2, **Reichweite**; *fig.* ~ *sich sein* be beside o.s. (*vor* with); ~ *sich geraten* lose control of o.s. **2.** apart from, except (for): *alle* ~ *dir* all except (*or* but) you. **3.** besides, in addition to. **II** *conj* **4.** ~ (*wenn*) unless; ~ *daß* except that.

'**außerberuflich** *adj* private.

'**außerbetrieblich** *adj* external.

'**außerdem** *adv* besides.

äußere ['ɔysərə] *adj* outer, outside, external, ✝, *pol.* foreign: *k-e* ~*n Verletzungen* no external injuries; *pol.* ~ *Angelegenheiten* foreign affairs.

'**Äußere** *n* (-n) outside, (outward) appearance, *s.o.'s* looks: *von angenehmem* ~*n* personable; *auf sein* ~*s achten* be particular about one's appearance.

'**außerehelich** *adj* illegitimate (*child*), extramarital (*relationship*).

'**außergerichtlich** *adj* extrajudicial: ~*er Vergleich* settlement out of court.

'**außergewöhnlich** *adj* exceptional, uncommon, ✝ extraordinary.

'**außerhalb** **I** *prep* (*gen*) out of: ~ *des*

Hauses outdoors, outside. **II** *adv* a) outside, b) out of town.

'**außerirdisch** *adj* (*a.* **~es Wesen**) extraterrestrial.

äußerlich ['ɔysərlıç] *adj. a. fig.* a) outward, external, b) superficial: **𝕱 nur zur ~en Anwendung** for external use only; **~ betrachtet** on the face of it.

'**Äußerlichkeit** *f* (-; -en) *fig.* superficiality: **bloße ~en** mere formalities.

äußern ['ɔysərn] (h) **I** *v/t* a) utter, express, b) voice (*criticism etc*). **II sich ~** a) (*über acc* on) express o.s., give one's opinion, b) (*in dat* in) be shown, *disease etc*: manifest itself.

'**außerordentlich I** *adj* extraordinary, unusual, remarkable, outstanding: **~er Professor** senior lecturer, *Am.* associate professor. **II** *adv* extremely.

'**außerparlamen,tarisch** *adj* extraparliamentary. '**außerplanmäßig** *adj* a) extraordinary, b) supernumerary (*official*). '**außersinnlich** *adj* **~e Wahrnehmung** extrasensory perception.

äußerst ['ɔysɐrst] **I** *adj* **1.** outermost, remotest: *pol. die ~e Linke* the extreme left. **2.** latest, final: **~er Termin** a deadline. **3.** *fig.* extreme, utmost: *von ~er Wichtigkeit* of utmost importance; *im ~en Fall* at worst; *mit ~er Kraft* by a supreme effort. **II** *adv* **4.** extremely.

'**Äußerste** *n* (-n) *fig.* a) the limit, the most, b) the worst: *sein ~s tun* do one's utmost; *zum ~n entschlossen sein* be desperate; *bis zum ~n gehen* go to the last extreme; *auf das ~ gefaßt sein* be prepared for the worst.

'**außerstande** *adj* **~ sein** be unable.

Äußerung ['ɔysərʊŋ] *f* (-; -en) **1.** statement, remark. **2.** *fig.* expression, sign.

'**aussetzen** (*sep*, -ge-, h) **I** *v/t* **1.** expose (*dat* to, *a. fig.* to danger, criticism, *etc*), abandon (*child*), release (*pet*). **2.** **⚓** lower (*boat*), disembark, *b.s.* maroon (*passengers*). **3.** offer *award etc* (*dat* to): *e-n Preis auf j-s Kopf ~* put a price on s.o.'s head. **4.** interrupt, **✝**, **⚖** suspend: **→ Bewährung** 2. **5. et. ~** (*or auszusetzen haben*) *an* (*dat*) object to, criticize; *was ist daran auszusetzen?* what's wrong with it?; *er hat an allem et. auszusetzen* he finds fault with everything. **II** *v/i* **6.** fail, *mot.* misfire, *heart:* miss a beat. **7.** a) stop, break off, b)

take a rest, c) *in a game:* sit out: **~ mit** interrupt (*treatment etc*); *ohne auszusetzen* without interruption; *at games:* (*e-e Runde*) **~** miss a turn.

'**Aussicht** *f* (-; -en) (*auf acc* of) **1.** *no pl* view: *ein Zimmer mit ~ auf das Meer* a room overlooking the sea. **2.** chance, prospect, *pl a.* outlook: *er hat ~en zu gewinnen* he stands a chance to win; *gute ~en auf Erfolg haben* stand a good chance of success. '**aussichtslos** *adj* hopeless: **~e Sache** lost cause; *e-n ~en Kampf führen* fight a losing battle. '**Aussichtslosigkeit** *f* (-; *no pl*) hopelessness.

'**aussichtsreich** *adj* promising.

'**Aussichtsturm** *m* observation tower.

'**aussiedeln** *v/t* (*sep*, -ge-, h) resettle.

'**Aussiedler(in** *f*) *m* → *Umsiedler(in)*.

aussöhnen ['aʊszø:nən] *v/t* (*sep*, -ge-, h) reconcile (*sich* o.s.) (*mit* with, to). '**Aussöhnung** *f* (-; -en) reconciliation.

'**aussondern** *v/t* (*sep*, -ge-, h), '**aussor,tieren** *v/t* (*sep*, -ge-, h) sort out.

'**ausspannen** (*sep*, -ge-, h) **I** *v/t* **1.** unharness: F *fig.* *j-m die Freundin ~* steal s.o.'s girl. **2.** spread out, stretch out. **II** *v/i* **3.** relax, (take a) rest.

'**aussparen** *v/t* (*sep*, -ge-, h) **1.** ⚙ leave open. **2.** leave out, avoid (*subject etc*).

'**aussperren** *v/t* (*sep*, -ge-, h) *j-n ~ a.* **✝** lock s.o. out (*aus* of).

'**Aussperrung** *f* (-; -en) **✝** lockout.

'**ausspielen** (*sep*, -ge-, h) **I** *v/t* play (*card*), *fig.* bring *one's skill etc* to bear: *j-n gegen j-n ~* play s.o. off against s.o. **II** *v/i* *cards:* lead: *fig.* *er hat ausgespielt* he's finished.

'**ausspinnen** *v/t* (*irr*, *sep*, -ge-, h, → *spinnen*) *fig.* spin out.

'**ausspio,nieren** *v/t* (*sep*, -ge-, h) spy out, spy on *s.o.*

'**Aussprache** *f* (-; -n) **1.** *no pl* pronunciation. **2.** discussion, *a. parl.* debate.

'**aussprechen** (*irr*, *sep*, -ge-, h, → *sprechen*) **I** *v/t* **1.** pronounce: → *ausgesprochen*. **2.** express (*one's sympathy*, *views*, *etc*): → *Vertrauen*. **3.** ⚖ grant (*divorce*). **II** *v/i* **4.** → *ausreden* I. **III** *sich ~* **5.** express one's views (*über acc* on, about), speak (*für* for, *gegen* against). **6.** a) *bei j-m* unburden o.s. to s.o., b) *mit j-m* F have it out with s.o.

'**Ausspruch** *m* (-[e]s, ⸗e) remark, saying.

'**ausspucken** v/t, v/i (sep, -ge-, h) spit out.

'**ausspülen** v/t (sep, -ge-, h) rinse.

'**ausstaf,fieren** v/t (sep, h) F rig out.

'**Ausstand** m (-[e]s; ⁎e) strike, F walkout: **in den ~ treten** go on strike, walk out.

'**ausstatten** ['aʊsʃtatən] v/t (sep, -ge-, h) (**mit** with) **1.** fit out, equip, a. furnish (flat), get up (book). **2.** ✝ endow (with capital, a. fig. with talent etc), 🜨 vest (with power etc). '**Ausstattung** f (-; -en) a) outfit, equipment, b) furnishing, décor, c) thea. etc sets and costumes, d) design, e) get-up. '**Ausstattungsstück** n thea. spectacular (show).

'**ausstechen** v/t (irr, sep, -ge-, h, → **stechen**) **1.** gastr. cut out. **2.** fig. outdo (s.o.), cut out (rival).

'**ausstehen** (irr, sep, -ge-, h, → **stehen**) **I** v/t stand, bear, suffer: **es ist noch nicht ausgestanden** it's not over yet; F **ich kann ihn nicht ~** I can't stand him. **II** v/i decision: be pending, payment: be outstanding: **s-e Antwort steht noch aus ~** he hasn't answered yet.

'**aussteigen** v/i (irr, sep, -ge-, sn, → **steigen**) (**aus**) get out (of, a. fig. an enterprise etc), get off (a train, bus, etc), ✈ disembark, F ✔ bail out (of), fig. opt out (of business venture, nuclear power, etc), drop out (of society etc).

'**Aussteiger** m (-s; -) F dropout.

'**ausstellen** (sep, -ge-, h) **I** v/t **1.** display, show, exhibit. **2.** make bill, cheque, etc out (**auf j-s Namen** in s.o.'s name), issue (passport), draw bill of exchange (**auf** acc on). **II** v/i **3.** exhibit.

'**Aussteller** ['aʊsʃtɛlər] m (-s; -) **1.** exhibitor. **2.** ✝ drawer.

'**Ausstellfenster** n mot. ventipane.

'**Ausstellung** f (-; -en) **1.** exhibition, show, fair. **2.** issue (of document etc). '**Ausstellungs|datum** n date of issue. **~gelände** n exhibition grounds. **~halle** f exhibition hall. **~raum** m show-room. **~stück** n exhibit.

'**ausstempeln** v/i (sep, -ge-, h) clock out.

'**aussterben** v/i (irr, sep, -ge-, sn, → **sterben**) die out: → **ausgestorben**.

'**Aussteuer** f (-; -n) trousseau.

'**aussteuern** v/t (sep, -ge-, h) modulate.

'**Ausstieg** m (-[e]s; -e) **1.** exit (door). **2.** (**aus**) exit (from), getting out (of), fig. a. opting out of (of nuclear energy, a business, etc). **~luke** f (escape) hatch.

'**ausstopfen** v/t (sep, -ge-, h) stuff.

'**Ausstoß** m (-es; rare ⁎e) ✝ output, production. '**ausstoßen** (irr, sep, -ge-, h, → **stoßen**) **1.** ⚙ eject, blow off, exhaust. **2.** ✝ turn out, produce. **3.** utter (words), give (yell etc), heave (a sigh). **4.** j-n ~ expel s.o. (**aus** from); **j-n aus der Gesellschaft ~** ostracize s.o.

'**ausstrahlen** v/t (sep, -ge-, h) **1.** a. fig. radiate. **2.** broadcast, TV a. televise. '**Ausstrahlung** f (-; -en) **1.** fig. radiation, of person: charisma. **2.** broadcast(ing).

'**ausstrecken** v/t (sep, -ge-, h) (a. **sich ~**) stretch out: **die Hand ~ nach** reach (out) for; → **Fühler** 1.

'**ausstreichen** v/t (irr, sep, -ge-, h, → **streichen**) cross out.

'**ausströmen** (sep, -ge-) **I** v/i (sn) (**aus** from) a. fig. radiate, smell: emanate, gas etc: escape. **II** v/t (h) radiate (a. fig.), give off (smell).

'**aussuchen** v/t (sep, -ge-, h) choose, select: → **ausgesucht**.

'**Austausch** m (-[e]s; no pl) (**im ~** in) exchange (**für** for). '**Austausch...** ped., univ. exchange (teacher, student, etc). '**austauschbar** adj interchangeable. '**austauschen** v/t (sep, -ge-, h) (**gegen**) a) exchange (for), b) replace (by). '**Austauschmotor** m replacement engine.

'**austeilen** v/t (sep, -ge-, h) distribute (**an** acc to, **unter** acc among), deal (out) (cards, blows).

Auster ['aʊstər] f (-; -n) oyster. '**Austernbank** f (-; ⁎e) oyster bed.

'**austoben: sich ~** (sep, -ge-, h) have one's fling, children: have a good romp.

'**austragen** (irr, sep, -ge-, h, → **tragen**) **I** v/t **1.** deliver (letters etc). **2.** ⚕ carry baby to (full) term, w.s. have. **3.** settle (dispute): **die Sache ~** F have it out. **4.** hold (tournament etc), play (match). **5.** cancel (data etc). **II** v/i ✍ sign out. '**Austragungsort** m sports: venue.

Australien [aʊsˈtraːliən] n (-s) Australia. **Au'stralier** m (-s; -), **Au'stralierin** f (-; -nen), **au'stralisch** adj Australian.

'**austreiben** (irr, sep, -ge-, h, → **treiben**) **I** v/t exorcize: fig. **j-m et. ~** cure s.o. of s.th. **II** v/i 🌱 sprout.

'**austreten** (irr, sep, -ge-, → **treten**) **I** v/t (h) **1.** stamp out (fire etc). **2.** tread (path). **3.** wear out (shoes), wear down (steps). **II** v/i (sn) **4.** (**aus**) come out (of,

81   **auswringen**

gas etc: escape (from). **5.** **~ aus** leave
(*club etc*). **6.** F (go and) spend a penny.
'**austricksen** *v/t* (*sep*, -ge-, h) F trick.
'**austrinken** *v/t, v/i* (*irr, sep*, -ge-, h, →
trinken) drink up, finish (one's drink).
'**Austritt** *m* [-[e]s; -e) (*aus dat*) leaving (*a
club etc*).
'**austrocknen** *v/t* (*sep*, -ge-, h) *and v/i*
(sn) dry up.
'**austüfteln** *v/t* (*sep*, -ge-, h) F work out.
'**ausüben** *v/t* (*sep*, -ge-, h) **1.** carry on
(*trade etc*), practise (*profession etc*),
perform (*function*), hold (*office*). **2.**
exercise (*power, right, etc*). **3.** (*auf acc
on*) exert (*influence etc*), have (*effect*),
use (*violence etc*): → **Druck**¹. '**Ausübung** *f*
(-; *no pl*) carrying on (*etc*), exercise: *in ~
s-r Pflicht* in the execution of his duty.
'**ausufern** *v/i* (*sep*, -ge-, sn) get out of
hand.
'**Ausverkauf** *m* (-[e]s; ⁓e) † a) selling off,
b) (*im ~ kaufen* buy at a) sale, c) *fig.*
sellout. '**ausverkaufen** *v/t* (*sep*, h) sell
off: *ausverkauft* sold out, *thea. etc a.*
full (*house etc*).
'**auswachsen** (*irr, sep*, -ge-, → **wachsen**) **I** *v/t* (h) grow out of. **II** *v/i* (sn) ⚭
go to seed: F *es ist zum* ⚹*!* a) it's
enough to drive you crazy, b) it's
dreadfully boring. **III** *sich ~* (h) *fig.*
develop (*zu* into): → **ausgewachsen**.
'**Auswahl** *f* (-; *no pl*) **1.** selection, † *a.*
choice, range: *... in großer ~* a large
assortment of ...; *... zur ~* ... to choose
from; *e-e ~ treffen* select (*aus* from). **2.**
→ **Auswahlmannschaft**. '**auswählen**
v/t (*sep*, -ge-, h) choose, select.
'**Auswahlmannschaft** *f* representative
team.
'**Auswanderer** *m* (-s; -) emigrant.
'**auswandern** *v/i* (*sep*, -ge-, sn) emigrate.
'**Auswanderung** *f* (-; -en) emigration.
auswärtig ['aʊsvɛrtɪç] *adj* **1.** nonlocal, *a.*
† out-of-town. **2.** *pol.* foreign (*affairs,
office, etc*).
auswärts ['aʊsvɛrts] *adv* **1.** out, away
(from home), out of town: *~ essen* eat
out; *sports*: *~ spielen* play away from
home; *~ wohnen* live out of town. **2.**
outward(s). ⚹**spiel** *n* away match.
'**auswaschen** *v/t* (*irr, sep*, -ge-, h, →
waschen) wash out.
auswechselbar ['aʊsvɛksəlbaːr] *adj*
(*gegen*) exchangeable (for), replace-

able (by). '**auswechseln** *v/t* (*sep*, -ge-,
h) (*gegen*) exchange (for), replace (by),
change (*tyre*), substitute (*player*).
'**Auswechselspieler(in** *f*) *m* substitute.
'**Auswechs(e)lung** *f* (-; -en) exchange,
replacement, *sports*: substitution.
'**Ausweg** *m* (-[e]s; -e) *fig.* way out (*aus
of*): *als letzter ~* as a last resort.
'**ausweglos** *adj* hopeless. '**Ausweglo-
sigkeit** *f* (-; *no pl*) hopelessness.
'**ausweichen** *v/i* (*irr, sep*, -ge-, sn, →
weichen) **1.** (*dat*) make way (for), get
out of the way (of), dodge: *j-s Blicken
~* avoid s.o.'s eyes; *e-r Frage ~* evade a
question. **2.** be evasive. **3.** *~ auf* (*acc*)
switch to. '**ausweichend** *adj* evasive.
'**Ausweich|ma,növer** *n fig.* evasive ac-
tion. ⚹**möglichkeit** *f* alternative.
'**ausweinen**: *sich ~* (*sep*, -ge-, h) have a
good cry (*bei j-m* on s.o.'s shoulder).
'**Ausweis** *m* (-es; -e) identity (*abbr.* ID)
card, (*membership*) card, pass.
'**ausweisen** (*irr, sep*, -ge-, h, → **weisen**)
I *v/t* **1.** (*aus* from) a) expel, b) deport
(*alien*). **2.** *fig. j-n ~ als* show s.o. to be
(*an expert etc*). **II** *sich ~* prove one's
identity: *sich als Experte etc ~* prove
o.s. an expert *etc*.
'**Ausweis|kon,trolle** *f* ID check. ⚹**pa-
piere** *pl* (identification *or* ID) papers.
'**Ausweisung** *f* (-; -en) (*aus* from) a)
expulsion, b) deportation (*of aliens*).
'**ausweiten** *v/t* (*sep*, -ge-, h) (*a. sich ~*)
expand (*a. fig. zu* into).
'**Ausweitung** *f* (-; -en) expansion.
'**auswendig** *adv* by heart: ♩ *~ spielen*
play from memory; *et. in- und ~ kennen* know s.th. inside out.
'**auswerfen** *v/t* (*irr, sep*, -ge-, h, → **werfen**) cast (*anchor etc*).
'**auswerten** *v/t* (*sep*, -ge-, h) **1.** evaluate.
2. utilize, † *a.* exploit. '**Auswertung** *f*
(-; -en) **1.** evaluation. **2.** utilization.
'**auswickeln** *v/t* (*sep*, -ge-, h) unwrap.
'**auswirken**: *sich ~* (*sep*, -ge-, h) a) have
consequences, b) *auf* (*acc*) affect, c) *in*
(*dat*) result in; *sich positiv* (*negativ*) *~*
have a favo(u)rable (negative) effect.
'**Auswirkung** *f* (-; -en) **1.** effect (*auf acc
on*). **2.** → **Rückwirkung**.
'**auswischen** *v/t* (*sep*, -ge-, h) wipe out:
F *j-m eins ~* play a nasty trick on s.o.
'**auswringen** *v/t* (*irr, sep*, -ge-, h, →
wringen) wring out.

'Auswuchs *m* (-es; ⸚e) **1.** ⚘ outgrowth. **2.** *fig.* a) *pl* excesses, b) product (*of the imagination*).

'Auswurf *m* (-[e]s; *no pl*) **1.** ⚘ sputum. **2.** → **Abschaum.**

'auszahlen (*sep*, -ge-, h) **I** *v/t* pay (out) (*sum*), pay *s.o.* off, buy out (*partner*). **II sich ~** *fig.* pay.

'auszählen *v/t* (*sep*, -ge-, h) count out.

'Auszahlung *f* (-; -en) payment.

'auszeichnen (*sep*, -ge-, h) **I** *v/t* **1.** distinguish, hono(u)r: *mit e-m Preis ~* award a prize to; (*mit e-m Orden*) ~ decorate. **2.** ✝ price (*goods*). **II sich ~** distinguish o.s. **'Auszeichnung** *f* (-; -en) **1.** a) (mark of) distinction, b) decoration, c) award: *mit ~ bestehen* pass *an exam* with distinction. **2.** ✝ pricing.

'ausziehbar *adj* pull-out, telescopic.

'ausziehen (*irr, sep*, -ge-, → **ziehen**) **I** *v/t* (h) **1.** take off (*clothes*): *j-n ~* undress s.o. **2.** pull out (*table etc*). **3.** 🜨, ⚗ extract. **II** *v/i* (sn) **4.** set out. **5.** (*aus e-r Wohnung*) ~ move out (of a flat). **III sich ~** (h) undress.

'Auszieh|feder *f* drawing pen. **~platte** *f* (*table*) leaf. **~tisch** *m* pull-out table. **~tusche** *f* drawing ink.

'Auszubildende *m, f* (-n; -n) trainee.

'Auszug *m* (-[e]s; ⸚e) **1.** departure, *demonstrative*: walkout: ~ (*aus e-r Wohnung*) move (from a flat). **2.** a) 🜨 extraction, b) *a. fig.* extract (*aus* from), c) ♪ arrangement. **3.** ✝ statement (of account). **'auszugsweise** *adv* in parts: *et. ~ vorlesen* read extracts from s.th.

'auszupfen *v/t* (*sep*, -ge-, h) pluck out.

autark [au'tark] *adj* ✝ autarkic.

Autarkie [autar'ki:] *f* (-; -en) autarky.

authentisch [au'tɛntɪʃ] *adj* authentic.

Auto ['auto] *n* (-s; -s) (motor)car, *esp. Am.* auto(mobile): ~ *fahren* drive (a car); *mit dem ~ fahren* go by car; *können Sie ~ fahren?, fahren Sie ~?* do you drive? → *mitnehmen* 1.

'Autoapo,theke *f* (driver's) first-aid kit.

'Autoatlas *m* road atlas.

'Autobahn *f* (-; -en) motorway, *Am.* expressway, freeway. **~auffahrt** *f* motorway *etc* approach, slip road. **~ausfahrt** *f* exit. **~gebühr** *f* toll. **~kreuz** *n* motorway *etc* intersection.

'Autobahnmeisterei [-maɪstəraɪ] *f* (-; -en) motorway maintenance area.

'Autobahn|raststätte *f* motorway service area. **~zubringer** *m* slip road.

Autobiographie [autobiogra'fi:] *f* (-; -n) autobiography.

'Autobus *m* bus, *Br. a.* coach.

Autodidakt [autodi'dakt] *m* (-en; -en), **Autodi'daktin** *f* (-; -nen) autodidact.

'Auto|dieb *m* car thief. **~diebstahl** *m* car theft. **~fähre** *f* car ferry. **~fahrer(in** *f*) *m* motorist, (car) driver. **~fahrt** *f* drive.

'autofrei *adj* traffic-free.

'Autofriedhof *m* F *fig.* car dump.

autogen [auto'ge:n] *adj* ⚙, ⚗ autogenous: **~es Training** autogenic training.

Autogramm [auto'gram] *n* (-[e]s; -e) autograph. **Auto'grammjäger(in** *f*) *m* F autograph hunter. **Auto'grammstunde** *f* autograph(ing) session. ♪

'Auto|händler *m* car dealer. **~indu,strie** *f* car industry. **~kino** *n* drive-in (cinema). **~knacker** *m* (-s; -) F car burglar. **~ko,lonne** *f* line of cars, convoy.

Automat [auto'ma:t] *m* (-en; -en) **1.** a) vending machine, b) slot machine, c) juke box, d) ⚙ automatic machine. **2.** *fig.* (*person*) robot.

Auto'matenrestau,rant *n* automat.

Automatik [auto'ma:tɪk] *f* (-; ⚙ -en) automatism, ⚙ automatic system, *mot.* automatic transmission. **Auto'matikgurt** *m* reel seat belt. **Automation** [automa'tsio:n] *f* (-; *no pl*) automation. **automatisch** [auto'ma:tɪʃ] *adj* automatic. **automatisieren** [automati'zi:rən] *v/t* (h) automate.

'Auto,me,chaniker *m* car mechanic.

Automobil [automo'bi:l] *n* (-s; -e) automobile. **~ausstellung** *f* motor show. **~klub** *m* automobile association.

autonom [auto'no:m] *adj* ✝ autonomous.

Autonomie [autono'mi:] *f* (-; -n) autonomy.

'Autonummer *f* (car) number.

'Autopi,lot *m* (-en; -en) ✈ autopilot.

Autopsie [auto'psi:] *f* (-; -n) ✞ autopsy, post-mortem.

Autor ['autor] *m* (-s; -en), **Autorin** [au'to:rɪn] *f* (-; -nen) author, writer.

'Auto|radio *n* car radio. **~reifen** *m* tyre, *Am.* tire. **~reisezug** *m* motorail train. **~rennen** *n* car (*or* motor) race. **~rennsport** *m* motor racing.

autorisieren [autori'zi:rən] *v/t* (h) authorize.

autoritär [autori'tɛ:r] *adj* authoritarian.
Autorität [autori'tɛ:t] *f* (-; -en) **1.** *no pl* authority. **2.** (*auf dem Gebiet gen*) authority (on), expert (of).
'**Auto|schalter** *m* of a bank: drive-up counter. ~**schlosser** *m* car mechanic. ~**schlüssel** *m* car key. ~**skooter** [-sku:tər] *m* (-s; -) dodgem. ~**stop(p)** *m* ~ **machen** hitchhike. ~**straße** *f* motor road, *Am.* highway.
Autosuggesti'on *f* autosuggestion.
'**Auto|tele|fon** *n* car telephone. ~**unfall** *m* car accident: *er kam bei e-m ~ ums Leben* he died in a car crash. ~**verleih** *m* car hire service, *esp. Am.* rent-a-car

(service). ~**waschanlage** *f* carwash. ~**werkstatt** *f* garage, repair shop.
Avantgarde [avā'gardə] *f* (-; -n), **avantgardistisch** [-'dıstıʃ] *adj* avant-garde.
Aversion [aver'zĭo:n] *f* (-; -en) aversion (*gegen* to).
Avitaminose [avitami'no:zə] *f* (-; -n) 🗲 avitaminosis.
Avocato [avo'ka:to] *f* (-; -s) 🍃 avocado.
Axt [akst] *f* (-; ⁓e) axe, *Am.* ax.
Azalee [atsa'le:ə] *f* (-; -n) 🍃 azalea.
Azteke [ats'te:kə] *m* (-n; -n) *hist.* Aztec.
Azubi [a'tsu:bi] *m* (-s; -s), *f* (-; -s) F → *Auszubildende.*
azurblau [a'tsu:r-] *adj* azure (blue).

B

B, b [be:] *n* (-; -) B, b, ♩ B flat.
babbeln ['babəln] *v/t, v/i* (h) F babble.
Baby ['be:bi] *n* (-s; -s) baby. ~**ausstattung** *f* layette. ~**nahrung** *f* baby food. ~**sitter** *m* (-s; -) babysitter. ~**speck** *m* F puppy fat. ~**sprache** *f* babytalk. ~**tragetasche** *f* carrycot.
Bach [bax] *m* (-[e]s; ⁓e) stream, brook.
Bache ['baxə] *f* (-; -n) *zo.* (wild) sow.
'**Bachfo,relle** *f* river trout.
'**Bachstelze** *f zo.* (water) wagtail.
'**Backblech** ['bak-] *n* baking tray.
'**backbord** *adv* ♣ to port.
'**Backbord** *n, m* (-s; *no pl*) ♣ port (side).
Backe ['bakə] *f* (-; -n) **1.** cheek. **2.** ⊙ a) jaw, b) die. **3.** *on ski*: toe piece.
backen ['bakən] (backte, † buk, gebakken, h) **I** *v/t, a. v/i a*) bake, b) *dial.* fry. **II** *v/i snow etc*: cake, stick.
'**Backen|bart** *m* sideburns. ~**knochen** *m* cheekbone. ~**zahn** *m* molar.
Bäcker ['bɛkər] *m* (-s; -) baker: *beim* ~ at the baker's. **Bäckerei** [bɛkə'raı] *f* (-; -en) **1.** baker's (shop). **2.** *no pl* a) baking, b) baker's trade. '**Bäckerladen** *m* → *Bäckerei* 1. '**Bäckermeister** *m* master baker.
'**Back|fett** *n gastr.* shortening. ~**form** *f* baking tin. ~**hefe** *f* baker's yeast. ~**obst** *n* dried fruit. ~**ofen** *m* oven. ~**pflaume** *f*

prune. ~**pulver** *n* baking powder. ~**röhre** *f* oven. ~**stein** *m* brick. ~**waren** *pl* bread, cakes and pastries.
Bad [ba:t] *n* (-[e]s; ⁓er) **1.** a) bath (*a.* 🗲 *and* 🗲), b) swim: *ein ~ nehmen* → *baden* 1. **2.** → a) *Badeanstalt,* b) *Badeort,* c) *Badezimmer.*
'**Bade|anstalt** *f* swimming pool, public baths. ~**anzug** *m* swimsuit. ~**gast** *m* **1.** bather. **2.** → *Kurgast.* ~**hose** *f* swimming trunks. ~**kappe** *f* bathing cap. ~**mantel** *m* bathrobe. ~**matte** *f* bath mat. ~**meister** *m* **1.** pool attendant. **2.** *at beaches:* lifeguard.
baden ['ba:dən] (h) **I** *v/i* **1.** have (*or* take) a bath. **2.** swim: ~ *gehen* a) go swimming, b) F *fig.* come a cropper, *thing:* go phut. **II** *v/t* **3.** bath, *Am.* bathe. **III** *sich* ~ **4.** → 1. **5.** *fig.* bask (*in dat* in).
'**Bade|ofen** *m* bathroom boiler. ~**ort** *m* **1.** seaside resort. **2.** health resort, spa. ~**salz** *n* bath salts. ~**schuhe** *pl* beach shoes. ~**strand** *m* beach. ~**tuch** *n* (-[e]s; ⁓er) bath towel. ~**wanne** *f* bath(tub). ~**zeug** *n* swimming things. ~**zimmer** *n* bathroom.
baff [baf] *adj* F ~ *sein* be flabbergasted.
Bagage [ba'ga:ʒə] *f* (-; *no pl*) *contp.* bunch, tot.
Bagatelle [baga'tɛlə] *f* (-; -n) trifle.

bagatellisieren [bagatɛli'ziːrən] *v/t* (h) play down.

Baga'tellschaden *m* petty damage(s).

Bagger ['bagər] *m* (-s; -) ⚙ excavator.

baggern ['bagərn] *v/i, v/t* (h) excavate, dredge. **'Baggersee** *m* flooded quarry.

Bahn [baːn] *f* (-; -en) **1.** path, course: *fig.* **sich ~ brechen** forge ahead; **auf die schiefe ~ geraten** go astray; **~ frei!** make way! **2.** a) road, b) lane, c) (*racing*) track, d) *skiing*: course, piste. **3.** a) trajectory, b) *astr.* course, c) orbit. **4.** a) (*skating*) rink, b) (*bowling*) alley. **5.** a) railway, *Am.* railroad, b) train, c) tram, *Am.* streetcar: *mit der ~* by train, ⚓ by rail; *j-n zur ~ bringen* see s.o. off (at the station). **6.** web (*of paper*), width (*of cloth*). **'Bahn...** railway (*Am.* railroad) (*official etc*). **'bahnbrechend** *adj* pioneer(ing), revolutionary. **'Bahndamm** *m* railway embankment. **bahnen** ['baːnən] *v/t* (h) clear (*path*): **sich e-n Weg ~** force one's way (*durch* through).

'Bahn|fahrt *f* train journey. **⊈fracht** *f* ⚓ rail carriage (*Am.* freight). **⊈frei** *adj and adv* ⚓ free on rail (*or* board) (*abbr.* f.o.r., f.o.b.). **⊷hof** *m* railway (*Am.* railroad) station: *auf dem ~* at the station; F *fig.* **großer ~** red-carpet treatment.

'Bahnhofs|halle *f* concourse. **⊷restaurant** *n* station restaurant. **⊷vorsteher** *m* stationmaster.

'Bahn|körper *m* permanent way. **⊈lagernd** *adv* ⚓ to be called for at the station. **⊷linie** *f* railway line. **⊷poli'zei** *f* railway police. **⊷reise** *f* train journey. **⊷steig** [-ʃtaɪk] *m* (-[e]s; -e) platform. **⊷strecke** *f* line, *Am.* track. **⊷übergang** *m* level (*Am.* grade) crossing. **⊷wärter** *m* level crossing attendant.

Bahre ['baːrə] *f* **1.** stretcher. **2.** bier.

Baiser [bɛ'zeː] *n* (-s; -s) *gastr.* meringue.

Baisse ['bɛːsə] *f* (-; -n) ⚓ slump.

Baissier [bɛ'sie̯] *m* (-s; -s) ⚓ bear.

Bajonett [bajo'nɛt] *n* (-[e]s; -e) bayonet.

Bajo'nettverschluß *m* ⚙ bayonet joint (*phot.* mount).

Bake ['baːkə] *f* (-; -n) beacon.

Bakterie [bak'teːri̯ə] *f* (-; -n) bacterium, germ. **bakteriell** [bakte'ri̯ɛl] *adj* bacterial. **Bakteriologe** [bakteri̯o'loːgə] *m* (-n; -n) bacteriologist.

Balance [ba'lãsə] *f* (-; -n) balance.

Ba'lanceakt *m* balancing act. **balancie-**

ren [balãˈsiːrən] *v/t, v/i* (h) balance.

bald [balt] *adv* **1.** soon: **~ darauf** shortly afterwards; **so ~ als möglich** as soon as possible; **bis ~!** see you soon! **2.** F almost, nearly.

Baldachin ['baldaxiːn] *m* (-s; -e) canopy.

baldig ['baldiç] *adj* speedy, early.

Baldrian ['baldria:n] *m* (-s; -e) valerian.

Balg¹ [balk] *m* (-[e]s; ⁓e) **1.** skin. **2.** (*organ*) bellows.

Balg² *m, n* (-[e]s; ⁓er) F brat.

balgen ['balgən] **sich ~** (h), **Balgerei** [-'raɪ] *f* (-; -en) (*um* for) scuffle, tussle.

Balken ['balkən] *m* (-s; -) **1.** beam: F *lügen, daß sich die ~ biegen* lie in one's teeth. **2.** crossbar. **3.** → **Schwebebalken**. **⊷decke** *f* timbered ceiling. **⊷überschrift** *f* banner headline.

Balkon [bal'kõ] *m* (-s; -e) **1.** balcony, *thea. a.* dress circle. **⊷tür** *f* French window(s).

Ball¹ [bal] *m* (-[e]s; ⁓e) ball: F *fig. am ~ bleiben* keep at it. **Ball²** *m* (-[e]s; ⁓e) (*auf e-m ~* at a) ball (*or* dance).

Ballade [ba'laːdə] *f* (-; -n) ballad.

Ballast [ba'last] *m* (-[e]s; -e) *a. fig.* ballast. **Bal'laststoffe** *pl* 💊 roughage.

ballen ['balən] (h) **I** *v/t* **1.** make into a ball. **2.** *die Faust ~* clench one's fist. **II** *sich ~* form into a ball, *clouds*: gather.

'Ballen *m* (-s; -) **1.** *anat.* ball (of one's foot *or* hand). **2.** ⚓ bale.

Ballerina [balə'riːna] *f* (-; -rinen) ballerina, ballet dancer.

Ballermann ['balərman] *m* (-s; ⁓er) F shooter, *Am. sl.* rod.

ballern ['balərn] *v/i* (h) F bang (away).

Ballett [ba'lɛt] *n* (-[e]s; -e) a) ballet, b) ballet company.

Bal'lettänzer(in *f*) *m* ballet dancer.

Bal'lettschule *f* ballet school.

Ballistik [ba'lɪstɪk] *f* (-; *no pl*) ballistics.

ballistisch [ba'lɪstɪʃ] *adj* ballistic.

'Balljunge *m* ball boy.

'Ballkleid *n* ball dress.

Ballon [ba'lõ] *m* (-s; -s) **1.** balloon. **2.** a) carboy, b) demijohn.

Bal'lonreifen *m* balloon tyre (*Am.* tire).

'Ballsaal *m* ballroom.

'Ballspiel *n* ball game.

'Ballung *f* (-; -en) concentration.

'Ballungs|gebiet *n*, **⊷raum** *m*, **⊷zentrum** *n* conurbation, ⚓ area of industrial concentration.

'Ballwechsel *m tennis*: exchange.

bannen

Balsam ['balza:m] *m* (-s; -e) *a. fig.* balm.

balsamieren [balza'mi:rən] *v/t* (h) embalm.

baltisch ['baltɪʃ] *adj* Baltic.

Balz [balts] *f* (-; -en) *zo.* a) courting, b) mating season.

'**balzen** *v/i* (h) *zo.* a) court, b) mate.

Bambus ['bambʊs] *m* (-[ses]; -se] bamboo. **~sprossen** *pl* bamboo sprouts.

Bammel ['baməl] *m* (-s; *no pl*) F **~ haben** (*vor dat*) be in a blue funk (of).

banal [ba'na:l] *adj* trite, banal.

Banalität [banali'tɛ:t] *f* (-; -en) banality.

Banane [ba'na:nə] *f* (-; -n) banana.

Ba'nanenstecker *m ⚡* banana plug.

Banause [ba'naʊzə] *m* (-n; -n) *contp.* Philistine, lowbrow.

band [bant] *pret of* **binden.**

Band[1] *m* (-[e]s; *⁻e*) volume: *fig. das spricht Bände* that speaks volumes.

Band[2] *n* (-[e]s; *⁻er*) **1.** a) ribbon, b) (apron) string, c) (hat) band. **2.** ⚙, *video etc, a. sports:* tape: *auf ~ aufnehmen* tape(-record). **3.** ⚙ a) (conveyor) belt, b) assembly line: *fig. am laufenden ~* one after the other, *w.s.* nonstop. **4.** *anat.* ligament. **5.** *radio:* wave band. **6.** (*pl -e*) *fig.* bond (*of love etc*).

Band[3] [bɛnt] *f* (-; -s) ♩ band, group.

Bandage [ban'da:ʒə] *f* (-; -n) bandage: *fig. mit harten ~n* with the gloves off.

bandagieren [banda'ʒi:rən] *v/t* (h) bandage.

'**Bandaufnahme** *f* tape recording.

'**Bandbreite** *f* **1.** ⚡ band width. **2.** *statistics etc:* spread. **3.** *fig.* spectrum.

Bande[1] ['bandə] *f*(-; -n) gang, F *contp. a.* bunch: *die ganze ~* the whole lot.

'**Bande**[2] *f* billiard, bowling: cushion, *ice hockey etc:* boards.

Bänderriß ['bɛndɐr-] *m 🦴* torn ligament.

'**Bänderzerrung** *f 🦴* pulled ligament.

'**Bandfilter** *n, m radio:* band(-pass) filter.

'**Bandförderer** *m* ⚙ belt conveyor.

bändigen ['bɛndɪgən] *v/t* (h) tame, *fig. a.* subdue, restrain, control.

'**Bändigung** *f* (-; *no pl*) taming (*etc*).

Bandit [ban'di:t] *m* (-en; -en) bandit.

'**Bandmaß** *n* measuring tape.

'**Bandnudeln** *pl* ribbon noodles.

'**Bandscheibe** *f anat.* (intervertebral) disc. '**Bandscheibenschaden** *m 🦴* **1.** damaged disc. **2.** → '**Bandscheibenvorfall** *m* slipped disc.

'**Bandwurm** *m* tapeworm. '**Bandwurmsatz** *m humor.* endless sentence.

bange ['baŋə] *adj* (*um* about) anxious, worried: *j-m* (*or j-s*) **~ machen** frighten s.o. '**Bange** *f* (*nur*) *k-e ~!* don't worry!

bangen ['baŋən] *v/i* (h) be worried (*um* about): *um j-s Leben ~* fear for s.o.'s life; *es bangt ihr vor* she is afraid of.

Bank[1] [baŋk] *f* (-; *⁻e*) a) bench, b) *ped.* desk, c) *eccl.* pew: *fig. et. auf die lange ~ schieben* put s.th. off; F *durch die ~* without exception, down the line.

Bank[2] *f* (-; -en) **1.** ✝ bank: *Geld auf der ~ haben* have money in the bank. **2.** bank: *die ~ halten* (*sprengen*) hold (break) the bank. **~angestellte** *m, f* bank clerk. **~anweisung** *f* banker's order. **~ausweis** *m* bank return (*Am.* statement). **~beamte** *m* bank clerk. **~di,rektor** *m* bank manager. **~dis,kont** *m* bank discount. **~einlage** *f* deposit.

Bankett [baŋ'ket] *n* (-[e]s; -e] **1.** banquet. **2.** ⚙ shoulder (*of road*).

'**Bank|fach** *n* (-[e]s; *⁻er*) **1.** *no pl* banking. **2.** safe(-deposit) box. **⌂fähig** *adj* bankable. **~geheimnis** *n* banker's secrecy. **~geschäft** *n* **1.** banking transaction. **2.** banking (business). **~guthaben** *n* **1.** bank balance. **2.** bank account. **~halter** *m* (-s; -) banker.

Bankier [baŋ'kie:] *m* (-s; -s) banker.

'**Bank|kaufmann** *m* bank clerk. **~konto** *n* bank account. **~leitzahl** *f* bank code (number). **~note** *f* (bank)note, *Am.* bill. **~raub** *m* bank robbery. **~räuber** *m* bank robber.

bankrott [baŋ'krot] *adj a. fig.* bankrupt.

Bank'rott *m* (-[e]s; -e) (*a. fig.* **den ~ erklären** declare) bankruptcy; *~ machen* go bankrupt. **Bank'rotterklärung** *f a. fig.* declaration of bankruptcy.

'**Bank|überfall** *m* bank holdup. **~überweisung** *f* bank transfer. **~verbindung** *f* **1.** bank account. **2.** correspondent. **~wesen** *n* (-s; *no pl*) banking.

Bann [ban] *m* (-[e]s; *no pl*) **1.** ban, *eccl.* excommunication: *in den ~ tun* outlaw, *eccl.* excommunicate. **2.** spell: *in s-n ~ schlagen* (*or ziehen*) → Bannen 3; *unter dem ~ stehen von* (*or gen*) be under the spell of. '**bannen** *v/t* (h) **1.** exorcize. **2.** ward off (*danger*). **3.** a) transfix, b) captivate, spellbind: → *gebannt*. **1.** *fig. ot. ~ auf* (*acc*) capture s.th. on *paper etc.* '**Banner** *n* (-s; -) banner (*a. fig.*), standard.

'**Bannkreis** *m fig.* sphere (of influence).

'**Bannmeile** *f* neutral zone.

Bantamgewicht ['bantam-] *n* (-[e]s; *no pl*) *sports:* bantamweight.

bar [ba:r] *adj* **1.** ~*es Geld* (ready) cash; (*in*) ~ *bezahlen* pay cash; *gegen* ~ for cash; ~ *ohne Abzug* net cash. **2.** pure (*gold etc*), *contp. a.* downright: ~*er Unsinn* sheer nonsense; → *Münze* 1. **3.** ~ *jeglicher Vernunft* devoid of any sense.

Bar *f* (-; -s) bar, nightclub: *an der* ~ at the bar.

Bär [bε:r] *m* (-en; -en) bear (*a.* ♈): *astr. der Große (Kleine)* ~ the Great (Little) Bear; F *fig. j-m e-n* ~*en aufbinden* tell s.o. a whopping lie.

Baracke [ba'rakə] *f* (-; -n) hut, *contp.* shack.

'**Barauszahlung** *f* cash payment.

Barbar [bar'ba:r] *m* (-en; -en) barbarian. **Barbarei** [barba'raı] *f* (-; -en) a) barbarism, b) barbarity. **barbarisch** [bar-'ba:rıʃ] *adj* barbarian, barbarous (*a. fig. contp.*), atrocious, F awful.

bärbeißig ['bε:rbaısıç] *adj* gruff.

'**Barbestand** *m* cash in hand, *of bank:* cash reserve.

'**Bardame** *f* barmaid.

'**Bareinnahmen** *pl* cash receipts.

'**Bärendienst** *m j-m e-n* ~ *erweisen* do s.o. a disservice. '**Bärenhunger** *m* F *e-n* ~ *haben* be ravenous.

Barett [ba'rεt] *n* (-[e]s; -e) beret.

'**barfuß, barfüßig** ['ba:rfy:sıç] *adj and adv* barefoot(ed).

barg [bark] *pret of* **bergen.**

'**Bargeld** *n* cash.

'**bargeldlos** *adj and adv* cashless.

'**barhäuptig** [-hɔyptıç] *adj* bareheaded.

'**Barhocker** *m* barstool.

Bärin ['bε:rın] *f* (-; -nen) she-bear.

Bariton ['ba:rıtɔn] *m* (-s; -e) baritone.

Barkasse [bar'kasə] *f* (-; -n) (motor) launch.

'**Barkauf** *m* cash purchase.

'**Barkeeper** *m* (-s; -) barman.

'**Barkre‚dit** *m* cash loan.

barmherzig [barm'hεrtsıç] *adj* (*gegen* to) a) merciful, b) charitable; → *Samariter.* **Barm'herzigkeit** *f* (-; *no pl*) a) mercy, b) charity.

'**Barmittel** *pl* cash.

'**Barmixer** *m* (-s; -) barman, bartender.

barock [ba'rɔk] *adj* baroque, *fig. a.* bizarre. **Ba'rock** *n*, *m* (-s; *no pl*) a) baroque period, b) baroque style.

Barometer [baro'me:tər] *n* (-s; -) *a. fig.* barometer.

Baron [ba'ro:n] *m* (-s; -e) baron. **Ba'ronin** *f* (-; -nen) baroness.

Barren ['barən] *m* (-s; -) **1.** bullion, ingot. **2.** *gym.* parallel bars.

Barriere [ba'riε:rə] *f* (-; -n) barrier.

Barrikade [bari'ka:də] *f* (-; -n) barricade: *auf die* ~*n gehen* mount the barricades (*für* for).

barsch [barʃ] *adj* gruff, brusque.

Barsch *m* (-[e]s; -e) *zo.* perch.

'**Barschaft** *f* (-; *no pl*) (ready) money, F cash.

'**Barscheck** *m* uncrossed cheque (*Am.* check).

barst [barst] *pret of* **bersten.**

Bart [ba:rt] *m* (-[e]s; ⤳e) **1.** beard: *sich e-n* ~ *wachsen lassen* (*or stehenlassen*) grow a beard; F *so ein* ~*!* that's an old one! **2.** bit (*of key*). **bärtig** ['bε:rtıç] *adj* bearded. '**Bartstoppeln** *pl* stubble.

'**Barvermögen** *n* liquid funds.

'**Barzahlung** *f* cash payment: *gegen* ~ cash down.

Basar [ba'za:r] *m* (-s; -e) bazaar.

Base[1] *f* (-; -n) female cousin.

Base[2] *f* (-; -n) ♞ base.

basieren [ba'zi:rən] *v/i* (h) ~ *auf* (*dat*) be based on.

Basilika [ba'zi:lika] *f* (-; -ken) basilica.

Basilikum [ba'zi:likʊm] *n* (-s; *no pl*) ♣ basil.

Basis ['ba:zıs] *f* (-; Basen) **1.** △, ⅋, ✕ *etc* base. **2.** *fig.* basis, foundation: *pol.* (*an der*) ~ (at the) grassroots.

basisch ['ba:zıʃ] *adj* ♞ basic.

'**Basisdemokra‚tie** *f* grassroots democracy. '**Basislager** *n mount.* base camp.

Baskenmütze ['baskən-] *f* beret.

Baß [bas] *m* (-sses; ⤳sse) bass. ~*geige* *f* (double) bass. ~*gi‚tarre* *f* bass guitar.

Bassin [ba'sε̃:] *n* (-s; -s) tank, basin.

Bassist [ba'sıst] *m* (-en; -en) ♪ **1.** bass (singer). **2.** bass player.

'**Baßregler** *m radio etc:* bass control. '**Baßschlüssel** *m* ♪ bass clef. '**Baßstimme** *f* bass (voice, ♪ *a.* part).

Bast [bast] *m* (-[e]s; -e) bast, raffia.

basta ['basta] *int* F (**und damit**) ~*!* and that's that!

Bastard ['bastart] *m* (-[e]s; -e) ♋, *zo.* hybrid, cross(breed), (*dog*) mongrel.

'**Bastelarbeit** *f* 1. handicraft (work). 2. → *Basteln*. **basteln** ['bastəln] (h) I *v/t* make, rig up, build. II *v/i* do handicrafts: ~ **an** (*dat*) *a. fig.* tinker at. '**Basteln** *n* (-s) handicrafts, home mechanics, *a. fig.* tinkering.

Bastion [bas'tǐo:n] *f* (-; -en) bastion.

'**Bastler** *m* (-s; -) home mechanic, hobbyist.

bat [ba:t] *pret of* **bitten**.

Bataillon [batal'jo:n] *n* (-s; -e) ✕ battalion.

Batik ['ba:tɪk] *f* (-; -en) batik.

batiken ['ba:tɪkən] *v/t, v/i* (h) batik.

Batist [ba'tɪst] *m* (-[e]s; -e) batiste, cambric.

Batterie [batə'ri:] *f* (-; -n) ⚡, ✕, ⚙, *a. fig.* battery. ⚡**betrieben** *adj* battery-operated. ~**ladegerät** *n* battery charger.

Bau [baʊ] *m* (-[e]s; Bauten) 1. *no pl* construction: **im** ~ under construction, being built. 2. building: → **Bauten**. 3. *no pl* ⚙ design, structure. 4. *no pl* building trade: F *fig.* **er ist vom** ~ he is an expert. 5. (*pl* Baue) earth (*of fox*), burrow (*of rabbits*). 6. *no pl* F ✕ detention: *3 Tage* ~ 3 days in the guardhouse.

'**Bau**|**amt** *n* Building Authorities. ~**arbeiten** *pl* construction work, roadworks. ~**arbeiter** *m* construction worker. ~**art** *f* a) style, ⚙ design, b) model, type. ~**aufsichtsbehörde** *f* building supervisory board.

Bauch [baʊx] *m* (-[e]s; ⸚e) belly (*a. fig.*), stomach, *anat.* abdomen, *contp.* paunch: *sich den* ~ *halten vor Lachen* split one's sides laughing; *fig. aus dem* ~ from the guts, guts (*reaction etc*).

'**Bauch**|**ansatz** *m* beginnings of a paunch. ~**fell** *n anat.* peritoneum. ~**fellentzündung** *f* ⚕ peritonitis.

bauchig ['baʊxɪç] *adj* bulbous.

'**Bauch**|**klatscher** *m* (-s; -) F belly flop. ~**landung** *f* ✈ belly landing: *e-e* ~ *machen* bellyland. ~**muskel** *m* stomach muscle. ~**nabel** *m* navel, F belly button. ⚥**reden** *v/i* (*only inf*) ventriloquize. ~**redner** *m* ventriloquist. ~**schmerzen** *pl* stomach-ache. ~**speicheldrüse** *f*

pancreas. ~**tanz** *m* belly dance. ~**tänzerin** *f* belly dancer.

'**Bauchweh** *n* (-s; *no pl*) F stomach-ache.

'**Baudenkmal** *n* historical monument.

bauen ['baʊən] (h) I *v/t* 1. build, construct, ⚙ *a.* make. 2. ✗ cultivate, grow. 3. F *fig.* a) make, take, pass (*exam*), c) cause: *e-n Unfall* ~ have an accident. II *v/i* 4. build (a house). 5. *fig.* ~ *auf* (*acc*) rely on, count on.

Bauer[1] ['baʊər] *n* (-s; -) (bird)cage.

Bauer[2] *m* (-n; -n) 1. farmer, *fig. contp.* peasant, boor. 2. *chess*: pawn, *cards*: jack. **Bäuerin** ['bɔʏərɪn] *f* (-; -nen) farmer's wife. '**bäuerlich** *adj* rustic.

'**Bauernbrot** *n* (coarse) brown bread.

'**Bauernfänger** *m* con man. **Bauernfängerei** [-fɛŋə'raɪ] *f* (-; *no pl*) con game.

'**Bauern**|**haus** *n* farmhouse. ~**hof** *m* farm. ~**möbel** *pl* rustic furniture. ~**regel** *f* F peasants' weather maxim.

'**bauernschlau** *adj* crafty.

'**Bauerwartungsland** *n* development area. '**Baufach** *n* (-[e]s; *no pl*) 1. architecture. 2. building trade.

'**baufällig** *adj* dilapidated.

'**Bau**|**firma** *f* builders and contractors. ~**gelände** *n* 1. building area. 2. → *Baustelle*. 1. ~**genehmigung** *f* planning (and building) permission. ~**genossenschaft** *f* cooperative building association. ~**gerüst** *n* scaffolding. ~**gewerbe** *n* building trade. ~**grund(stück** *n*) *m* (building) site. ~**handwerker** *m* workman in the building trade. ~**herr** *m* client, building owner. ~**ingeni,eur** *m* civic engineer. ~**jahr** *n* construction year: *mot.* ~ *1991* (a) 1991 model. ~**kasten** *m* 1. box of bricks. 2. construction set. ~**kastensy,stem** *n* ⚙ unit construction system. ~**klotz** *m* building block: F *da staunt man Bauklötze!* it's mind-boggling! ~**kunst** *f* (-; *no pl*) architecture. ~**land** *n* (-[e]s; *no pl*) building land. ~**leiter** *m* site manager.

'**baulich** *adj* architectural, structural: *in gutem* ~**en** *Zustand* in good repair.

Baum [baʊm] *m* (-[e]s; ⸚e) tree.

'**Bauma,schinen** *pl* construction (*or* building) machines.

'**Baumblüte** *f* **während der** ~ while the trees are in blossom.

'**Baumeister** *m* master builder, *w.s.* architect.

baumeln ['baʊməln] *v/i* (h) **1.** (*an dat* from) dangle, swing: *mit den Beinen* ~ dangle one's legs. **2.** F swing.

'**Baum|grenze** *f* timberline. **~krone** *f* tree-top. **~kuchen** *m* pyramid cake.

'**baumlos** *adj* treeless.

'**Baum|schere** *f* pruning shears. **~schule** *f* (tree) nursery. **~stamm** *m* a) trunk, b) log. **§stark** *adj fig.* (a̅s) strong as an ox. **~sterben** *n* (-s) death of trees.

'**Baumwolle** *f*, '**baumwollen** *adj* cotton.

'**Bau|plan** *m* architect's plan, ⊙ blueprint. **~platz** *m* (building) site. **~projekt** *n* building project.

'**baureif** *adj* a. ⊙ developed.

Bausch [baʊʃ] *m* (-[e]s; ⁓e) wad (a. ✷): *fig. in* ~ *und Bogen* lock, stock and barrel. '**bauschen** (h) **I** *v/i* (a. *sich* ~) billow. **II** *v/t* puff out.

'**bauschig** *adj* puffed out.

'**Bau|schlosser** *m* building fitter. **~sparkasse** *f* building society. **~sparvertrag** *m* building savings agreement. **~stahl** *m* structural steel. **~stein** *m* **1.** brick, stone (for building). **2.** *fig.* element, component, contribution. **3.** ⚡ module. **~stelle** *f* **1.** building site. **2.** roadworks. **~stil** *m* (architectural) style. **~stoff** *m* building material. **~stopp** *m* **e-n** ~ *verhängen* impose a halt on building. **~substanz** *f* fabric (of a building). **~techniker** *m* constructional engineer. **~teil** *n* structural member, component part.

Bauten ['baʊtən] *pl* **1.** buildings, structures. **2.** *thea. etc* setting.

'**Bau|träger** *m* **1.** builder. **2.** institution *etc* responsible for the building project. **~unternehmer** *m* building contractor. **~vorhaben** *n* building project. **~weise** *f* (method of) construction, style (of architecture). **~werk** *n* building. **~zeichnung** *f* construction drawing.

Bayer ['baɪər] *m* (-n; -n), '**Bayerin** *f* (-; -nen), '**bay(e)risch** *adj* Bavarian.

Bazillenträger(**in** *f*) *m* [ba'tsɪlən-] germ carrier. **Bazillus** *m* [ba'tsɪlʊs] *m* (-; -len) bacillus (*pl* -cilli), germ, F bug.

beabsichtigen [bə'ʔapzɪçtɪgən] *v/t* (h) intend (*zu tun* to, doing): *das war beabsichtigt* that was intentional.

be'achten *v/t* (h) a) pay attention to, note, b) take into account, consider, c) notice, d) observe (*rules etc*): *bitte*

zu ~ please note; *nicht* ~ ignore, disregard.

be'achtenswert *adj* noteworthy.

be'achtlich *adj* considerable.

Be'achtung *f* (-; *no pl*) (*gen*) a) attention (to), b) observing (of), c) consideration (of): ~ *schenken* (*dat*) → *beachten*.

Beamte [bə'ʔamtə] *m* (-n; -n) (government) official, *Br.* cɪvɪl (*Am.* publɪc) servant, (*police or customs*) officer.

Be'amtenlaufbahn *f* civil service career.

Be'amtin *f* (-; -nen) → *Beamte*.

be'ängstigend *adj* worrying, alarming.

be'anspruchen *v/t* (h) **1.** claim (*a right etc*). **2.** a) demand, require, b) take up (*room, time*): *j-n ganz* ~ keep s.o. busy. **3.** avail o.s. of (*s.o.'s help etc*). **4.** ⊙ stress. **Be'anspruchung** *f* (-; -en) (*gen* on) **1.** claim. **2.** demand (*on s.o.'s time etc*). **3.** a. ⊙ strain, stress.

beanstanden [bə'ʔanʃtandən] *v/t* (h) object to, criticize, a. ✚ complain about, reject (*goods*).

Be'anstandung *f* (-; -en) (*gen*) objection (to), complaint (about).

beantragen [bə'ʔantra:gən] *v/t* (h) **1.** apply for (*bei j-m* to s.o.). **2.** propose, ⚡₂, *parl.* move (for).

be'arbeiten *v/t* (h) **1.** work, ⚒ a. cultivate, till, ⊙ a. machine, process, treat. **2.** *fig.* a) work on, deal with, *adm.* a. process, b) be in charge of. **3.** edit, revise (*book*), adapt (*a play etc for the stage etc*). **4.** ♪ arrange. **5.** *j-n* ~ a) work on s.o., b) F give s.o. a working over.

Be'arbeitung *f* (-; -en) **1.** working (*etc*, → *bearbeiten*), treatment, ⚒ cultivation, *adm.* processing. **2.** a) revision, b) revised edition, *thea. etc* adaptation. **3.** ♪ arrangement.

Be'atmung *f* (-; *no pl*) (*künstliche*) ~ artificial respiration.

beaufsichtigen [bə'ʔaʊfzɪçtɪgən] *v/t* (h) supervise, look after. **Be'aufsichtigung** *f* (-; -en) supervision.

be'auftragen *v/t* (h) a) instruct, b) commission (*artist etc*), c) appoint: *j-n mit e-m Fall* ~ put s.o. in charge of a case. **Be'auftragte** *m, f* (-n; -n) representative, *adm.* commissioner.

be'bauen *v/t* (h) **1.** build on. **2.** ⚒ cultivate. **Be'bauung** *f* (-; -en) **1.** development. **2.** ⚒ cultivation.

beben ['be:bən] *v/i* (h) shake, tremble (*a.*

fig. **vor** *dat* with). '**Beben** *n* (-s; -) trembling, *geol.* tremor, earthquake.

bebildern [bə'bɪldərn] *v/t* (h) illustrate.

bebrillt [bə'brɪlt] *adj* spectacled.

Becher ['bɛçər] *m* (-s; -) **1.** tumbler, mug, beaker. **2.** tub (*of ice cream etc*). **3.** ♀ cup, calix. '**bechern** *v/i* (h) F booze.

Becken ['bɛkən] *n* (-s; -) **1.** bowl, basin (*a.* ⊙), (*kitchen*) sink. **2.** (swimming) pool. **3.** *anat.* pelvis. **4.** ♪ cymbal.

'**Becken...** pelvic (*bone etc*).

'**Beckenbruch** *m* ♂ fractured pelvis.

Becquerel [bɛkə'rɛl] *n* (-s; -) Becquerel.

bedacht [bə'daxt] **I** *pp* of **bedenken**. **II** *adj* **~ sein auf** (*acc*) be intent on; *darauf* **~ sein zu** *inf* be anxious to *inf*.

be'dachte *pret* of **bedenken**.

bedächtig [bə'dɛçtɪç] *adj* a) careful, b) circumspect, c) slow.

be'danken: sich ~ (h) say thank you, express one's thanks (*bei j-m* to s.o.); *ich bedanke mich!* thank you!; *iro.* *dafür bedanke ich mich!* no, thank you very much!

Bedarf [bə'darf] *m* (-[e]s; *no pl*) (*an dat*) need (of), *esp.* ♥ a) demand (for), b) consumption (of), c) requirements (of): *bei* (*nach*) **~** if (as required; **~ haben an** (*dat*) need; *den* **~ decken** meet the demand; *s-n* **~ decken** get everything one needs.

Be'darfs|ar,tikel *m* commodity, *pl* a. consumer goods. **~fall** *im* **~** in case of need, if required. **~güter** *pl* consumer goods. **~haltestelle** *f* request stop.

bedauerlich [bə'daʊərlɪç] *adj* regrettable, unfortunate. **be'dauerlicherweise** *adv* unfortunately. **be'dauern** *v/t* (h) regret (*s.th.*), feel sorry for (*s.o.*): *ich bedaure sehr, daß ...* I am very sorry that ...; *bedaure!* sorry! **Be'dauern** *n* (-s) regret (*über acc* for): *zu m-m* **~** to my regret. **be'dauernswert** *adj* **1.** pitiable. **2.** → **bedauerlich**.

be'decken (h) **I** *v/t* cover (up). **II** *sich* **~** cover o.s., *sky:* cloud over. **be'deckt** *adj* **1.** overcast (*sky*). **2.** *fig.* *sich* **~ halten** keep a low profile. **Be'deckung** *f* (-; -en) **1.** covering. **2.** escort, convoy.

be'denken *v/t* (bedachte, bedacht, h) **1.** a) consider, think *s.th.* over, b) bear *s.th.* in mind. **2.** *j-n mit et.* **~** give s.o. s.th.; *j-n in s-m Testament* **~** remember s.o. in one's will. **Be'denken** *n* (-s; -)

usu. pl a) objection, b) doubt: *k-e* **~ haben** have no reservations (*wegen* about). **be'denkenlos I** *adj* unscrupulous. **II** *adv* without hesitation (*or* scruple). **be'denklich** *adj* **1.** dubious. **2.** alarming, critical, serious, dangerous. **3.** worried, sceptical. **Be'denkzeit** *f* time to think it over: *ich gebe dir bis morgen* **~** I'll give you till tomorrow.

be'deuten *v/t* (h) **1.** mean, *symbol, word, etc: a.* stand for: *was soll das (denn)* **~?** what's the meaning of this?, *picture etc:* what's that supposed to be?, *contp.* what's the idea?; *das hat nichts zu* **~** a) it doesn't mean a thing, b) it doesn't matter; *das bedeutet nichts Gutes* that's a bad thing; *das bedeutet mir viel* that's very important to me. **2.** *j-m et.* **~** point s.th. out to s.o.; *j-m* **~**, *daß ...* give s.o. to understand that ... **be'deutend I** *adj* important, considerable, great, outstanding. **II** *adv* considerably, a great deal *better etc*.

be'deutsam → **bedeutungsvoll**.

Be'deutung *f* (-; -en) **1.** meaning. **2.** *no pl* importance, *w.s.* import: *von* **~** important, significant, relevant (*für* to); *nichts von* **~** nothing important; → *beimessen* b. **be'deutungsvoll** *adj* **1.** important, significant. **2.** meaningful.

be'dienen (h) **I** *v/t* **1.** serve: *iro.* *ich bin bedient!* I've had enough! **2.** operate. **3.** F *sports:* pass (the ball) to. **II** *sich* **~ 4.** help o.s.; **~** *Sie sich!* help yourself! **5.** *sich e-r Sache* **~** use s.th. **III** *v/i* **6.** serve, wait at (*Am.* on) table.

Be'dienung *f* (-; -en) **1.** *no pl* a) service, b) operation. **2.** waiter, waitress.

Be'dienungs|anleitung *f* instructions for use, operating instructions. **~knopf** *m* control knob. **~kom,fort** *m* easy operation.

bedingen [bə'dɪŋən] *v/t* (h) **1.** require. **2.** imply. **3.** entail. **4.** determine. **5.** cause. **be'dingt I** *adj* **1.** **~ durch**, **~ von** conditional on, dependent on; **~ sein durch** *a.* be determined by. **2.** qualified (*approval, success, etc*). **II** *adv* **3.** conditionally. **4.** up to a point, partly.

Be'dingung *f* (-; -en) condition: **~en** a) terms, b) conditions; **~en stellen** make stipulations; (*es*) *zur* **~ machen**, *daß ...* make it a condition that ...; *unter der* **~**, *daß ...* provided (that) ...; *unter diesen*

~en under these circumstances; *unter k-r* ~ on no account; *✝ zu günstigen ~en* on easy terms. **be'dingungslos** *adj* 1. unconditional. 2. unquestioning. **Be'dingungssatz** *m* conditional clause.

be'drängen *v/t* (h) 1. press *s.o.* hard: *(schwer) bedrängt sein* be in (bad) trouble, be hard-pressed. 2. pester *(mit Fragen etc* with questions *etc)*: *be drängt von* beset by *doubts etc:*

be'drohen *v/t* (h) threaten: *zo. bedrohte Arten* endangered species. **be'drohlich** *adj* a) threatening, menacing, b) alarming, c) ominous. **Be'drohung** *f* (-; -en) *(gen* to) a. *fig.* threat, menace.

be'drucken *v/t* (h) print.

be'drücken *v/t* (h) 1. oppress. 2. depress. **be'drückend** *adj* depressing. **Be'drückung** *f* (-; -en) 1. oppression. 2. depression.

be'dürfen *v/i* (bedurfte, bedurft, h) *(gen)* need, require, take: *es bedarf k-r weiteren Beweise* no further evidence is required. **Bedürfnis** [bəˈdʏrfnɪs] *n* (-sses; -sse) a) need *(nach* for), requirement, b) urge. **Be'dürfnisanstalt** *f* public convenience. **be'dürfnislos** *adj* *er ist* ~ he doesn't need much. **be'dürftig** *adj* needy, poor. **Be'dürftigkeit** *f* (-; *no pl)* neediness, poverty.

Beefsteak [ˈbiːfsteːk] *n* (-s; -s) steak: *deutsches* ~ beefburger.

be'ehren *v/t* (h) hono(u)r.

beeid(ig)en [bəˈʔaɪd(ɪg)ən] *v/t* (h) swear to. **be'eidigt** *adj* 🜍 sworn. **Be'eidigung** *f* (-; -en) confirmation by oath.

be'eilen: *sich* ~ (h) hurry; *beeil dich!* hurry up!, F get a move on!

beeindrucken [bəˈʔaɪndrʊkən] *v/t* (h) impress.

beeinflussen [bəˈʔaɪnflʊsən] *v/t* (h) influence. **Be'einflussung** *f* (-; -en) influence *(gen* on).

beeinträchtigen [bəˈʔaɪntrɛçtɪgən] *v/t* a) impair, affect, b) detract from *(beauty etc)*, c) impede, d) reduce. **Be'einträchtigung** *f* (-; -en) *(gen)* a) impairment (of), b) detraction (from), c) impeding (of), d) reduction (in).

beend(ig)en [bəˈʔɛnd(ɪg)ən] *v/t* (h) (bring *s.th.* to an) end, conclude, close. **Be'endigung** *f* (-; *no pl)* conclusion.

beengen [bəˈʔɛŋən] *v/t* (h) cramp.

be'erben *v/t* (h) *j-n* ~ be s.o.'s heir.

beerdigen [bəˈʔɛːrdɪgən] *v/t* (h) bury. **Be'erdigung** *f* (-; -en) burial, funeral. **Be'erdigungsinsti,tut** *n* undertaker's, funeral directors.

Beere [ˈbeːrə] *f* (-; -n) a) berry, b) grape. **'Beerenauslese** *f* quality wine made from selected grapes.

Beet [beːt] *n* (-[e]s; -e) bed.

Beete ▸ *Bete.*

befähigen [bəˈfɛːɪgən] *v/t* (h) enable, qualify *(für, zu* for): *j-n (dazu)* ~*, et. zu tun* enable s.o. to do s.th. **be'fähigt** *adj* *(zu)* 1. capable (of). 2. qualified (for). **Be'fähigung** *f* (-; -en) 1. qualification *(zu* for). 2. ability, competence. **Be'fähigungsnachweis** *m* certificate of qualification.

befahl [bəˈfaːl] *pret of* **befehlen.**

be'fahrbar *adj* passable, ⚓ navigable.

be'fahren¹ *v/t* (befuhr, befahren, h) drive on, use *(a road)*, cover *(distance)*.

be'fahren² I *pp of* **befahren¹.** II *adj* *sehr (or stark)* ~*e Straße* busy road.

be'fallen *v/t* (befiel, befallen, h) attack *(a. ⚔)*, *fig.* seize: ~ *werden von* a) be infested by *(insects etc)*, b) be seized by *(fear etc)*.

be'fand *pret of* **befinden.**

be'fangen *adj* 1. inhibited, shy, self-conscious. 2. a. 🜍 bias(s)ed: *in e-m Irrtum* ~ *sein* be labo(u)ring under a delusion. **Be'fangenheit** *f* (-; *no pl)* 1. shyness, self-consciousness. 2. 🜍 *etc* bias.

be'fassen: *sich* ~ *mit* (h) concern o.s. with, deal with *(a problem etc)*.

Befehl [bəˈfeːl] *m* (-[e]s; -e) order, command: *auf* ~ *von (or gen)* by order of; *(den)* ~ *haben zu inf* be under orders to *inf*; *den* ~ *haben (übernehmen)* be in (take) command *(über acc* of). **be'fehlen** (befahl, befohlen, h) I *v/t j-m et.* ~ order s.o. to do s.th. II *v/i* give the orders. **befehligen** [bəˈfeːlɪgən] *v/t* (h) be in command of. **Be'fehlsbereich** *m* ✕ (area of) command. **Be'fehlsform** *f ling.* imperative. **Befehlshaber** [bəˈfeːlsˌhaːbər] *m* (-s; -) commander. **Be'fehlsverweigerung** *f* refusal to obey an order.

be'festigen *v/t* (h) 1. *(an dat* to) fasten, fix. 2. pave. 3. ✕ fortify. **Be'festigung** *f* (-; -en) 1. fastening, fixing. 2. ✕ fortification.

befeuchten [bəˈfɔʏçtən] *v/t* (h) moisten.

be'finden (befand, befunden, h) I *v/t et.* **für gut** *etc* ~ think s.th. is good *etc*. II **sich** ~ a) be, *house etc*: a. be located, b) be, feel. III *v/i* decide.

Be'finden *n* (-s) (state of) health.

befindlich [bə'fɪntlɪç] *adj* **alle im Haus** ~**en Möbel** all furniture in the house.

befingern [bə'fɪŋərn] *v/t* (h) finger.

be'flaggen *v/t* (h) flag.

be'flecken *v/t* (h) stain, soil, *fig*. sully.

be'fliegen *v/t* (beflog, beflogen, h) fly.

beflügeln [bə'fly:gəln] *v/t* (h) inspire, spur *s.o.* on, fire (*s.o.'s imagination*).

befohlen [bə'fo:lən] *pp of* **befehlen**.

be'folgen *v/t* (h) a) follow, take (*advice*), b) observe (*rule*). **Be'folgung** *f* (-; *no pl*) following (*etc*), observance (*gen of*).

be'fördern *v/t* (h) **1.** convey, transport, ✝ forward, ship. **2.** promote: *er wurde zum Major befördert* he was promoted (to the rank of) major. **Be'förderung** *f* (-; -en) **1.** *no pl* conveyance, transport(ation), ✝ forwarding, shipment. **2.** promotion. **Be'förderungsmittel** *n* (means of) transport(ation).

befrachten [bə'fraxtən] *v/t* (h) load, ⚓, *a. fig.* freight.

be'fragen *v/t* (h) (*nach, über acc* about) **1.** question, ask. **2.** poll, interview. **3.** consult. **Be'fragung** *f* (-; -en) **1.** interview. **2.** (public opinion) poll.

befreien [bə'fraɪən] (h) (*von* from) I *v/t* **1.** a) free, liberate, b) rescue. **2.** excuse, exempt (*from taxes etc*), release (*from obligations*), relieve (*from burden, pain, etc*). II **sich** ~ free o.s., liberate o.s.: *sich von* ~ get rid of s.th. **Be'freier** *m* (-s; -) liberator. **Be'freiung** *f* (-; *no pl*) (*von* from) **1.** a) freeing, liberation, b) rescue. **2.** exemption, release.

Be'freiungs|bewegung *f* liberation movement. ~**kampf** *m* fight for independence. ~**krieg** *m* war of liberation.

befremden [bə'fremdən] *v/t* (h) *j-n* ~ take *s.o.* aback. **Be'fremden** *n* (-s) astonishment (*über acc* at).

befreunden [bə'frɔʏndən] **sich** ~ (h) become friends, **sich** ~ **mit** make friends with, *fig*. get used to s.th.

be'freundet *adj* friendly (*a. pol.*): ~ **sein** be friends (*mit* with).

be'frieden *v/t* (h) *pol*. pacify.

befriedigen [bə'fri:dɪɡən] *v/t* (h) satisfy (*s.o., s.o.'s curiosity etc*), please (*s.o.,*

meet (*demand etc*), come up to (*expectations*): **schwer zu** ~ hard to please. **be'friedigend** *adj* satisfactory (*a. ped. mark*). **be'friedigt** *adj and adv* satisfied, pleased. **Be'friedigung** *f* (-; *no pl*) satisfaction (*über acc* at, with).

be'fristen *v/t* (h) *et.* (*auf e-n Monat*) ~ set a time limit (of one month) on s.th. **be'fristet** *adj* limited (in time) (*auf acc* to). **Be'fristung** *f* (-; -en) **1.** setting of a time limit. **2.** time limit.

be'fruchten *v/t* (h) *biol*. fertilize (*a. fig.*), 🐝 pollinate, *fig*. stimulate: (*künstlich*) ~ inseminate (artificially).

Be'fruchtung *f* (-; -en) *biol*. fertilization (*a. fig.*), 🐝 pollination: *künstliche* ~ artificial insemination.

Befugnis [bə'fu:knɪs] *f* (-; -se) *a. pl* authority, power(s): ~ **erteilen** (*zu inf*) authorize s.o. (*to inf*).

befugt [bə'fu:kt] *adj* authorized.

be'fühlen *v/t* (h) feel, touch.

befuhr [bə'fu:r] *pret of* **befahren**[1].

Be'fund *m* (-[e]s; -e) findings: 🩺 *ohne* ~ negative. **be'funden** *pp of* **befinden**.

be'fürchten *v/t* (h) fear: *es ist zu* ~, *daß* ... it is feared that ...; *wir müssen das Schlimmste* ~ we must be prepared for the worst. **Be'fürchtung** *f* (-; -en) fear, *pl a.* misgivings.

befürworten [bə'fy:rvɔrtən] *v/t* (h) **1.** advocate, recommend. **2.** support. **Be'fürworter** *m* (-s; -) supporter, advocate. **Be'fürwortung** *f* (-; -en) recommendation, support.

begab [bə'ɡa:p] *pret of* **begeben**.

begabt [bə'ɡa:pt] *adj* gifted, talented.

Begabung [bə'ɡa:bʊŋ] *f* (-; -en) gift, (*a. person*) talent.

begangen [bə'ɡaŋən] *pp of* **begehen**.

begann [bə'ɡan] *pret of* **beginnen**.

begatten [bə'ɡatən] *v/t* (h) copulate with, *zo*. mate with. **Be'gattung** *f* (-; -en) copulation, *zo*. mating.

be'geben (begab, begeben, h) I **sich** ~ **1.** happen, occur. **2.** *sich* ~ *nach* (*or zu*) go to; *sich in ärztliche Behandlung* ~ have medical treatment; *sich an die Arbeit* ~ set to work; *sich auf die Reise* ~ set out (on one's journey); → **Gefahr**. II *v/t* **3.** ✝ negotiate (*bill*). **Be'gebenheit** *f* (-; -en) occurrence, incident.

begegnen [bə'ɡe:ɡnən] *v/i* (sn) (*dat*) **1.** meet, F bump into, come across: *sich* ~

meet. **2.** meet with (*difficulties*), face (*s.o.*, *situation*, *etc*), obviate (*danger etc*). **3.** be found (*bei* in). **4.** *j-m freundlich etc* ~ treat s.o. kindly etc.

Be'gegnung *f* (-; -en) **1.** meeting, encounter. **2.** *sports*: bout, match.

begehbar [bə'ge:ba:r] *adj* passable.

be'gehen *v/t* (beging, begangen, h) **1.** walk on. **2.** inspect. **3.** make (*mistake*), commit (*crime*). **4.** celebrate (*birthday etc*), observe (*holiday*).

begehren [bə'ge:rən] *v/t* (h) desire, crave for, demand: (**sehr**) **begehrt** (much) sought after, (very) much in demand. **Be'gehren** *n* (-s) desire (*nach* for). **be'gehrenswert** *adj* desirable. **be'gehrlich** *adj* covetous, greedy.

Be'gehung *f* (-; -en) **1.** inspection. **2.** commission (*of crime*). **3.** celebration.

begeistern [bə'gaɪstərn] **I** *v/t* (h) fill *s.o.* with enthusiasm (*für* about), inspire. **II** *sich* ~ *für* be (*or* get) enthusiastic about. **III** *v/i* arouse enthusiasm (*durch* by). **be'geisternd** *adj* rousing, inspiring, marvel(l)ous. **be'geistert I** *adj* (*von*) enthusiastic (about), keen (on): **~er Anhänger** (*gen or von*) fan (of); **...begeistert** ...-minded, F ...-mad. **II** *adv* enthusiastic(ally): ~ **sprechen von** *a.* rave about. **Be'geisterung** *f* (-; *no pl*) enthusiasm (*für* for, about): **mit** ~ *a.* enthusiastically.

Begierde [bə'gi:rdə] *f* (-; -n) (*nach* for) a) appetite, b) desire, lust. **be-'gierig** *adj* eager (*nach*, *auf acc* for): **ich bin** ~ **zu erfahren** I am anxious to know.

be'gießen *v/t* (begoß, begossen, h) **1.** pour water *etc* over (*or* on), water. **2.** F *fig.* celebrate (with a drink): **das müssen wir** ~*! that calls for a drink!

beging [bə'gɪŋ] *pret of* **begehen.**

Beginn [bə'gɪn] *m* (-[e]s; *no pl*) (**zu** ~ at the) beginning. **be'ginnen** *v/t*, *v/i* (begann, begonnen, h) begin, start.

beglaubigen [bə'glaʊbɪgən] *v/t* (h) **1.** certify (*document*). **2.** accredit *diplomat* (**bei** to). **be'glaubigt** *adj* (**öffentlich**) ~ certified (by a notary public): **~e Abschrift** certified copy, *as a note:* a true copy. **Be'glaubigung** *f* (-; -en) **1.** certification. **2.** accreditation. **Be'glaubigungsschreiben** *n* credentials.

be'gleichen *v/t* (beglich, beglichen, h) ✝

pay, settle. **Be'gleichung** *f* (-; *no pl*) settlement, payment.

be'gleiten *v/t* (h) accompany (*a.* ♪ *or fig.*), *a.* ♪, ✕, *mot.* escort.

Be'gleiter *m* (-s; -) **1.** companion. **2.** attendant. **3.** ♪ accompanist. **4.** escort. **Be'gleiterin** *f* (-; -nen) → **Begleiter** 1-3.

Be'gleit|erscheinung *f* concomitant, ✗ attendant symptom. **~flugzeug** *n* escort plane. **~mu̱si̱k** *f* incidental music, *fig.* accompaniment. **~peṟson** *f* escort. **~schein** *m* ✝ **1.** waybill. **2.** (custom's) permit. **~schiff** *n* escort vessel. **~schreiben** *n* covering letter. **~umstände** *pl* attendant circumstances.

Be'gleitung *f* (-; -en) **1.** a) company, *a.* ♪, ✕, escort, b) entourage: **ohne** ~ unaccompanied; **in** ~ **von** (*or gen*) accompanied by. **2.** ♪ accompaniment.

beglich [bə'glɪç] *pret of* **begleichen.**

be'glichen *pp of* **begleichen.**

be'glücken *v/t* (h) *j-n* ~ make s.o. happy.

be'glückwünschen *v/t* (h) *j-n* (**zu et.**) ~ congratulate s.o. (on s.th.).

begnadet [bə'gna:dət] *adj* inspired, highly gifted: ~ **mit** blessed with.

begnadigen [bə'gna:dɪgən] *v/t* (h), **Be'gnadigung** *f* (-; -en) pardon, *pol.* amnesty.

begnügen [bə'gny:gən] *sich* ~ (h) (**mit** with) be content, make do.

Begonie [be'go:niə] *f* (-; -n) ❀ begonia.

begonnen [bə'gɔnən] *pp of* **beginnen.**

begoß [bə'gɔs] *pret of* **begießen.**

be'gossen *pp of* **begießen.**

be'graben *v/t* (begrub, begraben, h) *a. fig.* bury. **Begräbnis** [bə'grɛ:pnɪs] *n* (-ses; -se) burial, funeral.

begradigen [bə'gra:dɪgən] *v/t* (h) straighten.

be'greifen *v/t* (begriff, begriffen, h) understand (*a. v/i*), grasp: **das begreife ich nicht!** that's beyond me!; **schnell** ~ F catch on quickly, be quick on the uptake. **be'greiflich** *adj* understandable: *j-m et.* ~ **machen** make s.th. clear to s.o. **be'greiflicherweise** *adv* understandably (enough).

be'grenzen *v/t* (h) **1.** mark off. **2.** form the boundary of. **3.** *fig.* (**auf** *acc* to) limit, restrict. **Be'grenztheit** *f* (-; *no pl*) limitations. **Be'grenzung** *f* (-; -en) **1.** (**auf** *acc* to) limiting, restriction. **2.** bounds, limit.

Be'grenzungslicht *n mot.* sidelight.

begriff [bə'grɪf] *pret of* **begreifen**.

Be'griff *m* (-[e]s; -e) **1.** a) idea, notion, *philos.* concept, b) term: **sich e-n ~ ma-chen von** get an idea of, imagine; **du machst dir k-n ~!** you have no idea!; **ist dir das ein ~?** does that mean anything to you?; **nach m-n ~en** as I see it. **2.** F **schwer von ~** slow (in the uptake). **3.** **im ~ sein, et. zu tun** be about to do s.th.

be'griffen I *pp of* **begreifen**. **II** *adj* **im Aufbruch ~ sein** be about to leave.

be'grifflich *adj* conceptual, abstract.

Be'griffsbestimmung *f* definition.

be'griffsstutzig *adj* dense, slow.

begrub [bə'gru:p] *pret of* **begraben**.

be'gründen *v/t* (h) **1.** give reasons for, explain, justify. **2.** found, establish, set up, *fig.* lay the foundations of.

be'gründet *adj* well-founded, justified: **~er Verdacht** reasonable suspicion.

Be'gründung *f* (-; -en) **1.** reason(s), argument(s), explanation: **mit der ~, daß ...** on the grounds that ...; **ohne jede ~** without giving any reasons. **2.** establishment, foundation, setting up.

be'grüßen *v/t* (h) greet, welcome: **es ist zu ~, daß** we welcome the fact that.

Be'grüßenswert *adj* welcome.

Be'grüßung *f* (-; -en) greeting, welcome.

Be'grüßungs|ansprache *f* welcoming speech. **~worte** *pl* words of welcome.

begünstigen [bə'gʏnstɪɡən] *v/t* (h) a) favo(u)r, b) promote. **Be'günstigte** *m, f* (-n; -n) ✝, ⚖ beneficiary. **Be'günsti-gung** *f* (-; -en) **1.** a) favo(u)ring, b) promotion. **2.** preferential treatment. **3.** *(financial)* benefit. **4.** ⚖ acting as accessory after the fact.

be'gutachten *v/t* (h) **1.** give an (expert's) opinion on: **et. ~ lassen** obtain an expert's opinion on s.th. **2.** examine.

begütert [bə'ɡy:tərt] *adj* rich, wealthy, well-off, well-to-do.

begütigen [bə'ɡy:tɪɡən] *v/t* (h) appease.

behaart [bə'ha:rt] *adj* hairy, hirsute.

behäbig [bə'hɛ:bɪç] *adj* **1.** sedate. **2.** portly.

behaftet [bə'haftət] *adj* **~ mit** full of (*mistakes*), afflicted with (*disease*), tainted with (*flaw*).

behagen [bə'ha:ɡən] *v/i* (h) **j-m ~** a) suit s.o., b) please s.o.; **das behagt mir (ganz und gar) nicht** I don't like that

(at all). **Be'hagen** *n* (-s) a) ease, comfort, b) pleasure. **be'haglich** *adj* comfortable, cosy. **Be'haglichkeit** *f* (-; *no pl*) comfort, cosiness.

be'halten *v/t* (behielt, behalten, h) **1.** keep: **recht ~** be right (in the end); **für sich ~** keep *secret* to o.s.; **behalte das für dich!** keep it under your hat! **2.** remember.

Behälter [bə'hɛltər] *m* (-s; -) container, tank.

be'handeln *v/t* (h) treat (*a.* ✚, ⚙), *fig. a.* deal with, handle. **Be'handlung** *f* (-; -en) treatment, handling: **in (ärztlicher) ~** under medical treatment.

be'hängen *v/t* (h) hang, drape, decorate: F *contp.* **mit Schmuck behängt** decked (out) with jewels.

be'harren *v/i* (h) (**auf** *dat*) persist (in), F stick (to): **darauf ~, daß ...** insist that ...

be'harrlich *adj* persistent, steadfast, stubborn. **Be'harrlichkeit** *f* (-; *no pl*) perseverance, stubbornness.

be'hauen *v/t* (h) hew.

behaupten [bə'hauptən] (h) **I** *v/t* **1.** maintain, claim, say (**daß** that): F **steif und fest ~, daß ...** insist that ... **2.** maintain, assert. **II** *sich ~* **3.** hold one's own. **4.** ✝ *prices etc*: remain firm. **Be'haup-tung** *f* (-; -en) **1.** claim, assertion. **2.** *no pl* maintenance, assertion.

Behausung [bə'hauzʊŋ] *f* (-; -en) dwelling.

be'heben *v/t* (behob, behoben, h) remove, repair (*damage*), remedy (*grievance*). **Be'hebung** *f* (-; *no pl*) removal.

beheimatet [bə'haima:tət] *adj* **~ in** (*dat*) resident in, living in, coming from.

be'heizbar *adj* heatable.

be'heizen *v/t* (h) heat.

Behelf [bə'hɛlf] *m* (-[e]s; -e) makeshift.

be'helfen: sich ~ (behalf, beholfen, h) (**mit** with) make do, manage.

Be'helfs..., be'helfsmäßig *adj* makeshift, temporary.

behelligen [bə'hɛlɪɡən] *v/t* (h) bother.

beherbergen [bə'hɛrbɛrɡən] *v/t* (h) put up, accommodate, *a. fig.* house.

be'herrschen (h) **I** *v/t* **1.** rule (over), govern. **2.** *fig.* control (*situation, market, one's feelings, etc*): **j-n ~** dominate s.o. **3.** have a good command of, speak (*German etc*), know: **sein Handwerk ~** know one's trade. **II** *sich ~* control o.s.

be'herrschend *adj* dominating.
Be'herrscher *m* ruler (*gen* over, of).
Be'herrschung *f* (-; *no pl*) **1.** rule, domination. **2.** *fig.* (*gen* of) control, b) mastery, command. **3.** self-control.
beherzigen [bə'hɛrtsɪgən] *v/t* (h) ~ bear s.th. in mind.
beherzt [bə'hɛrtst] *adj* courageous.
behielt [bə'hi:lt] *pret of* **behalten.**
behilflich [bə'hɪlflɪç] *adj* **j-m** ~ **sein** help (*or* assist) s.o. (*bei* in).
be'hindern *v/t* (h) (*bei* in) hinder, hamper, *a. sports*: obstruct.
be'hindert *adj* (*körperlich or geistig*) ~ (physically *or* mentally) handicapped. **Be'hinderte** *m*, *f* (-n; -n) handicapped person. **Be'hinderung** *f* (-; -en) **1.** hindrance, impediment, *a. sports*: obstruction. **2.** 🏃 handicap.
behob [bə'ho:p] *pret of* **beheben.**
behoben [bə'ho:bən] *pp of* **beheben.**
beholfen [bə'hɔlfən] *pp of* **behelfen.**
Be'hörde [bə'hø:rdə] *f* (-; -n) (public) authority: *die* ~*n* the authorities.
behördlich [bə'hø:rtlɪç] *adj* official.
be'hüten *v/t* (h) protect (*vor dat* from).
behutsam [bə'hu:tza:m] *adj* cautious, careful, gentle. **Be'hutsamkeit** *f* (-; *no pl*) caution, gentleness.
bei [baɪ] *prep* (*dat*) **1.** ~ *Berlin* near Berlin; *die Schlacht* ~ *Waterloo* the Battle of Waterloo; ~*m Bäcker* at the baker's; ~ *Familie Braun*, ~ *Brauns* at Braun's; ~ *Braun* c/o (= care of) Braun; ~ *Hofe* at court; ~ *j-m sitzen* sit with s.o.; *arbeiten* ~ work for; *e-e Stellung* ~ a job with; ~*m Heer* (~ *der Marine*) in the army (navy); ~ *uns* a) with us, b) (*zu Hause*) at home, c) (*in Deutschland*) in Germany, at home; *ich habe kein Geld* ~ *mir* I have no money one me; *er hatte s-n Hund* ~ *sich* he had his dog with him. **2.** ~ *s-r Geburt* (*Hochzeit*) at his birth (wedding); ~ *Tag* (*Nacht*) by day (day), during the night (day); ~ *Licht* by light; ~ *70 Grad* at 70 degrees; ~ *schönem Wetter* when the weather is fine; ~*m Arbeiten* while working; ~ *offenem Fenster* with the window open; ~ *Regen* (*Gefahr*) in case of rain (danger); F *er ist nicht ganz* ~ *sich* he's not all there. **3.** ~ *so vielen Problemen* with (*or* considering) all the problems; ~ *solcher Hitze* in such heat; ~ *all s-n Be-*

mühungen for all his efforts; → *a. corresponding headwords.*
'**beibehalten** *v/t* (*irr, sep,* h, → *behalten*) retain, maintain, keep.
'**Beiblatt** *n* supplement (*gen* to).
'**Beiboot** *n* dinghy.
'**beibringen** *v/t* (*irr, sep,* -ge-, h, → *bringen*) *j-m et.* ~ a) teach s.o. s.th., b) get s.th. across to s.o.; *j-m et. schonend* ~ break s.th. gently to s.o.
Beichte ['baɪçtə] *f* (-; -n) confession: *j-m die* ~ *abnehmen* confess s.o.
beichten ['baɪçtən] *v/t, v/i* (h) confess.
'**Beicht|geheimnis** *n* confessional secret. ~*kind* *n* penitent. ~*stuhl* *m* confessional. ~*vater* *m* (father) confessor.
beide ['baɪdə] *adj* a) both, b) the two, c) either: *m-e* ~*n Brüder* both my brothers, my two brothers; *wir* ~ both of us, we two; *alle* ~ both of them; *in* ~*n Fällen* in either case; *kein(e)s von* ~*n* neither (of the two).
'**beidemal** *adv* both times.
beiderlei ['baɪdərlaɪ] *adj* (of) both kinds: ~ *Geschlechts* of either sex. '**beiderseitig** [-zaɪtɪç] *adj and adv* a) on both sides, b) mutual(ly *adv*). '**beiderseits** [-zarts] **I** *adv* on both sides, *fig. a.* mutually. **II** *prep* (*gen*) on both sides (of).
beidhändig ['baɪthɛndɪç] *adj* ambidextrous, *sports*: two-handed.
'**beidrehen** *v/i* (*sep,* -ge-, h) ⚓ heave to.
beiein'ander *adv* together: (*dicht*) ~ next to each other. ~*haben* *v/t* (*irr, sep,* -ge-, h, → *haben*) F have got s.th. together: *du hast wohl nicht alle beieinander!* you must be out of your mind! ~*halten* *v/t* (*irr, sep,* -ge-, h, → *halten*) F keep s.th. together. ~*sein* *v/i* (*irr, sep,* -ge-, sn, → *sein*) F *gut* ~ be in good shape; *er ist nicht ganz beieinander* he's not all there.
'**Beifahrer** *m* *in car*: front passenger, *in truck*: driver's mate, *in races*: co-driver.
'**Beifahrersitz** *m* front-passenger seat.
'**Beifall** *m* (-[e]s; *no pl*) applause, (loud) cheers, *fig.* approval: ~ *ernten*, ~ *finden* draw applause, *fig.* meet with approval, be acclaimed; ~ *klatschen*, ~ *spenden* applaud (*j-m* s.o.).
'**beifällig** *adj* approving.
'**Beifallsruf** *m* cheer(s).
'**Beifallssturm** *m* thunderous applause.
'**Beifilm** *m* supporting film.

'**beifügen** v/t (sep, -ge-, h) (dat) a) add (to), b) enclose (with a letter).

'**Beifügung** f (-; -en) ling. apposition.

'**Beigabe** f (-; -n) **1.** addition, extra: **als ~** a. into the bargain. **2. → Beilage** 2.

beige [be:ʃ] adj, **Beige** n (-; no pl) beige.

'**beigeben** (irr, sep, -ge-, h, → **geben**) **I** v/t add (dat to). **II** v/i F **klein ~** knuckle under, climb down.

'**Beigeordnete** m, f (-n; -n) assistant, pol. town council(l)or.

'**Beigeschmack** m (-[e]s; no pl) (unpleasant) taste, fig. smack (von of).

'**Beihilfe** f **1.** a) aid, b) grant, c) subsidy. **2.** ⚖ aiding and abetting: (j-m) ~ **leisten** aid and abet (s.o.).

'**beikommen** v/i (irr, sep, -ge-, sn, → **kommen**) (dat) get at (s.o.), cope with.

Beil [baıl] n (-[e]s; -e) a) ax(e), hatchet, b) (meat) chopper.

'**Beilage** f (-; -n) **1.** supplement, insertion, inset. **2.** gastr. side dish: **Fleisch mit ~** meat and vegetables.

'**beiläufig** **I** adj casual. **II** adv casually, by the way: **et. ~ erwähnen** mention s.th. in passing.

'**beilegen** v/t (sep, -ge-, h) **1.** (dat) add (to), enclose (with). **2.** give (a name). **3.** settle (quarrel).

beileibe [baı'laıbə] adv ~ **nicht**(!) certainly not(!), by no means(!).

'**Beileid** n (-[e]s; no pl) (j-m sein ~ **aussprechen** offer s.o. one's condolences: (**mein**) **herzliches ~!** a. iro. my heartfelt sympathy!

'**Beileidsbesuch** m visit of condolence.

'**Beileidsbrief** m letter of condolence.

'**Beileidskarte** f condolence card.

'**beiliegen** v/i (irr, sep, -ge-, h, → **liegen**) be enclosed (dat with). '**beiliegend** adj and adv enclosed: ~ **übersenden wir Ihnen ...** enclosed please find ...

beim [baım] = **bei dem**.

'**beimessen** v/t (irr, sep, -ge-, h, → **messen**) (dat) a) **Glauben ~** give credence to, b) **Bedeutung** etc ~ attach importance etc to.

'**beimischen** v/t (sep, -ge-, h) (dat) **et. ~** mix s.th. with, add s.th. to.

'**Beimischung** f (-; -en) admixture.

Bein [baın] n (-[e]s; -e) leg (a. of pants, table, etc): (**früh**) **auf den ~en sein** be up and about (early); **dauernd auf den ~en sein** be always on the go; **wieder**

auf den ~en sein be back on one's feet (again); F **j-m ~e machen** make s.o. get a move on; **ich muß mich auf die ~e machen!** I must be off!; F **die ~e in die Hand nehmen** take to one's heels, run; fig. **auf eigenen ~en stehen** stand on one's own two feet; fig. **j-n** (et.) **auf die ~e stellen** set s.o. (s.th.) up; **j-m ein ~ stellen** a. fig. trip s.o. up; **sich die ~e vertreten** stretch one's legs; → **Grab**.

beinah(e) ['baına:(ə)] adv almost, nearly: **~ et. tun** come near doing s.th.

'**Beinahezusammenstoß** m near miss.

'**Beiname** m epithet.

'**Bein|arbeit** f boxing: footwork, swimming: legwork. **~bruch** m ⚕ fractured leg: F fig. **das ist kein ~!** that's no tragedy! **~freiheit** f mot. legroom.

beinhalten [bə'ʔınhaltən] v/t (h) contain, say, imply.

'**Beinpro,these** f artificial leg.

'**beiordnen** v/t (sep, -ge-, h) **1.** j-m j-n ~ assign s.o. to s.o. **2.** ling. coordinate.

'**Beipackzettel** m instructions.

'**beipflichten** ['baıpflıçtən] v/i (sep, -ge-, h) agree (dat to).

'**Beipro,gramm** n film: supporting program(me Br.).

'**Beirat** m (-[e]s; -e) advisory board.

beirren [bə'ʔırən] v/t (h) disconcert: **er läßt sich nicht ~** he stands firm.

beisammen [baı'zamən] adv together.

Bei'sammensein n (-s) being together: **geselliges ~** get-together.

'**Beischlaf** m ⚖ sexual intercourse.

'**Beisein** n: **im ~ von** (or gen) in the presence of.

bei'seite adv aside: ~ **lassen** disregard; ~ **legen** set aside; ~ **schaffen** remove, get rid of; ~ **schieben** push (argument: brush) aside; ~ **treten** step aside.

'**beisetzen** v/t (sep, -ge-, h) bury.

'**Beisetzung** f (-; -en) burial, funeral.

'**Beispiel** n (-[e]s; -e) a) example, b) model: (**wie**) **zum ~** for instance, for example (abbr. e.g.); **ein ~ geben, mit gutem ~ vorangehen** set an example; **sich ein ~ an j-m** (et.) **nehmen** take s.o. (s.th.) as an example. '**beispielhaft** adj exemplary, model. '**beispiellos** adj unprecedented, unheard-of. '**beispielsweise** adv for example, (as) for instance.

beißen ['baısən] v/t, v/i (biß, gebissen, h) bite (**auf** acc, **in** acc s.th.), smoke, pepper, etc: a. burn: **nach j-m ~** snap at s.o.; F **die Farben ~ sich** the colo(u)rs clash.; F **er wird dich schon nicht ~!** he won't eat you! '**beißend** adj biting (*wind, a. criticism etc*), acrid (*smell*).

'**Beißring** m teething ring.

'**Beistand** m (-[e]s; ~e) **1.** *no pl* help, aid, support: **j-m ~ leisten → beistehen. 2.** → **Rechtsbeistand.** '**Beistandspakt** m *pol.* mutual assistance pact.

'**beistehen** v/i (*irr, sep,* -ge-, h, → **stehen**) **j-m ~** help (*or* assist, stand by) s.o., come to s.o.'s aid, ♣ attend to.

'**beisteuern** v/t, v/i (*sep,* -ge-, h) contribute (**zu** to).

'**Beistrich** m comma.

'**Beitrag** ['baɪtraːk] m (-[e]s; ~e) a) contribution (*a. fig.*), b) subscription (fee), fee: **e-n ~ leisten** make a contribution (**zu** to). '**beitragen** v/t, v/i (*irr, sep,* -ge-, h, → **tragen**) contribute (**zu** to).

'**beitragsfrei** adj noncontributary.

'**beitragspflichtig** adj liable to contributions.

'**beitreiben** v/t (*irr, sep,* -ge-, h, → **treiben**) collect (*taxes etc*), recover (*debts*).

'**beitreten** v/i (*irr, sep,* -ge-, sn, → **treten**) (*dat*) join (*a club etc*), accede to (*treaty*).

'**Beitritt** m (-[e]s; -e) (**zu**) joining (*a club etc*). '**Beitrittserklärung** f application for membership.

'**Beiwagen** m *mot.* sidecar. **~ma‚schine** f (motorcycle) combination.

'**beiwohnen** v/i (*sep,* -ge-, h) (*dat*) **1.** a) be present at, attend, b) witness. **2.** ⚥ have sexual intercourse with.

'**Beiwort** n (-[e]s; ~er) epithet.

Beize[1] ['baɪtsə] f (-; -n) **1.** corrosive, *for wood:* stain, *for dies:* mordant, *metall.* pickle. **2.** (*tobacco*) sauce. **3.** *gastr.* marinade. '**Beize**[2] f (-; -n) hawking.

beizeiten [baɪ'tsaɪtən] adv in good time.

beizen ['baɪtsən] v/t (h) **1.** corrode, stain (*wood*), bate (*hides*), *metall.* pickle. **2.** sauce (*tobacco*). **3.** *gastr.* marinade.

bejahen [bə'jaːən] v/t (h) answer in the affirmative (*a. v/i*), *a. fig.* say yes to.

be'jahend adj affirmative.

Be'jahung f (-; -en) affirmation, *fig.* positive attitude (*gen* towards).

bejahrt [bə'jaːrt] adj advanced in years.

bekam [bə'kaːm] pret of **bekommen**.

be'kämpfen v/t (h) fight (against), com-

bat. **Be'kämpfung** f (-; *no pl*) fight (*gen* against).

bekannt [bə'kant] **I** pp of **bekennen**. **II** adj (well-)known (**wegen** for): **~ mit** acquainted with; **j-n ~ machen mit** introduce s.o. to; **sich mit et. ~ machen** familiarize o.s. with s.th.; **das ist mir ~** I know (that); **dafür ~ sein, daß ...** have a reputation for ger. **be'kannte** pret of **bekennen. Be'kannte** m, f (-n; -n) friend, acquaintance.

Be'kanntenkreis m (circle of) friends.

Be'kanntgabe f (-; *no pl*) announcement. **be'kanntgeben** v/t (*irr, sep,* -ge-, h, → **geben**) announce.

Be'kanntheitsgrad m (-[e]s; *no pl*) name recognition (rating).

be'kanntlich adv as everybody knows.

be'kanntmachen v/t (*sep,* -ge-, h) announce, make *s.th.* known.

Be'kanntmachung f (-; -en) announcement, publication, bulletin.

Be'kanntschaft f (-; -en) **1.** *no pl* (**bei näherer ~** on closer) acquaintance: **j-s ~ machen** become acquainted with s.o. **2.** (circle of) friends.

be'kanntwerden v/i (*irr, sep,* -ge-, sn, → **werden**) become known, come out.

be'kehren v/t (h) *a. fig.* convert (**zu** to): **sich ~** (**zu** to) become a convert, *fig. a.* come round. **Be'kehrte** m, f (-n; -n) convert. **Be'kehrung** f (-; -en) conversion.

be'kennen (bekannte, bekannt, h) **I** v/t confess (to). **II sich ~ zu** a) confess (*deed*), b) profess (*faith etc*); **sich zu j-m ~** stand by s.o., stand up for s.o.; → **Farbe** 3, **schuldig** 1.

Be'kenntnis n (-ses; -se) **1.** confession. **2.** *eccl.* a) creed, b) denomination. **~schule** f denominational school.

be'klagen (h) **I** v/t lament, deplore **II sich ~** complain (**über** acc of). **be'klagenswert** adj deplorable, sorry, *person:* pitiable. **Beklagte** [bə'klaːktə] m, f (-n; -n) ⚖ defendant.

be'klauen v/t (h) F **j-n ~** steal from s.o.

be'kleben v/t (h) **1.** paste *s.th.* over. **2.** **et. ~ mit** stick (*or* paste) *s.th.* on s.th.

be'kleckern (h) **I** v/t stain, mess up. **II sich ~ mit ...** spill ... over o.s.

be'kleiden v/t (h) **1.** dress: *fig.* **~ mit** (in)vest with. **2.** hold (*an office*).

Be'kleidung f (-; -en) clothing, clothes.

belegen

Be'kleidungsindu,strie *f* clothing industry.

be'klemmen *v/t* (h) oppress. **be'klemmend** *adj* oppressive, *fig. a.* eerie.

Beklemmung *f* (-; -en) oppression, *fig. a.* anxiety. **beklommen** [bə'klɔmən] *adj* uneasy, anxious. **Be'klommenheit** *f* (-; *no pl*) uneasiness, anxiety.

bekloppt [bə'klɔpt], **beknackt** [-'knakt] *adj* F nutty, batty, crazy, *pred* nuts.

be'kommen (bekam, bekommen) **I** *v/t* (h) get, *✗ a.* catch (*a.* F *bus etc*), have (*child, young*): **Hunger** (**Durst**) ~ get hungry (thirsty); *sie bekommt ein Kind* she's going to have a baby; *Zähne* ~ cut one's teeth; *et. geschenkt* ~ be given s.th. (as a present); *wieviel* ~ *Sie* (*von mir*)? how much do I owe you? **II** *v/i* (sn) *j-m* (*gut*) ~ agree with s.o.; *j-m nicht* (*or schlecht*) ~ disagree with s.o.; *wohl bekomm's!* cheers!; *fig.* **es wird ihm schlecht** ~ he will regret it.

bekömmlich [bə'kœmlıç] *adj* wholesome, *a.* easily digestible, light (*food*), salubrious (*air, climate*).

beköstigen [bə'kœstıgən] *v/t* (h) feed: *sich selbst* ~ cook for o.s. **Be'köstigung** *f* (-; *no pl*) a) feeding, b) food.

be'kräftigen *v/t* (h) confirm. **Be'kräftigung** *f* (-; -en) confirmation.

be'kreuzigen: *sich* ~ (h) cross o.s.

be'kriegen *v/t* (h) make war on: *sich* ~ be at war with one another.

be'kritteln *v/t* (h) *contp.* criticize.

be'kritzeln *v/t* (h) scribble on.

be'kümmern *v/t* (h) grieve, worry.

bekunden [bə'kʊndən] *v/t* (h) **1.** show, demonstrate. **2.** state, *🏛 a.* testify.

be'lächeln *v/t* (h) smile (condescendingly) at.

be'laden *v/t* (belud, beladen) (h) load, *fig. a.* burden.

Belag [bə'la:k] *m* (-[e]s; ⸚e) **1.** a) covering, ⚙ *a.* coating, b) surface (*of road*), c) (*brake*) lining. **2.** (*sandwich*) filling. **3.** *✗ a.* coating (*of tongue*), b) plaque.

be'lagern *v/t* (h) *a. fig.* besiege. **Be'lagerung** *f* (-; -en) siege.

Belang [bə'laŋ] *m* (-[e]s; -e) **1.** *no pl von* ~ of importance (*für* to); *ohne* ~ a) unimportant, b) irrelevant. **2.** *pl* interests.

be'langen *v/t* (h) *🏛 a.* sue, b) prosecute. **be'langlos** *adj* unimportant, irrelevant (*für* to), *a.* negligible. **Be'langlo-**

sigkeit *f* (-; -en) **1.** *no pl* a) insignificance, b) irrelevance. **2.** *pl* trivialities.

be'lassen *v/t* (beließ, belassen, h) *et. an s-m Platz* ~ leave s.th. in its place; *es dabei* ~ leave it at that; *alles beim alten* ~ leave things as they are.

belastbar [bə'lastba:r] *adj* **1.** ⚙ having a load capacity (*bis zu* of). **2.** *fig.* strong, resilient. **Be'lastbarkeit** *f* (-; *no pl*) **1.** ⚙ load(ing) capacity. **2.** ability to cope with pressure (*or* strain): *bis zur Grenze der* ~ to breaking point. **be'lasten** *v/t* (h) **1.** *⚡*, ⚙ load. **2.** *fig.* burden (*mit* with, *sich* o.s.), put (*or* be) a strain on, weigh on, worry: *das belastet mich sehr* that's a great burden (*or* worry) to me; *damit kann ich mich jetzt nicht* ~ I can't be bothered with that now; → *erblich*. **3.** *†* a) charge, b) encumber (*house etc*): *j-n* (*or j-s Konto*) (*mit e-m Betrag*) ~ charge a sum to s.o.'s account. **4.** *🏛, pol.* incriminate.

belästigen [bə'lɛstıgən] *v/t* (h) a) molest, b) (*mit* with) pester, bother.

Be'lästigung *f* (-; -en) **1.** molestation, pestering: *sexuelle* ~ sexual harassment. **2.** nuisance.

Be'lastung *f* (-; -en) **1.** loading (*etc*, → *belasten*). **2.** *⚡*, ⚙ load: *zulässige* ~ safe load. **3.** *fig.* (*gen or für*) a) (*financial etc*) burden (to, on), b) worry (to, on), c) trouble (to), d) (*mental*) strain (on), stress (on): *er ist zu e-r* ~ *geworden* he has become a liability. **4.** *†* (*gen*) a) charge (to *an account*), b) encumbrance (of *property*). **5.** *🏛, pol.* incrimination. **Be'lastungs|materi,al** *n* *🏛* incriminating evidence. **~probe** *f* **1.** ⚙ load test. **2.** *fig.* (severe) test. **~zeuge** *m*, **~zeugin** *f* witness for the prosecution.

belaubt [bə'laʊpt] *adj* leafy, in leaf.

be'laufen: *sich* ~ (belief, belaufen, h) (*auf acc*) amount (to), run up (to), total.

be'lauschen *v/t* (h) eavesdrop on.

be'leben [h] **I** *v/t* a) liven up, stimulate, *drink etc*: *a.* revive, b) brighten (*room*): *neu* ~ put new life into. **II** *sich* ~ *street etc*: come to life. **be'lebt** *adj* animated, lively, busy (*street etc*).

Beleg [bə'le:k] *m* (-[e]s; -e) **1.** *esp.* *†* a) record, b) proof, c) voucher, d) receipt. **2.** *ling.* a) example, b) reference.

be'legen *v/t* (h) **1.** a) cover, b) line (*a.*

brakes): **mit Teppichboden** ~ carpet; **mit Schinken** *etc* ~ put ham *etc* on; → **belegt** 4. **2.** a) occupy (*room etc*) b) reserve (*seat etc*). **3.** *univ.* enrol(l) for (*a subject*). **4.** *sports:* **den ersten** (**zweiten** *etc*) **Platz** ~ be placed (*or* come in) first (second *etc*). **5. mit e-r Strafe** (**Steuer** *etc*) ~ impose a penalty (tax *etc*) on. **6.** a) supply evidence for, verify, b) give a reference for (*text, word*); → **belegt** 5.

Be'legexem͵plar *n* author's copy.

Be'legschaft *f* (-; -en) personnel, staff, employees, workers, work force.

Be'legschein *m* (-[e]s; -e) voucher.

be'legt *adj* **1.** a) taken, occupied, b) full (up). **2.** ✈ husky (*voice*), coated (*tongue*). **3.** *teleph.* engaged, *Am.* busy. **4.** *gastr.* ~**es Brot** sandwich; ~**es Brötchen** filled roll. **5.** documented: **das ist nirgends** ~ there is no evidence for it.

be'lehren *v/t* (h) a) instruct, b) inform (**über** *acc* of): **er ist nicht zu** ~ he won't listen to reason; **j-n es Besseren** ~ set s.o. right, *w.s.* open s.o.'s eyes. **be'lehrend** *adj* instructive. **Be'lehrung** *f* (-; -en) a) instruction, b) advice.

beleibt [bə'laɪpt] *adj* corpulent, stout.

beleidigen [bə'laɪdɪɡən] *v/t* (h) offend (*a. fig.*), insult: **ich wollte Sie nicht** ~ **!** no offen/ce (*Am.* -se) meant! **be'leidigend** *adj* insulting. **Be'leidigung** *f* (-; -en) insult, ⚖ a) slander, b) libel.

be'lesen *adj* well-read.

Be'lesenheit *f* (-; *no pl*) wide reading.

be'leuchten *v/t* (h) light (up), illuminate, *fig.* throw light on.

Be'leuchter *m* (-s; -) *thea. etc* lighting technician.

Be'leuchtung *f* (-; -en) lighting, illumination (*a. fig.*), light(s). **Be'leuchtungskörper** *m* lighting fixture, lamp.

Belgien ['bɛlɡiən] *n* (-s) Belgium. **'Belgier** *m* (-s; -), **'Belgierin** *f* (-; -nen), **'belgisch** *adj* Belgian.

belichten [bə'lɪçtən] *v/t* (h) *phot.* expose. **Be'lichtung** *f* (-; -en) exposure. **Be'lichtungs|auto͵matik** *f* automatic exposure. ~**messer** *m* light meter. ~**zeit** *f* exposure (time).

be'lieben (h) **I** *v/t esp. iro.* deign. **II** *v/i* please: **wie es Ihnen beliebt** as you wish. **Be'lieben** *n* (-s) nach ~ at will; **ganz nach** ~ as you like. **be'liebig I** *adj* any ... (you like): **jeder** ~**e** anyone; **in**

~**er Reihenfolge** in any order (you *etc* like). **II** *adv* at will: ~ **viele** as many as you *etc* like. **be'liebt** *adj* popular (**bei** with), ♥ very much in demand: **sich** ~ **machen bei** ingratiate o.s. with. **Be'liebtheit** *f* (-; *no pl*) popularity (**bei** with). **Be'liebtheitsgrad** *m* (-[e]s; *no pl*) popularity (rating).

belief [bə'li:f] *pret of* **belaufen**.

be'liefern *v/t* (h) supply (**mit** with).

Be'lieferung *f* (-; -en) supply.

belieβ [bə'li:s] *pret of* **belassen**.

bellen ['bɛlən] *v/i, v/t* (h) *a. fig.* bark.

Belletristik [bɛlə'trɪstɪk] *f* (-; *no pl*) fiction. **belle'tristisch** *adj* belletristic.

belobigen [bə'lo:bɪɡən] *v/t* (h) praise.

Be'lobigung *f* (-; -en) praise.

belog [bə'lo:k] *pret of* **belügen**.

belogen [bə'lo:ɡən] *pp of* **belügen**.

be'lohnen *v/t* (h) reward (**für** for).

Be'lohnung *f* (-; -en) (**zur** ~ as a) reward.

belud [bə'lu:t] *pret of* **beladen**.

be'lüften *v/t* (h) ventilate.

Be'lüftung *f* (-; *no pl*) ventilation.

Be'lüftungsanlage *f* ventilation system.

be'lügen *v/t* (belog, belogen, h) **j-n** ~ lie to s.o.; **sich selbst** ~ deceive o.s.

belustigen [bə'lʊstɪɡən] *v/t* (h) amuse. **Be'lustigung** *f* (-; -en) amusement.

bemächtigen [bə'mɛçtɪɡən] **sich j-s** (**e-r Sache**) ~ seize s.o. (s.th.).

be'malen *v/t* (h) paint.

bemängeln [bə'mɛŋəln] *v/t* (h) criticize, fault: **daran ist nichts zu** ~ it can't be faulted.

bemannen [bə'manən] *v/t* (h) man: **bemannter Raumflug** manned space flight.

bemänteln [bə'mɛntəln] *v/t* (h) **1.** cover up. **2.** palliate.

bemaß [bə'ma:s] *pret of* **bemessen**.

bemerkbar [bə'mɛrkba:r] *adj* noticeable: **sich** ~ **machen** draw attention to o.s., show, make itself felt. **be'merken** *v/t* **1.** notice. **2.** remark. **be'merkenswert** *adj* remarkable (**wegen** for). **Be'merkung** *f* (-; -en) a) remark, comment, b) note, annotation.

be'messen (bemaß, bemessen, h) **I** *v/t* **1.** (**nach**) a) proportion (to), b) *fig.* measure (by). **2.** a) calculate, b) time. **3.** ⊙ a) dimension, b) rate (*performance*). **4.** fix (*penalty etc*). **II sich** ~ be proportioned (*etc*, → I). **III** *adj* (**knapp** ~

limited; *ihre Zeit ist knapp* ~ she is pressed for time.
bemitleiden [bəˈmɪtlaɪdən] *v/t* (h) pity.
be'mitleidenswert *adj* pitiable.
be'mogeln *v/t* (h) F cheat.
be'mühen (h) **I** *v/t* trouble (*mit* with, *um* for), call in (*doctor etc*). **II** *sich* ~ take trouble (*or* pains) (*mit* over), make an effort, try (hard); *sich ~ um* a) try to get (*a job etc*), apply for (*a post etc*), b) try to help *s.o.*; *sich um j-n* (*or j-s Gunst*) ~ court s.o.'s favo(u)r; *bemüht sein zu inf* endeavo(u)r to *inf*, be anxious to *inf*; ~ *Sie sich nicht!* don't trouble (*or* bother)! **Be'mühung** *f* (-; -en) effort(s), endeavo(u)r(s), trouble.
bemüßigt [bəˈmyːsɪçt] *adj sich ~ fühlen zu inf* feel bound (*or* obliged) to *inf*.
bemuttern [bəˈmʊtərn] *v/t* (h) mother.
be'nachbart *adj* neighbo(u)ring.
benachrichtigen [bəˈnaːxrɪçtɪɡən] *v/t* (h) *of* inform, notify, ✝ advise. **Be'nachrichtigung** *f* (-; -en) notification, ✝ advice.
benachteiligen [bəˈnaːxtaɪlɪɡən] *v/t* (h) a) put *s.o.* at a disadvantage, b) discriminate against: (*sozial*) *benachteiligt* underprivileged. **Be'nachteiligung** *f* (-; -en) 1. discrimination (*gen* against). 2. disadvantage, handicap.
benannt [bəˈnant] *pp of* **benennen**.
be'nannte *pret of* **benennen**.
benebelt [bəˈneːbəlt] *adj* F *fig.* fuddled.
Benefiz... [beneˈfiːts-] charity (*concert, match, etc*).
be'nehmen: *sich* ~ (benahm, benommen, h) behave (*gegenüber* towards): *sich gut* ~ behave well, behave o.s.; *sich schlecht* ~ behave badly, misbehave; *benimm dich!* behave yourself! **Be'nehmen** *n* (-s) 1. behavio(u)r, conduct, manners. 2. *adm. im* ~ *mit* in agreement with; *sich mit j-m ins* ~ *setzen* get in touch with s.o.
be'neiden *v/t* (h) *j-n* (*um et.*) ~ envy s.o. (s.th.). **be'neidenswert** *adj* enviable.
be'nennen *v/t* (benannte, benannt, h) 1. name, call. 2. fix (*date etc*), nominate (*candidate*): *j-n als Zeugen* ~ call s.o. as a witness. **Be'nennung** *f* (-; -en) a) naming, b) name.
be'netzen *v/t* (h) moisten, sprinkle.
Bengel [ˈbɛŋəl] *m* (-s; -) rascal.
benommen [bəˈnɔmən] *adj* dazed.

Be'nommenheit *f* (-; *no pl*) daze.
benoten [bəˈnoːtən] *v/t* (h) *ped.* mark, *Am.* grade.
benötigen [bəˈnøːtɪɡən] *v/t* (h) need: *dringend* ~ be in urgent need of.
Be'notung *f* (-; -en) a) marking, *Am.* grading, b) marks, *Am.* grades.
be'nutzen *v/t* (h) a) use, make use of, b) profit by. **Be'nutzer** *m* (-s; -) user.
be'nutzerfreundlich *adj* user-friendly.
Be'nutzung *f* (-; *no pl*) use.
Be'nutzungsgebühr *f* fee, charge.
Benzin [bɛnˈtsiːn] *n* (-s; -e) 1. *mot.* petrol, *Am.* gasoline, F gas. 2. 🜊 benzine. **~feuerzeug** *n* fuel lighter. **~fresser** *m* F *mot.* fuel guzzler. **~gutschein** *m* petrol (*Am.* gas) coupon. **~hahn** *m* fuel cock. **~ka͟nister** *m* petrol can, F jerry can. **~leitung** *f* fuel line. **~motor** *m* petrol (*Am.* gasoline) engine. **~pumpe** *f* fuel pump. **~tank** *m* fuel tank. **~uhr** *f* fuel ga(u)ge. **~verbrauch** *m* petrol (*Am.* gasoline) consumption.
Benzol [bɛnˈtsoːl] *n* (-s; -e) 🜊, ⊙ benzene, benzol.
beobachten [bəˈʔoːbaxtən] *v/t* (h) 1. watch, observe. 2. notice. 3. observe (*rule etc*). **Be'obachter** *m* (-s; -) a) observer (*a.* ✗, *pol. etc*), b) onlooker. **Be'obachtung** *f* (-; -en) 1. observation. 2. observance (*of rule*).
Be'obachtungsgabe *f* powers of observation. **Be'obachtungsstati͟on** *f* observation station (*🜊 ward*).
beordern [bəˈʔɔrdərn] *v/t* (h) a) order (*nach* [to go] to), b) summon.
be'packen *v/t* (h) load (*mit* with).
be'pflanzen *v/t* (h) plant (*mit* with).
be'quatschen *v/t* (h) F 1. thrash *s.th.* out. 2. *j-n* ~ talk s.o. into doing *s.th.*
bequem [bəˈkveːm] **I** *adj* 1. comfortable, easy (*a.* ✝ *terms etc*), convenient: *es sich ~ machen* make o.s. comfortable (*or* at home), *fig.* take the easy way out. 2. a) comfort-loving, b) lazy. **II** *adv* 3. easily. **be'quemen:** *sich ~* (h) deign (*or* bring o.s.) (*et. zu tun* to do s.th.); *sich zu e-r Antwort etc* ~ deign to give an answer *etc*. **Be'quemlichkeit** *f* (-; -en) 1. *no pl* comfort, ease. 2. *no pl* indolence. 3. convenience, *pl a.* amenities.
berappen [bəˈrapən] *v/t, v/i* (h) F pay.
be'raten (beriet, beraten, h) **I** *v/t* a) advise *s.o.* (*bei* on), b) discuss: *sich* ~

lassen von consult; *gut (schlecht)* ~ *sein* be well-(ill-)advised. **II sich mit j-m über et.** ~ discuss s.th. with s.o. **be'ratend** *adj* advisory. **Be'rater** *m* (-s; -), **Be'raterin** *f* (-; -nen) adviser: *fachmännischer (or fachärztlicher) Berater* consultant. **Be'ratung** *f* (-; -en) **1.** a) discussion *(über acc* of), b) consultation. **2.** → **Be'ratungsstelle** *f* information cent/re *(Am.* -er).

be'rauben *v/t* (h) *(gen* of) rob, *fig. a.* deprive.

be'rauschen *v/t* (h) intoxicate: *fig. sich* ~ get intoxicated *(an dat* with).

be'rauschend *adj a. fig.* intoxicating: *iro. nicht gerade* ~ not so hot.

berechenbar [bə'rɛçənbaːr] *adj* calculable, *fig.* predictable. **be'rechnen** *v/t* (h) a) calculate *(a. fig.),* b) estimate *(auf acc* at), c) ✝ charge *(j-m et.* s.o. s.th.).

be'rechnend *adj fig.* calculating.

Be'rechnung *f* (-; -en) calculation: *fig. mit* ~ with deliberation.

berechtigen [bə'rɛçtɪgən] (h) **I** *v/t j-n (zu e-r Sache)* ~ entitle s.o. (to [do] s.th.), authorize s.o. (to do s.th.). **II** *v/i zu e-r Sache* ~ entitle to s.th.; *zu der Annahme (Hoffnung)* ~, *daß* ... warrant the assumption (hope) that ... **be'rechtigt** *adj (zu* to) a) entitled, authorized, b) justified, c) legitimate *(claim etc).* **Be'rechtigung** *f* (-; *no pl)* right *(zu* to), authorization, authority, legitimacy.

be'reden *v/t* (h) **1.** discuss. **2.** → *überreden.* **Beredsamkeit** [bə'reːtzaːmkaɪt] *f* (-; *no pl)* eloquence. **beredt** [bə'reːt] *adj a. fig.* eloquent.

Be'reich *m* (-[e]s; -e) **1.** area. **2.** *fig.* field, sphere, sector: *im* ~ *des Möglichen liegen* be possible, be within the bounds of possibility; *im sozialen* ~ in the social sector, socially; *im persönlichen* ~ on the personal side, personally.

bereichern [bə'raɪçərn] *v/t* (h) *a. fig.* enrich *(sich* o.s.). **Be'reicherung** *f* (-; -en) *a. fig.* enrichment.

bereifen [bə'raɪfən] *v/t* (h) put tyres *(Am.* tires) on. **Be'reifung** *f* (-; -en) tyres, *Am.* tires.

be'reinigen *v/t* (h) settle *(quarrel,* ✝ *account),* iron out *(mistake etc), statistics:* adjust. **Be'reinigung** *f* (-; *no pl)* settlement, adjustment.

be'reisen *v/t* (h) travel around, tour.

bereit [bə'raɪt] *adj pred* ready, prepared, willing: *sich* ~ *erklären (or finden) zu inf* agree *(or* volunteer) to *inf; bist du* ~? (are you) ready?

be'reiten *v/t* (h) **1.** prepare, make *(tea etc).* **2.** cause *(trouble etc): j-m Vergnügen* ~ give s.o. pleasure.

be'reithalten *(irr, sep,* -ge-, h, → *halten)* **I** *v/t et.* ~ have s.th. ready. **II** *sich* ~ be ready *(für* for).

be'reitliegen *v/i (irr, sep,* -ge-, h, → *liegen)* be ready.

be'reitmachen *v/t (sep,* -ge-, h) *(a. sich* ~) *(zu* for) get ready, prepare (o.s.).

bereits [bə'raɪts] *adv* already.

Be'reitschaft *f* (-; -en) **1.** *no pl* readiness: *in* ~ *sein* → *bereitstehen; (sich) in* ~ *halten* → *bereithalten.* **2.** (police) squad. **Be'reitschafts|arzt** *m* duty doctor. **~dienst** *m* standby duty. **~poli,zei** *f* riot police. **~tasche** *f* carrying *(phot.* camera) case.

be'reitstehen *v/i (irr, sep,* -ge-, h, → *stehen)* **1.** be ready, ✕ stand by. **2.** be available.

be'reitstellen *v/t (sep,* -ge-, h) provide, make *s.th.* available.

Be'reitstellung *f* (-; *no pl)* provision.

be'reitwillig *adj* willing, eager.

Be'reitwilligkeit *f* (-; *no pl)* willingness.

bereuen [bə'rɔʏən] *v/t* (h) regret.

Berg [bɛrk] *m* (-[e]s; -e) mountain *(a. fig.),* hill: *fig.* ~ *e von* piles of; *~e versetzen* move mountains; *j-m goldene ~e versprechen* promise s.o. the moon; *über den* ~ *sein* be over the worst; *über alle ~e* off and away; *die Haare standen ihm zu ~e* his hair stood on end; *er hielt damit nicht hinterm* ~ he made no bones about it.

berg'ab *adv a. fig.* downhill.

'Bergarbeiter *m* miner.

berg'auf *adv* uphill: *fig. es geht wieder* ~ things are looking up.

'Berg|bahn *f* mountain railway. **~bau** *m* (-[e]s; *no pl)* mining (industry).

bergen ['bɛrgən] *v/t* (barg, geborgen, h) **1.** a) rescue, b) recover, salvage, c) ⚓ take in *(sails).* **2.** contain, hold, *a.* involve *(danger).*

'Bergführer *m* mountain guide.

bergig ['bɛrgɪç] *adj* mountainous.

'Berg|kette *f* mountain range. **~kri,stall**

m crystallized quartz. **~land** *n* mountainous country. **~mas|siv** *n* massif. **~predigt** *f bibl.* Sermon on the Mount. **~rücken** *m* (mountain) ridge. **~schuh** *m* mountaineering boot. **~spitze** *f* mountain peak. **~steigen** *n* (ɛ) mountaineering. **~steiger** *m* (-s; -) mountaineer. **~straße** *f* mountain road. **~tour** *f* mountain tour.

'Berg-und-'Tal-Bahn *f* switchback (railway), *Am.* roller coaster.

'Bergung *f* (-; -en) a) rescue, b) recovery, salvage.

'Bergungs|arbeiten *pl* rescue work, salvage operations. **~dienst** *m* recovery (*or* salvage) service. **~fahrzeug** *n* recovery (✈ crash) vehicle. **~mannschaft** *f* rescue party, ⚓ salvage crew.

'Berg|wacht *f* (-; *no pl*) mountain rescue service. **~wanderung** *f* mountain hike. **~werk** *n* (-[e]s; -e) mine.

Bericht [bə'rɪçt] *m* (-[e]s; -e) report (on), account (of): (*j-m*) **~ erstatten** report (to s.o.). **be'richten** *v/t*, *v/i* (h) report (*über acc* on, *j-m* to s.o.), relate: *j-m et.* **~** inform s.o. of s.th.

Be'richterstatter *m* (-s; -) reporter, *abroad:* correspondent, *radio, TV a.* commentator.

Be'richterstattung *f* (-; -en) a) reporting, *a.* coverage (*by the press*), b) report, *radio, TV a.* commentary.

berichtigen [bə'rɪçtɪgən] *v/t* (h) correct (*sich* o.s.), rectify (*s.th.*), ⚙ *a.* adjust.

Be'richtigung *f* (-; -en) correction, ⚙ *a.* adjustment.

Be'richtsjahr *n* ✝ year under review.

be'riechen *v/t* (beroch, berochen, h) sniff at.

berief [bə'riːf] *pret of* **berufen**.

be'rieseln *v/t* (h) irrigate, sprinkle.

Be'rieselung *f* (-; *no pl*) **1.** irrigation, sprinkling. **2.** *F fig.* constant exposure (*mit Musik etc* to music etc).

beriet [bə'riːt] *pret of* **beraten**.

beritten [bə'rɪtən] *adj* mounted.

Berliner[1] [bɛr'liːnər] **I** *m* (-s; -) Berliner. **II** *adj* (of) Berlin.

Ber'liner[2] *m* (-s; -) *gastr.* doughnut.

Bernhardiner [bɛrnhar'diːnər] *m* (-s; -) St. Bernard (dog).

Bernstein ['bɛrn-] *m* (-[e]s; *no pl*) amber.

beroch [bə'rɔx] *pret of* **beriechen**.

berochen [bə'rɔxən] *pp of* **beriechen**.

bersten ['bɛrstən] *v/i* (barst, geborsten, sn) burst (*fig. vor dat* with).

berüchtigt [bə'rʏçtɪçt] *adj* notorious (*wegen* for).

berücksichtigen [bə'rʏkzɪçtɪgən] *v/t* (h) consider, take s.th. into consideration, bear *s.th.* in mind, allow for. **Be'rücksichtigung** *f* (-; *no pl*) consideration: *unter ~ s-s Alters* considering his age.

Beruf [bə'ruːf] *m* (-[e]s; -e) a) occupation, F job, b) profession, c) trade, d) business, e) line: *von ~* by profession, by trade. **be'rufen** (berief, berufen, h) **I** *v/t j-n ~* appoint s.o. (*zu e-m Amt* to an office, *zum Vorsitzenden* chairman). **II** *sich ~ auf* (*acc*) cite: *sich auf et. ~* a) rely on, b) plead (*ignorance etc*); *sich darauf ~, daß ...* plead that ...; *darf ich mich auf Sie ~?* may I mention your name? **III** *adj* qualified: *sich ~ fühlen zu inf* feel called upon to *inf; aus ~em Munde* from a competent authority.

be'ruflich *adj* professional, vocational.

Be'rufs|ausbildung *f* vocational training. **~aussichten** *pl* career prospects. **~berater(in** *f*) *m* vocational adviser. **~beratung** *f* vocational guidance. **~bild** *n* job description. **~erfahrung** *f* (vocational) experience. **~fachschule** *f* vocational college. **~geheimnis** *n* professional secret (*as duty:* secrecy). **~krankheit** *f* occupational disease. **~leben** *n* professional (*or* active) life. **~risiko** *n* occupational hazard. **~schule** *f* vocational school. **~sol,dat** *m* regular (soldier). **~spieler** *m sports:* professional (player). **~sportler(in** *f*) *m* professional. **~stand** *m* profession. **2tätig** *adj* a) working, b) employed. **~tätige,** *m, f* (-n; -n) working person. **~verbot** *n* disqualification from a profession. **~verkehr** *m* rush-hour traffic.

Be'rufung *f* (-; -en) **1.** calling. **2.** appointment (*zu* to). **3.** *unter ~ auf* (*acc*) with reference to. **4.** ⚖ (*~ einlegen* file an) appeal (*bei* with, *gegen* from).

Be'rufungsgericht *n,* **Be'rufungs-in,stanz** *f* ⚖ court of appeal.

Be'rufungsverfahren *n* ⚖ **1.** appeal proceedings. **2.** appellate procedure.

be'ruhen *v/i* (h) **1. ~ auf** (*dat*) a) rest on, be based on, b) be due to. **2. et. auf sich ~ lassen** let s.th. rest; *lassen wir die Sache auf sich ~!* let's leave it at that!

beruhigen [bə'ruːɪgən] **I** v/t (h) a) reassure, b) calm (down): ~ **Sie sich doch!** calm down!; **seien Sie beruhigt, ich werde ...** rest assured I'll ...; **wenn Sie das beruhigt** if that puts your mind at rest. **II sich ~** calm down, situation: quieten down. **be'ruhigend** adj **1.** reassuring. **2.** ✲ sedative.
Be'ruhigung f (-; -en) **1.** no pl calming (down), of situation: a. stabilization: **sie braucht et. zur ~** she needs s.th. to calm her down. **2.** reassurance: **zu d-r ~** to put your mind at rest.
Be'ruhigungs|mittel n, **~pille** f ✲ sedative, fig. soporific. **~spritze** f sedative injection.
berühmt [bə'ryːmt] adj famous (**wegen** for): F fig. **das ist nicht gerade ~!** that's nothing to write home about!
Be'rühmtheit f (-; -en) **1.** no pl fame: ~ **erlangen** become famous. **2.** celebrity.
be'rühren [bə'ryːrən] **I** v/t **1.** touch, fig. a. affect: **j-n (un)angenehm ~** (dis)please s.o.; → **peinlich 3. 2.** fig. touch (up)on (subject), concern (s.o.'s interests). **II sich ~** touch, fig. a. meet. **Be'rührung** f (-; -en) **1.** touch. **2.** contact: **in ~ kommen mit** come into contact with.
Be'rührungspunkt m point of contact.
be'sagen v/t (h) say, mean: **das besagt (noch) gar nichts!** that doesn't mean anything! **be'sagt** adj adm. aforesaid.
besah [bə'zaː] pret of **besehen.**
besamen [bə'zaːmən] v/t (h) inseminate, 🐝 pollinate.
Besan [be'zaːn] m (-s; -e) ⚓ miz(z)en.
besänftigen [bə'zɛnftɪgən] v/t (h) (a. **sich ~**) calm down: **j-n ~** placate s.o.
besang [bə'zaŋ] pret of **besingen.**
besann [bə'zan] pret of **besinnen.**
besaß [bə'zaːs] pret of **besitzen.**
besät [bə'zɛːt] adj fig. covered (**mit** with).
Besatz [bə'zats] m (-es; ⁎e) trimming(s).
Be'satzung f (-; -en) **1.** ✕ a) occupying forces, b) garrison. **2.** ✈, ⚓ crew.
Be'satzungs|macht f occupying power. **~streitkräfte** pl occupying forces.
be'saufen: sich ~ (besoff, besoffen, h) F get sloshed. **Besäufnis** [bə'zɔyfnɪs] n (-ses; -se) F booze-up.
be'schädigen v/t (h) damage.
Be'schädigung f (-; -en) **1.** damaging. **2.** a. pl damage (**gen** to).

be'schaffen v/t (h) **j-m et. ~** get (or procure) s.o. s.th.; (**sich**) **et. ~** get s.th.
Be'schaffenheit f (-; no pl) condition, state, quality, nature.
Be'schaffung f (-; no pl) procurement.
beschäftigen [bə'ʃɛftɪgən] (h) **I** v/t **1. j-n ~** occupy s.o., keep s.o. busy. **2.** employ. **3.** occupy, problem: preoccupy, be on s.o.'s mind. **II sich ~** (**mit**) busy (with), work (at); **sich mit e-m Problem** etc ~ deal with a problem etc. **be'schäftigt** adj **1.** busy. **2.** employed (**bei** with). **Be'schäftigte** m, f (-n; -n) employee. **Be'schäftigung** f (-; -en) **1.** occupation, work, activity: **sie muß ~ haben** she must have s.th. to do. **2.** employment, job: **ohne ~** unemployed, out of work. **Be'schäftigungsthera,pie** f occupational therapy.
be'schälen v/t (h) cover (mare).
be'schämen v/t (h) **j-n ~** a) shame s.o., b) put s.o. to shame. **be'schämend** adj shameful. **be'schämt** adj ashamed (**über** acc of). **Be'schämung** f (-; no pl) shame: **zu m-r ~** to my shame.
be'schatten v/t (h) fig. shadow.
be'schauen v/t (h) (a. **sich et. ~**) (have a) look at. **be'schaulich** adj contemplative, tranquil.
Bescheid [bə'ʃaɪt] m (-[e]s; -e) answer, adm. notice, information (**über** acc about): ~ **bekommen** be informed; **j-m ~ geben** let s.o. know (**über** acc about); F **j-m ~ stoßen, j-m gehörig ~ sagen** give s.o. a piece of one's mind; ~ **wissen** a) be informed (**über** acc of), b) **mit, in** (dat) know all about, c) be in the know, iro. know the score.
bescheiden¹ [bə'ʃaɪdən] (beschied, beschieden, h) **I** v/t **1.** adm. notify: → **abschlägig. 2. es war ihm nicht beschieden zu** inf it was not granted to him to inf. **II sich ~** be content (**mit** with).
be'scheiden² adj a. fig. modest.
Be'scheidenheit f (-; no pl) modesty.
be'scheinen v/t (beschien, beschienen, h) shine on.
bescheinigen [bə'ʃaɪnɪgən] v/t (h) certify: **j-m et. ~** a. iro. attest s.o. s.th.; **den Empfang ~** (**gen** or **von**) a) acknowledge receipt of, b) give a receipt for; **hiermit wird bescheinigt, daß ...** this is to certify that ...

Be'scheinigung f (-; -en) **1.** no pl attestation, certification. **2.** certificate.

be'scheißen v/t (beschiß, beschissen, h) V j-n ~ cheat (or do) s.o. (**um** out of).

be'schenken v/t (h) j-n ~ give s.o. a present; **j-n mit et.** ~ give s.o. s.th.

be'scheren v/t (h) j-m et. ~ give (fig. bring) s.o. s.th. **Be'scherung** f (-; -en) distribution of (Christmas) presents: fig. **e-e schöne ~!** a fine mess!; **da haben wir die ~!** there you are!; F **die ganze ~** the whole bag of tricks.

bescheuert [bə'ʃɔyərt] → **bekloppt**.

be'schichten v/t (h) ⊕ coat.

be'schicken v/t(h) **1.** exhibit at (a fair). **2.** send delegates to. **3.** ⊕ charge.

beschied [bə'ʃiːt] pret, **beschieden** [bə'ʃiːdən] pp of **bescheiden¹**.

beschien [bə'ʃiːn] pret, **be'schienen** pp of **bescheinen**.

be'schießen v/t (beschoß, beschossen, h) a) fire at, b) bombard (a. phys.).

be'schildern v/t (h) signpost. **Be'schilderung** f (-; -en) **1.** signposting. **2.** signposts.

be'schimpfen v/t (h) call s.o. names. **Be'schimpfung** f (-; -en) abuse.

beschiß [bə'ʃis] V pret of **bescheißen**. **Be'schiß** m (-sses; no pl) V **1.** swindle, rip-off. **2.** frost. **be'schissen** V I pp of **bescheißen**. II adj lousy, rotten.

Be'schlag m (-[e]s; ⸚e) **1.** usu. pl metal fitting(s). **2.** a) condensation, b) film. **3.** in ~ nehmen, mit ~ belegen F grab, monopolize. **be'schlagen** (beschlug, beschlagen, h) I v/t **1.** put metal fittings on. **2.** shoe (a horse). **3.** steam up. II sich ~ a) mirror etc: steam up, b) metal: oxidize, c) go mo(u)ldy. III adj gut ~ sein in (dat) be well up in. **Be'schlagenheit** f (-; no pl) sound knowledge (**in** dat of).

Beschlagnahme [bə'ʃlaːknaːmə] f (-; -n) seizure, confiscation.

be'schlagnahmen v/t (h) **1.** seize, confiscate. **2.** → **Beschlag** 3.

beschleunigen [bə'ʃlɔynɪɡən] v/t, v/i (h) (a. sich ~) accelerate (a. mot., phys.), speed up: **s-e Schritte** ~ quicken one's steps; **das Tempo** ~ speed up. **Be'schleuniger** m (-s; -) ⊕, phys. accelerator. **Be'schleunigung** f (-; -en) acceleration (a. mot., phys.), speeding up. **Be'schleunigungs|spur** f mot. accele-

ration lane. **~vermögen** n (-s; no pl) mot. acceleration.

be'schließen v/t (beschloß, beschlossen, h) **1.** (zu inf to inf) decide, make up one's mind. **2.** close, end, settle.

be'schlossen adj agreed, settled.

beschlug [bə'ʃluːk] pret of **beschlagen**.

Be'schluß m (-sses; ⸚sse) decision, resolution: **e-n ~ fassen** parl. pass a resolution. **be'schlußfähig** adj ~ **sein** constitute a quorum; **die Versammlung** etc **ist (nicht)** ~ there is a (no) quorum.

be'schmieren v/t (h) smear.

be'schmutzen v/t (h) dirty, soil, fig. sully; → **Nest** 1.

be'schneiden v/t (beschnitt, beschnitten, h) **1.** trim, prune, cut. **2.** ✚ circumcise. **3.** fig. cut (down), curtail. **Be'schneidung** f (-; -en) **1.** trimming (etc). **2.** ✚ circumcision. **3.** fig. curtailment, cut, reduction.

be'schnüffeln v/t (h), **be'schnuppern** v/t (h) sniff at: F fig. sich (gegenseitig) ~ take stock of each other.

beschönigen [bə'ʃøːnɪɡən] v/t (h) palliate, gloss over: **~d** palliative.

Be'schönigung f (-; -en) palliation.

beschoß [bə'ʃɔs] pret, **be'schossen** pp of **beschießen**.

beschränken [bə'ʃrɛŋkən] (h) I v/t (auf acc to) limit, restrict. II sich ~ auf (acc) confine o.s. to, matter: be confined to. **be'schränkt** adj **1.** limited, restricted. **2.** contp. a) dense, b) narrow-minded. **Be'schränktheit** f (-; no pl) **1.** limitedness. **2.** contp. stupidity, narrow-mindedness. **Be'schränkung** f (-; -en) (auf acc to) limitation, restriction.

be'schreiben v/t (beschrieb, beschrieben, h) **1.** write on. **2.** describe (a. Å): **nicht zu ~** indescribable.

Be'schreibung f (-; -en) **1.** (das spottet jeder ~ that beggars) description. **2.** ⊕ specification.

be'schreiten v/t (beschritt, beschritten, h) walk on: fig. **neue Wege** ~ tread new paths.

beschrieb [bə'ʃriːp] pret, **beschrieben** [bə'ʃriːbən] pp of **beschreiben**.

beschriften [bə'ʃrɪftən] v/t (h) a) inscribe, b) mark (boxes), label (goods). **Be'schriftung** f (-; -en) inscription.

beschritt [bə'ʃrɪt] pret, **be'schritten** pp of **beschreiten**.

beschuldigen [bəˈʃʊldɪɡən] *v/t* (h) *j-n* ~
accuse s.o. (*gen* of). **Be'schuldigte** *m, f*
(-n; -n) accused. **Be'schuldigung** *f* (-;
-en) accusation, charge.

be'schummeln *v/t* (h) F *j-n* (*um et.*) ~
cheat s.o. (out of s.th.).

Be'schuß *m* (-sses; *no pl*) firc, bombard-
ment (*a. phys.*): *unter ~ geraten a. fig.*
come under fire; *unter ~ nehmen* a) →
beschießen, b) *fig.* attack.

be'schützen *v/t* (h) protect (*vor dat*,
gegen from). **Be'schützer** *m* (-s; -)
protector. **Be'schützerin** *f* (-; -nen)
protectress.

be'schwatzen *v/t* (h) *j-n* ~, *et. zu tun*
coax s.o. to do (*or* into doing) s.th.

Beschwerde [bəˈʃveːrdə] *f* (-; -n) **1.**
trouble, ☞ *usu. pl* complaint: *sein Herz
macht ihm ~n* his heart is giving him
trouble. **2.** complaint (*über acc* about),
⚖ appeal (*gegen* from). **~buch** *n* complaints book. ⚖**frei** ☞ free of pain.
~führer(in *f*) *m* ⚖ complainant.

beschweren [bəˈʃveːrən] (h) **I** *v/t* **1.**
weight. **2.** *fig.* weigh down. **II** *sich ~*
complain (*über acc* about, of, *bei* to).

be'schwerlich *adj* onerous, tiring.

beschwichtigen [bəˈʃvɪçtɪɡən] *v/t* (h)
appease (*a. pol.*), calm down, placate.
Be'schwichtigungspoli,tik *f* policy of
appeasement.

be'schwindeln *v/t* (h) *j-n* ~ lie to s.o.

beschwingt [bəˈʃvɪŋt] *adj* elated, buoy-
ant, lively, lilting (*melody*).

be'schwipst *adj* F tipsy, merry.

be'schwören *v/t* (beschwor, beschwo-
ren, h) **1.** *esp.* ⚖ swear to. **2.** a) conjure
up (*ghosts, a. fig.*), b) exorcise. **3.** *j-n* ~
implore s.o. **Be'schwörung** *f* (-; -en) **1.**
entreaty. **2.** a) invocation, b) exorcism.

beseelt [bəˈzeːlt] *adj* (*von* with) inspired,
filled.

be'sehen *v/t* (besah, besehen, h) (*a. sich
et. ~*) have a look at, examine.

beseitigen [bəˈzaɪtɪɡən] *v/t* (h) remove,
dispose of, *fig. a.* eliminate: *j-n ~* do
away with s.o. **Be'seitigung** *f* (-; *no pl*)
removal, disposal, *fig. a.* elimination.

Besen [ˈbeːzən] *m* (-s; -) **1.** broom,
brush: *fig. neue ~ kehren gut* a new
broom sweeps clean; F *ich fresse e-n ~,
wenn ...* I'll eat my hat if ... **2.** *contp.*
(old) hag. **'Besenstiel** *m* broomstick.

besessen [bəˈzɛsən] **I** *pp of* **besitzen**. **II**
adj **1.** (*von*) possessed (by), *fig. a.* obsessed (with). **2.** frantic: *wie ~* like mad.
Be'sessenheit *f* (-; *no pl*) *fig.* obsession.

be'setzen *v/t* (h) **1.** take (*a seat*), occupy
(*country, house, etc*). **2.** fill (*a post*): *wir
wollen diesen Posten mit e-r Frau ~*
we want to put a woman in this posi-
tion. **3.** *thea.* cast: *neu ~* recast. **4.** trim
(*dress* (*mit* with). **be'setzt** *adj* **1.** occupied (*a.* ✕, *pol.*), *seat:* a. taken, *bus etc:*
full (up). **2.** *thea.* **das Stück ist gut
besetzt** the play is well cast. **3.** *teleph.*
engaged, *Am.* busy. **4.** ⚖ *mit court etc*
composed of. **Be'setztzeichen** *n*
teleph. engaged (*Am.* busy) signal.

Be'setzung *f* (-; -en) **1.** occupation. **2.** a)
filling (*of post*), b) staff, c) composition
(*of court, team*), d) entrants. **3.** *thea.* a)
casting, b) cast.

besichtigen [bəˈzɪçtɪɡən] *v/t* (h) view,
inspect, visit, see: *zu ~ sein* be on view.
Be'sichtigung *f* (-; -en) inspection (*a.*
✕), visit (*gen* to): *~ von Sehenswürdigkeiten* sight-seeing.

be'siedeln *v/t* (h) settle, colonize: *dicht
(dünn) besiedelt* densely (sparsely)
populated. **Be'sied(e)lung** *f* (-; -en)
settlement, colonization.

be'siegeln *v/t* (h) *a. fig.* seal.

be'siegen *v/t* (h) defeat, beat, *fig.* overcome, conquer. **Be'siegte** *m, f* (-n; -n)
the defeated, loser.

be'singen *v/t* (besang, besungen, h) **1.**
sing (of). **2.** *e-e Platte etc ~* make a
record etc.

be'sinnen: *sich ~* (besann, besonnen, h)
1. reflect, think: *ohne sich zu ~* without thinking twice; *sich anders ~*
change one's mind; *sich e-s Besseren
~* think better of it. **2.** *sich auf j-n* (*et.*) *~*
remember s.o. (s.th.).

be'sinnlich *adj* contemplative.

Be'sinnung *f* (-; *no pl*) **1.** (*die ~ verlieren* lose) consciousness; *wieder zur ~
kommen* regain consciousness, *fig.*
come to one's senses; *fig. j-n zur ~ bringen* bring s.o. to his senses. **2.** (*auf acc*)
contemplation (of), reflection (on).

be'sinnungslos *adj* unconscious.

Be'sinnungslosigkeit *f* (-; *no pl*) unconsciousness.

Besitz [bəˈzɪts] *m* (-es; *no pl*) **1.** possession (*gen, an dat, von* of): *~ ergreifen
von* a) *a. in ~ nehmen* take possession

of, b) *fig.* take hold of *s.o.*; **im ~ sein von** (*or gen*) be in possession of; → **gelangen** 1. **2.** possession(s), property, estate. **be'sitzanzeigend** *adj* **~es Fürwort** possessive pronoun. **besitzen** *v/t* (besaß, besessen, h) possess, own, have. **Be'sitzer** *m* (-s; -), **Be'sitzerin** *f* (-; -nen) possessor, owner, holder (*of passport etc*): **den Besitzer wechseln** change hands. **Be'sitzergreifung** *f* (-; *no pl*) (**von**) (of) taking possession, seizure. **be'sitzlos** *adj* unpropertied.

Be'sitztum *n* (-s; ⸚er), **Be'sitzung** *f* (-; -en) possession(s), property, estate.

besoff [bə'zɔf] *pret of* **besaufen**.

be'soffen I *pp of* **besaufen**. II *adj* F sloshed, plastered.

besohlen [bə'zo:lən] *v/t* (h) sole.

besolden [bə'zɔldən] *v/t* (h) pay.

be'soldet *adj* salaried.

Be'soldung *f* (-; -en) pay, salary.

besonder [bə'zɔndər] *adj* **1.** a) special, particular, specific, b) exceptional, great (*joy, hono[u]r*): **nichts Besonderes** nothing unusual; **in diesem ~en Fall** in this particular case. **2.** separate. **Be'sonderheit** *f* (-; -en) special quality (*or feature*). **be'sonders** *adv* **1.** especially, particularly, above all. **2.** exceptionally. **3.** very much.

besonnen [bə'zɔnən] I *pp of* **besinnen**. II *adj* sensible, level-headed, calm.

Be'sonnenheit *f* (-; *no pl*) level-headedness, calmness.

be'sorgen *v/t* (h) **1.** *j-m et.* **~** get s.o. s.th., provide s.o. with s.th.; **sich et. ~** get (*or* buy) s.th.; F **dem werde ich's ~!** I'll give him what for! **2.** see to, deal with, manage (*household*): F **wird besorgt!** will do! **Besorgnis** [bə'zɔrknıs] *f* (-; -se) anxiety. **be'sorgniserregend** *adj* alarming, worrying. **be'sorgt** I *pp of* **besorgen**. II *adj* (**um** about) worried, concerned. **Be'sorgtheit** *f* (-; *no pl*) **1.** anxiety. **2.** (**um** for) solicitude, concern. **Be'sorgung** *f* (-; -en) **1.** *no pl* procurement. **2.** a) purchase, b) errand: **~en machen** go shopping. **3.** *no pl* (*gen*) dealing (with), management (of).

be'spannen *v/t* (h) **1.** cover (*with silk etc*). **2.** string (*violin etc*). **Be'spannung** *f* (-; -en) **1.** cover. **2.** strings.

be'spielen *v/t* (h) **ein Tonband** *etc* (**mit et.**) **~** record (*s.th.*) on tape *etc*.

be'spielt *adj* prerecorded (*cassette etc*).

be'spitzeln *v/t* (h) *j-n* **~** spy on s.o.

be'sprechen *v/t* (besprach, besprochen, h) **1.** discuss, talk about. Über: **sich mit** *j-m* **~** discuss the matter (*or* talk things over) with s.o. **2.** review. **3.** record *s.th.* on *tape etc*. **4.** 🖅 cure by magic formulas. **Be'sprechung** *f* (-; -en) **1.** discussion. **2.** meeting, conference: **er ist in e-r ~** he is in conference. **3.** review.

Be'sprechungsexem_plar *n* review copy.

be'sprengen *v/t* (h) sprinkle, spray.

be'spritzen *v/t* (h) spatter, splash.

besprochen [bə'ʃprɔxən] *pp of* **besprechen**.

be'spucken *v/t* (h) spit at, spit on.

besser ['bɛsər] *adj and adv* better (**als** than): *contp.* **e-e ~e Scheune** a glorified barn; **immer ~** better and better; **um so ~** so much the better; (**oder**) **~ gesagt** *or* rather; **~ ist** – let's keep on the safe side; **~ werden** improve, get better; **es geht ihm heute ~** he is better today; **es geht (wirtschaftlich) ~** things are looking up; **er ist ~ dran als ich** he is better off than me; **ich weiß es ~** I know better; **er täte ~ (daran) zu gehen** he had better go; **Besseres zu tun haben** have more important things to do; *j-n* **e-s Besseren belehren** set s.o. right, *w.s.* open s.o.'s eyes; → **besinnen** 1, **Hälfte**.

'bessergestellt *adj* better-off.

'bessern (h) I *v/t* **1.** improve. **2.** reform (*s.o.*). II **sich ~ 3.** improve. **4.** mend one's ways.

'Besserung *f* (-; *no pl*) improvement: 🖅 **auf dem Wege der ~** on the way to recovery; **gute ~!** hope you feel better soon!

'Besserwisser *m* (-s; -) know-(it-)all.

bestach [bə'ʃta:x] *pret of* **bestechen**.

bestahl [bə'ʃta:l] *pret of* **bestehlen**.

Bestallung [bə'ʃtaluŋ] *f* (-; -en) appointment.

bestand [bə'ʃtant] *pret of* **bestehen**.

Be'stand *m* (-[e]s; ⸚e) **1.** *no pl* a) (continued) existence, b) duration: **von ~ sein**, **~ haben** be lasting, last; **k-n ~ haben** be short-lived, ⚖ not to be valid (in law). **2.** (**an** *dat* of) stock, supplies, 🐾, *zo.* population; → **eisern. 3.** ✝ a) assets, b) (stock) holdings, c) cash in hand, d)

stock on hand, e) inventory. **4.** rolling stock, fleet. **5.** ✗ (effective) strength.
bestanden [bə'ʃtandən] *pp of* **bestehen.**
be'ständig *adj* **1.** constant, lasting. **2.** steady (*a.* ✝ *demand etc*), stable, settled (*weather*) **3.** resistant (**gegen** to).
Be'ständigkeit *f* (-; *no pl*) **1.** constancy, lastingness. **2.** steadiness, stability. **3.** resistance (**gegen** to).
Be'standsaufnahme *f* (-; -n) ✝ stock-taking, *Am.* inventory: **e-e ~ machen** *a. fig.* take stock.
Be'standteil *m* (-[e]s; -e) a) part, component, constituent (part), b) element, c) ingredient: → **auflösen** 1.
be'stärken *v/t* (h) **1.** (**in** *dat* in) a) confirm, strengthen, b) encourage.
bestätigen [bə'ʃtɛːtɪgən] (h) **I** *v/t* a) confirm (*a.* ✝ *an order*), b) acknowledge (receipt of), c) certify. **II sich ~** be confirmed, prove true.
Be'stätigung *f* (-; -en) **1.** confirmation, acknowledgement. **2.** a) letter of confirmation, b) certificate.
bestatten [bə'ʃtatən] *v/t* (h) bury.
Be'stattung *f* (-; -en) funeral, burial.
Be'stattungsinsti,tut *n* undertakers, *Am.* funeral home.
be'stäuben *v/t* (h) **1.** dust, spray. **2.** ⚘ pollinate. **Be'stäubung** *f* (-; -en) **1.** spraying, dusting. **2.** ⚘ pollination.
be'staunen *v/t* (h) marvel at.
beste ['bɛstə] *adj and adv* best: **mein ~r Freund** my best friend; **der (die) erste ~** the first comer; **das erste ~** the first thing; **am ~n wissen** *etc* know *etc* best; **am ~n, wir besuchen ihn** the best thing to do would be to call on him; **im ~n Fall** at best; **im ~n Alter, in den ~n Jahren** in the prime of life; **in ~m Zustand** in perfect condition; **mit ~m Dank** with many thanks; **(von) ~r Qualität** of first-class quality; **e-e Geschichte (ein Lied) zum ~n geben** tell a story (oblige with a song); **j-n zum ~n haben** pull s.o.'s leg; **sein Bestes tun** (*or* **geben**) do one's best; **das Beste daraus machen** make the best of it; **... sind nicht die ~ ...** are not of the best; → **bestens, Kraft** 1.
be'stechen *v/t* (bestach, bestochen, h) **1.** bribe: **sich ~ lassen** take bribes. **2.** *fig. a. v/i* impress (**durch** by). **be'stechend** *adj fig.* impressive, brilliant.

be'stechlich *adj* corrupt(ible).
Be'stechlichkeit *f* (-; *no pl*) corruptibility. **Be'stechung** *f* (-; -en) bribery: **passive ~** taking of bribes.
Be'stechungs|af,färe *f* corruption scandal. **~geld** *n* bribe money. **~versuch** *m* attempted bribery.
Besteck *n* (-[e]s; -e] **1.** knife, fork and spoon, *coll. or* **~e** cutlery. **2.** ✚ (set of) instruments.
be'stehen (bestand, bestanden, h) **I** *v/t* **1.** go (*or* come) through, win (*fight*), pass (*exam*): *fig. die Probe* **~** stand the test. **II** *v/i* **2.** a) exist, be, b) continue, last, c) remain, survive, have survived. **3.** ~ **aus** be composed of, consist of (*a. fig.*). **4.** ~ **auf** (*dat*) insist on; **ich bestehe darauf(, daß du kommst)** I insist (on your coming). **5.** pass.
Be'stehen *n* (-s) **1.** existence: **seit ~ der Firma** ever since the firm was founded; **das 50jährige ~ feiern** celebrate the fiftieth anniversary. **2.** passing. **3.** insistence (**auf** *dat* on).
be'stehenbleiben *v/i* (*irr, sep,* -ge-, sn, → **bleiben**) continue (to exist), survive.
be'stehend *adj* existing, present.
be'stehlen *v/t* (bestahl, bestohlen, h) rob, steal from.
be'steigen *v/t* (bestieg, bestiegen, h) climb (up), ascend (*mountain etc*), mount (*horse etc*), board (*train etc*).
Be'steigung *f* (-; -en) ascent.
Bestellbuch [bə'ʃtɛl-] *n* ✝ order book.
be'stellen *v/t* (h) **1.** order (*a.* ✝), book (*room*), call (*taxi*). **2. j-n** (**zu sich**) **~** ask s.o. to come, send for s.o. **3. j-m e-e Nachricht** *etc* **~** give (*or* send) s.o. a message *etc*; **kann ich et. ~?** can I take a message? **4.** ✗ cultivate. **5.** → **ernennen. 6. es ist schlecht um ihn** *etc* **bestellt** things are looking bad for him *etc*. **7.** F *fig.* **er hat nicht viel zu ~** he doesn't rate high (**bei** with).
Be'steller *m* (-s; -) ✝ orderer, buyer.
Be'stell|karte *f*, **~schein** *m* order form.
Be'stellung *f* (-; -en) **1.** order: **auf ~ gemacht** made to order, *Am.* custom-made. **2.** message. **3.** ✗ cultivation. **4.** → **Ernennung.**
'besten'falls *adv* at best.
'bestens *adv* extremely well: **(ich) danke ~!** thank you very much!; F **ist ja ~!** that's just great!

be'steuern v/t (h) tax.
Be'steuerung f (-; -en) taxation.
bestialisch [bɛsˈtiːaliʃ] adj atrocious, F fig. a. awful.
Bestie [ˈbɛstiə] f (-; -n) beast, fig. brute.
bestieg [bəˈʃtiːk] pret, **bestiegen** [bəˈʃtiːgən] pp of **besteigen**.
be'stimmen (h) **I** v/t **1.** a) determine, b) decide, c) fix (date, price, etc). **2.** order, decide: **er hat (dabei) nichts zu ~** he has no say (in this matter). **3.** contract, law: provide. **4.** determine (a policy etc): **bestimmt werden durch** (or **von**) be determined by, depend on. **5.** intend (**für**, **zu** for): **j-n zu s-m Nachfolger ~** name s.o. as one's successor; → **bestimmt** 3. **6.** a) a. ⚛, phys. etc: determine, b) define. **II** v/i **7.** give orders: **hier bestimme ich!** F I'm the boss here! **8.** ~ **über** (acc) dispose over.
be'stimmend adj determinant (factor etc), ling. determinative.
be'stimmt I pp of **bestimmen**. **II** adj **1.** a) certain (day, number, etc), b) special (plan etc), c) definite: **et. Bestimmtes** something (or anything) special (or definite). **2.** determined, firm. **3.** ~ **sein** a) **für** be meant for, b) **zu et.** be destined for (or to be). **4.** (**nach** for) ✈, destined, ✈, ⚓ bound. **II** adv **5.** certainly, for certain: (**ganz**) ~ definitely; ~ **wissen**, **daß** know for sure that; **er kommt** ~ he is sure to come; **ich kann es nicht** ~ **sagen** I can't tell with certainty. **6.** firmly, categorically.
Be'stimmtheit f (-; no pl) certainty, b) firmness: **mit** ~ → **bestimmt** II.
Be'stimmung f (-; -en) **1.** no pl (gen) decision (on), fixing of (date etc). **2.** regulation, rule, provision. **3.** a) a. ⚛, phys., etc: determination, b) definition. **4.** no pl intended purpose: **et. s-r** ~ **übergeben** inaugurate s.th., open s.th. to the public. **5.** ling. qualification: **adverbiale** ~ adverbial element. **6.** no pl fate, destiny.
Be'stimmungs|bahnhof m station of destination. **⚙gemäß** adj and adv as directed. **⚙flughafen** m airport of destination. **~ort** m (place of) destination.
'Bestleistung f sports: best performance: **persönliche** ~ personal best.
'Bestmarke f sports: record.
best'möglich adj best possible.

bestochen [bəˈʃtɔxən] pp of **bestechen**.
bestohlen [bəˈʃtoːlən] pp of **bestehlen**.
be'strafen v/t (h) punish (**wegen**, **für** for), a. sports: penalize, ⚖ a. sentence (**mit** to). **Be'strafung** f (-; -en) punishment, a. sports: penalty.
be'strahlen v/t (h) **1.** shine on, illuminate. **2.** phys. irradiate, ✦ a. give s.o. ray treatment. **Be'strahlung** f (-; -en) phys. irradiation, ✦ a. ray treatment.
bestrebt [bəˈʃtreːpt] adj ~ **sein zu** inf endeavo(u)r (or strive, be anxious) to inf. **Be'strebung** f (-; -en) effort, endeavo(u)r.
be'streichen v/t (bestrich, bestrichen, h) ~ **mit** spread s.th. on; **mit Butter** ~ butter.
be'streiken v/t (h) go out (or be) on strike against. **be'streikt I** pp of **bestreiken**. **II** adj strike-bound.
be'streiten v/t (bestritt, bestritten, h) **1.** a) dispute, contest, b) deny. **2.** bear, meet, pay (for) (expenses etc). **3.** fill (program[me]): **sie bestritt die Unterhaltung allein** she did all the talking.
be'streuen v/t (h) strew: **mit Salz** etc ~ sprinkle with salt etc.
bestrich [bəˈʃtrɪç] pret, **be'strichen** pp of **bestreichen**.
be'stritt [bəˈʃtrɪt] pret, **be'stritten** pp of **bestreiten**.
'Bestseller m (-s; -) best seller.
bestücken [bəˈʃtʏkən] v/t (h) ⚓, ✕ arm (with guns), w.s. equip (**mit** with).
Be'stuhlung f (-; -en) seating.
be'stürmen v/t (h) **1.** storm. **2.** fig. a) urge, b) implore, c) bombard (**mit** with questions etc).
be'stürzen v/t (h) dismay. **be'stürzend** adj dismaying. **be'stürzt** adj dismayed (**über** acc at). **Be'stürzung** f (-; no pl) (**zu s-r** etc ~ to his etc) dismay.
Besuch [bəˈzuːx] m (-[e]s; -e) **1.** a) visit (gen, **bei**, **in** dat to), call (**bei j-m** on s.o., at s.o.'s house etc), b) stay (**bei** at): **auf** ~, **zu** ~ on a visit; **bei j-m zu** ~ **sein** be staying with s.o.; **e-n** ~ **machen bei** → **besuchen** 1. **2.** (gen) attendance (at school etc). **3.** visitor(s), guest(s), company. **be'suchen** v/t (h) **1.** go and see, visit, pay a visit to, call on. **2.** a) visit (place), go to. b) frequent (restaurant etc), c) go to, attend (school, meeting, etc): **gut besucht** well attended.

Be'sucher *m* (-s; -), **Be'sucherin** *f* (-; -nen) a) visitor (*gen* to), caller, b) guest, c) spectator.

Be'suchszeit *f* visiting hours.

be'sudeln *v/t* (h) soil, *fig.* sully.

besungen [bə'zʊŋən] *pp of* besingen.

Betablocker ['be:tablɔkər] *m* (s; -) ⚙ beta blocker.

betagt [bə'ta:kt] *adj* aged, old.

be'tasten *v/t* (h) feel, touch.

betätigen [bə'tɛ:tɪgən] (h) **I** *v/t* ⚙ operate (*machine*), actuate (*button, lever, etc*), apply (*brake*). **II** *sich ~* (*in dat* in) be active, work, busy o.s.; *sich ~ als* act (*or* work) as; *sich politisch* (*sportlich*) *~* be active in politics (*do sports*). **Be'tätigung** *f* (-; -en) **1.** activity, work, job: *körperliche ~* (physical) exercise. **2.** ⚙ actuation, operation. **Be'tätigungsfeld** *n* field (of activity), *w.s.* outlet.

betäuben [bə'tɔybən] (h) **I** *v/t* a) *a. fig.* stun, daze, b) make *s.o.* unconscious, F knock *s.o.* out, c) deafen, d) intoxicate, e) ⚙ an(a)esthetize, deaden: *fig. wie betäubt* stunned. **II** *sich ~ fig.* seek consolation (*mit, durch* in). **Be'täubung** *f* (-; -en) **1.** stunning (*etc.*). **2.** daze. **3.** ⚙ a) an(a)esthetization, b) (*örtliche*) *~* (local) an(a)esthesia. **Be'täubungsmittel** *n* narcotic, ⚙ *a.* an(a)esthetic.

Bete ['be:tə] *f* (-; -n) ✿ beet: *rote ~* beetroot.

beteiligen [bə'taɪlɪgən] (h) **I** *v/t j-n ~* (*an dat* in) a) ✝ give *s.o.* a share, b) let *s.o.* take part; *beteiligt sein* (*an dat* in) a) participate (in), ✝ have a share (in), share (in *the profit*), be involved (in *an accident etc*), ☆☆ be a party (to). **II** *sich ~* (*an dat*) a) participate (in), b) contribute (to), help (in); *sich an den Kosten ~* share (in) the expenses. **Be'teiligte** *m, f* (-n, -n) person concerned (*or* involved). **Be'teiligung** *f* (-; -en) **1.** participation. **2.** (*an dat* in) interest, share. **3.** ✝ a) investment, b) holding(s), c) partnership. **4.** (*an dat* at) attendance, turnout (*at election etc*).

beten ['be:tən] *v/i* (h) pray (*um* for), say a prayer.

beteuern [bə'tɔyərn] *v/t* (h) protest (*s-e Unschuld* one's innocence), swear to, *a.* ☆☆ affirm (solemnly).

Be'teuerung *f* (-; -en) protestation, *a.* ☆☆ solemn affirmation.

betiteln [bə'ti:təln] *v/t* (h) **1.** entitle (*book etc*). **2.** F *contp. j-n ... ~* call *s.o.* ...

Beton [be'tɔŋ] *m* (-s; -s, -e) concrete.

betonen [bə'to:nən] *v/t* (h) *a. fig.* stress, emphasize.

betonieren [beto'ni:rən] *v/t* (h) concrete. **Be'tonklotz** *m* **1.** concrete block. **2.** *contp.* concrete pile. **Be'tonmischma,schine** *f* cement mixer.

be'tont I *pp of* **betonen. II** *adj fig.* emphatic, marked: *mit ~er Gleichgültigkeit* with studied (*or* marked) indifference. **III** *adv* markedly. **Be'tonung** *f* (-; -en) *a. fig.* stress, emphasis.

betören [bə'tø:rən] *v/t* (h) bewitch, turn *s.o.'s* head.

Betracht [bə'traxt] *in ~ ziehen* take into consideration; *außer ~ lassen* disregard; (*nicht*) *in ~ kommen* be a possibility (be out of the question).

be'trachten *v/t* (h) look at, *fig. a.* view: *j-n als Freund ~* look upon s.o. as (*or* consider s.o.) a friend; *genau betrachtet* strictly speaking. **Be'trachter** *m* (-s; -), **Be'trachterin** *f* (-; -nen) viewer, observer. **beträchtlich** [bə'trɛçtlɪç] *adj* considerable. **Be'trachtung** *f* (-; -en) **1.** *no pl* view (*gen* of). **2.** reflection: *~en anstellen über* (*acc*) reflect on; *bei näherer ~* on closer inspection.

betraf [bə'tra:f] *pret of* betreffen.

Betrag [bə'tra:k] *m* (-[e]s; ⸚e) amount, sum: *im ~e von* to the amount of.

be'tragen (betrug, betragen, h) **I** *v/i* amount to, total. **II** *sich ~* behave.

Be'tragen *n* (-s) behavio(u)r, conduct.

betrank [bə'traŋk] *pret of* betrinken.

betrat [bə'tra:t] *pret of* betreten².

be'trauen *v/t* (h) entrust (*mit* with).

be'trauern *v/t* (h) mourn.

Betreff [bə'trɛf] *m* (-[e]s; -e) ✝ reference, *in letters*: (*abbr. Betr.*) re: ... **be'treffen** *v/t* (betraf, betroffen, h) **1.** a) concern, b) refer to: *was mich betrifft* as for me, as far as I am concerned; *was das betrifft* as to that. **2.** affect: → **betroffen 2. be'treffend** *adj* **1.** concerning. **2.** concerned: *die ~e Person* the person concerned (*or* in question); *das ~e Buch* the book referred to.

be'treiben *v/t* (betrieb, betrieben, h) **1.** pursue, manage, run (*enterprise etc*),

go in for, do (*sports*). **2.** ⚙ operate, run. **Be'treiben** *n* (-s) **auf ~ von** (*or gen*) at the instigation of. **Be'treiber** *m* (-s; -) person (*pl* body) running an enterprise.
be'treten² *adj* embarrassed, awkward.
be'treten² *v/t* (betrat, betreten, h) **1.** step on (to). **2.** enter. **Be'treten** *n* (-s) **~ verboten!** keep off!, no entrance!
betreuen [bə'trɔyən] *v/t* (h) look after, attend to, *sports*: coach, ✝ serve (*area*).
Be'treuer *m* (-s; -), **Be'treuerin** *f* (-; -nen) s.o. who looks after s.o. (*or* s.th.), *sports*: coach. **Be'treuung** *f* (-; *no pl*) care (*von or gen* of, for).
betrieb [bə'tri:p] *pret of betreiben*.
Be'trieb *m* (-[e]s; -e) **1.** enterprise, company, business, firm, factory, works, plant: *öffentliche ~e* public utilities. **2.** *no pl* a) management, running, b) ⚙ operation: *in ~* working, in operation; *außer ~* a) not working, b) out of order; *in ~ setzen* put into operation, start; *außer ~ setzen* put out of action. **3.** *no pl* F a) activity, bustle, b) (heavy) traffic: *wir hatten heute viel ~* we were very busy today.
betrieben [bə'tri:bən] *pp of betreiben*.
be'trieblich *adj* internal, company.
be'triebsam *adj* active, busy. **Be'triebsamkeit** *f* (-; *no pl*) activity, bustle.
Be'triebs|angehörige *m, f* employee. **~anleitung** *f* operating instructions. **~ausflug** *m* (annual) work outing. **Ꝺblind** *adj* routine-blinded. **Ꝺeigen** *adj* company(-owned). **Ꝺfähig** *adj* in (good) working condition. **~ferien** *pl* works holidays. **~fest** *n* company fête. **Ꝺfremd** *adj* outside ...: **~e Person** outsider. **~geheimnis** *n* trade secret. **Ꝺin₁tern** *adj* internal. **~kapi₁tal** *n* working capital. **~klima** *n* work climate. **~kosten** *pl* running costs. **~leiter** *m* works (*or* production) manager. **~obmann** *m* works steward. **~rat** *m* (member of the) works council. **Ꝺsicher** *adj* fail-safe, reliable (in service). **~sicherheit** *f* safety (in operation), reliability. **~stillegung** *f* closure, shutdown. **~störung** *f* ⚙ stoppage, breakdown. **~sy₁stem** *n* computer: operating system. **~unfall** *m* industrial accident. **~verfassung** *f* industrial-relations scheme. **~versammlung** *f* works meeting. **~wirt** *m* graduate in business man-

agement. **~wirtschaft** *f* (-; *no pl*) business management. **~zugehörigkeit** *f* (period of) employment: *nach zehn-jähriger ~* after ten years(' employment) with the company.
be'trinken: sich ~ (betrank, betrunken, h) get drunk.
betroffen [bə'trɔfən] **I** *pp of betreffen*. **II** *adj* **1.** shocked, dismayed, *pred* taken aback. **2.** affected (*von* by): *die ~en Personen* the persons concerned.
Be'troffenheit *f* (-; *no pl*) (*über acc* at) dismay, shock.
betrog [bə'tro:k] *pret*, **betrogen** [bə-'tro:gən] *pp of betrügen*.
be'trüben *v/t* (h) sadden.
beträblich [bə'try:plıç] *adj* sad.
be'trübt *adj* sad (*über acc* at, about).
betrug [bə'tru:k] *pret of betragen*.
Be'trug *m* (-[e]s; *no pl*) cheat, swindle, ⚖ fraud, deception. **be'trügen** *v/t, v/i* (betrog, betrogen, h) cheat, swindle, ⚖ defraud, deceive (*wife etc*): *j-n um et. ~* cheat (*or* do) s.o. out of s.th.; *sich (selbst) ~* deceive o.s. **Be'trüger** *m* (-s; -), **Be'trügerin** *f* (-; -nen) swindler, fraud. **Betrüge'rei** *f* (-; -en) **1.** cheating. **2.** deceit, *a.* ⚖ fraud. **be'trügerisch** *adj* deceitful, fraudulent.
betrunken [bə'trʊŋkən] **I** *pp of betrinken*. **II** *adj* drunk(en), pred drunk.
Be'trunkene *m, f* (-n; -n) drunk.
Be'trunkenheit *f* (-; *no pl*) drunkenness.
Bett [bɛt] *n* (-[e]s; -en) bed (*a. geol.,* ⚙): *im ~* in bed; *j-n zu ~ bringen* put s.o. to bed; *ins ~ gehen* go to bed (F *mit j-m* with s.o.), F turn in; *das ~ hüten (müssen)* be laid up (*wegen* with).
'**Bettbezug** *m* duvet cover. '**Bettcouch** *f* bed settee. '**Bettdecke** *f* a) blanket, b) quilt, c) bedspread.
Bettel ['bɛtl] *m* (-s; *no pl*) *der ganze ~* the whole (wretched) business.
bettel'arm *adj* desperately poor. '**Bettelbrief** *m* begging letter. **betteln** ['bɛtln] *v/i* (h) beg (*um* for): *~ gehen* go begging. '**Bettelstab** *m j-n an den ~ bringen* reduce s.o. to poverty.
betten ['bɛtn] *v/t* (h) bed (*a.* ⚙): *wie man sich bettet, so liegt man* as you make your bed, so you must lie on it.
'**Bettjacke** *f* bed jacket. '**bettlägerig** ['bɛtlɛːgərɪç] *adj* laid up. '**Bettlaken** *n* sheet. '**Bettlek₁türe** *f* bedtime reading.

Bettler ['bɛtlər] *m* (-s; -), **'Bettlerin** *f* (-; -nen) beggar.

Bettnässer ['bɛtnɛsər] *m* (-s, -), **'Bettnässerin** *f* (-; -nen) bed-wetter.

'Bettruhe *f* (period of) bed rest: *j-m ~ verordnen* order s.o. to stay in bed.

'Bettung *f* (-; -en) ⊙ bed(ding).

'Bettvorleger *m* bedside rug.

'Bettwäsche *f*, **'Bettzeug** *n* bed linen.

betucht [bə'tu:xt] *adj* F well-heeled.

be'tupfen *v/t* (h) dab, 𝕤 swab.

beugen ['bɔyɡən] (h) **I** *v/t* **1.** bend (*a. fig. the law*), bow: *vom Alter gebeugt* bowed with age. **2.** *ling.* inflect, decline (*noun*), conjugate (*verb*). **II** *sich ~* **3.** bend. **4.** *fig.* (*dat* to) bow, submit.

Beule ['bɔylə] *f* (-; -n) **1.** bump, swelling. **2.** dent.

beunruhigen [bə'ʔʊnru:ɡən] (h) **I** *v/t* worry, alarm. **II** *sich ~* be worried (*über acc, wegen* about). **Be'unruhigung** *f* (-; -en) anxiety, worry.

beurkunden [bə'ʔu:rkʊndən] *v/t* (h) a) record, b) certify, c) register (*birth etc*). **Be'urkundung** *f* (-; -en) a) recording, b) certification, c) registration.

beurlauben [bə'ʔu:rlaʊbən] *v/t* (h) give *s.o.* leave (*or* time off), *w.s.* suspend *s.o.* (*from office*): *beurlaubt* a) on leave, b) temporarily suspended. **Be'urlaubung** *f* (-; -en) (granting of a) leave, *w.s.* suspension (*from office*).

be'urteilen *v/t* (h) judge (*nach* by): *das kann ich nicht ~!* I am no judge (of this)!; *falsch ~* misjudge. **Be'urteilung** *f* (-; -en) judg(e)ment, assessment, *in personal file*: confidential report.

Beute ['bɔytə] *f* (-; *no pl*) **1.** booty, loot. **2.** *zo.* prey (*a. fig. gen* to), *hunt.* bag: (*dat*) *zur ~ fallen a. fig.* fall a prey to.

Beutel ['bɔytəl] *m* (-s; -) bag, F purse, *zo.* pouch, sac. **'beuteln** *v/t* (h) F *fig.* shake (up). **'Beuteltier** *n* marsupial.

bevölkern [bə'fœlkərn] *v/t* (h) **1.** populate. **2.** inhabit.

Be'völkerung *f* (-; -en) population.

Be'völkerungs|dichte *f* population density. **~explosi,on** *f* population explosion. **~poli,tik** *f* population policy. **~rückgang** *m* decline in population. **~schicht** *f* social stratum (*or* class).

bevollmächtigen [bə'fɔlmɛçtɪɡən] *v/t* (h) *j-n ~* authorize s.o. (*et. zu tun* to do s.th.), 𝕤𝕥𝕥 give s.o. power of attorney.

Be'vollmächtigte *m, f* (-n; -n) authorized person (✝, 𝕤𝕥𝕥 representative), *pol.* plenipotentiary. **Be'vollmächtigung** *f* (-; -en) **1.** authorization. **2.** authority, power, 𝕤𝕥𝕥 power of attorney.

be'vor *adv* before: *nicht ~* not until.

bevormunden [bə'fo:rmʊndən] *v/t* (h) *j-n ~* keep s.o. in leading strings.

bevorrechtigt [bə'fo:rrɛçtɪçt] *adj* privileged.

be'vorstehen *v/i* (*irr, sep,* -ge-, h, → *stehen*) be approaching, *problems etc:* lie ahead, *crisis etc:* be imminent: *j-m ~* be in store for s.o., await s.o. **be'vorstehend** *adj* approaching, forthcoming, *pleasures etc:* to come, imminent.

bevorzugen [bə'fo:rtsu:ɡən] *v/t* (h) (*vor dat*) prefer (to), favo(u)r (above), give *s.o.* preferential treatment. **be'vorzugt** *adj* **1.** privileged: *~e Behandlung* preferential treatment. **2.** favo(u)rite. **3.** (most) popular. **Be'vorzugung** *f* (-; -en) preference (*gen* given to).

be'wachen *v/t* (h) guard, watch, *sports:* mark. **Be'wacher** *m* (-s; -) guard, *sports:* marker.

be'wachsen *adj ~ mit* overgrown with. **Be'wachung** *f* (-; -en) **1.** *no pl* guarding (*etc*). **2.** guard(s).

bewaffnen [bə'vafnən] *v/t* (h) arm (*sich* o.s., *a. fig.*). **be'waffnet** *adj* armed (*mit* with). **Be'waffnung** *f* (-; -en) **1.** *no pl* arming. **2.** arms, weapons.

be'wahren *v/t* (h) **1.** keep: *die Fassung ~* keep one's head, keep cool. **2.** (*vor dat* from) keep, preserve; → *Gott*.

bewähren [bə've:rən] *sich ~* (h) prove one's (*or* its) worth, stand the test, *principle:* hold good; *sich ~ als ...* prove to be ...; *sich nicht ~* prove a failure.

bewahrheiten [bə'va:rhaɪtən] *sich ~* (h) **1.** prove (*to be*) true. **2.** come true.

bewährt [bə've:rt] *adj* **1.** well-tried, reliable. **2.** experienced.

Be'wahrung *f* (-; *no pl*) (*vor dat* from) preservation, keeping.

Be'währung *f* (-; -en) **1.** trial, (crucial) test. **2.** 𝕤𝕥𝕥 (release on) probation: *drei Monate Gefängnis auf ~* a suspended sentence of three months; *die Strafe wurde zur ~ ausgesetzt* the defendant was placed on probation.

Be'währungs|frist *f* 𝕤𝕥𝕥 (period of)

probation. **~helfer(in** f) m probation officer. **~probe** f fig. (acid) test.

bewaldet [bə'valdət] adj wooded.

bewältigen [bə'vɛltɪgən] v/t (h) cope with, master, manage. **Be'wältigung** f (-; no pl) coping (gen with), mastering.

bewandert [bə'vandərt] adj (gut) **~ in** (dat) well versed (or well up) in.

Bewandtnis [bə'vantnɪs] f (-; -se) damit **hat es folgende ~** the case is this; das hat s-e eigene **~** thereby hangs a tale.

bewarb [bə'varp] pret of **bewerben**.

bewarf [bə'varf] pret of **bewerfen**.

be'wässern v/t (h) irrigate.

Be'wässerung f (-; -en) irrigation.

bewegen[1] [bə've:gən] (h) **I** v/t **1.** move, ⊛ a. work, set s.th. going: fig. et. ~ move s.th., get things moving. **2.** fig. move, touch: **sage mir, was dich be-wegt!** tell me what's on your mind! **II** sich ~ a. fig. move; **sich nicht von der Stelle ~ (lassen)** not to budge; **~ sich zwischen ... und ...** prices etc range between ... and ...

be'wegen[2] v/t (bewog, bewogen, h) **j-n ~ zu** inf prompt (or get) s.o. to inf; **was hat ihn (nur) dazu bewogen?** what(ever) made him do it?

be'wegend adj fig. moving.

Be'weggrund m (tieferer ~ real) motive.

beweglich [bə've:klɪç] adj **1.** movable (a. holiday), mobile, ⊛, a. fig. flexible: **~e Teile (~es Ziel)** moving parts (target); ⚖ **~e Sachen** movables. **2.** agile.

Be'weglichkeit f (-; no pl) **1.** mobility, flexibility. **2.** agility.

be'wegt adj **1.** rough. **2.** fig. turbulent. **3.** fig. moved, touched. **Be'wegung** f (-; -en) **1.** a) movement, motion (a. phys.), b) move: **k-e ~!** don't move!; **in ~** ⊛ in motion, fig. astir; **in ~ setzen** a. start; **sich in ~ setzen** start to move; fig. **in ~e Sache ~ bringen** get s.th. moving. **2.** (physical) exercise. **3.** pol. etc movement. **4.** emotion.

Be'wegungsfreiheit f (-; no pl) freedom of movement (⊛ motion, fig. action), fig. elbowroom.

be'wegungslos adj and adv motionless.

Be'wegungs|studie f motion study. **~thera,pie** f therapeutic exercises. **⦵unfähig** adj unable to move.

be'weinen v/t (h) mourn, lament.

Beweis [bə'vaɪs] m (-es; -e) (für of) proof, ⚖ a. pl evidence: **zum ~** (gen) in proof of, to prove s.th.; **bis zum ~ des Gegenteils** pending proof to the contrary; **den ~ erbringen** (or liefern) **für** et., et. unter **~ stellen** prove s.th.; **als s-r Zuneigung** as a token of his affection. **Be'weisaufnahme** f (-; no pl) ⚖ hearing of evidence. **be'weisbar** adj provable: **ist es ~?** can it be proved?

be'weisen v/t (bewies, bewiesen, h) **1.** prove (j-m et. s.th. to s.o.). **2.** show.

Be'weis|führung f (-; no pl) argumentation, ⚖ presentation of (the) evidence. **~kraft** f (-; no pl) conclusiveness. **⦵kräftig** adj conclusive. **~lage** f nach der **~** on the evidence. **~last** f die **~ obliegt dem Kläger** the onus (of proof) is on the plaintiff. **~materi,al** n evidence. **~mittel** n (piece of) evidence: **die ~** the evidence (**für** of). **~stück** n (piece of) evidence, in court: exhibit.

be'wenden v/i **es dabei ~ lassen** leave it at that.

be'werben: sich ~ (bewarb, beworben, h) (**um** for) a) apply (**bei** to), b) pol. stand, Am. a. run, a) compete.

Be'werber m (-s; -), **Be'werberin** f (-; -nen) **1.** applicant, candidate. **2.** competitor, sports: a. entrant.

Be'werbung f (-; -en) application (**um** for). **Be'werbungsschreiben** n (letter of) application.

be'werfen v/t (bewarf, beworfen, h) **j-n ~ mit** pelt s.o. with.

bewerkstelligen [bə'vɛrkʃtɛlɪgən] v/t (h) manage.

be'werten v/t (h) **1.** assess, judge, rate: **wird mit 7 Punkten bewertet** the jump etc rates (or scores) 7 points. **2.** ✝ (mit at) value, assess: **zu hoch (niedrig) ~** overrate (underrate).

Be'wertung f (-; -en) assessment, ✝ a. valuation, ped. mark(s), Am. grade(s), sports: point(s), score(s).

bewies [bə'vi:s] pret, **bewiesen** [bə'vi:zən] pp of **beweisen**.

bewilligen [bə'vɪlɪgən] v/t (h) **1.** allow (j-m et. s.o. s.th.). **2.** grant (funds etc), parl. appropriate. **Be'willigung** f (-; -en) **1.** grant(ing), parl. appropriation. **2.** permission.

be'wirken v/t (h) cause, bring s.th. about, give rise to, result in: **das Gegenteil ~** produce the opposite effect.

bewirten [bə'vɪrtən] *v/t* (h) entertain.

be'wirtschaften *v/t* (h) **1.** run (*estate etc*): **bewirtschaftet** *hotel etc*: open (to the public). **2.** ✍ cultivate. **3.** ✚ ration.

Be'wirtschaftung *f* (-; -en) **1.** running. **2.** ✍ cultivation. **3.** ✚ rationing.

Bewirtung [bə'vɪrtʊŋ] *f* (-; -en) **1.** entertainment. **2.** food and service.

bewog [bə'vo:k] *pret*, **bewogen** [bə'vo:gən] *pp of* **bewegen**.

bewohnbar [bə'vo:nba:r] *adj* (in)habitable. **be'wohnen** *v/t* (h) inhabit, live in. **Be'wohner** *m* (-s; -), **Be'wohnerin** *f* (-; -nen) a) occupant, b) tenant, c) inhabitant.

bewölken [bə'vœlkən] *sich* ~ (h) cloud over, get cloudy. **be'wölkt** *adj* cloudy. **Be'wölkung** *f* (-; *no pl*) **1.** clouding over. **2.** clouds. **Be'wölkungsauflockerung** *f* cloud dispersal. **Be'wölkungszunahme** *f* increasing cloudiness.

beworben [bə'vɔrbən] *pp of* **bewerben**.

beworfen [bə'vɔrfən] *pp of* **bewerfen**.

Bewunderer [bə'vʊndərər] *m* (-s; -), **Be'wunderin** *f* (-; -nen) admirer.

be'wundern *v/t* (h) admire (*wegen* for).

be'wundernswert, **be'wundernswürdig** *adj* admirable.

Be'wunderung *f* (-; *no pl*) admiration.

bewußt [bə'vʊst] *adj* **1.** conscious (*gen* of): *sich e-r Sache* ~ *sein* (*werden*) be aware of (realize) s.th. **2.** deliberate. **3.** said. **be'wußtlos** *adj* unconscious: ~ *werden* lose consciousness. **Be'wußtlosigkeit** *f* (-; *no pl*) unconsciousness.

Be'wußtsein *n* (-s) consciousness, *fig.* a. awareness: *bei* (*vollem*) ~ (fully) conscious; *das* ~ *verlieren* lose consciousness; *j-n zum* ~ *bringen* bring s.o. round; *j-m et. zum* ~ *bringen* bring s.th. home to s.o.; *wieder zu(m)* ~ *kommen* come round, regain consciousness; *j-m zum* ~ *kommen* dawn on s.o.; *im* ~ *zu inf* (*or daß*) conscious of ger.

be'wußtseinserweiternd *adj* mind-expanding (*drug*).

be'zahlen *v/t*, *v/i* (h) pay (for): *fig. et. teuer* ~ pay dearly for s.th.; *sich bezahlt machen* pay off. **Be'zahlung** *f* (-; *no pl*) (*gegen* ~ for) payment, pay.

be'zähmen *v/t* (h) restrain (*sich* o.s.).

be'zaubern *v/t* (h) bewitch, enchant, *fig. a.* charm: ~*d* charming, delightful.

be'zeichnen *v/t* (h) **1.** mark. **2.** a) describe (*als* as), call, b) indicate, c) stand for. **be'zeichnend** *adj* (*für* of) typical, characteristic. **be'zeichnenderweise** *adv* typically (enough). **Be'zeichnung** *f* (-; -en) **1.** *no pl* marking. **2.** designation, name, term.

bo'zeugen *v/t* (h) ✚, *a. fig.* testify (to).

bezichtigen [bə'tsɪçtɪgən] *v/t* (h) accuse (*gen* of).

beziehbar [bə'tsi:ba:r] *adj* **1.** ready for occupation. **2.** ✚ obtainable.

be'ziehen (bezog, bezogen, h) **I** *v/t* **1.** put clean sheets on (*bed*), (*neu* ~ re-)cover (*settee etc*). **2.** move into (*a flat etc*). **3. Posten** ~ take up one's post. **4.** a) get, obtain, b) draw (*salary etc*), c) take (*newspaper*). **5. et.** ~ *auf* (*acc*) relate (*or* apply) s.th. to; *er bezog es auf sich* he took it personally. **II** *sich* ~ **6.** *sky*: cloud over. **7.** *sich* ~ *auf* (*acc*) refer to, *matter*: relate to; *sich auf j-n* ~ use s.o.'s name (as a reference). **Be'zieher** *m* (-s; -) **1.** ✚ buyer, customer. **2.** subscriber (*gen* to *a newspaper*).

Be'ziehung *f* (-; -en) (*zu* relation (to), relationship (with), connection (with): *diplomatische* ~*en* diplomatic relations; *gute* ~*en haben* a) have good connections, b) *zu j-m* be on good terms with s.o.; *in dieser* (*jeder*) ~ in this (every) respect; *in gewisser* ~ in a way; *in politischer* ~ politically.

Be'ziehungskiste *f* F *fig.* relationship.

Be'ziehungssatz *m ling.* relative clause.

be'ziehungsvoll *adj* suggestive.

be'ziehungsweise *conj* **1.** or rather. **2.** or ... respectively; *mit dem Auto* ~ *mit der Bahn* by car or train respectively.

Be'ziehungswort *n ling.* antecedent.

beziffern [bə'tsɪfərn] *v/t* (h) **1.** number. **2.** estimate (*auf* acc at): *sich* ~ *auf* (*acc*) amount to.

Bezirk [bə'tsɪrk] *m* (-[e]s; -e) district.

bezog [bə'tso:k] *pret*, **bezogen** [bə'tso:gən] *pp of* **beziehen**.

Bezug [bə'tsu:k] *m* (-[e]s; ⁻e) **1.** cover, (pillow) slip. **2.** *no pl* moving in(to *a flat etc*). **3.** *no pl* a) purchase, b) subscription (*gen* to): *bei* ~ *von* ... on orders of *10 pieces*. **4.** *fig.* reference (*auf acc* to): *in* ♋ *auf* (*acc*) → *bezüglich* II; ~ *nehmen auf* (*acc*) refer to. **5.** *pl* income, salary. **bezüglich** [bə'tsy:klɪç] **I** *adj* ~ *auf* (*acc*) relating to; *ling.* ~*es Fürwort* relative pronoun. **II** *prep (gen)* concerning, with reference to.

Be'zugnahme *f adm.* **unter ~ auf** *(acc)* with reference to.

Be'zugs|bedingungen *pl* terms of sale. **~per͵son** *f j-s ~* person to whom s.o. relates most closely, parent person. **~preis** *m* purchase (*or* subscription) price. **~punkt** *m* reference point. **~quelle** *f* source (of supply).

bezwang [bə'tsvaŋ] *pret of bezwingen.*

bezwecken [bə'tsvɛkən] *v/t* (h) *et.* **~** be aiming at s.th.

be'zweifeln *v/t* (h) doubt, question.

be'zwingen *v/t* (bezwang, bezwungen, h) overcome, conquer, *a. sports*: defeat: **sich ~** restrain o.s. **Be'zwinger** *m* (-s; -) conqueror, *sports*: winner (*gen* over). **Be'zwingung** *f* (-; *no pl*) overcoming, defeat(ing), conquest.

Bibel ['bi:bəl] *f* (-; -en) Bible. **'bibelfest** *adj* well versed in the Scriptures. **'Bibelspruch** *m* verse from the Bible.

Biber ['bi:bər] *m* (-s; -) *zo.* beaver.

Bibliographie [bibliogra'fi:] *f* (-; -n) bibliography. **Bibliothek** [biblio'te:k] *f* (-; -en) library. **Bibliothekar** [bibliote'ka:r] *m* (-s; -e), **Bibliothe'karin** *f* (-; -nen) librarian. **Biblio'thekswissenschaft** *f* library science.

bieder ['bi:dər] *adj* honest, *iro.* simple.

biegen ['bi:gən] (bog, gebogen) **I** *v/t* (h) bend. **II sich ~** (h) bend; → *Lachen.* **III** *v/i* (sn) **nach links (rechts) ~** turn left (right); **um e-e Ecke ~** turn (round) a corner. **'Biegen** *n* (-s) bending: **auf ~ oder Brechen** by hook or by crook.

biegsam ['bi:kza:m] *adj* pliable, flexible, supple. **'Biegsamkeit** *f* (-; *no pl*) pliability, flexibility, suppleness.

'Biegung *f* (-; -en) bend, curve.

Biene ['bi:nə] *f* (-; -n) **1.** *zo.* bee. **2.** F chick.

'Bienen|fleiß *m* assiduity. **~haus** *n* beehouse, apiary. **~königin** *f* queen bee. **~korb** *m* beehive. **~schwarm** *m* swarm of bees. **~staat** *m* colony of bees. **~stich** *m* bee-sting. **~stock** *m* beehive. **~wabe** *f* honeycomb. **~wachs** *n* beeswax. **~zucht** *f* beekeeping. **~züchter** *m* beekeeper.

Bier [bi:r] *n* (-[e]s; -e) beer: **helles ~** lager, *Am.* light beer; **dunkles ~** *etwa* brown ale, *Am.* dark beer; **~ vom Faß**

beer on draught; F **das ist dein ~!** that's your problem!

'Bier|brauerei *f* brewery. **~deckel** *m* beer mat. **~dose** *f* beer can. **~faß** *n* beer barrel. **~flasche** *f* beer bottle. **~garten** *m* beer garden. **~glas** *n* beer glass. **~hefe** *f* brewer's yeast. **~keller** *m* beer tavern. **~krug** *m* beer mug, *Am.* stein. **~stube** *f* beer tavern. **~zelt** *n* beer tent.

Biest [bi:st] *n* (-[e]s; er) *a.* Γ *fig.* beast.

bieten ['bi:tən] (bot, geboten, h) **I** *v/t* **1.** offer (*j-m et.* s.o. s.th.), present (*sight, difficulties, etc*): **das läßt sie sich nicht ~** she won't stand for that; → **Stirn. 2.** **†** bid. **II sich ~** present itself. **'Bieter** *m* (-s; -), **'Bieterin** *f* (-; -nen) **†** bidder.

Bigamie [biga'mi:] *f* (-; -n) bigamy.

bigott [bi'gɔt] *adj contp.* bigoted.

Bikini [bi'ki:ni] *m* (-s; -s) bikini.

Bilanz [bi'lants] *f* (-; -en) a) balance, b) balance sheet: **die ~ ziehen** (*gen* of) strike the balance, *fig. a.* take stock; *fig.* **negative ~** negative record.

Bi'lanzjahr *n* financial year.

Bi'lanzposten *m* balance-sheet item.

Bild [bilt] *n* (-[e]s; -er) a) picture (*a. TV or fig.*), photo, illustration, image (*a. opt., TV*), painting, portrait, b) *fig.* sight, c) *fig.* idea, *rhet.* image, metaphor: **~ der Zerstörung** *etc* scene of destruction *etc*; **im ~e sein** be in the picture, **über** (*acc*) know about; **sich ein ~ machen von** get an idea of, visualize; **du machst dir kein ~!** you have no idea!; **j-n ins ~ setzen** inform s.o., put s.o. in the picture; **ein falsches ~ bekommen** get a wrong impression.

'Bildͺarchiv *n* photographic archives.

'Bildausfall *m TV* picture loss, blackout. **'Bildband** *m* (-[e]s; ~e) illustrated book. **'Bildbericht** *m* photo-report.

'bilden (h) **I** *v/t* **1.** form, shape (*a. fig.*), make up (*sentence*). **2.** create, establish, set up (*committee etc*), form (*government*). **3.** form, develop (*buds*). **4.** *fig.* form, be; → **Ausnahme. 5.** educate, cultivate; → **gebildet. II** *v/i* **6.** broaden the mind. **III sich ~ 7.** form, develop. **8.** educate o.s., improve one's mind.

'bildend *adj* educational, informative: **~e Künste** fine arts.

'Bilder|buch *n* picture book. **~buch...** F *fig.* storybook (*career, landing, etc*). **~gale͵rie** *f* picture gallery. **~rätsel** *n* picture puzzle. **~reich** *adj* richly illustrated (*book*), *fig.* language rich in images. **~schrift** *f* pictographic script. **~sprache** *f* imagery.

'**Bildfläche** *f* TV image area: F *fig.* **auf der ~ erscheinen** turn up; **von der ~ verschwinden** disappear.

'**Bildfunk** *m* radio picture transmission.
'**bildhaft** *adj fig.* graphic.
'**Bildhauer** *m* (-s; -) sculptor.
'**Bildhaue'rei** *f* (-; *no pl*) sculpture.
'**Bildhauerin** *f* (-; -nen) sculptress. '**bildhauern** [-hauərn] *v/i*, *v/t* (h) F sculpt.
'**bild'hübsch** *adj* (very) lovely.
'**bildlich** *adj* **1.** pictorial, graphic. **2.** *ling.* figurative (*expression etc*).
'**Bildnis** *n* (-ses; -se) portrait.
'**Bild|platte** *f* video disc. **~plattenspieler** *m* video disc player. **~quali,tät** *f phot.*, *TV* picture quality. **~redak,teur** *m* picture editor. **~re,gie** *f* camerawork. **~röhre** *f* picture tube. **~schärfe** *f* definition, sharpness.
'**Bildschirm** *m* screen. **~gerät** *n* visual display unit. **~text** *m* view data.
'**bild'schön** *adj* (very) beautiful.
'**Bildstörung** *f* TV image interference.
'**Bildtele,fon** *n* videophone.
'**Bildtonkamera** *f* sound-film camera.
'**Bildung** *f* (-; -en) **1.** a) forming, formation, b) development, c) creation, d) establishment, setting-up (*of committee etc*): **~ des Perfekts** forming (of) the perfect. **2.** *no pl* a) education, culture, b) *ped.*, *univ.* formal education: **et. für s-e ~ tun** improve one's mind. **3.** *no pl* (good) breeding.
'**Bildungs...** educational (*reform etc*). **♀fähig** *adj* educable. **~gang** *m* (course of) education. **~grad** *m* educational level. **~lücke** *f* gap in one's education. **♀po,litisch** *adj* politico-educational. **~urlaub** *m* educational leave. **~weg** *m* education: **der zweite ~** evening classes (*with a view to obtaining university qualification*); **auf dem zweiten ~** through evening classes. **~wesen** *n* (-s; *no pl*) education.

'**Billard** ['bɪljart] *n* (-s; -e) billiards. **~kugel** *f* billiard ball. **~stock** *m* cue.
Billiarde [bɪl'ɪardə] *f* (-; -n) trillion, *Am.* quadrillion.
billig ['bɪlɪç] *adj* **1.** a) cheap, inexpensive, b) low (*price*). **2.** *fig.* cheap, poor (*ad-*

vice etc), lame (*excuse etc*). **3.** fair.
'**Billig...** cut-price, *Am.* cut-rate.
billigen ['bɪlɪgən] *v/t* (h) approve of, sanction, *adm.* approve.
'**Billigkeit** *f* (-; *no pl*) cheapness.
'**Billigung** *f* (-; *no pl*) (*gen* of) approval, sanction.
Billion [bɪ'ljo:n] *f* (-; -en) trillion, *esp. Br.* million million.
bimmeln ['bɪməln] *v/i* (h) ring, tinkle.
Bimsstein ['bɪms-] *m* pumice (stone).
binär [bi'nɛ:r] *adj*, **Bi'när...** binary.
Binde ['bɪndə] *f* (-; -n) **1.** a) armband, bandage, b) sling, c) blindfold, d) F sanitary towel (*Am.* napkin). **2.** F *fig.* **e-n hinter die ~ gießen** hoist one.
'**Binde|gewebe** *n anat.* connective tissue. **~glied** *n* (connecting) link. **~haut** *f anat.* conjunctiva. **~hautentzündung** *f ♣* conjunctivitis. **~mittel** *n* **1.** ⊙ bonding agent. **2.** *gastr.* thickening.
'**binden** (band, gebunden, h) **I** *v/t* **1.** tie (**an** *acc* to), tie (up), make (*bouquet*), tie (*knot etc*). **2.** bind (*book*). **3.** *gastr.* bind, thicken. **4.** ♪ a) tie, b) slur. **5.** ♣ tie up (*funds*), fix (*prices*). **6.** *fenc.*, a. ✗ bind. **7.** *fig.* bind, commit (*s.o.*); → **gebunden** 4. **II** *v/i* **8.** bind. **9.** *gastr.* bind, thicken. **10.** ⊙ *cement etc*: harden, set, *plastic*: bond. **III** **sich ~** *fig.* commit o.s., tie o.s. down. '**bindend** *adj fig.* binding (**für** upon).
'**Bindestrich** *m* hyphen: **mit ~ schreiben** hyphen(ate).
'**Bindewort** *n* (-[e]s; **~**er) conjunction.
'**Bindfaden** *m* string.
'**Bindung** *f* (-; -en) **1.** a) (**an** *acc*) ties (to, with), bond (with), attachment (to), b) (lasting) relationship. **2.** *ski*: binding. **3.** ✈, *phys.* bond(ing). **4.** ♪ ligature.
binnen ['bɪnən] *prep* (*dat or gen*) within: **~ kurzem** before long.
'**Binnen|gewässer** *n* inland water. **~hafen** *m* inland port. **~handel** *m* domestic trade. **~land** *n* interior.
'**binnenländisch** [-lɛndɪʃ] *adj* inland.
'**Binnen|markt** *m* home (*EC*: single) market. **~meer** *n* inland sea. **~schiffahrt** *f* inland navigation. **~verkehr** *m* inland traffic.
Binse ['bɪnzə] *f* (-; -n) ♀ rush: F **in die ~n gehen** go to pot.
'**Binsenweisheit** *f* truism.
Biochemie [bioçe'mi:] *f* biochemistry.

Bio'chemiker(in *f)* *m* biochemist.
bio'chemisch *adj* biochemical.
'Biogas *n* biogas.
Bioge'netik *f* biogenetics.
Biograph [bio'gra:f] *m* (-en; -en),
Bio'graphin *f* (-; -nen) biographer.
Biographie [biogra'fi:] *f* (-; -n) biography. **bio'graphisch** *adj* biographical.
'Bioladen *m* F whole food shop.
Biologe [bio'lo:gə] *m* (-n; -n), **Bio'login**
f (-; -nen) biologist. **Biologie** [biolo'gi:]
f (-; *no pl)* biology. **bio'logisch** *adj* biological.
'Biomasse *f* (-; *no pl)* biomass.
Biophy'sik *f* biophysics.
Biopsie [biɔp'si:] *f* (-; -n) *℞* biopsy.
'Biorhythmus *m* biorhythm.
'Biotechnik *f* bioengineering.
Biotop [bio'to:p] *n* (-s; -e) biotope.
Birke ['bɪrkə] *f* (-; -n) birch(-tree).
'Birnbaum *m* pear-tree. **Birne** ['bɪrnə] *f*
1. ❀ pear. **2. ⚡** bulb. **3.** F noodle.
'birnenförmig *adj* pear-shaped.
bis [bɪs] **I** *prep* **1.** a) till, until, b) by: ~
heute so far, to date; ~ *jetzt* up to now;
~ *jetzt* *(noch)* *nicht* not as yet; ~ *auf*
weiteres for the present, until further
notice; ~ *in die Nacht* into the night; ~
vor einigen Jahren until a few years
ago; ~ *zum Ende* (right) to the end; *(in
der Zeit)* *vom ...* ~ *between ... and*; F ~
dann (morgen)! see you later (tomorrow)! **2.** (up) to, as far as: ~ *hierher* up
to here; ~ *wohin?* how far?; *(von hier)*
~ *London* from here to London. **3.** 7 ~
10 Tage from 7 to 10 days, between 7
and 10 days; ~ *zu 10 Meter hoch* as
high as ten metres; ~ *zu 100 Personen*
as many as 100 persons; ~ *drei zählen*
count up to three. **4.** ~ *auf das letzte
Stück* down to the last bit. **5.** ~ *auf (acc)*
except, but. **II** *conj* till, until.
Bisam ['bi:zam] *m* (-s; -e) **1.** *zo.* musk. **2.**
musquash. **Bisamratte** *f zo.* muskrat.
Bischof ['bɪʃɔf] *m* (-s; ⁀e) bishop.
bischöflich ['bɪʃœflɪç] *adj* episcopal.
'Bischofssitz *m* episcopal see.
bisexuell [bisɛ'ksüɛl] *adj* bisexual.
bis'her *adv* up to now, so far: ~ *(noch)
nicht* not (as) yet; *wie* ~ as before; *die* ~
beste Leistung the best performance
so far. **bisherig** [bɪs'he:rɪç] *adj* a) past,
previous, b) present: *die* ~*en Ergebnisse* results so far.

Biskuit [bɪs'kvi:t] *m* (-[s]; -s, -e) *gastr.*
sponge. **Bis'kuitrolle** *f* Swiss roll.
bis'lang → *bisher.*
biß [bɪs] *pret* of *beißen.*
Biß *m* (Bisses; Bisse) bite.
'bißchen *adj* and *adv* *ein (kleines)* ~ a
(little) bit, a little; *kein* ~ not a bit.
'Bissen *m* (-s; -) **1.** bite, morsel, mouthful. **2.** bite, snack.
'bissig *adj* **1.** vicious: *ein* ~*er Hund* a.
a dog that bites. **2.** *fig.* cutting (*remark*),
snappish (*person*). **'Bißwunde** *f* bite.
Bistum ['bɪstu:m] *n* (-s; ⁀er) bishopric.
Bit [bɪt] *n* (-[s]; -[s]) *computer:* bit.
bitte ['bɪtə] *adv* **1.** please: ~, *gib mir die
Zeitung!* hand me the paper, please!; ~
nicht! please don't!; *(aber)* ~*!* certainly!, go ahead! **2.** ~ *(sehr or schön)!* a)
after "danke": that's all right!, *esp. Am.*
(you are) welcome!, b) *after excuses:*
it's all right!, c) *when offering s.th.:*
there you are!, d) come in, please! **3.**
wie ~*?* (I beg your) pardon?, sorry? **4.**
(na) ~*!* there!, I told you so!
'Bitte *f* (-; -n) a) request, b) entreaty: *auf
j-s* ~ at s.o.'s request; *ich habe e-e* ~ *an
Sie* I have a favo(u)r to ask of you.
bitten ['bɪtən] *v/t*, *v/i* (bat, gebeten, h) a)
ask *(j-n um et.* s.o. for s.th.), request,
beg, b) implore: *um j-s Namen (Erlaubnis)* ~ ask s.o.'s name (permission); *j-n zu sich* ~ ask s.o. to come; *für
j-n* ~ intercede for s.o.; *es wird gebeten, daß ...* it is requested that ...; *darf
ich* ~*?* a) come in, please!, b) may I have
this dance?, c) dinner is served!
bitter ['bɪtər] *adj and adv* bitter: *fig.* *es ist
mein* ~*er Ernst* I mean it!; *er hat es* ~
nötig he badly needs it!; *das ist* ~*!* that's
hard! **bitter'böse** *adj* a) wicked, b) furious. **'Bitterkeit** *f* (-; *no pl)* a. *fig.* bitterness. **'bitterlich** *adv* ~ *weinen* weep
bitterly. **'bittersüß** *adj* bitter-sweet.
'Bittgesuch *n*, **'Bittschrift** *f* petition.
Bittsteller ['bɪt‚ʃtɛlər] *m* (-s; -), **'Bittstellerin** *f* (-; -nen) petitioner.
Biwak ['bi:vak] *n* (-s; -s, -e), **biwakieren**
[biva'ki:rən] *v/i* (h) bivouac.
bizarr [bi'tsar] *adj* bizarre.
Bizeps ['bi:tsɛps] *m* (-[es]; -e) biceps.
blähen ['blɛ:ən] (h) **I** *v/i* cause flatulence,
give you wind. **II** *v/t* (a. *sich* ~) fill out.
'Blähungen *pl* wind, flatulence.
blamabel [bla'ma:bəl] *adj* embarrass-

ing, disgraceful. **Blamage** [bla'ma:ʒə] f (-; -n) disgrace, fiasco.

blamieren [bla'mi:rən] (h) **I** v/t j-n ~ make s.o. look like a fool, w.s. compromise s.o. **II** sich ~ make a fool of o.s., w.s. compromise o.s.

blank [blaŋk] adj **1.** shining, polished, shiny. **2.** naked, bare (a. ⊙). **3.** F broke. **4.** F ~er Unsinn etc sheer nonsense etc.

blanko ['blaŋko] adj ✝ (adv in) blank.

'**Blankoscheck** m blank cheque (Am. check). '**Blankovollmacht** f full discretionary power, fig. carte blanche.

Bläschen ['blɛ:sçən] n (-s; -) **1.** small bubble. **2.** ✻ a) small blister, b) pustule.

Blase ['bla:zə] f (-; -n) **1.** (air) bubble, in glass etc: flaw. **2.** comics: balloon. **3.** a) anat. bladder, b) ✻ blister. **4.** F contp. bunch, lot. '**Blasebalg** m bellows.

blasen ['bla:zən] v/i, v/t (blies, geblasen, h) blow, ♪ a. play.

'**Blasen|entzündung** f, ~ka,tarrh m cystitis. ~leiden n bladder trouble.

Bläser ['blɛ:zər] m (-s; -) ♪ wind player: die ~ the wind (section).

blasiert [bla'zi:rt] adj conceited.

'**Blasinstru,ment** n ♪ wind instrument. '**Blaska,pelle** f brass band.

'**Blasmu,sik** f **1.** music for brass instruments. **2.** (playing of a) brass band.

Blasphemie [blasfe'mi:] f (-; -n) blasphemy.

blaß [blas] adj pale (vor with), fig. colo(u)rless: ~ werden (turn) pale; ~ vor Neid green with envy; → Ahnung.

Blässe ['blɛsə] f (-; no pl) paleness, pallor.

Blatt [blat] n (-[e]s; ⁻er) **1.** ♀ leaf: fig. kein ~ vor den Mund nehmen not to mince matters. **2.** a) leaf, sheet, b) page: ~ vom ~ spielen sight-read; fig. das steht auf e-m anderen ~ that's a different matter altogether; das ~ hat sich gewendet the tide has turned. **3.** (news)paper. **4.** art: a) print, b) drawing, c) engraving. **5.** (playing) card, w.s. a good etc hand. **6.** blade (of saw etc).

Blättchen ['blɛtçən] n (-s; -) **1.** small leaf (etc, → Blatt). **2.** anat., ♀, ✿ lamella. **3.** slip (of paper). **4.** local paper.

Blatter ['blatər] f (-; -n) ✻ pock.
'**Blattern** pl ✻ smallpox.

blättern ['blɛtərn] v/i (h) in e-m Buch etc ~ leaf through a book etc.

'**Blätterteig** m flaky pastry.

'**Blatt|feder** f ⊙ leaf spring. ~gold n gold leaf. ~grün n (-s; no pl) chlorophyll. ~laus f greenfly ~pflanze f green plant. ~sa,lat m green salad.

blau [blau] adj **1.** blue: ~er Fleck bruise; F ~er Brief a) (letter of) dismissal, b) ped. letter of warning; → Auge, Blut. **2.** F tight, sloshed. **Blau** n (-s; -) blue.

'**blauäugig** [-ɔygɪç] adj a. fig. blue-eyed.

'**Blaubeere** f ♀ bilberry, Am. blueberry.

'**blaublütig** [-bly:tɪç] adj blue-blooded.

'**Blaue** n Fahrt ins ~ mystery tour.

Bläue ['blɔyə] f (-; no pl) blue(ness).

bläuen ['blɔyən] v/t (h) dye blue.

'**Blaufuchs** m zo. arctic (✝ blue) fox.

'**blaugrau** adj bluish grey (Am. gray).

'**Blaukraut** n gastr. red cabbage.

bläulich ['blɔylɪç] adj bluish.

'**Blaulicht** n flashing light(s): mit ~ ambulance etc with its lights flashing.

'**blaumachen** v/i (sep, -ge-, h) F stay away (from work), sl. scive.

'**Blaumeise** f zo. blue tit. '**Blaupause** f blueprint. '**Blausäure** f 🜍 prussic acid. '**Blaustrumpf** m bluestocking.

Blech [blɛç] n (-[e]s; -e) **1.** a) sheet metal, b) metal sheet. **2.** baking tray. **3.** F rubbish. '**Blechbüchse** f, '**Blechdose** f tin, (tin) can.

blechen ['blɛçən] v/t, v/i (h) F cough up.

'**blechern** adj **1.** (of) tin. **2.** tinny (sound).

'**Blech|instru,ment** n ♪ brass instrument. ~schaden m mot. bodywork damage. ~schere f plate shears.

blecken ['blɛkən] v/t (h) die Zähne ~ animal: bare its fangs.

Blei [blai] n (-[e]s; no pl) **1.** lead: aus ~ (made of) lead; fig. (schwer) wie ~ leaden. **2.** hunt. shot.

Bleibe ['blaibə] f (-; -n) F place to stay.

bleiben ['blaibən] v/i (blieb, geblieben, sn) **1.** stay (im Bett in bed, zu Hause at home, zum Essen for dinner); wo bleibt er denn nur? what has taken him?; F fig. und wo bleibe ich? and where do I come in?; → Ball¹. **2.** ~ bei stick to (der Wahrheit the truth); → Sache 2. **3.** remain, keep: geschlossen (gesund etc) ~ stay closed (healthy etc); für sich ~ keep to o.s.; das bleibt unter uns! F keep it under your hat!; ~

Sie (**doch**) **sitzen!** don't get up!; **es bleibt dabei!** that's final!; **und dabei bleibt es!** and that's that! **4.** be left (*dat* to), remain. 'bleibend *adj* lasting, permanent. 'bleibenlassen *v/t* (*irr, sep, no* -ge-, h, → *lassen*) **et.** ∼ a) not to do s.th., b) stop (doing) s.th.; **laß das bleiben!** stop it!; **das werde ich schön** ∼**!** I'll do nothing of the kind!

bleich [blaiç] *adj* pale (**vor** with): ∼ **werden** (turn) pale.
bleichen ['blaiçən] *v/t, v/i* (h) bleach.
'**Bleichgesicht** *n* paleface.
'**Bleichmittel** *n* bleach(ing agent).
bleiern ['blaiərn] *adj a. fig.* leaden.
'**Bleifarbe** *f* lead paint. '**bleifrei** *adj* unleaded. '**bleihaltig** [-haltiç] *adj* containing lead, leaded (*petrol*). '**Bleikristall** *n* lead crystal. '**Bleistift** *m* (lead) pencil. '**Bleistiftspitzer** *m* pencil sharpener. '**Bleivergiftung** *f* lead poisoning.
'**Blendautomatik** ['blɛnt-] *f phot.* automatic aperture control.
Blende ['blɛndə] *f* (-; -n) **1.** screen. **2.** *phot.* a) diaphragm, b) aperture, c) f-stop: (**bei**) ∼ **8** at f-8. **3.** facing. '**blenden** (h) **I** *v/t* **1.** *a. fig.* dazzle. **2.** blind. **II** *v/i* **3.** dazzle, be dazzling (*a. fig.*). **4.** *fig.* deceive. '**Blenden** *n* (-s) *mot.* glare. '**blendend** *adj* dazzling, *fig. a.* brilliant: ∼ **aussehen** look great; **sich** ∼ **amüsieren** have a great time.
'**Blendeneinstellung** *f phot.* aperture setting. ∼**skala** *f* aperture ring. ∼**zahl** *f phot.* f-stop.
'**Blender** *m* (-s; -) *fig.* fake.
'**blendfrei** *adj* antiglare.
'**Blendschutzscheibe** *f mot.* antiglare screen. ∼**zaun** *m mot.* antiglare barrier.
'**Blendung** *f* (-; -en) **1.** blinding, *mot. etc* dazzle, glare. **2.** *fig.* deception.
Blick [blɪk] *m* (-[e]s; -e) **1.** (**auf** *acc* at) look, glance: **auf den ersten** ∼ at first sight; **mit einem** ∼ at a glance; **e-n** ∼ **werfen auf** (*acc*) have a look at. **2.** view (**auf** *acc* of): **mit** ∼ **auf** (*acc*) with a view of, overlooking *the lake etc.*
'**blicken** *v/i* (h) look (**auf** *acc* at): **um sich** ∼ look around; **sich** ∼ **lassen** show o.s.; **das läßt tief** ∼**!** that's very revealing!
'**Blickfang** *m* eyecatcher. ∼**feld** *n a. fig.* field of vision. ∼**kontakt** *m* eye contact. ∼**punkt** *m* **1.** *opt.* visual focus: *fig.* **im** ∼ **stehen** be in the centre of interest. **2.**

fig. point of view. ∼**richtung** *f* **1.** line of vision. **2.** *fig.* direction. ∼**winkel** *m* **1.** angle of view. **2.** *fig.* point of view.
blieb [bli:p] *pret of* **bleiben.**
blies [bli:s] *pret of* **blasen.**
blind [blɪnt] **I** *adj* **1.** blind (*a.* △, ☺, *a. fig.* **gegen, für** to, **vor** *dat* with): **auf einem Auge** ∼ blind in one eye; **j-n** ∼ **machen gegen** blind s.o. to; → **Passagier. 2.** cloudy (*mirror*), tarnished (*metal*). **II** *adv fly etc* blind, *fig. trust etc* blindly.
'**Blinddarm** *m* appendix. ∼**entzündung** *f* appendicitis. ∼**operation** *f* appendectomy.
'**Blinde** *m, f* (-[n]; -n) blind man (woman): **die** ∼**n** the blind; **das sieht doch ein** ∼**r!** you can see that with half an eye!
'**Blindenheim** *n* home for the blind. ∼**hund** *m* guide dog, *Am.* seeing-eye dog. ∼**schrift** *f* braille. ∼**stock** *m* white stick, (blind person's) cane.
'**Blindflug** *m* instrument flying.
'**Blindgänger** ['blɪntgɛŋər] *m* (-s; -) **1.** ✗ dud. **2.** F *fig.* dud, washout.
'**Blindheit** *f* (-; *no pl*) blindness.
'**blindlings** ['blɪntlɪŋs] *adv* blindly.
'**Blindschleiche** *f zo.* blindworm.
'**blindschreiben** *v/i* (*irr, sep,* -ge-, h, → *schreiben*) touch-type.
blinken ['blɪŋkən] *v/i* (h) **1.** sparkle. **2.** *a. v/t* (flash a) signal, flash. '**Blinker** *m* (-s; -) **1.** *mot.* indicator. **2.** spoon bait. '**Blinklicht** *n* (-[e]s; -er) *mot.* a) flashing light, b) → **Blinker** 1. '**Blinkzeichen** *n* flashing (*mot.* indicator) signal.
blinzeln ['blɪntsəln] *v/i* (h) blink.
Blitz [blɪts] *m* (-es; -e) **1.** a) lightning, b) flash of (lightning): **vom** ∼ **getroffen** struck by lightning; *fig.* **ein** ∼ **aus heiterem Himmel** a bolt from the blue; **wie vom** ∼ **getroffen** thunderstruck; **wie der** ∼ → **blitzschnell II. 2.** *phot.* flash. '**Blitzableiter** *m* lightning conductor. '**blitzartig** → **blitzschnell.**
'**Blitzaufnahme** *f phot.* flash shot.
'**Blitzbesuch** *m* lightning visit.
'**Blitzbirne** *f phot.* flashbulb.
'**blitzblank** *adj and adv* sparkling clean.
blitzen ['blɪtsən] **I** *v/i* (h) **1.** **es hat geblitzt** there was (a flash of) lightning. **2.** flash, *fig. a.* sparkle. **II** *v/t* **3.** *phot.* F flash. '**Blitzgerät** *n* (electronic) flash (gun). '**Blitzlampe** *f phot.* flashbulb. '**Blitzlicht** *n phot.* flashlight: **mit** ∼ **foto-**

grafieren (use a) flash. 'blitzsauber *adj* F (as) clean as a whistle. 'Blitzschlag *m* lightning. 'blitzschnell I *adj* lightning ... II *adv* with lightning speed, like a flash. 'Blitzstart *m* lightning start. 'Blitzwürfel *m phot.* flashcube.

Block [blɔk] *m* (-[e]s; ⸗e) **1.** block (*a.* of stamps, houses, *etc*), (writing) pad, book (of tickets). **2.** boulder. **3.** ⚥, *parl., pol.* bloc.

Blockade [blɔ'ka:də] *f* (-; -n) **1.** blockade. **2.** ⚓ block(ing).

'Blockbuchstabe *m* block letter.

'Blockflöte *f* recorder.

'blockfrei *adj pol.* nonaligned.

'Blockhaus *n* log cabin.

blockieren [blɔ'ki:rən] *v/t* (h) block, (*a. v/i* wheels) lock, ⚙ jam.

'Blockschoko,lade *f* cooking chocolate.

'Blockschrift *f* block letters.

'Blockstaat *m pol.* aligned state.

blöd [blø:t] *adj* **1.** ⚕ imbecile. **2.** F stupid, silly. **Blödel...** ['blø:dəl] slapstick (*show etc*). 'blödeln *v/i* (h) fool around. 'Blödheit *f* (-; -en) **1.** *no pl* ⚕ imbecility. **2.** F stupidity, silliness. 'Blödmann *m* (-[e]s; ⸗er) F idiot, silly ass. 'Blödsinn *m* (-s; *no pl*) **1.** ⚕ imbecility. **2.** F nonsense, rubbish. 'blödsinnig *adj* idiotic.

blöken ['blø:kən] *v/i* (h) *sheep:* bleat, *cow:* low.

blond [blɔnt] *adj* blond(e), fair(-haired). blondieren [blɔn'di:rən] *v/t* (h) dye *one's hair* blond. **Blon'dine** *f* (-; -n) blonde.

bloß [blo:s] I *adj* **1.** bare, naked: **mit ⸗en Füßen** barefoot(ed); **mit ⸗en Händen** with one's bare hands; **mit dem ⸗en Auge** with the naked eye. **2.** mere: *der ⸗e Gedanke* the mere thought. II *adv* **3.** only, simply, merely: **komm ⸗ nicht rein!** don't you dare come in!

Blöße ['blø:sə] *f* (-; -n) **1.** bareness, nakedness. **2.** *sports or fig.* opening: *sich e-e ⸗ geben* leave o.s. wide open.

'bloßlegen *v/t* (*sep*, -ge-, h) lay bare, expose (*a. fig.*). 'bloßstellen *v/t* (*sep*, -ge-, h) expose, show *s.o.* up.

'Bloßstellung *f* (-; -en) exposure.

Blouson [blu'zõ:] *m, n* (-s; -s) blouson.

Bluff [blʊf] *m* (-s; -s). 'bluffen *v/i, v/t* (h) *contp.* bluff.

blühen ['bly:ən] *v/i* (h) blossom (*a. fig.*), be in bloom, *fig.* thrive: F **wer weiß, was uns noch blüht!** who knows

what's in store for us!

'blühend *adj* **1.** flowering, blooming. **2.** *fig.* flourishing, glowing (*health*), lively (*imagination*): **⸗ aussehen** look the picture of health.

Blume ['blu:mə] *f* (-; -n) **1.** flower: *j-m et. durch die ⸗ sagen* hint to s.o. that. **2.** bouquet (*of wine*), head, froth (*on beer*).

'Blumen|beet *n* flower bed. **⸗erde** *f* garden mo(u)ld. **⸗händler(in** *f***)** *m* florist. **⸗kohl** *m* cauliflower. **⸗laden** *m* flower shop. **⸗muster** *n* floral design. **⸗strauß** *m* bunch of flowers, bouquet. **⸗topf** *m* flowerpot. **⸗zwiebel** *f* flower bulb.

blumig *adj* **1.** *fig.* flowery. **2.** *wine:* with a fine bouquet.

Bluse ['blu:zə] *f* (-; -n) blouse.

Blut [blu:t] *n* (-[e]s; *no pl*) blood: *sie kann kein ⸗ sehen* she can't stand the sight of blood; **⸗ spenden** donate (*or* give) blood; *fig.* **blaues** (*junges*) **⸗** blue (young) blood; *ruhig ⸗!* take it easy!; *j-n bis aufs ⸗ reizen* drive s.o. wild; F *⸗ (und Wasser) schwitzen* sweat blood; *⸗ vergießen* shed blood; *böses ⸗ machen* breed bad blood; *die Musik liegt ihm im ⸗* music is in his blood.

'Blut|alko,hol(gehalt) *m* blood alcohol. ⚥**arm** *adj* an(a)emic. **⸗armut** *f* an(a)emia. **⸗bad** *n fig.* massacre. **⸗bank** *f* (-; -en) ⚕ blood bank. **⸗bild** *n* ⚕ blood count. **⸗blase** *f* blood blister.

'Blutdruck *m* (-[e]s; *no pl*) blood pressure: *(j-s ⸗ messen* take s.o.'s) blood pressure.

'blutdrucksenkend *adj* hypotensive. 'blutdürstig [-dʏrstɪç] *adj* bloodthirsty.

Blüte ['bly:tə] *f* (-; -n) **1.** blossom, flower. **2.** *no pl* flowering time, blossom: *in voller ⸗* in (full) bloom. **3.** *no pl fig.* heyday, ⚥ time of prosperity: *in höchster ⸗ stehen* be flourishing; *in der ⸗ s-r Jahre* in his prime. **4.** *fig.* flower, élite. **5.** F dud, counterfeit money.

'Blutegel *m zo.* leech.

bluten ['blu:tən] *v/i* (h) bleed (*aus* from): F *fig. schwer ⸗ müssen* have to pay through the nose.

'Blüten|honig *m* honey made from blossoms and flowers. **⸗knospe** *f* (flower) bud. **⸗lese** *f fig.* anthology. **⸗staub** *m* pollen. ⚥**weiß** *adj* snow-white.

'Bluter *m* (-s; -) ⚕ h(a)emophiliac.

'Blut|erguß *m* ⚕ h(a)ematoma, bruise.

~**farbstoff** *m* h(a)emoglobin. ~**fleck** *m* bloodstain. ~**gefäß** *n* ✻ blood vessel. ~**gerinnsel** *n* ✻ blood clot. ~**gruppe** *f* blood group. ~**hochdruck** *m* ✻ high blood pressure. ~**hund** *m* bloodhound.
'**blutig** *adj* **1.** a) bloody (*a. fig.*), b) bloodstained: *fig.* ~**er Anfänger** rank beginner. **2.** *gastr.* rare (*steak*).
'**blutjung** *adj* very young.
'**Blut|kon,serve** *f* unit of stored blood. ~**körperchen** *n* blood corpuscle. ~**kreislauf** *m* (blood) circulation. ~**lache** *f* pool of blood. ⚥**leer** *adj a. fig.* bloodless. ~**o,range** *f* blood orange. ~**plasma** *n* blood plasma. ~**probe** *f* **1.** blood (🚗 alcohol) test. **2.** ✻ blood sample. ~**rache** *f* vendetta.
'**blutrot** *adj* (dark) crimson.
'**blutrünstig** ['blu:trʏnstɪç] *adj fig.* gory: ~**er Film** *etc* blood-curdling film *etc*.
'**Blutsauger** *m a. fig.* bloodsucker.
'**Blutschande** *f* incest. **blutschände-risch** ['blu:tʃɛndərɪʃ] *adj* incestuous.
'**Blutsenkung** *f* ✻ blood sedimentation.
'**Blutspender(in** *f*) *m* blood donor.
'**blutstillend** *adj* (*a.* ~**es Mittel**) styptic.
'**Blutstropfen** *m* drop of blood.
'**Blutsturz** *m* ✻ h(a)emorrhage.
'**blutsverwandt** *adj* related by blood (*mit* to). '**Blutsverwandte** *m, f* (-n; -n) blood relation. '**Blutsverwandtschaft** *f* consanguinity.
'**Bluttransfusi,on** *f* blood transfusion.
'**bluttriefend** *adj* dripping with blood.
'**blutüberströmt** *adj* covered with blood.
'**Blutübertragung** *f* blood transfusion.
'**Blutung** *f* (-; -en) bleeding, h(a)emorrhage.
'**blutunterlaufen** *adj* bloodshot.
'**Blut|vergießen** *n* (-s; *no pl*) bloodshed. ~**vergiftung** *f* blood poisoning. ~**verlust** *m* loss of blood. ~**wäsche** *f* ✻ (h(a)emo)dialysis. ~**wurst** *f gastr.* black pudding. ~**zucker(spiegel)** *m* ✻ blood sugar (level). ~**zufuhr** *f* blood supply.
Bö [bø:] *f* (-; -en) gust, squall.
Bob [bɔp] *m* (-s; -s) *sports:* bob(sleigh).
'**Bobbahn** *f* bob(sleigh) run.
Bock [bɔk] *m* (-[e]s; ⸚e) **1.** *zo.* a) buck, b) ram, c) he-goat: *fig.* **e-n ~ schießen** make a blunder; *den* ~ *zum Gärtner machen* set the fox to keep the geese; → *null*. **2.** ⊙ a) stand, b) jack. **3.** *gym.* buck. **4.** bock (beer).

'**bockbeinig** [-baɪnɪç] *adj* F stubborn.
'**Bockbier** *n* bock (beer).
'**bocken** *v/i* (h) **1.** *a. mot.* buck. **2.** be stubborn, sulk. '**bockig** *adj* stubborn.
'**Bockshorn** *n j-n ins* ~ *jagen* scare s.o.
'**Bockspringen** *n* (-s) leapfrog.
Boden ['bo:dən] *m* (-s; ⸚) **1.** ground, ✧ soil, bottom (*of a vessel, the sea*): floor: *am* ~, *auf dem* ~ on the ground (*or* floor); *sports:* **am** ~ **sein** be down; *zu* ~ *fallen* fall to the ground; F *fig.* **er war** (*völlig*) **am** ~ **zerstört** he was absolutely shattered; *auf britischem* ~ on British soil; *den* ~ *unter den Füßen verlieren a. fig.* get out of one's depth; (*an*) ~ *gewinnen* (*verlieren*) gain (lose) ground; *aus dem* ~ *schießen* mushroom (up); *et. aus dem* ~ *stampfen* conjure s.th. up. **2.** attic.
'**Boden|abstand** *m mot.* ground clearance. ~**belag** *m* floor covering. ~**fläche** *f* **1.** ✓ acreage. **2.** △ floor space. ~**frost** *m* ground frost. ~**haftung** *f mot.* road holding.
'**bodenlos** *adj* **1.** bottomless. **2.** F *fig.* incredible, shocking.
'**Boden|nebel** *m* ground fog. ~**perso,nal** *n* ✈ ground crew. ~**radar** *n* ground-based radar. ~**re,form** *f* land reform. ~**satz** *m* **1.** sediment. **2.** *fig. contp.* dregs. ~**schätze** *pl* mineral resources.
'**bodenständig** *adj* native, local.
'**Boden|stati,on** *f* earth (*or* tracking) station. ~**stewardeß** *f* ground hostess. ~**streitkräfte** *pl* ground forces. ~**turnen** *n* floor exercises.
bog [bo:k] *pret of* **biegen**.
Bogen ['bo:gən] *m* (-s; -/⸚) **1.** bow: *fig.* **den** ~ **überspannen** overdo it. **2.** curve, bend: *fig.* **e-n großen** ~ **um j-n machen** give s.o. a wide berth. **3.** ∡, ⚕ arc, △ arch, vault, ⊙ bend. **4.** *skating:* curve, *skiing:* turn. **5.** sheet (*of paper*).
'**Bogenfenster** *n* arched window.
'**bogenförmig** *adj* arched.
'**Bogen|gang** *m* arcade. ~**lampe** *f* arc lamp. ~**schießen** *n* archery. ~**schütze** *m* archer.
Bohemien [boe'mjɛ̃:] *m* (-s; -s) bohemian.
Bohle ['bo:lə] *f* (-; -n) plank.
Böhme ['bø:mə] *m* (-n; -n), '**Böhmin** *f* (-; -nen) Bohemian. '**böhmisch** *adj* Bohe-

mian: *das sind für mich* ~*e Dörfer*
that's (all) Greek to me.
Bohne ['boːnə] *f* (-; -n) &a) bean, b)
broad bean: *grüne* ~ French (*or*
string) beans; *weiße* ~*n* haricot beans;
F *nicht die* ~*!* not a bit!
'**Bohnenkaffee** *m* (F real) coffee.
'**Bohnenstange** *f* beanpole (*a.* F *person*).
'**Bohnenstroh** *n* F *dumm wie* ~ as thick
as two short planks.
Bohner ['boːnər] *m* (-s; -) floor polisher.
'**bohnern** *v/t* (h) polish.
'**Bohnerwachs** *n* floor polish.
bohren ['boːrən] (h) **I** *v/t* **1.** ⚙ a) drill, b)
bore. **II** *v/i* **2.** drill (*nach* for), bore: →
Nase. **3.** *fig. pain etc*: gnaw (*in dat* at).
4. *fig.* a) probe, b) keep at it (*bis* until).
III *sich* ~ *in* (*acc*) bore into.
'**bohrend** *adj fig.* gnawing (*pain etc*),
piercing (*look*), probing (*questions*).
'**Bohrer** *m* (-s; -) drill.
'**Bohrinsel** *f* oil rig. '**Bohrloch** *n* drill
hole. '**Bohrma,schine** *f* drill(ing machine). '**Bohrmeißel** *m*, '**Bohrstahl** *m*
boring tool. '**Bohrturm** *m* derrick.
'**Bohrung** *f* (-; -en) **1.** drilling. **2.** (drill)
hole. **3.** *mot.* bore.
'**Bohrversuch** *m* trial drilling.
böig ['bøːɪç] *adj* gusty, ✈ bumpy.
Boiler ['bɔylər] *m* (-s; -) water heater, ⚙
boiler.
Boje ['boːjə] *f* (-; -n) buoy.
Bollwerk ['bɔlvɛrk] *n a. fig.* bulwark.
Bolschewismus [bɔlʃə'vɪsmʊs] *m* (-; *no
pl*) Bolshevism. **Bolsche'wist** [-'vɪst] *m*
(-en; -en), **Bolsche'wistin** *f* (-; -nen),
bolsche'wistisch *adj* Bolshevist.
Bolzen ['bɔltsən] *m* (-s; -) ⚙ bolt.
bombardieren [bɔmbar'diːrən] *v/t* (h)
bomb, *a. phys. or fig.* bombard.
bombastisch [bɔm'bastɪʃ] *adj* bombastic.
Bombe ['bɔmbə] *f* (-; -n) **1.** bomb: →
einschlagen 6. **2.** F *soccer*: rocket.
'**Bomben|a,larm** *m* bomb alert. ~**an-**
griff *m* bomb attack. ~**anschlag** *m* **1.**
bomb attack. **2.** → ~**atten,tat** *n* bomb
attempt (*auf j-n* on s.o.'s life). ~**besetz-**
zung *f* F thea. *all-star cast.* ~**drohung** *f*
bomb threat. ~**erfolg** *m* F huge success,
smash hit. 2**fest** *adj* bombproof: F ~
überzeugt dead sure. ~**gehalt** *n* F fantastic salary. ~**geschäft** *n* F roaring
business. ~**sache** *f* F knockout. 2**si-**

cher *adj* **1.** bombproof. **2.** F sure-fire:
es ist e-e ~*e Sache* it's a dead cert.
~**stimmung** *f* F *es herrschte e-e* ~ eve-
rybody was in roaring high spirits.
'**Bomber** *m* (-s; -) bomber (*a.* F *fig.
soccer*). '**bombig** *adj* F great, terrific.
Bon [bɔŋ] *m* (-s; -s) **1.** voucher. **2.** receipt.
Bonbon [bɔŋ'bɔŋ] *m, n* (-s; -s) **1.** sweet,
Am. candy. **2.** F *fig.* bonbon.
Bonmot [bõ'moː] *n* (-s; -s) bon mot.
Bonus ['boːnʊs] *m* (-[ses]; -se) **1.** bonus,
premium. **2.** special dividend.
Bonze ['bɔntsə] *m* (-n; -n) *contp.* bigwig.
Boot [boːt] *n* (-[e]s; -e) boat: ~ *fahren* go
boating; *fig. wir sitzen alle im glei-*
chen ~ we are all in the same boat.
'**Bootsfahrt** *f* boat trip. '**Bootshaus** *n*
boathouse. '**Bootsmann** *m* (-[e]s; -leu-
te) ⚓ boatswain, ⚔ petty officer.
'**Bootsverleih** *m* boat hire.
Bord[1] [bɔrt] *n* (-[e]s; -e) shelf.
Bord[2] *m* (-[e]s; -e) **1.** ✈, ⚓ an ~ on
board, aboard; *an* ~ *gehen* go aboard,
✈ board the plane; *an* ~ *nehmen* take
aboard; *über* ~ *gehen a. fig.* go by the
board; *über* ~ *werfen a. fig.* throw
overboard. **2.** edge. '**Bordbuch** *n* ⚓
logbook. '**Bord,puter** *m* on-board
(*mot. a.* dashboard) computer.
Bordell [bɔr'dɛl] *n* (-s; -e) brothel.
'**Bord|funk** *m* a) ship's radio, b) aircraft
radio (equipment). ~**karte** *f* ✈ boarding pass. ~**me,chaniker** *m* ✈ flight mechanic. ~**radar** *n* airborne radar.
~**stein** *m* kerb(stone), *Am.* curb(stone).
~**verpflegung** *f* in-flight meals.
Borg [bɔrk] *m auf* ~ on credit. **borgen**
['bɔrgən] *v/t* (h) **1.** borrow: *sich et.* ~
borrow s.th. **2.** lend, *Am.* loan.
Borke ['bɔrkə] *f* (-; -n) bark, *a.* 🟤 crust.
borniert [bɔr'niːrt] *adj* narrow-minded.
Börse ['bœrzə] *f* (-; -n) **1.** purse. **2.** † (*an*
[*auf*] *der* ~ on the) stock exchange: *an*
die ~ *gehen firm*: go public.
'**Börsen|bericht** *m* market report.
~**blatt** *n* financial (news)paper. 2**fähig**
adj marketable, listed: ~*e Wertpapiere*
listed securities. ~**geschäft** *n* stock-
-market transaction. ~**krach** *m* F
(stock-exchange) crash. ~**kurs** *m* market price, quotation. ~**makler** *m* stockbroker. ~**no,tierung** *f* quotation.
~**speku,lant** *m* stock-exchange speculator. ~**zettel** *m* stock list.

Borste ['bɔrstə] f (-; -n) bristle.
'**borstig** adj **1.** bristly. **2.** F fig. gruff.
Borte ['bɔrtə] f (-; -n) border, braid.
bösartig ['bøːzˌaːrtic] adj **1.** vicious. **2.** ♣ malignant. '**Bösartigkeit** f (-; no pl) **1.** viciousness. **2.** ♣ malignancy.
Böschung ['bœʃʊŋ] f (-; -en) slope, embankment.
böse ['bøːzə] I adj **1.** bad, evil, wicked: *e-e ~ Sache* a bad business. **2.** vicious, nasty. **3.** naughty, bad. **4.** angry: *j-m (or auf j-n) ~ sein* be angry (F mad) at s.o., be cross with s.o.; *~ werden* get angry; *bist du mir ~, wenn ...?* would you mind terribly if ...? **5.** F ♣ bad, sore: *~ Erkältung* bad cold; *~r Finger* sore finger. II adv **6.** badly (etc): *es sieht ~ aus* things look bad; *ich habe es nicht ~ gemeint* I meant no harm.
'**Böse** I m, f (-n; -n) bad person. II n (-n) evil, harm: *~s im Sinn haben* be up to no good.
'**Bösewicht** m (-[e]s; -er) a. iro. villain.
boshaft ['boːshaft] adj malicious.
'**Bosheit** f (-; -en) **1.** no pl malice: *aus ~* out of spite. **2.** snide remark. **3.** nasty trick.
Boß [bɔs] m (Bosses; Bosse) F boss.
'**böswillig** adj malicious, ♣♣ a. wilful.
'**Böswilligkeit** f (-; no pl) malevolence, ♣♣ wilfulness.
bot [boːt] pret of **bieten**.
Botanik [boˈtaːnik] f (-; no pl) botany.
Bo'taniker m (-s; -) botanist.
bo'tanisch adj botanic(al).
Bote ['boːtə] m (-n; -n) messenger.
'**Botengang** m (e-n ~ machen run an) errand.
Botschaft ['boːtʃaft] f (-; -en) **1.** message (a. fig.), news. **2.** pol. embassy.
'**Botschafter** m (-s; -) ambassador.
'**Botschafterin** f (-; -nen) ambassadress.
Böttcher ['bœtçər] m (-s; -) cooper.
Bottich ['bɔtiç] m (-s; -e) vat, tub.
Bouillon [bʊlˈjɔŋ] f (-; -s) clear soup.
Boulevard [bʊləˈvaːr] m (-s; -s) boulevard. **~presse** f (-; no pl) gutter press. **~zeitung** f tabloid.
Boutique [buˈtiːk] f (-; -n) boutique.
Bowle ['boːlə] f (-; -n) **1.** punch bowl. **2.** gastr. (cold) punch.
Box [bɔks] f (-; -en) **1.** box (for horses). **2.** motor racing: pit. **3.** parking space. **4.** box camera. **5.** → **Lautsprecherbox**.

'**boxen** v/i (h) box, fight. '**Boxen** n (-s) boxing. '**Boxer** m (-s; -) boxer (a. dog). '**Boxhandschuh** m boxing glove. '**Boxkampf** m fight, boxing match. '**Boxring** m ring. '**Boxsport** m boxing.
Boykott [bɔyˈkɔt] m (-[e]s; -s, -e), **boykottieren** [-ˈtiːrən] v/t (h) boycott.
brach [braːx] pret of **brechen**.
Brachialgewalt [braˈxiaːl-] f (mit ~ by) brute force.
Brachland ['braːx-] n fallow (land).
'**brachliegen** v/i (irr, sep, -ge-, h, → liegen) **1.** lie fallow. **2.** fig. go to waste.
brachte ['braxtə] pret of **bringen**.
Brahmane [braˈmaːnə] m (-n; -n), **brah'manisch** adj Brahman.
Branche ['brãːʃə] f (-; -n) **1.** industrial sector, trade. **2.** line (of business). '**Branchen|kenntnis** f knowledge of the trade. **♣üblich** adj usual in the trade. **~verzeichnis** n classified directory.
Brand [brant] m (-[e]s; ♣e) **1.** (in ~ on) fire: *in ~ geraten* catch fire; *in ~ stecken* set fire to; F *e-n ~ haben* be dying of thirst. **2.** ♣ blight, mildew. **3.** ♣ gangrene. **~blase** f blister. **~bombe** f incendiary bomb.
branden ['brandən] v/i (sn) a. fig. surge.
'**Brand|gefahr** f fire hazard. **~geruch** m burnt smell. **~herd** m **1.** source of (the) fire. **2.** fig. trouble spot. **~kata**strophe f fire disaster. **~mal** n (-[e]s; -e) **1.** brand. **2.** fig. stigma.
brandmarken ['brantmarkən] v/t (insep, -ge-, h) brand.
'**Brand|mauer** f fire wall. **~schaden** m fire damage. **~sohle** f insole. **~stelle** f scene of the fire. **~stifter(in** f) m arsonist, incendiary. **~stiftung** f arson.
'**Brandung** f (-; no pl) surf, breakers.
'**Brand|ursache** f cause of the fire. **~wunde** f burn. **~zeichen** n brand.
brannte ['brantə] pret of **brennen**.
'**Branntwein** m spirits.
Brasilianer [braziˈliaːnər] m (-s; -), **Brasili'anerin** f (-; -nen), **brasili'anisch** adj Brazilian. **Brasilien** [braˈziːliən] n (-s) Brazil.
brassen ['brasən] v/t ♣ brace.
'**Bratapfel** m baked apple.
braten ['braːtən] v/t, v/i (briet, gebraten, h) roast, fry: *auf dem Rost ~* grill, broil; *am Spieß ~* barbecue; F *(in der Sonne) ~* roast (in the sun).

'Braten *m* (-s; -) roast, joint: F *fig. den ~ riechen* smell a rat; *fetter ~* fine catch.

'Bratenfett *n* dripping. **'Bratensoße** *f* gravy. **'bratfertig** *adj* oven-ready. **'Bratfett** *n* cooking fat. **'Bratfisch** *m* fried fish. **'Brathering** *m* grilled (and pickled) herring. **'Brathuhn** *n* roaster, broiler. **'Bratkar,toffeln** *pl* fried potatoes. **'Bratofen** *m* oven. **'Bratpfanne** *f* frying-pan. **'Bratröhre** *f* oven.

Bratsche ['braːtʃə] *f* (-; -n) ♪ viola. **'Bratscher** *m* (-s; -), **'Bratscherin** *f* (-; -nen) viola player.

'Bratspieß *m* spit.

'Bratwurst *f* fried (*or* grilled) sausage.

Brauch [braʊx] *m* (-[e]s; ▪e) custom, tradition, practice, ♥ usage. **'brauchbar** *adj* useful, serviceable. **'Brauchbarkeit** *f* (-; *no pl*) usefulness. **'brauchen** (h) I *v/t* **1.** need, require, take: *wie lange wird er ~?* how long will it take him? **2.** → a) *gebrauchen*, b) *verbrauchen*. II *v/aux* need, have to: *du brauchst es nicht zu tun* you needn't (*or* you don't have to) do it; *du brauchst es nur zu sagen!* just say so! **'Brauchtum** *n* (-s; *no pl*) custom(s), tradition.

Braue ['braʊə] *f* (-; -n) (eye)brow.

'brauen *v/t* (h) brew. **'Brauer** *m* (-s; -) brewer. **Braue'rei** *f* (-; -en) brewery.

braun [braʊn] *adj* brown, a. (sun)-tanned: *~ werden* tan, get a tan. **Bräune** ['brɔynə] *f* (-; *no pl*) **1.** brownness. **2.** (sun)tan. **'bräunen** (h) I *v/t* **1.** brown. **2.** tan (*skin*, *person*). II *v/i* (*a. sich ~*) a) get brown, b) tan, get a tan. **'braungebrannt** *adj* tanned.

'Braunkohle *f* brown coal, lignite. **bräunlich** ['brɔynlɪç] *adj* brownish. **'Bräunungs|creme** *f* liquid tan (make-up). **~studio** *n* solarium.

Brause ['braʊzə] *f* (-; -n) **1.** sprinkler, rose. **2.** → *Dusche*. **3.** F pop. **'Brausebad** *n* shower. **'Brauselimo,nade** *f* (fizzy) lemonade, *Am.* lemon soda.

'brausen *v/i* **1.** (h) *wind etc*: roar, *organ etc*: surge. **2.** (sn) F zoom. **3.** (h) (have a) shower.

'Brausepulver *n* sherbet powder.

Braut [braʊt] *f* (-; ▪e) a) bride, b) fiancée, c) F (*my etc*) girl. **Bräutigam** ['brɔytɪɡam] *m* (-s; -e) a) (bride)groom, b) fiancé. **'Brautjungfer** *f* bridesmaid. **'Brautkleid** *n* wedding dress. **'Braut-**

paar *n* a) engaged couple, b) bride and bridegroom. **'Brautschleier** *m* bridal veil.

brav [braːf] *adj* **1.** good, well-behaved: *sei ~!* be good!; *sei (schön) ~ und geh zu Bett!* go to bed like a good boy (*or* girl)! **2.** honest, good, *a. iro.* worthy. **bravo** ['braːvo] *int* well done!, bravo! **'Bravo** *n* (-s; -s), **~ruf** *m* bravo, *pl* cheers.

Bravour [bra'vuːr] *f* (-; *no pl*) **1.** dash: *mit ~* brilliantly. **2.** bravery. **bravou'rös** [bravuˈrøːs] *adj* brilliant. **Bra'vourstück** *n* **1.** brilliant feat. **2.** ♪ bravura.

Brech|durchfall *m* ✻ diarrh(o)ea with vomiting. **~eisen** *n* ⚒ crowbar.

brechen ['brɛçən] (brach, gebrochen) I *v/t* (h) **1.** break (*a. fig. oath, record, resistance, etc*), *fig.* violate (*contract, law*): (*sich*) *den Arm ~* break one's arm; *die Ehe ~* commit adultery. **2.** *phys.* break, refract (*rays*). **3.** F ✻ vomit. II *v/i* **4.** (sn) break (*a. fig. voice etc*). **5.** (sn) *~ aus* (*dat*) burst out of. **6.** (h) *fig. ~ mit* (*dat*) break with (*s.o., a habit, etc*). **7.** (h) F ✻ be sick, vomit. III *sich ~* (h) **8.** *waves*: break, *phys. light etc*: be refracted. **'Brecher** *m* (-s; -) breaker.

'Brech|mittel *n* **1.** ✻ emetic. **2.** F *fig.* **er** (**es**) *ist ein ~ sl.* he (it's) enough to make you want to puke. **~reiz** *m* ✻ nausea. **~stange** *f* ⚒ crowbar.

'Brechung *f* (-; -en) *phys.* refraction.

Brei [braɪ] *m* (-[e]s; -e) a) mush (*a. fig.*), b) porridge, c) mash, d) ☺ pulp: F *j-n zu ~ schlagen* beat s.o. to a pulp; → *Katze*, *Löffel*. **'breiig** *adj* mushy.

breit [braɪt] *adj* broad (*a. fig. accent etc*), *a.* ☺ wide, *fig.* widespread: *die ~e Öffentlichkeit* the public at large; *ein ~es Publikum* a wide public; → *Masse* 4. **'Breitband...** *radio*: wide-band ...

'breitbeinig [-baɪnɪç] *adj and adv* with legs apart.

'Breite *f* (-; -n) width, breadth (*a. fig.*), *astr.*, *geogr.* latitude: F *in die ~ gehen* put on weight.

'Breiten|grad *m* (degree of) latitude: *der 30. ~* the 30th parallel. **~kreis** *m* parallel. **~sport** *m* mass sport(s).

'breitgefächert *adj* wide-ranging.

'breitmachen: sich ~ (*sep, -ge-, h*) F a) spread o.s. out, b) *fig. fear etc*: spread.

'breitschlagen *v/t* (*irr, sep, -ge-, h,* →

schlagen) F **j-n** ~ talk s.o. round, **zu et.** talk s.o. into (doing) s.th.; **sich** ~ **lassen** give in.
breitschult(e)rig ['braɪtʃʊlt(ə)rɪç] *adj* broad-shouldered.
'**Breitseite** f 1. long side (*of table etc*). 2. ♻, ✗, *a. fig.* broadside.
'**breitspurig** *adj* 🚂 broad-gauge.
'**breittreten** *v/t* (*irr, sep*, -ge-, h, → **treten**) F *fig.* enlarge (up)on (*a subject*): **et. überall** ~ talk about s.th. too much.
'**Breitwandfilm** *m* wide-screen film.
Bremsbelag ['brɛms-] *m* brake lining.
Bremse[^1] ['brɛmzə] f (-; -n) *mot.* brake.
'**Bremse**[^2] f (-; -n) *zo.* horsefly.
'**bremsen** (h) **I** *v/t* 1. brake. 2. cushion (*fall*). 3. F *fig.* check, slow down. **II** *v/i* 4. brake, apply the brakes. **III sich** ~ F restrain o.s., **mit et.** cut down on s.th.
'**Brems|flüssigkeit** f brake fluid. ~**kraftverstärker** *m* brake booster. ~**leuchte** f, ~**licht** *n* stop light. ~**pe,dal** *n* brake pedal. ~**scheibe** f brake disc. ~**spur** f skid mark(s). ~**trommel** f brake drum.
'**Bremsung** f (-; -en) 1. braking. 2. *nucl.* retardation.
'**Bremsvorrichtung** f brake mechanism.
'**Bremsweg** *m* braking distance.
brennbar ['brɛnba:r] *adj* combustible.
brennen ['brɛnən] (brannte, gebrannt, h) **I** *v/t* 1. burn. 2. distil(l) (*spirits*), roast (*coffee*). 3. have the light etc on. **II** *v/i* 4. burn, *house etc*: *a.* be on fire: **es brennt!** fire!; F *fig.* **wo brennt's denn?** what's wrong?; **vor Ungeduld** ~ be burning with impatience; F **darauf** ~ **zu** *inf* be dying to *inf*. 5. *wound, nettle*: sting, *pepper etc*: be hot, *light, lamp*: be on. '**brennend** *adj* burning (*a. fig. question etc*): **es interessiert mich** ~ a) I'm terribly interested in it, b) **ob** I'm dying to know it.
'**Brenner** *m* (-s; -) 1. distiller. 2. ⚙ burner. **Brenne'rei** f (-; -en) distillery.
'**Brennessel** f 🌿 (stinging) nettle.
'**Brenn|holz** *n* firewood. ~**materi,al** *n* fuel. ~**ofen** *m* kiln, *metall.* furnace. ~**punkt** *m a. fig.* focal point, focus: *fig.* **in den** ~ **rücken** focus attention on; **im** ~ **des Interesses stehen** be in the focus of attention. ~**spiegel** *m* burning mirror. ~**spiritus** *m* methylated spirit. ~**stab** *m nucl.* fuel rod. ~**stoff** *m* fuel. ~**weite** f *opt.* focal distance.

brenzlig ['brɛntslɪç] *adj* F *fig.* ticklish.
Bresche ['brɛʃə] f (-; -n) breach: **e-e** ~ **schlagen** *a. fig.* clear the way (**für** for); **in die** ~ **springen** step into the breach.
Brett [brɛt] *n* (-[e]s; -er) a) board, b) shelf, c) tray, d) *sports*: springboard: **Schwarzes** ~ notice (*Am.* bulletin) board; F ~**er** skis; F *fig.* **ein** ~ **vor dem Kopf haben** be very dense.
'**Brettspiel** *n* board game.
Brevier [bre'vi:r] *n* (-s; -e) breviary.
Brezel ['bre:tsəl] f (-; -n) pretzel.
Brief [bri:f] *m* (-[e]s; -e) letter (**an** *acc* to). ~**beschwerer** *m* paperweight. ~**bogen** *m* sheet of writing paper. ~**bombe** f letter bomb. ~**freund(in** f) *m* penfriend. ~**geheimnis** *n* privacy of correspondence. ~**kasten** *m* 1. letterbox, *Am.* mailbox: **toter** ~ letter drop. 2. suggestion box, *newspaper*: Question and Answer Column. ~**kastenfirma** f letter-box company. ~**kopf** *m* letterhead. '**brieflich** *adj and adv* in writing, by letter(s).
'**Briefmarke** f (postage) stamp.
'**Briefmarken|album** *n* stamp album. ~**auto,mat** *m* stamp machine. ~**sammler(in** f) *m* stamp collector, philatelist. ~**sammlung** f stamp collection.
'**Brief|öffner** *m* letter opener. ~**pa,pier** *n* notepaper. ~**post** f mail, post, *Am.* first-class mail. ~**tasche** f wallet, *Am. a.* billfold. ~**taube** f *zo.* carrier pigeon. ~**tele,gramm** *n* letter telegram, *Am.* lettergram. ~**träger(in** f) *m* mailman, postman (postwoman). ~**umschlag** *m* envelope. ~**waage** f letter balance. ~**wahl** f postal vote, absentee voting. ~**wechsel** *m* correspondence.
Bries [bri:s] *n* (-es; -e) *gastr.* sweetbread.
briet [bri:t] *pret of* **braten**.
Brigade [bri'ga:də] f (-; -n) brigade.
Brikett [bri'kɛt] *n* (-s; -s) briquette.
brillant [brɪl'jant] *adj* brilliant.
Bril'lant *m* (-en; -en) diamond.
Brille ['brɪlə] f (-; -n) 1. (**e-e** ~ a pair of) glasses (*or* spectacles), F specs. 2. goggles. 3. toilet seat.
'**Brillen|e,tui** *n* spectacle case. ~**fassung** f, ~**gestell** *n* spectacle frame. ~**glas** *n* lens, glass. ~**schlange** f 1. *zo.* spectacled cobra. 2. F foureyes. ~**träger(in** f) *m* ~ **sein** wear glasses.
bringen ['brɪŋən] *v/t* (brachte, gebracht,

h) **1.** bring, get, fetch (*all: j-m et. s.o. s.th.*). **2.** take (*[zu] j-m* to s.o.): *j-n ins Krankenhaus* ~ take s.o. to the hospital; *j-n nach Hause* ~ take (*or* see) s.o. home. **3.** cause, bring (*luck, relief, etc*), bear (*interest*) **4.** *j-n dazu* ~, *daß er et. tut* make s.o. do s.th. **5.** show, present (*film etc*), *thea. a.* film, ♪ play, sing, *newspaper etc*: bring, have, carry (*an article etc*). **6.** do, manage: *es zu et.* ~ make one's mark (*in life*); F *das bringt's!* that's the stuff!; *das bringt's (auch) nicht!* that's no use!; *er bringt es nicht!* a) he just can't do it!, b) he's no good!; → *Leistung* 1, *weit* 6. **7.** *with prep an sich* ~ get hold of; *er brachte es auf 7 Punkte* he managed seven points; *es bis zum Major etc* ~ make it to major *etc*; *mit sich* ~ a) involve, b) require, make it necessary; *ich kann es nicht über mich* (*or* übers Herz) ~, *das zu tun* I can't bring myself to do it; *j-n um et.* ~ rob s.o. of s.th.; *j-n wieder zu sich* ~ bring s.o. round (*or* to); *j-n zum Lachen etc* ~ make s.o. laugh *etc*; → *hinter* I.

brisant [briˈzant] *adj* high-explosive, *fig.* explosive. **Brisanz** [briˈzants] *f* (-; *no pl*) explosive effect, *fig.* explosiveness.

Brise [ˈbriːzə] *f* (-; -n) breeze.

Brite [ˈbriːtə] *m* (-n; -n) British man, Briton, F *Brit: die* ~*n* the British. **'Britin** *f* (-; -nen) British woman. **'britisch** *adj* British: *die* 2*en Inseln* the British Isles.

bröck(e)lig [ˈbrœk(ə)lıç] *adj* crumbly.

bröckeln [ˈbrœkəln] *v/t, v/i* (h) crumble.

Brocken [ˈbrɔkən] *m* (-s; -) **1.** piece, chunk, lump: F *ein* ~ (*von Mann*) a hulk of a man; *fig. ein harter* ~ a toughie. **2.** *pl* scraps (*of German etc*), snatches (*of conversation*).

brodeln [ˈbroːdəln] *v/i* (h) bubble, simmer, *fig.* seethe (*vor dat* with).

Brokat [broˈkaːt] *m* (-[e]s; -e) brocade.

Brom [broːm] *n* (-s; *no pl*) bromine.

Brombeere [ˈbrɔmbeːrə] *f* blackberry.

Bromid [broˈmiːt] *n* (-[e]s; -e) bromide.

'Bromsilber *n* bromide of silver.

Bronchial... [brɔnˈçiaːl-] bronchial (*asthma etc*). **Bronchien** [ˈbrɔnçiən] *pl* bronchi. **Bronchitis** [brɔnˈçiːtıs] *f* (-; -tiden [-çiˈtiːdən]) bronchitis.

Bronze [ˈbrõːsə] *f* (-; -n) bronze.

'Bronzeme,daille *f* bronze medal.

'Bronzezeit *f archeol.* Bronze Age.

Brosame [ˈbroːzaːmə] (-; -n) *fig.* crumb.

Brosche [ˈbrɔʃə] *f* (-; -n) brooch.

broschiert [brɔˈʃiːrt] *adj* paperback.

Broschüre [brɔˈʃyːrə] *f* (-; -n) pamphlet.

Brot [broːt] *n* ([e]s; c) bread, loaf: (**belegtes**) ~ sandwich; *fig.* **das tägliche** ~ one's daily bread; *sein* ~ *verdienen* earn a living. **'Brotaufstrich** *m* spread.

Brötchen [ˈbrøːtçən] *n* (-s; -) roll.

'Brötchengeber(in *f) m* F boss.

'Brot|getreide *n* breadgrain. ~**kasten** *m* bread bin, *Am.* breadbox. ~**korb** *m* bread basket: *j-m den* ~ *höher hängen* put s.o. on short commons. ~**krume** *f*, ~**krümel** *m* (bread)crumb.

'brotlos *adj* **1.** jobless. **2.** unprofitable: *das ist e-e* ~*e Kunst!* there is no money in it!

'Brot|messer *n* bread knife. ~**neid** *m* professional jealousy. ~**röster** *m* (-s; -) toaster. ~**schneidema,schine** *f* bread slicer. ~**zeit** *f* (-; -en) *dial.* snack.

brr [br] *int* **1.** whoa! **2.** ugh!

Bruch [brʊx] *m* (-[e]s; ⁀e) **1.** a) breaking, b) breakage: *zu* ~ *gehen* break, be smashed; ~ *machen* crash; *zu* ~ *fahren* smash up (*a car*). **2.** *fig.* breaking-off, rupture, breach (*of oath, peace*), violation (*of a law*): ~ *mit der Vergangenheit* (clean) break with the past; *in die Brüche gehen* break up, *marriage: a.* go on the rocks. **3.** ♯ a) fracture, b) rupture, hernia: *sich e-n* ~ *heben* rupture o.s. **4.** F *contp.* junk. **5.** A fraction.

'Bruchband *n* (-[e]s; ⁀er) ♯ truss.

'Bruchbude *f* F *contp.* hovel, dump (*sl.*).

brüchig [ˈbrʏçıç] *adj* **1.** fragile, brittle. **2.** *fig.* cracked (*voice*), shaky (*marriage*).

'Bruch|landung *f* crash landing. ~**rechnung** *f* fractions. ~**schaden** *m* breakage. 2**sicher** *adj* breakproof. ~**stelle** *f* crack, ♯ point of fracture.

'Bruchstrich *m* A fraction stroke.

'Bruchstück *n* fragment (*a. fig.*), *pl fig. a.* snatches. **'Bruchstückhaft I** *adj* fragmentary. **II** *adv* in fragments.

'Bruch|teil *m* fraction: *im* ~ *e-r Sekunde* in a split second. ~**zahl** *f* fraction.

Brücke [ˈbrʏkə] *f* (-; -n) **1.** bridge (*a.* ⚡, ⚓, ♯, *gym.*): *e-e* ~ *bauen* (*or* schlagen) *über* (*acc*) build a bridge across; *fig. alle* ~*n hinter sich abbrechen* burn one's boats. **2.** rug.

'**Brückenkopf** m bridgehead.
'**Brückenpfeiler** m bridge pier.
Bruder ['bru:dər] m (-s; ⸚) brother (a. eccl., pl brethren), eccl. monk, F guy: F *unter Brüdern* among friends.
'**Bruderkrieg** m fratricidal war. **brüderlich** ['bry:dərlıç] adj brotherly. **Brüderlichkeit** f (-; no pl) brotherliness. '**Brudermord** m, '**Brudermörder(in** f) m fratricide. '**Brüderschaft** f (-; -en) **1.** brotherhood. **2.** (*mit j-m*) ~ *trinken* drink the pledge of close friendship.
Brühe ['bry:ə] f (-; -n) **1.** gastr. stock, broth. **2.** F contp. a) dirty water, b) slop, swill, dishwater. **3.** F sweat.
brühen ['bry:ən] v/t (h) scald.
'**brüh|heiß** adj scalding (hot). ~**warm** adj fig. hot (news etc): *j-n et. ~ wiedererzählen* tell s.th. straightaway to s.o.
'**Brühwürfel** m stock cube.
brüllen ['brʏlən] v/i, v/t (h) roar (a. fig. gun, engine, etc), cow: bellow, low, children: shout, bawl: *vor Lachen etc* ~ roar with laughter etc; F er (es) *ist zum* ⸚! he's (it's) a scream!
Brummbär ['brʊm-] m fig. grumbler.
brummen ['brʊmən] v/i (h) **1.** bear etc: growl. **2.** a. ⚡ hum: *mir brummt der Kopf* my head is throbbing. **3.** fig. (*über* acc about) growl, grumble. **4.** F in prison: do time. '**Brummer** m (-s; -) **1.** a) bluebottle, b) bumblebee. **2.** F (*dicker*) ~ → '**Brummi** m (-s; -s) F juggernaut. '**brummig** adj grumpy.
'**Brummkreisel** m humming top.
'**Brummschädel** m F **1.** headache. **2.** hangover.
brünett [bry'nɛt] adj, **Brü'nette** f (-n; -n) brunette.
Brunft [brʊnft] f (-; ⸚e), '**brunften** v/i (h) hunt. rut. '**Brunftzeit** f rutting season.
'**Brunnen** ['brʊnən] m (-s; -) well, spring, fountain (a. fig.), ⚕ (mineral) waters.
'**Brunnenkresse** f ⚕ watercress.
'**Brunnenkur** f mineral-water cure.
'**Brunnenvergiftung** f fig. calumny.
Brunst [brʊnst] f (-; ⸚e) zo. a) rut, b) heat, c) rutting season. **brünstig** ['brʏnstıç] adj zo. a) rutting, b) in heat.
brüsk [brʏsk] adj brusque.
Brust [brʊst] f (-; ⸚e) **1.** no pl breast, chest: *swimming*: **100 m** ~ 100 metres breaststroke; F fig. *e-n zur ~ nehmen*

have a quick one; *sich j-n zur ~ nehmen* give s.o. hell. **2.** bosom, breasts: (dat) *die ~ geben* breastfeed. **3.** → *Bruststück*. ~**bein** n **1.** anat. breastbone. **2.** wishbone. ~**beutel** m money bag. ~**bild** n head-and-shoulder portrait. ~**drüse** f anat. mammary gland.
brüsten ['brʏstən] *sich* ~ (h) boast (*mit* about).
'**Brust|fell** n anat. pleura. ~**fellentzündung** f ⚕ pleurisy. ~**kasten** m, ~**korb** m rib cage, chest. ~**krebs** m ⚕ breast cancer. ~**schwimmen** n breaststroke. ~**stimme** f ♪ chest voice. ~**stück** n gastr. a) brisket, b) breast. ~**tasche** f breast pocket. ~**ton** m fig. *im ~ der Überzeugung* with deep conviction.
'**Brüstung** f (-; -en) **1.** parapet. **2.** balustrade.
'**Brustwarze** f nipple.
'**Brustweite** f chest measurement, bust.
Brut [bru:t] f (-; -en) **1.** no pl brooding. **2.** a) brood, b) spawn. **3.** no pl F fig. a) (*children*) brood, b) scum.
brutal [bru'ta:l] adj brutal. **Brutalität** [brutali'tɛ:t] f (-; -en) brutality.
'**Brutappa,rat** m incubator.
brüten ['bry:tən] (h) **I** v/i brood (fig. *über* dat over), hatch, hen: sit: *die Hitze* sweltering heat. **II** v/t → **Rache**.
'**Brüter** m (-s; -) → *Brutreaktor:* phys. *schneller* ~ fast breeder (reactor).
'**Bruthenne** f sitting hen. '**Brutkasten** m incubator. '**Brutplatz** m zo. breeding ground. '**Brutre,aktor** m phys. breeder reactor. '**Brutstätte** f fig. hotbed.
brutto ['brʊto] adj, '**Brutto...** gross (income, weight, register ton, etc).
'**Bruttosozi,alpro,dukt** m gross national product.
Bub [bu:p] m (-en; -en) dial. boy. **Bube** ['bu:bə] m (-n; -n) cards: jack. **Bubi** ['bu:bi] m (-s; -s) F contp. pipsqueak.
Buch [bu:x] n (-[e]s; ⸚er) **1.** book (a. ✝): ~ *führen* keep accounts, do the bookkeeping; ~ *führen über* (acc) keep a record of; *fig. wie er* (es) *im ~e steht* typical. **2.** film: script. '**Buchbesprechung** f book review. '**Buchbinder** m (-s; -) bookbinder. '**Buchdruck** m (-[e]s; no pl) printing. '**Buchdrucker** m printer. '**Buchdruckerei** f (-; -en) **1.** printing plant, press. **2.** no pl printing.
Buche ['bu:xə] f (-; -n) beech (tree).

buchen ['bu:xən] *v/t* (h) **1.** book, reserve (*room, flight, etc*). **2.** ✝ fig: *fig.* als Erfolg ~ put s.th. down as a success.
Bücherei [by:çə'raɪ] *f* (-; -en) library.
'**Bücher|freund(in** *f*) *m* book lover. ~**gutschein** *m* book token. ~**narr** *m* bibliomaniac. ~**re,gal** *n* bookshelf. ~**revisi,on** *f* ✝ audit. ~**schrank** *m* bookcase. ~**ständer** *m* bookstand. ~**stütze** *f* bookend. ~**wand** *f* wall of bookshelves. ~**weisheit** *f* book knowledge. ~**wurm** *m* humor. bookworm.
'**Buchfink** *m* zo. chaffinch.
'**Buchforderungen** *pl* ✝ book claims.
'**Buchführung** *f* (-; *no pl*) ✝ bookkeeping, accountancy: doppelte ~ double-entry bookkeeping. '**Buchgemeinschaft** *f* book club. '**Buchhaltung** *f* (-; -en) **1.** accounts department. **2.** *no pl* → **Buchführung**. '**Buchhandel** *m* book trade. '**Buchhändler(in** *f*) *m* bookseller. '**Buchhandlung** *f* bookshop, Am. bookstore. '**Buchhülle** *f* jacket, wrapper. '**Buchmacher** *m* (-s; -) bookmaker. '**buchmäßig** *adj and adv* ✝ according to the books. '**Buchmesse** *f* book fair. '**Buchprüfer** *m* auditor, accountant. '**Buchprüfung** *f* audit.
Buchsbaum ['bʊksbaʊm] *m* (-s; *no pl*) ♀ box (tree).
Buchse ['bʊksə] *f* (-; -n) ⊙ bush(ing), liner, ⚡ socket.
Büchse ['bʏksə] *f* (-; -n) **1.** tin, can, box. **2.** gun, rifle.
'**Büchsen|bier** *n* canned beer. ~**fleisch** *n* tinned (*or* canned) meat. ~**milch** *f* tinned (*or* canned) milk. ~**öffner** *m* (-s; -) tin (*or* can) opener.
Buchstabe ['bu:xʃta:bə] *m* (-n; -n) letter: großer (kleiner) ~ capital (small) letter. '**buchstabengetreu** *adj* literal.
buchstabieren [bu:xʃta'bi:rən] *v/t* (h) a) spell, b) spell out: falsch ~ misspell.
Buchsta'bieren *n* (-s) spelling.
buchstäblich ['bu:xʃtɛ:plɪç] *adj* literal.
Bucht [bʊxt] *f* (-; -en) bay, inlet.
'**Buchumschlag** *m* dustjacket.
'**Buchung** *f* (-; -en) **1.** booking, reservation. **2.** ✝ a) booking, b) entry.
'**Buchweizen** *m* ♀ buckwheat.
Buckel ['bʊkəl] *m* (-s; -) **1.** a) hump (*a. fig.*), hunchback, b) stoop: e-n ~ machen stoop, cat: arch its back. **2.** F back. **3.** F hillock. '**buck(e)lig** *adj*

hunchbacked. '**Buck(e)lige** *m, f* (-n; -n) hunchback.
bücken ['bʏkən] sich ~ (h) bend (down) (nach et. to pick up s.th.).
Bückling ['bʏklɪŋ] *m* (-s; -e) **1.** gastr. smoked herring. **2.** Γ bow.
buddeln ['bʊdəln] *v/i, v/t* (h) F dig.
Buddhismus [bʊ'dɪsmʊs] *m* (-; *no pl*) Buddhism. **Buddhist** [bʊ'dɪst] *m* (-en; -en), **bud'dhistisch** *adj* Buddhist.
Bude ['bu:də] *f* (-; -n) **1.** kiosk, stall. **2.** F a) *contp.* hovel, dump, b) place, digs, Am. pad, c) *contp.* joint (*sl.*): Leben in die ~ bringen liven things up.
Budget [by'dʒe:] *n* (-s; -s) budget: et. im ~ vorsehen budget for s.th.
Büfett [by'fe:] *n* (-s; -s) **1.** sideboard. **2.** counter, bar. **3.** gastr. buffet.
Büffel ['bʏfəl] *m* (-s; -) zo. buffalo.
büffeln ['bʏfəln] *v/t, v/i* (h) F swot, cram.
Büffler ['bʏflər] *m* (-s; -), '**Büfflerin** *f* (-; -nen) F swot.
Bug [bu:k] *m* (-[e]s; -e) **1.** ⚓ bow, ✈ nose: *fig.* Schuß vor den ~ warning shot. **2.** zo. shoulder (*a. gastr.*).
Bügel ['by:gəl] *m* (-s; -) **1.** hanger. **2.** stirrup. **3.** ear piece (*of spectacles*). **4.** ⊙ bow, shackle. ~**brett** *n* ironing board. ~**eisen** *n* iron. ~**falte** *f* crease.
'**bügelfrei** *adj* noniron, drip-dry.
bügeln ['by:gəln] *v/t, v/i* (h) iron, press.
'**Bügelpresse** *f* (laundry) press.
Buggy ['bagi] *m* (-s; -s) (*car:* beach) buggy.
Bügler ['by:glər] *m* (-s; -), '**Büglerin** *f* (-; -nen) ironer, presser.
bugsieren [bʊ'ksi:rən] *v/t* **1.** ⚓ tow. **2.** F *fig.* steer.
buh [bu:] *int* boo! **Buh** *n* (-s; -s) F boo.
buhen ['bu:ən] *v/i* (h) F boo.
buhlen ['bu:lən] *v/i* (h) ~ um strive after; um j-s Gunst ~ court s.o.'s favo(u)r.
'**Buhmann** *m* (-[e]s; ⁻er) *fig.* bogey man.
Buhne ['bu:nə] *f* (-; -n) ⊙ groyne.
Bühne ['by:nə] *f* (-; -n) **1.** thea. stage, w.s. theat/re (*Am.* -er): hinter der ~ a. *fig.* backstage; F *fig.* et. über die ~ bringen bring s.th. off; glatt über die ~ gehen go off smoothly; von der politischen etc ~ abtreten quit the political etc scene. **2.** a. ⊙ platform.
'**Bühnen|anweisung** *f* stage direction. ~**arbeiter** *m* stage hand. ~**bearbeitung** *f* stage adaptation. ~**beleuchtung**

f stage lighting. **~bild** *n* (stage) set. **~bildner(in** *f*) *m* stage designer. **~fassung** *f* stage version. **~künstler(in** *f*) *m* stage artist. **~laufbahn** *f* stage career. **~meister** *m* stage manager. **~rechte** *pl* stage rights. **&reif** *adj* ready for the stage. **~stück** *n* (stage) play. **~werk** *n* drama. **~wirksam** *adj* stageworthy.
'**Buhrufe** *pl* boos.
Bukett [bu'kɛt] *n* (-s; -s, -e) bouquet.
Bulette [bu'lɛtə] *f* (-; -n) *gastr.* meatball.
Bulgare [bʊl'gaːrə] *m* (-n; -n) Bulgarian.
Bulgarien [bʊl'gaːriən] *n* (-s) Bulgaria.
Bul'garin *f* (-; -nen), **bul'garisch** *adj* Bulgarian.
'**Bullauge** *n* ↕ porthole.
'**Bulldogge** *f zo.* bulldog.
Bulle¹ ['bʊlə] *m* (-n; -n) **1.** *zo.* bull (*a.* F *contp. man*). **2.** F *contp.* cop, bull: **die ~n** *a.* the fuzz.
'**Bulle²** *f* (-; -n) *eccl.* (papal) bull.
'**Bullenhitze** *f* F scorching heat.
Bulletin [byl'tɛ̃ː] *n* (-s; -s) bulletin.
'**bullig** *adj* **1.** bull-like, hefty. **2.** F scorching (*heat*).
'**Bully** ['bʊli] *n* (-s; -s) **1.** *hockey*: bully. **2.** *icehockey*: face-off.
bum [bʊm] *int* bang!
Bumerang ['buːmərɑŋ] *m* (-s; -e, -s) boomerang.
Bummel ['bʊməl] *m* (-s; -) F stroll. **Bummelant** [bʊmə'lant] *m* (-en; -en), **Bumme'lantin** *f* (-; -nen) → **Bummler(in)** 2.
Bumme'lei *f* (-; *no pl*) F a) dawdling, b) loafing. '**bumm(e)lig** *adj* F dawdling, slow. '**bummeln** *v/i* (h) F **1.** (go for a) stroll: **~ gehen** go for a stroll, *w.s.* go on a binge. **2.** a) dawdle, b) loaf. '**Bummelstreik** *m* go-slow. '**Bummelzug** *m* F slow train. '**Bummler** *m* (-s; -), '**Bummlerin** *f* (-; -nen) F **1.** stroller. **2.** a) dawdler, b) loafer.
bums [bʊms] *int* bang! **Bums** *m* (-es; -e) bang, crash. **bumsen** ['bʊmzən] *v/i* (h) **1.** bang, crash. **2.** V *mit j-m* (*v/t j-n*) **~** bang s.o., screw s.o., have it off with s.o. '**Bumslo,kal** *n* F low dive.
Bund¹ [bʊnt] *n* (-[e]s; -e) bundle, bunch.
Bund² *m* (-[e]s; *·e) **1.** union, bond: **~ der Ehe** bond of marriage. **2.** pact: **im ~e mit** together with, *b.s.* in league with. **3.** *pol.* alliance, *n.s.* federation: **der ~** a) the Federal Government, b) →

Bundesrepublik, c) F → **Bundeswehr**. **4.** association, union.
Bund³ *m* (-[e]s; *·e) waistband.
Bündel ['byndəl] *n* (-s; -) bundle.
'**bündeln** *v/t* (h) bundle up, bunch, *phys.* focus.
'**bündelweise** *adv* in bundles.
'**Bundes...** *pol.* (German) Federal ... **~bahn** *f* Federal Railway(s). **~bank** *f* (; *no pl*) German Central Bank. **~behörde** *f* federal authority. **~bürger(in** *f*) *m* German citizen. **&deutsch** *adj* (German) Federal. **~ebene** *f auf* **~** on a national level. **~gebiet** *n* Federal territory. **~genosse** *m* ally. **~gerichtshof** *m* Federal Supreme Court. **~kabi,nett** *n* (German) federal cabinet. **~kanzler** *m* German (*or* Federal) Chancellor. **~kar,tellamt** *n* Federal Cartel Office. **~krimi,nalamt** *n* Federal Bureau of Criminal Investigation. **~land** *n* (federal) state, land, Land: **die neuen Bundesländer** the newly-formed German states. **~liga** *f sports*: **erste (zweite) ~** First (Second) Division. **~mi,nister(in** *f*) *m* minister (*for a*). **~post** *f* Federal Post Office. **~präsi,dent** *m* German (*or* Federal) President. **~presseamt** *n* Federal Information Agency. **~rat** *m* Bundesrat, Upper House (of the Federal parliament). **~re,gierung** *f* Federal Government. **~repu,blik** *f* **~ Deutschland** Federal Republic of Germany. **~staat** *m* a) federal state, b) (con)federation. **~straße** *f* major road. **~tag** *m* Bundestag, Lower House (of the German parliament). **~tagspräsi,dent(in** *f*) *m* speaker of the Bundestag. **~tagswahl** *f* parliamentary elections. **~trainer(in** *f*) *m* coach of the national team. **~verfassungsgericht** *n* Federal Constitutional Court. **~wehr** *f* (-; *no pl*) (German) armed forces.
'**bundesweit** *adj and adv* nation-wide.
'**bündig** ['byndɪç] *adj* a) concise, b) precise, c) curt: → **kurz** 4.
Bündnis ['byntnɪs] *n* (-ses; -se) alliance.
'**bündnisfrei** *adj pol.* nonaligned.
'**Bündnispartner** *m* ally.
'**Bundweite** *f* waist (size).
Bungalow ['bʊŋgalo] *m* (-s; -s) bungalow.
Bunker ['bʊŋkər] *m* (-s; -) ✗ a) bunker (*a. for coal, a. golf*), b) air-raid shelter.

Bunsenbrenner ['bʊnzən-] m 🜍 Bunsen burner.

bunt [bʊnt] adj **1.** colo(u)rful (a. fig.), (multi)colo(u)red, stained (glass); → **Hund.** **2.** fig. chequered, Am. checkered, motley, mixed, varied: **~er Abend** variety show; F **er treibt es zu ~** he goes too far.

'**Buntdruck** m (-[e]s; -e) **1.** colo(u)r printing. **2.** colo(u)r print. '**Buntstift** m crayon. '**Buntwäsche** f colo(u)reds.

Bürde ['byrdə] f (-; -n) a. fig. burden.

Burg [bʊrk] f (-; -en) castle.

Bürge ['byrgə] m (-n; -n) **1.** 🜲 guarantor (a. fig.), surety. **2.** reference.

'**bürgen** v/i (h) **~ für** 🜲 stand surety for, w.s. guarantee, vouch for.

'**Bürger** m (-s; -), '**Bürgerin** f (-; -nen) a) citizen, b) inhabitant, resident.

'**Bürgerinitia,tive** f civic action group.

'**Bürgerkrieg** m civil war.

'**bürgerlich** adj **1.** middle-class, contp. bourgeois: **~e Küche** home cooking. **2.** untitled. **3.** civil, civic: **~es Gesetzbuch** Civil Code; **~es Recht** civil law; **~rechtlich** civil-law, under civil law.

'**Bürgerliche** m, f (-n; -n) commoner.

'**Bürgermeister** m mayor. '**bürgernah** adj people-oriented, grassroots (politician, politics, etc.). '**Bürgerpflicht** f civic duty. '**Bürgerrecht** n usu. pl civil rights. '**Bürgerrechtler** [-rɛçtlər] m (-s; -), '**Bürgerrechtlerin** f (-; -nen) civil rights activist. '**Bürgerrechtsbewegung** f civil rights movement.

'**Bürgerschaft** f (-; -en) citizens.

'**Bürgersteig** m pavement, Am. sidewalk.

'**Bürgertum** n (-s; no pl) the middle classes.

'**Burgfriede** m fig. truce. '**Burggraben** m moat. '**Burggraf** m burgrave.

'**Bürgschaft** f (-; -en) 🜲 surety, guarantee (a. fig.), bail: **~ leisten, die ~ übernehmen** a) stand surety, b) go (or give) bail, c) **für e-n Wechsel** etc guarantee a bill etc.

Burgunder [bʊr'gʊndər] m (-s; -), **Bur'gunderwein** m burgundy.

burlesk [bʊr'lɛsk] adj burlesque, farcical. **Bur'leske** f (-; -n) burlesque, farce.

Büro [by'ro:] n (-s; -s) the office. **~angestellte** m, f office employee (or worker, clerk). **~arbeit** f office work.

~bedarf m office supplies. **~chef** m head clerk. **~gebäude** n office building. **~klammer** f paper clip.

Bürokrat [byro'kra:t] m (-en; -en) bureaucrat. **Bürokratie** [byrokra'ti:] f (-; -n) **1.** bureaucracy. **2.** › **Bürokratismus.** **büro'kratisch** adj bureaucratic. **Bürokratismus** [byrokra'tɪsmʊs] m (-; no pl) red tape.

Bü'ro|ma,schine f office machine. **~möbel** pl office furniture. **~perso,nal** n office staff. **~schluß** m (-sses; no pl) (office) closing time: **nach ~** after hours. **~stunden** pl office hours.

Bursche ['bʊrʃə] m (-n; -n) **1.** boy, lad. **2.** fellow, F guy: **ein übler ~** a bad egg. **Burschenschaft** f (-; -en) (students') fraternity.

burschikos [bʊrʃi'ko:s] adj pert.

Bürste ['byrstə] f (-; -n) brush (a. ⚡, ⊙).

'**bürsten** v/t (h) brush.

'**Bürstenschnitt** m crew cut.

Bürzel ['byrtsəl] m (-s; -) **1.** zo. rump. **2.** hunt. tail. **3.** F gastr. parson's nose.

Bus [bʊs] m (-ses; -se) F bus, coach: **mit dem ~ fahren** go by bus.

'**Busbahnhof** m bus terminal.

Busch [bʊʃ] m (-es; ⁓e) **1.** a) bush (a. primeval forest), shrub, b) copse, thicket: F **bei j-m auf den ~ klopfen** sound s.o.; **hinterm ~ halten mit** be quiet about; **et. ist im ~!** there's s.th. going on! **2.** bunch.

Büschel ['byʃəl] n (-s; -) **1.** bunch. **2.** tuft, wisp (of hair etc). **3.** cluster (of flowers etc). **4.** phys. pencil, brush.

'**Buschhemd** n jacket shirt.

'**buschig** adj bushy.

'**Buschwindröschen** n wood anemone.

Busen ['bu:zən] m (-s; -) breast(s), bust, bosom (a. fig.).

'**Busenfreund(in** f) m bosom friend.

'**Busfahrer(in** f) m bus driver.

'**Busfahrt** f bus ride, w.s. coach tour.

'**Bushaltestelle** f bus stop. '**Buslinie** f bus route: **die ~ 8** (bus) number 8.

Bussard ['bʊsart] m (-s; -e) zo. buzzard.

Buße ['bu:sə] f (-; -n) **1.** 🜲 penalty, fine. **2.** penance, atonement: **~ tun** → **büßen** ['by:sən] v/t, v/i (h) do penance: **~ für** atone for, fig. pay (or suffer) for; **du sollst du mir ~!** you'll pay for that!

'**Büßer** m (-s; -), '**Büßerin** f (-; -nen) penitent. '**bußfertig** adj penitent.

'**Bußgeld** f fine. **~bescheid** m notice of fine due. **~kata,log** m list of fines.
'**Buß- und** '**Bettag** m Day of Prayer and Repentance.
Büste ['byːstə] f (-; -n) bust.
'**Büstenhalter** m brassière, F bra.
Butan [buˈtaːn] n (-s; no pl) 🎵 butane.
Butt [bʊt] m (-[e]s; -e) flounder.
Bütte ['bʏtə] f (-; -n) tub, vat.
'**Büttenpa,pier** n handmade paper.
'**Büttenrede** f carnival speech.
Butter ['bʊtər] f (-; no pl) butter: F *alles in ~l* everything's okay! **~berg** m F fig. butter mountain. **~blume** f buttercup.

~brot n (slice of) bread and butter: F *für ein ~* a) *get s.th.* for a song, b) *work* for peanuts. **~brotpa,pier** n grease-proof paper. **~creme** f gastr. butter cream. **~dose** f butter dish. **~messer** n butter knife. **~milch** f buttermilk.
buttern ['bʊtərn] (h) **I** v/t **1.** (spread with) butter. **2.** F *Geld in et.* ~ sink money into s.th. **II** v/i **3.** make butter.
'**butterweich** adj a. F fig. very soft.
Butzenscheibe ['bʊtsən-] f bull's-eye (pane).
Byte [baɪt] n (-[s]; -[s]) *computer*: byte.

C

C, c [tseː] n (-; -) a. ♪ C, c.
Café [kaˈfeː] n (-s; -s) café. **Cafeteria** [kafeteˈriːa] f (-; -s) cafeteria.
campen ['kɛmpən] v/i (h) camp.
'**Camper** m (-s; -) camper (a. mot.).
Camping|ausrüstung ['kɛmpɪŋ-] f camping gear. **~bus** m camper. **~führer** m camping guide. **~platz** m camping site, campsite. **~tisch** m folding table.
Cape [keːp] n (-s; -s) cape.
Caravan ['ka(ː)ravan] m (-s; -s) a) estate car, *Am.* station wagon, b) caravan, *Am.* trailer.
Cäsium ['tsɛːzɪʊm] n (-s; no pl) 🎵 c(a)esium.
Catcher ['kɛtʃər] m (-s; -) all-in wrestler.
CB-Funk [tseːˈbeː-] m CB (= citizens' band) radio.
C-Dur ['tseː-] n (-; no pl) ♪ C major.
Cellist [tʃɛˈlɪst] m (-en; -en), **Cel'listin** f (-; -nen) cellist.
Cello ['tʃɛlo] n (-s; -s) cello.
Cellophan [tsɛloˈfaːn] n (-s; no pl) (TM) cellophane.
Celsius ['tsɛlzɪʊs] n undeclined celsius: *20 Grad ~* a. 20 degrees centigrade.
Cembalist [tʃɛmbaˈlɪst] m (-en; -en), **Cemba'listin** f (-; -nen) harpsichord-ist. **Cembalo** ['tʃɛmbalo] n (-s; -s, -li) harpsichord.
Ces [tsɛs] n (-; -) ♪ C flat.

Chalet [ʃaˈleː] n (-s; -s) chalet.
Chamäleon [kaˈmɛːleɔn] n (-s; -s) zo. or fig. chameleon.
Champagner [ʃamˈpanjər] m (-s; -) champagne.
Champignon ['ʃampɪnjɔn] m (-s; -s) (button) mushroom.
Chance ['ʃãːsə] f (-; -n) chance, pl a. prospects: *k-e ~, nicht die geringste ~* not a chance; *bei j-m ~n haben* stand a chance with s.o. '**Chancengleichheit** f equal opportunities.
Chanson [ʃãˈsõː] n (-s; -s) chanson.
Chaos ['kaːɔs] n (-; no pl) chaos.
Chaote [kaˈoːtə] m (-n; -n) F chaotic person, pol. violent anarchist, w.s. yob.
cha'otisch adj chaotic.
Charakter [kaˈraktər] m (-s; -e [-ˈteːrə]) character, nature: *vertraulichen ~s* talks etc of a confidential nature.
Cha'rakter|darsteller(in f) m character actor (actress). **~eigenschaft** f trait. **~fehler** m weakness, flaw.
cha'rakterfest adj of strong character.
charakterisieren [karaktəriˈziːrən] v/t (h) **1.** characterize, mark. **2.** describe (*als* as). **Charakteri'sierung** f (-; -en) **1.** characterization. **2.** description.
Charakteristik [karakteˈrɪstɪk] f (-; -en) **1.** characterization. **2.** ♣, ⊕ character-istic. **charakte'ristisch** adj (*für* of)

characteristic, typical. **cha'rakterlich
I** *adj* of (one's) character, moral. **II** *adv*
in character.

cha'rakterlos *adj* **1.** unprincipled, weak.
2. colo(u)rless. **Cha'rakterlosigkeit** *f*
(-; *no pl*) lack of character.

Cha'rakter|rolle *f thea*. character part.
~schwäche *f* weakness (of character).
~stärke *f* strength (of character). **2voll**
adj full of character. **~zug** *m* trait.

Charge ['ʃarʒə] *f* (-; -n) **1.** *thea*. supporting part. **2.** *metall*. charge.

Charisma ['ça:rɪsma] *n* (-s; -men, -mata)
charisma. **charismatisch** [çarɪs'ma:-tɪʃ] *adj* charismatic.

charmant [ʃar'mant] *adj* charming.

Charme [ʃarm] *m* (-s; *no pl*) (**s-n ~ spielen lassen** turn on the old) charm.

Charta ['karta] *f* (-; -s) *pol*. charter.

Charter ['(t)ʃartər] *m* (-s; -s) charter.
'Charterflug *m* charter flight.
'Chartermaschine *f* charter plane.

chartern ['(t)ʃartərn] *v/t* (h) charter.

Chassis [ʃa'si:] *n* (-; -) chassis.

Chauffeur [ʃɔ'fø:r] *m* (-s; -e) driver,
chauffeur.

Chauvi ['ʃo:vi] *m* (-s; -s) F male chauvinist (pig). **Chauvinismus** [ʃovi'nɪsmʊs] *m* (-; *no pl*) (**männlicher ~** male)
chauvinism. **Chauvi'nist** *m* (-en; -en)
1. chauvinist. **2.** → **Chauvi. chauvi'nistisch** *adj* chauvinistic.

checken ['tʃɛkən] *v/t* (h) check.
'Checkliste *f* check list.

Chef [ʃɛf] *m* (-s; -s) **1.** head, F boss. **2.**
gastr. chef. **'Chefarzt** *m* medical superintendent. **'Chefetage** *f* executive
floor. **'Chefideologe** *m* chief ideologue. **'Chefin** *f* (-; -nen) **1.** → **Chef. 2.**
F *the* boss's wife. **'Chefkonstrukteur**
m chief designer. **'Chefpilot** *m* chief
pilot. **'Chefredakteur(in** *f*) *m* editor in
chief. **'Chefsekretär(in** *f*) *m* executive
(*or* personal) assistant, *Am*. executive
(*or* private) secretary.

Chemie [çe'mi:] *f* (-; *no pl*) chemistry.
Che'miefaser *f* synthetic fibre (*Am*.
fiber). **Che'mieindustrie** *f* chemicals
industry. **Chemikalien** [çemi'ka:liən]
pl chemicals. **Chemiker** ['çe:mikər] *m* (-s;
-), **'Chemikerin** *f* (-; -nen) (analytical)
chemist. **chemisch** ['çe:mɪʃ] *adj* chemical: **~e Reinigung** dry cleaning; **et. ~
reinigen lassen** have s.th. dry-cleaned.

Chemotechniker(in *f*) *m* [çe:mo-]
laboratory technician.

Chicorée ['ʃɪkore] *m* (-s; *no pl*) chicory.

Chiffre ['ʃɪfrə] *f* (-; -n) **1.** cipher, code. **2.**
box number. **'Chiffreanzeige** *f* box--number advertisement.

chiffrieren [ʃɪ'fri:rən] *v/t* (h) (en)code.

Chile ['tʃi:le] *n* (-s) Chile. **Chilene**
[tʃi'le:nə] *m* (-n; -n), **Chi'lenin** *f* (-;
-nen), **chi'lenisch** *adj* Chilean.

China ['çi:na] *n* (-s) China. **Chinese**
[çi'ne:zə] *m* (-n; -n), **Chi'nesin** *f* (-;
-nen), **chi'nesisch** *adj* Chinese.

Chinin [çi'ni:n] *n* (-s; *no pl*) quinine.

Chip [tʃɪp] *m* (-s; -s) **1.** *a. computer*: chip.
2. *pl gastr*. (potato) crisps (*Am*. chips).

Chirurg [çi'rʊrk] *m* (-en; -en) surgeon.
Chirurgie [çirʊr'gi:] *f* (-; *no pl*) surgery.
Chir'urgin *f* (-; -nen) surgeon.
chir'urgisch [-gɪʃ] *adj* surgical.

Chlor [klo:r] *n* (-s; *no pl*) 🜨 chlorine.
'Chlorgas *n* 🜨 chloric gas.

Chlorid [klo'ri:t] *n* (-s; -e) 🜨 chloride.

chlorieren [klo'ri:rən] *v/t* (h) chlorinate.

Chlorophyll [kloro'fyl] *n* (-s; *no pl*) 🌿
chlorophyll.

Cholera ['ko:lera] *f* (-; *no pl*) 🦠 cholera.

cholerisch [ko'le:rɪʃ] *adj* choleric.

Cholesterin [çoleste'ri:n] *n* (-s; *no pl*) 🦠
cholesterol. **Choleste'rinspiegel** *m* 🦠
cholesterol level.

Chor [ko:r] *m* (-[e]s; ⸚e) choir (*a.* 🜨),
chorus (*a. thea.*): *fig. im ~* in chorus.

Choral [ko'ra:l] *m* (-s; ⸚e) 🜨 Choräle) hymn,
chorale.

Choreograph [koreo'gra:f] *m* (-en; -en),
Choreo'graphin *f* (-; -nen) choreographer. **Choreographie** [koreogra'fi:] *f*
(-; -n) choreography.

'Chorgesang *m* choral singing (*or* music). **~gestühl** *n* (choir) stalls. **~knabe**
m choirboy. **~sänger(in** *f*) *m* chorister.

Christ... [krɪst-] → **Weihnachts...**

Christ *m* (-en; -en), **'Christin** *f* (-; -nen)
Christian. **'Christenheit** *f* (-; *no pl*)
Christendom. **'Christentum** *n* (-s; *no
pl*) Christianity. **'Christkind** *n* (-[e]s; *no
pl*) **1.** infant Jesus. **2.** F Father Christmas, Santa Claus. **'christlich** *adj* (*adv*
like a) Christian.

Chrom [kro:m] *n* (-s; *no pl*) chromium.
chromatisch [kro'ma:tɪʃ] *adj* ♪ chromatic.

Chromosom [kromo'zo:m] *n* (-s; -en)
chromosome.

Chronik ['kro:nɪk] *f* (-; -en) chronicle.
chronisch ['kro:nɪʃ] *adj* ✂ chronic.
Chronist [kro'nɪst] *m* (-en; -en), **Chro'nistin** *f* (-; -nen) chronicler.
Chronologie [kronolo'gi:] *f* (-; -n) chronology. **chronologisch** [krono'lo:gɪʃ] *adj* chronological.
circa ['tsɪrka] *adv* about, approximately.
Cis [tsɪs] *n* (-; -) ♪ C sharp.
City ['sɪti] *f* (-; -s) (town) centre, *Am.* downtown.
Clique ['klɪkə] *f* (-; -n) clique, F crowd.
Clou [klu:] *m* (-s; -s) **1.** high spot, climax. **2.** point.
Cockpit ['kɔkpɪt] *n* ✈, ⚓, *mot.* cockpit.
Code [ko:t] *m* (-s; -s) code.
codieren [ko'di:rən] *v/t* (h) (en)code.
Co'dierung *f* (-; -en) (en)coding.
Collage [kɔ'la:ʒə] *f* (-; -n) collage.
Computer [kɔm'pju:tər] *m* (-s; -) computer. **com'putergesteuert** *adj* computer-controlled. **com'putergestützt** *adj* computer-aided. **computerisieren** [kɔmpju:təri'zi:rən] *v/t* (h) computerize. **Com'puterspiel** *n* computer game.
Conférencier [kõferã'sïe:] *m* (-s; -s) compère, *Am.* emcee.

Container [kɔn'te:nər] *m* (-s; -) container. **~schiff** *n* container ship.
Contergankind [kɔntɛr'ga:n-] *n* F thalidomide child.
Couch [kaʊtʃ] *f* (-; -es) couch.
'Couchgarni,tur *f* three-piece suite.
'Couchtisch *m* coffee table.
Coup [ku:] *m* (-s; -s) coup.
Coupé [ku'pe:] *n* (-s; -s) **1.** railway compartment. **2.** coupé (*a. mot.*).
Coupon [ku'põ:] *m* (-s; -s) coupon, counterfoil.
Courage [ku'ra:ʒə] *f* (-; *no pl*) F courage, pluck. **couragiert** [kura'ʒi:rt] *adj* F courageous, plucky.
Cousin [ku'zɛ̃:] *m* (-s; -s) (male) cousin.
Cousine [ku'zi:nə] *f* (-; -n) (female) cousin; → *a.* **Kusine.**
Creme [kre:m] *f* (-; -s) **1.** cream. **2.** *gastr.* crème. **'cremefarben** *adj* cream-colo(u)red. **'Cremetorte** *f* cream gateau. **'cremig** *adj* creamy.
Cup [kap] *m* (-s; -s) *sports*: Cup.
'Cupfi,nale *n* *sports*: Cup Final.
Curry ['kœri; 'kari] *n* (-s; -s) **1.** curry. **2.** curry powder.
Cutter ['katər] *m* (-s; -), **'Cutterin** *f* (-; -nen) *film etc*: cutter.

D

D, d [de:] *n* (-; -) D, d, ♪ D.
da [da:] **I** *adv* **1.** a) there, b) here; *der (die, das) ... ~* that ... (there); *~ und dort* here and there; *er ist ~* he's here, he has arrived; *~ kommt sie* here she comes; *~ liegt die Schwierigkeit* that's the difficulty; *~ (hast du)!* there you are!; *sieh ~!* look at that!; *~ haben wir's!* there (you are)!; *nichts ~!* nothing doing!; → *dasein.* **2.** then, at that time: *~ erst* only then; *hier und ~* now and then. **3.** (*in that case*) there, here: *~ bin ich Ihrer Meinung* I do agree with you there; *was kann man ~ machen?* what's to be done?; *was gibt's denn ~ zu lachen?* what's so funny about it?; *und ~ zögerst du noch?* and you still

hesitate? **II** *conj* as, since, because.
dabei [da'baɪ] **I** *adv* **1.** near, near by, close by: *ein Brief war nicht ~* there was no letter (with it). **2.** *~ sein, et. zu tun* be about to do, be on the point of doing. **3.** at the same time: *sie strickte und hörte Radio ~* while knitting she listened to the radio. **4.** as well, into the bargain. **5.** yet, nevertheless. **6.** on the occasion, as a result: *~ gab es Streit* this led to a quarrel; *alle ~ entstehenden Kosten* all costs incurred; *es kommt nichts ~ heraus* nothing will come of it. **7.** present, there: → *bleiben* 3, *dabeisein*. **8.** *ich dachte mir nichts ~* a) I meant no harm, b) I paid no particular attention to it; *es ist nichts ~!* a)

there's nothing to it!, b) there's no harm in it!; **was ist schon ~?** what of it?; **lassen wir es ~!** let's leave it at that! II *conj* but, (and) yet.

da'beibleiben *v/i* (*irr, sep,* -ge-, sn, → **bleiben**) stay (*or* remain) with it, them *etc*; → *a.* **bleiben** 3.

da'beihaben *v/t* (*irr, sep,* -ge-, h, → **haben**) F have *s.o., s.th.* there: **kein Geld ~** have no money on one.

da'beisein *v/i* (*irr, sep,* -ge-, sn, → **sein**) a) be present, be there, take part, b) be a witness: **ich bin dabei!** count me in!

da'beistehen *v/i* (*irr, sep,* -ge-, h, → **stehen**) stand by (*or* there).

'dableiben *v/i* (*irr, sep,* -ge-, sn, → **bleiben**) remain, stay.

Dach [dax] *n* (-[e]s; ‿er) roof, *mot. a.* top, *fig. a.* shelter: **unter ~ und Fach bringen** a) shelter, b) *fig.* complete; F *fig.* **eins aufs ~ kriegen** get it in the neck.

'Dach|an,tenne *f* roof (*mot.* over-car) aerial (*Am.* antenna). **~balken** *m* roof-tree. **~boden** *m* loft. **~decker** [-dɛkər] *m* (-s; -) roofer. **~fenster** *n* dormer (window). **~first** *m* ridge (of a roof). **~garten** *m* roof garden. **~gepäckhalter** *m mot.* roof rack. **~geschoß** *n* attic stor(e)y, loft. **~gesellschaft** *f* ‡ holding company. **~kammer** *f* attic, garret. **~luke** *f* skylight. **~pappe** *f* roofing (felt). **~rinne** *f* gutter, eaves.

Dachs [daks] *m* (-es; -e) *zo.* badger.

'Dachstuhl *m* roof truss, timbering.

dachte ['daxtə] *pret of* **denken**.

'Dach|ter,rasse *f* roof terrace. **~verband** *m* ‡ umbrella organization. **~wohnung** *f* attic flat. **~ziegel** *m* (roofing) tile.

Dackel ['dakəl] *m* (-s; -) *zo.* dachshund.

dadurch [da'dʊrç] I *adv* **1.** through it (*or* there), that way. **2.** a) by it, b) because of that: **alle ~ verursachten Schäden** all damages caused thereby; **sie verschlief und kam ~ zu spät** she overslept, and so she was late. II *conj* **3. ~, daß es regnete** because of the rain. **4. ~, daß er weniger ißt** by eating less.

dafür [da'fy:r] I *adv* **1.** for it (them, this, *etc*). **2.** in return (for it), instead (of it). **3. ~ sein** be for it, be in favo(u)r of it; **ich bin ~ zu bleiben** I'm for staying; **ich bin sehr ~!** I'm all for it!; *parl.* **die**

Mehrheit ist ~ the ayes have it; → **sprechen** I. **4. ~ wirst du ja bezahlt** that's what you are paid for. II *conj* **5. er wurde ~ bestraft, daß er gelogen hatte** he was punished for lying. **6. ~ sorgen, daß** see to it that. **7.** but (then): **sie arbeiten langsam, ~ aber sorgfältig** they are slow but diligent.

Da'fürhalten *n* (-s) **nach m-m** *etc* ~ in my *etc* opinion, as I *etc* see it.

da'türkönnen *v/t* (*irr, sep,* -ge-, h, → **können**) F **ich kann nicht dafür** it's not my fault, I cannot help it.

dagegen [da'ge:gən] I *adv* **1.** against it (*or* that): **~ hilft Wärme** warmth is good for it; **~ hilft nichts** there is no remedy (for it), *w.s.* it can't be helped; **~ sein** be against it; **ich bin ~, daß du allein gehst** I'm against your(r) going alone; **haben Sie et. ~, wenn ich rauche?** do you mind if I smoke?; **ich habe nichts ~** I don't mind. **2.** by (*or* in) comparison, compared with. **3.** in exchange (for it). II *conj* a) but, however, on the other hand, b) whereas, while.

da'gegenhalten *v/i* (*irr, sep,* -ge-, h, → **halten**) argue (against it). **da'gegensprechen** *v/i* (*irr, sep,* -ge-, h, → **sprechen**) speak against it. **da'gegenstellen: sich ~** (*sep,* -ge-, h) *fig.* oppose it.

daheim [da'haɪm] *adv dial.* a) at home, b) back home. **Da'heim** *n* (-s) home.

daher [da'he:r] I *adv* **1.** from there. **2.** a. **von ~** therefore; **~ kommt es, daß** that's why (*or* how); **~ ihr Mißtrauen** hence her suspicion. II *conj* a. **von ~** that's why, (and) so.

da'hergelaufen *adj* F *contp.* **jeder ~e Kerl** any guy who happens along.

dahin [da'hɪn] I *adv* **1.** there: **auf dem Weg ~** on the way there; **ist es noch weit bis ~?** is it much farther? **2. bis ~** a) until then, till then, b) by then; **bis ~ bin ich fertig** I'll be finished by then. **3.** to the effect: **sich ~ (gehend) einigen, daß** agree that. **4. es ~ bringen, daß** bring matters to the stage where; **j-n ~ bringen, daß** bring s.o. to the point of ger. II *adj* gone, lost.

da'hingestellt *adj* **et. ~ sein lassen** leave it open as to whether; **das bleibt ~** that remains to be seen.

da'hinreden, da'hinsagen *v/t* (*sep,* -ge-, h) say *s.th.* without thinking.

da'hinschleppen: *sich* ~ (*sep*, -ge-, h) **1.** drag o.s. along. **2.** *fig.* drag on.
da'hinsiechen *v/i* (*sep*, -ge-, sn) waste away.
dahinten [da'hɪntən] *adv* back there.
dahinter [da'hɪntər] *adv* behind it *etc*, at the back (of him *etc*): *fig.* **es ist nichts ~** there's nothing behind it.
da'hinterklemmen: *sich* ~ (*sep*, -ge-, h) F buckle down (to it).
da'hinterkommen *v/i* (*irr, sep*, -ge-, sn, → **kommen**) F find out (about it).
da'hinterstecken *v/i* (*sep*, -ge-, h) *fig.* be behind it, be at the bottom of it: *es steckt mehr dahinter* there's more to it than meets the eye.
da'hinvege,tieren *v/i* (*sep*, h) vegetate.
da'hinziehen *v/i* (*irr, sep*, -ge-, sn, → **ziehen**) move (*clouds*: drift) along.
Dahlie ['da:liə] *f* (-; -n) **❀** dahlia.
'dalassen *v/t* (*irr, sep*, -ge-, h, → **lassen**) F leave. **'daliegen** *v/i* (*irr, sep*, -ge-, h, → **liegen**) lie (there).
dalli ['dali] *adv* F ~, ~!, *ein bißchen* ~!, *mach* ~! get a move on!
damalig ['da:ma:lɪç] *adj* then, at that time: *in der* ~*en Zeit* → **damals** ['da:ma:ls] *adv* then, in those days.
Damast [da'mast] *m* (-[e]s; -e) damask.
Dame ['da:mə] *f* (-; -n) **1.** a) lady, b) (dancing) partner: ~ *des Hauses* hostess; *m-e* ~*n und Herren!* ladies and gentlemen! **2.** a) draughts, *Am.* checkers, b) king, c) *chess etc*: queen. ~**brett** *n* draughtboard, *Am.* checkerboard.
'Damen|binde *f* sanitary towel (*Am.* napkin). ~**doppel** *n* tennis: the women's doubles. ~**einzel** *n* tennis: the women's singles. ~**fahrrad** *n* lady's bicycle. ~**fri,seur** *m* ladies' hairdresser.
'damenhaft *adj* ladylike.
'Damen|konfekti,on *f* ladies' ready-made (*Am.* ready-to-wear) clothing. ~**mannschaft** *f* women's team. ~**schneider(in** *f*) *m* dressmaker. ~**toi,lette** *f* ladies' toilet (*Am.* restroom). ~**unterwäsche** *f* ladies' underwear, lingerie. ~**wahl** *f* ladies' choice.
'Damespiel *n* → **Dame** 2 a.
damit [da'mɪt] **I** *adv* with it (*or* them, *emphatic*: that, those), by it: *ich bin ~ fertig* I've finished with it; *was willst du ~?* what do you want it for?; *was soll ich ~?* what am I supposed to do

with it?; *was willst du ~ sagen?* what are you trying to say?; ~ *ist der Fall erledigt* so much for that. **II** *conj* so that: ~ *nichts passiert* lest anything should happen.
dämlich ['dɛ:mlɪç] *adj* F stupid, silly.
Damm [dam] *m* (-[e]s; ~e) **1.** a) bank, b) dike, c) dam, d) embankment, e) roadway: F *fig.* *ich bin nicht auf dem ~* I don't feel well; *sie ist wieder auf dem ~* she's fit again. **2.** *anat.* perineum.
'Dammbruch *m* bursting of a dam.
dämm(e)rig ['dɛm(ə)rɪç] *adj* **1.** *es ist ~* → **dämmern** I a. **2.** faint, dim (*light*).
'Dämmerlicht *n* (-[e]s; *no pl*) twilight.
dämmern ['dɛmərn] (h) **I** *v/impers es dämmert* a) it is getting light (*or* dark), b) F *fig.* (*bei*) *j-m* it's beginning to dawn on s.o. **II** *v/i vor sich hin* ~ doze, be half asleep. **'Dämmerung** *f* (-; -en) a) dawn, b) dusk, twilight: *in der* ~ at dawn, at dusk, at nightfall.
Dämmung ['dɛmʊŋ] *f* (-; -en) insulation.
Dämon ['dɛ:mɔn] *m* (-s; -en) demon.
dämonisch [dɛ'mo:nɪʃ] *adj* demoniac(al).
Dampf [dampf] *m* (-[e]s; ~e) a) steam, b) vapo(u)r, fume: F *fig.* ~ *ablassen* let off steam; ~ *dahinter machen* put on steam; *j-m* ~ *machen* make s.o. get a move on. **'Dampfbad** *n* steam bath. **'Dampfbügeleisen** *n* steam iron.
dampfen ['dampfən] *v/i* (h *or* sn) steam.
dämpfen ['dɛmpfən] *v/t* (h) **1.** *gastr.*, **☉** steam. **2.** deaden, silence, muffle (*sounds*), lower (*one's voice*), mute (*trumpet etc*). **3.** cushion, absorb (*shock*). **4.** soften (*colo[u]r, light*): → **gedämpft. 5.** *fig.* restrain, subdue (*feelings*), put a damper on (*mood*).
Dampfer ['dampfər] *m* (-s; -) steamer.
Dämpfer ['dɛmpfər] *m* (-s; -) damper, ♪ *a.* mute: F *fig.* *e-n* ~ *bekommen* be damp(en)ed; (*dat*) *e-n* ~ *aufsetzen* put a damper on.
'Dampf|heizung *f* steam heating. ~**kessel** *m* steam boiler. ~**kochtopf** *m* pressure cooker. ~**ma,schine** *f* steam engine. ~**schiff** *n* steamship. ~**walze** *f* a. *fig.* steamroller.
Damwild ['dam-] *n zo.* fallow deer.
danach [da'na:x] *adv* **1.** after (that), afterward(s), b) later on: *bald* ~ soon after. **2.** then, next, behind (*or* after)

him *etc.* **3.** according to it, accordingly: F *aber es war auch ~* the meal etc was cheap but it tasted like it, too; *mir ist nicht ~* I don't feel like it. **4.** *~ fragen* ask for it; *sich ~ sehnen zu inf* long to *inf*; *sich ~ erkundigen* inquire about it.

Däne ['dɛːnə] *m* (-n, -n) Dane.

daneben [da'neːbən] *adv* **1.** beside (or next to) it (or them): *im Haus ~* next door. **2.** *a. conj* a) besides, b) at the same time. **3.** beside it (or them *etc*), in comparison. **4.** off the mark: *~!* missed! *~benehmen:* *sich ~* (*irr, sep,* h, → **benehmen**) F behave badly. *~gehen v/i* (*irr, sep,* -ge-, sn, → **gehen**) **1.** *shot etc:* miss. **2.** F misfire, go wrong. *~greifen v/i* (*irr, sep,* -ge-, h, → **greifen**) **1.** ♩ strike a wrong (*fig.* false) note. **2.** miss. **3.** F *fig.* be wide of the mark. *~schießen v/i* (*irr, sep,* -ge-, h, → **schießen**) **1.** miss. **2.** F *fig.* be wide of the mark.

Dänemark ['dɛːnəmark] *n* (-s) Denmark. **Dänin** ['dɛːnɪn] *f* (-; -nen) Dane. **'dänisch** *adj* Danish.

dank [daŋk] *prep* (*gen, dat*) *a. iro.* thanks to. **Dank** *m* (-[e]s; *no pl*) thanks, gratitude, reward: *vielen* (or *herzlichen, besten, schönen*) *~!* many thanks!, thank you very much!; *als ~, zum ~* by way of thanks; *j-m s-n ~ abstatten* express one's thanks to s.o.; *j-m ~ schulden* owe s.o. a debt of gratitude; *das ist der* (*ganze*) *~!* that's gratitude for you!; → **Gott. 'dankbar** *adj* **1.** grateful (*j-m für et.* to s.o. for s.th.), appreciative: *ich wäre Ihnen ~, wenn Sie kämen* I'd be much obliged if you came. **2.** rewarding (*task etc*). **3.** F hard-wearing (*material etc*). **'Dankbarkeit** *f* (-; *no pl*) (*aus ~* out of) gratitude (*für* for).

danken ['daŋkən] (h) **I** *v/i* **1.** thank (*j-m für et.* s.o. for s.th.): *danke* (*schön*)! (many) thanks!, thank you (very much)!; (*nein*) *danke!* no, thank you!; no, thanks!; *nichts zu ~* you are welcome; *wie kann ich Ihnen nur ~?* how can I begin to thank you?; F *na, danke!* thank you for nothing! **2.** decline. **II** *v/t* **3.** *j-m et. ~* reward s.o. for s.th. **4.** → **verdanken.**

'dankenswerter'weise *adv* **1.** kindly. **2.** *fig.* commendably.

'Dankesbrief *m* thank-you letter.

'Dankeschön *n* (-s; *no pl*) thank-you.

'Dankesschuld *f* debt of gratitude.

'Dankesworte *pl* words of thanks.

'Dankgebet *n* thanksgiving (prayer).

'Dankschreiben *n* letter of thanks.

dann [dan] **I** *adv* **1.** then, after that: *~ und wann* every now and then; *was passierte ~?* what happened next?; F *bis ~!* see you (later)! **2.** then, in that case. **II** *conj* F (well) then, so: *~ eben nicht!* all right, forget it!

daran [da'ran] *adv* **1.** at (or on, in, to) it (or that): *halt dich ~ fest!* hold on to it!; *nahe ~* close to it; → **nahe II. 2.** *~ anschließend, im Anschluß ~* afterward(s). **3.** *es ist et. (nichts) ~* there's s.th. (nothing) in it; *~ ist kein wahres Wort* there's not a word of truth in it; *~ stirbt man nicht* you don't die of it; *du tust gut ~ zu gehen* you are wise to go; *das Schönste ~ war* the best thing about it was; → **denken** 3, **liegen** 4 *etc.*

dar'angehen *v/i* (*irr, sep,* -ge-, sn, → **gehen**) get down to it: *~, et. zu tun* get down to doing s.th. **dar'anmachen:** *sich ~* (*sep,* -ge-, h) F → **darangehen. dar'ansetzen** *v/t* (*sep,* -ge-, h) *alles ~, um zu inf* spare no effort to *inf*.

darauf [da'raʊf] *adv* **1.** on it *etc,* on top of it. **2.** after (that), then: *bald ~* soon after; *e-e Woche ~* a week later. **3.** *fig.* *ich freue mich ~* I'm looking forward to it; *~ wollen wir trinken!* let's drink to that!; *sie ging direkt ~ zu* she went straight for it; *~ steht Gefängnis* there is a prison penalty for that; *~ bin ich stolz* I'm proud of it; *wie kommt er nur ~?* whatever makes him think of that?; *ich komme nicht ~* (F *drauf*) I can't think of it!

daraufhin [darauf'hɪn] *adv* **1.** as a result, consequently. **2.** after that. **3.** *et. ~ prüfen, ob* examine s.th. to see if.

daraus [da'raʊs] *adv* **1.** from it *etc:* *~ lernen* (*vorlesen*) learn (read) from it. **2.** of it *etc:* *was ist ~ geworden?* what has become of it?; *~ wird nichts!* F nothing doing! **3.** for it *etc:* *ich mache mir nichts ~* a) I don't care for it, b) that doesn't worry me (a bit).

darben ['darbən] *v/i* (h) suffer want.

darbieten ['daːr-] *v/t* (*irr, sep,* -ge-, h, → **bieten**) **1.** present (*sich* offer). **2.** perform. **'Darbietung** *f* (-; -en) **1.** presentation. **2.** *thea. etc* performance.

135   **daß**

'darbringen v/t (irr, sep, -ge-, h, → **bringen**) (dat) present, give.

darin [da'rɪn] adv **1.** in it etc: *was ist ~?* what's in it (or inside)? **2.** there, in this (respect): *~ irren Sie sich!* there you are mistaken!; *~ liegt der Unterschied* that's the difference. **3.** at it, at that: *~ ist er sehr gut* he is very good at that.

'darlegen v/t (sep, -ge-, h) show, state: *j-m et. ~* explain s.th. to s.o.

'Darlegung f (-; -en) **1.** explanation. **2.** statement.

Darlehen ['da:rle:ən] n (-s; -) loan: *ein ~ aufnehmen* raise (or take up) a loan.

'Darlehens... loan (bank, contract, etc).

Darm [darm] m (-[e]s; -̈e) **1.** anat. intestine(s), bowel(s), gut(s): *den ~ entleeren* evacuate the bowels, defecate. **2.** (sausage) skin.

'Darm|entleerung f defecation. **~flora** f intestinal flora. **~geschwür** n intestinal ulcer. **~grippe** f gastroenteric influenza. **~krebs** m ♣ cancer of the intestine. **~saite** f ♪ catgut (string). **~spiegelung** f enteroscopy. **~trägheit** f constipation. **~verschluß** m ♣ ileus.

Darre ['darə] f ⚙ drying kiln.

'darstellen v/t (sep, -ge-, h) **1.** represent, describe (a. ♠), portray, show, express, constitute, mean: *falsch ~* misrepresent; *was soll das ~?* what's that supposed to be?; *e-e Belastung ~* be a burden. **2.** thea. etc act, play, w.s. interpret. **3.** ♣ prepare. **4.** computer: display. **'darstellend** adj: **~e Geometrie** descriptive geometry. **2.** → **Kunst** 1.

'Darsteller m (-s; -) player, actor: *der ~ des Faust* the actor playing Faust.

'Darstellerin f (-; -nen) actress, player.

'darstellerisch adj acting: *s-e ~e Leistung* his performance, his acting.

'Darstellung f (-; -en) **1.** representation, description, account: *graphische ~* graph, diagram. **2.** thea. etc acting, performance, w.s. interpretation. **3.** ♣ preparation. **4.** computer: display.

darüber [da'ry:bər] adv **1.** over it (or that) (a. time), above it etc: *das Zimmer ~* the room above; *ich bin ~ eingeschlafen* I fell asleep over it. **2.** more. **3.** *~ hinaus* a) beyond it etc, b) fig. over and above that, moreover; *fig. er ist ~ hinaus* he is past (all) that. **4.** fig. about it (or that), (on a subject) on that, on it:

ich freue mich ~ I'm glad about it; *~ vergißt er alle s-e Sorgen* that takes his mind off his problems; *~ kam sie nicht hinweg* she didn't get over it.

dar'überstehen v/i (irr, sep, -ge-, h, → **stehen**) fig. be above it.

darum [da'rum] adv **1.** (a)round it etc. **2.** *ich bat ihn ~* I asked him: a) for it, b) to do it; *~ geht es nicht!* that's not the point! **3.** → **deshalb**.

darunter [da'runtər] adv **1.** under it etc, underneath: *das Zimmer ~* the room below; *trug sie ...* underneath she was wearing ... **2.** less, under: *F ~ tut er es nicht* he won't do it for less. **3.** a) among them, b) including. **4.** *~ leiden, daß* suffer from ger; *was versteht man ~?* what do you understand by it?; *~ kann ich mir nichts vorstellen* that doesn't mean anything to me.

dar'unterfallen v/i (irr, sep, -ge-, sn, → **fallen**) fig. come under (a law etc).

dar'unterliegen v/i (irr, sep, -ge-, h, → **liegen**) fig. be below (standard).

dar'untersetzen v/t (sep, -ge-, h) put signature etc below.

Darwinismus [darvi'nɪsmʊs] m (-; no pl) Darwinism.

das [das] **I** def art the: *~ Buch des Monats* the book of the month. **II** dem pron this (one), that (one): *~ war sie!* that was her!; *~ sind s-e Bücher* those are his books; *~ ist es ja (gerade)!* that's the point!; *~ nur ~ nicht!* anything but that! **III** rel pron which: *~ Geschäft, ~ ich meine* the shop (which) I'm talking of. **IV** pers pron F for **es.**

'dasein v/i (irr, sep, -ge-, sn, → **sein**) **1.** a) be there, be present, b) exist: *bist du noch da?* are you still here?; *ist noch Brot da?* is there any bread left?; *ich bin gleich wieder da!* I'll be right back!; *ist j-d dagewesen?* has anyone been? fig. *noch nie dagewesen* unprecedented, unheard-of. **2.** F *(voll) ~* a) be all there, b) be in great shape, c) be conscious.

'Dasein n (-s; no pl) existence.

'dasitzen v/i (irr, sep, -ge-, h, → **sitzen**) sit there: fig. *~ ohne* be left without.

daß [das] conj that: *so ~* so that; *es sei denn, ~* unless; *ohne ~* without ger; *ich weiß, ~ ich recht habe* I know I'm right; *er entschuldigte sich, ~ er zu* *spät kam* he apologized for being late; *nicht, ~ ich wüßte* not that I know of; *es ist lange her, ~ ich sie gesehen habe* it's a long time since I saw her; F ~ *du ja hingehst!* be sure to go!

'**dastehen** *v/i (irr, sep,* -ge-, h, → *stehen)* stand there: *flg. gut ~* be in a good position, *firm:* be flourishing; *mittellos ~* be penniless; F *wie stehe ich jetzt da!* what a fool I look now!

Datei [da'taɪ] *f (-;* -en) data file.

Daten ['da:tən] *pl* data, facts, particulars. ~**ausgabe** *f* data output. ~**austausch** *m* data exchange. ~**bank** *f (-;* -en) data bank. ~**eingabe** *f* data input. ~**erfassung** *f* data collection. ~**mißbrauch** *m* data abuse. ~**netz** *n* data network. ~**schutz** *m* data protection. ~**schutzbeauftragte** *m, f* data protection commissioner. ~**sichtgerät** *n* (visual) display unit, (video) terminal. ~**speicher** *m* data memory. ~**speicherung** *f* data storage. ~**technik** *f* data systems engineering. ~**träger** *m* data medium. ~**typist** [-ty,pɪst] *m* (-en; -en), ~**ty,pistin** *f* (-; -nen) data typist. ~**übermittlung, ~übertragung** *f* data transfer (*or* communication). ~**umsetzung** *f* data conversion. 2**verarbeitend** *adj* data-processing. ~**verarbeitung** *f* data processing. ~**verarbeitungsanlage** *f* data-processing equipment.

datieren [da'ti:rən] *v/t, v/i* (h) date.

Dativ ['da:ti:f] *m* (-s; -e) dative (case). ~**ob,jekt** *n* dative (*or* indirect) object.

Dattel ['datəl] *f* (-; -n) 🌴 date.

Datum ['da:tʊm] *n* (-s; Daten) date: *ohne ~* undated; *welches ~ haben wir heute?* what's the date today?; *neueren ~s* of recent date. **Datumsgrenze** *f geogr.* date line. '**Datumsstempel** *m* a) date stamp, b) dater.

Dauer ['daʊər] *f (-; no pl)* duration (*a. ling.,* ♪), period (of time), *esp.* ⚖ term, length: *von ~* lasting; *von kurzer* (*or nicht von*) *~ sein* be short-lived, not to last long; *auf die ~ in* the long run; *der Lärm ist auf die ~ unerträglich* you can't stand the noise for long; *das kann die ~ nicht so weitergehen* that can't go on indefinitely; *für die ~ von* (*or gen*) for the duration (*or a* period) of.

'**Dauer|arbeitslosigkeit** *f* chronic un-

employment. ~**auftrag** *m* ✝ periodical payment order. ~**belastung** *f* **1.** ⊙ continuous load. **2.** *fig.* permanent stress. ~**brenner** *m* F long-running success (*or* hit). ~**gast** *m* permanent guest.

'**dauerhaft** *adj* permanent, lasting, durable, hard-wearing (*goods*): ~ *sein a.* wear well. '**Dauerhaftigkeit** *f* (-; *no pl*) durability, permanence.

'**Dauer|karte** *f* season ticket. ~**lauf** *m* jogging: *im ~* at a jog (trot). ~**lutscher** *m* (-s; -) F lollipop.

dauern ['daʊərn] *v/i* (h) last, go on, take: *zwei Stunden ~* take two hours; *wie lange dauert es denn noch?* how much longer will it take?; *es wird lange ~, bis* it will be a long time before; *das dauert mir zu lange!* that's too long for me! '**dauernd** *I adj* constant: ~**er Wohnsitz** permanent residence. **II** *adv* constantly: ~ *et. tun* keep doing; *er kommt ~ zu spät* he is always late; *das passiert ~* that happens all the time.

'**Dauer|parker** *m* long-term parker. ~**regen** *m* continuous rain. ~**stellung** *f* permanent post. ~**welle** *f* (**~n haben** F have a) perm. ~**zustand** *m zum ~ werden* become permanent (*b.s.* chronic).

Daumen ['daʊmən] *m* (-s; -) thumb: ~ *lutschen* suck one's thumb; F *j-m die ~ drücken* keep one's fingers crossed for s.o.; *(die) ~ drehen* twiddle one's thumbs; *über den ~ gepeilt* at a rough estimate. ~**nagel** *m* thumbnail.

Daunen ['daʊnən] *pl* down.

'**Daunendecke** *f* eiderdown.

davon [da'fɔn] *adv* **1.** *das Dorf liegt nicht weit ~* (*entfernt*) the village is not far away (*or* from it); ~ *zweigt ein Weg ab* a path branches off it. **2.** *ich wachte ~ auf* I was awakened by it; ~ *wird man dick* that makes you fat; F *das kommt ~!* that'll teach you!; *was habe ich ~?* what do I get out of it? **3.** *hast du schon ~ gehört?* have you heard about it yet?; *genug ~!* enough of that! **4.** *auf und ~* up and away.

da'vonfliegen *v/i* (*irr, sep,* -ge-, sn, → *fliegen*) fly off, fly away. **da'vonjagen** *v/t* (*sep,* -ge-, h) chase away.

da'vonkommen *v/i* (*irr, sep,* -ge-, sn, → *kommen*) get away, get off, escape: *mit dem Leben ~* survive; → *Schreck.*

da'vonlaufen *v/i* (*irr, sep,* -ge-, sn, →

laufen) run away. **da'vonmachen:**
sich ~ (*sep*, -ge-, h) F make off, beat it.
da'vonstehlen: *sich ~* (*irr, sep*, -ge-, h,
→ *stehlen*) steal away.
da'vontragen
v/t (*irr, sep*, -ge-, h, → *tragen*) **1.** *a. fig.*
carry off. **2.** sustain (*injury*), get, catch
(*disease*). **da'vonziehen** *v/i* (*irr, sep*,
-ge-, sn, → *ziehen*) move away (*or* off):
sports: j-m ~ pull away from s.o.

davor [da'fo:r] *adv* **1.** before (*or* in front
of) it *etc*: *mit e-m Garten ~* with a
garden in front. **2.** *time*: before that. **3.**
~ habe ich Angst I'm afraid of that; *ich
habe ihn ~ gewarnt* I warned him of it.

dazu [da'tsu:] *adv* **1.** in addition to it,
besides: *sie sang und spielte ~ Gitarre*
she sang and accompanied herself on
the guitar; *möchten Sie Reis ~?* would
you like rice with it?; *und sie ist noch ~
hübsch* and she is pretty into the bargain. **2.** for it, for that purpose: *~ ist er
ja da!* that's what he is there for! **3.** *wie
ist es ~ gekommen?* how did that
come about?; *~ darf es nicht kommen*
that must not happen; *ich kam nie ~* I
never got (a)round to it; F *wie komme
ich ~?* why on earth should I?

da'zugehören *v/i* (*sep*, -ge-, h) belong to
it *etc*; → *a.* **gehören. da'zugehörig** *adj*
belonging to it (*or* them).

da'zukommen *v/i* (*irr, sep*, -ge-, sn, →
kommen) **1.** (*gerade ~* happen to)
come along (*als* when). **2.** a) join *s.o.*,
b) be added. **da'zulernen** *v/t*, *v/i* (*sep*,
-ge-, h) learn (*s.th.* new). **da'zutun** *v/t*
(*irr, sep*, -ge-, h, → *tun*) F add: *ohne
sein etc* **2** without his *etc* help.

dazwischen [da'tsvɪʃən] *adv* between
(them), in between (*a.* time), among
them. **~fahren** *v/i* (*irr, sep*, -ge-, sn, →
fahren) a) step in, interfere, b) interrupt. **~kommen** *v/i* (*irr, sep*, -ge-, sn, →
kommen) intervene: *wenn nichts dazwischenkommt* if all goes well.
~liegen *v/i* (*irr, sep*, -ge-, h, → *liegen*)
intervene. **~reden** *v/i* (*sep*, -ge-, h) *j-m ~*
interrupt s.o. **~treten** *v/i* (*irr, sep*, -ge-,
sn, → *treten*) intervene.

Dealer ['di:lər] *m* (-s; -) dealer.
Debakel [de'ba:kəl] *n* (-s; -) débâcle.
Debatte [de'batə] *f* (-; -n) *a. parl.* debate:
zur ~ stehen be under discussion; *das
steht nicht zur ~* that's not the issue.
debattieren [deba'ti:rən] *v/t*, *v/i* (h)

(*über e-e Sache* s.th.) debate, discuss.
Debet ['de:bɛt] *n* (-s; -s) ✝ debit. **~saldo**
m debit balance. **~seite** *f* debit side.
debil [de'bi:l] *adj* 🖐 feebleminded.
Debüt [de'by:] *n* (-s; -s) debut: *sein ~
geben* → **debütieren** [deby'ti:rən] *v/i*
(h) make one's debut.
dechiffrieren [deʃɪ'fri:rən] *v/t* (h) decipher, decode.
Deck [dɛk] *n* (-[e]s; -s) ⚓ deck: *an* (*or*
auf) *~* on deck.
'Decka,dresse *f* cover (address).
'Deckanstrich *m* top (*or* finishing) coat.
'Deckbett *n* feather quilt.
'Deckblatt *n* wrapper (*of cigar*).
Deckchen ['dɛkçən] *n* (-s; -) doily.
Decke ['dɛkə] *f* (-; -n) **1.** a) blanket, b)
(bed)cover, c) (table)cloth: F *mit j-m
unter einer ~ stecken* be in league with
s.o.; *fig. sich nach der ~ strecken* cut
one's coat according to one's cloth. **2.**
ceiling: F *fig.* (*vor Freude*) *an die ~
springen* jump with joy; (*vor Wut*) *an
die ~ gehen* go through the roof; *mir
fiel die ~ auf den Kopf* I felt shut in. **3.**
🔘 cover(ing). **4.** *civ.eng.* surface, sur-
facing. **5.** tyre cover (*of car, bicycle*).
Deckel ['dɛkəl] *m* (-s; -) lid (*a. humor.
hat*), cover, (screw) cap: F *j-m eins auf
den ~ geben* tick s.o. off (properly).
decken ['dɛkən] **I** *v/t* **1.** *~ über* (*acc*)
cover *s.th.* with. **2.** roof: *mit Stroh* (*Ziegeln, Schiefer*) *~* thatch (tile, slate) *a
roof*. **3.** *den Tisch ~* lay (*or* set) the table
(*für drei Personen* for three). **4.** *a. fig.
or contp.* shield, protect: *j-n ~* cover up
for s.o., *sports:* mark s.o.; *den Rückzug ~* cover the retreat. **5.** cover (*costs*),
meet (*demand*). **6.** *zo.* cover, serve. **II** *v/i*
7. paint *etc*: cover (*well etc*). **8.** *sports:*
cover, mark, *boxer:* cover (up). **III** *sich
~* **9.** cover o.s., *boxer:* cover up. **10.** (*mit*
with) A coincide, *fig. a.* tally.
'Decken|balken *m* ceiling beam. **~be-
leuchtung** *f* ceiling lighting. **~gemäl-
de** *n* ceiling fresco. **~leuchte** *f* ceiling
lamp, *mot.* dome lamp.
'Deck|farbe *f* 🔘 body colo(u)r. **~fe-
der** *f* deck feather. **~mantel** *m fig.*
cloak. **~name** *m* pseudonym, ✗ code
name.
'Deckung *f* (-; *no pl*) **1.** (*in ~ gehen* take)
cover. **2.** ✝ a) cover, security, b) supply: *k-e ~* no funds. **3.** *sports:* covering,

marking, *boxing etc*: guard. **4.** ₳ *or fig.* coincidence.

'**deckungsgleich** *adj* ₳ congruent.

'**Deckweiß** *n* opaque white.

Defätismus [defɛ'tɪsmʊs] *m* (-; *no pl*) defeatism. **defä'tistisch** *adj* defeatist.

defekt [de'fɛkt] *adj* defective, faulty.

De'fekt *m* (-[e]s; -e) defect (**an** *dat* in).

defensiv [defɛn'zi:f] *adj* defensive.

Defensive [defɛn'zi:və] *f* (-; -n) (**in der ~** on the) defensive.

defilieren [defi'li:rən] *v/i* (sn) march past.

defi'nierbar *adj* definable: **schwer ~** difficult to define. **definieren** [defi'ni:rən] *v/t* (h) define. **Definition** [defini'tsi̯o:n] *f* (-; -en) definition. **definitiv** [-'ti:f] *adj* definite (*answer*), positive (*offer*): **es steht ~ fest, daß ...** it is definite that ...

Defizit ['de:fitsɪt] *n* (-s; -e) *a. fig.* deficit.

Deflation [defla'tsi̯o:n] *f* (-; -en) † deflation. **deflationär** [-tsi̯o'nɛ:r], **deflatorisch** [-'to:rɪʃ] *adj* † deflationary.

deflorieren [deflo'ri:rən] *v/t* (h) deflower. **⊘** *a.* distort.

deformieren [defɔr'mi:rən] *v/t* (h) deform, **⊘** *a.* distort.

deftig ['dɛftɪç] *adj* F solid (*meal*), earthy (*joke*), steep (*prices*), sound (*blow etc*).

Degen ['de:gən] *m* (-s; -) sword, *fenc.* épée.

Degeneration [degenera'tsi̯o:n] *f* (-; -en) degeneration. **degenerativ** [degenera'ti:f] *adj* degenerative.

degenerieren [degene'ri:rən] *v/i* (sn), **degene'riert** *adj* degenerate.

'**Degenfechten** *n sports*: épée fencing.

degradieren [degra'di:rən] *v/t* (h) ✕ demote, *esp. fig.* degrade.

'**dehnbar** *adj a. fig.* elastic. '**Dehnbarkeit** *f* (-; *no pl*) elasticity. **dehnen** ['de:nən] (h) **I** *v/t* **1.** stretch (*a. fig.*). **2.** lengthen (*vowels*), drawl (*words*). **II** *sich ~* stretch (o.s.). '**Dehnung** *f* (-; -en) **1.** stretch(ing). **2.** *ling.* lengthening.

dehydrieren [dehy'dri:rən] *v/t* (h) 🜊 dehydrate.

Deich [daɪç] *m* (-[e]s; -e) dike, dam, *of river*: embankment, *Am.* levee.

Deichsel ['daɪksəl] *f* (-; -n) a) pole, b) shaft. '**deichseln** *v/t* F (h) wangle.

dein [daɪn] **1.** your: *eccl.* **~ Wille geschehe** Thy will be done. **2.** *pred* **~er, ~e, ~(e)s, der (die, das) ~e** yours;

e-r ~er Freunde a friend of yours. **3. der (die, das) ~(ig)e** your own, yours; **die ♀(ig)en** your family, your people.

'**deiner** *pers pron* (*of*) you: **wir werden ~ gedenken** we shall remember you.

'**deinerseits** *adv* on your part.

'**deines'gleichen** *indef pron* people like you, *contp.* the likes of you.

deinetwegen ['daɪnətve:gən] *adv* a) for your sake, b) because of you.

deinig ['daɪnɪç] → **dein** 3.

Dekade [de'ka:də] *f* (-; -n) decade.

dekadent [deka'dɛnt] *adj* decadent. **Dekadenz** [deka'dɛnts] *f* (-; *no pl*) decadence.

Dekan [de'ka:n] *m* (-s; -e) dean. **Dekanat** [deka'na:t] *n* (-s; -e) dean's office.

deklamieren [dekla'mi:rən] *v/t, v/i* (h) declaim.

deklarieren [dekla'ri:rən] *v/t* (h) † declare.

deklassieren [dekla'si:rən] *v/t* (h) declass, *sports*: outclass.

Deklination [deklina'tsi̯o:n] *f* (-; -en) **1.** *ling.* declension. **2.** *phys.* declination.

dekli'nierbar *adj* declinable. **deklinieren** [dekli'ni:rən] *v/t* (h) decline.

Dékolleté [dekɔl'te:] *n* (-s; -s) (**tiefes ~** plunging) neckline.

dékolletiert [dekɔl'ti:rt] *adj* décolleté.

dekontaminieren [dekɔntami'ni:rən] *v/t* (h) decontaminate.

Dekor [de'ko:r] *m, n* (-s; -s) **1.** a) decoration, b) décor, c) pattern. **2.** *thea.* décor, set(s). **Dekorateur** [dekora'tø:r] *m* (-s; -e), **Dekora'teurin** *f* (-; -nen) **1.** window-dresser. **2.** interior designer. **3.** *thea. etc* scene painter. **Dekoration** [dekora'tsi̯o:n] *f* (-; -en) decoration, *a.* window display, furnishings, *thea. etc* set(s). **dekorativ** [-'ti:f] *adj* decorative.

dekorieren [deko'ri:rən] *v/t* (h) decorate (*a. with an order*), dress (*shop window*).

Dekret [de'kre:t] *n* (-[e]s; -e) decree.

Delegation [delega'tsi̯o:n] *f* (-; -en) delegation. **delegieren** [dele'gi:rən] *v/t* (h) delegate.

Dele'gierte *m, f* (-n; -n) delegate.

delikat [deli'ka:t] *adj* delicious, *a. fig.* delicate. **Delikatesse** [delika'tɛsə] *f* (-; -n) delicacy, *fig. a.* discretion.

Delika'teßgeschäft *n* delicatessen.

Delikt [de'lɪkt] *n* (-[e]s; -e) 🕮 offen/ce

(*Am.* -se). **Delinquent** [delɪŋˈkvɛnt] *m* (-en; -en) offender.

Delirium [deˈliːriʊm] *n a. fig.* delirium.

Delle [ˈdɛlə] *f* (-; -n) F dent.

Delphin [dɛlˈfiːn] *m* (-s; -e) *zo.* dolphin.

Del'phin(schwimmen) *n* (-s) butterfly.

Delta [ˈdɛlta] *n* (-s; -s) *geogr.* delta.

'Deltamuskel *m* deltoid (muscle).

dem [deːm] **I** *def art* **gib es ~ Jungen** give it to the boy. **II** *dem pron* **wie ~ auch sei** however that may be; **nach ~, was ich gehört habe** from what I've heard. **III** *rel pron* **der, ~ ich es gab** the one (*or* the person) I gave it to.

Demagoge [demaˈgoːgə] *m* (-n; -n) demagogue. **Demagogie** [demagoˈgiː] *f* (-; -n) demagogy. **demagogisch** [demaˈgoːgɪʃ] *adj* demagogic.

Demarkationslinie [demarkaˈtsǐoːns-] *f* demarcation line.

demaskieren [demasˈkiːrən] *v/t* (h) *a. fig.* unmask.

Dementi [deˈmɛnti] *n* (-s; -s) *pol.* (official) denial. **dementieren** [demɛnˈtiːrən] *v/t* (h) deny (officially).

'dementsprechend *adv* accordingly.

'demgegen'über *adv* in contrast to this.

'demge'mäß *adv* accordingly.

'demnach *adv* **1.** therefore. **2.** → *demgemäß.*

'dem'nächst *adv* shortly, soon: **~ erscheinend** *etc* forthcoming.

Demo [ˈdeːmo] *f* (-; -s) F demo.

Demograph [demoˈgraːf] *m* (-en; -en) demographer. **Demographie** [demograˈfiː] *f* (-; -n) demography. **demographisch** [-ˈgraːfɪʃ] *adj* demographic.

'Demokas,sette *f* F demo (tape).

Demokrat [demoˈkraːt] *m* (-en; -en), **Demo'kratin** *f* (-; -nen) *pol.* democrat. **Demokratie** [demokraˈtiː] *f* (-; -n) democracy. **demokratisch** [-ˈkraːtɪʃ] *adj* democratic. **demokratisieren** [demokratiˈziːrən] *v/t* (h) democratize.

demolieren [demoˈliːrən] *v/t* (h) demolish, wreck.

Demo'lierung *f* (-; -en) demolition.

Demonstrant [demɔnˈstrant] *m* (-en; -en), **Demon'strantin** *f* (-; -nen) demonstrator, protester. **Demonstration** [-straˈtsǐoːn] *f* (-; -en) (*pol.* **e-e ~ veranstalten** hold a) demonstration: *fig.* **e-e ~ der Macht** a show of force. **Demonstrati'ons|recht** *n* right to demonstrate. **~verbot** *n* ban on demonstrations. **~zug** *m* protest march.

demonstrativ [demɔnstraˈtiːf] *adj* demonstrative. **Demonstra'tivpro,nomen** *n* demonstrative (pronoun).

demonstrieren [demɔnˈstriːrən] *v/t*, *v/i* (h) demonstrate.

Demontage [demɔnˈtaːʒə] *f* (-; -n) ⊙ *or fig.* dismantling.

demontieren [demɔnˈtiːrən] *v/t* (h) dismantle (*a. fig.*), take down, take apart.

demoralisieren [demoraliˈziːrən] *v/t* (h) demoralize.

Demoskopie [demoskoˈpiː] *f* (-; -n) (public) opinion research. **demoskopisch** [demoˈskoːpɪʃ] *adj* **~e Umfrage** (public) opinion poll.

Demut [ˈdeːmuːt] *f* (-; *no pl*) humility.

demütig [ˈdeːmyːtɪç] *adj* humble.

demütigen [ˈdeːmyːtɪgən] *v/t* (h) humiliate: **sich ~** humble o.s.

'Demütigung *f* (-; -en) humiliation.

denaturieren [denatuˈriːrən] *v/t* (h) 🜂, *phys.* denature.

'Denkanstoß *m* impulse: **j-m e-n ~ geben,** (**bei j-m**) **als ~ wirken** set s.o. thinking. **'Denkart** *f* way of thinking. **'Denkaufgabe** *f* problem, brain teaser.

'denkbar *adj* thinkable, conceivable: **es ist durchaus ~, daß** it's quite possible that; **die ~ beste Methode** the best method imaginable.

denken [ˈdɛŋkən] *v/t*, *v/i* (dachte, gedacht, h) **1.** think, *a.* imagine, suppose, *Am.* F guess: **das gibt e-m zu ~** that makes you think; **ich denke schon** I (should) think so; **das habe ich mir gedacht** I thought as much; **das hättest du dir ~ können!** you should have known that!; **ich dachte mir nichts dabei** I thought nothing of it; **solange ich ~ kann** as long as I remember; F **denkste!** that's what you think! **2.** think of, consider: **er denkt daran zu kommen** he thinks of coming; **ich denke nicht daran!** I wouldn't dream of it! **3. ~ an** (*acc*) a) think of (*or* about), b) remember; **daran ist nicht zu ~** it's out of the question; **an Schlaf war nicht zu ~** sleep was out of the question; **wenn ich nur daran denke!** the mere thought of it! **4. ~ über** (*acc*) think about (*or* of).

'Denken *n* (-s) thinking, thought.

'Denker *m* (-s; -) thinker. **'Denkfa,brik** *f*

F think-tank. **'denkfähig** *adj* intelligent. **'denkfaul** *adj* mentally lazy. **'Denkfehler** *m* flaw in one's reasoning. **'Denkmal** *n* (-[e]s; ⸱er) monument: *j-m ein ~ setzen* put up a monument to s.o. **'Denkmalpflege** *f* preservation of historic buildings and monuments. **'Denkmalschutz** *m unter ~ stehen* be listed (as a historic monument). **'Denk|muster** *n* thought pattern. **~pause** *f* pause for reflection. **~pro,zeß** *m* thought process. **~schrift** *f* memorandum. **~vermögen** *n* (-s; *no pl*) intellectual capacity, intelligence. **~weise** *f* way of thinking. ⚥**würdig** *adj* memorable. **~zettel** *m* (*j-m e-n ~ verpassen* teach s.o. a) lesson.

denn [dɛn] **I** *conj* **1.** because, since. **2.** than: *mehr ~ je* more than ever. **3.** *sei ~* unless. **II** *adv* **4.** then: *war es ~ so schlimm?* was it really that bad?; *was ist ~?* what is it now?; *wieso ~?* (but) why?; *wo warst du ~ nur?* where on earth have you been?

dennoch ['dɛnɔx] *conj* (but) still, yet.

Dental [dɛn'ta:l] *m* (-[e]s; -e) *ling.* dental.

Denunziant [denʊn'tsĭant] *m* (-en; -en), **Denunzi'antin** *f* (-; -nen) informer.

denunzieren [denʊn'tsi:rən] *v/t* (h) *j-n ~* denounce s.o. (*bei* to).

Deodorant [deʔodo'rant] *n* (-s; -e, -s) deodorant.

deplaziert [depla'tsi:rt] *adj* out of place, *a.* misplaced (*remark etc*).

Deponie [depo'ni:] *f* (-; -n) dump, tip.

deponieren [depo'ni:rən] *v/t* (h) (*bei* with) deposit, leave.

Deportation [departa'tsĭo:n] *f* (-; -en) deportation. **deportieren** [depɔr'ti:-rən] *v/t* (h) deport. **Depor'tierte** *m, f* (-n; -n) deportee.

Depot [de'po:] *n* (-s; -s) depot, ✝ (*a. account*) deposit. **De'potwirkung** *f* 💊 controlled sustained release.

Depression [deprɛ'sĭo:n] *f* (-; -en) depression. **depressiv** [-'si:f] *adj psych.* depressive. **deprimieren** [depri'mi:-rən] *v/t* (h) depress; **~d** depressing.

der [de:r] **I** *art* the: ~ *arme Peter* poor Peter. **II** *dem pron* that (one), this (one): ~ *mit ~ Brille* the one with the glasses; *contp.* ~ *und sein Wort halten?* him keep his word? **III** *rel pron* who, which. **IV** *pers pron* F *for* **er.**

derart [de:rʔa:rt] *adv* so, in such a way. **'der'artig** *adj* such: *nichts Derartiges* nothing of the kind. **II** *adv* → **derart.**

derb [dɛrp] *adj* **1.** strong, sturdy, coarse (*food etc*). **2.** *fig.* coarse, crude (*joke etc*). **'Derbheit** *f* (-; -en) **1.** *no pl* coarseness. **2.** *pl* crude jokes (*or* remarks).

derentwegen ['de:rəntve:gən] **I** *adv* because of her (*or* that *etc*). **II** *rel pron* because of whom (*or* which).

'der'gleichen *dem pron* **1.** such. **2.** such a thing, the like: *nichts ~* no such thing; *und ~ mehr* and so on, and the like.

Derivat [deri'va:t] *n* (-[e]s; -e) 🧪, *ling.* derivative.

derjenige ['de:rje:nigə] *dem pron* that: **~, der** he (*or* the one) who.

dermaßen ['de:rma:sən] → **derart.**

Dermatologe [dɛrmato'lo:gə] *m* (-n; -n) 🩺 dermatologist. **Dermatose** [-'to:zə] *f* (-; -n) dermatosis, skin disease.

derselbe [de:r'zɛlbə] *dem pron* the same.

'der'zeit *adv* at present. **'der'zeitig** *adj* **1.** present. **2.** then, of (*or* at) the time.

Des [dɛs] *n* (-; -) ♪ D flat.

desensibilisieren [dezɛnzibili'zi:rən] *v/t* (h) 💊, *phot.* desensitize.

Deserteur [dezɛr'tø:r] *m* (-s; -e) deserter.

desertieren [-'ti:rən] *v/i* (sn) desert.

'des'gleichen *adv and conj* likewise.

'deshalb *adv and conj* therefore, that's why: *gerade ~!* that's just why!; *sie ist ~ nicht glücklicher* she isn't any happier for it.

designiert [dezɪ'gni:rt] *adj der ~e Präsident* the president designate.

desillusionieren [dɛsʔɪluzĭo'ni:rən] *v/t* (h) disillusion.

Desinfektion [dɛsʔɪnfɛk'tsĭo:n] *f* (-; -en) disinfection. **Desinfekti'onsmittel** *n* disinfectant, 🧪 *a.* antiseptic. **desinfizieren** [-fi'tsi:rən] *v/t* (h) disinfect.

Desinformati'on *f* (-; -en) disinformation.

'Desinter,esse *n* (-s; *no pl*) lack of interest, indifference (*an dat* to). **'desinter-es,siert** *adj* uninterested, indifferent.

desolat [dezo'la:t] *adj* desolate.

Desorganisati'on *f* disorganization.

desorien'tiert *adj psych.* confused.

Despot [dɛs'po:t] *m* (-en; -en) despot. **des'potisch** *adj* despotic(al).

Despotismus [dɛspo'tɪsmʊs] *m* (-; *no pl*) despotism.

141   Diagramm

dessen ['dɛsən] **I** *rel pron* whose, of which. **II** *dem pron* **sich ~ bewußt sein, daß ...** be aware (of the fact) that ...; ~ **bin ich sicher** I'm quite sure of that. **III** *poss pron* **mein Bruder und ~ Frau** my brother and his wife.

'dessenunge'achtet *adv* nevertheless.

Dessert [dɛ'sɛːr] *n* (-s; -s) *gastr.* dessert.

Destillat [dɛstɪ'laːt] *n* (-[e]s; -e) distillate.

destillieren [-'liːrən] *v/t, v/i* (h) distil(l).

desto ['dɛstoː] **I** *adv* (all) the: **~ besser!** all (*or* so much) the better!; **~ schlimmer** so much the worse. **II** *conj* the ... the: **je mehr** (*eher etc*), **~ besser** the more (sooner *etc*) the better.

destruktiv [dɛstrʊk'tiːf] *adj* destructive.

deswegen ['dɛs've:gən] → **deshalb.**

Detail [de'taɪ] *n* (-s; -s) detail.

detaillieren [dɛta'jiːrən] *v/t* (h) specify.

detail'liert I *adj* detailed. **II** *adv* in detail.

Detektiv [detɛk'tiːf] *m* (-s; -e) detective.

Detek'tivbü,ro *n* detective agency.

Detek'tivro,man *m* detective story.

Detonation [detona'tsi̯oːn] *f* (-; -en) detonation, blast. **detonieren** [deto-'niːrən] *v/i* (sn) detonate.

deuten ['dɔytən] (h) **I** *v/t* interpret, read: **falsch ~** misinterpret, *fig.* misconstrue. **II** *v/i* **~ auf** (*acc*) point at (*esp. fig.* to); **alles deutet darauf hin, daß** there is every indication that.

deutlich ['dɔytlɪç] *adj* clear, distinct, legible, plain: **~er Wink** broad hint; **~er Fortschritt** visible progress; *fig.* **~ werden** speak in very plain terms; **muß ich noch ~er werden?** do I have to spell it out (to you)?

'Deutlichkeit *f* (-; *no pl*) clarity, clearness: **in aller ~** in plain terms.

deutsch [dɔytʃ] *adj* (**auf ~, in ~** in) German: **~ reden** talk (in) German; F *fig.* **mit j-m ~ reden** speak plainly with s.o. **Deutsch, das ~** German: **er kann gut ~** he speaks German well.

'Deutsch|ameri,kaner(in *f*) *m*, **₂ame-ri,kanisch** *adj* German-American.

'deutsch-'deutsch *adj pol. hist.* inter--German, German-German.

Deutsche(r) *m* (-(n); -n) German.

'deutsch-'englisch *adj pol.* Anglo--German, *ling.* German-English.

'deutschfeindlich *adj* anti-German.

'deutsch-fran'zösisch *adj pol.* Franco-German, *ling.* German-French.

'deutschfreundlich *adj* pro-German.

'Deutschland *n* (-s) Germany.

'Deutschlehrer *m* German teacher.

'deutschsprachig [-ʃpraːxɪç] *adj* German-language (*text*), German-speaking (*area*).

'Deutschunterricht *m* German lessons.

'Deutung *f* (-; -en) interpretation.

Devise [de'viːzə] *f* (-; -n) **1.** motto. **2.** *pl* ✝ foreign exchange (*or* currency).

De'visen|abkommen *n* foreign exchange agreement. **~bestimmungen** *pl* currency regulations. **~börse** *f* foreign exchange market. **~geschäft** *n* foreign exchange transaction. **~händler** *m* foreign exchange dealer. **~knappheit** *f* (foreign) currency stringency. **~verge-hen** *n* currency offen/ce (*Am.* -se).

devot [de'voːt] *adj contp.* servile.

Devotionalien [devotsi̯o'naːli̯ən] *pl eccl.* devotional objects.

Dezember [de'tsɛmbər] *m* (-[s]; -) (**im ~** in) December.

dezent [de'tsɛnt] *adj* discreet, unobtrusive, soft (*colo[u]r, music, etc*).

dezentralisieren [detsɛntrali'ziːrən] *v/t* (h) decentralize.

Dezernat [detsɛr'naːt] *n* (-[e]s; -e) department. **Dezernent** [detsɛr'nɛnt] *m* (-en; -en) head of (a) department.

Dezibel [de'tsiːbɛl] *n* (-s; -) decibel.

Dezimal|bruch [detsi'maːl-] *m* ⅍ decimal (fraction). **~stelle** *f* decimal (place). **~sy,stem** *n* decimal system. **~zahl** *f* decimal.

Dezimeter ['deːtsimeːtər] *m, n* (-s; -) decimet/re (*Am.* -er). **dezimieren** [detsi'miːrən] *v/t* (h) decimate.

Dia ['diːa] *n* (-s; -s) F slide.

Diabetes [dia'beːtɛs] *m* (-; *no pl*) diabetes. **Diabetiker** [dia'beːtikər] *m* (-s; -), **Dia'betikerin** *f* (-; -nen) diabetic.

'Diabetrachter *m* slide viewer.

diabolisch [dia'boːlɪʃ] *adj* diabolic(al).

'Diafilm *m* dia film.

Diagnose [dia'gnoːzə] *f* (-; -n) (**e-e ~ stellen** make a) diagnosis.

diagnostizieren [diagnɔsti'tsiːrən] *v/t, v/i* (h) diagnose.

diagonal [diago'naːl] *adj*, **Diago'nale** *f* (-; -n) diagonal. **Diago'nalreifen** *m* *mot.* cross-ply tyre (*Am.* tire).

Diagramm [dia'gram] *n* (-s; -e) diagram, graph.

Diakon

Diakon [dia'ko:n] *m* (-s, -en; -e[n]) *eccl.* deacon. **Diakonisse** [diako'nɪsə] *f* (-; -n) Protestant (nursing) sister.

Dialekt [dia'lɛkt] *m* (-[e]s; -e) dialect.

Dialektik [dia'lɛktɪk] *f* (-; *no pl*) dialectics.

Dialog [dia'lo:k] *m* (-[e]s; -e) (*e-n ~ führen* carry on a) dialog(ue *Br.*).

Dialyse [dia'ly:zə] *f* (-; -n) *⚕* dialysis.

Diamant [dia'mant] *m* (-en; -en), **dia'manten** *adj* diamond.

diametral [diame'tra:l] *adj* diametric(al): *~ entgegengesetzt* diametrically opposed (*dat* to).

Diapositiv ['di:apoziti:f] *n* (-s; -e) slide. **'Diaprojektor** *m* slide projector.

'Diarahmen *m* slide frame.

Diät [di'ɛ:t] *f* (-; -en) (special) diet: *~ halten, ⚲ leben* (keep to a) diet; *j-n auf ~ setzen* put s.o. on a diet.

Di'ätassi̱stent(in *f*) *m* dietician.

Di'äten *pl parl.* attendance allowance.

Di'ätfahrplan *m* F dietary schedule.

Di'ätkost *f* dietary food.

Di'ätvorschrift *f* dietary.

dich [dɪç] **I** *pers pron* you. **II** *reflex pron* yourself: *schau ~ an!* look at yourself!

dicht [dɪçt] **I** *adj* **1.** dense (*wood, crowd, fog, etc*), *a.* heavy (*traffic*), thick (*hair, hedge*), close(ly-woven) (*fabric*). **2.** watertight, leakproof: F *fig. er ist nicht ganz ~* he's got a screw loose. **3.** compact, *fig.* tight (*plot*). **II** *adv* **4.** densely, thickly: *~ schließen* shut tightly; *~ gedrängt stehen* stand closely packed. **5.** *~ an* (*dat*), *~ bei* close to; *~ aufeinanderfolgen* follow closely (*or* in rapid succession); *~ hinter j-m* close (*or* hard) on s.o.'s heels.

'dichtbehaart *adj* (very) hairy.

'dichtbevölkert *adj* densely populated.

'Dichte *f* (-; *no pl*) density (*a. phys.*), denseness, thickness, tightness.

dichten¹ ['dɪçtən] *v/t* (h) *⊛* seal, pack.

'dichten² (h) **I** *v/t* write. **II** *v/i* write poetry (*or* plays *etc*).

'Dichter *m* (-s; -) poet, *w.s.* author, writer. **'Dichterin** *f* (-; -nen) poetess, *w.s.* authoress, writer.

'dichterisch *adj* poetic(al); → **Freiheit.**

'dichthalten *v/i* (*irr, sep*, -ge-, h, → *halten*) F keep one's mouth shut.

'Dichtkunst *f* (-; *no pl*) poetry.

'dichtmachen (*sep*, -ge-, h) F **I** *v/t* shut

(up). **II** *v/i* (*den Laden*) *~* shut up shop.

'Dichtung¹ *f* (-; -en) *⊛* seal, packing.

'Dichtung² *f* (-; -en) a) literature, b) poetry, c) poem, d) (literary *or* poetic) work(s): *fig. ~ und Wahrheit* fact and fiction.

'Dichtungs|masse *f* *⊛* sealing compound. *~ring m, ~scheibe f* washer.

dick [dɪk] **I** *adj* **1.** thick, *w.s. a.* a) dense, b) big, large, c) stout, fat: F *~er Verkehr* heavy traffic; *~ machen* be fattening; *~ werden* grow fat; *durch ~ und dünn* through thick and thin. **2.** F a) close, intimate, b) big: *sie sind ~e Freunde* they are (as) thick as thieves; *~es Lob ernten* reap lavish praise; *~er Auftrag* fat order; → *Ende* 1, *Luft* 1. **II** *adv* **3.** thick(ly). **4.** F very: *~ befreundet sein* be great pals (*mit j-m* with s.o.); *ich habe ihn* (*es*) *~* I'm sick of him (it); → *auftragen* 5.

'dickbäuchig [-bɔyçɪç] *adj* fat-bellied.

'Dickdarm *m anat.* colon.

'Dicke¹ *f* (-; *no pl*) thickness, *⊛ a.* diameter, *w.s. a.* a) denseness, b) bigness, c) stoutness, fatness.

'Dicke² *m, f* (-n; -n) F fat person.

'Dickerchen *n* (-s; -) F fatso.

'dickfellig [-fɛlɪç] *adj* thick-skinned.

'Dickfelligkeit *f* (-; *no pl*) F callousness.

'dickflüssig *adj* thick(-flowing).

'Dickhäuter ['dɪkhɔytər] *m* (-s; -) *zo.* pachyderm.

'Dickicht ['dɪkɪçt] *n* (-s; -e) **1.** thicket. **2.** *fig.* labyrinth.

'Dickkopf *m* F *fig.* pigheaded fellow: *e-n ~ haben → 'dickköpfig* [-kœpfɪç] *adj ~ sein* be pigheaded. **'Dickköpfigkeit** *f* (-; *no pl*) pigheadedness, stubbornness.

'dicklich *adj* **1.** plump. **2.** → *dickflüssig.*

'Dickmilch *f* soured milk.

'dickschalig [-ʃa:lɪç] *adj* thick-skinned.

'Dickwanst *m* F fatso.

Didaktik [di'daktɪk] *f* (-; *no pl*) didactics. **di'daktisch** *adj* didactic.

die [di:] **I** *def art* the. **II** *dem pron* this (one), that (one): *~ nicht!* not she! **III** *rel pron* who, which. **IV** *pers pron* F *for sie* 1.

Dieb [di:p] *m* (-[e]s; -e) thief.

'Diebes|bande ['di:bəs-] *f* gang of thieves. *~beute f, ~gut n* stolen goods. **Diebin** ['di:bɪn] *f* (-; -nen) thief.

diebisch ['di:bɪʃ] *adj* **1.** thievish. **2.** malicious (*joy*): **sich ~ freuen (über** *acc*) F be tickled pink (at), gloat (at, over).

Diebstahl ['di:pʃta:l] *m* (-[e]s; ⁓e) theft, ⚖️ larceny: **einfacher (schwerer) ~** petty (grand) larceny; **geistiger ~** plagiarism. ⚖️**sicher** *adj* theftproof. ⁓**sicherung** *f mot.* theft protection. ⁓**versicherung** *f* insurance against theft.

Diele ['di:lə] *f* (-; -n) **1.** floorboard. **2.** (entrance) hall, *Am.* hallway.

dienen ['di:nən] *v/i* (h) serve ([bei] *j-m* s.o., ✕ *bei* in, zu for, als as): **dazu ~ zu** *inf* serve to *inf*; **womit kann ich ~?** what can I do for you?; **damit ist mir nicht gedient** that's of no use to me; **wozu soll das ~?** what's the use of that?

Diener *m* (-s; -) *a. fig.* servant. '**Dienerin** *f* (-; -nen) maid(servant), *fig.* handmaid. '**Dienerschaft** *f* (-; *no pl*) servants. '**dienlich** *adj* useful (*dat* to), expedient: **~ sein (**a**) j-m** be of help (*or* use) to s.o., b) **e-r Sache** further s.th.

Dienst [di:nst] *m* (-es; -e) **1.** service (**an** *dat* to), ✕ *a.* duty: **öffentlicher ~** civil service; **im (außer) ~** on (off) duty; **~ haben** be on duty, *pharmacy:* be open; **j-m e-n guten (schlechten) ~ erweisen** do s.o. a good (bad) turn; **j-m gute ~e leisten** serve s.o. well; **in ~ stellen** put *ship etc* into service; (**j-m) den ~ versagen** fail (s.o.); **~ nach Vorschrift** work-to-rule (campaign). **2.** post, employment, work: **im ~e** (*gen*) **stehen** be employed by, work for, *contp.* be on s.o.'s payroll; **außer ~** retired; **den ~ quittieren** resign; → **antreten** 1.

Dienstag ['di:nsta:k] *m* (-[e]s; -e) (**am ~** on) Tuesday. '**dienstags** *adv* on Tuesdays: **~ abends** (on) Tuesday evenings. '**Dienst|alter** *n* (**nach dem ~** by) seniority. ⁓**älteste** *m, f* (-n; -n) senior. ⁓**antritt** *m* (**bei ~** on) taking up duty (*or* one's job). ⁓**auffassung** *f* work ethic. '**dienstbar** *adj* subservient (*dat* to): **sich et. ~ machen** utilize (*or* exploit) s.th. '**dienstbereit** *adj* **1.** a) on duty, b) open. **2.** helpful. '**Dienst|eid** *m* oath of office. ⁓**eifer** *m* zeal, *b.s.* officiousness. ⚖️**eifrig** *adj* zealous, *b.s.* officious. ⚖️**frei** *adj* ⁓**er Tag** day off; **~ haben** be off duty. ⁓**gebrauch** *m* **nur für den ~** for official use only. ⁓**geheimnis** *n* official secret (*or* secrecy). ⁓**gespräch** *n teleph.* official

call. ⁓**grad** *m* ✕ rank, *Am.* grade, ⚓ rating. ⚖️**habend** *adj* on duty. ⁓**herr** *m* employer. ⁓**jahre** *pl* years of service. ⁓**leistung** *f* service (rendered); ⁓**en** services.

'**Dienstleistungs|betrieb** *m* (**öffentlicher ~** public) services enterprise. ⁓**gewerbe** *n* service industries.

'**dienstlich** *adj* official: **~ verhindert** prevented by official duties.

'**Dienst|mädchen** *n* maid(servant), help. ⁓**marke** *f* identity disc. ⁓**pi,stole** *f* service pistol. ⁓**plan** *m* duty roster. ⁓**reise** *f* official trip. ⁓**schluß** *m* **nach ~** after (office) hours. ⁓**stelle** *f* office, department. ⁓**stunden** *pl* office hours. ⚖️**tauglich** *adj* fit for (✕ active) service. ⚖️**untauglich** *adj* unfit for (military) service. ⁓**verhältnis** *n* (contract of) employment. ⁓**vorschrift** *f* regulations. ⁓**wagen** *m* official car. ⁓**weg** *m* (**auf dem ~** through) official channels. ⁓**wohnung** *f* company, army *etc* flat (*or* house). ⁓**zeit** *f* **1.** office (*or* working) hours. **2.** (period of) service.

diesbezüglich ['di:s-] *adj and adv* concerning this, in this connection.

Dieselmotor ['di:zəl-] *m* Diesel engine.

dieser ['di:zər], **diese, dieses,** *a.* **dies** [di:s], *pl* **diese** *dem pron* **I** this, *pl* these: **dieser Tage** a) the other day, b) one of these days. **II** a) this one, *pl* these, b) he, she, it, *pl* they: **dieses und jenes, dies und das** this and that, various things.

diesig ['di:zɪç] *adj* hazy.

diesjährig ['di:sjɛ:rɪç] *adj* this year's.

'**diesmal** *adv* this time.

diesseitig ['di:szaɪtɪç] *adj* near, on this side. **diesseits** ['di:szaɪts] *adv* on this side (*gen* of).

Dietrich ['di:trɪç] *m* (-s; -e) a) picklock, b) skeleton key.

diffamieren [dɪfa'mi:rən] *v/t* (h) slander, defame.

Differential|getriebe [dɪfərɛn'tsĭa:l-] *n mot.* differential (gear). ⁓**rechnung** *f* 📐 differential calculus.

Differenz [dɪfe'rɛnts] *f* (-; -en) difference. **differenzieren** [dɪfərɛn'tsi:rən] *v/t, v/i* (h) differentiate. **differieren** [dɪfə'ri:rən] *v/i* (h) differ (**um** by).

diffus [dɪ'fu:s] *adj* **1.** *phys.* diffuse(d). **2.** *fig.* vague.

digital [digi'ta:l] *adj* digital.

Digi'talanzeige f digital display.
digitalisieren [digitali'ziːrən] v/t (h) digitize.
Digi'talrechner m digital computer.
Digi'taluhr f digital watch (or clock).
Diktat [dɪk'taːt] n (-[e]s; -e) **1.** (ped. ~ **schreiben** write or do) dictation; **das** ~ **aufnehmen** take the dictation. **2.** fig. dictate. **Diktator** [dɪk'taːtɔr] m (-s; -en [-taˈtoːrən]) dictator. **diktatorisch** [dɪkta'toːrɪʃ] adj dictatorial. **Diktatur** [dɪkta'tuːr] f (-; -en) dictatorship.
diktieren [dɪk'tiːrən] v/t, v/i (h) a. fig. dictate (**j-m** to s.o.).
Dik'tiergerät n dictating machine.
Dilemma [di'lɛma] n (-s; -s, -ta) dilemma, F fix.
Dilettant [dilɛ'tant] m (-en; -en), **dilet'tantisch** adj dilettante.
Dill [dɪl] m (-[e]s; -e) ♀ dill.
Dimension [dimɛn'zioːn] f (-; -en) **1.** ∆, phys. dimension. **2.** pl dimensions, fig. a. extent.
Ding [dɪŋ] n (-[e]s; -e, F -er) **1.** thing, a. object; **vor allen** ~**en** above all; F **die armen** ~**er!** the poor (little) things!; fig. **guter** ~**e sein** be cheerful. **2.** pl things, matters: **der Stand der** ~**e** the state of affairs; (**so,) wie die** ~**e liegen** as matters stand; **das geht nicht mit rechten** ~**en zu** F there's s.th. fishy about it. **3.** F **ein tolles** ~ a wow; **ein** ~ **drehen** pull a job; → **verpassen** 2.
'dingfest adj **j-n** ~ **machen** arrest s.o.
Dings [dɪŋs] m, f, n (-; no pl), **'Dingsbums** m, f, n (-; no pl), **'Dingsda** m, f, n (-; no pl) F what's-his(-her, -its)-name, thingumajig.
Dinosaurier [dino'zaʊriər] m (-s; -) dinosaur.
Diode [di'oːdə] f (-; -n) ∮ diode.
Dioxyd ['diˈʔɔksyːt] n (-s; -e) 🜂 dioxide.
Diözese [diø'tseːzə] f (-; -n) diocese.
Diphtherie [dɪfteˈriː] f (-; -n) diphtheria.
Diphthong [dɪf'tɔŋ] m (-s; -e) diphthong.
Diplom [di'ploːm] n (-[e]s; -e) diploma.
Di'plom... diplomaed, graduate (engineer etc), qualified (interpreter etc).
Di'plomarbeit f dissertation.
Diplomat [diplo'maːt] m (-en; -en) diplomat. **Diplo'matenkoffer** m attaché case. **Diplomatie** [diploma'tiː] f (-; no pl) a. fig. diplomacy. **Diplo'matin** f (-;

-nen) diplomat. **diplo'matisch** adj a. fig. diplomatic.
dir [diːr] **I** pers pron you, to you. **II** reflex pron yourself: **wasch** ~ **die Hände!** wash your hands!
direkt [di'rɛkt] **I** adj **1.** a) direct (a. ling.), b) immediate, c) plain: ~**e Informationen** a. firsthand information. **II** adv **2.** direct, a. fig. straight. **3.** directly, immediately: ~ **vor dir** right in front of you. **4.** directly, exactly: ~ **nach Süden liegen** face due south. **5.** F **das ist** ~ **lächerlich** etc that's downright ridiculous etc. **6.** radio, TV live.
Di'rektflug m direct flight.
Direktion [dirɛk'tsioːn] f (-; -en) **1.** management. **2.** manager's office. **3.** direction. **Direkti'onsassi,stent(in** f) m junior executive, assistant manager.
Direktive [dirɛk'tiːvə] f (-; -en) instruction(s).
Direktor [di'rɛktɔr] m (-s; -en [-'toːrən]) **1.** ♰ director, manager. **2.** ped. headmaster, principal. **Direktorat** [dirɛkto'raːt] n (-[e]s; -e) **1.** directorship. **2.** headmaster's office. **Direktorin** [dirɛk'toːrɪn] f (-; -nen) **1.** directress, manageress. **2.** ped. headmistress, principal. **Direktorium** [dirɛkto'riʊm] n (-s; -rien) board of directors.
Direktrice [dirɛk'triːsə] f (-; -n) textil. directress.
Di'rektsendung f live broadcast.
Di'rektwahl f teleph. direct dial(l)ing.
Dirigent [diri'gɛnt] m (-en; -en) ♪ conductor. **Diri'gentin** f (-; -nen) conductress. **dirigieren** [diri'giːrən] v/t, v/i (h) direct, ♰ a. control, ♪ conduct.
Dirigismus [diri'gɪsmʊs] m (-; no pl) ♰ planned economy.
Dirndl ['dɪrndəl] n (-s; -), ~**kleid** n dirndl.
Dirne ['dɪrnə] f (-; -n) prostitute, whore.
Dis [dɪs] n (-; -) ♪ D sharp.
Disharmo'nie f (-; -n) a. fig. discord.
dishar'monisch adj a. fig. discordant.
Diskant [dɪs'kant] m (-s; -e) ♪ treble.
Diskette [dɪs'kɛtə] f computer: disk(ette).
Diskjockey ['dɪsk-] m disc jockey.
Disko ['dɪsko] f (-; -s) F disco.
Diskont [dɪs'kɔnt] m (-s; -e) discount. **diskontieren** [-'tiːrən] v/t (h) ♰ discount. **Dis'kontsatz** m discount rate.
Diskothek [dɪsko'teːk] f (-; -en) discotheque.

Diskrepanz [dɪskreˈpants] f (-; -en) discrepancy.

diskret [dɪsˈkreːt] adj discreet.

Diskretion [dɪskreˈtsǐoːn] f (-; no pl) discretion.

diskriminieren [dɪskrimiˈniːrən] v/t (h) discriminate against.

Diskriminierung f (-; -en) discrimination (gen against).

Diskus [ˈdɪskʊs] m (-[ses]; -se, Disken) sports: discus.

Diskussion [dɪskʊˈsǐoːn] f (-; -en) discussion (über acc on).

Diskussions|leiter m (panel) chairman. **~teilnehmer(in** f) m panel(l)ist. **~veranstaltung** f forum.

'Diskuswerfen n (-s) discus throwing.

'Diskuswerfer(in f) m discus thrower.

diskutabel [dɪskuˈtaːbəl] adj debatable.

diskutieren [dɪskuˈtiːrən] v/t, v/i (h) discuss, debate.

dispensieren [dɪspenˈziːrən] v/t (h) **j-n ~** exempt s.o. (**von** from [doing]).

disponieren [dɪspoˈniːrən] v/i (h) make (one's) arrangements, plan ahead: **~ über** (acc) dispose of. **dispo'niert** adj **gut** etc **~ sein** be in good etc form. **Disposition** [dɪspoziˈtsǐoːn] f (-; -en) 1. a. ♣ disposition. 2. (s-e **~en treffen** make one's) arrangements. **Dispositi'onskre|dit** m ✝ overdraft facilities.

Disqualifikation [dɪskvalifikaˈtsǐoːn] f (-; -en) disqualification (**wegen** for).

disqualifizieren [dɪskvalifiˈtsiːrən] v/t (h) a. fig. disqualify (**wegen** for).

Dissertation [dɪsɛrtaˈtsǐoːn] f (-; -en) dissertation, thesis.

Dissident [dɪsiˈdɛnt] m (-en; -en), **Dissi'dentin** f (-; -nen) pol. dissident.

Dissonanz [dɪsoˈnants] f (-; -en) ♪ dissonance, fig. a. discord.

Distanz [dɪsˈtants] f (-; no pl) distance, fig. a. detachment: **~ wahren** keep one's distance (**gegenüber** from).

distanzieren [dɪstanˈtsiːrən] **sich ~** (h) keep one's distance; **sich ~ von** dis(as)sociate o.s. from. **distan'ziert** adj fig. distanced, reserved.

Distel [ˈdɪstəl] f (-; -n) ♣ thistle.

'Distelfink m zo. goldfinch.

Distrikt [dɪsˈtrɪkt] m (-[e]s; -e) district.

Disziplin [dɪstsiˈpliːn] f (-; -en) 1. no pl discipline. 2. branch, discipline. 3. sports: event. **disziplinarisch** [dɪstsi-

pliˈnaːrɪʃ] adj disciplinary. **Diszipli'narstrafe** f disciplinary punishment. **Diszipli'narverfahren** n disciplinary proceedings. **diszipli'niert** adj disciplined. **diszi'plinlos** adj undisciplined, unruly. **Diszi'plinlosigkeit** f (-; no pl) lack of discipline.

Diva [ˈdiːva] f (-; -s, Diven) star.

divergieren [divɛrˈgiːrən] v/i (h) a. fig. diverge.

divers [diˈvɛrs] adj various, sundry.

diversifizieren [divɛrzifiˈtsiːrən] v/t, v/i (h) ✝ diversify.

Dividend [diviˈdɛnt] m (-en; -en) A dividend. **Dividende** [diviˈdɛndə] f (-; -n) ✝ dividend. **dividieren** [diviˈdiːrən] v/t, v/i (h) A divide (**durch** by). **Division** [diviˈzǐoːn] f (-; -en) A, ✗ division.

Divisor [diˈviːzor] m (-s; -en [diviˈzoːrən]) A divisor.

doch [dɔx] **I** conj 1. but. **II** adv 2. yet, however, nevertheless: **bestimmt** polite yet firm; **also ~!** I knew it!; **er hat also ~ recht!** so he's right after all! 3. **du kommst nicht mit? – ~!** you won't come along? - Oh yes, I will!; **er kommt ~?** he will come, won't he?; **ja ~!** of course!; **nicht ~!** a) don't!, b) certainly not!; **setzen Sie sich ~!** do sit down, please!; **frag ihn ~!** just ask him!; **sei(d) ~ mal still!** be quiet, will you!; **das ist ~ Peter!** why, that's Peter!

Docht [dɔxt] m (-[e]s; -e) wick.

Dock [dɔk] n (-s; -s) dock. **Dockarbeiter** m docker. **'docken** v/i (h) dock.

Dogge [ˈdɔgə] f (-; -n) zo. **deutsche ~** Great Dane; **englische ~** mastiff.

Dogma [ˈdɔgma] n (-s; -men) dogma.

dogmatisch [dɔgˈmaːtɪʃ] adj dogmatic.

Dohle [ˈdoːlə] f (-; -n) zo. (jack)daw.

Doktor [ˈdɔktor] m (-s; -en [-ˈtoːrən]) doctor (a. F ♣): **s-n ~ machen** take (or work for) one's doctor's degree.

Doktorand [dɔktoˈrant] m (-en; -en) doctoral candidate.

'Doktor|arbeit f (doctoral) thesis. **~vater** m supervisor. **~würde** f doctorate.

Doktrin [dɔkˈtriːn] f (-; -en) doctrine.

Dokument [dokuˈmɛnt] n (-[e]s; -e) document (a. fig.), ⚖ a. deed: ✝ **~e gegen Zahlung** documents against payment.

Dokumentar... [dokumenˈtaːr-] documentary (report, play, etc). **Dokumen'tarfilm** m documentary (film).

dokumen'tarisch *adj* documentary.
Dokumentation [dokumɛnta'tsĭoːn] *f* (-; -en) documentation.
dokumentieren [dokumɛn'tiːrən] *v/t* (h) document, *fig. a.* demonstrate, show.
Dolch [dɔlç] *m* (-[e]s; -e) dagger. **~stoß** *m* dagger thrust, *fig.* stab in the back.
Dolde ['dɔldə] *f* (-; -n) ⚜ umbel.
Dollar ['dɔlar] *m* (-[s]; -s) dollar.
Dolle ['dɔlə] *f* (-; -n) ⚓ thole(pin).
dolmetschen ['dɔlmɛtʃən] *v/i* (h) interpret (*a. v/t*), act as interpreter.
'Dolmetscher *m* (-s;-), **'Dolmetscherin** *f* (-; -nen) interpreter.
'Dolmetscherinsti,tut *n* school (*univ.* institute) for interpreters.
Dom [doːm] *m* (-[e]s; -e) cathedral.
Domäne [doˈmɛːnə] *f* (-; -n) domain.
domestizieren [domɛsti'tsiːrən] *v/t* (h) domesticate.
dominant [domi'nant] *adj* dominant.
Domi'nante *f* (-; -n) ♪, *biol.* dominant.
dominieren [domi'niːrən] *v/t, v/i* (h) dominate. **~d** dominant, dominating.
Dominikaner [domini'kaːnər] *m* (-s; -), **Domini'kanerin** *f* (-; -nen), **domini'kanisch** *adj* Dominican.
Domini'kaner(mönch) *m* Dominican.
Domino ['doːmino] *n* (-s; -s), **~spiel** *n* (game of) dominoes. **~stein** *m* domino.
Domizil [domi'tsiːl] *n* (-s; -e) domicile.
Dompteur [dɔmp'tøːr] *m* (-s; -e), **Dompteuse** [-'tøːzə] *f* (-; -n) animal trainer.
Donner ['dɔnər] *m* (-s; -) thunder, *fig. a.* roar: **wie vom ~ gerührt** thunderstruck. **'donnern I** *v/impers* (h) **1. es donnert** it is thundering. **II** *v/i* (sn) *fig.* **2.** thunder, roar. **3.** F **~ gegen** crash against (*or* into). **III** *v/t* (h) *fig.* **4.** roar (*commands etc*). **5.** F slam. **'donnernd** *adj fig.* thunderous (*applause etc*).
'Donnerschlag *m a. fig.* thunderclap.
'Donnerstag *m* (**am ~** on) Thursday.
'donnerstags *adv* (on) Thursdays.
'Donnerwetter F **I** *n* (-s; -) row. **II** *int* **~!** wow!; **warum** (**wo** *etc*) **zum ~?** why (where *etc*) the hell?
doof [doːf] *adj* F dopey, dumb.
dopen ['dɔpən, 'doːpən] *v/t* (h) dope: **sich ~** take dope. **Doping** ['dɔpɪŋ, 'doːpɪŋ] *n* (-s; -s) doping.
'Dopingkon,trolle *f* dope test.
Doppel ['dɔpəl] *n* (-s; -) **1.** duplicate. **2.**

tennis: doubles. **~a,gent(in** *f*) *m* double agent. **~bett** *n* double bed.
Doppeldecker ['dɔpəldɛkər] *m* (-s; -) **1.** biplane. **2.** F (*bus*) double-decker.
'Doppelfehler *m tennis*: double fault.
'Doppelfenster *n* double window.
Doppelgänger ['dɔpəlɡɛŋər] *m* (-s; -), **'Doppelgängerin** *f* (-; -nen) double.
'Doppel|haushälfte *f* semi-detached (house). **~kinn** *n* double chin. **~name** *m* hyphenated name. **~punkt** *m* colon. **~rolle** *f a. fig.* double role.
'doppelseitig [-zaɪtɪç] **I** *adj* reversible (*cloth*). **II** *adv* on both sides.
'Doppelsieg *m sports*: double win.
'Doppelsinn *m* double meaning, ambiguity.
'doppelsinnig *adj* ambiguous.
'Doppelspiel *n* **1.** *contp.* ⊙ double play a) double game. **2.** → **Doppel** 2.
'Doppelstecker *m* ⚡ two-way adapter.
'doppelt I *adj* double, *esp.* ⊙ dual, twin, *esp.* ⚡ duplex: **den ~en Preis** (*or* **das 2e**) **zahlen** pay double the price; **in ~er Ausfertigung** in duplicate. **II** *adv* doubly (*painful etc*), double, twice: **~ so groß** (**viel**) twice as big (much).
'Doppel|tür *f* double doors. **~verdiener** *pl* dual-income family. **~vierer** *m* (-s; -) *rowing*: sculling four.
'doppelwandig [-vandɪç] *adj* double-walled.
'Doppel|zentner *m* quintal. **~zimmer** *n* double room. **~zweier** *m* (-s; -) *rowing*: double sculls.
Dorf [dɔrf] *n* (-[e]s; -er) village.
'Dorfbewohner(in *f*) *m* villager.
dörflich ['dœrflɪç] *adj* village (*life etc*).
Dorn [dɔrn] *m* (-[e]s; -en) **1.** ⚜ thorn, spine (*a. zo.*): **j-m ein ~ im Auge sein** be a thorn in s.o.'s side. **2.** ⊙ spike.
'Dornenkrone *f* crown of thorns.
'dornenlos *adj* thornless.
'dornenreich *adj fig.* thorny.
'Dornenstrauch *m* bramble.
Dorn'röschen *n* (-s) Sleeping Beauty.
dörren ['dœrən] *v/t* (h) dry.
'Dörrobst *n* dried fruit.
Dorsch [dɔrʃ] *m* (-es; -e) *zo.* cod.
dort [dɔrt] *adv* there: **~ drüben** over there; **von ~** → **'dorther** *adv* from there. **'dorthin** *adv* there.
Dose ['doːzə] *f* (-; -n) **1.** box. **2.** tin, can. **3.** ⚡ outlet.

dösen ['dø:zən] *v/i* (h) F **1.** doze. **2.** daydream.

'**Dosen-...** → *Büchsen...*

dosieren [do'zi:rən] *v/t* (h) dose, *fig.* give *s.th.* in small *etc* doses.

Do'sierung *f* (-; -en) *a. fig.* dosage.

Dosis ['do:zis] *f* (-; Dosen) *a. fig.* dose: **zu geringe ~** underdose.

dotieren [do'ti:rən] *v/t* (h) endow (**mit** with): **ein mit 100 000 DM dotiertes Turnier** a tournament carrying a 100,000 mark prize; **e-e gut dotierte Stellung** a well-paid position.

Do'tierung *f* (-; -en) **1.** endowment. **2.** payment, remuneration.

Dotter ['dɔtər] *n* (-s; -) yolk.

doubeln ['du:bəln] *v/t, v/i* (h) *film etc:* double. **Double** ['du:bəl] *n* (-s; -s) double, stand-in.

Dozent [do'tsɛnt] *m* (-en; -en), **Do'zentin** *f* (-; -nen) (university) lecturer, *Am.* assistant professor. **dozieren** [do'tsi:rən] *v/t, v/i* (h) lecture (**über** *acc* on).

Drache ['draxə] *m* (-n; -n) dragon.

Drachen ['draxn] *m* (-s; -) **1.** (**e-n steigen lassen** fly a) kite. **2.** *sports:* hang glider. **3.** F *contp.* battle-ax(e).

'**Drachen|fliegen** *n* (-s) hang gliding. **~flieger(in** *f)* *m* hang glider (pilot).

Dragée [dra'ʒe:] *n* (-s; -s) dragée, coated tablet.

Draht [dra:t] *m* (-[e]s; -̈e) wire: *pol.* **heißer ~** hot line; F **auf ~ sein** a) be in good form, b) be on the ball. **~bürste** *f* wire brush. **~esel** *m humor.* bike. **~funk** *m* wired radio. **~glas** *n* wire(d) glass.

'**Drahthaar...** *zo.* wirehaired (*terrier etc*).

'**drahtig** *adj fig. person:* wiry.

'**drahtlos** *adj* wireless, radio-...

'**Drahtsaite** *f ♪* wire.

'**Drahtseil** *n* wire rope, *circus:* tightrope.

'**Drahtseilakt** *m* tightrope act (*fig.* walk). '**Drahtseilbahn** *f* cable railway.

'**Drahtzaun** *m* wire fence.

'**Drahtzieher** *m* (-s; -) *fig.* wirepuller.

drakonisch [dra'ko:nɪʃ] *adj* Draconian.

drall [dral] *adj* buxom, strapping.

Drall *m* (-[e]s; -e) ⊚ twist, *a. sports:* spin.

Drama ['dra:ma] *n* (-s; -men) drama.

Dramatik [dra'ma:tɪk] *f* (-; *no pl*) drama. **Dramatiker** [dra'ma:tɪkər] *m* (-s; -) dramatist. **dra'matisch** *adj* dramatic. **dramatisieren** [dramati'zi:rən] *v/t* (h) dramatize.

Dramaturg [drama'tʊrk] *m* (-en; -en), **Drama'turgin** [-gɪn] *f* (-; -nen) dramaturge. **Dramaturgie** [dramatʊr'gi:] *f* (-; -n) dramaturgy.

dran [dran] *adv* F **1.** → *daran.* **2. ich bin ~** it's my turn; **jetzt ist er ~!** now he's (in) for it! **3. du bist gut ~!** you are lucky!; **er ist übel ~** he's in a bad way; **spät ~ sein** be late; **an der Sache ist was ~** there is s.th. in it; **man weiß nie, wie man mit ihr ~ ist** you never know what to make of her; **jetzt weiß ich, wie ich ~ bin** now I know where I stand; → **drauf** 2, **Drum**, **glauben** II.

'**dranbleiben** *v/i* (*irr, sep,* -ge-, sn, → *bleiben*) F *fig.* **~ an** (*dat*) stick to; **bleib dran!** a) keep at it!, b) hold the line!

drang [dran] *pret* of *dringen.*

Drang *m* (-[e]s; *no pl*) a) urge, impulse, b) desire (**nach** for).

Drängelei [drɛŋə'laɪ] *f* (-; -en) F pushing and shoving.

drängeln ['drɛŋəln] *v/t, v/i* (h) F **1.** push, shove. **2.** *fig.* pester. **3.** *mot.* tailgate.

drängen ['drɛŋən] (h) I *v/t* **1.** push: *fig.* **j-n ~, et. zu tun** urge s.o. to do s.th., pressure s.o. into doing s.th.; **ich lasse mich nicht ~** I won't be rushed. II *v/i* **2.** push, throng. **3.** *fig.* be urgent, be pressing: **die Zeit drängt** time is running short. **4. auf Zahlung ~** press for payment; **auf e-e Entscheidung ~** urge a decision. III *sich ~* crowd (**um** round); **sich nach vorne (zur Tür etc) ~** force one's way to the front (towards the door *etc*); *fig.* **sich nach et. ~** be keen on (doing) s.th. '**Drängen** *n* (-s) **auf sein** *etc* **~ hin** at his *etc* insistence. '**drängend** *adj* urgent.

'**Drängler** *m* (-s; -) F **1.** pusher. **2.** *mot.* tailgater.

drangsalieren [dranza'li:rən] *v/t* (h) torment.

'**dranhalten: sich ~** (*irr, sep,* -ge-, h, → *halten*) F a) hurry up, b) keep at it.

'**drankommen** *v/i* (*irr, sep,* -ge-, sn, → *kommen*) F **1. jetzt komme ich dran** now it's my turn; **als nächster ~** be next. **2.** *ped.* be asked (a question).

'**drankriegen** *v/t* (*sep,* -ge-, h) F get.

'**drannehmen** *v/t* (*irr, sep,* -ge-, h, → *nehmen*) F take (*patient*), ask (*pupil*).

drapieren [dra'pi:rən] *v/t* (h) drape.

drastisch ['drastɪʃ] *adj* drastic.

drauf [drauf] F *adv* **1.** → *darauf.* **2.** ~ *und dran sein, et. zu tun* be on the point of doing s.th.; *gut ~ sein* a) be in great form, b) *a.* (*schwer*) *was ~ haben* be (just) great (*in dat* at); *er hatte 150 Sachen ~* he was doing 100 miles.

Draufgänger ['draufɡɛŋɐr] *m* (s;) a) daredevil, b) go-getter, c) casanova, wolf. '**draufgängerisch** *adj* reckless.

'**draufgehen** *v/i* (*irr, sep,* -ge-, sn, → **gehen**) F **1.** be killed. **2.** a) be lost, *money:* go down the drain, b) go to pot.

'**draufkommen** *v/i* (*irr, sep,* -ge-, sn, → **kommen**) F *j-m ~* find s.o. out.

'**draufkriegen** *v/t* (*sep,* -ge-, h) F *eins ~* a) get it in the neck, b) *sports:* get a thrashing.

'**drauflegen** *v/t* (*sep,* -ge-, h) F pay an extra *100 marks etc.*

drauf'los F I *adv* straight ahead. II *int* (*feste*) ~! come on! **drauf'losgehen** *v/i* (*irr, sep,* -ge-, sn, → **gehen**) F make straight for it. **drauf'losreden** *v/i* (*sep,* -ge-, h) F start rattling away.

'**draufmachen** *v/t* (*sep,* -ge-, h) F *e-n ~* have a ball (*or* a booze-up), go to town.

'**draufstoßen** *v/t* (*irr, sep,* -ge-, h, → **stoßen**) F *j-n ~* spell it out to s.o.

'**draufzahlen** (*sep,* -ge-, h) F I *v/t* pay an extra *100 marks etc.* II *v/i* lose money.

draus [draus] F *for* **daraus.**

draußen ['drausən] *adv* outside, in the open (air), ♏ at sea: *~ im Garten* out in the garden; *bleib(t) ~!* keep out!

drechseln ['drɛksəln] *v/t* (h) turn: → *gedrechselt.* **Drechsler** ['drɛkslər] *m* (-s; -) wood turner.

Dreck [drɛk] *m* (-[e]s; *no pl*) **1.** dirt, filth, mud: *fig. im ~ sitzen* be in a mess; *j-n* (*et.*) *in den ~ ziehen* drag s.o.'s name (s.th.) in the mud; *j-n wie* (*den letzten*) *~ behandeln* treat s.o. like dirt; *er hat* (*viel*) *~ am Stecken* he has a lot to answer for. **2.** *fig.* rubbish, crap: *er kümmert sich e-n ~ darum* he doesn't care a damn; *das geht dich e-n ~ an!* that's none of your business!

'**Dreckding** *n* (-[e]s; -er) F damn thing.

'**dreckig** *adj* F dirty, filthy, *fig. a.* nasty, mean: *~e Witze* dirty jokes; *es geht ihm ~* he's having a bad time.

'**Dreckfink** *m contr.* dump, hole.

'**Drecksau** *f,* '**Dreckschwein** *n* V **1.** (dirty) pig. **2.** swine.

'**Dreckskerl** *m* F swine, bastard.

'**Dreckwetter** *n* F filthy weather.

Dreh [dre:] *m* (-[e]s; -e) F trick: *den richtigen ~ heraushaben* have got the hang of it.

'**Dreharbeiten** *pl film:* shooting.

'**Drehbank** *f* ⚙ lathe.

'**drehbar** *adj* rotatable.

'**Drehbleistift** *m* propelling pencil.

'**Drehbuch** *n* script, *a. fig.* scenario.

'**Drehbuchautor(in** *f*) *m* scriptwriter.

'**Drehbühne** *f* revolving stage.

drehen ['dre:ən] (h) I *v/t* **1.** a) turn, b) twist (*a. fig.*): *fig. man kann es ~ und wenden* (*wie man will*) whichever way you look at it. **2.** roll (*cigarette etc*). **3.** shoot (*film*). **4.** F *fig.* wangle: → *Ding* 3. **5.** ⚙ turn. II *v/i* **6.** turn (round): *~ an* (*dat*) turn, *a. fig.* fiddle with; F *daran ist nichts zu ~ und zu deuteln* that's a fact. III *sich ~* turn, go (*or* spin) round; *die Erde dreht sich um die Sonne* the earth revolves around the sun; *mir dreht sich alles* my head is spinning; *fig. sich ~ um* revolve round, talk: be about; *es dreht sich darum, ob* it's a question of whether.

'**Dreher** *m* (-s; -) ⚙ lathe operator.

'**Dreh|kraft** *f* rotatory force. **~kran** *m* slewing crane. **~kreuz** *n* turnstile. **~mo‚ment** *n* ⚙ torque. **~orgel** *f* barrel organ. **~pause** *f film:* shooting break. **~punkt** *m* ⚙ *or fig.* pivot. **~schalter** *m* rotary switch. **~scheibe** *f* 🚂 turntable.

'**Drehstrom** *m* ⚡ threephase current. **~motor** *m* threephase A.C. motor.

'**Drehstuhl** *m* swivel chair.

'**Drehtür** *f* revolving door.

'**Drehung** *f* (-; -en) turn(ing), rotation: *schnelle ~* spin.

'**Drehzahl** *f* revolutions per minute (*abbr.* r.p.m.). **~messer** *m* revolution counter. **~regelung** *f* speed control.

drei [drai] *adj* three: F *sie kann nicht bis ~ zählen* she is pretty dim(witted).

Drei *f* (-; -en) a) (number) three, b) *ped.* satisfactory.

'**dreibeinig** [-bainiç] *adj* three-legged.

'**dreidimensio‚nal** *adj* three-dimensional.

'**Dreieck** *n* (-[e]s; -e) triangle.

'**dreieckig** *adj* triangular.

'**Dreiecksverhältnis** *n* (love) triangle.

Drei'einigkeit *f* (-; *no pl*) *eccl.* Trinity.

'**dreifach** *adj* threefold, triple: *die ~e Menge* three times the amount; *in ~er Ausfertigung* in triplicate; *das Dreifache* three times as much, triple.

'**dreifarbig** *adj* tricolo(u)r.

'**Dreiganggetriebe** *n* three-speed gear.

'**dreihundert** *adj* three hundred.

'**dreijährig** [-jɛːrɪç] *adj* **1.** three-year-old. **2.** lasting (*or* of) three years.

'**Dreijährige** [-jɛːrɪgə] *m, f* (-n; -n) three- -year-old (child).

'**Dreiklang** *m* ♪ triad.

Drei'könige *pl eccl.* (**zu ~** on) Epiphany.

'**dreimal** *adv* three times.

'**Drei'meilenzone** *f* three-mile limit.

'**Dreimeterbrett** *n* three-metre (diving) board.

dreinblicken ['draɪn-] *v/i* (*sep*, -ge-, h) F look *sad etc.*

'**dreinschlagen** *v/i* (*irr, sep*, -ge-, h, → *schlagen*) F lay about one.

'**Dreirad** *n* tricycle.

'**Dreisatz** *m* (-es; *no pl*) ⅍ rule of three.

'**dreisilbig** [-zɪlbɪç] *adj* trisyllabic.

'**Dreisprung** *m sports:* triple jump.

'**dreispurig** [-ʃpuːrɪç] *adj* three-lane(d).

dreißig ['draɪsɪç] *adj* thirty. '**Dreißig** *f* (-) thirty: *sie ist Ende (der)* ~ *sh* in her late thirties. **dreißiger** ['draɪsɪgər] *adj* *die ~ Jahre* the thirties (*of a century*). '**Dreißiger** *m* (-s; -), '**Dreißigerin** *f* (-; -nen) man (woman) of thirty (*or* in his [her] thirties). '**dreißigst** *adj* thirtieth.

dreist [draɪst] *adj* impudent, imperti- nent, F cheeky, brazen (*lie etc.*).

'**dreistellig** [-ʃtɛlɪç] *adj* ⅍ three-digit.

'**Dreistigkeit** *f* (-; *no pl*) impudence, im- pertinence, F cheek.

'**dreistufig** [-ʃtuːfɪç] *adj* ◉ three-stage.

'**dreitägig** [-tɛːgɪç] *adj* three-day.

'**dreiteilig** [-taɪlɪç] *adj* three-piece.

'**drei'viertel** *adj* three-quarter: *es war ~ zwei* it was a quarter to two; ~ *voll* three-quarters full.

'**dreiwertig** [-veːrtɪç] *adj* ⚛ trivalent.

'**dreiwöchig** [-vœçɪç] *adj* three-week.

'**Dreizack** *m* (-s; -e) trident.

'**dreizehn** *adj* thirteen: F *jetzt schlägt's aber ~!* that's the limit!

'**dreizehnt** *adj* thirteenth.

Dresche ['drɛʃə] *f* (-; *no pl*) F hiding.

dreschen *v/t, v/i* (drosch, gedroschen, h) ✝ thresh: → *Phrase.*

'**Dreschma,schine** *f* threshing machine.

Dresseur [drɛˈsøːr] *m* (-s; -e) animal trainer. **dressieren** [drɛˈsiːrən] *v/t* (h) train (*animal*), drill (*child*).

Dressman ['drɛsmən] *m* (-s; -men) male model.

Dressur [drɛˈsuːr] *f* (-; -en) **1.** (animal) training. **2.** → **Dres'surreiten** *n* dres- sage.

Drift [drɪft] *f* (-; -en) ⚓ drift (current).

driften ['drɪftən] *v/i* (sn) ⚓ *or fig.* drift.

Drill [drɪl] *m* (-[e]s; *no pl*) ✂ *or fig.* drill.

drillen ['drɪlən] *v/t* (h) *a. fig.* drill.

Drilling ['drɪlɪŋ] *m* (-s; -e) triplet.

drin [drɪn] *adv* F **1.** → *darin:* **er ist** ~ he's inside. **2.** *es ist noch alles* ~ anything is still possible; *das ist (bei mir) nicht ~!* that's not on!, that's out!; *mehr war nicht* ~ that was the best I *etc* could do.

dringen ['drɪŋən] (drang, gedrungen) *v/i* **1.** (sn) ~ *durch* force one's way through, *light etc:* penetrate, *water etc:* seep through. **2.** (sn) ~ *aus* (*dat*) *sounds etc:* come from. **3.** (sn) ~ *in* (acc) pene- trate (into), *water: a.* seep into, *a. fig.* invade; *in die Öffentlichkeit* ~ leak out. **4.** (sn) ~ *bis zu* reach, get as far as. **5.** (h) ~ *auf* (acc) insist on, press for. **6.** (sn) (*mit Fragen etc.*) *in j-n* ~ press s.o. (with questions *etc*). '**dringend** *adj* urgent, pressing, strong (*suspicion etc*), com- pelling (*reasons*): ~ *brauchen* need ur- gently (*or badly*); ~ *empfehlen* recom- mend strongly; ~ *notwendig* impera- tive; ~ *verdächtig* highly suspect.

'**dringlich** *adj* urgent.

'**Dringlichkeit** *f* (-; *no pl*) urgency: *von größter* ~ of top (*or* first) priority.

'**Dringlichkeitsantrag** *m parl.* emergen- cy motion. '**Dringlichkeitsstufe** *f* prio- rity (class): *höchste* ~ top priority.

'**drinnen** ['drɪnən] *adv* inside, indoors.

'**drinstecken** *v/i* (sep, -ge-, h) F *da steckt viel Arbeit drin* a lot of work has gone into it.

dritt [drɪt] *adj* third: ~*er Klasse* third- -class; *wir gingen zu* ~ *hin* three of us went; *pol. die* 2*e Welt* the Third World. '**Dritte** *m, f* (-n; -n) third, ⅍ third party: ~*(r) werden sports:* finish third.

Drittel ['drɪtəl] *n* (-s; -) third.

drittens ['drɪtəns] *adv* third(ly).

'**drittklassig** [-klasɪç] *adj fig.* third-rate.

'**drittletzt** *adj* last but two.

Droge ['droːgə] *f* (-; -n) drug.

'drogenabhängig *adj* addicted to drugs. **'Drogenabhängige** *m, f* (-n; -n) drug addict. **'Drogenabhängigkeit** *f* (-; *no pl*) drug addiction.

'Drogen|handel *m* drug trafficking. **~händler** *m* drug dealer. **~kon,sum** *m* use of drugs. **~mißbrauch** *m* drug abuse. **~rausch** *m* F (*im ~* on a) trip. **~sucht** *f* drug addiction. **2süchtig** *adj* addicted to drugs. **~süchtige** *m, f* (-n; -n) drug addict. **~szene** *f* drug scene.

Drogerie [drogəˈriː] *f* (-; -n) chemist's (shop), *Am.* drugstore, pharmacy.

Drogist [droˈɡɪst] *m* (-en; -en), **Dro'gistin** *f* (-; -nen) chemist, *Am.* druggist.

'Drohbrief *m* threatening letter.

drohen [ˈdroːən] *v/i* (h) threaten (*j-m* s.o.); *j-m ~* a) *mit der Faust* shake one's fist at s.o.; b) *fig.* be in store for s.o.; *mit der Polizei ~* threaten to call the police; *er drohte zu ertrinken* he was in danger of drowning.

'drohend *adj* threatening, *fig. a.* imminent: *~e Gefahr* imminent danger.

Drohne [ˈdroːnə] *f* (-; -n) *a. fig.* drone.

dröhnen [ˈdrøːnən] *v/i* (h) a) boom, roar, b) resound (*von* with): *fig. mein Kopf dröhnt* my head is ringing.

Drohung *f* (-; -en) threat, menace.

drollig [ˈdrɔlɪç] *adj* droll, funny.

Dromedar [ˈdroːmedaːr] *n* (-s; -e) *zo.* dromedary.

Drops [drɔps] *m, n* (-; -) fruit drop.

drosch [drɔʃ] *pret of* **dreschen.**

Drossel[1] [ˈdrɔsəl] *f* (-; -n) *zo.* thrush.

Drossel[2] *f* (-; -n) ⊕ choke.

'Drosselklappe *f mot.* throttle (valve).

drosseln [ˈdrɔsəln] *v/t* (h) ⊕ throttle (*a. fig.*), turn down (*heating*).

drüben [ˈdryːbən] *adv* (*da*) *~* over there.

Druck[1] [drʊk] *m* (-[e]s; *no pl*) pressure, *fig. a.* stress, ✍ sensation of pressure: *auf j-n ~ ausüben, j-n unter ~ setzen* put s.o. under pressure; F *im ~ sein* be pressed for time.

Druck[2] *m* (-[e]s; -e) **1.** *no pl* printing: *in ~ gehen* go to press; *im ~ sein* be printing. **2.** *paint., print., textil.* print.

'Druck|abfall *m* drop in pressure. **~anstieg** *m* increase in pressure. **~ausgleich** *m* pressure compensation.

'Druckbuchstabe *m* block letter: *in ~n schreiben a.* print.

Drückeberger [ˈdrʏkəbɛrɡər] *m* (-s; -) F shirker.

'druckempfindlich *adj* sensitive to pressure, *fruit*: easily bruised.

drucken [ˈdrʊkən] *v/t* (h) print.

drücken [ˈdrʏkən] (h) **I** *v/t* **1.** press, squeeze, push (*button, key*): *j-m die Hand ~* shake hands with s.o.; *j-m et. in die Hand ~* put (*or* slip) s.th. into s.o.'s hand; *j-n* (*an sich*) *~* hug s.o.; → *Daumen.* **2.** *j-n ~ shoe:* pinch s.o., *fig. worries etc:* weigh heavily on s.o. **3.** bring (*or* force) down (*performance, prices*), better *a record* (*um* by). **4.** *sl.* shoot up (*drug*). **II** *v/i* **5.** press, *shoe:* pinch, *backpack etc:* a. hurt, *fig. heat etc:* be oppressive: *~ auf* (*acc*) press on, press, push (*button etc*); *auf die Stimmung ~* cast a gloom (*on everything*). **III** *sich ~* (*heat etc*).

'drückend *adj fig.* heavy (*debts*), oppressive (*heat etc*).

'Drucker *m* (-s; -) *a. computer:* printer.

'Drücker *m* (-s; -) a) latch, b) *on gun:* trigger: F *auf den letzten ~* at the last minute; *am ~ sitzen* be at the controls.

Drucke'rei *f* (-; -en) printing office.

'Druckerzeugnis *n* publication.

'Druckfehler *m* misprint.

'Druckfehlerverzeichnis *n* errata.

'druckfertig *adj* ready for (the) press: *~es Manuskript* fair copy.

'Druck|ka,bine *f* ✈ pressurized cabin. **~knopf** *m* press-stud, F popper, *Am.* snap fastener, ⊕ push button. **~luft** *f* compressed air. **~luftbremse** *f* air brake. **~ma,schine** *f* printing machine. **~messer** *m* ⊕ pressure ga(u)ge. **~mittel** *n fig.* lever. **~posten** *m* F cushy job. **2reif** → *druckfertig.* **~sache** *f* **1.** ✉ printed (*Am. a.* second-class) matter. **2.** *parl.* Document. **~schrift** *f* **1.** block letters: *in ~ schreiben a.* print. **2.** printing type. **3.** publication. **~stelle** *f* tender spot, *on fruit:* bruise. **~verband** *m* ✍ compression bandage. **~welle** *f* blast, shock wave. **~zeile** *f* printline.

drum [drʊm] *adv* F → *darum.*

Drum: *das ganze ~ und Dran* everything that goes with it; *mit allem ~ und Dran* with all the trimmings.

drunter [ˈdrʊntər] *adv* F **1.** → *darunter.* **2.** *es ging alles ~ und drüber* it was absolutely chaotic.

Drüse ['dry:zə] f (-; -n) gland.

Dschungel ['dʒʊŋəl] m (-s; -) jungle.

Dschunke ['dʒʊŋkə] f (-; -n) junk.

du [du:] *pers pron* you: **bist ~ es?** is that you?; **~ Glückliche(r)!** lucky you!; **mit j-m per ~ sein** → **duzen** b.

Dübel ['dy:bəl] m (-s; -), **'dübeln** v/t (h) dowel, peg.

Dublee... [du'ble:-] gold-plated.

ducken ['dʊkən] (h) **I** v/t **den Kopf ~** duck one's head. **II sich ~** a) crouch (down), b) duck, c) *fig.* cringe (**vor** before). **Duckmäuser** ['dʊkmɔʏzər] m (-s; -) F *contp.* **1.** cringer. **2.** hypocrite.

dudeln ['du:dəln] v/t, v/i (h) F tootle. **'Dudelsack** m bagpipe(s).

Duell [du'ɛl] n (-s; -e) duel (**auf Pistolen** with pistols), *fig. a.* fight. **duellieren** [due'li:rən] **sich ~** (h) fight a duel.

Duett [du'ɛt] n (-[e]s; -e) ♪ duet.

Duft [dʊft] m (-[e]s; ⁓e) smell, scent, fragrance, aroma. **'dufte** *adj* F great, super. **'duften** v/i (h) smell (**nach** of): **süß ~** smell sweet. **'duftend** *adj* fragrant.

duftig ['dʊftɪç] *adj* gossamer, filmy.

'Duftnote f special scent.

'Duftstoff m scent, aroma.

dulden ['dʊldən] v/t (h) **1.** tolerate: **ich dulde es nicht** I won't have it (**daß** that); → **Aufschub. 2.** endure, suffer. **'Dulder** m (-s; -), **'Dulderin** f (-; -nen) (patient) sufferer. **'Duldermiene** f *iro.* **mit ~** with a martyred expression. **'duldsam** *adj* (**gegen**) tolerant (of), patient (with). **'Duldsamkeit** f (-; *no pl*) tolerance (**gegen** of), forbearance. **'Duldung** f (-; *no pl*) toleration.

dumm [dʊm] *adj* stupid, F dumb, *a.* silly, *fig. a.* awkward: **zu ~!**, **so et. ⁓es!** how stupid!, what a nuisance!; F **~es Zeug** rubbish; **sich ~ stellen** act the fool; **ich lasse mich nicht für ~ verkaufen** I'm not that stupid; **die Sache wird mir zu ~** I'm sick and tired of it; **j-m ~ kommen** get fresh with s.o. **'Dumme** m, f (-n; -n) fool: **der ~ sein** be left holding the baby. **'dummerweise** *adv* F **1. ~ habe ich es vergessen** like a fool I forgot it. **2.** unfortunately. **'Dummheit** f (-; -en) **1.** *no pl* stupidity. **2.** stupid thing: **was für e-e ~!** what a stupid thing to do!; **(mach) k-e ⁓en!** don't do anything stupid!, none of your tricks! **'Dummkopf** m fool, idiot.

dumpf [dʊmpf] *adj* **1.** dull, muffled: **~er Aufprall** thud. **2.** stuffy, musty. **3.** *fig.* dark (*feeling etc*), dull (*pain*), gloomy (*silence etc*).

Düne ['dy:nə] f (-; -n) dune.

Dung [dʊŋ] m (-[e]s; *no pl*) manure, dung. **'Düngemittel** n → **Dünger.**

düngen ['dyŋən] v/t, v/i (h) fertilize. **'Dünger** m (-s; -) a) fertilizer, b) manure, dung. **'Düngrube** f manure pit.

dunkel ['dʊŋkəl] *adj* **1.** dark, *a. fig.* gloomy: **es wird ~** it is getting dark. **2.** deep (*voice etc*). **3.** *fig.* dark, vague, dim, mysterious, *b.s.* shady, dubious: **j-n im ⁓n lassen** leave s.o. in the dark (**über** *acc* about); F **im ⁓n tappen** grope in the dark; **sich ~ erinnern** remember dimly. **'Dunkel** n (-s) the dark.

Dünkel ['dyŋkəl] m (-s; *no pl*) conceit.

'dunkelblau *adj* dark blue. **'dunkelblond** *adj* dark blond. **'dunkelhaarig** *adj* dark(-haired). **'dunkelhäutig** [-hɔʏtɪç] *adj* dark(-skinned), swarthy.

'Dunkelheit f (-; *no pl*) darkness, *fig. a.* obscurity: → **Einbruch** 2.

'Dunkelkammer f *phot.* darkroom.

'dunkelrot *adj* dark red.

'Dunkelziffer f estimated number of unknown cases.

dünn [dyn] *adj* **1.** thin, *a.* flimsy (*dress etc*), *phys.* rare (*air*), weak (*tea etc*). **2.** *fig.* poor. **'dünnbesiedelt** *adj* sparsely populated. **'Dünndarm** m *anat.* small intestine. **'Dünndruck(ausgabe** f) m India-paper edition. **'dünnemachen: sich ~** (*sep*, -ge-, h) F make o.s. scarce. **'dünnflüssig** *adj* thin, liquid, thin-bodied (*oil*). **'dünngesät** F *fig.* scarce, rare. **'dünnhäutig** [-hɔʏtɪç] *adj a. fig.* thin-skinned. **'Dünnheit** f (-; *no pl*) thinness, weakness.

Dunst [dʊnst] m (-[e]s; ⁓e) a) haze, mist, b) vapo(u)r, fumes, steam: F *fig.* **er hat k-n (blassen) ~ davon** he hasn't the foggiest (idea) about it.

dünsten ['dynstən] v/t, v/i (h) stew.

'Dunstglocke f blanket of smog.

'dunstig *adj* hazy, misty.

'Dunstschleier m (veil of) haze.

Dünung ['dy:nʊŋ] f (-; -en) ♣ swell.

Duo ['du:o] n (-s; -s) ♪ duo.

Duplikat [dupli'ka:t] n (-[e]s; -e) duplicate, copy.

Dur [du:r] n (-; *no pl*) ♪ (**in ~** in) major.

durch [dʊrç] **I** *prep* **1.** through: *quer ~* across; *~ ganz Amerika travel etc* all over America. **2.** by, by means of, through: *~ Zufall* by chance. **3.** *₳ 10 ~ 2* 10 divided by 2. **4.** due to, through. **II** *adv* **5.** during, through(out): *das ganze Jahr ~* throughout the year; *die ganze Nacht ~* all night long; *F es ist 5 Uhr ~* it is past five. **6.** *F ~ und ~* through and through, completely.

'**durchackern** *v/t* (*sep*, -ge-, h) F *fig.* plough (*Am.* plow) through.

'**durcharbeiten** (*sep*, -ge-, h) **I** *v/t* work (*or* go) through. **II** *v/i* work through (without a break). **III** *sich ~ a. fig.* work one's way through.

'**durchatmen** *v/i* (*sep*, -ge-, h) (*tief*) ~ breathe deeply.

durch'aus *adv* **1.** thoroughly, quite: ~*!* absolutely!; *~ möglich!* quite possible!; *wenn er ~ kommen will* if he insists on coming. **2.** *~ nicht* by no means; *~ nicht!* absolutely not!; *er wollte ~ nicht gehen* he absolutely refused to go.

'**durchbeißen** (*irr*, *sep*, -ge-, h, → *beißen*) **I** *v/t* bite through. **II** *sich ~* F *fig.* struggle through.

'**durchbiegen**: *sich ~* (*irr*, *sep*, -ge-, h, → *biegen*) sag.

'**durchblättern** *v/t* (*sep*, -ge-, h) leaf through.

'**Durchblick** *m* **1.** view (*auf acc* of). **2.** F *fig.* grasp: *~ haben* → *durchblicken* 3; *sich den* (*nötigen*) *~ verschaffen* find out what's what. '**durchblicken** *v/i* (*sep*, -ge-, h) **1.** look through. **2.** *fig. ~ lassen* intimate (*daß* that). **3.** F a) get it, b) know the score: *da blicke ich nicht durch!* I don't get it!

durch'bluten *v/t* (h) supply with blood. **Durch'blutung** *f* (*-; no pl*) (blood) circulation. **durch'blutungsfördernd** *adj* 🞧 stimulating (blood) circulation. **Durch'blutungsstörung** *f* 🞧 circulatory disturbance.

durch'bohren *v/t* (*insep*, *no* -ge-, h) stab, pierce: *j-n mit Blicken ~* look daggers at s.o.; *~der Blick* piercing look.

'**durchbrechen¹** (*irr*, *sep*, -ge-, → *brechen*) **I** *v/t* (h) **1.** break *s.th.* in two. **II** *v/i* (sn) **2.** break (in two), break through (*a.* ✗ *or sports*). **3.** 🞧 burst, *teeth*: erupt. **4.** *fig.* reveal itself.

durch'brechen² *v/t* (*irr*, *insep*, *no* -ge-, h, → *brechen*) **1.** break through *s.th.* **2.** break (*rule etc*).

'**durchbrennen** *v/i* (*irr*, *sep*, -ge-, sn, → *brennen*) **1.** 🗲 *fuse*: blow, *bulb*: burn out. **2.** F *fig.* run away, make off.

'**durchbringen** (*irr*, *sep*, -ge-, h, → *bringen*) **I** *v/t* **1.** get *s.o.*, *s.th.* through, pull *a patient* through, support (*family etc*). **2.** squander, blue. **II** *sich ~* get by.

'**Durchbruch** *m* (*-[e]s; ⸚e*) **1.** breakthrough (*a. fig.*), 🞧 perforation, *of teeth*: eruption: *fig. zum ~ kommen* show, become manifest. **2.** opening.

durchdacht [-'daxt] *adj* reasoned.

durch'denken *v/t* (*irr*, *insep*, *no* -ge-, h, → *denken*) reason *s.th.* (out).

'**durchdrängen**: *sich ~* (*sep*, -ge-, h) force one's way through.

'**durchdrehen** (*sep*, -ge-, h) **I** *v/t* **1.** *gastr.* mince. **II** *v/i* **2.** *wheels*: spin. **3.** (*a.* sn) F *fig.* a) flip, b) panic.

durch'dringen¹ *v/t* (*irr*, *insep*, *no* -ge-, h, → *dringen*) **1.** go through, penetrate. **2.** *fig.* fill, pervade. '**durchdringen²** *v/i* (*irr*, *sep*, -ge-, sn, → *dringen*) **1.** penetrate, get through, *voice etc*: be heard: *fig. bis zu j-m ~* reach s.o. **2.** *fig. ~ mit* succeed with, get *s.th.* accepted.

durch'dringend *adj* penetrating, piercing, loud, shrill (*voice etc*), pungent (*smell*), biting (*cold etc*).

'**durchdrücken** *v/t* (*sep*, -ge-, h) **1.** straighten. **2.** F → **durchsetzen¹**.

durch'drungen I *pp* of **durchdringen¹**. **II** *adj fig.* filled (*von* with).

durchein'ander *adv* ~ *sein* be at sixes and sevens, be in a mess; *ganz ~ sein person*: a) be all mixed up, b) be in a flap. **Durchein'ander** *n* (*-s*) *a. fig.* confusion, mess.

durchein'ander|bringen *v/t* (*irr*, *sep*, -ge-, h, → *bringen*) jumble up, *a. fig.* mix up (*notions etc*), confuse, get *s.o.* all flustered: *alles ~* get everything mixed up. **~geraten** *v/i* (*sep*, -ge-, sn, → *geraten*) get mixed up. **~reden** *v/i* (*sep*, -ge-, h) talk all at once.

'**durchfahren¹** *v/i* (*irr*, *sep*, -ge-, sn, → *fahren*) pass (*or* go, drive) through, 🚆 *a.* go nonstop (*bis* to): *die Nacht ~* travel all night. **durch'fahren²** *v/t* (*irr*, *insep*, *no* -ge-, h, → *fahren*) pass (*or* go, drive, *fig.* flash) through.

'Durchfahrt f a) passage, b) gate(way): ~ **verboten!** no thoroughfare!

'Durchfahrtsstraße f through road.

'Durchfall m 1. ✻ diarrh(o)ea. 2. F thea. flop. **'durchfallen** v/i (irr, sep, -ge-, sn, → **fallen**) 1. fall through. 2. F a) ped., univ. (a. ~ **lassen**) fail, Am. flunk, b) in elections: be defeated, c) proposal etc: be turned down, d) thea. etc be a flop.

'Durchfallquote f ped. etc failure rate.

'durchfelern v/i (sep, -ge-, h) Γ make a night of it.

'durchfinden v/i (irr, sep, -ge-, h, → **finden**) (a. **sich** ~) find one's way through: fig. (**sich**) **nicht mehr** ~ be lost.

'durchfliegen v/i (irr, sep, -ge-, sn, → **fliegen**) 1. fly through, a. fly nonstop. 2. → **durchfallen** 2 a. **durch'fliegen²** v/t (irr, insep, no -ge-, h, → **fliegen**) 1. a) fly through, b) fly, cover (distance). 2. fig. skim (or glance) through.

'durchfließen v/i (irr, sep, -ge-, sn, → **fließen**) flow (or run) through.

'durchfragen: sich ~ (sep, -ge-, h) ask one's way (through).

durchfroren [-'fro:rən] adj frozen stiff.

'Durchfuhr [-fu:r] f (-; -en) ✝ transit.

'durchfuhrbar adj practicable, feasible: **schwer** ~ difficult to carry out.

'durchführen (sep, -ge-, h) **I** v/t 1. lead (or take) s.o., s.th. through. 2. carry out (or through) (work, plan, etc), realize (project), organize (event). 3. enforce (a law). **II** v/i 3. ~ **durch** lead through. **'Durchführung** f (-; -en) carrying out, realization, ⚖ enforcement.

'Durchfuhrzoll m ✝ transit duty.

'durchfüttern v/t (sep, -ge-, h) F feed.

'Durchgang m (-[e]s, ⁓e) 1. passage, alley: ~ **verboten!**, **kein** ~! no thoroughfare!; **den** ~ **versperren** block the passage. 2. astr., ✝ transit. 3. stage, of vote, a. sports: round, of race: heat.

'durchgängig adj general.

'Durchgangs|lager n transit camp. **~straße** f through road. **~verkehr** m 1. through traffic. 2. ✝ transit.

'durchgeben v/t (irr, sep, -ge-, h, → **geben**) pass on: **telefonisch** ~ phone; (**im Radio**) ~ announce (on the radio).

'durchgebraten adj gastr. well done.

'durchgefroren → **durchfroren**.

'durchgehen (irr, sep, -ge-, sn, → **gehen**) **I** v/i 1. go through, motion, bill,

etc: a. be passed: **et.** ~ **lassen** let s.th. pass, tolerate s.th.; F **j-m et.** ~ **lassen** let s.o. get away with s.th. 2. F run away, make off, horse: bolt: fig. **mit j-m** ~ **imagination** etc: run away with s.o.; **ihm gingen die Nerven durch** he lost his head. **II** v/t 3. go over, go through.

'durchgehend I adj through (train etc), continuous (operation etc, a. ⊛). **II** adv throughout: ~ **geöffnet** open all day.

durch'geistigt adj spiritual

'durchgreifen v/i (irr, sep, -ge-, h, → **greifen**) (**gegen**) take steps (against), F crack down (on). **'Durchgreifen** n (-s) (**hartes** etc) ~ (**gegen**) (rigorous etc) action (against), F crackdown (on). **'durchgreifend** adj drastic (measures), radical, sweeping (changes etc).

'durchhalten (irr, sep, -ge-, h, → **halten**) **I** v/i hold out (to the end), F stick it out. **II** v/t keep s.th. up, stand (the pace).

'Durchhaltevermögen n (-s; no pl) staying power, stamina.

'durchhängen v/i (irr, sep, -ge-, h, → **hängen**) 1. sag. 2. F fig. a) feel low, b) show etc: be dull. **'Durchhänger** m (-s; -) F **e-n** ~ **haben** feel low.

'durchhecheln v/t (sep, -ge-, h) F fig. gossip about, run s.o., s.th. down.

'durchkämmen¹ v/t (sep, -ge-, h) 1. comb out (hair). 2. → durch'kämmen² v/t (insep, no -ge-, h) comb (**nach** for).

'durchkämpfen (sep, -ge-, h) **I sich** ~ a. fig. fight one's way through. **II** v/t fight s.th. through.

'durchkauen v/t (sep, -ge-, h) chew s.th. well: F fig. **et.** ~ go over s.th. again and again.

'durchkommen v/i (irr, sep, -ge-, sn, → **kommen**) 1. come through, patient: a. pull through, teleph. get through, ped. pass. 2. (**mit** on) manage, get by: **mit dieser Ausrede kommt er nicht durch** he won't get away with this excuse.

durch'kreuzen v/t (insep, no -ge-, h) fig. thwart.

'durchkriechen v/i (irr, sep, -ge-, sn, → **kriechen**) creep (or crawl) through.

Durchlaß ['dʊrçlas] m (-sses; ⁓sse) passage. **'durchlassen** v/t (irr, sep, -ge-, h, → **lassen**) let s.o., s.th. through (or pass), transmit (light): **Wasser** ~ leak; F fig. **et.** ~ let s.th. pass, overlook s.th.

'durchlässig adj pervious (**für** to).

'Durchlauf *m* (-[e]s; ⁓e) **1.** ⊙, *computer*: pass. **2.** *sports*: heat. 'durchlaufen¹ (*irr, sep,* -ge-, → *laufen*) **I** *v/i* (sn) run through, *computer*: (a. ⁓ *lassen*) pass (through). **II** *v/t* (h) wear *s.th.* through. durch'laufen² *v/t* (*irr, insep, no* -ge-, h, → *laufen*) run (*fig. a.* pass) through, cover (*distance*). 'durchlaufend *adj a.* ⊙ continuous. 'Durchlauferhitzer *m* instantaneous water heater.

durch'leben *v/t* (*insep, no* -ge-, h) go (or live) through: (*im Geiste*) *noch einmal* ⁓ relive.

'durchlesen *v/t* (*irr, sep,* -ge-, h, → *lesen*) read *s.th.* through, peruse.

durch'leuchten¹ *v/t* (*insep, no* -ge-, h) **1.** 💉 screen, x-ray. **2.** investigate, probe into *s.o.'s past etc.* 'durchleuchten² *v/i* (*sep,* -ge-, h) shine through.

Durch'leuchtung *f* (-; -en) x-ray examination, screening.

durch'löchern *v/t* (*insep, no* -ge-, h) **1.** make holes in, perforate: *von Kugeln durchlöchert* riddled with bullets. **2.** F *fig.* shoot holes in (*argument etc*).

'durchmachen (*sep,* -ge-, h) **I** *v/t* go through, undergo: *er hat viel durchgemacht* he has been through a lot. **II** *v/i* F (*die Nacht*) ⁓ make a night of it.

'Durchmesser *m* (-s; -) diameter.

'durchmogeln: *sich* ⁓ F wangle one's way through.

durch'nässen *v/t* (*insep, no* -ge-, h) soak, drench.

'durchnehmen *v/t* (*irr, sep,* -ge-, h, → *nehmen*) *ped.* do, go through.

'durchpausen *v/t* (*sep,* -ge-, h) trace.

'durchpeitschen *v/t* (*sep,* -ge-, h) *parl.* rush *s.th.* through, F railroad.

durch'queren *v/t* (*insep, no* -ge-, h) cross, traverse.

'durchrasen *v/i* (*sep,* -ge-, sn) race (or tear) through.

'durchrechnen *v/t* (*sep,* -ge-, h) check.

'Durchreiche *f* (-; -n) (service) hatch.

'Durchreise *f* (*auf der* ⁓ on one's way through. **⁓visum** *n* transit visa.

'durchringen: *sich* ⁓ (*irr, sep,* -ge-, h, → *ringen*) make up one's mind: *sich* ⁓*, et. zu tun* finally bring *s.o.* to do *s.th.*

'durchrosten *v/i* (*sep,* -ge-, sn) rust through.

'durchrutschen *v/i* (*sep,* -ge-, sn) F slip through (*a. fig.*).

'durchrütteln *v/t* (*sep,* -ge-, h) shake (up), jolt.

'durchsacken *v/i* (*sep,* -ge-, sn) ✈ pancake.

'Durchsage *f* (-; -n) announcement.

'durchsagen *v/t* (*sep,* -ge-, h) pass on, *radio*: announce.

'durchsägen *v/t* (*sep,* -ge-, h) saw through.

durch'schaubar *adj* obvious, transparent (*motives etc*): *schwer* ⁓ puzzling.

durch'schauen *v/t* (*insep, no* -ge-, h) see through: *du bist durchschaut!* F I've got your number!

'durchscheinen *v/i* (*irr, sep,* -ge-, h, → *scheinen*) shine through: ⁓*d* transparent, translucent.

'durchscheuern *v/t* (*sep,* -ge-, h) wear through.

'durchschlafen *v/i* (*irr, sep,* -ge-, h, → *schlafen*) sleep through.

'Durchschlag *m* (-[e]s; ⁓e) **1.** strainer. **2.** (carbon) copy, F carbon. **3.** ⚡ blowout.

'durchschlagen¹ (*irr, sep,* -ge-, → *schlagen*) **I** *v/t* (h) **1.** cut in two. **2.** *gastr.* pass *s.th.* through a strainer. **II** *v/i* **3.** (sn) *wetness*: come through, *colo(u)r*: show through. **4.** (sn) ⚡ *fuse*: blow. **5.** (h) *law etc*: have its effect: ⁓ *auf* (*acc*) affect. **III** *sich* ⁓ (h) fight one's way through: *sich mühsam* ⁓ scrape through; *sich allein* ⁓ fend for o.s. durch'schlagen² *v/t* (*irr, insep, no* -ge-, h, → *schlagen*) penetrate.

'durchschlagend *adj fig.* sweeping (*success*), conclusive (*evidence*): *mit* ⁓*em Erfolg* very effectively.

'Durchschlagpa,pier *n* copy paper.

'Durchschlagskraft *f* (-; *no pl*) penetration, *fig.* force (*of an argument etc*).

'durchschlängeln: *sich* ⁓ (*sep,* -ge-, h) thread one's way (*fig.* wriggle) through.

'durchschleusen *v/t* (*sep,* -ge-, h) **1.** ⚓ lock. **2.** *fig.* get *s.o., s.th.* through.

'durchschlüpfen *v/i* (*sep,* -ge-, sn) slip through.

'durchschmoren *v/i* (*sep,* -ge-, sn) F ⚡ char, scorch.

'durchschneiden¹ *v/t* (*irr, sep,* -ge-, h, → *schneiden*) cut (in two).

durch'schneiden² *v/t* (*irr, insep, no* -ge-, h, → *schneiden*) **1.** cut. **2.** intersect, cut through (*road*), cleave (*air, waves*).

'**Durchschnitt** m (-[e]s; -e) average: **im ~**
→ **durchschnittlich** II; **über (unter) ~**
above (below) (the) average; **(guter) ~**
sein be (a good) average.
'**durchschnittlich** I adj a) average, b)
ordinary, c) contp. mediocre. II adv on
(an or the) average: **~ verdienen** etc a.
average.
'**Durchschnitts...** average (age, income,
speed, temperature, etc).
'**Durchschreibeblock** m carbon-copy
pad. '**durchschreiben** v/t (irr, sep,
-ge-, h, → **schreiben**) make a (carbon)
copy of. '**Durchschrift** f (carbon) copy.
durch'schwimmen v/t (irr, insep, no
-ge-, h, → **schwimmen**) swim (through
or across).
'**durchschwitzen** v/t (sep, -ge-, h) soak
with sweat.
'**durchsehen** (irr, sep, -ge-, h, → **sehen**)
I v/i see (or look) through. II v/t look
s.th. over, go through, check.
'**durchsetzen**[1] (sep, -ge-, h) I v/t et. **~** get
s.th. through (or accepted); **~, daß et.**
geschieht succeed in getting s.th.
done; **s-n Kopf** (or **Willen**) **~** have one's
way. II **sich ~** a) assert o.s., have one's
way, b) idea etc: be accepted, catch on,
party, candidate: be successful; **sich ~**
gegen prevail against, F win out over
(a. sports); **er kann sich nicht ~** he has
no authority. **durch'setzen**[2] v/t (insep,
no -ge-, h) intersperse (**mit** with).
'**Durchsetzungsvermögen** n (-s; no pl)
self-assertion, authority: **~ haben** a. be
able to assert o.s.
'**Durchsicht** f (-; no pl) examination, inspection: **bei ~ der Akten** on looking
through (or on checking) the papers.
durchsichtig ['dʊrçsɪçtɪç] adj transparent, fig. a. obvious. '**Durchsichtigkeit** f
(-; no pl) a. fig. transparency.
'**durchsickern** v/i (sep, -ge-, sn) seep out,
fig. a. leak out.
'**durchspielen** v/t (sep, -ge-, h) 1. thea.
etc play s.th. right through. 2. fig. rehearse, go through.
'**durchsprechen** v/t (irr, sep, -ge-, h, →
sprechen) talk s.th. over, discuss.
'**durchstarten** v/i (sep, -ge-, sn) ✈ climb
and reaccelerate, F go round again.
'**durchstechen** v/t (sep, -ge-, h) put (or
pass) s.th. through.
'**durchstehen** v/t (irr, sep, -ge-, h, →

stehen) 1. fig. get through. 2. →
durchhalten II.
'**durchstellen** v/t (sep, -ge-, h) teleph. **ein**
Gespräch ~ put a call through.
'**durchstoßen**[1] v/i (irr, sep, -ge-, sn, →
stoßen) break (or push) through.
durch'stoßen[2] v/t (irr, insep, no -ge-, h,
→ **stoßen**) pierce, break through.
'**durchstreichen** v/t (irr, sep, -ge-, h, →
streichen) cross out, cancel.
durch'strömen v/t (insep, no -ge-, h) a.
fig. flow through.
durch'suchen v/t (insep, no -ge-, h) a)
search, b) comb. **Durch'suchung** f (-;
-en) search. **Durch'suchungsbefehl** m
search warrant.
'**durchtrai,niert** adj top fit.
'**durchtreten** v/t (irr, sep, -ge-, h, →
treten) mot. step on, Am. floor (pedal),
kick (starter).
durchtrieben [dʊrç'triːbən] adj sly.
durch'wachsen adj 1. streaky (bacon).
2. pred F fig. so-so, mixed.
'**Durchwahl** f (-; no pl) direct dial(l)ing.
'**durchwählen** v/i (sep, -ge-, h) **~ nach**
dial through to, dial ... direct.
durchweg ['dʊrçvɛk] adv all of it (or
them), without exception.
durch'weicht adj drenched, soaked.
durch'wühlen v/t (insep, no -ge-, h) rummage through.
'**durchwursteln: sich ~** (sep, -ge-, h) F
muddle through.
'**durchzählen** v/t (sep, -ge-, h) count off.
'**durchziehen**[1] (irr, sep, -ge-, → **ziehen**)
I v/t (h) 1. pull s.th. through. 2. F push
(or see) project etc through. II v/i (sn) 3.
pass (or march) through. 4. gastr. **gut ~**
lassen soak well. III **sich ~** (h) motif
etc: run through.
durch'ziehen[2] v/t (irr, insep, no -ge-, h,
→ **ziehen**) pass through, river etc, a.
motif etc: run through, smell: fill, pain
etc: shoot through.
durch'zucken v/t (insep, no -ge-, h) a.
fig. flash through.
'**Durchzug** m (-[e]s; ⁻e) 1. passage,
march through. 2. no pl draught, Am.
draft: **~ machen** air room thoroughly.
dürfen ['dyrfən] I v/aux (durfte, dürfen,
h) **et. tun ~** be allowed to do s.th.; **darf**
ich es behalten? may I keep it?; **ja, Sie**
~ yes, you may; **nein, Sie ~ es nicht** no,
you can't; **wir ~ stolz auf ihn sein** we

can be proud of him; *was darf es sein?* shop assistant: what can I do for you?, hostess: what would you like?; *das dürfte genügen* that should be enough. **II** *v/i* (durfte, gedurft, h) *er darf (es)* he is allowed to; *wenn ich nur dürfte* if only I were allowed to.

dürftig ['dyrftiç] *adj* poor, meag/re (*Am.* -er), scanty: *~e Kenntnisse* scanty knowledge. **'Dürftigkeit** *f* (-; *no pl*) poorness, meag/reness (*Am.* -er).

dürr [dyr] *adj* **1.** a) dry, b) barren (*soil*). **2.** thin, skinny, scrawny (*neck*), spindly (*legs*): *fig. in ~en Worten* in plain terms. **'Dürre** *f* (-; -n) drought. **'Dürrekatastrophe** *f* disastrous drought. **'Dürreschäden** *pl* drought damage.

Durst [dʊrst] *m* (-es; *no pl*) thirst (*fig. nach* for): *~ haben* (get) thirsty; *F er hat e-n über den ~ getrunken* he has had one too many. **dürsten** ['dyrstən] *v/i* (h) thirst (*nach* for). **'durstig** *adj* thirsty (*fig. nach* for). **'durstlöschend** *adj* thirst-quenching. **'Durststrecke** *f* hard slog, hard times.

Duschbad *n* shower bath. **Dusche** ['dʊʃə; 'duːʃə] *f* (-; -n) shower, douche (*a. ✱*): *wie e-e kalte ~ auf j-n wirken* bring s.o. down to earth with a bump. **'duschen** *v/i* (h) (*a. sich ~*) (have a) shower. **'Duschgel** *n* shower foam. **'Duschka,bine** *f* shower cubicle. **'Duschraum** *m* shower room. **'Duschvorhang** *m* shower curtain.

Düse ['dyːzə] *f* (-; -n) nozzle.

Dusel ['duːzəl] *m* (-s; *no pl*) F fluke, luck: *~ haben* be lucky; *mit ~* by a fluke.

düsen ['dyːzən] *v/i* (sn) F zoom.

'Düsen\antrieb *m* jet propulsion: *mit ~* jet-propelled. **~flugzeug** *n* jet plane. **~jäger** *m* ✗ jet fighter. **~pi,lot** *m* jet pilot. **~triebwerk** *n* jet engine. **~verkehrsflugzeug** *n* jetliner.

Dussel ['dʊsəl] *m* (-s; -) F dope.

düster ['dyːstər] *adj a. fig.* dark, gloomy, dismal: *~e Aussichten* bleak prospects; *~e Stimmung* black mood.

Dutzend ['dʊtsənt] *n* (-s; -e) dozen: *~e von Leuten* dozens of people; *zu ~en* in dozens. **'dutzendmal** *adv* dozens of times. **'dutzendweise** *adv* in dozens.

duzen ['duːtsən] *v/t* (h) *j-n ~* a) address s.o. with "du", b) *a. sich mit j-m ~* be on first-name terms with s.o. **'Duzfreund(in** *f*) *m* intimate friend.

Dynamik [dyˈnaːmɪk] *f* (-; *no pl*) dynamics, *fig. a.* dynamism. **dy'namisch** *adj a. fig.* dynamic: *~e Rente* index-linked pension. **dynamisieren** [dynamiˈziːrən] *v/t* (h) **1.** speed *s.th.* up. **2.** index-link (*pensions etc*).

Dynamit [dynaˈmiːt] *n* (-s; *no pl*) dynamite.

Dynamo [dyˈnaːmo] *m* (-s; -s) dynamo.

Dynastie [dynasˈtiː] *f* (-; -n) dynasty.

Dystonie [dystoˈniː] *f* (-; -n) ✱ dystonia: *vegetative ~* neurodystonia.

D-Zug *m* fast train.

E

E, e [eː] *n* (-; -) E, e (*a. ♪*).

Ebbe ['ɛbə] *f* (-; -n) low tide: *es ist ~* the tide is out.

eben ['eːbən] **I** *adj* **1.** even, level, flat, smooth. **II** *adv* **2.** just (now): *~ erst* only just; *ich wollte ~ gehen* I was just going to leave. **3.** just, exactly: (*das ist es ja*) *~!* that's it!; *~ nicht!* on the contrary! **4.** *~ noch* only just. **5.** just: *es taugt ~ nichts* it's just no good; *er ist ~*

der Bessere he's better, that's all; *so ist es ~!* that's the way it is!; *dann ~ nicht!* all right, forget it!

'Ebenbild *n* image: *das ~ s-s Vaters* the spit and image of his father.

ebenbürtig ['eːbənbyrtɪç] *adj* equal: *j-m ~ sein* be s.o.'s equal, match s.o.

'ebender('selbe), **'ebendie('selbe)**, **'ebendas('selbe) I** *dem pron* the very same. **II** *adj* that very *man*, *woman*, *thing*. 'eben'deswegen *adv* for that very reason.

Ebene ['e:bənə] *f* (-; -n) **1.** *geogr.* plain. **2.** ⚤ plane. **3.** *fig.* level: *auf staatlicher (höchster)* ~ at government (top) level.

'ebenerdig *adj* at ground level.

'ebenfalls *adv* likewise, too, as well: *er hat ~ kein Geld* he has no money either.

'Ebenheit *f* (-; *no pl*) evenness, flatness.

'Ebenholz *n* ebony.

'Ebenmaß *n* (-es; *no pl*) harmony, symmetry. 'ebenmäßig *adj* well-proportioned, regular (*face, features*).

'ebenso *adv* **1.** just as *good etc.* **2.** (in) the same way. **3.** likewise. 'ebensogut *adv* (just) as well. 'ebensoviel *indef pron* just as much (*or* many).

Eber ['e:bər] *m* (-s; -) *zo.* boar.

'Eberesche *f* ⚤ mountain ash.

ebnen ['e:bnən] *v/t* (h) level: → *Weg*.

Echo ['ɛço] *n* (-s; -s) echo: *fig. ein lebhaftes ~ finden* meet with a lively response. **'Echolot** *n* echo sounder.

echt [ɛçt] **I** *adj* genuine (*a. fig.*), authentic (*document*), fast (*colo[u]r*), natural (*hair*), pure, real (*gold, leather, etc*): *~er Engländer (Freund)* true Englishman (friend). **II** *adv* really: F ~ *gut!* real good!; *das ist ~ Paul!* that's Paul all over! **'Echtheit** *f* (-; *no pl*) genuineness (*etc*), authenticity.

'Eckball *m sports*: corner.

Ecke ['ɛkə] *f* (-; -n) **1.** corner (*a. sports*): *an der ~ at* (*house*: on) the corner; *fig. an allen ~n und Enden* everywhere; *es fehlte an allen ~n und Enden* we were short on everything; F *j-n um die ~ bringen* bump s.o. off. **2.** F a) piece, b) stretch, c) corner, region.

'Eckfahne *f sports*: corner flag. **'Eckhaus** *n* corner house.

eckig ['ɛkɪç] *adj* square, angular, *fig.* awkward. ...**eckig** ...-cornered.

'Ecklohn *m* basic wage. **'Eckpfeiler** *m* **1.** △ corner pillar. **2.** *fig.* cornerstone. **'Eckplatz** *m* corner seat. **'Eckstoß** *m sports*: corner kick. **'Eckzahn** *m* eyetooth. **'Eckzins** *m* basic interest rate.

edel ['e:dəl] *adj* (*a. fig.*) noble. **2.** exquisite (*wine etc*), precious (*stone, metal*).

'Edel|gas *n* inert gas. **~holz** *n* rare wood. **~kitsch** *m* glorified trash. **~mann** *m* (-[e]s; -leute) nobleman. **~me,tall** *n* precious metal. **~pilzkäse** *m* blue cheese.

~stahl *m* high-grade steel. **~stein** *m* precious stone, gem. **~tanne** *f* silver fir.

'Edelweiß *n* (-[e]s; -e) ⚤ edelweiss.

EDV-Anlage [e:de:'vaʊ-] *f* electronic data-processing equipment.

Efeu ['e:fɔy] *m* (-s; *no pl*) ⚤ ivy.

Eff-eff [ɛf'?ɛf] *n* F *et. aus dem ~ können* be a real wizard at s.th.

Effekten [ɛ'fɛktən] *pl* ♠ a) securities, b) stocks and bonds. **~börse** *f* stock exchange. **~händler** *m* stock dealer. **~makler** *m* stockbroker.

Ef'fekthascherei [-haʃərai] *f* (-; *no pl*) sensationalism, (cheap) showmanship.

effektiv [ɛfɛk'ti:f] *adj* actual.

ef'fektvoll *adj* effective, striking.

Effet [ɛ'fe:] *m sports*: spin.

Effizienz [ɛfi'tsiɛnts] *f* (-; -en) efficiency.

egal [e'ga:l] *adj pred* **1.** F *das ist (ganz) ~* it doesn't matter; *das ist mir (ganz) ~* I don't care; *das ist mir nicht ~* I do care; *ganz ~, wer (warum etc)* no matter who (why *etc*). **2.** the same.

Egel ['e:gəl] *m* (-s; -) *zo.* leech.

Egge ['ɛgə] *f* (-; -n) harrow.

eggen ['ɛgən] *v/t* (h) harrow.

Egoismus [ego'ɪsmʊs] *m* (-; *no pl*) egoism. **Egoist** [ego'ɪst] *m* (-en; -en), **Ego'istin** *f* (-; -nen) ego(t)ist.

ego'istisch *adj* egotistic(al), selfish.

ego'zentrisch *adj* self-centred.

eh [e:] *adv* **1.** *dial.* → *ohnehin*. **2.** *seit ~ und je* always; *wie ~ und je* as ever.

ehe ['e:ə] *conj* before: *nicht ~* not until; → *eher, ehest*.

'Ehe *f* (-; -n) marriage: *sie hat e-e Tochter aus erster ~* she has a daughter by her first marriage; *die ~ brechen* commit adultery; *sie führen e-e glückliche ~* they are happily married.

'Eheberater(in *f)* *m* marriage guidance counsel(l)or. **'Eheberatung(sstelle)** *f* marriage guidance (bureau). **'Ehebett** *n* marriage bed. **'Ehebrecher(in** *f)* *m* adulterer(-ess). **'ehebrecherisch** *adj* adulterous. **'Ehebruch** *m* adultery. **'Ehefrau** *f* wife, *w.s.* married woman. **'Eheleben** *n* married life. **'Eheleute** *pl* husband and wife. **'ehelich** *adj* **1.** marital. **2.** 🕱 legitimate (*child*).

ehelichen ['e:əlɪçən] *v/t* (h) marry.

'Ehelichkeit *f* (-; *no pl*) 🕱 legitimacy.

'Ehelosigkeit *f* (-; *no pl*) unmarried state, *eccl.* celibacy.

ehemalig ['e:əma:lıç] *adj* **1.** former, ex-... **2.** late.

ehemals ['e:əma:ls] *adv* formerly.

'**Ehemann** *m* (-[e]s; ⁓er) husband, *w.s.* married man. '**ehemündig** *adj* 🏛 marriageable. '**Ehepaar** *n* married couple: *das* ⁓ *Brown* Mr. and Mrs. Brown. '**Ehepartner(in** *f*) *m* (marriage) partner.

eher ['e:ər] *adv* **1.** earlier, sooner: *je* ⁓, *desto besser* the sooner the better. **2.** a) rather, b) more easily, c) more, d) more likely.

'**Eherecht** *n* (-[e]s; *no pl*) matrimonial law. '**Ehering** *m* wedding ring.

ehern ['e:ərn] *adj* **1.** (of) brass. **2.** *fig.* iron (*law, rule, will*).

'**Ehescheidung** *f* divorce.

'**Eheschließung** *f* marriage.

ehest ['e:əst] **I** *adj* earliest. **II** *adv* am ⁓**en** a) (the) earliest, (the) first, b) best; *er kann uns am ⁓en helfen* if anyone can help us, it's him.

'**Ehestand** *m* (-[e]s; *no pl*) matrimony.

'**Ehestreit** *m* marital row. '**Ehevermittlungsinsti,tut** *n* marriage bureau.

'**ehrbar** *adj* hono(u)rable, respectable.

Ehre ['e:rə] *f* (-; -n) hono(u)r: *zu* ⁓*n* (*gen or von*) in hono(u)r of; *ihm zu* ⁓*n* in his hono(u)r; *j-m die letzte* ⁓ *erweisen* pay one's last respects to s.o.; *j-m* (*k-e*) ⁓ *machen* be (be no) credit to s.o.; *in* ⁓*n halten* hold in hono(u)r.

'**ehren** *v/t* (h) a) hono(u)r, b) respect: *das ehrt ihn* that does him credit.

'**Ehren|amt** *n* honorary post. **2amtlich I** *adj* honorary. **II** *adv* in an honorary capacity. ⁓**bürger(in** *f*) *m* honorary citizen. ⁓**doktor** *m* honorary doctor. ⁓**gast** *m* guest of hono(u)r. ⁓**gericht** *n* disciplinary court.

'**ehrenhaft** *adj* hono(u)rable, upright.

'**ehrenhalber** [-halbər] *adv* for hono(u)r's sake: *Doktor* ⁓ doctor honoris causa.

'**Ehren|kodex** *m* code of hono(u)r. ⁓**legi,on** *f* Legion of Hono(u)r. ⁓**mann** *m* (-[e]s; ⁓er) man of hono(u)r. ⁓**mitglied** *n* honorary member. ⁓**platz** *m* place of hono(u)r. ⁓**rechte** *pl* 🏛 bürgerliche ~ civil rights. ⁓**runde** *f sports*: (*e-e* ⁓ *laufen or drehen* do a) lap of hono(u)r. ⁓**sache** *f* matter of hono(u)r. ⁓**tag** *m* great day. ⁓**titel** *m* hono-

rary title. ⁓**treffer** *m sports*: consolation goal. ⁓**tri,büne** *f* VIP lounge. **2voll** *adj* hono(u)rable. **2wert** *adj* respectable. ⁓**wort** *n* word of hono(u)r: *sein* ⁓ *geben* give one's word; ⁓*! I* promise (you)! ⁓**zeichen** *n* decoration.

ehrerbietig ['e:rʔerbi:tıç] *adj* (*gegen* towards) respectful, deferential.

'**Ehrfurcht** *f* (-; *no pl*) (*vor dat*) respect (for), awe (of). '**ehrfurchtgebietend** *adj* awe-inspiring. **ehrfürchtig** ['e:rfyrçtıç] *adj* respectful, reverential.

'**Ehrgefühl** *n* (-[e]s; *no pl*) sense of hono(u)r.

'**Ehrgeiz** *m* (-es; *no pl*) ambition.

'**ehrgeizig** *adj* ambitious.

'**ehrlich I** *adj* honest, sincere, frank: ⁓ *währt am längsten* honesty is the best policy; *seien wir ehrlich!* let's face it! **II** *adv* honestly (*etc*): ⁓ *gesagt* truth to tell; F ⁓*?* really?

'**Ehrlichkeit** *f* (-; *no pl*) honesty.

'**ehrlos** *adj* disgraceful.

'**Ehrung** *f* (-; -en) hono(u)r (*gen* conferred on).

'**Ehrwürden** *eccl. Seine* ⁓ the Reverend.

'**ehrwürdig** *adj* venerable, *eccl.* Reverend.

ei [aı] *int* oh.

Ei *n* (-[e]s; -er) **1.** egg, *physiol.* ovum: *fig.* *wie ein* ⁓ *dem anderen gleichen* be as like as two peas; F *wie aus dem* ⁓ *gepellt* spick and span; *j-n wie ein rohes* ⁓ *behandeln* handle s.o. with kid gloves. **2.** *pl* F quid, *Am.* bucks. **3.** *pl* V (*testicles*) nuts, balls.

Eibe ['aıbə] *f* (-; -n) 🌿 yew (tree).

Eiche ['aıçə] *f* (-; -n) a) oak (tree), b) oak.

Eichel ['aıçəl] *f* (-; -n) **1.** 🌿 acorn. **2.** *anat.* glans.

'**eichen** *v/t* (h) ⚙ adjust, calibrate.

'**Eichhörnchen** *n* (-s; -) *zo.* squirrel.

Eid [aıt] *m* (-[e]s; -e) oath: *e-n* ⁓ *ablegen* (*or leisten, schwören*) take an oath, swear (*auf die Bibel* by the Bible); *j-m e-n* ⁓ *abnehmen* administer an oath to s.o.; *unter* ⁓ *aussagen* testify on oath; 🏛 *an* ⁓*es Statt* → *eidesstattlich*.

Eidechse ['aıdeksə] *f* (-; -n) *zo.* lizard.

'**eidesstattlich** *adj and adv* in lieu of (an) oath: ⁓*e Erklärung* affidavit.

'**Eidgenosse** *m* Swiss (citizen). **eidgenössisch** ['aıtgənœsıʃ] *adj* Swiss.

'**eidlich I** *adj* ⁓*e Aussage,* ⁓*e Erklärung*

a) sworn statement, b) affidavit. **II** *adv* on (*or* under) oath.

'**Eidotter** *m* (egg) yolk.

'**Eier|becher** *m* eggcup. **∼kocher** *m* egg boiler. **∼kopf** *m* F egghead. **∼kuchen** *m* pancake. **∼löffel** *m* egg spoon. **∼schale** *f* eggshell. **∼speise** *f* egg dish. **∼stock** *m* anat. ovary. **∼wärmer** *m* egg cosy.

Eifer ['aɪfər] *m* (-s; *no pl*) zeal, eagerness, enthusiasm, fervo(u)r: *blinder ∼* rashness; *blinder ∼ schadet nur* haste is waste; *im ∼ des Gefechts* in the heat of the moment. '**Eiferer** *m* (-s; -) fanatic.

'**eifern** *v/i* (h) **1.** **∼ nach** strive for. **2.** **∼ gegen** rail against. **3.** → *wetteifern*.

'**Eifersucht** *f* (-; *no pl*) jealousy (*auf acc* of).

'**eifersüchtig** *adj* jealous (*auf acc* of).

eifrig ['aɪfrɪç] *adj* a) keen, ardent, b) busy: **∼ bemüht zu** *inf* anxious to *inf*.

eigen ['aɪgən] *adj* **1.** own, of one's own: *sich zu ∼ machen* make *s.th.* one's own, adopt; *ein ∼es Zimmer* a room of one's own. **2.** own, personal, private: *für den ∼en Gebrauch* for one's own use; *∼e Ansichten* personal views. **3.** characteristic, typical: *mit dem ihr ∼en Charme* with her characteristic charm. **4.** particular, fussy.

...eigen ...-owned: *staats∼* state-owned.

'**Eigenart** *f* (-; -en) peculiarity.

'**eigenartig** *adj* peculiar. '**eigenartigerweise** *adv* strangely enough.

'**Eigenbedarf** *m* a) one's personal needs, b) domestic requirements.

Eigenbrötler ['aɪgənbrø:tlər] *m* (-s; -) **1.** eccentric. **2.** solitary (person).

'**Eigenfinan,zierung** *f* self-financing.

'**Eigengewicht** *n* dead (⊙ net) weight.

'**eigenhändig** [-hɛndɪç] **I** *adj* personal: *∼e Unterschrift* one's own signature. **II** *adv* personally, oneself.

'**Eigenheim** *n* house of one's own.

'**Eigenheit** *f* (-; -en) peculiarity.

'**Eigen|initia,tive** *f* one's own initiative. **∼kapi,tal** *n* capital resources. **∼leben** *n* (-s; *no pl*) one's own (*or* private) life: *ein ∼ entwickeln* take on a life of its own. **∼liebe** *f* self-love, narcissism. **∼lob** *n* self-praise. 2**mächtig** *adj* **1.** high-handed. **2.** unauthorized. **∼mächtigkeit** *f* (-; -en) **1.** *no pl* high-handedness. **2.** arbitrary act. **∼name** *m* proper name (*or* noun).

'**Eigennutz** *m* (-es; *no pl*) self-interest.

'**eigennützig** [-nʏtsɪç] *adj* selfish.

eigens ['aɪgəns] *adv* (e)specially.

'**Eigenschaft** *f* (-; -en) quality, characteristic, feature, 🐾, *phys.*, ⊙ property: *in s-r ∼ als* in his capacity of (*or* as).

'**Eigenschaftswort** *n* (-[e]s; **∼er**) *ling.* adjective.

'**Eigensinn** *m* (-[e]s; *no pl*) stubbornness. '**eigensinnig** *adj* stubborn.

'**eigenständig** *adj* independent.

eigentlich ['aɪgəntlɪç] **I** *adj* real, actual: *im ∼en Sinne* in the true sense of the word. **II** *adv* a) actually, really, b) by rights.

'**Eigentor** *n* a. *fig.* own goal.

'**Eigentum** *n* (-s; *no pl*) property, ownership. **Eigentümer** ['aɪgənty:mər] *m* (-s; -), **Eigentümerin** *f* (-; -nen) owner, proprietor (proprietress).

'**eigentümlich** [-ty:mlɪç] *adj* **1.** characteristic (*dat* of). **2.** peculiar, strange. '**Eigentümlichkeit** *f* (-; -en) peculiarity.

'**Eigentums|recht** *n* (right of) ownership, title (*an dat* of). **∼wohnung** *f* freehold flat, *Am.* condominium.

'**Eigenwille** *m* self-will. '**eigenwillig** *adj* **1.** self-willed, headstrong. **2.** *fig.* very individual. '**Eigenwilligkeit** *f* (-; *no pl*) *fig.* (strong) individualism.

eignen ['aɪgnən] *sich ∼* (h) (*als* as, *zu* as, for) be suitable, *person:* be suited; *sich als* (*or zum*) *Lehrer ∼* a. make a good teacher. '**Eigner** *m* (-s; -) owner.

'**Eignung** *f* (-; *no pl*) (*zu, für*) suitability (for), *of a person:* a. qualification (for, to be). '**Eignungstest** *m* aptitude test.

'**Eilauftrag** *m* ⚓ rush order. '**Eilbote** *m* *durch ∼n* express, *Am.* (by) special delivery. '**Eilbrief** *m* express letter, *Am.* special delivery (letter).

Eile ['aɪlə] *f* (-; *no pl*) hurry, rush: *in ∼* in a hurry; *es hat k-e ∼* there's no hurry.

'**Eileiter** *m* anat. Fallopian tube.

eilen ['aɪlən] *v/i* **1.** (sn) hurry. **2.** (h) be urgent: *Eilt!* urgent!; *es eilt nicht* there's no hurry. **eilends** ['aɪlənts] *adv* in a hurry, hurriedly, hastily.

'**Eilfracht** *f* express goods, *Am.* fast freight.

eilig ['aɪlɪç] *adj* a) hurried, b) urgent: *es ∼ haben* be in a hurry.

'**eiligst** *adv* in a hurry, hurriedly.

'**Eiltempo** *n im ∼* in double quick time.

'Eilzug *m* fast train.

'Eilzustellung *f* 🐝 special delivery.

Eimer ['aɪmər] *m* (-s; -) bucket (*a.* ⊕), pail: F *die Uhr ist im* ~ the watch has had it. **'eimerweise** *adv* in bucketfuls.

ein[1] [aɪn] **I** *adj* one: ~ *für allemal* once and for all; ~ *und derselbe* (*Mann*) one and the same person. **II** *indef art* a, an: ~ (*gewisser*) *Herr Brown* a (*or* one) Mr. Brown; ~*es Tages* one day. **III** *indef pron* a) one (*Mr. X etc*), b) one thing: ~*er von beiden* one of them.

ein[2] *adv* **1.** *switch*: on: ~ *- aus* on - off. **2.** ~ *und aus gehen* come and go (*bei j-m* at s.o.'s place); *ich weiß nicht mehr* ~ *noch aus* I'm at my wits' end.

Einakter ['aɪn͡ʔaktər] *m* (-s; -) *thea.* one-act play.

einander [aɪ'nandər] *adv* each other, one another.

'einarbeiten (*sep*, -ge-, h) **I** *v/t* **1.** *j-n* ~ acquaint s.o. with his (new) work, F break s.o. in. **2.** *et.* ~ *in* (*acc*) work s.th. into. **II** *sich* ~ get into the (new) job (*or* subject *etc*).

einarmig ['aɪn͡ʔarmɪç] *adj* one-armed.

'einäschern ['aɪn͡ʔɛʃərn] *v/t* (*sep*, -ge-, h) **1.** burn to ashes. **2.** cremate. **'Einäscherung** *f* (-; -en) cremation.

'einatmen *v/t, v/i* (*sep*, -ge-, h) breathe in, inhale: *tief* ~ take a deep breath.

einäugig ['aɪn͡ʔɔygɪç] *adj* one-eyed.

'Einbahn... one-way (*street, traffic*).

'einbalsamieren *v/t* (*sep*, h) embalm.

'Einband *m* (-[e]s; ~e) binding, cover.

'einbändig [-bɛndɪç] *adj* in one volume.

'Einbau *m* (-[e]s; -ten) installation, fitting. **'Einbau...** built-in, fitted (*kitchen, cupboard, etc*). **'einbauen** *v/t* (*sep*, -ge-, h) build in, install, fit: *fig. ein Zitat etc* ~ work in a quotation *etc*.

'einbegriffen *adj* (*mit*) ~ included.

'einbehalten *v/t* (*irr, sep*, h, → *behalten*) keep back, withhold, deduct.

'einberufen *v/t* (*irr, sep*, h, → *berufen*) **1.** call (*assembly*), *parl.* convoke. **2.** ✕ (*zu*) call up (for), *Am.* draft (to). **'Einberufung** *f* (-; -en) **1.** calling, *parl.* convocation. **2.** ✕ conscription, *Am.* draft. **'Einberufungsbescheid** *m* ✕ call-up order, *Am.* draft papers.

'einbetten *v/t* (*sep*, -ge-, h) embed.

'Einbettkabine *f* ⚓ single-berth cabin.

'Einbettzimmer *n* single room.

'einbeziehen *v/t* (*irr, sep*, h, → *beziehen*) include (*in acc* in).

'einbiegen *v/i* (*irr, sep*, -ge-, sn, → *biegen*) turn (*in acc* into *a street etc*): *links* ~ turn left.

'einbilden: sich ~ (*sep*, -ge-, h) **1.** imagine, think · *bilde dir ja nicht ein, daß* ... don't think that ...; *das bildest du dir nur ein* you're imagining things; *was bildest du dir eigentlich ein?* who do you think you are? **2.** *sich et.* ~ (*auf acc*) be (very) conceited (about).

'Einbildung *f* (-; *no pl*) **1.** illusion: *das ist reine* ~ you're (he is *etc*) imagining things. **2.** conceit. **'Einbildungskraft** *f* (-; *no pl*) imagination.

'einbinden *v/t* (*irr, sep*, -ge-, h, → *binden*) **1.** bind (*book*). **2.** *fig.* integrate.

'einblenden (*sep*, -ge-, h) **I** *v/t* film, radio, TV fade in. **II** *sich* ~ *in* (*acc*) tune in to. **'Einblendung** *f* (-; -en) fade-in.

einbleuen ['aɪnblɔyən] *v/t* (*sep*, -ge-, h) *j-m et.* ~ drum s.th. into s.o.'s head.

'Einblick *m* (-[e]s; -e) *fig.* insight (*in acc* into): ~ *nehmen in* (*acc*) inspect.

'einbrechen (*irr, sep*, -ge-, → *brechen*) **I** *v/i* (sn) **1.** *in ein Haus etc* ~ break into a house *etc*; *bei ihm wurde eingebrochen* his house was burgled. **2.** ~ *in* (*acc*) invade (*a country etc*). **3.** collapse, *fig.* break down, *sports: a.* wilt. **4.** (*ins Eis*) ~ break through the ice. **5.** *frost etc*: set in, *night*: fall. **6.** ✝ suffer heavy losses, *prices*: slump. **II** *v/t* (h) **7.** break down (*door etc*).

'Einbrecher *m* (-s; -) burglar.

'einbringen *v/t* (*irr, sep*, -ge-, h, → *bringen*) **1.** bring in (*harvest etc*). **2.** invest (*capital*), *a. fig.* contribute (*in an etc*). **3.** bring (in), yield (*profit etc*): *es bringt mir ... ein* it gets me ...; *das bringt nichts ein!* it doesn't pay! **4.** make up (for *time etc*). **5.** *e-e Gesetzesvorlage* ~ introduce a bill. **6.** 🜨 bring in, file (*action*). **7.** *print.* take in (*line*).

'einbrocken *v/t* (*sep*, -ge-, h) F *sich et.* ~ let o.s. in for s.th.; *das hat er sich selbst eingebrockt!* it's his own fault!

'Einbruch *m* (-[e]s; ~e) **1.** break-in, burglary. **2.** *bei* ~ *der Dunkelheit* at nightfall; *bei* ~ *der Kälte* when the cold (weather) sets in; ~ *von Kaltluft* influx of cold air. **3.** invasion (*in acc of a country*). **4.** collapse, *fig.* setback. **5.** ✝

slump. '**Einbruchdiebstahl** m burglary. '**einbruchsicher** adj burglar-proof.

einbürgern ['aɪnbʏrɡərn] v/t (sep, -ge-, h) ♞, 🐾, zo. naturalize: fig. **sich ~ word**: be adopted; **es hat sich (bei uns) so eingebürgert** it has become a custom (with us).

'**Einbürgerung** f (-; -en) naturalization.

'**Einbuße** f (-; -n) loss (**an** dat of).

'**einbüßen** (sep, -ge-, h) **I** v/t lose. **II** v/t ~ **an** (dat) lose some of.

'**einchecken** v/t, v/i (sep, -ge-, h) ✈ check in.

'**eincremen** v/t (sep, -ge-, h) cream.

'**eindämmen** v/t (sep, -ge-, h) dam up, fig. a. check, get fire etc under control, pol. contain. '**Eindämmungspoli,tik** f policy of containment.

'**eindecken** (sep, -ge-, h) **I** v/t j-n ~ **mit** supply s.o. with; **gut eingedeckt** well stocked; F **mit Arbeit eingedeckt sein** be swamped with work. **II sich ~** stock up (**mit** on).

eindeutig ['aɪndɔɪtɪç] adj clear, plain. '**Eindeutigkeit** f (-; no pl) clearness.

eindeutschen ['aɪndɔɪtʃən] v/t (sep, -ge-, h) Germanize.

'**eindimensio,nal** adj one-dimensional.

'**eindrängen: sich ~** (sep, -ge-, h) (**in** acc) a) push one's way in(to), b) intrude (into).

'**eindringen** v/i (irr, sep, -ge-, sn, → **dringen**) (**in** acc) get in(to), force one's way in(to), bullet etc: penetrate (s.th.), ✗ a. invade (a country): **auf j-n ~** a) attack s.o., b) press s.o. (**mit** with questions etc). '**eindringlich** adj urgent (warning etc), forceful (speech etc). '**Eindringlichkeit** f (-; no pl) urgency.

'**Eindruck** m (-[e]s; ᵉe) **1.** impression: ~ **machen** be impressive; **auf j-n ~ machen** impress s.o.; **e-n schlechten ~ machen** make a bad impression (**auf** acc on); **den ~ erwecken, daß ...** give the impression that ...; **ich habe den ~, daß ...** I have a feeling that ...; ~ **schinden** 2. **2.** imprint.

'**eindrücken** v/t (sep, -ge-, h) break (window), force (door), dent (car body).

'**eindrucksvoll** adj impressive.

'**einebnen** v/t (sep, -ge-, h) flatten, level (out fig.).

'**Einehe** f monogamy.

eineiig ['aɪn'aɪɪç] adj ~**e Zwillinge** identical twins.

'**einengen** v/t (sep, -ge-, h) narrow down, restrict: **sich eingeengt fühlen** feel cramped.

'**einer** pron someone, somebody; → a. **ein**[1] III. '**Einer** m (-s; -) **1.** A digit. **2.** ⬧ single (sculler). '**einerlei** adj pred all the same, all one: **das ist mir ~!** I don't care!; ~ **wer** (**wo** etc) no matter who (where etc). **Einerlei** n (-s; no pl) monotony: (**ewiges**) ~ routine.

'**einerseits** adv on the one hand.

einfach ['aɪnfax] **I** adj **1.** simple, a. easy (task), a. plain (food). **2.** single: ~**e Fahrkarte** single (ticket), Am. one-way ticket. **II** adv **3.** simply, just: **ich mußte ~ lachen** I couldn't help laughing.

'**Einfachheit** f (-; no pl) simplicity, plainness: **der ~ halber** to simplify matters.

'**einfädeln** (sep, -ge-, h) **I** v/t **1.** thread. **2.** fig. arrange, contrive. **II sich ~** mot. filter (**in** acc into): **sich links ~** filter to the left.

'**einfahren** (irr, sep, -ge-, → **fahren**) **I** v/i (sn) **1.** come in, arrive. **2.** ✗ descend into a mine. **II** v/t (h) **3.** bring in (harvest). **4.** run in (car). **5.** retract (landing gear etc). **6.** crash into.

'**Einfahrt** f (-; -en) **1.** drive(way), entrance, to motorway: approach: ~ **freihalten!** keep clear of the gate(s)! **2.** no pl entry (in an area): **der Zug aus ... hat ~ auf Gleis 1** the train from ... is now coming in on track 1; **Vorsicht bei der ~!** please stand back! **3.** ✗ descent.

'**Einfall** m (-[e]s; ᵉe) **1.** idea. **2.** ✗ invasion (**in** acc of). **3.** no pl phys. incidence (of light).

'**einfallen** v/i (irr, sep, -ge-, sn, → **fallen**) **1.** j-m ~ occur to s.o.; **mir fällt eben ein, daß ...** a. I've just remembered that ...; **es fällt mir (jetzt) nicht ein** I can't think of it now; **was fällt dir ein?** a) how dare you!, b) you must be joking!; **sich et. ~ lassen** come up with s.th.; **das fällt mir nicht im Traum ein!** I wouldn't dream of (doing) it! **2.** ✗ **in ein Land ~** invade a country; F fig. **bei j-m ~** descend on s.o. **3.** light: enter. **4.** ♪ enter, join in.

'**einfallslos** adj unimaginative, dull. '**Einfallslosigkeit** f (-; no pl) lack of ideas. '**einfallsreich** *adj* imaginative, inventive. '**Einfallsreichtum** *m* (-s; *no pl*) wealth of ideas.

'**Einfallswinkel** *m* angle of incidence.

einfältig ['aınfɛltıç] *adj* naive, simple.

'**Einfa,milienhaus** *n* detached house.

'**einfangen** *v/t* (*irr*, *sep*, -ge-, h, → **fangen**) *a. fig.* catch, capture.

'**einfarbig** *adj* unicolo(u)red, plain.

'**einfassen** *v/t* (*sep*, -ge-, h) **1.** a) surround, b) edge, border (*dress etc*). **2.** set (*diamond etc*), frame (*lens etc*).

'**Einfassung** *f* (-; -en) **1.** a) enclosure, b) border, edge. **2.** setting.

'**einfetten** *v/t* (*sep*, -ge-, h) grease.

'**einfinden**: **sich** ~ (*irr*, *sep*, -ge-, h, → **finden**) assemble, arrive, F turn up.

'**einflechten** *v/t* (*irr*, *sep*, -ge-, h, → **flechten**) *fig. et.* ~ mention s.th. in passing; *et.* ~ **in** (*acc*) work s.th. into.

'**einfliegen** (*irr*, *sep*, -ge-, → **fliegen**) **I** *v/t* (h) fly in, test(-fly). **II** *v/i* (sn) approach: ~ **in** (*acc*) fly into, enter.

'**einfließen** *v/i* (*irr*, *sep*, -ge-, sn, → **fließen**) flow in(to *in acc*): *fig.* ~ **lassen** slip s.th. in, give s.th. to understand.

'**einflößen** *v/t sep*, -ge-, h) *j-m et.* ~ a) give s.o. s.th. (to drink), b) fill (*or* inspire) s.o. with admiration, courage, *etc*; *j-m Angst* ~ fill s.o. with fear.

'**Einflugschneise** *f* approach corridor.

'**Einfluß** *m* (-sses; -sse) influence (*auf acc* on): ~ **haben auf** (*acc*) a) have an influence on, influence, b) have an effect on, affect; → **geltend**. '**Einflußbereich** *m* sphere of influence. '**Einflußnahme** *f* (-; *no pl*) intervention (*auf acc* in).

'**einflußreich** *adj* influential.

einförmig ['aınfœrmıç] *adj* uniform, monotonous. '**Einförmigkeit** *f* (-; *no pl*) uniformity, monotony.

'**einfrieren** (*irr*, *sep*, -ge-, → **frieren**) **I** *v/i* (sn) **1.** *water*: freeze over, *pipe etc*: freeze (up), *ship*: become icebound. **2.** *fig.* freeze. **II** *v/t* (h) **3.** (deep-)freeze (*food*). **4.** *fig.* freeze (*wages, assets, etc*).

'**einfügen** (*sep*, -ge-, h) **I** *v/t* (*in acc*) fit in(to), insert (into). **II sich** ~ (*in acc*) *fig.* fit in (with), *person*: adjust (to).

'**Einfügung** *f* (-; -en) insertion, addition.

'**einfühlen**: **sich** ~ (*sep*, -ge-, h) empathize (*in acc* with). '**einfühlsam** *adj* sensitive. '**Einfühlungsvermögen** *n* (-s; *no pl*) empathy.

Einfuhr ['aınfu:r] *f* (-; -en) ✝ **1.** *no pl* import. **2.** imports. ~**ar,tikel** *m* imported article, *pl* imports. ~**bestimmungen** *pl* import regulations.

'**einführen** *v/t* (*sep*, -ge-, h) **1.** introduce, *a.* adopt (*method etc*). **2.** *j-n* ~ introduce s.o. (*in acc* into, *bei* to); *j-n* (**in ein Amt**) ~ inaugurate s.o. **3.** (*in acc* into) insert, introduce. **4.** ✝ import.

'**Einfuhr|genehmigung** *f* import licence (*Am.* license). ~**hafen** *m* port of entry. ~**handel** *m* import trade. ~**land** *n* importing country. ~**stopp** *m* import ban.

'**Einführung** *f* (-; -en) (*in acc*) introduction (to), inauguration (into).

'**Einführungs...** introductory (*course, price, offer, etc*).

'**Einfuhrverbot** *n* import ban (*für* on).

'**Einfuhrzoll** *m* import duty.

'**einfüllen** *v/t* (*sep*, -ge-, h) pour in(to *in acc*).

'**Eingabe** *f* (-; -n) **1.** application (*bei* to, *um*, *für* for). **2.** *computer*: input. '**Eingabedaten** *pl computer*: input data.

'**Eingang** *m* (-[e]s; ~e) **1.** entrance, way in, entry. **2.** (*zu* to) access, entry, admission. **3.** *no pl* arrival (*of goods*), receipt (*of mail*): *bei* ~, *nach* ~ on receipt. **4.** *pl* ✝ a) arrivals, b) incoming mail, *pl* receipts. **5.** *no pl* (*zu* ~ at the) beginning (*gen of*). **6.** ⚡ input.

'**eingängig** *adj* catchy (*tune, slogan*).

eingangs ['aıngaŋs] **I** *adv* at the beginning. **II** *prep* (*gen*) at the beginning of.

'**Eingangs|datum** *n* date of receipt. ~**halle** *f* entrance hall. ~**stempel** *m* date stamp. ~**worte** *pl* opening words.

'**eingebaut** *adj* built-in, ⊙ *a.* integrated.

'**eingeben** *v/t* (*irr*, *sep*, -ge-, h, → **geben**) (*dat*) **1.** (to) give, administer (*drug*): *fig. j-m e-n Gedanken* ~ give s.o. an idea. **2.** feed *data* (into).

'**eingebildet** *adj* **1.** imaginary. **2.** conceited (*auf acc* about), arrogant.

'**Eingeborene** *m, f* (-n; -n) native.

'**Eingebung** *f* (-; -en) inspiration.

eingedenk ['aıngədɛŋk] *adj pred* mindful (*gen of*).

'**eingefallen** *adj fig.* hollow (*cheeks*).

'**eingefleischt** ['aıngəflaıʃt] *adj* inveterate, confirmed (*bachelor etc*).

'**eingehen** (*irr*, *sep*, -ge-, sn, → **gehen**) **I** *v/i* **1.** *goods, mail, etc*: come in, arrive: ~**d** incoming. **2.** ~ **in** (*acc*) enter (*a lan-*

guage etc): → **Geschichte** 2. **3. bei j-m ein- und ausgehen** be a frequent visitor at s.o.'s place. **4. ~ auf** (*acc*) a) accept, agree to, b) deal with (*details etc*), go into (*a question etc*), go along with (*a joke*): **auf j-n ~** listen (*or* respond) to s.o., humo(u)r s.o. **5.** *animal, plant*: die (*a.* F *person*: **vor** *dat* with), F *athlete etc*: go under, *business etc*: fold up. **6.** *fabric*: shrink. **7.** F **das geht ihm nicht ein** he can't grasp it. **II** *v/t* enter into (*contract, marriage, etc*); → **Risiko, Wette.**

'**eingehend I** *adj fig.* thorough, detailed. **II** *adv* thoroughly, in detail.

'**eingeklemmt I** *pp of* **einklemmen.** **II** *adj* ❦ strangulated (*hernia*), trapped (*nerve*).

'**eingemacht I** *pp of* **einmachen.** **II** *adj* preserved (*fruit*), pickled (*gherkins etc*).

eingemeinden ['aɪŋɡəmaɪndən] *v/t* (*sep, -ge-, h*) incorporate (*in acc* into).

'**eingenommen I** *pp of* **einnehmen.** **II** *adj*: **~ sein von** be taken with; *contp.* **von sich ~ sein** be full of o.s.

'**eingerostet** *adj a. fig.* rusty.

'**eingeschnappt I** *pp of* **einschnappen.** **II** *adj* F cross: **~ sein** be in a huff.

'**eingespielt I** *pp of* **einspielen.** **II** *adj* (**gut**) **aufeinander ~ sein** *a. fig.* make a good team.

'**Eingeständnis** *n* (*-ses; -se*) admission.

'**eingestehen** *v/t* (*irr, sep, h,* → **gestehen**) admit.

'**eingestellt I** *pp of* **einstellen.** **II** *adj* **1. ~ gegen** opposed to. **2. ~ auf** (*acc*) geared to, prepared for. **3. sozial ~** socially *etc* minded.

'**eingetragen I** *pp of* **eintragen.** **II** *adj* ♱ registered.

Eingeweide ['aɪŋɡəvaɪdə] *pl* a) insides, F innards, b) intestines, guts.

'**Eingeweihte** *m, f* (*-n; -n*) initiate, insider.

'**eingewöhnen: sich ~** (*sep, h*) (*in dat*) get accustomed (to), settle (into).

'**eingießen** *v/t* (*irr, sep, -ge-, h,* → **gießen**) pour (out).

'**eingipsen** *v/t* (*sep, -ge-, h*) ❦ put in plaster.

eingleisig ['aɪnɡlaɪzɪç] *adj* single-track.

'**eingliedern** (*sep, -ge-, h*) **I** *v/t* (*in acc* into) integrate, incorporate: **j-n wieder**

~ rehabilitate s.o. **II sich ~** (*in acc*) fit in (with), *person*: adjust (to).

'**Eingliederung** *f* (*-; -en*) integration.

'**eingraben** (*irr, sep, -ge-, h,* → **graben**) **I** *v/t* **1.** bury, dig in. **2.** engrave (*in acc* on). **II sich ~** dig (o.s.) in, entrench o.s., *zo.* burrow itself (*in acc* into).

'**eingra‚vieren** *v/t* (*sep, h*) engrave (*in acc* on).

'**eingreifen** *v/i* (*irr, sep, -ge-, h,* → **greifen**) **1.** step in, intervene, *a.* ✗ interfere (*in acc* with *rights*), ✗ go into action: **in ein Gespräch ~** cut in on a conversation; **in die Debatte ~** interfere in the debate; **in j-s Leben ~** affect s.o.'s life. **2.** ⚙ mesh (*in acc* with). '**Eingreifen** *n* (*-s*) intervention, interference, action.

'**eingreifend** *adj fig.* drastic, far-reaching. '**Eingriff** *m* (*-[e]s; -e*) **1.** ❦ operation. **2.** (*in acc* in) intervention, interference (*a.* with).

'**einhacken** *v/i* (*sep, -ge-, h*) **~ auf** (*acc*) hack at; *fig.* **auf j-n ~** keep on at s.o.

'**einhaken** (*sep, -ge-, h*) **I** *v/t* hook *s.th.* in. **II sich ~** link arms (**bei j-m** with s.o.). **III** *v/i fig.* cut in (**bei** on): **bei e-r Sache ~** take s.th. up.

'**Einhalt:** (*dat*) **~ gebieten** put a stop to.

'**einhalten** *v/t* (*irr, sep, -ge-, h,* → **halten**) keep (*promise*), keep to, observe (*contract, deadline, rule, etc*), meet (*obligation*). '**Einhaltung** *f* (*-; no pl*) (*gen*) adherence (to), observance (of).

'**einhämmern** → **einbleuen.**

'**Einhand...** ⚓ single-handed.

'**einhandeln** *v/t* (*sep, -ge-, h*) **et. für** (*or* **gegen**) **et. ~** exchange s.th. for s.th.; F *fig.* **sich et. ~** land o.s. with s.th.

einhändig ['aɪnhɛndɪç] *adj and adv* single-handed.

'**einhängen** (*sep, -ge-, h*) **I** *v/t* **1.** put *door* on its hinges. **2. den Hörer ~** hang up, replace the receiver. **II sich bei j-m ~** take s.o.'s arm. **III** *v/i* → 2.

'**einheimisch** *adj* local, native, *a.* ❧, *zo.* indigenous, ♱ domestic: **~e Mannschaft** home team. '**Einheimische** *m, f* (*-n; -n*) a) native, b) resident, local.

einheimsen ['aɪnhaɪmzən] *v/t* (*sep, -ge-, h*) F rake in (*money*), win (*praise*).

'**einheiraten** *v/i* (*sep, -ge-, h*) **~ in** (*acc*) marry into.

Einheit ['aɪnhaɪt] *f* (*-; -en*) **1.** unit: **e-e**

geschlossene ~ bilden form an integrated whole. **2.** *a. pol.* unity.
'**einheitlich** *adj* a) uniform, homogeneous, b) standard(ized), c) united.
'**Einheitlichkeit** *f* (-; *no pl*) **1.** uniformity. **2.** unity.
'**Einheits**|**front** *f pol.* united front. **~liste** *f pol.* single list (*Am.* ticket). **~preis** *m* a) standard price, b) flat-rate price. **~staat** *m* centralized state. **~wert** *m* *taxation:* rateable value.
'**einheizen** *v/i* (*sep*, -ge-, h) F *fig. **j-m** ~* give s.o. hell.
'**einhellig** ['aɪnhɛlɪç] *adj* unanimous.
'**ein'her...** *walk etc* along.
'**einholen** (*sep*, -ge-, h) **I** *v/t* **1.** catch up with (*a. fig.*), make up for (*lost time etc*). **2.** get, obtain: ***Auskünfte** ~* make inquiries (*über acc* about); ***Rat** ~* seek advice (*bei* from). **3.** ⚓ strike (*sails*), tow in (*ship*). **II** *v/i* **4.** F *~ gehen* go shopping.
'**Einhorn** *n* (-[e]s; **~**er) unicorn.
'**einhüllen** *v/t* (*sep*, -ge-, h) (*in acc*) wrap up (in), cover (with): *fig. **eingehüllt in Nebel** etc* enveloped in fog *etc*.
'**einhundert** *adj* a (*or* one) hundred.
'**einig** ['aɪnɪç] *adj* **1.** united. **2.** in agreement (*mit* with): (*sich*) *~ werden* come to an agreement (*über acc* about); *sich ~ sein, daß ...* be agreed that ...; *sich nicht ~ sein* (*über acc*) disagree (on).
einige ['aɪnɪɡə] *indef pron* **I** *adjectival* **1.** a few, some, several. **2.** a) quite a (bit of), b) some, c) quite a few: *es besteht ~ Hoffnung, daß ...* there is some hope that ...; *~s Aufsehen erregen* cause quite a stir. **3.** some *hundred marks etc.* **II** *substantival* **4.** *pl* a few, some, several. **5.** → *einiges*.
'**einigemal** *adv* several times.
'**einigen** (h) **I** *v/t* unite. **II** *sich ~* (*über acc, auf acc*) agree (on), reach an agreement (about).
'**einiger'maßen** *adv* a) to some extent, somewhat, b) quite, fairly, c) fairly well, F so-so.
'**einiges** *indef pron* a) something, some things, b) quite a bit: *~ davon* some of it; *er hat ~ gelernt* he has learned a thing or two; *sein Plan hat ~ für sich* there is s.th. to be said for his plan.
'**Einigkeit** *f* (-; *no pl*) **1.** unity, harmony. **2.** agreement, consensus: *es herrschte*

~ darüber, daß ... we (*or* they) all agreed that ...
'**Einigung** *f* (-; -en) **1.** unification. **2.** agreement: *es wurde k-e ~ erzielt* no agreement was reached (*über acc* on).
'**einimpfen** *v/t* (*sep*, -ge-, h) *fig. j-m et. ~* a) indoctrinate s.o. with s.th., b) → *einbleuen*.
'**einjagen** *v/t* (*sep*, -ge-, h) *j-m e-n Schreck ~* give s.o. a fright.
'**einjährig** ['aɪnjɛːrɪç] *adj* **1.** one-year-old. **2.** one-year (*course etc*). **3.** ♀ annual.
'**einkalku,lieren** *v/t* (*sep*, h) take *s.th.* into account, allow for.
'**Einkauf** *m* (-[e]s; **~**e) **1.** purchase: *Einkäufe machen* → *einkaufen* II. **2.** purchasing, buying. **3.** *no pl* ♆ purchasing department. '**einkaufen** (*sep*, -ge-, h) **I** *v/t* buy, purchase. **II** *v/i ~ gehen* go (*or* do one's) shopping. '**Einkäufer**(**in** *f*) *m* ♆ buyer.
'**Einkaufs**|**bummel** *m e-n ~ machen* go on a shopping spree. **~liste** *f* shopping list. **~preis** *m* (*zum ~* at the) purchase price. **~tasche** *f* shopping bag. **~zentrum** *n* shopping cent/re (*Am.* -er).
'**einkehren** *v/i* (*sep*, -ge-, sn) stop off (*in dat* at).
'**einkeilen** *v/t* (*sep*, -ge-, h) wedge in.
'**einkellern** *v/t* (*sep*, -ge-, h) put down.
'**einkerben** *v/t* (*sep*, -ge-, h), '**Einkerbung** *f* (-; -en) notch.
'**einklagen** *v/t* (*sep*, -ge-, h) *et.* (*gegen j-n*) *~* sue (s.o.) for s.th.
'**einklammern** *v/t* (*sep*, -ge-, h) put *s.th.* in brackets.
'**Einklang** *m* (-[e]s; *no pl*) ♪ unison, *fig. a.* harmony: *fig. in ~ bringen* reconcile (*mit* with); *nicht im ~ stehen* be at variance (*mit* with).
'**einkleben** *v/t* (*sep*, -ge-, h) stick *s.th.* in(to *in acc*).
'**einkleiden** (*sep*, -ge-, h) **I** *v/t j-n ~ a.* ✕ fit s.o. out. **II** *sich* (*neu*) *~* fit o.s. out with a new set of clothes.
'**einklemmen** *v/t* (*sep*, -ge-, h) (*sich*) *den Finger ~* get one's finger caught (*in dat* in); → *eingeklemmt*.
'**einkochen** *v/t* (*sep*, -ge-, h) **1.** boil down. **2.** preserve.
'**Einkommen** *n* (-s; -) **1.** income, earnings. **2.** revenue. '**Einkommensgruppe** *f* income bracket. '**einkommensschwach** *adj* low-income.

'**Einkommenssteuer** f income tax. **~erklärung** f income-tax return.
'**einköpfen** v/t (sep, -ge-) soccer: head in.
'**einkreisen** v/t (sep, -ge-, h) **1.** surround, encircle. **2.** narrow down (problem etc).
Einkünfte ['aɪnkʏnftə] pl **1.** income, earnings. **2.** revenue.
'**einkuppeln** v/i (sep, -ge-, h) mot. let in the clutch.
'**einladen** (irr, sep, -ge-, h, → **laden**) **I** v/t **1.** load (in). **2.** j-n ~ invite s.o. (**zum Essen** to lunch etc), ask s.o. (round); **ich lade dich (dazu) ein!** that's my treat!, this is on me! **II** v/i **3.** a. fig. invite. '**einladend** adj fig. a) inviting, b) tempting, c) delicious(-looking).
'**Einladung** f (-; -en) invitation: **auf ~ von** (or gen) at the invitation of.
'**Einlage** f (-; -n) **1.** in letter: enclosure, in newspaper etc: insert. **2.** a) (arch) support, b) insole. **3.** in panties etc: liner. **4.** padding. **5.** in tooth: temporary filling. **6.** in soups: garnish. **7.** ✝ a) in bank: deposit, b) (capital) contribution. **8.** thea. etc interlude, extra.
Einlaß ['aɪnlas] m (-sses; no pl) admittance (zu to): **sich ~ verschaffen** get in; **~ ab 18 Uhr** opening at 18:00 hours.
'**einlassen** (irr, sep, -ge-, h, → **lassen**) **I** v/t **1.** let s.o., s.th. in, admit: **Wasser (in die Wanne) ~** run a bath. **2.** (in acc in) set (diamond etc), ⚙ embed. **II sich ~ auf** (acc) a) get involved in, b.s. let o.s. in for, b) agree to (a proposal), c) go into (a question); **laß dich nicht darauf ein!** leave it alone!; **sich mit j-m ~** get involved with s.o. (a. amorously); **sich mit j-m auf e-n Kampf (ein Wortgefecht) ~** F tangle with s.o.
'**Einlauf** m (-[e]s; ⸚e) **1.** ✿ (**e-n ~ machen** give s.o.) an enema. **2.** sports: finish.
'**einlaufen** (irr, sep, -ge-, → **laufen**) **I** v/i (sn) **1.** come in (a. sports), ⚓ put in. **2.** water: run in: **Badewasser ~ lassen** run a bath. **3.** fabric: shrink: **nicht ~d** nonshrink. **II** v/t (h) break in (shoes). **III sich ~** (h) sports: warm up.
'**einläuten** v/t (sep, -ge-, h) ring in.
'**einleben** → **eingewöhnen**.
'**Einlegearbeit** f inlaid work.
'**einlegen** v/t (sep, -ge-, h) **1.** put in, insert (film etc): **et. ~ in** (acc) a. enclose s.th. in (or with); fig. **e-e Pause ~** have

a break; **e-n Spurt ~** put in a spurt; → **Wort** 2. **2.** deposit (money in bank). **3.** gastr. (in Essig) ~ pickle. **4.** ⚙ inlay (mit with). **5.** lodge, file (appeal etc): **Berufung** 4, **Protest**, **Veto**. **6.** j-m (sich) **die Haare ~** set s.o.'s (one's) hair.
'**Einleger** m (-s; -) ✝ depositor.
'**Einlegesohle** f insole.
'**einleiten** v/t (sep, -ge-, h) **1.** start, begin, a. open (negotiations), initiate (reforms etc), introduce (a. ltng. clause). **2.** ✿ induce. **3.** ⚖ institute: **e-n Prozeß ~ gegen** bring an action against. '**einleitend I** adj introductory, opening, preliminary. **II** adv by way of introduction. '**Einleitung** f (-; -en) **1.** opening, start, introduction (a. ling.). **2.** preface. **3.** ✿ induction. **4.** ⚖ institution.
'**einlenken** v/i (sep, -ge-, h) fig. relent.
'**einlesen** v/t (irr, sep, -ge-, h, → **lesen**) computer: read in.
'**einleuchten** v/i (sep, -ge-, h) make sense (j-m to s.o.). '**einleuchtend** adj clear, convincing.
'**einliefern** v/t (sep, -ge-, h) **1.** j-n ins Krankenhaus (Gefängnis) ~ take s.o. to (the) hospital (to prison). **2.** post, mail. '**Einlieferung** f (-; -en) **1.** (in acc) admission to (hospital), committal to (prison etc). **2.** posting, mailing.
'**Einlieferungsschein** m postal receipt.
'**einlochen** v/t (sep, -ge-) **1.** golf: put(t). **2.** F j-n ~ put s.o. in clink.
'**einlösen** v/t (sep, -ge-, h) **1.** redeem (pawn, securities), cash (cheque). **2.** fig. keep (promise etc).
'**einlullen** v/t (sep, -ge-, h) F fig. lull.
'**einmachen** v/t (sep, -ge-, h) preserve.
'**einmal** adv **1.** once: ~ **im Jahr** once a year; ~ **und nie wieder** never again; **noch** ~ once more; **erst** ~ first; **auf** ~ a) at one go, b) at the same time, c) suddenly. **2.** once, before: **das war** ~ that's all in the past; **es war** ~ once upon a time there was; **ich war schon** ~ **da** a) I've been there before, b) I was there once; **haben Sie schon** ~ ...? have you ever ...? **3.** one day, some day (or other), later on: **wenn du** ~ **groß bist** when you grow up. **4.** **nicht** ~ not even, not so much as. **5.** **ich bin** ~ **so!** I can't help it!; **es ist nun** ~ **so** that's the way it is; **laßt ihn doch** ~ **reden!** let him talk, will you!; **stell dir** ~ **vor!** just imagine!

Einmal'eins n (-; no pl) **1.** (multiplication) table. **2.** fig. basics.

'**einmalig** adj **1.** single, nonrecurring: ~e **Abfindung** single payment. **2.** unique, singular, unparallel(l)ed, F fantastic: **e-e ~e Chance** the chance of a lifetime; ~ **schön** absolutely beautiful.

'**Einmannbetrieb** m one-man business.

'**Einmarsch** m marching in, a. invasion.

'**einmar,schieren** v/i (sep, sn) march in: **in ein Land** ~ invade a country.

'**einmieten: sich** ~ (sep, -ge-, h) take a room (or rooms) (**in** dat at, **bei** with).

'**einmischen: sich** ~ (**in** acc in, with) meddle, interfere; **sich in ein Gespräch** ~ join in (or F butt in on) a conversation; **misch dich da nicht ein!** just keep out of it!

'**Einmischung** f (-; -en) interference.

'**einmo,torig** adj single-engined.

einmotten ['aɪnmɔtən] v/t (sep, -ge-, h) put s.th. in mothballs, fig. a. mothball.

'**einmünden** v/i (sep, -ge-, sn) a) flow into, b) road: lead into, c) fig. lead to.

'**Einmündung** f (-; -en) a) estuary, mouth, b) (road) junction.

einmütig ['aɪnmy:tɪç] adj unanimous.

'**Einmütigkeit** f (-; no pl) unanimity.

Einnahme ['aɪnnaːmə] f (-; -n) **1.** taking, ✕ a. capture, occupation. **2.** pl a) receipts, b) proceeds, c) income, earnings, d) revenue.

'**Einnahmequelle** f source of income.

'**einnehmen** v/t (irr, sep, -ge-, h, → **nehmen**) **1.** have (lunch etc), take (medicament). **2.** take in, earn (money). **3.** ✕ capture, occupy. **4.** take up (space): **s-n Platz** ~ take one's seat. **5.** hold (position etc). **6.** fig. **j-n für sich** ~ win s.o. over, charm s.o.; **j-n gegen sich** ~ set s.o. against o.s. '**einnehmend** adj fig. winning, engaging.

'**einnicken** v/i (sep, -ge-, sn) F nod off.

'**einnisten: sich** ~ (sep, -ge-, h) nest, fig. person: install o.s.

'**Einöde** f (-; -n) wilderness.

'**einölen** v/t (sep, -ge-, h) a) oil, b) rub oil into.

'**einordnen** (sep, -ge-, h) **I** v/t **1.** arrange (**nach** according to), file. **2.** a) classify, b) integrate (**in** acc into a system etc), c) place, date (work of art), d) class (**unter** acc with). **II** sich ~ **3.** → **einfügen** II. **4.**

mot. get in lane: **sich links** ~ get into the left lane, Br. filter to the left.

'**einpacken** (sep, -ge-, h) **I** v/t pack (up), wrap up, do up. **II** v/i pack: F fig. **da können wir ~!** we might as well pack up and leave!

'**einparken** v/t, v/i (sep, -ge-, h) park (between two cars).

'**einpendeln: sich** ~ (sep, -ge-, h) fig. find its (own) level.

'**einpferchen** v/t (sep, -ge-, h) coop up.

'**einpflanzen** v/t **1.** ✓ plant. **2.** ✿ implant (organ).

Ein'phasen..., einphasig ['aɪnfaːzɪç] adj ∮ single-phase.

'**einplanen** v/t (sep, -ge-, h) **1.** include (in the plan), plan. **2.** allow for.

einpolig ['aɪnpoːlɪç] adj ∮ single-pole.

'**einprägen** (sep, -ge-, h) **I** v/t imprint (**in** acc on): **j-m et.** ~ impress s.th. on s.o.; **sich et.** ~ a) remember, b) memorize. **II** sich **j-m** ~ stick in s.o.'s mind.

'**einprägsam** adj easily remembered, catchy (tune).

'**einquar,tieren** (sep, h) **I** v/t ✕ billet (**bei** on). **II** sich ~ **bei** move in with.

'**Einquar,tierung** f (-; -en) ✕ billeting.

'**einrahmen** v/t (sep, -ge-, h) frame.

'**einrammen** v/t (sep, -ge-, h) ram s.th. in(**to in** acc).

'**einrasten** v/i (sep, -ge-, sn) **1.** ✿ click into place, engage. **2.** F go into a huff.

'**einräumen** v/t (sep, -ge-, h) **1.** a) put away, b) put the furniture in a room: **e-n Schrank** ~ put (the) things into a cupboard. **2.** fig. **j-m et.** ~ grant s.th. to s.o. '**einräumend** adj ling. concessive.

'**Einrede** f (-; -n) ⚖ plea, demurrer.

'**einreden** (sep, -ge-, h) **I** v/t **j-m** (**sich**) **et.** ~ talk s.o. (o.s.) into (believing) s.th.; **j-m** (**sich**) ~, **daß ...** persuade s.o. (o.s.) that ...; **das redest du dir** (**doch**) **nur ein!** you're imagining it! **II** v/i **auf j-n** ~ a) talk insistently to s.o., b) urge s.o.

'**einregnen** (sep, -ge-) **I** v/i (sn) **eingeregnet sein** be caught by the rain; fig. **auf j-n** ~ rain on s.o. **II** v/impers (h) **es regnet sich ein** the rain is settling in.

'**einreiben** v/t (irr, sep, -ge-, h, → **reiben**) rub s.th. in: ~ **mit** rub with.

'**Einreibemittel** n liniment.

'**einreichen** v/t (sep, -ge-, h) (**bei** to) send in, hand in, submit: ⚖ **e-e Klage** ~ file (or bring) an action.

'einreihen (*sep*, -ge-, h) **I** *sich* ~ (*in acc*) take one's place (in), join (*s.th.*). **II** *v/t* class (*in acc* with): *j-n* ~ *unter* (*acc*) rank s.o. with.

'Einreiher *m* (-s; -) single-breasted suit.

'Einreise *f* (-; -n) entry. ~**genehmigung** *f* entry permit. ~**visum** *n* entry visa.

'einreißen (*irr*, *sep*, -ge-, → *reißen*) **I** *v/t* (h) **1.** tear. **2.** demolish, pull *house etc* down. **II** *v/i* (sn) **3.** tear. **4.** F *nuisance etc*: spread.

einrenken]'aınrɛŋkən] (*sep*, -ge-, h) **I** *v/t* **1.** ⚕ set. **2.** F *fig.* straighten *s.th.* out. **II** *sich* ~ F *fig.* sort itself out.

'einrichten (*sep*, -ge-, h) **I** *v/t* **1.** furnish (*room etc*), fit *kitchen*, *shop*, *etc* out, equip, install. **2.** set up, found, establish. **3.** arrange: *es* ~*, daß ... a.* see (to it) that ...; *wenn du es* ~ *kannst* if you can (manage to). **4.** ⚕ set (*broken bone*). **II** *sich* ~ **5.** *sich* (*neu*) ~ (re)furnish one's flat (*or* house); → *häuslich*. **6.** make ends meet. **7.** *sich* ~ *auf* (*acc*) prepare for; *auf so et. sind wir nicht eingerichtet* we're not prepared for that sort of thing.

'Einrichtung *f* (-; -en) **1.** furniture, fittings, equipment. **2.** installation: *die sanitären* ~*en a.* sanitation. **3.** *no pl* setting up, foundation. **4.** (*öffentliche* ~ public) institution, *w.s.* facility: *zu e-r ständigen* ~ *werden* become a permanent institution. **5.** → *Vorrichtung*.

'Einrichtungsgegenstände *pl* equipment, fixtures.

'einrosten *v/i* (*sep*, -ge-, sn) get rusty.

'einrücken (*sep*, -ge-) **I** *v/t* (h) **1.** indent (*line*). **2.** put *an advertisement* in *a newspaper etc*. **II** *v/i* **3.** ⚔ a) be called up, b) march in: ~ *in* (*acc*) march into.

eins [aıns] **I** *adj* **1.** one: *um* ~ at one (o'clock); *sports*: ~ *zu zwei* one two; F *fig.* ~ *zu null für dich!* score one for you! **2.** *es ist mir alles* ~ I couldn't care less; *das ist doch alles* ~ it all amounts to the same thing. **II** *indef pron* one thing: ~ *nach dem andern!* one thing at a time!; *noch* ~*!* another thing!

Eins *f* (-; -en) (number) one, *ped.* A: *e-e* ~ *schreiben* get an A; F *wie e-e* ~ just super.

'einsacken (*sep*, -ge-, h) **I** *v/t* (h) bag, F *fig. a.* pocket. **II** *v/i* (sn) sag.

einsam ['aınza:m] *adj* lonely, isolated, secluded. **'Einsamkeit** *f* (-; *no pl*) loneliness, seclusion, isolation.

'einsammeln *v/t* (*sep*, -ge-, h) gather, collect.

'Einsatz *m* (-es; ~e) **1.** insert, *on dress*: inset, (*filter*) element. **2.** stake (*a. fig.*): *den* ~ *verdoppeln* double the stake(s). **3.** risk: *unter* ~*s-s Lebens* at the risk of one's life. **4.** ♪ entry: *den* ~ *geben* give the cue. **5.** effort(s), hard work, zeal, dedication: *harter* ~ *sports*: hard tackling; *mit vollem* ~ all out. **6.** use, employment, ⚔ deployment: *im* ~ ◎ in operation. **7.** ⚔, *police etc*: action, (*combat*) mission: *im* ~ *stehen* be on duty, ⚔ be in action; *zum* ~ *kommen* be brought in(to action).

'Einsatz|befehl *m* ⚔ combat order. **2bereit** *adj* ready for duty (⚔ action, ◎ use): *sich* ~ *halten* stand by; *et.* ~ *halten* have s.th. ready. ~**besprechung** *f before a mission*: briefing, *after a mission*: debriefing. **2fähig** *adj* a) available, usable, ⚔ operational, b) fit to work (*or* play *etc*). **2freudig** *adj* keen, zealous. ~**gruppe** *f*, ~**kom**,**mando** *n* task force. ~**wagen** *m* police car (*or* van).

'einsaugen *v/t* (*sep*, -ge-, h) suck in.

'einschalten (*sep*, -ge-, h) **I** *v/t* **1.** switch on, turn on, ◎ *a.* connect: *e-n Sender* ~ tune in to; *den Motor* ~ start the engine; *den dritten Gang* ~ shift into third gear. **2.** *fig.* put in, insert: *e-e Pause* ~ have a break. **3.** *fig.* call in: *in e-n* (*or bei e-m*) *Fall Sachverständige* ~ call (*or* bring) in experts in a case. **II** *sich* ~ **4.** *fig.* step in, intervene: *sich in ein Gespräch* ~ join in a conversation. **5.** *TV* tune in (*in acc* to). **6.** ◎ switch itself on (automatically).

'Einschaltquote *f* radio, *TV* viewing figures, ratings.

'einschärfen *v/t* (*sep*, -ge-, h) *j-m* ~ *zu inf* urge (*or* warn) s.o. to *inf.*

'einschätzen *v/t* (*sep*, -ge-, h) **1.** judge, assess: *falsch* ~ misjudge; *zu hoch* (*niedrig*) ~ overrate (underrate). **2.** assess, estimate. **'Einschätzung** *f* (-; -en) **1.** assessment. **2.** estimation, judg(e)-ment: *nach m-r* ~ in my estimation.

'einschenken *v/t* (*sep*, -ge-, h) pour (out).

'einschicken *v/t* (*sep*, -ge-, h) send in.

'einschieben *v/t* (*irr*, *sep*, -ge-, h, →

schieben) **1.** put in, insert. **2.** *fig.* fit in.

'**Einschiebung** *f* (-; -en) insertion.
'**einschießen: sich ~** (*irr*, *sep*, -ge-, h, → **schießen**) *a. fig.* zero in (**auf** *acc* on).
'**einschiffen: sich ~** (*sep*, -ge-, h) embark (**nach** for), board a (*or* the) ship.
'**einschlafen** *v/i* (*irr*, *sep*, -ge-, sn, → **schlafen**) **1.** fall asleep, *a. leg etc*: go to sleep. **2.** *fig. correspondence etc*: peter out. **3.** *fig.* die peacefully, pass away.
'**einschläfern** *v/t* (*sep*, -ge-, h) **1.** a) lull (*🗡* put) *s.o.* to sleep, b) make *s.o.* drowsy: *fig.* **j-n ~** lull s.o. (into a false sense of security). **2.** put down (*dog etc*). '**einschläfernd** *adj* soporific.
'**Einschlag** *m* (-[e]s; ⸚e) **1.** impact (*of bomb etc*), striking (*of lightning*). **2.** *fig.* touch: **ein südländischer ~** an element of the Mediterranean. **3.** *mot.* lock.
'**einschlagen** (*irr*, *sep*, -ge-, h, → **schlagen**) **I** *v/t* **1.** drive nail in(to in *acc*). **2.** break, smash (in): **j-m den Schädel ~** F bash s.o.'s head in; **sich die Zähne ~** knock one's teeth out. **3.** wrap up. **4.** take (*direction, road*). **5.** *fig.* enter (*a career*), adopt (*a policy etc*): **e-n anderen Weg ~** adopt a different method. **II** *v/i* **6.** (**in** *acc*) bomb *etc*: hit (*lightning*: strike) (*the house etc*): *fig.* **wie e-e Bombe ~** fall like a bombshell, cause a sensation. **7.** *fig.* (**gut**) **~** be a (great) success, be a (big) hit. **8. ~ auf** (*acc*) beat. **III** *sich ~* (h) *tennis*: warm up.
einschlägig ['aɪnʃlɛːgɪç] *adj* relevant: **ein ~er Fall** a case in point; **~ vorbestraft** previously convicted for the same offence.
'**einschleichen: sich ~** (*irr*, *sep*, -ge-, h, → **schleichen**) creep in(to in *acc*); **sich in j-s Vertrauen ~** worm one's way into s.o.'s confidence.
'**einschleppen** *v/t* (*sep*, -ge-, h) bring a disease *etc* in(to in *acc*).
'**einschleusen** *v/t* (*sep*, -ge-, h) (**in** *acc*) infiltrate *s.o.* (into), smuggle *s.o.*, *s.th.* in(to).
'**einschließen** *v/t* (*irr*, *sep*, -ge-, h, → **schließen**) **1.** lock (*or* shut) *s.o.*, *s.th.* (**sich** o.s.) up (*or* in). **2.** enclose, *a.* ✗ surround, encircle. **3.** *fig.* include (**in** *acc* in). '**einschließlich I** *prep* (*gen*) including, inclusive of: **~ Porto** postage included. **II** *adv* **bis Seite 7 ~** up to and

including page 7; **von Montag bis ~ Freitag** from Monday to Friday inclusive, *Am.* Monday through Friday.
'**einschmeicheln: sich ~** (*sep*, -ge-, h) ingratiate o.s. (**bei j-m** with s.o.).
'**einschmeichelnd** *adj* ingratiating.
'**einschmelzen** *v/t* (*irr*, *sep*, -ge-, h, → **schmelzen**) melt *s.th.* (down).
'**einschnappen** *v/i* (*sep*, -ge-, sn) **1.** catch, click. **2.** F *fig.* go into a huff: → **eingeschnappt.**
'**einschneiden** (*irr*, *sep*, -ge-, h, → **schneiden**) **I** *v/t* (**in** *acc* into) cut, carve. **II** *v/i* cut into. '**einschneidend** *adj fig.* incisive, drastic, crucial, decisive.
'**einschneien** *v/t* (*sep*, -ge-, sn) **eingeschneit sein** be snowed in (*or* up).
'**Einschnitt** *m* **1.** cut, incision, notch. **2.** *fig.* a) crucial event, b) turning point.
'**einschränken** [-ʃrɛŋkən] (*sep*, -ge-, h) **I** *v/t* **1.** (**auf** *acc* to) restrict, reduce (*production etc*), cut down (*expenditure etc*): **das Rauchen ~** cut down on smoking. **2.** qualify (*statement etc*). **II sich ~** economize (**in** *dat* in), cut down expenses. '**einschränkend** *adj* restrictive (*a. ling.*), qualifying (*remark*).
'**Einschränkung** *f* (-; -en) **1.** restriction, reduction, cut. **2.** qualification: **ohne ~** without reservation.
'**einschrauben** *v/t* (*sep*, -ge-, h) screw in(to **in** *acc*).
'**Einschreibe|brief** *m* registered letter. **~gebühr** *f* registration fee.
'**einschreiben** (*irr*, *sep*, -ge-, h, → **schreiben**) **I** *v/t* **1. e-n Brief ~ lassen** have a letter registered; *Σ!* registered! **2.** enter, *as a member*: enrol(l): **sich ~ lassen** → **II sich ~** sign up, *univ.* register, enrol(l). '**Einschreibung** *f* (-; -en) signing up, *univ.* enrol(l)ment.
'**einschreiten** *v/i* (*irr*, *sep*, -ge-, sn, → **schreiten**) intervene, step in: **~ gegen** take action against.
'**Einschub** *m* (-[e]s; ⸚e) insertion, ⚙ insert, ⚡ slide-in module.
'**einschüchtern** *v/t* (*sep*, -ge-, h) intimidate. '**Einschüchterung** *f* (-; -en) intimidation.
'**einschulen** *v/t* (*sep*, -ge-, h) **ein Kind ~** put a child to school.
'**Einschuß** *m* (-sses; ⸚sse) bullet hole, *🗡* entry wound.

'**einschweißen** v/t (sep, -ge-, h) shrink-wrap.

'**einschwenken** v/i (sep, -ge-, sn) turn (in acc into): nach links ~ turn (to the) left; fig. ~ (auf acc) come round (to).

'**Einsegnung** f (-; -en) eccl. **1.** consecration. **2.** confirmation.

'**einsehen** v/t (irr, sep, -ge-, h, → **sehen**) **1.** have a look at, inspect. **2.** see, ✕ observe (terrain). **3.** fig. understand, see, realize: ich sehe nicht ein, weshalb I don't see why. '**Einsehen** n (-s) ein ~ haben a) show some consideration (mit for), b) be reasonable.

'**einseifen** v/t (sep, -ge-, h) **1.** lather, soap. **2.** F fig. j-n ~ take s.o. in.

einseitig ['aɪnzaɪtɪç] adj **1.** one-sided (a. fig.), pol. unilateral, ⚕ a. on one side: ~e Ernährung unbalanced diet; ~ beschrieben written on one side (only). **2.** bias(s)ed: et. sehr ~ darstellen give a one-sided description of s.th. '**Einseitigkeit** f (-; no pl) one-sidedness, fig. a. bias, partiality.

'**einsenden** v/t (irr, sep, -ge-, h, → **senden**) send in. '**Einsender(in** f) m **1.** sender. **2.** contributor. '**Einsendeschluß** m closing date (for entries). '**Einsendung** f (-; -en) a) sending in, b) at competition: entry.

Einser ['aɪnzər] m (-s; -) F → **Eins**.

'**einsetzen** (sep, -ge-, h) I v/t **1.** put in, insert. **2.** set up (committee). **3.** use, employ, apply, bring influence etc into play. **4.** put into action, call in (the police), employ (work force etc): j-n ~ in (dat (or bei)) assign s.o. to; j-n als Erben ~ appoint s.o. one's heir. **5.** stake, bet: fig. sein Leben ~ risk one's life. II **6.** sich ~ exert o.s.; sich voll ~ go all out; sich ~ für support, speak up for, champion; sich bei j-m für j-n ~ intercede with s.o. for s.o. III v/i **7.** start (off), rain etc: set in. **8.** ♪ come in.

'**Einsetzung** f (-; -en) **1.** insertion. **2.** appointment.

'**Einsicht** f (-; -en) **1.** no pl examination (in Akten of records): ~ nehmen in (acc) examine. **2.** insight, understanding: zur ~ kommen listen to reason.

'**einsichtig** adj reasonable.

'**Einsichtnahme** f (-; no pl) inspection.

'**einsickern** v/i (sep, -ge-, sn) seep in: ~ in (acc) seep into, a. fig. infiltrate into.

'**Einsiedler** m (-s; -) hermit.

einsilbig ['aɪnzɪlbɪç] adj monosyllabic, fig. a. taciturn. '**Einsilbigkeit** f (-; no pl) fig. taciturnity.

'**einsinken** v/i (irr, sep, -ge-, sn, → **sinken**) a) sink in(to in acc), b) cave in.

'**einsitzen** v/i (irr, sep, -ge-, h, → **sitzen**) ⚖ serve a sentence.

Einsitzer ['aɪnzɪtsər] m (-s; -) ✈, mot. single-seater.

'**einsor,ticren** v/t (sep, h) sort in(to in acc).

'**einspannen** v/t (sep, -ge-, h) **1.** harness. **2.** ⚙ clamp, fix: e-n Bogen (in die Schreibmaschine) ~ insert a sheet of paper into the typewriter. **3.** F fig. j-n ~ rope s.o. in.

'**einsparen** v/t (sep, -ge-, h) **1.** save. **2.** eliminate (jobs). '**Einsparung** f (-; -en) **1.** saving. **2.** (job) elimination.

'**einspeichern** v/t (sep, -ge-, h) computer: read in.

'**einspeisen** v/t (sep, -ge-, h) ⚙ feed (in acc into).

'**einsperren** v/t (sep, -ge-, h) lock up.

'**einspielen** (sep, -ge-, h) I v/t **1.** bring in (money). **2.** TV a) show, b) fade in. **3.** ♪ play in. **4.** record. II sich ~ **5.** get into practice, sports: warm up, fig. get going (properly): sich aufeinander ~ get used to one another; → eingespielt.

'**Einspielergebnisse** pl box-office returns.

einsprachig ['aɪnʃpraːxɪç] adj monolingual.

'**einspringen** v/i (irr, sep, -ge-, sn, → **springen**) fig. help out, step in(to the breach): für j-n ~ fill in for s.o.

'**Einspritz...** mot. (fuel) injection (engine, pump, etc). '**einspritzen** v/t (sep, -ge-, h) inject (in acc into): j-m et. ~ inject s.o. with, give s.o. an injection of.

'**Einspruch** m (-[e]s; ⸚e) (gegen) objection (to) (a. ⚖), protest (against), esp. pol. veto (against), ⚖ appeal (against): ~ erheben (gegen) object (to), ⚖ (file an) appeal (against), pol. veto (s.th.).

'**Einspruchsfrist** f appeal period.

'**Einspruchsrecht** n **1.** ⚖ right to appeal. **2.** pol. (power of) veto.

einspurig ['aɪnʃpuːrɪç] adj a) single-track, b) single-lane.

einst [aɪnst] adv **1.** once. **2.** one day.

'**einstampfen** v/t (sep, -ge-, h) pulp.

'Einstand *m* (-[e]s; *no pl*) **1.** (*s-n ~ geben* celebrate the) start of one's new job. **2.** *fig.* debut. **3.** *tennis*: deuce.

'einstecken *v/t* (*sep*, -ge-, h) **1.** put in. **2.** put *s.th.* in one's pocket (*or* bag *etc*), take. **3.** F *fig.* pocket (*profit etc*), swallow (*reprimand etc*), take (*a blow*): *er kann viel ~* he can take a lot.

'einstehen *v/i* (*irr, sep*, -ge-, h, → *stehen*) *~ für* a) answer for, take reponsibility for, b) vouch for.

'einsteigen *v/i* (*irr, sep*, -ge-, sn, → *steigen*) get in(to *in acc*): *alle(s) ~!* all aboard!; *~ in* (*acc*) a) get on (*a bus, train, plane*), b) F*fig.* get in on (*a project etc*), start on (*or* in); *er ist in die Politik eingestiegen* he went into politics; *hart ~ sports*: play rough.

'einstellbar *adj* adjustable.

'einstellen (*sep*, -ge-, h) **I** *v/t* **1.** put s.th. in(to *in acc*), store (*furniture*), put *car* in the garage. **2.** take on (*workers etc*). **3.** (*auf acc*) ⊙ set (to), adjust (to) (*a. fig.*), tune *radio etc* in (to), *opt.* focus (on). **4.** stop, discontinue: **'vorübergehend**) *~* suspend; ⚖ *die Klage ~* drop the action; *das Verfahren ~* dismiss the case; *die Arbeit ~* a) stop work, b) (go on) strike, walk out; *den Betrieb ~* shut down; ✕ *das Feuer ~* cease fire. **5.** tie, equal (*a record*). **II sich ~ 6.** appear, turn up, *fig. fever etc*: set in, *problems etc*: arise. **7. sich ~ auf** (*acc*) a) adjust (to), b) prepare (o.s.) for; *sich ganz auf j-n ~* give s.o. one's undivided attention.

'einstellig *adj* ℞ one-digit.

'Einstellknopf *m* control knob.

'Einstellung *f* (-; -en) **1.** employment (*of personnel*). **2.** ⊙ adjustment, setting, *opt., phot.* focus(s)ing, focus. **3.** *film*: a) (camera) angle, b) take. **4.** discontinuance, cessation (*a.* ✕ *of hostilities*), stoppage (*of work, operation*), suspension (*of payments*): ⚖ *~ des Verfahrens* dismissal of a case; *~ e-r Klage* withdrawal of an action. **5.** *fig.* adjustment (*auf acc* to). **6.** (*zu*) attitude (towards), opinion (of): *s-e politische ~* his political views, F his politics.

Einstieg ['aɪnʃtiːk] *m* (-[e]s; -e) **1.** way in, entrance. **2.** *fig.* (*in acc*) entry (into), start (in *or* on), getting in (on): *~ in die Kernenergie* opting for nuclear ener-

gy. **'Einstiegluke** *f* (access) hatch.

'Einstiegsdroge *f* gateway drug.

einstig ['aɪnstɪç] *adj* former.

'einstimmen (*sep*, -ge-, h) **I** *v/i* **1.** *in ein Lied* (*das Gelächter*) *~* join in a song (the laughter). **II** *v/t* **2.** ♪ tune (up). **3.** *fig.* **j-n (sich)** *~* (*auf acc*) get s.o. (o.s.) in the proper mood (for).

einstimmig ['aɪnʃtɪmɪç] *adj* **1.** ♪ for one voice. **2.** unanimous (*decision etc*).

'Einstimmigkeit *f* (-; *no pl*) unanimity, consensus.

einstöckig ['aɪnʃtœkɪç] *adj* one-stor(e)y.

'einstöpseln *v/t* (*sep*, -ge-, h) plug in.

'einstreuen *v/t* (*sep*, -ge-, h) *fig.* insert: *Zitate etc in s-e Rede ~* intersperse one's speech with quotations *etc*.

'einströmen *v/i* (*sep*, -ge-, sn) flow in(to *in acc*).

'einstu,dieren *v/t* (*sep*, h) learn *s.th.* (by heart), *thea.* rehearse. **'Einstu,dierung** *f* (-; -en) *thea.* production.

'einstufen *v/t* (*sep*, -ge-, h) class, grade, rate: *hoch ~* rate high. **'einstufig** *adj* single-stage. **'Einstufung** *f* (-; -en) classification, rating.

einstündig ['aɪnʃtʏndɪç] *adj* one-hour.

'einstürmen *v/i* (*sep*, -ge-, sn) *~ auf* (*acc*) rush at, ✕ attack; *fig. auf j-n ~* assail s.o. (*mit Fragen* with questions).

'Einsturz *m* (-es; *~e*) collapse. **'einstürzen** *v/i* (*sep*, -ge-, sn) collapse, cave in.

einst'weilen *adv* **1.** meanwhile, in the meantime. **2.** for the time being. **einst'weilig** *adj* temporary: ⚖ *~e Verfügung* a) interim order, b) injunction.

eintägig ['aɪntɛːgɪç] *adj* one-day.

'Eintagsfliege *f* **1.** *zo.* day fly, ephemera. **2.** *fig.* nine days' wonder.

'eintasten *v/t* (*sep*, -ge-, h) *computer*: key in.

'eintauchen (*sep*, -ge-, h) **I** *v/t* dip in(to *in acc*). **II** *v/i* dive in(to *in acc*).

'eintauschen *v/t* (*sep*, -ge-, h) (*gegen* for) **1.** exchange. **2.** trade *s.th.* in.

'einteilen *v/t* (*sep*, -ge-, h) **1.** a) divide (up) (*in acc* into), b) rate (*nach* according to). **2.** organize (*one's time*), budget (*money*), use *material etc* sparingly. **3.** *j-n ~ zu* asssign s.o. to, ✕ detail s.o. for.

'Einteiler *m* (-s; -), **einteilig** ['aɪntaɪlɪç] *adj* one-piece. **'Einteilung** *f* (-; -en) **1.** (*in acc* into) a) division, b) classification. **2.** planning, organization (*of work, time, etc*), budgeting (*of money*).

'**eintippen** *v/t* (*sep*, -ge-, h) type in(to *in acc*), *computer:* key in.

eintönig ['aɪntøːnɪç] *adj* monotonous.

'**Eintönigkeit** *f* (-; *no pl*) monotony.

'**Eintopf** *m* (-[e]s; ⁓e) *gastr.* stew.

'**Eintracht** *f* (-; *no pl*) harmony.

'**einträchtig** *adj* harmonious, peaceful.

Eintrag ['aɪntraːk] *m* (-[e]s; ⁓e) entry.

'**eintragen** (*irr*, *sep*, -ge-, h, → **tragen**) *v/t* **1.** enter (*a.* ✝), *adm.* register, enrol(l) (**als Mitglied** as a member): **sich ⁓ lassen** (*bei*) register (with), enrol(l) (in); → **eingetragen. 2.** *j-m et.* ⁓ earn s.o. *praise, sympathy, etc.* **II sich ⁓** a) register, b) put one's name down: **sich in e-e Anwesenheitsliste ⁓** sign in.

einträglich ['aɪntrɛːklɪç] *adj* profitable.

'**Eintragung** *f* (-; -en) **1.** registration, enrol(l)ment. **2.** → **Eintrag.**

'**eintreffen** *v/i* (*irr*, *sep*, -ge-, sn, → **treffen**) **1.** arrive (*in dat, auf dat* at). **2.** *fig.* a) happen, b) prove (*or* come) true.

'**Eintreffen** *n* (-s) arrival.

'**eintreiben** *v/t* (*irr*, *sep*, -ge-, h, → **treiben**) collect.

'**eintreten** (*irr*, *sep*, -ge-, → **treten**) **I** *v/i* **1.** (sn) go in, come in: **er trat ins Haus ein** he went into (*or* entered) the house; **bitte, treten Sie ein!** do come in, please! **2.** (sn) ⁓ **in** (*acc*) join, enter (*club, firm, etc*); **in den Krieg ⁓** enter the war; **in Verhandlungen ⁓** enter into negotiations. **3.** (sn) take place, happen, *a. death:* occur, *case etc:* arise: **es trat Stille ein** silence fell; **es ist e-e Besserung eingetreten** there has been an improvement. **4.** (sn) ⁓ **für** stand up for *s.o.*, support *s.th.* **5.** (h) ⁓ **auf** (*acc*) kick. **II** *v/t* (h) **6.** kick in (*or* down). **7.** break in (*shoes*). **8. ich habe mir e-n Dorn (in den Fuß) eingetreten** I've run a thorn into my foot.

'**eintrichtern** → **einbleuen.**

'**Eintritt** *m* (-[e]s; -e) **1.** (*in acc* into) entry, entrance: **bei s-m ⁓ in den Klub** on his joining the club. **2.** beginning, onset (*of winter etc*): **nach ⁓ der Dunkelheit** after dark. **3.** occurrence. **4.** admission: ⁓ **frei!** admission free!; ⁓ **verboten!** no entry! **5.** → '**Eintrittsgebühr** *f*, '**Eintrittsgeld** *n* admission (fee).

'**Eintrittskarte** *f* (admission) ticket.

'**eintrocknen** *v/i* (*sep*, -ge-, sn) dry up.

'**eintrudeln** *v/i* (*sep*, -ge-, sn) F turn up.

'**einüben** *v/t* (*sep*, -ge-, h) practi/se (*Am.* -ce), learn.

einverleiben ['aɪnfɛrlaɪbən] *v/t* (*sep*, *no* -ge-, h) **1.** (*dat, in acc* to) add, annex (*territory*). **2.** F **sich et.** ⁓ put away (*food, drink*).

'**Einvernehmen** *n* (-s; *no pl*) agreement, (good) understanding: **in gutem** ⁓ on good terms; **im** ⁓ **mit** in agreement with.

'**einverstanden** *adj* ⁓ **sein** agree; **mit et.** ⁓ **sein** agree to (*or* approve of) s.th.; ⁓! all right!, okay! '**Einverständnis** *n* (-ses; *no pl*) **1.** (*zu*) approval (of), consent (to): **sein** ⁓ **erklären** (give one's) consent. **2.** → **Einvernehmen.**

'**einwachsen** *v/i* (*irr*, *sep*, -ge-, sn, → **wachsen**) grow in(to *in acc*).

Einwand ['aɪnvant] *m* (-[e]s; ⁓e) objection (**gegen** to).

'**Einwanderer** *m* (-s; -), '**Einwanderin** *f* (-; -nen) immigrant. '**einwandern** *v/i* (*sep*, -ge-, sn) immigrate (**in** *acc* to). '**Einwanderung** *f* (-; -en) immigration. '**Einwanderungs...** immigration (*quota, country, etc*).

'**einwandfrei** *adj* impeccable, flawless, perfect: ⁓ **der Beste** undoubtedly the best; **es steht** ⁓ **fest** it is beyond question.

einwärts ['aɪnvɛrts] *adv* inward(s).

'**einwechseln** *v/t* (*sep*, -ge-, h) **1.** change money (**in** *acc*, **gegen** into). **2.** *sports:* **j-n** ⁓ send s.o. on the field.

'**einwecken** → **einmachen.**

'**Einwegflasche** *f* nonreturnable bottle.

'**Einwegspritze** *f* ✚ disposable syringe.

'**einweichen** *v/t* (*sep*, -ge-, h) soak.

'**einweihen** *v/t* (*sep*, -ge-, h) **1.** open, inaugurate, *eccl.* consecrate. **2.** F *fig.* christen (*a. dress etc*). **3.** **j-n** ⁓ **in** (*acc*) initiate s.o. into; **j-n in ein Geheimnis** ⁓ let s.o. into a secret; **eingeweiht sein** be in the know; → **Eingeweihte.**

'**Einweihung** *f* (-; -en) (formal) opening, *eccl.* consecration.

'**Einweihungsfeier** *f* opening ceremony.

'**einweisen** *v/t* (*irr*, *sep*, -ge-, h, → **weisen**) **1.** **j-n** ⁓ **in** (*acc*) send s.o. to, ⚖ commit s.o. to (*a mental institution*); **j-n in ein Krankenhaus** ⁓ hospitalize s.o. **2.** **j-n** ⁓ **in** (*acc*) brief s.o. in, introduce s.o. to (*a task etc*), inaugurate s.o. into (*an office*). **3.** direct *car, driver* (*in acc* into). '**Einweisung** *f* (-; -en) **1.** ⚖ committal (*in acc* to *an institution*); ~ **ins Krankenhaus** hospitalization. **2.** (*in acc*) briefing (in), introduction (to).

'**einwenden** *v/t* (*irr, sep,* -ge-, h, → **wenden**) **et.** ~ (**gegen**) object (to); ~ **daß** ... argue that ...; *ich habe nichts dagegen einzuwenden* I have no objections; *es läßt sich nichts dagegen* ~ there is nothing to be said against it.

'**Einwendung** *f* (-; -en) → **Einwand**.

'**einwerfen** *v/t* (*irr, sep,* -ge-, h, → **werfen**) **1.** throw in (*a. fig. remark*). **2.** smash (*window etc*). **3.** post, *Am.* mail (*letter etc*). **4.** insert, put in (*coin*).

einwertig ['aɪnveːrtɪç] *adj* monovalent.

'**einwickeln** *v/t* (*sep,* -ge-, h) **1.** wrap up. **2.** F *j-n* ~ a) take s.o. in, b) softsoap s.o.

einwilligen ['aɪnvɪlɪɡən] *v/i* (*sep,* -ge-, h) (*in acc* to) agree, consent. '**Einwilligung** *f* (-; -en) approval, consent.

'**einwirken** *v/i* (*sep,* -ge-, h) ~ **auf** (*acc*) a) have an effect on, b) affect (*a.* 🎨), c) influence; *auf j-n* ~ work on s.o.; *et.* ~ *lassen* let s.th. take effect.

'**Einwirkung** *f* (-; -en) (**auf** *acc* on) a) effect, b) influence.

Einwohner ['aɪnvoːnər] *m* (-s; -), '**Einwohnerin** *f* (-; -nen) inhabitant, resident. '**Einwohnermeldeamt** *n* residents' registration office. '**Einwohnerschaft** *f* (-; *no pl*) inhabitants, population.

'**Einwurf** *m* **1.** *sports*: throw-in. **2.** a) insertion (*of coins*), b) *for letters etc*: slit, opening, *for coins*: slot. **3.** *fig.* remark.

'**Einzahl** *f* (-; *no pl*) *ling.* singular.

'**einzahlen** *v/t* (*sep,* -ge-, h) pay in: *Geld bei der Bank* ~ deposit money at the bank; *Geld* (*auf ein Konto*) ~ pay money into an account. '**Einzahlung** *f* (-; -en) payment, *at bank*: deposit.

'**Einzahlungsschein** *m* paying-in (*or* deposit) slip.

einzäunen ['aɪntsɔʏnən] *v/t* (*sep,* -ge-, h) fence in. '**Einzäunung** *f* (-; -en) fence.

'**einzeichnen** *v/t* (*sep,* -ge-, h) a) sketch in, b) mark (*in, auf dat* on): *... ist nicht eingezeichnet* ... isn't on the map.

Einzel ['aɪntsəl] *n* (-s; -) *n tennis*: singles.

'**Einzel|anfertigung** *f* special design: *es ist e-e* ~ it was custom-built. ~**antrieb**

m 🔧 separate drive. ~**aufstellung** *f* ⚖ itemized list. ~**beispiel** *n* isolated case. ~**betrag** *m* (single) item. ~**bett** *n* single bed. ~**diszi,plin** *f* *sports*: individual event. ~**exem,plar** *n* unique specimen (*book*: copy). ~**fall** *m* isolated case.

Einzelgänger ['aɪntsəlɡɛŋər] *m* (-s; -), '**Einzelgängerin** *f* (-; -nen) loner.

'**Einzel|haft** *f* solitary confinement. ~**handel** *m* retail trade. ~**handelspreis** *m* retail price. ~**händler** (*in* f) *m* retailer. ~**haus** *n* detached house.

'**Einzelheit** *f* (-; -en) detail: *bis in alle* ~**en** down to the last detail; *auf* ~**en eingehen** go into detail.

'**Einzelkind** *n* only child.

einzellig ['aɪntsɛlɪç] *adj* monocellular.

'**einzeln** ['aɪntsəln] **I** *adj* **1.** a) single, individual, b) separate, isolated: *ein* ~*er Schuh* an odd shoe. **2.** ~**e** several, some, a few; *meteor.* ~**e Schauer** scattered showers. **II** *adv* **3.** a) singly, individually, b) separately: ~ *eintreten* enter one by one (*or* one at a time); ~ *aufführen* specify, itemize. '**einzelne I** *m, f* (-n; -n) individual: ~ *pl* some, a few; *jeder* ~ (*von uns*) every (single) one (of us). **II** *das* ~ (-n; *no pl*) the detail(s): *im* ~*n* a) in detail, b) in particular; *ins* ~ *gehen* go into detail; ~*s gefällt mir nicht* I don't like some things (*or* points).

'**Einzel|spiel** *n tennis*: singles (match). ~**stück** *n* **1.** odd piece. **2.** unique specimen. ~**teil** *n* 🔧 (component) part. ~**unterricht** *m* private lessons. ~**wesen** *n* individual (being). ~**zelle** *f* ⚖ solitary cell. ~**zimmer** *n* single room.

'**einziehbar** *adj* **1.** 🔧 retractable. **2.** ✝ collectible. '**einziehen** (*irr, sep,* -ge-, → **ziehen**) **I** *v/t* (h) **1.** draw *s.th.* in, 🔧 retract, haul *flag* down: *den Kopf* ~ duck; *die Segel* ~ take in sail; *die Riemen* ~ ship the oars. **2.** draw in, inhale, breathe. **3.** put in. **4.** ✗ call up, draft. **5.** ⚖ seize, confiscate, withdraw *banknotes* (from circulation). **6.** collect (*taxes etc*). **7.** → *Erkundigung*. **II** *v/i* (*sn*) **8.** enter, march in(to *in acc*), *lodger*: move in(to *in acc, bei* with): *er zog ins Parlament ein* he took his seat in Parliament. **9.** *liquid*: soak in.

einzig ['aɪntsɪç] **I** *adj* **1.** only, single, sole: *kein* ~*es Auto* not a single car; *sein* ~*er Halt* his sole support; *nicht ein* ~*es Mal* not once. **2.** *der (die)* **~e** the only one; *nicht ein* **~er** not (a single) one; *das* **~e** the only thing. **3.** → *einzigartig* I. **II** *adv* **4.** only, *(a. ~ und allein)* solely, entirely: *das ist das ~ Richtige* that's the only thing to do.

'einzigartig *adj* unique, singular, unequal(l)ed, fantastic, marvel(l)ous.

'Ein|zimmerwohnung *f* one-room flat (*Am.* apartment).

'Einzug *m* (-[e]s; *ⸯe*) **1.** a) entry, b) moving in(to *in a house etc*), c) *fig.* coming. **2.** *print.* indent.

'Einzugsermächtigung *f* standing order for a direct debit.

'Einzugsgebiet *n geol.* catchment area.

'Eipulver *n* dried egg.

E-is ['e:ɪs] *n* (-; -) ♪ E sharp.

Eis [aɪs] *n* (-es; *no pl*) a) ice, b) ice cream: F *fig. et. auf ~ legen* put s.th. on ice; *das ~ brechen* break the ice. **~bahn** *f* (ice-)skating rink. **~bär** *m* polar bear. **~becher** *m gastr.* sundae. **~bein** *n gastr.* pickled knuckle of pork. **~berg** *m* iceberg: → *Spitze*¹ 1. **~beutel** *m* ♣ ice bag. **~blumen** *pl* frostwork. **~bombe** *f gastr.* bombe glacée.

'Eischnee *m gastr.* beaten egg white.

'Eisdiele *f* ice-cream parlo(u)r.

Eisen ['aɪzən] *n* (-s; *no pl*) iron: *fig. ein heißes ~ anfassen* tackle a hot issue; *j-n zum alten ~ werfen* throw s.o. on the scrap heap, shelve s.o.; *er gehört zum alten ~* he's past it; *zwei ~ im Feuer haben* have more than one string to one's bow; *(man muß) das ~ schmieden, solange es heiß ist* strike while the iron is hot.

'Eisenbahn *f* a) railway, *Am.* railroad, b) train: *mit der ~* by rail, by train.

Eisenbahner ['aɪzənba:nər] *m* (-s; -) F railwayman, *Am.* railroadman.

'Eisenbahn|knotenpunkt *m* (railway, *Am.* railroad) junction. **~netz** *n* railway (*Am.* railroad) network. **~schaffner** *m* guard, conductor. **~wagen** *m* railway carriage, coach, *Am.* railroad car.

'Eisen|erz *n* iron ore. **~gehalt** *m* iron content. **~gießerei** *f* iron foundry. **~guß** *m* (-sses; *no pl*) **1.** iron casting. **2.** cast iron.

'eisenhaltig *adj* **1.** *~ sein* contain iron. **2.** *min.* ferruginous.

'Eisen|hut *m* (-[e]s; *no pl*) ♣ monkshood.

~hütte *f*, **~hüttenwerk** *n* ironworks. **~mangel** *m* ♣ iron deficiency. **~o,xyd** *n* 🜍 ferric oxide.

'Eisenwaren *pl* ironware, hardware. **~geschäft** *n* hardware store.

'Eisenzeit *f* (-; *no pl*) *hist.* the Iron age.

eisern ['aɪzərn] *adj* a) *fig.* iron, of iron, *nerves* of steel, b) adamant, firm: **~e Sparsamkeit** rigorous economy; **~e Gesundheit** cast-iron constitution; **~er Bestand** permanent stock; **~e Regel** hard and fast rule; **s-e ~e Ruhe** his imperturbability; **~ festhalten an** (*dat*) adhere rigidly to; **~ sparen** save rigorously; → *Lunge* 1.

'Eiseskälte *f* icy cold.

'eisfrei *adj* free of ice. **'eisgekühlt** *adj* chilled. **'Eisglätte** *f* icy roads.

'Eishockey *n* ice hockey. **~schläger** *m* ice-hockey stick. **~spieler** *m* ice-hockey player.

eisig ['aɪzɪç] *adj a. fig.* icy.

'Eiskaffee *m gastr.* iced coffee.

'eiskalt *adj* **1.** ice-cold. **2.** *gastr.* chilled. **3.** *fig.* a) icy (*look etc*), b) cold (as ice), c) cool, d) brazen.

'Eiskübel *m* ice bucket.

'Eiskunstlauf *m* (-[e]s; *no pl*) figure skating. **'Eiskunstläufer(in** *f*) *m* figure skater. **'Eislauf** *m* (-[e]s; *no pl*) ice-skating. **'eislaufen** *v/i* (*sep, -ge-, sn*) ice-skate. **'Eisläufer(in** *f*) *m* ice-skater.

'Eismeer *n* polar sea: *Nördliches (Südliches) ~* Arctic (Antarctic) Ocean.

'Eispickel *m* ice pick.

'Eisprung *m physiol.* ovulation.

'Eis|re,vue *f* ice show. **~sa,lat** *m* iceberg lettuce. **~schnellauf** *m* (-[e]s; *no pl*) speed skating. **~schnelläufer(in** *f*) *m* speed skater. **~scholle** *f* ice floe. **~schrank** *m* refrigerator, F fridge, *Am.* icebox. **~stadion** *n* ice stadium. **~tanz** *m* ice dancing. **~torte** *f* ice-cream gateau. **~waffel** *f* ice-cream wafer. **~wasser** *n* ice water. **~würfel** *m* ice cube. **~zapfen** *m* icicle.

'Eiszeit *f* (-; *no pl*) ice age, glacial period.

'Eiszeitmensch *m* glacial man.

eitel ['aɪtəl] *adj* **1.** vain, conceited. **2.** vain, futile: *eitle Hoffnung* idle hope.

'Eitelkeit *f* (-; *no pl*) vanity, *a.* futility.

Eiter ['aɪtər] *m* (-s; *no pl*) ♣ pus. **'Eiterbeule** *f* abscess, boil, *fig.* festering sore.

'Eiterbläschen *n* pustule. **'eit(e)rig**

adj suppurative, festering. **'eitern** *v/i* (h) fester, suppurate. **'Eiterpfropf** *m* core. **'Eiterung** *f* (-; -en) suppuration.
'Eiweiß *n* (-es; -e) white of egg, (egg) white, *biol.* albumen, protein. **♀arm** *adj* low in protein, low-protein (*diet*). **~bedarf** *m* protein requirement. **~mangel** *m* protein deficiency. **♀reich** *adj* rich in protein, high-protein (*diet*).
'Eizelle *f biol.* egg cell, ovum.
Ejakulation [ejakula'tsĭo:n] *f* (-; -en) *physiol.* ejaculation.
Ekel¹ ['e:kəl] *m* (-s; *no pl*) (*vor dat*) disgust (at), revulsion (against): **~ empfinden → ekeln; F ... ist (sind) mir ein ~** I can't stand ..., I loathe ...
'Ekel² *n* (-s; -) F nasty person, beast.
'ekelerregend *adj* repulsive. **'Ekelgefühl** *n* revulsion. **'ekelhaft, 'ek(e)lig** *adj* revolting, disgusting. **'ekeln: sich ~** (h) **ich ekle mich davor (vor ihm)** it (he) makes me sick.
Eklat [e'kla:] *m* (-s; -s) a) stir, sensation, b) scandal, c) row.
eklatant [ekla'tant] *adj* a) striking, b) *contp.* flagrant, blatant.
Eklipse [ɛk'lɪpsə] *f* (-; -n) *astr.* eclipse.
Ekstase [ɛk'sta:zə] *f* (-; -n) ecstasy: **in ~ geraten** go into ecstasies (**über** *acc* over). **ek'statisch** [-tɪʃ] *adj* ecstatic.
Ekzem [ɛk'tse:m] *n* (-s; -e) 🔬 eczema.
Elan [e'la:n] *m* (-s; *no pl*) verve, zest.
Elastik [e'lastɪk] *n* (-s; -s) elastic.
elastisch [e'lastɪʃ] *adj* elastic (*a. fig.*), springy, *mot.*, ⚙ flexible (*a. fig.*).
Elastizität [elastitsi'tɛ:t] *f* (-; *no pl*) *a. fig.* elasticity, flexibility.
Elch [ɛlç] *m* (-[e]s; -e) *zo.* elk, moose.
Elefant [ele'fant] *m* (-en; -en) elephant: **wie ein ~ im Porzellanladen** like a bull in a china shop.
Ele'fanten|bulle *m zo.* bull elephant. **~hochzeit** *f* 🔩 giant merger. **~kuh** *f zo.* cow elephant. **~rüssel** *m* trunk.
elegant [ele'gant] *adj* elegant (*a. fig.*), smart: **e-e ~e Lösung** a neat (*or* clever) solution. **Eleganz** [ele'gants] *f* (-; *no pl*) *a. fig.* elegance.
Elegie [ele'gi:] *f* (-; -n) elegy. **elegisch** [e'le:gɪʃ] *adj* elegiac, *fig. a.* melancholy.
elektrifizieren [elɛktrifi'tsi:rən] *v/t* (h) electrify. **Elektrifi'zierung** *f* (-; *no pl*) electrification. **Elektrik** [e'lɛktrɪk] *f* (-; *no pl*) **1.** electricity. **2.** electrical system.

Elektriker [e'lɛktrɪkər] *m* (-s; -) electrician. **elektrisch** [e'lɛktrɪʃ] **I** *adj* electric(al): **~er Schlag (Strom, Stuhl)** electric shock (current, chair). **II** *adv* electrically, by electricity. **elektrisieren** [elɛktri'zi:rən] *v/t* (h) *a. fig.* electrify. **Elektrizität** [elɛktritsi'tɛ:t] *f* (-; *no pl*) electricity, (electric) current.
Elektrizi'tätsversorgung *f* electricity (*or* power) supply. **Elektrizi'tätswerk** *n* (electric) power station.
Elektroauto [e'lɛktro-] *n* electric car.
E'lektrobohrer *m* electric drill.
E'lektroche,mie *f* electrochemistry.
Elektrode [elɛk'tro:də] *f* (-; -n) electrode: **negative ~** cathode; **positive ~** anode.
E'lektro|enzephalo,gramm *n* 🔬 (*abbr.* EEG) electroencephalogram. **~fahrzeug** *n* electric vehicle. **~gerät** *n* electrical appliance. **~geschäft** *n* electrical shop. **~herd** *m* electric cooker. **~ingeni,eur** *m* electrical engineer. **~kardio,gramm** *n* 🔬 (*abbr.* EKG) electrocardiogram.
Elektrolyse [elɛktro'ly:zə] *f* (-; -n) electrolysis.
E'lektromotor *m* (electric) motor.
Elektron ['e:lɛktron] *n* (-s; -en [elɛk'tro:nən]) *phys.* electron.
Elek'tronen|blitz(gerät) *n) m phot.* electronic flash (gun). **~gehirn** *n* electronic brain. **~mikro,skop** *n* electron microscope. **~rechner** *m* computer. **~röhre** *f* electronic valve (*Am.* tube).
Elektronik [elɛk'tro:nɪk] *f* (-; *no pl*) **1.** electronics. **2.** electronic system.
elek'tronisch [-nɪʃ] *adj* electronic.
E'lektro|ofen *m* electric stove. **~ra,sierer** *m* electric razor. **~schock** *m* 🔬 electroshock.
Elektro|'technik *f* electrical engineering. **~'techniker** *m* electrical engineer. **♀'technisch** *adj* electrotechnical, electrical (*component, industry, etc*).
Elektrothera'pie *f* 🔬 electrotherapy.
Element [ele'mɛnt] *n* (-[e]s; -e) element, ⚡ *a.* battery, cell: *fig.* **in s-m ~ sein** be in one's element; *contp.* **asoziale ~e** antisocial elements.
elementar [elemɛn'ta:r] *adj* **1.** elemental. **2.** elementary (*duty, mistake, etc*).
Elemen'tar|begriff *m* fundamental idea. **~gewalt** *f* elemental force. **~teil-**

Empfangsbestätigung

chen *n phys.* elementary particle. **~unterricht** *m* elementary instruction.

elend ['e:lɛnt] **I** *adj* **1.** *a. fig. contp.* miserable, wretched: **~ aussehen** look ill; **sich ~ fühlen** feel wretched (*or* terrible). **2.** poverty-stricken, pitiable. **3.** F *fig.* terrible, awful. **II** *adv* **4.** miserably. **5.** F *fig.* terribly, awfully. **'Elend** *n* (-s; *no pl*) misery, poverty: → **stürzen** 3.

'Elendsquar,tier *n* hovel.

'Elendsviertel *n* slum(s).

elf [ɛlf] *adj* eleven. **Elf[1]** *f* (-; -en) **1.** (number) eleven. **2.** *soccer:* team.

Elf[2] *m* (-en; -en), **Elfe** ['ɛlfə] *f* (-; -n) elf.

'Elfenbein *n* (-[e]s; *no pl*), **'elfenbeinern** *adj*, **'elfenbeinfarbig** *adj* ivory.

'Elfenbeinturm *m fig.* ivory tower.

'Elf'meter *m soccer:* penalty (kick). **~schießen** *n* (penalty) shoot-out.

elft [ɛlft] *adj*, **Elfte** ['ɛlftə] *m, f* (-n; -n) eleventh. **elftens** ['ɛlftəns] *adv* in the eleventh place.

eliminieren [elimi'niːrən] *v/t* (h) eliminate.

elitär [eli'tɛːr] *adj* elitist. **Elite** [e'liːtə] *f* (-; -n) élite. **E'litedenken** *n* elitism.

Elixier [elɪˈksiːr] *n* (-s; -e) elixir.

'Ellbogen *m* (-s; -) elbow. **~freiheit** *f* elbow room. **~gesellschaft** *f* dog-eat-dog society. **~mensch** *m* ruthless go-getter.

ellenlang ['ɛlən-] *adj* F *fig.* endless.

Ellipse [ɛ'lɪpsə] *f* (-; -n) ℞ ellipse. **elliptisch** [ɛ'lɪptɪʃ] *adj* ℞ elliptic(al).

Elsässer ['ɛlzɛsər] *m* (-s; -), **'Elsässerin** *f* (-; -nen), **'elsässisch** *adj* Alsatian.

Elster ['ɛlstər] *f* (-; -n) *zo.* magpie.

elterlich ['ɛltərlɪç] *adj* parental (*duty*, *love, etc*), parents' (*bedroom etc*).

Eltern ['ɛltərn] *pl* parents: F *fig.* **nicht von schlechten ~** terrific.

'Elternabend *m* parent-teacher meeting. **'Elternbeirat** *m ped.* parents' council. **'Elternhaus** *n* (one's parents') home. **'elternlos** *adj* orphan(ed).

'Elternschaft *f* (-; *no pl*) **1.** parenthood. **2.** parents. **'Elternsprechtag** *m ped.* open day. **'Elternteil** *m* parent.

Email [e'maːi(l)] *n* (-s; -s), **Emaille** [e'maljə] *f* (-; -n), **emaillieren** [ema(l)'jiːrən] *v/t* (h) enamel.

Emanze [e'mantsə] *f* (-; -n) F *contp.* women's libber. **Emanzipation** [emantsipa'tsioːn] *f* (-; -en) emancipation: **die**

~ der Frau *a.* women's liberation. **emanzipatorisch** [emantsipa'toːrɪʃ] *adj* emancipatory. **emanzipieren** [emantsi'piːrən] (h) **I** *v/t* emancipate. **II sich ~** become emancipated.

Embargo [ɛm'bargo] *n* (-s; -s) embargo. **Emblem** [ɛm'bleːm] *n* (-s; -e) emblem. **Embolie** [ɛmboˈliː] *f* (-; -n) ✝ embolism. **Embryo** ['ɛmbryo] *m* (-s; -s, -nen [ɛmbry'oːnən]) embryo. **embryonal** [ɛmbry'oˈnaːl] *adj* embryonic, embryo.

emeritieren [emeri'tiːrən] *v/t* (h) retire. **Emigrant** [emi'grant] *m* (-en; -en), **Emi'grantin** *f* (-; -nen) emigrant. **Emigration** [emigra'tsioːn] *f* (-; -en) emigration: **in der (die) ~** in(to) exile. **emigrieren** [emi'griːrən] *v/i* (sn) emigrate.

Emission [emɪˈsioːn] *f* (-; -en) **1.** *phys.* emission. **2.** ✝ issue.

Emotion [emo'tsioːn] *f* (-; -en) emotion. **emotional** [emotsio'naːl] *adj* emotional. **emotionalisieren** [emotsionali'ziːrən] *v/t* (h) emotionalize.

emotionell [emotsio'nɛl] *adj* emotional.

empfahl [ɛm'pfaːl] *pret of* **empfehlen**.

empfand [ɛm'pfant] *pret of* **empfinden**.

Empfang [ɛm'pfaŋ] *m* (-[e]s; ⸚e) **1.** *no pl* receipt: **nach ~, bei ~** on receipt; **in ~ nehmen** a) receive, b) meet (*s.o.*). **2.** *no pl* reception (*a. radio etc*), welcome: **j-m e-n begeisterten ~ bereiten** give s.o. an enthusiastic reception. **3.** *hotel etc:* reception (desk). **4.** reception.

emp'fangen (empfing, empfangen, h) **I** *v/t* receive (*a. radio etc*), welcome: **sie empfängt niemanden** she refuses to see anybody; **wir wurden sehr freundlich ~** we met with a friendly reception. **II** *v/i biol.* conceive.

Empfänger [ɛm'pfɛŋər] *m* (-s; -) receiver (*a. radio etc*), recipient, ✆ addressee. **empfänglich** [ɛm'pfɛŋlɪç] *adj* (**für** to) receptive, susceptible (*a.* ✒), ✒ prone. **Emp'fänglichkeit** *f* (-; *no pl*) (**für** to) receptivity, *a.* ✒ susceptibility.

Empfängnis [ɛm'pfɛŋnɪs] *f* (-; *no pl*) *biol.* conception. **℞verhütend** *adj* (*a.* **~es Mittel**) contraceptive. **~verhütung** *f* contraception.

Emp'fangs|an,tenne *f* reception aerial (*Am.* antenna). **~bereich** *m radio etc:* **1.** range of reception. **2.** frequency range. **~bescheinigung** *f* receipt. **~be-**

stätigung *f* acknowledg(e)ment of receipt. **~chef(in** *f*) *m* reception (*Am.* room) clerk. **~dame** *f* receptionist.

empfehlen [ɛm'pfeːlən] (empfahl, empfohlen, h) **I** *v/t* **1.** recommend (*j-m et.* s.th. to s.o.): *nicht zu ~* not to be recommended; *es empfiehlt sich zu inf* it is advisable to *inf.* **II** *sich ~* **2.** recommend itself. **3.** take one's leave.

emp'fehlenswert *adj* a) recommendable, b) advisable. **Emp'fehlung** *f* (-; -en) (*auf ~* on) recommendation: *gute ~en haben* have good references.

Emp'fehlungsschreiben *n* letter of recommendation.

empfinden [ɛm'pfɪndən] *v/t* (empfand, empfunden, h) feel (*a. v/i*): *et. als lästig ~* find s.th. a nuisance. **Emp'finden** *n* (-s) a) feeling, b) opinion, c) sense: *nach m-m ~* the way I see it.

empfindlich [ɛm'pfɪntlɪç] *adj* **1.** sensitive (*gegen* to) (a. ♥, *phot.*, ⚙), delicate: *fig. ~e Stelle* tender spot. **2.** touchy, irritable (*a. stomach*): *~ reagieren* overreact. **3.** severe (*cold, penalty, etc*), bad (*loss*): *~ kalt* bitterly cold; *fig. er war ~ getroffen* he was badly hit.

Emp'findlichkeit *f* (-; *no pl*) **1.** a) sensitivity (*gegen* to), *phot. a.* speed, b) delicacy. **2.** touchiness, irritability.

emp'findsam *adj* **1.** sensitive. **2.** sentimental. **Emp'findsamkeit** *f* (-; *no pl*) sensitivity, sentimentality.

Emp'findung *f* (-; -en) a) sensation, perception, b) feeling, emotion.

emp'findungslos *adj* insensitive (*für, gegen* to), numb (*limb*).

empfing [ɛm'pfɪŋ] *pret of* **empfangen**.

empfohlen [ɛm'pfoːlən] **I** *pp of* **empfehlen**. **II** *adj* recommended.

empfunden [ɛm'pfʊndən] *pp of* **empfinden**.

empirisch [ɛm'piːrɪʃ] *adj* empirical.

empor [ɛm'poːr] *adv lit.* up, upward(s).

Empore [ɛm'poːrə] *f* (-; -n) △ gallery.

empören [ɛm'pøːrən] (h) **I** *v/t* **1.** shock, outrage. **II** *sich ~* **2.** be outraged (*über acc* at). **3.** rebel (*gegen* against).

em'pörend *adj* outrageous, shocking.

Emporkömmling [ɛm'poːrkœmlɪŋ] *m* (-s; -e) upstart, parvenu.

em'pört **I** *pp of* **empören**. **II** *adj* indignant (*über acc* at).

Em'pörung *f* (-; -en) **1.** *no pl* indignation

(*über acc* at). **2.** revolt, rebellion.

emsig ['ɛmzɪç] *adj* busy, industrious, hard-working. **'Emsigkeit** *f* (-; *no pl*) **1.** bustle. **2.** industry, zeal.

Emulsion [emʊl'zioːn] *f* (-; -en) emulsion.

'E-Mu₁sik *f* (-; *no pl*) serious music.

'Endabrechnung *f* final account.

'Endbahnhof *m* terminus.

'Endbetrag *m* (sum) total.

Ende ['ɛndə] *n* (-s; -n) **1.** *no pl* end, *a.* ending (*of film etc*): *~ (der Durchsage)!* end of the message!, *radio*: over (and out)!; *~ Mai* at the end of May; *~ der dreißiger Jahre* in the late thirties; *am ~* a) in the end, after all, b) eventually, c) maybe; *letzten ~s* when all is said and done; *ich bin am ~* I'm finished; *bis zum bitteren ~* to the bitter end; *e-r Sache ein ~ machen* (*or bereiten*) put an end to s.th.; *et. zu ~ führen* finish s.th., see s.th. through; *zu ~ gehen* a) → *enden*, b) run short; *zu ~ sein* be over, *time*: be up; *ein böses ~ nehmen* come to a bad end; *~ gut, alles gut* all's well that ends well; F *das dicke ~ kommt nach* there will be hell to pay; *die Arbeit geht ihrem ~ entgegen* the work is nearing completion; *es geht mit ihm zu ~* he's going fast; → *Latein, Lied, Weisheit*. **2.** F a) (small) piece, b) *no pl* (long) distance (*or* way).

'Endef₁fekt *n* [-ɛnt-] *m* final result: *im ~* in the final analysis, in the end.

endemisch [ɛn'deːmɪʃ] *adj* ✿ endemic.

enden ['ɛndən] *v/i* (h) (come to an) end, draw to a close, finish, stop, *contract etc*: expire: *mit e-r Prügelei ~* end in a brawl; *ling. ~ auf* (*acc*) end with; *nicht ~ wollend* unending; *das Stück endet tragisch* the play has a tragic ending.

'Endergebnis *n* final result.

'Endgeschwindigkeit *f* final velocity.

'endgültig I *adj* final: *e-e ~e Antwort* a definite answer. **II** *adv* a) finally, b) for good: *das steht ~ fest* that's final.

'Endgültigkeit *f* (-; *no pl*) finality.

Endivie [ɛn'diːviə] *f* (-; -n) ♣ endive.

'Endkampf *m sports*: (*in den ~ kommen* reach the) final(s). **'Endlagerung** *f* ultimate disposal (*of nuclear waste*).

endlich ['ɛntlɪç] **I** *adj* final, ultimate, ⚛, *philos.* finite. **II** *adv* finally, at last.

'endlos *adj* endless.

'**Endlosigkeit** f (-; no pl) endlessness.
'**Endlösung** f pol. hist. Final Solution.
endogen [ɛndo'geːn] adj endogenous.
Endoskop [ɛndo'skoːp] n (-s; -e) 🕮 endoscope.
'**End|phase** f final stage. ~**preis** m retail price. ~**produkt** n end product. ~**reim** m end rhyme. ~**resul,tat** n final result. ~**runde** f sports: final(s). ~**silbe** f final syllable. ~**spiel** n sports: final(s): **ins ~ einziehen** go to the finals. ~**spurt** m a. fig. final sprint, finish. ~**stati,on** f 1. terminus. 2. fig. end of the road. ~**summe** f (sum) total.
'**Endung** f (-; -en) ling. ending.
'**Endverbraucher** m end user. ~**verstärker** m 🕮 output amplifier. ~**ziel** n final objective, ultimate goal. ~**ziffer** f last number. ~**zweck** m final purpose.
Energie [enɛr'giː] f (-; -n) energy (a. fig.), 🕮 a. power. **Ener'giebedarf** m energy demand. **ener'giegeladen** adj fig. bursting with energy. **Ener'giekrise** f energy crisis. **ener'gielos** adj lacking energy, weak. **Ener'gielosigkeit** f (-; no pl) lack of energy.
Ener'gie|poli,tik f energy policy. ~**quelle** f source of energy. 🄴**sparend** adj energy-saving. ~**verbrauch** m energy consumption. ~**verschwendung** f waste of energy (fig. of effort). ~**versorgung** f power supply. ~**wirtschaft** f (-; no pl) energy industry.
energisch [e'nɛrgɪʃ] adj energetic, firm (words etc), strong (protest etc): ~ **werden** put one's foot down.
eng [ɛŋ] adj 1. narrow (a. fig.), crowded, cramped, tight (skirt etc): ~**er werden** narrow; **ein Kleid ~er machen** take a dress in; **auf ~em Raum zs.-leben** live crowded together; fig. **in ~en Grenzen** within narrow bounds; F **das wird zeitlich sehr ~ für mich** I've got a tight schedule already; F **das darf man nicht so ~ sehen!** let's be (more) broadminded!; → **Sinn** 5, **Wahl** 2. 2. fig. close (cooperation etc): ~ **befreundet sein** be close friends; → **Kreis** 1.
Engagement [ãɡaʒə'mãː] n (-s; -s) 1. thea. etc engagement. 2. pol. or fig. commitment. **engagieren** [ãɡa'ʒiːrən] (h) **I** v/t engage, employ, take s.o. on. **II sich ~** pol. or fig. get (or be) involved (in

dat in). **enga'giert** adj fig. dedicated, pol. committed.
'**enganliegend** adj tight(-fitting).
Enge ['ɛŋə] f (-; -n) 1. no pl narrowness (a. fig.), tightness: **in großer ~ leben** live in very cramped conditions; fig. **j-n in die ~ treiben** drive s.o. into a corner. 2. narrow passage, (of sea) strait.
Engel ['ɛŋəl] m (-s; -) angel: F **die ~ im Himmel singen hören** see stars.
'**engelhaft** adj angelic.
'**Engelsgeduld** f endless patience.
'**engherzig** adj small-minded. '**Engherzigkeit** f (-; no pl) small-mindedness.
Engländer ['ɛŋlɛndər] m (-s; -) 1. Englishman: **er ist ~** he is English; **die ~** the English. 2. 🕮 monkey wrench.
'**Engländerin** f (-; -nen) Englishwoman.
englisch ['ɛŋlɪʃ] adj English: **die ~e Staatskirche** the Anglican Church; (**gut**) ~ **sprechen** speak English (well); ~ **geschrieben** (written) in English.
'**Englisch** n (-[s]) English, the English language: **aus dem ~en übersetzt** translated from (the) English; **im ~en** in English; **er spricht gut(es)** ~ he speaks good English.
'**englisch-'deutsch** adj 1. pol. Anglo-German. 2. ling. English-German.
'**Englischhorn** n ♪ cor anglais.
'**englischsprachig** adj English-language. '**englischsprechend** adj English-speaking. '**Englischunterricht** m English lesson(s).
'**engmaschig** [-maʃɪç] adj fine-meshed, fig. close-meshed.
'**Engpaß** m (-sses; ~sse) fig. a) bottleneck, b) supply shortfall.
en gros [ã'ɡro] adv 🕮 wholesale.
engstirnig ['ɛŋʃtɪrnɪç] adj narrow-minded. '**Engstirnigkeit** f (-; no pl) narrow-mindedness.
Enkel ['ɛŋkəl] m (-s; -) a) grandchild, b) grandson.
'**Enkelin** f (-; -nen) granddaughter.
Enklave [ɛn'klaːvə] f (-; -n) enclave.
enorm [e'nɔrm] adj enormous, huge, F terrific: ~ **schnell** incredibly fast.
en passant [ãpa'sãː] adv in passing.
Ensemble [ã'sãːbl] n (-s; -s) 1. ♪, fashion: ensemble. 2. thea. a) company, b) cast.
entarten [ɛnt'ʔartən] v/i (sn) degenerate.

ent'artet I *pp of* **entarten. II** *adj* degenerate, *fig. a.* decadent.

Ent'artung *f* (-; -en) degeneration.

entband [ɛnt'bant] *pret of* **entbinden.**

entbehren [ɛnt'be:rən] *v/t* (h) **1.** do without: *kannst du ... ?* can you spare ...? **2.** miss. **ent'behrlich** *adj* dispensable, expendable.

Ent'behrung *f* (-; -en) privation, want.

ent'binden (entband, entbunden, h) *v/t* **1.** ⚕ deliver *woman* (**von** of): *entbunden werden von ...* a. give birth to ... **2.** *fig.* (**von** from) release, excuse. **II** *v/i* **3.** ⚕ give birth to a child.

Ent'bindung *f* (-; -en) **1.** ⚕ delivery. **2.** *fig.* release (**von** from).

Ent'bindungsklinik *f* maternity clinic.

Ent'bindungsstati,**on** *f* maternity ward.

ent'blättern (h) **I** *v/t* **1.** strip *s.th.* of leaves. **II sich ~ 2.** shed (its) leaves. **3.** *humor.* shed one's clothes, strip.

entblöden [ɛnt'blø:dən] (h) **sich nicht ~ zu** *inf* have the nerve to *inf.*

entblößen [ɛnt'blø:sən] *v/t* (h) bare.

ent'blößt I *pp of* **entblößen. II** *adj* bare.

ent'brennen *v/i* (entbrannte, entbrannt, sn) *fight etc:* break out, *a. rage etc:* flare up.

ent'decken *v/t* (h) **a)** discover, find out, **b)** see, spot: *zufällig ~* stumble (up)on.

Ent'decker *m* (-s; -) discoverer.

Ent'deckung *f* (-; -en) discovery.

Ent'deckungsreise *f a. fig.* expedition.

Ente ['ɛntə] *f* (-; -n) **1.** *zo.* duck: *junge ~* duckling; F *fig.* **lahme ~** slowpoke. **2.** *gastr.* a) roast duck, b) *kalte ~* white wine cup with champagne. **3.** canard, hoax. **4.** ⚕ (bed) urinal.

ent'ehren *v/t* (h) dishono(u)r, disgrace, degrade. **Ent'ehrung** *f* (-; -en) dishono(u)r(ing), degradation.

ent'eignen *v/t* (h) expropriate.

Ent'eignung *f* (-; -en) expropriation.

ent'eisen *v/t* (h) clear of ice, ⚙ defrost, de-ice. **Ent'eisung** *f* (-; *no pl*) ⚙ defrosting, de-icing.

'Enten|braten *m* roast duck. **~ei** *n* duck's egg. **~jagd** *f* duck shooting.

ent'erben *v/t* (h) disinherit.

Enterich ['ɛntərɪç] *m* (-s; -e) *zo.* drake.

entern ['ɛntərn] *v/t* (h) board.

entfachen [ɛnt'faxən] *v/t* (h) **1.** kindle (*fire*). **2.** *fig.* a) rouse, b) provoke.

ent'fallen *v/i* (entfiel, entfallen, sn) **1.** *es

ist mir ~* it has slipped my memory; *der Name ist mir ~* the name escapes me. **2.** be cancel(l)ed: *entfällt* not applicable. **3.** *auf j-n ~* fall to s.o.

ent'falten (h) **I** *v/t* **1.** unfold (*a. fig.*), open, spread out. **2.** *fig.* develop (*talents etc*), launch into (*activity etc*), display (*pomp etc*). **II sich ~ 3.** blossom *etc:* open, unfold. **4.** *fig.* develop (**zu** into). **Ent'faltung** *f* (-; -en) **1.** unfolding. **2.** *fig.* a) development, b) display.

ent'färben *v/t* (h) remove the colo(u)r from, 🔧, ⚙ decolo(u)rize, bleach.

entfernen [ɛnt'fɛrnən] (h) **I** *v/t a. fig.* remove: *j-n von der Schule ~* expel s.o. from school. **II sich ~** leave, go away.

ent'fernt *adj a. fig.* remote, distant, *a.* faint (*similarity etc*): **e-e Meile ~** von a mile away from; *zwei Meilen voneinander ~* two miles apart; (*weit*) *~ far* away; *fig.* **weit davon ~** *zu inf* far from *ger*; *~ verwandt* distantly related; *nicht im ~esten* not in the least.

Ent'fernung *f* (-; -en) **1.** a) distance, b) range: *in e-r ~ von* at a distance of; *aus der (einiger) ~* from the (a) distance; *aus kurzer ~* at close range. **2.** removal.

Ent'fernungs|messer *m phot.* range finder. **~skala** *f phot.* focus(s)ing scale.

ent'fesseln *v/t* (h) unleash, provoke: *e-n Krieg ~* start a war.

ent'fesselt *adj* raging (*elements etc*).

ent'fetten *v/t* (h) remove the grease (*or* fat) from, ⚙ degrease.

entfiel [ɛnt'fi:l] *pret of* **entfallen.**

ent'flammbar *adj* inflammable.

ent'flammen I *v/t* (h) **1.** ⚙ ignite. **2.** *fig.* inflame, rouse, kindle. **II** *v/i* (sn) → 1.

ent'flechten *v/t* (entflocht, entflochten, h) ✝ decartelize.

ent'fliegen *v/i* (entflog, entflogen, sn) fly away (*dat* from).

entfliehen *v/i* (entfloh, entflohen, sn) (*[aus]* *dat* from) flee, escape.

entfremden [ɛnt'frɛmdən] (h) **I** *v/t* alienate (*dat* from). **II sich (j-m) ~** become estranged (from s.o.).

Ent'fremdung *f* (-; -en) estrangement, *a. sociol.* alienation.

ent'frosten *v/t* (h) ⚙ defrost.

Ent'froster *m* (-s; -) ⚙ defroster.

ent'führen *v/t* (h) kidnap, abduct, ✈ hijack. **Ent'führer** *m* (-s; -) kidnap-

(p)er, ✔ hijacker. **Ent'führung** *f* (-; -en) kidnap(p)ing, ✔ hijacking.

entgalt [ɛntˈgalt] *pret of* **entgelten.**

entgangen [ɛntˈgaŋən] *pp of* **entgehen.**

ent'gegen I *prep* (*dat*) contrary to, against: **~ allen Erwartungen** contrary to all expectations. **II** *adv* towards.

ent'gegenbringen *v/t* (*irr, sep, -ge-, h,* → **bringen**) *j-m Vertrauen (Zueignung)* ~ show trust in (affection for) s.o.; *e-r Sache Interesse* ~ show an interest in s.th.

ent'gegengehen *v/i* (*irr, sep, -ge-, sn,* → **gehen**) (*dat*) **1.** walk towards, go to meet. **2.** *fig.* face (*danger, the future, etc*), be heading for (*disaster etc*): **dem Ende** ~ be drawing to a close.

ent'gegengesetzt *adj* **1.** opposite. **2.** *fig.* contrary, opposed (*dat* to), opposing.

ent'gegenhalten *v/t* (*irr, sep, -ge-, h,* → **halten**) *fig.* object (*dat* to): **dem ist nichts entgegenzuhalten** there is no objection to that.

ent'gegenkommen *v/i* (*irr, sep, -ge-, sn,* → **kommen**) *j-m* ~ come towards s.o., *fig.* oblige s.o., make s.o. concessions; *j-m auf halbem Wege* ~ esp. *fig.* meet s.o. halfways; *j-s Wünschen* ~ comply with s.o.'s wishes. **Ent'gegenkommen** *n* (-s) obligingness: ~ **zeigen** be willing to make concessions. **ent'gegenkommend** *adj* oncoming, *fig.* obliging.

ent'gegenlaufen *v/i* (*irr, sep, -ge-, sn,* → **laufen**) *j-m* ~ run towards s.o.

Ent'gegennahme [-na:mə] *f* (-; *no pl*) acceptance.

ent'gegennehmen *v/t* (*irr, sep, -ge-, h,* → **nehmen**) accept, take.

ent'gegensehen *v/i* (*irr, sep, -ge-, h,* → **sehen**) (*dat*) a) await, b) look forward (to), c) face.

ent'gegensetzen *v/t* (*sep, -ge-, h*) **Widerstand** ~ offer resistance (*dat* to).

ent'gegenstehen *v/i* (*irr, sep, -ge-, h,* → **stehen**) *fig.* stand in the way (*dat* of): **dem steht nichts entgegen** there's nothing to be said against that.

ent'gegenstellen: sich ~ (*sep, -ge-, h*) *fig.* (*dat*) resist, oppose.

ent'gegentreten *v/i* (*irr, sep, -ge-, sn,* → **treten**) **1.** *j-m* ~ step (*or* walk) up to s.o., *fig.* oppose s.o. **2.** take steps against (*abuses etc*), contradict (*rumo[u]r*).

ent'gegenwirken *v/i* (*sep, -ge-, h*) (*dat*) work against, counteract, fight.

entgegnen [ɛntˈge:gnən] *v/i* (h) a) reply (*auf acc* to), b) retort.

ent'gehen *v/i* (entging, entgangen, sn) escape (*a. death etc*): *fig. j-m* ~ escape s.o.('s notice); *sich et.* ~ *lassen* let s.th. slip; *er ließ sich die Gelegenheit nicht* ~ he seized the opportunity.

entgeistert [ɛntˈgaistərt] *adj and adv* dum(b)founded, aghast.

Entgelt [ɛntˈgɛlt] *n* (-[e]s; -e) a) remuneration, payment, b) pay, c) fee, 🏛 consideration, d) reward: *gegen* ~ against payment; *als* ~ *für* in consideration of.

ent'gelten *v/t* (entgalt, entgolten, h) *j-m et.* ~ pay s.o. for s.th.

entgiften [ɛntˈgiftən] *v/t* (h) a) detoxicate, b) decontaminate (*toxic waste etc*), c) *fig.* clear (*the atmosphere*).

entging [ɛntˈgiŋ] *pret of* **entgehen.**

entgleisen [ɛntˈglaizən] *v/i* (sn) **1.** 🚃 run off the rails, be derailed. **2.** *fig.* go too far, make a faux pas.

Ent'gleisung *f* (-; -en) **1.** 🚃 derailment. **2.** *fig.* faux pas, gaffe.

ent'gleiten *v/i* (entglitt, entglitten, sn) *j-m* ~ slip out of s.o.'s hand(s), *fig.* slip away from s.o.

entgolten [ɛntˈgɔltən] *pp of* **entgelten.**

entgräten [ɛntˈgrɛ:tən] *v/t* (h) bone.

ent'haaren *v/t* (h) depilate. **Ent'haarungscreme** *f* depilatory cream.

ent'halten (enthielt, enthalten, h) **I** *v/t* a) contain, hold, b) comprise: *mit* ~ *sein* be included (*in dat* in). **II sich** ~ abstain (*gen* from); *sich der Stimme* ~ abstain.

ent'haltsam *adj* abstinent, abstemious, *sexually:* continent.

Ent'haltsamkeit *f* (-; *no pl*) abstinence.

ent'haltung *f* (-; *parl.* -en) abstention.

ent'härten *v/t* (h) soften (*water*).

enthaupten [ɛntˈhauptən] *v/t* (h) behead, decapitate. **Ent'hauptung** *f* (-; -en) beheading, decapitation.

ent'häuten *v/t* (h) skin.

ent'heben *v/t* (enthob, enthoben, h) (*gen*) relieve (of), release (*or* exempt) (from), remove (from *office*).

enthielt [ɛntˈhi:lt] *pret of* **enthalten.**

enthüllen [ɛntˈhʏlən] (h) **I** *v/t* **1.** unveil, bare, show. **2.** *fig.* reveal, bring *s.th.* to light, expose. **II sich** ~ *fig.* reveal o.s., *matter:* be revealed (*dat* to). **Ent'hüllung** *f* (-; -en) **1.** unveiling. **2.** *fig.* dis-

closure, exposure. **Ent'hüllungsjourna͵lismus** *m* investigative journalism.
Enthusiasmus [ɛntu'ziːasmʊs] *m* (-; *no pl*) enthusiasm. **Enthusiast** [ɛntu'ziast] *m* (-en; -en), **Enthusi'astin** *f* (-; -nen) enthusiast, F fan. **enthusi'astisch** *adj* enthusiastic.
entjungfern [ɛnt'jʊŋfərn] *v/t* (h) deflower.
ent'kalken *v/t* (h) descale.
ent'kernen *v/t* (h) stone, core.
ent'kleiden *v/t* (h) **1.** (*a. sich* ~) undress. **2.** *fig.* (*gen* of) divest, strip.
ent'kommen *v/i* (entkam, entkommen, sn) ([*aus*] *dat* from) get away, escape. **Ent'kommen** *n* (-s) escape, F getaway.
ent'korken *v/t* (h) uncork.
entkräften [ɛnt'krɛftən] *v/t* (h) **1.** weaken, exhaust. **2.** *fig.* invalidate (*a.* 🏛), refute. **Ent'kräftung** *f* (-; -en) **1.** a) weakening, b) weakness, exhaustion. **2.** *fig.* invalidation (*a.* 🏛), refutation.
ent'laden (entlud, entladen, h) **I** *v/t* (h) **1.** unload, *a.* ⚡ discharge. **2.** *fig.* give vent to, vent (*one's rage*). **II** *sich* ~ **3.** *storm:* break. **4.** ⚡ discharge. **5.** *rifle etc:* go off. **6.** *fig. suspense:* be released, *rage:* erupt. **Ent'ladung** *f* (-; -en) **1.** unloading, *a.* ⚡ discharge. **2.** *fig.* explosion.
ent'lang *adv and prep* along: **die Straße** ~ along (*or* down) the street; **hier** ~, **bitte!** this way, please! **ent'langgehen** *v/t* (*irr, sep,* -ge-, sn, → **gehen**) (*v/i* ~ *an dat*) go (*or* walk) along.
entlarven [ɛn'larfən] *v/t* (h) unmask, expose. **Ent'larvung** *f* (-; -en) unmasking, exposure.
ent'lassen (entließ, entlassen, h) *v/t* (h) a) dismiss, b) pension off: *j-n fristlos* ~ dismiss s.o. without notice. **2.** (*aus dat* from) discharge (*patient etc*), release (*prisoner*). **Ent'lassung** *f* (-; -en) **1.** dismissal. **2.** (*aus dat* from) discharge, release. **Ent'lassungspa͵piere** *pl* discharge papers.
ent'lasten *v/t* (h) relieve (*fig. von* of), 🏛 exonerate, clear *s.o.* of a charge, ✝ give *s.o.* a release. **ent'lastend** *adj* 🏛 exonerating. **Ent'lastung** *f* (-; -en) relief, 🏛 exoneration, ✝ release.
Ent'lastungs͵materi͵al *n* 🏛 exonerating evidence. **~straße** *f* bypass. **~zeuge** *m* 🏛 witness for the defen/ce (*Am.* -se). **~zug** *m* 🚂 relief train.

entlaubt [ɛnt'laʊpt] *adj* leafless, bare.
ent'laufen *v/i* (entlief, entlaufen, sn) run away (*dat* from).
entlausen [ɛnt'laʊzən] *v/t* (h) delouse.
entledigen [ɛnt'leːdɪgən] *sich* ~ (h) (*gen*) **1.** get rid of, take off (*clothing*). **2.** carry out, discharge (*a task*), fulfil(l), meet (*an obligation*).
ent'leeren *v/t* (h) empty: **den Darm** ~ evacuate (the bowels).
ent'legen *adj* remote, out-of-the-way.
ent'lehnen *v/t* (h) borrow *word etc* (*dat, aus, von* from).
ent'leihen *v/t* (entlieh, entliehen, h) borrow (*aus, von* from).
entlief [ɛnt'liːf] *pret of* **entlaufen**.
entließ [ɛnt'liːs] *pret of* **entlassen**.
ent'loben: *sich* ~ (h) break off one's engagement.
ent'locken *v/t* (h) (*dat* from) elicit, draw.
ent'lohnen *v/t* (h) pay. **Ent'lohnung** *f* (-; -en) pay, payment, remuneration.
entlud [ɛnt'luːt] *pret of* **entladen**.
ent'lüften *v/t* (h) deaerate, bleed (*brake*). **Ent'lüfter** *m* (-s; -) deaerator. **Ent'lüftung** *f* (-; -en) aeration, airing. **Ent'lüftungsschraube** *f* vent screw.
entmachten [ɛnt'maxtən] *v/t* (h) *j-n* (*et.*) ~ deprive s.o. (s.th.) of his (its) power.
entmenscht [ɛnt'mɛnʃt] *adj* inhuman, brutish.
entmilitarisieren [ɛntmilitari'ziːrən] *v/t* (h) demilitarize. **Entmilitari'sierung** *f* (-; -en) demilitarization.
entmündigen [ɛnt'mʏndɪgən] *v/t* (h) (legally) incapacitate. **Ent'mündigung** *f* (-; -en) (legal) incapacitation.
entmutigen [ɛnt'muːtɪgən] *v/t* (h) discourage, dishearten. **Ent'mutigung** *f* (-; -en) discouragement, disheartening.
entnahm [ɛnt'naːm] *pret of* **entnehmen**.
Ent'nahme *f* (-; -n) taking (*of samples*), withdrawal (*of money*).
entnazifizieren [ɛntnatsifi'tsiːrən] *v/t* (h) *hist.* denazify. **Entnazifi'zierung** *f* (-; -en) denazification.
ent'nehmen *v/t* (entnahm, entnommen, h) (*dat*) take (from, out of), borrow (from *a book etc*), quote (from): *fig. et.* ~ *aus* (*or dat*) learn (*or* gather) s.th. from.
ent'nerven *v/t* (h) enervate.
ent'ölen *v/t* (h) remove the oil from.
entper'sönlichen *v/t* (h) depersonalize.

entpoliti'sieren *v/t* (h) depoliticize.

entprivati'sieren *v/t* (h) deprivatize.

entpuppen [ɛnt'pʊpən] (h) *sich ~ als fig.* turn out to be.

ent'rahmen *v/t* (h) skim (*milk*).

entrann [ɛnt'ran] *pret of* **entrinnen**.

ent'rätseln *v/t* (h) a) solve, unravel, b) decipher.

entrechten [ɛnt'rɛçtən] *v/t* (h) *j-n* ~ deprive s.o. of his rights.

ent'reißen *v/t* (entriß, entrissen, h) *j-m et. ~ a. fig.* snatch s.th. from s.o.

ent'richten *v/t* (h) pay.

entriegeln [ɛnt'ri:gəln] *v/t* (h) unlock.

ent'rinnen *v/i* (entrann, entronnen, sn) (*dat* from) escape, get away.

Ent'rinnen *n* (-s) escape.

entriß [ɛnt'rɪs] *pret*, **ent'rissen** *pp of* **ent'reißen**.

ent'rollen *v/t* (h) unroll, unfurl.

ent'rosten *v/t* (h) remove the rust from.

ent'rücken *v/t* (h) (*dat* from) carry away. **ent'rückt** *adj* enraptured.

entrümpeln [ɛnt'rʏmpəln] *v/t* (h) clear out.

ent'rüsten (h) **I** *v/t* fill *s.o.* with indignation, shock, scandalize. **II** *sich ~* (*über acc*) get indignant (at *s.th.*, with *s.o.*), be shocked (at). **ent'rüstet** *adj* indignant, shocked. **Ent'rüstung** *f* (-; -en) indignation: *Schrei der ~* outcry.

entsaften [ɛnt'zaftən] *v/t* (h) extract the juice from. **Ent'safter** *m* (-s; -) juice extractor, juicer.

ent'sagen *v/i* (h) *e-r Sache ~* renounce s.th. **Ent'sagung** *f* (-; -en) renunciation. **ent'sagungsreich** *adj ein ~es Leben* a life full of privations.

entsann [ɛnt'zan] *pret of* **entsinnen**.

ent'schädigen *v/t* (h) (*für* for) compensate (*a. fig.*), reimburse: *die Aussicht entschädigte uns für den langen Aufstieg* the view made up for the long climb. **Ent'schädigung** *f* (-; -en) compensation (*a. fig.*), reimbursement.

ent'schärfen *v/t* (h) defuse (*a. fig. crisis etc*), deactivate (*ammunition*), *fig.* take the edge off (*a speech etc*).

Entscheid [ɛnt'ʃaɪt] *m* (-[e]s; -e) decree, decision. **ent'scheiden** (entschied, entschieden, h) **I** *v/t* decide, settle, **rɪ̃t** rule (*über acc* on): *damit war die Sache entschieden* that settled it; *das mußt du ~* that's up to you. **II** *v/i* (*über*

acc) a) decide (on), b) be decisive (for). **III** *sich ~* be decided, *person:* decide, make up one's mind; *sich ~ für* decide on, settle for; *er entschied sich dagegen* he decided against it. **ent'scheidend** *adj* a) decisive, b) crucial (*moment etc*): *~e Stimme* casting vote.

Ent'scheidung *f* (-; -en) (*über acc* on) decision, **rɪ̃t** *a.* ruling: *e-e ~ treffen* (*or fällen*) make (*or* come to) a decision.

Ent'scheidungs|bedarf *m es besteht ~* this calls for a decision. **~freiheit** *f* freedom of choice. **~kampf** *m* **1.** ✕ decisive battle. **2.** *fig.* showdown. **~spiel** *n sports:* a) deciding match, decider, b) final. **~träger** *m* decision-maker.

entschied [ɛnt'ʃi:t] *pret of* **entscheiden**.

entschieden [ɛnt'ʃi:dən] **I** *pp of* **entscheiden**. **II** *adj* **1.** a) determined, firm, b) sta(u)nch (*supporter*), declared, decided (*enemy etc*). **2.** decided, definite. **II** *adv* **3.** firmly, decidedly, definitely: *ich bin* (*ganz*) *~ dafür* I'm strongly in favo(u)r of it, I'm all for it. **Ent'schiedenheit** *f* (-; *no pl*) determination, firmness: *mit* (*aller*) *~* categorically.

entschlacken [ɛnt'ʃlakən] *v/t* (h) **1.** ⚙ remove the slag from. **2.** 🎲 a) purify, b) purge. **Ent'schlackung** *f* (-; -en) 🎲 a) purification, b) purge.

ent'schlafen *v/i* (sn) *fig.* pass away.

ent'schließen: *sich ~* (entschloß, entschlossen, h) (*zu, für* on, *zu tun* to do) decide, make up one's mind; *sich anders ~* change one's mind. **Ent'schließung** *f* (-; -en) *pol.* resolution.

entschloß [ɛnt'ʃlɔs] *pret of* **entschließen**. **ent'schlossen I** *pp of* **entschließen**. **II** *adj* determined, firm, resolute: *zu allem ~ sein* be ready for anything; *kurz ~* without a moment's hesitation. **Ent'schlossenheit** *f* (-; *no pl*) determination, resolution, firmness.

Ent'schluß *m* (-sses; ⸚sse) decision: *e-n ~ fassen, zu e-m ~ kommen* make (*or* reach) a decision, make up one's mind.

entschlüsseln [ɛnt'ʃlʏsəln] *v/t* (h) decipher, decode.

entschuldbar [ɛnt'ʃʊltbaːr] *adj* excusable. **entschuldigen** [ɛnt'ʃʊldɪgən] (h) **I** *v/t* excuse: *das ist nicht zu ~* that is impardonable; *bitte, ~ Sie mich* (*für heute abend*) I beg to be excused (for tonight). **II** *v/i ~ Sie!* a) excuse me!, b)

sorry! **III** *sich* ~ a) apologize (*bei j-m für et.* to s.o. for s.th.), b) excuse o.s.
ent'schuldigend *adj* apologetic.
Ent'schuldigung *f* (-; -en) a) excuse, b) apology: *j-n um* ~ *bitten* apologize to s.o. (*wegen* for); *als* ~, *zur* ~ as an excuse (*für* for); *~! → entschuldigen* **II. Ent'schuldigungsgrund** *m* (*et. als* ~ *anführen* offer s.th. as an) excuse.
Entschwefelungsanlage [ɛntˈʃveːfəluŋs-] *f* ⊙ desulphurization plant.
ent'setzen (h) **I** *v/t* horrify, shock, appal(l). **II** *sich* ~ (*über acc* at) be horrified, be shocked. **Ent'setzen** *n* (-s) horror, terror. **entsetzlich** [ɛntˈzɛtslɪç] **I** *adj* horrible, terrible, atrocious. **II** *adv* terribly, F *a.* awfully (*cold, boring, etc*).
Ent'setzlichkeit *f* (-; -en) a) terribleness, horribleness, b) atrocity.
entseuchen [ɛntˈzɔʏçən] *v/t* (h) decontaminate. **Ent'seuchung** *f* (-; -en) decontamination.
ent'sichern *v/t* (h) release the safety catch of (*a gun*), cock.
ent'sinnen: *sich* ~ (entsann, entsonnen, h) (*gen*) recall, recollect; *wenn ich mich recht entsinne* if I remember rightly.
ent'sorgen *v/t* (h) dispose of the nuclear (*or toxic etc*) waste (of a plant *etc*).
Ent'sorgung *f* (-; -en) disposal of nuclear (*or toxic etc*) waste.
entspann [ɛntˈʃpan] *pret of* **entspinnen.**
ent'spannen (h) **I** *sich* ~ relax, *person: a.* take it easy, *fig. situation etc:* ease off. **II** *v/t* relax. **III** *v/i* be relaxing.
Ent'spannung *f* (-; -en) relaxation (*a. fig.*), *pol.* détente, ✝ easing.
Ent'spannungs|poli,tik *f* policy of détente. **~übung** *f* relaxation exercise.
ent'spiegelt *adj opt.* antireflection.
ent'spinnen: *sich* ~ (entspann, entsponnen, h) (*aus* from) arise, develop.
ent'sprechen *v/i* (entsprach, entsprochen, h) (*dat*) **1.** a) correspond (to, with), agree (with), b) be equivalent (to): *er entspricht nicht der Beschreibung* he doesn't answer the description. **2.** a) meet, come up (to *expectations etc*), b) comply (with *a request*): *den Anforderungen nicht* ~ fail to meet the requirements. **ent'sprechend I** *adj* (*dat* to) a) corresponding, b) appropriate, c) adequate, d) equivalent, e) respective. **II** *adv* correspondingly,

accordingly. **III** *prep* (*dat*) according to: *den Umständen* ~ as can be expected under the circumstances.
ent'springen *v/i* (entsprang, entsprungen, sn) **1.** have its source (*in dat* in). **2.** (*dat, aus* from) spring, arise, come.
entstaatlichen [ɛntˈʃtaːtlɪçən] *v/t* (h) denationalize. **Ent'staatlichung** *f* (-; -en) denationalization.
ent'stammen *v/i* (sn) (*dat* from) descend, *fig.* come, derive.
ent'stehen *v/i* (entstand, entstanden, sn) **1.** come into being, develop (*aus* from). **2.** arise, come about, *costs, problems, etc:* (*aus, durch*) arise (*or* result) (from), be caused (by). **3.** be created (*or* built, produced, written, composed, painted). **Ent'stehen** *n* (-s) → *Entstehung: im* ~ *begriffen* in the making.
Ent'stehung *f* (-; -en) a) coming into being, development, emergence, b) origin, beginning, c) creation.
Ent'stehungsgeschichte *f* genesis.
ent'steigen *v/i* (entstieg, entstiegen, sn) (*dat*) get out of.
entsteinen [ɛntˈʃtaɪnən] *v/t* (h) stone.
ent'stellen *v/t* (h) disfigure, *fig.* distort (*facts*), garble (*report*). **Ent'stellung** *f* (-; -en) disfigurement, *fig.* distortion.
ent'stören *v/t* (h) ⚡ radioshield, screen.
Ent'störung *f* (-; -en) screening, *radio:* interference suppression.
ent'tarnen *v/t* (h) unmask, expose (*spy*).
ent'täuschen (h) **I** *v/t* disappoint, let s.o. down. **II** *v/i* be disappointing. **Ent'täuschung** *f* (-; -en) disappointment.
ent'thronen *v/t* (h) *a. fig.* dethrone.
entvölkert [-ˈfœlkərt] *adj* depopulated.
ent'wachsen *v/i* (entwuchs, entwachsen, sn) *e-r Sache* ~ grow out of s.th., outgrow s.th.
entwaffnen [ɛntˈvafnən] *v/t* (h) disarm: *fig. ~des Lächeln* disarming smile.
entwand [ɛntˈvant] *pret of* **entwinden.**
entwarf [ɛntˈvarf] *pret of* **entwerfen.**
ent'warnen *v/i* (h) give the all-clear.
Ent'warnung *f* (-; -en) all-clear (signal).
ent'wässern *v/t* (h) **1.** drain. **2.** 🩺 dehydrate. **Ent'wässerung** *f* (-; -en) **1.** draining. **2.** 🩺 dehydration. **Ent'wässerungsanlage** *f* drainage system.
entweder [ˈɛntveːdər] *conj* ~ ... *oder* either ... or; ~ *oder!* take it or leave it!
'Entweder-'Oder *n* hier gibt es nur

ein ~ you've got to decide one way or the other.

ent'weichen *v/i* (entwich, entwichen, sn) escape (*dat*, *aus* from).

ent'weihen *v/t* (h) desecrate.

Ent'weihung *f* (-; -en) desecration.

ent'wenden *v/t* (h) *j-m et.* ~ steal (*or* purloin) s.th. from s.o.

ent'werfen *v/t* (entwarf, entworfen, h) **1.** sketch, outline (*a. fig. a plan etc*), design. **2.** plan (*program[me] etc*), work out, devise (*plan*). **3.** draw up, draft (*contract*). **Ent'werfer(in** *f*) *m* designer.

ent'werten *v/t* (h) **1.** cancel (*ticket, stamp, etc*). **2.** ✝ a) demonetize, b) → **abwerten.** **3.** *fig.* devalue: (*völlig*) ~ invalidate. **Ent'wertung** *f* (-; -en) **1.** cancel(l)ation. **2.** *fig.* devaluation.

entwich [ɛntˈvɪç] *pret*, **ent'wichen** *pp* of **entweichen.**

ent'wickeln (h) **I** *v/t* **1.** develop (*a. phot., ⊗), phys.-a.* generate, evolve, work out (*plan, method, etc*): *er entwickelte mir s-e Theorie* he expounded his theory to me. **2.** display, show (*energy, an interest, etc*). **II** *sich* ~ (*aus, zu*) develop (from, into), grow (out of, into): *sich gut* ~ be shaping well.

Ent'wickler *m* (-s; -) *phot.* developer.

Ent'wicklung *f* (-; -en) development (*a. fig.*), *a.* trend, *a. biol.* evolution.

Ent'wicklungs|abteilung *f* planning department, Development. **~alter** *n* formative years, *n.s.* age of puberty. **~fähig** *adj* capable of development, progressive (*post etc*). **~geschichte** *f* history, *biol.* genesis. **~helfer(in** *f*) *m* development aid worker, *Br.* member of the Voluntary Service Overseas, *Am.* Peace Corps Worker. **~hilfe** *f* development aid. **~jahre** *pl* → **Entwicklungsalter.** **~land** *n* developing country. **~poli₁tik** *f* third world policy. **~pro₁zeß** *m* (process of) development. **~stufe** *f* stage of development, phase. **~zeit** *f* **1.** period of development. **2.** → **Entwicklungsalter. 3.** *phot.* developing time.

ent'winden *v/t* (entwand, entwunden, h) *j-m et.* ~ wrest s.th. from s.o.

ent'wirren *v/t* (h) disentangle, unravel.

ent'wischen *v/i* (sn) F (*dat* from) escape, slip away: *j-m* ~ a. give s.o. the slip.

entwöhnen [ɛntˈvøːnən] *v/t* (h) **1.** wean (*a baby*). **2.** *j-n* ~ cure s.o. (*gen of an*

addiction etc). **Ent'wöhnung** *f* (-; -en) **1.** weaning. **2.** curing, cure.

entworfen [ɛntˈvɔrfən] *pp* of **entwerfen.**

ent'würdigen *v/t* (h) degrade (*sich* o.s.).

ent'würdigend *adj* degrading.

Ent'würdigung *f* (-; -en) degradation.

Ent'wurf *m* (-[e]s; ¨e) **1.** a) (first) draft, sketch, b) plan, blueprint, c) design, d) model. **2.** ✝, ⚖ draft, *parl.* bill.

Ent'wurfsstadium *n* planning stage.

ent'wurzeln *v/t* (h) *a. fig.* uproot.

ent'ziehen (entzog, entzogen, h) **I** *v/t* **1.** *j-m et.* ~ withdraw s.th. from s.o. (*a. 🔬*), withhold s.th. from s.o., deprive (*or* strip) s.o. of *rights etc*; *j-m den Führerschein* (*die Lizenz etc*) ~ revoke s.o.'s licen/ce (*Am.* -se); *et. j-s Zugriff* (*Einfluß*) ~ remove s.th. from s.o.'s reach (influence); *parl. etc j-m das Wort* ~ rule s.o. out of order. **2.** 🔬 extract (*dat* from). **II** *sich* ~ (*dat*) evade, avoid; → **Kenntnis.** **Ent'ziehung** *f* (-; -en) withdrawal (*a. 🔬*), deprivation.

Ent'ziehungs|anstalt *f* drying-out cent/re (*Am.* -er). **~erscheinung** *f* withdrawal symptom. **~kur** *f* withdrawal treatment.

entziffern [ɛntˈtsɪfərn] *v/t* (h) **1.** decipher, *w.s.* make out. **2.** decode.

Ent'zifferung *f* (-; -en) **1.** deciphering. **2.** decoding.

entzücken [ɛntˈtsʏkən] *v/t* (h) charm, delight. **Ent'zücken** *n* (-s) delight (*über acc* at). **ent'zückend** *adj* charming, delightful, lovely, F sweet. **ent'zückt** *adj* delighted (*über acc* at, *von* with).

Ent'zug *m* (-[e]s; *no pl*) → **Entziehung.**

entzündbar [ɛntˈtsʏndbaːr] *adj* inflammable. **ent'zünden** (h) **I** *v/t* **1.** light. **II** *sich* ~ **2.** catch fire (*an dat* from). **3.** 🔥, ⊗ ignite. **4.** 🩹 become inflamed. **5.** *fig.* (*an dat* by) *passion etc*: be roused, *argument*: be sparked off. **ent'zündet** *adj* 🩹 inflamed, red (*eyes*). **ent'zündlich** *adj* 🩹 inflammatory. **Ent'zündung** *f* (-; -en) 🩹 inflammation. **ent'zündungshemmend** *adj* 🩹 antiphlogistic.

ent'zwei *adj pred* **1.** in two, in half. **2.** in pieces, broken. **ent'zweibrechen** (*irr, sep, -ge-,* → **brechen**) *v/t* (h), *v/i* (sn) break in two. **entzweien** [ɛntˈtsvaiən] (h) **I** *v/t* divide: *Freunde* ~ turn friends against each other. **II** *sich* ~ fall out (*mit* with). **ent'zweigehen** *v/i* (*irr, sep,*

-ge-, sn, → *gehen*) break, go to pieces.
Ent'zweiung f (-; -en) split, rupture.
Enzephalitis [ɛntsefa'li:tɪs] f (-; -litiden [-li'ti:dən]) ✠ encephalitis.
Enzian ['ɛntsia:n] m (-s; -e) ❀ gentian.
Enzyklopädie [ɛntsyklopɛ'di:] f encyclop(a)edia. **enzyklopädisch** [ɛntsyklo'pɛ:dɪʃ] adj encyclop(a)edic.
Enzym [ɛn'tsy:m] n (-s; -e) biol. enzyme.
Epen ['e:pən] pl of **Epos**.
ephemer [efe'me:r] adj ephemeral.
Epidemie [epide'mi:] f (-; -n) epidemic. **epidemisch** [epi'de:mɪʃ] adj epidemic.
Epidermis [epi'dɛrmɪs] f (-; -men) ✠ epidermis.
Epigone [epi'go:nə] m (-n; -n) epigone.
Epigramm [epi'gram] n (-s; -e) epigram.
Epik ['e:pɪk] f (-; no pl) 1. epic poetry. 2. narrative literature. **'Epiker** m (-s; -) 1. epic poet. 2. narrative author.
Epilepsie [epilɛp'si:] f (-; -n) ✠ epilepsy. **Epileptiker** [epi'lɛptɪkər] m (-s; -), **Epi'leptikerin** f (-; -nen), **epileptisch** [epi'lɛptɪʃ] adj epileptic.
Epilog [epi'lo:k] m (-s; -e) epilog(ue Br.).
episch ['e:pɪʃ] adj epic.
Episode [epi'zo:də] f (-; -n) episode.
epi'sodenhaft adj episodic.
Epoche [e'pɔxə] f (-; -n) epoch.
e'pochemachend adj epoch-making.
Epos ['e:pɔs] n (-; Epen) epic (poem).
er [e:r] pers pron he, it: *~ ist es!* it's him!
Er m (-; -s) *F es ist ein ~* it's a he.
Er'achten [ɛr-] n *m-s ~s* in my opinion.
er'arbeiten v/t (h) 1. (a. *sich ~*) work (hard) for, acquire. 2. a) compile, b) develop.
Erbadel ['ɛrp-] m hereditary nobility.
'Erbanlage f genetic make-up, ✠ hereditary disposition.
'Erbanspruch m hereditary title.
erbarmen [ɛr'barmən] (h) I v/t *j-n ~* move s.o. to pity. II *sich ~* (gen) take pity (on). **Er'barmen** n (-s) pity, compassion: *kein ~ kennen* be merciless.
erbärmlich [ɛr'bɛrmlɪç] I adj 1. pitiful, a. miserable, wretched, a. paltry 2. mean, vile. 3. F terrible, awful. II adv 4. pitifully (etc). 5. F awfully: *~ wenig* precious little. **Er'bärmlichkeit** f (-; no pl) pitifulness, miserableness (etc).
er'barmungslos adj merciless.
er'bauen (h) I v/t 1. build, erect. 2. fig. edify: *F er ist nicht besonders erbaut*

davon he's not exactly enthusiastic about it. II *sich ~* (an dat by) be delighted, be uplifted. **Er'bauer** m (-s; -) a) builder, b) founder. **er'baulich** adj edifying (a. iro.), eccl. devotional.
Er'bauung f (-; no pl) 1. building, construction, erection, 2. fig. edification.
Erbe¹ ['ɛrbə] m (-n; -n) heir, successor (j-s of or to s.o., a. fig.): *~ e-s Vermögens* heir (or successor) to an estate; *j-n zum ~n einsetzen* make s.o. one's heir. **'Erbe²** n (-s; no pl) inheritance, fig. heritage. **'erben** v/t (h) inherit (a. fig.), a. come into (money). **'Erbengemeinschaft** f ⚖ community of heirs.
er'betteln v/t (h) (*sich*) et. ~ get s.th. by begging, b.s. scrounge s.th. (von off).
erbeuten [ɛr'bɔytən] v/t (h) ✗ capture.
'Erbfaktor m gene. **'Erbfehler** m hereditary defect. **'Erbfeind** m sworn enemy. **'Erbfolge** f (*gesetzliche ~* intestate) succession. **Erbgut** n biol. genotype.
Erbin ['ɛrbɪn] f (-; -nen) heiress.
erbittern [ɛr'bɪtərn] v/t (h) anger. **erbittert** adj 1. fierce (enemy, fight, etc). 2. embittered (über acc at, by). **Er'bitterung** f (-; no pl) 1. bitterness. 2. anger.
'Erbkrankheit f hereditary disease.
'Erblasser ['ɛrplasər] m (-s; -), **'Erblasserin** f (-; -nen) ⚖ a) the deceased, b) testator (testatrix). **'Erblast** f fig. (evil) legacy. **erblich** ['ɛrplɪç] adj hereditary, inheritable (title etc): *~ belastet* ✠ subject to a(n) hereditary taint.
er'blicken v/t (h) see, catch sight of.
erblinden [ɛr'blɪndən] v/i (sn) go blind. **Er'blindung** f (-; -en) going blind, loss of (one's) sight.
er'blühen v/i (sn) blossom (fig. zu into).
'Erbmasse f 1. ⚖ estate. 2. biol. genetic make-up. **'Erbonkel** m F rich uncle.
er'brechen (erbrach, erbrochen, h) I v/t 1. break open, force (door), open (letter). 2. ✠ vomit, bring up. II v/i a. *sich ~*) ✠ vomit, be sick. **Er'brechen** n (-s) ✠ vomiting: fig. *bis zum ~* ad nauseam.
'Erbrecht n ⚖ 1. law of succession. 2. hereditary title.
'Erbschaft f (-; -en) inheritance: *e-e ~ machen* inherit; *e-e ~ antreten* succeed to an estate.
'Erbschaftssteuer f death duties.
'Erbschein m certificate of heirship.

Erbschleicher ['ɛrpʃlaɪçər] *m* (-s; -) *contp.* legacy-hunter.

Erbse ['ɛrpsə] *f* (-; -n) pea.

'Erbsensuppe *f* pea soup.

'Erbstück *n* heirloom. **'Erbsünde** *f eccl.* original sin. **'Erbtante** *f* F rich aunt. **'Erbteil** *n* share of the inheritance.

Erd\|achse ['e:rt-] *f* earth's axis. **\~anziehungskraft** *f* gravity. **\~arbeiten** *pl* excavations. **\~atmo\|sphäre** *f* (earth's) atmosphere. **\~bahn** *f* earth's orbit. **\~ball** *m* (-[e]s; *no pl*) globe, *w.s.* earth. **'Erdbeben** *n* (-s; -) earthquake. **\~gebiet** *n* **1.** earthquake area. **2.** area hit by an earthquake. **\~herd** *m* seismic focus.

'Erdbeere *f* (-; -n) strawberry.

'Erd\|bevölkerung *f* population of the earth. **\~bewohner** *m* inhabitant of the earth. **\~boden** *m* ground, earth: *dem \~ gleichmachen* raze *s.th.* to the ground; *es (er) war wie vom \~ verschluckt* it (he) had vanished (into thin air).

Erde ['e:rdə] *f* (-; -n) **1.** earth, soil, ground: *über der \~* above ground. **2.** *no pl* (planet) earth: *auf \~n* on earth; *auf der ganzen \~* all over the world. **3.** *ϟ* (*a. an \~ legen*) earth, *Am.* ground.

'erden *v/t* (h) *ϟ* earth, *Am.* ground.

erdenklich [ɛr'dɛŋklɪç] *adj* imaginable, conceivable: *sich alle \~e Mühe geben* do one's utmost.

'Erdgas *n* natural gas.

'Erdgeschichte *f* history of the earth.

'Erdgeschoß *n* ground (*Am.* first) floor.

er'dichten *v/t* (h) make up, invent.

erdig ['e:rdɪç] *adj* earthy.

'Erdinnere *n* interior of the earth.

'Erdkabel *n* underground cable.

'Erdkruste *f* crust of the earth.

'Erdkugel *f* globe, *w.s.* earth.

'Erdkunde *f* (-; *no pl*) geography.

'erdkundlich *adj* geographic(al).

'Erdnuß\(butter\) *f* peanut (butter).

'Erdoberfläche *f* surface of the earth.

'Erdöl *n* (mineral) oil, petroleum.

erdolchen [ɛr'dɔlçən] *v/t* (h) *j-n \~* stab *s.o.* to death.

'Erdreich *n* (-[e]s; *no pl*) earth, soil.

erdreisten [ɛr'draɪstən] *sich \~* (h) dare (*or* have the cheek) (*zu inf* to *inf*).

erdrosseln [ɛr'drɔsəln] *v/t* (h) strangle.

er'drücken *v/t* (h) crush *s.o.* to death, *fig.* crush, overwhelm: *von Arbeit erdrückt werden* be swamped with work.

er'drückend *adj fig.* overwhelming (*majority etc*), damning (*evidence*).

'Erdrutsch *m a. pol.* landslide.

'Erdschicht *f* layer of the earth, stratum.

'Erdstoß *m* seismic shock.

'Erdteil *m* continent.

er'dulden *v/t* (h) endure, suffer.

'Erdumdrehung *f* rotation of the earth.

'Erdumkreisung *f* orbit around the earth.

'Erdung *f* (-; -en) *ϟ* earth(ing), *Am.* ground(ing).

'Erdwärme *f* geothermal energy.

er'eifern: sich \~ (h) get excited (*or* worked up) (*über acc* about).

ereignen [ɛr'ʔaɪgnən] *sich \~* (h) happen, occur, take place. **Ereignis** [ɛr'ʔaɪgnɪs] *n* (-ses; -se) a) event, b) incident, c) great event, sensation. **er'eignislos** *adj* uneventful. **er'eignisreich** *adj* very eventful, exciting.

er'eilen *v/t* (h) *j-n \~* catch up with s.o.

Erektion [erɛk'tsi̯o:n] *f* (-; -en) erection.

Eremit [ere'mi:t] *m* (-en; -en) hermit.

er'erbt *adj* inherited, *biol. a.* hereditary.

er'fahren (erfuhr, erfahren, h) **I** *v/t* **1.** hear, be told, find out. **2.** a) experience, b) suffer, c) receive. **II** *v/i* **3.** *~ von* get to know about, hear about (*or* that). **III** *adj* **4.** experienced, seasoned: *\~ sein in* (*dat*) be well versed in, be at first hand at. **Er'fahrenheit** *f* (-; *no pl*) experience.

Er'fahrung *f* (-; -en) experience: *technische \~ a.* know-how; *aus (eigener) \~* from experience; *durch \~ klug werden* learn the hard way; *in \~ bringen* learn, find out; *die \~ machen, daß ...* find that ...; *die \~ hat gezeigt, daß ...* past experience has shown that ...

Er'fahrungs\|austausch *m* exchange of experience. **⎵gemäß** *adv* as experience shows, we know from experience.

erfand [ɛr'fant] *pret of* **erfinden**.

er'fassen *v/t* (h) **1.** seize, grasp, take: *er wurde vom Auto erfaßt* he was hit by the car; *Furcht erfaßte sie* she was seized with fear. **2.** grasp, understand: *er hat's erfaßt!* he's got it! **3.** a) register, record, b) include, cover: *zahlenmäßig \~* count; *steuerlich \~* tax.

Er'fassung *f* (-; -en) a) registration, b) inclusion, coverage.

er'finden *v/t* (erfand, erfunden, h) a) invent, b) make *s.th.* up. **Er'finder** *m*

Erfindergeist 186

inventor. **Er'findergeist** m (-[e]s; *no pl*) inventiveness. **er'finderisch** *adj* inventive, imaginative, resourceful: → *Not* 2. **Er'findung** f (-; -en) invention, *fig. contp. a.* fabrication. **Er'findungsgabe** f inventive talent, imagination.

Erfolg [ɛr'fɔlk] m (-[e]s; -e) a) success, achievement, b) result, outcome, effect: *guter* ~ good result; *es war ein großer* ~ it was a great success; ~ *haben* succeed, be successful; *k-n* ~ *haben* be unsuccessful, fail; *es zu e-m* ~ *gestalten* make a success of it; *mit dem* ~, *daß* ... with the result that ...

er'folgen v/i (sn) **1.** follow. **2.** take place, happen, *payment*: be made.

er'folglos *adj* unsuccessful, fruitless. **Er'folglosigkeit** f (-; *no pl*) failure. **er'folgreich** *adj* successful.

Er'folgs|aussichten *pl* chances of success. ~**autor** m best-selling author. ~**beteiligung** f profit-sharing. ~**chance** f chance (of success). ~**erlebnis** n **1.** success experience. **2.** → ~**gefühl** n sense of achievement. ~**kurs** m *auf* ~ on the road to success (*or* victory). ~**mensch** m go-getter. ~**quote** f success rate. ~**ro**,**man** m best-selling novel. ~**typ** m born winner, achiever. ~**zwang** m *unter* ~ *stehen* be under pressure to succeed (*or* do well).

er'folgversprechend *adj* promising. **erforderlich** [ɛr'fɔrdərlɪç] *adj* necessary, required: *unbedingt* ~ essential.

er'fordern v/t (h) require, call for, *a.* take (*time, courage, etc*).

Erfordernis [ɛr'fɔrdərnɪs] n (-ses; -se) requirement, demand, prerequisite.

er'forschen v/t (h) investigate, study, research, explore. **Er'forscher** m explorer. **Er'forschung** f (-; -en) (*gen*) investigation (of, into), research (into), exploration (of).

er'fragen v/t (h) ask (for).

er'freuen (h) **I** v/t please. **II** *sich* ~ *an* (*dat*), *sich* ~ (*gen*) enjoy. **erfreulich** [ɛr'frɔylɪç] *adj* a) pleasant, pleasing, welcome (*news etc*), b) encouraging.

er'freulicherweise *adv* fortunately.

er'frieren (erfror, erfroren) **I** v/i (sn) freeze to death, *plants*: be killed by frost: *ihm sind zwei Finger erfroren* he lost two fingers through frostbite. **II**

v/t (h) *sich die Ohren erfroren haben* have frostbitten ears.

Er'frierung f (-; -en) 🦴 frostbite.

erfrischen [ɛr'frɪʃən] v/t (h *and*) refresh (*sich* o.s.). **er'frischend** *adj* refreshing.

Er'frischung f (-; -en) refreshment.

Er'frischungs|getränk n **1.** soft drink **2.** cool drink. ~**raum** m refreshment room. ~**tuch** n moistened tissue.

erfuhr [ɛr'fuːr] *pret of* **erfahren**.

er'füllen (h) **I** v/t **1.** *a. fig.* fill (*mit* with): *ein erfülltes Leben* a full life; *s-e Arbeit erfüllt ihn* he finds his work very satisfying. **2.** fulfil(l) (*duty, contract, etc*), grant (*a wish*), meet (*conditions, expectations, etc*), keep (*promise*): *s-n Zweck* ~ serve its purpose. **II** *sich* ~ come true. **Er'füllung** f (-; -en) fulfil(l)ment: *in* ~ *gehen* come true.

Er'füllungsort m ⚖, ⚒ place of fulfil(l)ment.

erfunden I *pp of* **erfinden**. **II** *adj* imaginary, *contp.* fictitious, (all) made up.

ergangen [ɛr'ɡaŋən] *pp of* **ergehen**.

ergänzen [ɛr'ɡɛntsən] v/t (h) **1.** complement (*sich or einander* one another). **2.** a) complete, b) supplement, add: *et. laufend* ~ keep s.th. up to date. **3.** replenish (*supplies etc*). **er'gänzend I** *adj* a) complementary, b) supplementary, c) additional. **II** *adv* in addition.

Er'gänzung f (-; -en) **1.** a) completion, b) supplementation, c) addition. **2.** complement (*a. ling., ♫*), supplement, addition, *parl.* amendment. **Er'gänzungsband** m (-[e]s; ⁓e) supplement.

ergattern [ɛr'ɡatərn] v/t (h) F (manage to) get hold of.

er'geben (ergab, ergeben, h) **I** v/t **1.** a) result in, b) come to, c) yield. **2.** show, prove. **II** *sich* ~ **3.** a) (*dat* to) *esp.* ✗ surrender, capitulate, b) (*in dat*) resign o.s. (to), c) (*dat*) take to (*drink[ing] etc*). **4.** *problems etc*: arise, *discussion etc*: ensue: *sich* ~ *aus* result (*or* arise) from; *daraus ergibt sich, daß* ... it follows that ...; *es hat sich so* ~ it just happened that way. **III** *adj* **5.** (*dat* to) a) loyal, devoted, b) resigned, c) addicted. **Er'gebenheit** f (-; *no pl*) a) devotion, loyalty, b) resignation.

Ergebnis [ɛr'ɡeːpnɪs] n (-ses; -se) result, outcome, *a.* findings (*of investigation*), *sports: a.* score.

er'gebnislos *adj* without result: ~ *bleiben* (*or* **verlaufen**) come to nothing.

Er'gebung *f* (-; *no pl*) **1.** *esp.* ✕ surrender. **2.** resignation (*in acc* to).

er'gehen (erging, ergangen) **I** *v/i* (sn) **1.** (*an acc* to) *order etc*: be issued, *invitation etc*: be sent. **2.** ⚖ *law*: come out, *decision, judg(e)ment*: be passed. **3.** *et. über sich ~ lassen* endure s.th. **II** *sich ~* (h) a) hold forth (*über acc* on *a subject*), b) indulge (*in dat* in *conjectures etc*). **III** *v/impers* **es ist ihm schlecht ergangen** he had a bad time of it; *wie ist es dir ergangen?* how did you fare?; *mir ist es genauso ergangen* it was the same with me.

ergiebig [ɛr'giːbɪç] *adj* **1.** productive (*a. fig.*), rich (*deposits etc*), lucrative (*business etc*), fruitful (*subject etc*). **2.** economical.

er'gießen: sich ~ (ergoß, ergossen, h) (*in, über acc*) pour (into, over).

er'götzen [ɛr'gœtsən] *sich ~* (h) (*an dat*) a) be amused (by), b) gloat (over).

er'grauen *v/i* (sn) (turn) grey (*Am.* gray): *im Dienst ergraut* grown old in service.

er'greifen *v/t* (ergriff, ergriffen, h) **1.** seize, a. arrest (*criminal*). **2.** take (*measures etc*): → *Besitz* 1, *Flucht¹*, *Wort* 2. **3.** a) overcome, seize, b) move: *Angst ergriff sie* she was seized with fear. **er'greifend** *adj* moving.

ergriffen [ɛr'grɪfən] **I** *pp of* **ergreifen**. **II** *adj* moved.

Er'griffenheit *f* (-; *no pl*) emotion.

er'gründen *v/t* (h) get to the bottom of.

Er'guß *m* (-sses; ⁻sse) **1.** ⚕ a) effusion (of blood), b) ejaculation. **2.** *fig.* effusion, *a. iro.* outpouring.

Er'gußgestein *n geol.* effusive rock.

er'haben *adj* **1.** ⊙ raised, embossed. **2.** *fig.* lofty, sublime, grand. **3.** *fig. ~ über* (*acc*) above, beyond (*reproach etc*).

Er'habenheit *f* (-; *no pl*) grandeur.

er'halten (erhielt, erhalten, h) **I** *v/t* **1.** get, receive, obtain: *e-n Preis ~* be awarded (*or* given) a prize. **2.** keep, maintain, preserve: *j-n am Leben ~* keep s.o. alive; *das erhält (e-n) jung* that keeps you young; *j-m das Augenlicht ~* save s.o.'s eyesight. **3.** keep, support (*family etc*). **II** *sich ~* a) survive, b) subsist (*von* on). **III** *adj* **gut ~ sein** be in good condition; *~ bleiben* survive; *noch ~ sein* remain, be left.

erhältlich [ɛr'hɛltlɪç] *adj* obtainable, available: *schwer ~* hard to get hold of.

Er'haltung *f* (-; *no pl*) preservation, maintenance, upkeep.

er'hängen *v/t* (h) hang (*sich* o.s.).

er'härten *v/t* (h) corroborate, confirm.

er'haschen *v/t* (h) catch.

er'heben (erhob, erhoben, h) **I** *v/t* **1.** raise (*a. fig. one's voice, objections, etc*), lift (up): *j-n in den Adelsstand ~* raise s.o. to the peerage; → *Anklage, Anspruch*. **2.** levy, impose (*duties, taxes*), charge (*a fee*). **II** *sich ~* **3.** rise (to one's feet), get up. **4.** *hill, house, etc*: rise (*über dat* above). **5.** *wind, fig. doubts, shouting, etc*: arise. **6.** rise (*in arms*), revolt. **er'hebend** *adj* edifying.

erheblich [ɛr'heːplɪç] **I** *adj* a) considerable, b) important. **II** *adv* considerably: *~ besser* much better.

Er'hebung *f* (-; -en) **1.** elevation, rise (in the ground). **2.** elevation (*in den Adelsstand* to a peerage). **3.** levy (*of duties, taxes*), charge (*of fees*). **4.** *statistics*: survey: *~en anstellen* (*über acc*) make investigations (about), investigate (into). **5.** uprising, revolt.

erheitern [ɛr'haɪtərn] *v/t* (h) amuse.

Er'heiterung *f* (-; *no pl*) amusement.

erhellen [ɛr'hɛlən] (h) **I** *v/t* light up, illuminate, *fig.* shed light (up)on. **II** *sich ~* brighten.

erhielt [ɛr'hiːlt] *pret of* **erhalten**.

erhitzen [ɛr'hɪtsən] (h) **I** *v/t* heat (up): *die Gemüter ~* make feelings run high. **II** *sich ~* get hot, *fig.* get heated (*person*: excited). **er'hitzt** *adj* hot, *person*: a. flushed, *fig.* heated (*debate etc*).

erhob [ɛr'hoːp] *pret of* **erheben**.

erhoben [ɛr'hoːbən] *pp of* **erheben**.

er'hoffen *v/t* (h) (*a. sich ~*) hope for.

er'hofft *adj* hoped-for.

erhöhen [ɛr'høːən] (h) **I** *v/t* raise (*a. fig. auf acc* to, *um* by), *fig. a.* increase, intensify, enhance, heighten. **II** *sich ~* increase, *price etc*: rise, go up.

Er'höhung *f* (-; -en) **1.** raising. **2.** rise, increase (*gen* in), *fig. a.* intensification, enhancement, heightening; → *Gehalts-, Lohnerhöhung*.

er'holen: sich ~ (h) a) recover (*von* from, *a.* ✝), b) take a rest, relax: *du* *siehst sehr erholt aus* you look very rested (*or* fit). **er'holsam** *adj* restful, relaxing. **Er'holung** *f* (-; *no pl*) **1.** a) recovery (**von** from, *a.* ✝), b) rest, relaxation. **2.** holiday, *Am.* vacation.

Er'holungs|aufenthalt *m* holiday, *Am.* vacation. **⸠bedürftig** *adj* in need of a rest (*or* holiday). **⸠gebiet** *n* recreation area. **⸠heim** *n* rest home. **⸠ort** *m* (health *or* holiday) resort. **⸠pause** *f* rest, breather. **⸠reise** *f* holiday (*Am.* vacation) trip. **⸠urlaub** *m* holiday (*Am.* vacation), ✕ convalescent leave. **⸠wert** *m* recreational value. **⸠zentrum** *n* recreation park.

er'hören *v/t* (h) hear, answer (*prayer*).
erigieren [eri'giːrən] (sn) become erect.
Erika ['eːrika] *f* (-; -s, -ken) ♣ heather.
erinnern [ɛr'ʔɪnərn] (h) **I** *v/t j-n ~* remind s.o. (*an acc* of); *j-n daran ~, daß* remind s.o. that. **II** *sich ~* (*an acc*) remember, recall; *wenn ich mich recht erinnere* if I remember rightly; *soviel ich mich ~ kann* as far as I remember. **III** *v/i ~ an* (*acc*) remind one of, *fig. a.* be suggestive of. **Er'innerung** *f* (-; -en) a) memory, recollection, reminiscence (*all: an acc* of), b) memento, souvenir, keepsake, c) reminder; *⸠en* reminiscences, memoirs; *zur ~ an* (*acc*) in memory of; *in guter ~ behalten* have fond memories of.

Er'innerungstafel *f* memorial tablet.
Er'innerungsvermögen *n* memory.
Er'innerungswert *m* sentimental value.
erkalten [ɛr'kaltən] *v/i* (sn) **1.** get cold. **2.** *fig.* cool (off).

erkälten [ɛr'kɛltən] *sich ~* (h) catch a cold; (*stark*) *erkältet sein* have a (bad) cold. **Er'kältung** *f* (-; -en) cold.

er'kämpfen *v/t* (h) gain (*or* win) (after a hard struggle): *sich et. hart ~ müssen* have to struggle hard for s.th.

er'kaufen *v/t* (h) buy: *et. teuer ~ müssen* (have to) pay a high price for s.th.; *j-s Schweigen ~* bribe s.o. into silence.

er'kennbar *adj* **1.** recognizable. **2.** discernible, to be seen.

erkennen (erkannte, erkannt, h) **I** *v/t* **1.** a) recognize (*an dat* by), b) make out, see, c) detect, F spot, d) identify, ✗ diagnose: *~ an* (*dat*) a. know by; *~ lassen* show, reveal; *zu ~ geben* indicate, give to understand; *sich zu ~ geben*

disclose one's identity; ✗ *j-n für schuldig ~* find s.o. guilty. **2.** realize, see. **II** *v/i* **3.** ✗ *~ über* (*acc*) decide on; *~ auf* (*acc*) pass a sentence of.

er'kenntlich *adj* *sich (j-m) ~ zeigen* show (s.o.) one's gratitude.

Er'kenntnis *f* (-; se) a) knowledge, b) realization, c) idea, d) discovery: *neueste ~se* the latest findings; *zu der ~ gelangen, daß* (come to) realize that.

Er'kennung *f* (-; *no pl*) a) recognition, b) identification.

Er'kennungs|dienst *m* criminal identification department. **⸠marke** *f* identity disc, *Am.* identification tag. **⸠melo,die** *f* signature tune. **⸠wort** *n* password. **⸠zeichen** *n* **1.** sign to be recognized by. **2.** ✓ identification sign.

Erker ['ɛrkər] *m* (-s; -) △ oriel.
'Erkerfenster *n* bay window.

erklärbar [ɛr'klɛːrbaːr] *adj* explainable.
er'klären (h) **I** *v/t* **1.** explain (*j-m et.* s.th. to s.o.): *kannst du mir ~, warum?* can you tell me why?; *ich kann es mir nicht ~* I don't understand it. **2.** a) interpret, b) illustrate (*an e-m Beispiel* by an example). **3.** declare, pronounce: *j-n für gesund ~* pronounce s.o. healthy; ✗ *er wurde für tot erklärt* he was declared dead; → *Einverständnis* 1, *Rücktritt* 1. **II** *sich ~* a) declare o.s., explain o.s., b) be explained; *sich ~ für* (*gegen*) declare for (against); *sich einverstanden ~* consent (*mit* to); *sich solidarisch ~* declare one's solidarity (*mit* with). **er'klärend** *adj* explanatory.

er'klärlich *adj* **1.** explainable. **2.** understandable. **er'klärlicherweise** *adv* understandably (enough).

er'klärt *adj* declared (*enemy etc*).
Er'klärung *f* (-; -en) **1.** (*zur ~* by way of) explanation (*für* of). **2.** *a. pol.* declaration, statement: *e-e ~ abgeben* make a statement (*zu* on).

er'klettern *v/t* (h) climb (up).
er'klingen *v/i* (erklang, erklungen, sn) be heard, sound, ring out.

er'kranken *v/i* (sn) fall ill (*or* sick) (*an dat* with), *organ:* be diseased: *~ an* (*dat*) a. get, come down with; *erkrankt sein an* (*dat*) a. have. **Er'krankung** *f* (-; -en) illness, sickness, disease (*of an organ*).

erkunden [ɛr'kundən] *v/t* (h) explore, ✕ reconnoit/re (*Am.* -er), find out.

erkundigen [ɛrˈkʊndɪɡən] *sich ~* (h) (*über acc* about) ask, inquire, make inquiries; *sich nach dem Weg ~* ask the way; *sich nach j-m* (*or ~s Befinden*) *~* inquire after s.o. **Er'kundigung** *f* (-; -en) inquiry: *~en einziehen* make inquiries (*über acc* about).

Er'kundung *f* (-; -en) ✗ reconnaissance.

erlag [ɛrˈlaːk] *pret of* **erliegen**.

er'lahmen *v/i* (sn) **1.** grow weary, tire. **2.** *fig.* interest, zeal, *etc*: flag, wane.

er'langen *v/t* (h) a) get, obtain, b) attain, reach, c) gain, acquire.

Erlaß [ɛrˈlas] *m* (-sses, -sse) **1.** (*gen*) release (from *debts etc*), remission (of *penalty etc*). **2.** a) issuing, enactment (of *a law*), b) decree.

er'lassen *v/t* (erließ, erlassen, h) **1.** issue, publish (*ordinance*), enact (*a law*). **2.** remit (*penalty*), waive (*fees*): *j-m et. ~* release s.o. from s.th.

er'lauben [ɛrˈlaʊbən] *v/t* (h) allow, permit (*j-m et.* s.o. to do s.th.): *j-m ~, et. zu tun a.* give s.o. permission to do s.th.; *~ Sie, daß ich rauche?* may I smoke?; *wenn Sie ~* if you don't mind; *sich ~ zu inf* take the liberty of *ger*, *b.s. a.* dare (to) *inf*; *~ Sie mal!, was ~ Sie sich?* who do you think you are?; *er kann sich das ~ w.s.* he can get away with it.

Erlaubnis [ɛrˈlaʊpnɪs] *f* (-; *no pl*) permission: *j-n um ~ bitten* ask s.o.'s (*or* s.o.s for) permission (*et. zu tun* to do s.th.); *die ~ erhalten* be given permission.

er'läutern *v/t* (h) explain, comment (up)on: *durch Beispiele ~* illustrate. **er'läuternd** *adj* explanatory, illustrative. **Er'läuterung** *f* (-; -en) a) explanation, b) illustration, c) note.

Erle [ˈɛrlə] *f* (-; -n) ♣ alder.

er'leben *v/t* (h) a) experience, b) have (*adventures etc*), c) go through (*bad times etc*), d) live to see, e) see: *ich habe* (*es*) *selbst erlebt, was es heißt, arm zu sein* I know from experience what it means to be poor; *ich habe es oft erlebt*(*, daß*) I've often seen it happen (that); *wir werden es ja ~!* we'll see!

Erlebnis [ɛrˈleːpnɪs] *n* (-ses; -se) a) experience, b) event, c) adventure.

er'lebnisreich *adj* eventful.

er'ledigen [ɛrˈleːdɪɡən] (h) **I** *v/t* **1.** a) finish (off), b) deal with, take care of, c) settle (*problem, deal, etc*), d) carry out

(*order, task*): *würden Sie das für mich ~?* would you do that for me? **2.** dismiss. **3.** F *j-n ~* finish s.o. (*a. sports*), *a.* do s.o. in. **II** *sich selbst ~* take care of itself, F sort itself out. **er'ledigt** *adj* **1.** settled, finished: *das wäre ~!* that's that!; *das ist für mich ~* the matter's closed as far as I'm concerned; F *du bist für mich ~!* I'm through with you! **2.** F *person*: a) finished, b) done in, whacked: *der ist ~!* he's done for!

Er'ledigung *f* (-; -en) **1.** *no pl* settlement: *zur umgehenden ~* for immediate attention. **2.** *pl* errands, shopping.

er'legen I *pp of* **erliegen**. **II** *v/t* (h) *hunt.* shoot, kill.

erleichtern [ɛrˈlaɪçtərn] *v/t* (h) a) make *a task* easier, facilitate, b) lighten (*a burden*), c) relieve (*need, pain, etc*), ease (*one's conscience*): *sich das Herz ~* unburden one's heart; *das erleichterte mich sehr* that was a great relief to me; F *j-n ~ um ...* relieve s.o. of *wallet etc*.

er'leichtert *adj* relieved: *ich war ~, als ...* it was a relief to me when ...; *~ aufatmen* breathe a sigh of relief.

Er'leichterung *f* (-; -en) **1.** *no pl* facilitation, lightening, easing. **2.** *no pl* relief (*über acc* at): *zu m-r ~* to my relief. **3.** *pl* ✞, *pol.* relief, facilities.

er'leiden *v/t* (erlitt, erlitten, h) a) suffer, go through, b) sustain: *den Tod ~* die.

erlernbar [ɛrˈlɛrnbaːr] *adj* learnable.

er'lernen *v/t* (h) learn.

er'lesen *adj* select, choice, exquisite.

er'leuchten *v/t* (h) **1.** light (up), illuminate. **2.** *fig.* enlighten. **Er'leuchtung** *f* (-; -en) **1.** illumination. **2.** *fig.* a) enlightenment, b) idea, inspiration.

er'liegen *v/i* (erlag, erlegen, sn) (*dat*) succumb (to *temptation etc*), be the victim (of *a mistake etc*). **Er'liegen** *n* (-s) *zum ~ kommen* break down; *et. zum ~ bringen* bring s.th. to a standstill.

erließ [ɛrˈliːs] *pret of* **erlassen**.

erlitt [ɛrˈlɪt] *pret of* **erleiden**.

erlogen [ɛrˈloːɡən] *adj* made(-)up: *das ist ~* that's a lie.

Erlös [ɛrˈløːs] *m* (-es; -e) proceeds.

erloschen [ɛrˈlɔʃən] **I** *pp of* **erlöschen**. **II** *adj* **1.** extinct. **2.** *fig.* dead. **3.** *contract etc*: expired.

er'löschen *v/i* (erlosch, erloschen, sn)

Erlöschen

190

go out, *a. fig. life*: be extinguished, *contract etc*: expire.

Er'löschen *n* (-s) a) extinction, b) expiry.

er'lösen *v/t* (h) (**von** from) a) release, free, b) rescue: *j-n ~ iro.* put s.o. out of his (her) misery, *eccl.* save (*or* redeem) s.o.; *er ist erlöst* his sufferings are over. **er'lösend** *adj das ~e Wort sprechen* break the tension; *ein ~es Gefühl* a great relief. **Er'lösung** *f* (-; -en) **1.** release. **2.** *eccl.* salvation. **3.** relief.

ermächtigen [ɛr'mɛçtɪɡən] *v/t* (h) authorize (*j-n zu et.* s.o. to do s.th.). **Er'mächtigung** *f* (-; -en) **1.** authorization. **2.** authority.

er'mahnen *v/t* (h) admonish (*j-n zur Vorsicht etc* s.o. to be careful *etc*), caution, warn (*a. sports*). **Er'mahnung** *f* (-; -en) admonition, warning, *esp. sports*: (first) caution.

er'mangelung: *in ~* (*gen*) for want of.

er'mäßigen (h) **I** *v/t* reduce, cut: *zu ermäßigten Preisen* at reduced prices. **II** *sich ~* be reduced (*auf acc* to).

er'messen *v/t* (ermaß, ermessen, h) a) estimate, assess, b) judge, c) appreciate, realize. **Er'messen** *n* (-s) judg(e)ment, discretion: *ich stelle es in Ihr ~* I leave it to you(r discretion); *das liegt ganz in Ihrem ~ a.* it's entirely up to you. **Er'messensfrage** *f* matter of opinion. **Er'messensspielraum** *m* latitude.

ermitteln [ɛr'mɪtəln] (h) **I** *v/t* a) find out, establish, locate (*place etc*), b) determine. **II** *v/i police*: investigate, carry out investigations (*gegen* concerning). **Er'mittlung** *f* (-; -en) **1.** a) finding out *s.th.*, b) determination. **2.** investigation, inquiry: *~en anstellen* a) make inquiries (*über acc* about), b) → *ermitteln* II. **3.** *pl* findings. **Er'mittlungs|ausschuß** *m* fact-finding committee. **~beamte** *m* investigating officer. **~verfahren** *n* ᵗᵗᵗ preliminary proceedings.

ermöglichen [ɛr'møːklɪçən] *v/t* (h) a) make *s.th.* possible, b) allow: *j-m ~, et. zu tun* make it possible for (*or* enable) s.o. to do s.th.

er'morden *v/t* (h) murder. **Er'mordete** *m, f* (-n; -n) (murder) victim. **Er'mordung** *f* (-; -en) murder.

ermüden [ɛr'myːdən] *v/t* (h), *v/i* (sn) tire. **er'müdend** *adj* tiring. **er'müdet** *adj*

tired. **Er'müdung** *f* (-; *no pl*) tiredness, *a.* ⊚ fatigue. **Er'müdungserscheinung** *f a.* ⊚ sign of fatigue.

ermuntern [ɛr'mʊntərn] *v/t* (h) **1.** encourage *s.o.* (*zu et., et. zu tun* to do s.th.). **2.** stimulate. **er'munternd** *adj* encouraging. **Er'munterung** *f* (-; -en) **1.** encouragement. **2.** stimulation.

ermutigen [ɛr'muːtɪɡən] *v/t* (h) encourage *s.o.* (*zu et., et. zu tun* to do s.th.). **er'mutigend** *adj* encouraging, reassuring. **Er'mutigung** *f* (-; -en) (*zur ~* as an) encouragement.

er'nähren (h) **I** *v/t* a) feed, nourish, b) support: *schlecht ernährt* malnourished. **II** *sich ~* (*von*) live (on), *fig.* make a living (by). **Er'nährer** *m* (-s; -), **Er'nährerin** *f* (-; -nen) supporter, breadwinner. **Er'nährung** *f* (-; *no pl*) **1.** a) feeding, ⊛ nutrition, b) food: *schlechte ~* malnutrition. **2.** support. **Er'nährungs|weise** *f* eating habits. **~wissenschaft** *f* (-; *no pl*) dietetics. **~wissenschaftler(in** *f)* *m* dietician.

er'nennen *v/t* (ernannte, ernannt, h) appoint (*j-n zu et.* s.o. s.th.). **Er'nennung** *f* (-; -en) appointment (*zum* as *or* to the post of).

erneuern [ɛr'nɔʏərn] (h) **I** *v/t* renew (*contract, offer, etc*), ⊛ *a.* replace, *fig. a.* revive. **II** *sich ~* be renewed, revive. **Er'neuerung** *f* (-; -en) renewal, ⊛ *a.* replacement, *fig. a.* revival. **erneut** [ɛr'nɔʏt] **I** *adj* renewed, new, repeated, fresh. **II** *adv* again, once more.

erniedrigen [ɛr'niːdrɪɡən] (h) **I** *v/t* **1.** a) degrade, b) humiliate. **2.** → *herabsetzen* 2. **II** *sich ~* degrade o.s.; *sich (so weit) ~, et. zu tun* lower o.s. to do s.th. **er'niedrigend** *adj* degrading, humiliating. **Er'niedrigung** *f* (-; -en) a) degradation, b) humiliation.

ernst [ɛrnst] **I** *adj* serious, a) *a.* earnest, b) *a.* grave, solemn, c) *a.* severe, d) *a.* weighty: *~e Musik* serious music. **II** *adv* seriously (*etc*), in earnest: *ich meine es ~* I'm serious about it, I mean it; *j-n* (*et.*) *~ nehmen* take s.o. (s.th.) seriously; *das war nicht ~ gemeint!* I (*etc*) didn't mean it!

Ernst *m* (-es; *no pl*) seriousness, *a.* earnestness, gravity, severity: *allen ~es* in all seriousness; *~ machen mit* go ahead with; *ich meine es im ~, es ist mein voller ~* I'm dead serious.

'**Ernstfall** *m* emergency: *im ~* a) in case of emergency, b) if things come to the worst, c) ✕ in the event of a war. '**ernstgemeint** *adj* serious, sincere. '**ernsthaft** *adj* serious: *sich ~e Sorgen machen um* be seriously worried about. '**Ernsthaftigkeit** *f* (-; *no pl*) seriousness. '**ernstlich I** *adj* serious. **II** *adv ~ krank* seriously ill; *~ böse* really angry. '**ernstzunehmend** *adj* serious.

Ernte ['ɛrntə] *f* (-; -n) **1.** *a. fig.* harvest. **2.** crop. '**Ernteausfall** *m* crop failure. '**Erntedankfest** *n* harvest festival. **ernten** ['ɛrntən] *v/t, v/i* (h) harvest, reap (*a. fig.*). '**Ernteschäden** *pl* crop damage. '**Erntezeit** *f* harvest time.

er'nüchtern *v/t* (h) sober: *fig. j-n ~ a.* bring s.o. down to earth again. **Er'nüchterung** *f* (-; -en) **1.** sobering-up. **2.** *fig.* disillusionment.

Er'oberer *m* (-s; -) conqueror. **erobern** [ɛr'ʔoːbərn] *v/t* (h) *a. fig.* conquer: *~ Sturm* **2.** **Er'oberung** *f* (-; -en) (*fig. e-e ~ machen* make a) conquest.

er'öffnen I *v/t* **1.** open, inaugurate: ✕ *das Feuer ~* open fire. **2.** *fig.* open (up), offer (*prospects etc*). **3.** *j-m et. ~* disclose s.th. to s.o., inform s.o. of s.th. **II** *v/i* open (*a. at chess*). **III** *sich ~ opportunity etc*: present itself. **Er'öffnung** *f* (-; -en) **1.** opening (*a. at chess*), inauguration. **2.** disclosure. **Er'öffnungs|ansprache** *f* inaugural address. **~beschluß** *m* ⚖ **1.** order to proceed. **2.** bankruptcy order. **~feier** *f* opening ceremony. **~kurs** *m* ✝ opening quotation.

erogen [ero'geːn] *adj* erogenous. **erörtern** [ɛr'ʔœrtərn] *v/t* (h) discuss. **Er'örterung** *f* (-; -en) discussion (*gen* of). **Erosion** [ero'zi̯oːn] *f* (-; -en) erosion. **Erotik** [e'roːtɪk] *f* (-; *no pl*) eroticism. **erotisch** [e'roːtɪʃ] *adj* erotic. **erpicht** [ɛr'pɪçt] *adj ~ sein auf* (*acc*) be very (F dead) keen on, be bent on. **er'preßbar** *adj* open to blackmail. **er'pressen** *v/t* (h) *j-n* blackmail s.o. (*et. zu tun* into doing s.th.); *et. ~* extort s.th. (*von* from). **Er'presser** *m* (-s; -), **Er'presserin** *f* (-; -nen) blackmailer. **Er'presserbrief** *m* blackmail letter.

Er'pressung *f* (-; -en) blackmail. **Er'pressungsversuch** *m* blackmail attempt.

er'proben *v/t* (h) try (out), test. **er'probt** *adj* **1.** well-tried. **2.** experienced. **Er'probung** *f* (-; -en) trial, test. **errang** [ɛr'raŋ] *pret of* **erringen**. **er'raten** *v/t* (erriet, erraten, h) guess. **er'rechnen** *v/t* (h) work out, calculate: *sich ~ aus* be calculated from.

erregbar [ɛr'reːkbaːr] *adj* a) excitable, b) irritable. **Er'regbarkeit** *f* (-; *no pl*) a) excitability, b) irritability. **er'regen** (h) **I** *v/t* **1.** excite (*a. ⚥, a. sexually*), *b.s.* irritate, infuriate. **2.** *fig.* cause: *j-s Zorn ~* provoke s.o.'s anger; *Bewunderung ~* excite admiration; → *Ärgernis, Aufsehen.* **II** *sich ~* (*über acc* about) a) get excited, get all worked up, b) get angry. **er'regend** *adj* exciting. **Er'reger** *m* (-s; -) **1.** *a. ⚥* exciter. **2.** 🎗 pathogen, germ. **er'regt** *adj* excited (*a. sexually*), heated (*debate etc*). **Er'regung** *f* (-; -en) **1.** creation, excitation (*a. ⚥*), causing. **2.** excitement, *sexually:* a. (state of) arousal. **3.** anger.

erreichbar [ɛr'raɪçbaːr] *adj* a) within reach, *fig.* attainable, b) available: *leicht ~* within easy reach; *zu Fuß (mit dem Wagen) leicht ~* within easy walking (driving) distance; *er ist nie ~* you just can't get hold of him. **er'reichen** *v/t* (h) **1.** a) reach, catch (*bus, train, etc*), b) catch up with: *j-n telefonisch ~* get s.o. on the phone; *ein hohes Alter ~* live to an old age; *leicht zu ~* within easy reach. **2.** *fig.* a) achieve, b) obtain, get: *et. ~* get somewhere; (*es*) *~, daß ...* succeed in *ger;* *haben Sie (bei ihm) et. erreicht?* did you get anywhere (with him)? **Er'reichung** *f* (-; *no pl*) attainment: *nach ~ der Altersgrenze* on reaching the retirement age.

er'richten *v/t* (h) **1.** build, erect, put up. **2.** *fig.* found, *esp.* ✝ set up. **Er'richtung** *f* (-; *no pl*) **1.** building, erection. **2.** *fig.* foundation.

erriet [ɛr'riːt] *pret of* **erraten**. **er'ringen** *v/t* (errang, errungen, h) gain, *a.* win (*prize*), *a.* achieve (*success*). **er'röten** *v/i* (sn) blush (*vor* with, *über acc* at).

Errungenschaft [ɛr'rʊŋənʃaft] *f* (-; -en) **1.** acquisition. **2.** *fig.* achievement.

ersah [ɛr'za:] *pret of* **ersehen.**

Ersatz [ɛr'zats] *m* (-es; *no pl*) **1.** substitute, replacement(s ✕): **als ~ für j-n** to replace s.o.; **er (das) ist kein ~ für ...** he (that) can't replace ... **2.** ✝, ⚔ a) compensation, b) damages: **als ~ für** by way of compensation, in exchange (*or* return) for. **~anspruch** *m* claim for compensation. **~bank** *f sports:* substitutes' bench. **~batte‚rie** *f* spare battery. **~befriedigung** *f psych.* compensation. **~handlung** *f psych.* displacement activity, *w.s.* compensation. **~kasse** *f* health insurance society. **~leistung** *f* compensation. **~mann** *m* substitute (*a. sports*), replacement (*a.* ✕). **~mine** *f* refill. **~mittel** *n* substitute, ersatz. **~mutter** *f* mother-substitute.

er'satzpflichtig *adj* liable for damages. **Er'satzreifen** *m* spare tyre (*Am.* tire). **Er'satzspieler(in** *f*) *m sports:* substitute. **Er'satzteil** *n, m* ⚙ replacement part, spare (part). **~chirur‚gie** *f* spare parts surgery. **~lager** *n* spare parts store.

er'satzweise *adv* alternatively.

er'saufen *v/i* (ersoff, ersoffen, sn) F drown.

ersäufen [ɛr'zɔyfən] *v/t* (h) drown.

er'schaffen *v/t* (erschuf, erschaffen, h) create, make.

Er'schaffung *f* (-; *no pl*) creation.

er'scheinen *v/i* (erschien, erschienen, sn) **1.** appear (*a. ghost*: *j-m* to s.o.), come, F turn up: **vor Gericht ~** appear in court. **2.** appear, come out, be published: **soeben erschienen** just published. **3.** (*j-m* to s.o.) seem, appear: **es erscheint ratsam** it would seem advisable. **Er'scheinen** *n* (-s) **1.** appearance, *a.* publication. **2.** attendance (**bei** at). **Er'scheinung** *f* (-; -en) **1.** a) appearance, b) apparition, c) vision: **in ~ treten** appear, *fig.* a. make itself felt; **stark (kaum) in ~ treten** be very (not) much in evidence; **er tritt kaum in ~** he keeps very much in the background. **2.** *fig.* sign, symptom (*a.* ⚕). **3.** a) (outward) appearance, b) figure. **Er'scheinungsjahr** *n* year of publication.

er'schießen (erschoß, erschossen, h) **I** *v/t* shoot (dead): **j-n ~ lassen** have s.o. shot. **II** *sich ~* shoot o.s.

Er'schießung *f* (-; -en) shooting, ✕ execution (by a firing squad).

erschlaffen [ɛr'ʃlafən] *v/i* (sn) *muscles etc:* grow tired, *skin:* begin (to) sag.

er'schlagen (erschlug, erschlagen, h) **I** *v/t* kill. **II** *adj* F **wie ~** a) dum(b)found-ed, b) dead-beat, whacked.

er'schleichen *v/t* (erschlich, erschli-chen, h) **sich et. ~** obtain s.th. by trick-ery; **sich j-s Vertrauen ~** worm o.s. into s.o.'s confidence.

er'schließen (erschloß, erschlossen, h) **I** *v/t* open (up) (*a. market etc*), develop (*area, building estates*). **II** *sich j-m ~** *mystery etc:* be revealed to s.o., *opportunities etc:* open up before s.o.

Er'schließung *f* (-; -en) opening (up), development.

er'schöpfen (h) **I** *v/t a. fig.* exhaust. **II** *sich ~* exhaust o.s., *fig.* be exhausted: **sich ~ in** (*dat*) *activity etc:* be limited to. **er'schöpfend** *adj* **1.** exhausting. **2.** exhaustive. **er'schöpft** *adj* a) exhausted (**von** by), b) spent. **Er'schöpfung** *f* (-; *no pl*) exhaustion (**bis zur ~** to the point of) exhaustion. **Er'schöpfungszustand** *m* (state of) exhaustion.

erschoß [ɛr'ʃɔs] *pret,* **er'schossen** *pp of* **erschießen.**

er'schrecken¹ *v/t* (h) frighten, scare, startle: → **Tod. er'schrecken²** *v/i* (erschrak, erschrocken, sn) be frightened (**über** *acc* at). **Er'schrecken** *n* (-s) fright. **er'schreckend** *adj* frightening, appalling: **~ wenige** alarmingly few.

erschrocken [ɛr'ʃrɔkən] **I** *pp of* **erschrecken².** **II** *adj and adv* frightened.

erschuf [ɛr'ʃu:f] *pret of* **erschaffen.**

erschüttern [ɛr'ʃʏtərn] *v/t* (h) **1.** *a. fig.* shake. **2.** *fig.* a) shock, b) move *s.o.* deeply. **er'schütternd** *adj* a) shocking, b) deeply moving. **Er'schütterung** *f* (-; -en) **1.** shock (*a. fig.*), b) *fig.* emotion.

erschweren [ɛr'ʃve:rən] *v/t* (h) a) make *s.th.* (more) difficult, complicate, impede, b) *a.* ⚖ aggravate.

er'schwerend *adj* ⚖ aggravating.

er'schwindeln *v/t* (h) **sich et. von j-m ~** cheat s.th. out of s.o.

erschwinglich [ɛr'ʃvɪŋlɪç] *adj* within s.o.'s means: **zu ~en Preisen** at reasonable prices.

er'sehen *v/t* (ersah, ersehen, h) (**aus** from) see, gather.

er'sehnen *v/t* (h) long for.

ersetzbar [ɛr'zɛtsba:r] *adj* replaceable

(a. ⚙), reparable (*damage*), recoverable (*loss*). **er'setzen** *v/t* (h) a) replace (*durch* by), a. take the place of *s.o.*, b) compensate for, make up for: *j-m den Schaden (die Auslagen)* ~ compensate s.o. for the damage (reimburse s.o. for expenses). **Er'setzung** *f* (-; -en) a) replacement, b) compensation, reimbursement (*of expenses*).

er'sichtlich *adj* apparent, evident, clear: *ohne* ~*en Grund* for no apparent reason; *daraus wird* ~ hence it appears.

ersoff [ɛr'zɔf] *pret of* **ersaufen.**

ersoffen [ɛr'zɔfən] *pp of* **ersaufen.**

er'spähen *v/t* (h) F spot.

er'sparen *v/t* (h) **1.** (a. *sich* ~) save. **2.** *fig. sich et.* ~ spare o.s. s.th.; *j-m Arbeit (Kosten etc)* ~ save s.o. work (money etc); *ihr bleibt nichts erspart* she gets all the bad breaks.

Ersparnis [ɛr'ʃpaːrnɪs] *f* (-; -se) **1.** saving (*an dat* in). **2.** *pl* savings.

ersprießlich [ɛr'ʃpriːslɪç] *adj* fruitful, profitable.

erst [eːrst] *adv* a) (at) first, b) first, c) only, just, d) only, not till, not until: (*eben*) ~ just (now); ~ *als* (*dann, jetzt*) only when (then, now); ~ *nächste Woche* not before next week; ~ *nach* only (or not until) after; *es ist* ~ *fünf Uhr* it's only five o'clock; *ich muß* ~ *telefonieren* I've got to make a phone call first.

erstach [ɛr'ʃtaːx] *pret of* **erstechen.**

erstand [ɛr'ʃtant] *pret of* **erstehen.**

erstanden [ɛr'ʃtandən] *pp of* **erstehen.**

erstarken [ɛr'ʃtarkən] *v/i* (sn) grow strong(er).

er'starren *v/i* (sn) a) grow stiff, stiffen, go numb (*with cold*), b) 🜺 *etc* solidify, *blood*: coagulate, c) freeze (*a. fig. vor dat* with), *fig.* run cold: *vor Schreck* ~ a. be paralysed with fear. **er'starrt** *adj* stiff, numb, *fig.* paralysed. **Er'starrung** *f* (-; *no pl*) a) stiffness, numbness, b) 🜺 solidification, c) *fig.* paralysis, rigidity.

erstatten [ɛr'ʃtatən] *v/t* (h) **1.** refund (*j-m* to s.o.). **2.** *Anzeige* ~ *gegen* report s.o. to the police; → *Bericht.*

Er'stattung *f* (-; -en) refund(ing).

'Erstaufführung *f thea. etc* première, *film*: a. first run.

er'staunen *I* *v/t* (h) astonish, amaze. *II* *v/i* → **staunen** I. **Er'staunen** *n* (-s) astonishment, amazement: *in* ~ *setzen*

astonish, amaze; (*sehr*) *zu m-m* ~ (much) to my surprise. **er'staunlich** *adj* astonishing, amazing. **er'staunlicherweise** *adv* astonishingly, to my *etc* surprise (*or* amazement). **er'staunt** *adj* (*über acc* at) astonished, amazed.

'Erstausgabe *f* first edition.

'erst'beste *I* *adj the* first, F any (old). *II* *der* (*die*) ~ the first person one happens to see, just anyone; *das* ~ the next best (F any old) thing *etc.*

erste ['eːrstə] *adj* first: *Karl der* 2 (*Karl I.*) Charles the First (Charles I); ~ *Qualität* prime quality; *der* 2 *des Monats* the first (day) of the month; ~ *beste* → **erstbeste**; *als* ~(*r*), *als* ~ first; *er war der* ~ he was first; *er war der* ~, *der ...* he was the first to *inf*; *fürs* ~ for the moment; → **Blick** 1, **Geige, Hand, Hilfe** 1 *etc.*

er'stechen *v/t* (erstach, erstochen, h) stab *s.o.* (to death).

er'stehen (erstand, erstanden) *I* *v/i* (sn) rise, be built. *II* *v/t* (h) buy, get.

er'steigen *v/t* (erstieg, erstiegen, h) climb (up to), ascend.

er'steigern *v/t* (h) buy at an auction.

Er'steigung *f* (-; -en) ascent, climbing.

er'stellen *v/t* (h) **1.** erect, build. **2.** prepare, draw up (*report etc*).

erstemal ['eːrstəmaːl] *adv das* ~ the first time; *beim erstenmal* the first time; *zum erstenmal* for the first time.

erstens ['eːrstəns] *adv* first(ly), first of all.

'erster → **erste.**

erstere ['eːrstərə] *adj the* former.

'erstgeboren *adj* first-born.

'Erstgeburtsrecht *n* birthright.

'erstgenannt *adj* first-mentioned.

ersticken [ɛr'ʃtɪkən] *I* *v/t* (h) suffocate, choke, a. smother, stifle: → **Keim** 1. *II* *v/i* (sn) suffocate (*durch, an dat* from): *an e-r Gräte* ~ choke (to death) on a bone; *fig. in Arbeit* ~ be swamped with work. **Er'sticken** *n* (-s) suffocation: *zum* ~ (*heiß*) stifling(ly) hot. **er'stickend** *adj a. fig.* stifling. **Er'stickung** *f* (-; *no pl*) suffocation. **Er'stickungs|anfall** *m* choking fit. ~**tod** *m* death from suffocation.

erstieg [ɛr'ʃtiːk] *pret of* **ersteigen.**

erstiegen [ɛr'ʃtiːgən] *pp of* **ersteigen.**

'erstklassig *adj* first-class, first-rate, top-quality (*goods etc*).

Erstling ['e:rstlɪŋ] *m* (-s; -e) **1.** first-born child. **2.** *fig.* first work.

erstmalig ['e:rstma:lɪç] **I** *adj* first. **II** *adv*, **a. 'erstmals** for the first time.

'Erstmeldung *f* exclusive report, F scoop.

erstochen [ɛr'ʃtɔxən] *pp of* **erstechen.**

er'strahlen *v/i* (sn) shine.

erstrangig ['e:rstraŋɪç] *adj* first-rate.

er'streben *v/t* (h) strive after, aim for.

er'strebenswert *adj* desirable.

er'strecken: sich ~ a) (*bis zu* to) extend, stretch, b) *fig.* (*über acc*) cover (*area etc*), c) *fig.* (*auf acc*) concern, apply to.

'Erstschlag *m* ✗ first strike.

er'stürmen *v/t* (h) (take by) storm.

Er'stürmung *f* (-; -en) storming.

'Erstwähler(in *f*) *m* first-time voter.

er'suchen *v/t* (h) *j-n ~ zu inf* ask (or request) s.o. to *inf*; *j-n um et. ~* request s.th. from s.o. **Er'suchen** *n* (-s; -) (*auf sein ~ hin* at his) request.

er'tappen *v/t* (h) catch (*bei* at): *j-n beim Stehlen ~* catch s.o. stealing.

er'teilen *v/t* **1.** give (*lessons, advice, etc*): ✝ *j-m e-n Auftrag ~* place an order with s.o.; *j-m das Wort ~* ask s.o. to speak. **2.** (*dat*) grant (*s.o. a patent etc*), confer (*a right etc on s.o.*).

Ertrag [ɛr'tra:k] *m* (-[e]s; ~e) **1.** yield, ✗ *etc* output. **2.** (*aus* from) proceeds, returns.

er'tragen *v/t* (ertrug, ertragen, h) a) endure, bear, stand, b) put up with: *das ist kaum noch zu ~* that is hardly bearable; *ich kann den Gedanken nicht ~, daß ...* I can't bear to think that ...

er'tragfähig *adj* **1.** 🌱 productive. **2.** ✝ profit-yielding.

erträglich [ɛr'trɛ:klɪç] **I** *adj* bearable, tolerable. **II** *adv* tolerably well.

er'tragreich *adj* productive, profitable.

Er'tragslage *f* ✝ profit situation.

er'tränken *v/t* (h) drown (*sich* o.s.).

er'träumen *v/t* (h) *sich et. ~* dream of.

er'trinken *v/i* (ertrank, ertrunken, sn) drown, be drowned.

ertrug [ɛr'tru:k] *pret of* **ertragen.**

Ertüchtigung [ɛr'tʏçtɪɡʊŋ] *f* (-; -en) physical training.

erübrigen [ɛr'ʔy:brɪɡən] (h) **I** *v/t* save (*money*), spare (*time*). **II** *sich ~* be unnecessary, be superfluous.

eruieren [eru'i:rən] *v/t* (h) find out.

Eruption [erʊp'tsĭo:n] *f* (-; -en) eruption.

er'wachen *v/i* (sn) wake up (*a. fig.*), awake, *fig. feelings etc*: be awakened, *suspicion etc*: be aroused. **Er'wachen** *n* (-s) (*fig. unsanftes ~* rude) awakening.

er'wachsen¹ *v/i* (erwuchs, erwachsen, sn) arise (*aus* from).

er'wachsen² *adj*, **Er'wachsene** *m*, *f* (-n; -n) grown-up, adult. **Er'wachsenenbildung** *f* adult education.

erwägen [ɛr'vɛ:ɡən] *v/t* (erwog, erwogen, h) consider, think *s.th.* over: *den Kauf e-s Autos ~* consider buying a car. **Er'wägung** *f* (-; -en) (*et. in ~ ziehen* take s.th. into) consideration.

er'wähnen *v/t* (h) mention.

er'wähnenswert *adj* worth mentioning.

Er'wähnung *f* (-; -en) mention.

erwarb [ɛr'varp] *pret of* **erwerben.**

er'wärmen (h) **I** *v/t* warm (up): *fig. j-n für et. ~* get s.o. interested in s.th. **II** *sich ~* get warm(er); *fig. sich für et. ~* warm to s.th.

er'warten *v/t* (h) a) expect, b) wait for: *fig. j-n ~ surprise etc*: be in store for s.o.; *ein Kind ~* be expecting (a baby); *ich kann es kaum ~ (zu inf)* I can hardly wait (to *inf*); *das war zu ~* that was to be expected. **Er'warten** *n* (-s) *über alles ~* beyond all expectation; *wider ~* contrary to all expectations.

Er'wartung *f* (-; -en) a) expectation, b) expectancy, anticipation: *in ~* (*gen*) awaiting; *den* (*j-s*) *~en entsprechen* come up to (s.o.'s) expectations; *hinter den* (*j-s*) *~en zurückbleiben* fall short of (s.o.'s) expectations.

er'wartungsgemäß *adv* as expected.

Er'wartungs|haltung *f* expectancy, expectations. *~hori,zont m* (-[e]s; *no pl*) horizon of expectations.

er'wartungsvoll *adj* expectant.

er'wecken *v/t* **1.** *a. fig. wieder zum Leben ~* revive. **2.** *fig.* arouse (*interest, suspicion, etc*), bring back (*memories*), raise (*hopes*), inspire (*trust*): → *Anschein, Eindruck* 1 *etc.*

er'wehren: sich ~ (h) (*gen*) ward off, resist; *sich nicht ~ können* (*gen*) be helpless against; *man konnte sich des Eindrucks nicht ~, daß ...* you couldn't help feeling that ...

er'weichen *v/t* (h) soften, *fig. a.* move: *sich ~ lassen* give in.

er'weisen (erwies, erwiesen, h) **I** v/t **1.** prove, show. **2.** do (*a good turn etc*), grant (*a favo[u]r*), show (*respect*): → **Ehre. II** *sich* ~ *als* prove (*or turn out*) to be; *sich (j-m gegenüber) dankbar* ~ show one's gratitude (towards s.o.).

erweitern [ɛr'vaɪtərn] (h) **I** v/t widen (*road etc*), extend (*building, business, etc, a. fig. powers etc*), enlarge (*book*), broaden (*knowledge, etc*), 🖋 dilate. **II** *sich* ~ a) a. fig. widen, expand, b) 🖋 dilate. **Er'weiterung** f (-; -en) widening (*etc*), extension, enlargement, 🖋 dilatation.

Erwerb [ɛr'vɛrp] m (-[e]s; -e) acquisition, purchase. **er'werben** v/t (erwarb, erworben, h) a) acquire (*a. fig. rights, knowledge, etc*), purchase, b) earn, *fig.* gain, win (*fame, wealth, etc*): *sich Verdienste* ~ *um* render great service(s) to.

er'werbsfähig adj fit for work: *im* ~*en Alter* of employable age. **Er'werbsfähigkeit** f (-; *no pl*) ability to work. **Er'werbsleben** n working life.

er'werbslos = **arbeitslos. Er'werbsminderung** f (-; *no pl*) reduction in earning capacity. **Er'werbsquelle** f source of income. **er'werbstätig** adj (gainfully) employed. **Er'werbstätige** m, f (-n; -n) employed person. **Er'werbstätigkeit** f gainful employment. **er'werbsunfähig** adj unfit for work. **Er'werbsunfähigkeit** f incapacity to work. **Er'werbszweig** m a) branch of industry, b) line (of business). **Er'werbung** f (-; -en) acquisition.

erwidern [ɛr'vi:dərn] v/t (h) **1.** (*auf acc* to) reply, answer: *auf m-e Frage erwiderte er ...* in reply to my question he said ... **2.** return (*greeting, visit, etc,* ✕ *fire*). **Er'widerung** f (-; -en) **1.** (*auf acc* to) reply, answer. **2.** *fig.* return.

erwies [ɛr'vi:s] *pret,* **erwiesen** [ɛr'vi:zən] *pp of* **erweisen. er'wiesenermaßen** *adv* as has been proved.

er'wirken v/t (h) obtain, secure.

er'wirtschaften v/t (h) make (*profit*).

er'wischen v/t (h) catch (*a. fig.*): *sich* ~ *lassen* get caught; F *ihn hat's bös erwischt!* he's got it bad!

erwog [ɛr'vo:k] *pret of* **erwägen.**

erwogen [ɛr'vo:gən] *pp of* **erwägen.**

erworben [ɛr'vɔrbən] *pp of* **erwerben.**

erwuchs [ɛr'vu:ks] *pret of* **erwachsen¹.**

erwünscht [ɛr'vʏnʃt] adj a) desired, b) welcome, c) desirable.

er'würgen v/t (h) strangle.

Erz [e:rts] n (-es; -e) ore.

er'zählen (h) **I** v/t tell, narrate: *man hat mir erzählt* I've been told; *man erzählt sich* they say; F *das kannst du mir nicht* ~*!* pull another one! **II** v/i tell a story (*or stories*): ~ *von,* ~ *über* (*acc*) tell (s.o.) of (*or about*); *erzähl mal!* do tell! **er'zählenswert** adj worth telling. **Er'zähler** m (-s; -), **Er'zählerin** f (-; -nen) **1.** narrator, storyteller. **2.** narrative writer. **Er'zählung** f (-; -en) a) narration, story, tale, b) account, c) *literature:* (short) story.

Erzbischof [ˈɛrts-] m archbishop. **'erzbischöflich** adj archiepiscopal. **'Erzbistum** n, **'Erzdiö,zese** f archbishopric. **'Erzengel** m archangel.

er'zeugen v/t (h) produce, ☉ a. make, ✒ a. grow, 🐄, *phys.* generate, *fig.* a. cause, create. **Er'zeuger** m (-s; -) **1.** father. **2.** producer, a. ☉ manufacturer, ✒ a. grower. **Er'zeugerland** n country of origin. **Er'zeugnis** n (-ses; -se) product (*a. fig.*), ✒ *usu. pl* produce, (*novel etc*) production: *eigenes* ~ my etc own make. **Er'zeugung** f (-; *no pl*) production, ☉ a. manufacture, 🐄, *phys.* generation, *fig.* creation. **Er'zeugungskosten** pl production costs.

'Erzfeind m archenemy. **'Erzfeindschaft** f archrivalry, deadly feud. **'Erzherzog** m archduke.

'Erzherzogin f archduchess.

'Erzhütte f smelting works.

er'ziehbar adj educable: *schwer* ~*es Kind* problem child. **er'ziehen** v/t (erzog, erzogen, h) a) bring *s.o.* up, raise, b) educate: *j-n zu et.* ~ train (*or teach*) s.o. to be (*or do*) s.th.; → **erzogen. Er'zieher** m (-s; -) a) educator, b) teacher, c) tutor. **Er'zieherin** f (-; -nen) a) (lady) teacher, b) nursery-school teacher, c) governess. **er'zieherisch** adj educational. **Er'ziehung** f (-; *no pl*) **1.** a) upbringing, b) education, c) training. **2.** a) breeding, b) manners. **Er'ziehungs|anstalt** f approved (*Am.* reform) school. ~**berater(in** f) m educational adviser. ~**beratung** f child guidance. ~**berechtigte** m, f (-n; -n) a) parent, b) (legal) guardian. ~**wis-**

senschaft *f* (-; *no pl*) educational science.

er'zielen *v/t* (h) a) obtain, get, achieve (*success etc*), b) reach (*an agreement etc*), c) make (*a profit*), fetch (*a prize*), d) *sports*: score (*goals, points*).

er'zittern *v/i* (sn) tremble.

'erzkonserva,tiv *adj* ultra-conservative.

erzog [ɛr'tso:k] *pret of* **erziehen.**

erzogen [ɛr'tso:gən] **I** *pp of* **erziehen. II** *adj* **gut ~** well-bred; **schlecht ~** ill-bred.

er'zürnen (h) **I** *v/t* anger, infuriate. **II** **sich ~** get angry (**über** *acc* at).

er'zürnt *adj* angry, furious.

erzwungen [ɛr'tsvʊŋən] *pp of* **erzwingen.**

es [ɛs] *pers pron* a) it, b) he, she: **ich bin ~!** it's me!; **bist du ~?** is it you?; **~ gibt** there is, there are; **ich hoffe ~** I hope so; **ich weiß ~ (nicht)** I (don't) know; **er kann nicht schwimmen, aber ich kann ~** he can't swim, but I can; **du bist müde, ich bin ~ auch** you are tired, so am I; **ich will ~** I want to; **ich will ~ versuchen** I'll try; **~ wurde getanzt** there was dancing, we (they) danced.

Es *n* (-; -) ♪ E flat.

Esche ['ɛʃə] *f* (-; -n) ♀ ash (tree).

Esel ['e:zəl] *m* (-s; -) **1.** donkey, jackass. **2.** F *fig.* (silly) ass: **alter ~** old fool.

Eselin *f* (-; -nen) she-ass.

'Eselsbrücke *f* F mnemonic (aid): **j-m e-e ~ bauen** give s.o. a hint.

Eskalation [ɛskala'tsĭo:n] *f* (-; -en) escalation. **eskalieren** [ɛska'li:rən] *v/i, v/t* (h) escalate.

Eskapade [ɛska'pa:də] *f* (-; -n) escapade.

Eskimo ['ɛskimo] *m* (-s; -s) Eskimo.

Eskorte [ɛs'kɔrtə] *f* (-; -n) escort. **eskortieren** [ɛskɔr'ti:rən] *v/t* (h) escort.

Espe ['ɛspə] *f* (-; -n) ♀ asp. **'Espenlaub** *n* **zittern wie ~** tremble like an aspen leaf.

Espresso [ɛs'prɛso] *m* (-[s]; -s) espresso.

Esprit [ɛs'pri:] *m* (-s; *no pl*) wit.

Essay ['ɛsə] *m* (-s; -s) essay (**über** *acc* on). **Essayist** [ɛsɛ'ɪst] *m* (-en; -en), **Essay'istin** *f* (-; -nen) essayist.

'eßbar *adj* a) eatable, b) edible: **~er Pilz** (edible) mushroom.

'Eßbesteck *n* cutlery (set).

Esse ['ɛsə] *f* (-; -n) **1.** chimney. **2.** forge.

essen ['ɛsən] *v/t, v/i* (aß, gegessen, h) eat: *et.* **gern ~** like; **man ißt dort ganz**

gut the food is quite good there; → **Abend, Mittag** *etc.*

'Essen *n* (-s; -) **1.** *no pl* eating. **2.** a) food, b) dish, c) meal, d) dinner (party): **~ und Trinken** food and drink. **~marke** *f* meal ticket, *Br. a.* luncheon voucher.

'Essenszeit *f* mealtime, *n.s.* lunchtime, dinnertime.

Essenz [ɛ'sɛnts] *f* (-; -en) *a. fig.* essence.

'Esser *m* (-s; -) eater: → **stark** 1.

'Eßgeschirr *n* crockery, dinner service.

'Eßgewohnheiten *pl* eating habits.

Essig ['ɛsɪç] *m* (-s; -e) vinegar: F **damit ist es ~!** it's all off! **'Essiggurke** *f* gherkin. **'Essigsäure** *f* acetic acid.

'Essig- und 'Ölständer *m* cruet stand.

'Eßka,stanie *f* (sweet) chestnut. **'Eßlöffel** *m* tablespoon: **zwei ~** two tablespoonfuls. **'Eßlo,kal** *n* restaurant. **'Eßstäbchen** *pl* chopsticks. **'Eßtisch** *m* dining table. **'Eßwaren** *pl* food. **'Eßzimmer** *n* dining room.

Estragon ['ɛstragɔn] *m* (-s; *no pl*) ♀ tarragon.

etablieren [eta'bli:rən] **sich ~** (h) a) *a. fig.* establish o.s., become established, b) set (o.s.) up (**als** as), start a business.

Etablissement [etablɪs(ə)'mã:] *n* (-s; -s) establishment.

Etage [e'ta:ʒə] *f* (-; -n) floor, stor(e)y. **E'tagen,bett** *n* bunk bed. **~heizung** *f* single-stor(e)y heating (system). **~wohnung** *f* flat, *Am.* apartment.

Etappe [e'tapə] *f* (-; -n) *a. sports*: stage, leg: **in ~n** in stages.

Etat [e'ta:] *m* (-s; -s) budget. **E'tatansatz** *m* budgetary estimate. **E'tatentwurf** *m* draft budget. **E'tatjahr** *n* fiscal year.

e'tatmäßig *adj* a) budgetary (*expenditure*), b) permanent (*civil servant*).

etepetete [e:təpe'te:tə] *adj* F **1.** la-di-da. **2.** fussy, finicky.

Ethik ['e:tɪk] *f* (-; -en) ethics.

ethisch ['e:tɪʃ] *adj* ethical.

ethnisch ['ɛtnɪʃ] *adj* ethnic.

Ethnographie [ɛtnogra'fi:] *f* (-; -n) ethnography. **ethnographisch** [ɛtno'gra:fɪʃ] *adj* ethnographic.

Ethnologe [ɛtno'lo:gə] *m* (-n; -n) ethnologist. **Ethnologie** [ɛtnolo'gi:] *f* (-; -n) ethnology.

Ethos ['e:tɔs] *n* (-; *no pl*) ethos, *w.s.* ethics.

Etikett [eti'kɛt] *n* (-[e]s; -e) **1.** label. **2.**

price tag. **Etikette** [eti'kɛtə] f (-; -n) (*Verstoß gegen die* ~ breach of) etiquette. **etikettieren** [etikɛ'ti:rən] v/t (h) put a label on, *fig.* label.

etliche ['ɛtliçə] *indef pron pl* several: ~s a number of things.

'etlichemal *adv* several times.

Etmal ['ɛtma:l] n (-[e]s; -e) ♩ run.

Etüde [e'ty:də] f (-; -n) ♩ étude.

Etui [et'vi:] n (-s; -s) case.

etwa ['ɛtva] *adv* **1.** *a.* in ~ about, approximately, F around; *in* ~ *dasselbe* more or less the same; *wann* ~? approximately when?, *a.* F around what time? **2.** a) by any chance, b) for instance, (let's) say: *nicht* ~, *daß* ... not that *it mattered etc*; *ist das* ~ *besser?* is that any better?; *du glaubst doch nicht* ~ ...? surely you don't think ...?

etwaig ['ɛtva:iç] *adj* any.

etwas ['ɛtvas] **I** *indef pron* something, anything: ~ *anderes* something (anything) else. **II** *adj* some, any, a little: *ich brauche* ~ *Geld* I need some money. **III** *adv* a little: *es erscheint* ~ *merkwürdig* it seems a bit funny.

'Etwas n (-; -) something: F *das gewisse* ~ the certain something.

Etymologie [etymolo'gi:] f (-; -n) etymology. **etymologisch** [etymo'lo:gɪʃ] *adj* etymological.

euch [ɔʏç] *pers pron* (to) you, *reflexive*: yourselves; *after prep*: you: *setzt* ~! sit down!

Eucharistie [ɔʏçarıs'ti:] f (-; -n) *the* Eucharist.

euer ['ɔʏər] **I** *adj* **1.** your: *eu(e)re Mutter* your mother; *unser und* ~ *Haus* our house and yours. **2.** *der* (*die, das*) *eu(e)re* yours. **II** *pers pron* (*gen of ihr*) of you.

Eugenik [ɔʏ'ge:nɪk] f (-; *no pl*) eugenics.

Eule ['ɔʏlə] f (-; -n) owl: *fig.* ~*n nach Athen tragen* carry coals to Newcastle.

Eunuch [ɔʏ'nu:x] m (-en; -en) eunuch.

Euphemismus [ɔʏfe'mɪsmʊs] m (-; -men) euphemism. **euphemistisch** [ɔʏfe'mɪstɪʃ] *adj* euphemistic.

Euphorie [ɔʏfo'ri:] f (-; -n) euphoria.

eure ['ɔʏrə] → *euer*. **'eurerseits** *adv* for (or on) your part. **'eures'gleichen** *pron* people like yourselves, *contp.* the likes of you. **'eurethalben**, **'euretwe-**

gen, (*um*) **'euretwillen** *adv* a) because of you, b) for your sake.

Eurhythmie [ɔʏryt'mi:] f (-; *no pl*) eurhythmics.

eurig ['ɔʏrɪç] → *euer*.

Europa [ɔʏ'ro:pa] n (-s) Europe. **Europäer** [ɔʏro'pɛ:ər] m (-s; -), **Euro'päerin** f (-; -nen) European. **euro'päisch** *adj* European: *Europäische Gemeinschaft* (*abbr.* **EG**) European (Economic) Community (*abbr.* E[E]C).

Eu'ropa|meister(in f) m *sports*: European champion. ~**meisterschaft** f European championships. ~**po,kal** m European cup. ~**poli,tik** f Euro-politics. ~**rat** m (-[e]s; *no pl*) Council of Europe.

Euroscheck ['ɔʏro-] m Eurocheque.

Eurovisi'on f TV Eurovision.

Euter ['ɔʏtər] n (-s; -) udder.

Euthanasie [ɔʏtana'zi:] f (-; *no pl*) euthanasia.

evakuieren [evaku'i:rən] v/t (h) a. ✗ *and phys.* evacuate.

Evaku'ierung f (-; -en) evacuation.

evangelisch [evaŋ'ge:lɪʃ] *adj* Protestant. **Evangelist** [evaŋge'lɪst] m (-en; -en) evangelist. **Evangelium** [evaŋ'ge:liʊm] n (-s; -lien) gospel (*a. fig.*): *das* ~ *des Matthäus* the Gospel according to St. Matthew.

'Evasko,stüm ['efa:s-] n F *im* ~ in the nude.

Eventualität [evɛntuali'tɛ:t] f (-; -en) eventuality. **eventuell** [evɛn'tʊɛl] **I** *adj* possible. **II** *adv* a) possibly, b) if necessary, c) should the occasion arise.

evident [evi'dɛnt] *adj* obvious.

Evolution [evolu'tsio:n] f (-; -en) evolution.

ewig ['e:vɪç] **I** *adj* **1.** eternal, everlasting: ~*er Schnee* perpetual snow; *die* 2e *Stadt* (*Rome*) the Eternal City; *seit* ~*en Zeiten* from time immemorial, F for ages. **2.** F eternal, constant, endless. **II** *adv* **3.** eternally, forever: *auf immer und* ~ for ever and ever; F *es ist* ~ *schade* it's just too bad; ~ (*lange*) for ages; *es dauert* ~ it's taking ages.

'Ewigkeit f (-; -en) eternity: *bis in alle* ~ to the end of time; F *es ist e-e* ~, *seit* ... it's ages since ...; *ich habe e-e* ~ *gewartet* I've waited for ages.

Ex... [ɛks...] ex-...

exakt [ɛ'ksakt] *adj* precise, exact: **~e Wissenschaften** exact sciences.

Ex'aktheit *f* (-; *no pl*) precision.

Examen [ɛ'ksa:mən] *n* (-s; -) examination, F exam: **(s)ein ~ machen** take one's exams.

exekutieren [ɛkseku'ti:rən] *v/t* (h) execute. **Exekution** [ɛkseku'tsio:n] *f* (-; -en) execution.

exekutiv [ɛkseku'ti:f] *adj*, **Exekutive** [ɛkseku'ti:və] *f* (-; -n) executive.

Exeku'tivgewalt *f* executive power.

Exempel [ɛ'ksɛmpəl] *n* (-s; -) **ein ~ statuieren** set a warning example.

Exemplar [ɛksɛm'pla:r] *n* (-s; -e) **1.** specimen, sample. **2.** a) copy (*of book*), b) number, issue (*of magazine etc*).

exem'plarisch I *adj* exemplary. **II** *adv* **j-n ~ bestrafen** make an example of s.o.

exerzieren [ɛksɛr'tsi:rən] *v/t, v/i* (h) ✗ drill.

Exhibitionismus [ɛkshibitsio'nɪsmʊs] *m* (-; *no pl*) exhibitionism, ⚖ indecent exposure. **Exhibitionist** [-'nɪst] *m* (-en; -en) exhibitionist.

exhumieren [ɛkshu'mi:rən] *v/t* (h) exhume.

Exil [ɛ'ksi:l] *n* (-s; -e) (**im ~** in) exile: **ins ~ gehen** go into exile.

E'xilre,gierung *f* government in exile.

Existentialismus [ɛksɪstɛntsia'lɪsmʊs] *m* (-; *no pl*) existentialism. **Existentialist** [-'lɪst] *m* (-en; -en), **existentialistisch** [-'lɪstɪʃ] *adj* existentialist.

existentiell [ɛksɪstɛn'tsiɛl] *adj* **1.** existential. **2.** **von ~er Bedeutung** vitally important.

Existenz [ɛksɪs'tɛnts] *f* (-; -en) **1.** a) existence, b) livelihood: **gesicherte ~** secure position. **2.** *contp*. character: → **verkracht** 2. **~angst** *f psych*. existential anxiety, *w.s.* economic fears. **~berechtigung** *f* **1.** right to exist. **2.** raison d'être. **~kampf** *m* struggle for existence. **~minimum** *n* subsistence level.

existieren [ɛksɪs'ti:rən] *v/i* (h) **1.** exist, be: **nur wenige ~ noch** there are only a few left. **2.** (**von** on) exist, live.

Exitus ['ɛksitʊs] *m* (-; *no pl*) 💊 exitus, death.

exklusiv [ɛksklu'zi:f] *adj* exclusive.

Exklu'sivbericht *m* exclusive (story).

Exklu'sivrechte *pl* exclusive rights.

exkommunizieren [ɛkskɔmuni'tsi:rən] *v/t* (h) excommunicate.

Exkrement [ɛkskre'mɛnt] *n* (-[e]s; -e) excrement.

Exkursion [ɛkskʊr'zio:n] *f* (-; -en) excursion, field trip.

exmatrikulieren [ɛksmatriku'li:rən] *v/t* (h) **j-n (sich) ~** take s.o.'s (one's) name off the (university) register.

Exodus ['ɛksodʊs] *m* (-; *no pl*) exodus.

Exot [ɛ'kso:t] *m* (-en; -en), **E'xotin** *f* (-; -nen) exotic. **e'xotisch** *adj* exotic.

Expander [ɛks'pandər] *m* (-s; -) *sports*: expander.

Expansion [ɛkspan'zio:n] *f* (-; -en) expansion.

Expansi'onspoli,tik *f* expansionism.

expedieren [ɛkspe'di:rən] *v/t* (h) dispatch. **Expedition** [ɛkspedi'tsio:n] *f* (-; -en) **1.** expedition. **2.** ✝ forwarding (department).

Experiment [ɛksperi'mɛnt] *n* (-[e]s; -e) experiment. **Experimental...** [ɛksperimɛn'ta:l-], **experimentell** [-'tɛl] *adj* experimental. **experimentieren** [-'ti:rən] *v/i* (h) experiment (**an dat** on, **mit** with).

Experte [ɛks'pɛrtə] *m* (-n; -n) expert. **Expertise** [ɛkspɛr'ti:zə] *f* (-; -n) **1.** expertise. **2.** expert's opinion.

explodieren [ɛksplo'di:rən] *v/i* (sn) explode. **Explosion** [ɛksplo'zio:n] *f* (-; -en) explosion, blast.

explosi'onsartig *adj a. fig.* explosive.

Explosi'onsgefahr *f* danger of explosion. **~kraft** *f* explosive force.

explosiv [ɛksplo'zi:f] *adj* explosive.

Exponat [ɛkspo'na:t] *n* (-[e]s; -e) exhibit.

Exponent [ɛkspo'nɛnt] *m* (-en; -en) ⅍, *a. fig.* exponent.

exponieren [ɛkspo'ni:rən] *v/t* (h) expose (**sich** o.s.). **expo'niert** *adj* exposed.

Export [ɛks'pɔrt] *m* (-[e]s; -e) **1.** *no pl* exportation, exporting. **2.** exports.

Ex'port|abteilung *f* export department. **~ar,tikel** *m* export article (*or* item), *pl a.* exports. **~ausführung** *f* export model. **Exporteur** [ɛkspɔr'tø:r] *m* (-s; -e) exporter. **Ex'portgeschäft** *n*, **Ex'porthandel** *m* export trade. **exportieren** [ɛkspɔr'ti:rən] *v/t* (h) export (**nach** to).

Ex'portland *n* exporting country.

Ex'portleiter *m* export manager.

Exposé [ɛkspo'ze:] *n* (-s; -s) exposé.

expreß [ɛks'prɛs] *adv* ~ *schicken* send express (*Am.* by special delivery).

Expressionismus [ɛksprɛsĭo'nɪsmʊs] *m* (-; *no pl*) expressionism. **Expressionist** [-'nɪst] *m* (-en; -en), **expressionistisch** [-'nɪstɪʃ] *adj* expressionistic.

extern [ɛks'tɛrn] *adj* external.

extra ['ɛkstra] **I** *adj* extra. **II** *adv* a) extra, *a.* separately, b) specially, c) F on purpose: ~ *für dich* just for you.

'**Extra** *n* (-s; -s) extra. ~**blatt** *n* extra.

extrahieren [ɛkstra'hi:rən] *v/t* (h), **Extrakt** [ɛks'trakt] *m* (-[e]s; -e) extract.

extravagant [ɛkstrava'gant] *adj* flamboyant.

extravertiert [ɛkstravɛr'ti:rt] *adj* (*a.* ~*er Mensch*) extrovert.

extrem [ɛks'tre:m] *adj* extreme.

Ex'trem *n* (-s; -e) extreme. **Extremismus** [ɛkstre'mɪsmʊs] *m* (-; *no pl*) extremism. **Extremist** [-'mɪst] *m* (-en; -en), **extre'mistisch** *adj* extremist.

Extremitäten [ɛkstremi'tɛːtən] *pl* extremities.

extrover'tiert [ɛkstro-] → **extravertiert**.

Exzellenz [ɛktsɛ'lɛnts] *f* (-; -en) (*Eure, Seine* ~ your, his) Excellency.

Exzentriker [ɛks'tsɛntrɪkər] *m* (-s; -), **Ex'zentrikerin** *f* (-; -nen) eccentric.

ex'zentrisch [-trɪʃ] *adj a.* A, ⊕ eccentric.

Exzeß [ɛks'tsɛs] *m* (-sses; -sse) excess.

F

F, f [ɛf] *n* (-; -) F, f (*a.* ♪).

Fabel ['fa:bəl] *f* (-; -n) a) fable, *fig. a.* story, b) plot (*of drama etc*).

'**fabelhaft** *adj* fantastic.

Fabrik [fa'bri:k] *f* (-; -en) factory, works, mill. **Fa'brikanlage** *f* (manufacturing) plant. **Fabrikant** [fabri'kant] *m* (-en; -en) **1.** factory owner. **2.** manufacturer. **Fa'brikarbeit** *f* **1.** factory work. **2.** → **Fabrikware**. **Fa'brikarbeiter(in** *f*) *m* factory worker. **Fabrikat** [fabri'ka:t] *n* (-[e]s; -e) product, make. **Fabrikation** [fabrika'tsĭo:n] *f* (-; -en) production.

Fabrikati'ons|nummer *f* serial number. ~**pro,gramm** *n* production schedule.

Fa'brik|besitzer(in *f*) *m* factory owner. ~**gebäude** *n* factory building. ~**gelände** *n* factory site. 2**neu** *adj* brand-new. ~**schiff** *n* factory ship. ~**ware** *f* manufactured product(s).

fabrizieren [fabri'tsi:rən] *v/t* (h) **1.** manufacture, make, *fig.* concoct. **2.** *fig.* get up to.

Facette [fa'sɛtə] *f* (-; -n) facet.

Fa'cettenauge *n zo.* compound eye.

Fach [fax] *n* (-[e]s; ⸚er) **1.** a) compartment, partition, b) shelf. **2.** field, line: *er ist vom* ~ he is an expert; *das*

schlägt nicht in mein ~ that's not in my line. **3.** *ped., univ.* subject.

...**fach** *in cpds.* ...fold, times.

'**Fach|arbeit** *f* skilled work. ~**arbeiter(in** *f*) *m* skilled worker, *pl* skilled labo(u)r. ~**arzt** *m*, ~**ärztin** *f* specialist (*für* in). 2**ärztlich** *adj* (*adv* by a) specialist. ~**ausbildung** *f* special(ized) training. ~**ausdruck** *m* technical term. ~**bereich** *m* **1.** → **Fachgebiet**. **2.** *univ.* department. ~**buch** *n* specialist book.

Fächer ['fɛçər] *m* (-s; -) **1.** fan. **2.** *fig.* range, spectrum. '**fächerförmig** *adj* fan-like: *sich* ~ *ausbreiten* fan out. '**fächern** *v/t* (h) (*a. sich* ~) fan out.

'**Fach|frau** *f* (woman) expert. ~**gebiet** *n* (special) field. 2**gerecht** *adj* expert, professional. ~**geschäft** *n* specialist shop (*Am.* store). ~**handel** *m* specialized trade (*or* dealers). ~**hochschule** *f* college. ~**idi,ot** *m* F *contp.* specialist borné. ~**jar,gon** *m* technical jargon. ~**kenntnis(se** *pl*) *f* specialized knowledge, know-how. ~**kräfte** *pl* qualified personnel. ~**kreis** *m in* ~**en** among the experts. 2**kundig** *adj* competent, expert. ~**lehrer(in** *f*) *m* subject teacher. ~**leute** *pl* experts.

'**fachlich** *adj* technical, professional.

'Fachlitera,tur f specialized literature.
'Fachmann m (-[e]s; -leute) (*in dat* in, at, *für* on) expert, specialist.
fachmännisch ['faxmɛnɪʃ] adj expert, specialist, professional (*work*): **~es Urteil** expert opinion.
'Fach|perso,nal n qualified personnel.
~presse f trade press. **~richtung** f field. **~schule** f technical college.
Fachsimpelei [faxzɪmpə'laɪ] f (-; -en) F shoptalk. **'fachsimpeln** v/i (*insep, pp* gefachsimpelt, h) talk shop.
'Fach|sprache f technical language (*or* terminology). **~studium** n special(ized) studies. **~übersetzer(in** f) m specialized translator. **~verband** m professional (*or* trade) association. **~werk** n (-[e]s; *no pl*) half-timbering. **~werkhaus** n half-timbered house. **~wissen** n → **Fachkenntnis(se)**. **~wörterbuch** n specialized dictionary. **~zeitschrift** f (professional *or* trade) journal.
Fackel ['fakəl] f (-; -n) a. fig. torch.
'fackeln v/i (h) F *nicht lange* ~ waste no time.
fade ['fa:də] adj 1. tasteless, stale, flat (*beer*). 2. fig. boring, dull.
Faden ['fa:dən] m (-s; -) thread (*a. fig.*), ⚡, ❂ filament; ♯ stitch, string (*of puppets etc*): ♯ **die Fäden ziehen** remove the stitches; **der rote** ~ the thread (running through the story *etc*); **den** ~ **verlieren** lose the thread (of one's speech *etc*); **es hing an e-m** ~ it hang by a thread; **er hält alle Fäden in der Hand** he pulls the strings. **'Fadenkreuz** n opt. reticule. **'Fadennudeln** pl vermicelli.
fadenscheinig ['fa:dənʃaɪnɪç] adj threadbare, fig. a. flimsy (*excuse etc*).
Fagott [fa'gɔt] n (-[e]s; -e) ♪ bassoon.
Fagottist [fagɔ'tɪst] m (-en; -en), **Fagot'tistin** f (-; -nen) bassoonist.
fähig ['fɛ:ɪç] adj a) able, capable, b) gifted, talented, c) qualified: ~ **sein zu** be capable of; *b.s.* **zu allem** ~ capable of anything, desperate; (*dazu*) ~ **sein, et. zu tun** be capable of doing s.th., be able (*or* qualified) to do s.th.
'Fähigkeit f (-; -en) a) ability, capability, b) talent.
fahl [fa:l] adj pale, ashen (*face*).
Fähnchen ['fɛ:nçən] n (-s; -) 1. pennant, *sports*: marker. 2. F cheap, flimsy dress.
fahnden ['fa:ndən] v/i (h) ~ **nach** search

for. **'Fahnder** m (-s; -) investigator.
'Fahndung f (-; -en) search.
'Fahndungs|akti,on f (police) search.
~dienst m tracing and search department. **~liste** f wanted list.
Fahne ['fa:nə] f (-; -n) 1. flag, fig. banner, ⚓, ✗ colo(u)rs. 2. fig. *mit fliegenden* ~n with flying colo(u)rs. 2. F **e-e** ~ **haben** reek of the bottle. 3. print. galley (proof).
'Fahneneid m ✗ oath of allegiance.
'Fahnenflucht f (-; *no pl*) desertion.
'fahnenflüchtig adj ~ **sein** be a deserter; ~ **werden** desert.
'Fahnen|mast m, **~stange** f flagpole.
Fähnrich ['fɛ:nrɪç] m (-s; -e) ✗ cadet: ⚓ ~ **zur See** midshipman.
'Fahrausweis m ticket. **'Fahrbahn** f road, carriageway, lane. **'fahrbar** adj mobile. **'Fahrbereitschaft** f car pool.
Fähre ['fɛ:rə] f (-; -n) ferry.
'Fahreigenschaften pl mot. road performance.
fahren ['fa:rən] (fuhr, gefahren) **I** v/i (sn) 1. a) go (*mit* by bus, train, *etc*), ride (on bicycle, *etc*), mot. drive, ⚓ sail, b) run, c) leave, depart, go, d) be moving: *der Zug fährt zweimal am Tag* the train runs (*or* goes) twice a day; *über e-e Brücke* ~ cross a bridge; *rechts* ~! keep to the right!; *mit Diesel* ~ run on diesel, be diesel-driven; fig. *mit der Hand* ~ *über* (acc) run one's hand over; *in et.* ~ bullet, knife, *etc*: go into; *gut (schlecht)* ~ *bei* fare well (ill) with, do well (badly) by; *es (der Gedanke) fuhr mir durch den Kopf* it flashed through my mind; *was ist in ihn gefahren?* what has got into him?; F *e-n* ~ *lassen* fart, let go; → **Haut. II** v/t 2. (h) a) drive, b) take (*s.o. or s.th. somewhere*), transport, ⚓ sail. 3. (sn) drive, cover (*distance etc*), do: *das Auto fährt 150 km/h* the car does 150 km/h. 4. (h *or* sn) *sports*: make, clock (*ten minutes etc*): *ein Rennen* ~ participate in a race. 5. (h) ❂ a) work (*a shift*), b) run (*a line*), operate (*plant, unit*). 6. (h) TV run.
fahrend adj travel(l)ing, itinerant.
'Fahrer m (-s; -), **'Fahrerin** f (-; -nen) a) driver, b) chauffeur (chauffeuse).
'Fahrerflucht f ~ *begehen* commit a hit-and-run offen/ce (*Am.* -se).
'Fahrersitz m driver's seat.

'**Fahr|gast** *m* passenger, *of taxi*: fare. **~geld** *n* fare. **~gelegenheit** *f* (means of) transport(ation). **~gemeinschaft** *f* car pool. **~gestell** *n* **1.** *mot.* chassis, ✈ undercarriage. **2.** F (*legs*) pins.

fahrig ['faːrɪç] *adj* a) nervous, jumpy, b) inattentive.

'**Fahrkarte** *f* ticket (*nach* to).

'**Fahrkarten|auto,mat** *m* ticket machine. **~kon,trolle** *f* ticket inspection. **~kontrol,leur** *m* ticket inspector. **~schalter** *m* ticket office.

'**Fahrkom,fort** *m mot.* driving comfort.

'**fahrlässig** *adj* careless, *a.* ⚖ negligent; **~e Tötung** manslaughter (*Am.* in the second degree). '**Fahrlässigkeit** *f* (-; -en) carelessness, *a.* ⚖ negligence.

'**Fahrlehrer(in** *f*) *m* driving instructor.

'**Fährmann** *m* ferryman.

'**Fahrplan** *m* timetable (*a. fig.*), schedule. **~änderung** *f* change in the timetable.

'**fahrplanmäßig I** *adj* scheduled. **II** *adv* according to schedule, on time.

'**Fahr|praxis** *f* driving experience. **~preis** *m* fare. **~prüfung** *f* driving test. **~rad** *n* bicycle, F bike. **~rinne** *f* ⚓ lane. **~schein** *m* ticket. **~schule** *f* driving school. **~schüler(in** *f*) *m mot.* learner (driver). **~spur** *f* lane. **~stuhl** *m* lift, *Am.* elevator. **~stunde** *f* driving lesson.

'**Fahrt** [faːrt] *f* (-; -en) **1.** a) drive, ride, b) journey, trip, ⚓ *a.* voyage, cruise: *auf ~ gehen* go on a trip; *auf der ~ nach X* on the way to X; *gute ~!* have a good trip! **2.** speed (*a.* ⚓): *in voller ~* at full speed; *in ~ kommen* a) get under way, b) F *fig.* get going; F *j-n in ~ bringen* a) get s.o. going, b) make s.o. wild; F *in ~ sein* *person*: a) be going it strong, b) be wild.

'**Fahrtdauer** *f* length of the trip: *die ~ beträgt 3 Stunden* it will take 3 hours (to get there).

'**Fährte** ['fɛːrtə] *f* (-; -n) *a. fig.* trail, track: *fig. auf der falschen ~ sein* be on the wrong track.

'**Fahrtenbuch** *n mot.* logbook.

'**Fahrtenschreiber** *m mot.* tachograph.

'**Fahrtrichtungsanzeiger** *m mot.* direction indicator.

'**fahrtüchtig** *adj car*: roadworthy, *driver*: fit to drive.

'**Fahrtunterbrechung** *f* stop.

'**Fahrtwind** *m* airstream.

'**Fahr|verbot** *n j-n mit ~ belegen* sus-

pend s.o.'s driving licence (*Am.* driver's license). **~verhalten** *n mot.* road behavio(u)r. **~wasser** *n* (-s; *no pl*) **1.** → *Fahrrinne*. **2.** F *fig.* track: *im richtigen ~ sein* be in one's element. **~weise** *f* (way of) driving. **~werk** *n mot.* chassis, ✈ undercarriage. **~zeit** *f* → *Fahrtdauer*.

'**Fahrzeug** *n* (-[e]s; -e) vehicle, ⚓ vessel. **~brief** *m mot.* (vehicle) registration document. **~halter(in** *f*) *m* car owner. **~pa,piere** *pl* documents.

Faible ['fɛːbəl] *n* (-s; -s) → *Schwäche* 3.

fair [fɛːr] *adj* fair.

Fairneß ['fɛːrnɛs] *f* (-; *no pl*) fairness.

Fäkalien [fɛ'kaːliən] *pl* f(a)eces.

Fakir ['faːkɪr] *m* (-s; -e) fakir.

Faksimile [fak'ziːmile] *n* (-s; -s) facsimile.

faktisch ['faktɪʃ] *adj* actual(ly *adv*), *adv a.* in fact. **Faktor** ['faktɔr] *m* (-s; -ren [-'toːrən]) *a. biol.*, ⚑ factor. '**Faktum** *n* (-s; -ten) a) fact, b) *pl* facts, data.

fakturieren [faktu'riːrən] *v/t* (h) invoice. **Fakultät** [fakʊl'tɛːt] *f* (-; -en) *univ.* faculty, *esp. Am.* department.

fakultativ [fakʊlta'tiːf] *adj* optional.

Falke ['falkə] *m* (-n; -n) *zo.* falcon, *hunt. and pol. a.* hawk.

Fall [fal] *m* (-[e]s; ⸚e) **1.** fall (*a.* 🎾), ♱ *a.* drop, *fig.* downfall: *zu ~ bringen* a) *j-n* cause s.o. to fall, *in a fight or fig.* bring s.o. down, trip s.o. up, b) thwart (*plans etc*), defeat (*bill, motion, etc*); *fig. zu ~ kommen* fall, be ruined. **2.** case (*a.* ⚖, *ling.*, ♬), matter, affair: *auf alle Fälle* a) in any case, b) definitely, c) *a. für alle Fälle* just in case, to be on the safe side; *für den* (*or im*) *~, daß er kommt* in case he should come; *im ~e* (*gen*) in the event of; *gesetzt den ~* suppose, supposing; *in diesem ~* in that case; F *klarer ~!* sure (thing)!; *das ist* (*nicht*) *ganz mein ~* that's right up my street (not my cup of tea); *das ist auch bei ihr der ~* it's the same with her.

Falle ['falə] *f* (-; -n) trap (*a. fig.*), snare: *fig. j-m in die ~ gehen* walk into the trap set by s.o.; *j-m e-e ~ stellen* set a trap for s.o.

fallen ['falən] *v/i* (fiel, gefallen, sn) **1.** fall (*von* from, off), fall down, drop: *~ lassen a. fig.* let fall, drop; *von der Leiter ~* fall off a ladder; *ich bin gefallen* I had a fall; *er ließ sich in e-n Sessel ~* he dropped into a chair. **2.** ✕ fall, *soldier: a.* be killed (in action). **3.** *temperature, prices, etc:* fall, drop, go down. **4.** *name, remark, etc:* fall, *decision etc: a.* be made: *sein Name fiel auch* his name was mentioned too; *es fielen harte Worte* there were harsh words; *die Entscheidung ist noch nicht gefallen* the matter is still undecided. **5.** *sports:* goal *etc:* be scored: *die Entscheidung fiel in der letzten Minute* the decider came in the last minute. **6.** *Schüsse fielen* shots were fired. **7.** *obstacle etc:* be removed, go. **8. an j-n ~** *inheritance etc:* fall (*or* go) to s.o. **9. ~ auf** (*acc*) *a. fig.* fall on; *die Wahl fiel auf sie* she was chosen. **10. ~ unter** come under. **11. ~ in** (*acc*) fall into; *in Schlaf ~* fall asleep; *fig. j-m in den Arm ~* restrain s.o.; → *Ohnmacht* 2.

fällen ['fɛlən] *v/t* (h) **1.** cut down (*tree etc*). **2.** ⚖ *ein Urteil ~* (*über acc on*) pass sentence, *a. fig.* pass judg(e)ment; → *Entscheidung.*

'fallenlassen *v/t* (*irr, sep,* h, → *lassen*) drop (*plan, friend, hint, etc*).

'Fallgeschwindigkeit *f phys.* rate of fall. **'Fallgrube** *f* pit, *a. fig.* trap.

fällig ['fɛlɪç] *adj* ✝ due, payable: *längst ~* (long) overdue; *~ werden* a) become due (*or* payable), b) expire.

'Fälligkeit *f* (-; *no pl*) (*bei ~* at) maturity. **'Fallobst** *n* windfall.

Fallout ['fɔ:laʊt] *m* (-s; -s) *nucl.* fallout.

'Fallrückzieher *m soccer:* falling overhead kick.

falls [fals] *conj* if, in case: *~ nicht* unless.

'Fallschirm *m* parachute. **~absprung** *m* parachute jump (*or* descent). **~abwurf** *m* airdrop. **~jäger** *m* ✕ paratrooper. **~springen** *n* parachute jumping, *sports:* skydiving. **~springer(in** *f*) *m* parachutist, *sports:* skydiver.

'Fallstrick *m fig.* trap. **'Fallstudie** *f* case study. **'Falltreppe** *f* foldaway stairs. **'Falltür** *f* trapdoor.

falsch [falʃ] **I** *adj* **1.** a) wrong, b) untrue, *pred* not true: *~e Darstellung* misrepresentation. **2.** a) false, artificial, b) forged, fake(d), counterfeit: *~er Name* fictitious name. **3.** false, insincere. **II** *adv* **4.** wrongly, falsely (*etc*): *~ aussprechen* mispronounce; *~ gehen* *watch:*

be wrong; *~ geraten!* wrong guess!; *~ schreiben* misspell; *~ singen* sing out of tune; *~ spielen* cheat; *~ verbunden!* sorry, wrong number!; *~ verstehen* misunderstand.

'Falschaussage *f* ⚖ false testimony. **'Falscheid** *m* ⚖ false oath.

fälschen ['fɛlʃən] *v/t* (h) fake, forge, counterfeit, ✝ tamper with (*books etc*).

'Fälscher *m* (-s; -) forger, counterfeiter.

'Falschgeld *n* counterfeit money.

'Falschheit *f* (-; *no pl*) falseness.

fälschlich ['fɛlʃlɪç] **I** *adj* wrong, false. **II** *adv* → **'fälschlicherweise** *adv* a) wrongly, falsely, b) by mistake.

'Falschmeldung *f* false report, hoax.

'Falschmünzer [-mʏntsər] *m* (-s; -) counterfeiter.

'Falschspieler *m* cardsharper, cheat.

'Fälschung *f* (-; -en) **1.** forging, counterfeiting. **2.** fake, forgery.

'Faltbett *n* folding bed. **'Faltblatt** *n* leaflet. **'Faltboot** *n* folding canoe.

Fältchen ['fɛltçən] *n* (-s; -) wrinkle, *pl* crow's-feet.

Falte ['faltə] *f* (-; -n) a) fold, b) crease, c) pleat (*in skirt etc*), d) wrinkle, line (*in face*): *~n werfen* pucker.

fälteln ['fɛltəln] *v/t* (h) pleat.

falten ['faltən] *v/t* (h) a) fold, b) crease.

'Faltenrock *m* pleated skirt.

Falter ['faltər] *m* (-s; -) *zo.* butterfly.

faltig ['faltɪç] *adj* creased, *a.* wrinkled (*skin*), *a.* lined (*face*).

'Faltkarte *f* folding (*or* pull-out) map. **'Faltkar,ton** *m* collapsible cardboard box. **'Falttür** *f* folding door.

Falz [falts] *m* (-es; -e), **'falzen** *v/t* (h) **1.** fold. **2.** ⚙ rabbet.

familiär [fami'liɛːr] *adj* **1.** family (*affairs etc*). **2.** a) familiar, b) informal. **3.** *ling.* familiar, colloquial.

Familie [fa'mi:liə] *f* (-; -n) family: (*die*) *~ Miller* the Miller family; *e-e ~ gründen* start a family; *~ haben* have children; *es liegt in der ~* it runs in the family.

Fa'milien|angehörige *m, f* member of the family. **~angelegenheit** *f* family affair. **~anschluß** *m* *~ haben* live (there) as one of the family. **~betrieb** *m* family business (*or* farm). **~fest** *n* family celebration. **~gericht** *n* ⚖ family court. **~kreis** *m* family circle: *im engsten ~ celebrate etc* with the immediate family. **~leben** n family life. **~mitglied** n member of the family. **~name** m surname, last name. **~oberhaupt** n head of the family. **~packung** f family pack. **~planung** f family planning. **~ro,man** m roman fleuve. **~sinn** m (-[e]s; no pl) sense of family. **~stand** m (-[e]s; no pl) marital status. **~unterhalt** m upkeep of the family. **~vater** m 1. head of the family. 2. family man. **~verhältnisse** pl family background. **~zuwachs** m addition to the family.

Fan [fɛn] m (-s; -s) fan.

Fanatiker [faˈnaːtikər] m (-s; -), **Faˈnatikerin** f (-; -nen) fanatic. **fanatisch** [faˈnaːtɪʃ] adj fanatic(al). **Fanatismus** [fanaˈtɪsmʊs] m (-; no pl) fanaticism.

fand [fant] pret of **finden**.

Fanfare [fanˈfaːrə] f (-; -n) 1. fanfare. 2. mot. multitone horn.

Fang [faŋ] m (-[e]s; ⁓e) 1. a. fig. catch, haul. 2. zo. usu. pl a) claw, b) fang, tusk (of boar). **Fangarm** m zo. tentacle.

fangen [ˈfaŋən] (fing, gefangen, h) I v/t 1. catch, fig. a. trap: **sich ~ lassen** get caught; → **Feuer** 1. II **sich ~** 2. be caught. 3. catch o.s. stumbling etc. 4. fig. **sich (wieder) ~** rally (a. sports), recover, w.s. get a grip on o.s. (again).

Fangen n (-s) catch, Am. tag.

Fänger [ˈfɛŋər] m (-s; -) catcher.

Fangfrage f trick question.

Fangopackung [ˈfaŋgo-] f ✽ mud pack.

Fangzahn m zo. fang.

Fanklub m fan club.

Farbabzug m phot. colo(u)r print.

Farbaufnahme f colo(u)r photo.

Farbband n typewriter ribbon.

Farbe [ˈfarbə] f (-; -n) 1. a) colo(u)r, b) shade, c) paint, d) dye: **in** ~ TV in colo(u)r; → **leuchtend**. 2. complexion, colo(u)r. 3. cards: suit: ~ **bekennen** follow suit, fig. show one's true colo(u)rs. 4. pl colo(u)rs (of club etc).

farbecht adj colo(u)rfast, nonfading.

Färbemittel n dye.

färben [ˈfɛrbən] (h) I v/t 1. a) dye (hair, cloth), stain (glass, paper), b) tint, colo(u)r (a. fig.): **gefärbter Bericht** colo(u)red report. 2. lose colo(u)r, stain. II **sich ~** (leaves: change) colo(u)r: **sich rot etc** ~ turn red etc.

farbenblind adj colo(u)r-blind.

farben|freudig, ~froh adj colo(u)rful.

Farben(kunst)druck m colo(u)r plate.

Farbenlehre f theory of colo(u)rs.

farbenprächtig adj colo(u)rful.

Farbenskala f colo(u)r chart.

Farbenspiel n play of colo(u)rs.

Färber [ˈfɛrbər] m (-s; -) dyer.

Färberei [fɛrbəˈraɪ] f (-; -en) dyeworks.

Farb|fernsehen n colo(u)r television (or TV). **~fernseher** m, **~fernsehgerät** n colo(u)r television (or TV) set. **~film** m colo(u)r film. **~filter** n, m phot. colo(u)r filter. **~foto** n colo(u)r photo. **~fotogra,fie** f 1. colo(u)r photography. 2. colo(u)r photo.

farbig [ˈfarbɪç] adj colo(u)red (a. race), fig. colo(u)rful. **Farbige** m, f (-n; -n) colo(u)red person (or man, woman), nonwhite: **die ~n** the colo(u)reds, the colo(u)red people, the nonwhites.

Farbko,pierer m colo(u)r copier.

farblich adj colo(u)r, a. adv in colo(u)r.

farblos adj a. fig. colo(u)rless.

Farb|skala f colo(u)r chart. **~stift** m colo(u)red pencil, crayon. **~stoff** m ⊕ dye, in foods: colo(u)ring. **~ton** m hue, tint, shade, paint., phot. tone.

Färbung f (-; -en) colo(u)ring, hue.

Farbwiedergabe f colo(u)r fidelity.

Farbzusammenstellung f colo(u)r scheme.

Farce [ˈfarsə] f (-; -n) thea. burlesque, a. fig. farce.

Farm [farm] f (-; -en) farm.

Farmer [ˈfarmər] m (-s; -) farmer.

Farn [farn] m (-[e]s; -e), **~kraut** n ✿ fern.

Färse [ˈfɛrzə] f (-; -n) zo. heifer.

Fasan [faˈzaːn] m (-[e]s; -e) zo. pheasant.

Fasching [ˈfaʃɪŋ] m (-s; -e, -s) carnival.

Faschings... carnival...

Faschismus [faˈʃɪsmʊs] m (-; no pl) fascism. **Faschist** [faˈʃɪst] m (-en; -en), **Faˈschistin** f (-; -nen), **faschistisch** adj [faˈʃɪstɪʃ] fascist.

faseln [ˈfaːzəln] v/i (h) F drivel.

Faser [ˈfaːzər] f (-; -n) fibre, Am. fiber.

faserig adj fibrous, stringy (meat etc).

fasern [ˈfaːzərn] v/i (h) fray.

Faserplatte f fib/reboard (Am. -er-).

Faß [fas] n (Fasses; Fässer) a) barrel, b) vat, tub: **Bier vom** ~ → **Faßbier**; **(frisch) vom** ~ beer on tap (or draught), wine from the wood; fig. **das ist ein ~ ohne Boden** there is no end to it; **das**

schlägt dem ~ den Boden aus! that's the last straw!

Fassade [fa'sa:də] *f* (-; -n) façade, front.

Fas'sadenkletterer *m* cat burglar.

Fas'sadenreiniger *m* exterior cleaner.

'**faßbar** *adj* comprehensible: *schwer ~* difficult (to understand).

'**Faßbier** *n* draught beer.

Fäßchen ['fɛsçən] *n* (-s; -) keg.

fassen ['fasən] **I** *v/t* **1.** take hold of, grasp, seize, a. ⚙ grip: F *zu ~ kriegen* get hold of; *j-n an* (or *bei*) *der Hand ~* take s.o. by the hand. **2.** apprehend, catch (*criminal etc*). **3.** mount (*in silver etc*), set (*jewel*). **4.** a) *room etc*: hold, *a.* accommodate, seat (*persons*), b) contain. **5.** *fig.* grasp, understand, b) believe: *nicht zu ~* unbelievable, incredible. **6.** put, formulate: *et. in Worte ~* put s.th. into words. **7.** *e-n Gedanken ~* form an idea; → *Beschluß, Entschluß, Fuß* 1, *Plan* 1. **II** *v/i* **8.** ~ *an* (*acc*) touch; ~ *nach* grasp at. **III** *sich ~* **9.** regain one's composure, compose o.s.: → *gefaßt* 1. **10.** *sich kurz ~* be brief; *fasse dich kurz!* make it brief!; → *Geduld.*

'**faßlich** *adj* comprehensible: *leicht* (*schwer*) ~ easy (hard) to understand.

Fasson [fa'sõ:] *f* (-; -s) **1.** a) shape, b) cut: *fig. nach s-r* (*eigenen*) ~ after one's own fashion. b → **Fas'sonschnitt** *m* trim, short back and sides.

'**Fassung** *f* (-; -en) **1.** frame (*of spectacles*), socket (*of lamp*), setting (*of diamond etc*). **2.** a) formulation, b) text, wording, c) version (*of book, film, etc*). **3.** *no pl* composure: *j-n aus der ~ bringen* put s.o. out; *die ~ bewahren* keep one's head; *die ~ verlieren* lose one's composure (*or* temper); *s-e ~ wiedergewinnen* → *fassen* 9; *er war ganz außer ~* he was completely beside himself; → *ringen* I.

'**Fassungskraft** *f* (-; *no pl*) (powers of) comprehension, mental capacity.

'**fassungslos** *adj* stunned, speechless: ~ *vor Glück etc* beside o.s. with joy *etc*.

'**Fassungslosigkeit** *f* (-; *no pl*) shock.

'**Fassungsvermögen** *n* **1.** capacity. **2.** → *Fassungskraft.*

fast [fast] *adv* a) almost, nearly, b) hardly: ~ *nie* hardly ever.

fasten ['fastən] *v/i* (h) fast. '**Fasten** *n* (-s

fast(ing). '**Fastenkur** *f* starvation cure.

'**Fastentag** *m* day of fasting.

'**Fastenzeit** *f* Lent.

'**Fastnacht** *f* (-; *no pl*) **1.** Shrove Tuesday, Mardi gras. **2.** → *Fasching(s...).*

Faszination [fastsina'tsio:n] *f* (-; *no pl*) fascination. **faszinieren** [fastsi'ni:rən] *v/t* (h) fascinate.

fatal [fa'ta:l] *adj* **1.** fatal, disastrous. **2.** (very) awkward.

Fatalismus [fata'lɪsmʊs] *m* (-; *no pl*) fatalism. **Fatalist** [fata'lɪst] *m* (-en; -en) fatalist. **fata'listisch** *adj* fatalistic(ic).

fauchen ['fauxən] *v/i* (h) snarl, *cat*: hiss.

faul [faul] *adj* **1.** a) rotten, bad (*egg, tooth, etc*), b) putrid: F *fig.* ~*er Kompromiß* hollow compromise; ~*er Kunde* shady customer; ~*e Sache* fishy business; ~*er Witz* bad joke; *an der Sache ist et.* ~ there is s.th. fishy about it; → *Ausrede.* **2.** lazy, idle.

Fäule ['fɔylə] *f* (-; *no pl*). ✗ rot. **2.** → *Fäulnis.* '**faulen** *v/i* (sn, h) go bad, rot.

faulenzen ['faulɛntsən] *v/i* (h) loaf, laze around, *contp. a.* be lazy.

'**Faulenzer** *m* (-s; -) idler, lazybones.

'**Faulheit** *f* (-; *no pl*) laziness.

faulig ['faulɪç] *adj* a) rotten, b) mo(u)ldy, c) rotting. **Fäulnis** ['fɔylnɪs] *f* (-; *no pl*) a) rottenness, decay (*a.* 🞔), b) putrefaction: *in ~ übergehen* (begin to) rot.

'**Faulpelz** *m* (-es; -e) F *contp.* lazybones.

'**Faultier** *n* **1.** *zo.* sloth. **2.** → *Faulpelz.*

Faun [faun] *m* (-[e]s; -e) faun.

Fauna ['fauna] *f* (-; Faunen) fauna.

Faust [faust] *f* (-; ⸚e) fist: *fig. auf eigene ~* F off one's own bat; *mit eiserner ~* with an iron hand; *mit der ~ auf den Tisch schlagen* put one's foot down; *das paßt wie die ~ aufs Auge* a) it goes together like chalk and cheese, b) *iro.* it fits (perfectly); → *ballen* 2.

Fäustchen ['fɔystçən] *n* (-s; -) *fig. sich ins ~ lachen* laugh up one's sleeve.

'**faust'dick** *adj* as big as your fist: F *fig.* ~*e Lüge* whopping great lie; *er hat es ~ hinter den Ohren* he's a sly one.

'**fausten** *v/t* (*v/i*) (h) *sports*: fist (the ball).

'**faustgroß** *adj* as big as your fist.

'**Faust|handschuh** *m* mitt(en). ~*regel* f rule of thumb, general rule. ~*schlag* *m* punch. ~*skizze* f rough sketch.

favorisieren [favori'zi:rən] *v/t* (h)

favo(u)r. **Favorit** [favo'ri:t] *m* (-en; -en), **Favo'ritin** *f* (-; -nen) favo(u)rite.

Fax [faks] *n* (-; -[e]), **'faxen** *v/t* (h) fax.

Faxen ['faksən] *pl* nonsense: **~ machen** a) pull faces, b) clown about.

Fazit ['fa:tsıt] *n* (-s; -s) a) result, upshot, b) conclusion: **das ~ ziehen aus** sum *s.th.* up, draw one's conclusion from.

Februar ['fe:bruar] *m* (-[s]; *rare* -e) (**im ~** in) February.

Fccht... fencing (*glove, mask, etc*).

fechten ['feçtən] *v/i* (focht, gefochten, h) **1.** fence, a. *fig.* fight. **2.** F beg: **~ gehen** go begging. **'Fechten** *n* (-s) fencing. **'Fechter** *m* (-s; -), **'Fechterin** *f* (-; -nen) fencer. **'Fechtsport** *m* fencing.

Feder ['fe:dər] *f* (-; -n) **1.** a) feather, b) plume: **sich mit fremden ~n schmükken** adorn o.s. with borrowed plumes; F **noch in den ~n liegen** be still in bed; **~n lassen müssen** not to escape unscathed. **2.** a) nib, b) pen. **3.** ⚙ spring. **'Federball** *m* (-[e]s; ⁓e) **1.** shuttlecock. **2.** *no pl* badminton.

'Federbett *n* duvet, featherbed.

'federführend *adj* responsible.

'Federgewicht *n sports:* featherweight.

'Federhalter *m* fountain pen.

'federleicht *adj* (as) light as a feather.

'Federlesen *n* **nicht viel ~s machen mit** make short work of.

federn ['fe:dərn] (h) **I** *v/i* **1.** be springy, be elastic, bounce. **2.** *gym.* flex. **II** *v/t* **3.** *a.* ⚙ spring, cushion: **gut gefedert sein** be well sprung.

'federnd *adj* springy, elastic, resilient.

'Federschmuck *m zo.* plumage.

'Federstrich *m* stroke of the pen.

'Federung *f* (-; -en) springs, *mot.* suspension.

'Federwolke *f* cirrus (cloud).

'Federzeichnung *f* pen-and-ink drawing.

Fee [fe:] *f* (-; -n) fairy.

'Fegefeuer *n* (-s; *no pl*) purgatory.

fegen ['fe:gən] **I** *v/t* (h) sweep: **Schnee ~** clear away the snow; → **Platz** 5. **II** *v/i* (sn) *fig.* sweep, F *a.* flit, rush.

Feh [fe:] *n* (-[e]s; -e) *zo.* squirrel.

Fehde ['fe:də] *f* (-; -n) feud.

fehl [fe:l] *adv* → **Platz** 2.

'Fehlanzeige *f* ✕, ⚙ nil return: F **~!** negative!

'fehlbar *adj* fallible.

'Fehlbarkeit *f* (-; *no pl*) fallibility.

'Fehlbesetzung *f* **1.** *thea.* miscast. **2.** *sports etc:* wrong choice.

'Fehlbetrag *m* deficit.

'Fehlbezeichnung *f* misnomer.

'Fehldia,gnose *f* ✚ wrong diagnosis.

'Fehleinschätzung *f* misjudg(e)ment.

fehlen ['fe:lən] *v/i* (h) **1.** be absent (**in der Schule, bei e-r Sitzung** *etc* from school, a meeting, *etc*). **2.** be missing: **ihm ~ zwei Zähne** he has two teeth missing; **du hast uns sehr gefehlt!** we really missed you! **3.** be lacking: **ihm fehlt (es an) Mut** he is lacking (in) courage; **uns fehlt es am nötigen Geld** we haven't got the money; **es ~ uns immer noch einige Helfer** we still need some helpers; **es fehlt uns an nichts** we have got everything we want; **es fehlte an jeder Zs.-arbeit** there was no cooperation whatsoever; **das fehlte gerade noch!** that's all we needed!; **wo fehlt's denn?** what's the trouble?; **fehlt Ihnen etwas?** is anything wrong with you?; **es fehlte nicht viel und er ... he** very nearly ... **4.. weit gefehlt!** far from it!

'Fehlen *n* (-s) **1.** a) absence (**bei, in** *dat* from), b) absenteeism. **2.** lack, absence.

'fehlend *adj* **1.** absent. **2.** missing. **3.** outstanding.

'Fehlentscheidung *f* wrong decision.

'Fehlentwicklung *f* undesirable development.

Fehler ['fe:lər] *m* (-s; -) **1.** mistake, error, *sports:* fault: **grober ~** blunder; **e-n ~ machen** make a mistake; **dein (eigener) ~!** (that's) your (own) fault! **2.** fault, defect, flaw.

'fehlerfrei *adj* faultless, perfect, flawless.

'fehlerhaft *adj* faulty (*a.* ⚙), incorrect, full of mistakes: ⚙ **~e Stelle** flaw.

'fehlerlos → **fehlerfrei**.

'Fehler|quelle *f* source of error (⚙ trouble). **~quote** *f* error rate. **~verzeichnis** *n* errata.

'Fehlgeburt *f* ✚ miscarriage.

'fehlgeleitet *adj fig.* misguided.

'Fehlgriff *m* mistake, *a.* wrong choice.

'Fehlinvestiti,on *f* bad investment.

'Fehlkalkulati,on *f* miscalculation.

'Fehlkonstrukti,on *f* **e-e ~ sein** be badly designed.

'Fehlleistung *f* (**Freudsche ~** Freudian) slip.

'**Fehlpaß** m sports: bad pass.
'**Fehlplanung** f bad planning.
'**Fehlschlag** m fig. failure, F washout.
'**fehlschlagen** v/i (irr, sep, -ge-, sn, → **schlagen**) fail, go wrong.
'**Fehlschluß** m fallacy.
'**Fehlstart** m false start: **e-n ~ verursachen** sports: jump the gun.
'**Fehlurteil** n misjudg(e)ment.
'**Fehlverhalten** n lapse.
'**Fehlversuch** m unsuccessful attempt.
'**Fehlzeit** f time debit.
'**Fehlzündung** f mot. misfire, backfire.
Feier ['faɪər] f (-; -n) a) celebration, party, fête, b) ceremony: **zur ~ des Tages** to mark the occasion.
'**Feierabend** m ~ **machen** finish (work), F knock off, shop: close; **nach ~** after work.
'**feierlich** adj a) solemn, b) ceremonious.
'**Feierlichkeit** f (-; -en) **1.** no pl solemnity, ceremoniousness. **2.** ceremony.
feiern ['faɪərn] (h) **I** v/t celebrate, a. keep, observe (holiday), a. commemorate (anniversary). **II** v/i celebrate, have a party.
'**Feiertag** m (gesetzlicher ~ public) holiday; **kirchlicher ~** religious holiday.
feige ['faɪɡə] adj cowardly.
'**Feige** f (-; -n) 🍃 fig.
'**Feigenbaum** m fig tree.
'**Feigenblatt** n a. fig. fig leaf.
'**Feigheit** f (-; no pl) cowardice.
Feigling ['faɪklɪŋ] m (-s; -e) coward.
Feile ['faɪlə] f (-; -n) file. '**feilen** v/t, v/i (h) file: fig. ~ **an** (dat) polish.
'**feilschen** ['faɪlʃən] v/i (h) haggle (um about).
fein [faɪn] **I** adj **1.** fine, a. delicate: **~es Gebäck** fancy cakes; **~er Regen** (light) drizzle. **2.** a) fine, a. choice, excellent (quality), b) elegant, c) refined: **~e Art, ~er Ton** good form; **nur vom Feinsten** only of the best. **3.** keen, sharp (ear etc), fine, sensitive: **~er Humor** subtle humo(u)r; **~er Unterschied** subtle (or fine) distinction. **4.** a. iro. nice, fine: **~!** fine!, good! **II** adv **5.** finely (etc): **er ist ~ heraus** he's sitting pretty.
'**Feinabstimmung** f 🎵, ⊙ fine tuning.
'**Feinarbeit** f precision work.
Feind [faɪnt] m (-[e]s; -e) enemy, adversary: **Feund und ~** friend and foe; **sich ~e**

machen make enemies; **sich j-n zum ~ machen** antagonize s.o.
Feindin ['faɪndɪn] f (-; -nen) enemy.
'**feindlich** adj ✕ enemy (troops etc), a. hostile (attitude etc **gegen** to[wards]).
'**Feindlichkeit** f (-; -en) hostility.
'**Feindschaft** f (-; -en) enmity, hostility.
'**feindselig** adj hostile (**gegen** to).
'**Feindseligkeit** f (-; -en) **1.** no pl hostility (**gegen** to). **2.** pl ✕ hostilities.
'**Feindstaat** m enemy state.
'**feinfühlig** [-fy:lɪç] adj sensitive, delicate, tactful. '**Feingefühl** n (-[e]s; no pl) sensitiveness, a. tact.
'**Feingehalt** m standard.
'**Feingold** n fine gold.
'**Feinheit** f (-; -en) **1.** no pl a) fineness, a. delicacy, a. exquisiteness, b) refinement, c) elegance. **2.** subtlety: **die ~en** the finer points, the niceties; **die letzten ~en** the finishing touches.
'**Feinkostladen** m delicatessen (shop).
'**feinmachen: sich ~** (sep, -ge-, h) F dress up.
'**feinmaschig** adj fine-meshed.
'**Feinme,chanik** f precision mechanics.
'**Feinschmecker** m (-s; -) gourmet. **~lo,kal** n gourmet restaurant.
'**Feinschnitt** m (-[e]s; no pl) fine cut.
'**feinsinnig** adj sensitive, subtle.
'**Feinwäsche** f delicate fabrics.
'**Feinwaschmittel** n washing powder for delicate fabrics.
feist [faɪst] adj fat, stout.
feixen ['faɪksən] v/i (h) F smirk.
Feld [fɛlt] n (-[e]s; -er) field (a. fig.), ⊿ a. panel, chess: square: **auf dem ~** in the field; **das ~ anführen** sports: lead the field; **das ~ behaupten** stand one's ground; **das ~ räumen** beat a retreat; **zu ~e ziehen gegen** fight against.
'**Feld|arbeit** f **1.** ✎ work in the fields. **2.** research etc: fieldwork. **~bett** n camp-bed. **~flasche** f ✕ water bottle. **~forschung** f field research, fieldwork. **~küche** f field kitchen. **~lager** n bivouac, camp. **~laza,rett** n casualty clearing station, Am. evacuation hospital. **~marschall** m field marshal. **~sa,lat** m 🍃 lamb's lettuce. **~spieler(in** f) m sports: outfield player.
'**Feldstecher** m (-s; -) field glasses.
Feld-Wald-und-'Wiesen... F common-or-garden ..., run-of-the-mill ...

'**Feldwebel** [-ve:bəl] *m* (-s; -) sergeant.
'**Feldweg** *m* country lane.
'**Feldzug** *m* ✕ campaign.
Felge ['fɛlgə] *f* (-; -n) **1.** ⚙ rim. **2.** *gym.* circle. '**Felgenbremse** *f* rim brake.
Fell [fɛl] *n* (-[e]s; -e) **1.** *zo.* coat. **2.** a) hide, skin, b) pelt, c) fur: *das ~ abziehen* (*dat*) skin; *fig. ein dickes ~ haben* have a thick skin; F *j-m das ~ über die Ohren ziehen* fleece s.o.; *s-e ~e davonschwimmen sehen* see one's hopes dashed.
Fels [fɛls] *m* (-en; -en) rock.
Felsblock *m* boulder.
Felsen ['fɛlzən] *m* (-s; -) rock, cliff.
'**felsenfest** *adj* unshakable: *~ davon überzeugt* absolutely convinced of it.
'**Felsenküste** *f* rocky coast.
felsig ['fɛlzɪç] *adj* rocky.
'**Felsklettern** *n* (-s) rock climbing.
'**Felsspalte** *f* crevice. '**Felswand** *f* wall of rock, rock face. '**Felszacke** *f* crag.
feminin [femi'ni:n] *adj* feminine (*a. ling.*), *contp.* effeminate. **Feminismus** [femi'nɪsmʊs] *m* (-; *no pl*) feminism. **Femi'nist** *m* (-en; -en), **Femi'nistin** *f* (-; -nen), **femi'nistisch** *adj* feminist.
Fenchel ['fɛnçəl] *m* (-s; *no pl*) ♣ fennel.
Fenster ['fɛnstər] *n* (-s; -) window: *das Geld zum ~ hinauswerfen* throw one's money away; F *er ist weg vom ~* he has had his chips.
'**Fenster|bank** *f* (-; ⸚e), **~brett** *n* windowsill. **~briefumschlag** *m* window envelope. **~glas** *n* window glass. **~laden** *m* shutter. **~leder** *n* chamois (leather). **~platz** *m* window seat. **~rahmen** *m* window frame. **~scheibe** *f* windowpane. **~tür** *f* French window.
Ferien ['fe:riən] *pl* holidays, *📖 univ.* or *Am.* vacation, *parl.* recess: *die großen ~* the long vacation; *~ machen* go on holiday (*Am.* vacation).
'**Ferien...** holiday (*camp, flat, etc*). **~ort** *m* holiday resort. **~reise** *f* holiday (*Am.* vacation) trip. **~reisende** *m, f* (-n; -n) holidaymaker. **~zeit** *f* holiday period.
Ferkel ['fɛrkəl] *n* (-s; -) *zo.* young pig, piglet; *fig. contp. du ~!* you (dirty) pig!
Ferke'lei *f* (-; -en) F *contp.* obscenity, dirty joke. '**ferkeln** *v/i* (h) *zo.* farrow.
Fermate [fɛr'ma:tə] *f* (-; -n) ♪ pause, fermata.

Ferment [fɛr'mɛnt] *n* (-s; -e) enzyme, ferment.
fern [fɛrn] **I** *adj* a) far (*a. adv*), b) far-off, *a. fig.* distant, remote: *der 2e Osten* the Far East; *von ~* from (*or* at) a distance, from afar; *in nicht allzu ~er Zukunft* in the not too distant future; *nichts liegt mir ~er* (*als*) nothing is further from my mind (than). **II** *prep* (*dat*) far (away) from. **fern'ab** *adv* far away.
'**Fernauslöser** *m phot.* cable release.
'**Fernbedienung** *f* remote control.
'**fernbleiben** *v/i* (*irr, sep, -ge-, sn, → bleiben*) (*dat* from) stay away from, be absent. '**Fernbleiben** *n* (-s) a) absence, b) absenteeism.
'**Fernbrille** *f* distance glasses.
Ferne ['fɛrnə] *f* (-; *no pl*) distance: *aus der ~* from (*or* at) a distance, from afar; *in der ~* far away, far off; *fig.* (*noch*) *in weiter ~* (still) a long way off.
ferner ['fɛrnər] **I** *adj* further: → *a. fern-liegen.* **II** *adv* further(more), besides: F *fig. er erschien unter ~ liefen* he was among the also rans.
'**fernerhin** *adv* for the (*or* in) future: *auch ~ tun* continue to do.
'**Fern|fahrer** *m mot.* long-distance lorry driver, *Am.* long-haul truck driver, F trucker. **~fahrt** *f* long-distance trip. **~flug** *m* long-distance flight. **2gelenkt** *adj* remote-controlled, ✕ guided (*missile etc*). **~gespräch** *n* long-distance call. **~glas** *n* binoculars.
'**fernhalten** *v/t* (*irr, sep, -ge-, h, → halten*) keep away (*a. sich ~, von* from): *j-n von sich ~* keep s.o. at a distance; *et. von j-m ~* keep s.th. from s.o.
'**Fernheizung** *f* district heating.
fern'her *adv* (*von*) ~ from afar.
'**Fern|ko,pierer** *m* telecopier. **~kursus** *m* correspondence course. **~laster** [-lastər] *m* (-s; -) F, **~lastwagen** *m* long-distance lorry, *Am.* long-haul truck. **~leitung** *f teleph.* long-distance line, ⚡ transmission line, ⚙ pipeline. **~lenkung** *f* remote control. **~lenkwaffe** *f* guided weapon (*or* missile). **~licht** *n mot.* full (*or* high) beam.
'**fernliegen** *v/i* (*irr, sep, -ge-, h, → liegen*) *es liegt mir fern zu inf* far be it from me to *inf*; *nichts lag mir ferner* nothing was farther from my mind.
'**Fernmelde|amt** *n* telephone exchange.

Fernmeldesatellit

~satel‚lit m (tele)communication satellite. **~technik** f (-; no pl) (tele)communications. **~turm** m radio and TV tower. **~wesen** n (-s; no pl) (tele)communications.

'**fernmündlich** → telefonisch.
'**Fern'ost...**, '**fern'östlich** adj Far Eastern.
'**Fernrohr** n (-[e]s; -e) telescope.
'**Fernschreiben** n (-s; -) (per ~ by) telex.
'**Fernschreiber** m telex machine.
'**Fernseh...** television (or TV) (aerial, camera, interview, studio, network, etc).
'**Fernseh|ansager(in** f) m television (or TV) announcer. **~ansprache** f television (or video) address. **~anstalt** f television company. **~appa‚rat** m → Fernsehgerät. **~diskussi‚on** f (TV) panel discussion. **~empfänger** m → Fernsehgerät.

'**fernsehen** v/i (irr, sep, -ge-, h, → sehen) watch television. '**Fernsehen** n (-s) (im ~ on) television (or TV): im ~ bringen (or übertragen) telecast, televise. '**Fernseher** m (-s; -) F 1. → Fernsehgerät. 2. → Fernsehzuschauer.
'**Fernseh|fassung** f television (or TV) adaptation. **~gerät** n television (set), TV (set). **~pro‚gramm** n 1. television (or TV) program(me Br.). 2. TV guide. **~publikum** n television audience. **~röhre** f television tube. **~satel‚lit** m TV (or television) satellite. **~schirm** m (television) screen. **~sender** m 1. television transmitter. 2. television (broadcasting) station. 3. television channel. **~sendung** f (television or TV) program(me Br.), telecast. **~spiel** n television (or TV) play. **~teilnehmer** m 1. TV licen/ce (Am. -se) holder. 2. → Fernsehzuschauer. **~turm** m television (or TV) tower. **~übertragung** f television (or TV) broadcast. **~zeitschrift** f TV guide. **~zuschauer** m a) (television or TV) viewer, b) pl → Fernsehpublikum.

'**Fernsicht** f view.
'**Fernsprech|amt** n telephone exchange. **~auftragsdienst** m answering service. **~auto‚mat** m pay phone. **~buch** n telephone directory, F phone book.
'**Fernsprecher** m (-s; -) (öffentlicher ~ public) telephone, F phone.
'**Fernsprech|gebühren** pl telephone

charges. **~teilnehmer** m telephone subscriber.
'**fernstehen** v/i (irr, sep, -ge-, h, → stehen) j-m ~ have no contact with s.o.
'**fernsteuern** v/t (sep, -ge-, h) operate s.th. by remote control.
'**Fern|steuerung** f remote control. **~straße** f 1. major road. 2. motorway, Am. freeway. **~trans‚port** m long-distance (Am. long-haul) transport. **~unterricht** m correspondence course. **~verkehr** m long-distance traffic. **~wärmenetz** n long-distance heating system. **~ziel** n long-term objective. **~zug** m long-distance train.
Ferse ['fɛrzə] f (-; -n) heel: j-m auf den ~ n a) sein be hard on s.o.'s heels, b) folgen dog s.o.'s footsteps.
fertig ['fɛrtɪç] adj 1. ready: (Achtung,) ~, los! ready, steady, go! 2. finished, completed: ~ sein mit have finished (with); fig. ~ werden mit a) cope (or deal) with, b) get over (grief etc); (gut) ohne ... ~ werden manage (or get along) (quite well) without ... 3. a) ⊙ finished, prefabricated, b) ready-to-eat, precooked, instant (food), c) ready-made (clothes). 4. fig. accomplished, mature. 5. F fig. a) a. fix und ~ bushed, b) done for, c) flabbergasted: der ist ~! he has had it!; → fertigmachen.
'**Fertigbauweise** f ⊙ prefabricated construction.
'**fertigbringen** v/t (irr, sep, -ge-, h, → bringen) et. ~ get s.th. done, manage s.th., bring s.th. off; es ~ zu inf manage to inf; ich brachte es nicht fertig I couldn't (w.s. bring myself to) do it.
fertigen ['fɛrtɪgən] v/t (h) produce, make.
'**Fertig|erzeugnis** n finished product. **~gericht** n gastr. instant meal. **~haus** n prefabricated house, F prefab.
'**Fertigkeit** f (-; -en) a) skill, b) talent, c) proficiency (in dat in).
'**fertigmachen** v/t (sep, -ge-, h) 1. get s.o., s.th. ready. 2. finish. 3. F j-n ~ a) finish s.o. (off), b) get s.o. down, c) slam s.o., d) sl. clobber s.o. (a. sports).
'**Fertigmon‚tage** f final assembly.
'**Fertigpro‚dukt** n finished product.
'**fertigstellen** v/t (sep, -ge-, h) finish, complete.
'**Fertigstellung** f (-; no pl) completion.

'**Fertigteil** *n* prefabricated part, *pl* assembly units.

'**Fertigung** *f* (-; *no pl*) manufacture, production.

'**Fertigungsstraße** *f* ✪ production line.

'**Fertigwaren** *pl* finished products.

Fes [fɛs] *m* (-[es]; -[e]) fez.

fesch [fɛʃ] *adj* F smart, chic.

Fessel¹ ['fɛsəl] *f* (-; -n) *a. fig.* shackle, fetter: *j-m ~n anlegen* → **fesseln** 1.

Fessel² *f* (-; -n) **1.** ankle. **2.** *zo.* pastern.

fesseln ['fɛsəln] *v/t* (h) **1.** *j-n ~* tie s.o. up (*an acc* to): *fig.* **ans Bett gefesselt** confined to one's bed, bedridden. **2.** *fig.* a) fascinate, captivate, b) catch (*s.o.'s eye, attention, etc*). '**fesselnd** *adj fig.* fascinating, riveting, gripping.

fest [fɛst] **I** *adj* **1.** a) firm (*a. fig. decision, prices, etc*), solid (*a. phys.*), ✪ *a.* tight, (firmly) fixed, b) strong, sturdy: *~ werden* harden, solidify, *cement etc*: set. **2.** *fig.* fixed (*costs, date, income, prices, etc*), a. binding (*agreement etc*), regular (*customer*), permanent (*domicile, position, etc*), F steady (*girlfriend etc*): *~er Wohnsitz* ⚖️ *a.* fixed abode; *~er Schlaf* sound sleep; *~e Freundschaft* lasting friendship. **II** *adv* **3.** firmly (*etc*): *~ schlafen* sleep soundly; *et. ~ abmachen* settle s.th. definitely; *Kapital ~ anlegen* tie up capital; *j-n ~ anstellen* employ s.o. on a permanent basis; *ich bin ~ davon überzeugt, daß ...* I'm absolutely convinced that ...; *das habe ich ihr ~ versprochen* I gave her my word for it. **4.** F *a. ~e* properly; *immer ~e!* go at it!

Fest *n* (-[e]s; -e) **1.** a) celebration, festivities, b) party, fête: *ein ~ feiern* celebrate. **2.** holiday, *eccl.* feast.

'**Festakt** *m* ceremony.

'**festangelegt** *adj* tied-up (*funds*). '**festangestellt** *adj* permanently employed.

'**Festaufführung** *f* gala performance.

'**festbinden** *v/t* (*irr, sep,* -ge-, h, → *binden*) tie (*an dat* to), tie *s.o., s.th.* up.

'**festbleiben** *v/i* (*irr, sep,* -ge-, sn, → *bleiben*) remain firm.

'**Festessen** *n* dinner, banquet.

'**festfahren: sich ~** (*irr, sep,* -ge-, h, → *fahren*) *a. fig.* get stuck, *talks:* reach a deadlock.

'**festfressen: sich ~** (*irr, sep,* -ge-, h, → *fressen*) ✪ seize, jam.

'**Festgeldkonto** *n* fixed-term deposit account.

'**festgelegt**, '**festgesetzt** *adj* fixed.

'**festhalten** (*irr, sep,* -ge-, h, → *halten*) **I** *v/t* **1.** hold on to, grasp. **2.** hold, keep, *a.* detain. **3.** *fig.* a) record, b) photograph, film, capture: *e-n Gedanken ~* make a (mental) note of an idea; *et. schriftlich ~* put s.th. down in writing. **II** *sich ~* a) hold tight, b) *a. fig.* hold on (*an dat* to).

festigen ['fɛstɪɡən] (h) **I** *v/t* strengthen, consolidate, *a.* stabilize (*currency*). **II** *sich ~* strengthen, grow stronger, *currency etc: a.* stabilize, *knowledge:* improve.

'**Festiger** *m* (-s; -) setting lotion.

'**Festigkeit** *f* (-; *no pl*) firmness, strength, steadiness, stability.

'**Festigung** *f* (-; -en) strengthening, consolidation, stabilization.

'**festklammern: sich ~** (*sep,* -ge-, h) cling (*an dat* to).

'**festkleben** *v/t, v/i* (*sep,* -ge-, h) stick (*an dat* to).

'**festklemmen** (*sep,* -ge-, h) **I** *v/t* clamp (fast), wedge. **II** *v/i* stick (fast), get stuck, jam, be jammed.

'**Festkon,zert** *n* gala concert.

'**Festkörper** *m phys.* solid.

'**Festkurs** *m* ✝ fixed rate.

'**Festland** *n* a) mainland, b) land, c) continent. '**Festland(s)...** continental.

'**festlegen** (*sep,* -ge-, h) **I** *v/t* **1.** → *festsetzen* 1. **2.** lay down, define (*principles etc*). **3.** ♣ plot (*course*). **4.** ✝ tie up (*capital*). **5.** *j-n auf e-e Sache ~* pin s.o. down to s.th. **II** *sich ~ auf* (*acc*) a) commit o.s. to, b) decide on.

'**festlich I** *adj* festive, splendid. **II** *adv* festively (*etc*): *~ begehen* celebrate; *~ gestimmt* in a festive mood.

'**Festlichkeit** *f* (-; -en) **1.** festivity. **2.** *no pl* festive atmosphere.

'**festliegen** *v/i* (*irr, sep,* -ge-, h, → *liegen*) **1.** be fixed, *capital:* be tied up. **2.** *mot.* be stuck, ♣ be grounded.

'**festmachen** (*sep,* -ge-, h) **I** *v/t* **1.** (*an dat* to) fix, fasten, ♣ moor. **2.** *fig.* fix, settle, *a.* clinch (*a deal*). *et. ~ an* (*dat*) fix s.th. on. **II** *v/i* **3.** ♣ moor.

'**Festmeter** *m, n* cubic met/re (*Am.* -er).

'**festnageln** *v/t* (*sep,* -ge-, h) nail down (*a. fig. auf acc* to).

Festnahme ['fɛstnaːmə] *f* (-; -n) arrest.

festnehmen 210

'festnehmen v/t (irr, sep, -ge-, h, → **nehmen**) arrest.
'Festplatte f computer: hard disc.
'Festpreis m fixed price.
'Festrede f (ceremonial) address.
'Festredner(in f) m official speaker.
'Festsaal m (banqueting) hall.
'Festschrift f commemorative publication.
'festsetzen (sep, -ge-, h) **I** v/t **1.** a) (auf acc for) fix, arrange (place, time, etc), b) (auf acc at) fix (price, penalty, salary, etc), c) assess (damage, tax), d) lay down, agree on (conditions). **2.** arrest. **II** sich ~ settle (in dat in).
'festsitzen v/i (irr, sep, -ge-, h, → **sitzen**) mot. be stuck (a. F fig.), ♻ be stranded.
'Festspeicher m computer: read-only memory (abbr. ROM).
'Festspiel n festival performance: ~e pl → **Festspielwoche** f festival.
'feststehen v/i (irr, sep, -ge-, h, → **stehen**) a) be fixed, b) be certain, be a fact.
'feststehend adj **1.** ⚙ stationary. **2.** fig. established (fact etc).
'feststellbar adj **1.** ascertainable. **2.** noticeable. **3.** ⚙ lock-type.
'Feststellbremse f parking brake.
'feststellen v/t (sep, -ge-, h) **1.** a) find out, discover, establish, b) locate (fault, place, etc), c) ✽ diagnose. **2.** realize, see, notice. **3.** state, say. **4.** ⚙ lock.
'Feststellung f (-; -en) **1.** establishing (etc, → **feststellen**), discovery. **2.** observation: **er machte die ~, daß ...** he found (or realized) that ... **3.** a) remark, b) statement.
'Feststoffra,kete f solid-fuel rocket.
'Festtag m (eccl.) religious) holiday.
'festtäglich adj festive.
'Festung f (-; -en) fortress, fort.
'festverzinslich adj ✝ fixed interest (bearing): ~e Anlagepapiere investment bonds.
'Festwoche f, a. pl festival.
'Festzelt n marquee.
'festziehen v/t (irr, sep, -ge-, h, → **ziehen**) tighten.
'Festzug m procession.
Fetisch ['feːtɪʃ] m (-s; -e) fetish.
Fetischismus [fetiˈʃɪsmʊs] m (-; no pl) fetishism.
Fetischist [-ˈʃɪst] m (-en; -en) fetishist.
fett [fɛt] adj **1.** fat, a. obese (person), fatty

(food): ~ machen fatten; ~ essen eat fatty food. **2.** F fig. fat, rich, big: ~e Beute big haul. **3.** print. bold.
Fett n (-[e]s; -e) **1.** fat: F sein ~ weghaben have caught it. **2.** of body: fat, F flab: ~ ansetzen put on (a lot of) weight. **3.** ⚙ grease.
'fettarm adj low-fat ..., pred low in fat.
'Fettauge n blob of fat.
'Fettcreme f rich oil-based cream.
'Fettdruck m print. bold(-faced) type.
fetten ['fɛtən] (h) **I** v/t grease. **II** v/i be greasy.
'Fettfleck m grease spot.
'fettgedruckt adj in bold type.
'Fettgehalt m (-[e]s; -e) fat content.
'Fettgewebe n fatty tissue.
'fetthaltig adj containing fat, fatty, oil-based (lotion).
fettig ['fɛtɪç] adj fat, fatty, oily, greasy (hair, skin, etc).
'Fettleber f 🐟 fatty liver.
fettleibig ['fɛtlaɪbɪç] adj obese.
'Fettleibigkeit f (-; no pl) obesity.
'Fettnäpfchen n F (bei j-m) ins ~ treten put one's foot in it. **'Fettsack** m F contp. fatso. **'Fettsalbe** f greasy ointment. **'Fettschicht** f layer of fat. **'Fettsucht** f (-; no pl) 🐟 obesity. **'Fettwanst** m F contp. **1.** paunch. **2.** fatso.
Fetus ['feːtʊs] m (-[ses]; -se) f(o)etus.
Fetzen ['fɛtsən] m (-s; -) **1.** rag (a. humor. dress), scrap (of paper), shred (of cloth): in ~ in shreds and tatters; F daß die ~ fliegen like crazy. **2.** pl F fig. snatches (of conversation etc).
fetzig ['fɛtsɪç] adj F wild.
feucht [fɔʏçt] adj damp, moist (a. eyes, lips, skin, etc), wet (climate), humid (air): ~e Hände sweaty palms.
'feucht'fröhlich adj F (very) merry.
'Feuchtigkeit f (-; no pl) damp(ness), moisture, humidity: vor ~ schützen! keep in a dry place!
'Feuchtigkeits|creme f moisturizing cream, moisturizer. **~gehalt** m moisture content, of air: a. humidity.
feudal [fɔʏˈdaːl] adj **1.** hist. feudal. **2.** F fig. a) sumptuous, b) posh.
Feudalismus [fɔʏdaˈlɪsmʊs] m (-; no pl) hist. feudalism.
Feuer ['fɔʏɐ] n (-s; -) **1.** fire: ✗ ~! fire!; haben Sie ~? have you got a light?; ~ fangen catch fire; j-m ~ geben give s.o.

a light; *das Olympische* ~ the Olympic flame; *fig. durchs* ~ *gehen für* go through fire and water for; *mit dem* ~ *spielen* play with fire; *zwischen zwei* ~ *geraten* be caught between the devil and the deep blue sea; → *eröffnen* 1. 2. ⚓ beacon. 3. *fig.* fire, *a.* fervo(u)r, spirit: ~ *und Flamme sein* be all for it.

'Feuer|a₁larm *m* fire alarm. ~anzünder *m* fire lighter. ~bestattung *f* cremation. ~eifer *m* zeal. ~einstellung *f* ✕ cessation of fire. ℒfest *adj* 1. fireproof. 2. incombustible. ~gefahr *f* danger of fire. ℒgefährlich *adj* flammable. ~gefecht *n* ✕ gun battle. ~haken *m* poker. ~kraft *f* (-; *no pl*) ✕ fire power. ~leiter *f* 1. fire ladder. 2. *m* fire escape. ~löscher *m* fire extinguisher. ~melder *m* (-s; -) fire alarm.

feuern ['fɔyərn] *v/t* (h) **1.** fire (*stove*, ✕ *salute*), *a.* burn (*wood*, *coal*). **2.** F hurl, *sports*: slam (*the ball*): *j-m e-e* ~ land s.o. one. **3.** F fire, sack.

'Feuer|probe *f fig.* acid test. ℒrot *adj* fiery (red), flaming red. ~schaden *m* damage caused by fire. ~schiff *n* lightship. ~schlucker *m* fire-eater. ~schutz *m* **1.** fire prevention. **2.** ✕ covering fire. ~stein *m* flint. ~stelle *f* fireplace, hearth. ~taufe *f* fig. baptism of fire. ~teufel *m* F fire bug. ~treppe *f* fire escape.

'Feuerung *f* (-; -en) **1.** heating. **2.** *no pl* fuel.

'Feuer|versicherung *f* fire insurance. ~wache *f* fire station. ~waffe *f* firearm.

'Feuerwehr *f* (-; -en) fire brigade: F *wie die* ~ like a flash. ~mann *m* fireman.

'Feuerwerk *n* (-s; -e) fireworks (*a. fig.*).

'Feuerwerkskörper *m* firework.

'Feuerzangenbowle *f* burnt punch.

'Feuerzeug *n* (-[e]s; -e) (cigarette) lighter. 'Feuerzeugben₁zin *n* lighter fluid.

Feuilleton [fœjə'tõ:] *n* (-s; -s) feature pages. Feuilletonist [fœjəto'nɪst] *m* (-en; -en) feature writer.

feurig ['fɔyrɪç] *adj fig.* **1.** fiery, ardent, passionate. **2.** rich, heady (*wine*).

Fiasko [fi'asko] *n* (-s; -s) fiasco.

Fibel ['fi:bəl] *f* (-; -n) *ped.* primer.

Fiber ['fi:bər] *f* (-; -n) fibre, *Am.* fiber. 'Fiberglas *n* fibre (*Am.* fiber) glass.

Fichte ['fɪçtə] *f* (-; -n) ♣ spruce, F pine (tree). 'Fichtenholz *n* deal.

ficken ['fɪkən] *v/t, v/i* (h) V fuck.

fidel [fi'de:l] *adj* cheerful.

Fieber ['fi:bər] *n* (-s; *no pl*) fever (*a. fig.*), (high) temperature: ~ *haben* → *fiebern* 1; *j-m* (*or* *j-s*) ~ *messen* take s.o.'s temperature.

'Fieberanfall *m* attack of fever.

'fieberfrei *adj sie ist* ~ her temperature is back to normal again.

'fieberhaft *adj a. fig.* feverish.

'Fieberkranke *m*, *f* (-n; -n) fever case.

'Fieberkurve *f* temperature curve.

'Fiebermittel *n* antipyretic.

fiebern ['fi:bərn] *v/i* (h) **1.** a) have (*or* be running) a temperature, b) be delirious. **2.** *fig.* be feverish (*vor* with): ~ *nach* yearn for.

'Fieber|ta₁belle *f* temperature chart. ~thermo₁meter *n* (clinical) thermometer. ~traum *m* feverish dream.

fiebrig ['fi:brɪç] → *fieberhaft*.

Fiedel ['fi:dəl] *f* (-; -n) fiddle.

fiedeln ['fi:dəln] *v/t, v/i* (h) F fiddle.

fiel [fi:l] *pret of fallen*.

fies [fi:s] *adj* F nasty, mean.

Fiesling ['fi:slɪŋ] *m* (-s; -e) F meanie.

Figur [fi'gu:r] *f* (-; -en) **1.** figure (*a.* ♞, ♪), *a.* build: *fig. e-e gute* (*schlechte*) ~ *machen* cut a fine (poor) figure. **2.** *in film, novel, etc*: figure, character: *komische* ~ a) figure of fun, b) strange character. **3.** *chess*: piece, *pl a.* chessmen. **4.** *arts*: figure, statue, b) figurine.

figurativ [figura'ti:f] *adj* fig. figurative.

figurieren [figu'ri:rən] *v/i* (h) figure (*als* as). figürlich [fi'gy:rlɪç] *adj* **1.** paint. etc figured. **2.** ling. figurative.

Fiktion [fɪk'tsio:n] *f* (-; -en) fiction.

fiktiv [fɪk'ti:f] *adj* fictitious.

Filet [fi'le:] *n* (-s; -s) *gastr.* fillet. ~steak *n* fillet steak. ~stück *n* piece of sirloin.

Filiale [fi'lia:lə] *f* (-; -n) **1.** branch (office), subsidiary. **2.** chain store.

Fili'alleiter(in *f*) *m* branch manager.

Filigran [fili'gra:n] *n* (-s; -e), Fili'granarbeit *f* filigree.

Film [fɪlm] *m* (-[e]s; -e) **1.** *phot.* film. **2.** film, *esp. Am. a.* movie: *e-n* ~ *drehen* (*über acc*) shoot (*or* make a film (of), film *s.th.*; F *fig. mir ist der* ~ *gerissen* I had a blackout. **3.** *the* cinema, *esp. Am. the* movies: *beim* ~ *sein* a) be in the film (*esp. Am. a.* movie) business, b) be a film (*esp. Am. a.* movie) actor (*or* actress). **4.** film, coat(ing). **~ar¦chiv** n film library. **~ateli¦er** n film studio. **~aufnahme** f **1.** shooting (of a film). **2.** shot, take. **~bericht** m film report.

'**Filmemacher(in** f) m film (esp. Am. a. movie) maker.

filmen ['fɪlmən] (h) **I** v/t film, shoot. **II** v/t be filming, make a film, a. be on location.

'**Film¦festspiele** pl film festival. **~gelände** n studio lot. **~gesellschaft** f film (Am. motion-picture) company. **~in¦du¦strie** f film (Am. motion-picture) industry.

filmisch ['fɪlmɪʃ] adj cinematic.

'**Film¦kamera** f **1.** film (or movie) camera. **2.** cinecamera. **~kri¦tik** f film review. **~kritiker(in** f) m film critic. **~kunst** f (-; no pl) cinematography. **~materi¦al** n footage. **~mu¦sik** f **1.** film music. **2.** the music to the film. **~pack** m film pack. **~preis** m film (esp. Am. a. movie) award. **~produ¦zent(in** f) m (film) producer. **~pro¦jektor** m film (esp. Am. a. movie) projector. **~regis¦seur(in** f) m film (esp. Am. a. movie) director. **~re¦klame** f screen advertising. **~schauspieler(in** f) m film (or screen, esp. Am. a. movie) actor (actress). **~star** m film (esp. Am. a. movie) star. **~streifen** m reel, w.s. strip. **~studio** n film studio. **~the¦ater** n cinema, Am. movie theater. **~verleih** m **1.** film distribution. **2.** film distributors. **~vorführer** m projectionist. **~vorführung** f film (esp. Am. a. movie) show. **~vorschau** f a) preview, b) trailer, c) in newspaper: forthcoming films. **~welt** f film world, Am. a. movieland.

Filter ['fɪltər] m, n (-s; -) filter. **~anlage** f filtration plant. **~einsatz** m filter element. **~kaffee** m filtered coffee.

filtern ['fɪltərn] v/t (h) filter, a. percolate.

'**Filter¦pa¦pier** n filter paper. **~ziga¦rette** f filter(-tipped) cigarette.

Filtrat [fɪl'traːt] n (-[e]s; -e) filtrate.

filtrieren [fɪl'triːrən] v/t (h) filter.

Filz [fɪlts] m (-es; -e) **1.** felt. **2.** F felt hat. **3.** F contp. a) skinflint, b) corruption. **filzen** ['fɪltsən] (h) **I** v/t F fig. frisk. **II** v/t wool: felt. '**Filzhut** m felt hat.

filzig ['fɪltsɪç] adj **1.** a) felted, b) matted (hair). **2.** F fig. mean, stingy.

'**Filzlaus** f zo. crab louse.

'**Filzpan¦toffel** m felt slipper.

'**Filzstift** m felt(-tipped) pen.

Fimmel ['fɪməl] m (-s; -) F craze: **e-n ~ haben für** be mad about.

Finale [fi'naːlə] n (-s; -) **1.** finale. **2.** sports: final (round), finals,

Finalist [fina'lɪst] m (-en; -en), **Fina¦listin** f (-; -nen) sports: finalist.

Fi¦nalsatz m ling. final clause.

Finanz... [fi'nants-] financial (adviser, paper, etc). **~amt** n inland (Am. internal) revenue (office), fig. contp. the Tax Man. **~ausschuß** m finance committee. **~beamte** m revenue officer.

Fi¦nanzen pl finances.

Fi¦nanzgericht n tax tribunal. **Fi¦nanzgeschäft** n financial transaction.

finanziell [finan'tsi̯εl] adj financial.

finanzieren [finan'tsiːrən] v/t (h) finance: → **frei** 12. **Finan¦zierung** f (-; -en) financing. **Finan¦zierungsgesellschaft** f finance company.

Fi¦nanzjahr n fiscal (or financial) year. **2kräftig** adj financially strong, potent. **~lage** f financial situation. **~mann** m financier. **~mi¦nister** m minister of finance, Br. Chancellor of the Exchequer, Am. Secretary of the Treasury. **~mini¦sterium** n ministry of finance, Br. Treasury, Am. Treasury Department. **~poli¦tik** f financial (or fiscal) policy. **2schwach** adj financially weak. **~spritze** f F shot in the arm. **~welt** f financial world. **~wesen** n (-s; no pl) (public) finance.

finden ['fɪndən] (fand, gefunden, h) **I** v/t find, fig. a. think: **nirgends zu ~** nowhere to be found; fig. **ein Ende ~** come to an end; **ich fand k-e Worte** I was at a loss for words; **ich finde es gut (, daß ...)** I think it's good (that ...); **wie ~ Sie das Buch?** how do you like (or what do you think of) the book?; **~ Sie (nicht)?** do (don't) you think so?; **ich weiß nicht, was sie an ihm findet** I don't know what she sees in him. **II** sich **~** a) be found, b) find o.s.; **das wird sich ~** we'll see. **III** v/i nach Hause **~** find one's way home; **zu sich selbst ~** sort o.s out.

'**Finder** m (-s; -), '**Finderin** f (-; -nen) finder. '**Finderlohn** m finder's reward.

Findling ['fɪntlɪŋ] m (-s; -e) geol. erratic block.

Finesse [fiˈnɛsə] *f* (-; -n) finesse, *pl* tricks: *mit allen ~n car etc* with all the refinements.

fing [fɪŋ] *pret of* **fangen.**

Finger [ˈfɪŋər] *m* (-s; -) finger: *sich die ~ verbrennen a. fig.* burn one's fingers; *sich in den ~ schneiden* a) cut one's finger, b) *fig.* make a big mistake; *j-m auf die ~ klopfen a. fig.* rap s.o.'s knuckles; *laß die ~ davon!* a) hands off!, b) *fig.* leave well alone!; *fig. sich et. aus den ~n saugen* make s.th. up; *j-m auf die ~ sehen* keep a sharp eye on s.o.; *j-n um den kleinen ~ wickeln* twist s.o. round one's little finger; *k-n ~ rühren* not to lift a finger; *er hat überall s-e ~ im Spiel* he's got a finger in every pie; → **abzählen.**

'Finger|abdruck *m* fingerprint: → **abnehmen.** *b,) fig.* **~alpha,bet** *n* finger alphabet.

'fingerfertig *adj* nimble-fingered.

'Fingerfertigkeit *f* (-; *no pl*) dexterity.

'Fingerhut *m* **1.** ❀ foxglove. **2.** thimble.

fingern [ˈfɪŋərn] (h) **I** *v/i ~ an* (*dat*) finger. **II** *v/t* F wangle.

'Finger|nagel *m* fingernail. **~ring** *m* ring. **~schale** *f* finger bowl. **~spitze** *f* fingertip. **~spitzengefühl** *n* a) sure instinct, b) tact. **~sprache** *f* finger language. **~übung** *f* finger exercise.

'Fingerzeig *m* (-[e]s; -e) hint, pointer.

fingieren [fɪnˈɡiːrən] *v/t* (h) **1.** fake: *fingiert* fake(d), fictitious. **2.** fabricate.

Finish [ˈfɪnɪʃ] *n* (-s; -s) *sports*, ☼ finish.

Fink [fɪŋk] *m* (-en; -en) *zo.* finch.

Finne¹ [ˈfɪnə] *f* (-; -n) fin.

'Finne² *m* (-n; -n), **'Finnin** *f* (-; -nen) Finn. **finnisch, 'Finnisch** [ˈfɪnɪʃ] *adj* Finnish. **'Finnland** *n* (-s) Finland.

finster [ˈfɪnstər] *adj* **1.** *a. fig.* dark, black, gloomy. **2.** a) grim, b) evil, sinister: *~er Blick* black look; *j-n ~ ansehen* glower at s.o. **3.** F *fig.* a) shady, b) bad: *es sieht ~ aus!* things are looking bad!

'Finsternis *f* (-; -se) *a. fig.* darkness, gloom(iness).

Finte [ˈfɪntə] *f sports*: feint, *fig. a.* trick.

Firlefanz [ˈfɪrləfants] *m* (-es; *no pl*) F *contp.* a) frippery, junk, b) nonsense.

Firma [ˈfɪrma] *f* (-; -men) firm, company: *die ~ Bosch* (the) Bosch (Company).

Firmament [fɪrmaˈmɛnt] *n* (-[e]s; -e) firmament, sky.

firmen [ˈfɪrmən] *v/t* (h) *eccl.* confirm.

'Firmen|inhaber(in *f)* *m* owner of a (*or* the) firm. **~name** *m* company name. **~schild** *n* company name, facia, *on machine etc*: nameplate. **~sitz** *m* (company) headquarters. **~stempel** *m* firm('s) stamp. **~verzeichnis** *n* trade directory. **~wagen** *m* company car. **~wert** *m* (-[e]s; *no pl*) goodwill. **~zeichen** *n* F logo.

firmieren [fɪrˈmiːrən] *v/i* (h) **~ als** have the company name of.

'Firmling *m* (-s; -e) *eccl.* confirmand.

'Firmung *f* (-; -en) *eccl.* confirmation.

Firn [fɪrn] *m* (-[e]s; -e) corn snow.

Firnis [ˈfɪrnɪs] *m* (-ses; -se) varnish.

firnissen [ˈfɪrnɪsən] *v/t* (h) varnish.

First [fɪrst] *m* (-[e]s; -e) ridge.

Fis [fɪs] *n* (-; -) ♪ F sharp.

Fisch [fɪʃ] *m* (-[e]s; -e) **1.** fish: *F fig. ein großer* (*or dicker*) *~* a big fish; *kleine ~e* peanuts, small beer. **2.** *pl astr.* Pisces. **'Fischauge** *n phot.* fish-eye (lens).

fischen [ˈfɪʃən] *v/t, v/i* (h) fish (*nach* for): → **trübe** 1. **'Fischen** *n* (-s) fishing.

'Fischer *m* (-s; -) fisherman. **~boot** *n* fishing boat. **~dorf** *n* fishing village.

Fische'rei *f* (-; *no pl*) **1.** fishing. **2.** fishing industry. **~flotte** *f* fishing fleet. **~grenze** *f* fishing limit. **~hafen** *m* fishing port. **~recht** *n* fishing right(s).

'Fisch|fang *m* fishing. **~fi,let** *n gastr.* fish fillet. **~gabel** *f* fish fork. **~gericht** *n gastr.* fish dish. **~geruch** *m* fishy smell. **~geschäft** *n* fishmonger('s). **~grätenmuster** *n* herringbone (pattern). **~gründe** *pl* fishing grounds, fishery. **~händler(in** *f) m* fishmonger, *Am.* fish dealer. **~indu,strie** *f* fish-processing industry. **~kon,serven** *pl* tinned (*or* canned) fish. **~kunde** *f* (-; *no pl*) ichthyology. **~kutter** *m* (fishing) trawler. **~laich** *m* (fish) spawn. **~markt** *m* fish market. **~mehl** *n* fishmeal. **~messer** *n* fish knife. **~otter** *m zo.* otter. **~reiher** *m zo.* heron. **~restau,rant** *n* fish (*or* seafood) restaurant. **~schuppe** *f* scale. **~stäbchen** *n gastr.* fish finger, *Am.* fish stick. **~sterben** *n* fish kill. **~vergiftung** *f* fish poisoning. **~zucht** *f* fish farming. **~zug** *m* catch, *fig. a.* haul.

Fiskus [ˈfɪskʊs] *m* (-; *no pl*) **1.** Treasury. **2.** government.

Fistel [ˈfɪstəl] *f* (-; -n) ✚ fistula.

'**Fistelstimme** f **1.** ♪ falsetto. **2.** contp. squeaky voice.

fit [fit] adj (sich ~ halten keep) fit.

Fitneß ['fitnɛs] f (-; no pl) fitness.

'**Fitneßcenter** n health club, gym.

'**Fitneßraum** m exercise room.

Fittich ['fitiç] m (fig. j-n unter ᴣ-e ~e nehmen take s.o. under one's) wing.

fix [fiks] **I** adj **1.** fixed (salary, costs, etc): ~e Idee fixed idea, obsession. **2.** F a) quick (in dat at), b) smart, sharp. **3.** ~ und fertig a) all ready, b) → fertig 5 a. **II** adv **4.** F quickly, in a flash.

fixen ['fiksən] v/i (h) sl. fix, shoot, mainline. **Fixer** ['fiksər] m (-s; -), '**Fixerin** f (-; -nen) sl. junkie.

Fi'xierbad n phot. fixer.

fixieren [fi'ksi:rən] v/t (h) **1.** a. phot, ↗ fix, fig. a. determine: schriftlich ~ formulate, record. **2.** psych. fixiert sein auf (acc) be fixated on. **3.** stare at.

Fi'xiermittel n phot. fixative.

Fi'xierung f (-; -en) **1.** fixing (a. phot. etc). **2.** psych. fixation.

'**Fixstern** m fixed star.

Fixum ['fiksʊm] n (-s; Fixa) ♱ fixed sum (or salary).

Fjord [fjɔrt] m (-[e]s; -e) fjord, fiord.

FKK [ɛfka:'ka:] → Freikörperkultur. **FK'K-Strand** m nudist beach.

flach [flax] adj **1.** flat, a. level, even: ~ machen (klopfen etc) flatten; ~ werden flatten (out); mit der ~en Hand with the flat of one's hand. **2.** a. fig. shallow: ~er Teller shallow (w.s. dinner) plate. **3.** low (a. sports: shot).

'**Flachboot** n flat-bottomed boat.

'**Flachdach** n flat roof.

Fläche ['flɛçə] f (-; -n) a) surface (a. A), b) area, space: (weite) ~ expanse.

'**Flächen|ausdehnung** f area. ~**brand** m extensive fire. **²deckend** adj overall, global. ~**inhalt** m A area. ~**maß** n A surface measurement.

'**flachfallen** v/i (irr, sep, -ge-, sn, → fallen) F fall through.

'**Flachheit** f (-; no pl) flatness, fig. shallowness.

'**Flachmann** m (-[e]s; ⸚er) F hip flask. '**Flachland** n flat country. '**Flachpaß** m soccer: low pass. '**Flachreli,ef** n bas-relief. '**Flachrennen** n flat race.

Flachs [flaks] m (-es; no pl) **1.** ♣ flax. **2.** F kidding: ohne ~! no kidding!

'**Flachschuß** m soccer: low ball.

flachsen ['flaksən] v/i (h) F kid.

flackern ['flakərn] v/i (h) flicker.

Fladen ['fla:dən] m (-s; -) flat cake.

'**Fladenbrot** n round flat loaf.

Flagge ['flagə] f (-; -n) flag: fig. unter falscher ~ segeln sail under false colo(u)rs; ~ zeigen make a stand.

flaggen ['flagən] (h) **I** v/i fly (or hoist) a flag (or flags). **II** v/t flag, signal.

'**Flaggschiff** n a. fig. flagship.

Flair [flɛ:r] n (-s; no pl) **1.** aura. **2.** flair.

Flak [flak] f (-; -, -s) **1.** → Flakgeschütz. **2.** → '**Flakartille,rie** f antiaircraft artillery. '**Flakfeuer** n antiaircraft fire, F flak. '**Flakgeschütz** n antiaircraft gun.

Flakon [fla'kõ:] n, m (-s; -s) small bottle.

flambieren [flam'bi:rən] v/t (h) flame.

Flamingo [fla'mɪŋɡo] m (-s; -s) zo. flamingo.

flämisch ['flɛ:mɪʃ] adj Flemish.

Flamme ['flamə] f (-; -n) a. fig. flame: in (hellen) ~n stehen be ablaze; auf kleiner ~ cook on a low heat. '**flammend** adj fig. fiery, stirring (speech etc).

'**Flammenmeer** n sea of flames.

Flanell [fla'nɛl] m (-s; -e) flannel.

Flanke ['flaŋkə] f (-; -n) **1.** flank, side. **2.** a) soccer: cent/re (Am. -er), b) gym. (flank) vault.

'**flanken** v/i (h) soccer: cent/re (Am. -er).

flankieren [flaŋ'ki:rən] v/t (h) flank: fig. ~de Maßnahme supporting measure.

Flansch [flanʃ] m (-[e]s; -e) ✪ flange.

flapsig ['flapsiç] adj loutish.

Fläschchen ['flɛʃçən] n (-s; -) **1.** small bottle, pharm. phial. **2.** (baby) bottle.

Flasche ['flaʃə] f (-; -n) **1.** bottle: e-e ~ Wein a bottle of wine; e-m Baby die ~ geben give a baby its bottle; mit der ~ aufziehen bottle-feed. **2.** F dud, flop.

'**Flaschen|bier** n bottled beer. ~**gas** n bottled gas. **²grün** adj bottle-green. ~**kind** n bottle-fed baby. ~**milch** f bottled milk. ~**öffner** m bottle opener. ~**pfand** n deposit (on a bottle). ~**post** f bottle post. ~**wein** m bottled wine.

'**flaschenweise** adv by the bottle.

'**Flaschenzug** m ✪ block and pulley.

'**flatterhaft** adj flighty, fickle.

flattern ['flatərn] v/i **1.** (sn) flutter. **2.** (h) flutter (a. ✿, ✪), flap, wheels: wobble.

flau [flaʊ] adj **1.** a) queasy, b) faint, c)

fliegerisch

listless. **2.** stale (taste). **3.** phot. flat, fuzzy, weak. **4.** ✝ slack.

Flaum [flaʊm] m (-[e]s; no pl) down.

'**flaumig** adj downy.

Flausch [flaʊʃ] m (-es; -e) textil. coating.

'**flauschig** adj fluffy.

Flausen ['flaʊzən] pl F silly ideas.

Flaute ['flaʊtə] f (-; -n) **1.** ♣ lull. **2.** ✝ slack period.

Flechte ['flɛçtə] f (-; -n) **1.** ♣ lichen. **2.** ♣ eczema. **3.** braid.

'**flechten** v/t (flocht, geflochten, h) plait (hair), bind (wreath), weave (basket).

Fleck [flɛk] m (-[e]s; -e) **1.** spot, stain: ♣ **blauer** ~ bruise. **2.** fig. blemish. **3.** F a) spot, place, b) patch: **am falschen** ~ a. fig. in the wrong place; fig. **nicht vom** ~ **kommen** not to make any headway; **sich nicht vom** ~ **rühren** not to budge.

'**Fleckchen** n (-s; -) **1.** speck. **2.** fig. (**ein schönes** ~ [**Erde**] a lovely) spot.

flecken ['flɛkən] v/i (h) stain.

'**Flecken** m (-s; -) → **Fleck.**

'**Fleckenentferner** m stain remover.

'**fleckenlos** adj a. fig. spotless.

'**fleckig** adj a) spotted, b) stained.

'**Flecktyphus** m ♣ (epidemic) typhus.

Fledermaus ['fle:dər-] f zo. bat.

Flegel ['fle:gəl] m (-s; -) lout. **Flege'lei** f (-; -en) loutish behavio(u)r. '**flegelhaft** adj loutish. '**Flegeljahre** pl (**in den** ~ **sein** be at an) awkward age.

flehen ['fle:ən] v/i (h) ~ **um** beg for, implore. '**Flehen** n (-s) entreaty.

'**flehend, 'flehentlich** adj imploring, urgent (request): ~ **bitten um** → **flehen.**

Fleisch [flaɪʃ] n (-es; no pl) **1.** a. fig. flesh: **das eigene** ~ **und Blut** one's own flesh and blood; **j-m in** ~ **und Blut übergehen** become second nature to s.o.; **sich ins eigene** ~ **schneiden** cut off one's nose to spite one's face; **vom** ~ **fallen** grow thin. **2.** gastr. a) meat, b) flesh (of fruit). **~brühe** f a) consommé, beef tea, b) (beef) stock.

'**Fleischer** m (-s; -) butcher.

Fleische'rei f (-; -en), '**Fleischerladen** m butcher's shop.

'**fleischfarben** adj flesh-colo(u)red.

'**fleischfressend** adj ♣, zo. carnivorous.

'**Fleischfresser** m zo. carnivore.

'**Fleischgericht** n meat dish.

'**fleischig** adj **1.** fleshy. **2.** meaty.

'**Fleisch|kloß** m **1.** gastr. meatball. **2.** F

fig. mound of flesh. **~kon,serven** pl tinned (or canned) meat.

'**fleischlich** adj carnal.

'**fleischlos** adj meatless (diet).

'**Fleisch|to,mate** f beef tomato. **~vergiftung** f ♣ meat poisoning. **~waren** pl meat products. **~wolf** m mincer, Am. meat grinder. **~wunde** f ♣ flesh wound. **~wurst** f pork sausage.

Fleiß [flaɪs] m (-es; no pl) diligence, industry, hard work: **viel** ~ **verwenden auf** (acc) take great pains over; **ohne** ~ **kein Preis** no sweet without sweat.

'**fleißig I** adj diligent, hard-working, busy. **II** adv diligently, F a lot.

flektieren [flɛk'tiːrən] v/t (h) ling. inflect.

fletschen ['flɛtʃən] v/t (h) **die Zähne** ~ snarl.

flexibel [flɛ'ksiːbəl] adj a. fig. flexible.

Flexibilität [flɛksibili'tɛːt] f (-; no pl) a. fig. flexibility.

Flexion [flɛ'ksioːn] f (-; -en) inflection.

flicken ['flɪkən] v/t (h) a) mend, b) a. F fig. patch up. '**Flicken** m (-s; -) patch.

'**Flickwerk** n (-[e]s; no pl) fig. patch-up job(s). '**Flickzeug** n **1.** sewing kit. **2.** mot. etc repair kit.

Flieder ['fliːdər] m (-s; -) ♣ lilac.

Fliege ['fliːgə] f (-; -n) **1.** zo. fly: **er tut k-r** ~ **was zuleide** he wouldn't hurt a fly; **sterben wie die** ~n die like flies; **zwei** ~n **mit einer Klappe schlagen** kill two birds with one stone. **2.** bow tie.

fliegen ['fliːgən] (flog, geflogen) **I** v/i (sn) **1.** fly, a. go by air: ~ **lassen** fly; → **Luft** 3. **2.** fig. fly, rush. **3.** F fig. be fired, get the sack: **aus der Schule** etc ~ be kicked out of school etc. **4.** F fig. ~ **auf** (acc) really go for; **auf j-n** ~ a. fall for s.o. **II** v/t (h) **5.** fly (persons, plane, etc).

'**Fliegen** n (-s) a) flying, b) aviation.

'**fliegend** adj flying (a. sports): **~er Händler** hawker.

'**Fliegen|fänger** m flypaper. **~gewicht** n (-s; no pl) sports: flyweight. **~klatsche** f fly swatter. **~pilz** m toadstool.

'**Flieger** m (-s; -) **1.** zo., horse racing: flier, flyer. **2.** airman (a. ✕), pilot. **3.** ✕ Br. aircraftman 2nd class, Am. airman basic. **4.** F plane. **5.** cycling: sprinter. **~a,larm** m air-raid warning. **~angriff** m air raid. **~horst** m air base.

'**Fliegerin** f (-; -nen) airwoman, woman pilot. '**fliegerisch** adj flying.

'**Fliegerjacke** f bomber jacket.

fliehen ['fliːən] (floh, geflohen) **I** v/i (sn) (*vor dat* from, *nach, zu* to) flee, run away, escape. **II** v/t (h) avoid, shun.

'**fliehend** adj fig. receding (*chin etc*).

'**Fliehkraft** f phys. centrifugal force.

Fliese ['fliːzə] f (-; -n) tile.

'**Fliesenboden** m tiled floor.

'**Fliesenleger** m (-s; -) tiler.

'**Fließarbeit** f (-; no pl) assembly-line work.

'**Fließband** n (-[e]s; ⸚er) **1.** assembly line. **2.** conveyor belt. **⸚arbeiter** m assembly-line worker. **⸚fertigung** f assembly-line production.

fließen ['fliːsən] v/i (floß, geflossen, sn) flow (a. fig.), river, water, etc: run.

'**fließend** adj **1.** flowing: **⸚es Wasser** running water. **2.** fast-moving (*traffic*). **3.** fig. fluid, fluent: **er spricht ⸚ Englisch** he speaks fluent English.

'**Fließ|heck** n mot. fastback. **⸚komma** n computer: floating decimal point.

flimmern ['flɪmərn] v/i (h) shimmer, TV flicker.

flink [flɪŋk] adj quick, nimble.

Flinte ['flɪntə] f (-; -n) gun: F fig. **die ⸚ ins Korn werfen** throw in the towel.

Flipper ['flɪpər] m (-s; -) pinball machine.

flippern ['flɪpərn] v/i (h) F play pinball.

Flirt [flœrt] m (-s; -s) **1.** flirtation. **2.** flirt.

flirten ['flœrtən] v/i (h) flirt.

'**Flittchen** ['flɪtçən] n (-s; -) F hussie.

Flitter ['flɪtər] m (-s; no pl) **1.** coll. sequins. **2.** fig. a) a. '**Flitterglanz** m glitter, b) a. '**Flitterkram** m tinsel.

'**Flitterwochen** pl honeymoon.

flitzen ['flɪtsən] v/i (sn) F **1.** flit. **2.** streak.

Flitzer ['flɪtsər] m (-s; -) F **1.** nippy little car. **2.** streaker.

floaten ['floutən] v/t, v/i (h) ✝ float.

flocht [flɔxt] pret of **flechten**.

Flocke ['flɔkə] f (-; -n) **1.** flake. **2.** fluff.

flocken ['flɔkən] v/i (h) flake. '**flockig** adj **1.** flaky. **2.** fluffy. **3.** 🌼 flocculent.

flog [floːk] pret of **fliegen**.

floh [floː] pret of **fliehen**.

Floh m (-[e]s; ⸚e) zo. flea: F fig. **j-m e-n ⸚ ins Ohr setzen** put ideas into s.o.'s head. '**Flohmarkt** m flea market.

Flor¹ [floːr] m (-s; no pl) **1.** bloom. **2.** mass of flowers (*or blossoms*).

Flor² m (-s; -e) textil. **1.** gauze. **2.** pile.

Flora ['floːra] f (-; Floren) flora.

floral [floˈraːl] adj floral.

Florett [floˈrɛt] n (-[e]s; -e) foil.

Flo'rettfechten n foil fencing.

florieren [floˈriːrən] v/i (h) flourish.

Floskel ['flɔskəl] f (-; -n) empty phrase.

'**floskelhaft** adj meaningless, empty.

Floß [floːs] n (-es; ⸚e) raft.

Flosse ['flɔsə] f (-; -n) **1.** zo. a) fin, b) flipper (*a. sports*). **2.** ✈ stabilizer fin. **3.** F a) paw, mitt, b) trotter.

flößen ['fløːsən] v/t (h) float.

Flöte ['fløːtə] f (-; -n) **1.** ♩ flute. **2.** flute glass. **3.** cards: flush. '**flöten** v/t, v/i ♩ play the flute, a. fig. flute, bird: sing.

'**flötengehen** v/i (irr, sep, -ge-, sn, → **gehen**) F go down the drain.

Flötist [fløˈtɪst] m (-en; -en), **Flö'tistin** f (-; -nen) flautist, flute-player.

flott [flɔt] adj **1.** F brisk, lively, zippy. **2.** F a) smart, snazzy, b) dashing, c) gay: **ein ⸚es Leben führen** live it up. **3.** ⚓ **⸚ sein** be afloat; → **flottmachen** 1.

Flotte ['flɔtə] f (-; -n) ✈, ⚓ fleet.

'**Flottenstützpunkt** m ⚓ naval base.

Flottille [flɔˈtɪl(j)ə] f (-; -n) ⚓ flotilla.

'**flottmachen** v/t (sep, -ge-, h) **1.** ⚓ float, set s.th. afloat. **2.** get car going again.

Flöz [fløːs] n (-es; -e) ⚒, geol. seam.

Fluch [fluːx] m (-[e]s; ⸚e) **1.** curse. **2.** curse, oath, swearword.

fluchen ['fluːxən] v/i (h) curse, swear: **auf** (*or* **über**) **j-n** (*et.*) **⸚** curse s.o. (s.th.).

Flucht¹ [fluːxt] f (-; -en) a) flight (**vor** *dat* from, a. fig.), b) escape: **auf der ⸚ erschossen** etc shot etc while fleeing (*or* attempting to escape); **auf der ⸚ sein** be on the run (*vor dat* from); **die ⸚ ergreifen** → **flüchten** 1; **in die ⸚ schlagen** put s.o. to flight; fig. **die ⸚ nach vorn antreten** seek refuge in attack.

Flucht² f (-; -en) △, ◎ alignment, row.

'**fluchtartig I** adj hasty. **II** adv hastily, in a hurry.

flüchten ['flʏçtən] v/i (sn) **1.** flee (**nach, zu** to), run away, prisoner: escape (**aus** from), 🏃 abscond (**vor** dat from). **2.** (a. **sich ⸚**) take shelter (*or* refuge) (**in** acc in): fig. **sich in Ausreden ⸚** resort to excuses.

'**Fluchthelfer(in** f**)** m escape agent.

'**flüchtig I** adj **1.** a) hasty, b) brief, flying, c) cursory, superficial, d) careless, slapdash: **⸚e Bekanntschaft** passing acquaintance. **2.** fleeting (*glance etc*). **3.**

fugitive, escaped, ⚖ absconding: **∼er Fahrer** hit-and-run driver. **4.** 🎇 volatile. **II** *adv* **5.** hastily (*etc*): **∼ durchlesen** skim over; **∼ kennen** know *s.o.*, *s.th.* vaguely; **∼ sehen** catch a glimpse of.

'**Flüchtige** *m, f* (-n; -n) fugitive.

'**Flüchtigkeitsfehler** *m* slip.

'**Flüchtling** ['flʏçtlɪŋ] *m* (-s; -e) fugitive, *pol.* refugee.

'**Flüchtlingslager** *n* refugee camp.

'**Fluchtversuch** *m* attempt to escape.

'**Fluchtwagen** *m* getaway car.

'**Fluchtweg** *m* escape route.

'**Flug** [fluːk] *m* (-[e]s; ∼e) flight: *fig.* (**wie**) **im ∼(e)** very quickly. **∼bahn** *f* trajectory, ✈ flight path. **∼ball** *m* tennis: volley. **∼begleiter(in** *f*) *m* flight attendant. **♀bereit** *adj* ready for take-off. **∼betrieb** *m* (-[e]s; *no pl*) air traffic. **∼blatt** *n* leaflet. **∼boot** *n* flying boat, seaplane.

'**Flügel** ['flyːgəl] *m* (-s; -) **1.** wing (*a. pol. or sports*), ✗ *a.* flank, blade (*of propeller etc*), panel (*of altar etc*): *fig.* **j-m die ∼ stutzen** clip *s.o.*'s wings; (*dat*) **∼ verleihen** lend wings to; → **link. 2.** ♩ grand (piano): **am ∼ ...** accompanied by ...

'**Flügelfenster** *n* casement (window).

'**flügellos** *adj* wingless.

'**Flügelmutter** *f* ⚙ wing nut. **∼schlag** *m* flapping of wings. **∼schraube** *f* ⚙ thumbscrew. **∼stürmer(in** *f*) *m* sports: wing, winger. **∼tür** *f* folding door(s).

'**flugfähig** *adj* airworthy.

'**Fluggast** *m* (air) passenger.

'**Fluggastabfertigung** *f* **1.** passenger clearance. **2.** check-in desk.

flügge ['flʏgə] *adj* fully fledged: **∼ werden** a) fledge, b) *fig.* begin to stand on one's own two feet.

'**Fluggeschwindigkeit** *f* flying speed. **∼gesellschaft** *f* airline. **∼hafen** *m* airport. **∼höhe** *f* (flying) altitude. **∼kapitän** *m* (flight) captain. **∼karte** *f* **1.** (air) ticket. **2.** aeronautical map. **∼körper** *m* flying object, ✗ missile. **∼lehrer(in** *f*) *m* flying instructor. **∼leitung** *f* air traffic control. **∼linie** *f* **1.** (air) route. **2.** F airline (company). **∼lotse** *m* air traffic controller. **∼nummer** *f* flight number. **∼objekt** *n* **unbekanntes ∼** unidentified flying object. **∼passagier** *m* (air) passenger. **∼personal** *n* aircrew, *coll.* flying personnel. **∼plan** *m* timetable. **∼platz** *m* a) airfield, b) airport. **∼preis**

m (air) fare. **∼reise** *f* journey by air. **∼schalter** *m* flight desk. **∼schein** *m* **1.** (air) ticket. **2.** pilot's licen|ce (*Am.* -se). **∼schneise** *f* approach corridor. **∼schreiber** *m* flight recorder, black box. **∼sicherung** *f* air traffic control. **∼steig** *m* gate. **∼strecke** *f* **1.** (air) route. **2.** distance flown. **3.** leg. **∼stunde** *f* **1.** flying hour. **2.** **nach zwei ∼n** after a two-hour flight; **sechs ∼n entfernt** six flight-hours away. **♀tauglich** *adj* fit to fly, airworthy. **∼ticket** *n* (air) ticket. **∼überwachung** *f* air traffic control. **∼verbindung** *f* air connection. **∼verkehr** *m* **1.** air traffic. **2.** air services. **∼wetter** *n* flying weather. **∼zeit** *f* flying time.

'**Flugzeug** *n* (-[e]s; -e) (aero)plane, *Am.* (air)plane, aircraft: **mit dem ∼** by air, by plane. **∼absturz** *m* air (or plane) crash. **∼bau** *m* (-[e]s; *no pl*) aircraft construction. **∼besatzung** *f* aircrew. **∼entführer(in** *f*) *m* hijacker, skyjacker. **∼entführung** *f* hijacking, skyjacking. **∼fabrik** *f* aircraft factory. **∼führer** *m* pilot. **∼halle** *f* hangar. **∼industrie** *f* aircraft industry. **∼konstrukteur** *m* aircraft designer. **∼träger** *m* ⚓, ✗ aircraft carrier. **∼unglück** *n* air disaster, air (or plane) crash.

'**Flugziel** *n* destination.

Fluidum ['fluːidʊm] *n* (-s; -da) aura, air, atmosphere.

fluktuieren [flʊktuˈiːrən] *v/i* (h) fluctuate.

Flunder ['flʊndər] *f* (-; -n) *zo.* flounder.

flunkern ['flʊŋkərn] *v/i* (h) fib.

Fluor ['fluːɔr] *n* (-s; *no pl*) fluorine: **mit ∼ anreichern** fluoridate.

fluoreszieren [fluɔrɛsˈtsiːrən] *v/i* (h) fluoresce: **∼d** fluorescent.

Flur¹ [fluːr] *m* (-[e]s; -e) **1.** hall. **2.** corridor.

Flur² *f* (-; -en) open fields: *fig.* **allein auf weiter ∼** all alone. **∼bereinigung** *f* consolidation (of farmland). **∼schaden** *m* crop damage.

Fluse ['fluːzə] *f* (-; -n) fluff, *Am.* lint.

Fluß [flʊs] *m* (-sses; ∼sse) **1.** river. **2.** *no pl* flow(ing): **in ∼ kommen** get going.

fluß'ab(wärts) *adv* down the river, downstream.

'**Flußarm** *m* arm of a river.

fluß'auf(wärts) *adv* up the river, upstream.

'Flußbett n riverbed.
Flüßchen ['flʏsçən] n (-s; -) small river.
'Flußdia**gramm** n flowchart.
flüssig ['flʏsıç] **I** adj **1.** a) liquid, b) molten: ~ **werden** liquefy, melt. **2.** fig. flowing, fluent: → a. **fließend 3. 3.** ✝ liquid, available. **II** adv **4.** in liquid form. **5.** write, speak fluently, traffic etc go smoothly. **'Flüssiggas** n liquid gas.
'Flüssigkeit f (-; -en) **1.** no pl liquidity (a. ✝), a. fig. fluidity. **2.** liquid, fluid.
'Flüssigkeitsbremse f mot. hydraulic brake. ~**getriebe** n mot. fluid drive. ~**maß** n liquid measure.
'Flüssigkristall-Sichtanzeige f computer: liquid crystal display (LCD).
'flüssigmachen v/t (sep, -ge-, h) ✝ realize, convert into cash.
'Flußkrebs m zo. freshwater crayfish. ~**lauf** m course of a river. ~**mündung** f mouth (of a river), estuary. ~**pferd** n hippopotamus, F hippo. ~**ufer** n riverbank, riverside.
flüstern ['flʏstərn] v/t, v/i (h) (speak in a) whisper: F **dem werde ich was** ~! I'll tell him a thing or two! **Flüstern** (-s) whisper(ing). **'Flüsterpropa**ganda f whispering campaign. **'Flüsterton** m **im** ~ in a whisper.
Flut [fluːt] f (-; -en) **1.** high tide: **es ist** ~ the tide is in. **2.** often pl waters, waves. **3.** fig. flood (of tears, letters, etc), a. torrent (of words etc).
fluten ['fluːtən] **I** v/i (sn) a. fig. flood, stream, pour. **II** v/t (h) flood.
'Flutkata**strophe** f flood disaster. ~**licht** n (-[e]s; no pl) floodlights: **bei** ~ under floodlight. ~**welle** f tidal wave.
focht [fɔxt] pret of **fechten**.
Fock [fɔk] f (-; -en) ⚓ **1.** foremast. **2.** a. **Focksegel** n foresail.
Föderalismus [fœdera'lɪsmʊs] m (-; no pl) federalism. **föderalistisch** [fœdera'lɪstıʃ] adj a) federal, b) federalistic (efforts etc). **Föderation** [fœdera-'tsǐoːn] f (-; -en) (con)federation.
fohlen ['foːlən] v/i (h) zo. foal.
'Fohlen n (-s; -) a) foal, b) colt, c) filly.
Föhn [føːn] m (-[e]s; -e) ~**wind** m föhn.
Föhre ['føːrə] f (-; -n) ♀ pine (tree).
Fokus ['foːkʊs] m (-; -se) focus.
fokussieren [foku'siːrən] v/t (h) focus.
Folge ['fɔlɡə] f (-; -en) **1.** succession, sequence: **in der** ~ subsequently; **dreimal**

etc **in** ~ three times etc running (or in a row); **in rascher** ~ in rapid succession. **2.** a) instal(l)ment, TV part, sequel, serial, b) number, issue. **3.** a) consequence, b) aftermath, aftereffect: **als** ~ **davon** as a consequence; **zur** ~ **haben** result in, lead to; (**üble**) ~**n haben** have (dire) consequences; **die** ~**n tragen** bear the consequences. **4.** (dat) ~ **leisten** → **folgen** 2.
'Folgeerscheinung f → **Folge** 3.
'Folgekosten pl follow-up costs.
folgen ['fɔlɡən] v/i (sn) **1.** (dat) follow (s.o., s.th.): ~ **auf** (acc) a. succeed (s.o.), a. come after (s.o., s.th.); **Brief folgt!** letter will follow!; **wie folgt** as follows; **daraus folgt, daß** (from this) it follows that; **j-s Beispiel** ~ follow s.o.'s example; **können Sie mir** ~? do you follow me?; **ich kann Ihnen da(rin) nicht** ~ I can't agree with you there. **2.** (dat) obey (an order), comply with a request etc, accept (an invitation). **3.** F obey (j-m s.o.). **'folgend** adj following, next, subsequent: **am** ~**en Tage** the following (or next) day; **im** ~**en** in the following; **es handelt sich um** ~**es** the matter is as follows.
'folgendermaßen adv as follows.
'folgenschwer adj momentous, grave.
'folgerichtig adj logical, consistent.
folgern ['fɔlɡərn] v/t (h) (**aus** from) conclude, deduce. **'Folgerung** f (-; -en) (e-e ~ **ziehen** draw a) conclusion.
'Folgesatz m **1.** ling. consecutive clause. **2.** ♈, philos. corollary. **'Folgeschäden** pl ♣ secondary (⚒ consequential) damage. **'Folgezeit** f (in der ~ in the) period following.
folglich ['fɔlklıç] conj a) thus, b) consequently, therefore.
folgsam ['fɔlkzaːm] adj obedient, good.
Folie ['foːlǐə] f (-; -n) foil (a. fig.), film.
'Folienkartoffeln pl baked potatoes.
Folklore [fɔlk'loːrə] f (-; no pl) folklore.
folkloristisch [fɔlklo'rıstıʃ] adj folkloristic.
Follikel [fɔ'liːkəl] m (-s; -) follicle.
Fol'likelsprung m physiol. ovulation.
Folter ['fɔltər] f (-; -n) torture, fig. a. torment: **j-n auf die** ~ **spannen** keep s.o. on tenterhooks. **foltern** v/t (h) torture. **'Folterung** f (-; -en) torture.
Fön [føːn] m (-[e]s; -e) TM hair drier.

Fond [fõ:] *m* (-s; -s) **1.** background. **2.** *mot.* back (of the car).

Fonds [fõ:] *m* (-; - [fõ:s]) **♦ 1.** fund. **2.** funds. **3.** government stocks.

Fondue [fõ'dy:] *n* (-s; -s) *gastr.* fondue.

fönen ['fø:nən] *v/t* (h) (blow-)dry.

Fontäne [fɔn'tɛ:nə] *f* (-; -n) **1.** fountain. **2.** jet of water.

forcieren [fɔr'si:rən] *v/t* (h) force.

'**Förderanlage** *f* conveyor (system).

'**Förderband** *n* conveyor belt.

'**Förderer** *m* (-s; -), '**Förderin** *f* (-; -nen) a) promoter, supporter, b) patron(ess), sponsor. '**förderlich** *adj* (*dat* to) conducive, useful, beneficial.

'**Fördermenge** *f* ⚒ output.

fordern ['fɔrdərn] *v/t* (h) **1.** demand (*von j-m* of s.o.), a. call for, ♦ *a.* claim, ask (for *a price*): **zuviel ~** a) ask (*or* expect) too much, b) overcharge (*von j-m* s.o.). **2.** challenge, *sports: a.* push *s.o.* to the limit: **er war voll gefordert** he was fully stretched; **nun ist der Minister gefordert** now it's for the minister to act. **3.** claim (*human lives etc*).

fördern ['fœrdərn] *v/t* (h) **1.** a) promote, support, b) patronize, sponsor, c) encourage, d) help, be good for: **~des Mitglied** supporting member. **2.** ⚒ produce, → **zutage.**

'**Förderpreis** *m* (literary *etc*) award.

'**Forderung** *f* (-; -en) **1.** demand (*nach* for, *an acc* on), ♈ claim: **~en stellen** make demands, enter claims. **2.** ♦ a) call, b) charge.

'**Förderung** *f* (-; -en) **1.** a) promotion, b) patronage, sponsorship, c) encouragement. **2.** production, output (*of oil etc*).

Forelle [fo'rɛlə] *f* (-; -n) *zo.* trout.

Forke ['fɔrkə] *f* (-; -n) ✐ pitchfork.

Form [fɔrm] *f* (-; -en) **1.** form (a. ling., phys., a. fig.), shape (a. fig.): ling. **aktive (passive) ~** active (passive) voice; *in aller ~* formally; *in ~ von (or gen)* in the form of; *in höflicher (netter) ~* politely (in a nice way); *der ~ halber* a) pro forma, b) to keep up appearances; *die ~ wahren* observe the proprieties; *fig.* **(greifbare) ~(en)** annehmen take shape. **2.** ◉ a) model, b) mo(u)ld, c) die. **3.** a) cake tin, b) pastry cutter. **4.** *esp. sports:* form, condition: *in (guter) ~* in good form (*or* shape); *in bester ~* in top form; *nicht in ~* off

form; *in ~ bleiben, sich in ~ halten* keep in trim, keep fit; *in ~ kommen* a) get into shape, b) *fig.* get going.

formal [fɔr'ma:l] *adj* formal.

Formaldehyd [fɔrm'aldəhy:t] *m* (-s; *no pl*) ♞ formaldehyde.

Formalien [fɔr'ma:liən] *pl* formalities.

Formalität [fɔrmali'tɛ:t] *f* (-; -en) formality.

Format [fɔr'ma:t] *n* (-[e]s; -e) **1.** format, size. **2.** *fig.* stature, calib*re* (*Am.* -er).

Formation [fɔrma'tsĭo:n] *f* (-; -en) formation. **Formati'ons...** formation (*flying, dancing, etc*).

'**formbar** *adj metall.* malleable.

'**Formblatt** *n* form.

Formel ['fɔrməl] *f* (-; -n) **1.** ♞, ♈, *a.* fig. formula. **2.** a) (set) formula, b) (set) phrase. **Formel-I-Rennen** *n mot.* formula-one race.

formell [fɔr'mɛl] *adj* formal.

'**Formelwagen** *m mot.* formula car.

formen ['fɔrmən] *v/t* (h) form, shape (*both a. sich ~*), ◉ mo(u)ld (*a. fig. s.o.*).

'**Formenlehre** *f* **1.** *ling.* morphology. **2.** ♪ theory of musical forms.

'**Formfehler** *m* a) irregularity, ♈ formal defect, b) faux pas.

'**Formgebung** *f* (-; -en), '**Formgestaltung** *f* ◉ styling, design.

formieren [fɔr'mi:rən] *v/t* (*a. sich ~*) form up.

'**Formkrise** *f sports: in e-r ~ stecken* be off form.

förmlich ['fœrmlɪç] **I** *adj* **1.** formal, ceremonious. **2.** F regular. **II** *adv* **3.** F literally. '**Förmlichkeit** *f* (-; -en) formality.

'**formlos** *adj* **1.** shapeless. **2.** informal.

'**Formsache** *f* matter of form, (*reine ~* mere) formality.

'**formschön** *adj* ◉ very stylish.

Formular [fɔrmu'la:r] *n* (-s; -e) form.

formulieren [fɔrmu'li:rən] *v/t* (h) formulate, phrase, word: *wie soll ich es ~?* how shall I put it?

Formu'lierung *f* (-; -en) **1.** formulation, wording, phrasing. **2.** phrase.

'**Formung** *f* (-; -en) forming, shaping.

'**formvollendet** *adj* a) perfect (*manners etc*), b) perfectly shaped, finished.

forsch [fɔrʃ] *adj* spirited, brisk, F peppy.

forschen ['fɔrʃən] *v/i* (h) **1.** do research (work). **2.** *~ nach* search for.

'**forschend** *adj* inquiring, searching.

Forscher 220

'**Forscher** *m* (-s; -) **1.** researcher, *a.* (research) scientist. **2.** explorer. **~drang** *m*, **~geist** *m* inquiring mind.
'**Forscherin** *f* (-; -nen) → **Forscher**.
'**Forschheit** *f* (-; *no pl*) spirit(edness), dash, F pep.
'**Forschung** *f* (-; -en) research (*auf dem Gebiet* gen on).
'**Forschungs...** research (*work, institute, etc*). **~auftrag** *m* research assignment. **~reise** *f* **1.** expedition. **2.** research trip. **~reisende** *m, f* (-n; -n) explorer.
Forst [fɔrst] *m* (-[e]s; -e[n]) forest.
Förster ['fœrstər] *m* (-s; -) forester.
'**Forsthaus** *n* forester's house.
'**Forstre‚vier** *n* forest district.
'**Forstwirtschaft** *f* (-; *no pl*) forestry.
fort [fɔrt] *adv* **1.** away, off, gone: *sie sind schon ~* they have already gone (*or* left); *ich muß ~* I must be going. **2.** gone, lost. **3.** *und so ~* and so on.
Fort [foːr] *n* (-s; -s) ✕ fort.
Fort..., fort... → *a. Weg..., weg..., Weiter..., weiter...*
'**Fortbestand** *m* (-[e]s; *no pl*) continued existence. '**fortbestehen** *v/i* (*irr, sep, h, → bestehen*) continue (to exist).
'**fortbewegen** (*sep, h*) **I** *v/t* move. **II** *sich ~* move, walk. '**Fortbewegung** *f* movement, (loco)motion.
'**fortbilden: sich ~** (*sep, h*) a) continue one's education (*or* training), b) do a course, c) improve one's knowledge. '**Fortbildung** *f* further education (*or* training). '**Fortbildungskurs** *m* (continuation) course.
'**fortbleiben** *v/i* (*irr, sep, -ge-, sn, → bleiben*) stay away.
'**fortdauern** *v/i* (*sep, -ge-, h*) continue, last: **~d** continuous, lasting.
forte ['fɔrtə] *adv*, '**Forte** *n* (-s; -s) ♪ forte.
'**fortfahren** *v/i* (*irr, sep, -ge-, sn, → fahren*) **1.** leave, *mot. a.* drive away. **2.** *a.* (h) continue: *~ zu reden* continue (*or* go on) talking; *~ mit* continue (with) (*one's story etc*); *fahren Sie fort!* go on!
'**fortfliegen** *v/i* (*irr, sep, -ge-, sn, → fliegen*) fly away, fly off.
'**fortführen** *v/t* (*sep, -ge-, h*) **1.** lead *s.o.* away. **2.** continue, carry on.
'**Fortführung** *f* (-; *no pl*) continuation.
'**Fortgang** *m* (-[e]s; *no pl*) **1.** departure. **2.** progress. '**fortgehen** *v/i* (*irr, sep, -ge-,*

sn, → *gehen*) **1.** go (away), leave. **2.** go on, continue.
'**fortgeschritten** *adj* advanced: *Kurs für Fortgeschrittene* advanced course.
'**fortgesetzt I** *adj* continued, constant. **II** *adv* continually, constantly.
'**fortlaufen** *v/i* (*irr, sep, -ge-, sn, → laufen*) **1.** run away ([*vor*] *j-m* from s.o.). **2.** continue. '**fortlaufend** *adj* a) continuous, b) consecutive (*numbers*): *~ numeriert* numbered consecutively.
'**fortpflanzen** (*sep, -ge-, h*) **I** *v/t* propagate, *biol. a.* reproduce, *phys. a.* transmit, *fig. a.* spread. **II** *sich ~ biol.* reproduce, *phys.* be propagated, travel, *fig.* spread. '**Fortpflanzung** *f* (-; *no pl*) propagation, *biol. a.* reproduction, *phys. a.* transmission, *fig. a.* spread(ing). '**Fortpflanzungsor‚gan** *n* reproductive organ.
'**Fortsatz** *m anat.* process, appendix.
'**fortschreiben** *v/t* (*irr, sep, -ge-, h, → schreiben*) **1.** update (*statistics etc*), reassess (*value*). **2.** *fig.* perpetuate.
'**fortschreiten** *v/i* (*irr, sep, -ge-, sn, → schreiten*) *fig.* advance, progress.
'**fortschreitend** *adj* progressive.
'**Fortschritt** *m* progress, improvement: *~e machen* make progress (*or* headway); *große ~e machen* make great strides. '**fortschrittlich** *adj* progressive, advanced, (very) modern, up-to-date.
'**Fortschrittsglaube** *m* belief in progress.
'**fortsetzen** *v/t* (*sep, -ge-, h*) continue (*a. sich ~*), resume. '**Fortsetzung** *f* (-; -en) continuation, sequel: *~ folgt* to be continued; *~ auf (von) Seite 2* continued on (from) page 2.
'**Fortsetzungsro‚man** *m* serial.
Fortuna [fɔr'tuːna] *f* (-; *no pl*) fortune.
'**fortwährend** → *ständig*.
'**Fortzahlung** *f* continued payment.
Forum ['foːrʊm] *n* (-s; Foren, Fora) forum, *fig. a.* platform.
fossil [fɔ'siːl] *adj* fossil.
Fossil [fɔ'siːl] *n* (-s; -ien [-liən]) fossil.
Foto ['foːto] *n* (-s; -s) F photo. **~album** *n* photo album. **~appa‚rat** *m* camera. **~ausrüstung** *f* photographic equipment. **~finish** *n sports*: photo finish.
fotogen [foto'geːn] *adj* photogenic.
Fotograf [foto'graːf] *m* (-en; -en) photographer. **Fotografie** [fotogra'fiː] *f* (-; -n)

1. no pl photography. **2.** photograph, picture. **fotografieren** [fotogra'fi:rən] v/i, v/t (h) photograph, take a picture (or pictures) (of). **Foto'grafin** f (-; -nen) photographer. **fotografisch** [foto-'gra:fiʃ] adj photographic.

Foto|ko'pie f, **2ko'pieren** v/t (h) photocopy. **~ko'piergerät** n photocopier. **~la,bor** n photographic laboratory. **~mo,dell** n (photographer's) model. **~mon,tage** f photomontage. **~repor,tage** f photographic reportage. **~satz** m print. photocomposition: **im ~ herstellen** photocompose.

Fotothek [foto'te:k] f (-; -en) photographic library.

'Fotozelle f ⚡ photocell.

Fötus ['fø:tʊs] m (-ses; -se) f(o)etus.

Foul [faʊl] n (-s; -s) sports: foul.

foulen ['faʊlən] v/i, v/t (h) sports: foul.

Foxtrott ['fɔkstrɔt] m (-s; -e, -s) (a. ~ tanzen) foxtrot.

Foyer [fŏa'je:] n (-s; -s) foyer, lounge, Am. lobby.

Fracht [fraxt] f (-; -en) **1.** load, freight, cargo. **2.** carriage, Am. freight(age), ⚓ freightage. **'Frachtbrief** m consignment note, Am. waybill.

'Frachter m (-s; -) freighter, cargo ship.

'Fracht|flugzeug n (air) freighter. **2frei** adj carriage paid, Am. freight prepaid. **~führer** m carrier. **~gebühr** f, **~geld** n → **Fracht** 2. **~gut** n freight, cargo: **als ~** by goods (Am. freight) train. **~kosten** pl freight charges (or costs). **~raum** m **1.** cargo hold. **2.** freight capacity. **~sätze** pl freight rates. **~schiff** n cargo ship, freighter. **~verkehr** m freight traffic.

Frack [frak] m (-[e]s; ⁻e) tailcoat, tails: **im ~** in evening dress, in tails.

'Frackhemd n dress shirt.

Frage ['fra:gə] f (-; -n) **1.** a) question, b) query, c) inquiry: **e-e ~ an j-n haben** have a question to ask s.o.; **(j-m) e-e ~ stellen** ask (s.o.) a question; **die ~ stellt sich nicht** the question does not arise; **ohne ~** undoubtedly; **das ist eben die ~** that's just the point; **in ~ stellen** a) question, doubt, b) jeopardize; **F gar k-e ~!** of course! **2.** matter, question: **e-e ~ der Zeit** a matter of time; **das ist e-e andere ~** that's a different matter. **3.** in ~ kommen be a possibility, person:

a. be eligible; **das kommt gar nicht in ~** that's out of the question.

'Frage|bogen m form, questionnaire. **~form** f ling. interrogative form. **~fürwort** n ling. interrogative (pronoun).

fragen ['fra:gən] v/t, v/i (h) ask, question: **nach et. (j-m) ~** inquire about s.th. (after s.o.); **(j-n) et. ~** ask (s.o.) a question; **(j-n) ~ nach** ask (s.o.) for; **j-n nach s-m Namen (dem Weg) ~** ask s.o. his name (the way); **es fragt sich, ob ...** it's a question of whether ...; **ich frage mich, warum** I (just) wonder why; **niemand fragte danach** nobody bothered about it; **↑ (sehr) gefragt** in (great) demand; **da fragst du mich zuviel** I'm afraid I can't tell you that. **'Fragen** n (-s) **~ kostet nichts** there's no harm in asking. **'fragend** adj questioning, inquiring, ling. interrogative.

Frager ['fra:gər] m (-s; -), **'Fragerin** f (-; -nen) questioner.

'Frage|satz m ling. interrogative clause (or sentence). **~stellung** f a. fig. question. **~stunde** f parl. question time.

'Frage-und-'Antwort-Spiel n quiz, a. fig. question and answer game.

'Frage|wort n ling. interrogative. **~zeichen** n question mark, a. fig. query.

fraglich ['fra:klɪç] adj **1.** doubtful. **2.** in question. **'fraglos** adv undoubtedly.

Fragment [fra'gmɛnt] n (-[e]s; -e) fragment. **fragmentarisch** [fragmɛn'ta:-rɪʃ] **I** adj fragmentary. **II** adv fragmentarily, in fragmentary form.

fragwürdig ['fra:kvʏrdɪç] adj questionable, dubious, F shady.

Fraktion [frak'tsĭo:n] f (-; -en) **1.** parl. a) parliamentary party, b) faction. **2.** 🜍 fraction. **frakti'onslos** adj independent. **Frakti'onsvorsitzende** m, f (-n; -n) party (Am. floor) leader. **Frakti'onszwang** m obligation to vote according to party policy.

Fraktur [frak'tu:r] f (-; -en) 🜍 fracture.

Franke ['fraŋkə] m (-n; -n) Franconian.

'Franken m (-s; -) (Swiss) franc.

frankieren [fraŋ'ki:rən] v/t (h) ⚑ prepay, stamp, frank. **fran'kiert** adj prepaid, post paid: **der Brief ist nicht ausreichend ~** they didn't put enough stamps on this letter.

franko ['fraŋko] adv prepaid.

Franse ['franzə] f (-; -n) fringe.

'**fransen** (h) **I** v/i fray. **II** v/t fringe.
'**fransig** adj **1.** fringed. **2.** frayed.
Franziskaner [frantsɪs'kaːnər] m (-s; -) Franciscan (friar).
Franzose [fran'tsoːzə] m (-n; -n) Frenchman: **die ~n** the French; **er ist ~** he is a Frenchman, he is French.
Französin [fran'tsøːzɪn] f (-; -nen) Frenchwoman: **sie ist ~** she is French.
fran'zösisch I adj French: **~es Bett** (double) divan. **II** ⚥ n ling. French: **aus dem** ⚥e **(ins** ⚥e) from (into) French.
frappieren [fra'piːrən] v/t (h) amaze: **~d** striking, amazing, remarkable.
Fräse ['frɛːzə] f (-; -n) **1.** ⚘ rotary hoe. **2.** milling machine. '**fräsen** v/t, v/i ⊙ mill.
fraß [fraːs] pret of **fressen**.
Fraß m (-es; no pl) **1.** F contp. muck. **2.** feed (for animals). **3.** ⚘ corrosion.
Fratze ['fratsə] f (-; -n) **1.** grimace: **~n schneiden** pull faces. **2.** F mug (sl.).
Frau [frau] f (-; -en) **1.** a) woman, adm. female, b) Mrs, Ms Brown etc: **die ~ von heute** modern woman. **2.** wife: **wie geht es Ihrer ~?** how is Mrs X? **3.** lady: **gnädige ~!** madam!
'**Frauen|arzt** m, **~ärztin** f gyn(a)ecologist. **~beauftragte** f women's representative. **~beruf** m female profession. **~bewegung** f (-; no pl) women's movement. ⚥**feindlich** adj anti-women. **~frage** f question of women's rights. **~fußball** m women's soccer. **~haus** n women's refuge (Am. shelter). **~heilkunde** f gyn(a)ecology. **~held** m ladykiller. **~leiden** n gyn(a)ecological disorder. **~rechte** pl women's rights.
Frauenrechtler ['frauənrɛçtlər] m (-s; -), '**Frauenrechtlerin** f (-; -nen) feminist.
'**Frauen|sport** m women's sport(s). **~stimmrecht** n votes for women. **~zeitschrift** f women's magazine.
Fräulein ['frɔʏlaɪn] n (-s; -) **1.** a) (young) lady, girl, b) Miss Brown etc. **2.** F a) salesgirl, b) waitress.
'**fraulich** adj womanly, feminine.
'**Fraulichkeit** f (-; no pl) womanliness.
frech [frɛç] adj a) impudent, F cheeky, saucy, Am. fresh, b) bold, brazen.
'**Frechheit** f (-; -en) impudence, F cheek: **so e-e ~!** what (a) cheek!
Fregatte [fre'gatə] f (-; -n) frigate.
frei [fraɪ] **I** adj **1.** free (von from, of), a. clear (road etc): **ist dieser Platz noch**

~? is this seat taken?; **Zimmer ~!** room(s) to let (Am. rent)!; **ein ~er Tag** a) a free day, b) a day off; **den Oberkörper ~ machen** strip to the waist; **~e Fahrt** mot. clear road, 🚦 green light; **~e Fahrt haben** a. fig. have the green light; → **Fuß** 1, **Hand, Stück** 1. **2.** a) free, independent, unattached, b) free and easy, c) liberal: **~er Beruf** independent profession; **~e Künste** liberal arts; **die ~e Wirtschaft** free enterprise; **ein ~er Mensch** a free agent. **3.** free, frank, open. **4.** blank: **e-n ~en Platz lassen** leave a blank. **5.** open, vacant: **~e Stelle** vacancy. **6.** open: **in der ~en Natur, im** ⚥en **in** the open (country); → **Himmel. 7.** a) free (of charge), b) prepaid: **Eintritt ~** admission free. **8.** freelance (journalist etc). **9.** phys. free, 🜁 a. uncombined: **Wärme wird ~** heat is released. **10.** teleph. vacant, Am. not busy. **11.** sports: unmarked. **II** adv **12.** freely (etc): **~ sprechen** a) speak openly, b) speak without notes; **~ erfunden** entirely fictitious, made(-)up; 🕈 **an Bord** free on board (f.o.b.); **Lieferung ~ Haus** no delivery charge; **~ finanziert** privately financed.
'**Freiaktie** f bonus share.
'**Freibad** n open-air swimming pool.
'**freibekommen** v/t (irr, sep, h, → **bekommen**) **1.** F **e-n Tag** etc ~ get a day etc off. **2.** j-n ~ get s.o. released; **et. ~** free s.th.
'**Freiberufler** m (-s; -), '**Freiberuflerin** f (-; -nen) freelance. '**freiberuflich** adj self-employed, freelance, lawyer, doctor, etc in private practice: **~ tätig sein** a. work (as a) freelance.
'**Freibetrag** m tax allowance.
'**Freibier** n (-[e]s; no pl) free beer.
'**freibleibend** adj and adv 🕈 without engagement.
'**Freibrief** m fig. excuse (**für** for).
'**Freidenker(in** f) m freethinker.
Freier ['fraɪər] m (-s; -) **1.** suitor. **2.** customer (of a prostitute).
'**Freiexem,plar** n free copy.
'**Freifahrschein** m free ticket.
'**Freiflug** m free flight.
'**Freifrau** f, '**Freifräulein** n baroness.
'**Freigabe** f (-; no pl) release, 🕈 floating (of exchange rate), 🛈 clearance.
'**freigeben** v/t (irr, sep, -ge-, h, → **ge-**

ben) 1. j-m e-n Tag etc ~ give s.o. a day etc off. **2.** release, ✈ float (*exchange rate*), ✔ *etc* clear: **et. für den Verkehr ~** open s.th. to traffic; **et. zur Veröffentlichung ~** release s.th. for publication.

freigebig ['fraɪge:bɪç] *adj* generous.

'**Freigebigkeit** *f* (-; *no pl*) generosity.

'**Freigehege** *n* open-air enclosure.

'**Freigepäck** *n* baggage allowance.

'**Freigrenze** *f* tax exemption limit.

'**freihaben** *v/i* (*irr, sep*, -ge-, h) F have the day off: **Freitag habe ich frei** Friday is my day off.

'**Freihafen** *m* free port.

'**freihalten** *v/t* (*irr, sep*, -ge-, h, → **halten**) **1.** keep (*seat*). **2.** keep *entrance etc* clear. **3.** keep *a post etc* open. **4.** *j-n ~* treat s.o., pay for s.o.

'**Freihandel** *m* free trade.

'**Freihandelszone** *f* free trade area.

freihändig ['fraɪhɛndɪç] *adj and adv* *shooting* without support, *cycling etc* with no hands. '**Freihandzeichnung** *f* freehand drawing.

'**Freiheit** *f* (-; -en) freedom, liberty: **dichterische ~** poetic licen/ce (*Am.* -se); **in ~ sein** be free; **sich die ~ nehmen zu** *inf* take the liberty of *ger*; **sich ~en erlauben** take liberties (**gegenüber** with).

'**freiheitlich** *adj* free, liberal.

'**Freiheits|beraubung** *f* deprivation of liberty, ⅔⅔ illegal detention. **~bewegung** *f* *pol.* freedom movement. **~entzug** *m* imprisonment. **~kampf** *m* struggle for freedom, revolt. **~kämpfer(in** *f*) *m* freedom fighter. **~krieg** *m* war of liberation. **~liebe** *f* love of freedom. **~strafe** *f* ⅔⅔ prison sentence: **zu e-r ~ von 5 Jahren verurteilt werden** be sentenced to 5 years' imprisonment.

freiher'aus *adv* frankly, point-blank.

'**Freiherr** *m* baron.

'**Freikarte** *f* free ticket.

'**freikaufen** (*sep*, -ge-, h) **I** *v/t* pay for s.o.'s release. **II sich ~** pay to be set free, *fig.* buy a clear conscience.

'**freikommen** *v/i* (*irr, sep*, -ge-, sn, → **kommen**) **1.** get free, get away. **2.** ⅔⅔ a) be released, b) be acquitted.

'**Freikörperkul,tur** *f* (-; *no pl*) nudism: **Anhänger(in)** *der* **~** nudist.

'**Freilandgemüse** *n* outdoor vegetables.

'**freilassen** *v/t* (*irr, sep*, -ge-, h, → **lassen**), '**Freilassung** *f* (-; -en) release.

'**Freilauf** *m* (*a.* **im ~ fahren**) freewheel.

'**freilaufend** *adj* **~e Hühner** free-running chicken.

'**freilegen** *v/t* (*sep*, -ge-, h) lay open, expose, uncover.

'**freilich** *adv* of course.

'**Freilicht|bühne** *f*, **~the,ater** *n* open-air theat/re (*Am.* -er). **~kino** → **Autokino**.

'**freiliegen** *v/i* (*irr, sep*, -ge-, h, → **liegen**) lie exposed, lie open.

'**Freilos** *n* **1.** free (lottery) ticket. **2.** *sports*: (**ein ~ ziehen** draw a) bye.

'**Freiluft...** open-air ..., outdoor ...

'**freimachen** (*sep*, -ge-, h) **I** *v/t* ✉ stamp, prepay. **II sich ~** free o.s. (**von** from), F arrange to be free.

'**Freimaurer** *m* freemason. **~loge** *f* freemason's (*or* Masonic) lodge.

'**Freimut** *m* cando(u)r, openness.

freimütig ['fraɪmy:tɪç] *adj* candid, open.

'**freinehmen** *v/t* (*irr, sep*, -ge-, h, → **nehmen**) (**sich**) **e-n Tag ~** take a day off.

'**Freiplastik** *f* free-standing sculpture.

'**freischaffend** *adj* freelance.

'**freischwimmen: sich ~** (*irr, sep*, -ge-, h, → **schwimmen**) a) pass one's 15-minute swimming test, b) *fig.* learn to stand on one's own two feet.

'**freisetzen** *v/t* (*sep*, -ge-, h) 🜚, *phys.* release (*a. fig.*): *j-n ~* make s.o. redundant; **freigesetzte Arbeitskräfte** redundant workers. '**Freisetzung** *f* (-; -en) a) release (*a. fig.*), b) redundancy.

'**freispielen: sich ~** (*sep*, -ge-, h) *sports*: break clear.

'**freisprechen** *v/t* (*irr, sep*, -ge-, h, → **sprechen**) **1.** (**von**) ⅔⅔ acquit (of), exonerate (from), clear (of *a suspicion*), *eccl.* absolve (from). **2.** release *apprentice* from his (*or her*) articles.

'**Freispruch** *m* (-[e]s; -e) ⅔⅔ acquittal.

'**Freistaat** *m* free state, republic.

'**Freistatt** *f*, '**Freistätte** *f* sanctuary.

'**freistehen** *v/i* (*irr, sep*, -ge-, h, → **stehen**) **1.** *sports*: be unmarked. **2.** *j-m ~* be up to s.o.; **es steht Ihnen frei zu** *inf* you are at liberty (*or* free) to *inf*.

'**freistellen** *v/t* (*sep*, -ge-, h) **1.** *j-n ~ a.* ✗ exempt s.o. (**von** from). **2.** *j-m et.* **~** leave s.th. (up) to s.o. '**Freistellung** *f* (-; -en) exemption (**von** from).

'**Freistil** *m* (-[e]s; *no pl*), '**Freistil...** *sports*: freestyle.

'**Freistoß** *m* *soccer*: free kick.

'**Freistunde** f ped. free period.
'**Freitag** m (-[e]s; -e) (**am ~** on) Friday.
'**freitags** adv on Friday(s).
'**freitragend** adj △, ⚙ cantilever, self-supporting.
'**Freitreppe** f (outdoor) steps.
'**Freiübungen** pl exercises.
'**Freiumschlag** m stamped addressed envelope.
'**Freiverkehr** m ✝ **im ~** in the open market, Am. over the counter.
'**Freiverkehrsbörse** f ✝ kerb market.
frei'weg adv F straight out.
'**Freiwild** n fig. fair game.
'**freiwillig I** adj a) voluntary, b) spontaneous. **II** adv voluntarily, of one's own free will: **sich ~ melden** volunteer (**zu** for).
'**Freiwillige** m, f (-n; -n) volunteer.
'**Freiwilligkeit** f (-; no pl) voluntariness.
'**Freiwurf** m sports: free throw.
'**Freizeichen** n teleph. dial(l)ing tone.
'**Freizeit** f (-; -en) **1.** no pl free (or leisure, spare) time. **2.** ped. holiday (or weekend) course.
'**Freizeit|beschäftigung** f leisure-time activity (or activities), n.s. hobby. **~gestaltung** f leisure-time activities. **~kleidung** f casual (or leisure) wear. **~zentrum** n leisure cent/re (Am. -er).
'**Freizone** f free zone.
'**freizügig** adj **1.** ✝ unrestricted. **2.** generous, liberal. **3.** permissive, free.
'**Freizügigkeit** f (-; no pl) **1.** ✝ free(dom of) movement. **2.** generosity. **3.** permissiveness.
fremd [frɛmt] adj **1.** strange, a. a) unfamiliar, unknown, b) odd: **~e Leute** strangers; **~e Hilfe** outside help; **~es Eigentum** other people's property; **ich bin hier ~** I'm a stranger here. **2.** a. fig. foreign, alien.
'**Fremdarbeiter(in** f) m foreign worker.
'**fremdartig** adj a. fig. foreign, strange, exotic.
'**Fremdartigkeit** f (-; no pl) strangeness.
'**Fremde¹** m, f (-n; -n) a) stranger, b) foreigner, c) tourist.
'**Fremde²** f (-; no pl) foreign parts: **in die (der) ~** away from home, abroad.
'**Fremden|führer(in** f) m (tourist) guide. **~haß** m xenophobia. **~heim** n guesthouse. **~industrie** f tourist industry. **~legion** f Foreign Legion. **~verkehr**

m tourism. **~verkehrsbü,ro** n tourist office. **~zimmer** n room (to let).
'**fremdgehen** v/i (irr, sep, -ge-, sn, → **gehen**) be unfaithful (to one's husband or wife).
'**Fremd|herrschaft** f foreign rule. **~kapi,tal** n loan capital. **~körper** m **1.** 🩺 foreign body. **2.** fig. alien element.
'**fremdländisch** [-lɛndɪʃ] adj foreign, exotic.
'**Fremdling** m (-s; -e) stranger.
'**Fremdsprache** f foreign language.
'**Fremdsprachen|korrespon,dent(in** f) m foreign correspondence clerk. **~sekre,tär(in** f) m linguist-secretary. **~unterricht** m foreign-language teaching (or lessons).
'**fremdsprachig** adj **1.** speaking a foreign language. **2.** → '**fremdsprachlich** adj foreign-language.
'**Fremdwort** n (-[e]s; ⸚er) foreign word.
frequentieren [frekvɛn'tiːrən] v/t frequent. **Frequenz** [fre'kvɛnts] f (-; -en) **1.** 🎵, phys. frequency. **2.** 🩺 (pulse) rate. **3.** number of visitors. **4.** density of traffic. **Fre'quenzbereich** m 🎵 frequency range.
Fresko ['frɛsko] n (-s; -ken) fresco.
Fressalien [frɛ'saːliən] pl F grub.
Fresse ['frɛsə] f (-; -n) V mug, kisser.
fressen ['frɛsən] (fraß, gefressen, h) **I** v/t **1.** eat, a. a) devour, F person: a. stuff o.s. with, b) feed on: **e-m Tier (...) zu ~ geben** feed an animal (on ...); F **er wird dich schon nicht ~** he won't bite you; → **Besen** 1, **Narr.** **2.** F fig. gobble up (money), guzzle (fuel etc). **II** v/i **3.** eat, F person: guzzle, eat like a pig. **4.** fig. **~ an** (dat) eat away, corrode. **III** sich ~ in (acc) fig. eat into.
'**Fressen** n (-s) food, feed, F grub: F fig. **das war ein gefundenes ~ für ihn** that was just what he was waiting for.
'**Fresser** m (-s; -) F guzzler, glutton.
'**Freßgier** f voraciousness.
'**Freßsack** m F glutton.
Frettchen ['frɛtçən] n (-s; -) zo. ferret.
Freude ['frɔydə] f (-; -n) joy (**über** acc at), pleasure, delight: **~ haben** (or **finden**) **an** (dat) enjoy; **j-m ~ bereiten** make s.o. happy; **ich hoffe, es macht dir ~!** I hope it will give you pleasure; **es macht mir k-e ~** I don't enjoy it; **zu m-r großen ~** much to my delight.

'**Freuden|fest** n celebration. **~feuer** n bonfire. **~geschrei** n cheers, cheering. **~schrei** m cry of joy. **~tag** m red-letter day. **~taumel** m in e-n ~ geraten go into ecstasies. **~tränen** pl tears of joy.
'**freudestrahlend** adj radiant (with joy).
'**freudig** adj joyful, cheerful, happy (event): **j-n ~ begrüßen** be happy to see s.o.; ~ **überrascht** pleasantly surprised.
freudlos ['frɔytloːs] adj cheerless, bleak.
Freudsch [frɔytʃ] adj → **Fehlleistung**.
freuen ['frɔyən] (h) **I sich ~** be glad (or happy, pleased) (über acc about); sich ~ **an** (dat) enjoy; **sich ~ auf** (acc) be looking forward to. **II** v/t please: **das freut mich sehr** I'm glad to hear that; **ich hoffe, es freut dich** I hope it will give you pleasure. **III** v/impers **es freut mich, Sie zu sehen** nice to see you; **es würde mich ..., wenn ...** I'd be very pleased if ...
Freund [frɔynt] m (-[e]s, -e) friend (a. fig.), boyfriend: **~ und Feind** friend and foe; fig. **ein ~ sein von** be fond of; **ein ~ der Musik** a music lover; → **dick** 2.
'**Freundchen** n (-s; -) iro. laddie, Am. buddy.
'**Freundeskreis** m (circle of) friends.
'**Freundin** ['frɔyndɪn] f (-; -nen) friend (a. fig.), girlfriend.
'**freundlich** adj **1.** friendly (gegen to), kind, nice: **~e Grüße** kind regards (an acc to); **bitte seien Sie so ~ und ...** (will you) be so kind as to ...; **sehr ~!** very kind of you! **2.** fig. mild, pleasant (climate etc), cheerful (room etc).
'**freundlicherweise** adv kindly.
'**Freundlichkeit** f (-; no pl) friendliness, kindness.
'**Freundschaft** f (-; -en) friendship: ~ **schließen mit** make friends with; **aus ~** because we etc are friends.
'**freundschaftlich** adj amicable, friendly: ~ **verbunden** on friendly terms.
'**Freundschafts|besuch** m pol. goodwill visit. **~dienst** m (j-m e-n ~ erweisen do s.o. a) good turn. **~spiel** n sports: friendly (game).
Frevel ['freːfəl] m (-s; -) **1.** sacrilege. **2.** (an dat, gegen against) crime, outrage.
'**frevelhaft** adj sacrilegious, w.s. outrageous. '**Freveltat** f outrage, crime.
Frevler ['freːflər] m (-s; -), '**Frevlerin** f (-; -nen) offender, esp. eccl. sinner.

Frieden ['friːdən] m (-s; no pl) a) peace, b) tranquil(l)ity: **innerer ~** peace of mind; **im ~** in peacetime; ~ **schließen** make peace, **mit j-m** make it up with s.o.; **laß mich in ~!** leave me alone!
'**Friedens|bedingungen** pl peace terms. **~bewegung** f pol. peace movement. **~bruch** m ᵗᵗ breach (pol. violation) of the peace. **~forschung** f peace research. **~gespräche** pl peace talks. **~initia,tive** f peace initiative. **~konfe,renz** f peace conference. **~kundgebung** f peace rally. **~no,belpreis** m Nobel Peace Prize. **~poli,tik** f policy of peace. **~schluß** m conclusion of the peace treaty. **~taube** f a. fig. dove of peace. **~truppe** f peacekeeping force. **~verhandlungen** pl peace negotiations. **~vertrag** m peace treaty. **~zeit** f often pl peacetime, time of peace.
friedfertig ['friːt-] adj peaceable.
Friedhof ['friːthoːf] m cemetery.
friedlich ['friːtlɪç] adj peaceful.
'**Friedlichkeit** f (-; no pl) peacefulness.
friedliebend ['friːt-] adj peace-loving.
frieren ['friːrən] v/i and v/impers (fror, gefroren, h) freeze: **ich friere, mich friert, es friert mich** I am cold; **es friert** it is freezing.
frigide [fri'giːdə] adj frigid. **Frigidität** [frigidi'tɛːt] f (-; no pl) frigidity.
Frikadelle [frika'dɛlə] f (-; -n) meatball.
Frikassee [frika'seː] n (-s; -s) fricassee.
Friktion [frɪk'tsioːn] f (-; -en) friction.
frisch [frɪʃ] **I** adj **1.** fresh, a. freshly-laid (egg), a. new (bread): **~e Farbe** (adv wet) paint; **~e Luft schöpfen** get some fresh air; **noch in ~er Erinnerung** fresh in my etc mind. **2.** a) clean (linen etc), b) fresh, new (page etc): **sich ~ machen** freshen up; fig. **mit ~en Kräften** with renewed strength. **3.** fresh, cool, chilly. **4.** fresh, brisk, lively: ~ **und munter** F alive and kicking. **5.** fresh (complexion etc), bright (colo[u]r). **II** adv freshly (etc): ~ **gestrichen!** wet paint!; ~ **gebacken** fresh from the oven.
'**Frische** f (-; no pl) **1.** freshness, fig. a. vigo(u)r, briskness, liveliness: fig. **in alter ~** as alive and well as ever. **2.** coolness, chilliness.
'**Frischei** n fresh(ly laid) egg.
'**Frischfleisch** n fresh meat.

'**Frischhalte|beutel** *m* polythene bag. **~packung** *f* keep-fresh package.

'**Frischmilch** *f* fresh milk.

'**Frischzellenthera,pie** *f* 🝚 living-cell therapy.

Friseur [fri'zøːr] *m* (-s; -e) hairdresser: *beim ~* at the hairdresser's. **Fri'seur-sa,lon** *m* hairdresser's shop.

Friseuse [fri'zøːzə] *f* (-; -n) hairdresser.

frisieren [fri'ziːrən] (h) **I** *v/t* **1.** *j-n ~* do s.o.'s hair. **2.** F doctor (*accounts etc*), soup up (*engine*). **II** *sich ~* do one's hair. **Fri'siersa,lon** *m* hairdresser's salon. **Fri'siertisch** *m* dresser.

Frist [frɪst] *f* (-; -en) a) (fixed) period of time, time limit, b) deadline, c) 🝚 respite: *e-e ~ setzen* (*einhalten*) fix (meet) a deadline; *innerhalb e-r ~ von 10 Tagen* within a ten-day period; *in kürzester ~* at very short notice.

fristen ['frɪstən] *v/t* (h) *sein Leben* (*or Dasein*) *~* scrape a (bare) living.

'**fristgemäß**, '**fristgerecht** *adj and adv* in time, within the prescribed time limit.

'**fristlos** *adj and adv* without notice.

'**Fristverlängerung** *f* extension (of the deadline).

Frisur [fri'zuːr] *f* (-; -en) a) hairstyle, b) haircut.

Friteuse [fri'tøːzə] *f* (-; -n) deep fryer.

fritieren [fri'tiːrən] *v/t* (h) deep-fry.

frivol [fri'voːl] *adj* **1.** frivolous. **2.** risqué.

Frivolität [frivoli'tɛːt] *f* (-; -en) **1.** *no pl* frivolity. **2.** frivolous remark.

froh [froː] *adj* glad (*über acc* of, about), cheerful: *sei ~, daß du nicht dabei warst* be thankful you weren't there.

fröhlich ['frøːlɪç] *adj* cheerful, merry.

'**Fröhlichkeit** *f* (-; *no pl*) cheerfulness.

froh'locken *v/i* (h) (*über acc*) a) rejoice (in, at), b) gloat (over). **Froh'locken** *n* (-s) a) jubilation, b) gloating.

'**Frohna,tur** *f* (-; -en) cheerful person.

'**Frohsinn** *m* (-[e]s; *no pl*) cheerfulness.

fromm [frɔm] *adj* **1.** pious, devout: *fig. ~er Betrug* pious fraud; *~e Lüge* white lie; *~er Wunsch* wishful thinking. **2.** gentle, steady (*horse*). **Frömmelei** [frœmə'laɪ] *f* (-; -en) sanctimoniousness. **Frömmigkeit** ['frœmɪçkaɪt] *f* (-; *no pl*) piety.

Fron [froːn] *f* (-; -en) *fig.* drudgery.

frönen ['frøːnən] *v/i* (h) (*dat*) indulge in.

Fron'leichnam *m* (-[e]s) Corpus Christi.

Front [frɔnt] *f* (-; -en) front, ✕ *a.* front line: *an der ~* at the front; *hinter der ~* behind the lines; *fig. ~ machen gegen* turn against, resist; *sports: in ~ gehen* (*liegen*) take (be in) the lead.

Frontal... [frɔn'taːl-] head-on, frontal. **~angriff** *m* frontal attack. **~zusammenstoß** *m* head-on collision.

'**Frontantrieb** *m mot.* front-wheel drive.

'**Frontkämpfer** *m* **1.** front-line soldier. **2.** ex-serviceman, *Am.* veteran.

'**Frontlader** *m* (-s; -) a) 🝚 loading shovel, b) 🖉 front loader.

'**Frontwechsel** *m fig.* about-face.

fror [froːr] *pret of* **frieren.**

Frosch [frɔʃ] *m* (-[e]s; ⸚e) **1.** *zo.* frog: F *sei kein ~!* don't be a spoilsport! **2.** squib. **~laich** *m* frog spawn. **~mann** *m* (-[e]s; ⸚er) frogman. **~perspek,tive** *f* (*aus der ~ sehen* have a) worm's-eye view. **~schenkel** *m gastr.* frog's leg.

Frost [frɔst] *m* (-[e]s; ⸚e) frost.

'**frostbeständig** *adj* frost-resistant.

'**Frostbeule** *f* chilblain.

'**Frosteinbruch** *m* sudden frost.

frösteln ['frœstəln] *v/i* (h) shiver (with cold): *mich fröstelt* I feel shivery.

'**Frösteln** *n* (-s) shivering.

frosten ['frɔstən] *v/t* (h) freeze.

'**frostfrei** *adj* free of frost, frost-free.

'**Frostgrenze** *f* frost line.

frostig ['frɔstɪç] *adj* frosty, *fig. a.* icy.

'**Frostsalbe** *f* chilblain ointment.

'**Frostschaden** *m* frost damage.

'**Frostschutz** *m* frost protection. **~mittel** *n* antifreeze. **~scheibe** *f mot.* defrosting screen.

'**Frostwetter** *n* frosty weather.

Frottee [frɔ'teː] *m*, *n* (-[s]; -s) towel(l)ing, terry(cloth).

frottieren [frɔ'tiːrən] *v/t* (h) rub down.

Frot'tier(hand)tuch *m* terry towel.

Frucht [frʊxt] *f* (-; ⸚e) **1.** 🝚 fruit: *Früchte tragen a. fig.* bear fruit. **2.** *pl fig.* fruit(s). '**fruchtbar** *adj a. fig.* fertile, fruitful, prolific: *auf ~en Boden fallen* fall on fertile ground. '**Fruchtbarkeit** *f* (-; *no pl*) *a. fig.* fertility, fruitfulness. '**Fruchtbon,bon** *m, n* fruit drop. '**Fruchteis** *n* fruit-flavo(u)red ice cream. **fruchten** ['frʊxtən] *v/i* (h) be of use, have an effect: *nichts ~* be no use, be in vain. '**Fruchtfleisch** *n* (fruit) flesh. '**fruchtlos** *adj* fruitless, *fig. a.* futile.

'**Frucht|presse** f juicer. **~saft** m fruit juice. **~wasser** n physiol. amniotic fluid. **~zucker** m fructose.

frugal [fru'ga:l] adj frugal.

früh [fry:] **I** adj early: **ein ~er van Gogh** an early (work by) van Gogh; → **früher, frühest, frühestens. II** adv early: **heute ~** this morning; (**schon**) ~ early on; ~ **genug** soon enough; **von ~ bis spät** from morning till night; **zu ~ kommen** be early.

'**Frühaufsteher** m (-s; -), '**Frühaufsteherin** f (-; -nen) early riser (F bird).

'**Frühe** f (-; no pl) (early) morning: **in aller ~** early in the morning.

'**früher I** adj a) earlier, b) former, c) past: **der ~e Besitzer** the previous owner. **II** adv a) earlier, a. sooner, b) in the past: ~ **oder später** sooner or later; ~ **habe ich geraucht** I used to smoke; **ich kenne sie von ~** I know her from way back.

'**Früherkennung** f ♣ early diagnosis.

'**frühest** adj earliest: **in ~er Kindheit** at a very early age.

'**frühestens** adv at the earliest.

'**Früh|geburt** f premature birth. **~geschichte** f (-; no pl) early history. **~jahr** n (-s; -e) (**im ~** in [the]) spring. '**Frühjahrs|mode** f spring fashions. **~müdigkeit** f spring tiredness.

'**Frühkar,toffeln** pl new potatoes.

'**Frühling** ['fry:lɪŋ] m (-s; -e) a. fig. spring(time): **im ~** in (the) spring. '**frühlingshaft** adj springlike, spring. '**Frühlingsrolle** f gastr. spring roll.

'**Frühmesse** f eccl. matins.

'**früh'morgens** adv early in the morning.

'**Früh|nebel** m early morning fog. ♀**reif** adj a. fig. precocious. **~reife** f precociousness, fig. a. precocity. **~schicht** f early shift. **~schoppen** m pre-lunch drink(s). **~sommer** m early summer. **~sport** m early morning exercises. **~stadium** n early stage.

'**Frühstück** n (-s; -e) breakfast: **zweites ~** mid-morning snack, Br. elevenses.

'**frühstücken** (h) **I** v/i (have) breakfast. **II** v/t have s.th. for breakfast.

'**Frühstückspause** f morning break.

'**Früh|warnsy,stem** n early warning system. **~zeit** f **1.** early period. **2.** prehistoric times. ♀**zeitig I** adj a) early, b) untimely, premature. **II** adv early, in good time. **~zug** m early train. **~zün-**

dung f mot. advanced ignition.

Frust [frʊst] m (-[e]s; no pl) F, **Frustration** [frʊstra'tsĭo:n] f (-; -en) psych. frustration. **frustrieren** [frʊs'tri:rən] v/t (h) frustrate.

Fuchs [fʊks] m (-es; ⁻e) **1.** zo. a) fox, b) sorrel. **2.** → **Fuchspelz. 3.** fig. **alter ~** cunning old devil; **schlauer ~** sly fox.

'**Fuchsbau** m (-[e]s; -e) fox's den.

Fuchsie ['fʊksĭə] f (-; -n) ♀ fuchsia.

Füchsin ['fʏksɪn] f (-; -nen) zo. vixen.

'**Fuchs|jagd** f fox hunt(ing). **~pelz** m fox (fur). ♀**rot** adj ginger. **~schwanz** m **1.** zo. foxtail. **2.** ⊙ pad saw.

'**fuchs'teufels'wild** adj F hopping mad.

Fuchtel ['fʊxtəl] f (-; -n) F **unter j-s ~ stehen** be under s.o.'s thumb.

fuchteln ['fʊxtəln] v/i (h) ~ **mit** wave s.th. around, brandish; **mit den Händen ~** gesticulate wildly.

Fug [fu:k] **mit ~ und Recht** rightly.

Fuge¹ ['fu:gə] f (-; -n) ♪ fugue.

'**Fuge²** f (-; -n) ⊙ a) joint, b) seam, c) groove: **aus den ~n gehen** fall apart, fig. be thrown out of joint.

fugen ['fu:gən] v/t (h) joint.

fügen ['fy:gən] (h) **I** v/t ⊙ joint. **II** sich ~ (dat or in acc to) a) submit, give in, b) resign o.s.; **sich e-m Befehl ~** comply with an order; → **unabänderlich. III** v/impers **es fügt sich, daß ...** it so happens that ... **fügsam** ['fy:kza:m] adj obedient. '**Fügung** f (-; -en) (act of) providence, (stroke of) fate: **durch e-e glückliche ~** by a lucky coincidence.

'**fühlbar** adj fig. noticeable, considerable: **sich ~ machen** make itself felt.

fühlen ['fy:lən] (h) **I** v/t feel, sense. **II** v/i feel: ~ **nach** feel for; **mit j-m ~** feel with s.o. **III** sich glücklich etc ~ feel happy etc; **sich ~ als** see o.s. as.

'**Fühler** m (-s; -) **1.** zo. feeler, antenna, tentacle; fig. **die ~ ausstrecken** put out one's feelers. **2.** ⊙ sensor.

'**Fühlung** f (-; no pl) contact: ~ **haben mit** be in touch with; ~ **nehmen mit** contact, get in touch with; **die ~ verlieren** lose touch (**mit** with). '**Fühlungnahme** [-na:mə] f (-; -n) contact.

fuhr [fu:r] pret of **fahren.**

Fuhre ['fu:rə] f (-; -n) a) loaded cart, b) (cart)load.

führen ['fy:rən] (h) **I** v/t **1.** lead (**nach, zu** to), take, guide: **j-n in ein Zimmer**

(*durchs Haus*) ~ show s.o. into a room (over the house); → **Leine**. **2.** a) lead, head, ✗ *a.* command, b) be in charge of, manage, run, c) hold (*an office*), d) keep (*books etc*), e) conduct (*business, lawsuit, etc*), carry on (*negotiations etc*): → **Gespräch, Klage** 2. **3.** bear (*a name*), go by (*the name of*), hold (*a title*), have (*coat of arms*): → **Schild**¹ 1. **4.** ✝ a) carry (*in stock*), b) sell, deal in. **5.** use, wield (*brush etc*). **6.** have *s.th.* with (*or* on) one, carry (*weapon etc*): ⚡ **Strom** ~ a) be live, b) conduct current. **7.** e-n **Schlag** ~ strike a blow. **8.** ~ **durch** (**um** *etc*) pass *line, tool, etc* through (*around etc*). **II** *v/i* lead, *sports: a.* be in the lead: ~ **nach,** *a. fig.* ~ **zu** lead to; *das führt zu nichts* that won't get us anywhere; *sports: mit zwei Toren* ~ be two goals ahead. **III** *sich gut etc* ~ conduct o.s. well *etc.*

'**führend** *adj* leading, prominent: ~ *sein* lead, rank in first place.

'**Führer** *m* (-s; -) **1.** leader, head. **2.** guide. **3.** *mot.* driver, ✈ pilot, ⚙ operator. **4.** guide(book). '**Führerin** *f* (-; -ncn) → **Führer** 1-3. '**führerlos** *adj* **1.** without a leader (*or* guide *etc*). **2.** *mot.* driverless, ✈ pilotless.

'**Führerna,tur** *f* born leader.

'**Führerschaft** *f* (-; *no pl*) **1.** leadership. **2.** *coll.* the leaders.

'**Führerschein** *m mot.* driving licence, *Am.* driver's license: *s-n* ~ *machen* take one's driving test. ~**entzug** *m* revocation of s.o.'s driving licence (*etc*).

'**Fuhrpark** *m* car pool, fleet (of vehicles).

'**Führung** (-; -en) *f* **1.** *no pl* guidance, *pol. etc* leadership, ✗ command, ✝ management, *coll.* the leaders: *unter der* ~ *von* headed by; *die* ~ *übernehmen* take charge (→ *a.* 5). **2.** (guided) tour. **3.** *no pl* conduct (*of negotiations etc*). **4.** *no pl* conduct, behavio(u)r. **5.** *no pl sports:* lead: *in* ~ *gehen, die* ~ *übernehmen* take the lead; *in* ~ *liegen* be in the lead. **6.** *no pl* use (*of title*).

'**Führungs|aufgabe** *f* executive function. ~**e,tage** *f* executive floor. ~**gremium** *n* executive committee. ~**kraft** *f* ✝ executive, *pl* executive personnel, *pol.* leaders. ~**schicht** *f* ruling class(es). ~**schwäche** *f* weak leadership. ~**spitze** *f* top echelons. ~**stil** *m* style of leader-

ship. ~**tor** *n,* ~**treffer** *m* goal that puts a team into the lead. ~**zeugnis** *n* certificate of (good) conduct.

'**Fuhrunternehmen** *n* haulage company. '**Fuhrunternehmer** *m* haulage contractor. '**Fuhrwerk** *n* wag(g)on.

Fülle ['fylə] *f* (-; *no pl*) **1.** fullness, *fig. a.* richness: → **Hülle** 4. **2.** wealth, abundance. **3.** corpulence.

füllen ['fylən] *v/t* (h) **1.** (*a. sich* ~) fill: *in Flaschen* ~ bottle; *der Aufsatz füllte drei Seiten* the essay took up three pages. **2.** *gastr.* stuff.

Füller ['fylər] *m* (-s; -) F, **Füll-(feder)halter** *m* fountain pen.

füllig ['fylɪç] *adj* full, plump.

Füllsel ['fylzəl] *n* (-s; -) filler.

'**Füllung** *f* (-; -en) **1.** filling (*a. of tooth*), *gastr. a.* stuffing, cent/re (*Am.* -er) (*of chocolates*). **2.** padding.

'**Füllwort** *n* (-[e]s; ~er) filler.

fummeln ['fʊməln] *v/i* (h) F **1.** fiddle around (*an dat* with). **2.** pet.

Fund [fʊnt] *m* (-[e]s; -e) a) discovery, finding, b) (*e-n* ~ *machen* make a) find.

Fundament [fʊndaˈmɛnt] *n* (-[e]s; -e) △ foundations. **fundamental** [fʊndamɛnˈtaːl] *adj* fundamental, basic.

Fundamentalismus [fʊndamɛntaˈlɪsmʊs] *m* (-; *no pl*) fundamentalism.

'**Fundbü,ro** *n* lost property office.

'**Fundgrube** *f fig.* (gold)mine.

fundieren [fʊnˈdiːrən] *v/t* (h) **1.** substantiate. **2.** ✝ fund. **fun'diert** *adj* **1.** sound (*knowledge etc*). **2.** ✝ founded.

fündig ['fyndɪç] *adj* ~ *werden a. fig.* strike gold.

'**Fundort** *m* (-[e]s; -e) site (of discovery).

'**Fundsache** *f* lost article, *pl a.* lost property.

Fundus ['fʊndʊs] *m* (-; -) **1.** *thea.* general equipment. **2.** store (*von, an dat* of).

fünf [fynf] *adj* five, *ped.* poor, *Br.* E, *Am.* F. **Fünfeck** *n* (-[e]s; -e) pentagon.

'**fünfeckig** *adj* pentagonal.

'**Fünfer** *m* (-s; -) **1.** five-pfennig (*or* five-mark) piece. **2.** → **Fünf.**

'**fünffach** *adj and adv* fivefold.

'**fünfhundert** *adj* five hundred.

fünfjährig ['fynfjɛːrɪç] *adj* **1.** five-year-old: *ein* ~*es Kind a.* a child of five. **2.** five-year, *period etc* of five years.

'**Fünfkampf** *m sports*: pentathlon.
'**Fünfkämpfer(in** *f*) *m* pentathlete.
'**Fünflinge** *pl* quintuplets, F quins.
'**fünfmal** *adv* five times.
Fünfpro'zentklausel *f parl.* five per cent
 hurdle.
fünfstellig ['fʏnfʃtɛlɪç] *adj* five-digit.
Fünf'tagewoche *f* five-day working
 week.
fünfte ['fʏnftə] *adj* fifth: → *Kolonne*,
 Rad 1. '**Fünftel** (-s; -) fifth.
'**fünfzehn** *adj* fifteen.
fünfzig ['fʏnftsɪç] *adj* fifty. '**Fünfzig** *f* (-;
 no pl) fifty: **sie ist Mitte (der)** ~ she is in
 her mid-fifties. '**fünfziger** *adj die* ~
 Jahre the fifties (*of a century*).
'**Fünfziger** *m* (-s; -) **1.** man of fifty: *er ist
 in den* ~*n* he is in his fifties. **2.** F a)
 fifty-pfennig piece, b) fifty-mark note
 (*Am.* bill). '**Fünfzigerin** *f* (-; -nen)
 woman of fifty (*or* in her fifties).
fungieren [fʊŋ'giːrən] *v/i* (h) ~ *als* act
 (*thing*: serve) as.
Funk [fʊŋk] *m* (-s; *no pl*) radio; → *a.
 Rundfunk, Radio.* ~**ama|teur** *m* radio
 ham. ~**ausstellung** *f* radio and TV exhibition. ~**bild** *n* photo-radiogram.
Fünkchen ['fʏŋkçən] *n* (-s; -) → **Funke**
 ['fʊŋkə] *m* (-n; -n) *a. fig.* spark: *ein* ~
 (**von**) **Verstand** a modicum of sense;
 kein ~ *Hoffnung* not a flicker of hope.
funkeln ['fʊŋkəln] *v/i* (h) sparkle (*a. fig.*).
'**funkel'nagel'neu** *adj* F brand-new.
funken ['fʊŋkən] *v/t* (h) radio (*a. v/i*),
 send out: F *zwischen uns hat es sofort gefunkt* we clicked the moment we
 met.
'**Funken** *m* (-s; -) → **Funke**.
'**funkentstört** *adj* radio-screened.
Funker ['fʊŋkər] *m* (-s; -) radio operator.
'**Funk|gerät** *n* transmitter. ~**haus** *n*
 broadcasting cent/re (*Am.* -er). ~**meldung** *f* radio message. ~**peilgerät** *n*
 radio direction finder. ~**rufempfänger**
 m bleep(er). ~**si|gnal** *n* radio signal.
'**Funksprech|gerät** *n* walkie-talkie.
 ~**verkehr** *m* radio telephony.
'**Funk|spruch** *m* radio message. ~**sta-
ti|on** *f*, ~**stelle** *f* radio station. ~**stille** *f*
 radio silence. ~**streife** *f* **1.** radio patrol.
 2. → ~**streifenwagen** *m* radio patrol
 car. ~**taxi** *n* radio cab. ~**technik** *f* radio
 engineering. ~**tele|gramm** *n* radiotele-
gram, radiogram.

Funktion [fʊŋk'tsɪoːn] *f* (-; -en) function,
 a. position: *in* ~ *treten* go into action.
Funktionär [fʊŋktsɪo'nɛːr] *m* (-s; -e),
 Funktio'närin *f* (-; -nen) official.
funktionell [fʊŋktsɪo'nɛl] *adj* functional.
funktionieren [fʊŋktsɪo'niːrən] *v/i* (h)
 function, work (*a.* F *fig.*).
funkti'onsfähig *adj* functioning.
Funkti'onsstörung *f* ✷ malfunction.
'**Funk|turm** *m* radio tower. ~**verbin-
dung** *f* radio contact. ~**verkehr** *m* radio communication(s). ~**wagen** *m* **1.**
 radio van. **2.** → **Funkstreifenwagen**.
für [fyːr] *prep* for, *a.* a) in exchange (*or*
 return) for, b) in favo(u)r of, c) instead
 of: *Jahr* ~ *Jahr* year after year; ~ *mich*
 for me, to me, in my opinion; *ich* ~ *m-e
 Person* I myself; ~*s erste* for the moment; ~ *sich leben* live by o.s.; *an und
~ sich* actually; *e-e Sache* ~ *sich* another matter entirely; *das hat viel* ~
 sich there's a lot to be said for it; *was* ~
 (*ein*) ...*?* what (kind of) ...?
Für *n das* ~ *und Wider* the pros and cons.
'**Fürbitte** *f a. eccl.* intercession.
Furche ['fʊrçə] *f* (-; -n) **1.** 🖊, *anat.* fur-
row, *geol.*, ⚙ *a.* groove. **2.** rut.
Furcht [fʊrçt] *f* (-; *no pl*) (*vor dat* of) fear,
 dread: *aus* ~ *vor* for fear of; *j-m* ~
 einflößen (*or einjagen*) frighten s.o.
'**furchtbar I** *adj* terrible, dreadful. **II** *adv*
 terribly, F *a.* awfully.
'**furchteinflößend** *adj* frightening.
fürchten ['fʏrçtən] (h) **I** *v/t* be afraid of,
 dread: *ich fürchte, wir schaffen es
 nicht* I fear we're not going to make it.
 II *v/i für j-n* ~ fear for s.o. **III** *sich* ~ (*vor
 dat* of) be afraid, be scared, be fright-
ened; *sich* ~ *vor* (*dat*) *a.* dread; *sich
 (davor)* ~ *zu inf* be afraid of *ger.*
fürchterlich ['fʏrçtərlɪç] → *furchtbar.*
'**furchterregend** *adj* frightening.
'**furchtlos** *adj* fearless, intrepid.
'**Furchtlosigkeit** *f* (-; *no pl*) fearlessness.
'**furchtsam** *adj* timorous.
'**Furchtsamkeit** *f* (-; *no pl*) timorousness.
fürein'ander *adv* for each other, for one
 another.
Furie ['fuːrɪə] *f* (-; -n) *fig.* hellcat, virago.
Furnier [fʊr'niːr] *n* (-s; -e) veneer.
furnieren [fʊr'niːrən] *v/t* (h) veneer.
Furore [fu'roːrə] ~ *machen* cause a
 sensation.
'**Fürsorge** *f* (-; *no pl*) **1.** a) care (*für* for),

b) solicitude: **ärztliche ~** medical care. **2. öffentliche ~** public welfare.

'**fürsorglich** *adj* considerate, solicitous.

'**Fürsprache** *f* (*-; no pl*) **1.** intercession (**für** for, **bei** with). **2.** recommendation.

'**Fürsprecher(in** *f*) *m* a) intercessor, b) advocate.

Fürst [fyrst] *m* (*-en; -en*) a) prince, b) ruler: **F leben wie ein ~** live like a king.

'**Fürstenhaus** *n* dynasty. '**Fürstentum** *n* (*-s; ⸚er*) principality. '**Fürstin** *f* (*-; -nen*) princess. '**fürstlich** *adj* princely (*a. fig.*), prince's, *fig.* sumptuous, generous (*tip etc*): **j-n ~ bewirten** (**belohnen**) entertain (reward) s.o. royally.

Furt [furt] *f* (*-; -en*) fjord.

Furunkel [fu'ruŋkəl] *m* (*-s; -*) ♣ boil.

'**Fürwort** *n* (*-[e]s; ⸚er*) *ling.* pronoun.

Furz [furts] *m* (*-es; ⸚e*) V fart.

furzen ['furtsən] *v/i* (h) V fart.

Fusel ['fu:zəl] *m* (*-s; -*) F rotgut.

Fusion [fu'zĭo:n] *f* (*-; -en*) **1.** ⚛ fusion. **2.** ✝ merger. **fusionieren** [fuzĭo'ni:rən] *v/t, v/i* (h) ✝ merge.

Fuß [fu:s] *m* (*-es; ⸚e*) **1.** foot: **zu ~** on foot; **zu ~ gehen** walk; **zu ~ erreichbar** within walking distance; **gut zu ~ sein** be a good walker; *fig.* (**festen**) **~ fassen** gain a foothold; (*dat*) **auf dem ~e folgen** follow on the heels of; *fig.* **auf die Füße fallen** fall on one's feet; **auf freiem ~** at large; **j-n auf freien ~ setzen** release s.o.; **auf eigenen Füßen stehen** stand on one's own two feet; **auf großem ~e leben** live in grand style; **auf gutem ~e stehen mit** be on good terms with; **auf schwachen Füßen stehen** be shaky; **mit beiden Füßen auf der Erde stehen** have both feet firmly on the ground; **kalte Füße bekommen** *a.* F *fig.* get cold feet; → **link. 2.** foot, bottom (*of list, page, etc*), leg (*of chair etc*), stem (*of wineglass etc*), stand (*of lamp*): **am ~e des Berges** at the bottom of the mountain. **3.** foot (= 30,48 cm): **10 ~** ten feet.

'**Fußabdruck** *m* footprint.

'**Fußangel** *f* mantrap, *fig.* trap.

'**Fußbad** *n* footbath.

'**Fußball** *m* (*-[e]s; ⸚e*) **1.** football, *Am.* soccer ball. **2.** *no pl* football, *esp. Am.* soccer. '**Fußball...** football (*club etc*).

'**Fußballen** *m* *anat.* ball of the foot.

'**Fußballer** [-balər] *m* (*-s; -*) F footballer.

'**Fußballänderspiel** *n* (*getr.* -ll‚l-) international (football) match.

'**Fußball|platz** *m* football pitch. **~spieler** *m* football player. **~toto** *m, n* football pools, F *the* pools. **~verband** *m* football association. **~weltmeister** *m* World Cup holders. **~weltmeisterschaft** *f* World Cup.

'**Fußbank** *f* footstool.

'**Fußboden** *m* **1.** floor. **2.** → **~belag** *m* floor covering, flooring. **~heizung** *f* underfloor heating.

'**Fußbreit** *m k-n ~ weichen** not to budge an inch.

'**Fußbremse** *f* *mot.* footbrake.

Fussel ['fusəl] *f* (*-; -n*) F fluff, *Am.* lint.

'**fusselig** *adj* F covered in fluff: *fig.* **sich den Mund ~ reden** talk one's head off.

fußen ['fu:sən] *v/i* (h) **~ auf** (*dat*) be based (up)on.

'**Fußende** *n* (**am ~** at the) foot.

'**Fußgänger** ['fu:sgɛŋər] *m* (*-s; -*) pedestrian. **~brücke** *f* footbridge.

'**Fußgängerin** *f* (*-; -nen*) pedestrian.

'**Fußgänger|übergang** *m*, **~überweg** *m* pedestrian crossing. **~unterführung** *f* (pedestrian) underpass, *Br. a.* subway. **~zone** *f* pedestrian precinct.

'**Fuß|gelenk** *n* *anat.* ankle. **♀hoch** ankle-deep. **~matte** *f* doormat, *mot.* floor mat. **~note** *f* footnote. **~pfad** *m* footpath. **~pflege** *f* pedicure. **~pfleger(in** *f*) *m* pedicurist, chiropodist. **~pilz** *m* ♣ athlete's foot. **~puder** *m* foot powder. **~sohle** *f* sole (of the foot). **~spur** *f* footprint. **~stapfe** *f* (*-; -n*) footstep: *fig.* **in j-s ~n treten** follow s.o.'s footsteps. **~tritt** *m* **1.** footstep. **2.** footprint. **3.** kick: **j-m e-n ~ geben** *a.* kick s.o. **~volk** *n* *fig.* rank and file. **~weg** *m* **1.** footpath. **2.** *e-e Stunde etc* **~** an hour's *etc* walk.

futsch [futʃ] *adj pred* F a) gone, b) broken, *sl.* bust: **es ist ~** *a.* it has had it.

Futter¹ ['futər] *n* (*-s; no pl*) **1.** ✿ fodder, feed, food. **2.** F grub (*sl.*), chow (*sl.*).

'**Futter²** *n* (*-s; -*) lining, △ casing.

Futteral [futə'ra:l] *n* (*-s; -e*) case, cover.

'**Futtermittel** *n* feed, fodder.

futtern ['futərn] *v/i* (h) F tuck in(to *v/t*).

füttern¹ ['fytərn] *v/t* (h) feed.

'**füttern²** *v/t* (h) line.

'**Futternapf** *m* feeding bowl.

'**Futterneid** *m fig.* envy, jealousy.
'**Futterstoff** *m* lining (material).
'**Fütterung** *f* (-; -en) feeding.
Futur [fu'tu:r] *n* (-s; *no pl*) *ling.* (*a.* **erstes** ~) future (tense); **zweites** ~ future perfect (tense).

Futurismus [futu'rɪsmʊs] *m* (-; *no pl*) futurism. **Futurist** [futu'rɪst] *m* (-en; -en), **futu'ristisch** *adj* futurist.
Futurologe [futuro'lo:gə] *m* (-n; -n) futurologist. **Futurologie** [futurolo-'gi:] *f* (-; *no pl*) futurology.

G

G, g [ge:] *n* (-; -) *a.* ♪ G, g.
gab [ga:p] *pret of* **geben**.
Gabardine ['gabardi:n] *m* (-s; *no pl*), *a. f* (-; *no pl*) gabardine.
Gabe ['ga:bə] *f* (-; -n) **1.** (**an** *acc* to) a) gift, present, b) contribution: **milde** ~ charity. **2.** gift, talent.
Gabel ['ga:bəl] *f* (-; -n) **1.** a) fork (*a. on bike*), b) ↗ (pitch)fork. **2.** *teleph.* rest, cradle. **3.** *zo.* spire. **gabeln** ['ga:bəln] (h) **I** *sich* ~ fork (off *or* out). **II** *v/t* fork.
'**Gabelstapler** *m* (-s; -) forklift (truck).
'**Gabelung** *f* (-; -en) fork.
'**Gabentisch** *m* table with (the) presents.
gackern ['gakərn] *v/i* (h) cluck.
gaffen ['gafən] *v/i* (h) gape, stare.
Gag [gɛk] *m* (-s; -s) gag.
Gage ['ga:ʒə] *f* (-; -n) fee.
gähnen ['gɛ:nən] *v/i* (h) *a. fig.* yawn: ~*d leer* completely empty.
'**Gähnen** *n* (-s) yawn(ing).
Gala ['ga:la] *f* (-; *no pl*) gala dress.
'**Gala...** gala (*concert, performance, etc*).
galant [ga'lant] *adj* gallant. **Galanterie** [galantə'ri:] *f* (-; -n) gallantry.
Galeere [ga'le:rə] *f* (-; -n) galley.
Galerie [galə'ri:] *f* (-; -n) gallery.
Galerist [galə'rɪst] *m* (-en; -en), **Gale'ristin** *f* (-; -nen) gallery owner.
Galgen ['galgən] *m* (-s; -) gallows.
'**Galgenhu,mor** *m* gallows humo(u)r.
Gali'onsfi,gur [ga'lio:ns-] *f* figurehead.
gälisch ['gɛ:lɪʃ] *adj* Gaelic.
'**Gallapfel** *m* oakapple.
Galle ['galə] *f* (-; -n) **1.** *anat.* gall bladder. **2.** *physiol., a. fig.* bile, *a.* 🐝, *zo.* gall: *mir kam die* ~ *hoch* my blood was up.
'**Gallen|blase** *f* *anat.* gall bladder. ~**gang** *m* bile (*or* gall) duct. ~**kolik** *f*

bilious attack. ~**leiden** *n* bilious complaint. ~**stein** *m* 🝙 gallstone.
Gallert ['galərt] *n* (-[e]s; -e) jelly.
'**gallertartig** *adj* jelly-like, gelatinous.
Gallier ['galiər] *m* (-s; -) *hist.* Gaul.
gallig ['galɪç] *adj a. fig.* bilious.
Galopp [ga'lɔp] *m* (-s; -s, -e) gallop: *im* ~ at a gallop, *fig. a.* in a hurry.
galoppieren [galɔ'pi:rən] *v/i* (sn) gallop.
galt [galt] *pret of* **gelten**.
galvanisch [gal'va:nɪʃ] *adj* galvanic.
galvanisieren [galvani'zi:rən] *v/t* (h) galvanize (*a.* ↗), ⊕ *a.* electroplate.
Galvanotechnik [gal'va:no-] *f* electroplating.
Gamasche [ga'maʃə] *f* (-; -n) a) gaiter, b) puttee.
Gamet [ga'me:t] *m* (-en; -en) gamete.
Gammaglobulin [gamaglobu'li:n] *n* (-s; *no pl*) 🝙 gamma globulin.
'**Gammastrahl** *m phys.* gamma ray.
'**Gammastrahlung** *f* gamma radiation.
Gamme'lei *f* (-; *no pl*) F loafing around.
'**gammelig** *adj* F **1.** old (*meat etc*), rotten (*fruit etc*). **2.** scruffy. **gammeln** ['ga-məln] *v/i* (h) F loaf (*or* bum) around.
Gammler ['gamlər] *m* (-s; -), '**Gammlerin** *f* (-; -nen) F layabout, loafer, bum.
gang [gaŋ] *adj ~ und gäbe sein* be quite common (*or* usual).
Gang *m* (-[e]s; ⁓e) **1.** → **Gangart**. **2.** a) walk, b) errand, c) way, d) visit. **3.** course: *s-n* ~ *gehen* take its course. **4.** ⊕ a) running, working, action, b) operation: *in* ~ *setzen* (*or* **bringen**) *a. fig.* start, get *s.th.* going; *in* ~ *kommen a. fig.* get going (*or* started); *im* ~ *(e) sein* ⊕ be running, be working, *fig.* be under way, be in progress; *es ist et. im* ⁓*e*

s.th. is going on; *in vollem ~e sein* be in full swing. **5.** *mot.* gear, *a.* ☉ speed: *erster ~* first (*or* bottom) gear; *in den dritten ~ schalten* change (*Am.* shift) into third (gear); *den ~herausnehmen* put the car in neutral. **6.** a) corridor (*a.* 🚂), hall(way), b) passage(way), c) aisle, d) walkway, e) tunnel. **7.** *anat.* duct. **8.** *gastr.* course: *ein Essen mit fünf Gängen* a five-course meal.

'**Gangart** *f* gait, walk, pace (*of horse*).
'**gangbar** *adj* passable (*road etc*), practicable (*a. fig.*).
gängeln ['gɛŋəln] *v/t* (h) F *j-n ~* keep s.o. in leading strings.
gängig ['gɛŋɪç] *adj* **1.** current (*expression*), (very) common (*method etc*). **2.** 📈 saleable, fast-selling.
'**Gangschaltung** *f mot.* gear change, *Am.* gearshift.
Gangster ['gɛŋstər] *m* (-s; -) gangster.
'**Gangsterbande** *f* gang of criminals.
'**Gangsterbraut** *f* moll.
'**Gangstertum** *n* (-s; *no pl*) gangsterism.
Gangway ['gæŋweɪ] *f* (-; -s) **1.** ✈ steps. **2.** ⚓ gangway.
Ganove [ga'noːvə] *m* (-n; -n) F crook.
Gans [gans] *f* (-; e) goose: *junge ~* gosling; *dumme ~* stupid thing (*or* girl).
Gänschen ['gɛnsçən] *n* (-s; -) gosling.
Gänse|**blümchen** ['gɛnzə-] *n* daisy. **~braten** *m* roast goose. **~füßchen** *pl* F quotation marks, inverted commas. **~haut** *f* gooseflesh, goose pimples: *ich kriege e-e ~* it gives me the creeps. **~leberpa,stete** *f* pâté de foie gras. **~marsch** *m im ~* in single file.
Gänserich ['gɛnzərɪç] *m* (-s; -e) gander.
'**Gänseschmalz** *n* goose dripping.
ganz [gants] **I** *adj* **1.** whole, complete: *~ Deutschland* all (*or* the whole) of Germany; *die ~e Stadt* the whole town; *in der ~en Welt* all over the world; *~e Länge* total (*or* overall) length; *~e Zahl* whole number; *~e zwei Stunden* a) for two solid hours, b) for just two hours; *von ~em Herzen* with all my *etc* heart; *den ~en Tag* all day; *die ~e Nacht (hindurch)* all night long; *die ~e Zeit* all the time; F *ihr ~es Geld* all her money. **2.** F intact, in one piece: *~ machen* mend. **II** *adv* **3.** (*a. ~ und gar*) completely, totally: *~ aus Holz etc* all wood *etc*; *das ist et. ~ anderes* that's a

different matter altogether; *nicht ~* not quite; *nicht ~ zehn Minuten* just under ten minutes; *~ und gar nicht* not at all; *~ gewiß* certainly; *~ naß* wet through; *wie du willst* just as you like; (*ich bin*) *~ Ihrer Meinung* I quite agree; *er ist ~ der Vater* he's just like his father; → *Ohr.* **4.** a) quite, F pretty, b) very, really: *~ gut* quite good, not bad; *~ wenig* a tiny bit; *~ besonders, weil* (e)specially since. **5.** *im ~en* altogether, in all, 📈 wholesale: → *groß* 6, 7.
Ganze ['gantsə] *n* (-n; *no pl*) whole: *einheitliches ~s* integral whole; *als ~s* as a whole, in its entirety; *das ~* the whole thing; *aufs ~ gehen* go all out; *jetzt geht es ums ~* it's all or nothing now.
'**Ganzheit** *f* (-; *no pl*) (*in s-r ~* as a) whole.
'**Ganzheitsme,thode** *f* **1.** whole-word method. **2.** *a.* '**Ganzheitsunterricht** *m* integrated curriculum.
ganzjährig ['gantsjɛːrɪç] *adj* all-year: *~ geöffnet* open all year round.
gänzlich ['gɛntslɪç] *adj and adv* total(ly), complete(ly), entire(ly).
'**Ganzme,tall...** ☉ all-metal.
ganzseitig ['gantszaɪtɪç] *adj* full-page.
ganztägig ['gantstɛːgɪç] *adj* all-day: *~ geöffnet* open all day.
'**Ganztags**|**beschäftigung** *f* full-time job. **~schule** *f* all-day school(ing).
gar[1] [gaːr] *adj gastr.* done, cooked.
gar[2] *adv* **1.** *~ nicht* not at all; *~ nichts* not a thing, nothing at all, absolutely nothing; *~ nicht so schlecht (viel)* not all that bad (much); *~ keiner* nobody at all; *es besteht ~ kein Zweifel* there's no doubt whatsoever. **2.** a) perhaps, b) even: *oder ~ ... ...* let alone ...
Garage [ga'raːʒə] *f* (-; -n) garage.
Garant [ga'rant] *m* (-en; -en) guarantor.
Garantie [garan'tiː] *f* (-; -n) guarantee: *die Uhr hat ein Jahr ~* the watch has got a year's guarantee; *die Reparatur geht noch auf ~* the repair is covered by the guarantee; *dafür kann ich k-e ~ übernehmen* I can't guarantee that; F *er fällt unter ~ durch* he's bound to fail.
garantieren [garan'tiːrən] *v/t* (h) (*v/i ~ für*) guarantee (*a. fig.*).
Garan'tieschein *m* guarantee.
Garan'tiezeit *f* guarantee.
Garbe ['garbə] *f* (-; -n) ⚹ sheaf.

Garde ['gardə] *f* ✗ *the* Guards: *fig.* **die alte ~** the Old Guard.

Garderobe [gardə'ro:bə] *f* (-; -n) **1.** cloakroom, *Am.* checkroom. **2.** *thea.* dressing room. **3.** coat rack. **4.** *no pl* a) coat (and hat), b) clothes, wardrobe.

Garde|robenfrau *f* cloakroom (*Am.* checkroom) attendant. **~marke** *f* cloakroom ticket, *Am.* check. **~ständer** *m* coat rack.

Garderobier [gardəro'bĭe:] *m* (-s; -s), **Garderobiere** [gardəro'bĭe:rə] *f* (-; -n) *thea.* dresser.

Gardine [gar'di:nə] *f* (-; -n) curtain.

gären ['gɛːrən] *v/i* (gärte, gor, gegoren, h) **1.** (*a.* **~ lassen**) ferment. **2.** seethe: *im Volk gärte es* there was unrest among the people.

Garn [garn] *n* (-[e]s; -e) thread, cotton: *fig.* **j-m ins ~ gehen** fall into the (or s.o.'s) trap; *ein ~ spinnen* spin a yarn.

Garnele [gar'ne:lə] *f* (-; -n) shrimp, prawn.

garnieren [gar'ni:rən] *v/t* (h) decorate, *a.* trim (*hat etc*), *gastr. a.* garnish.

Garnison [garni'zo:n] *f* (-; -en) garrison.

Garnitur [garni'tu:r] *f* (-; -en) **1.** set. **2.** trimmings. **3.** *fig.* **zur ersten (zweiten) ~ gehören** be first-rate (second-rate).

Garten ['gartən] *m* (-s; ⁓) garden: *botanischer ~* botanical gardens. **~arbeit** *f* gardening. **~archi,tekt(in** *f)* *m* landscape gardener. **~bau** *m* (-[e]s; *no pl)* horticulture. **~bau...** horticultural (*show etc*). **~fest** *n* garden party. **~geräte** *pl* gardening tools. **~haus** *n* summerhouse. **~lo,kal** *n* beer garden. **~möbel** *pl* garden furniture. **~schere** *f* pruning shears, *esp. Br.* secateurs. **~stadt** *f* garden city. **~zaun** *m* garden fence. **~zwerg** *m* **1.** (garden) gnome. **2.** F *fig.* little squirt.

Gärtner ['gɛrtnər] *m* (-s; -), **'Gärtnerin** *f* (-; -nen) gardener.

Gärtne'rei *f* (-; -en) **1.** *no pl* F gardening. **2.** market garden, *Am.* truck farm.

Gärung *f* (-; -en) **1.** fermentation. **2.** *fig.* (state of) unrest. **'Gärungspro,zeß** *m* (process of) fermentation.

Gas [ga:s] *n* (-es; -e) gas: *mot.* **~ geben** step on the gas (*a.* F *fig.*); **~ wegnehmen** throttle back (*or* down); *mit ~ vergiften* gas. **'Gasableser** *m* (-s; -) gasman. **'Gasanzünder** *m* gaslighter.

'Gasbehälter *m* gasholder, gas tank. **'gasbeheizt** *adj* gas-fired. **'Gasflasche** *f* gas cylinder. **'gasförmig** *adj* gaseous. **'Gashahn** *m* gas tap. **'Gasheizung** *f* gas heating. **'Gasherd** *m* gas stove. **'Gaskammer** *f* gas chamber. **'Gasleitung** *f* gas mains. **'Gasmaske** *f* gas mask. **'Gaspe,dal** *n* *mot.* accelerator, *Am.* gas pedal.

Gasse ['gasə] *f* (-; -n) alley, *a. fig.* lane.

Gast [gast] *m* (-[e]s; ⁓e) **1.** a) guest, b) customer, c) visitor: *Gäste haben a.* have company. **2.** *thea.* guest (artist *or* performer). **~arbeiter(in** *f)* *m* foreign worker. **~diri,gent** *m* guest conductor. **~do,zent(in** *f)* *m* guest lecturer.

Gästebuch ['gɛstə-] *n* visitors' book.

'Gästehaus *n* guesthouse.

'Gästezimmer *n* guestroom.

'gastfreundlich *adj* hospitable. **'Gastfreundschaft** *f* (-; *no pl)* hospitality.

'Gast|geber *m* **1.** host. **2.** *pl sports:* home team. **~geberin** *f* hostess. **~haus** *n*, **~hof** *m* restaurant, inn. **~hörer(in** *f)* *m* *univ.* guest student, *Am.* auditor.

gastieren [gas'ti:rən] *v/i* (h) *thea.* give a guest performance, *esp. Am.* guest.

'Gastland *n* host country.

'gastlich *adj* hospitable.

'Gastlichkeit *f* (-; *no pl)* hospitality.

'Gast|mannschaft *f* visiting team. **~pro,fessor** *m* visiting professor. **~recht** *n* (~ **genießen**) enjoy) hospitality.

Gastritis [gas'tri:tıs] *f* (-; -tiden [-tri'ti:dən]) 𝒮 gastritis.

'Gastrolle *f* *thea.* guest part.

Gastronom [gastro'no:m] *m* (-en; -en) restaurant proprietor (*cook:* chef).

Gastronomie [gastrono'mi:] *f* (-; *no pl)* **1.** catering trade. **2.** gastronomy.

gastronomisch [gastro'no:mıʃ] *adj* **1.** catering. **2.** gastronomic(al).

'Gastspiel *n* *thea.* guest performance.

'Gaststätte *f* restaurant.

'Gaststättengewerbe *n* catering trade.

'Gaststube *f* lounge, taproom.

'Gastur,bine *f* gas turbine.

'Gastvorlesung *f*, **'Gastvortrag** *m* guest lecture. **'Gastvorstellung** *f* *thea.* guest performance.

'Gastwirt *m* landlord, proprietor.

'Gastwirtin *f* landlady, proprietress.

'Gastwirtschaft *f* restaurant.

'Gasvergiftung *f* gas poisoning.

'**Gaswerk** n gasworks.
'**Gaszähler** m gasmeter.
Gatte ['gatə] m (-n; -n) husband, ♂♀ spouse.
Gatter ['gatər] n 1. gate. 2. fence.
'**Gattersäge** f ⊙ gate (or frame) saw.
Gattin ['gatɪn] f (-; -nen) wife, ♂♀ spouse.
Gattung ['gatʊŋ] f (-; -en) 1. biol. genus. 2. species, kind, type. 3. a) (art) form, b) literature: genre.
'**Gattungsbegriff** m generic term.
'**Gattungsname** m 1. biol. generic name. 2. ling. collective (or common) noun.
gaukeln ['gaʊkəln] v/i (sn) flutter around. **Gaukler** ['gaʊklər] m (-s; -) 1. tumbler. 2. clown.
Gaul [gaʊl] m (-[e]s; ⸚e) horse, contp. nag: alter ~ (old) jade; fig. **e-m geschenkten ~ sieht man nicht ins Maul** never look a gift horse in the mouth.
Gaumen ['gaʊmən] m (-s; -) palate.
'**Gaumenlaut** m ling. palatal.
'**Gaumenzäpfchen** n anat. uvula.
Gauner ['gaʊnər] m (-s; -) 1. swindler, crook, sl. con man. 2. rascal.
'**Gaunersprache** f thieves' Latin.
'**Gaunerstück** n swindle.
Gaze ['ga:zə] f (-; -n) gauze (a. ✗).
Gazelle [ga'tsɛlə] f (-; -n) zo. gazelle.
geachtet [gə'ʔaxtət] adj esteemed.
Geächtete [gə'ʔɛçtətə] m, f (-n; -n) outlaw.
Geäder [gə'ʔɛːdər] n (-s; -) veins.
geädert [gə'ʔɛːdərt] adj veined.
geartet [gə'ʔartət] adj disposed: **er ist so ~, daß ...** he is the kind of person that ...; **anders ~ sein** be different.
Gebäck [gə'bɛk] n (-[e]s; -e) a) (fancy) cakes, b) biscuits, Am. cookies.
ge'backen pp of **backen**.
Gebälk [gə'bɛlk] n (-[e]s; -e) beams.
geballt [gə'balt] adj 1. clenched. 2. fig. concentrated.
gebannt [gə'bant] adj and adv spellbound.
gebar [gə'baːr] pret of **gebären**.
Gebärde [gə'bɛːrdə] f (-; -n) gesture.
ge'bärden: sich ~ (h) behave, act.
Ge'bärden|spiel n gestures, gesticulation, pantomime (a. fig.). **~sprache** f 1. sign language. 2. thea. mimicry.
Gebaren [gə'baːrən] n (-s; no pl) behavio(u)r, ✝ conduct.
gebären [gə'bɛːrən] (gebar, geboren, h)

I v/t give birth to: **geboren werden** be born; → **geboren**. II v/i give birth.
Ge'bärmutter f (-; ⸚) anat. womb.
Ge'bärmutter|krebs m ✗ cancer of the womb. **~vorfall** m (uterine) prolapse.
Gebäude [gə'bɔydə] n (-s; -) building, edifice (a. fig.), fig. structure. **~kom- ,plex** m complex (of buildings).
'**gebefreudig** adj open-handed.
Gebein [gə'baɪn] n (-[e]s; -e) 1. bones. 2. pl (mortal) remains.
Gebell [gə'bɛl] n (-[e]s; no pl) barking.
geben ['geːbən] (gab, gegeben, h) I v/t 1. (j-m et.) s.o. s.th., s.th. to s.o.) give, a. hand, b) grant: **laß dir e-e Quittung ~!** ask for a receipt!; **~ Sie mir bitte Frau X** teleph. can I speak to Mrs X, please; F fig. **es j-m ~** let s.o. have it; → **Anlaß** 2, **Bescheid, gegeben. 2.** give (lessons etc), teach. **3.** give (a concert etc), a. have (a party etc), perform (play etc), show (a film): **was wird heute abend gegeben?** what's on tonight? **4.** yield, produce: **Milch ~** give milk; **zweimal fünf gibt zehn** two times five makes ten; **das gibt e-e gute Suppe** that will make a good soup; **Flecken ~** make (or leave) stains; **das gibt k-n Sinn** that doesn't make sense; **ein Wort gab ein andere** one word led to another. **5. von sich ~** a) ✗ give off, emit, b) make (remark etc), give, let out (shout etc), c) bring up, vomit; **sie gab k-n Ton von sich** she didn't utter a sound. **6. viel ~ auf** (acc) set great store by s.th., think highly (or a lot) of s.o.; **ich gebe nicht viel auf** (acc) I don't think much of. II v/i 7. give (mit vollen Händen freely). **8.** cards: deal: **wer gibt?** whose deal is it? **9.** tennis: serve. III **sich ~ 10.** act, behave: **sich gelassen ~** pretend to be calm; **er gibt sich gern als Experte** he likes to act the expert. **11.** a) pass, F blow over, b) come right: **das wird sich alles ~** everything will be all right. IV v/impers **es gibt** there is, there are; **der beste Spieler, den es je gab** the best player of all time; **es gab viel zu tun** there was a lot to do; F **was gibt's?** what's up?; **was gibt's Neues?** what's new?; **was gibt es zum Mittagessen?** what's for lunch?; **was gibt's heute abend im Fernsehen?** what's on in television tonight?; **das gibt es (bei**

mir) *nicht!* that's out!; *das gibt's doch nicht!* you're joking!; *heute wird's noch was* ~ I think we're in for s.th.; *er hat recht, da gibt's nichts!* he's right, and no mistake about it!

'**Geben** *n* (-s) **1.** giving: ~ *ist seliger denn Nehmen* it is more blessed to give than to receive. **2.** *cards:* *am* ~ *sein* be dealing; *er ist am* ~ it's his deal.

Geber ['ge:bər] *m* (-s; -) **1.** giver, *cards:* dealer. **2.** *tel.* transmitter. '**Geberin** *f* (-; -nen) → **Geber** 1. '**Geberlaune** *f in* ~ *sein* be in a generous mood.

Gebet [gə'be:t] *n* (-[e]s; -e) prayer: F *fig.* *j-n ins* ~ *nehmen* give s.o. a good talking-to. **Ge'betbuch** *n* prayerbook.

ge'beten *pp of* **bitten.**

Gebiet [gə'bi:t] *n* (-[e]s; -e) **1.** a) region, area, b) district, zone, c) territory. **2.** *fig.* field, sphere: *er ist Fachmann auf dem* ~ (*gen*) he is an authority on.

ge'bieten (gebot, geboten, h) **I** *v/t* **1.** *j-m* ~ *et. zu tun* order s.o. to do s.th. **2.** command (*respect etc*). **3.** require, call for: *die Vernunft gebietet uns zu inf* reason demands of us to *inf*. **II** *v/i* **4.** ~ *über* (*acc*) a) control, rule over, b) have at one's disposal; → *geboten.*

Ge'bieter *m* (-s; -) **1.** master, lord. **2.** ruler. **Ge'bieterin** *f* (-; -nen) mistress.

ge'bieterisch *adj* domineering, peremptory (*tone*).

Ge'biets|anspruch *m* territorial claim. **~hoheit** *f* (-; *no pl*) territorial sovereignty. **~leiter** *m* ✝ regional manager.

Gebilde [gə'bɪldə] *n* (-s; -) a) thing, object, b) work, creation, c) structure.

gebildet [gə'bɪldət] *adj* a) educated, (well-)informed, b) cultured, refined.

Gebinde [gə'bɪndə] *n* (-s; -) arrangement.

Gebirge [gə'bɪrgə] *n* (-s; -) mountains.

gebirgig [gə'bɪrgɪç] *adj* mountainous.

Ge'birgskette *f* mountain range.

Gebiß [gə'bɪs] *n* (-sses; -sse) **1.** a) (set of) teeth, b) dentures. **2.** bit.

Ge'bißabdruck *m* (dental) impression.

gebissen [gə'bɪsən] *pp of* **beißen.**

Gebläse [gə'blɛ:zə] *n* (-s; -) ⊗ a) fan, b) blower. **Ge'bläsemotor** *m mot.* supercharger engine.

ge'blasen *pp of* **blasen.**

geblieben [gə'bli:bən] *pp of* **bleiben.**

geblümt [gə'bly:mt] *adj* floral, flowered.

Geblüt [gə'bly:t] *n* (-[e]s; *no pl*) blood.

gebogen [gə'bo:gən] *pp of* **biegen.**

gebongt [gə'bɔŋt] *adj* F *ist* ~*!* I will do!

geboren [gə'bo:rən] **I** *pp of* **gebären.** **II** *adj* born: ~*er Deutscher* (*Berliner*) *sein* be German (a Berliner) by birth; *Frau X,* ~*e Braun* Mrs X, née Braun; *sie ist e-e* ~*e Braun* her maiden name is Braun; *fig.* ~ *sein zu* be born to be (*or* to do), be cut out for (*a job*); *er ist zum* ~*e Geschäftsmann* he is a born businessman; → *a.* **gebären.**

geborgen [gə'bɔrgən] **I** *pp of* **bergen. II** *adj* safe, secure. **Ge'borgenheit** *f* (-; *no pl*) safety, security.

geborsten [gə'bɔrstən] *pp of* **bersten.**

gebot [gə'bo:t] *pret of* **gebieten.**

Ge'bot *n* (-[e]s; -e) **1.** *bibl.* commandment. **2.** rule. **3.** requirement, necessity: *das* ~ *der Vernunft* (*des Herzens, der Stunde*) the dictates of reason (of one's heart, of the moment). **4.** ✝ bid. **5.** *j-m zu* ~*e stehen* be at s.o.'s disposal.

ge'boten **I** *pp of* **bieten** *and* **gebieten.** **II** *adj* a) necessary, b) imperative, c) due.

Ge'botsschild *n* mandatory sign.

gebracht [gə'braxt] *pp of* **bringen.**

gebrannt [gə'brant] **I** *pp of* **brennen. II** *adj* burnt, roasted, fired; → **Kind.**

ge'braten *pp of* **braten.**

Gebräu [gə'brɔʏ] *n* (-[e]s; -e) *contp.* brew, *fig. a.* concoction.

Ge'brauch *m* (-[e]s; ⸚e) **1.** *no pl* use, ⚕ *a.* application, *ling.* usage: ~ *machen von* use, make use of; *guten* ~ *machen von* put *s.th.* to good use; *außer* ~ *kommen* pass out of use; *im* ~ *sein* be in use, be used; *et. in* ~ *nehmen* put s.th. into use; *der* ~ *s-s linken Arms* the use of his left arm; *zum persönlichen* ~ for personal use; *vor* ~ *schütteln!* shake before use! **2.** *usu. pl* practice, custom.

ge'brauchen *v/t* (h) **1.** use: *kannst du das* ~*?* can you make use of that?; *das kann ich gut* ~ I can make good use of that; F *er ist zu nichts zu* ~ he is hopeless. **2.** F use, do with (*a drink etc*).

gebräuchlich [gə'brɔʏçlɪç] *adj* common (*a. ling.*), normal: *allgemein* ~ in common use; *nicht mehr* ~ no longer used.

Ge'brauchs|anleitung *f,* **~anweisung** *f* directions for use, instructions (for use). **~ar,tikel** *m* article of daily use. **2fähig** *adj* usable. **~fahrzeug** *n* utility vehicle. **2fertig** *adj* ready for use. **~graphik** *f* commercial art. **~güter** *pl* (consumer) durables. **~muster** *n* registered design. **~wert** *m* practical value.

ge'braucht I *pp of* **brauchen. II** *adj* used, ✝ *a.* second-hand.

Ge'brauchtwagen *m* used (*or* second-hand) car. **~händler** *m* used car dealer.

gebräunt [gə'brɔʏnt] *adj* tanned.

Ge'brechen *n* (-s; -) disability, (physical) handicap, infirmity. **gebrechlich** [gə'brɛçlıç] *adj* frail, infirm. **Ge'brechlichkeit** *f* (-; *no pl*) frailty, infirmity.

gebrochen [gə'brɔxən] **I** *pp of* **brechen. II** *adj* broken (*a.* ling.), *fig. a.* broken-hearted: **sie spricht nur ~ Englisch** she speaks only broken English.

Gebrüder [gə'bryːdər] *pl* ~ (*abbr.* **Gebr.**) **Wolf** Wolf Brothers (*abbr.* Bros.).

Gebrüll [gə'brʏl] *n* (-[e]s; *no pl*) roar(ing), bellow(ing) (*a. zo.*).

gebückt [gə'bʏkt] *adj* stooping.

Gebühr [gə'byːr] *f* (-; -en) **1.** a) charge, fee, b) rate, c) postage, d) *mot.* toll: **ermäßigte ~** reduced rate. **2.** **nach ~** duly; **über ~** unduly, excessively.

ge'bühren *v/i* (h) *j-m* ~ be due to s.o. **ge'bührend I** *adj* due (*dat* to), proper. **II** *adv* duly, properly.

Ge'bühren|einheit *f* unit. **~erlaß** *m* remission of fees. **2frei** *adj* free of charge. **~ordnung** *f* scale of fees (*or* charges).

ge'bührenpflichtig *adj* subject to charges: **~e Straße** toll road; **~e Verwarnung** summary fine.

gebündelt [gə'bʏndəlt] *adj* bundled.

gebunden [gə'bʊndən] **I** *pp of* **binden. II** *adj* **1.** *print.* bound. **2.** 🔒 bound (*a. phys.*), fixed: **~e Wärme** latent heat. **3.** ♩ legato. **4.** *fig.* bound, tied, engaged: **vertraglich ~** bound by contract; **sich ~ fühlen an** (*acc*) feel committed to. **5.** tied (up) *(capital)*. **6.** *gastr.* thickened.

Geburt [gə'buːrt] *f* (-; -en) **1.** birth (*a. fig.*), descent: **er ist von ~ Deutscher** he is German by birth. **2.** a) (child)-birth, b) delivery: **von ~ an** from birth; F *fig.* **e-e schwere ~** a tough job.

Ge'burten|kon,trolle *f*, **~regelung** *f* birth control. **~rückgang** *m* decline in the birthrate (*year etc*). **2schwach** *adj* low-birth-rate (*year etc*). **2stark** *adj* high-birth-rate (*year etc*). **~überschuß** *m* excess of births. **~ziffer** *f* birthrate.

gebürtig [gə'bʏrtɪç] *adj* **er ist ~er Engländer** he was born in England.

Ge'burts|anzeige *f* birth announcement. **~datum** *n* date of birth. **~haus** *n* **mein** *etc* ~ the house where I *etc* was born. **~helfer** *m* obstetrician. **~helferin** *f* midwife. **~hilfe** *f* a) obstetrics, b) midwifery. **~jahr** *n* year of birth. **~jahrgang** *m* cohort. **~land** *n* native country. **~ort** *m* birthplace: ~ **und Geburtstag** place and date of birth. **~stadt** *f* native town. **~stunde** *f* **1.** hour of birth. **2.** *fig.* birth.

Ge'burtstag *m* birthday, *adm.* date of birth: **sie hat heute ~** it's her birthday today; **(ich) gratuliere zum ~** many happy returns of the day.

Ge'burtstags... birthday (*present etc*).

Ge'burtstagskind *n* birthday boy (girl).

Ge'burtsurkunde *f* birth certificate.

Gebüsch [gə'bʏʃ] *n* (-[e]s; -e) bushes, shrubbery.

gedacht [gə'daxt] **I** *pp of* **denken** *and* **gedenken. II** *adj* assumed: ~ **als** intended as (*or* to be).

ge'dachte *pret of* **gedenken.**

Gedächtnis [gə'dɛçtnıs] *n* (-ses; -se) **1.** memory: **aus dem ~** a) from memory, b) by heart; **sich et. ins ~ zurückrufen** recall s.th. **2.** *no pl* commemoration: **zum ~** an (*acc*) *a.* in memory of. **~hilfe** *f* mnemonic (aid). **~lücke** *f* lapse of memory. **~schwund** *m* amnesia, loss of memory. **~störung** *f* partial amnesia. **~training** *n* memory training.

gedämpft [gə'dɛmpft] *adj* **1.** muffled (*sound*), subdued (*colo[u]r, light, voice, etc, fig. mood etc*): **~er Optimismus** guarded optimism. **2.** *gastr.* steamed.

Gedanke [gə'daŋkə] *m* (-n; -n) thought (**an** *acc* of, **über** *acc* on), idea: **kein schlechter ~!** not a bad idea!; **in ~n** absent-mindedly; **in ~n versunken** lost in thought; **s-e ~n beisammen halten** keep one's wits about one; **j-n auf andere ~n bringen** get s.o.'s mind on to other things; **j-n auf den ~n bringen zu** *inf* give s.o. the idea of *ger*; **j-n auf dumme ~n bringen** give s.o. silly ideas; **j-s ~n lesen** read s.o.'s mind; **sich ~n machen über** (*acc*) a) think about, b) be worried about; **wie kommst du auf den ~n?** what makes you think of that?; → **spielen** 1, **tragen** 9.

Ge'danken|austausch *m* exchange of ideas. **~blitz** *m* sudden inspiration, F brainwave. **~freiheit** *f* (-; *no pl*) freedom of thought. **~gang** *m* train of thought. **~leser(in** *f*) *m* mind-reader.
ge'dankenlos *adj* a) thoughtless, inconsiderate, b) careless. **Ge'dankenlosigkeit** *f* (-; *no pl*) thoughtlessness.
ge'dankenreich *adj* full of ideas.
Ge'danken|sprung *m* jump (from one idea to the other). **~strich** *m* dash. **~übertragung** *f* telepathy.
ge'dankenvoll *adj* pensive.
ge'danklich *adj* intellectual.
Gedärm [gə'dɛrm] *n* (-[e]s, -e) *usu. pl* intestines, *zo.* entrails.
Gedeck [gə'dɛk] *n* (-[e]s, -e) **1.** cover: *ein ~ mehr auflegen* set another place. **2.** set meal. **3.** cover charge.
Gedeih [gə'daɪ]: *auf ~ und Verderb* come what may. **ge'deihen** *v/i* (gedieh, gediehen, sn) thrive, prosper, develop well, *fig. a.* progress: *so weit gediehen sein, daß* have reached a point where. **Ge'deihen** *n* (-s) thriving, prosperity.
ge'denken (gedachte, gedacht, h) **I** *v/i* (*gen*) a) think of, remember, b) mention, c) commemorate. **II** *v/t zu tun ~* think of doing, intend to do.
Ge'denken *n* (-s) (*zum ~ an acc* in) memory of; → *a.* **Andenken.**
Ge'denk|feier *f* commemoration (ceremony). **~gottesdienst** *m* memorial service. **~mi,nute** *f* a minute's silence (*für* in memory of). **~münze** *f* commemorative coin. **~rede** *f* commemorative address. **~stätte** *f* memorial (place). **~stein** *m* memorial (stone). **~stunde** *f* hour of remembrance. **~tafel** *f* commemorative plaque. **~tag** *m* day of remembrance.
Gedicht [gə'dɪçt] *n* (-[e]s, -e) poem: *das Kleid ist ein ~* the dress is a (perfect) dream. **Ge'dichtsammlung** *f* a) collection of poems, b) anthology.
gediegen [gə'di:gən] *adj* **1.** *metall.* solid (*a. fig. character etc*), pure. **2.** ✝ a) good-quality, b) tasteful.
Ge'diegenheit *f* (-; *no pl*) solidity.
gedieh [gə'di:] *pret of* **gedeihen.**
ge'diehen *pp of* **gedeihen.**
Gedränge [gə'drɛŋə] *n* (-s; *no pl*) **1.** crowd, F crush: F *fig.* **damit wir nicht ins ~ kommen** so that we don't get

pushed for time. **2.** rush (*nach, um* for). **3.** *rugby:* scrummage.
Ge'drängel *n* (-s; *no pl*) F pushing.
ge'drängt *adj* **1.** (*a. ~ voll*) crowded, F (jam-)packed. **2.** concise (*style etc*).
gedrechselt [gə'drɛksəlt] *adj fig.* stilted.
gedroschen [gə'drɔʃən] *pp of* **dreschen.**
gedruckt [gə'drʊkt] *adj* printed: F *lügen wie ~* lie through one's teeth.
gedrückt [gə'drʏkt] *adj a.* ✝ depressed: *~er Stimmung sein a.* be in low spirits; *die Stimmung war ~* spirits were low.
gedrungen [gə'drʊŋən] **I** *pp of* **dringen.** **II** *adj* stocky.
Geduld [gə'dʊlt] *f* (-; *no pl*) patience: *~ haben mit* be patient with; *jetzt reißt mir aber die ~!* that's done it!; *sich in ~ fassen* have patience.
gedulden [gə'dʊldən] *sich ~* (h) have patience, be patient; *~ Sie sich bitte e-n Augenblick!* wait a minute, please!
geduldig [gə'dʊldɪç] *adj* patient.
Ge'dulds|probe *f* e-e ~ *für j-n sein* be a test of s.o.'s patience. **~spiel** *n* puzzle.
gedungen [gə'dʊŋən] *adj* hired (*killer*).
gedunsen [gə'dʊnzən] *adj* bloated.
gedurft [gə'dʊrft] *pp of* **dürfen.**
geehrt [gə'e:rt] *adj* hono(u)red: *in letter:* **Sehr ~er Herr X!** Dear Mr X; **Sehr ~e Herren!** Dear Sirs, Gentlemen.
geeignet [gə'aɪgnət] *adj* (*für* for) suited, suitable, right, qualified: *er ist nicht dafür ~* he's not the right man for it; *im ~en Augenblick* at the right moment; *~e Maßnahmen* appropriate measures.
Gefahr [gə'fa:r] *f* (-; -en) danger, threat (*both:* **für** for, to), risk: *auf eigene ~* at one's own risk; *außer ~* out of danger; *auf die ~ hin zu inf* at the risk of *ger*; *sich e-r ~ aussetzen, sich in ~ begeben* expose o.s. to danger, take risks; *~ laufen zu inf* run the risk of *ger*; *in ~ bringen → gefährden; es besteht k-e ~* it's perfectly safe; → *schweben* 1.
gefährden [gə'fɛ:rdən] *v/t* (h) endanger, threaten, (put at) risk, jeopardize.
ge'fährdet *adj* endangered: *~ sein a.* be in danger, be at risk. **Ge'fährdung** *f* (-; -en) **1.** endangering (*etc, → gefährden*). **2.** (*gen* to) danger, threat.
ge'fahren *pp of* **fahren.**
Ge'fahren|herd *m* (constant) source of danger, *pol.* trouble spot. **~stelle** *f*

danger spot. **~zone** f danger zone. **~zu-lage** f danger money.

gefährlich [gəˈfɛːrlɪç] adj dangerous (dat, für to), risky, grave, critical: **~e Krankheit** serious illness.

Ge'fährlichkeit f (-; no pl) danger(ousness), risk, gravity, seriousness.

ge'fahrlos adj not dangerous, safe.

Gefährte [gəˈfɛːrtə] m (-n; -n), **Ge'fährtin** f (-; -nen) companion.

ge'fahrvoll adj dangerous, risky.

Gefälle [gəˈfɛlə] n (-s; -) **1.** fall, slope, incline, gradient, esp. Am. grade. **2.** ⚡, ₳, phys. gradient. **3.** a) difference(s), b) (wage etc) differential.

ge'fallen¹ v/i (gefiel, gefallen, h) **1.** please: **es gefällt mir (nicht)** I (don't) like it; F **er gefällt mir nicht** he doesn't look too well; **solche Filme ~ der Masse** films like that appeal to the masses; **hat dir das Konzert ~?** did you enjoy the concert?; **wie gefällt es Ihnen in Berlin?** how do you like Berlin? **2.** **sich et. ~ lassen** put up with s.th.; **das lasse ich mir nicht ~!** I'm not going to put up with it!; **sie läßt sich von ihm nichts ~** she won't stand any nonsense from him; **das lasse ich mir ~!** now you're talking! **3.** **sich ~ in** (dat) indulge in; **sich in der Rolle des Fachmanns ~** fancy o.s. as an expert.

ge'fallen² I pp of **fallen** and **gefallen¹**. II adj fallen, ⚔ a. killed in action: **die Gefallenen** the dead.

Ge'fallen¹ m (-s; -) (**j-m e-n ~ tun** do s.o. a) favo(u)r; **j-n um e-n ~ bitten** ask a favo(u)r of s.o.

Ge'fallen² n (-s; no pl) pleasure: **~ finden an** a) enjoy, take pleasure in (s.th.), b) like, take a (fancy) to (s.o.).

Ge'fallenendenkmal n war memorial.

ge'fällig adj **1.** agreeable, pleasant. **2.** obliging, kind: **j-m ~ sein** oblige s.o., help s.o.; F **et. zu trinken ~?** would you like s.th. to drink?; → **gefälligst**.

Ge'fälligkeit f (-; -en) **1.** favo(u)r. **2.** → **Gefälligkeit¹**.

ge'fälligst adv iro. if you don't mind: **sei ~ still!** be quiet, will you!

ge'fangen I pp of **fangen**. II adj a) caught, b) ⚔ captive, b) imprisoned, in prison, c) fig. captivated. **Ge'fangene** m, f (-n; -n) prisoner, convict.

Ge'fangenenlager n prison camp, ⚔ prisoner-of-war camp.

ge'fangenhalten v/t (irr, sep, -ge-, h, → **halten**) **j-n ~** keep (or hold) s.o. prisoner, fig. have s.o. spellbound.

Ge'fangennahme f (-; no pl) arrest, ⚔ capture. **ge'fangennehmen** v/t (irr, sep, -ge-, h, → **nehmen**) arrest, ⚔ capture, take s.o. prisoner, fig. captivate.

Ge'fangenschaft f (-; no pl) (**in ~** in) captivity (a. zo.), imprisonment: **in ~ geraten** be taken prisoner.

Gefängnis [gəˈfɛŋnɪs] n (-ses; -se) prison, jail, Br. a. gaol: **ins ~ kommen** be sent (or go) to prison. **~di,rektor** m governor, Am. warden. **~strafe** f → **Freiheitsstrafe**. **~zelle** f prison cell.

Gefasel [gəˈfaːzəl] n (-s; no pl) F drivel.

Gefäß [gəˈfɛːs] n (-es; -e) a) vessel (a. anat., biol.), receptacle, b) bowl, c) jar.

ge'fäßerweiternd adj ⚕ vasodilating.

Ge'fäßkrankheit f vascular disease.

gefaßt [gəˈfast] adj **1.** calm, composed. **2.** **~ sein auf** (acc) be prepared for; **sich ~ machen auf** (acc) prepare for; F **er kann sich auf et. ~ machen** he's in for it now. **Ge'faßtheit** f (-; no pl) calmness, composure.

Gefecht n (-[e]s; -e) **1.** fight, battle: **außer ~ setzen** a. fig. put s.o., s.th. out of action; → **Eifer, Hitze**. **2.** fencing bout.

Ge'fechtskopf m ⚔ warhead.

gefeit [gəˈfait] adj immune (**gegen** to).

Gefieder [gəˈfiːdər] n (-s; -) plumage, feathers. **ge'fiedert** adj feathered.

gefiel [gəˈfiːl] pret of **gefallen**.

Geflecht [gəˈflɛçt] n (-[e]s; -e) **1.** a. fig. network, mesh. **2.** anat. plexus.

gefleckt [gəˈflɛkt] adj spotted.

geflochten [gəˈflɔxtən] pp of **flechten**.

geflogen [gəˈfloːgən] pp of **fliegen**.

geflohen [gəˈfloːən] pp of **fliehen**.

geflossen [gəˈflɔsən] pp of **fließen**.

Ge'flügel n (-s; no pl) poultry (a. in cpds. disease, farm, farming etc).

Ge'flügelhändler(in f) m poulterer.

Ge'flügelsa,lat m gastr. chicken salad.

Ge'flügelschere f poultry shears.

ge'flügelt adj winged: **~es Wort** saying.

Geflunker [gəˈflʊŋkər] n (-s; no pl) fibbing, fibs.

Geflüster [gəˈflʏstər] n (-s; no pl) whispering, whispers.

gefochten [gəˈfɔxtən] pp of **fechten**.

Gefolge [gə'fɔlgə] *n* (-s; -) **1.** entourage, attendants. **2.** cortège, mourners. **3.** *fig.* **im ~ von** (*or gen*) in the wake of.

Ge'folgschaft *f* (-; -en) followers, adherents. **Ge'folgsmann** *m* **1.** *hist.* vassal. **2.** *esp. pol.* follower, supporter.

gefräßig [gə'frɛːsɪç] *adj* greedy, *zo.* voracious. **Ge'fräßigkeit** *f* (-; *no pl*) greediness, *zo.* voracity.

Gefreite [gə'fraɪtə] *m* (-n; -n) ✗ lance corporal, *Am.* private first class, ✈ aircraftman first class, *Am.* airman third class.

ge'fressen *pp of* **fressen**.

Ge'frieranlage *f* refrigeration plant.

Ge'frierbeutel *m* freezer bag.

ge'frieren *v/i* (gefror, gefroren, sn) freeze.

Ge'frier|fach *n* freezer, freezing compartment. **~punkt** *m* (*auf dem ~* at) freezing point. **~schrank** *m* freezer. **~schutzmittel** *n* ⊙ antifreeze.

Ge'friertrocknen *v/t* (h) freeze-dry.

Ge'friertruhe *f* deep freeze, freezer.

gefror [gə'froːr] *pret of* **gefrieren**.

ge'froren *pp of* **frieren** and **gefrieren**.

Gefüge [gə'fyːgə] *n* (-s; -) structure.

gefügig [gə'fyːgɪç] *adj* docile, compliant; *j-n ~ machen* bring s.o. to heel.

Gefühl [gə'fyːl] *n* (-[e]s; -e) **1.** feeling, sentiment: *für mein ~, m-m ~ nach* my feeling is that, I think that; *ich habe das ~, daß ...* I have a feeling that ...; *mit ~ → gefühlvoll* II. **2.** *no pl* sensation, touch, feel: *ein ~ der Kälte* a cold sensation. **3.** *no pl* (*für*) a sense (of), b flair (for *languages etc*): *sich auf sein ~ verlassen* rely on one's instinct. **4.** *usu. pl* feeling, emotion: *j-s ~e verletzen* hurt s.o.'s feelings.

ge'fühllos *adj* **1.** numb. **2.** *fig.* insensitive (*gegen* to), unfeeling, heartless. **Ge'fühllosigkeit** *f* (-; *no pl*) **1.** numbness. **2.** *fig.* heartlessness, cruelty.

ge'fühlsarm *adj* (emotionally) cold.

Ge'fühlsausbruch *m* outburst.

ge'fühlsbetont *adj* emotional.

Gefühlsduse'lei *f* (-; -en) F sentimentality.

Ge'fühlsleben *n* emotional life.

ge'fühlsmäßig *adj* emotional, *w.s.* intuitive, instinctive.

ge'fühlvoll I *adj* full of feeling, emotional, *a. contp.* sentimental. **II** *adv* feelingly (*etc*), *sing etc* with feeling.

ge'füllt *adj* filled, *gastr. a.* stuffed.

gefunden [gə'fʊndən] *pp of* **finden**.

gegangen [gə'gaŋən] *pp of* **gehen**.

ge'geben I *pp of* **geben**. **II** *adj* given: *als ~ voraussetzen* take *s.th.* for granted; *unter den ~en Umständen* under the circumstances; *zu ~er Zeit* a) when the occasion arises, b) at some future time.

ge'gebenenfalls *adv* **1.** should the occasion arise. **2.** if necessary.

Ge'gebenheit *f* (-; -en) given fact: *~en* a) circumstances, b) reality.

gegen ['geːgən] **I** *prep* **1.** toward(s), *time: a.* at about: *~ Osten* toward(s) the east, eastward(s); *~ zehn (Uhr)* (at) about ten o'clock. **2.** against (*a. fig.*): *~ die Wand lehnen* lean against the wall; *ein Mittel ~* a remedy for; *~ die Vernunft* contrary to reason. **3.** toward(s), to: *freundlich ~* kind to. **4.** compared with. **5.** in return for: ✝ *~ Bezahlung* against payment; *~ bar* for cash. **6.** ⚖, *sports*: versus. **II** *adv* **7.** about, around.

'Gegen|angebot *n* counteroffer. **~angriff** *m a. fig.* counterattack. **~argu,ment** *n* counterargument. **~beispiel** *n* counterexample. **~besuch** *m* return visit: *j-m e-n ~ machen* return s.o.'s visit. **~bewegung** *f esp. fig.* countermovement. **~beweis** *m* (*den ~ antreten* furnish) proof to the contrary.

Gegend ['geːgənt] *f* (-; -en) region (*a. anat.*), area, b) countryside, c) neighbo(u)rhood: *in der ~ von* (*or gen*) near, around, in the *Munich etc* area; *in unserer ~* where we live.

'Gegendarstellung *f* correction, reply.

'Gegendemonstrati,on *f* counterdemonstration.

gegenein'ander *adv* **1.** against (*or* toward[s]) each other (*or* one another). **2.** mutually.

'Gegen|einladung *f* return invitation. **~erklärung** *f* counterstatement. **~fahrbahn** *f* opposite lane. **~frage** *f* counterquestion. **~gerade** *f sports*: back straight, *Am.* backstretch. **~gewicht** *n* counterweight: *fig. das ~ bilden zu* counterbalance. **~gift** *n* antidote. **~kandi,dat(in** *f*) *m* rival (candidate). **~klage** *f* ⚖ cross action. **~leistung** *f* return (service): *als ~ in return* (*für* for).

'**Gegenlicht** n back light(ing): *bei ~* against the light. **~aufnahme** f contre-jour shot. **~blende** f lens hood.

'**Gegen|liebe** f *er stieß mit s-m Vorschlag auf wenig ~* his suggestion didn't go down particularly well. **~maßnahme** f countermeasure: *~n ergreifen* take steps (*gegen* against). **~mittel** n a. fig. antidote. **~offen,sive** f counteroffensive. **~par,tei** f opposite (*or other*) side, pol. opposition, sports: opponents. **~pol** m fig. counterpart. **~probe** f (*a. die ~ machen*) crosscheck. **~revoluti,on** f counterrevolution. **~richtung** f the opposite direction: *aus der ~* oncoming (*traffic etc*).

'**Gegensatz** m (-es; ÷e) **1.** contrast: *im ~ zu* in contrast to (*or* with), as opposed to, unlike the British etc; *im ~ dazu* by way of contrast. **2.** *the* opposite. **3.** pl differences. '**gegensätzlich** [-zɛtsliç] adj contrary, opposite, different.

'**Gegenschlag** m a. fig. counterblow: *zum ~ ausholen* get ready to hit back.

'**Gegenseite** f opposite (*or other*) side.

'**gegenseitig** [-zaitiç] adj mutual, reciprocal: *~e Abhängigkeit* interdependence; *~es Interesse* mutual interest; *sich ~ helfen* help one another (*or each* other). '**Gegenseitigkeit** f (-; *no pl*) reciprocity, mutuality: *auf ~ beruhen* be mutual; iro. *das beruht auf ~!* the feeling is mutual!

'**Gegen|sinn** m *im ~* in the opposite direction. **~spieler** m antagonist, a. sports: opponent, a. pol. opposite number. **~spio,nage** f counterespionage. **~sprechanlage** f intercom (system).

'**Gegenstand** m (-[e]s; ÷e) **1.** object (*a. fig.*), thing, item, article: *~ des Mitleids* object of pity; *~ des Spottes* figure of fun. **2.** a) subject, b) subject-matter, c) matter, affair, d) issue: *zum ~ haben* deal with. '**gegenständlich** [-ʃtɛntliç] adj **1.** a. ling. concrete. **2.** graphic. **3.** paint. etc: representational.

'**gegenstandslos** adj **1.** abstract, paint. etc: a. nonrepresentational. **2.** fig. a) invalid, b) unfounded.

'**Gegen|stimme** f **1.** parl. vote against. **2.** fig. objection. **~strömung** f **1.** countercurrent. **2.** fig. countermovement. **~stück** n (*zu*) counterpart (of), paint. etc pendant (to). **~teil** n opposite (*von*

of): (*ganz*) *im ~* on the contrary.

'**gegenteilig** adj contrary, opposite: *~er Meinung sein* disagree; ⚖ *~ entscheiden* come to a different decision.

'**Gegen|tor** n, **~treffer** m goal against.

gegen'über I adv **1.** opposite, across the way (*or* street), person: a. face to face: *sie saßen einander ~* they sat facing one another. II prep (dat) **2.** opposite, facing. **3.** fig. to, toward(s): *er war mir ~ sehr höflich* he was very polite to me. **4.** compared with, as against. **5.** in contrast to. **6.** in view of, in the face of. **Gegen'über** n (-s; -) **1.** person opposite, vis-à-vis, sports: opponent, pol. etc opposite number. **2.** house opposite.

gegen'überliegen v/i (irr, sep, -ge-, h, → *liegen*) (dat) be opposite, face.

gegen'übersehen: *sich ~* (irr, sep, -ge-, h, → *sehen*) be confronted with.

gegen'überstehen v/i (irr, sep, -ge-, h, → *stehen*) **1.** j-m ~ face s.o.; *sich* (*or einander*) ~ be facing each other, *feindlich* be enemies. **2.** (dat) be faced (*or* confronted) with, F be up against.

gegen'überstellen v/t (sep, -ge-, h) fig. (dat) with) confront (s.o.), compare (s.th.). **Gegen'überstellung** f (-; -en) **1.** a. ⚖ confrontation. **2.** comparison.

gegen'übertreten v/i (irr, sep, -ge-, sn, → *treten*) j-m ~ face s.o.

'**Gegenverkehr** m oncoming traffic.

'**Gegenvorschlag** m counterproposal.

Gegenwart ['geːgənvart] f (-; *no pl*) **1.** *the* present (time): *... der ~* present-day, contemporary. **2.** (*in ihrer etc ~* in her etc) presence. **3.** ling. present (tense).

gegenwärtig ['geːgənvɛrtiç] I adj present, current, present-day, contemporary, today's. II adv a) at the moment, at present, b) nowadays, these days.

'**Gegenwarts|litera,tur** f contemporary literature. ❷**nah(e)** adj topical. **~pro,bleme** pl present-day problems.

'**Gegenwehr** f (-; *no pl*) resistance.

'**Gegenwert** m equivalent (value).

'**Gegenwind** m headwind.

'**Gegenwirkung** f countereffect.

'**gegenzeichnen** v/i, v/t (sep, -ge-, h) countersign.

'**Gegenzug** m **1.** chess: countermove: fig. *im ~ zu* as a countermove. **2.** train coming from the other direction.

gegessen [gəˈgɛsən] pp *of* essen.

geglichen [gə'glɪçən] *pp of* **gleichen**.
ge'gliedert *adj* **1.** jointed. **2.** *fig.* a) organized, structured, b) subdivided.
geglitten [gə'glɪtən] *pp of* **gleiten**.
Gegner ['ge:gnər] *m* (-s; -) **1.** opponent (*a. sports*), adversary, enemy, rival: *ein ~ sein von* be against. 🏛 opposing party. **'Gegnerin** *f* (-; -nen) → **Gegner**. **'gegnerisch** *adj* opposing (*a.* 🏛 *or sports*), antagonistic, *a.* ✕ enemy, hostile: *die ~e Partei a.* the other side. **'Gegnerschaft** *f* (-; -en) **1.** opposition, opponents. **2.** *no pl* opposition (*gegen* to).
gegolten [gə'gɔltən] *pp of* **gelten**.
gegoren [gə'go:rən] *pp of* **gären**.
gegossen [gə'gɔsən] *pp of* **gießen**.
ge'graben *pp of* **graben**.
gegriffen [gə'grɪfən] *pp of* **greifen**.
Ge'habe *n* (-s; *no pl*) affectation, airs.
gehabt [gə'ha:pt] *pp of* **haben**.
Ge'hackte *n* (-n; *no pl*) → *Hackfleisch*.
Ge'halt¹ *m* (-[e]s; -e) *fig.* a) content, b) substance. **2.** (*an dat* of) content, 🔬 *a.* concentration: *~ an Öl* oil content.
Gehalt² *n* (-[e]s; ⁓er) salary, pay: *bei vollem ~* on full pay.
ge'halten *pp of* **halten**.
ge'haltlos *adj* **1.** unsubstantial (*food*). **2.** *fig.* empty, lacking substance.
Ge'halts|abzug *m* deduction from salary. **~ansprüche** *pl* salary expectations. **~empfänger** *m* salaried employee. **~erhöhung** *f* salary increase, (pay) rise, *esp. Am.* raise. **~forderung** *f* salary claim. **~gruppe** *f*, **~klasse** *f* salary bracket. **~kürzung** *f* salary cut. **~liste** *f* payroll. **~streifen** *m* pay slip. **~stufe** *f* salary bracket. **~zahlung** *f* payment of salary. **~zulage** *f* **1.** bonus. **2.** → *Gehaltserhöhung*.
ge'haltvoll *adj* **1.** substantial (*food*). **2.** *fig.* rich in content, profound.
gehangen [gə'haŋən] *pp of* **hängen¹**.
ge'harnischt *adj fig.* sharp, withering.
gehässig [gə'hɛsɪç] *adj* spiteful, venomous. **Ge'hässigkeit** *f* (-; -en) **1.** *no pl* spite(fulness), venom, venomousness. **2.** spiteful words (*or* act).
ge'hauen *pp of* **hauen**.
Gehäuse [gə'hɔyzə] *n* (-s; -) **1.** ⚙ case, casing, cabinet, *phot.* body. **2.** *zo.* shell.
'gehbehindert *adj* *sie ist ~* she can't walk properly.

Gehege [gə'he:gə] *n* (-s; -) enclosure, pen, *hunt.* preserve: *fig. j-m ins ~ kommen* get in s.o.'s way, cross s.o.
geheim [gə'haɪm] *adj* **1.** secret, *a.* a) confidential, b) hidden: *im ~en* secretly; *in ~er Wahl* by closed ballot; *streng ~!* top-secret! **2.** occult.
Ge'heim... a) secret (*agent, agreement, order, etc*), b) occult. **~akte** *f* classified document, *pl* secret files. **~dienst** *m* secret service. **~fach** *n* secret drawer.
ge'heimhalten *v/t* (*irr, sep,* -ge-, h, → **halten**) keep *s.th.* secret (*vor dat* from).
Ge'heimhaltung *f* (-; *no pl*) secrecy.
Ge'heimkonto *n* secret account.
Ge'heimnis *n* (-ses; -se) secret (*vor dat* from), *a.* mystery: *kein ~ machen aus* make no secret out of. **Ge'heimniskrämer** [-krɛːmər] *m* (-s; -) mystery-monger. **Ge'heimnisträger** *m* bearer of official secrets. **ge'heimnisumwittert** *adj* shrouded in mystery, mysterious. **Ge'heimnisverrat** *m* betrayal of a state (*or* trade) secret. **ge'heimnisvoll** *adj* mysterious.
Ge'heim|nummer *f* secret (*teleph.* ex-directory) number. **~poli,zei** *f* secret police. **~poli,zist** *m* member of the secret police. **~sache** *f* secret (✕, *pol.* security) matter. **~tip** *m* F hot tip.
ge'heißen *pp of* **heißen**.
ge'hemmt *adj* inhibited.
gehen ['ge:ən] (ging, gegangen, sn) **I** *v/i* **1.** (*zu Fuß ~*) walk, go (on foot): *schwimmen ~* go swimming; *auf die (or zur) Bank (Post) ~* go to the bank (post office); *auf die Straße ~* a) go out into the street, b) *fig.* take to the streets; *über die Brücke ~* cross the bridge; *fig. an die Arbeit ~* get down to work; *das geht zu weit* that is going too far; *wie ich ging und stand* a) as I was, b) at once. **2.** go, leave, *adm. a.* resign: *er ist gegangen* he's gone, he has left; *j-n ~ lassen* let s.o. go. **3.** 🚂 *etc* (*nach, bis* to, as far as) go, run: *über München ~* go via Munich. **4.** (*nach* to) go, lead: *~ um* go round. **5.** ⚙ 🔧 go, work, *machine:* a. run, *bell:* go, ring, *radio etc:* be on: *fig. das Gedicht geht so ...* the poem goes like this ... **6.** ✝ (*gut*) *~* sell (well); *wie ~ die Geschäfte?* how's business? **7.** *dough:* rise. **8.** *wind:* blow. **9.** *~ an (acc) fig.* a) go as far as, reach to, b)

inheritance etc: fall to, go to. **10. das Fenster geht auf die Straße** the window looks out on(to) the street. **11. das geht gegen dich** this is meant for you. **12. in die Industrie (Politik** *etc*) ~ go into industry (politics *etc*); **in den Saal ~100 Personen** the hall holds (*or* seats) 100 persons; **der Schaden geht in die Millionen** the damage runs into millions; **wie oft geht 2 in 10?** how many times goes 2 into 10?; **in sich ~** do a bit of soul-searching. **13.** F **~ mit** go out with (*a boy or girl*); **fest ~** go steady. **14. die Fenster ~ nach Westen** the windows face (*or* look) west; **nach s-n Worten zu ~** to go by his words; **wenn es nach ihr ginge** if she had her way. **15. ~ über** (*acc*) go beyond; **es geht nichts über ...** there's nothing like ...; **ihre Familie geht ihr über alles** her family means everything to her. **16. vor sich ~** happen; **wie geht das vor sich?** how does it go (*or* work)? **II** *v/impers* **17.** *fig.* **es geht** a) it works, b) I can manage; **es geht nicht** a) it doesn't work, b) it can't be done, it's impossible; **es wird schon ~** it'll be all right; **es geht (eben) nicht anders** it can't be helped. **18.** be, feel: **wie geht es Ihnen?,** F **wie geht's?** a) how are you?, b) how are you feeling?; **es geht mir gut** a) I'm fine, b) ✝ I'm doing fine; **es geht mir schlecht** a) I'm not feeling too good, b) ✝ things aren't going too well; **mir geht es genauso** F same here; **ihm ist es genauso gegangen** it was the same with him; **so geht es, wenn man lügt** that's what comes of lying; **es sich gut ~ lassen** have a good time, enjoy o.s. **19. es geht auf 10 (Uhr)** it is getting on for ten. **20. es geht über m-e Kraft** it's too much for me. **21. es geht um den Frieden (sein Leben)** peace (his life) is at stake; **ihr geht es nur ums Geld** she's just interested in the money; **worum geht es?** what's it all about?, what's the problem?; **es geht darum zu** *inf* it's a question of *ger*; **darum geht es (ja)!** that's the (whole) point!; **darum geht es hier gar nicht** that's not the point. **III** *v/t* **22.** walk (*distance etc*), go (on foot): *humor.* **er ist gegangen worden** he was sacked.

¹Gehen *n* (-s) walking: **50 km ~** *sports*: 50 kilomet/res (*Am.* -ers) walk.

¹gehenlassen: sich ~ (*irr, sep, no* -ge-, h, → **lassen**) **1.** let o.s. go, lose one's temper. **2.** relax.

Geher [ˈgeːər] *m* (-s; -) *sports*: walker.

geheuer [gəˈhɔyər] *adj nicht* (**ganz**) **~** a) creepy, b) fishy, c) a bit risky; **er** (**die Sache**) **ist mir nicht ~** I've got a funny feeling about him (it).

Geheul [gəˈhɔyl] *n* (-[e]s; *no pl*) F howling, howls.

Gehilfe [gəˈhɪlfə] *m* (-n; -n), **Ge'hilfin** *f* (-; -nen) **1.** helper, assistant. **2.** clerk. **3.** ✝ˇ accessory before the fact.

Gehirn [gəˈhɪrn] *n* (-[e]s; -e) **1.** *a. fig.* brain. **2.** F brain(s), mind.

Ge'hirn... cerebral; **~blutung** *f* cerebral h(a)emorrhage. **~chirur,gie** *f* brain surgery. **~erschütterung** *f* concussion. **~hautentzündung** *f* meningitis. **~tumor** *m* cerebral tumo(u)r. **~wäsche** *f* *pol.* brainwashing: **j-n e-r ~ unterziehen** brainwash s.o.

gehoben [gəˈhoːbən] **I** *pp of* **heben. II** *adj* high, senior, elevated, ✝ up-market (*article, shop, etc*); **~e Ansprüche** expensive tastes; **in ~er Stimmung** in high spirits.

Gehöft [gəˈhœft] *n* (-[e]s; -e) farm(stead).

geholfen [gəˈhɔlfən] *pp of* **helfen.**

Gehölz [gəˈhœlts] *n* (-es; -e) copse, coppice, small wood.

Gehör [gəˈhøːr] *n* (-[e]s; *no pl*) **1.** (sense of) hearing, ear(s): **feines ~** sensitive ear; **♪ absolutes ~** perfect pitch; **nach dem ~** by ear. **2.** (~ **finden** get a) hearing: **e-r Bitte kein ~ schenken** turn a deaf ear to a request; **sich ~ verschaffen** make o.s. heard.

ge'horchen *v/i* (h) **j-m** (**e-m Befehl** *etc*) (**nicht**) **~** (dis)obey s.o. (an order *etc*).

gehören [gəˈhøːrən] (h) **I** *v/i* **1.** belong (*dat* to): **wem gehört das Buch?** whose book is this?; **gehört es dir?** is it yours?; **es gehört mir** it belongs to me, it is mine; *fig.* **das gehört nicht hierher** that's beside the point; **der Raumfahrt gehört die Zukunft** the future belongs to space travel. **2. ~ zu** a) belong to, be part of, b) rank (*or* be) among; **er gehört zu den besten Spielern** he is one of the best players; **es gehört zu s-r Arbeit** it is part of his job; **dazu gehört**

a) **Geld** you need money for that, b) **Zeit** that kind of thing takes time, c) (**viel**) **Mut** it takes (a lot of) courage; **dazu gehört schon einiges!** that takes a lot of doing!; **es gehört nicht viel dazu!** there's nothing to it! **3.** ~ **unter** (*acc*) come under. **4.** ~ **in** (*acc*) belong in; **f du gehörst ins Bett!** you should be in bed! **II sich** ~ be proper; **wie es sich gehört** properly; **er weiß, was sich gehört** he knows how to behave; **das gehört sich nicht!** it's not done!

Ge'hörfehler *m* hearing defect.

Ge'hörgang *m* auditory canal.

gehörig [gə'høːrɪç] **I** *adj* **1.** ~ **zu** belonging to; (**nicht**) **zur Sache** ~ (ir)relevant. **2.** right, due, proper. **3.** F good, sound: **j-m e-n** ~**en Schrecken einjagen** put the fear of God into s.o. **II** *adv* **4.** duly, properly: → **Meinung.**

ge'hörlos *adj* deaf. **Ge'hörlosenschule** *f* school for the deaf.

Ge'hörnerv *m* auditory nerve.

gehörnt [gə'hœrnt] *adj* horned: ~**er Ehemann** cuckolded husband.

gehorsam [gə'hoːrzaːm] *adj* obedient (**gegen** to). **Ge'horsam** *m* (-s; *no pl*) obedience (**gegen**[**über**] to): **j-m den** ~ **verweigern** disobey s.o.

Ge'hörsinn *m* (-[e]s; *no pl*) → **Gehör.**

'Gehsteig *m* pavement, *Am.* sidewalk.

Ge'hupe *n* (-s; *no pl*) F blaring horns.

'Gehversuch *m* attempt to walk.

Geier ['gaɪər] *m* (-s; -) *a. fig.* vulture.

Geifer ['gaɪfər] *m* (-s; *no pl*) **1.** slaver, foam. **2.** *fig.* venom. **'geifern** *v/i* (h) **1.** dribble, slaver. **2.** *fig.* ~ **gegen** rail at.

Geige ['gaɪgə] *f* (-; -n) violin: (**auf der**) ~ **spielen** play (on) the violin; (**die**) **erste** (**zweite**) ~ **spielen** play first (second) violin (*fig.* fiddle).

geigen ['gaɪgən] *v/i* (h) play the violin.

'Geigen|bauer *m* (-s; -) violin-maker. ~**harz** *n* resin. ~**kasten** *m* violin case. ~**strich** *m* stroke of the bow.

Geiger ['gaɪgər] *m* (-s; -), **'Geigerin** *f* (-; -nen) violinist.

'Geigerzähler *m* Geiger counter.

geil [gaɪl] *adj* **1.** F *contp.* a) randy, V horny, b) lecherous: *fig.* ~ **sein auf** (*acc*) be hot for, be dead keen on. **2.** rank (*plant*). **3.** F (**echt**) ~ hot, terrific.

Geisel ['gaɪzəl] *f* (-; -n) (**j-n als** ~ **nehmen** take s.o.) hostage. **'Geiseldrama**

---

n hostage drama. **'Geiselnahme** *f* (-; -n) taking of hostages. **'Geiselnehmer** *m* (-s; -) hostage-taker.

Geiß [gaɪs] *f* (-; -en) *zo.* **1.** (nanny) goat. **2.** doe.

Geißel ['gaɪsəl] *f* (-; -n) **1.** whip. **2.** *biol.* flagellum. **3.** *fig.* scourge. **'geißeln** *v/t* (h) whip, *eccl.* flagellate, *fig.* castigate.

'Geißeltierchen *n* flagellate.

'Geißelung *f* (-; -en) **1.** flagellation. **2.** *fig.* castigation.

Geist [gaɪst] *m* (-[e]s; -er) **1.** *no pl* a) mind, intellect, b) spirit, c) wit: ~ **und Körper** mind and body; **ein Mann von** ~ a (man of) wit; **im** ~**e** a) see s.th. in one's mind's eye, b) be with s.o. in one's thoughts; *humor.* **den** ~ **aufgeben** give up the ghost, *engine etc:* a. conk out; F **j-m auf den** ~ **gehen** get on s.o.'s nerves; → **scheiden** III. **2.** *no pl* spirit, morale: **der** ~ **der Zeit** the spirit of the times; **wes** ~**es Kind er ist** what sort of person he is. **3.** spirit, ghost: **böser** ~ evil spirit, demon; **der Heilige** ~ the Holy Ghost. **4.** mind: **ein großer** ~ a great mind (*or* thinker).

'Geister|bahn *f* ghost train. ~**beschwörung** *f* exorcism. ~**bild** *n* *TV* double image. ~**erscheinung** *f* apparition. ~**fahrer** *m* wrong-way driver, *Am.* ghost driver.

'geisterhaft *adj* ghostly.

'Geisterhand *f* **wie von** ~ as if by magic.

'Geisterstadt *f* ghost town.

'Geisterstunde *f* witching hour.

'geistesabwesend *adj* absent-minded.

'Geistesabwesenheit *f* (-; *no pl*) absent-mindedness.

'Geistes|arbeit *f* brainwork. ~**blitz** *m* (flash of) inspiration, brainwave.

'Geistesgegenwart *f* presence of mind.

'geistesgegenwärtig *adv* ~ **sprang er zur Seite** he had the presence of mind to jump aside.

'Geistesgeschichte *f* (-; *no pl*) history of thought (*or* ideas): **die deutsche** ~ the history of German thought.

'geistesgestört *adj* mentally disturbed.

'geisteskrank *adj* mentally ill, *a. contp.* insane. **'Geisteskranke** *m, f* (-n; -n) insane person, mental case (*or* patient), *pl the* mentally ill. **'Geisteskrankheit** *f* insanity, mental disease (*or* illness).

'Geistes|leben *n* (-s; *no pl*) intellectual

life. **₂schwach** *adj* feeble-minded. **₂schwäche** *f* (-; *no pl*) feeble-mindedness. **₂störung** *f* mental disorder. **₂verfassung** *f* frame of mind. **₂verwandt** *adj* congenial. **₂verwirrung** *f* confused state of mind. **₂wissenschaft** *f* arts subject, *pl the* arts, *the* humanities. **₂wissenschaftler** *m* 1. scholar. 2. arts student. **₂wissenschaftlich** *adj* arts ... **₂zerrüttung** *f* mental derangement, dementia. **₂zustand** *m* (-[e]s; *no pl*) mental state.

'geistig¹ *adj* a) mental (*a. psych.*), b) intellectual, c) spiritual: **~es Eigentum** intellectual property; **~ anspruchsvoll** demanding, highbrow; **~ behindert** mentally handicapped; → **Diebstahl**.

'geistig² *adj* **~e Getränke** spirits, alcoholic drinks.

'geistlich *adj* 1. religious, spiritual, sacred (*music etc*): **~er Orden** religious order. 2. clerical, ecclesiastical: **der ~e Stand** the clergy; **~es Amt** ministry.

'Geistliche *m* (-n; -n) clergyman, (*Protestant*) minister, (*Catholic*) priest, ✗ chaplain, padre.

'Geistlichkeit *f* (-; *no pl*) the clergy.

'geistlos *adj* trivial, dull, insipid, stupid.

'Geistlosigkeit *f* (-; -en) 1. *no pl* lack of wit, dullness, insipidity. 2. platitude.

'geistreich *adj* witty, clever, brilliant.

'geisttötend *adj* soul-destroying.

'geistvoll *adj* 1. witty. 2. profound.

Geiz [gaɪts] *m* (-es; *no pl*) stinginess, meanness. **'geizen** *v/i* (h) be stingy (**mit** with); **mit Lob ~** be sparing with one's praise. **'Geizhals** *m* miser, F meanie.

'geizig *adj* miserly, stingy, mean.

Ge'jammer *n* (-s; *no pl*) F *contp.* moaning, (endless) lamentation.

Gejohle [gə'joːlə] *n* (-s; *no pl*) F howling.

gekannt [gə'kant] *pp of* **kennen**.

Gekicher [gə'kɪçər] *n* (-s; *no pl*) F *contp.* giggling, giggle, titter.

Gekläff [gə'klɛf] *n* (-[e]s; *no pl*) F *contp.* yapping.

Ge'klapper *n* (-s; *no pl*) F rattling.

Geklimper [gə'klɪmpər] *n* (-s; *no pl*) F *contp.* tinkling.

geklungen [gə'klʊŋən] *pp of* **klingen**.

geknickt [gə'knɪkt] *adj* F *fig.* crestfallen.

gekniffen [gə'knɪfən] *pp of* **kneifen**.

Geknister [gə'knɪstər] *n* (-s; *no pl*) F *contp.* rustling.

ge'kommen *pp of* **kommen**.

gekonnt [gə'kɔnt] **I** *pp of* **können**. **II** *adj* competent, masterly.

gekränkt [gə'krɛŋkt] *adj* offended, hurt.

Gekreisch [gə'kraɪʃ] *n* (-[e]s; *no pl*) screaming, shrieking.

Gekritzel [gə'krɪtsəl] *n* (-s; *no pl*) *contp.* scrawl(ing), scribbling, scribble.

gekrochen [gə'krɔxən] *pp of* **kriechen**.

gekünstelt [gə'kʏnstəlt] *adj* affected.

gekürzt [gə'kʏrtst] *adj* abridged.

Gel [geːl] *n* (-s; -e) 🜛, *cosmetics*: gel.

Gelächter [gə'lɛçtər] *n* (-s; -) laughter.

ge'laden *pp of* **laden¹** *and* **laden²**. **II** *adj* 1. loaded, ✗ *a.* charged. 2. F *auf j-n* **~ sein** be furious (*or* mad) at s.o.

Ge'lage *n* (-s; -) feast, banquet.

ge'lagert *adj fig.* anders **~** different; **in besonders ~en Fällen** in special cases.

Gelände [gə'lɛndə] *n* (-s; -) country, ground, terrain, site. **Ge'lände...** cross-country (*car, race, etc*).

ge'ländegängig *adj mot.* all-terrain.

Geländer [gə'lɛndər] *n* (-s; -) a) railing, b) banisters, c) balustrade.

gelang [gə'laŋ] *pret of* **gelingen**.

ge'langen *v/i* (sn) 1. **~ an** (*acc*) (*or* **nach, zu, auf** *acc*) reach, arrive at, get (*or* come) to; **ans Ziel ~** a) reach one's destination, b) *fig.* achieve one's end, F make it; **in den Besitz ~ von** (*or* gen) get hold of, acquire; **in j-s Hände ~** get into (*or* reach) s.o.'s hands. 2. **zu et. ~** win (*or* gain, achieve) s.th.; **zu Reichtum ~** become rich; → **Ansicht** 1, **Erkenntnis, Macht** 1. 3. **zur Aufführung ~** be performed.

ge'langweilt *adj and adv* bored.

ge'lassen I *pp of* **lassen**. **II** *adj* calm, composed. **Ge'lassenheit** *f* (-; *no pl*) calmness, composure: **mit ~** calmly.

Gelatine [ʒela'tiːnə] *f* (-; -n) gelatine.

ge'laufen *pp of* **laufen**.

ge'läufig *adj* 1. a) common, current (*expression etc*), b) familiar: **das ist mir ~** I'm familiar with that. 2. fluent.

Ge'läufigkeit *f* (-; *no pl*) 1. familiarity. 2. fluency.

gelaunt [gə'laʊnt] *adj* **gut** (**schlecht**) **~ sein** be in a good (bad) mood.

Geläut [gə'lɔʏt] *n* (-[e]s; *no pl*) ringing.

gelb [gɛlp] *adj*, **Gelb** *n* (-s; -, -, -) yellow, *traffic lights*: amber: **bei Gelb** at amber; **Gelbe Seiten** Yellow Pages.

Gelbe [ˈgɛlbə] *n* (-n; *no pl*) yolk: F *auch nicht das ~ vom Ei!* not all that good!
'Gelbfilter *n, m phot.* yellow filter.
'gelblich *adj* yellowish.
'Gelbsucht *f* (-; *no pl*) 🙖 jaundice.
Geld [gɛlt] *n* (-[e]s; -er) money: *~er* funds, money; *bares ~* cash; *großes ~* notes, *Am.* bills; *kleines ~* change; F *das große ~ machen* make big money, make a packet; *et. zu ~ machen* turn s.th. into cash, sell s.th. off; *um ~ spielen* play for money; F *im ~ schwimmen* be rolling in money; *das geht ins ~* that costs a packet; *~ spielt k-e Rolle* money is no object; → *Heu.*
'Geld|abwertung *f* (currency) devaluation. **~angelegenheiten** *pl* money (or financial) matters. **~anlage** *f* investment. **~anweisung** *f* money order, remittance. **~aufwertung** *f* (currency) revaluation. **~ausgabe** *f* (financial) expenditure. **~auto͜mat** *m* cash dispenser. **~betrag** *m* amount (or sum) of money. **~beutel** *m* purse. **~buße** *f* fine. **~einwurf** *m* **1.** insertion of coins. **2.** (coin) slot. **~entwertung** *f* currency depreciation, inflation. **~geber** *m* financial backer, investor. **~geschäfte** *pl* money transactions. **~geschenk** *n* gift of money. **~gier** *f* greed for money, avarice. **2gierig** *adj* greedy for money, avaricious. **~knappheit** *f* lack of money, (financial) stringency.
'geldlich *adj* financial, pecuniary.
'Geld|mangel *m* lack of money. **~mann** *m* (-[e]s; -leute) financier. **~markt** *m* money market. **~mittel** *pl* funds. **~prämie** *f* a) bonus, b) reward, c) award, (cash) prize. **~quelle** *f* source of money (or income). **~schein** *m* (bank)note, *Am.* bill. **~schrank** *m* safe. **~sendung** *f* (cash) remittance. **~sorgen** *pl* financial worries. **~spende** *f* donation, contribution. **~strafe** *f* (*a. j-n mit e-r ~ belegen*) fine. **~stück** *n* coin. **~umtausch** *m* exchange of money, conversion. **~verdienen** *n* (-s) moneymaking. **~verdiener(in** *f*) *m* moneymaker, breadwinner. **~verlegenheit** *f* financial embarrassment: *in ~ sein* be short of money, F be hard up. **~verschwendung** *f* waste of money. **~wäsche** *f* money laundering. **~wechsel** *m* **1.** → *Geldumtausch.* **2.** (*office*) Change. **~wechsler** *m* change

machine. **~wert** *m* cash (or currency) value.
Gelee [ʒeˈleː] *n* (-s; -s) jelly.
ge'legen I *pp of liegen.* **II** *adj* **1.** situated, located. **2.** convenient, suitable: *es kommt mir sehr ~* it suits me fine.
Ge'legenheit *f* (-; -en) **1.** opportunity, chance: *die ~ nutzen* (or *beim Schopf packen*) seize the opportunity; *die ~ verpassen* miss the chance; *bei der ersten besten ~* at the first opportunity; → *passend* **2. 2.** occasion: *bei ~* sometime; *bei dieser ~* on this occasion. **3.** 🙖 bargain.
Ge'legenheits|arbeit *f* casual work (or job). **~arbeiter** *m* casual labo(u)rer.
gelegentlich [gəˈleːgəntlɪç] **I** *adj* occasional. **II** *adv* a) occasionally, *a.* sometimes, b) sometime.
gelehrig [gəˈleːrɪç] *adj* clever, quick to learn. **gelehrt** [gəˈleːrt] *adj* learned. **Ge'lehrte** *m, f* (-n; -n) learned man (woman), scholar, scientist.
Geleit [gəˈlaɪt] *n* (-[e]s; -e) *a.* ✕ escort, ♣ *a.* convoy: *freies ~* 🙖 safe-conduct.
ge'leiten *v/t* (h) escort (*a.* ✕, ♣).
Ge'leit|schiff *n* escort ship. **~schutz** *m* escort, ♣ *a.* convoy. **~zug** *m* ♣ convoy.
Gelenk [gəˈlɛŋk] *n* (-[e]s; -e) joint, ⚙ *a.* link. **Ge'lenk...** ⊙ articulated.
Ge'lenkentzündung *f* 🙖 arthritis.
ge'lenkig *adj* flexible (*a.* ⊙), supple, lithe. **Ge'lenkigkeit** *f* (-; *no pl*) flexibility, suppleness, litheness.
Ge'lenkrheuma͜tismus *m* 🙖 articular rheumatism.
gelernt [gəˈlɛrnt] *adj* trained.
ge'lesen *pp of lesen.*
geliebt [gəˈliːpt] *adj* dear, beloved. **Ge'liebte¹** *m* (-n; -n) lover. **Ge'liebte²** *f* (-n; -n) a) love(r), sweetheart, b) mistress.
geliehen [gəˈliːən] *pp of leihen.*
gelieren [ʒeˈliːrən] *v/i* (h) jell.
gelinde [gəˈlɪndə] *adv ~ gesagt* to put it mildly.
gelingen [gəˈlɪŋən] *v/i and v/impers* (gelang, gelungen, sn) succeed, be successful, be a success, turn out well: *nicht ~* not to succeed (*etc*), fail; *ihm gelang die Flucht, es gelang ihm zu fliehen* he succeeded in escaping, he managed to escape; *es gelang ihm nicht(, das zu tun)* he failed (to bring it

off); *endlich ist es mir gelungen* at last I managed (*or* made) it.

Ge'lingen n (-s) success: *gutes ~!* good luck!; *auf gutes ~!* to success!

gelitten [gə'lɪtən] *pp of* **leiden**.

gellend ['gɛlənt] *adj* piercing, shrill: *~er Schrei* scream; *~ aufschreien* shriek (*vor dat* with).

ge'loben *v/t* (h) promise, vow, ˈswear.

Ge'löbnis [gə'lø:pnɪs] n (-ses; -se) vow.

gelobt [gə'lo:pt] *adj das Gelobte Land Bibl.* the Land of Promise.

gelogen [gə'lo:gən] *pp of* **lügen**.

gelöst [gə'lø:st] *adj fig.* relaxed.

gelten ['gɛltən] (galt, gegolten, h) **I** *v/t* **1.** be worth (*10 dollars etc*): *fig. wenig ~* count for little (*bei* with); *was er sagt, gilt* what he says goes; → *Wette*. **II** *v/i* **2.** be valid, be good, *contract etc:* be effective: (*weiterhin*) ~ hold (good); *für* apply to (*or*): *das gilt für alle* that applies to (F goes for) all of you; *~ lassen* allow (*a. sports*), (*als*) accept (as), let *s.o., s.th.* pass (for); *das lasse ich ~!* I'll agree to that!; *es gilt!* done!, it's a deal!; *das gilt nicht!* a) that's not allowed (*or* fair), b) *sports etc:* that doesn't count!; *mein Angebot gilt noch!* my offer still stands! **3.** ~ *als* be regarded as, be considered to be. **4.** *j-m ~ remark etc:* be meant for (*or* aimed at) s.o. **III** *v/impers es gilt zu inf* it is necessary (*for us etc*) to *inf*; *es gilt als sicher, daß* ... it seems certain that ...

'**geltend** *adj* a) current(ly valid), *a.* effective (*law etc*), b) accepted, prevailing: ~ *machen* assert, enforce (*claims, rights*), plead (*illness etc*); ~ *machen, daß* ... maintain that ...; (*bei j-m*) *s-n Einfluß ~ machen* bring one's influence to bear (on s.o.).

'**Geltung** *f* (-; *no pl*) **1.** validity: ~ *haben* → *gelten* **2. 2.** a) value, b) prestige: *an ~ verlieren* lose prestige. **3.** weight, influence, *of person:* a. authority: (*dat*) ~ *verschaffen* enforce; *sich ~ verschaffen* make o.s. respected; *et. zur ~ bringen* show s.th. (off) to advantage; *zur ~ kommen* show to advantage.

'**Geltungsbedürfnis** n, '**geltungsbedürftig** *adj* craving for admiration.

Gelübde [gə'lypdə] n (-s; -) vow: *ein ~ ablegen* take (*or* make a) vow.

gelungen [gə'lʊŋən] **I** *pp of* **gelingen**. **II**

adj successful: *die Party war ~* the party was a success.

Gelüst [gə'lʏst] n (-[e]s; -e) craving (*nach* for). **ge'lüsten** *v/impers* (h) *es gelüstet mich nach* I am craving for, I feel like.

gemächlich [gə'mɛ:çlɪç] *adj* leisurely, unhurried.

gemacht [gə'maxt] *adj ein ~er Mann* a made man; *sie waren ~e Leute* they had got it made.

ge'mahlen *pp of* **mahlen**.

Gemälde [gə'mɛ:ldə] n (-s; -) painting, picture. *~ausstellung f* exhibition of paintings. *~gale,rie f* picture gallery.

gemäß [gə'mɛ:s] (*dat*) **I** *adj* appropriate (to). **II** *prep* according to, in accordance with, pursuant to, under (*a law*).

gemäßigt [gə'mɛ:sɪçt] *adj* **1.** moderate (*a. pol.*). **2.** *geogr.* temperate.

Gemecker [gə'mɛkər] n (-s) F *contp.* grouch, *sl.* bellyaching.

ge'mein *adj* **1.** *contp.* a) low, mean, nasty, F awful (*job etc*), b) vulgar, dirty, filthy (*joke etc*): *~er Trick* dirty trick. **2.** *et. ~ haben* have s.th. in common (*mit* with). **3.** common (*a.* ♀, ♈, *zo.*), general: *das ~e Volk* the common people.

Gemeinde [gə'maɪndə] f (-; -n) **1.** *pol.* a) municipality, b) local government (*or* authority), c) community. **2.** *eccl.* a) parish, b) parishioners, c) congregation. **3.** *fig.* following, audience.

Ge'meinde|amt n **1.** local authority. **2.** municipal office. *~bezirk m* district. *~haus n* **1.** parish hall. **2.** → *Gemeindezentrum. ~rat m* municipal council (*person:* council[l]or). *~schwester f* district nurse. *~steuern pl* (local) rates, *Am.* local taxes. *~verwaltung f* → *Gemeinde* 1 b. *~vorstand m* local board. *~wahl f* local election. *~zentrum n* community cent/re (*Am.* -er).

ge'meingefährlich *adj* dangerous: ~ *sein a.* be a public danger.

Ge'meingut n (-[e]s; *no pl*) *a. fig.* common property.

Ge'meinheit f (-; -en) **1.** *no pl* meanness, nastiness. **2.** mean thing (to do *or* say): *so e-e ~!* a) what a dirty trick!, b) what rotten luck!

ge'meinhin *adv* generally.

Ge'meinkosten *pl* overhead (cost).

gemeinnützig [gə'maɪnnʏtsɪç] *adj* for

the public benefit, public welfare ..., nonprofit(-making) (*organization etc*).
Ge'meinplatz *m* commonplace.

ge'meinsam I *adj* common (*a.* A), joint (*account, ownership, etc*), mutual: *~e Sache machen* make common cause (*mit* with); *vieles ~ haben* have a great deal in common; → *Nenner.* **II** *adv* jointly, together: *et. ~ tun* do s.th. together; *~ vorgehen* take joint action.

Ge'meinsamkeit *f* (*-; -en*) **1.** common ground: *~en entdecken* discover things in common. **2.** *no pl* a) mutuality, b) solidarity.

Ge'meinschaft *f* (*-; -en*) a) community (*a. pol.*), b) team, c) association: *eheliche ~* 🔀 matrimony: *in enger ~ leben* live close together (*mit* with).

ge'meinschaftlich → *gemeinsam.*

Ge'meinschafts|anschluß *m teleph.* party line. **~an|tenne** *f* communal aerial (*Am.* antenna). **~arbeit** *f* teamwork. **~erziehung** *f* **1.** *ped.* coeducation. **2.** social education. **~geist** *m* community spirit. **~produkti|on** *f* coproduction. **~raum** *m* communal room. **~sendung** *f* simultaneous broadcast, hookup.

Ge'mein|schuldner *m* bankrupt. **~sinn** *m* (*-[e]s; no pl*) public spirit. **2verständlich** *adj* intelligible to all, popular. **~wesen** *n* **1.** community. **2.** polity.

ge'messen I *pp of* **messen. II** *adj fig.* **1.** measured. **2.** formal. **3.** solemn, grave.

Gemetzel [gə'mɛtsəl] *n* (*-s; -*) slaughter.

gemieden [gə'mi:dən] *pp of* **meiden.**

Gemisch [gə'mɪʃ] *n* (*-[e]s; -e*) mixture.

ge'mischt *adj a. fig.* mixed. **ge'mischtwirtschaftlich** *adj* 🔀 mixed-type.

Gemme ['gɛmə] *f* (*-; -n*) gem.

gemocht [gə'mɔxt] *pp of* **mögen.**

gemolken [gə'mɔlkən] *pp of* **melken.**

'Gemsbock *m zo.* chamois buck.

Gemse ['gɛmzə] *f* (*-; -n*) *zo.* chamois.

Gemüse [gə'my:zə] *n* (*-s; -*) vegetable, *coll.* vegetables, greens. **~(an)bau** *m* (*-[e]s; no pl*) vegetable gardening, *Am.* truck farming. **~garten** *m* kitchen garden. **~händler** *m* greengrocer. **~konserven** *pl* tinned (*or* canned) vegetables. **~laden** *m* greengrocer's shop.

gemußt [gə'mʊst] *pp of* **müssen** II.

ge'mustert *adj* (*a. in sich ~*) patterned.

Gemüt [gə'my:t] *n* (*-[e]s; -er*) **1.** *no pl* mind, soul, heart, feeling, disposition,

nature: F *sich e-e Flasche Wein zu ~e führen* get outside a bottle of wine. **2.** soul: *die ~er bewegen* cause quite a stir; → *erhitzen* I.

ge'mütlich *adj* **1.** comfortable, snug, cosy, pleasant: *mach es dir ~!* a) make yourself at home!, b) *a. sei ~!* relax! **2.** good-natured, pleasant (*person*). **3.** leisurely, unhurried. **Ge'mütlichkeit** *f* (*-; no pl*) **1.** cosiness (*etc*). **2.** cosy (*or* relaxed) atmosphere. **3.** leisure(liness).

Ge'müts|art *f* disposition, nature. **~bewegung** *f* emotion. **2krank** *adj* emotionally disturbed. **~krankheit** *f* emotional disturbance, mental disorder. **~mensch** *m* F a) warm-hearted person, b) *iro.* callous beast. **~ruhe** *f* peace of mind: F *in aller ~* calmly, *iro.* as cool as you please. **~verfassung** *f,* **~zustand** *m* frame of mind, (mental) state.

ge'mütvoll *adj* a) soulful, sentimental, b) warm(-hearted) (*person*).

Gen [ge:n] *n* (*-s; -e*) *biol.* gene.

genannt [gə'nant] *pp of* **nennen.**

genas [gə'na:s] *pret of* **genesen.**

genau [gə'nau] **I** *adj* a) exact, accurate, precise, b) detailed (*report etc*), c) careful, d) strict: *Genaueres* particulars, further details; *man weiß nichts Genaues* we don't know anything definite. **II** *adv* exactly (*etc*): *~ das Gegenteil* exactly (*or* just) the opposite; *~ das, was ich brauche* just what I need; *~ in der Mitte* right in the middle; *~ (um) 10 Uhr* (at) ten o'clock sharp; *~ zuhören* listen closely; *ich weiß es ~* I know it for sure; *sich ~ an die Regeln halten* keep strictly to the rules; *es nicht sehr ~ nehmen* not to be particular (*mit* about); (*stimmt*) *~!* exactly!

ge'naugenommen *adv* strictly speaking, to be exact.

Ge'nauigkeit *f* (*-; no pl*) exactness, accuracy, precision, thoroughness.

ge'nauso → *ebenso.*

ge'nausogut → *ebensogut.*

Genealogie [genealo'gi:] *f* (*-; no pl*) genealogy.

genehm [gə'ne:m] *adj j-m ~ sein* suit s.o.

genehmigen [gə'ne:mɪgən] *v/t* (h) approve (*a. adm.,* 🔀), permit, *adm.* authorize: F *sich e-n ~* have a drink.

Ge'nehmigung *f* (*-; -en*) **1.** approval, permission, authorization. **2.** permit,

geneigt [gə'naıkt] *adj* inclined (**zu** to).
General [gene'ra:l] *m* (-s; -e) general.
Gene'ral... general (*agency, amnesty, etc*). **~baß** *m* ♩ basso continuo. **~bevollmächtigte** *m, f* (-n; -n) **1.** *pol.* plenipotentiary. **2.** ✝ general representative. **~di,rektor** *m* general manager. **~konsul** *m* consul general. **~konsu,lat** *n* consulate general. **~leutnant** *m* lieutenant general. **~ma,jor** *m* major general. **~probe** *f a. fig.* dress rehearsal. **~sekre,tär(in** *f)* *m* secretary-general. **~staatsanwalt** *m* Chief State Prosecutor. **~stab** *m* ✕ General Staff. **~stabskarte** *f* (*1:100 000*) ordnance survey map, *Am.* strategic map. **~streik** *m* general strike. **~überholung** *f* ⊙ complete overhaul. **~versammlung** *f* **1.** ✝ general meeting. **2.** *pol.* General Assembly (of the UN). **~vertreter** *m* general agent. **~vollmacht** *f* general power of attorney.
Generation [genera'tsıo:n] *f* (-; -en) generation. **Generati'onskon,flikt** *m* generation gap.
Generator [gene'ra:tɔr] *m* (-s; -en [-ra'to:rən]) ⚡ generator.
generell [gene'rɛl] *adj* general.
genesen [gə'ne:zən] *v/i* (genas, genesen, sn) recover (**von** from), get well.
Ge'nesung *f* (-; *no pl*) a) convalescence, b) recovery. **Ge'nesungs...** convalescent (*home, leave, etc*).
Genetik [ge'ne:tık] *f* (-; *no pl*) genetics. **Genetiker** [ge'ne:tıkər] *m* (-s; -) genetic scientist. **ge'netisch** *adj* genetic.
genial [ge'nıa:l] *adj* of genius, inspired, brilliant, ingenious: *e-e ~e Idee a. iro.* a brilliant idea. **Genialität** [genıalı'tɛ:t] *f* (-; *no pl*) genius, brilliancy, ingenuity.
Genick [gə'nık] *n* (-[e]s; -e) (back of the) neck: (**sich**) *das ~ brechen* break one's neck; *fig. das brach ihm das ~* that was his undoing.
Ge'nickschuß *m* shot in the neck.
Genie [ʒe'ni:] *n* (-s; -s) genius.
genieren [ʒe'ni:rən] (h) **I** *v/t j-n ~* a) embarrass s.o., b) bother s.o. **II sich ~** be embarrassed, be shy; *~ Sie sich nicht!* don't be shy!
ge'nießbar *adj* edible, eatable, drinkable. **genießen** [gə'ni:sən] *v/t* (genoß, genossen, h) **1.** enjoy. **2.** have, eat, drink. **3.** *fig.* enjoy, have (*reputation*

etc), receive, get (*education etc*): *j-s Vertrauen ~* be in s.o.'s confidence.
Ge'nießer *m* (-s; -) bon vivant.
Genitalien [geni'ta:lıən] *pl* genitals.
Genitiv ['ge:niti:f] *m* (-s; -e) *ling.* genitive (case), possessive (case).
Genius ['ge:nıʊs] *m* (-; *no pl*) genius.
genommen [gə'nɔmən] *pp of* **nehmen.**
genormt [gə'nɔrmt] *adj* standardized.
genoß [gə'nɔs] *pret of* **genießen.**
Genosse [gə'nɔsə] *m* (-n; -n), **Ge'nossin** *f* (-; -nen) **1.** *pol.* comrade. **2.** F pal.
genossen [gə'nɔsən] *pp of* **genießen.**
Ge'nossenschaft *f* (-; -en), **ge'nossenschaftlich** *adj* ✝ cooperative.
Genre [ʒã:r] *n* (-s; -s) genre.
'**Gentechnolo,gie** *f* genetic engineering.
genug [gə'nu:k] *adj and adv* enough, sufficient(ly): *mehr als ~* more than enough; *ich habe nicht ~ Zeit* I haven't enough time (*or* time enough) *to do it; ~* (**davon**)*!* enough (of that)!; *ich habe ~ davon!* I've had enough of that!
Genüge [gə'ny:gə] **1.** *zur ~* a) enough, sufficiently, b) only too well, c) often enough. **2.** *~ tun* (*dat*) → **genügen** 2.
ge'nügen *v/i* (h) **1.** be enough, be sufficient: *das genügt* (**mir**)*!* that's enough (for me)!, that'll do (for me)!, *fig. a.* that's good enough (for me)! **2.** satisfy, meet (*requirements etc*). **ge'nügend** *adj* **1.** *a. adv* → **genug. 2.** satisfactory.
genügsam [gə'ny:kza:m] *adj* content with little, modest, frugal. **Ge'nügsamkeit** *f* (-; *no pl*) modesty, frugality.
Ge'nugtuung *f* (-; *no pl*) (**über** *acc* at) satisfaction, gratification: *mit ~ hören, daß ...* be gratified to hear that ...
Genuß [gə'nʊs] *m* (-sses; ⸚sse) **1.** *no pl* a) consumption, eating, drinking, b) taking (*of drugs*). **2.** pleasure: *mit ~* with relish; *ein wahrer ~* a real treat. **3.** *a.* ⚖ enjoyment: *in den ~ e-r Sache kommen* get (the benefit of) s.th.
Ge'nußmittel *n* **1.** semiluxury food, drink, and tobacco. **2.** stimulant.
Ge'nußsucht *f* (-; *no pl*) hedonism.
ge'nußsüchtig *adj* hedonistic.
Geodäsie [geodɛ'zi:] *f* (-; *no pl*) geodesy.
Geograph [geo'gra:f] *m* (-en; -en) geographer. **Geographie** [geogra'fi:] *f* (-; *no pl*) geography. **geographisch** [geo-'gra:fıʃ] *adj* geographic(al).
Geologe [geo'lo:gə] *m* (-n; -n) geologist.

Geologie [geolo'gi:] f (-; no pl) geology.
geologisch [geo'lo:gɪʃ] adj geological.
Geometer [geo'me:tər] m (-s; -) surveyor. **Geometrie** [geome'tri:] f (-; -) geometry. **geometrisch** [geo'me:trɪʃ] adj geometric(al).
Geophy'sik f geophysics.
Geopoli'tik f geopolitics.
geopo'litisch adj geopolitical.
Gepäck [gə'pɛk] n (-[e]s; no pl) luggage, esp. Am. baggage. **~abfertigung** f 1. 🚄 luggage (esp. Am. baggage) processing, ✈ checking-in of luggage (esp. Am. baggage). 2. luggage (esp. Am. baggage) office, ✈ check-in counter. **~ablage** f luggage (esp. Am. baggage) rack. **~aufbewahrung** f left-luggage office, Am. baggage room. **~kon,trolle** f luggage (esp. Am. baggage) check. **~schein** m luggage ticket, Am. baggage check. **~stück** n piece of luggage (esp. Am. baggage). **~träger** m 1. porter. 2. on bike: carrier, mot. roof rack. **~wagen** m 🚄 luggage van, Am. baggage car.
ge'panzert adj armo(u)red.
Gepard ['ge:part] m (-s; -e) zo. cheetah.
ge'pfeffert adj steep (prices etc), tough (test etc), sharp (letter etc), juicy (joke).
gepfiffen [gə'pfɪfən] pp of **pfeifen**.
ge'pflegt adj 1. well-groomed. 2. select, excellent (wine). 3. cultured, refined.
Gepflogenheit [gə'pflo:gənhaɪt] f (-; -en) habit, custom, † etc practice.
Geplänkel [gə'plɛŋkəl] n (-s; -) a. fig. skirmish.
Ge'plapper n (-s; no pl) F babbling, contp. a. chatter(ing).
Ge'plauder n (-s; no pl) chatting, chat.
Ge'polter n (-s; no pl) rumbling.
Gepräge [gə'prɛ:gə] n (-s; no pl) fig. stamp, character.
gepriesen [gə'pri:zən] pp of **preisen**.
ge'quält adj pained, forced (smile).
Ge'quassel n (-s; no pl), **Ge'quatsche** n (-s; no pl) F blather.
gequollen [gə'kvɔlən] pp of **quellen**.
gerade [gə'ra:də] I adj 1. a) straight, b) upright, erect, c) even (a. number). 2. fig. straight, sincere, upright. II adv 3. just: **~ erst** only just; **nicht ~ schön** etc not exactly beautiful etc; **er wollte ~ gehen** he was just about to leave; **ich war ~ dort als ...** I happened to be there

when ...; **nun ~!** now more than ever!; **~ du!** especially you!; **warum ~ ich?** why me of all people?; **~ an diesem Tag** on that very day.
Ge'rade f (-n; -n) 1. ⅄ straight line. 2. sports: straight: **linke (rechte) ~** boxing: straight left (right).
gerade'aus adv straight ahead (or on).
ge'radebiegen v/t (irr, sep, -ge-, h, → **biegen**) F fig. straighten out.
geradeher'aus adv openly, bluntly.
gerädert [gə'rɛ:dərt] adj F fig. (wie) ~ whacked.
ge'radeso etc → **ebenso** etc.
ge'radestehen v/i (irr, sep, -ge-, h, → **stehen**) fig. answer (**für** for).
ge'radewegs adv a) straight, directly, b) straightaway.
ge'radezu¹ adv almost, next to, really.
gerade'zu² adv openly, bluntly.
Geradheit [gə'ra:thaɪt] f (-; no pl) straightness, fig. a. uprightness.
geradlinig [gə'ra:tli:nɪç] adj 1. straight (a. adv), lineal, direct (descent etc), linear (motion). 2. fig. straight(forward).
gerammelt [gə'raməlt] adj F **~voll (von)** chock-full (of), jam-packed (with).
Gerangel [gə'raŋəl] n (-s; no pl) (**um** over) F tussle, fig. a. wrangling.
gerann [gə'ran] pret of **gerinnen**.
gerannt [gə'rant] pp of **rennen**.
Gerät [gə'rɛ:t] n (-[e]s; -e) 1. ⚙ device, instrument, appliance, apparatus (a. gym.), F gadget, (radio or TV) set. 3. coll. a) equipment, gear, b) tools, c) utensils. 4. (motorbike etc) machine.
ge'raten¹ v/i (geriet, geraten, sn) 1. turn out (**zu kurz** too short etc). 2. **~ an** (acc) come across s.o., come by (or get) s.th.; **an e-n Betrüger ~** fall into the hands of a swindler; **in Schwierigkeiten ~** get into difficulties; **in e-n Sturm ~** be caught in a storm; → **Abweg, Adresse, außer** 1, **Bahn** 1, **Brand** 1 etc. 3. **~nach** take after (one's father etc)
ge'raten² pp of **raten** and **geraten¹**. II adj advisable.
Ge'räteschuppen m toolshed.
Ge'räteturnen n apparatus gymnastics.
Gerate'wohl n F **aufs ~** at random.
Ge'rätschaften f pl → **Gerät** 3.
Ge'ratter n (-s; no pl) rattling, rattle.
geräumig [gə'rɔʏmɪç] adj roomy, spa-

Geräumigkeit

Geräusch [gə'rɔʏʃ] n (-[e]s; -e) sound, a. ⚙ noise. **ge'räuscharm** adj noiseless, silent. **Ge'räuschdämpfung** f (-; -en) silencing. **Ge'räuschku,lisse** f background noise. **ge'räuschlos** adj a. ⚙ noiseless, silent, quiet. **Ge'räuschlosigkeit** f (-; no pl) noiselessness. **Ge'räuschpegel** m decibel (or noise) level. **ge'räuschvoll** adj noisy, loud.

gerben ['gɛrbən] v/t (h) tan. **'Gerber** m (-s; -) tanner. **'Gerbe'rei** f (-; -en) tannery. **Gerbsäure** ['gɛrp-] f tannic acid.

ge'recht adj **1.** just, fair. **2.** (dat) ~ **werden** do justice to (s.o., s.th.), meet, fulfil(l) (requirements etc), come up to (expectations). **ge'rechterweise** adv **1.** justly. **2.** to be fair.

ge'rechtfertigt adj justified. **Ge'rechtigkeit** f (-; no pl) justice, fairness: → **widerfahren.** **Ge'rechtigkeitssinn** m sense of justice.

Ge'rede n (-s; no pl) F **1.** (leeres ~ idle) talk. **2.** gossip: **ins ~ kommen** get o.s. talked about, set tongues wagging.

ge'regelt adj regular.

ge'reizt adj irritable, irritated (a. 🎴). **Ge'reiztheit** f (-; no pl) irritation.

Geriatrie [geria'tri:] f (-; no pl) geriatrics.

Gericht¹ [gə'rɪçt] n (-[e]s; -e) gastr. **1.** dish. **2.** course.

Ge'richt² n (-[e]s; -e) a) (law) court, fig. tribunal, b) the court, c) courthouse: **das Jüngste ~** eccl. the Last Judgement; **vor ~ bringen** bring s.o. to court; **vor ~ gehen** go to court; **vor ~ aussagen** testify in court; **j-n vor ~ stellen** bring s.o. to trial; fig. **mit j-m ins ~ gehen** take s.o. to task; **zu ~ sitzen über** (acc) sit in judg(e)ment on.

ge'richtlich adj judicial, legal.

Ge'richtsbarkeit f (-; no pl) jurisdiction.

Ge'richts|beschluß m court order: **durch ~** by order of the court. **~gebäude** n law court, courthouse. **~hof** m court of justice, law court. **~kosten** pl costs (of an action). **~medi,zin** f forensic medicine. **~medi,ziner** m medical expert (Am. examiner). **~referen,dar(in** f) m junior lawyer (who has passed his/her first State Examination). **~saal** m courtroom. **~stand** m venue,

legal domicile, place of jurisdiction. **~urteil** n a) sentence, b) judg(e)ment. **~verfahren** n **1.** a) (legal) proceedings, lawsuit, b) trial. **2.** court procedure. **~verhandlung** f a) (judicial) hearing, b) trial. **~vollzieher** m bailiff, Am. marshal. **~weg** m **auf dem ~** by legal proceedings; **den ~ einschlagen** take legal action.

gerieben [gə'ri:bən] pp of **reiben.**

geriet [gə'ri:t] pret of **geraten¹.**

gering [gə'rɪŋ] adj a) little, small, slight, b) low (price etc), a. poor (opinion etc), slim (chance, hope, etc), minor (importance etc): **in ~erem Maße** to a less degree; **kein 2erer als** no less a person than; **nicht im ~sten** not in the least; **das soll m-e ~ste Sorge sein!** that's the least of my worries!; → **Chance.**

ge'ringachten v/t (sep, -ge-, h) **1.** think little of. **2.** disregard (danger etc).

ge'ringfügig [-fy:gɪç] adj insignificant, negligible, slight, minor, small, petty. **Ge'ringfügigkeit** f (-; no pl) insignificance, slightness, smallness.

ge'ringschätzig [-ʃɛtsɪç] adj contemptuous, disparaging.

Ge'ringschätzung f (-; no pl) (für, gen) disdain (of), low regard (for).

ge'rinnen v/i (gerann, geronnen, sn) coagulate, clot, milk: curdle.

Gerinnsel [gə'rɪnzəl] n (-s; -) 🎴 clot.

Ge'rinnung f (-; no pl) coagulation, clotting, curdling.

Gerippe [gə'rɪpə] n (-s; -) a. fig. skeleton.

ge'rippt adj ribbed.

gerissen [gə'rɪsən] I pp of **reißen.** II adj F fig. cunning, crafty.

geritten [gə'rɪtən] pp of **reiten.**

Germane [gɛr'ma:nə] m (-n; -n), **Ger'manin** f (-; -nen) Teuton.

ger'manisch adj Germanic (a. ling.), Teutonic. **Germanist** [gɛrma'nɪst] m (-en; -en), **Germa'nistin** f (-; -nen) Germanist, a. student of German.

Germanistik [gɛrma'nɪstɪk] f (-; no pl) German (studies or philology).

gern [gɛrn], **'gerne** adv gladly, with pleasure: **(ja,** ~**!** a) yes, certainly!, b) I'd love to!; **(aber)** ~**!** of course!, gladly!; **herzlich** (or liebend) ~**!** with great pleasure!; ~ **geschehen!** not at all!, (you're) welcome!; ~ **haben** like, be fond of; **(sehr)** ~ **tun** a) like (love) to do *(or doing)*, b) tend to do; **~ essen (trinken)** like; **~ lesen** like reading; **ich hätte ~ e-e Tasse Tee** I'd like a cup of tea; **ich möchte ~ wissen, ob ...** a) I'd like to know if ..., b) I wonder if ...; **er kann ~ kommen!** a) he's welcome!, b) I don't mind if he comes!; **das kannst du ~ haben!** you're welcome to it!; **er sieht es nicht ~** he doesn't like it; F **du kannst mich ~ haben!** go to blazes!

'**Gernegroß** *m* (-; -e) F show-off.

gerochen [gə'rɔxən] *pp of* **riechen**.

Geröll [gə'rœl] *n* (-[e]s; -e) scree, rubble.

geronnen [gə'rɔnən] *pp of* **rinnen and rinnen**.

Gerste ['gɛrstə] *f* (-; -n) ♣ barley.

'**Gerstenkorn** *n* **1.** barleycorn. **2.** ♂ sty.

Gerte ['gɛrtə] *f* (-; -n) switch, twig.

'**gertenschlank** *adj* (slim and) willowy.

Geruch [gə'rʊx] *m* (-[e]s; ⁓e) smell, scent, *b.s.* odo(u)r (*a. fig.*).

ge'ruchlos *adj* odo(u)rless.

Ge'ruchs|nerv *m* olfactory nerve. **~sinn** *m* (-[e]s; *no pl*) (sense of) smell.

Gerücht [gə'rʏçt] *n* (-[e]s; -e) rumo(u)r: **es geht das ~** it is rumo(u)red that.

gerufen [gə'ruːfən] *pp of* **rufen**.

ge'ruhen *v/t* (h) **~, et. zu tun** deign to do s.th.

ge'rührt *adj fig.* touched, moved.

Gerümpel [gə'rʏmpəl] *n* (-s; *no pl*) junk.

Gerundium [ge'rʊndiʊm] *n* (-s; -dien) *ling.* gerund.

gerungen [gə'rʊŋən] *pp of* **ringen**.

Gerüst [gə'rʏst] *n* (-[e]s; -e) **1.** a) scaffold(ing), b) stage, c) frame. **2.** *fig.* frame(work).

ge'rüttelt *adj fig.* **ein ~ Maß an** (*dat*) a fair amount of.

ges, Ges [gɛs] *n* (-; -) ♪ G flat.

ge'salzen I *pp of* **salzen**. **II** *adj* **1.** salted. **2.** → **gepfeffert**.

ge'sammelt *adj* **1. ~e Werke** collected works. **2.** *fig.* concentrated.

gesamt [gə'zamt] *adj* **1.** whole, entire, all. **2.** total (*amount etc*).

Ge'samt|ansicht *f* general view. **~auflage** *f* a) total circulation, b) total number of copies published. **~ausgabe** *f* **1.** complete edition. **2.** *pl* † total expenditure. **~betrag** *m* total (amount). **~bevölkerung** *f* total population. **~bild** *n* overall picture. **2deutsch** *adj* all-German. **~eindruck** *m* general impression.

Ge'samtheit *f* (-; *no pl*) totality, *the* whole: **die ~ der Arbeiter** all the workers; **in s-r ~** in its entirety, as a whole.

Ge'samt|hochschule *f* comprehensive university. **~kosten** *pl* overall (*or* total) cost. **~länge** *f* overall length. **~note** *f* *ped.* aggregate mark. **~schule** *f* comprehensive school. **~sieger(in** *f*) *m* overall winner. **~summe** *f* (sum) total, total amount. **~werk** *n* complete works. **~zahl** *f* total (number).

gesandt [gə'zant] *pp of* **senden²**.

Gesandte [gə'zantə] *m*, *f* (-n; -n) envoy.

Ge'sandtschaft *f* (-; -en) legation.

Gesang [gə'zaŋ] *m* (-[e]s; ⁓e) **1.** *no pl* singing: **~ studieren** study voice. **2.** song, **Ge'sangbuch** *n eccl.* hymnbook.

Ge'sanglehrer(in *f*) *m* singing teacher. **~sanglich** *adj* vocal. **Ge'sangunterricht** *m* singing lessons. **Ge'sangverein** *m* choral society.

Gesäß [gə'zɛːs] *n* (-es; -e) buttocks, F bottom. **~sättasche** *f* back pocket.

ge'schaffen *pp of* **schaffen**.

Geschäft [gə'ʃɛft] *n* (-[e]s; -e) **1.** a) business, b) trade, c) (business) deal, transaction: **ein gutes (schlechtes) ~** a good (bad) deal; **ein gutes ~ machen** make a good profit (F a packet) (**mit** out of); **~e machen mit** deal in, *w.s.* make money out of; **mit j-m ~e machen, mit j-m ins ~ kommen** do business with s.o.; **gut im ~ sein** be doing well; **~ ist ~!** business is business!; **er versteht sein ~!** he knows his business (*or* stuff)! **2.** a) enterprise, firm, b) office, c) shop, store. **3.** *fig.* business, affair.

ge'schäftehalber *adv* on business.

Ge'schäftemacher *m contp.* profiteer.

ge'schäftig *adj* busy, active.

Ge'schäftigkeit *f* (-; *no pl*) activity.

ge'schäftlich *adj* business, commercial: **~ verreist** away on business; **~ zu tun haben** have (some) business (**mit** with); **~ verhindert** prevented by business.

Ge'schäfts|abschluß *m* (business) transaction (*or* deal). **~bedingungen** *pl* terms of business. **~bereich** *m* sphere of activity, scope, *pol.* portfolio, ⚖️ jurisdiction. **~bericht** *m* business report. **~beziehungen** *pl* business connections. **~brief** *m* business letter. **~fähig** *adj* competent, having legal capacity. **~fähigkeit** *f* (-; *no pl*) legal capacity.

⹋frau f businesswoman. ⹋freund m business friend. 2führend adj managing, executive, acting. ⹋führer(in f) m manager(ess), secretary (of a club etc). ⹋führung f management. ⹋gebaren n business methods. ⹋geheimnis n business secret. ⹋haus n 1. office building. 2. commercial firm, company. ⹋inhaber(in f) m owner (of a business), proprietor (proprietress). ⹋jahr n financial year. ⹋kosten pl business expenses: auf ~ on expense account. ⹋lage f business situation. ⹋leben n (im ~ in) business (life). ⹋leitung f management. ⹋mann m (-[e]s; -leute) businessman. ge'schäftsmäßig adj businesslike. Ge'schäfts|ordnung f rules of procedure, parl. standing orders: zur ~ on a point of order. ⹋partner(in f) m (business) partner. ⹋räume pl business premises, offices. ⹋reise f (auf ~ on a) business trip. 2schädigend adj damaging to business. ⹋schädigung f 🏠 injurious malpractice, w.s. trade libel (gen on). ⹋schluß m closing time: nach ~ a. after business hours. ⹋sinn m (-[e]s; no pl) business sense. ⹋sitz m place of business. ⹋stelle f office(s). ⹋straße f shopping street. ⹋träger m pol. chargé d'affaires. 2tüchtig adj smart, efficient (in business). ⹋tüchtigkeit f (-; no pl) business efficiency, smartness. 2unfähig adj 🏠 legally incapacitated. ⹋unfähigkeit f (-; no pl) 🏠 legal incapacity. ⹋verbindung f business connection. ⹋verkehr m business (dealings). ⹋viertel n commercial district, Am. a. downtown. ⹋wert m goodwill. ⹋zweig m branch (of business).

geschehen [gə'ʃeːən] v/i (geschah, geschehen, sn) happen, occur, take place: ihm wird nichts ~ nothing will happen to him; was soll damit ~? what's to be done with it?; es muß et. ~! s.th. must be done!; da war es um ihn ~ he was done for; → recht 3.

Ge'schehen n (-s) happenings, events.

gescheit [gə'ʃaɪt] adj 1. clever, intelligent, bright. 2. wise, sensible.

Geschenk [gə'ʃɛŋk] n (-[e]s; -e) present, gift: j-m et. zum ~ machen give s.o. s.th. (as a present); als ~ verpacken gift-wrap. ⹋ar,tikel m gift. ⹋packung f gift box.

Geschichte [gə'ʃɪçtə] f (-; -n) 1. story, a. narrative. 2. no pl history: die ~ der Neuzeit modern history; ~ machen make history; in die ~ eingehen go down in history. 3. F business, thing: die ganze (iro. e-e schöne) ~ the whole (a nice) business.

ge'schichtlich adj historical, historic. Ge'schichts|buch n history book. ⹋forscher(in f) m historian. ⹋forschung f historical research. ⹋lehrer(in f) m history teacher. ⹋unterricht m history.

Geschick¹ [gə'ʃɪk] n (-[e]s; -e) fate, lot.
Ge'schick² (-[e]s; no pl) skill.

Ge'schicklichkeit f (-; no pl) 1. skill, dexterity. 2. cleverness.

ge'schickt adj skil(l)ful (zu at, in dat in), a. clever.

geschieden [gə'ʃiːdən] I pp of scheiden. II adj person: divorced, marriage: dissolved: m-e ~e Frau my ex-wife.

Ge'schiedene¹ m (-n; -n) divorcé, divorced man. Ge'schiedene² f (-n; -n) divorcée, divorced woman.

geschienen [gə'ʃiːnən] pp of scheinen.

Geschirr [gə'ʃɪr] n (-[e]s; -e) 1. no pl a) dishes, tableware, b) kitchenware, pots and pans: das ~ abräumen clear the table; ~ spülen do the dishes, wash up. 2. china. 3. harness.

Ge'schirr|schrank m (china) cupboard. ⹋spüler m (-s; -) F, ⹋spülma,schine f dishwasher. ⹋tuch n tea towel.

geschissen [gə'ʃɪsən] pp of scheißen.
ge'schlafen pp of schlafen.

ge'schlagen I pp of schlagen. II adj 1. beaten, defeated: sich ~ geben admit defeat. 2. F full: zwei ~e Stunden (lang for) two solid hours.

Geschlecht [gə'ʃlɛçt] n (-[e]s; -er) 1. biol. sex: beiderlei ~s of both sexes; das andere (schwache, schöne) ~ the opposite (weaker, fair) sex. 2. ling. gender. 3. a) race, b) lineage, c) family: das menschliche ~ the human race.

ge'schlechtlich adj sexual.

Ge'schlechts|akt m sexual act. ⹋hor,mon n sex hormone. 2krank adj suffering from a venereal disease, having VD. ⹋krankheit f venereal disease (abbr. V.D.). ⹋leben n sex life.

ge'schlechtslos adj sexless, asexual.

Ge'schlechts|merkmal n sex characteristic. ⹋or,gan n sex(ual) organ. ⹋reife f

geschwommen

sexual maturity. **~teile** *pl* genitals. **~trieb** *m* sexual urge. **~umwandlung** *f* sex change. **~verkehr** *m* sexual intercourse. **~wort** *n ling.* article.

geschlichen [gəˈʃlɪçən] *pp of* **schleichen.**

geschliffen [gəˈʃlɪfən] **I** *pp of* **schleifen¹.** **II** *adj* **1.** cut (*glass*). **2.** *fig.* polished.

geschlossen [gəˈʃlɔsən] **I** *pp of* **schließen.** **II** *adj* **1.** closed, *ling.*, ✕ close: (**in sich**) **~** *a.* ☉ self-contained, *fig.* compact; **~e Gesellschaft** a) closed society, b) private party; **~e Veranstaltung** private meeting; **~e Ortschaft** built-up area. **2.** united: **~ stimmen für** vote unanimously for, be solid for; **~ hinter j-m stehen** be solidly behind s.o.

geschlungen [gəˈʃlʊŋən] *pp of* **schlingen.**

Geschmack [gəˈʃmak] *m* (-[e]s; ⁓e, F ⁓er) taste (*a. fig.* **an** *dat* for), flavo(u)r: **~ finden an** (*dat*) develop a taste for; **e-n guten ~ haben** a) taste good, b) *fig.* have good taste; **für m-n ~** for my taste; **das ist nicht nach m-m ~** that's not to my taste; **über ~ läßt sich nicht streiten** there's no accounting for tastes.

ge'schmacklos *adj* tasteless: **~ sein** *fig. a.* be in bad taste. **Ge'schmacklosigkeit** *f* (-; *no pl*) *a. fig.* tastelessness: **das war e-e ~** that was in bad taste.

Ge'schmacks|richtung *f* taste. **~sache** *f* (**es ist ~** it's a) matter of taste. **~sinn** *m* (-[e]s; *no pl*) (sense of) taste. **~verirrung** *f* lapse of taste.

ge'schmackvoll *adj* tasteful: **~ sein** *fig. a.* be in good taste.

Geschmeide [gəˈʃmaɪdə] *n* (-s; -) jewels, jewel(le)ry.

geschmeidig [gəˈʃmaɪdɪç] *adj* **1.** supple, pliant, sleek, soft. **2.** *fig.* flexible.

geschmissen [gəˈʃmɪsən] *pp of* **schmeißen.**

geschmolzen [gəˈʃmɔltsən] *pp of* **schmelzen.**

Geschmuse [gəˈʃmuːzə] *n* (-s; *no pl*) F smooching.

Ge'schnatter *n* (-s; *no pl*) **1.** cackling. **2.** F *fig.* chatter(ing).

geschnitten [gəˈʃnɪtən] *pp of* **schneiden.**

geschoben [gəˈʃoːbən] *pp of* **schieben.**

gescholten [gəˈʃɔltən] *pp of* **schelten.**

Geschöpf [gəˈʃœpf] *n* (-[e]s; -e) **1.** creature. **2.** *fig.* creation.

geschoren [gəˈʃoːrən] *pp of* **scheren.**

Geschoß¹ [gəˈʃɔs] *n* (-sses; -sse) projectile, bullet, missile.

Ge'schoß² *n* (-sses; -sse) stor(e)y, floor.

geschossen [gəˈʃɔsən] *pp of* **schießen.**

geschraubt [gəˈʃraʊpt] *adj fig.* stilted.

Ge'schrei *n* (-[e]s; *no pl*) **1.** a) shouting, yelling, bawling, b) shouts, screams. **2.** F *fig.* (**um** about) fuss, noise.

geschrieben [gəˈʃriːbən] *pp of* **schreiben.**

geschrie(e)n [gəˈʃriː(ə)n] *pp of* **schreien.**

geschritten [gəˈʃrɪtən] *pp of* **schreiten.**

ge'schult *adj* trained (*a. eye*).

geschunden [gəˈʃʊndən] *pp of* **schinden.**

Geschütz [gəˈʃyts] *n* (-es; -e) gun: *fig.* **schweres ~ auffahren** bring up one's heavy guns. **~feuer** *n* gunfire, shelling.

ge'schützt *adj* protected.

Ge'schützturm *m* turret.

Geschwader [gəˈʃvaːdər] *n* (-s; -) ⚓ squadron, ✈ group, *Am.* wing.

Ge'schwafel *n* (-s; *no pl*) F *contp.* waffle.

Geschwätz [gəˈʃvɛts] *n* (-es; *no pl*) F *contp.* **1.** twaddle. **2.** gossip.

ge'schwätzig *adj contp.* **1.** talkative, F gabby. **2.** gossipy. **Ge'schwätzigkeit** *f* (-; *no pl*) *contp.* talkativeness.

ge'schweige *conj* (**~ denn**) not to mention, let alone, much less.

geschwiegen [gəˈʃviːgən] *pp of* **schweigen.**

Geschwindigkeit [gəˈʃvɪndɪçkaɪt] *f* (-; -en) speed, pace, rate, *phys.* velocity: **mit e-r ~ von** at a speed (*or* rate) of.

Ge'schwindigkeits|beschränkung *f* speed limit. **~messer** *m* tachometer, *mot. a.* speedometer. **~re�** *m* speed record. **~überschreitung** *f* speeding.

Geschwister [gəˈʃvɪstər] *pl* brother(s) and sister(s), siblings.

ge'schwisterlich *adj* a) brotherly, b) sisterly.

Ge'schwisterpaar *n* a) brother and sister, b) two brothers (*or* sisters).

geschwollen [gəˈʃvɔlən] **I** *pp of* **schwellen.** **II** *adj* **1.** swollen. **2.** *fig.* pompous, bombastic.

geschwommen [gəˈʃvɔmən] *pp of* **schwimmen.**

geschworen [gə'ʃvoːrən] II *pp of*
schwören. II *adj* sworn (*enemy*).
Ge'schworene *m, f* (-n; -n) ⚖ juror: *die*
∼n the (members of the) jury.
Ge'schworenenbank *f* 1. jury box. 2.
the jury.
Ge'schwulst *f* (-; ⸚e) 🩺 tumo(u)r.
geschwunden [gə'ʃvʊndən] *pp of*
schwinden.
geschwungen [gə'ʃvʊŋən] I *pp of*
schwingen. II *adj* curved.
Geschwür [gə'ʃvyːr] *n* (-[e]s; -e) 🩺 ulcer,
abscess, boil.
ge'sehen *pp of* **sehen.**
Geselle [gə'zɛlə] *m* (-n; -n) journeyman.
ge'sellen: (h) *sich zu j-m ∼* join s.o.
ge'sellig *adj* social, gregarious (*a. fig.*),
sociable (*person*): *∼es Leben* social life.
Ge'selligkeit *f* (-; *no pl*) 1. sociability. 2.
social life: *die ∼ lieben* be fond of company.
Gesellschaft [gə'zɛlʃaft] *f* (-; -en) 1. *no pl*
society: *die vornehme ∼* high society;
Dame der ∼ society lady. 2. *no pl* company: *in s-r ∼* in his company; *j-m ∼
leisten* a) keep s.o. company, b) join
s.o. (*bei* in). 3. a) party, b) guests: *e-e ∼
geben* give a party. 4. company; →
*Haftung*2. 5. *no pl* F bunch.
Ge'sellschafter *m* (-s; -), **Ge'sellschaf-
terin** *f* (-; -nen) 1. companion. 2. †
partner. **ge'sellschaftlich** *adj* social.
Ge'sellschafts|anzug *m* formal dress.
⃝**fähig** *adj* 1. socially acceptable. 2.
presentable. **∼kri,tik** *f* social criticism.
⃝**kritisch** *adj* socio-critical. **∼ordnung** *f*
social order. **∼recht** *n* (-[e]s; *no pl*) company law. **∼reise** *f* package (*or* conducted) tour. **∼schicht** *f* (social) class,
social stratum. **∼spiel** *n* parlo(u)r
game. **∼sy,stem** *n* social system. **∼tanz**
m ballroom dance. **∼wissenschaft** *f* 1.
sociology. 2. *pl* social sciences.
Gesenk [gə'zɛŋk] *n* (-[e]s; -e) ⚙ swage.
gesessen [gə'zɛsən] *pp of* **sitzen.**
Gesetz [gə'zɛts] *n* (-es; -e) law, *parl.* act:
nach dem ∼ under the law (*über acc*
on); *vor dem ∼* in the eyes of the law.
Ge'setz|blatt *n* law gazette. **∼buch** *n*
code (of law). **∼entwurf** *m* (draft) bill.
Ge'setzeskraft *f* legal force: *∼ erhalten*
pass into law; (*dat*) *∼ verleihen* enact.
Ge'setzeslücke *f* loophole in the law.
Ge'setzesvorlage *f* (draft) bill.

ge'setzgebend *adj* legislative.
Ge'setzgeber *m* (-s; -) legislator.
Ge'setzgebung *f* (-; *no pl*) legislation.
ge'setzlich *adj* legal, statutory, lawful,
legitimate: *∼ geschützt* protected (by
law), patented (*invention etc*), registered (*trademark etc*), copyright (*book
etc*). **Ge'setzlichkeit** *f* (-; *no pl*) legality, lawfulness.
Ge'setzlosigkeit *f* (-; *no pl*) lawlessness.
ge'setzmäßig *adj* 1. ⚖ legal, lawful,
legitimate. 2. regular. **Ge'setzmäßig-
keit** *f* (-; *no pl*) 1. ⚖ legality, lawfulness,
legitimacy. 2. regularity.
ge'setzt I *adj* 1. sedate: *∼en Alters, in
∼em Alter* of mature age. 2. *sports:*
seeded: *∼er Spieler* seed. II *conj* →
Fall 2. **Ge'setztheit** *f* (-; *no pl*) sedate-
ness.
ge'setzwidrig *adj* unlawful, illegal.
Ge'setzwidrigkeit *f* (-; -en) 1. *no pl* un-
lawfulness, illegality. 2. offen/ce (*Am.*
-se), illegal act.
Gesicht [gə'zɪçt] *n* (-[e]s; -er) 1. face, *a.*
look: *ein trauriges ∼ machen* look
sad; *ein langes ∼ machen* pull a long
face; *das ∼ verziehen* make a face; *j-m
et. ins ∼ sagen* tell s.o. s.th. to his (her)
face; *j-m wie aus dem ∼ geschnitten
sein* be the spit and image of s.o.; *fig.
sein wahres ∼ zeigen* show one's true
face; *das ∼ verlieren (wahren)* lose
(save one's) face; *das gibt der Sache
ein ganz anderes ∼* that puts a different complexion on the matter. 2. (eye)-
sight: *das zweite ∼* second sight; *zu ∼
bekommen* catch sight of, see; *aus
dem ∼ verlieren* lose sight of.
Ge'sichts|ausdruck *m* (facial) expres-
sion, face. **∼creme** *f* face cream. **∼far-
be** *f* complexion. **∼feld** *n* *opt.* field of
vision. **∼kreis** *m* horizon.
ge'sichtslos *adj fig.* featureless.
Ge'sichts|maske *f* face mask.
∼mas,sage *f* facial massage, F facial.
∼muskel *m* facial muscle. **∼packung** *f*
face pack. **∼pflege** *f* care of one's face.
∼punkt *m* 1. point of view, viewpoint,
angle: *von diesem ∼ aus (gesehen)*
(looked at) from this point of view. 2.
point, aspect. **∼wasser** *n* face lotion.
∼winkel *m* *opt.* visual angle. **∼züge** *pl*
features.
Gesindel [gə'zɪndəl] *n* (-s; *no pl*) riffraff.

gesinnt [gə'zɪnt] *adj* **1.** disposed (*dat* toward). **2.** *in cpds.* ...-minded.

Gesinnung [gə'zɪnʊŋ] *f* (-; -en) **1.** mind, character. **2.** convictions, views.

ge'sinnungslos *adj* unprincipled.

Ge'sinnungswandel *m* change of heart.

gesittet [gə'zɪtət] *adj* civilized.

Gesöff [gə'zœf] *n* (-[e]s; -e) F *contp.* awful stuff.

gesoffen [gə'zɔfən] *pp of* **saufen.**

gesondert [gə'zɔndərt] *adj* separate.

gesonnen [gə'zɔnən] *pp of* **sinnen.**

ge'spalten I *pp of* **spalten. II** *adj* split.

Gespann [gə'ʃpan] *n* (-[e]s; -e) **1.** team. **2.** *mot.* combination. **3.** *fig.* pair.

gespannt *adj* **1.** tight, taut. **2.** *fig.* tense (*nerves, situation*), strained (*relations*), close (*attention*). **3. a)** eager, anxious, **b)** curious, **c)** excited: **~ sein auf** (*acc*) be anxious to see (*or* know); **ich bin ~, ob (wie)** ... I wonder if (how) ...; **da bin ich aber ~!** I can't wait to see that!

Ge'spanntheit *f* (-; *no pl*) **1.** tension (*a. fig.*), tenseness. **2. a)** eagerness, intentness, **b)** (anxious) anticipation.

Gespenst [gə'ʃpɛnst] *n* (-[e]s; -er) ghost, *a. fig.* spect/re (*Am.* -er).

ge'spenstisch *adj* **1.** ghostly, F spooky. **2.** *fig.* eerie, nightmarish.

Gespinst [gə'ʃpɪnst] *n* (-[e]s; -e) tissue.

gesponnen [gə'ʃpɔnən] *pp of* **spinnen.**

Gespött [gə'ʃpœt] *n* (-[e]s; *no pl*) derision, mockery: **j-n zum ~ machen** make a laughingstock of s.o.

Gespräch [gə'ʃprɛːç] *n* (-[e]s; -e) talk (*a. pol.*), conversation, discussion, *teleph.* call: **ein ~ führen mit** have a talk *etc* with; **das ~ bringen auf** (*acc*) steer the conversation round to; **im ~ sein** be under discussion; **ins ~ kommen** get talking (*mit* to); **mit j-m im ~ bleiben** stay in contact (*or* touch) with s.o.

ge'sprächig *adj* **1.** talkative. **2.** communicative. **Ge'sprächigkeit** *f* (-; *no pl*) talkativeness.

Ge'sprächs|partner(in *f*) *m* interlocutor, *w.s interesting etc* person to talk to. **~pause** *f* lull in the conversation. **~runde** *f pol.* round of talks. **~stoff** *m* topic(s) (of conversation).

ge'spreizt *adj fig.* affected.

gesprochen [gə'ʃprɔxən] *pp of* **sprechen.**

gesprossen [gə'ʃprɔsən] *pp of* **sprießen.**

gesprungen [gə'ʃprʊŋən] *pp of* **springen.**

Gespür [gə'ʃpyːr] *n* (-s; *no pl*) (**für**) flair, nose.

ge'staffelt *adj* staggered, graduated.

Gestalt [gə'ʃtalt] *f* (-; -en) **1.** form, shape: **in ~ von** in the form (*or* shape) of; (**feste**) **~ annehmen** take shape. **2.** (*literary etc*) figure, character. **3.** build.

ge'stalten (h) **I** *v/t* **a)** shape, fashion, design, **b)** decorate (*room etc*), **c)** create: **et. interessant ~** make s.th. interesting. **2.** arrange, organize. **II** *sich ~* develop; **sich ~ zu** become, turn into, (turn out to) be (*a success etc*); **sich anders ~** turn out differently.

Ge'stalter *m* (-s; -), **Ge'stalterin** *f* (-; -nen) **1. a)** designer, stylist, **b)** creator. **2.** organizer. **ge'stalterisch** *adj* designing, stylistic, *b.s* creative, artistic.

Ge'staltung *f* (-; *no pl*) **1. a)** shaping (*a. fig.*), forming, design, **b)** creation. **2.** arrangement, organization.

Ge'stammel *n* (-s; *no pl*) stammering.

gestand [gə'ʃtant] *pret of* **gestehen.**

gestanden [gə'ʃtandən] **I** *pp of* **stehen** *and* **gestehen. II** *adj* **ein ~er Mann** a man who has made his mark (in life).

geständig [gə'ʃtɛndɪç] *adj* confessing (one's guilt): **~ sein** confess.

Geständnis [gə'ʃtɛntnɪs] *n* (-ses; -se) *a.* 🏛 confession: **ein ~ ablegen** confess; **j-m ein ~ machen** confess s.th. to s.o.

Gestank [gə'ʃtaŋk] *m* (-[e]s; *no pl*) stench, F stink.

gestatten [gə'ʃtatən] *v/t* (h) allow, permit: **~ Sie, daß ich ...?** may I ...?, do you mind if I ...?; **~ Sie e-e Frage**, may I ask you s.th.; **wenn Sie ~** with your permission.

Geste ['ɡɛstə] *f* (-; -n) *a. fig.* gesture.

ge'stehen *v/t, v/i* (gestand, gestanden, h) confess: → **offen.**

Ge'stehungskosten *pl* 🕇 production costs, prime cost.

Ge'stein *n* (-[e]s; -e) rock.

Gestell [gə'ʃtɛl] *n* (-[e]s; -e) **a)** stand, rack, shelve, **b)** trestle, **c)** frame.

gestellt [gə'ʃtɛlt] *adj* **1.** *phot.* posed, unnatural. **2.** → **stellen** 5.

Ge'stellungsbefehl *m* ✗ call-up (*Am.* induction) order.

gestern ['ɡɛstərn] *adv* yesterday: **~ abend** yesterday evening, last night;

256

von ~ yesterday's (*paper etc*); F **er ist nicht von ~** he wasn't born yesterday.

gestiegen [gə'ʃtiːɡən] *pp of* **steigen**.

gestielt [gə'ʃtiːlt] *adj* stemmed.

Gestik ['gɛstɪk] *f* (-; *no pl*) gestures.

gestikulieren [gɛstiku'liːrən] *v/i* (h) gesticulate.

Gestirn [gə'ʃtɪrn] *n* (-[e]s; -e) star.

Gestöber [gə'ʃtøːbər] *n* (-s; -) drift(ing).

gestochen [gə'ʃtɔxən] **I** *pp of* **stechen**. **II** *adj* **wie** ~ very neat (*hand*); *phot.* ~ **scharf** very sharp.

gestohlen [gə'ʃtoːlən] *pp of* **stehlen**.

gestorben [gə'ʃtɔrbən] *pp of* **sterben**.

gestört [gə'ʃtøːrt] *adj* disturbed, disordered, *psych.* unbalanced, ☉ faulty.

ge'stoßen *pp of* **stoßen**.

Gestotter [gə'ʃtɔtər] *n* (-s; *no pl*) stuttering, stammering.

gesträhnt [gə'ʃtrɛːnt] *adj* streaked-in.

Gesträuch [gə'ʃtrɔʏç] *n* (-[e]s; -e) shrubbery, bushes.

gestreift [gə'ʃtraɪft] *adj* striped.

gestrichen [gə'ʃtrɪçən] **I** *pp of* **streichen**. **II** *adj* **1.** painted. **2.** deleted. **3.** ~ **voll** a) level, b) brimful(l); **drei ~e Teelöffel (voll)** three level teaspoons (full).

gestrig ['gɛstrɪç] *adj* of yesterday: **die ~e Zeitung** yesterday's paper.

gestritten [gə'ʃtrɪtən] *pp of* **streiten**.

Gestrüpp [gə'ʃtrʏp] *n* (-[e]s; -e) **1.** undergrowth, brushwood. **2.** *fig.* jungle.

Gestühl [gə'ʃtyːl] *n* (-[e]s; -e) seats, *eccl.* pews.

gestunken [gə'ʃtʊŋkən] *pp of* **stinken**.

Gestüt [gə'ʃtyːt] *n* (-[e]s; -e) a) stud farm, b) stud.

Gesuch [gə'zuːx] *n* (-[e]s; -e) application, request, petition. **ge'sucht** *adj* **1.** wanted (*a.* 🖙), much sought-after, in (great) demand. **2.** *fig.* studied.

gesund [gə'zʊnt] *adj* healthy, *fig. a.* sound (*firm, sleep, views, etc*): ~ **sein** *a.* be in good health, be well; **geistig** ~ sane; ~ **und munter** (as) fit as a fiddle; **(wieder) ~ werden** get well (again), recover; **Gemüse ist** ~ vegetables are good for you(r health); *iro.* **das ist (ganz) ~ für ihn!** that's good for him!; → **Menschenverstand**.

Ge'sundbeter(in *f*) *m* faith healer.

gesunden [gə'zʊndən] *v/i* (sn) recover (*a. fig.*), get well (again).

Ge'sundheit *f* (-; *no pl*) a) health, b)

healthiness: **geistige** ~ sanity; **bei guter** ~ **sein** be in good health; **auf j-s** ~ **trinken** drink to s.o.'s health; **~!** *at a sneeze:* bless you!

ge'sundheitlich *adj* physical: **aus ~en Gründen** for health reasons; ~ **geht es ihm gut** he is in good health; **ich bin ~ nicht auf der Höhe** I don't feel too well.

Ge'sundheits|amt *n* public health office. **~a,postel** *m iro.* health freak. **2fördernd** *adj* healthy. **~pflege** *f* (personal) hygiene, health care. **2schädlich** *adj* injurious to health, unhealthy. **~wesen** *n* (-s; *no pl*) Public Health (Service). **~zeugnis** *n* health certificate. **~zustand** *m* (state of) health.

ge'sundschrumpfen *v/t, a.* **sich** ~ (*sep*, -ge-, h) F slim down.

ge'sundstoßen: **sich** ~ (*irr, sep*, -ge-, h, → **stoßen**) F make a pile.

Ge'sundung *f* (-; *no pl*) *a. fig.* recovery.

gesungen [gə'zʊŋən] *pp of* **singen**.

gesunken [gə'zʊŋkən] *pp of* **sinken**.

getan [gə'taːn] *pp of* **tun**.

geteilt [gə'taɪlt] *adj* **1.** divided: **~er Meinung sein** disagree; **darüber kann man ~er Meinung sein** that's a matter of opinion. **2.** shared.

Getöse [gə'tøːzə] *n* (-s; *no pl*) din.

ge'tragen I *pp of* **tragen**. **II** *adj* **1.** second-hand, old (*clothes*). **2.** *fig.* solemn, measured, slow.

Ge'trampel *n* (-s; *no pl*) F trampling.

Getränk [gə'trɛŋk] *n* (-[e]s; -e) drink, beverage.

Ge'tränkeauto,mat *m* drinks dispenser.

Ge'tränkekarte *f* list of beverages.

Ge'tränkesteuer *f* alcohol tax.

Getrappel [gə'trapəl] *n* (-s; *no pl*) patter.

Getreide [gə'traɪdə] *n* (-s; -) cereal(s), grain. **~(an)bau** *m* (-[e]s; *no pl*) cultivation of cereals. **~arten** *pl* cereals. **~ernte** *f* a) grain harvest, b) grain crop. **~feld** *n* grain field. **~land** *n* **1.** grain-growing country (*or* land). **2.** *no pl* grain fields. **~pflanze** *f* cereal plant. **~silo** *m* (grain) silo.

ge'treten *pp of* **treten**.

getreu [gə'trɔʏ] *adj* true, faithful.

Getriebe [gə'triːbə] *n* (-s; -) **1.** ☉ gear(ing), mechanism, *mot.* transmission, gearbox. **2.** *fig.* wheels. **3.** *fig.* bustle, rush.

getrieben [gə'triːbən] *pp of* **treiben**.

Ge'triebeschaden m mot. gearbox trouble.

getroffen [gə'trɔfən] pp of **treffen**.

getrogen [gə'tro:gən] pp of **trügen**.

ge'trost adj confidently, safely.

getrunken [gə'trʊŋkən] pp of **trinken**.

Getto ['gɛto] n (-s; -s) ghetto.

Getue [gə'tu:ə] n (-s; no pl) F fuss (*um* about).

Getümmel [gə'tyməl] n (-s; -) turmoil.

geübt [gə'y:pt] adj practised, trained (*eye etc*), experienced.

Gewächs [gə'vɛks] n (-es; -e) 1. plant. 2. ✝ produce, growth. 3. a) wine, b) vintage. 4. ✍ growth.

ge'wachsen I pp of **wachsen**[1]. II adj j-m ~ **sein** be a match for s.o.; **e-r Sache ~ sein** be up (or equal) to s.th.; **sich der Lage ~ zeigen** rise to the occasion.

Ge'wächshaus n greenhouse, hothouse.

gewagt [gə'va:kt] adj a) daring (*a. fig.*), risky, b) risqué (*joke etc*).

gewählt [gə'vɛ:lt] adj fig. refined.

Gewähr [gə'vɛ:r] f (-; no pl) guarantee: **ohne** ~ a) without guarantee, b) subject to change; **für et. ~ bieten** (or **leisten**) guarantee s.th. **ge'währen** v/t (h) a) grant (*j-m e-e Bitte* s.o. a request), b) give, afford (*an insight, protection, etc*): **j-n ~ lassen** let s.o. have his way.

ge'währleisten v/t (h) guarantee.

Ge'wahrsam m (-s; no pl) **in ~ nehmen** a) take s.th. in safe keeping, b) take s.o. into custody.

Ge'währsmann m informant, source.

Gewalt [gə'valt] f (-; -en) 1. no pl force, violence: **mit ~** by force; **mit aller ~** a) with all one's strength, b) fig. at all costs; **~ anwenden** use force; → **roh** 3. 2. a) power, adm., ⚖ authority, b) control (**über** acc of): **höhere ~** act of God; **die gesetzgebende ~** the legislature; **et. in s-e ~ bringen** gain control of s.th.; **et.** (**sich**) **in der ~ haben** have s.th. (o.s.) under control; **in j-s ~ sein** be in s.o.'s power (or hands); **die ~ verlieren über** (acc) lose control over.

Ge'waltakt m act of violence.

Ge'waltanwendung f (use of) force.

Ge'waltenteilung f pol. separation of powers.

Ge'waltherrschaft f tyranny. **Ge'waltherrscher(in** f) m despot, tyrant.

ge'waltig adj 1. powerful, mighty. 2. enormous, huge.

ge'waltlos I adj nonviolent. II adv without violence. **Ge'waltlosigkeit** f (-; no pl) nonviolence.

Ge'waltmaßnahme f drastic measure.

ge'waltsam I adj forcible, violent: **~er Tod** violent death. II adv forcibly, by force: **et. ~ öffnen** force s.th. (open).

Ge'waltsamkeit f (-; no pl) violence.

Ge'walttat f act of violence, outrage.

ge'walttätig adj violent, brutal.

Ge'walttätigkeit f (-; -en) 1. no pl violence, brutality. 2. act of violence.

Ge'waltverbrechen n crime of violence.

Ge'waltverbrecher m violent criminal.

Ge'waltverzichtsabkommen n pol. nonaggression treaty.

Gewand [gə'vant] n (-[e]s; ⸚er) robe.

gewandt [gə'vant] I pp of **wenden**[2]. II adj a) agile, nimble, b) elegant, c) clever. **Ge'wandtheit** f (-; no pl) a) agility, nimbleness, b) elegance, c) cleverness.

gewann [gə'van] pret of **gewinnen**.

gewappnet [gə'vapnət] adj fig. prepared (**für** for).

gewärtig [gə'vɛrtɪç] adj ~ **sein** (gen) → **ge'wärtigen** [-tɪgən] v/t (h) expect, reckon with: **zu ~ haben** be in for s.th.

Gewäsch [gə'vɛʃ] n (-[e]s; no pl) F contp. blather.

ge'waschen pp of **waschen**.

Gewässer [gə'vɛsər] n (-s; -) (stretch of) water, pl waters, rivers and lakes.

Ge'wässerschutz m prevention of water pollution.

Gewebe [gə'veːbə] n (-s; -) a) (woven) fabric, b) tissue (*a. anat. or fig.*), c) weave. **~probe** f ✍ tissue sample.

Gewehr [gə'veːr] n (-[e]s; -e) gun, rifle. **~kolben** m (rifle) butt. **~kugel** f (rifle) bullet. **~lauf** m (rifle) barrel.

Geweih [gə'vaɪ] n (-[e]s; -e) antlers, horns.

Gewerbe [gə'vɛrbə] n (-s; -) trade, business, occupation: **Handel und ~** trade and industry. **~freiheit** f freedom of trade. **~lehrer(in** f) m teacher at a trade school. **~ordnung** f industrial code. **~schein** m trade licen/ce (*Am.* -se). **~schule** f trade school. **~steuer** f trade tax. ⚲**treibend** adj carrying on a trade, industrial. **~treibende** m, f (-n; -n) person carrying on a trade, trader. **~zweig** m (branch of) trade (or industry).

gewerblich [gə'vɛrplɪç] *adj* commercial, industrial, trade. **ge'werbsmäßig** *adj* professional, gainful, *adv a.* for gain.
Gewerkschaft [gə'vɛrkʃaft] *f* (-; -en) trade (*Am.* labor) union.
Ge'werkschaftler *m* (-s; -) (trade, *Am.* labor) unionist. **ge'werkschaftlich** *adj* trade (*Am.* labor) union: ~ *organisiert* unionized, organized.
Ge'werkschafts... (trade, *Am.* labor) union (*boss*, *member*, *etc*). **~bund** *m* federation of trade (*Am.* labor) unions.
ge'wesen *pp of* **sein**[1].
gewichen [gə'vɪçən] *pp of* **weichen**.
Gewicht [gə'vɪçt] *n* (-[e]s; -e) *a.* fig. weight: *ein ~ von ... haben* weigh ...; *nach ~ verkaufen* sell by weight; *fig. ~ haben* carry weight (*bei* with); (*nicht*) *ins ~ fallen* be of (no) importance; ~ *legen auf* (*acc*) stress, emphasize; (*dat*) ~ *beimessen* attach importance to; (*dat*) ~ *verleihen* lend weight to; → *spezifisch.* **ge'wichten** *v/t* (*h*) *statistics*: weigh: *fig.* (*neu*) ~ (re)assess.
Ge'wichtheben *n* (-s) weight lifting.
Ge'wichtheber *m* (-s; -) weight lifter.
gewichtig [gə'vɪçtɪç] *adj a.* fig. weighty.
Ge'wichts|klasse *f* *sports*: weight (class). **~verlust** *m* loss of weight. **~zunahme** *f* increase in weight.
gewiesen [gə'vi:zən] *pp of* **weisen**.
gewillt [gə'vɪlt] *adj ~ sein, et. zu tun* be willing (*or* ready) to do s.th.
Gewimmel [gə'vɪməl] *n* (-s; *no pl*) a) swarm(ing), swarming mass (*of insects etc*), b) milling crowd.
Gewinde [gə'vɪndə] *n* (-s; -) ⊕ thread.
Ge'windebohrer *m* (screw) tap.
Gewinn [gə'vɪn] *m* (-[e]s; -e) **1.** † profit, gain(s): *mit ~* at a profit; ~ *ziehen aus* profit by. **2.** *fig. a*) profit, gain, advantage, *b*) asset (*für* to). **3.** *a*) prize, *b*) winnings. **4.** → *Gewinnlos.* **~anteil** *m* share in (the) profits, dividend. **~beteiligung** *f* profit sharing. **⌂bringend** *adj* profitable. **~chance** *f* chance (of winning).
gewinnen [gə'vɪnən] (gewann, gewonnen, h) **I** *v/t fig. a*) win, *fig. a.* gain: *Höhe ~* ✈ gain height; *j-n für sich ~* win s.o. over; *j-n für et. ~* win s.o. to s.th.; → *Spiel* 2. **b**) produce, ⚒ mine, win, recover (*aus* from *scrap etc*). **II** *v/i* **3.** (*bei*, *in dat* at) win, be the winner,

number, ticket, etc: come up a winner. **4.** *gain: fig. an Bedeutung ~* gain in importance; *sie hat sehr gewonnen* she has greatly improved.
ge'winnend *adj a. fig.* winning, engaging. **Ge'winner** *m* (-s; -), **Ge'winnerin** *f* (-; -nen) winner.
Ge'winn|los *n* winning ticket, winner. **~maxi,mierung** *f* ✝ maximization of profits. **~spanne** *f* profit margin. **~sucht** *f* (-; *no pl*) (*aus* ~ from) greed.
Ge'winn-und-Ver'lust-Rechnung *f* profit and loss account.
Ge'winnung *f* (-; *no pl*) winning, production.
Ge'winnzahl *f* winning number.
Gewinsel [gə'vɪnzəl] *n* (-s; *no pl*) *contp.* whining.
Gewirr [gə'vɪr] *n* (-[e]s; -e) tangle (*a. fig.*).
gewiß [gə'vɪs] **I** *adj* certain: *in gewissem Sinne* in a sense; *ich bin mir m-r Sache ~* I am sure of my ground; → *Etwas.* **II** *adv* certainly, for certain: ~*!* certainly!, sure!; *aber ~!* but of course!
Ge'wissen *n* (-s; -) conscience: *j-m ins ~ reden* reason with s.o.
ge'wissenhaft *adj* conscientious.
Ge'wissenhaftigkeit *f* (-; *no pl*) conscientiousness.
ge'wissenlos *adj* unscrupulous.
Ge'wissenlosigkeit *f* (-; *no pl*) unscrupulousness.
Ge'wissens|bisse *pl* twinges of remorse. **~frage** *f* matter of conscience. **~freiheit** *f* (-; *no pl*) freedom of conscience. **~gründe** *pl aus ~n* for reasons of conscience. **~kon,flikt** *m*, **~not** *f* moral dilemma.
gewissermaßen [gə'vɪsɐ'ma:sən] *adv* in a way, so to speak.
Ge'wißheit *f* (-; *no pl*) certainty: *mit ~* for certain; *sich ~ verschaffen* make sure (*über acc* of); (*zur*) ~ *werden* become a certainty.
Gewitter [gə'vɪtɐ] *n* (-s; -) thunderstorm, *fig.* storm. **ge'wittern** *v/impers* (*h*) *es gewittert* there is a thunderstorm. **Ge'witterwolke** *f* thundercloud. **ge'wittrig** [-trɪç] *adj* thundery.
gewitzt [gə'vɪtst] *adj* F smart, clever.
gewogen [gə'vo:gən] **I** *pp of* **wiegen**[2]. **II** *adj fig. j-m ~ sein* be well disposed to (*or* toward[s]) s.o.
gewöhnen [gə'vø:nən] *v/t, a. sich ~ (h)*

get used (**an** *acc* to); **man gewöhnt sich an alles** you get used to anything.

Gewohnheit [gə'vo:nhaɪt] *f* (-; -en) (**aus** ~ from) habit: **die ~ haben, et. zu tun** be in the habit of doing s.th.; **sich et. zur ~ machen** make a habit of s.th.

Ge'wohnheits... habitual (*drinker etc*).

ge'wohnheitsmäßig *adj* and *adv* habitual(ly), *adv a.* out of habit.

Ge'wohnheitssache *f* matter of habit.

Ge'wohnheitstier *n* F creature of habit.

gewöhnlich [gə'vø:nlɪç] **I** *adj* **1.** a) common, ordinary, b) usual. **2.** common, vulgar. **II** *adv* **3.** commonly (*etc*): (**für**) ~ usually, normally; **wie** ~ as usual.

gewohnt [gə'vo:nt] *adj* usual: **et.** (**zu tun**) ~ **sein** be used to (doing) s.th.

Ge'wöhnung *f* (-; *no pl*) (**an** *acc* to) **1.** habituation. **2.** addiction.

Gewölbe [gə'vœlbə] *n* (-s; -) vault.

gewölbt [gə'vœlpt] *adj* **1.** △ arched, vaulted. **2.** domed.

gewollt [gə'vɔlt] *pp of* **wollen²**.

gewonnen [gə'vɔnən] *pp of* **gewinnen**.

geworben [gə'vɔrbən] *pp of* **werben**.

geworden [gə'vɔrdən] *pp of* **werden**.

geworfen [gə'vɔrfən] *pp of* **werfen**.

gewrungen [gə'vrʊŋən] *pp of* **wringen**.

Gewühl [gə'vy:l] *n* (-[e]s; *no pl*) milling crowd.

gewunden [gə'vʊndən] **I** *pp of* **winden**. **II** *adj* winding, *a. fig.* tortuous.

Gewürz [gə'vʏrts] *n* (-es; -e) spice, condiment, seasoning.

Ge'würz|gurke *f* pickled gherkin. **~mischung** *f* mixed herbs (*or* spices). **~nelke** *f* clove. **~ständer** *m* spice rack.

gewußt [gə'vʊst] *pp of* **wissen**.

ge'zahnt, ge'zähnt *adj* toothed, serrated (*a.* ⚙), perforated (*stamp*).

Ge'zeiten *pl* tide(s).

Ge'zeiten... tidal (*power plant etc*). **~wechsel** *m* turn of the tide.

Ge'zeter *n* (-s; *no pl*) *contp.* nagging.

ge'zielt *adj fig.* specific (*measure etc*), calculated (*indiscretion etc*).

ge'ziert *adj* affected.

gezogen [gə'tso:gən] *pp of* **ziehen**.

Ge'zwitscher *n* (-s; *no pl*) chirping, twitter(ing).

gezwungen [gə'tsvʊŋən] **I** *pp of* **zwingen**. **II** *adj fig.* forced (*smile etc*), stiff, constrained (*manner etc*): ~ **lachen** force a laugh.

ge'zwungenermaßen *adv* of necessity: ~ **et. tun** be forced to do s.th.

Gicht [gɪçt] *f* (-; *no pl*) ✚ gout. **'Gichtknoten** *m* gouty node. **'Gichtkranke** *m, f* (-n; -n) gout patient, gouty person.

Giebel ['gi:bəl] *m* (-s; -) gable. **'Giebelseite** *f*, **'Giebelwand** *f* gable end.

Gier [gi:r] *f* (-; *no pl*) greed(iness) (**nach** for). **'gierig** *adj* greedy (**nach** for).

gießen ['gi:sən] (goß, gegossen, h) **I** *v/t* **1.** pour. **2.** water. **3.** ⚙ found, *art:* cast. **II** *v/i* **4.** pour: **es gießt** (**in Strömen**) it is pouring (with rain). **'Gießer** *m* (-s; -) ⚙ founder. **Gießerei** [gi:sə'raɪ] *f* (-; -en) ⚙ **1.** *no pl* casting. **2.** fig.

'Gießkanne *f* watering can.

Gift [gɪft] *n* (-[e]s; -e) *a.* ✚ poison, *zo.* venom: F **darauf kannst du ~ nehmen!** you bet your life on it! **'Giftgas** *n* poison gas. **'giftig** *adj* a) poisonous, *fig. a.* venomous, ♜, ✚ toxic, b) poisoned. **'Giftmischer** *m* (-s; -), **'Giftmischerin** *f* (-; -nen) F poisoner. **'Giftmüll** *m* toxic waste. **'Giftpilz** *m* poisonous mushroom, toadstool. **'Giftschlange** *f* venomous (*or* poisonous) snake, *fig.* snake. **'Giftstoff** *m* poisonous (*or* toxic) substance. **'Giftzahn** *m* (poison) fang.

Gigant [gi'gant] *m* (-en; -en) *fig.* giant. **gi'gantisch** *adj* gigantic.

Gilde ['gɪldə] *f* (-; -n) guild.

ging [gɪŋ] *pret of* **gehen**.

Ginster ['gɪnstər] *m* (-s; -) ♣ broom.

Gipfel ['gɪpfəl] *m* (-s; -) summit (*a. fig. pol.*), top, peak: *fig.* **auf dem ~ der Macht** at the height (*or* peak) of power; F **das ist** (**doch**) **der ~!** that's the limit. **~konferenz** *f pol.* summit conference. **'gipfeln** *v/i* (h) ~ **in** (*dat*) culminate in. **'Gipfeltreffen** *n pol.* summit (meeting).

Gips [gɪps] *m* (-es; -e) ⚗ plaster, *art,* ✚ *a.* plaster of Paris, ♞ gypsum. **~abdruck** *m* plaster cast. **~bein** *n* F leg in plaster. **'gipsen** *v/t* (h) ⚗ (F put in) plaster. **'Gipsverband** *m* ✚ plaster cast.

Giraffe [gi'rafə] *f* (-; -n) *zo.* giraffe.

girieren [ʒi'ri:rən] *v/t* (h) ✝ endorse.

Girlande [gɪr'landə] *f* (-; -n) garland.

Giro|bank ['ʒi:ro-] *f* (-; -en) ✝ clearing bank. **~konto** *n* current (*Am.* checking) account. **~zen,trale** *f* clearing house.

Gis, gis [gɪs] *n* (-; -) ♩ G sharp.

Gischt [gɪʃt] *m* (-[e]s; *no pl*) (sea) spray.

Gitarre [gi'tarə] *f* (-; -n) guitar.

Gitarrist [gita'rɪst] *m* (-en; -en), **Gitar'ristin** *f* (-; -nen) guitarist.

Gitter ['gɪtər] *n* (-s; -) **1.** a) lattice, grille, b) bars, c) (wire) screen, d) grate: *hinter ~n* behind bars. **2.** *opt.* grating. **3.** *⚡, a. maps:* grid. **~bett** *n* cot, *Am.* crib. **~fenster** *n* lattice (*or* barred) window. **~mast** *m* ⚡ pylon. **~netz** *n* maps: grid.

Glacéhandschuhe [gla'se:-] *pl* (*fig. j-n mit ~n anfassen* handle s.o. with) kid gloves.

Gladiole [gla'djo:lə] *f* (-; -n) ⚘ gladiolus.

Glanz [glants] *m* (-es; *no pl*) **1.** lust/re (*Am.* -er) (*a. fig.*), shine, gloss, glitter, brilliance (*a. fig.*). **2.** *fig.* glamo(u)r, splendo(u)r.

glänzen ['glɛntsən] *v/i* (h) shine (*a. fig.*), gleam, *fabric, nose, etc:* be shiny.

glänzend *adj* **1.** lustrous, glossy, shining, shiny. **2.** *fig.* brilliant, splendid: *sich ~ amüsieren* have a great time.

Glanzleistung *f* brilliant performance (*or* feat). **glanzlos** *adj* dull. **Glanznummer** *f* star turn. **Glanzpa‚pier** *n* glazed paper. **Glanzpunkt** *m* highlight, high spot. **Glanzstück** *n* pièce de résistance. **glanzvoll** *adj* splendid, magnificent. **Glanzzeit** *f* heyday.

Glas [gla:s] *n* (-es; ·er) *no pl* glass. **2.** a) glass, *or* jar: *drei ~ Wein* three glasses of wine. **3.** *opt.* a) lens, glass, b) glasses.

Glasbläser *m* glass blower.

Glaser ['gla:zər] *m* (-s; -) glazier.

Glase'rei *f* (-; -en) glazier's (work)shop.

gläsern ['glɛːzərn] *adj* **1.** (of) glass. **2.** *fig.* glassy.

Glas|faser *f*, **~fiber** *f* glass fib/re (*Am.* -er). **~haus** *n wer im ~ sitzt, soll nicht mit Steinen werfen* people who live in glass houses should not throw stones. **~hütte** *f* ⚙ glassworks.

glasieren [gla'zi:rən] *v/t* (h) **1.** ⚙ glaze. **2.** *gastr.* ice, *Am.* frost.

glasig ['gla:zɪç] *adj* glassy (*a. fig.*), vitreous.

Glas|kasten *m* glass case. ⚪**klar** *adj a. fig.* crystal-clear. **~körper** *m anat.* vitreous body. **~malerei** *f* glass painting. **~scheibe** *f* (glass) pane. **~scherben** *pl* (pieces of) broken glass. **~schneider** *m* glass cutter. **~schrank** *m* glass-fronted cupboard.

Glasur [gla'zu:r] *f* (-; -en) **1.** ⚙ glaze, enamel. **2.** *gastr.* icing, *Am.* frosting.

Glaswaren *pl* glassware.

glasweise *adv* by the glass.

Glaswolle *f* glass wool.

glatt [glat] **I** *adj* **1.** a) smooth (*a. fig.*), b) even, c) polished: ~*es Haar* straight hair. **2.** slippery. **3.** F *fig.* plain, clear: ~*e Absage* flat refusal; ~*e Lüge* downright (*or* outright) lie; *das ist ~er Wahnsinn* that's sheer madness. **II** *adv* **4.** a) smoothly (*etc*), b) clean: ~ (*anliegend*) ⚙ flush; ~ *durchschneiden* cut clean through; ~ *gestrickt* plainly knit; *fig.* ~ *gewinnen* win clearly, win hands down. **5.** F *fig.* ~ *ablehnen* (*leugnen*) refuse (deny) flatly; *das bringt er ~ fertig* I wouldn't put it past him; *et.* ~ *vergessen* clean forget (about) s.th.

Glätte ['glɛtə] *f* (-; *no pl*) **1.** a) smoothness, b) slipperiness (*a. contp.*).

Glatteis *n* a) (black, *Am.* glare) ice, b) icy ground, icy roads: *fig. j-n aufs ~ führen* trip s.o. up.

glätten ['glɛtən] (h) **I** *v/t* a) smooth, b) polish (*a. fig.*). **II** *sich ~* smooth down.

glattgehen *v/i* (*irr, sep,* -ge-, sn, → *gehen*) go smoothly.

glattra‚siert *adj* clean-shaven.

glattstellen *v/t* (*sep,* -ge-, h) ✝ square, even up.

glattweg *adv* F → *glatt* 5.

Glatze ['glatsə] *f* (-; -n) bald head: *e-e ~ haben* (*bekommen*) be (go) bald.

Glatzkopf *m* **1.** → **Glatze**. **2.** F bald-head, baldy. **glatzköpfig** ['glatskœpfɪç] *adj* bald(headed).

Glaube ['glaʊbə] *m* (-ns; *no pl*) (*an acc* in) belief, faith: ~*n schenken* (*dat*) believe, give credence to; *in gutem ~n* in good faith; *den ~n verlieren* lose faith.

glauben (h) **I** *v/t* believe, *a.* think, suppose: *das glaube ich dir nicht!* I don't believe you!; *es ist nicht zu ~!* it's incredible! **II** *v/i* believe (*an acc* in): *an j-n ~ a.* have faith in s.o., trust s.o.; *ich glaube, ja!* I think so!; F *er* (*es*) *hat dran ~ müssen* he (it) has had it; *er wird dran ~ müssen* he's for it.

Glaubens|bekenntnis *n* creed (*a. fig.*), confession. **~freiheit** *f* (-; *no pl*) religious freedom. **~gemeinschaft** *f* denomination, church. **~genosse** *m* fellow believer. **~krieg** *m* religious war. **~lehre** *f*, **~satz** *m* dogma.

glaubhaft ['glaʊphaft] *adj* a) credible,

plausible, b) convincing: *et. ~ machen* a. ✂ substantiate s.th.

gläubig ['glɔybɪç] *adj* believing, *eccl. a.* religious, devout. **Gläubige** ['glɔybɪgə] *m, f* (-n; -n) believer: *die ~n* the faithful. **Gläubiger** ['glɔybɪgər] *m* (-s; -) creditor.

glaublich ['glauplɪç] *adj das ist kaum ~* that's hard to believe.

glaubwürdig ['glaupvyrdɪç] *adj* credible, reliable. **'Glaubwürdigkeit** *f* (-; *no pl*) credibility, reliability.

gleich [glaɪç] **I** *adj* **1.** same, equal (*a.* Å), identical: *3 mal 3 ist ~ 9* three times three equals (*or* is) nine; *in ~er Höhe mit* level with; *auf ~e Weise* (in) the same way; *zur ~en Zeit* at the same time; *das ist mir ~!* it's all the same to me!, *contp.* I don't care!; *ganz ~, wann* (*wer etc*) no matter when (who *etc*); *das* ≙e the same (thing). **II** *adv* **2.** equally, alike: *~ alt (groß)* of the same age (size); *~ schnell* just as fast; *~ aussehen* look alike; *alle ~ behandeln* treat everybody the same way. **3.** at once, right away, in a moment: *~ darauf* immediately afterwards; *~ nach ...* right after ...; *es ist ~ 11 (Uhr)* it's almost eleven (o'clock); *ich komme ~!* (I'm) coming!, just a minute!; *ich bin ~ wieder da!* I'll be right back!; F *bis ~!* see you soon (*or* later)! **4.** immediately, directly: *~ neben ...* right next to ...; *~ gegenüber* just (*or* directly) opposite.

'gleichaltrig [-ʔaltrɪç] *adj* (of) the same age. **'gleichartig** *adj* **1.** of the same kind, homogeneous. **2.** like, similar. **'gleichbedeutend** *adj* (*mit*) synonymous (with) (*a. ling.*), equivalent (to). **'Gleichbehandlung** *f* equal treatment.

'gleichberechtigt *adj* having equal rights. **'Gleichberechtigung** *f* (-; *no pl*) equal rights, equality.

'gleichbleiben *v/i* (*irr, sep,* -ge-, sn, → *bleiben*) (*a. sich ~*) stay the same (*or* unchanged); F *das bleibt sich gleich!* that makes no difference!

gleichen ['glaɪçən] *v/i* (*glich, geglichen, h*) (*dat*) be (*or* look) like: *sich* (*or einander*) *~* be (*or* look) alike, be similar; *j-m ~ an* (*dat*) equal s.o. in.

'gleicher'maßen *adv* **1.** equally. **2.** → **~'weise** *adv* in like manner, likewise.

'gleichfalls *adv* also, likewise: *danke, ~!* (thanks), the same to you!

'gleichförmig *adj* **1.** uniform, monotonous. **2.** regular. **'Gleichförmigkeit** *f* (-; *no pl*) **1.** uniformity, monotony. **2.** regularity.

'gleichgesinnt *adj* like-minded.

'Gleichgewicht *n* (-[e]s; *no pl*) *a. fig.* balance, equilibrium: *das ~ verlieren* (*halten*) lose (keep) one's balance; *j-n aus dem ~ bringen a. fig.* throw s.o. off balance; *seelisches ~* (mental) equilibrium; *das ~ der Kräfte pol.* the balance of power.

'gleichgültig *adj* **1.** indifferent (*gegen* to): *er ist mir ~* I don't care for him. **2.** unimportant, trivial: *es ist mir ~* I don't care; *es ist ~, ob ...* it doesn't matter whether ...; *~, wann* no matter when. **'Gleichgültigkeit** *f* (-; *no pl*) **1.** indifference (*gegen* to). **2.** apathy.

'Gleichheit *f* (-; *no pl*) **1.** equality, identity. **2.** uniformity.

'Gleichheitszeichen *n* Å equality sign.

'gleichkommen *v/i* (*irr, sep,* -ge-, sn, → *kommen*) (*dat*) **1.** equal (*an dat* in). **2.** amount to.

'gleichlautend *adj* identical: *~es Wort* homonym.

gleichmachen *v/t* (*sep,* -ge-, h) make equal (*dat* to): → *Erdboden*. **Gleichmache'rei** *f* (-; *no pl*) egalitarianism.

'gleichmäßig *adj* a) regular, even, b) constant: *et. ~ verteilen* distribute s.th. evenly. **'Gleichmäßigkeit** *f* (-; *no pl*) a) regularity, evenness, b) constancy.

'Gleichmut *m* (-[e]s; *no pl*) equanimity, calmness. **gleichmütig** ['glaɪçmy:tɪç] *adj* calm, imperturbable.

gleichnamig ['glaɪçna:mɪç] *adj* **1.** of the same name. **2.** Å with a common denominator.

'Gleichnis *n* (-ses; -se) parable.

gleichrangig ['glaɪçraŋɪç] *adj* **1.** of the same rank. **2.** *fig.* of equal importance.

'Gleichrichter *m* (-s; -) ⚡ rectifier.

'gleichschalten *v/t* (*sep,* -ge-, h) *fig.* coordinate, *pol.* bring into line.

'gleichseitig *adj* equilateral.

'gleichsetzen *v/t* (*sep,* -ge-, h) **1.** equate (*dat, mit* with). **2.** → *gleichstellen* 2.

'Gleichstand *m* (-[e]s; *no pl*) level score.

'gleichstellen *v/t* (*sep,* -ge-, h) **1.** → *gleichsetzen* 1. **2.** *j-n ~* put s.o. on an equal footing (*dat* with).

'Gleichstellung *f* (-; *no pl*) equalization.

'Gleichstrom *m* ⚡ direct current (DC).
'gleichtun *v/t* (*irr, sep*, -ge-, h, → *tun*) **es j-m** ~ equal s.o. (**an** *or* **in** *dat* in).
'Gleichung *f* (-; -en) equation.
'gleichwertig *adj* **1.** of the same value, equivalent. **2.** equally good: **~e Gegner** evenly matched opponents.
'gleichzeitig *adj and adv* simultaneous(ly), *adv a.* at the same time.
'gleichziehen *v/i* (*irr, sep*, -ge-, h, → *ziehen*) a) *a. fig.* (**mit** with) catch up, draw level, b) equalize, level the score.
Gleis [glaıs] *n* (-es; -e) rail(s), track(s), line: *fig. auf ein totes ~ schieben* put *s.o.,s.th.* on ice; *das ausgefahrene ~* a) the beaten track, b) *a. das alte ~* the same old rut.
'Gleiskörper *m* permanent way.
'Gleitboot *n* hydroglider, hydroplane.
gleiten ['glaıtən] *v/i* (glitt, geglitten, sn) **1.** glide, slide, slip, *hand etc:* pass. **2.** F *employee:* make use of flex(i)time.
'gleitend *adj fig.* sliding (*scale*): **~e Arbeitszeit** → **Gleitzeit.**
'Gleit|fläche *f* sliding surface. **~flug** *m* glide. **~flugzeug** *n* glider. **~klausel** *f* ⚖ escalator clause. **~komma** *n* floating point. **~mittel** *n* lubricant. **~schirm** *m* paraglider. **~schutz** *m mot.* antiskid device. **~sichtgläser** *pl* multifocal lenses. **~wachs** *n* skiing: gliding wax.
'Gleitzeit *f* (-; *no pl*) flexible working hours, flex(i)time. **~karte** *f* time card.
Gletscher ['glɛtʃər] *m* (-s; -) glacier.
'Gletscherbrand *m* glacial sunburn.
'Gletscherspalte *f* crevasse.
glich [glıç] *pret of* **gleichen.**
Glied [gli:t] *n* (-[e]s; -er) **1.** limb, member (*a. fig.*): *der Schreck fuhr ihr in die ~er* she had a bad shock. **2.** penis, (male) member. **3.** *a. fig.* link. **4.** ✕ rank.
gliedern ['gli:dərn] (h) **I** *v/t* a) arrange, organize, b) (sub)divide (*in acc* into). **II sich ~ in** (*acc*) be (sub)divided into.
'Glieder|puppe *f* jointed doll, *art:* lay figure. **~schmerz** *m* rheumatism.
Gliederung ['gli:dərʊŋ] *f* (-; -en) a) arrangement, organization, structure, b) (sub)division.
'Gliedmaßen *pl* limbs.
'Glimmer *m* (-s; -) *min.* mica.
'Glimmstengel *m* F fag.
glimpflich ['glımpflıç] *adj* mild, light: **~ mit j-m verfahren** be lenient with s.o.;

~ davonkommen get off lightly.
glitschig ['glıtʃıç] *adj* F slippery.
glitt [glıt] *pret of* **gleiten.**
glitzern ['glıtsərn] *v/i* (h) glitter.
global [glo'ba:l] *adj* global.
Globus ['glo:bʊs] *m* (-[ses]; -ben) globe.
'Glöckchen ['glœkçən] *n* (-s; -) little bell.
Glocke ['glɔkə] *f* (-; -n) **1.** bell: F **et. an die große ~ hängen** shout s.th. from the housetops. **2.** (*cheese etc*) cover.
'Glocken|blume *f* bellflower. **~geläut** *n* bell ringing. **~gießer** *m* bell founder. **~rock** *m* flared skirt. **~schlag** *m* stroke (of the clock). **~spiel** *n* chime(s), carillon. **~stuhl** *m*, **~turm** *m* belfry.
Glorie ['glo:riə] *f* (-; -n) **1.** glory. **2.** → **'Glorienschein** *m fig.* halo.
glorreich ['glo:rraıç] *adj* glorious.
Glossar [glɔ'sa:r] *n* (-s; -e) glossary.
Glosse ['glɔsə] *f* (-; -n) **1.** gloss. **2.** commentary. **3.** *pl* snide remarks: **s-e ~n machen über** (*acc*) remark on, jeer at.
'Glotzaugen *pl* F goggle-eyes.
Glotze ['glɔtsə] *f* (-; -n) F gogglebox, *Am.* tube. **'glotzen** *v/i* (h) F goggle, gawp.
Glück *n* **1.** fortune, (good) luck: *auf gut ~* a) on the off-chance, b) at random; *zum ~* fortunately; *zu m-m* luckily for me; *~ haben* be lucky; *er hatte kein ~* he had no luck; *das ~ haben zu inf* have the good fortune to *inf*; *~ gehabt!* that was lucky!; *nochmal ~ gehabt!* that was close!; *viel ~!* good luck!; *j-m ~ wünschen* a) wish s.o. luck, b) congratulate s.o. (*zu et.* on s.th.), *zum Geburtstag* wish s.o. (a) happy birthday; (*es ist) ein ~, daß ...* (it's a) good thing that ...; *er kann von ~ sagen, daß ...* he may thank his lucky stars that ... **2.** happiness, bliss.
'glückbringend *adj* lucky.
Glucke ['glʊkə] *f* (-; -n) **1.** *zo.* sitting hen. **2.** *fig.* (mother-)hen.
'glucken *v/i* (h) a) sit, b) cluck.
'glücken *v/i, v/impers* (sn) → **gelingen** I.
gluckern ['glʊkərn] *v/i* (h) glug, gurgle.
'glücklich **I** *adj* a) happy, b) lucky, fortunate: *sich ~ preisen* (*or* **schätzen**) count o.s. lucky; *ein ~er Einfall* a happy thought. **II** *adv* a) happily, b) luckily, c) safely, d) F finally, at (long) last.
'glücklicherweise *adv* luckily, fortunately, as luck would have it.

'**Glücksache** f es ist ~ it is a matter of luck.

'**Glücksbringer** m mascot, lucky charm.

glück'selig adj blissful, very happy.

Glück'seligkeit f (-; no pl) bliss.

glucksen ['glʊksən] v/i (h) **1.** gurgle. **2.** chuckle.

'**Glücks|fall** m lucky chance (F break), stroke of luck. **~göttin** f Fortune. **~kind** n child of Fortune. **~klee** m four-leaf clover. **~pfennig** m lucky penny. **~pilz** m F fig. lucky dog. **~ritter** m soldier of fortune. **~spiel** n **1.** game of chance, coll. gambling. **2.** fig. gamble. **~spieler(in** f) m gambler. **~stern** m lucky star. **~strähne** f streak of luck. **~tag** m lucky (or happy) day.

'**glückstrahlend** adj radiant (with happiness).

'**Glückstreffer** m **1.** sports: fluke (hit or shot). **2.** fig. stroke of luck.

'**Glückwunsch** m congratulations (zu on), good wishes (für for): m-n (or herzlichen) ~! congratulations!, zum Geburtstag happy birthday!

'**Glückwunsch|karte** f greetings card. **~tele,gramm** n greetings telegram.

'**Glühbirne** f (incandescent) bulb.

glühen ['glyːən] (h) **I** v/i (vor dat with) glow, fig. a. burn. **II** v/t ⊕ anneal.

'**glühend** adj glowing (a. fig.), red-hot (metal), live (coals): ~ heiß scorching. **2.** fig. burning, ardent.

'**Glühkerze** f mot. heater plug.

'**Glühlampe** f incandescent lamp.

'**Glühwein** m mulled claret.

'**Glühwürmchen** n (-s; -) glow-worm.

Glut [gluːt] f (-; -en) **1.** (blazing) heat. **2.** (glowing) fire. **3.** a) embers, b) live coals. **4.** fig. ardo(u)r, glow.

Glutaminsäure [glutaˈmiːn-] f glutamic acid.

Glyzerin [glytseˈriːn] n (-s; no pl) glycerin(e).

Gnade ['gnaːdə] f (-; no pl) **1.** mercy: j-m auf ~ und Ungnade ausgeliefert sein be at s.o.'s mercy; ~ vor Recht ergehen lassen show mercy. **2.** favo(u)r. **3.** eccl. grace: 'gnaden v/i dann gnade dir Gott! (then) God help you!

'**Gnaden|akt** m ⚖ act of grace. **~frist** f reprieve: ⊕-⊕ ~ von drei Tagen three days' grace. **~gesuch** n ⚖ petition for mercy.

'**gnadenlos** adj merciless.

'**Gnadenstoß** m coup de grâce.

gnädig ['gnɛːdɪç] adj a) gracious, b) merciful: ~e Frau madam.

Gnom [gnoːm] m (-en; -en) gnome.

Gobelin [gobəˈlɛ̃ː] m (-s; -s) Gobelin (tapestry).

Gold [gɔlt] n (-[e]s; no pl) gold: ~ waschen pan for gold; ~ gewinnen sports: win gold; treu wie ~ good as gold; das ist nicht mit ~ aufzuwiegen that is priceless; es ist nicht alles ~, was glänzt all that glitters is not gold.

'**Goldader** f vein of gold.

'**Goldbarren** m ingot of gold.

golden ['gɔldən] adj **1.** a) (of) gold, b) gilt. **2.** fig. golden (wedding, disc, etc)

'**Gold|fisch** m goldfish. 2**gelb** adj golden(-yellow). **~gräber** [-grɛbər] m gold digger. **~grube** f F fig. goldmine. **~hamster** m zo. golden hamster.

goldig ['gɔldɪç] adj F sweet, Am. a. cute.

'**Gold|krone** f ⚒ gold cap. **~medaille** f gold medal. **~me,daillengewinner(in** f) m gold medal(l)ist. **~mine** f ⚒ goldmine. **~münze** f gold coin. **~plombe** f gold filling. **~rahmen** m gilt frame. 2**richtig** adj and adv F dead right: er ist ~ he is okay. **~schmied** m goldsmith. **~schnitt** m gilt edge(s): Buch mit ~ gilt-edged book. **~stück** n **1.** gold coin. **2.** F fig. jewel. **~waage** f jedes Wort auf die ~ legen weigh every word. **~währung** f gold standard. **~waren** pl gold articles.

Golf[1] [gɔlf] m (-[e]s; -e) geogr. gulf.

Golf[2] n (-s; no pl) sports: golf.

'**Golfplatz** m golf course, (golf) links.

'**Golfschläger** m golf club.

'**Golfspiel** n **1.** golf. **2.** game of golf.

'**Golfspieler(in** f) m golfer.

'**Golfstrom** m geogr. Gulf Stream.

Gondel ['gɔndəl] f (-; -n) gondola.

Gong [gɔŋ] m (-s; -e) gong.

gönnen ['gœnən] v/t (h) **1.** j-m et. ~ not to (be)grudge s.o. s.th.; j-m et. nicht ~ → mißgönnen. **2.** j-m (sich) et. ~ allow s.o. (o.s.) s.th.

'**Gönner** m (-s; -) patron.

'**gönnerhaft** adj patronizing.

'**Gönnerin** f (-; -nen) patroness.

Gonokokken [gonoˈkɔkən] pl ⚕ gonococci.

gor [goːr] pret of gären.

Gör [gø:r] n (-[e]s; -en) F contp. brat.

Gorilla [go'rıla] m (-s; -s) gorilla (a. sl. bodyguard).

goß [gɔs] pret of gießen.

Gosse ['gɔsə] f (-; -n) a. fig. gutter.

Gotik ['go:tık] f a) Gothic (style), b) Gothic period. **'gotisch** adj Gothic.

Gott [gɔt] m (-es; ⁓er) a) no pl God, the god, deity: **der liebe ⁓** the good Lord; **⁓ sei Dank!** thank God!; **leider ⁓es** unfortunately; **⁓ bewahre!, ⁓ behüte!** God forbid!; **weiß ⁓(, was** etc) God knows (what etc); **um ⁓es Willen!** for God's sake!; **großer ⁓!, lieber ⁓!** good Lord!; → **gnaden, wahr.**

'gottähnlich adj godlike.

'gottbegnadet adj god-gifted, inspired.

Götterbild ['gœtər-] n idol.

'Götterspeise f gastr. jelly.

Gottesdienst ['gɔtəs-] m (divine) service.

'gottesfürchtig [-fyrçtıç] adj godfearing.

'Gottes|haus n house of God, church. **⁓lästerer** m (-s; -) blasphemer. **⁓lästerung** f (-; -en) blasphemy. **⁓mutter** f (-; no pl) Mother of God. **⁓sohn** m (-[e]s; no pl) Son of God.

'Gottheit f (-; -en) deity, god, goddess.

Göttin ['gœtın] f (-; -nen) goddess.

'göttlich adj divine, godlike.

'gottlos adj godless, ungodly, wicked.

'gottser'bärmlich adj F awful.

'gottverdammt adj V (god)damned.

'gottverlassen adj F godforsaken.

'Gottvertrauen n trust in God.

'gottvoll adj F fig. capital, very funny.

Götze ['gœtsə] m (-n; -n) idol.

Gouverneur [guvɛr'nø:r] m (-s; -e) governor.

Grab [gra:p] n (-[e]s; ⁓er) grave, tomb: **mit einem Bein im ⁓e stehen** have one foot in the grave; **sich im ⁓e umdrehen** turn in one's grave; **verschwiegen wie das ⁓** (as) silent as the grave.

graben ['gra:bən] (grub, gegraben, h) **I** v/t dig, burrow (hole etc), sink (shaft etc). **II** v/i dig (nach for). **III** v/i (in acc into) dig, zo. burrow itself, fig. bury itself; **sich in j-s Gedächtnis ⁓** engrave itself on s.o.'s memory.

'Graben m (-s; ⁓) ditch, ✕ trench, hist. moat, geol. graben, rift.

Grabesstille ['gra:bəs-] f deathly silence. **'Grabesstimme** f (mit ⁓ in a) sepulchral voice.

'Grab|fund m grave find. **⁓gewölbe** n (burial) vault, tomb. **⁓inschrift** f epitaph. **⁓kammer** f burial chamber. **⁓mal** n (-[e]s; ⁓er) a) tomb, b) monument. **⁓rede** f funeral oration. **⁓stätte** f burial place, tomb. **⁓stein** m tombstone, gravestone.

Grad [gra:t] m (-[e]s; -e) degree (a. univ. or fig.), ✕ etc rank, grade: **10 ⁓ Wärme (Kälte)** ten degrees above (below) zero (or freezing point); **Verbrennungen dritten ⁓es** third-degree burns; **Verwandte(r) zweiten (dritten) ⁓es** relative once (twice) removed; **bis zu e-m gewissen ⁓** to a certain degree, up to a point; **im höchsten ⁓e** in the highest degree, extremely.

'Gradeinteilung f graduation.

gradieren [gra'di:rən] v/t (h) graduate.

'Gradmesser m fig. ga(u)ge, barometer.

'Gradnetz n (map) grid.

graduell [gra'dɥɛl] adj gradual.

graduieren [gradu'i:rən] (h) **I** v/t **1.** ❂ graduate. **2.** univ. confer a degree upon. **II** v/i **3.** univ. graduate.

Gradu'ierte m, f (-n; -n) graduate.

Graf [gra:f] m (-en; -en) count, Br. earl.

Graffito [gra'fi:to] m, n (-[s]; -ti) graffito.

Gräfin ['grɛ:fın] f (-; -nen) countess.

'Grafschaft f (-; -en) county.

gram [gra:m] adj **j-m ⁓ sein** bear s.o. a grudge (**wegen** gen because of s.th.).

Gram m (-[e]s; no pl) grief, sorrow.

grämen ['grɛ:mən] (h) **I** v/t grieve. **II sich ⁓ (über** acc, **wegen)** a) grieve (over), b) worry (about).

Gramm [gram] n (-s; -e) gram, Br. a. gramme: **100 ⁓** 100 grams.

Grammatik [gra'matık] f (-; -en) **1.** no pl grammar. **2.** grammar book. **grammatikalisch** [gramati'ka:lıʃ], **grammatisch** [gra'matıʃ] adj grammatical.

Grammophon [gramo'fo:n] n (-s; -e) TM gramophone, Am. phonograph.

Granat [gra'na:t] m (-[e]s; -e) min. garnet. **Gra'natapfel** m ❦ pomegranate.

Granate [gra'na:tə] f (-; -n) **1.** ✕ a) shell, b) grenade. **2.** F sports: cannonball.

Gra'nat|feuer n shellfire. **⁓splitter** m shell splinter. **⁓werfer** m mortar.

grandios [gran'diˈo:s] adj grandiose, F terrific.

Granit [gra'ni:t] m (-s; -e) granite.

Granne ['granə] *f* (-; -n) **1.** ✼ beard, awn. **2.** *zo.* kemp.

Graphik ['gra:fɪk] *f* (-; -en) **1.** *no pl* a) graphic arts, b) art(work). **2.** a) graphic (*a. computer*), print, b) ⚙ graph, diagram, c) illustration(s). **~dia,gramm** *n computer*: graphic drawing.

Graphiker ['gra:fɪkər] *m* (-s; -), **'Graphikerin** *f* (-; -nen) **1.** (graphic) artist. **2.** commercial artist, (graphic) designer.

'graphisch *adj* **1.** graphic, art ... **2.** ⚙ graphic, diagrammatic: **~e Darstellung** → **Graphik** 2.

Graphit [gra'fi:t] *m* (-s; -e) graphite.

Graphologe [grafo'lo:gə] *m* (-n; -n), graphologist. **Graphologie** [grafolo'gi:] *f* (-; *no pl*) graphology. **graphologisch** [grafo'lo:gɪʃ] *adj* graphological.

Gras [gra:s] *n* (-es; ⁓er ['grɛ:zər]) grass: F **ins ~ beißen** bite the dust; **das ~ wachsen hören** hear the grass grow; **über et. ~ wachsen lassen** let the grass grow over s.th. **'grasbedeckt** *adj* grassy.

grasen ['gra:zən] *v/i* (h) graze.

'grasfressend *adj zo.* graminivorous. **'grasgrün** *adj* grass-green. **'Grashalm** *m* blade of grass. **'Grashüpfer** *m zo.* grasshopper. **'Grasnarbe** *f* turf.

grassieren [gra'si:rən] *v/i* (h) be rife, *disease: a.* rage: **es ~ Gerüchte, daß ...** there are rumo(u)rs that ...

gräßlich ['grɛslɪç] *adj* horrible, ghastly, dreadful, monstrous, atrocious.

Grat [gra:t] *m* (-[e]s; -e) **1.** ⚙ bur(r). **2.** ridge.

Gräte ['grɛ:tə] *f* (-; -n) (fish)bone.

Gratifikation [gratifika'tsio:n] *f* (-; -en) gratuity, bonus.

gratis ['gra:tɪs] *adv* free (of charge). **'Gratisaktie** *f* bonus share, *pl* scrip issues. **'Gratisprobe** *f* free sample.

Grätsche ['grɛ:tʃə] *f* (-; -n) *gym.* a) straddle, b) straddle vault.

'grätschen *v/t, v/i* (h) *gym.* straddle.

Gratulant [gratu'lant] *m* (-en; -en) congratulator, well-wisher. **Gratulation** [gratula'tsio:n] *f* (-; -en) congratulations (**zu** on). **gratulieren** [gratu'li:rən] *v/i* (h) congratulate (**j-m zu et.** s.o. on s.th.): **j-m zum Geburtstag ~** wish s.o. many happy returns (of the day); (**ich**) **gratuliere!** congratulations!

'Gratwanderung *f fig.* tightrope walk.

grau [grau] *adj* grey, *Am.* gray, *fig. a.*

bleak: **der ~e Alltag** the drab monotony of everyday life; → **Haar, Vorzeit.**

'Graubrot *n* rye bread.

grauen ['grauən] *v/i, v/impers* (h) **mir graut** (*or* **es graut mir**) **vor** (*dat*) I dread the thought of), I am terrified of. **'Grauen** *n* (-s; -) horror (**vor** *dat* of).

'grauenhaft, 'grauenvoll *adj* horrible.

'grauhaarig *adj* grey-(*Am.* gray-)haired.

graulen ['graulən] (h) F **I sich ~** be afraid (**vor** *dat* of). **II** *v/t* **j-n aus dem Haus ~** freeze s.o. out.

gräulich ['grɔylɪç] *adj* greyish, *Am.* grayish.

'graume,liert *adj* greying, *Am.* graying.

Graupe ['graupə] *f* (-; -n) pearl barley.

Graupel ['graupəl] *f* (-; -n) soft hail.

'graupeln *v/impers* (h) **es graupelt** a soft hail is falling.

'grausam *adj* **1.** cruel. **2.** F *fig.* awful. **'Grausamkeit** *f* (-; -en) cruelty.

grausen ['grauzən] → **grauen.**

'Grausen *n* (-s; *no pl*) horror.

grausig ['grauzɪç] → **grauenhaft.**

Grauzone *f fig.* grey (*Am.* gray) area.

Graveur [gra'vø:r] *m* (-s; -e) engraver.

gravieren [gra'vi:rən] *v/t* (h) engrave.

gra'vierend *adj fig.* serious.

Gra'vierung *f* (-; -en) engraving.

Gravitation [gravita'tsio:n] *f* (-; *no pl*) *phys.* gravitation. **gravitieren** [gravi'ti:rən] *v/i* (h) a. *fig.* (**zu, auf** *acc* towards) gravitate, tend.

Grazie ['gra:tsiə] *f* (-; *no pl*) grace.

graziös [gra'tsiø:s] *adj* graceful.

'greifbar *adj* **1.** handy, available: **in ~er Nähe, ~ nahe** *a. fig.* within reach, near at hand. **2.** tangible, concrete: **~e Formen annehmen** be taking shape.

greifen ['graifən] (griff, gegriffen, h) **I** *v/t* **1.** seize, take hold of, grab: **um 2 nah** within reach; *fig.* **zu hoch gegriffen** *figure etc*: too high. **2.** ♩ stop (*string*), strike (*note etc*). **II** *v/i* **3.** **~ an** (*acc*) touch; **~ nach** reach for, grasp at, grab for; **~ in** (*acc*) reach into; **~ zu** reach for, *fig.* resort to; *fig.* **um sich ~** spread; → **Arm, Tasche** 2. **4.** ⚙ grip, grab. **5.** *fig.* be effective, F bite.

'Greifer *m* (-s; -) ⚙ grab, gripper.

'Greifvogel *m* bird of prey.

'Greifzange *f* gripping tongs.

'Greifzirkel *m* cal(l)ipers.

greis [grais] *adj* (very) old. **Greis** *m* (-es;

-e) (very) old man. '**Greisenalter** *n* old age. '**greisenhaft** *adj* senile. '**Greisenhaftigkeit** *f* (-; *no pl*) senility. **Greisin** ['graɪzɪn] *f* (-; -nen) (very) old woman.

grell [grɛl] *adj* glaring (*a. fig.*), a. loud (*colo[u]r*), shrill, strident (*sound*).

Gremium ['grɛːmiʊm] *n* (-s; -mien) body (*of experts etc*), group.

'**Grenzbereich** *m* **1.** border area. **2.** *fig.* borderland. '**Grenzbewohner(in** *f*) *m* inhabitant of the border area.

Grenze ['grɛntsə] *f* (-; -n) **1.** border, frontier, boundary (*a. fig.*): **an der ~** on the border, at the frontier; *fig.* **die ~ ziehen bei** draw the line at. **2.** *fig.* a) borderline, b) limit (*gen* to), bounds (*gen* of): **in ~n** within limits, up to a point; **ohne ~n → grenzenlos**; **sich in ~n halten** keep within (reasonable) limits, *iro. success etc*: be rather limited; **~n setzen** set limits (*dat* to); **alles hat s-e ~n** there is a limit to everything. '**grenzen** *v/i* (h) border (**an** *acc* on).

'**grenzenlos** *adj* boundless, immense, infinite (*misery, patience, etc*), unlimited (*power*): **~ dumm** incredibly stupid. '**Grenzfall** *m fig.* borderline case.

Grenzgänger ['grɛntsgɛŋər] *m* (-s; -) frontier commuter.

'**Grenz|gebiet** *n* **1.** border area. **2.** *fig.* borderland. **~kon|flikt** *m* border dispute. **~kon|trolle** *f* border control. **~kosten** *pl* † marginal cost. **~linie** *f* boundary (line), borderline (*a. fig.*), *pol.* demarcation line, *sports*: line. **~pfahl** *m* boundary post. **~posten** *m* border guard. **~schutz** *m* **1.** frontier protection. **2.** border police. **~stadt** *f* frontier town. **~stein** *m* boundary stone. **~übergang** *m* checkpoint, border crossing(-point). ²**überschreitend** *adj* border-crossing, across the border(s). **~verkehr** *m* (*kleiner ~* local) border traffic. **~wert** *m* limit(ing value), threshold value. **~zwischenfall** *m* border incident.

Greuel ['grɔyəl] *m* (-s; -) **1.** horror: **er (es) ist mir ein ~** I loathe him (it). **2.** atrocity. '**Greuelmärchen** *n* atrocity story. '**Greueltat** *f* atrocity.

greulich ['grɔylɪç] → **gräßlich**.

Grieben ['griːbən] *pl gastr.* greaves.

Grieche ['griːçə] *m* (-n; -n) Greek. '**Griechenland** *n* (-s) Greece.

'**Griechin** *f* (-; -nen) Greek (woman).

'**griechisch** *adj* Greek, *art:* a. Grecian: **~römisch** Gr(a)eco-Roman; **~orthodox** Greek (Orthodox).

'**Griechisch** *n* (-[s]) *ling.* Greek.

griesgrämig ['griːsgrɛːmɪç] *adj* F sullen, grumpy, grouchy.

Grieß [griːs] *m* (-es; -e) **1.** *gastr.* semolina. **2.** ⚙ grit. **3.** ⚒ gravel. '**Grießbrei** *m* semolina pudding.

griff [grɪf] *pret of* **greifen**.

Griff *m* (-[e]s; -e) **1.** *no pl* (**nach**) grasp (at), grab (for), reaching (for): **~ nach der Macht** bid for power; **e-n guten ~ tun** make a good choice (*mit* with); **im ~ haben (in den ~ bekommen**) have (get) *s.th.* under control, have (get) a (good) grip on; **mit sicherem ~** right away, *fig.* with a sure touch. **2.** grip (*a. gym.*), *wrestling*: hold, ♪ stop. **3.** a) handle, b) grip, c) *in bus etc*: strap. **4.** *textil.* feel.

'**griffbereit** *adj* (ready) to hand, handy. '**Griffbrett** *n* ♪ fingerboard.

Griffel ['grɪfəl] *m* (-s; -) style.

griffig ['grɪfɪç] *adj* **1.** handy. **2.** *road:* having a good grip, nonskid (*wheels*).

Grill [grɪl] *m* (-s; -s) *gastr.* grill.

Grille ['grɪlə] *f* (-; -n) **1.** *zo.* cricket. **2.** F *fig.* silly idea, whim.

grillen ['grɪlən] *v/t* (h) grill, barbecue. '**Grillparty** *f* barbecue.

Grimasse [grɪ'masə] *f* (-; -n) grimace: **~n schneiden** pull faces, grimace.

grimmig ['grɪmɪç] *adj a. fig.* grim, fierce.

Grind [grɪnt] *m* (-[e]s; -e) ⚕ scab.

grinsen ['grɪnzən] *v/i* (h), '**Grinsen** *n* (-s) (*über acc* at) a) grin, b) sneer.

grippal [grɪ'paːl] *adj* **~er Infekt** influenza(l) infection. **Grippe** ['grɪpə] *f* (-; -n) influenza, F 'flu. '**Grippe...** influenza (*epidemic, virus, etc*). '**grippekrank** *adj* down with influenza, F having the 'flu. '**Grippewelle** *f* wave of influenza.

grob [groːp] *adj* **1.** coarse (*a.* ⚙), rough (*a. fig. sketch, work, etc*): **~ behauen** rough-hewn; **in ~en Zügen** roughly; F **wir sind aus dem Gröbsten heraus** we are over the worst; → **schätzen 1. 2.** *fig.* gross (*lie, mistake, etc*). **3.** *fig.* rude, coarse: **~ werden gegen** be rude to. '**grobgemahlen** *adj* coarse-ground.

'**Grobheit** *f* (-; -en) **1.** *no pl* coarseness, roughness, *fig. a.* rudeness. **2.** *pl* rude words: *j-m* **~***en an den Kopf werfen* be rude to s.o., insult s.o.

Grobian ['gro:bĭa:n] *m* (-s; -e) rude fellow.

'**grobkörnig** *adj* coarse-grained.

'**grobmaschig** *adj* wide-meshed.

'**Grobschnitt** *m* (*tobacco*) coarse cut.

grölen ['grø:lən] *v/i, v/t* (h) bawl, roar.

Groll [grɔl] *m* (-[e]s; *no pl*) ranco(u)r, resentment, anger. '**grollen** *v/i* (h) **1.** be angry: *j-m* **~** have a grudge against s.o. (*wegen* because of). **2.** *fig.* rumble.

Gros [gro:] *n* (- [gro:(s)]; - [gro:s]) main body.

Groschen ['grɔʃən] *m* (-s; -) ten-pfennig piece, *fig.* penny, *Am.* cent: F *der* **~** *ist gefallen!* the penny has dropped!

'**Groschenro,man** *m* F penny dreadful, *Am.* dime novel.

groß [gro:s] **I** *adj* **1.** big, large, *a.* capital (*letter*): *wie* **~** *ist es?* what size is it? **2.** tall, high: *wie* **~** *sind Sie?* what is your height?; *sie sind gleich* **~** they are of equal height. **3.** great (*distance*), long (*trip etc*). **4.** a) elder, F big (*brother, sister*), b) grown-up: *die Großen* the grown-ups. **5.** *fig.* great, big, bad (*mistake etc*), severe (*loss etc*): *Friedrich der Große* Frederick the Great; *e-e größere Sache* a major affair; **~***e Worte* big words; *Großes leisten* achieve great things; → *Ferien, Geld, Los* 1, *Rede* 1, *Welt.* **6.** great, grand: F *ganz* **~** super, terrific; *in et.* **~** *sein* be great at (doing) s.th.; *er ist kein* **~***er Tänzer* he's no great dancer. **7.** *im* **~***en* on a large scale, ✝ wholesale, in bulk; *im* **~***en (und) ganzen* on the whole, by and large. **II** *adv* **8.** **~** *schreiben* capitalize; F *et.* **~** *feiern* celebrate s.th. in great style; **~** *in Mode sein* be all the rage; **~** *ankommen* be a big success (*bei* with); *er kümmert sich nicht* **~** *darum* he doesn't bother much about it; → *herausbringen, herauskommen* 1.

'**Großabnehmer** *m* ✝ bulk purchaser.

'**Großaktio,när** *m* major shareholder.

'**großangelegt** *adj* large-scale.

'**Großangriff** *m* ✗ large-scale attack.

'**großartig** *adj* grand, great, marvel-(l)ous, fantastic.

'**Großaufnahme** *f* film: close-up.

'**Großauftrag** *m* ✝ large (*or* big) order.

'**Großbank** *f* (-; -en) big (*or* major) bank.

'**Großbetrieb** *m* large-scale enterprise.

'**Großbuchstabe** *m* capital (letter).

Größe ['grø:sə] *f* (-; -n) **1.** a) size, b) height, c) dimensions, area: *welche* **~** *haben Sie?* what size do you take? **2.** Å, *phys.* quantity, *astr.* magnitude. **3.** *no pl fig.* a) extent, b) greatness. **4.** F *fig.* great figure, celebrity, *film, sports, etc*: star: *e-e* **~** *auf dem Gebiet* (*gen*) an authority on.

'**Großeinkauf** *m* ✝ bulk purchase.

'**Großeinsatz** *m* large-scale operation.

'**Großeltern** *pl* grandparents.

'**Großenkel** *m etc* → *Urenkel etc*.

'**Größenordnung** *f* **1.** *astr. etc* order (of magnitude). **2.** *fig.* scale: *dieser* **~** of this order.

'**großenteils** *adv* mostly, largely.

'**Größenverhältnisse** *pl* proportions.

'**Größenwahn** *m* megalomania.

'**größenwahnsinnig** *adj* megalomaniac.

'**Großfahndung** *f* dragnet operation.

'**Großfa,milie** *f* extended family.

'**Großfeuer** *n* big blaze, four-alarm fire.

'**Großflughafen** *m* major airport.

'**Großfor,mat** *n* large size.

'**Großgrundbesitz** *m* large land holdings, large estates. '**Großgrundbesitzer**(in *f*) *m* big landowner.

'**Großhandel** *m* wholesale trade: *im* **~** wholesale. '**Großhandels...** wholesale.

'**Großhändler**(in *f*) *m* wholesaler.

'**Großhandlung** *f* wholesale firm.

'**Großherzog**(in *f*) *m* grand duke (duchess).

'**Großhirn** *n anat.* cerebrum.

'**Großindu,strie** *f* big industry.

'**Großindustri,elle** *m* big industrialist.

Grossist [grɔ'sɪst] *m* (-en; -en) wholesaler.

'**großjährig** → *volljährig.*

'**Großkapi,tal** *n* big business.

'**Großkaufmann** *m* large merchant.

'**Großkon,zern** *m* big concern.

großkotzig ['gro:skɔtsɪç] *adj* F a) flash, b) show-off(ish), arrogant.

'**Großkraftwerk** *n* super power station.

'**Großküche** *f* canteen kitchen.

'**Großkundgebung** *f* mass rally.

'**Großmacht** *f* super power.

'**Großmama** *f* F grandma.

'**Großmaul** *n* F bigmouth.

'**Großmut** *f* (-; *no pl*) magnanimity, generosity. **großmütig** ['gro:smy:tɪç] *adj* magnanimous, generous.

'**Großmutter** f grandmother.
'**Großneffe** m grandnephew.
'**Großnichte** f grandniece.
'**Großonkel** m great-uncle.
'**Großpapa** m F grandpa.
'**Groß,pro,jekt** n large-scale project.
'**Großraum** m der ~ München Greater Munich. ~**bü,ro** n open-plan office.
'**Großrechner** m large(-scale) computer.
'**Großschreibung** f capitalization.
'**großsprecherisch** adj boastful.
'**großspurig** ['gro:sʃpu:rɪç] adj arrogant.
'**Großstadt** f big city.
'**Großstädter(ln** f) m city-dweller.
'**großstädtisch** adj of a big city, urban.
'**Großtante** f great-aunt.
'**Großtat** f great feat.
'**Großteil** m large part. '**größtenteils** adv for the most part, mostly.
'**großtun** v/i (irr, sep, -ge-, h, → **tun**) talk big: ~ **mit** brag about, show off with.
'**Großunternehmen** n ✝ large-scale (or big) enterprise.
'**Großvater** m grandfather.
'**Großveranstaltung** f big event.
'**Großverdiener(in** f) m big earner.
'**Großwildjagd** f big game hunt(ing).
'**großziehen** v/t (irr, sep, -ge-, h, → **ziehen**) raise, rear, bring up (child).
'**großzügig** adj 1. generous. 2. broad-minded. 3. spacious. 4. large-scale.
'**Großzügigkeit** f (-; no pl) 1. generosity. 2. broad-mindedness. 3. large scale.
grotesk [gro'tɛsk] adj grotesque.
Grotte ['grɔtə] f (-; -n) grotto.
grub [gru:p] pret of **graben**.
Grübchen ['gry:pçən] n (-s; -) dimple.
Grube ['gru:bə] f (-; -n) pit, ✖ mine.
Grübelei [gry:bə'laɪ] f (-; -en) brooding.
grübeln ['gry:bəln] v/i (h) (**über** acc over, on) brood, muse.
'**Grubenarbeiter** m miner.
'**Grubenunglück** n mine disaster.
Grübler ['gry:blər] m (-s; -) brooder.
Gruft [gruft] f (-; -̈e) tomb, vault, crypt.
grün [gry:n] adj green (a. fig.): ~**er Hering** fresh herring; ~**er Salat** lettuce; F ~**er Junge** greenhorn; **die Grünen** pol. the Green (Party); fig. ~**es Licht geben** (**bekommen**) give s.o. (get) the green light (**für** for); **e-e Entscheidung vom** ~**en Tisch** an armchair decision; ~ **vor Neid** green with envy; **j-n** ~ **und blau schlagen** beat s.o. black and blue; **auf**

k-n ~**en Zweig kommen** get nowhere; F **er ist dir nicht** ~ he has it in for you.
Grün n (-s; -) green (a. golf): **bei** ~, **auf** ~ mot. at green; F **das ist dasselbe in** ~ it's practically the same thing.
Grund [grʊnt] m (-[e]s; -̈e) **1.** no pl a) ground, b) bottom (a. fig.): **am** ~, **auf dem** ~ at the bottom; **auf** ~ **laufen** ⚓ run aground; **e-r Sache auf den** ~ **gehen** (**kommen**) go (get) to the bottom of s.th. **2.** no pl ~ (**und Boden**) land, property; **sich in** ~ **und Boden schämen** be terribly ashamed; **in** ~ **und Boden verdammen** condemn s.o., s.th. outright. **3.** no pl fig. basis, foundation(s): **auf** ~ **von** (or gen) a) on the basis (or strength) of, b) because of; **von** ~ **auf** change etc entirely (or radically); **im** ~**e** (**genommen**) actually, basically. **4.** reason, cause: **aus diesem** ~ for this reason; **aus persönlichen Gründen** for personal reasons; **aus gutem** ~ for good reason, justly; **allen** ~ **haben zu** inf have every reason to inf; **ich frage aus e-m bestimmten** ~ I ask for a reason; (**k-n**) ~ **zur Klage haben** have (no) cause for complaint.
'**Grund|anstrich** m priming coat. ~**ausbildung** f ✖ basic training. ~**bedeutung** f primary meaning. ~**bedingung** f basic condition, prerequisite. ~**begriff** m basic concept, pl fundamentals.
'**Grund|besitz** m landed property, real estate. ~**besitzer(in** f) m landowner.
'**Grundbestandteil** m basic component.
'**Grundbuch** n land register. ~**amt** n land registry. ~**auszug** m extract from the land register.
'**grund'ehrlich** adj thoroughly honest.
gründen ['grʏndən] (h) **I** v/t found, establish, set up: fig. **et.** ~ **auf** (acc) base (or found) s.th. on. **II sich** ~ **auf** (acc) fig. be based on. **III** v/i ~ **auf** (dat) a) rest (or be based) on, b) be due to.
Gründer ['grʏndər] m (-s; -), '**Gründerin** f (-; -nen) founder.
'**grund'falsch** adj absolutely wrong.
'**Grund|farbe** f phys. primary colo(u)r. ~**fläche** f area, ⚒ base, △ floor space. ~**gebühr** f basic rate. ~**gedanke** m basic idea. ~**gehalt** n (-[e]s; -̈er) basic salary. ~**gesetz** n basic (constitutional) law.
grundieren [grʊn'di:rən] v/t (h) ground,

⊕ prime. **Grun'dierfarbe** f primer. **Grun'dierung** f (-; -en) priming coat.

'Grund|kapi,tal n initial capital, stock. **~kenntnisse** pl basic knowledge. **~lage** f foundation, fig. a. basis: *jeder ~ entbehren* be completely unfounded. **~lagenforschung** f basic research.

'grundlegend adj basic, fundamental, definitive (book etc).

gründlich ['grʏntlɪç] adj thorough, careful: *F sich ~ irren* be jolly well mistaken.

'Gründlichkeit f (-; no pl) thoroughness.

'Grundlinie f A, sports: base line.

'Grundlohn m basic wage(s).

'grundlos I adj fig. groundless, unfounded. II adv for no reason (at all).

'Grund|mauer f foundation wall. **~nahrungsmittel** pl basic food(stuff).

Grün'donnerstag m Maundy Thursday.

'Grund|pfeiler m 1. △ supporting pillar. 2. fig. cornerstone. **~prin,zip** n basic principle. **~rechnungsart** f die vier **~en** the four fundamental operations of arithmetics. **~rechte** pl pol. basic rights. **~regel** f ground rule. **~riß** m 1. △ ground plan. 2. fig. outline(s).

'Grundsatz m principle: *es sich zum ~ machen zu* inf make it a rule to inf.

'grundsätzlich [-zɛtslɪç] I adj fundamental. II adv in principle: *ich bin ~ dagegen* I am absolutely against it.

'Grund|schule f primary (Am. a. grade) school. **~schüler(in** f) m primary pupil. **~stein** m △ foundation stone: fig. *den ~ legen zu* lay the foundations of. **~steinlegung** f (-; -en) laying (of) the foundation stone. **~stock** m (-[e]s; no pl) basis. **~stoff** m 1. 🐟 element. 2. raw material. **~stoffindu,strie** f basic industry. **~stück** n 1. plot (of land), ✝, ⚖ property, real estate. 2. (building) site.

'Grundstücks|makler(in f) m (real) estate agent, Am. realtor. **~markt** m property market. **~preis** m land price.

'Grund|studium n basic study. **~stufe** f ped. elementary classes. **~ton** m 1. ♪ keynote. 2. paint. ground shade. **~umsatz** m 🐟 basal metabolic rate.

'Gründung f (-; -en) foundation.

'grund|ver'kehrt adj utterly wrong. **~ver'schieden** adj entirely different.

'Grundwasser n (-s; no pl) ground water. **~spiegel** m ground-water level.

'Grund|wehrdienst m basic military service. **~wortschatz** m basic vocabulary. **~zahl** f cardinal number. **~zug** m characteristic (feature), pl outline(s), basics: *in s-n Grundzügen schildern* outline.

'Grün|fläche f a) green space, lawn, b) park area. **~futter** n 🐄 green fodder. **~gürtel** m green belt. **~kohl** m kale.

'grünlich adj greenish.

'Grünschnabel m F whippersnapper.

'Grünspan m (-[e]s; no pl) verdigris.

'Grünspecht m zo. green woodpecker.

'Grünstreifen m → **Mittelstreifen.**

grunzen ['grʊntsən] v/i, v/t (h) grunt.

'Grünzeug n F a) greens, b) herbs.

Gruppe ['grʊpə] f (-; -n) **1.** group (a. ✈). **2.** team. **3.** ⚔ squad.

'Gruppen|arbeit f teamwork. **~dy,namik** f group dynamics. **~reise** f group travel. **~sex** m group sex. **~thera,pie** f group therapy.

'gruppenweise adv in groups.

gruppieren [grʊ'piːrən] (h) I v/t group: *neu ~* regroup. II sich **~** form a group (or groups) (um [a]round).

Grup'pierung f (-; -en) **1.** grouping, formation. **2.** group(s).

Grusel... ['gruːzəl...] horror (film, story, etc). **'gruselig** adj creepy, spooky. **'gruseln** v/t, v/i, v/impers *es gruselt mir* (or *mich*), *mich gruselt* it gives me the creeps; *es war zum Gruseln* it was enough to give you the creeps.

Gruß [gruːs] m (-es; ﹖e) greeting(s) (aus from), ⚔ salute: *viele Grüße* (or *e-n schönen*) *~ an* ... give my regards (or my love) to ...; in letter: *mit besten* (or *freundlichen*) *Grüßen* Yours sincerely; *herzliche Grüße* love, best wishes.

grüßen ['gryːsən] (h) I v/t greet, esp. ⚔ salute, F say hello: F *grüß dich!* hello (there)!, hi!; **~** *Sie ihn von mir!* give my regards (or my love) to him! II v/i say good morning (etc), say hello, esp. ⚔ salute.

'Grußwort n (-[e]s; -e) greeting.

gucken ['gʊkən] v/i (h) look, peep.

'Guckloch n peephole.

Guerillakrieg [ge'rɪlja-] m guer(r)illa war(fare).

Gulasch ['gʊlaʃ] n (-[e]s; -e, -s) goulash.

'Gulaschsuppe f goulash soup.

Gulden ['gʊldən] *m* (-s; -) guilder.

gültig ['gʏltɪç] *adj* valid (*a. fig.*), good (*a. sports*), effective (**ab, vom** as from), in force, legal: **~ werden** become valid, *contract etc*: become effective.

'Gültigkeit *f* (-; *no pl*) validity, 🏛 *pol.* legal force.

'Gültigkeitsdauer *f* (period of) validity, *a.* term (*of contract*).

Gummi ['gʊmi] **1.** *m, n* (-s; -[s]) ⚙ a) rubber, b) gum. **2.** *m* (-s; -s) F rubber. **3.** *n* (-s; -s) → **Gummiband. 4.** *m* (-s; -s) → **Radiergummi.**

'gummiartig *adj* rubbery.

'Gummi|band *n* rubber band, elastic. **~bärchen** *n gastr.* jelly baby. **~baum** *m* **1.** rubber tree. **2.** rubber plant.

gummieren [gʊ'miːrən] *v/t* (h) gum, ⚙ rubberize.

'Gummi|handschuh *m* rubber glove. **~linse** *f phot.* zoom lens. **~para,graph** *m* F elastic clause. **~stiefel** *m* wellington (boot), *Am.* rubber boot. **~strumpf** *m* elastic stocking. **~waren** *pl* rubber goods. **~zug** *m* elastic.

Gunst [gʊnst] *f* (-; *no pl*) favo(u)r.

günstig ['gʏnstɪç] *adj* **1.** favo(u)rable (**für** to): **~e Gelegenheit** opportunity; **im ~sten Fall** at best; **zu ~en Bedingungen** on easy terms; **~es Angebot, ~er Kauf** bargain. **2.** convenient.

Günstling ['gʏnstlɪŋ] *m* (-s; -e) favo(u)rite. **'Günstlingswirtschaft** *f* (-; *no pl*) favo(u)ritism.

Gurgel ['gʊrgəl] *f* (-; -n) a) throat, b) gullet. **'Gurgelmittel** *n* gargle.

'gurgeln *v/i* (h) **1.** gargle. **2.** gurgle.

Gurke ['gʊrkə] *f* (-; -n) **1.** a) cucumber, b) gherkin. **2.** F *contp.* lemon.

'Gurkenhobel *m* cucumber slicer.

'Gurkensa,lat *m* cucumber salad.

gurren ['gʊrən] *v/i* (h) coo.

Gurt [gʊrt] *m* (-[e]s; -e) **1.** belt, ✈, *mot.* seat belt. **2.** strap.

'Gurtband *n* (-[e]s; ∙er) waistband.

Gürtel ['gʏrtəl] *m* (-s; -) belt: **den ~ enger schnallen** *a. fig.* tighten one's belt. **~linie** *f* waist(line): **unter der** (*or* **die**) **~** *a. fig.* below the belt. **~reifen** *m* mot. radial(-ply) tyre (*Am.* tire). **~rose** *f* (-; *no pl*) 🩺 shingles. **~schnalle** *f* belt buckle. **~tier** *n* armadillo.

Guß [gʊs] *m* (-sses; ∙sse) **1.** ⚙ a) casting, founding, b) cast iron: *fig.* (**wie**) **aus**

einem ~ of a piece. **2.** a) gush, jet, b) downpour. **3.** *gastr.* icing.

'Gußbe,ton *m* cast concrete. **'Gußeisen** *n* cast iron. **'gußeisern** *adj* cast-iron. **'Gußform** *f* casting mo(u)ld. **'Gußstahl** *m* cast steel. **'Gußstück** *n* casting.

gut [guːt] **I** *adj* good, fine: **ganz ~** quite good, not bad; *also ~!* all right (then)!; **schon ~!** never mind!; (**es ist**) **~, daß ...**, **nur ~, daß ...** (it's a) good thing that ...; **auch ~!, es ist ganz ~ so!** it's just as well!; (**wieder**) **~ werden** come right (again), be all right; **sei** (**bitte**) **so ~ und ...** would you be good enough to ...; **~ sein in** (*dat*) be good at (doing *s.th.*); **das ist ~ gegen** (*or* **für**) **Erkältungen** that's good for colds; **mir ist nicht ~!** I don't feel (so) well!; **wozu soll das ~ sein?** what's that in aid of?; **laß** (**mal** *or* **es**) **~ sein!** that'll do!; **Gut und Böse** good and evil; **im ~en** in a friendly way, amicably. **II** *adv* well, look, taste, *etc* good: **er spricht ~ Englisch** he speaks good English; **es ~ haben** have it good, have a good time; **du hast es ~!** you are lucky!; **es ist ~ möglich, es kann ~ sein** it may well be; **es gefällt mir ~** I (do) like it; **~ gemacht!** well done!; **so ~ wie gewonnen** as good as won; **so ~ wie nichts** hardly anything; **so ~ wie unmöglich** practically impossible; **~ zwei Stunden** a good two hours; **~** (**und gern**) easily; **ich kann ihn doch nicht ~ fragen** I can't very well ask him; F **mach's ~!** a) good luck, b) so long!, take care (of yourself)!; → **Gute, gutgehen** *etc*, **Reise.**

Gut *n* (-[e]s; Güter) **1.** good(s), property, possession(s): *fig.* **das höchste ~** the greatest good. **2.** *usu. pl* a) ✝ goods, b) 🚂 goods, *Am.* freight. **3.** estate. **4.** ⚙ material, stock.

'Gutachten *n* (-s; -) (expert) opinion.

'Gutachter *m* (-s; -), **'Gutachterin** *f* (-; -nen) expert, 🏛 expert witness.

'gutartig *adj* **1.** good-natured. **2.** 🩺 benign. **'Gutartigkeit** *f* (-; *no pl*) **1.** good nature. **2.** 🩺 benignity.

'gutaussehend *adj* good-looking.

'gutbezahlt *adj* well-paid.

'gut'bürgerlich *adj* solid middle-class: **~e Küche** good plain cooking.

Gutdünken ['guːtdʏŋkən] *n* (-s; *no pl*)

Haar

discretion: *handle nach (eigenem)* ~ use your own discretion.

'**Gute** n (-n) the good: *das ~ an der Sache* the good thing about it; *~s tun* do good; *des ~n zuviel tun* overdo it; *das ist des ~n zuviel* that's too much of a good thing; *alles ~!* all the best!

Güte ['gy:tə] f (-; *no pl*) **1.** goodness, kindness: *würden Sie die ~ haben zu* inf would you be so kind as to inf; F *(du) m-e ~!* good gracious! **2.** quality: *erster ~* a) first-class, b) iro. of the first water. '**Güteklasse** f ✝ grade, quality.

'**Gute**'**nachtgeschichte** f bedtime story.

'**Gute**'**nachtkuß** m goodnight kiss.

Güter|bahnhof ['gy:tər-] m goods station, Am. freight depot. **~gemeinschaft** f ⚖ community of property. **~trennung** f ⚖ separation of property. **~verkehr** m goods (Am. freight) traffic. **~wagen** m 🚃 (goods) waggon, Am. freight car. **~zug** m goods (Am. freight) train.

'**Gütezeichen** n mark of quality.

'**gutgebaut** adj well-built.

'**gutgehen** v/i (irr, sep, -ge-, sn, → *gehen*) **1.** go (off) well, work out well: *das kann nicht ~!* that's bound to go wrong!; *wenn alles gutgeht* if nothing goes wrong. **2.** *mir geht es gut* a) I'm fine, b) I'm doing fine.

'**gutgelaunt** adj in a good mood.

'**gutgemeint** adj well-meant.

'**gutgläubig** adj **1.** credulous. **2.** acting (or done) in good faith, bona fide.

'**Gutgläubigkeit** f (-; *no pl*) credulity, gullibility.

'**Guthaben** n (-s; -) **1.** credit (balance). **2.** account.

'**gutheißen** v/t (irr, sep, -ge-, h, → *heißen*) et. ~ approve (of) s.th.

'**gutherzig** adj kind(-hearted).

gütig ['gy:tɪç] adj kind (**zu** to).

gütlich ['gy:tlɪç] **I** adj **1.** amicable. **II** adv **2.** amicably. **3.** *sich ~ tun an* (dat) help o.s. to, take (or eat, drink) one's fill of.

'**gutmachen** v/t (sep, -ge-, h) make good, make up for.

'**gutmütig** ['-my:tɪç] adj good-natured.

'**Gutmütigkeit** f (-; *no pl*) good nature.

'**Gutschein** m coupon, voucher.

'**gutschreiben** v/t (irr, sep, -ge-, h, → *schreiben*) j-m et. ~ credit s.o. with s.th., pass s.th. to s.o.'s credit.

'**Gutschrift** f **1.** credit (entry). **2.** credit voucher. **~anzeige** f credit note.

'**Gutshaus** n manor (house).

'**Gutsherr(in** f) m lord (lady) of the manor. '**Gutshof** m estate.

'**gutsituiert** adj well-to-do, well-off.

'**guttun** v/i (irr, sep, -ge-, h, → *tun*) j-m ~ do s.o. good.

guttural [gʊtu'raːl] adj guttural.

'**gutunterrichtet** adj well-informed.

'**gutwillig** adj willing (to oblige).

'**Gutwilligkeit** f (-; *no pl*) willingness.

Gymnasialbildung [gʏmna'ziaːl-] f secondary school education. **Gymnasiast** [gʏmna'ziast] m (-en; -en) grammar-school (Am. high-school) student.

Gymnasium [gʏm'naːziʊm] n (-s; -ien) (*humanistisches* ~ classical) secondary school, Br. a. grammar school.

Gymnastik [gʏm'nastɪk] f (-; *no pl*) gymnastics, (physical) exercises, callisthenics. **Gymnastikanzug** m leotard.

gym'**nastisch** adj gymnastic.

Gynäkologe [gʏnɛko'loːgə] m (-n; -n) gyn(a)ecologist. **Gynäkologie** [gʏnɛkolo'giː] f (-; *no pl*) gyn(a)ecology.

gynäko'**logisch** adj gyn(a)ecological.

H

H, h [haː] n (-; -) **1.** H, h. **2.** ♪ B.

ha [ha(ː)] int ha, ah.

Haar [haːr] n (-[e]s; -e) hair: *sich die ~e kämmen* (F *machen*) comb (do) one's hair; *sich die ~e schneiden lassen* get a haircut; *sich die ~e raufen* tear one's hair; fig. *aufs ~* to a T; *sich aufs ~ gleichen* be absolutely identical; *um ein ~* by a hair's breadth; *um ein ~ wäre er überfahren worden* he just missed being run over, he had a narrow escape; **er (es) ist um kein ~ besser** he (it) is not a bit better; **~e spalten** split hairs; **ein ~ in der Suppe finden** find a fly in the ointment; **sich in die ~e geraten** quarrel, clash; **sich in den ~en liegen** be at loggerheads, be quarrel(l)ing; **sie hat ~e auf den Zähnen** she's a tough customer; **das ist bei den ~en herbeigezogen** that's (pretty) far-fetched; **ihr wurde kein ~ gekrümmt** they did not touch a hair on her head; F **~e lassen müssen** not to escape unscathed; **kein gutes ~ an j-m lassen** pull s.o. to pieces; **ihm standen die ~e zu Berge, ihm sträubten sich die ~e** it made his hair stand on end; **laß dir deshalb k-e grauen ~e wachsen!** don't lose any sleep over it!

'**Haar|ansatz** m hairline. **~ausfall** m loss of hair. **~bürste** f hairbrush.

'**haaren** v/i (h) **1.** a. **sich ~** zo. lose its hair. **2.** fur etc: shed (hairs).

'**Haarentferner** m (-s; -) hair remover.

'**Haaresbreite** f **er entging um ~ e-m Unfall** he escaped an accident by a hair's breadth; **sie ging nicht um ~ von ihrer Meinung ab** she didn't budge from her opinion one little bit.

'**Haar|farbe** f hair colo(u)r. **~färbemittel** n hair dye. **~festiger** m setting lotion. **~gefäß** n anat. capillary (vessel).

'**haarge'nau** adj F precise: (**stimmt**) **~!** dead right!

haarig ['haːrɪç] adj hairy (a. F fig.).

...**haarig** ...-haired.

'**haar'klein** adj (down) to the last detail.

'**Haarklemme** f hair clip.

'**haarlos** adj **1.** hairless. **2.** bald.

'**Haar|mittel** n hair restorer. **~nadel** f hairpin. **~nadelkurve** f mot. hairpin bend. **~netz** n **1.** hairnet. **2.** hair lacquer. **~öl** n hair oil. **~pflege** f hair care. **~riß** m hairline crack. **~scharf I** adj very precise, exact. **II** adv by a hair's breadth. **~schleife** f (hair) ribbon, bow. **~schnitt** m a) haircut, b) hairstyle. **~schuppen** pl dandruff.

Haarspalte'rei f (-; -en) (**das ist ~** that's just) splitting hairs.

'**Haar|spange** f (hair) slide, Am. barrette. **~spitzen** pl hair tips. **~spray** m, n hairspray. **~strähne** f strand of hair.

'**haarsträubend** adj hair-raising.

'**Haar|teil** n hairpiece. **~trockner** m hair-drier. **~wäsche** f shampoo. **~waschmittel** n shampoo. **~wasser** n hair tonic. **~wuchs** m **1.** growth of (the) hair. **2.** hair. **~wuchsmittel** n hair restorer. **~wurzeln** pl roots of one's hair.

Hab [haːp] (**all sein**) **~ und Gut** all one's possessions.

Habe ['haːbə] f (-; no pl) possessions.

haben ['haːbən] (hatte, gehabt, h) **I** v/t have (got), own, possess: **et. ~ wollen** want (to have) s.th.; **er will es so ~** that's the way he wants it; (**noch**) **zu ~ sein** be (still) available; Γ **sie ist noch zu ~** she's still to be had; **was hast du?** what's wrong?; F **er hat es im Hals** he has a bad throat; **wir ~ schönes Wetter** the weather is fine (here); **wir ~ Winter!** it's winter!; dial. **es hat viel Schnee** there's a lot of snow; possess: **et. ~ wollen**; **welche Farbe hat das Kleid?** what colo(u)r is the dress?; **da hast du's!** there you are!, fig. a. I told you so!; **das hätten wir!** well, that's that!; F **er hat's ja!** he can (well) afford it!; **woher hast du das?** a) where did you get that from?, b) who told you?; **was hast du gegen ihn?** what have you got against him?; **was habe ich davon?** a) what do I get out of it?, b) **wenn ...?** what's the good if ...?; **ich habe nicht viel davon gehabt** I didn't get much out of it; **das hast du nun davon!** there (you are)!; F **ich hab's!** (I've) got it!; **das werden wir gleich ~!** (that's) no problem!; **wie gehabt** as had, same as ever; F **sie ~ et. miteinander** they are lovers; **die Prüfung hatte es in sich** the exam was pretty tough; **er hat et. Überspanntes** there's s.th. eccentric about him; **das hat er so an sich** that's the way he is; **ich habe viel zu erzählen** I have a lot to tell; **dafür bin ich nicht zu ~!** count me out!; **hab dich nicht so!** a) don't make a fuss!, b) don't take on so! **II** v/aux have: **hast du ihn gesehen?** have you seen him?; **du hättest es mir sagen sollen!** you should (or might) have told me!; **er hätte es tun können** he could have done it.

'**Haben** n (-s; -) ✝ credit: → **Soll.**

'**Habenichts** m (-[e]s; -e) have-not.

'**Habenseite** f ✝ credit side.

Habgier ['haːpgiːr] f (-; no pl) greed.

'habgierig adj greedy.
habhaft ['ha:phaft] adj ~ **werden** (gen) get hold of, a. catch (criminal etc).
Habicht ['ha:bɪçt] m (-[e]s; -e) zo. hawk.
Habilitation [habilita'tsio:n] f (-; -en) university lecturing qualification.
habilitieren [habili'ti:rən] sich ~ (h) qualify to give lectures at a university.
Habitat [habi'ta:t] n (-s; -e) zo. habitat.
Habseligkeiten ['ha:p-] pl belongings.
Habsucht ['ha:p-] f (-; no pl) greed.
'habsüchtig adj greedy.
Hachse ['haksə] f (-; -n) **1.** zo. hock. **2.** gastr. knuckles. **3.** F leg, pl pins.
Hackbeil n chopper. **'Hackbraten** m meat loaf. **'Hackbrett** n **1.** chopping board. **2.** ♪ dulcimer.
Hacke¹ ['hakə] f (-; -n) **1.** ✗ hoe. **2.** pickax(e). **Hacke²** f (-; -n) dial. heel.
'hacken (h) **I** v/t **1.** hack, ✗ a. hoe. **2.** chop. **II** v/i **3.** (nach at) pick, peck.
'Hackepeter m (-s; no pl) raw minced meat mixed with onions and spices.
'Hacker m (-s; -) F computer: hacker.
'Hackfleisch n minced (Am. ground) meat: F **aus dir mache ich ~!** I'll make mincemeat of you!
'Hackmesser n chopper.
'Hackordnung f a. fig. pecking order.
Häcksel ['hɛksəl] m, n (-s; no pl) ✗ chaff.
'Hacksteak n gastr. beefburger.
Hader ['ha:dər] m (-s; no pl) quarrel.
'hadern v/i (h) quarrel (mit with).
Hafen m **1.** a.) harbo(u)r, b) port, c) dock(s): **in den ~ einlaufen** put into port. **2.** fig. (ruhiger) ~ haven.
'Hafen|anlagen pl docks. **~arbeiter** m docker. **~becken** n harbo(u)r basin, (wet) dock. **~einfahrt** f harbo(u)r entrance. **~gebühren** pl harbo(u)r dues. **~meister** m harbo(u)r master. **~rundfahrt** f boat tour of a harbo(u)r. **~stadt** f (sea)port. **~viertel** n dockland(s).
Hafer ['ha:fər] m (-s; -) oats: F **ihn sticht der ~** he's getting cocky. **'Haferbrei** m porridge. **'Haferflocken** pl rolled oats. **'Hafergrütze** f groats. **'Hafermehl** n oatmeal. **'Haferschleim** m gruel.
Haff [haf] n (-[e]s; -s) lagoon.
Haft [haft] f (-; no pl) **1.** custody: **in ~** under arrest, in custody; **j-n in ~ nehmen** take s.o. into custody. **2.** imprisonment. **'Haftanstalt** f prison.
'haftbar adj (für for) responsible, ⚖

liable: **j-n ~ machen** make s.o. liable.
'Haftbefehl m arrest warrant: **~ gegen j-n** warrant for s.o.'s arrest.
'haften¹ v/i (h) (an dat) cling, stick: **im Gedächtnis ~** stick (in one's mind).
'haften² v/i (h) (für for) be (held) responsible, ⚖ be liable: **~ für** guarantee.
'Haftfähigkeit f (-; no pl) **1.** → **Haftvermögen. 2.** ⚖ fitness to undergo detention.
'Häftling ['hɛftlɪŋ] m (-s; -e) prisoner.
'Haftpflicht f (legal) liability.
'haftpflichtig adj liable (für for).
'Haftpflichtversicherung f third party (liability) insurance.
'Haftrichter(in f) m magistrate.
'Haftschale f opt. contact lens.
'Haftstrafe f imprisonment.
'Haftung¹ f (-; no pl) ⊙ adhesion.
'Haftung² f (-; -en) a) (legal) liability, b) guarantee: **beschränkte ~** limited liability; **Gesellschaft mit beschränkter ~** private limited (liability) company; **~ übernehmen** accept liability (für for).
'Haftvermögen n (-s; no pl) adhesive power(s).
Hagebutte ['ha:gəbutə] f (-; -n) rose hip.
Hagel ['ha:gəl] m (-s; -) **1.** hail. **2.** fig. hail, shower (of blows etc), torrent (of invective etc). **'Hagelkorn** n hailstone.
hager ['ha:gər] adj gaunt.
haha [ha'ha(:)] int ha ha.
Häher ['hɛ:ər] m (-s; -) zo. jay.
Hahn [ha:n] m (-[e]s; -e) **1.** zo. cock, rooster: F **~ im Korbe sein** be cock of the walk; **es kräht kein ~ danach** nobody cares (two hoots) about it. **2.** ⊙ a) tap, Am. faucet, b) spigot. **3.** of gun: hammer.
Hähnchen ['hɛ:nçən] n (-s; -) chicken.
'Hahnenkamm m a. ♣ cockscomb.
'Hahnenkampf m cockfight.
Hahnrei ['ha:nrai] m (-[e]s; -e) cuckold.
Hai [hai] m (-[e]s; -e), **'Haifisch** m shark.
'Haifischflosse f shark fin.
Häkchen ['hɛ:kçən] n (-s; -) **1.** small hook. **2.** on list etc: tick, Am. check. **3.** ling. apostrophe.
Häkelarbeit f, **Häke'lei** f (-; -en) crochet work. **häkeln** ['hɛ:kəln] v/t, v/i (h) crochet. **'Häkelnadel** f crochet needle.
haken ['ha:kən] v/t (h) hook (an acc onto).
'Haken m (-s; -) **1.** hook, peg: **~ und Öse**

hook and eye; *boxing*: **rechter (linker)** ~ right (left) hook. **2.** → **Häkchen** 2. **3.** F *fig. der ~ an der Sache* the snag; *die Sache hat e-n ~* there is a catch to it.

'Hakenkreuz *n* swastika.

'Hakennase *f* hooked nose.

Halali [ha'laːliː] *n* (-s; -[s]) *hunt.* mort.

halb [halp] **I** *adj* half: *e-e ~e Stunde* half an hour; *~ drei* half past two; *~ Europa* half of Europe; *~e Note ♩* half note; *~er Ton ♩* semitone; *auf ~er Höhe* halfway (up); *die ~e Summe* half the sum; *zum ~en Preis* for half the price, (at) half-price; *nur die ~e Wahrheit* only half the truth; *fig. e-e ~e Sache* a half-measure; *er macht k-e ~en Sachen* he doesn't do things by halves; *nichts Halbes und nichts Ganzes* neither one thing nor the other; *j-m auf ~em Wege entgegenkommen* meet s.o. halfway; *sich auf ~em Wege einigen* split the difference. **II** *adv* half: *~ soviel* half as much; *~ und ~* a) half and half, b) partly; F *(mit j-m) halbe-halbe machen* go halves (*or* fifty-fifty) (with s.o.); *es ist ~ so schlimm* it's not as bad as all that; *das ist ja ~ geschenkt* that's a giveaway; *damit war die Sache ~ gewonnen* that was half the battle.

'halbamtlich *adj* semiofficial.

'Halbärmel *m* half-sleeve.

'halbauto,matisch *adj* semiautomatic.

'Halbbildung *f* superficial knowledge.

'halbbitter *adj* plain (*chocolate*).

'Halbblut *n* **1.** half-caste. **2.** half-breed.

'Halbblut..., **'Halbblüter** [-bly:tər] *m* (-s; -), **'halbblütig** *adj zo.* half-breed.

'Halbbruder *m* half brother.

'halbdunkel *adj* dusky, dimly-lit (*room*).

'Halbdunkel *n* semidarkness, twilight.

Halbe ['halbə] *m, f, n* (-n; -n) pint (of beer).

'Halbedelstein *m* semiprecious stone.

...halben, **...halber** *in cpds.* a) on account of, due to, b) for the sake of, c) for.

'Halbfabri,kat *n* semifinished product.

'halbfertig *adj* half-finished, ✝ semifinished.

'halbfett *adj* **1.** semibold. **2.** medium-fat.

'Halbfi,nale *n sports*: semifinal.

'halbgar *adj gastr.* underdone, rare.

'halbgebildet *adj* semiliterate.

'Halbgott *m* (**~göttin** *f*) demigod(dess).

'Halbheit *f* (-; -en) half measure.

'halbherzig *adj* half-hearted.

'halbhoch *adj* medium-high, *sports etc*: shoulder-high.

halbieren [hal'biːrən] *v/t* (h) halve, cut (*or* divide) in half, ♈ bisect. **Hal'bierung** *f* (-; -en) halving, ♈ bisection.

'Halbinsel *f* peninsula.

'Halbjahr *n* half-year, (period of) six months. **'Halbjahr(e)s...** half-yearly, six-month ... **'halbjährig** [-jɛ:rɪç] *adj* a) half-yearly, six-month ..., of six months, b) six-month-old. **'halbjährlich** *adj and adv* half-yearly, semiannual(ly), *adv a.* every six months.

'Halbkreis *m* semicircle.

'Halbkugel *f a. geogr.* hemisphere.

'halblang *adj* a) medium-length, b) knee-length (*skirt etc*), c) *ling.* half-long (*vowel*): F *mach mal ~!* draw it mild!

'halblaut **I** *adj* low. **II** *adv* in an undertone.

'Halbleder *n print.* half-leather: *in ~ gebunden* half-bound.

'Halbleinen *n* half-linen (cloth): *in ~ gebunden* print. half-cloth.

'Halbleiter *m ⚡* semiconductor.

Halb'linke *m, f* (-n; -n), **halb'links** *adv sports*: inside left.

'halbmast *adv* (*auf ~* at) half-mast.

Halbmesser *m* (-s; -) radius.

'Halbmittelgewicht *n sports*: light middleweight.

'Halbmond *m* half moon, crescent: *wir haben ~* there's a half moon.

'halbmondförmig *adj* crescent-shaped.

'halbnackt *adj* half-naked.

'halboffen *adj* a. *ling.* half-open.

'halboffizi,ell *adj* semiofficial.

'halbpart [-part] *adv* F (*mit j-m*) *~ machen* go halves (*or* fifty-fifty) with s.o.

'Halbpensi,on *f* half-board.

'Halbpro,fil *n* semiprofile.

Halb'rechte *m, f* (-n; -n), **halb'rechts** *adv sports*: inside right.

'Halbreli,ef *n* half relief, mezzo-relievo.

'halbrund *adj* semicircular.

'Halbrund *n* (-[e]s; *no pl*) semicircle.

'Halbschlaf *m* doze: *im ~* half asleep.

'Halbschuh *m* (low) shoe.

'Halbschwergewicht *n sports*: light heavyweight.

'Halbschwester *f* half sister.

'**halbseiden** *adj* **1.** half-silk. **2.** *contp.* (*a.* ~*es Milieu*) demimonde.

'**halbseitig** *adj* **1.** *print.* half-page. **2.** ⚕ unilateral: ~*e Lähmung* hemiplegia.

'**Halbstarke** *m*, *f* (-*n*; -*n*) F yob(bo).

'**Halbstiefel** *m* ankle boot.

'**halbstündig** [-ʃtʏndɪç] *adj* half-hour.

'**halbstündlich** *adj* and *adv* half-hourly, *adv a.* every half-hour.

'**halbtägig** [-tɛ:gɪç] *adj* half a day's, half-day. '**halbtags** *adv* ~ *arbeiten* work part-time. '**Halbtags...** half-day, part-time (*job etc*). '**Halbtagskraft** *f* part-time worker, part-timer.

'**Halbton** *m* **1.** ♪ semitone. **2.** *phot.*, *print.* half-tone.

'**halbtot** *adj* half-dead.

'**halbverhungert** *adj* starving.

'**Halbvo̱kal** *m* *ling.* semivowel.

'**halbvoll** *adj* half-full.

'**halbwach** *adj* half-awake, dozing.

'**Halbwahrheit** *f* (-; -en) half-truth.

'**Halbwaise** *f* half-orphan.

'**Halbwelt** *f* (-; *no pl*) demimonde.

'**Halbwertszeit** *f* *nucl.* half-life.

'**Halbwissen** *n* superficial knowledge.

Halbwüchsige ['halpvy:ksɪgə] *m*, *f* (-*n*; -*n*) adolescent, teenager.

'**Halbzeit** *f* **1.** half(-time): *erste* (*zweite*) ~ first (second) half. **2.** → ~*pause* *f* half-time. ~*stand* *m* half-time score.

Halde ['haldə] *f* (-; -*n*) **1.** a) dump, b) slag heap, c) coal stocks. **2.** † (surplus) stocks: *auf* ~ *legen* stockpile; *auf* ~ *liegen* be (excessively) stockpiled.

half [half] *pret of* **helfen.**

Hälfte ['hɛlftə] *f* (-; -*n*) half: *die* ~ *der Leute* (*Zeit*) half the people (time); *um die* ~ *teurer sein* cost half as much again; *Kinder zahlen die* ~ children pay half(-price); *zur* ~ half (of it *or* them); F *m-e bessere* ~ my better half.

Halfter ['halftər] *n* (-*s*; -) **1.** *a. m* halter. **2.** *a. f* (-; -*n*) (pistol) holster.

Halle ['halə] *f* (-; -*n*) **1.** a) hall, b) foyer, lounge, c) entrance hall. **2.** ⚙ shop, ✈ hangar. **3.** a) gymnasium, F gym, b) covered court(s), c) indoor (swimming) pool: *in der* ~ indoors. **4.** 🏉 concourse.

Halleluja [hale'lu:ja] *n* (-*s*; -*s*) hallelujah.

hallen ['halən] *v/i* (h) (*von* with) reverberate, echo.

'**Hallen...** indoor (*handball, tennis, etc*).

'**Hallenfußball** *m* five-a-side football.

'**Hallen(schwimm)bad** *n* indoor (swimming) pool.

hallo ['halo] *int* a) hello, F hi, b) hey: ~ (, *Sie*)*!* excuse me!, F hey, you! **Hallo** [ha'lo:] *n* (-*s*; -*s*) *fig.* hullabaloo. **Hallodri** [ha'lo:dri] *m* (-*s*; -[*s*]) F scallywag.

Halluzination [halutsina'tsǐo:n] *f* (-; -*en*) hallucination. **halluzinatorisch** ['to:-rɪʃ] *adj* hallucinatory. **halluzinieren** [-'ni:rən] *v/i* (h) hallucinate. **Halluzinogen** [-no'ge:n] *n* (-*s*; -*e*) hallucinogenic.

Halm [halm] *m* (-[*e*]*s*; -*e*) blade, stalk.

Halogenscheinwerfer [halo'ge:n-] *m* *mot.* halogen headlight.

Hals [hals] *m* (-*es*; *⸚e*) a) neck, b) throat: ⚕ *steifer* ~ stiff neck; *aus vollem* ~(*e*) a) *yell etc* at the top of one's voice, b) *lachen* roar with laughter; ~ *über Kopf* headlong, helter-skelter; *sich* ~ *über Kopf verlieben* fall in love head over heels; *bis an den* ~ up to one's neck (*fig. a.* ears); F *auf dem* (*or am*) ~ *haben* have *s.o.*, *s.th.* on one's back, be stuck with; *j-m die Polizei etc auf den* ~ *hetzen* get the police *etc* onto s.o.; *sich j-n* (*et.*) *vom* ~(*e*) *schaffen* get rid of s.o. (s.th.); *j-m um den* ~ *fallen* fling one's arms round s.o.'s neck; *sich j-m an den* ~ *werfen* throw o.s. at s.o.; *sich den* ~ *brechen* break one's neck; *fig. das bricht ihm den* ~ that'll be his undoing; F *e-r Flasche den* ~ *brechen* crack a bottle; F *er hat es in den falschen* ~ *bekommen* he took it the wrong way; F *es hängt mir zum* ~(*e*) *heraus!* I'm fed up (to the teeth) with it!; *bleib mir damit vom* ~(*e*)*!* don't bother me with that!; → *umdrehen*, *Wasser*. '**Halsabschneider** *m* (-*s*; -) F *fig.* cutthroat. '**Halsband** *n* (-[*e*]*s*; *⸚er*) **1.** necklace. **2.** (dog) collar.

'**halsbrecherisch** *adj* breakneck.

'**Halsentzündung** *f* ⚕ sore throat.

'**Halskette** *f* necklace.

'**Hals-'Nasen-'Ohren[-Arzt** *m*, ~*Ärztin* *f* ear, nose and throat specialist.

'**Halsschlagader** *f* carotid (artery).

'**Halsschmerzen** *pl* ~ *haben* have a sore throat.

halsstarrig ['halsʃtarɪç] *adj* stubborn.

'**Halstuch** *n* a) neckerchief, b) scarf.

'**Hals- und 'Beinbruch** F break a leg!

'**Halsweite** *f* collar size.

'**Halswirbel** *m* *anat.* cervical vertebra.

halt¹ [halt] *int* a) stop, *esp.* ✕ halt, b) wait (a minute), c) that'll do.

halt² *adv dial.* → **eben** 5.

Halt *m* (-[e]s; -e, -s) **1.** *no pl* hold, *a.* foothold, *a. fig.* support, *fig.* (moral) stability. **2.** stop: **ohne ~** nonstop; *fig.* **~ gebieten** (*dat*) call a halt to, stop; → **haltmachen**.

'haltbar *adj* **1.** durable, hard-wearing, ⊕ *a.* wear-resistant. **2.** not perishable: **begrenzt ~** perishable; **~ sein** keep (well); **~ machen** preserve; **~ bis ...** best before ... *3. fig.* tenable. **'Haltbarkeit** *f* (-; *no pl*) **1.** durability, ⊕ *a.* (long *etc*) service life, ⊤ shelf life. **2.** keeping quality: **von geringer ~** perishable. **3.** *fig.* tenability.

'Haltbarkeitsdatum *n* best-by (*or* best-before, *Am.* pull) date.

'Haltebucht *f mot.* lay-by, *Am.* rest stop.

'Haltegriff *m* strap.

'Haltelinie *f mot.* stop line.

halten ['haltən] (hielt, gehalten, h) **I** *v/t* **1.** a) hold, b) hold (up), support: **er hielt ihr den Mantel** he held her coat for her; **et. gegen das Licht ~** hold s.th. to the light; → **Stellung** 1. **2.** hold back, stop, keep: **er war nicht zu ~** there was no holding him; **mich hält hier nichts mehr** there is nothing holding me here any more; **haltet den Dieb!** stop thief! **3.** a) keep (**sauber, trocken** *etc* clean, dry, *etc*), b) keep (up), maintain, hold: **der Raum war ganz in Weiß gehalten** everything in the room was done in white; **der Film hielt nicht, was er versprach** the film did not live up to its promise; → **Diät, Ordnung, Schritt** 1, **Takt¹** 1, **Wort** 3. **4.** *sports:* a) stop, block, save, b) hold (*a record*): **s-n Vorsprung ~** stay in the lead. **5.** hold, contain. **6.** make, deliver (*speech etc*), give (*lecture*): → **Predigt, Rede** 1, **Vorlesung.** **7.** *sich ~* keep (*car, dog, personnel, etc*), take (*newspaper*). **8.** treat: **er hielt s-e Kinder sehr streng** he was very strict with his children. **9.** ~ **für** (mis)take *s.o., s.th.* for, consider *s.o., s.th.* (to be): **ich halte es für ratsam** I think it advisable; **man sollte es nicht für möglich ~, aber ...** you wouldn't believe it but ...; **wofür ~ Sie mich (eigentlich)?** who do you think I am?; **für wie alt hältst du ihn?** how old do you think he is? **10.** **viel ~ von** think highly

(*or* the world) of; **nicht viel ~ von** not to think much of; **er hält nichts vom Sparen** he doesn't believe in saving; **was ~ Sie von ...?** a) what do you think of ...?, b) **e-r Tasse Tee** *etc?* how about a cup of tea *etc?* **11.** do, handle: **wie hältst du es mit ...?** what do you usually do about ...?; **das kannst du ~, wie du willst!** please yourself! **12.** *et. auf sich ~* → 19. **II** *v/i* **13.** hold (*a. fig. weather*), last, *flowers, food, etc*: keep. **14.** stop, *mot. a.* draw up, pull up. **15.** *sports:* save. **16.** *an sich ~* restrain o.s., control o.s. **17.** ~ **auf** (*acc*) a) pay attention to, b) set great store by, c) insist on. **18.** ~ **auf** (*acc*) ⚓ *a.* ~ **nach** head for, b) aim at; **nach Süden ~** be heading south; **mehr nach links ~** keep (aim) more to the left. **19.** **auf sich ~** a) be particular about one's appearance, b) be self-respecting. **20.** **zu j-m ~** a) stand by s.o., F stick to s.o., b) side with s.o. **III** *sich ~* **21.** hold on (**an** *dat* to): *fig.* **sich ~ an** (*acc*) keep to, F stick to (*facts, rules, etc*); **sich an j-n ~** a) rely on s.o., b) hold s.o. liable. **22.** wear well, last long, *food, flowers, etc*: keep, *weather:* hold: F **sie hat sich gut gehalten** she is well-preserved. **23.** **sich ~ für** think (*or* consider) o.s. (to be); **sie hält sich für et. Besonderes** she thinks she's s.th. special. **24.** **sich aufrecht ~** hold (*or* carry) o.s. upright; **ich kann mich kaum noch auf den Beinen ~** I'm ready to drop. **25.** keep, stay: **sich warm ~** keep warm; **halte dich mehr links** keep more to the left; **er hat sich bei der Firma nicht lange gehalten** he didn't last long with the firm.

'Halten *n* (-s) **1.** *mot.* **zum ~ bringen** stop, bring *s.th.* to a standstill; *fig.* **da gab es kein ~ mehr** there was no holding them (*etc*). **2.** → **Haltung** 4.

'Haltepunkt *m* stop.

'Halter *m* (-s; -) **1.** ⊕ a) holder, b) handle, c) rest. **2.** ⚕⚕ owner.

'Halterung *f* (-; -en) ⊕ holding device.

'Halteschild *n* stop sign. **'Haltesignal** *n* stop signal. **'Haltestelle** *f* stop. **'Halteverbot** *n* no stopping (zone). **'Halteverbotsschild** *n* no stopping sign.

'haltlos *adj* **1.** unstable, weak. **2.** untenable, unfounded. **'Haltlosigkeit** *f* (-; *no* *pl)* **1.** weakness, instability. **2.** untenableness, unfoundedness.

'**haltmachen** *v/i (sep,* -ge-, h) (make a) stop; *fig.* **vor nichts ~** stop at nothing.

'**Haltung** *f* (-; -en) **1.** a) posture, b) *a. sports:* position, c) pose: **~ annehmen** ✕ stand to attention. **2.** *no pl a)* deportment, behavio(u)r, b) attitude (**gegenüber** towards): *politische ~* political outlook (*or* views). **3.** *no pl* composure: **~ bewahren** a) control o.s., b) *a.* **~ zeigen** bear up well. **4.** *no pl* keeping (*animals etc).*

Halunke [haˈlʊŋkə] *m* (-n; -n) scoundrel.

Hamburger [ˈhambʊrgər] I *m* (-s; -) **1.** *a.* '**Hamburgerin** *f* (-; -nen) Hamburgian. **2.** *gastr.* hamburger. II *adj* **3.** (of) Hamburg.

Häme [ˈhɛːmə] *f* (-; *no pl)* F sneers, snide remarks: *voller ~* sneeringly.

'**hämisch** *adj* malicious, sneering.

Hammel [ˈhaməl] *m* (-s; -) **1.** *zo.* wether. **2.** *gastr.* mutton. **3.** F *fig.* idiot.

'**Hammelbraten** *m* roast mutton.

'**Hammelfleisch** *n* mutton.

'**Hammelkeule** *f* leg of mutton.

'**Hammelsprung** *m parl.* division.

Hammer [ˈhamər] *m* (-s; ⸚) **1.** hammer (*a.* ♪, *sports or at auctions*), mallet, *parl. etc:* gavel: **~ und Sichel** hammer and sickle; *unter den ~ kommen* come under the hammer. **2.** F *fig.* whammy: *das ist ein ~!* that beats everything!

'**Hammerkla,vier** *n* piano(forte).

hämmern [ˈhɛmərn] (h) I *v/i* **1.** hammer, *fig. heart etc:* a. pound. **2. ~ auf** (*acc*), **~ gegen** hammer away at, pound (at). II *v/t* **3.** ⚙ a) hammer, beat, b) forge.

'**Hammer|werfen** *n* (-s) *sports:* hammer throwing. **~werfer** *m* hammer thrower.

Hämoglobin [hɛmogloˈbiːn] *n* (-s; *no pl)* h(a)emoglobin.

Hämophile [hɛmoˈfiːlə] *m* (-n; -n) ⚕ h(a)emophiliac.

Hämorrhoiden [hɛmoroˈiːdən] *pl* ⚕ h(a)emorrhoids, F piles.

Hampelmann [ˈhampəlman] *m* (-[e]s; ⸚er) **1.** jumping Jack. **2.** F *contp.* clown.

Hamster [ˈhamstər] *m* (-s; -) *zo.* hamster.

'**Hamsterer** *m* (-s; -) hoarder.

'**Hamsterkäufe** *pl* panic buying.

hamstern [ˈhamstərn] *v/t, v/i* (h) hoard.

Hand [hant] *f* (; ⸚e) hand (*u. cards*): *j-m die ~ geben* (*or* **reichen, schütteln**)

shake hands with s.o.; **~ in ~ gehen** walk (*fig.* go) hand in hand (*mit* with); *Hände hoch* (**weg**)*!* hands up (off)!; **~***!* *soccer:* hands!; *fig. die öffentliche ~* the public authorities, the State; *j-s rechte ~* s.o.'s right-hand man; *an ~ von* (*or gen*) by means of, on the basis of; *aus erster* (**zweiter**) **~** buy, know, *etc* firsthand (secondhand); *bei der ~, zur ~* at hand, handy; *mit der ~, von ~ make etc* by hand; *unter der ~* on the quiet; *zu Händen* c/o (= care of), *adm.* Attention *Mr Smith etc*; *mit leeren Händen abziehen* go away empty-handed; (*mit*) **~ anlegen** lend a hand; *et. in die Hände bekommen* get hold of s.th.; *j-m in die Hände fallen* fall into s.o.'s hands; *j-m et. an die ~ geben* furnish s.o. with s.th.; *aus der ~ geben* part with; *j-n in der ~ haben* have s.o. in one's grip (F over a barrel); **~ und Fuß haben** make sense; *j-m freie ~ lassen* give s.o. a free hand; *von der ~ in den Mund leben* live from hand to mouth; *letzte ~ an et. legen* put the finishing touches to s.th.; *fig. die Hände in den Schoß legen* twiddle one's thumbs; *aus der ~ legen* lay aside; *s-e ~ ins Feuer legen für* put one's hand into the fire for; *es liegt in s-r ~* it's up to him; *es liegt klar auf der ~* it's obvious; *fig. et. in die ~ nehmen* take charge of s.th.; *j-m (et.) in die Hände spielen* play (s.th.) into s.o.'s hands; *alle Hände voll zu tun haben* have one's hands full; *in andere Hände übergehen* change hands; *das war von langer ~ vorbereitet* that was carefully planned long beforehand; *e-e ~ wäscht die andere* you scratch my back and I'll scratch yours; *sich mit Händen und Füßen* (**gegen et.**) *wehren* fight (s.th.) tooth and nail; *es läßt sich nicht von der ~ weisen, daß ...* it can't be denied that ...; *mit beiden Händen zugreifen* jump at the chance; → *Spiel* 2.

'**Handarbeit** *f* **1.** *no pl* manual work. **2.** a) *no pl* handiwork, handicraft, b) handmade article: *diese Vase ist ~* this vase is handmade. **3.** needlework.

'**Handarbeiter(in** *f) m* manual worker.

'**Handaufheben** *n* (-s) *parl.* **durch ~** by a show of hands.

'**Handball** *m* (-[e]s; *no pl*) handball.

'**Handballen** *m anat.* ball of the thumb.

'**Handballer** [-balər] *m* (-s; -), '**Handballerin** *f* (-; -nen) F, '**Handballspieler(in** *f*) *m* handball player.

'**handbetätigt** *adj* ⊕ hand-operated, manual.

'**Handbetrieb** *m* (-[e]s; *no pl*) manual operation: *mit* ~ → **handbetätigt**.

'**Handbewegung** *f* gesture.

'**Handbiblio,thek** *f* reference library.

'**Handbohrma,schine** *f* hand drill.

'**handbreit** *adj* a few inches wide.

'**Handbreit** *f* (-; -) hand's breadth.

'**Handbremse** *f* handbrake.

'**Handbuch** *n* manual, handbook, guide.

Händen ['hɛntɕən] *n* (-s; -) little hand: F ~ **halten** hold hands.

'**Handcreme** *f* hand cream.

Hände|druck ['hɛndə-] *m* handshake. ~**klatschen** *n* (-s) clapping, applause.

Handel ['handəl] *m* (-s; *no pl*) **1.** commerce, business, trade (*mit* *s.th.*, with *s.o.*), *a. contp.* traffic: ~ *und Gewerbe* trade and industry; ~ *mit Waffen* (*Drogen etc*) trade (*or* traffic) in arms (drugs *etc*); *im* ~ on the market; *nicht mehr im* ~ off the market; *in den* ~ *bringen* (*kommen*) put (be) on the market; ~ *treiben mit* a) *et.* deal in *s.th.*, b) *j-m* trade (*or* do business) with *s.o.* **2.** (business) transaction, F deal, *fig. a.* bargain.

Händel ['hɛndəl] *pl* quarrel, fight.

handeln ['handəln] (h) **I** *v/i* **1.** act, take action. **2.** ✝ trade, do business (*mit j-m* with *s.o.*): ~ *mit* trade (*or* deal, *contp.* traffic) in. **3.** (*um*) bargain (for), haggle (over): *er läßt sich mit sich* ~ he is open to an offer (*w.s.* a suggestion). **4.** ~ *von book*, *film*, *etc*: be about, deal with. **II** *v/t* **gehandelt werden** a) ✝ be sold, *on the stock exchange*: be traded, be listed, b) *name etc*: be mentioned. **III** *v/impers* **es handelt sich um** it concerns, it is a question of, it is about; *worum handelt es sich?* what is it (all) about?, what's the problem?; *es handelt sich darum, ob* (*wer etc*) the question is whether (who *etc*); *darum handelt es sich* (*nicht*)*!* that's just (not) the point!; *bei dem Opfer handelt es sich um e-n Ausländer* the victim is a foreigner.

'**Handeln** *n* (-s) acting (*etc*): *gemeinsa-*

mes (*rasches*) ~ joint (quick) action.

'**Handels|abkommen** *n* trade agreement. ~**atta,ché** *m* commercial attaché. ~**bank** *f* (-; -en) merchant bank. ~**beschränkungen** *pl* trade restrictions. ~**betrieb** *m* commercial enterprise. ~**bezeichnung** *f* trade name. ~**beziehungen** *pl* trade relations. ~**bi,lanz** *f* (*aktive* ~ surplus, *passive* ~ adverse) balance of trade. ~**defizit** *n* trading deficit. 2**einig** *adj* ~ *werden* come to terms (*mit* with). ~**em,bargo** *n* (trade) embargo. ~**flotte** *f* merchant fleet. ~**genossenschaft** *f* traders' cooperative. ~**gericht** *n* commercial court. ~**gesellschaft** *f* (trading) company, *Am.* (business) corporation: *offene* ~ general partnership. ~**gesetzbuch** *n* Commercial Code. ~**hafen** *m* trading port. ~**kammer** *f* Chamber of Commerce. ~**klasse** *f Äpfel der* ~ *A* grade one apples. ~**korrespon,denz** *f* commercial correspondence. ~**lehrer** *m* teacher at a commercial school. ~**macht** *f* (great) trading nation. ~**ma,rine** *f* merchant navy. ~**marke** *f* brand. ~**mi,nister** *m* minister of commerce, *Br.* Secretary of State for Trade and Industry, *Am.* Secretary of Commerce. ~**mini,sterium** *n* ministry of commerce, *Br.* Board of Trade, *Am.* Department of Commerce. ~**name** *m* trade name. ~**nati,on** *f* trading nation. ~**niederlassung** *f* **1.** business establishment. **2.** registered seat. **3.** branch. ~**partner** *m* trading partner. ~**platz** *m* trading cent/re (*Am.* -er). ~**poli,tik** *f* trade policy. ~**recht** *n* (-[e]s; *no pl*) commercial law. ~**re,gister** *n* trade register: *ins* ~ *eintragen* (*lassen*) register, *Am.* incorporate. ~**reisende** *m, f* (-n; -n) commercial travel(l)er. ~**schiff** *n* trading vessel. ~**schiffahrt** *f* merchant shipping. ~**schranke** *f* trade barrier. ~**schule** *f* commercial school. ~**spanne** *f* trade margin. 2**üblich** *adj* usual in the trade: ~**e** *Qualität* commercial quality. ~**verkehr** *m* trade, trading. ~**vertrag** *m* trade agreement. ~**vertreter(in** *f*) *m* commercial representative. ~**vertretung** *f* commercial agency, *pol.* trade mission. ~**vo,lumen** *n* volume of trade. ~**ware** *f* commodity: ~*n* merchandise. ~**weg** *m* trade route. **~wert** m market value. **~zweig** m line of business.

'**handeltreibend** adj trading.

'**händeringend** adv a) imploringly, b) despairingly.

'**Händeschütteln** n (-s) shaking of hands, handshake.

'**Handfertigkeit** f manual skill.

'**handfest** adj 1. sturdy, strong. 2. fig. huge (scandal etc), solid (proof etc), whopping (lie).

'**Hand|feuerlöscher** m fire extinguisher. **~feuerwaffe** f hand gun, pl small arms. **~fläche** f palm. ⚥**gearbeitet**, ⚥**gefertigt** adj handmade. **~gelenk** n wrist: F **aus dem ~** off the cuff, just like that. ⚥**gemalt** adj handpainted. **~gemenge** n (-s; -) fray, brawl. **~gepäck** n hand luggage (Am. baggage). ⚥**geschrieben** adj handwritten. ⚥**gestrickt** adj 1. handknitted. 2. F contp. home-made. ⚥**gewebt** adj handwoven. **~gra͵nate** f hand grenade.

handgreiflich ['hantgraɪflɪç] adj 1. **er wurde ~** a) he got violent, b) he started to paw. 2. fig. obvious, plain.

'**Handgreiflichkeiten** pl violence.

'**Handgriff** m 1. handle, grip. 2. fig. a) movement of the hand, b) manipulation: **mit wenigen ~en** do s.th. in no time (or deftly).

'**Handhabe** f (-; -n) a) proof, b) lever: **er hat keinerlei ~** he hasn't got a leg to stand on. '**handhaben** v/t (handhabte, gehandhabt, h) 1. use, handle, operate. 2. fig. a) handle, deal with, b) apply. '**Handhabung** f (-; -en) handling (a. fig.), use, operation.

Handicap ['hɛndikɛp] n (-s; -s) a. fig. handicap (für to).

'**Hand|kante** f side of the hand: **Schlag mit der ~** → **~kantenschlag** m (karate) chop. **~karren** m handcart. **~koffer** m small suitcase. **~kuß** m **j-m e-n ~ geben** kiss s.o.'s hand; F fig. **mit ~** gladly.

'**Handlanger** m (-s; -) odd-job man, contp. dogsbody, pol. etc henchman.

'**Händler** ['hɛndlɐ] m (-s; -), '**Händlerin** f (-; -nen) trader, merchant, dealer.

'**Handlesekunst** f (-; no pl) palmistry.

'**handlich** adj handy.

'**Handlichkeit** f (-; no pl) handiness.

'**Handlung** f (-; -en) 1. act, action. 2. of film etc: action, story, plot: **Ort der ~** scene (of action). 3. ✝ shop.

'**Handlungs|bedarf** m **es besteht (kein) ~** this calls (there is no need) for action. **~bevollmächtigte** m, f (authorized) agent, proxy. ⚥**fähig** adj 1. ⚖ having disposing capacity. 2. functioning, working (government etc). **~fähigkeit** f (-; no pl) 1. ⚖ legal capacity. 2. capacity to act. **~freiheit** f freedom of action: **j-m ~ geben** give s.o. a free hand. **~gehilfe** m, **~gehilfin** f 1. (commercial) clerk. 2. shop assistant. ⚥**reich** adj full of action, action-packed. **~reisende** m, f commercial travel(l)er. **~spielraum** m room for manoeuvre (Am. maneuver). **~vollmacht** f limited authority to act and sign. **~weise** f 1. way of acting, conduct. 2. procedure.

Hand|pflege f manicure. **~puppe** f glove puppet. **~rücken** m back of the hand. **~schelle** f handcuff: **j-m ~n anlegen** handcuff s.o. **~schlag** m (-[e]s; no pl) handshake: **durch ~ bekräftigen** shake hands on; F **er tut k-n ~** he doesn't lift a finger. **~schrift** f 1. handwriting, hand. 2. manuscript. ⚥**schriftlich** I adj handwritten. II adv in writing, correct etc by hand. **~schuh** m glove. **~schuhfach** n mot. glove compartment. **~spiegel** m hand mirror. **~spiel** n soccer: hands. **~stand** m gym. handstand. **~standüberschlag** m handspring. **~steuerung** f manual control. **~streich** m coup (de main). **~tasche** f handbag, Am. purse.

'**Handtuch** n (das ~ werfen a. F fig. throw in the) towel. **~auto͵mat** m towel dispenser. **~halter** m towel rack.

'**Handumdrehen** n **im ~** in no time.

'**handverlesen** adj a. fig. handpicked.

'**Handvoll** f (-; -) a. fig. handful.

'**handwarm** adj lukewarm.

'**Handwaschbecken** n hand basin.

'**Handwerk** n (-[e]s; -e) trade, craft: **das ~** the trade; **ein ~ lernen** learn a trade; fig. **j-m das ~ legen** put a stop to s.o.('s game); **j-m ins ~ pfuschen** botch at s.o.'s trade; **er versteht sein ~** he knows his stuff. '**Handwerker** m (-s; -) (skilled) workman, craftsman.

'**handwerklich** adj craftsman's, craft: **~er Beruf** skilled trade; **~es Können** craftsmanship, craft skills.

Handwerkskammer 280

'**Handwerks|kammer** *f* chamber of handicrafts. **~meister** *m* master craftsman. **~zeug** *n* tools (*a. fig.*).
'**Hand|wörterbuch** *n* concise dictionary. **~wurzel** *f anat.* wrist, carpus. **~zeichen** *n* **1.** sign. **2.** *parl.* show of hands. **~zettel** *m* leaflet.
Hanf [hanf] *m* (-[e]s; *no pl*) hemp.
Hang [haŋ] *m* (-[e]s; ⸱e) **1.** slope. **2.** *gym.* hang. **3.** *fig.* (**zu**) a) bent (for), tendency (to), b) proneness (to).
Hangar ['haŋgar] *m* (-s; -s) hangar.
'**Hängebacken** *pl* flabby cheeks.
'**Hängebrücke** *f* suspension bridge.
'**Hängebusen** *m* sagging breasts.
'**Hängelampe** *f* hanging lamp.
hangeln ['haŋəln] *v/i* (h) *gym.* climb (*or* travel) hand over hand.
'**Hängematte** *f* hammock.
'**Hangen:** *mit ~ und Bangen* in anxious anticipation.
hängen¹ ['hɛŋən] *v/i* (hing, gehangen, h) **1.** hang (*an dat* from *or* on): *voller Äpfel etc ~* be full of apples *etc*; *über j-m ~ a. fig.* hang over s.o.; *fig.* **die ganze Arbeit hängt an mir** I am stuck with all the work; → *Tropf.* **2.** (*an dat* to) *mud etc*: cling, stick. **3.** be stuck, be caught: F *fig.* **woran hängt's?** what's the problem?; *er hängt in Latein* he's bad at Latin. **4.** *~ an* (*dat*) love (*life, money, etc*), cling to (*a custom etc*); *an j-m ~* be fond of (*or* devoted to) s.o. **5.** be lopsided.
'**hängen²** (h) **I** *v/t* **1.** *j-n ~* hang s.o.; *gehängt werden* be hanged. **2.** *et. ~ an* (*acc*) hang s.th. from (*or* on); *fig.* **sein Herz ~ an** (*acc*) set one's heart on. **II** *sich ~ an* (*acc*) hang on to; F *sich ans Telefon ~* get on the phone; *sich an j-n ~* a) cling to s.o., b) trail s.o., c) *runner*: drop in behind s.o.
'**Hängen** *n* (-s) F *mit ~ und Würgen* only just, barely.
'**hängenbleiben** *v/i* (*irr, sep*, -ge-, sn, → *bleiben*) F **1.** (*an dat*) get (*or* be) caught (by), catch (on, in), get (*or* be) stuck (in): *fig. im Gedächtnis ~* stick in one's mind. **2.** *fig.* be held up, *sports*: be stopped (*an dat* by).
'**hängenlassen** (*irr, sep, no* -ge-, h, → *lassen*) **I** *v/t* **1.** let *s.th.* hang, (let *s.th.*) dangle. **2.** F *j-n ~* leave s.o. in the lurch. **II** *sich ~* let o.s. go.

'**Hängeohren** *pl* floppy ears.
'**Hängepar|tie** *f chess:* adjourned game.
'**Hängepflanze** *f* hanging plant.
'**Hänger** *m* (-s; -) loose dress (*or* coat).
'**Hängeschrank** *m* wall cabinet.
Hans'dampf *m* (-[e]s; -e) F *~ in allen Gassen* jack-of-all-trades.
hanseatisch [hanze'a:tɪʃ] *adj* Hanseatic.
Hänse'lei *f* (-; -en) teasing, F kidding.
hänseln ['hɛnzəln] *v/t* (h) tease, F kid.
Hansestadt ['hanzə-] *f* Hanse town.
'**Hanswurst** *m* (-[e]s; -e) *a. contp.* clown.
Hantel ['hantəl] *f* (-; -n) dumbbell.
hantieren [han'ti:rən] *v/i* (h) **1.** potter around. **2.** *~ mit* work with, handle; *~ an* (*dat*) work on, *contp.* fiddle with.
hapern ['ha:pərn] *v/impers* (h) F *es hapert mit* (*or bei*) there are problems with; *es hapert an* (*dat*) there isn't (*or* aren't) enough; *im Englischen hapert es bei ihm* English is his weak point.
Häppchen ['hɛpçən] *n* (-s; -) a) morsel, b) titbit, snack) canapé.
Happen ['hapən] *m* (-s; -) **1.** bite (to eat): *e-n ~ essen* have a bite. **2.** *fig.* (*ein fetter ~* a fine) catch.
happig ['hapɪç] *adj* F steep (*prices etc*).
Härchen ['hɛːrçən] *n* (-s; -) little hair.
Harem ['ha:rɛm] *m* (-s; -s) harem.
Harfe ['harfə] *f* (-; -n) ♪ harp. **Harfenist** [harfə'nɪst] *m* (-en; -en), **Harfe'nistin** *f* (-; -nen) harpist.
Harke ['harkə] *f* (-; -n) rake: F *j-m zeigen, was e-e ~ ist* show (*or* tell) s.o. what's what.
harmlos ['harmlo:s] *adj* harmless.
'**Harmlosigkeit** *f* (-; *no pl*) harmlessness.
Harmonie [harmo'ni:] *f* (-; -n) harmony.
Harmo'nielehre *f* (-; *no pl*) ♪ harmony.
harmonieren [harmo'ni:rən] *v/i* (h) harmonize (*mit* with). **harmonisch** [har'mo:nɪʃ] *adj* ♪, ♪ harmonic(al), *a. fig.* harmonious. **harmonisieren** [harmoni'zi:rən] *v/t* (h) *a. fig.* harmonize.
Harn [harn] *m* (-[e]s; -e) ♂ urine.
'**Harnblase** *f anat.* bladder.
'**harnen** *v/i* (h) pass water, urinate.
'**Harnflasche** *f* urinal.
'**Harngrieß** *m* ♂ gravel.
Harnisch ['harnɪʃ] *m* (-s; -e) a) (suit of) armo(u)r, b) cuirass: F *j-n in ~ bringen* get s.o.'s back up; *in ~ geraten* get (really) furious; *in ~ sein* be up in arms.
'**Harn|leiter** *m anat.* ureter. **~probe** *f* ♂

urine sample. **~röhre** *f anat.* urethra.
~säure *f* ✷ uric acid. **✷treibend** *adj*
diuretic. **~untersuchung** *f* urinalysis.
~wege *pl anat.* urinary tract.

Harpune [har'puːnə] *f* (-; -n) harpoon.

harren ['harən] *v/i* (h) (*gen or auf acc*)
wait (for), await (*s.o., s.th.*).

Harsch [harʃ] *m* (-es; *no pl*) crusted
snow. **'harschig** *adj* crusted.

hart [hart] **I** *adj* **1.** hard: **~ werden** harden (*a. fig.*); **~es Ei** hard-boiled egg;
fig. **~e Währung** (*Droge*) hard currency
(drug). **2.** *fig.* a) hard, b) hardened,
tough, *sports:* rough: **er ist ~ im Nehmen** he can take a lot of punishment;
er blieb ~ he stood firm. **3.** *fig.* hard
(*work, life, winter, etc*), severe (*criticism, punishment, etc*), harsh (*words
etc*), heavy (*blow, loss, etc*), tough (*policy etc*): **~e Tatsachen** hard facts; *das
war ~!* that was tough!; *das war ~ für
ihn* that was hard on him; → *Nuß,
Schule.* **II** *adv* **4.** hard, severely: **~ arbeiten** work hard; *es ging ~ auf ~* it
was either do or die; *wenn es ~ auf ~
geht* when it comes to the crunch. **5.** **~
an** (*dat*) close to; ⚓ **~ am Wind** close-
hauled.

Härte ['hɛrtə] *f* (-; -n) **1.** hardness. **2.** *fig.*
toughness, *sports:* roughness, rough
play. **3.** *fig.* hardness, harshness, severity: ⚖ (*unbillige ~*) undue) hardship. **4.**
phot. contrast. **~fall** *m* hardship case.

härten ['hɛrtən] (h) **I** *v/t* a) harden, b)
temper (*steel*). **II** *v/i* harden, grow hard.

'Hartfaserplatte *f* hardboard, *Am.*
fiberboard.

'hartgefroren *adj* frozen hard.

'hartgekocht *adj* hard-boiled.

'Hartgeld *n* (-es; *no pl*) coins.

'hartgesotten [-gəzɔtən] *adj fig.* hard-
-boiled.

'Hartgummi *n, m* hard rubber.

'hartherzig *adj* hard-hearted.

'Hartkäse *m* hard cheese.

'hartnäckig [-nɛkɪç] *adj* stubborn, persistent, ✷ refractory. **'Hartnäckigkeit** *f*
(-; *no pl*) stubbornness, persistence.

'Hartplatz *m* hard pitch (*tennis:* court).

'Härtung *f* (-; -en) hardening, tempering.

'Hartwurst *f* hard sausage.

Harz [harts] *n* (-es; -e) resin, rosin.

'harzig *adj* resinous.

Hasardspiel [ha'zart-] *n fig.* gamble.

Hasch [haʃ] *n* (-s; *no pl*) F hash.

Haschee [ha'ʃeː] *n* (-s; -s) *gastr.* hash.

haschen¹ ['haʃən] (h) **I** *v/t* (*sich ~* play)
catch. **II** *v/i* **~ nach** snatch at, *fig.* seek:
nach Komplimenten ~ fish for compli-
ments.

'haschen² *v/i* (h) F smoke hash.

Häschen ['hɛːsçən] *n* (-s; -) **1.** young
hare. **2.** F bunny.

Hascherl ['haʃərl] *n* (-s; -[n]) *dial.* (*armes*) ~ poor little thing, poor creature.

Haschisch ['haʃɪʃ] *n* (-; *no pl*) hashish.

Hase ['haːzə] *m* (-n; -n) hare: *fig. alter ~*
old hand; *sehen, wie der ~ läuft* see
how things develop; *da liegt der ~ im
Pfeffer* that's the real problem; *mein
Name ist ~(, ich weiß von nichts)!*
search me!

Haselnuß ['haːzəl-] *f* **1.** hazelnut. **2.** →
'Haselnußstrauch *m* hazelnut (tree).

'Hasenbraten *m* roast hare.

'Hasenfuß *m* F *fig.* coward.

'Hasenpfeffer *m gastr.* jugged hare.

'Hasenscharte *f* ✷ hare lip.

Häsin ['hɛːzɪn] *f* (-; -nen) female hare,
doe.

Haspel ['haspəl] *f* (-; -n) ⚙ hasp, reel.

haspeln ['haspəln] *v/t* (h) **1.** ⚙ reel,
wind. **2.** *a. v/i* splutter.

Haß [has] *m* (-sses; *no pl*) (*auf acc, gegen*
of, for) hatred, hate: **aus ~** out of hatred; **e-n ~ haben auf** (*acc*) → **hassen**
['hasən] *v/t* (h) hate: → *Pest.*

'hassenswert *adj* hateful. **'haßerfüllt**
adj full of hate, venomous (*look etc*).

häßlich ['hɛslɪç] *adj* ugly, *fig. a.* nasty.

'Haßliebe *f* love-hate relationship.

Hast [hast] *f* (-; *no pl*) hurry, rush.

hasten ['hastən] *v/i* (sn) hurry.

'hastig I *adj* **1.** hasty, hurried: *nicht so ~!*
just a minute! **2.** slapdash. **3.** nervous.
II *adv* **4.** hastily, in a hurry.

hätscheln ['hɛːtʃəln] *v/t* (h) **1.** cuddle. **2.**
fig. pamper.

hatte ['hatə] *pret of* **haben.**

Haube ['haʊbə] *f* (-; -n) **1.** a) bonnet, b)
hood (*a.* ⚙), c) cap, d) *eccl.* cornet: *fig.
unter die ~ bringen* find a husband for.
2. (hair-)drier. **3.** *zo.* crest. **4.** *mot.* bonnet, *Am.* hood.

Hauch [haʊx] *m* (-[e]s; *no pl*) **1.** a) breath,
b) breath (of wind), c) whiff. **2.** *ling.*
aspiration. **3.** *fig.* touch. **'hauch'dünn**
adj **1.** a) wafer-thin, b) flimsy. **2.** *fig.*

very slim (*chance etc*), bare (*majority etc*): **~er Sieg** knife-edge victory.
hauchen ['haʊxən] *v/i*, *v/t* (h) breathe, *ling*. aspirate.
'**Hauchlaut** *m ling*. aspirate.
'**Haudegen** *m* (-s; -) *alter* **~** F warhorse.
'**Haue¹** ['haʊə] *f* (-; -n) *dial*. hoe.
'**Haue²** *f* (-; *no pl*) F (**~ kriegen** get a) spanking.
hauen ['haʊən] (haute *or* hieb, gehauen, h) **I** *v/t* **1.** F hit, slap, thrash, spank: *sich* **~** fight, scrap; → *Ohr, Pauke*. **2.** F bang, slam. **3.** *dial*. a) hew, cut, b) chop (*wood*), c) chop down (*tree*). **II** *v/i* **4.** hit (out) (*nach* at). '**Hauer** *m* (-s; -) **1.** *zo*. tusk. **2.** ⚒ face worker.
Häufchen ['hɔʏfçən] *n* (-s; -) small heap (*or* pile): *wie ein* **~** *Unglück* (looking) the picture of misery.
Haufen ['haʊfən] *m* (-s; -) **1.** heap, pile: F *über den* **~** *rennen* (*fahren*) knock *s.o.*, *s.th.* down; *j-n über den* **~** *schießen* shoot s.o. down; *über den* **~** *werfen* a) upset (*plan etc*), b) explode (*theory etc*). **2.** F loads of, a lot (*or* lots) of (*friends, money, etc*): *e-n* **~** *Geld kosten* (*verdienen*) cost (make) a packet. **3.** F crowd, bunch, ⚔ outfit. **4.** V turd.
häufen ['hɔʏfən] (h) **I** *v/t* heap up, *fig. a*. accumulate: → *gehäuft*. **II** *sich* **~** *fig.* a) accumulate, pile up, *debts*: a. mount, b) increase (in number).
'**haufenweise** *adv* F a) in piles, b) in crowds, c) a lot of, lots of, loads of.
'**Haufenwolke** *f* cumulus (cloud).
häufig ['hɔʏfɪç] **I** *adj* frequent, *a.* widespread. **II** *adv* frequently, often: **~** *besuchen* a. frequent. '**Häufigkeit** *f* (-; *no pl*) frequency, (high) incidence.
'**Häufung** *f* (-; -en) accumulation, increase, spreading, frequent occurrence.
Haupt [haʊpt] *n* (-[e]s; ⁓er) *a. fig.* head: *et. an* **~** *und Gliedern reformieren* reform s.th. root and branch.
'**Haupt...** main, chief, principal. **~abteilungsleiter** *m* senior head of department. **~aktio̱när** *m* principal shareholder (*Am.* stockholder). **~ak̩zent** *m ling.* primary stress. ⚥**amtlich** *adj and adv* full-time. **~angeklagte** *m, f* principal defendant. **~anschluß** *m teleph*. main line. **~anteil** *m* principal (*fig.* lion's) share. **~attrakti̩on** *f* main attraction, highlight. **~auf-**

~gabe *f* main duty (*or* work). **~augenmerk** *n sein* **~** *richten auf* (*acc*) give one's special attention to. **~bahnhof** *m* main station. ⚥**beruflich** *adj and adv* full-time, *adv a.* as one's main job. **~beschäftigung** *f* main job. **~bestandteil** *m* main constituent. **~betrieb** *m* ✝ a) head office, b) central works. **~buch** *n* ✝ main ledger. **~darsteller(in** *f*) *m* leading actor (actress), lead. **~einfahrt** *f*, **~eingang** *m* main entrance. **~erbe** *m* chief (*or* principal) heir. **~fach** *n ped.*, *univ.* main subject, *Am.* major: *als* (*or im*) **~** *studieren* study s.th. as a main subject, *Am.* major in. **~feldwebel** *m* ⚔ sergeant major, *Am.* first sergeant. **~fi̩gur** *f* central figure, *thea. etc* main character. **~film** *m* feature film. **~gang** *m gastr.* main course. **~gebäude** *n* main building. **~gericht** *n gastr.* main course. **~geschäft** *n* **1.** main business. **2.** → **~geschäftsstelle** *f* a) head office, b) main store. **~geschäftszeit** *f* peak business hours. **~gewicht** *n fig.* main emphasis. **~gewinn** *m* first prize. **~grund** *m* main reason. **~hahn** *m* ⊙ main tap. **~kasse** *f* main cash desk, *thea.* box office. **~last** *f* main burden: *die* **~** *tragen* bear the brunt (*gen* of).
Häuptling ['hɔʏptlɪŋ] *m* (-s; -e) **1.** chieftain. **2.** F boss.
'**Haupt|mahlzeit** *f* main meal. **~mangel** *m* main fault (*or* weakness). **~mann** *m* (-[e]s; -leute) ⚔ captain. **~merkmal** *n* chief characteristic. **~nahrung** *f* staple (food). **~nenner** *m* ✝ common denominator. **~niederlassung** *f* ✝ head office, headquarters. **~per̩son** *f* most important person, central figure (*thea. a.* character). **~postamt** *n* main post office. **~probe** *f thea.* dress (*♪* general) rehearsal. **~quar̩tier** *n* headquarters. **~reisezeit** *f* peak tourist season. **~rolle** *f thea. etc* leading role, main part, lead: *fig. die* **~** *spielen* a) be all-important, b) be the central figure. **~sache** *f* (-; *no pl*) main (*or* most important) thing: **~** *du bist da!* (the) main thing (is), you're here! ⚥**sächlich** *adj and adv* main(ly), chief(ly), *adv a.* above all. **~sai̩son** *f* peak season. **~satz** *m ling.* main clause. **~schalter** *m* ⚡ master switch. **~schlagader** *f anat.* aorta. **~schlüssel** *m* master key. **~schuld** *f er trägt die* **~** *daran*

it's mainly his fault. **~schuldige** *m, f* chief culprit, 𝄞𝄞 principal. **~schule** *f* secondary modern school. **~sendezeit** *f TV* prime time. **~sitz** *m* head office, headquarters. **~sorge** *f* main concern. **~speicher** *m computer*: main memory. **~stadt** *f* capital (city). **~straße** *f* main street. **~stütze** *f fig.* mainstay. **~täter** *m* 𝄞𝄞 principal (in the first degree). **~teil** *m* main part, most of it. **~thema** *n* main subject. **~ton** *m* 1. *ling.* main stress. 2. ♩ keynote. **~tor** *n* main gate. **~treffer** *m* first prize, F jackpot. **~tri,büne** *f* grandstand. **~unterschied** *m* main difference. **~verfahren** *n*, **~verhandlung** *f* 𝄞𝄞 trial. **~verkehrsstraße** *f* main road. **~verkehrszeit** *f* rush hour. **~versammlung** *f* general meeting. **~vertreter** *m* general agent. **~verwaltung** *f* head office. **~wort** *n* (-[e]s; ⸚er) noun. **~zeuge** *m*, **~zeugin** *f* chief witness. **~ziel** *n* main objective. **~zweck** *m* main object, chief purpose.

hau ruck ['haʊ 'rʊk] *int* heave-ho.

Haus [haʊs] *n* (-es; ⸚er) a) house (*a. astr.*, ♱, *thea.*), building, b) family, c) dynasty: *pl.* **das (Hohe) ~** the House; *aus gutem ~(e) sein* come from a good family; *außer ~* out, not in; *im ~* inside, ♱ on the premises; *ins ~* in(doors); *fig. ins ~ stehen* be forthcoming; *das steht uns noch ins ~* we are yet in for that; *j-n nach ~(e) bringen* take (*or* see) s.o. home; *nach ~(e) kommen* come (*or* get) home; *zu ~(e) a. sports*: at home; *er ist nicht zu ~e a.* he is not in; *bei uns zu ~(e)* where I come from, at home; *fig. in e-r Sache zu ~e sein* be at home in s.th.; *sich wie zu ~(e) fühlen* feel at home; *fühl dich (ganz) wie zu ~e!* make yourself at home! *fig. von ~e aus* originally, actually; *thea. vor vollem ~(e) spielen* play to a full house. **Haus|al,tar** *m* family altar. **~angestellte** *f* domestic (servant). **~an,tenne** *f* roof aerial (*Am.* antenna). **~apo,theke** *f* medicine cabinet. **~arbeit** *f* 1. housework. 2. *a. pl ped.* homework. **~ar,rest** *m* (*j-n unter ~ stellen* place s.o. under) house arrest. **~arzt** *m*, **~ärztin** *f* family doctor, *at spa etc*: resident doctor. **~aufgabe(n** *pl*) *f* (s-e *~ machen a. fig.* do one's) homework. **~aufsatz** *m ped.* essay to be written at home. **~ball** *m*

private dance, house party. **~bar** *f* a) cocktail cabinet, b) bar. **~bau** *m* (-[e]s; *no pl*) house building. **~besetzer** *m* squatter. **~besetzung** *f* (-; -en) squatting. **~besitzer(in** *f*) *m* 1. house owner. 2. landlord (landlady). **~besuch** *m* home visit. **~bewohner** *m* a) occupant, b) tenant. **~boot** *n* houseboat. **~brand** *m* (-[e]s; *no pl*) domestic fuel.

Häuschen ['hɔʏsçən] *n* (-s; -) 1. small house, cottage: F (*ganz*) *aus dem ~ geraten* get into a flap (*wegen* about, *vor dat* with); *ganz aus dem ~ sein* F be wild (*vor* with). 2. F too, *Am.* john.

'Hausdetek,tiv(in *f*) *m* store detective.

hausen ['haʊzən] *v/i* (h) F 1. live. 2. (*übel*) *~* wreak havoc (*unter dat* among).

Häuserblock ['hɔʏzərblɔk] *m* block (of houses).

'Haus|flur *m* hall(way). **~frau** *f* housewife. **~freund** *m iro.* (secret) lover. **~friedensbruch** *m* 𝄞𝄞 illegal entry of *s.o.'s* house, *w.s.* violation of *s.o.'s* privacy. **~gebrauch** *m für den ~* for use in the home; F *fig. für den ~ reichen* be enough to get by on. **♀gemacht** *adj a. fig.* home-made. **~gemeinschaft** *f* 1. house community. 2. household.

'Haushalt *m* (-[e]s; -e) 1. household: (*j-m*) *den ~ führen* run the household (for s.o.); *im ~ helfen* help in the house. 2. *pol.* budget. 3. *biol.* balance. **'haushalten** *v/i* (*irr, sep*, -ge-, h, → **halten**) economize: *~ mit* be economical with; *mit s-n Kräften ~* husband one's energies. **'Haushälterin** [-hɛltərɪn] *f* (-; -nen) housekeeper. **'haushälterisch** *adj* economical.

'Haushalts... a) household (*article etc*), b) ♱, *pol.* budget (*committee, debate, etc*), budgetary (*deficit, policy, etc*). **~führung** *f* (-; *no pl*) housekeeping. **~geld** *n* housekeeping money. **~gerät** *n* household appliance. **~jahr** *n* fiscal year. **~mittel** *pl* budgetary means: (*gebilligte*) *~* appropriations. **~packung** *f* economy pack. **~plan** *m parl.* budget: *im ~ vorsehen* budget for.

'Hausherr *m* 1. head of (the) house. 2. landlord. 3. host. **'Hausherrin** *f* 1. lady of the house. 2. landlady. 3. hostess.

'haushoch *adj* huge: *haushoher Sieg*

smashing victory; **haushohe Niederla-**
ge crushing defeat; **~ gewinnen** win
hands down; **~ schlagen** trounce; **~**
verlieren get an awful drubbing; **j-m ~**
überlegen sein be streets ahead of s.o.

hausieren [hau'zi:rən] *v/i* (h) **mit et. ~**
(gehen) hawk s.th., *a. fig.* peddle s.th.

Hausierer *m* (-s; -) hawker, peddler.

'Hauslehrer(in *f*) *m* private tutor(ess).

häuslich ['hɔyslɪç] *adj* a) household, domestic, b) family, c) homekeeping, domesticated; ♒ **~e Gemeinschaft** joint
household; **im ~en Kreis** in the family
circle; **er ist sehr ~** he's a real house
body; **sich ~ einrichten** (*or* **niederlas-**
sen) settle down, *iro.* **bei j-m** come to
stay with s.o.

'Häuslichkeit *f* (-; *no pl*) domesticity.

'Hausmacherart *f gastr.* **nach ~** home-
-made, traditional-style ...

'Haus|mädchen *n* maid. **~mann** *m*
(-[e]s; **-**er) house husband. **~manns-**
kost *f* good plain cooking. **~marke** *f* a)
own brand, b) house wine, c) F *one's*
favo(u)rite brand. **~meister** *m* caretak-
er. **~mittel** *n* household remedy. **~müll**
m household waste. **~mu͵sik** *f* music-
-making in the home. **~nummer** *f*
house number. **~ordnung** *f* house
rules. **~pflege** *f* home nursing (*or* care).

'Hausrat *m* (-[e]s; *no pl*) household ef-
fects. **'Hausratversicherung** *f* household contents insurance.

'Haus|sammlung *f* door-to-door collec-
tion. **~schlüssel** *m* front-door key.
~schuh *m* slipper.

Hausse ['ho:s(ə)] *f* (-; -n) bull market,
boom; **auf ~ spekulieren** bull the market. **'Haussespeku͵lant** *m* bull.

'Haussuchung *f* (-; -en) house search.

'Haus|tele͵fon *n* intercom. **~tier** *n* do-
mestic animal, pet. **~tür** *f* front door.
~verwalter *m* 1. → *Hausmeister.* 2.
property manager. **~verwaltung** *f*
property management. **~wirt** *m* landlord. **~wirtin** *f* landlady. **~wirtschaft** *f*
(-; *no pl*) 1. housekeeping. 2. → **~wirt-**
schaftslehre *f* domestic science, *Am.*
home economics. **~zelt** *n* frame tent.

Haut [haut] *f* (-; **-**e) skin (*a. fig.*), *a.* hide,
anat., ♒ *a.* membrane, ♒ *a.* peel, *on milk*
etc: *a.* film; **bis auf die ~ durchnäßt**
soaked to the skin; F **mit ~ und Haar**

sich auf die faule ~ legen loaf; **e-e**
dicke ~ haben *a. fig.* have a thick skin;
mit heiler ~ davonkommen come out
of it unscathed; F **aus der ~ fahren** go
through the roof; **s-e (eigene) ~ retten**
save one's skin; **sich s-r ~ wehren**
defend o.s.; **ich möchte nicht in s-r ~**
stecken I wouldn't like to be in his
shoes; **er ist nur noch ~ und Knochen**
he's just skin and bones; **es kann eben**
k-r aus s-r ~ a leopard can't change his
spots; **das geht e-m unter die ~** it gets
under your skin.

'Hautabschürfung *f* abrasion, graze.

'Hautarzt *m* dermatologist.

'Hautausschlag *m* (skin) rash: **e-n ~**
bekommen come out in a rash.

Häutchen ['hɔytçən] *n* (-s; -) *anat.*, ♒
membrane, cuticle, *on milk etc*: skin.

'Hautcreme *f* skin cream.

haute ['haute] *pret of* **hauen.**

häuten ['hɔytən] (h) **I** *v/t* skin, flay. **II**
sich ~ *zo.* shed its skin, slough off.

'hauteng *adj* skin-tight.

Hautevolee [(h)o:tvo'le:] *f* (-; *no pl*) *a.*
iro. upper crust (F).

'Hautfarbe *f* colo(u)r (of one's skin),
complexion. **'hautfarben** *adj* flesh-
-colo(u)red, skin-colo(u)red.

'Hautkrankheit *f* skin disease.

'Hautkrebs *m* ♣ skin cancer.

'hautnah *adj* 1. *a. sports:* (very) close. 2.
F *fig.* vivid, realistic.

'Hautpflege *f* skin care.

'Hautpflegemittel *n* skin-care product.

'Hautpilz *m* ♣ fungal infection.

'Hautschere *f* cuticle scissors.

'Hauttransplantati͵on *f* skin graft(ing).

'Häutung *f* (-; -en) *zo.* sloughing.

'Hautunreinheit *f* (skin) blemish.

'Hautwunde *f* (skin) lesion.

Havarie [hava'ri:] *f* (-; -n) a) accident, b)
damage: ♣ **(große) ~** (general) average; **(kleine) ~** (petty) average.

he [he:] *int* F hey.

Hebamme ['he:p²amə] *f* (-; -n) midwife.

Hebebaum *m* ☉ heaver. **'Hebebühne** *f*
☉ lifting platform, *mot.* car lift.

Hebel ['he:bəl] *m* (-s; -) lever: **den ~**
ansetzen apply the lever, *fig.* tackle it;
fig. **alle ~ in Bewegung setzen** move
heaven and earth; **am längeren ~ sit-**
zen be in the stronger position; **an den**
~n der Macht sitzen be at the controls.

~arm m lever arm. **~griff** m lever hold. **~kraft** f, **~mo‚ment** n phys. leverage.

heben ['he:bən] (hob, gehoben, h) **I** v/t **1.** lift, raise, ⚙ a. hoist: *ein Wrack (e-n Schatz)* ~ raise a wreck (treasure); F *fig.* *e-n* ~ have a drink, hoist one. **2.** *fig.* raise (*eyes, voice, morale, etc*), improve, enhance. **II** *sich* ~ **4.** *cur-tain etc:* rise, go up, *fog:* lift: *sich* ~ *und senken* rise and fall. **5.** *fig.* rise.

'**Heben** n (-s) lifting (*etc*). '**Heber** m (-s; -) **1.** 🜂 siphon. **2.** → *Gewichtheber*.

'**Hebezeug** n (-[e]s; -e) ⚙ hoist.

hebräisch ['he:brɛ:ɪʃ] adj Hebrew.

'**Hebung** f (-; -en) **1.** lifting, a. raising (of *treasure, wreck*). **2.** no pl fig. improve-ment, rise, increase, promotion. **3.** metr. stress(ed syllable).

hecheln ['hɛçəln] v/i (h) pant.

Hecht [hɛçt] m (-[e]s; -e) **1.** zo. pike: F *fig.* *toller* ~ some guy; *er ist (wie) der* ~ *im Karpfenteich* he really stirs things up. **2.** F fug. '**hechten** v/i (h) do a pike-dive, *gym.* do a long-fly, *soccer etc:* dive full-length.

'**Hechtsprung** m pike-dive, *gym.* long-fly, *soccer etc:* (flying) dive.

Heck [hɛk] n (-[e]s; -e, -s) ⚓ stern, *mot.* rear, back, ✈ tail.

'**Heckantrieb** m mot. rear-wheel drive.

Hecke ['hɛkə] f (-; -n) hedge.

'**Hecken|rose** f dogrose. **~schere** f hedge clippers. **~schütze** m sniper.

'**Heckfenster** n mot. rear window. '**Heckklappe** f mot. tailgate. '**heckla-stig** adj ✈, mot. tailheavy. '**Hecklicht** n ✈, mot. taillight. '**Heckmotor** m rear engine. '**Heckscheibe** f mot. rear win-dow. '**Heckscheibenheizung** f rear--window defroster. '**Heckscheiben-wischer** m rear window wiper. **Heckspoiler** m mot. back spoiler.

heda ['he:da] int hey (there).

Hedonismus [hedo'nɪsmʊs] m (-; no pl) hedonism. **Hedonist** [hedo'nɪst] m (-en; -en) hedonist. **hedo'nistisch** adj hedonistic.

Heer [he:r] n (-[e]s; -e) army, fig. host. '**Heeres...** army (*command, group, etc*). '**Heerschar** f fig. host.

Hefe ['he:fə] f (-; -n) **1.** yeast. **2.** fig. dregs. '**Hefeteig** m yeast dough.

Heft¹ [hɛft] n (-[e]s; -e) **1.** ped. exercise book. **2.** number, issue. **3.** booklet.

Heft² n (-[e]s; -e) handle, of dagger etc: hilt: *fig.* *das* ~ *in der Hand haben (be-halten)* hold the rein (stay in control).

Heftchen ['hɛftçən] n (-s; -) book.

heften ['hɛftən] (h) **I** v/t **1.** (*an acc to*) fix, pin. **2.** baste, tack. **3.** print. stitch: *geheftet* in sheets. **II** *sich an j-s Fersen* ~ stick hard on s.o.'s heels; *sich* ~ *auf* (*acc*) *eyes etc:* be fixed (*or* riveted) on.

Hefter ['hɛftər] m (-s; -) file.

'**Heft|faden** m, **~garn** n tacking thread.

heftig ['hɛftɪç] adj **1.** violent, severe, fierce (*argument*), heavy (*rain*), acute (*pain*), splitting (*headache*), heated (*de-bate etc*): *et.* ~ *verteidigen* defend s.th. vehemently. **2.** irascible, vehement: *er wird schnell* ~ he flares up quickly.

'**Heftigkeit** f (-; no pl) **1.** violence, fierce-ness, vehemence. **2.** hot temper.

'**Heft|klammer** f paper clip, ⚙ staple. **~ma‚schine** f ⚙ stapler. **~pflaster** n ⚕ (sticking) plaster. **~zwecke** f drawing pin, *Am.* thumbtack.

Hegemonie [hegemo'ni:] f (-; -n) hege-mony.

hegen ['he:gən] v/t (h) **1.** preserve (*wild-life etc*), tend (*plants*), protect: ~ *und pflegen* a. fig. take loving care of. **2.** fig. have (*doubts, a suspicion, etc*), cher-ish (*hope, love, etc*).

Hehl [he:l] *kein(en)* ~ *machen aus* make no secret of.

Hehler ['he:lər] m (-s; -) ⚖ receiver, *sl.* fence. **Hehle'rei** f (-; -en) ⚖ receiving, *sl.* fencing.

hehr [he:r] adj sublime, noble.

Heide¹ ['haɪdə] m (-n; -n) heathen, pagan.

'**Heide²** f (-; -n) **1.** heath(land). **2.** → '**Heidekraut** n (-[e]s; no pl) 🌿 heather.

Heidelbeere ['haɪdəlˌbe:rə] 🌿 bilberry, *Am.* blueberry.

'**Heiden...** F → *Mords...* '**Heidengeld** n F *ein* ~ a fortune, a packet.

'**Heidentum** n (-s; no pl) heathenism, paganism.

Heidin ['haɪdɪn] f (-; -nen) → *Heide¹*.

heidnisch ['haɪdnɪʃ] adj heathen, pagan.

Heidschnucke ['haɪtˌʃnʊkə] f (-; -n) zo. moorland sheep.

heikel ['haɪkəl] adj **1.** delicate, tricky: *ein heikler Punkt* a sore point. **2.** dial. a) fussy, b) squeamish.

heil [haɪl] adj person: unharmed, safe

and sound, *thing*: undamaged, whole, intact: **wieder ~** a) healed(-up), mended, b) repaired; *fig.* **e-e ~e Welt** an intact world. **Heil** *n* (-s; *no pl*) well--being, good, *eccl.* salvation: **sein ~ versuchen** try one's luck; **sein ~ in der Flucht suchen** take flight, run for it.

Heiland ['haɪlant] *m* (-[e]s; *no pl*) *eccl.* Savio(u)r.

'**Heilanstalt** *f* **1.** sanatorium. **2.** (mental) home.

'**heilbar** *adj* curable.

'**Heilbarkeit** *f* (-; *no pl*) curability.

'**Heilbutt** ['haɪlbʊt] *m* (-[e]s, -e) halibut.

heilen ['haɪlən] **I** *v/t* (h) cure, heal: **j-n ~ von** *a. fig.* cure s.o. of. **II** *v/i* (sn) heal (up). '**heilend** *adj* healing, curative.

'**Heilerde** *f* healing earth.

'**heilfroh** *adj* F **~ sein** be really glad.

heilig ['haɪlɪç] *adj* a) holy, b) sacred (*a. fig.*), c) sacrosanct, d) saintly, pious: **der ~e** (*abbr. hl.*) **Paulus** Saint (*abbr.* St.) Paul; **der ~e Abend** Christmas Eve; **die ~e Jungfrau** the Blessed Virgin; **die ~e Nacht** Holy Night; **der ~e Vater** the Holy Father; **das ~e Land** the Holy Land; *fig.* **~e Kuh** sacred cow; **ihm ist nichts ~** nothing is sacred to him; → **Geist** 3, **Schrift** 2, **Stuhl** 1.

'**Heilige** *m, f* (-n; -n) *a. fig.* saint.

heiligen ['haɪlɪgən] *v/t* (h) **1.** hallow, sanctify; → **Zweck. 2.** → **heilighalten.**

'**Heiligenschein** *m* halo, gloriole.

'**heilighalten** *v/t* (*irr, sep, -ge-*, h, → **halten**) a) hold *s.th.* sacred, b) keep *s.th.* (holy), observe (*Sunday etc*).

'**Heiligkeit** *f* (-; *no pl*) a) holiness, *a. fig.* sacredness, sanctity, b) saintliness: **Seine ~** (*the Pope*) His Holiness.

'**heiligsprechen** *v/t* (*irr, sep, -ge-*, h, → **sprechen**) canonize. '**Heiligsprechung** *f* (-; -en) canonization.

'**Heiligtum** *n* (-s; -*wer*) **1.** shrine. **2.** (sacred) relic, F s.th. sacred: **das ist sein ~!** that's sacred to him!

'**Heiligung** *f* (-; *no pl*) **1.** *a. fig.* sanctification. **2.** observance (*of Sunday etc*).

'**Heilklima** *n* healthy climate.

'**Heilkraft** *f* healing power(s).

'**heilkräftig** *adj* curative.

'**Heilkunde** *f* (-; *no pl*) medicine.

'**heillos** *adj* F hopeless, unholy (*mess etc*), *a.* frightful (*scare etc*).

'**Heil|me,thode** *f* cure, treatment. **~mit-**

tel *n* (**gegen** for) a) *a. fig.* cure, remedy, b) medicine. **~päda,gogik** *f* therapeutic pedagogy. **~pflanze** *f* medicinal herb. **~praktiker(in** *f*) *m* nonmedical practitioner. **~quelle** *f* mineral spring.

'**heilsam** *adj a. fig.* salutary, healthy: **~ sein (für)** *a.* be good (for).

'**Heilsar,mee** *f* Salvation Army.

'**Heilschlaf** *m* ✄ hypnotherapy.

'**Heilserum** *n* ✄ antiserum.

'**Heilung** *f* (-; -en) a) (**von** of) curing, cure (*a. fig.*), b) healing, c) recovery.

'**Heilungs|aussichten** *pl* chances of recovery. **~pro,zeß** *m* healing process.

'**Heilverfahren** *n* treatment, therapy.

'**Heilwirkung** *f* therapeutic effect.

heim [haɪm] *adv* home.

Heim *n* (-[e]s; -e) **1.** *no pl* home. **2.** home, hostel. '**Heimarbeit** *f* homework.

'**Heimarbeiter(in** *f*) *m* homeworker.

Heimat ['haɪmaːt] *f* (-; *no pl*) home (*a. fig.*), ✄, *zo.* habitat: **zweite ~** second home, F home from home; **in der ~** at home; **in m-r ~** *a.* where I come from. **~dichtung** *f* regional literature. **~film** *m* (sentimental) film with a regional background. **~hafen** *m* ⚓ home port. **~kunde** *f* (-; *no pl*) *ped.* local studies. **~land** *n* home country.

'**heimatlich** *adj* a) home, native, b) homelike, *pred* like home, *Am.* hom(e)y. '**heimatlos** *adj* homeless.

'**Heimat|mu,seum** *n* museum of local history. **~ort** *m* home town (*or village*). **~stadt** *f* home town. **~vertriebene** *m, f* (-n; -n) expellee.

'**heimbegleiten** *v/t* (*sep*, h) **j-n ~** see s.o. home.

Heimchen ['haɪmçən] *n* (-s; -) *zo.* (house) cricket.

'**Heimcom,puter** *m* home computer.

heimelig ['haɪməlɪç] *adj* cosy, F hom(e)y.

'**heimfahren** *v/i* (*irr, sep, -ge-*, sn, → **fahren**) go home, (*a. v/t*) drive home.

'**Heimfahrt** *f* journey home.

'**heimfinden** *v/i* (*irr, sep, -ge-*, h, → **finden**) find one's way home.

'**heimgehen** *v/i* (*irr, sep, -ge-*, sn, → **gehen**) **1.** go home. **2.** pass away, die.

'**Heimindu,strie** *f* cottage industry.

'**heimisch** *adj* a) domestic, home, b) ✄, *zo.* native, indigenous, c) inland: **~e Gewässer** home waters; **~ sein in** (*dat*) *a. fig.* be at home in; **~ werden** settle (down), become acclimatized (*in dat* to); *sich ~ fühlen* feel at home.

Heimkehr ['haimke:r] *f* (-; *no pl*) return (home). **'heimkehren** *v/i* (*sep*, -ge-, sn) return home, come back. **'Heimkehrer** *m* (-s; -) homecomer, *pol.* repatriate.

'Heimkind *n* institution child.

'Heimkino *n* home movies.

'heimkommen *v/i* (*irr, sep*, -ge-, sn, → *kommen*) return (*or* come, get) home.

'Heimleiter(in *f*) *m* head of a home (*or* hostel).

'heimleuchten *v/t* (*sep*, -ge-, h) F *j-m ~* send s.o. packing.

'heimlich I *adj* a) secret, b) clandestine, c) furtive. **II** *adv* secretly (*etc*), in secret, (*a.* **~, still und leise**) F on the quiet. **'Heimlichkeit** *f* (-; -en) **1.** *no pl* secrecy, furtiveness. **2.** *pl* secrets.

Heimlichtue'rei *f* (-; *no pl*) secretiveness.

'heimlichtun *v/i* (*irr, sep*, -ge-, h, → *tun*) be secretive (*mit* about).

'Heimmannschaft *f* sports: home team.

'Heimniederlage *f* sports: home defeat.

'Heimorgel *f* ♪ electric organ.

'Heimreise *f* journey home: *auf der ~* on the way home. **'heimreisen** *v/i* (*sep*, -ge-, sn) go (*or* travel) home.

'Heimsieg *m* sports: home victory.

'Heimspiel *n* sports: home game.

'Heimstärke *f* sports: home strength.

'Heimstätte *f a. fig.* home.

'heimsuchen *v/t* (*sep*, -ge-, h) **1.** strike, visit (*a. bibl.*), plague, afflict, *premonitions etc*, *a. ghost:* haunt: *heimgesucht von* struck (*etc*) by; *von Dürre (Krieg) heimgesucht* drought-ridden (war-torn). **2.** F descend on. **'Heimsuchung** *f* (-; -en) visitation, affliction, trial.

'Heimtrainer *m* home exerciser.

'Heimtücke *f* (-; *no pl*) perfidy, treachery. **'heimtückisch** *adj* insidious (*a.* ♪), treacherous.

'Heimvorteil *m* sports: home advantage.

heimwärts ['haimvɛrts] *adv* homeward(s), home.

'Heimweg *m* way home.

'Heimweh *n* (-[e]s; *no pl*) homesickness: *~ haben* be homesick (*nach* for).

Heimwerker ['haimvɛrkər] *m* (-s; -) do-it-yourselfer, home mechanic. **Heimwerker...** do-it-yourself (*kit etc*).

'heimzahlen *v/t* (*sep*, -ge-, h) *j-m et. ~* repay s.o. for s.th.

'heimzu *adv* F on the way home.

Heini ['haini] *m* (-s; -s) F *contp.* twerp.

Heinzelmännchen ['haintsəlmɛnçən] *n* (-s; -) brownie.

Heirat ['haira:t] *f* (-; -en) marriage.

heiraten ['haira:tən] *v/t, v/i* (h) *(j-n) ~* marry (s.o.), get married (to s.o.).

'Heirats|an,nonce *f* marriage ad. **~antrag** *m* (marriage) proposal: *e-n ~ machen* propose (*dat* to). **~anzeige** *f* **1.** marriage announcement. **2.** marriage ad. ♀fähig *adj* marriageable: *im ~en Alter* of marriageable age. **~markt** *m* marriage market. **~schwindler** *m* marriage impostor. **~urkunde** *f* marriage certificate. **~vermittlung** *f* **1.** marriage brokerage. **2.** marriage bureau.

heiser ['haizər] *adj* hoarse.

'Heiserkeit *f* (-; *no pl*) hoarseness.

heiß [hais] **I** *adj* **1.** hot, *fig. a.* a) ardent, passionate, b) fierce (*battle etc*), heated (*discussion etc*): *~e Zone* torrid zone; *et. ~ machen* heat s.th. up; *mir ist (wird) ~* I'm (getting) hot; → *Draht, Eisen, Hölle, Ofen* **2.** F *fig.* hot: *~e Ware* hot goods; *~er Tip* hot tip. **II** *adv* **3.** hotly (*etc*): *et. ~ ersehnen* long for s.th. (fervently); *sich ~ und innig lieben* adore each other; → *hergehen*.

'heißblütig [-bly:tiç] *adj* hot-blooded, passionate.

heißen ['haisən] (hieß, geheißen, h) **I** *v/i* **1.** be called (*nach* after): *wie ~ Sie?* what's your name?; *wie heißt das?* a) what's that called?, b) *auf Englisch?* what's that (called) in English. **2.** *text:* read, be. **3.** mean: *was heißt das?*, *was soll das ~?* a) what does it mean?, b) what do you mean (by this)?, c) what's the (big) idea?; *das hieße, das würde ~* that would mean; *das will (et)was ~!* that's saying something!; *das will nichts ~!* that doesn't mean a thing!; *soll das ~, daß ...?* do you mean to say that ...?; *das soll nicht ~, daß* that doesn't mean that; *das heißt* that is (*abbr.* i.e.). **II** *v/impers* **4.** es heißt, daß they say that; *in dem Brief heißt es, daß* the letter says that. **5.** *jetzt heißt es handeln!* now it's time to act! **III** *v/t* **6.** call. **7.** *j-n et. tun ~* tell s.o. to do s.th.; → *willkommen*.

'heißersehnt adj longed-for.
'heißgeliebt adj dearly loved.
'Heißhunger m ☞ b(o)ulimia, a. fig. (sudden) craving (**nach** for).
'heißlaufen v/i (irr, sep, -ge-, sn, → **laufen**) (a. **sich ~** [h]) ⊕ overheat, F tele-phone lines: be buzzing.
'Heißluft... hot-air ...
'heißumkämpft adj fiercely embattled.
'heißumstritten adj **1.** highly controversial. **2.** hotly debated.
heiter ['haɪtər] adj **1.** a) cheerful, gay, b) serene, c) funny, amusing: F iro. (**das**) **kann ja ~ werden!** nice prospects! **2.** bright, sunny: → **Himmel. 3.** ♪ scherzando. **'Heiterkeit** f (-; no pl) **1.** a) cheerfulness, b) serenity: **~ erregen** cause amusement. **2.** brightness.
'Heizanlage f heating system.
'heizbar adj heatable, with heating.
'Heizdecke f electric blanket.
'Heizele,ment n heating element.
heizen ['haɪtsən] (h) **I** v/t heat (room etc), fire (stove). **II** v/i put (or have) the heating on.
Heizer m (-s; -) boilerman, ♻, 🚂 stoker.
'Heizgas n fuel gas. **'Heizgerät** n heater.
'Heizkessel m boiler. **'Heizkissen** n electric pad. **'Heizkörper** m radiator, ⚡ heater. **'Heizkosten** pl heating costs. **'Heizlüfter** m fan heater. **'Heizmateri,al** n fuel. **'Heizöl** n (fuel) oil.
'Heizung f (-; -en) **1.** (central) heating. **2.** → **Heizkörper.**
'Heizungsanlage f heating system.
'Heizungsmon,teur m heating engineer.
Hektar ['hɛkta:r] n, m (-s; -e) hectare.
Hektik ['hɛktɪk] f (-; no pl) a) hectic atmosphere, mad rush, b) nervy state: F **nur k-e ~!** take it easy!
'hektisch adj hectic.
Hektoliter ['hɛktoliːtər] m, n hectolit/re (Am. -er).
Held [hɛlt] m (-en; -en) hero.
'heldenhaft ['hɛldən-] adj heroic.
'Heldensage f saga. **'Heldentat** f heroic deed. **'Heldente,nor** m ♪ heroic tenor.
'Heldentum n (-s; no pl) heroism.
'Heldenverehrung f hero worship.
'Heldin ['hɛldɪn] f (-; -nen) heroine.
helfen ['hɛlfən] v/i (half, geholfen, h) **1.** (dat) help, assist, aid, lend s.o. a hand: **j-m bei et. ~** help s.o. with s.th.; **j-m aus dem (in den) Mantel ~** help s.o. off (on)

with his etc coat; fig. **j-m aus e-r Verlegenheit ~** help s.o. out of a difficulty; **ihm ist nicht zu ~** there is no help for him, iro. he's hopeless; **er weiß sich zu ~** a) he can look after himself, b) he is resourceful; **sich nicht mehr zu ~ wissen** be at one's wits' end; **ich kann mir nicht ~** a) I can't help it, b) **...**, **ich muß einfach lachen** I can't help laughing. **2.** help: **das half** that worked; **das hilft gegen Schnupfen** that's good for colds; **das hilft mir wenig!** that's not much help!, F a fat lot it helps!; **es hilft nichts** it's no use; **da hilft kein Jammern!** it's no use complaining!; **da hilft nur eines** there's only one thing for it.
'Helfer m (-s; -), **'Helferin** f (-; -nen) helper, assistant: **ein Helfer in der Not** a friend in need.
'Helfershelfer(in f) m accomplice.
Helium ['he:li̯ʊm] n (-s; no pl) 🧪 helium.
hell [hɛl] adj **1.** light, bright (sunshine etc), fair (hair, complexion, etc), light-colo(u)red (clothes), clear (voice etc): **~es Bier** lager; **~es Blau** light blue; fig. **~es Gelächter** loud laughter; **es wird schon ~** it is getting light already. **2.** fig. bright, intelligent. **3.** F great, utter (nonsense etc), pure (envy etc): **~er Wahnsinn** sheer madness; **~ begeistert** (absolutely) enthusiastic.
'hellblond adj very fair.
helle ['hɛlə] adj pred F bright, intelligent.
'Helle¹ f, n (-; no pl) brightness, (bright) light. **'Helle²** n (-n; -n) F (glass of) beer (Br. lager): **zwei ~!** two beers!
Heller ['hɛlər] m (-s; -) F **k-n (roten) ~ wert** not worth a cent; **auf ~ und Pfennig** to the last penny.
'hellgrün adj light-green.
'hellhörig adj **1.** fig. **das machte ihn ~** that made him prick up his ears. **2.** poorly soundproofed.
'hellicht ['hɛlɪçt] adj **am ~en Tage** in broad daylight.
Helligkeit ['hɛlɪçkaɪt] f (-; no pl) brightness (a. TV), light, phys. luminosity.
Helling ['hɛlɪŋ] f (-; -en) ♻ slip(way), (building) cradle.
'hellrot adj light-red.
'hellsehen v/i (only inf) have second sight, be clairvoyant. **'Hellsehen** n (-s) clairvoyance. **'Hellseher(in** f) m, **'hellseherisch** adj clairvoyant.

'hell'wach *adj a. fig.* wide-awake.
Helm [hɛlm] *m* (-[e]s; -e) helmet.
Hemd [hɛmt] *n* (-[e]s; -en) a) shirt, b) vest, *Am.* undershirt: *fig.* **j-n bis aufs ~ ausziehen** fleece s.o.
'**Hemdbluse** *f* shirt.
'**Hemdblusenkleid** *n* shirtwaister.
'**Hemdsärmel** *m* shirtsleeve: *in ~n* in (one's) shirtsleeves. '**hemdsärm(e)lig** [-ɛrm(ə)lɪç] *adj a. fig.* shirtsleeve.
Hemisphäre [hemi'sfɛːrə] *f* (-; -n) hemisphere.
hemmen ['hɛmən] *v/t* (h) **1.** *a. fig. a.* stop, check, b) hinder, impede. **2.** *psych.* inhibit: → **gehemmt**.
Hemmnis ['hɛmnɪs] *n* (-ses;-se) obstacle.
'**Hemmschuh** *m fig.* drag (**für** on).
'**Hemmung** *f* (-; -en) **1.** hindrance, check. **2.** *psych.* inhibition, *w.s.* scruple: *~en haben* be inhibited; *nur k-e ~en!* don't be shy! **3.** ⚙ stop, escapement (*of watch*). '**hemmungslos** *adj* **1.** unrestrained, uncontrollable (*weeping etc*). **2.** unscrupulous. '**Hemmungslosigkeit** *f* (-; *no pl*) **1.** lack of restraint, recklessness. **2.** unscrupulousness.
Hengst [hɛŋst] *m* (-[e]s; -e) a) stallion, b) stud. '**Hengstfohlen** *n* colt.
Henkel ['hɛŋkəl] *m* (-s; -) handle.
henken ['hɛŋkən] *v/t* (h) hang.
'**Henker** *m* (-s; -) executioner: F *wer* (*wo etc*) *zum ~?* who (where *etc*) the hell?
Henna ['hɛna] *n* (-; *no pl*) henna.
Henne ['hɛna] *f* (-; -n) *zo.* hen.
Hepatitis [hepa'tiːtɪs] *f* (-; -titiden [-tiˈtiːdən] ⚕ hepatitis.
her [heːr] *adv* **1.** ago: *wie lange ist es ~?* how long ago was it?; *das ist lange ~* that was a long time ago; *es ist ein Jahr ~, daß ...* it's a year since ... **2.** *von ... ~* from; *von oben ~* from above; *von weit ~* from afar; *um mich ~* around me; *~ damit!* give (it) to me)!; → *herhaben etc*, *hinter* I. **3.** *fig. von ... ~* from the point of view of; *vom Technischen ~* from a technical point of view, technically (speaking).
herab [hɛˈrap] *adv* down: *fig. von oben ~* condescendingly.
her'ab... down; → *a. herunter*.
her'abgehen, her'abhängen, her'abkommen → *heruntergehen etc.*
her'ablassen (*irr, sep, -ge -, h, ›* **lassen**) **I** *v/t* let down, lower. **II** *fig. sich ~*

zu antworten *etc* deign to answer *etc.*
her'ablassend *adj* condescending (*zu* towards). **Her'ablassung** *f* (-; *no pl*) condescension.
her'absehen *v/i* (*irr, sep, -ge-, h, →* **sehen**) *~ auf* (*acc*) *a. fig.* look down on.
her'absetzen *v/t* (*sep, -ge-, h*) **1.** reduce, lower, cut (back): (*im Preis*) *~* reduce (in price); *zu herabgesetzten Preisen* at reduced prices, cut-price ... **2.** *fig.* disparage, belittle.
her'absetzend *adj fig.* disparaging.
Her'absetzung *f* (-; -en) **1.** reduction, cut. **2.** *fig.* disparagement.
her'absteigen *v/i* (*irr, sep, -ge-, sn, →* **steigen**) **1.** descend, climb (*or come*) down. **2.** dismount.
her'abwürdigen *v/t* (h) degrade (*sich* o.s.).
Heraldik [heˈraldɪk] *f* (-; *no pl*) heraldry.
heran [hɛˈran] *adv* near, close: *~ an* (*acc*) up to; *nur ~!* come closer!
her'anbilden *v/t* (*sep, -ge-, h*) (*a. sich ~*) train (*zu* to be).
her'anbringen *v/t* (*irr, sep, -ge-, h, →* **bringen**) bring up (*an acc* to).
her'anführen *v/t* (*sep, -ge-, h*) lead (*or* bring) up (*an acc* to): *fig. j-n an et. ~* introduce s.o. to s.th.
her'angehen *v/i* (*irr, sep, -ge-, sn, →* **gehen**) *~ an* (*acc*) a) go up to, b) *fig.* approach, tackle (*a task etc*).
her'anholen *v/t* (*sep, -ge-, h*) **1.** fetch, get. **2.** *phot.* zoom in on.
her'ankämpfen: *sich ~* (*sep, -ge-, h*) (*an acc*) *sports*: close in (on), pull up (to).
her'ankommen *v/i* (*irr, sep, -ge-, sn, →* **kommen**) **1.** draw near, approach. **2.** *~ an* (*acc*) a) come up to (*a. fig.*), approach, come near (*a standard etc*), b) get at, get hold of; *er* (*es*) *kommt nicht an ... heran a.* he (it) can't touch ...; *fig. an j-n ~* get through to s.o.; *die Sache* (*or es*) *an sich ~ lassen* wait and see.
her'anmachen: *sich ~* (*sep, -ge-, h*) (*an acc*) F a) set to work (on), b) sidle up (to *s.o.*): *fig. sich an j-n ~* a) approach s.o., b) make up to s.o., c) start working on s.o.
her'anreichen *v/i* (*sep, -ge-, h*) *~ an* (*acc*) come up to, *fig. a.* touch.
her'anreifen *v/i* (*sep, -ge-, sn*) (*zu* into) ripen, *fig. plan etc*: *a.* mature, *person*: *a.* grow up.

her'anrücken v/i (sep, -ge-, sn) **1.** come close(r) (**an** acc to): **an j-n ~** move up (close) to s.o. **2.** draw near, approach.

her'antreten v/i (irr, sep, -ge-, sn, → **treten**) **an j-n ~** go up to s.o., a. fig. approach s.o., fig. confront s.o.

her'anwachsen v/i (irr, sep, -ge-, sn, → **wachsen**) grow up: **~ zu** grow into.

Her'anwachsende m, f (-n; -n) young person, adolescent.

her'anwagen: sich ~ (sep, -ge-, h) (**an** acc) venture near, dare to approach (s.o.), fig. dare to tackle (a task etc).

her'anziehen (irr, sep, -ge-, → **ziehen**) **I** v/t (h) **1.** pull s.th. up (**an** acc to). **2.** a) raise, b) train. **3.** **j-n** (**zu**) call on s.o. (to do s.th.), enlist s.o.('s services) (for s.th.); **e-n Fachmann ~** call in an expert. **4.** cite, invoke. **II** v/i (sn) **5.** draw near, approach.

herauf [hɛ'raʊf] adv up, upwards: (**hier**) **~** up here; **den Berg ~** up the hill, uphill; **den Fluß ~** up the river, upstream; **die Treppe ~** up the stairs, upstairs; in cpds. → a. **empor...**

her'aufbeschwören v/t (irr, sep, h, → **beschwören**) **1.** conjure up (memories etc). **2.** bring on (disaster etc).

her'aufkommen v/i (irr, sep, -ge-, sn, → **kommen**) come up (**zu** to).

her'aufsetzen v/t (sep, -ge-, h) raise.

her'aufsteigen v/i (irr, sep, -ge-, sn, → **steigen**) climb, mount (stairs etc).

her'aufziehen (irr, sep, -ge-, → **ziehen**) **I** v/t (h) pull s.o., s.th. up. **II** v/i (sn) draw near, approach.

heraus [hɛ'raʊs] adv out (**aus** of): **zum Fenster ~** out of the window; fig. **aus e-m Gefühl der Verlassenheit** etc **~** from (or out of) a sense of loneliness etc; **~ damit!** out with it!; **~ mit der Sprache!** F spit it out!; F **jetzt ist es ~!** now the secret's out!

her'ausarbeiten (sep, -ge-, h) **I** v/t a. fig. work out. **II sich ~ aus** work one's way out of, fig. a. manage to get out of.

her'ausbekommen v/t (irr, sep, h, → **bekommen**) **1.** get stain etc out (**aus** of). **2.** fig. a) F work out, solve, figure out, get, b) find s.th. out: **et. aus j-m ~** get s.th. out of s.o. **3. Sie bekommen noch 10 Mark heraus** you get ten marks change.

her'ausbringen v/t (irr, sep, -ge-, h, →

bringen) **1.** bring out (a. fig.), print. a. publish, thea. produce: **sie brachte kein Wort heraus** she couldn't say a word; **j-n** (**et.**) **groß ~** give s.o. (s.th.) a big buildup.

her'ausfahren (irr, sep, -ge-, → **fahren**) **I** v/i (sn) **1.** come (or drive) out (**aus** of). **2.** remark etc: slip out. **II** v/t (h) **3.** drive out (**aus** of): sports: **er hat e-e gute Zeit** (**den Sieg**) **herausgefahren** he made good time (won the race).

her'ausfallen v/i (irr, sep, -ge-, sn, → **fallen**) (**aus** of) fall out, drop out.

her'ausfiltern v/t (sep, -ge-, h) a. fig. filter out.

her'ausfinden (irr, sep, -ge-, h, → **finden**) **I** v/t a) find, b) find out, discover. **II** v/i find one's way out (**aus** of).

Her'ausforderer m (-s; -) challenger, pol. rival (candidate). **her'ausfordern** (sep, -ge-, h) **I** v/t challenge, defy, provoke: **das Schicksal ~** court disaster, F ask for it; **Kritik** (**Protest**) **~** → **II**. **II** v/i **zur Kritik** (**zum Protest**) **~** invite (or provoke) criticism (protest). **her'ausfordernd** adj challenging, defiant, provocative. **Her'ausforderung** f (-; -en) challenge (a. fig.), provocation.

Her'ausgabe f (-; no pl) **1.** surrender, delivery. **2.** print. editing, publication. **her'ausgeben** (irr, sep, -ge-, h, → **geben**) **I** v/t **1.** (dat to) hand s.th. over, give s.th. back, return. **2.** a) publish, b) edit, c) issue (stamps, a. rules etc). **3. j-m zehn Mark ~** give s.o. ten marks change. **II** v/i **4.** (**j-m**) **~** give (s.o.) change (**auf** acc for). **Her'ausgeber(in** f) m a) publisher, b) editor.

her'ausgehen v/i (irr, sep, -ge-, sn, → **gehen**) **1. ~ hinausgehen** 1; fig. **aus sich ~** come out of one's shell. **2.** stain etc: come out (**aus** of).

her'ausgreifen v/t (irr, sep, -ge-, h, → **greifen**) a) pick out, b) cite (examples).

her'aushaben v/t (irr, sep, -ge-, h, → **haben**) F fig. have found s.th. out, have got, have solved (problem etc): **er hat es heraus** he has got the hang of it.

her'aushalten v/t (irr, sep, -ge-, h, → **halten**) F **j-n** (**sich**) **aus der Sache ~** keep s.o. (o.s.) out of it.

her'ausheben v/t (irr, sep, -ge-, h, → **heben**) **1.** lift (or take) s.o., s.th. out (**aus** of). **2.** → **hervorheben**.

her'aushelfen *v/i (irr, sep, -ge-, h, →* *helfen) j-m ~* help s.o. out (**aus** of).

her'ausholen *v/t (sep, -ge-, h) a. fig.* get *s.o., s.th.* out (**aus** of): **das Letzte aus sich ~** make a supreme effort.

her'aushören *v/t (sep, -ge-, h)* hear, *fig.* detect (**aus** in *s.o.'s words etc*).

her'auskehren *v/t (sep, -ge-, h) fig.* act, play *the expert etc,* show, display.

her'auskommen *v/i (irr, sep, -ge-, sn, →* *kommen)* **1.** (**aus**) emerge (from), come out (of), *a. fig.* get out (of): **er kam aus dem Lachen nicht heraus** he couldn't stop laughing; F **groß ~** be a great success. **2.** *fig.* come out, *book: a.* be published, *stamps etc:* be issued: ↑ **mit e-m neuen Modell ~** come out with a new model; F **~ mit** come out with, admit. **3.** (**aus** of) a) ↕ be the result, b) *fig.* come out (out): **es kommt nichts dabei heraus** it doesn't pay; **es kommt auf eins** (*or* **dasselbe**) **heraus** it boils down to the same thing; → *a. herausspringen 2.*

her'auskristalli,sieren *v/t (sep, -ge-, h)* (*a. sich ~*) *a. fig.* crystallize (**aus** out of).

her'auslassen *v/t (irr, sep, -ge-, →* *lassen)* let out (**aus** of).

her'auslaufen *(irr, sep, -ge-, →* *laufen) I* *v/i* (sn) run out (**aus** of). **II** *v/t* (h) *sports:* gain (*lead, victory, etc*).

her'auslocken *v/t (sep, -ge-, h)* **1.** *j-n ~* lure s.o. out (**aus** of). **2.** *et. aus j-m ~* draw (*or* worm) s.th. out of s.o.

her'ausmachen: *sich ~ (sep, -ge-, h) fig.* be coming on well.

her'ausnehmen *v/t (irr, sep, -ge-, h, →* *nehmen)* (**aus**) take *s.o., s.th.* out (of), remove (from): *fig.* **sich Freiheiten ~** take liberties (**gegenüber** with).

her'ausplatzen *v/i (sep, -ge-, sn)* F **1.** burst out laughing. **2.** *~ mit* blurt out.

her'ausputzen *v/t (sep, -ge-, h)* (**sich**) ~ dress (o.s.) up, F spruce (o.s.) up.

her'ausragen *v/i (sep, -ge-, h)* (**aus** from) a) jut out, b) *fig.* stand out.

her'ausragend *adj fig.* outstanding.

her'ausreden: *sich ~ (sep, -ge-, h)* talk one's way out (**aus** of).

her'ausreißen *v/t (irr, sep, -ge-, h, →* *reißen)* **1.** pull (*or* tear) out. **2.** *fig.* *j-n ~ aus* tear s.o. away from (*surroundings etc*), rouse s.o. from (*sleep etc*),

interrupt s.o. in (*one's work etc*); F *j-n ~ performance etc:* save s.o.

her'ausrücken *(sep, -ge-)* F **I** *v/t* (h) → **II** b. **II** *v/i* (sn) **~ mit** a) come out with, b) fork out, cough up (*money*); **mit der Sprache ~** talk, come out with it.

her'ausrutschen *v/i (sep, -ge-, sn)* F *fig.* slip out: **das ist mir einfach so herausgerutscht** it just slipped out.

her'ausschinden *v/t (irr, sep, -ge-, h, →* *schinden)* manage to get (**aus** out of).

her'ausschlagen *v/t (irr, sep, -ge-, h, →* *schlagen)* (**aus** of) **1.** knock s.th. out. **2.** F get s.th. out: **Geld ~ aus** make money out of; **möglichst viel ~** make the most of it.

her'ausschneiden *v/t (irr, sep, -ge-, h, →* *schneiden)* cut s.th. out (**aus** of).

her'aussehen *v/i (irr, sep, -ge-, h, →* *sehen)* look out (**aus** of).

her'ausspringen *v/i (irr, sep, -ge-, sn, →* *springen)* **1.** jump out (**aus** of). **2.** F *fig.* be gained (**bei** by): **was springt für Sie dabei heraus?** what's in it for you?

her'ausstellen *v/t (sep, -ge-, h)* **1.** put s.th. out(side). **2.** *fig.* a) point out, b) emphasize, underline: **groß ~** highlight, feature (*a. thea.*). **3.** → *hinausstellen 2.* **II** *sich ~* turn out (**als** to be), come to light: **es stellte sich heraus, daß sie recht hatte** she turned out to be right.

her'ausstrecken *v/t (sep, -ge-, h)* stick out (**aus** of): → **Zunge.**

her'ausstreichen *v/t (irr, sep, -ge-, h, →* *streichen)* **1.** cross out (**aus** of). **2.** *fig.* praise *s.o., s.th.* (to the skies).

her'aussuchen *v/t (sep, -ge-, h)* (**aus**) choose (from), pick out (of).

her'auswinden: *sich ~ (irr, sep, -ge-, h, →* *winden)* wriggle out (**aus** of).

herb [hɛrp] *adj* **1.** sour, tart, dry (*wine*), tangy (*smell*). **2.** *fig.* harsh (*words, criticism, etc*), bitter (*disappointment, loss, etc*), austere (*beauty, style, etc*).

herbei [hɛr'baɪ] *adv* here, up, over; → *a.* **her...,** **heran... herbeieilen** *v/i (sep, -ge-, sn)* come running up.

her'beiführen *v/t (sep, -ge-, h) fig.* bring about, cause, lead to, *esp.* ✍ induce.

her'beilassen: *sich ~ (irr, sep, -ge-, h, →* *lassen)* condescend (**zu** to).

her'beischaffen *v/t (sep, -ge-, h)* bring (up), fetch, get.

her'beisehnen *v/t (sep, -ge-, h)* long for.

'**herbemühen** (*sep*, h) **I** *v/t* j-n ~ ask s.o. to come (here). **II** *sich* ~ take the trouble to come.

Herberge ['hɛrbɛrgə] *f* (-; -n) youth hostel. '**Herbergsmutter** *f*, '**Herbergsvater** *m* (hostel) warden.

'**herbeten** *v/t* (*sep*, -ge-, h) rattle off.

'**Herbheit** *f* (-; *no pl*) **1.** sourness, *of wine*: dryness. **2.** *fig.* austerity.

'**herbitten** *v/t* (*irr, sep*, -ge-, h, → *bitten*) j-n ~ ask s.o. to come.

'**herbringen** *v/t* (*irr, sep*, -ge-, h, → *bringen*) bring *s.o., s.th.* (along).

Herbst [hɛrpst] *m* (-[e]s; -e) autumn, *Am. a.* fall. '**Herbstfärbung** *f* autumnal tints. '**Herbstferien** *pl* autumn break. '**herbstlich** *adj* autumn(al). '**Herbstzeitlose** *f* (-; -n) ♀ meadow saffron.

Herd [hɛrt] *m* (-[e]s; -e) **1.** a) (kitchen) stove, cooker, b) oven. **2.** *fig.* hearth. **3.** *fig.* cent|re (*Am.* -er), seat, focus (*a.* ✷).

Herde ['hɛrdə] *f* (-; -n) **1.** herd, flock. **2.** *fig. contp.* the (common) herd.

'**Herdentier** *n zo.* gregarious animal: *fig. contp.* **ein ~ sein** follow the herd.

'**Herdentrieb** *m a. fig.* herd instinct.

'**Herdplatte** *f* hotplate.

herein [hɛˈraɪn] *adv zo*: **von draußen ~** from outside; **~!** come in!; → *a.* **ein...**, **hinein...**, F **rein...**

her'einbekommen *v/t* (*irr, sep*, h, → *bekommen*) F ✝ get *s.th.* in.

her'einbitten *v/t* (*irr, sep*, -ge-, h, → *bitten*) j-n ~ ask s.o. (to come) in.

her'einbrechen *v/i* (*irr, sep*, -ge-, sn, → *brechen*) *night*: fall, *storm*: break, *winter*: set in: **~ über** (*acc*) *misfortune etc*: befall.

her'einbringen *v/t* (*irr, sep*, -ge-, h, → *bringen*) bring in, get in.

her'einfallen *v/i* (*irr, sep*, -ge-, sn, → *fallen*) F *fig.* **~ auf** (*acc*) be taken in by (*or* fall for) *s.o., s.th.*; **~ mit** make a (bad) mistake with.

her'einführen *v/t* (*sep*, -ge-, h) j-n ~ show s.o. in(to **in** *acc*).

her'einholen *v/t* (*sep*, -ge-, h) **1.** bring *s.o., s.th.* in. **2.** ✝ get (in *orders*).

her'einkommen *v/i* (*irr, sep*, -ge-, sn, → *kommen*) a) come in (*a.* ✝ *orders*), b) get in: **~ in** (*acc*) come into (*or* inside).

her'einlassen *v/t* (*irr, sep*, -ge-, h, → *lassen*) let *s.o., s.th.* in.

her'einlegen *v/t* (*sep*, -ge-, h) F *fig.* j-n ~

take s.o. for a ride, take s.o. in; **man hat uns hereingelegt** we have been had.

her'einplatzen *v/i* (*sep*, -ge-, sn) F burst in(to **in** *acc*).

her'einschauen *v/i* (*sep*, -ge-, h) F (**bei** j-m) ~ drop by (at s.o.'s place).

her'einschneien *v/i* (*sep*, -ge-, sn) F *fig.* (**bei** j-m) ~ blow in (at s.o.'s place).

'**herfahren** (*irr, sep*, -ge-, → *fahren*) **I** *v/i* (sn) travel (*or* come, drive) here: **hinter** j-m ~ drive behind s.o., follow s.o.'s car. **II** *v/t* (h) j-n ~ drive s.o. here.

'**Herfahrt** *f* (**auf der ~** on the) journey (*or* way) here.

'**herfallen** *v/i* (*irr, sep*, -ge-, sn, → *fallen*) **~ über** (*acc*) fall upon, attack.

'**herfinden** *v/i* (*irr, sep*, -ge-, h, → *finden*) find one's way.

'**herführen** *v/t* (*sep*, -ge-, h) j-n ~ bring s.o. here; **was führt Sie her?** what brings you here?

'**Hergang** *m* (-[e]s; *no pl*) course of events, *the* way s.th. happened, *the* circumstances: **schildern Sie** (**mir**) **den** ~! tell me what (*or* how it) happened!

'**hergeben** *v/t* (*irr, sep*, -ge-, h, → *geben*) *et.* ~ hand s.th. over, give s.th. away; *et.* **wieder** ~ give s.th. back; **gib** (**es**) **her!** give (it to me)!; **sich** (*or* **s-n Namen**) ~ lend one's name (**zu, für** to).

'**hergehen** *v/impers* (*irr, sep*, -ge-, h, → *gehen*) **es ging hoch** (**heiß**) **her** things were pretty lively (the sparks flew).

'**herhaben** *v/t* (-s; -e-) h, → *haben*) F **wo hast du das her?** a) where did you get that (from)?, b) *fig.* who told you that?

'**herhalten** *v/i* (*irr, sep*, -ge-, h, → *halten*) F **~ müssen** a) have to suffer (for it), b) have to serve (**als** as).

'**herholen** *v/t* (*sep*, -ge-, h) fetch: *fig.* **weit hergeholt** far-fetched.

Hering ['heːrɪŋ] *m* (-s; -e) **1.** *zo.* herring: *humor.* **wie die ~e** packed like sardines. **2.** tent peg.

'**herkommen** *v/i* (*irr, sep*, -ge-, sn, → *kommen*) come (here): **komm her!** come here!; *fig.* **~ von** come from; **wo kommen Sie her?** where do you come from?

herkömmlich ['hɛːrkœmlɪç] *adj* conventional, customary, traditional.

Herkunft ['hɛːrkʊnft] *f* (-; *no pl*) origin, *of person*: *a.* birth, descent, *w.s.* origins, background: *er ist deutscher ~* he is of German extraction.

'Herkunftsland n country of origin.

'herlaufen v/i (irr, sep, -ge-, sn, → *laufen*) run here: *hinter j-m ~ a. fig.* run after s.o.

'herleiten v/t (sep, -ge-, h) (a. *sich*) ~ *von* derive from.

'hermachen: sich ~ (sep, -ge-, h) F (*über acc*) set about, tackle (*task etc*), attack (*food, fig. s.o.*).

Hermelin [hɛrmə'liːn] (-s; -e) **1.** n zo. ermine. **2.** m ermine (fur).

hermetisch [hɛr'meːtɪʃ] adj hermetic.

'hernehmen v/t (irr, sep, -ge-, h, → *nehmen*) (*von*) from) take, get.

hernieder [hɛr'niːdər] → *herab(...)*, *herunter(...)*.

Heroin [hero'iːn] n (-s; no pl) heroin.

Hero'insüchtig adj heroin-addicted.

Hero'insüchtige m, f heroin addict.

heroisch [he'roːɪʃ] adj heroic.

Heroismus [hero'ɪsmʊs] m (-; no pl) heroism. **Heros** ['heːrɔs] m (-; Heroen [he'roːən]) adj heroic.

Herr [hɛr] m (-en; -en) a) gentleman, b) master, c) ruler (*über acc* over, of): *mein ~!* Sir!; *m-e ~en!* gentlemen!; ~ *Miller* Mr Miller; ~ *Doktor* (*Professor etc*) Doctor (Professor *etc*); *Ihr ~ Vater* your father; *sports:* ~*en* men; (*Gott*) *der ~* the Lord (God); *der ~ Jesus* Our Lord Jesus; *sein eigener ~ sein* be one's own boss; ~ *werden* (gen) master, (get *s.th.* under) control; ~ *der Lage sein* have the situation well in hand; → *Land* 3.

'Herrchen n (-s; -) master (*of a dog*).

Herren|ausstatter ['hɛrən-] m (-s; -) men's outfitter, *Am.* haberdasher. ~**bekleidung** f men's wear. ~**doppel** n *tennis:* men's doubles. ~**einzel** n *tennis:* men's singles. ~**fahrrad** n man's bicycle. ~**fri,seur** m barber, men's hairdresser. ~**haus** n mansion. ~**konfekti,on** f men's ready-to-wear clothes.

'herrenlos adj ownerless, stray (*dog*).

'Herren|mode f men's fashion. ~**schneider** m men's tailor. ~**toi,lette** f men's toilet (*Am.* restroom).

'Herrgott m (-s; no pl) the Lord (God), God; V ~ *noch mal!* for God's sake!

'Herrgottsfrühe f *in aller ~* at an unearthly hour.

'herrichten v/t (sep, -ge-, h) **1.** get *s.th.* ready. **2.** do up. **3.** tidy (*room*).

Herrin ['hɛrɪn] f (-; -nen) **1.** mistress, lady. **2.** ruler. **'herrisch** adj **1.** imperious. **2.** peremptory.

herrlich ['hɛrlɪç] adj marvel(l)ous, wonderful, magnificent, F fantastic.

'Herrschaft f (-; -en) **1.** no pl (*über acc* over) a) power, control, b) rule, reign: *fig.* **die ~ verlieren über** (acc) lose control of. **2.** *m-e ~en!* ladies and gentlemen!, F folks! **'herrschaftlich** adj a) nobleman's, *hist.* manorial, b) stately.

herrschen ['hɛrʃən] v/i (h) **1.** rule (*über acc* over): *über e-n Staat etc ~* rule a state *etc*. **2.** *fig.* prevail, reign: *es herrschte Frieden* a. there was peace; *es herrschte Stille* silence reigned. **'herrschend** adj **1.** ruling (*class etc*). **2.** *fig.* prevailing, current (*opinion etc*). **Herrscher** ['hɛrʃər] m (-s; -) ruler, sovereign, monarch. **'Herrscherhaus** n a) dynasty, b) ruling house. **'Herrscherin** f (-; -nen) → *Herrscher*.

'Herrschsucht f (-; no pl) domineering (F bossy) nature. **'herrschsüchtig** adj domineering, F bossy.

'herrühren v/i (sep, -ge-, h) ~ *von* come (or date) from, be due to.

'hersehen v/i (irr, sep, -ge-, h, → *sehen*) look (here).

'herstellen v/t (sep, -ge-, h) **1.** ⚕, ⚙ produce (a. *film*), manufacture, make. **2.** *fig.* establish (*order, contact, etc*)

Hersteller ['heːrʃtɛlər] m (-s; -) maker, manufacturer, producer (a. *film*).

'Herstellerfirma f manufacturers.

'Herstellerin f (-; -nen) → *Hersteller*.

'Herstellung f (-; no pl) **1.** a) manufacture, production (a. *print. and film*), b) Production (Department). **2.** *fig.* establishment, making (*of contacts etc*).

'Herstellungs|kosten pl production cost(s). ~**land** n producer country. ~**verfahren** n manufacturing process.

Hertz [hɛrts] n (-; -) *phys.* hertz.

herüber [hɛ'ryːbər] adv **1.** over (here), across: *hier ~!* over here!, this way! **2.** F → *hinüber.* **her'überkommen** v/i (irr, sep, -ge-, sn, → *kommen*) come over (a. *on a visit*), come across.

'Herübersetzung f translation from the foreign language.

herum [hɛ'rʊm] adv **1.** around: *immer*

um et. ~ round and round s.th. **2.** about, (a)round (*the room, town, etc*). **3.** around, near(by): (*irgendwo*) *hier* ~ somewhere around here, hereabouts. **4. um die Ecke** ~ (a)round the corner; *rechts* ~ (to the) right; *anders (falsch, so)* ~ the other (the wrong, this) way round. **5.** F *um ...* ~ around, about (*two o'clock, ten dollars, etc*); *um Ostern* ~ around Easter. **6.** *time etc*: over, up.

her'um... dance, move, travel, walk, etc (a)round, about.

her'umärgern: sich ~ (*sep*, -ge-, h) be plagued (*mit* with).

her'umdrehen (*sep*, -ge-, h) **I** *v/t a*) (*a. sich* ~) turn round, b) F turn over. **II** *v/i* F ~ *an* (*dat*) fiddle with.

her'umdrücken: sich ~ (*sep*, -ge-, h) F **1.** hang around. **2.** *um et.* dodge s.th.

her'umfahren (*irr, sep*, -ge-, → *fahren*) **I** *v/i*(sn) **1.** drive (*or* go, travel) around: *um et.* ~ drive round s.th. **2.** spin round. **II** *v/t* (h) **3.** drive (*or* take) *s.o., s.th.* around.

her'umfragen *v/i* (*sep*, -ge-, h) ask around.

her'umführen (*sep*, -ge-, h) **I** *v/t j-n* ~ lead s.o. around; *j-n im Haus etc* ~ show s.o. around the house *etc*; → *Nase*. **II** *v/i um et.* ~ *road, fence, etc*: run (a)round s.th.

her'umfuhrwerken *v/i* (*sep*, -ge-, h) F bustle around.

her'umgehen *v/i* (*irr, sep*, -ge-, sn, → *gehen*) **1.** walk (*or* go) around (*im Park etc* the park *etc*): *j-m im Kopf* ~ go round and round in s.o.'s head. **2.** *um et.* ~ *a*. F *belt etc*: go round s.th. **3.** be passed around. **4.** *rumo[u]r etc*: make the round. **5.** *time, day, etc*: pass.

her'umhängen *v/i* (*irr, sep*, -ge-, h, → *hängen*) F *fig*. hang around (*mit* with).

her'umkomman,dieren *v/t* (*sep*, h) *j-n* ~ order s.o. around.

her'umkommen *v/i* (*irr, sep*, -ge-, sn, → *kommen*) **1.** *um et.* ~ come (*fig*. get) round s.th., *fig. a.* avoid s.th.; *um diese Tatsache kommen wir nicht herum* we can't get away from that (fact). **2.** get around: *er ist weit herumgekommen* he has seen a lot of the world.

her'umkriegen *v/t* (*sep*, -ge-, h) F **1.** *j-n* ~ get s.o. round; *j-n dazu* ~, *daß er et. tut*

talk s.o. into doing s.th. **2.** get through (*time, day, etc*).

her'umlaufen *v/i* (*irr, sep*, -ge-, sn, → *laufen*) (*um et.*) ~ run (*or* go) around (s.th.); *frei* ~ *criminal etc*: be at large, *dog etc*: run free.

her'umliegen *v/i* (*irr, sep*, -ge-, h, → *liegen*) F lie around, lie about.

her'umlungern *v/i* (*sep*, -ge-, h) loiter (*or* hang, loaf) around.

her'umpfuschen *v/i* (*sep*, -ge-, h) ~ *an* (*dat*) monkey (about) with.

her'umreichen (*sep*, -ge-, h) **I** *v/t* hand (*or* pass) *s.th.* (a)round: F *j-n* ~ introduce s.o. to (all) one's friends. **II** *v/i* (*um et.*) ~ *belt etc*: go (a)round (s.th.).

her'umreiten *v/i* (*irr, sep*, -ge-, → *reiten*) (*um et.*) ~ ride (a)round (s.th.): F *fig.* ~ *auf* (*dat*) keep harping on.

her'umschlagen: sich ~ (*irr, sep*, -ge-, h, → *schlagen*) a) *mit j-m* fight with s.o., b) *mit e-r Sache* struggle with s.th.

her'umschnüffeln *v/i* (*sep*, -ge-, h) F *fig.* snoop around.

her'umsein *v/i* (*irr, sep*, -ge-, sn, → *sein*) *time etc*: be over.

her'umstehen *v/i* (*irr, sep*, -ge-, h, → *stehen*) ~ *um* stand (a)round.

her'umstoßen *v/t* (*irr, sep*, -ge-, h, → *stoßen*) F *fig. j-n* ~ push s.o. around.

her'umtragen *v/t* (*irr, sep*, -ge-, → *tragen*) **1.** carry *s.o., s.th.* around (*mit sich* with one). **2.** *fig.* spread (*news etc*).

her'umtrampeln *v/i* (*sep*, -ge-, h) trample (*auf dat* on): *fig. auf j-m* ~ treat s.o. like a doormat.

her'umtreiben: sich ~ (*irr, sep*, -ge-, h, → *treiben*) F **1.** knock around. **2.** → *herumlungern*. **Her'umtreiber** *m* (-s; -) **1.** loiterer, loafer. **2.** tramp.

her'umzeigen *v/t* (*sep*, -ge-, h) *et.* ~ show (*or* pass) s.th. round.

herunter [hɛ'rʊntər] *adv* **1.** a) down, b) off: ~ *damit!* down (*or* off) with it!; *die Treppe* ~ down the stairs, downstairs; → *heruntersein*. **2.** F → *hinunter*.

herunter... [hɛ'rʊntər] down; → *a. her-ab...,* F *hinab...,* *hinunter....*

her'unterbekommen *v/t* (*irr, sep*, h, → *bekommen*) F get *s.th.* down (*or* off).

her'unterfallen *v/i* (*irr, sep*, -ge-, sn, → *fallen*) fall down (*or* off).

her'untergehen *v/i* (*irr, sep*, -ge-, sn, → *gehen*) go down (*a.* ✓), *fig. a.* fall, drop: *mit der Geschwindigkeit (den Preisen)* ~ slow down (reduce prices).

her'untergekommen I *pp of* **heruntergekommen. II** *adj* F a) seedy, shabby, down-at-heel, b) run-down, *pred* in bad shape, c) dissolute, d) dilapidated.

her'unterhandeln *v/t* (*sep*, -ge-, h) beat *price etc* down (*um* by).

her'unterholen *v/t* (*sep*, -ge-, h) **1.** get *s.o.* down. **2.** F shoot *s.th.* down.

her'unterklappen *v/t* (*sep*, -ge-, h) turn *s.th.* down.

her'unterkommen *v/i* (*irr*, *sep*, -ge-, sn, → **kommen**) **1.** come (*or* get) down. **2.** F a) go to seed, b) get into bad shape, c) go downhill, go to rack and ruin, d) sink low; → **heruntergekommen. 3.** ~ **von** F get over, *sl.* kick (*drugs etc*).

her'untermachen *v/t* (*sep*, -ge-, h) F **1.** knock, pull *s.o.*, *s.th.* to pieces. **2.** → **her'unterputzen** *v/t* (*sep*, -ge-, h) F *j-n* ~ blow s.o. up.

her'unterrasseln *v/t* (*sep*, -ge-, h) F rattle off.

her'unterschalten *v/i* (*sep*, -ge-, h) *mot.* (*in den ersten Gang*) ~ change (*or* shift) down (into first [gear]).

her'unterschrauben *v/t* (*sep*, -ge-, h) *fig.* lower.

her'untersein *v/i* (*sep*, -ge-, sn, → **sein**) F *fig.* be run down, be in bad shape: *er ist mit den Nerven ganz herunter* he is a nervous wreck.

her'unterspielen *v/t* (*sep*, -ge-, h) F *fig.* *et.* ~ play s.th. down.

her'unterwirtschaften *v/t* (*sep*, h) F *et.* ~ run s.th. down, mismanage s.th.

hervor [hɛr'foːr] *adv* out of, (out) from, forth: *hinter ... ~* from behind *a tree etc*; *unter ... ~* from under *the bed etc*.

her'vorbringen *v/t* (*irr*, *sep*, -ge-, h, → **bringen**) produce.

her'vorgehen *v/i* (*irr*, *sep*, -ge-, sn, → **gehen**) **1.** (*aus* from) follow, result: *daraus geht hervor, daß* from this follows that; *aus dem Brief geht nicht hervor, ob* the letter doesn't say whether; *als Sieger* ~ emerge victorious; *aus der Ehe gingen drei Kinder hervor* there were three children of this marriage.

her'vorheben *v/t* (*irr*, *sep*, -ge-, h, → **heben**) **1.** *paint.*, *print.* set *s th* off. **2.** *fig.* a) emphasize, stress, b) point out.

her'vorholen *v/t* (*sep*, -ge-, h) *et.* ~ (*aus*) get s.th. out (of), produce s.th. (from).

her'vorragen *v/i* (*sep*, -ge-, h) **1.** project, stick out. **2.** *fig.* stand out (*unter dat* among). **her'vorragend I** *adj* **1.** projecting. **2.** *fig.* outstanding, excellent, superior, prominent. **II** *adv* **3.** excellently, outstandingly (well).

her'vorrufen *v/t* (*irr*, *sep*, -ge-, h, → **rufen**) **1.** *thea.* call for. **2.** *fig.* cause, give rise to, provoke.

her'vorstechen *v/i* (*irr*, *sep*, -ge-, h, → **stechen**) stand out (*aus* from).

her'vorstechend *adj* **1.** → **hervorragend** 2. **2.** striking.

her'vortreten *v/i* (*irr*, *sep*, -ge-, sn, → **treten**) **1.** step forth, (*aus dat*) step out (of), emerge (from). **2.** a) stand out, b) *fig.* emerge, become evident: *et.* ~ **lassen** set s.th. off, *fig.* bring s.th. out, show s.th. **3.** *veins*, *eyes*: protrude. **4.** → **her'vortun:** *sich* ~ (*irr*, *sep*, -ge-, h, → **tun**) distinguish o.s. (*als* as, *durch* by).

'**herwagen:** *sich* ~ (*sep*, -ge-, h) dare to come (here).

'**Herweg** *m* (*auf dem* ~ on the) way here.

Herz [hɛrts] *n* (-ens; -en) heart (*a. fig.*), *cards*: hearts: *aus ganzem ~ens* s-s ~ens at heart; *leichten ~ens* with a light heart; *schweren ~ens* with a heavy heart, very reluctantly; *von ~en gern* with (the greatest) pleasure, gladly; *j-m von (ganzem) ~en danken* thank s.o. with all one's heart; *von ~en kommend* heartfelt; *auf ~ und Nieren prüfen* put *s.th.* to the acid test, F vet *s.o.*, *s.th.* (thoroughly); *j-m das ~ brechen* break s.o.'s heart; *sich ein ~ fassen* take heart, pluck up courage; *j-m zu ~en gehen* move s.o. deeply; *er ist mir sehr ans ~ gewachsen* I have grown very fond of him; *was haben Sie auf dem ~en?* a) what's on your mind?, b) what can I do for you?; *j-m et. ans ~ legen* enjoin s.th. on s.o.; *das liegt mir sehr am ~en* that's very important to me; *s-m ~en Luft machen* give vent to one's feelings; *j-n ins ~ schließen* take s.o. to one's heart; *sie sind ein ~ und eine Seele* they are very close, F they are as thick as thieves; → **ausschütten** 1, **bringen** 7, **Stoß** 1, **tief** I.

'**Herzanfall** *m* heart attack.

'**Herzas** *n cards*: ace of hearts.

'**Herzasthma** n ♣ cardiac asthma.
'**Herzbeschwerden** pl heart trouble.
'**Herzbeutel** m anat. pericardium.
'**Herzchen** ['hɛrtsçən] n (-s; -) darling.
'**Herzchir,urg** m heart surgeon.
'**Herzdame** f cards: queen of hearts.
'**herzeigen** v/t (sep, -ge-, h) F show: **zeig (mal) her!** let me see!
herzen ['hɛrtsən] v/t (h) hug, cuddle.
'**Herzens|brecher** m (-s; -) F ladykiller. **~lust** f **nach** ~ to one's heart's content. **~wunsch** m dearest wish.
'**herzerfrischend** adj (very) refreshing.
'**herzergreifend** adj (deeply) moving.
'**Herzfehler** m ♣ cardiac defect.
'**Herzflimmern** n (-s) ♣ heart flutter.
'**herzförmig** [-fœrmɪç] adj heart-shaped.
'**herzhaft** adj **1.** hearty. **2.** → **beherzt.**
'**herziehen** (irr, sep, -ge-, → **ziehen**) **I** v/t (h) **1. hinter sich** ~ drag s.o., s.th. along (behind one). **II** v/i (sn) **2.** move here. **3.** F ~ **über** (acc) run s.o., s.th. down.
herzig ['hɛrtsɪç] adj sweet, lovely.
'**Herz|in,farkt** m ♣ cardiac infarction, F heart attack, coronary. **~kammer** f anat. ventricle. **~ka,theter** m ♣ cardiac catheter. **~klappe** f anat. cardiac valve. **~klappenfehler** m ♣ valvular (heart) defect. **~klopfen** n (-s) beating (♣ palpitation) of the heart: **er hatte** ~ his heart was thumping (**vor** dat with). **♀krank** adj suffering from a heart condition, cardiac. **~kranke** m, f cardiac. **~kranzgefäß** n anat. coronary vessel. **~leiden** n heart disease (or condition).
'**herzlich** **I** adj a) cordial, warm, friendly, b) sincere, heartfelt: **~e Grüße, mit ~en Grüßen** kind regards (**an** acc to), (with) love; → **Beileid, Dank, Gruß.** '**Herzlichkeit** f (-; no pl) a) warmth, cordiality, b) sincerity.
'**herzlos** adj heartless.
'**Herzlosigkeit** f (-; no pl) heartlessness.
'**Herz-'Lungen-Ma'schine** f ♣ heart--lung machine.
'**Herzmas,sage** f ♣ heart massage.
Herzog ['hɛrtsoːk] m (-s; ⸰e) duke. **Herzogin** [hɛrtsoːgɪn] f (-en; -en) duchess. '**herzoglich** adj ducal. '**Herzogtum** n (-s; ⸰er) dukedom, duchy.
'**Herz|operati,on** f heart operation. **~rhythmusstörung** f arrythmia. **~schlag** m **1.** heartbeat. **2.** heart attack

(or failure). **~schrittmacher** m cardiac pacemaker. **~schwäche** f cardiac insufficiency. **~spezia,list** m heart specialist. **♀stärkend** adj cardiotonic. **~stillstand** m cardiac arrest. **~stück** n fig. core. **~tod** m death by heart failure.
herzu(...) ['hɛr'tsuː] → **heran(...), herbei(...), hinzu(...).**
'**Herzversagen** n ♣ heart failure.
'**Herzverpflanzung** f heart transplant.
'**herzzerbrechend** adj heartbreaking.
'**herzzerreißend** adj heartrending.
Hesse ['hɛsə] m (-n; -n), '**Hessin** f (-; -nen), '**hessisch** adj Hessian.
heterogen [hetᵉroˈgeːn] adj heterogeneous.
heterosexu'ell adj, **Heterosexu'elle** m, f (-n; -n) heterosexual.
Hetze ['hɛtsə] f (-; -n) **1. (gegen** against) agitation, smear campaign. **2.** F (mad) rush. **3.** → **Hetzjagd** 1, 2.
'**hetzen** **I** v/t (h) **1.** a. fig. hunt, hound. **2. e-n Hund** etc ~ **auf** (acc) set a dog etc on. **3.** (a. **sich** ~) rush. **II** v/i **4.** (h) **(gegen** against) agitate, stir up hatred. **5.** (sn) F rush, hurry.
'**Hetzer** m (-s; -) agitator.
Hetze'rei f (-; no pl) → **Hetze** 1, 2.
'**hetzerisch** adj inflammatory.
'**Hetzjagd** f **1.** hunt(ing) (with hounds). **2.** fig. chase. **3.** → **Hetze** 1, 2.
'**Hetzrede** f inflammatory speech.
Heu [hɔy] n (-[e]s; no pl) hay: F **er hat Geld wie** ~ he's rolling in money.
'**Heuboden** m hayloft.
Heuche'lei f (-; -en) **1.** no pl hypocrisy, dissimulation. **2.** cant. **heucheln** ['hɔyçəln] (h) **I** v/t simulate, feign. **II** v/i a) play the hypocrite, b) dissemble, c) cant. '**Heuchler** m (-s; -), '**Heuchlerin** f (-; -nen) hypocrite. '**heuchlerisch** adj hypocritical.
heuen ['hɔyən] v/i (h) make hay.
Heuer ['hɔyər] f (-; -n) ♣ pay.
heuern ['hɔyərn] v/t (h) ♣ hire.
'**Heuernte** f hay harvest.
'**Heugabel** f hayfork, pitchfork.
heulen ['hɔylən] v/i (h) **1.** zo. howl. **2.** F bawl, a. fig. siren: wail: fig. **es ist zum ♀** it's a (great) shame.
'**Heuler** m (-s; -) **1.** F **das ist (ja) der letzte ~!** a) would you believe it, b) it's absolutely super. **2.** zo. baby seal.
'**Heulsuse** f (-; -n) F crybaby.

Heurige ['hɔyrɪgə] *m* (-n; *no pl*) *Austrian* new wine.

'**Heuschnupfen** *m* hay fever.

'**Heuschober** *m* haystack.

Heuschrecke ['hɔyʃrɛkə] *f* (-; -n) *zo.* grasshopper, locust.

heute ['hɔytə] **I** *adv* today, this day: ~ *abend* this evening, tonight; ~ *in acht Tagen* a week from now, *Br. a.* today week; ~ *vor acht Tagen* a week ago (today); *von* ~ → *heutig*; *von* ~ *an* from today; *fig. von* ~ *auf morgen* overnight. **II** *das Heute* the present, today.

heutig ['hɔytɪç] *adj* today's, of today, *a.* present(-day), modern: *bis auf den ~en Tag* to this day.

'**heutzutage** *adv* nowadays, today.

Hexe ['hɛksə] *f* (-; -n) witch (*a. fig.*), sorceress, *fig.* hellcat: (*alte* ~) (old) hag.

hexen ['hɛksən] *v/i* (h) practise witchcraft: F *ich kann doch nicht* ~*!* I can't work miracles!

'**Hexen**|**jagd** *f fig.* witch-hunt. ~**kessel** *m fig.* inferno. ~**meister** *m* sorcerer. ~**schuß** *m* (-sses; *no pl*) ♣ F lumbago.

Hexe'rei *f* (-; -en) witchcraft, magic (*a. fig.*): *das ist k-e* ~*!* there's nothing to it!

hieb [hi:p] *pret of* **hauen**.

Hieb *m* (-[e]s; -e) **1.** stroke, blow, punch: F ~*e bekommen* get a thrashing; *auf einen* ~ at one go. **2.** *fig.* dig (*auf acc* at). '**hieb- und 'stichfest** *adj* watertight (*argument*), cast-iron (*proof etc*).

hielt [hi:lt] *pret of* **halten**.

hier [hi:r] *adv* here (*a. fig. in this case*), *a.* present: ~ *drinnen* (*draußen, oben*) in (out, up) here; ~ *und da* a) here and there, b) now and then; ~ *und heute* here and now; *von* ~ *an* (*or ab*) from here (on); ~*, bitte!* here you are!

hieran ['hi:'ran] *adv* **1.** ~ *kann man sehen, daß* you can see from this that; ~ *ist kein wahres Wort* there is not a word of truth in this. **2.** ~ *schließt sich ... an* this is followed by ...

Hierarchie [hiɛrar'çi:] *f* (-; -n) hierarchy.

hieraus ['hi:'raʊs] *adv* from it (*or* this).

'**hier'bei** *adv* a) here, b) on this occasion, c) in this connection.

'**hierbleiben** *v/i* (*irr, sep*, -ge-, sn, → *bleiben*) stay here.

'**hier'durch** *adv* by this, hereby.

'**hicr'für** *adv* for this, for it.

'**hier'her** *adv* here, this way, over here:

bis ~ up to here, *a. time*: so far; *bis* ~ *und nicht weiter* this far and no further; (*komm*) ~*!* come here!

hier'hergehören *v/i* (*sep*, h) belong here: *fig. das gehört nicht hierher* that's irrelevant.

hierherum ['hi:'rhɛ'rʊm] *adv* **1.** this way (a)round. **2.** F hereabout(s).

'**hier'hin** *adv* here. '**hierhin'auf** *adv* up here. '**hierhin'ein** *adv* in here.

hierin ['hi:'rɪn] *adv a. fig.* in this, here.

'**hier'mit** *adv* with this, herewith.

'**hier'nach** *adv* **1.** after this (*or* it). **2.** according to this.

Hieroglyphe [hiɛro'gly:fə] *f* (-; -n) hieroglyph.

'**hiersein** *v/i* (*irr, sep*, -ge-, sn, → *sein*) be here, be present: *während s-s Hierseins* during his stay here.

hierüber ['hi:'ry:bər] *adv fig.* about this.

hierum ['hi:'rʊm] *adv* **1.** (a)round this. **2.** → *hierherum* **2. 3.** *fig.* about this (*or* it): ~ *geht es nicht* that's not the point.

hierunter ['hi:'rʊntər] *adv* **1.** under this, among these. **2.** *fig. understand etc*: by this, by that: ~ *fällt ...* this includes ...

'**hier'von** *adv* of (*or* from) this.

'**hier'zu** *adv* **1.** for this. **2.** to this (*or* these): *im Gegensatz* ~ in contrast to this.

hierzu'lande *adv* in this country, here.

hiesig ['hi:zɪç] *adj* local, here, of this place (*or* country).

hieß [hi:s] *pret of* **heißen**.

hieven ['hi:fən] *v/t* (h) *a. fig.* heave.

Hi-Fi ['haɪfi] *abbr. of* **High Fidelity**.

'**Hi-Fi-'Anlage** *f* hi-fi set.

Hilfe ['hɪlfə] *f* (-; -n) **1.** help, aid, assistance, relief: *ärztliche* ~ medical assistance; *Erste* ~ first aid; *j-m* ~ *leisten* help s.o., aid s.o.; *j-m zu* ~ *kommen* come to s.o.'s aid; *zu* ~ *nehmen* make use of, use; *um* ~ *rufen* call for help; *mit* ~ *von* (*or gen*) with the help of, *fig. a.* by means of; *ohne* ~ unaided, without help; (*zu*) ~*!* help! **2.** (*person*) help.

'**hilfeflehend** *adj* imploring.

'**Hilfeleistung** *f* aid, assistance, help.

'**Hilferuf** *m a. fig.* cry for help.

'**Hilfestellung** *f* (-; *no pl*) *a. fig.* support.

'**hilfesuchend** *adj* seeking (for) help.

'**hilflos** *adj* helpless.

'**Hilflosigkeit** *f* (-; *no pl*) helplessness.

'**hilfreich** *adj a. fig.* helpful.

'**Hilfs|akti,on** f relief (or rescue) action.
~arbeiter(in f) m unskilled worker.
2bedürftig adj a) in need (of help), b) needy. **~bedürftigkeit** f (-; no pl) neediness, need. **2bereit** adj ready to help, helpful. **~bereitschaft** f (-; no pl) readiness to help. **~fonds** m relief fund. **~kraft** f **1.** assistant, help. **2.** temporary worker. **~mittel** n aid. **~motor** m auxiliary engine (⚡ motor). **~organisati,on** f relief organization. **~quelle** f source of help, pl resources. **~verb** n auxiliary verb. **~werk** n relief organization. **~wissenschaft** f auxiliary science.

Himbeere ['hɪmbeːrə] f (-; -n) raspberry.
'**Himbeersaft** m raspberry juice.
'**Himbeerstrauch** m raspberry bush.

Himmel ['hɪməl] m (-s; -) sky, eccl. or fig. heaven: **der ~ auf Erden** heaven on earth; **am ~** in the sky; fig. (**wie**) **aus heiterem ~** out of the blue; **unter freiem ~** in the open air; **zum ~** (**empor**) skyward(s), heavenward(s); **im ~ sein** in heaven; **in den ~ heben** praise s.o., s.th. to the skies; F **weiß der ~(, wo)!** God knows (where)!; **das schreit zum ~** it's a crying shame; F **das stinkt zum ~** that stinks to high heaven; **um ~s willen!** a) a. (**ach,**) **du lieber ~!** good heavens!, b) a. **~ (noch mal)!** for Heaven's sake!

'**Himmel|angst** adj **mir war** (or **wurde**) **~** I was scared to death.
'**Himmelbett** n four-poster.
'**himmelblau** adj sky-blue.
'**Himmelfahrt** f (-; no pl) **Christi ~** a) the Ascension of Christ, b) Ascension Day; **Mariä ~** a) the Assumption of the Virgin Mary, b) Assumption Day.
'**Himmelfahrtstag** m (**am ~** on) Ascension Day.
'**Himmelreich** n kingdom of heaven.
'**Himmelschlüssel** m ♣ primrose.
'**himmelschreiend** adj outrageous, terrible: **~e Schande** crying shame.
'**Himmelskarte** f star map.
'**Himmelskörper** m celestial body.
'**Himmelsrichtung** f direction.
'**himmelweit** adj fig. vast: **es ist ein ~er Unterschied zwischen ...** there is a world of difference between ...; **~ verschieden sein** differ enormously.

himmlisch ['hɪmlɪʃ] adj heavenly, divine.

hin [hɪn] **I** adv **1.** there: **nichts wie ~!** let's

go!; **~ zu** to, towards; **bis ~ zu** a) as far as, b) fig. (even) including, c) till; **über** (acc) **~** over; **~ und her** to and fro, back and forth; **~ und zurück** a) there and back, b) return (Am. round-trip) (ticket); **~ und her gerissen sein** a) zwischen be torn between, b) F **von** be gone over. **2. auf e-e Sache ~** a) as a result of, b) on the basis of, c) because of, d) in reply to, on; **auf s-e Bitte ~** at his request; **auf s-n Rat ~** at his advice. **3. ~ und wieder** now and then. **4.** F **~ oder her** a) more or less, give or take (ten dollars, years, etc), b) a. **... ~, her** I don't care; **Anstand ~, Anstand her** fairness or no. **II** adj pred → **hinsein**.

Hin n → **Hin und Her**.

hinab(...) [hɪ'nap] → **hinunter(...)**, **herab(...)**, **herunter(...)**.

'**hinarbeiten** v/i (sep, -ge-, h) **auf** (acc) work towards, aim at.

hinauf [hɪ'naʊf] adv up: **da ~** up there; **bis ~ zu** up to; **den Berg ~** up the hill, uphill; (**die Treppe**) **~** upstairs.

hin'auf... climb, drive, look, etc up, → a. **empor...**, **hoch...**

hin'aufgehen (irr, sep, -ge-, sn, → **gehen**) **I** v/i go up (a. fig.): **mit dem Preis ~** raise the price. **II** v/t go up: **die Treppe ~** a. go upstairs.

hinaus [hɪ'naʊs] adv **1.** out, outside: **aus** out of; **da ~!** this way (out)!; **zum Fenster ~** out of the window; **nach vorn** (**hinten**) **~ wohnen** live at the front (back); **~ (mit dir or euch)!** out (with you)!, get out!; **~ damit!** out with it! **2. über** (acc) **~** a. fig. a) beyond, b) above, over; **auf Jahre ~** for years (to come); → **darüber** 3, **hinaussein**.

hin'ausbegleiten v/t (sep, h) **j-n ~** see s.o. out (**aus** of).

hin'ausekeln v/t (sep, -ge-, h) F **j-n ~** freeze s.o. out (**aus** of).

hin'ausfliegen v/i (irr, sep, -ge-, sn, → **fliegen**) **1.** fly out. **2.** F fig. get kicked out, a. get the sack.

hin'ausgehen v/i (irr, sep, -ge-, sn, → **gehen**) **1.** go out (**aus** of). **2.** fig. **~ auf** (acc) window etc: open on(to). **3.** fig. **~ über** (acc) go beyond, a. exceed.

hin'auslaufen v/i (irr, sep, -ge-, sn, → **laufen**) **1.** run out (**aus** of). **2.** fig. **~ auf** (acc) come to, amount to, lead to; **es**

läuft auf dasselbe hinaus it comes (*or* amounts) to the same thing.

hin'ausschieben *v/t* (*irr, sep*, -ge-, h, → **schieben**) *fig.* put *s.th.* off, postpone.

hin'aussein *v/i* (*irr, sep*, -ge-, sn, → **sein**) ~ *über* (*acc*) be beyond, be past; *über das Alter* (*or darüber*) *ist er hinaus* he is past that age.

hin'ausstellen *v/t* (*sep*, -ge-, h) **1.** put *s.th.* out(side). **2.** *sports:* **j-n** ~ send (*or* order) s.o. off the field.

hin'auswachsen *v/i* (*irr, sep*, -ge-, sn, → **wachsen**) *fig.* ~ *über* (*acc*) surpass.

hin'auswagen: *sich* ~ (*sep*, -ge-, h) venture (to go) out (*aus* of).

hin'auswerfen *v/t* (*irr, sep*, -ge-, h, → **werfen**) **1.** throw *s.th.* out (*aus* of): → *Fenster.* **2.** F throw (*or* kick) *s.o.* out (*aus* of), ~ a. sack, fire.

hin'auswollen *v/i* (*irr, sep*, -ge-, h, → **wollen**) **1.** want to go (*or* get) out (*aus* of). **2.** *fig.* **worauf will er hinaus?** what is he driving at?; *hoch* ~ be aiming high.

hin'ausziehen (*irr, sep*, -ge-, → **ziehen**) **I** *v/t* (h) **1.** pull *s.o.*, *s.th.* out (*aus* of). **2.** *fig. et.* ~ drag s.th. out. **II** *v/i* (sn) go out, march out. **III** *sich* ~ (h) a) drag on, b) take longer than expected.

hin'auszögern *v/t* (*sep*, -ge-, h) delay: *sich* ~ be delayed.

'hinbiegen *v/t* (*irr, sep*, -ge-, h, → **biegen**) F *fig. et.* ~ wangle s.th.

'Hinblick *m im* ~ *auf* (*acc*) with regard to.

'hinbringen *v/t* (*irr, sep*, -ge-, h, → **bringen**) **1.** take *s.o.*, *s.th.* there. **2.** pass, spend (*time*). **3.** → **fertigbringen**.

hinderlich ['hɪndərlɪç] *adj* troublesome: ~ *sein* (*dat*) hamper, impede, be a handicap to. **hindern** ['hɪndərn] *v/t* (h) a) hamper, impede, b) interfere (*bei* with): *j-n am Arbeiten* ~ prevent (*or* keep) s.o. from working.

'Hindernis *n* (-ses; -se) obstacle (*für* to): *j-m* ~*se in den Weg legen* put obstacles in s.o.'s way; *auf* ~*se stoßen* run into difficulties. ~*lauf m sports:* obstacle race. ~*rennen n* steeplechase.

'hindeuten *v/i* (*sep*, -ge-, h) ~ *auf* (*acc*) point at, *fig.* point to, indicate.

Hindu ['hɪndu] *m* (-[s]; -[s]) Hindu.

Hinduismus [hɪndu'ɪsmʊs] *m* (-; *no pl*) Hinduism.

hin'durch *adv* **1.** through. **2.** through-(out): *die Nacht* ~ all night (long); *das*

ganze Jahr ~ throughout the year.

hinein [hɪ'naɪn] *adv* in, inside, *a.* into (*May etc*): *da* ~ in there; *bis tief in die Nacht* ~ far into the night; F ~*!* let's go!

hin'einbekommen *v/t* (*irr, sep*, h, → **bekommen**) get *s.o.*, *s.th.* in(to *in acc*).

hin'eindenken: *sich* ~ (*irr, sep*, -ge-, h, → **denken**) *in* (*acc*) go into; *sich in j-n* ~ put o.s. into s.o.'s position.

hin'eingehen *v/i* (*irr, sep*, -ge-, sn, → **gehen**) **1.** (*in acc*) go in(to), enter (*the house etc*). **2.** hold (*two litres etc*), seat, accommodate (*500 persons etc*).

hin'einknien: *sich* ~ (*sep*, -ge-, h) F *fig.* buckle down (*in acc* to).

hin'einkommen *v/i* (*irr, sep*, -ge-, sn, → **kommen**) come (*or* get) in(to *in acc*).

hin'einleben *v/i* (*sep*, -ge-, h) *in den Tag* ~ take it easy.

hin'einlegen *v/t* (*sep*, -ge-, h) **1.** put *s.th.* in(to *in acc*). **2.** → **hereinlegen**.

hin'einpassen *v/i* (*sep*, -ge-, h) **1.** fit in(to *in acc*). **2.** → **hineingehen** 2.

hin'einreden *v/i* (*sep*, -ge-, h) *j-m* ~ interrupt s.o.; *j-m in s-e Angelegenheiten*) ~ interfere with s.o.'s affairs.

hin'einstecken *v/t* (*sep*, -ge-, h) F *a. fig.* put *s.th.* in(to *in acc*): → **Nase**.

hin'einsteigern: *sich* ~ (*sep*, -ge-, h) get worked up (*in acc* over); *sich in s-e Wut* ~ work o.s. up into a rage.

hin'einziehen (*irr, sep*, -ge-, → **ziehen**) **I** *v/t* (h) pull *s.o.*, *s.th.* in(to *in acc*): *j-n in e-e Sache* ~ involve s.o. in s.th. **II** *v/i* (sn) march (*or* move) in(to *in acc*).

'hinfahren (*irr, sep*, -ge-, → **fahren**) **I** *v/t* (h) take (*or* drive) *s.o.*, *s.th.* there. **II** *v/i* (sn) go (*mot. a.* drive) there.

'Hinfahrt *f* journey there: *auf der* ~ on the (*or our etc*) way there.

'hinfallen *v/i* (*irr, sep*, -ge-, sn, → **fallen**) fall (down). **'hinfällig** *adj* **1.** frail. **2.** *fig.* invalid: *et.* ~ *machen* invalidate s.th.

'hinfinden *v/i* (*irr, sep*, -ge-, h, → **finden**) (*a. sich* ~) find one's way there.

'Hinflug *m* outward flight: *auf dem* ~ *a.* on the flight there.

'hinführen (*sep*, -ge-, h) **I** *v/t* *j-n* ~ lead (*or* take) s.o. there (*or zu* to). **II** *v/i* lead (*or* go) there: *fig.* **wo soll das** (*noch*) ~*?* where is this leading to?

hing [hɪŋ] *pret of* **hängen¹**.

'Hingabe *f* (-; *no pl*) **1.** (*an acc* to) devotion, dedication: *mit* ~ *a.* lovingly. **2.**

sacrifice. **'hingeben** (*irr, sep*, -ge-, h, → **geben**) **I** *v/t* give away, sacrifice, give up. **II sich ~** (*dat*) devote (*or* dedicate) o.s. to *a task etc*, abandon o.s. to *despair etc*; **sich j-m ~** give o.s. to s.o.; **sich Hoffnungen** (**Illusionen**) **~** have hopes (illusions).

'hingebungsvoll *adj and adv* devoted(ly), *adv a.* with dedication.

hin'gegen *conj* however, on the other hand.

'hingehen *v/i* (*irr, sep*, -ge-, sn, → **gehen**) **1.** go (there): **wo gehst du hin?** where are you going? **2.** pass, go by. **3.** *fig.* pass, do: **et. ~ lassen** let s.th. pass.

'hingehören *v/i* (*sep*, h) belong: **wo gehört das hin?** *a.* where does this go?

'hingeraten *v/i* (*irr, sep*, sn, → **geraten**) get (*irgendwo* somewhere): **wo ist es ~?** what has become of it?

'hingerissen **I** *adj* (**von**) enraptured (by), ecstatic (*pred* in raptures, **F** gone) (over). **II** *adv* in raptures, ecstatically.

'hinhalten *v/t* (*irr, sep*, -ge-, h, → **halten**) **1.** *j-m et.* ~ hold s.th. out to s.o.; → **Kopf** 1. **2.** *fig. j-n* ~ put s.o. off, keep s.o. on a string.

'Hinhaltetaktik *f* delaying tactics.

'hinhauen (*irr, sep*, -ge-, h, → **hauen**) **F I** *v/t* **1.** slam *s.th.* down. **2.** *fig.* knock off (*essay, sketch, etc*). **II** *v/i fig.* a) work, b) be okay, c) be right, d) do. **III sich ~** a) hit the ground, b) hit the sack.

'hinhören *v/i* (*sep*, -ge-, h) listen.

hinken ['hɪŋkən] *v/i* (h) (walk with a) limp: **der Vergleich hinkt** that's a lame comparison.

'hinkommen *v/i* (*irr, sep*, -ge-, sn, → **kommen**) **1.** come (*or* get) there: **wo kämen wir denn hin, wenn ...** where would we be if ... **2.** **F** go, belong: **wo kommt das hin?** where does that go? **3.** **F** manage (**mit** with). **4.** **F** be right: **wieder ~** come right.

'hinkriegen *v/t* (*sep*, -ge-, h) **F** manage: **das hat er prima hingekriegt** he's made a first-rate job of it; **j-n wieder ~** put s.o. right again.

'hinlangen *v/i* (*sep*, -ge-, h) **F** (**kräftig**) **~** a) let go with a wallop, b) *fig.* (really) go to town (**bei** on).

'hinlänglich *adj* sufficient.

'hinlegen (*sep*, -ge-, h) **I** *v/t* **1.** put (*or* lay) down. **2.** **F** fork out (*money*). **3.** **F**

do *s.th.* brilliantly: **sie haben ein tolles Spiel hingelegt** they played a fantastic game. **II sich ~** lie down.

'hinmachen (*sep*, -ge-, h) **F I** *v/t* **1.** fix. **2.** a) kill, b) wreck, break. **II** *v/i* **3.** *dial.* hurry up: **mach(t) hin!** get a move on!

'hinnehmen *v/t* (*irr, sep*, -ge-, h, → **nehmen**) **1.** accept, *fig. a.* take, put up with. **2.** **F** **mit ~** take *s.o.*, *s.th.* along.

'hinreichend *adj* sufficient.

'Hinreise *f* journey there (*or* out), **⚓** voyage out: **auf der ~** on the way there.

'hinreißen *v/t* (*irr, sep*, -ge-, h, → **reißen**) **1.** enrapture, thrill: → **hingerissen**. **2. sich ~ lassen** (let o.s.) be carried away (**von** by, **zu** into *doing*).

'hinreißend *adj* breathtaking, fantastic.

'hinrichten *v/t* (*sep*, -ge-, h) execute.

'Hinrichtung *f* (-; -en) execution.

'hinsehen *v/i* (*irr, sep*, -ge-, h, → **sehen**) look: **ohne hinzusehen** without looking; **bei näherem ♀** at a closer look.

'hinsein *v/i* (*irr, sep*, -ge-, sn, → **sein**) **F** **1.** a) be wrecked, *a. fig.* be ruined, b) be gone, c) be dead(-beat), d) be done for: **es** (**er**) **ist hin** a. it (he) has had it; **hin ist hin!** gone is gone! **2.** (**ganz**) **~** (**von**) → **hingerissen I**.

'hinsetzen (*sep*, -ge-, h) **I** *v/t* a) set (*or* put) *s.th.* down, b) seat (*s.o.*), sit *child* down. **II sich ~** sit down, take a seat.

'Hinsicht *f* **in dieser** (**in jeder**) **~** in this (in every) respect; **in mancher** (**vieler**) **~** in some (many) respects (*or* ways); **in politischer ~** politically. **'hinsichtlich** *prep* (*gen*) with regard to, concerning.

'Hinspiel *n sports*: first leg.

'hinstellen (*sep*, -ge-, h) **I** *v/t* **1.** a) put, place, b) put down. **2.** **F** put up (*a house etc*). **3.** *fig. j-n* (**et.**) **~ als** make s.o. (s.th.) out to be. **II sich ~ 4.** stand (**vor** *j-n* in front of s.o.). **5.** *fig. sich ~ als* claim (*or* pretend) to be.

hintan'setzen [hɪnt''an-], **hint'anstellen** *v/t* (*sep*, -ge-, h) *fig.* a) put *s.th.* last, b) neglect.

hinten ['hɪntən] *adv* a) at the back (*or* rear), b) in the background: **~ im Garten** at the back of the garden; **~ am Auto** at the rear of the car; **~ im Buch** at the end of the book; **nach ~** a) to the back, b) back, c) backwards; **von ~** from the back, from behind; **F das reicht ~ und vorn nicht** that's not nearly enough; *das stimmt ~ und vorn nicht* that's all wrong.

'**hintenherum** *adv* F **1.** (a)round the back. **2.** *fig.* on the quiet.

'**hinten'über** *adv* backwards.

hinter ['hɪntər] **I** *prep* (*dat or acc*) behind: *~ dem Haus* behind (*or* at the back of) the house; *et. ~ sich bringen* a) get s.th. over (with), b) cover (*distance*); *~ et. kommen* a) find out about s.th., b) get (the hang of) s.th.; *j-n* (*et.*) *~ sich lassen* leave s.o. (s.th.) behind; *et. ~ sich haben* have s.th. behind one; *er hat schon viel ~ sich* he has been through a lot; *fig. ~ j-m stehen* be behind s.o., *a. sich ~ j-n stellen* back s.o. (up); *~ j-m* (*et.*) *her sein* be after s.o. (s.th.) → *hintere.* **II** *adj* → *hintere.*

'**Hinterachse** *f mot.* rear axle.

'**Hinterausgang** *m* rear exit.

'**Hinterbacke** *f* F buttock.

Hinterbänkler ['hɪntərbɛŋklər] *m* (-s; -) *parl.* backbencher.

'**Hinterbein** *n* hind leg: F *fig. sich auf die ~e stellen* put up a fight.

Hinterbliebene [hɪntər'bliːbənə] *m*, *f* (-n; -n) surviving dependant: *die ~n* the bereaved.

hinter'bringen *v/t* (*irr, insep, no* -ge-, h, → *bringen*) *j-m et. ~* inform s.o. of s.th.

'**Hinterdeck** *n* ♣ afterdeck.

hintere ['hɪntərə] *adj* back, rear: *die ~n Reihen* the back rows, the rows at the back; *am ~n Ende* at the far end.

hinterein'ander *adv* a) one behind the other, b) one after the other: *drei Tage* (*dreimal*) *~* three days (times) running (*or* in a row). **2.** → *nacheinander.* *~gehen v/i* (*irr, sep,* -ge-, sn, → *gehen*) walk one behind the other. *~schalten v/t* (*sep,* -ge-, h) ∮ connect in series.

'**Hintereingang** *m* back entrance.

hinter'fragen *v/t* (*insep, no* -ge-, h) scrutinize (closely).

'**Hinterfuß** *m* hind foot.

'**Hintergedanke** *m* ulterior motive.

hinter'gehen *v/t* (*irr, insep, no* -ge-, h, → *gehen*) deceive, cheat.

'**Hintergrund** *m* (*fig. vor dem ~* against the) background (*gen* of); *in den ~ drängen* push *s.o., s.th.* into the background; *sich im ~ halten* keep a low profile; *die Hintergründe* the background (*of a deed etc*). '**Hinter-**

grund... background (*information, music, etc*).

'**hintergründig** [-gryndɪç] *adj* a) enigmatic, cryptic, b) profound, c) subtle (*humo[u]r etc*).

'**Hinterhalt** *m* (-[e]s; -e) **1.** (*a. aus dem ~ angreifen*) ambush. **2.** *fig. et. im ~ haben* have s.th. in reserve.

'**hinterhältig** [-hɛltɪç] → *hinterlistig.*

'**Hinterhand** *f* (-; *no pl*) **1.** *zo.* hindquarters. **2.** *fig.* (*noch*) *et. in der ~ haben* have s.th. up one's sleeve.

'**Hinterhaus** *n* back building.

hinter'her *adv* **1.** behind, after. **2.** afterwards, after the event.

hinter'hersein *v/i* (*irr, sep,* -ge-, sn, → *sein*) F **1.** *j-m ~* be after s.o. **2.** *~, daß* see (to it) that, make sure that.

'**Hinterhof** *m* backyard.

'**Hinterkopf** *m* back of one's head: F *et. im ~ haben* have s.th. at the back of one's mind.

'**Hinterland** *n* (-[e]s; *no pl*) hinterland.

hinter'lassen (*irr, insep, no* -ge-, h, → *lassen*) **I** *v/t* leave (behind), *testator: a.* bequeath (*dat* to). **II** *adj* posthumous (*works*). **Hinter'lassenschaft** *f* (-; -en) ♨ estate, *fig.* legacy.

Hinter'lassung *f unter ~ von* (*or gen*) leaving *s.th.* behind.

hinter'legen *v/t* (*insep, no* -ge-, h) deposit (*bei* with). **Hinter'legung** *f gegen ~ von* (*or gen*) on depositing *s.th.*

'**Hinterlist** *f* (-; *no pl*) **1.** a) cunning, b) underhandedness. **2.** underhand(ed) trick. '**hinterlistig** *adj* a) crafty, cunning, b) underhand(ed).

'**Hintermann** *m* (-[e]s; ⁻er) **1.** *mein etc ~* the man (*or* car) behind me *etc*. **2.** *fig. usu. pl the* man behind it.

'**Hintermannschaft** *f* defen/ce (*Am.* -se).

'**Hintern** *m* (-s; -) F bottom, backside, behind: *j-m in den ~ kriechen* suck up to s.o.

'**Hinterrad** *n* rear wheel. '**Hinterradantrieb** *m mot.* rear-wheel drive.

hinterrücks ['hɪntərryks] *adv* **1.** from behind. **2.** *fig.* behind *s.o.'s* back.

'**Hinterseite** *f* back.

'**Hintersitz** *m* back seat.

'**hinterste** *adj* (very) last, hindmost: *am ~n Ende* at the very end.

'**Hinterteil** *n* → *Hintern.*

'**Hintertreffen** *n* **Ins ~ geraten** a) fall behind, b) be losing out.

hinter'treiben v/t (irr, insep, no -ge-, h, → **treiben**) prevent, foil.

'Hintertreppe f back stairs.

'Hintertür f **1.** back door. **2.** a. **'Hintertürchen** n fig. loophole.

'Hinterwäldler [-vɛltlər] m (-s; -) backwoodsman, Am. a. hick.

hinter'ziehen v/t (irr, insep, no -ge-, h, → **ziehen**) Steuern ~ evade taxes.

'Hinterzimmer n back room.

'hintun v/t (irr, sep, -ge-, h, → **tun**) F put: fig. ich weiß nicht, wo ich ihn ~ soll I can't place him.

hinüber [hi'ny:bər] adv over, across: **da** ~**!** over there! **~fahren** (irr, sep, -ge-, → **fahren**) **I** v/t (h) take (or drive) s.o., s.th. over (or across) (**über** acc a bridge etc). **II** v/i (sn) go (or travel, drive) across (or over) (**nach, zu** to). **~sein** v/i (irr, sep, -ge-, sn, → **sein**) F a) be dead, be gone, b) be dead to the world, c) be ruined, have had it, d) food: have gone bad.

'Hinübersetzung f translation into the foreign language.

Hin und Her: das ~ the coming and going, a. fig. the to-and-fro; **nach langem** ~ after endless discussions.

'Hin- und 'Rück|fahrkarte f return (Am. round-trip) ticket. **~fahrt** f return journey, Am. round trip. **~flug** m return (Am. round-trip) flight.

hinunter [hi'nʊntər] adv down: **die Treppe** ~ down the stairs, downstairs; **die Straße** ~ down the street.

hin'unter... fall, look, walk, etc down; → a. **herunter...**

hin'unterspülen v/t (sep, -ge-, h) a. fig. wash down.

hin'unterstürzen (sep, -ge-) **I** v/t **1.** (h) throw s.o., s.th. down. **2.** (sn) rush down (the stairs etc). **3.** (h) gulp down. **II** v/i **4.** (sn) crash down.

'hinwagen: sich ~ (sep, -ge-, h) venture there.

hinweg [hin'vɛk] adv **1.** away, off. **2.** ~ **über** (acc) over, across; fig. **über j-n** (or **j-s Kopf**) ~ over s.o.'s head; **darüber ist er** ~ he has got over that.

'Hinweg m (auf dem ~ on the) way there.

hin'weggehen v/i (irr, sep, -ge-, sn, → **gehen**) fig. ~ **über** (acc) pass over, ignore; **lachend** (**achselzuckend**) **über et.** ~ laugh (shrug) s.th. off.

hin'weghelfen v/t (irr, sep, -ge-, h, →

helfen) **j-m über et.** ~ a. fig. help s.o. to get over s.th.

hin'wegkommen v/i (irr, sep, -ge-, sn, → **kommen**) **über et.** ~ a. fig. get over s.th.

hin'wegsehen v/i (irr, sep, -ge-, h, → **sehen**) **über et.** ~ a) see (or look) over s.th., b) fig. ignore s.th., overlook s.th.

hin'wegsetzen (sep, -ge-) **I** v/i (h, sn) ~ **über** (acc) jump over. **II** sich ~ (h) → **hinweggehen.**

Hinweis ['hɪnvaɪs] m (-es; -e) (**auf** acc) **1.** a) tip, hint (as to), b) a. pl information (on, about), c) indication (of), clue (as to), d) note (about), comment (on): **sachdienliche** ~**e** relevant information; ~**e zur Benutzung** directions for use. **2.** reference (to). **3.** allusion (to).

'hinweisen (irr, sep, -ge-, h, → **weisen**) **I** v/t ~ **auf et.** ~ point s.th. out to s.o. **II** v/i ~ **auf** (acc) a) point to, fig. a. indicate, b) refer to; **darauf** ~, **daß** point out that. **'hinweisend** adj ~**es Fürwort** demonstrative pronoun.

'Hinweis|schild n, ~**tafel** f sign.

'hinwerfen v/t (irr, sep, -ge-, h, → **werfen**) **1.** throw s.th. down, F drop (a. fig. remark etc): **sich** ~ throw o.s. down; **j-m et.** ~ throw s.th. to s.o. **2.** F chuck (job). **3.** F dash off (letter etc).

'hinwirken v/i (sep, -ge-, h) ~ **auf** (acc) work towards.

'hinwollen v/i (irr, sep, -ge-, h, → **wollen**) F want to go: **wo willst du hin?** where are you going?

'hinziehen (irr, sep, -ge-, → **ziehen**) **I** v/t (h) **1.** draw s.o., s.th. (**zu** to; towards): fig. **sich hingezogen fühlen zu** feel drawn towards. **2.** fig. drag s.th. out. **II** v/i (sn) **3.** a) move (**über** acc across, **zu** towards), b) move there. **III** sich ~ (h) **4.** drag on (**über Wochen** etc for weeks etc). **5.** stretch (**bis zu** to, as far as).

hinzu [hin'tsu:] adv in addition, besides.

hin'zufügen v/t (dat to) add, append.

Hin'zufügung f (-; no pl) addition: **unter** ~ **von** (or gen) (by) adding.

hin'zukommen v/i (irr, sep, -ge-, sn, → **kommen**) **1.** come (along): ~ **zu** join (s.o., s.th.). **2.** a) be added, b) follow: **hinzu kommt, daß ...** add to this ..., besides ...; **es kommt noch hinzu, daß er ...** what is more he ...

hin'zuziehen v/t (irr, sep, -ge-, h, → **ziehen**) **j-n** ~ call s.o. in, consult s.o.

Hiobsbotschaft ['hi:ɔps-] *f* bad news.

Hirn [hırn] *n* (-[e]s; -e) **1.** *anat.* brain. **2.** *gastr.* brains. **3.** *fig.* brain(s), head, mind: **sich das ~ zermartern** rack one's brains.

'**Hirngespinst** *n* (**ein reines ~** a mere) fantasy, *w.s.* pipe dream.

'**Hirnhaut** *f anat.* meninges. '**Hirnhautentzündung** *f* 🔊 meningitis.

'**hirnlos** *adj a.* F *fig.* brainless.

'**Hirnrinde** *f anat.* cerebral cortex.

'**hirnrissig,** '**hirnverbrannt** *adj* F mad.

Hirsch [hırʃ] *m* (-es; -e) stag. **~braten** *m* roast venison. **~fänger** *m* hunting knife. **~kalb** *n* fawn. **~keule** *f gastr.* haunch of venison. **~kuh** *f* hind. **~leder** *n,* ⊇**ledern** *adj* buckskin.

Hirse ['hırzə] *f* (-; -n) 🌿 millet.

Hirte ['hırtə] *m* (-n; -n) herdsman, shepherd (*a. eccl.*). '**Hirtenbrief** *m eccl.* pastoral letter. '**Hirtenvolk** *n* pastoral tribe. '**Hirtin** *f* (-; -nen) shepherdess.

his, His [hıs] *n* (-; -) ♪ B sharp.

hissen ['hısən] *v/t* (h) hoist.

Historiker [hıs'to:rikər] *m* (-s; -) historian. **historisch** [hıs'to:rıʃ] *adj a)* historical, *b)* historic (*figure, moment, etc*).

Hit [hıt] *m* (-[s]; -s) ♪ *or* F *fig.* hit.

'**Hitliste** *f* ♪ *the* top ten *etc* (of the week *etc*). '**Hitpa,rade** *f* ♪ hit parade.

Hitze ['hıtsə] *f* (-; *no pl*) (**bei dieser ~** in this) heat: 🔊 **fliegende ~** hot flushes; **in der ~ des Gefechts** in the heat of the moment. ⊇**beständig** *adj* heat-resistant. ⊇**empfindlich** *adj* sensitive to heat. ⊇**frei** *adj* **~ haben** have time off from school because of very hot weather. **~grad** *m* degree of heat. **~schild** *m* heat shield. **~welle** *f* heat wave.

'**Hitzkopf** *m* hothead.

'**hitzköpfig** [-kœpfıç] *adj* hotheaded.

'**Hitzschlag** *m* heat stroke.

H-Milch ['ha:mılç] *f* long-life milk.

hob [ho:p] *pret of* **heben.**

Hobby ['hɔbi] *n* (-s; -s) hobby.

Hobel ['ho:bəl] *m* (-s; -) plane. **hobeln** ['ho:bəln] *v/t, v/i* (h) plane.

hoch [ho:x] I *adj* **1.** high (*a. fig. costs, income, etc*), *a.* tall (*tree etc*), deep (*snow, water*), *a.* great (*speed etc, a. hono[u]r, value, etc*), heavy (*penalty*), high(-pitched) (*sound, voice*): **ein hohes Alter erreichen** live to a ripe old age; **hohe Niederlage** *sports:* crushing

defeat; ♪ **das hohe C** top C; *parl. das Hohe Haus* the House; **der hohe Norden** the far North; *fig. das ist mir zu ~!* that's above me!; → **Maß**[1] 3, **Roß, Tier** *etc.* **II** *adv* **2.** high, *fig.* highly: **~ oben** high up, on high; **~ gewinnen** win high; **~ verlieren** *sports:* get trounced; **~ spielen** play (*a. fig.* gamble) high; **sie kamen drei Mann ~** there were three of them; **j-m et. ~ und heilig versprechen** promise s.o. s.th. solemnly; **wenn es ~ kommt** at (the) most; **Hände ~!** hands up!; **~ lebe ...!** long live ...!; **~ soll er leben!** three cheers for him!; → **hinauswollen** 2. **3.** → a) **hinauf,** b) **herauf.** **4.** ♣ **fünf ~ zwei** five (raised) to the second power; **sechs ~ drei** six cubed.

Hoch *n* (-s; -s) **1.** *meteor.* high(-pressure area). **2.** cheers. **3.** *fig.* high.

'**Hochachtung** *f* deep respect: **alle ~!** my compliment!; **mit vorzüglicher ~** → '**hochachtungsvoll** *adv* Yours faithfully, Sincerely yours.

'**Hochadel** *m* high nobility.

'**hochaktu,ell** *adj* highly topical.

'**hochal,pin** *adj* (high) alpine.

'**Hochal,tar** *m* high altar.

'**hochangesehen** *adj* highly esteemed.

'**Hochan,tenne** *f* overhead aerial (*Am.* antenna).

'**hocharbeiten: sich ~** (*sep, -ge-,* h) work one's way up.

'**Hochbahn** *f* elevated railway (*Am.* railroad).

'**Hochbau** *m* (-[e]s; -ten) structural engineering.

'**hochbegabt** *adj* highly gifted.

'**hochbetagt** *adj* very old, aged.

'**Hochbetrieb** *m* (-[e]s; *no pl*) intense activity, rush: **es herrschte ~** they (*or* we) were extremely busy.

'**hochbezahlt** *adj* highly paid.

'**hochbringen** *v/t* (*irr, sep, -ge-,* h, → **bringen**) **1.** bring *s.o., s.th.* up. **2.** F get *s.th.* up. **3.** make *a firm* a going concern: **e-e Firma wieder ~** put a firm back on its feet.

'**Hochburg** *f* stronghold.

'**hochdeutsch** *adj,* '**Hochdeutsch** *n* standard (*or* High) German.

'**hochdo,tiert** *adj a)* highly paid, *b)* tournament *etc* carrying a high prize.

'**Hochdruck** *m* (-[e]s; *no pl*) **1.** *meteor., phys.* high pressure: *fig. mit ~ arbeiten* work (at) full blast. **2.** ⚡ high blood pressure. **'Hochdruckgebiet** *n meteor.* high-pressure area.

'Hochebene *f* plateau.

'hochempfindlich *adj* highly sensitive, *phot.* high-speed (*film*).

'hochentwickelt *adj* highly developed, ⊚ sophisticated.

'hocherfreut *adj* (most) delighted (*über acc* at).

'Hochfi,nanz *f* (-; *no pl*) high finance.

'hochfliegen *v/i* (*irr, sep*, -ge-, sn, → *fliegen*) fly up, soar. **'hochfliegend** *adj fig.* ambitious, high-flown (*plans*).

'Hochform *f* (-; *no pl*) (**in ~** in) top form.

'Hochfor,mat *n* upright format.

'Hochfre,quenz *f* high frequency.

'Hochga,rage *f* multistor(e)y car park.

'Hochgebirge *n* high mountain region.

'Hochgebirgs... alpine, mountain.

'hochgehen (*irr, sep*, -ge-, → *gehen*) **I** *v/i* **1.** go up, *curtain, prices*: *a.* rise. **2.** F *bomb etc*: explode, blow up, *fig. person*: *a.* hit the ceiling: **et. ~ lassen** blow s.th. up. **3.** F *criminal etc*: be caught: **~ lassen** a) expose, b) nab, c) round up, *sl.* bust (*gang*). **II** *v/t* → *hinaufgehen* II.

'Hochgenuß *m* (real) treat.

'hochgeschlossen *adj* high-necked.

'Hochgeschwindigkeits... high-speed ...

'hochgespannt *adj* high (*expectations etc*), ambitious (*plans*).

'hochgestellt *adj fig.* high-ranking.

'hochgestochen *adj* F **1.** stuck-up. **2.** jumped-up, very highbrow.

'hochgewachsen *adj* tall.

'Hochglanz *m* high polish (*or* gloss).

'Hochglanzpa,pier *n* high-gloss paper. ⊚

'hochgradig [-gra:dıç] *adj* **1.** extreme, ⊚ high-grade. **2.** F utter (*nonsense etc*).

'hochhackig [-hakıç] *adj* high-heeled.

'hochhalten *v/t* (*irr, sep*, -ge-, h, → *halten*) **1.** hold *s.o., s.th.* up. **2.** *fig.* uphold, hono(u)r (*s.o.'s memory*).

'Hochhaus *n* tower block, high rise.

'hochheben *v/t* (*irr, sep*, -ge-, h, → *heben*) lift (up), raise.

'hochinteres,sant *adj* most interesting.

'hochjubeln *v/t* (*sep*, -ge-, h) F glorify.

'hochkant *adv* on end: **~ stellen** up-end.

'hochka,rätig *adj* **1.** high-carat. **2.** *fig.* 24-carat, top-flight.

'hochklappen *v/t* (*sep*, -ge-, h) turn up (*collar etc*), tip (*seat etc*).

'hochkommen *v/i* (*irr, sep*, -ge-, sn, → *kommen*) **1.** come up: (*wieder*) **~** get up (again), *fig.* get back on one's feet. **2.** *fig.* get ahead, F make it. **3. wenn es hochkommt** at the most, at best.

'Hochkonjunk,tur *f* ↑ boom.

'hochkrempeln *v/t* (*sep*, -ge-, h) roll up.

'Hochland *n* highland(s).

'hochleben *v/i* (*sep*, -ge-, h) **~ lassen** a) give three cheers for, b) toast; **er lebe hoch!** three cheers for him!

'Hochleistung *f* high performance.

'Hochleistungs... ⊚ high-power(ed), high-speed ..., heavy-duty ... **~sport** *m* high-performance sport(s). **~sportler(in** *f*) *m* top athlete.

'hochmo,dern *adj* ultramodern.

'Hochmut *m* arrogance: **~ kommt vor dem Fall** pride goes before a fall.

hochmütig ['ho:xmy:tıç] *adj* arrogant.

hochnäsig ['ho:xnɛ:zıç] *adj* stuck-up.

'hochnehmen *v/t* (*irr, sep*, -ge-, h, → *nehmen*) **1.** pick *s.o., s.th.* up. **2.** F *fig. j-n* **~** a) pull s.o.'s leg, b) fleece s.o., take s.o. for a ride, c) nab s.o.

'Hochofen *m* ⊚ (blast) furnace.

'hochpro,zentig *adj* **1.** 🔥 highly concentrated. **2.** high-proof (*spirits*).

'hochqualifi,ziert *adj* highly qualified.

'hochrechnen *v/t* (*sep*, -ge-, h) project.

'Hochrechnung *f* projection, *a.* (computer) forecast.

'Hochruf *m* cheer.

'Hochsai,son *f* peak season.

'hochschätzen *v/t* (*sep*, -ge-, h) *j-n* **~** esteem s.o. highly.

'hochschaukeln *v/t* (*sep*, -ge-, h) F *fig.* play up: **sich** (*gegenseitig*) **~** get each other all worked up.

'hochschnellen *v/i* (*sep*, -ge-, sn) **1.** bounce up. **2.** *fig. prices*: rocket.

'hochschrauben *v/t* (*sep*, -ge-, h) force up (*prices*), raise (*expectations*).

'Hochschulabsol,vent *m* (university *or* college) graduate. **~ausbildung** *f* university (*or* college) education.

'Hochschule *f* a) university, b) college; → *technisch*. **'Hochschüler(in** *f*) *m* university (*or* college) student.

'Hochschullehrer(in *f*) *m* university (*or* college) teacher (*or* lecturer). **~reife** *f* university entrance qualification(s).

'hochschwanger *adj* far advanced in pregnancy.

'Hochsee f (-; no pl) high sea(s).
'Hochseefische,rei f deep-sea fishing.
'Hochseejacht f ocean-going yacht.
'Hochseilakt m tight-rope act.
'Hochsitz m hunt. (raised) hide.
'Hochsommer m (im ~ in) midsummer.
'Hochspannung f (-; -en) **1.** ∮ high tension (or voltage). **2.** no pl fig. a) high tension, b) great suspense: **politische ~** high political tension. **'Hochspannungskabel** n high-voltage cable.
'hochspielen v/t (sep, -ge-, h) fig. et. ~ play s.th. up.
'Hochsprache f standard language: **die deutsche ~** Standard German.
'hochsprachlich adj standard: **nicht ~** substandard.
'Hochspringer(in f) m high jumper.
'Hochsprung m (-[e]s) high jump.
höchst [høːçst] adv highly, extremely, most: → **höchste.**
'Höchstalter n maximum age.
'Hochstape'lei f (-; -en) **1.** a. fig. imposture. **2.** (gross) overstatement.
'hochstapeln v/i (sep, -ge-, h) **1.** be an impostor. **2.** exaggerate.
'Hochstapler m (-s; -), **'Hochstaplerin** f (-; -nen) impostor, fig. fraud.
'Höchstbelastung f ⊙ maximum load.
'Höchstbetrag m maximum (amount).
höchste [ˈhøːçstə] adj highest, †, ⊙ a. maximum, top, a. tallest, a. uppermost, a. extreme, utmost: **am ~n** highest; → **Instanz, Zeit.**
'höchstens adv **1.** at (the) most, at best: adm. **von ~** not exceeding. **2.** except.
'Höchstfall m im ~ → **höchstens 1.**
'Höchstform f sports: top form.
'Höchstgeschwindigkeit f maximum (or top) speed: **mit ~** at top speed; **zulässige ~** speed limit.
'Höchstgrenze f upper limit.
'Höchstleistung f top performance, sports: a. record, ⊙ a. maxium output, research etc: supreme achievement.
'Höchstmaß n ein ~ **an Sicherheit** etc a maximum of safety etc.
'Höchstpreis m maximum price: **zum ~** at the highest price.
'Höchststand m highest level: **e-n ~ erreichen** peak.
'Höchststrafe f maximum penalty.
'höchstwahr'scheinlich adv in all probability.

'Höchstwert m maximum value.
'höchstzulässig adj maximum (permissible).
'Hochtouren pl **auf ~ bringen** a) rev engine up to full speed, b) fig. get s.o., s.th. really going; **auf ~ laufen** run at full speed, a. fig. go at full blast.
'hochtrabend adj pompous.
'Hoch- und 'Tiefbau m (-[e]s; no pl) structural and civil engineering.
'hochverdient adj a) well-deserved (success etc), b) person of great merit.
'hochverehrt adj a) highly esteemed, b) Dear Mr Brown etc.
'Hochverrat m high treason.
'hochverräterisch adj treasonable.
'hochverzinslich adj high-interest-bearing.
'Hochwald m timber forest.
'Hochwasser n (-s; -) **1.** high tide (or water). **2.** flood: **der Fluß führt ~** the river is in flood. **~gefahr** f danger of flooding. **~kata,strophe** f flood disaster. **~stand** m high-water level.
'hochwerfen v/t (irr, sep, -ge-, h, → **werfen**) throw s.o., s.th. up.
'hochwertig adj a) high-grade, high-quality, b) highly nutritious.
'Hochwild n big game.
Hochzeit [ˈhɔxtsaıt] f (-; -en) wedding, marriage: **~ haben, ~ feiern** get married; **zur ~ schenken** (**bekommen**) give (get) as a wedding present.
'Hochzeits... wedding (present, dress, etc). **~nacht** f wedding night. **~reise** f honeymoon (trip): **auf ~** honeymooning. **~tag** m a) wedding day, b) wedding anniversary.
'hochziehen v/t (irr, sep, -ge-, h, → **ziehen**) draw up, pull up (a. ≯), hoist (flag, sail): **sich ~ an** (dat) a) pull o.s. up by, b) F fig. get an ego-boost out of.
Hocke [ˈhɔkə] f (-; -n) **1.** squat, crouch: **in der ~** in a crouch; **in die ~ gehen** squat down. **2.** diving: tuck (position).
hocken [ˈhɔkən] v/i (h) **1.** squat, crouch. **2.** dial. sit, bird: perch: **über s-n Büchern ~** pore over one's books.
'Hocker m (-s; -) stool.
Höcker [ˈhœkər] m (-s; -) zo. hump.
Hockey [ˈhɔkɛ] n (-s; no pl) hockey.
'Hockeyschläger m hockey stick.
'Hockeyspieler(in f) m hockey player.

'**Hocksprung** m a) gym. squat jump, squat vault, b) diving: tuck(ed) jump.

Hode ['ho:də] f (-; -n), '**Hoden** m (-s; -) anat. testicle. '**Hodensack** m scrotum.

Hof [ho:f] m (-[e]s, ⁓e) **1.** a) yard, b) court(yard), c) backyard, d) schoolyard. **2.** farm. **3.** court: **am** ⁓, **bei** ⁓e at court; **j-m den** ⁓ **machen** court s.o. **4.** astr., ⁂, opt. halo.

'**Hofdame** f lady-in-waiting.

hoffen ['hɔfən] v/i (h) (**auf** acc) a) hope (for), b) trust (in): **ich hoffe** I hope so; **ich hoffe nicht** I hope not; **ich hoffe es** I hope so; **das will ich nicht** ⁓ I hope not; ⁓ **wir das Beste!** let's hope for the best!; **verzweifelt** ⁓ hope against hope.

hoffentlich ['hɔfəntlɪç] adv I (or we) hope so, let's hope so, F hopefully: ⁓ **nicht!** I hope not!

Hoffnung ['hɔfnʊŋ] f (-; -en) hope (**auf** acc of): **die** ⁓ **aufgeben** abandon hope; **j-m** ⁓**en machen** raise s.o.'s hopes; **er machte mir k-e** ⁓**en** he didn't hold out any hopes for me; **sich** ⁓**en machen** have hopes (**auf** acc of ger); **mach dir k-e (falschen)** ⁓**en!** don't be too hopeful!; **s-e** ⁓ **setzen auf** (acc) pin one's hopes on; **j-n in s-n** ⁓**en enttäuschen** dash s.o.'s hopes; **(neue)** ⁓ **schöpfen** have new hopes; **es besteht k-e** ⁓ there is no hope; **in der** ⁓ **zu** inf hoping to inf; **er ist m-e einzige** ⁓ he is my only hope; pol., sports etc **die große** ⁓ the great white hope.

'**Hoffnungslauf** m sports: repechage.

'**hoffnungslos** adj hopeless, pred a. past (all) hope: fig. **er ist ein** ⁓**er Fall** he's hopeless. '**Hoffnungslosigkeit** f (-; no pl) hopelessness, despair.

'**Hoffnungsschimmer** m glimmer of hope. '**Hoffnungsträger** m pol., sports etc: the great white hope.

'**hoffnungsvoll** adj hopeful, pred full of hope (a. adv), promising (talent etc).

höfisch ['hø:fɪʃ] adj courtly.

höflich ['hø:flɪç] adj (**zu** to) polite, courteous. '**Höflichkeit** f (-; -en) **1.** no pl (**aus** ⁓ out of) politeness: **in aller** ⁓ very politely. **2.** usu. pl compliment. '**Höflichkeitsbesuch** m courtesy visit.

'**Hofnarr** m hist. or iro. court jester.

hohe ['ho:ə] → **hoch 1.**

Höhe ['hø:ə] f (-; -n) **1.** height, astr., ⁇, geogr. altitude, level: **in e-r** ⁓ **von ...** at a height (or an altitude) of ...; **in die** ⁓ up (→ a. cpds. with **hoch**...); **an** ⁓ **verlieren** lose height; **auf der** ⁓ **von** a) geogr. in the latitude of London etc, b) ⚓ off Dover etc; **auf gleicher** ⁓ (fig. on a) level (**mit** with); fig. **auf der** ⁓ **s-s Ruhms (s-r Macht)** at the height of his fame (power); F **auf der** ⁓ **sein** be in good form; **auf der** ⁓ **(der Zeit) sein** be up to date; **ich bin nicht ganz auf der** ⁓ I'm not feeling up to the mark; F **das ist doch die** ⁓**!** that's the limit!; → **treiben 1. 2.** amount: **e-e Summe in** ⁓ **von** a sum (to the amount) of; **bis zu e-r** ⁓ **von** up to, not exceeding. **3.** → **Anhöhe.**

Hoheit ['ho:haɪt] f (-; -en) **1.** no pl pol. sovereignty. **2.** (**Seine, Ihre**) ⁓ (His, Her) Highness. **3.** no pl fig. grandeur, majesty. '**hoheitlich** adj sovereign.

'**Hoheits**|**abzeichen** n national emblem. ⁓**gebiet** n territory. ⁓**gewässer** pl territorial waters.

'**Höhen**|**flosse** f ✈ tail plane. ⁓**flug** m **1.** high-altitude flight. **2.** fig. (intellectual etc) flight. ⁓**krankheit** f altitude sickness. ⁓**kurort** m mountain (health) resort. ⁓**lage** f altitude. ⁓**leitwerk** n ✈ elevator unit. ⁓**sonne** f **1.** mountain sun. **2.** ⚕ sunray lamp, sunlamp. ⁓**unterschied** m difference in altitude. ⁓**zug** m range of hills, mountain range.

'**Höhepunkt** m peak, height, climax (a. orgasm), highlight (of event etc): **auf dem** ⁓ (gen) at the height of ([one's] power, fame, etc).

höher ['hø:ər] adj and adv higher (a. fig.), a. senior: ⁓**er Dienst** senior service; ⁓**e Bildung** higher education; ⁓**e Schule** secondary school; **in** ⁓**em Maße** to a greater extent, more; **nach Höherem streben** strive for higher things.

hohl [ho:l] adj a. fig. hollow: **in der** ⁓**en Hand** in the hollow of one's hand.

'**hohläugig** ['-ɔʏgɪç] adj hollow-eyed.

'**Hohlblock(stein)** m cavity block.

Höhle ['hø:lə] f (-; -n) **1.** cave. **2.** zo. hole: fig. **sich in die** ⁓ **des Löwen wagen** beard the lion in his den. **3.** anat. cavity, (eye) socket. **4.** F hole, hovel.

'**Höhlen**|**forscher** m spel(a)eologist, potholer. ⁓**forschung** f spel(a)eology. ⁓**mensch** m cave man.

'**Hohlheit** f (-; no pl) a. fig. hollowness.

'Hohl|kehle *f* ◉ groove. **~kopf** *m* F numskull. **~körper** *m* A- hollow body. **~kreuz** *n* ☞ hollow back. **~kugel** *f* hollow sphere. **~maß** *n* measure of capacity, dry measure. **~raum** *m* cavity, hollow. **~saum** *m* hemstitch. **~schliff** *m* hollow grinding: **mit ~** hollow-ground. **~spiegel** *m* concave mirror.

'Höhlung *f* (-; -en) hollow, cavity.

'Hohl|weg *m* ravine. **~ziegel** *m* a) cavity brick, b) hollow tile.

Hohn [ho:n] *m* (-[e]s; *no pl*) a) scorn, b) derision: **nur ~ und Spott ernten** earn but scorn and derision; **der rein(st)e** (*or blanke*) **~** sheer mockery. höhnen ['hø:nən] *v/i* (h) (**über** *acc* at) sneer, jeer. 'Hohngelächter *n* derisive laughter. 'höhnisch *adj* sneering: **~e Bemerkung, ~es Lächeln** sneer.

'hohnlächeln *v/i* (*sep or insep*, -ge-, h), 'Hohnlächeln *n* (-s) sneer.

'hohnsprechen *v/i* (*irr*, *sep*, -ge-, h, → **sprechen**) make a mockery (*dat* of).

Hokuspokus [ho:kus'po:kus] *m* (-; *no pl*) hocus-pocus, *contp. a.* mumbo jumbo: **~!** hey presto!

hold [hɔlt] *adj* 1. lovely, sweet. 2. **das Glück war ihm ~** he was lucky.

Holdinggesellschaft ['hoːldɪŋ-] *f* ☆ holding company.

holen ['hoːlən] *v/t* (h) 1. get, fetch: **j-m et. ~** get s.th. for s.o.; **et. aus der Tasche ~** take (*or draw*) s.th. out of one's pocket; F **da ist nichts zu ~!** there's nothing in it (for us)!; **bei ihm ist nichts zu ~!** you won't get anything out of him!; → **Atem, Luft** 2. 2. call: **j-n lassen** send for s.o. 3. come for, pick *s.o.*, *s.th.* up. 4. **sich et. ~** a) get o.s., fetch, b) F catch (*a cold etc*); **du wirst dir noch et. ~!** you'll catch it yet!; **sich bei j-m e-n Rat ~** ask s.o.'s advice; F **sich e-n Preis ~** win (*or* get) a prize; → **Abfuhr** 2.

Holland ['hɔlant] *n* (-s) Holland, the Netherlands. Holländer ['hɔlɛndər] *m* (-s; -) Dutchman: **die ~** the Dutch. 'Holländerin *f* (-; -nen) Dutchwoman. 'holländisch [-dɪʃ] *adj*, ♀ *n* (-[s]) Dutch.

Hölle ['hœlə] *f* (-; -n) hell: **in der ~** in hell; **die ~ auf Erden** hell on earth; F **j-m die ~ heiß machen** give s.o. hell; **j-m das Leben zur ~ machen** make a life a perfect hell for s.o.; **zur ~ damit!** to hell

with it!; **die ~ ist los!** all hell has broken loose!

'Höllen|angst *f* F **e-e ~ haben** be scared stiff (*vor dat* of). **~lärm** *m* infernal noise: **e-n ~ machen** make a hell of a noise. **~qual** *f* F agony: **~en ausstehen** suffer hell. **~tempo** *n* F (*mit e-m ~ at*) breakneck speed.

höllisch ['hœlɪʃ] *adj* infernal, F hellish: **~ aufpassen** watch out like a hawk, be damn careful; **~ weh tun** hurt like hell.

Holm [hɔlm] *m* (-[e]s; -e) beam, *gym.* bar, ☞ spar.

Hologramm [holo'gram] *n* (-s; -e) *opt.* holograph.

holp(e)rig ['hɔlp(ə)rɪç] *adj* 1. bumpy. 2. *fig.* clumsy. holpern ['hɔlpərn] *v/i* 1. (sn) bump, jolt. 2. (h) *fig.* stumble.

Holunder [ho'lundar] *m* (-s; -) ♀ elder.

Ho'lunderbeere *f* elderberry.

Ho'lundertee *m* elderflower tea.

Holz [hɔlts] *n* (-es; ⸚er) 1. a) *no pl* wood, b) timber: **aus ~** wooden, (made of) wood; *fig.* **klopf auf ~!** touch wood!; **aus e-m anderen ~ geschnitzt** of a different stamp; **aus härterem ~ geschnitzt** made of sterner stuff; F **sie hat ~ vor der Hütte** she's well stacked. 2. (nine)pin: **Gut ~!** good bowling! 3. *no pl* ♪ the woodwind. **~bauweise** *f* timber construction. **~bearbeitung** *f* woodworking. **~bläser** *m* ♪ woodwind player, *pl* the woodwind (section).

holzen ['hɔltsən] *v/i* (h) F *soccer:* clog, play rough.

hölzern ['hœltsərn] *adj* wooden, *fig. a.* clumsy.

'Holzfäller [-fɛlər] *m* (-s; -) woodcutter, *Am.* lumberjack.

'Holzfaser *f* wood fibre (*Am.* fiber). **~platte** *f* wood fibreboard (*Am.* fiberboard). **~stoff** *m* a) wood cellulose, b) wood pulp.

'holzfrei *adj* wood-free (*paper*).

'Holz|hacken *n* (-s) wood chopping. **~hammer** *m* mallet: F *fig.* **mit dem ~** with a sledgehammer. **~handel** *m* timber (*Am.* lumber) trade. **~haus** *n* wooden house.

holzig ['hɔltsɪç] *adj* a) woody, b) stringy.

'Holz|kitt *m* plastic wood. **~kohle** *f* charcoal. **~scheit** *n* log. **~schnitt** *m* wood engraving. **~stoß** *m* stack of wood. **~täfelung** *f* wood(en) panel(l)ing. ♀**verar-**

beitend *adj*, **~verarbeitung** *f* wood processing. **~weg** *m* F **auf dem ~ sein** a) be on the wrong track, b) be very much mistaken. **~wolle** *f* wood wool, excelsior. **~wurm** *m* woodworm.

Homo ['ho:mo] *m* (-s; -s) F homo, queer, gay.

homogen [homo'ge:n] *adj* homogeneous.

Homonym [homo'ny:m] *n* (-s; -e) *ling.* homonym.

Homöopath [homøo'pa:t] *m* (-en; -en) ♯ hom(o)eopath. **Homöopathie** [-pa'ti:] *f* (-; *no pl*) hom(o)eopathy. **homöopathisch** [-'pa:tɪʃ] *adj* hom(o)eopathic.

Homosexuali'tät [homo-] *f* homosexuality. **homosexu'ell** *adj*, **Homosexu'elle** *m*, *f* (-n; -n) homosexual, F gay.

Honig ['ho:nɪç] *m* (-s; -e) honey: F **j-m ~ ums Maul schmieren** soft-soap s.o. **~kuchen** *m* gingerbread. **~lecken** *n* F **das war kein ~!** that was no picnic! **~me‚lone** *f* honeydew melon. **♀süß** *adj* (as) sweet as honey, *fig.* honeyed.

Honorar [hono'ra:r] *n* (-s; -e) fee, *of author:* royalty.

Honoratioren [honora'tsi̯o:rən] *pl* notabilities, local dignitaries.

honorieren [hono'ri:rən] *v/t* (h) **1.** *j-n* ~ pay (a fee to) s.o. **2.** *et.* ~ pay for s.th. **3.** ♯ hono(u)r, *fig. a.* reward.

honoris causa [ho'no:rɪs 'kaʊza] *Professor etc* ~ honorary professor *etc.*

Hopfen ['hɔpfən] *m* (-s; *no pl*) ♀ hop: F **an ihm ist ~ und Malz verloren** he's hopeless, he's a dead loss.

hopp [hɔp] *int* a) hop!, b) quick!

hoppeln ['hɔpəln] *v/i* (sn) hop.

hoppla ['hɔpla] *int* a) (wh)oops!, b) hey!

hops [hɔps] *int* jump! **Hops** *m* (-es; -e) hop. **hopsa** ['hɔpsa] *int* (wh)oops!

hopsen ['hɔpsən] *v/i* (sn) F hop.

Hopser ['hɔpsər] *m* (-s; -) F hop.

'hopsgehen *v/i* (*irr, sep*, -ge-, sn, → *gehen*) F a) get broken, b) go down the drain, c) get nabbed, d) kick the bucket. **'hopsnehmen** *v/t* (*irr, sep*, -ge-, h, → *nehmen*) F *j-n* ~ nab s.o.

'hörbar *adj* audible. **'Hörbehinderte** *m*, *f* hearing-impaired person. **'Hörbild** *n* radio feature. **'Hörbrille** *f* earglasses. **'Hörbuch** *n* talking book.

horchen ['hɔrçən] *v/i* (h) listen (**auf** *acc* to), *a.* eavesdrop: **horch!** listen!

'Horcher *m* (-s; -) eavesdropper.

Horde ['hɔrdə] *f* (-; -n) *a. fig.* horde, *contp. a.* mob, gang.

hören ['hø:rən] (h) **I** *v/t* **1.** a) hear, b) listen (**auf** *acc* to): *univ.* ~ **bei** attend the lectures of; F **mir verging ♀ und Sehen** I was stunned; ~ **Sie mal!** listen!, look here!; **na**, ~ **Sie mal!** well, really!; **das läßt sich eher** ~ that sounds more like it; **ich lasse von mir** ~ I'll be in touch; **man hörte nie wieder von ihm** he was never heard of again; → **schwer** 4. **2.** F obey, listen. **II** *v/t* **3.** a) hear, b) listen to (*concert etc*): **et.** ~ **von** hear s.th. about (*or* of); **er ließ nichts von sich** ~ he sent no news; **er wollte nichts davon** ~ he would not hear of it; **wie ich höre, will er kommen** I understand he wants to come; **soviel man hört** from all accounts; → **Radio. 4.** *univ.* attend (*lectures*), take (*subject*).

'Hörensagen *n* (-s) (**vom** ~ **by**) hearsay.

'Hörer *m* (-s; -) **1.** listener, *univ.* student. **2.** *teleph.* receiver: **den** ~ **auflegen** hang up. **'Hörerin** *f* (-; -nen) → **Hörer** 1.

'Hörerschaft *f* (-; -en) **1.** the listeners, audience. **2.** (number of) students.

'Hörfolge *f* radio series (*or* serial).

'Hörfunk *m* radio.

'Hörgerät *n*, **'Hörhilfe** *f* hearing aid.

hörig ['hø:rɪç] *adj* **j-m** ~ **sein** be enslaved to s.o. **'Hörigkeit** *f* (-; *no pl*) bondage.

Horizont [hori'tsɔnt] *m* (-[e]s; -e) (**am** ~ on the) horizon (*a. fig.*): **s-n** ~ **erweitern** broaden one's mind; F **das geht über m-n** ~ that's beyond me.

horizontal [horitsɔn'ta:l] *adj* horizontal. **Horizon'tale** *f* (-; -n) horizontal.

Hormon [hɔr'mo:n] *n* (-s; -e) hormone. **Hor'mon...**, **hormonal** [hɔrmo'na:l] *adj* hormonal.

'Hörmuschel *f teleph.* earpiece.

Horn [hɔrn] *n* (-[e]s; ⁓er) **1.** *zo.* horn, *a.* feeler (*of snail*): **aus** ~ (made of) horn; *fig.* **sich die Hörner abstoßen** sow one's wild oats; F **j-m Hörner aufsetzen** cuckold s.o.; → **Stier** 1. **2.** ♪ horn, ✗ bugle: F **ins gleiche** ~ **stoßen** chime in with s.o.

'Hornbläser(in *f*) *m* ♪ horn player.

'Hornbrille *f* horn-rimmed spectacles.

'Hörnerv *m* auditory nerve.

'Hornhaut *f* **1.** callus. **2.** *of eye:* cornea.

Hornisse [hɔr'nɪsə] *f* (-; -n) *zo.* hornet.

Hornist [hɔrˈnɪst] *m* (-en; -en) ♩ hornist.
'Hornvieh *n* (-s; *no pl*) horned cattle.
Horoskop [horoˈsko:p] *n* (-s; -e) (*j-m das ~ stellen* cast s.o.'s) horoscope.
Horror [ˈhɔrɔr] *m* (-s; *no pl*) horror (*vor dat* of). **'Horrorfilm** *m* horror film.
'Hörsaal *m* lecture hall.
'Hörspiel *n* radio play.
Horst [hɔrst] *m* (-es; -e) nest, eyrie.
'Hörsturz *m* ♪ aural attack.
Hort [hɔrt] *m* (-[e]s; -e) **1.** hoard, treasure. **2.** (safe) refuge. **3.** *fig.* stronghold. **4.** day nursery. **'horten** *v/t* (h) hoard.
Hortensie [hɔrˈtɛnziə] *f* (-; -n) ♣ hydrangea.
'Hörtest *m* hearing test: *e-n ~ machen lassen* have one's ears tested.
'Hörvermögen *n* (-s; *no pl*) hearing.
'Hörweite *f* (-; *no pl*) hearing range: *in (außer) ~* within (out of) earshot.
Höschen [ˈhøːsçən] *n* (-s; -) panties.
Hose [ˈhoːzə] *f* (-; -n) (*a. ein Paar ~n*) (a pair of) trousers *pl* (*Am.* pants): *kurze ~(n)* shorts; *zwei ~n* two pairs of trousers (*etc*); (*sich*) *in die ~(n) machen* make a mess in one's pants, F *fig.* be scared stiff; F *die ~n anhaben* wear the trousers (*Am.* pants); *das ging in die ~* that was a complete flop; *e-e tote ~ sein* be a complete washout.
'Hosen|anzug *m* trouser suit, *Am.* pantsuit. *~bein* *n* trouser leg. *~boden* *m* (trouser) seat: F *sich auf den ~ setzen* buckle down to work. *~bügel* *m* trouser hanger. *~bund* *m* waistband. *~klammer* *f* trouser clip. *~rock* *m* culottes. *~schlitz* *m* fly. *~tasche* *f* trouser(s) pocket. *~träger* *pl* (pair of) braces (*Am.* suspenders).
hospitieren [hɔspiˈtiːrən] *v/i* (h) sit in on classes (*or* lectures) (*bei* with).
Hospiz [hɔsˈpiːts] *n* (-es; -e) hospice.
Hostess [hɔsˈtɛs] *f* (-; -en) hostess.
Hostie [ˈhɔstiə] *f* (-; -n) *eccl.* host.
Hotel [hoˈtɛl] *n* (-s; -s) hotel: *~ garni* bed and breakfast hotel.
Ho'telfach *n* (-[e]s; *no pl*) hotel business.
Ho'telgewerbe *n* hotel industry.
Hotelier [hoteˈliːe] *m* (-s; -s) hotelier.
Ho'telverzeichnis *n* list of hotels.
Ho'telzimmer *n* hotel room.
Hub [huːp] *m* (-[e]s; ⸚e) *mot.*, ⚙ stroke.
hüben [ˈhyːbən] *adv* over here, on this side: *~ wie drüben* on both sides.

'Hubraum *m* *mot.* cubic capacity.
hübsch [hypʃ] *adj* a) pretty, good-looking, b) nice, F *fig. a.* fine: *ein ~es Sümmchen* a tidy sum; *das wirst du ~ bleiben lassen!* you're not going to do anything of the sort!
'Hubschrauber *m* (-s; -) helicopter.
'Hubschrauberlandeplatz *m* heliport.
'Hubstapler [-ʃtaːplər] *m* (-s; -) stacker truck.
huch [hʊx] *int* ooh!
'huckepack *adv* F pick-a-back. **'Huckepackverkehr** *m* pick-a-back traffic.
hudeln [ˈhuːdəln] *v/i* (h) F work sloppily.
Huf [huːf] *m* (-[e]s; -e) hoof.
'Hufeisen *n* horseshoe. **'Hufeisenform** *f* (*in ~* arranged in a) horseshoe.
'hufeisenförmig [-fœrmɪç] *adj* horseshoe-shaped.
'Huflattich *m* ♣ coltsfoot.
'Hüftbein *n* hipbone. **Hüfte** [ˈhyftə] *f* (-; -n) hip. **'Hüftgelenk** *n* hip joint. **'Hüftgürtel** *m*, **'Hüfthalter** *m* suspender (*Am.* garter) belt. **'hüfthoch** *adj and adv* waist-high, *water:* waist-deep. **'Hüftweite** *f* hip measurement.
Hügel [ˈhyːgəl] *m* (-s; -) a) hill, *a.* hillock, b) mound. **'hüg(e)lig** *adj* hilly.
Huhn [huːn] *n* (-[e]s; ⸚er) fowl, chicken (*a. gastr.*), hen: *mit den Hühnern aufstehen (zu Bett gehen)* get up with the lark (go to bed early); F *da lachen ja die Hühner!* that's a laugh!; *dummes ~* silly goose; *verrücktes ~* crazy thing.
Hühnchen [ˈhyːnçən] *n* (-s; -) **1.** (young) chicken: F *mit j-m ein ~ zu rupfen haben* have a score to settle with s.o. **2.** *gastr.* (roast) chicken.
Hühnerauge [ˈhyːnər-] *n* corn: F *fig. j-m auf die ~n treten* tread on s.o.'s corns.
'Hühneraugenpflaster *n* corn plaster.
'Hühner|brühe *f* chicken broth. *~brust* *f* **1.** *gastr.* chicken breast. **2.** ♪ pigeon breast. *~ei* *n* hen's egg. *~farm* *f* chicken farm. *~futter* *n* chickenfeed. *~hof* *m* chicken yard. *~leiter* *f* chicken ladder. *~pest* *f* *vet.* fowl pest. *~stall* *m* henhouse. *~zucht* *f* chicken farming.
huldigen [ˈhʊldɪgən] *v/i* (h) *j-m ~* pay homage to s.o. **'Huldigung** *f* (-; -en) homage (*an acc* to).
Hülle [ˈhylə] *f* (-; -n) **1.** wrap(ping), cover, (*record*) sleeve, *Am.* jacket (*a.* of *book*), envelope: *die sterbliche ~* the

mortal remains. **2.** F clothes. **3.** *fig.* veil, cloak. **4.** *in* ~ *und Fülle* in abundance, plenty of, *whisky etc* galore.

hüllen ['hʏlən] *v/t* (h) (*in acc*) wrap *s.o.*, *s.th.* (up) (in), cover (with): *sich in Schweigen* ~ remain silent (*über acc* about); *in Dunkel (Nebel) gehüllt* shrouded in darkness (fog).

'**hüllenlos** *adj* naked.

Hülse ['hʏlzə] *f* (-; -n) **1.** ⚘ a) hull, husk, b) pod. **2.** ⚙ a) sleeve, socket, b) case.

'**Hülsenfrucht** *f* legume(n), *pl* pulse.

human [hu'ma:n] *adj* humane, F *a.* decent, ♂ human. **Hu'mange,netik** *f* ♂ human genetics.

Humanismus [huma'nɪsmʊs] *m* (-; *no pl*) humanism: *hist. der* ~ Humanism. **Humanist** [-'nɪst] *m* (-en; -en) humanist, *ped., univ.* classicist, *hist.* Humanist. **huma'nistisch** *adj* humanist(ic), *ped., univ.* classical: → *Gymnasium.*

humanitär [humani'tɛ:r] *adj* humanitarian. **Humanität** [humani'tɛ:t] *f* (-; *no pl*) humaneness, humanity.

Hu'manmedi,zin *f* human medicine.

Humbug ['hʊmbʊk] *m* (-s; *no pl*) humbug.

Hummel ['hʊməl] *f* (-; -n) bumblebee.

Hummer ['hʊmər] *m* (-s; -) lobster.

Humor [hu'mo:r] *m* (-s; *no pl*) humo(u)r: *k-n Sinn für* ~ *haben* have no sense of humo(u)r; *den* ~ *behalten* keep one's sense of humo(u)r; *et. mit* ~ *nehmen* take s.th. in good humo(u)r; *du hast (vielleicht)* ~*!* you've got a nerve!

Humoreske [humo'rɛskə] *f* (-; -n) humoresque, humorous sketch (*or* story).

Humorist [humo'rɪst] *m* (-en; -en) humorist. **humo'ristisch** *adj* humorous.

hu'morlos *adj* humo(u)rless: *er ist völlig* ~ *a.* he has absolutely no sense of humo(u)r. **hu'morvoll** *adj* humorous.

humpeln ['hʊmpəln] *v/i* (h *or* sn) limp.

Humpen ['hʊmpən] *m* (-s; -) tankard.

Humus ['hu:mʊs] *m* (-; *no pl*) humus.

'**Humusschicht** *f* humus layer, topsoil.

Hund [hʊnt] *m* (-[e]s; -e) dog, *hunt.* hound: *junger* ~ puppy; *fig. schlauer (feiger)* ~ sly (yellow) dog; F (*gemeiner*) ~ bastard; *der arme* ~*!* (the) poor sod!; *das ist ja ein dicker* ~*!* that takes the cake!; *auf den* ~ *kommen* go to the dogs; (*ganz*) *auf dem* ~ *sein* be down and out, *a.* be a wreck; *vor die* ~*e*

gehen a) go to the dogs, b) kick the bucket; *wie* ~ *und Katze leben* lead a cat-and-dog life; *er ist bekannt wie ein bunter* ~ he's known all over the place; *da liegt der* ~ *begraben!* that's it (*or* why)!; *damit kann man k-n* ~ *hinterm Ofen hervorlocken!* that won't tempt anybody!; ~*e, die bellen, beißen nicht* barking dogs seldom bite.

'**Hundeausstellung** *f* dog show.

'**hunde'elend** *adj* F *mir ist* ~ I feel lousy.

'**Hunde|futter** *n* dog food. ~**halsband** *n* dog collar. ~**hütte** *f* (dog) kennel.

'**hunde'kalt** *adj* F freezing cold.

'**Hunde|kuchen** *m* dog biscuit. ~**leben** *n* F dog's life. ~**leine** *f* dog lead, dog leash. ~**marke** *f* dog licence disc, *Am.* dog tag.

'**hunde'müde** *adj* F dog-tired.

hundert ['hʊndərt] *adj* a (*or* one) hundred: *einige* (*or ein paar*) ~ *Leute* a few hundred people. '**Hundert**[1] *n* (-s; -e) hundred: *zu* ~*en* in hundreds; *zehn von* ~ ten in a hundred, ten per cent. '**Hundert**[2] *f* (-; -en) hundred.

Hunderter ['hʊndərtər] *m* (-s; -) **1.** ♈ a) (the) hundred, b) three-figure number. **2.** F one-hundred-mark *etc* note (*Am.* bill). '**hunderter'lei** [-'laɪ] *adj* a hundred and one. '**hundertfach I** *adj* hundredfold. **II** *adv* a hundred times.

Hundert'jahrfeier *f* centenary, *Am.* centennial. '**hundertjährig** [-jɛ:rɪç] *adj* **1.** one-hundred-year-old. **2.** of a hundred years, hundred years' ...

'**hundertmal** *adv* a hundred times.

Hundert'markschein *m* one-hundred-mark note (*Am.* bill). **Hundert'meterlauf** *m* the 100-metres (*Am.* meters).

'**hundertpro,zentig** *adj* a hundred per cent (*a. fig.*), pure (*alcohol, wool, etc*), *fig.* out-and-out (*conservative etc*): F *das weiß ich* ~ I'm dead sure.

'**hundertst** *adj* hundredth. '**hundertstel** *adj*, '**Hundertstel** *n* (-s; -) hundredth.

'**hundert'tausend** *adj* a (*or* one) hundred thousand.

'**Hundesa,lon** *m* dog parlo(u)r.

'**Hundezucht** *f* **1.** dog breeding. **2.** (breeding) kennel(s).

'**Hundezüchter(in** *f*) *m* dog breeder.

Hündin ['hʏndɪn] *f* (-; -nen) bitch.

hündisch ['hʏndɪʃ] *adj fig.* cringing.

'**hundsge'mein** *adj* F a) dirty, low-down, nasty, b) hellish (*job etc*).
'**hundsmise,rabel** *adj* F lousy.
'**Hundstage** *pl* dog days.
Hüne ['hy:nə] *m* (-n; -n) giant.
'**Hünengrab** *n* megalithic grave.
'**hünenhaft** *adj* gigantic.
Hunger ['huŋər] *m* (-s; *no pl*) **1.** hunger (*a. fig.* **nach** for): ~ **haben** (**bekommen**) be (get) hungry; ~ **leiden** go hungry; **vor** ~ **sterben** starve to death; *ich sterbe vor* ~ I'm starving; ~ *ist der beste Koch* hunger is the best sauce. **2.** → *Hungersnot.*
'**Hungerleider** [-laidər] *m* (-s; -) starveling.
'**Hungerlohn** *m* starvation wages.
hungern ['huŋərn] (h) **I** *v/i* a) go hungry, starve, *fig.* hunger (**nach** for), b) starve o.s., go without food. **II** *sich zu Tode* ~ starve o.s. to death.
'**hungernd** *adj* hungry, starving.
'**Hungerö,dem** *n* 𝕏 famine (o)edema.
'**Hungersnot** *f* famine.
'**Hungerstreik** *m* (*in den* ~ *treten* go on a) hunger strike. **Hungertod** *m* (-[e]s; *no pl*) death from starvation. '**Hungertuch** *n* F *fig.* **am** ~ **nagen** be starving.
hungrig ['huŋrɪç] *adj a. fig.* hungry (**nach** for): ~ *sein* be (*or* feel) hungry; *das macht* ~ that makes you hungry.
Hunne ['hunə] *m* (-n; -n) *hist.* Hun.
Hupe ['hu:pə] *f* (-; -n) horn: *auf die* ~ *drücken* → **hupen** ['hu:pən] *v/i* (h) hoot, honk, sound the horn.
hüpfen ['hypfən] *v/i* (sn) hop, skip, *ball:* bounce.
'**Hupsi,gnal** *n* honk, hoot.
Hürde ['hyrdə] *f* (-; -n) **1.** (*a. fig.* **e-e** ~ *nehmen* take a) hurdle. **2.** fold.
'**Hürdenlauf** *m sports:* hurdles.
'**Hürdenläufer(in** *f*) *m sports:* hurdler.
Hure ['hu:rə] *f* (-; -n) whore.
hurra [hʊ'ra:] *int* hurray!, hurrah!
Hurrikan ['hʊrika:n] *m* (-s; -e) hurricane.
husch [hʊʃ] *int* a) whoosh!, b) shoo!
huschen ['hʊʃən] *v/i* (sn) flit.
hüsteln ['hy:stəln] *v/i* (h) cough slightly.
husten ['hu:stən] (h) **I** *v/i* cough (*a. fig. engine*): *stark* ~ have a bad cough; F ~ *auf* (*acc*) not to give a damn for. **II** *v/t* cough up: F *dem werde ich was* ~*!* to hell with him!

'**Husten** *m* (-s; -) cough. ~**anfall** *m* coughing fit. ~**bon,bon** *m, n* cough drop. ~**reiz** *m* tickle in one's throat. ~**saft** *m* cough syrup. ~**tee** *m* bronchial tea. ~**tropfen** *pl* cough drops.
Hut[1] *m* (-[e]s; *ᵘe*) **1.** hat: F *fig. ein alter* ~ old hat; *den* ~ *abnehmen* (*or ziehen*) take off one's hat (*fig.* **vor** *j-m* to s.o.); ~ *ab* (*vor dir*)! I'll take my hat off to you!; *alles unter einen* ~ *bringen* reconcile things; F *damit habe ich nichts am* ~ I can't be bothered with that!; *ihm ging der* ~ *hoch* he blew his top; F *fig. den* ~ *nehmen müssen* have to go (*or* resign); *das kannst du dir an den* ~ *stecken!* (you can) keep it! **2.** 𝔅 cap.
Hut[2] *f* (-; *no pl*) **1.** *in j-s* ~ in s.o.'s care; *in guter* (*or sicherer*) ~ *sein* be safe (*bei* with). **2.** *auf der* ~ *sein* be on one's guard (*vor dat* against).
'**Hutablage** *f* hat rack.
hüten ['hy:tən] (h) **I** *v/t* look after, mind (*children etc*), guard (*a. secret etc*): → *Bett.* **II** *sich* ~ (*vor dat*) be on one's guard (against), watch out (for); *sich* ~, *et. zu tun* take care not to do s.th.; *ich werde mich* ~*!* I'll do nothing of the sort!; *hüte dich vor* ...*!* beware of ...!
'**Hüter** *m* (-s; -), '**Hüterin** *f* (-; -nen) guardian, keeper: *humor. der Hüter des Gesetzes* (the arm of) the Law.
'**Hutgeschäft** *n* hat shop. '**Hutgröße** *f* hat size. '**Hutkrempe** *f* (hat) brim.
'**Hutmacher** *m* (-s; -) hatter.
'**Hutmacherin** *f* (-; -nen) milliner.
'**Hutschnur** *f* hat string: F *fig. das geht mir über die* ~*!* that's going too far!
Hütte ['hytə] *f* (-; -n) **1.** a) hut, cabin, b) *contp.* shack, shanty, c) refuge. **2.** → *Hüttenwerk.*
'**Hüttenindu,strie** *f* iron and steel industry. '**Hüttenwerk** *n* metallurgical plant.
Hyäne [hy'ɛ:nə] *f* (-; -n) *zo.* hyena.
Hyazinthe [hya'tsɪntə] *f* (-; -n) hyacinth.
Hybride [hy'bri:də] *f* (-; -n) hybrid.
Hydrant [hy'drant] *m* (-en; -en) hydrant.
Hydrat [hy'dra:t] *n* (-[e]s; -e) 🜍 hydrate.
Hydraulik [hy'draʊlɪk] *f* (-; *no pl*) hydraulics. **hy'draulisch** *adj* hydraulic.
hydrieren [hy'dri:rən] *v/t* (h) hydrogenate.
'**Hy'drierwerk** *n* hydrogenation plant.
Hydrody'namik [hydro-] *f* hydrodynamics.

Hydrokul,tur ['hy:dro-] *f* hydroponics.
Hydrolyse [hydro'ly:zə] *f* (-; -n) 🜊 hydrolysis.
Hygiene [hy'ǧie:nə] *f* (-; *no pl*) hygiene.
hygi'enisch *adj* hygienic.
Hygrometer [hygro'me:tər] *n* (-s; -) hygrometer.
Hymne ['hymnə] *f* (-; -n) hymn (**an** *acc* to).
Hyperbel [hy'pɛrbəl] *f* (-; -n) **1.** 𝔸 hyperbola. **2.** *ling.* hyperbole.
hypermo'dern [hypər-] *adj* ultramodern.
Hypertonie [hypərto'ni:] *f* (-; -n) 🞇 hypertension.
Hypnose [hyp'no:zə] *f* (-; -n) (*in* ~ under) hypnosis. **hyp'notisch** [-tɪʃ] *adj* hypnotic. **Hypnotiseur** [hypnoti'zø:r] *m* (-s; -e) hypnotist. **hypnotisieren** [hypnoti'zi:rən] *v/t* (h) hypnotize.
Hypochonder [hypo'xɔndər] *m* (-s; -),

hypo'chondrisch *adj* hypochondriac.
Hypotenuse [hypote'nu:zə] *f* (-; -n) 𝔸 hypotenuse.
Hypothek [hypo'te:k] *f* (-; -en) 🌳 mortgage: *e-e* ~ *aufnehmen* raise a mortgage (*auf acc* on); *mit e-r* ~ *belasten* (encumber *s.th.* with a) mortgage.
hypothekarisch [hypote'ka:rɪʃ] *adj and adv* by (*or* on) mortgage.
Hypo'theken|bank *f* mortgage bank. **~brief** *m* mortgage deed. **𝔩frei** *adj* unmortgaged. **~gläubiger(in** *f*) *m* mortgagee. **~pfandbrief** *m* mortgage bond. **~schuldner(in** *f*) *m* mortgagor.
Hypothese [hypo'te:zə] *f* (-; -n) hypothesis. **hypo'thetisch** *adj* hypothetical.
Hypotonie [hypoto'ni:] *f* (-; -n) 🞇 hypotension.
Hysterie [hyste'ri:] *f* (-; *no pl*) 🞇 hysteria.
hysterisch [hys'te:rɪʃ] *adj* hysterical: **~er Anfall** hysterics.

I

I, i [i:] *n* (-; -) I, i: *i wo!* not a bit of it!
iberisch [i'be:rɪʃ] *adj geogr.* Iberian.
ich [ɪç] *pers pron* I: ~ *bin's!* it is I!, F it's me!; ~ *selbst* (I) myself; ~ *Idiot!* what a fool I am!
Ich *n* (-[s]; -[s]) self, *psych.* ego: *mein besseres* ~ my better self; *zweites* ~ alter ego. **'ichbezogen** *adj* egocentric. **'Ichform** *f* (-; *no pl*) (*in der* ~ *geschrieben* written in the) first person.
ideal [ide'a:l] *adj*, **Ide'al** *n* (-s; -e) ideal. **Ide'alfall** *m* ideal case: *im* ~ ideally.
idealisieren [ideali'zi:rən] *v/t* (h) idealize. **Idealismus** [idea'lɪsmʊs] *m* (-; *no pl*) idealism. **Idealist** [idea'lɪst] *m* (-en; -en), **Idea'listin** *f* (-; -nen) idealist. **idea'listisch** *adj* idealistic.
Idee [i'de:] *f* (-; -n) **1.** idea, *a.* thought, concept: *gute* ~*!* good idea!; *ich kam auf die* ~ *zu inf* it occurred to me to *inf*; *wie kamst du auf die* ~? what gave you the idea?; *wie kamst du auf die* ~ *ihn einzuladen?* what made you invite him? **2.** F *e-e* ~ (just) a bit.

ideell [ide'ɛl] *adj* a) ideal (*a.* 𝔸), b) idealistic: ~*er Wert* sentimental value.
i'deenarm, i'deenlos *adj* lacking in ideas, unimaginative. **i'deenreich** *adj* full of ideas, imaginative. **I'deenreichtum** *m* (-s; *no pl*) wealth of ideas.
identifi'zierbar *adj* identifiable.
identifizieren [idɛntifi'tsi:rən] *v/t* (h) identify: *sich* ~ *mit* identify (o.s.) with. **Identifi'zierung** *f* (-; -en) identification.
identisch [i'dɛntɪʃ] *adj* identical.
Identität [idɛnti'tɛ:t] *f* (-; *no pl*) identity. **Identi'täts|krise** *f* identity crisis. **~nachweis** *m* proof of (one's) identity.
Ideologe [ideo'lo:gə] *m* (-n; -n) ideologue. **Ideologie** [ideolo'gi:] *f* (-; -n) ideology. **ideo'logisch** *adj* ideological.
Idiom [i'dĭo:m] *n* (-s; -e) **1.** idiom. **2.** language.
Idiomatik [idĭo'ma:tɪk] *f* (-; *no pl*) **1.** phraseology. **2.** idioms (and phrases). **idiomatisch** [idĭo'ma:tɪʃ] *adj* idiomatic.
Idiot [i'dĭo:t] *m* (-en; -en) idiot.
Idi'otenhügel *m* F nursery slope.

idi'otensicher adj F foolproof.
Idiotie [idi̯o'tiː] f (-; -n) **1.** ♂ idiocy. **2.** F imbecility, idiocy: *pure* ~ sheer lunacy.
idiotisch [i'diːotiʃ] adj idiotic.
Idol [i'doːl] n (-s; -e) idol.
Idyll [i'dʏl] n (-s; -e) idyll. **Idylle** [i'dʏlə] f (-; -n) **1.** idyll. **2.** pastoral poem (*paint.* scene). **idyllisch** [i'dʏlɪʃ] adj idyllic.
Igel ['iːgəl] m (-s; -) zo. hedgehog.
ignorant [ɪgno'rant] adj ignorant.
Igno'rant m (-en; -en) ignorant person.
Ignoranz [ɪgno'rants] f (-; no pl) ignorance.
ignorieren [ɪgno'riːrən] v/t (h) ignore.
ihm [iːm] pers pron (dat of *er* and *es*) (to) him, (to) it: *ich glaube (es)* ~ I believe him; *ein Freund von* ~ a friend of his.
ihn [iːn] pers pron (acc of *er*) him, of *things*: it.
ihnen ['iːnən] **I** pers pron (dat pl of *er, sie, es*) (to) them: *ich habe es* ~ *gesagt* I've told them; *ein Freund von* ~ a friend of theirs. **II Ihnen** (dat of *Sie*) (to) you: *ist er ein Freund von Ihnen?* is he a friend of yours?
ihr [iːr] **I** pers pron **1.** (dat of *sie sg*) (to) her, of *things*: (to) it: *e-e Tante von* ~ an aunt of hers; → *a. ihm*. **2.** (nom pl of *du,* in *letters*: *Ihr*) you. **II** adj **3.** sg her, of *things*: its, pl their: *e-r* ~*er Brüder* one of her (or their) brothers, a brother of hers (or theirs). **4.** *Ihr address*: your. **III** pos pron **5.** *der* (*die, das*) *ihr(ig)e* hers (pl theirs, address: *Ihr(ig)e* yours).
'ihrer'seits [-'zaɪts] adv as far as she's (pl they're, address: *Ihrerseits* you're) concerned.
'ihres'gleichen indef pron **1.** the likes of her (pl them), her (pl their) equals. **2.** *Ihresgleichen* the likes of you, your equals.
'ihret'wegen adv **1.** for her (pl their) sake. **2. 'Ihret'wegen** for your sake.
'ihrig → *ihr* III.
Ikone [i'koːnə] f (-; -n) icon.
illegal ['ɪlegaːl] adj illegal.
illegitim ['ɪlegitiːm] adj illegitimate.
Illusion [ɪlu'zi̯oːn] f (-; -en) illusion: *sich* ~*en hingeben* delude o.s.; *darüber mache ich mir k-e* ~*en* I have no illusions about that. **illusi'onslos** adj and adv without (any) illusions.
illusorisch [ɪlu'zoːrɪʃ] adj illusory.
Illustration [ɪlʊstra'tsi̯oːn] f (-; -en) illus-

tration, picture. **illustrieren** [ɪlʊs'triːrən] v/t illustrate, *fig. a.* demonstrate.
Illu'strierte f (-n; -n) magazine, F mag.
im [ɪm] = *in dem* → *in*[1].
Image ['ɪmɪtʃ] n (-[s]; -s) image. **'Imagepflege** f (-; no pl) image cultivation.
imaginär [imagi'nɛːr] adj imaginary.
Imbiß ['ɪmbɪs] m (-sses; -sse) snack.
'Imbiß halle f, **~stube** f snack bar.
Imitation [imita'tsi̯oːn] f (-; -en) imitation, copy.
imitieren [imi'tiːrən] v/t (h) imitate.
Imker ['ɪmkər] m (-s; -) beekeeper.
immanent [ɪma'nɛnt] adj inherent (dat in).
Immatrikulation [ɪmatrikula'tsi̯oːn] f (-; -en) univ. enrolment.
immatrikulieren [ɪmatriku'liːrən] v/t (h) (*a. sich* ~ *lassen*) enrol (*an dat* at).
immens [ɪ'mɛns] adj immense.
immer ['ɪmər] adv **1.** always, constantly, all the time, *a.* every time: *noch* ~ still; *noch* ~ *nicht* not yet; ~ *wenn* whenever; ~ *wieder* over and over again, time and again; ~ *wieder tun* keep doing; *sie redete* ~ *weiter* F she went on and on. **2.** *before comp:* ~ *besser* better and better; ~ *schlimmer* worse and worse; ~ *größer werdend* ever increasing. **3.** F ~ *zwei* two at a time. **4.** *wann (auch)* ~ whenever; *was (auch)* ~ whatever; *wer (auch)* ~ whoever; *wie (auch)* ~ however; *wo (auch)* ~ wherever.
'immergrün adj evergreen.
'immer'hin adv **1.** still, after all: ~*!* not too bad! **2.** at least.
'immer'während adj everlasting.
Immigrant [ɪmi'grant] m (-en; -en), **Immi'grantin** f (-; -nen) immigrant.
Immigration [ɪmigra'tsi̯oːn] f (-; -en) immigration. **immigrieren** [ɪmi'griːrən] v/i (sn) immigrate.
Immobilien [ɪmo'biːli̯ən] pl real estate, (real) property. ~**händler(in** f) m, ~**makler(in** f) m estate agent, Am. realtor. ~**markt** m property market.
immun [ɪ'muːn] adj immune (*gegen* to): ~ *machen* → **immunisieren** [ɪmuni'ziːrən] v/t immunize (*gegen* against).
Immunität [ɪmuni'tɛːt] f (-; no pl) immunity (*gegen* to, against, from).
Im'munkörper m ♂ antibody.
Immunologe [ɪmuno'loːgə] m (-n; -n)

immunologist. **Immunologie** [ɪmunolo'giː] f (-; no pl) immunology.

Im'mun|schwäche f ⚕ immunodeficiency. **~sy,stem** n immune system.

Impedanz [ɪmpe'dants] f (-; -en) ⚡ impedance.

Imperativ ['ɪmperatiːf] m (-s; -e) ling. imperative.

Imperfekt ['ɪmpɛrfɛkt] n (-s; -e) ling. imperfect (tense).

Imperialismus [ɪmperĭa'lɪsmʊs] m (-; no pl) imperialism.

imperia'listisch adj imperialist(ic).

Imperium [ɪm'peːrĭʊm] n (-s; -rien) a. fig. empire.

'Impf|akti,on f ⚕ vaccination program(me Br.). **~arzt** m vaccinator.

impfen ['ɪmpfən] v/t (h) vaccinate, inoculate: **sich ~ lassen (gegen** against) be vaccinated, get a vaccination.

'Impf|paß m vaccination card. **~pi,stole** f vaccination gun. **~schein** m vaccination certificate. **~stoff** m vaccine.

'Impfung f (-; -en) vaccination, inoculation.

Implantat [ɪmplan'taːt] n (-[e]s; -e), **implantieren** [-'tiːrən] v/t (h) ⚕ implant.

implizieren [ɪmpli'tsiːrən] v/t (h) imply.

implodieren [ɪmplo'diːrən] v/i (sn) implode. **Implosion** [ɪmplo'zĭoːn] f (-; -en) implosion.

imponieren [ɪmpo'niːrən] v/i (h) j-m ~ a) impress s.o., b) command s.o.'s respect. **impo'nierend** adj impressive.

Impo'niergehabe n **1.** zo. display behavio(u)r. **2.** fig. attempt to impress.

Import [ɪm'pɔrt] m (-[e]s; -e) **1.** no pl importing. **2.** imports. **Im'port...** import (agency, trade, etc) **Importeur** [ɪmpɔr'tøːr] m (-s; -e) importer. **Im'portgeschäft** n **1.** import trade. **2.** import company. **importieren** [ɪmpɔr-'tiːrən] v/t (h) import.

imposant [ɪmpo'zant] adj imposing, impressive.

impotent ['ɪmpotɛnt] adj impotent.

'Impotenz [-tɛnts] f (-; no pl) impotence.

imprägnieren [ɪmprɛ'gniːrən] v/t (h) impregnate, a. waterproof.

Imprä'gnierung f (-; -en) impregnation, waterproofing.

Impression [ɪmprɛ'sĭoːn] f (-; -en) impression. **Impressionismus** [ɪmprɛsĭo-'nɪsmʊs] m (-; no pl) impressionism.

Impressionist [-'nɪst] m (-en; -en) impressionist. **impressio'nistisch** adj impressionist(ic).

Impressum [ɪm'prɛsʊm] n (-s; -sen) imprint, of newspaper: a. masthead.

Improvisation [ɪmproviza'tsĭoːn] f (-; -en) improvisation. **improvisieren** [ɪmprovi'ziːrən] v/t, v/i (h) improvise, speaker etc: a. extemporize, F ad-lib.

Impuls [ɪm'pʊls] m (-es; -e) impulse: **e-m ~ folgend** on (an) impulse; fig. **neue ~e geben** give a fresh impetus (dat to).

impulsiv [ɪmpʊl'ziːf] adj impulsive: **~ handeln** act on impulse.

Im'pulskauf m ✝ impulsive buying.

im'stande adj pred zu et. ~ sein be capable of (doing) s.th.; **(nicht) ~ sein, et. zu tun** be (un)able to do s.th.; **dazu ist er glatt ~** iro. I wouldn't put it past him.

in¹ [ɪn] prep **1.** a) in, at, b) within, c) into, in: **~ England** in England; **waren Sie schon einmal ~ England?** have you ever been to England?; **im Haus** in(side) the house, indoors; **~ der (die) Schule** at (to) school; **er ist Kassierer ~ e-r Bank** he is a cashier in (or at) a bank. **2.** a) in, b) during, c) within: **im Mai** in May; **~ diesem Jahr** this year; **~ diesem Alter** at this age. **3.** ~ **größter Eile** in a great rush; **im Kreis** in a circle; **~ Behandlung sein** be having treatment; **ein Mann ~ s-r Stellung** a man in his position; **gut ~ Chemie** good at chemistry.

in² adj ~ **sein** F be in.

'inaktiv adj inactive, 🔬 a. inert.

'Inaktivi,tät f (-; no pl) inactivity.

'inakzep,tabel adj unacceptable.

In'angriffnahme [-na:mə] f (-; -n) adm. (gen) starting (on), tackling (of).

In'anspruchnahme [-na:mə] f (-; -n) (gen, von) **1.** use (of). **2.** demands (on).

'Inbegriff m (-[e]s; -e) epitome.

'inbegriffen adj ~ **sein** be included.

Inbe'sitznahme [-na:mə] f (-; -n) (gen of) taking possession, occupation.

Inbe'triebnahme [-na:mə] f (-; -n) (gen of) opening, starting: **bei ~ der Anlage** when the plant is put into operation.

'Inbrunst f (-; no pl) ardo(u)r, fervo(u)r.

'inbrünstig adj ardent, fervent.

in'dem conj **1.** by: **er entkam, ~ er aus dem Fenster sprang** he escaped by jumping out of the window. **2.** while.

Inder ['ɪndər] *m* (-s; -), **'Inderin** *f* (-; -nen) Indian.

in'dessen I *adv* 1. meanwhile. 2. however. II *conj* → **wohingegen**.

Index ['ɪndɛks] *m* (-es; -e, -dizes [-ditsɛs]) index. **~lohn** *m* index-linked wages.

Indianer [ɪn'dīa:nər] *m* (-s; -), **Indi'anerin** *f* (-; -nen), **indi'anisch** *adj* (Red) Indian.

Indien ['ɪndīən] *n* (-s) India.

Indikation [ɪndika'tsīo:n] *f* (-; -en) ♣ indication: **soziale ~** social grounds for termination of pregnancy.

Indikativ ['ɪndikati:f] *m* (-s; -e) *ling.* indicative (mood).

'indirekt *adj* indirect: **~e Rede** *ling.* indirect (*or* reported) speech.

indisch ['ɪndɪʃ] *adj* Indian.

'indiskret *adj* indiscreet.

Indiskreti'on *f* (-; -en) indiscretion.

indiskutabel ['ɪndɪskuta:bəl] *adj* impossible: **~ sein** *a.* be out of the question.

'indisponiert *adj* indisposed.

individualisieren [ɪndividuáli'zi:rən] *v/t* (h) individualize. **Individualismus** [-'lɪsmʊs] *m* (-; *no pl*) individualism. **Individualist** [-'lɪst] *m* (-en; -en) individualist. **individua'listisch** *adj* individualist(ic). **Individualität** [-'tɛ:t] *f* (-; *no pl*) individuality. **individuell** [ɪndivi'dŭɛl] *adj* individual: **~ gestalten** individualize; **das ist ~ verschieden** that varies from person to person.

Individuum [ɪndi'vi:duʊm] *n* (-s; -duen [-dŭən]) individual.

Indiz [ɪn'di:ts] *n* (-es; -zien [-tsīən]) 1. indication, sign. 2. *usu. pl* → **In'dizienbeweis(e** *pl*) *m* ⚖ circumstantial evidence.

indoeuro'päisch [ɪndo-], **indoger'manisch** *adj* Indo-European.

indoktrinieren [ɪndɔktri'ni:rən] *v/t* (h) indoctrinate.

Indonesien [ɪndo'ne:zīən] *n* (-s) Indonesia. **Indonesier** [ɪndo'ne:zīər] *m* (-s; -), **Indo'nesierin** *f* (-; -nen), **indo'nesisch** [-zɪʃ] *adj* Indonesian.

Indossament [ɪndɔsa'mɛnt] *n* (-s; -e) ✝ endorsement. **Indossant** [ɪndɔ'sant] *m* (-en; -en) endorser. **Indossat** [ɪndɔ'sa:t] *m* (-en; -en) endorsee. **indossieren** [ɪndɔ'si:rən] *v/t* (h) endorse.

Induktion [ɪndʊk'tsīo:n] *f* (-; -en) induc-

tion. **Induktivität** [ɪndʊktivi'tɛ:t] *f* (-; *no pl*) inductivity.

industrialisieren [ɪndʊstrīali'zi:rən] *v/t* (h) industrialize. **Industriali'sierung** *f* (-; *no pl*) industrialization.

Industrie [ɪndʊs'tri:] *f* (-; -n) a) industry, b) → **Industriezweig.**

Indu'strie... industrial (*nation, diamond, product, etc*). **~anlage** *f* industrial plant. **~arbeiter(in** *f*) *m* industrial worker. **~betrieb** *m* industrial company (*or* plant). **~gebiet** *n* industrial area. **~gelände** *n* industrial estate. **~gesellschaft** *f* industrial society. **~gewerkschaft** *f* industry-wide union: **~ Metall** metalworkers' union. **~kaufmann** *m* officer (*or* clerk) in an industrial company.

industriell [ɪndʊstri'ɛl] *adj* industrial.

Industri'elle *m, f* (-n; -n) industrialist.

Indu'strie|macht *f* industrial power. **~messe** *f* industrial fair. **~müll** *m* industrial waste. **~park** *m* industrial park. **~spio,nage** *f* industrial espionage. **~stadt** *f* industrial town. **~- und Handelskammer** *f* chamber of industry and commerce. **~verband** *m* federation of industries. **~zweig** *m* (branch of) industry.

induzieren [ɪndu'tsi:rən] *v/t* (h) induce.

inein'ander *adv* in(to) one another (*or* each other), *in cpds. a.* inter...: **~ verliebt** in love (with each other).

inein'anderfließen *v/i* (*irr, sep, -ge-, sn*, → **fließen**) merge into one another, *colo(u)rs: a.* run.

inein'andergreifen *v/i* (*irr, sep, -ge-, h*, → **greifen**) 1. ⚙ interlock, *gears etc:* mesh. 2. *fig.* interlink.

inein'anderschieben *v/t* (*irr, sep, -ge-, h*, → **schieben**) (*a. sich ~ lassen*) telescope.

infam [ɪn'fa:m] *adj* infamous, disgraceful. **Infamie** [ɪnfa'mi:] *f* (-; -n) infamy.

Infanterie [ɪnfantə'ri:] *f* (-; -n) infantry. **Infanterist** [ɪnfantə'rɪst] *m* (-en; -en) infantryman.

infantil [ɪnfan'ti:l] *adj* infantile.

Infarkt [ɪn'farkt] *m* (-[e]s; -e) ♣ infarct.

Infekt [ɪn'fɛkt] *m* (-[e]s; -e), **Infektion** [ɪnfɛk'tsīo:n] *f* (-; -en) infection. **Infekti'ons|gefahr** *f* risk of infection. **~herd** *m* focus of infection. **~krankheit** *f* infectious disease.

infektiös 316

infektiös [ɪnfɛk'tsiøːs] *adj* infectious, contagious.
Inferno [ɪn'fɛrno] *n* (-s; *no pl*) inferno.
infiltrieren [ɪnfɪl'triːrən] *v/t* (h), *v/i* (sn) infiltrate.
Infinitesimalrechnung [ɪnfinitezi'maːl-] *f* infinitesimal calculus.
Infinitiv ['ɪnfinitiːf] *m* (-s; -e) infinitive.
infizieren [ɪnfi'tsiːrən] (h) **I** *v/t* infect. **II sich ~** catch an infection, become infected: *er hat sich bei ihr infiziert* he caught the disease from her.
in flagranti [ɪn fla'ɡranti] *adv* **~ ertappen** catch *s.o.* in the act (*or* red-handed).
Inflation [ɪnfla'tsioːn] *f* (-; -en) inflation.
inflationär [ɪnflatsio'nɛːr], **inflationistisch** [-'nɪstɪʃ] *adj* inflationary.
Inflati'onspoli,tik *f* inflationary policy.
Inflati'onsrate *f* inflation rate.
Info ['ɪnfo] *n* (-s; -s) F → *Informationsblatt.*
in'folge *prep* (*gen*) as a result of, owing to. **infolge'dessen** *adv* as a result (of this), consequently.
Informant [ɪnfɔr'mant] *m* (-en; -en), **Infor'mantin** *f* (-; -nen) informant.
Informatik [ɪnfɔr'maːtɪk] *f* (-; *no pl*) computer science, informatics. **Infor'matiker** [-tikər] *m* (-s; -) computer specialist.
Information [ɪnfɔrma'tsioːn] *f* (-; -en) (*zu Ihrer ~* for your) information.
Informati'ons|blatt *n* newssheet. **~bü,ro** *n* information office. **~fluß** *m* (-sses; *no pl*) flow of information. **~materi,al** *n* information(al material). **~schalter** *m*, **~stand** *m* information desk.
informativ [ɪnfɔrma'tiːf] *adj* informative.
informieren [ɪnfɔr'miːrən] (h) **I** *v/t* (*über acc*) inform (of, about), *a.* notify (of), let *s.o.* know (about), *a.* instruct (as to), brief (on): *falsch ~* misinform. **II sich ~** (*über acc* about) inform o.s., find out. **infor'miert** *adj* informed: **~e Kreise** well-informed circles.
'Infostand *m* F → *Informationsstand.*
infrarot ['ɪnfra-] *adj*, **'Infrarot...** infrared.
'Infraschall *m* infrasound.
'Infraschall... infrasonic.
'Infrastruk,tur *f* infrastructure.
Infusion [ɪnfu'zioːn] *f* (-; -en) infusion.
Infusorien [ɪnfu'zoːriən] *pl zo.* infusoria.
Inge'brauchnahme [-na:mə] *f* (-; *no pl*)

adm. **vor ~** (*gen*) before using *s.th.*
Ingenieur [ɪnʒe'niøːr] *m* (-s; -e) engineer.
Ingeni'eurbü,ro *n* **1.** (firm of) consulting engineers. **2.** engineering office.
Ingwer ['ɪŋvər] *m* (-s; *no pl*) ginger.
Inhaber ['ɪnhaːbər] *m* (-s; -), **'Inhaberin** *f* (-; -nen) a) owner, proprietor (-tress), b) occupant (*of flat*), c) holder (*of title, office, patent, record, etc*), ✝ *a.* bearer.
'Inhaber|aktie *f* bearer share. **~scheck** *m* cheque (*Am.* check) to bearer.
inhaftieren [ɪnhaf'tiːrən] *v/t* (h) arrest, take *s.o.* into custody. **Inhaf'tierung** *f* (-; -en) **1.** arrest(ing). **2.** detention.
Inhalation [ɪnhala'tsioːn] *f* (-; -en) inhalation. **Inhalati'onsappa,rat** *m* inhaler. **inhalieren** [-'liːrən] *v/t* (h) inhale.
Inhalt ['ɪnhalt] *m* (-[e]s; -e) **1.** a) contents, b) capacity, volume. **2.** *fig.* a) content(s), subject matter, b) meaning: *des ~s, daß* to the effect that; *wesentlicher ~* essence; *mein Leben hat k-n ~* my life is meaningless (*or* empty).
'inhaltlich *adv* in content.
'Inhaltsangabe *f* summary, synopsis.
'Inhaltserklärung *f* ✝ list of contents.
'inhaltslos *adj* empty, meaningless, lacking in substance. **'inhaltsreich** *adj* rich in substance, full, rich (*life*).
'Inhaltsverzeichnis *n* list (*book:* table) of contents.
'inhuman *adj* inhuman.
Initiale [ini'tsiaːlə] *f* (-; -n) initial.
Initiative [initsia'tiːvə] *f* (-; -n) **1.** (*die ~ ergreifen* take the) initiative: *auf s-e ~ hin* on his initiative; *aus eigener ~* on one's own initiative. **2.** action group.
Initiator [ini'tsiaːtɔr] *m* (-s; -en [-tsia'toːrən]), **Initia'torin** *f* (-; -nen) initiator.
Injektion [ɪnjɛk'tsioːn] *f* (-; -en) injection, F shot. **Injekti'onsnadel** *f* hypodermic needle. **Injekti'onsspritze** *f* (hypodermic) syringe.
injizieren [ɪnji'tsiːrən] *v/t* (h) inject.
Inkasso [ɪn'kaso] *n* (-s; -s) ✝ collection.
In'kasso... collection (*agency, business, etc*). **~vollmacht** *f* authority to collect.
inklusive [ɪnklu'ziːvə] **I** *prep* (*nom, gen*) including, inclusive of: **~ Verpackung** packing included. **II** *adv* **bis zum 4. Mai ~** up to and including May 4th.
inkognito [ɪn'kɔɡnito] *adv* incognito.
In'kognito *n* (-s; -s) incognito.
'inkompetent *adj* incompetent.

'**inkonsequent** *adj* inconsistent.
'**Inkonsequenz** *f* (-; -en) inconsistency.
In'krafttreten *n* (-s) coming into force:
bei ~ upon taking effect; **Tag des ~s**
effective date.
inkriminieren [ɪnkrimi'niːrən] *v/t* (h)
incriminate.
Inkubationszeit [ɪnkuba'tsɪoːns-] *f* 🐍
incubation period.
Inkubator [ɪnku'baːtər] *m* (-s; -en
[-ba'toːrən]) 🐍 incubator.
'**Inland** *n* (-[e]s; *no pl*) **1.** home: **im In-
und Ausland** at home and abroad. **2.**
inland, interior. '**Inland...** → **inländisch**. **Inländer** ['ɪnlɛndər] *m* (-s; -),
'**Inländerin** *f* (-; -nen) native. '**inländisch** *adj* home, domestic, internal.
'**Inlands|absatz** *m* ✝ domestic sales.
~flug *m* domestic (*or* internal) flight.
~markt *m* home (*or* domestic) market.
~post *f* inland (*Am.* domestic) mail.
Inlett ['ɪnlɛt] *n* (-[e]s; -e) ticking.
in'mitten *prep* (*gen*) in the middle of.
innehaben ['ɪnə-] *v/t* (*irr, sep, -ge-,* h, →
haben) hold.
'**innehalten** *v/i* (*irr, sep, -ge-,* h, → **halten**) stop, pause.
innen ['ɪnən] *adv* inside, *a.* indoors: ~
und außen inside and out(side); **nach ~**
(**zu**) inwards; **von ~** from (the) inside.
'**Innen|ansicht** *f* interior view. **~archi-
tekt(in** *f*) *m* interior designer. **~archi-
tektur** *f* interior design. **~aufnahme** *f*
phot. indoor (*film*: studio) shot. **~aus-
stattung** *f* a) interior decoration, b)
décor, furnishings, *mot.* trim. **~bahn** *f*
sports: inside lane. **~dienst** *m* office
work: **im ~ tätig sein** work in the office.
~durchmesser *m* inside diameter.
~einrichtung *f* interior decoration.
~hof *m* (inner) courtyard. **~leben** *n* (-s;
no pl) inner life. **~leuchte** *f mot.* interior light. **~minister** *m* minister of the
interior, *Br.* Home Secretary, *Am.* Secretary of the Interior. **~mini,sterium** *n*
ministry of the interior, *Br.* Home Office, *Am.* Department of the Interior.
~poli,tik *f* domestic politics (*or* policy),
home affairs. 2**po,litisch** *adj* domestic,
internal: ~ (**gesehen**) concerning domestic policy. **~raum** *m* interior. **~sei-
te** *f* inside. **~spiegel** *m mot.* inside mirror. **~stadt** *f* inner city, (town) cent/re
(*Am.* -er), *Am. a.* downtown: **in der ~**

von Chicago in downtown Chicago.
~tasche *f* inside pocket. **~tempera,tur**
f internal (*or* indoor) temperature.
~wand *f* inside wall.
inner ['ɪnər] *adj* a) inside, ✝, *pol.* domestic, *a.* 🐍 internal, b) *fig.* inner, mental:
~er Halt moral backbone; **~e Ruhe**
peace of mind; **ein ~er Widerspruch** an
inconsistency.
'**innerbetrieblich** *adj* ✝ internal.
'**innerdeutsch** *adj* **1.** German, (German)
domestic, internal. **2.** *hist.* German-
German (*relations, traffic, etc*)
Innere ['ɪnərə] *n* (-n; *no pl*) **1.** interior (*a.
geogr.*), inside, heart, cent/re (*Am.* -er):
im ~n inside, *geogr.* in the interior. **2.**
fig. heart, soul, mind, core: **in ihrem
tiefsten ~n** deep down; → *a.* **Innerste.**
Innereien [ɪnə'raɪən] *pl* innards, guts.
'**innerhalb I** *prep* (*gen*) **1.** inside, within:
~ der Familie within the family. **2.** a)
in, within, b) during: **~ der Arbeitszeit**
during working hours; **~ weniger Tage**
within a few days. **II** *adv* **~ von** within.
'**innerlich I** *adj* **1.** inner, *a.* 🐍 internal. **2.**
fig. a) inward(-looking), b) emotional,
c) thoughtful. **II** *adv* **3.** internally: ~
(**anzuwenden**) *pharm.* for internal use
(only). **4.** *fig.* inwardly, *a.* secretly.
'**Innerlichkeit** *f* (-; *no pl*) a) inwardness,
b) sensitivity, depth of feeling.
'**innerpar,teilich** *adj* inner-party ..., internal.
innerst ['ɪnərst] *adj* innermost, inmost.
'**innerstaatlich** *adj* internal.
'**innerstädtisch** *adj* urban.
'**Innerste** *n* (-n; *no pl*) *the* innermost
part, *a.* heart, midst.
'**innewohnen** *v/i* (*sep, -ge-,* h) be inherent (*dat* in).
innig ['ɪnɪç] *adj* a) tender, b) ardent, fervent, *a.* devout, c) heartfelt, sincere, d)
close, intimate: **j-n ~ lieben** love s.o.
dearly, be devoted to s.o.
'**Innigkeit** *f* (-; *no pl*) a) tenderness, b)
ardo(u)r, c) sincerity.
Innovation [ɪnova'tsɪoːn] *f* (-; -en) innovation. **innovati'onsfreudig, innova-
tiv** [ɪnova'tiːf] *adj* innovative.
Innung ['ɪnʊŋ] *f* (-; -en) guild.
'**inoffizi,ell** *adj* **1.** unofficial. **2.** informal.
in petto [ɪn 'pɛto] *adv* **et. ~ haben** have
s.th. up one's sleeve.
in puncto [ɪn 'pʊŋkto] *prep* as regards.

Insasse ['ınzasə] *m* (-n; -n), **'Insassin** *f* (-; -nen) **1.** passenger. **2.** inmate.
'Insassenversicherung *f mot.* passenger insurance (cover).
'Inschrift *f* (-; -en) inscription.
Insekt [ın'zɛkt] *n* (-[e]s; -en) insect, bug.
In'sekten|bekämpfungsmittel *n* insecticide. **~fresser** *m zo.* insectivore. **~kunde** *f* (-; *no pl*) entomology. **~stich** *m* insect bite.
Insektizid [ınzɛkti'tsi:t] *n* (-s; -e) insecticide.
Insel ['ınzəl] *f* island (*a. fig.*), *poet. or before proper names:* isle: **die ~ Wight** the Isle of Wight; **die Britischen ~n** the British Isles. **~bewohner** *m* islander. **~gruppe** *f* archipelago. **~staat** *m* island state. **~volk** *n* islanders. **~welt** *f* islands.
Inserat [ınze'ra:t] *n* (-[e]s; -e) advertisement, F ad. **Inserent** [ınze'rɛnt] *m* (-en; -en), **Inse'rentin** *f* (-; -nen) advertiser. **inserieren** [ınze'ri:rən] (h) **I** *v/t* advertise. **II** *v/i ~ in* (*dat*) advertise in, put an advertisement (F ad) into.
insge'heim *adv* secretly.
insge'samt *adv* a) altogether, in all, b) as a whole: **~ betragen** total.
in'sofern² *adv* as far as that goes.
inso'fern² *conj* **~** (*als*) in so far as.
Insolvenz ['ınzɔlvɛnts] *f* (-; -en) ✝ insolvency.
Inspekteur [ınspɛk'tø:r] *m* (-s; -e) inspector. **Inspektion** [ınspɛk'tsi̯o:n] *f* (-; -en) **1.** inspection. **2.** (*das Auto zur ~ bringen* put the car in for a) service.
Inspektor [ın'spɛktɔr] *m* (-s; -en [-'to:rən]), **Inspektorin** [ınspɛk'to:rın] *f* (-; -nen) inspector.
Inspiration [ınspira'tsi̯o:n] *f* (-; -en) inspiration. **inspirieren** [ınspi'ri:rən] *v/t* (h) *j-n zu et.* ~ inspire s.o. to (do) s.th.: **sich ~ lassen** be inspired (**von** by).
Inspizient [ınspi'tsi̯ɛnt] *m* (-en; -en) *thea. etc* stage manager. **inspizieren** [ınspi'tsi:rən] *v/t* (h) inspect, examine.
Installateur [ınstala'tø:r] *m* (-s; -e) **1.** plumber. **2.** electrician. **3.** gas fitter.
Installation [ınstala'tsi̯o:n] *f* (-; -en) installation. **installieren** [ınsta'li:rən] (h) **I** *v/t* install. **II** *sich ~* install o.s.
instand [ın'ʃtant] *adv* **~ halten** keep s.th. in good condition, maintain, service; **~ setzen** a) repair, b) renovate. **In'standhaltung** *f* (-; -en) maintenance.

in'ständig *adj* urgent: *j-n ~ um et. bitten* implore s.o. for s.th.
In'standsetzung *f* (-; -en) a) repair, b) renovation. **In'standsetzungsarbeit** *f* repair work, repairs.
Instanz [ın'stants] *f* (-; -en) authority, 🏛 instance: **höhere ~en** higher authorities (🏛 courts); **in erster ~** 🏛 at first instance; **Gericht erster ~** court of first instance; **in letzter ~** *a. fig.* in the last instance. **In'stanzenweg** *m* 🏛 (successive) stages of appeal; **auf dem ~** through the prescribed channels.
Instinkt [ın'stıŋkt] *m* (-[e]s; -e) instinct, *w.s.* feeling: **aus ~** from (*or* by) instinct, instinctively. **instinktiv** [ınstıŋk'ti:f] *adj* instinctive. **in'stinktlos** *adj fig.* showing a sad lack of flair.
Institut [ınsti'tu:t] *n* (-s; -e) institute.
Institution [ınstitu'tsi̯o:n] *f* (-; -en) *a. fig.* institution. **institutionalisieren** [ınstitutsi̯onali'zi:rən] *v/t* (h) institutionalize. **institutionell** [ınstitutsi̯o'nɛl] *adj* institutional.
instruieren [ınstru'i:rən] *v/t* (h) a) give s.o. instructions, *a.* ✗ brief, b) inform.
Instruktion [ınstrʊk'tsi̯o:n] *f* (-; -en) instruction.
instruktiv [ınstrʊk'ti:f] *adj* instructive.
Instrument [ınstru'mɛnt] *n* (-[e]s; -e) instrument.
Instrumentalmu,sik [ınstrumɛn'ta:l-] *f* instrumental music.
Instrumentarium [ınstrumɛn'ta:ri̯ʊm] *n* (-s; -rien) instruments.
Instru'menten|bau *m* (-[e]s; *no pl*) ♪ instrument making. **~brett** *n* instrument panel, *mot. a.* dashboard. **~flug** *m* instrument flying.
instrumentieren [ınstrumɛn'ti:rən] *v/t* (h) ♪ orchestrate.
Insuffizienz ['ınzʊfitsi̯ɛnts] *f* (-; -en) *a.* ⚕ insufficiency.
Insulaner [ınzu'la:nər] *m* (-s; -) islander.
Insulin [ınzu'li:n] *n* (-s; *no pl*) insulin.
inszenieren [ıntse'ni:rən] *v/t* (h) *thea.* a) stage (*a. fig.*), *a. film, TV* produce, b) direct. **Insze'nierung** *f* (-; -en) production: **in der ~ von X** produced by X.
intakt [ın'takt] *adj* intact.
Intarsien [ın'tarzi̯ən] *pl* inlaid work.
integer [ın'te:gər] *adj man* of integrity.
integral [ınte'gra:l] *adj* integral.
Inte'gral *n* (-s; -e) Å integral.

Inte'gralrechnung f integral calculus.
Integration [ɪntegraˈtsĭoːn] f (-; -en) integration. **integrieren** [ɪnteˈɡriːrən] v/t (h) (a. **sich ~**) integrate (**in** acc into, within). **inte'griert** adj integrated.
Integrität [ɪntegriˈtɛːt] f (-; no pl) integrity.
Intellekt [ɪnteˈlɛkt] m (-[e]s; no pl) intellect. **intellektuell** [ɪntelɛkˈtŭɛl] adj, **Intellektu'elle** m, f (-n; -n) intellectual, F highbrow.
intelligent [ɪnteliˈɡɛnt] adj intelligent.
Intelligenz [ɪnteliˈɡɛnts] f (-; no pl) **1.** intelligence. **2.** intelligentsia.
Intelli'genz|quoti,ent m intelligence quotient, I.Q. **~test** m intelligence test.
Intendant [ɪntɛnˈdant] m (-en; -en) thea. etc director.
Intensität [ɪntɛnziˈtɛːt] f (-; no pl) intensity. **intensiv** [ɪntɛnˈziːf] adj **1.** intensive. **2.** intense, strong. **intensivieren** [ɪntɛnzivˈiːrən] v/t (h) intensify. **Intensi'vierung** f (-; no pl) intensification.
Inten'sivkurs m crash course.
Inten'sivstati,on f ✚ intensive-care unit: **auf der ~ liegen** be in intensive care.
Intercity-Zug [ɪntərˈsɪti-] m inter-city train.
interessant [ɪntərɛˈsant] adj interesting.
Interesse [ɪntəˈrɛsə] n (-s; -n) interest (**an** dat, **für** in): **~ haben an** (or **für**) → **interessieren** II; **~ zeigen** show an interest (**an** dat, **für** in); **im öffentlichen ~** in the public interest; **ich tat es in d-m ~** I did it for your sake; **es liegt in d-m eigenen ~** it's in your own interest; **j-s ~n vertreten** (or **wahrnehmen**) look after (or represent) s.o.'s interests; **es besteht kein ~ an** (dat) nobody is interested in, ✚ there is no demand for. **inter'essehalber** [-halbər] adv out of interest. **inter'esselos** adj uninterested, indifferent. **Inter'esselosigkeit** f (-; no pl) indifference.
Inter'essen|gebiet n field (or area) of interest. **~gemeinschaft** f community of interests, ✚ combine, pool. **~kolli-si,on** f clash of interests. **~sphäre** f sphere of influence.
Interessent [ɪntərɛˈsɛnt] m (-en; -en) person interested, interested party, ✚ prospective buyer: **~en werden gebeten** those interested are requested.
interessieren [ɪntərɛˈsiːrən] (h) **I** v/t in-

terest (**für** in): **das Buch interessiert mich nicht** the book doesn't interest me, I'm not interested in the book; **das interessiert mich (überhaupt) nicht!** a) I'm not (a bit) interested!, b) I couldn't care less!; **es wird dich ~ (zu hören), daß** you'll be interested to know that; **wen interessiert das schon?** who cares? **II sich ~ für** be interested in, take (or show) an interest in. **III** v/i be of interest: **das interessiert hier nicht!** that's irrelevant!
interes'siert I adj interested (**an** dat in). **II** adv with interest, interestedly.
Interimsˌgierung [ˈɪntərɪms-] f interim government.
interkonfessio'nell [ɪntərkɔnfɛsĭoˈnɛl] adj interdenominational.
Interkontinentalflug [ɪntərkɔntinɛnˈtaːl-] m intercontinental flight.
Interkontinen'talraˌkete f intercontinental ballistic missile.
Intermezzo [ɪntərˈmɛtso] n (-s; -s or -zi) ♩ intermezzo, interlude (a. fig.).
intern [ɪnˈtɛrn] adj internal.
Internat [ɪntərˈnaːt] n (-[e]s; -e) boarding school.
international [ɪntərnatsĭoˈnaːl] adj international. **internationalisieren** [-nali-ˈziːrən] v/t (h) internationalize.
Inter'natsschüler(in f) m boarder.
internieren [ɪntərˈniːrən] v/t (h) intern. **Inter'nierte** m, f (-n; -n) internee. **Inter'nierung** f (-; -en) internment.
Inter'nierungslager n internment camp.
Internist [ɪntərˈnɪst] m (-en; -en), **Inter'nistin** f (-; -nen) ✚ internist.
interparlamen'tarisch adj interparliamentary.
Interpret [ɪntərˈpreːt] m (-en; -en), **Inter'pretin** f (-; -nen) interpreter, ♩ a. performer, singer. **Interpretation** [ɪntərpretaˈtsĭoːn] f (-; -en) interpretation. **interpretieren** [ɪntərpreˈtiːrən] v/t (h) interpret, a. read, 𝕤 construe.
Interpunktion [ɪntərpʊŋkˈtsĭoːn] f (-; no pl) punctuation. **Interpunkti'onszei-chen** n punctuation mark.
Interrogativ... [ɪntəroɡaˈtiːf] interrogative (pronoun, sentence, etc).
Intervall [ɪntərˈval] n (-s; -e) interval. **~training** n sports: interval training.
intervenieren [ɪntərveˈniːrən] v/i (h) in-

tervene. **Intervention** [ɪntərvɛn'tsĭoːn] f (-; -en) intervention.

Interview [ɪntər'vjuː] n (-s; -s) interview.

interviewen [-'vjuːən] v/t (h) interview.

Inter'viewer m (-s; -) interviewer.

intim [ɪn'tiːm] adj intimate, a. cosy (*room* etc): **mit j-m ~e Beziehungen haben** (or **~ sein**) have intimate relations with s.o.; **ein ~er Kenner sein von** (or gen) have an intimate knowledge of.

In'tim|bereich m **1.** anat. genitals. **2.** → **Intimsphäre. ~feind** m archenemy.

Intimität [ɪntimi'tɛːt] f (-; -en) intimacy: **es kam zu ~en zwischen ihnen** they became intimate.

In'timsphäre f (-; no pl) (**in j-s ~ eindringen** violate s.o.'s) privacy.

In'timspray m vaginal spray.

'intolerant adj intolerant.

'Intoleranz f intolerance.

Intonation [ɪntona'tsĭoːn] f (-; -en) ling., ♪ intonation.

intonieren [ɪnto'niːrən] v/t (h) intonate.

'intransitiv adj ling. intransitive.

intrave'nös [ɪntra-] adj ♣ intravenous.

Intrigant [ɪntri'gant] m (-en; -en), **Intri'gantin** f (-; -nen) schemer.

Intrige [ɪn'triːgə] f (-; -n) plot, intrigue, scheme. **intrigieren** [ɪntri'giːrən] v/i (h) (plot and) scheme.

introvertiert [ɪntrovɛr'tiːrt] adj introverted: **~er Mensch** introvert.

intuitiv [ɪntui'tiːf] adj intuitive.

Intuition [ɪntui'tsĭoːn] f (-; -en) intuition.

Invalide [ɪnva'liːdə] m (-n; -n) invalid.

Inva'lidenversicherung f disability insurance.

Invalidität [ɪnvalidi'tɛːt] f (-; no pl) disablement, disability.

Invasion [ɪnva'zĭoːn] f (-; -en) invasion.

Inventar [ɪnvɛn'taːr] n (-s; -e) a) inventory, b) stock: **festes ~** fixture(s); **totes ~** dead stock; **lebendes ~** livestock; **ein ~ aufnehmen** → **inventarisieren** [ɪnvɛntari'ziːrən] (h) **I** v/i take inventory (or stock). **II** v/t take an inventory of.

Inventur [ɪnvɛn'tuːr] f (-; -en) inventory, stocktaking: **~ machen** ♣ take inventory (or stock).

Inversion [ɪnvɛr'zĭoːn] f (-; -en) inversion.

investieren [ɪnvɛs'tiːrən] v/t, v/i (h) invest (**in** acc or dat in).

Inve'stierung f (-; -en) investment.

Investition [ɪnvɛsti'tsĭoːn] f (-; -en) **1.** investment. **2.** capital expenditure.

Investiti'ons... investment (*bank*, *loan*, etc). **~anreiz** m investment incentive. **~güter** pl capital goods. **~pro,gramm** n capital expenditure program(me Br.).

In'vestmentfonds m investment fund. **~gesellschaft** f investment company.

Investor [ɪn'vɛstor] m (-s; -en [-'toːrən]) ♣ investor.

'inwendig adj inwardly: F **in- und auswendig kennen** know s.th. inside out.

inwie'fern conj in what way, how.

inwie'welt conj to what extent.

In'zahlungnahme [-na:mə] f (-; no pl) part exchange, trade-in.

Inzest [ɪn'tsɛst] m (-[e]s; -e) incest.

inzestuös [ɪntsɛstu'øːs] adj incestuous.

'Inzucht f (-; no pl) intermarriage, a. zo. inbreeding.

in'zwischen adv meanwhile.

Ion [i'oːn] n (-s; -en) phys. ion.

ionisieren [ioni'ziːrən] v/t (h) ionize.

Iono'sphäre [iono-] f (-; no pl) ionosphere.

'I-Punkt m dot over the i: **bis auf den ~** fig. down to the last detail.

Irak [i'raːk] m (-s) Iraq, Irak. **I'raker** m (-s; -), **I'rakerin** f (-; -nen), **i'rakisch** adj Iraqi, Iraki.

Iran [i'raːn] m (-s) Iran. **I'raner** m (-s; -), **I'ranerin** f (-; -nen), **i'ranisch** adj Iranian.

irdisch ['ɪrdɪʃ] adj a) earthly, b) worldly, c) mortal.

Ire ['iːrə] m (-n; -n) Irishman: **die ~n** the Irish.

irgend ['ɪrgənt] adv **1.** **~ jemand** someone, anyone, somebody, anybody. **2.** **~ etwas** something, anything; **wir müssen ~ etwas tun** we've got to do something; **F ~ so ein ...** some sort of ... **3.** **wann (wo) es ~ geht** whenever (wherever) it might be possible; **wenn ich ~ kann** if I possibly can; **so rasch wie ~ möglich** as soon as at all possible.

'irgend'ein indef pron some, any: **auf ~e Weise** somehow; **besteht noch ~e Hoffnung?** is there any hope at all?

'irgend'einer → **irgend** 1.

'irgend'wann adv **1.** some time (or other). **2.** any time.

'irgend'was F → **irgend** 2.

'irgend'welche *indef pron* any: *ohne ~ Kosten* without any expense at all.

'irgend'wie *adv* somehow, some way (or other).

'irgend|'wo *adv* somewhere, anywhere: *~ anders* somewhere else. **~wo'her** *adv* from somewhere, from anywhere. **~wo'hin** *adv* somewhere, anywhere.

Irin ['i:rɪn] *f* (-; -nen) Irishwoman: *sie ist ~* she is Irish.

Iris ['i:rɪs] *f* (-; -) *anat.*, ⚜ iris.

irisch ['i:rɪʃ] *adj* Irish: ♀e *Republik* Irish Republic, Eire. **'Irisch** *n ling.* Irish.

Irland ['ɪrlant] *n* (-s) Ireland.

Irländer ['ɪrlɛndər] *m* (-s; -) Irishman.

'Irländerin *f* (-; -nen) Irishwoman.

Ironie [iro'ni:] *f* (-; -n) irony.

ironisch [i'ro:nɪʃ] *adj* ironic.

ironisieren [ironi'zi:rən] *v/t* (h) *et. ~* treat s.th. with irony.

irrational ['ɪratsīona:l] *adj* irrational.

irre ['ɪrə] **I** *adj* **1.** mad, insane, crazy: *~s Zeug reden* be raving. **2.** F *fig.* mind-blowing, crazy, mad: *~ (gut)* fantastic, super, wild; *ein ~r Typ* a super guy; *es war e-e ~e Hitze* it was awfully hot; *wie ~* work *etc* like crazy. **II** *adv* **3.** F a) awfully (*big, hot, etc*), b) *work etc* like crazy: *~ viel(e)* an awful lot of.

'Irre[1] *m, f* (-n; -n) madman (madwoman), lunatic, F *fig.* nutcase: F *wie ein ~r* work, drive, *etc* like crazy.

'Irre[2] *f* (-) *j-n in die ~ führen* → *irreführen.*

irreal *adj* **1.** unreal. **2.** unrealistic.

'irreführen *v/t* (*sep*, -ge-, h) *fig.* mislead, *a.* deceive: *sich ~ lassen* be deceived (*von* by). **'irreführend** *adj* misleading.

'irregeleitet *adj fig.* misguided.

irregulär *adj* irregular.

irrelevant *adj* irrelevant.

irren ['ɪrən] **I** *sich ~* (h) **1.** (*in dat* about *s.o.*, *in s.th.*) be wrong, be mistaken: *ich habe mich im Datum geirrt* I got the date wrong; *er hat sich in der Tür geirrt* he went to the wrong door; *ich kann mich (auch) ~* (of course,) I may be wrong; *da irrst du dich aber (gewaltig)!* you're very much mistaken there!; *wenn ich mich nicht irre* if I'm not mistaken. **II** *v/i* **2.** (sn) *a. fig.* wander, err, stray. **3.** (h) be wrong, be mistaken: *Irren ist menschlich* we all make mistakes.

'Irrenanstalt *f* mental home.

'Irrenhaus *n* F *fig.* madhouse.

'irreparabel *adj* irreparable.

'Irrfahrt *f* odyssey. **'Irrgarten** *m* maze, labyrinth. **'Irrglaube** *m* **1.** heresy. **2.** erroneous belief.

'irrig(er'weise *adv*)) *adj* wrong(ly).

irritieren [ɪri'ti:rən] *v/t* (h) irritate, *a.* annoy, *a.* confuse.

'Irrläufer *m* stray letter *etc.*

'Irrlehre *f* false doctrine, heresy.

'Irrlicht *n* (-[e]s, -er) will-o'-the-wisp.

'Irrsinn *m* (-[e]s; *no pl*) *a. fig.* madness.

irrsinnig ['ɪrzɪnɪç] → *irre.* **Irrsinnige** ['ɪrzɪnɪgə] *m, f* (-n; -n) → **Irre**[1].

'Irrtum *m* (-s; ⸚er) a) mistake, error (*a.* 🛠️🛠️), b) misunderstanding: *im ~ sein* be mistaken, be wrong; *da muß ein ~ vorliegen!* there must be some mistake!; F *~!* you're wrong there!

irrtümlich ['ɪrty:mlɪç] *adj* wrong(ly *adv*).

'irrtümlicher'weise *adv* by mistake.

Ischias ['ɪʃĩas] *m, n, ⚕* *f* (-; *no pl*) sciatica.

'Ischiasnerv *m* sciatic nerve.

Islam [ɪs'la:m; 'ɪslam] *m* (-s; *no pl*) Islam.

islamisch [ɪs'la:mɪʃ] *adj* Islamic.

Island ['i:slant] *n* (-s) Iceland. **Isländer** ['i:slɛndər] *m* (-s; -), **'Isländerin** *f* (-; -nen) Icelander. **'isländisch** [-dɪʃ] *adj* Icelandic.

Isobare [izo'ba:rə] *f* (-; -n) isobar.

Isolation [izola'tsĭo:n] *f* (-; -en) **1.** isolation. **2.** ⚡, 🔧 insulation.

Iso'lierband *n* (-[e]s; ⸚er) insulating tape.

isolieren [izo'li:rən] (h) **I** *v/t* **1.** isolate. **2.** ⚡, 🔧 insulate (*gegen* against). **II** *sich ~* isolate o.s., cut o.s. off.

Iso'lier|materi,al *n* insulating material, insulant. **~schicht** *f* insulating layer. **~stati,on** *f* isolation ward.

Iso'lierung *f* (-; -en) **1.** isolation. **2.** ⚡, 🔧 insulation.

Isotop [izo'to:p] *n* (-s; -e) isotope.

Israel ['ɪsrael] *n* (-s) Israel. **Israeli** [ɪsra'e:li] *m* (-[s]; -[s]), *f* (-; -[s]) Israeli. **isra'elisch** [-lɪʃ] *adj* Israeli.

Israelit [ɪsrae'li:t] *m* (-en; -en), **Israe'litin** *f* (-; -nen), **israe'litisch** *adj* Israelite.

'Ist-Bestand *m* ✝ a) actual amount, b) actual stock.

Italien [i'ta:lĭən] *n* (-s) Italy. **Italiener** [ita'lĭe:nər] *m* (-s; -), **Itali'enerin** *f* (-; -nen) Italian. **itali'enisch** *adj* Italian. **Itali'enisch** *n ling.* Italian.

J

J, j [jɔt] *n* (-; -) J, j.

ja [ja] *adv* **1.** yes, *parl.* aye, *Am.* yea, *at wedding:* I do: **~?** a) really?, b) right?, c) *teleph.* hello; *nun* **~** well (yes); **~ doch!, aber ~!** yes, of course!, sure!; **~ sagen (zu)** to say yes, *fig. a.* agree; *ich glaube* **~!** I think so! **2.** after all: *du kennst ihn* **~** you know what he's like. **3.** *da bist du* **~!** there you are!; *ich hab's dir* **~ gesagt** didn't I tell you?; *das ist* **~ schrecklich!** but that's just terrible!; *es regnet* **~!** oh dear, it's raining! **4.** *sei* **~ vorsichtig!** do be careful!; *bring es* **~ mit!** make sure you bring it!; *sag's ihm* **~ nicht!** don't tell him! **5.** **~, weißt (or wußtest) du denn (das) nicht?** do you mean to say you didn't know? **6.** *ich würde es* **~ gern tun, aber ...** I'd really like to do it, but ...

Ja *n* (-[s]; -[s]) yes, *parl.* aye, *Am.* yea: *mit* **~ oder Nein antworten** answer yes or no.

Jacht [jaxt] *f* (-; -en) yacht.

'Jachtklub *m* yacht club.

Jacke ['jakə] *f* (-; -n) jacket, coat, *a.* cardigan: F *das ist* **~ wie Hose** it's much of a muchness.

'Jackenkleid *n* two-piece dress.

Jacketkrone ['dʒækɪt-] *f* jacket crown.

Jackett [ʒa'kɛt] *n* (-s; -s) jacket, coat.

Jade ['jaːdə] *m* (-[s]; *no pl*) *min.* jade.

Jagd [jaːkt] *f* (-; -en) **1.** hunt(ing), shoot(ing): *auf (die)* **~ gehen** go hunting. **2.** *fig.* (*nach*) chase (after), pursuit (of): **~ machen auf** (*acc*) chase (after), pursue; *wilde* **~ nach** mad rush for.

'Jagd|beute *f* bag. **~bomber** *m* fighter bomber. **~flieger** *m* fighter pilot. **~flugzeug** *n* fighter (plane). **~hund** *m* **1.** hound. **2.** short-haired pointer. **~hütte** *f* (hunting) lodge. **~rennen** *n* steeplechase. **~re͵vier** *n* hunting ground. **~schein** *m* hunting licen/ce (*Am.* -se). **~zeit** *f* hunting season.

jagen ['jaːgən] **I** *v/t* (h) **1.** hunt, shoot. **2.** *fig.* a) chase (after), b) hunt (for): *ein Ereignis jagte das andere* things happened really fast; F *damit kannst du mich ~!* I just hate that! **3.** F *j-m (sich) e-e Kugel durch den Kopf ~* blow s.o.'s (one's) brains out; *den Ball ins Netz ~* slam the ball home; *et. in die Luft ~* blow s.th. up. **II** *v/i* **4.** (h) go hunting, go shooting, hunt. **5.** (sn) *fig.* race. **6.** (h) **~ nach** *fig.* chase after, hunt for.

'Jagen *n* (-s) hunt(ing), shoot(ing).

Jäger ['jɛːgər] *m* (-s; -) **1.** huntsman, hunter. **2.** → **Jagdflieger, -flugzeug**

Jaguar ['jaːguaːr] *m* (-s; -e) *zo.* jaguar.

jäh [jɛː] **I** *adj* **1.** sudden, abrupt: *fig. ein* **~es Erwachen** a rude awakening. **2.** steep: **~er Abhang** precipice. **II** *adv* **3.** all of a sudden, abruptly. **4. ~abfallend** precipitous.

Jahr [jaːr] *n* (-[e]s; -e) year: *ein halbes* **~** half a year, six months; *das Kind ist zwei* **~e** alt the child is two (years old); *mit 20* **~en** at the age of twenty; *alle* **~e** every year; **~ für ~** year after year; *im* **~e 1989** in (the year of) 1989; *in diesem (im nächsten)* **~** this (next) year; *heute vor einem* **~** a year ago today; *von* **~ zu ~** from year to year; *auf* **~e hinaus** for years to come; *seit* **~en (nicht)** (not) for years; *im Lauf der* **~e** through (or over) the years; *in die* **~e kommen** be getting on; *in den besten* **~en** in the prime of life; → *jünger* 1.

jahr'aus *adv* **~, jahrein** year in, year out.

'Jahrbuch *n* yearbook, almanac.

'jahrelang I *adj* longstanding, lasting for years: **~e Erfahrung** years of experience. **II** *adv* for years.

jähren ['jɛːrən] *heute jährt sich ...* it's a year today since (*or* that) ...

'Jahres... annual (*balance sheet, report, ring, etc*), yearly. **~abrechnung** *f*, **~abschluß** *m* † annual accounts. **~beginn** *m* (*zum* **~** at the) beginning of the year. **~bestleistung** *f sports:* record of the year. **~einkommen** *n* yearly income. **~ende** *n* (*zum* **~, am** at the) end of the year. **~gehalt** *n* (-[e]s; *-er*) annual salary. **~hälfte** *f erste (zweite)* **~** first (second) half of the year. **~hauptversammlung** *f* annual general meeting. **~tag** *m* anniversary. **~zahl** *f* year. **~zeit** *f* season: *in dieser* **~** at this time of year. **⌂zeitlich** *adj* seasonal.

'Jahrgang *m* **1.** age group, *ped.* year: *sie*

ist ~ 1900 she was born in 1900; *er ist mein ~* we were born in the same year; *die Jahrgänge 1970-80* the 1970-80 age group. **2.** *gastr.* vintage, year. **3.** volume (*of magazine etc*).

Jahr'hundert *n* (-s; -e) century.

jahr'hunderte|alt *adj* centuries old. **~lang** *adv* (*adj* lasting) for centuries.

Jahr'hundert|feier *f* centenary, centennial. **~wende** *f* turn of the century.

...jährig [-jɛ:rɪç] *in cpds.* ...-year-old.

jährlich ['jɛ:rlɪç] **I** *adj* yearly, annual. **II** *adv* a) yearly, every year, once a year, b) *1000 marks* a year (*or* per annum).

'Jahrmarkt *m* (*auf dem ~* at the) fair.

Jahr'tausend *n* (-s; -e) millennium.

Jahr'tausendfeier *f* millenary.

Jahr'zehnt *n* (-[e]s; -e) decade, ten years.

jahr'zehntelang I *adj* lasting for decades: **~e Forschungsarbeit** decades of research. **II** *adv* for decades.

'Jähzorn *m* (*im ~* in a fit of) violent temper. **'jähzornig** *adj* irascible: *er ist ~ a.* he has a violent temper.

Jalousie [ʒalu'zi:] *f* (-; -n) (Venetian) blind(s).

Jammer ['jamər] *m* (-s; *no pl*) **1.** misery: F *es ist ein ~, daß* it's such a shame (*or* too bad) that. **2.** lamentation, wailing.

jämmerlich ['jɛmərlɪç] **I** *adj* **1.** miserable, wretched, pitiful, *fig. contp. a.* deplorable: *mir war ~ zumute* I felt (just) miserable. **2.** heart-rending, piteous. **II** *adv* **3.** miserably (*etc*): *~ weinen* cry piteously; *~ (schlecht)* sing *etc* terribly; *~ versagen* fail miserably.

jammern ['jamərn] *v/i* (h) moan, wail: *~ nach* cry for; *~ über* (*acc*) a) moan (about), b) complain (of).

'Jammern *n* (-s) moaning, wailing.

'jammerschade *adj* (*es ist*) *~, daß* ... it's such a shame (*or* too bad) that ...

Januar ['janua:r] *m* (-[s]; -e) (*im ~* in) January.

Japan ['ja:pan] *n* (-s) Japan. **Japaner** [ja'pa:nər] *m* (-s; -), **Ja'panerin** *f* (-; -nen) Japanese. **ja'panisch** *adj*, **Ja'panisch** *n ling.* Japanese.

Jargon [ʒar'gõ:] *m* (-s; -s) jargon.

'Jasager *m* (-s; -) *contp.* yes-man.

Jasmin [jas'mi:n] *m* (-s; -e) 🌸 jasmin.

'Ja-Stimme *f* aye, *Am.* yea.

jäten ['jɛ:tən] *v/t, v/i* (h) weed.

Jauche ['jaʊxə] *f* (-; -n) liquid manure.

'Jauchegrube *f* cesspool.

jauchzen ['jaʊxtsən] *v/i* (h) shout for joy.

jaulen ['jaʊlən] *v/i* (h) *a. fig.* howl.

ja'wohl *adv* a) yes, ✕ yes, Sir, b) that's right.

Jazz [dʒɛs] *m* (-; *no pl*) jazz.

'Jazzband *f*, **'Jazzka,pelle** *f* jazz band.

'Jazzmu,sik *f* jazz (music).

'Jazzsänger(in *f*) *m* jazz singer.

je [je:] **I** *adv* **1.** ever: *ohne ihn ~ gesehen zu haben* without ever having seen him. **2.** → *eh* 2, *jeher*. **3.** *sie kosten ~ e-n Dollar* they cost a dollar each; *für ~ 10 Personen* for every ten persons; *es gibt sie in Schachteln mit ~ 10 Stück* they come in boxes of ten. **4.** *~ nach* according to; *~ nachdem* it (all) depends (→ 6). **II** *conj* **5.** *~ eher, desto besser* the sooner the better; *~ länger, ~ lieber* the longer the better. **6.** *~ nachdem* according to *what he says*, depending on *how you do it* (→ 4).

'jeden'falls *adv* **1.** in any case, at any rate, anyway. **2.** be that as it may. **3.** at least.

'jedermann *indef pron* everyone, everybody: *das ist nicht ~s Sache* it's not everyone's cup of tea.

'jeder'zeit *adv* any time, always.

'jedes'mal *adv* a) every time, b) always.

je'doch *adv* however, still.

je'her *adv von ~* always.

jein [jaɪn] *adv* F yes and no.

jemals ['je:ma:ls] *adv* ever.

jemand ['je:mant] *indef pron* a) somebody, someone, b) anybody, anyone: *es kommt ~* somebody's coming; *ist ~ hier?* is anybody here?; *~ anders* someone (*or* anyone) else; *sonst noch ~?* anyone else?

jene ['je:nə], **'jener**, **'jenes** *dem pron* **1.** that, *pl* those: *seit ~m Tag* from that day on. **2.** that one, *pl* those.

jede ['je:də], **'jeder**, **'jedes** *indef pron* **1.** a) each, b) any, c) either, d) every: *ich hörte ~s (einzelne) Wort* I heard every (single) word; *~s zweite Auto* every other car; *ohne ~n Zweifel* without any doubt; *(zu) ~r Zeit* any time; *bei ~m Wetter* in any weather. **2.** each (*or* every) one, everyone: *~(r) von ihnen* each (*or* all) of them.

jenseitig ['jɛːnzaɪtɪç] *adj* on the other side: *das ~e Ufer* the opposite bank.

jenseits ['jeːnzaɪts] **I** *prep (gen)* on the other side of, beyond, across. **II** *adv* on the other side: *~ von* beyond. **'Jenseits** *n (-; no pl)* the hereafter: F *j-n ins ~ befördern* send s.o. to kingdom come.

Jesus ['jeːzʊs] *m* (Jesu; *no pl*) Jesus: *~ Christus* Jesus Christ.

'Jesuskind *n* the infant Jesus.

Jet [dʒɛt] *m* (-[s]; -s) ✈ jet. **'Jet-set** *m* (-s; -s) jet set. **'jetten** *v/i* (sn) F jet.

jetzig ['jɛtsɪç] *adj* a) present(-day), current, b) existing.

jetzt [jɛtst] *adv* now, *a.* nowadays: *erst ~* only now; *noch ~* even now; *bis ~* so far, *negative*: *a.* (as) yet.

Jetzt *n* (-; *no pl*) the present (time).

jeweilig ['jeːvaɪlɪç] **I** *adj* a) respective, b) prevailing: *der ~e Präsident* the president then in office; *der ~en Mode entsprechend* according to the fashion (at the time). **II** *adv* → **jeweils** 4.

jeweils ['jeːvaɪls] *adv* **1.** *~ zwei* two at a time. **2.** always: *sie kommt ~ am Montag* she comes every Monday; *er trainiert ~ zwei Stunden* he does two hours of training a time. **3.** each: *mit ~ 20 Fragen* exercises *etc* with 20 questions each. **4.** in each case.

jiddisch ['jɪdɪʃ] *adj* Yiddish

'Jiddisch *n ling.* Yiddish.

Job [dʒɔp] *m* (-s; -s) F job.

jobben ['dʒɔbən] *v/i* (h) F job.

Joch [jɔx] *n* (-[e]s; -e) yoke.

'Jochbein *n anat.* cheekbone.

Jockei, Jockey ['dʒɔke] *m* (-s; -s) jockey.

Jod [joːt] *n* (-[e]s; *no pl*) 🜍 iodine.

jodeln ['joːdəln] *v/t, v/i* (h) yodel.

'jodhaltig *adj* containing iodine.

jodieren [jo'diːrən] *v/t* (h) **1.** 🜍 iodinate. **2.** ✄, *phot.* iodize.

'Jodsalbe *f* iodine ointment. **'Jodsalz** *n* iodized salt. **'Jodtablette** *f* iodine tablet. **'Jodtinktur** *f* tincture of iodine.

Joga → **Yoga.**

joggen ['dʒɔgən] *v/i* (h) jog, go jogging. **Jogger** ['dʒɔgər] *m* (-s; -), **'Joggerin** *f* (-; -nen) jogger.

Jogging ['dʒɔgɪŋ] *n* (-s) jogging.

Joghurt ['joːgʊrt] *m, n* (-[s]; *no pl*) yog(h)urt.

Johannisbeere [jo'hanɪs-] *f rote ~* redcurrant; *schwarze ~* blackcurrant.

johlen ['joːlən] *v/i* (h) bawl, yell.

Jolle ['jɔlə] *f* (-; -n) ⚓ dinghy.

Jongleur [ʒõ'gløːr] *m* (-s; -e) juggler.

jonglieren [ʒõ'gliːrən] *v/t, v/i* (h) *a. fig.* juggle (*mit* [with] *s.th.*).

Jordanien [jɔr'daːniən] *n* (-s) Jordan. **Jor'danier** [-niər] *m* (-s; -), **Jor'danierin** *f* (-; -nen), **jor'danisch** *adj* Jordanian.

Jota ['joːta] *n* (-[s]; -s) iota.

Joule [dʒuːl] *n* (-[s]; -) *phys.* joule.

Journalismus [ʒʊrna'lɪsmʊs] *m* (-; *no pl*) journalism. **Journalist** [ʒʊrna'lɪst] *m* (-en; -en), **Journa'listin** *f* (-; -nen) journalist. **journalistisch** [ʒʊrna'lɪstɪʃ] *adj* journalistic.

jovial [jo'vi̯aːl] *adj* affable.

Jubel ['juːbəl] *m* (-s; *no pl*) jubilation, cheers. **'Jubeljahr** *n eccl.* jubilee: F *alle ~e einmal* once in a blue moon.

jubeln ['juːbəln] *v/i* (h) cheer: (*vor Freude*) ~ shout for joy, rejoice.

Jubilar [jubi'laːr] *m* (-s; -e), **Jubi'larin** *f* (-; -nen) person celebrating his (her) jubilee. **Jubiläum** [jubi'lɛːʊm] *n* (-s; -läen) jubilee, anniversary.

Jubi'läumsausgabe *f* jubilee edition.

jucken ['jʊkən] *v/t, v/i, v/impers* (h) itch: *mich juckt's* I'm itching; *sich ~* scratch o.s.; *es juckt mich am Arm, mein Arm juckt* my arm's itchy; *der Pullover juckt* the pullover's scratchy; F *fig.* *es juckt mich zu inf* I'm itching to *inf*; *das juckt mich nicht!* what do I care.

'Jucken *n* (-s) itch, itching.

'Juckreiz *m* itch, itching.

Jude ['juːdə] *m* (-n; -n) Jew. **'Judenhaß** *m* anti-Semitism. **'Judentum** *n* (-s; *no pl*) **1.** Judaism. **2.** *the* Jews, Jewry. **3.** Jewishness. **'Judenverfolgung** *f* persecution of (the) Jews. **Jüdin** ['jyːdɪn] *f* (-; -nen) Jewess. **'jüdisch** *adj* Jewish.

Judo ['juːdo] *n* (-s; *no pl*) judo.

Judoka [ju'doːka] *m* (-s; -s) judoka.

Jugend ['juːgənt] *f* (-; *no pl*) **1.** youth: *von ~ an* from childhood, from a child; *in m-r ~* when I was young. **2.** youth, youthfulness. **3.** youth, young people: *die ~ von heute* the young people of today; *die deutsche ~* the young Germans (of today). **4.** → **Jugendklasse, Jugendmannschaft.**

'Jugend|amt *n* youth welfare department. **~arbeitslosigkeit** *f* youth unemployment. **~ar₁rest** m ⚖ short-term detention for young offenders. **~buch** n book for young people. **2frei** adj film: U-certificate, Am. G-rated; **nicht ~** for adults only. **~freund(in** f) m friend from one's youth. **2gefährdend** adj harmful to young persons. **~gericht** n juvenile court. **~herberge** f youth hostel. **~klasse** f sports: youth class. **~kriminali,tät** f juvenile delinquency. **~lager** n youth camp.

'**jugendlich** adj youthful (a. clothes, look), young; ⚤ juvenile.

'**Jugendliche** m, f (-n; -n) young person, m a. youth, ⚤ a. juvenile.

'**Jugendlichkeit** f (-; no pl) youthfulness. '**Jugend|liebe** f a) puppy love, b) old flame. **~mannschaft** f sports: youth team. **~meister(in** f) m sports: youth champion. **~richter(in** f) m judge of a juvenile court. **~schutz** m legal protection for children and young persons. **~stil** m (-s; no pl) Jugendstil, art nouveau. **~strafanstalt** f remand home. **~zeit** f (-; -en) youth.

Jugoslawe [jugo'slaːvə] m (-n; -n) Yugoslav. **Jugoslawien** [jugo'slaːviən] n (-s) Yugoslavia. **Jugo'slawin** f (-; -nen), **jugo'slawisch** adj Yugoslav.

Juli ['juːli] m (-[s]; -s) (im ~ in) July.

jung [jʊŋ] adj a) young, b) youthful: **ziemlich ~** youngish; **~es Unternehmen** new company; **~er Wein** new wine; **von ~ auf** from childhood; **~ werfen** (or **bekommen**) → **jungen** ['jʊŋən] v/i (h) zo. have young (or puppies or kittens).

'**jungenhaft** adj boyish.

jünger ['jʏŋər] adj **1.** younger: **sie sieht ~ aus als sie ist** she doesn't look her age; **das macht sie um Jahre ~** that takes years off her age. **2.** more recent, later: **ein Foto ~en Datums** a more recent photograph.

'**Jünger** m (-s; -) disciple, fig. a. follower.

Jungfer ['jʊŋfər] f (-; -n) **alte ~** old maid.
'**Jungfern|fahrt** f maiden voyage. **~flug** m maiden flight. **~häutchen** n anat. hymen. **~rede** f maiden speech.

'**Jungfrau** f **1.** virgin: **die Heilige ~, die ~ Maria** the Holy Virgin, the Virgin Mary. **2.** astr. (**er ist ~** he is [a]) Virgo.

jungfräulich ['jʊŋfrɔylɪç] adj virginal, fig. virgin.

'**Jungfräulichkeit** f (-; no pl) virginity.

'**Junggeselle** m (-n; -n) bachelor.

'**Junggesellin** f (-; -nen) bachelor girl.

Jüngling ['jʏŋlɪŋ] m (-s; -e) youth.

jüngst [jʏŋst] adj **1.** youngest. **2.** latest (events etc): **der Jüngste Tag** the Day of Judg(e)ment; **der ~en Vergangenheit** of the recent past.

'**Jüngste** m, f, n (-n; -n) the youngest: **unser ~r, unsere ~** our youngest (child); **sie ist auch nicht mehr die ~** she is no spring chicken any more.

'**Jungsteinzeit** f (-; no pl) Neolithic age.

'**jungverheiratet** adj newly-wed.

'**Jungvieh** n young stock.

Juni ['juːni] m (-[s]; -s) (im ~ in) June.

junior ['juːniɔr] adj **1. Herr X ~** (abbr. jun., jr.) Mr. X, Junior (abbr. jr.).

'**Junior** m (-s; -en [ju'nioːrən]) **1.** F and sports: junior. **2.** ✝ a) son of the owner, b) a. '**Juniorchef** m junior partner.

Juni'oren... sports: junior (team etc).

Junktim ['jʊŋktɪm] n (-s; -s) pol. package deal.

Junta ['xʊnta] f (-; -ten) pol. junta.

Jura[1] ['juːra] m (-; no pl) geol. Jurassic (period).

Jura[2]: **~ studieren** study (Br. a. read) law. '**Jurastu,dent(in** f) m law student. '**Jurastudium** n law studies.

Jurist [ju'rɪst] m (-en; -en) **1.** lawyer. **2.** law student. **Ju'ristensprache** f legalese. **Ju'ristin** f (-; -nen) → **Jurist. ju'ristisch** adj legal: **~e Fakultät** faculty of law, Am. a. law school; **~e Person** legal entity, juristic person.

Jury [ʒy'riː] f (-; -s) **1.** a) jury, (panel of) judges, b) selection committee. **2.** ⚖ jury.

ju'stierbar adj adjustable.

justieren [jʊs'tiːrən] v/t (h) adjust.

Ju'stierung f (-; -en) adjustment.

Justitiar [jʊsti'tsiaːr] m (-s; -e), **Justiti'arin** f (-; -ncn) legal adviser.

Justiz [jʊs'tiːts] f (-; no pl) justice, the

law. **~beamte** *m*, **~beamtin** *f* judicial officer. **~behörde** *f* judicial authority. **~gewalt** *f* judiciary (power). **~irrtum** *m* judicial error, miscarriage of justice. **~mi‚nister** *m* minister of justice, *Br.* Lord Chancellor, *Am.* Attorney General. **~mini‚sterium** *n* ministry of justice, *Am.* Department of Justice. **~mord** *m* judicial murder. **~verwal-**

tung *f* a) administration of justice, b) legal administrative body.
Jute ['ju:tə] *f* (-; *no pl*) jute.
Juwel [ju've:l] *n* (-s; -en) *a. fig.* jewel: **~en** jewel(le)ry, precious stones.
Juwelier [juvə'li:r] *m* (-s; -e) jewel(l)er.
Juwe'liergeschäft *n* jewel(l)er's shop.
Jux [jʊks] *m* (-es; -e) F (practical) joke.

K

K, k [ka:] *n* (-; -) K, k.
Kabarett [kaba'rɛt] *n* (-s; -s, -e) cabaret (show), (satirical) revue.
Kabarettist [kabarɛ'tɪst] *m* (-en; -en), **Kabaret'tistin** *f* (-; -nen) cabaret artist.
kabbelig ['kabəlɪç] *adj* choppy (*sea*).
Kabel ['ka:bəl] *n* (-s; -) cable. **'Kabelfernsehen** *n* cable television (*or* TV).
Kabeljau ['ka:bəljaʊ] *m* (-s; -e, -s) cod(fish).
Kabine [ka'bi:nə] *f* (-; -n) **1.** ✈, ⚓ cabin. **2.** a) cage (*of lift*), b) cable car. **3.** cubicle, *sports:* a. locker room.
Kabinett [kabi'nɛt] *n* (-s; -e) *pol.* cabinet. **Kabi'netts|beschluß** *m* decision of the cabinet. **~bildung** *f* formation of a (*or* the) cabinet. **~krise** *f* cabinet crisis. **~liste** *f* list of cabinet members. **~sitzung** *f* cabinet meeting. **~umbildung** *f* cabinet reshuffle.
Kabrio ['ka:brio] *n* (-s; -s), **Kabriolett** [ka:brio'lɛt] *n* (-s; -s) *mot.* convertible.
Kachel ['kaxəl] *f* (-; -n) tile. **'kacheln** *v/t* (h) tile. **'Kachelofen** *m* tiled stove.
Kacke ['kakə] *f* (-; *no pl*), **'kacken** *v/t, v/i* (h) V crap, shit. **'Kacker** *m* (-s; -) V shit.
Kadaver [ka'da:vər] *m* (-s; -) carcass. **~gehorsam** *m contp.* blind obedience.
Kadenz [ka'dɛnts] *f* (-; -en) ♩ cadence, cadenza.
Kader ['ka:dər] *m* (-s; -) ✕, *pol.* cadre, *sports:* a. pool.
Kadett [ka'dɛt] *m* (-en; -en) ⚓, ✕ cadet.
Kadi ['ka:di] *m* (-s; -s) F (**j-n vor den ~ schleppen** haul s.o. before the) judge.
Kadmium *n* (-s; *no pl*) ♨ cadmium.

Käfer ['kɛ:fər] *m* (-s; -) **1.** *zo.* beetle (*a. mot.* F *VW*). **2.** F *fig.* chick, girlie.
Kaff [kaf] *n* (-s; -s, -e) *n* F *contp.* dump, awful hole.
Kaffee ['kafe:, ka'fe:] *m* (-s; -s) coffee: **~ kochen** (*or* **machen**) make coffee; **zwei ~, bitte!** two coffees, please!; **~ mit Milch** white coffee; F *fig.* **das ist doch kalter ~!** that's old hat!
'Kaffee|auto‚mat *m* coffee machine. **~bohne** *f* coffee (bean). **~haus** *n* café, coffee house. **~kanne** *f* coffee pot. **~klatsch** *m* F coffee (*or* hen) party, *Am.* coffee klatsch. **~löffel** *m* coffee spoon. **~ma‚schine** *f* coffeemaker, percolator, (*coffee urn.* **~mühle** *f* coffee grinder. **~pause** *f* coffee break. **~satz** *m* coffee grounds. **~ser‚vice** *n* coffee set. **~strauch** *m* coffee shrub. **~tasse** *f* coffee cup. **~weißer** *m* coffee whitener (*Am.* creamer).
Käfig ['kɛ:fɪç] *m* (-s; -e) cage.
kahl [ka:l] *adj* **1.** (**~ werden** go *or* grow) bald. **2.** *fig.* bare, *a.* leafless (*tree*), *a.* barren, bleak (*region etc*).
'kahlgeschoren *adj* shaven.
'Kahlheit *f* (-; *no pl*) **1.** baldness. **2.** *fig.* bareness (*etc*, *→* **kahl** 2).
'Kahlkopf *m* F baldhead(ed person).
'kahlköpfig [-kœpfɪç] *adj* bald(headed).
'Kahlschlag *m* **1.** a) deforestation, b) clearing. **2.** *fig.* demolition. **~sa‚nierung** *f* wholesale redevelopment.
Kahn [ka:n] *m* (-[e]s; *‑e) **1.** (rowing *or* fishing) boat: **~ fahren** go boating. **2.** barge. **3.** F tub. **'Kahnfahrt** *f* boat trip.

Kai [kaɪ] *m* (-s; -s) quay, wharf.
'**Kaimauer** *f* quay wall.
Kaiser ['kaɪzər] *m* (-s; -) emperor.
'**Kaiserin** *f* (-; -nen) empress.
'**Kaiserkrone** *f* imperial crown.
'**kaiserlich** *adj* imperial.
'**Kaiserreich** *n* empire.
'**Kaiserschnitt** *m* ☞ C(a)esarean section.
Kajak ['ka:jak] *m* (-s; -s) *a.* sports: kayak.
Ka'jütboot *n* cabin boat.
Kajüte [ka'jy:tə] *f* (-; -n) cabin.
Kakadu ['kakadu] *m* (-s; -s) cockatoo.
Kakao [ka'kaʊ, ka'ka:o] *m* (-s; -s) cocoa: F *fig. durch den ~ ziehen* make fun of, roast. **Ka'kaobaum** *m* cacao (tree).
Kaktee [kak'te:] *f* (-; -n), **Kaktus** ['kaktʊs] *m* (-; -teen) ♣ cactus.
Kalauer ['ka:laʊər] *m* (-s; -) dreadful pun, corny joke.
Kalb [kalp] *n* (-[e]s; ⁻er) calf. **kalben** ['kalbən] *v/i* (h) calve. '**Kalbfell** *n* calfskin. '**Kalbfleisch** *n* veal.
'**Kalbs|braten** *m* roast veal. **~haxe** *f* knuckle of veal. **~keule** *f* leg of veal. **~kopf** *m* calf's head. **~leder** *n* calf(skin). **~schnitzel** *n* escalope of veal.
Kaleidoskop [kalaɪdo'sko:p] *n* (-s; -e) *a.* fig. kaleidoscope.
Kalender [ka'lɛndər] *m* (-s; -) calendar.
Ka'lenderjahr *n* calendar year.
Kali ['ka:li] *n* (-s; -s) ♣ potash.
Kaliber [ka'li:bər] *n* (-s; -) calib/re (*Am.* -er), F *fig. a.* sort, type.
Kalium ['ka:liʊm] *n* (-s; *no pl*) ♣ potassium.
Kalk [kalk] *m* (-[e]s; -e) **1.** ♣ a) lime, b) quicklime. **2.** ♂ calcium. **3.** *min.* limestone. **4.** → **~dünger** *m* lime fertilizer.
'**kalken** *v/t* (h) **1.** whitewash. **2.** ✎ lime.
'**kalkig** *adj* limy.
'**Kalkmangel** *m* (-s; *no pl*) ♂ calcium deficiency. '**Kalkstein** *m* limestone.
Kalkül [kal'ky:l] *n* (-s; -e) calculation: *et. ins ~ ziehen* take s.th. into consideration.
Kalkulation [kalkula'tsɪo:n] *f* (-; -en) *a. fig.* calculation.
kalkulieren [kalku'li:rən] *v/t, v/i* (h) *a. fig.* calculate: *falsch ~* miscalculate.
Kalorie [kalo'ri:] *f* (-; -n) calorie.
kalo'rienarm *adj* low-calorie: *~ sein* be low in calories. **Kalo'rienbedarf** *m* calorie requirement. **Kalo'riengehalt** *m* caloric content. **kalo'rienreich** *adj*

high-calorie: *~ sein* be rich in calories.
kalt [kalt] **I** *adj* cold, *fig. a.* frigid: *mir ist ~* I'm cold; *es (mir) wird ~* it's (I'm) getting cold; **~er Krieg** Cold War; *gastr.* **~e Platte** cold meats; F *j-m die ~e Schulter zeigen* give s.o. the cold shoulder. **II** *adv* coldly: *et. ~ stellen* put s.th. to cool; *~ essen* have a cold meal; *es überlief mich ~* a cold shiver ran down my spine.
'**kaltbleiben** *v/i* (*irr, sep,* -ge-, sn, → *bleiben*) F *fig.* keep cool, keep one's head.
'**Kaltblüter** [-bly:tər] *m* (-s; -) cold-blooded animal. '**kaltblütig** [-bly:tɪç] **I** *adj* cold-blooded, *fig. a.* cool. **II** *adv* a) coolly, b) *kill etc* in cold blood. '**Kaltblütigkeit** *f* (-; *no pl*) a) coolness, sangfroid, b) cold-bloodedness.
Kälte ['kɛltə] *f* (-; *no pl*) cold, *a. fig.* coldness, frigidity: *es sind 10 Grad ~* the temperature is ten degrees below zero; *bei dieser ~* in this cold.
'**kältebeständig** *adj* cold-resistant.
'**Kälte|einbruch** *m* cold snap. **~grad** *m* degree of frost. **~peri\|ode** *f* cold spell. **~pol** *m* cold pole. **~welle** *f* cold wave.
'**kaltlächelnd** *adv* F (as) cool as you please, without turning a hair.
'**kaltlassen** *v/t* (*irr, sep,* -ge-, h, → *lassen*) F *das läßt mich kalt* that leaves me cold.
'**Kaltluft** *f* (-; *no pl*) cold air: *polare ~* polar air.
'**kaltmachen** *v/t* (*sep,* -ge-, h) F *j-n ~* bump s.o. off, do s.o. in.
'**Kaltmiete** *f* rent exclusive of heating charges.
'**kaltschnäuzig** [-ʃnɔytsɪç] *adj* F cool.
'**Kaltstart** *m mot.* cold start.
'**kaltstellen** *v/t* (*sep,* -ge-, h) F neutralize.
Kalzium ['kaltsɪʊm] *n* (-s; *no pl*) calcium.
kam [ka:m] *pret of* **kommen.**
Kamel [ka'me:l] *n* (-[e]s; -e) **1.** *zo.* camel. **2.** F idiot, blockhead.
Ka'melhaar... camel-hair.
Kamelie [ka'me:liə] *f* (-; -s) ♣ camellia.
Kamera ['kaməra] *f* (-; -s) camera.
Kamerad [kamə'ra:t] *m* (-en; -en) comrade, companion, fellow, mate, F pal, buddy. **Kame'radschaft** *f* (-; *no pl*) comradeship, fellowship. **kame'radschaftlich** *adj and adv* comradely.
'**Kameraführung** *f film:* camerawork.
'**Kameramann** *m* cameraman.

'Kameratasche *f* camera case.

Kamille [ka'mɪlə] *f* (-; -n) camomile.

Kamin [ka'mi:n] *m* (-s; -e) **1.** chimney (*a. mount.*). **2. (offener)** ~ fireside, fireplace; **am** ~ by the fireside.

Kamm [kam] *m* (-[e]s; ᵚe) **1.** comb: *fig.* **alle über einen** ~ **scheren** lump them all together. **2.** *zo.* comb, crest. **3.** crest (*of wave*). **4.** (mountain) ridge.

kämmen ['kɛmən] (h) **I** *v/t* comb (*a.* ⊙): **j-n** ~, **j-m die Haare** ~ comb s.o.'s hair; **sich die Haare** ~ → **II sich** ~ comb (*or* do) one's hair.

Kammer ['kamər] *f* (-; -n) **1.** chamber (*a. anat.*, ⊙), small room, closet. **2.** *parl.* chamber, house. **3.** association.

'Kammer|diener *m* valet. ~**mu,sik** *f* chamber music. ~**or,chester** *n* chamber orchestra. ~**ton** *m* ♩ concert pitch.

'Kammgarn *n*, **'Kammgarn...** worsted.

Kampagne [kam'panjə] *f* (-; -n) campaign.

Kampf [kampf] *m* (-[e]s; ᵚe) **1.** a) *a. fig.* fight, battle, struggle (**gegen** against, **um** for), b) conflict, controversy: **den** ~ **ansagen** declare war (*dat* on); **j-m den** ~ **ansagen** challenge s.o.; ~ **dem Hunger!** war on hunger!; **sich zum** ~ **stellen** give battle; **innere Kämpfe** inner conflicts; → **Dasein. 2.** ✕ combat, fight. **3.** *sports*: contest, fight, bout, match. ~**abstimmung** *f* **1.** *parl.* crucial vote. **2.** strike ballot. ~**ansage** *f* challenge (**an** *acc* to). ⚲**bereit** *adj fig.* ready for battle (*sports*: to fight).

kämpfen ['kɛmpfən] (h) **I** *v/i* (**für, um** for) *a. fig.* fight, battle, struggle: **mit Schwierigkeiten zu** ~ **haben** have (to struggle against) difficulties; **mit j-m** ~ *sports*: fight (with) s.o.; **ich habe lange mit mir gekämpft** I had a long battle with myself; **sie kämpfte mit den Tränen** she was fighting back her tears. **II** *v/t* fight. **III sich** ~ struggle (*or* fight one's way) (**durch** through, **nach oben** *a. fig.* up). **'kämpfend** *adj* fighting: ~**e Truppen** combatant troops.

Kampfer ['kampfər] *m* (-s; *no pl*) 🜍 camphor.

Kämpfer ['kɛmpfər] *m* (-s; -) fighter, ✕ *a.* combatant. **'kämpferisch** *adj* fighting, *fig. a.* aggressive.

Kampf|flugzeug *n* tactical (*or* combat) aircraft. ~**geist** *m* (-[e]s; *no pl*) fighting

spirit: ~ **zeigen** show fight. ~**gericht** *n* *sports*: the judges. ~**handlung** *f* ✕ fighting, action. ~**hubschrauber** *m* (helicopter) gunship.

'kampflos *adj and adv* without a fight: ~ **gewinnen** *sports*: win by default.

'kampflustig *adj* belligerent.

'Kampf|maßnahme *f* militant action. ~**platz** *m* battlefield, *sports*: arena (*a. fig.*). ~**richter(in** *f*) *m* judge, *tennis etc*: umpire. ~**schwimmer** *m* ✕ frogman. ~**sport** *m* combative sports, (*carate etc*) martial arts. ~**stoff** *m* ✕ agent, chemical *etc* weapon. ~**truppe** *f* ✕ combat troops. ⚲**unfähig** *adj* disabled, out of action: **j-n** ~ **machen** put s.o. out of action. ~**verband** *m* ✕ combat unit.

kampieren [kam'pi:rən] *v/i* (h) camp.

Kanada ['kanada] *n* (-s) Canada.

Kanadier¹ [ka'na:diər] *m* (-s; -) Canadian (canoe).

Kanadier² *m* (-s; -), **Ka'nadierin** *f* (-; -nen), **ka'nadisch** *adj* Canadian.

Kanal [ka'na:l] *m* (-s; ᵚe) **1.** a) channel, b) canal, duct, c) conduit: *fig.* **dunkle Kanäle** secret channels; F **den** ~ **voll haben** a) be sloshed, b) be fed up to here. **2.** *anat.* duct. **3.** *radio, TV*: channel.

Kanalisation [kanaliza'tsio:n] *f* (-; -en) **1.** canalization. **2.** drains (*in house*), sewage system (*of town*). **kanalisieren** [kanali'zi:rən] *v/t* (h) **1.** canalize. **2.** provide with sewers. **3.** *fig.* channel.

Ka'nalküste *f* the Channel coast.

Ka'nalwähler *m* *radio, TV* tuner.

Kanarienvogel [ka'na:riən-] *m* canary.

kanarisch [ka'na:rɪʃ] *adj* die **Zen Inseln** the Canaries, the Canary Islands.

Kandare [kan'da:rə] *f* (-; -n) curb (bit): **j-n an die** ~ **nehmen** take s.o. in hand.

Kandelaber [kandə'la:bər] *m* (-s; -) candelabrum.

Kandidat [kandi'da:t] *m* (-en; -en), **Kandi'datin** *f* (-; -nen) *a. fig.* candidate. **Kandi'datenliste** *f* list of candidates, *pol. Am. a.* ticket. **Kandidatur** [kandida'tu:r] *f* (-; -en) candidacy.

kandidieren [kandi'di:rən] *v/i* (h) be a candidate, stand, run: **für das Amt des Präsidenten** ~ run for president.

kandiert [kan'di:rt] *adj* candied (*fruit*).

Kandiszucker ['kandɪs-] *m* candy.

Känguruh ['kɛŋguru] *n* (-s; -s) kangaroo.

Kaninchen [ka'ni:nçən] *n* (-s; -) rabbit.
Ka'ninchenstall *m* rabbit hutch.
Kanister [ka'nɪstər] *m* (-s; -) can(ister).
Ännchen ['kɛnçən] *n* (-s; -) jug: *ein ~ Kaffee gastr.* a pot of coffee.
Kanne ['kanə] *f* (-; -n) a) can, b) pot.
Kannibale [kani'ba:lə] *m* (-n; -n) cannibal. **kanni'balisch** *adj* cannibal.
kannte ['kantə] *pret of* **kennen**.
Kanon ['ka:nɔn] *m* (-s; -s) canon.
Kanone [ka'no:nə] *f* (-; -n) **1.** ✕ cannon, gun: *unter aller ~* just lousy. **2.** F gun, shooter. **3.** F (*in dat* at) wizard, ace.
Kanonier [kano'ni:r] *m* (-s; -e) gunner.
kanonisch [ka'no:nɪʃ] *adj eccl.* canonical: *~es Recht* canon law.
Kantate [kan'ta:tə] *f* (-; -n) ♪ cantata.
Kante ['kantə] *f* (-; -n) **1.** edge, *a.* border: F *et. auf die hohe ~ legen* save some money; *et. auf der hohen ~ haben* have saved some money. **2.** selvage.
kanten ['kantən] *v/t* (h) **1.** cant, tilt, carve (*ski*). **2.** ⊙ edge.
'Kanten *m* (-s; -) crust (*of bread*).
Kanter ['kantər] *m* (-s; -) canter.
kantig ['kantɪç] *adj* squared, angular.
Kantine [kan'ti:nə] *f* (-; -n) canteen.
Kanton [kan'to:n] *m* (-s; -e) canton.
Kanu ['ka:nu, ka'nu:] *n* (-s; -s) canoe.
Kanüle [ka'ny:lə] *f* (-; -n) ✿ cannula, (drain) tube.
Kanute [ka'nu:tə] *m* (-n; -n) canoeist.
Kanzel ['kantsəl] *f* (-; -n) **1.** (*auf der ~* in the) pulpit. **2.** ✈ cockpit. **3.** ✕ turret.
Kanzlei [kants'laɪ] *f* (-; -en) office.
Kanzler ['kantslər] *m* (-s; -) **1.** *pol.* chancellor. **2.** *univ.* vice-chancellor. **~amt** *n* **1.** chancellor's office. **2.** chancellorship. **~kandi,dat** *m* candidate for the chancellorship.
Kap [kap] *n* (-s; -s) *geogr.* cape.
Kapazität [kapatsi'tɛ:t] *f* (-; -en) **1.** *no pl* capacity (*a. fig.*), ⚡ capacitance. **2.** *fig.* (leading) authority (*auf dem Gebiet gen* on the subject of).
Kapelle [ka'pɛlə] *f* (-; -n) **1.** *eccl.* chapel. **2.** ♪ band. **Ka'pellmeister** *m* a) director of music, b) conductor, c) bandmaster (*a.* ✕), bandleader.
Kaper ['ka:pər] *f* (-; -n) ❀ caper.
kapern ['ka:pərn] *v/t* (h) ⚓ capture, seize, F *fig.* nab.
kapieren [ka'pi:rən] (h) F **I** *v/t* get. **II** *v/i*

get it, catch on to: *kapiert?* (have you) got it?
Kapillargefäß [kapɪl'la:r-] *n anat.* capillary (vessel).
kapital [kapi'ta:l] *adj* F capital (*error*).
Kapi'tal *n* (-s; -e, -ien) a) capital, b) capital stock: *~ und Zinsen* principal and interest; *~ schlagen aus* capitalize on.
Kapi'talabwanderung *f* capital outflow. **~anlage** *f* investment. **~anlagegesellschaft** *f* investment trust. **~anleger(in** *f*) *m* investor. **~bildung** *f* accumulation of capital. **~einkommen** *n* investment income. **~erhöhung** *f* increase of capital. **~ertragsteuer** *f* capital yields tax. **~flucht** *f* flight of capital. **~geber(in** *f*) *m* financier. **~gesellschaft** *f* joint-stock company, *Am.* (stock) corporation.
kapitalisieren [kapitali'zi:rən] *v/t* (h) capitalize. **Kapitalismus** [-'lɪsmʊs] *m* (-; *no pl*) capitalism. **Kapitalist** [-'lɪst] *m* (-en; -en) capitalist. **kapita'listisch** *adj* capitalist(ic).
kapi'talkräftig *adj* (financially) powerful, potent.
Kapi'talmarkt *m* capital market.
Kapi'talverbrechen *n* capital crime.
Kapitän [kapi'tɛ:n] *m* (-s; -e) captain.
Kapi'tänspa,tent *n* master's certificate.
Kapitel [ka'pɪtəl] *n* (-s; -) chapter (*a. eccl.*): *fig. ein ~ für sich* another story.
Kapitell [kapi'tɛl] *n* (-s; -e) △ capital.
Kapitulation [kapitula'tsio:n] *f* (-; -en) *a. fig.* capitulation, surrender.
kapitulieren [kapitu'li:rən] *v/i* (h) (*vor dat* to) *a. fig.* capitulate, surrender.
Kaplan [ka'pla:n] *m* (-s; Kapläne) chaplain.
Kappe ['kapə] *f* (-; -n) **1.** cap: F *et. auf s-e ~ nehmen* take the responsibility for s.th. **2.** ⊙ top, cap. **3.** (toe) cap.
kappen ['kapən] *v/t* (h) **1.** cut (*rope etc*). **2.** lop (*tree etc*).
Käppi ['kɛpi] *n* (-s; -s) cap, ✕ *a.* kepi.
Kapriole [kapri'o:lə] *f* (-; -n) caper.
kaprizieren [kapri'tsi:rən] *sich ~* (h) *auf* (*acc*) set one's heart on, insist on.
kapriziös [kapri'tsiö:s] *adj* capricious.
Kapsel ['kapsəl] *f* (-; -n) **1.** case, container. **2.** *anat.*, ✿, *pharm.* capsule.
kaputt [ka'pʊt] *adj* F *~ sein* **1.** be broken, be bust, be torn, ⊙ be out of order, ✿ *heart etc*: be ruined, be bad, *nerves*: be

shattered, *fig. marriage etc*: be broken; *mein Auto ist ~* my car has broken down (*or* has had it). **2.** *person*: a) be ruined, be finished, b) be worn out, be all in: *~er Typ* complete wreck.

ka'puttfahren *v/t* (*irr, sep*, -ge-, h, → *fahren*) F smash up, wreck.

ka'puttgehen *v/i* (*irr, sep*, -ge-, sn, → *gehen*) F **1.** break, tear, *car etc*: break down, *fig. marriage etc*: break up. **2.** *person*: crack (up), go to pieces.

ka'puttlachen: *sich ~* (*sep*, -ge-, h) F kill o.s. laughing.

ka'puttmachen (*sep*, -ge-, h) F I *v/t* **1.** break, smash, *fig.* ruin, bust. **2.** *j-n ~* a) ruin s.o., b) get s.o. down, wear s.o. out, c) kill s.o. **II** *sich ~* wear o.s. out, kill o.s. (*mit* over, doing *s.th.*).

Kapuze [ka'pu:tsə] *f* (-; -n) **1.** hood. **2.** cowl.

Karabiner [kara'bi:nər] *m* (-s; -) **1.** ✕ carbine. **2.** → *~haken* m spring hook.

Karaffe [ka'rafə] *f* carafe, *a.* decanter.

Karambolage [karambo'la:ʒə] *f* (-; -n) **1.** *billiards*: cannon, *Am.* carom. **2.** F crash, collision.

Karamel [kara'mɛl] *n* (-s; *no pl*) caramel.

Karat [ka'ra:t] *n* (-[e]s; -e) carat.

Karate [ka'ra:tə] *n* (-e[s]; *no pl*) karate.

Ka'ratekämpfer *m* karateka.

Ka'rateschlag *m* karate chop.

...karätig [karɛtɪç] *...-carat*.

Karawane [kara'va:nə] *f* (-; -n) caravan.

Kardangelenk [kar'da:n-] *n* ✿ cardan (*or* universal) joint.

Kar'danwelle *f* ✿ cardan shaft.

Kardinal [kardi'na:l] *m* (-s; ⸚e) cardinal.

Kardi'nal... cardinal (*fault, question, etc*). *~zahl* f cardinal (number).

Kardiologe [kardiọ'lo:gə] *m* (-n; -n) ✻ cardiologist.

Karenzzeit [ka'rɛnts-] *f insurance*: waiting period, ✝ period of restriction.

Kar'freitag [ka:r-] *m eccl.* Good Friday.

karg [kark] *adj* **1.** meagre, *Am.* meager, scanty, poor, frugal (*meal, life*), barren (*soil*). **2.** austere. **3.** sparing: *~ bemessen* (very) meagre, *fig.* (very) limited.

kargen ['kargən] *v/i* (h) *~ mit* be sparing of *praise etc*, be stingy with *money*.

'Kargheit *f* (-; *no pl*) meag/reness (*Am.* -er-), poorness.

kärglich ['kɛrklɪç] *adj* → *karg* 1.

kariert [ka'ri:rt] *adj* checked, chequered, *Am.* checkered.

Karies ['ka:riɛs] *f* (-; *no pl*) ✻ tooth decay, dental caries.

Karikatur [karika'tu:r] *f* (-; -en) cartoon, caricature (*a. fig.*). **Karikaturist** [karikatu'rɪst] *m* (-en; -en) cartoonist, caricaturist. **karikieren** [kari'ki:rən] *v/t* (h) cartoon, caricature.

kariös [ka'riø:s] *adj* ✻ carious, decayed.

karitativ [karita'ti:f] *adj* charitable.

Karmin [kar'mi:n] *n* (-s; *no pl*) crimson.

kar'minrot *adj* crimson.

Karneval ['karnəval] *m* (-s; -e) carnival.

Karo ['ka:ro] *n* (-s; -s) **1.** check, square. **2.** *cards*: diamonds.

Karosserie [karɔsə'ri:] *f* (-; -n) *mot.* (car) body.

Karotin [karo'ti:n] *n* (-s; *no pl*) carotene.

Karotte [ka'rɔtə] *f* (-; -n) carrot.

Karpfen ['karpfən] *m* (-s; -) carp.

Karre ['karə] *f* (-; -n) **1.** F (*alte*) ~ bus, crate, banger. **2.** → *Karren*.

Karren ['karən] *m* (-s; -) cart, (wheel)barrow: F *fig. j-m an den ~ fahren* step on s.o.'s toes; *den ~ in den Dreck fahren* mess things up; *den ~ wieder aus dem Dreck ziehen* clear up the mess; *j-n vor s-n ~ spannen* rope s.o. in.

Karriere [ka'riɛ:rə] *f* (-; -n) career: *~ machen* make a career for o.s.

Karri'erefrau *f* career woman (*or* girl).

Karri'eremacher *m contp.* careerist.

Karte ['kartə] *f* (-; -n) a) card, b) map, ✿ chart, c) 🎫, *thea. etc*: ticket, d) menu, wine list: *nach der ~ speisen* dine à la carte; *die gelbe (rote) ~ soccer*: the yellow (red) card; *~n spielen* play cards; *gute ~n haben* have a good hand; *s-e ~n auf den Tisch legen a. fig.* show one's hand, put one's cards on the table; *alles auf eine ~ setzen* put all one's eggs in one basket; → *legen* 6.

Kartei [kar'taɪ] *f* (-; -en) (*~ führen* keep a) card index (*über* acc on).

Kar'teikarte *f* file (*or* index) card.

Kar'teikasten *m* card-index box.

Kartell [kar'tɛl] *n* (-s; -e) cartel, ✝ *a.* combine, trust.

'Karten|haus *n* **1.** ✿ chartroom. **2.** house of cards. *~kunststück* n card trick. *~leger* m (-s; -), *~legerin* f (-; -nen) fortune-teller. *~spiel* n **1.** a) card playing, b) card game. **2.** pack (*Am. a.*

deck) of cards. **~verkauf** m sale of tickets. **~vorverkauf** m advance booking. **~zeichen** n conventional sign.

Kartoffel [kar'tɔfəl] f (-; -n) potato. **Kar'toffel|brei** m mashed potatoes. **~chips** pl potato crisps (Am. chips). **~käfer** m potato beetle (Am. bug). **~puffer** m potato fritter. **~sa‚lat** m potato salad. **~schäler** m potato peeler.

Kartograph [karto'graːf] m (-en; -en) cartographer. **Kartographie** [kartogra'fiː] f (-; no pl) cartography.

Karton [kar'tɔŋ, kar'toːn] m (-s; -s) **1.** cardboard. **2.** cardboard box, carton. **kartoniert** [karto'niːrt] adj print. paperback(ed).

Karussell [karʊ'sɛl] n (-s; -s, -e) roundabout, merry-go-round, whirligig.

'Karwoche f eccl. Holy Week.

karzinogen [kartsino'geːn] adj ❦ carcinogenic. **Karzinom** [kartsi'noːm] n (-s; -e) ❦ carcinoma, cancer.

kaschieren [ka'ʃiːrən] v/t (h) conceal.

Kaschmir ['kaʃmɪr] m (-s; -e) cashmere.

Käse ['kɛːzə] m (-s; -) **1.** cheese. **2.** F a) rubbish, b) stupid business.

'Käse|blatt n F rag. **~gebäck** n cheese biscuits. **~glocke** f cheese cover. **~kuchen** m cheesecake. **~platte** f gastr. cheese platter. **~rinde** f cheese rind.

Kaserne [ka'zɛrnə] f (-; -n) barracks.

Ka'sernenhof m barrack square.

kasernieren [kazɛr'niːrən] v/t (h) quarter in barracks.

'Käsestange f cheese straw.

käsig ['kɛːzɪç] adj **1.** caseous, cheesy. **2.** F pale, pasty (face).

Kasino [ka'ziːno] n (-s; -s) **1.** casino, club. **2.** a) (officers') mess, b) cafeteria, canteen.

Kaskoversicherung ['kasko-] f mot. insurance against damage to one's own vehicle; → **Teilkaskoversicherung, Vollkaskoversicherung.**

Kasper ['kaspər] m (-s; -) **1.** Punch. **2.** fig. clown. **'Kasperlethe‚ather** n Punch and Judy (show).

Kassageschäft ['kasa-] n ✝ cash transaction. **'Kassara‚batt** m cash discount.

Kasse ['kasə] f (-; -n) **1.** a) cashbox, b) till, c) cash register: **der Film hat volle ~n gebracht** the film was a box-office success. **2.** in shop, bank, etc: cash desk, in supermarket: checkout (counter), in

cinema etc: ticket window, thea. etc a. box office: **zahlen Sie bitte an der ~!** pay at the desk, please!; fig. **j-n zur ~ bitten** make s.o. pay up. **3.** ✝ cash (payment): **gegen ~** for cash; **netto ~** net cash. **4.** cash: **~ machen** a) cash up, b) F count one's cash, c) F fig. cash in heavily, make a packet; F **gut bei ~ sein** be flush; **knapp bei ~ sein** be (a bit) hard up; **gemeinsame ~ machen** split the expenses; **getrennte ~ machen** go Dutch. **5.** F (**er ist in k-r ~** he has no) health insurance. **6.** F (savings) bank.

'Kassen|abschluß m balancing of the (cash) accounts. **~anweisung** f cash order. **~arzt** m health-plan doctor. **~bestand** m cash balance. **~bon** m sales check (Am. slip), receipt. **~buch** n cashbook. **~erfolg** m thea. etc box-office hit. **~ma‚gnet** m F crowd-puller. **~pati‚ent(in** f) m health-plan patient. **~prüfung** f cash audit: **e-e ~ vornehmen** audit the cash. **~schlager** m F **1.** crowd-puller. **2.** moneymaker. **~sturz** m **~ machen** count one's cash. **~wart** m (-[e]s; -e) treasurer. **~zettel** m sales check (Am. slip), receipt.

Kasserolle [kasə'rɔlə] f (-; -n) casserole.

Kassette [ka'sɛtə] f (-; -n) **1.** a) box, b) casket, c) cashbox. **2.** slipcase (for books), box set (for records). **3.** phot., TV etc cassette, cartridge. **4.** △ coffer.

Kas'setten|deck n cassette deck. **~re‚corder** m cassette recorder.

kassieren [ka'siːrən] (h) **I** v/t **1.** collect (rent etc). **2.** F a) collect, take (fees etc), b) seize (property), c) nab, catch (criminal), d) suffer (loss etc), take, get (beating, etc). **3.** ⚖ quash (sentence). **II** v/i **4.** collect (the money): F fig. **kräftig ~** cash in (heavily) (**bei** on); **darf ich bei Ihnen ~?** would you mind paying now?

Kassierer [ka'siːrər] m (-s; -), **Kas'siererin** f (-; -nen) cashier, esp. Am. teller.

Kastagnette [kastan'jɛtə] f (-; -n) castanet.

Kastanie [kas'taːniə] f (-; -n) chestnut: fig. **für j-n die ~n aus dem Feuer holen** pull the chestnuts out of the fire for s.o.

Ka'stanienbaum m chestnut (tree).

ka'stanienbraun adj chestnut.

Kästchen ['kɛstçən] n **1.** small box (or case), casket. **2.** print. square, box.

Kaste ['kastə] f (-; -n) caste.

kasteien [kas'taɪən] *sich* ~ (h) **1.** *eccl.* mortify the flesh. **2.** *fig.* deny o.s.

Kasten ['kastən] *m* (-s; ⁈) **1.** box (*a. print.*), case, chest, (*beer etc*) crate: F **er hat was auf dem** ~ he's brainy, he's on the ball. **2.** F (*goal, house, TV set*) box, (*car, plane*) bus, crate, (*ship*) tub.

'**Kastengeist** *m* (-[e]s; *no pl*) caste spirit.

'**Kastenwesen** *n* (-s; *no pl*) caste system.

Kastration [kastra'tsɪoːn] *f* (-; -en) castration.

kastrieren [kas'triːrən] *v/t* (h) castrate.

Kasus ['kaːzʊs] *m* (-; -) *ling.* case.

Kat [kat] *m* (-s; -s) → **Katalysator** 2.

Katakomben [kata'kɔmbən] *pl* catacombs.

Katalog [kata'loːk] *m* (-[e]s; -e) catalog(ue *Br.*). **katalogisieren** [katalogi'ziːrən] *v/t* (h) catalog(ue *Br.*).

Katalysator [kataly'zaːtɔr] *m* (-s; -en [-za'toːrən]) **1.** ⚗ *or fig.* catalyst. **2.** *mot.* catalytic converter.

Katapult [kata'pʊlt] *n, m* (-[e]s; -e), **katapultieren** [-'tiːrən] *v/t* (h) catapult.

Kata'pultstart *m* ✈ catapult takeoff.

Katarrh [ka'tar] *m* (-s; -e) ⚕ catarrh.

Kataster [ka'tastər] *m, n* (-s; -) land register.

katastrophal [katastro'faːl] *adj* catastrophic, *a.* F *fig.* disastrous.

Katastrophe [kata'stroːfə] *f* (-; -n) *a.* F *fig.* catastrophe, disaster.

Kata'strophen|a,larm *m* red alert. ~**einsatz** *m* (*im* ~ on) duty in a disaster area. ~**fall** *m* (*im* ~ in an) emergency. ~**film** *m* disaster film. ~**gebiet** *n* disaster area. ~**hilfe** *f* disaster relief. ~**schutz** *m* disaster control (*or* prevention).

Katechismus [kate'çɪsmʊs] *m* (-; -men) *eccl.* catechism.

Kategorie [katego'riː] *f* (-; -n) category.

kategorisch [kate'goːrɪʃ] *adj* categorical: ~ **ablehnen** a. refuse flatly.

Kater ['kaːtər] *m* (-s; -) **1.** *zo.* tom(cat). **2.** F hangover: *e-n* ~ *haben* a. be hung over.

Katheder [ka'teːdər] *n, a. m* (-s; -) (teacher's *or* lecturer's) desk.

Kathedrale [kate'draːlə] *f* (-; -n) cathedral.

Katheter [ka'teːtər] *m* (-s; -) ⚕ catheter.

Kathode [ka'toːdə] *f* (-; -n) cathode.

Katholik [kato'liːk] *m* (-en; -en), **Katho'likin** *f* (-; -nen), **katholisch**

[ka'toːlɪʃ] *adj* (Roman) Catholic.

Katholizismus [katoli'tsɪsmʊs] *m* (-; *no pl*) Catholicism.

Kätzchen ['kɛtsçən] *n* (-s; -) **1.** *zo.* kitten. **2.** ⚘ catkin.

Katze ['katsə] *f* (-; -n) cat: F *fig.* **das ist für die Katz** that's all for nothing; *Katz und Maus spielen mit* play cat and mouse with; *die* ~ *im Sack kaufen* buy a pig in a poke; *die* ~ *aus dem Sack lassen* let the cat out of the bag; *wie die* ~ *um den heißen Brei gehen* beat about the bush.

'**Katzenauge** *n* **1.** cat's eye (*a. min.*). **2.** F rear reflector.

'**katzenhaft** *adj* catlike, feline.

'**Katzen|jammer** *m* F hangover: (*moralischen*) ~ *haben* a. have the blues. ~**klo** *n* cat tray. ~**sprung** *m fig.* **ein** ~ *von hier* a stone's throw from here. ~**streu** *f* cat litter. ~**wäsche** *f* F *fig.* (~ *machen* have a) cat's lick.

Kauderwelsch ['kaʊdərvɛlʃ] *n* (-[s]; *no pl*) double Dutch, lingo.

kauen ['kaʊən] *v/t, v/i* (h) chew: *an den Nägeln* ~ bite one's nails; *fig. an e-r Sache* ~ chew s.th. over.

kauern ['kaʊərn] *v/i* (*a. sich* ~) (h) crouch (*or* squat) (down).

Kauf [kaʊf] *m* (-[e]s; ⁈e) **1.** buying, purchase: *zum* ~ for sale; *beim* ~ when buying; *et. in* ~ *nehmen* put up with s.th.; *leichten* ~*es davonkommen* get off cheaply. **2.** purchase, F buy: *ein guter* ~ a good bargain (*or* buy).

'**kaufen** *v/t, v/i* (h) buy (*a.* F *fig.*), purchase: *bei* ~ go to, buy at; *sich ein Auto* ~ buy (o.s.) a car; F *dafür kann ich mir nichts* ~! that's no use to me!; *den kaufe ich mir!* I'll tell him what's what!

Käufer ['kɔyfər] *m* (-s; -), '**Käuferin** *f* (-; -nen) buyer, purchaser.

'**Kauf|frau** *f* businesswoman. ~**halle** *f* small department store. ~**haus** *n* department store. ~**kraft** *f* (-; *no pl*) purchasing power (*of money*), spending power (*of consumers*). ²**kräftig** *adj* a) well-to-do, b) hard (*currency*).

käuflich ['kɔyflɪç] *adj* **1.** purchasable: (*nicht*) ~ *sein* (not to) be for sale; ~*e Liebe* prostitution; ~ *erwerben* purchase. **2.** *fig.* venal, corrupt.

'**Käuflichkeit** *f* (-; *no pl*) *fig.* venality.

'**Kaufmann** *m* (-[e]s; -leute) **1.** businessman, merchant, trader, dealer. **2.** shop-keeper, *Am. a.* storekeeper, *n.s.* grocer.

kaufmännisch ['kaʊfmɛnɪʃ] *adj* commercial, business: **~e(r) Angestellte(r)** (commercial) clerk.

'Kaufpreis *m* (purchase) price.

'Kaufvertrag *m* contract of sale.

'Kaufzwang *m* obligation (to buy).

'Kaugummi *m, a. n* (-s; -s) chewing gum.

Kaulquappe ['kaʊlkvapə] *f* (-; -n) *zo.* tadpole.

kaum [kaʊm] *adv* a) hardly, scarcely, b) barely, only just: **~ zu glauben** hard to believe; **~ möglich** hardly possible; **wohl ~(!)** hardly(!); **ich glaube ~, daß** I hardly think that; **~ war sie gegangen, als ...** no sooner had she gone than ...

'Kaumuskel *m* masticatory muscle.

kausal [kaʊ'zaːl] *adj* causal. **Kausalität** [kaʊzali'tɛːt] *f* (-; -en) causality.

Kau'sal|satz *m ling.* causal clause. **~zusammenhang** *m* causal connection.

Kaution [kaʊ'tsi̯oːn] *f* (-; -en) ⚖ security, ⚖ bail: **~ stellen** ⚖ furnish security, ⚖ stand bail; **gegen ~** ⚖ on bail.

Kautschuk ['kaʊtʃʊk] *m* (-s; -e) caoutchouc, India rubber.

'Kauwerkzeuge *pl* masticatory organs.

Kauz [kaʊts] *m* (-es; **~e**) **1.** *zo.* screech-owl. **2.** F (*komischer*) **~** odd (*or* queer) fellow, *Am.* oddball.

kauzig ['kaʊtsɪç] *adj* F queer, odd.

Kavalier [kava'liːr] *m* (-s; -e) gentleman.

Kava'liersde,likt *n* peccadillo.

Kavallerie [kavalə'riː] *f* (-; -n) cavalry.

Kavallerist [kavalə'rɪst] *m* (-en; -en) cavalryman, trooper.

Kaviar ['kaːvi̯ar] *m* (-s; -e) caviar(e).

keck [kɛk] *adj* pert, saucy.

Kegel ['keːgəl] *m* (-s; -) **1.** Å, ☀ cone. **2.** ninepin, skittle(pin): → **Kind.**

'Kegelbahn *f* skittle (*or* bowling) alley.

'kegelförmig [-fœrmɪç] *adj* conical.

'Kegelklub *m* skittles (*or* bowling) club.

'Kegelkugel *f* skittle (*or* bowling) ball.

kegeln ['keːgəln] *v/i* (h) play (at) skittles (*or* ninepins), bowl, go bowling.

'Kegelsport *m* skittles, bowling.

'Kegelstumpf *m* Å truncated cone.

Kegler ['keːglər] *m* (-s; -), **'Keglerin** *f* (-; -nen) skittles player, bowler.

Kehle ['keːlə] *f* (-; -n) **1.** *anat.* throat: **j-m die ~ durchschneiden** cut s.o.'s throat; *fig.* **et. in die falsche ~ bekommen** take

s.th. the wrong way. **2.** ⚙ flute.

'Kehlkopf *m anat.* larynx. **~entzündung** *f* 🩺 laryngitis. **~krebs** *m* 🩺 cancer of the larynx, F throat cancer.

'Kehllaut *m* guttural (sound).

Kehre ['keːrə] *f* (-; -n) **1.** (sharp) bend. **2.** *skating etc:* turn, *gym.* rear vault.

kehren¹ ['keːrən] (h) **I** *v/t* **1.** *et. nach oben* (*unten, außen etc*) **~** turn s.th. upwards (down, outside, *etc*); **den Rücken ~** *a. fig.* turn one's back (*dat* on); **in sich gekehrt** withdrawn, *psych.* introvert(ed); → **oberst. II sich ~ 2.** → **wenden 4. 3. sich nicht ~ an** (*dat*) ignore. **III** *v/i* **4. kehrt!** ✕ about turn!

'kehren² ['keːrən] *v/t, v/i* (h) sweep.

Kehricht ['keːrɪçt] *m, n* (-s; *no pl*) **1.** sweepings. **2.** rubbish, *Am.* garbage.

'Kehrma,schine *f* road sweeper.

'Kehrreim *m* burden, refrain.

'Kehrseite *f* **1.** reverse. **2.** *humor.* back. **3.** *fig.* a) *the* other side, b) drawback.

kehrtmachen ['keːrt-] *v/i* (*sep*, -ge-, h) **1.** turn round, ✕ face about. **2.** turn back.

'Kehrtwendung *f a. fig.* about-face.

keifen ['kaɪfən] *v/i* (h) nag, bicker.

Keil [kaɪl] *m* (-[e]s; -e) **1.** wedge. **2.** gore, gusset. **'Keilabsatz** *m* wedge heel.

keilen ['kaɪlən] (h) **I** *v/t j-n* **~** rope s.o. in (**für** for). **II sich ~** fight.

Keiler ['kaɪlər] *m* (-s; -) *zo.* wild boar.

'keilförmig [-fœrmɪç] *adj* wedge-shaped.

'Keilriemen *m* ⚙ V-belt.

'Keilschrift *f* cuneiform (script).

Keim [kaɪm] *m* (-[e]s; -e) **1.** *biol.* germ, embryo (*both a. fig.*), ☘ *a.* bud, *fig. a.* seed(s): *im* **~** in embryo; *im* **~ ersticken** nip *s.th.* in the bud. **2.** 🩺 germ, bacillus. **~blatt** *n* **1.** ☘ cotyledon. **2.** *biol.* germ layer. **~drüse** *f physiol.* gonad.

keimen ['kaɪmən] *v/i* (h) **1.** *biol.* germinate. **2.** *fig.* grow, stir.

'keimfähig *adj* germinable.

'keimfrei *adj* sterile: **~ machen** sterilize.

'Keimling *m* (-s; -e) *biol.* embryo.

'keimtötend *adj* germicidal, antiseptic: **~es Mittel** germicide.

'Keimträger *m* 🩺 (germ) carrier.

'Keimzelle *f* **1.** germ cell. **2.** *fig.* nucleus.

kein [kaɪn] *indef pron* no, not any, not a: **ich habe ~ Geld** I haven't (got) any money; **du bist ~ Kind mehr** you are not a child any more; **~ Wort mehr!** not another word!; **~ anderer als X** none other than X; *es kostet ~e 100 Mark* it costs less than 100 marks.

'**keine**, '**keiner**, '**keines** (*or* **keins**) *indef pron* **1.** no one, nobody, not one, none: *~(r) von uns* a) neither of us, b) none of us. **2.** not any, none, not one: *keins von beiden* neither (of the two).

'**keinerlei** *adj* no ... what(so)ever, no ... at all.

'**keines'falls** *adv* on no account, under no circumstances. '**keines'wegs** *adv* by no means, not at all, not in the least.

'**keinmal** *adv* not once, never.

Keks [ke:ks] *m* [-es]; -e) biscuit, *Am.* cookie.

Kelch [kɛlç] *m* (-[e]s; -e) **1.** goblet, *eccl.* chalice, cup (*a. fig.*). **2.** ♀ calyx, cup. *~blatt n* ♀ sepal. *~hülle f* ♀ calycle.

Kelle ['kɛlə] *f* (-; -n) **1.** *gastr.* ladle. **2.** △ trowel. **3.** ⚏ *etc* signal(l)ing disc.

Keller ['kɛlər] *m* (-s; -) cellar.

Kellerei ['kɛləraɪ] *f* (-; -en) wine cellars.

'**Kellergeschoß** *n* basement.

'**Kellermeister** *m* cellarman.

Kellner ['kɛlnər] *m* (-s; -) waiter.

'**Kellnerin** *f* (-; -nen) waitress.

Kelte ['kɛltə] *m* (-n; -n) Celt.

Kelter ['kɛltər] *f* (-; -n) (wine)press.

keltern ['kɛltərn] *v/t* (h) press.

Keltin *f* (-; -nen) Celt.

keltisch ['kɛltɪʃ] *adj* Celtic.

kennen ['kɛnən] *v/t* (kannte, gekannt, h) know, *a.* be acquainted (*or* familiar) with, *a.* recognize (*an dat* by): *wir ~ uns* we know each other, *schon a.* we have already met; *ich kenne sie von der Schule* we were at school together; *kennst du mich noch?* do you remember me?; *das ~ wir!* we know all about that!; *er kennt nichts als s-e Arbeit* he lives only for his work; *sie kennt k-e Müdigkeit* she never gets tired; *kein Erbarmen ~* know no mercy.

'**kennenlernen** *v/t* (*sep*, -ge-, h) become acquainted with, get (*or* come) to know: *j-n ~* meet s.o.; *j-n näher ~* (get to) know s.o. better; *wir haben uns in B. kennengelernt* we first met in B.

Kenner ['kɛnər] *m* (-s; -), '**Kennerin** *f* (-; -nen) **1.** connoisseur. **2.** (*gen*) expert (at, in, of), authority (on).

'**Kennerblick** *m* (*mit ~* with an) expert's eye. '**Kennermiene** *f* (*e-e ~ aufsetzen* assume the) air of an expert.

'**Kennmelo,die** *f* signature tune.

kenntlich ['kɛntlɪç] *adj* recognizable (*an dat* by): *~ machen* mark.

Kenntnis ['kɛntnɪs] *f* (-; -se) knowledge: *gute ~se haben in* (*dat*) have a good knowledge of, be well grounded in; *das entzieht sich m-r ~* I don't know anything about it; *von et. ~ haben* know (about) s.th., be aware of s.th.; *et. zur ~ nehmen* take note of (*or* note) s.th.; *j-n in ~ setzen von* inform s.o. of.

'**Kenntnisnahme** [-na:mə] *f* *zu Ihrer etc ~* for your *etc* attention.

'**Kennwort** *n* code word, ✗ *a.* password (*a. computer*).

'**Kennzeichen** *n* **1.** a) (distinguishing) mark, characteristic, b) sign, symptom (*a.* 🐾): *besondere ~* distinguishing marks. **2.** *fig.* hallmark. **3.** (*polizeiliches*) ~ *mot.* registration (*Am.* license) number. **4.** *computer:* flag.

'**Kennzeichen|leuchte** *f* *mot.* number-plate (*Am.* license-plate) light. *~schild n* number (*Am.* license) plate.

'**kennzeichnen** *v/t* (h) **1.** mark. **2.** *fig.* characterize, (go to) show. '**kennzeichnend** *adj* characteristic (*für* of).

'**Kennziffer** *f* code number, ✝ reference number, *of ad:* box number.

kentern ['kɛntərn] *v/i* (sn) capsize.

Keramik [ke'ra:mɪk] *f* (-; -en) **1.** *no pl* ceramics, pottery. **2.** ceramic (article), piece of pottery. **Ke'ramiker** *m* (-s; -), **Ke'ramikerin** *f* (-; -nen) ceramist.

Kerbe ['kɛrbə] *f* (-; -n) notch.

Kerbel ['kɛrbəl] *m* (-s; *no pl*) ♀ chervil.

kerben ['kɛrbən] *v/t* (h) notch.

Kerbholz ['kɛrp-] *n* F **et. auf dem ~ haben** have done s.th. wrong; *er hat einiges auf dem ~* he has quite a record.

Kerl [kɛrl] *m* (-s; -e) F fellow, bloke, chap, *Am.* guy, *contp.* type: *er ist ein anständiger ~* he is a decent sort; *ein feiner ~* a splendid fellow, *Am.* a great guy; *ein lieber* (*or* netter) *~* a dear; *ein (ganzer) ~* a real man; *ein übler ~* a nasty customer.

Kern [kɛrn] *m* (-[e]s; -e) **1.** ♀ a) pip, b) stone, *Am.* pit, c) kernel: *fig. sie hat e-n guten ~* she is good at heart. **2.** *fig.* core (*a.* ⚡, *phys.*, ⚙), nucleus (*a. phys.*), essence: *der ~ der Sache* the heart of the matter; *pol.* harter *~* hard core. *~brennstoff m* nuclear fuel. *~ener,gie* *f* nuclear energy. **explosi,on** *f* nuclear explosion. **fach** *n* ped., univ. basic subject. **fa,milie** *f* sociol. nuclear family. **forschung** *f* nuclear research. **frage** *f* crucial question. **fusi,on** *f* nuclear fusion. **gehäuse** *n* ❀ core.

'kerngesund adj thoroughly healthy, F (as) sound as a bell.

'kernig adj fig. a) robust, b) pithy, c) earthy, d) F super, terrific.

'Kernkraft *f* nuclear power. **gegner(in** *f*) *m* antinuclear campaigner. **werk** *n* nuclear power station.

'kernlos adj ❀ seedless.

'Kern|obst *n* pome. **phy,sik** *f* nuclear physics. **physiker** *m* nuclear physicist. **punkt** *m* central point (or issue). **re,aktor** *m* nuclear reactor. **schmelze** *f* (-; no pl) (nuclear core) meltdown. **seife** *f* curd soap. **spaltung** *f* nuclear fission. **stück** *n* fig. essential part, main item. **waffe** *f* nuclear weapon. **waffenverbot** *n* ban on nuclear weapons. **waffenversuch** *m* nuclear weapons test. **zeit** *f* core time. **zerfall** *m* nuclear disintegration.

Kerosin [kero'zi:n] *n* (-s; no pl) kerosene.

Kerze ['kɛrtsə] *f* (-; -n) **1.** candle (a. ⚡, phys.). **2.** mot. spark(ing) plug.

'kerzengerade adv bolt upright.

'Kerzenhalter *m* candlestick.

'Kerzenlicht *n* (bei ~ by) candlelight.

'Kerzenschlüssel *m* mot. plug wrench.

keß [kɛs] adj F pert, saucy.

Kessel ['kɛsəl] *m* (-s; -) **1.** kettle, cauldron, ⊙ vat, boiler. **2.** geol. basin, hollow. **3.** ✗ pocket.

'Kesselstein *m* (-[e]s; no pl) scale, fur.

'Kesseltreiben *n* (-s) fig. (gegen) hunt (for), pol. witch hunt (against).

Kette ['kɛtə] *f* (-; -n) **1.** chain (a. 🐒, ♈, ♈), a. necklace: j-n an die ~ legen put s.o. on a short leash. **2.** fig. a) chain, series (of accidents, events, etc), b) string, line: e-e ~ bilden form a cordon (or line). **3.** hunt. covey. **4.** mot. track. **5.** textil. warp: ~ und Schuß warp and weft.

ketten ['kɛtən] *v/t* (h) chain (an acc to).

'Ketten|brief *m* chain letter. **fahrzeug** *n* tracked vehicle. **glied** *n* chain link. **karus,sell** *n* chairoplane. **laden** *m* chain store. **raucher(in** *f*) *m* chain-smoker. **reakti,on** *f* chain reaction.

Ketzer ['kɛtsər] *m* (-s; -) heretic.

Ketzerei [kɛtsə'raɪ] *f* (-; -en) heresy.

'Ketzerin *f* (-; -nen) heretic.

'ketzerisch adj heretical.

keuchen ['kɔɥçən] *v/i* (h) pant, puff (a. 🚂), a. *v/t* gasp.

'Keuchhusten *m* 🐾 whooping cough.

Keule ['kɔɥlə] *f* (-; -n) **1.** club. **2.** chemische ~ Mace (TM). **3.** gastr. leg.

'Keulenschlag *m* **1.** blow with a club. **2.** fig. crushing blow.

keusch [kɔɥʃ] adj chaste.

'Keuschheit *f* (-; no pl) chastity.

Kibbuz [kɪ'bu:ts] *m* (-; -e) kibbutz.

kichern ['kɪçərn] *v/i* (h) (über acc at) giggle, snigger.

kicken ['kɪkən] *v/t*, *v/i* (h) kick.

Kiebitz ['ki:bɪts] *m* (-es; -e) **1.** zo. peewit, lapwing. **2.** F fig. kibitzer.

Kiefer¹ ['ki:fər] *f* (-; -n) ❀ pine.

'Kiefer² *m* (-s; -) anat. jaw.

'Kieferhöhle *f* anat. maxillary sinus.

'Kiefernzapfen *m* ❀ pine cone.

'Kieferortho,päde *m* 🐾 orthodontist.

Kiel [ki:l] *m* (-[e]s; -e) ⚓ keel. kiel'oben adv ⚓ bottom up. **'Kielraum** *m* ⚓ bilge. **'Kielwasser** *n* (-s; -) (fig. in j-s ~ segeln sail in s.o.'s) wake.

Kieme ['ki:mə] *f* (-; -n) gill.

Kies [ki:s] *m* (-es; -e) **1.** (a. mit ~ bestreuen) gravel. **2.** F fig. lolly, Am. bread.

Kiesel ['ki:zəl] *m* (-s; -) flint, pebble.

'Kieselerde *f* 🌿 silica, siliceous earth.

'Kieselsäure *f* 🌿 silicic acid.

'Kieselstein *m* → Kiesel.

'Kies|grube *f* gravel pit. **strand** *m* shingle (beach). **weg** *m* gravel path.

Kiez [ki:ts] *m* (-es; -e) F district, area.

kiffen ['kɪfən] *v/i* (h) F smoke pot (or hash).

killen ['kɪlən] *v/t* (h) F kill.

Killer ['kɪlər] *m* (-s; -) F killer.

Kilo ['ki:lo] *n* (-s; -[s]), **Kilogramm** [kilo'gram] *n* kilogram(me Br.).

Kilo'hertz [kilo-] *n* ⚡, phys. kilohertz.

Kilo'joule *n* phys. kilojoule.

Kilo'meter *m* kilomet/re (Am. -er). **geld** *n* mileage allowance. **pau,schale** *f* flat mileage allowance. **stand** *m* mileage (reading). **stein** *m* milestone. ²**weit** adv for miles (and miles). **zähler** *m* mileage indicator.

Kilo'volt *n* kilovolt.

Kilo'watt(stunde *f*) *n* kilowatt(-hour).

Kimm [kɪm] f (-; no pl) ♻ visual horizon.
Kimme ['kɪmə] f (-; -n) ✕ notch.
Kind [kɪnt] n (-[e]s; -er) child (a. fig.), F
kid, a. baby: **ein ~ erwarten** (**bekommen**) be expecting (going to have) a
baby; **von ~ auf** from childhood; F **mit
~ und Kegel** (with) bag and baggage;
fig. **das ~ mit dem Bade ausschütten**
throw the baby out with the bathwater;
das ~ beim rechten Namen nennen
call a spade a spade; (**ein**) **gebranntes
~ scheut das Feuer** once bitten, twice
shy; → **Geist** 2, **lieb.**
'**Kindbettfieber** n ☞ puerperal fever.
'**Kinder|arbeit** f child labo(u)r. **~arzt** m,
~ärztin f p(a)ediatrician. **~bett**(chen)
n cot, Am. crib. **~buch** n children's
book. **~dorf** n children's village. **~ermäßigung** f reduction for children.
~erziehung f bringing up children.
~fahrrad n child's bicycle. ♀**feindlich**
adj hostile to children, antichildren.
♀**freundlich** adj **1.** fond of children. **2.**
suitable for children. **~garten** m kindergarten. **~gärtner**(**in**) f(m) kindergarten teacher. **~geld** n children's allowance. **~heim** n children's home. **~hort**
m day nursery. **~kleidung** f children's
wear. **~krankheit** f children's disease,
fig. teething troubles. **~krippe** f crèche,
day nursery. **~lähmung** f ☞ (spinale) ~
polio(myelitis). ♀**leicht** adj dead easy.
♀**lieb** adj very fond of children. **~lied** n
children's song.
'**kinderlos** adj childless.
'**Kinder|mädchen** n nurse(maid), nanny. **~pflege** f child care. **~psychologie** f child psychology. ♀**reich** adj
with many children: **~e Familie** large
family. **~schuhe** pl children's shoes:
fig. **noch in den ~n stecken** be still in
its infancy. **~sendung** f children's program(me Br.). ♀**sicher** adj childproof.
~sicherung f mot. childproof lock.
~spiel n fig. **das ist ein ~** (**für ihn**) that's
child's play (for him). **~spielplatz** m
children's playground. **~stube** f fig.
upbringing. **~tagesstätte** f day nursery, day-care cent/re (Am. -er). **~wagen**
m pram, Am. baby carriage. **~zimmer**
n children's room, nursery. **~zulage** f
children's allowance.
'**Kindes|alter** n a) infancy, b) childhood.
~liebe f filial love. **~mißhandlung** f

child abuse. **~tötung** f ☞ infanticide.
'**Kindheit** f (-; no pl) childhood: **von ~ an**
from a child.
'**kindisch** adj childish.
'**kindlich** adj **1.** childlike, childish. **2.**
filial (love etc).
'**Kindlichkeit** f (-; no pl) childishness.
'**Kindskopf** m F fig. (big) child, silly.
'**Kindtaufe** f christening.
Kinetik [ki'ne:tɪk] f (-; no pl) kinetics.
ki'netisch adj kinetic.
Kinkerlitzchen ['kɪŋkərlɪtsçən] pl F **1.**
gimcrackery, frills. **2.** trivia.
Kinn [kɪn] n (-[e]s; -e) chin.
'**Kinnlade** [-la:də] f (-; -n) jaw(bone).
'**Kinnhaken** m boxing: hook to the chin.
Kino ['ki:no] n (-s; -s) **1.** cinema, Am.
motion-picture (F movie) theater. **2.**
cinema, esp. Am. the movies: **ins ~
gehen** go to the pictures (or movies).
'**Kinogänger** [-gɛŋər] m (-s; -) cinemagoer, esp. Am. moviegoer.
Kiosk [ki'ɔsk] m (-[e]s; -e) kiosk.
Kippe[1] ['kɪpə] f (-; -n) F stub, fag end,
butt.
'**Kippe**[2] f (-; -n) **1.** ✕ tip, (a. rubbish)
dump. **2.** gym. upstart, Am. kip. **3.** F
fig. **es** (**er**) **steht auf der ~** it is touch
and go (with him).
kippen ['kɪpən] **I** v/t (h) **1.** a) tilt, tip over,
b) tip out: F **e-n ~** have a quick one. **2.** F
fig. overturn (government, project, etc),
drop (program[me]), sack (s.o.), sports:
turn (the match). **II** v/i (sn) **3.** a) tip
(over), b) overturn, capsize.
'**Kipper** m (-s; -) mot. tipper, Am. dump
truck.
'**Kippfenster** n tilting window.
'**Kippfre,quenz** f ☇ sweep frequency.
'**Kippschalter** m ☇ toggle switch.
'**kippsicher** adj stable.
Kirche ['kɪrçə] f (-; -n) (**in der ~** at)
church: **zur ~ gehen** go to church; F
wir wollen doch die ~ im Dorf lassen!
let's not exaggerate things!
'**Kirchen|buch** n parish register. **~chor**
m church choir. **~diener** m sexton.
~gemeinde f parish. **~geschichte** f
church history. **~jahr** n ecclesiastical
year. **~lied** n hymn. **~mu,sik** f sacred
music. **~rat** m (member of the) consistory. **~recht** n (-[e]s; no pl) canon law.
~schiff n ⌂ nave. **~steuer** f church tax.
~stuhl m pew. **~tag** m Church congress.

'**Kirchgang** *m* churchgoing. '**Kirch-gänger** [-gɛŋər] *m* (-s; -) churchgoer.
'**Kirchhof** *m* churchyard, graveyard.
'**kirchlich** *adj* church ..., ecclesiastical: **sich ~ trauen lassen, ~ heiraten** have a church wedding; **~ bestattet werden** be given a Christian burial.
'**Kirchturm** *m* church tower, steeple.
'**Kirschbaum** *m* cherry tree.
'**Kirschblüte** *f* a) cherry blossom, b) (**zur Zeit der ~** at) cherry-blossom time.
Kirsche ['kɪrʃə] *f* (-; -n) cherry: *fig.* **mit ihm ist nicht gut ~n essen** it's best not to tangle with him.
'**Kirsch|kern** *m* cherry stone. **~kuchen** *m* cherry cake. **~li|kör** *m* cherry brandy. **2rot** *adj.* cherry(-red). **~saft** *m* cherry juice. **~torte** *f* cherry gateau. **~wasser** *n* (-s; ~) kirsch.
Kissen ['kɪsən] *n* (-s; -) a) cushion, b) pillow. '**Kissenbezug** *m* a) cushion slip, b) pillowcase.
Kiste ['kɪstə] *f* (-; -n) **1.** box, ✝ case, chest, crate. **2.** → **Kasten** 2.
Kitsch [kɪtʃ] *m* (-es; *no pl*) kitsch, trash. '**kitschig** *adj* kitschy, trashy.
Kitt [kɪt] *m* (-[e]s; -e) **1.** cement. **2.** putty.
Kittchen ['kɪtçən] *n* (-s; -) → **Knast**.
Kittel ['kɪtəl] *m* (-s; -) a) smock, b) overall, c) (*doctor's*) (white) coat.
kitten ['kɪtən] *v/t* (h) cement, putty, *fig.* patch up (*marriage etc*).
Kitz [kɪts] *n* (-es; -e) *zo.* a) kid, b) fawn.
Kitzel ['kɪtsəl] *m* (-s; *no pl*) **1.** tickle, itch. **2.** *fig.* thrill, kick. '**kitzeln** *v/t, v/i* (h) tickle. **Kitzler** ['kɪtslər] *m* (-s; -) *anat.* clitoris, F clit. '**kitzlig** *adj a. fig.* ticklish.
Kiwi[1] ['kiːvi] *m* (-s; -s) *zo.* kiwi.
'**Kiwi**[2] *f* (-; -s) ❀ kiwi.
Klacks [klaks] *m* (-es; -e) F dollop, blob: *fig.* **das ist ein ~** that's nothing.
Kladde ['kladə] *f* (-; -n) **1.** scribbling pad, b) ✝ waste book. **3.** rough copy.
klaffen ['klafən] *v/i* (h) gape, *fig. a.* yawn: **~de Wunde** gaping wound.
kläffen ['klɛfən] *v/i* (h) *a.* F *fig.* yap.
Klage ['klaːgə] *f* (-; -n) **1.** lament(ation) (**um, über** *acc* for, over). **2.** complaint (**über** *acc* about): **~ führen über** (*acc*) make complaints (*or* complain) about; **es sind ~n laut geworden** there have been complaints. **3.** ⚖ action (*auf acc* for), lawsuit, b) statement of claim: **~ erheben** institute proceedings (**ge-**

gen against, **wegen** for) (→ *a.* **klagen** 3); **e-e ~ abweisen** dismiss an action.
'**Klagegrund** *m* ⚖ cause of action.
'**Klagelied** *n* lamentation.
klagen ['klaːgən] (h) **I** *v/i* **1.** lament (**um, über** *acc* over, about). **2. ~ über** (*acc*) complain of (*a.* ✍) (*or* about); **ohne zu ~** without complaining; **ich kann nicht ~** I have no cause for complaint. **3.** ⚖ go to court: **gegen j-n ~** (**wegen** for) sue s.o., bring an action against s.o. **II** *v/t* → **Leid** 1.
Kläger ['klɛːgər] *m* (-s; -), '**Klägerin** *f* (-; -nen) ⚖ plaintiff.
'**Klageschrift** *f* ⚖ statement of claim.
'**Klageweg** *m* ⚖ **auf dem** (*or* **im**) **~** by entering legal action.
'**klaglos** *adv* without complaining.
Klamauk [kla'maʊk] *m* (-s; *no pl*) F **1.** racket. **2.** to-do. **3.** *thea. etc* slapstick.
klamm [klam] *adj* **1.** clammy. **2.** numb (with cold). **3.** F *fig.* **~ sein** be hard up.
Klamm *f* (-; -en) *geol.* narrow gorge.
Klammer ['klamər] *f* (-; -n) **1.** a) clip, ⚙ *a.* clamp, cramp, b) clothes peg, *Am.* clothespin. **2.** ✍ brace(s). **3.** A, *print.* parenthesis, bracket, brace: **in ~n setzen** put s.th. in parentheses, bracket; **~ auf (zu)** open (close) brackets; **die ~(n) auflösen** A remove the brackets.
klammern ['klamərn] (h) **I** *v/t* (**an** *acc* to) a) clip, ⚙ *a.* clamp, b) peg, pin. **II** *sich ~ an* (*acc*) *a. fig.* cling to.
'**klamm'heimlich** *adv* F on the quiet.
Klamotte [kla'mɔtə] *f* (-; -n) F **1.** (*alte*) ~ (*film etc*) oldie. **2.** *pl* a) rags, togs, b) things, junk.
klang [klaŋ] *pret of* **klingen**.
Klang *m* (-[e]s; ⁻e) a) sound, ring, b) tone, c) timbre: **unter den Klängen von** (*or gen*) to the strains of.
'**Klangfarbe** *f* timbre.
'**Klangfülle** *f* sonority.
'**klanglich** *adj* tonal.
'**klanglos** *adj* toneless.
'**Klangregler** *m radio etc*: tone control.
'**klangrein** *adj* **~ sein** have a pure sound.
'**Klangtreue** *f* fidelity.
'**klangvoll** *adj* **1.** sonorous, melodious. **2.** *fig.* illustrious (*name etc*).
'**Klangwiedergabe** *f* sound reproduction.
'**klappbar** *adj* **1.** collapsible, folding. **2.**

hinged. '**Klappbett** *n* folding bed. '**Klappdeckel** *m* snap lid.

Klappe ['klapə] *f* (-; -n) **1.** flap (*a.* ⚙), leaf (*of table*). **2.** *anat.* valve. **3.** (eye) patch. **4.** ♪ key. **5.** F *fig.* mouth, trap: *e-e große ~ haben* have a big mouth; *halt die ~!* shut up!

klappen ['klapən] (h) **I** *v/t* **1.** *nach oben ~ → hochklappen; nach unten ~ → herunterklappen; der Sitz läßt sich nach hinten ~* the seat folds back. **II** *v/i* **2.** a) clack, bang, b) click shut. **3.** F *fig.* work, go off well: *~ wie am Schnürchen* go like clockwork; *es klappt nicht* it won't work; *nichts klappte* nothing worked; *wenn alles klappt* if all goes well; *es wird schon ~!* it'll work out all right!; *hat es mit dem Job geklappt?* did you get the job all right?

'**Klappentext** *m* blurb. '**Klappen,ven,til** *n* ⚙ flap valve.

Klapper ['klapər] *f* (-; -n) rattle. **~kasten** *m*, **~kiste** *f* F rattletrap, old banger.

klappern ['klapərn] *v/i* (h) **1.** clatter, rattle, *knitting needles*: clack: *mit dem Geschirr ~* rattle the dishes; *auf der Schreibmaschine ~* clatter away on the typewriter. **2.** shiver: *er klapperte vor Kälte (Angst) mit den Zähnen* his teeth were chattering with cold (fear).

'**Klappern** *n* (-s) clatter(ing) (*etc*).

'**Klapperschlange** *f zo.* rattlesnake.

'**Klapp(fahr)rad** *n* folding bicycle.

'**Klappfenster** *n* top-hung window.

'**Klappmesser** *n* jackknife.

klapprig ['klapriç] *adj* F **1.** rattly, rickety. **2.** *fig.* shaky, doddering.

'**Klappsitz** *m* folding (*or* jump) seat.

'**Klappstuhl** *m* folding (*or* camp) chair.

'**Klapptisch** *m* folding table.

'**Klappverdeck** *n mot.* folding hood (*Am.* top).

Klaps [klaps] *m* (-es; -e) **1.** (*a. j-m e-n ~ geben*) slap, smack. **2.** F *e-n ~ haben* be nuts, have a screw loose.

'**Klapsmühle** *f* F funny farm, nut-house.

klar [kla:r] *adj* clear (*a. fig.*), *a.* distinct, *fig. a.* clear-cut (*aim, decision, etc*), *a.* lucid (*moments etc*), *a.* plain, obvious: **~er Sieg** clear victory; *~ zum Start* ready for takeoff; *e-n ~en Kopf behalten* keep one's wits about one; *sich ein ~es Bild machen von* get a clear idea of; *~e Verhältnisse schaffen* get things

straight; *es ist ~, daß* it is clear (*or* evident) that; *es ist mir ~* (*or ich bin mir darüber im ~en*), *daß* I realize (*or* I'm aware) that; *ist das ~?* is that clear?; *das ist mir (nicht ganz) ~* I (don't quite) understand; *(na) ~!* of course!, sure!; *alles ~?* a) everything o.k.?, b) got it?; *~ und deutlich* a) clearly, distinctly, b) *fig.* straight; *et. ~ zum Ausdruck bringen* make s.th. plain; *~ a. klargehen, klarkommen etc.*

'**Kläranlage** *f* sewage (purification) plant. '**Klärbecken** *n* settling basin.

klären ['klɛ:rən] (h) **I** *v/t* **1.** purify, clear. **2.** *fig.* clear up, clarify, sort *s.th.* out. **II** *sich ~* **3.** *weather*: clear (up). **4.** *fig. issue*: be settled, *problem*: be solved.

'**klargehen** *v/i* (*irr, sep, -ge-, sn, → gehen*) F be all right.

'**Klarheit** *f* (-; *no pl*) *a. fig.* clearness, clarity: *sich ~ verschaffen über* (*acc*) find out about.

Klarinette [klari'nɛtə] *f* (-; -n) clarinet.

'**klarkommen** *v/i* (*irr, sep, -ge-, sn, → kommen*) F manage: *mit j-m ~* get along (fine) with s.o.; *kommst du damit klar?* can you manage?

'**klarmachen** *v/t* (*sep, -ge-, h*) **1.** F *j-m et. ~* make s.th. clear (*or* explain s.th.) to s.o.; *sich ~, daß* realize that. **2.** ♣ clear, get s.th. ready. **3.** F *alles ~* settle it.

'**Klärschlamm** *m* sewage sludge.

'**Klarschrift** *f computer*: (*a. in ~*) clear. **~leser** *m* (optical) character reader.

'**klarsehen** *v/i* (*irr, sep, -ge-, h, → sehen*) F *fig.* see (the light).

'**Klarsicht**|**folie** *f* cling film, transparent sheet. **~packung** *f* transparent packing. **~scheibe** *f mot.* antimist panel.

'**klarstellen** *v/t* (*sep, -ge-, h*) *et.* ~ a) get s.th. straight, b) state s.th. clearly.

'**Klartext** *m* clear text: *im ~* a) in clear, b) *fig.* in plain language.

'**Klärung** *f* (-; -en) **1.** purification. **2.** *fig.* clarification, clearing up.

'**klarwerden** *v/i* (*irr, sep, -ge-, sn, → werden*) become clear (*dat* to): *sich ~ über* (*acc*) a) get *s.th.* clear in one's mind, b) make up one's mind about; *es wurde mir klar, daß* I realized that.

Klasse ['klasə] *f* (-; -n) **1.** class, *ped. a.* form, *Am.* grade. **2.** † class, quality, grade, (*tax, age*) bracket: *erster ~* a. F *fig.* first-class; *nach ~n ordnen* class,

classify; F **~!** super!, great!; **große** (*or* **einsame**) **~ sein** be super (*or* fantastic).
'Klassen|arbeit *f ped.* (class) test. **~bewußtsein** *n* class consciousness. **~buch** *n* (class) register, *Am.* classbook. **~gesellschaft** *f* class society. **~kame,rad(in** *f*) *m* classmate. **~kampf** *m pol.* class struggle. **~lehrer(in** *f*) *m* class (*Am. a.* homeroom) teacher.

'klassenlos *adj* classless.
'Klassen|lotte,rie *f* class lottery. **~sprecher(in** *f*) *m ped.* class representative, *Br.* form captain. **~unterschied** *m* class difference. **~zimmer** *n* classroom.

klassifizieren [klasifi'tsi:rən] *v/t* (h) classify. **Klassifi'zierung** *f* (-; -en) classification.

Klassik ['klasɪk] *f* (-; *no pl*) **1.** classical period. **2.** classical music. **Klassiker** ['klasɪkər] *m* (-s; -) **1.** classic(al author). **2.** a) great artist (*etc*), b) (*work*) classic.
'klassisch *adj* **1.** classical. **2.** *fig.* classic. **Klassizismus** [klasi'tsɪsmʊs] *m* (-; *no pl*) classicism. **klassizistisch** [klasi'tsɪstɪʃ] *adj* classicist.

Klatsch [klatʃ] *m* (-es; -e) **1.** splash. **2.** smack, slap. **3.** *no pl* F gossip.
'Klatschbase *f* F gossip(monger).
Klatsche ['klatʃə] *f* (-; -n) **1.** (fly)swatter. **2.** F *ped.* crib. **3.** F gossip(monger).
klatschen ['klatʃən] (h) **I** *v/i* **1.** applaud, clap: **in die Hände ~** clap one's hands. **2.** (**an** *acc* against) *rain etc*: splash, *waves*: crash. **3.** F gossip (**über** *acc* about). **II** *v/t* **4.** *et.* **~ auf** (*acc*) (*or* **gegen, an** *acc*) slap (*or* bang) s.th. on (*or* against). **5. Beifall ~** applaud, clap.
Klatsche'rei *f* (-; -en) clapping.
'Klatsch|kolum,nist(in *f*) *m* F gossip columnist. **~maul** *n* F real gossip.
'klatschnaß *adj* F dripping wet.
'Klatschspalte *f* F gossip column.

Klaue ['klaʊə] *f* (-; -n) **1.** *zo.* claw (*a.* ⚙), *a.* talon: *fig.* **in j-s ~n geraten** fall into s.o.'s clutches. **2.** F *fig.* scrawl.
klauen ['klaʊən] *v/t, v/i* (h) F swipe, pinch, filch: steal, borrow (*ideas etc*).
Klause ['klaʊzə] *f* (-; -n) hermitage.
Klausel ['klaʊzəl] *f* (-; -n) ⚖ a) clause, stipulation, b) proviso.
Klaustrophobie [klaʊstrofo'bi:] *f* (-; *no pl*) claustrophobia.
Klausur [klaʊ'zu:r] *f* (-; -en) **1.** *no pl* seclusion. **2.** *ped., univ.* test, paper.

Klau'surarbeit *f* → **Klausur** 2.
Klau'surtagung *f* closed meeting.
Klaviatur [klavia'tu:r] *f* (-; -en) ♪ keyboard.
Klavier [kla'vi:r] *n* (-s; -e) piano(forte): **auf dem** (**am**) **~** on (at) the piano; **~ spielen** (**können**) play the piano.
Kla'vier|abend *m* piano recital. **~auszug** *m* piano score. **~begleitung** *f* piano accompaniment. **~kon,zert** *n* **1.** piano concert. **2.** → **Klavierabend**. **~lehrer(in** *f*) *m* piano teacher. **~schemel** *m* piano stool. **~schule** *f* (*book*) piano tutor. **~so,nate** *f* piano sonata. **~spieler(in** *f*) *m* pianist. **~stimmer** *m* (piano) tuner. **~stunde** *f* piano lesson. **~unterricht** *m* piano lessons.

'Klebeband *n* adhesive (*or* sticky) tape.
'Klebefolie *f* adhesive film.
kleben ['kle:bən] (h) **I** *v/t* **1.** (**an** *acc* to) glue, paste. **2.** F *j-m* **e-e ~** paste s.o. one. **II** *v/i* **3.** be sticky. **4.** (**an** *dat* to) adhere, stick: *fig.* **an j-m ~** remain glued to s.o.; **an s-m Posten ~** hang on to one's job.
'klebenbleiben *v/i* (*irr, sep,* -ge-, sn, → **bleiben**) **1.** stick (**an** *dat* to). **2.** F *fig.* get stuck (**in** *dat* in, at).
'Klebepresse *f film:* splicer.
'Kleber *m* (-s; -) **1.** gluten. **2.** F adhesive, glue.
'Klebe|stelle *f film:* splice. **~stift** *m* glue stick. **~streifen** *m* adhesive (*or* sticky) tape. **~zettel** *m* gummed label.
klebrig ['kle:brɪç] *adj* sticky.
'Klebrigkeit *f* (-; *no pl*) stickiness.
Klebstoff ['kle:p-] *m* adhesive, glue.
kleckern ['klɛkərn] (h) F **I** *v/i* **1.** make a mess. **2.** drip. **II** *v/t* **3.** *et.* **~ auf** (*acc*) spill s.th. on.
'kleckerweise *adv* F in dribs and drabs.
Klecks [klɛks] *m* (-es; -e) F **1.** stain, blot. **2.** blob. **'klecksen** *v/i* (h) F **1.** make blots (*or* stains), make a mess. **2.** daub.
Klee [kle:] *m* (-s; *no pl*) ♣ clover: F **über den grünen ~ loben** praise s.o., s.th. to the skies. **'Kleeblatt** *n* **1.** cloverleaf: **vierblättriges ~** four-leaf(ed) clover. **2.** *mot.* cloverleaf (intersection).
Kleiber ['klaɪbər] *m* (-s; -) *zo.* nut hatch.
Kleid [klaɪt] *n* (-es; -er) **1.** dress (*a. fig.*), frock, gown. **2.** *pl* clothes, clothing: **~er machen Leute** fine feathers make fine birds. **3.** *hunt.* a) fur, coat, b) plumage.
kleiden ['klaɪdən] (h) **I** *v/t* **1.** clothe,

dress: *fig. et. in Worte* ~ couch s.th. in words. **2.** *j-n (gut)* ~ suit (*or* become) s.o., look well on s.o. **II** *sich* ~ dress; *sich* ~ *in (acc)* wear.

Kleider|bügel ['klaɪdər-] *m* coat hanger. **~bürste** *f* clothes brush. **~haken** *m* coat hook. **~puppe** *f* dummy, mannequin. **~schrank** *m* wardrobe. **~ständer** *m* clothes tree (*or* rack). **~stoff** *m* dress material.

'**kleidsam** *adj* becoming.

Kleidung ['klaɪdʊŋ] *f* (-; *no pl*) clothing, clothes, garments. '**Kleidungsstück** *n* article of clothing, garment.

Kleie ['klaɪə] *f* (-; -n) bran.

klein [klaɪn] **I** *adj* **1.** small, little (*finger, toe, house, etc*): *sehr* ~, *winzig* ~ very small, tiny, F teeny; *ziemlich* ~ rather small, smallish; *von* ~ *auf* from a child; *im* ~*en* in miniature; *mein* ~*er Bruder* my little (*or* young) brother; *die Welt ist (doch)* ~*!* it's a small world! **2.** *fig.* small, little, *a.* ♫ minor, petty: *aus* ~*en Verhältnissen kommen* have a humble background; *~e Geister* small minds; *der* ~*e Mann* the man in (*Am.* on) the street; *das* ~*ere Übel* the lesser evil; *bis ins* ~*ste* (down to the last detail; *das ist m-e* ~*ste Sorge* that's the least of my worries. **II** *adv* small: *ein Wort* ~ *schreiben* write a word with a small (initial) letter; F *ein (ganz)* ~ *wenig* a little (*or* tiny) bit; ~ *anfangen* start in a small way; → *beigeben* II.

'**Klein|aktie** *f* baby share (*Am.* stock). **~aktio,när(in** *f*) *m* small shareholder (*Am.* stockholder). **~anzeige** *f* classified advertisement (F ad). **~arbeit** *f a. mühevolle* ~ painstaking and detailed work. **~auto** *n* small car. **~bauer** *m* small farmer. **~betrieb** *m* small enterprise. **~bildkamera** *f* 35 mm camera. **~buchstabe** *m* small letter. **~bürger(in** *f*) *m*, ⚭**bürgerlich** *adj* petty bourgeois. **~bus** *m* minibus.

'**Kleine**¹ *m*, *f* (-n; -n) little one.

'**Kleine**² *n* (-n; -n) F baby.

'**Klein|fa,milie** *f sociol.* nuclear family. **~for,mat** *n* small size: *im* ~ small-format. **~garten** *m* allotment (garden). **~gärtner(in** *f*) *m* allotment gardener.

'**Kleingedruckte** *n das* ~ *lesen* read the small print.

'**Kleingeld** *n* (small) change: *fig. das nö-*

---

tige ~ *haben* have the wherewithal.

'**kleingläubig** *adj* of little faith.

'**Kleinhandel** *m* → *Einzelhandel.*

'**Kleinheit** *f* (-; *no pl*) smallness (*a. fig.*).

'**Kleinhirn** *n anat.* cerebellum.

'**Kleinholz** *n* (-es; *no pl*) firewood: F *fig.* ~ *machen aus* a) *j-m* make mincemeat of s.o., b) *e-r Sache* smash s.th. to pieces.

'**Kleinigkeit** *f* (-; -en) a) trifle, small thing, b) (*gift*) little something, c) minor detail: *e-e* ~ *essen* have a bite; *das war e-e (k-e)* ~ that was (not) easy.

'**Kleinindu,strie** *f* small industry.

'**kleinka,riert** *adj* **1.** small-check(ed). **2.** Γ *fig.* small-minded

'**Klein|kind** *n* infant. **~kram** *m* trifles. **~kre,dit** *m* small(-scale) credit. **~krieg** *m* guer(r)illa warfare: *fig. e-n* ~ *führen mit* keep up a running battle with.

'**kleinkriegen** *v/t* (*sep*, -ge-, h) F (manage to) break: *fig. j-n* ~ a) wear s.o. out, b) get s.o. down; *nicht kleinzukriegen a. person:* indestructible.

'**kleinlich** *adj* **1.** pedantic. **2.** narrow-minded. **3.** mean.

'**Kleinlichkeit** *f* (-; *no pl*) **1.** pedantry. **2.** narrow-mindedness. **3.** meanness.

Kleinod ['klaɪno:t] *n* (-[e]s; -e) jewel.

'**Kleinrentner(in** *f*) *m* person receiving a small pension.

'**kleinschneiden** *v/t* (*irr, sep,* -ge-, h, → *schneiden*) cut up, chop (up).

'**kleinschreiben** *v/t* (*irr, sep,* -ge-, h, → *schreiben*) F *Ordnung etc wird bei ihm kleingeschrieben* he isn't a great one for order *etc.*

'**Kleinstaat** *m* minor state.

'**Klein|stadt** *f* small town. **~städter(in** *f*) *m*, ⚭**städtisch** *adj* provincial.

'**Kleinst|bildkamera** *f* subminiature camera. **~lebewesen** *n biol.* microorganism. ⚭**möglich** *adj* smallest possible. **~wagen** *m* minicar, midget car.

'**Klein|tier** *n* small (domestic) animal. **~vieh** *n* small domestic animals: F *fig.* ~ *macht auch Mist* many a little makes a mickle. **~wagen** *m* small car.

kleinwüchsig ['klaɪnvy:ksɪç] *adj* small, short.

Kleister ['klaɪstər] *m* (-s; -) paste.

'**kleistern** *v/t* (h) paste (*an, auf acc* on).

Klematis [kle'maːtɪs] *f* (-; -) ♀ clematis.

Klemme ['klɛmə] *f* (-; -n) **1.** clamp (*a.* ✄, ◉), clip, ⚡ terminal. **2.** F *fig. in der* ~

sein (*or* *sitzen*) be in a fix (*or* tight spot); *j-m aus der ~ helfen* help s.o. out of a fix.

klemmen ['klɛmən] (h) **I** *v/t* **1.** a) jam (*a.* ⚙), b) squeeze, pinch, c) stick: *ich habe mir den Finger geklemmt* → 3. **II** *v/i* **2.** be jammed, be stuck: F *wo klemmt's?* what's wrong?, where's the snag? **III** *sich ~* **3.** jam one's finger (*etc*), get one's finger (*etc*) caught. **4.** squeeze o.s. (*in acc* into, *hinter acc* behind): F *sich ~ hinter* a) *e-e Sache* get down to s.th., b) *j-n* get to work on s.o.

Klempner ['klɛmpnər] *m* (-s; -) **1.** tinsmith. **2.** plumber. **Klempnerei** [klɛmpnə'raɪ] *f* (-; -en) tinsmith's (*or* plumber's) workshop. **'Klempnermeister** *m* master tinsmith (*or* plumber).

Kleptomane [klɛpto'maːnə] *m* (-n; -n) kleptomaniac. **Kleptomanie** [-maˈniː] *f* (-; *no pl*) kleptomania. **Klepto'manin** *f* (-; -nen) kleptomaniac.

klerikal [kleriˈkaːl] *adj* clerical.

Kleriker ['kleːrikər] *m* (-s; -) cleric.

Klerus ['kleːrʊs] *m* (-; *no pl*) clergy.

Klette ['klɛtə] *f* (-; -n) ❀ bur(r) (*a. fig.*): *sich wie e-e ~ an j-n hängen* cling to s.o. like a leech.

'Kletterer *m* (-s; -) climber.

'Klettergerüst *n* climbing frame.

klettern ['klɛtərn] *v/i* (sn) climb, ❀ *a.* creep, *fig. a.* go up (*auf acc* to): *auf e-n Baum ~* climb a tree.

'Kletter|pflanze *f* climber. **~rose** *f* rambler. **~stange** *f* climbing pole.

'Klettverschluß *m* Velcro (*TM*).

klicken ['klɪkən] *v/i* (h) click.

Klient [kliˈɛnt] *m* (-en; -en) ⚖ client.

Kliff [klɪf] *n* (-[e]s; -e) *geol.* cliff.

Klima ['kliːma] *n* (-s; -s) *climate, fig. a.* atmosphere: *soziales ~* social climate.

'Klimaanlage *f* air-conditioning: *mit e-r ~ ausrüsten* air-condition.

Klimakterium [klimak'teːriʊm] *n* (-s; *no pl*) menopause, climacteric.

klimatisch [kliˈmaːtɪʃ] *adj* climatic.

klimatisieren [klimatiˈziːrən] *v/t* (h) air-condition.

Klimatologie [klimatoloˈgiː] *f* (-; *no pl*) climatology.

'Klimaveränderung *f*, **'Klimawechsel** *m* change in climate.

Klimmzug ['klɪm-] *m gym.* chin-up: *e-n ~ machen* do a chin-up, chin o.s. up.

klimpern ['klɪmpərn] *v/i* (h) **1.** (*a. ~ mit*) jingle. **2.** *~ auf* (*dat*) strum on *the guitar*, tinkle on *the piano*.

Klinge ['klɪŋə] *f* (-; -n) blade.

Klingel ['klɪŋəl] *f* (-; -n) bell.

'Klingelknopf *m* bell push, call button.

klingeln ['klɪŋəln] (h) **I** *v/i* **1.** ring ([*nach*] *j-m* for s.o., *bei j-m* at s.o.'s doorbell): *es klingelt* a) the doorbell is ringing, b) there's the bell. **2.** *engine:* ping. **II** *v/t* **3.** *j-n aus dem Bett ~* get s.o. out of bed.

'Klingelzeichen *n* ring, bell (signal).

klingen ['klɪŋən] *v/i* (klang, geklungen, h) sound (*a. fig.*), ring, *glasses:* clink, *metal:* clank: *fig. das klingt schon besser* that sounds better; *das klingt nach Neid* that sounds like envy.

'klingend *adj* melodious.

Klinik ['kliːnɪk] *f* (-; -en) clinic, nursing home. **Klinikum** ['kliːnikʊm] *n* (-s; -ka, -ken) clinical cent/re (*Am.* -er).

klinisch ['kliːnɪʃ] *adj* clinical: *~ tot* clinically dead.

Klinke ['klɪŋkə] *f* (-; -n) (door) handle.

Klinker ['klɪŋkər] *m* (-s; -) △ clinker.

klipp [klɪp] *adv* *~ und klar* clearly, plainly; *ich habe ihm ~ und klar gesagt, daß* ... I told him straight out that ...

Klippe ['klɪpə] *f* (-; -n) *geol.* reef, rock: *fig. e-e ~ umschiffen* clear an obstacle.

klirren ['klɪrən] *v/i* (h) **1.** a) rattle, clatter, b) clink, chink, jingle: *~ mit* rattle (*one's chains, keys, etc*). **2.** *radio:* produce harmonic distortion.

'Klirrfaktor *m radio:* distortion factor.

Klischee [klɪˈʃeː] *n* (-s; -s) *fig.* cliché. **~vorstellung** *f* stereotyped idea.

Klistier [klɪsˈtiːr] *n* (-s; -e) ✚ enema.

Kli'stierspritze *f* enema syringe.

Klitoris ['kliːtorɪs] *f* (-; -) *anat.* clitoris.

klitschig ['klɪtʃɪç] *adj* doughy (*bread etc*).

klitzeklein ['klɪtsə-] *adj* F teeny-(weeny).

Klo [kloː] *n* (-s; -s) F loo, *Am.* john.

Kloake [kloˈaːkə] *f* (-; -n) sewer.

Kloben ['kloːbən] *m* (-s; -) **1.** ⚙ block. **2.** log.

'klobig *adj* bulky, *a. fig.* clumsy.

klönen ['kløːnən] *v/i* (h) F have a natter.

'Klopa,pier *n* F toilet (*Br. a.* loo) paper.

klopfen ['klɔpfən] (h) **I** *v/i* **1.** (*an acc* at, on) knock, tap: *es klopft* there's somebody (knocking) at the door; → *Busch* 1, *Finger, Schulter.* **2.** *heart etc:* beat, throb: *fig. mit ~dem Herzen* with (a) beating heart. **3.** *engine*: knock. **II** *v/t* **4.** beat (*carpet etc*): **den Takt ~** beat time.

'Klopfer *m* (-s; -) **1.** doorknocker. **2.** carpet-beater.

'klopffest *adj mot.* knockproof.

Klöppel ['klœpəl] *m* (-s; -) **1.** clapper (*of bell*). **2.** *textil.* (lace) bobbin. **'Klöppelkissen** *n* lace pillow. **'klöppeln** *v/i* (h) make lace. **'Klöppelspitze** *f* bone lace.

Klosett [klo'zɛt] *n* (-s; -s) lavatory, toilet. **~deckel** *m* toilet lid. **~pa,pier** *n* toilet paper. **~sitz** *m* toilet seat.

Kloß [klo:s] *m* (-es; ⸚e) dumpling: *fig.* **ich hatte e-n ~ im Hals** I had a lump in my throat.

Kloster ['klo:stər] *n* (-s; ⸚) a) monastery, b) convent, nunnery: **ins ~ gehen** enter a monastery (*etc*), become a monk (*or* nun). **~bruder** *m* friar. **~frau** *f* nun. **~leben** *n* monastic life.

klösterlich ['klø:stərlıç] *adj* monastic.

Klotz [klɔts] *m* (-es; ⸚e) **1.** block (*of* wood), log: F **er ist mir nur ein ~ am Bein** he is just a millstone round my neck. **2.** F *contp.* oaf, *Am. sl.* klutz.

'klotzig *adj* bulky, heavy.

Kluft¹ [klʊft] *f* (-; ⸚e) *fig.* gap.

Kluft² *f* (-; -en) F togs, gear.

klug [klu:k] **I** *adj* **1.** a) intelligent, clever, smart, bright, shrewd, b) sensible, wise, judicious, c) prudent: **ein ~er Rat** a sound advice; **so ~ wie zuvor** none the wiser; **der Klügere gibt nach** the wiser head gives in. **2.** F **ich werde aus ihr (der Sache) nicht ~** I can't make her (it) out; **wirst du daraus ~?** does it make sense to you? **II** *adv* intelligently (*etc*): **du hättest klüger daran getan zu** *inf* you would have been wise to *inf.*

klugerweise ['klu:gər-] *adv* wisely, sensibly: **~ hat sie geschwiegen** *a.* she had the good sense to keep quiet.

'Klugheit *f* (-; *no pl*) a) intelligence, brightness, b) good sense, c) prudence.

'Klugscheißer *m* F smart aleck, smarty.

klumpen ['klʊmpən] *v/i* (h) clot, become lumpy. **'Klumpen** *m* (-s; -) lump, clot, clod. **'Klumpfuß** *m* clubfoot. **klumpig** ['klʊmpıç] *adj* lumpy, clotted.

Klüngel ['klʏŋəl] *m* (-s; -) *contp.* clique.

Klunkern ['klʊŋkərn] *pl* F rocks, ice.

Klüver ['kly:vər] *m* (-s; -) ⚓ jib.

knabbern ['knabərn] *v/i, v/t* (h) (**an** *dat* at) nibble, gnaw: F *fig.* **ich hatte lange**

daran zu ~ a) I didn't get over it easily, b) it took me some time to figure it out.

Knabe ['kna:bə] *m* (-n; -n) boy, lad. **'Knabenalter** *n* boyhood. **'Knabenchor** *m* boys' choir. **'knabenhaft** *adj* boyish.

Knäckebrot ['knɛkə-] *n* crispbread.

knacken ['knakən] (h) **I** *v/t a. fig.* crack: F **ein Auto ~** break into a car. **II** *v/i* a) crack, b) snap. **'Knacker** *m* (-s; -) F **alter ~** old fog(e)y. **Knacki** ['knaki] *m* (-s; -s) F jailbird. **'knackig** *adj* **1.** crisp, crunchy. **2.** F *fig.* dishy.

'Knacklaut *m ling.* glottal stop.

'Knackpunkt *m* F *fig.* crunch (point).

Knacks [knaks] *m* (-es; -e) **1.** crack. **2.** F *fig.* defect: **er hat e-n ~ (weg)** a) his health is shaken, b) his nerves are all shot, c) he is badly hit, d) he's slightly cracked; **ihre Ehe hat e-n ~** their marriage is cracking up.

Knall [knal] *m* (-[e]s; -e) **1.** bang, pop (*of a cork*). **2.** *fig.* quarrel, row. **3.** F **e-n ~ haben** be nuts. **4.** F **~ und Fall** (all) of a sudden; *j-n ~* **und Fall entlassen** dismiss s.o. on the spot.

'Knallbon,bon *m, n* (party) cracker.

'Knallef,fekt *m* F clou, sensation.

knallen ['knalən] F **I** *v/i* **1.** (*a. ~ mit*) *door etc*: bang, slam, *whip*: crack, *cork*: pop: **es knallte zweimal** there were two loud bangs. **2.** F bang, fire. **3.** F crash (**gegen** into): **mit dem Kopf an die Windschutzscheibe ~** hit one's head on the windscreen; F **sonst knallt's!** or else! **4.** *sun*: beat down. **II** *v/t* **5.** bang, slam: **den Ball ins Tor ~** slam the ball home; F *j-m e-e ~* paste s.o. one.

'Knaller *m* (-s; -) F **1.** → *Knallkörper.* **2.** → *Knüller.*

'Knallerbse *f* (toy) torpedo.

'Knallfrosch *m* jumping cracker.

'Knallgas *n* 🔥 oxyhydrogen (gas).

'knall'hart *adj* F **1.** smashing, powerful (*blow etc*). **2.** *fig.* tough, brutal: **~ fragen** *etc* ask *etc* with brutal frankness.

'knallig F I *adj* **1.** loud, glaring (*colo[u]r*). **2.** skintight. **II** *adv* **~ bunt** gaudy; **~ heiß** scorching.

'Knallkopf *m* F idiot.

'Knallkörper *m* banger.

'knall'rot *adj* bright red, crimson.

'knall'voll *adj* F **1.** jam-packed. **2.** dead drunk, paralytic.

knapp [knap] **I** *adj* **1.** scanty, meag/re

(*Am.* -er): ~ *sein* be scarce, be in short supply; ~ *werden* run short; → *Kasse* 4. **2.** *fig.* narrow: ~*e Mehrheit* bare majority. **3.** *fig.* concise, terse (*style etc*), brief, short (*answer etc*): *in ~en Worten* in a few words. **4.** ~(*e*) *zwei Stunden* just under two hours; *in e-m ~en Jahr* in less than a year; ~ *10 Minuten* barely (*or* just) ten minutes. **5.** tight (*skirt etc*). **II** *adv* **6.** only just: ~ *gewinnen* win by a narrow margin; *e-e Prüfung ~ bestehen* scrape through an examination; *(aber) nicht zu ~!* a) you bet!, b) plenty of it!, c) and how! **7.** ~ *sitzen* fit tightly; *fig. m-e Zeit ist ~ bemessen* I'm pushed for time.

'knapphalten *v/t* (*irr, sep,* -ge-, h, → *halten*) **F** *j-n* ~ keep s.o. short.

'Knappheit *f* (-; *no pl*) **1.** a) scantincss, b) scarcity, shortage. **2.** *fig.* narrowness. **3.** *fig.* terseness, conciseness, shortness. **4.** tightness.

'Knappschaft *f* (-; -en) miners' association.

Knarre ['knarə] *f* (-; -n) **F** gun.

knarren ['knarən] *v/i* (h) creak.

Knast [knast] *m* (-[e]s; -e, ~e) **F** (*im* ~ *in*) clink: ~ *schieben* do time.

'Knastbruder *m* **F** jailbird.

knattern ['knatərn] *v/i* (h) rattle, *motorbike etc*: roar, flag, *sail*: flap.

Knäuel ['knɔʏəl] *m, n* (-s; -) **1.** ball (*of wool*). **2.** tangle. **3.** cluster (*of people*).

Knauf [knaʊf] *m* (-[e]s; ~e) **1.** knob. **2.** △ capital. **3.** pommel.

Knauser ['knaʊzər] *m* (-s; -) **F** miser.

Knause'rei f (-; -en) **F** stinginess.

'knauserig *adj* **F** stingy.

knausern ['knaʊzərn] *v/i* (h) **F** be stingy.

knautschen ['knaʊtʃən] *v/i* (h) **F** crease, crumple.

'Knautschzone *f mot.* crumple zone.

Knebel ['kne:bəl] *m* (-s; -) gag.

knebeln ['kne:bəln] *v/t* (h) *a. fig.* gag.

Knecht [knɛçt] *m* (-[e]s; -e) **1.** farmhand. **2.** *fig.* slave. **knechten** ['knɛçtən] *v/t* (h) enslave. **'Knechtschaft** *f* (-; *no pl*) slavery. **'Knechtung** *f* (-; -en) enslavement.

kneifen ['knaɪfən] (kniff, gekniffen, h) **I** *v/t* **1.** pinch: *j-n* (*or j-m*) *in den Arm* ~ pinch s.o.'s arm. **II** *v/i* **2.** pinch. **3.** **F** (*vor dat*) dodge (*s.th.*), back out (of), chicken out (of, on).

'Kneifzange *f* (*e-e* ~ a pair of) pincers.

Kneipe ['knaɪpə] *f* (-; -n) **F** pub, *Am.* bar.

'Kneipenbummel *m* (*a.* *e-n* ~ *machen*) pub-crawl.

Kneippkur ['knaɪp-] *f* ♨ Kneipp('s) cure.

Knete ['kne:tə] *f* (-; *no pl*) **F** **1.** → *Knetmasse*. **2.** lolly, *Am.* bread. **'kneten** *v/t* (h) a) knead, *a.* massage, b) mo(u)ld.

'Knetmasse *f* plasticine.

Knick [knɪk] *m* (-[e]s; -e) **1.** (sharp) bend: *die Straße macht e-n* ~ *a.* the road bends sharply. **2.** a) crease, fold, b) kink. **3.** *fig.* (sharp) drop, falling off.

knicken ['knɪkən] *v/t* (h) **1.** (*a. v/i*) break, snap: → *geknickt*. **2.** crease, fold: *nicht ~!* do not bend! (*a. v/i*) buckle, bend.

knickerig ['knɪkərɪç] *adj* stingy, mean.

Knicks [knɪks] *m* (-es; -e) curtsy: *e-n ~ machen* → **knicksen** ['knɪksən] *v/i* (h) (drop a) curtsy (*vor j-m* to s.o.).

Knie [kni:] *n* (-s; - ['kni:(ə)]) **1.** knee: *bis an die* ~ up to one's knees, knee-deep; *j-n auf den ~n bitten* beg s.o. on bended knees; *in die* ~ *brechen* collapse; *in die* ~ *gehen* a) sag at the knees, b) *fig.* go to the wall; *j-n in die* ~ *zwingen* a. *fig.* force s.o. on his knees; *fig. et. übers* ~ *brechen* rush s.th.; **F** *weiche ~ bekommen* go weak at the knees, become scared; *j-n übers* ~ *legen* give s.o. a spanking. **2.** ⊙ elbow, bend.

'Kniebeuge *f gym.* knee bend. **'Kniefall** *m eccl.* genuflection. **'kniefrei** *adj* above-the-knee. **'Kniegelenk** *n a.* ⊙ knee joint. **'Kniekehle** *f anat.* hollow of the knee. **'knielang** *adj* knee-length.

knien [kni:n, 'kni:ən] (h) **I** *v/i* (*vor dat* before) kneel, be on one's knees. **II** *sich* ~ kneel down; **F** *fig. sich* ~ *in* (*acc*) get down to.

'Kniescheibe *f anat.* kneecap.

'Knieschützer *m sports:* kneepad.

'Kniestrumpf *m* knee-length sock.

'knietief *adj* knee-deep.

kniff [knɪf] *pret of* **kneifen.**

Kniff *m* (-[e]s; -e) **1.** crease, fold. **2.** *fig.* trick. **kniffelig** ['knɪfəlɪç] *adj* tricky.

kniffen ['knɪfən] *v/t* (h) fold, crease.

knipsen ['knɪpsən] (h) **I** *v/t* **1.** punch (*ticket*). **2.** **F** *j-n* ~ take s.o.'s picture, snap s.o. **II** *v/i* **3.** **F** take photos, snap.

Knirps [knɪrps] *m* (-es; -e) little chap (*Am.* guy), *contp.* squirt.

knirschen ['knɪrʃən] *v/i* (h) grate, *snow,*

sand, etc: crunch: *mit den Zähnen ~* grind (*or* gnash) one's teeth.

knistern ['knɪstərn] *v/i* (h) crackle, *silk, paper, etc*: rustle: *fig. der Saal knisterte vor Spannung* the atmosphere in the hall was electric.

'Knitterfalte *f* crease. **'knitterfrei** *adj* creaseproof, noncrease. **knittern** ['knɪtərn] *v/i, v/t* (h) crease, wrinkle.

knobeln ['kno:bəln] *v/i* (h) **1.** (*um* for) throw dice, toss. **2.** F puzzle (*an dat* over).

Knoblauch ['kno:p-] *m* & garlic. **~kapsel** *f* garlic pill. **~zehe** *f* clove of garlic.

Knöchel ['knœçəl] *m* (-s; -) a) knuckle, b) ankle. **'Knöchelbruch** *m* & ankle fracture. **'knöchellang** *adj* ankle-length.

Knochen ['knɔxən] *m* (-s; -) bone: *Fleisch mit (ohne) ~* meat on (off) the bone; *bis auf die ~* a) *abgemagert* just skin and bones, b) *naß* soaked to the skin; *F der Schreck fuhr mir in die ~* I was shaken to the core; *das ist ihm in die ~ gefahren* it really got to him; *sich bis auf die ~ blamieren* make an absolute fool of o.s.

'Knochen|arbeit *f* hard slog, gruel(l)ing work. **~bau** *m* (-[e]s; *no pl*) bone structure. **~bruch** *m* fracture. **~gerüst** *n* skeleton. **2hart** *adj* F (as) hard as stone. **~haut** *f* periosteum. **~krebs** *m* & bone cancer. **~mark** *n* (bone) marrow. **~mehl** *n* ✹ bone meal. **~mühle** *f* F sweatshop. **~splitter** *m* bone splinter. **'knochentrocken** *adj* F bone-dry.

knöchern ['knœçərn] *adj* bone ..., bony.

knochig ['knɔxɪç] *adj* bony.

Knödel ['knø:dəl] *m* (-s; -) dumpling.

Knolle ['knɔlə] *f* (-; -n) ✹ tuber, bulb.

Knollen ['knɔlən] *m* (-s; -) lump.

'Knollenblätterpilz *m* death cap.

'Knollennase *f* F bulbous nose.

knollig ['knɔlɪç] *adj* ✹ tuberous, bulbous.

Knopf [knɔpf] *m* (-[e]s; ⁓e) **1.** button: ☺ *auf e-n ~ drücken* push a button. **2.** → *Knauf* 1, 3. **'Knopfdruck** *m auf* (*or per*) *~* at the touch of a button.

knöpfen ['knœpfən] *v/t* (h) button: *zum 2 buttoned*.

'Knopfloch *n* buttonhole.

Knorpel ['knɔrpəl] *m* (-s; -) **1.** *anat.* cartilage. **2.** *gastr.* gristle. **'knorpelig** *adj* **1.** *anat.* cartilaginous. **2.** *gastr.* gristly.

Knorren ['knɔrən] *m* (-s; -) knot, snag.

'knorrig *adj* **1.** gnarled, knotty. **2.** *fig.* gruff.

Knospe ['knɔspə] *f* (-; -n) bud.

knospen ['knɔspən] *v/i* (h) bud.

knospig ['knɔspɪç] *adj* full of buds.

knoten ['kno:tən] *v/t* (h) knot, tie a knot.

'Knoten *m* (-s; -) **1.** knot: *e-n ~ machen* tie a knot (*in acc* into); F *bei ihm ist endlich der ~ geplatzt* he has caught on at last. **2.** bun, knot. **3.** & knot: *10 ~ machen* do ten knots. **4.** ✹, ✿ knot, *a. astr., phys.* node. **'Knotenpunkt** *m* **1.** ✹ *etc* junction. **2.** *fig.* cent/re (*Am.* -er).

knotig ['kno:tɪç] *adj a. fig.* knotty.

Knuff [knʊf] *m* (-[e]s; ⁓e) F poke, nudge: *j-m e-n ~ geben* → **knuffen** ['knʊfən] *v/t* (h) *j-n* punch (*or* nudge) s.o.

Knülch [knʏlç] *m* (-[e]s; -e) F bloke, *Am.* guy, *sl.* creep.

knüllen ['knʏlən] *v/t, v/i* (h) crumple.

Knüller ['knʏlər] *m* (-s; -) F sensation, (big) hit, scoop.

knüpfen ['knʏpfən] (h) **I** *v/t* tie, make, knot (*carpet*): *~ an* (*acc*) fasten (*fig.* attach *conditions, hopes, etc* to). **II** *sich ~ an* (*acc*) *fig. condition etc*: be attached to, *memories etc*: be connected with.

Knüppel ['knʏpəl] *m* (-s; -) **1.** a) (heavy) stick, club, b) truncheon, *Am.* billy: *j-m e-n ~ zwischen die Beine werfen* put a spoke in s.o.'s wheels. **2.** ✈ stick.

'Knüppeldamm *m* corduroy road.

knüppeln ['knʏpəln] *v/t* (h) beat, club.

'Knüppelschaltung *f mot.* floor shift, floor-mounted gear change

knurren ['knʊrən] *v/i* (h) **1.** (*a. v/t*) growl, snarl. **2.** *fig.* grumble (*über acc* at). **3.** *stomach*: rumble: *mir knurrt der Magen* I'm famished.

knurrig ['knʊrɪç] *adj* F *fig.* grumpy.

knusp(e)rig ['knʊsp(ə)rɪç] *adj* crisp.

Knute ['knu:tə] *f* (-; -n) knout: *fig. unter j-s ~ stehen* be under s.o.'s thumb.

knutschen ['knu:tʃən] *v/i* (h) F (*a. sich ~*) neck, smooch, snog.

'Knutschfleck *m* F love bite.

k.o. [ka:'ʔo:] *adj pred boxing*: knocked out: *j-n ~ schlagen* knock s.o. out; F *fig. ich bin ~* I'm all in, I'm bushed.

K.'o. *m* (-; -) *boxing*: knockout.

Koalition [ko'ali'tsïo:n] *f* (-; -en) *pol.* coalition.

Kobalt ['ko:balt] *m* (-[e]s; *no pl*) cobalt.

'Kobaltblau *n* cobalt blue.

Kobold ['ko:bɔlt] *m* (-[e]s; -e) goblin.
Koch [kɔx] *m* (-[e]s; ⁻e) cook: *viele Köche verderben den Brei* too many cooks spoil the broth.
'**Kochbuch** *n* cookery book, cookbook.
'**kochecht** *adj* (boil)fast.
kochen ['kɔxən] (h) **I** *v/t* **1.** a) cook, b) boil, c) make (*tea etc*). **II** *v/i* **2.** cook, do the cooking: *sie kocht gut* she is a good cook. **3.** *food:* be cooking, *water:* be boiling: *leicht ~, auf kleiner Flamme ~* simmer; *fig.* **er kochte innerlich** (*or vor Wut*) he was seething with rage.
'**Kochen** *n* (-s) cooking: *et. zum ~ bringen* bring s.th. to the boil; *fig. j-n zum ~ bringen* make s.o.'s blood boil.
'**kochendheiß** *adj* boiling hot, scalding.
Kocher ['kɔxər] *m* (-s; -) cooker.
Köcher ['kœçər] *m* (-s; -) **1.** quiver. **2.** *phot.* lens case.
'**kochfertig** *adj* ready-to-cook, instant.
'**Kochgelegenheit** *f* cooking facilities.
'**Kochgeschirr** *n* ✗ mess tin (*Am.* kit).
Köchin ['kœçɪn] *f* (-; -nen) cook.
'**Koch|kunst** *f* **1.** *no pl* gastronomy. **2.** *ihre Kochkünste* her cooking (ability). **~kurs(us)** *m* cookery course. **~löffel** *m* spoon. **~nische** *f* kitchenette. **~platte** *f* hot plate. **~re,zept** *n* recipe.
'**Kochsalz** *n* **1.** table salt. **2.** 🜪 sodium chloride. **~lösung** *f* 💊 saline (solution).
'**Kochtopf** *m* cooking pot, saucepan.
'**Kochwäsche** *f* boil wash.
Köder ['kø:dər] *m* (-s; -) bait.
ködern ['kø:dərn] *v/t* (h) *a. fig.* bait: *er läßt sich mit Geld nicht ~* he is not tempted by money.
Koeffizient [ko°ɛfi'tsiɛnt] *m* (-en; -en) ⅄ coefficient.
Koexistenz ['ko:°ɛksɪstɛnts] *f* (-; *no pl*) coexistence.
Koffein [kɔfe'i:n] *n* (-s; *no pl*) caffeine.
koffe'infrei *adj* decaffeinated.
Koffer ['kɔfər] *m* (-s; -) a) bag, case, suitcase, b) trunk: *~ packen* pack one's bags; F *fig. die ~ packen* leave; *aus dem ~ leben* live out of a suitcase. **~anhänger** *m* luggage tag. **~gerät** *n*, **~radio** *n* portable. **~raum** *m mot.* boot, *Am.* trunk: *viel ~ haben* have much luggage space.
Kognak ['kɔnjak] *m* (-s; -s) cognac, brandy.
Kohl [ko:l] *m* (-[e]s; -e) **1.** 🌱 cabbage. **2.** F

fig. (*red k-n ~* don't talk) rubbish.
'**Kohldampf** *m* F *~ haben* be starving.
Kohle ['ko:lə] *f* (-; -n) **1.** a) coal, b) charcoal (*a. paint.*): *ausgeglühte ~* cinders; *glühende ~* ember; *fig. weiße ~* white coal, waterpower; *ich saß* (*wie*) *auf* (*glühenden*) *~n* I was on tenterhooks. **2.** F *fig.* lolly, *Am.* bread: *Hauptsache, die ~n stimmen!* it's all right as long as the money is right!
'**kohlehaltig** *adj* carboniferous.
'**Kohlehy,drat** *n* carbohydrate.
'**Kohlekraftwerk** *n* coal power plant.
'**Kohlenbergbau** *m* coal mining.
'**Kohlenbergwerk** *n* coal mine.
Kohlen'dio,xyd *n* 🜪 carbon dioxide.
'**Kohlen|eimer** *m* coal scuttle. **~flöz** *n* coal seam. **~grube** *f* coal mine. **~händler(in** *f*) *m* coal merchant.
Kohlen'mono,xyd *n* 🜪 carbon monoxide.
'**Kohlen|re,vier** *n* coalfield. **~säure** *f* 🜪 carbonic acid. **~staub** *m* coal dust. **~stoff** *m* 🜪 carbon. **~wasserstoff** *m* 🜪 hydrocarbon.
'**Kohle|pa,pier** *n* carbon (paper). **~stift** *m* charcoal. **~ta,blette** *f* charcoal tablet. **~vorkommen** *n* coal deposit(s). **~zeichnung** *f* charcoal (drawing).
'**Kohlkopf** *m* 🌱 cabbage.
'**Kohlmeise** *f zo.* great titmouse.
'**kohl'raben'schwarz** *adj* coal-black.
Kohlrabi [ko:l'ra:bi] *m* (-[s]; -[s]) 🌱 kohlrabi.
'**Kohlrübe** *f* 🌱 swede.
Kohlweißling ['ko:lvaɪslɪŋ] *m* (-s; -e) *zo.* cabbage butterfly.
Koitus ['ko:itʊs] *m* (-; -) coitus, coition.
Koje ['ko:jə] *f* (-; -n) ⚓ berth, bunk.
Kokain [koka'i:n] *n* (-s; *no pl*) cocaine.
Kokarde [ko'kardə] *f* (-; -n) ✗ cockade.
kokett [ko'kɛt] *adj* coquettish, flirtatious. **Koketterie** [kokɛtə'ri:] *f* (-; -n) coquetry. **kokettieren** [kokɛ'ti:rən] *v/i* (h) *a. fig.* flirt (*mit* with).
Kokken ['kɔkən] *pl* 💊 cocci.
Kokolores [koko'lo:rəs] *m* (-; *no pl*) F rubbish.
Kokon [ko'kõ:] *m* (-s; -s) cocoon.
Kokos|faser ['ko:kɔs-] *f* coconut fibre (*Am.* fiber), coir. **~fett** *n* coconut fat. **~milch** *f* coconut milk. **~nuß** *f* coconut. **~palme** *f* coconut palm.

Koks¹ [ko:ks] *m* (-es; -e) **1.** ⚙ coke. **2.** F *fig.* lolly, *Am.* bread.

Koks² *m* (-es; *no pl*) *sl.* coke.

koksen ['ko:ksən] *v/i* (h) *sl.* take coke.

Kolben ['kɔlbən] *m* (-s; -) **1.** ⚙ a) piston, b) plunger (*a.* ⚡). **2.** 🦋 flask. **3.** (*rifle*) butt. **4.** ♀ spike. **5.** F conk.

'Kolben|fresser *m mot.* F jamming of the piston. **~hub** *m* piston stroke. **~ring** *m* piston ring. **~stange** *f* piston rod.

Kolchos ['kɔlçɔs] *m* (-; -e [kɔl'çɔːzə]), **Kolchose** [kɔl'çoːzə] *f* (-; -n) kolkhoz, collective farm.

Kollbak,torie ['kɔ:li-] *f* ⚕ colibacillus.

Kolibri ['ko:libri] *m* (-s; -s) *zo.* hummingbird.

Kolik ['ko:lɪk] *f* (-; -en) ⚕ colic.

Kollaborateur [kɔlaborate̩ːr] *m* (-s; -e) *pol.* collaborator.

Kollaps [kɔ'laps] *m* (-es; -e) ⚕ (*a.* **e-n ~ erleiden**) collapse.

Kolleg [kɔ'le:k] *n* (-s; -s, -ien [-'giːən]) *univ.* a) (single) lecture, b) course of lectures, c) → **Kollegstufe: ein ~ halten über** (*acc*) lecture on.

Kollege [kɔ'le:gə] *m* (-n; -n) colleague.

kollegial [kɔle'giɑːl] *adj* cooperative, helpful: **sich ~ verhalten** be loyal (**gegenüber** to[wards]).

Kollegin [kɔ'le:gɪn] *f* (-; -nen).

Kollegium [kɔ'le:giʊm] *n* (-s; -ien) *ped.* (teaching) staff, *Am. a.* faculty.

Kol'legmappe *f* (underarm) briefcase.

Kol'legstufe *f ped.* sixth-form college.

Kollekte [kɔ'lɛktə] *f* (-; -n) collection.

Kollektion [kɔlɛk'tsioːn] *f* (-; -en) a) collection, ✝ *a.* range, b) samples, c) selection.

kollektiv [kɔlɛk'tiːf] *adj*, **Kollek'tiv** *n* (-s; -e) collective. **kollektivieren** [kɔlɛkti-'viːrən] *v/t* (h) collectivize.

Kollek'tivschuld *f* collective guilt.

Kollektivum [kɔlɛk'tiːvʊm] *n ling.* (-s; -va) collective (noun).

Kollektor [kɔ'lɛktɔr] *m* (-s; -en [-'to:rən]) ⚡ commutator, collector.

Koller ['kɔlər] *m* (-s; -) F (**e-n ~ kriegen**) fly into a) tantrum.

kollern ['kɔlərn] *v/i* **1.** (sn) roll. **2.** (h) *turkey:* gobble.

kollidieren [kɔli'diːrən] *v/i* **1.** (sn) collide. **2.** (h) *fig.* collide, clash.

Kollier [kɔ'lieː] *n* (-s; -s) necklace.

Kollision [kɔli'zioːn] *f* (-; -en) collision,

fig. a. clash, conflict. **Kollisi'onskurs** *m a. fig.* (**auf ~** on a) collision course.

Kolloquium [kɔ'lo:kviʊm] *n* (-s; -ien) colloquium.

Kölner ['kœlnər] **I** *m* (-s; -) inhabitant of Cologne. **II** *adj* (of) Cologne: **der ~ Dom** Cologne Cathedral.

'Kölnerin *f* (-; -nen) → **Kölner** I.

Kölnischwasser ['kœlnɪʃ-] *n* (-s; *no pl*) eau-de-Cologne.

Kolonial... [kolo'nĭaːl] colonial (*empire, power, etc*). **Kolonialismus** [koloniă-'lɪsmʊs] *m* (-; *no pl*) colonialism.

Kolonie [kolo'niː] *f* (-; -n) colony.

Kolonisation [koloniza'tsioːn] *f* (-; -en) colonization. **kolonisieren** [koloni-'ziːrən] *v/t* (h) colonize. **Kolonist** [kolo'nɪst] *m* (-en; -en) colonist, settler.

Kolonnade [kolɔ'na:də] *f* (-; -n) △ colonnade.

Kolonne [ko'lɔnə] *f* (-; -n) column (*a.* ♟, *print.*), *a. mot.* line, ✕ convoy: **~ fahren** drive in line (*or* convoy); *pol.* **die Fünfte ~** the Fifth Column.

Ko'lonnenspringer *m mot.* F queue jumper.

Kolophonium [kolo'fo:niʊm] *n* (-s; *no pl*) colophony, rosin.

Koloratur [kolora'tuːr] *f* (-; -en) coloratura. **~so,pran** *m* coloratura soprano.

kolorieren [kolo'riːrən] *v/t* (h) colo(u)r.

Kolorit [kolo'riːt, -'rɪt] *n* (-[e]s; -e) **1.** ♪ colo(u)r. **2.** *paint.* colo(u)ring. **3.** *fig.* (local) colo(u)r, atmosphere.

Koloß [ko'lɔs] *m* (-sses; -sse) colossus.

kolossal [kolɔ'saːl] *adj* colossal, huge, gigantic, F *fig. a.* enormous: **~ viel** an enormous amount (of).

Kolportage [kɔlpɔr'ta:ʒə] *f* (-; -n) **1.** sensationalism. **2.** → **Kolpor'tagelitera,tur** *f* trashy (*or* sensational) literature. **kolportieren** [kɔlpɔr'tiːrən] *v/t* (h) spread.

Kolumne [ko'lʊmnə] *f* (-; -n) *print.* column. **Ko'lumnentitel** *m* (**lebender ~** running) head(line). **Kolumnist** [kolʊm'nɪst] *m* (-en; -en) columnist.

Kombi ['kɔmbi] *m* (-[s]; -s) → **Kombiwagen. 'Kombikarte** *f* combi-ticket.

Kombinat [kɔmbi'na:t] *n* (-[e]s; -e) ✝ combined collective.

Kombination [kɔmbina'tsioːn] *f* (-; -en) **1.** combination (*a.* chess, *of lock etc*), *soccer etc:* (combined) move. **2.** *fig.* a) deduction, b) conjecture. **3.** *fashion*: set, ensemble. **4.** a) overalls, b) flying suit. **5.** *skiing*: **Alpine (Nordische)** ~ Alpine (Nordic) Combined.

Kombinati'ons|gabe *f* power(s) of deduction. **~schloß** *n* combination lock.

kombinieren [kɔmbi'niːrən] (h) **I** *v/t* **1.** combine (**mit** with). **II** *v/i* **2.** *sports*: combine: **gut** ~ show excellent teamwork. **3.** *fig.* a) deduct, b) conjecture.

'**Kombiwagen** *m* estate car, *Am.* station wagon.

Kombüse [kɔm'byːzə] *f* (-; -n) ⚓ galley.

Komet [ko'meːt] *m* (-en; -en) comet.

ko'metenhaft *adj* comet-like, meteoric.

Komfort [kɔm'foːr] *m* (-s; *no pl*) a) comfort, b) luxury, c) conveniences: **mit allem** ~ *flat etc* with all modern conveniences, *car etc* with all the extras.

komfortabel [kɔmfɔr'taːbəl] *adj* a) comfortable, b) luxurious.

Kom'fortwohnung *f* luxury flat.

Komik ['koːmɪk] *f* (-; *no pl*) a) *the* comic, b) comic effect (*or* touch): **e-r gewissen** ~ **nicht entbehren** have a comic side. '**Komiker** *m* (-s; -) comedian (*a.* F *fig.*), comic actor. '**Komikerin** *f* (-; -nen) comedienne, comic actress.

komisch ['koːmɪʃ] *adj* **1.** comic(al), funny: ~**e Oper** comic opera; **was ist daran so** ~? what's so funny about it? **2.** F *fig.* funny, queer: **ich habe so ein** ~**es Gefühl** I feel funny; **das kam mir sehr** ~ **vor** I found that very strange; **das Komische daran ist** the funny thing about it is; ..., **daß** ... (it's) funny that ...

'**komischerweise** *adv* funnily enough.

Komitee [komi'teː] *n* (-s; -s) committee.

Komma ['kɔma] *n* (-s; -s, -ta) a) comma, b) ⒜ (decimal) point: **vier** ~ **fünf** (4,5) four point five; **null** ~ **drei** point three.

Kommandant [kɔman'dant] *m* (-en; -en) commander. **Kommandantur** [kɔmandan'tuːr] *f* (-; -en) (garrison, *Am.* post) headquarters. **Kommandeur** [kɔman-'døːr] *m* (-s; -e) commanding officer.

kommandieren [kɔman'diːrən] (h) **I** *v/t* **1.** command, be in command of: **j-n** ~ **zu** detach (*or* detail) s.o. to. **II** *v/i* **2.** (be in) command: **~der General** commanding general. **3.** F give the orders.

Kommanditgesellschaft [kɔman'diːt-] *f* ✝ limited partnership.

Kommanditist [kɔmandi'tɪst] *m* (-en; -en) ✝ limited partner.

Kommando [kɔ'mando] *n* (-s; -s) a) command, order, b) command ⒮ commando (unit), c) detachment: (**wie**) **auf** ~ (as if) by command. **~brücke** *f* ⚓ bridge. **~kapsel** *f* command module. **~raum** *m* control room. **~sprache** *f computer*: command language. **~zen,trale** *f* control cent/re (*Am.* -er).

kommen ['kɔmən] (kam, gekommen, sn) **I** *v/i* **1.** come (*a.* F *orgasmically*), *a.* arrive, *a.* approach, *a.* get (**bis** to): **angelaufen** ~ come running; **j-n** ~ **sehen** see s.o. coming (*or* come); **ich habe es** ~ **sehen** I saw it coming; ~ **lassen** a) send for, call (*s.o.*), b) order (*s.th.*); **weit** ~ *a. fig.* get far; **er wird bald** ~ he won't be long; **wann kommt der nächste Zug?** when is the next train due (to arrive)?; **zur Schule** ~ start school; **komme, was wolle** come what may; **mir kam der Gedanke** it occurred to me; **ihr kamen die Tränen** her eyes filled with tears; **später kamen mir Zweifel** afterwards I started to have doubts; (**na**), **komm schon!** come on!; **ich komme (schon)!** (I'm) coming!; F ~ **Sie mir nicht so!** don't (you) try that on me!; → **Gefängnis, spät II. 2.** ~ **auf** (*acc*) a) hit on, b) think of, c) amount to, come to; **ich komme nicht darauf!** I just can't think of it!; **darauf komme ich gleich** (**zu sprechen**)**!** I'll be coming to that!; **wie kommst du darauf?** what makes you think (*or* say) that?; **auf jeden von uns** ~ **zwei Äpfel** each of us will get two apples; **er kommt auf 3000 Mark im Monat** he makes 3,000 marks a month; → **Schliche, Sprache** 2 *etc.* **3.** **hinter** *et.* ~ find out. **4.** F **er kommt nach s-r Mutter** he takes after his mother. **5.** **was ist über dich gekommen?** what has come over (*or* got into) you? **6.** ~ **um** (*acc*) a) lose, b) miss. **7.** ~ **von** come from, *fig. a.* be due to. **8.** ~ **zu** come by, get; **zu Geld** ~ come into money; (**wieder**) **zu sich** ~ come round (*or* to), *w.s.* recover; **sie ist nicht dazu gekommen, den Brief zu schreiben** she didn't get round to writing the letter; **wie** ~ **Sie dazu?** how dare you? **II** *v/impers* **9.** **es kommt j-n** s.o. is coming. **10.** happen, come (about): **so mußte**

es ja ~! it was bound to happen that way!; *wie kommt es, daß ...?* why is it that ...?, F how come ...?; *daher kommt es, daß ...* that's why ...; *es kam zum Krieg* there was a war; *es ist so weit gekommen, daß ...* things have got to a stage where ...

'Kommen *n* (-s) a) coming, b) arrival: *fig. ... sind wieder im ~* ... are coming (*or* are on the way in) again.

'kommend *adj* coming, *a.* future: *~e Woche* next week; *in den ~en Jahren* in the years to come; *die ~e Generation* the rising generation; *er ist der ~e Mann* he is the coming man.

Kommentar [kɔmɛn'taːr] *m* (-s; -e) (*zu* on) a) commentary, b) (*kein ~!* no) comment(!). **kommen'tarlos** *adv* without comment. **Kommentator** [-'taːtɔr] *m* (-s; -en [-ta'toːrən]) commentator. **kommentieren** [kɔmɛn'tiːrən] *v/t* (h) comment (on).

kommerzialisieren [kɔmɛrtsiali'ziːrən] *v/t* (h) commercialize. **kommerziell** [kɔmɛr'tsiɛl] *adj* commercial.

Kommilitone [kɔmili'toːnə] *m* (-n; -n), **Kommili'tonin** *f* (-; -nen) *univ.* fellow student.

Kommiß [kɔ'mɪs] *m* (-sses; *no pl*) F (*beim ~* in the) army.

Kommissar [kɔmɪ'saːr] *m* (-s; -e) **1.** commissioner. **2.** → *Kriminalkommissar.*

kommissarisch [kɔmɪ'saːrɪʃ] *adj* **1.** temporary. **2.** deputy.

Kommission [kɔmɪ'sioːn] *f* (-; -en) (*a. ✝ in ~* on) commission, committee.

Kommissionär [kɔmɪsio'nɛːr] *m* (-s; -e) ✝ commission agent.

Kommissi'onsbuchhändler(in *f*) *m* wholesale bookseller.

Kommode [kɔ'moːdə] *f* (-; -n) chest of drawers.

Kommodore [kɔmo'doːrə] *m* (-s; -n, -s) ⚓ commodore.

kommunal [kɔmu'naːl] *adj* local, municipal.

Kommu'nal|abgaben *pl* local rates (*Am.* taxes). **~beamte** *m* municipal officer. **~poli,tik** *f* local politics. **~verwaltung** *f* local government. **~wahlen** *pl* local elections.

Kommune [kɔ'muːnə] *f* (-; -n) **1.** community. **2.** commune.

Kommunikation [kɔmunika'tsioːn] *f* (-; -en) communication.

Kommunikati'ons|mittel *n* means of communication, *pl a.* (mass) media. **~schwierigkeiten** *pl ~ haben* have difficulty communicating. **~technik** *f* communications technology. **~wissenschaft** *f* communication(s) science.

kommunikativ [kɔmunika'tiːf] *adj* communicative.

Kommunion [kɔmu'nioːn] *f* (-; -en) *eccl.* (Holy) Communion.

Kommuniqué [kɔmyni'keː] *n* (-s; -s) communiqué.

Kommunismus [kɔmu'nɪsmʊs] *m* (-; *no pl*) communism.

Kommunist [kɔmu'nɪst] *m* (-en; -en), **Kommu'nistin** *f* (-; -nen) communist.

kommu'nistisch *adj* communist(ic).

kommunizieren [kɔmuni'tsiːrən] *v/i* (h) communicate.

kommutieren [kɔmu'tiːrən] *v/t* (h) ⚡ commutate.

Komödiant [kɔmø'diant] *m* (-en; -en), **Komödi'antin** *f* (-; -nen) actor (actress), *fig. contp.* play-actor. **Komödie** [ko'møːdiə] *f* (-; -n) comedy, *fig.* farce.

Kompagnon [kɔmpan'jõ:] *m* (-s; -s) ✝ partner.

kompakt [kɔm'pakt] *adj* compact.

Kompanie [kɔmpa'niː] *f* (-; -n) ✗ company. **~chef** *m* company commander.

Komparativ ['kɔmparatiːf] *m* (-s; -e) *ling.* comparative (degree).

Komparse [kɔm'parzə] *m* (-n; -n), **Kom'parsin** *f* (-; -nen) *film etc*: extra.

Kompaß ['kɔmpas] *m* (-sses; -sse) compass. **~haus** *n* ⚓ binnacle. **~nadel** *f* compass needle. **~rose** *f* compass card.

kompatibel [kɔmpa'tiːbəl] *adj* compatible.

Kompensation [kɔmpɛnza'tsioːn] *f* (-; -en) compensation.

kompensieren [kɔmpɛn'ziːrən] *v/t* (h) compensate (for) (*a. psych.*).

kompetent [kɔmpe'tɛnt] *adj* competent, *a.* responsible (*für* for), *a.* authorized.

Kompetenz [kɔmpe'tɛnts] *f* (-; -en) competence, *a.* responsibility (*für* for), *a.* authority: *s-e ~en überschreiten* exceed one's authority. **~bereich** *m* sphere of authority. **~streit** *m*, **~streitigkeit** *f usu. pl* demarcation dispute.

kompilieren [kɔmpiˈliːrən] *v/t* (h) compile.

Komplementärfarbe [kɔmplemɛnˈtɛːr-] *f* complementary colo(u)r.

komplett [kɔmˈplɛt] *adj* complete.

komplex [kɔmˈplɛks] *adj* complex.

Kom'plex *m* (-es; -e) *psych.* (*wegen* about) complex, F hangup.

Komplikation [kɔmplikaˈtsɪoːn] *f* (-; -en) complication.

Kompliment [kɔmpliˈmɛnt] *n* (-[e]s; -e) (*j-m ein ~ machen* pay s.o. a) compliment; *~!* congratulations!

Komplize [kɔmˈpliːtsə] *m* (-n; -n), **Kom'plizin** *f* (-; -nen) accomplice.

komplizieren [kɔmpliˈtsiːrən] *v/t* (h) complicate. **kompli'ziert** *adj* complicated, complex (*character etc*), intricate (*problem etc*): ✿ *~er Bruch* compound fracture. **Kompli'ziertheit** *f* (-; *no pl*) complexity.

Komplott [kɔmˈplɔt] *n* (-[e]s; -e) (*a. ein ~ schmieden* plot (*gegen* against).

Komponente [kɔmpoˈnɛntə] *f* (-; -n) component.

komponieren [kɔmpoˈniːrən] *v/t, v/i* (h) *a. fig.* compose. **Komponist** [-ˈnɪst] *m* (-en; -en) composer. **Komposition** [kɔmpoziˈtsɪoːn] *f* (-; -en) composition.

Kompositum [kɔmˈpoːzitʊm] *n* (-s; -ta) *ling.* compound (word).

Kompost [kɔmˈpɔst] *m* (-[e]s; -e), **kompostieren** [-ˈtiːrən] *v/t* (h) compost.

Kompott [kɔmˈpɔt] *n* (-[e]s; -e) stewed fruit.

Kompresse [kɔmˈprɛsə] *f* (-; -n) ✿ compress. **Kompressor** [kɔmˈprɛsɔr] *m* (-s; -en [-ˈsoːrən]) ✿ compressor, *mot.* supercharger. **komprimieren** [kɔmpriˈmiːrən] *v/t* (h) compress.

Kompromiß [kɔmproˈmɪs] *m* (-sses; -sse) compromise: *e-n ~ schließen* (make a) compromise (*über acc* on). *~bereitschaft* *f* willingness to compromise.

kompro'mißlos *adj* uncompromising. **Kompro'miß** **lösung** *f* compromise solution. *~vorschlag* *m* compromise proposal: *e-n ~ machen* suggest a compromise.

kompromittieren [kɔmprɔmɪˈtiːrən] *v/t* (h) compromise (*sich* o.s.).

Kondensat [kɔndɛnˈzaːt] *n* (-[e]s; -e) condensate. **Kondensation** [-zaˈtsɪoːn] *f* (-; -en) condensation. **Kondensator**

[-ˈzaːtɔr] *m* (-s; -en [-zaˈtoːrən]) **1.** ✿ condenser. **2.** ⚡ capacitor. **kondensieren** [-ˈziːrən] *v/t, v/i* (h) condense.

Kondens **milch** [kɔnˈdɛns-] *f* evaporated milk. *~streifen* *m* ✈ condensation trail. *~wasser* *n* condensation water.

Kondition [kɔndiˈtsɪoːn] *f* (-; -en) **1.** *no pl sports:* condition, trim, shape: *e-e ausgezeichnete ~ haben* be very fit. **2.** *usu. pl* ✝ condition.

Konditional [kɔnditsɪoˈnaːl] *m* (-s; -e) *ling.* conditional (mood).

Konditio'nalsatz *m* conditional clause.

Konditi'ons **schwäche** *f sports:* lack of stamina, poor shape. **²stark** *adj* very fit. *~training* *n* fitness training.

Konditor [kɔnˈdiːtɔr] *m* (-s; -en [-diˈtoːrən]) pastry cook. **Kondltorei** [kɔndito'raɪ] *f* (-; -en) a) cake shop, b) café.

Kondolenz(...) [kɔndoˈlɛnts-] → **Beileid(s...). kondolieren** [kɔndoˈliːrən] *v/i* (h) *j-m ~* express one's condolences to s.o. (*zu* on).

Kondom [kɔnˈdoːm] *n, m* (-s; -e) condom, *Am. a.* prophylactic.

Konfekt [kɔnˈfɛkt] *n* (-[e]s; -e) a) sweets, *Am.* (soft) candy, b) chocolates.

Konfektion [kɔnfɛkˈtsɪoːn] *f* (-; -en) (manufacture of) ready-to-wear (*or* ready-made) clothing (*or* clothes).

Konfekti'ons... ready-to-wear (*clothes, suit, etc*). *~größe* *f* size.

Konferenz [kɔnfeˈrɛnts] *f* (-; -en) meeting, conference. **Konfe'renzschaltung** *f radio etc:* conference system.

konferieren [kɔnfeˈriːrən] *v/i* (h) **1.** confer (*über acc* on). **2.** *a. v/t* compère.

Konfession [kɔnfɛˈsɪoːn] *f* (-; -en) (*welcher ~ gehören Sie an?* what is your [religious] denomination(?). **konfessionell** [kɔnfɛsɪoˈnɛl] *adj* denominational. **konfessi'onslos** *adj* nondenominational. **Konfessi'onsschule** *f* denominational school.

Konfetti [kɔnˈfɛti] *n* (-[s]; *no pl*) confetti.

Konfirmand [kɔnfɪrˈmant] *m* (-en; -en), **Konfir'mandin** [-dɪn] *f* (-; -nen) confirmand. **Konfirmation** [kɔnfɪrmaˈtsɪoːn] *f* (-; -en) confirmation. **konfirmieren** [kɔnfɪrˈmiːrən] *v/t* (h) confirm.

konfiszieren [kɔnfɪsˈtsiːrən] *v/t* (h) confiscate, seize.

Konfitüre [kɔnfiˈtyːrə] *f* (-; -n) jam.

Konflikt

Konflikt [kɔn'flɪkt] *m* (-[e]s; -e) (*in ~ geraten* come into) conflict (*mit* with).

Kon'fliktstoff *m* matter for conflict.

Konföderation [kɔnfødera'tsi̯oːn] *f* (-; -en) confederation.

konform [kɔn'fɔrm] *adj* conforming, Ⓐ conformal: *mit j-m ~ gehen* agree with s.o. (*in dat* about).

Konformist [kɔnfɔr'mɪst] *m* (-en; -en), **komfor'mistisch** *adj* conformist.

Konfrontation [kɔnfrɔnta'tsi̯oːn] *f* (-; -en) confrontation. **konfrontieren** [-'tiːrən] *v/t* (h) confront (*mit* with).

konfus [kɔn'fuːs] *adj* confused: *ich bin ganz ~ a.* I'm in a muddle. **Konfusion** [kɔnfu'zi̯oːn] *f* (-; -en) confusion.

Konglomerat [kɔnglome'raːt] *n* (-[e]s; -e) *a. fig.* conglomerate.

Kongreß [kɔn'grɛs] *m* (-sses; -sse) congress, convention: *pol. Am. der ~* Congress. **Kon'greßmitglied** *n pol. Am.* Congressman (Congresswoman).

kongruent [kɔngru'ɛnt] *adj* Ⓐ congruent (*a. fig.*). **Kongruenz** [-'ɛnts] *f* (-; -en) Ⓐ congruence (*a. fig.*). **kongruieren** [-'iːrən] *v/i* (h) Ⓐ be congruent (*a. fig.*).

Konifere [koni'feːrə] *f* (-; -n) ⚘ conifer.

König ['køːnɪç] *m* (-s; -e) king.

Königin ['køːnɪgɪn] *f* (-; -nen) *a. zo.* queen. **'Königinmutter** *f* queen mother. **'Königinwitwe** *f* queen dowager.

königlich ['køːnɪklɪç] *adj* royal, *a.* regal (*insignia, power, etc*), *fig. a.* kingly: F *sich ~ amüsieren* have great fun.

Königreich ['køːnɪk-] *n* kingdom.

'Königs|haus *n* royal house (*or* dynasty). **~krone** *f* royal crown. **~sohn** *m* king's son, prince. **~tiger** *m zo.* Bengal tiger. **~tochter** *f* king's daughter, princess. **🕀treu** *adj* a) loyal (to the king), b) royalist.

'Königtum *n* (-s; *no pl*) monarchy.

konisch ['koːnɪʃ] *adj* conic(al).

Konjugation [kɔnjuga'tsi̯oːn] *f* (-; -en) *ling.* conjugation. **konjugieren** [kɔnju-'giːrən] *v/t* (h) *ling.* conjugate.

Konjunktion [kɔnjʊŋk'tsi̯oːn] *f* (-; -en) *ling.* conjunction.

Konjunktiv ['kɔnjʊŋktiːf] *m* (-s; -e) *ling.* subjunctive (mood).

'Konjunktivsatz *m* subjunctive clause.

Konjunktur [kɔnjʊŋk'tuːr] *f* (-; -en) 🕀 a) business cycle, b) boom, c) economic trend (*or* situation). **~abschwächung** *f*

downswing. **~aufschwung** *m* upswing. **🕀bedingt** *adj* cyclic(al). **~bericht** *m* economic report. **🕀dämpfend** *adj* countercyclical.

konjunkturell [kɔnjʊŋktu'rɛl] *adj* cyclical, economic, business (*trend etc*).

Konjunk'tur|poli,tik *f* trade-cycle policy. **~schwankungen** *pl* cyclical fluctuations. **~spritze** *f* F shot in the arm. **~verlauf** *m* economic trend.

konkav [kɔn'kaːf] *adj* concave.

Konkordat [kɔnkɔr'daːt] *n* (-[e]s; -e) concordat.

konkret [kɔn'kreːt] *adj* concrete, *a.* definite, specific, precise.

konkretisieren [kɔnkreti'ziːrən] *v/t* (h) put *s.th.* in concrete form (*or* terms).

Konkurrent [kɔnkʊ'rɛnt] *m* (-en; -en) competitor, (🕀 *a.* business) rival.

Konkurrenz [kɔnkʊ'rɛnts] *f* (-; -en) 1. *no pl* competition, rivalry: *j-m ~ machen* compete with s.o. 2. *no pl* competitor(s), rival(s), *coll. a.* competition: *die ~ ausschalten* eliminate one's competitors. 3. competition, contest, *sports: a.* event: *außer ~* hors concours.

Konkur'renz|erzeugnis *n* rival product. **🕀fähig** *adj* competitive. **~firma** *f*, **~geschäft** *n* rival firm. **~kampf** *m* (*mörderischer ~* cutthroat) competition; *endloser ~* F rat race. **~klausel** *f* restraint clause.

konkur'renzlos *adj* unrival(l)ed.

konkurrieren [kɔnkʊ'riːrən] *v/i* (h) *mit j-m ~* compete with s.o. (*um* for).

Konkurs [kɔn'kʊrs] *m* (-es; -e) bankruptcy: *in ~ gehen, ~ machen* go bankrupt. **~antrag** *m* petition in bankruptcy. **~erklärung** *f* declaration of insolvency. **~masse** *f* bankrupt's estate. **~verfahren** *n* (*das ~ eröffnen* institute) bankruptcy proceedings. **~verwalter** *m* a) trustee in bankruptcy, b) 🕀 receiver.

können ['kœnən] *v/aux*, *v/i*, *v/t* (konnte, gekonnt, h) 1. be able to: *kannst du es?* can you do it?; *er hätte es tun ~* he could have done it; *ich habe nicht arbeiten ~* I was unable to work; *ich kann nicht mehr!* a) I can't go on!, F I've had it!, b) I can't take any more!, c) I can't manage (*or* eat) any more!; F *da kann man nichts machen!* there's nothing to be done!; *du kannst mich mal!* go to hell! 2. know: *~ Sie tanzen?*

do you (know how to) dance?, can you dance?; **sie kann kein Spanisch** she doesn't know (*or* speak) Spanish; F **er kann etwas (*ganz nichts*)** he is a capable fellow (he's absolutely incapable). **3.** be allowed to: **kann ich jetzt gehen?** can I go now?; **Sie ~ (es) mir glauben!** (you may) believe me!; F **das kann doch nicht wahr sein!** but that's impossible! **4. es kann sein, daß er noch kommt** he may (*or* might) come yet; **ich kann mich irren** I may be mistaken; **wann könnte das gewesen sein?** when might that have been?; **du könntest recht haben** you may (*or* could) be right; F **kann sein!** maybe! **5. ich kann nichts für ...** I'm not responsible for ...; **ich konnte doch nichts dafür!** it wasn't my fault! **6.** F **mit j-m (gut) ~** get on with s.o. (like a house on fire).

'**Können** *n* (-s) skill, ability.

Könner ['kœnər] *m* (-s; -), '**Könnerin** *f* (-; -nen) expert, *sports*: ace.

Konsekutivsatz [kɔnzeku'ti:f-] *m ling.* consecutive clause.

konsequent [kɔnze'kvɛnt] *adj* a) consistent, logical, b) firm, resolute, c) uncompromising: ~ **bleiben** remain firm.

Konsequenz [kɔnze'kvɛnts] *f* (-; -en) **1.** consequence: **die ~en ziehen** draw the conclusions (**aus** from), act accordingly. **2.** consistency.

konservativ [kɔnzɛrva'ti:f] *adj,* **Konservative** [kɔnzɛrva'ti:və] *m* (-*n*; -n) conservative, *pol. Br. a.* Tory.

Konservator [kɔnzɛr'va:tɔr] *m* (-s; -en [-va'to:rən]) curator.

Konservatorium [kɔnzɛrva'to:rĭʊm] *n* (-s; -rien) conservatory.

Konserve [kɔn'zɛrvə] *f* (-; -n) **1.** a) preserve(d food), b) tin, can: ~**n** tinned (*or* canned) food; **von ~n leben** live out of tins (*or* cans); F *fig.* **Musik aus der ~** canned music. **2.** → **Blutkonserve.**

Kon'serven|büchse *f,* ~**dose** *f* tin, can. ~**fa,brik** *f* canning factory, cannery.

konservieren [kɔnzɛr'vi:rən] *v/t* (h) preserve. **Konser'vierung** *f* (-; -en) preservation. **Konser'vierungsmittel** *n* preservative.

Konsistenz [kɔnzɪs'tɛnts] *f* (-; -en) consistency.

Konsole [kɔn'zo:lə] *f* (-; -n) console.

konsolidieren [kɔnzoli'di:rən] *v/t* (*a.* **sich ~**) (h) consolidate.

Konsonant [kɔnzo'nant] *m* (-en; -en) consonant. **konso'nantisch** *adj* consonant(al).

Konsortium [kɔn'zɔrtsĭʊm] *n* (-s; -tien) ✝ syndicate.

Konspiration [kɔnspira'tsĭo:n] *f* (-; -en) conspiracy, plot. **konspirativ** [-'ti:f] *adj* conspiratorial. **konspirieren** [kɔnspi-'ri:rən] *v/i* (h) conspire, plot.

konstant [kɔn'stant] *adj* constant.

Kon'stante *f* (-; -n) *a. fig.* constant.

Konstellation [kɔnstɛla'tsĭo:n] *f* (-; -en) constellation.

konstituieren [kɔnstitu'i:rən] *v/t* (h) constitute: *parl.* **sich ~ als ...** resolve itself into ...; **konstituierende Versammlung** constituent assembly.

Konstitution [kɔnstitu'tsĭo:n] *f* (-; -en) ✻, *pol.* constitution. **konstitutionell** [kɔnstitutsĭo'nɛl] *adj* constitutional.

konstruieren [kɔnstru'i:rən] *v/t* (h) construct (*a. ling.,* ℞), ⊕ *a.* design, build, *fig. contp.* fabricate. **Konstrukteur** [kɔnstrʊk'tø:r] *m* (-s; -e) design engineer. **Konstruktion** [kɔnstrʊk'tsĭo:n] *f* (-; -en) a) construction (*a. ling.,* ℞), b) design, c) structure. **Konstrukti'ons-fehler** *m* constructional fault, faulty design. **konstruktiv** [kɔnstrʊk'ti:f] *adj* **1.** *fig.* constructive. **2.** ⊕ constructional, structural, design.

Konsul ['kɔnzʊl] *m* (-s; -n) consul.

Konsular... [kɔnzu'la:r-] consular.

Konsulat [-'la:t] *n* (-[e]s; -e) consulate.

Konsultation [kɔnzʊlta'tsĭo:n] *f* (-; -en) consultation. **konsultieren** [kɔnzʊl-'ti:rən] *v/t* (h) consult.

Konsum¹ ['kɔnzu:m] *m* (-s; -s) cooperative (store), F co-op.

Konsum² [kɔn'zu:m] *m* (-s; *no pl*) *a. fig.* consumption. **Kon'sumdenken** *n* (-s) consumerism. **Konsument** [kɔnzu-'mɛnt] *m* (-en; -en) *a. fig.* consumer. **Kon'sumgesellschaft** *f* consumer society. **Kon'sumgüter** *pl* consumer goods. **konsumieren** [kɔnzu'mi:rən] *v/t* (h) *a. fig.* consume. **Kon'sumterror** *m* F pressure to buy.

Kontakt [kɔn'takt] *m* (-[e]s; -e) contact: **mit j-m in ~ stehen** be in contact (*or* touch) with s.o.; **mit j-m ~ aufnehmen** get in touch with s.o., contact s.o. ~**ab-**

zug *m phot.* contact print. **♀arm** *adj* unsociable: *er ist ~ a.* F he is a bad mixer. **♀freudig** *adj* sociable: *er ist ~ a.* F he is a good mixer. **~gespräche** *pl* initial talks. **~gift** *n* contact poison. **~linse** *f opt.* contact lens. **~mann** *m* contact. **~per₁son** *f a.* ♣ contact. **~schalter** *m* touch sensitive switch.

Kontamination [kɔntamina'tsĭoːn] *f* (-; -en) contamination. **kontaminieren** [kɔntami'niːrən] *v/t* (h) contaminate.

Konteradmi₁ral ['kɔntər-] *m* ♣ rear admiral.

kontern ['kɔntərn] *v/i, v/t* (h) counter.

'Konterrevolutiˌon *f* counterrevolution.

Kontext ['kɔntɛkst] *m* (-[e]s; -e) context.

Kontinent [kɔnti'nɛnt] *m* (-[e]s; -e) continent. **kontinental** [kɔntinɛn'taːl] *adj* continental.

Kontingent [kɔntɪŋ'gɛnt] *n* (-[e]s; -e) contingent (*a.* ✕), ✝ *a.* quota.

kontingentieren [kɔntɪŋgɛn'tiːrən] *v/t* (h) **1.** fix a quota for. **2.** ration.

kontinuierlich [kɔntinu'iːrlɪç] *adj* continuous. **Kontinuität** [kɔntinui'tɛːt] *f* (-; *no pl*) continuity.

Konto ['kɔnto] *n* (-s; -ten) account: *ein ~ haben bei* have (*or* keep) an account with (*or* at); F *fig. das geht auf sein ~* that's his doing. **~auszug** *m* bank statement. **~führungsgebühr** *f* service charge. **~inhaber(in** *f)* *m* account holder. **~nummer** *f* account number.

Kontorist [kɔnto'rɪst] *m* (-en; -en), **Konto'ristin** *f* (-; -nen) (office) clerk.

'Kontostand *m* balance: *wie ist der ~?* how does the account stand?; *Ihr ~ beläuft sich auf ...* you have ... to your credit.

kontra ['kɔntra] **I** *prep* contra, ⚖ *or fig.* versus (*abbr.* vs.). **II** *adv* *sie ist immer ~ (eingestellt)* she's against everything.

'Kontra *n* (-s; -s) *fig.* objection: *~ geben cards:* double; F *j-m ~ geben* hit back at s.o.; → **Pro.**

'Kontrabaß *m* ♪ double bass.

Kontrahent [kɔntra'hɛnt] *m* (-en; -en) ⚖ contracting party, *fig.* opponent, *a. sports:* rival.

'Kontraindikatiˌon *f* contraindication.

Kontraktion [kɔntrak'tsĭoːn] *f* (-; -en) contraction.

'kontraprodukˌtiv *adj* counterproductive.

'Kontrapunkt *m* (-[e]s; *no pl*) ♪ counterpoint.

konträr [kɔn'trɛːr] *adj* contrary.

Kontrast [kɔn'trast] *m* (-[e]s; -e) contrast: *e-n ~ bilden (zu)* → **kontrastieren.** **kon'trastarm** *adj* phot. flat. **kontrastieren** [-'tiːrən] *v/i* (h) (*mit*) contrast (with), form a contrast (to). **Kon'trastˌmittel** *n* ✱ radiopaque material. **♀reich** *adj phot.,* TV contrasty.

Kon'trollabschnitt *m* stub.

Kon'trollbehörde *f* control authority.

Kontrolle [kɔn'trɔlə] *f* (-; -n) a) control (*über acc* of), *a.* ⊙ inspection, check, b) supervision: *unter (außer) ~* under (out of) control; *unter ärztlicher ~* under medical supervision; *er verlor die ~ über s-n Wagen* he lost control of his car; *... steht unter ständiger ~* a constant check is kept on ...

Kon'trolleuchte *f* pilot lamp.

Kontrolleur [kɔntrɔ'løːr] *m* (-s; -e) inspector, supervisor.

Kon'trollˌfunktiˌon *f* controlling function. **~gang** *m* round.

kontrollieren [kɔntrɔ'liːrən] *v/t* (h) a) control, check, b) supervise.

Kon'trolliste *f* checklist.

Kon'trollˌpunkt *m* checkpoint. **~turm** *m* ✈ control tower. **~uhr** *f* time clock.

Kontroverse [kɔntro'vɛrzə] *f* (-; -n) controversy, argument.

Kontur [kɔn'tuːr] *f* (-; -en) contour, outline.

Konus ['koːnʊs] *m* (-; -se) ⚙ cone.

Konvention [kɔnvɛn'tsĭoːn] *f* (-; -en) convention.

Konventionalstrafe [kɔnvɛntsĭona'l-] *f* (contractual) penalty.

konventionell [kɔnvɛntsĭo'nɛl] *adj* conventional.

konvergieren [kɔnvɛr'giːrən] *v/i* (h) ⚿ converge.

Konversation [kɔnvɛrza'tsĭoːn] *f* (-; -en) conversation. **Konversatiˈonslexikon** *n* encyclop(a)edia.

konver'tierbar *adj* convertible.

konvertieren [kɔnvɛr'tiːrən] *v/t* (h), *v/i* (sn) convert (✝ *in acc* into, *eccl.* **zu** to): *er ist (or hat) konvertiert a.* he was converted.

Konvertit [kɔnvɛr'tiːt] *m* (-en; -en), **Konver'titin** *f* (-; -nen) *eccl.* convert.

konvex [kɔn'vɛks] *adj* ⚿ convex.

Konvoi ['kɔnvɔi] *m* (-s; -s) convoy.
Konzentrat [kɔntsɛn'traːt] *n* (-[e]s; -e) 🜊 concentrate. **Konzentration** [kɔntsɛntra'tsɪoːn] *f* (-; -en) *a.* 🜊 concentration.
Konzentrati'ons|fähigkeit *f* power(s) of concentration. **~lager** *n pol.* concentration camp. **~schwäche** *f* lack of concentration.
konzentrieren [kɔntsɛn'triːrən] *v/t* (*a. sich ~*) (h) concentrate (*auf acc* on).
konzen'triert *adj* concentrated: *in ~er Form a.* in tabloid form; *~ arbeiten etc a.* work *etc* with concentration.
konzentrisch [kɔn'tsɛntrɪʃ] *adj* concentric.
Konzept [kɔn'tsɛpt] *n* (-[e]s; -e) a) rough draft (*or* copy), *a.* notes, b) plan(s): *fig. j-n aus dem ~ bringen* put s.o. off his stroke, F rattle s.o.; *aus dem ~ kommen* lose the thread; F *j-m das ~ verderben* thwart s.o.'s plans; *das paßte ihr nicht ins ~* that didn't suit her at all.
Konzeption [kɔntsɛp'tsɪoːn] *f* (-; -en) conception.
Konzern [kɔn'tsɛrn] *m* (-s; -e) ✝ group, combine.
Konzert [kɔn'tsɛrt] *n* (-[e]s; -e) **1.** a) concert, b) recital: *ins ~ gehen* go to a concert. **2.** ♪ concerto. **~agen,tur** *f* concert agency. **~besucher** *m* concertgoer. **~flügel** *m* concert grand. **~führer** *m* concert guide.
konzer'tiert [kɔntsɛr'tiːrt] *adj* ✝, *pol.* **~e Aktion** concerted action.
Kon'zert|meister *m* leader, *Am.* concertmaster. **~saal** *m* concert hall.
Konzession [kɔntsɛ'sɪoːn] *f* (-; -en) **1.** concession (*an acc* to). **2.** licen/ce (*Am.* -se). **Konzessivsatz** [kɔntsɛ'siː-f-] *m* concessive clause.
Konzil [kɔn'tsiːl] *n* (-s; -e) council.
konzipieren [kɔntsi'piːrən] *v/t* (h) a) conceive, b) draft: *konzipiert für a.* ⊙ designed for.
Kooperation [koʔopera'tsɪoːn] *f* (-; no pl) cooperation. **kooperativ** [koʔopera'tiːf] *adj* cooperative. **kooperieren** [koʔope'riːrən] *v/i* (h) cooperate.
Koordinate [koʔordi'naːtə] *f* (-; -n) ✦ coordinate. **Koordination** [-na'tsɪoːn] *f* (-; -en) coordination. **koordinieren** [koʔordi'niːrən] *v/t* (h) coordinate.
Kopf [kɔpf] *m* (-[e]s; ⸚e) **1.** a) head (*a.* 🜊,

♪, ⊙), b) (letter)head, c) (pipe) bowl, d) top: *~ hoch!* cheer up!, chin up!; *~ an ~ in race, election:* neck to neck; *von ~ bis Fuß* from head to foot, from top to toe; *mit bloßem ~* bare-headed; *über j-s ~ hinweg a. fig.* over s.o.'s head; *fig. pro ~* per person, a head; *sie ist nicht auf den ~ gefallen* she is no fool; *ich war wie vor den ~ geschlagen* I was thunderstruck; *den ~ hängen lassen a. fig.* hang one's head; F *sein Geld auf den ~ hauen* blow one's money; *den ~ hinhalten* take the blame (*für* for); *~ und Kragen riskieren* risk one's neck; *ich weiß nicht, wo mir der ~ steht* I don't know whether I'm coming or going; *j-m zu ~e steigen* go to s.o.'s head; *auf den ~ stellen* turn *s.th.* upside down; F *und wenn du dich auf den ~ stellst!* and if it kills you!; *j-n vor den ~ stoßen* offend s.o.; *j-m über den ~ wachsen* a) outgrow s.o., b) *fig.* be too much for s.o.; *j-m den ~ waschen* a) wash s.o.'s hair, b) *a. j-m den ~ zurechtrücken* straighten s.o. out; *sie will immer mit dem ~ durch die Wand* she always wants to have her own way regardless; *j-m et. auf den ~ zusagen* tell s.o. straight out; → *Nagel, schütteln.* **2.** *fig.* head, *a.* mind, brains, *a.* leader, brain: *er war der ~ des Unternehmens* he was the head (*or* brain) of the enterprise; *aus dem ~* by heart; *et. im ~ rechnen* work s.th. out in one's head; F *das hältst du ja im ~ nicht aus!* it's incredible!; *e-n kühlen (klaren) ~ bewahren* keep a cool (clear) head; *sich et. durch den ~ gehen lassen* think s.th. over; *ich habe die Zahlen nicht im ~* I can't give you the figures off the cuff; *er hat andere Dinge im ~* he has other things on his mind; *er hat nur Fußball im ~* he thinks of nothing but football; *schlag dir das aus dem ~!* forget it!; *sich et. in den ~ setzen* take s.th. into one's head; *j-m den ~ verdrehen* turn s.o.'s head; *den ~ verlieren* lose one's head; *sich den ~ zerbrechen* rack one's brains (*über acc* over); → *herumgehen* 1, *richtig* 1.
'Kopf|-an-Kopf-Rennen *n sports:* neck-and-neck race. **~arbeit** *f* brainwork. **~arbeiter(in** *f)* *m* brainworker. **~bahnhof** *m* terminal. **~ball** *m* header.

Köpfchen ['kœpfçən] *n* (-s; -) **1.** small head. **2.** F ~ *haben* have brains.

köpfen ['kœpfən] *v/t* (h) **1.** behead. **2.** head (*ball*).

'**Kopf|ende** *n* head. ~**haar** *n* hair (on the head). ~**haut** *f* scalp. ~**hörer** *m* headphone, *pl a.* headset. ~**kissen** *n* pillow.

'**kopflastig** [-lastiç] *adj* top-heavy.

'**kopflos** *adj* **1.** headless. **2.** *fig.* panicky: ~ *werden* lose one's head, panic.

'**Kopf|nicken** *n* nod. ~**rechnen** *n* mental arithmetic. ~**sa, lat** *n* lettuce. ⚲**scheu** *adj* ~ *machen* confuse, intimidate; ~ *werden* become confused. ~**schmerzen** *pl* (~ *haben* have a) headache. ~**schuß** *m* shot in the head. ⚲**schütteind** *adv* with a shake of the head. ~**sprung** *m* header. ~**stand** *m* headstand.

'**kopfstehen** *v/i* (*irr, sep,* -ge-, h, → *stehen*) F *fig.* be in a flap.

'**Kopf|steinpflaster** *n* cobblestone pavement. ~**steuer** *f* poll tax. ~**stimme** *f* ♪ head voice, falsetto. ~**stütze** *f* headrest. ~**tuch** *n* (head)scarf.

kopf|über *adv* head first, headlong.

'**Kopf|verletzung** *f* head injury. ~**zerbrechen** *n j-m* ~ *machen* puzzle s.o.

Kopie [ko'pi:] *f* (-; -n) copy, *phot. a.* print, *a.* duplicate. **kopieren** [ko'pi:rən] *v/t* (h) copy (*a. fig.*), *a.* ⊕ duplicate, *phot. a.* print, *fig. a.* imitate.

Ko'pier|gerät *n* copier. ~**pa, pier** *n* copying paper. ~**stift** *m* indelible pencil.

Kopi, lot ['ko:-] *m* copilot.

Koppel¹ ['kɔpəl] *f* (-; -n) **1.** a) enclosure, b) paddock. **2.** e-e ~ a leash (*of dogs*), a string (*of horses*).

'**Koppel²** *n* (-s; -) ✗ belt.

koppeln ['kɔpəln] *v/t* (h) couple (*an acc* to) link, couple: *Raumschiffe* ~ dock spaceships; *fig. et.* ~ *mit* couple (*or combine*) s.th. with.

'**Kopplung** *f* (-; -en) coupling (*a. fig.*), docking (*of spaceships*).

Koralle [ko'ralə] *f* (-; -n) coral.

Ko'rallenbank *f* coral reef.

Koran [ko'ra:n] *m* (-s; *no pl*) Koran.

Korb [kɔrp] *m* (-[e]s; ⸚e ['kœrbə]) **1.** basket (*a. sports*): *ein* ~ (*voll*) *Äpfel* a basketful of apples; → *Hahn* 1. **2.** F *fig. j-m e-n* ~ *geben* turn s.o. down; *e-n* ~ *bekommen* be turned down.

'**Korbball** *m* (-[e]s; *no pl*) netball.

'**Korbblüter** [-bly:tər] *m* (-s; -) ⚘ composite.

Körbchen ['kœrpçən] *n* (-s; -) **1.** basket. **2.** cup (*of bra*).

'**Korbmöbel** *pl* wicker furniture.

'**Korbwaren** *pl* wickerwork.

Kord [kɔrt] *m* (-[e]s; -e) corduroy.

Kordel ['kɔrdəl] *f* (-; -n) cord.

'**Kordhose** *f* cords, corduroys.

Kordon [kɔr'dõː] *m* (-s; -s) cordon.

Kordsamt *m* corduroy, cord velvet.

Korea [ko're:a] *n* (-s) Korea. **Koreaner** [kore'a:nər] *m* (-s; -), **Kore'anerin** *f* (-; -nen) Korean. **kore'anisch** *adj* Korean.

Korinthe [ko'rɪntə] *f* (-; -n) currant.

Kork [kɔrk] (-[e]s; -e) *m* cork.

Korken ['kɔrkən] *m* (-s; -) cork.

'**Korkenzieher** *m* (-s; -) corkscrew.

Korn¹ [kɔrn] *n* (-[e]s; ⸚er) **1.** *no pl* grain, cereals: → *Flinte*. **2.** grain.

Korn² *n* (-[e]s; *no pl*) **1.** ✗ front sight: F *fig. aufs* ~ *nehmen* attack, go for. **2.** *phot.,* ⊕ grain.

Korn³ *m* (-[e]s; -) F grain whisky.

'**Kornblume** *f* cornflower.

Körnchen ['kœrnçən] *n* (-s; -) granule: *fig. ein* ~ *Wahrheit* a grain of truth.

'**Kornfeld** *n* cornfield, *Am.* grainfield.

körnig ['kœrnıç] *adj* grainy, granular, *rice etc:* al dente, *in cpds.* ...-grained.

'**Kornkammer** *f a. fig.* granary.

Koronar... [koro'na:r-] *anat.*, ⚕ coronary (*artery, vessel, sclerosis*).

Körper ['kœrpər] *m* (-s; -) body (*a. of wine*), 🅰, *phys. a.* solid: ~ *und Geist* body and mind; *am ganzen* ~ all over one's body; *am ganzen* ~ *zittern* tremble all over. ~**bau** *m* (-[e]s; *no pl*) build, physique. ~**behinderte** *m, f* (-n; -n) physically disabled (*or handicapped*) person: *die* ~*n a.* the handicapped. ~**behinderung** *f* physical handicap.

'**Körperchen** *n* (-s; -) corpuscle, particle.

'**körpereigen** *adj biol.* endogenous.

'**Körper|geruch** *m* body odo(u)r. ~**haltung** *f* posture. ~**kon, takt** *m* physical contact. ~**kraft** *f* physical strength.

'**körperlich** *adj* a) physical, bodily, b) corporeal (*a.* 🕮): ~*e Arbeit* manual work; → *Züchtigung*.

'**Körperpflege** *f* care of the body, personal hygiene. ~**mittel** *n* cosmetic.

'**Körperschaft** *f* (-; -en) corporation, (corporate) body: *gesetzgebende* ~

legislative (body). '**Körperschafts-
steuer** f corporation tax.
'**Körper|sprache** f body language. **~teil**
m part (or member) of the body. **~ver-
letzung** f (schwere ~ grievous) bodily
harm. **~wärme** f body heat.
Korps [ko:r] n (-s; -) corps.
korpulent [kɔrpu'lɛnt] adj corpulent,
stout. **Korpulenz** [kɔrpu'lɛnts] f (-; no
pl) corpulence, stoutness.
korrekt [kɔ'rɛkt] adj correct.
Kor'rektheit f (-; no pl) correctness.
Korrektor [kɔ'rɛktɔr] m (-s; -en [-'to:-
rən]) (proof)reader.
Korrektur [kɔrɛk'tu:r] f (-,-en) a) correction, b) print. proofreading: ~ lesen
proofread. **~bogen** m, **~fahne** f proof.
~zeichen n proofreader's mark.
Korrespondent [kɔrɛspɔn'dɛnt] m (-en;
-en) **1.** correspondent. **2.** ✝ correspondence clerk. **Korrespondenz** [-'dɛnts] f
(-; -en) correspondence. **korrespondieren** [-'di:rən] v/i (h) correspond.
Korridor ['kɔrido:r] m (-s; -e) corridor.
korrigieren [kɔri'gi:rən] v/t (h) correct,
ped. a. mark, a. change, alter.
korrodieren [kɔro'di:rən] v/t (h), v/i (sn)
corrode. **Korrosion** [kɔro'zio:n] f (-;
-en) corrosion. **korrosi'onsbeständig**
adj corrosion-resistant. **Korrosi'ons-
schutz** m corrosion prevention, in
cpds. anticorrosive (agent, paint, etc).
korrumpieren [kɔrum'pi:rən] v/t (h)
corrupt. **korrupt** [kɔ'rupt] adj corrupt.
Korruption [kɔrup'tsio:n] f (-; -en) corruption.
Korse ['kɔrzə] m (-n; -n) Corsican.
Korsett [kɔr'zɛt] n (-[e]s; -e) corset.
Korsika ['kɔrzika] n (-s) Corsica.
Korsin ['kɔrzin] f (-; -nen), '**korsisch** adj
Corsican.
Kortison [kɔrti'zo:n] n (-s; no pl) corti-
sone.
Koryphäe [kory'fɛ:ə] f (-; -n) (eminent)
authority.
koscher ['ko:ʃər] adj a. F fig. kosher.
Kosename ['ko:zə-] m pet name.
Kosinus ['ko:zinus] m (-; -, -se) ⅋ cosine.
Kosmetik [kɔs'me:tik] f (-; no pl) **1.**
beauty care. **2.** fig. cosmetics.
Kosmetikerin [kɔs'me:tikərin] f (-; -nen)
cosmetician, beautician.
Kos'metik|koffer m vanity box (or case).
~sa,lon m beauty parlo(u)r.

Kosmetikum [kɔs'me:tikum] n (-s; -ka)
cosmetic. **kos'metisch** adj cosmetic.
kosmisch ['kɔsmiʃ] adj cosmic.
Kosmonaut [kɔsmo'naut] m (-en; -en),
Kosmo'nautin f (-; -nen) cosmonaut.
Kosmopolit [kɔsmopo'li:t] m (-en; -en),
kosmopo'litisch adj cosmopolitan.
Kosmos ['kɔsmɔs] m (-; no pl) cos-
mos.
Kost [kɔst] f (-; no pl) a) food, fare (a.
fig.), diet, b) cooking, c) board: fleisch-
lose ~ meatless diet; (freie) ~ und Logis
(free) board and lodging.
'**kostbar** adj precious, valuable (a. fig.
time etc), a. expensive: jede Minute ist
~ every minute counts.
'**Kostbarkeit** f (-; -en) **1.** no pl precious-
ness, valuableness. **2.** precious object,
treasure, pl a. valuables.
kosten¹ ['kɔstən] v/t (v/i von) (h) taste
(a. fig.), try.
'**kosten²** v/t (h) cost, fig. a. take (time
etc): was kostet das? how much is
that?; F er hat es sich et. ~ lassen he
spent a lot of money on it; es hat mich
viel Mühe gekostet it gave me a lot of
trouble; es kostete ihn das Leben it
cost him his life; koste es, was es wolle at all costs; F das kostet Nerven!
that's hard on the nerves.
'**Kosten** pl cost(s), expenses, expenditure: die ~ tragen bear (or meet) the
cost(s); auf ~ von (or gen) a. fig. at the
expense of; auf m-e ~ at my expense;
k-e ~ scheuen spare no expense; ⚖ j-n
zu den ~ verurteilen award costs
against s.o.; fig. auf s-e ~ kommen get
one's money's worth. **~anstieg** m increase in costs. **~aufwand** m expenditure, cost: mit e-m ~ von ... at a cost of
... **~beteiligung** f cost sharing. ⚷**dämp-
fend** adj cost-cutting. **~dämpfung** f
curbing (of) costs. ⚷**deckend** adj cost-
-covering. **~explosi,on** f runaway
costs. **~faktor** m cost factor. **~frage** f
es ist e-e ~ it is a question of cost (or of
what it costs). ⚷**günstig** adj cost-effec-
tive. ⚷**inten,siv** adj cost-intensive.
~la,wine f escalating costs.
kostenlos adj and adv free, gratis.
'**Kosten-'Nutzen-Ana'lyse** f cost-bene-
fit analysis.
'**kostenpflichtig** adj a) liable to pay the
costs, b) tow away etc at the owner's

expense: **e-e Klage ~ abweisen** dismiss a case with costs.

'**Kosten|punkt** *m* F costs: **~?** how much? **~rechnung** *f* ✝ cost accounting. ⚥**senkend** *adj* cost-cutting. **~senkung** *f* reduction in costs. ⚥**sparend** *adj* cost-saving. **~steigerung** *f* cost increase. **~voranschlag** *m* estimate, quotation.

'**Kostgeld** *n* board (allowance).

köstlich ['kœstlɪç] *adj* a) delicious (*food etc*), b) *fig.* delightful (*humo[u]r etc*): **sich ~ amüsieren** have great fun.

'**Köstlichkeit** *f* (-; -en) **1.** *no pl* deliciousness. **2.** *gastr.* titbit, delicacy.

'**Kostprobe** *f a. fig.* sample, taste.

kostspielig ['kɔst[pi:lɪç] *adj* expensive.

Kostüm [kɔs'ty:m] *n* (-s; -e) **1.** (woman's) suit. **2.** costume (*a. thea.*), dress.

Ko'stümball *m* fancy-dress ball.

kostümieren [kɔsty'mi:rən] *v/t* (h) dress *s.o.* up: **sich ~** dress up (**als** as).

Ko'stümprobe *f thea.* dress rehearsal.

Ko'stümverleih *m* costume rental.

Kot [ko:t] *m* (-[e]s; *no pl*) excrement, f(a)eces.

Kotelett [kɔt'lɛt] *n* (-s; -s) *gastr.* chop, cutlet. **Kote'letten** *pl* sideboards, *Am.* sideburns.

Köter ['kø:tər] *m* (-s; -) *contp.* cur.

'**Kotflügel** *m* mudguard, *Am.* fender.

kotzen ['kɔtsən] *v/i* (h) V throw up, *sl.* puke: **ich finde ihn zum Kotzen** he makes me sick!; **das ist ja zum Kotzen!** that's enough to make one puke!

Krabbe ['krabə] *f* (-; -n) shrimp, prawn.

krabbeln ['krabəln] **I** *v/i* (sn) crawl. **II** *v/t* (h) tickle.

Krach [krax] *m* (-[e]s; ⁼e) **1.** crash, bang. **2.** *no pl* (loud) noise, din, F row, racket: **~ machen** make a racket, be noisy. **3.** F row, quarrel: **mit j-m ~ haben** have a row with s.o.; **~ schlagen** raise hell.

krachen ['kraxən] **I** *v/i* **1.** F (h) crash, crack. **2.** (sn) slam, bang: **~ gegen** (*or* **in** *acc*) crash into. **II sich ~** (h) F have a row.

krächzen ['krɛçtsən] *v/t*, *v/i* (h) croak.

kraft [kraft] *prep* (*gen*) ⚖ by virtue of.

Kraft *f* (-; ⁼e) **1.** *a. fig.* strength, a. *phys.* force, energy, ⚡, *phys.*, ⚙ power: **mit aller ~** with all one's might; **mit frischer** (*letzter*) **~** with renewed (one's last ounce of) strength; ⚓ **volle ~ voraus** full speed ahead; **Kräfte sammeln**

build up one's strength; **m-e Kräfte lassen nach** my strength fails; **das geht über m-e ~** that's too much for me; **ich bin am Ende m-r Kräfte** I can't take any more; **nach** (**besten**) **Kräften** to the best of one's ability; **~ schöpfen** gain strength (**aus** from); **er tat, was in s-n Kräften stand** he did everything within his power; → **vereinen. 2.** *pol. etc:* force. **3.** ⚖ **in ~ sein** (**setzen**) be in (put into) force; **in ~ treten** come into force, become effective; **außer ~ setzen** a) annul, invalidate, repeal (*law*), cancel (*contract*), b) suspend; **außer ~ treten** expire. **4.** worker, employee, *pl a.* personnel, staff.

'**Kraft|akt** *m* stunt. **~anstrengung** *f*, **~aufwand** *m* (strenuous) effort. **~ausdruck** *m* swearword. **~brühe** *f* beef tea.

'**Kräfteverfall** *m* loss of strength.

'**Kräfteverschleiß** *m* waste of energy.

'**Kraftfahrer(in** *f*) *m* driver, motorist.

'**Kraftfahrzeug** *n* motor vehicle. **~brief** *m* vehicle registration document. **~mechaniker** *m* car mechanic. **~schein** *m* vehicle registration document. **~steuer** *f* road (*Am.* automobile) tax.

'**Kraftfeld** *n phys.* field of force.

'**Kraftfutter** *n* 🌾 concentrated feed.

kräftig ['krɛftɪç] **I** *adj* **1.** a) *a.* ⚙ strong, robust, sturdy, b) powerful (*a. blow etc*): F **er nahm e-n ~en Schluck** he took a good swig; *fig.* **~e Farbe** deep (*or* rich) colo(u)r; ✝ **~er Aufschwung** sharp upswing. **2.** substantial, nourishing. **II** *adv* **3.** strongly (*etc*), F soundly, heartily: **er ist ~ gebaut** he is powerfully built; **~ zuschlagen** hit hard.

kräftigen ['krɛftɪgən] *v/t* (h) strengthen.

'**Kräftigungsmittel** *n* ⚕ tonic.

'**kraftlos** *adj* weak, feeble.

'**Kraft|probe** *f* trial of strength. **~protz** *m* F muscleman. **~rad** *n* motorcycle.

'**Kraftstoff** *m* fuel. **~anzeiger** *m* fuel ga(u)ge. **~leitung** *f* fuel pipe (*or* line). **~-'Luft-Gemisch** *n* fuel(-air) mixture. **~pumpe** *f* fuel pump. **~verbrauch** *m* fuel consumption.

'**kraftstrotzend** *adj* bursting with strength, vigorous, powerful.

'**Kraft|übertragung** *f* power transmission. **~verkehr** *m* motor traffic. **~verschwendung** *f* waste of energy.

'**kraftvoll** *adj* powerful, vigorous, strong.

'**Kraftwagen** *m* motor vehicle.
'**Kraftwerk** *n* power station.
Kragen ['kra:gən] *m* (-s; ⁻) collar: F *ihm platzte der ~* he blew his top; *jetzt geht es ihm an den ~* he is in for it now.
'**Kragenweite** *f* collar size: *welche ~ haben Sie?* what size collar do you take?; F *sie (das) ist genau m-e ~!* she's (it's) just my cup of tea!
Krähe ['krɛ:ə] *f* (-; -n) *zo.* crow: *fig.* *e-e ~ hackt der anderen kein Auge aus* dog does not eat dog.
krähen ['krɛ:ən] *v/i* (h) crow.
'**Krähenfüße** *pl fig.* crow's-feet.
Krake ['kra:kə] *m* (-n; -n) *zo.* octopus.
Krakeel [kra'ke:l] *m* (-s; *no pl*) F row.
kra'keelen *v/i* (h) F make a row.
Kra'keeler *m* (-s; -) F roisterer.
Krakel ['kra:kəl] *m* (-s; -) F scrawl.
'**krak(e)lig** *adj* F scrawly.
krakeln ['kra:kəln] *v/t, v/i* (h) F scrawl.
Kral [kra:l] *m* (-s; -e) kraal.
Kralle ['kralə] *f* (-; -n) claw: *fig.* *j-m die ~n zeigen* show s.o. one's claws.
krallen ['kralən] **I** *v/t* *s-e Finger ~ in* (*acc*) dig one's fingers into. **II** *sich ~ an* (*acc*) cling to, b) *in* (*acc*) dig one's claws (*person:* nails) into.
Kram [kra:m] *m* (-[e]s; *no pl*) F **1.** a) things, stuff, b) junk, rubbish. **2.** *fig.* business: *den ganzen ~ hinschmeißen* chuck the whole thing; *j-m nicht in den ~ passen* not to suit s.o.'s plans.
kramen ['kra:mən] (h) F **I** *v/i* rummage (about) (*nach* for): *in Erinnerungen ~* take a trip down memory lane. **II** *v/t et. ~ aus* fish s.th. out of *one's bag etc.*
Krampe ['krampə] *f* (-; -n) ⊙ cramp.
Krampf [krampf] *m* (-[e]s; ⁻e) **1.** ♪ a) cramp, b) spasm, convulsion: *e-n ~ bekommen* get a cramp. **2.** *no pl* F *fig.* (*das ist doch alles ~* that's just a lot of) rubbish. '**Krampfader** *f* varicose vein.
'**krampfartig** *adj* convulsive.
krampfen ['krampfən] *v/t* (*a. sich ~*) (h) clench (*hand etc*).
'**krampfhaft** *adj* **1.** ♪ convulsive, spasmodic. **2.** *fig.* desperate, frantic, forced (*laughter*): *sich ~ festhalten an* (*dat*) cling desperately to.
'**krampflösend** *adj* spasmolytic.
Kran [kra:n] *m* (-[e]s; ⁻e) ⊙ crane.
'**Kranführer** *m* crane driver.
Kranich ['kra:nɪç] *m* (-s; -e) *zo.* crane.

krank [kraŋk] *adj* a) sick (*a. fig.*), *pred* ill, diseased (*organ*), bad (*tooth*), b) invalid, suffering, ailing (*a. fig.*): *~ werden* fall ill (*or* sick), be taken ill; *sich ~ fühlen* feel ill; *sich ~ melden* report sick; *j-n ~ schreiben* write s.o. off sick, ✕ put s.o. on the sick list; *er macht mich ganz ~!* he's driving me crazy!
'**Kranke** *m, f* (-n; -n) sick person, patient.
kränkeln ['krɛŋkəln] *v/i* (h) be in poor health, be sickly, be ailing (*a. fig.*).
kranken ['kraŋkən] *v/i* (h) *a. fig.* *~ an* (*dat*) suffer from.
kränken ['krɛŋkən] *v/t* (h) hurt, wound, offend: *j-n ~* hurt s.o.('s feelings).
'**Kranken|anstalt** *f* hospital. **~auto** *n* ambulance. **~besuch** *m* visit (to a sick person), *of doctor:* sick call: *~e machen* a. visit patients. **~bett** *n* sickbed. **~blatt** *n* medical record. **~geld** *n* sick pay. **~geschichte** *f* case (*or* medical) history. **~gym.nast(in** *f*) *m* physiotherapist. **~gym,nastik** *f* remedial gymnastics.
'**Krankenhaus** *n* hospital. **~aufenthalt** *m* stay in (a) hospital. **~einweisung** *f* hospitalization. **~kosten** *pl* hospital expenses. **~tagegeld** *n* sum paid by a private sickness insurance fund for each day in hospital.
'**Kranken|kasse** *f* a) health insurance scheme, b) health insurance company. **~lager** *n* sickbed: *nach langem ~* after a long illness. **~pflege** *f* nursing. **~pfleger** *m* male nurse. **~pflegerin** *f* nurse. **~schein** *m* health insurance certificate. **~schwester** *f* nurse. **~stand** *m* number of sick persons. **~träger** *m* stretcher-bearer. **~versicherung** *f* health insurance. **~wagen** *m* ambulance. **~zimmer** *n* sickroom.
'**krankfeiern** *v/i* (*sep*, -ge-, h) F go sick, malinger, *Br.* skive off.
'**krankhaft** *adj* **1.** ♪ pathological. **2.** *fig.* morbid, abnormal.
'**Krankheit** *f* (-; -en) illness, sickness, disease: *nach langer ~* after a long illness.
'**Krankheits|bild** *n* clinical picture. **~erscheinung** *f* symptom.
'**krankheitshalber** [-halbər] *adv* owing to illness.
'**Krankheits|herd** *m* focus of a disease. **~keim** *m* germ. **~überträger** *m* carrier.
'**kranklachen:** *sich ~* (*sep*, -ge-, h) F nearly die with laughter.

kränklich ['krɛŋklɪç] *adj* sickly.
'Krankmeldung *f* notification of illness (to one's employer): **zehn ~en** ten persons reported sick.
'Kränkung *f* (-; -en) insult.
Kranz [krants] *m* (-es; ⁓e) **1.** garland, (**e-n ~ niederlegen** lay a) wreath. **2.** *fig.* circle, ring. **3.** *gastr.* ring. **4.** *astr.* corona. **Kränzchen** ['krɛntsçən] *n* (-s; -) *fig.* (ladies') circle, coffee (F hen) party.
'Kranzgefäß *n anat.* coronary artery.
Krapfen ['krapfən] *m* (-s; -) doughnut.
kraß [kras] *adj* crass, gross: *krasser Egoist (Außenseiter)* crass egotist (rank outsider); *krasser Widerspruch (Unterschied)* flagrant contradiction (huge difference); *krasse Lüge* blatant lie; *sich ~ ausdrücken* be very blunt.
Krater ['kra:tər] *m* (-s; -) crater.
Krätze ['krɛtsə] *f* (-; *no pl*) ✻ scabies.
kratzen ['kratsən] *v/t, v/i* (h) a) scratch, b) scrape: *sich ~* scratch o.s.; *sich am Ohr ~* scratch one's ear; *den Rest aus dem Topf ~* scrape the last bit from the pot; *der Pullover kratzt (mich am Hals)* the pullover scratches (my neck); *fig. mein Hals kratzt* I've got a sore throat; F *das kratzt mich nicht!* that doesn't worry me!; → *Kurve.* **'Kratzer** *m* (-s; -) F scratch. **'kratzfest** *adj* scratch-resistant. **'kratzig** *adj* scratchy.
'Kratzwunde *f* scratch.

Kraul [kraʊl] *n* (-s; *no pl*) crawl.
kraulen¹ ['kraʊlən] *v/t, v/i* (h, sn) crawl.
'kraulen² *v/t* (h) ruffle (*fur etc*).
'Kraulschwimmen *n* crawl.
'Kraulschwimmer(in *f*) *m* crawler.
kraus [kraʊs] *adj* **1.** frizzy, curly (*hair*), wrinkled (*brow*): *~ ziehen* → *krausen.* **2.** *fig.* confused, muddled (*ideas*).
Krause ['kraʊzə] *f* (-; -n) frill, ruffle.
kräuseln ['krɔʏzəln] (h) **I** *v/t* **1.** gather (*cloth*). **2.** friz(z), crimp (*hair*). **3.** ruffle, ripple (*water*). **4.** *die Lippen ~* curl one's lips; → *a.* **krausen. II** *sich ~* **5.** → 2. *smoke etc*: curl up.
krausen ['kraʊzən] *v/t* (h) wrinkle, pucker: *die Nase ~* wrinkle one's nose.
'kraushaarig *adj* curly-haired.
Kraut [kraʊt] *n* (-[e]s; ⁓er) **1.** *no pl* (stem and) leaves, tops: *ins ~ schießen* run to leaf, *fig.* run wild; F *wie ~ und Rüben (durcheinander)* in a jumble (*or* mess). **2.** herb: *fig. gegen ... ist kein ~ ge-*

wachsen there is no remedy for ... **3.** *no pl dial.* a) cabbage, b) sauerkraut. **4.** F weed, tobacco.
Kräuter|butter ['krɔʏtər-] *f* herb butter.
~essig *m* aromatic vinegar. **~käse** *m* green cheese. **~li,kör** *m* herb-fla-vo(u)red liqueur. **~tee** *m* herb tea.
Krawall [kra'val] *m* (-s; -e) **1.** riot. **2.** F (*~ machen or schlagen* kick up a) row.
Kra'wallmacher *m* rioter, rowdy.
Krawatte [kra'vatə] *f* (-; -n) tie, *Am.* necktie.
Kra'watten|muffel *m* (-s; -) *er ist ein ~* he's no tie man. **~nadel** *f* tiepin.
kraxeln ['kraksəln] *v/i* (sn) F *dial.* climb.
Kreation [krea'tsi̯o:n] *f* (-; -en) creation.
kreativ [krea'ti:f] *adj* creative. **Kreativi-tät** [kreativi'tɛ:t] *f* (-; *no pl*) creativity.
Kreatur [krea'tu:r] *f* (-; -en) creature.
Krebs [kre:ps] *m* (-es; -e) **1.** a) crayfish, *Am.* crawfish, b) crab. **2.** *astrol.* (**ich bin [ein] ~** I am [a]) Cancer. **3.** ✻ cancer. **'krebsartig** *adj* ✻ cancerous.
krebserregend, krebserzeugend *adj* carcinogenic: *~ wirken* cause cancer.
'Krebs|forschung *f* ✻ cancer research.
~früherkennung *f* early cancer diagnosis. **~geschwulst** *f* carcinoma, cancerous tumo(u)r. **~geschwür** *n* **1.** cancerous ulcer. **2.** *fig.* canker. **~knoten** *m* cancerous lump. **~kranke** *m, f* (-n; -n) person suffering from cancer, cancer patient. **~krankheit** *f*, **~leiden** *n* cancer. **~tiere** *pl* crustaceans.
'Krebsvorsorge *f* ✻ cancer prevention.
~untersuchung *f* cancer screening.
'Krebszelle *f* ✻ cancer(ous) cell.
Kredit¹ ['kre:dɪt] *m* (-s; -s) ✝ credit (side).
Kredit² [kre'di:t] *m* (-[e]s; -e) ✝ credit, *a.* loan: *e-n ~ aufnehmen (überziehen)* raise (overdraw) a credit; *ich habe bei der Bank ~* my credit with the bank is good; *auf ~ kaufen* buy on credit.
Kre'dit|aufnahme *f* borrowing. **~brief** *m* letter of credit. **~geber** *m* lender. **~hai** *m* F *contp.* loan shark.
kreditieren [kredi'ti:rən] *v/t* (h) *j-m et. ~* credit s.o.('s account) with s.th.
Kre'dit|insti,tut *n* credit bank. **~karte** *f* credit card. **~kauf** *m* purchase on credit. **~markt** *m* credit market. **~nehmer** *m* borrower. **~spritze** *f* credit injection.
kre'ditwürdig *adj* creditworthy.
kregel ['kre:gəl] *adj* F chirpy, chipper.

Kreide ['kraɪdə] f (-; -n) chalk, *paint. a.* crayon: F *bei j-m in der ~ stehen* owe s.o. money. ♀'**bleich**, ♀'**weiß** *adj* (as) white as a sheet. **~zeichnung** f chalk drawing. **~zeit** f (-; *no pl*) the Cretaceous period.

kreieren [kre'i:rən] *v/t* (h) create.

Kreis [kraɪs] m (-es; -e) **1.** a) circle (*a. fig. of friends etc*), b) cycle, c) ⚡ circuit, d) *fig.* sphere, field: *sich im ~ drehen a. fig.* move in a circle; *der Skandal zog weite ~e* the scandal involved more and more persons; *hier schließt sich der ~* we've come full circle; *im engsten ~ feiern* celebrate within the family circle (*or* with one's close friends); *im ~e der Familie* in the family (circle); *weite ~e der Bevölkerung* wide sections of the population; *aus gutunterrichteten ~en* from well-informed quarters. **2.** *pol.* district, *Am.* county.

'**Kreis|abschnitt** m ♐ segment. **~ausschnitt** m ♐ sector. **~bahn** f orbit. **~bogen** m ♐ arc of a circle.

kreischen ['kraɪʃən] *v/i* (h) shriek.

'**Kreischen** n (-s) shrieking, shrieks *pl.*

Kreisel ['kraɪzəl] m (-s; -) **1.** (peg)top. **2.** *phys.* gyro(scope).

'**Kreiselkompaß** m gyrocompass.

kreisen ['kraɪzən] I *v/i* (sn) (move in a) circle, *esp.* ⊙ rotate, revolve (*a. fig. thoughts etc*), blood, money: circulate, ✈ orbit: *et. ~ lassen* pass s.th. round; *die Erde kreist um die Sonne* the earth revolves (a)round the sun. II *v/t* (h) *gym. die Arme etc ~* swing one's arms *etc* around.

'**Kreisfläche** f ♐ area of a circle.

'**kreisförmig** *adj* circular.

'**Kreislauf** m cycle (*a.* ⊙), *of blood, money:* circulation, ⚡, ⊙ *a.* circuit, *astr.* revolution. **~störung** f ♣ circulatory disturbance, *pl* bad circulation. **~versagen** n ♣ circulatory collapse.

'**kreisrund** *adj* circular.

'**Kreissäge** f circular saw.

Kreißsaal ['kraɪs-] m ♣ delivery room.

'**Kreisstadt** f district town, *Am.* county seat.

'**Kreisverkehr** m roundabout, *Am.* rotary (traffic).

Krem [kre:m] f (-; -s) → *Creme etc.*

Krematorium [krema'to:rɪʊm] n (-s; -rien) crematorium, *Am.* crematory.

Kreml ['kre:məl; 'krɛməl] m (-s; *no pl*) the Kremlin.

Krempe ['krɛmpə] f (-; -n) brim.

krepieren [kre'pi:rən] *v/i* (sn) **1.** F die, perish. **2.** *bomb etc:* burst, explode.

Krepp [krɛp] m (-s; -s) crepe.

'**Kreppa,pier** n crepe paper.

Kresse ['krɛsə] f (-; -n) ♣ cress.

Kreta ['kre:ta] n (-s) Crete. **Kreter** ['kre:tər] m (-s; -), '**Kreterin** f (-; -nen), '**kretisch** *adj* Cretan.

kreuz [krɔʏts] *adv* ~ *und quer, a.* ~ *und quer durchziehen* crisscross.

Kreuz n (-es; -e) **1.** cross (*a. fig.*), *print.* dagger, obelisk: *astr. das ~ des Südens* the Southern Cross; *über ~* crosswise; *ein ~ schlagen* make the sign of the cross; *es ist ein ~ mit ihm* he is a real problem; F *zu ~e kriechen* knuckle under (*vor j-m* to s.o.). **2.** (small of the) back: *mir tut das ~ weh* my back aches; F *j-n aufs ~ legen* take s.o. for a ride. **3.** ♪ sharp. **4.** *cards:* club(s).

'**Kreuz|band** n (-[e]s; *÷er*) *anat.* crucial ligament. **~bein** n *anat.* sacrum.

kreuzen ['krɔʏtsən] (h) I *v/t* **1.** cross, ⊙ *a.* intersect, *biol. a.* crossbreed. II *v/i* **2.** ⚓ cruise. III *v/i* ~ **3.** → **1. 4.** *fig.* cross, *interests etc:* clash: *ihre Blicke kreuzten sich* their eyes met.

'**Kreuzer** m (-s; -) ⚓ **1.** ✕ cruiser. **2.** *sports:* (cabin) cruiser.

'**Kreuzfahrer** m *hist.* crusader.

'**Kreuzfahrt** f **1.** *hist.* crusade. **2.** ⚓ (*e-e ~ machen*) go on a) cruise.

'**Kreuzfeuer** n *a. fig.* crossfire: *ins ~ der öffentlichen Meinung* (*or der Kritik*) *geraten* come under fire from all sides.

'**Kreuzgang** m △ cloister.

kreuzigen ['krɔʏtsɪgən] *v/t* (h) crucify.

'**Kreuzigung** f (-; -en) crucifixion.

'**Kreuzotter** f *zo.* common viper.

'**Kreuzritter** m *hist.* Knight of the Cross.

'**Kreuzstich** m cross-stitch.

'**Kreuzung** f (-; -en) **1.** crossing, *biol. a.* crossbreeding. (*race*) crossbreed. **2.** crossing, intersection, junction.

'**Kreuzverhör** n cross-examination, F grilling: *j-n ins ~ nehmen* cross-examine (F grill) s.o.

'**Kreuzweg** m *eccl.* Way of the Cross.

'**kreuzweise** *adv* crosswise.

'**Kreuzworträtsel** n crossword (puzzle).

Kreuzzug

'Kreuzzug *m hist. or fig.* (a. **e-n ~ unternehmen**) crusade (**gegen** against).
kribbelig ['krɪbəlɪç] *adj* F a) nervous, jittery, b) edgy: **sie macht mich ganz ~** she gets terribly on my nerves.
kribbeln ['krɪbəln] *v/i* **1.** (h) itch, tickle, tingle: **F es kribbelte mir in den Fingern, et. zu tun** I was itching to do s.th. **2.** (sn) crawl, swarm.
Kricket ['krɪkət] *n* (-s; *no pl*) cricket.
'Kricketspieler *m* cricketer.
kriechen ['kri:çən] *v/i* (kroch, gekrochen, sn) creep, crawl: *fig. contp. vor j-m ~* toady to s o. **'Kriecher** *m* (-s; -) *contp.* crawler, toady. **'kriecherisch** *adj contp.* crawling, toadying.
'Kriechspur *f* **1.** trail. **2.** *mot.* slow (*or* creeper) lane. **'Kriechstrom** *m ⚡* leak current. **'Kriechtier** *n* reptile.
Krieg [kri:k] *m* (-[e]s; -e) a) war, b) warfare: *kalter ~* cold war; *im ~ mit* at war with; (*dat*) *den ~ erklären a. fig.* declare war on; *~ führen gegen* be at war against; *in den ~ ziehen* go to war.
kriegen ['kri:gən] *v/t* (h) F get: a. catch; → *a. bekommen* I; *es mit j-m zu tun ~* get into trouble with s.o.
Krieger ['kri:gər] *m* (-s; -) warrior.
'Kriegerdenkmal *n* war memorial.
'kriegerisch *adj* warlike, martial, *a. fig.* belligerent: **~e Auseinandersetzung** armed conflict.
'Kriegerwitwe *f* war widow.
'kriegführend *adj* belligerent.
'Kriegführung *f* (-; *no pl*) warfare.
'Kriegs|ausbruch *m* outbreak of (the) war: *bei ~* when the war broke out. **~berichterstatter** *m* war correspondent. **~beschädigte** *m, f* (-n; -n) wardisabled person. **~dienst** *m* military service. **~dienstverweigerer** *m* conscientious objector. **~ende** *n* end of (the) war: *bei ~ a.* when the war ended. **~entschädigungen** *pl* reparations. **~erklärung** *f* declaration of war. **~fall** *m im ~* in case of war. **~film** *m* war film. **~flotte** *f* navy, fleet. **~freiwillige** *m* (war) volunteer. **~fuß** *m auf ~ stehen mit j-m* be at daggers drawn with s.o., b) *e-r Sache* have (great) trouble with s.th. **~gebiet** *n* war zone. **~gefahr** *f* threat of war. **~gefangene** *m* prisoner of war, P.O.W. **~gefangenenlager** *n* prisoner-of-war (*or* P.O.W.) camp. **~gefan-

genschaft *f* captivity: *in ~ geraten* be taken prisoner. **~gegner** *m* **1.** pacifist. **2.** *the* enemy. **~gericht** *n* (*a. vor ein ~ stellen*) court-martial.
'Kriegsgewinnler [-gəvɪnlər] *m* (-s; -) war profiteer.
'Kriegs|gräberfürsorge *f* War Graves Commission. **~hafen** *m* naval port. **~held** *m* war hero. **~hetzer** *m* warmonger. **~hinterbliebenen** *pl* war widows and orphans. **~kamerad** *m* fellow soldier. **~marine** *f* navy. **~material** *n* matériel. **~opfer** *n* war victim. **~pfad** *m auf dem ~ sein a.* F *fig.* be on the warpath. **~recht** *n* (-[e]s; *no pl*) martial law. **~schauplatz** *m* theat/re (*Am.* -er) of war. **~schiff** *n* warship. **~schulden** *pl* war debts. **~schuld(frage)** *f* (question of) war guilt. **~spielzeug** *n* war toys. **~tanz** *m* war dance. **~teilnehmer** *m* **1.** combatant. **2.** ex-serviceman, *Am.* (war) veteran. **~trauung** *f* wartime wedding. **~treiber** *m* warmonger. **~verbrechen** *n* war crime.
'Kriegsverbrecher *m* war criminal. **~pro‚zeß** *m* war crimes trial.
'Kriegs|waise *f* war orphan. **²wichtig** *adj* essential to the war effort: **~e Ziele** strategic targets. **~zeit** *f* wartime: *in ~en* in time(s) of war. **~zustand** *m* (state of) war: *im ~* at war.
Krimi ['kri:mi; 'krɪmi] *m* (-[s]; -[s]) F thriller (*a. fig.*), whodun(n)it.
Kriminal|beamte [krimi'na:l-] *m* detective, C.I.D. officer. **~fall** *m* criminal case. **~film** *m* crime film (*or* thriller).
kriminalisieren [krimina'li'zi:rən] *v/t* (h) criminalize.
Kriminalist [krimina'lɪst] *m* (-en; -en) **1.** criminologist. **2.** detective.
Kriminalität [kriminali'tɛ:t] *f* (-; *no pl*) **1.** criminality. **2.** crime: *ansteigende ~* increasing crime rate.
Krimi‚nal|kommis‚sar *m* detective superintendent, *Am.* captain of police. **~poli‚zei** *f* criminal investigation department (C.I.D.), plain-clothes police. **~poli‚zist** *m* → **Kriminalbeamte.** **~ro‚man** *m* detective (*or* crime) novel.
kriminell [krimi'nɛl] *adj* criminal.
Krimi'nelle *m, f* (-n; -n) criminal.
Krippe ['krɪpə] *f* (-; -n) **1.** 🐴 manger, crib. **2.** (Christmas) crib, *Am.* crèche. **3.** crèche, day nursery.

'**Krippenspiel** n Nativity play.
Krise ['kri:zə] f (-; -n) crisis: *in e-e ~ geraten* enter a state of crisis.
kriseln ['kri:zəln] v/impers (h) *es kriselt* a) there is trouble brewing, b) *in ihrer Ehe* they seem to be going through a crisis, c) *in der Regierung* a government crisis is looming.
'**krisenanfällig** adj crisis-prone.
'**krisenfest** adj stable.
'**Krisengebiet** n crisis area.
'**krisengeschüttelt** adj crisis-ridden.
'**Krisen|herd** m trouble spot. **~manage-ment** n crisis management. **~situati,on** f crisis (situation). **~sitzung** f crisis meeting. **~stab** m crisis management group. **~zeit** f time of crisis.
Kristall[1] [krɪs'tal] m (-[e]s; -e) crystal.
Kri'stall[2] n (-[e]s; no pl) 1. crystal (glass), cut glass. 2. crystal (goods).
kri'stallen adj crystalline, a. fig. crystal.
kristallinisch [krɪsta'li:nɪʃ] adj crystal-line. **Kristallisation** [krɪstaliza'tsi̯o:n] f (-; -en) crystallization. **kristallisieren** [krɪstali'zi:rən] v/i (h) crystallize.
kri'stallklar adj crystal-clear.
Kristallographie [krɪstalogra'fi:] f (-; no pl) crystallography.
Kriterium [kri'te:ri̯ʊm] n (-s; -rien) 1. criterion (*für* of). 2. sports: circuit race.
Kritik [kri'ti:k] f (-; -en) a) criticism (*an dat* of), b) review, c) the critics: ~ *hervorrufen* give rise to criticism; ~ *üben an* (dat) criticize; *e-e ~ schreiben über* (acc) a. review; *gute ~en haben* get (or have) good reviews, have a good press; F *unter aller ~ sein* be beneath contempt. **Kritiker** ['kri:tikər] m (-s; -), '**Kritikerin** f (-; -nen) a) critic, b) reviewer. **kri'tikfähigkeit** f critical faculties. **kri'tiklos** adj uncritical. **kritisch** ['kri:tɪʃ] adj a. phys., ⊙ critical (*gegenüber* of), fig. a. crucial. **kritisieren** [kriti'zi:rən] v/t, v/i (h) criticize.
kritteln ['krɪtəln] v/i (h) carp (*an dat* at).
Kritzelei [krɪtsə'laɪ] f (-; -en) scribble.
kritzeln ['krɪtsəln] v/t, v/i (h) scribble.
kroch [krɔx] pret of **kriechen**.
Krocket ['krɔkət] n (-s; no pl) croquet.
Krokant [kro'kant] m (-[e]s; no pl) brittle.
Krokette [kro'kɛtə] f (-; -n) croquette.
Kroko ['kro:ko] n (-[s]; -s) �璽 → **Krokodil-leder**. **Krokodil** [kroko'di:l] n (-s; -e) crocodile. **Kroko'dilleder** n crocodile

(skin or leather). **Kroko'dilstränen** pl F (~ *vergießen* shed) crocodile tears.
Krokus ['kro:kʊs] m (-; -[se]) ⍟ crocus.
Krone ['kro:nə] f (-; -n) 1. crown (*a. fig.*), coronet: *die ~ der Schöpfung* the pride of creation; F *das setzt allem die ~ auf!* that beats everything!; *e-n in der ~ haben* be tight. 2. ⊙ a) cap, top, b) crown, crest. 3. crown (*of tooth*). 4. (*Swedish coin*) krona, (*Danish or Norwegian coin*) krone. 5. chandelier.
krönen ['krø:nən] v/t (h) crown (*j-n zum König* s.o. king), fig. a. climax: *von Erfolg gekrönt* crowned with success.
'**Kronenkorken** m crown cork.
'**Kronju,welen** pl crown jewels.
'**Kronleuchter** m chandelier.
'**Kronprinz** m crown prince (*a. fig.*), Br. Prince of Wales. **Kronprin,zessin** f crown princess, Br. Princess Royal.
'**Krönung** f (-; -en) 1. coronation. 2. fig. crowning (event): *die ~ s-r Laufbahn* the climax of his career; *die ~ des Abends* the highlight (F high spot) of the evening.
'**Kronzeuge** m, '**Kronzeugin** f chief witness: ~ *werden* turn Queen's (King's, Am. State's) evidence.
Kropf [krɔpf] m (-[e]s; ⍨e) 1. zo. crop. 2. ⍩ goitre, Am. goiter.
kroß [krɔs] adj crisp.
Kröte ['krø:tə] f (-; -n) 1. zo. toad. 2. pl F dough, pennies.
Krücke ['krʏkə] f (-; -n) 1. crutch: *an ~n gehen* walk on crutches. 2. crook (*of walking stick etc*). 3. F contp. a) washout, b) *alte ~* rattletrap.
Krug [kru:k] m (-[e]s; ⍨e) 1. jug, pitcher. 2. → **Maßkrug**. 3. dial. pub, inn.
Krume ['kru:mə] f (-; -n) 1. ⍫ topsoil. 2. → **Krümel**. **Krümel** ['kry:məl] m (-s; -) crumb.
krümelig ['kry:məlɪç] adj crumbly.
krümeln ['kry:məln] v/t, v/i (h) crumble.
krumm [krʊm] **I** adj crooked (*a. F fig. dishonest*), hooked, a. bent: **~e Haltung** stoop; **~er Schnabel** curved beak; ~ *biegen* bend; *ganz ~ und schief* awry, lopsided; F *sich ~ und schief lachen* laugh one's head off; **~e Sache**, **~e Tour** crooked business; *ein ~es Ding drehen* pull a fast one; *et. auf die ~e Tour versuchen* try to wangle s.th. **II** adv ~ *gewachsen* crooked; *sich ~ halten*, ~ *gehen* stoop.

'**krummbeinig** [-bainiç] *adj* bow-legged.

krümmen ['krymən] (h) **I** *v/t* bend, crook. **II sich ~** bend, *road:* a. curve, *worm etc:* squirm: **sich ~ vor** (*dat*) writhe with *pain etc*, squirm with *embarrassment*; **sich vor Lachen ~ →** *krummlachen*.

Krümmer ['krymər] *m* (-s; -) **1.** *mot.* manifold. **2.** ⚙ bend, elbow.

'**krummlachen:** **sich ~** (*sep*, -ge-, h) F laugh one's head off. '**krummlegen:** **sich ~** (*sep*, -ge-, h) F pinch and scrape. '**krummnehmen** *v/t* (*irr*, *sep*, -ge-, h, → *nehmen*) F *et.* ~ take s.th. amiss.

Krümmung *f* (-; -en) bend, curve, turn, ⚼, 🔬, *phys.*, ⚙ curvature.

Kruppe ['krupə] *f* (-; -n) croup (*of horse*).

Krüppel ['krypəl] *m* (-s; -) (a. **zum ~ machen**) cripple: **zum ~ werden** be crippled. '**krüpp(e)lig** *adj* crippled.

Kruste ['krustə] *f* (-; -n) crust, *gastr. a.* crackling. '**Krustentier** *n* crustacean. **krustig** ['krustiç] *adj* crusty.

Kruzifix ['kru:tsifiks] *n* (-es; -e) crucifix. **Krypta** ['krypta] *f* (-; -ten) ⛪ crypt.

Kuba ['ku:ba] *n* (-s) Cuba. **Kubaner** [ku'ba:nər] *m* (-s; -), **Ku'banerin** *f* (-; -nen), **ku'banisch** *adj* Cuban.

Kübel ['ky:bəl] *m* (-s; -) a) bucket (a. ⚙), pail, b) tub: F **es gießt wie aus ~n** it's coming down in buckets.

Kubik|inhalt [ku'bi:k-] *m* cubic content. **~maß** *n* cubic measure. **~meter** *m, n* cubic metre (*Am.* meter). **~wurzel** *f* ⚼ cube root. **~zahl** *f* cube.

kubisch ['ku:biʃ] *adj* cubic(al).

Kubismus [ku'bismus] *m* (-; *no pl*) cubism. **Ku'bist** *m* (-en; -en) cubist. **ku'bistisch** *adj* cubist(ic).

Kubus ['ku:bus] *m* (-; Kuben) ⚼ cube.

Küche ['kyçə] *f* (-; -n) **1.** kitchen, kitchenette; → *Teufel*. **2.** a) cooking, cookery, cuisine, b) meals, food: **kalte** (**warme**) ~ cold (hot) meals; **die chinesische ~** Chinese cooking; → *gutbürgerlich*. **3.** F → *Küchenpersonal*.

Kuchen ['ku:xən] *m* (-s; -) cake.

'**Küchenbenutzung** *f* **mit ~** with use of kitchen.

'**Kuchenblech** *n* baking sheet (*or* tin).

'**Küchenchef** *m* chef (de cuisine).

'**Kücheneinrichtung** *f* kitchen furniture and fittings.

'**Kuchenform** *f* cake tin.

'**Kuchengabel** *f* pastry fork.

'**Küchen|gerät** *n* kitchen utensil (*or* appliance). **~geschirr** *n* kitchenware. **~herd** *m* kitchen range. **~hilfe** *f* kitchenmaid. **~kraut** *n* potherb. **~messer** *n* kitchen knife. **~perso,nal** *n* kitchen staff. **~schrank** *m* (kitchen) cupboard.

'**Kuchenteig** *m* cake mixture.

'**Kuchenteller** *m* dessert plate.

'**Küchen|tisch** *m* kitchen table. **~waage** *f* kitchen scales. **~wecker** *m* (kitchen) timer. **~zettel** *m* menu.

Kuckuck ['kukuk] *m* (-s; -e) **1.** cuckoo: F **wo** (**wer** *etc*) **zum ~!** where (who *etc*) the devil! **2.** *humor.* bailiff's seal.

'**Kuckucks|ei** *n* F *fig.* **ein ~** a cuckoo in the nest. **~uhr** *f* cuckoo clock.

Kufe ['ku:fə] *f* (-; -n) runner, 🎿 skid.

Küfer ['ky:fər] *m* (-s; -) cooper.

Kugel ['ku:gəl] *f* (-; -n) **1.** ball (a. ⚙), globe, *astr.*, ⚼ sphere: **die Erde ist e-e ~** the earth is a sphere. **2.** bullet; → **jagen 3.** *sports:* a) shot, b) bowl: **er stieß die ~ auf 22 m** he put the shot at 22 metres; F *fig.* **e-e ruhige ~ schieben** have a cushy job.

'**Kugelabschnitt** *m* ⚼ spherical segment.

'**Kugelfang** *m* butt.

'**kugelförmig** *adj* globular, spherical.

'**Kugelgelenk** *n* (ball-and-)socket joint.

'**Kugelhagel** *m* hail of bullets.

'**Kugelkopf(schreibma,schine** *f*) *m* golfball (typewriter).

'**Kugellager** *n* ⚙ ball bearing.

kugeln ['ku:gəln] (h) **I** *v/t, v/i* roll. **II sich ~** roll about (**im Schnee** in the snow).

'**kugel'rund** *adj* (as) round as a ball.

'**Kugelschreiber** *m* ballpoint (pen), *Br. a.* Biro (*TM*). **~mine** *f* refill.

'**kugelsicher** *adj* bulletproof.

'**Kugelstoßen** *n* shot put. '**Kugelstoßer** *m* (-s; -), '**Kugelstoßerin** *f* (-; -nen) shot-putter.

Kuh [ku:] *f* (-; ~e) cow: *fig.* **heilige ~** sacred cow; F *contp.* **dumme ~!** silly cow! **~fladen** *m* cowpat. **~glocke** *f* cowbell. **~handel** *m* F *fig.* horse trading. **~haut** *f* cowhide: F *fig.* **das geht auf k-e ~!** it's just incredible!

kühl [ky:l] *adj a. fig.* cool, chilly: **es wird ~** it's getting (I feel) chilly; (*j-m gegenüber*) **~ bleiben** remain cool (toward[s] s.o.); *et.* **~ lagern** store s.th.

cool; **j-n ~ empfangen** give s.o. a cool reception; → **Kopf** 2.
'**Kühl|anlage** f cooling plant (*mot.* system). **~appa,rat** m cooling apparatus. **~con,tainer** m (-s; -) cooltainer.
'**Kühle** f (-; *no pl*) coolness (*a. fig.*), cool.
'**kühlen** (h) **I** *v/t* cool (*a.* ⚙), chill **II** have a cooling effect.
'**Kühler** m (-s; -) **1.** ⚙ cooler. **2.** *mot.* radiator. **~block** m *mot.* radiator core. **~fi,gur** f *mot.* radiator mascot.
'**Kühl|haus** n cold-storage house. **~mittel** n coolant. **~raum** m cold-storage chamber, ♨ refrigerating hold. **~schiff** n refrigerator ship. **~schlange** f cooling coil. **~schrank** m refrigerator, F fridge. **~tasche** f cool box (*or* bag). **~truhe** f (chest) freezer, deep-freeze. **~turm** m cooling tower.
'**Kühlung** f (-; -en) **1.** ⚙ cooling. **2.** ⚙ cooling system. **3.** *no pl* coolness.
'**Kühlwagen** m 🚃 refrigerator wagon (*Am.* car), *mot.* refrigerator truck.
'**Kühlwasser** n cooling water.
'**Kuhmilch** f cow's milk.
kühn [ky:n] *adj a. fig.* bold, daring: **das übertrifft m-e ~sten Träume** that goes beyond my wildest dreams.
'**Kühnheit** f (-; *no pl*) boldness.
'**Kuhpocken** pl 🦠 cowpox.
'**Kuhstall** m cowshed.
Küken ['ky:kən] n (-s; -) *a. fig.* chick.
kulant [ku'lant] *adj* 🕊 accommodating, fair (*price etc*).
Kuli ['ku:li] m (-s; -s) coolie.
kulinarisch [kuli'naːrɪʃ] *adj* culinary.
Kulisse [ku'lɪsə] f (-; -n) *usu. pl thea. etc* scenery, set, wing, *a. fig.* background: **hinter den ~n** *a. fig.* behind the scenes, backstage.
kulminieren [kʊlmi'niːrən] *v/i* (h) *astr.* culminate (*fig.* **in** *dat* in).
Kult [kʊlt] m (-[e]s; -e) cult: **e-n ~ treiben** make a cult (**mit** out of). '**Kultfi,gur** f cult figure. '**Kulthandlung** f ritual act. '**kultisch** *adj* ritual, cultic.
kultivieren [kʊlti'viːrən] *v/t* (h) cultivate. **kulti'viert** *adj* cultured, cultivated, *a.* civilized (*person*), refined (*taste*).
Kultur [kʊl'tuːr] f (-; -en) **1.** *no pl* a) culture, *a.* refinement, b) civilization: **die abendländische ~** (the) Western civilization; **er hat (k-e) ~** he is (un)cultured; F **in ~ machen** be into culture. **2.**

no pl 🌱 cultivation. **3.** 🌱, 🧫 culture.
Kul'tur|abkommen n *pol.* cultural agreement. **~austausch** m cultural exchange. **~ba,nause** m F philistine. **~betrieb** m (-[e]s *no pl*) F cultural activities. **~beutel** m toilet bag. **~denkmal** n cultural monument.
kulturell [kʊltuˈrɛl] *adj* cultural.
Kul'tur|erbe n cultural heritage. **~film** m documentary. **~geschichte** f **1.** history of civilization (*a. book*). **2.** *no pl* a) cultural history *of France etc*, b) history of culture. **2geschichtlich** *adj* cultural-historical. **~gut** n cultural asset(s). **~landschaft** f **1.** land developed and cultivated by man. **2.** *fig.* cultural scene. **~leben** n cultural life.
kul'turlos *adj* uncultured, uncivilized.
Kul'tur|mensch m civilized man. **~pessi,mismus** m cultural pessimism. **~pflanze** f cultivated plant. **~poli,tik** f cultural and educational policy. **2po,litisch** *adj* politico-cultural. **~revoluti,on** f cultural revolution. **~schock** m cultural shock. **~sprache** f cultural (*or* civilized) language. **~stätte** f place of cultural interest. **~stufe** f stage (*or* level) of civilization. **~szene** f (-; *no pl*) cultural scene. **~volk** n civilized people (*or* nation, race).
Kultusmi,nister ['kʊltʊs-] m Minister of Culture, Education, and Church Affairs.
Kümmel ['kʏməl] m (-s; -) **1.** 🌿 caraway: **Echter ~** cumin. **2.** *gastr.* kümmel.
Kummer ['kʊmər] m (-s; *no pl*) a) grief, sorrow, b) trouble, worry, worries, problems: **~ haben** have problems; **j-m viel ~ machen** cause s.o. a lot of worry (*or* trouble); F **ich bin ~ gewöhnt!** I'm used to this sort of thing!
kümmerlich ['kʏmərlɪç] *adj* miserable, *a.* poor, meagre, *Am.* meager, sparse (*vegetation etc*): **sich ~ durchschlagen** (**mit Stundengeben** *etc*) eke out a bare existence (by giving lessons *etc*).
kümmern ['kʏmərn] (h) **I sich ~ um** a) look after, take care of, b) care about, c) pay attention to, d) see to: **ich muß mich um das Mittagessen ~** I must see to our lunch; **kümmere dich um d-e eigenen Angelegenheiten!** mind your own business!; **sich nicht ~ um** a) not to bother about, ignore, b) neglect. **II**

v/t **was kümmert mich ...** what do I care about ...; **was kümmert's mich?** that's not my problem!; **was kümmert dich das?** what concern is that of yours? **III** *v/i* develop poorly.

'**kummervoll** *adj* woebegone, sad.

Kumpan [kʊm'paːn] *m* (-s; -e) F a) companion, fellow, b) *b.s.* accomplice.

Kumpel ['kʊmpəl] *m* (-s; -) **1.** ⚒ pitman, miner. **2.** F mate, pal, chum, *Am.* buddy. '**kumpelhaft** *adj* chummy.

kündbar ['kʏntbaːr] *adj* terminable (*contract*), *capital* at call, redeemable (*loan*), *lease, position*, etc subject to notice: **er ist jederzeit ~** he can be given notice at any time.

Kunde ['kʊndə] *m* (-n; -n) customer, client: **fester ~** regular customer.

'**Kunden|beratung** *f* (customer) advisory service (*or* office). **~dienst** *m* a) service (to the customer), b) after-sales service, c) service department. **~fang** *m* (-[e]s; *no pl*) contp. (**auf ~ ausgehen**) touting. **~kar,tei** *f* list of customers. **~kreis** *m* customers, clientele. **~nummer** *f* client code. **~stamm** *m* regular customers (*or* clientele). **~werbung** *f* canvassing (of customers).

Kundgebung ['kʊntgeːbʊŋ] *f* (-; -en) *pol.* meeting, rally.

kundig ['kʊndɪç] *adj* experienced, expert, *a.* practised (*eye, hand*).

kündigen ['kʏndɪgən] (h) **I** *v/t* terminate (*contract* etc), cancel (*subscription* etc), call in (*capital*): **s-e Stellung ~** quit one's job; **die Wohnung ~** give notice of one's intention to leave, **j-m** give s.o. notice to quit; F **j-n ~** dismiss s.o., sack s.o. **II** *v/i* **j-m** (**zum 1. Mai**) ~ give s.o. notice (*landlord*: to quit) (for May 1st), dismiss s.o. (as of May 1st); (**j-m**) **drei Monate im voraus ~** give (s.o.) three months' notice; **bei e-r Firma ~** hand in one's notice to a firm; **mir ist** (**zum 1. Mai**) **gekündigt worden** I'm under notice to leave (on May 1st).

'**Kündigung** *f* (-; -en) a) notice, notice of withdrawal (*of loan etc*), termination (*of contract*), cancel(l)ation (*of subscription etc*), b) dismissal: **~** (**e-r Wohnung**) by landlord: notice to quit, by tenant: notice of one's intention to leave; **vierteljährliche ~ vereinbaren** agree on three months' notice.

'**Kündigungs|frist** *f* period of notice: **mit halbjähriger ~** at six months' notice. **~grund** *m* grounds for giving notice (*or* for dismissal). **~schreiben** *n* a) (written) notice, b) letter of dismissal. **~schutz** *m* protection against unlawful dismissal (*or* unwarrranted eviction).

Kundin ['kʊndɪn] *f* (-; -nen) (female) customer (*etc*); → **Kunde.**

Kundschaft ['kʊntʃaft] *f* (-; *no pl*) a) customers, clientele, b) F customer, c) patronage.

'**Kundschafter** *m* (-s; -) scout, spy.

künftig ['kʏnftɪç] **I** *adj* future, coming: **~e Generationen** *a.* generations to come. **II** *adv* in future, from now on.

Kunst [kʊnst] *f* (-; ːe) **1.** art: **die schönen Künste** the fine arts; **die bildende ~** graphic art; **die darstellenden Künste** a) the performing arts, b) the pictorial arts; **die ~ der Gegenwart** contemporary art; F **was macht die ~?** how are things?; → **schön** 1. **2.** a) skill, art, b) trick: **die ~ des Schreibens** the art of writing; **ärztliche ~** medical skill; F **das ist k-e ~!** that's easy!; **das ist e-e brotlose ~** there's no money in it; **die ganze ~ besteht darin zu** inf the whole trick is to inf; **sie ließ alle ihre Künste spielen** she used all her wiles.

'**Kunst|akade,mie** *f* academy of arts. **~auge** *n* artificial eye. **~ausstellung** *f* art exhibition. **~band** *m* (-[e]s; ːe) art book. **~betrieb** *m* (-[e]s; *no pl*) contp. cultural activities. **~denkmal** *n* monument of art. **~druck** *m* (-[e]s; -e) **1.** *no pl* art printing. **2.** art print. **~dünger** *m* artificial fertilizer. **~eisbahn** *f* artificial ice rink. **~erzieher(in** *f*) *m* art teacher. **~erziehung** *f* art (education). **~faser** *f* synthetic fibre (*Am.* fiber). **~fehler** *m* ⚕ professional blunder.

'**kunstfertig** *adj* skil(l)ful, skilled.

'**Kunst|flieger** *m* stunt flyer. **~flug** *m* aerobatics, stunt flying. **~flug...** aerobatic (*figure, team*, etc). **~freund(in** *f*) *m* art lover. **~gale,rie** *f* art gallery. **~gegenstand** *m* objet d'art.

'**kunstgerecht** *adj* skil(l)ful, expert.

'**Kunst|geschichte** *f* (*no pl*) art history. **~gewerbe** *n* (-s; *no pl*) arts and crafts, applied art(s). **~glied** *n* artificial limb. **~griff** *m* trick. **~handel** *m* art trade. **~händler** *m* art dealer. **~hand-**

lung f art dealer('s shop). **~handwerk** n → **Kunstgewerbe**. **~handwerker(in** f) m artisan. **~herz** n 🐝 artificial heart. **~hi,storiker** m art historian. **~hochschule** f art college. **~honig** m artificial honey. **~kritiker** m art critic. **~leder** n imitation leather.

Künstler ['kʏnstlər] m (-s; -), '**Künstlerin** f (-; -nen) artist, ♪, thea. performer, (circus etc) artiste. '**künstlerisch** adj artistic: **~er Leiter** art director; **ein ~ wertvoller Film** a film of artistic merit; **~ begabt sein** have an artistic talent. '**Künstlername** m thea. etc stage name. '**Künstlertum** n (-s; no pl) artistry, coll. the artistic world. '**Künstlerviertel** n artists' quarter.

künstlich ['kʏnstlɪç] adj artificial (a. fig.), a. false (teeth etc), man-made, synthetic (fibres): **~e Niere** kidney machine; **~ ernähren** feed s.o. artificially. '**Kunstlicht** n phot. artificial light. '**Kunstliebhaber(in** f) m art lover. '**kunstlos** adj simple, plain. '**Kunst|maler(in** f) m artist, painter. **~pause** f iro. **e-e ~ machen** pause for effect. **~reiter(in** f) m trick rider. **~sammler(in** f) m art collector. **~sammlung** f art collection. **~schätze** pl art treasures. **~schule** f art school. **~schwimmen** n water ballet. **~seide** f artificial silk, rayon. 2**seiden** adj (of) rayon. **~sprache** f artificial language. **~springen** n (fancy) diving. **~springer(in** f) m (fancy) diver.

'**Kunststoff** m synthetic material, plastic (material): **~e** plastics; **aus ~** (of) plastic. 2**beschichtet** adj plastic-laminated. **~indu,strie** f plastics industry. **~rasen** m artificial lawn. '**Kunst|stopfen** n (-s) invisible mending. **~stück** n a) trick, b) stunt, fig. a. (great) feat: iro. **~!** small wonder!, big deal!; **das ist doch kein ~!** anyone can do that! **~stu,dent(in** f) m art student. **~tischler** m cabinetmaker. **~turnen** n gymnastics. **~turner(in** f) m gymnast. 2**verständig** adj 1. artistic. 2. expert. **~verständnis** n appreciation (or expert knowledge) of art. '**kunstvoll** adj a) (highly) artistic, b) elaborate, c) ingenious. '**Kunst|werk** n work of art. **~wort** n coinage. **~zeitschrift** f art magazine.

kunterbunt ['kʊntər-] adv **~ durcheinander** higgledy-piggledy, in a jumble.

Kupfer ['kʊpfər] n (-s; no pl) copper. '**Kupferblech** n sheet copper. '**Kupferdraht** m copper wire. '**kupferhaltig** adj containing copper. **kupfern** ['kʊpfərn] adj (of) copper. '**Kupferstecher** m (-s; -) copperplate engraver. '**Kupferstich** m (-[e]s; -e) copperplate (engraving).

kupieren [ku'piːrən] v/t (h) dock.

Kupon [ku'põː] m (-s; -s) coupon.

Kuppe ['kʊpə] f (-; -n) **1.** (hill)top. **2.** (finger)tip.

Kuppel ['kʊpəl] f (-; -n) dome. '**kuppelförmig** adj dome-shaped.

Kuppelei [kʊpə'laɪ] f (-; -en) ⚖ procuration. **kuppeln** ['kʊpəln] **I** v/t **1.** ⚙ (an acc) couple (with), connect (to). **II** v/i **2.** mot. a) (let in the) clutch, b) declutch. **3.** matchmake. '**Kuppler** m (-s; -), '**Kupplerin** f (-; -nen) a) ⚖ procurer (procuress), b) matchmaker.

'**Kupplung** f (-; -en) **1.** 🚂 coupling. **2.** mot. clutch: **die ~ treten (loslassen)** → **kuppeln** 2. '**Kupplungs|belag** m mot. clutch facing. **~pe,dal** n clutch pedal. **~scheibe** f clutch disc. **~stecker** m ⚡ coupler plug.

Kur [kuːr] f (-; -en) cure, (course of) treatment: **e-e ~ machen** take a cure (or a course of treatment); **zur ~ fahren** go to a health resort (or spa).

Kür [kyːr] f (-; -en) a) gym. free (or voluntary) exercise(s), b) free skating (etc).

Kurator [ku'raːtɔr] m (-s; -en [kura-'toːrən]) trustee. **Kuratorium** [kura-'toːriʊm] n (-s; -rien) board of trustees.

'**Kuraufenthalt** m stay at a health resort.

Kurbel ['kʊrbəl] f (-; -n) crank, handle. **kurbeln** ['kʊrbəln] **I** v/i crank, F mot. turn the steering wheel. **II** v/t et. in die Höhe ~ wind s.th. up. '**Kurbelwelle** f mot. crankshaft.

Kürbis ['kʏrbɪs] m (-ses; -se) **1.** 🌱 pumpkin. **2.** F nut.

Kurde ['kʊrdə] m (-n; -n), '**Kurdin** f (-; -nen), '**kurdisch** adj Kurd.

Kurfürst(in f) m elector (electress). '**Kurgast** m visitor (to a health resort). '**Kurhaus** n kurhaus, casino. '**Kurho,tel** n health-resort hotel. **Kurie** ['kuːriə] f (-; -n) eccl. Curia. **Kurier** [ku'riːr] m (-s; -e) courier. **kurieren** [ku'riːrən] v/t (h) cure (**von** of).

Ku'riergepäck *n* diplomatic bag.

kurios [ku'rĭo:s] *adj* curious, odd. **Kuriosität** [kurĭozi'tɛ:t] *f* (-; -en) **1.** curiosity. **2.** curio. **Kuriosum** [ku'rĭo:zʊm] *n* (-s; -sa) odd thing, odd fact.

'Kurort *m* spa, health resort.

'Kurpfuscher(in *f*) *m* quack. **Kurpfusche'rei** *f* (-; *no pl*) quackery.

Kurs [kʊrs] *m* (-es; -e) **1.** ✝ a) rate (of exchange), exchange rate, b) price, quotation: *zum ~ von* at a rate of; *außer ~ setzen* withdraw from circulation; *die ~e geben nach (ziehen an)* prices are softening (hardening); *hoch im ~ stehen* a) be high, b) *fig.* be popular (*bei* with). **2.** ✓, ⚓ course, *fig. a.* line: *~ nehmen auf (acc)* set course for, *a. fig.* head for; *e-n falschen ~ einschlagen* take the wrong course (*fig.* a wrong line); *pol. harter (weicher) ~* hard (soft) line; → *abweichen*. **3.** class, course: *e-n ~ für Englisch besuchen* attend a course in English.

'Kursänderung *f* **1.** ✓, ⚓ change of course (*a. fig.*). **2.** ✝ change in the exchange rate. **'Kursanstieg** *m* ✝ rise (in rates *or* prices). **'Kursbericht** *m* ✝ (stock) market report. **'Kursbuch** *n* (railway, *Am.* railroad) timetable.

Kürschner ['kʏrʃnər] *m* (-s; -) furrier. **Kürschnerei** [kʏrʃna'raɪ] *f* (-; -en) **1.** *no pl* furrier's trade. **2.** furrier's shop.

'Kurseinbruch *m* ✝ fall in prices, slump.

'Kursgewinn *m* ✝ a) (price) gains, b) exchange profits.

kursieren [kʊr'zi:rən] *v/i* (h) circulate, *fig. rumo(u)r etc: a.* go round.

'Kursindex *m* ✝ share price index.

kursiv [kʊr'zi:f] *adj* italic: *et. ~ drucken* print s.th. in italics.

'Kurskorrek,tur *f* course correction: *e-e ~ vornehmen* correct the course.

'Kursleiter *m* instructor, teacher.

'Kursno,tierung *f* ✝ quotation.

'Kursrückgang *m* ✝ decline in prices.

'Kursschwankung *f* a) exchange rate fluctuation, b) price fluctuation.

Kursus ['kʊrzʊs] *m* (-; Kurse) → *Kurs* 3.

'Kursverlust *m* ✝ a) exchange loss, b) (stock price) loss.

'Kurswechsel *m pol.* change of policy.

'Kurswert *m* ✝ market value.

'Kurszettel *m* ✝ price list, stock list.

'Kurtaxe *f* health resort tax.

'Kürübung *f sports*: free exercise.

Kurve ['kʊrvə] *f* (-; -n) curve, Å *a.* graph, *a.* bend, turn (*of road etc*), *pl* F curves (*of woman*): *die Straße macht e-e ~* the road bends; *unübersichtliche ~* blind bend; *mot. die ~ schneiden* cut the curve; *e-e ~ fliegen* bank; F *fig. die ~ kratzen* beat it, push off; *der kriegt die ~ nie!* he'll never make it!

kurven ['kʊrvən] *v/i* (sn) curve, ✓ bank.

'Kurven|bild *n* diagram, graph. **~festigkeit** *f*, **~lage** *f mot.* cornering stability. **~line,al** *n* (French) curve. **~reich** *adj* **1.** *road:* full of bends, winding. **2.** F *fig.* curvaceous. **~technik** *f mot.* cornering technique. **~vorgabe** *f sports:* stagger.

kurz [kʊrts] **I** *adj* **1.** short (*a. fig.*), brief: *kürzer werden (machen)* get (make) shorter, shorten; *5 m zu ~ sein* be five metres short; *den kürzeren ziehen* come off worst, lose out; F *et. ~ und klein schlagen* smash s.th. to bits; *~es Gedächtnis* short memory; *mit ein paar ~en Worten* in a few words, briefly; *in kürzester Zeit* in no time; *binnen ~em* shortly; *seit ~em* for some little time (now); *bis vor ~em* until quite recently; F *mach's ~!* be brief! **2.** short, curt (*gegen j-n* with s.o.). **II** *adv* **3.** short: *~ vor ...* just before ... ; *~ hinter dem Bahnhof* just after the station; *zu ~ werfen* throw (too) short; *er wird ~ Tom genannt* he is called Tom for short; *zu ~ kommen* get a bad deal, *matter:* be neglected. **4.** a) briefly, b) for a while, c) for a moment; *~ vor ...*, *~ zuvor* shortly before (...); *~ nach ...*, *~ darauf* shortly after (...); *über ~ oder lang* sooner or later; *j-n ~ abweisen* be short with s.o.; *sich ~ ausruhen* take a short rest; *~ entschlossen* without the slightest hesitation; *~ (gesagt), um es ~ zu machen* to cut a long story short; *~ und gut* in short; *fasse dich ~!* please be brief!; *~ und bündig* brief(ly), concise(ly); *~ angebunden* short, curt (*gegen* with).

'Kurzarbeit *f* short time, short-time working. **'kurzarbeiten** *v/i* (sep, -ge-, h) be on (*or* work) short time. **'Kurzarbeiter(in** *f*) *m* short-time worker.

'kurzärm(e)lig [-ɛrm(ə)lɪç] *adj* short-sleeved.

'**kurzatmig** [-a:tmɪç] *adj* short-winded.
'**kurzbeinig** [-baɪnɪç] *adj* short-legged.
'**Kurzbericht** *m* brief report, summary.
'**Kurzbiogra,phie** *f* profile.
'**Kürze** ['kʏrtsə] *f* (-; *no pl*) shortness (*a. fig.*), *a.* briefness, brevity, *fig.* conciseness: **in** ~ shortly, before long; **in aller** ~ very briefly. **Kürzel** ['kʏrtsəl] *n* (-s; -) shorthand symbol. '**kürzen** *v/t* (h) shorten (**um** by), *a.* abridge (*book etc*), cut (*wages etc*), ♣ reduce (*fraction*): **drastisch** ~ F slash; *j-s Lohn um 50 Mark* ~ dock 50 marks off s.o.'s wages.
'**kurzerhand** *adv* without further ado: ~ **ablehnen** refuse flatly.
'**kürzertreten** *v/i* (*irr, sep,* -ge-, h, → **treten**) F a) tighten one's belt, b) take things easy, go slow.
'**Kurzfassung** *f* abridged version.
'**Kurzfilm** *m* short (film).
'**Kurzform** *f* short(ened) form.
'**kurzfristig** [-frɪstɪç] **I** *adj* **1.** ♣ short--term. **2.** *fig.* a) short-range (*plans etc*), b) sudden, c) immediate. **II** *adv* **3.** a) at short notice, b) for a short period.
'**Kurzgeschichte** *f* short story.
'**kurzgeschnitten** *adj* cropped.
'**Kurzhaar...** *esp. zo.*, '**kurzhaarig** *adj* short-haired.
'**kurzhalten** *v/t* (*irr, sep,* -ge-, h, → **halten**) F *j-n* ~ keep s.o. very short (**mit Geld** of money).
'**kurzlebig** [-le:bɪç] *adj* short-lived.
'**Kurzlehrgang** *m* short (*or* crash) course.
'**kürzlich** ['kʏrtslɪç] *adv* recently, not long ago: (**erst**) ~ (just) the other day.
'**Kurzmeldung** *f* news flash.
'**Kurznachrichten** *pl* news bulletin.
'**kurzschließen** *v/t* (*irr, sep,* -ge-, h, → **schließen**) ⚡ short(-circuit).
'**Kurzschluß** *m* **1.** ⚡ short circuit: **e-n** ~ **verursachen in** (*dat*) short-circuit. **2.** → ~**handlung** *f* panic action: **e-e** ~ **begehen** a) do s.th. rash, b) panic.
'**Kurzschrift** *f* (**in** ~ in) shorthand.
'**kurzsichtig** *adj* shortsighted (*a. fig.*), nearsighted. '**Kurzsichtige** *m,f* (-n; -n) shortsighted (*or* nearsighted) person. '**Kurzsichtigkeit** *f* (-; *no pl*) shortsightedness (*a. fig.*), nearsightedness.
'**Kurzstrecke** *f* short distance.
'**Kurzstrecken...** short-distance, short-

-range. ~**läufer(in** *f*) *m* sprinter. ~**ra,kete** *f* short-range missile.
'**kurztreten** → **kürzertreten.**
kurz'um *adv* in short.
'**Kürzung** *f* (-; -en) shortening, *a.* abridg(e)ment (*of book etc*), cut (*gen in expenses etc*), ♣ reduction (*of fraction*).
'**Kurzurlaub** *m* short holiday.
'**Kurzwaren** *pl* haberdashery, *Am.* dry goods, notions.
'**Kurzwelle** *f* **1.** *radio*: short wave. **2.** ♣ radiothermy.
'**Kurzwellen...** short-wave (*transmitter, range, etc*). ~**thera,pie** *f* radiothermy.
'**kurzwellig** *adj* short-wave.
'**Kurzwort** *n* (-[e]s; ⁻er) contraction.
'**Kurzzeitgedächtnis** *n* short-term memory. '**kurzzeitig** *adj* brief, short.
kuschelig ['kʊʃəlɪç] *adj* F a) (soft and) cuddly, b) cosy.
kuscheln ['kʊʃəln] **sich** ~ (h) snuggle (**an** *acc* up to *s.o.*, **in** *acc* down in *bed etc*).
'**Kuscheltier** *n* cuddly toy.
kuschen ['kʊʃən] *v/i* (h) **1.** *dog*: lie down. **2.** F (**vor** *j-m*) ~ knuckle under (to *s.o.*).
Kusine [ku'zi:nə] *f* (-; -n) (female) cousin.
Kuß [kʊs] *m* (Kusses; Küsse) kiss: **flüchtiger** ~ peck; **sich mit e-m** ~ **(von** *j-m*) **verabschieden** kiss s.o. goodbye.
'**kußecht** *adj* kissproof.
küssen ['kʏsən] *v/t, v/i* (h) kiss: **sie küßten sich (zum Abschied)** they kissed (goodbye); *j-m die Hand* ~ kiss s.o.'s hand.
'**Kußhand** *f j-m e-e* ~ *zuwerfen* blow s.o. a kiss; F *fig.* **mit** ~ gladly.
'**Küste** ['kʏstə] *f* (-; -n) coast, shore: **an der** ~ **leben** live at the seaside.
'**Küsten|bewohner(in** *f*) *m* coastal inhabitant. ~**fischerei** *f* inshore fishing. ~**gebiet** *n* coastal area. ~**gewässer** *pl* coastal waters. ~**linie** *f* coast line. ~**schiffahrt** *f* coastal shipping. ~**schutz** *m* shore protection. ~**straße** *f* coast(al) road. ~**streifen** *m*, ~**strich** *m* coastal strip. ~**wache** *f* coast guard (station).
Küster ['kʏstər] *m* (-s; -) *eccl.* sexton.
Kutsche ['kʊtʃə] *f* (-; -n) carriage, coach; *humor.* **alte** ~ (old) rattletrap.
'**Kutscher** *m* (-s; -) coachman, driver.
Kutte ['kʊtə] *f* (-; -n) cowl.

Kutter ['kʊtər] *m* (-s; -) ♣ cutter.
Kuwait [ku'vaɪt] *n* (-s) Kuwait. **Ku'waiter** *m* (-s; -), **Ku'waiterin** *f* (-; -nen), **ku'waitisch** *adj* Kuwaiti.
Kybernetik [kybɛr'neːtɪk] *f* (-; *no pl*) cybernetics.

Kyber'netiker *m* (-s; -) cyberneticist.
kyber'netisch *adj* cybernetic.
kyrillisch [ky'rɪlɪʃ] *adj* Cyrillic.
KZ [kaː'tsɛt] *n* (-[s]; -[s]) concentration camp. **K'Z-Häftling** *m* concentration camp prisoner.

L

L, l [ɛl] *n* (-; -) L, l.
labberig ['labərɪç] *adj* F *a. fig.* **1.** a) sloppy, b) insipid, c) stale. **2.** limp.
Labial [la'biːal] *m* (-s; -e) labial (sound).
labil [la'biːl] *adj* unstable, labile.
Labilität [labili'tɛːt] *f* (-; *no pl*) instability, lability.
Labor [la'boːr] *n* (-s; -s, -e) F lab: *im ~ untersuchen* lab-examine.
Laborant [labo'rant] *m* (-en; -en), **Labo'rantin** *f* (-; -nen) laboratory assistant. **Laboratorium** [labora'toːriʊm] *n* (-s; -rien) laboratory.
La'borbefund *m* test result(s).
laborieren [labo'riːrən] *v/i* (h) F ♬ suffer (*an dat* from).
La'bortechniker(in *f*) *m* laboratory technician.
Labyrinth [laby'rɪnt] *n* (-[e]s; -e) *a. fig.* labyrinth, maze.
'Lachanfall *m* laughing fit.
Lache¹ ['laxə] *f* (-; -n) pool, puddle.
'Lache² *f* (-; -n) F laugh.
lächeln ['lɛçəln] *v/i* (h) (*über acc* at) smile, grin: *sie lächelte freundlich* she gave a friendly smile; *immer nur ~!* keep smiling! **'Lächeln** *n* (-s) smile.
lachen ['laxən] *v/i* (h) laugh (*über acc* at): *er lachte schallend* he roared with laughter; *sie lachte verlegen* she gave an embarrassed laugh; F *daß ich nicht lache!* don't make me laugh!; *sie hat nichts zu ~* her life is no bed of roses; *du hast gut ~!* you can laugh!; *da kann ich nur ~!* excuse me while I laugh!; *es wäre ja gelacht, wenn ...* it would be ridiculous if ...; *wer zuletzt lacht, lacht am besten* he who laughs last laughs loudest; → *Fäustchen.*

'Lachen *n* (-s) laughing, laugh(ter): *j-n zum ~ bringen* make s.o. laugh; *sich vor ~ biegen* nearly die laughing; *~ ist gesund* laughter is the best medicine; F *das ist nicht zum ~* that's no joke; → *zumute.*
'lachend *adj* laughing: *~e Erben* joyful heirs; *der ~e Dritte* the real winner.
'Lacher *m* (-s; -) **1.** laugher: *er hatte die ~ auf s-r Seite* he had the laugh on his side. **2.** F laugh.
'Lacherfolg *m* *e-n ~ ernten* (*or haben*) raise a laugh.
lächerlich ['lɛçərlɪç] *adj* **1.** ridiculous, absurd, funny: *~ machen* make fun of, ridicule; *sich ~ machen* make a fool of o.s.; *das ♀e daran* the ridiculous thing about it; *et. ins ♀e ziehen* turn s.th. into a joke; *sich ~ vorkommen* feel ridiculous. **2.** *fig.* trifling, petty: *für e-e ~e Summe* for a ridiculously low sum.
'Lächerlichkeit *f* (-; -en) **1.** *no pl* ridiculousness. **2.** *usu. pl* trifles.
'Lachfältchen *pl* laughter lines.
'Lachgas *n* ♬ laughing gas.
'lachhaft *adj* laughable, ridiculous.
Lachs [laks] *m* (-es; -e) salmon.
'Lachsalve *f* burst of laughter.
'Lachsfang *m* salmon fishing.
'lachs|farben, ~rosa *adj* salmon-pink.
'Lachsschinken *m* smoked, rolled fillet of ham.
Lack [lak] *m* (-[e]s; -e) a) varnish, b) lacquer, c) enamel, d) *mot.* paint(work): F *fig. der ~ ist ab!* all the glamo(u)r is gone! *~farbe f* varnish (paint).
lackieren [la'kiːrən] *v/t* (h) **1.** varnish, lacquer, enamel, *mot.* paint: *sich die Fingernä-*

gel ~ paint one's nails. **2.** F *fig.* dupe: *er war der Lackierte* he was the dupe.

Lac'kierer m (-s; -) ⊙ varnisher, painter.

Lac'kierung f (-; -en) → *Lack.*

'Lackleder n patent leather.

'Lackmuspa,pier ['lakmʊs-] n 🌿 litmus paper.

'Lackschaden m *mot.* damage to the paintwork.

'Lackschuhe pl patent-leather shoes.

'Lackstift m *mot.* touch-up applicator.

'Lade|baum m ⚓ beam. **~fläche** f loading area. **~gerät** n ⚡ battery charger. **~hemmung** f ✕ (a. ~ **haben**) jam. **~klappe** f *mot.* tailboard. **~kon,trolleuchte** f *mot.* charge control lamp.

laden¹ ['la:dən] v/t (lud, geladen, h) **1.** load. **2.** ⚡, *phys.* charge. **3.** *fig. et.* **auf sich ~** burden (*or* saddle) o.s. with.

laden² v/t (lud, geladen, h) **1.** invite, cite. ⚖ summon, cite.

'Laden m (-s; -ⁿ) **1.** shop, *Am.* store: → *dichtmachen* II. **2.** F *fig.* shop, outfit: → *schmeißen* 3. **3.** shutter.

'Laden|dieb(in f) m shoplifter. **~diebstahl** m shoplifting. **~hüter** m shelf warmer, drug in (*Am.* on) the market. **~inhaber** m shopkeeper, *Am.* storekeeper. **~kasse** f till. **~kette** f chain (of shops). **~mädchen** n F shopgirl. **~preis** m retail price. **~schild** n shop sign. **~schluß** m closing time. **~straße** f shopping street. **~tisch** m (*fig. unter dem* ~ under the) counter.

'Laderampe f loading ramp.

'Laderaum m loading space, (ship's) hold, ✈ cargo bay.

lädieren [lɛ'di:rən] v/t (h) a) damage, b) injure, c) *a. fig.* batter, *fig.* dent.

'Ladung¹ f (-; -en) **1.** ✈ load, freight, ✈, ⚓ cargo, b) shipment: F **e-e** ~ *Sand* a load of sand. **2.** ⚡, ✕, *phys.* charge.

'Ladung² f (-; -en) ⚖ summons.

lag [la:k] *pret of liegen.*

Lage ['la:gə] f (-; -n) **1.** a) *a. fig.* position, situation, b) site, location: *in zentraler* ~ centrally situated; *die politische* ~ the political situation; *die rechtliche* ~ the legal position; *unangenehme* ~ predicament; *nach* ~ *der Dinge* as matters stand; *in der* ~ *sein, et. zu tun* be in a position to do s.th.; → *Herr, peilen* 1, *versetzen* 5, 9. **2.** layer, *geol. a.* stratum, ✕ bed, ⊙ ply. **3.** ♪ register. **4.** F

e-e ~ *Bier ausgeben* buy a round of beer.

'Lagenstaffel f swimming: medley relay.

'Lageplan m site plan.

Lager ['la:gər] n (-s; -, ✕ *a.* ⁿ) **1.** bed, *hunt.* lair. **2.** *a. fig.* camp: *ein* ~ *aufschlagen* pitch camp; *ins gegnerische* ~ *überwechseln* change sides. **3.** ✈ a) stock, store(s), b) storehouse, warehouse: *et. auf* ~ *haben* have s.th. in store (*or* stock, F *fig. a.* up one's sleeve). **4.** ✕ bed, deposit. **5.** ⊙ a) support, b) bearing.

'Lagerarbeiter m warehouseman.

'Lagerbier n lager.

'lagerfähig *adj* storable.

'Lagerfähigkeit f (-; *no pl*) shelf life.

'Lagerfeuer n campfire.

'Lagergebühr f storage (fee).

'Lagerhaltung f (-; *no pl*) storekeeping.

'Lagerhaus n warehouse.

Lagerist [la:gə'rɪst] m (-en; -en), **Lage'ristin** f (-; -nen) storekeeper.

'Lagerleben n camp life.

'Lagerleiter(in f) m camp leader.

lagern ['la:gərn] (h) **I** v/i **1.** rest, lie down (*both a. sich* ~), ✕ camp. **2.** ✈ be stored. **3.** mature. **II** v/t **4.** ✈ store, keep. **5.** lay, rest: ✚ *das Bein hoch* ~ put the leg up; → *gelagert.* **6.** ⊙ rest.

'Lager|raum m storeroom. **~stätte** f **1.** bed, *hunt.* lair. **2.** ✕, *geol.* deposit.

'Lagerung f (-; *no pl*) **1.** storage, warehousing. **2.** seasoning. **3.** ⊙ bearing application.

'Lagerverwalter(in f) m storekeeper.

'Lageskizze f sketch map.

Lagune [la'gu:nə] f (-; -n) lagoon.

lahm [la:m] *adj* **1.** lame. **2.** F stiff, tired, limp. **3.** F *fig.* lame (*excuse etc*), tame, dull (*film etc*): → *Ente* 1. **'Lahmarsch** m V drip. **'lahmarschig** *adj* V slow, lame, listless. **'lahmen** v/i ✚ limp.

lähmen ['lɛ:mən] v/t (h) paralyze: *wie gelähmt vor ...* paralyzed with *fear etc.*

'Lahmheit f (-; *no pl*) lameness, F *fig. a.* dullness, slowness.

'lahmlegen v/t (*sep,* -ge-, h) paralyze, *a.* bring *traffic etc* to a standstill, knock out (*machine etc*).

'Lähmung f (-; -en) **1.** ✚ paralysis. **2.** *fig.* paralyzing.

Laib [laɪp] m (-[e]s; -e) loaf.

Laich [laɪç] m (-[e]s; -e) spawn.

laichen ['laiçən] *v/i* (h) spawn.
Laie ['laiə] *m* (-n; -n) layman: *da bin ich absoluter ~* I don't know the first thing about it. **'Laien...** 1. lay (*priest etc*). 2. amateur (*actor etc*).
'laienhaft *adj* amateurish.
Lakai [la'kai] *m* (-en; -en) *a. fig. contp.* lackey.
Lake ['la:kə] *f* (-; -n) *gastr.* brine.
Laken ['la:kən] *n* (-s; -) sheet.
lakonisch [la'ko:niʃ] *adj* laconic.
Lakritze [la'krıtsə] *f* (-; -n) liquorice.
lallen ['lalən] *v/t, v/i* (h) speak thickly.
Lama¹ ['la:ma] *m* (-[s]; -s) *eccl.* Lama.
'Lama² *n* (-s; -s) *zo.* llama.
Lamelle [la'mɛlə] *f* (-; -n) 1. ♀, ⚙ lamella. 2. *mot.* a) rib, b) disc.
lamentieren [lamɛn'ti:rən] *v/i* (h) F (*über acc* about) complain, moan.
Lametta [la'mɛta] *n* (-s; *no pl*) tinsel.
Lamm [lam] *n* (-[e]s; ⁀er) lamb.
'Lammbraten *m* roast lamb.
Lämmchen ['lɛmçən] *n* (-s; -) lambkin.
lammen ['lamən] *v/i* (h) lamb.
'Lamm|fell *n* lambskin. **~fleisch** *n* lamb. **~keule** *f gastr.* leg of lamb.
Lampe ['lampə] *f* (-; -n) 1. lamp, light. 2. bulb.
'Lampenfieber *n* stagefright.
'Lampenschirm *m* lampshade.
Lampion [lam'pĩɔŋ] *m* (-s; -s) Chinese lantern.
lancieren [lã'si:rən] *v/t* (h) *fig.* launch.
Land [lant] *n* (-es; ⁀er) 1. land: *zu ~e* by land; *ans ~* ashore; F *e-n Job an ~ ziehen* land a job; *wieder ~ sehen* see daylight again. 2. a) country, b) soil, c) land: *auf dem ~e* in the country; *aufs ~* (in)to the country. 3. *pol.* a) country, b) territory, c) *FRG:* (Federal) Land, d) *Austria:* Province: *außer ~es gehen* go abroad; *aus aller Herren Länder* from all four corners of the earth.
'Landarbeiter(in *f*) *m* farm hand.
'Landarzt *m* country doctor.
'Landbesitz *m* landed property.
'Landbevölkerung *f* rural population.
'Lande|anflug *m* ✈ landing approach. **~bahn** *f* runway. **~brücke** *f* ⚓ landing stage. **~deck** *n* ⚓ flight deck. **~erlaubnis** *f* landing clearance, permission to land. **~fähre** *f* landing module.
land'einwärts *adv* (further) inland.
'Landeklappe *f* ✈ landing flap.

landen ['landən] *v/i* (sn), *v/t* (h) land (*a. fig. blow, success, etc*), ⚓ *a.* disembark, F *fig. a.* end up (*in dat* in): *weich ~* make a soft landing; *sports: auf dem 4. Platz ~* come in fourth; F *damit kannst du bei ihr nicht ~* with that you won't get anywhere with her.
'Landenge *f geogr.* isthmus.
'Lande|piste *f* landing strip. **~platz** *m* 1. ✈ airstrip. 2. ⚓ quay, wharf.
Ländereien [lɛndə'raiən] *pl* lands, estates.
'Länderkampf *m sports*: 1. international competition. 2. → **'Länderspiel** *n* international match.
'Landes... a) national, b) regional, *FRG:* (of the) Land, *in Austria:* Provincial. **~farben** *pl* national colo(u)rs. **~innere** *n* interior. **~meister(in** *f*) *m sports:* national champion. **~sprache** *f* national language. **~tracht** *f* national costume. **~verrat** *m* treason. **~verteidigung** *f* national defen/ce (*Am.* -se). **~währung** *f* national currency.
'landesweit *adj and adv* nationwide.
'Landeverbot *n* ✈ *~ erhalten* be refused permission to land.
'Land|fahrzeug *n* land vehicle. **~flucht** *f* rural exodus. **~friedensbruch** *m* breach of the public peace. **~gemeinde** *f* rural community. **~gericht** *n* ⚖ district (*or* superior) court.
'landgestützt *adj* ✗ land-based *missile*.
'Land|gewinnung *f* land reclamation. **~haus** *n* country house. **~karte** *f* map. **~kreis** *m* (administrative) district.
'landläufig *adj* common, general.
'Landleben *n* country life.
ländlich ['lɛntlıç] *adj* a) rural, b) rustic.
'Landluft *f* country air.
'Landma,schine *f* agricultural machine.
'Landmesser *m* (-s; -) surveyor.
'Landpfarrer *m* country parson.
'Landrat *m* district administrator.
'Landratsamt *n* district administration (office).
'Landregen *m* persistent rain.
'Landschaft *f* (-; -en) 1. landscape (*a. paint.*), scenery, countryside: *die politische ~* the political scene. 2. region, country. **'landschaftlich** *adj* 1. *geogr.* regional. 2. scenic (*beauty etc*): *~ schöne Strecke* scenic road.
'Landschafts|gärtner(in *f*) *m* landscape

gardener. **~maler(in** *f*) *m* landscape painter. **~pflege** *f*, **~schutz** *m* conservation. **~schutzgebiet** *n* (natural) preserve.

'**Landsitz** *m* country seat.

'**Landsmann** *m* (-[e]s; -leute) (fellow) countryman, compatriot.

'**Landsmannschaft** *f* (-; -en) *FRG*: expellee organization.

'**Landstraße** *f* country road.

'**Landstreicher(in** *f*) *m* tramp.

Landstreiche'rei *f* (-; *no pl*) vagrancy.

'**Landstreitkräfte** *pl* land forces.

'**Landtag** *m FRG*: Landtag, parliament of a Land.

'**Landung** *f* (-; -en) landing, ✈ *a.* touchdown, ⚓ *a.* disembarkation: ✈ **zur ~ ansetzen** come in to land.

'**Landungsbrücke** *f* landing stage, jetty.

'**Landurlaub** *m* ⚓ shore leave.

'**Landvermessung** *f* (land) surveying.

'**Landweg** *m* **1.** country road. **2.** overland route: **auf dem ~** by land.

'**Landwirt** *m* farmer.

'**Landwirtschaft** *f* (-; -en) **1.** *no pl* agriculture, farming. **2.** farm.

'**landwirtschaftlich** *adj* agricultural.

'**Landwirtschafts...** agricultural (*show, school, etc*). **~mi,nister** *m* Minister of Agriculture. **~mini,sterium** *n* Ministry of Agriculture.

'**Landzunge** *f geogr.* promontory.

lang [laŋ] **I** *adj* **1.** long, *a.* lengthy, F tall: **über kurz oder ~** sooner or later; **seit ~em** for a long time; → **Bank**[1] **1**, **Gesicht 1**, **Hand**, **Sicht 1** *etc.* **II** *adv* **2.** long: **4 Fuß ~** 4 feet long; **~ entbehrt** long missed; **länger werden** lengthen; **die Zeit wird mir ~** time hangs heavy on my hands; **F ~ und breit** at great length; **e-e Woche ~** for a week; **die ganze Woche ~** all week, the whole week long; **mein ganzes Leben ~** all my life. **3.** along: *fig.* **wissen, wo's ~ geht** know the score; **j-m zeigen, wo's ~ geht** tell s.o. what's what. **4.** → **lange**.

'**langärm(e)lig** [-ɛrm(ə)lıç] *adj* long-sleeved. '**langatmig** [-a:tmıç] *adj fig.* lengthy, long-winded. '**langbeinig** [-baınıç] *adj* long-legged, F leggy.

lange ['laŋə] *adv* long, a long time: **das ist (schon) ~ her** that was a long time ago (→ *a.* **her 1**); **das ist noch ~ hin** that's still a long way off; **wie ~ noch?**

how much longer?; **wie ~ lernen Sie schon Englisch?** how long have you been learning English?; **noch ~ nicht** not for a long time (yet); **noch ~ nicht fertig (gut genug** *etc*) not nearly ready (good enough *etc*); **bis ~ nach Mitternacht** until well past midnight; **ich bleibe nicht ~ (weg)** I won't be long.

Länge ['lɛŋə] *f* (-; -n) **1.** *no pl* length: **von 10 Metern ~** ten metres long (*or* in length); **der ~ nach** lengthwise; **in die ~ ziehen** stretch, *fig.* drag *s.th.* out; *fig.* **sich in die ~ ziehen** drag on. **2.** *sports:* **er gewann mit zwei ~n Vorsprung** he won by two lengths. **3.** *fig., usu. pl* dull passage, longueur. **4.** *geogr.* longitude. **5.** *ling., metr.* long.

'**längelang** *adv* (at) full length.

langen ['laŋən] (h) F **I** *v/t* **1.** *j-m et.* hand s.o. s.th.; *j-m e-e* ~ land s.o. one. **II** *v/i* **2.** ~ **nach** reach for; ~ **in** (*acc*) reach into. **3.** reach (*bis* to *or* as far as). **4.** a) be enough (**für** for), b) manage (**mit** with, on): **langt das?** will that do?; **das langt mir** that will do for me; *fig.* **mir langt's!, jetzt langt's mir!** I've had enough!, I'm sick of it!; → *a.* **reichen 3**.

'**Längen|grad** *m geogr.* degree of longitude. **~kreis** *m geogr.* meridian. **~maß** *n* linear (*or* long) measure.

'**längerfristig** [-frıstıç] *adj and adv* covering (*or* for) a prolonged period.

'**langersehnt** *adj* long-awaited.

'**Langeweile** *f* (-; *no pl*) boredom: ~ **haben** be (*or* feel) bored; F **ich sterbe vor ~** I'm bored to death.

'**langfristig** [-frıstıç] **I** *adj* long-term. **II** *adv* on a long-term basis: ~ **(gesehen)** in the long term.

'**Langhaar...,** '**langhaarig** *adj* long-haired.

'**langjährig** [-jɛ:rıç] *adj* of many years, long-standing (*friendship etc*), long: **~e Erfahrung** many years of experience.

'**Langlauf** *m* (-[e]s; *no pl*) cross-country skiing.

'**Langläufer(in** *f*) *m* cross-country skier.

'**langlebig** [-le:bıç] *adj* long-lived, ✝ durable, *nucl.* long-life. '**Langlebigkeit** *f* (-; *no pl*) longevity, ✝ durability.

länglich ['lɛŋlıç] *adj* long(ish), oblong.

'**langmütig** [-my:tıç] *adj* forbearing.

längs [lɛŋs] **I** *prep* along: ~ **der Küste** alongshore. **II** *adv* lengthwise.

'Längsachse f longitudinal axis.
'langsam I adj a. fig. slow: **~er werden**
(fahren etc) slow down; F fig. **~ treten**
slow down, a. take it easy. **II** adv slowly: (immer schön) **~!** not so fast!; **er**
wird ~ alt he's getting old; F **es wurde ~**
Zeit! it was about time!; **~ reicht's mir!**
I'm getting fed up with this!
'Langsamkeit f (-; no pl) slowness.
'Langschläfer(in f) m late riser.
'Langspielplatte f long-playing record.
'Längsschnitt m longitudinal section.
'längsseits adv alongside.
längst [lɛŋst] adv long ago, long since:
am ~en longest; **~ nicht so gut** not
nearly as good; **das ist ~ vorbei (vergessen)** that's long past (forgotten);
ich weiß es ~ I've known it for a long
time; **er sollte ~ dasein** he should have
been here long ago; → **fällig**.
längstens ['lɛŋstəns] adv **1.** at the longest (or most). **2.** at the latest.
'langstielig [-ʃti:lɪç] adj long-stemmed.
'Langstrecke f long range, sports:
(long) distance.
'Langstrecken... long-range (flight,
missile, etc), sports: long-distance.
~lauf m (long-)distance run (or race).
~läufer(in f) m (long-)distance runner.
langweilen ['laŋvaɪlən] v/t (h) bore: **sich**
~ be (or get) bored; **sich zu Tode ~** F be
bored stiff. **'Langweiler** m (-s; -) F
bore. **'langweilig** adj boring, dull: **~**
sein a. be a bore.
'Langwelle f radio: long wave.
'Langwellen|bereich m long-wave
band. **~sender** m long-wave radio
station (or transmitter).
langwierig ['laŋvi:rɪç] adj lengthy, pro-
tracted (a. 🐟).
'Langwierigkeit f (-; no pl) lengthiness.
'Langzeit... long-term (memory, effect).
Lanze ['lantsə] f (-; -n) lance.
lapidar [lapi'da:r] adj terse, succinct.
Lappalie [la'pa:liə] f (-; -n) (mere) trifle.
Lappe ['lapə] m (-n; -n) Lapp.
Lappen ['lapən] m (-s; -) **1.** (piece of)
cloth, rag: F **j-m durch die ~ gehen** a)
slip through s.o.'s fingers, b) person:
give s.o. the slip. **2.** anat., 🫁 lobe. **3.** F
(bank)note, Am. bill. **4.** F (dress) rag.
läppern ['lɛpərn] v/impers (h) F **es läp-
pert sich** it all adds up.
lappig ['lapɪç] adj F limp, flabby.

Lappin ['lapɪn] f (-; -nen) Lapp.
läppisch ['lɛpɪʃ] adj F silly, childish.
Lapsus ['lapsʊs] m (-; -) slip, lapse.
Lärche ['lɛrçə] f (-; -n) 🌳 larch.
Lärm [lɛrm] m (-[e]s; no pl) **1.** noise, din,
racket, roar (of engine etc): **~ machen**
make much noise, be noisy; F **~ schlagen** raise a hue and cry (**gegen**
against). **2.** fig. fuss (**um** about).
'Lärmbekämpfung f noise abatement.
'Lärmbelästigung f noise pollution.
'lärmempfindlich adj sensitive to noise.
lärmen ['lɛrmən] v/i (h) make much
noise, be noisy. **'lärmend** adj noisy.
'Lärmpegel m noise (or decibel) level.
'Lärmschutzwand f noise barrier.
Larve ['larfə] f (-; -n) zo. larva.
las [la:s] pret of lesen¹ and lesen².
lasch [laʃ] adj F **1.** limp (handshake). **2.**
fig. lax, slack (discipline etc). **3.** insipid.
Lasche ['laʃə] f (-; -n) flap, on shoe:
tongue, ⊙ fishplate, flat link.
Laser ['le:zər] m (-s; -) phys. laser.
'Laserchirur,gie f laser surgery.
'Laserstrahl m laser beam.
'Lasertechnik f laser technology.
lassen ['lasən] (ließ, gelassen, h) **I** v/aux
1. let: **laß mich sehen** let me see; **das**
Licht brennen ~ leave the light(s) on;
j-n warten ~ keep s.o. waiting; **er läßt**
sich nicht zwingen he won't be forced.
2. j-n et. tun ~ have (or make) s.o. do
s.th.; **den Arzt kommen ~** send for the
doctor. **3.** machen ~ have s.th. made
(or done); **sich die Haare schneiden ~**
have one's hair cut; **ich ließ es mir
zuschicken** I had it sent to me. **4.** ich
habe mir sagen ~ I have been told; **der
Wein läßt sich trinken** the wine is
drinkable; **dies Wort läßt sich nicht
übersetzen** this word is untranslatable; **das läßt sich nicht mehr ändern**
it's too late now to do anything about
it; **das läßt sich nicht beweisen** it can't
be proved; **die Tür ließ sich leicht öffnen** the door opened easily; → **ma-
chen** 13, **sagen** etc. **II** v/t **5.** leave: **laß
alles, wie es ist!** leave everything as it
is!; **wo soll ich mein Gepäck ~?** where
shall I leave (or put) my luggage? **6.** j-m
et. ~ leave s.o. s.th., let s.o. have s.th.;
laß mir das Buch noch e-e Weile! let
me keep the book a while longer!; F fig.
das muß man ihm ~! you've got to

hand it to him! **7.** stop: *laß das!* don't!, stop that!; *~ wir das!* enough of that!; *du solltest das Rauchen ~!* you ought to stop smoking! **III** *v/i* **8.** *von j-m (e-r Sache)* ~ part from s.o. (with s.th.).

lässig ['lɛsɪç] **I** *adj* a) casual, nonchalant, F cool, b) careless. **II** *adv* F easily: *er gewann ~* he won hands down.

'Lässigkeit *f* (-; *no pl*) nonchalance.

Lasso ['laso] *n*, *m* (-s; -s) lasso.

Last [last] *f* (-; -en) **1.** *a. fig.* a) load, burden, b) weight: ⚖ *~ der Beweise* weight of the evidence; *j-m zur ~ fallen* be a burden to s.o.; *j-m et. zur ~ legen* charge s.o. with s.th. **2.** ✝ burden, charge: *öffentliche ~en* public charges; *soziale ~en* social burdens; *zu ~en von ...* to the debit of ... **3.** ⚡ load.

'Lastauto *n* lorry, *Am.* truck.

lasten ['lastən] *v/i* (h) *~ auf* (*dat*) *a. fig.* weigh (heavily) on, rest on.

'Lasten|aufzug *m* goods lift, *Am.* freight elevator. **~ausgleich** *m* equalization of burdens.

'lastend *adj fig.* oppressive.

Laster¹ ['lastər] *m* (-s; -) F *mot.* lorry, *Am.* truck.

'Laster² *n* (-s; -) vice. **'lasterhaft** *adj* depraved, corrupt, wicked, dissolute. **'Lasterhöhle** *f* F *contp.* den of iniquity. **'Lasterleben** *n* dissolute life.

lästerlich ['lɛstərlɪç] *adj* a) abusive, b) blasphemous.

lästern ['lɛstərn] *v/i* (h) *~ über* (*acc*) run s.o., s.th. down; *Gott ~* blaspheme.

lästig ['lɛstɪç] *adj* troublesome, annoying: *j-m ~ fallen* (*or sein*) be a nuisance to s.o., get on s.o.'s nerves.

'Lastkahn *m* barge.

'Lastkraftwagen *m* lorry, *Am.* truck.

'Lastschrift *f* ✝ **1.** debit entry. **2.** → **'Lastschriftanzeige** *f* debit note.

'Lasttier *n* pack animal.

'Lastwagen *m* lorry, *Am.* truck. **~fahrer** *m* lorry (*Am.* truck) driver.

'Lastzug *m* *mot.* truck trailer.

Lasur [la'zuːr] *f* (-; -en) glaze.

Latein [la'taɪn] *n* (-s; *no pl*) Latin: *fig. ich bin mit m-m ~ am Ende!* I give up!

La'teinameri|kaner(in *f*) *m*, **la'tein-ameri|kanisch** *adj* Latin-American.

la'teinisch *adj* Latin: *auf ♌ in Latin.

latent [la'tɛnt] *adj* latent.

Latenzzeit [la'tɛnts-] *f biol.*, ⚕ latency period, *nucl. etc* latency time.

Laterne [la'tɛrnə] *f* (-; -n) lantern, lamp.

La'ternenpfahl *m* lamppost.

Latinum [la'tiːnʊm] *n* (-s; *no pl*) *ped. hist.* *großes* (*kleines*) *~* Latin proficiency (intermediate Latin) certificate.

Latrine [la'triːnə] *f* (-; -n) latrine.

Latsche ['latʃə] *f* (-; -n) ⚘ dwarf pine.

latschen ['laːtʃən] F **I** *v/i* (sn) slouch (along), trudge: *~ auf* (*acc*) step on. **II** *v/t* (h) *j-m e-e ~* paste s.o. one.

'Latschen *m* (-s; -) F a) slipper, b) (old) shoe: *aus den ~ kippen* keel over.

Latte ['latə] *f* (-; -n) **1.** lath, slat, picket. **2.** *sports*: (cross-)bar: *die ~ überqueren* clear the bar. **3.** F *fig.* **e-e ganze ~ von** a whole string of; *j-n auf der ~ haben* have it in for s.o.

'Lattenkiste *f* crate.

'Lattenzaun *m* paling, picket fence.

Latz [lats] *m* (-es; ⁓e) bib: F *fig. j-m e-e vor den ~ knallen* zap s.o.

'Lätzchen ['lɛtsçən] *n* (-s; -) bib.

'Latzhose *f* (pair of) dungarees.

lau [laʊ] *adj* lukewarm (*a. fig.*), tepid, mild (*air, weather*).

Laub [laʊp] *n* (-[e]s; *no pl*) foliage, leaves.

'Laubbaum *m* deciduous tree.

Laube ['laʊbə] *f* (-; -n) a) arbo(u)r, b) summerhouse.

'Laubengang *m* arcade.

'Laubenkolo,nie *f* allotment gardens.

'Laubfrosch *m* tree frog.

'Laubsäge *f* fretsaw. **~arbeit** *f* fretwork.

'Laubwald *m* deciduous forest.

'Laubwerk *n* (-[e]s; *no pl*) foliage.

Lauch [laʊx] *m* (-[e]s; -) ⚘ leek.

Lauer ['laʊər] *f auf der ~ liegen* be lying in wait.

lauern ['laʊərn] *v/i* (h) lurk: *~ auf* (*acc*) a) be lying in wait for, b) be watching out for *an opportunity etc*.

'lauernd *adj* **1.** lurking. **2.** watchful.

Lauf [laʊf] *m* (-[e]s; ⁓e) **1.** *no pl* run(ning): *sie ließ ihren Tränen freien ~* she let her tears flow freely; *s-n Gefühlen freien ~ lassen* give vent to one's feelings. **2.** *sports*: run, race: *100-Meter-~* 100 metre run (*or* dash). **3.** *no pl* course: *im ~ der Zeit* (*des Gesprächs*) in the course of time (of the conversation); *im ~e der letzten Jahre* during the last few years; *den Dingen ihren ~ lassen* let things ride. **4.** *no pl* ⚙ movement, run, action, working, operation. **5.** barrel (*of rifle etc*). **6.** *hunt*. leg. **7.** ♪ run, passage. **'Laufbahn** *f* (*e-e ~ einschlagen* take up a) career. **'Laufdiszi,plin** *f sports*: running event.

laufen ['laʊfən] (lief, gelaufen) **I** *v/i* (sn) **1.** a) run (*a. fig.*), b) walk, go, c) run, flow: *er ließ Wasser in die Wanne ~* he ran water into the tub; F *m-e Nase läuft* my nose is running; *mir lief ein Schauer über den Rücken* a shudder ran down my spine. **2.** ⚙ work, *engine etc*; run: *Kamera läuft!* camera on! **3.** *film, play, etc*: run, show, be on: *läuft der Hauptfilm schon?* has the main film started yet? **4.** *fig*. go: F *wie ist es denn gelaufen?* how did it go?; *die Sache ist gelaufen* a) it's all over, b) it's in the bag; *da läuft nichts!* nothing doing!; *so läuft das!* that's the name of the game!; *was da in Berlin so läuft* what's going on in Berlin. **5.** a) *trial etc*: be in progress, b) *application etc*: be under consideration. **6.** ♈, ⚕ run, be valid: *der Mietvertrag läuft 5 Jahre* the lease runs for five years; *auf j-s Namen ~* be (made out) in s.o.'s name; *unter dem Namen X ~* go by the name of X. **7.** leak. **II** *v/t* **8.** (sn) walk. **9.** (h or sn) *sports*: run, do: *e-n neuen Rekord ~* run a new record; *e-e Zeit von 20 Sekunden ~* clock a time of 20 seconds. **10.** (h) *sich Blasen ~* get blisters (from walking). **III** *v/impers* (h) *hier läuft es sich schlecht* walking *etc* is bad here. **IV** *sich warm ~* (h) warm up.

'laufend I *adj* **1.** current: *im ~en Monat* this month; *~e Berichterstattung* running commentary; *~e Kosten* overheads; ♈ *~er Meter* running metre; *~e Nummern* serial numbers; *~e Kontrolle* regular inspection. **2.** *auf dem ~en sein* be up to date, *a*. be fully informed; *j-n* (*sich*) *auf dem ~en halten* keep s.o. (o.s.) informed. **3.** *mit ~em Motor* with the engine running. **II** *adv* **4.** constantly, continually.

'laufenlassen *v/t* (*irr, sep, no* -ge-, h, → *lassen*) F *j-n ~* let s.o. go (*or* off); *die Dinge ~* let things ride.

Läufer ['lɔyfər] *m* (-s; -) **1.** a) runner, b) skater, c) skier. **2.** *chess*: bishop. **3.** runner, rug. **4.** ⚙ slide, cursor, ⚡ rotor.

Lauferei [laʊfə'raɪ] *f* (-; -en) F running around, *fig. a.* trouble.

'Läuferin *f* (-; -nen) → **Läufer** 1.

'Lauf|feuer *n* (*sich verbreiten wie ein ~* spread like) wildfire. **~gitter** *n* playpen.

läufig ['lɔyfiç] *adj zo*. in heat, on heat.

'Lauf|junge *m* errand boy. **~kran** *m* ⚙ travel(l)ing crane. **~kundschaft** *f* casual customers. **~masche** *f* ladder, *Am.* run. **~paß** *m* F *j-m den ~ geben* send s.o. packing, ditch s.o. **~planke** *f* ⚓ gangway. **~schritt** *m im ~* at the double. **~schuhe** *pl* running (*or* track) shoes. **~sport** *m* running. **~steg** *m* catwalk, ⚓ gangway. **~zeit** *f* **1.** life, term (*of contract etc*). **2.** run (*of film etc*). **3.** ⚙, *a*. of tape *etc*: running time. **~zettel** *m* inter-office slip, tracer.

Lauge ['laʊgə] *f* (-; -n) **1.** lye. **2.** suds.

'Lauheit *f* (-; *no pl*) *a. fig*. lukewarmness.

Laune ['laʊnə] *f* (-; -n) **1.** mood, temper: *schlechte ~ haben, schlechter ~ sein* be in a bad mood (*or* temper); *bester ~ sein* be in a great mood; *j-n bei* (*guter*) *~ halten* *a. iro*. keep s.o. happy; *~n haben* be moody. **2.** whim, caprice.

'launenhaft *adj* moody, *fig*. capricious, fickle, *weather*: changeable.

launig ['laʊniç] *adj* humorous.

launisch ['laʊnɪʃ] *adj* **1.** → **launenhaft.** **2.** ill-tempered, peevish.

Laus [laʊs] *f* (-; *pl* Läuse) louse (*pl* lice).

lauschen ['laʊʃən] *v/i* (h) listen (*dat, auf acc* to): (*heimlich*) ~ eavesdrop (*dat* on). **'Lauscher** *m* (-s; -), **'Lauscherin** *f* (-; -nen) listener, eavesdropper.

'lauschig *adj* snug, cosy.

lausen ['laʊzən] *v/t* (h) louse: F *mich laust der Affe!* did you ever!

lausig ['laʊzɪç] *adj* F **1.** lousy, bad. **2.** dreadful, awful (*cold etc*): *~ wehtun* hurt awfully; *~ kalt* beastly cold.

laut¹ [laʊt] *adj* loud (*a. fig.*), noisy: *~ werden* a) become audible, b) *fig*. become known, *wishes etc*: be expressed, c) *person*: begin to shout; *es wurde das Gerücht ~, daß ...* it was rumo(u)red that ... **II** *adv* loud(ly): *et. ~ sagen* say s.th. out loud; *~* (*vor*)*lesen* read aloud; *~ und deutlich* loud and clear.

laut² *prep* according to, ♈ as per.

Laut *m* (-[e]s; -e) sound (*a. ling*.), noise: *hunt*. *~ geben* give tongue; *sie gab k-n ~ von sich* she didn't utter a sound.

Laute ['lautə] f (-; -n) ♪ lute.
lauten ['lautən] v/i (h) **1.** run, read, go: *der Text lautet wie folgt* the text reads as follows. **2.** ~ *auf* (acc) ⚖ *sentence etc*: be; *auf* (*den Namen*) **X** ~ *passport etc*: be (made out) in the name of X.
läuten ['lɔytən] v/i, v/t (h) ring, toll: *es läutet* there is a ring at the door, *ped.* the bell is ringing; F *ich habe davon* ~ *hören* I've heard s.th. to that effect.
lauter ['lautər] **I** adj **1.** pure (*gold etc*). **2.** *fig.* sincere, hono(u)rable. **II** adv **3.** nothing but: *aus* ~ *Bosheit* from sheer spite; *vor* ~ *Lärm* for all the noise; *das sind* ~ *Lügen* it's all lies.
'Lauterkeit f (-; *no pl*) *fig.* integrity.
läutern ['lɔytərn] (h) **I** v/t purify, *fig. a.* chasten. **II** *sich* ~ *fig.* reform.
'Läuterung f (-; -en) *fig.* reformation.
'lauthals adv at the top of one's voice: ~ *lachen* roar with laughter.
'Lautheit f (-; *no pl*) loudness, noisiness.
'Lautlehre f phonetics.
'lautlos adj soundless, noiseless, silent: ~*e Stille* hushed silence.
'Lautschrift f phonetic transcription.
'Lautsprecher m 🔊 (loud)speaker. ~**anlage** f public-address system. ~**box** f loudspeaker (cabinet). ~**wagen** m loudspeaker van, *Am.* sound truck.
'lautstark adj a. fig. loud: ~*e Minderheit* vocal minority.
'Lautstärke f loudness, 🔊 a. (sound) volume: *mit voller* ~ (at) full blast.
'Lautstärkeregler m volume control.
'Lautverschiebung f *ling.* sound shift.
'Lautzeichen n phonetic symbol.
'lauwarm adj lukewarm (a. fig.), tepid.
Lava ['laːva] f (-; Laven) lava.
Lavendel [la'vɛndəl] m (-s; -) 🌿 lavender.
lavieren [la'viːrən] v/i (h) *fig.* manoeuvre, *Am.* maneuver.
Lawine [la'viːnə] f (-; -n) avalanche.
la'winenartig adj and adv avalanche-like: ~ *anwachsen* snowball.
La'winen|gefahr f danger of avalanches. ₂**sicher** adj avalanche-proof. ~(**such**)**hund** m avalanche search dog. ~**warnung** f avalanche warning.
lax [laks] adj lax, loose.
Layout [leɪ'aʊt] n (-s; -s) layout.
Lay'outer m (-s; -) layout man.
Lazarett [latsa'rɛt] n (-[e]s; -e) (military) hospital. ~**schiff** n hospital ship.

leasen ['liːzən] v/t (h) lease.
Leasing ['liːzɪŋ] n (-s; -s) leasing.
'Lebemann m (-[e]s; ⸚er) playboy.
leben ['leːbən] (h) **I** v/i **1.** live, a. be alive, exist: *hier lebt es sich gut* it's not a bad life here; *lebt er noch?* is he still alive?; *bescheiden* ~ lead a modest life; ~ *von* live on; *er lebt vom Stundengeben* he makes a living by teaching; ~ *für* live for, devote one's life to; ~ *und* ~ *lassen* live and let live; *es lebe ...!* long live ...! **2.** live, reside: *sie lebt bei ihrer Mutter* she lives with her mother. **II** v/t **3.** live.
'Leben¹ n (-s) living (*etc*): *zum* ~ *zuwenig, zum Sterben zuviel* barely enough to keep body and soul together.
'Leben² n (-s; -) **1.** life: *das* ~ *in Kanada* life in Canada; *ein Kampf auf* ~ *und Tod* a life-and-death struggle; *aus dem* ~ *gegriffen* taken from life; *am* ~ *sein* live, be alive; *am* ~ *bleiben* (*erhalten*) stay (keep) alive; *sich das* ~ *nehmen* kill o.s., commit suicide; *ums* ~ *kommen* lose one's life, be killed; *mit dem* ~ *davonkommen* escape (alive); *ein neues* ~ *beginnen* turn over a new leaf; *ins* ~ *rufen* call into being, launch; *im öffentlichen* ~ *stehen* be a public figure; *mein* ~ *lang* all my life; *ich tanze für mein* ~ *gern* I just love to dance; *ich würde für mein* ~ *gern ...* I would give anything to *inf*; F *nie im* ~!, *im* ~ *nicht!* not on your life!; *so ist das* ~ (*eben*)! such is life!; → *Hölle*, *schwermachen*. **2.** a) life, activity, b) liveliness, vitality: ~ *bringen in* (*acc*) liven up; → *Bude* 2.
'lebend adj living, *ling. a.* modern (*language*), alive, *biol.* live: ~*es Inventar* livestock; *die Lebenden* the living; *die noch Lebenden* those still alive.
'lebendgebärend adj *biol.* viviparous.
'Lebendgewicht n live weight.
lebendig [le'bɛndɪç] adj **1.** living, *pred* alive: *bei* ~*em Leibe* alive; *wieder* ~ *werden* memories etc: come back. **2.** lively, alert. **3.** vivid. **Le'bendigkeit** f (-; *no pl*) **1.** liveliness. **2.** vividness.
'Lebens|abend m old age. ~**abschnitt** m period of (one's) life. ~**ader** f *fig.* lifeline. ~**alter** n age. ~**angst** f existential dread. ~**anschauung** f view of life, approach to life. ~**arbeitszeit** f working life. ~**art** f **1.** way of life. **2.** manners. ~**auffassung** f philosophy (of life).

~aufgabe f life task: *sich et. zur ~ machen* devote one's life to s.th. **~bedingungen** pl (living) conditions. **'lebensbedrohlich** adj life-threatening. **'Lebens|bedürfnisse** pl necessaries of life. **~bejahung** f positive approach to life. **~bereich** m sphere of life. **~beschreibung** f life, biography. **~dauer** f duration of life, lifespan, ✿ life. **~ende** n *bis an mein* etc **~** to the end of my etc days. **~erfahrung** f experience of life. **~erhaltungssy‚stem** n ✿, ✿ life-support system. **~erinnerungen** pl memoirs. **~erwartung** f life expectancy. **'lebensfähig** adj a. fig. viable. **'Lebens|form** f **1.** way of life. **2.** biol. form of life. **~frage** f vital question. **~freude** f joy of life, zest (for life). **'Lebensgefahr** f danger to life: *~l* danger!; *in ~ schweben* be in danger of one's life, ✿ be in a critical condition; *außer ~ sein* be out of danger, ✿ be off the critical list; *unter ~* at the risk of one's life. **'lebensgefährlich** adj extremely dangerous, perilous, very serious (*disease, injury*). **'Lebens|gefährte** m, **~gefährtin** f (life) companion, partner in life. **~gemeinschaft** f life partnership. **~geschichte** f life story. **'lebensgroß** adj life-size(d). **'Lebensgröße** f *in ~* a) life-size(d), in its actual size, b) F *fig.* large as life. **'Lebenshaltung** f (-; *no pl*) standard of living. **'Lebenshaltungskosten(index** m) pl cost of living (index). **'Lebens|inter‚essen** pl vital interests. **~jahr** n year of one's life: *im 20. ~* at the age of 20. **~kampf** m struggle for survival. **~kraft** f vigo(u)r, vitality. **'lebenslang** I adj lifelong. II adv all one's life. **'lebenslänglich** adj ☒ (for) life: *~e Freiheitsstrafe* life imprisonment; F *er hat ~ bekommen* he got a life term. **'Lebenslauf** m **1.** (course of) life, career. **2.** personal record, curriculum vitae. **'lebenslustig** adj fond of life, merry. **'Lebensmittel** pl food(stuffs), groceries, provisions. **~ab‚teilung** f food department. **~geschäft** n grocery, food shop (*Am.* store). **~händler(in** f) m grocer. **~indu‚strie** f food industry. **~vergiftung** f food poisoning.

'lebensmüde adj weary of life. **'lebensnotwendig** adj vital, essential. **'Lebens|quali‚tät** f quality of life. **~raum** m living space. **~retter(in** f) m life-saver, rescuer. **~rhythmus** m rhythm (of life). **~standard** m standard of living. **~stellung** f permanent position. **~stil** m life style. **'lebensunfähig** adj nonviable. **'Lebens|unterhalt** m (*s-n ~ verdienen* earn one's) living (*or* livelihood) (*mit* out of). **~versicherung** f life insurance. **~wandel** m life, conduct. **~weise** f **1.** way of life: *gesunde ~* a) healthy living, b) regimen. **2.** habits. **~weisheit** f **1.** worldly wisdom. **2.** maxim. **~werk** n lifework. **'lebenswert** adj worth living. **'lebenswichtig** adj vital, essential. **'Lebens|wille** m will to live. **~zeichen** n sign of life. **~zeit** f lifetime: *auf ~* for life. **~ziel** n, **~zweck** m aim in life.

Leber ['le:bər] f (-; -n) liver: *frisch (or frei) von der ~ weg* frankly. **'Leber|fleck** m mole. **~knödel** m gastr. liver dumpling. **~krankheit** f liver disease. **~krebs** m ✿ cancer of the liver. **~pa‚stete** f gastr. liver pâté. **~tran** m cod-liver oil. **~wurst** f liver sausage, *Am.* liverwurst. **~zir‚rhose** f ✿ cirrhosis of the liver.

'Lebewesen n (-s; -) living being, creature, biol. organism.

lebhaft ['le:phaft] adj lively, fig. a. vivid (*imagination etc*), a. keen (*interest*), busy (*traffic etc*), a. gay (*colours*), animated (*discussion etc*), ✝ brisk: *et. ~ bedauern* regret s.th. very much; *das kann ich mir ~ vorstellen* I can just imagine. **'Lebhaftigkeit** f (-; *no pl*) liveliness, fig. a. vividness.

'Lebkuchen m gingerbread (cake). **'leblos** adj lifeless (a. fig.), inanimate. **'Lebzeiten** pl *zu s-n ~* a) in his (life)time, b) when he was still alive.

leck [lɛk] adj leaky: *~ sein → lecken¹*; ✿ *~ werden* spring a leak. **Leck** n (-[e]s; -s) leak. **lecken¹** ['lɛkən] v/i (h) leak, ✿ have sprung a leak.

'lecken² v/t (h) a) lick, b) lap (up); → *Arsch* 1.

lecker ['lɛkər] adj delicious, tasty, F yummy. **'Leckerbissen** m a. fig. titbit,

Am. tidbit. **Leckerei** [lɛkə'raɪ] *f* (-; -en) dainty, sweet.

Leder ['le:dər] *n* (-s; -) leather: F *vom ~ ziehen* let go (*gegen* against).

'Leder... leather (*coat, glove, etc*). **~fett** ⚙ dubbing. **2gebunden** *adj* leather-bound. **~hose** *f* leather trousers.

ledern¹ ['le:dərn] *adj* 1. leather. 2. *fig.* leathery. 3. *fig.* dull.

ledern² *v/t* (h) polish with a chamois.

'Lederwaren *pl* leather goods.

ledig ['le:dɪç] *adj* single, unmarried: *~e Mutter* unmarried mother.

lediglich ['le:dɪklɪç] *adv* only, merely.

Lee [le:] *f* (-; *no pl*) ⚓ lee: *nach ~* leeward.

leer [le:r] *adj* empty (*a. fig.*), *a.* vacant (*house, post, etc*), blank (*cassette, page*): *die Batterie ist ~* the battery has run out (*mot.* is dead); *~es Gerede* idle talk, F hot air; *~ laufen* (*lassen*) ⚙ idle; *~ stehen* *house etc*: be empty, be unoccupied; *ins Leere starren* stare into space; *ins Leere gehen* *blow etc*: miss; → *ausgehen* 8, *Hand, Magen*.

Leere ['le:rə] *f* (-; *no pl*) *fig.* emptiness, void. **'leeren** *v/t* (h) empty (*a. sich ~*), *a.* drain (*glass*).

'Leer|gewicht *n* dead weight. **~gut** *n* ✝ empties. **~kas,sette** *f* blank cassette.

'Leerlauf *m* (-[e]s; *no pl*) 1. a) ⚙ idle running, b) *mot.* neutral (gear): *im ~ fahren* coast. 2. *fig.* a) wastage (of energy), b) running on the spot.

'leerlaufen *v/i* (*irr, sep, -ge-, sn*, → *laufen*) 1. (*a. ~ lassen*) drain, run dry. 2. *sports: j-n ~ lassen* sell s.o. a dummy.

'Leerpackung *f* ✝ dummy.

'leerstehend *adj* unoccupied, vacant.

'Leertaste *f typewriter:* space bar.

'Leerung *f* (-; -en) emptying (*etc*): ✉ *nächste ~* next collection.

Lefzen ['lɛftsən] *pl* flews.

legal [le'ga:l] *adj* legal, lawful: *auf ~em Wege* by legal means, lawfully.

legalisieren [legali'zi:rən] *v/t* (h) legalize.

Legali'sierung *f* (-; -en) legalization.

Legalität [legali'tɛ:t] *f* (-; *no pl*) legality, lawfulness: *außerhalb der ~* outside the law.

Legasthenie [legaste'ni:] *f* (-; *no pl*) dyslexia. **Legastheniker** [legas'te:nikər] *m* (-s; -) dyslexic.

Legat¹ [le'ga:t] *m* (-en; -en) legate.

Le'gat² *n* (-[e]s; -e) ⚖ legacy.

legen ['le:gən] (h) I *v/t* 1. a) put, place, b) lay *s.o., s.th.* down: *ein Kind ins Bett ~* put a child to bed; *er legte die Entscheidung in m-e Hände* he placed the decision in my hands. 2. lay (*carpet, cable, mines, etc*), plant (*bomb*). 3. fold. 4. set (*hair*): *bitte, waschen und ~* shampoo and set, please. 5. *zo.* lay (*eggs*). 6. *Karten ~* tell fortunes by the cards. 7. *sports: j-n ~* bring s.o. down. II *sich ~* 8. lie down: *sich ins Bett ~* go to bed. 9. *wind, rage, noise, etc:* die down, blow over, *pain, enthusiasm, etc:* wear off, *tension:* ease off. 10. *fig. sich ~ auf* (*acc*) take up, go in for (*activity etc*). 11. *sich j-m aufs Gemüt ~* (begin to) depress s.o. III *v/i* 12. *zo.* lay (*eggs*).

legendär [legɛn'dɛ:r] *adj* legendary.

Legende [le'gɛndə] *f* (-; -n) legend.

leger [le'ʒe:r] *adj* casual, informal.

legieren [le'gi:rən] *v/t* (h) 1. ⚙ alloy. 2. *gastr.* thicken.

Le'gierung *f* (-; -en) ⚙ alloy.

Legion [le'gio:n] *f* (-; -en) legion. **Legio-när** [legio'nɛ:r] *m* (-s; -e) legionnaire.

Legislative [legɪsla'ti:və] *f* (-; -n) 1. legislative body, legislature. 2. legislative power.

Legisla'turperi,ode *f* legislative period.

legitim [legi'ti:m] *adj* legitimate.

Legitimation [legitima'tsio:n] *f* (-; -en) 1. legitimation, proof of identity, credentials. 2. authority.

legitimieren [legiti'mi:rən] (h) I *v/t* 1. legitimate. 2. authorize. II *sich ~* prove one's identity.

Legitimität [legitimi'tɛ:t] *f* (-; *no pl*) legitimacy.

Leguan [le'gŭa:n] *m* (-s; -e) *zo.* iguana.

Lehen ['le:ən] *n* (-s; -) *hist.* fief.

Lehm [le:m] *m* (-[e]s; -e) a) loam, b) clay, c) F mud. **'Lehmboden** *m* loamy soil. **'lehmig** *adj* a) loamy, b) F muddy.

Lehne ['le:nə] *f* (-; -n) a) back(rest), b) arm(rest). **'lehnen** *v/t, v/i* (*a. sich ~*) (h) lean (*an acc, gegen* against): *sich aus dem Fenster ~* lean out of the window.

'Lehnsherr *m hist.* feudal lord.

'Lehnsmann *m hist.* vassal.

'Lehnwort *n* (-[e]s; *~er*) loan (word).

'Lehramt *n* a) teaching (profession), b) teaching post. **'Lehranstalt** *f* educational establishment, school. **'Lehrauf-**

trag *m univ.* teaching assignment, lectureship. **'Lehrbeauftragte** *m, f* (-n; -n) *univ.* assistant (*Am.* associate) lecturer. **'Lehrberuf** *m* **1.** *ped.* teaching profession. **2.** ⚲ skilled trade. **'Lehrbrief** *m* a) certificate of apprenticeship, b) indentures. **'Lehrbuch** *n* textbook.

Lehre¹ ['le:rə] *f* (-; -n) **1.** teaching(s), doctrine: *die ~ Hegels* the teachings of Hegel; *die christliche ~* the Christian doctrine. **2.** theory, science: *die ~ vom Schall* acoustics. **3.** a) lesson, b) (piece of) advice, c) moral (*of a tale etc*): *e-e ~ ziehen aus* draw a lesson from. **4.** (*e-e ~ machen* serve one's) apprenticeship (*bei* with).

'Lehre² *f* (-; -n) ⊗ **1.** ga(u)ge. **2.** model.

lehren ['le:rən] *v/t, v/i* (h) teach: *j-n lesen ~* teach s.o. (how) to read; *er lehrt Recht univ. a.* he lectures on law; *fig. das wird die Zukunft ~* time will tell. **'Lehrer** *m* (-s; -) a) teacher, *Br. a.* master, b) instructor. **~ausbildung** *f* teacher training. **~beruf** *m* teaching profession. **~fortbildung** *f* in-service training for teachers.

Lehrerin ['le:rərɪn] *f* (-; -nen) (lady) teacher, *Br. a.* mistress. **'Lehrer|kol,legium** *n* (teaching) staff, *Am. a.* faculty. **~konfe,renz** *f* staff (*Am. a.* faculty) meeting. **~mangel** *m* teacher shortage. **~zimmer** *n* staff room, *Am. a.* teacher's room.

'Lehrfach *n* **1.** subject. **2.** → *Lehramt* a. **'Lehrfilm** *m* educational film. **'Lehrgang** *m* course (*für* in). **'Lehrgeld** *n* ~ *zahlen müssen* learn it the hard way. **'Lehrherr** *m* master. **'Lehrjahre** *pl* (years of) apprenticeship. **'Lehrkörper** *m* teaching (*univ.* academic) staff, *Am. a.* faculty. **'Lehrkraft** *f* teacher.

Lehrling ['le:rlɪŋ] *m* (-s; -e) apprentice, trainee.

'Lehrmeister *m* master. **'Lehrme,thode** *f* teaching method. **'Lehrmittel** *pl* teaching aids. **'Lehrplan** *m* syllabus, curriculum. **'lehrreich** *adj* instructive, informative. **'Lehrsatz** *m* Ⓐ theorem, *eccl.* dogma. **'Lehrstelle** *f* apprenticeship: *offene ~* vacancy for an apprentice. **'Lehrstoff** *m* **1.** a) subject, b) subject matter. **2.** → *Lehrplan*. **'Lehrstuhl** *m* chair (*für* of *law etc*), professorship. **'Lehrveranstaltung** *f* lecture, sem-

inar. **'Lehrvertrag** *m* articles of apprenticeship. **'Lehrwerkstatt** *f* training workshop. **'Lehrzeit** *f* apprenticeship.

Leib [laip] *m* (-[e]s; -er) a) body, b) abdomen, c) womb: *am ganzen ~e zittern* tremble all over; *et. am eigenen ~ erfahren* experience s.th. for o.s.; F *zu ~e rücken* a) *j-m* press s.o. hard, attack s.o., b) *e-m Problem* tackle a problem; *sich j-n vom ~e halten* keep s.o. at arm's length; *~ und Leben riskieren* risk life and limb; *die Rolle war ihr auf den ~ geschrieben* she was made for the part; *mit ~ und Seele* heart and soul; → *lebendig* 1. **'Leibeigene** *m, f* (-n; -n) serf. **'Leibes|erben** *pl* ⚖ issue. **~frucht** *f* ⚖, ♔ f(o)etus. **~kräfte** *pl aus ~n* a) with all one's might, b) *schreien etc* at the top of one's voice. **~übungen** *pl* physical exercise (*ped.* education). **~visitati,on** *f* body search.

'Leibgarde *f* bodyguard. **'Leibgericht** *n* favo(u)rite dish.

leib|'haftig I *adj* real, true: *~es Ebenbild* living image; *der ~e Teufel* the devil incarnate. **II** *adv* in person, in the flesh. **'leiblich** *adj* **1.** bodily, physical: *das ~e Wohl* a) physical well-being, b) creature comforts. **2.** natural (*parents etc*), full, own: *~er Bruder* blood brother. **'Leibrente** *f* life annuity. **'Leibschmerzen** *pl* stomach-ache. **'Leib|wache** *f*, **~wächter** *m* bodyguard.

Leiche ['laiçə] *f* (-; -n) corpse, (dead) body: *über ~n gehen* stop at nothing; F *nur über m-e ~!* over my dead body! **'Leichen|beschauer** *m* doctor testifying a death. **~bestatter** *m* undertaker, *Am.* mortician. ☿**'blaß** *adj* deathly pale. **~gift** *n* ptomaine. **~halle** *f* mortuary. **~rede** *f* funeral oration. **~schauhaus** *n* morgue. **~starre** *f* ♔ rigor mortis. **~tuch** *n a. fig.* shroud. **~verbrennung** *f* cremation. **~wagen** *m* hearse. **~zug** *m* funeral procession.

Leichnam ['laiçna:m] *m* (-s; -e) (dead) body, corpse.

leicht [laiçt] **I** *adj* **1.** light (*a. fig. food, music, rain, reading, wine, work, etc*), ⊗ *a.* lightweight: *~e Erkältung* slight cold; *e-e ~e Bronchitis* a mild case (*f* a touch) of bronchitis; *~e Steigung* gentle slope; F *~es Mädchen* hussy;

mit **~er Hand** effortlessly; *et.* **auf die ~e Schulter nehmen** make light of s.th. **2.** easy, simple: **~er Sieg** walkover; *das ist* **~** that's easy; **nichts ~er als das!** no problem at all!; **sie hat es nicht ~ (mit ihm)** she is having a rough time (with him); **es war ihm ein ~es** it was easy for him. **3.** slight, minor (*a.* 🎵), mild (*penalty*): **~er Fehler** slight (*or* minor) mistake; **~e Verletzung** minor injury. **II** *adv* **4.** lightly (*etc*): **~ berühren** touch s.th. gently (*or* lightly). **5.** easily: **sie lernt ~** she is a good learner; **es ist ~ möglich** it is well possible; **das ist ~ gesagt** it's not as easy as that; **~er gesagt als getan** easier said than done; **nimm's ~!** take it easy! **6.** slightly: **ich bin ~ erkältet** I've (got) a slight cold.

'Leichtath,let(**in** *f*) *m* (track-and-field) athlete. **'Leichtath,letik** *f* (track-and--field) athletics.

'Leichtbauweise *f* lightweight construction.

'leichtbekleidet *adj* lightly (*or* scantily) dressed.

'Leichtben,zin *n* light petrol (*Am.* gasoline).

'leichtblütig [-bly:tɪç] *adj* lighthearted.
'leichtentzündlich *adj* inflammable.

Leichter ['laɪçtər] *m* (-s; -) ⚓ lighter.

'leichtfallen *v/i* (*irr, sep, -ge-*, sn, → *fallen*) **so et. fällt ihm leicht** he finds that sort of thing easy; **es fällt ihm nicht leicht** it isn't easy for him.

'leichtfertig *adj* **1.** light, frivolous. **2.** a) careless, b) irresponsible.

'Leichtfertigkeit *f* (-; *no pl*) **1.** frivolity. **2.** carelessness.

'leichtfüßig [-fy:sɪç] *adj* light-footed.
'Leichtgewicht *n* (-[e]s; *no pl*) *sports*: lightweight.

'leichtgläubig *adj* gullible.
'Leichtgläubigkeit *f* (-; *no pl*) gullibility.
'leicht'hin *adv* airily, casually.

'Leichtigkeit *f* (-; *no pl*) lightness, *fig. a.* easiness, ease: **mit ~** easily.

'leichtlebig [-le:bɪç] *adj* easy-going.

'Leichtlohngruppe *f* low-wage unskilled labo(u)r.

'leichtmachen *v/t* (*sep, -ge-*, h) *j-m et.* **~** make s.th. easy for s.o.; **sich das Leben ~** take it easy; **du machst es dir zu leicht!** it's not as easy as that!

'Leichtma,trose *m* ordinary seaman.

'Leichtme,tall *n* light metal.

'Leichtsinn *m* (-[e]s; *no pl*) **1.** carelessness, recklessness: **sträflicher ~** criminal negligence. **2.** frivolity, flightiness.

'leichtsinnig *adj* **1.** careless, reckless, rash. **2.** frivolous, flighty. **'leichtsinniger'weise** *adv* carelessly (enough).

'leichttun: *sich* **~** (*irr, sep, -ge-*, h, → *tun*) F *sich mit e-r Sache* **~** find s.th. easy.

'leicht|verdaulich *adj* easily digestible, light. **~verderblich** *adj* perishable: **~e Waren** perishables. **~verletzt** *adj* slightly injured. **~verständlich** *adj* easy to understand.

leid [laɪt] *adj pred* (**es**) **tut mir ~!** (I'm) sorry!; **es tut mir ~ um** I feel sorry for, b) **daß ...** I am (so) sorry that ...; **das tut mir aber ~!** I'm sorry to hear that!; **es tut mir (ja) ~, aber ich kann nicht kommen** *etc* I'm afraid I can't come *etc*; **sie tut mir ~** I feel sorry for her; **das wird dir noch ~ tun!** you'll regret it!; **ich bin es ~** a) I'm tired of it, b) *et. zu tun* I'm tired of doing s.th.

Leid *n* (-[e]s; *no pl*) **1.** a) grief, sorrow, b) misfortune; *j-m sein* **~** *klagen* pour out one's heart to s.o. **2.** a) harm, b) wrong: *j-m ein* **~** *zufügen* harm s.o.

leiden ['laɪdən] (litt, gelitten, h) **I** *v/t* **1.** suffer, bear, endure: **Hunger ~** *a.* starve; → *Not* **1.** **2.** (*nicht*) **~ können** (dis)like; *ich kann ihn nicht* **~** *a.* I can't stand him. **II** *v/i* **3.** a) suffer (**an** *or* **unter** *dat* from), b) be suffering, be in pain: *s-e Gesundheit hat darunter gelitten* it told on his health.

'Leiden *n* (-s; -) **1.** suffering. **2.** 🩺 illness, disease, complaint.

'leidend *adj* a) suffering, b) ailing, sickly: **~ aussehen** look ill.

'Leidenschaft *f* (-; -en) passion.

'leidenschaftlich *adj* passionate, ardent: *ich esse* **~** *gern Pizza* I just love pizza. **'Leidenschaftlichkeit** *f* (-; *no pl*) passionateness, ardo(u)r.

'leidenschaftslos *adj* dispassionate.

'Leidensgenosse *m* fellow sufferer.

'Leidensgeschichte *f* **1.** *no pl* **die ~** (**Christi**) Christ's Passion. **2.** *fig.* sad story, *iro.* tale of woe.

'Leidensmiene *f iro.* doleful expression.

'Leidensweg *m* **ihr Leben war ein einziger ~** hers was a life of suffering.

leider ['laɪdər] *adv* unfortunately: **~!** a.

alas!; *ich muß ~ gehen* (I am) sorry, but I must be going; I am afraid I have to go; *ja, ~!* I'm afraid so; *~ nein, ~ nicht* unfortunately not, I'm afraid not.

'**leidgeprüft** *adj* sorely tried.

leidig ['laɪdɪç] *adj* tiresome, unpleasant.

'**leidlich** *adj* tolerable, passable: *mir geht es ~* I'm not too bad.

'**Leidtragende** *m, f* (-n; -n) **1.** mourner: *die ~n* the bereaved. **2.** *er ist (immer) der ~* he is (always) the one to suffer.

'**Leidwesen** *n zu m-m ~* to my regret.

Leier ['laɪər] *f* (-; -n) **♩** *hist.* lyre: F *die alte ~* the same old story.

'**Leierkasten** *m* barrel-organ.

leiern ['laɪərn] *v/t, v/i* (h) drone.

'**Leihbiblio,thek** *f*, '**Leihbüche,rei** *f* lending library.

leihen ['laɪən] *v/t* (lieh, geliehen, h) **1.** *j-m et. ~* lend (*Am.* loan) s.o. s.th. **2.** *sich et. ~* borrow s.th. (*bei, von* from).

'**Leihgabe** *f art:* loan. '**Leihgebühr** *f* hire charge, *for books:* lending fee. '**Leihhaus** *n* pawnshop. '**Leihmutter** *f* surrogate mother. '**Leihwagen** *m* hire car. '**leihweise** *adv* on loan.

Leim [laɪm] *m* (-[e]s; -e) glue: F *aus dem ~ gehen* a) come apart, b) grow fat; *j-m auf den ~ gehen* be taken in by s.o.

leimen ['laɪmən] *v/t* (h) **1.** glue. **2.** F *j-n ~* take s.o. for a ride.

'**Leimfarbe** *f* glue colo(u)r.

Lein [laɪn] *m* (-[e]s; -e) **♣** flax.

Leine ['laɪnə] *f* (-; -n) a) string, cord, b) clothesline, c) leash, lead, d) (fishing) line: *den Hund an die ~ nehmen* (*an der ~ führen*) put (keep) the dog on the lead; *j-n an der ~ halten* keep s.o. on a short lead; F *~ ziehen* push off, scram.

leinen ['laɪnən] *adj* linen.

'**Leinen** *n* (-s; -) a) linen, b) canvas, c) *print.* cloth: *in ~ gebunden* clothbound. '**~kleid** *n* linen dress. '**~pa,pier** *n* linen paper. '**~schuh** *m* canvas shoe.

'**Leinöl** *n* linseed oil.

'**Leinsamen** *m* ♣ linseed.

'**Leinwand** *f* **1.** *a. paint.* canvas. **2.** *film etc:* screen.

leise ['laɪzə] *adj* quiet, low, soft (*voice etc*): *sei(d) ~!* be quiet!, don't make such a noise!; *das Radio ~(r) stellen* turn the radio down; *auf ~n Sohlen* treading softly; *ich habe nicht die leiseste Ahnung* I haven't the faintest

idea; *(sprich) ~(r)!* not so loud!

'**Leisetreter** *m* (-s; -) F pussyfoot(er).

Leiste ['laɪstə] *f* (-; -n) **1.** *anat.* groin. **2.** lath, strip of wood. **3.** △ fillet.

leisten ['laɪstən] *v/t* (h) **1.** a) do, manage, b) achieve, accomplish, c) *a.* ⚙ perform: *gute Arbeit ~* do a good job; *Erstaunliches ~* achieve amazing things. **2.** render: *für geleistete Dienste* for services rendered; *Ersatz ~* provide a replacement; *Zahlungen ~* make payments; → *Beitrag, Eid etc.* **3.** F *sich ~* a) afford, b) treat o.s. to, c) *fig.* get up to (do); *ich kann mir kein Auto ~* I can't afford a car; *fig.* *ich kann mir das nicht ~* I can't afford to do that; *er darf sich k-n Fehler mehr ~* he can't afford another mistake; *was hat er sich da wieder geleistet?* what has he been up to again?

'**Leisten** *m* (-s; -) last: F *fig.* *alles über einen ~ schlagen* measure everything by the same yardstick.

'**Leistenbruch** *m* ⚕ inguinal hernia.

'**Leistung** *f* (-; -en) **1.** a) *a.* ♦, *ped.*, *sports,* ⚙ *etc* performance, b) achievement, feat, c) work, d) output, e) result(s), ⚡, *phys.,* ⚙ *a.* power, ⚡ wattage, output, input: *schulische ~en* achievements at school; *nach ~ bezahlt werden* be paid by results; *e-e gute ~ bringen* make a good showing; F *e-e reife ~!* (*iro.* jolly) good show!; *schwache ~!* poor show! **2.** ♦ a) service(s) rendered, b) contribution, c) benefit, d) payment.

'**leistungs**|**berechtigt** *adj* ♦ entitled to claim. '**~bezogen** *adj* performance-oriented.

'**Leistungs**|**bi,lanz** *f* balance of current transactions. '**~denken** *n* performance-oriented outlook. '**~druck** *m* (-[e]s; *no pl*) pressure (to perform). '**leistungsfähig** *adj* a) efficient, ⚙ *a.* powerful, b) ♦ productive, c) fit. '**Leistungsfähigkeit** *f* (-; *no pl*) a) efficiency, ⚙ *a.* power, capacity, b) ♦ productivity, c) *ped. etc* ability, d) fitness. '**leistungsgerecht** *adj and adv* according to performance. '**Leistungs**|**gesellschaft** *f* achievement-oriented society. '**~knick** *m* sudden drop in performance. '**~kon,trolle** *f* *ped.* achievement control. '**~kurs** *m* *ped.* (*ich bin im ~ Geschichte* I am taking histo-

ry as a) special subject. **~lohn** m ✝ achievement wage(s). **~ni‚veau** n standard (of performance), *ped. a.* achievement level. **~prin‚zip** n performance principle. **~prüfung** f performance *(ped.* achievement) test.
'**leistungsschwach** *adj* inefficient, low--performance *(both a.* ◎), weak.
'**Leistungs|sport** m competitive sport(s). **~sportler(in** f) m competitive athlete. **~stand** m performance level.
'**leistungsstark** *adj* (highly) efficient, *a.* ◎ high-performance, powerful.
'**leistungssteigernd** *adj* performance--enhancing. '**Leistungssteigerung** f increase in performance *(or* efficiency).
'**Leistungs|träger(in** f) m top performer. **~wettbewerb** m ✝ efficiency contest. **~wille** m will to achieve. **~zentrum** n *sports:* training cent/re *(Am.* -er). **~zuschlag** m efficiency bonus.
'**Leitar‚tikel** m editorial, *esp. Br.* leader.
'**Leitbild** n model, example.
leiten ['laɪtən] *v/t* (h) **1.** a) lead, *a.* guide *(s.o.),* b) head, run, be in charge of, manage, c) direct, route *traffic (über acc* over): *e-e Sitzung (Diskussion)* ~ chair a meeting (discussion); *sports: das Spiel* ~ (be the) referee; *ein Orchester* ~ conduct an orchestra; *wer leitet die Delegation?* who is the head of the delegation? **2.** pass on *(an acc* to). **3.** *(a. v/i)* phys. conduct.
'**leitend** *adj* **1.** a) leading, guiding, b) ✝ managing, executive: **~e(r)** *Angestellte(r)* executive; **~e** *Stellung* managerial *(Am.* executive) post. **2.** phys. (*nicht*) ~ (non)conductive.
'**Leiter¹** ['laɪtər] f (-; -n) ladder.
'**Leiter²** m (-s; -) **1.** a) leader, b) ✝ head, managing director, manager, c) *ped.* headmaster, *Am.* principal, d) ♪ conductor. **2.** phys. conductor.
'**Leiterin** f (-; -nen) a) leader, b) ✝ head, manageress, c) *ped.* headmistress, *Am.* principal, d) ♪ conductress.
'**Leiterwagen** m (hand)cart.
'**Leitfaden** m textbook, manual, guide.
'**leitfähig** *adj phys.* conductive.
'**Leitfähigkeit** f (-; *no pl)* conductivity.
'**Leit|gedanke** m central theme. **~hammel** m *a. fig. contp.* bellwether. **~linie** f **1.** *mot.* white line. **2.** *pl fig.* guidelines. **~planke** f *mot.* crash barrier. **~satz** m

guiding principle. **~stelle** f central office. **~strahl** m ✈ guide beam. **~studie** f pilot study. **~tier** n leader.
'**Leitung** f (-; -en) **1.** *no pl* a) leadership, b) ✝ management, *(a. artistic)* direction, c) organization, d) administration, e) supervision, control: *die ~ haben von (or gen)* be in charge of, be the head of, head; *unter s-r* ~ under his direction; **♪** *unter der ~ von X* conducted by X. **2.** *the* leaders, management. **3.** a) *no pl phys.* conduction, ⚡ transmission, b) ⚡, ◎ line, c) *(gas, water, etc)* main(s), d) ⚡ lead. **4.** *teleph.* line: *die ~ ist besetzt* the line is busy *(or* engaged); F *e-e lange ~ haben* be slow in the uptake.
'**Leitungs|mast** m pole, pylon. **~netz** n a) supply network, b) mains system. **~schnur** f ⚡ cord, *Br.* flex. **~wasser** n tap water.
'**Leitwährung** f ✝ key currency.
'**Leitwerk** n ✈ tail unit.
'**Leitzins** m central bank discount rate.
Lektion [lɛk'tsĭoːn] f (-; -en) *ped.* unit: F *j-m e-e ~ erteilen* teach s.o. a lesson.
Lektor ['lɛktɔr] m (-s; -en ['-toːrən]), **Lektorin** [lɛk'toːrɪn] f (-; -nen) **1.** *univ.* lecturer. **2.** *(publisher's)* reader.
Lektüre [lɛk'tyːrə] f (-; -n) **1.** *no pl* reading. **2.** reading matter.
Lende ['lɛndə] f (-; -n) *anat., gastr.* loin.
'**Lenden|gegend** f *anat.* lumbar region. **~schurz** m loincloth. **~stück** n *gastr.* sirloin. **~wirbel** m lumbar vertebra.
Leninist [leni'nɪst] m (-en; -en) Leninist.
leni'nistisch *adj* Leninist.
'**lenkbar** *adj* **1.** ◎ manoeuvrable, *Am.* maneuverable, guided *(missile).* **2.** tractable *(child).*
lenken ['lɛŋkən] *v/t* (h) **1.** steer, *mot. a.* drive. **2.** *fig.* direct, guide, govern, control. **3.** *j-s Aufmerksamkeit ~ auf (acc)* direct *(or* draw) s.o.'s attention to; *die Unterhaltung ~ auf (acc)* steer the conversation round to; *den Verdacht ~ auf (acc)* throw suspicion on.
Lenker ['lɛŋkər] m (-s; -) **1.** driver. **2.** a) steering wheel, b) handlebar.
'**Lenkflugkörper** m ✗ guided missile.
'**Lenkrad** n *mot.* steering wheel. **~schaltung** f (steering-)column gear change *(Am.* shift). **~schloß** n steering-column *(or* steering-wheel) lock.

'Lenksäule f mot. steering column.
'Lenkstange f handlebar.
'Lenkung f (-; -en) **1.** no pl a) steering (etc, → **lenken**), b) ⚙ guidance, control (a. ✈). **2.** mot. steering mechanism.
lenzen ['lɛntsən] (h) ⚓ **I** v/t pump out. **II** v/i scud.
Leopard [leo'part] m (-en; -en) leopard.
Lepra ['le:pra] f (-; no pl) ⚕ leprosy.
Leprakranke m, f (-n; -n) leper.
Lerche ['lɛrçə] f (-; -n) zo. lark.
'lernbar adj learnable.
'lernbegierig adj eager to learn, keen.
'lernbehindert adj learning-disabled.
'Lerneifer m eagerness to learn.
lernen ['lɛrnən] v/t, v/i (h) learn (aus, bei, von from), study: kochen ~ learn (how) to cook; er lernt gut (schlecht) he is a good (slow) learner; et. auswendig ~ learn s.th. by heart; F er lernt Autoschlosser he's training as a car mechanic (bei a); aus s-n Fehlern ~ learn from one's mistakes; j-n (et.) schätzen ~ come to appreciate s.o. (s.th.); das will gelernt sein! that's not so easy!; F manche ~'s nie! some people never learn; → gelernt.
'Lernende m, f (-n; -n) learner.
'lernfähig adj able to learn.
'Lern|hilfe f learning aid. **~mittelfreiheit** f (-; no pl) free learning aids. **~pro,gramm** n computer: educational program(me Br.). **~pro,zeß** m learning process. **~schwester** f ⚕ student nurse. **~spiel** n educational game. **~stoff** m subject matter. **~ziel** n educational objective.
'Lesart f reading, version (a. fig.).
'lesbar adj a) legible, b) readable.
Lesbe ['lɛsbə] f (-; -n) F dike (sl.).
Lesbierin ['lɛsbĭərɪn] f (-; -nen) lesbian.
lesbisch ['lɛsbɪʃ] adj lesbian.
Lese ['le:zə] f (-; -n) ✂ **1.** gathering. **2.** vintage.
'Lesebrille f reading glasses.
'Lesebuch n reading book, reader.
'Lesekopf m computer: reading head.
'Leselampe f reading lamp.
lesen¹ ['le:zən] (las, gelesen, h) **I** v/t **1.** read: falsch ~ misread; flüchtig ~ skim (through); s-e Schrift ist kaum zu ~ his handwriting is hard to decipher; das Buch liest sich gut the book reads well; da war (or stand) zu ~, daß ... it said

there that ...; et. in j-s Gesicht ~ see s.th. in s.o.'s face; → **Messe¹**. **2.** univ. lecture on. **II** v/i **3.** read (in dat in, aus from). **4.** univ. lecture (über acc on).
'lesen² v/t (las, gelesen, h) a) gather, b) glean, c) vintage.
'lesenswert adj worth reading.
Leser ['le:zər] m (-s; -) reader.
'Leseratte f F bookworm.
'Leserbrief m a) reader's letter, b) letter to the editor.
'Leserin f (-; -nen) reader.
'Leserkreis m readers: e-n großen ~ haben be widely read.
'leserlich adj legible.
'Leserlichkeit f (-; no pl) legibility.
'Lesesaal m reading room.
'Lesestift m computer: scanner.
'Lesestoff m reading (matter).
'Lesestück n ped. reading (selection).
'Lesezeichen n bookmark.
'Lesung f (-; -en) reading: parl. in zweiter ~ on second reading.
letal [le'ta:l] adj ⚕ lethal.
Lethargie [letar'gi:] f (-; no pl) lethargy.
Lette ['lɛtə] m (-n; -n), **'Lettin** f (-; -nen), **'lettisch** adj Latvian. **'Lettland** n (-s) Latvia.
letzt [lɛtst] adj **1.** last, a. final, a. latter, a. former: ~e Nachrichten late(st) news; m-e ~en Ersparnisse the last of my savings; (am) ~en Sonntag last Sunday; in ~er Zeit lately, recently; ~er Endes after all; ~e(r) sein be last; als ~e(r) gehen go last, be the last to go; er wäre der Letzte, dem ich vertrauen würde he is the last person I would trust; das wäre das Letzte, was ich tun würde that's the last thing I would do; F das (er) ist doch das Letzte! that (he) is the absolute end!; → **Augenblick, Hand, Mal², Schrei** etc. **2.** last, extreme: bis ins ~e down to the last detail; bis aufs ~e completely, totally; → **Ehre, herausholen, Kraft** 1, **Ölung** 2. **3.** F poorest, worst: der ~e Mist! absolute rubbish!; → **Dreck** 1.
Letzt: zu guter ~ in the end.
'letztemal adv das ~ the last time.
'letztens adv lately.
'letztere adj der (die, das) ~ the latter.
'letztgenannt adj the last-mentioned.
'letzthin adv lately.

'**letztjährig** [-jɛ:rɪç] *adj das ~e Festival* last year's festival *etc.*

'**letztlich** *adj* **1.** ultimately, in the end. **2.** after all.

'**letztmals** *adv* for the last time.

'**letztwillig** *adj* ⚖ testamentary, *a. adv* by will: *~e Verfügung* last will (and testament).

'**Leuchtbombe** *f* flare (bomb).

Leuchte ['lɔʏçtə] *f* (-; -n) **1.** lamp, light. **2.** F luminary: *k-e ~ sein* be no genius.

leuchten ['lɔʏçtən] *v/i* (h) a) shine, b) flash, *fig. eyes:* light (up), c) gleam, sparkle: *mit e-r Lampe ~* shine a light; *j-m ~* light the way (*or* shine the torch) for s.o.; *j-m ins Gesicht ~* shine the (*or* a) lamp (*or* torch) in s.o.'s face.

'**leuchtend** *adj* shining (*eyes etc*), luminous, bright (*colour etc*): *~es Beispiel* shining example; *in ~en Farben schildern* paint s.th. in glowing colo(u)rs.

'**Leuchter** *m* (-s; -) a) candlestick, b) sconce, c) chandelier.

'**Leucht|farbe** *f* luminous paint. *~feuer* n beacon. *~gas* n → *Stadtgas*. *~kraft* f (-; *no pl*) luminosity. *~kugel* f (signal) flare. *~pi₁stole* f flare pistol. *~re₁klame* f luminous advertising, neon lights. *~röhre* f neon tube (*or* lamp). *~schirm* m fluorescent screen. *~spurgeschoß* n tracer bullet. *~stofflampe* f, *~stoffröhre* f fluorescent lamp (*or* tube). *~turm* m lighthouse. *~zeiger* m luminous hand. *~zifferblatt* n luminous dial.

leugnen ['lɔʏɡnən] (h) **I** *v/t* deny (*et. getan zu haben* having done s.th.): *es läßt sich nicht ~, es ist nicht zu ~* it cannot be denied, it is undeniable. **II** *v/i* deny everything, ⚖ deny the charge.

Leukämie [lɔʏkɛ'mi:] *f* (-; -n) ⚕ leuk(a)emia.

Leumund ['lɔʏmʊnt] *m* (-[e]s; *no pl*) reputation. '**Leumundszeugnis** *n* certificate of good character.

Leute ['lɔʏtə] *pl* people, ✕ *etc* men: *die ~* people; *m-e ~* my people, F my folks; F *hallo, ~!* hi, folks!; *es waren etwa 20 ~ da* there were about 20 persons present; *et. unter die ~ bringen* make s.th. public, spread s.th.

Leutnant ['lɔʏtnant] *m* (-s; -s) ✕ second lieutenant (*a.* ✈ *Am.*), ✈ pilot officer: *~ zur See* acting sublieutenant, *Am.* ensign.

'**leutselig** *adj* affable.

'**Leutseligkeit** *f* (-; *no pl*) affability.

Leviten [le'vi:tən] *pl j-m die ~ lesen* read s.o. the riot act.

Levkoje [lɛf'ko:jə] *f* (-; -n) ♣ stock.

lexikalisch [lɛksi'ka:lɪʃ] *adj* lexical.

Lexikograph [lɛksiko'gra:f] *m* (-en; -en) lexicographer. **Lexikographie** [lɛksikogra'fi:] *f* (-; *no pl*) lexicography. **lexiko'graphisch** *adj* lexicographical.

Lexikon ['lɛksikɔn] *n* (-s; -ka) **1.** encyclop(a)edia. **2.** → *Wörterbuch.*

Libanese [liba'ne:zə] *m* (-n; -n), **Liba'nesin** *f* (-; -nen), **liba'nesisch** *adj* Lebanese. **Libanon** ['li:banɔn] *m* (-s) *der ~* the Lebanon.

Libelle [li'bɛlə] *f* (-; -n) **1.** *zo.* dragonfly. **2.** ⊕ water level, bubble level.

liberal [libe'ra:l] *adj*, **Libe'rale** *m, f* (-n; -n) liberal, *pol.* Liberal. **liberalisieren** [liberali'zi:rən] *v/t* (h) liberalize.

Liberalismus [libera'lɪsmʊs] *m* (-; *no pl*) liberalism. **liberalistisch** [libera'lɪstɪʃ] *adj* liberalistic. **Liberalität** [liberali'tɛ:t] *f* (-; *no pl*) liberality.

Libero ['li:bero] *m* (-s; -s) *soccer:* libero.

Libido ['li:bido] *f* (-; *no pl*) *psych.* libido.

Libretto [li'brɛto] *n* (-s; -s, -tti) libretto.

Libyen ['li:byən] *n* (-s) Libya. '**Libyer** ['li:byər] *m* (-s; -), '**Libyerin** *f* (-; -nen), **libysch** ['li:byʃ] *adj* Libyan.

licht [lɪçt] *adj* **1.** bright: *~er Augenblick* lucid interval. **2.** thin, open (*woods*), *a.* thinning (*hair*). **3.** ⊕ *~e Höhe* clear height, overhead clearance; *~e Weite* inside width.

Licht *n* (-[e]s; -er) **1.** *no pl* a) light, b) daylight: *fig. bei ~(e) besehen* a) on closer inspection, b) strictly speaking; *ans ~ bringen (kommen)* bring (come) to light; *~ bringen in (acc)* throw light on; *das ~ der Welt erblicken* see the light of day, be born; *et. in e-m anderen ~ erscheinen lassen* reveal s.th. in a different light; F *j-n hinters ~ führen* deceive (*or* dupe) s.o.; *et. ins rechte ~ rücken* put s.th. in its true light; *das ~ scheuen* shun the light; *ein schlechtes* (*or schiefes*) *~ werfen auf (acc)* show s.o., s.th. in a bad light. **2.** a) light, b) lamp, c) candle: *~ machen, das ~ anmachen* turn on the light(s), *bei ~ arbeiten* work by lamplight; *die ~er der Großstadt* the lights of the city; F *er ist* *kein großes* ~ he is no genius; *mir geht ein* ~ *auf* I see (daylight); *j-m ein* ~ *aufstecken* open s.o.'s eyes; → *grün, Scheffel.* **3.** *paint.* (high)light. **4.** *pl hunt.* eyes.

'**Licht|anlage** *f* lighting system. ~**bild** *n* a) photo(graph), b) slide. ~**bildervortrag** *m* slide lecture. ~**blick** *m fig.* a) ray of hope, b) comfort: *der einzige* ~ (*in m-m Leben*) the only bright spot (in my life). ~**bogen** *m* ⚡ arc. ⚡**brechend** *adj opt.* refractive. ~**druck** *m* (-[e]s; *no pl*) phototype. ⚡**durchlässig** *adj* permeable to light. ⚡**echt** *adj* lightproof, nonfading. ⚡**empfindlich** *adj* sensitive to light, *opt., phot.* (photo)sensitive: ~ **machen** *phot.* sensitize. ~**empfindlichkeit** *f* sensitivity to light, *phot.* speed.

lichten¹ ['lɪçtən] (h) **I** *v/t* **1.** thin (out) (*trees etc*). **II** *sich* ~ **2.** *fog etc:* clear, lift. **3.** *trees, ranks, hair, etc:* be thinning (out), *supplies etc:* dwindle.

'**lichten²** *v/t* (h) *den Anker* ~ weigh anchor.

lichterloh ['lɪçtɐloː] *adv* ~ *brennen* be ablaze.

'**Licht|filter** *n, m phot.* light filter. ~**geschwindigkeit** *f* (*mit* ~ at) speed of light. ~**griffel** *m computer:* light pen. ~**hof** *m* **1.** ⌂ atrium. **2.** *astr., phot., TV* halo. ~**hupe** *f mot.* (headlamp) flasher: *die* ~ *betätigen* flash one's lights. ~**jahr** *n* light year. ~**kegel** *m* cone of light. ~**leitung** *f* ⚡ light circuit (*or* mains). ~**maschine** *f mot.* dynamo. ~**orgel** *f* colo(u)r organ. ~**quelle** *f* source of light. ~**schacht** *m* ⌂ light well. ~**schalter** *m* ⚡ light switch.

'**lichtscheu** *adj* **1.** shunning the light. **2.** *fig.* shady.

'**Lichtschranke** *f* photoelectric barrier.

'**Lichtschutzfaktor** *m* protection factor.

'**lichtstark** *adj* fast (*lens*). '**Lichtstärke** *f* luminous intensity, *phot.* speed.

'**Lichtstift** *m computer:* light pen.

'**Lichtstrahl** *m* ray (*or* beam) of light.

'**lichtundurchlässig** *adj* opaque.

'**Lichtung** *f* (-; -en) clearing.

Lid [liːt] *n* (-[e]s; -er) (eye)lid.

'**Lidschatten** *m* eye-shadow.

lieb [liːp] *adj* a) dear, b) sweet, nice, kind, c) good: *Lieber Herr X in letters:* Dear Mr. X; *sei* ~*!* be good!; *sei so* ~*!* be a dear!, do you mind?; *sei so* ~ *und ...* do

me a favo(u)r and ...; *es ist mir* ~*, daß ...* I am glad that ...; *es ist mir nicht* ~*, daß ...* I don't like it that ...; *mehr als mir* ~ *war* more than I really wanted; *das* ~*e Geld* always the money; *sich bei j-m* ~ *Kind machen* ingratiate o.s. with s.o.; → *Gott, lieber, liebst.*

liebäugeln ['liːpˀɔygəln] *v/i* (*insep,* ge-, h) ~ *mit* have one's eye on.

'**Lieben** *n* (-s; -) love, sweetheart.

Liebe¹ ['liːbə] *f* (-; -n) **1.** *no pl* (*zu*) love (of, for), affection (for): *die große* ~ the love of one's life; *aus* ~ *zu* out of love for; *aus* ~ *heiraten* marry for love; *mit* ~ *decorate etc* with loving care; ~ *macht blind* love is blind; *die* ~ *geht durch den Magen* the way to a man's heart is through his stomach. **2.** *no pl (körperliche)* ~ love(making), sex. **3.** F sweetheart, love, flame.

'**Liebe²** *m, f* (-n; -n) dear (person): *m-e* ~*!* my dear (girl)!; *mein* ~*r!* my dear man!; *m-e* ~*n!* my dears!

'**liebebedürftig** *adj* ~ *sein* need a lot of affection.

Liebelei [liːbə'laɪ] *f* (-; -en) flirtation.

lieben ['liːbən] (h) **I** *v/t* **1.** love, *a.* like: *j-n* ~ a) love s.o., b) make love to s.o.; *sich* ~ a) love each other, b) make love; *er liebt es nicht, wenn ...* he doesn't like it if ...; *liebend gern!* gladly!; *ich würde liebend gern ...* I'd love to ... **II** *v/i* **2.** (be in) love. **3.** make love ...

'**Liebende** *m, f* (-n; -n) lover.

'**liebenswert** *adj* lovable, amiable.

'**liebenswürdig** *adj* kind, obliging: *sehr* ~ *von Ihnen!* very kind of you!

'**liebenswürdiger**'**weise** *adv* kindly.

'**Liebenswürdigkeit** *f* (-; -en) **1.** *no pl* kindness. **2.** *pl* a) compliments, b) *iro.* insults.

lieber ['liːbɐ] *adv* rather, sooner, better: ~ *haben* (*als*) prefer (to), like *s.o., sth.* better (than); *du solltest* ~ *gehen* you had better go; *ich wüßte nicht, was ich* ~ *täte!, nichts* ~ *als das!* there's nothing I'd like better; (*ich möchte*) ~ *nicht!* I would (*or* I'd) rather not!

'**Liebes|abenteuer** *n,* ~**af**,**färe** *f* love affair. ~**brief** *m* love letter. ~**entzug** *m psych.* deprivation. ~**erklärung** *f* declaration of love: (*j-m*) *e-e* ~ *machen* declare one's love (to s.o.). ~**erlebnis** *n* **1.** experience of love. **2.** love (affair)

liegen

~**gabe** f (charitable) gift. ~**gedicht** n love poem. ~**geschichte** f love story. ~**heirat** f love match. ~**kummer** m lovesickness: ~ **haben** be lovesick. ~**leben** n love life. ~**lied** n love song. ~**mühe** f **das ist verlorene** ~! that's a waste of time! ~**paar** n (pair of) lovers, courting couple. ~**ro**|**man** m romance. ~**spiel** n loveplay. ~**szene** f love scene.

'**liebevoll** adj loving, affectionate: ~ **pflegen** take loving care of.

'**liebgewinnen** v/t (irr, sep, ge-, h, → **gewinnen**) grow (very) fond of.

'**liebhaben** v/t (irr, sep, ge-, h, → **haben**) love, be fond of.

Liebhaber ['li:pha:bər] m (-s; -) 1. lover. 2. a) (art etc) lover, enthusiast, fan, b) collector, c) at auctions etc: taker. 3. thea. jugendlicher ~ juvenile lead.

'**Liebhaber...** collector's (value etc).

Liebhabe'rei f (-; -en) hobby.

'**Liebhaberin** f (-; -nen) 1. → **Liebhaber** 2. 2. thea. **jugendliche** ~ jeune première.

liebkosen [li:p'ko:zən] v/t (insep, ge-, h), **Lieb'kosung** f (-; -en) caress.

'**lieblich** adj 1. a) lovely, charming, sweet, b) delightful, pleasant. 2. mellow (wine), sweet (bouquet).

'**Lieblichkeit** f (-; no pl) loveliness, charm, sweetness.

'**Liebling** m a) darling, favo(u)rite, b) pet: ~! (my) love!, darling!

'**Lieblings...** favo(u)rite. ~**schüler(in** f) m teacher's pet. ~**thema** n pet subject.

'**lieblos** adj unkind (words etc), uncaring (parents): ~ **zubereitet** prepared carelessly (F any old how).

'**Lieblosigkeit** f (-; no pl) unkindness, coldness.

'**Liebschaft** f (-; -en) (love) affair.

liebst I adj a) dearest, b) favo(u)rite: **m-e** ~**e Sendung** etc a. the program(me) etc I like best. **II** adv **am** ~**en** best (or most) of all; **am** ~**en spiele ich Tennis** I like tennis best; **es wäre mir am** ~**en, wenn ...** it would suit me best if ...

'**Liebste** m, f (-n; -n) (**mein** ~**r, m-e** ~ my) darling (or love, sweetheart)

Lied [li:t] n (-[e]s; -er) song, air, tune, lied: **geistliches** ~ hymn; **es ist immer das alte** ~ it's the same old story every time; **das Ende vom** ~ the upshot; **ich**

kann ein ~ **davon singen** I can tell you a thing or two about it.

Liederabend ['li:dər-] m lieder recital.

'**Liederbuch** n songbook.

liederlich ['li:dərliç] adj 1. slovenly, sloppy. 2. dissolute (life etc).

'**Liederlichkeit** f (-; no pl) 1. slovenliness. 2. dissoluteness.

'**Liedermacher** m singer-songwriter.

Lieferant [lifə'rant] m (-en; -en) a) supplier, b) contractor: ~ **für Speisen und Getränke** caterer.

'**lieferbar** adj available: **die Ware ist sofort** ~ the article can be supplied (or delivered) at once.

liefern ['li:fərn] (h) **I** v/t 1. a. fig. **j-m et.** ~ supply s.o. with s.th. 2. deliver (dat to). 3. yield, give, a. fig. provide: **e-n harten Kampf** ~ put up a good fight; **ein gutes Spiel** ~ play well, make a good showing. 4. F **er ist geliefert!** he's done for!, he's had it! **II** v/i 5. supply, deliver.

'**Lieferschein** m delivery note.

'**Lieferter**|**min** m date of delivery.

'**Lieferung** f (-; -en) 1. a) supply, b) delivery: **zahlbar bei** ~ cash on delivery (abbr. C.O.D.). 2. consignment, Am. shipment. 3. print. instal(l)ment.

'**Liefer**|**vertrag** m supply contract. ~**wagen** m delivery van (Am. truck), pickup. ~**werk** n supplier's plant, suppliers. ~**zeit** f delivery time.

Liege ['li:gə] f (-; -n) 1. couch. 2. campbed. 3. sunbed.

'**Liegegeld** n ⚓ demurrage.

liegen ['li:gən] v/i (lag, gelegen, h) 1. lie, be: **laß das Buch** ~! leave the book alone!; **liegst du bequem?** are you comfortable?; (**krank**) **im Bett** ~ be (ill) in bed; F fig. **damit liegst du richtig!** (there) you are on the right track!; **an der Kette** ~ be chained up; **es lag Schnee** there was snow; **das Geld liegt auf der Bank** the money is in the bank; sports: **er lag auf dem dritten Platz** ~ he was (lying) in third place; **wie die Dinge** ~ as matters stand; **die Sache liegt so ...** the matter is as follows ...; **die Preise** ~ **bei ...** prices are at (or around) ...; **wo** ~ **s-e Schwächen?** what are his weak points?; **da liegt der Fehler!** that's where the trouble lies! 2. (an dat) lie (on), be (situated) (at, near): **das Hotel liegt zentral** the hotel is centrally situated; *nach Süden* ~ face south; → *fern* I. 3. *fig. j-m* ~ a) suit s.o., b) appeal to s.o.; *die Rolle liegt ihr* the part suits her; *er (es) liegt mir nicht* he (it) isn't my cup of tea. **4.** *fig. woran liegt es?* what's the reason (for it)?; *woran liegt es, daß er nie gewinnt?* why is it (that) he never wins?; *daran liegt es* that's (the reason) why; *es liegt daran, daß ...* the reason is that ...; *was liegt daran?* who cares?; *mir liegt viel (wenig) daran* it means a lot (it doesn't mean much) to me; *es liegt nicht an ihr (wenn)* it's not her fault (if); *an mir soll's nicht ~!* a) it's all right by me!, b) I'll do my best!; *es liegt bei (or an) dir (zu entscheiden)* it is up to you (to decide).

'liegenbleiben *v/i (irr, sep,* -ge-, sn, → *bleiben)* **1.** remain lying: *(im Bett)* ~ stay in bed; *bleib liegen!* don't get up! **2.** *car etc:* break down, *driver etc:* be (or get) stranded. **3.** *snow:* settle. **4.** *work etc:* be left unfinished: *das kann ~!* that can wait! **5.** *goods:* be left unsold. **6.** be left behind.

'liegenlassen *v/t (irr, sep,* -ge-, h, → *lassen)* **1.** leave *s.th.* behind. **2.** leave *task etc* unfinished. **3.** leave *things* lying around: *alles stehen- und ~* drop everything; → *links* 1.

'Liegenschaften *pl* real estate.

'Liege|platz *m* ⚓ berth. **~sitz** *m mot.* reclining seat. **~stuhl** *m* deckchair. **~stütz** [-ʃtʏts] *m* (-es; -e) *gym.* *(e-n ~ machen* do a) press-up. **~wagen** *m* 🚃 couchette. **~wiese** *f* lawn.

lieh [liː] *pret of* **leihen.**

ließ [liːs] *pret of* **lassen.**

Lift [lɪft] *m* (-[e]s; -e, -s)) lift, *Am.* elevator. **'liften** *v/t* (h) 🎨 lift: *sich (das Gesicht)* ~ *lassen* have a facelift.

Liga ['liːga] *f* (-; Ligen) league, *sports:* a. division.

liieren [li'iːrən] *sich* ~ (h) team up *(mit* with); *mit j-m liiert sein* have an affair with s.o.

Likör [li'køːr] *m* (-s; -e) liqueur.

lila ['liːla] *adj,* **'Lila** *n* (-s; -) lilac, mauve.

Lilie ['liːli̯ə] *f* (-; -n) 🌸 lily.

Liliputaner [lilipu'taːnər] *m* (-s; -), **Liliputanerin** *f* (-; -nen) Lilliputian.

Limonade [limo'naːdə] *f* (-; -n) fizzy drink, *Am.* soda pop.

Limousine [limu'ziːnə] *f* (-; -n) *mot.* limousine, saloon (car), *Am.* sedan.

Linde ['lɪndə] *f* (-; -n) 🌳 lime (tree).

'Lindenblütentee *m* lime-blossom tea.

lindern ['lɪndərn] *v/t* (h) relieve, alleviate, ease. **'Linderung** *f* (-; *no pl)* relief, alleviation, easing: *(j-m)* ~ *verschaffen* bring (s.o.) relief.

Lineal [line'aːl] *n* (-s; -e) ruler.

linear [line'aːr] *adj* ✝, ⚗ linear.

Linguist [lɪŋˈɡʊɪst] *m* (-en; -en) linguist.

Linguistik [lɪŋˈɡʊɪstɪk] *f* (-; *no pl)* linguistics.

Linie ['liːni̯ə] *f* (-; -n) line (*a. fig.*), a. route, *pol. etc* course, policy: *auf die (schlanke)* ~ *achten* watch one's figure; *mit der* ~ *2 fahren* take the number two; *fig. auf der ganzen* ~ all along (or down) the line; *auf gleicher* ~ *mit* on a level with; *in erster* ~ in the first place.

'Linien|bus *m* regular bus. **~dienst** *m* regular service. **~flug** *m* scheduled flight. **~flugzeug** *n* 🛩 scheduled plane. **~ma,schine** *f* scheduled plane. **~netz** *n* (rail *etc*) network: *das* ~ *der U-Bahn* the underground (system). **~pa,pier** *n* ruled paper. **~richter** *m sports:* linesman. **⚲treu** *adj pol.* loyal (to the line): ~ *sein* follow the party line. **~treue** *m, f* (-n; -n) party liner. **~verkehr** *m* regular service (or traffic).

linieren [li'niːrən], **liniieren** [lini'iːrən] *v/t* (h) rule, line.

link [lɪŋk] *adj* left: *die* ~*e Seite of cloth:* the reverse (side); *auf die* ~*en Seite, ~er Hand* on the left; *~er Hand sehen Sie ...* on your left you see ...; *pol., sports:* ~*er Flügel* left wing; *pol. dem* ~*en Flügel angehören* be left-wing; *fig. er ist wohl mit dem* ~*en Fuß zuerst aufgestanden!* he must have got out of bed on the wrong side; *~e Masche* a) purl (stitch), b) a. ~*e Tour* F dirty trick; F *ein ganz* ~*er Typ* a real bastard.

'Linke¹ *f* (-n; -n) **1.** left hand, *boxing:* left. **2.** *pol. the* Left. **3.** left (side): *zu ihrer* ~*n* on her left.

'Linke² *m, f* (-n; -n) *pol.* leftist.

'linken *v/t* (h) F con, take *s.o.* for a ride.

'linkisch *adj* awkward, clumsy.

links *adv* **1.** on (*or* to) the left; *nach* ~ (to the) left; *von* ~ from the left; ~ *von* (on *or* to the) left of; ~ *von mir* (on *or* to) my left; ~ *abbiegen* turn left; *sich* ~

halten keep (to the) left; *fig.* ~ *liegenlassen* ignore; F ~ *sein* a) be left-handed, b) *a.* ~ *stehen pol.* be left-wing; ~ *stricken* purl; F *fig.* **das mache ich mit** ~ that's kid's stuff (for me). **2.** on the wrong side, inside out.

'**Linksabbieger** *m* (-s; -) *mot.* vehicle (*pl* traffic) turning left.

'**Linksaußen** *m sports*: outside left.

'**Linksextre,mist(in** *f*) *m pol.* left-wing extremist. '**linksextre,mistisch** *adj pol.* (of the) extreme left.

'**linksgerichtet** *adj pol.* left-wing.

'**Linkshänder** [-hɛndər] *m* (-s; -) left-hander: ~ *sein* be left-handed.

'**linksherum** *adv* **1.** ⚙ anticlockwise. **2.** inside out.

'**Linkskurve** *f* left turn.

'**linksradi,kal** *adj pol.* (of the) extreme left: *die Linksradikalen* the left-wing radicals.

'**linksrheinisch** *adj* and *adv* on the left bank of the Rhine.

'**Linksruck** *m pol.* swing to the left.

'**Linkssteuerung** *f mot.* left-hand drive.

'**Linksverkehr** *m in Großbritannien ist* ~ in Great Britain they drive on the left.

Linoleum [li'no:leʊm] *n* (-s; *no pl*) linoleum, F lino.

Linse ['lɪnzə] *f* (-; -n) **1.** ♀ lentil. **2.** *opt.* lens.

Lippe ['lɪpə] *f* (-; -n) lip: *von den ~n ablesen* lip-read; *ich bringe es nicht über die ~n* I can't bring myself to say it; *sich auf die ~n beißen* bite one's lip.

'**Lippenbekenntnis** *n* (*ein ~ ablegen* pay) lip service (*zu* to).

'**Lippenblütler** [-bly:tlər] *m* (-s; -) ♀ labiate.

'**Lippenlaut** *m ling.* labial (sound).

'**Lippenstift** *m* lipstick.

liquid [li'kvi:t] *adj* ✝ liquid, solvent.

Liquidation [likvida'tsjo:n] *f* (-; -en) **1.** ✝ liquidation (*a. pol. murder*), winding up. **2.** fee, charge, bill.

liquidieren [likvi'di:rən] *v/t* (h) **1.** ✝ liquidate (*a. pol. kill*), wind up. **2.** charge.

Liquidität [likvidi'tɛ:t] *f* (-; *no pl*) ✝ liquidity, solvency.

lispeln ['lɪspəln] *v/t, v/i* (h) lisp.

List [lɪst] *f* (-; -en) ruse, trick, cunning: *zu e-r* ~ *greifen* resort to a ruse.

Liste ['lɪstə] *f* (-; -n) list: *j-n auf die* ~ *setzen* put s.o.'s name on the list; F

schwarze ~ black list; *j-n auf die schwarze* ~ *setzen* blacklist s.o.

'**Listenpreis** *m* ✝ list price.

'**listig** *adj* cunning, sly, crafty.

Litanei [lita'naɪ] *f* (-; -en) litany.

Liter ['li:tər] *n, m* (-s; -) litre, *Am.* liter.

literarisch [lɪtə'ra:rɪʃ] *adj* literary.

Literat [lɪtə'ra:t] *m* (-en; -en) man of letters, literary man. **Literatur** [lɪtəra'tu:r] *f* (-; *no pl*) literature.

Litera'tur... literary. **~angaben** *pl* bibliography. **~gattung** *f* literary genre. **~geschichte** *f* history of literature. **~kritiker(in** *f*) *m* literary critic. **~preis** *m* literary award. **~wissenschaft** *f* literature, literary studies.

'**literweise** *adv fig.* by the gallon.

Litfaßsäule ['lɪtfas-] *f* advertising pillar.

Lithographie [litogra'fi:] *f* (-; -n) lithography.

litt [lɪt] *pret of leiden*.

Liturgie [lɪtʊr'gi:] *f* (-; -n) liturgy.

Litze ['lɪtsə] *f* (-; -n) **1.** braid, lace. **2.** ⚡ cord, flex, stranded conductor.

live [laɪf] *adj* and *adv* live.

'**Live-Sendung** *f* live broadcast.

Livree [li'vre:] *f* (-; -n) livery: *in* ~ → *livriert* [li'vri:rt] *adj* liveried.

Lizenz [li'tsɛnts] *f* (-; -en) licen/ce (*Am.* -se): *in* ~ *produce etc* under licence.

Li'zenz|ausgabe *f print.* edition printed under licence. **~geber** *m* (-s; -) licenser, licensor. **~gebühr** *f* royalty. **~inhaber** *m*, **~nehmer** *m* (-s; -) licensee. **~vertrag** *m* licensing agreement.

LKW-Fahrer ['ɛlkave-] *m* lorry driver, *Am.* truck driver.

Lob [lo:p] *n* (-[e]s; *no pl*) (*über jedes* ~ *erhaben* beyond) praise: *j-s* ~ *singen* sing s.o.'s praises.

Lobby ['lɔbi] *f* (-; -bys, -bies) lobby.

Lobbyist [lɔbi'ɪst] *m* (-en; -en) lobbyist.

loben ['lo:bən] *v/t, v/i* (h) (*wegen gen, dat* for) praise, commend: *das lobe ich mir!* that's what I like!; *da lobe ich mir ... an* ~ say any time; *j-n ~d hervorheben* single s.o. out for praise.

'**lobenswert** *adj* laudable.

Lobhudelei [lo:phudə'laɪ] *f* (-; -en) base flattery.

löblich ['lø:plɪç] *adj esp. iro.* laudable.

'**Loblied** *n fig. ein ~ auf j-n singen* sing s.o.'s praises.

'**Lobrede** *f* eulogy.

Loch [lɔx] *n* (-[e]s; ˈer) **1.** hole, *in tooth:* a. cavity, *in tyre:* puncture, *in fence etc:* gap: *fig.* **ein ~ reißen in** (*acc*) make a hole in; **ein ~ im Haushalt stopfen** stop a gap in the budget; F **er pfeift auf dem letzten ~** he's on his last legs. **2.** F *fig.* a) hole, dump, b) jug (*sl.*).

lochen ['lɔxən] *v/t* (h) a) punch, b) stamp, c) perforate.

'Locher *m* (-s; -) ⚙ punch, perforator.

löcherig ['lœçərɪç] *adj a. fig.* full of holes.

löchern ['lœçərn] *v/t* (h) F pester.

'Lochstreifen *m* punched tape.

'Lochung *f* (-; -en) perforation.

'Lochzange *f* punch pliers, 🎫 ticket punch.

Locke ['lɔkə] *f* (-; -n) curl: **~n haben** have curly hair.

locken¹ ['lɔkən] *v/t* (h) (*a.* **sich ~**) curl.

'locken² *v/t* (h) **1.** lure, bait, call (*animal*). **2.** *fig.* lure, tempt: **es lockt mich sehr zu** *inf* I'm very much tempted to *inf*; **~des Angebot** tempting offer.

'Lockenkopf *m* curly-head.

'Lockenwickler *m* curler.

locker ['lɔkər] *adj* **1.** a) loose (*a. fig. morals etc*), a) slack (*soil, dough, etc*): → **Schraube 1. 2.** *fig.* easy, relaxed, *person:* a. cool: F **es geht sehr ~ zu** it's all very relaxed; **das schafft er ~** he can do that easily. **'Lockerheit** *f* (-; *no pl*) **1.** a) looseness, slackness, b) lightness. **2.** *fig.* easy manner.

'lockerlassen *v/i* (*irr, sep,* -ge-, h, → **lassen**) F **nicht ~** not to let up, keep (on) trying.

'lockermachen *v/t* (*sep,* -ge-, h) F (**bei j-m**) **Geld ~** (make s.o.) fork out (*or* come across with) money.

lockern ['lɔkərn] (h) **I** *v/t* loosen, slacken (*rope etc*), relax (*grip, fig. discipline etc*): **s-e Muskeln ~** loosen up one's muscles. **II sich ~** become loose (*a. fig. morals etc*), slacken, *sports:* limber up, *fig. mood etc:* relax. **'Lockerung** *f* (-; *no pl*) loosening, slackening, *fig.* relaxation. **'Lockerungsübung** *f sports:* limbering-up exercise.

lockig ['lɔkɪç] *adj* curly.

'Lockmittel *n a. fig.* bait. **'Lockruf** *m zo.* (mating) call. **'Lockspitzel** *m pol.* stool pigeon, agent provocateur.

'Lockung *f* (-; -en) lure, temptation. **'Lockvogel** *m a. fig.* decoy. **~werbung** *f*

🎯 loss-leader selling.

Lodenmantel ['lo:dən-] *m* loden (coat).

lodern ['lo:dərn] *v/i* (h) *a. fig.* blaze.

Löffel ['lœfəl] *m* (-s; -) **1.** a) spoon, b) spoonful: **zwei ~** (**voll**) **Zucker** two spoonfuls of sugar; F *fig.* **den ~ weglegen** peg out. **2.** *hunt. or* F *ear:* **schreib dir das hinter die ~!** get that into your thick head once and for all!

'Löffelbagger *m* (power) shovel.

'Löffelbis,kuit *m* spongefinger.

löffeln ['lœfəln] *v/t* (h) spoon.

'Löffelstiel *m* spoon handle.

'löffelweise *adv* by the spoonful.

log [lo:k] *pret of* **lügen**.

Loga'rithmentafel *f* ⅄ log table.

Logarithmus [loga'rɪtmʊs] *m* (-; -men) ⅄ logarithm.

Logbuch ['lɔk-] *n* ⚓ log(book).

Loge ['lo:ʒə] *f* (-; -n) **1.** *thea.* box. **2.** (*freemason's*) lodge.

Logik ['lo:gɪk] *f* (-; *no pl*) logic.

logisch ['lo:gɪʃ] *adj* logical: F (**das ist doch**) **~!** naturally!, of course!

'logischerweise *adv* logically.

Logistik [lo'gɪstɪk] *f* (-; *no pl*) logistics.

logo ['lo:go] *adj pred* F sure (thing).

'Logo *m, n* (-s; -s) F logo.

Logopäde [logo'pɛ:də] *m* (-n; -n), **Logo'pädin** *f* (-; -nen) speech therapist. **Logopädie** [logopɛ'di:] *f* (-; *no pl*) logop(a)edics, speech therapy.

Lohn [lo:n] *m* (-[e]s; ˈe) **1.** wages, pay. **2.** *fig.* (**zum ~**) reward (**für** for): **s-n wohlverdienten ~ erhalten** a. *iro.* get one's just deserts. **~abschluß** *m* wage agreement. **~anteil** *m* wages. **~ausfall** *m* loss of wages. **~ausgleich** *m* **bei vollem ~** without cuts in pay. **~buchhalter(in** *f) m* wages clerk. **~bü,ro** *n* pay office. **~empfänger(in** *f) m* wage earner.

lohnen ['lo:nən] (h) **I sich ~ 1.** be worth(while), pay; **die Mühe lohnt sich** it's worth the trouble; **es lohnt sich zu** *inf* it's worth *ger*, it pays to *inf*; **der Film lohnt sich** the film is worth seeing; **Verbrechen lohnt sich nicht** crime doesn't pay. **II** *v/t* **2.** reward: **j-m et. schlecht ~** ill repay s.o. **3.** **die Mühe (e-n Besuch) ~** be worth the trouble (a visit). **'lohnend** *adj* **1.** paying, profitable. **2.** worthwhile, rewarding, a. worth seeing (*etc*).

'**Lohn|erhöhung** f wage increase, (pay) rise, Am. raise. **~forderung** f wage claim. **~fortzahlung** f continued pay (to sick workers). **~gefälle** n wage differential. **~gruppe** f pay bracket.

'**lohninten,siv** adj wage-intensive.

'**Lohn|kampf** m wage dispute. **~kosten** pl wage costs: **sehr hohe ~ haben** have a huge payroll. **~kürzung** f wage cut. **~runde** f round of wage negotiations.

'**Lohnsteuer** f wage(s) tax. **~jahresausgleich** m annual adjustment of income tax. **~karte** f wage(s) tax card.

'**Lohn|stopp** m pay freeze. **~streifen** m pay slip. **~ta,rif** m wage rate.

'**Löhnung** ['løːnʊŋ] f (-; -en) ✕ pay.

'**Loipe** ['lɔypə] f (-; -n) cross-country (skiing) trail.

'**Lok** [lɔk] f (-; -s) 🚂 F engine.

'**lokal** [loˈkaːl] adj local.

'**Lo'kal** n (-s; -e) a) restaurant, b) pub, Am. saloon. **Lo'kal...** local (newspaper, reporter, press, etc).

'**Lo'kalanästhe,sie** f local an(a)esthesia.

'**lokalisieren** [lokaliˈziːrən] v/t (h) locate, a. ⚕ localize (**auf** acc to).

'**Lo'kal|kolo,rit** n local colo(u)r. **~ter,min** m ⚖ visit to the scene (of the crime).

'**Lokomotive** [lokomoˈtiːvə] f (-; -n) engine. **Lokomo'tivführer** m engine driver, Am. engineer.

'**Lokus** ['loːkʊs] m (-[ses]; -[se]) F loo, Am. john.

'**Lombardkre,dit** ['lɔmbart-] m † collateral loan. '**Lombardsatz** m rate for (central bank) loans on securities.

'**Londoner** ['lɔndoːnər] I m (-s; -) Londoner. II adj (of) London.

'**Lorbeer** ['lɔrbeːr] m (-s; -en) **1.** ♣ laurel (tree), bay (tree). bay leaf. **3.** pl fig. laurels: **sich auf s-n ~en ausruhen** rest on one's laurels; **damit kannst du (bei ihr) k-e ~en ernten** that won't get you anywhere (with her).

'**Lore** ['loːrə] f (-; -n) 🚂 tipper.

'**los¹** [loːs] adj pred **1.** off: **der Knopf ist ~** the button is off; **der Hund ist ~** the dog is loose. **2.** F **~ sein** be rid of s.o., s.th.; **den wären wir ~!** good riddance!; **mein Geld bin ich ~** my money is gone; → a. **losgehen, loslegen** etc. **3.** F **was ist ~** a) (**mit dir**)? what's the matter (with you)?, b) (**hier**)? what's going on (here)?, c) **in Berlin** events etc: what's

on in Berlin?, politically etc: what's going on in Berlin?; **da war (schwer) was ~** a) things were really happening, b) the sparks were flying; **hier ist nichts** (or **nie was**) **~!** nothing doing (or no action) around here!; **wo ist hier was ~?** where can you go around here?; **mit ihm ist nicht viel ~** he isn't up to much. **4.** F **er hat (schwer) was ~** he's very good (**in** dat at), he's on the ball.

los² int a) let's go!, b) go!: fig. **schieß ~!** fire away!; sports: **Achtung, fertig, ~!** ready, steady, go!; **nun aber ~!** let's get going (or cracking)!; **nun mal ~!** here goes!; **~, sag schon!** come on, tell me!

Los n (-es; -e) **1.** a) lot, ticket, number: **ein ~ ziehen** draw a lot (or ticket); **das große ~ ziehen** win the first prize, fig. hit the jackpot; **mit j-m (et.) das große ~ ziehen** strike it lucky with s.o. (s.th.); **et. durch das ~ entscheiden** decide s.th. by drawing lots (or by a toss-up); **das ~ fiel auf ihn zu** inf it fell upon him to inf. **2.** fig. lot, fate: **ein schweres ~** a hard lot. **3.** † lot.

'**lösbar** adj soluble (a. 🜊), solvable.

'**losbinden** v/t (irr, sep, -ge-, h, → **binden**) untie.

'**losbrechen** (irr, sep, -ge-, → **brechen**) **I** v/t (h) break off. **II** v/i (sn) storm etc: break, laughter etc: break out.

löschen¹ ['lœʃən] v/t (h) **1.** extinguish, put out (fire, light, etc): **den Durst ~** quench one's thirst. **2.** 🜊 quench, slake (lime). blot (ink). **4.** strike out, cancel (a. mortgage), a. computer: delete, erase (a. tape recording etc), settle (debt), close (account). **5.** fig. efface.

'**löschen²** v/t (h) ⚓ unload.

'**Lösch|fahrzeug** n fire engine. **~gerät** n fire extinguisher, coll. fire-fighting equipment. **~kopf** m erasing head. **~mannschaft** f fire brigade. **~pa,pier** n blotting paper. **~taste** f erase button, computer: cancel key.

lose ['loːzə] adj a. fig. loose.

'**Lösegeld** n ransom.

'**loseisen: sich** (v/t **j-n**) ~ (sep, -ge-, h) F get (s.o.) away (**von** from).

losen ['loːzən] v/i (h) draw lots (or toss up) (**um** for).

lösen ['løːzən] (h) **I** v/t **1.** remove, detach. **2.** a) undo (hair, tie, etc) b) a. 🜊 loosen, relax, c) release (brake etc). **3.**

fig. solve (*a.* A), answer (*question*), resolve, settle (*conflict etc*). **4.** *fig.* dissolve (*marriage etc*), break off (*engagement*), sever (*relations etc*), terminate (*contract*). **5.** buy, get (*ticket*). **6.** 🔧 dissolve. **II sich ~ 7.** a) come loose (*or* undone), b) open, c) loosen (*a.* 🎾). **8. sich ~** (*von* from) free o.s., *a. sports:* break away. **9.** *·problem etc:* solve itself, *conflict etc:* resolve itself. **10.** *tension etc:* ease; → **gelöst. 11.** 🔧 dissolve.

'losfahren *v/i* (*irr, sep, -ge-, sn,* → **fahren**) a) leave, b) drive off.

'losgehen *v/i* (*irr, sep, -ge-, sn,* → **gehen**) **1.** leave, *a.* rifle, shot, *etc* go off. **2.** F start, begin: **gleich geht's los!** it's just about to begin!; **jetzt geht's los!** here goes!, here we go!; **es kann ~!** we're (*or* I'm *etc*) ready!; **jetzt geht's schon wieder los!** here we go again! **3.** F come off. **4. ~ auf** (*acc*) head (*or* make) for; **mit dem Messer auf j-n ~** go for s.o. with a knife.

'losheulen *v/i* (*sep, -ge-, h*) F burst into tears.

'losketten *v/t* (*sep, -ge-, h*) unchain.

'loskommen *v/i* (*irr, sep, -ge-, sn,* → **kommen**) *a. fig.* get away (*von* from).

'loslassen (*irr, sep, -ge-, h,* → **lassen**) **I** *v/t* **1.** let go of, let s.o. go, release: F **j-n auf die Menschheit ~** let s.o. loose on humanity; **das Buch läßt e-n nicht mehr los** the book is quite unputdownable; **der Gedanke läßt mich nicht (mehr) los** I can't get it out of my mind. **2.** let go with a blow *etc*, let off fireworks, launch (*protest etc*), let fly with a letter *etc*, crack (*joke etc*). **II** *v/i* **3.** let go: **nicht ~!** a. hang on!

'loslegen *v/i* (*sep, -ge-, h*) F **1.** get cracking. **2.** let fly (*gegen* at): **dann legte er los** then he really got going; **leg schon los!** fire away!

'löslich *adj* 🔧 soluble.

'losmachen (*sep, -ge-, h*) **I** *v/t* **1.** untie, undo. **2.** ⚓ cast off. **II sich ~** *a. fig.* free o.s. (*von* from).

'losrasen *v/i* (*sep, -ge-, sn*) zoom off.

'losreißen: sich ~ (*irr, sep, -ge-, h,* → **reißen**) (*von* from) break away, *fig.* tear o.s. away.

'losrennen *v/i* (*irr, sep, -ge-, sn,* → **rennen**) dash off, run off.

'lossagen: sich ~ von (*sep, -ge-, h*) break with.

'losschlagen *v/i* (*irr, sep, -ge-, h,* → **schlagen**) ⚔ strike.

'losschnallen *v/t* (*sep, -ge-, h*) unbuckle: ✈, *mot.* **sich ~** undo one's seat belt.

'lossteuern *v/i* (*sep, -ge-, sn*) **~ auf** (*acc*) *a. fig.* make (*or* head) for.

Losung¹ ['lo:zʊŋ] *f* (-; -en) ⚔ password, *fig.* watchword, *pol. a.* slogan.

'Losung² *f* (-; *no pl*) *hunt.* droppings.

'Lösung *f* (-; -en) 🔧 *or fig.* solution.

'Lösungsmittel *n* 🔧 solvent.

'Lösungswort *n* answer.

'loswerden *v/t* (*irr, sep, -ge-, sn,* → **werden**) **1.** get rid of: **ich werde das Gefühl nicht los, daß ...** I can't help feeling that ...; **das mußte ich mal ~!** I had to get that off my chest! **2.** *money:* a) lose, b) spend.

'losziehen *v/i* (*irr, sep, -ge-, sn,* → **ziehen**) **1.** set out, march off. **2.** *fig.* **~ gegen** lay into, let fly at.

Lot [lo:t] *n* (-[e]s; -e) **1.** A (**ein ~ fällen** drop a) perpendicular: **aus dem ~** out of plumb; *fig.* **im ~ sein** be in good order; *et.* **wieder ins ~ bringen** set s.th. right again. **2.** ⚙ plumb (bob). **3.** ⚙ solder.

'loten ['lo:tən] *v/t, v/i* (*h*) plumb, sound.

'löten ['lø:tən] *v/t* (*h*) ⚙ solder.

Lotion [lo'tsi̯o:n] *f* (-; -en) lotion.

'Lötkolben *m* soldering iron. **'Lötlampe** *f* soldering lamp, *Am.* blowtorch. **'Lötnaht** *f* soldered joint.

'lotrecht *adj* perpendicular, vertical.

Lotse ['lo:tsə] *m* (-n; -n) ⚓ pilot.

'lotsen ['lo:tsən] *v/t* (*h*) **1.** ⚓ pilot. **2.** F *j-n ~* a) guide s.o. (*durch* through), b) drag s.o. off (*in acc* to).

'Lotsendienst *m* *mot.* driver-guide service. **'Lotsengebühr** *f* ⚓ pilotage.

Lotterie [lɔtə'ri:] *f* (-; -n) lottery. **~gewinn** *m* (lottery) prize. **~los** *n* (lottery) ticket. **~spiel** *n* lottery, *fig.* gamble.

Lotto ['lɔto] *n* (-s; -s) **1.** lotto, bingo. **2.** Lotto, (West German numbers pool) lottery: **im ~ spielen** do Lotto.

'Lottoannahme(stelle) *f* Lotto ticket agency. **'Lottoschein** *m* Lotto ticket.

Löwe ['lø:və] *m* (-n; -n) **1.** *zo.* lion. **2.** *astr.* Leo: **er ist (ein) ~** he's (a) Leo.

'Löwen|anteil *m* *fig.* lion's share.

~mähne f fig. (thick) mane. **~maul** n (-[e]s; no pl) ♣ snapdragon. **~zahn** m (-[e]s; no pl) ♣ dandelion.

Löwin ['løːvɪn] f (-; -nen) zo. lioness.

loyal [lõaˈjaːl] adj loyal.

Loyalität [lõajaliˈtɛːt] f (-; no pl) loyalty.

Luchs [lʊks] m (-es; -e) zo. lynx: fig. **Augen haben (aufpassen) wie ein ~** have eyes (watch) like a hawk.

Lücke ['lʏkə] f (-; -n) gap, fig. a. loophole: fig. **e-e ~ schließen** fill a gap.

'Lückenbüßer(in f) m stopgap.

'lückenhaft adj 1. full of gaps, gappy. 2. fig. incomplete: **~es Wissen** a. sketchy knowledge.

'lückenlos adj 1. without gaps. 2. fig. complete, full, unbroken (line etc).

lud [luːt] pret of **laden**[1] and **laden**[2].

Luder ['luːdər] n (-s; -) F 1. (gemeines) ~ beast, bitch; (ordinäres) ~ hussy. 2. armes ~ poor creature; dummes ~ silly fool. 3. (kleines) ~ brat, (little) devil.

Luft [lʊft] f (-; ⸚e) 1. no pl air: **die ~ ablassen aus** deflate; F fig. **da war die ~ raus** all the steam was gone; **an die (frische) ~ gehen**, F **~ schnappen** get some (fresh) air; F fig. **j-n an die (frische) ~ setzen** chuck s.o. out, a. fire s.o.; fig. **sich in ~ auflösen** a) vanish into thin air, b) plan etc: go up in smoke; **j-n wie ~ behandeln** cut s.o. dead; (völlig) **aus der ~ gegriffen sein** be (totally) unfounded; **es liegt et. in der ~** there is s.th. in the wind; **die ~ ist rein** the coast is clear; F **es ist dicke ~** there is trouble brewing. 2. no pl breath: **die ~ anhalten** hold one's breath; F **halt (mal) die ~ an!** a) pipe down!, b) come off it!; **tief ~ holen** take a deep breath, fig. swallow hard; **nach ~ ringen** gasp for air; F **mir blieb die ~ weg** I was dumbfounded, **vor Schreck** I was breathless with shock. 3. sky, air: **in die ~ jagen, in die ~ fliegen** blow up; F fig. **in die ~ gehen** blow one's top, hit the roof; **das hängt (alles) noch in der ~** it's all (still) up in the air. 4. breeze. 5. no pl F space, room: **ich muß erst et. ~ schaffen** I must make some room first; fig. **sich (or s-m Herzen, Zorn etc) ~ machen** let off steam.

'Luft|abwehr f air defen/ce (Am. -se). **~angriff** m air raid. **~bal‚lon** m balloon. **~bild** n aerial view. **~bildkarte** f

aerial map. **~blase** f air bubble.

'Luft-'Boden-... ✗ air-to-ground ...

'Luftbrücke f airlift.

'luftdicht adj (a. ~ **machen**) airproof: ~ **verschließen** airseal.

'Luftdruck m (-[e]s; no pl) meteor. atmospheric pressure, ⊙ air pressure.

'Luftdruck... ⊙ air-pressure.

'luftdurchlässig adj permeable to air.

lüften ['lʏftən] v/t (h) 1. (a. v/i) air, ventilate: **s-e Kleidung ~** give one's clothes an airing. 2. lift, raise. 3. fig. **ein Geheimnis ~** reveal (or disclose) a secret.

Lüfter ['lʏftər] m (-s; -) ⊙ a) ventilator, b) exhaustor, c) blower.

'Luft|fahrt f (-; no pl) aviation. **~fahrtgesellschaft** f airline. **~fahrtindu‚strie** f aircraft industry. **~fahrzeug** n aircraft. **~feuchtigkeit** f (atmospheric) humidity. **~filter** n, m air filter. **~flotte** f air fleet. **~fracht** f airfreight. **~frachtbrief** m air waybill. ⸘gekühlt adj air-cooled. ⸘getrocknet adj air-dried. **~gewehr** n air gun. **~herrschaft** f (-; no pl) air supremacy. **~hoheit** f (-; no pl) air sovereignty. **~hülle** f atmosphere.

'luftig adj 1. airy, breezy: in ~er Höhe high up. 2. fig. flimsy, light (clothes).

'Luft|kammer f biol., ⊙ air chamber. **~kampf** m air combat. **~kissenfahrzeug** n air-cushion vehicle, hovercraft. **~korridor** m air corridor. ⸘krank adj airsick. **~kühlung** f air cooling. **~kurort** m climatic health resort. **~landetruppen** pl airborne troops. ⸘leer adj air-void: ~ **machen** evacuate; **~er Raum** vacuum. **~linie** f **100 km** ~ 100 km as the crow flies. **~loch** n airhole, ✈ a. air pocket. **~mangel** m (-s; no pl) ✈ want of air. **~ma‚tratze** f air mattress, air bed. **~pi‚rat** m hijacker, skyjacker. **~pi‚stole** f air pistol.

'Luftpost f (mit or per ~ by) airmail. **~brief** m air letter. **~pa‚ket** n air parcel.

'Luft|pumpe f air pump. **~raum** m air space. **~reinhaltung** f air-pollution control. **~rettungsdienst** m air rescue service. **~röhre** f anat. windpipe. **~sack** m ✈ windsock, mot. airbag. **~schiff** n airship, dirigible. **~schlauch** m air tube, mot. etc inner tube. **~schlösser** pl castles in the air. **~schraube** f ✈ airscrew.

'Luftschutz m air-raid precautions.

~**keller** *m*, ~**raum** *m* air-raid shelter. ~**übung** *f* air-raid drill.

Luft|spiegelung *f* mirage. ~**sprung** *m vor Freude an* a *e* **machen** jump for joy. ~**streitkräfte** *pl* air force. ~**strom** *m*, ~**strömung** *f* air current. ~**stützpunkt** *m* ✕ air base. ~**taxi** *n* air taxi. ~**trans,port** *m* air transport, airlift.

'**Lüftung** *f* (-; -en) ventilation.

'**Luftverkehr** *m* air traffic.

'**Luftverkehrs|gesellschaft** *f* airline (company). ~**linie** *f* airline, airway.

'**Luft|verschmutzung** *f* air pollution. ~**verteidigung** *f* air defen/cc (*Am.* -sc). ~**waffe** *f* ✕ air force. ~**weg** *m* **1.** air route: *auf dem* a *e* by air. **2.** *pl anat.* respiratory tracts. ~**widerstand** *m* air resistance, ✔, ⊙ a. drag. ~**zufuhr** *f* air supply. ~**zug** *m* draught, *Am.* draft.

Lüge ['ly:gə] *f* (-; -n) lie: ~**n strafen** belie.

lügen ['ly:gən] *v/i* (log, gelogen, h) lie, tell a lie (*or* lies): *das ist gelogen!* that's a lie!

'**Lügen|de,tektor** *m* lie detector. ~**ge-schichte** *f* cock-and-bull story.

Lügner ['ly:gnər] *m* (-s; -) liar.

'**lügnerisch** *adj* a) lying, b) untrue, false.

Luke ['lu:kə] *f* (-; -n) **1.** hatch. **2.** skylight.

lukrativ [lukra'ti:f] *adj* lucrative.

lukullisch [lu'kʊlɪʃ] *adj* sumptuous.

Lümmel ['lyməl] *m* (-s; -) lout.

'**lümmelhaft** *adj* loutish.

lümmeln ['lyməln] **sich** ~ (h) F sprawl.

Lump [lʊmp] *m* (-en; -en) scoundrel.

lumpen ['lʊmpən] *v/t* (h) F *sich nicht* ~ *lassen* come down handsomely.

'**Lumpen** *m* (-s; -) **1.** rag. **2.** *pl* rags.

'**lumpig** *adj* F *fig.* **1.** shabby. **2.** paltry, measly (*ten dollars etc*).

Lunchpa,ket ['lanʃ-] *n* packed lunch.

Lunge ['lʊŋə] *f* (-; -n) **1.** *anat.* lungs: 𝅘 *eiserne* ~ iron lung; *die grünen* ~*n e-r Stadt* the lungs of a city. **2.** *gastr.* lights.

'**Lungen...** pulmonary (*artery, embo-lism, etc*). ~**entzündung** *f* pneumonia. ~**flügel** *m anat.* lung. ~**heilstätte** *f* sanatorium, *Am.* sanitarium.

'**lungenkrank** *adj* ('**Lungenkranke** *m, f* person) suffering from (a) lung dis-ease.

'**Lungen|krankheit** *f* lung disease. ~**krebs** *m* 𝅘 lung cancer. ~**tuberku-,lose** *f* pulmonary tuberculosis. ~**zug** *m* **e-n** ~ **machen** inhale.

Lunte ['lʊntə] *f* (-; -n) fuse: F *fig.* ~ *rie-chen* smell a rat.

Lupe ['lu:pə] *f* (-; -n) magnifying glass: F *fig. unter die* ~ *nehmen* scrutinize *s.o.*, *s.th.* closely.

'**lupenrein** *adj* **1.** flawless (*diamond*). **2.** F clean, perfectly honest.

Lupine [lu'pi:nə] *f* (-; -n) 🌺 lupine.

Lust [lʊst] *f* (-; ⁀e) **1.** *no pl* a) inclination, b) desire, c) interest: *hätten Sie* ~ *zu kommen?* would you like to come?; *ich hätte große* ~ *zu kommen* I'd love to come; *ich habe* ~ *zu tanzen* I feel like dancing; Γ *ich hätte* ~ *auf ein Bier* I feel like a beer; *ich hätte nicht übel* ~ *zu inf* I have half a mind to *inf*; *ich habe k-e* ~ (*dazu or darauf*) I don't feel like it, I'm not in the mood (for it); *die* (*or alle*) ~ *verlieren* (*an dat*) lose all interest (in). **2.** *psych.* a) pleasure, b) (sexual) desire (*or* appetite, pleasure), *contp.* lust.

'**lustbetont** *adj psych.* hedonistic.

lüstern ['lʏstərn] *adj* **1.** greedy (*nach* for). **2.** lecherous, lewd.

'**Lüsternheit** *f* (-; *no pl*) **1.** greediness. **2.** lecherousness, lewdness.

'**Lustgefühl** *n* pleasurable sensation.

'**Lustgewinn** *m psych.* pleasure gain.

'**lustig** *adj* a) merry, cheerful, jolly, b) funny, amusing: *er* (*es*) *ist sehr* ~ he (it) is great fun; *sich* ~ *machen über* (*acc*) make fun of; *iro. das kann ja* ~ *werden!* nice prospects!; F *sie unter-hielten sich* ~ *weiter* they blithely went on talking (regardless).

'**Lustigkeit** *f* (-; *no pl*) **1.** gaiety, cheerful-ness. **2.** funniness, fun.

Lüstling ['lʏstlɪŋ] *m* (-s; -e) lecher.

'**lustlos** *adj* listless, ♣ a. slack.

'**Lust|molch** *m* F (old) lecher. ~**mord** *m* sex murder. ~**mörder** *m* sex killer. ~**ob,jekt** *n* sex object. ~**schloß** *n* sum-mer residence. ~**spiel** *n thea.* comedy.

lutschen ['lʊtʃən] *v/t, v/i* (h) suck (*an dat s.th.*): → *Daumen.* '**Lutscher** *m* (-s; -) **1.** lollipop. **2.** F dummy, *Am.* pacifier.

Luv [lu:f] *n* (-s; *no pl*), '**Luvseite** *f*, '**luv-wärts** *adv* ⚓ windward.

luxuriös [lʊksu'riø:s] *adj* luxurious.

Luxus ['lʊksʊs] *m* (-; *no pl*) a. *fig.* luxury.

'**Luxus...** luxury, de luxe. ~**ar,tikel** *m* luxury (article), *pl* a. luxury goods. ~**ausführung** *f* de luxe model. ~**leben** *n* life of luxury. ~**restau,rant** *n* first-

-class restaurant. **~wagen** *m mot.* luxury car.

'Lymphdrüse *f anat.* lymph gland.

Lymphe ['lymfə] *f* (-; -n) **1.** *physiol.* lymph. **2.** *#* vaccine.

'Lymphgefäß *n anat.* lymphatic (vessel).

'Lymphknoten *m anat.* lymph node.

lynchen ['lynçən] *v/t* (h) lynch. **'Lynchju,stiz** *f* (~ **üben** resort to) lynch law. **'Lynchmord** *m* lynching.

Lyrik ['ly:rɪk] *f* (-; *no pl*) **1.** poetry. **2.** lyricism. **'Lyriker** *m* (-s; -), **'Lyrikerin** *f* (-; -nen) (lyric) poet(ess), lyricist.

'lyrisch *adj* lyric, *a. fig.* lyrical.

M

M, m [ɛm] *n* (-; -) M, m.

Maat [ma:t] *m* (-[e]s; -e[n]) (ship's) mate.

'Machart *f* make, style, type.

'machbar *adj* practicable, possible.

Mache ['maxə] *f* (-; *no pl*) F **1.** make-believe, show. **2.** *j-n* **in die ~ nehmen** work s.o. over.

machen ['maxən] (h) **I** *v/t* **1.** make, *a.* prepare (*dinner etc*), *a.* do (*one's homework etc*), take (*snapshot, examination, etc*): *et.* **~ aus** (*dat*) make s.th. of (*or* from); *aus dem Keller e-e Werkstatt ~* turn the cellar into a workshop; *aus j-n e-n Star ~* make a star of s.o.; *j-n zum Abteilungsleiter ~* make s.o. head of the department; → **gemacht. 2.** put in order, *a.* fix, repair, make (*bed*), do, tidy up (*room*). **3.** do: *was macht er?* a) what is he doing?, b) what does he do for a living?, c) how is he (getting on)?; *was machst du morgen?* what are you doing tomorrow?; *wird gemacht!* okay, I'll do it!, *sl.* will do!; *gut gemacht!* well done!; *mach's gut!* take care (of yourself)!; *das läßt sich ~* that can be made (*or* arranged); *so et. macht man nicht!* that isn't done!; *da ist nichts zu ~* nothing doing; *da(gegen) kann man nichts ~* it can't be helped; F *er wird es nicht mehr lange ~* he (*the engine etc*): it) won't last much longer; *der Wagen macht 160 km/h* the car does 160 mph. **4.** give (*appetite, pleasure, etc*): *das macht Durst* that makes you thirsty. **5.** *j-n gesund ~* cure s.o.; *j-n glücklich ~* make s.o. happy. **6.** matter: *das macht nichts!* that doesn't matter!, never mind!; *das macht mir*

nichts I don't mind (*contp.* care). **7.** *sich et.* (*nichts*) **~ aus** (*dat*) (not to) care about (*gastr.* for); *mach dir nichts daraus!* don't worry (about it)!; *ich mache mir nichts aus ihm* I don't care (much) for him. **8.** F be: *4 mal 5 macht 20* four times five is twenty; *was* (*or wieviel*) *macht das?* how much is that?; *das macht 10 Mark* that will be ten marks. **9.** F be, act as: *den Schiedsrichter ~* be (the) referee. **II** *sich ~* **10.** F come along (well), be getting on (well): *wie macht sich der Neue?* how is the new man coming along?; *die Sache macht sich* things are shaping up well; *das Bild macht sich gut dort* the picture looks nice there. **11.** *sich an e-e Sache ~* get down to (doing) s.th.; *sich an die Arbeit ~* get down to work. **III** *v/i* **12.** F *mach, daß du fortkommst!* off with you!, get lost!; *mach schnell!, mach schon!* hurry up!, get a move on! **13.** do: *laß ihn nur ~!* a) let him (do as he pleases)!, b) just leave it to him!; *das läßt sich ~* that can be done. **14.** F *er macht in Radios* he deals in (*or* sells) radios; *sie macht jetzt in moderner Kunst* she's into modern art now.

'Machenschaften *pl* machinations.

Macher ['maxər] *m* (-s; -) *fig.* doer.

Macho ['matʃo] *m* (-s; -s) F macho.

Macht [maxt] *f* (-; ⁻e) **1.** *no pl* power (*über acc* of), *a.* might, force: *mit aller ~* with all one's might; *die ~ der Gewohnheit* the force of habit; *die ~ ergreifen* seize power, take over, *an die ~ kommen* (*or* **gelangen**) come into power; *an der ~ sein* be in power; *es*

steht nicht in m-r ~ it is not within my power. **2.** *pol. etc* power.
'Machtbefugnis f power, authority.
'Machtbereich m sphere of influence.
'Machtergreifung f seizure of power.
'machtgierig adj power-hungry.
'Machthaber [-ha:bər] m (-s; -) ruler.
mächtig ['mɛçtɪç] **I** adj powerful, mighty (*both a.* blow, voice, *etc*), *a.* enormous. **II** adv F tremendously, awfully: ~ **gewachsen sein** have grown a lot.
'Machtkampf m power struggle.
'machtlos adj powerless, helpless.
'Machtpoli,tik f power politics.
'Machtübernahme f assumption of power, takeover. **'machtvoll** adj a. fig. powerful. **'Machtwechsel** m transition of power. **'Machtwort** n *ein* ~ *sprechen* put one's foot down.
'Machwerk n concoction, F lousy job.
Macke ['makə] f (-; -n) F kink: *e-e* ~ *haben* a) be nuts, b) ◎ be acting up.
Mädchen ['mɛːtçən] n (-s; -) **1.** girl. **2.** maid: *fig.* ~ *für alles* dogsbody. **'mädchenhaft** adj girlish. **'Mädchenname** m **1.** girl's name. **2.** maiden name.
Made ['ma:də] f (-; -n) maggot, worm: F *wie die* ~ *im Speck leben* be in clover.
Mädel ['mɛːdəl] n (-s; -s) F girl(ie).
madig ['ma:dɪç] adj maggoty, worm-eaten: F ~ *machen* knock (*s.o., s.th.*); *j-m et.* ~ *machen* spoil s.th. for s.o.
Madonna [ma'dɔna] f (-; -en) Madonna.
Maf(f)ia ['mafia] f (-; -s) a. F fig. mafia.
Mafioso [ma'fio:zo] m (-[s]; -si) mafioso.
Magazin [maga'tsi:n] n (-s; -e) **1.** depot (a. ✕), warehouse. **2.** phot., ◎ magazine (a. of gun etc). **3.** print. magazine.
Magd [ma:kt] f (-; ⸚e) maid.
Magen ['ma:gən] m (-s; ⸚) stomach: *auf nüchternen* (*or leeren*) ~ on an empty stomach; *j-m schwer im* ~ *liegen* lie heavily on s.o.'s stomach, F worry s.o. terribly; *sich den* ~ *verderben* upset one's stomach. **~beschwerden** pl stomach trouble. **~bitter** m gastr. bitters. **~geschwür** n (stomach) ulcer. **~grube** f pit of the stomach. **⸗krank** adj ~ *sein* suffer from a stomach complaint. **~krebs** m ✽ stomach cancer. **~leiden** n gastric complaint. **~säure** f ✽ gastric acid.
'Magenschleimhaut f stomach lining. **~entzündung** f gastritis.

'Magenschmerzen pl stomach-ache.
'Magenverstimmung f indigestion.
mager ['ma:gər] adj **1.** lean (a. fig.), a. thin, a. low-fat: ~e Kost a. fig. slender fare. **2.** fig. meag/re (Am. -er), poor. **3.** print. light-faced.
'Magermilch f skimmed milk.
'Magerquark m low-fat curd cheese.
'Magersucht f (-; no pl) ✽ anorexia.
Magie [ma'gi:] f (-; no pl) magic.
Magier ['ma:giər] m (-s; -) magician.
magisch ['ma:gɪʃ] adj magic(al).
Magister [ma'gɪstər] m (-s; -) univ. Master (**Artium** of Arts, abbr. M.A.)
Magistrat [magɪs'tra:t] m (-[e]s; -e) town council.
Magnat [ma'gna:t] m (-en; -en) magnate, tycoon.
Magnesium [ma'gne:ziʊm] n (-s; no pl) 🜍 magnesium.
Magnet [ma'gne:t] m (-en; -e) magnet. **Ma'gnet...** magnetic (field, needle, etc).
ma'gnetisch adj magnetic: fig. *j-n* ~ *anziehen* have a magnetic effect on s.o.
magnetisieren [magneti'zi:rən] v/t (h) magnetize. **Magnetismus** [magne'tɪsmʊs] m (-; no pl) magnetism.
Ma'gnetkarte f magnetic card.
Ma'gnetzündung f magneto ignition.
Mahagoni [maha'go:ni] n (-s; no pl), **Maha'goniholz** n mahogany.
mähen¹ ['mɛːən] v/t, v/i (h) mow, cut.
'mähen² v/i (h) sheep: bleat.
mahlen ['ma:lən] v/t, v/i (h) grind.
Mahlzeit ['ma:ltsaɪt] f (-; -en) meal: F (*na dann*) *prost* ~! good night!
'Mähma,schine f reaper.
'Mahnbescheid m (court) order to pay.
Mähne ['mɛːnə] f (-; -n) mane.
mahnen ['ma:nən] v/t, v/i (h) **1.** admonish, urge (*j-n zur Vorsicht etc* s.o. to be careful etc). **2.** a) a. fig. remind (*an acc, wegen* of), b) ✝ send s.o. a reminder.
'Mahnmal n memorial.
'Mahnschreiben n (-s; -) ✝ reminder.
'Mahnung f (-; -en) **1.** admonition, warning. **2.** ✝ reminder.
'Mahnwache f pol. protest vigil.
Mai [maɪ] m (-[e]s; no pl) (im ~ in) May: *der Erste* ~ May Day.
'Mai|baum m maypole. **~feier** f May Day celebrations. **~glöckchen** n 🌼 lily of the valley. **~käfer** m cockchafer.
Mais [maɪs] m (-es; -e) maize, Am. corn.

Mais|flocken *pl* cornflakes. **~kolben** *m* (corn)cob, *gastr.* corn on the cob. **~mehl** *n* Indian (*Am.* corn) meal.

Maison(n)ette [mɛzɔ'nɛt] *f* (-; -s) maison(n)ette, *Am.* duplex.

Majestät [majɛs'tɛ:t] *f* (-; *no pl*) *a. fig.* majesty: **Seine ~** His Majesty.

maje'stätisch *adj* majestic.

Major [ma'jo:r] *m* (-s; -e) ✕ major.

Majoran ['ma:joran] *m* (-s; -e) ♀ marjoram.

makaber [ma'ka:bər] *adj* macab/re (*Am.* -er).

Makel ['ma:kəl] *m* (-s; -) *a. fig.* flaw.

'makellos *adj* immaculate, perfect.

mäkeln ['mɛ:kəln] *v/i* (h) carp (**an** *dat* at).

Makkaroni [maka'ro:ni] *pl* macaroni.

Makler ['ma:klər] *m* (-s; -) **1.** (stock)broker. **2.** (*Am.* real) estate agent.

Makrele [ma'kre:lə] *f* (-; -n) mackerel.

Makro... ['ma:kro-], **'makro...** macro...

Makrone [ma'kro:nə] *f* (-; -n) macaroon.

mal [ma:l] *adv* **1.** ஃ times, multiplied by: **der Raum ist 6 ~ 4 Meter** the room is six metres by four. **2.** F → **einmal.**

Mal¹ *n* (-[e]s; -e) **1.** a) mark, sign, b) spot; → **Muttermal** *etc.* **2.** *baseball etc:* base, *rugby:* in-goal.

Mal² *n* (-[e]s; -e) time: **dieses ~** this time; **dieses eine ~** this once; **ein anderes ~** some other time; **das erste ~, beim ersten ~** the first time; **zum letzten ~** for the last time; **das nächste ~** the next time; **mit einem ~** all of a sudden; **ein für alle ~** once and for all; **von ~ zu ~ besser** better every time.

Malaria [ma'la:rĭa] *f* (-; *no pl*) ஃ malaria.

malen ['ma:lən] (h) **I** *v/t* paint (*a. fig.*), portray: **et. zu schwarz ~** paint too black a picture of s.th. **II sich ~** *fig.* be reflected (*in s.o.'s face etc*).

'Maler *m* (-s; -) painter, artist. **Male'rei** *f* (-; -en) painting. **'Malerin** *f* (-; -nen) (woman) painter, artist. **'malerisch** *adj* **1.** picturesque. **2.** artistic (*talent*).

maliziös [mali'tsĭø:s] *adj* malicious.

'malnehmen *v/t* (*irr, sep,* -ge-, h, → **nehmen**) ஃ multiply (*mit* by).

Malve ['malvə] *f* (-; -n) ♀ mallow.

Malz [malts] *n* (-es; *no pl*) malt.

'Malzbier *n* malt beer.

'Malzeichen *n* ஃ multiplication sign.

'Malzkaf,fee *m* malt coffee.

Mama ['mama] *f* (-; -s) F mummy, mum, *Am.* mom.

Mammographie [mamogra'fi:] *f* (-; -n) ஃ mammography.

Mammon ['mamɔn] *m* (-s; *no pl*) *contp.* mammon: **schnöder ~** filthy lucre.

Mammut ['mamʊt] *n* (-s; -s) mammoth.

man [man] *indef pron* **1.** one, you, we: **~ kann nie wissen** you never can tell; **~ muß es tun** it must be done; **~ nehme** take. **2.** they, people: **~ hat mir gesagt** I have been told; **~ sagt** people say; **~ holte ihn** he was fetched.

managen ['mɛnɪdʒən] *v/t* (h) F manage.

'Manager *m* (-s; -) manager.

'Managerkrankheit *f* stress disease.

manch [manç] *indef pron* many a: **~ eine(r)** many (people); **in ~em hat er recht** he's right about some things; **so ~er (~es)** a good many people (things).

'manche *pl* some, quite a few.

'mancherlei *adj* a) various, many, a number of, b) a number of things.

'manchmal *adv* sometimes.

Mandant [man'dant] *m* (-en; -en), **Man'dantin** *f* (-; -nen) ⚖ client.

Mandarine [manda'ri:nə] *f* (-; -n) ♀ tangerine.

Mandat [man'da:t] *n* (-[e]s; -e) ⚖, *parl.*, *pol.* mandate, *of lawyer:* brief: *parl.* **sein ~ niederlegen** resign one's seat.

Mandel ['mandəl] *f* (-; -n) **1.** ♀ almond. **2.** *anat.* tonsil. **~baum** *m* almond (tree). **~entzündung** *f* ஃ tonsillitis.

Mandoline [mando'li:nə] *f* (-; -n) ♪ mandolin(e).

Manege [ma'ne:ʒə] *f* (-; -n) (circus) ring.

Mangan [maŋ'ga:n] *n* (-s; *no pl*) 🔬 manganese.

Mangel¹ ['maŋəl] *f* (-; -n) mangle: F **in die ~ nehmen** put *s.o.* through the mill.

'Mangel² *m* (-s; ⸚) **1.** a) defect, fault, flaw, b) drawback. **2.** (*an dat*) shortage, lack, scarcity (*all:* of), deficiency (in): **aus ~ an → mangels. ~beruf** *m* understaffed occupation. **~erscheinung** *f* ஃ deficiency symptom.

'mangelhaft *adj* a) faulty, defective, b) insufficient, inadequate, deficient, unsatisfactory (*a. ped.*), poor.

Mängelhaftung ['mɛŋəl-] *f* ⚖ responsibility for defects.

mangeln¹ ['maŋəln] *v/t* (h) press.

'mangeln² *v/i, v/impers* (h) be wanting,

be lacking: **es mangelt an** (*dat*) there is a lack (*or* want, shortage) of; **es mangelt mir an Geld** *etc* I am short of money *etc*; **es mangelt ihm an** (*or der*) **Mut** he lacks courage; **ihr ~des Selbstvertrauen** her lack of self-confidence.
'**Mängelrüge** *f* ✝ notice of defects.
'**mangels** *prep* (*gen*) for lack (*or* want) of: ~ **Beweisen** for lack of evidence.
'**Mangelware** *f* scarce commodity: ~ **sein** *a*. F *fig.* be in short supply.
Manie [ma'niː] *f* (-; -n) mania.
Manier [ma'niːr] *f* (-; -en) **1.** *no pl* manner, way (of doing *s.th.*), *art*: style. **2.** *pl* manners. **ma'nierlich** *adj* a) well-mannered, b) good, well-behaved: **sich ~ benehmen** behave o.s., be good.
Manifest [mani'fɛst] *n* (-[e]s; -e) *pol.* manifesto. **manifestieren** [manifɛs'tiːrən] *v/t* (h) manifest.
Maniküre [mani'kyːrə] *f* (-; -n) **1.** *no pl* manicure. **2.** manicurist.
mani'küren *v/t*, *v/i* (h) manicure.
Manipulation [manipula'tsĭoːn] *f* (-; -en) manipulation. **manipulieren** [manipu'liːrən] *v/t* (h) manipulate.
manisch ['maːnɪʃ] *adj psych.* manic. **~depres'siv** *adj* manic-depressive.
Manko ['maŋko] *n* (-s; -s) **1.** ✝ a) deficiency, b) deficit. **2.** *fig.* shortcoming.
Mann [man] *m* (-[e]s; ⸚er) a) man, b) husband: **100 ~** a hundred men; F *der kleine ~* the man in the street; **ein ~ von Welt** a man of the world; **ein Gespräch von ~ zu ~** a man-to-man talk; **wie ein ~** as one man; **bis auf den letzten ~** to a man; **ein Kampf ~ gegen ~** a hand-to-hand fight; **s-n ~ stehen** stand one's ground; ⚓ **alle ~ an Deck!** all hands on deck!; **mit ~ und Maus sinken** go down with all hands (on board); F **an den ~ bringen** get rid of (*goods, a joke, etc*); **den starken ~ markieren** throw one's weight about; **ein ~, ein Wort!** a promise is a promise; F **10 Mark pro ~** 10 marks per head; **wir gingen alle ~ (hoch) hin** all of us went; F (**mein lieber**) **~!** (oh) boy!, wow!
Männchen ['mɛnçən] *n* (-s; -) **1.** little man, manikin: ~ **malen** doodle. **2.** *zo.* male, cock: F **~ machen** sit up and beg.
Mannequin ['manəkɛ̃] *n* (-s; -s) mannequin, model.
Männer ['mɛnər] *pl of* **Mann**: ~ *on WC*:

Men, Gentlemen. '**Männer...** man's, men's ... '**Männerchor** *m* male(-voice) choir. '**männerfeindlich** *adj* hostile towards men.
'**Mannesalter** *n* manhood: **im besten ~** in the prime of life.
'**mannhaft** *adj* manly, *a.* brave.
mannigfach ['manɪçfax], '**mannigfaltig** *adj* diverse, manifold.
männlich ['mɛnlɪç] *adj* **1.** *biol.*, ⚢, ⚙ male. **2.** manly, masculine (*a. ling.*), mannish. '**Männlichkeit** *f* (-; *no pl*) masculinity, manliness, virility.
'**Mannsbild** *n* F man, fellow.
'**Mannschaft** *f* (-; -en) *sports*: team, ✈, ⚓, ✕ crew, ✕ detail, (*rescue etc*) party: ✕ **die ~en** the ranks.
'**Mannschafts|aufstellung** *f sports*: line-up. **~führer(in** *f*) *m sports*: (team) captain. **~geist** *m* (-[e]s; *no pl*) team spirit. **~kapi,tän** *m sports*: (team) captain. **~sport** *m* team sport. **~wagen** *m* a) ✕ personnel carrier, b) police van. **~wertung** *f sports*: team classification. **~wettbewerb** *m* team event.
'**mannshoch** *adj and adv* head-high.
'**mannstoll** *adj* F *contp.* man-crazy.
'**Mannweib** *n contp.* mannish woman.
Manometer [mano'meːtər] *n* (-s; -) ⚙ pressure ga(u)ge.
Manöver [ma'nøːvər] *n* (-s; -) **1.** *a. fig.* manoeuvre, *Am.* maneuver. **2.** ✕ manoeuvres, *Am.* maneuvers, exercise.
Ma'növerkri,tik *f fig.* post-mortem.
manövrieren [manø'vriːrən] *v/i* (h) *a. fig.* manoeuvre, *Am.* maneuver.
manö'vrierunfähig *adj* disabled.
Mansarde [man'zardə] *f* (-; -n) attic room.
Mansch [manʃ] *m* (-es; *no pl*) F **1.** slush. **2.** *contp.* mush. **manschen** ['manʃən] *v/i* (h) F mess about.
Manschette [man'ʃɛtə] *f* (-; -n) **1.** cuff: F **~n bekommen** get the wind up; **~n haben vor** be scared stiff of. **2.** ⚙ sleeve.
Man'schettenknopf *m* cuff-link.
Mantel ['mantəl] *m* (-s; ⸚) **1.** coat, cloak: *fig.* **den ~ nach dem Wind hängen** trim one's sails to the wind. **2.** ⚙ casing.
'**Manteltа,rif(vertrag)** *m* collective agreement (on working conditions).
manuell [ma'nŭɛl] *adj* manual.
Manuskript [manu'skrɪpt] *n* (-[e]s; -e) manuscript, *film*: script, *print.* copy.

Mappe ['mapə] f (-; -n) a) briefcase,
schoolbag, c) folder, file, d) portfolio.
Marathon ['ma:ratɔn] m (-s; -s), **'Mara-
thonlauf** m marathon (race).
Märchen ['mɛ:rçən] n (-s; -) fairytale,
fig. (tall) story, yarn.
'Märchenbuch n book of fairytales.
'märchenhaft adj magical, fairytale ..., F
fig. fantastic.
'Märchen|land n, **~welt** f fairyland.
Marder ['mardər] m (-s; -) zo. marten.
Margarine [marga'ri:nə] f (-; -n) margarine.
Marienbild [ma'ri:ən-] n Madonna.
Ma'rienkäfer m zo. ladybird.
Marihuana [mari'hŭa:na] n (-s; no pl)
marijuana, sl. pot.
Marinade [mari'na:də] f (-; -n) gastr.
marinade.
Marine [ma'ri:nə] f (-; -n) a) merchant
navy, b) navy.
Ma'rine|blau n, ♀**blau** adj navy blue.
~offi,zier m naval officer. **~sol,dat** m
marine. **~stützpunkt** m naval base.
marinieren [mari'ni:rən] v/t (h) gastr.
marinade.
Marionette [mario'nɛtə] f (-; -n) a. fig.
marionette, puppet.
Mario'netten|re,gierung f fig. puppet
government. **~spiel** n puppet show.
~the,ater n puppet theat/re (Am. -er).
Mark¹ [mark] n (-[e]s; no pl) marrow, fig.
a. core: **j-m durch ~ und Bein gehen**
set s.o.'s teeth on edge; **j-n bis ins ~
treffen** cut s.o. to the quick.
Mark² f (-; -) mark: **zehn ~** ten marks; F
jede ~ umdrehen count every penny.
Mark³ f (-; -en) hist. march.
markant [mar'kant] adj striking, prominent: **~e Persönlichkeit** outstanding
personality.
Marke ['markə] f (-; -n) **1.** ♱ make, type,
brand. **2.** mark, sign, computer: flag,
label. **3.** a) voucher, b) coupon, c)
stamp; → **Dienstmarke, Essenmarke,
Spielmarke** etc. **4.** F character.
'Marken|ar,tikel m ♱ proprietary arti-
cle. **~ben,zin** n brand name petrol (Am.
gasoline). **~butter** f best quality butter.
~fabri,kat n proprietary make. **~name**
m trade (or brand) name. **~zeichen** n
trademark.
'markerschütternd adj bloodcurdling.
markieren [mar'ki:rən] v/t (h) **1.** a)

mark (a. fig.), b) accentuate, underline.
2. act, play: → **Mann. 3.** sports: mark
(player), score (goal).
Mar'kierung f (-; -en) mark(ing).
'markig adj fig. pithy.
Markise [mar'ki:zə] f (-; -n) sunblind,
awning.
'Markstein m fig. milestone.
Markt [markt] m (-[e]s; ⁀e) **1.** market: **auf
dem ~** in (or on) the market; **et. auf den
~ bringen** market s.th. **2.** marketplace.
~ana,lyse f market analysis. **~anteil** m
share of the market. **~bericht** m market report. **~entwicklung** f market
trend. **~forscher** m market researcher.
~forschung f market research. **~führer**
m market leader. ♀**gängig** adj marketable, b) current (price). **~halle** f covered market. **~lücke** f opening: **in e-s ~
stoßen** fill a gap in the market. **~platz**
m marketplace.
'marktschreierisch adj fig. loud.
'Markt|stand m (market) stall. **~studie** f
market analysis. **~wert** m market
value. **~wirtschaft** f market economy:
freie ~ a. free enterprise; **soziale ~** social market economy.
Marmelade [marmə'la:də] f (-; -n) jam.
Marme'ladenglas n jam jar.
Marmor ['marmɔr] m (-s; -e), **marmo-
rieren** [marmo'ri:rən] v/t (h) marble.
Marokkaner [marɔ'ka:nər] m (-s; -), **Marok'kanerin** f (-; -nen), **marok'kanisch** adj Moroccan. **Marokko** [ma'rɔ-
ko] n (-s) Morocco.
Marone [ma'ro:nə] f (-; -n) ♀ (sweet)
chestnut.
Marotte [ma'rɔtə] f (-; -n) quirk.
Mars [mars] m (-; no pl) Mars.
'Marsmensch m Martian.
marsch [marʃ] int **1.** ✕ (**vorwärts ~!**
forward) march! **2.** F **~!** get a move on!
Marsch¹ m (-[e]s; ⁀e) walk, ✕ march (a.
♪): **sich in ~ setzen** move off.
Marsch² f (-; -en) geol. marsh.
'Marschbefehl m ✕ marching orders.
'Marschflugkörper m ✕ cruise missile.
'Marschgepäck n ✕ field kit.
marschieren [mar'ʃi:rən] v/i (sn) (a. ~
lassen) march.
'Marsch|mu,sik f military marches.
~ordnung f ✕ march formation.
~route f **1.** ✕ route. **2.** fig. strategy.
~verpflegung f ✕ marching rations.

Marstall ['mar-] *m* royal stables.
Marter ['martər] *f* (-; -n) torture, *fig. a.* ordeal. **'martern** *v/t* (h) torture, *fig. a.* torment. **'Marterpfahl** *m* stake.
Martinshorn ['marti:ns-] *n* F (police, ambulance *or* fire-engine) siren.
Märtyrer ['mɛrtyrər] *m* (-s; -) martyr: *iro.* **sich zum ~ machen** make a martyr of o.s. **Martyrium** [mar'ty:riʊm] *n* (-s; -rien) martyrdom.
Marxismus [mar'ksɪsmʊs] *m* (-; *no pl*) Marxism. **Marxist** [mar'ksɪst] *m* (-en; -en), **mar'xistisch** *adj* Marxist.
März [mɛrts] *m* (-[es]; *no pl*) (*im ~ in*) March.
Marzipan [martsi'pa:n] *n* (-s; -e) marzipan.
Masche ['maʃə] *f* (-; -n) **1.** a) stitch, b) mesh: *fig.* **durch die ~n des Gesetzes schlüpfen** find a loophole in the law. **2.** F a) trick, ploy, b) fad, craze.
'Maschendraht *m* wire netting.
Maschine [ma'ʃi:nə] *f* (-; -n) **1.** a) machine, b) F engine. **2.** plane, jetliner. **3.** F motorcycle. **4.** typewriter: *mit der ~ schreiben* type. **5.** sewing machine. **6.** washing machine.
maschinell [maʃi'nɛl] **I** *adj* machine ..., mechanical. **II** *adv* machine-..., by machine: *~ bearbeiten* machine; *~ hergestellt* machine-made.
Ma'schinen|bau *m* (-[e]s; *no pl*) mechanical engineering. **~bauer** *m* (-s; -), **~bauingeni,eur** *m* mechanical engineer. **~befehl** *m* computer: machine--code instruction. **~fa,brik** *f* engineering works. **2geschrieben** *adj* typewritten, typed. **~gewehr** *n* machine-gun. **~park** *m* machinery. **~pi,stole** *f* submachine-gun. **~raum** *m* engine-room. **~schaden** *m* mechanical breakdown, ♣, *mot.* engine trouble. **~schlosser** *m* engine fitter. **~schreiben** *n* (-s) typewriting, typing. **~schrift** *f* typescript. **2waschbar** *adj* machine-washable.
Maschinerie [maʃinə'ri:] *f* (-; -n) a) machinery, b) mechanism.
ma'schineschreiben *v/i* (*schrieb Maschine, hat maschinegeschrieben*) type.
Maschinist [maʃi'nɪst] *m* (-en; -en) machinist, machine operator, ♣ engine driver, *Am.* engineer.
Maser ['ma:zər] *f* (-; -n) wood etc: vein.

Masern ['ma:zərn] *pl* ♣ measles.
'Maserung *f* (-; -en) of wood: grain.
Maske ['maskə] *f* (-; -n) mask (*a. ♣, computer, phot.*), a. person), thea. make--up, *fig. a.* guise: *in der ~* (gen) under the guise of; *fig.* **die ~ fallen lassen** show one's true face.
'Maskenball *m* fancy-dress ball.
'Maskenbildner [-bɪldnər] *m* (-s; -) make-up artist.
'maskenhaft *adj* mask-like.
'Maskenko,stüm *n* fancy dress.
Maskerade [maskə'ra:də] *f* (-; -n) a. *fig.* masquerade.
maskieren [mas'ki:rən] (h) **I** *v/t* **1.** *j-n ~* a) mask s.o., b) dress s.o. up. **2.** a. ❂ conceal. **II** *sich ~* a) dress up, disguise o.s., b) put on a mask. **mas'kiert** *adj* masked. **Mas'kierung** *f* (-; -en) a) disguise, b) mask.
Maskottchen [mas'kɔtçən] *n* (-s; -) mascot.
maskulin [masku'li:n] *adj*, **Maskulinum** [-'li:nʊm] *n* (-s; -na) *ling.* masculine.
Masochismus [mazo'xɪsmʊs] *m* (-; *no pl*) masochism. **Masochist** [-'xɪst] *m* (-en; -en) masochist. **maso'chistisch** *adj* masochistic.
maß [ma:s] *pret of* **messen.**
Maß¹ *n* (-es; -e) **1.** measure: *~e und Gewichte* weights and measures; *mit zweierlei ~ messen* apply double standards; *das ~ überschreiten* overshoot the mark. **2.** *pl* measurements, of room etc: a. dimensions: *bei j-m ~ nehmen* take s.o.'s measurements; *nach ~ (angefertigt)* made-to-measure (→ a. *maßgeschneidert*). **3.** *fig.* degree, extent: *ein gewisses (hohes) ~ an* (dat) a certain degree (a high measure) of; *in hohem ~e* to a high degree, highly; *in höchstem ~e* extremely; *in gleichem ~e* to the same extent, equally; *in zunehmendem ~e* increasingly; *in dem ~e, wie ...* as ... (accordingly); *über alle ~en* exceedingly. **4.** moderation: *in ~en* a) *a.* **mit ~ und Ziel** in moderation, b) to some extent; *ohne ~ und Ziel* immoderately; → *maßhalten.*
Maß² *f* (-; -e) a) litre (*Am.* liter) of beer, b) → *Maßkrug.*
Massage [ma'sa:ʒə] *f* (-; -n) massage.
Massaker [ma'sa:kər] *n* (-s; -), **massa-**

krieren [masa'kri:rən] *v/t* (h) massacre, slaughter.

'**Maßanzug** *m* tailor-made (*Am.* custom-made) suit.

'**Maßarbeit** *f fig.* precision work.

'**Maßband** *n* (-[e]s; ⸗er) tape measure.

Masse ['masə] *f* (-; -n) **1.** mass (*a. phys.*), *a.* substance, *gastr.* mixture, ⚡ compound. **2.** F *e-e* ~ (*von*), *n von* masses (*or* lots, loads) of; *e-e* ~ *Geld* loads of money. **3.** bulk, majority. **4.** crowd: *die* (*breite*) ~ *a. contp.* the masses. **5.** ♰ estate, assets. **6.** ⚡ (*a. an* ~ *legen*) earth, *Am.* ground.

'**Maßeinheit** *f* unit of measure(ment).

'**Massen...** mass (*demonstration, production, tourism, etc.*). *abfertigung f a. contp.* mass processing. *andrang m* huge crowd, F terrible crush. *arbeitslosigkeit* *f* mass unemployment. *artikel m* ♰ mass-produced article. *entlassungen pl* mass dismissals. *erzeugung f, fabrikati*on *f, fertigung f* mass production. *flucht f* mass exodus, stampede. *grab n* mass grave. *güter pl* bulk goods.

'**massenhaft** *adv* ~ Massen (*or* lots, heaps) of: *sich* ~ *vermehren* multiply in huge numbers.

'**Massen|karambo,lage** *f* mot. (multiple) pile-up. *medium n* mass medium (*pl* media). *mensch m* mass man. *mord m* mass murder. *mörder m* mass murderer. *psy,chose f* mass hysteria. *quar,tier n* mass accommodation. *schläge,rei f* F free-for-all. *sport m* popular sport. *sterben n* widespread deaths (*zo.* dying-off). *veranstaltung f* mass meeting.

Masseur [ma'sø:r] *m* (-s; -e) masseur.

Mas'seurin *f* (-; -nen) masseuse.

Masseuse [ma'sø:zə] *f* (-; -n) *esp. sex*: masseuse.

'**Maßgabe** *f nach* ~ (*gen*) in accordance with; *mit der* ~, *daß* ... provided that ...

'**maßgebend** *adj* **1.** decisive, authoritative (*opinion etc*), leading, prominent (*personality etc*): *das ist* (*für mich*) *nicht* ~ that's no criterion for me); *s-e Meinung ist nicht* ~ his opinion does not count (here). **2.** a) competent, b) standard, definitive (*book etc*).

maßgeblich ['ma:sge:pliç] *adj* decisive: *en Anteil haben* (*or* ~ *beteiligt sein*)

an (*dat*) play a decisive role in, be instrumental in; ~*e Kreise* influential circles.

'**maßgerecht** *adj* true-to-size.

'**maßgeschneidert** *adj* tailor-made (*a. fig.*), made-to-measure, *Am.* custom-made.

'**maßhalten** *v/i* (*irr, sep,* -ge-, h, → *halten*) be moderate.

massieren[1] [ma'si:rən] *v/t* (h) massage.

mas'sieren[2] *v/t* (*a. sich* ~) (h) mass, concentrate.

massig ['masiç] *adj* massive, bulky.

mäßig ['mɛ:sɪç] I *adj* **1.** moderate, *a.* temperate. **2.** mediocre, (rather) poor, F (fair to) middling. II *adv* **3.** moderately, in moderation. **mäßigen** ['mɛ:sɪgən] (h) I *v/t* moderate, *a.* curb, control (*one's rage etc*); → *gemäßigt*. II *sich* ~ restrain (*or* control) o.s.; *sich beim Trinken etc* ~ cut down on drinks *etc*. '**Mäßigung** *f* (-; *no pl*) moderation.

massiv [ma'si:f] *adj* **1.** solid (*gold, wood, etc*). **2.** *fig.* massive (*threat, attack, etc*): F ~ *werden* cut up rough.

Mas'siv *n* (-s, -e) *geol.* massif. *bau(weise f) m* △ massive construction.

'**Maßkrug** *m* beer mug, stein.

'**maßlos I** *adj* immoderate, excessive (*demands etc*). II *adv* immoderately (*etc*): ~ *übertrieben* grossly exaggerated; ~ *eifersüchtig* extremely jealous.

'**Maßlosigkeit** *f* (-; *no pl*) immoderateness, lack of restraint, excess.

'**Maßnahme** [-na:mə] *f* (-; -n) measure.

'**maßregeln** *v/t* (*insep,* ge-, h) (*wegen* for) a) reprimand, b) punish, discipline, *sports*: penalize.

'**Maßregelung** *f* (-; -en) a) reprimand, b) disciplinary action, *sports*: penalty.

'**Maßschneider** *m* bespoke (*Am.* custom) tailor.

'**Maßstab** *m* **1.** scale: *im* ~ *1:10* on a scale of 1:10; *im verkleinerten* (*vergrößerten*) ~ on a reduced (an enlarged) scale; *in großem* ~ *a. fig.* large-scale. **2.** *fig.* standard, yardstick: *hohe Maßstäbe anlegen* apply strict standards (*an acc* to); *das ist kein* ~ that's no criterion.

'**maßstabgerecht** *adj* (true) to scale.

'**maßvoll** *adj* a) moderate, reasonable, b) restrained.

Mast[1] [mast] *m* (-[e]s; -e[n]) a) ♻ mast, b) ⚡ pylon, c) pole.

Mast² f (-; -en) ✔ **1.** fattening. **2.** mast.
'**Mastdarm** m anat. rectum.
mästen ['mɛstən] (h) **I** v/t fatten. **II** sich
~ gorge o.s. (**an** dat on).
Masturbation [masturba'tsĭo:n] f (-;
-en) masturbation. **masturbieren**
[mastur'bi:rən] v/i masturbate.
'**Mastvieh** n fat stock.
Match [mɛtʃ] n, a. m (-[e]s; -s, -e) match,
game. ~**ball** m tennis: match point.
Material [mate'rĭa:l] n (-s; -ien) material
(a. fig.), ◉ coll. materials.
Materi'alfehler m material defect.
Materialismus [materĭa'lısmʊs] m (-; no
pl) materialism. **Materialist** [materĭa-
'lıst] m (-en; -en) materialist.
materia'listisch adj materialist(ic).
Materi'alkosten pl cost of materials.
Materi'alprüfung f material test(ing).
Materie [ma'te:rĭə] f (-; -n) **1.** no pl a.
phys. matter. **2.** fig. subject (matter).
materiell [mate'rĭɛl] adj **1.** material. **2.**
→ **materialistisch**. **3.** financial.
Mathe ['matə] f (-; no pl) F maths, Am.
math. **Mathematik** [matema'ti:k] f (-;
no pl) mathematics. **Mathematiker**
[mate'ma:tikər] m (-s; -) mathemati-
cian. **mathematisch** [mate'ma:tıʃ] adj
mathematical.
Matinee [mati'ne:] f (-; -n) thea. morning performance.
Matjeshering ['matjəs-] m gastr. young
salted herring.
Matratze [ma'tratsə] f (-; -n) mattress.
Mätresse [mɛ'trɛsə] f (-; -n) mistress.
Matriarchat [matriar'ça:t] n (-[e]s; -e)
matriarchate.
Matrize [ma'tri:tsə] f (-; -n) **1.** (a. **auf** ~
schreiben) stencil. **2.** print. matrix. **3.**
◉ a) die, b) stencil.
Matrose [ma'tro:zə] m (-n; -n) sailor,
seaman.
Matsch [matʃ] m (-[e]s; no pl) F a) mush,
b) mud, c) slush. '**matschig** adj F **1.**
muddy, slushy. **2.** fruit etc: mushy.
matt [mat] adj **1.** dull (shine, colour, eyes,
etc), a. phot. mat(t), frosted (glass),
opal (bulb), dim (light). **2.** faint, weak,
feeble (a. fig. voice, applause, etc), exhausted. **3.** ♙ slack. **4.** (check)mate.
Matte ['matə] f (-; -n) mat.
'**Mattglas** n frosted glass.
mattieren [ma'ti:rən] v/t (h) a) mat(t), b)
frost (glass).

Mattigkeit ['matıç-] f (-; no pl) fatigue.
'**Mattscheibe** f **1.** phot. focus(s)ing
screen. **2.** a) TV screen, b) F telly, Am.
tube. **3.** F ~ **haben** have a blackout.
Mätzchen ['mɛtsçən] pl F **1.** nonsense. **2.**
tricks: **k-e** ~**!** none of your tricks!
Mauer ['mauər] f (-; -n) wall: hist. **die**
(**Berliner**) ~ the (Berlin) Wall.
'**Mauerblümchen** n F fig. wallflower.
mauern ['mauərn] (h) **I** v/i **1.** build a
wall etc, lay bricks. **2.** F cards: stone-
wall, sports: shut up shop. **II** v/t build.
'**Mauer|stein** m (building) brick. ~**werk**
n (-[e]s; no pl) masonry, brickwork.
Maul [maul] n (-[e]s; ◄er) **1.** zo. mouth,
jaws. **2.** V trap (sl.): **das** ~ **aufreißen**
brag; **halt's** ~**!** shut up!
maulen ['maulən] v/i (h) F grumble.
'**Maulesel** m mule. '**Maulheld** m F braggart. '**Maulkorb** m (a. dat **e-n** ~ **anlegen**) muzzle (a. fig.). '**Maultier** n mule.
'**Maul- und 'Klauenseuche** f vet.
foot-and-mouth disease.
'**Maulwurf** m (-[e]s; ◄e) zo. mole.
'**Maulwurfshügel** m molehill.
Maurer ['maurər] m (-s; -) bricklayer.
'**Maurerkelle** f trowel.
Maurermeister m master mason.
maurisch ['maurıʃ] adj Moorish.
Maus [maus] f (-; ◄e) mouse: humor.
weiße ~ traffic policeman; F **graue**
~ nondescript person; → **Katze**, **Mäuse**.
mäuschenstill ['mɔysçən-] adj a) (as)
quiet as a mouse, b) stockstill: **es war** ~
not a sound was to be heard.
Mäuse ['mɔyzə] pl **1.** mice: F **weiße** ~
sehen see pink elephants. **2.** F lolly,
Am. bread.
'**Mausefalle** f **1.** mousetrap. **2.** fig.
deathtrap. '**Mauseloch** n mousehole.
mausern ['mauzərn] v/i (a. **sich** ~) (h)
moult: F fig. **sich** ~ **zu** develop into.
'**mause'tot** adj F stone-dead.
Mausoleum [mauzo'le:ʊm] n (-s; -leen)
mausoleum.
Maut [maut] f (-; -en) toll. '**Mautstraße** f
toll road, Am. turnpike (road). '**Maut-
stelle** f tollhouse, Am. turnpike.
maximal [maksi'ma:l] **I** adj maximum.
II adv maximally, at (the) most.
Maxime [ma'ksi:mə] f (-; -n) maxim.
Maximum ['maksimʊm] n (-s; -xima)
maximum.

Mayonnaise [majɔ'nɛ:zə] f (-; -n) gastr. mayonnaise.

Mäzen [mɛ'tse:n] m (-s; -e) patron, sponsor.

Mechanik [me'ça:nɪk] f (-; -en) **1.** no pl mechanics. **2.** mechanism. **Mechaniker** [me'ça:nikər] m (-s; -) mechanic. **mechanisch** [me'ça:nɪʃ] adj mechanical, fig. a. automatic. **mechanisieren** [meçani'zi:rən] v/t (h) mechanize. **Mechani'sierung** f (-; -en) mechanization. **Mechanismus** [meça'nɪsmʊs] m (-; -men) mechanism.

Meckerer ['mɛkərər] m (-s; -) F grumbler. **meckern** ['mɛkərn] v/i (h) **1.** zo. bleat. **2.** F grumble (über acc about).

Medaille [me'daljə] f (-; -n) medal: → **Kehrseite.**

Me'daillengewinner(in f) m sports: medal(l)ist.

Medaillon [medal'jõ:] n (-s; -s) **1.** art, gastr. medallion. **2.** locket.

Medien ['me:diən] pl media.

'Medienforschung f media research.

'Medienverbund m multimedia system.

Medikament [medika'mɛnt] n (-[e]s; -e) drug, medicament.

Mediothek [medio'te:k] f (-; -en) media library.

Meditation [medita'tsio:n] f (-; -en) meditation.

meditieren [medi'ti:rən] v/i (h) meditate (über acc on).

Medium ['me:diʊm] n (-s; -ien) medium.

Medizin [medi'tsi:n] f (-; -en) **1.** no pl medicine: **Doktor der** ~ doctor of medicine (abbr. M.D.). **2.** medicine, medicament.

Medi'ziner m (-s; -) **1.** medical student, F medic. **2.** physician, doctor.

medi'zinisch adj a) medical, b) medicinal. **~-technische Assi'stentin** (abbr. MTA) medical laboratory assistant.

Medi'zinmann m (-[e]s; ⸚er) medicine man.

Meer [me:r] n (-[e]s; -e) sea (a. fig.), ocean: **das offene** ~ the high seas; **am** ~ by the sea, a. holidays etc at the seaside.

'Meer|busen m gulf. **~enge** f strait(s).

'Meeres|arm m arm of the sea, inlet. **~biolo,gie** f marine biology. **~boden** m → **Meeresgrund. ~früchte** pl seafood. **~grund** m seafloor, bottom of the sea. **~kunde** f (-; no pl) oceanography.

~spiegel m (über dem ~ above) sea level.

'Meerrettich m (-s; -e) ⚘ horseradish.

'Meersalz n sea salt.

'Meerschweinchen n zo. guinea pig.

'Meerwasser n sea water.

Mega... [mega-] mega (ton, volt, etc). **Mega'hertz** n megahertz, megacycle.

Megaphon [mega'fo:n] n (-s; -e) megaphone.

Mehl [me:l] n (-[e]s; -e) flour. **'mehlig** adj mealy. **'Mehlspeise** f **1.** farinaceous food. **2.** Austrian sweet dish.

mehr [me:r] **I** indef pron more: ~ **als 50 Autos** more than (or over) 50 cars; **und dergleichen** ~ and the like; (immer) ~ **und** ~ more and more; **was willst du noch ~?** what more do you want? **II** adj more: ~ **und** ~ (or **immer** ~) **Leute** more and more people. **III** adv more: **um so** ~, **nur noch** ~ all the more; **um so** ~ (**als**) all the more (as); **nicht** ~ a) no more, b) no longer, not any longer; **nie** ~ never again; **ich habe keins** (or **keine**) ~ I haven't got any more; **ich habe nichts** ~ I've got nothing left; **kein Wort** ~ (**davon**)! not another word (about it)!; **ich kann nicht** ~! a) I'm finished!, b) I couldn't eat another thing!; **er ist** ~ **praktisch veranlagt** he is more of a practical man.

Mehr n (-[s]; no pl) **ein** ~ **an Zeit** (Erfahrung etc) more time (experience etc).

'Mehrarbeit f (-; no pl) **1.** extra work. **2.** overtime. **'Mehraufwand** m extra (or additional) cost(s), time, etc. **'Mehrausgaben** pl additional expenditure.

'mehrbändig [-bɛndɪç] adj in several volumes.

'Mehrbedarf m extra (or increased) demand. **'Mehrbelastung** f additional load (fig. burden). **'Mehrbetrag** m **1.** surplus. **2.** extra charge.

'mehrdeutig [-dɔytɪç] adj ambiguous.

'Mehreinkommen n additional revenue.

mehren ['me:rən] v/t (a. **sich** ~) (h) increase.

mehrere ['me:rərə] adj or indef pron several.

'mehrfach I adj a) several, b) repeated, c) esp. ⊕ etc multiple: **~e Verletzungen** multiple injuries; **in ~er Hinsicht** in several respects; **~er deutscher Mei-**

ster several times German champion.
II *adv* a) several times, b) repeatedly:
ein Mehrfaches der Summe several
times the amount; *er ist ~ vorbestraft*
he has several previous convictions.

'**Mehrfachstecker** *m* multiple plug.
'**Mehrfa,milienhaus** *n* multiple dwell-
ing. '**Mehrgepäck** *n* excess luggage.
'**Mehrgewicht** *n* excess weight.

'**Mehrheit** *f* (-; -en) majority: *mit absoluter* (*einfacher, knapper, großer*) *~*
by an absolute (a simple, a narrow, a
large) majority; *mit zehn Stimmen ~*
by a majority of ten; → *schweigend*.
'**mehrheitlich** *adj und adv* (by the) majority.

'**Mehrheits|beschluß** *m* majority deci-
sion. *~beteiligung* *f ✝* controlling interest. *~wahlrecht* *n* majority vote system.

'**mehrjährig** [-jɛːrɪç] *adj* of (*or* lasting)
several years, several years' ...
'**Mehrkosten** *pl* a) additional (*or* extra)
cost(s), b) extra charge.
'**mehrmalig** [-maːlɪç] *adj* repeated.
'**mehrmals** *adv* several times.
'**Mehrpar,teiensy,stem** *n* multiparty
system.
'**mehrseitig** [-zaɪtɪç] *adj* **1.** ✚ polygonal.
2. *pol.* multilateral.
'**mehrsilbig** [-zɪlbɪç] *adj* polysyllabic.
'**mehrsprachig** [-ʃpraːxɪç] *adj* polyglot,
multilingual.
'**mehrstellig** [-ʃtɛlɪç] *adj* multidigit.
'**mehrstimmig** [-ʃtɪmɪç] *adj* polyphonic,
for several voices: *~er Gesang* part
singing. **2.** *mus* as I (*or* has been) mine, b)
'**mehrstöckig** [-ʃtœkɪç] *adj* multi-
stor(e)y.
'**mehrstündig** [-ʃtyndɪç] *adj* of (*or* lasting) several hours.
'**mehrtägig** [-tɛːgɪç] *adj* of (*or* lasting)
several days.
'**mehrteilig** [-taɪlɪç] *adj* consisting of several parts, *film etc*: in several parts.
'**Mehrverbrauch** *m* increased consumption. '**Mehrwertsteuer** *f* value-added
tax (*abbr.* VAT). '**Mehrzahl** *f* (-; *no pl*)
1. majority. **2.** *ling.* plural.
'**Mehrzweck...** multipurpose ...
meiden ['maɪdən] *v/t* (mied, gemieden,
h) avoid.
Meile ['maɪlə] *f* (-; -n) mile.
'**Meilenstein** *m a. fig.* milestone.

'**meilenweit** *adv* for miles (and miles): *~
entfernt von a. fig.* miles (away) from.
mein [maɪn] *pos pron* my: *~er, ~e, ~(e)s,
der* (*die, das*) *mein(ig)e* mine; *die
Mein(ig)en* my family, F my people,
my folks; *ich habe das Mein(ig)e getan* I've done my share (*or* bit).
'**Meineid** *m* (*e-n ~ leisten* commit) perjury. '**meineidig** *adj* perjured: *~ werden* perjure o.s., commit perjury.
meinen ['maɪnən] *v/i* (h) **1.** think, believe: *was ~ Sie dazu?* what do you
think?; *~ Sie* (*wirklich*)? do you (really)
think so? **2.** mean: *wie ~ Sie das?* a)
how do you mean?, b) what do you
mean by that?; *~ Sie das ernst?* do you
really mean it?; *so war es nicht gemeint* I (he *etc*) didn't mean it (like
that); *sie meint es gut* she means well
(*mit dir* by you); *es war gut gemeint* it
was well-meant; *er hat es nicht böse
gemeint* he meant no harm. **3.** refer to,
mean: *~ Sie ihn?* do you mean him? **4.**
mean, signify. **5.** *wenn du meinst* if
you say so; *wie Sie ~* as you wish; *ich
meine ja nur!* it was just a thought!
meiner ['maɪnər] *pers pron* (*gen of ich*)
(of) me: *erinnerst Sie sich ~?* do you
remember me? '**meinerseits** [-zaɪts]
adv for my part: *ich ~* I for one; *ganz ~*
a) the pleasure is (*or* has been) mine, b)
humor. same here!
'**meines'gleichen** *indef pron* people like
me, F the likes of me.
meinet'wegen ['maɪnət-] *adv* **1.** a) on
my account, because of me, b) for my
sake. **2.** *~ kann er gehen* I don't mind if
he goes, *iro.* he can go for all I care. **3.**
let's say.
meinige ['maɪnɪgə] → *mein*.
'**Meinung** *f* (-; -en) opinion (*über acc* of,
about, on): *e-e schlechte ~ haben von*
have a low opinion of; *m-r ~ nach* in
my opinion; *der ~ sein* think, believe,
be of the opinion; *derselben* (*anderer*)
~ sein (dis)agree; *ganz m-r ~!* I quite
agree!; F *j-m gehörig die ~ sagen* give
s.o. a piece of one's mind; → *geteilt*.
'**Meinungs|äußerung** *f* expression of
one's opinion, statement. *~austausch*
m exchange of views (*über acc* on).
⊖bildend *adj* opinion-forming. *~bil-
dung* *f* forming of an opinion: *öffentliche ~* forming of public opinion. *~for-*

scher *m* pollster. **~forschung** *f* opinion research. **~freiheit** *f* (-; *no pl*) freedom of opinion (*or* speech). **~führer** *m* opinion-leader. **~umfrage** *f* (public) opinion poll. **~umschwung** *m* swing of opinion. **~verschiedenheit** *f* **1.** difference of opinion. **2.** disagreement, argument (*über acc* about).

Meise ['maɪzə] *f* (-; -n) **1.** tit(mouse). **2.** F *du hast wohl 'ne ~?* you must be nuts!

Meißel ['maɪsəl] *m* (-s; -) chisel.

meißeln ['maɪsəln] *v/t, v/i* (h) chisel.

Meißner ['maɪsnər] **~ Porzellan** Dresden china.

meist [maɪst] **I** *adj* **1.** most, most of: *die ~en Leute* most people; *die ~e Zeit* most of the time. **II** *indef pron* **2.** *das ~e* (*davon*) most of it; *die ~en* most (of them), a) most people. **III** *adv* **3.** → *meistens.* **4.** *am ~en* most.

'meistbietend *adj* **~er Interessent** highest bidder: *~ verkaufen* sell to the highest bidder.

meistens ['maɪstəns], **'meistenteils** *adv* mostly, usually, most of the time.

Meister ['maɪstər] *m* (-s; -) **1.** master (craftsman): *s-n ~ machen* take one's master craftsman's diploma. **2.** foreman. **3.** *a. fig. or iro.* master: → *Übung* 1. **4.** *sports:* champion(s). **'Meisterbrief** *m* master craftsman's diploma.

'meisterhaft I *adj* masterly. **II** *adv* brilliantly; *iro. es ~ verstehen zu lügen etc* be an expert liar *etc.*

'Meisterin *f* (-; -nen) **1.** master craftswoman. **2.** forewoman. **3.** master's wife. **4.** → *Meister* 3, 4.

'Meisterleistung *f* masterly performance, great feat.

meistern ['maɪstərn] *v/t* (h) master.

'Meisterprüfung *f* examination for the master craftsman's diploma.

'Meisterschaft *f* (-; -en) **1.** *no pl* mastery. **2.** *sports:* championship, *a.* title.

'Meisterstück *n fig.* masterstroke.

'Meisterwerk *n* masterpiece.

Melancholie [melaŋko'li:] *f* (-; -n) melancholy. **melancholisch** [melaŋ'ko:lɪʃ] *adj* melancholy.

Melanom [mela'no:m] *n* (-s; -e) *☞* melanoma.

melden ['mɛldən] (h) **I** *v/t* **1.** a) report, register (*birth etc*), b) announce: *j-m et. ~* notify s.o. of s.th.; F *er hat nichts zu ~*

he has no say (in the matter), *w.s.* he has no chance (*gegen j-n* against s.o.). **2.** *sports:* enter. **II** *sich ~* **3.** report (*bei* to, *zur Arbeit* for work): *sich polizeilich ~* register with the police; → *krank.* **4.** get in touch (*bei* with): *sich freiwillig ~* volunteer (*zu* for); *ich werde mich (wieder) ~* I'll be in touch; *wenn du et. brauchst, melde dich!* if you need anything, let me know!; *sich auf ein Inserat ~* answer an advertisement. **5.** answer (the phone): *es meldet sich niemand* there is no reply. **6.** *ped.* put up one's hand. **7.** *sports:* enter (one's name) (*für* for). **8.** *fig.* make itself felt.

'Meldepflicht *f* obligatory registration, *☞* duty of notification.

'meldepflichtig *adj* subject to registration, *☞* notifiable.

'Meldung *f* (-; -en) **1.** report, a. news (item), announcement, notification, (*radio etc*) message. **2.** registration (*bei* with). **3.** (*zu* for) application, *for exam etc, a.* *sports:* entry.

melken ['mɛlkən] *v/t, v/i* (melkte/molk, gemelkt/gemolken, h) a. *fig.* milk.

'Melkmaschine *f* milking machine.

Melodie [melo'di:] *f* (-; -n) melody, tune.

melodiös [melo'diø:s], **melodisch** [me'lo:dɪʃ] *adj* melodic.

Melodrama [melo'dra:ma] *n* (-s; -en) *a.* F *fig.* melodrama. **melodra'matisch** *adj a.* F *fig.* melodramatic.

Melone [me'lo:nə] *f* (-; -n) ♀ melon.

Membran [mɛm'bra:n] *f* (-; -en) *anat.* membrane, *a.* ⊙ diaphragm.

Memoiren [me'mŏa:rən] *pl* memoirs.

Memorandum [memo'randʊm] *n* (-s; -den, -da) memorandum.

Menge ['mɛŋə] *f* (-; -en) **1.** quantity, amount, Å set: *e-e (große) ~ von* a lot of, F lots of; *e-e ~ Bücher* a. a great many books; *F jede ~ Geld, Geld in rauhen ~n* heaps of money. **2.** crowd.

mengen ['mɛŋən] (h) **I** *v/t* mix (*in acc* into). **II** *sich ~* → *mischen* II.

'Mengenangabe *f* (indication of) quantity. **'Mengenlehre** *f* (-; *no pl*) Å set theory. **'mengenmäßig** *adj* quantitative. **'Mengenra,batt** *m* ♯ bulk (*or* quantity) discount.

Meniskus [me'nɪskʊs] *m* (-; -ken) *anat.* meniscus.

Mensa ['mɛnza] *f* (-; -s, Mensen) (university) canteen.

Mensch [mɛnʃ] *m* (-en; -en) **1.** human being: *der* ~ man; *ich bin auch nur ein* ~*!* I'm only human! **2.** → *Menschheit.* **3.** person, man (woman): *kein* ~ not a soul, nobody; *(die)* ~*en* people; *gern unter* ~*en sein* enjoy human company; *F* ~*!* → *Menschenskind.*

Mensch, ärgere dich nicht! *n* ludo.

'**Menschen|affe** *m* ape. ~*alter n* **1.** generation. **2.** lifetime. ~*feind m* misanthropist. ~*fresser m* **1.** cannibal. **2.** *zo.* man-eater. ~*freund m* philanthropist. ~*gedenken n seit* ~ within living memory. ~*gestalt f in* ~ in human form; *ein Teufel in* ~ a devil incarnate. ~*hand f von* ~ *geschaffen* man-made. ~*handel m* slave trade. ~*haß m* misanthropy. ~*kenner m* good judge of character. ~*kenntnis f* (-; *no pl*) knowledge of human nature. ~*leben n* **1.** (human) life: ~ *sind nicht zu beklagen* there were no fatalities. **2.** lifetime. ♀*leer adj* deserted. ~*menge f* crowd (of people). ♀*möglich adj das* ~ everything that is humanly possible. ~*raub m* kidnapping. ~*rechte pl* human rights. ♀*scheu adj* shy, unsociable. ~*schlag m* (-[e]s; *no pl*) breed (of people). ~*seele f* **1.** human soul. **2.** *k-e* ~ not a living soul.

'**Menschenskind** *int* a) good heavens!, b) for heaven's sake!

'**menschenunwürdig** *adj* a) degrading, b) *dwelling etc*: unfit for human beings.

'**Menschenverstand** *m gesunder* ~ common sense.

'**Menschenwürde** *f the* dignity of man.

'**Menschheit** *die* ~ (-; *no pl*) man(kind).

'**menschlich** *adj* **1.** human: *die* ~*e Natur* human nature; *nach* ~*em Ermessen* as far as one can possibly judge. **2.** humane. **3.** F tolerable.

'**Menschlichkeit** *f* (-; *no pl*) humaneness, humanity: *Verbrechen gegen die* ~ crime against humanity.

Menstruation [mɛnstrua'tsi̯oːn] *f* (-; -en) ♣ menstruation. **menstruieren** [mɛnstru'iːrən] *v/i* (h) ♣ menstruate.

Mentalität [mɛntali'tɛːt] *f* (-; -en) mentality.

Menthol [mɛn'toːl] *n* (-s; *no pl*) ♣ menthol: *mit* ~ mentholated.

Menü [me'nyː] *n* (-s; -s) **1.** *gastr.* set meal,

set lunch. **2.** *computer*: menu.

Menuett [me'nu̯ɛt] *n* (-[e]s; -e) ♪ minuet.

Meridian [meri'di̯aːn] *m* (-s; -e) *astr.*, *geogr.* meridian.

'**Merkblatt** *n* leaflet.

merken ['mɛrkən] *v/t* (h) **1.** a) notice, b) feel, sense, c) realize, see, d) discover: *et.* ~ a. become aware of s.th.; *man merkte an s-r Stimme, daß* you could tell by his voice that. **2.** ~ *lassen* show, let on. **3.** *sich* ~ a) remember, b) make a mental note of; *merk dir das!* remember that!

'**merklich I** *adj* a) noticeable, b) marked, c) considerable. **II** *adv* noticeably *(etc).*

'**Merkmal** *n* (-[e]s; -e) characteristic: *besondere* ~*e* distinguishing marks.

Merkur [mɛr'kuːr] *m* (-s; *no pl*) *astr.* Mercury.

'**merkwürdig** *adj* strange, odd. '**merkwürdigerweise** *adv* oddly enough.

'**Meßband** *n* (-[e]s; ~er) tape measure.

'**meßbar** *adj* measurable.

'**Meßbecher** *m* measuring cup.

'**Meßdiener** *m eccl.* server.

Messe¹ ['mɛsə] *f* (-; -n) *eccl.* mass: *(die)* ~ *lesen* say Mass.

'**Messe²** *f* (-; -n) ✕ mess.

'**Messe³** *f* (-; -n) (trade) fair.

'**Messe|besucher(in** *f*) *m* visitor to a (or the) fair. ~*gelände n* exhibition cent/re *(Am.* -er). ~*halle f* exhibition hall.

messen ['mɛsən] (maß, gemessen, h) **I** *v/t* measure, ♣ a. ga(u)ge: *die Zeit* ~ time; *j-n mit Blicken* ~ size s.o. up. **II** *sich mit j-m* ~ match o.s. against s.o., *sports*: compete with s.o.; *sich nicht* ~ *können mit* a) *j-m* be no match for s.o., b) *e-r Sache* not to stand comparison with s.th. **III** *v/i* measure, be ... long *(or* high, wide, *etc)*, *person*: be ... (tall).

Messer ['mɛsər] *n* (-s; -) knife, ♣ *a.* scalpel, ♣ *a.* blade: *Kampf bis aufs* ~ fight to the death; *auf (des)* ~*s Schneide stehen* be on a razor's edge; F *j-n ans* ~ *liefern* betray s.o.

'**messerscharf** *adj a. fig.* razor-sharp.

'**Messerspitze** *f* knife point: *e-e* ~ *Salz* a pinch of salt.

Messerstecherei *f* (-; -en) knifing.

'**Messerstich** *m* **1.** stab. **2.** stab wound.

'**Messestand** *m* exhibition stand.

'**Meßgerät** *n* measuring instrument.

'**Meßglas** *n* graduated measuring glass.

Messias [mɛˈsiːas] m (-; no pl) Messiah.
Messing [ˈmɛsɪŋ] n (-s; no pl) brass.
'Meßinstru,ment n → **Meßgerät.**
'Meßuhr f meter, dial ga(u)ge.
'Meßtischblatt n ordnance map.
'Messung f (-; -en) measurement.
Metall [meˈtal] n (-s; -e) metal.
Me'tall|arbeiter m metalworker. **~in-du,strie** f metalworking industry.
me'tallisch adj metal, a. fig. metallic.
Metallurgie [metalʊrˈgiː] f (-; no pl) metallurgy. **metallurgisch** [metaˈlʊr-gɪʃ] adj metallurgic(al).
Me'tall|verarbeitung f metal processing. **~waren** pl metal goods, hardware.
Metamorphose [metamɔrˈfoːzə] f (-; -n) metamorphosis.
Metapher [meˈtafər] f (-; -n) metaphor.
Meta'phy'sik [meta-] f metaphysics.
meta'physisch adj metaphysical.
Metastase [metaˈstaːzə] f (-; -n) ✱ metastasis.
Meteor [meteˈoːr] m (-s; -e) meteor.
Meteorit [meteoˈriːt] m (-s; -e) meteorite.
Meteorologe [meteoroˈloːgə] m (-n; -n) meteorologist. **Meteorologie** [meteoroloˈgiː] f (-; no pl) meteorology.
meteoro'logisch adj meteorological.
Meter [ˈmeːtər] n, m (-s; -) metre, Am. meter. **'meterlang** adj very long.
'Meterware f yard goods.
Methode [meˈtoːdə] f (-; -n) method.
Methodik [meˈtoːdɪk] f (-; -en) **1.** no pl methodology. **2.** method(s).
me'thodisch adj methodical.
Methylalkohol [meˈtyːl-] m (-s; no pl) methyl alcohol.
Metier [meˈtĭeː] n (-s; -s) profession, job.
Metrik [ˈmeːtrɪk] f (-; -en) metre, Am. meter. **metrisch** [ˈmeːtrɪʃ] adj **1.** metric. **2.** ♪ etc metrical.
Metropole [metroˈpoːlə] f (-; -n) metropolis.
Metzger [ˈmɛtsgər] m (-s; -) butcher.
Metzge'rei f (-; -en) butcher's shop.
Meute [ˈmɔytə] f (-; -n) **1.** hunt. pack (of hounds). **2.** F mob.
Meute'rei f (-; -en) mutiny. **'Meuterer** m (-s; -) mutineer. **meutern** [ˈmɔytərn] v/i (h) a) mutiny, b) F rebel. **'meuternd** adj mutinous.
Mexikaner [mɛksiˈkaːnər] m (-s; -), **Mexi'kanerin** f (-; -nen), **mexi'ka-**

nisch [-nɪʃ] adj Mexican. **Mexiko** [ˈmɛksiko] n (-s) Mexico.
miau [miˈaʊ] int, **mi'auen** v/i (h) miaow.
mich [mɪç] **I** pers pron me. **II** reflex pron myself.
mick(e)rig [ˈmɪk(ə)rɪç] adj F **1.** measly (pay etc). **2.** puny, sickly.
mied [miːt] pret of **meiden.**
Mieder [ˈmiːdər] n (-s; -) bodice.
'Miederhöschen n panty girdle.
'Miederwaren pl foundation garments.
Mief [miːf] m (-[e]s; no pl) F fug, pong.
Miene [ˈmiːnə] f (-; -n) expression, face: **überlegene ~** superior air; **e-e ernste ~ aufsetzen** look serious; **gute ~ zum bösen Spiel machen** put on a brave face, grin and bear it; **~ machen, et. zu tun** make as if to do s.th.; **ohne e-e ~ zu verziehen** without batting an eyelid.
'Mienenspiel n facial expressions.
mies [miːs] F **I** adj bad, lousy: **~e Laune haben** be in a foul mood; **j-n** (et.) **~ machen** run s.o. (s.th.) down; **~er Kerl** bastard; **~e Sache** awful mess. **II** adv **sich ~ fühlen** feel lousy; **es geht ihm ~** he's in a bad way.
Miesepeter [ˈmiːzəpeːtər] m (-s; -) F sourpuss.
Miesmuschel [ˈmiːs-] f zo. mussel.
Miete [ˈmiːtə] f (-; -n) rent: **zur ~ wohnen** live in a rented flat.
'Mieteinnahme f rental income.
mieten [ˈmiːtən] v/t (h) rent, a. hire (car).
Mieter [ˈmiːtər] m (-s; -), **'Mieterin** f (-; -nen) tenant. **'Mieterschutz** m (legal) protection of tenants.
'mietfrei adj rent-free.
'Miet|gebühr f rental (charge). **~kauf** m hire purchase. **~preis** m rent.
'Mietshaus n block of flats, Am. apartment house.
'Miet|verhältnis n tenancy. **~vertrag** m a) lease, b) hire contract. **~wagen** m hire(d) car. **~wohnung** f (rented) flat, Am. apartment.
Migräne [miˈgrɛːnə] f (-; -n) ✱ migraine.
Mikro [ˈmiːkro] n (-s; -s) F mike.
Mikrobe [miˈkroːbə] f (-; -n) microbe.
Mikroche'mie [mikro-] f microchemistry. **Mikrochirur'gie** f microsurgery.
Mikrocom,puter [ˈmiːkro-] m microcomputer. **'Mikroelek,tronik** f microelectronics. **'Mikrofilm** m microfilm.
Mikro'kosmos m microcosm.

Mikroorga'nismus *m* microorganism.
Mikrophon [mikro'fo:n] *n* (-s; -e) microphone.
'Mikropro,zessor *m* microprocessor.
Mikroskop [mikro'sko:p] *n* (-s; -e) microscope. **mikro'skopisch** *adj* (*a.* ~ *klein*) microscopic(al).
'Mikrowelle *f* microwave.
'Mikrowellenherd *m* microwave oven.
Milbe ['mɪlbə] *f* (-; -n) *zo.* mite.
Milch [mɪlç] *f* (-; *no pl*) **1.** (*dicke or saure* ~ curdled) milk. **2.** *zo.* (soft) roe.
'Milch|bar *f* milk bar. **~brel** *m* milk pudding. **~flasche** *f* milk bottle. **~geschäft** *n* dairy. **~glas** *n* ⊚ frosted glass.
'milchig *adj* milky.
'Milch|kaf,fee *m* white coffee. **~känn-chen** *n* milk jug. **~kanne** *f* milk can. **~kuh** *f* milcher. **~mädchenrechnung** *f* F naive reasoning. **~mixgetränk** *n* milk shake. **~pro,dukte** *pl* dairy products. **~pulver** *n* powdered milk. **~reis** *m* rice pudding. **~schorf** *m* ✸ milk crust. **~straße** *f* Milky Way. **~wirtschaft** *f* dairy farming. **~zahn** *m* milk tooth.
mild [mɪlt] *adj* mild, *a.* gentle (*climate, reproof, etc*), *a.* lenient (*judge, penalty, etc*), *a.* light (*food*), soft (*light*): ~ *ge-sagt* to put it mildly; *et.* ~*e beurteilen* take a lenient view of s.th.
Milde ['mɪldə] *f* (-; *no pl*) **1.** mildness (*etc,* → *mild*). **2.** leniency.
mildern ['mɪldərn] (h) **I** *v/t* soften (*blow, contrast, etc*), ease (*pain etc*), soothe, alleviate (*a.* grief *etc*), moderate (*one's views etc*), mitigate (*sentence etc*), reduce (*effect*): ⚖ ~*de Umstände* extenuating circumstances. **II** *sich* ~ grow milder, *pain:* ease, *views etc:* soften.
'Milderung *f* (-; *no pl*) alleviation, mitigation, moderation. **'Milderungs-grund** *m* ⚖ extenuating circumstance.
Milieu [mi'liø:] *n* (-s; -s) environment (*a. biol.,* 🐾), *a.* (social) background.
mili'eubedingt *adj* due to environmental factors.
mili'eugeschädigt *adj* deprived.
militant [mili'tant] *adj* militant.
Militär [mili'tɛ:r] *n* (-s; *no pl*) **1.** (*beim* ~ in the) armed forces (*or* army). **2.** military personnel, soldiers. **~arzt** *m* medical officer. **~atta,ché** *m* military attaché. **~dikta,tur** *f* military dictatorship. **mili'tärisch** *adj* **1.** military. **2.** martial.

Militarismus [milita'rɪsmʊs] *m* (-; *no pl*) militarism. **Militarist** [milita'rɪst] *m* (-en; -en) militarist. **milita'ristisch** *adj* militaristic.
Mili'tär|ka,pelle *f* military band. **~mis-si,on** *f* military mission. **~poli,zei** *f* military police. **~putsch** *m* military putsch. **~re,gierung** *f* military government.
Military ['mɪlɪtəri] *f* (-; -s) three-day event. **~reiter** *m* three-day eventer.
Mili'tärzeit *f* time of (military) service.
Miliz [mi'li:ts] *f* (-; -en) militia.
Milliardär [mɪlĭar'dɛ:r] *m* (-s; -e) multimillionaire.
Milliarde [mɪ'lĭardə] *f* (-; -n) billion.
Milli'meter [mɪli-] *n*, *m* millimet/re (*Am.* -er). **~arbeit** *f* F *das war* ~ that was a precision job. **~pa,pier** *n* graph paper.
Million [mɪ'lĭo:n] *f* (-; -en) million: *5* ~*en Dollar* five million dollars. **Millionär** [mɪlĭo'nɛ:r] *m* (-s; -e) millionaire.
Milli'onengeschäft *n* multimillion dollar *etc* deal. **Milli'onenstadt** *f* city of over a million inhabitants.
milli'onstel *adj* millionth.
Milz [mɪlts] *f* (-; -en) *anat.* spleen.
Mime ['mi:mə] *m* (-n; -n) actor. **'mimen** *v/t* (h) act, play. **Mimik** ['mi:mɪk] *f* (-; *no pl*) mimic art. **'mimisch** *adj* mimic.
Mimose [mi'mo:zə] *f* (-; -n) **1.** ♀ mimosa. **2.** *fig.* oversensitive person.
Minarett [mina'rɛt] *n* (-s; -e) minaret.
minder [mɪndər] **I** *adv* less: *nicht* ~ no less. **II** *adj* a) less(er), b) minor, c) inferior (*quality*). **'minderbegabt** *adj* less gifted. **'minderbemittelt** *adj* less well-off: F *geistig* ~ not very bright.
'Minderheit *f* (-; -en) minority; → *a. Minderzahl.* **'Minderheitsre,gierung** *f* minority(-party) government.
'minderjährig [-jɛ:rɪç] *adj* ⚖ minor, under age. **'Minderjährige** [-jɛ:rɪgə] *m*, *f* (-n; -n) minor.
'Minderjährigkeit *f* (-; *no pl*) minority.
mindern ['mɪndərn] (h) **I** *v/t* a) lessen, reduce, lower, b) detract from. **II** *sich* ~ diminish, decrease.
'Minderung *f* (-; -en) a) (*gen*) decrease (in), reduction (in, of), b) depreciation.
'minderwertig *adj* ✝ *a.* of inferior quality. **'Minderwertigkeit** *f* (-; *no pl*) inferiority, ✝ inferior quality.

'**Minderwertigkeitskom,plex** *m* inferiority complex.

'**Minderzahl** *f* (-; *no pl*) **in der ~ sein** a) be in the minority, b) be outnumbered.

mindest ['mɪndəst] *adj* least, slightest: *nicht im ~en* not in the least, not at all; *zum ~en* at least; *das ~e* the least.

'**Mindest...** minimum (*age, price, wage, etc*). **~betrag** *m* minimum (amount).

mindestens ['mɪndəstəns] *adv* at least.

'**Mindestmaß** *n* (*auf das ~ beschränken* keep *s.th.* down to a) minimum.

Mine ['mi:nə] *f* (-; -n) **1.** ✕, ✕ mine. **2.** *of pencil*: lead, *of ball pen*: refill.

'**Minen|feld** *n* ✕ minefield. **~leger** *m* (-s; -) ⚓, ✕ minelayer. **~räumboot** *n*, **~suchboot** *n* ✕ minesweeper.

Mineral [minə'ra:l] *n* (-s; -e, -ien) mineral. **Mineralogie** [minəralo'gi:] *f* (-; *no pl*) mineralogy.

Mine'ral|öl *n* mineral oil. **~quelle** *f* mineral spring. **~wasser** *n* mineral water.

Miniatur [minĭa'tu:r] *f* (-; -en) miniature.

miniaturisieren [minĭaturi'zi:rən] *v/t* (h) ⚙ miniaturize.

Minigolf ['mi:ni-] *n* miniature golf.

'**Minikleid** *n* minidress.

minimal [mini'ma:l] *adj* minimal, minimum, *fig.* negligible. **Minimum** ['mi:nimɔm] *n* (-s; -ma) minimum.

'**Minirock** *m* miniskirt.

Minister [mi'nɪstər] *m* (-s; -) minister, *Br.* Secretary (of State), *Am.* Secretary.

Ministerialbeamte [ministe'rĭa:l-] *m* ministry official.

Ministerium [minɪs'te:rĭom] *n* (-s; -rien) ministry, *Am.* department.

Mi'nisterpräsi,dent *m* Prime Minister.

Mi'nisterrat *m* **1.** cabinet (council). **2.** *EC*: Council of Ministers.

Ministrant [minɪs'trant] *m* (-en; -en) *eccl.* altar server.

Minnesänger ['mɪnə-] *m* minnesinger.

minus ['mi:nʊs] **I** *prep* minus. **II** *adv* **~ 10 Grad** ten degrees below zero.

'**Minus** *n* (-; *no pl*) **1.** deficit. **2.** *fig.* disadvantage. '**Minuspunkt** *m* **1.** *sports*: penalty point. **2.** *fig.* minus, drawback. '**Minuszeichen** *n* A minus sign.

Minute [mi'nu:tə] *f* (-; -n) minute (*a. astr., ⚙*): *auf die ~ pünktlich* on the dot; *in letzter ~* at the last moment; *es klappte auf die ~* it was perfectly timed.

mi'nutenlang I *adj* lasting several min-

utes, several minutes of ... **II** *adv* for (several) minutes.

Mi'nutenzeiger *m* minute-hand.

minuziös [minu'tsĭø:s] *adj* detailed, meticulous.

Minze ['mɪntsə] *f* (-; -n) ⚘ mint.

mir [mi:r] *pers pron* a) me, to me, b) (to) myself: *gib es ~!* give it to me!; *ich wusch ~ die Hände* I washed my hands; *ein Freund von ~* a friend of mine; *von ~ aus* → *meinetwegen*; F ~ *nichts, dir nichts* just like that; *wie du ~, so ich dir* tit for tat.

Mirabelle [mira'bɛlə] *f* (-; -n) ⚘ yellow plum.

'**Mischehe** *f* mixed marriage.

mischen ['mɪʃən] (h) **I** *v/t* mix (*a. radio, film, etc*), blend (*tea, tobacco, etc*), shuffle (*cards*), *computer*: merge. **II** *sich ~ unter* (*acc*) mix (*or* mingle) with; *sich ~ in* (*acc*) interfere (*or* meddle) in; *sich in ein Gespräch ~* join in (*or* butt in on) the conversation. **III** *v/i* shuffle.

'**Mischer** *m* (-s; -) *a. TV* mixer.

'**Mischling** *m* (-s; -e) **1.** *biol.* hybrid. **2.** half-caste, half-breed.

'**Mischmasch** ['mɪʃmaʃ] *m* (-[e]s; -e) F hotchpotch.

'**Mischpult** *n* radio, *TV* mixer.

'**Mischrasse** *f* mixed race.

'**Mischung** *f* (-; -en) mixture (*a. fig.*), blend (*of tea etc*), assortment (*of chocolates etc*).

'**Mischwald** *m* mixed forest.

'**Mischwort** *n* (-[e]s; ⸗er) hybrid (word).

miserabel [mizə'ra:bəl] *adj* F lousy.

Misere [mi'ze:rə] *f* (-; -n) calamity.

miß'achten [mɪs-] *v/t* (*insep, no* -ge-, h) **1.** ignore. **2.** disdain, despise.

'**Mißachtung** *f* **1.** disregard. **2.** disdain: ~ *des Gerichts* contempt of court.

'**Mißbehagen** *n* feeling of uneasiness.

'**Mißbildung** *f* (-; -en) deformity.

miß'billigen *v/t* (*insep, no* -ge-, h) disapprove (of).

'**Mißbilligung** *f* (-; *no pl*) disapproval.

'**Mißbrauch** *m* abuse, misuse. **miß'brauchen** *v/t* (*insep, no* -ge-, h) abuse.

miß'deuten *v/t* (*insep, no* -ge-, h) misinterpret.

'**Mißdeutung** *f* misinterpretation.

'**Mißerfolg** *m* failure, F flop.

'**Mißernte** *f* crop failure.

miß'fallen *v/i* (*irr, insep, no* -ge-, h, →

fallen) er (es) mißfällt mir I don't like him (it). '**Mißfallen** n (-s) disapproval: **j-s ~ erregen** incur s.o.'s displeasure. '**Mißfallensäußerung** f expression of disapproval.

'**mißgebildet** adj deformed.

'**Mißgeburt** f freak.

'**Mißgeschick** n (-[e]s; -e) a) bad luck, misfortune, b) mishap.

miß'gönnen v/t (insep, no -ge-, h) **j-m et. ~** begrudge s.o. s.th.

'**Mißgriff** m mistake.

'**Mißgunst** f resentment.

'**mißgünstig** adj resentful.

miß'handeln v/t (insep, no -ge-, h) maltreat. **Miß'handlung** f maltreatment, ⚖ assault and battery.

Mission [mɪ'sĭo:n] f (-; -en) mission.

Missionar [mɪsĭo'na:r] m (-s; -e), **missio'narisch** adj missionary.

missionieren [mɪsĭo'ni:rən] (h) I v/i do missionary work. II v/t convert.

'**Mißklang** m a. fig. dissonance.

'**Mißkre,dit** m **in ~ bringen (geraten)** bring discredit upon (get a bad name).

'**mißlich** adj awkward, difficult.

mißlingen [mɪs'lɪŋən] (mißlang, mißlungen, sn) v/i fail, be unsuccessful.

'**mißmutig** adj disgruntled, morose.

miß'raten I v/i (mißriet, mißraten, sn) fail, turn out a failure: **das ist mir ~** I've bungled it. II adj wayward (child).

'**Mißstand** m deplorable state of affairs: **Mißstände abschaffen** remedy abuses.

miß'trauen v/i (insep, no -ge-, h) (dat) distrust, mistrust. '**Mißtrauen** n (-s) (**gegen** of) distrust, mistrust: **j-s ~ erregen** arouse s.o.'s suspicion.

'**Mißtrauensantrag** m parl. motion of no confidence. '**Mißtrauensvotum** n parl. vote of no confidence.

'**mißtrauisch** [-traʊɪʃ] adj (**gegen** of) a) distrustful, b) suspicious, c) doubtful: **j-n ~ machen** arouse s.o.'s suspicion.

'**Mißverhältnis** n disproportion: **in e-m ~ stehen** be out of proportion (**zu** to).

'**mißverständlich** adj misleading.

'**Mißverständnis** n (-ses; -se) misunderstanding. '**mißverstehen** v/t (mißverstand, mißverstanden, h) misunderstand, mistake.

'**Mißwahl** f beauty contest.

'**Mißwirtschaft** f mismanagement.

Mist [mɪst] m (-[e]s; no pl) **1.** a) dung, manure, b) droppings. **2.** F rubbish, crap: **~ machen** mess it up; **~ verzapfen** talk rot; (**so ein**) **~!** damn it!

Mistel ['mɪstəl] f (-; -n) ❧ mistletoe.

'**Mistelzweig** m sprig of mistletoe.

'**Mistgabel** f pitchfork. '**Misthaufen** m manure heap. '**Mistkäfer** m dungbeetle. '**Mistkerl** m V bastard. '**Miststück** n V a) bastard, b) bitch.

mit [mɪt] I prep **1.** with: **ein Haus ~ Garten** a house with a garden; **Zimmer ~ Frühstück** bed and breakfast; **ein Korb ~ Obst** a basket of fruit. **2.** by, with: **~ der Bahn** etc by train etc; **~ Bleistift** in pencil; **~ Gewalt** by force. **3. ~ Absicht** intentionally; **~ lauter Stimme** in a loud voice; **~ Verlust** at a loss; **~ einem Wort** in a word; **~ 8 zu 11 Stimmen** by 8 votes to 11; **was ist ~ ihm?** what's the matter with him?; **wie steht's ~ dir?** how about you? **4. ~ 20 Jahren** at (the age of) twenty; **~ dem 3. Mai** as of May 3rd; → **Zeit** 1. II adv **5.** also, too: **~ dabeisein** be there too; **das gehört ~ dazu** that's part (and parcel) of it; **er war ~ der beste** he was one of the best.

'**Mitangeklagte** m, f co-defendant.

'**Mitarbeit** f (-; no pl) cooperation, collaboration, a. assistance (**bei** in): **unter ~ von** (or gen) in collaboration with.

'**mitarbeiten** v/i (sep, -ge-, h) a) (**an** dat, **bei**) a) cooperate (in), collaborate (on), b) contribute (to a paper etc), c) ped. take an active part in the lessons.

'**Mitarbeiter(in** f) m **1.** a) employee, pl staff, b) collaborator (**bei** on), c) contributor (**bei** to a paper etc): **freier Mitarbeiter** freelance(r). **2.** colleague.

'**Mitarbeiterstab** m staff.

'**mitbekommen** v/t (irr, sep, h, → **bekommen**) **1.** get. **2.** F a) catch, get (joke etc), b) pick up: **hast du das mitbekommen?** did you get that?

'**mitbenutzen** v/t (sep, h) share.

'**mitbestimmen** v/i (sep, h) (**bei e-r Sache**) **~** have a say in the matter.

'**Mitbestimmung** f (-; no pl) codetermination, a. worker participation.

'**Mitbewerber(in** f) m competitor.

'**Mitbewohner(in** f) m fellow occupant.

'**mitbringen** v/t (irr, sep, -ge-, h, → **bringen**) **1.** bring s.o., s.th. along (with one). **2.** fig. have, possess (talents etc).

Mitbringsel ['mɪtbrɪŋzəl] n (-s; -) little present.

'**Mitbürger(in** f) m fellow citizen.

'**Miteigentümer(in** f) m joint owner.

mitein'ander adv a) with each other, b) together: **alle ~** one and all.

Mitein'ander n (-[-s]; no pl) togetherness.

'**Mit|erbe** m co-heir. **~erbin** f co-heiress.

'**miterleben** v/t (sep, h) witness.

'**Mitesser** m (-s; -) ♂ blackhead.

'**mitfahren** v/i (irr, sep, -ge-, sn, → **fahren**) **mit j-m ~** ride (or go) with s.o.

'**Mitfahrgelegenheit** f **biete ~ nach Köln** lift offered to Cologne.

'**mitfühlen** v/i (sep, -ge-, h) **mit j-m ~** sympathize with s.o.; **~d** sympathetic.

'**mitführen** v/t (sep, -ge-, h) carry with one.

'**mitgeben** v/t (irr, sep, -ge-, h, → **geben**) **j-m et. ~** give s.o. s.th. (to take with him).

'**Mitgefangene** m, f fellow-prisoner.

'**Mitgefühl** n (-[e]s; no pl) sympathy: **j-m sein ~ ausdrücken** offer one's sympathies (or condolences) to s.o.

'**mitgehen** v/i (irr, sep, -ge-, sn, → **gehen**) **1.** go along (**mit j-m** with s.o.): F **et. ~ lassen** pinch (or lift) s.th. **2.** fig. audience: respond (**mit** to).

'**mitgenommen** I pp of **mitnehmen**. II adj worn out, exhausted: **~ aussehen** look the worse for wear.

'**Mitgift** f (-; -en) dowry.

'**Mitglied** n (-[e]s; -er) member.

'**Mitglieder|versammlung** f general meeting. **~zahl** f membership.

'**Mitgliedsausweis** m membership card.

'**Mitgliedsbeitrag** m (membership) fee (Am. dues).

'**Mitgliedschaft** f (-; -en) membership.

'**Mitgliedstaat** m member state.

'**mithalten** v/i (irr, sep, -ge-, h, → **halten**) **1.** a. fig. keep up (**mit** with). **2.** cards: stay in the bidding.

'**Mitherausgeber(in** f) m co-editor.

'**Mithilfe** f (-; no pl) aid, help, assistance.

'**mithören** (sep, -ge-, h) I v/t a) listen (in) to, b) overhear, c) eavesdrop on, d) monitor, e) intercept. II v/i listen.

'**Mitinhaber(in** f) m joint owner, copartner.

'**mitkommen** v/i (irr, sep, -ge-, sn, → **kommen**) **1.** come along. **2.** ped. keep up (with the class): **gut ~** get on well;

nicht ~ do badly; F **da komme ich (einfach) nicht mit!** that's beyond me!

'**mitlaufen** v/i (irr, sep, -ge-, sn, → **laufen**) run (along) with, sports: run (in the race). '**Mitläufer(in** f) m pol. contp. **1.** hanger-on. **2.** fellow-travel(l)er.

'**Mitlaut** m ling. consonant.

'**Mitleid** n (-[e]s; no pl) (**aus ~** out of) pity (**für** for); **mit j-m ~ haben** have pity on s.o., be sorry for s.o.

'**Mitleidenschaft** f in **~ gezogen werden** be (adversely) affected (**durch** by).

'**mitleiderregend** adj pitiful, pitiable.

'**mitleidig** [-laɪdɪç] adj compassionate, sympathetic: **ein ~es Lächeln** a contemptuous smile.

'**mitleid(s)los** adj pitiless.

'**mitmachen** (sep, -ge-, h) I v/i **1.** a) take part, join in, b) cooperate: F **da mache ich nicht mit!** count me out on that! II v/t **2.** take part in, a. attend (course etc), go with (the fashion), join in (game etc). **3.** F **j-s Arbeit ~** do s.o.'s job as well. **4.** F live (or go) through, suffer: **das mache ich nicht mehr lange mit!** I won't take that much longer!

'**Mitmensch** m fellow (man, being).

'**mitmischen** v/i (sep, -ge-, h) F be in on the action: **bei et. ~** take part in s.th.

'**mitnehmen** v/t (irr, sep, -ge-, h, → **nehmen**) **1.** a) take along, take with one, b) borrow: **j-n im Auto ~** give s.o. a lift. **2.** take away. F take, buy. **4.** F take in (sights etc). **5.** fig. profit (**aus** from). **6.** F fig. **j-n (sehr) ~** take it out of s.o.; → **mitgenommen** II.

'**mitreden** v/t (sep, -ge-, h) **et. mitzureden haben** have a say (**bei** in).

'**Mitreisende** m, f fellow-passenger.

'**mitreißen** v/t (irr, sep, -ge-, h, → **reißen**) carry along, fig. carry away.

'**mitreißend** adj fig. thrilling, rousing.

mit'samt prep (dat) together with.

'**mitschleppen** v/t (sep, -ge-, h) drag along (with one).

'**mitschneiden** v/t (irr, sep, -ge-, h, → **schneiden**) tape(-record).

'**mitschreiben** (irr, sep, -ge-, h, → **schreiben**) I v/t write down. II v/i take notes.

'**Mitschuld** f (-; no pl) joint guilt, complicity (**an** dat in). '**mitschuldig** adj **an e-r Sache ~ sein** be implicated in s.th.

'**Mitschuldige** m, f accessory (**an** dat to).

'**Mitschüler(in** f) m classmate.
'**mitschwingen** v/i (irr, sep, -ge-, h, →
  schwingen) 1. phys. resonate. 2. fig.
  have overtones of.
'**mitsingen** v/t, v/i (irr, sep, -ge-, h, →
  singen) join in the singing (of).
'**mitspielen** v/i (sep, -ge-, h) 1. join in,
  sports: play, be on the team, thea. appear. 2. F fig. (bei) person: go along
  (with), matter: play a part (in): **ich
  spiele nicht mehr mit!** count me out! 3.
  F **j-m übel ~** a) treat s.o. badly, b) play a
  nasty trick on s.o.
'**Mitspieler(in** f) m player, partner, thea.
  etc member of the cast.
'**Mitspracherecht** n (-[e]s; no pl) right to
  a say: **ein ~ haben** have a say (**bei** in).
'**Mitstreiter(in** f) m comrade-in-arms.
Mittag ['mɪta:k] m (-[e]s; -e) midday,
  noon: **heute ♀** at noon today; **zu ~
  essen** have lunch. '**Mittagessen** n
  (**beim** [**zum**] **~** at [for]) lunch.
'**mittags** adv a) at noon, b) at lunchtime.
'**Mittags|pause** f lunch break. **~schlaf**
  m, **~schläfchen** n siesta, afternoon
  nap. **~zeit** f (-; no pl) lunchtime.
'**Mittäter(in** f) m ⚖ accomplice.
Mitte ['mɪtə] f (-; -n) middle, cent/re (Am.
  -er): **die goldene ~** the golden mean;
  pol. **die ~** the centre; **in unserer ~** in our
  midst; **in der ~ zwischen** halfway between; **~ Juli** in the middle of July, in
  mid-July; **in der ~ des 18. Jhs.** in the
  mid-18th-century; **~ Dreißig sein** be in
  one's mid-thirties; F **ab durch die ~!** a)
  off you go!, b) let's go!
'**mitteilen** (sep, -ge-, h) I v/t **j-m et. ~** a)
  inform (or notify) s.o. of s.th., tell s.o.
  s.th., b) impart knowledge to s.o. II
  sich j-m ~ a) confide in s.o., b) fig. joy
  etc: communicate itself to s.o.
'**mitteilsam** adj communicative.
'**Mitteilung** f (-; -en) information, communication, report, notification, message, news.
mittel ['mɪtəl] I adj → **mittler**. II adv F
  middling, so-so.
'**Mittel** n (-s; -) 1. a) means, b) method,
  way, c) expedient: **~ und Wege finden**
  find ways and means; **~ zum Zweck
  sein** be a means to an end; **als letztes ~**
  as a last resort; **ihm ist jedes ~ recht** he
  stops at nothing. 2. ✶ remedy (**gegen**
  for). 3. pl a) resources, b) funds, means:

aus öffentlichen ~n from the public
  purse. 4. (**im ~** on an) average.
'**Mittelalter** n (-s; no pl) Middle Ages.
'**mittelalterlich** adj medi(a)eval.
'**mittelbar** adj indirect.
'**Mittelding** n cross, s.th. in between.
'**Mitteleuro,päisch** adj **~e Zeit** (abbr.
  MEZ) Central European Time.
'**Mittelfeld** n (-[e]s; no pl) soccer: midfield. **~spieler** m midfield player.
'**Mittelfinger** m middle finger.
'**mittelfristig** adj ✝ medium-term.
'**Mittelgebirge** n highlands.
'**Mittelgewicht** n (-[e]s; no pl) sports:
  middleweight.
'**mittelgroß** adj medium-sized, person:
  of medium height.
'**Mittelklasse** f 1. ✝ medium price
  range. 2. → **Mittelstand** 1. **~wagen** m
  medium-range car.
'**Mittellinie** f 1. a. sports: cent/re (Am.
  -er) line, tennis: cent/re (Am. -er) service line. 2. ✚ median line.
'**mittellos** adj destitute, poor, penniless.
'**Mittelmaß** n (-es; no pl) average, contp.
  mediocrity.
'**mittelmäßig** adj average, mediocre.
'**Mittelmäßigkeit** f (-; no pl) mediocrity.
'**Mittelmeer...** Mediterranean.
'**Mittelohrentzündung** f inflammation
  of the middle ear.
'**Mittelpunkt** m cent/re (Am. -er), fig. a.
  heart, hub: **im ~ des Interesses stehen**
  be the focus of interest.
'**mittels** prep by (means of), through.
'**Mittelschiff** n ⌂ nave.
'**Mittelstand** m (-[e]s; no pl) 1. middle
  classes: **gehobener ~** upper middle
  class. 2. ✝ medium-sized and small
  enterprises. '**mittelständisch** [-ʃtɛndɪʃ]
  adj, '**Mittelstands...** middle-class: ✝
  mittelständische Betriebe → **Mittelstand** 2.
'**Mittelstrecken|flugzeug** n medium-
  -range plane. **~läufer(in** f) m sports:
  middle-distance runner. **~ra,kete** f ✕
  medium-range missile.
'**Mittel|streifen** m central reservation,
  Am. median strip. **~stück** n middle. **~
  stufe** f ped. middle school, Am. junior
  high. **~stürmer** m sports: cent/re (Am.
  -er) forward. **~weg** m (**e-n ~ einschlagen** steer a) middle course: **der goldene ~** the golden mean. **~welle** f ⚡ medi-

um wave. **~wert** *m* ✝, *Å* mean (value). **~wort** *n* (-[e]s; ᵘer) *ling.* participle.

mitten ['mɪtən] *adv* **~ in** (*an, auf, unter dat*) in the middle of; **~ in** *a.* in the thick of; **~ unter uns** in our midst; **~ durch** clean through; **~ hinein** right into it; **~ ins Herz** right into the heart.

mitten'drin *adv* F right in the middle (of it). **mitten'durch** *adv* right through (*or* across), *a.* cut *etc* clean through.

Mitternacht ['mɪtər-] *f* (-; *no pl*) midnight.

mittler ['mɪtlər] *adj a)* middle, central, b) average, medium, c) middling, d) *phys.,* ⊛ mean: **~en Alters** middle-aged; **~er Beamter** lower-grade civil servant; **~es Management** middle management; **der ~e Osten** the Middle East; **von ~er Qualität** of medium quality; → *Reife* 2.

'Mittler *m* (-s; -) mediator.

'mittler'weile *adv* meanwhile, (in the) meantime, since, by now.

'Mittsommer *m* midsummer.

Mittwoch ['mɪtvɔx] *m* (-[e]s; -e) (**am ~** on) Wednesday.

'mittwochs *adv* on Wednesday(s).

mit'unter *adv* now and then.

'mitverantwortlich *adj* jointly responsible. **'Mitverantwortung** *f* joint responsibility.

'mitverdienen *v/i* (*sep*, h) be earning as well.

'Mitverfasser(in *f*) *m* coauthor.

'Mitverschulden *n* (-s) ⚖ contributory negligence.

'mitwirken *v/i* (*sep*, -ge-, h) (*bei*) *a)* cooperate (in), *a. thea.* take part (in), ♪ perform, b) *matter:* contribute (to). **'Mitwirkende** *m, f* (-n; -n) *thea.* actor, player (*a.* ♪), *pl* cast: **~ sind ...** the cast includes ... **'Mitwirkung** *f* (-; *no pl*) *a)* cooperation, b) participation: **unter ~ von** (*or gen*) assisted by, *thea.* starring.

'Mitwisser *m* (-s; -) person who is in on the secret, ⚖ accessory.

'Mixbecher *m* shaker. **mixen** ['mɪksən] *v/t* (h) mix. **'Mixer** *m* (-s; -) **1.** barman, *Am.* bartender. **2.** *TV etc:* mixer. **3.** → **'Mixgerät** *n* mixer, liquidizer.

'Mixgetränk *n* mixed drink.

Mixtur [mɪks'tu:r] *f* (-; -en) mixture.

Mob [mɔp] *m* (-s; *no pl*) mob.

Möbel ['mø:bəl] *n* (-s; -) a) → **Möbelstück**, b) *pl* furniture.

'Möbel|geschäft *n* furniture shop. **~händler** *m* furniture dealer. **~poli,tur** *f* furniture polish. **~spediti,on** *f* removal firm. **~stoff** *m* furniture fabric. **~stück** *n* piece of furniture. **~tischler** *m* cabinet-maker. **~wagen** *m* furniture van, *Am.* moving truck.

mobil [mo'bi:l] *adj* **1.** mobile: ✕ **~ machen** mobilize. **2.** F active.

Mobile ['mo:bilə] *n* (-s; -s) mobile.

Mobiliar [mobi'lĭa:r] *n* (-s; *no pl*) furniture.

mobilisieren [mobili'zi:rən] *v/t* (h) mobilize. **Mobili'sierung** *f* (-; -en) mobilization. **Mo'bilmachung** *f* (-; -en) ✕ mobilization.

möblieren [mø'bli:rən] *v/t* (h) furnish: **neu ~** refurnish; **möbliertes Zimmer** furnished room, bed-sitter; F **möbliert wohnen** live in lodgings.

mochte ['mɔxtə] *pret of* **mögen.**

Möchtegern... ['mœçtə-] *iro.* would-be.

modal [mo'da:l] *adj* modal. **Modalität** [modali'tɛ:t] *f* (-; -en) modality.

Mode ['mo:də] *f* (-; -n) fashion: *contp.* **neue ~n** new-fangled ideas; (*die*) **große ~ sein** be (all) the fashion (*or* rage); **in** (**aus der**) **~ kommen** come into (go out of) fashion; **mit der ~ gehen** follow the latest fashion.

'Modear,tikel *n* novelty.

'modebewußt *adj* fashion-conscious.

'Mode|farbe *f* fashionable colo(u)r. **~geschäft** *n* fashion shop. **~haus** *n* **1.** fashion house. **2.** fashion shop.

Modell [mo'dɛl] *n* (-s; -e) *a)* model, b) design, type, c) mock-up: **j-m ~ stehen** sit (*or* pose) for s.o.

Mo'dell|ath,let(in *f*) *m* model athlete. **~bauer** *m* (-s; -) ⊛ model(l)er, model builder. **~eisenbahn** *f* model railway. **~flugzeug** *n* model airplane.

modellieren [modɛ'li:rən] *v/t* (h) model.

Mo'dellkleid *n* model (dress).

Modem ['mo:dɛm] *n* (-s; -s) ⚡ modem.

'Modenschau *f* fashion show.

Moder ['mo:dər] *m* (-s; *no pl*) mo(u)ld.

Moderation [modera'tsĭo:n] *f* (-; *no pl*) *TV* presentation, *Am.* moderation.

Moderator [mode'ra:tɔr] *m* (-s; -en [-ra'to:rən]), **Moderatorin** [modera'to:rɪn] *f* (-; -nen) *TV* presenter, *Am.* moderator. **moderieren** [mode'ri:rən] *v/t* (h) *TV* present, *Am.* moderate.

'mod(e)rig *adj* mo(u)ldy, *a.* musty.

modern¹ ['moːdɛrn] *v/i* (h) mo(u)lder.

modern² [moˈdɛrn] *adj* a) modern, up-to-date, b) fashionable.

Moˈderne *f* (-; *no pl*) **1.** modern age. **2.** *Kunst etc der ~* modernist art *etc.*

modernisieren [modɛrniˈziːrən] *v/t* (h) modernize. **Moderniˈsierung** *f* (-; -en) modernization.

'Modesaˌlon *m* fashion house.

'Modeschmuck *m* costume jewel(le)ry.

'Modeschöpfer *m* couturier.

'Modeschöpferin *f* couturière.

'Modewort *n* vogue word.

'Modezeichner *m* fashion designer.

'Modezeitschrift *f* fashion magazine.

modifizieren [modifiˈtsiːrən] *v/t* (h) modify, *a.* qualify (*expression*).

Modifiˈzierung *f* (-; -en) modification, qualification.

'modisch *adj* fashionable, stylish.

Modul [moˈduːl] *n* (-s; -n) ⊕ module.

modulieren [moduˈliːrən] *v/t* (h) modulate.

'Modultechnik *f* modular technique.

Modus ['moːdʊs] *m* (-; Modi) **1.** way, method, *a.* ♪ mode. **2.** *ling.* mood.

Mofa ['moːfa] *n* (-s; -s) → **Motorfahrrad.**

mogeln ['moːgəln] *v/i* (h) F cheat.

'Mogelpackung *f* deception package.

mögen ['møːgən] (mochte, gemocht, h) **I** *v/t* like, be fond of: *nicht ~* dislike; *ich möchte gern ein Bier* I'd like (to have) a beer; *ich mag k-n Kaffee* I don't like (or care for) coffee; *lieber ~* like better, prefer; *ich möchte lieber ...* I would rather ...; *ich mochte noch nicht nach Hause* I didn't want to go home yet. **II** *v/aux* (*pp* mögen) *ich mag nicht essen* I don't want to eat; *ich möchte ihn sehen* I want (or would like) to see him; *ich möchte wissen* I should like to know, I wonder; *mag er sagen, was er will* let him say what he wants; *das mag (wohl) sein* that may be so; *mag sein, daß* perhaps; *wie dem auch sein mag* be that as it may; *wo er auch sein mag* wherever he may be; *was mag das bedeuten?* I wonder what it could mean?

Mogler ['moːglər] *m* (-s; -) F cheat.

möglich ['møːklɪç] *adj* possible, *a.* practicable: *~er Käufer* potential buyer; *alle ~en* all sorts of; *alles ~e* all sorts of

things; *sein möglichstes tun* do one's utmost; *es ~ machen* → *ermöglichen; nicht ~!* impossible!, F no kidding?; *das ist eher ~!* that's more likely!; *es ist ~, daß er kommt* he may come; *so bald wie ~* as soon as possible.

'möglicherweise *adv* possibly, perhaps.

'Möglichkeit *f* (-; -en) possibility, *a.* opportunity, *a.* chance: *nach ~* if possible, as far as possible; *es besteht die ~, daß* it is possible that; *ich sehe k-e ~ zu* *inf* I cannot see any chance of *ger*; *ist das die ~!* that's not possible!

'möglichst *adv ~ bald etc* as soon *etc* as possible; *~ klein* as small as possible, *attr* the smallest possible.

Mohammedaner [mohameˈdaːnər] *m* (-s; -), **Mohammeˈdanerin** *f* (-; -nen), **mohammeˈdanisch** *adj* Moslem.

Mohn [moːn] *m* (-[e]s; -e) **1.** ♣ poppy. **2.** → **'Mohnsamen** *m* poppy-seed.

Möhre ['møːrə] *f* (-; -n), **Mohrrübe** ['moːr-] *f* ♣ carrot.

Mokka ['mɔka] *m* (-s; -s) mocha.

Molch [mɔlç] *m* (-[e]s; -e) *zo.* newt.

Mole ['moːlə] *f* (-; -n) ⚓ mole, jetty.

Molekül [moleˈkyːl] *n* (-s; -e) molecule.

molekular *adj*, **Molekular...** [molekuˈlaːr-] molecular.

molk [mɔlk] *pret* of **melken.**

Molke ['mɔlkə] *f* (-; *no pl*) whey.

Molkerei [mɔlkəˈraɪ] *f* (-; -en) dairy.

Moll [mɔl] *n* (-; *no pl*) ♪ minor (key).

mollig ['mɔlɪç] *adj* F **1.** cosy. **2.** plump.

Molotowcocktail ['moːlotɔf-] *m* (-s; -s) Molotov cocktail, petrol bomb.

Moment¹ [moˈmɛnt] *m* (-[e]s; -e) (*im ~ at* the) moment.

Moˈment² *n* (-[e]s; -e) **1.** factor, element, aspect. **2.** *phys.* momentum.

momentan [momɛnˈtaːn] **I** *adj* **1.** momentary. **2.** present. **II** *adv* **3.** momentarily. **4.** at the moment.

Monarch [moˈnarç] *m* (-en; -en), **Monˈarchin** *f* (-; -nen) monarch, sovereign. **Monarchie** [monarˈçiː] *f* (-; -n) monarchy. **Monarchist** [monarˈçɪst] *m* (-en; -en), **Monarˈchistin** *f* (-; -nen), **monarˈchistisch** *adj* monarchist.

Monat ['moːnat] *m* (-[e]s; -e) month: *im ~ Mai* in (the month of) May; *im ~, pro ~* a month, monthly; *F sie ist im dritten ~* she is three months gone. **'monatelang** **I** *adj* months of. **II** *adv* for months.

413

Mordkommission

'**monatlich** adj monthly, adv a. a month.
'**Monats|gehalt** n monthly salary (or pay). **~karte** f monthly season ticket, Am. monthly ticket. **~rate** f monthly instal(l)ment. **~schrift** f monthly.
Mönch [mœnç] m (-[e]s; -e) monk.
'**Mönchskloster** n monastery.
'**Mönchsorden** m monastic order.
Mond [moːnt] m (-[e]s; -e) moon, a. satellite: F **auf** (or **hinter**) **dem ~ leben** be behind the times.
mondän [mɔnˈdɛːn] adj fashionable.
'**Mond|aufgang** m moonrise. **~finsternis** f lunar eclipse. **~gestein** n moon rocks. **~landefähre** f lunar module. **~landschaft** f a. fig. moonscape. **~landung** f moon landing. **~nacht** f moonlit night. **~schein** m (-[e]s; no pl) moonlight. **~sichel** f crescent (of the moon). **~stein** m min. moonstone.
Moneten [moˈneːtən] pl F dough.
Mongole [mɔŋˈgoːlə] m (-n; -n), **Mon'golin** f (-; -nen), **mon'golisch** adj Mongol(ian). **Mongolismus** [mɔŋgoˈlɪsmʊs] m (-; no pl) 🎗 Down's syndrome. **mongoloid** [mɔŋgoloˈiːt] adj 🎗 mongoloid.
Monitor ['moːnitɔr] m (-s; -en [moniˈtoːrən]) TV monitor.
mono ['moːno] adj F (a. **~ abspielbar**) mono.
monogam [monoˈgaːm] adj monogamous.
Monogramm [monoˈgram] n (-s; -e) monogram.
Monographie [monograˈfiː] f (-; -n) monograph.
Monolog [monoˈloːk] m (-s; -e) monolog(ue Br.).
Monopol [monoˈpoːl] n (-s; -e) monopoly (**auf** acc on). **monopolisieren** [monopoliˈziːrən] v/t (h) monopolize.
monoton [monoˈtoːn] adj monotonous. **Monotonie** [monotoˈniː] f (-; -n) monotony.
Monster ['mɔnstər] n (-s; -) monster.
'**Monster...** F mammoth (enterprise, film, trial, etc).
Monstranz [mɔnˈstrants] f (-; -en) eccl. monstrance.
monströs [mɔnˈstrøːs] adj monstrous.
Monstrum ['mɔnstrʊm] n (-s; Monstren) monster.
Monsun [mɔnˈzuːn] m (-s; -e) monsoon.

Montag ['moːntaːk] m (-[e]s; -e) (**am ~** on) Monday.
Montage [mɔnˈtaːʒə] f (-; -n) 1. 🎗 a) mounting, fitting, installation, b) assembly: **auf ~ sein** be away on a construction job. 2. phot. etc montage.
Mon'tageband n assembly line.
Mon'tagehalle f assembly shop.
'**montags** adv on Monday(s).
Montanindu,strie [mɔnˈtaːn-] f coal, iron, and steel industries.
Monteur [mɔnˈtøːr] m (-s; -e) 🎗 fitter, ✔, mot. mechanic. **montieren** [mɔnˈtiːrən] v/t (h) a) mount (a. phot. etc), fit, instal(l), b) assemble.
Montur [mɔnˈtuːr] f (-; -en) F get-up.
Monument [monuˈmɛnt] n (-[e]s; -e) monument (**für** to). **monumental** [monumɛnˈtaːl] adj monumental.
Moor [moːr] n (-[e]s; -e) fen, bog, moor.
Moos [moːs] n (-es; -e) 1. 🌿 moss. 2. F dough, sl. lolly.
Moped ['moːpɛt] n (-s; -s) moped.
Mops [mɔps] m (-es; Möpse) zo. pug.
Moral [moˈraːl] f (-; no pl) a) morals, b) ethics, c) (working etc) morale: **doppelte ~** double standards; **die ~ heben** raise the morale; **~ predigen** moralize.
moralisch [moˈraːlɪʃ] adj moral.
Moralist [moraˈlɪst] m (-en; -en) moralist.
Morast [moˈrast] m (-[e]s; -e) morass.
morbid [mɔrˈbiːt] adj morbid.
Morchel ['mɔrçəl] f (-; -n) 🌿 morel.
Mord [mɔrt] m (-[e]s; -e) murder (**an** dat of): **e-n ~ begehen** commit murder; F **es gibt ~ und Totschlag** there will be a hell of a row.
'**Mordanklage** f murder charge: **unter ~ stehen** be charged with murder.
'**Mordanschlag** m attempted murder: **e-n ~ auf j-n verüben** make an attempt on s.o.'s life.
morden ['mɔrdən] (h) **I** v/i commit murder, kill. **II** v/t murder, kill.
Mörder ['mœrdər] m (-s; -) murderer.
'**Mörderin** f (-; -nen) murderess.
'**mörderisch** adj murderous, a. deadly (fight etc), a. terrible (heat etc), a. gruel(l)ing (job etc), a. breakneck (pace etc), cutthroat (competition etc).
'**Mordfall** m murder case.
'**Mordkommissi,on** f murder (Am. homicide) squad.

Mords... 414

'**Mords...** F a) great, terrific, fantastic, b) terrible. **~angst** *f e-e ~ haben* be in a flat panic, be scared stiff. **~ding** *n* whopper, humdinger. **~glück** *n* fantastic stroke of luck. **~kerl** *m* great guy. **~krach** *m* F terrific noise, awful racket: *e-n ~ schlagen* raise hell.

'**mordsmäßig** F **I** *adj* terrific. **II** *adv* terribly, awfully.

'**Mordverdacht** *m* suspicion of murder.

'**Mordversuch** *m* attempted murder.

'**Mordwaffe** *f* murder weapon.

morgen ['mɔrgən] *adv* tomorrow: *~ früh* tomorrow morning; *~ mittag* at noon tomorrow; *heute ~* this morning; *~ in 14 Tagen* a fortnight tomorrow; *~ in e-r Woche* a week from tomorrow; *~ um diese Zeit* this time tomorrow.

'**Morgen¹** *m* (-s; -) morning: *am (frühen) ~* (early) in the morning.

'**Morgen²** *m* (-s; -) acre.

'**Morgen|andacht** *f* morning prayer. **~dämmerung** *f* dawn, daybreak. **~grauen** *n beim ~* at dawn. **~gym,nastik** *f s-e ~ machen* do one's daily dozen. **~luft** *f* morning air: *fig. ~ wittern* see a chance. **~muffel** *m* F *ein ~ sein* be grumpy in the morning. **~rock** *m* dressing gown. **~rot** *n* (-s; *no pl*) **1.** red sky. **2.** *fig.* dawn.

'**morgens** *adv* in the morning(s): *~ um 4 (Uhr)* at four (o'clock) in the morning; *von ~ bis abends* from morning till midnight.

'**Morgen|sonne** *f* (*~ haben* get the) morning sun. **~stunde** *f* morning hour: *in den frühen ~n* in the small hours.

morgig ['mɔrgɪç] *adj* tomorrow's: *der ~e Tag* tomorrow.

Mormone [mɔr'moːnə] *m* (-n; -n), **Mor'monin** *f* (-; -nen), **mor'monisch** *adj* Mormon.

Morphium ['mɔrfiʊm] *n* (-s; *no pl*) morphine.

morsch [mɔrʃ] *adj* rotten, *fig. a.* shaky.

Morsealpha,bet ['mɔrzə-] *n* (-[e]s; *no pl*) Morse (code).

morsen ['mɔrzən] *v/t, v/i* (h) morse.

Mörser ['mœrzər] *m* (-s; -) mortar.

'**Morsezeichen** *n* Morse signal.

Mörtel ['mœrtəl] *m* (-s; -) mortar.

Mosaik [moza'iːk] *n* (-s; -en) mosaic.

Mosa'ikfußboden *m* tessellated floor.

Moschee [mɔ'ʃeː] *f* (-; -n) mosque.

Moschus ['mɔʃʊs] *m* (-; *no pl*) musk.

Mosel ['moːzəl] *m* (-s; -) Moselle.

Moskito [mɔs'kiːto] *m* (-s; -s) (tropical) mosquito. **~netz** *n* mosquito net.

Moslem ['mɔslɛm] *m* (-s; -s) Moslem, Muslim.

Most [mɔst] *m* (-[e]s; -e) must.

Mostrich ['mɔstrɪç] *m* (-s; *no pl*) *gastr.* mustard.

Motel ['moːtɛl] *n* (-s; -s) motel.

Motiv [mo'tiːf] *n* (-s; -e) **1.** motive (*zu* fọr). **2.** *art:* motif, *film etc:* a. theme, *phot.* subject. **Motivation** [motiva-'tsioːn] *f* (-; -en) motivation.

motivieren [moti'viːrən] *v/t* (h) **1.** motivate. **2.** explain, give reasons for.

Motor ['moːtor, mo'toːr] *m* (-s; -en [mo'toːrən]) engine, *⚡* motor (*a. fig.*). **~boot** *n* motorboat. **~fahrrad** *n* motorized bicycle. **~haube** *f* a) *mot.* bonnet, *Am.* hood, b) ✈ (engine) cowling.

motorisch [mo'toːrɪʃ] *adj* ✈ motor.

motorisieren [motori'ziːrən] *v/t* (h) motorize, *esp.* ✕ mechanize.

'**Motorpumpe** *f* power pump.

'**Motorrad** *n* (*~ fahren* ride a) motorcycle (F motorbike): *~ mit Beiwagen* combination. **~fahrer(in** *f*) *m* motorcyclist.

'**Motor|roller** *m* (motor) scooter. **~säge** *f* power saw. **~schaden** *m* engine trouble. **~schlitten** *m* snowmobile. **~sport** *m* motor sport.

Motte ['mɔtə] *f* (-; -n) *zo.* moth.

'**Mottenkugel** *f* mothball.

'**mottenzerfressen** *adj* motheaten.

Motto ['mɔto] *n* (-s; -s) motto.

motzen ['mɔtsən] *v/i* (h) F *person:* grouse.

Möwe ['møːvə] *f* (-; -n) *zo.* (sea)gull.

Mücke ['mʏkə] *f* (-; -n) *zo.* mosquito, midge: *aus e-r ~ e-n Elefanten machen* make a mountain out of a molehill. '**Mückenstich** *m* mosquito bite.

Mucks [mʊks] *m* (-es; -e) F *k-n ~ sagen* not to a utter a) sound. '**mucksen** *v/i* (*a. sich ~*) (h) stir, make a sound.

'**mucksmäuschen'still** *adj* F *person:* as quiet as a mouse: *es war ~* you could have heard a pin drop.

müde [myːdə] *adj* (*~ werden* get) tired: *zum Umfallen ~* ready to drop; *fig. nicht ~ werden zu inf* not to tire of ger.

'**Müdigkeit** *f* (-; *no pl*) tiredness.

Muff [mʊf] *m* (-[e]s; -e) muff.

Muffe ['mʊfə] *f* (-; -n) ⚙ sleeve, socket.

Muffel ['mʊfəl] *m* (-s; -) F sourpuss.
...muffel *m* → **Krawatten-, Partymuffel.**
muffig ['mʊfɪç] *adj* **1.** musty (*air etc*). **2.** *fig.* a) stuffy, b) grumpy.
Mühe ['my:ə] *f* (-; -n) a) trouble, pains, b) effort, c) difficulties (*mit* with, in doing): *vergebliche ~* waste of time (*or* energy); *mit ~ und Not* barely, with (great) difficulty; (*nicht*) *der ~ wert* (not) worth the trouble; *sich (große) ~ geben* take (great) trouble (*or* pains) (*mit* over), try hard; *sich die ~ machen zu inf* go to the trouble of *ger*; *k-e ~ scheuen* spare no effort (*or* pains); *gib dir k-e ~!, spar dir die ~!* save yourself the trouble!, don't bother!
'**mühelos** *adj* effortless, easy.
'**mühevoll** *adj* hard, difficult, laborious.
Mühle ['my:lə] *f* (-; -n) **1.** mill: → **Wasser. 2.** F *contp.* ✈, *mot.* crate, bus. **3.** *a.* '**Mühlespiel** *n* (nine men's) morris.
'**Mühlrad** *n* millwheel.
'**Mühlstein** *m* millstone.
Mühsal ['my:za:l] *f* (-; *no pl*) a) toil, trouble(s), b) strain.
'**mühsam I** *adj* a) troublesome, b) hard, c) tiring. **II** *adv* with difficulty: *sich et. ~ verdienen* work hard for s.th.; *sich ~ erheben* struggle to one's feet.
Mulatte [mu'latə] *m* (-n; -n), **Mu'lattin** *f* (-; -nen) mulatto.
Mulde ['mʊldə] *f* (-; -n) hollow.
Mull [mʊl] *m* (-[e]s; -e) muslin, ✚ gauze.
Müll [myl] *m* (-s; *no pl*) rubbish, refuse, *Am.* garbage. '**Müllabfuhr** *f* refuse (*Am.* garbage) collection.
'**Mullbinde** *f* ✚ gauze bandage.
'**Mülleimer** *m* rubbish bin, *Am.* garbage can.
'**Müller** ['mylər] *m* (-s; -) miller.
'**Müll|fahrer** *m* dustman, *Am.* garbage man. **~platz** *m* dump. **~schlucker** *m* rubbish chute. **~tonne** *f* dustbin, *Am.* garbage can. **~verbrennungsanlage** *f* incinerating plant. **~verwertungsanlage** *f* waste utilization plant. **~wagen** *m* dustcart, *Am.* garbage truck.
mulmig ['mʊlmɪç] *adj* F **1.** ticklish. **2.** *mir ist ganz ~ zumute* a) I feel queasy (*or* funny), b) I've got an uneasy feeling, c) I am scared.
Multi ['mʊlti] *m* (-s; -s) F multinational (concern).
'**Multimillio,när** *m* multimillionaire.

Multiplikation [mʊltiplika'tsĭo:n] *f* (-; -en) ✕ multiplication. **Multiplikator** [mʊltipli'ka:tɔr] *m* (-s; -en [-ka'to:rən]) multiplier. **multiplizieren** [mʊltipli-'tsi:rən] *v/t* (h) multiply (*mit* by).
Mumie ['mu:mĭə] *f* (-; -n) mummy.
Mumm [mʊm] *m* (-s; *no pl*) F spunk, guts.
Mumps [mʊmps] *m* (-; *no pl*) ✚ mumps.
Mund [mʊnt] *m* (-[e]s; ⁺er) mouth: *wie aus einem ~e* as one man; *~ und Nase aufsperren* be dum(b)founded; *den ~ halten* keep one's mouth shut; *halt den ~!* shut up!; F *den ~ voll nehmen* talk big; *du nimmst mir das Wort aus dem ~e* you are taking the very words out of my mouth; F *j-m über den ~ fahren* cut s.o. short; *in aller ~e sein* be the talk of the town; *nicht auf den ~ gefallen sein* have a ready (*or* glib) tongue; → *absparen, Blatt* 1, *stopfen* 3, *verbrennen* 1, *wässerig etc.*
'**Mundart** *f* dialect.
'**Munddusche** *f* oral spray.
Mündel ['myndəl] *n* (-s; -) ⚖ ward.
'**mündelsicher** *adj* ✝ *~e Papiere* gilt-edged securities.
münden ['myndən] *v/i* (sn) *~ in* (*acc*) a) *river:* flow into, b) (*a. auf acc*) *road etc:* lead into, c) *fig.* lead to, end in.
'**Mundgeruch** *m* ✚ bad breath, halitosis.
'**Mundhar,monika** *f* mouth organ.
mündig ['myndɪç] *adj* **1.** ⚖ (*~ werden* come) of age. **2.** *fig.* responsible.
mündlich ['myntlɪç] *adj* verbal (*statement etc*), oral (*exam*): *~e Überlieferung* oral tradition; *alles weitere ~* I'll tell you the rest when I see you.
'**Mund|pflege** *f* oral hygiene. **~schutz** *m* ✚ mask, *boxing:* gumshield. **~stück** *n* **1.** ♪, ⚙ mouthpiece. **2.** (cigarette) tip.
'**mundtot** *adj* *~ machen* (reduce to) silence, *pol.* gag, muzzle.
'**Mündung** ['myndʊŋ] *f* (-; -en) **1.** *river:* a) mouth, b) estuary. **2.** *anat.*, ⚙ mouth, ✗ muzzle.
'**Mund|wasser** *n* (-s; ⁺) mouthwash. **~werbung** *f* word-of-mouth advertising. **~werk** *n* (-[e]s; *no pl*) F *ein loses (gutes) ~ haben* have a loose tongue (the gift of the gab). **~winkel** *m* corner of one's mouth.
'**Mund-zu-'Mund-Beatmung** *f* mouth-to-mouth resuscitation, F kiss of life.

Munition [muni'tsĩo:n] f (-; no pl) ammunition.
Muniti'onslager n ammunition dump.
munkeln ['mʊŋkəln] v/i, v/t (h) whisper: **man munkelt, daß ...** it is rumo(u)red that ...
Münster ['mʏnstər] n (-s; -) minster, cathedral.
munter ['mʊntər] adj **1.** a) awake, b) up (and about). **2.** a) lively, b) cheerful, chirpy, c) vigorous; → **frisch** 4, **gesund. 'Munterkeit** f (-; no pl) liveliness.
'Muntermacher m (-s; -) F pick-me-up.
'Münzauto,mat m slot machine.
Münze ['mʏntsə] f (-; -n) **1.** coin: fig. **et. für bare ~ nehmen** take s.th. at face value. **2.** medal. **3.** mint.
'Münzeinwurf m coin slot.
münzen ['mʏntsən] v/t, v/i (h) coin, mint: fig. **gemünzt sein auf** (acc) be meant for.
'Münz|fernsprecher m pay phone. **~sammlung** f coin collection. **~tank-(auto,mat)** m coin-operated petrol (Am. gas) pump. **~wechsler** m (-s; -) change machine.
mürbe ['mʏrbə] adj **1.** a) crumbly (pastry etc), mellow, very ripe (fruit), tender (meat), b) rotten (wood). **2.** fig. worn out: **j-n ~ machen** wear s.o. down; **~ werden** give in, wilt.
'Mürbekuchen m shortcake.
'Mürbeteig m short pastry.
Murks [mʊrks] m (-es; no pl) F botch-up: **~ machen** → **'murksen** v/i (h) F make a hash of things.
Murmel ['mʊrməl] f (-; -n) marble.
murmeln ['mʊrməln] v/i, v/t (h) murmur, mutter.
'Murmeltier n marmot: fig. **schlafen wie ein ~** sleep like a top (or log).
murren ['mʊrən] v/i (h) grumble (über acc about).
mürrisch ['mʏrɪʃ] adj surly, grumpy.
Mus [mu:s] n (-es; -e) puree, mash.
Muschel ['mʊʃəl] f (-; -n) **1.** zo. a) mussel, b) shell. **2.** teleph. a) earpiece, b) mouthpiece.
'muschelförmig adj shell-shaped.
Muse ['mu:zə] f (-; -n) fig. muse.
Museum [mu'ze:ʊm] n (-s; Museen) museum.
Musik [mu'zi:k] f (-; no pl) **1.** music. **2.** F band. **musikalisch** [muzi'ka:lɪʃ] adj

musical: **~e Untermalung** incidental music. **Musikalität** [muzikali'tɛ:t] f (-; no pl) musicality.
Musiker ['mu:zikər] m (-s; -), **'Musikerin** f (-; -nen) musician.
Mu'sik|festspiele pl music festival. **~hochschule** f conservatory. **~instru,ment** n musical instrument. **~ka,pelle** f band. **~lehrer(in** f) m music teacher **~stück** n piece of music. **~stunde** f music lesson. **~unterricht** m music lessons. **~wissenschaft** f (-; no pl) musicology.
musisch ['mu:zɪʃ] adj artistic (talent etc): ped. **~e Fächer** fine arts (subjects).
musizieren [muzi'tsi:rən] (h) **I** v/i make music. **II** v/t play.
Muskat [mʊs'ka:t] m (-[e]s; -e) nutmeg. **~blüte** f mace. **~nuß** f nutmeg apple.
Muskel ['mʊskəl] m (-s; -n) muscle: **die ~n spielen lassen** flex one's muscles. **~faser** f muscular fib/re (Am. -er). **~kater** m (-s; no pl) F sore muscles: **~ haben** feel stiff and aching. **~pa,ket** n, **~protz** m F muscleman. **~riß** m torn muscle. **~zerrung** f pulled muscle.
Muskulatur [mʊskula'tu:r] f (-; -en) muscular system, muscles.
muskulös [mʊsku'lø:s] adj muscular.
Müsli ['my:sli] n (-s; -) muesli.
Muß [mʊs] **es ist ein ~** is a must.
Muße ['mu:sə] f (-; no pl) leisure.
'Mußehe f shotgun wedding.
müssen ['mʏsən] (mußte, müssen, h) **I** v/aux have to: **du mußt nicht hingehen** you needn't (or don't have to) go; **sie ~ bald kommen** they are bound to come soon; **der Zug müßte längst hier sein** the train is (long) overdue; **ich mußte (einfach) lachen** I couldn't help laughing; **muß das sein?** is that really necessary?, do you have to?; **wenn es unbedingt sein muß** if it can't be helped. **II** v/i (pp gemußt) **ich muß** I must, I have (got) to; **ich mußte** I had to; **ich müßte (eigentlich)** I ought to.
'Mußestunde f leisure hour.
müßig ['my:sɪç] adj **1.** idle. **2.** pointless.
'Müßiggang m (-[e]s; no pl) idleness.
'Müßiggänger [-gɛŋər] m (-s; -) idler.
mußte ['mʊstə] pret of **müssen.**
Muster ['mʊstər] n (-s; -) **1.** pattern, model: **sie ist das ~ e-r guten Haus-**

frau she's a model housewife. **2.** sample, specimen. **3.** *textil.* pattern, design.
'**Muster|beispiel** *n* classic example (*für* of). **~betrieb** *m* model plant. **~exem,plar** *n* **1.** ✝ sample specimen. **2.** *print.* specimen copy. **3.** *a. iro.* perfect example. **~gatte** *m iro.* model husband.
'**mustergültig, 'musterhaft** *adj* exemplary, model: *sich ~ benehmen* behave perfectly.
'**Muster|haus** *n* show house. **~knabe** *m iro.* paragon, *contp.* prig. **~koffer** *m* ✝ sample case. **~kollekti,on** *f* ✝ sample collection.
mustern ['mʊstərn] *v/t* (h) **1.** a) study, scrutinize, b) eye, look *s.o.* up and down, c) size *s.o.* up. **2.** ✕ inspect (*troops*), examine (*conscripts*): *gemustert werden* F have one's medical. **3.** pattern: → **gemustert.**
'**Musterpro,zeß** *m* ⚖ test case.
'**Musterung** *f* (-; -en) **1.** scrutiny. **2.** ✕ a) review (*of troops*), b) medical examination (for military service).
Mut [muːt] *m* (-[e]s; *no pl*) courage, F pluck: *~ fassen* pluck up courage; *j-m den ~ nehmen* discourage s.o.; *den ~ sinken lassen* (*or verlieren*) lose heart, despair; *nur ~!* cheer up!
Mutation [muta'tsi̯oːn] *f* (-; -en) **1.** *biol.* mutation. **2.** → **Stimmbruch.**
mutieren [mu'tiːrən] *v/i* (h) mutate.
'**mutig** *adj* courageous, brave.
'**mutlos** *adj* discouraged, disheartened, despondent. '**Mutlosigkeit** *f* (-; *no pl*) discouragement, despondency.
mutmaßlich ['muːtmaːslɪç] *adj* probable, ⚖ putative.
'**Mutmaßung** *f* (-; -en) (*über acc* about) conjecture, speculation.
'**Mutprobe** *f* test of courage.
Mutter¹ ['mʊtər] *f* (-; ") mother: *werdende ~* expectant mother; *e-e ~ von vier Kindern* a mother of four.
'**Mutter²** *f* (-; -n) ⚙ nut.
'**Mütterberatungsstelle** *f* child welfare centre, *Am.* maternity center.
'**Mutter|bindung** *f psych.* mother tie. **~boden** *m*, **~erde** *f* 🌱 topsoil. **~gesell-**

schaft *f* ✝ parent company.
Mutter'gottes *f* (-; *no pl*) (Virgin) Mary.
'**Mutter|haus** *n eccl.* mother house. **~herz** *n* mother's heart. **~in,stinkt** *m* maternal instinct. **~kom,plex** *m* mother fixation. **~kuchen** *m* 🪢 placenta. **~leib** *m* (-[e]s; *no pl*) womb.
mütterlich ['mʏtərlɪç] *adj* motherly, maternal. '**mütterlicherseits** *adv* on one's mother's side: *Onkel ~* maternal uncle.
'**Mütterlichkeit** *f* (-; *no pl*) motherliness.
'**Mutter|liebe** *f* motherly love. **~mal** *n* 🩸 birthmark. **~milch** *f* mother's milk: *mit ~ genährt* breast-fed. **~mund** *m* (-[e]s; *no pl*) *anat.* uterine orifice.
'**Mutterschaft** *f* (-; *no pl*) motherhood, maternity.
'**Mutterschafts|hilfe** *f* maternity benefits. **~urlaub** *m* maternity leave.
'**Mutterschutz** *m* legal (job-)protection for expectant and nursing mothers.
'**mutter'seelenal'lein** *adj pred* all alone.
'**Muttersöhnchen** [-zøːnçən] *n* (-s; -) F mummy's darling.
'**Muttersprache** *f* mother tongue.
'**Muttersprachler** [-ʃpraːxlər] *m* (-s; -) native speaker.
'**Muttertag** *m* (-[e]s; *no pl*) Mother's Day.
'**Muttertier** *n* mother, dam.
'**Mutterwitz** *m* (-es; *no pl*) **1.** common sense. **2.** natural wit.
Mutti ['mʊti] *f* (-; -s) F mum(my), *Am.* mom.
'**mutwillig** *adj* wilful, wanton.
Mütze ['mʏtsə] *f* (-; -n) cap.
Myrrhe ['mʏrə] *f* (-; -n) myrrh.
mysteriös [mʏste'ri̯øːs] *adj* mysterious.
Mystik ['mʏstɪk] *f* (-; *no pl*) mysticism.
Mystiker ['mʏstɪkər] *m* (-s; -) mystic.
mystisch ['mʏstɪʃ] *adj* **1.** a) mystic, b) mystical. **2.** mysterious.
Mythe ['myːtə] *f* (-; -n) myth.
'**mythisch** *adj* mythical.
Mythologie [mytolo'giː] *f* (-; -n) mythology. **mythologisch** [myto'loːgɪʃ] *adj* mythological. **mythologisieren** [mytologi'ziːrən] *v/t* (h) mythologize.
Mythos ['myːtɔs] *m* (-; Mythen) myth.

N

N, n [ɛn] *n* (-; -) N, n.

na [na] *int* F a) well, b) hey: ~, ~! come on (now)!; ~ *also!* there you are!; ~ *schön!* all right then!; ~, *so* (**et**)*was!* just fancy that!; → *warten¹, und.*

Nabe ['na:bə] *f* (-; -n) ⚙ hub.

Nabel ['na:bəl] *m* (-s; -) navel.

'**Nabelschnur** *f* umbilical cord.

nach [na:x] **I** *prep* (*dat*) **1.** to, toward(s), for. ~ *England gehen* (*abreisen*) go to (leave for) England; *der Zug ~ Paris* the train for Paris; *das Schiff fährt ~ Singapur* the ship is bound for Singapore. **2.** after: *e-r ~ dem anderen* one after the other, one by one. **3.** a) after, b) within, in (*three days etc*): *zehn Minuten ~ drei* ten minutes past three. **4.** according to, by, from: ~ *deutschem Recht* under German law; ~ *e-m Roman von Balzac* after a novel by Balzac; *wenn es ~ mir ginge* if I had my way; → *Ansicht 1, Natur, Uhr etc.* **5.** for: ~ *Gold graben* dig for gold; ~ *j-m fragen* ask for s.o. **II** *adv* **6.** after: *mir ~!* after me!, follow me! **7.** ~ *und* ~ little by little, gradually; ~ *wie vor* (now) as ever.

'**nachäffen** [-ɛfən] *v/t* (*sep*, -ge-, h) F ape.

'**nachahmen** [-a:mən] *v/t* (*sep*, -ge-, h) a) imitate, copy, b) take off, parody.

'**nachahmenswert** *adj* exemplary.

'**Nachahmung** *f* (-; -en) imitation.

Nachbar ['naxba:r] *m* (-n; -n) neighbo(u)r: *die ~n* a. the neighbo(u)rhood.

'**Nachbar...** neighbo(u)ring (*district, house, town, etc*).

'**Nachbarin** *f* (-; -nen) neighbo(u)r.

'**nachbarlich** *adj* **1.** a. *gut* ~ neighbo(u)rly. **2.** next-door (*garden etc*).

'**Nachbarschaft** *f* (-; *no pl*) neighbo(u)rhood, a. the neighbo(u)rs.

'**nachbauen** *v/t* (*sep*, -ge-, h) ⚙ copy.

'**Nachbehandlung** *f* ✚ subsequent treatment, a. 🎗 after-treatment.

'**nachbessern** *v/t* (*sep*, -ge-, h) touch up.

'**nachbestellen** *v/t* (*sep*, -ge-, h) order some more, ✝ place a repeat order for.

'**Nachbestellung** *f* ✝ repeat order (*gen* for).

'**nachbeten** *v/t* (*sep*, -ge-, h) F parrot.

'**nachbilden** *v/t* (*sep*, -ge-, h) copy, reproduce.

'**Nachbildung** *f* (-; -en) copy, replica.

'**nachda,tieren** *v/t* (*sep*, h) postdate.

nach'dem *conj* **1.** after, when. **2.** → *je* 4. **3.** since.

'**nachdenken** *v/i* (*irr, sep*, -ge-, h, → *denken*) think (*über acc* about): *denk mal nach!* think a little!; *Zeit zum* ⚶ *brauchen* need time to think (it over).

'**nachdenklich** *adj* thoughtful, pensive: *j-n ~ machen* set s.o. thinking.

'**Nachdruck¹** *m* (-[e]s; *no pl*) stress, emphasis: *mit ~* a) emphatically, b) energetically; ~ *legen auf* (*acc*), (*dat*) ~ *verleihen* stress, emphasize.

'**Nachdruck²** *m* (-[e]s; -e) reprint: ~ *verboten!* all rights reserved!

'**nachdrucken** *v/t* (*sep*, -ge-, h) reprint: *unerlaubt ~* pirate.

'**nachdrücklich** [-dryklɪç] *adj* emphatic (*warning etc*), forceful (*claim etc*): **et.** ~ *empfehlen* recommend s.th. strongly; ~ *verlangen* insist on.

'**Nachdrucksrecht** *n* right of reproduction.

'**nacheifern** *v/i* (*sep*, -ge-, h) *j-m* ~ emulate s.o.

nachein'ander *adv* **1.** one after another, a. in succession. **2.** by turns.

'**Nacherzählung** *f* ped. summary.

'**nachfahren** *v/i* (*irr, sep*, -ge-, sn, → *fahren*) *j-m* ~ follow s.o.

'**Nachfaß\|schreiben** *n* follow-up letter.

~**werbung** *f* follow-up advertising.

'**Nachfolge** *f* (-; *no pl*) succession: *j-s ~ antreten* → '**nachfolgen** *v/i* (*sep*, -ge-, sn) *j-m* (*im Amt*) ~ succeed s.o. (in office). '**nachfolgend** *adj* following. '**Nachfolger** *m* (-s; -) successor.

'**Nachforderung** *f* additional claim.

'**nachforschen** *v/i* (*sep*, -ge-, h) (*dat*) investigate. '**Nachforschung** *f* (-; -en) investigation: *~en anstellen* (*über acc*) investigate (*s.th.*).

'**Nachfrage** *f* (-; -n) **1.** ✝ demand (*nach* for). **2.** inquiry. '**nachfragen** *v/i* (*sep*, -ge-, h) inquire, ask.

'**nachfühlen** *v/i* (*sep* , -ge-, h) *j-m et.* ~

(können) feel with s.o., understand s.o.'s feelings about s.th.

'**nachfüllen** v/t (sep, -ge-, h) **1.** fill up, refill, top up. **2.** add (water etc).

'**nachgeben** v/i (irr, sep, -ge-, h, → **ge-ben**) **1.** ground etc: give (way). **2.** prices etc: drop. **3.** (dat) give in, yield.

Nachgebühr f † surcharge.

'**Nachgeburt** f ✻ afterbirth.

'**nachgehen** v/i (irr, sep, -ge-, sn, → **ge-hen**) (dat) **1.** follow. **2.** fig. look into (a matter), follow, check up on (rumour, tip, etc), attend to (business etc), pursue (one's studies): **s-r Arbeit ~** go about one's work. **3.** indulge in, seek, pursue (pleasure etc). **4.** be slow, lose: **m-e Uhr geht (e-e Minute) nach** my watch loses (a minute). **5.** fig. j-m ~ haunt s.o.

'**nachgemacht I** pp of **nachmachen. II** adj a) counterfeit, b) imitation.

'**nachgerade** adv **1.** really. **2.** by now.

'**Nachgeschmack** m a. fig. aftertaste.

'**nachgiebig** [-gi:bɪç] adj **1.** compliant, soft. **2.** ⚙ flexible, pliant. '**Nachgie-bigkeit** f (-; no pl) compliance, softness.

'**nachhaken** v/i (sep, -ge-, h) F follow (it) up: **bei j-m in e-m Punkt ~** press s.o. on a point.

'**nachhaltig** adj a) lasting (effect etc), sustained (efforts etc), b) strong, effective: **~ wirken** have a lasting effect; **~ beeinflussen** influence strongly.

'**nachhelfen** v/i (irr, sep, -ge-, h, → **hel-fen**) help: **e-r Sache ~** help s.th. along.

nach'her adv a) afterward(s), b) later (on): **bis ~!** see you later!, so long!

'**Nachhilfe** f private lessons. '**~lehrer(in** f) m (private) tutor. '**~stunde** f **1.** private lesson. **2.** pl → **~unterricht** m private lessons.

'**nachhinein** adv im **~** after the event.

'**nachhinken** v/i (sep, -ge-, sn) fig. lag behind.

'**Nachholbedarf** m **1.** † backlog demand. **2.** fig. deficit.

'**nachholen** v/t (sep, -ge-, h) **1.** make up for lost time etc, catch up on work, sleep, etc. **2.** fetch s.o., s.th. later.

'**Nachhut** f (-; -en) ✕ rearguard: **die ~ bilden** a. bring up the rear.

'**nachjagen** v/i (sep, -ge-, sn) (dat) chase after, a. fig. pursue.

'**Nachklang** m fig. echo, reminiscence.

'**Nachkomme** m (-n; -n) descendant, off-

spring: **ohne ~n** ⚖ without issue.

'**nachkommen** v/i (irr, sep, -ge-, sn, → **kommen**) **1.** come later, follow. **2.** a. fig. keep up (mit with). **3.** (dat) comply with (order, wish, etc), meet (obligation), keep (promise).

'**Nachkommenschaft** f descendants, ⚖ issue. '**Nachkömmling** [-kœmlɪŋ] m (-s; -e) late arrival.

'**Nachkriegs...** post-war ~.

'**Nachlaß** [-las] m (-sses; -lässe) **1.** estate: **literarischer ~** unpublished works. **2.** † reduction: **e-n ~ gewähren** allow a discount (auf acc on).

'**nachlassen** (irr, sep, -ge-, h, → **lassen**) **I** v/i **1.** decrease, weaken, wind: drop, rain, storm etc: let up, noise etc: subside, pain: ease, effect, strength, etc: wear off, performance, demand, etc: drop (off), interest etc: flag, slacken. **2.** a) deteriorate, grow weaker, fail, b) go off, be slowing down, runner etc: wilt, c) mentally: lose one's grip; **nicht ~!** hang on! **II** v/t **3.** leave (behind): **nach-gelassene Werke** unpublished works. **4.** et. vom Preis **~** allow a discount.

'**Nachlaßgericht** n ⚖ probate court.

'**nachlässig** adj careless, negligent, sloppy. '**Nachlässigkeit** f (-; no pl) carelessness, negligence, sloppiness.

'**nachlaufen** v/i (irr, sep, -ge-, sn, → **lau-fen**) j-m **~** run after s.o.; **den Mädchen ~** chase (after) the girls.

'**nachlesen** v/t (sep, -ge-, h, → **lesen**) read up, look s.th. up.

'**nachliefern** v/t (sep, -ge-, h) supply s.th. later (or in addition).

'**nachlösen** v/i, v/t (sep, -ge-, h) (e-e **Fahrkarte) ~** buy a ticket on the train.

'**nachmachen** v/t (sep, -ge-, h) a) copy, imitate, b) forge: **j-m et. ~** copy s.th. s.o. does; **das soll ihm erst mal e-r ~!** I'd like to see anyone do better!

'**nachmessen** v/t (irr, sep, -ge-, h, → **messen**) check.

'**Nachmittag** m (am **~** in the) afternoon; **heute ~** this afternoon. '**nachmittags** adv in the afternoon. '**Nachmittags-vorstellung** f thea. etc matinée.

'**Nachnahme** [-na:mə] f (-; -n) et. als (or per) **~ schicken** send s.th. cash (Am. collect) on delivery (abbr. C.O.D.).

'**Nachnahmesendung** f C.O.D. parcel.

'**Nachname** m surname, last name.

'**nachplappern** v/t (sep, -ge-, h) F parrot.

'**Nachporto** n surcharge.

'**nachprüfbar** adj verifiable.

'**nachprüfen** v/t (sep, -ge-, h) **1.** check. **2.** a) re-examine, b) examine at a later date. '**Nachprüfung** f (-; -en) **1.** check(ing). **2.** examination at a later date.

'**nachrechnen** v/t (sep, -ge-, h) check.

'**Nachrede** f üble ~ defamation.

Nachricht ['naːxrɪçt] f (-; -en) a) (e-e ~ a piece of) news, b) message, c) news (item; in radio, TV news; ~**en** hear from; j-m ~ geben let s.o. know; e-e ~ hinterlassen leave a message.

'**Nachrichten|agen,tur** f, **~bü,ro** n press agency. **~dienst** m **1.** radio, TV news service. **2.** ✕ intelligence service. **~satel,lit** m communications satellite. **~sendung** f radio, TV newscast, news broadcast. **~sperre** f pol. news blackout. **~sprecher(in** f) m news reader, newscaster. **~technik** f (tele)communication(s) (engineering). **~wesen** n (-s; no pl) communications.

'**nachrücken** v/i (sep, -ge-, sn) **1.** a. fig. move up. **2.** ✕ follow on.

'**Nachruf** m (-[e]s; -e) obituary.

'**nachrüsten** v/i (sep, -ge-, h) **1.** pol. close the armament gap. **2.** a. v/t ⊚ retrofit. '**Nachrüstsatz** m ⊚ retrofit kit.

'**nachsagen** v/t (sep, -ge-, h) **1.** repeat. **2.** j-m et. ~ say s.th. of s.o.

'**Nachsai,son** f off season.

'**Nachsatz** m **1.** postscript. **2.** ling. final clause.

'**nachschenken** v/t, v/i (sep, -ge-, h) j-m (et.) ~ top s.o. up (with s.th.).

'**nachschlagen** (irr, sep, -ge-, h, → schlagen) **I** v/t **1.** look s.th. up. **II** v/i **2.** im Lexikon ~ consult a dictionary. **3.** F j-m ~ take after s.o.

'**Nachschlagewerk** n reference book.

'**Nachschlüssel** m duplicate key.

'**Nachschrift** f postscript.

'**Nachschub** m (-[e]s; no pl) (an dat of) supply (a. fig.), coll. supplies.

'**Nachschuß** m soccer: follow-up shot.

'**nachsehen** (irr, sep, -ge-, h, → sehen) **I** v/i **1.** gaze after. **2.** have a look: ~ ob ... (go and) see whether ... **II** v/t **3.** inspect, check, ped. correct. **4.** → nachschlagen **1. 5.** j-m et. ~ forgive s.o. s.th.

'**Nachsehen:** das ~ haben be the loser.

'**nachsenden** v/t (irr, sep, -ge-, h, → senden²) forward.

'**Nachsicht** f a) forbearance, b) leniency: ~ üben be lenient; mit j-m ~ haben be lenient towards s.o.

'**nachsichtig** adj lenient, forbearing.

'**Nachsilbe** f ling. suffix.

'**nachsitzen** v/i (irr, sep, -ge-, h, → sitzen) ~ müssen be kept in.

'**Nachsommer** m late (or Indian) summer. '**Nachsorge** f (; no pl) ✿ aftercare. '**Nachspeise** f dessert.

'**Nachspiel** n **1.** ♪ postlude. **2.** thea. epilog(ue Br.). **3.** sex: afterplay. **4.** fig. sequel: die Sache wird ein ~ haben there are bound to be consequences.

'**nachspielen** v/i (sep, -ge-, h) sports: play (~ lassen allow) extra time.

nächst [nɛːçst] **I** sup of nahe. **II** adj **1.** nearest (a. fig. relatives etc), a. shortest: die ~e Umgebung the immediate vicinity; aus ~er Entfernung at close range. **2.** next: am ~en Tage the next day; in den ~en Tagen in the next few days; Mittwoch ~er Woche Wednesday week; in ~er Zeit in the near future; bei ~er Gelegenheit at the first opportunity; im ~en Augenblick the next moment. **III** adv **3.** am ~en (dat to) next, nearest, closest; fig. j-m am ~en stehen be closest to s.o.; (dat) am ~en kommen come closest to. **4.** fürs ~e for the time being. **IV** prep **5.** (dat) next to.

'**nächst'best** adj **1.** (comer etc). **2.** second-best, next-best.

'**Nächstbeste 1.** m, f the next best, the first person. **2.** n the next best (thing).

'**Nächste 1.** m, f (-n; -n) a) neighbo(u)r, one's fellow, b) the next (one): jeder ist sich selbst der ~ charity begins at home; der ~, bitte! next (one) please! **2.** n (-n; -n) the next (or first) thing.

'**nachstehen** v/i (irr, sep, -ge-, h, → stehen) j-m ~ in (or an dat) be inferior to s.o. in; j-m in nichts ~ be in no way inferior to s.o. '**nachstehend I** adj following. **II** adv in the following.

'**nachstellen** (sep, -ge-, h) **I** v/t **1.** put back (clock etc). **2.** ⊚ (re)adjust. **II** v/i (dat) a) be after, b) persecute. '**Nachstellung** f (-; -en) fig. persecution. '**Nächstenliebe** f (-; no pl) charity.

nächstens ['nɛːçstəns] adv (very) soon.

'**nächstliegend** *adj* nearest: *fig.* **das Nächstliegende** the obvious thing.

Nacht [naxt] *f* (-; ⁓e) (*bei* ⁓ at) night: *gute ⁓! a. iro.* good night!; *heute* ⁓ tonight; *die* ⁓ *zum Tage machen* turn night into day; *es wird* ⁓ it is getting dark; *zu ⁓ essen* have supper; *bis spät* (*or tief*) *in die* ⁓ till late in the night; *über* ⁓ *a. fig.* overnight; *die ganze* ⁓ (*hindurch or lang*) all night (long); *im Schutze* (*or Dunkel*) *der* ⁓, *bei* ⁓ *und Nebel* under the cover of night, *w.s.* secretly.

'**Nacht|arbeit** *f* nightwork. ⁓**blind** *adj* night-blind. ⁓**creme** *f* night cream. ⁓**dienst** *m* night duty: ⁓ *haben* be on night duty, *chemist's shop etc*: be open all night.

Nachteil *m* (-[e]s; -e) disadvantage, *a.* drawback, *sports, a. fig.* handicap: *zum* ⁓ *von* to the disadvantage of; *im* ⁓ *sein* be at a disadvantage.

'**nachteilig** *adj* disadvantageous, detrimental (*für* to): *nichts Nachteiliges* nothing unfavo(u)rable; ⁓ *beeinflussen* affect adversely.

nächtelang ['nɛçtə-] **I** *adj* ⁓*e Diskussionen etc* night after night of discussions *etc*. **II** *adv* night after night.

'**Nacht|essen** *n* supper. ⁓**frost** *m* night frost. ⁓**hemd** *n* a) nightshirt, b) nightdress, F nightie.

Nachtigall ['naxtɪɡal] *f* (-; -en) *zo.* nightingale.

'**Nachtisch** *m* (-[e]s; -e) dessert, sweet, F afters.

'**Nachtklub** *m* nightclub.

'**Nachtleben** *n* nightlife.

nächtlich ['nɛçtlɪç] *adj* nocturnal, nightly: *der* ⁓*e Park* the park at night.

'**Nacht|lo,kal** *n* nightclub. ⁓**porti,er** *m* night porter. ⁓**quar,tier** *n* place for the night, ⚔ night quarters.

'**Nachtrag** [-tra:k] *m* (-[e]s; ⁓e [-trɛ:ɡə]) supplement. '**nachtragen** *v/t* (*irr, sep, -ge-, h, → tragen*) **1.** *j-m et.* ⁓ *fig.* bear s.o. a grudge for s.th. **2.** add (*in writing*). '**nachtragend** *adj* unforgiving.

'**nachträglich** [-trɛ:klɪç] **I** *adj* a) additional, b) belated, c) later. **II** *adv* subsequently, later: ⁓ *herzlichen Glückwunsch!* belated best wishes!

'**Nachtragshaushalt** *m* supplementary budget.

'**nachtrauern** *v/i* (*sep, -ge-, h*) *j-m* (*e-r Sache*) ⁓ mourn s.o. (s.th.).

'**Nachtruhe** *f* sleep.

nachts *adv* at (*or* during) the night.

'**Nacht|schicht** *f* night shift. ⁓**schwärmer** *m* night owl. ⁓**schwester** *f* night nurse. ⁓**speicherofen** *m* night storage heater. ⁓**strom** *m* off-peak electricity. ⁓**tisch** *m* bedside table. ⁓**topf** *m* chamber pot. ⁓**tre,sor** *m* night safe. ⁓**und-'Nebel-Akti,on** *f* undercover operation. ⁓**wache** *f* night watch. ⁓**wächter** *m* **1.** night watchman. **2.** F *contp.* dope. ⁓**zug** *m* night train.

'**Nachuntersuchung** *f* checkup.

'**nachvollziehen** *v/t* (*irr, sep, h, → vollziehen*) understand, duplicate.

'**nachwachsen** *v/i* (*irr, sep, -ge-, sn, → wachsen*) grow again.

'**Nachwahl** *f parl.* by-election, *Am.* special election.

'**Nachwehen** *pl fig.* aftermath.

'**nachweinen** (*sep, -ge-, h*) **I** *v/i → nachtrauern*. **II** *v/t → Träne*.

Nachweis ['na:xvaɪs] *m* (-es; -e) **1.** a) proof, evidence, b) certificate: *den* ⁓ *führen* (*or erbringen*) prove, show. **2.** detection. '**nachweisbar** *adj* demonstrable, detectable: *... sind* ⁓ *a. ...* can be proved. '**nachweisen** *v/t* (*irr, sep, -ge-, h, → weisen*) prove, establish: *man konnte ihm nichts* ⁓ nothing could be proved against him; *j-m e-n Fehler* ⁓ show that s.o. has made a mistake. '**nachweislich I** *adj* demonstrable. **II** *adv* demonstrably: *er war* ⁓ *da* there is evidence that he was there.

'**Nachwelt** *f* (-; *no pl*) posterity.

'**nachwirken** *v/i* (*sep, -ge-, h*) have a lasting effect. '**Nachwirkung** *f* after-effect: ⁓*en fig. a.* aftermath.

'**Nachwort** *n* (-[e]s; -e) epilog(ue *Br.*).

'**Nachwuchs** *m* (-es; *no pl*) **1.** a) *the* young generation, b) young talent (*a. sports*), F new blood, ⚕ junior staff, trainees, ⚔ *etc* recruits: *der ärztliche* ⁓ the new generation of doctors. **2.** F a) offspring, b) addition to the family.

'**Nachwuchs...** a) talented, young, up-and-coming (*author, actor, etc*), b) ⚕ junior, trainee (*salesman etc*).

'**Nachwuchssorgen** *pl* ⁓ *haben* have difficulty (in) finding young talent.

'**nachzahlen** *v/t, v/i* (*sep, -ge-, h*) pay extra, pay later.

'**nachzählen** v/t (sep, -ge-, h) check.
'**Nachzahlung** f additional payment.
'**nachziehen** (irr, sep, -ge-, → **ziehen**) **I** v/t (h) **1.** drag (or pull) behind one, drag (foot etc). **2.** trace (line etc), pencil (eyebrows): **die Lippen ~** touch up one's lips. **3.** ⚙ tighten (screw etc). **II** v/i **4.** (sn) follow. **5.** (h) **F** fig. follow suit.
'**Nachzügler** [-tsy:glər] m (-s; -) **1.** straggler, latecomer. **2.** F late arrival.
Nacken ['nakən] m (-s; -) (nape of the) neck: **j-m im ~ sitzen** a) be hard on s.o.'s heels, b) fig. be breathing down s.o.'s neck; fig. **den ~ steifhalten** keep a stiff upper lip; → **steifen**.
'**Nackenschlag** m fig. blow.
'**Nackenwirbel** m cervical vertebra.
nackt [nakt] adj naked, bare (a. fig.), esp. art: **völlig ~** stark naked; **~ baden** (malen) swim (paint) in the nude; **sich ~ ausziehen** strip; **~e Tatsachen** hard facts; **die ~e Wahrheit** the plain truth; **das ~e Leben retten** escape with one's bare life.
'**Nacktbadestrand** m nudist beach.
'**Nacktheit** f (-; no pl) nakedness, fig. a. bareness.
'**Nacktkul,tur** f (-; no pl) nudism.
Nadel ['na:dəl] f (-; -n) a) needle, b) of record player: stylus, c) pin. **~baum** m conifer(ous tree). **~öhr** n **1.** eye of a needle. **2.** fig. bottleneck. **~stich** m (fig. pin)prick. **~streifen** m Anzug etc mit ~ pinstripe(d) suit etc. **~wald** m coniferous forest.
Nagel ['na:gəl] m (-s; ~) nail: fig. **et. an den ~ hängen** give s.th. up; **Nägel mit Köpfen machen** do things properly; **den ~ auf den Kopf treffen** hit the nail on the head; **er ist ein ~ zu m-m Sarg** he is a nail in my coffin. **~bett** n anat. nail bed. **~bürste** f nail brush. **~feile** f nail file. **~häutchen** n cuticle.
'**Nagellack** m nail varnish (or polish, Am. enamel). **~entferner** m nail-varnish (or nail-polish) remover.
nageln ['na:gəln] v/t (h) nail (**an** acc to).
'**nagel'neu** adj F brand-new.
'**Nagelschere** f (pair of) nail scissors.
nagen ['na:gən] v/t, v/i (h) a. fig. gnaw: **~ an** (dat) a. fig. gnaw at. '**nagend** adj fig. gnawing, nagging (doubt etc).
'**Nager** m (-s; -), '**Nagetier** n rodent.
'**Nahaufnahme** f film etc: close-up.

nahe ['na:ə] **I** adj a) near, close (both a. fig.), nearby, b) approaching, imminent (death etc): **der Nahe Osten** the Middle East; **in ~r Zukunft** in the near future; **den Tränen ~** on the verge of tears. **II** adv near, close, nearby: **~ bei** near (to), close to; **~ beieinander** close together; **~ verwandt** closely related; **von nah und fern** from far and near; **von ~m** up close, at close range; **j-m zu ~ treten** offend s.o.; **ich war ~ daran, ihn zu ohrfeigen** I very nearly slapped his face. **III** prep (dat) near, close to.
Nähe ['nɛ:ə] f (-; no pl) a) nearness (a. fig.), b) vicinity, neighbo(u)rhood: **aus der ~** at close range; **ganz in der ~** quite near; **in der ~ bleiben** stay around; **in d-r ~** near you; **in greifbare ~ gerückt** near at hand.
'**nahe'bei** adv nearby.
'**nahebringen** v/t (irr, sep, -ge-, h, → **bringen**) fig. **j-m et.** ~ make s.o. appreciate s.th.
'**nahegehen** v/i (irr, sep, -ge-, sn, → **gehen**) fig. **j-m** ~ affect s.o. deeply.
'**nahegelegen** **I** pp of **naheliegen**. **II** adj nearby.
'**nahekommen** v/i (irr, sep, -ge-, sn, → **kommen**) fig. come close (dat to): **sich** (or **einander**) ~ become close.
'**nahelegen** v/t (sep, -ge-, h) fig. **j-m et.** ~ suggest s.th. to s.o.; **j-m ~, et. zu tun** urge s.o. to do s.th.
'**naheliegen** v/i (irr, sep, -ge-, h, → **liegen**) fig. a) seem (very) likely, b) be the obvious thing: **die Vermutung liegt nahe, daß ...** it is fair to assume that ...
'**naheliegend** adj obvious.
nähen ['nɛ:ən] (h) **I** v/t sew, a. ✚ stitch: **sich ein Kleid ~** make a dress for o.s. **II** v/i sew.
näher ['nɛ:ər] **I** comp of **nahe**. **II** adj **1.** nearer, closer: **die ~e Umgebung** the (immediate) vicinity. **2.** further (data etc), more detailed: **bei ~er Betrachtung** on closer inspection. **III** adv **3.** (an dat, bei to) nearer, closer: **~ kommen** come (or draw) nearer. **4.** more closely: **ich kenne ihn ~** I know him quite well; **sich mit e-r Sache ~ befassen** go into a matter (more closely); **et. ~ erläutern** explain s.th. at greater detail.
'**näherbringen** v/t (irr, sep, -ge-, h, → **bringen**) fig. **j-m et.** ~ make s.th. acces-

sible to s.o.; **Menschen einander ~** bring people closer together.

'**Nähere** n (-n; no pl) the details, (further) particulars: **ich weiß nichts ~s** I don't know any details.

Näherei [nɛːəˈraɪ] f (-; -en) sewing.

'**Naherholungsgebiet** n recreation area in the immediate vicinity of a big city.

'**näherkommen** v/i (irr, sep, -ge-, sn, → **kommen**) get (or be) nearer (dat to): fig. **j-m ~** become closer to s.o.; **jetzt kommen wir der Sache schon näher!** now we're getting somewhere!

'**näherliegen** v/i (irr, sep, -ge-, h, → **liegen**) fig. be more obvious.

nähern ['nɛːərn] sich ~ (h) approach, a. draw near; **sich j-m ~** approach s.o.

'**Näherungs...** & approximate (calculation, value, etc).

'**nahestehen** v/i (irr, sep, -ge-, h, → **stehen**) fig. **j-m ~** be close to s.o.

'**nahezu** adv almost, nearly, next to.

'**Nähgarn** n sewing thread.

'**Nahkampf** m 1. ✗ close combat. 2. boxing: infighting.

nahm [naːm] pret of **nehmen.**

'**Näha,schine** f sewing machine.

'**Nährboden** m 1. culture medium (for bacteria). 2. fig. breeding ground.

'**Nährcreme** f nutrient cream.

nähren ['nɛːrən] (h) I v/t feed, fig. nourish (hope etc), a. harbo(u)r (hatred etc): **sich ~ von** live on. II v/i be nourishing.

'**nahrhaft** adj nutritious, nourishing.

'**Nährmittel** pl cereal products.

'**Nährstoff** m nutrient.

Nahrung ['naːrʊŋ] f (-; no pl) food, diet: **geistige ~** food for the mind.

'**Nahrungsaufnahme** f food intake.

'**Nahrungskette** f biol. food chain.

'**Nahrungsmangel** m lack of food.

'**Nahrungsmittel** n food(stuff), pl foodstuffs. **~chemiker** m food chemist.

'**Nährwert** m nutritional value.

'**Nähseide** f sewing silk.

Naht [naːt] f (-; ⸚e) seam, ⊚ a. joint: F **aus den** (or **allen**) **Nähten platzen** a. fig. be bursting at the seams.

'**nahtlos** adj 1. seamless. 2. fig. smooth.

'**Nahverkehr** m local traffic.

'**Nahverkehrszug** m commuter train.

'**Nähzeug** n (-[e]s; no pl) sewing kit.

'**Nahziel** n immediate objective.

naiv [naˈiːf] adj naive: **~er Maler** primitive.

Naivität [naiviˈtɛːt] f (-; no pl) naivety.

Name ['naːmə] m (-n; -n) name, a. reputation: **wie ist Ihr ~?** what is your name?; **im ~n** (gen), **in j-s ~n → namens** II; (**nur**) **dem ~n nach** by name (only); **sich e-n ~n machen** make a name for o.s.; **das Kind beim rechten ~n nennen** call a spade a spade.

'**Namenliste** f list of names.

'**namenlos** adj 1. nameless, a. anonymous. 2. fig. unspeakable.

'**namens** I adv by the name of, called. II prep (gen) in the name of, on behalf of.

'**Namens|aktie** f registered share (Am. stock). **~schild** n name plate. **~tag** m name day. **~vetter** m namesake. **~zug** m signature.

namentlich ['naːməntlɪç] I adj 1. by name: **~e Abstimmung** roll-call vote. II adv 2. by name. 3. (e)specially.

'**namhaft** adj 1. considerable (sum etc). 2. well-known (artist etc). 3. **~ machen** name.

nämlich ['nɛːmlɪç] adv 1. namely, that is (to say). 2. for, you see, you know.

nannte ['nantə] pret of **nennen.**

nanu [naˈnuː] int hey.

Napalm ['naːpalm] n (-s; no pl) napalm.

Napf [napf] m (-[e]s; ⸚e) bowl.

'**Napfkuchen** m deep-dish cake.

Nappa ['napa] n (-[s]; -s), '**Nappaleder** n nap(p)a (leather).

Narbe ['narbə] f (-; -n) 1. ⚕ scar: fig. **~n hinterlassen** leave a scar. 2. ⚕ stigma.

'**narbig** adj scarred.

Narkose [narˈkoːzə] f (-; -n) (in ~ under) an(a)esthesia: **aus der ~ aufwachen** come round. **Nar'kosefacharzt** m an(a)esthetist. **Narkotikum** [narˈkoːtikʊm] n (-s; -ka), **narkotisch** [narˈkoːtɪʃ] adj narcotic. **narkotisieren** [narkotiˈziːrən] v/t (h) an(a)esthetize.

Narr [nar] m (-en; -en) fool: F **e-n ~en gefressen haben an** (dat) be crazy about; **j-n zum ~en halten → 'narren** v/t **j-n ~** make a fool of s.o., fool s.o.

'**Narrenfreiheit** f fool's licen/ce (Am. -se). '**narrensicher** adj F foolproof.

Närrin ['nɛrɪn] f (-; -nen) fool.

'**närrisch** adj a) foolish, b) mad, c) odd.

Narzisse [narˈtsɪsə] f (-; -n) ⚘ narcissus: **Gelbe ~** daffodil.

Narzißmus 424

Narzißmus [nar'tsɪsmʊs] *m* (-; *no pl*)
psych. narcissism. **nar'zißtisch** [-tɪʃ]
adj narcissistic.

nasal [na'za:l] *adj* nasal.
nasalieren [naza'li:rən] *v/t* (h) nasalize.
Na'sallaut *m* nasal (sound).

naschen ['naʃən] *v/i, v/t* (h) nibble (*an
dat, von* at): *gern ~* have a sweet tooth.
Nasche'rei *f* (-; -en) sweets, F goodies.
'naschhaft *adj* sweet-toothed.

Nase ['na:zə] *f* (-; -n) nose: F *pro ~ e-n
Dollar* one dollar each; *fig. e-e gute (or
feine) ~ haben für* have a good nose
for; *in der ~ bohren* pick one's nose; F
fig. auf die ~ fallen come a cropper; *j-m
et. auf die ~ binden* tell (s.th. to) s.o.;
j-n an der ~ herumführen lead s.o. up
the garden path; *j-m auf der ~ herum-
tanzen* do what one likes with s.o.; *auf
der ~ liegen* be laid up; *man sieht es
dir an der ~ an* it's written all over your
face; *es j-m unter die ~ reiben* rub it
in; *s-e ~ in alles (hinein)stecken* poke
one's nose into everything; *die ~ voll
haben* be fed up (*von* with); *die ~ vorn
haben* be one step ahead (of one's competitors); *j-m et. vor der ~ wegschnappen* take s.th. away from under s.o.'s
nose; *der Zug fuhr mir vor der ~ weg* I
missed the train by an inch; → *zuhalten* 2.

näseln ['nɛ:zəln] *v/i* (h) speak through
one's nose. 'Näseln *n* (-s) (nasal)
twang. 'näselnd *adj* nasal.

'Nasen|bein *n* nasal bone. **~bluten** *n*
nosebleed. **~flügel** *m* nostril. **~länge** *f*
um e-e ~ gewinnen win by a whisker.
~loch *n* nostril. **~rücken** *m* bridge of
the nose. **~scheidewand** *f* nasal sep-
tum. **~schleimhaut** *f* nasal mucous
membrane. **~spitze** *f* tip of the nose.
~spray *m, n* nose spray. **~tropfen** *pl*
nose drops. **~wurzel** *f* root of the nose.

Nashorn ['na:s-] *n* rhinoceros, F rhino.

naß [nas] *adj* wet: ~ *machen* wet (*sich
o.s.*); ~ *werden* get wet; *durch und
durch ~, ~ bis auf die Haut* wet
through, wet to the skin; → *triefen*.

Nassauer ['nasaʊər] *m* (-s; -) F sponge.
'nassauern *v/i* (h) F sponge (*bei* on).

Nässe ['nɛsə] *f* (-; *no pl*) wet, wetness:
„vor ~ schützen!" "keep dry!"

'nässen (h) **I** *v/t* wet. **II** *v/i wound*: weep.

'naßkalt *adj* damp and cold, clammy.

'Naßra,sur *f* wet shave.
'Naßzelle *f* (prefab) bathroom unit.
Nation [na'tsĭo:n] *f* (-; -en) nation.
national [natsĭo'na:l] *adj* national.
Natio'nalfeiertag *m* national holiday.
Natio'nalflagge *f* national flag.
Natio'nalheld *m* national hero.
Natio'nalhymne *f* national anthem.
nationalisieren [natsĭonali'zi:rən] *v/t*
(h) nationalize. **Nationali'sierung** *f* (-;
-en) nationalization.
Nationalismus [natsĭona'lɪsmʊs] *m* (-;
no pl) nationalism. **Nationalist** [-'lɪst]
m (-en; -en) nationalist.
nationa'listisch *adj* nationalist(ic).
Nationalität [natsĭonali'tɛ:t] *f* (-; -en)
nationality.
Natio'nal|mannschaft *f sports*: national
team. **~park** *m* national park. **~sozia-
lismus** *m pol. hist.* National Socialism, *contp.* Nazism. **~sozia,list** *m*,
2sozia,listisch *adj pol. hist.* National
Socialist, *contp.* Nazi. **~spieler(in** *f*) *m*
sports: international. **~stolz** *m* national
pride.
Natrium ['na:trĭʊm] *n* (-s; *no pl*) sodium.
Natron ['na:trɔn] *n* (-s; *no pl*) bicarbo-
nate of soda.
Natter ['natər] *f* (-; -n) *zo.* adder.
Natur [na'tu:r] *f* (-; -en) **1.** *no pl* nature: *in
der freien ~* in the open country; *nach
der ~ zeichnen* draw from nature (*or*
life); *von ~ (aus)* by nature; *Fragen
grundsätzlicher ~* fundamental questions; *die Sache ist ernster ~* it's a
serious matter; *er hat e-e gesunde ~*
he has a healthy constitution. **2.** character, person.
Naturalien [natu'ra:lĭən] *pl* natural
produce: *in ~ zahlen* pay in kind.
naturalisieren [naturali'zi:rən] *v/t* (h)
naturalize.
Naturalismus [natura'lɪsmʊs] *m* (-; *no
pl*) naturalism.
natura'listisch *adj* naturalist(ic).
Na'turdenkmal *n* natural monument.
Naturell [natu'rɛl] *n* (-s; -e) disposition,
temperament.
Na'tur|ereignis *n*, **~erscheinung** *f* nat-
ural phenomenon. **~forscher** *m* natu-
ralist. **~forschung** *f* natural science.
~freund(in *f*) *m* nature lover. **2gemäß**
adj natural. **~geschichte** *f* natural history. **~gesetz** *n* law of nature. **2getreu**

adj true to nature, lifelike. **~gewalt** *f* force of nature. **~heilkunde** *f* naturopathy. **~kata,strophe** *f* natural disaster. **~kunde** *f* (-; *no pl*) natural history. **~lehrpfad** *m* nature trail.

natürlich [na'ty:rlıç] **I** *adj* natural: **~e Größe** actual size. **II** *adv* naturally, *int a.* of course.

Na'türlichkeit *f* (-; *no pl*) naturalness.

Na'tur|park *m* wildlife park. **~pro,dukt** *n* natural product. **~schutz** *m* conservation: **unter ~ stehen** be protected. **~schützer** *m* (-s; -) conservationist. **~schutzgebiet** *n* nature reserve. **~ta,lent** *n* **ein ~ sein** be a natural. **2ver-bunden** *adj* nature-loving. **~volk** *n* primitive race. **~wissenschaft** *f* (natural) science. **~wissenschaftler** *m* (natural) scientist. **2wissenschaftlich** *adj* scientific. **~wunder** *n* natural wonder. **~zustand** *m* (-[e]s; *no pl*) natural state, (**im ~** in a) state of nature.

nautisch ['naʊtɪʃ] *adj* nautical.

Navigation [naviga'tsio:n] *f* (-; *no pl*) navigation. **Navigator** [-'ga:tɔr] *m* (-s; -en [-ga'to:rən]) navigator. **navigieren** [-'gi:rən] *v/t, v/i* (h) navigate.

Nazi ['na:tsi] *m* (-s; -s) *pol. hist. contp.* Nazi. **Nazismus** [na'tsɪsmʊs] *m* (-; *no pl*) *pol. hist. contp.* Nazism. **na'zistisch** [-tɪʃ] *adj pol. hist. contp.* Nazi.

Nebel ['ne:bəl] *m* (-s; -) **1.** fog (*a. fig.*), mist, haze. **2.** *astr.* nebula.

nebelhaft *adj fig.* nebulous, hazy.

'Nebelscheinwerfer *m mot.* fog lamp.

'Nebelschlußleuchte *f* rear fog lamp.

neben ['ne:bən] *prep (dat)* **1.** (*a. acc*) a) beside, by (*or* at) the side of, by, b) close to, near, next to: **setzen Sie sich ~ mich** sit beside (*or* next to) me. **2.** apart from, besides: **~ anderen Dingen** among other things. **3.** compared with (*or* to). **4.** simultaneously with.

'Neben|absicht *f* secondary objective. **~ak,zent** *m ling.* secondary stress.

'nebenamtlich *adj* part-time (*job etc*).

neben'an *adv* a) next door, b) in the next room.

'Neben|anschluß *m teleph.* extension. **~arbeit** *f* **1.** extra work. **2.** minor job. **~ausgaben** *pl* incidental expenses, extras. **~ausgang** *m* side exit. **~bedeu-tung** *f ling.* connotation.

neben'bei *adv* **1.** besides, in addition. **2.**

in passing: **~ bemerkt** incidentally.

'Nebenberuf *m* sideline: **im ~** → **neben-beruflich II. 'nebenberuflich I** *adj* sideline. **II** *adv* as a sideline.

'Nebenbeschäftigung *f* sideline.

'Nebenbuhler [-bu:lər] *m* (-s; -) rival.

nebenein'ander *adv* side by side: **~ be-stehen** coexist. **Nebenein'ander** *n* (-s; *no pl*) coexistence.

nebenein'anderstellen *v/t (sep, -ge-, h)* **1.** put (*or* place) side by side (*or* next to each other). **2.** compare.

'Neben|eingang *m* side entrance. **~ein-kommen** *n*, **~einkünfte** *pl*, **~einnah-men** *pl* incidental earnings, extra income. **~erscheinung** *f* side effect (🞄 symptom). **~fach** *n ped.* subsidiary subject, *Am.* minor (subject). **~fluß** *m* tributary. **~gebäude** *n* **1.** adjoining building. **2.** annex(e). **~handlung** *f* subplot.

neben'her *adv* **1.** → **nebenbei** 1. **2.** by his (*or* her) side, beside.

'Neben|höhle *f anat.* sinus. **~kosten** *pl* extras. **~linie** *f* **1.** 🞄 branch line. **2.** *descent:* collateral line. **~mann** *m* **mein** *etc* **~** the person next to me *etc.* **~pro,dukt** *n (gen)* by-product (of), spin-off (from). **~rolle** *f thea.* minor part, *fig.* minor role. **~sache** *f* minor matter: **das ist ~!** that's quite unimportant (here)! **2sächlich** *adj* a) minor, unimportant, b) irrelevant. **~satz** *m ling.* subordinate clause. **~sai,son** *f* low season. **2stehend** *adj* in the margin: **~ (abgebildet)** opposite. **~stelle** *f* a) branch (office), b) *teleph.* extension. **~straße** *f* side street, byroad. **~tisch** *m* (**am ~** at the) next table. **~wirkung** *f* side effect. **~zimmer** *n* next (*or* adjoining) room.

neblig ['ne:blıç] *adj* foggy, misty.

Necessaire [nese'sɛ:r] *n* (-s; -s) **1.** toilet bag. **2.** manicure set.

necken ['nɛkən] *v/t* (h) tease.

'neckisch *adj* playful.

Neffe ['nɛfə] *m* (-n; -n) nephew.

Negation [nega'tsio:n] *f* (-; -en) negation. **negativ** *adj*, **Negativ** [ne'gati:f] *n* (-s; -e) 🙰, *phot., phys.* negative.

Neger ['ne:gər] *m* (-s; -) **1.** negro. **2.** F *fig.* a) ghostwriter, b) *TV* idiot board.

'Negerin *f* (-; -nen) negress.

negieren [ne'gi:rən] *v/t* (h) negate, deny.

Negligé [negli'ʒe:] *n* (-s; -s) néglité.

nehmen ['ne:mən] *v/t* (nahm, genommen, h) **1.** take (*a.* **an sich ~**, *a.* **bus**, *curve*, *obstacle*, etc), *at table*: help o.s. to, *a.* accept, *a.* buy, *a.* engage, hire (*s.o.*): **et. zu sich ~** eat s.th.; **ich nehme Wein** I'll have wine; **(sich)** *e-n* **Anwalt ~** retain counsel; **er versteht es, die Kunden zu ~** he has a way with the customers; **wie man's nimmt!** that depends!; F **er ist hart im Nehmen** he can take a lot (of punishment); → **Angriff, Anspruch, Beispiel, ernst** II, **Hürde** I etc. **2.** *j-m et.* **~** take *s.th.* away from s.o., free s.o. of (*pain*, *inhibitions*, etc), deprive s.o. of (*hope*, *rights*, etc); **es sich nicht ~ lassen** zu *inf* insist on *ger*. **3.** *fig.* **auf sich ~** take upon o.s., assume (*office*, *task*, etc), accept (*responsibility* etc). **4.** take, charge (**für** for).

Nehrung ['ne:rʊŋ] *f* (-; -en) *geogr.* spit.

Neid [naɪt] *m* (-[e]s; *no pl*) envy (**auf** *acc* of), jealousy; **aus ~** out of envy; **blaß** (*or* **gelb, grün**) **vor ~** green with envy; F **das muß ihm der ~ lassen** you have to hand it to him.

neiden ['naɪdən] *v/t* (h) *j-m et.* **~** envy s.o. s.th.

'Neider *m* (-s; -) **viele ~ haben** be envied by many people.

'neidisch I *adj* (**auf** *acc* of) envious, jealous. II *adv* enviously, with envy.

'neidlos *adj and adv* without envy.

Neige ['naɪɡə] *f* (-; -en) rest, dregs: *fig.* **bis zur bitteren ~** to the bitter end.

neigen ['naɪɡən] (h) I *v/t* a) incline, b) bend, bow, c) tilt. II *sich* **~** a) incline, *terrain*: slope, b) bend, bow (**vor** *dat* to). III *v/i* **~ zu** have a tendency to, be inclined to, *esp.* ✷ be prone to; **ich neige zu der Ansicht, daß ...** I am inclined to think that ...

'Neigung *f* (-; -en) **1.** inclination, slope, gradient. **2.** *fig.* (**zu**) a) inclination, tendency (to, towards), trend (to), *esp.* ✷ proneness (to), b) liking (for, of), penchant, predilection (for), c) affection (for), love (of).

'Neigungswinkel *m* angle of inclination.

nein [naɪn] *adv* no: **~, so was!** well, I never!; **aber ~!** of course (*or* certainly) not!; *fig.* **er kann nicht ~ sagen** he can't refuse anything.

Nein *n* (-[s]; -[s]) no: **mit (e-m) ~ antwor-**

ten answer in the negative, say no.

'Neinstimme *f no* (*pl* noes), *Am.* nay.

Nektar ['nɛktar] *m* (-s; -e) nectar.

Nektarine [nɛkta'ri:nə] *f* (-; -n) ✿ nectarine.

Nelke ['nɛlkə] *f* (-; -n) **1.** ✿ carnation. **2.** *gastr.* clove.

nennen ['nɛnən] (nannte, genannt, h) I *v/t* **1.** call, name: **das nenne ich ...** that's what I call ... **2.** name, mention, give (*example*, *one's name*, etc), nominate (*candidate*), *sports*: enter (**für** for). II *sich* **~** call o.s. (*a. iro.*), be called: **und das nennt sich Fachmann!** and he is supposed to be an expert!

'nennenswert *adj* worth mentioning.

'Nenner *m* (-s; -) Å (*a. fig.* **et. auf** *e-n* **gemeinsamen ~ bringen** reduce s.th. to a common) denominator; *fig.* **e-n gemeinsamen ~ finden** reach an agreement (on the matter).

'Nennleistung *f* ✺ rated output (✦ power). **'Nennspannung** *f* ✦ rated voltage.

'Nennung *f* (-; -en) naming, mention, *pol.* nomination, *sports etc*: entry.

'Nennwert *m* ✝ nominal (*or* face) value: **zum ~** at par; **unter dem ~** below par.

Neofa'schismus [neo-] *m* neo-fascism.

Neofa'schist *m* (-en; -en), **neofa'schistisch** *adj* neo-fascist.

Neon ['ne:ɔn] *n* (-s; *no pl*) neon.

'Neonleuchte *f* neon light.

Nepp [nɛp] *m* (-s; *no pl*) F rip-off.

'neppen *v/t* (h) F fleece, rip *s.o.* off.

'Neppo,kal *n* clip joint.

Nerv [nɛrf] *m* (-s; -en, ✿ *a.* vein: **er hat ~en wie Drahtseile** he's got nerves of steel; **die ~en behalten** (**verlieren**) keep (lose) one's head; F *j-m auf die* **~en gehen** get on s.o.'s nerves; **sie ist mit den ~en am Ende** (F **völlig fertig**) she's a nervous wreck; **~en zeigen** get nervy; F **du hast vielleicht ~en!** you've got a nerve!

nerven ['nɛrfən] *v/t* (h) F *j-n* **~** get on s.o.'s nerves.

'Nerven|arzt *m* neurologist. **☌aufreibend** *adj* nerve-racking. **☌belastung** *f* (nervous) strain. **☌bündel** *n* F **sie ist ein ~** she is a bundle of nerves. **☌entzündung** *f* neuritis. **☌gas** *n* ✗ nerve gas. **☌kitzel** *m fig.* thrill. **☌klinik** *f* mental hospital, psychiatric clinic. **☌krank** *adj* mentally ill. **☌krankheit** *f* nervous disease. **~krieg** *m fig.* war of nerves. **~probe** *f fig.* ordeal. **~sache** *f* F *das ist reine ~!* that's just a question of nerves! **~säge** *f* F pain in the neck. **~schmerz** *m* neuralgia. **2stark** *adj* strong-nerved. **~stärke** *f* strong nerves: **~ beweisen** remain cool. **~sy¦stem** *n* nervous system. **~zentrum** *n* nerve cent/re (*Am.* -er). **~zusammenbruch** *m* nervous breakdown.

'nervlich *adj* nervous.

nervös [nɛr'vøːs] *adj* nervous: **~ werden** get nervous; **j-n ~ machen** a) make s.o. nervous, b) get on s.o.'s nerves.

Nervosität [nɛrvozi'tɛːt] *f* (-; *no pl*) nervousness.

'nervtötend *adj* F nerve-racking (*noise etc*), soul-destroying (*work etc*).

Nerz [nɛrts] *m* (-es; -e) **1.** *zo.* mink. **2.** → **'Nerzmantel** *m* mink (coat).

Nessel ['nɛsəl] *f* (-; -n) ⚕ nettle: F *sich in die ~ setzen* get o.s. into trouble.

'Nesselfieber *n* ⚕ nettle rash.

Nest [nɛst] *n* (-[e]s; -er) **1.** nest: *fig. das eigene ~ beschmutzen* foul one's own nest; F *das ~ war leer* the bird(s) had flown. **2.** F small place, dump.

'Nesthäkchen *n* pet of the family.

'Nestwärme *f fig.* warmth and security.

nett [nɛt] *adj* nice (*a. iro.*): **sei so ~ und hilf mir** be so kind as to help me; F *ein ~es Sümmchen* a nice (*or* tidy) sum.

netto ['nɛto] *adv* ✝ net, clear.

'Netto¦einkommen *n* net income. **~gewicht** *n* net weight. **~lohn** *m* take-home pay. **~preis** *m* net price.

Netz [nɛts] *n* (-es; -e) **1.** net: *fig. j-m ins ~ gehen* walk into s.o.'s net. **2.** *fig.* network, system, ⚡ mains: *ans ~ gehen* power station: go into operation.

'Netz¦anschluß *m* ⚡ mains connection. **~ausfall** *m* ⚡ power failure. **~ball** *m* tennis: net (ball). **~haut** *f anat.* retina. **~hemd** *n* string vest. **~kabel** *n* ⚡ mains cable. **~karte** *f* runaround ticket. **~plan** *m* network. **~plantechnik** *f* network analysis. **~schalter** *m* ⚡ power switch. **~stecker** *m* ⚡ mains plug. **~strumpf** *m* net (*or* mesh) stocking. **~teil** *n* ⚡ power supply unit. **~werk** *n* network.

neu [nɔy] **I** *adj* a) new, *a.* fresh (*a. fig.*), *a.* novel, b) recent, modern, c) renewed: *ganz ~* brand-new; *wie ~* as good as new; *~er Anfang* fresh start; *neueren*

Datums of recent date; *~e Schwierigkeiten* more problems; *neuere Sprachen* modern languages; *neueste Nachrichten* latest news; *das ist mir ~!* that's new to me! **II** *adv* a) newly, b) recently, c) anew, afresh: *~ anfangen* start anew; *~ beleben* revive; *~ eröffnen* reopen; *~ gestalten* reorganize, ⚙ remodel; *~ schreiben* rewrite.

'Neuankömmling *m* newcomer.

'Neuanschaffung *f* new acquisition.

'neuartig *adj* novel, new (type of).

'Neuauflage *f* **1.** a) new edition, b) reprint. **2.** *fig.* repeat (performance).

'Neuausgabe *f* new edition.

'Neubau *m* (-[e]s; -ten) new building.

'Neubaugebiet *n* new housing estate.

'Neubearbeitung *f* **1.** a) revised edition, b) revision. **2.** *thea. etc* adaptation.

'Neubildung *f* **1.** (new) formation, reorganization. **2.** a) *physiol.* regeneration, b) ⚕ tumo(u)r. **3.** *ling.* neologism.

'Neudruck *m* reprint.

'Neue¹ *n* (-n) **1.** s.th. new: *das ~ daran* what's new about it; *das Neueste* the latest thing; *was gibt's Neues?* what's new?; *das ist mir nichts Neues* that's no news to me. **2.** *aufs neue, von neuem* afresh, anew; *seit neuem* of late.

'Neue² *m, f* (-n; -n) new man (woman).

'Neueinstellung *f* **1.** taking on (new) labo(u)r. **2.** new employee.

'Neuentdeckung *f* **1.** recent discovery. **2.** rediscovery.

'neuerdings *adv* recently, lately, of late.

Neuerer ['nɔyərər] *m* (-s; -) innovator.

'Neuerscheinung *f* new publication.

'Neuerung *f* (-; -en) innovation.

'neuestens *adv* quite recently, lately.

'Neufassung *f* **1.** revision. **2.** revised version.

'neugebacken *adj* F *fig.* newly-fledged.

'neugeboren *adj* newborn: *fig. ich fühle mich wie ~* I feel a different person.

'Neugeborene *n* (-n; -n) newborn (child).

'Neugestaltung *f* reshaping, reorganization, ⚙ remodel(l)ing.

'Neugier *f* (-; *no pl*) curiosity.

'neugierig *adj* (*auf acc*) curious (about, of), inquisitive (after, about): *ich bin ~, ob ...* I wonder if ...

'Neugliederung *f* reorganization.

'neugotisch *adj* neo-Gothic.

'**Neugründung** f (new) foundation.
'**Neuheit** f (-; -en) **1.** no pl newness, novelty. **2.** novelty, ⊕ a. innovation.
'**Neuigkeit** f (-; -en) (piece of) news.
'**Neuinsze,nierung** f new production.
'**Neujahr** n New Year('s Day): *Prosit ~!* Happy New Year!
'**Neujahrstag** m New Year's Day.
'**Neuland** n (-[e]s; no pl) fig. ~ *erschlie-*
ßen break new ground; *das ist ~ für*
mich that is new territory to me.
'**neulich** adv the other day, recently.
'**Neuling** m (-s; -c) (in dat, auf e-m Ge-
biet) newcomer (to), novice (at).
'**neumodisch** adj contp. newfangled.
'**Neumond** m new moon.
neun [nɔyn] adj nine: *alle ~e!* strike!
Neun f (-; -en) (number) nine.
'**neunhundert** adj nine hundred.
'**neunjährig** [-jɛ:rɪç] adj **1.** nine-year-old.
2. nine-year, of nine years.
'**neunmalklug** adj iro. smart-alecky.
neunt adj **1.** ninth. **2.** zu ~ (the) nine of us
(or them etc). '**Neunte** m, f (-n; -n)
ninth. '**neuntens** adv ninth(ly).
'**neunzehn** adj nineteen.
'**neunzehnt** adj nineteenth.
neunzig ['nɔyntsɪç] adj **1.** ninety.
'**Neunzig** f (-; -en) (number) ninety: *er*
ist Anfang ~ he is in his early nineties.
neunziger ['nɔyntsɪɡər] adj *die ~ Jahre*
the nineties. '**Neunziger** m (-s; -),
'**Neunzigerin** f (-; -nen) man (woman)
of ninety, nonagenarian.
'**Neuordnung** f reorganization.
'**Neuorien,tierung** f reorientation.
'**Neuphilo,loge** m teacher (or student) of
modern languages.
'**Neuphilolo,gie** f modern philology.
Neuralgie [nɔyral'gi:] f (-; -en) 🞄 neural-
gia. **neuralgisch** [nɔy'ralgɪʃ] adj 🞄
neuralgic: fig. ~*er Punkt* critical point,
pol. trouble spot.
'**Neuregelung** f revision.
'**Neureiche** m, f (-n; -n) parvenue: *die*
~n the nouveau riches.
Neurochir'urg m neurosurgeon.
Neurologe [nɔyro'lo:ɡə] m (-n; -n) neu-
rologist.
Neurose [nɔy'ro:zə] f (-; -n) 🞄 neurosis.
Neurotiker [nɔy'ro:tikər] m (-s; -),
neu'rotisch [-tɪʃ] adj neurotic.
'**Neuschnee** m fresh-fallen snow.
Neu'seeland n (-s) New Zealand.

Neu'seeländer m (-s; -), **Neu'seelän-**
derin f (-; -nen) New Zealander.
neu'seeländisch adj New Zealand.
'**neusprachlich** adj modern-language.
neutral [nɔy'tra:l] adj neutral.
neutralisieren [nɔytrali'zi:rən] v/t (h)
neutralize. **Neutralität** [nɔytrali'tɛ:t] f
(-; no pl) neutrality.
Neutron ['nɔytrɔn] n (-s; -en [nɔy'tro:-
nən]) neutron. **Neu'tronenbombe** f
neutron bomb.
Neutrum ['nɔytrʊm] n (-s; -tra) neuter.
'**Neuverfllmung** f remake.
'**Neuwahl** f new election.
'**neuwertig** adj practically new.
'**Neuwort** n (-[e]s; -er) neologism.
'**Neuzeit** f (-; no pl) modern times.
'**neuzeitlich** adj modern.
nicht [nɪçt] adv not: ~ *besser* no better; ~
(*ein*)*mal* not even; ~ *mehr* no longer; ~
(*bitte*) ~*!* (please) don't!; ~, *daß ich*
wüßte! not that I know of!; *er ist*
krank, ~ wahr? he is ill, isn't he?; *du*
tust es doch, ~ wahr? you will do it,
won't you?; → *auch* 1, *gar²* 1, *nur.*
'**Nicht|achtung** f disregard. ~*angriffs-*
pakt m nonaggression treaty. ~*beach-*
tung f (gen of) a) disregard, b) nonob-
servance (of rules etc).
Nichte ['nɪçtə] f (-; -n) niece.
'**Nicht|einhaltung** f noncompliance (gen
with). ~*einmischung* f pol. noninter-
ference, nonintervention. ~*erfüllung* f
🞄🞄 nonperformance. ~*erscheinen* n
nonappearance, 🞄🞄 a. default.
'**nichtexi,stent** adj nonexisting.
'**nichtig** adj **1.** trivial, vain: ~*er Vorwand*
flimsy excuse. **2.** 🞄🞄 (*null und*) ~ (null
and) void.
'**Nichtigkeit** f (-; -en) **1.** no pl a) triviality,
vanity, b) 🞄🞄 nullity. **2.** pl trifles.
'**Nichtmitglied** n nonmember.
'**Nichtraucher(in** f) m nonsmoker.
'**nichtrostend** adj rustproof, stainless.
nichts indef pron nothing, not ... anything: ~ *als Ärger* nothing but trouble;
~ *weniger als das* anything but that; ~
da! nothing doing!; *so gut wie* ~ next
to nothing; *das ist ~ für mich!* that's
not my thing!; *mir ~, dir ~* just like that,
quite coolly; *weiter ~?* is that all?; F
wie ~ in a flash; F ~ *wie hin!* let's go
(there fast)!; → *dergleichen* 2, *gar²* 1,
Nähere etc.

Nichts n (-; *no pl*) **1.** nothing(ness), void: *aus dem ~* appear etc from nowhere, *make etc* out of nothing; *vor dem ~ stehen* be left with nothing. **2.** *ein ~* a) a trifle, nothing, b) *contp.* a nobody.

'**nichtsahnend** *adj* unsuspecting.

'**Nichtschwimmer(in** f) m nonswimmer.

nichtsdesto|'**trotz** *adv* F, **~'weniger** *adv* nevertheless, none the less.

'**Nichtskönner** m (-s; -) incompetent person, F washout.

'**nichtssagend** *adj* empty (*words etc*), meaningless, vague (*answer*).

'**Nichtstuer** m (-s; -) idler, loafer.

'**Nichtstun** n idling, loafing, inactivity.

'**Nichtswisser** m (-s; -) ignoramus.

'**Nichtvorhandensein** n nonexistence.

'**Nichtzahlung** f ✝ *bei ~* in default of payment.

'**Nichtzutreffende** n *~s streichen!* delete where inapplicable!

Nickel n (-s; *no pl*) nickel.

'**Nickelbrille** f steel-rimmed spectacles.

nicken ['nɪkən] v/i (h) nod (one's head).

Nickerchen ['nɪkərçən] n (-s; -) F nap.

nie [ni:] *adv* never: *fast ~* hardly ever; *noch ~* never (before); *~ wieder* never again; *~ und nimmer* never ever.

nieder ['ni:dər] **I** *adj* low (*a. fig.*), inferior (*rank, value*), lower (*echelon etc*). **II** *adv* low, down: *~ mit ...!* down with ...!

'**niederbrennen** v/t, v/i (irr, sep, -ge-, h, → **brennen**) burn down.

'**niederbrüllen** v/t (sep, -ge-, h) *j-n ~* shout s.o. down.

'**niederdeutsch** *adj* Low German.

'**niederdrücken** v/t (sep, -ge-, h) **1.** press *s.th.* down. **2.** *fig.* depress (*s.o.*).

'**Niederfre,quenz** f ⚡ low frequency.

'**Niedergang** m (-[e]s; *no pl*) decline.

'**niedergehen** v/i (irr, sep, -ge-, sn, → **gehen**) come down (*a.* ✈), rain: fall, *storm*: burst.

'**niedergeschlagen I** *pp of* **niederschlagen**. **II** *adj fig.* depressed, dejected. '**Niedergeschlagenheit** f (-; *no pl*) depression, dejection.

'**niederknien** v/i (sep,-ge-,sn) kneel down.

'**Niederlage** f (-; -n) **1.** defeat: *e-e ~ erleiden* be defeated. **2.** ✝ a) depot, warehouse, b) → **Niederlassung** 2.

'**Niederlande** pl the Netherlands.

'**Niederländer** m (-s; -) Dutchman, Netherlander: *die ~* the Dutch.

'**Niederländerin** f (-; -nen) Dutch woman, Netherlander.

'**niederländisch** *adj* Dutch.

'**niederlassen** (irr, sep, -ge-, h, → **lassen**) **I** v/t **1.** lower, let s.th. down. **II** *sich ~* **2.** sit down. **3.** settle (*in dat* in, at). **4.** set up in business (*or* as a doctor, lawyer, *etc*), establish o.s. (*als* as).

'**Niederlassung** f (-; -en) **1.** establishment, settling. **2.** ✝ a) place of business, b) branch (office).

'**niederlegen** (sep, -ge-, h) **I** v/t lay down (*one's arms etc*): *ein Amt ~* resign an office; *die Arbeit ~* (go on) strike, walk out; *et. schriftlich ~* put s.th. down in writing. **II** *sich ~* lie down.

'**Niederlegung** f (-; *no pl*) (gen) **1.** laying down (of). **2.** resignation (from).

'**niedermachen** v/t (sep, -ge-, h) **1.** massacre, slaughter. **2.** → **fertigmachen**.

'**niederreißen** v/t (irr, sep, -ge-, h, → **reißen**) pull down (*a. fig.*), demolish.

'**Niederschlag** m **1.** *meteor.* precipitation, rain(fall). **2.** 🜊 a) precipitate, b) sediment: *radioaktiver ~* (nuclear) fallout; *fig. s-n ~ finden in* (dat) be reflected in. **3.** *boxing:* a) knockdown, b) knockout. '**niederschlagen** (irr, sep, -ge-, h, → **schlagen**) **I** v/t **1.** *j-n ~* knock s.o. down, *boxing:* knock s.o. out. **2.** cast down (one's eyes). **3.** *fig.* suppress, put down (*revolt etc*). **4.** ⚖ quash (*proceedings*). **II** *sich ~* **5.** 🜊 precipitate. **6.** *fig.* be reflected (*in dat* in).

'**niederschlagsreich** *adj* rainy, wet.

'**niederschmettern** v/t (sep, -ge-, h) *j-n ~* knock s.o. down, *fig.* shatter s.o.

'**niederschmetternd** *adj fig.* shattering.

'**Niederschrift** f (-; -en) **1.** writing down. **2.** notes, record, minutes.

'**Niederspannung** f ⚡ low tension.

'**niederstrecken** v/t (sep, -ge-, h) fell.

'**Niedertracht** f (-; *no pl*) **1.** baseness. **2.** perfidy, F dirty trick.

'**niederträchtig** *adj* low, perfidious.

'**Niederung** f (-; -en) lowland(s).

'**niederwerfen:** *sich ~* (irr, sep, -ge-, h, → **werfen**) throw o.s. down; *sich vor j-m ~* throw o.s. at s.o.'s feet.

niedlich ['ni:tlɪç] *adj* sweet, cute.

niedrig ['ni:drɪç] *adj* low, inferior (*quality etc*), lowly, humble (*origin etc*), *b.s. a.* base: *~ fliegen* fly low; *~ halten* keep *prices etc* down.

'**Niedrigkeit** f (-; *no pl*) lowness.
'**niemals** → **nie.**
niemand ['ni:mant] *indef pron* nobody, no one: *ich habe* **~(en) gesehen** I didn't see anybody; **~ anders** nobody else; **~ anders als** none other than; *es ist sonst* **~ da** nobody else is present.
'**Niemand** *m* (-s; *no pl*) *contp.* nobody.
'**Niemandsland** *n a. fig.* no man's land.
Niere ['ni:rə] f (-; -n) kidney: *künstliche* **~** kidney machine; *f das geht mir an die* **~n** that really gets me down.
'**Nierenbeckenentzündung** f pyelitis.
'**nierenförmig** *adj* kidney-shaped.
'**Nieren|leiden** *n* kidney disease. **~spender(in** f) *m* kidney donor. **~stein** *m* 🖈 kidney stone. **~verpflanzung** f kidney transplant.
nieseln ['ni:zəln] *v/i* (h) drizzle.
'**Nieselregen** *m* drizzle.
niesen ['ni:zən] *v/i* (h) sneeze.
Nießbrauch ['ni:s-] *m* (-[e]s; *no pl*) 🖈🖈 usufruct.
Niet [ni:t] *m* (-[e]s; -e) stud, 🔧 rivet.
Niete ['ni:tə] f (-; -n) **1.** (*e-e* **~ ziehen** draw a) blank. **2.** F flop, washout.
nieten ['ni:tən] *v/t, v/i* (h) 🔧 rivet.
'**Nietenhose** f jeans (with studs).
Nihilismus [nihi'lɪsmʊs] *m* (-; *no pl*) nihilism. **Nihilist** [nihi'lɪst] *m* (-en; -en) nihilist. **nihi'listisch** -[tɪʃ] *adj* nihilist(ic).
Nikolaustag ['ni:kolaʊs-] *m* St. Nicholas' Day.
Nikotin [niko'ti:n] *n* (-s; *no pl*) nicotine.
niko'tinarm *adj* low-nicotine.
niko'tinfrei *adj* nicotine-free.
Niko'tinvergiftung f nicotine poisoning.
Nilpferd ['ni:l-] *n zo.* hippopotamus.
Nimbus ['nɪmbʊs] *m* (-; -se) nimbus, halo, *fig. no pl a.* aura.
'**Nimmerwiedersehen** *n auf* **~** for good.
Nippel ['nɪpəl] *m* (-s; -) 🔧 nipple.
nippen ['nɪpən] *v/t, v/i* (h) sip (*an dat* at).
Nippsachen ['nɪp-] *pl* knick-knacks.
nirgends ['nɪrgənts] *adv* nowhere.
'**nirgendwo,** '**nirgendwohin** *adv* nowhere, not ... anywhere.
Nische ['ni:ʃə] f (-; -n) niche, recess.
nisten ['nɪstən] *v/i* (h) nest.
'**Nistplatz** *m* nesting place.
Nitrat [ni'tra:t] *n* (-[e]s; -e) 🧪 nitrate.
Nitroglyze'rin [nitro-] *n* nitroglycerine.
Niveau [ni'vo:] *n* (-s; -s) level, *a.* standard: **~ haben** have class; *ein hohes* **~**

haben have high standards; *das ist unter m-m* **~** that's beneath me; *geistiges* **~** level of intelligence (*or* education).
nivellieren [nivɛ'li:rən] *v/t* (h) level.
Nixe ['nɪksə] f (-; -n) water-nymph.
nobel ['no:bəl] *adj* **1.** noble(-minded). **2.** F generous. **3.** high-class, F posh, ritzy.
'**Nobelherberge** f F posh hotel.
Nobelpreis [no'bel-] *m* Nobel prize. **~träger(in** f) *m* Nobel prize winner.
noch [nɔx] **I** *adv* **1.** still: *immer* **~** still; **~** *nicht* not yet; **~** *nie* never before; **~** *gestern* only yesterday; **~** *heute* even today; **~** *lange nicht* not by a long chalk; **~** *im 18. Jahrhundert* as late as the 18th century; *wie heißt sie* **~**? what's her name again?; F **~** *und* **~** a) oodles of, piles of, b) awfully. **2.** more: **~** *einer* one more, another; **~** *einmal* once more; **~** *einmal so viel* as much again; **~** *etwas!* and another thing!; **~** *etwas?* anything else?; **~** *besser* even better; *nur* **~** *5 Minuten* only five minutes more. **3.** *sei es* **~** *so klein* no matter how small (it is). **II** *conj* → **weder.**
'**nochmalig** *adj* repeated, second, new.
nochmals ['nɔxma:ls] *adv* once more.
Nocke ['nɔkə] f (-; -n) 🔧 cam.
'**Nockenwelle** f *mot.* camshaft.
Nomade [no'ma:də] *m* (-n; -n) nomad. **No'maden...,** *no'madisch adj* nomadic.
Nominativ ['no:minati:f] *m* (-s; -e) *ling.* nominative (case).
nominell [nomi'nɛl] *adj* nominal.
nominieren [nomi'ni:rən] *v/t* (h) nominate, name.
Nonne ['nɔnə] f (-; -n) nun.
'**Nonnenkloster** *n* nunnery, convent.
Nonsens ['nɔnzɛns] *m* (-[es]; *no pl*) nonsense.
Nonstop... [nɔn'stɔp-] nonstop.
Noppe ['nɔpə] f (-; -n) nap.
Nord [nɔrt] *inv* North.
'**Nord'afrika** *n* (-s) North Africa. **Nord-afri'kaner(in** f) *m*, '**nordafri'kanisch** *adj* North African.
'**Norda'merika** *n* (-s) North America. '**Nordameri'kaner(in** f) *m*, '**nordame-ri'kanisch** *adj* North American.
'**norddeutsch** *adj*, '**Norddeutsche** *m, f* (-n; -n) North German.
Norden ['nɔrdən] *m* (-s; *no pl*) north, North: *nach* **~** to(wards) the north; **~** *von* (*or gen*) north of.

nordisch ['nɔrdɪʃ] *adj* a) northern, b) Nordic; → **Kombination** 5.

nördlich ['nœrtlɪç] **I** *adj* a) northern (*hemisphere etc*), b) northerly (*direction etc*), c) arctic (*ocean*). **II** *adv* ~ **von** (*or gen*) (to the) north of.

'Nordlicht *n* northern lights.

Nord'ost(en) *m*, **nord'östlich** *adj and adv* northeast.

'Nordpol *m* North Pole.

'Nordsee *f* North Sea.

'nordwärts *adv* north(wards).

Nord'west(en) *m*, **nord'westlich** *adj and adv* northwest.

'Nordwind *m* north wind.

Nörge'lei *f* (-; -en) grumbling, niggling. **nörgeln** ['nœrgəln] *v/i* (h) (**an** *dat* about) grumble, niggle. **Nörgler** ['nœrglər] *m* (-s; -) grumbler, niggler.

Norm [nɔrm] *f* (-; -en) norm, standard.

normal [nɔr'maːl] *adj* normal, ⊙ standard. **Nor'malben,zin** *n* regular (grade) petrol (*Am.* gasoline).

nor'malerweise *adv* normally.

Nor'malfall *m im* ~ normally.

normalisieren [nɔrmali'ziːrən] (h) **I** *v/t* normalize. **II** *sich* ~ return to normal.

Nor'malverbraucher *m* average consumer: F **Otto** ~ Mr. Average.

Nor'malzustand *m* normal state.

normen ['nɔrmən], **normieren** [nɔr'miːrən] *v/t* (h) standardize.

'Normung *f* (-; -en) standardization.

Norwegen ['nɔrveːgən] *n* (-s) Norway. **'Norweger** *m* (-s; -), **'Norwegerin** *f* (-; -nen), **'norwegisch** [-gɪʃ] *adj* Norwegian.

Nostalgie [nɔstal'giː] *f* (-; *no pl*) nostalgia. **nost'algisch** [-gɪʃ] *adj* nostalgic.

Not [noːt] *f* (-; ˝e) **1.** *no pl* need, misery: ~ **leiden** suffer want; **in** ~ **geraten** become destitute (→ 3). **2.** *no pl* necessity: ~ **macht erfinderisch** necessity is the mother of invention; **zur** ~, F **wenn** ~ **am Mann ist** if need be; **es tut not, daß** it is necessary that (→ 3). **3.** distress (*a.* ⚓), difficulty, trouble: **in** ~ (*or* **Nöten**) **sein** be in trouble; **in** ~ **geraten** run into difficulties (→ 1); F **s-e** (**liebe**) ~ **haben mit** really have problems with.

Notar [no'taːr] *m* (-s; -e), **No'tarin** *f* (-; -nen) notary. **Notariat** [nota'riːaːt] *n* (-[e]s; -e) notary's office. **notariell**

[nota'riɛl] *adj* notarial: ~ **beglaubigt** attested by a notary.

'Not|arzt *m* doctor on call. ~**arztwagen** *m* emergency ambulance. ~**aufnahmelager** *n* transit camp. ~**ausgang** *m* emergency exit. ~**behelf** *m* makeshift. ~**beleuchtung** *f* emergency lighting. ~**bremse** *f* emergency brake. ~**dienst** *m* (~ **haben** be on) emergency duty.

'notdürftig *adj* **1.** scanty: ~ **bekleidet** scantily dressed. **2.** makeshift: **et.** ~ **reparieren** patch s.th. up.

Note ['noːtə] *f* (-; -n) **1.** *ped.* mark, *Am.* grade. **2.** ♪ note: **ganze** ~ semibreve, *Am.* whole note; **halbe** ~ minim, *Am.* half note; **nach** ~**n singen** *etc* sing *etc* from music. **3.** *pol.* note, memorandum. **4.** *no pl fig.* touch: **e-r Sache e-e besondere** ~ **verleihen** add a special touch to s.th. **5.** → **Banknote**.

'Noten|bank *f* (-; -en) bank of issue. ~**blatt** *n* sheet of music. ~**heft** *n* music book. ~**pult** *n* music stand. ~**sy,stem** *n* *ped.* marking (*Am.* grading) system.

'Notfall *m* emergency: **für den** ~ (just) in case; **im** ~ → **'notfalls** *adv* if necessary, if need be, in an emergency.

'notgedrungen *adv* of necessity.

'Notgroschen *m* nest egg.

notieren [no'tiːrən] (h) **I** *v/t* **1.** make a note of. **2.** ♥ quote (**zu** at). **II** *v/i* **3.** ♥ be quoted (**mit** at, with).

No'tierung *f* (-; -en) ♥ quotation.

nötig ['nøːtɪç] *adj* necessary: **et.** (**dringend**) ~ **haben** need s.th. (badly); *iro.* **du hast es** (**gerade**) ~! you of all people!; **mit dem** ~**en Respekt** with due respect; (**nur**) **das Nötigste** (just) what is absolutely necessary.

nötigen ['nøːtɪgən] *v/t* (h) force, compel, urge, press (*guest*): **lassen Sie sich nicht** ~! help yourself!; **er ließ sich nicht lange** ~ he needed no coaxing.

'Nötigung *f* (-; -en) coercion.

Notiz [no'tiːts] *f* (-; -en) **1.** note: **sich** ~**en machen** take notes. **2.** (news) item. **3.** (**k-e**) ~ **nehmen von** take (no) notice of.

No'tizblock *m* notepad, *Am.* memo pad.

No'tizbuch *n* notebook.

'Notlage *f* predicament, plight.

'Notlager *n* shakedown.

'notlanden *v/i* (*insep*, -ge-, sn) make a forced landing.

'Notlandung *f* forced landing.

'notleidend adj needy.

'Notlösung f temporary solution.

'Notlüge f white lie.

'Notmaßnahme f emergency measure.

notorisch [no'to:rɪʃ] adj notorious.

'Notruf m teleph. emergency call.

'Notrufsäule f emergency telephone.

'Notschrei m a. fig. cry for help.

'Notsi‚gnal n distress signal.

'Notsitz m jump seat.

'Notstand m **1.** → **Notlage. 2.** pol. state of emergency: **den nationalen ~ ausrufen** declare a state of national emergency. **'Notstandsgebiet** n **1.** ✝ depressed area. **2.** disaster area.

'Notstromaggre‚gat n emergency generator.

'Notunterkunft f provisional accommodation.

'Notverband m 🗡 emergency dressing.

'Notwehr f (-; no pl) **(aus ~, in ~ in)** self-defen/ce (Am. -se).

'notwendig adj necessary **(für** to, for): **unbedingt ~** imperative.

'notwendiger'weise adv of necessity.

'Notwendigkeit f (-; -en) necessity.

'Notzucht f (-; no pl) ⚖ rape.

Nougat ['nu:gat] m, n (-s; -s) chocolate nut cream.

Novelle [no'vɛlə] f (-; -n) **1.** novella. **2.** parl. amendment.

November [no'vɛmbər] m (-s; -) **(im ~** in) November.

Novize [no'vi:tsə] m (-n; -n) novice.

Novum ['no:vʊm] n (-s; -va) s.th. new.

Nu [nu:] F **im ~** in no time, in a jiffy.

Nuance [ny'ã:sə] f (-; -n) nuance, shade.

nüchtern ['nʏçtərn] adj **1.** with an empty stomach: → **Magen. 2.** sober: **wieder ~ werden** sober up. **3.** bland (food). **4.** fig. a) sober, matter-of-fact, a. unemotional, b) austere, functional (building etc). **'Nüchternheit** f (-; no pl) sobriety, fig. a. austerity.

Nudel ['nu:dəl] f (-; -n) **1.** noodle. F **sie ist e-e ulkige ~** she is a funny bird.

nuklear [nukle'a:r] adj nuclear.

Nukle'ar... nuclear (medicine etc).

null [nʊl] adj nought, esp. Am. or phys., ⊕ etc zero, teleph. 0, Am. zero, sports: nil, Am. zero: **~ Grad** zero degrees; **~ Komma drei** (nought) point three; **~ Fehler** no (Am. zero) mistakes; **zwei zu ~** two-nil, Am. two-zero; tennis: **15:0**

fifteen love; **das Spiel endete 0:0** the match was a scoreless draw; F **er hat ~ Ahnung (davon)** he doesn't know a thing about it; **ich habe ~ Bock darauf** I'm not a bit keen on that; → **nichtig** 2.

Null f (-; -en) nought, esp. Am. or phys., ⊕ etc zero: F **er ist e-e ~** he's a cipher (or nobody); **in ~ Komma nichts** in a jiffy; **gleich ~ sein** be nil.

nullacht'fünfzehn adj F run-of-the-mill.

'Nulldi‚ät f no-calorie (or crash) diet.

'Nullmenge f ↋ null set.

Nullösung f zero option.

'Nullpunkt m zero, ↯, ⊕ neutral point: **auf dem ~** a. fig. at zero.

'Nullta‚rif m a) free transport, b) free admission: **zum ~** free.

'Nullwachstum n ✝ zero growth.

numerieren [nume'ri:rən] v/t number. **Nume'rierung** f (-; -en) numbering. **Nummer** ['nʊmər] f (-; -n) **1.** a) number, a. issue, copy (of newspaper etc), b) size (of shoes etc): F **auf ~ Sicher gehen** play it safe. **2.** thea. etc act. **3.** V fuck, trick, screw.

'Nummernkonto n numbered account.

'Nummernschild n mot. number plate.

nun [nu:n] **I** adv **1.** a) now, b) then: **von ~ an** from now on, from that time (onward). **2.** well: **~ ja** well(, you see); **~ gut!** all right!; **was ~?** what now (or next)?; **es geht ~ mal nicht!** it's just not on! **II** conj **3.** ~ **(da)** now that, since.

nur [nu:r] adv a) only, just, simply, b) nothing but, c) except: **~ einmal** just once; **~ noch** only; **~ daß** except (that); **~ weil** just because; **wenn ~** if only; **nicht ~ ..., sondern auch ~** not only ..., but also ...; **~ zu!** go on!; **warum hat er das ~ gesagt?** F why on earth did he say that?; **was meint er ~?** whatever does he mean?; **~ das nicht!** anything but that!; **du weißt ~ zu gut, daß** you know very well that; **soviel ich ~ kann** as much as I possibly can; **ohne auch ~ zu lächeln** without so much as a smile.

nuscheln ['nʊʃəln] v/i (h) mumble.

Nuß [nʊs] f (-; Nüsse) nut: fig. **e-e harte ~** a hard nut to crack.

'Nußbaum m **1.** walnut tree. **2.** no pl → **'Nußbaumholz** n walnut.

'nußbraun adj hazel.

'Nußknacker m nutcracker.

'Nußschale f nutshell.

Nüster ['nystər] *f* (-; -n) *zo.* nostril.

Nut [nu:t] *f* (-; -en) ◎ groove.

Nutte ['nʊtə] *f* (-; -n) F tart, *Am.* hooker.

'Nutzanwendung *f* practical use.

'nutzbar *adj* useful: ~ **machen** utilize, ✓ cultivate.

'Nutzbarkeit *f* (-; *no pl*) usefulness.

'Nutzbarmachung *f* (-; *no pl*) utilization, ⚒ *etc* exploitation, ✓ cultivation.

'nutzbringend *adj* profitable, useful: ~ **anwenden** turn *s.th.* to good account.

nütze ['nytsə] *adj* **zu et.** (*nichts*) ~ **sein** be useful, be of use (be [of] no use).

'Nutzef,fekt *m* ◎ *etc* efficiency.

nutzen ['nʊtsən], **nützen** ['nytsən] (h) **I** *v/i* a) be useful, be of use (**zu** for, *j-m* to s.o.), b) *j-m* be of advantage to s.o., benefit s.o.: **was nützt das?** what good is that?; **das nützt nichts!** that's no use! **II** *v/t* use, make use of. **'Nutzen** *m* (-s; *no pl*) a) use, b) profit, c) advantage, *a.*

⚒ benefit: ~ **ziehen aus** profit (*or* benefit) from; **von** ~ **sein** → **nutzen** I.

Nutzer ['nʊtsər] *m* (-s; -) *adm.* user.

'Nutz|fahrzeug *n* utility vehicle. **~fläche** *f* **1.** usable area. **2.** floor space. **~holz** *n* timber. **~last** *f* payload. **~leistung** *f* effective output (*or* power).

nützlich ['nytslıç] *adj* useful, helpful.

'Nützlichkeit *f* (-; *no pl*) usefulness.

'nutzlos *adj* useless.

'Nutzlosigkeit *f* (-; *no pl*) uselessness.

Nutznießer ['nʊtsni:sər] *m* (-s; -), **'Nutznießerin** *f* (-; -nen) beneficiary.

'Nutzpflanze *f* useful plant.

'Nutzung *f* (-; -en) use, utilization.

'Nutzungsrecht *n* usufruct, right to use.

Nylon ['naɪlɔn] *TM n* (-s; *no pl*) nylon.

'Nylonstrümpfe *pl* nylons.

Nymphe ['nymfə] *f* (-; -n) nymph.

Nymphomanin [nymfo'ma:nın] *f* (-; -nen) ⚥, *psych.* nymphomaniac.

O

O, o [o:] *n* (-; -) O, o.

o *int* oh: **o ja!** oh yes!

Oase [o'a:zə] *f* (-; -n) oasis.

ob [ɔp] *conj* whether, if: **als** ~ as if; **so tun als** ~ make as if; F (*na*) **und** ~**!** you bet!; ~ **er wohl geht?** I wonder if he will go.

Obacht ['o:baxt] *f dial.* ~ **geben auf** (*acc*) pay attention to; ~**!** look out!

'Obdach *n* (-[e]s; *no pl*) shelter.

'obdachlos *adj* (~ **werden** be left) homeless. **'Obdachlose** *m, f* (-n; -n) homeless person. **'Obdachlosena,syl** *n* shelter for the homeless.

Obduktion [ɔpdʊk'tsjo:n] *f* (-; -en) postmortem (examination), autopsy.

obduzieren [ɔpdu'tsi:rən] *v/t* (h) *j-n* ~ carry out an autopsy on s.o.

'O-Beine *pl* F bow legs, bandy legs.

'O-beinig [-baınıç] *adj* F bow-legged.

oben ['o:bən] *adv* a) at the top, b) upstairs, c) (~ **schwimmen** float) on the surface; **ganz** ~ a.fig. right at the top; **hier** ~ up here; **hoch** ~ high up; **nach** ~ up(wards), *a.* upstairs; **von** ~ *a. fig.*

from above; **von** ~ **bis unten** from top to bottom; *fig.* **von** ~ **herab** condescendingly; F ~ **ohne** topless.

oben'an *adv* at the top (*or* head).

oben'auf *adv* on top: F *fig.* ~ **sein** be fit and well, be on top of the world.

obendrein [-'draın] *adv* on top of it (all).

'obenerwähnt *adj* above(-mentioned).

oben'hin *adv* superficially, casually.

'Oben-'ohne-... topless (*bar etc*).

ober ['o:bər] *adj* upper; ~ → **oberst.**

'Ober *m* (-s; -) waiter.

'Ober|arm *m* upper arm. **~arzt** *m*, **~ärztin** *f* assistant medical director. **~befehl** *m* supreme command (*über acc* of). **~befehlshaber** *m* ✕ commander-in--chief. **~begriff** *m* generic term. **~bekleidung** *f* outer garments. **~bürgermeister** *m* (*Br.* Lord) Mayor. **~deck** *n* ⚓ upper deck. **~feldwebel** *m* staff sergeant, *Am.* sergeant 1st class.

'Oberfläche *f* surface: **an** (*or* **auf**) **der** ~ on the surface; **an die** ~ **kommen** (come to) the surface.

'oberflächlich [-fleçlıç] *adj* superficial, *fig. a.* shallow: **~e Bekanntschaft** casual acquaintance; **~ (betrachtet)** on the face of it. **'Oberflächlichkeit** *f* (-; *no pl*) superficiality.

'Ober|gefreite *m* lance corporal, *Am.* private 1st class. **~geschoß** *n* upper floor. **~grenze** *f* upper limit, ceiling.

'oberhalb *prep* (*gen*) above.

'Oberhand *f* **die ~ gewinnen** get the upper hand (*über acc* of).

'Ober|haupt *n* head, chief. **~haus** *n parl.* upper house, *Br.* House of Lords. **~haut** *f* epidermis. **~hemd** *n* shirt. **~herrschaft** *f* supremacy.

Oberin ['o:bərın] *f* (-; -nen) **1.** *eccl.* Mother Superior. **2.** *matron*.

'oberirdisch *adj* and *adv* overground, *overhead.*

'Ober|kellner *m* head waiter. **~kiefer** *m* upper jaw. **~körper** *m* upper part of the body: **den ~ freimachen** strip to the waist. **~landesgericht** *n* regional court of appeal. **~lauf** *m* upper course (*or* reaches). **~leder** *n* upper. **~leitung** *f* **1.** overall control. **2.** overhead cable. **~leutnant** *m* (*Am.* first) lieutenant. **~licht** *n* skylight. **~liga** *f sports*: third division. **~lippe** *f* upper lip. **~priester** *m* high priest. **~schenkel** *m* thigh. **~schicht** *f sociol.* upper class(es). **~schwester** *f* senior nursing officer. **~seite** *f* upper side, top (side).

oberst ['o:bərst] *adj* uppermost, top(most), *a.* highest, *fig. a.* supreme, chief: **das Oberste zuunterst kehren** turn everything upside down.

'Oberst *m* (-en; -en) colonel.

'Oberstaatsanwalt *m* senior public prosecutor.

'Oberstimme *f* ♪ upper part.

'Oberstleutnant *m* lieutenant colonel.

Ober'studien|di,rektor *m* headmaster, *Am.* principal. **~direk,torin** *f* headmistress, *Am.* principal. **~rat** *m* senior assistant master. **~rätin** [-rɛ:tın] *f* (-; -nen) senior assistant mistress.

'Oberstufe *f* (-; *no pl*) *ped.* upper school (*Am.* grades).

'Oberteil *m*, *n* top.

'Oberwasser *n fig.* (*wieder*) **~ bekommen** (*or* **haben**) be on top (again).

ob'gleich *conj* (al)though, even though.

Obhut ['ɔphu:t] *f* (-; *no pl*) care: **in s-e ~**

nehmen take care (*or* charge) of.

obig ['o:bıç] *adj* above.

Objekt [ɔp'jɛkt] *n* (-[e]s; -e) object (*a. ling. or art*), ♥ *a.* property.

objektiv [ɔpjɛk'ti:f] *adj* objective, *a.* impartial. **Objek'tiv** *n* (-s; -e) *opt.* (object) lens. **objektivieren** [ɔpjɛkti'vi:rən] *v/t* (h) objectify. **Objektivität** [ɔpjɛktivi-'tɛ:t] *f* (-; *no pl*) objectiveness.

Oblate [o'bla:tə] *f* (-; -n) wafer.

obligat [obli'ga:t] *adj iro.* inevitable.

Obligation [obliga'tsio:n] *f* (-; -en) ♥ bond, debenture.

obligatorisch [obliga'to:rıʃ] *adj* (*für*) obligatory (on), compulsory (for).

'Obmann *m* **1.** chief. **2.** *arbitration*: umpire, *of jury*: foreman.

Oboe [o'bo:ə] *f* (-; -n) oboe.

Oboist [obo'ıst] *m* (-en; -en) oboist.

Observatorium [ɔpzɛrva'to:riʊm] *n* (-s; -rien) observatory. **observieren** [-'vi:-rən] *v/t* (h) put under surveillance.

obskur [ɔps'ku:r] *adj* **1.** obscure, dubious, F shady.

Obst [o:pst] *n* (-[e]s; *no pl*) fruit. **~bau** *m* (-[e]s; *no pl*) fruit-growing. **~baum** *m* fruit tree. **~ernte** *f* a) fruit-gathering, b) fruit crop. **~garten** *m* orchard. **~händler(in** *f*) *m* fruiterer, *Am.* fruit seller. **~kon,serven** *pl* tinned (*or* canned) fruit. **~kuchen** *m* fruit tart. **~messer** *n* fruit knife.

Obstruktion [ɔpstrʊk'tsio:n] *f* (-; *no pl*) *pol.* obstruction.

'Obst|saft *m* (fruit) juice. **~sa,lat** *m* fruit salad. **~wasser** *n* fruit brandy.

obszön [ɔps'tsø:n] *adj* obscene, filthy.

Obszönität [ɔpstsøni'tɛ:t] *f* (-; -en) obscenity.

Obus ['o:bʊs] *m* (-ses; -se) trolley bus.

ob'wohl *conj* (al)though, even though.

Ochse ['ɔksə] *m* (-n; -n) **1.** ox, bullock. **2.** F ass. **'ochsen** *v/t, v/i* (h) F cram, swot.

'Ochsenschwanzsuppe *f* oxtail soup.

Ocker ['ɔkər] *m* (-s; -) ochre, *Am.* ocher.

Ode ['o:də] *f* (-; -n) ode.

öde ['ø:də] *adj* **1.** a) deserted, desolate, b) barren, waste. **2.** *fig.* dreary, dull.

'Öde *f* (-; -n) **1.** desert, waste(land). **2.** *no pl fig.* dreariness, tedium, emptiness.

Ödem [ø'de:m] *n* (-s; -e) ♥ (o)edema.

oder ['o:dər] *conj* or: **~ (aber)** (or) else, otherwise; **~ ...!** or else!; F **du kommst**

doch, ~? you are coming, aren't you?
→ **entweder, nicht.**

Odyssee [ody'se:] f (-; -n) fig. odyssey.

Ofen ['o:fən] m (-s; ~) **1.** a) stove, b) oven,
c) furnace, d) kiln: F *jetzt ist der ~ aus!*
it's curtains (for us *etc*)! **2.** F *heißer ~* a)
hot rod, b) (big motor)bike. **~heizung**
f stove heating. **~rohr** n stovepipe.

offen ['ofən] adj open (a. fig.), a. frank,
outspoken: **~e Rechnung** outstanding
account; **~e Stelle** vacant post, vacancy; **~er Wein** wine served by the glass;
die ~e See the open (sea); **mit ~en
Augen** with one's eyes open; **zu j-m ~
sein** be open with s.o.; **für Vorschläge
~ sein** be open to suggestions; **s-e Meinung ~ sagen** speak one's mind freely;
~ gestanden, ~ gesagt frankly (speaking); → **Handelsgesellschaft, Straße**
1, **Tür.**

'**offenbar I** adj → **offensichtlich. II** adv
evidently, it seems ...

offenbaren [ofən'ba:rən] v/t (offenbarte,
offenbart, h) reveal.

Offen'barung f (-; -en) revelation.

Offen'barungseid m 🛡 or fig. declaration of bankruptcy.

'**offenbleiben** v/i (irr, sep, -ge-, sn, →
bleiben) a. fig. remain open.

'**offenhalten** v/t (irr, sep, -ge-, h, →
halten) a. fig. keep s.th. open.

'**Offenheit** f (-; no pl) openness, frankness.

'**offenherzig** adj **1.** open-hearted, candid, frank. **2.** fig. revealing (dress etc).

'**offenkundig** adj obvious.

'**offenlassen** v/t (irr, sep, -ge-, h, →
lassen) a. fig. leave s.th. open.

'**offensichtlich** adj evident, obvious.

offensiv [ofən'zi:f] adj offensive.

Offensive [ofən'zi:və] f (-; -n) (**die ~ ergreifen** take the) offensive.

'**offenstehen** v/i (irr, sep, -ge-, h, →
stehen) **1.** be open (fig. j-m to s.o.): *es
steht ihm offen zu gehen* he is free to
go. **2.** accounts: be outstanding.

öffentlich ['œfəntlɪç] adj public: **~er
Dienst** a) public sector, b) civil service;
~e Mittel public funds; **~e Schulen**
state (Am. public) schools; 🛡 **in ~er
Sitzung** in open court; **~ auftreten** appear in public; **~ bekanntmachen**
make public, publicize; → **Ärgernis,
beglaubigt, Persönlichkeit** etc.

'**Öffentlichkeit** f (-; no pl) a) the (general)
public, b) a. 🛡 publicity: **an die ~ treten** appear before the public; **et. an die
~ bringen** bring s.th. before the public;
an (or in) die ~ dringen leak out; **in die
~ flüchten** resort to publicity; → **Ausschluß.** '**Öffentlichkeitsarbeit** f (-; no
pl) public relations.

'**öffentlich-'rechtlich** adj under public
law, public.

Offerte [o'fɛrtə] f (-; -n) 🛡 offer.

offiziell [ofi'tsi̯ɛl] adj official.

Offizier [ofi'tsi:r] m (-s; -e) ✕ officer.

Offi'ziersanwärter m officer cadet.

offizinell [ofitsi'nɛl] adj pharm. officinal.

offiziös [ofi'tsi̯ø:s] adj semiofficial.

öffnen ['œfnən] v/t (a. **sich** ~) (h) open.
'**Öffner** m (-s; -) opener. '**Öffnung** f (-;
-en) opening, a. gap, a. aperture.

'**Öffnungszeiten** pl opening hours.

Offsetdruck ['ɔfset-] m offset (printing).

oft [ɔft] adv often, frequently.

öfter ['œftər] adv a. **des öfteren** often.

oh [o:] int oh.

Ohm [o:m] n (-[s]; -) ⚡ ohm.

ohmsch [o:mʃ] adj ⚡ ohmic: **Ohmsches
Gesetz** Ohm's law.

ohne ['o:nə] **I** prep (acc) without: **~ s-e
Verletzung hätte er gewonnen** but for
his injury he would have won; F **~
mich!** count me out!; **nicht ~** not half
bad; → **Frage** 1 etc. **II** conj without.

ohne'gleichen adj unparallel(l)ed: **e-e
Frechheit ~** (an) incredible impudence.

ohne'hin adv anyhow, anyway.

'**Ohnmacht** f (-; -en) **1.** no pl fig. power-
lessness. **2.** 💊 unconsciousness, faint:
in ~ fallen faint.

'**ohnmächtig** adj **1.** powerless, helpless.
2. 💊 unconscious: **~ werden** faint.

Ohr [o:r] n (-[e]s; -en) ear: **ganz ~ sein** be
all ears; **nur mit halbem ~ zuhören**
listen only with half an ear; F **j-m in
den ~en liegen** pester s.o. (**mit** for,
with); **viel um die ~en haben** have a lot
on one's plate; **sich aufs ~ legen** get
some shut-eye; **schreib dir das hinter
die ~en!** now don't forget that!; **ich
traute m-n ~en nicht!** I couldn't believe
my ears!; **j-n übers ~ hauen** cheat s.o.;
j-m zu ~en kommen come to s.o.'s
ears; **halt die ~en steif!** chin up; **bis
über die ~en in Arbeit (Schulden)
stecken** be up to one's (or the) ears

ordinär [ɔrdi'nɛːr] *adj* vulgar, common.

Ordinariat [ɔrdina'ri̯aːt] *n* (-[e]s; -e) **1.** *univ.* (full) professorship. **2.** *eccl.* diocesan authorities.

Ordinarius [ɔrdi'naːri̯ʊs] *m* (-; -rien) *univ.* (full) professor.

Ordination [ɔrdina'tsi̯oːn] *f* (-; -en) **1.** *eccl.* ordination. **2.** *Austrian* ⚕ surgery.

ordnen ['ɔrdnən] *v/t* (h) **1.** a) put *s.th.* in order, b) file (*documents*), c) sort (out), d) arrange: **nach Klassen ~** classify; **s-e Gedanken ~** marshal one's thoughts; **~ alphabetisch. 2.** settle.

'Ordner *m* (-s; -) **1.** steward. **2.** file.

'Ordnung *f* (-; -en) order (*a. biol.*, ⚛), orderliness: **in alphabetischer ~** in alphabetical order; **Straße erster ~** primary road; F *fig.* **erster ~** of the first order; F (**das ist**) **in ~!** all right!, okay!, o.k.!; **es** (**er**) **ist in ~** it's (he's) all right; **nicht in ~ sein** a) be out of order, *fig. a.* be wrong, b) *person:* be out of sorts; **et. ist nicht in ~** (**damit**) s.th. is wrong (with it); **in ~ bringen** a) put *s.th.* right, *fig. a.* straighten *s.th.* out, b) tidy up (*room etc*), c) repair, F fix; **~ halten** keep order; **et. in ~ halten** keep s.th. in order; **~ schaffen** establish order; *parl.* **j-n zur ~ rufen** call s.o. to order.

'ordnungsgemäß I *adj* regular, orderly. **II** *adv* duly.

'ordnungshalber [-halbər] *adv* (only) as a matter of form.

'ordnungsliebend *adj* orderly.

'Ordnungsruf *m parl.* call to order.

'Ordnungsstrafe *f* fine.

'ordnungswidrig *adj* irregular.

'Ordnungszahl *f* ordinal (number).

Organ [ɔr'gaːn] *n* (-s; -e) **1.** *anat.* organ: *fig.* **kein ~ haben für** have no feeling for. **2.** *fig.* organ, publication. **3.** *fig.* organ, authority: **ausführendes ~** executive body. **4.** F voice. **~bank** *f* (-; -en) ⚕ organ bank. **~empfänger(in** *f*) *m* ⚕ organ recipient. **~erkrankung** *f* organic disease. **~handel** *m* sale of (transplant) organs.

Organisation [ɔrganiza'tsi̯oːn] *f* (-; -en) organization.

Organisati'onsta,lent *n* **er hat** (*or* **er ist ein**) **~** he has organizing ability.

Organisator [ɔrgani'zaːtɔr] *m* (-s; -en [-za'toːrən]) organizer. **organisatorisch** [-iza'toːrɪʃ] *adj* organizational:

~e Fähigkeit(en) organizing ability.

organisch [ɔr'gaːnɪʃ] *adj* organic.

organisieren [ɔrgani'ziːrən] *v/t* (h) **1.** organize: (**nicht**) **organisierter Arbeiter** (non)unionist. **2.** F rustle up.

Organismus [ɔrga'nɪsmʊs] *m* (-; -men) organism.

Organist [ɔrga'nɪst] *m* (-en; -en), **Orga'nistin** *f* (-; -nen) organist.

Or'gan|spende *f* donation of an organ. **~spender(in** *f*) *m* organ donor. **~verpflanzung** *f* organ transplant(ation).

Orgasmus [ɔr'gasmʊs] *m* (-; -men) orgasm, climax.

Orgel ['ɔrgəl] *f* (-; -n) organ. **~bauer** *m* (-s; -) organ builder. **~kon,zert** *n* organ recital. **~pfeife** *f* organ pipe: F *fig.* **wie die ~n** in order of size. **~re,gister** *n* organ stop.

Orgie ['ɔrgi̯ə] *f* (-; -n) orgy: **~n feiern** have orgies.

Orient ['oːri̯ɛnt] *m* (-s) Orient, East: **der Vordere ~** the Near East.

Orientale [oːri̯ɛn'taːlə] *m* (-n; -n), **Orien'talin** *f* (-; -nen) Oriental.

orien'talisch [-lɪʃ] *adj* oriental.

orientieren [oːri̯ɛn'tiːrən] (h) **I** *v/t* **1.** orient(ate) (**nach** according to). **2.** inform (**über** *acc* about, of): **gut orientiert** well informed. **II sich ~ 3.** (**an** *dat* by) orient(ate) o.s., be guided. **4.** inform o.s. (**über** *acc* of, about). **Orien'tierung** *f* (-; *no pl*) **1.** orientation: **die ~ verlieren** lose one's bearings. **2.** information: **zu Ihrer ~** for your guidance.

Orien'tierungs|punkt *m* point of reference. **~sinn** *m* sense of direction. **~stufe** *f ped.* orienteering term.

original [origi'naːl] *adj* original: **~ französisch** genuine French; **et. ~ übertragen** broadcast s.th. live.

Origi'nal *n* (-s; -e) original, F (*person*) *a.* character: **im ~ read** in the original. **~fassung** *f* original version: **in der deutschen ~** in the original German version. **getreu** *adj* faithful.

Originalität [originali'tɛːt] *f* (-; *no pl*) *a. fig.* originality.

Origi'nal|ko,pie *f film etc:* master copy. **~übertragung** *f* live broadcast. **~verpackung** *f* original packing.

originell [origi'nɛl] *adj* **1.** original, novel. **2.** F funny, quaint.

Orkan [ɔr'kaːn] *m* (-[e]s; -e) hurricane.

or'kanartig *adj* of hurricane force.
Ornament [ɔrna'mɛnt] *n* (-[e]s; -e) ornament.
Ornat [ɔr'na:t] *m* (-[e]s; -e) ☨ robe(s), *eccl.* vestments.
Ornithologe [ɔrnito'lo:gə] *m* (-n; -n) ornithologist.
Ort¹ [ɔrt] *m* (-[e]s; -e) place (→ *a.* **Ortschaft**), spot, locality, scene: (*hier*) *am* ~ (here) in this place; ~ *und Zeit* place and time; ~ *der Handlung* scene (of action); *an* ~ *und Stelle* on the spot; *höheren* ~(*e*)*s* at high quarters.
Ort² *n* (-[e]s; Örter) *vor* ~ ⚒ at the pit face, *fig.* on the scene (of action); *Besichtigung* ~ on-site inspection.
orten ['ɔrtən] *v/t* (h) ⚓ *etc* locate.
orthodox [ɔrto'dɔks] *adj* orthodox.
Orthographie [ɔrtogra'fi:] *f* (-; -n) orthography, spelling. **orthographisch** [ɔrto'gra:fiʃ] *adj* orthographic(al): ~ *richtig schreiben* spell correctly.
Orthopäde [ɔrto'pɛ:də] *m* (-n; -n) orthop(a)edist. **Orthopädie** [-pɛ'di:] *f* (-; *no pl*) orthop(a)edics. **orthopädisch** [-diʃ] *adj* orthop(a)edic.
örtlich ['œrtlɪç] *adj a.* ⚕ local: ~ *begrenzen* localize (*auf acc* to); ~ *verschieden sein* vary from place to place.
Örtlichkeit *f* (-; -en) locality.
'Ortsangabe *f* statement of place.
'ortsansässig *adj*, **'Ortsansässige** *m, f* (-n; -n) resident, local.
'Ortschaft *f* (-; -en) place, village, (small) town: *geschlossene* ~ built-up area.
'ortsfest *adj* stationary.
'Ortsgespräch *n teleph.* local call.
'Ortskenntnis *f* knowledge of a place: ~ *besitzen* → **'ortskundig** *adj* ~ *sein* know (one's way around) the place.
'Orts|name *m* place name. **~netz** *n teleph.* local exchange. **~schild** *n* place-name sign. **~sinn** *m* sense of direction. **~teil** *m* district. **Ǫüblich** *adj* customary, local. **~wechsel** *m* change (of place). **~zeit** *f* (-; *no pl*) local time. **~zuschlag** *m* ♰ weighting (allowance).
Ortung *f* (-; -en) ⚓ *etc* location.
Öse ['ø:zə] *f* (-; -n) eye.
Osmose [ɔs'mo:zə] *f* (-; -n) osmosis.
Ost [ɔst] *invar geogr.* east, *pol.* East.
'Ostblock *m pol.* Eastern bloc.
'ostdeutsch *adj*, **'Ostdeutsche** *m, f* (-n; -n) East German.

Osten ['ɔstən] *m* (-s; *no pl*) east, *of town*: East End, *geogr., pol. the* East: *der Ferne* (*Nahe*) ~ the Far (Middle) East; *im* ~ in the east; *nach* ~ (to the) east, eastward(s); *von* ~, *aus* ~ from the east, easterly (*wind*).
ostentativ [ɔstɛnta'ti:f] *adj* pointed: **~er Beifall** demonstrative applause.
Osteoporose [ɔsteopo'ro:zə] *f* (-; -n) ⚕ osteoporosis.
Osterei ['o:stər¹ai] *n* Easter egg.
'Osterfest *n* → **Ostern.**
'Osterglocke *f* ⚘ (yellow) daffodil.
'Osterhase *m* Easter bunny.
österlich ['ø:stərlɪç] *adj* (of) Easter.
Oster'montag *m* Easter Monday.
Ostern ['o:stərn] *n* (-; -) (*zu* ~ at) Easter.
Österreich ['ø:stəraɪç] *n* (-s) Austria. **'Österreicher** *m* (-s; -), **'Österreicherin** *f* (-; -nen), **'österreichisch** *adj* Austrian.
Oster'sonntag *m* Easter Sunday.
'Osteu,ropa *n* Eastern Europe.
östlich ['œstlɪç] **I** *adj* eastern, easterly. **II** *adv* ~ *von* (to the) east of.
Östrogen [œstro'ge:n] *n* (-s; -e) *biol.* (o)estrogen.
'Ostsee *f* Baltic (Sea).
ostwärts ['ɔstvɛrts] *adv* east(wards).
'Ostwind *m* east wind.
Oszillograph [ɔstsilo'gra:f] *m* (-en; -en) oscilloscope, oscillograph.
Otter¹ ['ɔtər] *m* (-s; -) *zo.* otter.
'Otter² *f* (-; -n) *zo.* viper.
Ouvertüre [uvɛr'ty:rə] *f* (-; -n) overture.
oval [o'va:l] *adj*, **O'val** *n* (-s; -e) oval.
Ovation [ova'tsi̯o:n] *f* (-; -en) ovation.
Ovulation [ovula'tsi̯o:n] *f* (-; -en) *biol.* ovulation.
Oxyd [ɔ'ksy:t] *n* (-[e]s; -e) 🜍 oxide.
Oxydation [ɔksyda'tsi̯o:n] *f* (-; -en) oxidation. **oxydieren** [ɔksy'di:rən] *v/i* (h, sn) oxidize.
Ozean ['o:tsea:n] *m* (-s; -e) ocean.
'Ozeandampfer *m* ocean liner.
ozeanisch [otse'a:nɪʃ] *adj* oceanic.
Ozeanographie [otseanogra'fi:] *f* (-; *no pl*) oceanography.
Ozelot ['o:tselɔt] *m* (-s; -e) *zo.* ocelot.
Ozon [o'tso:n] *n* (-s; *no pl*) ozone.
o'zonhaltig *adj* ozoniferous.
O'zon|loch *n* hole in the ozone layer. **~schicht** *f* ozone layer, ozonosphere. **~werte** *pl* ozone levels.

P

P, p [pe:] *n* (-; -) P, p.

paar [pa:r] *indef pron* **ein ~** a few, some, F a couple of. **Paar** *n* (-[e]s; -e) pair, couple: **ein ~ (neue) Schuhe** a (new) pair of shoes. **'paaren** *v/t* (h) **1.** (*a. sich ~*) *zo.* pair, couple, mate. **2.** *sports:* match. **3.** *fig.* (*a. sich ~*) combine.

'Paarlaufen *n* pair skating.

'paarmal *adv* **ein ~** several (*or* a few, F a couple of) times.

'Paarung *f* (-; -en) **1.** *zo.* pairing, mating. **2.** *sports:* a) matching, b) match.

'Paarungszeit *f zo.* mating season.

'paarweise *adv* in pairs, two by two.

Pacht [paxt] *f* (-; -en) a) lease, b) rent. **'pachten** *v/t* (h) (take on) lease: F *fig.* **er meint, er habe es (für sich) gepachtet** he thinks he has got a monopoly on that. **Pächter** ['pɛçtər] *m* (-s; -) lessee, leaseholder, tenant. **'Pachtung** *f* (-; -en) lease. **'Pachtvertrag** *m* lease.

Pack¹ [pak] *m* (-[e]s; -e, ⁻e) a) pack, pile, b) bundle: → **Sack**.

Pack² *n* (-[e]s; *no pl*) F *contp.* riffraff.

Päckchen ['pɛkçən] *n* (-s; -) small parcel (*a.* ✽), packet, *esp. Am.* pack (*a. of cigarettes*).

'Packeis *n* pack ice.

packen ['pakən] (h) **I** *v/t* **1.** pack (*one's clothes, suitcase, etc*), make up (*parcel etc*): F *pack dich!* beat it! **2.** (*an dat* by) grab, seize. **3.** *fig. j-n ~* a) *fear etc:* seize s.o., b) *novel etc:* grip s.o., thrill s.o.; F *es hat ihn gepackt* he's got it bad. **4.** F *fig.* lick (*problem etc*): **es ~** a) make it, manage, b) get it. **II** *v/i* **5.** pack (up).

'Packen *m* (-s; -) pack, pile (*a. fig.*).

'packend *adj fig.* gripping, thrilling.

'Packer *m* (-s; -), **'Packerin** *f* (-; -nen) packer.

'Packesel *m* pack-mule, pack-horse.

'Packpapier *n* wrapping paper.

'Packung *f* (-; -en) **1.** packet, *esp. Am.* pack (*a. of cigarettes*). **2.** ✽ pack. **3.** ⚙ packing, gasket. **4.** F *sports:* **e-e ~ bekommen** take a hammering.

Pädagoge [pɛda'go:gə] *m* (-n; -en), **Päda'gogin** *f* (-; -nen) a) teacher, b) education(al)ist, educator. **Pädagogik** [-'go:gɪk] *f* (-; *no pl*) pedagogy, educa-

tion. **päda'gogisch** [-gɪʃ] *adj* pedagogical, educational.

Paddel ['padəl] *n* (-s; -) paddle. **'Paddelboot** *n* canoe.

paddeln ['padəln] *v/t, v/i* (h) paddle.

paffen ['pafən] *v/i, v/t* (h) F puff (away) (*at one's pipe etc*), smoke.

Page ['pa:ʒə] *m* (-n; -n) **1.** *hist.* page. **2.** page, *Am.* bellboy, bellhop.

Pagode [pa'go:də] *f* (-; -n) pagoda.

pah [pa:] *int* bah, pshaw.

Paket [pa'ke:t] *n* (-[e]s; -e) package (*a. fig. pol. etc*), packet, ✽ parcel: **ein ~ Aktien** a parcel (*or* block) of shares.

Pa'ket|karte *f* (parcel) mailing form. **~post** *f* parcel post. **~schalter** *m* parcels counter. **~zustellung** *f* parcel delivery.

Pakistan ['pa:kista:n] *n* (-s) Pakistan. **Pakistaner** [pakis'ta:nər] *m* (-s; -), **Paki'stanerin** *f* (-; -nen), **paki'stanisch** *adj* Pakistani.

Pakt [pakt] *m* (-[e]s; -e) pact, agreement. **paktieren** [pak'ti:rən] *v/i* (h) make a deal (*mit* with).

Palast [pa'last] *m* (-[e]s; -läste) palace.

Palästina [palɛ'sti:na] *n* (-s) Palestine. **Palästinenser** [palɛsti'nɛnzər] *m* (-s; -), **Palästi'nenserin** *f* (-; -nen), **palästi'nensisch** [-zɪʃ] *adj* Palestinian.

Palatschinke [pala'tʃɪŋkə] *f* (-; -n) *Austrian gastr.* pancake.

Palaver [pa'la:vər] *n* (-s; -) F palaver.

Palette [pa'lɛtə] *f* (-; -n) **1.** *paint.* palette. **2.** *fig.* range. **3.** ⊙ pallet.

Palisade [pali'za:də] *f* (-; -n) palisade.

Palme ['palmə] *f* (-; -n) palm (tree): F *j-n auf die ~ bringen* drive s.o. up the wall.

Palm'sonntag *m eccl.* Palm Sunday.

'Palm|wedel *m*, **~zweig** *m* palm branch.

Pampe ['pampə] *f* (-; *no pl*) F mush.

Pampelmuse [pampəl'mu:zə] *f* (-; -n) ✿ grapefruit.

Pamphlet [pam'fle:t] *n* (-[e]s; -e) pamphlet, lampoon.

pampig *adj* F **1.** mushy. **2.** stroppy.

panieren [pa'ni:rən] *v/t* (h) bread.

Pa'niermehl *n* breadcrumbs.

Panik ['pa:nɪk] *f* (-; -en) panic: *in ~* panic-stricken, F panicky; *in ~ geraten* (*versetzen*) panic; F *nur k-e ~!* don't panic! **'Panikmache** f (-; *no pl*) scaremongering. **'panisch** *adj* panic: *von ~er Angst erfaßt* panic-stricken; *e-e ~e Angst haben vor* be terrified of.

Panne ['panə] f (-; -n) **1.** a) breakdown, b) puncture: *ich hatte e-e ~* my car broke down, I had a puncture. **2.** *fig.* a) mishap, b) F slip-up: *böse ~* foul-up.

'Pannendienst m breakdown service.

Panorama [pano'ra:ma] n (-s; -men) panorama. **~fenster** n picture window.

panschen ['panʃən] (h) **I** v/i F splash (about). **II** v/t water down, adulterate.

Pansen ['panzən] m (-s; -) zo. rumen.

Panther ['pantər] m (-s; -) panther.

Pantoffel [pan'tɔfəl] m (-s; -n) slipper: F *unter dem ~ stehen* be henpecked.

Pan'toffelheld m F henpecked husband.

Pan'toffelkino n F telly, *Am.* the tube.

Pantomime¹ [panto'mi:mə] f (-; -n) (panto)mime, dumb show.

Panto'mime² m (-n; -n) mime.

panto'mimisch *adj* pantomimic: *~ darstellen* mime.

Panzer ['pantsər] m (-s; -) **1.** *hist.* armo(u)r. **2.** ✕ tank. **3.** zo. shell. **~abwehr...** ✕ antitank (*rocket, gun, etc*). **~divisi,on** f ✕ armo(u)red division. **~faust** f antitank grenade launcher. **~glas** n bulletproof glass. **~kreuzer** m ⚓ ✕ armo(u)red cruiser.

panzern ['pantsərn] v/t (h) armo(u)r: *fig. sich ~* arm o.s.; → *gepanzert.*

'Panzer|schrank m safe. **~sperre** f ✕ antitank obstacle. **~truppe** f ✕ tank force. **~tür** f armo(u)red door. **~wagen** m ✕ armo(u)red car.

Papa ['papa] m (-s; -s) F daddy, dad, pa.

Papagei [papa'gai] m (-en; -e[n]) parrot.

Papa'geienkrankheit f psittacosis.

Papier [pa'pi:r] n (-s; -e) paper: *~e* a) (identity) papers, b) ✝ securities, papers; (*nur*) *auf dem ~* on paper (only); *zu ~ bringen* commit to paper; *s-e ~e bekommen* get one's cards, be sacked.

pa'pieren *adj* **1.** (of) paper. **2.** *fig.* prosy.

Pa'pier|fa,brik f paper mill. **~geld** n paper money. **~korb** m waste-paper basket. **~krieg** m F red tape, paper warfare. **~schlange** f paper streamer. **~schnipsel** m scrap of paper. **~servi,ette** f paper napkin. **~taschentuch** n tissue. **~tiger** m iro. paper tiger.

Pa'pierwaren pl stationery. **~geschäft** n stationer's (shop *or* store).

'Pappband m **1.** pasteboard (binding). **2.** paperback. **'Pappbecher** m paper cup. **'Pappdeckel** m pasteboard.

Pappe ['papə] f (-; -n) cardboard, pasteboard: F *nicht von ~* quite something, *person:* quite formidable.

Pappel ['papəl] f (-; -n) ♀ poplar.

'Pappenstiel m F *für e-n ~ buy etc s.th.* for a song; *k-n ~ wert* not worth a bean.

'Pappkar,ton m cardboard box.

Pappmaché [papma'ʃe:] n (-s; -s) papier mâché.

'Pappteller m paper plate.

Paprika ['paprika] m (-s; -[s]) **1.** *no pl* paprika. **2.** → **'Paprikaschote** f green (*or* sweet) pepper.

Papst [pa:pst] m (-[e]s; ⁻e) pope.

päpstlich ['pɛ:pstlɪç] *adj* papal.

'Papsttum n (-s; *no pl*) papacy.

Parabel [pa'ra:bəl] f (-; -n) **1.** parable. **2.** ⅄ parabola.

Parabolan,tenne [para'bo:l-] f *TV* parabolic aerial (*Am.* antenna), F dish.

Parade [pa'ra:də] f (-; -n) **1.** ✕ parade, review: F *j-m in die ~ fahren* cut s.o. short. **2.** *boxing, fenc.* parry, *soccer:* save. **~beispiel** n classic example.

Paradeiser [para'daizər] m (-s; -) *Austrian* tomato.

Paradies [para'di:s] n (-es; -e) (*im ~* in) paradise. **paradiesisch** [para'di:zɪʃ] *adj* paradisal(l), *fig.* heavenly.

paradox [para'dɔks] *adj* **1.** paradoxical. **2.** F strange, absurd.

para'doxerweise *adv* **1.** paradoxically. **2.** F strangely enough.

Paraffin [para'fi:n] n (-s; -e) 🜍 paraffin.

Paragraph [para'gra:f] m (-en; -en) **1.** section, article. **2.** paragraph. **3.** (*symbol* §) section mark.

parallel [para'le:l] *adj and adv* parallel (*mit, zu* to). **Paral'lele** f (-; -n) parallel (line): *fig. e-e ~ ziehen* draw a parallel (*zu* to). **Parallelogramm** [paralelo-'gram] n (-s; -e) ⅄ parallelogram.

paramili,tärisch ['pa:ra-] *adj* paramilitary.

Paranoia [para'nɔya] f (-; *no pl*) ⚕ paranoia. **Paranoiker** [para'nɔ:ikər] m (-s; -), **paranoisch** [-'nɔ:ıʃ] *adj* paranoiac.

Paranuß ['pa:ra-] f Brazil nut.

paraphieren [para'fi:rən] v/t (h) initial.

Parapsycholo'gie *f* parapsychology.
Parasit [para'zi:t] *m* (-en; -en) parasite.
para'sitisch [-tɪʃ] *adj* parasitic(al).
parat [pa'ra:t] *adj pred* ready.
Pärchen ['pɛːrçən] *n* (-s; -) (courting) couple, twosome.
pardon [par'dõ:] *int* sorry.
Parenthese [parɛn'te:zə] *f* (-; -n) *ling.* parenthesis.
Parfüm [par'fy:m] *n* (-s; -e, -s) perfume, scent. **Parfümerie** [parfymə'ri:] *f* (-; -n) perfumery.
Par'fümfläschchen *n* scent bottle.
parfümieren [parfy'mi:rən] (h) **I** *v/t* perfume, scent. **II sich** ~ put on perfume.
parieren [pa'ri:rən] (h) **I** *v/t* **1.** *sports or fig.* parry. **2.** pull up (*horse*). **II** *v/i* **3.** parry. **4.** F obey.
Pariser [pa'ri:zər] *m* (-s; -), **Pa'riserin** *f* (-; -nen) Parisian.
Parität [pari'te:t] *f* (-; *no pl*) parity.
pari'tätisch *adj* proportional, pro rata.
Park [park] *m* (-s; -e) park. **~anlage** *f* park. **~bank** *f* (-; -e) park bench. **~bucht** *f mot.* lay-by. **~deck** *n mot.* parking level.
parken ['parkən] *v/t, v/i* (h) park: **~de Autos** parked cars; **Parken verboten!** no parking!; **schräg** ~ angle-park; **in zweiter Reihe** ~ double-park.
Parkett [par'kɛt] *n* (-[e]s; -e) **1.** parquet. **2.** (dance) floor. **3.** *thea.* stalls, *Am.* parquet. **~(fuß)boden** *m* parquet floor.
'Park|gebühr *f* parking fee. **~hochhaus** *n* multistor(e)y car park, *Am.* parking garage. **~licht** *n* parking light. **~lücke** *f* parking space. **~platz** *m* a) car park, *Am.* parking lot, b) parking space. **~scheibe** *f* parking disc. **~sünder(in** *f)* *m* F parking offender. **~uhr** *f* parking meter. **~verbot** *n hier ist* ~ there's no parking here; *im* ~ *stehen* be parked in a towaway zone. **~wächter** *m* **1.** park keeper. **2.** *mot.* car park attendant.
Parlament [parla'mɛnt] *n* (-[e]s; -e) (*im* ~ *sitzen* be or sit in) parliament.
Parlamentarier [parlamɛn'ta:riər] *m* (-s; -) parliamentarian.
parlamen'tarisch *adj* parliamentary.
Parlamentarismus [parlamenta'rɪsmʊs] *m* (-; *no pl*) parliamentarianism.
Parla'ments|ausschuß *m* parliamentary committee. **~ferien** *pl* recess. **~mitglied** *n* member of parliament.

~sitzung *f* sitting (of parliament).
~wahlen *pl* parliamentary elections.
Parmesan [parme'za:n] *m* (-s; *no pl*) Parmesan.
Parodie [paro'di:] *f* (-; -n) parody, F take-off. **parodieren** [paro'di:rən] *v/t* (h) parody, F take *s.o.* off. **Parodist** [paro'dɪst] *m* (-en; -en) parodist.
Parodontose [parodɔn'to:zə] *f* (-; -n) 🦷 paradontosis.
Parole [pa'ro:lə] *f* (-; -n) ✗ password, *fig.* watchword, *pol. a.* slogan.
Partei [par'tai] *f* (-; -en) a) *a. pol. or* 🏛 party, b) *sports:* side, c) tenant: *j-s* ~ **ergreifen, für j-n** ~ **nehmen** side with s.o.; **gegen j-n** ~ **ergreifen** take sides against s.o.; ~ **sein** be biassed; **die** ~ **wechseln** change sides (*pol.* parties). **~appa¦rat** *m* party machine. **~basis** *f* rank and file (of a party). **~buch** *n* party membership book. **~freund** *m* fellow-member (of a party). **~führer** *m* party leader. **~führung** *f* **1.** party leadership. **2.** *coll.* party leaders. **~gänger** [-gɛŋər] *m* (-s; -) partisan, party man. **~genosse** *m* party member.
par'teiisch, par'teilich *adj* partial.
Par'teilinie *f* party line.
par'teilos *adj* independent.
Par'teilose *m, f* (-n; -n) independent.
Par'teimitglied *n* party member.
Par'teinahme *f* (-; -) partisanship.
Par'tei|poli¦tik *f* party politics. 💲**po¦litisch** *adj* party-political. **~pro¦gramm** *n* (party) platform. **~spende** *f* party donation. **~tag** *m* party conference (*Am.* convention). **~versammlung** *f* party meeting. **~vorsitzende** *m* party leader. **~vorstand** *m* executive committee (of a party). **~zugehörigkeit** *f* party membership.
Parterre [par'tɛrə] *n* (-s; -s) ground (*Am.* first) floor.
Partie [par'ti:] *f* (-; -n) **1.** part. **2.** 🌱 lot. **3.** 🎵 *etc* part. **4.** game, *sports: a.* match. **5.** F *ich bin mit von der* ~*! count me in!* **6.** F *e-e gute* ~ *sein* be a good match (*or* catch); *e-e gute* ~ *machen* marry a fortune.
partiell [par'tsiɛl] *adj* partial.
Partikel [par'ti:kəl] *f* (-; -n) particle.
Partisan [parti'za:n] *m* (-s, -en; -en) partisan, guerilla.
Partitur [parti'tu:r] *f* (-; -en) 🎵 score.

Partizip [parti'tsi:p] *n* (-s; -ien) *ling.* participle.
Partner ['partnɐ] *m* (-s; -), **'Partnerin** *f* (-; -nen) partner. **'Partnerschaft** *f* (-; -en) partnership. **'partnerschaftlich** *adj and adv* as (equal) partners, joint(ly). **'Partnerstadt** *f* twin town.
Party ['pa:rti] *f* (-; -s, -ties) (*auf e-e ~ gehen* go to a) party. **~muffel** *m* F party pooper. **~raum** *m* party room.
Parzelle [par'tsɛlə] *f* (-; -n) plot, lot.
parzellieren [partsɛ'li:rən] *v/t* (h) parcel out.
Pascha ['paʃa] *m* (-s; *no pl*) *hist.* pasha.
Paß [pas] *m* (Passes; Pässe) **1.** (mountain) pass. **2.** passport. **3.** *sports:* pass.
passabel [pa'sa:bəl] *adj* passable.
Passage [pa'sa:ʒə] *f* (-; -n) **1.** passage (*a. ♪, in book etc*). **2.** (shopping) arcade.
Passagier [pasa'ʒi:r] *m* (-s; -e) passenger: *blinder ~* ♣ stowaway. **~liste** *f* passenger list. **~schiff** *n* passenger ship.
Passant [pa'sant] *m* (-en; -en), **Pas'santin** *f* (-; -nen) passer-by.
Passat [pa'sa:t] *m* (-[e]s; -e) trade wind.
'Paßbild *n* passport photo(graph).
Passe ['pasə] *f* (-; -n) *dress:* yoke.
passen ['pasən] (h) **I** *v/i* **1.** *a. fig.* fit (*j-m, auf j-n* s.o., *für or zu et.* s.th.): *~ zu in colo(u)r etc:* go well with, match; *fig. sie ~ (gut) zueinander* they are well suited to each other; *das paßt (nicht) zu ihm!* that's just like him (not like him)! **2.** *j-m ~* suit s.o.; *paßt es dir morgen?* would tomorrow suit you (*or* be all right [with you])?; *das paßt mir gut* that suits me fine; *das (er) paßt mir gar nicht!* I don't like it (him) at all!; F *das könnte dir so ~!* nothing doing! **3.** *cards, a. passen:* ich passe! pass!; *fig. da muß ich ~!* you've got me there! **II** *v/t* **4.** *den Ball ~ zu* pass (the ball) to.
'passend *adj* **1.** fitting (*a. fig.*), in *colo(u)r etc:* matching: *e-e dazu ~e Krawatte* a (neck)tie to match. **2.** suitable, right: *die ~en Worte* the right words; *bei ~er Gelegenheit* at the right moment. **3.** F *haben Sie es ~?* have you got the right money?
Passepartout [paspar'tu:] *n* (-s; -s) mount.
'Paßform *f* (-; *no pl*) fit.
pas'sierbar *adj* passable, practicable.
passieren [pa'si:rən] **I** *v/i* (sn) **1.** take

place, happen: *j-m ~* happen to s.o.; *was ist passiert?* what's happened?; *mir ist nichts passiert* I'm all right. **II** *v/t* (h) **2.** pass (by *or* through). **3.** *gastr.* pass (through a sieve *etc*), strain.
Pas'sierschein *m* pass, permit.
Pas'sierschlag *m tennis:* passing shot.
Passion [pa'sio:n] *f* (-; -en) **1.** passion. **2.** *eccl.*, *♪ etc* Passion. **passioniert** [pasio'ni:rt] *adj* enthusiastic, keen.
Passi'onsspiel *n* Passion play.
passiv ['pasi:f] *adj* passive: *~es Mitglied* nonactive member; *~er Wortschatz* recognition vocabulary; → **Bestechung.**
'Passiv *n* (-s; -e) *ling.* passive (voice).
Passiva [pa'si:va] *pl* ✝ liabilities.
Passivität [pasivi'tɛ:t] *f* (-; *no pl*) passivity, passiveness, inaction.
'Passivposten *m* ✝ debit item.
'Passivseite *f* ✝ liability side.
'Paßkon,trolle *f* passport control.
'Paßstelle *f* passport office.
'Paßstraße *f* (mountain) pass.
'Paßstück *n* ◎ fitting piece, adapter.
Passus ['pasʊs] *m* (-; -) passage.
'Paßwort *n a. computer:* password.
Paste ['pastə] *f* (-; -n) paste.
Pastell [pas'tɛl] *n* (-[e]s; -e) pastel. **~farben** *pl* pastel shades. **~stift** *m* crayon.
Pastete [pas'te:tə] *f* (-; -n) pie, pâté.
pasteurisieren [pastøri'zi:rən] *v/t* (h) pasteurize.
Pastille [pas'tɪlə] *f* (-; -n) lozenge.
Pastor ['pasto:r] *m* (-s; -en) pastor.
Pate ['pa:tə] *m* (-n; -n) a) godfather, b) → *Patin,* c) → *Patenkind: ~ stehen bei* be godfather (*or* godmother) to, *fig.* sponsor, *w.s.* be behind.
'Patenkind *n* godchild, godson, goddaughter. **'Patenonkel** *m* godfather.
Patenschaft *f* (-; -en) sponsorship: *fig. die ~ übernehmen für* sponsor.
patent [pa'tɛnt] *adj* F ingenious, clever.
Pa'tent *n* (-[e]s; -e) **1.** patent (*auf acc* for): *ein ~ anmelden* apply for a patent; (*zum*) *~ angemeldet* patent pending. **2.** ✕ commission. **~amt** *n* Patent Office. **~anmeldung** *f* patent application. **~anspruch** *m* patent claim. **~anwalt** *m* patent attorney. **~beschreibung** *f* patent specification.
patentieren [patɛn'ti:rən] *v/t* (h) patent: *et. ~ lassen* take out a patent for s.th.

Pa'tent|inhaber *m* patentee. **~lösung** *f* F *fig.* ready-made solution. **~recht** *n* a) patent law, b) patent right. **2rechtlich** *adj and adv* under patent law: **~ ge-schützt** patented. **~schrift** *f* patent specification. **~schutz** *m* protection of patent.

Pater ['pa:tər] *m* (-s; -, Patres) father.

pathetisch [pa'te:tɪʃ] *adj* lofty, emotional, *contp.* pompous.

Pathologe [pato'lo:gə] *m* (-n; -n) pathologist. **Pathologie** [patolo'gi:] *f* (-; *no pl*) pathology. **pathologisch** [pato-'lo:gɪʃ] *adj* pathological.

Pathos ['pa:tɔs] *n* (-; *no pl*) emotion(al style or tone).

Patience [pa'sĩã:s] *f* (-; -n) (**e-e ~ legen** play a) patience (*Am.* solitaire).

Patient [pa'tsĩɛnt] *m* (-en; -en), **Pati'en-tin** *f* (-; -nen) patient.

Patin ['pa:tɪn] *f* (-; -nen) godmother.

Patina ['pa:tina] *f* (-; *no pl*) (**~ ansetzen** *a. fig.* develop a) patina.

Patriarch [patri'arç] *m* (-en; -en) patriarch. **patriarchalisch** [patriar'ça:lɪʃ] *adj* patriarchal.

Patriot [patri'o:t] *m* (-en; -en), **Patri'otin** *f* (-; -nen) patriot. **patri'otisch** [-tɪʃ] *adj* patriotic. **Patriotismus** [patrio'tɪsmʊs] *m* (-; *no pl*) patriotism.

Patron [pa'tro:n] *m* (-s; -e) **1.** *eccl.* patron saint. **2.** F fellow: *contp.* **übler ~** nasty customer.

Patrone [pa'tro:nə] *f* (-; -n) cartridge.

Pa'tronenhülse *f* cartridge case.

Pa'tronin *f* (-; -nen) *eccl.* patron saint.

Patrouille [pa'trʊljə] *f* (-; -n), **patrouil-lieren** [patrʊl'ji:rən] *v/i* (h) ✕ patrol.

patsch [patʃ] *int* splat!, smack!

Patsche ['patʃə] *f* F **in der ~ sitzen** be in a scrape; *j-m aus der ~ helfen* help s.o. out of a (tight) spot.

'patschen *v/i* (h, sn) a) splash, b) smack.

Patt [pat] *n chess:* stalemate (*a. fig. pol.*).

patzen ['patsən] *v/i* (h), **Patzer** ['patsər] *m* (-s; -) F blunder, boob.

patzig ['patsɪç] *adj* F snotty, stroppy.

Pauke ['paʊkə] *f* (-; -n) a) bass drum, b) kettledrum: F *fig.* **auf die ~ hauen** paint the town red; *mit ~n und Trom-peten durchfallen* *iro.* fail gloriously.

'pauken *v/i* (h) **1.** play the kettledrum(s). **2.** F *ped.* (*a. v/t*) cram, swot.

'Paukenschlag *m* drumbeat: *fig.* **wie ein ~** like a bombshell.

Pauker ['paʊkər] *m* (-s; -) **1.** ♪ drummer. **2.** F teacher.

pausbäckig ['paʊsbɛkɪç] *adj* chubby.

pauschal [paʊ'ʃa:l] **I** *adj* **1.** all-in(clusive) (*price etc*). **2.** *fig.* sweeping. **II** *adv* **3.** in a lump sum. **4.** *fig.* wholesale.

Pau'schale *f* (-; -n) lump sum.

Pau'schal|gebühr *f* flat rate. **~reise** *f* package tour. **~urteil** *n fig.* sweeping judg(e)ment.

'Pause¹ ['paʊzə] *f* (-; -n) pause, rest (*a.* ♪), *ped.* break, *Am.* recess, *thea. etc* interval, *Am.* intermission: *e-e ~ machen* a) take a break (*or* rest), b) pause.

'Pause² *f* (-; -n) ⚙ tracing, copy, blueprint. **'pausen** *v/t* (h) trace.

'pausenlos *adj* uninterrupted, nonstop.

'Pausenzeichen *n radio, TV* interval signal.

pausieren [paʊ'zi:rən] *v/i* (h) a) pause, b) take a break (*or* rest).

'Pauspa,pier *n* tracing paper.

Pavian ['pa:via:n] *m* (-s; -e) *zo.* baboon.

Pavillon ['pavɪljõ:] *m* (-s; -s) pavilion.

Pazifismus [patsi'fɪsmʊs] *m* (-; *no pl*) pacifism. **Pazifist** [patsi'fɪst] *m* (-en; -en), **pazi'fistisch** [-tɪʃ] *adj* pacifist.

Pech [pɛç] *n* (-s; -e) **1.** pitch: *fig.* **wie ~ und Schwefel zs.-halten** be as thick as thieves. **2.** *no pl* F bad luck: **~ gehabt!** tough luck!; **~ haben** be unlucky (*bei* with). **'pechschwarz** *adj* F jet-black (*hair etc*), pitch-dark (*night*).

'Pechsträhne *f* run of bad luck.

'Pechvogel *m* F unlucky fellow (*or* girl).

Pedal [pe'da:l] *n* (-s; -e) pedal.

Pedant [pe'dant] *m* (-en; -en) pedant. **Pedanterie** [-tə'ri:] *f* (-; *no pl*) pedantry. **pe'dantisch** [-tɪʃ] *adj* pedantic.

Pediküre [pedi'ky:rə] *f* (-; -) pedicure.

Pegel [pe:gəl] *m* (-s; -) *a. fig.* level.

'Pegelstand *m* water level.

peilen ['paɪlən] (h) **I** *v/t* take the bearings of: *fig.* **die Lage ~** see how the land lies; → **Daumen**. **II** *v/i* take the bearings.

'Peilfunk *m* directional radio.

'Peilgerät *n* radio direction finder.

'Peilung *f* (-; -en) a) locating, b) bearing.

Pein [paɪn] *f* (-; *no pl*) pain, agony.

peinigen ['paɪnigən] *v/t* (h) torment.

'Peiniger *m* (-s; -) tormentor.

'peinlich I *adj* **1.** embarrassing, *a.* awkward (*silence, situation, etc*): **es ist mir sehr ~** I feel awful about it. **2.** meticulous, scrupulous. **II** *adv* **3.** *j-n ~ berühren* pain s.o.; *~ berührt* embarrassed, pained. **4.** *~* (**genau**) meticulously; *~ sauber* scrupulously clean; *et. ~st vermeiden* take great care to avoid s.th.

'**Peinlichkeit** *f* (-; -en) **1.** *no pl* awkwardness. **2.** awkward situation (*or* remark).

Peitsche ['paɪtʃə] *f* (-; -n) whip.

'**peitschen** *v/i, v/t* (h) whip, *a. fig.* lash.

'**Peitschenhieb** *m* (whip)lash.

Pekinese [peki'ne:zə] *m* (-n; -n) *zo.* Pekin(g)ese.

Pelargonie [pelar'go:niə] *f* (-; -n) ♀ pelargonium.

Pelikan ['pe:lika:n] *m* (-s; -e) *zo.* pelican.

Pelle ['pɛlə] *f* (-; -n) *dial.* skin, peel.

'**pellen** *v/t* (h) skin, peel; → *Ei* 1.

'**Pellkartoffeln** *pl* potatoes (boiled) in their skins, jacket potatoes.

Pelz [pɛlts] *m* (-es; -e) *a.* fur, b) skin, hide; F *j-m auf den ~ rücken* press s.o. hard. **♫gefüttert** *adj* fur-lined. **~handel** *m* fur trade. **~händler** *m* furrier.

pelzig ['pɛltsɪç] *adj* **1.** furry. **2.** 🌶 furred, coated (*tongue etc*).

'**Pelz|jacke** *f* fur jacket. **~kragen** *m* fur collar. **~mantel** *m* fur coat. **~mütze** *f* fur hat.

'**Pelztier** *n* fur-bearing animal. **~farm** *f* fur farm. **~jäger** *m* trapper. **~zucht** *f* fur farming.

Pendel ['pɛndəl] *n* (-s; -) pendulum.

'**pendeln** *v/i* **1.** (h) swing, oscillate. **2.** (sn) 🚃 *etc* shuttle, *person*: commute.

'**Pendel|tür** *f* swing door. **~uhr** *f* pendulum clock. **~verkehr** *m* **1.** 🚃 shuttle service. **2.** commuter traffic.

Pendler ['pɛndlər] *m* (-s; -) commuter.

penetrant [pene'trant] *adj* **1.** penetrating (*smell etc*). **2.** *contp.* pushy (*person*).

peng [pɛŋ] *int* bang!

penibel [pe'ni:bəl] *adj* fussy.

Penis ['pe:nɪs] *m* (-; -se) *anat.* penis.

Penizillin [penitsɪ'li:n] *n* (-s; -e) penicillin.

Penne ['pɛnə] *f* (-; -n) F **1.** school. **2.** *contp. sl.* dosshouse, *Am.* flophouse.

'**pennen** *v/i* (h) F *contp.* a) *sl.* (have a) kip, b) *fig.* sleep. '**Penner** *m* (-s; -) F *contp.* **1.** *sl.* dosser, bum. **2.** sleepyhead.

Pension [pã'zioːn] *f* (-; -en) **1.** (old-age) pension: *in ~ gehen* retire; *in ~ sein* be retired. **2.** boarding-house, private hotel. **3.** board. **Pensionär** [pãzio'nɛːr] *m* (-s; -e) pensioner. **pensionieren** [-'ni:rən] *v/t* (h) pension (off): *sich ~ lassen* retire. **pensio'niert** *adj* retired. **Pensio'nierung** *f* (-; -en) retirement. **Pensi'onsalter** *n* retirement age.

pensi'ons|berechtigt *adj* eligible for a pension. **~reif** *adj* F due for retirement.

Pensum ['pɛnzʊm] *n* (-s; Pensen) (allotted) task, *w.s.* workload.

Peperoni [pepe'ro:ni] *pl* red peppers.

Pepsin [pɛ'psi:n] *n* (-s; -e) 🌶, ♫ pepsin.

per [pɛr] *prep* per, by: *~ Adresse* care of (*abbr.* c/o); *~ Bahn* by train; → *du.*

Perestroika [pere'strɔyka] *f* (-; *no pl*) *pol.* perestroika.

perfekt [pɛr'fɛkt] *adj* **1.** perfect. **2.** F settled: *et. ~ machen* clinch s.th.

'**Perfekt** *n* (-s; -e) *ling.* perfect (tense).

Perfektion [pɛrfɛk'tsioːn] *f* (-; *no pl*) perfection. **perfektionieren** [-tsio'ni:rən] *v/t* (h) (make) perfect. **Perfektionist** [-tsio'nɪst] *m* (-en; -en) perfectionist.

perforieren [pɛrfo'i:rən] *v/t* (h) perforate.

Pergament [pɛrga'mɛnt] *n* (-[e]s; -e) parchment. **Perga'mentpa,pier** *n* greaseproof paper.

Periode [pe'rioːdə] *f* (-; -n) period (*a. physiol.*), ♫ cycle. **peri'odisch** [-dɪʃ] *adj* periodic(al), ♫ recurring (*decimal*).

Peripherie [perife'ri:] *f* (-; -n) periphery, *a.* outskirts (*of a town*).

Periskop [peri'skoːp] *n* (-s; -e) periscope.

Perle ['pɛrlə] *f* (-; -n) **1.** a) pearl, b) bead: F *~n vor die Säue werfen* cast (one's) pearls before swine. **2.** bead, drop. **3.** *fig.* jewel, gem.

perlen ['pɛrlən] *v/i* **1.** (h) *drink*: sparkle. **2.** (sn) *sweat, water*: trickle (down).

'**Perlen|kette** *f* pearl (*or* bead) necklace. **~schnur** *f* string of pearls (*or* beads).

'**Perlhuhn** *n* *zo.* guinea fowl.

'**Perlmuschel** *f* pearl oyster.

'**Perlmutt** [-mʊt] *n* (-s; *no pl*), '**Perlmutter** *f* (-; *no pl*) mother-of-pearl.

perplex [pɛr'plɛks] *adj* F bewildered.

Persenning [pɛr'zɛnɪŋ] *f* (-; -e[n]) ⚓ tarpaulin.

Perser ['pɛrzər] *m* (-s; -), **~teppich** *m* Persian carpet.

Persianer [pɛr'ziaːnər] *m* (-s; -) **1.** Per-

sian lamb(skin). **2.** → **Persi'anermantel** *m* Persian lamb coat.
persisch ['pɛrzɪʃ] *adj* Persian.
Person [pɛr'zo:n] *f* (-; -en) person, *thea.* character: *ling.* **erste ~** first person; **in eigener ~** personally; **ich für m-e ~** I for my part; **pro ~** each; **ein Tisch für sechs ~en** a table for six; **sie ist die Güte in ~** she is kindness personified; → **juristisch.**
Personal [pɛrzo'na:l] *n* (-s; *no pl*) personnel, staff: **zuwenig ~ haben** be understaffed. **~abbau** *m* personnel reduction. **~abˌteilung** *f* personnel department. **~akte** *f* personal file. **~ausweis** *m* identity card. **~chef** *m* personnel manager. **~comˌputer** *m* personal computer.
Personalien [pɛrzo'na:liən] *pl* particulars, personal data.
Perso'nalˌpoliˌtik *f* personnel policy. **~proˌnomen** *n ling.* personal pronoun.
personell [pɛrzo'nɛl] *adj* **1.** personal. **2.** personnel.
Per'sonenˌbeförderung *f* passenger transport. **~beschreibung** *f* personal description. **~gesellschaft** *f* ✝ partnership. **~kraftwagen** *m* (*abbr.* PKW) motor car, *Am. a.* auto(mobile). **~kreis** *m* circle. **~kult** *m* personality cult. **~schaden** *m* personal injury. **~stand** *m* marital status. **~wagen** *m* **1.** 🚋 passenger coach (*Am.* car). **2.** → **Personenkraftwagen. ~zug** *m* slow train.
personifizieren [pɛrzonifi'tsi:rən] *v/t* (h) personify.
persönlich [pɛr'zø:nlɪç] **I** *adj* personal. **II** *adv* personally, *a.* in person.
Per'sönlichkeit *f* (-; -en) personality: **e-e ~ des öffentlichen Lebens** a public figure.
Perspektive [pɛrspɛk'ti:və] *f* (-; -n) perspective, *fig. a.* a) prospect, b) point of view: **das eröffnet neue ~n** that opens up new vistas. **perspek'tivisch** [-vɪʃ] *adj* perspective, *drawing* in perspective.
Peru [pe'ru:] *n* (-s) Peru. **Peruaner** [pe'rŭa:nər] *m* (-s; -), **Peru'anerin** *f* (-; -nen), **peru'anisch** *adj* Peruvian.
Perücke [pe'rʏkə] *f* (-; -n) wig.
pervers [pɛr'vɛrs] *adj* perverse.
Perversität [pɛrvɛrzi'tɛ:t] *f* (-; -en) perversity. **pervertieren** [pɛrvɛr'ti:rən] *v/t* (h) pervert.

Peseta [pe'ze:ta] *f* (-; Peseten) peseta.
Pessar [pɛ'sa:r] *n* (-s; -e) 🩺 pessary.
Pessimismus [pɛsi'mɪsmʊs] *m* (-; *no pl*) pessimism. **Pessimist** [-'mɪst] *m* (-en; -en), **Pessi'mistin** *f* (-; -nen) pessimist. **pessi'mistisch** *adj* pessimistic.
Pest [pɛst] *f* (-; *no pl*) plague: **j-n hassen wie die ~** hate s.o.'s guts; F **stinken wie die ~** stink to high heaven.
Petersilie [pe:tər'zi:liə] *f* (-; -n) parsley.
Petition [peti'tsĭo:n] *f* (-; -en) petition.
Petroche'mie [petro-] *f* petrochemistry.
petro'chemisch *adj* (*a.* **~es Produkt**) petrochemical.
Petroleum [pe'tro:leʊm] *n* (-s; *no pl*) **1.** → **Erdöl. 2.** paraffin, *Am.* kerosene.
petto ['pɛto] *et. in ~ haben* have s.th. up one's sleeve.
Petze ['pɛtsə] *f* (-; -n) F *ped.* telltale, sneak. '**petzen** *v/i* (h) F *ped.* sneak.
Pfad [pfa:t] *m* (-[e]s; -e) path.
'**Pfadfinder** *m* boy scout. '**Pfadfinderin** *f* girl guide, *Am.* girl scout.
Pfaffe ['pfafə] *m* (-n; -n) F *contp.* cleric, Holy Joe.
Pfahl [pfa:l] *m* (-[e]s; ⁓e) a) stake, b) post, △ pile, c) pole. '**Pfahlbau** *m* (-[e]s; -ten) pile dwelling. '**Pfahlwurzel** *f* tap-root.
Pfand [pfant] *n* (-[e]s; ⁓er ['pfɛndər] *f*) security, b) pledge, *in games*: forfeit, c) deposit: **als ~ geben** *a. fig.* pledge; **~ zahlen** pay a deposit (**für** on).
pfändbar ['pfɛntba:r] *adj* distrainable.
'**Pfandbrief** *m* ✝ bond.
pfänden ['pfɛndən] *v/t* (h) distrain (up)on, seize, attach (*claim etc*).
'**Pfänderspiel** *n* (game of) forfeits.
'**Pfandflasche** *f* returnable bottle.
'**Pfandhaus** *n*, '**Pfandleihe** *f* (-; -n) pawnshop. '**Pfandleiher** *m* (-s; -), '**Pfandleiherin** *f* (-; -nen) pawnbroker.
'**Pfandschein** *m* pawn ticket.
'**Pfändung** *f* (-; -en) (*gen*) seizure (of), distraint (upon).
'**Pfändungsbefehl** *m* distress warrant.
Pfanne ['pfanə] *f* (-; -n) **1.** pan: F *j-n in die ~ hauen* a) clobber s.o., b) give s.o. a roasting. **2.** *anat.* socket. **3.** pantile.
'**Pfannkuchen** *m* pancake: *Berliner ~* doughnut.
'**Pfarramt** *n* rectory. '**Pfarrbezirk** *m* parish. **Pfarrei** [pfa'raɪ] *f* (-; -en) rectory, vicarage. **Pfarrer** ['pfarər] *m* (-s; -) a)

pastor, minister, b) (parish) priest. '**Pfarrerin** f (-; -nen) woman pastor.
'**Pfarr|gemeinde** f parish. **~haus** n rectory, vicarage. **~kirche** f parish church.

Pfau [pfaʊ] m (-[e]s; -e) zo. peacock.
'**Pfauenauge** n zo. peacock (butterfly).

Pfeffer ['pfɛfər] m (-s; -) **1.** pepper: → **Hase. 2.** F pep. **~gurke** f gastr. gherkin. **~kuchen** m gingerbread.

'**Pfefferminz** n (-es; -e) peppermint (drop). '**Pfefferminze** f **&** peppermint.

'**Pfeffermühle** f pepper mill.

pfeffern ['pfɛfərn] v/t (h) **1.** a. fig. pepper: → **gepfeffert. 2.** F chuck.

'**Pfefferstreuer** m pepper caster.

Pfeife ['pfaɪfə] f (-; -n) **1.** a) whistle, b) (organ) pipe: fig. **nach j-s ~ tanzen** dance to s.o.'s tune. **2.** pipe: **~ rauchen** a) smoke a pipe, b) be a pipe smoker. **3.** F idiot, dope.

pfeifen ['pfaɪfən] (pfiff, gepfiffen, h) **I** v/i **1.** whistle (**j-m** to s.o.), referee etc: blow the whistle, spectator: boo: F **ich pfeife auf das Geld** I don't give a damn about the money. **II** v/t **2.** whistle: F **ich werd' dir was ~**! to hell with you! **3.** sports: **ein Spiel ~** referee a match.

'**Pfeifen|kopf** m bowl. **~raucher** m pipe smoker. **~reiniger** m pipe cleaner. **~stiel** m pipe stem. **~stopfer** m tamper.

'**Pfeifkon,zert** n (hail of) catcalls.

Pfeil [pfaɪl] m (-[e]s; -e) a) arrow, b) dart: **mit ~ und Bogen** with bow and arrow.

Pfeiler ['pfaɪlər] m (-s; -) pillar (a. fig.), pier.

'**pfeilförmig** [-fœrmɪç] adj V-shaped.

'**pfeilgerade I** adj (as) straight as an arrow. **II** adv straight. '**pfeilschnell** adj and adv (as) quick as lightning.

'**Pfeilspitze** f arrowhead.

Pfennig ['pfɛnɪç] m (-s; -e) pfennig, fig. penny, Am. cent: F **jeden ~ umdrehen** count every penny; **k-n ~ wert** not worth a thing. **~absatz** m stiletto heel.

Pferch [pfɛrç] m (-[e]s; -e) pen, fold.
'**pferchen** v/t pen, cram (**in** acc into).

Pferd [pfe:rt] n (-[e]s; -e) **1.** horse: **zu ~e** on horseback; F fig. **das beste ~ im Stall** the number one; **aufs falsche ~ setzen** back the wrong horse; **das ~ beim Schwanze aufzäumen** put the cart before the horse; **mit ihr kann man ~e stehlen** she's a good sport. **2.** gym. (vaulting-)horse. **3.** chess: knight.

Pferde|äpfel ['pfe:rdə-] pl horse droppings. **~fleisch** n horse-meat. **~fuß** m fig. snag. **~koppel** f paddock. **~länge** f sports: **um zwei ~n** by two lengths. **~rennbahn** f racecourse, racetrack. **~rennen** n a) horse racing, b) horse race. **~schwanz** m **1.** zo. horse's tail. **2.** ponytail. **~stall** m stable. **~stärke** f (abbr. PS) horsepower (abbr. H.P.). **~wagen** m horse-drawn vehicle. **~zucht** f **1.** horse breeding. **2.** stud farm.

pfiff [pfɪf] pret of **pfeifen.**

Pfiff m (-[e]s; -e) **1.** whistle. **2.** F pep: **mit ~** film etc with a difference; **der Mantel hat ~** the coat's got real style; **der richtige ~** that extra something.

Pfifferling ['pfɪfərlɪŋ] m (-s; -e) chanterelle: **k-n ~ wert** not worth a damn.

'**pfiffig** adj smart. '**Pfiffigkeit** f (-; no pl) smartness. **Pfiffikus** ['pfɪfikʊs] m (-[ses]; -se) F smart fellow.

Pfingsten ['pfɪŋstən] n (-; -) Whitsun.
'**Pfingst|fest** n → **Pfingsten.** **~'montag** m Whit Monday. **~rose** f **&** peony. **~'sonntag** m Whitsunday.

Pfirsich ['pfɪrzɪç] m (-s; -e) peach.

Pflanze ['pflantsə] f (-; -n) **1.** plant. **2.** F type, character. '**pflanzen** v/t (h) plant.

'**Pflanzen|faser** f plant fibre (Am. fiber). **~fett** n vegetable fat. **~fresser** m zo. herbivore. **~kost** f vegetable foodstuffs. **~kunde** f botany. **~öl** n vegetable oil. **~reich** n (-[e]s; no pl) vegetable kingdom, flora. **~schutzmittel** n pesticide. **~welt** f (-; no pl) flora.

'**pflanzlich** adj plant, vegetable.

'**Pflanzung** f (-; -en) plantation.

Pflaster ['pflastər] n (-s; -) **1.** pavement: fig. **ein heißes (teures) ~** a dangerous (an expensive) place. **2.** **&** (sticking) plaster, Am. band-aid.

'**Pflastermaler(in** f) m pavement artist.
'**pflastern** v/t (h) **1.** pave. **2.** F **&** plaster.
'**Pflasterstein** m paving stone.

Pflaume ['pflaʊmə] f (-; -n) **1.** a) plum, b) prune. **2.** F contp. dope, twit.
'**Pflaumen|baum** m plum (tree). **~kuchen** m plum tart. **~mus** n plum jam.

Pflege ['pfle:gə] f (-; no pl) care, **&** nursing, **⊚** maintenance, servicing, fig. cultivation (of the arts etc): **in ~ geben** put into care; **in ~ nehmen** a) look after, take into care, b) foster (child).

⌢**bedürftig** *adj* in need of care. **⌣eltern** *pl* foster parents. **⌣fall** *m* nursing case. **⌣heim** *n* nursing home. **⌣kind** *n* foster child. ⌢**leicht** *adj* easy-care. **⌣mutter** *f* foster mother.

pflegen ['pfle:gən] (h) **I** *v/t* a) look after, care for, **⚘** *a.* nurse, b) *fig.* cultivate (*the arts, a friendship, etc*), c) keep *s.th.* in good condition, **☉** *a.* service, groom: → **gepflegt. II** *v/i* (*et.*) **zu tun ⌣** be in the habit of doing (s.th.), usually do (s.th.); *sie pflegte zu sagen* she used to say, she would say. **III** *sich ⌣* a) take care of one's appearance, b) look after o.s.

'**Pflegeperso,nal** *n* **⚘** nursing staff.

Pfleger ['pfle:gər] *m* (-s; -) **1.** **⚘** (male) nurse. **2.** ⚖ curator.

'**Pflegerin** *f* (-; -nen) **⚘** nurse.

'**Pflege|sohn** *m* foster son. **⌣stelle** *f* foster home. **⌣tochter** *f* foster daughter. **⌣vater** *m* foster father.

pfleglich ['pfle:klɪç] *adj* careful: *et. ⌣ behandeln* take good care of s.th.

'**Pflegschaft** *f* (-; -en) ⚖ curatorship.

Pflicht [pflɪçt] *f* (-; -en) duty: *die ⌣ ruft!* duty calls! **2.** → *Pflichtübung.*

'**pflichtbewußt** *adj* conscientious, dutiful. '**Pflichtbewußtsein** *n* conscientiousness, sense of duty.

'**Pflicht|eifer** *m* zeal. **⌣fach** *n ped.* compulsory subject. **⌣gefühl** *n* sense of duty. ⌢**gemäß I** *adj* dutiful, due. **II** *adv* duly. ⌢**getreu** *adj* dutiful. **⌣lek,türe** *f* required reading, set books. **⌣teil** *m, n* ⚖ legal portion. **⌣übung** *f sports:* compulsory (*or* set) exercise: *fig.* **e-e reine ⌣** purely a matter of duty. ⌢**vergessen** *adj* derelict of duty. **⌣versäumnis** *n* dereliction of duty. **⌣versicherung** *f* compulsory insurance. **⌣verteidiger** *m* ⚖ assigned counsel.

Pflock [pflɔk] *m* (-[e]s; �⌣e) **1.** peg. **2.** stake.

pflücken ['pflʏkən] *v/t* (h) pick.

Pflug [pflu:k] *m* (-[e]s; �⌣e), **pflügen** ['pfly:gən] *v/t, v/i* (h) plough, *Am.* plow.

Pforte ['pfɔrtə] *f* (-; -n) gate, door, *fig.* gateway.

Pförtner ['pfœrtnər] *m* (-s; -) gatekeeper, porter, *Am.* doorman. **⌣haus** *n* lodge. **⌣loge** *f* porter's office (*or* lodge).

Pfosten ['pfɔstən] *m* (-s; -) **1.** post. **2.** jamb.

Pfote ['pfo:tə] *f* (-; -n) *zo.* paw, F (*hand*) *a. sl.* mitt.

Pfropf [pfrɔpf] *m* (-[e]s; -e) **⚘** clot.

pfropfen ['pfrɔpfən] *v/t* (h) **1.** stopper. **2.** F cram. **3.** ⚘ graft.

'**Pfropfen** *m* (-s; -) stopper, cork, plug. '**Pfropf|messer** *n* grafter. **⌣reis** *n* ⚘ graft.

Pfründe ['pfrʏndə] *f* (-; -n) a) *eccl.* living, b) *fig.* sinecure.

Pfuhl [pfu:l] *m* (-[e]s; -e) murky pool.

pfui [pfʊi] *int* a) (for) shame!, *sports etc:* boo!, b) ugh!, *to child or dog:* no!: *⌣ Teufel!* ugh!, how disgusting!

Pfund [pfʊnt] *n* (-[e]s; -e) **1.** pound (*abbr.* lb.): *3 ⌣ Mehl* three pounds of flour. **2. ⌣** (*Sterling*) pound (sterling) (*abbr.* L).

'**pfundweise** *adj* and *adv* by the pound.

Pfusch [pfʊʃ] *m* (-[e]s; *no pl*), '**Pfuscharbeit** *f* F bad job, botch-up.

pfuschen ['pfʊʃən] *v/i, v/t* (h) F bungle: → *Handwerk.*

'**Pfuscher** *m* (-s; -) F bungler.

Pfusche'rei *f* (-; -en) F bungling.

Pfütze ['pfʏtsə] *f* (-; -n) puddle.

Phallus ['falʊs] *m* (-; Palli) phallus.

'**Phallussym,bol** *n* phallic symbol.

Phänomen [fɛno'me:n] *n* (-s; -e) phenomenon. **phänomenal** [fɛnome'na:l] *adj* phenomenal.

Phantasie [fanta'zi:] *f* (-; -n) **1.** a) imagination, b) mind: *schmutzige ⌣* dirty mind; *nur in s-r ⌣* only in his mind; *ohne ⌣* → *phantasielos.* **2.** *usu. pl* fantasy. **3.** ♪ fantasia. **phantasieren** [fanta'zi:rən] *v/i* (h) **1.** fantasize, dream. **2.** ⚘ be delirious, *a. fig.* rave (*von* about). **3.** ♪ improvise. **phanta'sievoll** *adj* imaginative.

Phantast [fan'tast] *m* (-en; -en) dreamer, visionary. **Phantasterei** [fantastə'rai] *f* (-; -en) fantasy. **phan'tastisch** [-tʃ] *adj* fantastic, F *a.* terrific, incredible.

Phantom [fan'to:m] *n* (-s; -e) phantom. **Phan'tombild** *n* identikit (*or* photofit) picture (*TM*).

'**Pharmaindu,strie** ['farma-] *f* pharmaceutical industry.

Pharmakologe [farmako'lo:gə] *m* (-n; -n) pharmacologist. **Pharmakologie** [-lo'gi:] *f* (-; *no pl*) pharmacology.

'**Pharmakon,zern** *m* pharmaceutical company.

Pharmazeut [farma'tsɔyt] *m* (-en; -en)

Pharma'zeutin *f* (-; -nen) pharmacist. **pharma'zeutisch** *adj* pharmaceutical.
Pharmazie [farma'tsi:] *f* (-; *no pl*) pharmacy.
Phase ['fa:zə] *f* (-; -n) *a.* ⚡ phase.
Philanthrop [filan'tro:p] *m* (-en; -en) philanthropist. **Philanthropie** [filantro'pi:] *f* (-; *no pl*) philanthropism. **philan'thropisch** *adj* philanthropic.
Philatelie [filate'li:] *f* (-; *no pl*) philately.
Philatelist [-'lɪst] *m* (-en; -en) philatelist.
Philharmonie [filharmo'ni:] *f* (-; -n) philharmonic orchestra (*or* society).
Philologe [filo'lo:gə] *m* (-n; -n) teacher (*or* scholar) of language and literature, *Am.* philologist. **Philologie** [-lo'gi:] *f* (-; -n) study of language and literature, *Am.* philology. **philo'logisch** [-gɪʃ] *adj* language and literature ..., *Am.* philological.
Philosoph [filo'zo:f] *m* (-en; -en) philosopher. **Philosophie** [-zo'fi:] *f* (-; -n) philosophy. **philosophieren** [-zo'fi:rən] *v/i* (h) philosophize. **philo'sophisch** [-fɪʃ] *adj* philosophic(al).
Phlegma ['flɛgma] *n* (-s; *no pl*) phlegm. **Phlegmatiker** [flɛ'gma:tikər] *m* (-s; -) phlegmatic person. **phleg'matisch** [-tɪʃ] *adj* phlegmatic.
Phobie [fo'bi:] *f* (-; -n) *psych.* phobia.
Phon [fo:n] *n* (-s; -s) *phys.* phon: **50** ~ **50** phons.
Phonem [fo'ne:m] *n* (-s; -e) phoneme.
Phonetik [fo'ne:tɪk] *f* (-; *no pl*) phonetics. **Pho'netiker** [-tikər] *m* (-s; -) phonetician. **pho'netisch** [-tɪʃ] *adj* phonetic.
Phonotypistin [fonoty'pɪstɪn] *f* (-; -nen) audio typist.
Phosphat [fɔs'fa:t] *n* (-[e]s; -e) 🜨 phosphate.
Phosphor ['fɔsfɔr] *m* (-s; *no pl*) 🜨 phosphorus.
phosphoreszieren [fɔsforɛs'tsi:rən] *v/i* (h) phosphoresce. **~d** phosphorescent.
Photo(...) → *Foto(...)*.
Photoche'mie [foto-] *f* photochemistry.
Photosyn'these *f* photosynthesis.
Phrase ['fra:zə] *f* (-; -n) phrase (*a.* ♪), *contp. a.* cliché, *pol.* catchphrase: F **~n dreschen** talk in platitudes.
'Phrasendrescher *m* F phrasemonger.
'phrasenhaft *adj* empty, meaningless.
Physik [fy'zi:k] *f* (-; *no pl*) physics.
physikalisch [fyzi'ka:lɪʃ] *adj* physical.

Physiker ['fy:zikər] *m* (-s; -) physicist.
Physikum ['fy:zikɔm] *n* (-s; -ka) preliminary (medical) examination.
Physiognomie [fyziogno'mi:] *f* (-; -n) physiognomy.
Physiologie [fyzio'lo:gi:] *f* (-; *no pl*) physiology. **physiologisch** [fyzio'lo:gɪʃ] *adj* physiological.
Physiothera'peut(in *f)* *m* [fyzio-] 🜨 physiotherapist.
Physiothera'pie *f* physiotherapy.
physisch ['fy:zɪʃ] *adj* physical.
Pianist [pia'nɪst] *m* (-en; -en), **Pia'nistin** *f* (-; -nen) pianist.
Pickel¹ ['pɪkəl] *m* (-s; -) a) ⊗ pick(axe), b) ice-pick.
Pickel² *m* (-s; -) 🜨 pimple, spot.
pick(e)lig ['pɪk(ə)lɪç] *adj* pimply, spotty.
picken ['pɪkən] *v/t, v/i* (h) peck (*nach* at).
Picknick ['pɪknɪk] *n* (-s; -s) picnic.
'picknicken *v/i* (h) (have a) picnic.
pieken ['pi:kən] *v/t, v/i* (h) F prick.
'piek'fein *adj* F posh, very smart.
piepen ['pi:pən] *v/i* (h) *bird:* cheep, chirp, *mouse:* squeak, ⚡ bleep: F *bei dir piept's wohl?* are you off your rocker?
piepsen ['pi:psən] → *piepen*.
Pier [pi:r] *f* (-; -s) ⚓ jetty, pier.
Pietät [pie'tɛ:t] *f* (-; *no pl*) reverence: *aus* ~ out of respect (*gegenüber* of).
pie'tätlos *adj* irreverent.
pie'tätvoll *adj* reverent.
Pigment [pɪ'gmɛnt] *n* (-[e]s; -e) pigment.
Pik¹ [pi:k] *m* F *e-n* ~ *auf j-n haben* have it in for s.o.
Pik² *n* (-s; -s) *cards:* spade(s).
pikant [pi'kant] *adj a. fig.* piquant, spicy.
Pike ['pi:kə] *f* F *et. von der* ~ *auf lernen* learn s.th. from the bottom up.
pikiert [pi'ki:rt] *adj fig.* piqued (*über acc* about).
Pikkolo ['pɪkolo] *m* (-s; -s) **1.** apprentice waiter. **2.** F champagne miniature.
'Pikkoloflöte *f* ♪ piccolo.
Pilger ['pɪlgər] (-s; -) pilgrim. **'Pilgerfahrt** *f* pilgrimage. **'pilgern** *v/i* (sn) **1.** go on a pilgrimage. **2.** F wander.
Pille ['pɪlə] *f* (-; -n) pill: F *die* ~ *nehmen* be on the pill; *fig. e-e bittere* ~ a bitter pill (to swallow).
'Pillenknick *m* F sudden drop in birthrates. **'Pillenschachtel** *f* pillbox.
Pilot [pi'lo:t] *m* (-en; -en) **1.** ✈ pilot. **2.** (racing) driver. **~film** *m* pilot (film).

~pro,jekt n pilot project. **~sendung** f pilot broadcast.

Pilz [pɪlts] m (-es; -e) a) fungus (a. ☀), b) mushroom, c) toadstool: **~e suchen (gehen)** go mushrooming; **wie ~e aus dem Boden schießen** mushroom (up).

'Pilzvergiftung f mushroom poisoning.

pingelig ['pɪŋəlɪç] adj, **'Pingeligkeit** f (-; no pl) F nitpicking.

Pinguin ['pɪŋɡuːin] m (-s; -e) penguin.

Pinie ['piːnĭə] f (-; -n) ♣ (stone) pine.

Pinkel ['pɪŋkəl] m (-s; -) F **feiner ~** toff.

'pinkeln v/i (h) F (**~ gehen** go for a) pee.

Pinne ['pɪnə] f (-; -n) ♣ helm.

'Pinnwand f pinboard.

Pinscher ['pɪnʃər] m (-s; -) zo. pinscher.

Pinsel ['pɪnzəl] m (-s; -) brush.

'pinseln v/i, v/t (h) paint (a. ☀).

'Pinselstrich m stroke of the brush.

Pinzette [pɪn'tsɛtə] f (-; -n) tweezers.

Pionier [pĭoˈniːr] m (-s; -e) **1.** ✗ engineer. **2.** fig. pioneer. **~arbeit** f (-; no pl) pioneering work: **~ leisten für a.** pioneer s.th. **~geist** m pioneering spirit.

Pipette [pi'pɛtə] f (-; -n) 🜆 pipette.

Pipi [pi'pi:] n (-s; no pl) F **~ machen** wee.

Pirat [pi'ra:t] m (-en; -en) pirate.

Pi'ratensender m radio: pirate station.

Pirouette [pi'rŭɛtə] f (-; -n) pirouette.

Pirsch [pɪrʃ] f (-; no pl) stalk, still hunt: **auf die ~ gehen** go (deer-)stalking.

'pirschen v/i (h) **~ auf** (acc) stalk.

Pisse ['pɪsə] f (-; no pl) V piss.

'pissen v/i (h) V piss.

Pistazie [pɪs'ta:tsĭə] f (-; -n) pistachio.

Piste ['pɪstə] f (-; -n) **1.** a) (racing) track, course, b) piste, ski-run. **2.** ✈ runway.

'Pistenrowdy m terror of the slopes.

Pistole [pɪs'to:lə] f (-; -n) pistol: **mit vorgehaltener ~** at pistol-point; fig. **j-m die ~ auf die Brust setzen** hold a pistol to s.o.'s head; **wie aus der ~ geschossen** like a shot.

Pi'stolentasche f holster.

Pizza ['pɪtsa] f (-; -s) gastr. pizza.

Pizzeria [pɪtse'ri:a] f (-; -s) pizzeria.

Plackerei [plakə'raɪ] f (-; -en) F grind.

plädieren [plɛ'di:rən] v/i (h) 🜨 plead (**für, auf** acc for). **Plädoyer** [plɛdŏa'je:] n (-s; -s) final speech, fig. plea.

Plage ['pla:ɡə] f (-; -n) a) trouble, bother, b) nuisance, a. bibl. plague.

plagen ['pla:ɡən] (h) **I** v/t a) trouble, worry, b) torment, harass, F plague

pester (**mit** with requests etc): **geplagt von** troubled by. **II sich ~** toil away, take pains (**mit** with).

Plagiat [pla'ɡĭa:t] n (-[e]s; -e) plagiarism.

plagiieren [plaɡi'i:rən] v/i, v/t (h) plagiarize.

Plakat [pla'ka:t] n (-[e]s; -e) a) poster, b) placard. **plakatieren** [plaka'ti:rən] v/t (h) placard. **plakativ** [plaka'ti:f] adj fig. slogan-like, graphic.

Plakette [pla'kɛtə] f (-; -n) badge.

plan [pla:n] adj plane, level.

Plan m (-[e]s; -e) **1.** plan, a. schedule, a. project, scheme (a. b.s.): **e-n ~ fassen** make a plan; **Pläne schmieden** make plans; **was steht heute auf dem ~?** what's on today? **2.** a) plan, a. design, b) diagram. **3.** map.

Plane ['pla:nə] f (-; -n) tarpaulin.

planen ['pla:nən] v/t (h) plan, a. schedule, a. design. **Planer** m (-s; -) planner.

Planet [pla'ne:t] m (-en; -en) planet.

planetarisch [plane'ta:rɪʃ] adj planetary. **Planetarium** [plane'ta:rĭom] n (-s; -rien) planetarium.

planieren [pla'ni:rən] v/t (h) level, grade. **Pla'nierraupe** f ⚙ bulldozer.

Planke ['plaŋkə] f (-; -n) plank, board.

Plankton ['plaŋktɔn] n (-s; no pl) plankton.

'planlos adj without plan, aimless, unsystematic. **'Planlosigkeit** f (-; no pl) aimlessness, lack of system.

'planmäßig I adj **1.** planned, systematic. **2.** scheduled (arrival, flight, etc). **II** adv as planned, according to plan (or schedule), arrive etc on schedule.

'Planschbecken n paddle pond.

planschen ['planʃən] v/i (h) splash (about).

'Planstelle f permanent post.

Plantage [plan'ta:ʒə] f (-; -n) plantation.

'Planung f (-; -en) **1.** → **Plan 2.** planning: **in der ~** → **'Planungsstadium** n **im ~** in the planning stage.

'planvoll adj methodical, systematic.

'Planwirtschaft f planned economy.

'Plappermaul n F chatterbox.

plappern ['plapərn] v/i, v/i (h) F chatter.

plärren ['plɛrən] v/i (h) a) blubber, cry, b) bawl, c) radio etc: blare.

Plasma ['plasma] n (-s; -men) plasma.

Plastik[1] ['plastɪk] f (-; -en) **1.** sculpture. **2.** 🜨 plastic surgery.

plombieren

'**Plastik²** *n* (-s; *no pl*) plastic.
'**Plastik|bombe** *f* plastic bomb. **~folie** *f*
polythene sheet. **~geld** *n* F plastic
money. **~tüte** *f* plastic bag.
plastisch ['plastɪʃ] *adj* **1.** plastic. **2.** *fig.*
vivid, graphic. **3. ~e Chirurgie** plastic
surgery; *Facharzt für ~e Chirurgie*
plastic surgeon.
Platane [pla'ta:nə] *f* (-; -n) plane (tree).
Plateau [pla'to:] *n* (-s; -s) plateau.
Platin ['pla:ti:n] *n* (-s; *no pl*) platinum.
platonisch [pla'to:nɪʃ] *adj* a) Platonic, b)
platonic.
platsch *int*, **platschen** ['platʃən] *v/i* (h,
sn) F splash.
plätschern ['plɛtʃərn] *v/i* (h) ripple,
brook etc: murmur, *waves*: lap.
platt [plat] *adj* **1.** a) flat, b) level: **~ drük-
ken** flatten; F **e-n Platten haben** have a
flat tyre (*Am.* tire). **2.** *fig.* trite, banal. **3.**
F **~ sein** be flabbergasted.
Platt *n* (-[e]s; *no pl*) Low German.
'**plattdeutsch** *adj*, '**Plattdeutsch(e)** *n*
Low German.
Platte ['platə] *f* (-; -n) **1.** a) (stone) slab,
b) flag(stone), c) board, d) panel, e) tile,
f) sheet (*of glass, metal*). **2.** (rock) ledge.
3. (table) top. **4.** hotplate. **5.** dish: *kalte
~* cold cuts. **6.** record, disc, *Am.* disk: F
fig. die ~ kenn' ich! I know that line! **7.**
(dental) plate. **8.** F bald pate.
'**Platten|album** *n* record album. **~hülle** *f*
record sleeve. **~laufwerk** *n* computer:
disk drive. **~spieler** *m* record player.
~teller *m* turntable. **~wechsler** *m* record changer.
'**Plattform** *f* a. *pol.* platform.
'**Plattfuß** *m* **1.** flatfoot. **2.** F *mot.* flat.
'**plattfüßig** [-fy:sɪç] *adj* flat-footed.
'**Plattheit** *f* (-; -en) **1.** *no pl* a) flatness, b)
fig. triteness. **2.** platitude.
plattieren [pla'ti:rən] *v/t* (h) ⊛ plate.
Platz [plats] *m* (-es; ⁔e) **1.** *no pl* room,
space: *~ machen* (für for) a) make
room, b) make way (*a. fig.*); *~ sparen*
save space; *fig. ~ greifen* spread, arise.
2. place, spot, position, (*camp, building, etc*) site: *fig. fehl am ~e sein* be out
of place. **3.** (public) square. **4.** seat: *~
nehmen* take a seat, sit down. **5.**
(sports) field, (tennis) court, (golf)
course: F *j-n vom ~ fegen* play s.o. into
the ground; *j-n vom ~ verweisen* send
s.o. off; *auf eigenem (gegnerischem)*

~ spielen play at home (out of town).
6. *sports*: place: *auf ~ drei* in third
place; → *belegen* 4.
'**Platzangst** *f* **1.** *psych.* agoraphobia. **2.** F
claustrophobia.
'**Platzanweiser** *m* (-s; -) usher. '**Platzanweiserin** *f* (-; -nen) usherette.
Plätzchen ['plɛtsçən] *n* (-s; -) **1.** little
place, spot. **2.** biscuit, *Am.* cookie.
platzen ['platsən] *v/i* (sn) **1.** burst, *bomb
etc*: a. explode: *fig.* **vor Wut ~** explode
(with rage), blow up; **vor Neid ~** be
bursting with envy; F *ins Zimmer ~*
burst into the room; **~ Kragen, Naht**.
2. F *fig.* come to nothing, *sl.* bust, go
phut, *plan etc*: fall through, *engagement*: be broken off, **↑ cheque etc**:
bounce: *~ lassen* bust up (*gang etc*).
'**Platz|karte** *f* reservation card. **~man-
gel** *m* lack of space. **~pa,trone** *f* blank
cartridge. **⊝raubend** *adj* space-con-
suming. **~regen** *m* cloudburst. **⊝spa-
rend** *adj* space-saving. **~verweis** *m*
sports: *e-n ~ erhalten* be sent off.
~wunde *f* laceration.
Plauderei [plaudə'raɪ] *f* (-; -en) chat.
'**Plauderer** *m* (-s; -) conversationalist.
plaudern ['plaudərn] *v/i* (h) a) (have a)
chat, b) blab; *~ Schule*.
plausibel [plau'zi:bəl] *adj* plausible: *j-m
et. ~ machen* make s.th. clear to s.o.
plazieren [pla'tsi:rən] *v/t* (h) *place*: *sich
~* position o.s.; *sports*: *sich als Dritter ~*
be placed third.
Pla'zierung *f* (-; -en) *sports*: place.
Plebiszit [plebɪs'tsi:t] *n* (-[e]s; -e) plebis-
cite.
pleite ['plaitə] *adj* F **~ sein** be broke.
'**Pleite** *f* (-; -n) F **1.** bankruptcy: *~ machen* go bust. **2.** *fig.* flop: *so 'ne ~!*
what a frost!
Plenarsaal [ple'na:r-] *m* *parl.* (plenary)
assembly room.
Ple'narsitzung *f* plenary session.
Plenum ['ple:nʊm] *n* (-s; *no pl*) plenum.
Pleuelstange ['plɔyəl-] *f* ⊛ connecting
rod.
Plissee [plɪ'se:] *n* (-s; -s) pleats.
Plis'seerock *m* pleated skirt.
plissieren [plɪ'si:rən] *v/t* (h) pleat.
Plombe ['plɔmbə] *f* (-; -n) **1.** ⊛ (lead)
seal. **2.** ⚕ filling.
plombieren [plɔm'bi:rən] *v/t* (h) **1.** seal
(with lead). **2.** fill (*tooth*).

plötzlich ['plœtslıç] **I** *adj* sudden. **II** *adv* suddenly: *ganz ~* all of a sudden.
plump [plʊmp] *adj* **1.** a) plump, b) clumsy. **2.** *fig.* clumsy, tactless, gross (*lie etc*), crude (*joke etc*): *plump-vertraulich* chummy.
'**Plumpheit** *f* (-; *no pl*) **1.** plumpness. **2.** *fig.* clumsiness, grossness, *etc.*
plumps [plʊmps] *int*, **Plumps** *m* (-es; -e) F thud. '**plumpsen** *v/i* (sn) F thud.
Plunder ['plʊndər] *m* (-s; *no pl*) F junk, rubbish.
'**Plünderer** *m* (-s; -) looter.
plündern ['plʏndərn] *v/t, v/i* (h) plunder, loot, pillage, F raid (*fridge etc*).
'**Plünderung** *f* (-; -en) plundering, looting, pillage.
Plural ['plu:ra:l] *m* (-s; *no pl*) *ling.* plural (number). **Pluralismus** [plura'lɪsmʊs] *m* (-; *no pl*) pluralism. **plura'listisch** [-tɪʃ] *adj* pluralistic.
plus [plʊs] *prep* plus.
Plus *n* (-; -) **1.** & plus sign. **2.** a) surplus, b) profit. **3.** *fig.* plus, asset, advantage.
Plüsch [ply:ʃ] *m* (-[e]s; -e) plush.
'**Plüschtier** *n* cuddly toy.
'**Pluspunkt** *m* **1.** credit point. **2.** *fig.* plus, asset, advantage.
Plusquamperfekt ['plʊskvampɛrfɛkt] *n* (-s; -e) pluperfect (tense), past perfect.
'**Pluszeichen** *n* & plus sign.
pneumatisch [pnɔʏ'ma:tɪʃ] *adj* pneumatic.
Po [po:] *m* (-s; -s) F bottom, bum.
Pöbel ['pø:bəl] *m* (-s; *no pl*) rabble.
'**pöbelhaft** *adj* vulgar.
pochen ['pɔxən] *v/i* (h) **1.** (*an dat* at) knock, rap. **2.** *blood etc:* throb, *heart: a.* beat. **3.** *fig. ~ auf* (*acc*) insist on.
pochieren [pɔ'ʃiːrən] *v/t* (h) poach.
Pocke ['pɔkə] *f* (-; -n) 🌹 **1.** pock. **2.** *pl* smallpox.
'**Pockenimpfung** *f* 🌹 (smallpox) vaccination. '**Pockennarbe** *f* pockmark.
'**pockennarbig** *adj* pockmarked, pitted.
Podest [po'dɛst] *n, m* (-[e]s; -e) platform, *fig.* pedestal.
Podium ['po:diʊm] *n* (-s; -dien) rostrum, platform.
'**Podiumsdiskussi̦on** *f*, '**Podiumsgespräch** *n* panel discussion.
Poesie [poe'zi:] *f* (-; *no pl*) poetry.
Poet [po'e:t] *m* (-en; -en) poet.
Poetin [po'e:tɪn] *f* (-; -nen) poetess.

poetisch [po'e:tɪʃ] *adj* poetic(al).
Pogrom [po'gro:m] *n* (-s; -e) pogrom.
Pointe ['põɛ̃:tə] *f* (-; -n) point, *a.* punch line. **pointiert** [põɛ̃'ti:rt] *adj* pointed.
Pokal [po'ka:l] *m* (-s; -e) cup (*a. sports*), goblet. **~endspiel** *n* cup final. **~sieger** *m* cup winner. **~spiel** *n* cup tie.
Pökelfleisch ['pø:kəl-] *n* salt meat.
pökeln ['pø:kəln] *v/t* (h) salt.
pokern ['po:kərn] *v/i* (h) play poker.
'**Pokerspiel** *n* game of poker.
Pol [po:l] *m* (-s; -e) pole, ⚡ *a.* terminal: *fig. ruhender ~* stabilizing element.
polar [po'la:r] *adj*, **Po'lar...** polar.
polarisieren [polari'zi:rən] *v/t* (*a. sich ~*) (h) polarize.
Polarität [polari'tɛ:t] *f* (-; -en) polarity.
Po'larkreis *m* **nördlicher** (**südlicher**) **~** Arctic (Antarctic) Circle.
Po'larlicht *n* **nördliches** (**südliches**) **~** northern (southern) lights.
Po'larstern *m* Pole Star.
Pole ['po:lə] *m* (-n; -n) Pole.
Polemik [po'le:mɪk] *f* (-; -en) polemic(s).
polemisch [po'le:mɪʃ] *adj* polemic.
polemisieren [pole:mi'zi:rən] *v/i* (h) polemize.
polen ['po:lən] *v/t* (h) ⚡ pole.
'**Polen** (-s) Poland.
Police [po'li:sə] *f* (-; -n) policy.
Polier [po'li:r] *m* (-s; -e) foreman.
polieren [po'li:rən] *v/t* (h) polish.
Poliklinik ['po:li-] *f* outpatients' clinic.
Polin ['po:lɪn] *f* (-; -nen) Pole, Polish woman.
Po'litbü̦ro [po'li:t-] *n* politburo.
Politesse [poli'tɛsə] *f* (-; -n) (woman) traffic warden, F meter maid.
Politik [poli'ti:k] *f* (-; -en) **1.** politics: *in der ~* in politics; *in die ~ gehen* go into politics; *über ~ reden* talk politics. **2.** policy. **Politiker** [po'li:tikər] *m* (-s; -), **Po'litikerin** *f* (-; -nen) politician.
Politikum [po'li:tikʊm] *n* (-s; -ka) political issue.
politisch [po'li:tɪʃ] *adj* **1.** political: *~er Berater* policy adviser; *er ist ~ tätig* he is in politics; *~ interessiert sein* be politically minded. **2.** politic.
politisieren [politi'zi:rən] (h) **I** *v/i* talk politics. **II** *v/t* politicize. **Politi'sierung** *f* (-; -en) politicization.
Politologe [polito'lo:gə] *m* (-n; -n) polit-

ical scientist. **Politologie** [politolo'gi:] *f* (-; *no pl*) political science.
Politur [poli'tu:r] *f* (-; -en) polish.
Polizei [poli'tsai] *f* (-; -en) police: *die ~ rufen* call the police; F *er ist bei der ~* he is in the police force. **~aufgebot** *n* police detachment. **~aufsicht** *f* police supervision. **~beamte** *m* police officer. **~behörde** *f* police (authorities). **~dienststelle** *f* police station. **~einsatz** *m* police operation. **~es,korte** *f* police motorcade. **~funk** *m* police radio. **~hund** *m* police dog. **~knüppel** *m* truncheon, *Am.* billy. **~kommis,sar** *m* police inspector. **~kon,trolle** *f* police check.

poli'zeilich *adj and adv* a) (of the) police, b) by the police.

Poli'zei|präsi,dent *m* chief of police, *Br.* chief constable. **~prä,sidium** *n* police headquarters. **~re,vier** *n* **1.** (police) district, *Am.* precinct. **2.** police station, *Am.* station house. **~schüler** *m* police cadet. **~schutz** *m* police protection. **~staat** *m* police state. **~streife** *f* a) police patrol, b) patrolman. **~stunde** *f* closing time. **~wache** *f* police station, *Am.* station house.

Polizist [poli'tsɪst] *m* (-en; -en) policeman, constable.
Poli'zistin *f* (-; -nen) policewoman.
Pollen ['pɔlən] *m* (-s; -) 🌿 pollen.
polnisch ['pɔlnɪʃ] *adj* Polish.
Polo ['po:lo] *n* (-s; -s) *sports:* polo.
'Polohemd *n* polo (shirt).
Polster ['pɔlstər] *n* (-s; -) **1.** a) upholstery, b) cushion. **2.** pad(ding). **3.** F flab, layer of fat. **4.** *fig.* bolster, reserves.
'Polsterer *m* (-s; -) upholsterer.
'Polster|garni,tur *f* three-piece suite. **~möbel** *pl* upholstered furniture.
polstern ['pɔlstərn] *v/t* (h) a) upholster, b) pad: F *gut gepolstert* well padded.
'Polsterpflanze *f* cushion plant.
'Polstersessel *m* easy chair, armchair.
'Polsterstuhl *m* upholstered chair.
'Polsterung *f* (-; -en) **1.** upholstery. **2.** padding.
'Polterabend *m* eve-of-the-wedding party. **poltern** ['pɔltərn] *v/i* (h) **1.** make a racket, crash about. **2.** bluster.
Polyamid [poly'a'mi:t] *n* (-[e]s; -e) polyamide.
Polyäthy'len *n* polythene.

polygam [poly'ga:m] *adj* polygamous.
polyglott [poly'glɔt] *adj* polyglott.
Polyp [po'ly:p] *m* (-en; -en) **1.** *zo.* polyp. **2.** 🅰 polypus, *pl* adenoids. **3.** F cop (*sl.*).
polyphon [poly'fo:n] *adj* ♪ polyphonic.
Polytechnikum [poly'tɛçnikʊm] *n* (-s; -ka) polytechnic.
Pomade [po'ma:də] *f* (-; -n) pomade.
Pommes frites [pɔm'frit] *pl* chips, *Am.* French fries.
Pomp [pɔmp] *m* (-[e]s; *no pl*) pomp.
pompös [pɔm'pø:s] *adj* pompous.
Pontifikat [pɔntifi'ka:t] *n* (-[e]s; -e) pontificate.
Pontius ['pɔntsiʊs] *von ~ zu Pilatus laufen* F run from pillar to post.
Ponton [pɔ̃'tõ:] *m* (-s; -s) pontoon.
Pony¹ ['pɔni:] *n* (-s; -s) *zo.* pony.
'Pony² *m* (-s; -s) fringe, *Am.* bangs.
Popel ['po:pəl] *m* (-s; -) F bogey.
'popelig *adj* F piffling, miserable.
Popelin [popə'li:n] *m* (-s; -e) poplin.
popeln ['po:pəln] *v/i* (h) F pick one's nose.
Popgruppe ['pɔp-] *f* pop group.
'Popmu,sik *f* pop music.
Popo [po'po:] *m* (-s; -s) F bottom, bum.
populär [popu'lɛ:r] *adj* popular.
popularisieren [populari'zi:rən] *v/t* (h) popularize. **Popularität** [populari'tɛ:t] *f* (-; *no pl*) popularity.
Pore ['po:rə] *f* (-; -n) pore.
Porno ['pɔrno] *m* (-s; -s), **'Pornofilm** *m* porn (or blue) movie.
Pornographie [pɔrnogra'fi:] *f* (-; *no pl*) pornography. **pornographisch** [pɔrno'gra:fɪʃ] *adj* pornographic.
'Pornoheft *n* porn (or girlie) magazine.
Porree ['pɔre] *m* (-s; -s) 🌿 leek.
Portal [pɔr'ta:l] *n* (-s; -e) portal.
Portemonnaie [pɔrtmɔ'nɛ:] *n* (-s; -s) purse.
Portier [pɔr'tie:] *m* (-s; -s) **1.** porter. **2.** → *Pförtner.*
Portion [pɔr'tsio:n] *f* (-; -en) a) portion, b) helping, c) *pot of tea etc:* F *fig.* **halbe ~** shrimp; *e-e gehörige ~ Frechheit* a good deal of impudence.
Porto ['pɔrto] *n* (-s; -s, Porti) postage.
'portofrei *adj* postage paid.
'Portokasse *f* 🅲 petty cash.
Porträt [pɔr'trɛ:] *n* (-s; -s) portrait.
porträtieren [pɔrtrɛ'ti:rən] *v/t* (h) *j-n ~* paint s.o.'s portrait, *fig.* portray s.o.

Por'trätmaler(in *f)* *m* portraitist.

Portugal ['portugal] *n* (-s) Portugal.

Portugiese [portu'giːzə] *m* (-n; -n), **Por-tu'giesin** *f* (-; -nen), **portu'giesisch** *adj* Portuguese.

Portwein ['port-] *m* port.

Porzellan [portse'laːn] *n* (-s; -e) porcelain, china: F *fig.* **~ zerschlagen** do a lot of damage. **~laden** *m* china shop: → **Elefant**. **~waren** *pl* chinaware.

Posaune [po'zaʊnə] *f* (-; -n) **1.** (**~ blasen** play the) trombone. **2.** *fig.* trumpet.

Posaunist [pozaʊ'nɪst] *m* (-en; -en) trombonist.

Pose ['poːzə] *f* (-; -n) pose, *fig. a.* air, act.

posieren [po'ziːrən] *v/i* (h) pose (**als** as).

Position [pozi'tsioːn] *f* (-; -en) **1.** position, *sports: a.* place: *fig.* **~ beziehen** take one's stand. **2.** ✝ item.

positiv ['poːzitiːf] **I** *adj* positive, *a.* affirmative. **II** *adv* F for certain.

Positur [pozi'tuːr] *f* (-; -en) posture: *sich in ~ setzen* strike an attitude.

Posse ['posə] *f* (-; -n) farce, burlesque.

possessiv ['posɛsiːf] *adj ling.* possessive.

Posses'sivpro,nomen *n* possessive pronoun.

possierlich [po'siːrlɪç] *adj* droll, funny.

Post [post] *f* (-; *no pl*) *a)* post, mail, *b)* postal service, *c)* post office: *mit der ~* by post, by mail; *mit gleicher* (*or ge-trennter*) *~* under separate cover; *mit der ~ schicken* post, *Am.* mail; *ist ~ für mich da?* are there any letters for me?

postalisch [pos'taːlɪʃ] *adj* postal.

'**Post|amt** *n* post office. **~anschrift** *f* postal (*or* mailing) address. **~anwei-sung** *f* postal (*or* money) order. **~auto** *n* post-office van, mail van. **~bar-scheck** *m* postal cheque (*Am.* check). **~beamte** *m* post-office (*Am.* postal) clerk. **~bote** *m* postman, *Am.* mailman. **~botin** *f* postwoman. **~bus** *m* post bus.

Posten ['postən] *m* (-s; -) **1.** ✕ post: *fig.* *auf dem ~ sein a)* be on one's toes, *b)* be in good shape; *nicht* (*ganz*) *auf dem ~ sein* be a bit under the weather; → *beziehen* 3, *verloren* II. **2.** ✕ guard, sentry: *~ stehen* be on guard, stand sentry. **3.** post, position, job. **4.** ✝ *a)* lot, *b)* item, *c)* entry.

'**Post|fach** *n* post-office box, PO box. **~flugzeug** *n* mail plane. **~gebühr** *f* postage, *pl a.* postal charges. **~geheim-**

~nis *n* secrecy of the mails. **~giroamt** *n* postal giro office. **~girokonto** *n* (post--office) giro account, *Br.* national giro account.

posthum [pos'tuːm] *adj* posthumous.

postieren [pos'tiːrən] *v/t* (h) place.

'**Post|karte** *f* postcard, *Am.* postal card. **~lagernd** *adj* and *adv* poste restante, *Am.* (in care of) general delivery. **~leit-zahl** *f* postcode, *Am.* zip code. **~mi,nister** *m* postmaster general. **~scheck** *m* (post-office) giro cheque (*Am.* check). **~sparbuch** *n* post-office savings book. **~sparkasse** *f* post-office savings bank. **~stempel** *m* postmark. **~ver-sandhaus** *n* mail-order house. **~wa-gen** *m* 🚂 mail van, *Am.* postal car. **~wendend** *adv* by return (of post), by return mail, F *fig.* right away. **~wert-zeichen** *n* (postage) stamp. **~wurfsen-dung** *f* direct mail. **~zug** *m* mail train. **~zustellung** *f* postal delivery.

potent [po'tɛnt] *adj* potent.

Potential [potɛn'tsiaːl] *n* (-s; -e), **poten-tiell** [potɛn'tsiɛl] *adj* potential.

Potenz [po'tɛnts] *f* (-; -en) **1.** *no pl* potency. **2.** 🅐 power: *zweite ~* square; *dritte ~* cube. **3.** *fig.* power, strength.

potenzieren [potɛn'tsiːrən] *v/t* (h) **1.** 🅐 raise to a higher power. **2.** *fig.* magnify.

Potpourri ['potpuri] *n* (-s; -s) ♪ potpour-ri, medley.

Präambel [prɛ'ʔambəl] *f* (-; -n) preamble.

Pracht [praxt] *f* (-; *no pl*) splendo(u)r: F *es war e-e wahre ~* it was just great.

'**Prachtexem,plar** *n* F splendid speci-men, *a.* beauty.

prächtig ['prɛçtɪç] *adj* **1.** *a)* splendid, magnificent, *b)* glorious (*weather*). **2.** F *fig.* great, super.

'**Prachtkerl** *m* F great guy.

'**Prachtstraße** *f* boulevard.

'**prachtvoll** → **prächtig**.

prädestinieren [prɛdɛsti'niːrən] *v/t* (h) predestine.

Prädikat [prɛdi'kaːt] *n* (-[e]s; -e) **1.** *ling.* predicate. **2.** title. **3.** rating, attribute, *ped.* mark, grade.

Prädi'kats|nomen *n ling.* predicate complement. **~wein** *m* quality-tested wine (with special attributes).

Präfix [prɛ'fiːks] *n* (-es; -e) *ling.* prefix.

prägen ['prɛːgən] *v/t* (h) **1.** *a)* stamp, *b)*

mint (*coin*), c) emboss (*leather, metal, etc*). **2.** *fig.* a) coin (*word etc*), b) form, shape, determine, characterize.
Pragmatiker [pra'gma:tikər] *m* (-s; -) pragmatist. **prag'matisch** [-tɪʃ] *adj* pragmatic(al). **Pragmatismus** [pragma'tɪsmʊs] *m* (-; *no pl*) pragmatism.
prägnant [prɛ'gnant] *adj* terse, pithy.
'**Prägung** *f* (-; -en) **1.** stamping, coining. **2.** *fig.* a) stamp, character, b) forming.
prähi'storisch [prɛ-] *adj* prehistoric.
prahlen ['pra:lən] *v/i* (h) talk big: **mit et.** ~ brag about s.th., show off (with) s.th.
'**Prahler** *m* (-s; -) braggart, F show-off.
Prahlerei [pra:lə'raɪ] *f* (-; -en) a) showing-off, boasting, b) boast(s).
Praktik ['praktɪk] *f* (-; -en) practice, method, *pl b.s.* (sharp) practices.
Praktikant [prakti'kant] *m* (-en; -en), **Prakti'kantin** *f* (-; -nen) trainee.
'**Praktiker** *m* (-s; -) practical man.
Praktikum ['praktikʊm] *n* (-s; -ka) (period of) practical training.
praktisch ['praktɪʃ] **I** *adj* practical, *a.* handy: ~*er Arzt* general practitioner; ~*e Ausbildung* on-the-job training; ~*es Beispiel* concrete example; ~*er Versuch* field test. **II** *adv* a) practically, as good as (*done etc*), b) in practice.
praktizieren [prakti'tsi:rən] *v/t, v/i* (h) practise.
Prälat [prɛ'la:t] *m* (-en; -en) *eccl.* prelate.
Praline [pra'li:nə] *f* (-; -n), **Praliné** [prali'ne:] *n* (-s; -s) chocolate.
prall [pral] *adj* **1.** bulging (*bag etc*), hard (*ball etc*), full (*sails*), firm, taut (*muscles*). **2.** blazing (*sun*).
prallen ['pralən] *v/i* (sn) **1.** bounce (*auf acc* against), crash (*an acc, gegen* into). **2.** *sun*: blaze down (*auf acc* on).
'**prallvoll** *adj* F (full to) bursting.
Präludium [prɛ'lu:diʊm] *n* (-s; -dien) prelude.
Prämie ['prɛ:miə] *f* (-; -n) **1.** a) award, prize, b) reward, c) bonus. **2.** premium.
'**prämienbegünstigt** *adj* bonus-linked: ~*es Sparen* → '**Prämiensparen** *n* saving under the (Federal) bonus system.
prämieren [prɛ'mi:rən], **prämiieren** [prɛmi'i:rən] *v/t* (h) **1.** award a prize to. **2.** give a bonus for.
Pranger ['praŋər] *m* (-s; -) *hist.* stocks: *a. fig.* **an den ~ stellen** pillory.
Pranke ['praŋkə] *f* (-; -n) *zo.* paw.

Präparat [prɛpa'ra:t] *n* (-[e]s; -e) **1.** preparation. **2.** *biol.*, ♣ specimen.
präparieren [prɛpa'ri:rən] *v/t* (h) **1.** prepare (*a. sich ~, auf acc* for). **2.** dissect. **3.** preserve.
Präposition [prɛpozi'tsĭo:n] *f* (-; -en) *ling.* preposition.
Prärie [prɛ'ri:] *f* (-; -n) prairie.
Präsens ['prɛ:zɛns] *n* (-; Präsentia [prɛ'zɛntsĭa]) *ling.* present (tense).
präsentieren [prɛzɛn'ti:rən] (h) **I** *v/t* present (*j-m et.* s.o. with s.th.) **II** *v/i* ✗ present arms. **III** *sich* ~ present o.s.
Präsenz [prɛ'zɛnts] *f* (-; *no pl*) presence. ~*biblio,thek* *f* reference library.
Präserva'tiv [prɛzɛrva'ti:f] *n* (-s; -e) condom, sheath, *Am. a.* prophylactic.
Präsident [prɛzi'dɛnt] *m* (-en; -en) president, chairman, *parl.* presiding judge. **Präsi'dentenwahl** *f* presidential election. **Präsi'dentschaft** *f* (-; -en) presidency. **Präsi'dentschaftskandi,dat** *m* presidential candidate.
präsidieren [-'di:rən] *v/i* (h) preside (over). **Präsidium** [prɛ'zi:dĭʊm] *n* (-s; -dien) **1.** presidency. **2.** (presiding) committee. **3.** → *Polizeipräsidium*.
prasseln ['prasəln] *v/i* (h) *rain, hail*: patter, *fire*: crackle.
prassen ['prasən] *v/i* (h) feast.
Präteritum [prɛ'te:ritʊm] *n* (-s; -ta) *ling.* preterite, past tense.
präventiv [prɛvɛn'ti:f] *adj*, **Präven'tiv...** preventive, ♣ prophylactic.
Praxis ['praksɪs] *f* (-; Praxen) **1.** *no pl* practice, experience: **in der** ~ in practice; **et. in die** ~ *umsetzen* put s.th. into practice. **2.** 🏛, ♣ practice.
Präzedenzfall [prɛtse'dɛnts-] *m* (**e-n** ~ *schaffen* set a precedent).
präzis [prɛ'tsi:s] *adj* precise, exact.
präzisieren [prɛtsi'zi:rən] *v/t* (h) specify. **Präzision** [prɛtsi'zǐo:n] *f* (-; *no pl*) precision.
predigen ['pre:dɪɡən] *v/t, v/i* (h) preach.
Prediger ['pre:dɪɡər] *m* (-s; -) preacher.
Predigt ['pre:dɪçt] *f* (-; -en) sermon: **e-e** ~ *halten* preach (a sermon); F *fig. j-m e-e* ~ *halten* lecture s.o.
Preis [praɪs] *m* (-es; -e) **1.** a) price, b) fare: **zum** ~*e von* at a price of; **im** ~ *steigen* (*fallen*) go up (drop); *fig.* **um jeden** ~ at all costs; **um k-n** ~ not at any price. **2.** prize, award: **e-n** ~ *erringen*

win a prize. **3.** prize, reward. **4.** praise. **~absprache** f price agreement. **~änderung** f change in price: **~en vorbehalten** subject to change. **~angabe** f quotation (of prices): **ohne ~** not priced, not marked. **~anstieg** m rise in prices. **~aufschlag** m extra charge. **~ausschreiben** n competition. **⚥bewußt** adj price-conscious. **~bindung** f price maintenance.

Preiselbeere ['praɪzəl-] f 🌿 cranberry.

preisen ['praɪzən] v/t (pries, gepriesen, h) praise; → **glücklich** I.

'Preis|entwicklung f price trend. **~erhöhung** f price increase. **~ermäßigung** f price reduction. **~frage** f price question. **⚥gekrönt** adj prize-winning. **~gericht** n jury. **~gestaltung** f price formation. **~grenze** f price limit. **⚥günstig** → **preiswert**. **~klasse** f price range. **~lage** f price range: **in mittlerer (jeder) ~** medium-priced (in all prices).

'preislich adj and adv in price.

'Preis|liste f price list. **~nachlaß** m discount. **~poli,tik** f price policy. **~rätsel** n competition. **~richter(in** f) m judge. **~schild** n price tag. **~schwankung** f price fluctuation. **~senkung** f price reduction. **~steigerung** f rise in prices. **~stopp** m price freeze. **~sturz** m sudden drop in price(s). **~träger(in** f) m prize winner.

Preistreibe'rei f forcing up of prices.

'Preis|vergleich m price comparison. **~verleihung** f presentation (of prices).

'preiswert adj cheap, low-priced: **~ sein** a. be good value, be a bargain.

prekär [prɛ'kɛːr] adj precarious.

'Prellbock m 🚆 buffer stop, fig. buffer.

prellen ['prɛlən] v/t (h) **1.** 🚑 bruise. **2.** fig. cheat (**um** of).

'Prellung f (-; -en) 🚑 contusion, bruise.

Premiere [prə'mĭɛːrə] f (-; -n) thea. etc first night.

Premiermi,nister [prə'mĭɛ:-] m prime minister.

Presse¹ ['prɛsə] f (-; -n) ⚙ press.

'Presse² f (-; no pl) the press: **er hatte e-e gute ~** he got (or had) a good press. **~agen,tur** f press agency. **~amt** n press office. **~ausweis** m press card. **~bericht** m press report. **~chef** m chief press officer. **~dienst** m news service. **~empfang** m

press reception. **~erklärung** f press release. **~feldzug** m press campaign. **~foto,graf** m press photographer. **~freiheit** f freedom of the press. **~konfe,renz** f press conference. **~meldung** f a) press report, b) news item.

pressen ['prɛsən] v/t (h a) press (a. v/i), b) squeeze.

'Presse|refe,rent m press officer. **~schau** f press review. **~sprecher** m press spokesman. **~stelle** f public relations department. **~stimmen** pl press commentaries. **~tri,büne** f press box (parl. gallery). **~vertreter** m reporter. **~zen,sur** f censorship of the press. **~zentrum** n press cent/re (Am. -er).

'Preßluft f compressed air. **~bohrer** m pneumatic drill. **~hammer** m pneumatic hammer.

'Preßwehen pl 🚑 bearing-down pains.

Prestige [prɛs'tiːʒə] n (-s; no pl) prestige.

Pre'stigeverlust m loss of prestige.

Preuße ['prɔʏsə] m (-n; -n), **'Preußin** f (-; -nen), **'preußisch** adj Prussian.

prickeln ['prɪkəln] v/i (h) **1.** tingle, prickle. **2.** champagne: sparkle. **'prickelnd** adj **1.** tingling, prickly. **2.** fig. thrilling: **~er Reiz** thrill.

pries [priːs] pret of **preisen.**

Priester ['priːstər] m (-s; -) priest.

'Priesteramt n priesthood.

'Priesterin f (-; -nen) priestess.

'Priesterschaft f (-; no pl), **'Priestertum** n (-s; no pl) priesthood.

'Priesterweihe f ordination.

prima ['priːma] adj **1.** 🕇 prime, first-rate. **2.** F (a. int) great, super.

primär [pri'mɛːr] adj primary.

Primaten [pri'maːtən] pl zo. primates.

Primel ['priːməl] f (-; -n) 🌿 primrose.

primitiv [primi'tiːf] adj primitive.

Primitivität [primitivi'tɛːt] f (-; no pl) primitiveness.

Primzahl ['priːm-] f ➗ prime number.

Prinz [prɪnts] m (-en; -en) prince.

Prinzessin [prɪn'tsɛsɪn] f (-; -nen) princess.

'Prinzgemahl m prince consort.

Prinzip [prɪn'tsiːp] n (-s; -ien) (**aus ~** on, **im ~** in) principle. **prinzipiell** [prɪntsi'pĭɛl] adj and adv on principle.

Prior ['priːɔr] m (-s; -en [pri'oːrən]) eccl. prior. **Pri'orin** f (-; -nen) prioress.

Priorität [priori'tɛːt] f (-; -en) priority

(*über, vor* *dat* over): **~en setzen** establish priorities.

Prise ['pri:zə] *f* (-; -n) **1.** e-e ~ *Salz* a pinch of salt. **2.** ♣ prize.

Prisma ['prɪsma] *n* (-s; -men) prism.

prismatisch [prɪs'ma:tɪʃ] *adj* prismatic.

'**Prismensucher** *m* *phot.* prismatic viewfinder.

Pritsche ['prɪtʃə] *f* (-; -n) **1.** plank bed. **2.** *mot.* platform. **3.** slapstick.

privat [pri'va:t] **I** *adj* private, *a.* personal. **II** *adv* privately, in private.

Pri'vat|a,dresse *f* home address. **~besitz** *m* private (*or* personal) property: **in** ~ privately owned. **~do,zent** *m* (unsalaried) lecturer, *Am.* associate professor. **~gespräch** *n* *teleph.* private call. **~initia,tive** *f* private venture.

privatisieren [privati'zi:rən] (h) **I** *v/t* privatize. **II** *v/i* live on one's private income.

Pri'vat|klinik *f* private clinic. **~leben** *n* private (*or* personal) life. **~pati,ent(in** *f) m* private patient. **~recht** *n* (-[e]s; *no pl*) private (*or* civil) law. **~sache** *f* private matter (*or* affair): **das ist m-e ~!** that's my (own) business! **~schule** *f* private school. **~sekre,tär(in** *f) m* private secretary. **~stunden** *pl*, **~unterricht** *m* private lessons. **~wirtschaft** *f* (-; *no pl*) private enterprise.

Privileg [privi'le:k] *n* (-[e]s; -ien [-ɡiən]) privilege. **privilegieren** [privile'gi:rən] *v/t* (h) privilege.

pro [pro:] *prep* per: ~ *Jahr* per annum, a year; ~ *Kopf* per head, each; ~ *Stück* a piece; ~ *Stunde* per hour.

Pro das ~ und Kontra the pros and cons.

Probe ['pro:bə] *f* (-; -n) **1.** ♥, ♣ *etc* sample, *a.* ⊙ specimen, *iro. a.* taste: **e-e** ~ *ablegen* (*gen*) give a sample (*iro.* taste) of *one's courage etc.* **2.** a) test, try-out, b) check: **auf** ~, ~ *probeweise*; **j-n auf die** ~ *stellen* put s.o. to the test, test s.o.; **et. auf e-e harte** ~ *stellen* put s.th. to a severe test. **3.** *thea.* rehearsal. **~abzug** *m* print. proof. **~a,larm** *m* practice alarm. **~aufnahme** *f* **1.** *film:* screen test: **~n machen** von screen-test s.o. **2.** ♪ test recording. **~auftrag** *m* trial order. **~bohrung** *f* trial drill. **~exem,plar** *n* specimen copy. **2fahren** *v/t* (*only inf and pp* probegefahren, h) test-drive. **~fahrt** *f* test (*or* trial) run.

~flug *m* test (*or* trial) flight. **~jahr** *n* year of probation. **~lauf** *m* ⊙ test run.

proben ['pro:bən] *v/t*, *v/i* (h) rehearse.

'**Probenummer** *f* specimen copy.

'**probeweise** *adv* on a trial basis.

'**Probezeit** *f* trial period: **nach e-r** ~ *von 3 Monaten* at the end of three months' probation.

probieren [pro'bi:rən] *v/t* (h) **1.** try, *a.* taste, *a.* test: **es** ~ *mit* try; **F es bei j-m** ~ try it on with s.o. **2.** → **anprobieren**.

Problem [pro'ble:m] *n* (-s; -e) (*vor e-m* ~ *stehen* be faced with a problem).

Problematik [proble'ma:tɪk] *f* (-; *no pl*) problematic nature, problems.

proble'matisch *adj* problematic(al).

Pro'blemkind *n* problem child.

Pro'blemkreis *m* complex of problems.

pro'blemlos *adj* unproblematic(ally *adv*), *adv a.* without (any) difficulties.

Pro'blemstellung *f* **1.** formulation of a problem. **2.** problem.

Pro'blemstück *n* *thea.* thesis play.

Produkt [pro'dʊkt] *n* (-[e]s; -e) a) *a.* ℞ product, b) produce. **Pro'duktenwerbung** *f* ♥ product advertising.

Produktion [prodʊk'tsio:n] *f* (-; -en) (*in* ~ *gehen* go into) production.

Produkti'ons|anlage *f* production plant(s). **~ausfall** *m* loss of production. **~güter** *pl* producer goods. **~kapazi,tät** *f* production capacity. **~kosten** *pl* production costs. **~leiter** *m* production manager. **~mittel** *pl* means of production. **~rückgang** *m* fall in production. **~steigerung** *f* increase in production. **~ziel** *n* production target. **~zweig** *m* line of production.

produktiv [prodʊk'ti:f] *adj* productive.

Produktivität [prodʊktivi'tɛ:t] *f* (-; *no pl*) productivity.

Produzent [produ'tsɛnt] *m* (-en; -en) producer, *a.* grower.

produzieren [produ'tsi:rən] (h) **I** *v/t* produce, *a.* grow. **II** *sich* ~ F show off.

profan [pro'fa:n] *adj* **1.** profane, secular. **2.** mundane, trivial.

professionell [profɛsio'nɛl] *adj* professional.

Professor [pro'fɛsɔr] *m* (-s; -en [-'so:-rən]) professor. **Professorin** [profɛ-'so:rɪn] *f* (-; -nen) (woman) professor.

Professur [profɛ'su:r] *f* (-; -en) professorship, chair.

Profi ['pro:fi] *m* (-s; -s) F pro.
'Profi... professional (*football etc*).
Profil [pro'fi:l] *n* (-s; -e) profile (*a. fig.*), ⊙ *a.* section, *mot.* (tyre) tread: **im ~** in profile; *fig.* **~ haben** have personality; **an ~ gewinnen** improve one's image.
profilieren [profi'li:rən] (h) **I** *v/t* **1.** ⊙ profile, contour. **2.** *fig.* present in clear outline. **II** *sich ~* distinguish o.s.
profi'liert *adj fig.* distinguished.
Pro'fil|neu|rose *f* obsession with one's image. **~sohle** *f* profiled sole. **~stahl** *m* ⊙ section steel.
Profit [pro'fi:t] *m* (-[e]s; -e) profit: **~ schlagen aus** profit from (*or* by).
profitabel [profi'ta:bəl] *adj* profitable.
profitieren [profi'ti:rən] *v/i, v/t* (h) profit (**von** by, from).
Pro'fitjäger *m contp.* profiteer.
pro forma [pro: 'fɔrma] *adv* as a matter of form.
profund [pro'funt] *adj* profound.
Prognose [pro'gno:zə] *f* (-; -n) forecast, *esp.* ℱ prognosis.
Programm [pro'gram] *n* (-s; -e) **1.** program(me *Br.*), *pol. a.* platform, *thea. a.* bill, *TV a.* channel: **was steht heute auf dem ~?** what's the program(me) for today?; F **das paßt mir gar nicht ins ~!** that doesn't suit me at all! **2.** *computer:* program. **3.** ⊙ cycle. **~änderung** *f* change of program(me *Br.*).
programmatisch [progra'ma:tɪʃ] *adj* programmatic.
pro'grammgemäß *adv* according to plan.
Pro'gramm|gestaltung *f* program(me *Br.*) planning, program(m)ing. **℘ge-steuert** *adj computer:* program-controlled. **~heft** *n* program(me *Br.*). **~hin-weis** *m* program(me *Br.*) note.
program'mierbar *adj* program(m)able.
programmieren [progra'mi:rən] (h) program(me *Br.*): *fig.* **programmiert sein auf** (*acc*) be conditioned to (*do*) *s.th.* **Program'mierer** *m* (-s; -) program(m)er. **Program'miersprache** *f* program(m)ing language. **Program-'mierung** *f* (-; -en) program(m)ing.
Pro'gramm|punkt *m* item, *pol.* plank. **~steuerung** *f computer:* program control. **~taste** *f* program(me *Br.*) button. **~vorschau** *f* program(me *Br.*) roundup, *film:* trailer(s). **~wahl** *f* **1.** *TV* channel selec-

tion. **2.** ⊙ cycle selection. **~zeitschrift** *f* program(me *Br.*) guide.
Progression [progrɛ'sïo:n] *f* (-; -en) progression. **progressiv** [-'si:f] *adj* progressive. **Progressive** [-'si:və] *m, f* (-n; -n) progressive.
Projekt [pro'jɛkt] *n* (-[e]s; -e) project.
Pro'jektgruppe *f* task force.
Projektion [projɛk'tsïo:n] *f* (-; -en) projection. **Projekti'onsapparat** *m*, **Projektor** [pro'jɛktɔr] *m* (-s; -en [-'to:rən]) projector. **projizieren** [proji'tsi:rən] *v/t* (h) project.
Proklamation [proklama'tsïo:n] *f* (-; -en) proclamation. **proklamieren** [prokla'mi:rən] *v/t* (h) proclaim.
Pro-'Kopf-Einkommen *n* per capita income.
Prokura [pro'ku:ra] *f* (-; -ren) ✝ (power of) procuration. **Prokurist** [proku'rɪst] *m* (-en; -en), **Proku'ristin** *f* (-; -nen) authorized representative.
Prolet [pro'le:t] *m* (-en; -en) *contp.* prole. **Proletariat** [proleta'rïa:t] *n* (-[e]s; -e) proletariat(e). **Proletarier** [prole'ta:riər] *m* (-s; -), **prole'tarisch** [-rɪʃ] *adj* proletarian.
Prolog [pro'lo:k] *m* (-[e]s; -e) prolog(ue).
prolongieren [prolɔŋ'gi:rən] *v/t* (h) ✝ renew.
Promenade [prome'na:də] *f* (-; -n) promenade.
Promille [pro'mɪlə] *n* (-[s]; -) per mil, F *mot.* blood alcohol. **Pro'millegrenze** *f mot.* (blood) alcohol limit.
prominent [promi'nɛnt] *adj* prominent. **Promi'nente** *m, f* (-n; -n) public figure, celebrity. **Prominenz** [promi'nɛnts] *f* (-; -en) public figures, celebrities.
Promotion [promo'tsïo:n] *f* (-; -en) *univ.* doctorate. **promovieren** [promo'vi:-rən] (h) **I** *v/t* confer a doctorate on. **II** *v/i* take one's (doctor's) degree.
prompt [prɔmpt] *adj* prompt, quick.
Pronomen [pro'no:mən] *n* (-s; -, -mina) *ling.* pronoun.
Propaganda [propa'ganda] *f* (-; *no pl*) **1.** *pol.* propaganda. **2.** ✝ publicity.
Propagandist [propagan'dɪst] *m* (-en; -en), **Propagan'distin** *f* (-; -nen), **propagan'distisch** *adj* propagandist.
propagieren [propa'gi:rən] *v/t* (h) propagate.
Propan [pro'pa:n] *n* (-s; *no pl*) propane.

Propeller [pro'pɛlər] m (-s; -) propeller.
Prophet [pro'fe:t] m (-en; -en) prophet. **pro'phetisch** [-tɪʃ] adj prophetic.
prophezeien [profe'tsaɪən] v/t (h) prophesy, predict. **Prophe'zeiung** f (-; -en) prophecy, prediction.
prophylaktisch [profy'laktɪç] adj ℱ prophylactic. **Prophylaxe** [profy'laksə] f (-; -n) prophylaxis.
Proportion [propɔr'tsi̯o:n] f (-; -en) proportion. **proportional** [propɔrtsio'na:l] adj proportional (**zu** to).
Proporz [pro'pɔrts] m (-es; -e) proportional representation.
'Prorektor m univ. vice-chancellor.
Prosa ['pro:za] f (-; no pl) prose.
'Prosadichtung f prose writing.
Prosaiker [pro'za:ikər] m (-s; -) **1.** prose writer, prosaist. **2.** fig. prosaic person.
prosaisch [pro'za:ɪʃ] adj fig. prosaic, matter-of-fact, dull.
prosit ['pro:zɪt] int your health!, cheers!
Prospekt [pro'spɛkt] m (-[e]s; -e) **1.** a) brochure, b) leaflet. **2.** thea. backdrop.
prost [pro:st] → **prosit.**
Prostata ['prɔstata] f (-; no pl) prostate (gland).
prostituieren [prostitu'i:rən] **sich ~** (h) prostitute o.s. **Prostitu'ierte** f (-n; -n) prostitute. **Prostitution** [prostitu-'tsi̯o:n] f (-; no pl) prostitution.
protegieren [prote'ʒi:rən] v/t (h) patronize, sponsor: **von j-m protegiert werden** be s.o.'s protégé.
Protein [prote'i:n] n (-s; -e) protein.
Protektion [protɛk'tsi̯o:n] f (-; -en) patronage. **Protektionismus** [protɛk-tsi̯o'nɪsmʊs] m (-; no pl) ♥ protectionism. **protekti'onistisch** [-tɪʃ] adj ♥ protectionist.
Protektorat [protɛkto'ra:t] n (-[e]s; -e) **1.** pol. protectorate. **2.** fig. patronage.
Protest [pro'tɛst] m (-[e]s; -e) protest (a. ♥): **aus ~** in protest; **~ einlegen** enter a protest (**gegen** against).
Protestant [protɛs'tant] m (-en; -en), **Prote'stantin** f (-; -nen), **prote'stantisch** adj Protestant.
Protestantismus [protɛstan'tɪsmʊs] m (-; no pl) Protestantism.
protestieren [protɛs'ti:rən] v/i (h) protest (**gegen et.** against s.th., Am. s.th.).
Pro'testkundgebung f protest rally.
Pro'testmarsch m protest march.

Prothese [pro'te:zə] f (-; -n) **1.** artificial limb. **2.** denture(s).
Protokoll [proto'kɔl] n (-s; -e) **1.** record, minutes: **~ führen** take the minutes; **zu ~ geben** ⚖ depose, state (in evidence); **zu ~ nehmen** take down. **2.** protocol.
protokollarisch [protokɔ'la:rɪʃ] adj **1.** on record, minuted: **~ festhalten →** **protokollieren. 2.** (of) protocol.
Proto'koll|chef m chief of protocol. **~führer(in** f) m keeper of the minutes, recording clerk, ⚖ clerk of the court.
protokollieren [protokɔ'li:rən] v/t (h) record, enter in the minutes, take s.th. down.
Proton ['pro:tɔn] n (-s; -en [-'to:nən]) phys. proton.
Proto'plasma [proto-] n protoplasm.
Prototyp ['pro:to-] m prototype.
protzen ['prɔtsən] v/i (h) F show off (**mit** [with] s.o., s.th.). **'protzig** adj F showy.
Proviant [pro'vi̯ant] m (-s; -e) provisions.
Provinz [pro'vɪnts] f (-; -en) **1.** province. **2.** the provinces, fig. contp. backwater: **finsterste ~ sein** be utterly provincial.
provinziell [provɪn'tsi̯ɛl] adj provincial.
Pro'vinzler m (-s; -) contp. provincial.
Provision [provi'zi̯o:n] f (-; -en) ♥ (**auf ~** on) commission.
provisorisch [provi'zo:rɪʃ] adj provisional, temporary. **Provisorium** [provi'zo:ri̯ʊm] n (-s; -rien) **1.** provisional agreement. **2.** makeshift.
Provokation [provoka'tsi̯o:n] f (-; -en) provocation. **provozieren** [provo'tsi:-rən] v/t (h) provoke. **~d** provocative.
Prozedur [protse'du:r] f (-; -en) procedure, iro. ritual.
Prozent [pro'tsɛnt] n (-[e]s; -e) **1.** per cent, percent: **zu 5 ~** at five per cent (or percent); **zu wieviel ~?** at what percentage? **2.** pl F a) percentage, b) discount. **...pro,zentig** in cpds. per cent, percent. **Pro'zentsatz** m percentage.
prozentual [protsɛn'tǔa:l] adj proportional: **~er Anteil** percentage; **~ am Gewinn beteiligt sein** receive a percentage of the profit.
Prozeß [pro'tsɛs] m (-sses; -sse) **1.** process. **2.** ⚖ a) lawsuit, b) trial: **e-n ~ anstrengen gegen** bring an action against; **gegen j-n e-n ~ führen** be engaged in a lawsuit with s.o.; **e-n ~ ver-**

lieren lose a case; *j-m den ~ machen* put s.o. on trial; *fig. kurzen ~ machen* make short work (*mit* of).

prozessieren [protsɛ'si:rən] *v/i* (h) go to court, litigate: *gegen j-n ~* bring an action against s.o.

Prozession [protsɛ'sĭo:n] *f* (-; -en) procession.

Pro'zeßkosten *pl* (legal) costs.

Pro'zeßkostenhilfe *f* (-; *no pl*) legal aid.

Prozessor [pro'tsɛsɔr] *m* (-s; -en [-'so:rən]) *computer*: processor.

Pro'zeßordnung *f* code of procedure.

Pro'zeßsteuerung *f* ⊙ process control.

prüde ['pry:də] *adj* prudish: (*nicht*) ~ *sein* be a (no) prude.

Prüderie [prydə'ri:] *f* (-; -n) prudery.

prüfen ['pry:fən] *v/t* (h) **1.** a) examine, *a.* ⊙ inspect, test, check, ✝ audit, ⚖ review, b) investigate, look into *a matter etc*, c) consider (*proposal etc*): *~der Blick* searching glance. **2.** *ped., univ.* examine, test: → *geprüft*. **3.** afflict.

'Prüfer *m* (-s; -) *ped., univ.* examiner, ⊙ tester, ✝ auditor.

'Prüfling *m* (-s; -e) examinee, candidate.

'Prüf|stand *m* ⊙ test bed: *fig. auf dem ~* being tested. **~stein** *m fig.* touchstone.

'Prüfung *f* (-; -en) **1.** *ped.* examination, test, F exam: → *ablegen* 6. **2.** a) examination, inspection, check(ing), ⊙ test, trial, ✝ audit, ⚖ review, b) investigation, c) consideration. **3.** trial, affliction. **4.** *sports*: event.

'Prüfungs|angst *f* F exam nerves. **~arbeit** *f*, **~aufgabe** *f* examination (*or* test) paper. **~ausschuß** *m*, **~kommissi,on** *f* board of examiners. **~ordnung** *f* examination regulations.

'Prüfverfahren *n* method of testing.

Prügel ['pry:gəl] *m* (-s; -) **1.** cudgel. **2.** *pl* F ~ *beziehen* get a (sound) thrashing, *a. sports*: get clobbered.

Prüge'lei *f* (-; -en) fight, brawl.

'Prügelknabe *m* scapegoat.

prügeln ['pry:gəln] *v/t* (h) thrash, clobber: *sich ~* (have a) fight.

'Prügelstrafe *f* corporal punishment.

Prunk [prʊŋk] *m* (-[e]s; *no pl*) splendo(u)r, *contp.* pomp. **'Prunkgemach** *n* stateroom. **'Prunkstück** *n* F showpiece.

'prunkvoll *adj* splendid, magnificent.

prusten ['pru:stən] *v/i* (h) snort.

Psalm [psalm] *m* (-s; -e) psalm.

Pseudonym [psɔydo'ny:m] *n* (-s; -e) pseudonym, *a.* pen name.

pst [pst] *int* a) shh!, b) psst!

Psyche ['psy:çə] *f* (-; -n) psyche.

Psychiater [psy'çĭa:tər] *m* (-s; -) psychiatrist, F shrink. **Psychiatrie** [psyçĭa'tri:] *f* (-; *no pl*) **1.** psychiatry. **2.** psychiatric ward. **psychi'atrisch** [-trɪʃ] *adj* psychiatric.

psychisch ['psy:çɪʃ] *adj* a) psychic(al), b) psychological, mental: *~e Erkrankung* mental illness.

Psycho|ana'lyse [psyço-] *f* psychoanalysis. **~ana'lytiker** *m* psychoanalyst.

Psychogramm [psyço'gram] *n* (-s; -e) psychograph, *fig. a.* profile.

Psychologe [psyço'lo:gə] *m* (-n; -n) psychologist. **Psychologie** [psyçolo'gi:] *f* (-; *no pl*) psychology. **psycho'logisch** [-gɪʃ] *adj* psychological.

Psychopath [psyço'pa:t] *m* (-en; -en) psychopath. **psycho'pathisch** [-tɪʃ] *adj* psychopathic.

Psychopharmakon [psyço'farmakɔn] *n* (-s; -ka) psychochemical.

Psychose [psy'ço:zə] *f* (-; -n) psychosis.

psychoso'matisch *adj* psychosomatic.

Pychothera'peut *m* psychotherapist. **psychothera'peutisch** *adj* psychotherapeutic. **Psychothera'pie** *f* psychotherapy.

Pubertät [pubɛr'tɛ:t] *f* (-; *no pl*) puberty.

pubertieren [pubɛr'ti:rən] *v/i* (h) go through puberty.

publik [pu'bli:k] *adj* ~ *sein* (*werden*) be (become) common knowledge; *et. ~ machen* make s.th. public.

Publikation [publika'tsĭo:n] *f* (-; -en) publication.

Publikum ['pu:blikʊm] *n* (-s; *no pl*) a) the public, audience, *TV a.* viewers, *radio*: *a.* listeners, b) *sports*: spectators, c) customers, visitors.

'Publikums|erfolg *m* great (popular) success. **~geschmack** *m* public taste. **~liebling** *m* darling of the public.

publizieren [publi'tsi:rən] *v/t* (h) publish. **Publizist** [publi'tsɪst] *m* (-en; -en) publicist, journalist. **Publizistik** [publi'tsɪstɪk] *f* (-; *no pl*) journalism.

Pudding ['pʊdɪŋ] *m* (-s; -e) pudding, blancmange.

Pudel ['pu:dəl] *m zo.* poodle: F *daste-*

hen *wie ein begossener* ~ look crestfallen. **'Pudelmütze** f bobble hat.
'pudelnaß adj F soaking wet. **'pudelwohl** adj F *sich ~ fühlen* feel great.
Puder ['pu:dər] m, F a. n (-s; -) powder.
'Puderdose f powder compact.
pudern ['pu:dərn] v/t (h) powder.
'Puderquaste f puff.
'Puderzucker m icing (*Am.* confectioner's) sugar.

Puff [pυf] m (-[e]s; ⸚e) **1.** a) thump, b) poke, dig, nudge: F *fig. er* (*es*) *kann schon e-n ~ vertragen* he (it) can stand a knock. **2.** pop, bang.
Puff m, a. n (-s; -s) brothel.
'Puffärmel m puffed sleeve.
puffen ['pυfən] v/t (h) thump, nudge.
Puffer ['pυfər] m (-s; -) **1.** buffer. **2.** potato fritter. **'Pufferstaat** m buffer state.
'Puffmais m popcorn.
Pulle ['pυlə] f (-; -n) F bottle: *fig. volle ~* full blast.
Pulli ['pυli] m (-s; -s) F (light) sweater.
Pullover [pυ'lo:vər] m (-s; -) sweater, pullover.
Puls [pυls] m (-es; -e) pulse: *j-m den ~ fühlen* feel s.o.'s pulse, *fig.* sound s.o. out. **'Pulsader** f artery. **pulsieren** [pυl'zi:rən] v/i (h) pulsate. **'Pulsschlag** m pulse beat. **'Pulszahl** f pulse rate.
Pult [pυlt] n (-[e]s; -e) a) desk, b) lectern: *♩ am ~ XY* XY conducting.
Pulver ['pυlvər] n (-s; -) a) powder, b) gunpowder: F *er hat das ~ nicht erfunden* he is no great light; → *Schuß* 1.
'Pulverfaß n powder keg: *wie auf e-m ~ sitzen* be sitting on top of a volcano.
pulverisieren [pυlveri'zi:rən] v/t (h) pulverize.
'Pulverkaf,fee m instant coffee.
'Pulverschnee m powdery snow.
Puma ['pu:ma] m (-s; -s) zo. puma.
pummelig ['pυmǝliç] adj F plump.
Pump [pυmp] F *auf ~* on tick.
Pumpe ['pυmpə] f (-; -n) **1.** pump. **2.** F ticker. **'pumpen** v/t, v/i (h) **1.** pump. **2.** F lend, *Am.* loan: *sich et. ~ borrow* s.th. (*bei j-m* from s.o.).
Pumps [pœmps] m (-; -) court shoe.
Punker ['paŋkər] m (-s; -) punk.
Punkt [pυŋkt] m (-[e]s; -e) **1.** point (a. *A*, *sports etc*), dot, *ling.*, *print.* full stop, *Am.* period: *nach ~en siegen* win on points; *~ 10 Uhr* at ten o'clock sharp. **2.**

spot: *fig. bis zu e-m gewissen ~* up to a point; → *tot, wund.* **3.** *fig.* a) point, item, b) subject: *in vielen ~en* in many respects; F *der springende ~* the crux (of the matter), the whole point; *die Sache auf den ~ bringen* put it in a nutshell; → *strittig.*
punkten ['pυŋktən] **I** v/t dot. **II** v/i *sports:* score (points).
punktieren [pυŋk'ti:rən] v/t (h) *♣* puncture.
pünktlich ['pyŋktlıç] **I** adj punctual: *sei ~!* be on time! **II** adv punctually, on time: *~ um 10 Uhr* at ten o'clock sharp.
'Pünktlichkeit f (-; *no pl*) punctuality.
'Punkt|richter(in f) m *sports:* judge. *~sieg* m win on points. *~sieger(in* f) m winner on points. *~spiel* n league match. *~streik* m strike at selective sites. *~sy,stem* n points system.
punktuell [pυŋk'tŭɛl] adj selective(ly adv), adv a. at certain points.
Punsch [pυnʃ] m (-[e]s; -e) *gastr.* punch.
Pupille [pu'pılə] f (-; -n) pupil.
Püppchen ['pypçən] n (-s; -) dolly.
Puppe ['pυpə] f (-; -n) **1.** doll (*a.* F *girl*), b) *a. fig.* puppet, c) dummy: F *bis in die ~n schlafen* sleep till all hours. **2.** *zo.* a) chrysalis, pupa, b) cocoon.
'Puppen|spiel n puppet show. *~spieler(in* f) m puppeteer. *~stube* f doll's house. *~the,ater* n puppet theat/re (*Am.* -er). *~wagen* m doll's pram.
pur [pu:r] adj pure, a. sheer, *whisky:* neat, *Am.* straight.
Püree [py're:] n (-s; -s) purée, mash.
puritanisch [puri'ta:nıʃ] adj a) *hist.* Puritan, b) *contr.* puritanical.
purpurrot ['pυrpυr-] adj purple.
Purzelbaum ['pυrtsəl-] m forward roll.
purzeln ['pυrtsəln] v/i (h) tumble.
Puste ['pu:stə] f (-; *no pl*) F breath: *außer ~ sein* be puffed.
Pustel [pυstəl] f (-; -n) *♣* pustule.
pusten ['pu:stən] v/i, v/t (h) puff: F *mot. er mußte ~* he was breathalyzed.
Pute ['pu:tə] f (-; -n) *zo.* turkey (hen): F *dumme ~* silly goose.
Puter ['pu:tər] m (-s; -) *zo.* turkey (cock). **'puterrot** adj (~ *werden* turn) scarlet.
Putsch [pυtʃ] m (-[e]s; -e) *pol.* putsch, coup (d'état), revolt. **'putschen** v/i (h) *pol.* stage a putsch (*or* coup), revolt.
Putte ['pυtə] f (-; -n) putto.

Putz [pʊts] *m* (-es; *no pl*) **1.** △ plaster: ⚡ *unter* ~ buried, concealed; F *auf den* ~ *hauen* a) paint the town red, b) show off. **2.** F row: ~ *machen* raise hell.

putzen ['pʊtsən] (h) **I** *v/t* clean, polish, *Am.* shine (*shoes*), preen (*one's feathers*): *sich die Nase* ~ blow one's nose; *sich die Zähne* ~ brush one's teeth. **II** *v/i* clean: ~ (*gehen*) work as a cleaner. **III** *sich* ~ *a. fig.* preen o.s.

'Putzfrau *f* cleaning lady.

'putzig *adj* F funny.

'Putzlappen *m* cloth.

'Putzmacherin *f* (-; -nen) milliner.

'Putzmittel *n* cleaning agent.

'Putzwaren *pl* millinery.

'Putzzeug *n* cleaning things.

puzzeln ['pazəln] *v/i* (h) do a puzzle.

Puzzle ['pazəl] *n* (-s; -) (jigsaw) puzzle.

Pygmäe [pyˈgmɛːə] *m* (-n; -n) pygmy.

Pyjama [pyˈdʒaːma] *m* (-s; -s) (pair of) pyjamas (*Am.* pajamas).

Pyramide [pyraˈmiːdə] *f* (-; -n) pyramid.

pyraˈmidenförmig *adj* pyramidal.

Q

Q, q [kuː] *n* (-; -) Q, q.

Quacksalber ['kvak-] *m* (-s; -) quack.

Quadrat [kvaˈdraːt] *n* (-[e]s; -e) square: *2 Fuß im* ~ 2 feet square; *zum* ~ *erheben* square; *3 zum* (*or im*) ~ three squared.

Quaˈdrat... square (*metre, root, etc*).

quaˈdratisch *adj* square, Å quadratic.

Quadratur [kvadraˈtuːr] *f* (-; -en) quadrature: *die* ~ *des Kreises* the squaring of the circle.

quadrieren [kvaˈdriːrən] *v/t* (h) square.

quadrophon [kvadroˈfoːn] *adj* quadrophonic.

quaken ['kvaːkən] *v/i* (h) quack, croak.

quäken ['kvɛːkən] *v/i* (h) squawk.

Qual [kvaːl] *f* (-; -en) a) *a. pl* agony, (mental) anguish, b) ordeal: *unter* ~*en* in (great) pain, *fig.* with great difficulty; *es war e-e* ~ it was hell.

quälen ['kvɛːlən] (h) **I** *v/t* a) torment, torture, *fig. a.* haunt, b) pester; → *gequält.* **II** *sich* ~ (*mit*) a) torment o.s. (with), b) struggle hard (with), c) suffer (badly) (from). **'quälend** → *qualvoll.*

Quäleˈrei *f* (-; -en) **1.** tormenting (*etc*, → *quälen* I). **2.** torment, torture.

'Quälgeist *m* (-es; -er) pest, tormentor.

Qualifikation [kvalifikaˈtsĭoːn] *f* (-; -en) qualification. **Qualifikatiˈonsrunde** *f sports*: qualifying round.

qualifizieren [kvalifiˈtsiːrən] *v/t* (*a. sich* ~) (h) qualify (*für* for).

Qualität [kvaliˈtɛːt] *f* (-; -en) quality.

qualitativ [kvalitaˈtiːf] *adj* qualitative.

Qualiˈtätskonˌtrolle *f* quality control. ~*ware* *f* high-quality article, *coll.* quality goods. ~*wein* *m* quality-tested wine.

Qualle ['kvalə] *f* (-; -n) *zo.* jellyfish.

Qualm [kvalm] *m* (-[e]s; *no pl*) smoke.

qualmen ['kvalmən] *v/i, v/t* (h) smoke.

'qualmig *adj* smoky, full of smoke.

'qualvoll *adj* agonizing, very painful, excruciating (*pains*).

Quantenphyˌsik ['kvantən-] *f* quantum physics.

Quantität [kvantiˈtɛːt] *f* (-; -en) quantity.

quantitativ [kvantitaˈtiːf] *adj* quantitative.

Quantum ['kvantʊm] *n* (-s; Quanten) **1.** quantum, amount. **2.** share, quota.

Quarantäne [karanˈtɛːnə] *f* (-; -n) (*unter* ~ *stellen* put in) quarantine.

Quark [kvark] *m* (-s; *no pl*) **1.** *gastr.* curd cheese. **2.** → *Quatsch.*

Quartal [kvarˈtaːl] *n* (-s; -e) quarter (year).

Quartett [kvarˈtɛt] *n* (-[e]s; -e) **1.** ♪ quartet(te). **2.** *fig.* foursome. **3.** (*game*) happy families.

Quartier [kvarˈtiːr] *n* (-s; -e) accommodation, *esp.* ✕ quarters.

Quarz [kvaːrts] *m* (-es; -e) quartz.

quasi ['kvaːzi] *adv* as it were.

quasseln ['kvasəln] *v/i* (h) blather.

Quaste ['kvastə] *f* (-; -n) tassel.

Quatsch [kvatʃ] *m* (-es; *no pl*) F rubbish,

rot: ~ **machen** a) fool around, b) do s.th. stupid; **red k-n ~!** a) don't talk rubbish!, b) you're kidding!
quatschen ['kvatʃən] v/i (h) F **1.** talk rubbish. **2.** gossip. **3.** chat, waffle. **4.** blab. '**Quatschkopf** m F silly ass.
Quecke ['kvɛkə] f (-; -n) ♀ couch grass.
Quecksilber ['kvɛk-] n quicksilver, mercury. **~säule** f mercury column. **~vergiftung** f mercury poisoning.
Quelle ['kvɛlə] f (-; -n) a) spring, b) source (of river etc, a. fig.), c) well: **et. aus sicherer ~ wissen** have s.th. on good authority. '**quellen** v/i (quoll, gequollen, sn) **1.** (aus from) pour (a. fig.), blood, water: well, gush. **2.** swell: **~ lassen** soak (peas etc).
'**Quellen|angabe** f reference, pl bibliography. **~materi,al** n source material. **~steuer** f withholding tax. **~studium** n basic research.
'**Quellgebiet** n headwaters.
'**Quellwasser** n spring water.
quengelig ['kvɛŋəlıç] adj whining.
quengeln ['kvɛŋəln] v/i (h) whine.
quer [kve:r] adv a) crosswise, across, b) diagonally, c) at right angles (**zu** to): ~ **über** (acc) across.
'**Querbalken** m crossbeam.
Quere ['kve:rə] f **j-m in die ~ kommen** get in s.o.'s way.
querfeld'ein adv across country. **Querfeld'einlauf** m cross-country race.
'**Querflöte** f transverse flute.
'**Querfor,mat** n horizontal format.
'**quergestreift** adj horizontally striped.
'**Querkopf** m F pigheaded fellow.
'**querlegen: sich ~** (sep, -ge-, h) F fig. make trouble.
'**Querpaß** m sports: cross pass.
'**querschießen** v/i (irr, sep, -ge-, h, → **schießen**) F fig. make trouble.
'**Querschiff** n △ transept.
'**Querschläger** m ✕ ricochet.
'**Querschnitt** m cross-section (a. fig. **durch** of).

'**querschnitt(s)gelähmt** adj, '**Querschnitt(s)gelähmte** m,f ✚ paraplegic.
'**Querschnittzeichnung** f sectional drawing.
'**Querstraße** f intersecting road: **zweite ~ rechts** second turning on the right.
'**Querstrich** m horizontal line, dash.
'**Quersumme** f ♣ sum of the digits.
'**Quertreiber** m (-s; -) F obstructionist.
Querulant [kveru'lant] m (-en; -en) troublemaker.
'**Querverbindung** f cross connection.
'**Querverweis** m cross reference.
quetschen ['kvɛtʃən] v/t (h) a) squeeze (a. fig. **sich** o.s.), b) ✚ bruise, crush.
'**Quetschung** f (-; -en) ✚ bruise.
quickle'bendig ['kvɪk-] adj F very lively, active.
quieken ['kvi:kən] v/i (h) squeak.
quietschen ['kvi:tʃən] v/i (h) squeal, squeak.
'**quietschvergnügt** adj F chirpy.
Quinte ['kvɪntə] f (-; -n) ♪ fifth.
'**Quintes,senz** f (-; -en) essence.
Quintett [kvɪn'tɛt] n (-[e]s; -e) quintet(te).
Quirl [kvɪrl] m (-[e]s; -e) **1.** gastr. beater. **2.** ♀ whorl. **3.** fig. live wire.
'**quirlen** v/t (h) whisk, beat.
'**quirlig** adj fig. lively.
quitt [kvɪt] adj **mit j-m ~ sein** (**werden**) be (get) quits with s.o.
Quitte ['kvɪtə] f (-; -n) ♀ quince.
quittieren [kvɪ'ti:rən] v/t (h) give a receipt for: **et. mit e-m Lächeln ~** meet s.th. with a smile.
Quittung ['kvɪtʊŋ] f (-; -en) (**gegen ~** on) receipt: **das ist die ~ für d-n Leichtsinn** that's what you get for being so careless. '**Quittungsblock** m receipt book.
Quiz [kvɪz] n (-; -) quiz.
'**Quizmaster** m (-s; -) quizmaster.
'**Quizsendung** f quiz program(me Br.).
quoll [kvɔl] pret of **quellen.**
Quote ['kvo:tə] f (-; -n) quota, share.
Quotient [kvo'tsiɛnt] m (-en; -en) ♣ quotient.

R

R, r [ɛr] *n* (-; -) R, r.

Rabatt [ra'bat] *m* (-[e]s; -e) discount.

Rabbi ['rabi] *m* (-[s]; -nen [ra'bi:nən]), **Rabbiner** [ra'bi:nər] *m* (-s; -) rabbi.

Rabe ['ra:bə] *m* (-n; -n) raven.

'Rabenmutter *f* uncaring mother.

'raben'schwarz *adj* jet-black.

'Rabenvater *m* uncaring father.

rabiat [ra'bɪa:t] *adj* a) furious, b) rough, brutal, c) ruthless.

Rache ['raxə] *f* (-; *no pl*) revenge, vengeance: *aus* ~ in revenge (*für* for); ~ *schwören* vow vengeance; ~ *nehmen* (*or üben*) → *rächen* II.

'Rache,akt *m* act of revenge.

Rachen ['raxən] *m* (-s; -) **1.** *anat*. throat. **2.** *zo.*, *a. fig.* jaws, maw: F *j-m et. in den* ~ *schmeißen* cast s.th. into s.o.'s hungry maw; *er kann den* ~ *nicht voll kriegen* he can't get enough.

rächen ['rɛçən] (h) **I** *v/t* (*an dat* on, upon) avenge. **II** *sich* ~ take revenge, get one's own back; *sich an j-m* ~ revenge o.s. (*or* take revenge) on s.o.; *es rächte sich* (*bitter*), *daß* ... he had to pay dearly for ger.

'Rachenka,tarrh *m* **♥** pharyngitis.

Rächer ['rɛçər] *m* (-s; -) avenger.

Rachitis [ra'xi:tɪs] *f* (-; *no pl*) **♥** rickets.

ra'chitisch [-tɪʃ] *adj* **♥** rickety.

'Rachsucht *f* (-; *no pl*) vindictiveness.

'rachsüchtig *adj* vindictive, revengeful.

rackern ['rakərn] *v/i* (h) F slave away.

Rad [ra:t] *n* (-[e]s; -er ['rɛ:dər]) **1.** wheel: *ein* ~ *schlagen* a) *peacock*: spread the tail, b) → *radschlagen*; *das fünfte* ~ *am Wagen sein* be the fifth wheel; F *unter die Räder kommen* go to the dogs. **2.** bicycle, F bike.

Radar [ra'da:r] *m*, *n* (-s; *no pl*) radar. ~*falle* *f mot*. F radar (speed) trap. ~*ge,rät* *n* radar (set). ~*kon,trolle* *f* radar control. ~*schirm* *m* radar screen.

Radau [ra'dau] *m* (-s; *no pl*) F row.

'Raddampfer *m* paddle steamer.

radeln ['ra:dəln] *v/i* (sn) F cycle, pedal.

Rädelsführer ['rɛ:dəls-] *m* ringleader.

'Räderwerk *n* a) wheels, b) clockwork, c) gear(ing), d) *fig.* machinery.

'radfahren *v/i* (*irr, sep, -ge-, sn*, → *fah-*

ren) **1.** cycle, (ride a) bicycle, F bike. **2.** F *contp.* toady. **'Radfahrer(in** *f*) *m* **1.** cyclist. **2.** F *contp.* toady.

'Radfahrweg *m* cycle track.

radieren [ra'di:rən] *v/t*, *v/i* (h) **1.** erase, rub *s.th.* out. **2.** *art:* etch.

Ra'diergummi *m* eraser, *Br. a.* rubber.

Ra'dierung *f* (-; -en) *art:* etching.

Radieschen [ra'di:sçən] *n* (-s; -) radish.

radikal [radi'ka:l] *adj*, **Radi'kale** *m*, *f* (-n; -n) radical. **radikalisieren** [-kali-'zi:rən] *v/t* (h) radicalize. **Radikalismus** [-ka'lɪsmʊs] *m* (-; *no pl*) radicalism. **Radi'kalkur** *f* drastic cure.

Radio ['ra:dio] *n* (-s; -s) radio, *Br. a.* wireless: *im* ~ on the radio; ~ *hören* listen to the radio, listen in.

radioak'tiv *adj* radioactive: ~*er Niederschlag* fallout.

Radioaktivi'tät *f* (-; *no pl*) radioactivity.

'Radioappa,rat *m* radio (set).

Radiologe [radio'lo:gə] *m* (-n; -n) **♪** radiologist.

'Radiore,corder *m* radio cassette recorder. **'Radiowecker** *m* clock radio.

Radium ['ra:dɪʊm] *n* (-s; *no pl*) radium.

Radius ['ra:dɪʊs] *m* (-; Radien) radius.

'Radkappe *f* hub cap. **'Radrennbahn** *f* cycling track. **'Radrennen** *n* cycle race. **'radschlagen** *v/i* (*irr, sep, -ge-, h*, → *schlagen*) turn cartwheels. **'Radsport** *m* cycling. **'Radtour** *f* cycle tour. **'Radweg** *m* cycle track.

raffen ['rafən] (h) *v/t* **1.** snatch up, gather up (*skirt etc*). **2.** *fig.* condense, tighten.

Raffinade [rafi'na:də] *f* (-; -n) refined sugar. **Raffinerie** [rafinə'ri:] *f* (-; -n) **☉** refinery. **Raffinesse** [rafi'nɛsə] *f* (-; -n) cleverness, subtlety, sophistication, *a.* refinement (*of taste etc*). **raffinieren** [rafi'ni:rən] *v/t* (h) **☉** refine. **raffi'niert** *fig.* clever, ingenious (*plan etc*), subtle, sophisticated (*taste etc*).

Rage ['ra:ʒə] *f* (-; *no pl*) rage, fury: *j-n in* ~ *bringen* make s.o. furious.

ragen ['ra:gən] *v/i* (h) tower, loom: ~ *aus* (*dat*) rise (*or* project) from.

Raglanärmel ['ragla(:)n-] *pl* raglan sleeves.

Ragout [ra'gu:] *n* (-s; -s) *gastr.* ragout.

Rahe ['raːə] *f* (-; -n) ⚓ yard.
Rahm [raːm] *m* (-[e]s; *no pl*) cream; → **abschöpfen**.
rahmen ['raːmən] *v/t* (h) frame (*picture etc*), mount (*slides*).
'Rahmen *m* (-s; -) frame (*a. mot.*, ⚙), *fig. a.* framework, scope, limits, setting: *im ~ von* (*or gen*) within the scope of; *im ~ des Festes* in the course of the festival; *im ~ der Ausstellung finden ... statt* the exhibition will include ...; *im ~ des Möglichen* within the bounds of possibility; *in großem ~* on a large scale; *aus dem ~ fallen* a) be unusual, be off-beat, b) F get out of line, misbehave; *den ~ sprengen* go beyond the scope (*gen* of). **~abkommen** *n* skeleton agreement. **~bedingungen** *pl* general conditions. **~erzählung** *f* framework story. **~gesetz** *n* skeleton law. **~handlung** *f* frame (story). **~kampf** *m* boxing: supporting fight. **~pro,gramm** *n* fringe events.
rahmig ['raːmɪç] *adj* creamy.
'Rahmkäse *m* cream cheese.
'Rahsegel *n* square sail.
Rakete [ra'keːtə] *f* (-; -n) rocket, ✕ *a.* missile.
Ra'keten|abschußbasis *f* rocket launching site, ✕ missile base. **~antrieb** *m* rocket propulsion: *mit ~* rocket-propelled. **~start** *m* rocket-assisted takeoff. **~stützpunkt** *m* ✕ missile base.
Rallye ['rali] *f* (-; -s) (motor) rally.
Ramme ['ramə] *f* (-; -n) pile-driver.
rammen ['ramən] *v/t* (h) ram.
Rampe ['rampə] *f* (-; -n) **1.** ramp. **2.** *thea.* apron.
'Rampenlicht *n* thea. footlights: *fig. im ~ stehen* be in the limelight.
ramponieren [rampo'niːrən] *v/t* (h) F *a. fig.* batter.
Ramsch [ramʃ] *m* (-es; -e) *a.* ♣ rejects, pl F *contp.* junk, trash.
ran [ran] F let's go!; *in cpds.* → **heran...**
Rand [rant] *m* (-[e]s; ⸚er) **1.** edge, rim (*of plate etc*), brim (*of hat, glass, etc*), margin (*of page etc*), brink (*of wound*), brink (*of abyss, fig. of ruin etc*): *bis zum ~ voll* brimful; *e-n ~ lassen* leave a margin; *am ~e des Waldes* (*der Stadt*) on the edge of the wood (on the outskirts of the town); *am ~e* a) *note etc* in the margin, b) *mention etc* in passing; (*nur*

am ~e (only) marginally; *am ~e bemerkt* by the way. **2.** mark, *a.* tidemark. **3.** F *außer ~ und Band* a) completely out of hand, b) quite beside o.s. (*vor* with *joy etc*). **4.** F *er kommt* (*damit*) *nicht zu ~e* he can't cope (with it).
randalieren [randa'liːrən] *v/i* (h) raise hell, riot. **Randa'lierer** *m* (-s; -) hooligan, rioter.
'Rand|bemerkung *f* a) marginal note, b) passing remark. **~erscheinung** *f* side issue. **~gebiet** *n* borderland (*a. fig.*), outskirts (*of town*). **~gruppe** *f* fringe group.
'randlos *adj* rimless (*glasses*).
'Randpro,blem *n* side issue.
'Randstreifen *m* mot. shoulder.
rang [raŋ] *pret of* **ringen**.
Rang *m* (-[e]s; ⸚e) **1.** a) rank (*a.* ✕), status, position, b) quality: *fig. ersten ~es* first-class, first-rate; *j-m den ~ ablaufen* outstrip s.o.; *j-m den ~ streitig machen* compete with s.o.; *alles, was ~ und Namen hat* all the notables (F VIPs). **2.** *thea.* **erster ~** dress circle, *Am.* first balcony; **zweiter ~** upper circle, *Am.* second balcony; **dritter ~** gallery; *sports*: **die Ränge** the terraces. **3.** *lottery etc*: (dividend) class.
'Rangabzeichen *pl* insignia.
'rangehen *v/i* (irr, sep, -ge-, sn, → **gehen**) F go it.
rangeln ['raŋəln] *v/i* (h) F scuffle: *fig. um et. ~* wrangle for s.th.
'Rangfolge *f* order of precedence.
rangieren [rãˈʒiːrən] (h) **I** *v/t* 🚆 shunt, *Am.* switch. **II** *v/i fig.* rank (*vor* before).
Ran'giergleis *n* siding.
'Rangliste *f* sports: ranking list, table.
'Rangordnung *f* order of precedence.
'ranhalten: sich ~ (irr, sep, -ge-, h, → **halten**) F a) get on with it, b) dig in.
rank [raŋk] *adj.* **~ und schlank** slim.
Ranke ['raŋkə] *f* (-; -n) tendril. **'ranken** *v/i* (*a. sich ~*) (h) climb, creep.
'ranlassen *v/t* (irr, sep, -ge-, h, → **lassen**) F *j-n ~ an* (*acc*) let s.o. (have a go) at; *laß mich mal ran!* let me have a go!
rann [ran] *pret of* **rinnen**.
'rannehmen *v/t* (irr, sep, -ge-, h, → **nehmen**) F *j-n ~* ride s.o. hard.
rannte ['rantə] *pret of* **rennen**.
Ranzen ['rantsən] *m* (-s; -) a) knapsack, b) satchel.

ranzig ['rantsıç] *adj* rancid.
rapide [ra'piːdə] *adj* rapid.
Rappe ['rapə] *m* (-n; -n) black horse.
Rappel ['rapəl] *m* (-s; -) F cazy mood:
e-n ~ kriegen flip (one's lid).
Raps [raps] *m* (-es; -e) & rape(-seed).
rar [raːr] *adj* rare (*a. fig.*), scarce: F **sich ~
machen** make o.s. scarce. **Rarität**
[rari'tɛːt] *f* (-; -en) rarity, *a.* curiosity.
rasant [ra'zant] *adj* **1.** flat (*trajectory*). **2.**
F a) fast (*car etc*), b) rapid (*development
etc*), c) terrific, d) snazzy.
rasch [raʃ] *adj* quick, swift, speedy, fast:
mach ~! be quick!
rascheln ['raʃəln] *v/i* (h) rustle.
rasen ['raːzən] *v/i* **1.** (h) rage: *fig.* (*vor
Begeisterung*) **~** be wild with enthusiasm. **2.** (sn) F race, tear.
Rasen ['raːzən] *m* a) grass, b) lawn.
'rasend I *adj* **1.** raging (*fury etc*), agonizing (*pains*): **~e Kopfschmerzen** a splitting headache; **~e Wut** towering rage; **~
werden** (*machen*) go (drive *s.o.*) mad.
2. breakneck. **II** *adv* **3.** F madly (*in love
etc*): **et. ~ gern tun** just love to do s.th.
'Rasenmäher *m* lawn mower.
'Rasensprenger *m* sprinkler.
Raser ['raːzər] *m* (-s; -) F speeder.
Rase'rei *f* (-; -en) **1.** F *mot.* speeding. **2.**
no pl a) fury, b) frenzy: *j-n zur ~ brin-
gen* drive s.o. mad.
Ra'sierappa,rat *m* (safety) razor: *elektrischer ~* electric shaver (*or* razor).
Ra'siercreme *f* shaving cream.
rasieren [ra'ziːrən] (h) **I** *v/t* (*sich ~ lassen* get a) shave. **II** *sich ~* (have a)
shave: *sich elektrisch ~* use an electric
shaver.
Ra'sier|klinge *f* razor blade. **~messer** *n*
razor. **~pinsel** *m* shaving brush. **~seife**
f shaving soap. **~wasser** *n* aftershave
(lotion). **~zeug** *n* shaving things.
raspeln ['raspəln] *v/t* (h) grate.
Rasse ['rasə] *f* (-; -n) race, *zo.* breed.
'Rassehund *m* pedigree dog.
Rassel ['rasəl] *f* (-; -n) rattle.
'rasseln *v/i* (sn) rattle: F *durch e-e Prüfung ~* fail (*Am.* flunk) (an exam).
'Rassen... racial (*discrimination, problem, policy, etc*). **~kra,wall** *m* race riot.
~mischung *f* mixture of races, *zo.*
crossbreed. **~schranke** *f* colo(u)r bar.
~trennung *f* segregation, *South Africa:*
apartheid. **~unruhen** *pl* race riots.

'Rassepferd *n* thoroughbred (horse).
'rasserein *adj* purebred, thoroughbred.
rassig ['rasıç] *adj* thoroughbred.
Rassismus [ra'sısmus] *m* (-; *no pl*) racism. **Rassist** [ra'sıst] *m* (-en; -en),
ras'sistisch *adj* racist.
Rast [rast] *f* (-; *no pl*) rest, *a.* break: (*e-e*)
~ machen → **rasten**.
Raste ['rastə] *f* (-; -n) ⚙ catch.
rasten ['rastən] *v/i* (h) (take a) rest.
Raster ['rastər] *m* (-s; -) *phot., print.*
screen, *TV a.* raster, ⚡ grid.
'Rasthaus *n* motorway restaurant.
'rastlos *adj* restless.
'Rastlosigkeit *f* (-; *no pl*) restlessness.
'Rastplatz *m* resting place, *mot.* layby,
Am. rest stop.
'Raststätte *f mot.* service area.
Rasur [ra'zuːr] *f* (-; -en) shave.
Rat [raːt] *m* (-[e]s; **~e**) **1.** *no pl* (piece of)
advice, suggestion, recommendation:
auf s-n ~ hin on his advice; *j-n um ~
fragen* (*j-s ~ folgen*) ask (take) s.o.'s
advice; **~ schaffen** find a way out; **~
suchen** seek advice; *zu ~e ziehen* consult; **~ wissen** know what to do; *k-n ~
mehr wissen* be at a loss. **2.** a) council,
board, b) council(l)or.
Rate ['raːtə] *f* (-; -n) **1.** instal(l)ment: *in
~n zahlen* pay by (*or* in) instal(l)ments.
2. (*birth, growth, etc*) rate.
raten ['raːtən] *v/t, v/i* (riet, geraten, h) **1.**
j-m (*zu et.*) **~** advise s.o. (to do s.th.); **~
et. zu tun** recommend doing s.th.; *zur
Vorsicht ~* recommend caution; *wozu
~ Sie mir?* what do you advise me to
do?, what would you recommend? **2.**
guess, *a.* solve (*puzzle*): F *rate mal!* just
guess!; *falsch geraten!* wrong guess!
'Ratenzahlung *f* payment by in-
stal(l)ments.
'Ratespiel *n* guessing (*TV panel*) game.
'Ratgeber *m* (-s; -) **1.** adviser. **2.** reference book.
'Rathaus *n* townhall, *Am.* city hall.
Ratifikation [ratifika'tsioːn] *f* (-; -en),
Ratifi'zierung *f* (-; -en) ratification.
ratifizieren [ratifi'tsiːrən] *v/t* (h) ratify.
Ration [ra'tsioːn] *f* (-; -en) ration.
rational [ratsio'naːl] *adj* rational.
rationalisieren [ratsionali'ziːrən] *v/t* (h)
rationalize. **Rationali'sierung** *f* (-;
-en) rationalization. **Rationali'sie-
rungsfachmann** *m* efficiency expert.

467   **Raumfahrt**

Rationalismus [ratsĭona'lɪsmʊs] *m* (-; *no pl*) rationalism.

rationell [ratsĭo'nɛl] *adj* a) rational, b) efficient.

rationieren [ratsĭo'ni:rən] *v/t* (h) ration. **Ratio'nierung** *f* (-; -en) rationing.

'ratlos *adj* helpless: ~ *sein a.* be at a loss. **'Ratlosigkeit** *f* (-; *no pl*) helplessness.

'ratsam *adj* advisable, wise.

'Ratschlag *m* (piece of) advice: *einige gute Ratschläge* some good advice.

Rätsel ['rɛ:tsəl] *n* (-s; -) riddle, puzzle, *fig. a.* mystery: *es ist mir ein ~ (völliges)* ~ it's a (complete) mystery to me, F it beats me; *er ist mir ein ~* I can't make him out; *vor e-m ~ stehen* be baffled. **'rätselhaft** *adj* a) baffling, puzzling, b) mysterious.

'Rätselraten *n* (-s) *fig.* speculation.

'Ratsherr *m hist.* council(l)or.

Ratte ['ratə] *f* (-; -n) *zo.* rat.

'Rattenfänger *m* ratcatcher, *fig.* Pied Piper. **'Rattengift** *n* rat poison.

rattern ['ratərn] *v/i* (h and sn), **'Rattern** *n* (-s) rattle, clatter.

Raub [raʊp] *m* (-[e]s; *no pl*) **1.** a) (armed) robbery, b) kidnap(p)ing. **2.** a) loot, b) prey: *ein ~ der Flammen werden* be destroyed by fire.

'Raubbau *m* (-[e]s; *no pl*) ruinous exploitation: *~ treiben mit* a) exploit ruthlessly, b) *s-r Gesundheit* ruin one's health.

'Raubdruck *m* (-[e]s; -e) pirate edition.

rauben ['raʊbən] *v/t* (h) a) rob, b) kidnap: *j-m et.~ a. fig.* rob s.o. of s.th.

Räuber ['rɔʏbər] *m* (-s; -) robber, highwayman. **~bande** *f* gang of robbers, holdup gang. **~geschichte** *f* F cock-and-bull story.

'räuberisch *adj* rapacious, predatory: **~er Überfall** (armed) robbery, holdup.

'Raub|fisch *m* predatory fish. **~gier** *f* rapacity. **ℓgierig** *adj* rapacious. **~mord** *m* murder with robbery. **~mörder** *m* murderer and robber. **~ritter** *m hist.* robber baron. **~tier** *n* beast of prey. **~überfall** *m* (armed) robbery, holdup. **~vogel** *m* bird of prey. **~zug** *m* raid.

Rauch [raʊx] *m* (-[e]s; *no pl*) (*fig. sich in* ~ *auflösen* go up in) smoke.

rauchen ['raʊxən] *v/i, v/t* (h) smoke, 🚭 fume: F *e-e ~ have* a smoke; *Rauchen verboten!* No smoking!; → *Pfeife* 2.

Raucher ['raʊxər] *m* (-s; -) **1.** (*starker ~* heavy) smoker. **2.** → *Raucherabteil*.

Räucher... ['rɔʏçər-] *gastr.* smoked.

'Raucher|ab,teil *n* smoking compartment. **~husten** *m* 🚬 smoker's cough.

'Raucherin *f* (-; -nen) → *Raucher* 1.

räuchern ['rɔʏçərn] *v/t* (h) smoke(-dry).

'Räucherstäbchen *n* joss stick.

'Rauchfahne *f* trail of smoke.

'rauchig *adj* smoky (*a. fig. voice*).

'Rauch|pilz *m* mushroom cloud. **~säule** *f* column of smoke. **~verbot** *n* ban on smoking: *~!* No smoking! **~vergiftung** *f* smoke poisoning. **~waren** *pl* **1.** furs. **2.** tobacco products. **~wolke** *f* cloud of smoke. **~zeichen** *n* smoke signal.

Räude ['rɔʏdə] *f* (-; -n) *vet.* mange.

'räudig *adj* mangy.

rauf(...) [raʊf] F → *herauf(...), hinauf(...)*.

'Raufbold [-bɔlt] *m* (-[e]s; -e) brawler.

raufen ['raʊfən] (h) **I** *v/t sich die Haare* ~ tear one's hair. **II** *v/i* (*a. sich ~*) brawl, fight (*um* for).

Raufe'rei *f* (-; -en) brawl, fight.

rauh [raʊ] *adj* rough, *a.* harsh (*climate, treatment, voice, etc*), *a.* raw (*air etc*), sore (*throat*), wild, bleak (*region etc*), coarse (*cloth etc*): **~e Hände** chapped hands; **~e See** stormy sea; **~e Stimme** hoarse (*or* husky) voice; **~e Sitten** rough practices; **~, aber herzlich** pretty rough; *die ~e Wirklichkeit* (the) harsh reality; F *in ~en Mengen* lots of.

'Rauheit *f* (-; *no pl*) roughness (*a. fig.*).

'Rauhfaserta,pete *f* woodchip paper.

'Rauhhaar... *zo.* wirehaired.

'Rauhreif *m* hoarfrost.

Raum [raʊm] *m* (-[e]s; ⁓e) **1.** room. **2.** *no pl* room, space (*a. philos., phys.*), *fig. a.* scope: *auf engstem ~ leben* live in cramped surroundings; *fig. im ~ stehen problem etc*: be there; → *luftleer*. **3.** area, region: *im ~ (von) München* in the Munich area. **4.** *no pl* (outer) space. **~anzug** *m* space suit. **~ausstatter** *m* (-s; -) interior decorator. **~deckung** *f* *sports*: zone defen|ce (*Am.* -se).

räumen ['rɔʏmən] *v/t* (h) **1.** leave, a. ✗ evacuate, quit, vacate (*house etc*), clear (*hall, street, etc, a.* ✝ *stores*); → *Feld* 2. **2.** remove: *Minen ~* sweep mines; → *Weg*.

'Raumfähre *f* space shuttle.

'Raumfahrt *f* (-; *no pl*) space travel (*or*

flight), astronautics. **'Raumfahrt...** space (medicine, programme, etc).
'Räumfahrzeug n **1.** bulldozer. **2.** snow clearer.
'Raumflug m space flight.
'Rauminhalt m volume, capacity.
'Raumkapsel f space capsule.
räumlich ['rɔʏmlɪç] adj a) (of) space, spatial, three-dimensional, b) stereophonic, c) opt. stereoscopic: ~ **(sehr) beengt** cramped (for space).
'Räumlichkeit f (-; -en) **1.** room, pl premises. **2.** no pl three-dimensionality.
'Raummaß n solid measure. **'Raummeter** n, a. m cubic metre (Am. meter).
'Raumpflegerin f cleaning lady.
'Raumschiff n spacecraft, spaceship.
'Raumsonde f space probe.
'raumsparend adj space-saving.
'Raumstati|on f space station.
'Räumung f (-; -en) clearing, a. ✝ clearance, a. ⚔ evacuation, ⚖ eviction. **'Räumungs|befehl** m ⚖ eviction order. **~klage** f ⚖ action for eviction. **~verkauf** m ✝ clearance sale.
raunen ['raʊnən] v/i, v/t (h) whisper.
Raupe ['raʊpə] f (-; -n) zo. caterpillar.
'Raupen|fahrzeug n crawler (truck). **~kette** f crawler. **~schlepper** m tracklaying (or crawler) tractor.
raus [raʊs] int F get out!
raus(...) F → heraus(...), hinaus(...).
Rausch [raʊʃ] m (-[e]s; ⁼e) intoxication (a. fig.), drunkenness, F high, fig. ecstasy: **e-n ~ haben** be drunk; **s-n ~ ausschlafen** sleep it off.
'rauscharm adj low-noise.
rauschen ['raʊʃən] v/i **1.** (h) leaves, silk: rustle, water, stream, etc: rush, surge etc: roar. **2.** (sn) sweep. **'Rauschen** n (-s) rustling (etc), ⚡ noise. **'rauschend** adj **1.** rustling (etc). **2.** fig. glittering (parties), thunderous (applause).
'Rauschgift n drug(s pl coll). **~bekämpfung** f fight against drugs. **~handel** m drug traffic. **~händler** m drug trafficker, F pusher, sl. dealer. **~sucht** f drug addiction. **~süchtig** adj drug-addicted: **~ sein** a. be a drug addict, on drugs. **~süchtige** m, f (-n; -n) drug addict.
'rausfliegen F → hinausfliegen 2.
'rausgeben F → herausgeben.
räuspern ['rɔʏspərn] sich ~ (h) clear one's throat.

'rausreißen F → herausreißen.
'rausschmeißen v/t (irr, sep, -ge-, h, → schmeißen) F kick s.o. out, a. fire. **'Rausschmeißer** m (-s; -) F **1.** bouncer. **2.** get-out dance.
Raute ['raʊtə] f (-; -n) **1.** lozenge, esp. ♣ rhomb. **2.** ♣ rue.
Razzia ['ratsia] f (-; -ien) (police) raid.
Reagenzglas [re⁹a'gɛnts-] n test tube.
reagieren [re⁹a'giːrən] v/i (h) (auf acc to) react, fig. a. respond.
Reaktion [re⁹ak'tsioːn] f (-; -en) (auf acc to) reaction, fig. a. response.
reaktionär [re⁹aktsio'nɛːr] adj, **Reaktio'när** m (-s; -e) reactionary.
Reakti'ons|fähigkeit f (-; no pl) reactions. **~schnell** adj ~ **sein** have fast reactions. **~zeit** f reaction time.
Reaktor [re⁹'aktɔr] m (-s; -en [-'toːrən]) phys. reactor.
real [re'aːl] adj **1.** real. **2.** realistic.
Re'aleinkommen n real income.
realisieren [reali'ziːrən] v/t (h) realize.
Realismus [rea'lɪsmʊs] m (-; no pl) realism. **Realist** [-'lɪst] m (-en; -en) realist. **rea'listisch** [-tɪʃ] adj realistic.
Realität [reali'tɛːt] f (-; -en) reality.
Re'allohn m real wages.
Re'alschule f secondary school (leading to O-levels), Am. junior high school.
Rebe ['reːbə] f (-; -n) a) vine, b) tendril.
Rebell [re'bɛl] m (-en; -en) rebel.
rebellieren [rebɛ'liːrən] v/i (h) rebel.
Rebellion [rebɛ'lioːn] f (-; -en) rebellion. **re'bellisch** [lɪʃ] adj rebellious.
Rebhuhn ['reːp-] n zo. partridge.
'Rebstock m ♣ vine.
Rechen ['rɛçən] m (-s; -) rake.
'Rechen|anlage f computer. **~aufgabe** f (arithmetical) problem, sum. **~buch** n arithmetic book. **~fehler** m miscalculation, mistake. **~ma|schine** f calculator: **elektronische ~** computer.
'Rechenschaft f **~ ablegen über** (acc) answer for; **j-n zur ~ ziehen** call s.o. to account (wegen for); **j-m ~ schuldig sein** be answerable to s.o. (über acc for). **'Rechenschaftsbericht** m **1.** report. **2.** statement (of accounts).
'Rechen|schieber m slide rule. **~zentrum** n computer cent/re (Am. -er).
Recherche [re'ʃɛrʃə] f (-; -n) investigation. **recherchieren** [reʃɛr'ʃiːrən] v/i (h) investigate.

rechnen ['rɛçnən] (h) **I** v/t **1.** ☞ calculate, work out. **2.** a) estimate, b) count, allow for: *die Kinder nicht gerechnet* not counting the children. **3.** *j-n ~ zu* count s.o. among. **II** v/i **4.** calculate, *esp. ped.* do sums: *falsch ~* miscalculate; *gut ~ können* be good at figures. **5.** *fig.* **~ zu** count among; **~ mit, ~ auf** (acc) a) count on, b) expect, reckon with; *mit mir kannst du nicht ~!* count me out! **6.** economize. **'Rechnen** n (-s) calculation, *ped.* arithmetic.

'Rechner m (-s; -) **1.** calculator: *er ist ein guter ~* he is good at figures. **2.** ☺ a) calculator, b) computer. **'rechnergesteuert** adj computer-controlled.

'Rechnung f (-; -en) **1.** a) calculation, b) problem, sum: *die ~ ging nicht auf a. fig.* it didn't work out; → *Strich* 1. **2.** † account, bill, invoice, *in restaurant:* bill, *Am.* check: *die ~, bitte!* can I have the bill, please!; *auf ~* on account; *auf ~ kaufen* buy on credit; *das geht auf m-e ~* that's on me!; *fig.* **das geht auf s-e ~** that's his doing; F *auf s-e ~ kommen* get one's money's worth; *laut ~* as per invoice; *e-r Sache ~ tragen* take s.th. into account; *j-m et. in ~ stellen* charge s.th. to s.o.'s account.

'Rechnungs|betrag m invoice total. **~führung** f accountancy. **~hof** m audit division. **~jahr** n financial year. **~prüfer** m auditor. **~prüfung** f audit. **~wesen** n (-s; no pl) accountancy.

recht [rɛçt] **I** adj **1.** right, right-hand, *pol.* right(-wing), rightist: *~er Hand* on the right; *~er Hand sehen Sie ...* on your right you see ...; *im ~en Winkel* (zu) at right angles (to); → *Hand.* **2.** right, *a.* correct, *a.* suitable, *a.* just, fair: *das ist nur ~ und billig* that's only fair; *so ist's ~!* that's it!; *ganz ~!* quite right!, exactly!; *zur ~en Zeit* at the right moment; *mir ist's ~* that's all right with me, I don't mind; *mir ist alles ~* I don't care; *ist es Ihnen ~, wenn ...?* would you mind if ...?; *schon ~!* it's all right!; → *Ding* 2, *Mittel* 1. **3.** real, true, regular: *er hat k-n ~en Erfolg* he is not much of a success. **4.** **~ haben** be right; **~ behalten** be right in the end; *j-m ~ geben* agree with s.o. **II** adv **5.** a) right(ly), well, correctly, b) properly, c) very, d) rather, quite: *~ gut* not bad; *es gefällt*

mir ~ gut I rather like it; *erst ~* all the more; *(nun) erst ~ nicht* (now) less than ever; *wenn ich es ~ überlege* (when I) come to think of it; *ich weiß nicht ~* I wonder; *~ daran tun zu inf* do right to *inf*; *es geschieht ihm ~* it serves him right; *das kommt mir gerade ~* that comes in handy; *man kann es nicht allen ~ machen* you can't please everybody; *verstehen Sie mich ~* don't get me wrong.

Recht n (-[e]s; -e) **1.** no pl law, justice: *~ und Ordnung* law and order; *nach deutschem ~* under German law; *von ~s wegen* by law, *fig.* by rights; *gleiches ~ für alle* equal rights for all; *~ sprechen* administer justice; *im ~ sein* be in the right; → *a.* **recht** 4. **2.** a) right, *a.* claim, title (*all: auf* acc to), b) privilege, c) power, authority: *mit ~, zu ~* justly, rightly; *das ~ haben zu inf* have the right (or be entitled to) *inf*; *zu s-m ~ kommen* come into one's own; *er hat es mit vollem ~ getan* he had every right to do so; *alle ~e vorbehalten* all rights reserved.

'Rechte¹ f (-n; -n) **1.** right (hand or side): *zur ~n* on the right (hand); *zu s-r ~n* on (or to) his right. **2.** boxing: right. **3.** pol. the Right.

'Rechte² n (-[e]s) the right thing: *nicht das ~, nichts ~s* not the real thing; *nach dem ~n sehen* look after things.

'Rechteck n (-[e]s; -e) rectangle.
'rechteckig adj rectangular.
'rechtfertigen v/t (h) justify (*sich* o.s.).
'Rechtfertigung f (-; -en) justification: *zu m-r ~* in my defen|ce (*Am.* -se).
'rechtgläubig adj orthodox.
'rechthaberisch [-ha:bərɪʃ] adj dogmatic, opinionated, pigheaded.
'rechtlich I adj legal, *a.* lawful. **II** adv legally: *~ verpflichtet* bound by law.
'rechtlos adj without rights.
'rechtmäßig adj lawful, legitimate (*heir, claim, etc*), legal: *das steht ihm ~ zu* he is (legally) entitled to it.
'Rechtmäßigkeit f (-; no pl) lawfulness, legitimacy, legality.

rechts [rɛçts] adv on the right (hand side): *nach ~* to the right; *~ von ihm* on his right; *~ abbiegen* turn off right; *sich ~ halten* keep to the right; *pol. ~ stehen* belong to the Right.

'**Rechtsabbieger** m mot. vehicle (pl traffic) turning right.

'**Rechts|anspruch** m legal claim (auf acc to). **~anwalt** m, **~anwältin** f lawyer, Br. a. solicitor, in court: counsel, barrister, Am. attorney(-at-law).

'**Rechtsaußen** m (-; -) outside right.

'**Rechts|behelf** m legal remedy. **~beistand** m legal adviser, in court: counsel. **~beratungsstelle** f legal aid office. **~beugung** f perversion of justice. **~bruch** m breach of law.

'**rechtschaffen** adj honest, upright.

'**Rechtschreibfehler** m spelling mistake. '**Rechtschreibung** f spelling

'**Rechtsextre,mist(in** f) m right-wing extremist.

'**rechtsfähig** adj having legal capacity.

'**Rechts|fall** m (law) case. **~frage** f question of law. **~geschäft** n legal transaction. **♀gültig** adj legal(ly valid): **~ machen** validate. **~gutachten** n legal opinion.

'**Rechtshänder** [-hɛndər] m (-s; -) right-hander: **~ sein** be right-handed.

'**rechtsherum** adv to the right.

'**Rechtskraft** f legal force, validity: **~ erlangen** become effective.

'**rechtskräftig** adj legal(ly binding), final (judg[e]ment), effective (law).

'**Rechtskurve** f right-hand bend.

'**Rechts|lage** f legal position. **~mittel** n legal remedy: **ein ~ einlegen** lodge an appeal. **~nachfolger(in** f) m successor in interest. **~norm** f legal norm.

'**rechtsorien,tiert** adj pol. right-wing.

'**Rechtspar,tei** f right-wing party.

'**Rechtspflege** f (-; no pl) administration of justice. '**Rechtsprechung** f (-; -en) jurisdiction, administration of justice.

'**Rechts|radi,kale** m, f right-wing extremist. **~ruck** m pol. swing to the right.

'**Rechtsschutz** m legal protection. **~versicherung** f legal costs insurance.

'**Rechts|spruch** m legal decision, in civil matters: judg(e)ment, in criminal cases: sentence. **~staat** m constitutional state. **♀staatlich** adj constitutional. **~staatlichkeit** f (-; no pl) rule of law.

'**Rechtssteuerung** f right-hand drive.

'**Rechts|streit** m lawsuit, action. **~titel** m legal title. **♀unfähig** adj (legally) disabled. **♀unwirksam** adj ineffective. **♀verbindlich** adj (legally) binding (für

on). **~verfahren** n **1.** legal procedure. **2.** (legal) proceedings.

'**Rechtsverkehr** m right-hand traffic: **in ... ist ~** in ... they drive on the right.

'**Rechts|verletzung** f infringement. **~vertreter** m legal representative, (authorized) agent. **~weg** m course of law: **auf dem ~** by legal action; **den ~ beschreiten** go to law. **♀widrig** adj illegal. **~widrigkeit** f (-; -en) **1.** no pl illegality. **2.** unlawful act. **~wissenschaft** f (-; no pl) jurisprudence, law.

'**rechtwink(e)lig** adj right-angled, rectangular.

'**rechtzeitig I** adj punctual. **II** adv a) in time (zu for), b) on time: **gerade** (or **genau**) **~** in the nick of time.

Reck [rɛk] n (-[e]s; -e) horizontal bar.

recken ['rɛkən] v/t (h) stretch: **den Hals ~** crane one's neck.

'**Reckturnen** n bar exercises.

Redakteur [redak'tøːr] m (-s; -e) editor. **Redak'teurin** f (-; -nen) (woman) editor. **Redaktion** [-'tsjoːn] f (-; -en) **1.** no pl editing. **2.** a) editorial staff, b) editorial office. **redaktionell** [-tsjoˈnɛl] adj editorial: **~ bearbeiten** edit.

Rede ['reːdə] f (-; -n) **1.** speech, address: **e-e ~ halten** make a speech; F **große ~n schwingen** talk big. **2.** a) talk(ing), speech (a. ling.), b) conversation, talk, c) words, language: **direkte** (**indirekte**) **~** direct (reported or indirect) speech; **es geht die ~, daß** it is rumo(u)red (that); **die ~ kam auf** (acc) the conversation (or talk) turned to; (j-m) **~** (**und Antwort**) **stehen** account (to s.o.) (**über** acc for); **j-n zur ~ stellen** take s.o. to task (**wegen** gen for); **davon kann k-e ~ sein!** that's out of the question!; (**aber**) **k-e ~!** by no means!; **es ist nicht der ~ wert** a) it is not worth mentioning, b) don't mention it!, c) never mind!; **der langen ~ kurzer Sinn** to cut a long story short; → **verschlagen¹** 4.

'**Rede|freiheit** f (-; no pl) freedom of speech. **~gabe** f (-; no pl) eloquence.

'**redegewandt** adj eloquent.

'**Redekunst** f rhetoric.

reden ['reːdən] (h) **I** v/t, v/i (**mit** to, **über** acc about, of) speak, talk: **über Politik ~** talk politics; **von sich ~ machen** cause a stir; **j-m ins Gewissen ~** appeal to s.o.'s conscience; **ich habe mit dir zu**

~ I'd like a word with you; **laß uns vernünftig darüber ~!** let's talk sense!; **sie läßt nicht mit sich ~** she won't listen to reason; **nicht zu ~ von ...** not to mention ...; **~ wir von et. anderem!** let's change the subject!; **du hast gut ~!** you can talk!; **darüber läßt sich ~!** that's a possibility! II **sich heiser (in Wut)** ~ talk o.s. hoarse (into a rage).

'**Reden** n (-s) talking: **j-n zum ~ bringen** make s.o. talk.

'**Redensart** f a) phrase, b) saying, c) pl empty talk: **das ist nur so e-e ~!** it's just a way of speaking.

'**Rede|schwall** m flood of words. **~ver-bot** n ban on speaking: **j-m ~ erteilen** ban s.o. from speaking. **~weise** f s-e etc ~ the way he etc talks. **~wendung** f figure of speech, idiom.

redigieren [redi'gi:rən] v/t (h) edit.

redlich ['re:tlıç] adj honest, upright: **sich ~(e) Mühe geben** do one's best.

'**Redlichkeit** f (-; no pl) honesty, probity.

Redner ['re:dnər] m (-s; -) speaker. **~bühne** f rostrum, (speaker's) platform. **~pult** n lectern.

'**redselig** adj talkative.

'**Redseligkeit** f (-; no pl) talkativeness.

reduzieren [redu'tsi:rən] v/t (h) reduce (**auf** acc to): sich.

Reede ['re:də] f (-; -n) ⚓ roadstead, road(s): **das Schiff liegt auf der ~** the ship is (lying) in the roads. **Reeder** ['re:dər] m (-s; -) shipowner. **Reede'rei** f (-; -en) shipping company.

reell [re'ɛl] adj **1.** real (chance etc). **2.** honest, decent, ✝ good, fair (price etc).

Reep [re:p] n (-[e]s; -e) ⚓ rope.

Reetdach ['re:t-] n thatched roof.

Referat [refe'ra:t] n (-[e]s; -e) **1.** report, a. lecture, ped., univ. (seminar) paper: **ein ~ halten → referieren. 2.** department.

Referendar [referɛn'da:r] m (-s; -e), **Referen'darin** f (-; -nen) → **Gerichts-, Studienreferendar(in).**

Referendum [refe'rɛndʊm] n (-s; -den, -da) referendum.

Referent [refe'rɛnt] m (-en; -en) **1.** official in charge: **er ist persönlicher Referent** he is personal assistant (gen to). **2.** speaker, 🎓 referee.

Referenz [refe'rɛnts] f (-; -en) reference.

referieren [refe'ri:rən] v/t, v/i (h) (**über**

acc on) a) report, b) (give a) lecture, univ. give a paper.

reffen ['rɛfən] v/t (h) ⚓ reef.

reflektieren [reflɛk'ti:rən] (h) **I** v/t phys. reflect. **II** v/i F **~ auf** (acc) have one's eye on. **Reflektor** [re'flɛktɔr] m (-s; -en [-'to:rən]) reflector.

Reflex [re'flɛks] m (-es; -e) reflex.

Re'flexbewegung f reflex action.

Reflexion [reflɛ'ksio:n] f (-; -en) reflection.

reflexiv [reflɛ'ksi:f] adj ling. reflexive.

Refle'xivpro,nomen n reflexive pronoun.

Reform [re'fɔrm] f (-; -en) reform.

Reformation [reforma'tsio:n] f (-; -en) reformation. **Reformator** [refor'ma:-tɔr] m (-s; -en [-'ma'to:rən]) reformer.

re'formbedürftig adj in need of reform.

Re'formhaus n health food shop.

reformieren [refor'mi:rən] v/t (h) reform. **Refor'mierte** m, f (-n; -n) member of the Reformed Church.

Re'formkost f health food(s).

Refrain [rə'frɛ:] m (-s; -s) refrain.

Regal [re'ga:l] n (-s; -e) shelves. **Re'gal-wand** f wall lined with shelve units.

Regatta [re'gata] f (-; -ten) regatta.

rege ['re:gə] adj lively, a. active, vivid (imagination), busy (traffic etc): **~n Anteil nehmen an** (dat) show an active interest in; **~ Nachfrage** keen demand.

Regel ['re:gəl] f (-; -n) **1.** rule: **in der ~** as a rule; **zur ~ werden** become a rule (or habit); **es sich zur ~ machen zu** inf make it a rule to inf; **nach allen ~n der Kunst** in superior style. **2.** ✚ period.

'**regelbar** adj adjustable.

'**Regelblutung** f ✚ menstruation.

'**Regelfall** m **im ~** as a rule.

'**regellos** adj **1.** irregular. **2.** disorderly.

'**Regellosigkeit** f (-; no pl) irregularity.

'**regelmäßig** adj a) regular, a. periodical, b) regulated, orderly.

'**Regelmäßigkeit** f (-; no pl) regularity.

'**regeln** ['re:gəln] v/t (h) regulate, ⚙ a. adjust, a. direct (traffic), settle (matter etc): **das wird sich (schon) alles ~** that will sort itself out.

'**regelrecht I** adj **1.** proper. **2.** F regular, real. **II** adv **3.** properly. **4.** F downright.

'**Regelstudienzeit** f time limit for a course of study.

'**Regelung** f (-; -en) **1.** regulation, ⚙ a.

adjustment, settlement. **2.** provision, rule. '**Regelungstechnik** f control engineering.

'**Regelverstoß** m sports: foul.

'**regelwidrig** adj irregular, sports: against the rules, foul. '**Regelwidrigkeit** f (-; -en) irregularity, sports: foul.

regen ['reːgən] v/t (a. **sich** ~) (h) move, stir: fig. **sich** ~ feelings etc: stir, arise.

'**Regen** m (-s; -) rain, fig. a. shower: **saurer** ~ acid rain; **ich bin in den** ~ **gekommen** I was caught in the rain; F **vom** ~ **in die Traufe kommen** jump out of the frying-pan into the fire; F fig. **ein warmer** ~ a windfall.

'**regenarm** adj with low rainfall.

'**Regenbogen** m rainbow. ~**farben** pl colo(u)rs of the rainbow. ~**haut** f anat. iris. ~**presse** f trashy weeklies.

Regeneration [regenera'tsĭoːn] f (-; -en) regeneration. **Regenerati'onsfähigkeit** f regenerative power.

regenerieren [regene'riːrən] v/i (a. **sich** ~) (h) regenerate.

'**Regen|fälle** pl rain(fall). ~**guß** m downpour. ~**haut** f plastic mac. ~**mantel** m raincoat. 2**reich** adj rainy. ~**rinne** f gutter, mot. roof rail. ~**schauer** m shower. ~**schirm** m umbrella.

Regent [re'gɛnt] m (-en; -en) regent.

'**Regen|tag** m rainy day. ~**tonne** f water butt. ~**tropfen** m raindrop. ~**wald** m rain forest. ~**wasser** n rainwater. ~**wetter** n rainy weather. ~**wolke** f raincloud. ~**wurm** m earthworm. ~**zeit** f rainy season, the rains.

Regie [re'ʒiː] f (-; no pl) **1.** thea. etc direction: **unter der** ~ **von** a. directed by; ~ **führen** (**bei**) direct (s.th.). **2.** a) management, b) administration: fig. **in eigener** ~ on one's own. ~**anweisung** f stage direction. ~**assi**|**stent** m assistant director. ~**fehler** m humor. slip-up. ~**raum** m TV central control room.

regieren [re'giːrən] (h) **I** v/t a) govern (a. ling.), rule, b) manage, control. **II** v/i rule, monarch: a. reign (a. fig.).

Re'gierung f (-; -en) **1.** reign: **unter der** ~ **von** (or gen) under the reign of; **an der** ~ **sein** be in power; **an die** ~ **kommen** take over, come into power. **2.** government.

Re'gierungs|beamte m government official. ~**bezirk** m administration dis-

trict. ~**bildung** f formation of the government. ~**chef** m head of government. ~**erklärung** f policy statement. 2**fähig** adj in a position to govern the country: ~**e Mehrheit** etc working majority etc. ~**par,tei** f ruling party. ~**sitz** m seat of government. ~**sprecher** m government spokesman. ~**umbildung** f (government) reshuffle. ~**vorlage** f government bill. ~**wechsel** m change of government. ~**zeit** f a) reign, b) term of office.

Regime [re'ʒiːm] n (-s; - [-məˈ]) regime.

Re'gimekritiker m pol. dissident.

Regiment [regi'mɛnt] n (-[e]s) **1.** (-e) (a. **das** ~ **führen**) rule. **2.** (-er) ✕ regiment.

Region [re'giŏːn] f (-; -en) region.

regional [regĭo'naːl] adj, **Regio'nal...** regional.

Regisseur [reʒɪ'søːr] m (-s; -e), **Regis'seurin** f (-; -nen) thea., film: director, TV producer.

Register [re'gɪstər] n (-s; -) register (a. ♪), in book: index: F **alle** ~ **ziehen** pull all the stops.

Registratur [regɪstra'tuːr] f (-; -en) registry. **registrieren** [regɪs'triːrən] v/t (h) register (a. fig.), record (a. ☺), fig. note.

Regi'strierkasse f cash register.

Reglement [reglə'mãː] n (-s; -s) regulation(s).

Regler ['reːglər] m (-s; -) ☺ controller.

'**reglos** adj motionless.

regnen ['reːgnən] v/impers (h) rain: **es regnete in Strömen** it was pouring (with rain); fig. **es regnete Anfragen** there was a flood of inquiries.

'**regnerisch** adj rainy.

Regreß [re'grɛs] m (-sses; -sse) ✝, ⚖ recourse.

re'greßpflichtig adj liable to recourse.

'**regsam** adj active.

'**Regsamkeit** f (-; no pl) activity.

regulär [regu'lɛːr] adj regular.

regu'lierbar adj ☺ adjustable.

regulieren [regu'liːrən] v/t (h) **1.** a) regulate, b) adjust. **2.** settle (account etc).

Regung ['reːgʊŋ] f (-; -en) a) movement, b) emotion, c) impulse.

'**regungslos** adj motionless.

Reh [reː] n (-[e]s; -e) **1.** zo. (roe) deer. **2.** gastr. venison.

Rehabilitation [rehabilita'tsĭoːn] f (-; -en) rehabilitation.

Rehabilitati'onszentrum n (l) ~ rehabilitation centre (*Am.* -er).

rehabilitieren [ʔ, ɪlɪ'tiːrən] v/t (h) rehabilitate. **Rehabili'tierung** f (-; -en) rehabilitation.

'Reh|bock m roebuck. **~braten** m roast venison. **~geiß** f doe. **~keule** f gastr. leg of venison. **~kitz** n fawn. **~rücken** m gastr. saddle of venison.

Reibach ['raɪbax] m (-s; no pl) F **e-n ~ machen** make one's pile.

'Reibe f (-; -n), **'Reibeisen** n grater.

reiben ['raɪbən] (rieb, gerieben, h) I v/t **1.** rub: **sich die Hände ~** rub one's hands; → **Nase. 2.** grate. II v/i **3.** chafe.

Reibe'reien pl (constant) friction.

'Reibfläche f striking surface.

'Reibung f (-; -en) a. fig. friction.

'reibungslos adj a. fig. smooth.

'Reibungspunkt m fig. cause of friction.

'Reibungsverlust m ⊕ friction(al) loss.

'Reibungswärme f ⊕ frictional heat.

reich [raɪç] I adj rich (**an** dat in), a. wealthy, a. abundant, copious, a. sumptuous: **e-e ~e Auswahl** a wide selection (**an** dat, **von** of). II adv richly, copiously: **~ beschenkt** loaded with gifts.

Reich n (-[e]s; -e) empire, kingdom (a. eccl. or fig.), rhet. or fig. realm: hist. **das Dritte ~** the Third Reich; **das ~ der Tiere** animal kingdom.

reichen ['raɪçən] (h) I v/t **1.** j-m et. ~ hand (or pass) s.o. s.th.; **sich die Hände ~** shake hands. **2.** offer, serve. II v/i **3. ~ bis** (or an acc) reach to, extend to, come up (or go down) to; **soweit das Auge reicht** as far as the eye can see. **4.** last (out), do, be enough: **das reicht!** that will do!; **das Brot reicht nicht** there isn't enough bread; **damit ~ wir bis Mai** it will last us till May; **es reicht für alle** there is enough to go round; F **mir reicht's!** I've had enough!

'reichhaltig adj extensive, large: **~e Auswahl** wide selection; **~es Programm** varied program(me Br.).

'reichlich I adj ample, abundant, plentiful, plenty of (time, food, etc), generous (pay etc). II adv F rather, pretty: **~ versehen sein mit** have plenty of.

'Reichtum m (-s; ⁻er) (**an** dat of) riches, a. fig. wealth, abundance.

'Reichweite f reach, ✈, ✗ range: **in** (**außer**) ~ within (out of) reach.

~ 't [ɪıl] adj ripe, a. fig. mature: **~ werden** → **reifen**.

Reif[1] m (-[e]s; no pl) hoarfrost.

Reif[2] m (-[e]s; -e) ring, bracelet, circlet.

Reife ['raɪfə] f (-; no pl) **1.** ripeness, esp. fig. maturity. **2. mittlere ~** intermediate high school certificate, GCE O-levels.

reifen ['raɪfən] v/i (sn) ripen, mature (a. fig.): **~ lassen** mature.

'Reifen m (-s; -) **1.** mot. etc tyre, Am. tire: **die ~ wechseln** change tyres. **2.** hoop. **~panne** f puncture, blowout, Am. flat. **~pro,fil** n tyre (Am. tire) engraving. **~wechsel** m tyre (Am. tire) change.

'Reifeprüfung f → **Abitur.**

'Reifglätte f mot. slippery frost.

'reiflich I adj **nach ~er Überlegung** after careful consideration. II adv (**sich**) **et. ~ überlegen** consider s.th. carefully.

Reigen ['raɪgən] m (-s; -) round dance: **den ~ eröffnen** a. fig. lead off.

Reihe ['raɪə] f (-; -n) a) row, b) line, c) row (of seats), d) series, number, e) succession: **geometrische ~** geometric progression; **sich in e-r ~ aufstellen** line up; F **e-e ganze ~ von** a whole string of; **aus den ~n** (gen) from among; **Kritiker aus den eigenen ~n** critics from among the own ranks; (**immer**) **der ~ nach** in turn, one after the other; **außer der ~** out of turn; **ich bin an der ~** it's my turn; **warten, bis man an die ~ kommt** wait one's turn; F fig. **aus der ~ sein** be out of sorts; **aus der ~ tanzen** step out of line; **wieder in die ~ bringen** straighten s.o., s.th. out.

'Reihen|folge f order, sequence: **in zeitlicher ~** in chronological order. **~haus** n terrace (Am. row) house. **~untersuchung** f ✚ mass screening.

'reihenweise adv **1.** in rows. **2.** F fig. by the dozen.

Reiher ['raɪər] m (-s; -) zo. heron.

Reim [raɪm] m (-[e]s; -e) rhyme.

reimen ['raɪmən] v/t, v/i (a. **sich ~**) (h) rhyme (**auf** acc with).

rein [raɪn] I adj **1.** pure (a. biol., 🐑, a. fig.), clean, clear (a. skin, conscience, etc), net, clear (profit), fig. mere, sheer: **~e Wolle** pure wool; **e-e ~e Formalität** a mere formality; **~er Wahnsinn** sheer madness; **die ~e Wahrheit** the (plain) truth; **durch ~en Zufall** by pure accident; **et. ins ~e bringen** sort s.th. out;

mit j-m ins ~e kommen get things straightened out with s.o.; *ins ~e schreiben* make a fair copy of; → *Luft* 1, *Tisch*, *Wein* 2 *etc.* **II** *adv* **2.** purely: *aus ~ persönlichen Gründen* for purely personal reasons; → *zufällig.* **3.** F absolutely.

rein(...) F → *herein(...)*, *hinein(...)*.

Reineclaude [rɛ:nə'klo:də] *f* (-; -n) 🍒 greengage.

'**Reinertrag** *m* net proceeds.

'**Reinfall** *m* F a) flop, b) letdown, frost.

'**reinfallen** F → *hereinfallen* 2.

'**Reingewicht** *n* net weight.

'**Reingewinn** *m* net (*or* clear) profit.

'**reinhängen** (*sep*, *-ge-*, *h*) F *fig.* **I** *v/t j-n ~* set s.o. up, frame s.o. **II** *sich* (*voll*) *~* go flat out.

'**reinhauen** *v/i* (*irr*, *sep*, *-ge-*, *h*, → *hauen*) F dig in, tuck in.

'**Reinheit** *f* (-; *no pl*) purity (*a. fig.*), cleanness.

reinigen ['raɪnɪgən] *v/t* (*h*) clean, dry-clean (*clothes*), *a.* 🔬 cleanse (*von* of), purify (*a. fig.*), *metall.* refine.

'**Reinigung** *f* (-; *-en*) **1.** cleaning (*etc.*). **2.** dry cleaners: *et. in die ~ geben* send s.th. to the cleaners.

'**Reinigungs|milch** *f cosmetics:* cleansing milk. **~mittel** *n* detergent.

'**Reinkul,tur** *f* F *Kitsch in ~* pure unadulterated trash.

'**reinlegen** F → *hereinlegen.*

'**reinlich** *adj* clean, *person:* cleanly, *a.* neat, tidy. '**Reinlichkeit** *f* (-; *no pl*) cleanliness, neatness, tidiness.

'**reinrassig** *adj* pedigree (*dog etc*), thoroughbred (*horse*).

'**Reinschrift** *f* fair copy.

'**reinseiden** *adj* (of) pure silk.

'**reinwaschen** *v/t* (*irr*, *sep*, *-ge-*, *h*, → *waschen*) *fig.* clear (*von* of).

Reis[1] [raɪs] *n* (*-es*; *-er*) 🍃 **1.** twig. **2.** scion.

Reis[2] *m* (*-es*; *no pl*) rice.

'**Reisauflauf** *m* rice pudding.

Reise ['raɪzə] *f* (-; *-n*) journey, travel, trip, *a.* tour, ✈, ⚓ voyage: *gute ~!* have a nice trip!, bon voyage!; *e-e ~ mit dem Auto* a journey by car; *ich plane e-e ~ durch Amerika* I'm planning to travel through America; *auf ~n sein* be travel(l)ing; → *antreten* 1.

'**Reise|andenken** *n* souvenir. **~apo,theke** *f* first-aid kit. **~bekanntschaft** *f* travel(l)ing acquaintance. **~bericht** *m* travelog(ue *Br.*). **~beschreibung** *f* book of travels. **~bü,ro** *n* travel agency. **~bus** *m* coach. **~diploma,tie** *f pol.* shuttle-diplomacy. **2fertig** *adj* ready to start. **~führer** *m* **1.** guide. **2.** guide(book). **~gefährte** *m* travel companion. **~geschwindigkeit** *f* cruising speed. **~gesellschaft** *f* **1.** tourist party. **2.** → *Reiseveranstalter.*

'**Reisekosten** *pl* travel(l)ing expenses. **~zuschuß** *m* travel([l]ing) allowance.

'**Reiseland** *n* tourist country.

'**Reiseleiter(in** *f*) *m* courier.

'**reiselustig** *adj* fond of travel(l)ing.

'**Reisemo,bil** *n* (-[*e*]s; -e) camper, *Am.* mobile home.

reisen ['raɪzən] *v/i* (*sn*) (*nach* to) travel, go, make a trip: *zu s-n Verwandten ~* go to visit one's relatives; *er ist weit gereist* he has travel(l)ed a lot; *ins Ausland ~* go abroad; F *fig.* **~** *auf* (*acc*) coast on. '**Reisen** *n* (-s) travel, travel(l)ing. '**Reisende** *m*, *f* (-n; -n) **1.** a) travel(l)er, b) tourist, c) passenger. **2.** → *Handlungsreisende.*

'**Reise|neces,saire** *n* sponge bag. **~paß** *m* passport. **~pro,spekt** *m* travel brochure. **~provi,ant** *m* provisions for the journey. **~route** *f* route, itinerary. **~scheck** *m* traveller's cheque, *Am.* traveler's check. **~schreibma,schine** *f* portable typewriter. **~tasche** *f* travel(l)ing (*or* overnight) bag, holdall. **~unterlagen** *pl* travel documents. **~veranstalter** *m* tour operator. **~verkehr** *m* holiday traffic. **~wecker** *m* travel(l)ing (alarm) clock. **~zeit** *f* holiday season. **~ziel** *n* destination.

'**Reißaus:** *~ nehmen* take to one's heels.

'**Reißbrett** *n* drawing-board.

reißen ['raɪsən] (*riß*, *gerissen*) **I** *v/t* (*h*) **1.** tear (*in Stücke* to pieces), *a.* snatch (*off*), pull (*off*, *out*, *etc*): *mit sich ~* drag, *flood:* sweep; *an sich ~* snatch; *die Macht an sich ~* seize power; *sich ~* tear o.s. (*an dat* on); F *fig. sich ~ um* fight over; F *ich reiße mich nicht darum* I can do without; → *Witz* 1. **2.** *sports:* a) knock down (*the bar*), b) snatch (*the weight*). **3.** *zo.* kill. **II** *v/i* **4.** (*sn*) tear, burst, split, 🔬 rupture, *rope etc:* break, snap; → *Geduld.* **5.** (*h*) *~ an* (*dat*) tear at. **6.** (*h*) *sports:* knock down the bar. '**Reißen** n (-s) F ✷ rheumatism. '**reißend** adj **1.** rapid, torrential (river etc): → **Absatz** 3. **2.** rapacious (animal). **3.** searing (pain).

'**Reißer** m (-s; -) F **1.** thriller. **2.** hit.

'**reißerisch** adj sensational, loud: **~e Werbung** a. F ballyhoo.

'**Reiß|feder** f drawing-pen. **~leine** f rip cord. **~nagel** m drawing-pin, Am. thumbtack. **~verschluß** m zip(per): **den ~ e-r Jacke zumachen (aufmachen)** zip up (unzip) a jacket. **~zahn** m zo. fang, canine tooth. **~zwecke** f drawing-pin, Am. thumbtack.

reiten ['raɪtən] v/i (ritt, geritten, sn) ride (a. v/t), go on horseback. '**Reiten** n (-s) riding. '**Reiter** m (-s; -) **1.** rider, horseman. **2.** tab. **Reite'rei** f (-; -en) cavalry.

'**Reiterin** f (-; -nen) rider, horsewoman.

'**Reit|gerte** f riding crop. **~hose** f (riding) breeches. **~peitsche** f riding crop. **~pferd** n saddle horse. **~schule** f riding school. **~sport** m riding. **~stiefel** pl riding boots. **~tur,nier** n horse show. **~weg** m bridle path.

Reiz [raɪts] m (-es; -e) **1.** physiol., psych. or fig. stimulus, ✷ irritation. **2.** a) charm, b) appeal, attraction, c) lure, d) thrill: **der ~ des Neuen** the novelty; **s-n ~ (für j-n) verlieren** pall (on s.o.); **s-e ~e spielen lassen** display one's charms; **das hat k-n ~ für mich** that does not appeal to me.

'**reizbar** adj irritable, touchy.

'**Reizbarkeit** f (-; no pl) irritability.

reizen ['raɪtsən] (h) **I** v/t **1.** irritate (a. ✷), a. annoy, provoke. **2.** a) stimulate, b) (a)rouse (curiosity etc). **3.** a) tempt, b) appeal to: **es reizte ihn zu** inf he was tempted to inf; **es würde mich ~ zu** inf I wouldn't mind ger; **das reizt mich gar nicht** that doesn't appeal to me at all. **4.** cards: bid. '**reizend** adj charming, delightful, a. lovely, sweet.

'**Reizhusten** m ✷ dry cough.

'**reizlos** adj **1.** a) unattractive, a. plain, b) boring. **2.** ✷ bland (food).

'**Reizschwelle** f stimulus threshold.

'**Reizüberflutung** f stimulus satiation.

'**Reizung** f (-; -en) a. ✷ irritation, stimulation.

'**reizvoll** adj charming, attractive, fascinating, challenging (task etc).

'**Reizwäsche** f sexy underwear.

'**Reizwort** n emotive word.

rekapitulieren [rekapitu'liːrən] v/t (h) recapitulate.

rekeln ['rɛːkəln] **sich ~** (h) loll (about).

Reklamation [reklama'tsǐoːn] f (-; -en) complaint.

Reklame [re'klaːmə] f (-; -n) a) advertising, b) advertisement, F ad: **für et. ~ machen** advertise (F plug) s.th. **~rummel** m F contp. ballyhoo. **~tafel** f hoarding, esp. Am. billboard.

reklamieren [rekla'miːrən] (h) **I** v/i complain (**wegen** about), esp. sports: protest (**gegen** against). **II** v/t complain about.

rekonstruieren [rekɔnstru'iːrən] v/t (h) reconstruct.

Rekonvaleszent [rekɔnvalɛs'tsɛnt] m (-en; -en) convalescent.

Rekonvaleszenz [rekɔnvalɛs'tsɛnts] f (-; no pl) convalescence.

Rekord [re'kɔrt] m (-[e]s; -e) (**e-n ~ aufstellen** set up a) record. **~besuch** m record attendance. **~ernte** f bumper crop. **~halter(in** f) m, **~inhaber(in** f) m record holder. **~versuch** m attempt on the record. **~zeit** f record time.

Rekrut [re'kruːt] m (-en; -en), **rekrutieren** [rekru'tiːrən] v/t (h) recruit.

rektal [rɛk'taːl] adj ✷ rectal.

Rektion [rɛk'tsǐoːn] f (-; -en) ling. government: **die ~ e-s Verbs** the case governed by a verb.

Rektor ['rɛktɔr] m (-s; -en [-'toːrən]) **1.** ped. headmaster, principal. **2.** univ. rector. **Rektorat** [rɛkto'raːt] n (-[e]s; -e) **1.** rectorship, rectorate. **2.** headmaster's (or principal's, univ. rector's) office.

Rektorin [rɛk'toːrɪn] f (-; -nen) ped. headmistress, principal.

Relais [rə'lɛː] n (-; -[rə'lɛːs]) ⚡ relay.

Relation [rela'tsǐoːn] f (-; -en) relation(ship): **in k-r ~ stehen zu** be out of all proportion to.

relativ [rela'tiːf] adj relative(ly adv), adv a. comparatively. **Relativität** [relativi'tɛːt] f (-; no pl) relativity. **Relativi-'tätstheo,rie** f theory of relativity.

Rela'tivsatz m ling. relative clause.

relevant [rele'vant] adj relevant (**für** to).

Relief [re'lǐɛf] n (-s; -s, -e) relief.

Religion [reli'gǐoːn] f (-; -en) **1.** religion. **2.** no pl ped. religious instruction.

Religi'ons... → **Glaubens... ~freiheit** f

freedom of worship. **~gemeinschaft** f a) confession, b) religious community.

religi'onslos adj irreligious.

Religi'ons|unterricht m → **Religion** 2. **~zugehörigkeit** f religious affiliation.

religiös [reli'giø:s] adj religious.

Relikt [re'lɪkt] n (-[e]s; -e) **1.** relic. **2.** biol. relict.

Reling ['re:lɪŋ] f (-; -s) ⚓ rail.

Reliquie [re'li:kviə] f (-; -n) relic. **Re'liquienschrein** m reliquary.

Remis [rə'mi:] n (-; - [rə'mi:s]) draw.

Remittenden [remɪ'tɛndən] pl returns.

Remoulade [remu'la:də] f (-; -n) gastr. tartar sauce.

rempeln ['rɛmpəln] v/t (h) F jostle, push.

Ren [rɛn, re:n] n (-s; -s) zo. reindeer.

Renaissance [rənɛ'sã:s] f (-; -n) a) no pl hist. Renaissance, b) fig. renaissance.

Rendezvous [rãde'vu:] n (-; - [-'vu:s]) rendezvous (a. space travel), date.

Rendite [rɛn'di:tə] f (-; -n) ✝ (net) yield.

'Rennbahn f a) racecourse, racetrack (a. mot.), b) (cycling) track.

'Rennboot n speedboat.

rennen ['rɛnən] (rannte, gerannt) **I** v/i (sn) a) run, rush, dash, b) race: **~ gegen** run into; **schneller ~ als** outrun; **sie rannten um die Wette** they raced each other; → **Verderben. II** v/t (h) F **j-m ein Messer** etc **in die Brust ~** run a knife etc into s.o.'s chest; **j-n über den Haufen ~** knock s.o. down. **'Rennen** n (-s; -) a) running (etc), b) race, c) heat: **totes ~** dead heat; **das ~ machen** come in first, win, fig. come out on top.

'Renner m (-s; -) F fig. (great) hit.

'Renn|fahrer m a) racing driver, b) racing cyclist. **~läufer** m ski racer. **~pferd** n racehorse. **~rad** n racing cycle. **~schi** m racing ski. **~schuhe** pl spikes. **~sport** m racing ski. **~stall** m **1.** (racing) stable. **2.** F mot. racing team. **~strecke** f mot. racing course. **~wagen** m racing car.

renommiert [renɔ'mi:rt] adj (wegen for) famous, noted.

renovieren [reno'vi:rən] v/t (h) a) renovate (building), b) redecorate (room). **Reno'vierung** f (-; -en) a) renovation, b) redecoration.

rentabel [rɛn'ta:bəl] adj profitable.

Rentabilität [rɛntabili'tɛ:t] f (-; no pl) profitability.

Rente ['rɛntə] f (-; -n) **1.** pension: F **auf**

(or **in**) **~ gehen** retire; **auf** (or **in**) **~ sein** be retired; → **dynamisch. 2.** annuity.

'Renten|alter n retirement age. **~anpassung** f index-linked adjustment of pensions. **~empfänger(in** f) m → **Rentner(in). ~markt** m ✝ bond market. **~pa,piere** pl fixed interest bonds. **~versicherung** f pension scheme.

rentieren [rɛn'ti:rən] **sich ~** (h) be profitable, a. pay, be worthwhile.

Rentner ['rɛntnər] m (-s; -), **'Rentnerin** f (-; -nen) pensioner.

reorgani'sieren v/t (h) reorganize.

reparabel [repa'ra:bəl] adj repairable.

Reparation [repara'tsio:n] f (-; -en) reparation.

Reparatur [repara'tu:r] f (-; -en) repair(s): **in ~** being repaired; **zur ~ geben** have s.th. repaired. **✝bedürftig** adj in need of repair. **~kosten** pl cost of repairs. **~werkstatt** f mot. garage.

reparieren [repa'ri:rən] v/t (h) mend, F fix: **nicht mehr zu ~** beyond repair.

repatriieren [repatri'i:rən] v/t (h) repatriate.

Repertoire [reper'tŏa:r] n (-s; -s) a. fig. repertoire.

Reportage [repɔr'ta:ʒə] f (-; -n) report, commentary: **s-e ~ über** (acc) a. his coverage of. **Reporter** [re'pɔrtər] m (-s; -), **Re'porterin** f (-; -nen) reporter.

Repräsentant [reprɛzɛn'tant] m (-en; -en) representative.

Repräsen'tantenhaus n parl. Am. House of Representatives.

Repräsentation [reprɛzɛnta'tsio:n] f (-; no pl) representation: **der ~ dienen** be a status symbol. **repräsentativ** [reprɛzɛnta'ti:f] adj **1.** representative (**für** of). **2.** impressive. **repräsentieren** [reprɛzɛn'ti:rən] v/t (h) represent.

Repressalie [reprɛ'sa:liə] f (-; -n) reprisal.

repressiv [reprɛ'si:f] adj repressive.

reprivati'sieren v/t (h) ✝ denationalize.

Reproduktion [reprodʊk'tsio:n] f (-; -en) reproduction, a. print. **reproduzieren** [-du'tsi:rən] v/t (h) reproduce.

Reptil [rɛp'ti:l] n (-[e]s; -ien) reptile.

Republik [repu'bli:k] f (-; -en) republic.

Republikaner [republi'ka:nər] m (-s; -), **republi'kanisch** [-nɪʃ] adj republican, pol. Am. Republican.

Requiem ['re:kviɛm] n (-s; -s) requiem.

requirieren [rekvi'ri:rən] *v/t* (h) ✕ requisition.

Requisiten [rekvi'zi:tən] *pl thea. etc* properties, F props.

Reservat [rezɛr'va:t] *n* (-[e]s; -e) **1.** (nature) reserve. **2.** reservation.

Reserve [re'zɛrvə] *f* (-; -n) **1.** reserve (*a.* ✕ *or fig.*): ✝ **stille ~n** hidden reserves; F *j-n aus der ~* (*heraus*)*locken* bring s.o. out of his shell. **2.** *sports:* reserve team. **~bank** *f* (-; ~e) *sports:* (substitutes') bench. **~ka,nister** *m* spare can. **~rad** *n mot.* spare wheel. **~spieler(in** *f*) *m sports:* substitute.

reservieren [rezɛr'vi:rən] *v/t* (h) (*a. ~ lassen*) reserve, *a.* book. **reser'viert** *adj a. fig.* reserved: *sich ~ verhalten* keep one's distance.

Reservist [rezɛr'vɪst] *m* (-en; -en) ✕ reservist.

Reservoir [rezɛr'vŏa:r] *n* (-s; -e) *a. fig.* reservoir.

Residenz [rezi'dɛnts] *f* (-; -en) residence.

residieren [rezi'di:rən] *v/i* (h) reside.

Resignation [rezɪgna'tsĭo:n] *f* (-; *no pl*) resignation.

resignieren [rezɪ'gni:rən] *v/i* (h) resign, give up. **resi'gniert** *adj* resigned.

resistent [rezɪs'tɛnt] *adj biol.*, ✳ resistent (*gegen* to).

resolut [rezo'lu:t] *adj* resolute, determined, forceful.

Resolution [rezolu'tsĭo:n] *f* (-; -en) resolution.

Resonanz [rezo'nants] *f* (-; -en) *a. fig.* resonance.

resorbieren [rezɔr'bi:rən] *v/t* (h) resorb.

Resorption [rezɔrp'tsĭo:n] *f* (-; -en) resorption.

resoziali'sieren *v/t* (h) rehabilitate.

Resoziali'sierung *f* (-; -en) rehabilitation.

Respekt [re'spɛkt] *m* (-[e]s; *no pl*) respect (*vor* for): *sich ~ verschaffen* make o.s. respected; *bei allem ~* with all due respect. **respektabel** [respɛk'ta:bəl] *adj* respectable. **respektieren** [respɛk'ti:rən] *v/t* (h) respect. **re'spektlos** *adj* irreverent. **re'spektvoll** *adj* respectful.

Ressentiment [rɛsãti'mã:] *n* (-s; -s) resentment.

Ressort [rɛ'so:r] *n* (-s; -s) (*das fällt nicht in mein ~* that is not my) department.

Rest [rɛst] *m* (-[e]s; -e) rest, *a.* ✳ remain-

der, *a. textil.* remnant, 🐾, ♒, ⊙ residue, *gastr.* leftovers, ✝ balance, *fig.* vestige, *pl* remains: *der letzte ~* the last bit(s); *sterbliche ~e* mortal remains; F *das gab ihm den ~* that finished him (off). **~alkohol** *m* residual alcohol.

Restaurant [rɛsto'rã:] *n* (-s; -s) restaurant.

Restaurator [rɛstaʊ'ra:tɔr] *m* (-s; -en [-ra'to:rən] restorer. **restaurieren** [-'ri:rən] *v/t* (h) restore.

'Restbestand *m* ✝ remaining stock.

'Restbetrag *m* ✝ balance.

'restlich *adj* 🐾, ♒, Ƥ residual: *die ~e Zeit a.* the rest of his *etc* time. **'restlos I** *adj* complete, total. **II** *adv* completely, perfectly.

'Restrisiko *n* residual risk.

Resultat [rezʊl'ta:t] *n* (-[e]s; -e) result, *sports:* score, results. **resultieren** [rezʊl'ti:rən] *v/i* (h) result (*aus* from).

Resümee [rezy'me:] *n* (-s; -s) summary.

Retorte [re'tɔrtə] *f* (-; -n) retort.

Re'tortenbaby *n* test-tube baby.

Retourkutsche [re'tu:r-] F *e-e-e* tit for tat.

Retrospektive [retrospɛk'ti:və] *f* (-; -n) retrospective.

retten ['rɛtən] (h) **I** *v/t* (*aus, vor dat* from) save, rescue, *a.* deliver, *a.* recover, salvage (*a. fig.*): *j-m das Leben ~* save s.o.'s life; *sich ~* escape; *sich nicht mehr ~ können vor* (*dat*) be swamped with; F *der Abend war gerettet* the evening was saved. **II** *v/i sports:* save. **'Retter** *m* (-s; -), **'Retterin** *f* (-; -nen) rescuer.

Rettich ['rɛtɪç] *m* (-s; -e) ♧ radish.

'Rettung *f* (-; -en) a) rescue, b) escape, c) recovery, *esp.* ♦ salvage, d) *eccl.* salvation: *das war s-e ~* that saved him; *es gab k-e ~ für ihn* he was past help; *du bist m-e einzige (or letzte) ~* you are my last hope.

'Rettungs|akti,on *f a. fig.* rescue operation. **~anker** *m* sheet anchor. **~boje** *f* life-buoy. **~boot** *n* lifeboat. **~dienst** *m* rescue service. **~gerät** *n* life-saving equipment. **~hubschrauber** *m* rescue helicopter.

'rettungslos *adj* hopeless: *~ verloren sein* be beyond all hope.

'Rettungs|mannschaft *f* rescue party. **~ring** *m* lifebelt. **~schwimmer** *m* lifeguard. **~wagen** *m* ambulance.

retuschieren [retu'ʃiːrən] *v/t* (h) touch up.

Reue ['rɔyə] *f* (-; *no pl*) (*über acc* for) remorse, *esp. eccl.* repentance. **'reuen** (h) **I** *v/t s-e Tat* (*das Geld*) *reute ihn* he regretted what he had done (the money). **II** *v/impers es reut mich, daß* I regret that. **'reuevoll, reuig, 'reumütig** [-my:tɪç] *adj* repentant, remorseful.

Revanche [re'vãːʃə] *f* (-; -n) revenge.

Re'vanchespiel *n sports:* return match.

revanchieren [revã'ʃiːrən] *sich ~* (h) **1.** take one's revenge (*an dat* on), F get one's own back. **2.** return the favo(u)r.

Revanchismus [revã'ʃɪsmʊs] *m* (-; *no pl*) *pol.* revanchism.

Revers [re'vɛːr] *m, n* (-; - [-'vɛːrs]) lapel.

revidieren [revi'diːrən] *v/t* (h) **1.** revise. **2.** check, audit.

Revier [re'viːr] *n* (-s; -e) a) district, b) police station, c) (policeman's) beat, (postman's) round, d) *a. fig.* territory.

Revision [revi'zi̯oːn] *f* (-; -en) **1.** checking), ✝ audit(ing), (custom's) examination. **2.** revision. **3.** 🜊 (*~ einlegen* lodge an) appeal (*bei* with). **4.** *print.* final proofreading.

Revolte [re'vɔltə] *f* (-; -n) revolt.

revoltieren [revɔl'tiːrən] *v/i* (h) revolt.

Revolution [revolu'tsi̯oːn] *f* (-; -en) revolution. **revolutionär** [revolutsi̯o'nɛːr] *adj,* **Revolutio'när** *m* (-s; -e) revolutionary. **revolutionieren** [revolutsi̯o'niːrən] *v/t* (h) revolutionize.

Revolver [re'vɔlvər] *m* (-s; -) revolver.

Re'volverblatt *n contp.* sensational rag.

Re'volverheld *m contp.* gunslinger.

Revue [rə'vyː] *f* (-; -n) **1.** *thea.* revue. **2.** (*publication*) review.

Rezensent [retsɛn'zɛnt] *m* (-en; -en), **Rezen'sentin** *f* (-; -nen) critic, reviewer. **rezensieren** [retsɛn'ziːrən] *v/t* (h), **Rezension** [-'zi̯oːn] *f* (-; -en) review.

Rezept [re'tsɛpt] *n* (-[e]s; -e) a) 💊 prescription, b) *gastr. or fig.* recipe.

Rezeption [retsɛp'tsi̯oːn] *f* (-; -en) *hotel:* reception, Am. check-in desk.

re'zeptpflichtig *adj* available only on prescription, prescription(-only) ...

Rezession [retsɛ'si̯oːn] *f* (-; -en) ✝ recession.

Rezitativ [retsita'tiːf] *n* (-s; -e) recitative.

rezitieren [retsi'tiːrən] *v/t, v/i* (h) recite.

'R-Gespräch *n teleph.* reversed-charge call, *Am.* collect call.

Rhabarber [ra'barbər] *m* (-s; *no pl*) 🌿 rhubarb.

Rhapsodie [rapso'diː] *f* (-; -n) rhapsody.

Rheinwein ['raɪn-] *m* Rhine wine, hock.

Rhesus|affe ['reːzʊs-] *m* rhesus (monkey). **~faktor** *m* (-s; *no pl*) rhesus factor.

Rhetorik [re'toːrɪk] *f* (-; *no pl*) rhetoric. **rhetorisch** [re'toːrɪʃ] *adj* rhetorical.

Rheuma ['rɔyma] *n* (-s; *no pl*) F 🦴 rheumatism. **rheumatisch** [rɔy'maːtɪʃ] *adj* 🦴 rheumatic. **Rheumatismus** [rɔyma-'tɪsmʊs] *m* (-; -men) 🦴 rheumatism.

Rhinozeros [ri'noːtserɔs] *n* (-[ses]; -se) *zo.* rhinoceros.

Rhombus ['rɔmbʊs] *m* (-; -ben) △ rhomb(us).

rhythmisch ['rʏtmɪʃ] *adj* rhythmical.

Rhythmus ['rʏtmʊs] *m* (-; -men) rhythm.

'Richtantenne *f* directional aerial (*Am.* antenna).

richten¹ ['rɪçtən] (h) **I** *v/t* **1.** direct (*auf acc* to, *gegen* against): *~ auf* (*acc*) a. point (*or* level, aim) *weapon, camera* at, *a.* turn *one's eyes* on, *a.* concentrate *attention, efforts, etc* on; *~ an* (*acc*) address *letter etc* to, put *question* to. **2.** a) fix, get *s.th.* ready, prepare, b) bring *s.th.* in order, tidy *s.th.* (up), *a.* do (*one's hair, room, etc*), c) repair, mend, fix, d) align, adjust, trim (*sails*), straighten (out *fig.*): *sich die Zähne ~ lassen* have one's teeth done. **II** *sich ~ an* (*acc*) address o.s. to; *sich ~ auf* (*acc*) *attention etc:* focus on; *sich ~ gegen* be directed against, *remark etc:* be aimed at; *sich ~ nach* a) orient(ate) o.s. by, comply with *s.o.'s wishes*, a. keep to *rules,* go by *s.o.'s judgment*, follow *the fashion,* follow *s.o.'s example*, b) *matter:* be model(l)ed on, depend on, be determined by, *a. ling.* agree with; *ich richte mich nach dir* I leave it to you.

richten² *v/t, v/i* (h) judge.

'Richter *m* (-s; -) judge. **'Richteramt** *n* judicial office. **'Richterin** *f* (-; -nen) judge. **'richterlich** *adj* judicial.

'Richtfest *n* topping-out ceremony.

'Richtfunk *m* directional radio.

'Richtgeschwindigkeit *f mot.* recommended speed.

richtig ['rɪçtɪç] **I** *adj* **1.** right, correct, true, accurate: (*sehr*) *~!* (quite) right!, exactly!; F *er ist nicht ganz ~ im Kopf* he is not quite right in the head. **2.** a) right, suitable, appropriate, proper, b) fair, just: **es war ~, daß du ihnen geholfen hast** you did right to help them; **so ist's ~!** that's it! **3.** real, true: **ein ~er Engländer** a true Englishman; **s-e ~e Mutter** his real mother; **ein ~er Feigling** a regular coward. **II** adv **4.** a) right(ly), correctly (etc), b) F thoroughly, properly: **et. ~ machen** do s.th. right; **~ böse** really (F real) angry; **geht d-e Uhr ~?** is your watch right?

Richtige¹ ['rıçtıgə] m, f (-n; -n) the right man (woman), F Mr. (Mrs.) Right: iro. **Ihr seid mir die ~n!** a fine lot you are!; F **sechs ~ haben** Lotto: have six right.

Richtige² (-n; -n) the right thing: **er hat nichts ~s gelernt** he hasn't really learnt anything; **das ist für sie genau das ~** that's just right for her.

'richtiggehend adj real, regular.

'Richtigkeit f (-; no pl) correctness, rightness: **das hat schon s-e ~** it's all right.

'richtigstellen v/t (sep, -ge-, h) put s.th. right, correct.

'Richtlinien pl guidelines.

'Richtpreis m ✝ recommended price.

'Richtschnur f fig. guiding principle.

'Richtung f (-; -en) **1.** direction, course (a. ✒, ⚓), fig. a. line, trend: **in ~ auf** (acc) in the direction of; **aus allen ~en** from all directions; fig. **et. in dieser ~** s.th. along these lines. **2.** a) line (of thought), views, b) movement, school.

'richtungweisend adj trendsetting.

'Richtwert m, **'Richtzahl** f index.

Ricke ['rıkə] f (-; -n) zo. doe.

rieb [ri:p] pret of **reiben**.

riechen ['ri:çən] (roch, gerochen, h) **I** v/i smell (**nach** of, **an** dat at): **schlecht ~** smell (bad); **es riecht nach Gas** I can smell gas. **II** v/t smell: F **ich kann ihn nicht ~!** I can't stand him!; **er hat es gerochen** he got wind of it; **das konnte ich doch nicht ~!** how was I to know?; → **Braten, Lunte.**

'Riecher m (-s; -) F nose: fig. **e-n guten ~ haben für** have a good nose for.

Ried [ri:t] n (-[e]s; -e) **1.** reed. **2.** marsh.

rief [ri:f] pret of **rufen**.

Riege ['ri:gə] f (-; -n) gym. squad.

Riegel ['ri:gəl] m (-s; -) **1.** a) bolt, bar, b) latch: **e-r Sache e-n ~ vorschieben** put

a stop to s.th. **2.** bar (of soap), row, Am. strip (of chocolate).

Riemen¹ ['ri:mən] m (-s; -) strap, sling (of rifle), ⚙ belt: **sich am ~ reißen** pull o.s. together.

'Riemen² m (-s; -) oar.

Riese ['ri:zə] m (-n; -n) **1.** giant. **2.** F thousand-mark etc note, sl. grand.

rieseln ['ri:zəln] v/i (sn) water, sand, etc: trickle, run, rain: drizzle, snow: fall softly: **es rieselte mir kalt über den Rücken** a shiver ran down my spine.

'Riesen... giant, gigantic, enormous. **~erfolg** m huge success, a. film etc: smash hit. **~felge** f gym. giant swing.

'riesengroß, **'riesenhaft** → **riesig** 1.

'Riesen|rad n Ferris wheel. **~schlange** f boa constrictor. **~schritt** m giant stride. **~slalom** m skiing: giant slalom.

riesig ['ri:zıç] **I** adj **1.** a. fig. gigantic, colossal, enormous, huge. **2.** F a) tremendous, b) terrific, super. **II** adv **3.** F tremendously, terribly, enormously.

Riesin ['ri:zın] f (-; -nen) giantess.

riet [ri:t] pret of **raten**.

Riff [rıf] n (-[e]s; -e) reef.

rigoros [rigo'ro:s] adj rigorous.

Rigorosum [rigo'ro:zʊm] n (-s; -sa) univ. viva (voce).

Rille ['rılə] f (-; -n) groove.

Rind [rınt] n (-[e]s; -er) **1.** a) cow, b) bull, c) ox: **~er** cattle. **2.** gastr. beef.

Rinde ['rındə] f (-; -n) **1.** bark. **2.** (bread) crust, (cheese) rind.

Rinder|braten ['rındər-] m roast beef. **~fi,let** n fillet of beef. **~lende** f beef tenderloin. **~zucht** f cattle farming. **~zunge** f gastr. ox tongue.

'Rindfleisch n beef.

'Rind(s)leder n cowhide.

'Rindvieh n **1.** cattle. **2.** F contp. idiot.

Ring [rıŋ] m (-[e]s; -e) ring, circle (a. fig.).

'Ringbuch n ring (or loose-leaf) binder. **~einlage** f loose-leaf pages.

ringeln ['rıŋəln] **I** v/t (h) a) curl, b) coil (um around). **II** sich ~ a) curl, coil, b) wind, meander.

'Ringelnatter f zo. grass snake.

ringen ['rıŋən] (rang, gerungen, h) **I** v/i wrestle (**mit** with), fig. a. struggle (**um**, **nach** for): **nach Atem ~** gasp for breath; **nach Fassung ~** try to regain one's composure; **nach Worten ~** struggle for words. **II** v/t wring.

'**Ringen** n (-s) wrestling, *fig.* struggle:
'**Ringer** m (-s; -) *sports:* wrestler.
'**Ringfinger** m ring finger.
'**ringförmig** *adj* ring-shaped, annular.
'**Ringkampf** m wrestling (match).
'**Ringrichter** m *boxing:* referee.
rings [rɪŋs], '**ringsher'um**, '**rings'um**
adv all around.
Rinne ['rɪnə] f (-; -n) a) groove (*a. anat.,*
&), b) gutter, c) conduit, channel.
rinnen ['rɪnən] (rann, geronnen, sn) *v/i* **1.**
a) run, flow, b) drip, trickle: *das Geld*
rinnt ihr durch die Finger money just
slips through her fingers. **2.** leak.
'**Rinnstein** m gutter.
Rippchen ['rɪpçən] n (-s; -) rib (of pork).
Rippe ['rɪpə] f (-; -n) **1.** *anat.* rib. **2.** ⊙ rib,
fin. **3.** row, *Am.* strip (*of chocolate*).
rippen ['rɪpən] *v/t* (h) rib.
'**Rippenfell** n *anat.* pleura.
'**Rippenfellentzündung** f ✻ pleurisy.
'**Rippenstoß** m dig in the ribs.
Rips [rɪps] m (-es; -e) *textil.* rep.
Risiko ['riːziko] n (-s; -s, -ken) risk: *auf*
eigenes ~ at one's own risk; *mit vol-*
lem ~ at all risks; *ein* ~ *eingehen* take a
risk. '**risikofrei** *adj* safe. '**risikofreudig**
adj risk-taking, prepared to take a risk
(*or* risks). '**Risikogruppe** f high-risk
group. '**risikoreich** *adj* risky.
riskant [rɪs'kant] *adj* risky.
riskieren [rɪs'kiːrən] *v/t* (h) risk.
Rispe ['rɪspə] f (-; -n) & panicle.
riß [rɪs] *pret of* **reißen.**
Riß m (Risses; Risse) **1.** a) tear, rent, *in*
dry skin: chap, b) cleft, crevice, *fig.* rift,
split; *e-n* ~ *bekommen* friendship *etc:*
begin to break up. **2.** △, ⊙ draft.
rissig ['rɪsɪç] *adj* cracked, fissured, chap-
py, chapped (*skin etc*): ~ *werden* crack,
skin: chap; ~*e Hände* chapped hands.
'**Rißwunde** f laceration.
Rist [rɪst] m (-es; -e) **1.** instep. **2.** back of
the hand.
ritt [rɪt] *pret of* **reiten.**
Ritt m (-[e]s; -e) ride.
Ritter ['rɪtər] m (-s; -) (*a. zum* ~ *schla-*
gen) knight. '**Rittergut** n manor.
'**ritterlich** *adj* knightly, *fig.* chivalrous.
'**Ritterorden** m order (of knights).
'**Rittersporn** m (-[e]s; -e) & larkspur.
rittlings ['rɪtlɪŋs] *adv* astride: ~ *auf e-m*
Stuhl sitzen sit astride a chair.
Ritual [ri'tuːaːl] n (-s; -e, -lien) ritual.

rituell [ri'tŭɛl] *adj* ritual. ⊙
Ritus ['riːtʊs] m (-; Riten) rite.
Ritz [rɪts] m (-es; -e) scratch.
Ritze ['rɪtsə] f (-; -n) crack, gap, chink.
Ritzel ['rɪtsəl] n (-s; -) ⊙ pinion.
ritzen ['rɪtsən] *v/t* (h) **1.** scratch. **2.** carve.
Rivale [ri'vaːlə] m (-n; -n), **Ri'valin** f (-;
-nen) rival.
rivalisieren [rivali'ziːrən] *v/i* (h) rival.
Rivalität [rivali'tɛːt] f (-; -en) rivalry.
Rizinusöl ['riːtsinʊs-] n castor oil.
Robbe ['rɔbə] f (-; -n) *zo.* seal.
Robe ['roːbə] f (-; -n) gown, robe.
Roboter ['roːbɔtər] m (-s; -) robot.
'**Robotertechnik** f robotics.
robust [ro'bʊst] *adj a. fig.* robust.
roch [rɔx] *pret of* **riechen.**
röcheln ['rœçəln] *v/i* (h) breathe sterto-
rously, rattle.
Rochen ['rɔxən] m (-s; -) *zo.* ray.
Rock[1] [rɔk] m (-[e]s; ⁓e) **1.** skirt. **2.** jacket,
coat.
Rock[2] m (-[s]; *no pl*) rock (music).
Rocker ['rɔkər] m (-s; -) F rocker.
'**Rockmu,sik** f rock (music).
'**Rodelbahn** f toboggan run.
rodeln ['roːdəln] *v/i* (h *or* sn) toboggan.
roden ['roːdən] *v/t* (h) **1.** root out. **2.**
clear, stub (*land, woods*).
Rodler ['roːdlər] m (-s; -) tobogganist.
Rodung f (-; -en) clearing.
Rogen ['roːgən] m (-s; -) roe.
Roggen ['rɔgən] m (-s; -) rye.
'**Roggenbrot** n rye-bread.
roh [roː] *adj* **1.** raw, *a.* crude, *a.* rough
(*diamond, draft, etc*). **2.** ✞ gross. **3.** *fig.*
crude, rough, *a.* brutal: *mit* ~*er Gewalt*
with brute force.
'**Rohbau** m shell. '**Rohbi,lanz** f ✞ trial
balance. '**Rohdia,mant** m rough diamond. '**Roheisen** n pig iron.
'**Roheit** f (-; -en) **1.** *no pl* roughness, *a.*
brutality. **2.** brutal act.
'**Roherz** n crude ore. '**Rohfaser** f crude
fibre (*Am.* fiber). '**Rohfassung** f rough
draft. '**Rohgewinn** m ✞ gross profit.
'**Rohkost** f raw vegetables and fruit.
'**Rohköstler** [-kœstlər] m (-s; -) vegetarian. '**Rohleder** n rawhide.
Rohling ['roːlɪŋ] m (-s; -e) **1.** brute. **2.** ⊙
blank.
'**Rohmateri,al** n raw material. '**Rohöl** n
crude oil. '**Rohpro,dukt** n raw product.
Rohr [roːr] n (-[e]s; -e) **1.** & a) reed, b)

cane. **2.** ◎ a) tube, pipe, b) duct. **3.** (gun) barrel: F *fig. volles* ~ flat out.

'**Rohrbruch** *m* burst pipe.

Röhrchen ['rø:rçən] *n* (small) tube: *j-n ins* ~ *blasen lassen* breathalyze s.o.

Röhre ['rø:rə] *f* (-; -n) **1.** a) tube, b) pipe. **2.** ⚡, *radio, TV* valve, *Am.* tube: F *in die* ~ *gucken* a) *TV* sit in front of the box, b) *fig.* be left out in the cold. **3.** oven. **4.** *hunt.* gallery.

röhren ['rø:rən] *v/i* (h) *stag:* bell.

'**Röhrenknochen** *m* long bone.

'**Rohr|kolben** *m* ♣ reed mace. ~**leitung** *f* a) conduit, b) plumbing, c) pipeline. ~**netz** *n* (water *etc*) mains. ~**post** *f* pneumatic post. ~**spatz** *m* F *schimpfen wie ein* ~ rant and rave. ~**stock** *m* cane. ~**zange** *f* ◎ pipe wrench. ~**zucker** *m* cane sugar.

'**Rohseide** *f* raw silk. '**Rohstahl** *m* crude steel. '**Rohstoff** *m* raw material. '**Rohzucker** *m* unrefined sugar.

'**Rohzustand** *m* (*im* ~ in the) crude state.

'**Rolladen** *m* shutters.

'**Rollbahn** *f* ✈ runway.

Rolle[1] ['rɔlə] *f* (-; -n) a) roll (*a.* ✈, *gym.*), ◎ a. roller, *a.* pulley, b) castor, c) reel, coil: *e-e* ~ *Garn* a reel of cotton.

'**Rolle**[2] *f* (-; -n) *thea.* part, role (*a. psych.*): *e-e* ~ *spielen* play a part (*a. fig. bei, in dat* in), *fig. a.* figure (in); *das spielt k-e* ~ that doesn't make any difference; *Geld spielt k-e* ~ money is no object; *aus der* ~ *fallen* forget s.o.; *fig. die* ~*n* (*ver*)*tauschen* reverse roles.

rollen ['rɔlən] *v/i* (sn), *v/t* (h) roll, wheel, ✈ taxi: ~*des Material* 🚃 rolling stock; *fig. ins Rollen kommen* get under way.

'**Rollen|besetzung** *f thea.* casting. ~**lager** *n* ◎ roller bearing. ~**spiel** *n psych.* role-playing. ~**tausch** *m fig.* reversal of roles. ~**verteilung** *f* **1.** *thea.* casting. **2.** *fig.* respective roles.

'**Roller** *m* (-s; -) **1.** *mot. etc* scooter. **2.** *soccer:* daisy cutter.

'**Roll|feld** *n* ✈ taxiway, runway. ~**film** *m* roll film. ~**kom,mando** *n sl.* heavies. ~**kragen(pull,over)** *m* polo neck.

'**Rollschuh** *m* roller skate: ~ *laufen* roller-skate. ~**bahn** *f* roller-skating rink. ~**läufer** *m* roller skater.

'**Roll|stuhl** *m* wheelchair. ~**treppe** *f* escalator. ~**verdeck** *n* roller roof.

Roman [ro'ma:n] *m* (-[e]s; -e) novel.

~**held(in** *f*) *m* hero(ine) (of the novel).

Romanik [ro'ma:nɪk] *f* (-; *no pl*) Romanesque (style *or* period). **ro'manisch** *adj* **1.** *ling.* Romance. **2.** Romanesque.

Romanist [roma'nɪst] *m* (-en; -en) student of (*or* lecturer in) Romance languages and literature.

Ro'manlitera,tur *f* fiction.

Ro'manschriftsteller(in *f*) *m* novelist.

Romantik [ro'mantɪk] *f* (-; *no pl*) romanticism, *art:* Romanticism. **Ro'mantiker** *m* (-s; -) Romantic, *fig.* romantic. **ro'mantisch** *adj* romantic, *art etc:* Romantic. **romantisieren** [-ti'zi:rən] *v/t* (h) romanticize.

Romanze [ro'mantsə] *f* (-; -n) romance.

Römer ['rø:mər] *m* (-s; -) **1.** Roman. **2.** rummer. **römisch** ['rø:mɪʃ] *adj* Roman: ~-*katholisch* Roman Catholic.

Rommé [rɔ'me:] *n* (-s; -s) rummy.

röntgen ['rœntɡən] *v/t* (h) ☢ x-ray.

'**Röntgen|appa,rat** *m* x-ray unit. ~**arzt** *m* radiologist. ~**aufnahme** *f* x-ray (picture). ~**behandlung** *f*, ~**bestrahlung** *f* x-ray treatment, radiotherapy.

Röntgenologe [rœntɡeno'lo:ɡə] *m* (-n; -n) radiologist.

'**Röntgen|schirm** *m* (fluorescent) screen. ~**strahlen** *pl* x-rays. ~**untersuchung** *f* x-ray examination.

rosa ['ro:za] *adj* pink.

'**rosarot** *adj a. fig.* rose-colo(u)red.

Rose ['ro:zə] *f* (-; -n) **1.** ♣ rose. **2.** ☢ erysipelas.

Rosé [ro'ze:] *m* (-s; -s) rosé (wine).

'**Rosenkohl** *m* Brussels sprouts.

'**Rosenkranz** *m eccl.* (*den* ~ *beten* say the) rosary.

Rosen'montag *m* Monday before Lent.

'**Rosenstock** *m* rose-tree.

'**Rosenstrauß** *m* bunch of roses.

rosig ['ro:zɪç] *adj a. fig.* rosy.

Rosine [ro'zi:nə] *f* (-; -n) raisin: F (*große*) ~*n im Kopf haben* have big ideas.

Rosmarin ['ro:smari:n] *m* (-s; *no pl*) ♣ rosemary.

Roß [rɔs] *n* (Rosses; Rösser ['rœsər]) horse: *fig. sich aufs hohe* ~ *setzen* give o.s. airs. ~**äpfel** *pl* horse droppings.

'**Roßhaar** *n* horsehair.

Rost[1] [rɔst] *m* (-[e]s; *no pl*) *a. fig.* rust.

Rost[2] *m* (-[e]s; c) **1.** grate. **2.** grill.

'**Röstbrot** *n* toast.

rosten ['rɔstən] v/i (sn or h) rust: *nicht ~d* → *rostfrei.*

rösten ['rœstən] v/t (h) roast (*coffee*), toast (*bread*), fry (*potatoes*).

'rostfrei adj rustproof, stainless.

rostig ['rɔstiç] adj a. fig. rusty.

'Röstkar,toffeln pl fried potatoes.

'Rostschutzmittel n antirust agent.

'Roststelle f patch of rust.

rot [ro:t] adj red, pol. Red: *das Rote Kreuz* the Red Cross; *~ werden* a) go red, flush, b) blush; ✝ *in den ~en Zahlen stehen* be in the red; → *rotsehen, Faden, Tuch.*

Rot n (-s; -) red: *bei ~* at red; *die Ampel steht auf ~* the lights are at red.

Rotation [rota'tsi̯o:n] f (-; -en) rotation.

Rotati'onsdruck m rotary printing.

'rotblond adj sandy-haired, sandy (*hair*).

'rotbraun adj reddish brown.

'Rotbuche f copper beech.

'Rotdorn m (-[e]s; -e) pink hawthorn.

Rote ['ro:tə] m, f (-n; -n) pol. Red.

Röte ['rø:tə] f (-; -n) a) redness, b) blush.

Rötel ['rø:təl] m (-s; no pl) red chalk.

'Röteln pl 🞄 German measles.

röten ['rø:tən] v/t (h) redden: *sich ~* a. go red, flush.

'rotglühend adj red-hot.

'rothaarig adj red-haired.

'Rothaarige m, f (-n; -n) redhead.

rotieren [ro'ti:rən] v/i (h) a) rotate, b) F fig. flap: *am Rotieren sein* be in a flap.

Rotkäppchen ['ro:tkɛpçən] n (Little) Red Riding Hood.

'Rotkehlchen n zo. robin (redbreast).

'Rotkohl m, **'Rotkraut** n red cabbage.

rötlich ['rø:tlɪç] adj reddish.

'rotsehen v/i (irr, sep, -ge-, h, → sehen) F fig. see red.

'Rotstift m red pencil: fig. *den ~ ansetzen* make cuts (bei in).

Rotte ['rɔtə] f (-; -n) gang, horde.

'Rötung f (-; -en) reddening.

'Rotwein m red wine.

'Rotwild n red deer.

Rotz [rɔts] m (-es; no pl) V snot. **'Rotzfahne** f V snotrag. **'rotzfrech** adj F snotty.

Rouge [ru:ʒ] n (-s; -s [ru:ʒ]) rouge.

Roulade [ru'la:də] f (-; -n) roulade, roll.

Rouleau [ru'lo:] n (-s; -s) roller blind.

Roulett [ru'lɛt] n (-[e]s; -e) roulette.

Route ['ru:tə] f (-; -n) route, itinerary.

Routine [ru'ti:nə] f (-; no pl) routine, a. practice, experience.

rou'tinemäßig adj routine.

routiniert [ruti'ni:rt] adj experienced.

Rowdy ['raʊdi] m (-s; -s) hooligan.

'Rowdytum n (-s; no pl) hooliganism.

Rübe ['ry:bə] f (-; -n) **1.** *weiße ~* turnip; *rote ~* beetroot; *gelbe ~* carrot. **2.** F nut.

Rubel ['ru:bəl] m (-s; -) rouble.

rüber(...) ['ry:bər-] F → *herüber(...), hinüber(...).* **'rüberkommen** v/i (irr, sep, -ge-, sn, → kommen) F **1.** come over. **2.** thea. etc come across. **3.** *~ mit* come across with *money etc.*

Rubin [ru'bi:n] m (-s; -e) min. ruby.

Rubrik [ru'bri:k] f (-; -en) **1.** heading. **2.** column. **3.** category.

ruchbar ['ru:x-] adj *~ werden* become known.

Ruck [rʊk] m (-[e]s; -e) jerk, start, jolt (a. fig.), F pol. swing: *in einem ~* at one go; *sich e-n ~ geben* pull o.s. together.

'Rückansicht f back view.

'ruckartig I adj jerky. II adv a) with a jerk, b) abruptly.

'rückbezüglich adj ling. reflexive.

'Rückblende f film: flashback (*auf acc* to).

'Rückblick m review (*auf acc* of): *im ~* in retrospect, *auf* (acc) looking back on.

'rückda,tieren v/t (h) backdate.

rücken ['rʏkən] I v/t (h) move, a. shift, a. push (away). II v/i (sn) a) move, b) move over: *näher ~* draw near, approach; *an j-s Stelle ~* take s.o.'s place.

'Rücken m (-s; -) a) back, b) (*mountain*) ridge, c) bridge (*of nose*), d) gastr. saddle: *hinter j-s ~* behind s.o.'s back; *j-m in den ~ fallen* fig. stab s.o. in the back.

'Rücken|deckung f fig. backing, support. **~lehne** f back(-rest). **~mark** n anat. spinal cord. **~muskula,tur** f back muscles. **~schmerzen** pl backache. **~schwimmen** n backstroke. **~wind** m following wind. **~wirbel** m anat. dorsal vertebra.

'Rückeroberung f reconquest.

'rückerstatten v/t (only inf and rückerstattet, h) return, a. refund.

'Rückfahrkarte f return (ticket), Am. round-trip ticket.

'Rückfahrt f return journey (or trip): *auf der ~* a. on the way back.

'**Rückfall** *m* relapse (*a. fig.*), ⚖ *a.* recidivism. '**rückfällig** *adj* relapsing, ⚖ *a.* recidivist: ~ **werden** (have a) relapse.

'**Rückfenster** *n* rear window.

'**Rückflug** *m* return flight.

'**Rückfrage** *f* checkback.

'**rückfragen** *v/i* (*only inf and pp* rückgefragt, h) check (*bei* with).

'**Rückführung** *f* repatriation.

'**Rückgabe** *f* return, *sports*: pass back.

'**Rückgang** *m* (*gen in*) decline, drop, fall.

'**rückgängig** *adj* **1.** → *rückläufig*. **2.** ~ *machen* a) undo, b) cancel (*order etc*).

'**Rückgewinnung** *f* recovery.

'**Rückgrat** *n* spine, backbone (*a. fig.*).

'**rückgratlos** *adj fig.* spineless.

'**Rückhalt** *m* support. '**rückhaltlos I** *adj* unreserved, *a.* frank. **II** *adv* without reserve: *j-m ~ vertrauen* have complete confidence in s.o.

'**Rückhand** *f* (-; *no pl*) tennis: backhand.

'**Rückkampf** *m sports*: return match.

'**Rückkaufsrecht** *n* right of repurchase (*or* redemption).

'**Rückkehr** *f* (-; *no pl*) return.

'**Rückkopplung** *f* ⚡ feedback (*a. fig.*).

'**Rücklagen** *pl* reserve(s), savings.

'**rückläufig** *adj* dropping, declining: ~*e Tendenz* downward tendency.

'**Rücklicht** *n* (-[e]s; -er) *mot.* rear light, taillight.

'**rücklings** ['rʏklɪŋs] *adv* a) backwards, b) from behind.

'**Rückmarsch** *m* march back. '**Rückpaß** *m sports*: back pass. '**Rückporto** *n* return postage. '**Rückprall** *m* rebound. '**Rückreise** *f* → *Rückfahrt.* '**Rückruf** *m* **1.** ✆ recall. **2.** *teleph.* ring back.

'**Rucksack** *m* rucksack, *Am.* backpack. ~**tou,rismus** *m* backpacking. ~**tou,rist** *m* backpacker.

'**Rückschlag** *m fig.* setback.

'**Rückschluß** *m* conclusion.

'**Rückschritt** *m* step back(ward).

'**rückschrittlich** *adj pol.* reactionary.

'**Rückseite** *f* back, rear, reverse (*of coin etc*), B-side, F flip side (*of record*): *siehe ~!* see overleaf!

'**Rücksendung** *f* return.

'**Rücksicht** *f* (-; *no pl*) consideration: *mit ~ auf* (*acc*) out of consideration for; *ohne ~ auf* (*acc*) regardless of; (*k-e*) ~ *nehmen auf* (*acc*) show (no) consideration for, make (no) allowances for.

'**Rücksichtnahme** [-na:mə] *f* (-; *no pl*) consideration (*auf acc* for).

'**rücksichtslos** *adj* inconsiderate (*gegen* of), thoughtless, reckless (*driving etc*), *a.* ruthless. '**Rücksichtslosigkeit** *f* (-; *no pl*) lack of consideration, recklessness. '**rücksichtsvoll** *adj* considerate (*gegen* of).

'**Rücksitz** *m* a) backseat, b) pillion.

'**Rückspiegel** *m mot.* rearview mirror.

'**Rückspiel** *n sports*: return match.

'**Rücksprache** *f* (-; -n) consultation: *mit j-m ~ nehmen* consult (*with*) s.o.

'**Rückstand** *m* (-[e]s; ⁓e) **1.** 🧪 residue. **2.** ✝ arrears, *a.* backlog (*of work*): *im ~ sein mit* be behind with *one's payments etc*, *sports*: be down *one goal etc*.

'**rückständig** *adj* **1.** backward, *a.* underdeveloped. **2.** ~*e Miete* arrears of rent.

'**Rückständigkeit** *f* (-; *no pl*) backwardness.

'**Rückstau** *m mot.* tailback.

'**Rückstoß** *m* recoil (*of gun*).

'**Rückstrahler** *m* rear reflector.

'**Rücktaste** *f of typewriter*: back spacer, *of tape recorder etc*: rewind key.

'**Rücktritt** *m* **1.** (*von*) resignation (from *office*), withdrawal (from *contract*): *s-n ~ erklären* announce (*or* tender) one's resignation. **2.** F → '**Rücktrittbremse** *f* backpedal brake.

'**Rücktritts|gesuch** *n* (letter of) resignation. ~**recht** *n* right of rescission.

'**rückübersetzen** *v/t* (*only inf and pp* rückübersetzt, h) translate back (*in acc* into *English etc*).

'**Rückübersetzung** *f* retranslation.

'**rückvergüten** *v/t* (*only inf and pp* rückvergütet, h), '**Rückvergütung** *f* refund.

'**rückversichern** *v/t* (*only inf and pp* rückversichert, h) reinsure (*sich* o.s.): *fig. sich ~* play safe.

'**Rückversicherung** *f* reinsurance.

'**Rückwand** *f* back, back wall.

'**rückwärtig** ['rʏkvɛrtɪç] *adj* back, rear.

'**rückwärts** ['rʏkvɛrts] *adv* backwards: ~ *fahren in* (*acc*) (*or aus*) back into (*or* out of). '**Rückwärtsgang** *m mot.* (*im ~* in) reverse (gear).

'**Rückweg** *m* way back, return: *den ~ antreten* head for home.

'**ruckweise I** *adj* jerky. **II** *adv* jerkily, in jerks.

'**rückwirkend** *adj* ⚖ retroactive: ~ *ab*

backdated to. '**Rückwirkung** f (*auf acc* upon) reaction, repercussion.
'**rückzahlbar** adj repayable.
'**Rückzahlung** f repayment, refund.
'**Rückzieher** m (-s; -) **1.** soccer: overhead kick. **2.** F **e-n ~ machen** back down.
'**Rückzug** m retreat. '**Rückzugsgefecht** n a. fig. rearguard action.
rüde ['ry:də] adj rude, coarse.
'**Rüde** m (-n; -n) male dog (or wolf, fox).
Rudel ['ru:dəl] n (-s; -) pack (*of wolves* etc), herd (*of deer* etc), fig. swarm.
Ruder ['ru:dər] n (-s; -) a) oar, b) rudder (a. ✈), helm: **am ~** at the helm (a. fig.); fig. **ans ~ kommen** come into power.
'**Ruderboot** n rowing boat.
'**Ruderer** m (-s; -) rower, oarsman.
'**Ruderin** f (-; -nen) oarswoman.
'**Ruderklub** m rowing club.
rudern ['ru:dərn] v/t (h), v/i (h, sn) row.
'**Rudern** n (-s) rowing.
'**Ruderregatta** f boat race, regatta.
'**Rudersport** m rowing.
Ruf [ru:f] m (-[e]s; -e) **1.** call (a. teleph. or fig.), cry, shout: **e-n ~ erhalten nach** be offered an appointment (*univ.* a chair) at. **2.** no pl reputation: **von ~ artist** etc of high repute, noted *artist* etc.
rufen ['ru:fən] (rief, gerufen, h) **I** v/i a) call, b) cry, shout: **~ nach** call for (a. fig.); **um Hilfe ~** cry for help. **II** v/t call, a. summon: **~ lassen** send for; **du kommst mir wie gerufen** you're just the person I need. '**Rufen** n (-s) a) calling, b) calls. '**Rufer** m (-s; -) caller.
Rüffel ['ryfəl] m (-s; -) F dressing-down.
'**Ruf|mord** m character assassination.
~name m name by which one is called.
~nummer f telephone number. **~weite** f in ~ within calling distance.
Rüge ['ry:gə] f (-; -n) reprimand, rebuke.
'**rügen** v/t (h) (*wegen* for) reprimand, rebuke (s.o.), criticize, censure (s.th.).
Ruhe ['ru:ə] f (-; no pl) a) rest (a. phys.), b) quiet, silence, c) peace, d) calm(ness), composure: **~ und Ordnung** law and order; **die ~ vor dem Sturm** the calm before the storm; **in aller ~** very calmly, leisurely; **überlege es dir in aller ~** take your time about it; **~ bewahren** keep quiet, keep cool; **sich zur ~ setzen** retire; **zur ~ bringen** quieten down; **~, bitte!** quiet, please!; **laß mich in ~!** leave me alone!; **laß mich damit in**

~! I don't want to hear about it!; **er möchte s-e ~ haben** he wants to be left in peace; F **er hat die ~ weg!** he's (as) cool as a cucumber; **immer mit der ~!** take it easy!
'**ruhebedürftig** adj in need of (a) rest.
'**Ruhegehalt** n pension.
'**ruhelos** adj restless.
'**Ruhelosigkeit** f (-; no pl) restlessness.
ruhen ['ru:ən] v/i a) rest, work, traffic, etc: be at a standstill, negotiations etc: be suspended: **~ auf** (dat) fig. rest on; **er ruhte nicht, bis** he didn't rest until; **hier ruht** here lies; **laß die Vergangenheit ~!** let bygones be bygones!
'**Ruhe|pause** f break, rest. **~stand** m (-[e]s; no pl) (**vorzeitiger ~** early) retirement: **im ~** retired; **in den ~ treten** (**versetzen**) retire. **~stätte** f resting place. **~stellung** f ◎ neutral position. **~störer** m disturber of the peace. **~störung** f öffentliche ~ disturbance of the peace. **~tag** m a) day of rest, b) day off, c) closing day: **Montag ~!** closed on Mondays!
ruhig ['ru:ɪç] **I** adj **1.** a) quiet (a. fig.), a. silent, b) still, c) peaceful, restful, d) calm (sea, a. voice), steady (hand), smooth (a. ◎), e) leisurely: (**sei**) **~!** (be) quiet!; **sei ganz ~!** don't worry!; **~ bleiben** keep calm; **k-e ~e Minute haben** not to have a moment's peace. **II** adv **2.** quietly (etc): **das Haus liegt ~** the house is in a quiet area; **~ verlaufen** be uneventful. **3.** F easily, very well: **tu das ~!** go right ahead!; **du kannst ~ dableiben!** (you can) stay if you want!
Ruhm [ru:m] m (-[e]s; no pl) fame, glory.
rühmen ['ry:mən] v/t (h) praise (*wegen* for): **sich ~** (gen) pride o.s. (on), boast (s.th.). '**rühmenswert → rühmlich.**
'**Ruhmesblatt** n das ist kein ~ für ihn that's not exactly to his credit.
'**rühmlich** adj laudable, praiseworthy: **~e Ausnahme** noteworthy exception.
'**ruhmlos** adj inglorious.
'**ruhmreich, 'ruhmvoll** adj glorious.
Ruhr [ru:r] f (-; no pl) ✻ dysentery.
'**Rührbesen** m gastr. whisk.
'**Rühreier** pl scrambled eggs.
rühren ['ry:rən] (h) **I** v/t **1.** stir, a. move: **er hat k-n Finger gerührt** he did not lift a finger; → **Donner, Trommel. 2.** fig. touch, move (**zu Tränen** to tears): **das**

rührt mich wenig that leaves me cold. **II** *v/i* **3.** stir. **4. ~ an** *(acc)* a) touch, b) touch (up)on *a subject etc.* **III sich ~ 5.** stir, move: ✗ *rührt euch!* (stand) at ease!; *sich nicht (von der Stelle) ~* not to budge (an inch) **6.** F *fig.* do (*or* say) s.th. **'rührend** *adj* **1.** touching, moving. **2.** very kind.

'rührig *adj* active, busy, enterprising.
'Rührigkeit *f* (-; *no pl*) activity.
'rührselig *adj* sentimental, mawkish: *~e Geschichte* F sob story.
'Rührung *f* (-; *no pl*) emotion: *er brachte vor ~ kein Wort heraus* he was choked with emotion.
Ruin [ru'iːn] *m* (-s; *no pl*) (*vor dem ~ stehen* be on the brink of) ruin.
Ruine [ru'iːnə] *f* (-; -n) ruin(s).
ruinieren [rui'niːrən] *v/t* (h) ruin.
ruinös [rui'nøːs] *adj* ruinous.
rülpsen ['rʏlpsən] *v/i* (h) F belch.
Rum [rʊm] *m* (-s; -s) rum.
rum(...) F → *herum(...)*.
Rumäne [ru'mɛːnə] *m* (-n; -n) Romanian. **Ru'mänien** [-niən] *n* (-s) Romania. **Ru'mänin** *f* (-; -nen), **ru'mänisch** *adj* Romanian.
Rummel ['rʊməl] *m* (-s; *no pl*) F **1.** (hustle and) bustle. **2.** fuss, to-do: *großen ~ machen um* make a big fuss about. **3.** a) fun fair, b) → **'Rummelplatz** *m* fairground, amusement park.
rumoren [ru'moːrən] *v/i* (h) F bang around.
'Rumpelkammer *f* lumber room.
rumpeln ['rʊmpəln] *v/i* (h, sn) F rumble.
Rumpf [rʊmpf] *m* (-[e]s; ⸚e) **1.** *anat.* trunk. **2.** ⚓ hull, ✈ fuselage.
rümpfen ['rʏmpfən] *v/t* (h) *die Nase ~* turn up one's nose (*über acc* at).
rund [rʊnt] **I** *adj* **1.** round (*a. fig.*): *Gespräche am ~en Tisch* round-table talks; *~e 1000 Mark* 1,000 marks or so; *e-e ~e Leistung* a perfect performance. **II** *adv* **2.** about, roughly: *~ gerechnet* in round figures. **3. ~ um** (a)round.
'Rundbau *m* (-[e]s; -ten) rotunda.
'Rundblick *m* panorama.
Runde ['rʊndə] *f* (-; -n) **1.** circle. **2.** round: *s-e ~ machen* make one's rounds, *policeman*: be on one's beat; F *die ~ machen* story *etc*: go the round. **3.** boxing, golf, *etc*: round (*a. fig.* of negotiations), racing: lap: F *fig.* *gerade*

so über die ~n kommen just about make it, scrape by, *a. financially*: get by. **4.** round (*of beer etc*). **'runden: sich ~** (h) grow round, *fig.* take shape.
'runderneuern *v/t* (*only inf and pp* runderneuert, h) retread (*tyres*).
'Rundfahrt *f* tour (*durch* of).
'Rundflug *m* circuit.
'Rundfunk *m* (-s; *no pl*) **1.** broadcasting, radio: *im ~* on the radio; *~ hören* listen to the radio; *im ~ übertragen* (*or senden, bringen*) broadcast; *beim ~ sein* work in broadcasting. **2.** → **~anstalt** *f* broadcasting company, *Am.* radio corporation. **~gebühren** *pl* radio licen|ce (*Am.* -se) fees. **~gerät** *n* radio (set). **~hörer(in** *f*) *m* listener. **~pro₁gramm** *n* radio program(me Br.). **~sender** *m* → *Rundfunkstation*. **~sendung** *f* broadcast, radio program(me Br.). **~sprecher** *m* (radio) announcer. **~stati₁on** *f* radio station. **~zeitung** *f* radio journal.
'Rundgang *m* round, tour (*durch* of).
'rundher'aus *adv* flatly, straight out.
'rundher'um *adv* all (a)round.
'rundlich *adj* plump, chubby.
'Rundreise *f* tour (*durch* of).
'Rundschreiben *n* circular (letter).
'Rundstrecke *f* circuit.
'rund'um *adv* all (a)round.
'Rundung *f* (-; -en) curve.
'rund'weg *adv* flatly.
Rune ['ruːnə] *f* (-; -n) rune.
runter(...) ['rʊntər-] F → *herunter(...)*, *hinunter(...)*. **'runterhauen** *v/t* (*sep*, -ge-, h) F *j-m e-e ~* slap s.o.('s face).
Runzel ['rʊntsəl] *f* (-; -n) wrinkle, line. **'runz(e)lig** *adj* wrinkled, lined. **'runzeln** *v/t* (h) wrinkle: *die Stirn ~* frown.
Rüpel ['ryːpəl] *m* (-s; -) lout.
'rüpelhaft *adj* rude, loutish, uncouth.
rupfen ['rʊpfən] *v/t* (h) pluck (*chicken etc*): F *j-n ~* fleece s.o.; → *Hühnchen* 1.
ruppig ['rʊpɪç] *adj* **1.** shaggy. **2.** gruff.
Rüsche ['ryːʃə] *f* (-; -n) frill.
Ruß [ruːs] *m* (-es; *no pl*) soot.
Russe ['rʊsə] *m* (-n; -n) Russian.
Rüssel ['rʏsəl] *m* (-s; -) proboscis, *a.* (elephant's) trunk, (pig's) snout.
rußen ['ruːsən] *v/i* (h) smoke.
'rußig *adj* sooty.
'Russin *f* (-; -nen), **'russisch** *adj* Russian. **Rußland** ['rʊs-] *n* (-s) Russia.
rüsten ['rʏstən] (h) (*für, zu* for) **I** *v/i* ✗

arm: *fig.* **gerüstet** armed, ready. **II** *sich*
~ prepare, get ready.
Rüster ['ry:stər] *f* (-; -n) ♀ elm.
rüstig ['rʏstɪç] *adj* vigorous, sprightly.
rustikal [rʊsti'ka:l] *adj* rustic.
'Rüstung¹ *f* (-; -en) (knight's) armo(u)r.
'Rüstung² *f* (-; -en) ⚔ armament.
'Rüstungs|ausgaben *pl* defen/ce (*Am.*
-se) expenditure. **~begrenzung** *f* arms
limitation. **~indu,strie** *f* defen/ce (*Am.*
-se) industry. **~kon,trolle** *f* arms control. **~stopp** *m* arms freeze. **~wettlauf**
m arms race.
'Rüstzeug *n* *fig.* equipment.
Rute ['ru:tə] *f* (-; -n) **1.** a) switch, b) rod.
2. fishing rod. **3.** *hunt.* a) penis, b) tail,
(fox's) brush.

'Rutengänger [-gɛŋər] *m* (-s; -) diviner.
Rutsch [rʊtʃ] *m* (-[e]s; -e) **1.** slide, *a.*
landslide: F **in einem ~** in one go; **guten ~ (ins Neue Jahr)!** Happy New
Year! **2.** F (short) trip, jaunt.
'Rutschbahn *f* slide.
'Rutsche *f* (-; -n) slide, ⚙ *a.* chute.
'rutschen *v/i* (sn) slide, glide, slip, *mot.*
etc skid. **'rutschig** *adj* slippery.
'rutschsicher *adj* nonslip, *mot.* nonskid.
rütteln ['rʏtəln] (h) **I** *v/t* shake, ⚙ vibrate. **II** *v/i mot.* shake, jolt, ⚙ vibrate:
~ an (*dat*) a) rattle (at) *the door*, b) *fig.*
shake, *a.* question: **daran ist nicht zu ~!**
that's a fact!

S

S, s [s] *n* (-; -) S, s.
Saal [za:l] *m* (-[e]s; "e) hall.
Saat [za:t] *f* (-; -en)**1.** *no pl* sowing. **2.**
seed (*a. fig.*), *a.* crop(s). **~gut** *n* (-[e]s; *no
pl*) seed(s). **~kar,toffel** *f* seed potato.
Sabbat ['zabat] *m* (-s; -e) Sabbath.
sabbern ['zabərn] *v/i* (h) slaver, drool.
Säbel ['zɛ:bəl] *m* (-s; -) sab/re (*Am.* -er).
Sabotage [zabo'ta:ʒə] *f* (-; -n) sabotage.
Sabo'tageakt *m* act of sabotage.
Saboteur [zabo'tø:r] *m* (-s; -e) saboteur.
sabotieren [-'ti:rən] *v/t* (h) sabotage.
'Sach|bearbeiter(in *f*) *m* official (♰
clerk) in charge (**für** of). **~beschädi-
gung** *f* damage to property. ⅖**bezogen**
adj pertinent. **~buch** *n* nonfiction
book, *pl coll.* nonfiction.
'sachdienlich *adj* relevant, pertinent.
Sache ['zaxə] *f* (-; -n) **1.** a) thing, object,
b) F *pl* things (*a. food etc*), *a.* belongings; F *mot.* **mit 100 ~n** at 60 (miles per
hour). **2.** a) affair, matter, business, b)
problem, c) subject, d) case, ⚖ *or fig.*
cause: **e-e ~ für sich** a matter apart; **in
~n Umwelt** concerning the environment; **in eigener ~** on one's own behalf; **bei der ~ bleiben** stick to the
point; **er war nicht bei der ~** he was

inattentive; **für e-e gute ~ kämpfen**
fight for a good cause; **s-e ~ gut machen** do a good job; **(sich) s-r ~ sicher
sein** be sure of one's ground; **zur ~
kommen** get to the point, *w.s.* get down
to business; **das ist s-e ~!** that's his
problem (*or* affair)!; **es ist s-e ~ zu** *inf*
it's his business to *inf*; **es ist ~ des
Vertrauens** it's a matter of trust; **das
tut nichts zur ~** that makes no difference; **die ~ ist die, daß** the point is that;
F **j-m sagen, was ~ ist** tell s.o. what's
what; → **gemeinsam** I.
'Sach|frage *f* factual issue. ⅖**fremd** *adj*
irrelevant. **~gebiet** *n* subject, field.
⅖**gemäß**, ⅖**gerecht** *adj* proper, appropriate. **~kenner** *m* expert. **~kenntnis** *f*
expertise, know-how. **~kunde** *f* (-; *no
pl*) *ped.* general knowledge. ⅖**kundig**
adj expert: **sich ~ machen** inform o.s.
~lage *f* (-; *no pl*) state of affairs. **~lei-
stung** *f* payment in kind.
'sachlich *adj* **1.** factual, *a.* technical, *a.*
△, ⚙ functional: **aus ~en Gründen** for
technical (*or* practical) reasons; *a.* **richtig** factually correct. **2.** a) matter-of-
-fact, realistic, unemotional, b) objective, c) practical(-minded).

487   **Salat**

sächlich ['zɛçlıç] adj ling. neuter.
'Sachlichkeit f (-; no pl) matter-of-factness, objectivity, △, ◑ functionalism.
'Sachre,gister n (subject) index.
'Sachschaden m material damage.
Sachse ['zaksə] m (-n; -n), **Sächsin** ['zɛksın] f (-; -nen), **sächsisch** ['zɛksıʃ] adj Saxon.
'Sachspende f donation in kind.
sacht [zaxt] I adj soft, gentle. II adv a. ~e a) softly, gently, b) cautiously, c) slowly: F (immer) ~e! take it easy!
'Sachverhalt m the facts (of the case).
'Sachvermögen n tangible property.
'sachverständig adj expert, competent.
'Sachverständige m, f (-n; -n) expert, ⚖ expert witness. **'Sachverständigengutachten** n expert opinion.
'Sachwalter [-valtər] m (-s; -) 1. ⚖ trustee. 2. fig. advocate, champion.
'Sachwert m (-[e]s; -e) 1. no pl real value. 2. pl material assets.
Sack [zak] m (-[e]s; ~e) 1. sack, bag, anat., zo. sac: mit ~ und Pack with bag and baggage. 2. V balls.
sacken ['zakən] v/i (sn) sink, give way, sag, person: slump.
'Sack|**gasse** f 1. cul-de-sac. 2. fig. dead end, impasse. **~hüpfen** n sack race.
Sadismus [za'dısmʊs] m (-; no pl) sadism. **Sadist** [za'dıst] m (-en; -en) sadist. **sa'distisch** [-tıʃ] adj sadistic.
säen ['zɛːən] v/t, v/i (h) sow: fig. dünn gesät scarce, few and far between.
Safari [za'faːri] f (-; -s) safari.
Sa'faripark m wildlife reserve.
Safe [seıf] m, n (-s; -s) safe.
Safran ['zafran] m (-s; -e) saffron.
Saft [zaft] m (-[e]s; ~e) juice (a. F ⚡), ⚘ sap: fig. ohne ~ und Kraft → saftlos 2; → schmoren.
'saftig adj 1. juicy, ⚘ lush. 2. F fig. juicy, spicy (joke etc), resounding (slap), stiff, steep (prices), crushing (defeat etc).
'saftlos adj 1. juiceless, dry. 2. fig. a. saft- u. kraftlos lame, wishy-washy.
'Saftpresse f squeezer, juice extractor.
Sage ['zaːgə] f (-; -n) 1. legend. 2. fig. rumo(u)r.
Säge ['zɛːgə] f (-; -n) saw. **~blatt** n saw blade. **~bock** m sawhorse. **~fisch** m sawfish. **~mehl** n sawdust.
sagen ['zaːgən] v/t, v/i (h) say: j-m et. ~

say s.th. to s.o., tell s.o. s.th.; ich habe mir ~ lassen, daß I've been told that; et. (nichts) zu ~ haben have a (no) say (bei in); das hat nichts zu ~ that doesn't matter; ~ Sie ihm, er soll kommen tell him to come; was sagst du zu ...? a) what do you say to ...?, b) how about ...?; was willst du damit ~? what do you mean (by that)?; das Buch sagt mir nichts the book doesn't mean a thing to me; wie sagt man ... auf Englisch? what is the English for ...?; ich hab's dir ja gleich gesagt! I told you so!; laß dir das gesagt sein! put that in your pipe and smoke it!; man sagt, er sei krank he is said to be ill; was Sie nicht ~! you don't say!; F wem ~ Sie das! you're telling me!; (das) sagst du! F says you!; sage und schreibe no less than; es (or damit) ist nicht gesagt, daß that doesn't necessarily mean that; unter uns gesagt between you and me; gesagt, getan no sooner said than done; → Meinung etc, schwer II.
'Sagen n (-s) F das ~ haben be the boss, bei (or in dat) have the (final) say in.
sägen ['zɛːgən] v/t, v/i (h) saw.
'sagenhaft adj 1. legendary, mythical. 2. F fig. fantastic, terrific, incredible.
'Sägespäne pl wood shavings.
'Sägewerk n sawmill.
sah [zaː] pret of sehen.
Sahne ['zaːnə] f (-; no pl) cream.
'Sahnebon,bon m, n toffee, Am. taffy.
'Sahnetorte f cream gateau.
sahnig ['zaːnıç] adj creamy.
Saison [zɛ'zõː] f (-; -s) season. ⚲**abhängig** adj seasonal. **~arbeiter** m seasonal worker. **~schlußverkauf** m ♁ seasonal sale.
Saite ['zaıtə] f (-; -n) ♪ string, chord: → aufziehen 4. **'Saiteninstru,ment** n stringed instrument.
Sakko ['zako] m, n (-s; -s) jacket.
sakral [za'kraːl] adj eccl. sacred.
Sakrament [zakra'mɛnt] n (-[e]s; -e) eccl. sacrament.
Sakrileg [zakri'leːk] n (-s; -e) sacrilege.
Sakristei [zakrıs'taı] f (-; -en) vestry.
Salamander [zala'mandər] m (-s; -) zo. salamander.
Salami [za'laːmi] f (-; -[s]) salami.
Salat [za'laːt] m (-[e]s; -e) 1. gastr. salad: F da haben wir den ~! there you are! 2.

no pl ♀ lettuce. **~besteck** *n* salad servers. **~kopf** *m* (head of) lettuce. **~öl** *n* salad oil. **~soße** *f* salad dressing.

Salbe ['zalbə] *f* (-; -n) ointment.

Salbei ['zalbaɪ] *m* (-s; *no pl*) ♀ sage.

salben ['zalbən] *v/t* (h) anoint.

'**Salbung** *f* (-; -en) anointing, *a. fig.* unction. '**salbungsvoll** *adj* unctuous.

Saldo ['zaldo] *m* (-s; Salden) ✝ balance.

Saline [za'li:nə] *f* (-; -n) saltworks.

Salmiak [zal'mĭak] *m* (-s; *no pl*) 🜍 ammonium chloride.

Salmonellen [zalmo'nɛlən] *pl* salmonellae. **~erkrankung** *f* salmonellosis.

Salon [za'lõ:] *m* (-s; -s) drawing-room, salon (*a.* ✝), *Am.* parlor, ⚓ saloon.

sa'lonfähig *adj* a) presentable, b) respectable: *nicht* ~ risqué (*joke*).

salopp [za'lɔp] *adj* casual, off-hand.

Salpeter [zal'pe:tər] *m* (-s; *no pl*) 🜍 saltpet/re (*Am.* -er). **~säure** *f* nitric acid.

Salto ['zalto] *m* (-s, -s, -ti) somersault.

Salut [za'lu:t] *m* (-[e]s; -e) salute.

salutieren [zalu'ti:rən] *v/t*, *v/i* (h) salute.

Salve ['zalvə] *f* (-; -n) ✕ volley, salvo.

Salz [zalts] *n* (-es; -e) salt.

'**salzarm** *adj* **~e Kost** low-salt diet.

'**Salzbergwerk** *m* salt mine.

salzen ['zaltsən] *v/t* (salzte, gesalzen, h) salt, *fig. a.* season; → **gesalzen**.

'**Salzfäßchen** *n* salt cellar.

'**Salzgurke** *f* pickled gherkin.

'**salzhaltig** *adj* saline.

'**Salzhering** *m* salted herring.

salzig ['zaltsɪç] *adj* salty.

'**Salzkartoffeln** *pl* boiled potatoes.

'**salzlos** *adj* salt-free.

'**Salzsäure** *f* 🜍 hydrochloric acid.

'**Salzstange** *f* saltstick. '**Salzstreuer** *m* salt shaker. '**Salzwasser** *n* salt water.

Samariter [zama'ri:tər] *m* (-s; -) (*barmherziger* ~ good) Samaritan.

Samen ['za:mən] *m* (-s; -) **1.** ♀ *or fig.* seed. **2.** *physiol.* sperm, semen. **~bank** *f* (-; -en) ⚕, *vet.* sperm bank. **~erguß** *m* ejaculation. **~faden** *m* spermatozoon. **~flüssigkeit** *f* semen. **~kapsel** *f* ♀ seed capsule. **~leiter** *m anat.* vas deferens. **~spender** *m* (sperm) donor. **~strang** *m anat.* spermatic cord.

'**Sammel|akti,on** *f* **1.** fund-raising campaign. **2.** (salvage) collection. **~band** *m* (-[e]s; ⁻e) anthology. **~becken** *n* reservoir (*a. fig.*), *geogr.* catchment area.

~begriff *m* generic term. **~bestellung** *f* collective order. **~büchse** *f* collecting box. **~fahrschein** *m* group ticket. **~lager** *n* assembly camp. **~mappe** *f* folder.

sammeln ['zamǝln] (h) **I** *v/t* **1.** collect (*money, stamps, etc*), gather (*wood etc, fig. experience*); → **gesammelt** 1. **2.** assemble, gather: (*wieder*) ~ rally. **3.** *opt.* focus. **II** *v/i* **4.** (*für* for) collect money, pass the hat (around). **III** *sich* ~ **5.** gather, accumulate. **6.** assemble, meet, rally. **7.** *fig.* a) *a.* **s-e Gedanken** ~ collect one's thoughts, b) compose o.s.; → **gesammelt** 2. **8.** *opt.* focus.

'**Sammel|name** *m* collective (noun). **~platz** *m*, **~punkt** *m* **1.** assembly point. **2.** ~**stelle** *f* collecting point.

Sammelsurium [zaməl'zu:rĭʊm] *n* (-s; -rien) omnium gatherum.

'**Sammelvisum** *n* group visa.

Sammler¹ ['zamlər] *m* (-s; -) ⚡ accumulator. '**Sammler²** *m* (-s; -), '**Sammlerin** *f* (-; -nen) collector.

'**Sammlerwert** *m* collector's value.

'**Sammlung** *f* (-; -en) **1.** collection. **2.** anthology. **3.** museum. **4.** *fig.* a) concentration, b) composure.

Samstag ['zams-] *m* (*am* ~ on) Saturday.

'**samstags** *adv* on Saturdays.

samt [zamt] **I** *adv* ~ *und sonders* all of them, F the whole lot. **II** *prep* together with, along with.

Samt *m* (-[e]s; -e) a) velvet, b) velveteen.

'**samtartig** *adj* velvety.

'**Samthandschuh** *m fig. j-n mit ~en anfassen* handle s.o. with kid gloves.

sämtlich ['zɛmtlɪç] **I** *adj* all: **~e Werke** the complete works. **II** *adv* all of them.

Sanatorium [zana'to:rĭʊm] *n* (-s; -rien) sanatorium, *Am.* sanitarium.

Sand [zant] *m* (-[e]s; ⁻e) sand: F *wie* ~ *am Meer* any number of; *im* ~*e verlaufen* come to nothing; *j-m* ~ *in die Augen streuen* throw dust in s.o.'s eyes; F *in den* ~ *setzen* waste (*a project etc*).

Sandale [zan'da:lə] *f* (-; -n) sandal.

Sandalette [zanda'lɛtə] *f* (-; -n) high-heeled sandal.

'**Sand|bahn** *f mot.* dirt track. **~bank** *f* (-; ⁻e) sandbank. **~boden** *m* sandy soil.

'**Sanddorn** *m* (-[e]s; -e) ♀ sea buckthorn.

sandig ['zandɪç] *adj* sandy.

'**Sand|kasten** *m* sandpit, ✕ sandtable. **~männchen** *n* sandman. **~pa,pier** *n* sandpaper. **~sack** *m* sandbag. **~stein** *m* sandstone. **~strand** *m* sandy beach. **~sturm** *m* sandstorm.

sandte ['zantə] *pret of senden².*

'Sanduhr *f* hourglass.

sanft [zanft] *adj* soft, gentle, peaceful, easy (*death etc*). **'Sanftheit** *f* (-; *no pl*) softness, gentleness.

'sanftmütig [-my:tɪç] *adj* gentle, meek.

sang [zaŋ] *pret of singen.*

Sänger ['zɛŋər] *m* (-s; -) **1.** singer. **2.** *zo.* songbird. **~fest** *n* choral festival.

'Sängerin *f* (-; -nen) singer.

'sang- und 'klanglos *adv* F quietly.

sanieren [za'ni:rən] (h) **I** *v/t* redevelop, *a.* ✝ rehabilitate. **II** *sich ~ a*) ✝ get back on one's feet again, b) F line one's own pockets. **Sa'nierung** *f* (-; -en) redevelopment, *a.* ✝ rehabilitation. **Sa'nierungsgebiet** *n* redevelopment area.

sanitär [zani'tɛ:r] *adj* sanitary.

Sanitäter [zani'tɛ:tər] *m* (-s; -) **1.** ambulance (*or* first-aid) man. **2.** ✗ medical orderly.

Sani'täts|dienst *m* medical service. **~korps** *n* ✗ medical corps. **~wache** *f* first-aid post. **~wagen** *m* ambulance. **~zelt** *n* hospital tent.

sank [zaŋk] *pret of sinken.*

Sankt [zaŋkt] (*abbr.* St.) Saint (*abbr.* St.).

Sanktion [zaŋk'tsio:n] *f* (-; -en) sanction.

sanktionieren [zaŋktsio'ni:rən] *v/t* (h) sanction.

sann [zan] *pret of sinnen.*

Saphir ['za:fir] *m* (-s; -e) **1.** sapphire. **2.** *a.* **'Saphirnadel** *f* sapphire (needle).

Sardelle [zar'dɛlə] *f* (-; -n) anchovy.

Sardine [zar'di:nə] *f* (-; -n) sardine.

Sarg [zark] *m* (-[e]s; ⁓e) coffin, *Am. a.* casket.

Sarkasmus [zar'kasmʊs] *m* (-; *no pl*) sarcasm.

sarkastisch [zar'kastɪʃ] *adj* sarcastic.

saß [za:s] *pret of sitzen.*

Satan ['za:tan] *m* (-s; -e) Satan.

satanisch [za'ta:nɪʃ] *adj* satanic.

Satellit [zatɛ'li:t] *m* (-en; -en) satellite. **Satel'liten|bild** *n,* **~foto** *n* satellite picture. **~staat** *m pol.* satellite (state). **~stadt** *f* satellite town. **~übertragung** *f* TV satellite transmission.

Satin [za'tɛ̃] *m* (-s; -s) a) satin, b) sateen.

Satire [za'ti:rə] *f* (-; -n) satire (*auf acc*

on). **Satiriker** [za'ti:rikər] *m* (-s; -) satirist. **satirisch** [za'ti:rɪʃ] *adj* satirical.

satt [zat] *adj* **1.** satisfied, F full up: *ich bin ~* I've had enough; *sich ~ essen* eat one's fill; *das macht ~* that's very filling; *~ zu essen haben* have enough to eat; F *et. (j-n) (gründlich) ~ haben* be sick and tired of (*or* be fed up with) s.th. (s.o.). **2.** full (*sound*), deep, rich (*colour*). **3.** *fig.* complacent. **F** stiff, steep (*price etc*), powerful (*blow*).

Sattel ['zatəl] *m* saddle: *fig. j-n aus dem ~ heben* oust s.o.; *fest im ~ sitzen* be firmly in the saddle. **'sattelfest** *adj* well up (*in dat* in). **'satteln** *v/t* (h) saddle.

'Sattel|schlepper *m mot.* **1.** road tractor. **2.** articulated lorry, *Am.* semitrailer (truck). **~tasche** *f* saddle-bag. **~zeug** *n* saddle and harness.

sättigen ['zɛtɪgən] (h) **I** *v/t* **1.** satisfy, fill. **2.** ✽, *a.* ✝ saturate. **II** *v/i* **3.** be filling. **'Sättigung** *f* (-; *no pl*) a) satiation, b) satiety, c) ✽ *or fig.* saturation.

Sattler ['zatlər] *m* (-s; -) saddler.

Sattlerei [zatlə'raɪ] *f* (-; -en) saddlery.

saturieren [zatu'ri:rən] *v/t* (h) saturate.

Satyr ['za:tyr] *m* (-s, -n; -n) satyr.

Satz [zats] *m* (-es; ⁓e) **1.** *ling.* sentence, clause. **2.** principle, tenet, ₳ theorem. **3.** *print.* a) (type)setting, composition, b) (set) matter. **4.** ♪ movement. **5.** *tennis:* set. **6.** set (*of tools, stamps, etc*). **7.** sediment, dregs, (coffee) grounds. **8.** rate: *zum ~ von* at the rate of. **9.** leap: *e-n ~ machen* (take a) leap.

'Satz|aussage *f ling.* predicate. **~ball** *m tennis:* set point. **~bau** *m* (-[e]s; *no pl*) *ling.* syntax, construction. **~gefüge** *n ling.* compound sentence. **~gegenstand** *m ling.* subject. **~lehre** *f ling.* syntax. **~spiegel** *m print.* type area. **~teil** *m ling.* part of sentence, clause.

'Satzung *f* (-; -en) statute, *a. pl* statutes and articles.

'satzungsgemäß *adj* statutory, *a.* in accordance with the statutes.

'Satzzeichen *n* punctuation mark.

Sau [zaʊ] *f* (-; ⁓e) **1.** *zo.* sow. **2.** V *fig.* a) (dirty) pig, b) slut, c) *contp.* swine, *a.* bitch: *unter aller ~* lousy; *j-n (et.) zur ~ machen* let s.o. have it (tear s.th. to pieces); *die ~ rauslassen* let one's hair down.

sauber ['zaʊbər] *adj* **1.** *a. fig.* clean, neat:

~ *sein child*: be potty-trained; *e-e ~e Lösung* a neat solution. **2.** F *iro.* nice, (just) great.

säuberlich ['zɔybərlɪç] *adj* **1.** clean, neat. **2.** careful.

'**saubermachen** *v/t, v/i* (*sep*, -ge-, h) clean (up), tidy (up).

säubern ['zɔybərn] *v/t* (h) **1.** clean (up), tidy (up). **2.** clear (*von* of). **3.** *fig.* purge.

'**Säuberung** *f* (-; -en) **1.** cleaning (*etc*). **2.** *fig.* purge.

'**Saubohne** *f* ♣ broad bean.

Sauciere [zo'siɛ:rə] *f* (-; -en) gravy boat.

Saudi ['zaʊdi] *m* (-s; -s) ɛaʊdi.

Saudi-A'rabien *n* (-s) Saudi Arabia.

'**sau'dumm** *adj* V damned stupid.

sauer ['zaʊər] **I** *adj* **1.** sour, ♠ acid (*a. drops, rain*), *gastr.* pickled: ~ *werden milk*: turn (sour), curdle; *in den sauren Apfel beißen müssen* have to swallow the bitter pill. **2.** F sour, cross: ~ *werden* get cross; *j-m das Leben ~ machen* make life miserable for s.o. **II** *adv* **3.** ~ *verdientes Geld* hard-earned money; F ~ *reagieren auf* (*acc*) be annoyed (*or* mad) at.

'**Sauerampfer** *m* (-s; *no pl*) ♣ sorrel.

Saue'rei *f* (-; -en) → *Schweinerei*.

'**Sauerkirsche** *f* ♣ sour cherry.

säuerlich ['zɔyərlɪç] *adj* (a bit) sour.

'**Sauermilch** *f* curdled milk.

säuern ['zɔyərn] *v/t* (h) make sour.

'**Sauerstoff** *m* (-[e]s; *no pl*) oxygen. ~**fla-sche** *f* oxygen cylinder. ~**mangel** *m* lack of oxygen. ~**maske** *f* oxygen mask. ~**zelt** *n* ♠ oxygen tent.

'**Sauerteig** *m* leaven.

saufen ['zaʊfən] *v/t, v/i* (soff, gesoffen, h) **1.** *animal*: drink. **2.** F *person*: booze, guzzle. **Säufer** ['zɔyfər] *m* (-s; -) F alcoholic, boozer. **Saufe'rei** *f* (-; -en) F **1.** boozing. **2.** F drinking bout, booze-up. '**Säuferin** *f* (-; -nen) → *Säufer*.

saugen ['zaʊɡən] *v/t, v/i* (h) **1.** suck (*an dat* s.th.); → *Finger*. **2.** vacuum.

säugen ['zɔyɡən] *v/t* (h) suckle (*a. zo.*), nurse, breastfeed.

'**Sauger** *m* (-s; -) teat, *Am.* nipple.

'**Säugetier** *n* mammal.

saugfähig ['zaʊk-] *adj* absorbent.

Säugling ['zɔyklɪŋ] *m* (-s; -e) baby.

'**Säuglings|alter** *n* (*im* ~ in) infancy. ~**nahrung** *f* baby food. ~**pflege** *f* baby care. ~**schwester** *f* baby nurse.

~**sterblichkeit** *f* infant mortality.

'**Saugwirkung** *f* suction.

'**sau'kalt** *adj* V bloody cold.

Säule ['zɔylə] *f* (-; -n) column, pillar (*a. fig.*). '**Säulengang** *m* colonnade.

Saum [zaʊm] *m* (-[e]s; ⁓e) hem.

'**saumäßig** *adj* V awful, lousy.

säumen ['zɔymən] *v/t* (h) **1.** hem. **2.** *fig.* line, skirt.

säumig ['zɔymɪç] *adj* **1.** late, tardy. **2.** ✝ ~*er Zahler* (*Schuldner*) defaulter.

Sauna ['zaʊna] *f* (-; Saunen) sauna.

Säure ['zɔyrə] *f* (-; -n) **1.** *no pl* sourness, *a.* ♠ acidity. **2.** ♠ acid.

'**säure|beständig, ~fest** *adj* acid-proof.

Säure'gurkenzeit *f* F (-; *no pl*) a) ✝ off-season, b) *tn the press*: silly season.

'**säurehaltig** *adj* acid(ic).

'**säurelöslich** *adj* acid-soluble.

Saurier ['zaʊriər] *m* (-s; -) saurian.

Saus [zaʊs] *in* ~ *und Braus leben* live on (*or* off) the fat of the land.

säuseln ['zɔyzəln] *v/i, v/t* (h) whisper, *iro. person*: purr.

sausen ['zaʊzən] *v/i* **1.** (sn) F whiz, rush, dash. **2.** (h) *wind*: rush, *a. bullet etc*: whistle, *ears*: buzz. '**sausenlassen** *v/t* (*irr, sep, no* -ge-, h) F a) pass up, give *s.th.* a miss, b) drop (*s.o.*).

'**Saustall** *m* pigsty (*a.* F *fig.*).

'**Sauwetter** *n* F filthy weather.

'**sau'wohl** *adj* F *sich ~ fühlen* feel real good.

Saxophon [zakso'fo:n] *n* (-s; -e) saxophone.

'**S-Bahn** *f* suburban (fast) train(s).

Schabe ['ʃa:bə] *f* (-; -n) *zo.* cockroach.

schaben ['ʃa:bən] *v/t, v/i* (h) scrape.

Schabernack ['ʃa:bərnak] *m* (-[e]s; -e) practical joke, hoax.

schäbig ['ʃɛ:bɪç] *adj* shabby, *fig. a.* mean. '**Schäbigkeit** *f* (-; *no pl*) shabbiness, *fig. a.* meanness.

Schablone [ʃa'blo:nə] *f* (-; -n) **1.** stencil, ⚙ template. **2.** *fig. a* stereotype, cliché, b) (fixed) routine. **Scha'blonenden-ken** *n* stereotyped thinking.

scha'blonenhaft *adj* stereotyped.

Schach [ʃax] *n* (-s; -s) **1.** *no pl* chess: ~ *spielen* play (at) chess. **2.** check: ~ *und matt!* checkmate!; *j-m* ~ *bieten* check s.o., *fig.* stand up to s.o.; *in* ~ *halten* keep in check (*a. fig.*), *with gun*: *a.* cover. **⸰brett** *n* chessboard. **⸰com¡puter** *m* chess computer.

Schacher ['ʃaxər] *m* (-s; *no pl*) haggling.

'**schachern** *v/i* (h) haggle (**um** over).

'**Schach|fi¡gur** *f* chessman, (chess) piece. ♟'**matt** *adj* **1.** (check)mate: **~ setzen** *a. fig.* checkmate. **2.** F exhausted. **⸰par¡tie** *f* game of chess. **⸰spiel** *n* **1.** (game of) chess. **2.** chess set. **⸰spie-ler(in** *f*) *m* chess player.

Schacht [ʃaxt] *m* (-[e]s; ⸰e) a) shaft (*a.* ⚒), b) manhole.

Schachtel ['ʃaxtəl] *f* (-; -n) **1.** box, *a.* carton, packet. **2.** F *alte* **~** old bag.

'**Schachtelsatz** *m* involved sentence.

'**Schachtur¡nier** *n* chess tournament.

'**Schachzug** *m a. fig.* move.

schade ['ʃaːdə] *adj pred* (**es ist** [**sehr**]) **~** it's a (great) pity (**um** about, **daß** that), F it's too bad (*he couldn't come etc*); **wie ~!** what a pity!; **dafür ist es** (**er**) **zu ~** it (he) is too good for that!; **darum ist es nicht ~!** it is no great loss!

Schädel ['ʃɛːdəl] *m* (-s; -) skull, cranium. **⸰basisbruch** *m* fracture of the skull-base. **⸰bruch** *m* fracture of the skull. **⸰dach** *n anat.* skullcap, calvaria.

schaden ['ʃaːdən] *v/i* (h) (*dat*) damage, harm, be detrimental (to): **das schadet der Gesundheit** that's bad for your health; **das schadet nichts** a) it won't do any harm, b) it doesn't matter; *iro.* **das schadet ihr gar nichts!** that serves her right!; **ein Versuch kann nicht ~** there is no harm in trying.

'**Schaden** *m* (-s; ⸰) a) damage (**an** *dat* to), b) injury, harm, c) *a.* ♂ defect, d) disadvantage, e) loss: **~ nehmen** be damaged, *person:* be harmed; **durch ~ wird man klug** once bitten twice shy.

'**Schadenersatz** *m* a) compensation, indemnification, b) damages: **~ erhalten** (**fordern, leisten**) recover (claim, pay) damages; **auf ~** (**ver**)**klagen** sue for damages. **⸰klage** *f* action for damages.

'**schadenersatzpflichtig** *adj* liable for damages.

'**Schadenfreiheitsra¡batt** *m mot.* no--claims bonus.

'**Schadenfreude** *f* (-; *no pl*) malicious glee, gloating: **voller ~** → '**schaden-froh** *adj* gloating(ly *adv*): **~ sein** gloat.

'**Schadenversicherung** *f* indemnity insurance.

schadhaft ['ʃaːt-] *adj* defective.

schädigen ['ʃɛːdɪɡən] *v/t* (h) damage, *a.* injure, harm, impair (*a. fig.*): **wir sind schwer geschädigt worden** we have suffered heavy losses. '**Schädigung** *f* (-; -en) (*gen* to) damage, harm.

schädlich ['ʃɛːtlɪç] *adj* (*dat* to) harmful, injurious, *a.* detrimental: **~ für die Ge-sundheit** bad for your health.

'**Schädlichkeit** *f* (-; *no pl*) harmfulness.

Schädling ['ʃɛːtlɪŋ] *m* (-s; -e) *zo.* pest.

'**Schädlings|bekämpfung** *f* pest control. **⸰bekämpfungsmittel** *n* pesticide.

'**schadlos** *adj j-n* (**sich**) **~ halten** indemnify s.o. (recoup o.s.) (**für** for); **sich an j-m ~ halten** recoup one's losses from s.o.

'**Schadstoff** *m* a) harmful substance, b) pollutant.

Schaf [ʃaːf] *n* (-[e]s; -e) **1.** *zo.* sheep: *fig.* **schwarzes ~** black sheep. **2.** F ninny.

'**Schafbock** *m zo.* ram.

Schäfchen ['ʃɛːfçən] *n* (-s; -) lamb: *fig.* **sein ~ ins trockene bringen** feather one's nest.

Schäfer ['ʃɛːfər] *m* (-s; -) shepherd.

'**Schäferhund** (**deutscher**) **~** Alsatian, German shepherd (dog).

'**Schäferin** *f* (-; -nen) shepherdess.

schaffen ['ʃafən] (schuf, geschaffen, h) **I** *v/t* **1.** a) create, produce, *fig. a.* make, b) bring about, cause, c) found, set up, establish: **er ist zum Lehrer** (**für den Posten**) **wie geschaffen** he is a born teacher (cut out for the job); → **Ordnung. 2.** take (*in acc*, *nach*, *zu* to), put: → **Hals, Weg, Welt. 3.** a) manage, b) F catch (*bus, train, etc*), c) set up (*record*): **es ~** make it, *a.* succeed; **das hätten wir geschafft!** we've done it!; **~ wir es bis dorthin** (**in 3 Stunden**)? can we make it there (in three hours)? **4. ich habe da-mit nichts zu ~** that's no business of mine, I wash my hands of it; **mit ihm will ich nichts zu ~ haben** I don't want anything to do with him. **5.** F *j-n* **~** a) take it out of s.o., b) get s.o. down; **ich bin geschafft!** I've had it! **II** *v/i* **6.** *dial.* work. **7. sich zu ~ machen** potter about, **an** (*dat*) busy o.s. (*b.s.* tamper) with. **8. j-m** (**viel** *or* **schwer**) **zu ~ ma-chen** give (*or* cause) s.o. (no end of) trouble, *illness:* trouble s.o.

'**Schaffen** n (-s) a) work, (creative activity, b) work(s).
'**schaffend** adj **1.** creative. **2.** working.
'**Schaffensdrang** m **1.** creative urge. **2.** zest for work. '**Schaffenskraft** f (-; no pl) **1.** creative power. **2.** vigo(u)r.
Schaffner ['ʃafnər] m (-s; -) conductor, 🚋 guard.
'**Schaffnerin** f (-; -nen) conductress.
'**Schaffung** f (-; no pl) a) creation, b) foundation, setting-up (→ *schaffen* 1).
'**Schafherde** f flock of sheep. '**Schafhirt** m shepherd. '**Schafleder** n sheepskin.
Schafott [ʃa'fɔt] n (-[e]s; -e) scaffold.
'**Schafpelz** m sheepskin: fig. *Wolf im ~* wolf in sheep's clothing.
'**Schafschur** f sheep shearing.
'**Schafskäse** m sheep's milk cheese.
Schaft [ʃaft] m (-[e]s; ᴗe) shaft (of axe etc), stock (of rifle), shank (of tool etc), leg (of boot). **~stiefel** m high boot.
'**Schafwolle** f sheep's wool.
'**Schafzucht** f sheep breeding.
Schah [ʃɑː] m (-s; -s) Shah.
Schakal [ʃa'kaːl] m (-s; -e) zo. jackal.
schäkern ['ʃɛːkərn] v/i (h) **1.** joke around. **2.** flirt.
schal [ʃaːl] adj stale, flat, fig. a. empty.
Schal m (-s; -s, -e) scarf.
Schale¹ ['ʃaːlə] f (-; -n) a) bowl, b) dish.
Schale² f (-; -n) **1.** shell (of eggs, nuts, a. 🔘 and zo.), skin (of fruit etc), peel(ing) (of potatoes etc), husk. **2.** F *sich in ~ werfen* dress up.
schälen ['ʃɛːlən] (h) **I** v/t peel (orange, potatoes, etc), shell (eggs, nuts), husk (peas etc), skin (tomatoes etc). **II** *sich ~ skin*: peel off.
'**Schalensitz** m mot. bucket seat.
'**Schalheit** f (-; no pl) a. fig. staleness.
Schall [ʃal] m (-[e]s; -e) **1.** sound: *schneller als der ~* supersonic. **2.** echo.
'**schalldämpfend** adj sound-deadening.
'**Schalldämpfer** m sound absorber, mot. silencer (a. on guns), Am. muffler.
'**schalldicht** adj soundproof.
schallen ['ʃalən] v/i (h) resound, ring: *~de Ohrfeige* resounding slap; *~des Gelächter* peals of laughter; *er lachte ~d* he roared with laughter.
'**Schallgeschwindigkeit** f sonic speed.
'**Schallmauer** f sound barrier.
'**Schallplatte** f record, disc, disk.
'**Schallplattenaufnahme** f recording.

'**schallschluckend** adj sound-absorbing.
'**Schallwelle** f sound wave.
schalt [ʃalt] pret of *schelten*.
'**Schaltauto**|**matik** f mot. automatic gear change.
schalten ['ʃaltən] (h) **I** v/i **1.** ⚡, 🔘 switch (*auf* acc to), shift (the levers), mot. change (or shift) the gears: *in den dritten Gang ~* change (or shift) into third (gear). **2.** F get it, catch on: *schnell ~ a)* do some quick thinking, b) catch on quickly, be quick in the uptake. **3.** *~ und walten* be in charge (of things); *j-n ~ und walten lassen* give s.o. a free hand. **II** v/t **4.** ⚡ switch, turn, shift (gear, lever). **5.** ⚡ switch (*auf* acc to).
'**Schalter** m (-s; -) **1.** counter, 🚋 ticket window, ✉ desk. **2.** ⚡ switch. **~beamte** m counter (or booking) clerk. **~dienst** m counter duty. **~halle** f main hall. **~stunden** pl business hours.
'**Schalt**|**getriebe** n gear box. **~hebel** m mot. (gear)shift lever, ⚡ switch lever, 🔘 control lever: *an den ~n der Macht sitzen* be at the controls. **~jahr** n leap year: F *alle ~e (mal)* once in a blue moon. **~kasten** m ⚡ switchbox. **~knopf** m (control) button. **~kreis** m ⚡ circuit. **~plan** m wiring diagram. **~pult** n control desk. **~tafel** f ⚡ switchboard. **~tag** m intercalary day. **~uhr** f timer.
'**Schaltung** f (-; -en) **1.** mot. a) gearshift assembly, b) gear change (or shift). **2.** ⚡ a) circuit, b) wiring. **3.** 🔘 control(s).
Scham [ʃaːm] f (-; no pl) **1.** shame: *rot vor ~ →* **schamrot**. **2.** private parts, genitals. **~bein** n anat. pubic bone.
schämen ['ʃɛːmən] *sich ~* (h) be (or feel) ashamed ([*wegen*] gen, *für* of); *schäme dich!* shame on you!
'**Scham**|**gefühl** n (-[e]s; no pl) sense of shame. **~haare** n pl pubic hair.
'**schamhaft** adj bashful, modest.
'**Schamlippen** pl anat. labia.
'**schamlos** adj a) shameless, b) indecent: *~e Lüge* barefaced lie. '**Schamlosigkeit** f (-; no pl) shamelessness.
Schamottestein [ʃa'mɔtə-] m firebrick.
'**schamrot** adj red with shame: *~ werden* blush with shame.
Schande ['ʃandə] f (-; no pl) disgrace (*für* to), a. shame: *~ machen* (dat) be a disgrace to.

schänden ['ʃɛndən] v/t (h) a) dishon-o(u)r, b) violate, rape, c) desecrate.

'**Schandfleck** m blot, eyesore.

schändlich ['ʃɛntlɪç] adj disgraceful, scandalous.

Schandtat ['ʃant-] f outrage.

'**Schändung** f (-; -en) a) disgrace (gen to), b) violation, rape, c) desecration.

Schankstube ['ʃaŋk-] f (public) bar.

Schanze ['ʃantsə] f (-; -n) ski-jump.

'**Schanzentisch** m ski-jump platform.

Schar [ʃaːr] f (-; -en) crowd (of people), troop (of children), flock (of birds).

scharen ['ʃaːrən] v/t (h) (a. sich ~) gather (or rally) (um round); e-e Menge etc um sich ~ rally a crowd etc round one.

'**scharenweise** adv in droves.

scharf [ʃarf] I adj 1. sharp (a. fig. eye, criticism, tongue, etc), a. biting (wind etc, fig. words etc), a. piercing (sound), a. keen (mind, glance, etc). 2. live (ammunition), armed (bomb etc). 3. hot (food, pepper, etc), strong (spirits, vinegar, etc), pungent, acrid (smell), 🕳 or fig. caustic. 4. sharp, abrupt. 5. sharp, exact, clear: phot. ein ~es Bild a sharp(ly defined) picture. 6. a) sharp, severe, strict, b) hard, fierce: ~e Konkurrenz stiff competition; ~er Protest fierce protest; ~es Tempo hard pace; ~e Bewachung close guard(ing); ~er Hund savage dog, F fig. tough guy. 7. randy, hot, a. sexy: ~ sein auf (acc) be very keen on, sexually: be hot for. II adv 8. sharply (etc): ~ aufpassen pay close attention, watch out; ~ bremsen brake hard; phot. ~ einstellen focus; ~ nachdenken think hard; ~ schießen shoot with live ammunition; ~ verurteilen condemn severely.

'**Scharfblick** m [-(e)s; no pl] perspicacity.

Schärfe ['ʃɛrfə] f (-; no pl) 1. sharpness, fig. a. severity, a. keenness (of mind), a. fierceness: in aller ~ very severely. 2. a) gastr. hotness, b) pungency (of smell), c) 🕳 or fig. causticity. 3. acuteness (of sight, hearing), opt., phot. sharpness.

'**Scharfeinstellung** f opt., phot. a) focus(s)ing, b) focus(s)ing control.

schärfen ['ʃɛrfən] v/t (h) a. fig. sharpen.

'**Schärfentiefe** f phot. depth of focus.

'**scharfkantig** adj sharp-edged.

'**scharfmachen** v/t (sep, -ge-, h) F j-n ~ a) gegen set s.o. against, b) auf (acc)

make s.o. keen on, c) turn s.o. on.

'**Scharfmacher** m (-s; -) F agitator.

'**Scharfschießen** n live shooting.

'**Scharfschütze** m sharpshooter, sniper.

'**scharfsichtig** adj fig. perspicacious.

'**Scharfsinn** m (-[e]s; no pl) acumen.

'**scharfsinnig** adj astute, shrewd.

Scharlach ['ʃarlax] m (-s; no pl) 🕳 scarlet fever. '**scharlachrot** adj scarlet.

Scharlatan ['ʃarlatan] m (-s; -e) charlatan, F quack, fraud.

Scharnier [ʃar'niːr] n (-s; -e) hinge.

Schärpe ['ʃɛrpə] f (-; -n) sash.

scharren ['ʃarən] v/i (h) scrape (mit den Füßen one's feet), horse etc: paw.

Scharte ['ʃartə] f (-; -n) nick: fig. die ~ (wieder) auswetzen make up for it.

schartig ['ʃartɪç] adj jagged.

Schaschlik ['ʃaʃlɪk] m, n (-s; -s) shashlik.

Schatten ['ʃatən] m (-s; -) a. fig. shadow, b) shade: im ~ in the shade; fig. in den ~ stellen outshine, eclipse; in j-s ~ stehen live in s.o.'s shadow; man kann nicht über s-n (eigenen) ~ springen the leopard can't change its spots.

'**Schattendasein** n ein ~ führen live in the shadow.

'**schattenhaft** adj shadowy.

'**Schatten|kabi,nett** n pol. shadow cabinet. ~riß m silhouette. ~seite f shady (fig. seamy) side. ~spiel n shadow play.

schattieren [ʃa'tiːrən] v/t (h) shade.

Schat'tierung f (-; -en) a) shading, b) a. fig. shade.

schattig ['ʃatɪç] adj shady.

Schatulle [ʃa'tʊlə] f (-; -n) casket.

Schatz [ʃats] m (-es; ~e) 1. a. fig. treasure. 2. F darling, love.

'**Schatzamt** n pol. Treasury.

'**Schatzanweisung** f 🕳 treasury bond.

'**schätzbar** adj assessable.

Schätzchen ['ʃɛtsçən] n (-s; -) darling.

schätzen ['ʃɛtsən] v/t (h) 1. estimate, guess, a. assess (damage, value, etc) (auf acc at): wie alt ~ Sie ihn? how old would you say he is?; grob geschätzt at a rough guess. 2. suppose, Am. F guess. 3. a) esteem, think highly of, b) appreciate: → glücklich I.

'**Schätzer** m (-s; -) 🕳 valuer, assessor.

'**Schatzgräber** [-grɛːbər] m (-s; -) treasure seeker.

'**Schatz|kammer** f treasury. ~meister m treasurer. ~suche f treasure hunt.

'**Schätzung** f (-; -en) estimate, guess, ✝, ⚬⚬⚬ assessment.

'**schätzungsweise** adv approximately.

Schau [ʃaʊ] f (-; -en) **1.** show, exhibition: **zur ~ stellen** exhibit, display, fig. a. parade; fig. **nur zur ~** only for show. **2.** TV etc show: F **e-e ~ abziehen** put on a show; **j-m die ~ stehlen** steal the show from s.o., upstage s.o.

'**Schaubild** n chart, graph, diagram.

Schauder [ʃaʊdər] m (-s; -) shudder, shiver. '**schauderhaft** adj horrible, dreadful. '**schaudern** v/i (h) (**vor** dat with, **bei** at) shudder, shiver.

schauen [ʃaʊən] v/i (h) look (**auf** acc at, fig. upon): F **schau, daß du ...** mind you ...; iro. **schau, schau!** well, well!

Schauer [ʃaʊər] m (-s; -) **1.** meteor. shower. **2.** shudder, shiver, a. thrill; → **laufen** 1. '**schauerartig** adj **~e Regen-fälle** showers.

'**schauerlich** adj **1.** horrible, terrible (a. fig.). **2.** weird, F creepy.

'**Schauermärchen** n F horror story.

Schaufel [ʃaʊfəl] f (-; -n) **1.** a) shovel, b) scoop, c) ⚬ paddle (of water wheel), blade (of turbine). **2.** hunt. palm.

'**schaufeln** v/t, v/i (h) a) shovel, b) dig.

'**Schaufenster** n shop window, fig. showcase. **~bummel** m **e-n ~ machen** go window-shopping. **~dekorati on** f window dressing.

'**Schau|fliegen** n, **~flug** m air display.

'**Schaugeschäft** n show business.

'**Schaukampf** m exhibition bout.

'**Schaukasten** m showcase.

Schaukel [ʃaʊkəl] f (-; -n) swing.

schaukeln [ʃaʊkəln] v/t, v/i (h) swing, cradle, chair, ship: rock: F **die Sache ~** manage (or swing) it.

'**Schaukelpoli tik** f seesaw politics.

'**Schaukelstuhl** m rocking chair.

'**Schaulaufen** n exhibition skating.

'**Schaulustige**, m, f (-n; -n) curious on-looker, contp. gaper.

Schaum [ʃaʊm] m (-[e]s; ⸚e) foam (a. ⚬), froth (a. on beer), lather: gastr. **zu ~ schlagen** beat (to a froth).

'**Schaumbad** n bubble bath.

schäumen [ʃɔʏmən] v/i (h) foam, froth: (**vor Wut**) **~** foam (with rage).

'**Schaumgummi** m, n foam rubber.

schaumig [ʃaʊmɪç] adj frothy.

'**Schaum|krone** f white crest. **~löscher**

m foam extinguisher. **~schläger** m contp. hot-air artist. **~schläge'rei** f (-; no pl) contp. hot air. **~stoff** m ⚬ foamed material. **~teppich** m ⚬ foam carpet. **~wein** m sparkling wine.

'**Schaupackung** f ✝ dummy.

'**Schauplatz** m (am ~ at the) scene.

'**Schaupro,zeß** m ⚬⚬⚬ show trial.

schaurig [ʃaʊrɪç] → **schauerlich**.

'**Schauspiel** n **1.** play, drama. **2.** fig. spectacle, sight. '**Schauspieler** m (fig. play-)actor. **Schauspiele'rei** f (-; no pl) (fig. play-)acting. '**Schauspielerin** f actress. '**schauspielerisch** adj theat-rical, acting (talent etc). '**schauspie-lern** v/i (h) fig. play-act, F put on an act.

'**Schauspielhaus** n theat/re (Am. -er).

'**Schauspielschule** f drama school.

'**Schausteller** m (-s; -) exhibitor, at fairs etc: showman.

Scheck [ʃɛk] m (-s; -s) cheque, Am. check (**über** acc for). **~buch** n, **~heft** n chequebook, Am. checkbook. **~karte** f cheque (Am. check) card.

scheel [ʃeːl] **~ansehen** look askance at.

Scheffel [ʃɛfəl] m (-s; -) bushel: fig. **sein Licht unter den ~ stellen** hide one's light under a bushel.

'**scheffeln** v/t (h) rake in money.

Scheibe [ʃaɪbə] f (-; -n) **1.** disc (a. F record), ⚬ a. wheel, a. washer. **2.** (win-dow etc) pane, mot. windscreen, Am. windshield. **3.** target. **4.** ice hockey: puck. **5.** slice (of bread etc): F **da(von) kannst du dir e-e ~ abschneiden!** you can take a leaf out of his (her etc) book!

'**Scheiben|bremse** f mot. disc brake. **~kupplung** f disc clutch. **~schießen** n target practice. **~waschanlage** f mot. windscreen (Am. windshield) washers. **~wischer** m mot. windscreen (Am. windshield) wiper.

Scheich [ʃaɪç] m (-[e]s; -s, -e) sheik(h).

'**Scheichtum** n (-s; ⸚er) sheikhdom.

Scheide [ʃaɪdə] f (-; -n) **1.** sheath (a. ⚬), a. scabbard. **2.** anat. vagina.

scheiden [ʃaɪdən] (schied, geschieden) **I** v/t (h) separate, divide, ⚬⚬⚬ divorce (a married couple), dissolve (marriage): **sich ~ lassen**, a. **geschieden werden** get a divorce (**von** from). **II** v/i (sn) part (**von** from): **aus dem Dienst ~** retire from service, resign; **aus e-r Firma ~**

leave a firm. **III sich ~** (h) separate; *hier ~ sich die Geister* here opinions are divided.

'**Scheide|wand** f partition, *fig.* barrier. **~weg** m fig. **am ~** at a crossroads.

'**Scheidung** f (-; -en) **1.** separation. **2.** divorce (**von** from), dissolution (of *marriage*): *die ~ einreichen* file a petition for divorce.

'**Scheidungs|grund** m ground for divorce. **~klage** f petition for divorce.

Schein¹ [ʃaɪn] m (-[e]s; *no pl*) **1.** light, *a.* glow. **2.** appearance: *et. nur zum ~ tun* pretend to do s.th.; *dem ~ nach* (*zu urteilen*) to all appearances; *den ~ wahren* keep up appearances; *der ~ trügt* appearances are deceptive.

Schein² m (-[e]s; -e) **1.** a) slip, b) *a.* *univ.* certificate. **2.** (bank)note, *Am. a.* bill.

'**scheinbar** adj seeming, apparent: *er ging nur ~ darauf ein* he only pretended to agree.

'**Scheinehe** f fictitious marriage.

scheinen ['ʃaɪnən] v/i (schien, geschienen, h) **1.** a) shine, b) gleam. **2.** appear, seem: *wie es scheint* as it seems; *es scheint mir* it seems to me; *er scheint nicht zu wollen*; *mir scheint, er will nicht* he doesn't seem to want to.

'**Schein|firma** f dummy firm. **~friede** m hollow peace. **~geschäft** n fictitious transaction.

'**scheinheilig** adj F contp. hypocritical.

'**Scheinheiligkeit** f (-; *no pl*) hypocrisy.

'**Scheintod** m suspended animation.

'**scheintot** adj seemingly dead.

'**Scheinwerfer** m (-s; -) floodlight, searchlight, *mot.* headlight, *film:* klieg light, *thea.* (a. **~licht** n) spotlight.

Scheiß... [ʃaɪs-] V bloody, *sl.* fucking.

'**Scheißdreck** m → **Scheiße** 2.

'**Scheiße** f (-; *no pl*) V *a. fig.* shit, crap: *fig.* **in der ~ sitzen** be in the shit; *~!* shit!; *~ bauen* make a foul-up; *große ~ sein* be a load of crap. '**scheißen** v/i (schiß, geschissen, h) V shit, crap: *scheiß drauf!* to hell with it!, fuck it!

'**Scheißer** m (-s; -) V **1. kleiner ~** little shit. **2.** *a.* '**Scheißkerl** m bastard.

Scheit [ʃaɪt] n (-[e]s; -e) piece of wood, log.

Scheitel ['ʃaɪtəl] m (-s; -) parting: *vom ~ bis zur Sohle* from top to toe.

scheiteln ['ʃaɪtəln] v/t (h) (**sich**) **das Haar ~** part one's hair.

'**Scheitelpunkt** m *A* vertex, *astr.* zenith.

Scheiterhaufen ['ʃaɪtər-] m (funeral) pyre, *hist.* (**auf dem ~** at the) stake.

scheitern ['ʃaɪtərn] v/i (sn) (**an** dat) fail (because of), *negotiations: a.* break down, *sports:* be stopped (by): *daran ist er gescheitert* that was his undoing.

'**Scheitern** n (-s) failure, breakdown.

Schelle ['ʃɛlə] f (-; -n) **1.** (little) bell. **2.** ⊕ clamp, clip.

schellen ['ʃɛlən] *dial.* → **klingeln** 1.

'**Schellfisch** m haddock.

Schelm [ʃɛlm] m (-[e]s; -e) rogue.

'**schelmisch** adj roguish, impish.

schelten ['ʃɛltən] v/t (schalt, gescholten, h) scold, chide (a. *v/i*).

Schema ['ʃeːma] n (-s; -s, -ta) **1.** pattern, system: *nach e-m ~* schematically; F *nach ~ F* by rote. **2.** diagram, scheme.

schematisch [ʃeˈmaːtɪʃ] adj schematic, systematic, *contp.* mechanical.

schematisieren [ʃematiˈziːrən] v/t (h) schematize.

Schemel ['ʃeːməl] m (-s; -) (foot)stool.

Schemen ['ʃeːmən] n (-s; -) phantom.

'**schemenhaft** adj shadowy.

Schenke ['ʃɛŋkə] f (-; -n) tavern.

Schenkel ['ʃɛŋkəl] m (-s; -) **1.** *anat.* a) thigh, b) shank. **2.** *A* side, leg.

schenken ['ʃɛŋkən] v/t (h) a) give (as a present), *a.* 🕀 donate, b) grant: *j-m et. ~* give s.o. s.th. (as a present) (*zum Geburtstag* for his *etc* birthday); *fig.* *sich et. ~* skip s.th., give s.th. a miss; F *geschenkt!* forget it!; → *Aufmerksamkeit* 1, *Gehör* 2, *Glaube* etc.

'**Schenkung** f (-; -en) donation.

'**Schenkungsurkunde** f deed of donation.

scheppern ['ʃɛpərn] v/i (h) F rattle.

Scherbe ['ʃɛrbə] f (-; -n) broken piece, fragment.

Schere ['ʃeːrə] f (-; -n) **1.** (e-e ~ a pair of) scissors (✂ shears). **2.** *zo.* pincer. **3.** *sports:* scissors.

scheren ['ʃeːrən] **I** v/t (schor, geschoren, h) trim, cut (a. *hair*), shear (*sheep*), clip (*hedge*). **II** F *sich nicht ~ um* not to care about; *sich nach Hause* (*ins Bett*) **~** go home (to bed); *scher dich!* beat it!

'**Scherenschnitt** m silhouette.

Schere'rei f (-; -en) F trouble.

Scherflein ['ʃɛrflaɪn] n (-s; -) *sein ~ beitragen* give one's mite, *a.* do one's bit.

Scherz [ʃɛrts] m (-es; -e) joke: *(s-n) ~ treiben mit* make fun of; *im ~, zum ~* as a joke, for fun; *~ beiseite* joking apart.

scherzen ['ʃɛrtsən] v/i (h) joke: *damit ist nicht zu ~* that's not to be trifled with.

'**scherzhaft** *adj* joking, humorous.

scheu [ʃɔy] *adj* shy, timid: *~ machen* frighten (*horse etc*). **Scheu** f (-; *no pl*) a) shyness, timidity, b) awe.

scheuchen ['ʃɔyçən] v/t (h) chase.

scheuen ['ʃɔyən] (h) **I** v/i *horse etc*: shy, take fright (*vor dat* at). **II** v/t shun, avoid, shy away from: *k-e Kosten ~* spare no expense; → *Licht* 1. **III** *sich ~, et. zu tun* be afraid of (*or* shrink from) doing s.th.; *sich nicht ~ zu inf* not to be afraid to *inf*, *b.s.* have the nerve to *inf*.

'**Scheuerbürste** f scrubbing brush.

'**Scheuerlappen** m floor cloth.

scheuern ['ʃɔyərn] v/t (h) v/t **1.** scour, scrub. **2.** chafe. **3.** F *j-m e-e ~* slap s.o.('s face). **II** v/i **4.** chafe.

Scheuklappe f *a. fig.* blinker.

Scheune ['ʃɔynə] f (-; -n) barn.

Scheusal ['ʃɔyza:l] n (-s; -e) monster (*a. fig.*), F beast: *kleines ~* little horror.

scheußlich ['ʃɔyslɪç] *adj* horrible (*a.* F *fig.*), *a.* hideous, revolting: F *~es Wetter* filthy weather; *~ kalt* terribly cold.

Schi(...) [ʃi:] → *Ski(...)*.

Schicht [ʃɪçt] f (-; -en) **1.** layer, *a.* coat(ing), *geol.* stratum, bed, *phot.* emulsion. **2.** class, *pl a.* social strata: *breite ~en* large sections (*of the population*). **3.** shift: *~ arbeiten* do shift work.

'**Schichtarbeit** f shift work.

'**Schichtarbeiter(in** f) m shift worker.

schichten ['ʃɪçtən] v/t (h) pile up, stack.

'**Schichtunterricht** m teaching in shifts.

'**Schichtwechsel** m change of shift.

'**schichtweise** *adv* **1.** in layers. **2.** *work etc* in shifts.

schick [ʃɪk] *adj* **1.** a) smart, chic, stylish, b) posh, c) trendy. **2.** F great, super.

Schick m (-[e]s; *no pl*) chic, stylishness.

schicken ['ʃɪkən] (h) **I** v/t **1.** send (*nach, zu* to). **II** *sich ~ in* (*acc*) resign o.s. to. **3.** *sich ~ in* (*acc*) resign o.s. to. **4.** befit (*für j-n* s.o.): *es schickt sich nicht!* that is not the done thing! **3.** *sich ~ in* (*acc*) resign o.s. to.

Schickeria [ʃɪkə'ri:a] f (-; *no pl*) the chic set, *the* trendies. **Schickimicki** ['ʃɪkɪˈmɪkɪ] m (-s; -s) F trendy.

'**schicklich** *adj* proper, fitting.

Schicksal ['ʃɪkza:l] n (-s; -e) fate, destiny, *a.* lot: *das ~ herausfordern* tempt fate. '**schicksalhaft** *adj* fateful.

'**Schicksals|frage** f vital question. **~gefährte** m, **~genosse** m companion in distress. **~schlag** m (bad) blow.

'**Schiebedach** n *mot.* sliding roof, sunroof. '**Schiebefenster** n sliding (*or* sash) window.

schieben ['ʃi:bən] (schob, geschoben, h) **I** v/t **1.** a) push, b) slip, put (*in acc* into): *sich durch die Menge ~* push one's way through the crowd; → *Bank¹*. **II** v/i **2.** push. **3.** F *~ mit* traffic in.

'**Schieber** m (-s; -) **1.** a) slide, b) gate, c) bar, bolt. **2.** F racketeer.

'**Schiebesitz** m sliding seat.

'**Schiebetür** f sliding door.

'**Schiebung** f (-; -en) F put-up job, fix.

'**schied** [ʃi:t] *pret of* **scheiden**.

'**Schiedsgericht** ['ʃi:ts-] n court of arbitration, *sports etc*: jury.

'**Schiedsrichter** m arbitrator, *at competitions*: judge, *pl jury, sports*: umpire, referee: *als ~ fungieren* → *schiedsrichtern*.

'**schiedsrichterlich** *adj and adv sports*: of (*or* by) the umpire (*or* referee).

'**schiedsrichtern** v/i (h) referee, umpire.

'**Schiedsspruch** m award, arbitration.

schief [ʃi:f] **I** *adj* **1.** oblique, *a.* slanting, lop-sided: *~e Absätze* worn-down heels; *~e Ebene* inclined plane; *der ~e Turm von Pisa* the Leaning Tower of Pisa; *fig. ~es Lächeln* wry smile. **2.** *fig.* false, wrong, distorted, warped: → *Bahn* 1, *Licht* 1. **II** *adv* **3.** obliquely, aslant, at an angle: F *fig. j-n ~ ansehen* look askance at s.o.

Schiefer ['ʃi:fər] m (-s; -) slate. **~dach** n slate roof. **~platte** f, **~tafel** f slate.

'**schiefgehen** v/i (*irr, sep*, -ge-, sn, → *gehen*) F go wrong.

'**schieflachen**: *sich ~* (*sep*, -ge-, h) F laugh one's head off.

schielen ['ʃi:lən] v/i (h) **1.** (have a) squint, be cross-eyed: *auf dem rechten Auge ~* have a squint in one's right eye. **2.** F peer: *~ auf* (*acc*) (*or nach*) a) steal a glance at, b) have an eye on.

schien [ʃi:n] *pret of* **scheinen**.

'**Schienbein** n *anat.* shin(bone), tibia. **~schützer** m *sports*: shin-guard.

Schiene [ˈʃiːnə] f (-; -n) **1.** 🚆 *etc* rail, *pl a.* track. **2.** ⚙ bar. **3.** 🩹 splint.

schienen [ˈʃiːnən] v/t (h) 🩹 put in a splint (*or* in splints).

'**Schienen|bus** m rail bus. **~fahrzeug** n rail vehicle. **~netz** n railway (*Am.* railroad) system. **~strang** m track, railway line. **~verkehr** m rail traffic.

schier [ʃiːr] **I** *adj* sheer, pure. **II** *adv* almost, nearly.

Schierling [ˈʃiːrlɪŋ] m (-s; -e) ❧ hemlock.

'**Schießbefehl** m order to fire.

'**Schießbude** f shooting gallery.

schießen [ˈʃiːsən] (schoß, geschossen) **I** v/i **1.** (h) (*auf acc* at) shoot (*a. sports*), fire: *gut ~* be a good shot; *ein Tor ~* score (a goal); F *fig.* *~ Sie los!* fire away!; → *Pistole.* **2.** (sn) shoot (*durch* through): *ein Gedanke schoß durch m-n Kopf* a thought flashed through my mind. **3.** (sn) shoot (*or* gush) (*aus* from *or* out of). **4.** (sn) shoot up: → *Kraut* 1, *Pilz.* **5.** (h) *sl.* shoot, mainline. **II** v/t (h) **6.** shoot (*a. sports or phot.*).

'**Schießen** n (-s) a) shooting, b) shooting match: F *es* (*er*) *ist zum ~* it (he) is a scream. **Schieße'rei** f (-; -en) **1.** gunfight. **2.** (incessant) shooting.

'**Schieß|hund** m F *aufpassen wie ein ~* watch like a hawk. **~platz** m (shooting) range. **~pulver** n gunpowder. **~scharte** f embrasure. **~scheibe** f target. **~stand** m shooting range, ✕ rifle range.

'**schießwütig** [-vy:tɪç] *adj* trigger-happy.

Schiff [ʃɪf] n (-[e]s; -e) **1.** (*auf dem ~* on board) ship. **2.** △ a) nave, b) aisle.

'**Schiffahrt** f (-; *no pl*) navigation.

'**Schiffahrtslinie** f shipping line.

'**Schiffahrtsweg** m shipping route.

'**schiffbar** *adj* navigable.

'**Schiffbau** m (-[e]s; *no pl*) shipbuilding.

'**Schiffbruch** m shipwreck: *~ erleiden fig.* fail. '**Schiffbrüchige** m, f (-n; -n) shipwrecked person.

'**Schiffchen** n (-s; -) **1.** little ship (*or* boat). **2.** ✕ forage cap.

'**Schiffer** m (-s; -) a) bargee, *Am.* bargeman, b) (ship's) captain, F skipper.

'**Schifferkla,vier** n accordion.

'**Schifferknoten** m sailor's knot.

'**Schiffsarzt** m ship's doctor.

'**Schiffsbesatzung** f (ship's) crew.

'**Schiffschaukel** f swingboat.

'**Schiffs|eigner** m (-s; -) shipowner.

~junge m ship's boy. **~koch** m ship's cook. **~küche** f galley. **~ladung** f a) shipload, b) cargo, freight. **~rumpf** m hull. **~schraube** f screw. **~verkehr** m shipping. **~werft** f shipyard.

Schikane [ʃiˈkaːnə] f (-; -n) harassment, *pl a.* persecution, mob. racing: chicane: F *mit allen ~n* with all the trimmings.

schikanieren [ʃikaˈniːrən] v/t (h) harass.

schikanös [ʃikaˈnøːs] *adj* harassing.

Schild¹ [ʃɪlt] m (-[e]s; -e) **1.** ✕, *a.* ⚙ shield: *fig. et. im ~e führen* be up to s.th. **2.** peak, visor.

Schild² n (-[e]s; -er) a) sign, *a.* road (*or* street) sign, b) nameplate, c) label, tag.

'**Schildbürger** m Gothamite, *w.s.* simpleton. **~streich** m folly.

'**Schilddrüse** f *anat.* thyroid gland.

schildern [ˈʃɪldərn] v/t (h) describe, *a.* relate, *a.* outline. '**Schilderung** f (-; -en) description, account.

'**Schilderwald** m F jungle of road signs.

'**Schildkröte** f a) tortoise, b) turtle.

'**Schildpatt** [ˈʃɪltpat] n (-[e]s; *no pl*) tortoiseshell.

Schilf [ʃɪlf] n (-[e]s; -e) ❧ **1.** reed. **2.** reeds. '**schilfig** *adj* reedy. '**Schilfmatte** f rush mat. '**Schilfrohr** n ❧ reed.

schillern [ˈʃɪlərn] v/i (h) shine in various colo(u)rs, shimmer, sparkle.

'**schillernd** *adj* **1.** iridescent, opalescent. **2.** *fig.* (dazzling but) dubious.

Schimpanse [ʃɪmˈpanzə] m (-n; -n) *zo.* chimpanzee.

Schimmel¹ [ˈʃɪməl] m (-s; -) white horse.

Schimmel² m (-s; *no pl*) mo(u)ld, mildew. '**schimm(e)lig** *adj* mo(u)ldy.

'**schimmeln** v/i (h) go mo(u)ldy.

'**Schimmelpilz** m mo(u)ld.

Schimmer [ˈʃɪmər] m (-s; *no pl*) gleam, glimmer (*a. fig.*): F *k-n (blassen) ~ haben* not to have the foggiest (idea). '**schimmern** v/i (h) gleam, glisten.

Schimpf [ʃɪmpf] m *mit ~ und Schande* ignominiously.

schimpfen [ˈʃɪmpfən] (h) **I** v/i **1.** scold (*mit j-m* s.o.): *~ auf* (*acc*) complain about, rail at. **II** v/t **2.** scold. **3.** *j-n e-n Lügner etc ~* call s.o. a liar *etc*.

'**Schimpfname** m abusive name.

'**Schimpfwort** n swearword, *pl* abuse.

Schindel [ˈʃɪndəl] f (-; -n) shingle.

schinden [ˈʃɪndən] v/t (schindete, geschunden, h) **1.** drive *s.o.* hard, *a.* mal-

treat: *sich* ~ slave away. **2.** F wangle:
Eindruck ~ (*wollen*) try to impress,
show off; *Zeit* ~ play for time.

'**Schinder** *m* (-s; -) slave-driver.

'**Schinde'rei** *f* (-; -en) (real) grind.

'**Schindluder** *n* F ~ *treiben mit* play fast
and loose with.

Schinken ['ʃɪŋkən] *m* (-s; -) **1.** *gastr.*
ham. **2.** F a) (great) daub, b) fat tome,
c) slushy film. **~speck** *m* bacon.

'**Schippe** ['ʃɪpə] *f* (-; -n) shovel: F *j-n auf*
die ~ *nehmen* pull s.o.'s leg.

schippen ['ʃɪpən] *v/t, v/i* (h) shovel.

Schirm [ʃɪrm] *m* (-[e]s; -e) **1.** a) umbrella,
b) parasol, c) (lamp)shade, d) shield,
screen, e) peak. **2.** screen. **3.** parachute.
4. ♀ pileus. **5.** *fig.* protection.

schirmen ['ʃɪrmən] *v/t* (h) shield.

'**Schirmherr(in** *f*) *m* patron(ess).

'**Schirmherrschaft** *f* patronage: *unter*
der ~ *von* ... under the auspices of ...

'**Schirmmütze** *f* peaked cap.

'**Schirmständer** *m* umbrella stand.

schiß [ʃɪs] *pret of* **scheißen**.

Schiß *m* F ~ *haben* be scared stiff; ~
bekommen get the jitters (V shits).

schizophren [ʃitso'freːn] *adj*, **Schizo-**
'**phrene** *m, f* (-n; -n) schizophrenic.

Schizophrenie [ʃitsofre'niː] *f* (-; -n)
schizophrenia.

Schlacht [ʃlaxt] *f* (-; -en) battle (*bei of*):
e-e ~ *liefern* give battle (*dat* to).

'**schlachten** *v/t* (h) slaughter, kill.

'**Schlachtenbummler** *m* *sports:* fan,
supporter.

Schlächter ['ʃlɛçtər] *m* (-s; -) butcher.

Schlächte'rei *f* (-; -en) butcher's shop.

'**Schlacht|feld** *n* battlefield. **~hof** *m*
slaughterhouse, abattoir. **~plan** *m* a. F
fig. plan of action. **~schiff** *n* battleship.

'**Schlachtung** *f* (-; -en) slaughter(ing).

'**Schlachtvieh** *n* meat stock.

Schlacke ['ʃlakə] *f* (-; -en) **1.** a) *metall.*
dross, slag (*a. geol.*), b) cinders. **2.** *pl* ♣
a) waste products, b) roughage.

schlackern ['ʃlakərn] *v/i* (h) F wobble,
dress etc: flap, *knees:* tremble: *fig. mit*
den Ohren ~ be flabbergasted.

Schlaf [ʃlaːf] *m* (-[e]s; *no pl*) sleep: *e-n*
festen (*leichten*) ~ *haben* be a sound
(light) sleeper; F *das kann ich im* ~! I
can do that blindfold.

'**Schlafanzug** *m* pyjamas, *Am.* pajamas.

Schläfchen ['ʃlɛːfçən] *n* (-s; -) nap.

'**Schlafcouch** *f* studio couch, sofa bed.

Schläfe ['ʃlɛːfə] *f* (-; -n) *anat.* temple.

schlafen ['ʃlaːfən] *v/i* (schlief, geschlafen, h) *a.* F *fig.* a) sleep, b) be asleep: *tief*
(*or fest*) ~ be sound asleep; ~ *gehen* go
to bed; *im Hotel* ~ stay at a hotel; ~ *Sie*
darüber! sleep on it!

'**Schlafenszeit** *f* bedtime.

Schläfer ['ʃlɛːfər] *m* (-s; -), '**Schläferin** *f*
(-; -nen) sleeper.

schlaff [ʃlaf] *adj* a) slack (*rope, sail*), b)
flabby (*skin, muscles, etc*), c) limp (*body*
etc, a. handshake), d) F listless, lame:
~er Typ lame fellow.

'**Schlaffheit** *f* (-; *no pl*) slackness, flabbi-
ness, limpness, F lameness.

'**Schlaf|gelegenheit** *f* sleeping accom-
modation. **~krankheit** *f* sleeping sickness. **~lied** *n* lullaby.

'**schlaflos** *adj* sleepless: ~ *liegen* lie
awake; **~e Nächte** sleepless nights.

'**Schlaflosigkeit** *f* (-; *no pl*) insomnia.

'**Schlafmittel** *n* soporific (drug).

'**Schlafmütze** *f* F *fig.* sleepyhead.

schläfrig ['ʃlɛːfrɪç] *adj* sleepy, drowsy.

'**Schläfrigkeit** *f* (-; *no pl*) sleepiness.

'**Schlaf|rock** *m* dressing gown. **~saal** *m*
dormitory. **~sack** *m* sleeping bag.
~stadt *f* dormitory town. **~störungen**
pl disturbed sleep. **~ta,blette** *f* sleeping
pill. **~trunk** *m* F nightcap.

'**schlaftrunken** *adj* drowsy.

'**Schlafwagen** *m* 🚆 sleeping car, sleeper.

'**schlafwandeln** *v/i* (*insep*, ge-, h *or* sn)
sleepwalk. '**Schlafwandler** [-vandlər]
m (-s; -) sleepwalker, somnambulist.

'**Schlafzimmer** *n* bedroom. '**Schlafzim-**
merblick *m* *humor.* bedroom eyes.

Schlag [ʃlaːk] *m* (-[e]s; *·e*) **1.** a) blow (*a.*
fig.), stroke, *a.* punch, b) slap, c)
thump, thud: *j-m e-n* ~ *versetzen* deal
s.o. a blow, *fig.* hit s.o. hard; ~ *ins*
Gesicht a. fig. slap in the face; *das war*
ein ~ *für ihn* that was a blow to him;
ein ~ *ins Wasser* a flop; ~ *auf* ~ in rapid
succession; *auf einen* ~ at a (*or* one)
stroke, in one go; *mit einem* ~ abruptly. **2.** ⚔ strike. **3.** ⚙ impact, *a.* ⚡ shock.
4. *rowing, swimming:* stroke, *golf, tennis:* shot. **5.** stroke (of lightning). **6.**
beat (*of heart, pulse, etc*), stroke (*of
clock etc*). **7.** F 🚑 stroke: *ich dachte,*
mich trifft der ~! I was floored! **8.** F
helping. **9.** door (*of carriage etc*). **10.**

race, sort, breed: *Leute s-s ~es* men of his stamp (*contp.* his sort).
'**Schlag|abtausch** *m boxing*: exchange of punches, *fig.* crossing of swords. **~ader** *f* artery. **~anfall** *m* 🟥 stroke.
'**schlagartig** *adj* abrupt.
'**Schlagbaum** *m* turnpike.
'**Schlagbohrer** *m* ⊙ percussion drill.
'**Schlagbolzen** *m* ⚔ striking pin.
schlagen ['ʃlaːgən] (schlug, geschlagen) **I** *v/t* (h) **1.** strike, hit, beat, punch, slap: *e-n Nagel in die Wand ~* drive a nail into the wall; *die Trommel ~* beat the drum; *j-m et. aus der Hand ~* knock s.th. from s.o.'s hand; *j-n zu Boden ~* knock s.o. down; → *Alarm, Brücke* 1, *Flucht*[1], *geschlagen.* **2.** whip (*cream*), beat (*eggs etc*): *Eier in die Pfanne ~* break eggs into the frying pan. **3.** fell (*tree*), cut (*wood*). **4.** *fig.* beat (*in dat* at), *a.* defeat: *sich geschlagen geben* admit defeat, give up. **II** *v/i* **5.** (h) strike, hit: *nach j-m ~;* hit out at s.o.; *um sich ~* lash out. **6.** (sn) **~ an** (*acc*) (*or gegen*) beat against; *mit dem Kopf ~ an* (*acc*) strike (*or bump*) one's head against; *die Nachricht ist mir auf den Magen geschlagen* the news has affected my stomach; *Flammen schlugen aus dem Dach* flames leapt out of the roof; → *Art* 4, *Fach* 2 *etc.* **7.** (h) *heart, pulse*: beat, throb, *clock*: strike. **8.** (h) *bird*: sing. **III** *sich ~* (h) **9.** (have a) fight: *sich um et. ~* fight over s.th.; *sich gut ~* give a good account of o.s. **10.** *sich auf j-s Seite ~* side with s.o., *a.* go over to s.o.; *die Erkältung hat sich mir auf den Magen geschlagen* the cold has affected my stomach.
'**schlagend** *adj* **1.** *fig.* convincing, conclusive (*evidence*). **2.** → *Wetter* 2.
Schlager ['ʃlaːgər] *m* (-s; -) **1.** a) pop-song, b) hit (tune). **2.** *fig.* hit, sensation, 🟥 (sales) hit, moneymaker.
Schläger ['ʃlɛːgər] *m* (-s; -) **1.** tough, *boxing etc*: slugger. **2.** *sports*: a) batsman, b) (cricket, baseball, *etc*) bat, (tennis) racket, (golf) club, (hockey) stick. **Schläge'rei** *f* (-; -en) brawl, F punch-up: *allgemeine ~* free-for-all.
'**Schlagerfestival** *n* pop festival.
'**Schlagermu,sik** *f* pop music.
'**Schlagersänger(in** *f*) *m* pop singer.
'**schlagfertig** *adj* quick-witted: *~ sein*

quick at repartee. '**Schlagfertigkeit** *f* (-; *no pl*) quick-wittedness, ready wit.
'**Schlag|instru,ment** *n* ♪ percussion instrument. **~kraft** *f* (-; *no pl*) **1.** *boxing or fig.* punch. **2.** ⚔ combat effectiveness. 🟥**kräftig** *adj* **1.** powerful. **2.** convincing, conclusive. **~licht** *n* (-[e]s; -er) *paint.* (*a. fig. ein ~ werfen auf* [*acc*]) highlight. **~loch** *n* pothole. **~mann** *m* (-[e]s; ⸗er) *rowing*: stroke. **~obers** *n* (-; *no pl*) *Austrian*, **~rahm** *m* → *Schlagsahne.* **~ring** *m* **1.** knuckleduster. **2.** ♪ plectrum, F pick. **~sahne** *f* whipped cream. **~seite** *f* ⚓ list: *~ haben* be listing, F *fig.* be halfseas-over. **~stock** *m* **1.** truncheon, riot stick. **2.** ♪ drumstick. **~wechsel** *m* *boxing*: exchange of blows. **~werk** *n* ♪ striking mechanism.
'**Schlagwort** *n* **1.** catchword, slogan, *pl contp.* platitudes. **2.** (*pl* ⸗er) catchword. **~kata,log** *m* subject catalog(ue *Br.*).
'**Schlagzeile** *f* headline: *~n machen, in die ~n geraten* make the headlines.
'**Schlagzeug** *n* ♪ percussion, drums. '**Schlagzeuger** [-tsɔʏɡər] *m* (-s; -) ♪ percussionist, drummer.
schlaksig ['ʃlaːksɪç] *adj* gangling, lanky.
Schlamassel [ʃlaˈmasəl] *m, n* (-s; -) F mess.
Schlamm [ʃlam] *m* (-[e]s; -e, ⸗e) mud.
'**Schlammbad** *n* 🟥 mud bath.
'**schlammig** *adj* muddy.
'**Schlammpackung** *f* 🟥 mud pack.
Schlampe ['ʃlampə] *f* (-; -n) F slut.
'**schlampen** *v/i* (h) F do a sloppy job.
'**Schlamper** *m* (-s; -) F sloven, slouch.
Schlampe'rei *f* (-; -en) F a) sloppiness, b) mess, sloppy work.
'**schlampig** *adj* F slovenly, sloppy.
schlang [ʃlaŋ] *pret of* **schlingen**[1] *and* [2].
Schlange ['ʃlaŋə] *f* (-; -n) **1.** *zo.* snake: *fig. falsche ~* snake in the grass. **2.** queue, *Am.* line (*of people, cars*): F *~ stehen* (*nach* for) stand in a queue (*Am.* in line), queue up, *Am.* line up. **3.** ⊙ coil.
schlängeln ['ʃlɛŋəln] *sich ~* (h) wriggle, *fig. road etc*: wind, *river*: *a.* meander; *sich ~ durch* worm one's way through.
'**Schlangen|biß** *m* snakebite. **~gift** *n* snake poison. **~haut** *f*, **~leder** *n* snakeskin. **~linie** *f* wavy line: *in ~n fahren* zigzag (along the road).

schlank [ʃlaŋk] *adj* slender, slim: *auf die*
~e Linie achten watch one's weight.
'Schlankheit *f* (-; *no pl*) slimness.
'Schlankheitskur *f* slimming (diet): *e-e*
~ machen be slimming.

schlapp [ʃlap] *adj* **1.** → *schlaff.* **2.**
worn-out, listless.
'Schlappe *f* (-; -n) a) setback, b) beating.
'schlappmachen *v/i* (*sep*, -ge-, h) F
wilt.
'Schlappschwanz *m* F softie, sissy.
Schlaraffenland [ʃlaˈrafən-] *n* (-[e]s; *no
pl*) Cockaigne.
schlau [ʃlaʊ] *adj* a) clever, smart, b) sly,
cunning, crafty: F *~e Bücher* clever
books; *ich werde nicht ~ daraus* I
can't make head or tail of it.
Schlauberger ['ʃlaʊbɛrgər] *m* (-s; -) F
smartie.
Schlauch [ʃlaʊx] *m* (-[e]s; ~e) **1.** flexible
tube, (water) hose. **2.** *mot. etc* inner
tube. **3.** F hard slog. **4.** F (*room*) tunnel.
'Schlauchboot *n* rubber dinghy.
schlauchen ['ʃlaʊxən] (h) F **I** *v/t j-n ~*
take it out of s.o., *a.* go hard with s.o. **II**
v/i das schlaucht! that's tough going!
Schläue ['ʃlɔʏə] *f* → *Schlauheit.*
Schlaufe ['ʃlaʊfə] *f* (-; -n) loop.
'Schlauheit *f* (-; *no pl*) a) cleverness,
smartness, b) slyness, cunning.

schlecht [ʃlɛçt] **I** *adj* bad, poor (*eyes,
health, memory, quality, etc*), *a.* wicked:
nicht ~! not bad!; *~e Laune* bad mood;
~e Zeiten bad (*or* hard) times; *~ sein* in
(*dat*) be poor at; *~ werden* meat *etc*: go
bad, go off; *~er werden* get worse,
deteriorate; *mir ist ~* I feel sick; F *es
kann e-m ~ dabei werden!* it's enough
to make you sick!; → *Dienst* 1. **II** *adv*
bad(ly): *~ aussehen* look bad, *a.* look
ill; *~ und recht* after a fashion; *~ beraten sein* be ill-advised; *~ reden von*
speak ill of; *es steht ~ um ihn* he's in a
bad way; *~ daran sein* be badly off; *es
bekam ihm ~ food etc*: it didn't agree
with him, *fig.* it did him no good; *er
kann es sich ~ leisten zu inf* he can ill
afford to *inf*; *heute geht es ~* it's a bit
awkward today; *ich kann ~ ablehnen* I
can't very well refuse; *ich staunte nicht
~* F I wasn't half surprised.
'schlechtgelaunt *adj* bad-tempered.
'schlechthin *adv* **1.** absolutely. **2.** as
such.

'Schlechtigkeit *f* (-; *no pl*) badness,
wickedness, baseness.
'schlechtmachen *v/t* (*sep*, -ge-, h) run
s.o., s.th. down, knock.
Schlecht'wetter|front *f* bad weather
front. *~peri,ode* *f* spell of bad weather.
Schlehe ['ʃleːə] *f* (-; -n) ❦ sloe.
schleichen ['ʃlaɪçən] *v/i* (schlich, geschlichen, sn) creep, sneak, crawl (*a.
car, time*): *auf den Zehenspitzen ~* tip-
toe; *ums Haus ~* prowl around the
house; *dial. schleich dich!* *sl.* beat it!
'schleichend *adj* lingering (*illness*),
slow (*poison etc*), creeping (*inflation*).
'Schleich|handel *m* illicit trade. *~weg*
m secret path: *fig. auf ~en* by secret
means, surreptitiously. *~werbung* *f*
surreptitious advertising, F plugging.
Schleier ['ʃlaɪər] *m* (-s; -) **1.** *a. fig.* veil. **2.**
haze, *phot.* fog. *~eule* *f zo.* barn owl.
'schleierhaft *adj* mysterious: *das ist mir
~!* that's a mystery to me!
Schleife ['ʃlaɪfə] *f* (-; -n) **1.** bow, *a.* ribbon. **2.** *a.* ✄, ❂ loop.
schleifen¹ ['ʃlaɪfən] *v/t* (schliff, geschliffen, h) **1.** grind, whet. **2.** ❂ smooth,
sand (*wood*), cut (*glass, diamond*). **3.** ✕
F drill *s.o.* hard.
schleifen² (h) **I** *v/t* drag (along) (*a. fig.
s.o.*), trail (*skirt etc*). **II** *v/i ~ lassen*
drag; *die Kupplung ~ lassen* let the
clutch slip.
'Schleifer *m* (-s; -) **1.** ❂ grinder, *a.* cutter. **2.** ✕ F martinet.
'Schleif|lackausführung *f* egg-shell fin-
ish. *~ma,schine* *f* grinding machine.
~mittel *n* abrasive. *~pa,pier* *n* emery
paper. *~scheibe* *f* grinding wheel.
~stein *m* a) whetstone, b) grindstone.
Schleim [ʃlaɪm] *m* (-[e]s; -e) slime, ✿,
physiol. mucus, phlegm. *~beutel* *m
anat.* bursa. *~drüse* *f* mucous gland.
~haut *f* mucous membrane.
'schleimig *adj* slimy (*a. fig. contp.*).
'schleimlösend *adj* expectorant.
'Schleimsuppe *f* gruel.
schlemmen ['ʃlɛmən] *v/i* (h) feast.
'Schlemmer *m* (-s; -) gormandizer.
Schlemme'rei *f* (-; -en) F feasting.
schlendern ['ʃlɛndərn] *v/i* (sn) stroll.
Schlendrian ['ʃlɛndriaːn] *m* (-[e]s; *no pl*)
F *contp.* a) dawdling, b) rut.
Schlenker ['ʃlɛŋkər] *m* (-s; -) (*a. e-n ~
machen*) F swerve. **'schlenkern** *v/t, v/i*

(h) swing, dangle (*mit den Armen* one's arms).

schlenzen [ˈʃlɛntsən] v/t, v/i (h) scoop.

Schlepp [ʃlɛp] *m* **in ~ nehmen (im ~ haben)** a. fig. take (have) in tow.

'Schleppdampfer *m* tug.

Schleppe [ˈʃlɛpə] *f* (-; -n) train, trail.

'schleppen (h) **I** v/t a) drag (*a. fig. s.o.*), ⚓, ✈, *mot.* tow, b) carry, F tote: F **(Kunden)** ~ tout. **II sich** ~ a) drag on, b) drag o.s. (along), limp (along). **'schleppend** *adj* sluggish, slow (*a.* ✈), labo(u)red, slow, drawling (*speech*). **'Schlepper** *m* (-s; -) **1.** ⚓ tug. **2.** *mot.* tractor. **3.** F tout.

'Schlepp|flugzeug *n* towplane. **~kahn** *m* lighter, barge (in tow). **~lift** *m* ski tow. **~netz** *n* dragnet. **~schiff** *n* tug. **~tau** *n* tow-rope, tow-line: F fig. *j-n bis* **~ nehmen** take s.o. in tow. **~zug** *m* **1.** ⚓ train of barges. **2.** semitrailer truck.

Schleuder [ˈʃlɔydər] *f* (-; -n) **1.** catapult (*a.* ✈), sling, *Am.* slingshot. **2.** ⚙ a) → **Zentrifuge**, b) spin dryer.

'Schleudergefahr *f* slippery road.

schleudern [ˈʃlɔydərn] (h) **I** v/t **1.** fling, hurl, sling, ✈ catapult. **2.** ⚙ centrifuge, strain (*honey*), spin-dry (*laundry*). **II** v/i (*a.* sn) *mot.* skid, (*a.* **ins Schleudern geraten**) go into a skid (*a. fig.*).

'Schleuder|preis *m* knockdown price. **~sitz** *m* ✈ ejector seat, F *fig.* hot seat. **~ware** *f* cut-price article(s).

schleunig [ˈʃlɔynɪç] *I adj* quick, prompt, *a.* hasty. **II** *adv a.* **'schleunigst** quickly, promptly, *a.* hastily.

Schleuse [ˈʃlɔyzə] *f* (-; -n) sluice, floodgate (*a. fig.*), (canal) lock. **'schleusen** v/t (h) **1.** ⚓ lock. **2.** *fig.* a) channel, b) steer, *a.* smuggle (*s.o.*).

'Schleusentor *n* floodgate.

schlich [ʃlɪç] *pret of* **schleichen.**

Schliche [ˈʃlɪçə] *pl* tricks: *j-m auf die* **~ kommen** find s.o. out.

schlicht [ʃlɪçt] **I** *adj* simple, plain. **II** *adv* **~ (und einfach)** (quite) simply.

schlichten [ˈʃlɪçtən] **I** v/t settle (*dispute*). **II** v/i mediate (*zwischen* between).

'Schlichter *m* (-s; -) mediator.

'Schlichtheit *f* (-; *no pl*) simplicity, plainness.

'Schlichtung *f* (-; -en) a) settlement, b) arbitration.

'Schlichtungs|ausschuß *m* arbitration committee. **~versuch** *m* attempt at conciliation.

Schlick [ʃlɪk] *m* (-[e]s; -e) sludge, silt.

schlief [ʃliːf] *pret of* **schlafen.**

Schliere [ˈʃliːrə] *f* (-; -n) streak.

Schließe [ˈʃliːsə] *f* (-; -n) fastening, clasp.

schließen [ˈʃliːsən] (schloß, geschlossen, h) **I** v/t **1.** close (*a.* ⚡ *circuit*), shut, *a.* shut down (*factory etc*): → **Lücke. 2.** enter into *an alliance etc*, make, come to *a settlement*: → **Ehe, Freundschaft, Frieden** etc. **3.** close, conclude, end (*debate etc*), *a.* wind up (*letter, speech* *mit den Worten* by saying). **II** v/i **4.** shut, close, *factory etc*: *a.* shut down. **5.** (come to a) close: **er schloß mit den Worten** he wound up by saying. **6.** conclude (*aus* from): *von sich auf andere* ~ judge others by o.s.; *auf et.* ~ **lassen** suggest (*or* point to) s.th. **III** *sich* ~ close, shut; → **Kreis** 1.

'Schließfach *n* **1.** safe deposit box. **2.** ⚓ (left-luggage) locker. **3.** → **Postfach.**

'schließlich *adv* a) finally, b) eventually, c) after all.

'Schließmuskel *m* anat. sphincter.

'Schließung *f* (-; -en) **1.** closing, shutting, shutdown, closure (*of factory etc*). **2.** contraction (*of marriage etc*).

schliff [ʃlɪf] *pret of* **schleifen¹.**

Schliff [ʃlɪf] *m* (-[e]s; -e) **1.** *no pl* grinding, *a.* sharpening. **2.** cut (*of glass etc*). **3.** *fig.* polish, refinement: *den letzten* **~ geben** put the finishing touches (*dat* to).

schlimm [ʃlɪm] *adj* bad, F *a.* nasty (*wound etc*): F **~er Finger (Hals)** sore finger (throat); *das ist e-e* **~e Sache** that's a bad business; *es sieht* **~ aus** it looks bad; *das ist halb so* **~!** a) it's not as bad as all that!, b) it doesn't matter!, never mind!; F *ist es* **~, wenn ...?** would you mind terribly if ...?; **~er machen (werden) → verschlimmern; es wird immer ~er** things are going from bad to worse; *um so* **~er** so much the worse; *am* **~sten** worst of all; *auf das Schlimmste gefaßt sein* be prepared for the worst; *es gibt Schlimmeres* things could be worse.

'schlimmstenfalls *adv* if the worst comes to the worst.

Schlinge [ˈʃlɪŋə] *f* (-; -n) loop, noose (*a. fig.*), *a.* ⚕ sling, *hunt.* snare (*a. fig.*): *fig. sich aus der* **~ ziehen** wriggle out of it.

Schlingel ['ʃlɪŋəl] *m* (-s; -) rascal.

schlingen[1] ['ʃlɪŋən] (schlang, geschlungen, h) (**um** around) **I** *v/t* tie, wrap, wind. **II sich** ~ wind, coil.

'**schlingen**[2] (schlang, geschlungen, h) **I** *v/i* gobble, bolt one's food. **II** *v/t* gobble (up), gulp *s.th.* down.

schlingern ['ʃlɪŋərn] *v/i* ⚓ roll.

'**Schlingpflanze** *f* climbing plant.

Schlips [ʃlɪps] *m* (-es; -e) tie: *fig.* **j-m auf den** ~ **treten** tread on s.o.'s toes.

Schlitten ['ʃlɪtən] *m* (-s; -) **1.** a) sledge, *Am.* sled, b) sleigh, c) toboggan: ~ **fahren** sledge, toboggan; F *fig.* **mit j-m** ~ **fahren** give s.o. hell. **2.** F car: **alter** ~ crate, bus, jalopy.

'**Schlittenfahrt** *f* sledge (*or* sleigh) ride.

schlittern ['ʃlɪtərn] *v/i* (sn) slide (**in** *acc* into, *a. fig.*), *a.* slip, *mot.* skid.

'**Schlittschuh** *m* (ice-)skate: ~ **laufen** skate. **~laufen** *n* (ice-)skating. **~läufer(in** *f*) *m* (ice-)skater.

Schlitz [ʃlɪts] *m* (-es; -e) **1.** slit. **2.** slot. '**Schlitzauge** *n* **1.** slit eye: **~n haben** be slit-eyed. **2.** *contp.* slit-eye.

schlitzen ['ʃlɪtsən] *v/t*, *v/i* (h) slit, slash.

schloß [ʃlɔs] *pret of* **schließen**.

Schloß *n* (-sses; -sser) **1.** castle, palace. **2.** a) lock, b) clasp: **hinter** ~ **und Riegel** behind bars.

Schloße ['ʃloːsə] *f usu. pl* sleet.

Schlosser ['ʃlɔsər] *m* (-s; -) locksmith.

Schlosse'rei *f* (-; -en) **1.** *no pl* locksmith's trade. **2.** locksmith's shop.

Schlot [ʃloːt] *m* (-[e]s; -e) (F **rauchen wie ein** ~ smoke like a) chimney.

schlottern ['ʃlɔtərn] *v/i* (h) **1.** (**vor** with) shake, tremble: **mit ~den Knien** with shaking knees. **2.** *clothes:* hang loosely.

Schlucht [ʃlʊxt] *f* (-; -en) gorge, ravine, *a.* canyon.

schluchzen ['ʃlʊxtsən] *v/t*, *v/i* (h) sob.

'**Schluchzen** *n* (-s) sobbing, sobs.

Schluck [ʃlʊk] *m* (-[e]s; -e) swallow, gulp: **kräftiger** ~ F swig. '**Schluckauf** *m* (-s; *no pl*) (**e-n** ~ **haben** have the) hiccups. **Schlückchen** ['ʃlʏkçən] *n* (-s; -) sip. '**schlucken** (h) **I** *v/t* swallow (*a. fig.* insult etc, a. F believe), *fig.* swallow up (*savings etc*), absorb (*light, sound*). **II** *v/i* swallow. '**Schlucker** *m* (-s; -) **armer** ~ poor devil.

'**Schluckimpfung** *f* ⚕ oral vaccination.

schlud(e)rig ['ʃluːd(ə)rɪç] → **schlampig**.

schludern ['ʃluːdərn] → **schlampen**.

schlug [ʃluːk] *pret of* **schlagen**.

schlummern ['ʃlʊmərn] *v/i* (h) slumber, sleep, *fig.* lie dormant.

'**schlummernd** *adj fig.* dormant, latent.

Schlund [ʃlʊnt] *m* (-es; ⁓e) **1.** *anat.* (back of the) throat, pharynx. **2.** *zo.* maw. **3.** *fig.* abyss.

schlüpfen ['ʃlʏpfən] *v/i* (sn) **1.** slip (**in** *acc* into, **aus** out of). **2.** *zo.* hatch (out).

'**Schlüpfer** *m* (-s; -) briefs, panties.

Schlupfloch ['ʃlʊpf-] *n* **1.** gap. **2.** *fig.* loophole.

schlüpfrig ['ʃlʏpfrɪç] *adj* slippery, *fig.* lewd, risqué (*joke etc*).

'**Schlupfwinkel** *m* hideout, haunt.

schlurfen ['ʃlʊrfən] *v/i* (sn) shuffle.

schlürfen ['ʃlʏrfən] *v/t*, *v/i* (h) a) slurp, b) sip.

Schluß [ʃlʊs] *m* (-sses; ⁓sse) **1.** end, conclusion, ending (*of book, film, etc*): ~ (**damit**)! stop it!; F ~ **machen** a) call it a day, b) put an end to o.s.; ~ **machen mit** a) *et.* stop s.th., b) *j-m* break up with s.o.; **am** ~ at the end; **zum** ~ finally. **2.** conclusion: **voreilige Schlüsse ziehen** jump to conclusions. **~ak,kord** *m* ♪ final chord. **~akt** *m* *thea.* final act. **2.** closing ceremony. **~bemerkung** *f* final comment.

'**Schlüssel** ['ʃlʏsəl] *m* (-s; -) **1.** key (**zu**, **für** of, *fig.* to). **2.** ♪ clef. **3.** ratio. **4.** ⚙ spanner, *Am.* wrench. **~bein** *n* *anat.* collarbone. **~blume** *f* primrose, cowslip. **~bund** *m*, *n* bunch of keys. **~erlebnis** *n* crucial experience. **~fi,gur** *f* key figure. **~indu,strie** *f* key industry. **~kind** *n* latchkey child. **~loch** *n* keyhole. **~ring** *m* key ring. **~ro,man** *m* roman-à-clef. **~stellung** *f* key position. **~wort** *n* (-[e]s; ⁓er) code word, keyword, *computer:* a. password.

'**Schlußfeier** *f* closing ceremony, *ped.* speech day, *Am.* commencement.

'**Schlußfolgerung** *f* (-; -en) conclusion.

schlüssig ['ʃlʏsɪç] *adj* **1.** logical **2.** conclusive (*evidence*). **3. sich** ~ **werden** make up one's mind (**über** *acc* about).

'**Schluß|läufer(in** *f*) *m* anchor. **~licht** *n* (-[e]s; -er) **1.** *mot.* taillight. **2.** F *esp. sports:* tailender: **das** ~ **bilden** bring up the rear. **~pfiff** *m sports:* final whistle. **~satz** *m* **1.** closing sentence. **2.** ♪ final movement. **~strich** *m fig.* **e-n** ~ **unter**

et. ziehen consider the matter closed.
~verkauf *m* (end-of-season) sale.
~wort *n* (-[e]s; -e) closing words.

Schmach [ʃmaːx] *f* (-; *no pl*) disgrace.
schmächtig [ˈʃmɛçtɪç] *adj* slight, thin.
'schmachvoll *adj* disgraceful.
schmackhaft [ˈʃmakhaft] *adj* savo(u)ry, tasty: *fig. j-m et. ~ machen* make s.th. palatable to s.o.
schmal [ʃmaːl] *adj* narrow, *a.* thin, slender (*a. fig.*), *fig.* meag/re (*Am.* -er).
schmälern [ˈʃmɛːlərn] *v/t* (h) **1.** curtail, impair. **2.** detract from.
'Schmalfilm *m* cine-film.
'Schmalfilmkamera *f* cine-camera.
'Schmalspur *f* (-; *no pl*) narrow ga(u)ge.
'Schmalspur- F *fig.* small-time ...
Schmalz¹ [ʃmalts] *n* (-es; -e) lard.
Schmalz² *m* (-es; *no pl*) F schmaltz.
'schmalzig *adj* F schmaltzy.
schmarotzen [ʃmaˈrɔtsən] *v/i* (h) sponge (*bei* on). **Schma'rotzer** *m* (-s; -) parasite, *fig. a.* sponger.
schmatzen [ˈʃmatsən] *v/i* (h) eat noisily.
schmecken [ˈʃmɛkən] (h) I *v/t* taste. II *v/i* ~ *nach* taste of, *fig.* smack of; *es schmeckt* (*gut*) it tastes good; *sich et. ~ lassen* tuck in; *schmeckt es* (*Ihnen*)? do you like it?; *fig. das schmeckte ihm nicht* he didn't like it one bit.
Schmeichelei [ʃmaɪçəˈlaɪ] *f* (-; -en) flattery, (flattering) compliment.
'schmeichelhaft *adj a. fig.* flattering.
schmeicheln [ˈʃmaɪçəln] *v/i* (h) *j-m* ~ a) flatter s.o. (*a. fig.*), b) cajole s.o.; *sich geschmeichelt fühlen* feel flattered (*durch* by); *das Bild ist geschmeichelt* the picture is flattering.
Schmeichler [ˈʃmaɪçlər] *m* (-s; -) flatterer. **'schmeichlerisch** *adj* a) flattering, b) cajoling.
schmeißen [ˈʃmaɪsən] (schmiß, geschmissen, h) F I *v/t* **1.** a) throw, chuck, b) slam, bang (*door etc*). **2.** chuck up (*job etc*), *thea.* muff (*scene*). **3.** manage: *den Laden ~* run the show. **4.** *e-e Lage ~* stand a round of drinks. II *v/i* **5.** ~ *mit* throw; *mit Geld um sich ~* throw one's money around.
'Schmeißfliege *f* bluebottle.
Schmelz [ʃmɛlts] *m* (-es; -e) **1.** enamel. **2.** *fig.* mellowness, ♩ melodiousness.
'schmelzbar *adj* ⊙ fusible.
Schmelze [ˈʃmɛltsə] *f* (-; -n) ⊙ melting

molten mass. **'schmelzen** (schmolz, geschmolzen) I *v/i* (sn) liquefy, melt (*a. fig. supply etc*). II *v/t* (h) liquefy, melt, *metall.* smelt. **'schmelzend** *adj fig.* melting (*look*), sweet (*voice*).
'Schmelz|käse *m* soft cheese. **~punkt** *m* melting point. **~tiegel** *m a. fig.* melting pot. **~wasser** *n* melted snow and ice.
Schmerbauch [ˈʃmeːr-] *m* paunch.
Schmerz [ʃmɛrts] *m* (-es; -en) a) pain, ache, b) grief, sorrow, c) agony: *~en haben* be in pain. **'schmerzen** (h) I *v/i* hurt (*a. fig.*), ache. II *v/t* hurt (*a. fig.*), pain.
'Schmerzensgeld *n* compensation for personal suffering, *Am.* smart-money.
'Schmerzensschrei *m* scream of pain.
'schmerzfrei *adj* free of pain.
'Schmerzgrenze *f* pain threshold.
'schmerzhaft *adj a. fig.* painful.
'schmerzlich I *adj* painful, *fig.* sad (*loss, smile, etc*). II *adv* badly, sadly: *j-n ~ berühren* touch s.o.
'schmerzlindernd *adj* soothing, (*a. ~es Mittel*) analgesic.
'schmerzlos *adj* painless.
'schmerzstillend *adj* painkilling.
'Schmerzta,blette *f* painkiller.
'Schmetterball *m* tennis: smash.
Schmetterling [ˈʃmɛtərlɪŋ] *m* (-s; -e) *zo.* butterfly. **'Schmetterlingsstil** *m swimming:* butterfly (stroke).
schmettern [ˈʃmɛtərn] (h) I *v/t* **1.** smash (*a. tennis*), slam. **2.** belt out (*song*). II *v/i* **3.** ring (out), *trumpet:* blare, *bird:* warble.
Schmied [ʃmiːt] *m* (-[e]s; -e) a) smith, b) blacksmith. **Schmiede** [ˈʃmiːdə] *f* (-; -n) forge, smithy.
'Schmiedeeisen *n* wrought iron.
'schmiedeeisern *adj* wrought-iron.
schmieden [ˈʃmiːdən] *v/t*, *v/i* (h) *a. fig.* forge: → *Eisen, Plan* 1.
schmiegen [ˈʃmiːgən] *sich ~* (h) cling (*or* cuddle up) (*an acc* to). **schmiegsam** [ˈʃmiːk-] *adj* pliant, flexible.
Schmiere¹ [ˈʃmiːrə] *f* (-; -n) **1.** ⊙ grease, lubricant. **2.** F mess, goo.
'Schmiere² *f* F ~ *stehen* keep a lookout.
schmieren [ˈʃmiːrən] *v/t* (h) **1.** smear, *a.* butter (*bread*), spread (*butter etc*): F *wie geschmiert* like clockwork; *j-m e-e ~* slap s.o.('s face). **2.** ⊙ a) grease, b) lubricate, oil. **3.** *a. v/i* scrawl. **4.** F *j-n ~* grease s.o.'s palm.

'**Schmierenkomödi,ant** *m* ham actor.
Schmie·re'rei *f* (-; -en) **1.** scribble, scrawl. **2.** daub. **3.** *pl* graffiti.
'**Schmier|fett** *n* ⊕ (lubricating) grease. **~fink** *m* F **1.** a) scrawler, b) messy fellow. **2.** muckraker. **~geld** *n* F bribe (money), payoff, *pol.* slush fund.
schmierig ['ʃmiːrɪç] *adj* **1.** greasy. **2.** messy. **3.** *fig.* a) smutty, b) F smarmy.
'**Schmier|mittel** *n* ⊕ lubricant. **~öl** *n* ⊕ lubricating oil. **~pa,pier** *n* scribbling paper. **~seife** *f* soft soap.
'**Schmierung** *f* (-; -en) ⊕ a) lubrication, b) greasing.
Schminke ['ʃmɪŋkə] *f* (-; -n) make-up. '**schminken** (h) **I** *v/t* make up: *sich die Lippen* ~ put on lipstick. **II** *sich* ~ put on make-up, make one's face up.
schmirgeln ['ʃmɪrgəln] *v/t* (h), '**Schmirgelpa,pier** *n* ⊕ sandpaper.
schmiß [ʃmɪs] *pret of* **schmeißen.**
Schmiß *m* (-sses; -sse) **1.** (duelling) scar. **2.** *no pl* F *fig.* pep, zip.
'**schmissig** *adj* F zippy, rousing (*music*).
Schmöker ['ʃmøːkər] *m* (-s; -) F **1.** old book. **2.** light novel. '**schmökern** (h) a) do some light reading, b) browse.
schmollen ['ʃmɔlən] *v/i* (h) sulk.
'**Schmollmund** *m* pout.
schmolz [ʃmɔlts] *pret of* **schmelzen.**
'**Schmorbraten** *m* pot roast.
schmoren ['ʃmoːrən] *v/t, v/i* (h) *gastr.* braise: *j-n* (*in s-m eigenen Saft*) ~ *lassen* let s.o. stew (in his own juice); *in der Sonne* ~ roast in the sun.
Schmuck [ʃmʊk] *m* (-[e]s; *no pl*) **1.** decoration. **2.** jewel(le)ry, jewels.
schmücken ['ʃmʏkən] (h) **I** *v/t* decorate, *fig.* embroider (*speech etc*). **II** *sich* ~ dress up; → **Feder** 1.
'**Schmuckkästchen** *n* **1.** jewel(le)ry box. **2.** *fig.* jewel of a house.
'**schmucklos** *adj* plain, austere.
'**Schmuckstück** *n* **1.** piece of jewel(le)ry. **2.** *fig.* gem.
schmudd(e)lig ['ʃmʊd(ə)lɪç] *adj* F grubby, grimy, scruffy.
Schmuggel ['ʃmʊgəl] *m* (-s; *no pl*) smuggling. '**schmuggeln** *v/t, v/i* (h) smuggle. '**Schmuggelware** *f* smuggled goods, contraband. '**Schmuggler** *m* (-s; -) smuggler.
schmunzeln ['ʃmʊntsəln] *v/i* (h) smile to o.s., grin.

Schmus [ʃmuːs] *m* (-es; *no pl*) F blarney.
schmusen ['ʃmuːzən] *v/i* (h) F cuddle, *lovers:* a. smooch.
Schmutz [ʃmʊts] *m* (-es; *no pl*) dirt, filth, mud, *fig.* a. smut: *fig.* *in den* ~ *ziehen* drag *s.o., s.th.* through the mud.
'**schmutzen** *v/i* (h) soil, get dirty.
'**Schmutzfink** *m* F **1.** pig. **2.** *fig.* dirty fellow. '**Schmutzfleck** *m* smudge.
'**schmutzig** *adj* **1.** dirty, filthy, soiled: ~ *machen* dirty, soil; *sich* ~ *machen,* ~ *werden* get dirty; *fig.* ~*e Phantasie* dirty mind; → **Wäsche** 1. **2.** *contp.* a) dirty, shabby, b) smutty (*joke etc*).
Schnabel ['ʃnaːbəl] *m* (-s; ⁓) **1.** bill, beak. **2.** spout. **3.** F trap: *halt den* ~*!* shut up!
schnäbeln ['ʃnɛːbəln] *v/i* (h) *zo.* bill.
Schnake ['ʃnaːkə] *f* (-; -n) *zo.* mosquito.
Schnalle ['ʃnalə] *f* (-; -n) buckle, clasp.
schnallen ['ʃnalən] *v/t* (h) **1.** buckle, strap (*an acc* to): → **Gürtel.** **2.** F get: *ich schnalle das nicht!* I don't get it!
schnalzen ['ʃnaltsən] *v/i* (h) *mit der Zunge* ~ click one's tongue; *mit den Fingern* ~ snap one's fingers.
schnappen ['ʃnapən] (h) **I** *v/t* F catch, nab: (*sich*) *et.* ~ grab s.th.; → **Luft** 1. **II** *v/i* **2.** snap, click. **3.** ~ *nach* grab at, *dog:* snap at; *nach Luft* ~ gasp for breath.
'**Schnappschuß** *m phot.* snapshot: *e-n* ~ *machen von* take a snap of, snap.
Schnaps [ʃnaps] *m* (-es; ⁓e) spirits, schnapps. **~brenne'rei** *f* distillery.
Schnäpschen ['ʃnɛpsçən] *n* (-s; -) F snifter.
'**Schnapsi,dee** *f* F *fig.* crazy idea.
schnarchen ['ʃnarçən] *v/i* (h) snore.
schnarren ['ʃnarən] *v/i* (h) **1.** rattle. **2.** *bell etc:* buzz. **3.** a. *v/t* rasp, bark.
schnattern ['ʃnatərn] *v/i* (h) **1.** *goose:* cackle, *duck:* quack. **2.** F *fig.* gabble.
schnauben ['ʃnaʊbən] *v/i, v/t* (h) snort: *sich* (*die Nase*) ~ blow one's nose; *vor Wut* ~ foam with rage.
schnaufen ['ʃnaʊfən] *v/i* (h) **1.** breathe hard, puff, pant. **2.** *dial.* breathe.
'**Schnauzbart** *m* walrus m(o)ustache.
Schnauze ['ʃnaʊtsə] *f* (-; -n) **1.** *zo.* snout, muzzle, nose. **2.** lip (*of jug etc*), ⊕ nozzle, F ✗, *mot.* nose. **3.** V trap: *halt die* ~*!* shut up!; *die* ~ *voll haben* be fed up (to the teeth) (*von* with).
'**Schnauzer** *m* (-s; -) *zo.* schnauzer.

Schnecke ['ʃnɛkə] f (-; -n) **1.** zo. a) snail, b) slug: F j-n zur ~ machen give s.o. hell. **2.** ∆ scroll. **3.** gastr. Chelsea bun. **4.** pl earphones. '**Schneckenhaus** n (snail) shell. '**Schneckentempo** n im ~ at a snail's pace.

Schnee [ʃne:] m (-s; no pl) **1.** snow. **2.** Eiweiß zu ~ schlagen beat white of egg until stiff. **3.** sl. snow. ~ball m snowball. ~ballschlacht f snowball fight. 2bedeckt adj snow-covered. ~besen m egg-beater, whisk. 2blind adj snow-blind. ~brille f (e-e ~ a pair of) snow goggles. ~decke f (blanket of) snow. ~fall m snowfall. ~flocke f snowflake. ~gestöber n snow flurry. ~glätte f packed snow. ~glöckchen n ♀ snowdrop. ~grenze f snowline. ~kette f snowchain. ~mann m (-[e]s; ⁛er) snowman. ~matsch m slush. ~mo,bil n snowmobile. ~pflug m snowplough, Am. snowplow. ~regen m sleet. ~schleuder f snowblower. ~schmelze f thaw. ~schuh m snowshoe. ~sturm m snowstorm. ~treiben n snow flurry. ~verhältnisse pl snow conditions. ~verwehung f, ~wehe f snowdrift. 2weiß adj snow-white.

Schneid [ʃnaɪt] m (-[e]s; no pl) F guts.

'**Schneidbrenner** m cutting torch.

Schneide ['ʃnaɪdə] f (-; -n) edge.

schneiden ['ʃnaɪdən] (schnitt, geschnitten, h) **I** v/t **1.** a) cut (a. ball, curve), carve (meat), b) cut (lawn), mow (lawn), prune (tree), trim (hedge): in Stücke ~ cut up; F j-n → fig. cut s.o. dead, mot. cut in on s.o.; → Grimasse, Haar. **2.** edit (film, tape). **II** sich ~ a) cut o.s., b) lines: intersect; F da hat er sich aber geschnitten! he is very much mistaken there! '**schneidend** adj fig. sharp (pain, voice, etc), biting (cold, sarcasm, etc).

'**Schneider** m (-s; -) tailor: F aus dem ~ sein be out of the woods.

Schneide'rei f (-; no pl) tailoring, dressmaking.

'**Schneiderin** f (-; -nen) dressmaker.

schneidern ['ʃnaɪdərn] (h) **I** v/i do tailoring (or dressmaking). **II** v/t make.

'**Schneidetisch** m film etc: editing table.

'**Schneidezahn** m incisor.

'**schneidig** adj plucky, snappy, dashing, w.s. brisk (a. pace), rousing (music).

schneien ['ʃnaɪən] **I** v/impers (h) es

schneit it's snowing. **II** v/i (sn) F (j-m) ins Haus ~ drop in (on s.o.) unexpectedly.

Schneise ['ʃnaɪzə] f (-; -n) **1.** (forest) lane, fire-break. **2.** → Flugschneise.

schnell [ʃnɛl] **I** adj quick (movement, decision, etc), fast (car, runner, track, etc), a. rapid, a. prompt, speedy: in ~er Folge in rapid succession; ~es Handeln prompt action; ~e Fortschritte machen make rapid progress; F e-e ~e Mark machen make a fast buck; auf dem ~sten Wege as quickly as possible; F auf die Schnelle quickly, contp. slapdash; → Brüter. **II** adv fast, quick(ly), rapidly (etc): ~ fahren (handeln) drive (act) fast; das geht ~ that won't take long; das ist ~ gegangen that was quick; ~er geht es nicht I (we etc) couldn't do it any faster; so ~ wie möglich, schnellstens as quickly as possible; (mach) ~! hurry up!, F get a move on!; nicht so ~! easy!; sie ist ~ beleidigt she is quick to take offence; wie ~ die Zeit vergeht! how time flies!

'**Schnellboot** n ⚔ speedboat.

schnellebig [-le:bɪç] adj fast-moving (times, which see Leben), short-lived (fashion etc).

schnellen ['ʃnɛlən] **I** v/i (sn) bounce, pop: in die Höhe ~ → hochschnellen. **II** v/t (h) toss, flick.

'**Schnell|feuerwaffe** f automatic weapon. ~gang m mot. overdrive. ~gaststätte f cafeteria. ~gericht n **1.** ⚖ summary court. **2.** gastr. instant meal. ~hefter m (-s; -) letter file.

'**Schnelligkeit** f (-; no pl) a) quickness, fastness, rapidity, speediness, b) speed.

'**Schnell|imbiß** m **1.** snack. **2.** → imbißstube f snack bar. ~kochtopf m pressure cooker. ~reinigung f express dry-cleaning. ~straße f dual carriageway, Am. divided highway. ~verband m first-aid dressing. ~verfahren n **1.** ⚖ summary procedure (or proceedings). **2.** ⚙ high-speed process: fig. im ~ very quickly. 2wirkend adj pharm. fast-acting. ~zug m fast train.

Schnepfe ['ʃnɛpfə] f (-; -n) zo. snipe.

schneuzen ['ʃnɔʏtsən] sich ~ (h) blow one's nose.

schniefen ['ʃni:fən] v/i (h) F sniffle.

Schnippchen ['ʃnɪpçən] n j-m ein ~ schlagen outwit (or fool) s.o.

schnippeln 506

schnippeln ['ʃnɪpəln] v/t, v/i (h) snip
(away) (*an dat* at).
schnippen ['ʃnɪpən] (h) **I** v/i snip: (*mit
den Fingern*) ~ snap one's fingers. **II**
v/t flick (off).
schnippisch ['ʃnɪpɪʃ] adj pert, saucy.
Schnipsel ['ʃnɪpsəl] m, n (-s; -) shred.
schnitt [ʃnɪt] pret of **schneiden**.
Schnitt m (-[e]s; -e) **1.** no pl cutting, ✗ a.
mowing, *film etc*: editing. **2.** cut, ✗ a.
incision, gash: *film etc*: *harter* ~ jump
cut. **3.** cut (*of hair, dress, etc*), shape. **4.**
pattern, ⅋ intersection. **6.** ⚙ sec-
tion(al view). **7.** (a. *im* ~ *erreichen etc*)
average: *im* ~ on average. **8.** F profit.
Schnittblumen pl cut flowers.
Schnitte ['ʃnɪtə] f (-; -n) **1.** slice. **2.** (open)
sandwich.
schnittfest adj firm (*tomatoes etc*).
schnittig adj racy, sleek, streamlined.
Schnittlauch m ⚘ chives.
Schnittmuster n pattern.
Schnittpunkt m (point of) intersection.
Schnittwunde f cut, gash.
Schnittzeichnung f ⚙ section(al view).
Schnitzarbeit ['ʃnɪts-] f (wood-)carving.
Schnitzel ['ʃnɪtsəl] n (-s; -) gastr. a. *Wie-
ner* ~ escalope.
Schnitzel² n, m (-s; -) shred, scrap.
Schnitzeljagd f paper chase.
Schnitzelwerk n shredder.
schnitzen ['ʃnɪtsən] v/t, v/i (h) carve.
Schnitzer m (-s; -) **1.** (wood-)carver. **2.**
F blunder.
Schnitze'rei f (-; -en) (wood-)carving.
schnodd(e)rig ['ʃnɔd(ə)rɪç] adj F snotty.
Schnorchel ['ʃnɔrçəl] m (-s; -) snorkel.
Schnörkel ['ʃnœrkəl] m (-s; -) **1.** scroll. **2.**
flourish: *fig. ohne* ~ without frills.
schnorren ['ʃnɔrən] v/i, v/t (h) scrounge
(*bei j-m* off s.o.).
Schnorrer m (-s; -) scrounger.
Schnösel ['ʃnøːzəl] m (-s; -) snot-nose.
schnuck(e)lig ['ʃnʊk(ə)lɪç] adj F cuddly,
pretty, cute.
schnüffeln ['ʃnʏfəln] v/i (h) **1.** sniff (*an
dat* at). **2.** F snoop (around).
Schnüffler m (-s; -) F snooper, sleuth.
Schnuller ['ʃnʊlər] m (-s; -) comforter,
dummy, *Am.* pacifier.
Schnulze ['ʃnʊltsə] f (-; -n) F **1.** sobstuff,
tearjerker. **2.** schmaltzy song.
schnupfen ['ʃnʊpfən] v/i (h) take snuff.
Schnupfen m (-s; -) cold, F the sniffles.

Schnupftabak m snuff.
schnuppe ['ʃnʊpə] → **schnurz**.
schnuppern → **schnüffeln** 1.
Schnur [ʃnuːr] f (-; ⁐e) cord, (piece of)
string, ⚡ flex: F *über die* ~ *hauen* overdo it.
Schnürchen ['ʃnyːrçən] n F *das ging
wie am* ~ it went like clockwork.
schnüren ['ʃnyːrən] v/t (h) lace up.
schnurgerade adj and adv F (as)
straight as an arrow, dead straight.
Schnurrbart m m(o)ustache.
schnurren ['ʃnʊrən] v/i (h) purr.
Schnür|riemen m strap. **~schuh** m
lace-up shoe. **~senkel** [-zɛŋkəl] m (-s; -)
shoelace, bootlace.
schnurstracks ['ʃnuːrʃtraks] adv F a)
straight, b) straightaway.
schnurz [ʃnʊrts] adj F *das ist mir* ~ I
couldn't care less.
schob [ʃoːp] pret of **schieben**.
Schober ['ʃoːbər] m (-s; -) **1.** rick. **2.**
barn, shed.
Schock [ʃɔk] m (-[e]s; -s) a. ⚡ shock: *e-n*
~ *haben* be in (a state of) shock.
schocken v/t (h) F shock.
schockieren [ʃɔ'kiːrən] v/t (h) shock,
scandalize: **~d** shocking, scandalizing.
Schockthera,pie f ⚡ (electro-)shock
therapy.
schofel ['ʃoːfəl] adj F shabby, mean.
Schöffe ['ʃœfə] m (-n; -n) lay assessor.
Schokolade [ʃoko'laːdə] f (-; -n) (*e-e
Tafel* ~ a bar of) chocolate.
Scholle¹ ['ʃɔlə] f (-; -n) **1.** clod (*of earth*).
2. (ice) floe. **3.** *fig.* (native) soil.
Scholle² f (-; -n) zo. plaice.
schon [ʃoːn] adv **1.** a) already, yet, b)
before, c) ever, d) even: ~ *damals* even
then; ~ *früher* before; ~ *immer* always,
all along; ~ *oft* often (enough); ~ *wieder* again; (*nicht*) ~ *wieder!* not again!;
~ *am nächsten Tage* the very next day;
~ *im 16. Jahrhundert* as early as the
16th century; *ist er* ~ *da?* has he come
yet?; *hast du* ~ (*einmal*) *...?* have you
ever *...?*; *ich habe ihn* ~ *einmal gesehen* I have seen him before; *ich komme
(ja)* ~*!* (I'm) coming!; *das kennen wir
~!* that's an old story! **2.** *er wird* ~
kommen he is sure to come; don't worry, he'll come; *er wird es* ~ *machen*
leave it to him; *das ist* ~ *möglich* that's
quite possible; (*das ist*) ~ *wahr, aber ...*

that's (certainly) true, but ...; **er ist ~ ein guter Spieler** he really is a good player. **3. ~ gar nicht** least of all. **4. ~ der Anblick (Gedanke** etc) the very sight (idea etc); **~ deswegen** if only for that reason; **~ weil** if only because. **5.** F **na, wenn ~!** so what!; **was macht das ~?** what does it matter?; **wenn ~, denn ~!** if we do it at all, let's do it properly!

schön [ʃøːn] **I** adj **1.** beautiful: **das ~e Geschlecht** the fair sex; **die ~en Künste** the fine arts; **~es Wetter** good (or fine) weather. **2.** a) good, fine, b) pleasant, nice: **~!** all right!, okay!; **e-s ~en Tages** one of these days; **~es Wochenende!** have a nice weekend!; **~er Tod** easy death; **das ist alles ~ und gut, aber ...** that's all very well, but ...; **es war sehr ~** I (we etc) had a good time; **~wär's!** some hope!; **das wäre ja noch ~er!** F nothing doing!; iro. **du bist mir ein ~er Freund!** a fine friend you are!; → **Dank. 3.** F handsome, nice (gift etc). **II** adv **4.** beautifully, nicely, pleasantly: **sie war ~ braun** she had a beautiful tan. **5.** F very, really, pretty: **ganz ~ teuer** pretty expensive; iro. **da wärst du ~ dumm** you'd be a fool; **sei ~ brav!** be a good boy (or girl) now!; **~ warm** nice and warm.

'Schöne n (-n) the beautiful: **das ~ daran** the nice thing about it; **es gibt nichts Schöneres als** there's nothing nicer (or better) than.

schonen ['ʃoːnən] (h) **I** v/t spare (s.o., s.o.'s feelings), save (one's energy, supplies, etc), treat s.th. with care, detergent etc: a. be easy on (the carpet etc). **II** sich ~ take it easy; **sich für et. ~** save one's strength for s.th.; **sich nicht ~** drive o.s. (hard). **'schonend** adj gentle, careful, considerate, b) mild (detergent etc): **~ umgehen mit** go easy on; → **beibringen.**

'Schoner m (-s; -) ⚓ schooner.
'Schöngeist m (-[e]s; -er) (a)esthete.
'schöngeistig adj (a)esthetical.
'Schönheit f (-; -en) beauty.
'Schönheits|fehler m blemish, flaw. **~königin** f beauty queen. **~operati|on** f cosmetic operation. **~pflege** f beauty care. **~sa,lon** m beauty parlo(u)r. **~wettbewerb** m beauty contest.
'Schonkost f light food, bland diet.

'schönmachen (sep, -ge-, h) **I** v/i dog: sit up (and beg). **II** sich ~ a) dress up, b) make (o.s.) up.

'Schonung f (-; -en) **1.** no pl a) mercy, b) forbearance, c) good care, d) protection, e) rest: **sie braucht ~** she needs a rest; **zur ~** (gen) to protect (one's hands etc), to save (one's eyes, strength, etc). **2.** (young) forest plantation.

'schonungsbedürftig adj in need of rest. **'schonungslos** adj merciless.
'Schonwaschgang m program(me Br.) for delicate fabrics.
'Schön'wetterlage f period of fine weather.
'Schonzeit f hunt. close season.
Schopf [ʃɔpf] m (-[e]s; ⸚e) mop (of hair), of birds: tuft; → **Gelegenheit.**
schöpfen ['ʃœpfən] v/t (h) scoop, ladle; → **Hoffnung, Kraft** 1, **Verdacht** etc.
'Schöpfer m (-s; -) creator, bibl. the Creator. **~geist** m creative genius.
'schöpferisch adj creative.
'Schöpfkelle f, **'Schöpflöffel** m ladle.
'Schöpfung f (-; -en) **1.** creation, work. **2.** no pl bibl. the Creation.
'Schöpfungsgeschichte f Genesis.
schor [ʃoːr] pret of **scheren.**
Schorf [ʃɔrf] m (-[e]s; -e) 🗡 scab.
Schornstein ['ʃɔrn-] m chimney, smoke stack, ⚓, 🚂 funnel. **'Schornsteinfeger** m (-s; -) chimney sweep.
schoß [ʃɔs] pret of **schießen.**
Schoß [ʃoːs] m (-es; ⸚e) **1.** lap: → **Hand. 2.** a) womb, b) (woman's) sex.
Schößling ['ʃœslɪŋ] m (-s; -e) 🌱 shoot.
Schote ['ʃoːtə] f (-; -n) 🌱 husk, pod.
Schotte ['ʃɔtə] m (-n; -n) Scot, Scotsman: **die ~n** the Scots.
Schotter ['ʃɔtər] m (-s;) gravel, a. (road) metal. **'schottern** v/t (h) gravel, metal.
Schottin ['ʃɔtɪn] f (-; -nen) Scotswoman.
'schottisch adj Scottish: **~er Whisky** Scotch (whisky). **'Schottland** n (-s) Scotland.
schraffieren [ʃraˈfiːrən] v/t (h) hatch.
schräg [ʃrɛːk] **I** adj oblique, slanting, sloping (ground, roof, etc), diagonal (line). **II** adv cut, set, etc at an angle: **~ gegenüber** diagonally opposite.
Schräge ['ʃrɛːgə] f (-; -n) **1.** slant. **2.** incline, slope.
'Schrägstrich m slash, oblique.
Schramme ['ʃramə] f (-; -n) scratch.

'**schrammen** v/t (h) scratch, graze.
Schrank [ʃraŋk] m (-[e]s; ~e) a) cupboard, closet, wardrobe, b) locker: F *er ist ein ~* he's a hulking fellow.
'**Schrankbett** n foldaway bed.
Schranke ['ʃraŋkə] f (-; -n) **1.** barrier, 🚂 *a.* gate, ⚖️ barrier. **2.** *fig.* a) (social *etc, a. trade*) barrier, b) bounds, limits: *~n setzen* set bounds (*dat* to); *(sich) in ~n halten* keep within bounds, restrain (o.s.); *j-n in s-e ~n weisen* put s.o. in his place.
'**schrankenlos** *adj fig.* boundless.
'**Schrankenwärter** m 🚂 gatekeeper.
'**schrankfertig** *adj* washed and ironed.
'**Schrankwand** f wall-to-wall cupboard.
'**Schraubdeckel** m screw cap.
Schraube ['ʃraubə] f (-; -n) **1.** screw (*a.* ⚓), ✈ propeller: *~ und Mutter* bolt and nut; F *bei ihm ist e-e ~ locker* he has a screw loose. **2.** *gym. etc* twist.
'**schrauben** v/t (h) screw, *a.* twist: *fester ~* tighten the screw(s) of; *fig. niedriger ~* lower, scale down; *(sich) in die Höhe ~* → *hochschrauben*; → *geschraubt*.
'**Schraubendreher** m screwdriver.
'**schraubenförmig** *adj* helical, spiral.
'**Schrauben|schlüssel** m wrench, spanner. *~zieher* m (-s; -) screwdriver.
'**Schraubstock** m vice, *Am.* vise.
Schrebergarten ['ʃre:bər-] m allotment (garden).
Schreck [ʃrɛk] m (-[e]s; -e) fright, shock: F *krieg k-n ~!* don't be alarmed!; *ach du ~!* good God!, dear me! '**schrecken** v/t (h) frighten, startle: *das schreckt mich nicht* that can't scare me.
'**Schrecken** m (-s; -) fright, shock: *in ~en versetzen* frighten, terrify; *mit dem ~en davonkommen* get off with a bad fright; *zu m-m ~en* to my dismay; *die ~ des Krieges* the horrors of war.
'**Schreckens|herrschaft** f reign of terror. *~nachricht* f alarming (*or* dreadful) news. *~tat* f atrocity.
'**Schreckgespenst** n fig. nightmare.
'**schreckhaft** *adj* jumpy, nervous.
'**schrecklich I** *adj* terrible, dreadful, horrible. **II** *adv* F awfully, terribly.
'**Schreckschuß** m warning shot. *~pi,stole* f blank (cartridge) pistol.
'**Schrecksekunde** f *mot.* reaction time.
Schrei [ʃraɪ] m (-[e]s; -e) cry, shout, scream, yell: *fig. ~ der Entrüstung* out-

cry; F *der letzte ~* the latest rage.
Schreib|arbeit ['ʃraɪp-] f desk work, paperwork. *~block* m writing pad.
schreiben ['ʃraɪbən] v/t, v/i (schrieb, geschrieben, h) write (*über acc* about, on), write out (*bill etc*), ⊙ record: *j-m ~* write to s.o., *Am. a.* write s.o.; *j-m et. ~* write to s.o. about s.th.; *mit Bleistift etc ~* write in pencil *etc*; *mit der Maschine ~* type; *sich mit j-m ~* correspond with s.o.; *noch einmal ~* rewrite; *gut ~* a) write a good hand, b) be a good writer; *(richtig) ~* spell *word* (correctly); *falsch ~* misspell; *wie schreibt er sich?* how do you spell his name?; *an e-m Roman ~* be working on a novel; *ped. etc e-e Arbeit ~* do a test; → *Ohr, rein* 1 *etc.*
'**Schreiben** n (-s; -) **1.** *no pl* writing. **2.** letter. '**Schreiber** m (-s; -) writer.
Schreibe'rei f (-; -en) (endless) writing, paperwork. '**Schreiberin** f (-; -nen) writer. '**Schreiberling** m (-s; -e) *contp.* hack. '**schreibfaul** *adj* lazy about writing letters.
'**Schreib|feder** f pen. *~fehler* m a) spelling mistake, b) slip of the pen. *~gerät* n writing utensils, ⊙ recorder. *~heft* n exercise-book. *~kopf* m ⊙ daddball. *~kraft* f (shorthand) typist. *~mappe* f writing case. *~ma,schine* f typewriter: *~ schreiben* type; *mit ~ geschrieben* typewritten, typed. *~ma,schinen-pa,pier* n typing paper. *~pa,pier* n writing paper. *~stube* f ⚔️ orderly room. *~tisch* m (writing) desk. *~tisch-lampe* f desk lamp.
'**Schreibung** f (-; -en) spelling.
'**Schreibwaren** pl stationery. *~geschäft* n stationer's (shop).
'**Schreibweise** f **1.** style. **2.** spelling.
schreien ['ʃraɪən] v/i, v/t (schrie, geschrien, h) shout, yell, scream, *baby:* howl: *~ nach* cry for; F *es (er) ist zum Schreien!* it (he) is a scream!
'**schreiend** *adj fig.* loud (*colo[u]r*), flagrant (*injustice*), glaring (*contrast*).
'**Schreihals** m F **1.** loudmouth. **2.** brawler. **3.** (*baby*) bawler, (*child*) noisy brat.
Schrein [ʃraɪn] m (-[e]s; -e) shrine.
Schreiner ['ʃraɪnər] m (-s; -) *etc* → *Tischler etc.*
schreiten ['ʃraɪtən] v/i (schritt, geschritten, sn) **1.** walk, stride. **2.** *zu et.* ~ proceed to (do) s.th.; *zur Tat ~* set to work.

schrie [ʃriː] *pret of* **schreien.**

schrieb [ʃriːp] *pret of* **schreiben.**

Schrift [ʃrɪft] *f* (-; -en) **1.** writing, hand(writing), *print.* script, type: *in lateinischen ~* in Roman characters (*or* letters). **2.** publication, paper, pamphlet: *~en* writings, works; *die Heilige ~* the Holy Scripture(s). *~art f* script, type. *~bild n* typeface. *~deutsch n* standard German. *~führer(in f) m* secretary. *~gelehrte m bibl.* scribe. *~grad m* type size.

'**schriftlich I** *adj* written, in writing: *~e Prüfung* written examination. **II** *adv* in writing, *a.* by letter: F *das kann ich dir ~ geben!* I can guarantee you that!

'**Schrift|probe** *f* specimen of *s.o.'s* handwriting. *~satz m* 🜍 written statement. *~setzer m* (-s; -) typesetter. *~sprache f* standard language.

'**Schriftsteller** *m* (-s; -) writer.

Schriftstelle'rei *f* (-; *no pl*) writing.

'**Schriftstellerin** *f* (-; -nen) writer.

'**schriftstellerisch I** *adj* literary. **II** *adv* as a writer.

'**Schriftstück** *n* document, paper.

'**Schrifttum** *n* (-s; *no pl*) literature.

'**Schriftwechsel** *m* correspondence.

'**Schriftzeichen** *n* letter, character.

schrill [ʃrɪl] *adj* shrill, piercing.

schritt [ʃrɪt] *pret of* **schreiten.**

Schritt *m* (-[e]s; -e) **1.** a) step, stride, b) footstep, c) pace: *~ halten mit* keep pace with, *fig. a.* keep abreast of; *~ für ~ a. fig.* step by step; *auf ~ und Tritt* at every turn, everywhere. **2.** *no pl* walk, gait: *im ~* at a walking pace; *mot.* (*im*) *~ fahren!* dead slow! **3.** *a. f anat.* crotch. **4.** *fig.* step, *a.* measure, move: *diplomatischer ~* démarche; *Politik der kleinen ~e* step-by-step policy; *den ersten ~ tun* take the first step; *wir sind k-n ~ weitergekommen* we haven't made the slightest bit of progress.

'**Schrittmacher** *m* (-s; -) *sports:* pacemaker, *fig. a.* trendsetter. *~dienste pl j-m ~ leisten sports:* make the pace for s.o., *fig.* smooth the way for s.o.

'**schrittweise I** *adj* step-by-step, gradual. **II** *adv* step by step.

schroff [ʃrɔf] *adj* **1.** steep, precipitous. **2.** gruff, curt, abrupt: *~e Ablehnung* flat refusal; *~er Gegensatz* sharp contrast.

schröpfen ['ʃrœpfən] *v/t* (h) **1.** 🜍 bleed.

2. F *j-n ~* fleece s.o. (*um* for).

Schrot [ʃroːt] *m, n* (-[e]s; -e) **1.** wholemeal. **2.** *hunt.* (small) shot. **3.** *fig. von echtem ~ und Korn* true.

schroten ['ʃroːtən] *v/t* (h) bruise.

'**Schrot|flinte** *f* shotgun. *~korn n,* *~kugel f* pellet. *~säge f* crosscut saw.

Schrott [ʃrɔt] *m* (-[e]s; -e) **1.** scrap metal: *ein Auto zu ~ fahren* smash up a car. **2.** F a) junk, b) rubbish. *~händler m* scrap dealer. *~haufen m* scrap heap. *~platz m* scrap yard. 🜍**reif** *adj* ready for the scrap heap. *~wert m* scrap value.

schrubben ['ʃrʊbən] *v/t* (h) scrub.

'**Schrubber** *m* (-s; -) scrubbing brush.

'**Schrulle** ['ʃrʊlə] *f* (-; -n) quirk, (cranky) whim. '**schrullig** *adj* F cranky.

schrump(e)lig ['ʃrʊmp(ə)lɪç] *adj* shrivel(l)ed.

schrumpfen ['ʃrʊmpfən] *v/i* (sn) shrink (*a.* 🜍), 🜍 *a.* atrophy, *fig. a.* dwindle.

Schub [ʃuːp] *m* (-[e]s; *~e*) **1.** push, *phys. a.* thrust. **2.** batch. **3.** 🜍 phase, *a.* attack, rush (*of* adrenaline etc.): *in Schüben* intermittent(ly). *~fach n* drawer. *~kraft f phys.* thrust. *~lade f* (-; -n) drawer.

Schubs [ʃʊps] *m* (-es; -e) F (*a. dat e-n ~ geben*) push, shove.

'**schubsen** *v/t* (h) F push, shove.

'**schubweise** ['ʃuː-] *adv* in batches.

schüchtern ['ʃʏçtərn] *adj* shy, timid, bashful. '**Schüchternheit** *f* (-; *no pl*) shyness, timidity, bashfulness.

Schuft [ʃʊft] *m* (-[e]s; -e) scoundrel.

schuften ['ʃʊftən] *v/i* (h) F slave away.

Schufte'rei *f* (-; *no pl*) F drudgery, grind.

Schuh [ʃuː] *m* (-[e]s; -e) shoe (*a.* 🜍): *fig. j-m et. in die ~e schieben* put the blame for s.th. on s.o.; *wo drückt dich der ~?* what's the trouble? *~bürste f* shoe brush. *~creme f* shoe polish. *~geschäft n* shoe shop. *~größe f* shoe size: *welche ~ haben Sie?* what size shoe(s) do you take? *~löffel m* shoehorn. *~macher m* (-s; -) shoemaker. *~putzer m* (-s; -) shoeblack. *~sohle f* sole. *~spanner m* shoe tree. *~werk n* (-[e]s; *no pl*) footwear, shoes.

Schukostecker ['ʃuːkoː-] *m* (*TM*) 🜍 shockproof plug.

'**Schul|abgänger** [-gɛŋər] *m* (-s; -) school-leaver. *~alter n* school age. *~anfänger m* (-s; -) (school) beginner.

~arbeiten pl, ~aufgaben pl homework. ~ausflug m school outing. ~bank f (-; ‿e) desk: die ~ drücken go to school. ~behörde f education authority. ~beispiel n classic example (für of). ~besuch m (school) attendance. ~bildung f (-; no pl) education: höhere ~ secondary education. ~buch n textbook. ~buchverlag m educational publishers. ~bus m school bus.

Schuld [ʃʊlt] f (-; -en) **1.** no pl guilt (a. ⚖), blame, eccl. sin(s): ihn trifft die ~, er ist schuld he is to blame for it; die ~ auf sich nehmen take the blame; die ~ geben (dat) blame it on; ohne m-e ~ through no fault of mine; → zuschieben 2. **2.** usu. pl debt: ~en haben, in ~en stecken be in debt; in ~en geraten run into debt; fig. (tief) in j-s ~ stehen be (greatly) indebted to s.o.

'schuldbewußt adj guilty (look etc).

schulden ['ʃʊldən] v/t (h) j-m et. ~ owe s.o. s.th.; → Dank.

'Schuldenberg m F enormous debt(s).

'schuldenfrei adj a) free of debt, b) unencumbered (house etc).

'Schuldentilgung f liquidation of debts.

'Schuldforderung f claim, (active) debt.

'Schuldfrage f question of guilt.

'Schuldgefühl (pl -e) n guilty conscience.

'schuldhaft adj ⚖ culpable.

'Schuldienst m (-[e]s; no pl) teaching: im ~ sein be a teacher.

schuldig ['ʃʊldɪç] adj **1.** (gen) a. ⚖ guilty (of), responsible (for): j-n für ~ befinden find s.o. guilty (e-s Verbrechens of a crime, e-r Anklage on a charge); j-n ~ sprechen pronounce s.o. guilty; sich ~ bekennen plead guilty. **2.** j-m et. ~ sein owe s.o. s.th.; was bin ich Ihnen ~? how much do I owe you?; das ist man ihm ~ that's his due; j-m die Antwort ~ bleiben give s.o. no answer.

Schuldige ['ʃʊldɪgə] m, f (-n, -n) culprit, ⚖ guilty party, offender.

'Schuldigkeit f (-; no pl) duty.

'Schuldi‚rektor m headmaster, Am. principal.

'schuldlos adj innocent (an dat of).

Schuldner ['ʃʊldnər] m (-s; -) debtor.

'Schuldnerland n debtor nation.

'Schuld|schein m (-[e]s; -e) promissory note, IOU (= I owe you). ~spruch m

⚖ verdict of guilty, conviction. ~verschreibung f ✝ (debenture) bond.

Schule ['ʃuːlə] f (-; -n) school: höhere ~ secondary school, Am. senior high school; auf (or in) der ~ at school; in die (or zur) ~ gehen go to school; fig. aus der ~ plaudern tell tales out of school, blab; ~ machen set a precedent, be imitated, spread; durch e-e harte ~ gehen learn the hard way; → besuchen, schwänzen.

'schulen v/t (h) train; → geschult.

'Schulenglisch n school English.

Schüler ['ʃyːlər] m (-s; -) a) schoolboy, a. pupil, student, b) disciple.

'Schüleraustausch m school exchange.

'Schülerin f (-; -nen) schoolgirl (etc, → Schüler).

'Schüler|lotse m pupil acting as a school crossing warden. ~zeitung f school magazine.

'Schul|fach n subject. ~ferien pl holidays, Am. vacation. ~fernsehen n educational television. ~flugzeug n training aircraft, trainer. ♀frei adj ~ haben have a holiday; heute ist ~ there's no school today. ~freund(in f) m schoolmate. ~funk m school broadcasts. ~gelände n school grounds, Am. campus. ~geld n (-[e]s; no pl) school fees. ~heft n exercise book. ~hof m playground, schoolyard.

schulisch ['ʃuːlɪʃ] adj school (affairs etc); ~e Leistungen progress at school.

'Schul|jahr n school year: m-e ~e my school days. ~junge m schoolboy. ~kame‚rad(in f) m schoolmate. ~kenntnisse pl school knowledge. ~klasse f class, Br. a. form, Am. grade. ~leiter(in f) m headmaster (-mistress), Am. principal. ~mädchen n schoolgirl. ~mappe f schoolbag. ~medi‚zin f orthodox medicine. ~meinung f received opinion. ~ordnung f school regulations. ~pflicht f compulsory education.

'schulpflichtig adj school-age, of school age: ~es Alter school-(entering) age.

'Schul|psycho‚loge m educational psychologist. ~ranzen m satchel. ~rat m school inspector. ~schiff n training ship. ~schluß m (-sses; no pl) a) end of school, b) end of term: nach ~ after school. ~schwänzer m (-s; -) truant. ~speisung f school meals. ~spre-

cher(in f) m head boy (girl). **~stunde** f
lesson, class. **~tasche** f schoolbag.
Schulter [ˈʃʊltɐr] f (-; -n) shoulder: **~ an
~** shoulder to shoulder; **mit den ~n zuk-
ken** shrug one's shoulders; **j-m auf die
~ klopfen** slap s.o.'s back; → **kalt** I,
leicht 1. **~blatt** n anat. shoulder blade.
'**schulter|frei** adj off-the-shoulder
(dress). **~lang** adj shoulder-length.
schultern [ˈʃʊltɐrn] v/t (h) shoulder.
'**Schulung** f (-; -en) **1.** training, a. practice. **2.** pol. indoctrination.
'**Schulungskurs** m course of training.
'**Schul|unterricht** m lessons, classes.
~weg m (**auf dem ~** on one's way to
school). **~weisheit** f contp. book learning. **~wesen** n (-s; no pl) school system.
~zeit f school days. **~zeugnis** n
(school) report, report card.
schummeln [ˈʃʊməln] v/i (h) F cheat.
schumm(e)rig [ˈʃʊm(ə)rɪç] adj F dim.
Schund [ʃʊnt] m (-[e]s; no pl) trash, rub-
bish. '**Schundro|man** m trashy novel.
schunkeln [ˈʃʊŋkəln] v/i (h) rock, sway.
Schuppe [ˈʃʊpə] f (-; -n) **1.** scale: **es fiel
mir wie ~n von den Augen** the scales
fell from my eyes. **2.** pl dandruff.
schuppen [ˈʃʊpən] (h) **I** v/t scale (fish).
II sich ~ skin: peel.
'**Schuppen** m (-s; -) **1.** shed, ✓ a. hangar. **2.** F a) contp. hovel, b) joint.
schuppig [ˈʃʊpɪç] adj scaly.
Schur [ʃuːr] f (-; -en) a) shearing, b)
fleece.
schürfen [ˈʃʏrfən] (h) **I** v/i **1.** (**nach** for)
prospect, dig: fig. **tiefer ~** dig below the
surface. **II** v/t **2.** prospect (or dig) for
(ore etc). **3.** scrape, graze (skin).
'**Schürfwunde** f graze, abrasion.
Schurke [ˈʃʊrkə] m (-n; -n) villain.
'**Schurwolle** f virgin (or new) wool.
Schurz [ʃʊrts] m (-es; -e) apron.
Schürze [ˈʃʏrtsə] f (-; -n) apron.
schürzen [ˈʃʏrtsən] v/t (h) gather up
(skirt), purse (lips).
'**Schürzenjäger** m F womanizer.
Schuß [ʃʊs] m (-sses; -sse) **1.** shot (a.
phot. or sports), round (of ammunition):
ein ~ ins Schwarze a. fig. a bull's-eye;
e-n ~ abgeben fire (a shot); **weit vom ~**
well out of harm's way; **er (es) ist k-n ~
Pulver wert** he (it) is no good; fig. **der ~
ging nach hinten los** it backfired; →
Bug 1. **2.** → **Schußverletzung**. **3.** F

shot, sl. fix: **sich e-n ~ setzen** give o.s. a
fix. **4.** skiing: (a. **im ~ fahren**) schuss. **5.**
dash (a. fig.): **Tee mit e-m ~ Milch** tea
with a dash of milk; **e-e Cola mit ~** a
spiked coke. **6.** fig. (**gut**) **in** (or **im**) **~
sein** be in good shape; **in ~ bringen**
knock s.th. into shape, bring s.o. up to
the mark; **in ~ halten** keep s.o., s.th. in
good shape. **7.** textil. weft.
'**schußbereit** adj ready to shoot (a.
phot.), gun: at the ready.
Schussel [ˈʃʊsəl] m (-s; -) F scatterbrain.
Schüssel [ˈʃʏsəl] f (-; -n) bowl, basin, a.
F TV dish.
'**schusselig** adj F scatterbrained.
'**Schuß|fahrt** f skiing: schuss. **~linie** f
line of fire: fig. **in die ~ geraten** come
under fire (gen from). **~verletzung** f
gunshot wound. **~waffe** f firearm.
~wechsel m exchange of shots. **~weite**
f (firing) range: **außer ~** out of range.
Schuster [ˈʃuːstɐr] m (-s; -) shoemaker.
Schutt [ʃʊt] m (-[e]s; no pl) rubble, geol.
a. debris: **in ~ und Asche liegen** be in
ruins.
'**Schüttelfrost** m 🏥 shivering fit.
schütteln [ˈʃʏtəln] v/t (h) shake: **den
Kopf ~** shake one's head; **j-m die Hand
~** shake hands with s.o., shake s.o. by
the hand; → **Ärmel**.
schütten [ˈʃʏtən] v/t (h) pour: F **es
schüttet** it's pouring (with rain).
schütter [ˈʃʏtɐr] adj thin (hair etc).
'**Schutthaufen** m heap of rubble.
Schutz [ʃʊts] m (-es; no pl) protection
(**gegen, vor** against, from), a. shelter,
esp. ✗ cover, escort, (esp. legal) safeguard, a. preservation: **~ suchen** seek
refuge (**vor** from, **bei** with); **j-n in ~
nehmen** come to s.o.'s defence, back
s.o. up; **im ~e der Dunkelheit** under
cover of darkness.
'**Schütz** [ʃʏts] n (-es; -e) ⚡ contactor.
'**Schutzanzug** m protective suit.
'**Schutzbefohlene** m, f (-n; -n) charge.
'**Schutzblech** n mudguard, Am. fender.
'**Schutzbrille** f (safety) goggles.
Schütze [ˈʃʏtsə] m (-n; -n) **1.** shot,
marksman. **2.** sports: scorer. **3.** ✗ private. **4.** no pl astr. ([**ein**] **~ sein** be [a])
Sagittarius.
'**schützen** v/t (h) (**gegen, vor** dat) protect
(from, against), defend (against), shel-
ter (from), guard (against), a. fig. shield

(from), *esp.* ✕ cover (against): **sich ~ (vor)** guard (against), protect o.s. (from): **~des Dach** shelter; → **Nässe**.
'**Schutzengel** *m* guardian angel.
'**Schützen|graben** *m* ✕ trench. **~hilfe** *f j-m ~ geben* back s.o. up. **~könig** *m* champion shot, *sports:* top scorer. **~panzer** *m* ✕ armo(u)red personnel carrier.
'**Schutz|gebiet** *n* protectorate. **~geld** *n* protection money. **~haft** *f* protective custody. **~heilige** *m, f* (-n; -n) patron saint. **~helm** *m* helmet. **~herrschaft** *f* protectorate. **~hülle** *f* protective cover, ☺ sheath, *for passport etc:* holder. **~hütte** *f* shelter. **~impfung** *f* inoculation, vaccination. **~kappe** *f* protective cap, *phot.* lens cap. **~kleidung** *f* protective clothing.
Schützling ['ʃʏtslɪŋ] *m* (-s; -e) a) charge, b) protégé(e *f*).
'**schutzlos** *adj* unprotected, defenceless, *Am.* defenseless.
'**Schutz|macht** *f pol.* protecting power. **~marke** *f* (*eingetragene ~* registered) trademark. **~maske** *f* (protective) mask. **~maßnahme** *f* protective (*or* safety) measure, precaution. **~rechte** *pl* patent (*or* trademark) rights. **~schicht** *f* protective layer. **~schild** *m* shield. **~umschlag** *m* (dust) jacket. **~vorrichtung** *f* safety device. **~zoll** *m* protective duty.
schwabb(e)lig ['ʃvab(ə)lɪç] *adj* flabby.
Schwabe ['ʃvaːbə] *m* (-n; -n) Swabian. '**Schwaben** *n* (-s) Swabia. **Schwäbin** ['ʃvɛːbɪn] *f* (-; -nen) Swabian (girl *or* woman). '**schwäbisch** *adj* Swabian.
schwach [ʃvax] **I** *adj* **1.** weak (*a. ling.*), *a.* faint, *a.* infirm: *humor. das ~ we Geschlecht* the weaker sex; *~ werden* weaken; *schwächer werden* weaken, *eyesight:* fail, *sound, light:* fade, ♥ *demand:* fall off; F *nur nicht ~ werden!* don't weaken!; *~e Erinnerung* faint (*or* vague) recollection; *~e Hoffnung* faint hope; → *Trost.* **2.** *fig.* weak, *a.* poor (*hearing, memory, etc*), low (*battery*), low-powered (*engine*), slow (*pulse*), dim (*light*): *~e Leistung* poor performance; *~e Seite* weakness. **3.** ♔ dilute (*solution*). **II** *adv* **bevölkert** sparsely populated; *~ besucht* poorly attended.
Schwäche ['ʃvɛçə] *f* (-; -n) **1.** weakness,

faintness (*a. fig.*). **2.** *fig.* weakness, failing, shortcoming, weak point. **3.** *no pl* weakness (*für* for): *e-e ~ für j-n haben* F have a soft spot for s.o. **~anfall** *m*, **~gefühl** *n* (sudden feeling of) faintness.
schwächen ['ʃvɛçən] *v/t* (h) weaken.
'**Schwachheit** *f* (-; *no pl*) weakness.
'**Schwachkopf** *m* F idiot, twit.
schwächlich ['ʃvɛçlɪç] *adj* weakly, *a.* delicate, sickly.
'**Schwächling** *m* (-s; -e) weakling.
'**schwachsichtig** *adj* ✻ weak-sighted.
'**Schwachsinn** *m* (-[e]s; *no pl*) **1.** ✻ mental deficiency. **2.** F *contp.* a) idiocy, b) rubbish. '**schwachsinnig** *adj* **1.** ✻ mentally deficient. **2.** F *contp.* idiotic.
'**Schwachsinnige** *m, f* (-n; -n) *a.* F *contp.* imbecile.
'**Schwachstelle** *f* weak point.
'**Schwachstrom** *m* low-voltage current.
'**Schwachstromtechnik** *f* communications engineering.
'**Schwächung** *f* (-; -en) weakening.
Schwaden ['ʃvaːdən] *m* (-s; -) cloud.
schwafeln ['ʃvaːfəln] *v/i* (h) F blether.
Schwager ['ʃvaːgər] *m* (-s; ") brother-in-law. **Schwägerin** ['ʃvɛːgərɪn] *f* (-; -nen) sister-in-law.
Schwalbe ['ʃvalbə] *f* (-; -n) *zo.* swallow.
'**Schwalbennest** *n* swallow's nest.
Schwall [ʃval] *m* (-[e]s; -e) *a. fig.* gush, flood, torrent.
schwamm [ʃvam] *pret of* **schwimmen.**
Schwamm *m* (-[e]s; "e) **1.** sponge: *fig. ~ drüber!* (let's) forget it! **2.** a) fungus, b) → *Pilz*, c) dry rot. '**schwammig** *adj* **1.** spongy, flabby (*body*), puffy (*face*). **2.** *fig.* woolly (*idea, concept, etc*).
Schwan [ʃvaːn] *m* (-[e]s; "e) *zo.* swan.
schwand [ʃvant] *pret of* **schwinden.**
schwanen ['ʃvaːnən] *v/impers* (h) F *mir schwant s.th. tells me; ihr schwante nichts Gutes* she feared the worst.
schwang [ʃvaŋ] *pret of* **schwingen.**
Schwang *m im ~(e) sein* be in vogue.
schwanger ['ʃvaŋər] *adj* (*im vierten etc Monat ~* four months *etc*) pregnant.
'**Schwangere** *f* (-n; -n) pregnant woman, expectant mother.
schwängern ['ʃvɛŋərn] *v/t* (h) **1.** make *woman* pregnant. **2.** *fig.* impregnate.
'**Schwangerschaft** *f* (-; -en) pregnancy.
'**Schwangerschafts|abbruch** *m* termination of pregnancy, induced abor-

tion. **~gym͵nastik** *f* antenatal exercises. **~streifen** *pl* stretchmarks. **~test** *m* pregnancy test.

Schwank [ʃvaŋk] *m* (-[e]s; ⁼e) **1.** anecdote. **2.** *thea.* farce.

schwanken ['ʃvaŋkən] *v/i* **1.** (h) sway, *ground etc: a.* shake, rock. **2.** (sn) sway, stagger, totter. **3.** (h) (*zwischen* between) waver, vacillate: *ich schwanke noch* I'm still undecided. **4.** (h) *temperature, prices, etc:* fluctuate, *a.* vary, alternate: *die Preise ~ zwischen ... und ... a.* prices range from ... to ...

'Schwanken *n* (-s) **1.** swaying (*etc*). **2.** vacillation. **3.** → *Schwankung* 2.

'schwankend *adj* **1.** swaying (*etc*). **2.** a) undecided, wavering, b) unstable.

'Schwankung *f* (-; -en) **1.** → *Schwanken* 1. **2.** variation, *a.* 🕂 fluctuation.

Schwanz [ʃvants] *m* (-es; ⁼e) **1.** *zo.* tail (*a.* ✔ *etc*): F *kein ~* not a (blessed) soul. **2.** *fig.* tail end. **3.** ∨ cock, dick.

schwänzen ['ʃvɛntsən] *v/i, v/t* (h) F (*die Schule*) *~* play truant (*Am.* hooky).

'Schwanzfeder *f* tail feather.

'Schwanzflosse *f* tail fin.

'schwanzlastig *adj* ✔ tail-heavy.

schwappen ['ʃvapən] *v/i* **1.** (h) slosh around. **2.** (sn) slop, spill.

Schwarm [ʃvarm] *m* (-[e]s; ⁼e) **1.** swarm, *a.* crowd, flight (*of birds*), shoal (*of fish*). **2.** F a) heartthrob, b) dream.

schwärmen ['ʃvɛrmən] *v/i* **1.** swarm. **2.** enthuse (*or* rave) (*von* about): *~ für* be crazy about; *für j-n ~ a.* have a crush on s.o.; *ins Schwärmen geraten* go into raptures. **'Schwärmer** *m* (-s; -) **1.** enthusiast, dreamer. **2.** squib. **3.** *zo.* hawk moth. **Schwärme'rei** *f* (-; -en) **1.** enthusiasm, passion. **'schwärmerisch** *adj* enthusiastic, gushing.

Schwarte ['ʃvartə] *f* (-; -n) **1.** (bacon) rind. **2.** F old book, tome.

schwarz [ʃvarts] *adj* **1.** black (*a. coffee, tea*), *a.* swarthy, dark-skinned, F *a.* dirty, *a.* deeply tanned: *Schwarzer Erdteil* Black Continent; *~er Humor* black humo(u)r, *thea.* Black Comedy; *~ auf weiß* in black and white, in cold print; *mir wurde ~ vor den Augen* everything went black; F *sich ~ ärgern* be terribly annoyed; *da kann er warten, bis er ~ wird* he can wait till he's blue in the face; → *Brett, Liste, Schaf* 1 *etc*,

schwarzfahren, schwarzsehen. 2. *fig.* black, gloomy: *~er Tag* black day. **3.** F *fig.* black, illicit: *der ~e Markt* the black market. **4.** F Catholic(-Conservative).

Schwarz *n* (-[es]; -) black: *in ~ gehen* be dressed in black (*or* in mourning). **~arbeit** *f* illicit work, F moonlighting. **~arbeiter** *m* illicit worker, F moonlighter. **~brot** *n* brown bread.

'Schwarze¹ *m* (-n; -n) **1.** black: *die ~n* the Blacks. **2.** black-haired man (*or* boy). **3.** F Catholic(-Conservative).

'Schwarze² *f* (-n; -n) black (woman *or* girl). **2.** black-haired woman (*or* girl).

'Schwarze³ *n* (-n; -n) **1.** black dress. **2.** *a. fig. ins ~ treffen* hit the bull's-eye.

Schwärze ['ʃvɛrtsə] *f* (-; *no pl*) **1.** blackness. **2.** darkness.

schwärzen ['ʃvɛrtsən] *v/t* (h) blacken.

'schwarzfahren *v/i* (*irr, sep*, *-ge-*, sn, → *fahren*) a) go without paying, b) *mot.* drive without a licen/ce (*Am.* -se).

'Schwarzfahrer(in *f*) *m* fare dodger.

'schwarzhaarig *adj* black-haired.

'Schwarz|handel *m* black market(eering): *im ~* on the black market. **~händler** *m* black marketeer. **~hörer** *m* (radio) licen/ce (*Am.* -se) dodger.

'schwärzlich *adj* blackish, swarthy.

'Schwarz|markt *m* black market. **₂sehen** *v/i* (*irr, sep*, *-ge-*, h, → *sehen*) be pessimistic (*für* about): *ich sehe schwarz (für dich)!* things look bad (for you)! **~seher** *m* **1.** pessimist. **2.** TV-licen/ce (*Am.* -se) dodger. **~sender** *m* pirate (radio) station.

Schwarz'weiß... black-and-white (*film, television, etc*).

'Schwarzwild *n hunt.* wild boars.

Schwatz [ʃvats] *m* (-es; -e) chat.

'schwatzen, *dial.* **schwätzen** ['ʃvɛtsən] (h) **I** *v/i* a) chat, b) blab. **II** *v/t dummes Zeug ~* talk rubbish.

'Schwätzer *m* (-s; -), **'Schwätzerin** *f* (-; -nen) chatterbox, blab(ber), F gasbag.

'schwatzhaft *adj* talkative, chatty.

Schwebe ['ʃveːbə] *f in der ~ sein* be undecided, ⚖ be pending. **~bahn** *f* cableway. **~balken** *m* (balance) beam.

schweben ['ʃveːbən] *v/i* (sn) **1.** glide, float, sail (*all a. fig.*), *a.* hover (*a. fig.*), *a.* soar, *a.* be suspended, hang: *in Gefahr ~* be in danger; → *Ungewißheit.* **2.** be undecided, *esp.* ⚖ be pending.

'**schwebend** adj **1.** floating (etc, →
schweben 1). **2.** esp. ⚖ pending.

Schwede ['ʃve:də] m (-n; -n) Swede.
'**Schweden** n (-s) Sweden. '**Schwedin**
f (-; -nen) Swede. '**schwedisch** adj
Swedish.

Schwefel ['ʃve:fəl] m (-s; no pl) sulphur,
Am. sulfur. '**Schwefeldioxyd** n sulphur (Am. -f-) dioxide. '**schwefelhal-
tig** adj sulphur(e)ous (Am. -f-).
'**schwefeln** v/t (h) ☧ sulphurate (Am.
-f-), a. ☉ sulphurize (Am. -f-).
'**Schwefelsäure** f sulphuric (Am. -f-)
acid. **Schwefel**'**wasserstoff** m hydrogen sulphide (Am. -f-).

schweflig ['ʃve:flɪç] adj sulphur(e)ous
(Am. -f-).

Schweif [ʃvaɪf] m (-[e]s; -e) **1.** tail (a.
astr.). **2.** fig. train.

'**schweifen** v/i (sn) a. fig. wander, roam.

'**Schweige|geld** n hush money.
~marsch m silent protest march.
~mi,nute f one minute's silence (**zu
Ehren** gen in memory of).

schweigen ['ʃvaɪgən] (schwieg, geschwiegen, h) v/i (**über** acc, **zu**) be
silent (on), keep mum (on, about), say
nothing: **ganz zu ~ von ...** to say nothing of ..., let alone ... '**Schweigen** n (-s)
(a. **zum ~ bringen**) silence: → **hüllen**.
'**schweigend** adj silent(ly adv), adv a.
in silence: **~e Mehrheit** silent majority.
'**Schweigepflicht** f secrecy, professional
discretion.

'**schweigsam** adj quiet, silent, a. taciturn. '**Schweigsamkeit** f (-; no pl)
quietness, silence, taciturnity.

Schwein [ʃvaɪn] n (-[e]s; -e) **1.** zo. pig,
hog, swine, a. sow. **2.** gastr. pork. **3.**
contp. a) F (filthy) pig, b) V bastard,
swine, c) F soul: **kein ~** not a (blessed)
soul; **armes ~!** poor sod! **4.** F luck: **~
haben** be lucky.

'**Schweine|braten** m roast pork. **~fi,let**
n fillet of pork. **~fleisch** n pork. **~hund**
m V swine, bastard: F **den inneren ~
überwinden** conquer one's weaker
self. **~kote,lett** n pork chop.

Schweine'rei f (-; -en) F **1.** (awful) mess,
filth. **2.** a) dirty trick, b) crying shame.
3. → **Schweinigelei**.

'**Schweine|stall** m a. fig. pigsty. **~zucht**
f pig-breeding, hog raising.

Schweinigel ['ʃvaɪnˌʔiːgəl] m (-s; -) F filthy pig. **Schweinige'lei** f (-; -en) F
dirty joke, obscenity. '**schweinigeln**
v/i (h) F **1.** mess about. **2.** talk smut.

'**schweinisch** adj F filthy.
'**Schweins|haxe** f (-; -n) gastr. knuckle
of pork. **~leder** n pigskin.

Schweiß [ʃvaɪs] m (-es; -e) **1.** sweat, perspiration: **in ~ geraten** get into a sweat;
das hat viel ~ gekostet that was hard
work. **2.** hunt. blood. **~band** n (-[e]s;
~er) sweatband. **~blatt** n dress-shield.
~brenner m ☉ welding torch. **~drüse** f
anat. sweat gland.

schweißen ['ʃvaɪsən] v/t (h) ☉ weld.
'**Schweißer** m (-s; -) ☉ welder.
'**Schweißfüße** pl sweaty feet.
'**schweißgebadet** adj bathed in sweat.
'**Schweißgeruch** m smell of sweat.
schweißig ['ʃvaɪsɪç] adj sweaty.
'**Schweiß|naht** f (welding) seam. **~perle**
f bead of perspiration. **~stelle** f weld.
~triefend adj dripping with sweat.
~tropfen m bead of perspiration.

Schweiz [ʃvaɪts] f (-) Switzerland.
Schweizer ['ʃvaɪtsər] I m (-s; -) Swiss:
die ~ the Swiss. II adj Swiss: **~ Käse**
Swiss cheese. '**Schweizerdeutsch** n
Swiss German. '**Schweizerin** f (-;
-nen) Swiss (woman or girl).
'**schweizerisch** adj Swiss.

schwelen ['ʃve:lən] v/i (h) smo(u)lder.
schwelgen ['ʃvɛlgən] v/i (h) revel (**in** dat
in).

Schwelle ['ʃvɛlə] f (-; -n) **1.** threshold (a.
fig.). **2.** 🚆 sleeper, Am. tie.
schwellen ['ʃvɛlən] v/i, v/t (schwoll, geschwollen, sn) swell.

'**Schwellenland** n emergent nation.
'**Schwellung** f (-; -en) swelling.

Schwemme ['ʃvɛmə] f (-; -n) **1.** watering
place. **2.** pub. **3.** ✝ glut (**an** dat of).
schwemmen ['ʃvɛmən] v/t (h) wash.
'**Schwemmland** n alluvial land.

Schwengel ['ʃvɛŋəl] m (-s; -) handle.
Schwenk [ʃvɛŋk] m (-[e]s; -s) film: pan.
'**Schwenkarm** m ☉ swivel arm.
'**schwenkbar** adj swivel(l)ing, slewing.
schwenken ['ʃvɛŋkən] I v/t (h) **1.** a)
swing, ☉ a. turn, slew, b) wave (hat,
flag, etc), brandish (stick), c) film etc:
pan (camera). **2.** rinse. **3.** gastr. toss.
II v/i (sn) **4.** turn, swing (round), camera: pan, ✕ wheel. '**Schwenkung** f (-;
-en) **1.** turn, swing, ✕ wheel(ing), film

etc: pan. **2.** change of mind (*pol.* of front).

schwer [ʃveːr] **I** *adj* **1.** heavy: *100 Pfund ~ sein* weigh 100 pounds. **2.** *fig.* heavy (*storm, losses, etc*), bad (*mistake etc*), hard, difficult, F tough (*decision, struggle, work, etc*), serious (*illness, accident, etc*), onerous (*duty etc*), grave (*crime etc*): *ein ~er Schock* a bad (*or* terrible) shock; *~er Diebstahl* aggravated larceny; *~er Gegner* formidable opponent; *~es Schicksal* hard lot; *~er Tag* hard day; *~e Zeit(en)* hard times; *~en Herzens* with a heavy heart, reluctantly; *er hat es ~* he has a hard time; → *Begriff* 2 *etc*. **3.** rich, heavy (*food*), strong (*cigar, scent, etc*): *~er Wein* heady wine. **II** *adv* **4.** heavily (*etc*), F very much, awfully, badly: *~ arbeiten* work hard; F *~ aufpassen* watch (out) like hell; *~ zu bekommen* hard to get; F *~ beleidigt* deeply offended; *~ büßen müssen* have to pay dearly; *~ hören* be hard of hearing; *~ krank* seriously ill; *~ zu sagen* hard to say; *sie ist ~ gestürzt* she had a nasty fall; *~ zu verstehen* difficult to understand; F *da hat er sich aber ~ getäuscht* he's very much mistaken there.

ˈSchwer|arbeit *f* heavy labo(u)r. **~ath,let** *m* heavy athlete. **~behinderte** *m, f* ✠ severely handicapped person.

ˈschwerbeladen *adj* heavily laden.

ˈschwerbewaffnet *adj* heavily armed.

Schwere [ˈʃveːrə] *f* (-; *no pl*) **1.** weight, *phys.* gravity. **2.** *fig.* seriousness, gravity, severity, *a.* weightiness. **3.** heaviness (*of food etc*). ˈschwerelos *adj* weightless. ˈSchwerelosigkeit *f* (-; *no pl*) weightlessness.

Schwerenöter [ˈʃveːrənøːtər] *m* (-s; -) *humor.* philanderer.

ˈschwererziehbar *adj* difficult, recalcitrant: *~es Kind a.* problem child.

ˈschwerfallen *v/i* (*irr, sep, -ge-, sn,* → *fallen*) be difficult (*dat* for): *es fällt mir schwer a.* I find it hard.

ˈschwerfällig *adj* awkward, clumsy, heavy, ponderous (*a. fig.*), slow.

ˈSchwerfälligkeit *f* (-; *no pl*) clumsiness, heaviness, ponderousness.

ˈSchwergewicht *n* (-[e]s; *no pl*) **1.** *sports:* heavyweight. **2.** *fig.* emphasis.

ˈschwerhalten *v/impers* (*irr, sep, -ge-, h,* → *halten*) *es hält schwer* it is difficult.

ˈschwerhörig *adj* hard of hearing.

ˈSchwerhörigkeit *f* (-; *no pl*) partial deafness.

ˈSchwerindu,strie *f* heavy industry.

ˈSchwerkraft *f* (-; *no pl*) (force of) gravity.

ˈschwerlich *adv* hardly.

ˈschwermachen *v/t* (*sep, -ge-, h*) *j-m et. ~* make s.th. difficult (*or* hard) for s.o.; *j-m das Leben ~* make life difficult for s.o; *mach es mir nicht so schwer!* don't make it so hard for me!

ˈSchwermut *f* (-; *no pl*) melancholy.

ˈschwermütig [-myːtɪç] *adj* melancholy.

ˈschwernehmen *v/t* (*irr, sep, -ge-, h,* → *nehmen*) *et. ~* take s.th. hard.

ˈSchwerpunkt *m* **1.** cent/re (*Am. -er*) of gravity. **2.** *fig.* a) focal point, b) emphasis: *~e bilden* set up priorities.

ˈSchwerpunktstreik *m* pinpoint strike.

ˈschwerreich *adj* F exceedingly rich.

Schwert [ʃveːrt] *n* (-[e]s; -er) sword. **~fisch** *m* swordfish. **~lilie** *f* iris.

ˈschwertun: *sich ~* (*irr, sep, -ge-, h,* → *tun*) have a hard time (*mit* with).

ˈSchwerverbrecher *m* felon, dangerous criminal.

ˈschwerverdaulich *adj* indigestible (*a. fig.*), heavy.

ˈSchwerverletzte *m, f* (-n; -n) seriously injured person. ˈSchwerverwundete *m, f* (-n; -n) seriously wounded person.

ˈschwerwiegend *adj* weighty, grave.

Schwester [ˈʃvɛstər] *f* (-; -n) **1.** *a. fig.* sister. **2.** (hospital) nurse, sister. **3.** *eccl.* sister, nun. **4.** → ˈSchwesterfirma *f* sister company.

ˈschwesterlich *adj* sisterly.

schwieg [ʃviːk] *pret* of *schweigen*.

Schwieger|eltern [ˈʃviːgər-] *pl* parents-in-law. **~mutter** *f* mother-in-law. **~sohn** *m* son-in-law. **~tochter** *f* daughter-in-law. **~vater** *m* father-in-law.

Schwiele [ˈʃviːlə] *f* (-; -n) callus.

ˈschwielig *adj* horny, callused.

schwierig [ˈʃviːrɪç] *adj* difficult, hard, F tough. ˈSchwierigkeit *f* (-; -en) difficulty, trouble: (*j-m*) *~en machen* be a problem (to s.o.), *person:* make things difficult (for s.o.); *in ~en geraten*, *~en bekommen* get into trouble; *~en haben zu inf* find it difficult to *inf*.

'**Schwimm|bad** n swimming pool (or bath). **~dock** n floating dock.

schwimmen ['ʃvɪmən] v/i (schwamm, geschwommen, h and sn) **1.** swim (a. v/t distance, record, etc), object: float, F floor etc: be flooded: **~ gehen** go swimming; F **im Geld ~** be rolling in money. **2.** F fig. flounder.

'**Schwimmen** n (-s) swimming: F fig. **ins ~ kommen** (begin to) flounder.

Schwimmer ['ʃvɪmər] m (-s; -) **1.** swimmer. **2.** fishing, ☉ float.

'**Schwimmerin** f (-; -nen) swimmer.

'**Schwimm|gürtel** m swimming belt. **~halle** f indoor pool. **~haut** f zo. web. **~lehrer(in** f) m swimming instructor. **~sport** m swimming. **~verein** m swimming club. **~weste** f life jacket.

Schwindel ['ʃvɪndəl] m (-s; no pl) **1.** ✴ dizziness, vertigo. **2.** F a) swindle, b) lie. **3.** F **der ganze ~** the whole lot.

'**Schwindelanfall** m ✴ dizzy spell.

Schwinde|lei f (-; -en) **1.** → **Schwindel** 2. **2.** a) cheating, b) lying.

'**schwindelerregend** adj dizzy, giddy (a. fig.), fig. staggering (prices etc).

'**schwindelfrei** adj **~ sein** have a good head for heights; **nicht ~ sein** be afraid of heights.

schwind(e)lig ['ʃvɪnd(ə)lɪç] adj giddy, dizzy (a. fig.): **mir ist ~** I feel dizzy.

'**schwindeln** v/i (h) **1. mir schwindelt** I feel dizzy, my head reels. **2.** lie, F tell fibs. **3. in ~der Höhe** at a giddy height.

schwinden ['ʃvɪndən] v/i (schwand, geschwunden, sn) strength, supplies, etc: dwindle, colo(u)r, light, beauty, etc: fade: **~de Hoffnung** dwindling hope.

Schwindler ['ʃvɪndlər] m (-s; -) a) swindler, F con man, b) liar.

Schwinge ['ʃvɪŋə] f (-; -n) wing.

schwingen ['ʃvɪŋən] (schwang, geschwungen, h) **I** v/t **1.** swing, wave, brandish: **er schwang sich auf sein Rad** he swung himself on his bicycle; → **Rede.** **II** v/i **2.** a. (sn) swing. **3.** phys. oscillate, vibrate.

'**Schwinger** m (-s; -) boxing: swing.

'**Schwingkreis** m ⚡ resonant circuit.

'**Schwingung** f (-; -en) phys. vibration, oscillation: a. fig. et. in **~en versetzen** set s.th. vibrating. '**schwingungsfrei** adj free from vibration.

Schwips [ʃvɪps] m F **e-n ~ haben** be tipsy.

schwirren ['ʃvɪrən] v/i **1.** (sn) whir(r), insects etc: buzz, arrow etc: whizz: **Gerüchte ~ durch die Stadt** the town is buzzing with rumo(u)rs. **2.** (h) **mir schwirrt der Kopf** my head is in a whirl.

schwitzen ['ʃvɪtsən] v/i, v/t (h) sweat (a. ☉), perspire: a. fig. **ins Schwitzen kommen** get into a sweat.

Schwof [ʃvoːf] m (-[e]s; -e) F hop.

schwofen [ʃvoːfən] v/i (h) F shake a leg.

schwoll [ʃvɔl] pret of **schwellen.**

schwören ['ʃvøːrən] v/i, v/t (schwor, geschworen, h) swear (bei by), ✴ take the oath: F fig. **ich schwöre auf** (acc) I swear by ...; **ich schwöre dir, daß** I swear to you that; → **Eid, Rache.**

schwul [ʃvuːl] adj F gay, contp. queer.

schwül [ʃvyːl] adj a) **1.** sultry, muggy, oppressive. **2.** fig. sultry, sensuous.

'**Schwule** m (-n; -n) F gay, contp. queer.

'**Schwüle** f (-; no pl) a. fig. sultriness.

Schwulst [ʃvʊlst] m (-[e]s; no pl) bombast. **schwülstig** ['ʃvylstɪç] adj bombastic.

Schwund [ʃvʊnt] m (-es; no pl) dwindling, decline, ✴, ☉ shrinkage, ✴ atrophy, ⚡ fading.

Schwung [ʃvʊŋ] m (-[e]s; ⸚e) **1.** swing. **2.** no pl swing, impetus (a. fig.), speed: et. **(j-n) in ~ bringen** set s.th. (s.o.) going; **(richtig) in ~ kommen** get going; **im ~ sein** party etc: be in full swing, person: be in full stride. **3.** no pl verve, zest, drive, F pep. **4.** no pl F batch.

'**Schwungfeder** f zo. pinion.

'**schwunghaft** adj ✴ brisk, roaring.

'**schwunglos** adj spiritless, lifeless.

'**Schwungrad** n ☉ flywheel.

'**schwungvoll** I adj a) full of drive (F go), zestful, b) bold (handwriting), c) swinging (tune). **II** adv with a swing.

Schwur [ʃvuːr] m (-[e]s; ⸚e) a) oath, b) vow. '**Schwurgericht** n jury court.

sechs [zɛks] adj six. **Sechs** f (-; -en) **1.** six. **2.** ped. very poor (mark). '**Sechseck** n (-[e]s; -e) hexagon. '**sechseckig** adj hexagonal. **Sechs'tagerennen** n six-day (cycling) race. '**sechste** adj sixth. '**Sechstel** n (-s; -) sixth (part). '**sechstens** adv sixthly.

sechzehn(te) ['zɛçtseːn(tə)] adj sixteen(th). '**Sechzehntel** n (-s; -) sixteenth (part).

sechzig ['zɛçtsɪç] adj sixty. '**Sechzig** f (-;

no pl) **1.** sixty. **2. sie ist Anfang (der) ~** she is in her early sixties. **sechziger** ['zɛçtsɪɡər] *adj* **die ~ Jahre** the sixties. **'Sechziger** *m* (-s; -) man in his sixties, sexagenarian: **in den ~n sein** be in one's sixties. **'Sechzigerin** *f* (-; -nen) woman in her sixties, sexagenarian. **'sechzigst** *adj* sixtieth.

Sediment [zedi'mɛnt] *n* (-[e]s; -e) sediment.

See¹ [ze:] *m* (-s; -n) lake.

See² *f* (-; -n) **1.** *no pl* sea, ocean: **an der ~** by the seaside; **an die ~ fahren** go to the seaside; **auf ~** at sea; **auf hoher ~** on the high seas; **in ~ gehen (or stechen)** put to sea; **zur ~ gehen** go to sea; **e-e schwere ~** a heavy sea. **2.** ♻ big wave, surge, breaker. **~bad** *n* seaside resort. **~bär** *m humor.* **alter ~** old salt. **~beben** *n* (-s; -) seaquake. **~Ele,fant** *m zo.* elephant seal. **~fahrt** *f* (-; -en) **1.** *no pl* seafaring. **2.** voyage, cruise. **2fest** *adj* seaworthy: **(nicht) ~ sein** be a good (bad) sailor. **~fisch** *m* saltwater fish. **~fracht** *f* sea (*or* ocean) freight. **~frachtbrief** *m* bill of lading (B/L). **~gang** *m* (-[e]s; *no pl*) **hoher ~** rough sea; **schwerer ~** heavy sea. **2gestützt** *adj* ✕ sea-based. **~gras** *n* seaweed. **~hafen** *m* seaport. **~handel** *m* maritime trade. **~herrschaft** *f* (-; *no pl*) naval supremacy. **~hund** *m* seal. **~igel** *m* sea urchin. **~karte** *f* nautical chart. **2klar** *adj* ♻ ready to sail. **2krank** *adj* seasick: **leicht ~ werden** be a bad sailor. **~krankheit** *f* (-; *no pl*) seasickness. **~krieg(führung** *f) m* naval war(fare). **~lachs** *m zo.* pollack.

Seele ['ze:lə] *f* (-; -n) **1.** soul, mind, *a.* heart: **e-e gute (treue) ~** a good (faithful) soul; **k-e ~** not a (blessed) soul; **zwei ~n und ein Gedanke** two minds and but a single thought; **aus tiefster ~** wish *etc* with all one's heart, *thank etc* from the bottom of one's heart, *hate* like poison; **er ist die ~ des Betriebs** he is the life and soul of the firm; **es liegt mir auf der ~** it weighs heavily on me; **es tat mir in der ~ weh** it hurt me deeply; **du sprichst mir aus der ~** that's exactly how I feel (about it); **sich et. von der ~ reden** F get s th off one's chest; → **Leib** *etc.* **2.** core (*of cable*), bore (*of gun*).

'Seelen|arzt *m* F mind doctor, shrink. **~frieden** *m* peace of mind. **~größe** *f* magnanimity. **~heil** *n eccl.* salvation. **~leben** *n* (-s; *no pl*) inner life.

'seelenlos *adj* soulless.

'Seelen|mas,sage *f* F pep talk. **~messe** *f* requiem. **~qual** *f* mental anguish. **~ruhe** *f* a) peace of mind, b) calmness: **in aller ~** → **2ruhig** *adv* (quite) coolly. **2verwandt** *adj* congenial: **~ sein** be kindred souls. **2voll** *adj a. iro.* soulful. **~wanderung** *f* transmigration of souls. **~zustand** *m* emotional state.

'Seeleute *pl* seamen, sailors.

seelisch *adj* psychological, mental, emotional, *a.* soul: **~e Belastung (ᵗᵗ Grausamkeit)** mental strain (cruelty); **~ bedingt sein** have psychological causes; → **Gleichgewicht**.

'Seelöwe *m zo.* sea lion.

'Seelsorge *f* (-; *no pl*) pastoral care. **'Seelsorger** *m* (-s; -) pastor.

'Seeluft *f* sea air.

'Seemacht *f* naval (*or* sea) power. **'Seemann** *m* (-[e]s; -leute) seaman, sailor. **'seemännisch** [-mɛnɪʃ] *adj* a) sailor's ..., b) nautical. **'Seemannsgarn** *n* F **ein ~ spinnen** spin a yarn.

'See|meile *f* nautical mile. **~not** *f* distress at sea: **Schiffe in ~** distressed ships. **~not(rettungs)dienst** *m* sea rescue service. **~pferdchen** *n zo.* seahorse. **~räuber** *m* pirate. **~reise** *f* voyage, cruise. **~rose** *f* ♻ water lily. **~schiffahrt** *f* **1.** ocean shipping. **2.** ocean navigation. **~schlacht** *f* naval battle. **~stern** *m zo.* starfish. **~streitkräfte** *pl* naval forces. **~tang** *m* ♻ seaweed. **2tüchtig** *adj* seaworthy. **~wasser** *n* salt water. **~weg** *m* sea route: **auf dem ~** by sea. **~wind** *m* sea breeze. **~zunge** *f zo.* sole.

Segel ['ze:ɡəl] *n* (-s; -) sail: **~ setzen** set sail; **~ hissen** make sail; **die ~ streichen** strike sail, *fig. a.* give in; → **Wind**. **~boot** *n* sailing boat, *Am.* sailboat, *sports:* yacht. **~fliegen** *n* gliding. **~flieger** *m* glider pilot. **~flug** *m* **1.** glider flight. **2.** gliding. **~flugplatz** *m* gliding field. **~flugzeug** *n* glider. **2klar** *adj* ready to sail. **~klub** *m* yachting club.

segeln ['ze:ɡəln] **I** *v/i* **1.** (*sn and* h) sail, ✈ glide. **2.** (*sn*) *fig.* sail, *bird: a.* soar. **II** *v/t* **3.** (h *and sn*) sail.

'Segeln *n* (-s) sailing.

'Segel|schiff n sailing ship. ~sport m sailing, yachting. ~tuch n (-[e]s; -e) canvas. ~tuchschuhe pl canvas shoes.

Segen ['ze:gən] m (-s; -) **1.** blessing (a. fig.), eccl. a. benediction: **s-n ~ geben** give one's blessing (**zu** to); **ein wahrer ~** a real blessing, iro. (quite) a mercy. **2.** F **der ganze ~** the whole lot.

'segensreich adj beneficial: **~ sein** be a blessing.

'Segenswünsche pl good wishes.

Segler ['ze:glər] m (-s; -) **1.** yachtsman. **2.** → Segelboot, -schiff, -flugzeug.

'Seglerin f (-; -nen) yachtswoman.

segnen ['ze:gnən] v/t (h) bless.

'Segnung f (-; -en) blessing (a. fig.), eccl. a. benediction.

sehen ['ze:ən] (sah, gesehen, h) **I** v/i **1.** see, look: **gut (schlecht)** ~ have good (bad or weak) eyes; **sieh nur!, ~ Sie mal!** look!; **siehe da!** lo and behold!; **siehe oben (unten)!** see above (below)!; F **sieh mal e-r an!** what do you know!; F **na, siehst du!** there you are!, what did I tell you?; **wir werden (schon)** ~ we shall see, let's wait and see; **sich gezwungen ~ zu** inf find o.s. compelled to inf. **2.** ~ **auf** (acc) set great store by. **3.** ~ **nach** look after; **ich muß nach dem Essen** ~ I have to see to the dinner. **II** v/t **4.** see, a. watch (program etc), look at, a. notice: **gern** ~ like (to see); **zu ~ sein** a) show, b) be on show; **es war nichts zu** ~ there was nothing to be seen; **niemand war zu** ~ there was nobody in sight; **man sieht's (kaum)!** it (hardly) shows!; **ich habe es kommen** ~ I have seen it coming; **sich ~ lassen** show one's face, a. turn up; **sie (es) kann sich ~ lassen** it isn't half bad; **ich sehe die Sache anders** I see it differently; **wie ich die Dinge sehe** I see it; **ich kann ihn (es) nicht mehr ~!** I can't stand (the sight of him (it) any more! **5.** see, meet: **sich (or einander) häufig ~** see a lot of each other.

'Sehen n (-s) seeing: **vom ~** by sight.

'sehenswert, 'sehenswürdig adj worth seeing, worthwhile.

'Sehenswürdigkeit f (-; -en) object of interest, sight, pl sights: **die ~en besichtigen** go sightseeing.

'Sehfehler m eye defect.

'Sehkraft f (-; no pl) (eye)sight, vision.

Sehne ['ze:nə] f (-; -n) **1.** anat. sinew, tendon. **2.** string (of bow). **3.** A chord.

sehnen ['ze:nən] **sich** ~ (h) (**nach** for) long, yearn: **er sehnte sich danach zu** inf he was longing to inf.

'Sehnenzerrung f pulled tendon.

'Sehnerv m optic nerve.

sehnig ['ze:nıç] adj sinewy, wiry (a. person), stringy (meat).

sehnlich ['ze:nlıç] adj ardent.

'Sehnsucht f (-; ⁓e) (**nach** for) longing, yearning. 'sehnsüchtig adj longing, yearning, wistful.

sehr [ze:r] adv **1.** preceding adj und adv very, most, extremely: ~ **gern** with pleasure, gladly; ~ **viel** much, a lot (better etc). **2.** with verb: (very) much: ~ **vermissen** miss s.o., s.th. badly (or a lot); **ich freue mich** ~ I am very glad.

'Sehschärfe f visual power, (eye)sight.

'Sehschwäche f poor (eye)sight.

'Sehstörung f impaired vision.

'Sehtest m eye test: **e-n ~ machen lassen** have one's eyes tested.

seicht [zaıçt] adj a. fig. shallow.

Seide ['zaıdə] f (-; -n) (**reine** ~ pure) silk.

seiden ['zaıdən] adj (of) silk.

'Seiden|pa‚pier n tissue paper. ~raupe f zo. silkworm. ~raupenzucht f sericulture. ~strümpfe pl silk stockings.

'seiden'weich adj (as) soft as silk, silky.

seidig ['zaıdıç] adj silky.

Seife ['zaıfə] f (-; -n) soap.

seifen ['zaıfən] v/t (h) soap.

'Seifen|blase f **1.** soap bubble. **2.** fig. bubble. ~lauge f soapsuds. ~pulver n soap powder. ~schale f soap dish. ~schaum m lather. ~spender m soap dispenser.

seifig ['zaıfıç] adj soapy.

seihen ['zaıən] v/t (h) strain, filter.

Seil [zaıl] n (-[e]s; -e) rope: ~ **springen** skip. 'Seilbahn f cable railway.

'Seilschaft f (-; -en) **1.** mount. rope (team). **2.** F fig. team.

'Seiltänzer(in f) m tightrope walker.

sein¹ [zaın] v/i (war, gewesen, sn) be, as v/aux a. have: **bist du es?** is that you?; **ich bin's** it's me; **ich bin für e-e Reform** I am for a reform; **mir ist nicht nach Arbeiten** I don't feel like working; **mir ist, als höre ich ihn** I can hear him now; **wenn er nicht gewesen wäre** but for him; **er ist aus Mexiko** he

selbst

comes from Mexico; *ich bin bei m-m Anwalt gewesen* I have been to see my lawyer; *laß das ~!* stop it!; *laß es ~!* don't bother!; *muß das ~?* do I (you *etc*) have to?; *was soll das ~?* what's that supposed to be?; *(das) mag (or kann) ~* that may be; that's possible; *es sei denn, daß* unless; *nun, wie ist's?* w519ell, what about it?; *und das wäre?* and what might that be?

sein² *pos pron* **1.** *~(e)* his, her, its, *of countries, ships*: her, *indefinite*: one's: *~ Glück machen* make one's fortune; *all ~ Geld* what money he had; *es kostet (gut) ~e 100 Dollar* it will easily cost a hundred dollars. **2.** *~er, ~e, ~(e)s, der, die, das ~e* his, hers, its. **3.** *der, die, das Seine* his (own), hers, her own, its (own); *die Seinen pl* his family; *jedem das Seine* to each his own; *das Seine tun* do one's bit.

Sein *n* (-s; *no pl*) being, existence.

seinerseits ['zaɪnərzaɪts] *adv* as far as he is concerned.

seinerzeit *adv* then, in those days.

'seines'gleichen *indef pron* his (her) equals, F his (her) sort.

'seinet'wegen *adv* **1.** for his sake. **2.** on his behself.**talf.** **3.** because of him.

Seismograph [zaɪsmo'graːf] *m* (-en; -en) seismograph. **Seismologe** [zaɪsmo'loːɡə] *m* (-n; -n) seismologist.

seit [zaɪt] **I** *prep* **1.** since: *~ wann sind Sie hier?* how long have you been here?; *~ damals → seitdem* I. **2.** for: *~ drei Wochen* for (the last) three weeks; *~ langem* for a long time. **II** *conj* **3.** since: *es ist ein Jahr her, ~* it is a year since.

'seit'dem I *adv* since then, ever since. **II** *conj → seit* 3.

Seite ['zaɪtə] *f* (-; -n) **1.** side (*a. fig. aspect, descent, etc*), *a.* direction: *rechte (linke) ~* textil. right (wrong) side; *fig. starke (schwache) ~* weak (strong) point; *an j-s ~* at (or by) s.o.'s side; *~ an ~* side by side; *nach allen ~n* in all directions; *von allen ~n* on all sides; *auf der e-n ~* on the one side (*fig.* hand); *auf j-s ~ sein* side with s.o.; *j-n auf s-e ~ bringen* (or *ziehen*) win s.o. over to one's side; *et. auf die ~ legen* put s.th. by; *j-m nicht von der ~ gehen* stick to s.o. like a leech; *von dieser ~ betrachtet* seen from that angle (or in

that light); *sich von der besten ~ zeigen* show o.s. at one's best; *j-m zur ~ stehen* stand by s.o. **2.** page. **3.** *auf (or von) seiten (gen)* on the part of.

'Seiten|ansicht *f* side view. **~blick** *m* sidelong glance. **~eingang** *m* side entrance. **~flügel** *m* △ wing. **~hieb** *m* (*gegen* at) cut, F sideswipe. **⒉lang** *adj* pages (and pages) of. **~linie** *f* **1.** *sports*: sideline. **2.** → *Nebenlinie*.

'seitens *prep* (*gen*) on the part of, by.

'Seiten|schiff *n* △ aisle. **~sprung** *m* escapade. **~stechen** *n* (-s) (*~ haben* have a) stitch. **~straße** *f* side street. **~streifen** *m* verge (*of road*). **~tasche** *f* side pocket. **~tür** *f* side door. **2verkehrt** *adj* the wrong way round. **~wagen** *m mot.* sidecar. **~wechsel** *m sports*: change of ends. **~wind** *m* crosswind. **~zahl** *f* a) page number, b) number of pages.

'seitlich I *adj* lateral, side. **II** *adv* at the side: **✓ ~** *abrutschen* sideslip.

'seitwärts *adv* **1.** sideways. **2.** at the side.

Sekret [ze'kreːt] *n* (-[e]s; -e) secretion.

Sekretär [zekre'tɛːr] *m* (-s; -e) **1.** secretary. **2.** secretary, bureau. **Sekretariat** [zekreta'rĭaːt] *n* (-[e]s; -e) (secretary's) office. **Sekre'tärin** *f* (-; -nen) secretary.

Sekt [zɛkt] *m* (-[e]s; -e) sparkling wine.

Sekte ['zɛktə] *f* (-; -n) sect.

'Sektglas *n* champagne glass.

Sektierer [zɛk'tiːrər] *m* (-s; -), **sek'tiererisch** *adj* sectarian.

Sektion [zɛk'tsǐoːn] *f* (-; -en) **1.** section, division. **2.** ♂ dissection, autopsy.

Sektor ['zɛktɔr] *m* (-s; -en [-'toːrən]) sector, *fig. a.* field.

sekundär [zekʊn'dɛːr] *adj*, **Sekun'där...** secondary.

Sekunde [ze'kʊndə] *f* (-; -n) second (*a.* ♪ *or* ♪): *auf die ~ pünktlich* on the dot; F *(eine) ~!* just a second.

Se'kundenzeiger *m* second hand.

selb [zɛlp] *adj* same: *zur ~en Zeit* at the same time.

selber ['zɛlbər] → *selbst* I.

selbst [zɛlbst] **I** *pron ich ~* I myself; *sie will es ~ machen* she wants to do it herself (*or* on her own); *er möchte ~ kochen* he wants to do his own cooking; *er war die Höflichkeit ~* he was politeness itself; *von ~* a) (by) itself, automatically, b) of one's own accord; → *verstehen* 9. **II** *adv* even.

Selbst *n* (-; *no pl*) (one's own) self.
'**Selbstachtung** *f* self-respect.
'**selbständig I** *adj* independent, *a.* self-employed: *sich* ~ *machen* set up on one's own. **II** *adv* independently, on one's own: ~ *denken* think for o.s.
'**Selbständigkeit** *f* (-; *no pl*) independence.
'**Selbst|anklage** *f* self-accusation. ~**auslöser** *m phot.* selftimer. ~**bedienungsrestau,rant** *n* self-service restaurant, cafeteria. ~**befriedigung** *f* masturbation. ~**behauptung** *f* self-assertion. ~**beherrschung** *f* self-control. *die* ~ *verlieren a.* lose one's temper. ~**bestätigung** *f* ego-boost: *zu s-r* ~ to prove himself. ~**bestimmungsrecht** *n* right of self-determination. ~**beteiligung** *f insurance*: percentage excess. ~**betrug** *m* self-deception. ⚢**bewußt** *adj* self-confident. ~**bewußtsein** *n* self-confidence. ~**bildnis** *n* self-portrait. ~**darstellung** *f* promotion of one's public image, *contp.* showmanship. ~**diszi,plin** *f* self-discipline. ~**einschätzung** *f* self-assessment. ~**erhaltungstrieb** *m* survival instinct. ~**erkenntnis** *f* self-knowledge. ⚢**ernannt** *adj iro.* self-styled. ~**fahrer** *m* owner-driver.
'**selbstgebacken** *adj* home-made.
'**selbstgefällig** *adj* complacent.
'**Selbstgefälligkeit** *f* (-; *no pl*) complacency.
'**selbstgemacht** *adj* home-made.
'**selbstgerecht** *adj* self-righteous.
'**Selbstgespräch** *n* monologue: ~*e führen* talk to o.s.
'**selbstherrlich** *adj* high-handed.
'**Selbst|hilfe** *f* (-; *no pl*) self-help. ~**hilfegruppe** *f* self-help group. ⚢**klebend** *adj* (self-)adhesive. ~**kon,trolle** *f* self-control. ~**kostenpreis** *m* cost price. ~**kri,tik** *f* self-criticism. ~**laut** *m* vowel.
'**selbstlos** *adj* selfless, unselfish.
'**Selbst|mitleid** *n* self-pity. ~**mord** *m*, ~**mörder** *m* suicide. ⚢**mörderisch** *adj* suicidal. ~**mordversuch** *m* attempted suicide. ~**por,trät** *n* self-portrait. ⚢**sicher** *adj* self-confident. ~**sicherheit** *f* (-; *no pl*) self-confidence.
'**Selbstsucht** *f* (-; *no pl*) selfishness.
'**selbstsüchtig** *adj* selfish.
'**selbsttätig** *adj* automatic.
'**Selbst|täuschung** *f* self-deception.

~**überschätzung** *f* exaggerated opinion of o.s. ~**unterricht** *m* self-instruction. ~**verlag** *m im* ~ published by the author. ~**verleugnung** *f* self-denial. ⚢**verschuldet** *adj* brought about by o.s. ~**versorger** *m* self-supplier: *Bungalows für* ~ self-catering bungalows.
'**selbstverständlich I** *adj* self-evident, obvious, natural: *es ist* ~(*, daß*) it goes without saying (that); *et. als* ~ *betrachten* take s.th. for granted. **II** *adv* of course, naturally. '**Selbstverständlichkeit** *f* (-; -en) matter of course.
'**Selbst|verständnis** *n* self-image: *sein* ~ *a.* the way he sees himself. ~**verteidigung** *f* self-defen/ce (*Am.* -se). ~**vertrauen** *n* self-confidence. ~**verwaltung** *f* self-government. ~**verwirklichung** *f* self-realization. ~**wählferndienst** *m* subscriber trunk dialling, *Am.* direct dialing. ~**wertgefühl** *n* (-[e]s; *no pl*) self-esteem. ⚢**zerstörerisch** *adj* self-destructive. ⚢**zufrieden** *adj* complacent. ~**zufriedenheit** *f* complacency. ~**zweck** *m* end in itself.
selektiv [zelɛk'ti:f] *adj* selective.
Selen [ze'le:n] *n* (-s; *no pl*) 🜍 selenium.
selig ['ze:lıç] *adj* **1.** *eccl.* blessed. **2.** overjoyed, blissful. **3.** late. '**Seligkeit** *f* (-; -en) **1.** *no pl eccl.* salvation, everlasting life. **2.** bliss, ecstasy. '**Seligsprechung** *f* (-; -en) *eccl.* beatification.
Sellerie ['zɛləri] *m* (-s; -[s]) 🌿 a) celeriac, b) celery.
selten ['zɛltən] **I** *adj* rare (*a. fig. beauty etc*), scarce. **II** *adv* seldom, rarely: *höchst* ~ very rarely.
'**Seltenheit** *f* (-; -en) **1.** *no pl* rareness, scarcity. **2.** rarity.
Selterswasser ['zɛltərs-] *n* (-s; ⸚) soda water.
seltsam ['zɛltza:m] *adj* strange, odd.
'**seltsamer'weise** *adv* oddly enough.
'**Seltsamkeit** *f* (-; -en) **1.** *no pl* oddness. **2.** oddity.
Semantik [ze'mantık] *f* (-; *no pl*) semantics. **se'mantisch** [-tıʃ] *adj* semantic.
Semester [ze'mɛstər] *n* (-s; -) semester.
Se'mesterferien *pl* vacation.
Semikolon [zemi'ko:lɔn] *n* (-s; -s, -kola) semicolon.
Seminar [zemi'na:r] *n* (-s; -e) **1.** *univ.* a) seminar, b) department. **2.** *eccl.* seminary.

Semit [ze'mi:t] *m* (-en; -en), **Se'mitin** *f* (-; -nen) Semite.

se'mitisch *adj* Semitic.

Semmel ['zɛməl] *f* (-; -n) roll: F *weggehen wie warme ～n* be selling like hot cakes. **'Semmelbrösel** [-brø:zəl] *pl* breadcrumbs.

Senat [ze'na:t] *m* (-[e]s; -e) **1.** *pol., univ.* senate. **2.** ⚖ division(al court).

Senator [ze'na:tɔr] *m* (-s; -en [zena-'to:rən]) senator.

'Sende|anlage *f* transmitter. **～anstalt** *f* → *Sender* 2. **～bereich** *m* transmission range. **～folge** *f* program(me *Br.*). **～fre,quenz** *f* transmitting frequency. **～leiter(in** *f*) *m* producer.

senden¹ ['zɛndən] *v/t, v/i* (h) ⚡ transmit, *radio:* a. broadcast, *TV* a. telecast.

'senden² *v/t, v/i* (sandte, gesandt, h) send (*dat, an acc* to).

'Sender *m* (-s; -) **1.** transmitter. **2.** radio (*or* television) station.

'Sende|raum *m* studio. **～reihe** *f* series. **～schluß** *m* closedown. **～zeichen** *n* call sign. **～zeit** *f* broadcasting time: *zur besten ～* at prime time.

'Sendung¹ *f* (-; -en) a) transmission, b) program(me *Br.*), *radio:* a. broadcast, *TV* a. telecast: *auf ～ gehen* (*sein*) go (be) on the air.

'Sendung² *f* (-; -en) **1.** ✝ consignment, shipment. **2.** parcel. **3.** *no pl fig.* mission. **'Sendungsbewußtsein** *n* sense of mission.

Senf [zɛnf] *m* (-[e]s; -e) mustard. **～gurke** *f* gherkin (pickled with mustard seeds).

sengen ['zɛŋən] (h) **I** *v/t* singe. **II** *v/i* scorch: **～de Hitze** scorching heat.

senil [ze'ni:l] *adj* senile. **Senilität** [zenili'tɛ:t] *f* (-; *no pl*) senility.

senior ['ze:niɔr] *adj* senior (*abbr.* sen.).

'Senior *m* (-s; -en [ze'niŏ:rən]) a) senior (*a. sports*), b) senior citizen.

'Seniorchef *m* ✝ senior partner.

Senioren|heim [ze'niŏ:rən-] *n* (first--class) home for the aged. **～paß** *m* senior citizen's railcard.

Seniorin [ze'niŏ:rin] (-; -nen) → *Senior*.

'Senkblei *n* (-[e]s; -e) △ plumb-line.

Senke ['zɛŋkə] *f* (-; -n) *geogr.* depression. **'senken** (h) **I** *v/t* **1.** sink (*a.* ⚙), lower (*a. fig. blood pressure, voice, etc*), *fig.* a. reduce (*costs, prices, etc*): *den Kopf ～* bow one's head. **II** *sich ～* **2.**

drop (*a. voice*), ground, *building:* subside, *wall:* sag, *road etc:* dip. **3.** *fig. silence etc:* descend (*über acc* on).

'Senkfüße *pl* ⚕ fallen arches.

'Senkgrube *f* cesspool.

'senkrecht *adj,* **'Senkrechte** *f* (-n; -) vertical, ♉ perpendicular.

'Senkrechtstarter *m* (-s; -) **1.** ✈ vertical takeoff plane. **2.** F whiz(z) kid.

'Senkung *f* (-; -en) **1.** *no pl* a) lowering, *fig.* a. reduction, b) sag(ging) (*of wall*). **2.** dip. **3.** ⚕ descent (*of organ*), sedimentation (*of blood corpuscles*). **4.** *metr.* thesis.

Sensation [zɛnza'tsiŏ:n] *f* (-; -en) sensation. **sensationell** [zɛnzatsiŏ'nɛl] *adj* sensational.

Sensati'ons|gier *f contp.* sensation--seeking. **～mache** *f contp.* sensationalism. **～meldung** *f* sensational report, scoop. **～presse** *f* yellow press. **～pro,zeß** *m* sensational trial.

Sense ['zɛnzə] *f* (-; -n) scythe: F *damit war ～!* that was the end of that!

sensibel [zɛn'zi:bəl] *adj* sensitive (*a. fig. problem etc*). **Sensibilität** [zɛnzibili'tɛ:t] *f* (-; *no pl*) sensitiveness.

Sensor ['zɛnzɔr] *m* (-s; -en [-'zo:rən]) sensor.

sentimental [zɛntimɛn'ta:l] *adj* sentimental. **Sentimentalität** [zɛntimɛntali'tɛ:t] *f* (-; -en) sentimentality.

separat [zepa'ra:t] *adj* separate.

Separatismus [zepara'tɪsmʊs] *m* (-; *no pl*) separatism.

September [zɛp'tɛmbər] *m* (-[s]; -) (*im ～* in) September.

septisch ['zɛptɪʃ] *adj* septic.

serbokroatisch [zɛrbokro'a:tɪʃ] *adj ling.* Serbo-Croat(ian).

Serenade [zere'na:də] *f* (-; -n) serenade.

Serie ['ze:riə] *f* (-; -n) a) series, *TV etc* a. serial, b) set, line, range: ⚙ *in ～ gehen* go into production; *in ～ bauen* (*or herstellen*) produce in series.

seriell [ze'riɛl] *adj computer:* serial.

'Serienausstattung *f* standard fittings.

'Serienbau *m* (-[e]s; *no pl*) serial production.

'serienmäßig *adj* series(-produced), standard (*fittings etc*): *et. ～ herstellen* produce s.th. in series. **'serienreif** *adj* ready to go into production.

'Serienwagen *m* standard-type car.

seriös [zeˈriøːs] *adj* respectable, ✝ *a.* reliable, serious (*applicant, offer, etc*).

Serpentine [zɛrpɛnˈtiːnə] *f* (-; -n) a) serpentine, b) double bend.

Serum [ˈzeːrʊm] *n* (-s; Seren) 🩸 serum.

Service¹ [zɛrˈviːs] *n* (-; -[-ˈviːsə]) service.

Service² [ˈsœrvis] *m* (-; *no pl*) **1.** service. **2.** ◎ (after-sales) service.

servieren [zɛrˈviːrən] (h) **I** *v/t* serve: *es ist serviert!* dinner is served! **II** *v/i* serve, wait at (*Am.* on) table.

Ser'viererin *f* (-; -nen) waitress.

Ser'viertisch *m* serving table.

Ser'vierwagen *m* trolley.

Serviette [zɛrˈvi̯ɛtə] *f* (-; -n) napkin.

servil [zɛrˈviːl] *adj* servile.

Servobremse [ˈzɛrvo-] *f* servo (*or* power) brake. **Servolenkung** *f* servo(-assisted) steering.

Sessel [ˈzɛsəl] *m* (-s; -) easy chair, armchair. **Sessellift** *m* chairlift.

seßhaft [ˈzɛshaft] *adj* settled, *a.* resident: **~ werden** settle (down).

'Seßhaftigkeit *f* (-; *no pl*) settledness.

Set [sɛt] *n*, *m* (-[-s]; -s) **1.** set. **2.** place mat.

'Setzei *n gastr.* fried egg.

setzen [ˈzɛtsən] (h) **I** *v/t* **1.** put, place, *a.* seat (*s.o.*), put, make (*comma etc*), ✍ set, plant: *an Land* ~ put ashore; *das Glas an die Lippen* ~ raise (*or* set) the glass to one's lips; *s-e Unterschrift* ~ *unter* (*acc*) put one's signature to; → *Bild, Denkmal, Druck*¹, *Frist etc.* **2.** *et.* ~ stake (*or* bet) s.th. (*auf acc* on). **3.** *sports:* seed (*player, team*): → *gesetzt* 2. **4.** *print.* set. **II** *sich* ~ **5.** sit down, take a seat: *sich aufs Rad* ~ mount (*or* get on) one's bicycle; *sich ins Auto* ~ get into the car; *sich zu j-m* ~ sit down beside s.o. **6.** *fig.* sink, *grounds, dust, etc:* settle, *impression etc:* sink in. **III** *v/i* **7.** ~ *über* (*acc*) jump (over), clear (*ditch etc*), cross (*river etc*). **8.** place one's bet: ~ *auf* (*acc*) bet on, back, *fig. a.* bank on.

'Setzer *m* (-s; -) compositor, typesetter.

Setze'rei *f* (-; -en) composing room.

'Setzling *m* (-s; -e) ✍ seedling.

'Setzma,schine *f* typesetting machine.

Seuche [ˈzɔy̯çə] *f* (-; -n) epidemic.

'Seuchenbekämpfung *f* epidemic control.

seufzen [ˈzɔy̯ftsən] *v/i* (h) sigh (*über acc* at, *vor* with): ~d with a sigh.

'Seufzer *m* (-s; -) sigh.

Sex [zɛks, sɛks] *m* (-[es]; *no pl*) sex: F ~ *haben* (*or machen*) have sex. **~bombe** *f* F sexpot. **~film** *m* sex film.

Sexismus [zɛˈksɪsmʊs] *m* (-; *no pl*) sexism. **se'xistisch** [-tɪʃ] *adj* sexist.

'Sexprotz *m* F sexual athlete, sexpot.

Sextett [zɛksˈtɛt] *n* (-[e]s; -e) sextet(te).

sexual [zɛˈksǔaːl] → *sexuell*.

Sexu'al... sexual, sex (*life etc*).

Sexu'alerziehung *f* sex education.

Sexualität [zɛksǔaliˈtɛːt] *f* (-; *no pl*) sexuality.

Sexu'al‖kunde *f* (-; *no pl*) *ped.* sex education. **~täter** *m* sex offender. **~verbrechen** *n* sex crime.

sexuell [zɛˈksǔɛl] *adj* sexual.

sexy [ˈzɛksi, ˈsɛksi] *adj* F sexy.

sezieren [zeˈtsiːrən] *v/t* (h) a) dissect (*a. fig.*), b) perform an autopsy on.

Showmaster [ˈʃoːmaːstər] *m* (-s; -) *TV* compère, host.

Sibirien [ziˈbiːri̯ən] *n* (-s) Siberia.

Sibirier [ziˈbiːri̯ər] *m* (-s; -), **Si'birierin** *f* (-; -nen), **si'birisch** [-rɪʃ] *adj* Siberian.

sich [zɪç] *reflex pron* oneself, *3 sg* himself, herself, itself, *pl* themselves, *after prep* him, her, it, *pl* them, *a.* each other, one another: ~ *ansehen* a) look at o.s., b) look at each other; *sie blickte hinter* ~ she looked behind her.

Sichel [ˈzɪçəl] *f* (-; -n) sickle.

sicher [ˈzɪçər] **I** *adj* **1.** a) (*vor dat* from) safe, secure, b) safe (*a.* ◎), secure (*income etc*): *in ~em Abstand* at a safe distance; ~ *ist ~!* better safe than sorry! **2.** reliable, good, sure (*goalkeeper, marksman, etc*), *a.* safe (*driver, method, etc*). **3.** *fig.* sure (*instinct, judg[e]ment, sign, etc*): ~*es Auftreten* self-assurance; *mit ~em Blick* (*Griff*) with a sure eye (hand). **4.** certain, sure: *der ~e Sieg* (*Tod*) certain victory (death); *das ist* ~ a) so much is certain, b) that's a fact; *ist das ~?* is that for certain?; *der Erfolg* (*die Stellung*) *ist ihm* ~ he is sure to succeed (get the job). **5.** *pred* sure, certain: *sind Sie* (*sich dessen*) ~? are you sure (about that)?; → *Sache* 2. **II** *adv* **6.** securely, safely (*etc*): *er fährt sehr* ~ he is a safe driver. **7.** *a. int* certainly, surely, definitely: (*aber or ganz*) ~! (but) of course!, F sure thing!; *du hast* ~ *kein Geld bei dir* I'm sure you have no money on you.

'**sichergehen** *v/i* (*irr, sep*, -ge-, *sn*, → *gehen*) *er wollte ganz* ~ he wanted to be quite sure; *um sicherzugehen* to be on the safe side.

'**Sicherheit** *f* (-; -en) **1.** *no pl* safety (*a.* ⊚), security: *öffentliche (soziale, innere)* ~ public (social, internal) security; *im Flugverkehr* safety in flying; *in* ~ *bringen* get *s.o., s.th.* out of harm's way; *sich in* ~ *bringen* get out of danger, *durch e-n Sprung* jump to safety; *in* ~ *sein* be safe; *zur* ~ → *sicherheitshalber*; → *wiegen*¹ **II. 2.** certainty: *mit* ~ definitely, certainly; *man kann mit* ~ *sagen* it is safe to say. **3.** a) self-assurance, b) competence, skill, c) reliability. **4.** ✝, ✖ security (*gegen* on, against): ~ *leisten* give security, stand bail; *e-m Gläubiger* ~ *bieten* secure a creditor.

'**Sicherheits|abstand** *m* safe distance. ~**beamte** *m* security officer. ~**bindung** *f skiing*: safety binding. ~**faktor** *m* factor of safety. ~**glas** *n* (-es; ⸗er) safety glass. ~**gurt** *m* safety (✔, *mot. a.* seat) belt.

'**sicherheitshalber** *adv* as a precaution, to be on the safe side.

'**Sicherheits|kon,trolle** *f* security check. ~**maßnahme** *f* safety (*pol.* security) measure, precaution. ~**nadel** *f* safety pin. ~**poli,zei** *f* security police. ~**rat** *m* (-es; *no pl*) *pol.* Security Council. ~**risiko** *n* security risk. ~**schloß** *n* safety lock. ~**ven,til** *n* safety valve.

'**sicherlich** → *sicher* 7.

'**sichern** ['zıçərn] *v/t* (h) **1.** (*gegen, vor dat*) secure (*a.* ⊚ *or* ✝), (safe)guard (*both*: against), protect (from): *sich* ~ *vor* (*or gegen*) protect o.s. from, guard against. **2.** put *gun etc* at safety: *gesichert sein* be at safety. **3.** secure: *sich Karten* ~ secure tickets. **4.** → *sicherstellen* 1.

'**sicherstellen** *v/t* (*sep*, -ge-, h) **1.** guarantee, *a.* secure. **2.** seize.

'**Sicherung** *f* (-; -en) **1.** *no pl* a) securing (*etc*, → *sichern*), b) protection. **2.** ⊚ safety device, safety (catch) (*on gun etc*). **3.** ⚡ fuse.

'**Sicherungskasten** *m* ⚡ fuse box.

'**Sicht** [zıçt] *f* (-; *no pl*) **1.** a) sight (*a.* ⊚), b) view, c) visibility: *in* (*außer*) ~ in (out of) sight (*a. fig.*); *in* ~ *kommen* come into view; *fig. auf weite* (*or lange*) ~ on a long-term basis, *a.* in the long run; *auf kurze* ~ in the short term; *aus s-r* ~ from his point of view, as he sees it. **2.** ✝ (*fällig*) *bei* ~ (due) at sight; *60 Tage nach* ~ *payable* at sixty days' sight.

'**sichtbar** *adj* visible, *a.* noticeable, evident, *a.* marked: ~ *machen* show; ~ *werden* appear, become visible.

'**Sichtbe,ton** *m* fair-faced concrete.

'**sichten** ['zıçtən] *v/t* (h) **1.** sight. **2.** sift, look through, sort out.

'**Sichtflug** *m* contact flight.

'**Sichtgerät** *n* visual display unit.

'**sichtlich** *adj* visible, evident.

'**Sicht|verhältnisse** *pl* (*gute, schlechte* ~ high, low) visibility. ~**vermerk** *m* **1.** visa. **2.** ✝ endorsement. ~**wechsel** *m* ✝ sight draft. ~**weite** *f* visual range: *in* ~ (with)in sight.

sickern ['zıkərn] *v/i* (sn) seep, ooze.

sie [zi:] *pers pron* she, *thing*: it, *pl* they, (*acc*) her, it, *pl* them.

Sie¹ *polite address*: you.

Sie² *f* (-; -s) F she, female.

Sieb [zi:p] *n* (-[e]s; -e) sieve, strainer, ⊚ screen, ✂ filter: *ein Gedächtnis wie ein* ~ a memory like a sieve.

'**Siebdruck** *m* (-[e]s; -e) **1.** silk-screen print. **2.** *no pl* silk-screen printing.

sieben¹ ['zi:bən] *v/t* (h) **1.** sift, sieve. **2.** → *aussieben*.

'**sieben**² *adj*, '**Sieben** *f* (-; -) seven.

'**Sieben'sachen** *pl* F things, belongings.

'**siebente** *adj*, '**Siebentel** *n* (-s; -) seventh. '**siebentens** *adv* seventh.

siebte ['zi:ptə] → *siebente*.

siebzehn(t) ['zi:p-] *adj* seventeen(th).

siebzig ['zi:tsıç] *adj* seventy. '**Siebzig** *f* (-; -en) seventy: *er ist Mitte* (*der*) ~ he is in his mid-seventies. **siebziger** ['zi:ptsıgər] *adj* *die* ~ *Jahre* the seventies. '**Siebziger** *m* (-s; -) man in his seventies, septuagenarian. '**Siebzigerin** *f* (-; -nen) woman in her seventies, septuagenarian. '**siebzigst** *adj* seventieth.

Siechtum ['zi:çtu:m] *n* (-s; *no pl*) lingering illness, invalidism.

siedeln ['zi:dəln] *v/i* (h) settle.

sieden ['zi:dən] (h) **I** *v/i* boil: ~*d heiß* boiling hot. **II** *v/t* boil gently.

'**Siedepunkt** *m* (-[e]s; *no pl*) boiling point.

Siedler ['zi:dlər] *m* (-s; -), '**Siedlerin** *f* (-;

-nen) settler. **'Siedlung** f (-; -en) a) settlement, b) housing estate.

Sieg [zi:k] m (-[e]s; -e) (*über acc* over) victory, *sports etc*: win, *fig*. triumph: *den ~ davontragen* carry the day.

Siegel ['zi:gəl] n (-s; -) a) seal, b) signet: *fig. unter dem ~ der Verschwiegenheit* under the seal of secrecy.

'Siegellack m sealing wax.

siegeln ['zi:gəln] v/t (h) seal.

'Siegelring m signet ring.

siegen ['zi:gən] v/i (h) (*über acc*) be victorious (over), *sports etc*: win (against), *fig*. triumph (over), win (over).

Sieger ['zi:gər] m (-s; -) victor, *sport etc*: winner. **'Siegerehrung** f *sports*: presentation ceremony.

'Siegerin f (-; -nen) → *Sieger*.

'Siegermächte pl victorious powers.

'Siegerpo,dest n (victory) rostrum.

'sieges|bewußt, ~sicher adj confident of victory, *fig*. sure of one's success.

'Siegeszug m *fig*. triumphant advance.

'siegreich adj victorious, triumphant.

siezen ['zi:tsən] v/t (h) *j-n ~* address s.o. as "Sie".

Signal [zɪ'gna:l] n (-[e]s; -e) signal.

signalisieren [zɪgnali'zi:rən] v/t, v/i (h) signal.

Signatarmacht [zɪgna'ta:r-] f *pol*. signatory power (*e-s Vertrages* to a treaty).

Signatur [zɪgna'tu:r] f (-; -en) **1.** signature. **2.** shelfmark (*of book*). **3.** conventional sign. **signieren** [zɪ'gni:rən] v/t (h) sign, *author*: autograph.

Silbe ['zɪlbə] f (-; -n) syllable: *fig. k-e ~* not a word.

'Silbentrennung f syllabification.

Silber ['zɪlbər] n (-s; *no pl*) **1.** silver. **2.** silver plate.

'Silber|besteck n silver (cutlery). **~blick** m F (slight) squint. **~distel** f ❀ carline thistle. **~hochzeit** f silver wedding. **~me,daille** f silver medal. **~me,daillengewinner(in** f) m silver medal(l)ist.

'silbern adj (of) silver, *fig*. silvery.

'Silber|pa,pier n tin foil. **~streifen** m *~ am Horizont* silver lining. **~waren** pl silverware.

Silhouette [zi'lŭɛtə] f (-; -n) silhouette.

Silikat [zili'ka:t] n (-[e]s; -e) silicate.

Silikon [zili'ko:n] n (-s; -e) silicon.

Silo ['zi:lo] m (-s; -s) silo.

Silvester [zɪl'vɛstər] m, n (-s; -), **~abend** m New Year's Eve.

simpel ['zɪmpəl] adj simple.

Sims [zɪms] m, n (-es; -e) **1.** ledge. **2.** sill.

Simulant [zimu'lant] m (-en; -en) malingerer. **Simulator** [zimu'la:tor] m (-s; -en [-la'to:rən]) ❂, ✗ simulator.

simulieren [zimu'li:rən] (h) **I** v/t sham, feign, a. ❂ simulate. **II** v/i malinger.

simultan [zimul'ta:n] adj simultaneous.

Simul'tan|dolmetschen n (-s) simultaneous translation. **~dolmetscher** m simultaneous translator.

Sinfonie [zɪnfo'ni:] f (-; -n) symphony. **~or,chester** n symphony orchestra.

sinfonisch [zɪn'fo:nɪʃ] adj symphonic.

singen ['zɪŋən] v/t, v/i (sang, gesungen, h) sing.

Single¹ ['sɪŋl] f (-; -[s]) (*record*) single.

'Single² m (-[s]; -s) single (person).

'Single³ n (-[s]; -[s]) *tennis etc*: singles.

'Singstimme f singing voice.

Singular ['zɪŋgula:r] m (-s; -e) *ling*. (*im ~* in the) singular.

'Singvogel m songbird.

sinken ['zɪŋkən] v/i (sank, gesunken, sn) sink (*a. fig.*), *sun*: a. set, *fig. prices, temperature, etc*: drop (*auf acc* to), fall, go down: *fig. er ist tief gesunken* he has sunk very low; *~ lassen* lower, drop (*a. voice*); → *Mut, Wert* 1 *etc*.

Sinn [zɪn] m (-[e]s; -e) **1.** *physiol*. sense: *fig. sechster ~* sixth sense; *s-e fünf ~e beisammen haben* have one's wits about one. **2.** *pl* a) mind, b) consciousness: *sie war wie von ~en* she was quite beside herself (*vor* with); *bist du von ~en?* are you out of your mind? **3.** *no pl* mind: *et. im ~ haben* have s.th. in mind, intend (*to do*) s.th.; *damit habe ich nichts im ~* I don't want any of that; *j-m in den ~ kommen* occur to s.o. **4.** *no pl* (*für*) a) sense (of), appreciation (of), b) taste (of), c) interest (in): *~ für Musik* an ear for music; *~ für das Schöne* an eye for beauty; *~ für Humor* a sense of humo(u)r; *das ist ganz nach s-m ~* that's just what he likes; *das war ganz in m-m ~e* that was just what I would have done. **5.** *no pl* a) sense, meaning, b) (basic) idea: *im weiteren (engeren) ~(e)* in a wider (narrower) sense; *im wahrsten ~(e) des Wortes* literally; *in gewissem ~* in a sense; *im ~e des Ge-*

setzes as defined by the law; *der ~ des Lebens* the meaning of life; *das ergibt* (F *macht*) *k-n ~* that makes no sense; *dem ~ nach* → *sinngemäß.* **6.** *no pl* sense, purpose: *~ und Zweck* (aim and) object; *das hat k-n ~* it's no use, it's pointless; *das ist* (*nicht*) *der ~ der Sache!* that's (not) the idea!

'**Sinnbild** *n* symbol.

'**sinnbildlich** *adj* symbolic(al).

sinnen ['zɪnən] *v/i* (sann, gesonnen, h) (*über acc* [up]on) meditate, reflect: *~ auf* (*acc*) contemplate, plan, *b.s.* plot.

'**Sinnen** *n* (-s) thoughts: *all sein ~ und Trachten* his every thought and wish.

'**sinnenfroh** *adj* sensuous.

'**Sinnenlust** *f* (-; *no pl*) sensual pleasure.

'**sinnentstellend** *adj* distorting (the meaning): *~ sein* distort the meaning.

'**Sinnes|or,gan** *n* sense organ. *~reiz m* sense stimulus. *~täuschung* *f* hallucination. *~wahrnehmung* *f* sensory perception. *~wandel m* change of heart.

'**sinnfällig** *adj* obvious, clear.

'**sinngemäß** *adj* giving the gist (*of s.th.*), *esp.* ⚖ analogous: *et. ~ übersetzen* give the analogous meaning of s.th.

sinnieren [zɪ'niːrən] *v/i* (h) F ruminate (*über acc* on).

sinnig ['zɪnɪç] *adj a. iro.* clever.

'**sinnlich** *adj* sensual (*impression, pleasure, etc*), *a.* sensuous: *~e Wahrnehmung* sensory perception.

'**Sinnlichkeit** *f* (-; *no pl*) sensuality.

'**sinnlos** *adj* a) senseless, meaningless, b) absurd, c) useless: *~ betrunken* blind drunk. '**Sinnlosigkeit** *f* (-; *no pl*) senselessness (*etc*), absurdity.

'**sinnreich** *adj* ingenious, clever.

'**sinnverwandt** *adj* synonymous: *~es Wort* synonym.

'**sinnvoll** *adj* **1.** meaningful. **2.** a) useful, b) wise. **3.** ingenious, clever.

Sintflut ['zɪnt-] *f* (-; *no pl*) *bibl. the* Flood.

Sinus ['ziːnʊs] *m* (-; -, -se) **1.** Å sine. **2.** *anat.* sinus. '**Sinuskurve** *f* sine curve.

Siphon ['ziːfõ:] *m* (-s; -s) siphon.

Sippe ['zɪpə] *f* (-; -n) **1.** family, tribe. **2.** → '**Sippschaft** *f* (-; -en) *contp.* a) clan, b) gang, lot.

Sirene [zi're:nə] *f* (-; -n) siren.

Sirup ['ziːrʊp] *m* (-s; -e) syrup, treacle, *Am.* molasses.

Sitte ['zɪtə] *f* (-; -n) **1.** custom, *a.* practice,

habit: *~n und Gebräuche* manners and customs. **2.** *pl* a) morals, b) manners.

'**Sittenlehre** *f* ethics.

'**sittenlos** *adj* immoral, dissolute.

'**Sittenlosigkeit** *f* (-; *no pl*) immorality.

'**Sittenpoli,zei** *f* vice squad.

'**Sittenrichter** *m* moralizer.

'**sittenstreng** *adj* puritanical.

'**sittenwidrig** *adj* immoral.

Sittich ['zɪtɪç] *m* (-s; -e) *zo.* parakeet.

'**sittlich** *adj* moral, ethical.

'**Sittlichkeit** *f* (-; *no pl*) morality, morals.

'**Sittlichkeits|verbrechen** *n* sex crime. *~verbrecher* *m* sex offender.

Situation [zitŭa'tsĭoːn] *f* (-; -en) situation, position: *sich der ~ gewachsen zeigen* rise to the occasion.

Situati'onskomik *f* situational comedy.

Sitz [zɪts] *m* (-es; -e) **1.** a) seat (*a. fig.*), b) (place of) residence, ✝ headquarters: *Firma mit ~ in London* London-based firm; *die Zuschauer von den ~en reißen* electrify the audience. **2.** *no pl* fit.

'**Sitzecke** *f* corner unit.

sitzen ['zɪtsən] *v/i* (saß, gesessen, h) **1.** sit, *bird:* perch: *~ bleiben* remain seated; *sie saßen beim Essen* they were having lunch; *im Parlament ~* have a seat in Parliament; *an e-r Arbeit* (*bei e-m Glas Wein*) *~* be sitting over a task (a glass of wine); F *e-n ~ haben* be soused; *~de Lebensweise* sedentary life; → *Patsche etc.* **2.** be, *firm etc:* have one's headquarters (*in dat* in). **3.** sit, fit. **4.** F (*im Gefängnis*) *~* do time, be in jail. **5.** F *blow, remark, etc:* hit home. **6.** F stick (in the mind).

'**sitzenbleiben** *v/i* (*irr, sep, -ge-, sn,* → *bleiben*) F **1.** *ped.* have to repeat the year. **2.** *woman:* be left on the shelf. **3.** *~ auf* (*dat*) be left with *goods.*

'**sitzenlassen** *v/t* (*irr, sep, pp* sitzenlassen, h, → *lassen*) F **1.** *j-n ~* a) leave s.o. in the lurch, b) walk out on s.o., jilt s.o. **2.** *das lasse ich nicht auf mir sitzen!* I won't stand for that!

'**Sitz|gelegenheit** *f* seat. *~gruppe* *f* three-piece suite. *~ordnung* *f* seating plan. *~platz m* seat. *~streik m* sit-down strike.

'**Sitzung** *f* (-; -en) meeting, conference, *parl.* sitting, session, ⚖ hearing.

'**Sitzungs|bericht** *m* minutes (of the meeting). *~peri,ode* *f parl.* session.

~saal m conference room, parl. chamber. **~zimmer** n conference room.

Sizilianer [zitsi'liːanər] m (-s; -) Sicilian. **Sizili'anerin** f (-; -nen) Sicilian (woman or girl). **sizili'anisch** adj Sicilian.

Sizilien [zi'tsiːliən] n (-s) Sicily.

Skala ['skaːla] f (-; -len, -s) 1. ♩, ◉ scale. 2. fig. range.

Skalp [skalp] m (-s; -e) scalp.

Skalpell [skal'pɛl] n (-s; -e) ✻ scalpel.

skalpieren [skal'piːrən] v/t (h) scalp.

Skandal [skan'daːl] m (-s; -e) scandal, a. disgrace, shame. **~blatt** n scandal sheet.

skandalös [skanda'løːs] adj scandalous.

Skan'dalpresse f (-; no pl) gutter press.

Skandinavien [skandi'naːviən] n (-s) Scandinavia. **Skandi'navier** m (-s; -), **Skandi'navierin** f (-; -nen), **skandi'navisch** [-vɪʃ] adj Scandinavian.

Skat [skaːt] m (-[e]s; -e, -s) skat.

Skelett [ske'lɛt] n (-[e]s; -e) skeleton.

Skepsis ['skɛpsɪs] f (-; no pl) scepticism, Am. skepticism. **Skeptiker** ['skɛptikər] m (-s; -) sceptic, Am. skeptic. **'skeptisch** adj sceptical, Am. skeptic.

Ski [ʃiː] m (-s; -er, -) ski: **~ fahren, ~ laufen** ski.

'Ski|anzug m ski suit. **~ausrüstung** f skiing gear. **~bob** m skibob. **~fahren** n skiing. **~fahrer** m skier. **~fliegen** n, **~flug** m ski flying. **~gebiet** n skiing area. **~hütte** f ski hut, ski lodge. **~kurs** m skiing course. **~langlauf** m cross-country skiing. **~lauf** m, **~laufen** n skiing. **~läufer** m skier. **~lehrer** m skiing instructor. **~lift** m ski lift. **~piste** f ski run, piste. **~schuh** m ski boot. **~sport** m skiing. **~springen** n, **~sprung** m ski jumping. **~stiefel** m ski boot. **~stock** m ski pole. **~träger** m mot. ski rack. **~wandern** n ski hiking. **~zirkus** m F ski circus (or circuit).

Skizze ['skɪtsə] f (-; -n) sketch.

'Skizzenbuch n sketchbook.

'skizzenhaft adj sketchy.

skizzieren [skɪ'tsiːrən] v/t (h) sketch, fig. a. outline.

Sklave ['sklaːvə] m (-n; -n) slave. **'Sklavenhandel** m slave trade. **Sklave'rei** f (-; no pl) slavery. **'Sklavin** f (-; -nen) slave. **'sklavisch** adj slavish.

Sklerose [skle'roːzə] f (-; -n) ✻ sclerosis.

Skonto ['skɔnto] m, n (-s; -s) ✝ (cash) discount.

Skorbut [skɔr'buːt] m (-[e]s; no pl) ✻ scurvy.

Skorpion [skɔr'pioːn] m (-s; -e) 1. zo. scorpion. 2. no pl astr. ([ein] ~ sein be [a]) Scorpio.

Skrupel ['skruːpəl] m (-s; -) scruple. **'skrupellos** adj unscrupulous.

Skulptur [skʊlp'tuːr] f (-; -en) sculpture.

skurril [skʊ'riːl] adj bizarre.

Slalom ['slaːlom] m (-s; -s) skiing: slalom. **~läufer(in** f) m slalom racer.

Slawe ['slaːvə] m (-n; -n), **'Slawin** f (-; -nen), **'slawisch** adj Slav.

Slip [slɪp] m (-s; -s) briefs, panties. **'Slipeinlage** f panty liner.

Smaragd [sma'rakt] m (-[e]s; -e), **sma'ragdgrün** adj emerald.

Smog [smɔk] m (-[s]; -s) smog.

'Smog,larm m smog alert.

Smoking ['smoːkɪŋ] m (-s; -s) dinner jacket, Am. tuxedo.

Snob [snɔp] m (-s; -s) snob. **Snobismus** [sno'bɪsmʊs] m (-; -men) snobbery. **sno'bistisch** [-tɪʃ] adj snobbish.

so [zoː] **I** adv 1. so, so much: **nicht ~** einfach not so easy; **das hat ihn ~** gefreut, daß that pleased him so much that. 2. like this (or that), this (or that) way, thus: **~ ist es!** that's how it is!; **~** ist das Leben! such is life!; **~ oder ~** a) one way or another, b) anyway. 3. such: **~ etwas** such a thing; **~ ein** Trottel! what a fool! 4. about: **~ alle acht** Tage every week or so. **II** conj **~ daß** so that, so as to inf; **~ leid es mir tut** however much I regret it. **III** int **~!** a) (all) right!, okay!, b) that's that!; **~, ~!** well, well!; **~?** really?; **(na) ~ was!** you don't say!; **ach ~!** oh(, I see)!

so'bald conj as soon as.

Söckchen ['zœkçən] n (-s; -) ankle sock, Am. anklet.

Socke ['zɔkə] f (-; -n) sock: F **sich auf die ~n machen** buzz off; **von den ~n sein** be flabbergasted, be dum(b)founded.

Sockel ['zɔkəl] m (-s; -) pedestal, a. ♩, ◉ base. **~betrag** m basic allowance.

'Sockenhalter m suspender, Am. garter.

Soda ['zoːda] f (-; no pl), n (-s; no pl) soda. **'Sodawasser** n soda water.

Sodbrennen ['zoːt-] n (-s; no pl) ✻ heartburn.

so'eben adv just (now).

Sofa ['zoːfa] n (-s; -s) sofa, settee.

so'**fern** *conj* a) if, so far as, b) provided that: ~ *nicht* unless.

soff [zɔf] *pret of* **saufen**.

so'**fort** *adv* at once, instantly, immediately, right away: *ab ~* a) as of now, b) *a.* (*ab*) *~ gültig* effective immediately; ✝ *~zahlbar* spot cash; *er war ~ tot* he died instantaneously.

So'**fort|bildkamera** *f* instant camera. ~**hilfe** *f* immediate (*or* emergency) aid.

So'**fortig** *adj* immediate, prompt.

So'**fort|maßnahme** *f* immediate action. ~**pro,gramm** *n* crash program(me *Br.*).

Software ['sɔftwɛə] *f* (-; -s) software.

Sog *m* (-[e]s; -e) suction, ⚓, ⚓ *a.* wake (*a. fig.*).

so'**gar** *adv* even.

'**sogenannt** *adj* so-called.

Sohle ['zo:lə] *f* (-; -n) **1.** sole. **2.** bottom (*of valley etc*), ⚒ floor.

Sohn [zo:n] *m* (-[e]s; ⸚e) son.

Soja|bohne ['zo:ja-] *f* soybean. ~**mehl** *n* soybean flour. ~**soße** *f* soy sauce.

so'**lang(e)** *adv* as long as.

Solar,gie [zo'la:r-] *f* solar energy.

Solarium [zo'la:rĭʊm] *n* (-s; -rien) solarium.

So'**larzelle** *f* solar cell.

solch [zɔlç] *pron or adj* such.

'**solcher'lei** *adj* of such kind, such.

Sold [zɔlt] *m* (-[e]s; -e) pay.

Soldat [zɔl'da:t] *m* (-en; -en) soldier, *a.* serviceman.

Sol'**datenfriedhof** *m* war cemetery.

sol'**datisch** *adj* soldierlike, military.

'**Soldbuch** *n* ⚔ pay book.

Söldner ['zœltnər] *m* (-s; -) mercenary.

Sole ['zo:lə] *f* (-; -n) brine.

solidarisch [zoli'da:rɪʃ] **I** *adj* solidary, ✝, ⚎ joint (and several): *sich ~ erklären mit → solidarisieren.* **II** *adv* in solidarity, ✝, ⚎ jointly (and severally).

solidarisieren [zolidari'zi:rən] *sich ~ mit* (h) declare one's solidarity with, be solidly behind. **Solidarität** [zolidari-'tɛ:t] *f* (-; *no pl*) solidarity.

solide [zo'li:də] *adj* solid (*a. fig. person*), *fig. a.* steady (*person etc*), *a.* sound (*knowledge etc*), *a.* reliable (*firm*), reasonable (*price*), good (*profession*).

Solist [zo'lɪst] *m* (-en; -en), **So'listin** *f* (-; -nen) soloist.

Soll [zɔl] *n* (-[s]; -[s]) **1.** debit: *~ und Haben* debit and credit. **2.** (*production*

etc) target, quota: *sein ~ erfüllen* reach the target, *fig.* do one's bit.

sollen ['zɔlən] (sollte, sollen, h) **I** *v/aux* **1.** be to: *ich soll dir ausrichten* I am to tell you; *soll ich kommen?* shall I come?; *er soll nur kommen!* just let him come!; *was soll ich tun?* what should I do? **2.** *moral obligation:* *ich hätte hingehen ~* I ought to have gone; *ich hätte es wissen ~* I should have known; *du hättest das nicht tun ~* you shouldn't have done that! **3.** *intention:* *hier soll ein Schwimmbad entstehen* a swimming pool is to be built here; *es soll nicht wieder vorkommen* it won't happen again; *was soll das sein?* what's that supposed to be?; *es sollte ein Scherz sein* it was meant as (*or* supposed to be) a joke. **4.** *rumo(u)r:* *er soll reich sein* he is said to be rich; *die Rebellen ~ die Macht übernommen haben* the rebels are reported to have seized power. **5.** *possibility:* *sollte es wahr sein?* could it be true?; *sollte sie kommen* in case (*or* if) she should come. **6.** *fate:* *er sollte nie mehr zurückkehren* he was never to return again; *es sollte alles ganz anders kommen* things were to turn out quite differently; *ein Jahr sollte vergehen, bis ...* a year was to pass till ...; *es hat nicht ~ sein* it was not to be. **II** *v/i* (*pp* gesollt) *was soll ich hier?* what am I here for?; *was soll ich damit?* what am I to do with it?; *soll* (*sollte*) *ich?* shall (should) I?; *weshalb sollte ich* (*auch*)? why should I?; *was soll das?* a) what's the idea?, b) what's the use?, c) F *a.* *was soll's?* so what?

'**Soll-Leistung** *f* ⚙ nominal output.

'**Soll-Wert** *m* ⚙ rated value.

solo ['zo:lo] *adj* solo, F *fig. a.* alone.

'**Solo** *n* (-s; -s, Soli) solo, *sports:* solo attempt (*or* run).

'**Solostimme** *f* solo voice (*or* part).

'**Solotänzer(in** *f*) *m* solo dancer.

solvent [zɔl'vɛnt] *adj* ✝ solvent.

somatisch [zo'ma:tɪʃ] *adj* somatic.

so'**mit** *adv* consequently, thus.

Sommer ['zɔmər] *m* (-s; -) summer: *im ~* in (the) summer; *im nächsten ~* next summer. ~**ferien** *pl* summer holidays (*Am.* vacation). ~**kleidung** *f* summer clothes, ✝ summer wear.

'**sommerlich** *adj* summerly, summery.
'**Sommer|loch** *n* F *fig.* silly season. ~**reifen** *m mot.* normal tyre (*Am.* tire). ~**spiele** *pl Olympische* ~ Summer Olympics. ~**sprosse** *f* freckle.
'**sommersprossig** *adj* freckled.
'**Sommerzeit** *f* summer time, *a.* daylight saving time.
Sonate [zo'naːtə] *f* (-; -n) ♪ sonata.
Sonde ['zɔndə] *f* (-; -n) ♂, *astronautics*: probe, *meteor.*, *radar*: sonde.
Sonder... ['zɔndər-] special. ~**anfertigung** *f* special design, custom-made article (*etc*). ~**angebot** *n* special offer. ~**ausgabe** *f* **1.** special edition. **2.** extra (expenditure).
'**sonderbar** *adj* strange, odd, peculiar.
'**sonderbarer'weise** *adv* oddly enough.
'**Sonder|beauftragte** *m, f* special representative. ~**beilage** *f* (special) supplement, inset. ~**berichterstatter** *m* special correspondent. ~**bevollmächtigte** *m, f* plenipotentiary. ~**druck** *m* (-[e]s; -e) offprint. ~**fall** *m* special case. ~**interesse** *n* private interest.
'**sonderlich** **I** *adj* special: *ohne* ~*e Mühe* without any great effort. **II** *adv* **nicht** ~ not particularly, not much, not very.
Sonderling ['zɔndərlɪŋ] *m* (-s; -e) eccentric, crank.
'**Sonder|marke** *f* special issue. ~**maschine** *f* ✈ special flight. ~**meldung** *f* special announcement. ~**müll** *m* toxic waste.
sondern ['zɔndərn] *conj* but: *nicht nur ..., ~ auch ...* not only ..., but also ...
'**Sonder|nummer** *f* special edition. ~**recht** *n* privilege. ~**regelung** *f* special arrangement. ~**schule** *f* special school (for handicapped or maladjusted children). ~**sitzung** *f* special session. ~**stempel** *m* special postmark. ~**wunsch** *m* special request. ~**zug** *m* special train. ~**zulage** *f* special bonus.
sondieren [zɔn'diːrən] **I** *v/t* ♂ *or fig.* probe, sound (out). **II** *v/i fig.* put out feelers. **Son'dierungsgespräch** *n* exploratory talk.
Sonett [zo'nɛt] *n* (-[e]s; -e) sonnet.
'**Sonnabend** *m* (*am* ~ on) Saturday.
'**sonnabends** *adv* on Saturday(s).
Sonne ['zɔnə] *f* (-; *no pl*) sun: *an* (*or in*) *der* ~ in the sun.
sonnen ['zɔnən] *sich* ~ (h) sun o.s., bask

in the sun, *fig.* bask (*in dat* in).
'**Sonnenaufgang** *m* (*bei* ~ at) sunrise.
'**Sonnenbad** *n* sunbath: *ein* ~ *nehmen* → '**sonnenbaden** *v/i* (*only inf and pp* sonnengebadet, h) sunbathe.
'**Sonnen|bank** *f* sun bed. ~**blende** *f* *phot.* lens hood. ~**blume** *f* sunflower. ~**brand** *m* sunburn. ~**brille** *f* (*e-e* ~ a pair of) sunglasses. ~**creme** *f* sun(tan) cream. ~**dach** *n* sun blind, *mot.* sunshine roof. ~**deck** *n* ⚓ sun deck. ~**energie** *f* solar energy. ~**finsternis** *f* eclipse of the sun. ~**fleck** *m* sunspot. ~**hut** *m* sunhat. ~**kollektor** *m* solar panel. ~**kraftwerk** *n* solar power plant. ~**licht** *n* (*bei* ~ in) sunlight. ~**öl** *n* suntan oil. ~**schein** *m* sunshine. ~**schirm** *m* sunshade, *for ladies*: parasol. ~**schutzcreme** *f* sun (filter) cream. ~**seite** *f a. fig.* sunny side. ~**stich** *m* sunstroke. ~**strahl** *m* sunbeam. ~**system** *n* solar system. ~**uhr** *f* sundial. ~**untergang** *m* (*bei* ~ at) sunset. ~**wende** *f* solstice. ~**zelle** *f* solar cell.
'**sonnig** *adj a. fig.* sunny.
'**Sonntag** *m* (*am* ~ on) Sunday. '**sonntäglich** *adj* Sunday. '**sonntags** *adv* on Sunday(s), on a Sunday.
'**Sonntags|anzug** *m* Sunday best. ~**beilage** *f* Sunday supplement. ~**dienst** *m* ~ *haben* be on Sunday duty, *pharmacy*: be open on Sunday(s). ~**fahrer** *m contp.* Sunday driver. ~**kind** *n er ist ein* ~ he was born on a Sunday (*fig.* under a lucky star). ~**maler** *m* Sunday painter.
'**sonnverbrannt** *adj* (deeply) tanned.
sonor [zo'noːr] *adj* sonorous.
sonst [zɔnst] *adv* **1.** otherwise, or, or else. **2.** usually, normally: *wie* ~ as usual. **3.** otherwise, apart from that. **4.** else: *wer* ~? who else?; ~ *noch etwas?* anything else?; *nirgends* ~ nowhere else. **5.** always: *alles war wie* ~ everything was as it used to be. '**sonstig** *adj* other.
'**sonstjemand** *pron* F a) somebody else, b) anybody. '**sonstwas** *pron* F a) something else, b) anything. '**sonstwie** *adv* F some other way. '**sonstwo(hin)** *adv* F somewhere else.
so'oft *conj* whenever: ~ *du willst* as often as you like.
Sopran [zo'praːn] *m* (-s; -e) soprano.
Sopranist [zopra'nɪst] *m* (-en; -en), **Sopra'nistin** *f* (-; -nen) soprano.

Sorge ['zɔrgə] f (-; -n) **1.** a) worry, concern, b) trouble: *finanzielle (berufliche)* ~*n* financial (professional) worries (*or* problems); *j-m* ~*n machen* worry s.o., cause s.o. trouble; *sich* ~*n machen* a) *um* be worried about, b) *daß* be concerned about; *mach dir k-e* ~*n!*, *k-e* ~*!* don't worry!; *lassen Sie das m-e* ~ *sein!* leave that to me!; → *gering*. **2.** care: ~ *tragen für* → *sorgen* I.

sorgen ['zɔrgən] (h) I *v/i* ~ *für* a) see to, take care of, ensure, b) look after, c) provide; *dafür* ~*, daß* see to it that; *dafür werde ich* ~ I'll see to that; *für sich selbst* ~ fend for o.s.; *für ihn ist gesorgt* he's taken care of. II *sich* ~ *(um, wegen)* about be worried, worry.

'sorgenfrei *adj* free from care(s), carefree. **'Sorgenkind** *n* problem child.

'sorgenvoll *adj* life etc full of worries, *a.* worried (*face, look, etc*).

'Sorgerecht *n* (-[e]s; *no pl*) custody (*für* of).

'Sorgfalt ['zɔrkfalt] f (-; *no pl*) care: *große* ~ *verwenden auf* (*acc*) take great pains over. **'sorgfältig** [-fɛltɪç] *adj* careful.

'sorglos *adj* **1.** careless. **2.** carefree.
'Sorglosigkeit f (-; *no pl*) carelessness.

'sorgsam ~ *sorgfältig*.

Sorte ['zɔrtə] f (-; -n) sort, kind, type, ✝ brand, *a.* quality: ~*n* foreign exchange; *übelster* ~ of the worst kind.

sortieren [zɔr'ti:rən] *v/t* (h) sort, *a.* grade, *a.* size. **Sortiment** [zɔrti'mɛnt] *n* (-[e]s; -e) **1.** range. **2.** → **Sortimentsbuchhandel** *m* retail book trade.

so'sehr *conj* ~ *(auch)* however much.

Soße ['zo:sə] f (-; -n) **1.** a) sauce, b) gravy, c) dressing. **2.** F juice, goo.
'Soßenschüssel f sauceboat.

Souffleur [zu'flø:r] *m* (-s; -e) prompter.
Souf'fleurkasten *m* prompt box.
Souffleuse [zu'flø:zə] f (-; -n) prompter.
soufflieren [zu'fli:rən] *v/t, v/i* (h) *j-m* ~ prompt s.o.

'sound|'so *adv* F so and so: ~ *viel* so much; ~ *viele* so many; ~ *oft* time and again; *Herr* ♀ Mr what's-his-name. ~**so'vielt** *adj* F **1.** *am* ~*en* on such and such a date. **2.** umpteenth.

Soutane [zu'ta:nə] f (-; -n) cassock.
Souterrain [zutɛ'rɛ̃:] *n* (-s; -s) basement.
Souvenir [zuvə'ni:r] *n* (-s; -s) souvenir.
souverän [zuvə'rɛ:n] *adj* sovereign, fig.

superior, *a. adv* in superior style.
Souveränität [zuvərɛni'tɛ:t] f (-; *no pl*) sovereignty.

so'viel I *conj* ~ *ich weiß* as far as I know; ~ *ich gehört habe* from what I have heard. II *adj and adv* so much: ~ *wie* as much as; *doppelt* ~ twice as much; ~ *steht fest* one thing is certain.

so'weit I *conj* as far as (*I know etc*). II *adv* ~ *sein* be ready; *es ist* ~ *fertig* it's more or less finished; *es ist* ~*!* a) it's time!, b) here goes!

so'wenig I *adv* not more (*als* than): ~ *wie möglich* as little as possible. II *conj* however little.

so'wie *conj* **1.** as soon as. **2.** as well as.
sowie'so *adv* **1.** anyway, in any case. **2.** F *(das)* ~*!* that goes without saying!

Sowjet [zɔ'vjɛt] *m* (-s; -s) *hist.* Soviet.
sowjetisch [zɔ'vjɛtɪʃ] *adj hist.* Soviet.
So'wjetuni,on f *hist.* Soviet Union.

so'wohl *conj* ~ *... als (auch)* ... ... as well as ..., both ... and ...

sozial [zo'tsĭa:l] *adj* social: ~*e Stellung* social rank (*or* status); ~ *denken* be social-minded.

Sozi'al|abgaben *pl* social contributions. ~**amt** *n* social welfare office. ~**arbeit** f (-; *no pl*) social (*or* welfare) work. ~**arbeiter** *m* social (*or* welfare) worker. ~**demo,krat** *m* social democrat. ~**demokra,tie** f social democracy. ♀**demo,kratisch** *adj* social-democratic. ♀**denkend** *adj* social-minded. ~**einrichtungen** *pl* social services. ~**hilfe** f social security, *Am.* welfare: ~ *beziehen* be on social security (*Am.* welfare).

sozialisieren [zotsĭali'zi:rən] *v/t* (h) nationalize. **Sozialismus** [zotsĭa'lɪsmʊs] *m* (-; *no pl*) socialism. **Sozialist** [-'lɪst] *m* (-en; -en), **Sozia'listin** f (-; -nen) socialist. **sozia'listisch** *adj* socialistic.

sozi'alkritisch *adj* sociocritical.

Sozi'al|kunde f (-; *no pl*) *ped.* social studies. ~**lasten** *pl* social expenditure. ~**leistungen** *pl* **1.** social contributions. **2.** *of company*: fringe benefits. ~**poli,tik** f social policy. ♀**po,litisch** *adj* sociopolitical. ~**pre,stige** *n* social prestige. ~**pro,dukt** *n* (gross) national product. ~**staat** *m* welfare state. ~**versicherung** f social security. ~**wohnung** f council flat.

Soziologe [zotsĭo'lo:gə] *m* (-n; -n) sociologist. **Soziologie** [zotsīolo'giː] f (-; no pl) sociology. **sozio'logisch** adj sociological.

Sozius ['zoːtsīʊs] m (-; -se) **1.** ✝ partner. **2.** a. **~fahrer** m pillion rider. **~sitz** m (auf dem ~ mitfahren ride) pillion.

sozu'sagen adv so to speak, as it were.

Spachtel ['ʃpaxtəl] m (-s; -) **1.** spatula. **2.** → **~masse** f filler. **~messer** n putty knife.

spachteln ['ʃpaxtəln] v/t (h) surface.

Spagat [ʃpa'gaːt] m, n (-[e]s; -e) (~ machen do the) splits.

Spaghetti [ʃpa'gɛti] pl spaghetti.

spähen ['ʃpɛːən] v/i (h) peer, look out (nach for).

'Spähtrupp m ✕ reconnaissance patrol.

Spalier [ʃpa'liːr] n (-s; -e) **1.** ✗ trellis, espalier. **2.** a) guard of hono(u)r, b) lane, c) rows: **ein ~ bilden, ~ stehen** form a lane. **Spa'lierobst** n wall fruit.

Spalt [ʃpalt] m (-[e]s; -e) crack, gap, slit. **'spaltbar** adj phys. fissionable. **'Spalte** f (-; -n) **1.** crack, gap, split, geol. cleft, crevice, crevasse. **2.** print. column. **'spalten** v/t (spaltete, gespalten, h) split (a. atom), chop (wood), ❀ decompose, fig. split (up), divide; → **Haar.** **'Spaltung** f (-; -en) splitting, phys. fission, fig. split, division, eccl. schism.

Span [ʃpaːn] m (-[e]s; ⸚e) chip, pl shavings, (metal) filings: **wo gehobelt wird, da fallen Späne** you can't make an omelette without breaking eggs.

'Spanferkel n sucking pig.

Spange ['ʃpaŋə] f (-; -n) a) clasp, b) buckle, c) bangle, d) (hair) slide, e) (shoe) strap, f) (dental) brace.

Spanien ['ʃpaːnīən] n (-s) Spain.

'Spanier m (-s; -), **'Spanierin** f (-; -nen) Spaniard. **'spanisch** adj Spanish: **~e Wand** folding screen; F **das kommt mir ~ vor!** that's strange! **'Spanisch** n (auf ~ in) Spanish.

spann [ʃpan] pret of **spinnen.**

Spann m (-[e]s; -e) instep.

'Spannbe,ton m prestressed concrete.

Spanne ['ʃpanə] f (-; -n) **1.** span: fig. **e-e kurze ~** a short space (of time). **2.** ✝ margin. **'spannen** (h) **I** v/t stretch, tighten, put up (clothesline etc), cock (camera, gun), flex, tense (muscles), bend (bow), fig. strain (nerves): **e-n Bogen in die Schreibmaschine ~** insert a

sheet of paper into the typewriter; → **gespannt, Folter. II** sich ~ stretch; **sich ~ über** (acc) span. **III** v/i dress etc: be (too) tight, skin: be taut. **'spannend** adj exciting, thrilling, gripping, book, film full of suspense, suspense-packed.

'Spanner m (-s; -) **1.** (racket etc) press; → **Schuhspanner. 2.** F peeping Tom.

'Spannkraft f (-; no pl) energy, vigo(u)r.

'Spannung f (-; -en) **1.** ⊙ tension (a. ✷), ⚡ a. voltage, stress; ⚡ **unter ~ (stehend)** live. **2.** fig. a) excitement, suspense (a. of book etc), b) a. pol. tension: **mit** (or **voll**) **~ expect, watch, etc** with bated breath; **j-n in ~ halten** keep s.o. in suspense; **in ~ versetzen** thrill, excite.

'Spannungsgebiet n pol. area of tension, trouble spot.

'spannungsgeladen adj **1.** → **spannend. 2.** (extremely) tense (atmosphere etc).

'Spannungsmesser m ⚡ voltmeter.

'Spannweite f wingspan, △ span, fig. scope, range.

'Spanplatte f chipboard.

'Spar|buch n savings book. **~büchse** f money box. **~einlage** f savings depot.

sparen ['ʃpaːrən] (h) **I** v/t save: **das hättest du dir ~ können!** that was unnecessary. **II** v/i a) save (up) (auf acc for), b) economize (an dat, mit on): **mit Lob etc ~** be sparing of praise etc. **'Sparer** m (-s; -), **'Sparerin** f (-; -nen) saver.

Spargel ['ʃpargəl] m (-s; -) asparagus.

'Spar|groschen m F nest egg. **~guthaben** n savings balance. **~kasse** f savings bank. **~konto** n savings account.

spärlich ['ʃpɛːrlīç] adj scant(y), sparse, thin (a. hair), poor (attendance): **~ bekleidet** scantily dressed; **~ besucht** poorly attended.

'Spar|maßnahme f economy measure. **~prämie** f savings premium. **~programm** n **1.** pol. cuts (or austerity) program(me Br.). **2.** washing machine: energy-saving cycle.

Sparren ['ʃparən] m (-s; -) rafter.

'sparsam adj (mit) economical (of), thrifty (of, with): **~ im Verbrauch** economical; a. fig. **~ umgehen mit** be sparing of.

'Sparsamkeit f (-; no pl) economy, thrift, austerity, contp. parsimony.

'Sparschwein n F piggy bank.

spartanisch [ʃparˈtaːnɪʃ] *adj* Spartan, *fig.* spartan: **~ leben** lead a spartan life.
Sparte [ˈʃpartə] *f* (-; -n) field, line.
'**Sparvertrag** *m* savings agreement.
Spaß [ʃpaːs] *m* (-es; ∘e [ˈʃpɛːsə]) a) joke, b) fun: **aus** (*or* **im, zum**) **~** for fun; **er hat nur ~ gemacht!** he was only joking; **es macht** (*k-n*) **~** it's (no) fun; **es macht ihm viel ~** he really enjoys it; **er versteht k-n ~** he can't take a joke, *w.s.* he doesn't stand for any nonsense; **~ beiseite!** joking aside; **viel ~!** have fun!; **ein teurer ~** an expensive business.
'**spaßen** *v/i* (h) joke: **damit ist nicht zu ~!** that's no joking matter!; **er läßt nicht mit sich ~** he doesn't stand for any nonsense. **spaßeshalber** *adv* (just) for fun. '**spaßig** *adj* funny.
'**Spaßverderber** *m* (-s; -) spoilsport, killjoy. '**Spaßvogel** *m* joker, wag.
Spastiker [ˈʃpastikər] *m* (-s; -) *✚* spastic.
'**spastisch** *adj* (*a.* **~ gelähmt**) spastic.
spät [ʃpɛːt] **I** *adj* late: **am ~en Nachmittag** late in the afternoon; **wie ~ ist es?** what time is it?; **es ist** (**wird**) **~** it's (getting) late. **II** *adv* late, at a late hour (*a. fig.*): **zu ~ kommen** be late (**zu** for); **er kam 5 Minuten zu ~** he was five minutes late; **~ zu Abend essen** have a late dinner; **bis ~ in die Nacht** till late at night; **du bist ~ dran!** you are late!
Spatel [ˈʃpaːtəl] *m* (-s; -) *✚* spatula.
Spaten [ˈʃpaːtən] *m* (-s; -) spade.
'**Spätentwickler** *m* late developer.
'**später I** *adj* later. **II** *adv* later (**als** than), later on: **bis ~!** see you later!; → **früher II**. **spätestens** [ˈʃpɛːtəstəns] *adv* at the latest.
'**Spät|herbst** *m* F **1.** late autumn (*Am.* fall). **~lese** *f* late vintage (wine). **~schäden** *pl* (→ *haben* be on) late sequelae. **~schicht** *f* late shift. **~vorstellung** *f* late-night performance.
Spatz [ʃpats] *m* (-en, -es; -en) sparrow: F **das pfeifen die ~en von den Dächern** that's everybody's secret.
'**Spätzünder** *m* F **1. ein ~ sein** be slow on the uptake. **2.** → **Spätentwickler.**
'**Spätzündung** *f mot.* retarded ignition.
spazieren [ʃpaˈtsiːrən] *v/i* (sn) walk (around), stroll. **~fahren** (*irr, sep, -ge-, sn,* → *fahren*) **I** *v/i* take a ride. **II** *v/t* take *s.o.* for a ride. **~gehen** *v/i* (*irr, sep, -ge-, sn,* → *gehen*) go for a walk.

Spa'ziergang *m* **1.** walk, stroll: **e-n ~ machen** go for a walk. **2.** *sports etc*: walkover. **Spa'ziergänger** [-gɛŋər] *m* (-s; -) walker, stroller.
Spa'zierstock *m* walking stick.
Specht [ʃpɛçt] *m* (-[e]s; -e) woodpecker.
Speck [ʃpɛk] *m* (-[e]s; -e) **1.** *gastr.* bacon: → **Made. 2.** F flab: **~ ansetzen** get fat.
'**speckig** *adj* **1.** fat. **2.** *fig.* greasy.
'**Speckscheibe** *f* bacon rasher.
'**Speckschwarte** *f* bacon rind.
'**Speckseite** *f* flitch (of bacon).
Spediteur [ʃpediˈtøːr] *m* (-s; -e) **1.** forwarding (*✚* shipping) agent. **2.** (furniture) remover. **Spedition** [ʃpediˈtsioːn] *f* (-; -en) **1.** forwarding (*✚* shipping) (business). **2.** → **Speditionsfirma** *f* **1.** forwarding (*✚* shipping) agency. **2.** removal firm. **Spedi'tionskaufmann** *m* forwarding agent.
Speer [ʃpeːr] *m* (-[e]s; -e) spear, *sports*: javelin. '**Speerwerfen** *n sports*: javelin throw, *the* javelin. '**Speerwerfer(in** *f*) *m sports*: javelin thrower.
Speiche [ˈʃpaɪçə] *f* (-; -n) **1.** spoke. **2.** *anat.* radius.
Speichel [ˈʃpaɪçəl] *m* (-s; *no pl*) spittle, saliva. **~drüse** *f* salivary gland. **~lecker** *m contp.* toady, bootlicker.
Speicher [ˈʃpaɪçər] *m* (-s; -) **1.** a) granary, elevator, b) warehouse, c) reservoir. **2.** loft, attic. **3.** *computer*: store, memory. **~chip** *m computer*: memory chip. **~kapazi‚tät** *f* storage (*computer*: memory) capacity.
speichern [ˈʃpaɪçərn] *v/t* (h) store (*a. ⚡, computer*), **⚓** stockpile. **Speicherung** *f* (-; *no pl*) storage (*a. computer*).
Speise [ˈʃpaɪzə] *f* (-; -n) a) food, b) dish, meal. **~aufzug** *m* dumb waiter. **~eis** *n* ice cream. **~kammer** *f* larder, pantry. **~karte** *f* menu. **~leitung** *f ⚡* feeder.
speisen [ˈʃpaɪzən] (h) **I** *v/i* eat, dine: **zu Mittag ~** (have) lunch; **zu Abend ~** have dinner, dine. **II** *v/t* feed (*a. ⚡, ⊙*).
'**Speisenfolge** *f* order of courses.
'**Speise|öl** *n* cooking oil. **~röhre** *f anat.* gullet, (o)esophagus. **~saal** *m* dining hall (*in hotel*: room, *✚* saloon). **~wagen** *m ⚒* dining car, *Am.* diner. **~zettel** *m* menu. **~zimmer** *n* dining room.
'**Speisung** *f* (-; -en) feeding, *⊙ a.* supply.
Spektakel [ʃpɛkˈtaːkəl] *m* (-s; *no pl*) row, racket, *fig.* fuss.

Spektralana,lyse [ʃpɛk'tra:l-] *f* spectrum analysis. **Spektrum** ['ʃpɛktrʊm] *n* (-s; -tren) *a. fig.* spectrum.

Spekulant [ʃpeku'lant] *m* (-en; -en) speculator. **Spekulation** [ʃpekula'tsĭo:n] *f* (-; -en) speculation. **Spekulati'onsgeschäft** *n* speculative operation.

spekulieren [ʃpeku'li:rən] *v/i* (h) speculate (*über acc* on, *↑ mit* in): *~ auf* (*acc*) a) speculate on, b) F have one's eye on.

Spelunke [ʃpe'lʊŋkə] *f* (-; -n) F dive.

spendabel [ʃpɛn'da:bəl] *adj* F generous.

Spende ['ʃpɛndə] *f* (-; -n) donation, contribution. **'spenden** *v/t, v/i* (h) **1.** donate (*a.* blood etc), contribute. **2.** *machine:* dispense. **3.** *fig.* give (*praise etc*).

'Spenden|akti,on *f* collection campaign. **~konto** *n* account for donations.

'Spender *m* (-s; -) **1.** *a.* **'Spenderin** *f* (-; -nen) donator, contributor, *a.* ✱ donor. **2.** (*machine*) dispenser.

spendieren [ʃpɛn'di:rən] *v/t* (h) *j-m et. ~* treat s.o. to s.th.; *j-m ein Bier ~* stand s.o. a beer.

Sperber ['ʃpɛrbər] *m* (-s; -) *zo.* sparrow hawk.

Sperling ['ʃpɛrlɪŋ] *m* (-s; -e) *zo.* sparrow.

Sperma ['ʃpɛrma] *n* (-s; -men) sperm.

Sperre ['ʃpɛrə] *f* (-; -n) **1.** barrier, *a.* barricade, road block. **2.** ⊗ lock, stop, stoppage. **3.** *psych.* mental block. **4.** ✝ embargo, blockade: *e-e ~ verhängen über* (*acc*) impose a ban (✝ an embargo) on. **5.** *sports:* suspension. **'sperren** (h) **I** *v/t* **1.** shut, block (*road etc*), police *etc:* cordon off: *e-e Straße für den Verkehr ~* close a road to traffic. **2.** ⊗ a) lock, block, stop, b) cut off (*gas etc*). **3.** ✝ a) embargo, b) freeze (*payments etc*), block (*account*), stop (*cheque*). **4.** *sports: j-n ~* a) obstruct s.o. (unfairly), b) suspend s.o. **5.** *print.* space out: *gesperrt gedruckt* spaced out. **6.** *j-n ~ in* (*acc*) lock s.o. up in. **II** *sich ~* balk (*gegen* at).

'Sperr|feuer *n* ✕ barrage. **~frist** *f* blocking period. **~gebiet** *n* restricted area. **~gürtel** *m* cordon. **~holz** *n* plywood.

'sperrig *adj* bulky.

'Sperr|klausel *f* restrictive clause. **~konto** *n* blocked account. **~minori,tät** *f* blocking minority. **~müll** *m* bulk rubbish. **~sitz** *m* *thea.* orchestra stalls.

~stunde *f* closing time, ✕ curfew. **~taste** *f* locking key.

'Sperrung *f* (-; -en) **1.** closing (*etc,* → *sperren* I). **2.** blockage, obstruction, stoppage, ✝ embargo.

Spesen ['ʃpe:zən] *pl* expenses. **Ꝗfrei** *adj* free of charge(s). **~konto** *n* expense account. **~rechnung** *f* bill of expenses.

Spezi ['ʃpe:tsi] *m* (-s; -[s]) F chum, pal.

Spezial|ausbildung [ʃpe'tsĭa:l-] *f* special(ized) training. **~fach** *n* special subject. **~gebiet** *n* special field, speciality.

spezialisieren [ʃpetsĭali'zi:rən] *sich ~* (h) specialize (*auf acc* in). **Speziali'sierung** *f* (-; *no pl*) specialization. **Spezialist** [ʃpetsĭa'lɪst] *m* (-en; -en), **Spezia'listin** *f* (-; -nen) specialist. **Spezialität** [ʃpetsĭali'tɛ:t] *f* (-; -en) speciality.

speziell [ʃpe'tsĭɛl] *adj* special, specific.

Spezies ['ʃpe:tsĭes] *f* (-; -) species.

spezifisch [ʃpe'tsi:fɪʃ] *adj* specific: *phys. ~es Gewicht* specific gravity.

spezifizieren [ʃpetsifi'tsi:rən] *v/t* (h) specify, itemize.

Sphäre ['sfɛ:rə] *f* (-; -n) sphere.

'sphärisch *adj* spheric.

Sphinx [sfɪŋks] *f* (-; -e) *a. fig.* sphinx.

spicken ['ʃpɪkən] *v/t* (h) **1.** *gastr.* lard. **2.** F *fig.* interlard (*speech etc* (*mit* with): *gespickt mit Fehlern* full of mistakes.

Spiegel ['ʃpi:gəl] *m* (-s; -) **1.** mirror (*a. fig.*), ✱ speculum, *opt.*, ⊗ reflector. **2.** surface (*of water*), (*a.* blood sugar etc) level. **~bild** *n* **1.** mirror image. **2.** *fig.* reflection. **~ei** *n* *gastr.* fried egg.

'spiegel|frei *adj* nonglare. **~glatt** *adj* water (as) smooth as glass, *floor etc* like glass, *a.* icy (*road*).

spiegeln ['ʃpi:gəln] (h) **I** *v/i* shine, *a.* dazzle. **II** *v/t a. fig.* mirror, reflect. **III** *sich ~* be reflected, *fig. a.* be mirrored.

'Spiegel re,flexkamera *f* reflex camera.

Spiegelschrift *f* mirror writing.

'Spiegelung *f* (-; -en) **1.** reflection. **2.** mirage.

Spiel [ʃpi:l] *n* (-[e]s; -e) **1.** play (*a. fig.* of *colo[u]rs, muscles*), ♪ playing, *thea. a.* acting, performance. **2.** game, match, *a.* gamble: *wie steht das ~?* what's the score?; *fig. das ~ ist aus!* the game is up!; *gewagtes ~* gamble; *fig. ins ~ bringen* bring s.th. up; *gewonnenes ~ haben* have made it; *leichtes ~ haben* have little trouble (*mit* with); *die Hand im ~ haben* have one's (*or* a) finger in the pie; *ins ~ kommen* come into play; *aus dem ~ lassen* leave s.o., s.th. out of it; (*mit*) *im ~ sein* be at work, *bei et.* be involved in s.th.; *aufs ~ setzen* risk; *auf dem ~ stehen* be at stake; *mit j-m sein ~ treiben* play games with s.o.; *mit j-m ein falsches ~ treiben* doublecross s.o.; → *abgekartet*. **3.** *thea.*, *TV* play. **4.** ~ (*Karten*) pack (*Am.* deck) (of cards). **5.** ⚙ a) play, b) clearance.

'**Spiel**|**anzug** m playsuit. **~art** f *biol. or fig.* variety. **~auto,mat** m a) gaming machine, b) slot machine, F one-armed bandit. **~ball** m **1.** ball, *tennis:* game ball. **2.** *fig.* plaything. **~bank** f (-; -en) (gambling) casino.

spielen ['ʃpiːlən] (h) **I** v/i **1.** a) play (*a. fig.*), b) gamble: ~ *um* play for; *hoch* ~ play for high stakes; *sports:* **A.** *spielte gegen B.* A. played B.; *mit dem Gedanken* ~ *zu inf* toy with the idea of *ger*; *s-e Beziehungen* ~ *lassen* pull a few strings; *ins Rötliche* ~ have a reddish tinge; → *Charme, Feuer* 1, *Muskel*. **2.** *thea.* play, act: ~ *in* (*dat*) film, scene, *etc:* be set in. **II** v/t **3.** *Klavier* ~ play the piano; *sports:* *den Ball zu j-m* ~ pass (the ball) to s.o.; → *Geige, Hand*. **4.** *thea. or fig.* play, act: *fig. den Beleidigten* ~ act all offended; *mit gespielter Gleichgültigkeit* with studied indifference; F *fig. was wird hier gespielt?* what's going on here?; → *Rolle*[2]. **5.** *thea. etc* play, perform: *was wird heute abend gespielt?* what's on tonight?; → *Theater*.

'**spielend** *adv fig.* ~ (*leicht*) easily, effortlessly; *es ist* ~ *leicht* it's child's play; ~ *gewinnen* win hands down.

'**Spieler** m (-s; -) a) player, b) gambler. **Spiele'rei** f (-; -en) **1.** *no pl* playing around. **2.** pastime. **3.** *pl* a) gewgaws, b) gadgets. '**Spielerin** f (-; -nen) → *Spieler*. '**spielerisch** *adj* **1.** *sports:* playing, *thea.* acting. **2.** playful. **3.** *mit* ~*er Leichtigkeit* effortlessly.

'**Spiel**|**feld** n *sports:* field, pitch, *tennis: a.* court. **~film** m feature film. **~halle** f amusement arcade. **~hölle** f *contp.* gambling den. **~kame,rad(in** f) m playmate. **~karte** f playing card. **~ka,sino** n (gambling) casino. **~leiter(in** f) m →

Regisseur(in). **~macher** m *sports:* strategist. **~marke** f counter, chip. **~plan** m *thea. etc* program(me *Br.*). **~platz** m playground. **~raum** m *fig.* a) elbowroom, scope, b) time, c) margin. **~regel** f rule: *a. fig. sich an die ~n halten* play the game. **~sachen** pl toys. **~sa,lon** m amusement arcade. **~schuld** f gambling debt. **~stand** m score. **~tisch** m **1.** card table. **2.** gambling table. **~trieb** m play instinct. **~uhr** f musical clock. **~verbot** n *sports:* suspension: ~ *haben* have been suspended. **~waren** pl toys. **~warengeschäft** n toy shop (*or* store). **~zeit** f *sports, thea.* season, *of match:* playing time, *of film etc:* run. **~zeug** n toy(s), *fig.* toy. **~zeugpi,stole** f toy pistol.

Spieß [ʃpiːs] m (-es; -e) spear, *gastr.* spit, skewer: *am ~ braten* barbecue; F *fig. den ~ umdrehen* turn the tables (*gegen* on); *schreien wie am ~* scream blue murder. '**Spießbürger(in** f) m, '**spießbürgerlich** *adj* petty bourgeois, F square. '**Spießer** m (-s; -), '**Spießerin** f (-; -nen), '**spießig** *adj* petty bourgeois, F square. '**Spießruten** pl ~ *laufen a. fig.* run the gauntlet.

Spikes [ʃpaɪks] pl **1.** *sports:* spikes. **2.** *mot.* a) studs, b) → '**Spikesreifen** pl studded tyres (*Am.* tires).

spinal [ʃpiˈnaːl] *adj* spinal: ⚕ ~*e Kinderlähmung* polio(myelitis).

Spinat [ʃpiˈnaːt] m (-[e]s; -e) spinach.

Spind [ʃpɪnt] m, n (-[e]s; -e) locker.

Spindel ['ʃpɪndəl] f (-; -n) spindle.

Spinett [ʃpiˈnɛt] n (-[e]s; -e) spinet.

Spinne ['ʃpɪnə] f (-; -n) spider. '**spinnen** (spann, gesponnen, h) **I** v/t **1.** spin: *fig. Ränke* ~ hatch plots. **II** v/i **2.** spin. **3.** F a) be crazy, b) talk (a lot of) rubbish. '**Spinnennetz** n cobweb. '**Spinner** m (-s; -) **1.** spinner. **2.** F nut, crackpot, *Am.* screwball. **Spinne'rei** f (-; -en) **1.** *no pl* spinning. **2.** spinning mill. **3.** F a) crazy idea, b) rubbish. '**Spinnerin** f (-; -nen) → *Spinner*.

'**Spinn**|**gewebe** n cobweb. **~rad** n spinning wheel. **~webe** f (-; -n) cobweb.

Spion [ʃpiˈoːn] m (-s; -e) **1.** spy. **2.** a) spyhole, b) window mirror.

Spionage [ʃpioˈnaːʒə] f (-; *no pl*) espionage, spying. **~abwehr** f counterespio-

nage, counterintelligence. **~netz**´ *n*, **~ring** *m* spy ring. **~ro͵man** *m* spy story.
spionieren [ʃpio'ni:rən] *v/i* (h) spy, *fig. contp. a.* snoop (around).
Spi'onin *f* (-; -nen) spy.
Spirale [ʃpi'ra:lə] *f* (-; -n) spiral (*a.* ✝*etc*), ◉ coil (*a.* F *pessary*). **Spi'ralfeder** *f* coil spring, *of watch*: mainspring. **spi'ralförmig** *adj* spiral.
Spiritismus [ʃpiri'tɪsmʊs] *m* (-; *no pl*) spiritualism. **Spiri'tist** *m* (-en; -en), **spiri'tistisch** *adj* spiritualist.
Spirituosen [ʃpiri'tǔo:zən] *pl* spirits, liquor.
Spiritus ['ʃpi:ritʊs] *m* (-; -se) spirit.
Spirituskocher *m* spirit stove.
spitz [ʃpɪts] *adj* **1.** pointed, sharp: ~ **zulaufend** tapering. **2.** Å acute (*angle*). **3.** F peaky. **4.** *fig.* pointed (*remark etc*), sarcastic: **~e Zunge** sharp tongue.
Spitz *m* (-es; -e) (*dog*) Pomeranian.
Spitz|bart *m* goatee. **~bauch** *m* paunch.
'Spitze¹ *f* (-; -n) **1.** point, tip (*a. of finger, nose, etc*), peak, top, *a.* spire: *fig.* **die ~ des Eisbergs** the tip of the iceberg; **e-r Sache die ~ nehmen** take the edge off s.th.; **et. auf die ~ treiben** carry s.th. too far. **2.** head (*a. fig.*), ✕ (spear)head, *sports:* lead, *a.* leading group: F **~ spielen** *soccer:* be striker; **an der ~ der Tabelle** at the top of the table; *a. fig.* **an der ~ liegen** be in front; **sich an die ~ setzen** take the lead. **3.** peak, maximum: F **das Auto macht 220 km ~** the car does a maximum speed of 220 km per hour; F **das ist (einsame) ~!** that's super! **4.** *a.* top position, b) (top) management, c) *pl* leading figures, élite: **an der ~ der Firma** at the head of the firm. **5.** Å apex. **6.** F dig (**gegen** at).
'Spitze² *f* (-; -n) lace.
Spitzel ['ʃpɪtsəl] *m* (-s; -) a) informer, *sl.* nark, b) company spy.
spitzen ['ʃpɪtsən] *v/t* (h) point, sharpen: **die Ohren ~** prick up one's ears, *fig. a.* listen carefully.
'Spitzen|fabri͵kat *n* top-quality product (*or* make). **~gehalt** *n* top salary. **~geschwindigkeit** *f* maximum (*or* top) speed. **~gespräch** *n* top-level talks. **~kandi͵dat(in** *f*) *m* leading candidate, front-runner. **~klasse** *f* top class: **Läufer (Auto) der ~** top-class runner (car).
'Spitzenkleid *n* lace dress.

'Spitzen|kraft *f* highly qualified worker, top-level executive, *thea. etc* star performer. **~leistung** *f* **1.** ◉ maximum output, ⚡ peak power. **2.** *sports:* top performance, *fig. a.* great feat. **~lohn** *m* top wage(s). **~reiter** *m* front-runner, *sports:* leader, leading team, (*film, tune, etc*) (top) hit. **~sport** *m* high-performance sports. **~sportler(in** *f*) *m* top athlete. **~tanz** *m* toe-dancing. **~techno-lo͵gie** *f* high technology. **~verdiener(in** *f*) *m* top earner. **~wein** *m* vintage wine. **~zeit** *f* **1.** *sports:* record time. **2.** peak hours (*of traffic etc*).
'spitzfindig *adj* over-subtle.
'Spitzfindigkeit *f* (-; -en) subtlety: **das sind ~en** that's splitting hairs.
'Spitzhacke *f* pickax(e).
'spitzkriegen *v/t* (*sep*, -ge-, h) F **et. ~** cotton on to s.th.
'Spitzname *m* nickname.
'spitzwink(e)lig *adj* Å acute.
Spleen [ʃpli:n] *m* (-s; -e, -s) F tic, quirk.
splitten ['ʃplɪtən] *v/t* (h) ✝, *pol.* split.
Splitter ['ʃplɪtər] *m* (-s; -) splinter, fragment. **~bruch** *m* 🦴 chip fracture. **2frei** *adj* shatterproof. **~gruppe** *f* *pol.* splinter group.
splittern ['ʃplɪtərn] *v/i* **1.** (h) splinter. **2.** (sn) *glass:* shatter.
'splitternackt *adj* stark naked.
'Splitterpar͵tei *f* splinter party.
Spoiler ['ʃpɔylər] *m* (-s; -) *mot.* spoiler.
sponsern ['ʃpɔnzərn] *v/t* (h) sponsor.
Sponsor ['ʃpɔnzər] *m* (-s; -s, -en [-'zo:-rən]) sponsor.
spontan [ʃpɔn'ta:n] *adj* spontaneous.
sporadisch [ʃpo'ra:dɪʃ] *adj* sporadic.
Spore ['ʃpo:rə] *f* (-; -n) 🌿 spore.
Sporn [ʃpɔrn] *m* (-[e]s; Sporen ['ʃpo:rən]) spur (*a.* 🐎), ✈ (tail) skid: **s-m Pferd die Sporen geben** spur one's horse.
Sport [ʃpɔrt] *m* (-[e]s; *no pl*) **1.** sport, *coll.* sports, *ped. a.* physical education: **~ treiben** go in for sports; **viel ~ treiben** do a lot of sport. **2.** *fig.* (**als ~** as a) hobby. **~abzeichen** *n* sports badge. **~angler** *m* angler. **~anlage** *f* sports grounds (*or* facilities). **~art** *f* (kind of) sport. **~ar͵tikel** *m* sports article. **~arzt** *m* sports physician. **2begeistert** *adj* sporty. **~bericht** *m* sports report. **~fest** *n* sports day. **~flieger** *m* amateur pilot. **~geschäft** *n* sports shop (*or* store).

~**halle** f gymnasium. ~**hochschule** f physical education college. ~**kleidung** f sportswear. ~**klub** m sports club. ~**lehrer(in** f) m ped. PE (= physical education) teacher.

'**Sportler** m (-s; -) sportsman, athlete.

'**Sportlerin** f (-; -nen) sportswoman.

'**sportlich** adj sporting, sporty, a. fair (behavio[u]r, play), a. sports (meeting etc), athletic (person, figure, etc), casual (wear).

'**Sport|medi,zin** f sports medicine. ~**nachrichten** pl sports news. ~**platz** m sports ground. ~**repor,tage** f sports report, sportscast. ~**re,porter** m sports reporter, sportscaster. ~**sendung** f sports broadcast, sportscast.

'**Sportska,none** f F (sports) ace.

'**Sportsmann** m sportsman.

'**Sport|tauchen** n skin (or scuba) diving. ~**veranstaltung** f sporting event, sports meeting. ~**verein** m sports club. ~**wagen** m **1.** sports car. **2.** pushchair, Am. stroller. ~**zeitung** f sporting paper.

Spott [ʃpɔt] m (-[e]s; no pl) a. mockery, ridicule, b) derision, scorn. '**spottbillig** adj F dirt-cheap. **Spötte'lei** f (-; -en) mockery, a. gibe. **spötteln** ['ʃpœtəln] v/i (h) gibe (**über** acc at). '**spotten** v/t (h) (**über** acc) mock (at), scoff (at), make fun (of): → **Beschreibung** 1. **Spötter** ['ʃpœtər] m (-s; -) **1.** mocker. **2.** cynic. '**spöttisch** adj a) mocking, b) derisive, c) sarcastic.

'**Spottlied** n satirical song.

'**Spottpreis** m ridicule(ly low) price.

sprach [ʃpraːx] pret of **sprechen**.

'**sprachbegabt** adj good at languages.

'**Sprachbegabung** f gift for languages.

Sprache [ʃpraːxə] f (-; -n) **1.** no pl speech: → **verschlagen**[1] 4. **2.** language (a. fig.), a. vernacular, idiom, a. jargon, a. diction: **heraus mit der** ~ f out with it!, **et. zur** ~ **bringen** bring s.th. up; **ein Thema zur** ~ **bringen** raise a subject; **zur** ~ **kommen** come up (for discussion); → **herausrücken** II.

'**Sprach|ebene** f speech level. ~**eigenheit** f idiom(atic expression).

'**Sprachenschule** f language school.

'**Sprach|fehler** m speech defect. ~**führer** m phrasebook. ~**gebiet** n speech area: **deutsches** ~ German-speaking area. ~**gebrauch** m (-[e]s; no pl) (linguistic)

usage: **im gewöhnlichen** ~ in everyday usage. ~**gefühl** n (-[e]s; no pl) linguistic instinct. ⚲**gewandt** adj **1.** articulate. **2.** proficient in languages. ~**kenntnisse** pl knowledge of languages (or of a language): **gute deutsche** ~ **erwünscht** good command of German desirable. ⚲**kundig** adj proficient in languages, polyglot. ~**kurs** m language course. ~**la,bor** n language laboratory. ~**lehre** f **1.** grammar. **2.** grammar book. ~**lehrer** m language teacher.

'**sprachlich** adj a) linguistic, b) grammatical, c) stylistic.

'**sprachlos** adj speechless.

'**Sprach|regelung** f iro. (prescribed) phraseology. ~**rohr** n fig. mouthpiece. ~**störung** f ⚕ speech disorder. ~**studium** n language studies. ~**ta,lent** n gift for languages. ~**unterricht** m language teaching: **englischer** ~ English lessons. ~**wissenschaft** f philology. ~**wissenschaftler(in** f) m philologist, linguist. ⚲**wissenschaftlich** adj philological, linguistic.

sprang [ʃpraŋ] pret of **springen**.

Spray [ʃpreː] m, n (-s; -s) spray.

'**Sprech|anlage** f intercom. ~**blase** f in cartoons: balloon. ~**chor** m chorus: **im** ~ **rufen** chant.

sprechen ['ʃprɛçən] (sprach, gesprochen, h) **I** v/i speak, a. give a speech, a. talk (**mit** j-m to s.o., **über** acc, **von** about): ~ **mit** see (one's doctor etc); **über Geschäfte** (**Politik**) ~ talk business (politics); **von et. anderem** ~ change the subject; **j-n zum** ⚲ **bringen** make s.o. talk; ~ **für** a) speak on behalf of s.o., b) put in a good word for, c) plead for; **das spricht für ihn** that says s.th. for him; **das spricht für sich selbst** that speaks for itself; **vieles spricht dafür** (**dagegen**) there is much to be said for (against) it; **alles spricht dafür, daß** there is every indication that; **auf ihn ist sie nicht gut zu** ~ he's in her bad books; **wir kamen** (**man kam**) **auf ... zu** ~ the subject of ... came up. **II** v/t speak (language etc), say (prayer etc): **j-n** ~ speak to s.o., see s.o.; **j-n zu** ~ **wünschen** wish to see s.o.; **kann ich Sie kurz** ~? may I have a word with you?; **er ist nicht zu** ~ he is busy; → **Recht** 1, **schuldig** 1.

'**sprechend** *adj fig.* eloquent (*gesture etc*), striking (*resemblance*).
'**Sprecher** *m* (-s; -) **1.** speaker, *radio, TV* announcer. **2.** spokesman (*gen* for).
'**Sprecherin** *f* (-; -nen) **1.** → **Sprecher** 1. **2.** spokeswoman (*gen* for).
'**Sprecherziehung** *f* speech training.
'**Sprechfunk** *m* radiotelephony. **~gerät** *n* a) radiotelephone, b) walkie-talkie.
'**Sprechstunde** *f* a) office hours, b) (*doctor's*) consulting hours.
'**Sprechstundenhilfe** *f* receptionist.
'**Sprechzimmer** *n* a) office, b) (*doctor's*) consulting room, surgery.
spreizen ['ʃpraɪtsən] *v/t* (h) spread, *a.* straddle (*legs*).
'**Spreizfuß** *m* 🦶 splayfoot.
'**Sprengbombe** *f* high-explosive bomb.
sprengen¹ ['ʃprɛŋən] *v/t* (h) sprinkle, spray.
'**sprengen²** *v/t* (h) **1.** burst open, force (*door*), break (*fetters etc*). **2.** blast, blow up. **3.** *fig.* break up (*meeting*): **die Bank ~** break the bank; → **Rahmen**.
'**Spreng|kapsel** *f* detonator. **~kopf** *m* warhead. **~körper** *m*, **~ladung** *f*, **~satz** *m* explosive charge.
'**Sprengstoff** *m* explosive, *fig.* dynamite. **~anschlag** *m* bomb attack.
'**Sprengung** *f* (-; -en) **1.** blasting, blowing up. **2.** *fig.* breaking-up (*of meeting*).
sprenkeln ['ʃprɛŋkəln] *v/t* (h) dot.
Spreu [ʃprɔʏ] *f* (-; *no pl*) (*fig.* **die ~ vom Weizen trennen** separate the wheat from the) chaff.
'**Sprichwort** *n* proverb: **wie das ~ sagt** as the saying goes.
'**sprichwörtlich** *adj a. fig.* proverbial.
sprießen ['ʃpriːsən] *v/i* (sproß, gesprossen, sn) shoot up, sprout.
'**Springbrunnen** *m* fountain.
springen ['ʃprɪŋən] *v/i* (sprang, gesprungen, sn) **1.** a) jump, sports: *a.* (pole)vault, b) leap, hop, skip, *a. ball etc*: bounce; → **Auge** 1, **Punkt** 2. **2.** F run, nip. **3.** F *fig. etc.* **~ lassen** fork out, **für j-n** treat s.o. to s.th. **4.** crack, break.
'**Springen** *n* (-s) jumping, *sports:* diving. '**Springer** *m* (-s; -) **1.** sports: a) jumper, b) diver, c) vaulter. **2.** *chess:* knight. **3.** F ♟ stand-in. '**Springerin** *f* (-; -nen) → **Springer** 1, 3.
'**Spring|flut** *f* spring tide. **~reiter(in** *f*) *m* show jumper. **~seil** *n* skipping rope.

Sprinkleranlage ['ʃprɪŋklər-] *f* sprinkler system.
Sprint [ʃprɪnt] *m* (-s; -s), '**sprinten** *v/i, v/t* (sn, h) sprint. '**Sprinter** *m* (-s; -), '**Sprinterin** *f* (-; -nen) sprinter.
Sprit [ʃprɪt] *m* (-[e]s; -e) F **1.** spirit(s), alcohol. **2.** petrol, F juice, *Am.* gas.
Spritze ['ʃprɪtsə] *f* (-; -n) a) syringe, b) injection, F jab, *Am.* shot, c) → **Finanzspritze**.
spritzen ['ʃprɪtsən] **I** *v/t* (h) **1.** squirt, spray. **2.** → **sprengen¹**. **3.** F a) inject (*s.o.*), b) *sl.* shoot, mainline (*drugs*). **4.** mix *drink* with (soda) water. **5.** ⚙ inject (*plastic*). **II** *v/i* **6.** splash, spatter, *blood:* gush. **7.** spray. **8.** F mainline (*sl.*). '**Spritzer** *m* (-s; -) splash, *a.* dash (*of rum etc*). '**Spritzguß** *m* ⚙ a) die-casting, b) injection mo(u)lding.
'**spritzig** *adj* **1.** sparkling (*wine etc*). **2.** *fig.* lively, F peppy, nippy, zippy (*car*).
'**spritzlac̦kieren** *v/t* (h) spray(-paint).
'**Spritzmittel** *n* 🌱 spray. '**Spritzpi̦stole** *f* ⚙ spray gun. '**Spritztour** *f* F *mot.* (**e-e ~ machen** go for a) spin.
spröde ['ʃprøːdə] *adj* **1.** brittle (*a. voice*), rough, chapped (*skin*). **2.** *fig.* standoffish, demure, prim (*girl*).
sproß [ʃprɔs] *pret of* **sprießen.**
Sproß *m* (-sses; -sse) **1.** 🌱 shoot. **2.** *fig.* scion.
Sprosse ['ʃprɔsə] *f* (-; -n) **1.** *a. fig.* rung. **2.** *hunt.* tine.
'**Sprossenwand** *f gym.* wall bars.
'**Sprößling** ['ʃprœslɪŋ] *m* (-s; -e) F a) child, b) son, junior.
'**Sprotte** ['ʃprɔtə] *f* (-; -n) *zo.* sprat.
Spruch [ʃprʊx] *m* (-[e]s; ⁻e) **1.** saying, dictum, *a.* aphorism, epigram, (*bible*) quotation, verse: F (*große*) **Sprüche klopfen** talk big. **2.** decision.
'**Spruchband** *n* banner.
'**spruchreif** *adj* **die Sache ist noch nicht ~** nothing has been decided yet.
Sprudel ['ʃpruːdəl] *m* (-s; -) (carbonated) mineral water. '**sprudeln** *v/i* (sn) **1.** gush (forth). **2.** bubble, *drink: a.* fizz: *fig.* **~ vor** bubble (over) with.
'**Sprühdose** *f* spray can, aerosole (can).
sprühen ['ʃpryːən] (h) **I** *v/t* **1.** spray, sprinkle. **II** *v/i* **2.** spray. **3.** *a.* (sn) *sparks:* fly. **4.** *fig.* (**vor** *dat* with) bubble (over), *eyes:* flash: **vor Geist ~** sparkle

with wit. **'sprühend** *adj fig.* sparkling (*wit etc*). **'Sprühregen** *m* drizzle.

Sprung¹ [ʃprʊŋ] *m* (-[e]s; ⁓e) jump (*a. fig.*), leap, *gym., pole-vaulting*: vault, *high-diving*: dive: *fig.* **ein großer ⁓ nach vorn** a great leap forward; F **auf dem ⁓ sein zu** *inf* be about to *inf*; **j-m auf die Sprünge helfen** help s.o. along; **mit dem Gehalt kann er k-e großen Sprünge machen** he can't go far on that salary.

Sprung² *m* (-[e]s; ⁓e) crack: **e-n ⁓ haben** be cracked.

'Sprung|balken *m sports*: takeoff board. **⁓becken** *n* diving pool. **⁓brett** *n* springboard (*a. fig.*), *high-diving*: a. diving board. **⁓feder** *f* spring. **⁓federma,tratze** *f* spring (coil) mattress. **⁓grube** *f sports*: (jumping) pit.

'sprunghaft I *adj* **1.** erratic. **2.** rapid, *a.* sharp (*increase etc*). **II** *adv* rapidly: **⁓ ansteigen** go up by leaps and bounds, shoot up. **'Sprunghaftigkeit** *f* (-; *no pl*) **1.** *of person*: volatility. **2.** a) instability, b) rapidity.

'Sprung|lauf *m* ski-jumping. **⁓schanze** *f* ski jump. **⁓tuch** *n* jumping sheet. **⁓turm** *m* high-diving platforms.

Spucke ['ʃpʊkə] *f* (-; *no pl*) F spittle: **da blieb mir die ⁓ weg** I was flabbergasted. **'spucken** (h) **I** *v/i* **1.** spit, *engine*: splutter. **2.** F be sick, puke. **II** *v/t* **3.** spit *s.th.* out: **Blut ⁓** spit blood; → **Ton²** 1.

Spuk [ʃpuːk] *m* (-[e]s; -e) **1.** apparition, ghost, spectre, *Am.* specter, *w.s.* eerie happenings. **2.** *fig.* nightmare. **'spuken** (h) *v/i* haunt. **II** *v/impers* **in der Burg spukt es** the castle is haunted.

Spule ['ʃpuːlə] *f* (-; -n) **1.** ⊚ spool, reel. **2.** bobbin coil.

Spüle ['ʃpyːlə] *f* (-; -n) sink unit.

spulen ['ʃpuːlən] *v/t* (h) a) reel, spool, b) wind (*film etc*).

spülen ['ʃpyːlən] (h) **I** *v/t* **1.** rinse. **2.** wash (up): **Geschirr ⁓** → 4. **3.** *et. ans Ufer ⁓* wash s.th. ashore. **II** *v/i* **4.** wash up, wash (*or* do) the dishes. **5.** flush the toilet. **'Spülmittel** *n* washing-up liquid. **'Spülung** *f* (-; -en) **1.** rinse, ⚕ douche, irrigation. **2.** a) flushing, b) flush. **'Spülwasser** *n* rinsing water, washing-up water, *a.* dishwater (*a. fig. contp.*).

'Spulwurm *m* ♂, *zo.* roundworm.

Spur [ʃpuːr] *f* (-; -en) **1.** print, track(s),

trace(s), trail (*a. fig.*), *hunt. a.* scent: **e-e ⁓ aufnehmen** pick up a trail; *fig.* **auf die ⁓ kommen** (*dat*) get on to s.o., s.th.; **auf der falschen ⁓ sein** be on the wrong track; **s-e ⁓en verwischen** cover up one's tracks; (*bei j-m*) **s-e ⁓en hinterlassen** leave its mark (on s.o.). **2.** *fig.* trace, *esp.* ⚖ clue: **k-e ⁓ von ...** not a trace of ...; F **k-e ⁓!** not a bit! **3.** *fig.* trace, *gastr.* dash (*of pepper etc*). **4.** 🚗 a) ga(u)ge, b) track(s). **5.** *computer, tape*: track. **6.** *mot.* a) (**⁓ halten** keep) track, b) (**die ⁓ wechseln**) change lane.

'spürbar *adj* noticeable, marked, considerable: **⁓ sein** be felt; **⁓ werden** make itself felt.

spuren ['ʃpuːrən] *v/i* (h) **1.** *skiing*: lay a track. **2.** F toe the line.

spüren ['ʃpyːrən] *v/t* (h) feel, *a.* sense: **am eigenen Leibe zu ⁓ bekommen** have first-hand experience of; **von ... war nichts zu ⁓** there was no sign of ...

'Spurenele,ment *n* trace element.

'Spürhund *m* **1.** tracker dog. **2.** *humor.* sleuth.

'spurlos *adv* **⁓ verschwinden** disappear without a trace; **nicht ⁓ an j-m vorübergehen** leave its mark on s.o.

'Spürnase *f*, **'Spürsinn** *m* (-[e]s; *no pl*) (good) nose.

Spurt [ʃpʊrt] *m* (-[e]s; -s), **'spurten** *v/i* (h, sn) sprint, spurt.

'Spurwechsel *m mot.* changing lane.

'Spurweite *f* **1.** 🚗 ga(u)ge. **2.** *mot.* track.

Staat¹ [ʃtaːt] *m* (-[e]s; -en) **1.** *pol.* a) state, *a.* country, nation, b) government: F **die ⁓en** (*USA*) the States. **2.** *zo.* colony.

Staat² *m* (-[e]s; *no pl*) finery: *fig.* **damit kannst du k-n ⁓ machen!** that's nothing to write home about!

'Staatenbund *m* confederation.

'staatenlos *adj* stateless. **'Staatenlose** *m, f* (-n; -n) stateless person.

'staatlich *adj* state(-)...., government ..., national, public, *a.* state-owned (*plant etc*): **⁓e Mittel** government funds; **⁓ gefördert** state-sponsored; **⁓ gelenkt** state-run; **⁓ geprüft** qualified, registered.

'Staats|akt *m* a) act of state, b) state occasion. **⁓akti,on** *f* F **e-e ⁓ machen aus** (*dat*) make a big affair out of. **⁓angehörige** *m, f* national, citizen, *Br. a.* subject. **⁓angehörigkeit** *f* (**doppelte ⁓**

dual) nationality. **~angestellte** m, f state (or government) employee. **~anleihe** f government loan (or bond). **~anwalt** m ⚥ public prosecutor, Am. district attorney. **~anwaltschaft** f ⚥ a) the public prosecutor's office, b) the public prosecutors. **~beamte** m civil servant. **~begräbnis** n state funeral. **~besuch** m state visit. **~bürger** m citizen. **♀bürgerlich** adj civic: **~e Rechte** civil rights. **~bürgerschaft** f → **Staatsangehörigkeit**. **~chef** m head of state. **~dienst** m civil (Am. public) service. **♀eigen** adj state-owned. **~ex‚amen** n univ. state examination. **~feiertag** m national holiday. **~feind** m public enemy. **♀feindlich** adj subversive. **~form** f form of government. **~gebiet** n German etc territory. **~geheimnis** n state secret: F **das ist kein ~!** that's not top-secret. **~grenze** f border, frontier. **~haushalt** m national budget. **~hoheit** f (-; no pl) sovereignty. **~kasse** f (public) treasury. **~kosten** pl **auf ~** at (the) public expense.

'Staatsmann m (-[e]s; ⁻er) statesman. **'staatsmännisch** [-mɛnɪʃ] adj statesmanlike.

'Staats|mi‚nister m secretary of state, Am. secretary. **~mini‚sterium** n ministry. **~oberhaupt** n head of state. **~präsi‚dent** m president. **~rat** m a) council of state, Br. Privy Council, b) council(l)or of state. **~recht** n (-[e]s; no pl) constitutional law. **~religi‚on** f state religion. **~schulden** pl national debt. **~sekre‚tär** m permanent secretary. **~sicherheitsdienst** m DDR pol. hist. State Security (Service). **~streich** m coup (d'état). **♀tragend** adj supportive of the State. **~trauer** f national mourning. **~verbrechen** n political crime. **~vertrag** m (international) treaty. **~wesen** n (-s; no pl) 1. state, body politic. 2. political system. **~wissenschaft(en** pl) f political science. **~wohl** n public weal. **~zuschuß** m government grant, subsidy.

Stab¹ [ʃtaːp] m (-[e]s; ⁻e) a) staff, b) stick, c) rod, bar, d) wand, e) ♪, sports: baton, f) sports: pole: fig. **den ~ brechen über** (acc) condemn.

Stab² m (-[e]s; ⁻e) 1. a) (administrative etc) staff, b) team (of experts etc). 2. ✗

a) staff, b) staff officers, c) headquarters.

Stäbchen ['ʃtɛːpçən] n (-s; -) chopstick.

'Stabhochspringer m pole-vaulter.

'Stabhochsprung m pole-vault(ing).

stabil [ʃtaˈbiːl] adj 1. stable. 2. solid, sturdy. **stabilisieren** [ʃtabiliˈziːrən] v/t (h) stabilize: **sich ~ a.** become stabilized. **Stabili'sierung** f (-; -en) stabilization. **Stabilität** [ʃtabiliˈtɛːt] f (-; no pl) stability.

'Stabreim m alliteration.

'Stabs|arzt m captain (medical corps). **~chef** m chief of staff. **~feldwebel** m warrant officer, Am. master sergeant. **'Stabwechsel** m sports: baton change.

stach [ʃtaːx] pret of **stechen**.

Stachel ['ʃtaxəl] m (-s; -n) 1. prickle, zo. a. spine, sting, ⚘ a. thorn. 2. ⚙ spike.

'Stachelbeere f gooseberry.

'Stacheldraht m barbed wire.

'stach(e)lig adj 1. prickly, zo. a. spiny, ⚘ a. thorny. 2. fig. bristly (chin, beard).

'Stachelschwein n porcupine.

Stadion ['ʃtaːdiɔn] n (-s; -dien) stadium.

Stadium ['ʃtaːdiʊm] n (-s; -dien) stage, phase.

Stadt [ʃtat] f (-; ⁻e) 1. town, city: **in die ~ gehen** go to town. 2. adm. municipality. **~autobahn** f urban motorway (Am. expressway). **~bahn** f city railway. **♀bekannt** adj known all over town, notorious. **~bevölkerung** f urban population. **~bewohner** m city dweller. **~bezirk** m municipal district. **~bild** n townscape.

Städtchen ['ʃtɛːtçən] n (-s; -) small town.

Städte|bau ['ʃtɛːtə-] m (-[e]s; no pl) urban development. **~planung** f town planning.

Städter ['ʃtɛːtər] m (-s; -) city dweller.

'Stadt|gas n (-es; no pl) town gas. **~gebiet** n municipal area. **~gemeinde** f township. **~gespräch** n fig. **~ sein** be the talk of the town. **~gue‚rilla** f urban guer(r)illa. **~halle** f municipal hall.

städtisch ['ʃtɛːtɪʃ] adj town ..., city ..., urban, adm. municipal.

'Stadt|kern m town (or city) cent/re (Am. -er). **~leben** n city life. **~luft** f city air. **~mauer** f city wall. **~mitte** f → **Innenstadt**. **~plan** m city map. **~planung** f town planning.

'Stadtrand m (**am ~** at the) outskirts of

the town (*or* city). **~siedlung** *f* suburban estate (*or* housing development).

'Stadt|rat *m* **1.** municipal council. **2.** town (*Am.* city) council(l)or. **~rund-fahrt** *f* city sightseeing tour. **~sa,nie-rung** *f* urban renewal. **~staat** *m* city state. **~streicher** *m* (-s; -) city vagrant. **~teil** *m* district. **~tor** *n* town gate. **~ver-kehr** *m* town (*or* city) traffic. **~verwal-tung** *f* municipality. **~viertel** *n* district. **~zentrum** *n* → *Innenstadt.*

Staffage [ʃtaˈfaːʒə] *f* (-; -n) mere show.

Staffel ['ʃtafəl] *f* (-; -n) **1.** *sports:* relay (race *or* team). **2.** ✈, ✕ squadron.

Staffelei [ʃtafəˈlaɪ] *f* (-; -en) easel.

'Staffellauf *m* *sports:* relay race.

staffeln ['ʃtafəln] *v/t* (h) a) stagger, b) grade, graduate (*taxes, wages, etc*); → *gestaffelt.* **'Staffelung** *f* (-; -en) a) staggering, b) graduation (*of taxes etc*), progressive rates.

Stagnation [ʃtagnaˈtsjoːn] *f* (-; -en) stagnation.

stagnieren [ʃtaˈɡniːrən] *v/i* (h) stagnate.

stahl [ʃtaːl] *pret of stehlen.*

Stahl *m* (-[e]s; ⁓e) steel: *Nerven aus* ~ nerves of steel. **~arbeiter** *m* steelworker. **~bau** *m* steel(-girder) construction. **~be,ton** *m* reinforced concrete. **⚡blau** *adj* steel-blue. **~blech** *n* sheet steel.

stählen ['ʃtɛːlən] *v/t* (h) **1.** ⚙ steel-face. **2.** *fig.* steel (*sich* o.s.). **'stählern** *adj* **1.** (of) steel. **2.** *fig.* of steel, steely.

'Stahl|gürtelreifen *m* *mot.* steel breaker tyre (*Am.* tire). **⚡hart** *adj* (as) hard as steel, steely. **~helm** *m* steel helmet. **~(rohr)möbel** *pl* tubular steel furniture. **~stich** *m* steel engraving. **~waren** *pl* steel goods. **~werk** *n* steelworks. **~wolle** *f* steel wool.

Stall [ʃtal] *m* (-[e]s; ⁓e) stable (*a. fig.*), a cowshed: F *e-n ganzen* ~ *voll* a horde of *children etc.* **~bursche** *m* groom. **~gefährte** *m* *sports:* stable mate. **~mei-ster** *m* riding master.

'Stallungen *pl* stabling, stables.

Stamm [ʃtam] *m* (-[e]s; ⁓e) **1.** ♣ stem (*a. ling.*), (tree) trunk. **2.** a) race, tribe, b) family. **3.** *fig.* core, nucleus. **4.** permanent staff, ✝ regular customers, *sports:* regular players. **5.** *biol.* phylum. **~aktie** *f* ordinary share, *Am.* common stock. **~baum** *m* family tree, *zo.* pedigree, *biol.* phylogenetic tree. **~buch** *n* family

register. **~burg** *f* ancestral castle. **~da,tei** *f* master file.

stammeln ['ʃtaməln] *v/t, v/i* (h) stammer.

stammen ['ʃtamən] *v/i* (h) (*von, aus*) a) come (from), b) date (from), go back (to): *der Ausspruch stammt von ihm* the word was coined by him.

'Stammform *f* *ling.* principal form.

'Stammgast *m* regular (guest).

'Stammhalter *m* *humor.* son and heir.

'Stammhaus *n* ✝ parent firm.

stämmig ['ʃtɛmɪç] *adj* stocky, burly.

'Stamm|kapi,tal *n* ordinary share capital, *Am.* common capital stock. **~knei-pe** *f* F local. **~kunde** *m* regular customer, F regular. **~lo,kal** *n* favo(u)rite haunt. **~perso,nal** *n* permanent (*or* skeleton) staff. **~platz** *m* favo(u)rite seat: *sports: sich e-n* ~ *erobern* make the regular team. **~spieler** *m* *sports:* regular player. **~tafel** *f* genealogical table. **~tisch** *m* (table reserved for) regular guests. **~tischpo,litiker** *m* armchair politician. **~wähler** *m* *pol.* standing voter.

stampfen ['ʃtampfən] **I** *v/i* **1.** (sn) stamp, ⚓ pitch. **2.** (h) *mit dem Fuß* stamp one's foot. **II** *v/t* (h) a) pound, crush, mash, b) tamp: → *Boden* 1.

stand [ʃtant] *pret of stehen.*

Stand *m* (-[e]s; ⁓e) **1.** *no pl* a) (*aus dem* ~ from a) standing position, b) footing, foothold: *k-n* (*festen*) ~ *haben* be wobbly, *person:* have no firm foothold; *fig.* (*bei j-m*) *e-n schweren* ~ *haben* have a hard time of it (with s.o.). **2.** *no pl* a) state, condition, b) position (*a. astr.*), c) (*a. water etc*) level, standard, d) figure, (*barometer etc*) reading, e) *sports:* score: *beim* ~ *von 4:2* at 4:2; *nach dem* ~ *vom 1. Mai* as of May 1st; *den höchsten* ~ *erreichen* reach its peak; *et. auf den neuesten* ~ *bringen* bring s.th. up to date, update s.th.; *der* ~ *der Dinge* the state of affairs; *nach dem* ~ *der Dinge* as matters stand; *der neueste* ~ *der Technik* (*or Wissenschaft*) the state of the art. **3.** *no pl* social standing, rank, (*a. legal, marital*) status. **4.** a) class, b) profession.

Stand² *m* (-[e]s; ⁓e) stand.

Standard ['ʃtandart] *m* (-s; -s) standard.

standardisieren [ʃtandardiˈziːrən] *v/t*

(h) standardize. **Standardi'sierung** *f* (-; -en) standardization.

'**Standardwerk** *n* standard work.

Standarte [ʃtanˈdartə] *f* (-; -n) standard.

'**Standbild** *n* statue.

Ständchen ['ʃtɛntçən] *n* (-s; -) serenade: *j-m ein ~ bringen* serenade s.o.

Stander ['ʃtandər] *m* (-s; -) pennant.

Ständer ['ʃtɛndər] *m* (-s; -) **1.** stand, (*pipe, rifle, etc*) rack. **2.** V hard-on.

'**Standes|amt** *n* registry office. **⛣amtlich** *adj* **~e Trauung** registry office wedding. **~beamte** *m* registrar. **⛣gemäß** *adj and adv* in keeping with one's station. **~unterschied** *m* social difference.

'**standfest** *adj* steady, ⛣ stable.

'**Standfestigkeit** *f* (-; *no pl*) **1.** steadiness, ⛣ stability. **2.** → **Standhaftigkeit**.

'**Stand|foto** *n film*: still. **~gericht** *n* ✕ drumhead court martial.

'**standhaft** *adj* steadfast, firm.

'**Standhaftigkeit** *f* (-; *no pl*) steadfastness, firmness.

'**standhalten** *v/i* (*irr, sep,* -ge-, h, → **halten**) a) hold one's ground, stand firm, b) withstand, resist (*attack etc*), c) stand up to (*criticism etc*): → **Vergleich** 1.

ständig ['ʃtɛndɪç] **I** *adj* a) constant, continuous, b) permanent (*abode, personnel, etc*), c) fixed, regular (*income*), d) standing (*committee*): **~er Begleiter** constant companion. **II** *adv* permanently, constantly, always: *et. ~ tun* keep doing s.th.

'**Stand|licht** *n mot.* (-[e]s; *no pl*) parking light. **~ort** *m* position (*a.* ⚓ *or fig.*), location, site (*of firm etc*), ✕ garrison, *Am.* post, *biol.* habitat: **den ~** (*gen*) **bestimmen** locate. **~pauke** *f* F lecture: *j-m e-e ~ halten* lecture s.o. (*über acc* on). **~punkt** *m* **1.** post, point. **2.** *fig.* (*von s-m etc* **~ aus** from his *etc*) point of view: **den ~ vertreten, auf dem ~ stehen** take the view (*daß* that). **~quar,tier** *n* base. **~recht** *n* (-[e]s; *no pl*) martial law. **⛣rechtlich** *adj and adv* by order of a court martial. **~spur** *f mot.* hard shoulder. **~uhr** *f* grandfather clock.

Stange ['ʃtaŋə] *f* (-; -n) 1. pole (*a. sports*), (flag) staff, (metal) rod, bar, *for birds*: perch, (*sugar, celery, etc*) stick: *e-e ~* (*Zigaretten*) a carton (of cigarettes);

Kleidung von der ~ clothes off the peg; F *e-e ~ Geld* a packet; *bei der ~ bleiben* stick to it, *a.* stick it out; *j-n bei der ~ halten* keep s.o. at it; *j-m die ~ halten* stick up for s.o. **2.** branch (*on antlers*).

'**Stangen|bohne** *f* runner (*or* string) bean. **~spargel** *m* asparagus spears.

stank [ʃtaŋk] *pret of* **stinken**.

stänkern ['ʃtɛŋkərn] *v/i* (h) F *contp.* stir up trouble: **~ gegen** rail against.

Stanniol [ʃtaˈni̯oːl] *n* (-s; -e) tinfoil.

Stanze ['ʃtantsə] *f* (-; -n) ⛣ stamp(ing machine). '**stanzen** *v/t* (h) a) punch, b) stamp.

Stapel ['ʃtaːpəl] *m* (-s; -) **1.** pile, stack. **2.** ⚓ stocks: *auf ~ legen* lay down; *vom ~ lassen* launch (*a. fig.* project *etc*), *fig.* deliver (*speech*), crack (*joke*); *vom ~ laufen* be launched. '**Stapellauf** *m* launching. '**stapeln** *v/t* (h) **1.** stack, (*a. sich ~*) pile up. **2.** store, stockpile.

stapfen ['ʃtapfən] *v/i* (sn) trudge.

Star¹ [ʃtaːr] *m* (-[e]s; -e) *zo.* starling.

Star² *m* (-[e]s; -e) 🕯 *grauer ~* cataract; *grüner ~* glaucoma.

Star³ [staːr, ʃtaːr] *m* (-s; -s) *film etc*: star.

'**Staral,lüren** *pl contp.* airs and graces.

starb [ʃtarp] *pret of* **sterben**.

'**Stargast** *m* star guest.

stark [ʃtark] **I** *adj* **1.** strong (*a. ling. or fig.*), *w.s.* great, intense (*heat, cold, etc*), heavy (*rain, traffic,* 📈 *demand, etc*): *ein ~es Polizeiaufgebot* a strong force of police; *ein 20 Mann ~er Trupp* a group of 20; *er ist ein ~er Raucher* (*Esser*) he is a heavy smoker (big eater); *fig. ~e Seite* strong point; *sich ~ machen für* stand up for; F *das ist ein ~es Stück!* that's a bit thick! **2.** thick: *2 cm ~e Pappe* pasteboard two centimetres thick; *das Buch ist 150 Seiten ~* the book has 150 pages. **3.** *in performance, a.* opt., ⛣ strong, powerful, high-powered (*engine*): *ein ~es Medikament* a powerful (*or* potent) drug. **4.** stout, corpulent. **5.** bad, severe (*cold, pain, etc*). **6.** F (*echt*) *~* super, great. **II** *adv* strongly, highly, very much: *~ beschädigt* badly damaged; *~ übertrieben* grossly exaggerated; *~ erkältet*.

Stärke¹ ['ʃtɛrkə] *f* (-; -n) **1.** *no pl* strength, power. **2.** opt., ⛣ power, *a.* 💪 strength. **3.** thickness, diameter. **4.** intensity, force, *a.* heaviness (*of rain, traffic, etc*), *a.* severity (*of pain etc*). **5.** *fig.* **j-s ~** s.o.'s strong point (*or* forte).

'**Stärke**² *f* (-; -n) 🌾 starch.

stärken ['ʃtɛrkən] *v/t* (h) strengthen (*a. fig.*), invigorate: **sich ~** fortify o.s.

'**stärken**² *v/t* (h) starch.

'**stärkend** *adj* (*a.* **~es Mittel**) tonic.

'**Starkstrom** *m* ⚡ high-voltage (*or* heavy) current. **~leitung** *f* power line. **~technik** *f* heavy-current engineering.

'**Stärkung** *f* (-; -en) **1.** strengthening. **2.** refreshment, F pick-me-up.

'**Stärkungsmittel** *n* tonic.

starr [ʃtar] *adj* rigid (*a. fig.*), stiff, *a.* motionless: **~er Blick** (fixed) stare; **ich war ~** (**vor Staunen**) I was dum(b)-founded.

starren¹ ['ʃtarən] *v/i* (h) stare (**auf** *acc* at).

'**starren**² *v/i* (h) **~ vor** (*or* **von**) be full of; **vor Schmutz ~** be thick with dirt.

'**Starrheit** *f* (-; *no pl*) rigidity (*a. fig.*), stiffness.

'**starrköpfig** [-kœpfɪç] *adj* pigheaded.

'**Starrkopf** *m* (-[e]s; -s) pighead.

'**Starrsinn** *m* (-[e]s; *no pl*) obstinacy, pigheadedness.

Start [ʃtart] *m* (-[e]s; -s) start (*a. fig.*), ✈ takeoff, *of rocket etc*: liftoff: ✈ **zum ~ freigeben** clear for takeoff; *sports:* **an den ~ gehen** a) runner *etc*: take up one's starting position, b) take part. **~auto,matik** *f* *mot.* automatic choke (control). **~bahn** *f* ✈ runway.

'**startbereit** *adj* ready to start, ✈ ready for takeoff.

starten ['ʃtartən] **I** *v/i* (sn) **1.** *sports:* start, *a.* take part (**in** *dat*, **bei** in). **2.** ✈ take off, *rocket etc*: lift off. **II** *v/t* (h) start, F *fig. a.* launch. '**Starter** *m* (-s; -), '**Starterin** *f* (-; -nen) *sports:* starter.

'**Starterlaubnis** *f* **1.** *sports:* permission to take part. **2.** ✈ clearance for takeoff.

'**Starthilfe** *f* **1.** **j-m ~ geben** a) *mot.* give s.o. a jump-start, b) *fig.* give s.o. a start (in life). **2.** *Abflug mit ~* assisted takeoff. **~kabel** *n mot.* jump leads.

'**Startkapi,tal** *n* start-up capital.

'**Startschuß** *m* *sports:* starting shot.

'**Startverbot** *n* *sports:* suspension, ✈ grounding: **~ erhalten** a) be suspended, b) be grounded.

Stasi ['ʃta:zi] *f* (-; *no pl*) F DDR *pol. hist.* State Security (Service).

Statik ['ʃta:tɪk] *f* (-; *no pl*) △, ⚡, *phys.* statics. **Statiker** ['ʃta:tikər] *m* (-s; -) △ stress analyst.

Station [ʃta'tsĭo:n] *f* (-; -en) **1.** *radio, TV, etc:* station. **2.** 🚃 station, stop: **~ machen** break one's journey. **3.** (hospital) ward. **4.** *fig.* stage. **stationär** [ʃtatsĭo-'nɛ:r] *adj a.* ⚕ stationary: ✚ **~e Behandlung** in-patient treatment; **~er** (*or* **~ behandelter**) **Patient** in-patient.

stationieren [ʃtatsĭo'ni:rən] *v/t* (h) station, deploy (*rockets etc*). **Statio'nierung** *f* (-; -en) stationing, deployment.

Stati'ons|arzt *m* ward doctor. **~schwester** *f* ward sister. **~vorsteher** *m* 🚃 stationmaster.

statisch ['ʃta:tɪʃ] *adj* static.

Statist [ʃta'tɪst] *m* (-en; -en), **Sta'tistin** *f* (-; -nen) *thea., film:* extra.

Statistik [ʃta'tɪstɪk] *f* (-; -en) statistics. **Sta'tistiker** [-tikər] *m* (-s; -) statistician. **sta'tistisch** [-tɪʃ] *adj* statistical.

Stativ [ʃta'ti:f] *n* (-s; -e) tripod.

statt [ʃtat] → **anstatt**.

Statt *f* **an j-s ~** in s.o.'s place; **an Kindes ~ annehmen** adopt.

Stätte ['ʃtɛtə] *f* (-; -n) place, *a.* scene.

'**statt|finden** *v/i* (*irr, sep,* -ge-, h, → **finden**) take place, be held. **~geben** *v/i* (*irr, sep,* -ge-, h, → **geben**) *adm.* grant.

'**statthaft** *adj* admissible: **nicht ~** not allowed.

'**Statthalter** *m* (-s; -) governor.

'**stattlich** *adj* **1.** stately, impressive. **2.** large (*sum etc*). **3.** portly: **e-e ~e Erscheinung** a fine figure of a man *etc*.

Statue ['ʃta:tŭə] *f* (-; -n) statue.

statuieren [ʃtatu'i:rən] *v/t* (h) → **Exempel**.

Statur [ʃta'tu:r] *f* (-; -en) stature (*a. fig.*).

Status ['ʃta:tos] *m* (-; -) state, *a.* (legal) status. **~sym,bol** *n* status symbol.

Stau [ʃtaʊ] *m* (-[e]s; -s, -e) **1.** accumulation, pile-up. **2.** ✚ congestion. **3.** a) traffic jam (*or* congestion), b) tailback.

Staub [ʃtaʊp] *m* (-[e]s; *no pl*) dust: **~ wischen** do the dusting; F **sich aus dem ~(e) machen** clear off; → **aufwirbeln**. '**Staubbeutel** *m* **1.** ♣ anther. **2.** ⚙ dust bag. **Stäubchen** ['ʃtɔʏpçən] *n* (-s; -) speck of dust, dust particle.

'**Staubecken** *n* ⚙ reservoir.

stauben ['ʃtaʊbən] *v/i* (h) make a lot of dust: **es staubt** it's dusty. '**Staubflocke**

f piece of fluff. **'Staubgefäß** *n* ♀ stamen. **'staubig** *adj* dusty. **'staubsaugen** *v/t, v/i* (insep, -ge-, h) vacuum, *Br.* F hoover (*TM*). **'Staubsauger** *m* (-s; -) vacuum cleaner, *Br.* F hoover (*TM*). **'Staubwolke** *f* cloud of dust.

stauchen [ˈʃtauxən] *v/t* (h) ⊕ jolt, upset. **'Staudamm** *m* dam.

Staude [ˈʃtaudə] *f* (-; -n) herbaceous plant.

stauen [ˈʃtauən] (h) **I** *v/t* dam up (*water*), stop (the flow of *blood*). **II** *sich* ~ *water*: build up (*a. fig. anger, traffic, etc*), rise, *ice, fig. mail etc*: accumulate, pile up, ♣ be(come) congested.

'Stauer *m* (-s; -) ♣ stevedore.

staunen [ˈʃtaunən] *v/i* (h) (*über acc* at) be astonished, be amazed, marvel. **'Staunen** *n* (-s) astonishment, amazement: *in* ~ *versetzen* amaze; → *starr.* **'staunenswert** *adj* astonishing, amazing.

Staupe [ˈʃtaupə] *f* (-; -n) *vet.* distemper.

'Stausee *m* reservoir.

'Stauung *f* (-; -en) **1.** damming up. **2.** → *Stau.*

Steak [steːk] *n* (-s; -s) *gastr.* steak.

Stearin [ʃteaˈriːn] *n* (-s; -e) stearin.

stechen [ˈʃtɛçən] (stach, gestochen, h) **I** *v/t* **1.** prick, *wasp etc*: sting, *gnat*: bite: *sich* ~ prick o.s.; *sich in den Finger* ~ prick one's finger; → *Hafer, gestochen.* **2.** cut (*asparagus, peat, etc*), stick, kill (*pig etc*). **3.** punch (*time clock*). **4.** engrave (*picture*). **II** *v/i* **5.** prick, *wasp etc*: sting, *gnat*: bite. **6.** *nach j-m* ~ stab at s.o., cut: ~ *in* (acc) stick s.th. in(to). **7.** *sun*: burn. **8.** *pain*: stab, shoot. **9.** *sports*: jump (*or* shoot *etc*) off. **10.** *cards*: a) be trump, b) trump. **11.** F *fig. j-m in die Augen* ~ catch s.o.'s eye. **'Stechen** *n* (-s) **1.** stabbing (*or* shooting) pain. **2.** *show jumping*: jump-off. **'stechend** *adj fig.* piercing (*look*), pungent (*smell*), stabbing (*pain*), burning (*sun*).

'Stech|karte *f* time-punch card. **~mücke** *f* mosquito. **~palme** *f* holly. **~uhr** *f* time clock. **~zirkel** *m* dividers.

'Steckbrief *m* **1.** "wanted" circular. **2.** *fig.* description, fact file (*gen* of). **'steckbrieflich** *adv* ~ *gesucht werden* be wanted for arrest.

'Steckdose *f* ⚡ (wall) socket.

stecken [ˈʃtɛkən] (h) **I** *v/t* a) put, *secretly*: slip, b) stick (*pin etc*), c) pin (*fabric, paper*), d) ⊕ insert (*in acc* into): *fig. Geld* ~ *in* (acc) put money into, invest in; *j-n ins Gefängnis* (*Bett*) ~ put s.o. in prison (to bed); F *wer hat ihm das gesteckt?* who told him?; → *Brand* 1, *Nase.* **II** *v/i* be stuck, *bullet, splinter, etc*: be lodged, *person, thing*: be: *der Schlüssel steckt* the key is in the lock; F *wo steckst du denn* (*so lange*)? where have you been (all this time)?, *da steckt 'er dahinter* he's at the bottom of it; *sie steckt mitten in den Prüfungen* she's in the middle of her exams; → *Decke* 1.

'Stecken *m* (-s; -) stick: → *Dreck* 1. **'stecken|bleiben** *v/i* (irr, sep, -ge-, sn, → *bleiben*) *a. fig.* get stuck. **~lassen** *v/t* (irr, sep, -ge-, h, → *lassen*) *den Schlüssel* ~ leave the key in the lock.

'Steckenpferd *n* hobbyhorse, *fig. mst* hobby.

'Stecker *m* (-s; -) ⚡ plug. **'Steckkon|takt** *m* ⚡ plug (connection).

'Steckling *m* (-s; -e) ♀ cutting.

'Stecknadel *f* pin. **~kopf** *m* pinhead.

'Steckschlüssel *m* ⊕ box spanner.

'Steckschuh *m phot.* accessory shoe.

Steg [ʃteːk] *m* (-[e]s; -e) **1.** footpath. **2.** a) footbridge, b) landing stage, c) gangplank. **3.** bridge (of *spectacles, violin*).

'Stegreif *m aus dem* ~ off the cuff; *aus dem* ~ *spielen* improvise; *aus dem* ~ *sprechen* extemporize, F ad-lib.

stehen [ˈʃteːən] (stand, gestanden, h) **I** *v/i* **1.** stand, be: F *wie steht's?* a) how are things?, b) *mit dir?* how about you?, c) a. *wie steht das Spiel?* what's the score?; *wie steht's mit e-m Bier?* how about a beer?; *das Programm steht* the program(me *Br.*) is complete (*or* in the bag); *es steht zu befürchten, daß ...* it is to be feared that ...; F *mir steht's bis hier(her)!* I am fed up to here (with it); *gut* (*schlecht*) *mit j-m* ~ (not to) get on well with s.o.; *er steht sich gut* (*dabei*) he's not doing badly (out of it); *unter Alkohol* (*Drogen*) ~ be under the influence of alcohol (drugs); ~ *vor* be faced with (*decision, problem, etc*); *er steht vor s-r Prüfung* his exam is coming up; *zu j-m* ~ stand by s.o.; *zu s-m Versprechen etc* ~ keep one's promise; *wie stehst du dazu?* what do you think (of it)?; *pol.* **er steht links** he belongs to the left; *die Aktie (das Thermometer etc)* **steht auf ...** the share (the thermometer *etc*) is at ...; *auf Diebstahl* **steht e-e Freiheitsstrafe** theft is punishable by imprisonment; → *Debatte, teuer* II. **2.** stand still, *a. clock etc:* have stopped. **3.** be written, say: *in dem Brief* **steht** the letter says; *wo* **steht das?** where does it say so? **4.** *fig. j-m* ~ *dress etc:* suit s.o., look well on s.o. **II** *v/t* → *Mann, Modell, Posten* 2, *Wache etc.* '**Stehen** *n* (-s) (*a. im* ~) standing; *zum* ~ *bringen* a) (bring to a) stop, b) staunch (*bleeding*); *zum* ~ *kommen* come to a halt.

'**stehenbleiben** *v/i* (*irr, sep,* -ge-, sn, → *bleiben*) **1.** stop (*a. clock etc*), engine: stall, *heart:* stop (beating): *wo waren wir stehengeblieben?* where did we leave off? **2.** *umbrella etc:* be left (behind): *fig. der Satz kann so nicht* ~ the sentence cannot be left like this.

'**stehend** *adj* standing (*a. army, waters*), stationary: ~*e Redensart* stock phrase.

'**stehenlassen** *v/t* (*irr, sep,* -ge-, h, → *lassen*) **1.** leave (behind): *alles stehen- und liegenlassen* drop everything. **2.** leave *food etc* untouched. **3.** overlook (*mistake*): *fig. das kann man so nicht* ~ that's not quite correct. **4.** *j-n* ~ leave s.o. standing there. **5.** → *Bart* 1.

'**Steher** *m* (-s; -) *cycling:* stayer.

'**Steh|imbiß** *m* stand-up snack bar. ~**kragen** *m* stand-up collar. ~**lampe** *f* standard (*Am.* floor) lamp.

stehlen ['ʃteːlən] *v/t, v/i* (stahl, gestohlen, h) steal: *j-m et.* ~ steal s.th. from s.o.; *j-m die Zeit* ~ waste s.o.'s time; F *er kann mir gestohlen bleiben!* to hell with him!

'**Stehplatz** *m* standing room.

'**Stehvermögen** *n* (-s; *no pl*) stamina, staying power.

steif [ʃtaɪf] *adj* stiff (*a. fig.*), *a.* ⚙ rigid: ~ *vor Kälte* numb with cold; ~*e Brise* (~*er Grog*) stiff breeze (grog); *gastr.* ~ *schlagen* beat (until stiff); F ~ *und fest behaupten* insist, swear.

steifen ['ʃtaɪfən] *v/t* (h) *fig. j-m den Nacken* (or *Rücken*) ~ stiffen s.o.'s back.

'**Steifheit** *f* (-; *no pl*) *a. fig.* stiffness.

'**Steigbügel** *m* stirrup. '**Steigeisen** *n* climbing iron, *mount. a.* crampon.

steigen ['ʃtaɪgən] (stieg, gestiegen, sn) **I** *v/i* **1.** go up, climb (up), rise (*into the air*), ✈ climb (*auf acc* to): *auf e-n Baum* (*Berg*) ~ climb (up) a tree (mountain); *auf ein Pferd* ~ mount a horse; *vom Pferd* ~ dismount; *aus dem Bus etc* ~ get out of (or off) the bus *etc*; *in den Zug etc* ~ get on (or board) a train *etc*; ~ *lassen* fly (*kite*), send up (*balloon*); → *Kopf* 1. **2.** increase, grow, *temperature etc:* rise, *prices: a.* go up: → *Achtung* 1, *Wert* 1. **3.** F be on, take place: *e-e Party* ~ *lassen* throw a party. **II** *v/t* **4.** go up: *Treppen* ~ climb stairs. '**Steigen** *n* (-s) **1.** climbing (*etc,* → I). **2.** rise, increase: *das* ~ *und Fallen* the rise and fall; *im* ~ *begriffen sein* be rising. '**steigend** *adj fig.* rising, increasing: ~*e Tendenz* upward tendency.

'**Steiger** *m* (-s; -) ⚒ pit foreman.

steigern ['ʃtaɪgərn] (h) **I** *v/t* **1.** increase, *a.* heighten (*effect, suspense, etc*), step up (*pace, production, etc*), raise (*bet, offer, etc*): *s-e Leistung* ~ improve one's performance; *den Wert* ~ add to the value (*gen etc*). **2.** *ling.* compare. **II** *v/refl* *sich* ~ **3.** a) increase, *a.* grow, *interest, suspense, etc:* rise, b) improve (one's performance). **III** *v/i* a) *at auction:* bid, b) rise the amount (*auf acc* to). '**Steigerung** *f* (-; -en) **1.** a) increase, rise, b) improvement. **2.** *ling.* comparison.

'**Steigfähigkeit** *f* ✈ climbing power, *mot.* hill-climbing ability.

'**Steigung** *f* (-; -en) rise, ascent, gradient.

steil [ʃtaɪl] *adj a. fig.* steep: ~*e Karriere* meteoric career; ~ *ansteigen* rise steeply, *prices: a.* soar. '**Steilkurve** *f* steep turn. '**Steilküste** *f* steep coast. '**Steilpaß** *m soccer:* through pass.

Stein [ʃtaɪn] *m* (-[e]s; -e) a) stone (*a.* ♞, ♣), ⚙ *a.* brick, b) (precious) stone, gem, jewel, *of watch:* ruby, c) *board games:* piece: *fig. den* ~ *ins Rollen bringen* set the ball rolling; *bei j-m e-n* ~ *im Brett haben* be in s.o.'s good books; *mir fällt ein* ~ *vom Herzen* that takes a load off my mind; → *Tropfen* 1. ~**adler** *m zo.* golden eagle. ♀**alt** *adj* ancient. ~**bock** *m* **1.** *zo.* ibex. **2.** *no pl astr.* ([*ein*] ~ *sein* be [a]) Capricorn. ~**bruch** *m* quarry. ~**butt** *m zo.* turbot. ~**druck** *m*

(-[e]s; -e) **1.** *no pl* lithography. **2.** lithograph.

'**steinern** *adj* (of) stone, *fig.* stony.
'**Steinfrucht** *f* stone fruit.
'**Steingarten** *m* rock garden.
'**Steingut** *n* (-[e]s; -e) earthenware.
'**steinig** *adj* stony.
'**Steinkohle** *f* hard coal.
'**Steinmetz** [-mɛts] *m* (-en; -en) stonemason.
'**Steinobst** *n* stone fruit.
'**Steinpilz** *m* edible boletus.
'**steinreich** *adj* F filthy rich.
'**Steinschlag** *m* falling rocks.
'**Steinzeit** *f* (-; *no pl*) Stone Age.
Steiß [ʃtaɪs] *m* (-es; -e) buttocks, rump.
'**Steißbein** *n anat.* coccyx.
'**Stelldichein** *n* (-[s]; -[s]) rendezvous.
Stelle ['ʃtɛlə] *f* (-; -n) **1.** place, spot, point, position: **an dieser ~** here; **an anderer ~** elsewhere; **an erster ~** in the first place, first(ly); **an erster ~ stehen** come first; **an ~ von** (*or gen*) in place of, instead of; (**ich**) **an d-r ~** if I were you; **an die ~ treten von** (*or gen*) take the place of, *person:* **a.** take over from, replace; **auf der ~** on the spot; *fig.* **auf der ~ treten** mark time; **nicht von der ~ kommen** not to make any progress; **er rührte sich nicht von der ~** he didn't budge; **zur ~ sein** be at hand. **2.** passage (*a.* ♪). **3.** A a) digit, b) (decimal) place. **4.** situation, job, post: **freie** (*or* **offene**) **~** vacancy. **5.** → **Dienststelle**.
stellen ['ʃtɛlən] (h) **I** *v/t* **1.** put, place, set, arrange: → **Antrag** 1, **Bedingung**, **Bein**, **Falle**, **Frage** 1, **gestellt**. **2.** set *clock etc* (**auf** *acc* at), adjust: **leiser** (*or* **niedriger**) **~** turn down; **lauter** (*or* **höher**) **~** turn up. **3.** provide, supply. **4.** hunt down (*game, criminal*). **II** *sich* **~ 5.** place o.s.: **stell dich dorthin!** (go and) stand over there; **auf sich selbst gestellt sein** be on one's own; **gut** (**schlecht**) **gestellt sein** be well (badly) off; **sich gegen ~** oppose; **sich hinter** (**vor**) **j-n ~** back s.o. up (shield s.o.); **wie stellt er sich dazu?** what does he say (to this)? **6.** *sich* (**der Polizei**) **~** turn o.s. in; *sich* (**zum Wehrdienst**) **~** report for military service. **7.** (*dat*) take on *opponent*, face up to *criticism etc*, take up *challenge*: **sich der Presse ~** be prepared to meet (*or* face) the Press. **8.**

sich krank etc **~** pretend to be ill *etc*.
'**Stellen|angebot** *n* job offer: **~e** *newspaper:* vacancies. **~gesuch** *n* application (for a job): **~e** *newspaper:* situations wanted. **~markt** *m* job market. **~suche** *f* (**auf ~ sein** be) job-hunting. **~wechsel** *m* job change.
'**stellenweise** *adv* in places.
'**Stellenwert** *m* rating, (relative) importance: **e-n hohen ~ haben** rate high.
...stellig [-ʃtɛlɪç] *in cpds.* ...-digit.
'**Stellplatz** *m mot.* carport.
'**Stellschraube** *f* ☼ adjusting screw.
'**Stellung** *f* (-; -en) **1.** *a.* ✕ position: *fig.* **die ~ halten** hold the fort; **~ nehmen** (**zu**) take a stand (on), give one's view (on); **~ nehmen für** stand up for; **~ nehmen gegen** oppose. **2.** situation, job, post, position: **e-e leitende ~** an executive position. **3.** a) position, rank, b) status, standing.
'**Stellungnahme** *f* (-; -n) (**zu** on) opinion, comment, statement.
'**Stellungskrieg** *m* static warfare.
'**stellungslos** *adj* unemployed, jobless.
'**Stellungs|spiel** *n sports:* positional play. **~suche** *f* search for a post (*or* job): **auf ~ sein** be looking for a job, be job-hunting. **~suchende** *m, f* (-n; -n) person looking for a job, job-hunter. **~wechsel** *m* change of post (*or* job): **häufiger ~** job-hopping.
'**stellvertretend** *adj* acting, deputy: **~er Vorsitzender** vice-chairman; **~ für** a) acting for, b) on behalf of.
'**Stellvertreter(in** *f*) *m* representative, substitute, *of doctor etc:* locum (tenens), *adm.* deputy, ✝, ♟ proxy.
'**Stellvertretung** *f* representation, ✝, ♟ proxy: **j-s ~ übernehmen** act as representative of s.o.
'**Stellwerk** *n* 🚂 signal box.
Stelze ['ʃtɛltsə] *f* (-; -n) stilt.
stelzen ['ʃtɛltsən] *v/i* (sn) stalk (along).
'**Stemmbogen** *m skiing:* stem turn.
'**Stemmeisen** *n* ☼ mortise chisel.
stemmen ['ʃtɛmən] *v/t* (h) **1.** press: *sich* **~ gegen** press against, *fig.* resist. **2.** heave up, *sports:* lift.
Stempel ['ʃtɛmpəl] *m* (-s; -) **1.** stamp (*a. fig.*), *a.* seal. **2.** postmark. **3.** ☼ die. **4.** hallmark. **5.** ♣ pistil. **~farbe** *f* stamping ink. **~kissen** *n* ink pad.
'**stempeln** (h) **I** *v/t* **1.** a) stamp, b) cancel:

fig. j-n ~ zu stamp (*or* label, *b.s.* brand) s.o. as. **II** *v/i* **2.** *employee:* clock in (out). **3.** F ~ *gehen* be on the dole.
'**Stempeluhr** *f* time clock.
Stengel ['ʃtɛŋəl] *m* (-s; -) stalk, stem.
Stenogramm [ʃteno'gram] *n* (-s; -e) shorthand notes. **Stenograph** [-'gra:f] *m* (-en; -en) stenographer. **Stenographie** [-gra'fi:] *f* (-; -n) stenography, shorthand. **stenographieren** [-gra'fi:rən] (h) **I** *v/i* write shorthand. **II** *v/t* take down in shorthand. **stenographisch** [-'gra:fɪʃ] *adj* shorthand.
Stenotypistin [ʃtenoty'pɪstɪn] *f* (-; -nen) shorthand typist.
'**Steppdecke** *f* (continental) quilt.
Steppe ['ʃtɛpə] *f* (-; -n) steppe.
steppen¹ ['ʃtɛpən] *v/t* (h) backstitch.
'**steppen²** *v/i* (h) tap-dance.
'**Stepptanz** *m* tap dance.
'**Sterbe|bett** *n* (*auf dem ~* on one's) deathbed. **~fall** *m* (case of) death. **~hilfe** *f* euthanasia. **~klinik** *f* hospice.
sterben ['ʃtɛrbən] *v/i* (starb, gestorben, sn) die (*an dat, fig. vor dat* of).
'**Sterben** *n* (-s) dying, death: *im ~ liegen* be dying; *zum ~ langweilig* deadly dull.
'**sterbenskrank** *adj* mortally ill.
'**Sterbens|wort** *n*, **~wörtchen** *n kein ~ sagen** not to breathe a word.
'**Sterbesakra,mente** *pl* last rites.
'**Sterbeurkunde** *f* death certificate.
sterblich ['ʃtɛrplɪç] *adj* mortal: *iro. gewöhnliche* ²e ordinary mortals.
'**Sterblichkeit** *f* (-; *no pl*) mortality.
Stereo..., stereo... ['ʃte:reo] stereo.
'**Stereo|anlage** *f* stereo system. **~aufnahme** *f* stereo recording. **~bild** *n* stereoscopic picture. **~gerät** *n* stereo set.
stereophon [-'fo:n] *adj* stereophonic.
stereoskopisch [-'sko:pɪʃ] *adj* stereoscopic.
'**Stereoton** *m* stereo sound.
stereotyp [-'ty:p] *adj fig.* stereotyped.
steril [ʃte'ri:l] *adj* sterile. **sterilisieren** [ʃterili'zi:rən] *v/t* (h) sterilize. **Sterilisation** [ʃteriliza'tsio:n] *f* (-; -en) sterilization. **Sterilität** [ʃterili'tɛ:t] *f* (-; *no pl*) sterility.
Stern [ʃtɛrn] *m* (-[e]s; -e) *a. fig.* star: *unter e-m glücklichen (unglücklichen) ~ stehen* have fortune on one's side (be ill-fated); F *~e sehen* see stars.

'**Sternbild** *n* **1.** constellation. **2.** sign of the zodiac.
'**Sternchen** *n* **1.** little star, starlet (*a. fig. actress*). **2.** *print.* asterisk.
'**Sternenbanner:** *das ~* the Star-Spangled Banner, the Stars and Stripes.
'**Sternenhimmel** *m* starry sky.
'**Sternfahrt** *f mot.* car rally.
'**sternförmig** *adj* star-shaped.
'**sternhagel'voll** *adj* F rolling drunk.
'**sternhell, 'sternklar** *adj* starlit.
'**Sternmarsch** *m* demonstration march from different starting points.
'**Sternschnuppe** *f* (-; -n) shooting star.
'**Sternstunde** *f fig.* great moment.
'**Sternwarte** *f* (-; -n) observatory.
stet [ʃte:t] → *stetig, Tropfen* 1.
Stethoskop [ʃteto'sko:p] *n* (-s; -e) ⚕ stethoscope.
'**stetig** *adj* continual, constant, steady.
'**Stetigkeit** *f* (-; *no pl*) constancy, steadiness. **stets** *adv* always, constantly.
Steuer¹ ['ʃtɔyər] *n* (-s; -) ⚓ helm, rudder, *mot.* (steering) wheel, ✈ controls: *am ~* at the helm (*a. fig.*), at the wheel.
'**Steuer²** *f* (-; -n) (*auf acc* on) a) tax, b) duty, c) rate, *Am.* local tax: *vor (nach) Abzug der ~n* before (after) tax.
'**Steuer|abzug** *m* tax deduction. **~aufkommen** *n* tax yield. **~ausgleich** *m* tax equalization. **~befreiung** *f* tax exemption. ²**begünstigt** *adj* a) tax-privileged, b) tax-linked (*saving*). **~belastung** *f* tax burden. **~berater(in** *f*) *m* tax adviser. **~bescheid** *m* tax assessment.
'**Steuerbord** *n*, '**steuerbord(s)** *adv* ⚓ starboard.
'**Steuer|de,likt** *n* tax offen/ce (*Am.* -se). **~einnahmen** *pl* → *Steueraufkommen*. **~erklärung** *f* tax return. **~erleichterung** *f* tax relief. **~ermäßigung** *f* tax allowance. ²**frei** *adj* tax-free. **~freibetrag** *m* tax-free allowance. **~hinterzieher** *m* tax dodger. **~hinterziehung** *f* tax fraud. **~karte** *f* (wage) tax card. **~klasse** *f* tax bracket.
'**Steuerknüppel** *m* ✈ control stick, F joystick.
'**steuerlich** *adj* tax ...: *aus ~en Gründen* for tax purposes; *~ günstig* with low tax liability; *~ veranlagen* assess for taxation.
'**Steuermann** *m* **1.** ⚓ helmsman (*a. fig.*). **2.** *rowing:* coxswain.

'**Steuermarke** f revenue stamp.
steuern ['ʃtɔʏərn] **I** v/t (h) steer, *mot. a.* drive, ✈, ⚓ navigate, pilot, ☺ control. **II** v/i (h *or* sn) steer, *mot. a.* drive, ⚓ a. head (*nach Süden* southward).
'**Steuero**,**ase** f tax haven.
'**steuerpflichtig** adj taxable.
'**Steuer**|**poli**,**tik** f fiscal policy. **~pro-gressi,on** f progressive taxation.
'**Steuerpult** n ☺ control desk.
'**Steuerrad** n ⚓, *mot.* (steering) wheel.
'**steuerrechtlich** adj *and* adv under the tax laws.
Steuer|**rückerstattung** f tax refund. **~satz** m tax rate. **~schuld** f tax(es) due. **~senkung** f tax reduction.
'**Steuerung** f (-; -en) **1.** steering, ✈ piloting, ⚡, ☺ control (*a. fig.*). **2.** control system, *mot.* steering, ✈ controls.
'**Steuerveranlagung** f assessment.
'**Steuervorteil** m tax benefit.
'**Steuerzahler(in** f) m taxpayer.
Steward ['stju:ərt] m (-s; -s) steward.
Stewardeß ['stju:ərdɛs] f (-; -dessen) stewardess, air hostess.
Stich [ʃtɪç] m (-es; -e) **1.** *with knife:* stab, thrust, (*needle*) prick, (*wasp etc*) sting, (*gnat*) bite: *fig.* **es gab ihr e-n ~** it cut her to the quick. **2.** *sewing:* stitch. **3.** (*copper etc*) engraving. **4.** stitch, stabbing pain. **5.** *fig.* cut, dig. **6.** *im ~ lassen* abandon, desert, *j-n a.* leave s.o. in the lurch, let s.o. down; *sein Gedächtnis ließ ihn im ~* his memory failed him. **7.** *e-n ~ haben a.) milk etc:* be off, b) F *person:* be a bit touched. **8.** *ein ~ ins Blaue* a tinge of blue. **9.** *cards:* e-n ~ *machen* make a trick.
Stiche'lei f (-; -en) needling: *~en a.* gibe(s). **sticheln** ['ʃtɪçəln] v/i (h) *fig.* (*gegen* at) gibe, make snide remarks.
'**Stichflamme** f jet of flame, flash.
'**stichhaltig** adj valid, sound: *das Argument ist nicht ~* the argument doesn't hold water. '**Stichhaltigkeit** f (-; *no pl*) validity, soundness.
Stichling m (-s; -e) *zo.* stickleback.
'**Stichprobe** f *e-e ~ machen* carry out a spot check, ✈ take a random sample, *customs:* make a random search.
'**Stichtag** m a) effective day, b) deadline.
'**Stichwahl** f second ballot.
'**Stichwort** n (-[e]s) **1.** (*pl* -e) *esp. thea.* (*auf ~* on) cue: *~ "Umwelt"* à propos

"Environment". **2.** (*pl* ~er) headword. **3.** *~e pl* notes: *das Wichtigste in ~en* an outline of the main points; '**stichwort-artig** adj *and* adv in brief outlines. '**Stichwortverzeichnis** n index.
'**Stichwunde** f stab wound.
sticken ['ʃtɪkən] v/t, v/i (h) embroider. **Sticke'rei** f (-; -en) embroidery. **stickig** ['ʃtɪkɪç] adj stuffy, close.
'**Sticko,xyd** n 🜋 nitrogen oxide.
'**Stickstoff** m (-[e]s; *no pl*) 🜋 nitrogen. '**stickstoffhaltig** adj nitrogenous.
'**Stiefbruder** ['ʃti:f-] m stepbrother.
Stiefel ['ʃti:fəl] m (-s; -) boot. **Stiefelette** [ʃti:fə'lɛtə] f (-; -n) ankle boot, (*ladies'*) bootee. '**stiefeln** v/i (sn) F trudge.
'**Stiefmutter** f a. fig. stepmother. '**Stiefmütterchen** n (-s; -) ♣ pansy. '**stiefmütterlich** adv *~ behandeln* neglect badly. '**Stiefschwester** f stepsister.
'**Stiefsohn** m stepson. '**Stieftochter** f stepdaughter. '**Stiefvater** m stepfather.
stieg [ʃti:k] *pret of* **steigen.**
Stieglitz ['ʃti:glɪts] m (-es; -e) goldfinch.
Stiel [ʃti:l] m (-[e]s; -e) **1.** handle, stem (*of glass, pipe*), (*broom*)stick: *Eis am ~* ice lolly. **2.** ♣ stalk, stem.
'**Stielaugen** pl F *~ machen* goggle.
Stier [ʃti:r] m (-[e]s; -e) **1.** *zo.* bull: *fig.* **den ~ bei den Hörnern fassen** take the bull by the horns. **2.** *no pl astr.* ([*ein*] *~ sein* be [a]) Taurus.
'**stieren** v/i (h) stare (*auf* acc at).
'**Stierkampf** m bullfight. '**Stierkämpfer** m bullfighter.
'**stiernackig** [-nakɪç] adj bullnecked.
stieß [ʃti:s] *pret of* **stoßen.**
Stift[1] [ʃtɪft] m (-[e]s; -e) **1.** a) pin, b) peg, c) stud. **2.** a) pencil, b) crayon. **3.** *cosmetics:* stick. **4.** F apprentice.
Stift[2] n (-[e]s; -e) religious foundation.
stiften ['ʃtɪftən] v/t (h) **1.** found. **2.** give, donate. **3.** cause: → *Unfrieden etc.*
'**Stifter** m (-s; -) **1.** founder. **2.** donor.
'**Stiftung** f (-; -en) **1.** foundation. **2.** donation.
'**Stiftzahn** m pivot tooth.
Stil [ʃti:l] m (-[e]s; -e) style: *im großen ~, großen ~s* on a large scale, large-large; *das ist schlechter ~* that's bad style. '**Stilblüte** f howler. '**Stilbruch** m break in style. '**Stilebene** f ling. level of style.
'**stilecht** adj in period.
Stilett [ʃti'lɛt] n (-s; -e) stiletto.

'**Stilgefühl** *n* sense of style.
stilisieren [ʃtili'ziːrən] *v/t* (h) stylize.
Stilist [ʃti'lɪst] *m* (-en; -en) stylist (*a. sports etc*). **Sti'listik** [-tɪk] *f* (-; *no pl*) stylistics. **sti'listisch** *adj* stylistic.
'**Stilkunde** *f* → **Stilistik.**
still [ʃtɪl] *adj* a) quiet, silent, still, b) calm, peaceful, c) secret (*a. hope, love, etc*): **~e Jahreszeit** dead season; **~e Reserven** hidden reserves; **~er Teilhaber** sleeping (*Am.* silent) partner; **~e Übereinkunft** tacit understanding; (*sei*) **~!** (be) quiet!; **im ~en** inwardly, secretly; → **Wasser** 1. '**Stille** *f* (-; *no pl*) a) silence, b) quiet, calm, c) hush: **die ~ vor dem Sturm** the calm before the storm; **in aller ~** quietly, a. secretly.
'**Stilleben** *n* (-s; -) *paint.* still life.
'**stillegen** *v/t* (*sep*, -ge-, h) 1. shut down (*firm*), by *strike*: paralyse. 2. lay up (*car*), put *machine etc* out of operation. '**Stillegung** *f* (-; -en) 1. shutdown. 2. *mot.* laying-up.
stillen ['ʃtɪlən] *v/t* (h) 1. nurse, breast-feed: **~de Mutter** nursing mother. 2. stop, sta(u)nch (*bleeding*), quench (*thirst*), satisfy (*desire*), soothe (*pain*).
'**Stillhalteabkommen** *n pol.* standstill agreement. '**stillhalten** *v/i* (*irr*, *sep*, -ge-, h, → **halten**) 1. keep still. 2. *fig.* keep quiet. '**stilliegen** *v/i* (*irr*, *sep*, -ge-, h, → **liegen**) 1. lie still. 2. *fig.* lie dormant, *works*: lie idle.
'**stillos** *adj* in bad style, tasteless.
'**stillschweigen** *v/i* (*irr*, *sep*, -ge-, h, → **schweigen**) be silent, be quiet, say nothing. '**Stillschweigen** *n* (-s) silence: (*strengstes*) **~ bewahren** maintain (absolute) silence (**über** *acc* on). '**stillschweigend I** *adj* 1. silent. 2. *fig.* tacit. **II** *adv* 3. in silence, without a word. 4. *fig.* tacitly.
'**Stillstand** *m* (-[e]s; *no pl*) standstill, stoppage, *fig. a.* stagnation, *of negotiations*: deadlock: **zum ~ bringen** stop; **zum ~ kommen** come to a standstill, stop, *negotiations*: reach a deadlock.
'**stillstehen** *v/i* (*irr*, *sep*, -ge-, h, → **stehen**) 1. stand still, come to a standstill, stop, ⚙ be idle, be out of action: **~d a.** stagnant. 2. ✕ stand to attention: **stillgestanden!** attention!
'**Stillzeit** *f* nursing period.
'**Stilmöbel** *pl* period furniture.

'**stilvoll** *adj* stylish: **~ sein** have style.
'**Stimm|abgabe** *f* voting. **~band** *n anat.* vocal c(h)ord. ②**berechtigt** *adj* eligible to vote. **~bildung** *f* ♪ voice training. **~bruch** *m* (-[e]s; *no pl*) change of voice: **er ist im ~** his voice is breaking.
Stimme ['ʃtɪmə] *f* (-; -n) 1. (*mit lauter etc* **~** in a loud *etc*) voice. 2. ♪ a) voice, b) part: **gut bei ~ sein** be in good voice. 3. *fig.* voice, opinion: **die ~n mehren sich, die fordern ...** there is a growing number of people calling for ... 4. vote: **entscheidende ~** casting vote; **s-e ~ abgeben** (cast one's) vote; **sich der ~ enthalten** abstain (from voting).
stimmen ['ʃtɪmən] (h) **I** *v/t* 1. ♪ tune (**nach** to). 2. **j-n glücklich** (*traurig etc*) **~** make s.o. happy (sad *etc*). **II** *v/i* 3. be right, be correct, be true: **da stimmt et. nicht** a) there is sth. wrong here, b) there is sth. fishy going on. 4. **~ für** (**gegen**) vote for (against).
'**Stimmen|fang** *m* vote catching. **~gleichheit** *f* (**bei ~** in the event of a) tie. **~mehrheit** *f* majority (of votes).
'**Stimm|enthaltung** *f* abstention (from voting). **~gabel** *f* ♪ tuning fork.
'**stimmhaft** *adj ling.* voiced.
'**Stimmlage** *f* ♪ register, voice.
'**stimmlos** *adj ling.* voiceless, unvoiced.
'**Stimmrecht** *n* (right to) vote: **allgemeines ~** universal suffrage.
'**Stimmung** *f* (-; -en) 1. mood (*a.* ♪, *paint.*), spirits, *fig. a.* atmosphere, ✕ *etc*: morale: **in guter** (**gedrückter**) **~ sein** be in high (low) spirits; **festliche ~** festive mood (*or* atmosphere); **nicht in der ~ sein zu** *inf* not be in the mood to *inf*, not to feel like *ger*; **für ~ sorgen** liven things up. 2. opinion.
'**Stimmungs|baro,meter** *n* F barometer of opinion. **~mache** *f* (-; *no pl*) F *contp.* propaganda. **~mu,sik** *f* mood music. **~umschwung** *m* change of mood.
'**stimmungsvoll** *adj* atmospheric: **~e Musik** mood music.
'**Stimmzettel** *m* ballot paper.
Stimulans ['ʃtiːmulans] *n* (-; -lantia [ʃtiːmu'lantsĭa]) ⚕ *or fig.* stimulant. **stimulieren** [ʃtimu'liːrən] *v/t* (h) stimulate.
'**Stinkbombe** *f* stink bomb.
stinken ['ʃtɪŋkən] *v/i* (stank, gestunken, h) stink (**nach** of, *a. fig.*): F **das** (**er**) **stinkt mir!** I'm sick of it (him).

'**stink**|'**faul** *adj* F bone-lazy. ~'**langwei-lig** *adj* F deadly boring. ~'**reich** *adj* F stinking rich.

'**Stink**|**tier** *n* skunk. ~**wut** *f* F *e-e ~ haben* be hopping mad (*auf acc* with).

Stipendiat [ʃtipɛn'diaːt] *m* (-en; -en) scholarship holder. **Stipendium** [ʃti-'pɛndiʊm] *n* (-s; -dien) scholarship.

'**Stippvi**,**site** *f* F flying visit.

Stirn [ʃtɪrn] *f* (-; -en) forehead: *fig. die ~ haben zu inf* have the cheek to *inf*; *j-m die ~ bieten* face up to s.o. squarely; ~ *runzeln*. ~**band** *n* (-[e]s; ⸚er) headband. ~**höhle** *f anat.* (frontal) sinus. ~**höhlenentzündung** *f* frontal sinusitis. ~**runzeln** *n* (-s) frown(ing). ~**seite** *f* front (side *or* end). ~**wand** *f* front (*or* end) wall.

stöbern ['ʃtøːbərn] *v/i* (h) (*nach* for) rummage (around), *dog:* hunt about.

stochern ['ʃtɔxərn] *v/i* (h) ~ *in* (*dat*) poke; *in den Zähnen* (*s-m Essen*) ~ pick one's teeth (at one's food).

Stock [ʃtɔk] *m* (-[e]s; ⸚e) **1.** a) stick, b) cane, c) (billiard) cue, d) ♪ baton. **2.** ♀ stock: *über ~ und Stein* up hill and down dale. **3.** (bee)hive. **4.** → *Stock-werk*.

'**stockbe**'**soffen** *adj* F paralytic.

'**stock**'**dunkel** *adj* F pitch-dark.

Stöckelschuhe ['ʃtœkəl-] *pl* stilettos.

stocken ['ʃtɔkən] *v/i* (h) **1.** a) stop short, *voice:* falter, b) hesitate: ~*d sprechen* speak haltingly. **2.** *trade etc:* stagnate, slacken off, *negotiations etc:* reach a deadlock, *traffic:* be at a standstill: *ihr stockte das Herz* (*der Atem*) her heart missed a beat (she caught her breath).

'**Stocken** *n* (-s) *ins ~ geraten* → **stocken**.

'**Stockfisch** *m* dried cod.

...**stöckig** *-[stœkɪç] in cpds* ...-storied.

'**stock**|**konserva**'**tiv** *adj* F ultra-conservative. ~'**nüchtern** *adj* F stone-cold sober. ~'**sauer** *adj* F furious. ~'**steif** *adj* F (as) stiff as a poker, starchy. ~'**taub** *adj* F stone-deaf.

'**Stockung** *f* (-; -en) hold-up, interruption, *in negotiations etc:* a. deadlock, *in talks etc:* pause, ⸙ stagnation.

'**Stockwerk** *n* stor(e)y, floor: *im ersten ~* on the first (*Am.* second) floor.

Stoff [ʃtɔf] *m* (-[e]s; -e) **1.** ♠ substance, stuff (*a.* F alcohol, *drug*), agent. **2.** material, *a.* fabric, cloth. *fig.* a) subject

matter, b) topic (for discussion): ~ *zu e-m Roman* material for a novel. ~**muster** *n* pattern. ~**tier** *n* stuffed animal.

'**Stoffwechsel** *m* metabolism. ~**krankheit** *f* metabolic disorder.

stöhnen ['ʃtøːnən] *v/i* (h) groan.

'**Stöhnen** *n* (-s) groaning, groan(s).

stoisch ['ʃtoːɪʃ] *adj* stoical.

Stola ['ʃtoːla] *f* (-; Stolen) stole.

Stollen ['ʃtɔlən] *m* (-s; -) **1.** ⚒ tunnel. **2.** stud (*on shoe etc*). **3.** *gastr.* fruit loaf.

stolpern ['ʃtɔlpərn] *v/i* (h) (*über acc* over) *a. fig.* stumble, trip.

'**Stolperstein** *m fig.* stumbling block.

stolz [ʃtɔlts] *adj* **1.** proud (*auf acc* of). *2. fig.* proud, splendid: *iro.* ~*e Preise* (*Summe*) steep prices (tidy sum).

Stolz *m* (-es; *no pl*) pride (*a. fig.*): *voller ~*, *mit ~* proudly.

stolzieren [ʃtɔl'tsiːrən] *v/i* (sn) strut.

stopfen ['ʃtɔpfən] (h) **I** *v/t* **1.** darn, mend: → *Loch* 1. **2.** cram, stuff: *gestopft voll* crammed (full). **3.** fill (*hole, pipe, sausage, etc*): *fig. j-m den Mund ~* silence s.o. **4.** stuff (*geese etc*). **II** *v/i* **5.** ♣ cause constipation.

'**Stopfgarn** *n* darning cotton.

stopp [ʃtɔp] *int* stop. **Stopp** *m* (-s; -s) stop, *a.* (*price, wage, etc*) freeze.

Stoppel ['ʃtɔpəl] *f* (-; -n) stubble. ~**bart** *m* stubbly beard. ~**feld** *n* stubble field.

'**stopp(e)lig** *adj* stubbly.

stoppen ['ʃtɔpən] *v/t* (h) **1.** *a. v/i* stop. **2.** *sports etc:* time, clock.

'**Stopp**|**schild** *n mot.* stop sign. ~**taste** *f* stop button. ~**uhr** *f* stop watch.

Stöpsel ['ʃtœpsəl] *m* (-s; -) stopper, cork, *for bathtub etc,* a. ⚡ plug.

stöpseln ['ʃtœpsəln] *v/t* (h) *a.* ⚡ plug.

Stör [ʃtøːr] *m* (-[e]s; -e) *zo.* sturgeon.

'**Störakti**,**on** *f* disruptive action.

'**störanfällig** *adj* ⊙ sensitive, trouble-prone, ⚡ interference-prone.

Storch [ʃtɔrç] *m* (-[e]s; ⸚e) *zo.* stork.

Store [ʃtoːr] *m* (-s; -s) net curtain.

stören ['ʃtøːrən] (h) **I** *v/t* a) disturb, b) bother, c) disrupt (*meeting etc*), d) jam (*radio station*), interfere with (*reception*): *j-s Pläne ~* upset s.o.'s plans; *das* (*Gesamt*)*Bild ~* mar the picture; *was mich daran* (*an ihr*) *stört* what I don't like about it (her); *lassen Sie sich nicht ~!* don't let me disturb you; *darf ich Sie kurz ~?* may I trouble you for a minute?; **stört es Sie(, wenn ich rauche)?** do you mind (if I smoke)?; **das stört mich nicht** I don't mind (that); **er stört mich nicht** he doesn't bother me; → **gestört.** II *v/i* a) interfere, b) be in the way, d) be a nuisance, d) be an eyesore, e) *sports:* tackle: *„Bitte nicht ~!"* "please do not disturb!" **störend** *adj* disturbing, troublesome, annoying.

'**Störenfried** [-fri:t] *m* (-[e]s; -e) troublemaker.

'**Störfaktor** *m* disruptive element.

'**Störfall** *m* ⊚ breakdown, accident.

stornieren ['ʃtɔr'ni:rən] *v/t* (h) ✝ reverse (*entry*), cancel (*order*). **Stor'nierung** *f* (-; -en), **Storno** ['ʃtɔrno] *n* (-s; Storni) reversal, cancellation.

Störrigkeit ['ʃtœrɪçkaɪt] *f* (-; *no pl*) stubbornness, obstinacy, restiveness.

störrisch ['ʃtœrɪʃ] *adj* stubborn, obstinate, restive (*horse*).

'**Störsender** *m* jamming station.

'**Störung** *f* (-; -en) disturbance, 🟦 disorder, ⊚ trouble, defect, breakdown, interruption: *verzeihen Sie die ~!* sorry to disturb you; (**atmosphärische**) ~ a) statics, b) interference, c) jamming.

'**störungsfrei** *adj* undisturbed, ⊚ trouble-free, *radio, TV:* interference-free.

'**Störungsstelle** *f teleph. the* engineers.

Stoß [ʃto:s] *m* (-es; ˙e) **1.** a) push, b) kick, c) butt, d) dig, e) *a. fenc.* thrust, *swimming, billiards:* stroke, *shot-put:* put, f) jolt, bump, shock, *a. phys.* impact: *fig. j-m e-n ~ versetzen* shake s.o.; *sich (or s-m Herzen) e-n ~ geben* make an effort; *gib d-m Herzen e-n ~!* be a sport! **2.** 🔫 massive dose (*of vitamines etc*), rush (*of adrenaline*). **3.** pile, a. stack (*of wood etc*), a. batch (*of letters*).

'**Stoßdämpfer** *m mot.* shock-absorber.

Stößel ['ʃtø:səl] *m* (-s; -) **1.** pestle. **2.** *mot.* tappet.

stoßen ['ʃto:sən] (stieß, gestoßen, h) I *v/t* **1.** push, poke, *a.* kick, *a.* butt, *a.* jostle: *von sich ~* push away, *fig.* reject; *er stieß ihr das Messer in die Brust* he plunged his knife into her chest. **2.** *sports:* **die Kugel ~** put the shot. **3.** pound. II *v/i* → **4.** hurt o.s.; *sich ~ an* (*dat*) a) knock (*or bump*) against, b) *fig.* object to, take exception to. III *v/i* **5.** push (*etc*, → **1**). **6.** (sn) ~ *an* (*acc*) a) a. ~ *gegen* knock against, bump into, b)

border on; *er stieß mit dem Kopf an die Wand* he bumped his head against the wall; *fig.* ~ *auf* (*acc*) a) come across, stumble on, b) meet with (*opposition etc*); ~ *zu* join (up with) (*s.o., party, etc*); → **Horn** 2, **Kopf** 1.

'**stoßfest** *adj* shockproof.

'**Stoß|gebet** *n* quick prayer. **~kraft** *f* (-; *no pl*) *fig.* impetus, force. **~seufzer** *m* deep sigh. **~stange** *f mot.* bumper. **~trupp** *m* ✕ assault party. **~verkehr** *m* rush-hour traffic.

'**stoßweise** *adv* intermittently, sporadically, by fits and starts.

'**Stoß|zahn** *m zo.* tusk. **~zeit** *f* a) peak hours, b) rush hour.

'**Stotterer** *m* (-s; -) stutterer, stammerer.

stottern ['ʃtɔtərn] *v/i*, *v/t* (h) stutter, stammer: F *auf Stottern kaufen* buy on the never-never.

'**Straf|anstalt** *f* prison, penal institution. **~antrag** *m* **1.** private application (by the injured party). **2.** sentence demanded (by the public prosecutor). **~anzeige** *f* ~ *erstatten* bring a charge (*gegen* against). **~arbeit** *f ped.* extra work. **~bank** *f* (-; ˙e) *sports:* penalty bank.

'**strafbar** *adj* a) punishable, b) criminal: **~e Handlung** (criminal) offen/ce (*Am.* -se); *sich ~ machen* make o.s. liable to prosecution.

'**Strafbefehl** *m* ⚖ order of (summary punishment).

Strafe ['ʃtra:fə] *f* (-; -n) punishment (*a. fig.*), penalty (*a. sports*), *a.* fine, *a.* sentence: *bei ~ von* on pain (*or* penalty) of; *zur ~* as a punishment; ~ *zahlen* pay a fine; → **antreten** 1, **verbüßen.**

strafen ['ʃtra:fən] *v/t* (h) punish, *esp. sports:* penalize: **~der Blick** censorious look; → **Lüge, Verachtung.**

'**Straf|entlassene** *m, f* (-n; -n) ex-convict. **~erlaß** *m* remission (of sentence).

straff [ʃtraf] *adj* **1.** tight, taut, *a.* firm, erect (*posture*): ~ *anziehen* tighten; ~ *sitzen* fit tightly. **2.** *fig.* strict, tight.

'**straffällig** *adj* ~ *werden* commit an offen/ce (*Am.* -se). '**Straffällige** *m, f* (-n; -n) offender, delinquent.

straffen ['ʃtrafən] *v/t* (h) *a. fig.* tighten (up). '**Straffheit** *f* (-; *no pl*) tightness.

'**straffrei:** ~ *ausgehen* go unpunished. '**Straffreiheit** *f* (-; *no pl*) immunity.

'**Straf|gebühr** *f* fine. **~gefangene** *m, f*

(-n; -n) prisoner, convict. **~gericht** *n* **1.** criminal court. **2.** *fig.* punishment. **~gesetz** *n* penal law. **~gesetzbuch** *n* penal code.

sträflich ['ʃtrɛːflɪç] **I** *adj* punishable, *a. fig.* criminal. **II** *adv fig.* badly.

Sträfling ['ʃtrɛːflɪŋ] *m* (-s; -e) prisoner, convict.

'straflos → **straffrei.**

'Straf|man,dat *n* ticket. **~maß** *n* ♊ sentence. **⚥mildernd** *adj* mitigating. **⚥mündig** *adj* of responsible age. **~porto** *n* surcharge. **~predigt** *f* ⊢ lecture. **~pro,zeß** *m* trial, criminal case (*or* proceedings). **~pro,zeßordnung** *f* code of criminal procedure. **~punkt** *m* *sports*: penalty point. **~raum** *m* *soccer*: penalty area. **~recht** *n* (-[e]s; *no pl*) criminal law. **⚥rechtlich** *adj* criminal, penal: **~ verfolgen** prosecute. **~re,gister** *n* a) criminal records, b) *s.o.'s* criminal record. **~sache** *f* criminal case. **~stoß** *m* *soccer*: penalty kick. **~tat** *f* (criminal) offen/ce (*Am.* -se), crime. **~täter** *m* (criminal) offender. **~verfahren** *n* **1.** → **Strafprozeß. 2.** criminal procedure.

'strafverschärfend *adj* aggravating.

'strafversetzen *v/t* (*only inf and pp* strafversetzt, h), **'Strafversetzung** *f* (-; -en) transfer for disciplinary reasons.

'Straf|verteidiger(in *f*) *m* trial lawyer; → *a.* **Verteidiger(in** *f*). **~vollzug** *m* **1.** a) execution of the sentence, b) imprisonment. **2.** prison system. **~vollzugsbeamte** *m* prison officer. **⚥würdig** *adj* ♊ punishable. **~zettel** *m* ticket.

Strahl [ʃtraːl] *m* (-[e]s; -en) **1.** ray (*a. fig. of hope etc*), *a.* beam (*of light*), flash (*of fire etc*). **2.** stream, jet (*of water etc*).

'Strahlantrieb *m* ✈ jet propulsion.

strahlen ['ʃtraːlən] *v/i* (h) **1.** *phys.* radiate, emit radiation, be radioactive. **2.** shine, sparkle: **die Sonne strahlte** the sun shone brightly. **3.** *fig.* beam (*vor* with): **sie strahlte** (*vor Glück*) she was radiant (with happiness).

'Strahlen|belastung *f* ☢ exposure to radiation. **~bündel** *n* *opt.*, *phys.* pencil of rays. **~dosis** *f* ☢ radiation dose.

'strahlenförmig *adj* radial.

'Strahlen|krankheit *f* radiation sickness. **~schutz** *m* radiation protection. **~thera,pie** *f* radiotherapy. **~tod** *m* death by radiation.

'Strahler *m* (-s; -) **1.** radiator, *a.* heater. **2.** spotlight.

'Strahltriebwerk *n* ✈ jet engine.

'Strahlung *f* (-; -en) radiation.

'Strahlungs|ener,gie *f* radiation energy. **~wärme** *f* radiant heat.

Strähne ['ʃtrɛːnə] *f* (-; -n) a) strand, b) streak. **'strähnen** *v/t* (h) streak in (*hair*). **'strähnig** *adj* straggly.

stramm [ʃtram] **I** *adj* **1.** tight. **2.** strapping, sturdy, firm. **3.** strict (*discipline*), brisk (*pace*): F **~er Sozialist** sta(u)nch socialist. **II** *adv* **4.** tight(ly): **~ sitzen** fit tightly; F **~ arbeiten** work hard.

'strammstehen *v/i* (*irr, sep,* -ge-, h, → **stehen**) ✕ stand to attention.

'Strampelhöschen *n* rompers.

strampeln ['ʃtrampəln] *v/i* (h) **1.** a) kick, b) struggle. **2.** F pedal (away).

'Strampelsack *m* baby's sleeping bag.

Strand [ʃtrant] *m* (-[e]s; ⁓e) (sea)shore, beach. **~bad** *n* swimming area.

stranden ['ʃtrandən] *v/i* (sn) run aground: **gestrandet** *a. fig.* stranded.

'Strand|gut *n* (-[e]s; *no pl*) flotsam and jetsam (*a. fig.*). **~ho,tel** *n* seaside (*or* beach) hotel. **~kleidung** *f* beachwear. **~korb** *m* (canopied) beach chair. **~prome,nade** *f* promenade.

Strang [ʃtraŋ] *m* (-[e]s; ⁓e) **1.** rope: *fig.* **an 'einem ~ ziehen** pull together; **über die Stränge schlagen** kick over the traces; **wenn alle Stränge reißen** if all else fails. **2.** *anat.* cord. **3.** skein, hank.

strangulieren [ʃtraŋgu'liːrən] *v/t* (h) strangle.

Strapaze [ʃtra'paːtsə] *f* (-; -n) strain.

strapazieren [ʃtrapa'tsiːrən] *v/t* (h) wear *s.o.*, *s.th.* out, strain (*a. fig.*): F *j-s* **Geduld ~** tax *s.o.'s* patience. **strapa'zierfähig** *adj* hardwearing, tough.

strapaziös [ʃtrapa'tsiøːs] *adj* strenuous, F tough: **~ sein** be a (great) strain.

Straße ['ʃtraːsə] *f* (-; -n) **1.** road, street: **auf der ~** on the road, in (*Am.* on) the street; **der Mann auf der ~** the man in the street; *j-n auf die ~ setzen* a) turn *s.o.* out, b) sack *s.o.*; **auf offener ~** in broad daylight. **2.** *geogr.* **die ~ von Dover** the Strait(s) of Dover. **3.** ⚙ (production *etc*) line.

'Straßen|anzug *m* lounge (*Am.* business) suit. **~arbeiten** *pl* roadworks. **~arbeiter** *m* roadman.

'**Straßenbahn** f tram, Am. streetcar. **~haltestelle** f tram (Am. streetcar) stop. **~linie** f tram (Am. streetcar) line. **~wagen** m tram(car), Am. streetcar.

'**Straßen|bau** m (-[e]s; no pl) road construction. **~belag** m road surface. **~beleuchtung** f street lighting. **~ca,fé** n pavement (Am. sidewalk) café. **~fest** n street party. **~glätte** f slippery road(s). **~graben** m (road) ditch. **~händler** m street vendor. **~junge** m street urchin. **~kampf** m street fighting. **~karte** f road map. **~kehrer** m, **~kehrma,schine** f street sweeper. **~kreuzung** f crossroads. **~lage** f mot. roadholding. **~lärm** m noise from the street(s). **~la,terne** f street lamp. **~musi,kant** m street musician. **~name** m street name. **~netz** n road network. **~rand** m (am ~ on the) roadside. **~rennen** n road race. **~sammlung** f street collection. **~schild** n street sign. **~sperre** f road block. **~tunnel** m road tunnel. **~überführung** f flyover. **~unterführung** f underpass. **~verhältnisse** pl road conditions. **~verkehr** m (road) traffic. **~verkehrsordnung** f traffic regulations. **~zustand** m road condition(s).

Strategie [ʃtraˈteːgə] m (-n; -n) strategist. **Strategie** [ʃtrateˈgiː] f (-; -n) strategy. **stra'tegisch** [-gɪʃ] adj strategic(al).
Stratosphäre [ʃtratoˈsfɛːrə] f (-; no pl) stratosphere.

sträuben [ˈʃtrɔybən] (h) I v/t ruffle (up) (feathers), bristle (hair). II sich ~ hair: stand on end, fur: bristle up; fig. sich ~ gegen struggle against, resist; sich ~ zu inf refuse to inf.

Strauch [ʃtraʊx] m (-[e]s; ᵘer) shrub, bush.
straucheln [ˈʃtraʊxəln] v/i (sn) **1.** stumble, trip. **2.** fig. go astray.
Strauß¹ [ʃtraʊs] m (-es; ᵘe) bunch of flowers.
Strauß² m (-es; -e) zo. ostrich.
'**Straußenfeder** f ostrich feather.
Strebe [ˈʃtreːbə] f (-; -n) strut.
streben [ˈʃtreːbən] v/i **1.** (sn) ~ zu, ~ nach move towards, person: make for. **2.** (h) fig. ~ nach strive (for), aim (at).
'**Streben** n (-s) fig. efforts, (nach) striving (for), aspiration (for, after).
'**Streber** m (-s; -) contp. a) careerist, b) social climber, c) ped. swot.
'**Strebertum** n (-s; no pl) contp.

pushiness, ped. swotting.
strebsam [ˈʃtreːp-] adj industrious, ambitious. '**Strebsamkeit** f (-; no pl) industriousness, ambition.

Strecke [ˈʃtrɛkə] f (-; -n) **1.** stretch, a. leg, a. route (a. ✈, ⚓), a. distance (a. sports), sports: (racing) course, ♖, 🚂, teleph. line, ✗ roadway: 🚄 auf freier ~ between stations; auf e-r ~ von 10 km for a stretch of 10 km; fig. auf der ~ bleiben fail, come to grief. **2.** hunt. bag: zur ~ bringen kill, shoot down, bag, fig. hunt down, catch (criminal etc), defeat (opponent).
strecken [ˈʃtrɛkən] v/t (h) **1.** stretch: sich (or s-e Glieder) ~ stretch (o.s.) (or one's limbs); → Decke 1. **2.** eke out, spin out (supplies etc).
'**Streckennetz** n railway network.
'**streckenweise** adv a) in parts, in places, b) now and then, at times.
'**Streckmuskel** m extensor (muscle).
'**Streckverband** m ✚ im ~ in traction.
Streich [ʃtraɪç] m (-[e]s; -e) trick, prank: j-m e-n (bösen) ~ spielen play a (nasty) trick on s.o.
streicheln [ˈʃtraɪçəln] v/t, v/i (h) stroke.
streichen [ˈʃtraɪçən] (strich, gestrichen, h) I v/t **1.** spread (butter, bread, etc), apply, put ointment etc (auf acc on). **2.** paint: → gestrichen 1. **3.** stroke. **4.** a) cross out, delete, b) cancel (order etc), cut (funds): j-n von der Liste ~ strike s.o. off the list. **5.** strike, haul down (flag, sail). II v/i **6.** (mit der Hand) ~ über (acc) stroke, pass one's hand over. **7.** (sn) durch die Gegend ~ roam the countryside; ums Haus ~ prowl around the house.
'**Streicher** pl ♪ the strings.
'**Streichholz** n matches, matchstick.
'**Streichholzschachtel** f matchbox.
'**Streichinstru,ment** n string(ed) instrument: die ~ im ~ in traction.
'**Streichor,chester** n string orchestra.
'**Streichquar,tett** n string quartet.
'**Streichung** f (-; -en) cancel(l)ation (a. fig.), cut (of funds etc), print. deletion.
'**Streichwurst** f sausage spread.
'**Streifband** n (-[e]s; ᵘer) wrapper.
Streife [ˈʃtraɪfə] f (-; -n) ([auf] ~ gehen go on) patrol.
streifen [ˈʃtraɪfən] (h) I v/t **1.** touch, brush against, car: scrape against, bul-

let: graze: *ein Thema ~* touch (up)on a subject. **2.** *vom Finger (Leibe) ~* slip off *(ring, dress)*. **3.** *mit e-m Blick ~* glance at. **II** *v/i* (sn) **4.** *durch den Wald etc ~* roam the woods *etc*.
'**Streif|licht** *n fig.* sidelight. **~schuß** *m* grazing shot. **~zug** *m a. fig.* excursion.
Streik [ʃtraɪk] *m* (-[e]s; -s) strike: *wilder ~* wildcat strike; *e-n ~ ausrufen (abbrechen)* call (call off) a strike; *in den ~ treten* go on strike. **~aufruf** *m* strike call. **~brecher** *m* strikebreaker, F blackleg, *contp.* scab.
streiken [ˈʃtraɪkən] *v/i* (h) **1.** (be or go on) strike. **2.** F refuse, *a. stomach*: rebel, *machine etc*: refuse to work, pack up. **'Streikende** *m, f* (-n; -n) striker.
'**Streik|geld** *n* strike pay. **~posten** *m* (*a. ~ aufstellen vor, ~ stehen*) picket. **~recht** *n* right to strike. **~welle** *f* series of strikes.
Streit [ʃtraɪt] *m* (-[e]s; -e) a) quarrel, argument, F row, b) brawl, fight, c) controversy, dispute: *in ~ geraten mit* have an argument (*or* a fight) with; → *suchen, Zaun.* '**streitbar** *adj* belligerent.
'**streiten** *v/i* (stritt, gestritten, h) (*a. miteinander or sich ~*) a) quarrel, have an argument (F a row), b) fight: *darüber läßt sich ~* that's a moot point. '**Streiter** *m* (-s; -) *fig.* (*für*) fighter (for), champion (of). **Streite'rei** *f* (-; -en) (constant) quarrel(l)ing, fights, F rows.
'**Streitfall** *m* dispute, conflict, ⚖ case.
'**Streitfrage** *f* (controversial) issue.
'**Streitgespräch** *n* debate, dispute.
'**streitig** *adj* **1.** ⚖ contentious. **2.** *j-m (das Recht auf) et. ~ machen* dispute s.o.'s right to s.th.; → *Rang* 1.
'**Streitigkeit** *f* (-; -en) → **Streit.**
'**Streitkräfte** *pl* armed forces.
'**streitlustig** *adj* belligerent.
'**Streitpunkt** *m* (point at) issue.
'**Streitsache** *f* ⚖ a) case, b) lawsuit.
'**Streitsucht** *f* (-; *no pl*) quarrelsomeness.
'**streitsüchtig** *adj* quarrelsome.
'**Streitwert** *m* ⚖ value in dispute.
streng [ʃtrɛŋ] **I** *adj* severe (*a. cold, criticism, look, etc*), austere (*style*), strict (*discipline, regulation, etc*), harsh (*taste*), acrid (*smell etc*): *(mit j-m) ~ sein* be strict (with s.o.); *~es Stillschweigen* strict secrecy. **II** *adv* severely (*etc*): *sich ~ halten an* (*acc*) ad-

here strictly to; *~ geheim* top-secret; *~ vertraulich* strictly confidential.
'**Strenge** *f* (-; *no pl*) severity, austerity, strictness, harshness.
'**strenggläubig** *adj* orthodox.
Streß [ʃtrɛs] *m* (-sses; -sse) (*im ~* under) stress. '**stressen** *v/t* (h) F *j-n ~* put s.o. under stress. '**streßig** *adj* F stressful.
'**Streßkrankheit** *f* stress disease.
streuen [ˈʃtrɔɪən] (h) **I** *v/t* scatter, strew, spread, sprinkle: *den Gehweg ~* grit the sidewalk. **II** *v/i* ✕, *phys.* scatter.
streunen [ˈʃtrɔɪnən] *v/i* (sn) stray, roam about: *~de Katze* stray cat.
strich [ʃtrɪç] *pret of* **streichen.**
Strich *m* (-[e]s; -e) **1.** a) stroke, b) line, c) dash, d) mark, e) (compass) point, f) stroke (of the brush): *j-m e-n ~ durch die Rechnung machen* thwart s.o.'s plans; *unter dem ~* on balance; *e-n (dicken) ~ unter et. machen* make a clean break with s.th.; F *auf den ~ gehen* walk the streets, go on the game. **2.** *textiles*: nap: *gegen den ~* against the nap; F *das ging mir gegen den ~* it went against the grain with me; F *nach ~ und Faden* good and proper. **3.** F cut. **4.** ♪ a) stroke, b) bowing technique.
stricheln [ˈʃtrɪçəln] *v/t* (h) a) sketch in, b) hatch: *gestrichelte Linie* broken line.
'**Strich|junge** *m* F male prostitute. **~kode** *m* bar code. **~liste** *f* check list. **~mädchen** *n* F streetwalker, *Am. sl.* hooker. **~männchen** *n* matchstick man. **~punkt** *m* semicolon.
'**strichweise** *adv* in parts: *meteor. ~ Regen* scattered showers.
Strick [ʃtrɪk] *m* (-[e]s; -e) cord, rope: *fig. wenn alle ~e reißen* if all else fails; *j-m aus e-r Sache e-n ~ drehen (wollen)* use s.th. against s.o.
stricken [ˈʃtrɪkən] *v/t, v/i* (h) knit.
'**Stricker** *m* (-s; -), '**Strickerin** *f* (-; -nen) knitter.
'**Strick|jacke** *f* cardigan. **~leiter** *f* rope ladder. **~ma,schine** *f* knitting machine. **~nadel** *f* knitting needle. **~waren** *pl* knitwear. **~wolle** *f* knitting wool. **~zeug** *n* knitting (things).
striegeln [ˈʃtriːgəln] *v/t* (h) curry(comb).
Strieme [ˈʃtriːmə] *f* (-; -n), '**Striemen** *m* (-s; -) weal.
strikt [ʃtrɪkt] *adj* strict: *et. ~ ablehnen* refuse s.th. flatly.

Strippe ['ʃtrɪpə] f (-; -n) F cord, string: *fig. an der ~ hängen* be on the blower.
stritt [ʃtrɪt] *pret of* **streiten**.
strittig ['ʃtrɪtɪç] *adj* controversial: *der ~e Punkt* the point at issue.
Stroh [ʃtroː] n (-[e]s; *no pl*) **1.** straw. **2.** (*a. mit ~ decken*) thatch. **2blond** *adj* flaxen(-haired). **~blume** f immortelle. **~dach** n thatched roof. **~feuer** n *fig.* flash in the pan. **~halm** m straw: *nach e-m ~ greifen, sich an e-n ~ klammern* clutch at a straw. **~hut** m straw hat. **~mann** m (-[e]s; ⸚er) front. **~witwe(r** m) f F grass widow(er).
Strom [ʃtroːm] m (-[e]s; ⸚e) **1.** a) (large) river, b) torrent, c) stream, current (*a. fig.*), *fig.* flood (*of blood, tears, etc*), stream (*of people, cars, etc*): *mit dem (gegen den) ~ schwimmen* swim with (against) the current (*fig. a. tide*); *es gießt in Strömen* it is pouring with rain. **2.** a) (electrical) current, b) electricity: *unter ~ stehend* live.
strom'ab(wärts) *adv* downstream.
strom'auf(wärts) *adv* upstream.
'Stromausfall m power failure.
strömen ['ʃtrøːmən] *v/i* (sn) stream, pour, *air, gas, etc*: *a.* flow, *people*: *a.* throng, flock.
'Stromer m (-s; -) F *contp.* tramp.
'Strom|erzeuger m ⚡ **1.** generator. **2.** power station. **~erzeugung** f power generation. **2führend** *adj* live. **~kreis** m (electric) circuit. **~leitung** f power line.
'stromlinienförmig *adj* streamlined.
'Strom|netz n ⚡ power supply system. **~schnelle** f (-; -n) rapid. **~spannung** f ⚡ voltage. **~sperre** f power cut. **~stärke** f current intensity, amperage. **~stoß** m **1.** impulse. **2.** electric shock.
'Strömung f (-; -en) current, *fig. a.* trend.
'Strom|verbrauch m power consumption. **~versorgung** f power supply. **~zähler** m electric meter.
Strophe ['ʃtroːfə] f (-; -n) stanza, verse.
strotzen ['ʃtrɔtsən] *v/i* (h) *~ von, ~ vor* (*dat*) be full of, *a.* be teeming with (*mistakes*), be bursting with (*energy, health, etc*); *vor Dreck ~* be caked with dirt.
Strudel ['ʃtruːdəl] m (-s; -) **1.** *a. fig.* whirlpool, maelstrom. **2.** *gastr.* strudel.
strudeln ['ʃtruːdəln] *v/i* (h) swirl, whirl.
Struktur [ʃtrʊk'tuːr] f (-; -en) structure.

Struk'tur... structural (*change, policy, etc*). **strukturell** [ʃtrʊktuˈrɛl] *adj* (*a. ~ bedingt*) structural.
Strumpf [ʃtrʊmpf] m (-[e]s; ⸚e) stocking. **~band** n garter. **~halter** m suspender, *Am.* garter. **~hose** f (**e-e** ~ a pair of) tights, pantihose. **~maske** f stocking mask. **~waren** pl hosiery.
Strunk [ʃtrʊŋk] m (-[e]s; ⸚e) stalk.
struppig ['ʃtrʊpɪç] *adj* unkempt (*hair*), bristly (*beard*), shaggy (*dog*).
Strychnin [ʃtryç'niːn] n (-s; *no pl*) 🜍 strychnine.
Stube ['ʃtuːbə] f (-; -n) room.
'Stubenhocker m (-s; -) stay-at-home.
'Stubenmädchen n chambermaid.
'stubenrein *adj* house-broken (*dog*).
'Stubenwagen m bassinet.
Stuck [ʃtʊk] m (-s; *no pl*) stucco.
Stück [ʃtyk] n (-[e]s; -e) **1.** piece, *a.* slice (*of bread etc*), *a.* lump (*of sugar*), *a.* bar (*of soap*), *a.* head (*of cattle*): *ein ~ Land* a piece of land, a plot; *im ~, am ~* in one piece, *a.* unsliced (*cheese etc*); *50 Cent das ~* fifty cents each; *50 ~ Vieh* 50 head of cattle; *j-n ein ~ (Weges) begleiten* accompany s.o. part of the way; *~ für ~* piece by piece; *in ~e gehen* go to pieces; *in ~e schlagen* smash (to bits); *fig. aus freien ~en* of one's own free will; *große ~e halten auf* (*acc*) think highly of; *wir sind ein gutes ~ weitergekommen* we have made considerable headway; *das ist ein starkes ~!* that's a bit thick. **2.** piece (*of music*), *thea.* play, passage (*of book etc*).
'Stückchen n (-s; -) small piece (*etc*, → *Stück*).
'Stückelung f (-; -en) ✝ denomination.
'Stückeschreiber(in f) m playwright.
'Stück|gut n parcel(s). **~kosten** pl unit cost. **~liste** f ⊙ parts list. **~lohn** m piece rate. **~preis** m unit price.
'stückweise *adv* bit by bit.
'Stück|werk n (-[e]s; *no pl*) *contp.* patchwork. **~zahl** f number of pieces.
Student [ʃtu'dɛnt] m (-en; -en) student.
Stu'dentenausweis m student's identity card.
Stu'dentenschaft f (-; -en) *the* students.
Stu'denten|verbindung f fraternity. **~wohnheim** n students' hostel.
Stu'dentin f (-; -nen) student.

Studie ['ʃtuːdiə] *f* (-; -n) study (*a. paint. etc*) (*über acc* on), sketch.

'Studien|aufenthalt *m* study visit. **~beratung** *f* student advisory service. **~bewerber** *m* university applicant. **~di,rektor** *m* deputy headmaster. **~fach** *n* subject. **~gang** *m* course of studies. **~gebühren** *pl* tuition fees.

'studienhalber *adv* for study purposes.

'Studien|jahr *n* academic year: **~e** → *Studienzeit*. **~platz** *m* place at a university. **~rat** *m*, **~rätin** ['-rɛːtɪn] *f* (-; -nen) secondary school teacher. **~refe-ren,dar(in** *f*) *m* student teacher at a secondary school. **~reise** *f* study trip. **~zeit** *f* university (*Am.* college) days.

studieren [ʃtuˈdiːrən] (h) **I** *v/t* study, read: **er studiert Medizin** he studies medicine, he is a medical student. **II** *v/i* study, go to university: **wo hat er studiert?** which university did he go to?

Studio ['ʃtuːdio] *n* (-s; -s) studio.

Studium ['ʃtuːdiʊm] *n* (-s; -dien) studies, study (*gen* of).

Stufe ['ʃtuːfə] *f* (-; -n) **1.** step. **2.** *ling.*, ♪ degree. **3.** *fig.* a) stage, b) level, standard, c) rank: **j-n auf eine ~ stellen mit** place s.o. on a level with. **4.** (*income etc*) bracket. **5.** stage (*of rocket etc*).

'Stufen|barren *m* asymmetrical bars. **~heck** *n mot.* notchback. **~leiter** *f* stepladder: **~ des Erfolgs** ladder to success.

'stufenlos *adj* ⊙ continuous: **~ regelbar** infinitely variable. **'stufenweise I** *adj* gradual. **II** *adv* step by step, by degrees.

Stuhl [ʃtuːl] *m* (-[e]s; ⁓e) **1.** chair, (*piano etc*) stool: **der Heilige ~** the Holy See; *fig.* **sich zwischen zwei Stühle setzen** fall between two stools; → *elektrisch* I. **2.** ♣ a) stool, b) → *Stuhlgang*.

'Stuhl|bein *n* leg of a chair. **~gang** *m* (-[e]s; *no pl*) bowel movement.

stülpen ['ʃtʏlpən] *v/t* (h) put (**auf** *acc* on, **über** *acc* over): **et. nach außen ~** turn s.th. inside out.

stumm [ʃtʊm] *adj* dumb, mute, *fig. a.* silent (*a. ling.*), speechless (**vor** *dat* with).

Stummel ['ʃtʊməl] *m* (-s; -) stump, butt, stub (*a. of candle etc*).

'Stummfilm *m* silent film.

Stumpen ['ʃtʊmpən] *m* (-s; -) cheroot.

Stümper ['ʃtʏmpər] *m* (-s; -) bungler.

Stümpe'rei *f* (-; -en) **1.** *no pl* bungling.

---

2. botch. **'stümperhaft** *adj* bungling. **'stümpern** *v/i, v/t* (h) bungle, botch.

stumpf [ʃtʊmpf] *adj* **1.** blunt. **2.** ♠ obtuse (*angle*), truncated (*cone*). **3.** dull. **4.** *fig.* apathetic, dull, dulled (*senses*).

Stumpf *m* (-[e]s; ⁓e) stump: F **mit ~ und Stiel** root and branch.

'Stumpfheit *f* (-; *no pl*) **1.** bluntness. **2.** *a. fig.* dullness. **'Stumpfsinn** *m* (-[e]s; *no pl*) dullness, a. mindlessness (*of work etc*). **'stumpfsinnig** *adj* dull, a. mindless, soul-destroying (*work etc*).

'stumpfwink(e)lig *adj* ♠ obtuse.

Stunde ['ʃtʊndə] *f* (-; -n) **1.** hour: **zur ~** at this hour; **bis zur ~** as yet; *mot.* **50 Meilen in der ~** 50 miles per hour; **die ~ der Wahrheit** the moment of truth. **2.** *ped.* lesson, class, period: **bei j-m ~n nehmen** have lessons with s.o.

'stunden *v/t* (h) (*j-m*) (*die Zahlung* ~ extend the term of payment (to s.o.).

'Stunden|geschwindigkeit *f* (average) speed per hour: **e-e ~ von 60 Meilen** an average of 60 miles per hour (*abbr.* mph). **~kilo,meter** *pl* kilomet/res (*Am.* -ers) per hour. **⁓lang** *I adj* lasting (for) hours. **II** *adv* for hours (and hours). **~lohn** *m* hourly wage. **~plan** *m* timetable, *Am.* schedule.

'stundenweise *adj* and *adv* by the hour.

'Stundenzeiger *m* hour hand.

...stündig [-ʃtʏndɪç] *in cpds.* ...-hour.

'stündlich I *adj* hourly. **II** *adv* a) every hour, b) any time (now).

Stunk [ʃtʊŋk] *m* F – **machen** kick up a stink; **das gibt ~!** there will be trouble.

stupide [ʃtuˈpiːdə] *adj* dull, mindless.

Stups [ʃtʊps] *m* (-es; -e), **'stupsen** *v/t* (h) F prod. **'Stupsnase** *f* snub nose.

stur [ʃtuːr] *adj* F **1.** stubborn, pigheaded, stolid. **2.** → *stumpfsinnig*.

'Sturheit *f* (-; *no pl*) F **1.** stubbornness (*etc*). **2.** → *Stumpfsinn*.

Sturm [ʃtʊrm] *m* (-[e]s; ⁓e) **1.** storm (*a. fig.*), gale: **~ der Entrüstung** outcry; **~ im Wasserglas** storm in a teacup. **2.** ✕ storm, attack: *a. fig.* **im ~ erobern** take by storm; **~ laufen gegen** attack, assail; **✝ ~ auf** (*acc*) rush for (*goods*), run on (*a bank*). **3.** *sports:* forwards. **~an-griff** *m* ✕ assault. **~bö** *f* squall.

stürmen ['ʃtʏrmən] **I** *v/t* (h) **1.** ✕ storm: *fig.* **e-e Bank ~** make a run on a bank. **II** *v/i* **2.** (h) ✕ *or sports:* attack. **3.** (sn) *fig.* rush. **III** *v/impers* (h) **es stürmt** there's a gale blowing.

'**Stürmer** *m* (-s; -) *sports:* forward.

'**stürmisch** *adj* stormy (*a. fig. debate, love, etc*), passionate (*lover*), tumultuous (*applause etc*), vehement (*protest*), turbulent (*time*), rapid (*development etc*): **nicht so ~!** easy does it!

'**Sturm|lauf** *m* ✕ assault, *fig. a.* run (*auf acc* on). **~spitze** *f* soccer: spearhead. **~tief** *n* cyclone. **~warnung** *f* gale warning. **~wolke** *f* storm cloud.

Sturz [ʃtʊrts] *m* (-es; ⁼e) **1.** (sudden) fall, plunge (*a. fig.*), *fig.* (sudden) drop (*in temperature etc*), *a.* slump (*in prices etc*). **2.** (down)fall, overthrow (*of a government*). '**Sturzbach** *m* torrent.

stürzen [ʃtʏrtsən] **I** *v/i* (sn) **1.** fall, *a. fig.* plunge: **sie ist (mit dem Fahrrad) gestürzt** she had a fall (with her bicycle). **2.** rush, dash: **er kam ins Zimmer gestürzt** he burst into the room. **II** *v/t* (h) **3.** throw: **j-n ins Elend ~** plunge s.o. into misery. **4.** turn *s.th.* upside down, turn *pudding etc* out of the mo(u)ld: **Nicht ~!** this side up! **5.** bring down, overthrow (*government etc*). **III sich ~** (h) **6.** plunge (**ins Wasser** into the water); **sich aus dem Fenster ~** throw o.s. out of the window; *fig.* **sich in die Arbeit ~** throw o.s. into one's work; **sich in Schulden ~** plunge into debt; **sich in Unkosten ~** go to great expense. **7. sich ~ auf** (*acc*) pounce on, *a.* rush at (*s.o.*), *a.* make straight for.

'**Sturz|flug** *m* (nose)dive. **~helm** *m* crash helmet. **~regen** *m* (heavy) downpour.

Stute [ʃtuːtə] *f* (-; -n) mare.

'**Stutenfohlen** *n* filly.

'**Stützbalken** *m* supporting beam.

Stütze [ʃtʏtsə] *f* (-; -n) *a. fig.* support, prop, (*person*) mainstay.

stutzen[1] [ʃtʊtsən] *v/t* (h) cut, trim (*hair, beard*), lop (*tree*), clip (*hedge, wings*), crop (*ears*), dock (*tail*).

'**stutzen**[2] *v/i* (h) (**bei**) a) stop short (at), b) be puzzled (by), c) become suspicious (at).

'**Stutzen** *m* (-s; -) **1.** short rifle. **2.** ⚙ connecting piece. **3.** (football) sock.

stützen [ʃtʏtsən] *v/t* (h) support (*a. fig.*), prop, *fig.* back (up): **die Ellbogen auf den Tisch ~** prop (*or* rest) one's elbows on the table; *fig.* **et. ~ auf** (*acc*) base

s.th. on; **sich ~ auf** (*acc*) rely on, *opinion etc:* be based on.

stutzig [ʃtʊtsɪç] *adj* **j-n ~ machen** a) puzzle s.o., b) make s.o. suspicious; **~ werden** a) be puzzled, b) become suspicious.

'**Stütz|mauer** *f* retaining wall. **~pfeiler** *m* buttress. **~punkt** *m* ✕ *or fig.* base.

Styropor [ʃtyroˈpoːr] *n* (-s; *no pl*) (*TM*) polystyrene.

Subjekt [zʊpˈjɛkt] *n* (-[e]s; -e) **1.** *ling.* subject. **2.** F *contp.* fellow.

subjektiv [zʊpjɛkˈtiːf] *adj* subjective. **Subjektivität** [zʊpjɛktiviˈtɛːt] *f* (-; *no pl*) subjectivity.

'**Subkonti,nent** *m* subcontinent.

'**Subkul,tur** *f* (-; -en) subculture.

subkutan [zʊpkuˈtaːn] *adj* 💉 subcutaneous.

Sublimat [zubliˈmaːt] *n* (-[e]s; -e) 🜍 sublimate. **sublimieren** [zubliˈmiːrən] *v/t* (h) 🜍 *or fig.* sublimate.

Subskription [zʊpskrɪpˈtsi̯oːn] *f* (-; -en) subscription. **Subskripti,onspreis** *m* subscription price.

substantiell [zʊpstanˈtsi̯ɛl] *adj* substantial.

Substantiv [ʃʊpstantiːf] *n* (-s; -e) noun, substantive. **substantivieren** [zʊpstantiˈviːrən] *v/t* (h) use as a noun. '**substantivisch** [-tiːvɪʃ] *adj* substantival, *adv a.* as a noun.

Substanz [zʊpˈstants] *f* (-; -en) **1.** substance. **2.** † (**von der ~ leben** live on one's capital; F *fig.* **das geht an die ~** that really takes it out of you.

subtil [zʊpˈtiːl] *adj* subtle.

subtrahieren [zʊptraˈhiːrən] *v/t* (h) subtract. **Subtraktion** [zʊptrakˈtsi̯oːn] *f* (-; -en) subtraction.

'**subtropisch** *adj* subtropical.

Subvention [zʊpvɛnˈtsi̯oːn] *f* (-; -en) subsidy. **subventionieren** [zʊpvɛntsi̯oˈniːrən] *v/t* (h) subsidize.

'**Such|akti,on** *f* search (operation). **~dienst** *m* tracing service.

Suche [zuːxə] *f* (-; -n) (**nach** for) search, hunt: **auf der ~ nach** in search of; **auf der ~ sein nach** be looking for.

suchen [zuːxən] (h) **I** *v/t* a) look for, search for, b) seek (*advice, happiness, etc*), c) try to trace (*person, mistake, etc*): (**mit j-m**) **Streit ~** pick a quarrel (with s.o.); **Sie haben hier nichts zu ~!**

you have no business to be here; → **gesucht, Rat** 1, **Weite**[2]. **II** *v/i* look, search: **~ nach** → I; **nach Worten ~** be at a loss for words.

'**Sucher** *m* (-s; -) *phot.* viewfinder.

'**Sucherkamera** *f* rangefinder camera.

'**Such|gerät** *n* detector. **~hund** *m* tracker dog. **~lauf** *m video etc*: a) scanning, b) scanner. **~mannschaft** *f* search party. **~scheinwerfer** *m* searchlight.

Sucht [zʊxt] *f* (-; ⸚e) (*nach*) a) craving (for), b) *a.* ✻ addiction (to).

'**suchterzeugend** *adj* ✻ addictive.

'**süchtig** ['zʏçtɪç] *adj* addicted (*nach* to): **~ machen** be addictive; *fig.* **~ sein nach** a) have a craving for, b) be obsessed with. '**Süchtige** *m, f* (-n; -n) addict.

'**Suchtmittel** *n* addictive drug.

'**Suchtrupp** *m* search party.

Süd'afrika [zʊxt] *f* (-; ⸚e) *n* (-s) South Africa. '**Südafri'kaner(in** *f*) *m*, '**südafri'kanisch** *adj* South African.

'**Süda'merika** *n* (-s) South America. '**Südameri'kaner(in** *f*) *m*, '**südameri'kanisch** *adj* South American.

'**süddeutsch** *adj*, '**Süddeutsche** *m, f* (-n; -n) South German.

Sude'lei *f* (-; -en) F *contp.* mess. **sudeln** ['zuːdəln] *v/i* (h) F *contp.* make a mess.

Süden ['zyːdən] *m* (-s; *no pl*) south, South: **im ~** in the south; **im ~ von** (*or gen*) (to the) south of; **nach ~** south(ward).

'**Südfrüchte** *pl* tropical fruits.

'**Südküste** *f* (-s) south coast.

'**Südländer** [-lɛndər] *m* (-s; -), '**Südländerin** *f* (-; -nen) Mediterranean type, Latin. '**südländisch** *adj* Mediterranean, Latin (*temper etc*).

'**südlich I** *adj* southern, south, southerly (*wind, direction*). **II** *adv* south(wards). **III** *prep* **~ von** (*or gen*) (to the) south of.

Süd'osten *m* southeast.

süd'östlich I *adj* southeast(ern), southeasterly (*wind, direction*). **II** *adv* (to the) southeast. **III** *prep* **~ von** (*or gen*) (to the) southeast of.

'**Südpol** *m* South Pole.

Südpo'lar... Antarctic.

'**Südsee** *f* (-; *no pl*) South Sea.

'**südwärts** *adv* southward(s).

Süd'westen *m* southwest.

süd'westlich I *adj* southwest(ern), southwesterly (*wind, direction*). **II** *adv* (to the) southwest. **III** *prep* **~ von** (*or gen*) (to the) southwest of.

'**Südwind** *m* south wind.

Suff [zʊf] *m* (-[e]s; *no pl*) F boozing.

'**süffig** ['zʏfɪç] *adj* F pleasant (to drink).

'**süffisant** [zyfi'zant] *adj* smug.

suggerieren [zʊɡe'riːrən] *v/t* (h) suggest. **Suggestion** [zʊɡɛs'tǐoːn] *f* (-; -en) suggestion. **suggestiv** [zʊɡɛs'tiːf] *adj* suggestive. **Sugge'stivfrage** *f* leading question.

Sühne ['zyːnə] *f* (-; -n) atonement.

sühnen ['zyːnən] *v/t* (h) atone for.

Suite ['sviːt(ə)] *f* (-; -n) suite.

Sujet [zy'ʒeː] *n* (-s; -s) subject.

sukzessiv [zʊktsɛ'siːf] *adj* gradual.

Sulfat [zʊl'faːt] *n* (-[e]s; -e) ✻ sulphate (*Am.* -f-). **Sulfid** [zʊl'fiːt] *n* (-[e]s; -e) ✻ sulphide (*Am.* -f-).

Sulfonamid [zʊlfona'miːd] *n* (-[e]s; -e) sulphonamide (*Am.* -f-).

Sultan ['zʊltaːn] *m* (-s; -e) sultan. **Sultanine** [zʊlta'niːnə] *f* (-; -n) *gastr.* sultana.

Sülze ['zʏltsə] *f* (-; -n) jellied meat.

summarisch [zʊ'maːrɪʃ] *adj* summary.

Summe ['zʊmə] *f* (-; -n) a) sum, b) (sum) total, c) amount, d) *fig.* sum total.

summen ['zʊmən] (h) **I** *v/i* buzz, hum, drone. **II** *v/t* hum (*tune etc*).

'**Summer** *m* (-s; -) ⚡ buzzer.

summieren [zʊ'miːrən] *v/t* (*a.* **sich ~**) (h) add up.

Sumpf [zʊmpf] *m* (-[e]s; ⸚e) **1.** swamp. **2.** *fig.* (quag)mire. '**sumpfen** *v/i* (h) F live it up. '**sumpfig** *adj* marshy. '**Sumpfland** *n* (-[e]s; *no pl*) marshland.

Sund [zʊnt] *m* (-[e]s; -e) sound, strait(s).

Sünde ['zʏndə] *f* (-; -n) sin.

'**Sünden|erlaß** *m* absolution. **~fall** *m* the Fall (of Man). **~re, gister** *n humor. sein etc* **~** the list of his *etc* sins.

'**Sünder** *m* (-s; -), '**Sünderin** *f* (-; -nen) sinner. '**sündhaft** *adj* sinful: F **~ teuer** awfully expensive. '**sündig** *adj* sinful. **sündigen** ['zʏndɪɡən] *v/i* (h) **1.** sin (*gegen* against): **an j-m ~** wrong s.o. **2.** F indulge, overeat *etc*.

super ['zuːpər] *adj or int* F super.

'**Super** *n* (-s; *no pl*) F *mot.* super, four-star (petrol), *Am.* premium.

Superlativ ['zuːpɛrlatiːf] *m* (-s; -e) *ling. or fig.* superlative.

'**Supermacht** *f pol.* superpower.

'**Supermarkt** *m* supermarket.

'**supermo|dern** *adj* ultramodern.

Suppe ['zʊpə] *f* (-; -n) soup: F *die ~ auslöffeln müssen* have to face the music; *j-m* (*sich*) *e-e schöne ~ einbrocken* get s.o. (o.s.) into a nice mess. '**Suppen|fleisch** *n* meat for making soup. **~grün** *n* (bunch of) herbs and vegetables. **~huhn** *n* boiling fowl. **~kelle** *f* soup ladle. **~löffel** *m* soup spoon. **~schüssel** *f* soup tureen. **~teller** *m* soup plate. **~würfel** *m* stock cube.

Surfbrett ['sɛːf-] *n* surfboard. '**surfen** *v/i* (h, sn) do surfing, surf. '**Surfer** *m* (-s; -), '**Surferin** *f* (-; -nen) surfer.

Surrealismus [svrea'lɪsmʊs] *m* (-; *no pl*) surrealism.

surrea|listisch *adj* surrealist(ic).

surren ['zʊrən] *v/i* (h) whirr, hum, *insect etc*: buzz.

suspekt [zʊs'pɛkt] *adj* suspect.

suspendieren [zʊspɛn'diːrən] *v/t* (h) suspend.

Suspensorium [zʊspɛn'zoːriʊm] *n* (-s; -rien) *♣* suspensory, *sports*: jockstrap.

süß [zyːs] *adj* sweet. '**Süße¹** *f* (-; *no pl*) sweetness. '**Süße²** *m, f* (-n; -n) F sweetie. '**süßen** *v/t* (h) sweeten.

'**Süßigkeiten** *pl* sweets, *Am.* candy.

'**süßlich** *adj* **1.** sweetish. **2.** *fig.* a) sugary, b) mawkish.

'**süß-'sauer** *adj gastr.* sweet and sour: F *~ lächeln* smile sourly, force a smile.

'**Süßspeise** *f* sweet, dessert.

'**Süßstoff** *m* sweetener.

'**Süßwaren** *pl* sweets, *Am.* candy. **~geschäft** *n* sweet shop, *Am.* candy store.

'**Süßwasser** *n* fresh water.

Symbiose [zym'biˑozə] *f* (-; -n) *biol.* or *fig.* symbiosis.

Symbol [zym'boːl] *n* (-s; -e) symbol (*für* of), **🜪**, **𝄞** *etc a.* (conventional) sign. **Symbolik** [zym'boːlɪk] *f* (-; *no pl*) symbolism. **sym'bolisch** *adj* symbolic(al). **symbolisieren** [zymboli'ziːrən] *v/t* (h) symbolize.

Symmetrie [zyme'triː] *f* (-; -n) symmetry. **symmetrisch** [zy'meːtrɪʃ] *adj* symmetric(al).

Sympathie [zympa'tiː] *f* (-; -n) **1.** liking: *~ empfinden für* have a liking for. **2.** sympathy: *sich j-s ~n verscherzen* lose s.o.'s sympathies (*or* support).

Sympa'thiestreik *m* sympathetic strike.

Sympathisant [zympati'zant] *m* (-en; -en) sympathizer. **sympathisch** [zym-'paːtɪʃ] *adj* **1.** likeable, F nice: *er ist mir* (*nicht*) *~* I (don't) like him. **2.** *physiol.* sympathetic. **sympathisieren** [zympati'ziːrən] *v/i* (h) sympathize.

Symphonie [zymfo'niː] *f* (-; -n) *etc* → **Sinfonie** *etc.*

Symposium [zym'poːziʊm] *n* (-s; -sien) symposium.

Symptom [zymp'toːm] *n* (-s; -e) symptom. **symptomatisch** [zympto'maːtɪʃ] *adj* symptomatic (*für* of).

Synagoge [zyna'goːgə] *f* (-; -n) synagogue.

synchron [zyn'kroːn] *adj* synchronous, *ling.* synchronic: *~ laufen etc* be synchronized. **Syn'chron...** synchronizing. **synchronisieren** [zynkroni'ziːrən] *v/t* (h) synchronize, *film:* a. dub.

Syndikat [zyndi'kaːt] *n* (-[e]s; -e) syndicate.

Syndikus ['zyndikʊs] *m* (-; -se) company lawyer, in-house legal counsel.

Syndrom [zyn'droːm] *n* (-s; -e) *♣* syndrome.

Synkope *f* (-; -n) **1.** ['zynkope] *ling.* syncope. **2.** [zyn'koːpə] *♪* syncopation.

Synode [zy'noːdə] *f* (-; -n) *eccl.* synod.

synonym [zyno'nyːm] *adj ling.* synonymous. **Syno'nym** *n* (-s; -e) synonym.

syntaktisch [zyn'taktɪʃ] *adj ling.* syntactic(al).

Syntax ['zyntaks] *f* (-; -en) *ling.* syntax.

Synthese [zyn'teːzə] *f* (-; -n) synthesis.

synthetisch [zyn'teːtɪʃ] *adj* synthetic.

Syphilis ['zyːfilɪs] *f* (-; *no pl*) *♣* syphilis.

Syrien ['zyːriən] *n* (-s) Syria. **Syrier** ['zyːriər] *m* (-s; -), '**Syrierin** *f* (-; -nen), '**syrisch** *adj* Syrian.

System [zys'teːm] *n* (-s; -e) system, *of traffic etc:* a. network. **Systematik** [zyste'maːtɪk] *f* (-; -en) systematics, system. **syste'matisch** *adj* systematic.

Sy'stemkritiker(in *f*) *m* dissident.

sy'stemlos *adj* unmethodical.

Szenario [stse'naˑrio] *n* (-s; -s) scenario.

Szene ['stseːnə] *f* (-; -n) scene; *fig. sich in ~ setzen* put on a show; (*j-m*) *e-e ~ machen* make (s.o.) a scene.

'**Szenen|ap,plaus** *m* applause during the scene. **~wechsel** *m* scene change.

Szenerie [stsenə'riː] *f* (-; -n) scenery, *thea. a.* setting.

T

T, t [te:] *n* (-; -) T, t.
Tabak ['ta:bak] *m* (-s; -e) tobacco.
'Tabakpflanze *f* tobacco (plant).
'Tabakwaren *pl* tobacco goods.
'Tabakwarenladen *m* tobacconist's.
tabellarisch [tabɛ'la:rɪʃ] *adj* tabulated, tabular. **Tabelle** [ta'bɛlə] *f* (-; -n) table.
Ta'bellen|führer *m sports:* top team, leader. **~letzte** *m* bottom team. **~spitze** *f* (**an der** ~ at the) top of the table.
Tabernakel [tabɛr'na:kəl] *n, m* (-s; -) *eccl.* tabernacle.
Tablett [ta'blɛt] *n* (-[e]s; -e) tray.
Tablette [ta'blɛtə] *f* (-; -n) tablet, pill.
tabu [ta'bu:] *adj* taboo: **für ~ erklären** (put under a) taboo. **Ta'bu** *n* (-s; -s) taboo. **ta'bufrei** *adj* **~e Gesellschaft** permissive society.
Tabulator [tabu'la:tɔr] *m* (-s; -en [-la'to:-rən]) tabulator.
Tacho ['taxo] *m* (-s; -s) F, **Tachometer** [taxo'me:tər] *n* (-s; -) *mot.* speedometer.
Tadel ['ta:dəl] *m* (-s; -) reproach, rebuke, *ped.* bad mark: **ohne** ~ → **tadellos** *adj* faultless, flawless, blameless, perfect, impeccable (*a. clothing*). **'tadeln** *v/t* (h) (**wegen** for) a) rebuke, reprimand, blame, b) criticize, censure. **'tadelnswert** *adj* reprehensible.
Tafel ['ta:fəl] *f* (-; -n) **1.** *ped.* a) blackboard, b) slate. **2.** notice (*Am.* bulletin) board. **3.** plate (*a. in book*). **4.** a) slab, b) tablet, plaque, c) panel. **5.** bar (*of chocolate*). **6.** (dinner) table: **die ~ aufheben** rise from the table. **'tafelfertig** *adj* ready to serve. **'Tafelgeschirr** *n* dinner service.
tafeln ['ta:fəln] *v/i* (h) dine.
täfeln ['tɛ:fəln] *v/t* (h) panel.
'Tafelobst *n* dessert fruit.
'Tafelsilber *n* silver(ware).
'Täfelung *f* (-; -en) panel(l)ing.
'Tafelwasser *n* mineral (*or* table) water.
Taft [taft] *m* (-[e]s; -e) taffeta.
Tag [ta:k] *m* (-[e]s; -e) day: **am ~e, bei ~e** a) in the daytime, b) by daylight; ~ **für** ~ day after day, *get better etc* day by day; **am nächsten** ~ the day after; **am ~ zuvor** the day before; **dieser ~e** a) one of these days, b) the other day; **e-s ~es** one day, *a.* some day; **den ganzen** ~ all

day long; **alle paar ~e** every few days; **jeden zweiten** ~ every other day; ⚒ **unter (über) ~e** underground (above ground); **von e-m ~ auf den anderen** overnight; **guten ~!** a) good morning!, good afternoon!, F hello!, b) how do you do?; **j-m guten ~ sagen** say hello to s.o.; **an den ~ bringen (kommen)** bring (come) to light; **an den ~ legen** display, show; **welchen ~ haben wir heute?** what's (the date) today?; → **Abend, heute** I, **heutig.**
tag'aus → **tagein.**
Tage|bau ['ta:gə-] *m* (-[e]s; *no pl*) ⚒ opencast mining. **~buch** *n* diary. **~dieb** *m* idler. **~geld(er** *pl*) *n* daily allowance.
tag'ein ~, **tagaus** day in, day out.
'tagelang I *adj* lasting for days. **II** *adv* for day (and days).
'Tagelöhner [-lø:nər] *m* (-s; -), **'Tage-löhnerin** *f* (-; -nen) day labo(u)rer.
tagen ['ta:gən] *v/i* (h) have a meeting, sit (in conference), ⚖ be in session.
Tages|anbruch ['ta:gəs-] *m* (**bei** ~ at) daybreak. **~ausflug** *m* day trip. **~creme** *f* day cream. **~decke** *f* bedspread. **~einnahme(n** *pl*) *f* day's takings. **~gericht** *n gastr.* dish of the day. **~gespräch** *n* the talk of the day. **~karte** *f* **1.** day ticket. **2.** *gastr.* menu for the day. **~kasse** *f* **1.** *thea. etc* booking office. **2.** ✝ a) petty cash, b) → **Tageseinnahme(n).** **~kurs** *m* **1.** ✝ *foreign exchange:* current rate, *stock exchange:* current price. **2.** *ped.* day course. **~leistung** *f* daily output. **~licht** *n* (-[e]s; *no pl*) daylight: *fig.* **ans ~ bringen (kommen)** bring (come) to light. **~mutter** *f* child minder. **~ordnung** *f* (**auf der ~ stehen** be on the) agenda: *a. fig.* **zur ~ übergehen** proceed to the order of the day; *fig.* **an der ~ sein** be nothing unusual. **~presse** *f* daily press. **~raum** *m* dayroom. **~rückfahr-karte** *f* day return (ticket). **~satz** *m* **1.** daily rate. **2.** *med.* daily ration. **~stätte** *f* day-care cent/re (*Am.* -er). **~tour** *f* day trip. **~zeit** *f* **1.** time of day. **2.** daytime: **zu jeder** ~ at any time of the day. **~zeitung** *f* daily (newspaper).

'**tageweise** *adv* on a day-to-day basis.
'**taghell** *adj and adv* (as) light as day.
...**tägig** [-tɛ:ɡɪç] *in cpds.* ...-day.
täglich ['tɛ:klɪç] **I** *adj* a) daily, b) every-day. **II** *adv* every day, daily: **zweimal ~** twice a day.
tags [ta:ks] *adv* **~ darauf** (**zuvor**) the day after (before).
'**Tagschicht** *f* (**~ haben** be on) day shift.
'**tagsüber** *adv* during the day.
'**tag'täglich** *adv* day in, day out.
'**Tagung** *f* (-; -en) conference, convention. '**Tagungsbericht** *m* proceedings.
'**Tagungsort** *m* conference venue.
Taifun [tai'fu:n] *m* (-s; -e) typhoon.
Taille ['taljə] *f* (-; -n) waist, *a.* waistline.
tailliert [ta'ji:rt] *adj* waisted.
Takelage [takə'la:ʒə] *f* (-; -n) ⚓ rigging.
takeln ['ta:kəln] *v/t* (h) rig.
Takt¹ [takt] *m* (-[e]s; -e) **1.** ♪ a) bar, b) beat, c) (*waltz etc*) time: **3/4-~** three-four-time; **~ halten** keep time; **den ~ schlagen** beat the time; **aus dem ~ kommen** lose the beat, *fig.* be put off one's stroke. **2.** rhythm, (work *etc*) cycle, *mot.* stroke: **im 15-Minuten-Takt** at 15-minute intervals.
Takt² *m* (-[e]s; *no pl*), '**Taktgefühl** *n* (-[e]s; *no pl*) tact.
taktieren [tak'ti:rən] *v/i* (h) **geschickt ~** use clever tactics. **Taktik** ['taktɪk] *f* (-; -en) (**die ~ ändern** change) tactics. '**Taktiker** *m* (-s; -) tactician. '**taktisch** *adj a. fig.* tactical.
'**taktlos** *adj* tactless. '**Taktlosigkeit** *f* (-; *no pl*) tactlessness, indiscretion.
'**Takt|stock** *m* baton. **~strich** *m* ♪ bar.
'**taktvoll** *adj* tactful.
Tal [ta:l] *n* (-[e]s; ⸚er) valley.
Talar [ta'la:r] *m* (-s; -e) *univ.* gown, *eccl.* cassock, *fig.* robe.
Talent [ta'lɛnt] *n* (-[e]s; -e) **1.** talent (*für*, *zu* for). **2.** talent(ed person). **talentiert** [talɛn'ti:rt] *adj* talented, gifted. **ta'lentlos** *adj* untalented. **Ta'lentsucher** *m* (-s; -) talent scout. **ta'lentvoll** *adj* talented, gifted.
'**Talfahrt** *f* **1.** descent. **2.** ⸚ downswing.
Talg [talk] *m* (-[e]s; -e) **1.** *gastr.* a) suet, b) tallow. **2.** *physiol.* sebum.
'**Talgdrüse** *f* sebaceous gland.
Talisman ['ta:lɪsman] *m* (-s; -e) talisman, (lucky) charm, mascot.
Talk [talk] *m* (-[e]s; *no pl*) *min.* talc(um).

Talkmaster ['tɔ:kma:stər] *m* (-s; -) *TV* host. **Talk-Show** *f* (-; -s) *TV* chat (*esp. Am.* talk) show.
'**Talsohle** *f* **1.** bottom of the valley. **2.** ⸚ low. '**Talsperre** *f* dam.
Tamburin [tambu'ri:n] *n* (-s; -e) tambourine.
Tampon ['tampɔn] *m* (-s; -s), **tamponieren** [tampo'ni:rən] *v/t* (h) ✚ tampon.
Tamtam [tam'tam] *n* (-s; *no pl*) **F** *contp.* fuss (*um* about).
Tandem ['tandɛm] *n* (-s; -s) tandem.
Tang [taŋ] *m* (-[e]s; -e) ⚓ seaweed.
Tangahöschen ['taŋɡa-] *n* G-string.
Tangente [taŋ'ɡɛntə] *f* (-; -n) ⚥ tangent.
tangieren [taŋ'ɡi:rən] *v/t* (h) **1.** ⚥ be tangent to. **2.** *fig.* affect, concern.
Tango ['taŋɡo] *m* (-s; -s) tango.
Tank [taŋk] *m* (-[e]s; -e) tank. '**tanken** (h) **I** *v/t* **1.** a) fill up with, b) refill, refuel. **2.** **F** *fig.* get (*fresh air etc*) refuel. **II** *v/i* **3.** tank up (*a.* **F** *drink*), refuel.
'**Tanker** *m* (-s; -) ⚓ (oil) tanker.
'**Tank|schiff** *n* → **Tanker**. **~stelle** *f* filling (*or* petrol, *Am.* gas) station. **~verschluß** *m* *mot.* fuel cap. **~wagen** *m* *mot.* tanker. **~wart** *m* (-[e]s; -e) petrol pump (*Am.* gas station) attendant.
Tanne ['tanə] *f* (-; -n) fir (tree).
'**Tannen|baum** *m* fir (tree). **~nadel** *f* fir needle. **~zapfen** *m* fir cone.
Tante ['tantə] *f* (-; -n) **1.** aunt: **~ Helene** Aunt Helen. **2.** **F** woman, bird.
Tante-'Emma-Laden *m* **F** corner shop, *Am.* mom-and-pop store.
Tantieme [tã'tiɛ:mə] *f* (-; -n) royalty.
Tanz [tants] *m* (-es; ⸚e) **1.** dance. **2.** **F** *fig.* fuss. '**Tanzbein** *n* **F** *das ~ schwingen** shake a leg. **tänzeln** ['tɛntsəln] *v/i* **1.** (sn) skip. **2.** (h) *horse:* prance. '**tanzen** *v/t, v/i* (h) dance. **Tänzer** ['tɛntsər] *m* (-s; -), '**Tänzerin** *f* (-; -nen) dancer, *thea.* (ballet) dancer.
'**Tanz|fläche** *f* dance floor. **~kurs** *m* dancing course. **~lehrer(in** *f*) *m* dancing instructor. **~lo,kal** *n* dance hall. **~mu,sik** *f* dance music. **~or,chester** *n* dance band. **~partner(in** *f*) *m* dancing partner. **~saal** *m* dance hall, ballroom. **~schule** *f* dancing school. **~stunde** *f* **in die ~ gehen** go to a dancing class. **~tur,nier** *n* dancing contest.
Tapet [ta'pe:t] **F** *et.* **aufs ~ bringen** bring s.th. up.

Tapete [ta'pe:tə] f (-; -n) wallpaper. **Ta'petenwechsel** m F fig. change (of scenery). **tapezieren** [tape'tsi:rən] v/t, v/i (h) (wall)paper: **neu** ~ repaper.

tapfer ['tapfər] adj brave, courageous. **'Tapferkeit** f (-; no pl) bravery, courage.

tappen ['tapən] v/i **1.** (sn) a) pad, b) grope one's way. **2.** (h) grope (or fumble) (about) (nach for): a. fig. **im dunkeln** ~ be groping in the dark.

Tara ['ta:ra] f (-; Taren) ✝ tare.

Tarantel [ta'rantəl] f (-; -n) tarantula.

Tarif [ta'ri:f] m (-s; -e) a) scale of charges, b) rate, c) charge, d) pay scale, e) tariff. **~abschluß** m wage settlement. **~autono,mie** f free collective bargaining. **~kon,flikt** m pay dispute.

ta'riflich adj tariff ..., standard ...

Ta'rif|lohn m standard wage(s). **~partner** m party to a wage agreement, pl union(s) and management. **~runde** f pay round. **~satz** m **1.** (tariff) rate. **2.** (standard) wage rate. **~verhandlungen** pl wage negotiations. **~vertrag** m wage agreement.

tarnen ['tarnən] v/t (h) camouflage. **'Tarn|farbe** f camouflage colo(u)r. **~organisati,on** f cover organization. **'Tarnung** f (-; -en) camouflage, fig. a. cover.

Tasche ['taʃə] f (-; -n) **1.** a) (shopping etc) bag, b) (hand)bag, Am. purse. **2.** pocket: **et. aus der eigenen ~ bezahlen** pay for s.th. out of one's own pocket; **den Gewinn in die eigene ~ stecken** pocket the profit; F fig. **j-n in die ~ stecken** put s.o. in one's pocket; **den Auftrag haben wir in der ~!** the order is in the bag; F **j-m auf der ~ liegen** live off s.o.; **in die eigene ~ arbeiten** line one's (own) pockets; **tief in die ~ greifen (müssen)** have to) dig deep into one's pockets.

'Taschen|buch n paperback. **~dieb(in** f) m pickpocket. **~feuerzeug** n pocket lighter. **~for,mat** n pocket size: **im ~** pocket-size(d). **~geld** n pocket money. **~ka,lender** m pocket diary. **~lampe** f torch, Am. flashlight. **~messer** n penknife. **~rechner** m pocket calculator. **~spiegel** m pocket mirror. **~tuch** n handkerchief. **~uhr** f fob watch. **~wörterbuch** n pocket dictionary.

Tasse ['tasə] f (-; -n) cup: **e-e ~ Tee** a cup of tea; F contp. **trübe ~** drip.

Tastatur [tasta'tu:r] f (-; -en) keyboard, keys. **Taste** ['tastə] f (-; -n) key, a. push button.

tasten ['tastən] (h) **I** v/t touch, feel. **II** v/i (nach for) a. fig. grope, fumble. **III sich ~** grope one's way. **'tastend** adj groping, fig. a. tentative.

'Tasten|instru,ment n ♪ keyboard instrument. **~tele,fon** n push-button telephone.

'Taster m (-s; -) **1.** zo. feeler. **2.** ☺ a) key, b) sensor.

'Tastsinn m (-[e]s; no pl) sense of touch.

tat [ta:t] pret of **tun.**

Tat f (-; -en) **1.** a) deed, act, b) achievement, feat, c) action: **er ist ein Mann der ~** he is a man of action; → **umsetzen** 3. **2.** (criminal) offen/ce (Am. -se), crime: **auf frischer ~ ertappen** catch s.o. redhanded. **3. in der ~** indeed.

Tatar [ta'ta:r] n (-[s]; no pl) gastr. spiced raw minced beef.

'Tatbestand m state of affairs, ⚖ facts of the case.

'Tatendrang m thirst for action.

'tatenlos adj inactive.

Täter ['tɛ:tər] m (-s; -), **'Täterin** f (-; -nen) culprit, ⚖ offender.

tätig ['tɛ:tɪç] adj active (a. volcano), busy: **~ sein als** a) work as, b) act as; **~ sein bei** work for a firm, work at an institute etc; **~ werden** act, take action.

tätigen ['tɛ:tɪgən] v/t (h) effect, transact (business), make (purchases).

'Tätigkeit f (-; -en) a) activity, b) occupation, job, c) function, d) physiol., ☺ etc action: **in ~** in action; **welche ~ üben Sie aus?** what is your job?

'Tätigkeitsfeld n field of activity.

'Tatkraft f (-; no pl) energy, drive, enterprise. **'tatkräftig** adj energetic, active: **~e Hilfe** effective help.

tätlich ['tɛ:tlɪç] adj violent: ⚖ **~e Beleidigung** assault and battery; **~ werden** become violent; **gegen j-n ~ werden** assault s.o. **'Tätlichkeit** f (-; -en) (act of) violence, ⚖ assault (and battery).

'Tatort m scene of the crime.

tätowieren [tɛto'vi:rən] v/t (h) tattoo. **Täto'wierung** f (-; -en) tattoo.

'Tatsache f fact: **j-n vor vollendete ~n stellen** confront s.o. with a fait accompli; ~ **ist, daß** the fact is that; **das än-dert nichts an der ~, daß** that doesn't alter the fact that; **den ~n ins Auge blicken** face the facts.

'Tatsachenbericht m documentary.

'tatsächlich I adj actual, real. **II** adv actually, really, in fact: **~? really?**

tätscheln ['tɛ:tʃəln] v/t (h) pat.

tatterig ['tatərɪç] adj F doddery, shaky.

Tatze ['tatsə] f (-; -n) paw.

Tau¹ [taʊ] n (-[e]s; -e) rope.

Tau² m (-[e]s; no pl) dew.

taub [taʊp] adj **1.** deaf (fig. **gegen, für** to): **auf einem Ohr ~** deaf in one ear. **2.** empty (nut), dead (rock), numb (limbs).

Taube¹ ['taʊbə] m, f (-n; -n) deaf person: **die ~n** the deaf.

'Taube² f (-; -n) zo. pigeon, a. pol. dove.

'Taubenschlag m dovecote.

'Taubheit f (-; no pl) **1.** deafness. **2.** numbness. **'taubstumm** adj deaf and dumb. **'Taubstumme** m, f (-n; -n) deaf-mute. **'Taubstummensprache** f deaf-and-dumb language.

tauchen ['taʊxən] **I** v/i (sn) dive (nach for), a. skin-dive, submarine: a. submerge. **II** v/t (h) dip, immerse: **j-n ~** duck s.o.

'Taucher m (-s; -) (sports: skin) diver. **~anzug** m diving suit, a. wetsuit, **~bril-le** f diving goggles. **~glocke** f diving bell. **~maske** f diving mask.

'Tauch|sieder m (-s; -) ⚡ immersion heater. **~sport** m skin diving.

tauen ['taʊən] **I** v/i (sn) thaw, melt. **II** v/impers (h) **es taut** a) it is thawing, b) dew is falling.

'Taufbecken n font. **Taufe** ['taʊfə] f (-; -n) baptism, a. christening: **aus der ~ heben** stand godfather (or godmother) to, fig. launch. **'taufen** v/t (h) **1.** baptize, christen. **2.** call. **Täufling** ['tɔyflɪŋ] m (-s; -e) child (or person) to be baptized. **Taufname** m Christian (esp. Am. given) name. **'Taufschein** m certificate of baptism. **'Taufstein** m font.

'taugen ['taʊgən] v/i (h) (**zu, für** for) be suited, be of use: **nichts ~** be no good; **taugt es (et)was?** is it any good?

tauglich ['taʊklɪç] adj a) suitable (für, zu for), b) ✕ fit (for service). **'Tauglich-keit** f (-; no pl) a) suitability, b) fitness.

Taumel ['taʊməl] m (-s; no pl) **1.** dizzi-ness. **2.** fig. a) whirl, b) rapture, frenzy.

taum(e)lig ['taʊm(ə)lɪç] adj dizzy.

taumeln ['taʊməln] v/i (sn) reel, stagger.

Tausch [taʊʃ] m (-[e]s; -e) exchange, F swap, barter. **'tauschen** v/t, v/i (h) ex-change (a. looks etc), a. barter, F swap (**gegen** for): **ich möchte nicht mit ihr ~** I wouldn't like to be in her shoes.

täuschen ['tɔyʃən] (h) **I** v/t a) mislead, deceive, b) cheat, fool: **wenn mich nicht alles täuscht** if I am not very much mistaken; **wenn mich mein Ge-dächtnis nicht täuscht** if my memory serves me right; **sich ~ lassen** be taken in (von by). **II** v/i be deceptive, sports: feint, fake a blow etc. **III** sich ~ be mistaken, be wrong (in j-m about s.o.); **da täuscht er sich aber!** he's very much mistaken there! **'täuschend** adj a) deceptive, b) striking: **j-m ~ ähnlich sehen** look remarkably like s.o.

'Tausch|geschäft n, **~handel** m barter, F swap. **~ob,jekt** n object of exchange.

'Täuschung f (-; -en) a) deception, b) delusion, c) mistake, d) ⚖ deceit: **opti-sche ~** optical illusion.

'Täuschungs|ma,növer n feint, diver-sion. **~versuch** m attempt to deceive.

tausend ['taʊzənt] adj (a) thousand: **~ und aber ~** thousands and thousands of. **'Tausend** n (-s; -e) thousand: **zu ~en** by the thousand. **'Tausender** m (-s; -) F thousand mark note. **'tausend-fach I** adj thousandfold. **II** adv ~ mal **sendmal**. **'Tausendfüß(l)er** [-fy:s(l)ər] m (-s; -) zo. centipede. **'tausendjährig** adj of a thousand years, millennial. **'tausendmal** adv a thousand times. **'tausendst** adj, **'Tausendste** m, f (-n; -n) thousandth. **'Tausendstel** n (-s; -) thousandth (part).

'Tautropfen m dewdrop.

'Tauwetter n a. fig. pol. thaw.

'Tauziehen n f. tug-of-war.

Taxameter [taksa'me:tər] m (-s; -) taxi-meter.

Taxator [ta'ksa:tɔr] m (-s; -en [taksa'to:-rən]) †, ⚖ valuer, assessor.

Taxe ['taksə] f (-; -n) **1.** a) rate, fee, b) tax. **2.** → **Taxi** ['taksi] n (-s; -s) taxi, cab: **~ fahren** a) drive a taxi, b) go by taxi.

taxieren [ta'ksi:rən] v/t (h) **1.** estimate, †, ⚖ value, assess. **2.** F size up.

'Taxifahrer(in f) m taxi driver.

'**Taxistand** *m* taxi rank.

Teak [ti:k] *n* (-s; *no pl*), **~holz** *n* teak.

Technik ['tɛçnɪk] *f* (-; -en) **1.** *no pl* a) technology, technics, b) engineering. **2.** *a. art, sports, etc*: technique.

'**Techniker** *m* (-s; -) (technical) engineer, *a. sports etc*: technician.

'**technisch** *adj* engineering (*process etc*), *a. art, sports, etc*: technical, technological (*a. age, progress, etc*): *sports*: **~e Disziplin** field event; **~er K.o.** technical knockout; **~es Personal** technical staff; **~e Hochschule** college (*Am. institute*) of technology; **~ begabt** gifted technically.

technisieren [tɛçni'zi:rən] *v/t* (h) mechanize.

Technokrat [tɛçno'kra:t] *m* (-en; -en) technocrat.

Technologie [tɛçnolo'gi:] *f* (-; -n) technology. **Technolo'gietrans,fer** *m* technology transfer. **technologisch** [tɛçno'lo:gɪʃ] *adj* technological.

Teddybär ['tɛdi-] *m* teddy (bear).

Tee [te:] *m* (-s; -s) **1.** tea: **e-n ~ machen** make some tea; **e-n ~ trinken** have a cup of tea; **→ abwarten** II. **2.** tea party. **~beutel** *m* tea bag. **~büchse** *f* tea caddy. **~Ei** *n* infuser, tea egg, *esp. Am.* tea ball. **~gebäck** *n* biscuits, *Am.* cookies. **~haus** *n* teahouse. **~kanne** *f* teapot. **~kessel** *m* teakettle. **~löffel** *m* teaspoon. **~ma,schine** *f* tea-urn.

Teer [te:r] *m* (-[e]s; -e) tar.

teeren ['te:rən] *v/t* (h) tar.

'**Tee|sieb** *n* tea strainer. **~stube** *f* tearoom. **~tasse** *f* teacup. **~wagen** *m* tea trolley (*Am.* wagon).

Teich [taɪç] *m* (-[e]s; -e) pond, pool.

Teig [taɪk] *m* (-[e]s; -e) dough. **teigig** ['taɪgɪç] *adj* doughy, pasty (*a. fig.*).

'**Teigwaren** *pl* pasta.

Teil [taɪl] *m, n* (-[e]s; -e) part (*a.* ⚙), share, *a.* ⚙ component, element: *esp.* 🎲 **beide ~** both sides; **ein ~ davon** part of it; **zum ~** partly; **zum großen** (*or* **größten**) **~** largely, for the most part; **der größte ~** the greater part (*gen* of); **zu gleichen ~en** in equal shares; **sein ~ beitragen** do one's bit; **sich sein ~ denken** have one's own thoughts about it; **ich für mein ~** I for my part.

'**Teilansicht** *f* partial view.

'**teilbar** *adj* divisible.

'**Teilbetrag** *m* partial amount.

'**Teilchen** *n* (-s; -) *a. phys.* particle.

teilen ['taɪlən] (h) **I** *v/t* a) divide, b) distribute, share out, c) share: **die Kosten ~** share expenses; **Freud und Leid mit j-m ~** share s.o.'s joys and troubles. **II** *sich ~* divide, *curtain*: part; **sich in et. ~** share s.th.; **→ geteilt.**

'**Teiler** *m* (-s; -) 🅰 divisor.

'**Teilerfolg** *m* partial success.

'**teilhaben** *v/i* (*irr, sep*, -ge-, h, → **haben**) (*an dat* in) participate, share.

Teilhaber ['taɪlha:bər] *m* (-s; -) ♱ partner, associate. '**Teilhaberschaft** *f* (-; *no pl*) partnership.

'**Teilkaskoversicherung** *f mot.* partial coverage insurance.

'**Teillieferung** *f* part delivery.

Teilnahme ['taɪlna:mə] *f* (-; *no pl*) (*an dat*) **1.** a) participation (in), b) attendance (at). **2.** *fig.* a) interest (in), b) sympathy (with), c) condolence(s).

'**teilnahmeberechtigt** *adj* eligible.

'**teilnahmslos** *adj* indifferent, listless, apathetic. '**Teilnahmslosigkeit** *f* (-; *no pl*) indifference, listlessness, apathy.

'**teilnahmsvoll** *adj* sympathetic.

'**teilnehmen** *v/i* (*irr, sep*, -ge-, h, → **nehmen**) (*an dat*) **1.** a) take part (in), b) be present (at), attend (*s.th.*). **2.** *fig.* a) take an interest (in), b) sympathize (with).

'**Teilnehmer** *m* (-s; -), '**Teilnehmerin** *f* (-; -nen) participant, *sports etc*: competitor, entrant, *teleph.* subscriber.

'**Teilpro,these** *f* partial (denture).

teils [taɪls] *adv* partly.

'**Teilstrecke** *f bus etc*: (fare) stage, 🚃 section, *w.s.* stage, *a. sports*: leg.

'**Teilstrich** *m* ⊙ graduation mark.

'**Teilstück** *n* section.

'**Teilung** *f* (-; -en) division (*a. biol.*, 🅰).

'**teilweise I** *adj* partial. **II** *adv* partly, partially, in part.

'**Teilzahlung** *f* **1.** part payment. **2.** payment by instal(l)ments: **auf ~ kaufen** buy on instal(l)ment (*or* hire purchase).

'**Teilzahlungsvertrag** *m* hire-purchase contract.

'**Teilzeit|arbeit** *f*, **~beschäftigung** *f* part-time employment (*or* job).

Teint [tɛ:] *m* (-s; -s) complexion.

Tele ['te:lə] *n* (-[s]; -[s]) F telephoto lens.

Telefax ['te:lafaks] *n* (-; -[e]), '**telefaxen** *v/t* (h) telefax.

Telefon [tele'fo:n] *n* (-s; -e) (tele)phone: *am ~* on the (tele)phone; *ans ~ gehen* answer the (tele)phone; *~ haben* be on the (tele)phone. **~anschluß** *m* telephone connection: *~ haben* be on the (tele)phone. **~appa,rat** *m* telephone.

Telefonat [telefo'na:t] *n* (-[e]s; -e) → **Telefongespräch**.

Tele'fon|buch *n* phone book, telephone directory. **~gebühr** *f* telephone charge. **~gespräch** *n* telephone conversation, phone call. **~hörer** *m* receiver.

telefonieren [telefo'ni:rən] *v/i* (h) (tele)phone: *mit j-m ~* talk to s.o. over the (tele)phone; *sie telefoniert gerade* she is on the phone; *nach Amerika ~* make a (tele)phone call to America; *darf ich mal ~?* may I use your (tele)phone?

tele'fonisch **I** *adj* telephonic. **II** *adv* by (or over the) (tele)phone: *~ übermitteln* (tele)phone; *sind Sie ~ zu erreichen?* are you on the phone?, can I call you?

Telefonist [telefo'nɪst] *m* (-en; -en), **Telefo'nistin** *f* (-; -nen) switchboard operator.

Tele'fon|karte *f* phonecard. **~netz** *n* telephone network. **~nummer** *f* (tele)-phone number. **~verbindung** *f* telephone connection. **~zelle** *f* (tele)phone box (or booth), call box. **~zen,trale** *f* (telephone) exchange, *of firm:* switchboard.

Telegraf [tele'gra:f] *m* (-en; -en) telegraph. **Telegrafie** [telegra'fi:] *f* (-; no *pl*) telegraphy: *drahtlose ~* radiotelegraphy. **telegrafieren** [telegra'fi:rən] *v/t*, *v/i* (h) telegraph, wire. **tele'grafisch I** *adj* telegraphic: *~e Überweisung* telegraphic (or cable) transfer. **II** *adv* by telegram, by wire. **Telegrafist** [telegra'fɪst] *m* (-en; -en), **Telegra'fistin** *f* (-; -nen) telegraphist.

Telegramm [tele'gram] *n* (-s; -e) telegram. **~anschrift** *f* telegraphic address. **~stil** *m* (*im ~*) telegraphese.

'**Teleko,pierer** *m* (-s; -) telecopier.

'**Teleobjek,tiv** *n* telephoto lens.

Telepathie [telepa'ti:] *f* (-; no *pl*) telepathy.

telepathisch [tele'pa:tɪʃ] *adj* telepathic.

Teleskop [tele'sko:p] *n* (-s; -e) telescope. **tele'skopisch** *adj* telescopic.

Telespiel ['te:lə-] *n* TV game.

Telex ['te:lɛks] *n* (-; -[e]) telex. '**telexen** *v/t* (h) telex.

Teller ['tɛlər] *m* (-s; -) **1.** plate. **2.** ⊙, *a. on ski stick:* disc, disk.

'**Tellervoll** *m* (-s; -) plateful.

Tempel ['tɛmpəl] *m* (-s; -) temple.

Temperament [tɛmpera'mɛnt] *n* (-[e]s; -e) a) temperament, temper, b) verve, vivacity, F pep: *hitziges ~* hot temper.

tempera'mentlos *adj* lifeless.

tempera'mentvoll *adj* (high-)spirited.

Temperatur [tɛmpera'tu:r] *f* (-; -en) (*bei e-r ~ von* at a) temperature (of); ⚕ *~ haben* have (or run) a temperature; **~anstieg** *m* rise in temperature. **~sturz** *m* sudden drop in temperature.

temperieren [tɛmpə'ri:rən] *v/t* (h) *a.* ♪ temper.

Tempo ['tɛmpo] *n* (-s; -s, -pi) tempo (*a.* ♪), speed, rate, pace: *das ~ bestimmen (durchhalten, forcieren* or *steigern)* set (stand, force) the pace; *~! step on it!*, go! '**Tempolimit** *n mot.* speed limit.

Tempomat [tɛmpo'ma:t] *m* (-en; -en) *mot.* cruise control, speedhold.

Tendenz [tɛn'dɛnts] *f* (-; -en) tendency, trend (*a.* ✝), *contp.* bias, slant. **tendenziös** [tɛndɛn'tsjø:s] *adj* tendentious.

tendieren [tɛn'di:rən] *v/i* (h) tend (*nach, zu* to).

Tennis ['tɛnɪs] *n* (-; no *pl*) tennis. **~ball** *m* tennis ball. **~halle** *f* covered court. **~platz** *m* tennis court. **~schläger** *m* tennis racket. **~spieler(in** *f*) *m* tennis player. **~tur,nier** *n* tennis tournament.

Tenor[1] ['te:nɔr] *m* (-s; no *pl*) tenor, substance.

Tenor[2] [te'no:r] *m* (-s; ⸚e) ♪ **1.** (*a.* **~stimme** *f*, **~par,tie** *f*) tenor (voice, part). **2.** tenor (singer or player).

Teppich ['tɛpɪç] *m* (-s; -e) carpet: *fig. et. unter den ~ kehren* sweep s.th. under the carpet; F *bleib auf dem ~!* be reasonable. **~boden** *m* fitted carpet, wall-to-wall carpeting. **~fliese** *f* carpet tile. **~händler** *m* carpet dealer.

Termin [tɛr'mi:n] *m* (-s; -e) **1.** a) (set) date, time limit, b) deadline: *e-n ~ festsetzen* fix a date *etc*; *bis zu diesem ~* by this date. **2.** (*sich e-n ~ geben lassen* make an) appointment (*bei* with *one's doctor etc*). **3.** ⚖️ hearing.

Ter'mindruck *m* time pressure: *unter ~ stehen* be pressed for time.

ter'mingebunden *adj* scheduled (*work*).

ter'mingemäß *adj and adv* on schedule.

Ter'minka,lender *m* appointments book, 🏛 cause list, *Am.* calendar: **e-n vollen ~ haben** have a busy schedule.

Terminologie [tɛrminolo'giː] *f* (-; -n) terminology.

Ter'minplan *m* schedule.

Termite [tɛr'miːtə] *f* (-; -n) *zo.* termite.

Terpentin [tɛrpɛn'tiːn] *n, m* (-s; *no pl*) 🌿 turpentine.

Terrain [tɛ'rɛ̃ː] *n* (-s; -s) **1.** terrain. **2.** plot of land, (building) site.

Terrasse [tɛ'rasə] *f* (-; -n) terrace.

ter'rassenförmig *adj* terraced.

Ter'rassenhaus *n* stepped building.

Ter'rassentür *f* French window.

territorial [tɛrito'rĭaːl] *adj* territorial.

Territorium [tɛri'toːrĭʊm] *n* (-s; -rien) territory.

Terror ['tɛrɔr] *m* (-s; *no pl*) terror.

'Terroranschlag *m* terrorist attack.

terrorisieren [tɛrori'ziːrən] *v/t* (h) terrorize. **Terrorismus** [tɛro'rɪsmʊs] *m* (-; *no pl*) terrorism. **Terrorist** [-'rɪst] *m* (-en; -en), **Terro'ristin** *f* (-; -nen) terrorist. **terro'ristisch** *adj* terrorist.

Terz [tɛrts] *f* (-; -en) **1.** ♪ third. **2.** *fenc.* tierce.

Terzett [tɛr'tsɛt] *n* (-[e]s; -e) ♪ trio.

Tesafilm ['teːza-] *m* (TM) sellotape (*TM*), *esp. Am.* Scotch tape (*TM*).

Test [tɛst] *m* (-[e]s; -s, *a.* -e) test.

Testament [tɛsta'mɛnt] *n* (-[e]s; -e) **1.** (last) will, 🏛 last will and testament: **sein ~ machen** make a will. **2.** *eccl.* **Altes (Neues) ~** Old (New) Testament.

testamentarisch [tɛstamɛn'taːrɪʃ] **I** *adj* testamentary. **II** *adv* by will.

Testa'ments|eröffnung *f* opening of the will. **~vollstrecker** *m* executor.

testen ['tɛstən] *v/t* (h) test.

'Testper,son *f* (test) subject.

'Teststrecke *f* *mot.* test track.

Tetanus(schutz)impfung ['teːtanʊs-] *f* 🏥 tetanus vaccination.

teuer ['tɔyər] **I** *adj* expensive, dear: **wie ~ ist es?** how much is it?; *Fleisch ist teuer geworden* meat prices have gone up; *fig.* **j-m ~ sein** be dear to s.o. **II** *adv* dear(ly): **das wird ihn ~ zu stehen kommen** he will have to pay dearly for that. **'Teuerung** *f* (-; -en) high (*or* rising) prices, high cost of living.

'Teuerungsrate *f* rate of price increases.

Teufel ['tɔyfəl] *m* (-s; -) devil: **der ~** the Devil; F **wer (wo, was) zum ~?** who (where, what) the devil (*or* hell)?; **wie der ~, auf ~ komm raus** like blazes; **in (des) ~s Küche kommen** get into a hell of a mess; **j-n zum ~ jagen** send s.o. packing; **der ~ war los** all hell had broken loose; **das Geld ist zum ~** the money is down the drain; **mal' den ~ nicht an die Wand!** don't tempt fate; **scher dich zum ~!** go to hell!

'Teufelskerl *m* devil of a fellow.

'Teufelskreis *m* *fig.* vicious circle.

teuflisch ['tɔyflɪʃ] *adj* devilish, *fig.* hellish.

Text [tɛkst] *m* (-[e]s; -e) text, words, lyrics. **'Textbuch** *n* libretto. **'Texter** *m* (-s; -) **1.** copywriter. **2.** songwriter.

Textilien [tɛks'tiːlĭən] *pl* textiles.

Tex'tilindu,strie *f* textile industry.

'Text|kri,tik *f* textual criticism. **~verarbeitung** *f* word processing. **~verarbeitungssy,stem** *n* word processor.

Theater [te'aːtər] *n* (-s; -) **1.** theatre, *Am.* theater: **zum ~ gehen** go on the stage; **ins ~ gehen** go to the theatre. **2.** *fig.* a) play-acting, b) *contp.* farce, c) fuss: **~ spielen** put on an act; **mach kein ~!** don't make a fuss! **~abonne,ment** *n* theatre subscription. **~besuch** *m* visit to the theatre. **~besucher** *m* theat/re-goer (*Am.* -er-). **~karte** *f* theat/re (*Am.* -er) ticket. **~kasse** *f* box office. **~probe** *f* rehearsal. **~stück** *n* (stage) play. **~vorstellung** *f* theatrical performance. **~zettel** *m* playbill.

theatralisch [tea'traːlɪʃ] *adj* theatrical.

Theke ['teːkə] *f* (-; -n) bar, *a.* counter.

Thema ['teːma] *n* (-s; -men) subject, *a.* topic, ♪ *etc* theme: **beim ~ bleiben** stick to the point; **das ~ wechseln** change the subject. **Thematik** [te'maːtik] *f* (-; -en) subject (matter).

Themenkreis ['teːmən-] *m* subject area.

Theologe [teo'loːgə] *m* (-n; -n) theologian. **Theologie** [teolo'giː] *f* (-; -n) theology. **theo'logisch** *adj* theological.

Theoretiker [teo're:tikər] *m* (-s; -) theorist. **theo'retisch** *adj and adv* theoretical(ly), *adv a.* in theory. **theoretisieren** [teoreti'ziːrən] *v/i* (h) theorize. **Theorie** [teo'riː] *f* (-; -n) theory.

Therapeut [tera'pɔʏt] *m* (-en; -en), **The-ra'peutin** *f* (-; -nen) therapist.
thera'peutisch *adj* therapeutic.
Therapie [tera'pi:] *f* (-; -n) therapy.
Thermal|bad [tɛr'ma:l-] *n* **1.** thermal spa. **2.** thermal bath. **~quelle** *f* thermal spring.
Thermik ['tɛrmɪk] *f* (-; *no pl*) thermionics. **'thermisch** *adj* thermic.
Thermody'namik [tɛrmo-] *f* thermodynamics.
'Thermoele,ment *n* thermocouple.
Thermometer [tɛrmo'me:tər] *n* (-s; -) thermometer: *das ~ zeigt 5 Grad über (unter) Null* the thermometer is at (*or* shows) 5 degrees above (below) zero.
thermonukle'ar *adj* thermonuclear.
Thermosflasche ['tɛrmɔs-] *f* (*TM*) Thermos (flask) (*TM*).
Thermostat [tɛrmo'sta:t] *m* (-[e]s, -en; -e[n]) thermostat.
'Thermowäsche *f* thermal underwear.
These ['te:zə] *f* (-; -n) **1.** thesis. **2.** theory.
Thrombose [trɔm'bo:zə] *f* (-; -n) ♣ thrombosis.
Thron [tro:n] *m* (-[e]s; -e) throne.
thronen ['tro:nən] *v/i* (h) be enthroned.
'Thronerbe *m* heir to the throne.
'Thronfolge *f* succession to the throne.
'Thronfolger *m* (-s; -), **'Thronfolgerin** *f* (-; -nen) successor to the throne.
Thunfisch ['tu:n-] *m* **1.** tunny. **2.** ✝ tuna.
Thymian ['ty:mia:n] *m* (-s; -e) ✿ thyme.
Tibet ['ti:bɛt] *n* (-s) Tibet. **Tibeter** [ti'be:tər] *m* (-s; -), **Ti'beterin** *f* (-; -nen), **ti'betisch** *adj* Tibetan.
Tick [tɪk] *m* (-[e]s; -s) quirk, tic.
ticken ['tɪkən] *v/i* (h) tick.
tief [ti:f] **I** *adj* deep (*a. fig.*), low, *fig.* profound (*knowledge etc*): *aus ~stem Herzen* from the bottom of one's heart; *im ~sten Winter* in the dead of winter. **II** *adv* deep, low, *fig.* a) deeply, b) far: *~ in Gedanken* deep in thought; *~ enttäuscht* badly disappointed; *~ schlafen* be fast asleep, sleep soundly; *bis ~ in die Nacht* far into the night.
Tief *n* (-s; -s) *meteor.* low, depression.
'Tiefbau *m* (-[e]s; *no pl*) civil engineering. **~ingeni,eur** *m* construction engineer.
'tiefblau *adj* deep blue.
'Tiefdruck *m* (-[e]s; *no pl*) **1.** *meteor.* low pressure. **2.** intaglio (printing). **~gebiet** *n* cyclone, low-pressure area.

'Tiefe *f* (-; -n) **1.** depth, *fig. a.* profundity. **2.** *pl radio etc:* bass.
'Tiefebene *f* lowland(s).
'tiefempfunden *adj* heartfelt.
'Tiefen|inter,view *n* (in-)depth interview. **~psycholo,gie** *f* depth psychology. **~regler** *m radio etc:* bass control. **~schärfe** *f phot.* depth of focus.
'tiefernst *adj* very grave.
'Tief|flug *m* low-level flight. **~gang** *m* (-[e]s; *no pl*) **1.** ♦ draught. **2.** *fig.* depth. **~ga,rage** *f* underground car park.
'tiefgefroren *adj* deep-frozen.
'tiefgreifend *adj* far-reaching.
'tiefgründig [-ɡrʏndɪç] *adj* profound.
'Tiefkühlfach *n* freezing compartment.
'Tiefkühlkost *f* frozen foods.
'Tiefkühltruhe *f* freezer, deep-freeze.
'tiefliegend *adj* **1.** low(-lying). **2.** deep-set (*eyes*). **3.** *fig.* deep(-seated).
'Tiefpunkt *m fig.* low: *e-n seelischen ~ haben* feel very depressed.
'Tiefschlag *m a. fig.* hit below the belt.
'tiefschürfend *adj fig.* profound.
'tiefschwarz *adj* jet-black.
'Tiefsee *f* deep sea.
'tiefsinnig *adj* profound.
'Tiefstand *m* (-[e]s; *no pl*) low: *e-n absoluten ~ erreichen* hit an all-time low.
Tiegel ['ti:ɡəl] *m* (-s; -) saucepan.
Tier [ti:r] *n* (-[e]s; -e) animal (*a. fig.*), beast, *fig. contp.* brute: F *großes* (*or hohes*) *~* bigwig, big shot. **~art** *f* (animal) species. **~arzt** *m* veterinary surgeon, *Am.* veterinarian, F vet. **~freund** *m* animal lover. **~handlung** *f* pet shop. **~heim** *n* home for animals.
'tierisch I *adj* animal ..., *fig. contp. a.* brutish: **~e Fette** animal fats. **II** *adv* F *fig.* awfully, terribly.
'Tier|kreis *m* (-es; *no pl*) *astr.* zodiac. **~kreiszeichen** *n* sign of the zodiac. **♀lieb** *adj* fond of animals. **~medi,zin** *f* veterinary medicine. **~nahrung** *f* pet food. **~park** *m* zoological gardens, zoo. **~pfleger** *m* keeper. **~quäle'rei** *f* cruelty to animals. **~reich** *n* animal kingdom. **~schutzverein** *m* society for the prevention of cruelty to animals. **~versuch** *m* animal experiment. **~welt** *f* animal world.
Tiger ['ti:ɡər] *m* (-s; -) tiger. **'Tigerfell** *n* tiger skin. **'Tigerin** *f* (-; -nen) tigress.
tigern ['ti:ɡərn] *v/i* (sn) F traipse, trot.

Tilde ['tɪldə] f (-; -n) ling. tilde.

tilgbar ['tɪlk-] adj ✝ redeemable. **tilgen** ['tɪlgən] v/t (h) **1.** wipe out (a. fig.), blot out (a. fig. memories etc), print. delete, cancel, a. fig. efface, erase. **2.** ✝ a) pay off, b) redeem (loan). '**Tilgung** f (-; -en) ✝ repayment, redemption.

timen ['taɪmən] v/t (h) time: **gut (schlecht) getimt** well (badly) timed.

Tinktur [tɪŋk'tu:r] f (-; -en) tincture.

Tinnef ['tɪnɛf] m (-s; no pl) F rubbish.

Tinte ['tɪntə] f (-; -n) ink: F **in der ~ sitzen** be in the soup.

'**Tinten|fisch** m **1.** squid. **2.** octopus. **~klecks** m inkblot. **~kuli** m stylograph. **~stift** m indelible pencil.

Tip [tɪp] m (-s; -s) tip, a. hint: **ein sicherer ~** a sure bet; **j-m e-n ~ geben** a) give s.o. a tip, b) tip s.o. off.

tippen ['tɪpən] (h) **I** v/i **1.** **~ an** (acc) tap. **2.** F a) do the Lotto, b) do the pools. **3.** F **~ auf** (acc) tip; **ich tippe auf ihn** my bet is on him. **4.** F type. **II** v/t **5.** F type.

'**Tippfehler** m typing error.

Tippse ['tɪpsə] f (-; -n) F contp. typist.

'**tipp'topp** adj F first-class: **~ gekleidet** immaculately dressed; **~ sauber** spick and span.

'**Tippzettel** m lotto (or pools) coupon.

Tisch [tɪʃ] m (-[e]s; -e) table: **er ist zu ~** he's having his lunch hour; **am ~ sitzen** sit at the table; **bei ~ sitzen** sit at table; **den ~ decken (abräumen)** lay (clear) the table; fig. reinen ~ **machen** make a clean sweep (or make tabula rasa) (**mit** of); **unter den ~ fallen** fall flat; **die Sache ist auf dem (vom) ~** the matter is on (off) the table; **→ grün. ~dame** f partner at table. **~decke** f tablecloth. ⚥**fertig** adj ready(-)to(-)serve. **~gebet** n **das ~ sprechen** say grace. **~karte** f place card.

Tischler ['tɪʃlər] m (-s; -) **1.** joiner. **2.** cabinetmaker. **Tischle'rei** f (-; -en) **1.** no pl joinery. **2.** joiner's workshop. '**tischlern** (h) **I** v/t make. **II** v/i do joiner's work.

'**Tisch|ordnung** f seating plan. **~platte** f a) tabletop, b) leaf. **~rede** f after-dinner speech. **~rücken** n table turning.

'**Tischtennis** n table tennis. **~ball** m table tennis ball. **~schläger** m table tennis bat (Am. paddle).

'**Tisch|tuch** n tablecloth. **~wein** m table wine. **~zeit** f lunch hour (or break).

Titan [ti'ta:n] n (-s; no pl) 🜛 titanium.

Titel ['ti:təl] m (-s; -) title. **~bild** n frontispiece (of book), cover picture (of magazine). **~blatt** n title page (of book), front page (of magazine). **~geschichte** f cover story. **~halter** m sports: titleholder. **~kampf** m title match (boxing: bout). **~melo,die** f theme tune. **~rolle** f title role. **~seite** f → **Titelblatt**. **~verteidiger** m sports: titleholder.

Titten ['tɪtən] pl V tits, boobs.

Toast [to:st] m (-[e]s; -e, -s) **1.** toast: **e-n ~ ausbringen** → **toasten** II. **2.** gastr. toast. '**toasten** (h) **I** v/t toast (bread). **II** v/i propose (or drink) a toast (**auf** acc to). '**Toaster** m (-s; -) toaster.

toben ['to:bən] v/i (h) **1.** a. fig. rage. **2.** children: romp.

'**tobsüchtig** adj raving mad, frantic.

'**Tobsuchtsanfall** m F fig. **e-n ~ bekommen** fly into a tantrum.

Tochter ['tɔxtər] f (-; ⸚) **1.** daughter. **2.** → **~gesellschaft** f subsidiary (company).

Tod [to:t] m (-es; -e) death: **den ~ finden** be killed; fig. **et. zu ~e reiten** flog s.th. to death; F **j-n zu ~e erschrecken (langweilen)** frighten (bore) s.o. to death (or stiff); **auf den ~ nicht ausstehen können** loathe, hate like poison.

'**tod'ernst I** adj deadly serious. **II** adv in dead earnest.

Todes|angst ['to:dəs-] f **1.** fear of death. **2.** fig. mortal fear: **Todesängste ausstehen** be scared to death. **~anzeige** f obituary (notice). **~fall** m (**im ~** in case of) death. **~gefahr** f mortal danger. **~jahr** n year of s.o.'s death. **~kampf** m throes of death. **~kandi,dat** m doomed man, F goner. **~opfer** pl casualties, victims: **Zahl der ~ a.** death toll. **~stoß** m death blow. **~strafe** f death penalty, capital punishment: **bei ~** on penalty of death. **~stunde** f hour of death. **~tag** m day (w.s. anniversary) of s.o.'s death. **~ursache** f cause of death. **~urteil** n death sentence (fig. warrant). **~verachtung** f defiance of death: F **mit ~** unflinchingly. **~wunsch** m death wish. **~zelle** f death cell, pl a. death row.

'**Todfeind(in** f) m deadly enemy.

'**todgeweiht** adj doomed.

'**tod'krank** adj fatally ill.

tödlich ['tø:tlɪç] adj a) fatal, a. fig. mortal

(für to), lethal *(poison, dose, etc*), b) *fig.* deadly *(accuracy etc)*: **~ verunglücken** be killed in an accident; F **sich ~ lang- weilen** be bored stiff; **~ beleidigt** mor- tally offended.

'**tod'müde** *adj* dead tired. '**tod'schick** *adj* F snazzy: **~ angezogen** *a.* dressed to kill. '**tod'sicher** F **I** *adj* dead sure, sure-fire *(method, tip, etc)*: **e-e ~e Sa- che** a dead certainty, a cinch. **II** *adv* for sure: **er kommt ~** he is sure to come. '**Todsünde** *f* deadly *(or* mortal*)* sin.

Tohuwabohu [tohuva'bo:hu] *n* (-[s]; -s) complete chaos.

Toilette [tŏa'lɛtə] *f* (-; -n) **1.** lavatory, toilet, *Am.* bathroom, restroom: **öf- fentliche ~n** public conveniences. **2. ~ machen** make one's toilet. **3.** dress. **Toi'letten|ar,tikel** *m* toilet article. **~frau** *f*, **~mann** *m* lavatory attendant. **~pa,pier** *n* toilet paper. **~seife** *f* toilet soap. **~tisch** *m* dressing table.

toi, toi, toi ['tɔy'tɔy'tɔy] *int* F **1.** *(unberu- fen)* **~, ~, ~!** touch wood! **2.** good luck!

tolerant [tole'rant] *adj* tolerant (*gegen* of). **Toleranz** [tole'rants] *f* (-; *no pl*) tolerance (*gegen* of). **Tole'ranz- schwelle** *f* tolerance threshold.

tolerieren [tole'ri:rən] *v/t* (h) tolerate.

toll [tɔl] **I** *adj* **1.** *a. f fig.* a) crazy, mad, b) wild: **e-e ~e Sache** *or* **ein ~es Ding** a wild affair, a wow. **2.** F terrific, fantastic: **ein ~er Kerl** a terrific guy; **e-e ~e Frau** a smasher; **der** *(es) ist nicht so ~* he (it) is not so hot. **II** *adv* **3.** F *(wie)* **~** like mad; **er spielt** *(ganz)* **~** he's a fantastic player, he's a smasher; → **treiben** 5.

tollen ['tɔlən] *v/i* (h, sn) romp.

'**Tollkirsche** *f* ⚕ deadly nightshade.

'**tollkühn** *adj* foolhardy, daredevil.

'**Tollkühnheit** *f* (-; *no pl*) foolhardiness.

'**Tollwut** *f vet.* rabies. '**tollwütig** [-vy:tɪç] *adj* rabid.

Tolpatsch ['tɔlpatʃ] *m* (-[e]s; -e), **Tölpel** ['tœlpəl] *m* (-s; -) clumsy oaf.

Tomate [to'ma:tə] *f* (-; -n) tomato.

Tombola ['tɔmbola] *f* (-; -s) raffle.

Ton¹ [to:n] *m* (-[e]s; -e) *geol.* clay.

Ton² [to:n] *m* (-[e]s; ⁓e) **1.** tone, sound (*a. film, TV*): F **er hat k-n ~ gesagt** he didn't say a word; **in den höchsten Tönen loben** sing the praises of; **große Töne spuk- ken** talk big; **hat man Töne?** can you believe it? **2.** tone (of voice): **ich verbit-**

te mir diesen ~! don't take that tone with me; **e-n anderen ~ anschlagen** change one's tune; **den ~ angeben** call the tune, *in fashion etc*: set the trend; **es gehört zum guten ~ zu** *inf* it is good form to *inf*. **3.** *ling.* accent, stress: **den ~ legen auf** *(acc) a. fig.* emphasize. **4.** tone (*a. phot.*), shade: **~ in ~** in match- ing colo(u)rs; **rötlicher ~** tinge of red.

'**tonangebend** *adj* leading, *fashion:* trend-setting.

'**Ton|arm** *m* pickup (arm). **~art** *f* ♪ key. **~aufnahme** *f* (sound) recording. **~aus- fall** *m* TV loss of sound.

Tonband *n* tape: **auf ~ aufnehmen** tape(-record). **~aufnahme** *f* tape re- cording. **~gerät** *n* tape recorder.

tönen¹ ['tø:nən] *v/i* (h) **1.** sound. **2.** F *fig.* sound off.

tönen² *v/t* (h) a) tint, b) tone down.

'**Tonerde** *f* argillaceous earth: **essig- saure ~** alumin(i)um acetate.

'**tönern** *adj* (of) clay.

'**Ton|fall** *m* (-[e]s; *no pl*) intonation. **~film** *m* sound film. **~fre,quenz** *f* acoustic (*or* audio) frequency.

'**Tongeschirr** *n* earthenware, pottery.

'**Tonhöhe** *f* pitch.

Tonikum ['to:nikʊm] *n* (-s; -ka) ✳ tonic.

'**Ton|ingeni,eur** *m* sound engineer. **~ka- mera** *f* sound camera. **~kopf** *m* sound (*video:* audio) head. **~lage** *f* pitch. **~lei- ter** *f* ♪ scale.

'**tonlos** *adj fig.* toneless, flat.

'**Tonmeister** *m* sound engineer.

Tonnage [tɔ'na:ʒə] *f* (-; -n) ⚓ tonnage.

Tonne ['tɔnə] *f* (-; -n) **1.** barrel, cask. **2.** (metric) ton. **3.** ⚓ a) buoy, b) (register) ton.

'**Ton|regler** *m* tone control. **~spur** *f*, **~streifen** *m film:* sound track. **~studio** *n* recording studio.

Tonsur [tɔn'zu:r] *f* (-; -en) tonsure.

'**Tontaubenschießen** *n* trap shooting.

'**Tontechniker** *m* sound engineer.

'**Tonträger** *m* sound carrier.

'**Tönung** *f* (-; -en) tinge, shade, *a. phot.* tone.

'**Tonwaren** *pl* earthenware, pottery.

Topas [to'pa:s] *m* (-es; -e) *min.* topaz.

Topf [tɔpf] *m* (-[e]s; ⁓e) pot: *fig.* **in 'einen ~ werfen** lump together.

Töpfchen ['tœpfçən] *n* (-s; -) pot, potty.

Töpfer ['tœpfər] *m* (-s; -) potter. **Töp-**

it. '**Tramper** m (-s; -), '**Tramperin** f (-; -nen) F hitchhiker.
Trampolin ['trampoli:n] n (-s; -e) trampoline.
Tran [tra:n] m (-[e]s; -e) train oil.
Trance ['trã:s(ə)] f (-; -n [-sən]) trance.
tranchieren [trã'ʃi:rən] v/t (h) carve.
Tran'chiermesser n carving knife.
Träne ['trɛ:nə] f (-; -n) tear: **den ~n nahe** on the verge of tears; **unter ~n** in tears; **wir haben ~n gelacht** we laughed till we cried; **ihr werde ich k-e ~ nachweinen** I won't shed any tears over her; → **ausbrechen** 5. '**tränen** v/i (h) water.
'**Tränendrüse** f lachrymal gland: F **auf die ~ drücken** be a real tear-jerker.
'**Tränengas** n tear gas.
'**Tränensack** m anat. lachrymal sac.
trank [traŋk] pret of **trinken**.
Trank m (-[e]s; ⸚e) drink, ✿ potion.
Tränke ['trɛŋkə] f (-; -n) watering place. '**tränken** v/t (h) a) water, b) soak.
Transaktion [trans'ʔak'tsɪo:n] f (-; -en) transaction.
Transat'lantik..., transat'lantisch adj transatlantic.
Transfer [trans'fe:r] m (-s; -s), **transferieren** [transfe'ri:rən] v/t (h) transfer.
Transformator [transfɔr'ma:tɔr] m (-s; -en [-ma'to:rən]) ⚡ transformer. **transformieren** [-'mi:rən] v/t (h) transform.
Transfusion [transfu'zɪo:n] f (-; -en) transfusion.
Transistor [tran'zɪstɔr] m (-s; -en [-'to:rən]) transistor.
Tran'sistorradio n transistor (radio).
Transit [tran'zi:t] m (-s; -e) transit (a. in cpds. charge, goods, road, traffic, etc).
transitiv [tranzi'ti:f] adj ling. transitive.
Tran'sitraum m ✈ transit lounge.
Transmission [transmɪ'sɪo:n] f (-; -en) ⚙ transmission.
transparent [transpa'rɛnt] adj transparent. **Transpa'rent** n (-[e]s; -e) banner.
Transplantat [transplan'ta:t] n (-[e]s; -e) ✚ transplant, graft. **Transplantation** [transplanta'tsɪo:n] f (-; -en) transplantation, graft(ing). **transplantieren** [-'ti:rən] v/t (h) transplant, graft.
Transport [trans'pɔrt] m (-[e]s; -e) transport(ation), conveyance, ✈ shipment, haulage: **während des ~s** in transit.
transportabel [transpɔr'ta:bəl] adj transportable, ⚙ portable, mov(e)able.

Trans'portband n (-[e]s; ⸚er) ⚙ conveyor belt.
Trans'porter m (-s; -) → **Transportfahrzeug, -flugzeug, -schiff**.
Transporteur [transpɔr'tø:r] m (-s; -e) carrier.
trans'portfähig adj transportable.
Trans'portfahrzeug n transporter.
Trans'portflugzeug n transport plane.
transportieren [transpɔr'ti:rən] v/t (h) 1. transport. 2. **den Film ~** advance the film.
Trans'port|kosten pl transport(ation) charges, ⚓ freight (charges). **~mittel** n (means of) transport(ation). **~schaden** m damage in transit. **~schiff** n transport ship. **~unternehmen** n carriers, haulage contractors. **~versicherung** f transport insurance.
Transvestit [transvɛs'ti:t] m (-en; -en) transvestite.
transzendental [transtsɛndɛn'ta:l] adj transcendental.
Trapez [tra'pe:ts] n (-es; -e) 1. ⚬ trapezium, Am. trapezoid. 2. gym. trapeze.
trappeln ['trapəln] v/i (sn) horse etc: clatter, child: patter.
Trara [tra'ra:] n (-s; no pl) F fuss, to-do.
Trasse ['trasə] f (-; -n) ⚙ location line.
trassieren [tra'si:rən] v/t (h) 1. ⚙ trace (out). 2. ✝ draw bill (**auf** acc on).
trat [tra:t] pret of **treten**.
Tratsch [tra:tʃ] m (-[e]s; no pl), '**tratschen** v/i (h) F contp. gossip.
Tratte ['tratə] f (-; -n) ✝ draft.
Traube ['traubə] f (-; -n) 1. a) bunch of grapes, b) grap. cluster (of people). '**Traubensaft** m grape juice.
'**Traubenzucker** m glucose.
trauen ['trauən] v/t (h) marry: **sich ~ lassen** get married; → **kirchlich**.
'**trauen²** (h) I v/i (dat) trust (s.o., s.th.): **ich traute m-n Ohren nicht** I couldn't believe my ears; → **Weg**. II **sich ~ zu** inf dare (to) inf; **du traust dich nur nicht!** you're just scared.
Trauer ['trauər] f (-; no pl) a) mourning (**um** for), b) grief (**um, wegen** at, over): **~ tragen** be in mourning. **~fall** m death. **~feier** f funeral obsequies. **~flor** m mourning band, crape. **~kleidung** f mourning. **~marsch** m funeral march.
trauern ['trauərn] v/i (h) (**um**) a) mourn (for), b) grieve (for, over).

Trauer|rede f funeral oration. **~schleier** m mourning veil, weeper. **~spiel** n F fig. sorry affair. **~weide** f ♣ weeping willow. **~zug** m funeral procession.

Traufe ['traʊfə] f (-; -n) eaves, gutter: → **Regen.**

träufeln ['trɔʏfəln] v/t (h) drip, trickle.

traulich ['traʊlɪç] adj cosy, Am. cozy.

Traum [traʊm] m (-[e]s; ⁻e) dream (a. fig.): F **das fällt mir nicht im ~e ein!** I wouldn't dream of (doing) it; → **einfallen** 1, **kühn.**

Trauma ['traʊma] n (-s; -men, -mata) ♣, psych. trauma.

traumatisch [traʊ'ma:tɪʃ] adj traumatic.
'Traumberuf m dream job.
'Traumbild n a) dream vision, b) dream.
träumen ['trɔʏmən] (h) I v/t dream: **das hätte ich mir nicht ~ lassen** I never dreamt of such a thing. II v/i dream (**von** about, of), a. daydream: **schlecht ~** have a bad dream. **'Träumer** m (-s; -) dreamer. **Träume'rei** f (-; -en) reverie (a. ♪), (day)dream(s). **'träumerisch** adj dreamy.
'Traumfa,brik f dream factory.
'Traumfrau f F woman of one's dreams.
'traumhaft adj dreamlike, (a. ~ **schön**) absolutely beautiful, a dream.
'Traum|haus n F dream house. **~land** n dreamland. **~mann** m F man of one's dreams. **~welt** f dream world.

traurig ['traʊrɪç] adj sad (**über** acc at, about), a. sorry: ~ **stimmen** sadden; **~er Anblick** sorry sight; **~e Reste** sad remains.
'Traurigkeit f (-; no pl) sadness.
'Trauring m wedding ring (or band).
'Trauschein m marriage certificate.
'Trauung f (-; -en) marriage ceremony, wedding.
'Trauzeuge m, **'Trauzeugin** f witness to a marriage.

Travestie [traves'ti:] f (-; -n) travesty.
Treck [trɛk] m (-s; -s) trek. **'trecken** v/i (sn) trek. **'Trecker** m (-s; -) tractor.
Treff [trɛf] m (-s; -s) F a) meeting, b) meeting place.
treffen ['trɛfən] (traf, getroffen, h) I v/t 1. hit (**j-n am Arm** s.o.'s arm): **nicht ~** miss; F fig. **er ist gut getroffen** (**auf dem Bild**) that's a good photo (or painting) of him; → **Blitz** 1. **2.** a) concern, b) affect, hit s.o. hard, c) hurt:

das hat ihn hart getroffen he took it very hard, it's been a severe blow to him; → **Schuld** 1. **3.** reach, make (agreement etc); → **Anstalt** 3, **Entscheidung** etc. **4.** j-n meet s.o.; **j-n zufällig ~** come across s.o. II v/i **5.** hit: **nicht ~** miss. **6.** meet: **sich ~** meet s.o. **7.** auf (acc) a) meet with, b) strike (or hit) on. III **sich ~ 8.** meet (**mit j-m** s.o.). **9.** F **das trifft sich gut** (**schlecht**) that suits me (or us etc) fine (that's a bit awkward); **es trifft sich gut, daß** (it's a) good thing that; **das trifft sich ja großartig!** well, that's lucky. **'Treffen** n (-s; -) meeting, sports: meet. **'treffend** adj apt (remark etc): **kurz und ~** short and to the point; **~ gesagt!** well put.
'Treffer m (-s; -) **1.** hit, soccer etc: goal. **2.** win. **3.** fig. lucky strike.
'Treffpunkt m meeting place.
treiben ['traɪbən] (trieb, getrieben) I v/t (h) **1.** drive: **die Preise in die Höhe ~** force up prices; **j-n in den Selbstmord ~** drive s.o. to suicide; **was hat sie dazu getrieben?** what made her do that? **2.** sprout (leaves etc), force (plants). **3.** physiol. produce (urine, sweat). **4.** chase (metal). **5.** do, a. go in for (sports etc): **was treibst du** (**zur Zeit**)? what are you doing (these days)?; **was treibst du da?** what are you up to?; F **es toll ~** carry on like mad, live it up; **es zu weit ~** go too far; → **Aufwand** 2, **Enge** 1, **Spitze**¹ 1 etc. II v/i (sn) **6.** float, a. snow, smoke, etc: drift: **sich ~ lassen** a. fig. drift; **die Dinge ~ lassen** let things drift; **~de Kraft** driving force. **7.** ♣ sprout.
'Treiben n (-s) a) activity, F goings-on, b) (hustle and) bustle.
'Treiber m (-s; -) drover, hunt. beater.
'Treib|gas n fuel gas, for sprays: propellent. **~haus** n hothouse. **~hausef,fekt** m meteor. greenhouse effect. **~holz** n (-es; no pl) driftwood. **~jagd** f **1.** battue. **2.** fig. hunt (**auf** acc for), pol. witch hunt. **~rad** n ⊙ driving wheel. **~riemen** m ⊙ drive belt. **~satz** m propelling charge. **~stoff** m fuel.
Trend [trɛnt] m (-s; -s) trend (**zu** towards). **~wende** f change in trend.
'trennbar adj separable, detachable.
trennen ['trɛnən] (h) I v/t a) separate, b) divide, c) detach, cut off, ⚡, teleph. a. disconnect, d) undo, e) segregate. II v/i

~ zwischen distinguish between. **III sich ~** separate, *a. fig.* part (**von** with); **getrennt leben** be separated (**von** from), live apart; **getrennt schlafen** have separate bedrooms; → **Kasse** 4.

'**Trennschärfe** *f radio*: selectivity.

'**Trennung** *f* (-; -en) separation (*a.* ✆, ⚙), segregation (*of races*), division, ✄, *teleph.* disconnection; ⚖ **eheliche ~** judicial separation.

'**Trennungsstrich** *m* hyphen.

Trense ['trɛnzə] *f* (-; -n) snaffle (bit).

trepp'auf: ~, treppab up and down the stairs. '**Treppchen** *n F sports*: (victory) rostrum. **Treppe** ['trɛpə] *f* (-; -n) staircase, (*e-e* ~*a*) a flight of stairs (*or* steps): **zwei ~n hoch** on the second floor; **die ~ hinauf (hinab)** up (down) the stairs.

'**Treppen|absatz** *m* landing. **~geländer** *n* banisters. **~haus** *n* staircase.

Tresen ['tre:zən] *m* (-s; -) bar, *a.* counter.

Tresor [tre'zo:r] *m* (-s; -e) **1.** strongroom, vault. **2.** safe.

Tre'sorfach *n* safe deposit box.

'**Tret|auto** *n* pedal car. **~boot** *n* pedal boat. **~eimer** *n* pedal bin.

treten ['tre:tən] (trat, getreten) **I** *v/i* (sn) step, *cyclist etc*: pedal: **~ auf** (*acc*) step on, tread on; **aufs Gas(pedal) (auf die Bremse) ~** step on the gas (brake); **ins Zimmer ~** enter the room; **nach j-m ~** (take *a*) kick at s.o.; **bitte ~ Sie näher!** please come in!; **über die Ufer ~** overflow its banks; → **Kraft** 3, **nahe** II *etc*. **II** *v/t* (h) tread: **j-n (in den Bauch) ~** kick s.o. (in the stomach); *fig.* **et. mit Füßen ~** trample on s.th.

'**Tretmühle** *f a. fig.* treadmill.

treu [trɔy] *adj* (*dat* to) faithful (*a. fig.*), loyal, devoted: **sich j-m Grundsätzen ~ bleiben** remain true to o.s. (one's principles). '**Treue** *f* (-; *no pl*) faithfulness (*a. fig.*), loyalty, (*a. marital*) fidelity: **j-m die ~ halten** remain loyal to s.o.

'**Treueid** *m* oath of allegiance.

'**treuergeben** *adj* loyal, devoted.

'**Treuhänder** [-hɛndər] *m* (-s; -) trustee.

'**treuhänderisch** *adj* fiduciary: **et. ~ verwalten** hold s.th. in trust.

'**Treuhand|gesellschaft** *f* trust company. **~verwaltung** *f* trusteeship.

'**treuherzig** *adj* **1.** guileless. **2.** ingenuous, naive. **3.** trusting.

'**treulos** *adj* disloyal (**gegen** to).

'**Treulosigkeit** *f* (-; *no pl*) disloyalty.

Tribunal [tribu'na:l] *n* (-s; -e) tribunal.

Tribüne [tri'by:nə] *f* (-; -n) **1.** (*speaker's*) platform, rostrum. **2.** (grand)stand, *in stadium*: *a.* terraces.

Trichine [trɪ'çi:nə] *f* (-; -n) *vet.* trichina.

Trichter ['trɪçtər] *m* (-s; -) **1.** ⚙ funnel. **2.** flare, mouth. **3.** crater.

'**trichterförmig** *adj* funnel-shaped.

Trick [trɪk] *m* (-s; -s) trick. **~aufnahme** *f* **1.** *film*: trick shot, *pl* trick photography. **2.** *on tape*: trick recording. **~betrüger** *m* trickster. **~film** *m* a) trick film, b) animated cartoon.

'**trickreich** *adj* artful.

'**Trickskilaufen** *n* freestyle skiing.

trieb [tri:p] *pret of* **treiben.**

Trieb *m* (-[e]s; -e) **1.** ⚘ young shoot. **2.** a) instinct, b) sexual drive, c) impulse, d) urge. '**Triebfeder** *f fig.* mainspring.

'**triebhaft** *adj* a) instinctive, b) sexual, *a.* highly sexed (*person*).

'**Trieb|kraft** *f* **1.** motive force (*or* power). **2.** *fig.* driving force. **~täter** *m*, **~verbrecher** *m* sex offender. **~wagen** *m* tramcar, 🚃 railcar. **~werk** *n* a) driving gear, b) ➳ power unit, c) drive, gear.

triefen ['tri:fən] *v/i* (h) drip (**von** with), *eyes, nose*: run: **~d naß** dripping wet.

triftig ['trɪftɪç] *adj* **1.** valid, sound. **2.** weighty, convincing.

Trigonometrie [trigonome'tri:] *f* (-; *no pl*) trigonometry.

Trikot [tri'ko:] **1.** *m, n* (-s; -s) *textil.* tricot. **2.** *n* (-s; -s) a) leotard, tights, b) shirt, *sports*: *a.* jersey.

Triller ['trɪlər] *m* (-s; -) trill.

trillern ['trɪlərn] *v/t, v/i* (h) trill, warble.

Trillion [trɪ'lio:n] *f* (-; -en) trillion, *Am.* quintillion.

Trilogie [trilo'gi:] *f* (-; -n) trilogy.

Trimester [tri'mɛstər] *n* (-s; -) *ped., univ.* trimester.

trimmen ['trɪmən] (h) **I** *v/t* **1.** trim (*a.* ➳, ⚡, ⚓), F tune *engine* up (**auf** *acc* to). **2.** train. **II sich ~** keep fit, keep in (good) trim. '**Trimmpfad** *m* fitness trail.

'**trinkbar** *adj* drinkable. **trinken** ['trɪŋkən] *v/t, v/i* (trank, getrunken, h) drink, have (*tea etc*): **~ auf** (*acc*) drink to; **was ~ Sie?** what are you having?; **er trinkt** he drinks, he is a drinker. '**Trinker** *m* (-s; -), '**Trinkerin** *f* (-; -nen) drinker, alcoholic. '**trinkfest** *adj* **er** *etc* **ist** ~ he holds his liquor well.

'**Trink|geld** *n* tip: **j-m (5 Mark)** ~ **geben** tip s.o. (five marks). **~halle** *f* pump room. **~halm** *m* (drinking) straw. **~kur** *f* mineral water cure. **~milch** *f* certified milk. **~spruch** *m* toast. **~wasser** *n* drinking water.

Trio ['tri:o] *n* (-s; -s) ♩ *or* F *fig.* trio.

trippeln ['trɪpəln] *v/i* (sn) trip.

Tripper ['trɪpər] *m* (-s; -) ♂ gonorrh(o)ea, F clap.

trist [trɪst] *adj* dreary, bleak, dismal.

Tritt [trɪt] *m* (-[e]s; -e) **1.** a) step, b) footstep: ~ **fassen** fall in step; **aus dem ~ geraten (sein)** fall (be) out of step; → **Schritt** 1. **2.** footprint. **3.** kick: **j-m e-n ~ versetzen** give s.o. a kick, kick s.o. **4.** step (*of stairs etc*). **~brett** *n mot.* running board. **~leiter** *f* stepladder.

Triumph [tri'ʊmf] *m* (-[e]s; -e) triumph.

triumphal [triʊm'fa:l] *adj* triumphant.

triumphieren [triʊm'fi:rən] *v/i* (h) (**über** *acc* over) triumph, *contp. a.* gloat.

trivial [tri'vi̯a:l] *adj* trivial.

Trivi'allitera_tur *f* light fiction.

trocken ['trɔkən] **I** *adj* dry (*a.* wine *etc*, *fig.* remark, humo[u]r, *etc*), *fig. a.* dull: F *fig.* **auf dem trocknen sitzen** be in a fix; → **Schäfchen.** **II** *adv fig.* drily, dryly: **sich ~ rasieren** dry-shave.

'**Trocken|dock** *n* dry dock. **~eis** *n* dry ice. **~ele_ment** *n* ⚡ dry cell. **~gewicht** *n* dry weight. **~haube** *f* hairdrier.

'**Trockenheit** *f* (-; *no pl*) **1.** dryness (*a. fig.*). **2.** drought.

'**trockenlegen** *v/t* (*sep*, -ge-, h) **1.** drain (*land etc*). **2. ein Baby** ~ change a baby.

'**Trocken|milch** *f* dried milk. **~obst** *n* dried fruit. **~ra_sierer** *m* dry shaver. **~schleuder** *f* spin drier. **~skikurs** *m* dry skiing (course). **~zeit** *f* dry season.

trocknen ['trɔknən] *v/t, v/i* (h) dry.

'**Trockner** *m* (-s; -) drier.

Troddel ['trɔdəl] *f* (-; -n) tassel.

Trödel ['trø:dəl] *m* (-s; *no pl*) *a. contp.* junk. '**Trödelladen** *m* junk shop. '**Trödelmarkt** *m* flea market. '**trödeln** *v/i* F a) dawdle, b) (sn) saunter. **Trödler** ['trø:dlər] *m* (-s; -), '**Trödlerin** *f* (-; -nen) **1.** junk dealer. **2.** dawdler.

trog [tro:k] *pret of* **trügen.**

Trog *m* (-[e]s; ~e) trough.

trollen ['trɔlən] **sich ~** (h) toddle off.

Trommel ['trɔməl] *f* (-; -n) drum, ☉ *a.* cylinder: **die ~ rühren** beat the drum (**für** for). **~bremse** *f* drumbrake. **~fell** *n* **1.** drumskin. **2.** *anat.* eardrum. **~feuer** *n a. fig.* barrage.

trommeln ['trɔməln] (h) **I** *v/i* (**auf** *acc* at, on) drum, *rain:* beat. **II** *v/t* drum, beat.

'**Trommel|schlegel** *m*, **~stock** *m* drumstick. **~wirbel** *m* drum roll.

Trommler ['trɔmlər] *m* (-s; -) drummer.

Trompete [trɔm'pe:tə] *f* (-; -n) trumpet. **trom'peten** *v/t, v/i* (h) trumpet.

Tropen ['tro:pən] *pl the* tropics.

'**Tropen...** tropical (*suit, fever, etc*).

'**tropenfest** *adj* ♂ tropicalized.

'**Tropenhelm** *m* pith helmet, topee.

Tropf [trɔpf] *m* (-[e]s; -e) ♂ (**am ~ hängen** be on the) drip.

Tröpfchen ['trœpfçən] *n* (-s; -) droplet.

'**tröpfchenweise** *adv* drop by drop.

tröpfeln ['trœpfəln] *v/i* (h) drip (*a. v/t*), trickle: F **es tröpfelt** it's spitting.

tropfen ['trɔpfən] *v/i* (h) drop, drip.

'**Tropfen** *m* (-s; -) **1.** drop, *a.* bead (*of sweat*): **ein edler (or guter)** ~ a capital wine; **ein ~ auf den heißen Stein** a drop in the bucket; **steter ~ höhlt den Stein** little strokes fell big oaks. **2.** *pl* ♂ drops. '**tropfenweise** *adv* in drops, drop by drop.

'**Tropfflasche** *f* dropper bottle.

'**Tropfinfusi_on** *f* ♂ intravenous drip.

'**tropfnaß** *adj* dripping wet.

'**Tropfstein** *m* stalactite, stalagmite.

Trophäe [tro'fɛ:ə] *f* (-; -n) trophy.

tropisch ['tro:pɪʃ] *adj* tropical.

Trosse ['trɔsə] *f* (-; -n) cable, ⚓ hawser.

Trost [tro:st] *m* (-[e]s; *no pl*) comfort, consolation: **zum ~** as a consolation; **ein schwacher ~** cold comfort. **trösten** ['trø:stən] *v/t* (h) console (**sich** o.s.), comfort. '**tröstlich** *adj* comforting.

'**trostlos** *adj* a) disconsolate, b) hopeless (*state etc*), c) cheerless, dreary, bleak.

'**Trostlosigkeit** *f* (-; *no pl*) a) hopelessness, b) dreariness, bleakness.

'**Trost|pflaster** *n humor.* (small) consolation. **~preis** *m* consolation prize.

'**trostreich** *adj* comforting.

Trott [trɔt] *m* (-[e]s; -e) trot, *a. fig.* jogtrot: **in e-n ~ verfallen** get into a rut.

Trottel ['trɔtəl] *m* (-s; -) F dope, idiot.

trotten ['trɔtən] *v/i* (sn) trot, jog.

trotz [trɔts] *prep* (*gen*) in spite of, despite.

Trotz m (-es; no pl) defiance: **aus ~** out of spite; **mir zum ~** to spite me.

'**trotzdem I** adv nevertheless, all the same, still, anyway. **II** conj although.

trotzen ['trɔtsən] v/i (h) **1.** (dat) defy (s.o., s.th.), a. brave (danger etc). **2.** be obstinate.

'**trotzig** adj defiant, obstinate.

'**Trotzreakti,on** f act of defiance.

trübe ['try:bə] adj **1.** cloudy (liquid, glass, etc), muddy: F fig. **im trüben fischen** fish in troubled waters. **2.** dull, dim, murky. **3.** dreary (day). **4.** gloomy (mood, thoughts, etc), bleak (prospects etc), sad (experience etc).

Trubel ['tru:bəl] m (-s; no pl) (hustle and) bustle.

trüben ['try:bən] (h) **I** v/t **1.** (a. sich ~) cloud (liquid, glass, etc, a. mind, relations, etc). **2.** fig. spoil (joy etc), obscure (s.o.'s view), warp (judgement), blur (sight, mind). **II sich ~ 3.** become clouded, glass etc: cloud over. **4.** fig. relations etc: become strained.

trübselig ['try:p-] adj **1.** gloomy. **2.** dreary. '**Trübseligkeit** f (-; no pl) **1.** gloominess. **2.** dreariness.

'**Trübsinn** m (-[e]s; no pl) gloom, low spirits. '**trübsinnig** adj gloomy.

'**Trübung** f (-; -en) **1.** clouding (etc, → **trüben**). **2.** cloudiness, dullness.

trudeln ['tru:dəln] v/i (sn) ✈ spin: **ins ≥ geraten** go into a spin.

Trüffel ['tryfəl] f (-; -n) ⚭ truffle.

trug [tru:k] pret of **tragen**.

'**Trugbild** n illusion, hallucination.

trügen ['try:gən] (trog, getrogen, h) **I** v/t deceive: **wenn mein Gedächtnis mich nicht trügt** if my memory serves me right. **II** v/i be deceptive: → **Schein**[1] 2.

trügerisch ['try:gərɪʃ] adj deceptive, misleading, illusive (hope etc).

'**Trugschluß** m fallacy.

Truhe ['tru:ə] f (-; -n) chest.

Trümmer ['trymər] pl **1.** ruins, rubble. **2.** debris. **3.** fragments.

'**Trümmerhaufen** m heap of rubble.

Trumpf [trʊmpf] m (-[e]s; ⸚e) a) trump(s), b) trump card: **was ist ~?** what's trumps?; fig. **~ sein** be the thing; a. fig. **alle Trümpfe in der Hand haben** hold all the trumps; fig. **s-n letzten ~ ausspielen** play one's trump card.

Trunk [trʊŋk] m (-[e]s; no pl) drinking.

'**Trunkenheit** f (-; no pl) drunkenness: **~ am Steuer** drunken driving.

'**Trunksucht** f (-; no pl) alcoholism.

'**trunksüchtig** adj **~ sein** be an alcoholic.

Trupp [trʊp] m (-s; -s) troop, gang, ✕ detachment. '**Truppe** f (-; -n) **1.** ✕ a) troops, pl a. forces, b) unit. **2.** thea. company, troupe. **3.** sports: team.

'**Truppen|abbau** m reduction in forces. **~abzug** m withdrawal of troops, pull-out. **~gattung** f branch (of the service), arm. **~teil** m unit. **~trans,porter** m ⚓ transport, troopship, ✈ troop carrier. **~übungsplatz** m training area.

'**Truppführer** m squad leader.

Truthahn ['tru:t-] m turkey(-cock).

'**Truthenne** f turkey-hen.

Tscheche ['tʃɛçə] m (-n; -n), '**Tschechin** f (-; -nen), '**tschechisch** [-çɪʃ] adj Czech. **Tschechoslowakei** [tʃɛçoslova'kai] f (-) Czechoslovakia.

tschüs [tʃy:s] int F bye!, see you!

Tube ['tu:bə] f (-; -n) tube: F mot. or fig. **auf die ~ drücken** step on it.

tuberkulös [tubɛrku'lø:s] adj tubercular, tuberculous. **Tuberkulose** [tuberku'lo:zə] f (-; -n) tuberculosis.

Tuch [tu:x] n (-[e]s; ⸚er) **1.** textil. cloth, fabric. **2.** a) cloth, b) scarf: **das wirkt auf ihn wie ein rotes ~** that's a red rag to him. '**Tuchfühlung** f **~ haben mit** be in close contact with.

tüchtig ['tyçtɪç] **I** adj **1.** good (in dat at), capable, competent, efficient, hard-working. **2.** F good. **II** adv **3.** F tremendously, like hell: **~ arbeiten** work hard; **~ zulangen, ~ essen** tuck in.

'**Tüchtigkeit** f (-; no pl) ability, competence, efficiency, industry.

Tücke ['tʏkə] f (-; -n) malice, perfidy, trick: **s-e ~n haben** be tricky, river etc: be treacherous.

tuckern ['tʊkərn] v/i (sn) F chug.

tückisch ['tʏkɪʃ] adj **1.** malicious, insidious (a. ♘). **2.** treacherous (road etc).

tüfteln ['tyftəln] v/i (h) (an dat) **1.** tinker (with). **2.** puzzle (over).

'**Tüftler** ['tyftlər] m (-s; -) tinkerer.

Tugend ['tu:gənt] f (-; -en) virtue.

'**tugendhaft** adj virtuous.

Tüll [tʏl] m (-s; -e) textil. tulle.

Tülle ['tʏlə] f (-; -n) **1.** spout. **2.** ⚙ socket.

Tulpe ['tʊlpə] f (-; -n) tulip.

tummeln ['tʊməln] **sich ~** (h) disport o.s.

'Tummelplatz *m* **1.** playground. **2.** *fig.* stomping ground.

Tumor ['tu:mɔr] *m* ⟨-s; -en [tu'mo:rən]⟩ *✱* tumo(u)r.

Tümpel ['tympəl] *m* ⟨-s; -⟩ pool.

Tumult [tu'mʊlt] *m* ⟨-[e]s; -e⟩ tumult, uproar, riot.

tun [tu:n] *v/t, v/i* ⟨tat, getan, h⟩ a) do (→ *a.* **machen**), b) make (*vow etc*), take (*step etc*), c) put (*s.th. somewhere*), d) F *machine etc*: go, work: **höflich etc ~** act (*or* do) the polite *etc*; **so ~, als ob** pretend to *inf*; **er tut nur so** he's only pretending; **was hat er dir getan?** what has he done to you?; **dagegen müssen wir et. ~!** we must do s.th. about it!; **was (ist zu) ~?** what's to be done?; **wir haben zu ~** we have work to do, we are busy; **das tut nichts!** never mind!, it doesn't matter!; **was tut's!** what does it matter!; **das tut man nicht** that just isn't done!; **mit ihm (damit) habe ich nichts zu ~** I have nothing to do with him (it); **das hat nichts damit zu ~** that's nothing to do with it; **du wirst es mit ihm zu ~ bekommen** you'll get into trouble with him; F **es tut sich was!** there is s.th. going on.

Tun *n* ⟨-s⟩ doing, (*a.* **~ und Treiben, ~ und Lassen**) doings, activities.

Tünche ['tynçə] *f* ⟨-; -n⟩ **1.** whitewash. **2.** *fig.* veneer. **'tünchen** *v/t* ⟨h⟩ whitewash.

Tundra ['tʊndra] *f* ⟨-; -dren⟩ tundra.

tunen ['tju:nən] *v/t* ⟨h⟩ *mot.* tune (up).

Tunesien [tu'ne:ziən] *n* ⟨-s⟩ Tunisia. **Tu'nesier** *m* ⟨-s; -⟩, **Tu'nesierin** *f* ⟨-; -nen⟩, **tu'nesisch** *adj* Tunisian.

Tunke ['tʊŋkə] *f* ⟨-; -n⟩ sauce.

tunken ['tʊŋkən] *v/t* ⟨h⟩ dip.

Tunnel ['tʊnəl] *m* ⟨-s; -⟩ tunnel.

tüpfeln ['typfəln] *v/t* ⟨h⟩ dot.

tupfen ['tʊpfən] *v/t* ⟨h⟩ **1.** *✱* swab. **2.** dot. **'Tupfen** *m* ⟨-s; -⟩ dot, spot. **'Tupfer** *m* ⟨-s; -⟩ **1.** *✱* swab. **2.** dot.

Tür ['ty:r] *f* ⟨-; -en⟩ door: **Tag der offenen ~** Open Day; **in der ~** in the doorway; F *fig.* **offene ~en einrennen** force an open door; **mit der ~ ins Haus fallen** blurt it out; **(dat) ~ und Tor öffnen** open the door to; **j-n vor die ~ setzen** turn s.o. out.

Turban ['tʊrba:n] *m* ⟨-s; -e⟩ turban.

Turbine [tʊr'bi:nə] *f* ⟨-; -n⟩ turbine.

Turbo-Prop-Ma'schine ['tʊrbo'prɔp-] *f* *✈* turboprop (engine).

turbulent [tʊrbu'lɛnt] *adj* turbulent.

Turbulenz [tʊrbu'lɛnts] *f* ⟨-; -en⟩ *a. phys.* turbulence.

Türke ['tyrkə] *m* ⟨-n; -n⟩ **1.** Turk. **2.** F *press etc:* fake. **Türkei** [tyr'kaɪ] *f* ⟨-⟩ Turkey. **'türken** *v/t* ⟨h⟩ F fake. **'Türkin** *f* ⟨-; -nen⟩ Turk(ish woman).

Türkis [tyr'ki:s] *m* ⟨-es; -e⟩ *min.* turquoise.

'türkisch *adj* Turkish.

'Türklinke *f* doorhandle.

'Türklopfer *m* knocker.

Turm [tʊrm] *m* ⟨-[e]s; ⁎e⟩ **1.** a) tower (*a. fig.*), b) steeple. **2.** *sports:* (diving) platform. **3.** *chess:* castle.

Türmchen ['tyrmçən] *n* ⟨-s; -⟩ turret.

türmen¹ ['tyrmən] ⟨h⟩ **I** *v/t* pile (up). **II sich ~** *a. fig.* pile up.

'türmen² *v/i* ⟨sn⟩ F bolt, make off.

'Turmspitze *f* spire.

'Turmspringen *n* *sports:* high diving.

'Turmuhr *f* church clock.

'Turnanzug *m* gymsuit. **turnen** ['tʊrnən] ⟨h⟩ **I** *v/i* do gymnastics. **II** *v/t* do (*an exercise*). **'Turnen** *n* ⟨-s⟩ gymnastics. **'Turner** *m* ⟨-s; -⟩, **'Turnerin** *f* ⟨-; -nen⟩ gymnast.

'Turn|gerät *n* gymnastic apparatus. **~halle** *f* gymnasium, F gym. **~hemd** *n* singlet, gym top. **~hose** *f* gym shorts.

Turnier [tʊr'ni:r] *n* ⟨-s; -e⟩ tournament. **~tanz** *m* ballroom dancing.

'Turnschuhe *pl* gym shoes, trainers.

'Turnübung *f* gymnastic exercise.

Turnus ['tʊrnʊs] *m* ⟨-; -se⟩ rotation: **im ~** → **turnusmäßig** II. **'turnusmäßig I** *adj* a) rotational, b) regular. **II** *adv* in turns: **~ (aus)wechseln** rotate.

'Turnverein *m* gymnastics club.

'Tür|pfosten *m* door post. **~rahmen** *m* door frame. **~schild** *n* door plate. **~schließer** *m* ⊙ door closer.

'Turteltaube *f* turtledove.

Tusch [tʊʃ] *m* ⟨-[e]s; -e⟩ ♪ flourish.

Tusche ['tʊʃə] *f* ⟨-; -n⟩ **1.** a) Indian ink, b) drawing ink. **2.** mascara.

tuscheln ['tʊʃəln] *v/t, v/i* ⟨h⟩ whisper.

tuschen ['tʊʃən] *v/t* ⟨h⟩ draw in Indian ink: **sich die Wimpern ~** put some mascara on.

'Tuschkasten *m* paintbox.

'Tuschzeichnung *f* Indian drawing.

Tüte ['ty:tə] *f* (-; -n) **1.** (paper) bag. **2.** cone.

tuten ['tu:tən] *v/i* (h) F toot, *mot.* honk.

Tutor ['tu:tɔr] *m* (-s; -en [tu'to:rən]), **Tutorin** [tu'to:rɪn] *f* (-; -nen) *univ.* tutor.

Typ [ty:p] *m* (-s; -en) **1.** type, ⊙ *a.* model: F *sie ist mein* ~ she is my type. **2.** F fellow, chap.

Type ['ty:pə] *f* (-; -n) **1.** *print.* type. **2.** F *komische etc* ~ queer *etc* character.

'Typenrad *n* daisywheel.

'Typenschild *n* ⊙ type plate.

Typhus ['ty:fʊs] *m* (-; *no pl*) ✗ typhoid (*a. in cpds. epidemic, patient, etc*).

typisch ['ty:pɪʃ] *adj* typical (*für* of): F *das ist* ~ *John!* that's John all over.

typisieren [typi'zi:rən] *v/t* (h) typify.

Typographie [typogra'fi:] *f* (-; -n) typography.

Typus ['ty:pʊs] *m* (-; Typen) type.

Tyrann [ty'ran] *m* (-en; -en) tyrant.

Tyrannei [tyra'naɪ] *f* (-; -en) tyranny.

ty'rannisch *adj* tyrannical. **tyrannisieren** [tyrani'zi:rən] *v/t* (h) tyrannize.

U

U, u [u:] *n* (-; -) U, u.

'U-Bahn *f* → *Untergrundbahn.*

übel ['y:bəl] *adj* bad, *a.* nasty: F (*gar*) *nicht* ~ not bad (at all); *mir ist* (*wird*) ~ I'm feeling (getting) sick; F *fig. dabei kann e-m* ~ *werden!* it's enough to make you sick; *ein übler Kerl* a bad lot; *e-e üble Sache* a bad business; ~ *riechen* smell (terrible).

'Übel *n* (-s; -) a) evil, b) illness: *das kleinere* ~ the lesser of two evils; *zu allem* ~ to top it all.

'übelgelaunt *adj* bad-tempered.

'Übelkeit *f* (-; -en) nausea.

'übelnehmen *v/t* (*irr, sep*, -ge-, h, → *nehmen*) *et.* ~ take s.th. amiss, take offen/ce (*Am.* -se) at s.th.; *j-m et.* ~ hold s.th. against s.o.; *nimm es mir nicht übel, aber ...* don't be offended but ...

'übelriechend *adj* foul-smelling, foul.

'Übeltäter(in *f*) *m* malefactor.

üben ['y:bən] *v/t, v/i* (h) practi/se (*Am.* -ce) (*a. sich* ~ *in dat*), *a.* train: *Klavier* ~ practise the piano; *fig. Geduld* ~ have patience; → *Nachsicht, Rache.*

über ['y:bər] **I** *prep* **1.** over, *a.* above, *a.* across (*the river etc*): ~ *die Straße gehen* cross the street; ~ *München nach Rom reisen* go to Rome via Munich. **2.** over (*a period*): ~ *Nacht* overnight; ~ *das Wochenende* over the weekend; ~ *die Ferien* during the holidays; ~*s Jahr* (this time) next year; ~ *der Arbeit* over

one's work. **3.** a) over, more than, b) beyond, *adm.* exceeding (*a sum etc*): *er ist* ~ *siebzig* (*Jahre alt*) he is past (*or* over) seventy; *es geht nichts* ~ *Musik!* there's nothing like music; → *Verstand.* **4.** about (*a subject*), *essay, book, etc: a.* on: ~ *Geschäfte* (*Politik, den Beruf*) *reden* talk business (politics, shop). **5.** for: *e-e Rechnung* ~ *100 Mark* a bill for 100 marks. **6.** over, by: ~ *e-e Treppe* over (*or* by) a staircase; ~ *die Auskunft* from the information; ~ *e-n Makler* through a broker. **7.** *Fehler* ~ *Fehler* one mistake after the other. **II** *adv* ~ *und* ~ all over; *die ganze Zeit* ~ all along; → *überhaben.*

'überall *adv* everywhere, all over: ~ *wo* wherever. **'überallher** *adv* from everywhere. **'überallhin** *adv* everywhere.

über'altert *adj* overaged (*population*).

'Überangebot *n* oversupply.

'überängstlich *adj* overanxious.

über'anstrengen *v/t* (*insep, no* -ge-, h) overexert (*sich* o.s.), strain.

Über'anstrengung *f* (-; *no pl*) overexertion, strain.

über'arbeiten (*insep, no* -ge-, h) **I** *v/t* revise (*book etc*). **II** *sich* ~ overwork. **über'arbeitet** *adj* **1.** revised. **2.** overworked. **Über'arbeitung** *f* (-; -en) **1.** a) revision, b) revised edition. **2.** *no pl* overwork.

'überaus *adv* extremely.

über'backen adj gastr. au gratin.

'überbeanspruchen v/t (insep, no -ge-, h) **1.** ☉ overload, overstress. **2.** strain: j-n ~ overtax s.o.

'Überbein n ✱ node, exostosis.

'überbelegt adj overcrowded.

'überbelichten v/t (insep, no -ge-, h) phot. overexpose.

'überbesetzt adj overstaffed.

'überbewerten v/t (insep, no -ge-, h) overvalue, overrate.

über'bieten v/t (irr, insep, no -ge-, h, → bieten) **1.** ✝ outbid (um by). **2.** outdo, beat (record): sich (gegenseitig) ~ vie with each other (in dat in).

'Überbleibsel [-blaɪpsəl] n (-s; -) a. fig. remnant.

über'blenden v/t (insep, no -ge-, h) film etc: fade over.

'Überblick m **1.** view (über acc of). **2.** fig. overall view: e-n ~ gewinnen get a general idea (über acc of); den ~ verlieren lose track of things, be confused.

über'blicken v/t (insep, no -ge-, h) **1.** overlook, survey. **2.** a) grasp, b) assess.

über'bringen v/t (irr, insep, no -ge-, h, → bringen) j-m et. ~ deliver (or bring) s.th. to s.o. **Über'bringer** m (-s; -) bearer. **Über'bringung** f (-; no pl) delivery.

über'brücken v/t (insep, no -ge-, h) span, a. fig. bridge. **Über'brückungs,kre,dit** m ✝ bridging loan.

über'buchen v/t (insep, no -ge-, h) ✝ overbook.

über'dacht adj roofed, covered.

über'dauern v/t (insep, no -ge-, h) outlast, survive. **~'dehnen** v/t (insep, no -ge-, h) overstretch, pull (muscle). **~'denken** v/t (irr, insep, no -ge-, h, → denken) think s.th. over, reconsider.

'überdeutlich adj all too clear.

über'dies adv besides, moreover.

'überdimensio,nal adj outsize(d).

'Überdosis f overdose.

über'drehen v/t (insep, no -ge-, h) overspeed (engine).

'Überdruck m ☉ overpressure. **~ka,bine** f pressurized cabin. **~ven,til** n pressure relief valve.

'Überdruß [-drʊs] m (-sses; no pl) weariness: bis zum ~ ad nauseam.

'überdrüssig [-drʏsɪç] adj ~ sein be weary (or tired) (gen of).

'überdüngen v/t (insep, no -ge-, h) overfertilize.

'überdurchschnittlich adj above average.

'Übereifer m overzealousness.

'übereifrig adj overzealous, officious.

über'eignen v/t (insep, no -ge-, h) j-m et. ~ make s.th. over to s.o. **Über'eignung** f (-; -en) transfer (an acc to).

über'eilen v/t (h) rush: et. ~ a. rush things. **über'eilt** adj (over)hasty.

überein'ander adv **1.** one on top of the other. **2.** ~ sprechen, colo(u)rs etc: one another. **~schlagen** v/t (irr, sep, -ge-, h, → schlagen) cross (legs).

über'einkommen v/i (irr, sep, -ge-, sn, → kommen) (über acc on) agree, reach an agreement. **Über'einkommen** n (-s; -), **Über'einkunft** [-kʊnft] f (-; ⁻e) agreement.

über'einstimmen v/i (sep, -ge-, h) **1.** tally, correspond, colo(u)rs etc: match. **2.** mit j-m ~ agree with s.o. (über acc, in dat on). **über'einstimmend** adj corresponding, a. concurring, matching (colo[u]rs etc). **Über'einstimmung** f (-; -en) agreement, correspondence: in ~ mit in accordance (or keeping) with.

'überempfindlich adj hypersensitive, ✱ or fig. allergic (gegen to).

'überernährt adj overfed.

über'fahren v/t (irr, insep, no -ge-, h, → fahren) drive through (signal etc): j-n ~ run s.o. over, ☉ fig. bulldoze s.o., sports: clobber s.o. **'Überfahrt** f (-; -en) ⚓ crossing, passage.

'Überfall m (-[e]s; ⁻e) **1.** (auf acc) attack (on), raid (on), invasion (of). **2.** a) holdup, b) mugging. **3.** F surprise visit.

über'fallen v/t (irr, insep, no -ge-, h, → fallen) a) attack, assault, b) hold up, raid (bank etc), c) invade (country): F j-n ~ descend on s.o.; j-n mit e-r Frage etc ~ pounce on s.o. with a question etc.

'überfällig adj overdue.

'Überfallkom,mando n riot squad.

über'fliegen v/t (irr, insep, no -ge-, h, → fliegen) **1.** fly over. **2.** skim (letter etc).

'überfließen v/i (irr, sep, -ge-, sn, → fließen) overflow.

über'flügeln v/t (insep, no -ge-, h) j-n ~ outstrip s.o.

'Überfluß m (-sses; no pl) abundance (an dat of): ~ haben an (dat) abound in,

have plenty of; **zu allem ~** to top it all.
~gesellschaft f affluent society.
'überflüssig adj superfluous.
über'fluten v/t (insep, no -ge-, h) flood.
über'fordern v/t (insep, no -ge-, h) overtax, a. overstretch (staff etc): **j-n ~ a)**
expect too much of s.o., b) be too much
for s.o.; **damit war sie überfordert** this
was more than she could handle.
über'fragt adj F **da bin ich ~!** you've got
me there.
Über'fremdung f (-; -en) foreign infiltration, ⚑ control by foreign capital.
über'führen v/t (insep, no -ge-, h) **1.**
transport. **2.** find s.o. guilty (gen of).
Über'führung f (-; -en) **1.** transfer. **2.** ⚐
conviction. **3.** flyover, overpass.
'Überfülle f (-; no pl) (over)abundance.
über'füllt adj overcrowded, congested
(streets), (jam-)packed (bus, room, etc).
'Überfunkti,on f ⚕ hyperactivity.
über'füttert adj overfed.
'Übergabe f (-; -n) delivery, handing-
-over (a. of an office), ✗ surrender.
'Übergang m (-[e]s; ⸚e) **1.** crossing, passage. **2.** transition. **'übergangslos** adv
without transition, directly.
'Übergangs|re,gierung f caretaker
government. **~stadium** n transition(al
stage). **~zeit** f transition(al period).
über'geben (irr, insep, no -ge-, h, →
geben) **I** v/t (j-m et.) **~** hand over (s.th.
to s.o.), present (s.o. with s.th.); **dem
Verkehr ~** open s.th. to the traffic. **II
sich ~** vomit, be sick.
'übergehen¹ v/i (irr, sep, -ge-, sn, →
gehen) pass over (**zu** to): **~ auf** (acc)
devolve upon (successor etc); **~ in** (acc)
pass (or turn) into; **in j-s Besitz ~**
pass into s.o.'s possession; **in andere Hände ~** change hands; **in Verwesung ~**
begin to putrefy; **~ zu** proceed to (s.th.).
über'gehen² v/t (irr, insep, no -ge-, h, →
gehen) a) ignore, b) omit, skip, c) pass
s.o., s.th. over.
'übergeordnet adj **1.** higher (office etc).
2. of overriding importance.
'Übergepäck n ✈ excess baggage.
'übergeschnappt adj F crazy, mad.
'Übergewicht n (-[e]s; no pl) **1.** (**~ haben**
be) overweight. **2.** fig. preponderance:
das ~ haben predominate.
'überglücklich adj overjoyed.

'übergreifen v/i (irr, sep, -ge-, h, → **greifen**) fig. spread (**auf** acc to).
'Übergriff m (-[e]s; -e) (**in** acc) encroach-
ment ([up]on), infringement (of).
'übergroß adj outsize(d).
'Übergröße f outsize.
'überhaben v/t (irr, sep, -ge-, h, → **haben**) F **1.** have coat etc on. **2.** be fed up
with.
über'handnehmen v/i (irr, sep, -ge-, h,
→ **nehmen**) increase, spread.
'Überhang m (-[e]s; ⸚e) **1.** ✁, △, ☉ overhang. **2.** surplus (of money), backlog (of
orders etc). **'überhängen¹** v/i (irr, sep,
-ge-, h, → **hängen¹**) overhang, △ project. **'überhängen²** v/t (sep, h) throw
coat etc over one's shoulders.
über'häufen v/t (insep, no -ge-, h) **j-n ~
mit** swamp s.o. with work etc, shower
s.o. with presents etc, heap hono(u)rs
etc on s.o.
über'haupt adv at all, actually, really:
was willst du ~? what really do you
want?; **~ nicht** not at all; **~ nichts** nothing at all; **er versteht davon ~ nichts** he
doesn't know the first thing about it; **~
kein ...** no ... whatever; **wenn ~** if at all.
überheblich [-'he:plɪç] adj arrogant.
Über'heblichkeit f (-; no pl) arrogance.
über'hitzt adj a. fig. overheated.
über'höht adj excessive (prices etc).
über'holen v/t (insep, no -ge-, h) **1.** pass,
overtake, fig. outstrip. **2.** ☉ overhaul.
Über'holma,növer n overtaking manoeuvre, Am. passing maneuver.
Über'holspur f mot. passing lane.
Über'holung f (-; -en) ☉ overhaul.
Über'holverbot n "No Passing" sign.
über'hören v/t (insep, no -ge-, h) a) not
to hear, miss, not to catch, b) ignore.
'überirdisch adj supernatural.
'Überkapazi,tät f overcapacity.
über'kleben v/t (insep, no -ge-, h) **et. ~**
paste s.th. over.
'überkochen v/i (sep, sn) boil over.
über'kommen v/t (irr, insep, no -ge-, h,
→ **kommen**) **Furcht** etc **überkam ihn**
he was overcome by fear etc.
'überkonfessio,nell adj interdenominational.
über'kronen v/t (insep, no -ge-, h)
crown, cap (tooth).
über'laden (irr, insep, no -ge-, h, → **laden**) **I** v/t **1.** overload (a. ⚡), overbur-

den, swamp (**mit** with *work etc*). **II** *adj*
2. overloaded. **3.** *fig.* a) cluttered, b)
overladen, florid (*style*).

über'lagern *v/t* (*insep, no* -ge-, h) super-
impose, *partially*: overlap (*a.* **sich ~**),
radio: a) heterodyne, b) jam (*station*).

'**Überlandbus** *m* long-distance coach.

'**Überlänge** *f* exceptional length.

über'lassen *v/t* (*irr, insep, no* -ge-, h, →
lassen) **j-m et. ~** let s.o. have s.th., *a.*
fig. leave s.th. to s.o.; **j-n s-m Schicksal
~** leave s.o. to his fate; **sich selbst ~
sein** be left to one's own devices; **~ Sie
das mir!** leave it to me; **das bleibt ihm
~!** that's up to him.

über'lasten *v/t* (*insep, no* -ge-, h) **1.** *a. ⚡,
⚙* overload. **2.** *fig.* a) overtax, overbur-
den, b) overwork, overstretch.

Über'lastung *f* (-; -en) **1.** *a. ⚡, ⚙*
overload. **2.** *fig.* a) overburdening, b)
strain.

'**überlaufen¹** *v/i* (*irr, sep,* -ge-, sn, →
laufen) **1.** run over. **2.** (**zu** to) desert, go
over, defect. **über'laufen²** (*irr, insep,
no* -ge-, h, → **laufen**) **I** *v/t* seize: **Angst
überlief mich** I was seized with fear. **II**
v/impers **es überlief mich heiß und
kalt** I went hot and cold.

über'laufen³ *adj* overcrowded.

'**Überläufer** *m* deserter, defector.

über'leben *v/t, v/i* (*insep, no* -ge-, h)
survive. **Über'leben** *n* (-s) survival.

Über'lebende *m, f* (-n; -n) survivor.

Über'lebenschance *f* chance of survival.

'**überlebensgroß** *adj* larger than life,
larger-than-life ...

überlebt [-'le:pt] *adj* antiquated.

über'legen¹ *v/t, v/i* (*insep, no* -ge-, h)
think (*s.th.* over): **ich will es mir ~** I'll
think it over; **es sich anders ~** change
one's mind; **sich et. genau ~** think
carefully about it; **ohne zu ~** a) without
thinking, b) rashly, c) F like a shot; →
reiflich II.

über'legen² *I adj* superior (**dat** to, **an**
dat in), *contp. a.* supercilious: **j-m weit
~ sein** be head and shoulders above s.o.
II *adv* a) in superior style, b) supercili-
ously: **~ siegen** win in style.

Über'legenheit *f* (-; *no pl*) superiority.

überlegt [-'le:kt] *adj* (well-)considered.

Über'legung *f* (-; -en) consideration, reflection: **~en anstellen** a) **über** (*acc*)

think about, reflect on, b) **ob** consider
if; → **reiflich** I.

'**überleiten** *v/i* (*sep,* h) lead over (**zu**
to).

über'liefern *v/t* (*insep, no* -ge-, h) *et.* **~**
hand s.th. down (*dat* to). **über'liefert**
adj traditional. **Über'lieferung** *f* (-;
-en) tradition.

über'listen *v/t* (*insep, no* -ge-, h) outwit.

'**Übermacht** *f* (-; *no pl*) superiority.

'**übermächtig** *adj* too strong, *fig.* overpowering.

über'malen *v/t* (*insep, no* -ge-, h) *et.* **~**
paint s.th. over.

'**Übermaß** *n* (-es; *no pl*) excess (**an** *dat*
of). '**übermäßig** *adj* excessive.

'**Übermensch** *m* superman.

'**übermenschlich** *adj* superhuman.

über'mitteln *v/t* (*insep, no* -ge-, h) transmit (*dat* to).

Über'mittlung *f* (-; *no pl*) transmission.

'**übermorgen** *adv* the day after tomorrow.

über'müdet *adj* overtired.

'**Übermut** *m* (-[e]s; *no pl*) high spirits.

'**übermütig** [-my:tıç] *adj* high-spirited,
pred in high spirits.

'**übernächst** *adj the* next but one: **~e
Woche** the week after next.

über'nachten *v/i* (*insep, no* -ge-, h)
spend the night.

übernächtigt [-'nɛçtıçt] *adj* bleary-eyed.

Über'nachtung *f* (-; -en) overnight stay:
~ und Frühstück bed and breakfast.

Über'nachtungsmöglichkeit *f* overnight accommodation.

'**Übernahme** [-na:mə] *f* (-; -n) taking
over, takeover (*of firm, power*), assumption (*of office, responsibility*),
adoption (*of idea*). **~angebot** *n* ⚓ takeover bid.

'**übernatio̱nal** *adj* supranational.

'**überna̱türlich** *adj* supernatural.

über'nehmen (*irr, insep, no* -ge-, h, →
nehmen) **I** *v/t* take over (*firm, power,
etc*), *a.* accept (*goods*), take on (*responsibility, work, etc*), adopt (*ideas etc*): **es
~ zu** *inf* take it upon o.s. to *inf*; **et. ~**
take care of s.th. **II** *sich* **~** take on more
than one can handle, *financially*: over-
reach o.s., *physically*: overdo it; *iro.*
übernimm dich nur nicht! don't kill
yourself!

treten) 1. violate (*law etc*). **2. sich den Fuß ~** sprain one's ankle.

Über'tretung *f* (-; -en) ⚖ a) violation, b) (petty) offen/ce (*Am.* -se).

übertrieben [-'tri:bən] *adj* exaggerated, excessive (*demands etc*).

'Übertritt *m* (-[e]s; -e) (*zu* to) change, *pol.* defection, *eccl.* conversion.

über'trumpfen *v/t* (h) *fig.* outdo.

über'tünchen *v/t* (*insep, no* -ge-, h) *a. fig.* whitewash.

über'völkert *adj* overpopulated.

über'vorteilen *v/t* (*insep, no* -ge-) cheat.

über'wachen *v/t* (*insep, no* -ge-, h) supervise, *a.* ⚕ *etc* observe, *police:* keep under surveillance, ⚙ check, inspect, monitor. **Über'wachung** *f* (-; -en) supervision, observation, surveillance, ⚙ inspection, checking, monitoring.

überwältigen [-'vɛltɪgən] *v/t* (*insep, no* -ge-, h) *a. fig.* overpower, overwhelm. **über'wältigend** *adj fig.* overwhelming, *a.* stunning, breathtaking (*beauty*): **mit ~er Mehrheit** with an overwhelming majority; **nicht gerade ~!** nothing to write home about.

über'weisen *v/t* (*irr, insep, no* -ge-, h, → **weisen) 1.** transfer (**auf ein Konto** to an account, *j-m* to s.o.'s account). **2.** refer *case, patient, etc* (**an** *acc* to). **Über'weisung** *f* (-; -en) **1.** transfer, remittance. **2.** referral (**an** *acc* to).

'überwerfen¹ *v/t* (*irr, sep,* -ge-, h, → **werfen)** fling on *dress etc*.

über'werfen²: sich ~ (*irr, insep, no* -ge-, h, → **werfen)** fall out (**mit** with).

über'wiegen *v/i* (*irr, insep, no* -ge-, h, → **wiegen)** predominate, prevail.

über'wiegend I *adj* predominant, prevailing: **die ~e Mehrheit** the vast majority. **II** *adv* predominantly, mainly.

über'winden (*irr, insep, no* -ge-, h, → **winden) I** *v/t* overcome, get over, surmount (*crisis, illness, etc*). **II sich ~** *zu inf* bring o.s. to *inf.* **Über'windung** *f* (-; *no pl*) **1.** overcoming (*etc*). **2. es kostete mich ~** it cost me quite an effort.

über'wintern *v/i* (*insep, no* -ge-, h) spend the winter, *zo.* hibernate.

über'wuchern *v/t* (*insep, no* -ge-, h) overgrow.

'Überzahl *f* (-; *no pl*) (**in der ~ sein** be in the) majority.

'überzählig [-tsɛ:lıç] *adj* surplus, spare.

über'zeichnen *v/t* (*insep, no* -ge-, h) **1.** ✝ oversubscribe. **2.** *fig.* overdraw.

über'zeugen (*insep, no* -ge-, h) **I** *v/t* (**von**) convince (of), *esp.* ⚖ satisfy (as to). **II** *v/i* be convincing. **III sich ~** satisfy o.s. (**von** as to): → **Sie sich selbst!** go and see for yourself. **über'zeugend** *adj* convincing: **wenig ~** (rather) unconvincing. **über'zeugt** *adj* convinced (**von** of), ardent (*socialist etc*): **von sich selbst (sehr) ~ sein** have a high opinion of o.s. **über'zeugung** *f* (-; -en) conviction, (*political etc*) convictions: **der ~ sein, daß** be convinced that; **zu der ~ gelangen, daß** come to the conclusion that. **Über'zeugungskraft** *f* powers of persuasion.

'überziehen¹ *v/t* (*irr, sep,* -ge-, h, → **ziehen)** put on (*coat etc*).

über'ziehen² (*irr, insep, no* -ge-, h, → **ziehen) I** *v/t* **1.** a) cover, b) coat, c) line. **2.** put fresh linen on (*bed*). **3.** overdraw (*account*). **4.** overrun (*air time*). **5.** *fig.* exaggerate. **II** *v/i* exceed the time limit. **III sich ~** become covered (**mit** with), *sky:* become overcast. **Über'ziehung** *f* (-; *no pl*) ✝ overdraft. **Über'ziehungskre,dit** *m* overdraft credit.

'Überzug *m* a) cover, b) coat(ing).

üblich ['y:plıç] *adj* usual, customary, normal: **wie ~** as usual; **es ist bei uns (so) ~, daß** it is a custom with us that; **das Übliche** the usual (thing).

'U-Boot *n* submarine.

übrig ['y:brıç] *adj* remaining, left (over), other: **das ~e, alles ~e** the rest; **das ~e Geld** the rest of the money; **die ~en** the others, the rest; **im ~en** as for the rest, b) → **übrigens; et. ~ haben** have s.th. left (*fig. für* have a soft spot for); **nichts ~ haben für** have no time for.

'übrigbleiben *v/i* (*irr, sep,* -ge-, sn, → **bleiben)** be left, remain: **es blieb mir nichts anderes übrig (als)** I had no choice (but).

übrigens ['y:brıgəns] *adv* by the way, incidentally.

'übriglassen *v/t* (*irr, sep,* -ge-, h, → **lassen)** leave: **viel (nichts) zu wünschen ~** leave a lot (nothing) to be desired.

'Übung *f* (-; -en) **1.** practice: **aus der ~ sein (kommen)** be (get) out of practice; **in der ~ bleiben** keep one's hand in;

macht den Meister practice makes perfect. **2.** *gym.*, ✗, ♪ exercise.

'**Übungs|aufgabe** *f* exercise. **~buch** *n* book of exercises. **~hang** *m skiing:* nursery slope. **~sache** *f das ist reine ~!* it's just a matter of practice.

Ufer ['u:fər] *n* (-s; -) shore, b) bank: *am ~, ans ~* ashore; *über die ~ treten* overflow its banks. '**uferlos** *adj fig.* a) boundless, b) endless (*debate etc*): *ins ~e gehen* lead nowhere.

Ufo ['u:fo] *n* (-s; -s) UFO, unidentified flying object.

Uhr [u:r] *f* (-; -en) clock, watch: *wieviel ~ ist es?* what time is it?; *es ist zwei ~* it's two o'clock (*or* 2 p.m., 14.00 hours); *nach m-r ~* by my watch; *um wieviel ~?* (at) what time?; *sports: ein Rennen gegen die ~* a race against time; *F rund um die ~* around the clock. **~armband** *n* watch strap. **~macher** *m* (-s; -) clockmaker, watchmaker. **~werk** *n* clock mechanism, works. **~zeiger** *m* hand. **~zeigersinn** *m im ~* clockwise; *entgegen dem ~* anticlockwise. **~zeit** *f* time.

Uhu ['u:hu] *m* (-s; -s) *zo.* eagle-owl.

Ulk [ʊlk] *m* (-[e]s; -e) joke, lark: *aus ~* for a joke. '**ulkig** *adj* funny.

Ulme ['ʊlmə] *f* (-; -n) ♣ elm.

Ultimatum [ʊlti'ma:tʊm] *n* (-s; -ten) (*ein ~ stellen* deliver an) ultimatum.

Ultra ['ʊltra] *m* (-s; -s) *pol.* extremist.

Ultra'kurzwelle *f ⚡* very high frequency (*abbr.* VHF), *a.* ⚡ ultrashort wave.

'**ultrarot** *adj* ultrared, infrared.

'**Ultraschall** *m phys.* ultrasound.

'**Ultraschall...** ultrasonic, supersonic. **~untersuchung** *f ⚕* ultrasound scan.

'**ultravio,lett** *adj* ultraviolet.

um [ʊm] **I** *prep* **1.** *space:* (a)round, *time:* at, about, around: *~ Ostern* (*herum*) some time around Easter. **2.** *denoting difference:* by: *~ die Hälfte billiger sein* be only half the price; *~ so besser* so much the better; *~ so mehr* (*weniger*) (*als* as, *weil* because) all the more (less), (so much) the more (less). **3.** for, about: often (*schreien*) ~ ask (cry) for. **4.** *es steht schlecht ~ ihn* he's in a bad way; *schade ~ ...* it's too bad about ... **II** *conj* ~ *zu inf* (in order) to *inf*. **III** *adv* about, around (*100 persons etc*).

'**umadres,sieren** *v/t* (*sep*, h) redirect.

'**umarbeiten** *v/t* (*sep*, h) alter, remodel

(*dress etc*), revise (*book etc*), adapt (*for the screen etc*). '**Umarbeitung** *f* (-; -en) alteration, revision, adaptation.

um'armen *v/t* (*insep, no* -ge-, h) (*a. sich ~*), **Um'armung** *f* (-; -en) embrace, hug.

'**Umbau** *m* (-[e]s; -e, -ten) **1.** a) reconstruction, conversion (*in acc, zu* into), b) altered section. **2.** reorganization.

'**umbauen¹** (*sep*, h) **I** *v/t* alter, *a.* redesign, remodel, convert *flat etc* (*in acc, zu* into). **II** *v/i thea.* change the setting.

um'bauen² *v/t* (*insep, no* -ge-, h) build round: *umbauter Raum* interior space.

'**umbenennen** *v/t* (*irr, sep*, h, → *benennen*) rename.

'**umbesetzen** *v/t* (*sep*, h) *thea.* recast.

'**umbiegen** *v/t* (*irr, sep*, -ge-, h, → *biegen*) bend.

'**umbilden** *v/t* (*sep*, h) reorganize, *pol.* reshuffle (*cabinet etc*). '**Umbildung** *f* (-; -en) reorganization, *pol.* reshuffle.

'**umbinden** *v/t* (*irr, sep*, -ge-, h, → *binden*) tie round, (*a. sich ~*) put on (*tie, apron, etc*).

'**umblättern** *v/t* (*sep*, h) turn over (the page *v/i*).

'**umbrechen¹** *v/t* (*irr, sep*, -ge-, h, → *brechen*) break down.

um'brechen² *v/t* (*irr, insep, no* -ge-, h, → *brechen*) make up (into pages).

'**umbringen** (*irr, sep*, -ge-, h, → *bringen*) **I** *v/t* kill: *F fig. nicht umzubringen* indestructible. **II** *sich ~* kill o.s.; *F fig. sich (fast) ~* bend over backwards.

'**Umbruch** *m* (-[e]s; ⁺e) **1.** *print.* makeup, *on VSU:* formatting. **2.** *fig.* upheaval.

'**umbuchen** *v/t* (*sep*, h) **1.** change one's booking for. **2.** ✝ transfer (*auf acc* to)

'**umdenken** *v/i* (*irr, sep*, -ge-, h, → *denken*) ~ *müssen* have to do some rethinking. '**Umdenken** *n* (-s) rethink.

'**umdispo,nieren** *v/i* (*sep*, h) change one's plans.

'**umdrehen** *v/t* (*sep*, h) turn (round) (*a. sich ~*), twist (*arm*): *j-m den Hals ~* wring s.o.'s neck; → *Spieß*.

Um'drehung *f* (-; -en) turn, *phys.*, ⚙ revolution, rotation: *~en pro Minute* revolutions per minute (*abbr.* rpm).

umein'ander *adv sich ~ kümmern etc* take care *etc* of each other (*or* of one another).

'**Umerziehung** *f* (-; *no pl*) reeducation.

'umfahren¹ v/t (irr, sep, -ge-, h, → **fahren**) run (or knock) down.

um'fahren² v/t (irr, insep, no -ge-, h, → **fahren**) drive (or sail) round.

'umfallen v/i (irr, sep, -ge-, sn, → **fallen**) **1.** fall (down or over), collapse: **zum ♀ müde** ready to drop. **2.** F fig. cave in.

'Umfang m (-[e]s; no pl) a) circumference, girth, b) a. fig. extent, size, fig. scope, volume (of sales, traffic, etc): **10 Zoll im ~** 10 inches round; fig. **in vollem ~** fully; **in großem ~** on a large scale, large-scale. **'umfangreich** adj **1.** extensive. **2.** voluminous.

um'fassen v/t (insep, no -ge-, h) fig. **1.** comprise. **2.** cover (period).

um'fassend adj extensive, comprehensive (knowledge etc), complete, full (confession), sweeping (reforms etc).

'Umfeld n (-[e]s; -er) fig. surrounding(s).

'umformen v/t (sep, h) reshape (a. fig.), ⚡ transform, convert. **'Umformer** m (-s; -) ⚡ transformer, converter.

'Umfrage f (-; -n) a) inquiry, b) (public) opinion poll, survey.

'umfüllen v/t (sep, h) pour s.th. into another container (etc), decant (wine).

'umfunktio,nieren v/t (sep, h) **et. ~ in** (acc) convert (or turn) s.th. into.

'Umgang m (-[e]s; no pl) **1.** a) social intercourse, relations, b) company, friends: **~ haben mit** associate with; **guten (schlechten) ~ haben** keep good (bad) company. **2. der ~ mit Kindern** etc dealing with children etc; **im ~ mit ... (in)** dealing with ...

umgänglich ['ʊmgɛŋlɪç] adj affable, sociable, easy to get along with.

'Umgangs,formen pl manners. **~sprache** f colloquial language: **die englische ~** colloquial English. **'umgangssprachlich** adj colloquial.

um'garnen v/t (insep, no -ge-, h) fig. ensnare.

um'geben v/t (irr, insep, no -ge-, h, → **geben**) surround (**sich** o.s.) (**mit** with).

Um'gebung f (-; -en) environs, neighbo(u)rhood, vicinity, a. biol., sociol. environment, surroundings.

'Umgegend f (-; -en) environs, vicinity.

'umgehen¹ v/i (irr, sep, -ge-, sn, → **gehen**) **1.** disease, rumo(u)r, etc: circulate, go round. **2.** ghost: walk. **3. ~ mit** associate with (s.o.), treat, deal with, handle

(s.th., problem); **sie kann (gut) mit Leuten ~** she knows how to handle people; **er weiß mit Pferden umzugehen** he has a way with horses; **kannst du mit der Maschine ~?** do you know how to use (or handle) the machine?; → **schonend** II, **sparsam** II.

um'gehen² v/t (irr, insep, no -ge-, h, → **gehen**) **1.** bypass. **2.** fig. avoid, evade.

'umgehend adj immediate.

Um'gehung f (-; no pl) **1.** bypassing. **2.** fig. avoidance, a. ⚖ evasion.

Um'gehungsstraße f bypass, perimeter road.

'umgekehrt I adj a) reverse, b) inverse, opposite: **im ~en Falle** in the reverse case; **in ~er Reihenfolge** in reverse order; **(genau) ~!** (no,) it's exactly the other way round. **II** adv the other way round, conversely.

'umgestalten v/t (sep, h) reshape, fig. a. reorganize, ⚙ etc redesign.

'umgraben v/t (irr, sep, -ge-, h, → **graben**) dig (up), turn (over).

um'grenzen v/t (insep, no -ge-, h) define.

'umgrup,pieren v/t (sep, h) regroup, pol. reshuffle. **'Umgrup,pierung** f (-; -en) regrouping, pol. reshuffle.

'Umhang m (-[e]s; ⁀e) cape, wrap.

'umhängen v/t (sep, h) **1.** put on (coat etc), sling (rifle). **2.** rehang (picture).

'Umhängetasche f shoulder bag.

'umhauen v/t (irr, sep, -ge-, h, → **hauen**) **1.** fell, cut down. **2.** F fig. **j-n ~** drink etc: knock s.o. out, news etc: bowl s.o. over.

um'her adv about, (a)round.

um'hinkönnen v/i (irr, sep, -ge-, h, → **können**) **ich kann nicht umhin zu** inf I cannot help ger.

umhören: sich ~ (sep, h) keep one's ears open, ask around.

um'hüllen v/t (insep, no -ge-, h) (**mit**) wrap up (or envelop) (in), cover (with).

Um'hüllung f (-; -en) wrapping, cover.

'Umkehr f (-; no pl) **j-n zur ~ zwingen** force s.o. (to turn) back. **'umkehren** (sep) **I** v/i (sn) turn back. **II** v/t (h) turn round (a. **sich ~**), reverse (a. fig.).

'Umkehrfilm m reversal film.

'umkippen (sep) **I** v/t (h) **1.** tip over, upset. **II** v/i (sn) **2.** fall over, car etc: overturn, ⚓ a. capsize. **3.** F faint, keel over. **4.** F *fig.* turn, change completely, *river etc*: die, *wine*: turn sour.

um'**klammern** *v/t* (*insep, no* -ge-, h) clutch, clinch.

'**umklappen** *v/t* (*sep*, h) turn down.

'**Umkleideka,bine** *f* changing cubicle. '**umkleiden**: *sich* ~ (*sep*, h) change (one's clothes). '**Umkleideraum** *m* changing (*sports*: locker) room.

'**umknicken** *v/i* (*sep*, sn) (*mit dem Fuß*) ~ sprain one's ankle.

'**umkommen** *v/i* (*irr, sep*, -ge-, sn, → *kommen*) die (*a.* F *vor* with), be killed.

'**Umkreis** *m* (-es; *no pl*) vicinity: *im* ~ *von* within a radius of, for *three miles etc* round. **um'kreisen** *v/t* (*insep, no* -ge-, h) circle (*astr.* revolve) round.

'**umkrempeln** *v/t* (*sep*, h) **1.** roll up (*sleeve etc*). **2.** F *fig.* change completely.

'**umladen** *v/t* (*irr, sep*, -ge-, h, → *laden*) reload.

'**Umlage** *f* (-; -n) distribution of cost: *die* ~ *betrug ...* each person had to pay ...

'**Umland** *n* (-[e]s; *no pl*) environs, surrounding countryside.

'**Umlauf** *m* (-[e]s; ⸚e) **1.** circulation: *in* ~ *bringen* a) put *s.th.* in circulation, issue, b) start (*rumo[u]r*); *im* ~ *sein* circulate, *rumo(u)r*: *a.* be going round. **2.** *astr., phys.* a) revolution, b) cycle, c) orbit. **3.** circular (letter). '**Umlaufbahn** *f* (*in s-e* ~ *bringen* or *gelangen* put or get into) orbit. '**umlaufen** *v/i* (*irr, sep*, -ge-, sn, → *laufen*) circulate.

'**Umlaufkapi,tal** *n* ⸕ floating capital.

'**Umlaut** *m* (-[e]s; -e) a) umlaut, b) (vowel) mutation.

'**umlegen** *v/t* (*sep*, h) **1.** lay flat (*wheat etc*), fell (*tree*), tear down (*fence*). **2.** put on (*coat etc*). **3.** throw (*lever*). **4.** transfer (*a.* *teleph.*), *a.* move (*patient etc*), shift *appointment etc* (*auf acc* to). **5.** (*auf acc* among) apportion, divide (*costs etc*). **6.** *j-n* ~ a) F knock *s.o.* down, b) bump *s.o.* off, c) V lay *s.o.*

'**umleiten** *v/t* (*sep*, h) divert, detour.

'**Umleitung** *f* (-; -en) diversion, detour.

'**Umleitungsschild** *n* detour sign.

'**umlernen** *v/i* (*sep*, h) *wir müssen sehr* ~ we have a lot of relearning to do.

'**umliegend** *adj* surrounding.

'**ummelden** *v/t* (*sep*, h) (*a. sich* ~) register one's change of address (*bei* with).

'**ummodeln** *v/t* (*sep*, h) *fig.* change.

'**umorgani,sieren** *v/t* (*sep*, h) reorganize.

'**umpacken** *v/t* (*sep*, h) repack.

'**umpflanzen** *v/t* (*sep*, h) replant.

'**umquar,tieren** *v/t* (*sep*, h) move.

um'randen *v/t* (*insep, no* -ge-, h), **Um'randung** *f* (-; -en) border.

'**umräumen** *v/t* (*sep*, h) move *s.th.* (to another place), rearrange (*room*).

'**umrechnen** *v/t* (*sep*, h) convert (*in acc* into). '**Umrechnung** *f* (-; -en) conversion (*in acc* into).

'**Umrechnungs,kurs** *m* rate of exchange. ~**ta,belle** *f* conversion table.

'**umreißen**[1] *v/t* (*irr, sep*, -ge-, h, → *rei-ßen*) pull (*or* knock) down.

um'**reißen**[2] *v/t* (*irr, insep, no* -ge-, h, → *reißen*) *fig.* outline.

'**umrennen** *v/t* (*irr, sep*, -ge-, h, → *rennen*) run (*or* knock) down.

um'**ringen** *v/t* (*insep, no* -ge-, h) surround.

'**Umriß** *m* contour, *a. fig.* outline: *feste Umrisse annehmen* take shape.

'**umrühren** *v/t* (*sep*, h) stir.

'**umrüsten** *v/t* (*sep*, h) ⚙ change *s.th.* over (*auf acc* to).

'**umsatteln** *v/i* (*sep*, h) F change one's job (*student*: one's subject): ~ (*von ...*) *auf* (*acc*) switch (from ...) to.

'**Umsatz** *m* (-es; ⸚e) ⸕ turnover, sales. ~**beteiligung** *f* sales commission. ~**steuer** *f* turnover tax.

'**umschalten** (*sep*, h) **I** *v/t. a. v/i* ⚡, ⚙ *or fig.* switch (*or* change) (over) (*auf acc* to). **II** *v/i TV* change channels.

'**Umschalttaste** *f typewriter*: shift key.

'**umschichten** *v/t* (*sep*, h) **1.** rearrange. **2.** *fig.* regroup.

'**Umschichtung** *f* (-; -en) *fig.* regrouping: *soziale* ~ social upheaval.

um'**schiffen** *v/t* (*insep, no* -ge-, h) sail round, double: → *Klippe*.

'**Umschlag** *m* (-[e]s; ⸚e) **1.** a) envelope, b) cover, (*book or dust*) jacket. **2.** a) cuff, b) turnup. **3.** ⚕ (*feuchter*) ~ compress. **4.** *no pl* ⸕ a) handling (*of goods*), b) goods handled, c) transshipment. '**umschlagen** (*irr, sep*, -ge-, ~ *schlagen*) **I** *v/i* (sn) **1.** → *umkippen* **2. 2.** *weather, wind, mood, etc*: change (suddenly). **II** *v/t* **3.** turn up (*sleeve etc*). **4.** a) handle (*goods*), b) transship. '**Umschlag|hafen** *m* port of transshipment. **~platz** *m* trading cent/re (*Am.* -er), ♟ place of transshipment.

um'schließen *v/t* (*irr, insep, no* -ge-, h, → **schließen**) **1.** surround, enclose. **2.** *fig.* encompass.

'umschnallen *v/t* (*sep*, h) buckle on.

'umschreiben[1] *v/t* (*irr, sep,* -ge-, h, → **schreiben**) **1.** rewrite. **2.** transfer *property* (**auf** *acc* to). **um'schreiben**[2] *v/t* (*irr, insep, no* -ge-, h, → **schreiben**) **1.** paraphrase, circumscribe (*a.* Ⓐ). **2.** outline. **'Umschreibung**[1] *f* (-; -en) **1.** rewriting. **2.** ✝ transfer. **Um'schreibung**[2] *f* (-; -en) paraphrase, circumscription (*a.* Ⓐ).

'Umschrift *f* (-; -en) transcription.

'Umschuldung *f* (-; -en) ✝ conversion (of a debt).

'umschulen *v/t* (*sep*, h) **1.** retrain. **2.** transfer *student* to another school.

um'schwärmen *v/t* (*insep, no* -ge-, h) **1.** swarm round. **2.** *fig.* idolize.

'Umschweife: ohne ~ a) *say etc s.th.* straight out, b) *do s.th.* straightaway.

'umschwenken *v/i* (*sep*, sn) **1.** wheel round. **2.** *fig.* veer round.

'Umschwung *m* (-[e]s; ⸚e) change, reversal, *esp. pol.* swing, about-face.

um'segeln *v/t* (*insep, no* -ge-, h) sail round, double.

'umsehen: sich ~ (*irr, sep,* -ge-, h, → **sehen**) **1.** look back. **2.** look (a)round (**nach** for): **sich in der Stadt ~** (have a) look (a)round the city.

'umsein *v/i* (*irr, sep,* -ge-, sn, → **sein**) F be over: **s-e Zeit ist um** his time is up.

'umseitig [-zaitɪç] *adj and adv* overleaf.

'umsetzen *v/t* (*sep*, h) **1.** move, transfer, ✗ transplant. **2.** sell, turn over. **3. et. ~ in** (*acc*) *a.* 🜍, *phys.* convert (*or* transform) *s.th.* into; (**in die Praxis**) **~** realize; **et. in die Tat ~** put *s.th.* into action.

'Umsicht *f* (-; *no pl*) circumspection.

'umsichtig *adj* circumspect.

'umsiedeln *v/t* (*sep*, h) resettle.

'Umsiedler(in *f*) *m* resettler, *pol.* Ethnic German repatriate (from the East).

'Umsiedlung *f* (-; -en) resettlement.

um'sonst *adv* **1.** for nothing, free (of charge). **2.** in vain: **nicht ~** not without (good) reason, not for nothing.

um'spannen *v/t* (*insep, no* -ge-, h) span.

'Umspannwerk *n* transformer station.

um'spielen *v/t* (*insep, no* -ge-, h) soccer

etc: dribble round, *fig.* play (a)round.

'umspringen *v/i* (*irr, sep,* -ge-, sn, → **springen**) **1.** → **umschlagen** 2. **2. mit j-m grob** *etc* ~ treat s.o. roughly *etc.*

'Umstand *m* **1.** fact, circumstance. **2.** *pl* circumstances, conditions, situation: **unter Umständen** possibly, perhaps; **unter allen Umständen** at all events; **unter diesen (k-n) Umständen** under the (no) circumstances; F **in anderen Umständen sein** be in the family way; → **mildern** I. **3. ohne viel Umstände** without much fuss; **Umstände machen** a) cause trouble, b) make a fuss; **machen Sie (sich) k-e Umstände!** don't go to any trouble. **'umstände-halber** *adv* owing to circumstances.

umständlich ['ʊmʃtɛntlɪç] *adj* a) complicated, b) long-winded, c) awkward, d) fussy: **das ist (mir) viel zu ~** that's far too much trouble (for me).

'Umstandskleid *n* maternity dress.

'Umstandskrämer *m* (-s; -) F fusspot.

'Umstandswort *n* (-[e]s; ⸚er) adverb.

'umstehend *adj* next (*page*), *a. adv* overleaf: **die Umstehenden** the bystanders.

'Umsteige(fahr)karte *f* transfer ticket.

'umsteigen *v/i* (*irr, sep,* -ge-, sn, → **steigen**) **1.** change (**nach** for). **2.** F *fig.* switch (**auf** *acc* to).

um'stellen[1] *v/t* (*insep, no* -ge-, h) surround.

'umstellen[2] (*sep*, h) **I** *v/t* a) change, b) rearrange (*furniture etc*), c) regroup (*team*), d) reset (*watch*), e) Ⓖ change over (**auf** *acc* to), f) reorganize (*firm etc*): ~ **auf** (*acc*) switch to, convert to; **auf Computer ~** computerize; **s-e Lebensweise ~** readjust one's way of life. **II sich ~** get used to new conditions, adjust (**auf** *acc* to). **'Umstellung** *f* (-; -en) change, rearrangement, Ⓖ change-over (*or* switch) (**auf** *acc* to), reorganization, adjustment (**auf** *acc* to): **e-e große ~ sein** be quite a change.

'umstimmen *v/t* (*sep*, h) **j-n ~** bring s.o. round.

'umstoßen *v/t* (*irr, sep,* -ge-, h, → **stoßen**) **1.** knock over (*or* down). **2.** *fig.* change (*last will, plan, etc*), reverse (*judg[e]ment etc*), upset (*plan*).

umstritten [ʊm'ʃtrɪtən] *adj* contested.

'umstruktu,rieren *v/t* (*sep*, h) restructure.

'umstülpen *v/t* (*sep*, h) a) turn *s.th.* upside down, b) turn *s.th.* inside out.

'**Umsturz** *m* (-es; ¨e) overthrow, revolution. '**umstürzen** (*sep*) **I** *v/t* (h) upset, knock over, *pol.* overthrow. **II** *v/i* (sn) fall down (*or* over), overturn. '**Umstürzler** [-ʃtʏrtslər] *m* (-s; -) revolutionary. '**umstürzlerisch** *adj* subversive. '**Umsturzversuch** *m* attempted coup.

'**Umtausch** *m* (-[e]s; -e), '**umtauschen** *v/t* (*sep*, h) exchange (**gegen** for).

'**umtopfen** *v/t* (*sep*, h) ✿ repot.

'**Umtriebe** *pl contp.* activities, intrigues.

'**umtun:** *sich* ~ (*irr, sep,* -ge-, → *tun*) look around (**nach** for).

'**U-Mu,sik** *f* light music.

'**umwälzen** *v/t* (*sep*, h) **1.** ✪ circulate. **2.** *fig.* revolutionize.

'**umwälzend** *adj fig.* revolutionary.

'**Umwälzpumpe** *f* circulating pump.

'**Umwälzung** *f* (-; -en) **1.** ✪ circulation. **2.** *fig.* revolution, upheaval.

'**umwandeln** *v/t* (*sep*, h) change (**in** *acc*, **zu** into), *phys.* transform, convert (*a.* ⚡), ⚖ commute (*sentence*): **sie ist wie umgewandelt** she is a completely different person. '**Umwandler** *m* (-s; -) ⚡, ✪ converter. '**Umwandlung** *f* (-; -en) change, transformation, conversion, ⚖ commutation.

'**Umweg** *m* detour, roundabout way: **e-n ~ machen** make a detour; **das ist ein ~ für mich** that takes me out of my way; *fig.* **auf ~en** indirectly, in a roundabout way; **ohne ~e** straight.

'**Umwelt** *f* (-; *no pl*) environment: **unsere ~** *a.* the world around us.

'**Umwelt...** environmental. **~belastung** *f* (environmental) pollution. **2bewußt** *adj* environment-conscious. **2feindlich** → **umweltschädlich.** **~forscher** *m* ecologist. **~forschung** *f* (-; *no pl*) ecology. **2freundlich** *adj* ecologically friendly, nonpolluting, *a.* biodegradable. **~kata,strophe** *f* ecocatastrophe. **~kriminali,tät** *f* environmental crime. **~krise** *f* ecological crisis, ecocrisis. **~mini,sterium** *n* Department of the Environment. **~poli,tik** *f* ecopolicy. **2po,litisch** *adj* ecopolitical. **~schäden** *pl* damage done by pollution. **2schädlich** *adj* harmful (to the environment), polluting. **~schutz** *m* environmental (*or* pollution) control, conservation. **~schützer** *m* (-s; -) environmentalist, conservationist. **~sünder** *m* F polluter.

~**verbrechen** *n* environmental crime. ~**verschmutzung** *f* pollution. ~**zerstörung** *f* ecocide.

'**umwenden:** *sich* ~ (*irr, sep,* -ge-, h, → *wenden*) turn round.

um'**werben** *v/t* (*irr, insep, no* -ge-, h, → *werben*) court, *a. fig.* woo.

'**umwerfen** *v/t* (*irr, sep,* -ge-, h, → *werfen*) **1.** → **umstoßen. 2.** → **umhauen** 2.

'**umwerfend** *adj* fantastic, mind-blowing: ~ **komisch** too funny for words.

'**Umwertung** *f* (-; -en) revaluation.

um'**wickeln** *v/t* (*insep, no* -ge-, h) wind *s.th.* round, bandage *s.th.* (**mit** with).

'**umziehen** (*irr, sep,* -ge-, → *ziehen*) **I** *v/i* (sn) move (house). **II** *v/t* (h) **j-n** ~ change s.o.'s clothes; *sich* ~ change.

umzingeln [um'tsɪŋəln] *v/t* (*insep, no* -ge-, h) surround, encircle.

'**Umzug** *m* (-[e]s; ¨e) **1.** move. **2.** procession, *pol.* demonstration march.

unab**änderlich** [ʊnˀapˀɛndərlɪç] *adj* unalterable, irrevocable: *sich ins* **2e** *fügen* resign o.s. to the inevitable.

'**unabhängig** *adj* independent (**von** of): ~ **von** irrespective of; ~ **davon ob** regardless whether. '**Unabhängige** *m, f* (-n; -n) *pol.* independent. '**Unabhängigkeit** *f* (-; *no pl*) independence.

unab'**kömmlich** *adj* indispensable: **er ist** ~ he is busy, he can't get away.

unab**lässig** [ʊnˀapˀlɛsɪç] *adj* incessant.

unab'**sehbar** *adj* a) unforeseeable, b) incalculable, immense (*damage etc*): **auf ~e Zeit** for an indefinite period of time.

'**unabsichtlich** *adj* unintentional.

unab'**wendbar** *adj* unavoidable.

'**unachtsam** *adj* inattentive, careless. '**Unachtsamkeit** *f* (-; *no pl*) carelessness.

'**unähnlich** *adj* (*dat*) unlike (*s.o., s.th.*).

unan'**fechtbar** *adj* incontestable.

'**unangebracht** *adj* inappropriate: ~ **sein** *a.* be out of place.

'**unangefochten** *adj and adv* **1.** undisputed(ly). **2.** unhindered.

'**unangemeldet** *adj* unannounced.

'**unangemessen** *adj* **1.** inappropriate, inadequate. **2.** unreasonable (*price etc*).

'**unangenehm** *adj* unpleasant, *a.* nasty, awkward: **das 2e dabei ist** the unpleasant thing about it is.

'**unangetastet** *adj* untouched.

unan'**greifbar** *adj a. fig.* unassailable.

unan'nehmbar *adj* unacceptable.

'Unannehmlichkeiten *pl* (*j-m ~ berei-ten* cause s.o.) trouble: *~ bekommen* get into trouble.

'unansehnlich *adj* unsightly, plain.

'unanständig *adj* 1. indecent, obscene. 2. unfair.

unan'tastbar *adj* unimpeachable, invio-lable (*rights*), *iro.* sacrosanct.

'unappe,titlich *adj* unappetizing, *a. fig.* unsavo(u)ry.

'Unart *f* (-; -en) bad habit, bad trick.

'unartig *adj* naughty.

'unäs,thetisch *adj* un(a)esthetic, *w.s.* unpleasant, unsavo(u)ry, ugly.

'unaufdringlich *adj* unobtrusive.

'unauffällig *adj* 1. inconspicuous. 2. unobtrusive, discreet.

unauf'findbar *adj* untraceable, *pred* not to be found.

'unaufgefordert *adj and adv* unasked, *adv a.* of one's own accord.

unauf'haltsam [ʊnʔaʊf'haltza:m] *adj* unstoppable.

unauf'hörlich [ʊnʔaʊf'hø:rlıç] *adj* inces-sant, continuous.

unauf'lösbar, unauf'löslich *adj* indis-soluble, *a.* 🝆, 🝆 & insoluble.

'unaufmerksam *adj* 1. inattentive. 2. thoughtless, careless.

'Unaufmerksamkeit *f* (-; *no pl*) 1. inat-tention. 2. thoughtlessness.

'unaufrichtig *adj* insincere. 'Unaufrich-tigkeit *f* (-; *no pl*) insincerity.

unauf'schiebbar [ʊnʔaʊf'ʃi:pba:r] *adj* urgent.

unaus'bleiblich [ʊnʔaʊs'blaıplıç] *adj* inevitable.

unaus'führbar *adj* impracticable.

'unausgefüllt *adj* 1. blank (*form*). 2. *fig.* unfulfilled (*life, person*).

'unausgeglichen *adj* unbalanced, un-stable. Unausgeglichenheit *f* (-; *no pl*) imbalance, instability.

'unausgesprochen *adj* unspoken.

unaus'löschlich [ʊnʔaʊs'lœʃlıç] *adj fig.* indelible.

unaus'rottbar *adj* ineradicable.

unaus'sprechlich ['ʊnʔaʊsʃpreçlıç] *adj* unpronounceable, *fig.* unspeakable.

unaus'stehlich [ʊnʔaʊs'ʃte:lıç] *adj* insuf-ferable, intolerable.

unaus'weichlich [ʊnʔaʊs'vaıçlıç] *adj* unavoidable, inevitable.

unbändig ['ʊnbɛndıç] *adj* 1. unruly. 2. *fig.* tremendous (*rage, hate, etc*).

'unbarmherzig *adj* merciless. 'Unbarm-herzigkeit *f* (-; *no pl*) mercilessness.

'unbeabsichtigt *adj* unintentional.

'unbeachtet *adj and adv* (*~ bleiben* go) unnoticed: *~ lassen* disregard.

'unbeanstandet *adj* unobjected: *et. ~ lassen* let s.th. pass.

'unbeantwortet *adj* unanswered.

'unbearbeitet *adj* a) untreated, unfin-ished, b) undealt with, c) unedited.

'unbebaut *adj* 1. 🝆 untilled. 2. undevel-oped (*land*).

'unbedacht *adj* thoughtless, rash.

unbedarft ['ʊnbədarft] *adj* F naive.

'unbedenklich *adj* safe.

'unbedeutend *adj* insignificant, unim-portant, *a.* negligible.

'unbedingt I *adj* a) unconditional, b) absolute. II *adv* absolutely, at all costs: *et. ~ brauchen* need s.th. badly; *nicht ~* a) not necessarily, b) not exactly.

unbe'fahrbar *adj* impassable.

'unbefangen *adj* 1. unbias(s)ed, impar-tial. 2. uninhibited, free.

'Unbefangenheit *f* (-; *no pl*) 1. impar-tiality. 2. naturalness.

'unbefleckt *adj fig.* unsullied: *eccl. ~e Empfängnis* Immaculate Conception.

'unbefriedigend *adj* unsatisfactory.

'unbefriedigt *adj* unsatisfied.

'unbefristet I *adj* unlimited. II *adv* for an unlimited period.

'unbefugt *adj* unauthorized.

'Unbefugte *m, f* (-n; -n) unauthorized person: *Zutritt für ~ verboten!* no unauthorized entry!

'unbegabt *adj* untalented.

'unbegreiflich *adj* incomprehensible: *es ist mir völlig ~* it's beyond me.

'unbegrenzt I *adj* unlimited, boundless. II *adv* indefinitely: *ich habe ~ Zeit* I have unlimited time.

'unbegründet *adj* unfounded.

'Unbehagen *n* (-s; *no pl*) unease.

'unbehaglich *adj* uncomfortable, *fig. a.* uneasy: *sich ~ fühlen a.* feel ill at ease.

'unbehelligt *adj and adv* a) unmolested, b) unhindered.

'unbeherrscht *adj* unrestrained: *~ sein* have no self-control. 'Unbeherrscht-heit *f* (-; *no pl*) lack of self-control.

unbeholfen ['ʊnbəhɔlfən] *adj* clumsy.

'Unbeholfenheit *f* (-; *no pl*) clumsiness.
unbe'irrbar *adj* imperturbable.
unbe'irrt *adj* unswerving, unperturbed.
'unbekannt *adj* unknown: *das war mir ~* I didn't know that; *~e Größe* → 'Unbekannte *f* (-n; -n) *A̸ or fig.* unknown (quantity).
'unbekleidet *adj and adv* undressed.
'unbekömmlich *adj* indigestible.
'unbekümmert *adj* carefree: *~ um* unconcerned about.
'unbelastet *adj* **1.** carefree: *~ sein* be free from worries, *pol.* have a clean record. **2.** ✝ unencumbered (*property*).
unbe'lehrbar *adj* hopeless.
'unbeleuchtet *adj mot.* without lights.
'unbeliebt *adj* unpopular (*bei* with).
'Unbeliebtheit *f* (-; *no pl*) unpopularity.
'unbemannt *adj* unmanned, ✈ pilotless.
'unbemerkt *adj and adv* unnoticed.
'unbemittelt *adj* without means, poor.
unbenommen [ˈʊnbəˈnɔmən] *adj es ist Ihnen ~ zu inf* you are at liberty to *inf*.
'unbenutzt *adj* unused.
'unbeobachtet *adj and adv* unobserved.
'unbequem *adj* **1.** uncomfortable. **2.** *fig.* a) inconvenient, b) embarrassing (*question etc*), c) difficult (*person*). 'Unbequemlichkeit *f* (-; -en) **1.** *no pl* uncomfortableness. **2.** *fig.* inconvenience.
unbe'rechenbar *adj* incalculable, *fig. a.* unpredictable (*person*).
'unberechtigt *adj* **1.** unauthorized. **2.** unjustified, unfair.
'unberechtigter'weise *adv* **1.** without permission. **2.** without good reason.
unbe'rücksichtigt *adj* unconsidered: *et. ~ lassen* leave s.th. out of account.
unbe'rufen *int* touch wood!
'unberührt *adj* untouched (*a. fig.*), virgin (*girl, nature, etc*): *fig. ~ bleiben von* not to be affected by.
unbeschadet [ˈʊnbəˈʃaːdət] *adj* (*gen*) a) without prejudice to, b) irrespective of.
'unbeschädigt *adj* undamaged, intact.
'unbeschäftigt *adj* unemployed, idle.
'unbescheiden *adj* immodest. 'Unbescheidenheit *f* (-; *no pl*) immodesty.
unbescholten [ˈʊnbəˈʃɔltən] *adj* blameless: *𝕴̸ ~ sein* have no police record.
'unbeschränkt *adj* unrestricted, absolute (*power, right, etc*).
unbeschreiblich [ˈʊnbəˈʃraiplɪç] *adj* indescribable.

'unbeschrieben *adj* blank (*paper*): *fig. ~es Blatt* unknown quantity.
'unbeschwert *adj fig.* a) carefree, b) light (*conscience*): *~ von* free from.
'unbesehen *adv et. ~ kaufen* buy s.th. sight unseen; *das glaube ich dir ~* I well believe you.
'unbesetzt *adj* vacant (*post*), *a.* unoccupied, free (*seat etc*).
unbe'siegbar *adj* invincible.
unbe'siegt *adj* undefeated.
'unbesonnen *adj* imprudent, rash.
'Unbesonnenheit *f* (-; *no pl*) rashness.
'unbesorgt **I** *adj* unconcerned (*wegen* about): *seien Sie (deswegen) ~!* don't worry! **II** *adv* safely.
'unbespielt *adj* blank (*tape, cassette*).
'unbeständig *adj* unstable, changeable, unsettled (*weather etc*). 'Unbeständigkeit *f* (-; *no pl*) unstableness (*etc*).
'unbestätigt *adj* unconfirmed.
'unbestechlich *adj* **1.** incorruptible. **2.** unerring (*judgement etc*). 'Unbestechlichkeit *f* (-; *no pl*) incorruptibility.
'unbestimmt *adj* a) vague (*idea etc*), b) indeterminate, *a. ling.* indefinite: *auf ~e Zeit* for an indefinite period. 'Unbestimmtheit *f* (-; *no pl*) vagueness.
unbe'streitbar *adj* indisputable.
unbe'stritten **I** *adj* undisputed. **II** *adv* indisputably, without doubt.
'unbeteiligt *adj* **1.** not involved (*an dat* in). **2.** indifferent.
'unbetont *adj* unstressed.
'unbeträchtlich *adj* negligible, insignificant: *nicht ~* quite considerable.
unbeugsam [ˈʊnˈbɔykzaːm] *adj fig.* uncompromising.
'unbewacht *adj. a. fig.* unguarded.
'unbewaffnet *adj* unarmed.
'unbeweglich *adj* immobile, *a. 𝕴̸* immovable (*possessions, holiday, etc*), motionless, ⚙ fixed, rigid (*a. fig.*), (*mentally*) inflexible: *~e Güter* immovables. 'Unbeweglichkeit *f* (-; *no pl*) immobility, (*mental*) inflexibility.
'unbewegt *adj* a) expressionless, b) unmoved (*a. adv*).
unbe'weisbar *adj* unprovable.
unbe'wiesen *adj* unproved.
unbe'wohnbar *adj* uninhabitable. 'unbewohnt *adj* uninhabited, unoccupied.
'unbewußt *adj* unconscious.

unbe'zahlbar adj 1. too expensive. 2. fig. priceless (a. F funny).
'unbezahlt adj unpaid.
unbe'zähmbar adj fig. indomitable.
unbe'zwingbar adj invincible.
'Unbildung f (-; no pl) lack of education.
'unblutig I adj bloodless, ✚ nonoperative. **II** adv without bloodshed.
'unbrauchbar adj useless, unsuitable, impracticable (plan etc), unserviceable: et. ∼ machen render s.th. useless.
'Unbrauchbarkeit f (-; no pl) uselessness, impracticability, unserviceability.
un'brennbar adj nonflammable.
'unbüro,kratisch adj unbureaucratic.
'unchristlich adj unchristian.
und [unt] conj and: ∼? well?; F ∼ ob! you bet!; na ∼? so what?; ∼ so weiter (or fort) and so on; ∼ wenn (auch) even if.
'Undank m (-[e]s; no pl) ingratitude: F nur ∼ ernten get small thanks for it.
'undankbar adj 1. ungrateful (gegen to). 2. thankless (task etc).
'Undankbarkeit f (-; no pl) 1. ingratitude. 2. thanklessness.
'unda,tiert adj undated.
undefi'nierbar adj undefinable.
'undemo,kratisch adj undemocratic.
un'denkbar adj unthinkable.
undenklich [un'dɛŋklıç] adj seit ∼en Zeiten from time immemorial.
'undeutlich adj indistinct, pred not clear, inarticulate (speech), blurred (picture etc), vague (idea etc).
'undicht adj leaking, pred not tight: ∼e Stelle leak (a. fig. pol.).
'Unding n (-[e]s; no pl) absurdity: es ist ein ∼ it is preposterous (or absurd).
'undiszipli,niert adj undisciplined.
'unduldsam adj intolerant.
'Unduldsamkeit f (-; no pl) intolerance.
undurch'dringlich adj impenetrable, fig. a. inscrutable.
undurch'führbar adj impracticable.
'undurchlässig adj impermeable (für to).
'undurchsichtig adj 1. opaque. 2. fig. mysterious, inscrutable.
'uneben adj uneven, rough (road etc).
'unecht adj 1. a) a. fig. false, pred not genuine, b) artificial, c) counterfeit(ed), fake(d), F phon(e)y. 2. ✚ improper.
'unehelich adj illegitimate.
'unehrenhaft adj dishono(u)rable.

'unehrlich adj dishonest, insincere.
'Unehrlichkeit f (-; no pl) dishonesty.
'uneigennützig adj unselfish.
'uneingeschränkt adj unrestricted, unqualified (praise), absolute (trust etc).
'uneingeweiht adj uninitiated.
'uneinheitlich adj nonuniform, varied.
'uneinig adj divided: (sich) ∼ sein a. be at variance, disagree. **'Uneinigkeit** f (-; no pl) disagreement, discord.
unein'nehmbar adj impregnable.
'unempfänglich adj (für to) insusceptible, unreceptive.
'unempfindlich adj 1. insensitive (gegen to). 2. durable, rugged.
'Unempfindlichkeit f (-; no pl) 1. insensitiveness (gegen to). 2. durability.
un'endlich I adj ♀, ♪, phys. infinite (a. fig.), endless: phot. auf ∼ einstellen focus at infinity; fig. bis ins ∼e ad infinitum. **II** adv infinitely (etc), fig. a. immensely: ∼ klein infinitesimal; ∼ lang endless; ∼ viel a tremendous amount of; ∼ viele no end of.
Un'endlichkeit f (-; no pl) infinity.
unent'behrlich adj indispensable (dat, für to).
unent'geltlich adj and adv free (of charge), adv a. for nothing.
unent'rinnbar adj inescapable.
'unentschieden adj undecided (a. person), a. open (question), sports: drawn: ∼ enden end in a draw; ∼ spielen draw.
'Unentschieden n (-s; -) sports: draw.
'unentschlossen adj undecided, irresolute. **'Unentschlossenheit** f (-; no pl) irresolution, indecision.
unent'schuldbar adj inexcusable.
'unentschuldigt adj ∼es Fehlen unexcused absence.
unentwegt [un'ɛnt've:kt] adj incessant.
Unent'wegte m, f (-n; -n) pol. diehard.
unent'wirrbar adj inextricable.
unerbittlich [un'ɛr'bɪtlıç] adj merciless.
'unerfahren adj inexperienced. **'Unerfahrenheit** f (-; no pl) inexperience.
unerforschlich [un'ɛr'fɔrʃlıç] adj fig. unfathomable.
'unerforscht adj unexplored.
'unerfreulich adj unpleasant.
uner'füllbar adj unrealizable.
'unerfüllt adj unfulfilled.
'unergiebig adj unproductive.

'uner**gründlich** *adj* unfathomable, *fig. a.* inscrutable.

'un**erheblich** *adj* insignificant, *esp.* ⚖ irrelevant (**für** to).

uner'**hört** *adj* **1.** a) unheard-of, b) outrageous, scandalous: ~! what a cheek! **2.** F terrific, fantastic.

'un**erkannt** *adj* unrecognized.

'un**erklärlich** *adj* inexplicable.

un**erläßlich** [ʊn'ɛr'lɛslɪç] *adj* essential.

'un**erlaubt** I *adj* a) unauthorized, *pred* not allowed, b) illegal, illicit. II *adv* without permission.

'un**erledigt** *adj* not yet dealt with, unanswered (*mail*), unfulfilled (*orders etc*): ~**e Dinge** unfinished business.

uner**meßlich** [ʊn'ɛr'mɛslɪç] *adj* immeasurable, immense, vast.

uner**müdlich** [ʊn'ɛr'my:tlɪç] *adj* indefatigable, untiring.

'un**erquicklich** *adj* unpleasant.

uner'**reichbar** *adj* inaccessible, *fig.* unattainable (*goal etc*): **für j-n** ~ out of s.o.'s reach; **er war** ~ I (we *etc*) couldn't get hold of him. **'unerreicht** *adj fig.* unequal(l)ed, unrival(l)ed, record ...

uner**sättlich** [ʊn'ɛr'zɛtlɪç] *adj a. fig.* insatiable.

'un**erschlossen** *adj* undeveloped.

uner**schöpflich** [ʊn'ɛr'ʃœpflɪç] *adj* inexhaustible.

'un**erschrocken** *adj* undaunted.

uner**schütterlich** [ʊn'ɛr'ʃʏtɐlɪç] *adj* unshak(e)able, imperturbable.

uner'**schwinglich** *adj* unaffordable (*goods*), exorbitant (*price*): **für j-n** ~ **sein** be beyond s.o.'s means.

uner'**setzlich** *adj* **1.** irreplaceable. **2.** irreparable (*damage*).

uner'**träglich** *adj* unbearable.

'un**erwähnt** *adj* unmentioned: **et.** ~ **lassen** make no mention of s.th.

'un**erwidert** *adj* unrequited (*love*).

'un**erwünscht** *adj* undesirable.

'un**fähig** *adj* **1.** incapable, incompetent: ~ **zu** unqualified for (*a task etc*). **2.** ~ **zu** *inf.* unable to *inf.*, incapable of *ger.*

'Un**fähigkeit** *f* (-; *no pl*) **1.** incompetence. **2.** inability.

'un**fair** *adj* unfair.

'Un**fall** *m* (-[e]s; ⸚e) accident. ~**arzt** *m* casualty doctor. ~**flucht** *f* → **Fahrerflucht.** ⚲**frei** *adj* accident-free. ⚲**gefährdet** *adj* accident-prone. ~**krankenhaus**

n casualty hospital. ~**opfer** *n* accident victim. ~**quote** *f*, ~**rate** *f* accident rate. ~**stati,on** *f* a) first-aid station, b) casualty ward. ~**stelle** *f* scene of (the) accident. ~**tod** *m* accidental death. ⚲**trächtig** *adj* hazardous. ~**ursache** *f* cause of the accident. ~**verhütung** *f* prevention of accidents. ~**versicherung** *f* accident insurance. ~**wagen** *m* **1.** car damaged in an accident. **2.** ✓ crash tender.

un'**faßbar**, un'**faßlich** *adj* incomprehensible, inconceivable.

un'**fehlbar** I *adj* infallible (*a. eccl.*), unerring. II *adv* infallibly, without fail.

Un'**fehlbarkeit** *f* (-; *no pl*) infallibility.

'un**fein** *adj* indelicate, unrefined, *pred* not nice, bad form.

'un**fertig** *adj* **1.** unfinished. **2.** *fig.* immature (*person*).

un**flätig** ['ʊnflɛ:tɪç] *adj* filthy, obscene.

'un**folgsam** *adj* disobedient.

un**förmig** ['ʊnfœrmɪç] *adj* a) shapeless, b) bulky, c) misshapen.

'un**fran,kiert** *adj* unstamped (*letter*).

'un**frei** *adj* **1.** not free. **2.** *fig.* inhibited.

'un**freiwillig** *adj* a) involuntary, unintentional, b) unconscious (*humo[u]r*).

'un**freundlich** *adj* unfriendly, inclement (*climate, weather*), cheerless (*room etc*).

'Un**freundlichkeit** *f* (-; *no pl*) unfriendliness, inclemency, cheerlessness.

'Un**friede** *m* (-n; *no pl*) discord.

'un**fruchtbar** *adj* infertile, *a. fig.* barren, sterile, *fig.* fruitless. '**Unfruchtbarkeit** *f* (-; *no pl*) infertility, *fig.* fruitlessness.

Un**fug** ['ʊnfu:k] *m* (-[e]s; *no pl*) a) (~ **treiben** be up to) mischief, b) nonsense: ⚖ **grober** ~ disorderly conduct.

Un**gar** ['ʊŋɡar] *m* (-n; -n), '**Ungarin** *f* (-; -nen), '**ungarisch** *adj* Hungarian.

'Un**garn** *n* (-s) Hungary.

'un**gastlich** *adj* inhospitable.

un**geachtet** *prep* (*gen*) regardless of.

un**geahnt** ['ʊnɡə'a:nt] *adj* undreamt-of.

'un**gebeten** *adj* unasked, uninvited.

'un**gebildet** *adj* uneducated.

'un**geboren** *adj* unborn.

'un**gebräuchlich** *adj* unusual.

'un**gebraucht** *adj* unused.

'un**gebunden** *adj* **1.** *print.* unbound, in sheets. **2.** *fig.* unattached, independent.

'un**gedeckt** *adj* uncovered (*a. cheque*), unsecured (*credit*), *sports:* unmarked.

'Un**geduld** *f* (-; *no pl*) impatience.

'ungeduldig *adj* impatient.
'ungeeignet *adj* (**zu** for) unsuitable, *person: a.* unqualified, inopportune (*time*).
ungefähr ['ʊngəfɛːr] **I** *adj* approximate, rough. **II** *adv* approximately, about, around: **so ~** s.th. like that; **wo ~?** roughly where?
'ungefährlich *adj* harmless, safe.
'ungefällig *adj* unobliging.
'ungehalten *adj* annoyed (**über** *acc* at).
'ungehemmt **I** *adj* unchecked, *psych.* uninhibited. **II** *adv* without restraint.
'ungehcuchelt *adj* unfeigned.
'ungeheuer **I** *adj* **1.** immense, enormous. **2.** F tremendous, terrific. **II** *adv* **3.** enormously (*etc*). **Ungeheuer** *n* (-s; -) monster. **'ungeheuerlich** *adj* monstrous, outrageous. **'Ungeheuerlichkeit** *f* (-; -en) monstrosity, outrage.
'ungehindert *adj and adv* unhindered.
'ungehobelt *adj fig.* rude, uncouth.
'ungehörig *adj* improper, impertinent.
'ungehorsam *adj* disobedient. **'Ungehorsam** *m* (-s; *no pl*) disobedience.
'ungeklärt *adj* **1.** unsettled (*question etc*), unsolved (*case, problem, etc*). **2. ~e Abwässer** untreated sewage.
'ungekünstelt *adj* unaffected.
'ungekürzt *adj* unabridged (*book*), uncut (*film*).
'ungeladen *adj* **1.** uninvited (*guest*). **2.** unloaded (*gun*).
'ungelegen *adj* inconvenient: **das kommt mir sehr ~!** that doesn't suit me at all! **'Ungelegenheiten** *pl* **j-m ~ machen** put s.o. out, inconvenience s.o.
'ungelenk *adj* clumsy, stiff.
'ungelernt *adj* unskilled (*worker*).
'ungemein *adv* immensely.
'ungemischt *adj* unmixed.
'ungemütlich *adj* uncomfortable (*a. fig.*), cheerless (*room*): F **~ werden** get unpleasant, turn nasty. **'Ungemütlichkeit** *f* (-; *no pl*) uncomfortableness.
'ungenannt *adj* unnamed, anonymous.
'ungenau *adj* inaccurate, inexact, *fig.* vague, hazy.
'Ungenauigkeit *f* (-; -en) inaccuracy.
'unge,niert **I** *adj* uninhibited. **II** *adv* without inhibition, openly.
'ungenießbar *adj* **1.** a) inedible, b) undrinkable. **2.** F *person:* unbearable.
'ungenügend *adj* insufficient, *ped.* unsatisfactory, poor.

'ungenutzt *adj* unused: **e-e Gelegenheit ~ lassen** let an opportunity slip.
'ungepflegt *adj* unkempt, neglected.
'ungerade *adj* uneven, odd (*number*).
'ungerecht *adj* unjust. **'ungerechtfertigt** *adj* unjustified. **'Ungerechtigkeit** *f* (-; -en) injustice (**gegen** to).
'ungeregelt *adj* unregulated, irregular (*life, working hours, etc*).
'ungern *adv* unwillingly, reluctantly: **ich tue es ~** I don't like doing it.
'ungerührt *adj fig.* unmoved (**von** by).
'ungesagt *adj* (**~ bleiben** be left) unsaid.
'ungesalzen *adj* unsalted.
'ungeschehen *adj* **~ machen** undo.
'Ungeschick *n* (-[e]s; *no pl*), **'Ungeschicklichkeit** *f* (-; *no pl*) clumsiness.
'ungeschickt *adj* clumsy.
'ungeschlagen *adj fig.* undefeated.
'ungeschliffen *adj* **1.** rough (*diamond*). **2.** *fig.* unpolished (*behavio[u]r etc*).
'ungeschminkt *adj* **1.** not made up, without makeup. **2.** *fig.* unvarnished, *a.* plain (*truth*).
'ungeschoren *adj* **1.** unshorn. **2.** *fig.* unmolested: **j-n ~ lassen** leave s.o. in peace; **~ davonkommen** get off lightly (*or* F scot-free).
'ungeschrieben *adj* unwritten.
'ungeschützt *adj* unprotected.
'ungesehen *adj and adv* unseen.
'ungesellig *adj* unsociable. **'Ungeselligkeit** *f* (-; *no pl*) unsociableness.
'ungesetzlich *adj* illegal, illicit, unlawful.
'Ungesetzlichkeit *f* (-; *no pl*) illegality.
'ungesittet *adj* uncivilized.
'ungestört *adj and adv* undisturbed.
'ungestraft **I** *adj* unpunished. **II** *adv* with impunity: **~ davonkommen** go unpunished, F get off scot-free.
ungestüm ['ʊngəʃtyːm] *adj* impetuous.
'Ungestüm *n* (-s; *no pl*) impetuosity.
'ungesund *adj a. fig.* unhealthy.
'ungeteilt *adj a. fig.* undivided.
ungetrübt ['ʊngətryːpt] *adj fig.* unspoilt.
Ungetüm ['ʊngətyːm] *n* (-s; -e) monster.
'ungeübt *adj* untrained.
'ungewaschen *adj and adv* unwashed.
'ungewiß *adj* uncertain: **j-n im ungewissen lassen** keep s.o. guessing.
'Ungewißheit *f* (-; *no pl*) uncertainty: **in ~ schweben** be (kept) in suspense.
'ungewöhnlich *adj* unusual.

'**ungewohnt** *adj* strange, new (*für* to).
'**ungewollt** *adj* unintentional, unintended (*effect etc*), unwanted (*baby*).
'**ungezählt** *adj* uncounted, countless.
'**ungezähmt** *adj* untamed.
Ungeziefer ['ʊngətsiːfər] *n* (-s; *no pl*) *a. fig.* vermin.
'**ungezogen** *adj* naughty. '**Ungezogenheit** *f* (-; *no pl*) naughtiness.
'**ungezügelt** *fig.* **I** *adj* unbridled. **II** *adv* unrestrainedly.
'**ungezwungen** *adj* relaxed, informal.
'**Ungezwungenheit** *f* (-; *no pl*) ease.
'**ungiftig** *adj* nontoxic.
'**Unglaube** *m* unbelief. '**unglaubhaft** → **unglaubwürdig.** '**ungläubig** *adj* incredulous, disbelieving, *a. eccl.* unbelieving. **un'glaublich** *adj* incredible, unbelievable. '**unglaubwürdig** *adj* untrustworthy, implausible (*reasons etc*).
'**ungleich** **I** *adj* **1.** unequal, unlike, dissimilar. **II** *adv* **2.** ~ *lang* (*groß*) unequal in length (size); ~ *verteilt* unevenly distributed. **3.** far *better etc.*
'**Ungleichgewicht** *n* imbalance.
'**Ungleichheit** *f* (-; *no pl*) **1.** dissimilarity, unlikeness. **2.** inequality.
'**ungleichmäßig** *adj* uneven, irregular.
'**Unglück** *n* (-[e]s; -e) a) misfortune, b) bad luck, c) mishap, d) disaster: *es ist* (*weiter*) *kein* ~*!* it is no tragedy!; *zu allem* ~ to crown it all; ~ *bringen* bring ill (*or* bad) luck; *in sein* ~ *rennen* head for disaster. '**unglücklich** *adj* a) unfortunate, b) unlucky, c) unhappy, miserable: ~ *enden* end badly; ~ *verliebt* crossed in love. '**unglücklicher'weise** *adv* unfortunately. '**unglückselig** *adj* a) unfortunate, b) disastrous, fatal.
'**Unglücks|fall** *m* **1.** accident. **2.** misadventure. ~**rabe** *m* unlucky fellow. ~**tag** *m* black day. ~**zahl** *f* unlucky number.
'**Ungnade** *f* (-; *no pl*) disfavo(u)r: *in* ~ *fallen* fall out of favo(u)r (*bei* with).
'**ungnädig** *adj* ungracious.
'**ungültig** *adj* invalid, (null and) void, *coin*: not legal tender, *vote*: spoilt, *goal*: disallowed: ~ *machen* cancel (*ticket etc*); *et. für* ~ *erklären* invalidate s.th., declare s.th. null and void.
'**Ungültigkeit** *f* (-; *no pl*) invalidity.
'**Ungunst** *f* (-; *no pl*) *zu j-s* ~*en* to s.o.'s disadvantage. '**ungünstig** *adj* unfavo(u)rable, inconvenient (*date etc*).

'**ungut** *adj* bad: *ein* ~*es Gefühl haben* have misgivings (*bei* about); *nichts für* ~*!* no offen/ce (*Am.* -se) meant.
'**unhaltbar** *adj* **1.** untenable (*arguments etc*). **2.** intolerable (*conditions*). **3.** *sports*: unstoppable (*ball, shot, etc*).
'**unhandlich** *adj* unwieldy.
'**unhar,monisch** *adj a. fig.* discordant.
'**Unheil** *n* (-s; *no pl*) a) harm, b) disaster: ~ *anrichten* wreak havoc.
un'heilbar *adj* incurable: ~ *krank* suffering from an incurable disease.
'**unheilbringend** *adj* fatal. '**unheilvoll** *adj* **1.** disastrous. **2.** sinister (*look etc*).
'**unheimlich** **I** *adj* **1.** uncanny, weird (*both a. fig.*), eerie, F creepy. **2.** F *fig.* tremendous, terrific. **II** *adv* **3.** F *fig.* tremendously, awfully: ~ *gut* terrific, fantastic; ~ *viel* a tremendous lot of.
'**unhöflich** *adj* impolite.
'**Unhöflichkeit** *f* (-; *no pl*) impoliteness.
'**Unhold** *m* (-[e]s; -e) monster, fiend.
'**un'hörbar** *adj* inaudible.
'**unhygi,enisch** *adj* unhygienic.
Uni ['ʊni] *f* (-; -s) F university.
Uniform [uni'fɔrm] *f* (-; -en) uniform. **uniformiert** [-'miːrt] *adj* in uniform.
Unikum ['uːnikʊm] *n* (-s; -ka) **1.** unique specimen. **2.** (*pl* -s) F character.
'**uninteres,sant** *adj* uninteresting, not interesting. '**uninteres,siert** *adj* uninterested (*an dat* in).
Union [u'nioːn] *f* (-; -en) union: *die* ~ the Christian-Democrat Union (*or* Party).
universal [univɛr'zaːl] *adj* universal.
Univer'sal|erbe *m* sole heir. ~**mittel** *n* universal remedy, *a. fig.* panacea.
universell [univɛr'zɛl] *adj* universal.
Universität [univɛrzi'tɛːt] *f* (-; -en) (*auf or an der* ~ at the) university; *e-e* ~ *besuchen* go to university.
Universi'täts... university (*library, hospital, studies, etc*).
Universum [uni'vɛrzʊm] *n* (-s; *no pl*) universe.
unken ['ʊŋkən] *v/i* (h) F *fig.* croak.
'**unkenntlich** *adj* unrecognizable.
'**Unkenntnis** *f* (-; *no pl*) ignorance: *in* ~ (*gen*) unaware of *the danger etc*, ignorant of *the facts etc*; *j-n in* ~ *lassen* keep s.o. in the dark (*über acc* about).
'**unklar** *adj* unclear, *pred* not clear, *a.* vague, obscure, muddled; *im* ~*en sein* be in the dark (*über acc* about).

'**Unklarheit** *f* (-; *no pl*) unclearness, lack of clarity, vagueness.

'**unklug** *adj* unwise, imprudent.

'**unkompli,ziert** *adj* uncomplicated.

'**unkontrol,lierbar** *adj* uncontrollable.

'**unkontrol,liert** *adj* uncontrolled.

'**Unkosten** *pl* costs, expenses: *allgemeine (or laufende)* ∼ running expenses, ✝ overhead; → *stürzen* 6.

'**Unkraut** *n* (-[e]s; ∻er) weed(s): *fig.* ∼ *vergeht nicht* ill weeds grow apace. ∼*vertilgungsmittel* *n* weed killer.

'**unkritisch** *adj* uncritical.

'**unkulti,viert** *adj* uncultivated.

'**unkündbar** *adj* permanent (*post*), contract *etc*: not terminable: *er ist* ∼ F he can't be sacked.

'**unlängst** *adv* lately, recently.

'**unlauter** *adj fig.* dubious: ✝ ∼*er Wettbewerb* unfair competition.

'**unleserlich** *adj* illegible.

'**unlieb** *adj* *es ist mir nicht* ∼(, *daß*) it suits me quite fine (that). '**unliebenswürdig** *adj* unamiable, unfriendly. '**Unliebenswürdigkeit** *f* (-; *no pl*) unamiableness, unfriendliness.

unliebsam ['ʊnliːpzaːm] *adj* unpleasant.

'**unlini,iert** *adj* unruled.

'**unlogisch** *adj* illogical.

un'lösbar *adj* insoluble (*problem etc*).

un'löslich *adj* 🜊 insoluble.

'**Unlust** *f* (-; *no pl*) a) listlessness, b) aversion: *mit* ∼ with reluctance.

'**unlustig** *adj* listless, reluctant.

'**unma,nierlich** *adj* ill-mannered.

'**unmännlich** *adj* effeminate.

'**unmaßgeblich** *adj* unauthoritative: *iro. nach m-r* ∼*en Meinung* in my humble opinion.

'**unmäßig** *adj* excessive, immoderate. '**Unmäßigkeit** *f* (-; *no pl*) immoderateness, excess.

'**Unmenge** *f* (-; -n) (*von* of) vast (*or* enormous) amount (*or* number), F loads.

'**Unmensch** *m* monster, brute: F *sei kein* ∼*!* have a heart! '**unmenschlich** *adj* 1. inhuman, cruel. 2. F *fig.* awful. '**Unmenschlichkeit** *f* (-; *no pl*) inhumanity, cruelty.

'**unmerklich** *adj* imperceptible.

'**unme,thodisch** *adj* unmethodical.

'**unmißverständlich** I *adj* unmistakable. II *adv* a) unmistakably, b) plainly.

'**unmittelbar** I *adj* immediate, direct. II

adv immediately, directly: ∼ *vor* (*dat*) a) right in front of, b) *time*: just before; ∼ *bevorstehen* be imminent.

'**unmö,bliert** *adj* unfurnished.

'**unmo,dern** *adj* outmoded, dated.

'**unmöglich** I *adj* impossible (*a.* F *fig. person, dress, situation, etc*): ℒ*es leisten* (*verlangen*) do (ask) the impossible; *fig.* ∼ *aussehen* look a sight; *sich* ∼ *machen* a) compromise o.s., b) make a fool of o.s. II *adv* not possibly: *ich kann es* ∼ *tun* I can't possibly do it. '**Unmöglichkeit** *f* (-; *no pl*) impossibility.

'**unmo,ralisch** *adj* immoral.

'**unmoti,viert** *adj* unmotivated.

'**unmündig** *adj* under age, minor.

'**unmusi,kalisch** *adj* unmusical.

'**Unmut** *m* (-[e]s; *no pl*) annoyance (*über acc* at).

unnachahmlich ['ʊnnaːxˀaːmlɪç] *adj* inimitable.

'**unnachgiebig** *adj* unyielding.

'**unnachsichtig** *adj* strict, severe.

un'nahbar *adj* unapproachable.

'**unna,türlich** *adj* 1. unnatural (*a. fig.*). 2. affected.

'**unnötig** *adj* unnecessary.

unnütz ['ʊnnʏts] *adj* useless, pointless.

'**unordentlich** *adj* disorderly, untidy.

'**Unordnung** *f* (-; *no pl*) disorder, mess: *in* ∼ in a mess; *in* ∼ *bringen* mess s.th. up.

'**unor,ganisch** *adj* inorganic.

'**unpar,teilsch** *adj* impartial. '**Unpar,teiische** *m* (-n; -n) *sports*: referee.

'**unpassend** *adj* 1. inappropriate, unsuitable. 2. improper. 3. untimely.

'**unpas,sierbar** *adj* impassable.

unpäßlich ['ʊnpɛslɪç] *adj* ∼ *sein, sich* ∼ *fühlen* be indisposed, feel unwell. '**Unpäßlichkeit** *f* (-; -en) indisposition.

'**unpatri,otisch** *adj* unpatriotic.

'**Unper,son** *f* (-; -en) nonperson.

'**unper,sönlich** *adj* impersonal.

'**unpo,litisch** *adj* apolitical.

'**unpopu,lär** *adj* unpopular.

'**unpraktisch** *adj* impractical.

'**unproble,matisch** *adj* unproblematic.

'**unproduk,tiv** *adj* unproductive, ✝ nonproductive.

'**unpünktlich** *adj* unpunctual. '**Unpünktlichkeit** *f* (-; *no pl*) unpunctuality.

'**unqualifi,ziert** *adj* unqualified.

'**unra,siert** *adj* unshaven.

Unrat ['ʊnraːt] m (-[e]s; no pl) rubbish, Am. garbage: F ~ **wittern** smell a rat.
'**unratio,nell** adj inefficient.
'**unratsam** adj inadvisable.
'**unrecht** adj wrong: **et. Ωes tun** do s.th. wrong. '**Unrecht** n (-[e]s; no pl) wrong, injustice: **j-m Ω tun** do s.o. wrong; **im ~ sein, Ω haben** be (in the) wrong, a. be mistaken; **j-m Ω geben** disagree with s.o., fig. result etc: prove s.o. wrong; **j-n ins ~ setzen** put s.o. in the wrong; **zu ~** wrong(ful)ly, unjustly; **nicht zu ~** not without good reason.
'**unrechtmäßig** adj wrongful, unlawful.
'**unredlich** adj dishonest.
'**Unredlichkeit** f (-; no pl) dishonesty.
'**unre,ell** adj dishonest.
'**unregelmäßig** adj irregular. '**Unregelmäßigkeit** f (-; -en) irregularity.
'**unreif** adj 1. unripe. 2. fig. immature.
'**unrein** adj impure (a. fig.), bad (skin).
'**Unreinheit** f (-; -en) impurity.
'**unreinlich** adj unclean.
'**unren,tabel** adj unprofitable.
un'rettbar adj irrecoverable: ~ **verloren** irretrievably lost, person: beyond help.
'**unrichtig** adj incorrect, wrong.
'**Unrichtigkeit** f (-; -en) 1. no pl incorrectness. 2. mistake, error.
'**Unruh** f (-; -en) balance wheel.
'**Unruhe** f (-; no pl) 1. restlessness. 2. uneasiness, anxiety. 3. commotion, tumult: pol. **~n** unrest, disturbances.
'**Unruheherd** m fig. trouble spot.
'**Unruhestifter(in** f) m troublemaker.
'**unruhig** adj 1. restless. 2. fig. troubled (sleep, times). 3. fig. uneasy, worried. 4. fig. noisy. 5. fig. choppy (sea).
'**unrühmlich** adj inglorious.
uns [ʊns] I pers pron 1. us, to us: **ein Freund von ~** a friend of ours; **wir sehen ~ selten** we seldom see each other. II reflex pron 2. ourselves: **wir waschen ~** we wash (ourselves). 3. each other, one another.
'**unsachgemäß** adj improper, inexpert.
'**unsachlich** adj unobjective, irrelevant, pred beside the point: ~ **werden** become personal.
unsagbar [ʊn'zaːkbaːr], **unsäglich** [ʊn'zɛːklɪç] adj unspeakable.
'**unsanft** adj rough: fig. **ein ~es Erwachen** a rude awakening.
'**unsauber** adj 1. dirty. 2. fig. a) sloven-

ly, b) shady, dubious, c) sports: unfair.
'**unschädlich** adj harmless: ~ **machen** render harmless, neutralize, put s.o. out of action, lay criminal by the heels.
'**unscharf** adj 1. phot. blurred: opt. ~ **(eingestellt)** out of focus. 2. fig. hazy.
un'**schätzbar** adj invaluable.
'**unscheinbar** adj insignificant, inconspicuous, plain, Am. homely.
'**unschicklich** adj unseemly, improper.
un'**schlagbar** adj unbeatable.
'**unschlüssig** adj irresolute. '**Unschlüssigkeit** f (-; no pl) irresolution.
'**unschön** adj 1. unlovely, ugly. 2. fig. a) unkind, pred not nice, b) unpleasant.
'**Unschuld** f (-; no pl) innocence.
'**unschuldig** adj innocent (an dat of): 🏛 **sich für ~ erklären** plead not guilty.
'**unschwer** adv easily, without difficulty.
'**unselbständig** adj 1. dependent (on others), helpless. 2. employed: **Einkünfte aus ~er Arbeit** wage and salaries income. '**Unselbständigkeit** f (- no pl) lack of independence.
'**unselig** adj unfortunate, fatal.
unser ['ʊnzər] I pos pron ours, ours: **der (die, das) ~e** (or **uns[e]rige**) ours; **wir haben das ~e getan** we have done our bit. II gen of **wir**: of us.
'**unsereiner, unsereins, unseresgleichen** indef pron F people like us.
'**unser(e)twegen** adv 1. for our sake. 2. because of us.
'**unseri,ös** adj dubious.
'**unsicher** adj 1. unsafe, insecure, risky: F **die Gegend ~ machen** criminal etc: prowl (humor. tourists etc: infest) the place. 2. unsteady, shaky (a. fig. in dat in). 4. insecure, unsure (of o.s.): **j-n ~ machen** make s.o. feel insecure. '**Unsicherheit** f (-; no pl) 1. unsafeness, insecurity. 2. uncertainty. 3. unsteadiness. 4. unsureness (of o.s.), insecurity. '**Unsicherheitsfaktor** m element of uncertainty.
'**unsichtbar** adj invisible.
'**Unsichtbarkeit** f (-; no pl) invisibility.
'**Unsinn** m (-[e]s; no pl) 1. (~ **reden** talk) nonsense (or rubbish). 2. ~ **machen** fool around. '**unsinnig** adj 1. unreasonable, absurd. 2. F tremendous.
'**Unsitte** f (-; -n) bad habit.
'**unsittlich** adj immoral, indecent.
'**Unsittlichkeit** f (-; no pl) immorality.

'unso,lide *adj* 1. unsolid. 2. loose (*life, person, etc*). 3. dubious (*firm etc*).

'unsozi,al *adj* antisocial.

'unsportlich *adj* 1. unathletic. 2. *fig.* unfair, unsporting.

un'sterblich I *adj* immortal. II *adv* F awfully: ~ *verliebt* madly in love (*in acc* with). Un'sterblichkeit *f* (-; *no pl*) immortality.

'unstet *adj* 1. inconstant. 2. restless.

un'stillbar *adj* unquenchable (*thirst*), insatiable (*hunger*), *fig.* unappeasable.

'Unstimmigkeit *f* (-; -en) *usu. pl* 1. discrepancy. 2. disagreement, difference.

'unstreitig *adj* indisputable.

'Unsumme *f* (-; -n) enormous sum.

'unsym,metrisch *adj* asymmetrical.

'unsym,pathisch *adj* disagreeable, unpleasant: *er ist mir* ~ I don't like him.

'Untat *f* (-; -en) atrocity, outrage.

'untätig *adj* inactive, idle. 'Untätigkeit *f* (-; *no pl*) inactivity, idleness.

'untauglich *adj* unfit (*a.* ✕), unsuitable. 'Untauglichkeit *f* (-; *no pl*) unfitness.

un'teilbar *adj* indivisible.

unten ['ʊntən] *adv* a) below, b) downstairs: *da* ~ down there; *nach* ~ down(wards), *a.* downstairs; ~ *auf der Seite* at the bottom of the page; *was versteht man* ~ ...? what is meant by ...?; → *Bedingung, Hand, Träne etc.* 2. among: *einer* ~ *hundert* one in a hundred; ~ *anderem* among other things; ~ *uns gesagt* between you and me; *wir sind ganz* ~ *uns* we are quite alone. 3. during: ~ *s-r Regierung* under (*or* during) his reign.

below: *von oben bis* ~ from top to bottom (*person*: to toe); F *er ist bei mir* ~ *durch* I am through with him.

'untenerwähnt, 'untengenannt *adj* undermentioned, mentioned below.

unter ['ʊntər] *prep* (*dat*) 1. under, below, *a.* less than: ~ *Null* below zero; ~ *sich haben* be in charge of; *was versteht man* ~ ...? what is meant by ...?; → *Bedingung, Hand, Träne etc.* 2. among: *einer* ~ *hundert* one in a hundred; ~ *anderem* among other things; ~ *uns gesagt* between you and me; *wir sind ganz* ~ *uns* we are quite alone. 3. during: ~ *s-r Regierung* under (*or* during) his reign.

'Unter|abteilung *f* subdivision. ~arm *m* forearm. ~art *f* subspecies. ~ausschuß *m* subcommittee. ~bau *m* (-[e]s; -ten) 1. substructure, foundation. 2. *no pl fig.* base, ✝ *etc* infrastructure.

'unterbelichten *v/t* (*insep, no* -ge-, h) underexpose.

'unterbeschäftigt *adj* underemployed.

'unterbesetzt *adj* understaffed.

'unterbewerten *v/t* (*insep, no* -ge-, h) undervalue, *fig. a.* underrate.

'unterbewußt *adj* subconscious. 'Unterbewußtsein *n* (-s; *no pl*) the subconscious: *im* ~ subconsciously.

'unterbezahlt *adj* underpaid.

unter'bieten *v/t* (*irr, insep, no* -ge-, h, → *bieten*) underbid, undercut (*price*), undersell (*competitors*), beat (*record*).

unter'binden *v/t* (*irr, insep, no* -ge-, h, → *binden*) *fig.* stop, prevent.

unter'bleiben *v/i* (*irr, insep, no* -ge-, sn, → *bleiben*) 1. be left undone, not to take place. 2. stop, cease.

'Unter'bodenschutz *m* mot. underseal, *Am.* undercoat.

unter'brechen (*irr, insep, no* -ge-, h, → *brechen*) I *v/t* interrupt, *teleph.* cut off, hold up (*game*), ⚖ adjourn: *die Fahrt* (*or Reise*) ~ break one's journey. II *sich* ~ pause. Unter'brechung *f* (-; -en) interruption, break, *a.* stopover.

unter'breiten *v/t* (*insep, no* -ge-, h) submit (*dat* to).

'unterbringen *v/t* (*irr, sep,* -ge-, h, → *bringen*) 1. accommodate, *a.* put *s.o.* up: *j-n* ~ *in* put s.o. into (⚖ commit *s.o.* to) *an institution etc*; *j-n* ~ *in* (*or bei*) get s.o. a job with *a firm etc*; F *fig. ich kann ihn nicht* ~ I can't place him. 2. a) store, b) stow (away): *et.* ~ *in* (*dat*) get (*or* fit s.th. into, ◉ install s.th. in. 3. ✝ place *capital, orders* (*bei* with): *ein Buch bei e-m Verlag* ~ have a book accepted by publishers. Unter'bringung *f* (-; -en) accommodation, housing, ⚖ committal (*in dat* to). 'Unterbringungsmöglichkeit(en *pl*) *f* accommodation.

'unterbuttern *v/t* (*sep,* h) F *j-n* ~ push s.o. under.

'Unterdeck *n* ⚓ lower deck.

unterder'hand *adv* secretly, on the quiet: ~ *verkaufen* sell *s.th.* privately.

unter'dessen *adv* in the meantime.

unter'drücken *v/t* (*insep, no* -ge-, h) suppress (*a. publication*), *a.* stifle (*laughter, yawn, etc*), oppress (*people*), put down, quell (*rebellion*). Unter'drücker *m* (-s; -) oppressor. Unter'drückung *f* (-; -en) suppression, oppression.

'unterdurchschnittlich *adj* below average.

'untere *adj* lower.

'untereinander[1] *adv* one below the

other. **unterein'ander**[2] *adv* among one another (*or* each other, themselves, yourselves, *etc*).

'**unterentwickelt** *adj* underdeveloped (*a. phot.*), *a.* backward (*child, country, etc*), *psych.* subnormal.

'**unterernährt** *adj* underfed, undernourished. '**Unterernährung** *f* (-; *no pl*) malnutrition, undernourishment.

Unter'fangen *n* (-s; *no pl*) **1.** venture, undertaking. **2.** attempt.

Unter'führung *f* (-; -en) a) underpass, b) subway, *Am.* pedestrian underpass.

'**Unterfunkti,on** *f* ⚕ hypofunction.

'**Untergang** *m* (-[e]s; -e) **1.** *astr.* setting. **2.** ⚓ sinking. **3.** *fig.* (down)fall, decline.

'**Untergattung** *f* subgenus.

Unter'gebene *m, f* (-n; -n) subordinate.

'**untergehen** *v/i* (*irr, sep, -ge-, sn*, → **gehen**) go down, go under (*both a. fig.*), ⚓ *a.* sink, *astr. a.* set: *fig.* **im Lärm ~** be drowned out (*or* lost) by the noise.

'**untergeordnet** *adj* **1.** subordinate (*dat* to). **2.** *fig.* secondary (*importance etc*).

'**Unter|geschoß** *n* basement. **~gestell** *n mot.* underframe. **~gewicht** *n* (**~ haben** be) underweight.

unter|'gliedern *v/t* (*insep, no* -ge-, h) subdivide. **~'graben** *v/t* (*irr, insep, no* -ge-, h, → **graben**) *fig.* undermine.

'**Untergrund** *m* (-[e]s; -e) **1.** *geol.* subsoil. **2.** *paint.* ground(ing). **3.** *no pl pol.* (**in den ~ gehen** go) underground. **~bahn** *f* underground, *in London: a.* tube, *Am.* subway. **~bewegung** *f pol.* underground movement. **~kämpfer(in** *f*) *m pol.* underground fighter.

'**unterhalb** **I** *prep* (*gen*) below, under. **II** *adv* below, underneath.

'**Unterhalt** *m* (-[e]s; *no pl*) **1.** support, maintenance. **2.** → **Lebensunterhalt**.

unter'halten (*irr, insep, no* -ge-, h, → **halten**) **I** *v/t* **1.** maintain, support. **2.** keep up (*correspondence etc*). **3.** amuse, entertain. **II** **sich ~** **4.** talk (*mit* with, to). **5.** **sich** (*gut*) **~** enjoy o.s., have a good time. **unter'haltend** → **unterhaltsam**. **Unter'halter** *m* (-s; -) entertainer. **unter'haltsam** *adj* entertaining.

'**Unterhalts|anspruch** *m* maintenance claim. **~beihilfe** *f* maintenance grant. **⌀berechtigt** *adj* entitled to maintenance. **~kosten** *pl* maintenance costs.

Unter'haltung *f* (-; -en) **1.** entertain-

ment. **2.** conversation, talk. **3.** *no pl* upkeep, maintenance.

Unter'haltungs... entertainment (*concert, film, industry, etc*). **~branche** *f* (*in der ~* in) show business. **~elek,tronik** *f* video and audio systems. **~litera,tur** *f* light fiction. **~mu,sik** *f* light music. **~ro,man** *m* light novel. **~wert** *m* (-[e]s; *no pl*) entertainment value.

'**Unterhändler** *m* (-s; -) negotiator.

Unter'handlung *f* (-; -en) negotiation.

'**Unterhaus** *n* (-es; *no pl*) *parl. Br.* House of Commons.

'**Unterhemd** *n* vest, *Am.* undershirt.

unter'höhlen *v/t* (*insep, no* -ge-, h) *a. fig.* undermine.

'**Unterholz** *n* (-es; *no pl*) undergrowth.

'**Unterhose** *f* (**e-e ~** a pair of) underpants.

'**unterirdisch** *adj* subterranean, underground.

unter'jochen *v/t* (*insep, no* -ge-, h) subjugate.

'**unterjubeln** *v/t* (*sep*, h) F *j-m et.* **~** foist s.th. (off) on s.o.

'**Unterkiefer** *m anat.* lower jaw.

'**Unterkleid** *n* (full-length) slip.

'**Unterkleidung** *f* underwear.

'**unterkommen** *v/i* (*irr, sep, -ge-, sn*, → **kommen**) find accommodation (*or* lodgings): **~ in** (*dat*) find a place in; F **~ bei** find a job with *a firm etc*.

'**Unterkörper** *m* lower part of the body.

'**unterkriegen** *v/t* (*sep*, h) F *j-n* **~** get s.o. down.

Unter'kühlung *f* (-; -en) ⚕ hypothermia.

'**Unterkunft** *f* (-; -e) accommodation, lodging(s), quarters: **~ und Verpflegung** board and lodgings.

'**Unterlage** *f* (-; -n) **1.** ⚙ base, support. **2.** *fig.* basis. **3.** *pl* a) documents, records, b) data.

'**Unterlaß** *m* **ohne ~** incessantly.

unter'lassen *v/t* (*irr, insep, no* -ge-, h, → **lassen**) *et.* **~** a) omit (*or* fail) to do s.th., b) refrain from (doing) s.th.; *unterlaß das!* stop that!

Unter'lassung *f* (-; -en) omission.

Unter'lassungs|klage *f* ⚖ action for injunction. **~sünde** *f* sin of omission.

'**Unterlauf** *m* (-[e]s; -e) lower course.

unter'laufen (*irr, insep, no* -ge-, → **laufen**) **I** *v/t* (h) F dodge. **II** *v/i* (sn) *mir ist ein Fehler* **~** I've made a mistake.

'**unterlegen**¹ v/t (sep, h) lay (or put) s.th. under. **unter'legen**² adj **1.** inferior (dat to). **2.** losing, defeated.

Unter'legene m, f (-n; -n) loser.

Unter'legenheit f (-; no pl) inferiority.

'**Unterleib** m abdomen, belly.

'**Unterleibs...** abdominal (pain etc).

unter'liegen v/i (irr, insep, no -ge-, sn, → **liegen**) **1.** (dat) be defeated (or beaten) (by), lose (to), fig. succumb (to). **2.** be subject (dat to rule etc): **es unterliegt k-m Zweifel, daß** there is no doubt that.

'**Unterlippe** f lower lip.

Unter'malung f (-; -en) background.

unter'mauern v/t (insep, no -ge-, h) a. fig. underpin.

'**untermengen** v/t (sep, h) mix in.

'**Untermensch** m subhuman creature.

'**Untermiete** f (-; no pl) **1.** subtenancy: **in** (or **zur**) ~ **wohnen** be a subtenant (Am. roomer), lodge (**bei** with). **2.** sublease: → **untervermieten**. '**Untermieter(in** f) m subtenant, lodger, Am. roomer.

untermi'nieren v/t (insep, h) undermine.

unter'nehmen v/t (irr, insep, no -ge-, h, → **nehmen**) make, go on (a trip etc), do (s.th.): **et.** ~ **gegen** a. j-n take action against s.o., b) **et.** do s.th. about s.th.; **er unternahm nichts** he did nothing.

Unter'nehmen n (-s; -n) **1.** firm, business, enterprise, company. **2.** undertaking, enterprise, project: (**gewagtes**) ~ venture. **3.** ✕ operation.

Unter'nehmens|berater m management consultant. **~führung** f (-; no pl) management.

Unter'nehmer m (-s; -) a) entrepreneur b) contractor, c) employer, d) industrialist. **unter'nehmerisch** adj entrepreneurial. **Unter'nehmerschaft** f (-; no pl) die employers, the management. **Unter'nehmertum** n (-s; no pl) **1.** entrepreneurship: **freies** ~ free enterprise. **2.** → **Unternehmerschaft**.

Unter'nehmungsgeist m (spirit of) enterprise, initiative.

unter'nehmungslustig adj enterprising.

'**Unteroffi|zier** m a) noncommissioned officer (abbr. NCO), b) sergeant, ✓ corporal.

'**unterordnen** (sep, h) **I** v/t subordinate (dat to). **II sich** ~ submit (dat to).

'**Unterordnung** f (-; -en) **1.** no pl subordination. **2.** biol. suborder.

'**unterprivile,giert** adj underprivileged.

Unter'redung f (-; -en) talk, conversation.

Unterricht ['ʊntərɪçt] m (-[e]s; no pl) instruction, lessons, classes: **j-m** ~ (**in Deutsch**) **geben** teach s.o. (German), give (German) lessons to s.o.

unter'richten (insep, no -ge-, h) **I** v/t, v/i **1.** teach, give lessons (dat to): **j-n** (**in Deutsch**) ~ teach s.o. (German); **Mathematik** ~ teach mathematics. **2.** inform (**von, über** acc of): (**gut**) **unterrichtete Kreise** (well-)informed circles. **II sich** ~ inform o.s. (**über** acc about).

'**Unterrichts|einheit** f teaching unit. **~raum** m classroom. **~stunde** f lesson.

Unter'richtung f (-; no pl) **1.** instruction. **2.** (**zu Ihrer** ~) for your) information.

'**Unterrock** m slip.

unter'sagen v/t (insep, no -ge-, h) forbid, adm. prohibit: **j-m** ~ **zu inf** forbid s.o. to inf, prohibit s.o. from ger.

'**Untersatz** m (-es; ⁓e) stand, for glasses: mat, for flowerpots: saucer: F **fahrbarer** ~ wheels.

'**Unterschall** m subsonic (speed etc).

unter'schätzen v/t (insep, no -ge-, h) underestimate.

unter'scheiden (irr, insep, no -ge-, h, → **scheiden**) **I** v/t, v/i distinguish (**zwischen** between, **von** from): **et.** ~ **von** a. tell s.th. apart from; **das unterscheidet ihn von ...** that sets him apart from ... **II sich** ~ differ (**von** from, **dadurch daß** in ger). **unter'scheidend** adj distinctive.

Unter'scheidung f (-; -en) **1.** differentiation. **2.** difference. **Unter'scheidungsmerkmal** n distinguishing mark.

'**Unterschenkel** m anat. lower leg.

'**Unterschicht** f sociol. lower classes.

Unterschied ['ʊntərʃiːt] m (-[e]s; -e) difference: **e-n** ~ **machen** (**zwischen** between) distinguish, a. discriminate; **das macht k-n** ~ that makes no difference; **ohne** ~ indiscriminately; **zum** ~ **von** unlike, in contrast to; **das ist ein großer** ~ that makes a great difference.

'**unterschiedlich** adj different, varying, variable; ~ **behandeln** discriminate between. '**unterschiedslos I** adj indiscriminate. **II** adv without exception.

unter'schlagen v/t (irr, insep, no -ge-, h,

→ *schlagen*) embezzle (*money*), intercept (*letter*), suppress (*last will etc*), hold back (*facts*).

Unter'schlagung *f* (-; -en) embezzlement, interception, suppression.

'**Unterschlupf** *m* (-[e]s; -e) **1.** hiding place, F hideout. **2.** shelter, refuge.

'**unterschlüpfen** *v/i* (*sep*, sn) **1.** hide. **2.** take shelter (*bei* with).

unter'schreiben *v/t, v/i* (*irr, insep, no* -ge-, h, → *schreiben*) **1.** sign. **2.** F *fig.* subscribe (to).

unter'schreiten *v/t* (*irr, insep, no* -ge-, h, → *schreiten*) fall short of.

'**Unterschrift** *f* (-; -en) signature: → *setzen* 1. '**Unterschriftenmappe** *f* signature blotting book. '**unterschriftsberechtigt** *adj* authorized to sign.

'**unterschwellig** [-ʃvelɪç] *adj* subliminal.

'**Unterseeboot** *n* submarine.

'**unterseeisch** [-zeːɪʃ] *adj* submarine.

'**Unterseite** *f* underside, bottom.

untersetzt [-'zɛtst] *adj* stocky.

'**unterst** *adj* lowest: *das 2e zuoberst kehren* turn everything upside down.

'**Unterstand** *m* shelter, ✗ *a.* dugout.

unter'stehen (*irr, insep, no* -ge-, h, → *stehen*) **I** *v/i* **j-m ∼** be subordinate (*or* answerable) to s.o., be under s.o.'s supervision. **II** *sich ∼ zu inf* dare to *inf*: *was ∼ Sie sich?* how dare you?

'**unterstellen¹** (*sep*, h) **I** *v/t* put *s.th.* in(to *in dat*). **II** *sich ∼* take shelter.

unter'stellen² *v/t* (*insep, no* -ge-, h) **1.** *j-m j-n* (*et.*) ∼ put s.o. in charge of s.o. (s.th.). **2.** *fig. j-m et.* ∼ impute s.th. to s.o. **3.** suppose, assume. **Unter'stellung** *f* (-; -en) allegation, suggestion.

unter'streichen *v/t* (*irr, insep, no* -ge-, h, → *streichen*) *a. fig.* underline.

'**Unterstufe** *f* (-; -en) *ped.* lower grades.

unter'stützen *v/t* (*insep, no* -ge-, h) a) support, back (up), b) assist, aid, help. **Unter'stützung** *f* (-; -en) **1.** a) support, b) aid, grant, c) subsidy, d) benefit: ∼ *beziehen* be on social security. **2.** *fig.* support, backing, aid, assistance.

unter'suchen *v/t* (*insep, no* -ge-, h) examine (*a. ✚*), investigate (*a. ✚*), inspect, check, ✚ *or fig.* analy/se (*Am.* -ze): *et. ∼ auf* (*acc*) test s.th. for.

Unter'suchung *f* (-; -en) examination, ✚ *a.* checkup, investigation, inspection, test, ✚ *or fig.* analysis.

Unter'suchungs|ausschuß *m* fact-finding committee. **∼gefangene** *m, f* prisoner on remand. **∼gefängnis** *n* remand prison. **∼haft** *f* detention pending trial: *in ∼ sein* be on remand. **∼richter(in** *f*) *m* examining magistrate.

'**Untertan** [-taːn] *m* (-s, -en; -en) subject.

'**Untertasse** *f* saucer.

'**untertauchen** *v/i* (*sep*, sn) **1.** *a. v/t* (h) duck. **2.** *fig.* disappear, go into hiding, *esp. pol.* go underground.

'**Unterteil** *m, n* lower part, base.

unter'teilen *v/t* (*insep, no* -ge-, h) subdivide (*in acc* into). **Unter'teilung** *f* (-; -en) subdivision (*in acc* into).

'**Untertitel** *m* subtitle, *film: a.* caption.

'**Unterton** *m a. fig.* undertone.

unter'treiben *v/t, v/i* (*irr, insep, no* -ge-, h, → *treiben*) understate. **Unter'treibung** *f* (-; -en) understatement.

unter'tunneln *v/t* (*insep, no* -ge-, h) tunnel through.

'**untervermieten** *v/t* (*only inf and pp* untervermietet, h) sublet.

'**unterversichert** *adj* underinsured.

unter'wandern *v/t* (*insep, no* -ge-, h) infiltrate. **Unter'wanderung** *f* (-; -en) infiltration.

'**Unterwäsche** *f* (-; *no pl*) underwear.

'**Unterwasser...** underwater (*camera, massage, etc*).

unterwegs [ʊntɐ'veːks] *adv* on the (*or* one's) way (*nach* to), away: *immer ∼* always on the move.

unter'weisen *v/t* (*irr, insep, no* -ge-, h, → *weisen*) instruct. **Unter'weisung** *f* (-; -en) instruction.

'**Unterwelt** *f* (-; *no pl*) underworld.

unter'werfen (*irr, insep, no* -ge-, h, → *werfen*) **I** *v/t* **1.** subdue, subjugate. **2.** subject (*dat to test etc*). **II** *sich ∼ a. fig.* submit (*dat* to). **Unter'werfung** *f* (-; -en) **1.** subjugation, subjection. **2.** *fig.* submission (*unter acc* to). **unterworfen** [-'vɔrfən] *adj* subject (*dat* to).

unterwürfig [ʊntɐ'vʏrfɪç] *adj* submissive, servile. **Unter'würfigkeit** *f* (-; *no pl*) submissiveness, servility.

unter'zeichnen *v/t, v/i* (*insep, no* -ge-, h) sign. **Unter'zeichner** *m* (-s; -) signer, *the* undersigned, signatory (*gen* to). **Unter'zeichnete** *m, f* (-n; -n) the undersigned. **Unter'zeichnung** *f* (-; -en) signing.

'**unterziehen**¹ *v/t* (*irr, sep,* -ge-, h, → *ziehen*) put on underneath.

unter'ziehen² *v/t* (*irr, insep, no* -ge-, h, → *ziehen*) subject (*dat* to): *sich e-r Operation* ~ undergo an operation; *sich e-r Prüfung* ~ take an examination.

'**Untiefe** *f* (-; -n) shallow, shoal.

'**Untier** *n* (-[e]s; -e) *a. fig.* monster.

un'tragbar *adj* intolerable (*conduct etc*), prohibitive (*prices etc*).

un'trennbar *adj* inseparable.

'**untreu** *adj* (*dat* to) unfaithful, disloyal.

'**Untreue** *f* (-; *no pl*) unfaithfulness, disloyalty, (*marital*) infidelity.

un'tröstlich *adj* inconsolable.

untrüglich [ʊn'try:klɪç] *adj* **1.** unerring (*instinct etc*). **2.** sure (*sign etc*).

'**untüchtig** *adj* incapable, incompetent.

'**Untugend** *f* (-; -en) vice, bad habit.

unüber'brückbar *adj fig.* unbridgeable.

'**unüberlegt** *adj* ill-considered, unwise.

unüber'sehbar *adj* immense, vast.

unüber'setzbar *adj* untranslatable.

'**unübersichtlich** *adj* **1.** blind (*curve etc*). **2.** badly arranged, unclear, confused.

unübertrefflich [-'trɛflɪç] *adj* matchless, unsurpassable. **unübertroffen** [-'trɔfən] *adj* unsurpassed, unmatched.

unüberwindlich [-'vɪntlɪç] *adj* invincible, *fig.* insurmountable, insuperable.

'**unumgänglich** *adj* unavoidable: ~ (*notwendig*) indispensable.

'**unumschränkt** [-ʃrɛŋkt] *adj* unlimited, *pol.* absolute.

unumstößlich [-'ʃtøːslɪç] *adj* irrefutable (*fact etc*), irrevocable (*decision etc*).

unum'stritten *adj* undisputed.

'**unumwunden** [-vʊndən] *adv* straight out, frankly.

'**ununterbrochen** [-brɔxən] *adj* uninterrupted, incessant.

unver'änderlich *adj* unchanging, *ling.*, & invariable. '**unverändert** *adj* unchanged.

unver'antwortlich *adj* irresponsible.

unver'äußerlich *adj* inalienable.

unver'besserlich *adj* incorrigible.

'**unverbindlich** *adj offer etc* without obligation, noncommittal (*answer etc*).

'**unverblümt** *adj* plain, blunt.

'**unverbraucht** *adj* unused, *fig.* unspent.

'**unverbürgt** *adj* unconfirmed.

'**unverdächtig** *adj* unsuspicious.

'**unverdaulich** *adj a. fig.* indigestible.

'**unverdaut** *adj a. fig.* undigested.

'**unverdient** *adj* undeserved. '**unverdienter'maßen** *adv* undeservedly.

'**unverdorben** *adj* unspoilt, *fig. a.* uncorrupted.

'**unverdrossen** *adj* indefatigable.

'**unverdünnt** *adj* undiluted.

unver'einbar *adj* incompatible, irreconcilable.

'**unverfälscht** *adj* unadulterated, pure, *fig. a.* genuine.

unverfänglich *adj* harmless.

'**unverfroren** *adj* brazen, F cheeky. '**Unverfrorenheit** *f* (-; *no pl*) brazenness, impertinence, F cheek.

'**unvergänglich** *adj* immortal. '**Unvergänglichkeit** *f* (-; *no pl*) immortality.

'**unvergessen** *adj* unforgotten.

'**unvergeßlich** *adj* unforgettable.

unver'gleichlich *adj* incomparable.

'**unverhältnismäßig** *adv* disproportionately: ~ *hoch* excessive.

'**unverheiratet** *adj* unmarried, single.

'**unverhofft** [-hɔft] *adj a)* unhoped-for, b) unexpected.

'**unverhohlen** [-hoːlən] *adj* undisguised.

'**unverhüllt** *adj fig.* undisguised.

'**unverkäuflich** *adj* unsal(e)able, not for sale. '**unverkauft** *adj* unsold.

unver'kennbar *adj* unmistakable.

unver'letzlich *adj fig.* inviolable.

'**unverletzt** *adj* uninjured, unhurt.

unvermeidlich [-'maɪt-] *adj* unavoidable, inevitable (*a. iro.*): *sich ins Unvermeidliche fügen* bow to the inevitable.

'**unvermindert** *adj* undiminished.

'**unvermittelt** *adj* abrupt.

'**Unvermögen** *n* (-s; *no pl*) inability.

'**unvermutet** *adj* unexpected.

'**Unvernunft** *f* (-; *no pl*) unreasonableness, folly. '**unvernünftig** *adj* unreasonable, foolish.

'**unveröffentlicht** *adj* unpublished.

unver'richteter'dinge *adv* without having achieved anything.

'**unverschämt** *adj* **1.** impudent, impertinent. **2.** F barefaced (*lie*), outrageous (*demand, price, etc*).

'**Unverschämtheit** *f* (-; -en) impudence, impertinence: *die* ~ *haben zu inf* have the cheek to *inf.*

'**unverschuldet** *adj and adv* through no fault of one's own.

unversehens ['ʊnfɛrze:əns] *adv* unexpectedly, all of a sudden.
un'versehrt *adj* unharmed, intact.
unver'sichert *adj* uninsured.
unver'siegbar *adj* inexhaustible.
unver'söhnlich *adj a. fig.* irreconcilable.
unver'standen *adj* (*sich ~ fühlen* feel) misunderstood. **'unverständig** *adj* ignorant. **'unverständlich** *adj* (*dat* to) **1.** unintelligible. **2.** incomprehensible, obscure (*reasons etc*): *es ist mir ~, warum* (*wie etc*) I can't understand (F it beats me) why (how *etc*).
'unversteuert *adj* untaxed.
'unversucht *adj* **nichts ~ lassen** (*um zu inf*) try everything (to *inf*).
'unverträglich *adj* **1.** quarrelsome. **2.** indigestible. **3.** *a.* 🖝 incompatible.
unver'wechselbar *adj* unmistakable.
unver'wundbar *adj* invulnerable.
unver'wüstlich [-'vy:stlɪç] *adj* indestructible (*a. fig.*), irrepressible (*humo[u]r*).
'unverzagt *adj* undaunted.
unver'zeihlich *adj* inexcusable.
unver'zichtbar *adj* **1.** unrenounceable. **2.** indispensable.
unver'zinslich *adj* noninterest-bearing: *~es Darlehen* interest-free loan.
'unverzollt *adj* duty unpaid.
unverzüglich [ʊnfɛr'tsy:klɪç] *adj* immediate(ly *adv*), *adv a.* without delay.
'unvollendet *adj* unfinished.
'unvollkommen *adj* imperfect. **'Unvollkommenheit** *f* (-; -en) imperfection.
'unvollständig *adj* incomplete.
'unvorbereitet *adj* unprepared.
'unvoreingenommen *adj* unbias(s)ed, unprejudiced, objective.
'unvorhergesehen *adj* unforeseen.
'unvorschriftsmäßig *adj* irregular, contrary to (the) regulations, improper.
'unvorsichtig *adj* imprudent, rash, careless. **'Unvorsichtigkeit** *f* (-; *no pl*) imprudence, rashness, carelessness.
unvor'stellbar *adj* unimaginable, unthinkable, incredible.
'unvorteilhaft *adj* **1.** unprofitable. **2.** unbecoming (*dress etc*).
'unwahr *adj* untrue.
'Unwahrheit *f* (-; -en) untruth.
'unwahrscheinlich *adj* **1.** improbable, unlikely. **2.** F *fig.* incredible, fantastic. **'Unwahrscheinlichkeit** *f* (-; *no pl*) improbability.

un'wandelbar *adj* unchanging.
unwegsam ['ʊnve:kza:m] *adj* difficult.
'unweiblich *adj* unfeminine.
unweigerlich [ʊn'vaɪgərlɪç] **I** *adj* inevitable. **II** *adv* inevitably, without fail.
'unweit *prep* (*gen*) not far from.
'Unwesen *n* (-s; *no pl*) nuisance: *sein ~ treiben in* (*dat*) terrorize *a place etc*.
'unwesentlich *adj* **1.** irrelevant, unimportant. **2.** negligible.
'Unwetter *n* (-s; -) (thunder)storm.
'unwichtig *adj* unimportant, irrelevant.
unwider'legbar *adj* irrefutable.
unwiderruflich [-'ru:flɪç] **I** *adj* irrevocable. **II** *adv* irrevocably, definitely: *es steht ~ fest, daß* it is absolutely certain that.
unwider'stehlich [-'ʃte:lɪç] *adj* irresistible.
Unwider'stehlichkeit *f* (-; *no pl*) irresistibility.
unwiederbringlich [-'brɪŋlɪç] *adj* irretrievable.
'Unwille *m* (-ns; *no pl*) indignation.
'unwillig *adj* **1.** (*über acc* at) indignant, annoyed. **2.** unwilling, reluctant.
'unwillkommen *adj* unwelcome.
'unwillkürlich *adj* involuntary.
'unwirklich *adj* unreal.
'unwirksam *adj* ineffective, 🖝 inoperative, null and void.
'unwirsch ['ʊnvɪrʃ] *adj* disgruntled.
unwirtlich ['ʊnvɪrtlɪç] *adj* a) inhospitable, b) rough (*climate*).
'unwirtschaftlich *adj* uneconomic(al).
'unwissend *adj* ignorant.
'Unwissenheit *f* (-; *no pl*) ignorance.
'unwissenschaftlich *adj* unscientific.
'unwissentlich *adj* unknowing.
'unwohl *adj* **1.** unwell. **2.** *fig.* uneasy.
'Unwohlsein *n* (-s; *no pl*) indisposition.
'unwürdig *adj* unworthy (*gen* of): *das ist s-r ~* that is beneath him.
'Unzahl *f* e-e ~ *von* a host of.
unzählig [ʊn'tsɛ:lɪç] *adj* countless.
Unze ['ʊntsə] *f* (-; -n) ounce (*abbr.* oz.).
'unzeitgemäß *adj* old-fashioned.
unzer'brechlich *adj* unbreakable.
unzer'reißbar *adj* untearable.
unzer'störbar *adj* indestructible.
unzertrennlich [-'trɛnlɪç] *adj* inseparable.
unzivili̯siert *adj* uncivilized.
'Unzucht *f* (-; *no pl*) 🛪 sexual offen/ce

(*Am.* -se): **gewerbsmäßige ~** prostitution. '**unzüchtig** *adj* lewd, obscene.
'**unzufrieden** *adj* dissatisfied, discontented. '**Unzufriedenheit** *f* (-; *no pl*) dissatisfaction, discontent.
'**unzugänglich** *adj* inaccessible (*dat* to).
'**unzulänglich** *adj* inadequate.
'**Unzulänglichkeit** *f* (-; -en) **1.** *no pl* inadequacy. **2.** shortcoming.
'**unzulässig** *adj* inadmissible.
'**unzumutbar** *adj* unreasonable: **das ist für sie ~** a) you can't expect that of her, b) she will never accept that.
'**unzurechnungsfähig** *adj* irresponsible (for one's actions), insane.
'**Unzurechnungsfähigkeit** *f* (-; *no pl*) (**zeitweilige ~** temporary) insanity.
'**unzureichend** *adj* insufficient.
'**unzusammenhängend** *adj* a) disconnected, b) incoherent (*speech etc*).
'**unzuständig** *adj* 🏛 (**für**) incompetent (for), having no jurisdiction (over).
'**unzutreffend** *adj* incorrect: **Unzutreffendes bitte streichen!** please delete where inapplicable.
'**unzuverlässig** *adj* unreliable. '**Unzuverlässigkeit** *f* (-; *no pl*) unreliability.
'**unzweckmäßig** *adj* unsuitable.
'**unzweideutig** *adj* unequivocal.
'**unzweifelhaft I** *adj* indubitable. **II** *adv* doubtless, without a doubt.
üppig ['ʏpɪç] *adj* a) luxurious, b) luxuriant (*vegetation, fig. imagination etc*), c) opulent (*meal*), d) luscious, voluptuous (*figure etc*).
Ur [uːr] *m* (-[e]s; -e) *zo.* aurochs.
'**Urabstimmung** *f* strike ballot.
'**Urahn** *m* **1.** ancestor. **2.** great-grandfather. '**Urahne** *f* (-; -n) **1.** ancestress. **2.** great-grandmother.
'**uralt** *adj* ancient (*a. fig. iro.*), F as old as the hills, *fig.* age-old (*problem etc*).
Uran [uˈraːn] *n* (-s; *no pl*) ⚛ uranium.
u'ranhaltig *adj* uranium-bearing.
'**uraufführen** *v/t* (*only inf and pp* uraufgeführt, h) première, *a.* show *film* for the first time. '**Uraufführung** *f* première, first night (*or* showing).
urbar ['uːrbaːr] *adj* arable: **~ machen** cultivate, reclaim. '**Urbarmachung** *f* (-; -en) cultivation, reclamation.
'**Urbevölkerung** *f* → **Ureinwohner**.
'**Urbild** *n* model, prototype.

'**urdeutsch** *adj* German to the core, *iro.* very German.
'**ur'eigen** *adj* **in Ihrem ~sten Interesse** in your own best interest.
'**Ureinwohner** *pl* original inhabitants, *in Australia*: Aborigines.
'**Urenkel** *m* great-grandson.
'**Urenkelin** *f* great-granddaughter.
'**Urform** *f* archetype.
'**urge'mütlich** *adj* F very cosy.
'**Urgeschichte** *f* (-; *no pl*) primeval history. '**urgeschichtlich** *adj* prehistoric.
'**Urgestein** *n* *geol.* primary rock.
'**Urgewalt** *f* elemental force.
'**Urgroßeltern** *pl* great-grandparents.
'**Urgroßmutter** *f* great-grandmother.
'**Urgroßvater** *m* great-grandfather.
Urheber ['uːrheːbər] *m* (-s; -) author.
'**Urheberrecht** *n* copyright.
'**urheberrechtlich** *adj* copyright ...: **~ geschützt** (protected by) copyright.
'**Urheberschaft** *f* (-; *no pl*) authorship.
'**urig** ['uːrɪç] *adj* F → **urwüchsig**.
Urin [uˈriːn] *m* (-s; -e) urine.
urinieren [uriˈniːrən] *v/i* (h) urinate.
U'rinprobe *f* urine specimen.
U'rinuntersuchung *f* urine test.
'**Urknall** *m* (-[e]s; *no pl*) *phys.* big bang.
'**ur'komisch** *adj* F extremely funny.
'**Urkunde** *f* (-; -n) document, deed, record, *a. sports etc*: diploma. '**Urkundenfälschung** *f* forgery of documents.
'**urkundlich** *adj* documentary: **et. ~ belegen** document s.th.
'**Urkundsbeamte** *m* registrar.
Urlaub ['uːrlaʊp] *m* (-[e]s; -e) leave (of absence) (*a.* ✕), holiday(s), *esp. Am.* vacation: **auf ~ im ~** on holiday (vacation, ✕ leave); **in ~ gehen** (**sein**) go (be) on holiday (*etc*); **~ nehmen** go on leave; **e-n Tag ~ nehmen** take a day off. **Urlauber** ['uːrlaʊbər] *m* (-s; -) holidaymaker, *esp. Am.* vacationist.
'**Urlaubsanspruch** *m* holiday entitlement, *Am.* vacation privilege. **~geld** *n* holiday pay, *Am.* vacation money. **~tag** *m* (a day's) holiday (*esp. Am.* vacation). **~zeit** *f* holiday period.
'**Urmensch** *m* primitive man.
Urne ['ʊrnə] *f* (-; -n) **1.** urn. **2.** ballot box.
Urologe [uroˈloːgə] *m* (-n; -n) urologist.
Urologie [uroloˈgiː] *f* (-; *no pl*) urology.
'**ur'plötzlich I** *adj* sudden, abrupt. **II** *adv* all of a sudden.

'**Ursache** f (-; -n) a) cause, reason, b) occasion: *keine ~!* don't mention it, that's all right. '**ursächlich** adj causal: *~er Zusammenhang* causality.

'**Urschrift** f original (text or copy).

'**Ursprung** m (-[e]s; ⁀e) origin: *s-n ~ haben in* (dat) originate in (or from); *deutschen ~s* of German origin.

ursprünglich ['u:rʃprʏŋlıç] adj original.

'**Ursprungsland** n country of origin.

Urteil ['ʊrtaɪl] n (-s; -e) **1.** judg(e)ment, of jury: verdict (a. fig.), criminal court: sentence, divorce: decree: *das ~ verkünden* pronounce judg(e)ment (or sentence); → *fällen* 2. **2.** judg(e)ment, opinion: *sich ein ~ bilden* form a judg(e)ment (*über* acc about, on); *darüber kann ich mir kein ~ erlauben!* I am no judge (of that).

urteilen ['ʊrtaɪlən] v/i (h) judge: *über j-n (et.) ~* judge s.o. (s.th.); *ich urteile darüber anders* I take a different view (of it); *~ Sie selbst!* judge for yourself;

nach s-m Aussehen (s-n Worten) zu ~ judging by his looks (by what he says).

'**Urteils|begründung** f opinion. 2**fähig** adj discerning. ⁀**kraft** f (-; no pl) (power of) judg(e)ment. ⁀**spruch** m → **Urteil** 1.

'**Urtext** m original text.

'**Urtrieb** m basic instinct.

urtümlich ['u:rty:mlıç] adj **1.** original. **2.** archaic.

'**Urur...** great-great(-grandfather etc).

'**Urvolk** n **1.** pimitive people. **2.** → **Ureinwohner.**

'**Urwald** m **1.** primeval forest. **2.** jungle.

urwüchsig ['u:rvy:ksıç] adj **1.** original, natural. **2.** earthy, robust.

'**Urzeit** f primeval time: *vor ~en* a long, long time ago; *seit ~en* for ages.

'**Urzustand** m original state.

Utensilien [utɛn'zi:lɪən] pl utensils.

Uterus ['u:terʊs] m (-; -ri) anat. uterus.

Utopie [uto'pi:] f (-; -n) a) utopia, b) wild dream. **utopisch** [u'to:pıʃ] adj utopian, fantastic.

V

V, v [faʊ] n (-; -) V, v.

Vagabund [vaga'bʊnt] m (-en; -en) vagabond, tramp. **vagabundieren** [vagabʊn'di:rən] v/i (h) lead a vagabond life.

Vagina [va'gi:na] f (-; -nen) anat. vagina.

vakant [va'kant] adj vacant.

Vakuum ['va:kuʊm] n (-s; -kŭa) vacuum. 2**verpackt** adj vacuum-packed.

Vakzine [vak'tsi:nə] f (-; -n) ⚕ vaccine.

Valenz [va'lɛnts] f (-; -en) valence.

Valuta [va'lu:ta] f (-; -ten) ✝ valuta, foreign currency.

Vampir ['vampi:r] m (-s; -e) vampire.

Vandale m etc → **Wandale** etc.

Vanille [va'nıljə] f (-; no pl) ⚕ or gastr. vanilla. ⁀**zucker** m vanilla sugar.

variabel [va'rĭa:bəl] adj variable.

Variable [va'rĭa:blə] f (-; -n) variable.

Variante [va'rĭantə] f (-; -n) **1.** variant. **2.** version. **Variation** [varĭa'tsĭo:n] f (-; -en) variation.

Varieté [varĭe'te:] n (-s; -s) ⁀**the|ater** n

variety theatre, music hall, Am. vaudeville (theater).

variieren [vari'i:rən] v/t, v/i (h) vary.

Vasall [va'zal] m (-en; -en) vassal.

Va'sallenstaat m contp. satellite state.

Vase ['va:zə] f (-; -n) vase.

Vaseline [vazə'li:nə] f (-; no pl) vaseline.

Vater ['fa:tər] m (-s; ⁀) father (a. fig.), zo. sire: *er ist ~ von drei Kindern* he is a father of three (children); *er ist ganz der ~* he is a chip off the old block; humor. *~ Staat* the State.

'**Vaterfi|gur** f father figure.

'**Vaterland** n (-[e]s; ⁀er) one's native country. '**Vaterlandsliebe** f love of one's country, patriotism.

väterlich ['fɛ:tərlıç] **I** adj fatherly, paternal. **II** adv like a father. '**väterlicherseits** adv on one's father's side: *Großvater ~* paternal grandfather.

'**Vaterliebe** f paternal love.

'**vaterlos** adj fatherless.

'**Vater|mord** *m*, **~mörder** *m* patricide.
'**Vaterschaft** *f* (-; *no pl*) 👪 paternity: *Feststellung der ~* affiliation.
'**Vaterschaftsklage** *f* 👪 paternity suit.
'**Vater|stadt** *f* hometown. **~stelle** *f* ~ **vertreten** act as father (*bei* to).
Vater'unser *n* (-s; -) Lord's Prayer.
Vati ['fa:ti] *m* (-s; -s) F daddy, dad.
Vatikan [vati'ka:n] *m* (-s), **vati'kanisch** *adj* Vatican. **Vati'kanstadt** *f* Vatican City.
V-Ausschnitt ['fau-] *m* V-neck: *mit ~* V-neckcd.
Vegetarier [vege'ta:riər] *m* (-s; -) vegetarian. **vege'tarisch** [-rɪʃ] *adj* vegetarian: *~ leben* be a vegetarian.
Vegetation [vegeta'tsǐo:n] *f* (-; -en) vegetation. **vegetativ** [-'ti:f] *adj* vegetative: *~es Nervensystem* autonomous nervous system. **vegetieren** [vege'ti:rən] *v/i* (h) *fig.* vegetate.
Vehikel [ve'hi:kəl] *n* (-s; -) F rattletrap.
Veilchen ['faɪlçən] *n* (-s; -) **1.** 🌿 violet: F *blau wie ein ~* drunk as a lord. **2.** F *fig.* black eye. '**veilchenblau** *adj* violet.
Vektor ['vɛktɔr] *m* (-s; -en [-'to:rən]) 🅰 vector. **~rechnung** *f* vector analysis.
Velours [vəˈluːr] *m* (- [-vəˈluːrs]; - [vəˈluːrs]) velour(s).
Ve'loursleder *n* suede (leather).
Ve'loursteppich *m* velvet-pile carpet.
Vene ['ve:nə] *f* (-; -n) *anat.* vein.
'**Venenentzündung** *f* 💉 phlebitis.
venerisch [ve'ne:rɪʃ] *adj* 💉 venereal.
Venezianer [vene'tsǐa:nər] *m* (-s; -), **Vene'zianerin** *f* (-; -nen), **venezi'anisch** *adj* Venetian.
Venezolaner [venetso'la:nər] *m* (-s; -), **Venezo'lanerin** *f* (-; -nen), **venezo'lanisch** *adj* Venezuelan.
venös [ve'nø:s] *adj* 💉 venous.
Ventil [vɛn'ti:l] *n* (-s; -e) 🔧, ⚙ valve. **2.** *fig.* outlet. **Ventilation** [vɛntila'tsǐo:n] *f* (-; -en) a) ventilation, b) ventilating system. **Ventilator** [vɛnti'la:tɔr] *m* (-s; -en [-la'to:rən]) (ventilating) fan.
ver'abreden (h) **I** *v/t* agree upon, arrange, *a.* fix (*date, place*): *vorher ~* prearrange. **II** *sich ~* (*mit j-m*) arrange to meet (s.o.), make a date (*or* an appointment) (with s.o.): *ich bin leider schon verabredet* I'm afraid I have a previous engagement. **Ver'abredung** *f*

(-; -en) **1.** date, engagement, appointment. **2.** agreement, arrangement.
ver'abreichen *v/t* (h) *j-m et. ~* give s.o. s.th., *a.* administer s.th. to s.o.
ver'abscheuen *v/t* (h) abhor, detest.
verabschieden [vɛr'ʔapʃiːdən] (h) **I** *v/t* **1.** say goodbye to. **2.** discharge. **3.** *parl.* pass (*bill etc*), adopt (*budget*). **II** *sich ~ von* → 1. **Ver'abschiedung** *f* (-; -en) **1.** discharge. **2.** *parl.* passing (*of bill etc*), adoption (*of budget*).
ver'achten *v/t* (h) despise, disdain, *a.* scorn: F *nicht zu ~* not to be sneezed at.
ver'achtenswert *adj* contemptible, despicable. **Verächter** [vɛr'ʔɛçtər] *m* (-s; -) despiser. **ver'ächtlich** *adj* **1.** contemptuous, scornful: *~ machen* run *s.o.*, *s.th.* down. **2.** → *verachtenswert*. **Ver'achtung** *f* (-; *no pl*) contempt, disdain, *a.* scorn: *mit ~ strafen* ignore.
ver'albern *v/t* (h) F *j-n ~* pull s.o.'s leg.
verallgemeinern [fɛr'algə'maɪnərn] *v/t* (h) generalize. **Verallge'meinerung** *f* (-; -en) generalization.
ver'alten *v/i* (sn) become (out)dated (*or* obsolete), *views etc*: antiquated). **ver'altet** *adj* obsolete, (out)dated, *method etc*: antiquated: *~ sein* be out of date.
Veranda [ve'randa] *f* (-; -den) veranda(h).
ver'änderlich *adj* changeable, *a.* ling, 🅰 variable: 🅰 *~e Größe* variable.
Ver'änderlichkeit *f* (-; -en) changeability, *ling.*, 🅰 variability.
ver'ändern (h) **I** *v/t* **1.** (*an dat* on) alter, change. **II** *sich ~* **2.** change: *sich zu s-m Vorteil (Nachteil) ~* change for the better (worse); *hier hat sich vieles verändert* there have been many changes. **3.** change one's job. **ver'ändert** *adj* changed, different: *sie ist ganz ~* she has changed a lot. **Ver'änderung** *f* (-; -en) change.
verängstigt [-'ʔɛŋstɪçt] *adj* frightened.
ver'ankern *v/t* (h) ⚓, ⚙ anchor: *fig. in der Verfassung verankert* laid down in the constitution.
ver'anlagen *v/t* (h) *taxation*: assess.
ver'anlagt *adj* (*zu, für* to) (🎨 pre)disposed, (naturally) inclined: *künstlerisch ~ sein* have an artistic bent; *er ist praktisch ~* he is practical(ly minded); *romantisch ~ sein* have a romantic disposition. **Ver'anlagung** *f* (-; -en) **1.**

taxation: assessment. **2.** (⚕ pre)disposition. **3.** inclination, *a.* talent(s).

ver'anlassen *v/t* (h) **1.** *et.* ~; ~, *daß et. getan wird* order (*or* arrange) s.th., see (to it) that s.th. is done; *das Nötige* ~ take the necessary steps. **2.** *j-n* ~ *et. zu tun* cause (*or* get) s.o. to do s.th., make s.o. do s.th.; *sich veranlaßt sehen zu inf* feel compelled to *inf*; *was hat ihn bloß dazu veranlaßt?* whatever made him do that? **Ver'anlassung** *f* (-; -en) **1.** (*zu, für* for) cause, motive: *ohne jede* ~ without provocation. **2.** *auf* ~ *von* (*or gen*) at the instigation of.

ver'anschaulichen [fɛr'ʔanʃaʊlɪçən] *v/t* (h) illustrate: *sich et.* ~ visualize s.th. **Ver'anschaulichung** *f* (-; -en) (*zur* ~ by way of) illustration.

ver'anschlagen *v/t* (h) ✝ estimate (*auf acc* at): *zu hoch* ~ overestimate; *zu niedrig* ~ underestimate.

veranstalten [fɛr'ʔanʃtaltən] *v/t* (h) organize, arrange, stage (*a.* F *fig.*), give (*concert etc*). **Ver'anstalter** *m* (-s; -) organizer, *sports*: *a.* promoter. **Ver'anstaltung** *f* (-; -en) **1.** arrangement, organization, *fig.* staging. **2.** event, *a.* (public) function, *sports*: meeting, *Am.* meet, fixture. **Ver'anstaltungskalender** *m* calendar of events.

ver'antworten (h) **I** *v/t* answer for, take the responsibility for. **II** *sich* (*j-m gegenüber*) *für et.* ~ answer (to s.o.) for s.th. **ver'antwortlich** *adj* responsible (*für* for): *j-n* ~ *machen* hold s.o. responsible, *w.s.* blame s.o. (*für* for). **Ver'antwortlichkeit** *f* (-; only) responsibility. **Ver'antwortung** *f* (-; -en) (*die* ~ *tragen* bear [the] responsibility; *auf Ihre eigene* ~*!* at your own risk; *j-n zur* ~ *ziehen* call s.o. to account; → *abwälzen*. **ver'antwortungsbewußt** *adj* responsible. **Ver'antwortungsbewußtsein** *n* sense of responsibility.

ver'antwortungslos *adj* irresponsible.

ver'antwortungsvoll *adj* responsible.

ver'äppeln [fɛr'ʔɛpəln] *v/t* (h) F *j-n* ~ pull s.o.'s leg.

ver'arbeiten *v/t* (h) process (*a. data*), *physiol. or fig.* digest, use (*in dat, zu* in, for): *et.* ~ *zu* manufacture s.th. into; *~de Industrie* processing industries. **Ver'arbeitung** *f* (-; -en) **1.** processing, manufacture, treatment. **2.** *physiol. or*

fig. digestion. **3.** workmanship.

ver'ärgern *v/t* (h) annoy.

ver'armen *v/i* (sn) become poor. **ver'armt** *adj* impoverished. **Ver'armung** *f* (-; -en) *a. fig.* impoverishment.

ver'arschen *v/t* (h) ∨ *j-n* ~ take the mickey out of s.o., *by satire*: send s.o. up.

verarzten [fɛr'ʔartstən] *v/t* (h) F *j-n* ~ fix s.o. up.

verästeln [fɛr'ʔɛstəln] *sich* ~ (h) ramify. **Ver'ästelung** *f* (-; -en) ramification.

ver'ausgaben: sich ~ (h) **1.** overspend. **2.** *fig.* spend o.s.

ver'auslagen *v/t* (h) lay out.

ver'äußern *v/t* (h) sell, dispose of. **Ver'äußerung** *f* (-; -en) sale, disposal.

Verb [vɛrp] *n* (-s; -en) *ling.* verb.

verbal [vɛr'baːl] *adj* verbal. **verbalisieren** [vɛrbali'ziːrən] *v/t* (h) verbalize.

Verband [fɛr'bant] *m* (-[e]s; ⸰e) **1.** ⚕ bandage, dressing. **2.** union, federation. **3.** ✕ unit, ✈ formation. **Verband(s)|kasten** *m* ⚕ first-aid kit. **~materi̱al** *n* dressing material. **~mull** *m* surgical gauze.

ver'bannen *v/t* (h) (*aus* from) exile, banish (*a. fig.*). **Ver'bannte** *m, f* (-n; -n) exile. **Ver'bannung** *f* (-; -en) exile, banishment (*a. fig.*).

verbarrikadieren [fɛrbarika'diːrən] *v/t* (h) barricade (*sich* o.s.).

ver'bauen *v/t* (h) **1.** block up, obstruct: *fig. j-m* (*sich*) *den Weg* ~ bar s.o.'s (one's) way (*zu* to). **2.** build up (*area*). **3.** use (*material*).

ver'bauern *v/i* (sn) become countrified.

verbe'amten *v/t* (h) *j-n* ~ give s.o. the rank of a civil servant.

ver'beißen (*irr, no* -ge-, h, → *beißen*) **I** *v/t* **1.** suppress (*pain etc*), *a.* bite back (*laughter, tears, etc*): *er konnte sich ein Lächeln nicht* ~ he couldn't keep a straight face. **II** *sich* ~ *in* (*acc*) **2.** *dog etc*: sink its teeth into. **3.** *fig. person*: get set on, keep grimly at.

ver'bergen *v/t* (*irr, no* -ge-, h, → *bergen*) conceal, hide.

ver'bessern (h) **I** *v/t* **1.** improve, better (*record*). **2.** correct (*mistake etc*). **II** *sich* ~ **3.** improve: *sich finanziell* ~ better o.s. **4.** correct o.s. **Ver'besserung** *f* (-; -en) **1.** improvement, betterment. **2.** correction. **ver'besserungs|bedürftig** *adj* in need of improvement. **~fähig** *adj* capable of improvement. **2vorschlag** *m* suggestion for improvement.

ver'beugen: sich ~ (h) bow (**vor** *dat* to).

Ver'beugung *f* (-; -en) bow (**vor** *dat* to).

ver'beulen *v/t* (h) batter, dent.

ver'biegen *v/t* (*irr, no* -ge-, h, → **biegen**) twist, bend.

ver'bieten *v/t* (*irr, no* -ge-, h, → **bieten**) **j-m das Haus** (**das Rauchen**) **~** forbid s.o. the house (to smoke); → **verboten**.

ver'billigen *v/t* (h) reduce *s.th.* in price.

ver'billigt *adj* reduced (*price etc*), (*tickets etc*) at reduced prices.

ver'binden *v/t* (*irr, no* -ge-, h, → **binden**) **1. ∅** bandage: **j-n ~** dress s.o.'s wounds; **j-m die Augen ~** blindfold s.o.; → **verbunden 1. 2.** (*a.* **sich ~**) (**mit** with) connect (*a.* **⚛, ⊙,** *teleph. or fig.*), combine (*a.* **🐉**), unite: **teleph. ich verbinde Sie** I'll put you through (**mit** to); **das Angenehme mit dem Nützlichen ~** combine business with pleasure; **sich mit j-m ~** associate with s.o. **ver'bindend** *adj fig.* connecting (*text, words, etc*).

verbindlich [fɛr'bɪntlɪç] *adj* **1.** (**für** upon) obligatory, binding: **~e Zusage** definite promise. **2.** obliging, courteous, friendly. **Ver'bindlichkeit** *f* (-; -en) **1.** *no pl* obligation, binding character. **2.** *no pl* obligingness, friendliness. **3.** *pl* courtesies. **4.** *pl* ✝ liabilities.

Ver'bindung *f* (-; -en) **1.** connection (*a.* **⊙,** *teleph.*), combination: **in ~ mit a)** in conjunction with, **b)** in connection with: **in ~ bringen mit** connect (*or* associate) *s.o., s.th.* with. **2.** (*bus etc*) connection. **3. a)** union, association, **b)** students' society, *Am.* fraternity: **e-e ~ eingehen** join together (**mit** with). **4.** contact (*a.* **⚔**), *pl* connections: **mit j-m ~ aufnehmen** (*or* **in ~ treten**) contact s.o., get in touch with s.o.; **mit j-m in ~ stehen** (**bleiben**) be (keep) in touch with s.o.; **s-e ~en spielen lassen** pull a few strings.

Ver'bindungs... connecting (*cable, line, road, etc*). **~mann** *m* contact. **~offi‚zier** *m* liaison officer. **~stück** *n* **⊙** connecting piece, **⚡** connector, *a.* adaptor.

ver'bissen *adj* grim, dogged. **Ver'bissenheit** *f* (-; *no pl*) doggedness.

ver'bitten *v/t* (*irr, no* -ge-, h, → **bitten**) **sich et. ~** not to stand for s.th.; **das**

verbitte ich mir! I won't have that.

ver'bittert *adj* embittered, bitter.

Ver'bitterung *f* (-; *no pl*) bitterness.

verblassen [fɛr'blasən] *v/i* (sn) fade.

ver'bleiben *v/i* (*irr, no* -ge-, sn, → **bleiben**) **1.** remain: **verbleibe ich Ihr ...** in *letter*: (I remain,) Yours faithfully ... **2.** **wir sind so verblieben, daß** we agreed (*or* arranged) that.

verbleit [fɛr'blaɪt] *adj* leaded.

ver'blenden *v/t* (h) **1. ⚛** face, line. **2.** *fig.* blind: **von Haß verblendet** blind with hatred. **Ver'blendung** *f* (-; -en) **1. ⚛** facing. **2.** *no pl fig.* blindness.

verblichen [fɛr'blɪçən] *adj* faded.

verblöden [fɛr'blø:dən] F **I** *v/i* (sn) go dotty, go daft (**bei** with). **II** *v/t* (h) dull *s.o.'s* mind, stultify.

verblüffen [fɛr'blyfən] *v/t* (h) amaze, baffle. **ver'blüffend** *adj* amazing. **ver'blüfft** *adj* amazed, *pred* taken aback. **Ver'blüffung** *f* (-; *no pl*) amazement.

ver'blühen *v/i* (sn) *a. fig.* fade, wither.

ver'bluten *v/i* (sn) bleed to death.

ver'bocken *v/t* (h) F bungle, botch (up).

ver'bohren: sich ~ (h) F *fig.* become obsessed (**in** *acc* with). **ver'bohrt** *adj* F *fig.* stubborn, pigheaded.

ver'borgen¹ *v/t* (h) lend (out).

ver'borgen² *adj* hidden: **~ halten** conceal; **sich ~ halten** hide (o.s.); **im ~en** in secret, secretly.

Verbot [fɛr'bo:t] *n* (-[e]s; -e) prohibition (*gen* of), ban (*gen, von* on). **ver'boten** *adj* **a)** forbidden, prohibited, banned, **b)** illegal: **es war uns ~ zu** *inf* we were forbidden (*or* not allowed) to *inf*; **ist das etwa ~?** F is there a law against it?; **Rauchen ~!** no smoking!; F **sie sah ~ aus** she looked a sight. **ver'botenerweise** *adv* **~ et. tun** do s.th. although it is forbidden. **Ver'botsschild** *n* no parking (*or* no smoking *etc*) sign.

verbrämen [fɛr'brɛ:mən] *v/t* (h) **1. a)** border, trim, **b)** fur. **2.** *fig.* gloss over.

Ver'brauch *m* (-[e]s; *no pl*) consumption (**an** *dat* of).

ver'brauchen (h) **I** *v/t* consume, use up. **II sich ~** *fig.* exhaust o.s., wear o.s. out.

Ver'braucher *m* (-s; -) consumer. **~markt** *m* hypermarket. **~schutz** *m* consumer protection. **~umfrage** *f* consumer survey. **~verhalten** *n* consumer behavio(u)r.

Ver'brauchsgüter pl consumer goods.
ver'braucht adj a. fig. used(-)up, spent, worn(-)out: **~e Luft** stale air.
ver'brechen v/t (irr, no -ge-, h, → **brechen**) F humor. perpetrate: **was hat er verbrochen?** what has he done?
Ver'brechen n (-s; -) a. fig. crime.
Ver'brecher m (-s; -) criminal. **~album** n rogues' gallery. **~bande** f gang of criminals.
Ver'brecherin f (-; -nen) criminal.
ver'brecherisch adj criminal.
ver'breiten v/t (a. **sich ~**) (h) spread (**in** dat, **auf** dat, **über** acc over), a. disseminate (ideas etc): (weit) **verbreitet** widespread, a. widely read.
verbreitern [fɛr'braɪtɐn] v/t (a. **sich ~**) (h) widen.
Ver'breitung f (-; no pl) spread(ing), a. dissemination.
ver'brennen (irr, no -ge-, h, → **brennen**) **I** v/t burn, burn up (calories), cremate (corpse), scorch: **sich den Mund ~** burn one's mouth, fig. put one's foot in it; ✕ **verbrannte Erde** scorched earth. **II** v/i a) burn, b) be burnt to death.
Ver'brennung f (-; -en) **1.** burning, ⊙ combustion. **2.** cremation. **3.** ✵ burn: → **Grad**.
Ver'brennungs|motor m combustion engine. **~ofen** m incinerator.
verbrieft [fɛr'bri:ft] adj vested (right).
ver'bringen v/t (irr, no -ge-, h, → **bringen**) spend, pass.
verbrüdern [fɛr'bry:dɐn] **sich ~** (h) fraternize. **Ver'brüderung** f (-; -en) fraternization.
ver'brühen (h) **I** v/t scald (**sich die Hand** one's hand). **II sich ~** scald o.s.
ver'buchen v/t (h) **1.** ✝ book. **2.** fig. achieve, ✝ notch up (success etc).
ver'bummeln v/t (h) F **1.** waste, idle away. **2.** a) lose, b) clean forget.
Ver'bund m (-[e]s; -e) network, (integrated) system: **im ~ arbeiten** cooperate; → **Medien-, Verkehrsverbund. ~bauweise** f sandwich construction.
verbunden [fɛr'bʊndən] adj **1.** dressed (wound): **mit ~en Augen** blindfold. **2. ~ sein mit** a) be connected with, entail (difficulties, costs, etc), b) be attached to; **j-m ~ sein für** be obliged to s.o. for.
verbünden [fɛr'bʏndən] **sich ~** (h) (**mit** with) form an alliance, ally o.s. (a. to).

Ver'bundenheit f (-; no pl) (**mit**) attachment (to), bond(s), solidarity (with).
Ver'bündete m, f (-n; -n) a. fig. ally.
Ver'bundglas n laminated glass.
ver'bürgen v/t (h) guarantee: **sich ~ für** a. answer for. **verbürgt** [-'byrkt] adj authentic, established (fact etc).
ver'büßen v/t (h) serve (sentence).
ver'chromen v/t (h) chromium-plate.
Verdacht [fɛr'daxt] m (-[e]s; -e) (**~ erregen** arouse) suspicion: **j-n im ~ haben (et. getan zu haben)** suspect s.o. (of having done s.th.); **in ~ kommen** be suspected; **~ schöpfen** become suspicious, F smell a rat; **bei ihm besteht ~ auf Krebs** he is suspected of having cancer; F **auf ~** on spec; → **lenken** 3.
verdächtig [fɛr'dɛçtɪç] adj suspicious, suspect, a. dubious, F fishy: **des Diebstahls ~ sein** be suspected of theft.
Ver'dächtige m, f (-n; -n) suspect.
verdächtigen [fɛr'dɛçtɪgən] v/t (h) **j-n ~** cast suspicion on s.o., suspect s.o. (gen of; **et. getan zu haben** of having done s.th.). **Ver'dächtigung** f (-; -en) **1.** casting suspicion (gen on). **2.** suspicion.
Ver'dachtsmo,ment n suspicious fact.
verdammen [fɛr'damən] v/t (h) (**zu** to) condemn, a. eccl. damn. **ver'dammt I** adj **1.** damned: **dazu ~ sein zu** inf be condemned (or doomed) to inf. **2.** F damn(ed), blasted, Br. sl. a. bloody: **~ (nochmal)!** damn (it)!, blast it (all)! **II** adv F damn(ed), Br. sl. bloody: **~ kalt** a. beastly cold. **Ver'dammung** f (-; -en) condemnation, a. eccl. damnation.
ver'dampfen v/t (h), v/i (sn) evaporate.
ver'danken v/t (h) **j-m et. ~** owe s.th. to s.o., be indebted to s.o. for s.th.; **es ist ihr zu ~, daß** it is due to her that.
verdarb [fɛr'darp] pret of **verderben**.
verdattert [fɛr'datɐt] adj F dazed.
verdauen [fɛr'daʊən] v/t (h) digest.
ver'daulich adj (**leicht ~** easily) digestible; **schwer ~** hard to digest.
Ver'daulichkeit f (-; no pl) digestibility.
Ver'dauung f (-; no pl) digestion.
Ver'dauungs|appa,rat m digestive system. **~beschwerden** pl indigestion, digestive trouble.
Ver'deck n (-[e]s; -e) (folding) top, hood.
ver'decken v/t (h) cover, hide, a. ⊙ conceal: **verdeckte (Polizei)Aktion** undercover operation.

ver'denken v/t (irr, no -ge-, h, → **denken**) **ich kann es ihm nicht ~ (, daß)** I can't blame him (if).

verderben [fɛrˈdɛrbən] (verdarb, verdorben) **I** v/i (sn) spoil, go bad, perish. **II** v/t (h) spoil, a. ruin, morally: corrupt: **sich den Magen** (**die Augen**) **~** upset one's stomach (ruin one's eyes); **j-m die Freude** (**den Appetit**) **~** spoil s.o.'s fun (appetite); F **es mit j-m ~** fall out with s.o.; **er will es mit niemandem ~** he tries to please everybody.

Ver'derben n (-s; no pl) ruin: **in sein ~ rennen** rush (headlong) into disaster.

verderblich [fɛrˈdɛrplɪç] adj **1.** perishable (goods). **2.** fig. ruinous (effect etc), corrupting (influence etc).

ver'deutlichen v/t (h) **j-m et. ~** make s.th. clear (or explain s.th.) to s.o.

ver'dichten (h) **I** v/t **1. ⊙** compress, a. 🍃 condense. **II** sich **~ 2.** condense, fog: thicken. **3.** fig. suspicion etc: grow stronger. **Ver'dichtung** f (-; -en) condensation, mot. compression.

ver'dicken v/t (a. sich **~**) (h) thicken.

ver'dienen (h) **I** v/t **1.** earn, make (money): **sich et. nebenbei ~** make some money on the side. **2.** fig. deserve (punishment, praise, etc): **er hat es nicht besser verdient!** (it) serves him right!; → **verdient. II** v/i gut **~** earn a good salary (or wage); **an e-r Sache gut ~** make a good profit on s.th.

Ver'diener m (-s; -) (salary or wage) earner, breadwinner.

Ver'dienst¹ n (-[e]s; -e) fig. merit: **es ist ihr ~, daß** it is thanks to her that; → **erwerben.**

Ver'dienst² m (-[e]s; -e) income, earnings, wages, salary.

Ver'dienstausfall m lost earnings.

ver'dienstvoll adj deserving (person), commendable (deed etc).

ver'dient adj fig. **1.** deserving, man etc of merit: **sich ~ machen um** do s.o., s.th. a great service. **2.** a) well-deserved, due (punishment), b) well-earned (victory).

ver'dienter'maßen adv deservedly.

ver'dolmetschen v/t (h) **j-m et. ~** translate s.th. for (fig. explain s.th. to) s.o.

ver'donnern v/t (h) F condemn s.o. (**zu** to); **j-n ~, et. zu tun** make s.o. do s.th.

ver'doppeln v/t (a. sich **~**) (h) double. **Ver'dopplung** f (-; -en) doubling.

verdorben [fɛrˈdɔrbən] **I** pp of **verderben. II** adj spoiled (a. fig.), a. bad, fig. a. ruined, morally: a. corrupt: **~er Magen** upset stomach, indigestion.

verdorren [fɛrˈdɔrən] v/i (sn) wither.

verdrahten [fɛrˈdraːtən] v/t (h) ⚡ wire.

ver'drängen v/t (h) **1.** → **vertreiben** 1. **2.** fig. a) displace (a. ⚓, phys.), b) supersede, replace: **j-n ~** push s.o. out (sports: **vom ersten Platz** from first place); **j-n aus s-r Stellung ~** oust s.o. from his position. **3.** psych. repress, suppress. **4.** dismiss (a problem etc).

Ver'drängung f (-; -en) ousting, displacement (a. ⚓, phys.), fig. replacement, psych. repression, suppression.

verdreckt [fɛrˈdrɛkt] adj filthy, soiled.

ver'drehen v/t (h) **1.** twist (**j-m den Arm** s.o.'s arm): **die Augen ~** roll one's eyes; **j-m den Kopf ~** turn s.o.'s head. **2.** F fig. twist, distort (words etc), pervert (law). **ver'dreht** adj F fig. **1.** crazy, cranky. **2.** confused. **Ver'drehung** f (-; -en) twisting, fig. a. distortion (of facts etc).

ver'dreifachen v/t (h) treble.

verdrießen [fɛrˈdriːsən] v/t (verdroß, verdrossen, h) annoy.

verdrießlich adj morose, sullen.

verdrossen [fɛrˈdrɔsən] adj **1.** sullen. **2.** listless. **Ver'drossenheit** f (-; no pl) **1.** sullenness. **2.** listlessness.

ver'drücken (h) F **I** v/t polish off. **II** sich **~** slip away, beat it.

Verdruß [fɛrˈdrʊs] m (-sses; no pl) annoyance: **~ bereiten** cause s.o. trouble.

ver'duften v/i (sn) F beat it, scram.

verdummen [fɛrˈdʊmən] **I** v/t (h) dull s.o.'s mind, stultify, brainwash (the people). **II** v/i (sn) become stultified.

ver'dunkeln v/t (h) darken (a. sich **~**), black out, a. fig. cloud, fig. obscure. **Ver'dunklung** f (-; -en) a) darkening, b) blackout. **Ver'dunklungsgefahr** f ⚖ danger of collusion.

verdünnen [fɛrˈdʏnən] v/t (h) dilute, thin (down) (paint). **Ver'dünner** m (-s; -) thinner. **Ver'dünnung** f (-; -en) dilution, thinning (down).

ver'dunsten v/i (h), v/t (h) evaporate.

Ver'dunster m (-s; -) humidifier.

Ver'dunstung f (-; no pl) evaporation.

ver'dursten v/i (sn) die of thirst.

verdüstern [fɛrˈdyːstərn] sich **~** (h) a. fig. darken.

verdutzt [fɛr'dʊtst] *adj* nonplussed, *pred* taken aback.

ver'ebben *v/i* (sn) *a. fig.* ebb away.

veredeln [fɛr'?eːdəln] *v/t* (h) **1.** ennoble. **2.** refine, ⊙ *a.* process, finish. **3.** ✔ graft, bud. **Ver'edelungsindu,strie** *f* processing industry.

ver'ehren *v/t* (h) a) revere, *a. fig.* adore, worship, b) admire: *Verehrte Anwesende!* Ladies and Gentlemen! **Ver'ehrer** *m* (-s; -), **Ver'ehrerin** *f* (-; -nen) **1.** admirer. **2.** fan. **Ver'ehrerpost** *f* fan mail. **Ver'ehrung** *f* (-; *no pl*) a) (*~ zollen* pay) reverence (*dat* to), *a. fig.* worship, adoration, b) admiration. **ver'ehrungswürdig** *adj* venerable.

vereidigen [fɛr'?aɪdɪɡən] *v/t* (h) (*auf acc* on) put *s.o.* under an oath, swear *s.o.* in. **vereidigt** [fɛr'?aɪdɪçt] *adj* sworn. **Ver'eidigung** *f* (-; -en) swearing-in.

Ver'ein *m* (-[e]s; -e) **1.** club: F *contp.* **ein netter ~** a fine bunch. **2.** ✝ society, association. **3.** *im ~ mit* together with.

ver'einbar *adj* (*mit* with) compatible, consistent. **ver'einbaren** *v/t* (h) **1.** agree (up)on, arrange: *vorher ~* prearrange. **2.** reconcile (*mit* with). **Ver'einbarkeit** *f* (-; *no pl*) compatibility (*mit* with). **ver'einbart** *adj* agreed: *zur ~en Zeit* at the time agreed upon. **Ver'einbarung** *f* (-; -en) agreement, arrangement: *e-e ~ treffen* reach an agreement; *laut ~* as agreed; *nach ~* by agreement; *Gehalt nach ~* salary negotiable.

ver'einen *v/t* → **vereinigen**: *mit vereinten Kräften* in a combined effort.

ver'einfachen *v/t* (h) simplify. **Ver'einfachung** *f* (-; -en) simplification.

ver'einheitlichen *v/t* (h) standardize. **Ver'einheitlichung** *f* (-; -en) standardization.

ver'einigen *v/t* (*a. sich ~*) (h) a) unite (*zu* into), combine, join (together), ✝ amalgamate, b) assemble, *a.* rally: *Vereinigte Staaten (von Amerika)* United States (of America) (*abbr.* U.S.[A.]). **Ver'einigung** *f* (-; -en) **1.** *no pl* uniting (*etc*), *pol.* unification, ✝ merger. **2.** association, union.

ver'einnahmen *v/t* (h) F monopolize.

ver'einsamen *v/i* (sn) become isolated (*or* lonely). **Ver'einsamung** *f* (-; *no pl*) (growing) isolation.

Ver'eins|haus *n* clubhouse. **~kame,rad**

m clubmate. **~kasse** *f* club funds.

ver'einzelt I *adj* isolated, sporadic, *a.* scattered (*showers*). **II** *adv* a) sporadically, now and then, b) here and there.

ver'eisen I *v/t* (h) ✱ freeze. **II** *v/i* (sn) ice over, ✔ *etc* ice up, freeze over: *vereiste Straßen* icy roads.

ver'eiteln *v/t* (h) thwart, frustrate (*plan etc*), prevent (*deed*).

ver'eitert *adj* ✱ septic.

ver'ekeln *v/t j-m et.* ~ put s.o. off s.th.

verelenden [fɛr'?eːlɛndən] *v/i* (sn) be reduced to poverty. **Ver'elendung** *f* (-; *no pl*) impoverishment.

ver'enden *v/i* (sn) perish, die.

ver'engen *v/t* (*a. sich ~*) (h) narrow (*a. fig.*), *pupil:* contract. **Ver'engung** *f* (-; -en) **1.** narrowing, contraction. **2.** narrow part (*in dat* of).

ver'erben (h) **I** *v/t j-m et.* ~ leave (✱ transmit) s.th. to s.o. **II** *sich* ~ *a.* ✱ *or fig.* be passed on (*or* down) (*auf acc* to). **vererbt** [-'?ɛrpt] *adj biol.* inherited, hereditary. **Ver'erbung** *f* (-; *no pl*) *biol.* heredity, (hereditary) transmission.

Ver'erbungs|gesetze *pl* laws of heredity. **~lehre** *f* genetics.

verewigen [fɛr'?eːvɪɡən] *v/t* (h) immortalize.

ver'fahren¹ (*irr, no -ge-,* → *fahren*) **I** *v/i* (sn) (*nach* on) proceed, act: *~ mit* deal with, treat. **II** *v/t* (h) use up (*petrol*), spend *money, time* driving (around). **III** *sich* ~ get lost.

ver'fahren² *adj* muddled, tangled: *e-e ~e Sache* a (great) muddle.

Ver'fahren *n* (-s; -) **1.** procedure, method, process. **2.** ⚖ a) procedure, b) proceedings: *ein ~ einleiten* take (legal) proceedings (*gegen* against).

Ver'fahrens|frage *f* ⚖ procedural question. **~technik** *f* process technology. **~weise** *f* → *Verfahren* I.

Ver'fall *m* (-[e]s; *no pl*) **1.** decay, *a.* dilapidation, ruin, *a.* ✱ decline, (*moral*) degeneration, corruption. **2.** ✝ expiry.

ver'fallen¹ *v/i* (*irr, no -ge-, sn,* → *fallen*) **1.** decay, dilapidate, *building etc: a.* go to ruin, *culture, empire, etc: a.* decline, *patient:* waste away. **2.** become addicted (*dat* to): *j-m* ~ become s.o.'s slave. **3.** (*wieder*) ~ *in* (*acc*) fall (back) into. **4.** ~ *auf* (*acc*) hit (up)on (*an idea etc*); *wie ist er nur darauf* ~? what on earth made him think (or do) that? **5.** *ticket*: expire, *pawn*: become forfeited. **ver'fallen²** *adj* **1.** decayed, *a.* dilapidated. **2.** *ticket etc*: expired, *pawn*: forfeited. **3.** addicted (*dat* to); *j-m ~ sein* be s.o.'s slave.

Ver'falls|datum *n* best-before (*Am.* pull, *pharm.* sell-by) date. **~erscheinung** *f* sign of decay. **~tag** *m* ✝ expiry date.

ver'fälschen *v/t* (h) **1.** adulterate (*food etc*). **2.** falsify, distort (*facts etc*). **Ver'fälschung** *f* (-; -en) **1.** adulteration. **2.** falsification, distortion.

ver'fangen (*irr, no -ge-, h, → fangen*) **I** *v/i* work (*bei* with): *das verfängt bei mir nicht a.* that cuts no ice with me. **II** *sich ~ a. fig.* get caught (*in dat* in).

verfänglich [fɛr'fɛŋlɪç] *adj* trick (*question*), compromising, awkward (*situation etc*).

ver'färben: *sich ~* (h) change colo(u)r, *leaves*: turn.

ver'fassen *v/t* (h) write, compose, draw up. **Ver'fasser** *m* (-s; -), **Ver'fasserin** *f* (-; -nen) author, writer.

Ver'fassung *f* (-; -en) **1.** *no pl* a) state, condition, b) frame of mind: *in guter ~* in good condition (*or* shape), in a good state (of health). **2.** *pol.* constitution. **Ver'fassungs|änderung** *f* constitutional amendment. **~beschwerde** *f* constitutional complaint. **~bruch** *m* breach of the constitution. **2feindlich** *adj* anticonstitutional. **~gericht** *n* constitutional court. **~klage** *f* complaint of unconstitutionality. **2mäßig**, **2rechtlich** *adj* constitutional. **~schutz** *m* protection of the constitution. **2widrig** *adj* unconstitutional.

ver'faulen *v/i* (sn) rot, decay.

ver'fechten *v/t* (*irr, no -ge-, h, → fechten*) stand up for. **Ver'fechter** *m* (-s; -), **Ver'fechterin** *f* (-; -nen) advocate.

ver'fehlen *v/t* (h) miss (*um* by): *s-n Beruf verfehlt haben* have missed one's vocation; → *Wirkung* 1, *Zweck* 1.

ver'fehlt *adj* wrong, misguided.

Ver'fehlung *f* (-; -en) offen/ce (*Am.* -se).

verfeinden [fɛr'faɪndən] *sich ~* (h) become enemies; *sich mit j-m ~* make an enemy of s.o. **ver'feindet** *adj* hostile: *~ sein* be enemies.

verfeinern [fɛr'faɪnərn] *v/t* (h) refine. **Ver'feinerung** *f* (-; -en) refinement.

ver'femen *v/t* (h) **1.** ostracize. **2.** ban.

Ver'fettung *f* (-; -en) ✿ adiposis.

ver'feuern *v/t* (h) **1.** a) burn, b) use up. **2.** fire (*ammunition etc*).

ver'filmen *v/t* (h) film, adapt *novel etc* for the screen.

Ver'filmung *f* (-; -en) **1.** filming. **2.** film version, screen adaptation.

ver'filzen *v/i* (h) felt, *hair*: mat.

ver'finstern *v/t* (*a. sich ~*) (h) darken.

ver'flachen *v/i* (sn) **1.** flatten. **2.** *fig.* degenerate (*zu* into).

ver'flechten *v/t* (*irr, no -ge-, h, → flechten*) (*a. sich ~*) interweave (*a. fig.*), interlock: → *verflochten*. **Ver'flechtung** *f* (-; -en) interweaving (*a. fig.*), entanglement, ✝ interlocking.

ver'fliegen (*irr, no -ge-, → fliegen*) **I** *v/i* (sn) **1.** *alcohol etc*: evaporate. **2.** *fig.* vanish, *time etc*: fly. **II** *sich ~* get lost.

verflixt [fɛr'flɪkst] *adj* F blasted, damn(ed): *~!* blast!, damn (it)!

verflochten [fɛr'flɔxtən] *adj* interwoven (*a. fig.*), *fig.* (en)tangled, ✝ interlocked.

ver'flossen *adj* **1.** past (*time*). **2.** F ex-...

ver'fluchen *v/t* (h) curse.

ver'flucht → *verdammt*.

verflüchtigen [fɛr'flʏçtɪgən] *sich ~* (h) evaporate, *fig. a.* disappear.

verflüssigen [fɛr'flʏsɪgən] *v/t* (*a. sich ~*) (h) liquefy. **Ver'flüssigung** *f* (-; -en) liquefaction.

ver'folgen *v/t* (h) **1.** pursue (*a. fig. policy, career, etc*), chase, *a. hunt.* track: *j-n ~ thought etc*: haunt s.o.; *strafrechtlich ~* prosecute; *gerichtlich ~* take legal steps against. **2.** follow (*trail, a. fig. events, progress, etc*). **3.** *esp. pol.* persecute. **Ver'folger** *m* (-s; -) pursuer, *pol. etc* persecutor. **Ver'folgte** *m, f* (-n; -n) victim of persecution, (political) persecutee. **Ver'folgung** *f* (-; -en) pursuit (*a. cycling or fig.*), *pol. etc* persecution: *strafrechtliche ~* (criminal) prosecution. **Ver'folgungswahn** *m* persecution complex.

ver'formen *v/t* (*a. sich ~*) (h) deform. **Ver'formung** *f* (-; -en) deformation.

ver'frachten *v/t* (h) freight, ♦ *or Am.* ship: F *j-n in ein Taxi* (*ins Bett*) *~* bundle s.o. off into a taxi (to bed).

verfremden [fɛr'frɛmdən] *v/t* (h) alienate. **Ver'fremdung** *f* (-; -en) alienation.

ver'fressen *adj* F greedy.

ver'froren adj ~ sein feel the cold (very easily); ~ aussehen look frozen.

ver'früht adj premature.

verfügbar [fɛrˈfyːkbaːr] adj available.

Ver'fügbarkeit f (-; no pl) availability.

ver'fugen v/t (h) ✪ point.

ver'fügen (h) **I** v/t order: testamentarisch ~ decree by will. **II** v/i ~ über (acc) have s.o., s.th. at one's disposal, dispose of, possess, have; frei ~ können über (acc) be able to do what one wants with. **Ver'fügung** f (-; -en) **1.** order, adm. decree: laut ~ as ordered; → einstweilig, letztwillig. **2.** (über acc of) disposal, 🏛 disposition: zur ~ stehen (stellen) be (make) available, j-m be (place) at s.o.'s disposal; sich zur ~ stellen offer one's services, volunteer (für for); sein Amt zur ~ stellen tender one's resignation. **Ver'fügungsgewalt** f (-; no pl) control (über acc of).

ver'führen v/t (h) seduce. **Ver'führer** m (-s; -) seducer. **Ver'führerin** f (-; -nen) seductress. **ver'führerisch** adj **1.** seductive. **2.** fig. tempting. **Ver'führung** f (-; -en) **1.** seduction. **2.** fig. temptation. **Ver'führungskünste** pl powers of seduction.

ver'fünffachen v/t (a. sich ~) (h) quintuple.

ver'füttern v/t (h) feed.

Ver'gabe f (-; -n) placing (of orders etc), awarding (of prizes), allocation (of funds).

vergällen [fɛrˈɡɛlən] v/t (h) **1.** denature (alcohol). **2.** fig. sour, spoil.

ver'gammeln F **I** v/i (sn) rot, person: go to seed. **II** v/t (h) laze away (time). **ver'gammelt** adj F scruffy, seedy.

vergangen [fɛrˈɡaŋən] adj past: ~e Woche, in der ~en Woche last week. **Ver'gangenheit** f (-; no pl) past (a. fig.), ling. past tense: politische ~ political background; → ruhen.

Ver'gangenheitsbewältigung f coming to terms with the past.

vergänglich [fɛrˈɡɛŋlɪç] adj transitory, transient. **Ver'gänglichkeit** f (-; no pl) transitoriness, transience.

vergasen [fɛrˈɡaːzən] v/t (h) **1.** 🏭 gasify. **2.** gas.

Ver'gaser m (-s; -) mot. carburet(t)or.

vergaß [fɛrˈɡaːs] pret of **vergessen**.

Ver'gasung f (-; -en) **1.** 🏭 gasification. **2.** gassing.

ver'geben[1] (irr, no -ge-, h, → geben) **I** v/t **1.** (an acc) give s.th. away (to), place order etc (with), assign work etc (to), award prize (to), allocate funds (to), grant scholarship (to). **2.** j-m et. ~ forgive s.o. (for doing) s.th. **3.** e-e Chance ~ miss (or give away) the chance. **II** v/i **4.** j-m ~ forgive s.o. **5.** sports: give away the chance, shoot wide. **ver'geben**[2] adj post: filled, work etc: assigned: noch nicht ~ open, still vacant.

ver'gebens adj pred and adv in vain.

vergeblich [fɛrˈɡeːplɪç] **I** adj vain, futile, useless. **II** adv in vain.

Ver'geblichkeit f (-; no pl) futility.

Ver'gebung f (-; no pl) **1.** (j-n um ~ bitten ask s.o.'s) forgiveness. **2.** → **Vergabe**.

vergegenwärtigen [fɛrˈɡeːɡənvɛrtɪɡən] v/t (h) sich et. ~ visualize, picture.

ver'gehen (irr, no -ge-, h) **I** v/i (sn) pass (away) (a. fig.), time: a. go by, pain etc: wear off: wie die Zeit vergeht! how time flies; vor Ungeduld etc ~ be dying of impatience etc; er verging fast vor Angst he was frightened to death; mir ist der Appetit vergangen I've lost my appetite; F da vergeht einem alles! that turns you off completely. **II** sich ~ (h) a. an j-m commit indecent assault on s.o., rape s.o., b) gegen violate, offend against (law etc). **Ver'gehen** n (-s; -) offen/ce (Am. -se).

ver'gelten v/t (irr, no -ge-, h, → gelten) repay (j-m et. s.o. for s.th.).

Ver'geltung f (-; no pl) (als ~ in) retaliation (für for, of): ~ üben retaliate (an dat on). **Ver'geltungs...** retaliatory (measure, strike, etc).

verge'sellschaften v/t (h) ♀ socialize.

vergessen [fɛrˈɡɛsən] v/t (vergaß, vergessen, h) forget (sich o.s.), a. leave behind: ich habe es ~ a. it slipped my mind; ich habe ganz ~, wie I forget how; das vergesse ich dir nie I won't ever forget it; F das kannst du ~! forget it! **Ver'gessenheit** f (-; no pl) (in ~ geraten fall into) oblivion.

vergeßlich [fɛrˈɡɛslɪç] adj forgetful: ~ sein a. keep forgetting things.

Ver'geßlichkeit f (-; no pl) forgetfulness.

vergeuden [fɛrˈɡɔydən] v/t (h) waste,

squander. **Ver'geudung** f (-; -en) waste, squandering.

vergewaltigen [fɛrgə'valtɪgən] v/t (h) rape, a. fig. violate. **Verge'waltigung** f (-; -en) rape, a. fig. violation.

vergewissern [fɛrgə'vɪsərn] **sich ~** (h) make sure (**e-r Sache** of s.th.).

ver'gießen v/t (irr, no -ge-, h, → **gießen**) **1.** spill. **2.** shed (blood, tears).

ver'giften v/t (h) poison (**sich** o.s.), fig. a. contaminate. **Ver'giftung** f (-; -en) poisoning, fig. a. contamination.

vergilbt [fɛr'gɪlpt] adj yellowed.

Vergißmeinnicht [fɛr'gɪsmaɪnnɪçt] n (-[e]s; -[e]) ⚘ forget-me-not.

ver'gittern v/t (h) bar, a. lattice.

verglasen [fɛr'glaːzən] v/t (h) glaze.

Ver'gleich m (-[e]s; -e) **1.** (**im ~** in or by) comparison (**zu** with): **e-n ~ anstellen** draw a comparison; **dem ~ (nicht) standhalten** bear (no) comparison (**mit** with); → **hinken. 2.** ⚖ settlement, with creditors: composition: **gütlicher ~** amicable arrangement; **mit e-m Gläubiger e-n ~ schließen** compound with a creditor. **ver'gleichbar** adj comparable (**mit** to, with). **ver'gleichen** (irr, no -ge-, h, → **gleichen**) **I** v/t compare (**mit** to, with): **das ist nicht zu ~ mit ...** a) that cannot be compared to ..., b) it cannot compare with ... **II sich ~ mit** come to terms (or settle, compound) with. **ver'gleichend** adj comparative.

Ver'gleichs|kampf m sports: test. **~maßstab** m standard of comparison.

ver'gleichsweise adv comparatively.

Ver'gleichszahl f comparative figure.

ver'glühen v/i (sn) fire: smo(u)lder, meteor: burn out, rocket: burn up.

vergnügen [fɛr'gnyːgən] **sich ~** (h) enjoy o.s. **Ver'gnügen** n (-s; -) pleasure, fun: **mit ~** with pleasure; **viel ~!** a. iro. have fun!; (**nur**) **zum ~** (just) for fun; **vor ~ yell** etc with delight; **sein ~ haben an** (dat) enjoy; **j-m ~ machen** amuse s.o.; **ich wünsche dir viel ~** I hope you'll enjoy yourself; **es war kein (reines) ~** F it was no picnic; **ein teures ~** a costly affair. **vergnüglich** [-'gnyːklɪç] adj pleasant, amusing. **vergnügt** [-'gnyːkt] adj cheerful: **~ sein** a. be in high spirits. **Ver'gnügung** f (-; -en) usu. pl pleasure, amusement.

Ver'gnügungs|park m amusement

park, fun fair. **~reise** f pleasure trip. **~steuer** f entertainment tax. **⚖süchtig** adj pleasure-seeking. **~viertel** n night-life district.

ver'golden v/t (h) a. fig. gild.

ver'goldet adj gold-plated (watch etc).

ver'gönnen v/t (h) grant: **es war ihr nicht vergönnt zu** inf it was not granted to her to inf.

vergöttern [fɛr'gœtərn] v/t (h) idolize.

ver'graben v/t (irr, no -ge-, h, → **graben**) a. fig. bury (**sich** o.s.).

ver'grämt [fɛr'grɛːmt] adj careworn.

ver'graulen v/t (h) F scare off.

ver'greifen (irr, no -ge-, h, → **greifen**) **1. sich ~** make a mistake, ♪ play a wrong note: fig. **sich im Ton ~** strike a false note. **2. sich ~ an** (dat) misappropriate (s.th.); **sich an j-m ~** lay hands on s.o., (sexually) assault s.o.

vergreisen [fɛr'graɪzən] v/i (sn) become senile, a. population: age. **vergreist** [-'graɪst] adj senile. **Ver'greisung** f (-; no pl) (progressive) senility, ag(e)ing.

ver'griffen adj book: out of print.

vergrößern [fɛr'grøːsərn] (h) **I** v/t a) enlarge, phot. a. blow up, opt. magnify, b) expand, extend, c) a. fig. increase. **II sich ~** grow, a. enlarge, expand, increase, organ: become enlarged.

Ver'größerung f (-; -en) **1.** enlargement, expansion, increase. **2.** phot. enlargement, blow-up, opt. magnification.

Ver'größerungs|appa,rat m phot. enlarger. **~glas** n opt. magnifying glass.

Ver'günstigung f (-; -en) privilege, (tax) allowance, (social) benefit.

vergüten [fɛr'gyːtən] v/t (h) **1.** (j-m) et. ~ a) remunerate (or pay) (s.o.) (for) s.th., b) reimburse (s.o.) for s.th., c) compensate (s.o.) for s.th. **2.** ⊗ quench and temper (steel), opt. coat (lenses). **Ver'gütung** f (-; -en) **1.** remuneration, reimbursement, compensation. **2.** ⊗ quenching and tempering, opt. coating.

ver'haften v/t (h) arrest: **Sie sind verhaftet!** you are under arrest!

Ver'haftete m, f (-n; -n) person arrested.

Ver'haftung f (-; -en) arrest.

ver'hallen v/i (sn) die away.

ver'halten¹: sich ~ (irr, no -ge-, h, → **halten**) behave, a. conduct o.s., act, 🐾 a. react: **sich ruhig ~** keep quiet; **ich weiß nicht, wie ich mich ~ soll** I'm not sure what to do; *wenn sich die Sache so verhält* if that is the case.

ver'halten² I *adj* **1.** suppressed (*rage, laughter, etc*), restrained. **2.** → *gedämpft* 1. II *adv* with restraint: *~ fahren* drive cautiously; *sports*: *er lief ~* he didn't go all out; *~ spielen sports*: play a waiting game, *thea.* underact.

Ver'halten *n* (-s) behavio(u)r, conduct, attitude, reaction.

Ver'haltens|forscher *m* behavio(u)ral scientist. **~forschung** *f* behavio(u)ral science. **2gestört** *adj* disturbed, maladjusted. **~(maß)regeln** *pl* instructions. **~muster** *n* behavio(u)ral pattern. **~thera¸pie** *f* behavio(u)r therapy.

Verhältnis [fɛr'hɛltnɪs] *n* (-ses; -se) **1.** proportion, relation, ratio: *im ~ 1:10* in a ratio of 1:10; *in k-m ~ stehen* be out of all proportion (*zu* to). **2.** (*zu* with) relations, relationship: *ein gutes ~ zu j-m haben* get on well with s.o.; *er hat kein ~ zur Musik* he cannot relate to music. **3.** *pl* conditions, circumstances: *unter diesen ~sen* as matters stand; *in guten ~sen leben* be well off; *über s-e ~se leben* live beyond one's means. **4.** F (love) affair.

ver'hältnismäßig *adv* comparatively, relatively.

Ver'hältnis|wahl *f parl.* proportional representation. **~wort** *n* preposition.

ver'handeln (h) I *v/i* **1.** *~ über* (*acc*) a) negotiate (about, on, for), b) discuss. **2.** 🏛 hold a hearing (*or* trial). II *v/t* **1.** hear (*a case*), *criminal law*: try.

Ver'handlung *f* (-; -en) **1.** negotiation (*über acc* about, on, for). **2.** 🏛 a) hearing, b) trial: *zur ~ kommen* come up (for trial).

Ver'handlungs|basis *f* basis for negotiation: ✝ *~ 5000 DM* (price) DM 5,000 or nearest offer. **2bereit** *adj* ready to negotiate. **~partner** *m* negotiating partner. **~runde** *f* round of negotiations. **~tisch** *m* negotiating table.

verhangen [fɛr'haŋən] *adj* cloudy (*sky*).

ver'hängen *v/t* (h) **1.** (*mit* with) cover, drape. **2.** (*über acc*) impose *fine etc* (on), declare *state of emergency* (in a *country etc*). **3.** *sports*: award *penalty kick* (*gegen* against).

Ver'hängnis *n* (-ses; -se) a) fate, b) disaster: *j-m zum ~ werden* be s.o.'s un-

doing. **ver'hängnisvoll** *adj* a) fateful (*day etc*), b) disastrous, fatal.

verharmlosen [fɛr'harmloːzən] *v/t* (h) play *s.th.* down.

verhärmt [fɛr'hɛrmt] *adj* careworn.

ver'harschen *v/i* (sn) crust.

ver'härten *v/t* (h) *a. fig.* harden (*sich* o.s.). **Ver'härtung** *f* (-; -en) *esp. fig.* hardening, induration (*a.* 🩺).

ver'haspeln: sich ~ (h) F *fig.* get in a muddle.

ver'haßt *adj* hated, *matter*: *a.* hateful: *er hat sich bei allen ~ gemacht* he has turned everyone against him.

ver'hätscheln *v/t* (h) coddle, pamper.

ver'hauen *v/t* (h, *no* -ge-, h, → *hauen*) F **1.** beat *s.o.* up, spank. **2.** *fig.* muff.

verheddern [fɛr'hɛdərn] *sich ~* (h) F **1.** *a. fig.* tangle. **2.** → *verhaspeln*.

verheerend [fɛr'heːrənd] *adj* **1.** disastrous: *~ wirken auf* (*acc*) play havoc with. **2.** F dreadful. **Ver'heerungen** *pl* (*~ anrichten* cause) havoc.

ver'heilen *v/i* (sn) heal (up).

ver'heimlichen *v/t* (h) (*dat* from) hide, conceal, keep *s.th.* a secret.

ver'heiraten *v/t* (h) *j-n ~* marry s.o. (off) (*mit, an acc* to); *sich ~* marry, get married; *verheiratet sein* be married (*mit* to, *a.* F *fig.*). **Ver'heiratete** *m, f* (-n; -n) married man (woman).

ver'heißen *v/t* (*irr, no* -ge-, h, → *heißen*), **Ver'heißung** *f* (-; -en) promise.

ver'heißungsvoll *adj* promising.

ver'helfen *v/t* (*irr, no* -ge-, h, → *helfen*) *j-m ~ zu* help s.o. (to) find (*or* get *etc*).

ver'herrlichen *v/t* (h) glorify.

Ver'herrlichung *f* (-; -en) glorification.

ver'hexen *v/t* (h) bewitch, F jinx: *es ist wie verhext!* there is a jinx on it.

ver'hindern *v/t* (h) prevent: (*es*) ~, *daß j-d et. tut* prevent s.o. from doing s.th.

ver'hindert *adj* **1.** ~ *sein* be unable to come. **2.** F *fig.* would-be (*artist etc*).

Ver'hinderung *f* (-; -en) prevention.

ver'höhnen *v/t* (h) deride, mock. **Ver'höhnung** *f* (-; -en) derision, mockery.

verhökern [fɛr'høːkərn] *v/t* (h) F *contp.* flog, sell off.

Ver'hör [fɛr'høːr] *n* (-[e]s; -e) 🏛 interrogation, questioning.

ver'hören (h) I *v/t* 🏛 interrogate, question. II *sich ~* mishear.

ver'hüllen *v/t* (h) cover (up), *a. fig.* veil.

ver'hundertfachen v/t (h) centuple.

ver'hungern v/i (sn) die of starvation: *j-n ~ lassen* starve s.o. to death; F *ich bin am Verhungern!* I'm starving.

ver'hüten v/t (h) prevent.

ver'hütten v/t (h) ⚙ smelt (*ore*).

Ver'hütung f (-; *no pl*) **1.** prevention. **2.** ⚕ contraception.

Ver'hütungsmittel n ⚕ contraceptive.

verhutzelt [fɛr'hʊtsəlt] *adj* F wizened.

ver'innerlichen v/t (h) internalize.

ver'irren: sich ~ (h) lose one's way, get lost: *fig. verirrte Kugel* stray bullet.

Ver'irrung f (-; -en) *fig.* aberration.

ver'jagen v/t (h) a. *fig.* chase away.

ver'jähren v/i (sn) ⚖ come under the statute of limitation. **ver'jährt** *adj* statute-barred. **Ver'jährung** f (-; -en) **1.** limitation. **2.** (negative) prescription.

Ver'jährungsfrist f period of limitation.

ver'jubeln v/t (h) F blow.

verjüngen [fɛr'jʏŋən] (h) **I** v/t **1.** make s.o. (look) younger, rejuvenate: *sports: die Mannschaft ~* build up a younger team. **II** *sich ~* **2.** grow (*or* look) younger. **3.** ⚙ taper. **Ver'jüngung** f (-; -en) **1.** rejuvenation. **2.** ⚙ taper.

ver'kabeln v/t (h) connect to a cable TV network.

ver'kalken v/i (h) **1.** calcify, F *arteries: a.* harden, ⚕ *a.* fur up. **2.** F go senile: *er ist völlig verkalkt* a. he's gone completely gaga.

verkalku'lieren: sich ~ (h) miscalculate.

Ver'kalkung f (-; -en) **1.** calcification, F ⚕ *a.* hardening of the arteries, ⚕ *a.* furring up. **2.** F senility.

verkannt [fɛr'kant] *adj* unrecognized.

ver'kanten v/t (h) edge (*ski*).

ver'kappt *adj* disguised, in disguise.

Ver'kauf m (-[e]s; ⁓e) **1.** (*zum ~* for) sale. **2.** ⚓ sales department. **ver'kaufen I** v/t (*dat, an acc* to) sell (*a.* F *fig.*): *zu ~!* for sale! **II** *sich ~* sell *well, badly, etc, fig.* sell o.s. **Ver'käufer** m (-s; -) **1.** seller, vendor. **2.** shop assistant, *Am.* salesclerk. **Ver'käuferin** f (-; -nen) shop assistant, saleslady, *Am.* salesclerk. **ver'käuflich** *adj* a) marketable, sal(e)able, b) for sale: *gut ~* easy to sell; *⚕ frei ~* available without prescription.

Ver'kaufs|förderung f sales promotion. **~gespräch** n sales talk. **~leiter** m sales manager. **⚓offen** *adj* **~er Samstag**

all-day shopping on Saturday. **~preis** m selling price. **~schlager** m F money-spinner. **~stand** m stand. **~wert** m market value. **~ziffer** f sales figure.

Verkehr [fɛr'keːr] m (-s; *no pl*) **1.** traffic: *öffentlicher ~* public transport(ation). **2.** contact, dealings: *den ~ abbrechen* break off all contact(s). **3.** ⚓ a) trade, b) payments, c) circulation: *aus dem ~ ziehen* a. F *fig.* withdraw from circulation. **4.** (sexual) intercourse.

ver'kehren v/i (h) **1.** (*a.* sn) *bus etc*: run, operate. **2.** *~ in* (*dat*) frequent; *bei j-m ~* visit s.o. regularly. **3.** *~ mit* associate with; *geschäftlich ~ mit* have business dealings with. **4.** (*geschlechtlich*) *~ mit* have (sexual) intercourse with.

Ver'kehrs|ampel f traffic lights. **~amt** n tourist office. **~aufkommen** n volume of traffic. **~behinderung** f holdup, delay. **~betriebe** *pl* transport services. **~chaos** n traffic chaos. **~de,likt** n traffic offen/ce (*Am.* -se). **~dichte** f traffic density. **~durchsage** f traffic announcement. **~erziehung** f road safety education. **~flugzeug** n airliner. **~fluß** m (-sses; *no pl*) traffic flow. **⚓frei** *adj* traffic-free (*area etc*). **~funk** m information for motorists. **~günstig** *adv* **~ gelegen** conveniently placed as regards transport facilities. **~insel** f traffic island. **~kon,trolle** f vehicle spot check. **~lage** f situation on the roads. **~lärm** m traffic noise. **~meldungen** *pl* traffic news. **~mi,nister** m minister of transport. **~mini,sterium** n ministry of transport. **~mittel** n (means of) transportation: *öffentliche ~ pl* public transport(ation *Am.*). **~netz** n traffic system. **~opfer** n road casualty. **~ordnung** f traffic regulations. **~poli,zei** f traffic police. **~poli,zist** m traffic policeman. **~regel** f traffic regulation. **~regelung** f traffic control. **⚓reich** *adj* busy. **~schild** n road sign. **⚓sicher** *adj* roadworthy. **~sicherheit** f road safety, *mot.* roadworthiness. **~sprache** f lingua franca. **~stau** m, **~stockung** f traffic jam. **~streife** f traffic patrol. **~sünder** m traffic offender. **~teilnehmer** m road user. **~unfall** m traffic accident, (car) crash. **~unterricht** m traffic instruction. **~verbindung** f (road *or* rail) link. **~verbund** m (integrated) public transport system. **~verein** m tourist office. **~wert** m ✝ market value. **~wesen** n (-s; no pl) public transport(ation Am.). ♀**widrig** adj contrary to the traffic regulations. **~zählung** f traffic census. **~zeichen** n road sign.

ver'kehrt adj and adv wrong, adv a. the wrong way: **~ herum** a) the wrong way round, b) upside down, c) inside out.

ver'kennen v/t (irr, no -ge-, h, → **kennen**) misjudge; → **verkannt**.

ver'ketten v/t (h) a. fig. link.

Ver'kettung f (-; -en) fig. concatenation.

ver'ketzern v/t (h) denounce.

ver'klagen v/t (h) ⚖ sue (**wegen, auf** acc for).

ver'klappen v/t (h) dump into the sea.

ver'klären v/t (h) fig. idealize.

ver'klärt adj fig. beatific.

ver'kleiden (h) **I** v/t **1.** dress s.o. up, disguise. **2.** ⊛ a) cover, b) line, c) case, d) panel, e) ⚙ face, revet. **II** sich ~ dress (o.s.) up, disguise o.s.

Ver'kleidung f (-; -en) **1.** disguise. **2.** ⊛ covering, casing, lining, panel(l)ing, ⚙ facing, mot. cowling, ✈ fairing.

verkleinern [fɛr'klaɪnərn] v/t (h) **1.** make s.th. smaller, reduce (scale etc), diminish. **2.** fig. detract from, belittle.

Ver'kleinerung f (-; -en) reduction.

Ver'kleinerungsform f ling. diminutive.

ver'klemmen: sich ~ (h) get stuck.

ver'klemmt adj psych. inhibited.

ver'klingen v/i (irr, no -ge-, sn, → **klingen**) a. fig. die away.

ver'knacken v/t (h) F **j-n zu zwei Jahren ~** put s.o. inside for two years.

ver'knallen: sich ~ (h) F fall for (**in j-n** s.o.); **verknallt sein in** (acc) a. be madly in love with, have a crush on.

Ver'knappung f (-; -en) shortage.

ver'kneifen v/t (irr, no -ge-, h, → **kneifen**) F **sich et. ~** do (or go) without s.th.; **ich konnte mir ein Lächeln nicht ~** I couldn't help smiling.

ver'kniffen adj pinched (face, mouth).

ver'knöchern v/i (sn) a. fig. ossify: **er ist total verknöchert** F he's an old fossil.

ver'knoten v/t (h) knot, tie (up).

ver'knüpfen v/t (h) **1.** tie (or knot) together. **2.** fig. link: **verknüpft sein mit** involve (costs, difficulties, etc); **eng verknüpft sein mit** be bound up with.

ver'kochen v/i (sn) boil away: gastr. **verkocht sein** be overboiled.

ver'kohlen I v/i (sn) char. **II** v/t (h) F fig. **j-n ~** have s.o. on, pull s.o.'s leg.

ver'kommen¹ v/i (irr, no -ge-, sn, → **kommen**) go to rack and ruin, person: go to seed, morally: sink low, fruit etc: go to waste. **ver'kommen²** adj a) run-down, dilapidated, b) person: seedy, depraved. **Ver'kommenheit** f (-; no pl) seediness, depravity.

ver'korken v/t (h) cork (up).

verkorksen [fɛr'kɔrksən] v/t (h) F mess s.th. up; **sich den Magen ~** upset one's stomach; **verkorkste Sache** mess.

verkörpern [fɛr'kœrpərn] v/t (h) personify, embody, thea. impersonate, play.

Ver'körperung f (-; -en) personification, embodiment, thea. impersonation.

verköstigen [fɛr'kœstɪgən] v/t (h) feed.

ver'krachen: sich ~ (h) F fall out (**mit** with). **ver'kracht** adj F **1. mit j-n ~ sein** have fallen out with s.o. **2.** failed (artist etc): **~e Existenz** failure.

verkraften [fɛr'kraftən] v/t (h) cope with, handle, mentally: bear, take.

ver'krampfen: sich ~ (h) hands: clench, muscles etc: cramp, person: tense (up).

ver'kriechen: sich ~ (irr, no -ge-, h, → **kriechen**) a. fig. hide.

ver'krümeln: sich ~ (h) F sneak off.

ver'krümmt adj ✈ curved. **Ver'krümmung** f (-; -en) distortion: **~ der Wirbelsäule** curvature of the spine.

ver'krüppeln I v/t (h) cripple. **II** v/i (sn) become crippled (tree: stunted).

ver'krusten v/i (sn) become encrusted.

ver'kümmern v/i (sn) become stunted, a. fig. waste away, atrophy. **ver'kümmert** adj stunted, a. fig. atrophied.

verkünden [fɛr'kyndən] v/t (h) **1.** announce, adm. proclaim, ⚖ pronounce (sentence), promulgate (law etc). **2.** fig. herald. **ver'kündigen** v/t (h) **1.** lit. for **verkünden**. **2.** eccl. preach.

Ver'kündigung f (-; -en) eccl. preaching.

Ver'kündung f (-; -en) announcement, proclamation, ⚖ pronouncement, promulgation.

ver'kupfern v/t (h) copper.

ver'kuppeln v/t (h) F **j-n ~** marry s.o. off (**an** acc to).

ver'kürzen (h) **I** v/t shorten (**um** by), abridge, cut short: **verkürzte Arbeits-**

zeit reduced hours. **II** v/i ~ **auf** (acc) sports: shorten to.

Ver'ladebahnhof m shipping station.

ver'laden v/t (irr, no -ge-, h, → **laden**) **1.** load, ship, ♻ embark, ✈ emplane, 🚂 entrain, mot. entruck. **2.** F j-n ~ take s.o. for a ride, sell s.o.

Ver'ladung f (-; -en) loading (etc).

Verlag [fɛrˈlaːk] m (-[e]s; -e) publishing house (or company), publisher(s): **er-schienen im ~ L.** published by L.

ver'lagern v/t (h) **1.** (a. **sich ~**) a. fig. interest, emphasis, etc: shift (**auf** acc to). **2.** → **verlegen**¹ 1. **Ver'lagerung** f (-; -en) **1.** shift(ing). **2.** → **Verlegung**.

Ver'lags|anstalt f publishing house (or company). **~buchhandel** m publishing trade. **~buchhändler** m publisher. **~pro,gramm** n publisher's list. **~werk** n publication. **~wesen** n (-s; no pl) publishing.

ver'landen v/i (sn) silt up.

ver'langen (h) **I** v/t **1.** a) ask for, demand, b) expect ~ c) claim, d) charge: **die Rechnung ~** ask for the bill; **er verlangt viel** he's very demanding; **das ist (nicht) zuviel verlangt** that's (not) asking too much; **er verlangte den Geschäftsführer** he asked to speak to the manager; **Sie werden am Telefon verlangt** you are wanted on the phone. **2.** require, call for (patience, time, etc). **II** v/i ~ **nach** a) ask for, b) long for.

Ver'langen n (-s) **1.** (**nach** for) desire, longing: **heftiges ~** craving. **2.** demand, request: **auf ~** on request.

verlängern [fɛrˈlɛŋɐn] v/t (h) **1.** lengthen (a. **sich ~**), make s.th. longer, fig. prolong (life, period, etc), extend (a. credit, membership, etc), renew (contract etc). **2.** sports: touch ball etc on (**zu** to). **Ver'längerung** f (-; -en) **1.** a) lengthening, b) prolongation, extension, renewal. **2.** sports: a) pass, b) (**in die ~ gehen** go into) extra time (Am. overtime). **Ver'längerungsschnur** f ⚡ extension flex (Am. cord).

ver'langsamen v/t (a. **sich ~**) (h) slacken, slow down (a. fig. development etc).

Verlaß [fɛrˈlas] m **es ist (kein) ~ auf j-n (et.)** s.o. (s.th.) is reliable (unreliable).

ver'lassen¹ (irr, no -ge-, h, → **lassen**) **I** v/t leave, a. abandon, desert: **s-e Kräfte verließen ihn** his strength failed him.

II sich ~ auf (acc) rely (or count, depend) on; F **verlaß dich drauf!** take my word for it! **ver'lassen**² adj **1.** deserted, desolate (region etc). **2.** abandoned.

Ver'lassen n (-s) abandonment, desertion. **Ver'lassenheit** f (-; no pl) **1.** loneliness. **2.** desolation.

ver'läßlich adj reliable, dependable.

Ver'lauf m (-[e]s; ⁓e) **1.** course (of road etc). **2.** a) course, run, b) progress, development: **im ~ von** (or gen) in the course of; **im weiteren ~** in the sequel.

ver'laufen (irr, no -ge-, → **laufen**) **I** v/i (sn) **1.** road etc: run. **2.** go, run, come off: **alles verlief wie geplant** everything went according to plan; **normal ~** take its normal course; → **ergebnislos**. **3.** paint: run, bleed. **4.** trail: disappear: → **Sand**. **5.** → **zerlaufen**. **II sich ~** (h) get lost, lose one's way.

ver'laust adj full of lice.

ver'lauten v/i (sn) be reported: **wie verlautet** as reported; **~ lassen** give to understand, hint.

ver'leben v/t (h) spend: **e-e schöne Zeit ~ a.** have a nice time. **verlebt** [fɛrˈleːpt] adj dissipated, worn-out (by a fast life).

ver'legen¹ (h) **I** v/t **1.** (auch, in acc to) transfer, move. **2.** (auf acc) put off (to), postpone (until). **3.** mislay (key etc). **4.** lay (carpet, cable, etc). **5.** publish (book etc). **6.** → **verlagern** 1. **II sich ~ auf** (acc) a) take up, take to gardening etc, b) resort to pleading etc.

ver'legen² adj **1.** embarrassed: **~ machen** embarrass. **2.** (nie) **~ um** (never) at a loss for an answer, excuse, etc.

Ver'legenheit f (-; -en) **1.** no pl embarrassment: **j-n in ~ bringen** embarrass s.o. **2.** predicament, awkward situation: **j-m aus der ~ helfen** help s.o. out. **Ver'legenheits|lösung** f makeshift solution. **~pause** f awkward silence.

Ver'leger m (-s; -) publisher.

ver'legerisch adj publisher's (risk etc).

Ver'legung f (-; -en) **1.** transfer, removal. **2.** postponement. **3.** ⊙ laying.

ver'leiden v/t (h) j-m et. ~ spoil s.th. for s.o.

Verleih [fɛrˈlaɪ] m (-[e]s; -e) **1.** no pl hiring out, film: distribution: **~ von Autos** etc cars etc for hire. **2.** hire (or rental) service, film: distributors.

ver'leihen v/t (irr, no -ge-, h, → **leihen**)

1. (*an acc* to) a) lend (out), *esp. Am.* loan, b) hire (*Am.* rent) out. **2.** (*dat*) award *prize etc* (to), confer *title etc* (on), grant *s.o.* right etc. **3.** *fig.* give (*dat* to): **s-r Dankbarkeit Ausdruck ~** express one's gratitude. **Ver'leiher** *m* (-s; -) lender, *esp. Am.* loaner, *film:* distributor. **Ver'leihung** *f* (-; -en) **1.** lending (*etc*, → **verleihen** 1). **2.** award(ing), conferment, grant(ing).

ver'leimen *v/t* (h) glue together.

ver'leiten *v/t* (h) *j-n zu et. ~* make s.o. do s.th., lead *s.o.* to do s.th., seduce (*or* talk) s.o. into doing s.th.; **sich ~ lassen** (**zu** *inf*) be seduced (to *inf*).

ver'lernen *v/t* (h) unlearn, forget.

ver'lesen¹ (*irr, no* -ge-, h, → **lesen**) **I** *v/t* read out, call out: **die Namensliste ~** call the roll. **II sich ~** read it wrong.

ver'lesen² *v/t* (*irr, no* -ge-, h, → **lesen**) pick (through).

ver'letzbar, ver'letzlich *adj fig.* vulnerable, touchy. **verletzen** [fɛr'lɛtsən] (h) **I** *v/t* injure, hurt, wound, *fig. a.* offend (*s.o.*), violate (*law etc*), offend against (*good taste etc*): **er wurde tödlich verletzt** he was fatally injured; **j-n tief ~** cut s.o. to the quick; **s-e Pflicht ~** neglect one's duty. **II sich ~** hurt o.s., get hurt; **er hat sich am Arm verletzt** he hurt his arm. **ver'letzend** *adj fig.* offensive. **Ver'letzte** *m, f* (-n; -n) injured person: **die ~n** the injured; **es gab viele ~** many people were injured. **Ver'letzung** *f* (-; -en) **1.** injury, wound. **2.** *fig.* infringement, violation, breach.

Ver'letzungs|gefahr *f* danger of injuring o.s. **~pech** *n sports:* **vom ~ verfolgt** injury-ridden.

ver'leugnen *v/t* (h) deny (*fact etc*), renounce (*faith etc*), disown (*friend etc*): **es läßt sich nicht ~, daß** there's no denying that; **sich vor j-m ~ lassen** not to be at home to s.o.

Ver'leugnung *f* (-; -en) denial.

verleumden [fɛr'lɔymdən] *v/t* (h) calumniate, ⚖ slander, libel. **Ver'leumder** *m* (-s; -), **Ver'leumderin** *f* (-; -nen) slanderer, libel(l)er. **ver'leumderisch** *adj* slanderous, libel(l)ous. **Ver'leumdung** *f* (-; -en) calumny, slander, libel. **Ver'leumdungskam,pagne** *f* smear campaign. **Ver'leumdungsklage** *f* ⚖ action for slander (*or* libel).

ver'lieben: sich ~ (h) fall in love (**in** *acc* with). **verliebt** [fɛr'li:pt] *adj* in love (**in** *acc* with), amorous (*look etc*): **Verliebte** people in love, lovers. **Ver'liebtheit** *f* (-; *no pl*) being in love, amorousness.

verlieren [fɛr'li:rən] (verlor, verloren, h) **I** *v/t* lose, *a.* shed (*leaves, hair*); *fig.* **kein Wort darüber ~** not to say a word about it; F **er hat hier nichts verloren!** he's got no business (to be) here; → **Auge** 1, **Mut, Nerv.** **II** *v/i* lose (**gegen** to, against): *fig.* **an Wert ~** go down in value; → **Reiz** 2. **III sich ~** disappear. **Ver'lierer** *m* (-s; -), **Ver'liererin** *f* (-; -nen) loser. **Ver'liererseite** *f auf der ~ sein* be on the losing side.

Verlies [fɛr'li:s] *n* (-es; -e) dungeon.

ver'loben: sich ~ (h) get engaged (**mit** to). **verlobt** [fɛr'lo:pt] *adj* engaged (to be married) (**mit** to). **Ver'lobte** *m, f* (-n; -n) fiancé(e *f*): **die ~n** the engaged couple. **Ver'lobung** *f* (-; -en) engagement.

Ver'lobungs|anzeige *f* engagement announcement. **~feier** *f* engagement party. **~ring** *m* engagement ring.

ver'locken *v/t* (h) tempt (**zu et.** into doing s.th.). **ver'lockend** *adj* tempting. **Ver'lockung** *f* (-; -en) temptation.

verlogen [fɛr'lo:gən] *adj* a) lying, b) hypocritical (*morals etc*): **du ~er Kerl!** you damned liar! **Ver'logenheit** *f* (-; -en) a) lying, b) hypocrisy.

verlor [fɛr'lo:r] *pret of* **verlieren**.

ver'loren **I** *pp of* **verlieren**. **II** *adj* lost, *fig. a.* wasted, *a.* forlorn: *gastr.* **~e Eier** poached eggs; *bibl.* **der ~e Sohn** the prodigal son; **auf ~em Posten stehen** fight a losing battle.

ver'lorengehen *v/i* (*irr, sep,* -ge-, sn, → **gehen**) get lost, be lost: **an ihm ist ein Lehrer verlorengegangen** he would have made a good teacher.

ver'losen *v/t* (h) **1.** draw lots for. **2.** raffle (off). **Ver'losung** *f* (-; -en) **1.** drawing lots (*gen* for). **2.** raffle, lottery.

ver'löten *v/t* (h) ⚙ solder (up).

verlottern [fɛr'lɔtərn] → **verwahrlosen**.

Ver'lust *m* (-[e]s; -e) loss (**an** *dat* of, *fig.* **für** to). *a.* bereavement: **~e** losses, *at games:* losings, ✕ casualties; **mit ~** at a loss; **mit ~ arbeiten** *a.* be losing money.

Ver'lust|geschäft *n* losing deal. **~meldung** *f* report of loss, ✕ casualty report. **~ziffer** *f* ✕ casualty figure.

ver'machen v/t (h) leave (*dat* to).
Vermächtnis [fɛr'mɛçtnɪs] n (-ses; -se) ⚖️ 1. will. 2. a. fig. legacy.
vermählen [fɛr'mɛːlən] **sich ~** (h) get married (*mit* to). **Ver'mählte** m, f (-n; -n) newlywed: **die ~n** the newly-married couple. **Ver'mählung** f (-; -en) marriage, wedding.
ver'männlichen v/t (h) masculinize.
vermarkten [fɛr'marktən] v/t (h) market, a. fig. sell, fig. commercialize. **Ver'marktung** f (-; -en) marketing, fig. commercialization.
vermasseln [fɛr'masəln] v/t (h) F **et. ~** mess s.th. up; **j-m die Tour ~** queer s.o.'s pitch.
vermassen [fɛr'masən] **I** v/i (sn) lose one's individuality. **II** v/t (h) depersonalize. **Ver'massung** f (-; -en) loss of individuality, depersonalization.
ver'mehren (h) **I** v/t 1. (*um* by) increase, multiply. 2. *biol.* breed. **II sich ~** 3. → 1. 4. *biol.* reproduce, multiply, breed. **Ver'mehrung** f (-; -en) 1. increase. 2. *biol.* reproduction, breeding.
vermeidbar [fɛr'maɪtbaːr] adj avoidable. **ver'meiden** v/t (*irr, no* -ge-, h, → **meiden**) avoid, evade, shun: **es läßt sich nicht ~** it can't be helped.
vermeintlich [fɛr'maɪntlɪç] adj a) supposed, b) alleged.
ver'mengen v/t (h) mix, fig. mix up.
ver'menschlichen v/t (h) humanize.
Vermerk [fɛr'mɛrk] m (-[e]s; -e) note.
ver'merken v/t (h) make a note of.
ver'messen¹ v/t (*irr, no* -ge-, h, → **messen**) measure, survey (*land*).
ver'messen² adj presumptuous.
Ver'messenheit f (-; -en) presumption.
Ver'messung f (-; -en) survey(ing).
Ver'messungsingeni,eur m surveyor.
vermiesen [fɛr'miːzən] v/t (h) F **j-m et. ~** spoil s.th. for s.o.
ver'mieten v/t (h) (*an acc* to) let, ⚖️ lease, *esp. Am.* rent (out), hire (*Am.* rent) out (*car etc*): **zu ~** house: to let, *car*: for hire, *esp. Am.* for rent.
Ver'mieter m (-s; -) 1. landlord. 2. lessor. **Ver'mieterin** f (-; -nen) landlady.
Ver'mietung f (-; -en) letting, leasing, *esp. Am.* renting (out), hiring (out).
ver'mindern → **verringern**.
verminen [fɛr'miːnən] v/t (h) ✕ mine.
ver'mischen v/t (a. **sich ~**) (h) mix.

ver'mischt adj mixed, miscellaneous.
vermissen [fɛr'mɪsən] v/t (h) miss: **j-n sehr ~** miss s.o. badly; **vermißt werden** be missing; **ich vermisse m-e Uhr** my watch is missing; **~ lassen** lack.
Ver'mißte m, f (-n; -n) missing person.
ver'mitteln (h) **I** v/t 1. **j-m et. ~** get (*or* find) s.o. s.th.; **j-n ~ an** (*acc*) find s.o. a place with *a firm etc.* 2. arrange, negotiate (*deal etc*). 3. (*dat* to) impart (*knowledge etc*), convey (*impression etc*). **II** v/i (*zwischen* between, *in dat* in) a) mediate, b) intervene. **Ver'mittler** m (-s; -) 1. mediator. 2. go-between. 3. ✝ agent. **Ver'mittlung** f (-; -en) 1. procurement, negotiation (*of deal etc*), placement (*of worker etc*), arrangement (*of meeting etc*): **durch ~ von** (*or gen*) through. 2. imparting (*of knowledge etc*), conveyance (*of impression etc*). 3. a) mediation, b) intervention. 4. agency, office. 5. a) (telephone) exchange, *in firm etc*: switchboard, b) operator.
Ver'mittlungs|gebühr f ✝ agent's commission. **~versuch** m attempt at mediation.
ver'modern v/i (sn) mo(u)lder, rot.
Ver'mögen n (-s; -) 1. a) fortune, b) property, ✝ assets: **sie hat ~** she is wealthy; F fig. **ein ~ kosten** cost a fortune. 2. *no pl* (*nach bestem ~* to the best of one's) ability.
ver'mögend adj wealthy, well-to-do.
Ver'mögens|bildung f wealth formation. **~steuer** f property tax. **~verhältnisse** pl (financial) circumstances. **~verwalter** m custodian. **~werte** pl assets. **♀wirksam** adj **~e Leistung** (*employer's*) capital-forming payment *under the employees' saving scheme*.
vermummen [fɛr'mʊmən] v/t (h) 1. wrap up. 2. disguise.
ver'murksen v/t (h) F **et. ~** mess s.th. up.
vermuten [fɛr'muːtən] v/t (h) 1. think, suppose, assume, *Am.* F guess. 2. expect. 3. suspect. **ver'mutlich I** adj → **mutmaßlich. II** adv probably: **~! I** suppose so. **Ver'mutung** f (-; -en) a) supposition, F guess, b) suspicion, c) conjecture, speculation: **s-e ~ war richtig** his guess was right; **die ~ liegt nahe, daß** it is highly probable that; **das sind reine ~en** that's mere guesswork.

vernachlässigen [fɛr'naːxlɛsɪgən] *v/t* (h) **1.** neglect. **2.** ignore.

Ver'nachlässigung *f* (-; -en) neglect.

ver'nageln *v/t* (h) *mit Brettern* ~ board up. **ver'nagelt** *adj* F *fig.* dense, thick: *ich war wie* ~ my mind was a blank.

ver'nähen *v/t* (h) sew up.

ver'narben *v/i* (sn) **1.** scar over. **2.** *fig.* heal. **vernarbt** [-'narpt] *adj* scarred.

ver'narrt *adj* ~ *sein in* (acc) F be wild about, *ein Kind* dote on a child.

ver'naschen *v/t* (h) **1.** spend on sweets. **2.** F a) lay (*sl.*), b) *sports:* clobber.

ver'nebeln *v/t* (h) **1.** ⊕ atomize. **2.** ✕ screen. **3.** *fig.* obscure.

ver'nehmbar *adj* audible. **ver'nehmen** *v/t* (*irr, no* -ge-, h, → *nehmen*) **1.** hear, *fig. a.* learn. **2.** ⚖ interrogate, examine: *als Zeuge vernommen werden* be called into the witness box (*Am.* stand).

Ver'nehmen *n dem* ~ *nach* from what one hears; *sicherem* ~ *nach* according to reliable reports.

ver'nehmlich *adj* audible, distinct.

Ver'nehmung *f* (-; -en) ⚖ interrogation, examination. **ver'nehmungsfähig** *adj* fit to be examined.

ver'neigen: *sich* ~ (h) bow (*vor dat* to).

Ver'neigung *f* (-; -en) bow (*vor dat* to).

verneinen [fɛr'naɪnən] *v/t* (h) **1.** *a. v/i* answer in the negative. **2.** a) deny, reject. **ver'neinend** *adj a. ling.* negative. **Ver'neinung** *f* (-; -en) **1.** *a. ling.* negation. **2.** a) denial, b) rejection.

vernetzen [fɛr'nɛtsən] *v/t* (h) *computer:* network. **Ver'netzung** *f* (-; -en) networking.

vernichten [fɛr'nɪçtən] *v/t* (h) **1.** destroy, annihilate, *a. fig.* exterminate, wipe out. **2.** *fig.* dash, shatter (*hopes*).

ver'nichtend *adj fig.* scathing, devastating (*look, criticism, etc*), crushing (*blow, defeat, etc*): *j-n* ~ *schlagen sports:* beat s.o. hollow.

Ver'nichtung *f* (-; -en) destruction, annihilation, *a. fig.* extermination.

Ver'nichtungs|krieg *m* war of annihilation. **~lager** *n* extermination camp. **~potenti,al** *n* destructive potential. **~schlag** *m fig.* final blow. **~waffe** *f* weapon of destruction.

ver'nickeln *v/t* (h) nickel(-plate).

ver'niedlichen *v/t* (h) play down.

ver'nieten *v/t* (h) ⊕ rivet.

Vernissage [vɛrnɪ'saːʒə] *f* (-; -n) private view.

Vernunft [fɛr'nʊnft] *f* (-; *no pl*) reason: ~ *annehmen* listen to reason; *j-n zur* ~ *bringen* bring s.o. to his senses; *wieder zur* ~ *kommen* come back to one's senses. **ℒbegabt** *adj* rational. **~ehe** *f* marriage of convenience. **~gründe** *pl aus* ~*n* for reasons of common sense.

vernünftig [fɛr'nʏnftɪç] **I** *adj* **1.** sensible, reasonable, level-headed: *sie war* ~ *genug, nein zu sagen* she had the good sense to say no; *sei* (*doch*) ~! be sensible! **2.** F reasonable, decent: *e-n* ~*en Beruf ergreifen* take up a proper career. **II** *adv* sensibly, reasonably: ~ *reden* talk sense; F ~ *essen* eat properly.

Ver'nunftmensch *m* rational person.

ver'nunftwidrig *adj* irrational.

ver'öden I *v/t* (h) ⚕ sclerose, obliterate. **II** *v/i* (sn) become deserted.

ver'öffentlichen *v/t* (h) publish.

Ver'öffentlichung *f* (-; -en) publication.

ver'ordnen *v/t* (h) **1.** ⚕ a) order, b) prescribe (*j-m* for s.o.). **2.** *adm.* decree.

Ver'ordnung *f* (-; -en) **1.** ⚕ prescription. **2.** *adm.* ordinance, decree.

ver'pachten *v/t* (h) lease (*dat, an acc* to).

Ver'pächter(in *f*) *m* lessor.

Ver'pachtung *f* (-; -en) lease, leasing.

ver'packen *v/t* (h) pack (up), ✝ package, wrap up; → *Geschenk*.

Ver'packung *f* (-; -en) **1.** *no pl* packing, packaging. **2.** wrapping, packing material: ✝ *zuzüglich* ~ plus packing.

Ver'packungs|auto,mat *m* automatic packaging machine. **~materi,al** *n* packing material.

ver'passen *v/t* (h) **1.** miss (*bus etc*), *a.* lose, waste (*chance*). **2.** F *j-m e-e Uniform etc* ~ fit s.o. with a uniform *etc*; *j-m ein Ding* ~ land s.o. one, zap s.o.

ver'patzen *v/t* (h) F *et.* ~ mess s.th. up, *sports, thea.* muff s.th.

verpesten [fɛr'pɛstən] *v/t* (h) pollute: F *die Luft* ~ stink the place out.

ver'petzen *v/t* (h) F *j-n* ~ sneak on s.o.

ver'pfänden *v/t* (h) pawn, pledge (*a. fig. one's word*), mortgage.

ver'pfeifen *v/t* (*irr, no* -ge-, h, → *pfeifen*) F *j-n* ~ squeal on s.o.; *et.* ~ let s.th. out.

ver'pflanzen *v/t* (h) ⚘, ⚕ transplant.

Ver'pflanzung *f* (-; -en) transplant.

ver'pflegen v/t (h) feed, ✕ supply with rations: *sich selbst ~* cook for o.s.

Ver'pflegung f (-; -en) **1.** *no pl* catering, food supply. **2.** food, ✕ rations.

ver'pflichten (h) **I** v/t **1.** *j-n ~* oblige (*by contract*: obligate) s.o. (*zu inf* to *inf*); *j-n zum Schweigen ~* bind s.o. to silence; → *verpflichtet*. **2.** engage (*artist*), *sports*: sign on (*player etc*). **II** *sich ~* **3.** commit o.s. (*et. zu tun* to do[ing] s.th.). **4.** *artist, player, etc*: sign on (*für* for). **ver'pflichtet** *adj j-m zu Dank ~ sein* be indebted to s.o.; *ich fühle mich ~, ihr zu helfen* I feel obliged to help her; *gesetzlich ~* (*zu inf*) bound by law (to *inf*). **Ver'pflichtung** f (-; -en) a) obligation, duty, b) commitment, engagement, †, ♦♦♦ liability.

ver'pfuschen v/t (h) F botch, mess *s.th.* up, ruin (*a. fig. one's life etc*).

ver'planen v/t (h) F budget (*funds*), plan (*holidays etc*), book up (*time*).

ver'plappern: sich ~ (h) F blab.

verplempern [fɛr'plɛmpərn] v/t (h) F waste, fritter away.

verpönt [fɛr'pøːnt] *adj* disapproved-of: (*streng*) *~ sein a.* be frowned upon.

ver'prassen v/t (h) squander, F blow.

ver'puffen v/i (sn) **1.** 🔥 detonate, blow up. **2.** *fig.* fizzle out, fall flat.

ver'pulvern v/t (h) F blow (*money*).

ver'pumpen v/t (h) F (*an acc* to) lend, *esp. Am.* loan.

ver'puppen: sich ~ (h) *zo.* pupate.

ver'pusten: sich ~ (h) F get one's breath back.

ver'putzen v/t (h) **1.** △ roughcast. **2.** F polish off, put away.

ver'qualmt *adj* smoke-filled, *pred* full of smoke.

verquollen [fɛr'kvɔlən] *adj* puffed.

ver'ramschen v/t (h) F sell *s.th.* off dirt-cheap, remainder (*books*).

Ver'rat m (-[e]s; *no pl*) (*an dat*) betrayal (of), *a.* ♦♦♦, ✕ treason (to), treachery (to): *~ begehen an* (*dat*) betray.

ver'raten (*irr, no* -ge-, h, → *raten*) **I** v/t betray (*a. fig.*), give *s.o.*, *s.th.* away, *fig. a.* show, reveal: F *kannst du mir* (*mal*) *~, warum?* can you tell me why?; *nicht ~!* don't tell!; *~ und verkauft* sold down the river. **II** *sich ~* betray o.s., give o.s. away. **Verräter** [fɛr'rɛːtər] m (-s; -) traitor (*fig. an dat* to). **Ver'räterin** f (-;

-nen) traitress. **ver'räterisch** *adj* **1.** treacherous, traitorous, ♦♦♦ treasonable. **2.** *fig.* revealing, telltale.

ver'rauchen v/i (sn) *fig.* blow over.

ver'räuchert *adj* smoky.

ver'rechnen (h) **I** v/t charge (to account), clear (*cheque*): *et. ~ mit* offset s.th. against. **II** *sich ~ a. fig.* make a mistake; *sich um 10 Mark ~* be out by ten marks; *fig.* **da hast du dich aber leider verrechnet!** you are sadly mistaken there.

Ver'rechnung f (-; -en) offset, clearing: *nur zur ~ cheque*: for account only. **Ver'rechnungs|einheit** f clearing unit. **~konto** n offset account. **~scheck** m collection-only cheque (*Am.* check). **~verfahren** n clearing (system).

ver'recken v/i (sn) F perish, die, croak (*sl.*), *fig. engine etc*: conk out.

ver'regnet *adj* rainy.

ver'reiben v/t (*irr, no* -ge-, h, → *reiben*) spread *s.th.* by rubbing.

ver'reisen v/i (sn) go away: *~ nach* go to; *sie sind verreist* they are away.

ver'reißen v/t (*irr, no* -ge-, h, → *reißen*) F tear *s.o.*, *s.th.* to pieces, slate, pan.

verrenken [fɛr'rɛŋkən] v/t (h) contort, 🔥 dislocate (*sich den Arm* one's arm): F *sich den Hals ~* crane one's neck (*nach* to get a glimpse of), *Am.* rubberneck. **Ver'renkung** f (-; -en) contortion, 🔥 dislocation.

ver'rennen: sich ~ (*irr, no* -ge-, h, → *rennen*) *fig.* get stuck (*in acc* on).

ver'richten v/t (h) a) do, carry out, b) say (*prayer*).

ver'riegeln v/t (h) bolt, bar.

verringern [fɛr'rɪŋərn] v/t (h) reduce, lower, (*a. sich ~*) diminish, decrease, lessen: *das Tempo ~* slow down. **Ver'ringerung** f (-; -en) (*gen*) reduction (of), lowering (of), decrease (in).

verrohen [fɛr'roːən] v/i (sn) become brutalized. **Ver'rohung** f (-; -en) brutalization.

ver'rosten v/i (sn) rust. **ver'rostet** *adj* rusty.

verrotten [fɛr'rɔtən] v/i (sn) *a. fig.* rot.

ver'rücken v/t (h) move, disarrange.

ver'rückt *adj a.* F *fig.* mad, crazy, wild: *~ sein a.* be out of one's mind; *~ sein nach* (*or auf acc*) be wild about; *j-n ~ machen* drive s.o. mad; *mach dich* *doch nicht ~!* don't get all worked up!; *~ spielen* act up; *wie ~* like mad; *ich werd' ~!* I'll be blowed!; *es ist zum Verrücktwerden!* it's enough to drive you mad.

Ver'rückte *m, f* (-n; -n) *a.* F *fig.* lunatic, maniac, madman (madwoman).

Ver'rücktheit *f* (-; -en) **1.** *no pl* madness. **2.** folly, craze, F crazy idea (*or* thing).

Ver'ruf *m* in *~ bringen* (*kommen*) bring (fall) into disrepute.

ver'rufen *adj* disreputable, notorious.

ver'rutschen *v/i* (sn) slip.

Vers [fɛrs] *m* (-es; -e) a) verse, b) line.

ver'sachlichen *v/t* (h) de-emotionalize.

ver'sagen I *v/t j-m et. ~* refuse (*or* deny) s.o. s.th.; *sich et. ~* deny o.s. s.th., forgo s.th.; → *Dienst* 1. **II** *v/i* fail (*a. person*), ⊕ *a.* break down, *gun:* misfire: *ihr Gedächtnis versagte* her memory failed her. **Ver'sagen** *n* (-s) failure: *menschliches ~* human error. **Ver'sager** *m* (-s; -) failure, F flop.

ver'salzen *v/t* (h) **1.** oversalt. **2.** F *fig.* spoil.

ver'sammeln *v/t* (*a. sich ~*) (h) assemble (*a.* ✕), gather, meet. **Ver'sammlung** *f* (-; -en) assembly, gathering, meeting: *gesetzgebende ~* legislative assembly. **Ver'sammlungs|freiheit** *f* freedom of assembly. **~raum** *m* assembly room.

Versand [fɛr'zant] *m* (-[e]s; *no pl*) ✝ **1.** dispatch, forwarding, shipment. **2.** → **~abteilung** *f* forwarding department.

versanden [fɛr'zandən] *v/i* (sn) **1.** silt up. **2.** *fig.* peter out.

Ver'sandfertig *adj* ready for dispatch.

Ver'sand|geschäft *n*, **~handel** *m* mail--order business. **~haus** *n* mail-order firm. **~kosten** *pl* forwarding costs. **~pa,piere** *pl* shipping documents.

versauen [fɛr'zaʊən] *v/t* (h) F mess *s.th.* up, *fig. a.* ruin *s.th.* (*j-m* for s.o.).

ver'sauern *v/i* (sn) F *fig.* rot (away).

ver'saufen *v/t* (*irr, no* -ge-, h, → *saufen*) F spend on booze.

ver'säumen *v/t* (h) **1.** → *verpassen* 1. **2.** neglect (*duty etc*): (*es*) *~ zu inf* fail to *inf*. **Ver'säumnis** *n* (-ses; -se) omission, neglect. **Ver'säumnisurteil** *n* judg(e)-ment by default.

ver'schachern *v/t* (h) F flog.

ver'schachtelt *adj* interlocked, *fig.* complicated, *ling.* involved (*sentence*).

ver'schaffen *v/t* (h) **1.** *j-m et. ~* get (*or* find) s.o. s.th. (*or* s.th. for s.o.). **2.** *sich et. ~* get, obtain, secure, raise (*money*); → *Respekt*.

verschalen [fɛr'ʃaːlən] *v/t* (h) △ board, shutter (*concrete*). **Ver'schalung** *f* (-; -en) a) boarding, b) form(s).

verschämt [fɛr'ʃɛːmt] *adj* bashful.

verschandeln [fɛr'ʃandəln] *v/t* (h) F disfigure, spoil.

ver'schanzen: *sich ~* (h) *a. fig.* entrench (*hinter* behind, *in dat* in).

ver'schärfen *v/t* (*a. sich ~*) (h) increase, tighten (up) (*control, law, measures, etc*), aggravate (*crisis etc*), stiffen (*penalty*): *das Tempo ~* increase the pace; *die Spannungen ~ sich* tension is mounting. **Ver'schärfung** *f* (-; -en) increase, tightening (up), aggravation.

ver'scharren *v/t* (h) bury (hurriedly).

ver'schätzen: *sich ~* (h) be out (*um* by).

ver'schaukeln *v/t* (h) F *j-n ~* take s.o. for a ride, outtrick s.o.

ver'schenken *v/t* (h) *a. fig.* give away.

ver'scherzen *v/t* (h) forfeit.

ver'scheuchen *v/t* (h) chase away.

ver'scheuern *v/t* (h) F flog.

ver'schicken *v/t* (h) **1.** dispatch, send, ship. **2.** *j-n ~* send s.o. away.

verschiebbar [fɛr'ʃiːpbaːr] *adj* mov(e)able. **ver'schieben** (*irr, no* -ge-, h, → *schieben*) **I** *v/t* **1.** (re)move, shift. **2.** postpone (*auf später* to a later date): *et.* (*von e-m Tag zum anderen*) *~* put s.th. off (from one day to the next). **3.** F ✝ sell *s.th.* underhand. **II** *sich ~* **4.** shift, get out of place. **5.** be postponed, be put off. **Ver'schiebung** *f* (-; -en) **1.** shift(ing), moving. **2.** postponement.

verschieden [fɛr'ʃiːdən] *adj* **1.** different (*von* from): *~ sein a.* differ, vary; *die beiden Brüder sind sehr ~* the two brothers are quite unlike; *das ist ganz ~* it depends; *~ groß sein* vary in size. **2.** *~e pl* various, several; *~es* various things; *aus den ~sten Gründen* for a variety of reasons. **ver'schiedenartig** *adj* different (kinds of) ..., various. **Ver'schiedenartigkeit** *f* (-; *no pl*) **1.** difference. **2.** variety. **Ver'schiedenheit** *f* (-; -en) **1.** difference (*gen* of, in). **2.** dissimilarity. **3.** diversity, variety. **ver'schiedentlich** *adv* **1.** several times, repeatedly. **2.** occasionally.

ver'schießen (*irr, no* -ge-, → *schießen*) **I** *v/t* (h) **1.** shoot. **2.** *sports*: shoot wide. **II** *v/i* (sn) fade: → **verschossen** 1.

ver'schiffen *v/t* (h) ship.

Ver'schiffung *f* (-; -en) shipment.

ver'schimmeln *v/i* (sn) go mo(u)ldy.

ver'schlafen¹ (*irr, no* -ge-, h, → *schlafen*) **I** *v/i* **1.** oversleep. **II** *v/t* **2.** sleep through. **3.** F *fig.* miss (*chance etc*), forget (*appointment etc*).

ver'schlafen² *adj a. fig.* sleepy. **Ver'schlafenheit** *f* (-; *no pl*) *a. fig.* sleepiness.

Ver'schlag *m* (-[e]s; ⸚e) shed, shack.

ver'schlagen¹ *v/t* (*irr, no* -ge-, h, → *schlagen*) **1.** mishit (*ball*). **2.** lose (*page in book etc*). **3.** *fig.* **es hat mich nach X ~** I ended up in X. **4.** *fig.* **j-m die Stimme** (*or* **Rede, Sprache**) **~** leave s.o. speechless; **es verschlug mir den Atem** it took my breath away.

ver'schlagen² *adj* sly, shifty.

Ver'schlagenheit *f* (-; *no pl*) shiftiness.

ver'schlampen F *v/t* (h) a) go and lose, b) clean forget. **II** *v/i* (sn) go to seed.

verschlechtern [fɛr'ʃlɛçtərn] (h) **I** *v/t* make worse. **II** *sich ~* get worse, deteriorate; *sich (finanziell) ~* earn less. **Ver'schlechterung** *f* (-; -en) deterioration, *a.* change for the worse.

verschleiern [fɛr'ʃlaɪərn] *v/t* (h) veil.

ver'schleifen *v/t* (*irr, no* -ge-, h, → *schleifen¹*) *ling.*, ♪ slur.

ver'schleimt *adj* blocked with phlegm.

Verschleiß [fɛr'ʃlaɪs] *m* (-es; *no pl*) wear and tear (*a. fig.*), ⚙ *a.* attrition.

ver'schleißen (verschliß, verschlissen, h) **I** *v/t* wear out. **II** *sich ~* wear o.s. out. **III** *v/i* (sn) wear (out), become worn.

Ver'schleiß|erscheinung *f a. fig.* sign of wear. ⚙**fest** *adj* wear-resistant. **⸚teil** *n* ⚙ working (*or* expendable) part.

ver'schleppen *v/t* (h) **1.** carry off, *pol.* displace, 🚂 kidnap. **2.** delay, protract. **3.** ⚕ spread (*epidemic etc*), protract, neglect (*disease*). **Ver'schleppte** *m, f* (-n; -n) *pol.* displaced person.

Ver'schleppung *f* (-; -en) **1.** a) *pol.* displacement, b) kidnap(p)ing. **2.** protraction, delay(ing). **3.** ⚕ spreading (*of epidemic etc*), protraction (*of disease*).

Ver'schleppungstaktik *f* delaying tactics, *parl.* obstructionism.

ver'schleudern *v/t* (h) **1.** waste, squander (away). **2.** ✝ sell at a loss, dump.

ver'schließbar *adj* lockable.

ver'schließen (*irr, no* -ge-, h, → *schließen*) **I** *v/t* a) shut, close, b) lock (up), c) put *s.th.* under lock and key: *die Ohren ~ vor* (*dat*) turn a deaf ear to; → *Auge* 1. **II** *sich ~* (*dat*) shut o.s. off (from); *sich j-s Argumenten etc ~* remain inaccessible to s.o.'s arguments *etc.*

verschlimmern [fɛr'ʃlɪmərn] (h) **I** *v/t* make *s.th.* worse, aggravate. **II** *sich ~* get worse, deteriorate.

Ver'schlimmerung *f* (-; -en) deterioration, change for the worse.

ver'schlingen¹ *v/t* (*irr, no* -ge-, h, → *schlingen²*) wolf (down), devour (*a. book etc*), *fig.* swallow (up) (*money etc*).

ver'schlingen² *v/t* (*a. sich ~*) (*irr, no* -ge-, h, → *schlingen¹*) intertwine.

verschliß [fɛr'ʃlɪs] *pret,* **ver'schlissen** *pp of* **verschleißen**.

verschlossen [fɛr'ʃlɔsən] *adj* **1.** a) shut, closed, b) locked (up): *hinter ⸚en Türen* behind closed doors. **2.** reserved.

Ver'schlossenheit *f* (-; *no pl*) reserve.

ver'schlucken (h) **I** *v/t* swallow. **II** *sich ~* choke, swallow the wrong way.

verschlungen [fɛr'ʃlʊŋən] *adj fig.* intricate (*pattern etc*), tortuous (*path etc*).

Ver'schluß *m* (-sses; ⸚sse) **1.** a) fastener, clasp, b) stopper, c) ⚙ lock, seal: *unter ~* under lock and key, *customs*: in bond. **2.** *phot.* shutter. **3.** ✝ occlusion.

ver'schlüsseln *v/t* (h) encode: *verschlüsselter Text* code(d) text.

Ver'schluß|laut *m ling.* plosive. **⸚sache** *f pol.* classified matter.

ver'schmähen *v/t* (h) disdain, scorn.

ver'schmelzen (*irr, no* -ge-, → *schmelzen*) *v/t* (h), *v/i* (sn) (*mit, zu* into) fuse, merge (*both a.* ✝, *pol.*), *colo[u]rs etc*: blend. **Ver'schmelzung** *f* (-; -en) fusion, ✝, *pol. a.* merger.

ver'schmerzen *v/t* (h) **et. ~** get over s.th.

ver'schmieren *v/t* (h) smear.

verschmitzt [fɛr'ʃmɪtst] *adj* roguish.

ver'schmutzen *v/t* (h) **1.** dirty, soil. **2.** pollute (*air, water, etc*).

Ver'schmutzung *f* (-; -en) **1.** a) soiling, b) dirt. **2.** (*air, water, etc*) pollution.

ver'schnaufen *v/i* (*a. sich ~*) (h) F have a breather.

ver'schneiden *v/t* (*irr, no* -ge-, h, → *schneiden*) blend (*rum etc*).

verschneit [fɛr'ʃnaɪt] *adj* snow-covered.

Ver'schnitt *m* (-[e]s; -e) blend.
ver'schnörkelt *adj* a. *fig.* ornate.
verschnupft [fɛr'ʃnʊpft] *adj* ~ **sein** have a cold, F *fig.* be in a huff.
ver'schnüren *v/t* tie up.
verschollen [fɛr'ʃɔlən] *adj* **1.** missing, ⚖ presumed dead. **2.** (long-)forgotten.
ver'schonen *v/t* (h) spare: *von et. verschont bleiben* be spared s.th.; *verschone mich damit!* spare me that!
ver'schönen *v/t* (h) embellish, enhance.
verschönern [fɛr'ʃøːnərn] *v/t* (h) embellish, *a. fig.* brighten. **Ver'schönerung** *f* (-; -en) embellishment.
verschossen [fɛr'ʃɔsən] *adj* **1.** faded. **2.** F *in j-n ~ sein* have a crush on s.o.
verschränken [fɛr'ʃrɛŋkən] *v/t* (h) **1.** fold (*arms*), cross (*legs*). **2.** ⊙ cross.
ver'schrauben *v/t* (h) bolt, screw up.
ver'schreiben (*irr, no* -ge-, h, → *schreiben*) **I** *v/t* **1.** *j-m et. ~* a) ⚕ prescribe s.th. for s.o., b) ⚖ make s.th. over to s.o. **II** *sich ~* **2.** make a slip (of the pen). **3.** *fig.* devote o.s. (*dat* to).
Ver'schreibung *f* (-; -en) ⚕ prescription. **ver'schreibungspflichtig** *adj* ⚕ obtainable on prescription only.
verschroben [fɛr'ʃroːbən] *adj* eccentric. **Ver'schrobenheit** *f* (-; -en) eccentricity.
ver'schrotten *v/t* (h) scrap, *a.* junk (*car*).
ver'schrumpeln *v/i* (sn) F shrivel (up).
verschüchtert [fɛr'ʃʏçtərt] *adj* intimidated, shy.
ver'schulden (h) **I** *v/t* be responsible (*or* to blame) for. **II** *v/i* (*a.* **sich ~**) get into debt. **Ver'schulden** *n* (-s) fault: *ohne ihr ~* through no fault of hers; *uns trifft kein ~* it's not our fault. **ver'schuldet** *adj* indebted (*bei* to), *property:* encumbered. **Ver'schuldung** *f* (-; -en) indebtedness, debts, encumbrance.
ver'schütten *v/t* (h) **1.** spill. **2.** bury *s.o.* alive, block (*road*).
verschwägert [fɛr'ʃvɛːgərt] *adj* related by marriage.
ver'schweigen *v/t* (*irr, no* -ge-, h, → *schweigen*) (*dat* from) keep *s.th.* (a) secret, hide, withhold.
ver'schweißen *v/t* (h) weld together.
verschwenden [fɛr'ʃvɛndən] *v/t* (h) (*an acc, für, mit* on) waste, squander: *fig. du verschwendest d-e Worte* you are wasting your breath. **Ver'schwender** *m* (-s; -), **Ver'schwenderin** *f* (-; -nen)

spendthrift, squanderer. **ver'schwenderisch** *adj* wasteful, extravagant, lavish: *~ umgehen mit* be lavish with.
Ver'schwendung *f* (-; -en) waste, extravagance. **Ver'schwendungssucht** *f* extravagance, squandermania.
verschwiegen [fɛr'ʃviːgən] *adj* **1.** discreet. **2.** secret, secluded (*place*).
Ver'schwiegenheit *f* (-; *no pl*) **1.** discretion, secrecy; → *Siegel.* **2.** seclusion.
ver'schwimmen *v/i* (*irr, no* -ge-, sn, → *schwimmen*) *a. fig.* become blurred: *die Farben ~* the colo(u)rs merge.
ver'schwinden (*irr, no* -ge-, sn, → *schwinden*) *v/i* **1.** disappear, vanish: *spurlos ~* vanish into thin air; *~d klein* infinitely small. **2.** F make o.s. scarce: *verschwinde!* beat it!
Ver'schwinden *n* (-s) disappearance.
ver'schwitzen *v/t* (h) **1.** soak *s.th.* with sweat. **2.** F *et. ~* clean forget about s.th.
ver'schwitzt *adj* sweaty.
verschwollen [fɛr'ʃvɔlən] *adj* swollen.
verschwommen [fɛr'ʃvɔmən] *adj* **1.** *a. phot.* blurred. **2.** vague (*idea etc*), hazy, dim (*recollection etc*): *sich nur ~ erinnern* remember only dimly.
Ver'schwommenheit *f* (-; *no pl*) vagueness, haziness, dimness.
ver'schwören: *sich ~* (*irr, no* -ge-, ⟩ *schwören*) **1.** conspire (*or* plot) (*mit j-m* with s.o.) (*gegen* against). **2.** *fig.* devote o.s. (*dat* to). **Ver'schwörer** *m* (-s; -) conspirator, plotter. **Ver'schwörung** *f* (-; -en) conspiracy, plot.
ver'sehen (*irr, no* -ge-, h, → *sehen*) **I** *v/t* **1.** ~ *mit* provide (*or* furnish, equip) *o.s., s.th.* with; *mit Ratschlägen ~* armed with advice; *mit Vollmacht ~* authorize. **2.** perform, discharge (*duty etc*), *a.* hold (*office*): *er versieht auch das Amt des Richters a.* he acts as judge as well. **II** *sich ~* **3.** make a mistake. **4.** provide (*or* equip) o.s. (*mit* with). **5.** *ehe man sich's versieht* F before you know it.
Ver'sehen *n* (-s; -) oversight, mistake: *aus ~* → *versehentlich adv* inadvertently, by mistake.
versehrt [fɛr'zeːrt] *adj* disabled.
Ver'sehrte *m, f* (-n; -n) disabled person.
ver'senden *v/t* (*irr, no* -ge-, h, → *senden*) send, forward, ship. **Ver'sendung** *f* (-; -en) dispatch, shipment.
ver'sengen *v/t* (h) scorch, singe.

ver'senken (h) **I** *v/t* sink. **II** *sich ~ in* (*acc*) *fig.* become absorbed in.
Ver'senkung *f* (-; -en) **1.** sinking. **2.** *thea.* trapdoor: F *fig. in der ~ verschwinden* disappear from the scene. **3.** (*mental*) absorption.
versessen [fɛr'zɛsən] *adj ~ auf* (*acc*) mad about; *darauf ~ sein zu inf* be desperate to *inf*.
ver'setzen (h) **I** *v/t* **1.** remove, displace, shift, ✗ transplant. **2.** transfer (*in, auf acc, nach* to), *ped.* move *s.o.* up, *Am.* promote: *→ Ruhestand.* **3.** a) pawn, b) sell. **4.** *f j-n ~* a) stand *s.o.* up, b) *sports:* outtrick *s.o.* **5.** *j-n in die Lage ~ zu inf* put *s.o.* in a position (*or* enable *s.o.*) to *inf*; *j-n in Unruhe ~* disturb *s.o.*; *et. in Schwingungen ~* set s.th. vibrating; → *Angst.* **6.** F *j-m e-n Schlag etc. ~* give (*or* deal) *s.o.* a blow *etc.* **7.** mix (*mit* with). **8.** ✪ stagger. **II** *sich in j-n* (*j-s Lage*) *~* put *o.s.* in *s.o.'s* place (*or* position).
Ver'setzung *f* (-; -en) **1.** removal, ✗ transplanting. **2.** transfer (*in, auf acc, nach* to). **3.** *ped.* removal, *Am.* promotion.
Ver'setzungs|zeichen *n* ♪ accidental. **~zeugnis** *n ped.* end-of-year report.
ver'seuchen *v/t* (h) contaminate.
Ver'seuchung *f* (-; -en) contamination.
Ver'sicherer *m* (-s; -) ✝ insurer, ⚓ underwriter. **ver'sichern** *v/t* (h) **1.** ✝ insure (*sich* o.s.) (*bei* with, *gegen* against). **2.** declare, protest: *ich kann dir ~, daß* I (can) assure you that. **Ver'sicherte** *m, f* (-n; -n) the insured (party). **Ver'sicherung** *f* (-; -en) **1.** insurance: *e-e ~ abschließen* take out insurance (*or* an insurance policy). **2.** insurance company. **3.** assurance.
Ver'sicherungs|anstalt *f* insurance company. **~betrug** *m* insurance fraud. **~dauer** *f* time insured. **~gesellschaft** *f* insurance company. **~mathe,matiker** *m* actuary. **~nehmer** *m* (-s; -) insurant, *the* insured. **~nummer** *f* insurance policy number. **~po,lice** *f* insurance policy. **~prämie** *f* insurance premium. **~schutz** *m* insurance cover(age). **~summe** *f* sum insured. **~vertreter** *m* insurance agent. **~wesen** *n* (-s; *no pl*) insurance (business).
ver'sickern *v/i* (sn) trickle away.
ver'siegeln *v/t* (h) seal.

ver'siegen *v/i* (sn) dry up, run dry.
versiert [vɛr'ziːrt] *adj* (*in dat* in) experienced, (well-)versed.
ver'silbern *v/t* (h) **1.** ✪ silverplate. **2.** F *et. ~* turn s.th. into cash, sell s.th.
ver'sinken *v/i* (*irr, no* -ge-, sn, → *sinken*) *a. fig.* sink (*in acc* into).
Version [vɛr'zioːn] *f* (-; -en) version.
ver'sklaven *v/t* (h) enslave.
ver'slumen [fɛr'slamən] *v/i* (sn) become a slum.
'Versmaß *n* metre, *Am.* meter.
versnobt [fɛr'snɔpt] *adj* snobbish.
versoffen [fɛr'zɔfən] *adj* F boozy.
versöhnen [fɛr'zøːnən] (h) **I** *v/t* reconcile (*mit* with *s.o.*, to *one's fate etc.*). **II** *sich* (*wieder*) *~* be(come) reconciled, make it up. **ver'söhnlich** *adj* conciliatory; *~ stimmen* placate. **Ver'söhnung** *f* (-; -en) reconciliation.
versonnen [fɛr'zɔnən] *adj* pensive.
ver'sorgen *v/t* (h) **1.** (*mit* with) supply, provide. **2.** provide for (*family etc*). **3.** look after, take care of. **4.** ✗ attend to (*s.o.*), see to (*wound*). **Ver'sorgung** *f* (-; *no pl*) **1.** supply. **2.** (*gen*) support (of), provision (for). **3.** care.
Ver'sorgungs|betrieb *m* public utility. **~empfänger(in** *f*) *m* pensioner. **~güter** *pl* supplies. **~leitung** *f* supply line. **~lücke** *f* supply gap. **~netz** *n* supply system. **~technik** *f* utilities engineering.
ver'spannen *v/t* (h) ✪ stay, brace.
ver'spannt *adj* cramped, tense.
verspäten [fɛr'ʃpɛːtən] *sich ~* (h) be late.
ver'spätet *adj* late (*arrival etc*), belated (*thanks etc*).
Ver'spätung *f* (-; -en) delay: *bitte entschuldigen Sie m-e ~* please excuse my being late; *(e-e Stunde) ~ haben* be (an hour) late; *mit (e-r Stunde) ~ abfahren* leave (an hour) behind schedule.
ver'speisen *v/t* eat, consume.
ver'sperren *v/t* (h) bar, block (up), obstruct (*a. view*).
ver'spielen (h) **I** *v/t* lose (at play), *a. fig.* gamble away. **II** *v/i* lose: *fig. bei mir hat er verspielt!* I'm through with him.
ver'spielt *adj* playful.
ver'spotten *v/t* (h) make fun of, ridicule.
ver'sprechen (*irr, no* -ge-, h, → *sprechen*) **I** *v/t* **1.** *a. fig.* promise: *das Wetter verspricht schön zu werden* the weather looks promising. **2.** *sich et. ~*

von expect s.th. of; *ich hatte mir mehr davon versprochen* I had expected better of it. **II sich ~** make a slip (of the tongue). **Ver'sprechen** *n* (-s; -) promise. **Ver'sprecher** *m* (-s; -) slip (of the tongue). **Ver'sprechung** (-; -en) *f* promise; *j-m große ~en machen* promise s.o. the earth.

ver'spritzen, ver'sprühen *v/t* (h) spray.

ver'staatlichen *v/t* (h) nationalize. **Ver'staatlichung** *f* (-; -en) nationalization.

verstädtern [fɛr'ʃtɛːtərn] **I** *v/t* (h) urbanize. **II** *v/i* (sn) become urbanized. **Ver'städterung** *f* (-; -en) urbanization.

Ver'stand *m* (-[e]s; *no pl*) a) intellect, mind, b) reason, (common) sense, c) brain(s), intelligence: *scharfer ~* keen mind; *klarer (kühler) ~* clear (cool) head; *den ~ verlieren* go mad; F *hast du den ~ verloren?* are you out of your mind?; F *das geht über m-n ~!* that's beyond me; *all s-n ~ zs.-nehmen* keep all one's wits about one. **ver'standesmäßig** *adj* a) intellectual, b) rational. **Ver'standesmensch** *m* rationalist.

ver'ständig *adj* **1.** intelligent. **2.** reasonable, sensible, understanding.

verständigen [fɛr'ʃtɛndɪgən] *v/t* (h) **I** inform (*von* about, of), call (*police, doctor, etc*). **II sich mit j-m ~** a) make o.s. understood by s.o., b) come to an agreement with s.o. (*über acc* on). **Ver'ständigung** *f* (-; -en) **1.** information. **2.** communication: *teleph. die ~ war schlecht* the line was bad. **3.** agreement, understanding. **Ver'ständigungsschwierigkeiten** *pl* communication problems: *ich hatte ~* I had problems to make myself understood.

verständlich [fɛr'ʃtɛntlɪç] *adj* **1.** distinct, clear, audible. **2.** understandable, intelligible: *schwer ~* difficult to understand; *j-m et. ~ machen* explain s.th. to s.o.; *sich j-m ~ machen* make o.s. understood (*or* heard) by s.o. **ver'ständlicherweise** *adv* understandably.

Verständnis [fɛr'ʃtɛntnɪs] *n* (-ses; *no pl*) **1.** (*gen* of) understanding, comprehension: *zum besseren ~ des Textes* in order to understand the text better. **2.** a) understanding, insight, b) appreciation (*für* of), c) sympathy (*für* with): *(viel) ~ haben für* (fully) understand, *j-n* show (great) understanding for s.o.;

dafür fehlt mir jedes ~ that's beyond me. **ver'ständnislos** *adj* uncomprehending: *~e Blicke* blank looks; *e-r Sache ~ gegenüberstehen* have no understanding (*or* appreciation) of s.th. **Ver'ständnislosigkeit** *f* (-; *no pl*) lack of understanding (*or* appreciation).

ver'ständnisvoll *adj* understanding, sympathetic, *a.* knowing (*look*).

ver'stärken *v/t* (h) strengthen, *a.* ✗ reinforce (*both a.* ⊙), ♫ concentrate, ⚡ amplify, (*a.* **sich ~**) increase, intensify (*a. phot.*). **Ver'stärkung** *f* (-; -en) a) strengthening, reinforcement(s ✗), b) ⚡ amplification, c) increase, intensification (*a. phot.*).

ver'stauben *v/i* (sn) gather dust.

verstaubt [fɛr'ʃtaʊpt] *adj* **1.** dusty. **2.** *fig.* antiquated.

ver'stauchen *v/t* (h) ♠ sprain (*sich die Hand etc* one's wrist *etc*).

ver'stauen *v/t* (h) stow away.

Versteck [fɛr'ʃtɛk] *n* (-[e]s; -e) hiding place, hideaway: *~ spielen* play hide-and-seek. **ver'stecken** *v/t* (*a.* **sich ~**) (h) hide (*vor dat* from). **Ver'steckspiel** *n* (game of) hide-and-seek. **ver'steckt** *adj* hidden: *sich ~ halten* lie low; *~e Kamera* candid camera.

ver'stehen (*irr, no* -ge-, h, → **stehen**) **I** *v/t* **1.** hear, get, catch. **2.** understand, comprehend, grasp, catch, F get, realize, see, *a.* appreciate (*work of art etc*): *Spaß ~* take (*or* see) a joke; *falsch ~* misunderstand; *verstehe mich recht!* don't misunderstand me! **3.** understand, read, take: *was ~ Sie unter ...?* what do you understand by ...?; *wie ~ Sie das?* what do you make of it? **4.** know: *er versteht es zu inf* he knows how to *inf*; *sein Handwerk ~* know one's job; *davon versteht er gar nichts* he doesn't know the first thing about it. **5.** *j-m zu ~ geben* give s.o. to understand. **6.** *sich* (*or einander*) *~* get along (*or* on) (with each other). **II sich ~ 7.** *mit* get on (*or* along) with. **8.** *auf* (*acc*) be (very) good at *ger*. **9.** *das versteht sich von selbst* that goes without saying. **III** *v/i* *~ Sie?* you see?, F get me?; *ich verstehe!* I see; *verstanden?* F got it?; *wenn ich recht verstanden habe, willst du kommen?* I take it that you will come?

ver'steifen v/t (a. **sich ~**) (h) stiffen: *fig.* **sich ~ auf** (acc) insist on *ger.*

Ver'steigerer m (-s; -) auctioneer.

ver'steigern v/t (h) auction (off).

Ver'steigerung f (-; -en) (**zur ~ kommen** be put up for [*Am.* at]) auction.

ver'steinern v/i (a. **sich ~**) (h) petrify: *fig.* **wie versteinert vor Schreck** petrified with terror. **Ver'steinerung** f (-; -en) 1. petrifaction. 2. fossil.

ver'stellbar adj adjustable. **ver'stellen** (h) I v/t 1. move, shift. 2. disguise. 3. misadjust: **wer hat den Wecker verstellt?** who has tampered with the alarm? 4. obstruct, block. II **sich ~** *fig.* a) put on an act, b) hide one's feelings.

Ver'stellung f (-; *no pl*) 1. ⚙ adjustment. 2. *fig.* a) play-acting, b) disguise.

ver'steppen v/i (sn) turn into steppe.

ver'steuern v/t (h) pay tax on: **zu ~(d)** taxable. **ver'steuert** adj tax-paid.

Ver'steuerung f (-; -en) payment of tax (*gen*, **von** on).

verstiegen [fɛr'ʃtiːɡən] adj high-flown.

ver'stimmen v/t (h) 1. ♪ put s.th. out of tune. 2. 🎻 detune. 3. *j-n ~* annoy s.o., put s.o. in a bad mood. **ver'stimmt** adj 1. ♪ out of tune. 2. 🎻 off-tune. 3. annoyed (**über** *acc* at), in a bad mood. 4. 🎻 **~er Magen** upset stomach.

Ver'stimmung f (-; -en) 1. ill humo(u)r, ill feeling. 2. 🎻 (*stomach*) upset.

verstockt [fɛr'ʃtɔkt] adj stubborn, impenitent.

verstohlen [fɛr'ʃtoːlən] adj furtive, surreptitious.

ver'stopfen v/t (h) 1. stop (up), plug. 2. a) block (up), obstruct, b) congest, jam (*road*). 3. 🎻 a) clog, occlude, b) constipate: **m-e Nase ist verstopft** my nose is plugged up; **verstopft sein** be constipated. **Ver'stopfung** f (-; -en) 1. jam, block(age). 2. 🎻 constipation: **an ~ leiden** a. be constipated.

verstorben [fɛr'ʃtɔrbən] adj deceased, late. **Ver'storbene** m, f(-n; -n) *the* deceased: **die ~n** a. the dead.

verstört [fɛr'ʃtøːrt] adj badly upset, distraught, wild (*look etc*). **Ver'störtheit** f (-; *no pl*) distraction, distraught state.

Ver'stoß m (-es; -e) (**gegen**) offen/ce (*Am.* -se) (against), violation (of).

ver'stoßen (*irr, no* -ge-, h, → **stoßen**) I v/t reject: **j-n ~ aus** expel s.o. from, cast

s.o. out of. II v/i **~ gegen** offend against, infringe, violate.

ver'streben v/t (h) ⚙ strut.

Ver'strebung f (-; -en) ⚙ strut.

ver'streichen (*irr, no* -ge-, → **streichen**) I v/i (sn) *time:* pass, *set period:* expire. II v/t (h) spread (*butter, paint, etc*).

ver'streuen v/t (h) scatter.

ver'stricken (h) I v/t 1. use (up) (*wool*). 2. *j-n ~ in* (acc) involve s.o. in. II **sich ~ in** (acc) get entangled (*or* involved) in.

ver'stümmeln [fɛr'ʃtʏmln] v/t (h) mutilate, *fig. a.* garble (*text*).

Ver'stümmelung f (-; -en) mutilation.

ver'stummen [fɛr'ʃtʊmən] v/i (sn) become silent, *a.* stop talking, *conversation, noise, a. rumo(u)rs, etc:* stop, die down.

Versuch [fɛr'zuːx] m (-[e]s; -e) 1. attempt (a. ⚖️), trial (*both a. sports*), F try: **e-n ~ machen mit** try, give *s.o., s.th.* a try; **beim ersten ~** at the first attempt; **es käme auf e-n ~ an** we might as well try. 2. 🔬, 🎯, *phys.* experiment, *a.* ⚙ test, trial: **~e anstellen** experiment. 3. essay (**über** *acc* on).

ver'suchen v/t (h) 1. try, attempt (a. ⚖️): **et. ~** a) try s.th., b) experiment with s.th.; **es ~ mit** try, **j-m** give s.o. a try; **versuch's doch mal!** just (have a) try!, F have a go! *fig.* tempt: **ich war versucht zu inf** I was tempted to *inf.* 3. taste, try. **Ver'sucher** m (-s; -) tempter. **Ver'sucherin** f (-; -nen) temptress.

Ver'suchs,anstalt f research institute. **~bedingung** f test condition. **~bohrung** f trial drilling. **~gelände** n testing ground. **~ingeni,eur** m research engineer. **~ka,ninchen** n F *fig.* guinea pig. **~ob,jekt** n test object. **~per,son** f test subject (*or* person). **~pro,jekt** n pilot project. **~reihe** f series of tests. **~stadium** n experimental stage. **~strecke** f *mot.* test track. **~tier** n experimental (*or* laboratory) animal.

ver'suchsweise adv a) by way of trial, b) on trial, on a trial basis.

Ver'suchszwecke pl **zu ~n** for experimental purposes.

Ver'suchung f (-; -en) (*j-n in ~ führen* lead s.o. into) temptation: **in ~ sein** (*or* **kommen**) be tempted.

ver'sumpfen v/i (sn) 1. become marshy. 2. F *fig.* a) go to seed, b) end up boozing.

versunken [fɛr'zʊŋkən] *adj fig.* ~ **in** (*acc*) absorbed in, lost in.

ver'sündigen: sich ~ (h) sin (**an** *dat* against).

ver'süßen *v/t* (h) *fig.* sweeten.

ver'tagen *v/t* (*a.* **sich ~**) (h) adjourn (**auf** *acc* until). **Ver'tagung** *f* (-; -en) adjournment.

vertäuen [fɛr'tɔyən] *v/t* (h) ✥ moor.

ver'tauschen *v/t* (h) **1.** exchange (**mit**, **gegen** for): **mit vertauschten Rollen** with reversed roles. **2.** confuse, mix up.

verteidigen [fɛr'taɪdɪgən] (h) **I** *v/t* a) defend (**sich** o.s.) (**gegen** against, from), b) stand up for: **sich** (**vor Gericht**) **selbst ~** conduct one's own defen|ce (*Am.* -se). **II** *v/i sports:* defend.

Ver'teidiger *m* (-s; -) **1.** defender, *fig. a.* advocate, *soccer: a.* fullback. **2.** ⚖ counsel for the defence (*Am.* -se).

Ver'teidigung *f* (-; -en) defen|ce (*Am.* -se).

Ver'teidigungs|ausgaben *pl* defen|ce (*Am.* -se) expenditure. **~beitrag** *m* defen|ce (*Am.* -se) contribution. **~bereitschaft** *f* preparedness for defen|ce (*Am.* -se). **~bündnis** *n* defensive alliance. **~krieg** *m* defensive war. **~mi̱nister** *m* defen|ce (*Am.* -se) minister, *Br.* Defence Secretary, *Am.* Secretary of Defense. **~mini'sterium** *n* ministry of defence, *Am.* Department of Defense. **~rede** *f* (speech for the) defen|ce (*Am.* -se), *w.s.* apology. **~waffe** *f* defensive weapon.

ver'teilen (h) **I** *v/t* **1.** distribute, hand out, share out (**all: an** *acc* to, **unter** among), allocate, *thea.* cast (*rôles:*): **unter sich ~** share; **mit verteilten Rollen lesen** do a play reading of. **2.** (**auf**, **über** *acc* over) distribute, spread, *w.s.* scatter. **II sich ~** spread (**auf**, **über** *acc* over), *persons:* scatter, *a.* ✗ spread out.

Ver'teiler *m* (-s; -) **1.** distributor (*a.* ✝, ♫, *mot.*). **2.** *office:* distribution list. **~kasten** *m* ♫ distributing box. **~netz** *n* **1.** ♫ distribution system. **2.** ✝ distributing network. **~schlüssel** *m* ✝ **1.** distribution key. **2.** → *Verteiler* 2. **~tafel** *f* ♫ distribution switchboard.

Ver'teilung *f* (-; -en) distribution.

ver'teuern (h) **I** *v/t* raise the price of. **II sich ~** go up (in price). **Ver'teuerung** *f* (-; -en) rise in price(s) (*or* costs).

ver'teufeln *v/t* (h) denounce, demonize.

ver'teufelt *adj* F devilish, tricky: ~ **schwer** damned difficult.

ver'tiefen (h) **I** *v/t* **1.** (*a.* **sich ~**) deepen, *fig. a.* heighten. **2.** extend (*knowledge etc.*). **II sich ~ in** (*acc*) become absorbed (*or* engrossed) in. **Ver'tiefung** *f* (-; -en) **1.** deepening, *fig. a.* heightening, extension. **2.** depression. **3.** *fig.* absorption.

vertikal [vɛrti'kaːl] *adj* vertical.

Verti'kale *f* (-; -n) vertical (line).

ver'tilgen *v/t* (h) **1.** exterminate, kill. **2.** F polish off (*food*).

Ver'tilgung *f* (-; *no pl*) extermination.

ver'tippen: sich ~ (h) make a (typing) mistake.

vertonen [fɛr'toːnən] *v/t* (h) *et.* ~ set s.th. to music. **Ver'tonung** *f* (-; -en) setting.

vertrackt [fɛr'trakt] *adj* F tricky.

Vertrag [fɛr'traːk] *m* (-[e]s; ⸗e) contract, agreement, *pol.* treaty, pact: **mündlicher ~** verbal agreement; **e-n ~ (ab)schließen** make (*or* enter into) a contract; **j-n unter ~ nehmen** sign s.o. on.

ver'tragen (*irr, no* -ge-, h, → **tragen**) **I** *v/t* **1.** a) *a.* F *fig.* endure, bear, stand, F take, b) be able to eat (*or* drink), tolerate (*medicament*): **ich vertrage k-n Kaffee** coffee doesn't agree with me; **sie verträgt das Klima nicht** she can't stand the climate; **er kann e-e Menge ~** a) he can take a lot, b) he can hold his drink; **kannst du Kritik ~?** can you take criticism?; F **ich könnte e-e Tasse Tee ~** I could do with a cup of tea. **2. sich (miteinander) ~** a) get on (well) together, b) *colo(u)rs etc.:* go well together. **II sich ~ mit** a) *j-m* get on (well) with s.o., b) *fig.* go well with.

ver'traglich I *adj* contractual. **II** *adv* by contract: **sich ~ (zu et.) verpflichten** contract (for s.th. *or* to do s.th.).

verträglich [fɛr'trɛːklɪç] *adj* **1.** sociable: ~ **sein** *a.* be easy to get along with. **2.** (easily) digestible, light (*food*), (*a.* **gut** ~) well-tolerated (*medicament*).

Ver'trags|abschluß *m* conclusion of a contract: **bei ~** on entering into the contract. **~bedingungen** *pl* terms of the contract. **~bruch** *m* breach of contract. **⸗brüchig** *adj* defaulting: ~ **werden** commit a breach of contract.

ver'tragschließend *adj* contracting.

Ver'trags|entwurf *m* draft agreement.

2gemäß adv as stipulated. **~gemeinschaft** f pol. contractual union. **~händler** m authorized dealer. **~par,tei** f, **~partner** m party to an agreement. **~punkt** m article of a contract. **~spieler(in** f) m sports: player under contract. **~strafe** f (contractual) penalty. **~werkstatt** f authorized repairer.

ver'tragswidrig adj contrary to (the terms of) the contract.

ver'trauen v/i (h) (dat) trust: **~ auf** (acc) trust in, rely upon. **Ver'trauen** n (-s) (in, auf acc in) trust, faith, confidence: (ganz) **im ~** (gesagt) (strictly) confidentially, F between you and me; **im ~ auf** (acc) trusting in, relying on; **~ haben zu** have confidence in, trust; **er hat wenig ~ zu Ärzten** he has little faith in doctors; **j-n ins ~ ziehen** confide in s.o.; **der Regierung das ~ aussprechen** pass a vote of confidence.

ver'trauenerweckend adj inspiring confidence: (wenig) **~ aussehen** inspire (little) confidence.

Ver'trauens|arzt m (health insurance) medical examiner. **~beweis** m mark of confidence. **~bruch** m breach of trust. **~frage** f pol. **die ~ stellen** propose a vote of confidence. **~mann** m (-[e]s; -leute) a) representative, b) (pl a. **~er**) spokesman. **~per,son** f reliable person. **~sache** f confidential matter: **das ist ~** that's a matter of confidence. **2selig** adj (too) confiding, gullible. **~seligkeit** f (-; no pl) blind confidence, gullibility. **~stellung** f position of trust. **~verlust** m loss of confidence. **2voll** adj trustful, trusting. **~votum** n vote of confidence. **2würdig** adj trustworthy.

ver'traulich adj **1.** confidential: **~e Mitteilung** a. confidence. **2.** familiar, (a. plump **~**) F chummy.

Ver'traulichkeit f (-; -en) **1.** no pl confidentiality, confidence. **2.** familiarity, (a. plumpe **~**) F chumminess.

ver'träumt adj dreamy.

ver'traut adj **1.** close, intimate. **2.** familiar (dat to): **~ sein mit** be familiar with; **sich ~ machen mit** acquaint (or familiarize) o.s. with; **sich mit dem Gedanken ~ machen** get used to the idea.

Ver'traute m, f (-n; -n) confidant(e f).

Ver'trautheit f (-; no pl) familiarity.

ver'treiben v/t (irr, no -ge-, h, → trei-ben) **1.** drive s.o., s.th. away: **j-n ~ aus** (dat) drive s.o. out of, expel s.o. from; **sich die Zeit ~** while away the time. **2.** ✝ sell, distribute.

Ver'treibung f (-; -en) expulsion.

ver'tretbar adj justifiable, acceptable.

ver'treten¹ v/t (irr, no -ge-, h, → treten) **1.** substitute (or stand in, a. ⚖ act) for s.o. **2.** represent (s.o., country, etc), look after (s.o.'s interests): **j-s Sache ~** plead s.o.'s cause. **3.** support, advocate (idea etc), hold, take (view etc): **e-e andere Ansicht ~** take a different view (als from); → **Standpunkt** 2. **4. sich den Fuß ~** sprain one's ankle; F **sich die Beine ~** stretch one's legs.

ver'treten² adj ~ sein a) be represented, b) be present, esp. things: be found.

Ver'treter m (-s; -), **Ver'treterin** f (-; -nen) **1.** substitute, stand-in, deputy. **2.** a) representative, ✝ a. agent, b) sales representative, c) proxy. **3.** exponent. **4.** advocate.

Ver'tretung f (-; -en) **1.** representation, ✝ a. agency: **in ~** (gen) as representative of, b) (signed) for, c) by proxy: **diplomatische ~** diplomatic mission. **2.** a) substitution, b) stand-in, substitute: **j-s ~ übernehmen** stand in for s.o.

ver'tretungsweise adv as a stand-in.

Ver'trieb [fɛr'triːp] m (-[e]s; no pl) **1.** sale, distribution. **2.** sales department.

Ver'triebene [fɛr'triːbənə] m, f (-n; -n) expellee.

Ver'triebs|abteilung f sales department. **~kosten** pl marketing costs. **~leiter** m sales manager. **~organisati,on** f marketing organization. **~weg** m distribution channel.

ver'trimmen v/t (h) F thrash.

ver'trinken v/t (irr, no -ge-, h, → trinken) spend on drink.

ver'trocknen v/i (sn) dry up.

ver'trödeln v/t (h) dawdle away, waste.

ver'trösten v/t (h) **j-n ~** feed s.o. with hopes (auf acc of); **j-n auf später ~** put s.o. off until later.

ver'trotteln v/i (sn) F go gaga.

ver'trottelt adj F senile: **~ sein** go gaga.

ver'tun v/t (irr, no -ge-, h, → tun) waste.

ver'tuschen v/t (h) cover up, hush up.

verübeln [fɛr'ˀyːbəln] v/t (h) **j-m et. ~** take s.th. amiss; **j-m ~, daß** take it bad-

ly that; *ich kann es ihr nicht ~(, wenn)* I can't blame her (if).
ver'üben *v/t* (h) commit, perpetrate.
ver'ulken *v/t* (h) F make fun of.
verunglimpfen [fɛr'ʔʊnɡlɪmpfən] *v/t* (h) revile, disparage.
ver'unglücken *v/i* (sn) **1.** have an accident: *tödlich* ~ be killed in an accident; *mit dem Auto* ~ have a car accident. **2.** F go wrong, be a flop. **Ver'unglückte** *m, f* (-n; -n) injured person, casualty.
ver'unsichern *v/t* (h) *j-n* ~ make s.o. feel insecure, F rattle s.o.
verunstalten [fɛr'ʔʊnʃtaltən] *v/t* (h) deface, disfigure.
veruntreuen [fɛr'ʔʊntrɔyən] *v/t* (h) embezzle. **Ver'untreuung** *f* (-; -en) embezzlement.
ver'ursachen *v/t* (h) a) cause, create, give rise to b) entail.
ver'urteilen *v/t* (h) (**zu** to) ⚖ sentence, *a. fig.* condemn. **Ver'urteilte** *m, f* (-n; -n) convict. **Ver'urteilung** *f* (-; -en) *a. fig.* condemnation.
vervielfältigen [fɛr'fiːlfɛltɪɡən] *v/t* (h) **1.** (*a. sich*) multiply. **2.** duplicate, copy. **Ver'vielfältigung** *f* (-; -en) **1.** multiplication. **2.** a) duplication, b) duplicate, copy. **Ver'vielfältigungsappa,rat** *m* duplicator.
vervierfachen *v/t* (h) (*a. sich* ~) (h) quadruple.
vervollkommnen [fɛr'fɔlkɔmnən] (h) **I** *v/t* perfect. **II** *sich* ~ become perfect. **Ver'vollkommnung** *f* (-; -en) perfection.
vervollständigen [fɛr'fɔlʃtɛndɪɡən] *v/t* (h) complete. **Ver'vollständigung** *f* (-; -en) completion.
ver'wachsen¹ *v/i* (*irr, no* -ge-, sn, → **wachsen**) (*miteinander*) ~ grow together, *bones*: unite, *organs*: fuse: *fig.* ~ *mit* become bound up with *one's* job *etc*, feel at home in a *town etc*.
ver'wachsen² *adj* deformed, crippled.
ver'wachsen³ *v/t* (h) apply the wrong wax to *skis*.
ver'wackeln *v/t* (h) F *phot.* blur.
ver'wählen: sich ~ (h) F dial the wrong number.
ver'wahren (h) **I** *v/t* keep (**sicher** in a safe place). **II** *sich* ~ protest (**gegen** against).
verwahrlosen [fɛr'vaːrloːzən] *v/i* (sn) be neglected, *person*: go to seed: ~ *lassen*

neglect. **ver'wahrlost** [-loːst] *adj* a) neglected, run-down, dilapidated, b) seedy, *a.* dissolute. **Ver'wahrlosung** *f* (-; *no pl*) **1.** neglect. **2.** (moral) decline.
Ver'wahrung *f* (-; *no pl*) a) keeping, b) custody (*gen of s.o.*): *in* ~ *nehmen* take charge of; (*j-m*) *et. in* ~ *geben* deposit s.th. (with s.o.).
verwaisen [fɛr'vaɪzən] *v/i* (sn) become an orphan, be orphaned. **verwaist** [-'vaɪst] *adj* **1.** orphan (*child etc*). **2.** *fig.* a) deserted, b) vacant (*post*).
ver'walten *v/t* (h) administer, manage, conduct, run. **Ver'walter** *m* (-s; -) administrator, (*a.* estate) manager, trustee. **Ver'walterin** *f* (-; -nen) manageress. **Ver'waltung** *f* (-; -en) **1.** administration, ✝ management. **2.** administrative authority.
Ver'waltungs|angestellte *m, f* (-n; -n) employee in the administration. **~appa,rat** *m* administrative machinery. **~beamte** *m* civil servant. **~bezirk** *m* administrative district. **~gebäude** *n* administration building. **~gebühr** *f* administrative fee. **~gericht** *n* ⚖ administrative court. **~rat** *m* ✝ governing board. **²technisch** *adj* administrative. **~weg** *m auf dem ~e* through (the) administrative channels.
ver'wandeln *v/t* (h) (*in acc* into) change (*a. sich* ~), transform, turn, convert (*a. sports*): *wie verwandelt* completely changed. **Ver'wandlung** *f* (-; -en) change, transformation, conversion.
verwandt [fɛr'vant] *adj* (*mit*) *a. fig.* related (to), *ling. a.* cognate (with).
Ver'wandte *m, f* (-n; -n) relative, relation: *der nächste* ~ the next of kin.
Ver'wandtschaft *f* (-; *no pl*) **1.** relationship, *fig.* affinity. **2.** relations.
ver'wandtschaftlich *adj* relational: *~e Beziehung(en)* relations.
Ver'wandtschaftsgrad *m* degree of relationship.
verwanzt [fɛr'vantst] *adj* buggy.
ver'warnen *v/t* (h) warn, *a. sports*: caution. **Ver'warnung** *f* (-; -en) warning, *a. sports*: caution.
ver'waschen *adj* **1.** washed(-)out, *a.* faded. **2.** *fig.* vague, wool(l)y.
ver'wässern *v/t* (h) *a. fig.* water down.
ver'weben *v/t* (*irr, no* -ge-, h, → **weben**) interweave.

ver'wechseln v/t (h) (*mit* with) confuse, mix up: *j-n* (*mit j-m*) ~ mistake s.o. for s.o. else; *sie sehen sich zum ♀ ähnlich* they are as like as two peas (in a pod). **Ver'wechslung** f (-; -en) **1.** confusion, mistake, F mix-up. **2.** case of mistaken identity.

ver'wegen adj bold, daring, reckless.

ver'wehen v/t (h) **1.** blow s.th. away, scatter. **2.** cover (up) traces etc.

ver'wehren v/t (h) refuse: *j-m den Zutritt* ~ refuse s.o. admittance (*zu* to).

ver'weichlichen I v/t (h) *j-n* ~ make s.o. soft. **II** v/i (sn) go soft.

ver'weichlicht adj soft, effeminate.

ver'weigern (h) **I** v/t *j-m et.* ~ refuse (or deny) s.o. s.th.; *e-n Befehl* ~ disobey an order; *die Nahrung* ~ refuse to eat. **II** v/i horse: refuse. **Ver'weigerung** f (-; -en) refusal, denial.

Ver'weildauer f length of stay.

verweilen (h) **I** v/i (h) **1.** stay. **2.** fig. rest (*auf dat* on). **3.** ~ *bei* dwell on.

verweint [fɛr'vaɪnt] adj tear-stained (face), eyes red from crying.

Verweis [fɛr'vaɪs] m (-es; -e) **1.** reprimand, rebuke: *j-m e-n* ~ *erteilen* reprimand s.o. (*wegen* for). **2.** reference (*auf acc* to). **ver'weisen** v/t (irr, no -ge-, h, → **weisen**) **1.** refer (*an, auf acc* to). **2.** *j-n von der Schule* ~ expel s.o. from school; *j-n des Landes* ~ expel s.o. (from the country); → **Platz** 5.

ver'welken v/i (sn) a. fig. wither.

verwendbar [fɛr'vɛntbaːr] adj usable, suitable. **Ver'wendbarkeit** f (-; no pl) usability, suitability.

ver'wenden (irr, no -ge-, h, → **wenden**) **I** v/t **1.** use, employ, a. make use of, utilize. **2.** (*auf acc*) spend (on), a. devote effort, time, etc (to). **II** sich (*bei j-m*) *für j-n* ~ use one's influence (with s.o.) on s.o.'s behalf.

Ver'wendung f (-; -en) use, employment: *k-e* ~ *haben für* have no use for; ~ *finden* be used (*bei* in).

Ver'wendungs|bereich m range of use. **~möglichkeit** f use. **~zweck** m use, (intended) purpose.

ver'werfen (irr, no -ge-, h, → **werfen**) **I** v/t reject, turn down (plan etc), ⚖ dismiss (appeal, action, etc), overrule (motion), quash (sentence). **II** sich ~ a) geol. fault, b) wood: warp.

ver'werflich adj reprehensible.

Ver'werfung f (-; -en) **1.** rejection, ⚖ dismissal. **2.** a) geol. fault, b) warping.

ver'wertbar adj usable, ♦ realizable.

Ver'wertbarkeit f (-; no pl) usability.

ver'werten v/t (h) use, utilize, make use of, exploit (patent etc), ♦ realize (property etc). **Ver'wertung** f (-; -en) use, utilization, exploitation, ♦ realization.

ver'wesen v/i (sn) rot, decay: *halb verwest* putrefying. **Ver'wesung** f (-; no pl) decay, putrefaction.

ver'wetten v/t (h) spend s.th. on betting.

ver'wickeln (h) **I** v/t **1.** tangle s.th. **2.** fig. *j-n* ~ *in* (acc) involve s.o. in, a. drag s.o. into. **II** sich ~ **3.** tangle up. **4.** sich ~ *in* (acc) fig. get caught in, get tangled up in a web of contradictions etc.

ver'wickelt adj fig. **1.** complicated, complex, intricate. **2.** ~ *sein* (*werden*) *in* (acc) be (get) involved (or mixed up) in.

Ver'wicklung f (-; -en) fig. **1.** involvement (*in acc* in). **2.** entanglement, complication.

ver'wildern v/i (sn) run wild, morals etc: degenerate. **ver'wildert** adj wild, overgrown (garden), fig. degenerate.

Ver'wilderung f (-; no pl) (state of) neglect, fig. degeneration.

ver'wirken v/t (h) forfeit.

ver'wirklichen (h) **I** v/t realize. **II** sich ~ be realized, come true; sich (*selbst*) ~ fulfil(l) o.s. **Ver'wirklichung** f (-; -en) realization.

ver'wirren (h) **I** v/t **1.** tangle s.th. (up). **2.** fig. confuse, bewilder, muddle. **II** sich ~ **3.** get tangled up. **4.** fig. become muddled. **ver'wirrt** adj fig. confused, bewildered, muddled. **Ver'wirrung** f (-; -en) confusion, muddle, a. bewilderment: *es herrschte allgemeine* ~ there was general confusion; *in* ~ *bringen* → **verwirren** 2.

ver'wischen v/t (a. sich ~) (h) blur, fig. a. cover (up); → **Spur** 1.

ver'wittern v/i (sn) weather.

ver'wittert adj weather-beaten.

ver'witwet adj widowed.

verwöhnen [fɛr'vøːnən] v/t (h) spoil, pamper. **ver'wöhnt** adj **1.** spoilt. **2.** fastidious. **3.** demanding. **Ver'wöhnung** f (-; no pl) spoiling, pampering.

verworren [fɛr'vɔrən] adj confused,

muddled. **Ver'worrenheit** *f* (-; *no pl*) confusion, muddle.

verwundbar [fɛr'vʊntbaːr] *adj a. fig.* vulnerable. **Ver'wundbarkeit** *f* (-; *no pl*) *a. fig.* vulnerability. **verwunden** [fɛr'vʊndən] *v/t* (h) *a. fig.* wound.

ver'wunderlich *adj* surprising, astonishing. **ver'wundern** (h) **I** *v/t* surprise, astonish. **II** *sich ~* (*über acc* at) be surprised, be astonished. **ver'wundert** *adj* surprised, astonished: *j-n ~ ansehen* look at s.o. in surprise.

Ver'wunderung *f* (-; *no pl*) surprise, astonishment.

Ver'wundete *m, f* (-n; -n) casualty: *die ~n* the wounded.

Ver'wundung *f* (-; -en) wound, injury.

verwunschen [fɛr'vʊnʃən] *adj* enchanted.

ver'wünschen *v/t* (h) curse.

ver'wünscht *adj* cursed, confounded.

Ver'wünschung *f* (-; -en) curse.

ver'wurzelt *adj fig.* (deeply) rooted.

ver'wüsten *v/t* (h) devastate, ravage.

Ver'wüstung *f* (-; -en) devastation, ravage(s).

ver'zagen *v/i* (h) despair (*an dat* of), lose heart. **verzagt** [-'tsaːkt] *adj* disheartened, despondent.

ver'zählen: *sich ~ v/t* (h) miscount.

ver'zahnt *adj* ⊙ toothed: *miteinander ~ a. fig.* interlocked.

ver'zapfen *v/t* (h) **1.** ⊙ mortise. **2.** F dish out: *Unsinn ~* talk nonsense.

verzärteln [fɛr'tsɛːrtəln] *v/t* (h) pamper, (molly)coddle.

ver'zaubern *v/t* (h) cast a spell on, *fig. a.* enchant: *j-n ~ in* (*acc*) turn s.o. into.

ver'zehnfachen *v/t* (*a. sich ~*) (h) increase tenfold.

Verzehr [fɛr'tseːr] *m* (-[e]s; *no pl*) consumption. **ver'zehren** *v/t* (h) consume (*a. fig.*). **Ver'zehrzwang** *m* (-[e]s; *no pl*) obligation to order.

ver'zeichnen *v/t* (h) **1.** note (*or* write) down, register, record: *in e-r Liste ~* list; *er konnte e-n großen Erfolg ~* he achieved a great success; *Fortschritte sind nicht zu ~* no progress has been made. **2.** *fig.* distort, misrepresent.

Verzeichnis [fɛr'tsaɪçnɪs] *n* (-ses; -se) a) list, catalog(ue *Br.*), register, record, b) index, c) inventory.

verzeihen [fɛr'tsaɪən] (verzieh, verzie-

hen, h) **I** *v/t* forgive, excuse, pardon: *j-m et. ~* forgive s.o. s.th., excuse (*or* pardon) s.o. (for) s.th.; *~ Sie die Störung* excuse my interrupting you. **II** *v/i j-m ~* forgive s.o.; *~ Sie!* (I beg your) pardon!, sorry!, *Am.* excuse me!

ver'zeihlich *adj* pardonable.

Ver'zeihung *f* (-; *no pl*) pardon: *j-n um ~ bitten* a) ask s.o.'s forgiveness, b) apologize to s.o.; *~!* (I beg your) pardon!, sorry!, *Am.* excuse me!

ver'zerren (h) **I** *v/t a. fig.* distort. **II** *sich ~* become distorted.

Ver'zerrung *f* (-; -en) *a. fig.* distortion.

ver'zetteln (h) **I** *v/t* fritter away. **II** *sich ~* waste one's time (*or* energy) (*in dat, mit* on).

Verzicht [fɛr'tsɪçt] *m* (-[e]s; -e) (*auf acc* of) renunciation, ⚖ a. waiver.

ver'zichten *v/i* (h) *~ auf* (*acc*) do without, F cut out, *a.* give up, ⚖ renounce, waive; *zu j-s Gunsten ~* stand aside for s.o.'s benefit.

Ver'zichterklärung *f* ⚖ waiver.

verzieh [fɛr'tsiː] *pret of* verzeihen.

ver'ziehen¹ *pp of* verzeihen.

ver'ziehen² (*irr, no* -ge-, → ziehen) **I** *v/i* (sn) **1.** → *umziehen.* **II** *v/t* (h) **2.** distort, twist (*zu* into): *das Gesicht ~* (make a) grimace, pull a face; *→ Miene.* **3.** spoil: *→ verzogen.* **III** *sich ~* **4.** *mouth, face, etc:* twist (*zu* into). **5.** *wood:* warp. **6.** *clouds etc:* disperse, *storm etc:* blow over. **7.** F make *etc* scarce: *verzieht euch!* beat it!, get lost!

ver'zieren *v/t* (h) decorate.

Ver'zierung *f* (-; -en) decoration.

ver'zinken *v/t* (h) ⊙ galvanize.

ver'zinnen *v/t* (h) ⊙ tin(-plate).

verzinsen [fɛr'tsɪnzən] (h) **I** *v/t* pay interest on: *e-e Summe mit 5% ~* pay 5 per cent (*or* percent) interest on a sum. **II** *sich* (*mit 5%*) *~* yield (*or* bear) (5 per cent *or* percent) interest. **ver'zinslich** *adj* interest-bearing: *~ anlegen* put out at interest. **Ver'zinsung** *f* (-; -en) **1.** (*von, gen* on) a) payment of interest, b) interest yield. **2.** → *Zinssatz.*

verzogen [fɛr'tsoːgən] *adj fig.* spoilt.

ver'zögern (h) **I** *v/t* a) delay, b) slow down, c) protract. **II** *sich ~* be delayed.

Ver'zögerung *f* (-; -en) delay. **Ver'zögerungstaktik** *f* delaying tactics.

ver'zollen *v/t* (h) pay duty on: *haben*

Sie et. zu ~? have you anything to declare? **ver'zollt** *adj* duty-paid.
Ver'zollung *f* (-; -en) payment of duty (*gen on*).
verzückt [fɛr'tsʏkt] *adj* enraptured, ecstatic. **Ver'zückung** *f* (-; -en) rapture, ecstasy: *in ~ geraten* go into raptures (*or* ecstasies) (*über acc* over, about).
Ver'zug *m* (-[e]s; *no pl*) **1.** delay: *ohne ~* without delay, forthwith; *✝ im ~ sein* (*mit*) default (on), be in arrear(s) (for). **2.** *es ist Gefahr im ~* there is danger ahead.
Ver'zugszinsen *pl* interest on arrears.
ver'zweifeln *v/i* (sn) despair (*an dat* of): *es ist zum ℥* it's enough to drive you to despair; *ich bin am ℥* I'm desperate.
ver'zweifelt *adj* despairing (*look etc*), desperate (*fight, situation, etc*).
Ver'zweiflung *f* (-; *no pl*) (*j-n zur ~ bringen or treiben* drive s.o. to) despair.
Ver'zweiflungstat *f* act of desperation.
verzweigen [fɛr'tsvaɪɡən] *sich ~* (h) branch out, *esp. fig.* ramify.
ver'zweigt *adj* branching (*network etc*).
ver'zwickt *adj* F tricky, complicated.
Veteran [vete'ra:n] *m* (-en; -en) **1.** ✕ ex-serviceman, *Am.* and *fig.* veteran. **2.** *mot.* vintage car.
Veterinär [veteri'nɛ:r] *m* (-s; -e) veterinary surgeon, *Am.* veterinarian, F vet.
Veto ['ve:to] *n* (-s; -s) veto: (*s)ein ~ einlegen* put a veto on, veto.
'Vetorecht *n* veto (power).
Vetter ['fɛtər] *m* (-s; -n) cousin.
'Vetternwirtschaft *f* (-; *no pl*) nepotism.
Viadukt [vĭa'dʊkt] *m* (-[e]s; -e) viaduct.
Vibration [vibra'tsĭo:n] *f* (-; -en) vibration.
vibrieren [vi'bri:rən] *v/i* (h) vibrate.
Video ['vi:deo] *n* → **Videotechnik.**
'Video... video (*camera, film, system, etc*). **~aufzeichnung** *f* video recording. **~band** *n* video tape. **~gerät** *n* video recorder. **~kas‚sette** *f* video cassette. **~re‚corder** *m* video recorder. **~spiel** *n* video game. **~technik** *f* video technology. **~text** *m* teletext.
Videothek [video'te:k] *f* (-; -en) video-tape library.
Vieh [fi:] *n* (-[e]s; *no pl*) **1.** cattle, livestock. **2.** F *contp.* animal, beast. **~bestand** *m* livestock. **~futter** *n* fodder, feed. **~händler** *m* cattle dealer.

'viehisch *adj* bestial, brutal.
'Vieh|markt *m* cattle market. **~wagen** *m* 🚃 cattle truck, *Am.* stock car. **~zeug** *n* F animals. **~zucht** *f* stockbreeding. **~züchter** *m* stockbreeder, cattleman.
viel [fi:l] *adj and adv* a) a lot (of), plenty (of), F lots of, b) (*as, how, so, too, very, not*) much: (*sehr*) *~e* (a great) many; *sehr ~ Geld* a great deal (*or* plenty of) money; *ziemlich ~e* quite a lot (of); *das kommt vom ~en Rauchen* that comes from all that smoking; *ich halte nicht ~ davon* I don't think much of it; *~e hundert* hundreds and hundreds of; *~ besser* (*lieber*) much better (rather); *~ zuviel* far too much; *~ zu wenig* not nearly enough; *in ~em* in many ways.
'vielbeschäftigt *adj* very busy.
'vieldeutig *adj* ambiguous.
'vieldisku‚tiert *adj* much-discussed.
'Vieleck *n* (-[e]s; -e) Ⓐ polygon.
vielerlei ['fi:lər'laı] *adj* all sorts of.
vieler'orts *adv* in many places.
'vielfach I *adj* multiple: *er ist ~er Millionär* he is a millionaire many times over; *auf ~en Wunsch* by popular request. **II** *adv* a) in many cases, b) frequently.
'Vielfalt [-falt] *f* (-; *no pl*) (great) variety.
'vielfältig [-fɛltɪç] *adj* varied, manifold.
'Vielfraß *m* (-es; -e) a. F *fig.* glutton.
'vielgeliebt *adj* much-loved.
'vielgepriesen *adj* much-vaunted.
'vielköpfig [-kœpfɪç] *adj* large (*family*).
vielleicht [fi'laıçt] *adv* perhaps, maybe, possibly: *hast du ihn ~ gesehen?* have you seen him by any chance?; *~ kommen sie noch* they may yet come; *es ist ~ besser* it might be better; *könnten Sie ~ das Fenster schließen?* would you mind closing the window?; F *das ist ~ ein Trottel!* he really is an idiot!; *ich war ~ aufgeregt!* what a state I was in!; *das ist ~ ein Auto!* that's some car.
'vielmals *adv* many times: *danke ~* many thanks; *sie läßt ~ grüßen* she sends her best regards; *ich bitte ~ um Entschuldigung* I'm terribly sorry.
'vielmehr *adv* rather.
'vielsagend *adj* meaningful, knowing.
'vielschichtig [-ʃɪçtɪç] *adj fig.* complex.
'vielseitig [-zaıtıç] *adj* many-sided, versatile (*person*), varied (*interests etc*); *auf ~en Wunsch* by popular request; *sie ist ~ begabt* she has many talents;

er ist ~ *interessiert* he has varied interests; ~ *verwendbar* multi-purpose.
'Vielseitigkeit f (-; *no pl*) versatility.
'vielsprachig [-ʃpraːxɪç] *adj* polyglot.
'vielstimmig [-ʃtɪmɪç] *adj* ♪ polyphonic.
'vielversprechend *adj* (very) promising: *nicht (gerade)* ~ unpromising.
Viel'völkerstaat m multiracial state.
Vielweiberei [fiːlvaɪbəˈraɪ] f (-; *no pl*) polygamy.
'Vielzahl f (-; *no pl*) multitude.
vier [fiːr] *adj* four: *unter* ~ *Augen* in private; *Gespräch unter* ~ *Augen* private talk; F *auf allen* ~*en* on all fours.
Vier f (-; -en) four: *ped. e-e* ~ *bekommen* get a D.
'Vierbeiner [-baɪnər] m (-s; -) F quadruped. **'vierbeinig** *adj* four-legged.
'vierblätt(e)rig [-blɛt(ə)rɪç] *adj* four-leaf ..., four-leaved.
'Viereck n (-[e]s; -e) quadrangle, square.
'viereckig *adj* quadrangular, square.
Vierer ['fiːrər] m (-s; -) *rowing:* four, *golf:* foursome. ~**bob** m four-seater bob.
'vierfach *adj* fourfold.
Vier'farbendruck m four-colo(u)r printing (*picture:* print).
'Vierfüßer [-fyːsər] m (-s; -) *zo.* quadruped. **'vierfüßig** *adj* four-footed.
'Vierganggetriebe n *mot.* four-speed gear unit.
'vierhändig [-hɛndɪç] *adj* four-handed, for four hands: ~ *spielen* play a duet.
'vier'hundert *adj* four hundred.
'vierjährig [-jɛːrɪç] *adj* **1.** of four years, four-year (*period etc*). **2.** four-year-old.
'Vierjährige [-jɛːrɪgə] m, f (-n; -n) four-year-old.
'Vierkant m, n (-[e]s; -e) ⊕ square.
'vierkantig *adj* square.
'Vierlinge *pl* quadruplets.
'viermal *adv* four times.
'viermotorig [-mo,toːrɪç] *adj esp.* ✈ four-engine(d).
'Vierrad... four-wheel (*drive, brake*).
'vierrädrig [-rɛːdrɪç] *adj* four-wheeled.
'vierschrötig [-ʃrøːtɪç] *adj* square-built, burly.
'vierseitig [-zaɪtɪç] *adj* four-sided, ⋏ quadrilateral.
'viersilbig [-zɪlbɪç] *adj* four-syllable.
'Viersitzer m (-s; -) four-seater.
'vierspurig [-ʃpuːrɪç] *adj* four-lane.
'vierstellig [-ʃtɛlɪç] *adj* ⋏ four-digit.

'vierstimmig [-ʃtɪmɪç] *adj* ♪ four-part: ~ *singen* sing in four voices.
'vierstöckig [-ʃtœkɪç] *adj* four-storeyed, *Am.* four-storied.
'vierstündig [-ʃtʏndɪç] *adj* four-hour.
viert [fiːrt] *adj* fourth: *sie waren zu* ~ there were four of them.
'Viertaktmotor m four-stroke engine.
'vier'tausend *adj* four thousand.
'Vierte m, f (-n; -n) fourth.
Viertel ['fɪrtəl] n (-s; -) quarter, fourth: *es ist* ~ *vor eins* it is a quarter to one.
'Viertelfi,nale n *sports:* quarter final.
Viertel'jahr n three months, quarter.
'vierteljährlich *adj and adv* quarterly: ~*e Kündigung* three months' notice.
'Viertelliter m, n (-s; -) quarter of a litre (*Am.* liter).
vierteln ['fɪrtəln] v/t (h) quarter.
'Viertel|note f ♪ crotchet, *Am.* quarter note. ~**pause** f ♪ crotchet (*Am.* quarter note) rest. ~**pfund** n quarter of a pound. ~**stunde** f quarter of an hour.
'viertelstündlich *adj and adv* every quarter of an hour (*or* fifteen minutes).
'viertens *adv* fourthly.
Vier'vierteltakt m ♪ four-four (*or* common) time.
vierzehn ['fɪr-] *adj* fourteen: ~ *Tage* a fortnight, *Am.* fourteen days; *in* ~ *Tagen* in two weeks' time, in a fortnight. ~**jährig** [-jɛːrɪç] *adj* fourteen-year-old. ~**tägig** [-tɛːgɪç] *adj* two-week.
'Vierzeiler [-tsaɪlər] m (-s; -) quatrain.
vierzig ['fɪrtsɪç] *adj* forty. **'Vierzig** f (-; -en) forty: *sie ist Anfang (der)* ~ she is in her early forties. **'vierziger** *adj die* ~ *Jahre* the forties. **Vierziger** m (-s; -), **'Vierzigerin** f (-; -nen) man (woman) of forty (*or* in his [her] forties).
'vierzigst *adj* fortieth.
Vietnam [vĭɛtˈnam] n (-s) Vietnam.
Vietnamese [vĭɛtnaˈmeːzə] m (-n; -n), **Vietna'mesin** f (-; -nen), **vietna'mesisch** *adj* Vietnamese.
Vikar [viˈkaːr] m (-s; -e) curate.
Villa ['vɪla] f (-; Villen) villa.
'Villenviertel n residential area.
Viola ['vĭoːla] f (-; Violen) ♪ viola.
violett [vĭoˈlɛt] *adj* violet.
Violine [vĭoˈliːnə] f (-; -n) ♪ violin.
Violinist [vĭoliˈnɪst] m (-en; -en) violinist.
Vio'linschlüssel m ♪ treble clef.
Violon'cello [vĭolɔn-] n ♪ violoncello.

Viper ['vi:pər] *f* (-; -n) *zo.* viper, adder.

Virologie [virolo'gi:] *f* (-; *no pl*) virology.

virologisch [viro'lo:gɪʃ] *adj* virological.

virtuos [vɪr'tŭo:s] *adj* virtuoso. **Virtuose** [vɪr'tŭo:zə] *m* (-n; -n), **Virtu'osin** *f* (-; -nen) virtuoso. **Virtuosität** [vɪrtŭozi-'tɛ:t] *f* (-; *no pl*) virtuosity.

virulent [viru'lɛnt] *adj* virulent.

Virus ['vi:rʊs] *m, n* (-; Viren) ✴ virus. **~infekti,on** *f* virus (*or* viral) infection.

Visage [vi'za:ʒə] *f* (-; -n) F mug.

Visier [vi'zi:r] *n* (-s; -e) **1.** visor. **2.** *on rifle*: sight. **vi'sieren** *v/i* (h) take aim.

Vision [vi'zĭo:n] *f* (-; -en) vision.

visionär [vizĭo'nɛ:r] *adj* visionary.

Visite [vi'zi:tə] *f* (-; -n) (doctor's) round. **Vi'sitenkarte** *f* (visiting) card.

visuell [vi'zŭɛl] *adj* visual.

Visum ['vi:zʊm] *n* (-s; Visa, Visen) visa.

vital [vi'ta:l] *adj* **1.** vigorous, fit. **2.** vital.

Vitalität [vitali'tɛ:t] *f* (-; *no pl*) vitality.

Vitamin [vita'mi:n] *n* (-s; -e) vitamin: F *fig.* **~ B** contacts. **♀arm** *adj* low in vitamins. **~bedarf** *m* vitamin requirement. **~gehalt** *m* vitamin content.

vita'minhaltig *adj* containing vitamins.

vitaminieren [vitami'ni:rən] *v/t* (h) vitaminize.

Vita'min|mangel *m* vitamin deficiency. **~präpa,rat** *n* vitamin preparation. **♀reich** *adj* rich in vitamins. **~stoß** *m* massive dose of vitamins.

Vitrine [vi'tri:nə] *f* (-; -n) glass cupboard, ✝ showcase, display case.

Vize... ['fi:tsə-] vice-(*admiral, chancellor, president, etc*). **~könig** *m* viceroy. **~meister(in)** *f*) *m sports*: runner-up (*hinter dat* to).

Vogel ['fo:gəl] *m* (-s; ◆) **1.** bird: F *fig.* **e-n ~ haben** have a screw loose; **den ~ abschießen** take the cake; **j-m den ~ zeigen** tap one's forehead at s.o. **2.** F *fig.* bird, fellow: **ein komischer ~** a queer customer. **~beerbaum** *m* rowan-(-tree). **~beere** *f* rowanberry. **~futter** *n* birdseed. **~haus** *n* aviary. **~käfig** *m* birdcage. **~kunde** *f* (-; *no pl*) ornithology. **~mist** *m* bird droppings.

vögeln ['fø:gəln] *v/t, v/i* (h) V screw.

'**Vogel|nest** *n* bird's nest. **~perspek,tive** *f* Berlin aus der **~** a bird's-eye view of Berlin. **~scheuche** *f* (-; -n) scarecrow. **~schutzgebiet** *n* bird sanctuary.

Vogel-'Strauß-Poli,tik *f* ostrich policy.

'**Vogelwarte** *f* ornithological station.

'**Vogelzug** *m* migration of birds.

Vokabel [vo'ka:bəl] *f* (-; -n) word.

Vo'kabelheft *n* vocabulary book.

Vokal [vo'ka:l] *m* (-s; -e) vowel.

Vo'kalmu,sik *f* vocal music.

Volk [fɔlk] *n* (-[e]s; ◆er) **1.** a) people, nation, b) *the* masses, *contp.* mob, rabble, c) crowd: **ein Mann aus dem ~** a man of the people; **sich unters ~ mischen** mingle with the crowd. **2.** *zo.* swarm (*of bees*). **3.** *hunt.* covey.

Völker|kunde ['fœlkər-] *f* (-; *no pl*) ethnology. **~mord** *m* genocide. **~recht** *n* (-[e]s; *no pl*) international law. **♀rechtlich** *adj* relating to (*adv* under) international law. **~verständigung** *f* international understanding. **~wanderung** *f* **1.** migration of peoples. **2.** *fig.* exodus.

'**volkreich** *adj* populous.

'**Volks|abstimmung** *f* referendum. **~aufstand** *m* national uprising. **~befragung** *f* public opinion poll. **~begehren** *n* petition for a referendum. **~büche,rei** *f* public library. **~cha,rakter** *m* national character. **~demokra,tie** *f* people's democracy. **~deutsche** *m, f* (-n; -n) ethnic German. **♀eigen** *adj hist. DDR* state-owned. **~eigentum** *n* national property. **~einkommen** *n* national income. **~entscheid** *m* referendum. **~feind** *m* public enemy. **~fest** *n* public festival, fair. **~gruppe** *f* ethnic group. **~held(in** *f*) *m* folk hero(ine *f*). **~herrschaft** *f* democracy. **~hochschule** *f* adult evening classes. **~kammer** *f hist. DDR* People's Chamber. **~kunde** *f* (-; *no pl*) folklore. **~lauf** *m* open cross-country race. **~lied** *n* folk song. **~mund** *m* (*im ~* in the) vernacular. **~mu,sik** *f* folk music. **♀nah** *adj* popular, people-oriented, grassroots (*politician*). **~poli,zist** *m hist. DDR* member of the people's police. **~repu,blik** *f* people's republic. **♀eigen** *adj* of social class. **~schule** *f* → **Grund-, Hauptschule**. **~seele** *f iro.* **die ~ kocht** the populace is seething. **~sport** *m* popular sport. **~sprache** *f* vernacular. **~stamm** *m* tribe, race. **~stück** *n thea.* folk play. **~tanz** *m* folk dance. **~tracht** *f* national costume. **~trauertag** *m* day of national mourning.

'**Volkstum** *n* (-s; *no pl*) folklore.

'**volkstümlich** [-ty:mlıç] *adj* **1.** folkloristic. **2.** *ling.* vernacular. **3.** traditional. **4.** popular: *sich ~ geben* act folksy.

'**Volks|vermögen** *n* national wealth. **~versammlung** *f* public meeting. **~vertreter(in** *f*) *m* people's representative. **~vertretung** *f* representation of the people, parliament. **~wirt** *m* † (political) economist. **~wirtschaft** *f* **1.** political economy. **2.** → **~wirtschaftslehre** *f* economics. **~zählung** *f* census.

voll [fɔl] **I** *adj* **1.** full, *a.* filled, *a.* full up: ~(**er**), ~ **von**, ~ **mit** full of (*a.* fig.), filled (*or* loaded) with; *e-e Kanne* (~) *Tee* a pot of tea; *fig. aus dem ~en schöpfen* draw on plentiful resources; F ~ *sein* a) be full up, b) be tight. **2.** full, round (*figure*), thick, rich (*hair*): ~*er werden a.* fill out. **3.** *fig.* full, rich (*scent, voice, etc*). **4.** full, whole: *der Mond ist* ~ the moon is full; *e-e* ~*e Stunde* a full (*or* solid) hour; *~e drei Tage* full three days; *et. in* ~*er Höhe bezahlen* pay the full amount, pay the amount in full; *mit* ~*er Lautstärke* (at) full blast; *aus* ~*er Brust, aus* ~*em Halse* at the top of one's voice; *aus* ~*em Herzen* from the bottom of one's heart; ~*es Vertrauen* complete confidence; *die* ~*e Wahrheit* the whole truth. **II** *adv* fully, *a.* in full: ~ *und ganz* completely, wholly; ~ *arbeiten* work full time; ~ *beschäftigt* fully occupied; ~ *besetzt* full (up); *Sie müssen* ~ *bezahlen* you have to pay the full price; ~ *schlagen clock:* strike the full hour; *j-n nicht für* ~ *nehmen* not to take s.o. seriously; F *in die* ~*en gehen* go flat out.

'**vollauf** *adv* quite, perfectly.

'**vollauto,matisch** *adj* fully automatic.

'**Vollbad** *n* full bath.

'**Vollbart** *m* full beard.

'**vollbeschäftigt** *adj* employed full-time. '**Vollbeschäftigung** *f* (-; *no pl*) full employment.

'**Vollbesitz** *m im* ~ (*gen*) in full possession of.

'**Vollblut** *n* (-[e]s; *no pl*), '**Vollblüter** [-bly:tər] *m* (-s; -), '**Vollblutpferd** *n* thoroughbred.

'**Vollbremsung** *f* full braking, crash-halt: *e-e* ~ *machen* F slam on the brakes.

voll'bringen *v/t* (*irr, insep, no* -ge-, h) → *bringen*) a) accomplish, achieve, b) perform (*miracles etc*).

'**vollbusig** [-bu:zıç] *adj* bosomy, busty.

'**Volldampf** *m mit* ~ at full steam, *fig.* at full blast.

'**vollelek,tronisch** *adj* fully electronic.

voll'enden *v/t* (*insep, no* -ge-, h) **1.** finish, complete. **2.** perfect. **voll'endet** *adj* perfect, accomplished: ~ *schön* of perfect beauty; ~ *Tatsache.* **vollends** ['fɔlɛnts] *adv* completely. **Voll'endung** *f* (-; *no pl*) **1.** completion: *nach* (*or mit*) ~ (*gen*) on completion of. **2.** perfection.

'**voller** → **voll** I.

Völlerei [fœlə'raı] *f* (-; -en) gluttony.

Volleyball(spiel) ['vɔli-] *n* volleyball.

'**Vollfettkäse** *m* full-fat cheese.

voll'führen *v/t* (*insep, no* -ge-, h) perform.

'**vollfüllen** *v/t* (*sep,* h) fill (up).

'**Vollgas** *n mot.* full throttle: *mit* ~ F full tilt; ~ *geben* F step on the gas.

'**voll|gepackt,** ~**gepfropft,** ~**gestopft** *adj* crammed (full), F (jam-)packed.

'**vollgießen** *v/t* (*irr, sep,* -ge-, h, → *gießen*) fill (up).

'**Vollgummi** *m, n* solid rubber.

völlig ['fœlıç] **I** *adj* total, absolute, complete: ~*e Gleichberechtigung* full equality, ~*er Unsinn* utter (*or* perfect) nonsense; *ein* ~*er Versager* a complete failure. **II** *adv* quite, fully (*etc*): ~ *richtig* absolutely right; ~ *am Ende sein* be completely run down; *das ist mir* ~ *gleichgültig* I don't give a damn.

'**volljährig** [-jɛ:rıç] *adj* of (full legal) age, major: ~ *sein* (*werden*) be (come) of age; *noch nicht* ~ under age.

'**Volljährigkeit** *f* (-; *no pl*) full legal age, majority.

'**Vollju,rist** *m* fully qualified lawyer.

'**Vollkaskoversicherung** *f* comprehensive insurance.

voll'kommen I *adj* perfect, total, absolute. **II** *adv* F → **völlig** II.

Voll'kommenheit *f* (-; *no pl*) perfection.

'**Vollkornbrot** *n* wholemeal bread.

'**vollmachen** *v/t* (*sep,* h) F **1.** fill (up). **2.** dirty, soil: *die Hosen* ~ fill one's pants.

'**Vollmacht** *f* (-; -en) full power(s), authority, ⚖ a) power of attorney, b) proxy: ~ *haben* be authorized; *j-m* ~ *erteilen* authorize s.o.

'**Vollma,trose** *m* able-bodied seaman.

'**Vollmilch** f full-cream milk. **~schoko-
,lade** f milk chocolate.
'**Vollmond** m full moon: *heute ist ~*
there is a full moon tonight.
'**vollmundig** [-mʊndɪç] adj **1.** full-bodied
(*wine etc*). **2.** fig. iro. pompous.
'**Vollnar,kose** f general an(a)esthesia.
'**vollpacken** v/t (sep, h) pack s.th. full
(*mit* of).
'**Vollpensi,on** f (-; no pl) (full) board and
lodging.
'**vollsaugen: sich ~** (sep, h) become sat-
urated (*mit* with).
'**vollschlagen: sich ~** (irr, sep, -ge-, h, →
schlagen) fill one's belly.
'**vollschlank** adj *~ sein* have a full figure.
'**vollschreiben** v/t (irr, sep, -ge-, h, →
schreiben) fill.
'**vollständig I** adj complete, whole, entire: *~e Anschrift* full address. **II** adv →
völlig II. '**Vollständigkeit** f (-; no pl)
completeness.
'**vollstopfen** v/t (sep, h) stuff, cram.
voll'streckbar adj 🖫🖫 enforceable.
voll'strecken (h) **I** v/t **1.** execute, 🖫🖫 a.
enforce. **2.** sports: convert (*penalty kick
etc*). **II** v/i sports: score. **Voll'strecker**
m (-s; -) 🖫🖫 executor. **Voll'streckung** f
(-; -en) 🖫🖫 execution. **Voll'streckungs-
befehl** m 🖫🖫 writ of execution.
'**vollsyn,thetisch** adj all-synthetic.
'**volltanken** v/t, v/i (sep, h) fill up.
'**Volltreffer** m direct hit, a. fig. bull's-eye.
'**volltrunken** adj completely drunk.
'**Vollversammlung** f plenary assembly.
'**Vollwaise** f orphan. '**Vollwaschmit-
tel** n all-purpose washing powder.
'**vollwertig** adj full, adequate, of high
value. '**Vollwertkost** f natural food.
'**vollzählig** [-tseːlɪç] adj **1. ~ sein** be present in full number; *~ erscheinen* assemble in full strength. **2.** complete.
voll'ziehen (irr, insep, no -ge-, h, → *ziehen*) **I** v/t a) execute, carry out, b) perform (*marriage ceremony etc*), c) con-
summate (*marriage*): *de Gewalt* executive. **II** sich ~ take place. **Voll'zieher**
m (-s; -) executor. **Voll'ziehung** f (-; no
pl), **Voll'zug** m (-[e]s; no pl) execution,
performance (*of marriage ceremony
etc*), consummation (*of marriage*).
Voll'zugs|anstalt f penal institution,
prison. **~beamte** m prison officer.
Volontär [vɔlɔn'tɛːr] m (-s; -e), **Volon-**

'**tärin** f (-; -nen) unpaid trainee.
Volt [vɔlt] n (-, -[e]s; -) ⚡ volt.
'**Voltmeter** n (-s; -) voltmeter.
Volumen [vo'luːmən] n (-s; -, -mina) volume, a. capacity. **voluminös** [volu-
mi'nøːs] adj voluminous.
von [fɔn] prep **1.** from: *~ der Seite* from
the side; *~ morgen an* from (*adm.* as of)
tomorrow. **2.** a) of, b) by: *e-e Freundin
~ ihr* a friend of hers; *ein Bild ~ Picasso* a painting by Picasso; *sie nahm ~
dem Kuchen* she had some of the cake;
9 ~ 10 Leuten 9 out of (*or* in) 10 people;
→ *selbst* I. **3.** of: *ein Mann ~ Bildung* a
man of culture. **4.** of, about: *ich habe ~
ihm gehört* I have heard of him; *weißt
du ~ der Sache?* do you know about
this affair?
vonein'ander adv from each other.
vonstatten [fɔn'ʃtatən] adv *~ gehen* a)
take place, b) go, proceed (*well etc*).
vor [foːr] prep **1.** a) before, in front (*dat*
of), b) outside, c) in the presence (*dat*
of): *~ der Klasse* in front of the class; *~
der Tür* at the door; *~ dem Gesetz*
before the law. **2.** before, ago: *~ 10
Jahren (ein paar Tagen)* ten years (a
few days) ago; *~ dem Essen* before
dinner; *5 Minuten ~ 12* five minutes to
(*Am.* of) 12, *fig.* at the eleventh hour; *~
j-m liegen* be (*or* lie) ahead of s.o.; *et. ~
sich haben* have s.th. ahead of one, *b.s.*
be in for s.th.; *das haben wir noch ~
uns* that's still to come. **3.** for, with: *~
Angst* for fear; *~ Kälte* with cold; *~
lauter Arbeit* for all the work. **4.** above,
before: *~ allem, ~ allen Dingen* above
all. **5.** from, against: → *warnen*.
vor'ab adv **1.** first, to begin with. **2.** in
advance.
'**Vorabend** m (*am ~* on the) eve (*gen* of).
'**Vorahnung** f premonition, foreboding.
vor'an adv before, at the head, in front:
mit dem Kopf ~ head first.
vor'angehen v/i (irr, sep, -ge-, sn, →
gehen) **1.** lead the way, walk at the
front (*or* head) (*dat* of): *j-n ~ lassen*
let s.o. go first; → *Beispiel*. **2.** precede
(*e-r Sache* s.th.). **3.** fig. get on, get
ahead.
vor'ankommen v/i (irr, sep, -ge-, sn, →
kommen) make progress (*or* headway): *beruflich ~* get on in one's job.
'**Vorankündigung** f previous notice.

'**Voranmeldung** f booking: *teleph.* **Gespräch mit** ~ person-to-person call.

vor'antreiben v/t (*irr, sep,* -ge-, h, → *treiben*) *fig.* press ahead with.

'**Voranzeige** f preannouncement, *film:* trailer.

'**Vorarbeit** f preparatory work, preparations. '**vorarbeiten** v/i, v/t (*sep,* h) work in advance: *j-m* ~ pave the way for s.o. '**Vorarbeiter** m foreman. '**Vorarbeiterin** f forewoman.

vor'aus[1] *adv a. fig.* ahead (*dat* of).

'**voraus**[2] *adv im* ~ in advance.

vor'aus|ahnen v/t (*sep,* h) anticipate. **~berechnen** v/t (*sep,* h) precalculate. **~bezahlen** v/t (*sep,* h) prepay, pay *s.th.* in advance.

Vor'ausexem,plar n advance copy.

vor'aus|fahren v/i (*irr, sep,* -ge-, sn, → *fahren*) drive ahead (*dat* of). **~gehen** v/i (*irr,sep,*-ge-, sn,→ *gehen*)**1.** go ahead (*dat* of). **2.** precede (**e-r Sache** s.th.).

vor'ausgesetzt conj ~, **daß** provided (that), on condition that.

vor'aushaben v/t (*irr, sep,* -ge-, h, → *haben*) *j-m einige Erfahrung etc* ~ have the advantage of greater experience *etc* over s.o.

Vor'auskasse f ✝ *gegen* ~ cash before delivery.

vor'aus|laufen v/i (*irr, sep,* -ge-, sn, → *laufen*) run on ahead (*dat* of). **~planen** v/t, v/i (*sep,* h) plan *s.th.* ahead.

Vor'aussage f (-; -en) prediction, forecast. **voraus'sagen** v/t (*sep,* h) predict, forecast.

vor'ausschauend *adj fig.* foresighted.

vor'ausschicken v/t (*sep,* h) **1.** send on ahead. **2.** ~, **daß** first mention that.

vor'aussehen v/t (*irr, sep,* -ge-, h, → *sehen*) foresee, expect: *das war vorauszusehen* that was to be expected.

vor'aussetzen v/t (*sep,* h) **1.** require. **2.** assume, expect: *et. stillschweigend* ~ take s.th. for granted; *ich setze diese Tatsachen als bekannt voraus* I assume that these facts are known; → *vorausgesetzt.*

Vor'aussetzung f (-; -en) **1.** condition, prerequisite: *unter der* ~, **daß** on condition that; *die* ~**en erfüllen** meet the requirements. **2.** assumption.

Vor'aussicht f (*in weiser* ~ with wise) foresight; *aller* ~ *nach* in all probabili-

ty. **vor'aussichtlich I** *adj* prospective, expected. **II** *adv* probably: *er kommt* ~ *a.* he is likely (*or* expected) to come.

Vor'auszahlung f advance payment.

'**Vorbau** m (-[e]s; -ten) **1.** front part (of a building). **2.** porch. '**vorbauen** (*sep,* h) **I** v/t build *s.th.* in front (*or* out). **II** v/i *fig.* take precautions.

'**Vorbedeutung** f (-; -en) omen.

'**Vorbedingung** f (-; -en) condition.

'**Vorbehalt** m (-[e]s; -e) reservation, proviso: *unter dem* ~, **daß** provided (that); *ohne* ~ without reservation.

'**vorbehalten** v/t (*irr, sep,* h, → *behalten*) reserve: *Änderungen* ~ subject to change (without notice); *Irrtümer* ~ errors excepted; *alle Rechte* ~ all rights reserved; *sich (das Recht)* ~ *zu inf* reserve the right to *inf; j-m* ~ *sein* (*or bleiben*) be left to s.o.

'**vorbehaltlich** *prep* (*gen*) subject to.

'**vorbehaltlos** *adj* unreserved.

'**vorbehandeln** v/t (*sep,* h) pretreat.

vor'bei *adv* **1.** *a.* ~ *an* (*dat*) past, by: ~*!* missed! **2.** a) over, finished, b) gone, c) past: *5 Uhr* ~ past five (o'clock); *es ist aus und* ~ it's all over and done with.

vor'bei|fahren v/i (*irr, sep,* -ge-, sn, → *fahren*) ~ *an* (*dat*) drive past. **~gehen** v/i (*irr, sep,* -ge-, sn, → *gehen*) **1.** ~ *an* (*dat*) pass by, *fig.* miss, pass *s.th.* by: *im* ♀ in passing. **2.** *fig.* pass. **3.** *shot etc:* miss (the mark). **~kommen** v/i (*irr, sep,* -ge-, sn, → *kommen*) **1.** ~ *an* (*dat*) pass by, get past (*or* round), pass (*obstacle etc*). **2.** F drop in (*bei* on). **~lassen** v/t (*irr, sep,* -ge-, h, → *lassen*) let s.o., s.th. pass. **~mar,schieren** v/i (*sep,* sn) ~ *an* (*dat*) march past. **~reden** v/i (*sep,* h) *aneinander* ~ talk at cross-purposes; *am Thema* ~ miss the point. **~schießen** v/i (*irr, sep,* -ge-, h, → *schießen*) miss: (*am Tor*) ~ shoot wide. **~ziehen** v/i (*irr,sep,*-ge-, sn, → *ziehen*) *an j-m* ~ **1.** pass (*or* go past, *sports:* overtake) s.o. **2.** *fig.* go through s.o.'s mind.

'**vorbelastet** *adj erblich* ~ *sein* have a hereditary handicap.

'**Vorbemerkung** f preliminary remark.

'**vorbereiten** v/t (*a. sich* ~) (*sep,* h) (*für, auf acc* for) prepare, get ready: *sich auf das Schlimmste* ~ be prepared for the worst. '**vorbereitend** *adj* preparatory.

'**Vorbereitung** f (-; -en) preparation

(für, zu, auf acc for): **~en treffen** make preparations (*or* prepare) *(für* for); **in ~** in preparation, being prepared.

'**Vorbericht** *m* preliminary report.

'**vorberuflich** *adj* prevocational.

'**Vorbesprechung** *f* preliminary discussion (*or* talk).

'**vorbestellen** *v/t (sep,* h) book *room, tickets, etc* in advance, reserve.

'**Vorbestellung** *f* (-; -en) advance booking, reservation.

'**vorbestraft** *adj* **~ sein** have a police record.

'**vorbeugen** *(sep,* h) **I** *v/i* **e-r Sache ~** prevent (*or* guard against) s.th. **II** *sich ~* bend forward. '**vorbeugend** *adj* preventive, **#** *(a. ~es Mittel)* prophylactic.

'**Vorbild** *n* (-[e]s; -er) model, example: **leuchtendes ~** shining example; *sich j-n zum ~ nehmen* follow s.o.'s example; *(j-m) ein ~ sein* set an example (to s.o.). '**vorbildlich** *adj* exemplary, model: *er benahm sich ~* he behaved in an exemplary manner.

'**Vorbildung** *f* (-; *no pl*) (previous) training, education(al background).

'**Vorbote** *m* (-n; -n) *fig.* herald (*gen* of).

'**vorbringen** *v/t (irr, sep,* -ge-, h, → **bringen**) bring forward (*argument etc*), express, state (*wish, claim, etc*), offer (*excuse, reasons, etc*), raise (*objection*), enter (*protest*), **ﬆ** prefer (*charges*).

'**vorchristlich** *adj* pre-Christian.

'**Vordach** *n* canopy.

'**vorda,tieren** *v/t (sep,* h) a) postdate, b) antedate.

'**Vordenker** *m* (-s; -) thinker, brain.

'**vorder** ['fordər] *adj* front.

'**Vorder|achse** *f* front axle. **~ansicht** *f* front view. **~bein** *n zo.* foreleg. **~deck** *n* **♣** foredeck. **~fuß** *m zo.* forefoot, front paw (*of cat, dog, etc*).

'**Vordergrund** *m* (-[e]s; *no pl*) foreground: *fig. in den ~ rücken* come to the fore; *et. in den ~ stellen* give s.th. special emphasis. '**vordergründig** [-'gryndıç] *adj (adv* on the) surface.

'**Vorder|haus** *n* front building. **~lauf** *m hunt.* foreleg. **~mann** *m* (-[e]s; **~er**) *mein ~* the person in front of me; F *auf ~ bringen* a) *j-n* make s.o. pull his socks up, b) *et.* bring s.th. up to scratch. **~rad** *n* front wheel. **~rad...** front-wheel (*brake, drive, etc*). **~reihe** *f* front row.

~seite *f* front, **△**, **☉** *a.* face, obverse (*of coin*). **~sitz** *m* front seat.

'**vorderst** ['fordərst] *adj* front.

'**Vorder|teil** *m, n* front (part). **~tür** *f* front door. **~zahn** *m* front tooth.

'**vordrängen: sich ~** (*sep,* h) a) push forward, b) jump the queue, c) *fig.* put o.s. forward.

'**vordringen** *v/i (irr, sep,* -ge-, sn, → **dringen**) push (*or* forge) ahead: **~ in** (*acc) a. fig.* penetrate into; **~ (bis) zu** *a. fig.* work one's way through to. '**vordringlich** *adj* urgent, priority (*task etc*): **~ behandelt werden** be given priority.

'**Vordruck** *m* (-[e]s; -e) form, *Am.* blank.

'**vorehelich** *adj* premarital.

'**voreilig** *adj* hasty, rash: **~e Schlüsse ziehen** jump to conclusions. '**Voreiligkeit** *f* (-; *no pl*) rashness, hastiness.

vorein'ander *adv* **1.** one in front of the other. **2. *Achtung ~*** respect for each other; *sie haben Angst ~* they are afraid of each other.

'**voreingenommen** *adj (gegenüber* against) prejudiced, bias(s)ed.

'**Voreingenommenheit** *f* (-; *no pl*) prejudice, bias.

'**vorenthalten** *v/t (irr, sep,* h, → **enthalten**) *j-m et. ~* keep s.th. from s.o.

'**Vorentscheidung** *f* preliminary decision.

'**vorerst** *adv* for the time being.

'**Vorex,amen** *n* preliminary examination.

Vorfahr ['fo:rfa:r] *m* (-en; -en) ancestor.

'**vorfahren** *v/i (irr, sep,* -ge-, sn, → **fahren**) drive up (*vor dat* before). '**Vorfahrt** *f* (-; *no pl*) priority, right of way: **~ beachten!** give way! '**vorfahrt(s)berechtigt** *adj* having the right of way.

'**Vorfahrt(s)|schild** *n* sign regulating priority. **~straße** *f* priority road.

'**Vorfall** *m* (-[e]s; **~e**) **1.** incident, occurrence. **2. ♂** prolapse. '**vorfallen** *v/i (irr, sep,* -ge-, sn, → **fallen**) happen, occur.

'**Vorfeld** *n* **1. ✈** apron. **2.** *fig. im ~ (gen)* in the run-up to.

'**Vorfilm** *m* supporting film.

'**vorfinan,zieren** *v/t (sep,* h) prefinance.

'**vorfinden** *v/t (irr, sep,* -ge-, h, → **finden**) find.

'**Vorfreude** *f* (-; -n) anticipation.

vorfristig ['fo:rfrıstıç] *adj and adv* ahead of time.

'**Vorfrühling** *m* early spring.

'**vorfühlen** *v/i* (*sep*, h) *bei j-m ~* sound s.o. out.

'**vorführen** *v/t* (*sep*, h) **1.** show, present, model (*clothes*), demonstrate (*machine etc*), perform (*stunt*). **2.** *j-n ~* bring s.o. before (**e-m Richter** a judge *etc*), *fig.* make s.o. look like a fool.

'**Vorführer** *m* (-s; -) projectionist.

'**Vorführraum** *m* projection room.

'**Vorführung** *f* (-; -en) **1.** showing, presentation, ⊚ demonstration, performance (*of stunts etc*). **2.** *thea. etc* show.

'**Vorführwagen** *m* demonstration car.

'**Vorgabe** *f* (-; -n) **1.** *sports:* a) start, handicap, b) stagger. **2.** a) precondition, stipulation, b) target, c) given (*or* set) data. **3.** → *zeit f* ⊚ allowed time.

'**Vorgang** *m* (-[e]s; ⥨e) **1.** proceedings, *biol.*, 🜨, ⊚ process. **2.** occurrence, event. **3.** *adm.* file, record.

'**Vorgänger** ['foːrgɛŋər] *m* (-s; -), '**Vorgängerin** *f* (-; -nen) predecessor.

'**Vorgarten** *m* front garden, *Am.* frontyard.

'**vorgeben** *v/t* (*irr, sep*, -ge-, h, → **geben**) **1.** *sports:* give, allow. **2.** allege, claim, pretend. **3.** a) prescribe, stipulate, b) give, set (*data etc*).

'**Vorgebirge** *n* foothills.

'**vorgefaßt** *adj* preconceived.

'**vorgefertigt** *adj* a. *fig.* prefabricated.

'**vorgehen** *v/i* (*irr, sep*, -ge-, sn, → **gehen**) **1.** go forward, go up (**zu** to), ✗ advance, F lead the way: *m-e Uhr geht (e-e Minute) vor* my watch is (one minute) fast; F *geh schon mal vor!* you go on ahead! **2.** act: *~ gegen* take action against; *gerichtlich gegen j-n ~* proceed against s.o.; *hart ~ gegen* crack down on. **3.** happen, go on: *was geht hier vor?* what's going on here? **4.** come first, have priority. '**Vorgehen** *n* (-s) **1.** (line of) action. **2.** procedure.

'**vorgelagert** *adj ~e Inseln* offshore islands.

'**Vorgeschichte** *f* (-; *no pl*) **1.** prehistory. **2.** (past) history, 🖈 case history.

'**vorgeschichtlich** *adj* prehistoric.

'**Vorgeschmack** *m* (-[e]s; *no pl*) foretaste (*auf acc, von* of).

'**Vorgesetzte** *m, f* (-n; -n) superior.

'**Vorgespräche** *pl* preliminary talks.

'**vorgestern** *adv* the day before

yesterday: F *von ~* → '**vorgestrig** *adj* **1.** *paper etc* of the day before yesterday. **2.** *fig.* antiquated (*views etc*).

'**vorgreifen** *v/i* (*irr, sep*, -ge-, h, → **greifen**) *j-m* (**e-r Sache**) *~* anticipate s.o. (s.th.). '**Vorgriff** *m* (*im ~* in) anticipation (*auf acc* of).

'**vorhaben** *v/t* (*irr, sep*, -ge-, h, → **haben**) *~ zu inf* plan (*or* have in mind, intend) to *inf*; *e-e Reise ~* plan to go on a journey; *was habt ihr heute vor?* what are your plans for today?; *haben Sie heute abend etwas vor?* have you got anything planned for tonight?; *morgen habe ich e-e Menge vor* I've got a lot to do tomorrow; *was hast du damit vor?* what are you going to do with it?; *was hast du jetzt wieder vor?* what are you up to now? '**Vorhaben** *n* (-s; -) intention, plan(s), (*a. building*) project.

'**Vorhalle** *f* (entrance) hall, vestibule.

'**Vorhalt** *m* (-[e]s; -e) ♪ suspension.

'**vorhalten** *v/t* (*irr, sep*, -ge-, h, → **halten**) *j-m et. ~* a) hold s.th. (up) in front of s.o., b) *fig.* reproach s.o. with s.th.; *mit vorgehaltener Pistole* at pistol point. '**Vorhaltung** *f* (-; -en) reproach: *j-m ~en machen* remonstrate with s.o. (*über acc* about).

'**Vorhand** *f* (-; *no pl*) *tennis etc:* forehand.

vorhanden [foːr'handən] *adj* existing, available, 🜨 in stock: *~ sein* exist; *es ist nichts mehr ~* there is nothing left.

Vor'handensein *n* (-s) existence.

'**Vorhang** *m* (-[e]s; ⥨e) curtain, drapes.

'**Vorhängeschloß** *n* padlock.

'**Vorhaut** *f* *anat.* foreskin, prepuce.

'**vorher** *adv* before: *am Abend ~* the evening before, the previous evening.

vor'herbestimmen *v/t* (*sep*, h) a) predetermine, b) predestine.

vor'hergehen *v/i* (*irr, sep*, -ge-, sn, → **gehen**) *e-r Sache ~* precede s.th. **vor'hergehend, vorherig** [foːr'heːrɪç] *adj* preceding, previous.

'**Vorherrschaft** *f* (-; *no pl*) predominance, supremacy.

'**vorherrschen** *v/i* (*sep*, h) predominate, prevail. '**vorherrschend** *adj* predominant, prevailing (*opinion etc*).

Vor'hersage *f* (-; -n) prediction, *a.* 🜨, *meteor.* forecast.

vor'hersagen *v/t* (*sep*, h) predict.

vor'hersehen v/t (irr, sep, -ge-, h, → **sehen**) foresee.

'vorhin adv a (short) while ago.

'Vorhut f (-; -en) ✕ van(guard).

vorig ['fo:rɪç] adj former, previous: ~e **Woche** last week.

'vorindustri,ell adj pre-industrial.

'Vorjahr n previous (or last) year.

vorjährig ['fo:rjɛ:rɪç] adj of last year.

'Vorkämpfer(in f) m champion.

'vorkauen v/t (sep, h) F fig. **j-m et. ~** spoon-feed s.th. to s.o.

'Vorkaufsrecht n right of preemption: **das ~ haben** a. have the refusal.

'Vorkehrung f (-; -en) measure, precaution: **~en treffen** a. take measures (or precautions) (**gegen** against), b) make arrangements (**für** for).

'Vorkenntnisse pl previous knowledge (or experience).

'vorknöpfen v/t (sep, h) F **sich j-n ~** take s.o. to task.

'vorkommen v/i (irr, sep, -ge-, sn, → **kommen**) **1.** be found, occur. **2.** happen, occur: **so et. ist mir noch nicht vorgekommen!** F well, I never!; **das darf nicht wieder ~!** that must not (or don't let it) happen again! **3.** seem: **es kommt mir so vor, als ob** it seems to me as if; **sich dumm ~** feel silly; **er kommt sich sehr klug vor** he thinks he is very clever; **sie kommt mir bekannt vor** she looks familiar; **das kommt dir nur so vor** you are just imagining it; **es kommt mir merkwürdig vor** it strikes me as (rather) strange. **'Vorkommen** n (-s; -) **1.** occurrence. **2.** ✕ deposit(s).

'Vorkommnis n (-ses; -se) incident: **k-e besonderen ~se** no unusual occurrence(s).

'Vorkriegs... prewar ...

'vorladen v/t (irr, sep, -ge-, h, → **laden**) ⚖ summon. **'Vorladung** f (-; -en) (writ of) summons.

'Vorlage f (-; -n) **1.** model, pattern: **et. als ~ benutzen** copy from s.th. **2.** (**gegen ~** on) presentation (**gen** of). **3.** parl. bill. **4.** sports: pass.

'vorlassen v/t (irr, sep, -ge-, h, → **lassen**) **j-n ~** a) let s.o. go first, b) let s.o. pass, c) admit s.o. (**bei** to).

'Vorlauf m (-[e]s; ~e) **1.** sports: preliminary heat. **2.** ⊙ forward run.

'Vorläufer m forerunner (a. skiing).

'vorläufig I adj temporary, provisional. **II** adv for the time being.

'vorlaut adj pert, cheeky.

'Vorleben n (-s; no pl) former life, past.

'vorlegen (sep, h) **I** v/t **1.** a) (dat to) present, submit, b) produce, show (document etc), c) bring out, publish: pol. **den Haushalt ~** present the budget. **2.** put chain etc on. **3.** F **ein schnelles Tempo ~** set a fast pace. **II sich ~** lean forward. **'Vorleger** m (-s; -) rug, mat.

'vorlehnen: sich ~ (sep, h) lean forward.

'Vorleistung f (-; -en) **1.** ✝ advance (payment). **2.** pol. advance concession.

'vorlesen (irr, sep, -ge-, h, → **lesen**) **I** v/t (**j-m et. ~** read s.th. (out) (to s.o.). **II** v/i **j-m ~** read to s.o. (**aus** dat from, out of).

'Vorleser(in f) m reader.

'Vorlesung f (-; -en) (**e-e ~ halten** give a) lecture (**über** acc on, **vor** to): **~en halten** lecture (**über** acc on); **~en hören** go to lectures. **'Vorlesungsverzeichnis** n program(me Br.) of lectures.

vorletzt adj last but one: **~e Woche** the week before last.

'Vorliebe f (-; -n) (**für** for) preference, special liking: **et. mit ~ tun** love doing (or to do) s.th.

'vorliebnehmen v/i (irr, sep, -ge-, h, → **nehmen**) make do (**mit** with).

'vorliegen v/i (irr, sep, h, → **liegen**) **j-m ~** lie before s.o.; **der Antrag liegt vor** the application has been submitted; **es liegen k-e Beschwerden vor** there are no complaints; **liegt sonst noch et. vor?** is there anything else? **2.** be, exist: **es liegen Gründe vor** there are reasons; **es lag Notwehr vor** it was a case of self-defen/ce (Am. -se); **da muß ein Irrtum ~** there must be a mistake. **3.** be available, be out: **das Ergebnis liegt noch nicht vor** the result is not yet known. **'vorliegend** adj a) existing, present, b) available: **die ~en Probleme** the problems at issue; **im ~en Falle** in the present case.

'vorlügen v/t (irr, sep, -ge-, h, → **lügen**) **j-m et. ~** lie to s.o.

'vormachen v/t (sep, h) F **j-m et. ~** a) show s.o. how to do s.th., b) fool s.o.; **sich (selbst) et. ~** fool (F kid) o.s.

'Vormacht(stellung) f (-; no pl) supremacy.

vormalig ['fo:rma:lɪç] adj former.

'**vormals** *adv* formerly.

'**Vormarsch** *m* advance: **im** (*or* **auf dem**) ~ advancing, *fig.* on the march.

'**vormerken** *v/t* (*sep*, h) make a note of: **sich ~ lassen** put one's name down (**für** for).

'**Vormieter(in** *f*) *m* previous tenant.

'**vormittag** *adv* **heute** (**gestern**) ~ this (yesterday) morning. '**Vormittag** *m* (-s; -e) (**am** ~ in the) morning. '**vormittags** *adv* in the morning: **Montag** ~, **montags** ~ every Monday morning.

'**Vormund** *m* (-[e]s; -e, ⸚er) guardian.

'**Vormundschaft** *f* (-; -en) guardianship.

vorn [fɔrn] *adv* in front, before, ahead: **ganz** ~ a) right in front, up front, b) at the beginning; **nach** ~ to the front, forward; **von** ~ from the front; ~ **anfangen** begin at the beginning; (**nochmal**) **von** ~ **anfangen** start (all over) again; **noch einmal von** ~ all over again; **von** ~ **bis hinten** a) from front to back, b) from beginning to end.

'**Vorname** *m* Christian (*or* first, *esp. Am.* given) name.

vornehm ['foːrneːm] *adj* **1.** *a. fig.* noble: ~**e Gesinnung** high-mindedness. **2.** a) distinguished, b) elegant, fashionable, exclusive: **e-e** ~**e Dame** a distinguished lady; **e-e** ~**e Gegend** a fashionable quarter; F ~ **tun** give o.s. airs.

'**vornehmen** *v/t* (*irr*, *sep*, -ge-, h, → **nehmen**) **1.** make (*changes etc*), carry out (*work etc*). **2.** **sich et.** ~ plan, make plans for; **sich** ~ **zu** *inf* decide to *inf*; **sich zuviel** ~ take on too much; F **sich j-n** ~ take s.o. to task (**wegen** about).

'**Vornehmheit** *f* (-; *no pl*) **1.** nobility. **2.** a) distinction, b) elegance, refinement, exclusiveness: **ihre** ~ her distinguished appearance.

'**vornherein** *adv* **von** ~ from the start.

vorn'über *adv* forward.

'**Vorort** *m* (-[e]s; -e) suburb.

'**Vorort(s)...** suburban (*traffic etc*). ~**bewohner(in** *f*) *m* suburbanite. ~**zug** *m* suburban (*or* local, commuter) train.

'**Vorplatz** *m* forecourt, square.

'**Vorposten** *m* ✕ outpost.

'**Vorpro,gramm** *n film*: supporting program(me *Br.*). '**vorprogram,mieren** *v/t* (*sep*, h) (pre)program(me *Br.*).

'**Vorprüfung** *f* preliminary examination.

'**vorragen** *v/i* (*sep*, h) project, protrude.

'**Vorrang** *m* (-[e]s; *no pl*) precedence, priority: **den** ~ **haben vor** (*dat*) take (*or* have) priority (*or* precedence) over.

'**vorrangig** ['foːrraŋɪç] *adj* priority: ~ **behandeln** give s.th. priority treatment.

'**Vorrangstellung** *f* (-; *no pl*) (position of) pre-eminence.

'**Vorrat** *m* (-[e]s; ⸚e) (**an** *dat* of) stock (*a. fig.*), store, supply, provisions, stockpile (*of weapons etc*): **e-n** ~ **anlegen** lay in a stock (**von** of); **solange der** ~ **reicht** while stocks last.

'**vorrätig** ['foːrrɛːtɪç] *adj* available, ✝ in stock: **nicht** (**mehr**) ~ out of stock; **wir haben ... nicht mehr** ~ we are out of ...

'**Vorrats,behälter** *m* storage bin (*or* tank). ~**kammer** *f* pantry, larder.

'**Vorraum** *m* anteroom.

'**vorrechnen** *v/t* (*sep*, h) **j-m et.** ~ calculate s.th. for s.o.

'**Vorrecht** *n* privilege, prerogative.

'**Vorredner(in** *f*) *m* previous speaker.

'**Vorrichtung** *f* (-; -en) device, F gadget.

'**vorrücken** (*sep*) **I** *v/t* (h) move s.th. forward. **II** *v/i* (sn) move on, ✕ advance.

'**Vorrunde** *f sports*: preliminary round.

'**vorsagen** (*sep*, h) **I** *v/t* **j-m et.** ~ tell s.o. s.th. **II** *v/i* **j-m** ~ tell s.o. the answer.

'**Vorsai,son** *f* (-; -s) early season.

'**Vorsatz** *m* (-es; ⸚e) resolution, intention, 🏛 (criminal) intent: **mit** ~ with intent, will(ful)ly.

vorsätzlich ['foːrzɛtslɪç] *adj* intentional, deliberate, 🏛 will(l)ful: ~**er Mord** premeditated murder.

'**Vorschau** *f* (-; -en) preview (**auf** *acc* of), *film etc*: trailer(s).

'**Vorschein** *m* **zum** ~ **bringen** produce, *fig.* bring to light; **zum** ~ **kommen** come to light, appear, emerge.

'**vorschieben** *v/t* (*irr*, *sep*, -ge-, h, → **schieben**) **1.** push (*or* move) forward, advance. **2.** shoot (*bolt*): → **Riegel** 1. **3.** *fig. et.* ~ use s.th. as an excuse; **j-n** ~ use s.o. as a dummy.

'**vorschießen** *v/t* (*irr*, *sep*, -ge-, h, → **schießen**) advance (*sum*).

'**Vorschlag** *m* (-[e]s; ⸚e) suggestion, proposal (*a. parl.*), recommendation: **darf ich e-n** ~ **machen** may I offer a suggestion; **auf** ~ **von** (*or gen*) at the suggestion of. '**vorschlagen** *v/t* (*irr*, *sep*, -ge-, h, → **schlagen**) suggest, propose (*s.o.*): **ich schlage vor, nach**

Hause zu gehen I suggest going (*or* that we go) home.

'**Vorschlußrunde** *f sports:* semifinal.

'**vorschnell** *adj* hasty, rash.

'**vorschreiben** *v/t* (*irr, sep, -ge-, h,* → *schreiben*) *fig.* prescribe, dictate: *ich lasse mir nichts ~!* I won't be dictated to!; *das Gesetz schreibt vor, daß* the law provides that.

'**Vorschrift** *f* (-; -en) *a*) rule(s), regulation(s), b) direction, instruction: *nach ärztlicher ~* according to doctor's orders; *Dienst nach ~* work-to-rule; *streng nach ~ arbeiten* work to regulations.

'**vorschriftsmäßig I** *adj* correct, (as) prescribed, regulation .. **II** *adv* correctly, according to the regulations.

'**vorschriftswidrig** *adj and adv* contrary to the regulations.

'**Vorschub** *m* (-[e]s; ⸚e) **1.** ⊕ feed. **2.** *fig. ~ leisten* (*dat*) encourage (*s.th., s.o.*).

'**Vorschulalter** *n* preschool age.

'**Vorschule** *f* preschool.

'**vorschulisch** *adj* preschool.

'**Vorschuß** *m* (-sses; ⸚sse) advance (payment) (*auf acc* on).

'**vorschützen** *v/t* (*sep, h*) **et.** *~* plead s.th. (as an excuse).

'**vorschweben** *v/i* (*sep, h*) *mir schwebt ... vor* I'm thinking of ...

'**vorsehen** (*irr, sep, -ge-, h,* → *sehen*) **I** *v/t* **1.** plan, schedule: *das war nicht vorgesehen* that was not planned. **2.** intend, designate, *a.* earmark (*funds etc*): *j-n für e-n Posten ~* designate s.o. for a post. **II** *sich ~* be careful, watch out (*vor dat* against).

'**Vorsehung** *f* (-; *no pl*) *die ~* Providence.

'**vorsetzen** *v/t* (*sep, h*) *j-m et. ~* set s.th. before s.o., *a. fig.* offer s.o. s.th.

'**Vorsicht** *f* (-; *no pl*) caution, care: *~!* watch out!, careful!, (*inscription*) (handle) with care!; *~, Stufe!* mind the step!; *zur ~* as a precaution; *mit äußerster ~* with the utmost caution.

'**vorsichtig** *adj* cautious, careful: *~e Schätzung* conservative estimate; (*sei*) *~!* be careful!; *~ fahren* drive carefully.

'**vorsichtshalber** *adv* as a precaution.

'**Vorsichtsmaßnahme** *f* precaution(ary measure): *~n treffen* take precautions.

'**Vorsilbe** *f ling.* prefix.

'**vorsingen** (*irr, sep, -ge-, h,* → *singen*) **I** *v/t j-m et. ~* sing s.th. to s.o. **II** *v/i*

audition (*bei* with): *j-n ~ lassen* audition s.o.

'**vorsintflutlich** *adj* F *fig.* antediluvian.

'**Vorsitz** *m* (-es; *no pl*) chair(manship), presidency: *bei e-r Versammlung den ~ haben* (*or führen*) preside over (*or* chair, be in the chair at) a meeting; *unter dem ~ von ...* with ... in the chair.

'**Vorsitzende** *m, f* (-n; -n) **1.** president, chairman (chairwoman), chairperson. **2.** ⚖ presiding judge.

'**Vorsorge** *f* (-; *no pl*) provision, precaution: *~ treffen* take precautions (*daß* that), provide (*gegen* against).

'**vorsorgen** *v/i* (*sep, h*) (*für* for) make provisions, provide.

'**Vorsorgeuntersuchung** *f* (preventive) medical checkup.

'**vorsorglich** [-zɔrklɪç] **I** *adj* precautionary. **II** *adv* as a precaution.

'**Vorspann** *m* (-[e]s; -e) **1.** introduction. **2.** *film:* a) (title and) credits, b) pre-title sequence.

'**Vorspeise** *f* hors d'oeuvre, starter: *als ~ a.* for starters.

'**Vorspiegelung** *f* (-; -en) preten/ce (*Am.* -se): *unter ~ falscher Tatsachen* under false preten/ces (*Am.* -ses).

'**Vorspiel** *n* (-[e]s; -e) **1.** (*zu* to) *a. fig.* a) ♪ prelude, b) *thea.* curtain-raiser, prolog(ue *Br.*). **2.** foreplay. '**vorspielen** (*sep, h*) **I** *v/t* play: *j-m et. ~* play s.th. to s.o., *fig.* put on an act for s.o.'s benefit. **II** *v/i* a) play, b) audition (*bei* with): *j-n ~ lassen* audition s.o.

'**vorsprechen** (*irr, sep, -ge-, h,* → *sprechen*) **I** *v/t* **1.** *j-m et. ~* pronounce s.th. for s.o. to repeat. **2.** recite. **II** *v/i* **3.** *thea.* audition (*bei* with): *j-n ~ lassen* audition s.o. **4.** call (*bei* at).

'**vorspringen** *v/i* (*irr, sep, -ge-, sn,* → *springen*) **1.** leap forward. **2.** project, jut (out). '**vorspringend** *adj* projecting, jutting, prominent (*a. nose, chin*).

'**Vorsprung** *m* (-[e]s; ⸚e) **1.** △ projection, ledge. **2.** *a. sports:* a) start, b) lead: *ich gebe dir 5 Minuten ~* I'll give you a start of five minutes; *sein ~ beträgt 30 Sekunden* he has a lead of 30 seconds (*vor dat* on); *mit großem ~* by a wide margin; *e-n ~ haben a. fig.* be ahead (*vor dat* of).

'**Vorstadt** *f* suburb.

'**Vorstadtbewohner** *m* suburbanite.

'**vorstädtisch** *adj* suburban.

'**Vorstand** *m* (-[e]s; ⸚e) **1.** ⴕ board of directors: *im ~ sitzen* be on the board. **2.** managing committee (*of club etc*) **3.** chairman, *Am.* chief executive.

'**Vorstands|e,tage** *f* executive floor. **~mitglied** *n* member of the board. **~sitzung** *f* board meeting. **~vorsitzende** *m, f* (-n; -n) chairman (chairwoman) (*of the board*), *Am.* chief executive. **~wahl** *f* board elections.

'**vorstehen** *v/i* (*irr, sep, -ge-*, h, → *stehen*) **1.** project, jut out, *eyes*: protrude. **2.** (*dat*) direct, be at the head of, run (*institute etc*). '**vorstehend** *adj* projecting, protruding (*a. eyes, teeth, etc*): *~e Zähne* a. buckteeth. '**Vorsteher** *m* (-s; -) manager, director, head.

'**Vorsteherdrüse** *f anat.* prostate gland.

'**vorstellbar** *adj* conceivable, imaginable. '**vorstellen** (*sep*, h) **I** *v/t* **1.** move *s.th.* forward. **2.** put *clock etc* forward. **3.** *j-n j-m ~* introduce s.o. to s.o.; *darf ich Ihnen Herrn X ~?* may I introduce you to Mr X, I'd like you to meet Mr X. **4.** ⴕ present, introduce (*new product*). **5.** a) represent, b) mean: *was soll das Bild ~?* what's that picture supposed to be?; F *er stellt etwas vor* he's quite somebody. **6.** *sich et. ~* fancy, picture, have *s.th.* in mind; F *stell dir vor!* fancy!, just imagine!; *du kannst dir gar nicht ~ ...* you've no idea ...; *man kann sich ihre Enttäuschung ~* you can picture their disappointment; *so stelle ich mir ... vor* that's my idea of ...; *stellt euch das nicht so leicht vor!* don't think it's so easy; *darunter kann ich mir nichts ~* it doesn't mean anything to me. **II** *sich ~* introduce o.s. (*[bei] j-m* to s.o.), *bei* go for an interview with *a firm etc*.

'**Vorstellung** *f* (-; -en) **1.** introduction, ⴕ *a.* presentation (*of new product*). **2.** interview (*bei* with). **3.** *thea. etc* performance, show, *film:* show(ing). **4.** idea, notion, concept: *falsche ~* wrong idea, misconception; *sich e-e ~ machen* form an idea (*or* a picture) (*von* of); F *du machst dir k-e ~!* you've no idea; *das entspricht nicht m-n ~en* that's not what I expected (*or* had in mind). **5.** imagination.

'**Vorstellungsgespräch** *n* interview.

'**Vorstopper** *m* (-s; -) *soccer:* centre (*Am.* center) half.

'**Vorstoß** *m* (-es; ⸚e) ✕ advance, *sports:* attack (*a. fig.*), *pol. or fig.* démarche.

'**vorstoßen** *v/i* (*irr, sep, -ge-*, sn, → *stoßen*) ✕ advance, *sports:* attack: *fig. ~ in* (*acc*) venture into; *~ zu* reach.

'**Vorstrafe** *f* previous conviction. '**Vorstrafen(re,gister** *n*) *pl* police record.

'**vorstrecken** *v/t* (*sep*, h) **1.** stretch out, stick *one's* head out. **2.** advance (*sum*).

'**Vorstufe** *f* previous stage.

'**vorstürmen** *v/i* (*sep*, sn) rush forward.

'**Vortag** *m* previous day, day before.

'**vortasten:** *sich ~* (*sep*, h) grope one's way (*bis zu* to).

'**vortäuschen** *v/t* (*sep*, h) feign, simulate, fake, pretend: *Interesse ~* pretend to be interested.

Vorteil ['fɔrtail] *m* (-s; -e) a) advantage (*a. tennis*), b) benefit: *die Vor- und Nachteile e-r Sache gegeneinander abwägen* consider the pros and cons; *im ~ sein* have the advantage (*gegenüber* over); *auf s-n eigenen ~ bedacht sein* have an eye to the main chance; *~ ziehen aus* profit by; *sich zu s-m ~ verändern* change for the better.

'**vorteilhaft** *adj* advantageous, profitable, becoming (*dress etc*): *~ aussehen* look attractive; *sich ~ auswirken* have a favo(u)rable effect (*auf acc* on).

Vortrag ['fo:rtra:k] *m* (-[e]s; ⸚e) **1.** lecture (*über acc* on): *e-n ~ halten* (*vor dat* to) give a lecture (*or* talk), read a paper; F *j-m e-n ~ halten* lecture s.o. **2.** performance, recitation (*of poetry*), ♩ recital, execution. **3.** ⴕ carryover.

'**vortragen** *v/t* (*irr, sep, -ge-*, h, → *tragen*) **1.** state, present, express. **2.** perform, play, sing, recite. **3.** ⴕ carry forward. '**Vortragende** *m, f* (-n; -n) **1.** lecturer, speaker. **2.** ♩ *etc* performer.

'**Vortragsreihe** *f* series of lectures.

'**Vortragsreise** *f* lecture tour.

'**vortreten** *v/i* (*irr, sep, -ge-*, sn, → *treten*) **1.** step (*or* come) forward. **2.** protrude.

'**Vortritt** *m* (-[e]s; *no pl*) (*den ~ haben* take) precedence (*vor dat* over): *j-m den ~ lassen* let s.o. go first.

vor'über *adv ~ sein* be over.

vor'übergehen *v/i* (*irr, sep, -ge-*, sn, → *gehen*) pass, *fig. a.* go away. **vor'über-**

gehend I *adj* temporary, passing. **II** *adv* temporarily, for a short time.
'**Vorübung** *f* preliminary exercise.
'**Voruntersuchung** *f* ⚖, 🗲 preliminary examination.
'**Vorurteil** *n* prejudice: *~e haben gegen* be prejudiced against.
'**vorurteilsfrei**, '**vorurteilslos** *adj* unprejudiced, unbias(s)ed.
'**Vorvergangenheit** *f ling.* past perfect, pluperfect.
'**Vorverhandlung** *f* **1.** ⚖ preliminary trial. **2.** *pl* 🕇, *pol.* preliminary negotiations, preliminaries.
'**Vorverkauf** *m* (-[e]s; *no pl*) advance sale (*thea.* booking): *im ~ besorgen* buy (*or* book) *tickets* in advance.
'**Vorverkaufskasse** *f*, '**Vorverkaufsstelle** *f* (advance) booking office.
'**vorverlegen** *v/t* (*sep*, h) advance.
'**Vorverstärker** *m* 🔌 pre-amplifier.
'**Vorvertrag** *m* precontract.
'**vorvorig** *adj the year etc* before last.
'**Vorwahl** *f* **1.** *pol.* preliminary election, *Am.* primary (election). **2.** → **Vorwählnummer** *f teleph.* dialling (*Am.* area) code.
'**Vorwand** *m* (-[e]s; ⸚e) pretext, excuse: *unter dem ~ von* (*or daß*) on the pretext of (*or* that).
'**vorwärmen** *v/t* (*sep*, h) warm, preheat.
'**Vorwarnung** *f* (advance) warning.
'**vorwärts** *adv* forward, onward, on: *~!* let's go!
'**Vorwärtsgang** *m mot.* forward speed.
'**vorwärtsgehen** *v/i* (*irr, sep*, -ge-, sn, → **gehen**) F (make) progress.
'**Vorwäsche** *f* (-; -n), '**Vorwaschen** *n* (-s) prewash.
vor'**weg** *adv* beforehand.
Vor'wegnahme *f* (-; *no pl*) anticipation.
vor'**wegnehmen** *v/t* (*irr, sep*, -ge-, h, → **nehmen**) anticipate: *um es gleich vorwegzunehmen* to come to the point.
'**vorweihnachtlich** *adj* pre-Christmas.
'**Vorweihnachtszeit** *f* Advent season.
'**vorweisen** *v/t* (*irr, sep*, h, → **weisen**) produce, show.
'**vorwerfen** *v/t* (*irr, sep*, -ge-, h, → **werfen**) **1.** *e-m Tier et. ~* throw s.th. to an

animal. **2.** *j-m Faulheit etc ~* reproach s.o. with laziness (*or* for being lazy *etc*); *ich habe mir nichts vorzuwerfen* I have nothing to blame myself for.
'**vorwiegend** *adv* predominantly, mainly, chiefly: *~ sonnig* mainly sunny.
'**Vorwort** *n* (-[e]s; -e) foreword, preface.
'**Vorwurf** *m* (-[e]s; ⸚e) reproach: *j-m Vorwürfe machen* reproach s.o. (*wegen* for). '**vorwurfsvoll** *adj* reproachful.
'**vorzählen** *v/t* (*sep*, h) *j-m et. ~* count s.th. out to s.o.
'**Vorzeichen** *n* **1.** omen. **2.** ♪ accidental. **3.** ⅋ sign: *fig. mit umgekehrtem ~* the other way round.
'**vorzeichnen** *v/t* (*sep*, h) *j-m et. ~* draw (*fig.* trace out) s.th. for s.o.
vorzeigbar ['foːrtsaikbaːr] *adj* presentable. '**vorzeigen** *v/t* (*sep*, h) show.
'**Vorzeit** *f der Mensch der ~* prehistoric man; *fig. in grauer ~* ages and ages ago.
'**vorzeitig** *adj* premature.
'**Vorzen,sur** *f* precensorship: *e-r ~ unterziehen* precensor.
'**vorziehen** *v/t* (*irr, sep*, -ge-, h, → **ziehen**) **1.** pull out. **2.** *die Vorhänge ~* pull the curtains. **3.** advance (*date etc*), deal with *s.th.* first. **4.** prefer (*dat* to): *es ~ zu inf* prefer to *inf*; *j-n ~* favo(u)r s.o.
'**Vorzimmer** *n* anteroom, outer office.
'**Vorzimmerdame** *f* receptionist.
'**Vorzug** *m* (-[e]s; ⸚e) **1.** (*vor dat* over) priority, preference. **2.** advantage, merit. **3.** privilege. **vorzüglich** [foːr'tsyːklıç] *adj* excellent, exquisite, first-rate.
'**Vorzugs,aktien** *pl* preference shares, *Am.* preferred stock. *~milch* *f* full-cream milk. *~preis* *m* special price.
'**vorzugsweise** *adv* **1.** preferably. **2.** chiefly, mainly.
votieren [vo'tiːrən] *v/i* (h) vote.
Votum ['voːtʊm] *n* (-s; -ten, -ta) vote.
Voyeur [vŏa'jøːr] *m* (-s; -e) voyeur.
vulgär [vʊl'gɛːr] *adj* vulgar.
Vulkan [vʊl'kaːn] *m* (-s; -e) volcano. *~ausbruch* *m* (volcanic) eruption.
vul'kanisch *adj geol.* volcanic.
vulkanisieren [vʊlkani'ziːrən] *v/t* (h) ⚙ vulcanize, *mot. a.* recap.

W

W, w [ve:] *n* (-; -) W, w.
Waage ['va:gə] *f* (-; -n) **1.** (pair of) scales, balance (*a. fig.*): *fig.* **sich die ~ halten** balance each other; → *Zünglein.* **2.** *astr.* (*er ist* [e-e] ~ he is [a]) Libra.
'**waagerecht** *adj* horizontal.
Waagschale ['va:k-] *f* scale: *fig. in die ~ werfen* bring s.th. to bear; *s-e Worte auf die ~ legen* weigh one's words.
wabb(e)lig ['vab(ə)lıç] *adj* flabby.
wabbeln ['vabəln] *v/i* (h) wobble.
Wabe ['va:bə] *f* (-; -n) honeycomb.
'**Wabenhonig** *m* comb honey.
wach [vax] *adj* **1.** awake: ~ *werden a. fig.* wake up, awake; ~ *liegen* lie awake. **2.** *fig.* alert, wide-awake.
'**Wachablösung** *f* **1.** ✕ changing of the guard. **2.** *fig. pol.* change of power.
Wache ['vaxə] *f* (-; -n) **1.** guard: ~ *halten* → *wachen* **2.** ✕ a) guard, sentry, b) guardroom: *auf* ~ on guard, on duty; ~ *stehen*, F ~ *schieben* be on guard. **3.** police station.
'**wachen** *v/i* (h) **1.** ~ *über* (*acc*) watch (over), guard; *darüber* ~, *daß* see (to it) that. **2.** *bei j-m* ~ sit up with s.o.
'**Wachhabende** *m* (-n; -n) ✕ commander of the guard.
'**wachhalten** *v/t* (*irr, sep,* -ge-, h, → *halten*) *fig. et.* ~ keep s.th. alive.
'**Wachhund** *m a. fig.* watchdog.
'**Wachmannschaft** *f* guard.
Wacholder ['vaxɔldər] *m* (-s; -) **1.** ♀ juniper. **2.** → **Wa'cholderschnaps** *m* gin.
'**Wachposten** *m* guard, ✕ *a.* sentry.
'**wach|rufen** *v/t* (*irr, sep,* -ge-, h, → *rufen*) rouse, bring back (*memories etc*). **~rütteln** *v/t* (*sep,* h) rouse (*aus* from).
Wachs [vaks] *n* (-es; -e) wax.
'**Wachsabdruck** *m* wax impression.
'**wachsam** *adj* watchful, vigilant: *ein ~es Auge haben auf* (*acc*) keep a sharp eye on. '**Wachsamkeit** *f* (-; *no pl*) vigilance, watchfulness.
wachsen[1] ['vaksən] *v/i* (wuchs, gewachsen, sn) grow, *fig. a.* increase (*an dat* in): → *Bart* 1, *gewachsen* II.
'**wachsen**[2] *v/t* (h) wax (*a. ski*).
'**Wachs|fi,gur** *f* wax figure, *pl a.* waxwork. **~fi,gurenkabi,nett** *n* waxworks.

~kerze *f* wax candle. **~tuch** *n* oilcloth.
'**Wachstum** *n* (-s; *no pl*) growth (*a.* ♀), *fig. a.* increase, expansion: (*noch*) *im ~ begriffen* still growing.
'**wachstums|fördernd** *adj* **1.** ♀ growth-inducing. **2.** ♀ growth-stimulating. **~hemmend** *adj* growth-retarding.
'**Wachstums|indu,strie** *f* growth industry. **~rate** *f* rate of (economic) growth.
'**wachs'weich** *adj* **1.** *a. fig.* (as) soft as wax. **2.** medium boiled (*egg*).
Wachtel ['vaxtəl] *f* (-; -n) *zo.* quail.
Wächter ['veçtər] *m* (-s; -) a) guard, b) attendant, c) watchman.
'**Wachtraum** *m* daydream.
'**Wach(t)turm** *m* watchtower.
'**Wach- und Schließgesellschaft** *f* Security Corps.
wack(e)lig ['vak(ə)lıç] *adj* shaky, wobbly (*a.* F *fig.*), rickety (*chair etc*), loose (*tooth, screw*): *a. fig. auf ~en Beinen stehen* stand on shaky legs, be shaky.
'**Wackelkon,takt** *m* ♀ loose contact.
wackeln ['vakəln] *v/i* (h) a) wobble, *tooth, screw, etc*: *a.* be loose, b) totter, F *fig. government, job, etc*: be shaky: *mit den Ohren* ~ waggle one's ears.
Wade ['va:də] *f* (-; -n) calf.
'**Wadenkrampf** *m* cramp in the leg.
Waffe ['vafə] *f* (-; -n) weapon (*a. fig.*), *pl* arms: *~n tragen* bear arms; *j-n mit s-n eigenen ~n schlagen* beat s.o. at his own game.
Waffel ['vafəl] *f* (-; -n) waffle, wafer.
'**Waffeleisen** *n* waffle iron.
'**Waffen|besitz** *m* possession of firearms. **~fa,brik** *f* arms factory. **~gattung** *f* arm, branch (of the service). **~gewalt** *f* (*mit* ~ by) force of arms. **~handel** *m* arms trade. **~händler** *m* arms dealer. **~kammer** *f* armo(u)ry. **~lager** *n* **1.** ✕ ordnance depot. **2.** cache. **~lieferung** *f* supply of arms.
'**waffenlos** *adj* weaponless, unarmed.
'**Waffen|ruhe** *f* cease-fire. **~schein** *m* firearm certificate, *Am.* gun license. **~schmuggel** *m* gun-running. **~stillstand** *m* armistice, cease-fire, truce (*a. fig.*). **~sy,stem** *n* weapons system.
'**wagemutig** *adj* daring, bold.

wagen ['vaːgən] v/t (h) venture (a. **sich ~**), risk, dare: **es ~** take the plunge; **es ~ mit** try; **sich ~ an** (acc) venture on a task etc; **wie können Sie es ~, das zu sagen**? how dare you (say that)?; **wer nicht wagt, der nicht gewinnt** nothing ventured, nothing gained.

'Wagen m (-s; -) **1.** a) vehicle, b) car, c) lorry, Am. truck, d) van. **2.** wag(g)on, cart: F fig. **j-m an den ~ fahren** tread on s.o.'s toes. **3.** 🚂 carriage, Am. car. **4.** astr. **der Große ~** the Great Bear, Am. the Big Dipper. **5.** typewriter: carriage. **~heber** m mot. jack. **~ko₁lonne** f column of cars. **~ladung** f (cart)load, Am. truckload, 🚂 waggonload, Am. carload. **~pflege** f (car) maintenance. **~typ** m model. **~wäsche** f (-; -n) car wash.

Waggon [va'gõː, va'gɔŋ] m (-s; -s) **1.** a) (railway) carriage, Am. (railroad) car, b) goods waggon, Am. freight car. **2.** waggonload, Am. carload.

waghalsig ['vaːkhalzɪç] adj daring.

Wagnis ['vaːknɪs] n (-ses; -se) risk.

Wahl [vaːl] f (-; -en) **1.** a) choice, alternative, b) selection: ♥ **erste ~** top quality; **zweite ~** second-rate quality, seconds; **die ~ haben** have one's choice; **k-e (andere) ~ haben** have no choice (or alternative) (**als** but); **vor der ~ stehen zu** inf be faced with the choice of ger; **s-e ~ treffen** make one's choice; **e-e gute ~ treffen** choose well; **wer die ~ hat, hat die Qual** the wider the choice, the greater the trouble. **2.** pol. a) election, b) poll(ing): **~en abhalten** hold elections; **zur ~ gehen** go to the polls; **in die engere ~ kommen** be short-listed.

'Wahlalter n voting age.

'wählbar adj eligible (for election).

'wahlberechtigt adj entitled to vote.

'Wahl|beteiligung f turnout (at the election): **hohe (geringe) ~** heavy (poor) polling. **~bezirk** m ward, constituency, Am. electoral district.

wählen ['vɛːlən] (h) **I** v/t **1.** choose, select. **2.** esp. pol. elect, vote for: **j-n zum Präsidenten ~** elect s.o. president; ♥ **j-n in den Vorstand ~** vote s.o. on the board. **3.** teleph. dial. **II** v/i **4.** choose, make one's choice. **5.** pol. vote, (a. **~ gehen**) go to the polls.

'Wähler m (-s; -) voter.

'Wahlergebnis n election results.

'Wählerin f (-; -nen) voter.

'Wählerinitia₁tive f voters' initiative.

'wählerisch adj particular, choosy: iro. **nicht gerade ~** not too particular (**in** dat, about).

'Wählerschaft f (-; no pl) a) electorate, b) constituency, voters.

'Wahl|fach n ped. optional subject, Am. a. elective. **₂frei** adj ped. optional, Am. elective. **~gang** m (**im ersten ~** at the first) ballot. **~geschenk** n campaign promise. **~heimat** f adopted country. **~helfer(in** f) m campaign assistant. **~jahr** n election year. **~ka₁bine** f polling booth. **~kampf** m electoral battle, election campaign. **~kreis** m → **Wahlbezirk**. **~leiter** m returning officer. **~liste** f electoral register. **~lo₁kal** n polling station. **~lokomo₁tive** f F fig. (great) vote-catcher.

'wahllos adj indiscriminate.

'Wahl|niederlage f election defeat. **~ordnung** f election regulations. **~pflicht** f electoral duty. **~pla₁kat** n election poster. **~pro₁gramm** n election platform. **~recht** n (-[e]s; no pl) a) right to vote, franchise, b) eligibility: **allgemeines ~** universal suffrage. **~rede** f electoral address. **~redner** m election speaker.

'Wählscheibe f teleph. dial.

'Wahl|sieg m election victory. **~spende** f election (campaign) contribution. **~spruch** m motto. **~stimme** f vote. **~tag** m election day. **~urne** f ballot box: **zur ~ gehen** go to the polls. **~versammlung** f election meeting. **~versprechen** n campaign promise. **~vorschlag** m election proposal.

'wahlweise adv alternatively: **es gab ~ Fisch oder Fleisch** there was a choice of fish or meat.

Wahn [vaːn] m (-[e]s; no pl) delusion, mania: **in e-m ~ befangen sein** be under a delusion. **~bild** n hallucination.

'Wahnsinn m (-[e]s; no pl) a. F fig. insanity, madness. **'wahnsinnig I** adj **1.** mad, insane. **2.** F fig. a) mad, crazy, b) terrible (shock, pain, etc), c) terrific. **II** adv F fig. terribly, awfully: **~ verliebt** madly in love. **'Wahnsinnige** m, f (-n; -n) lunatic, madman (madwoman).

'Wahnvorstellung f delusion, idée fixe.

'wahnwitzig adj mad, crazy.

walzen

wahr [va:r] *adj* true, real, genuine: *ein ~er Freund* a true friend; *~e Liebe* true love; *ein ~es Wunder* a real wonder; *so ~ ich lebe!* as sure as I live!; *so ~ mir Gott helfe!* so help me God!; *~ werden* come true; F *das darf doch nicht ~ sein!* I can't believe it!; *das ist nicht das Wahre* that's not the real thing.

wahren ['va:rən] *v/t* (h) preserve, maintain, keep (*a. secret*), protect, safeguard (*interests*): → *Form* 1, *Schein*¹ 2.

während ['vɛ:rənt] **I** *prep* (*gen*) during, in the course of. **II** *conj* while.

'wahrhaben: nicht ~ wollen refuse to believe.

'wahrhaft I *adj* true, real. **II** *adv* → **wahr'haftig** *adv* truly, really, indeed.

'Wahrheit *f* (-; -en) truth: *in ~* in fact, in reality; *um die ~ zu sagen* to tell the truth; F *j-m mal die ~ sagen* give s.o. a piece of one's mind. **II** *adv* truthfully.

'wahrheitsgemäß, 'wahrheitsgetreu I *adj* truthful, true. **II** *adv* truthfully.

'Wahrheitsliebe *f* veracity. **'wahrheitsliebend** *adj* truthful, veracious.

'wahrlich *adv* truly, *bibl.* verily.

'wahrnehmbar *adj* perceptible, noticeable. **'wahrnehmen** *v/t* (*irr, sep,* -ge-, h, → *nehmen*) **1.** perceive, notice, *a.* see, *a.* hear. **2.** use, seize (*opportunity etc*), protect, safeguard (*interests etc*), observe (*deadline*). **'Wahrnehmung** *f* (-; -en) **1.** a) (*sinnliche ~* sense) perception, b) observation. **2.** *j-n mit der ~ s-r Geschäfte* (*Interessen*) *beauftragen* entrust s.o. with the care of one's business (the safeguarding of one's interests). **'Wahrnehmungsvermögen** *n* (-s; *no pl*) perceptive faculty.

'wahrsagen (*sep or insep,* h) **I** *v/t* prophesy. **II** *v/i* tell fortunes: *j-m ~* tell s.o.'s fortune. **'Wahrsager** *m* (-s; -), **'Wahrsagerin** *f* (-; -nen) fortune-teller.

wahrscheinlich [va:r'ʃaɪnlɪç] **I** *adj* probable, likely. **II** *adv* probably: *er wird ~ nicht kommen* he is not likely to come. **Wahr'scheinlichkeit** *f* (-; -en) (*aller ~ nach* in all) probability (*or* likelihood). **Wahr'scheinlichkeitsrechnung** *f* theory of probabilities.

'Wahrung *f* (-; *no pl*) maintenance, protection, safeguarding (*of interests etc*).

Währung ['vɛ:rʊŋ] *f* (-; -en) currency.

Währungs|abkommen *n* monetary

agreement. **~block** *m* monetary bloc. **~einheit** *f* unit of currency. **~krise** *f* monetary crisis. **~poli,tik** *f* monetary policy. **~re,form** *f* currency reform. **~sy,stem** *n* monetary system. **~uni,on** *f* monetary union.

'Wahrzeichen *n* **1.** symbol, emblem. **2.** landmark.

Waise ['vaɪzə] *f* (-; -n) orphan: (*zur*) *~ werden* be orphaned.

'Waisen|haus *n* orphanage. **~kind** *n* orphan. **~knabe** *m fig. gegen ihn sind wir die reinsten ~n* we are mere babes compared to him.

Wal [va:l] *m* (-[e]s; -e) *zo.* whale.

Wald [valt] *m* (-[e]s; -er) wood, forest (*a. fig.*): *er sieht den ~ vor lauter Bäumen nicht* he can't see the wood for the trees. **~bestand** *m* forest stand. **~brand** *m* forest fire. **~gebiet** *n*, **~gegend** *f* wooded area, woodland.

'Waldhorn *n* (-[e]s; -er) **♪** French horn.

waldig ['valdɪç] *adj* wooded.

'Wald|lauf *m* cross-country race. **~meister** *m* **♥** woodruff. **~rand** *m* (*am ~* at *or* on the) edge of the forest. **~schäden** *pl* forest damage. **~sterben** *n* dying of forests.

Waldung ['valdʊŋ] *f* (-; -en) wood(land), forest.

'Walfang *m* (-[e]s; *no pl*) whaling.

'Walfänger *m* (-s; -) whaler (*a. ship*).

'Walfisch *m* F whale.

Waliser [va'li:zər] *m* (-s; -) Welshman: *die ~* the Welsh. **Wa'liserin** *f* (-; -nen) Welshwoman. **wa'lisisch** *adj* Welsh.

walken ['valkən] *v/t* (h) **1.** mill. **2.** knead.

Wall [val] *m* (-[e]s; *+e*) *a. fig.* rampart.

Wallach ['valax] *m* (-[e]s; -e) *zo.* gelding.

'wallfahren *v/i* (*insep,* sn) (go on a) pilgrimage. **'Wallfahrer** *m* (-s; -), **'Wallfahrerin** *f* (-; -nen) pilgrim. **'Wallfahrt** *f* (-; -en) pilgrimage. **'Wallfahrtsort** *m* (-[e]s; -e) place of pilgrimage.

'Wallung *f* (-; -en) (*a.* **♥** hot) flush: *fig. j-n in ~ bringen* make s.o.'s blood boil.

Walnuß ['valnʊs] *f* (-; *+sse*) **♥** walnut.

Walroß ['valrɔs] *n* (-sses; -sse) *zo.* walrus.

walten ['valtən] *v/i* (h) be at work: *s-s Amtes ~* do one's duty; → *schalten* 3.

'Walzblech *n* rolled steel plate.

Walze ['valtsə] *f* (-; -n) **1.** ⚙ roll, roller, cylinder. **2.** *typewriter:* platen. **3.** *barrel organ:* barrel. **'walzen** *v/t* (h) ⚙ roll.

wälzen ['vɛltsən] (h) **I** v/t **1.** roll. **2.** F pore over *books etc*, turn *problem etc* over in one's mind. **II** *sich* ~ roll, a. wallow (*in mud etc*); *sich hin und her* ~ toss about, toss and turn.

'**walzenförmig** adj cylindrical.

'**Walzer** m (-s; -) (a. ~ **tanzen**) waltz.

'**Wälzer** m (-s; -) F huge tome.

'**Walzertakt** m waltz time.

'**Walz|ma,schine** f rolling machine. ~**stahl** m rolled steel. ~**straße** f (rolling) mill train. ~**werk** n (rolling) mill.

Wampe ['vampə] f (-; -n) F paunch.

wand [vant] pret of **winden**.

Wand f (-; ⸚e) a) wall (a. fig.), b) side, c) (rock) face: ~ **an** ~ wall to wall; *in s-n* *vier Wänden* within one's own four walls; F *fig.* *j-n an die* ~ **drücken** drive s.o. to the wall; *j-n an die* ~ **spielen** play s.o. into the ground; F *j-n an die* ~ *stellen* execute s.o.; *es ist, um die Wände hochzugehen* it's enough to drive you mad.

Wandale [van'da:lə] m (-n; -n) *hist.* Vandal, *fig.* vandal. **Wandalismus** [vanda'lɪsmʊs] m (-; *no pl*) vandalism.

'**Wandbehang** m wall hanging, tapestry.

Wandel ['vandəl] m (-s; *no pl*) change: *der* ~ *der Zeit* the changing times; *sich im* ~ *befinden* be changing.

'**wandelbar** adj changeable.

'**Wandelhalle** f at spa: pump room.

'**wandeln** v/t (a. *sich* ~) (h) change.

'**Wander|ausstellung** f touring exhibition. ~**büche,rei** f travel(l)ing library, *Am. a.* bookmobile. ~**bühne** f touring company. ~**düne** f shifting sand dune.

'**Wanderer** m (-s; -), '**Wanderin** f (-; -nen) wanderer, hiker, rambler.

'**Wanderkarte** f hiking map.

'**Wanderleben** n (-s; *no pl*) vagrant life.

wandern ['vandərn] v/i (sn) walk, hike, tramp, *a. fig.* thoughts etc: wander, *a. zo.* migrate: ~ **gehen** go hiking; F *fig.* ~ *in* (*acc*) end up in, go (in)to. '**Wandern** n (-s) hiking (*etc*), zo. migration.

'**Wanderpo,kal** m challenge cup.

'**Wanderpreis** m challenge trophy.

'**Wanderschaft** f (-; *no pl*) travels: *auf* ~ *sein* (**gehen**) be on (take to) the road.

'**Wandertag** m ped. school outing.

'**Wanderung** f (-; -en) walking tour, hike, ramble, *a. zo.* migration.

'**Wanderverein** m rambling club.

'**Wanderweg** m footpath.

'**Wand|gemälde** n mural. ~**ka,lender** m wall calendar. ~**karte** f wall map.

Wandler ['vandlər] m (-s; -) converter.

'**Wandleuchte** f wall lamp.

'**Wandlung** f (-; -en) change.

'**wandlungsfähig** adj flexible, versatile.

'**Wand|male,rei** f a) mural painting, b) mural. ~**schrank** m built-in cupboard (*Am.* closet). ~**spiegel** m wall mirror. ~**tafel** f blackboard.

wandte ['vantə] pret of **wenden**.

Wange ['vaŋə] f (-; -n) a. ⊕ cheek.: ~ **an** ~ cheek to cheek.

wankelmütig ['vaŋkəlmy:tɪç] adj fickle.

wanken ['vaŋkən] v/i (h) **1.** → **schwanken** 1. **2.** *fig.* falter, waver: *ins Wanken geraten* begin to rock (*fig.* falter *or* waver). **3.** → **weichen**[1] **2.**

wann [van] adv when, (at) what time: *seit* ~? (for) how long?, since when?; *bis* ~? till when?

Wanne ['vanə] f (-; -n) **1.** tub. **2.** bath(tub). '**Wannenbad** n (tub) bath.

Wanst [vanst] m (-[e]s; ⸚e) F paunch.

Wanze ['vantsə] f (-; -n) **1.** zo. bug, *Am.* bedbug. **2.** F *fig.* bug: ~*n anbringen in* (*dat*) bug (*a room etc*).

Wappen ['vapən] n (-s; -) coat of arms. ~**bild** n heraldic figure. ~**kunde** f (-; *no pl*) heraldry. ~**schild** m escutcheon, blazon. ~**spruch** m heraldic motto. ~**tier** n heraldic animal.

wappnen ['vapnən] *sich* ~ (h) (**gegen**) arm (against), prepare (*or* brace) o.s. (for); → **gewappnet**.

war [va:r] pret of **sein**[1].

warb [varp] pret of **werben**.

Ware ['va:rə] f (-; -n) product, article, *coll. a.* merchandise, *pl a.* goods, commodities.

'**Waren|angebot** n range of goods. ~**bestand** m stock (on hand). ~**börse** f commodity exchange. ~**haus** n department store. ~**lager** n **1.** stock (on hand). **2.** warehouse. ~**probe** f sample. ~**sendung** f consignment, ⓦ trade sample. ~**zeichen** n trademark.

warf [varf] pret of **werfen**.

warm [varm] **I** adj warm (a. fig.), hot (*meal, drink, etc*): *mir ist* ~ I feel warm; *et.* ~ *halten* keep s.th. warm; *sich* ~ *halten* keep warm; *et.* ~ *machen* warm s.th. up; ~ *werden* warm up; *es wird* *wärmer* it's getting warmer; F *ich kann mit ihr nicht ~ werden* I can't warm to her; → *warmhalten.* **II** *adv* warmly (*a. fig.*): F *die Wohnung kostet ~ ...* the rent for the flat is ... including heating.

'**Warmblüter** [-bly:tər] *m* (-s; -) warm-blooded animal.

Wärme ['vɛrmə] *f* (-; *no pl*) warmth (*a. fig.*), *meteor., phys.* heat: *zehn Grad ~* ten degrees above zero. **~behandlung** *f* **1.** ⊛ heat treatment. **2.** ✿ thermotherapy. **⌂beständig** *adj* heat-resistant. **~dämmung** *f* heat insulation. **~einheit** *f* thermal unit. **~grad** *m* degree above zero. **~kraftwerk** *n* thermoelectric power plant. **~lehre** *f* thermodynamics. **~leiter** *m phys.* heat conductor.

wärmen ['vɛrmən] (h) **I** *v/t* warm (up), heat (up) (*food etc*): *sich die Füße ~* warm one's feet. **II** *v/i* be warm: *Wolle wärmt* wool keeps you warm. **III** *sich ~* warm o.s. (up).

'**Wärme|pumpe** *f* heat pump. **~technik** *f* heat engineering. **~verlust** *m* heat loss.

'**Wärmflasche** *f* hot-water bottle.

'**warmhalten** *v/t* (*irr, sep,* -ge-, h, → *halten*) F *fig. sich j-n ~* keep in with s.o.

'**Warmhalteplatte** *f* plate warmer.

'**warmherzig** *adj* warm-hearted.

'**warmlaufen** *v/i* (*irr, sep,* -ge-, sn, → *laufen*) **~ lassen** run the engine up.

'**Warmluftfront** *f meteor.* warm front.

'**Warmmiete** *f* rent including heating.

Warm'wasser|bereiter *m* water heater. **~heizung** *f* hot-water heating. **~speicher** *m* hot-water tank. **~versorgung** *f* hot-water supply.

'**Warn|anlage** *f* warning device. **~blinkanlage** *f mot.* warning flasher. **~dreieck** *n mot.* warning triangle.

warnen ['varnən] *v/t, v/i* (h) warn (*vor* against): *davor ~ zu inf* warn against ger; *vor ... wird gewarnt!* beware of ...!

'**Warn|kreuz** *n* warning cross. **~leuchte** *f*, **~licht** *n* warning light. **~schild** *n* danger sign. **~schuß** *m* (e-n -) **a** abgeben fire a) warning shot. **~si,gnal** *n* warning signal. **~streik** *m* token strike.

'**Warnung** *f* (-; -en) warning.

'**Warnzeichen** *n* warning sign.

Warte ['vartə] *f fig. von hoher ~ aus* from a lofty standpoint; *von s-r ~ aus gesehen* from his point of view.

'**Warteliste** *f* (*auf der ~ stehen* be on

the) waiting list.

warten[1] ['vartən] *v/t* (h) ⊛ service.

'**warten**[2] *v/i* (h) wait (*auf acc* for): *j-n ~ lassen* keep s.o. waiting; *lange auf sich ~ lassen* be a long time in coming; *nicht lange auf sich ~ lassen* not to be long in coming; *warte (mal)!* wait a minute!; *na, warte!* you just wait!; *da kann er lange ~!* he's got a long wait coming; *das kann ~!* that'll keep!; *iro. auf ihn (darauf) haben wir gerade noch gewartet!* he (that) is all we needed. '**Warten** *n* (-s) wait(ing): *nach langem ~* after a long wait.

Wärter ['vɛrtər] *m* (-s, -), '**Wärterin** *f* (-; -nen) attendant, keeper.

'**Wartesaal** *m* 🚆 waiting room.

'**Wartezeit** *f* waiting period.

'**Wartezimmer** *n* waiting room.

'**Wartung** *f* (-; -en) maintenance, servicing.

'**Wartungsanleitung** *f* service manual.

'**wartungsfrei** *adj* maintenance-free.

warum [va'rʊm] *adv* why.

Warze ['vartsə] *f* (-; -n) **1.** ✿ wart. **2.** → Brustwarze.

was [vas] **I** *interrog pron* **1.** what (*a.* F *for wie bitte?, nanu!, nicht wahr?*): *~ gibt's?* what is it?, F what's up?; *~ gibt's zum Mittagessen?* what's for lunch?; *~ kostet das?* how much is it?; *~ für (ein) ...?* what sort of ...?; *~ für e-e Farbe?* what colo(u)r?; *~ für ein Unsinn!* what nonsense! **2.** F a) *~ mußte er auch lügen?* why did he have to lie?, b) *~ fährst er auch so e-n großen Wagen?* what does he need such a big car for? **II** *rel pron* **3.** what: *~ auch immer* whatever; *alles, ~ ich brauche* all I need; *ich weiß nicht, ~ ich tun soll* I don't know what to do. **4.** which: *er lachte nur, ~ mich ärgerte* he just laughed, which made me angry. **III** *indef pron* F something (*bad, better, etc*): *das ist ~ anderes* that's different; *ich will dir ~ sagen!* I'll tell you what; *sonst noch ~?* anything else?; *ist ~?* is anything wrong (*or* the matter)?

'**Wasch|anlage** *f mot.* car wash. **~anleitung** *f* washing instructions. **~automat** *m* washing machine.

'**waschbar** *adj* washable.

'**Waschbär** *m zo.* raccoon.

'**Waschbecken** *n* washbasin.

Wäsche ['vɛʃə] f (-; *no pl*) **1.** wash(ing), laundry; *in der* ~ in the wash; *fig.* *schmutzige* ~ *waschen* wash one's dirty linen in public. **2.** (*bed, table*) linen. **3.** (*die* ~ *wechseln* put on fresh) underwear. ~**beutel** *m* laundry bag.

'**waschecht** *adj* **1.** a) washable, nonshrink, b) fast. **2.** F *fig.* true, genuine.

'**Wäsche|klammer** f clothes peg. ~**korb** *m* laundry basket. ~**leine** f clothesline.

waschen ['vaʃən] (wusch, gewaschen, h) **I** *v/t* wash (*sich die Hände etc* one's hands *etc*), launder (*a.* F *fig. money*): *Waschen und Legen* shampoo and set. **II** *sich* ~ wash (o.s.).

Wäsche|rei f (-; -en) laundry.

'**Wäsche|schleuder** f spin-drier. ~**ständer** *m* clotheshorse. ~**tinte** f marking ink. ~**trockner** *m* drier.

'**Wasch|gang** *m* cycle. ~**gelegenheit** f washing facilities. ~**küche** f washhouse. **2.** F *fig.* pea soup. ~**lappen** *m* **1.** flannel, *Am.* washcloth. **2.** F *fig.* sissy. ~**lauge** f lye. ~**leder** *n* chamois (leather). ~**ma,schine** f washing machine. **2ma,schinenfest** *adj* machine-washable. ~**mittel** *n*, ~**pulver** *n* washing powder. ~**raum** *m* washroom. ~**sa,lon** *m* launderette, *Am.* laundromat. ~**schüssel** f washbowl. ~**straße** f car wash.

'**Waschung** f (-; -en) washing, *esp. eccl.*, ✝ ablution.

'**Wasch|wasser** *n* (-s; *no pl*) washing water. ~**zettel** *m* blurb.

Wasser ['vasər] *n* (-s; -, ⸗) water: *fließendes* (*stehendes*) ~ running (stagnant) water; *zu* ~ *und zu Land* by land and by water; ~ *lassen* pass water; *sich über* ~ *halten a. fig.* keep one's head above water; *unter* ~ *setzen* flood; *fig. ins* ~ *fallen* fall flat; *das ist* ~ *auf s-e Mühle* that's grist to his mill; *da läuft e-m das* ~ *im Munde zusammen* it makes your mouth water; *er kann ihr nicht das* ~ *reichen* he's not a patch on her; *er ist mit allen* ~*n gewaschen* he knows all the tricks (of the trade); *das* ~ *steht ihm bis zum Hals* he is in bad trouble; *er ist ein stilles* ~ he's a deep one; → *Schlag* 1.

'**wasser|abstoßend** *adj textil.* water-repellent. ~**arm** *adj* dry, arid.

'**Wasser|aufbereitungsanlage** f water-recycling plant. ~**bad** *n* **1.** 🐟, *phot.*

water bath. **2.** *gastr.* bain-marie. ~**ball** *m* **1.** beach ball. **2.** → ~**ballspiel** *n* water polo. ~**bau** *m* (-[e]s; *no pl*) hydraulic engineering. ~**behälter** *m* water container (👁 tank). ~**bett** *n* water bed. ~**bombe** f depth charge.

Wässerchen ['vɛsərçən] *n er sah aus, als könne er kein* ~ *trüben* he looked as though butter would not melt in his mouth.

'**Wasser|dampf** *m* steam. **2dicht** *adj* waterproof, ⚓, 👁 *a.* watertight. ~**enthärter** *m* water softener. ~**fahrzeug** *n* watercraft, vessel. ~**fall** *m* waterfall, falls: F *reden wie ein* ~ talk nineteen to the dozen. ~**farbe** f water colo(u)r. **2fest** *adj* waterproof. ~**flasche** f water bottle. ~**flugzeug** *n* seaplane. ~**gehalt** *m* water content. **2gekühlt** *adj* water-cooled. ~**glas** *n* **1.** 🐟 water glass. **2.** water glass, tumbler: → *Sturm* 1. ~**graben** *m* ditch, *sports:* water jump. ~**hahn** *m* tap, *Am.* faucet.

'**wasserhaltig** *adj* 🐟 hydrous.

'**Wasserhaushalt** *m* **1.** water supply. **2.** *biol.*, 🌿 water balance.

wässerig ['vɛsərɪç] *adj* watery, 🐟 aqueous: *j-m den Mund* ~ *machen* make s.o.'s mouth water (*nach* for).

'**Wasser|kessel** *m* **1.** kettle. **2.** 👁 boiler. ~**klo,sett** *n* water closet (*abbr.* W.C.). ~**kraft** f water power. ~**kraftwerk** *n* hydroelectric power plant. ~**kühlung** f water cooling (system). ~**lauf** *m* watercourse. ~**leitung** f water pipe(s). ~**linie** f ⚓ water line. **2löslich** *adj* water-soluble. ~**mangel** *m* water shortage.

'**Wassermann** *m* (-[e]s; *no pl*) *astr.* (*er ist* [*ein*] ~ he is [an]) Aquarius.

'**Wasserme,lone** f water melon.

wassern ['vasərn] *v/i* (h) ✈ touch down, *spacecraft:* splash down.

wässern ['vɛsərn] *v/t* (h) **1.** water, irrigate. **2.** soak.

'**Wasser|pfeife** f water pipe. ~**pflanze** f aquatic (plant). ~**pi,stole** f water pistol. ~**ratte** f **1.** *zo.* water rat. **2.** F enthusiastic swimmer. ~**rohr** *n* water pipe. ~**rutschbahn** f water chute. ~**schaden** *m* water damage. ~**scheide** f watershed, *Am. a.* divide. **2scheu** *adj* afraid of water. ~**schildkröte** f turtle.

'**Wasserschutz** *m* prevention of water

pollution. **~gebiet** n water reserve. **~poli,zei** f river police.

'**Wasser|ski** n (-s; no pl) water skiing: **~ laufen** go water-skiing, water-ski. **~speier** m △ gargoyle. **~spiegel** m **1.** surface of the water. **2.** water level. **~sport** m water (or aquatic) sports, aquatics. **~spülung** f a) flush, b) cistern. **~stand** m water level. **~standsanzeiger** m water ga(u)ge.

'**Wasserstoff** m (-[e]s; no pl) hydrogen. ♀**blond** adj F peroxide blond(e). **~bombe** f hydrogen bomb. **~'pero,xid** n, **~'supero,xid** n hydrogen peroxide.

'**Wasser|strahl** m jet of water. **~straße** f waterway. **~sucht** f (-; no pl) ♣ dropsy. **~tier** n aquatic (animal). **~tropfen** m drop of water. **~turm** m water tower.

'**Wasserung** f (-; -en) ➤ touchdown on water, of spacecraft: splashdown.

'**Wasser|verbrauch** m water consumption. **~verdrängung** f (water) displacement. **~verschmutzung** f water pollution. **~versorgung** f water supply. **~vogel** m water bird, pl a. waterfowl. **~waage** f spirit level. **~weg** m waterway: **auf dem ~** by water. **~welle** f (hairdo) water wave. **~werfer** m water cannon. **~werk(e pl)** n waterworks. **~zeichen** n watermark.

waten ['vaːtən] v/i (sn) wade.

watscheln ['vaːtʃəln] v/i (sn) waddle.

Watt¹ [vat] n (-[e]s; -en) geol. mud flats.

Watt² n (-s; -) ⚡ watt.

Watte ['vatə] f (-; -n) cotton wool.

'**Wattebausch** m cotton-wool swab.

'**Wattenmeer** n mud flats.

'**Wattestäbchen** n cotton bud.

wattieren [va'tiːrən] v/t (h) pad, wad.

weben ['veːbən] v/t, v/i (h) weave.

'**Weber** m (-s; -) weaver. **Webe'rei** f (-; -en) **1.** no pl weaving. **2.** weaving mill.

'**Weberknecht** m zo. daddy longlegs.

'**Web|fehler** m flaw. **~pelz** m woven imitation fur. **~stuhl** m loom. **~waren** pl woven goods.

Wechsel ['vɛksəl] m (-s; -) **1.** change, (a. ♪ crop) rotation. **2.** ♣ draft, bill (of exchange): **e-n ~ (auf j-n) ziehen** draw a bill (on s.o.). **3.** sports: a) (baton) change, b) change of ends. **4.** → **Wildwechsel.** **~bäder** pl ♣ alternating hot and cold baths. **~bank** f (-; -en) discount house. **~beziehung** f interrela-

tion. **~fälle** pl vicissitudes, F the ups and downs. **~geld** n (small) change.

'**wechselhaft** adj changeable.

'**Wechseljahre** pl physiol. menopause.

'**Wechselkurs** m rate of exchange.

wechseln ['vɛksəln] (h) **I** v/t **1.** a) change b) exchange (rings, glances, words, etc), c) vary, d) alternate, a. rotate: **den Arbeitsplatz (Arzt etc) ~** change jobs (doctors etc); → **Besitzer.** **II** v/i **2.** a) change, b) vary. **3.** (sn) deer etc: cross.

'**wechselnd** adj changing, varying.

'**Wechsel|rahmen** m interchangeable picture frame. **~schuld** f ♣ bill debt.

'**wechselseitig** [-zaɪtɪç] adj mutual, reciprocal: **~e Abhängigkeit** interdependence.

'**Wechselstrom** m ⚡ alternating current (abbr. A.C.). **~motor** m A.C. motor.

'**Wechselstube** f exchange office.

'**Wechselwähler(in** f) m floating voter.

'**wechselweise** adv alternately, in turn.

'**Wechselwirkung** f interaction.

wecken ['vɛkən] v/t (h) wake (up), call, a. fig. rouse, fig. awaken.

'**Wecker** m (-s; -) alarm (clock): F **j-m auf den ~ gehen** get on s.o.'s nerves.

'**Weckruf** m teleph. alarm call.

Wedel ['veːdəl] m (-s; -) ♣ frond.

'**wedeln** v/i (h) **1. ~ mit** wave (s.th.), **dem Schwanz** wag (its tail). **2.** skiing: wedel.

weder ['veːdər] conj **~ ... noch** neither ... nor.

weg [vɛk] adv F **1.** a) gone, b) not in, c) away: **~ (da)!** get away!, beat it!; **~ damit!** take it away!, w.s. off with it!; **Finger (or Hände) ~!** hands off!; **ich muß ~!** I must be off!; **nichts wie ~!** let's get out of here! **2. ~ sein** a) be out cold, b) be in raptures (**von** over); **über et. ~ sein** have got over s.th.

Weg [veːk] m (-[e]s; -e) way (a. fig.), path, route, F a. errand: **der ~ zum Erfolg** the road to success; **auf dem ~(e) der Besserung** on the road to recovery, F on the mend; **auf diesem ~e** this way; **auf diplomatischem ~e** through diplomatic channels; **auf friedlichem (legalem) ~e** by peaceful (legal) means; **auf dem besten ~e sein zu inf** be well on the way to ger; **auf dem richtigen ~e sein** be on the right track; **sich auf den ~ machen** set off; **j-m aus dem ~(e) gehen** get out of s.o.'s way; (dat) **aus**

dem ~e gehen steer clear of; *aus dem ~e räumen* (*or* **schaffen**) get rid of; *s-e eigenen ~e gehen* go one's own way; *den ~ ebnen* pave the way (*dat* for); *et. in die ~e leiten* initiate s.th., start s.th. off; *ich traue ihm nicht über den ~* I don't trust him an inch; *im ~(e) stehen* (*or* **sein**) *a*) *j-m* be in so.'s way, *b*) *e-r Sache* be an obstacle to s.th.; *dem steht nichts im ~e* there are no obstacles to that, F that's all right; → *bahnen, halb* I.

'wegbekommen *v/t* (*irr, sep,* h, → *bekommen*) F get *s.th.* off, move.

'Wegbereiter *m* (-s; -) pioneer: *der ~ sein für* pave the way for.

'wegblasen *v/t* (*irr, sep,* -ge-, h, → *blasen*) blow *s.th.* away: *fig. wie weggeblasen sein* be clean gone.

'wegbleiben *v/i* (*irr, sep,* -ge-, sn, → *bleiben*) F **1.** stay away. **2.** ☺ fail, *sl.* conk out: → *Luft* 2, *Spucke*.

'wegbringen *v/t* (*irr, sep,* -ge-, h, → *bringen*) take *s.o., s.th.* away.

wegen ['ve:ɡən] *prep* (*gen,* F *dat*) **1.** because of, on account of: *~ Diebstahls* for larceny; → *Amt* 1, *Recht* 1. **2.** for the sake of: *er hat es ~ s-r Kinder getan* he did it for his children's sake. **3.** due to. **4.** F *von ~* that's what you think!; *von ~ hübsch!* pretty, my foot!

'Wegerecht *n* (-[e]s; *no pl*) right of way.

Wegerich ['ve:ɡərɪç] *m* (-s; -e) plantain.

'wegfahren *v/i* (*irr, sep,* -ge-, sn, → *fahren*) leave, drive away.

'wegfegen *v/t* (*sep,* h) sweep *s.th.* away.

Weggang ['vɛk-] *m* (-[e]s; *no pl*) leaving.

'weggeben *v/t* (*irr, sep,* -ge-, h, → *geben*) give *s.th.* away.

'weggehen *v/i* (*irr, sep,* -ge-, sn, → *gehen*) **1.** go away (*a.* F *fig. pain etc*), leave: F *geh weg!* leave me alone!; *von Berlin* (*der Firma*) *~* leave Berlin (the firm). **2.** F *fig.* sell: → *Semmel*.

'weghaben *v/t* (*irr, sep,* -ge-, h, → *haben*) F **1.** *sein Teil etc ~* have got one's share *etc.* **2.** *et. ~ a*) have got the hang of it, *b*) be good (*in dat* at).

'wegkommen *v/i* (*irr, sep,* -ge-, sn, → *kommen*) F **1.** get away. **2.** get lost. **3.** *fig. gut* (*schlecht*) *~* come off well (badly) (*bei* at). **4.** *~ über* (*acc*) get over.

'weglassen *v/t* (*irr, sep,* -ge-, h, → *lassen*) **1.** let *s.o.* go. **2.** leave *s.th.* out.

Weglassung ['vɛk-] *f* (-; -en) omission.

'weglaufen *v/i* (*irr, sep,* -ge-, sn, → *laufen*) run away.

'weglegen *v/t* (*sep,* h) put *s.th.* aside.

'wegmüssen *v/i* (*irr, sep,* -ge-, h, → *müssen*) F *ich muß weg* I must be off; *es muß weg!* it must go!

'wegnehmen *v/t* (*irr, sep,* -ge-, h, → *nehmen*) remove, *fig.* take up (*room, time, etc*): (*j-m*) *et. ~* take s.th. away (from s.o.); → *Gas.*

'wegrationali,sieren *v/t* (*sep,* h) cut *jobs etc* (by rationalization).

'wegräumen *v/t* (*sep,* h) *a. fig.* remove.

'wegreißen *v/t* (*irr, sep,* -ge-, h, → *reißen*) tear *s.o., s.th.* away.

'wegscheren: sich ~ (*sep,* h) F clear off.

'wegschicken *v/t* (*sep,* h) send *s.o., s.th.* away (*or* off).

'wegschleppen *v/t* (*sep,* h) drag *s.o., s.th.* off.

'wegschließen *v/t* (*irr, sep,* -ge-, h, → *schließen*) lock *s.th.* away.

'wegschnappen *v/t* (*sep,* h) F (*j-m*) *et. ~* snatch s.th. away (from s.o.).

'wegsehen *v/i* (*irr, sep,* -ge-, h, → *sehen*) **1.** look away, *a. fig.* look the other way. **2.** → *hinwegsehen.*

'wegspülen *v/t* (*sep,* h) wash away.

'wegstecken *v/t* (*sep,* h) put *s.th.* away.

'wegtreten *v/i* (*irr, sep,* -ge-, sn, → *treten*) step aside, ⚔ break (the) ranks: *~ lassen* (*weggetreten!*) dismiss(!).

'Wegweiser *m* (-s; -) signpost, (road) sign, *in buildings:* directory.

'wegwerfen (*irr, sep,* -ge-, h, → *werfen*) **I** *v/t a. fig.* throw *s.th.* away. **II** *sich ~* throw o.s. away (*an acc* on).

'wegwerfend *adj* disparaging.

Wegwerf|flasche ['vɛk-] *f* throwaway (*or* disposable) bottle. *~gesellschaft* f *contp.* throwaway society.

'wegwischen *v/t* (*sep,* h) **1.** wipe *s.th.* off. **2.** *fig.* brush *objection etc* off.

'wegzaubern *v/t* (*sep,* h) spirit away.

'wegziehen (*irr, sep,* -ge-, sn, → *ziehen*) **I** *v/t* pull *s.o., s.th.* away. **II** *v/i* move.

weh [ve:] *adj* sore: (*j-m*) *~ tun* hurt (s.o., *fig.* s.o.'s feelings); *sich* (*am Kopf etc*) *~* hurt o.s. (one's head *etc*); *mir tut der Knöchel ~* my ankle hurts.

wehe ['ve:ə] *int* *~* (*dir*), *wenn ...* you'll be sorry if ...

'Wehe *f* (-; -n) (*sand, snow*) drift.

wehen ['ve:ən] *v/i, v/t* (h) *flag etc*: wave, *wind*: blow, *scent, tune, etc*: drift, waft.
'**Wehen** *pl* 🟥 pains, labo(u)r.
'**Wehgeschrei** *n a. fig.* wailing.
'**wehleidig** *adj* plaintive, whining: **sei nicht so ~!** don't be such a sissy!
'**Wehmut** *f* (-; *no pl*) melancholy, wistfulness, nostalgia. '**wehmütig** *adj* melancholy, wistful, nostalgic.
Wehr[1] [ve:r] *f* **sich zur ~ setzen** → **wehren** I.
Wehr[2] *n* (-[e]s; -e) weir, dam.
'**Wehr|beauftragte** *m* ombudsman (for the Armed Forces). **~bereich** *m* military district. **~bereichskom‚mando** *n* military district command. **~dienst** *m* (-[e]s; *no pl*) (**s-n ~ ableisten** do one's) military service. **~dienstverweigerer** *m* (-s; -) conscientious objector.
wehren ['ve:rən] (h) **I sich ~** defend o.s. (**gegen** against); **sich ~ gegen** a) resist, fight, b) refuse to accept. **II** *v/i* **den Anfängen ~** nip things in the bud.
'**Wehrersatzdienst** *m* (-[e]s; *no pl*) alternative service (for conscientious objectors).
'**wehrfähig** *adj* fit for military service.
'**wehrlos** *adj* defen/celess (*Am.* -se-), helpless. '**Wehrlosigkeit** *f* (-; *no pl*) defen/celessness (*Am.* -se-), helplessness.
'**Wehrmacht** *f* (-; *no pl*) *hist.* (German) Armed Forces, Wehrmacht.
'**Wehrpaß** *m* service record (book).
'**Wehrpflicht** *f* (-; *no pl*) (**allgemeine**) (universal) compulsory military service, (universal) conscription. '**wehrpflichtig** *adj* a) liable for military service, b) recruitable (*age*). '**Wehrpflichtige** *m* (-n; -n) a) person liable for military service, b) conscript, *Am.* draftee.
'**Wehrsold** *m* (service) pay.
'**Wehrübung** *f* reserve duty training.
Weib [vaip] *n* (-[e]s; -er) *a. contp.* woman.
'**Weibchen** *n* (-s; -) *zo.* female.
Weiber|feind ['vaibər-] *m* woman-hater. **~geschichten** *pl* F affairs, womanizing. **~held** *m contp.* ladykiller. **~regi‚ment** *n* petticoat government.
'**weibisch** ['vaibɪʃ] *adj* effeminate.
'**weiblich** *adj* female, feminine (*a. ling.*), womanly.
'**Weibsbild** *n* F *contp.* female, woman.
weich [vaiç] *adj* soft (*a. ling., phot. or fig.*), mellow (*voice, colo[u]r, etc*), ten-

der (*meat*), soft-boiled (*egg*): **~ machen** soften; **~ werden** give in, *fig. a.* give in.
'**Weiche**[1] *f* (-; -n) *anat.* flank, side.
'**Weiche**[2] *f* (-; -n) 🚆 points, *Am.* switch: *fig.* **die ~n stellen** set the course (**für** for).
weichen[1] ['vaiçən] *v/i* (wich, gewichen, sn) **1.** (*dat* to) *a. fig.* give way, yield. **2.** go (away): **j-m nicht von der Seite ~** not to leave s.o.'s side; **er wich und wankte nicht** he didn't budge.
'**weichen**[2] *v/i, v/t* (h) (*a. ~ lassen*) soak.
'**weichgekocht** *adj* soft-boiled (*egg*).
'**Weichheit** *f* (-; *no pl*) softness (*etc*, → **weich**).
'**weichherzig** *adj* soft-hearted.
'**Weichkäse** *m* soft cheese.
'**weichlich** *adj fig.* soft, effeminate.
'**Weichling** *m* (-s; -e) F softie, sissy.
'**Weich|macher** *m* (-s; -) 🟥, ⚙ softener. **~spüler** *m* (-s; -) (fabric) softener. **~teile** *pl anat.* soft parts. **~tier** *n* mollusc. **~zeichner** *m phot.* soft-focus lens.
Weide[1] ['vaidə] *f* (-; -n) 🌿 willow (tree).
'**Weide**[2] *f* (-; -n) (**auf der ~** at) pasture.
'**Weideland** *n* pastureage.
weiden (h) **I** *v/i* graze. **II** *v/t a.* **~ lassen** put out to pasture. **III sich ~ an** (*dat*) a) feast one's eyes on, b) gloat over.
'**Weidenbaum** *m* willow (tree).
'**Weidenkätzchen** *n* 🌿 catkin.
'**weidlich** ['vaitlɪç] *adv* thoroughly.
Weidmann ['vait-] *m* (-[e]s; ⸚er) huntsman. '**weidmännisch** [-mɛnɪʃ] **I** *adj* huntsmanlike. **II** *adv* in a huntsmanlike manner.
Weidmanns'heil *n* ~! good sport!
weigern ['vaigərn] **sich ~** (h) refuse.
'**Weigerung** *f* (-; -en) refusal.
'**Weihbischof** *m* suffragan (bishop).
Weihe ['vaiə] *f* (-; -n) **1.** *eccl.* a) consecration, b) ordination. **2.** *fig.* solemnity.
'**weihen** *v/t* (h) **1.** *eccl.* a) consecrate, b) ordain *as a priest.* **2.** (*dat* to) devote, dedicate (*both a.* **sich** o.s.): **dem Tode** (*or* **Untergang**) **geweiht** doomed.
'**Weihnacht** *f* (-; *no pl*) → '**Weihnachten** *pl* (**an ~, zu ~** at) Christmas (F Xmas); **Fröhliche ~!** Merry Christmas!
'**weihnachtlich** *adj* Christmas, F Christmassy.
'**Weihnachts|abend** *m* Christmas Eve. **~baum** *m* Christmas tree. **~einkäufe** *pl* Christmas shopping. **~feiertag** *m*

Christmas Day (*pl* holidays): **zweiter ~** Boxing Day. **~fest** *n* Christmas. **~geld** *n* Christmas bonus. **~lied** *n* Christmas carol. **~mann** *m* (-[e]s; ⸚er) **1.** Father Christmas, Santa Claus. **2.** F *contp.* dope. **~markt** *m* Christmas fair. **~zeit** *f* Christmas (season).

'Weihrauch *m* (-[e]s; *no pl*) incense.

'Weihwasser *n* (-s; *no pl*) holy water.

weil [vaɪl] *conj* **1.** because. **2.** since, as.

'Weilchen *n* (-s; *no pl*) **ein ~** a little while.

'Weile *f* (-; *no pl*) **e-e ~** a while, a time.

Wein [vaɪn] *m* (-[e]s; -e) **1.** ♀ vine. **2.** wine: *j-m reinen ~ einschenken* tell s.o. the truth. **~bau** *m* (-[e]s; *no pl*) wine growing, viticulture. **~bauer** *m* wine grower. **~baugebiet** *n* wine growing area. **~beere** *f* grape. **~berg** *m* vineyard. **~bergschnecke** *f* (edible) snail. **~blatt** *n* vine leaf. **~brand** *m* (-[e]s; ⸚e) brandy.

weinen ['vaɪnən] *v/i, v/t* (h) weep (*um* over), cry: *zum ♀ bringen* make s.o. cry; *es ist zum ♀* it's a (crying) shame.

weinerlich ['vaɪnərlɪç] *adj* tearful, F weepy, whining (*voice, child, etc*).

'Wein|essig *m* wine vinegar. **~faß** *n* wine cask. **~flasche** *f* wine bottle. **~geist** *m* spirit(s) of wine. **~glas** *n* wine glass. **~gut** *n* wine-growing estate. **~händler** *m* wine merchant. **~handlung** *f* wine shop. **~karte** *f* wine list. **~keller** *m* wine cellar. **~kelter** *f* wine press. **~kenner** *m* wine connoisseur.

'Weinkrampf *m* crying fit.

'Wein|lese *f* grape harvest. **~lo,kal** *n* wine tavern. **~probe** *f* wine tasting. **♀rot** *adj* wine-red. **~stock** *m* ♀ vine. **~stube** *f* wine tavern. **~traube** *f* a) bunch of grapes, b) *pl* grapes.

weise ['vaɪzə] *adj* wise.

'Weise¹ *m* (-n; -n) wise man, sage.

'Weise² *f* (-; -n) **1.** way: *auf diese ~* (in) this way; *auf jede ~* in every way; *auf die gleiche ~* the same way; *auf die e-e oder andere ~* (in) one way or another; *auf m-e (s-e) ~* my (his) way; *in k-r ~* in no way; *jeder auf s-e ~* everyone after his own fashion. **2.** ♪ tune.

weisen ['vaɪzən] (wies, gewiesen, h) **I** *v/t* **1.** *j-m den Weg ~* show s.o. the way. **2.** *j-n von der Schule ~* expel s.o. (from school). **3.** *et.* (*weit*) *von sich ~* repudiate s.th. (emphatically). **II** *v/i* → *zeigen* II.

'Weisheit *f* (-; -en) wisdom: *mit s-r ~ am Ende sein* be at one's wits' end.

'Weisheitszahn *m* wisdom tooth.

'weismachen *v/t* (*sep*, h) *j-m ~, daß* make s.o. believe that; *mir kannst du nichts ~!* you can't fool me!; *laß dir nichts ~!* don't be fooled!

weiß [vaɪs] *adj* **1.** white: *~ machen* whiten; *~ werden* go white; *~ gekleidet* dressed in white. **2.** *fig.* blank.

Weiß *n* (-[es]; -) *a.* chess *etc*: white.

'weissagen *v/t* (*insep*, h) prophesy, foretell. **'Weissager** *m* (-s; -) prophet. **'Weissagerin** *f* (-; -nen) prophetess. **'Weissagung** *f* (-; -en) prophecy.

'Weiß|blech *n* tinplate. **♀blond** *adj* silver-blond(e). **~brot** *n* white bread. **~buch** *n pol.* white paper (*Am.* book). **~dorn** *m* (-[e]s; -e) ♀ whitethorn.

'Weiße *m, f* (-n; -n) white man (woman): *die ~n* the whites, the white man.

weißen ['vaɪsən] *v/t* (h) **1.** whiten. **2.** whitewash.

'weißglühend *adj* white-hot.

'Weißglut *f* (-; *no pl*) white heat: F *j-n zur ~ bringen* make s.o. see red.

'weißhaarig *adj* white-haired.

'Weiß|kohl *m*, **~kraut** *n* white cabbage. **'weißlich** *adj* whitish.

'Weißwein *m* white wine.

'Weisung *f* (-; -en) instruction, order(s). **'Weisungs|befugnis** *f* authority to issue directives. **♀gemäß** *adv* as directed.

weit [vaɪt] **I** *adj* **1.** a) wide, a full (*skirt etc*) b) a. ⊙ loose. **2.** wide, extensive, vast, immense. **3.** *fig.* broad (*concept etc*): *im ~esten Sinne* in the widest sense. **4.** long: *auf ~e (or aus ~er) Entfernung* at a great distance. **II** *adv* **5.** wide(ly): *~ offen* wide open. **6.** far: *sie ist ~ über 60* she is well over sixty; *er ist ~ gereist* he has got around a good deal; *~ (or bei ~em) das beste* by far the best; *bei ~em nicht so gut* not nearly so good; *~ gefehlt!* far from it!; F *es ist nicht ~ her mit ihm* he is not up to much; *es ~ bringen* (*im Leben*) go far; *zu ~ gehen* go too far; *das geht zu ~* that's going too far; *ich bin so ~* I'm ready; *wie ~ bist du?* how far have you got?; *wenn es so ~ ist* when the time comes; → *entfernt, kommen* 1, 10.

'weit'ab *adv* far away (*von* from).

'weit'aus *adv* far *better etc*.

'**Weitblick** *m* (-[e]s; *no pl*) farsightedness.
'**weitblickend** *adj* farsighted, farseeing.
'**Weite**[1] *f* (-; -n) **1.** *a.* ⊛ a) width, b) breadth, c) size, extent: → *licht* **3. 2.** vastness, expanse. **3.** *sports*: distance.
'**Weite**[2]: *das* ~ *suchen* take to one's heels.
weiten ['vaɪtən] *v/t* (*a. sich* ~) (h) widen (*a. fig.*), stretch (*shoes etc*).
weiter ['vaɪtər] **I** *comp of* **weit. II** *adj* further: *nach e-r* ~*en Woche* after another week. **III** *adv* ~! go on!; *halt, nicht* ~! stop, no further!; *immer* ~ on and on; *nichts* (*niemand*) ~ nothing (no one) else; *und so* ~ and so on (*abbr.* etc); *das ist nicht* ~ *schlimm* that's no tragedy; *das störte sie* ~ *nicht* that didn't really bother her; → *weiterhin.*
'**weiter|arbeiten** *v/i* (*sep*, h) go on working. ~**befördern** *v/t* (*sep*, h) forward, send on. ~**bestehen** → *fortbestehen.*
'**weiterbilden** → *fortbilden.*
'**Weiterbildung** *f* → *Fortbildung.*
'**weiterbringen** *v/t* (*irr sep*, -ge-, h, → *bringen*) *das bringt mich* (*uns etc*) *nicht weiter* that's not much help.
'**Weitere, das** (-n) the rest: *bis auf weiteres* for the time being, *adm.* until further notice; *ohne weiteres* without further ado, easily.
'**weiter|empfehlen** *v/t* (*irr*, *sep*, h, → *empfehlen*) recommend (to others). ~**entwickeln** *v/t* (*a. sich* ~) (*sep*, h) develop (further). ~**erzählen** *v/t* (*sep*, h) tell others, repeat. ~**fahren** *v/i* (*irr*, *sep*, -ge-, sn, → *fahren*) go on, drive on. ~**führen** *v/t* (*sep*, h) continue, carry on. ~**geben** *v/t* (*irr*, *sep*, -ge-, h, → *geben*) *et.* ~ pass s.th. on. ~**gehen** *v/i* (*irr*, *sep*, -ge-, sn, → *gehen*) **1.** go on, walk on. **2.** *fig.* go on, continue: *das kann so nicht* ~*!* things can't go on like this!
'**weiter|hin I** *adv* ~ *et. tun* continue doing (*or* to do) s.th., go on doing s.th. **II** *conj* further(more), moreover.
'**weiter|kämpfen** *v/i* (*sep*, h) continue fighting. ~**kommen** *v/i* (*irr*, *sep*, -ge-, sn, → *kommen*) get on, *fig. a.* make headway, get somewhere: *nicht* ~ *a.* be stuck; *so kommen wir nicht weiter* this won't get us any further. ~**laufen** *v/i* (*irr*, *sep*, -ge-, sn, → *laufen*) payment *etc*: be continued. ~**leben** *v/i* (*sep*, h) live on, *fig. a.* survive. ~**leiten** *v/t* (*sep*,

h) (*an acc* to) pass s.th. on, refer. ~**lesen** *v/t*, *v/i* (*irr*, *sep*, -ge-, h, → *lesen*) go on (reading), continue to read. ~**machen** *v/i*, *v/t* (*sep*, h) continue, carry (*or* go) on (with). ~**sagen** *v/t* (*sep*, h) *et.* ~ pass s.th. on.
'**Weiterungen** *pl* complications.
'**weiterverarbeiten** *v/t* (*sep*, h) process.
'**Weiterverarbeitung** *f* (-; *no pl*) processing.
'**Weiterverkauf** *m* (-[e]s; *no pl*) resale.
'**weiterverkaufen** *v/t* (*sep*, h) resell.
'**weitgehend I** *adj* extensive, far-reaching, *a.* wide (*powers etc*): *es herrschte* ~*e Übereinstimmung* there was a large degree of consent. **II** *adv* largely, to a great extent.
'**weitgereist** *adj* widely travel(l)ed.
'**weit|her** *adv* from afar.
'**weit|hergeholt** *adj* *fig.* far-fetched.
'**weit|hin** *adv* **1.** far. **2.** to a large extent.
'**weitläufig I** *adj* **1.** extensive, vast, spacious. **2.** detailed, *contp.* long-winded. **3.** distant (*relatives*). **II** *adv* **4.** at great length. **5.** ~ *verwandt* distantly related.
'**weitreichend** *adj* **1.** far-reaching. **2.** ✕ long-range.
'**weitschweifig** [-'ʃvaɪfɪç] *adj* long-winded.
'**weitsichtig** *adj* long-sighted, *a. fig.* farsighted. '**Weitsichtigkeit** *f* (-; *no pl*) long-sightedness, *a. fig.* farsightedness.
'**Weitspringer(in** *f*) *m* longjumper, *Am.* broadjumper. '**Weitsprung** *m* (-[e]s; *no pl*) long (*Am.* broad) jump.
'**weit|verbreitet** *adj* widespread, common. ~**verzweigt** *adj* widely ramified.
'**Weitwinkelobjek,tiv** *n* wide-angle lens.
Weizen ['vaɪtsən] *m* (-s; -) wheat: *fig. sein* ~ *blüht* he is in clover.
welch [vɛlç] **I** *interrog pron* what, which: ~*er* (*von beiden*)? which (of the two)?; ~ *ein Anblick!* what a sight! **II** *rel pron* who, which, that. **III** *indef pron* some, any: *have you got money? ja, ich habe* ~*es* yes, I have some; *brauchen Sie* ~*es?* do you need any?
welk [vɛlk] *adj* withered, faded: ~*e Haut* wrinkled skin. '**welken** *v/i* (sn) wither.
'**Wellblech** *n* corrugated iron.
Welle ['vɛlə] *f* (-; -n) **1.** *a. fig.* wave: *fig.* (*hohe*) ~*n schlagen* cause quite a stir. **2.** ⊛ shaft. **3.** *gym.* circle.

'wellen (h) **I** *v/t* wave (*hair*). **II sich ~ hair**: be (*or* go) wavy.

'Wellen|bad *n* swimming pool with artificially produced waves. **~band** *n* ♫ wave band. **~bereich** *m* radio: wave range. **~brecher** *m* ♣ breakwater.

'wellenförmig *adj* wavy.

'Wellen|länge *f* (F *fig.* **die gleiche ~ haben** be on the same) wavelength. **~linie** *f* wavy line. **~reiten** *n* surfing.

'Wellensittich *m* zo. budgerigar.

wellig ['vɛlɪç] *adj* wavy.

'Wellpappe *f* corrugated board.

Welpe ['vɛlpə] *m* (-n; -n) zo. puppy, pup.

Welt [vɛlt] *f* (-; -en) world: **die große ~** a) the big wide world, b) high society; **alle ~** everybody; **auf der ganzen ~** all over the world; **der längste Fluß der ~** the longest river in the world, the world's longest river; **was in aller ~ ...?** what on earth ...?; **nicht um alles in der ~** not on your life; **aus der ~ schaffen** a) get rid of, b) settle (*problem etc*); **in die ~ setzen** a) put *children* into the world, b) start (*rumo[u]r*); **zur ~ bringen** give birth to; **zur ~ kommen** be born.

'Welt|all *n* (-s; *no pl*) universe. **2anschaulich** *adj* ideological. **~anschauung** *f* philosophy (of life), world view, *a.* ideology. **~ausstellung** *f* world fair. **~bank** *f* (-; *no pl*) World Bank.

'welt|bekannt, ~berühmt *adj* world-famous. **~bewegend** *adj* worldshaking: *iro.* **nichts Weltbewegendes** nothing to write home about.

'Weltbild *n* world view.

'Weltbürger(in *f*) *m* cosmopolitan.

'Weltbummler(in *f*) *m* globetrotter.

'Welterfolg *m* worldwide success.

Weltergewicht ['vɛltər-] *n* boxing: welterweight.

'Welt|firma *f* world-renowned firm. **2fremd** *adj* naive, unworldly, ivory-towered (*scholar etc*). **~frieden** *m* world peace. **~geschichte** *f* (-; *no pl*) world history. **2gewandt** *adj* urbane. **~handel** *m* international trade. **~herrschaft** *f* (-; *no pl*) world domination. **~karte** *f* map of the world. **~krieg** *m* world war: **der Zweite ~** World War II, the Second World War. **~kugel** *f* globe. **~lage** *f* (-; *no pl*) international situation.

'weltlich *adj* **1.** worldly. **2.** secular.

'Weltliteratur *f* world literature.

'Weltmacht *f* world power.

'weltmännisch [-mɛnɪʃ] *adj* man-of-the--world.

'Welt|markt *m* world market. **~meer** *n* ocean. **~meister(in** *f*) *m* world champion. **~meisterschaft** *f* world championship, *esp.* soccer: World Cup. **2offen** *adj* open-minded. **~öffentlichkeit** *f* world public. **~poli₁tik** *f* international (*or* world) politics. **~presse** *f* international press. **~rangliste** *f* world ranking list: **er steht an dritter Stelle der ~** he is ranked third in the world. **~raum** *m* (-[e]s; *no pl*) (outer) space. **~raum... → Raum...** **~reich** *n* empire. **~reise** *f* world trip. **~reisende** *m, f* globetrotter. **~re₁kord** *m* world record. **~re₁kordinhaber(in** *f*) *m*, **~re₁kordler(in** *f*) *m* world-record holder. **~religi₁on** *f* world religion. **~ruf** *m* (**von ~** of) worldwide renown. **~schmerz** *m* (-es; *no pl*) world-weariness. **~sicherheitsrat** *m* U.N. Security Council. **~sprache** *f* universal language. **~stadt** *f* metropolis. **~stadt...,** **2städtisch** *adj* metropolitan. **~untergang** *m* end of the world. **~uraufführung** *f* world première. **~verbesserer** *m* (-s; -) world changer. **~währungsfonds** *m* International Monetary Fund. **2weit** *adj* worldwide, global. **~wirtschaft** *f* (-; *no pl*) world economy. **~wirtschaftskrise** *f* worldwide economic crisis. **~wunder** *n* wonder of the world.

wem [ve:m] *pron* (to) whom: **von ~** of whom, by whom.

wen [ve:n] *pron* whom, F who.

Wende ['vɛndə] *f* (-; -n) **1.** *a.* sports: turn. **2.** change, *pol.* change of power. **~hals** *m* **1.** zo. wryneck. **2.** *pol. contp.* quick-change artist. **~kreis** *m* **1.** geogr. tropic. **2.** mot. turning circle.

Wendeltreppe ['vɛndəl-] *f* spiral staircase.

wenden¹ ['vɛndən] (h) **I** *v/t* a) turn, b) turn over (*page, roast, etc*). **II** *v/i* turn (around), sports: turn: **bitte ~!** please turn over (*abbr.* p.t.o.). **III** *sich zum Guten ~** take a turn for the better.

'wenden² (wandte, gewandt, h) **I** *v/t* **~ an** (*acc*) spend *money* on, devote *time etc* to. **II sich ~** turn (**nach** to, **gegen** on, against); **sich ~ gegen** oppose; **sich**

an j-n ~ ask (*or* see, consult, contact) s.o.; *sich um Rat (Hilfe) an j-n* ~ turn to s.o. for advice (help).

'**Wendepunkt** *m a. fig.* turning point.

wendig ['vɛndɪç] *adj* **1.** manoeuvrable, *Am.* maneuverable. **2.** nimble, agile.

'**Wendigkeit** *f* (-; *no pl*) **1.** manoeuvrability, *Am.* maneuverability. **2.** agility.

'**Wendung** *f* (-; -en) **1.** turn: *fig.* *e-e unerwartete* ~ *nehmen* take an unexpected turn. **2.** expression, phrase.

wenig ['ve:nɪç] *indef pron and adv* little, not much: *~e pl* few, not many, *su.* few (people); *nur ~e* only few; (*nur*) *einige ~e* (only) a few; *~er* less, *Å* minus; *immer ~er* less and less; *~er als* less than; *nicht ~er als* no less than, *pl* no fewer than; *nichts ~er als* anything but; *~er werden* decrease; *das ~e* the little; *das ~ste* the least; *am ~sten* least of all; *ein ~* a little; *nicht ~* quite a lot; *~ beliebt* not very popular; *~ bekannt* little known; *~ begeistert* (rather) unenthusiastic; *~ hilfreich* unhelpful.

'**Wenigkeit** *f* *F m-e ~* yours truly.

'**wenigstens** *adv* at least: *wenn sie ~ zuhörte* if only she would listen.

wenn [vɛn] *conj* **1.** a) when, b) whenever, c) as soon as: *~ man ihn so reden hört* to hear him (talk). **2.** if: *~ sie doch* (*or nur*) *käme* if only she would come; *~ du nicht bezahlst* unless you pay; *~ ich das gewußt hätte* had I (but) known. **3.** *~ auch, und* ~ even if; → *schon* 5.

Wenn *n ohne ~ und Aber* no ifs or buts.

wer [ve:r] **I** *interrog pron* who, which: *~ von euch?* which of you? **II** *rel pron* who, which: ~ (*auch immer*) whoever. **III** *indef pron* a) who, *adm.* any person who, b) F somebody, anybody.

'**Werbe**|ab,**teilung** *f* publicity department. *~***agen,tur** *f* advertising agency. *~***akti,on** *f* → *Werbekampagne*. *~***fachmann** *m* advertising expert. *~***fernsehen** *n* **1.** commercial television. **2.** television (*or* TV) commercials. *~***film** *m* promotion(al) film. *~***funk** *m* **1.** commercial radio. **2.** radio ads (*Am.* commercials). *~***geschenk** *n* promotional gift. *~***graphik** *f* commercial art. *~***graphiker** *m* commercial artist. *~***kam,pagne** *f* publicity (*or* advertising) campaign. *~***kosten** *pl* advertising costs.

*~***leiter** *m* publicity manager. *~***mittel** *pl* advertising media (*or* funds).

werben ['vɛrbən] (warb, geworben, h) **I** *v/t* **1.** enlist (*members*), *a.* recruit (*workers etc*), canvass, attract (*votes etc*): *j-n für e-e Sache* ~ win s.o. over to a cause. **II** *v/i* **2.** ~ *für* advertise, promote, F plug, *pol.* campaign (*or* canvass) for. **3.** ~ *um a. fig.* court, woo.

'**Werbe**|pro,**spekt** *m* publicity brochure. *~***psycholo,gie** *f* psychology of advertising. *~***spot** *m* commercial (spot). spot. *~***spruch** *m* (advertising) slogan. *~***texter** *m* copywriter. *~***trommel** *f* die *~ rühren* → *werben* 2.

'**werbewirksam** *adj* effective.

Werbung (-; *no pl*) *f* **1.** enlisting (*etc,* → *werben* 1), recruitment. **2.** advertising, publicity: *das ist e-e gute ~ für ...* that is good publicity for ... **3.** → *Werbeabteilung*. '**Werbungskosten** *pl* *taxation*: professional outlays.

'**Werdegang** *m* (-[e]s; *no pl*) development, *a. fig. or* ☉ history, *of person*: professional background, *a.* career.

werden ['ve:rdən] (wurde, geworden, sn) **I** *v/i* a) become, get, grow, b) turn, go (*sour etc*), turn out (*well etc*): *blaß ~* turn pale; *blind (verrückt) ~* go blind (mad); *böse ~* get angry; *gesund ~* get well; *wie sind die Fotos geworden?* how have the photos turned out?; *was will er (einmal) ~?* what does he want to be?; *was soll nun ~?* what are we going to do now?; *was ist aus ihm geworden?* what has become of him?; *daraus wird nichts!* a) nothing will come of it, b) nothing doing!; F *es wird schon (wieder) ~!* it will be all right!; F *wird's bald?* get a move on!; → *Mutter*[1]. **II** *v/aux* *ich werde fahren* I will (*or* I'll) drive, I am going to drive; *es wird gleich regnen* it's going to rain; *es ist uns gesagt worden* we have been told; *geliebt ~* be loved; *gebaut ~* be (being) built.

'**Werden** *n* (-s) development, growth, progress: *im ~ sein* be in the making.

werfen ['vɛrfən] (warf, geworfen, h) **I** *v/t* **1.** throw (*a. fig. or zo.*), cast (*a. anchor, glance, shadow*): (*v/i mit*) *a.* ~ *nach* throw s.th. at; *Bomben ~* drop bombs; → *Blick* 1, *Handtuch etc.* **II** *v/i* **2.** throw. **3.** → *schmeißen* 5. **III** *sich ~* **4.**

⊗ buckle, *wood:* warp. **5. sich ~ auf** (*acc*) throw o.s. on (*fig.* into); → *Hals.*

'**Werfer** *m* (-s; -), '**Werferin** *f* (-; -nen) *sports:* thrower.

Werft [vɛrft] *f* (-; -en) **1.** shipyard. **2.** ✈ hangar. **~arbeiter** *m* docker.

Werg [vɛrk] *n* (-[e]s; *no pl*) tow.

Werk [vɛrk] *n* (-[e]s; -e) **1.** work, *of writer etc:* a. works, *a.* deed: **am ~ sein** be at work; **ans ~ gehen** set to work; **ein gutes ~ tun** do a good deed; **vorsichtig zu ~e gehen** go about it cautiously; *b.s.* **es war sein ~** it was his work (*or* doing). **2.** factory, works, plant: ⚙ **ab ~** ex works. **3.** ⊗ works, mechanism.

'**Werk...** works ..., factory ... **~angehörige** *m, f* (-n; -n) (works) employee. **~arzt** *m* works doctor. **~bank** *f* (-; ⁓e) (work)bench. **≗eigen** *adj* works ..., company(-owned).

werkeln ['vɛrkəln] *v/i* (h) potter about.

werken ['vɛrkən] *v/i* (h) work, *ped.* do handicrafts.

'**Werken** *n* (-s) *ped.* handicrafts.

'**Werkleiter** *m* works manager.

'**Werkmeister** *m* foreman.

'**Werks...** → *Werk...*

'**Werk|schutz** *m* Security. **~spio nage** *f* industrial espionage. **~statt** *f* (-; ⁓en) workshop. **~stoff** *m* material. **~stück** *n* workpiece. **~tag** *m* workday, working day. **≗tags** *adv* on weekdays, during the week. **≗tätig** *adj* working. **~tätige** *m, f* (-n; -n) working person: **die ~n** the working population. **~unterricht** *m* *ped.* handicrafts.

'**Werkzeug** *n* (-[e]s; -e) tool (*a. fig.*), *coll.* tools. **~kasten** *m* tool box, tool kit. **~macher** *m* toolmaker. **~ma schine** *f* machine tool. **~tasche** *f* tool bag.

Wermut ['ve:rmu:t] *m* (-[e]s; *no pl*) **1.** ⚘ wormwood. **2.** vermouth. '**Wermutstropfen** *m* *fig.* drop of bitterness.

wert [ve:rt] *adj* worth: **et. ~ sein** be worth s.th.; **e-n Versuch (e-e Reise) ~** worth a try (a trip); **e-r Sache ~ sein** be worthy of s.th.; **viel ~** worth a lot, (very) valuable; **nicht viel ~** not up to much; **nichts ~** worthless, no good; **~ getan zu werden** worth doing; **das ist es (mir) nicht ~** it's not worth it.

Wert *m* (-[e]s; -e) **1.** a) value (*a.* ⚗, ⚕, *philos.*, *phys.*, ⊗), *fig. a.* merit(s), b) importance, c) F use: **im ~(e) von** to the

value of; **Waren im ~(e) von 400 Dollar** 400 dollars worth of goods; **im ~ sin ken (steigen)** lose (go up) in value; **e-r Sache großen ~ beimessen** attach great importance to s.th.; (**großen**) **~ legen auf** (*acc*) set (great) store by; **k-n besonderen ~ legen auf** (*acc*) not to care much for; *fig.* **sich unter ~ verkau fen** sell o.s. short; F **es hat k-n ~** that's no use! **2. ~e** *pl* a) data, readings, levels, b) ⯁ assets, securities, stocks.

'**Wertangabe** *f* **1.** declaration of value. **2.** declared value.

'**Wertarbeit** *f* (high-class) workmanship.

'**wertbeständig** *adj* stable, of stable (*fig.* lasting) value.

werten ['ve:rtən] *v/t* (h) assess, judge, *a. sports:* rate (**als Erfolg** as a success).

'**wertfrei** *adj and adv* value-free.

'**Wertgegenstand** *m* article of value, *pl* valuables.

Wertigkeit ['ve:rtɪç-] *f* (-; -en) ⚗ valency.

'**wertlos** *adj* worthless (*a. fig.*), valueless, useless, *pred* (of) no use, no good.

'**Wertlosigkeit** *f* (-; *no pl*) worthlessness.

'**Wertmaßstab** *m* standard (of value).

'**Wertminderung** *f* depreciation.

'**Wertpa piere** *pl* securities.

'**Wertsachen** *pl* valuables.

'**Wertsendung** *f* ✉ registered item.

'**Wertsteigerung** *f* ⯁ increase in value.

'**Wertung** *f* (-; -en) assessment, *a. sports:* rating, *sports:* score, points.

'**Werturteil** *n* value judgement.

'**Wertverlust** *m* ⯁ loss of value.

'**wertvoll** *adj* valuable.

'**Wertvorstellungen** *pl* values.

'**Wertzeichen** *n* (postage) stamp.

'**Wertzuwachs** *m* ⯁ increase in value.

Wesen ['ve:zən] *n* (-s; -) **1.** being, crea ture. **2.** *no pl* a) *philos.* essence, b) character, nature: **ihr heiteres ~** her cheerful disposition. **3.** F **viel ~s von et. machen** make a great fuss about s.th.

'**Wesensart** *f* (-; *no pl*) nature, character.

'**wesensfremd** *adj* alien (*dat* to).

'**Wesenszug** *m* (characteristic) trait.

wesentlich ['ve:zəntlɪç] **I** *adj* essential (**für** to), substantial: **das Wesentliche** the essence, the essential point; **nichts Wesentliches** nothing (very) impor tant; **im ~en** essentially, on the whole; **der ~e Inhalt** the substance (*of book*

659

wichtigtuerisch

etc). **II** *adv* essentially, considerably, a great deal, much: ~ **besser** far better.
weshalb [vɛs'halp] **I** *interrog pron* why. **II** *conj* and so, which is why.
Wespe ['vɛspə] *f* (-; -n) *zo.* wasp.
'**Wespennest** *n* wasps' nest: *fig.* **in ein ~ stechen** stir up a hornet's nest.
'**Wespenstich** *m* wasp sting.
wessen ['vɛsən] *interrog pron* **1.** *gen of* **wer**: whose. **2.** *gen of was*: ~ **beschuldigt man ihn?** what is he accused of?
West [vɛst] *m invar* **1.** West. **2.** west wind.
'**westdeutsch** *adj*, '**Westdeutsche** *m, f* (-n; -n) West German.
Weste ['vɛstə] *f* (-; -n) waistcoat, *Am.* vest: F *fig.* **e-e weiße ~ haben** have a clean record.
Westen ['vɛstən] *m* (-s; *no pl*) west, *of country*: West, *of town*: *a.* West End, *pol.* the West: **von ~** from the west; **nach ~** west(wards).
'**Westentasche** *f* waistcoat (*Am.* vest) pocket: F *et. wie s-e ~ kennen* know s.th. like the back of one's hand.
Westfale [vɛst'faːlə] *m* (-n; -n), **Westfälin** [vɛst'fɛːlɪn] *f* (-; -nen), **westfälisch** [vɛst'fɛːlɪʃ] *adj* Westphalian.
'**westlich** **I** *adj* western, west(erly) (*wind, direction*), *pol.* West(ern). **II** *adv* (to the) west (*von* of). **III** *prep* (*gen*) (to the) west of.
'**Westmächte** *pl pol.* Western powers.
'**westwärts** *adv* west(wards).
'**Westwind** *m* west wind.
'**Wettannahme** *f* betting office.
Wettbewerb ['vɛtbəvɛrp] *m* (-[e]s; -e) competition, *sports: a.* event: ✝ **freier (unlauterer) ~** free (unfair) competition; *in ~ stehen* be competing (*mit* with). '**Wettbewerber** *m* competitor.
'**wettbewerbsfähig** *adj* competitive.
'**Wettbü,ro** *n* betting office.
Wette ['vɛtə] *f* (-; -n) bet: *e-e ~ eingehen* (*or abschließen*) make a bet; *was gilt die ~?* what do you bet?; *mit j-m um die ~ laufen* (*or fahren*) race s.o.
'**Wetteifer** *m* competition, rivalry.
'**wetteifern** *v/i* (*insep*, ge-, h) (*mit* with, *um* for) vie, compete.
wetten ['vɛtən] *v/t*, *v/i* (h) bet: (*mit j-m*) *um et. ~* bet (s.o.) s.th.; *ich wette zehn zu eins, daß* I bet you ten to one that; ~ *auf* (*acc*) bet on, put one's money on, back (*horse*); F ~, *daß ...?* want to bet?

Wetter¹ ['vɛtər] *m* (-s; -) better.
'**Wetter²** *n* (-s; -) **1.** weather, *a.* storm: *bei diesem ~* in a weather like this; → **Wind. 2.** ⚒ **schlagende ~** firedamp.
'**Wetter|amt** *n* meteorological office. **~aussichten** *pl* weather outlook. **~bedingungen** *pl* weather conditions. **~bericht** *m* weather report. **~dienst** *m* weather service. **~fahne** *f* weather vane. **2fest** *adj* weatherproof. **~frosch** *m humor.* weatherman.
'**wetterfühlig** [-fy:lɪç] *adj* ~ *sein* be sensitive to changes in the weather.
'**Wetter|hahn** *m* weathercock. **2hart** *adj* weather-beaten. **~karte** *f* weather map. **~kunde** *f* (-; *no pl*) meteorology. **~lage** *f* weather situation. **~leuchten** *n* (-s) sheet lightning.
wettern ['vɛtərn] *v/i* (h) F storm (*gegen* at).
'**Wetter|satel,lit** *m* weather satellite. **~seite** *f* weather side. **~stati,on** *f* weather station. **~sturz** *m* sudden drop in temperature. **~umschwung** *m* (sudden) change in weather. **~vor,hersage** *f* (-; -n) weather forecast.
'**wetterwendisch** [-vɛndɪʃ] *adj* fickle.
'**Wett|fahrt** *f* race. **~kampf** *m* contest, competition, *sports: a.* event. **~kämpfer(in** *f*) *m* competitor, contestant. **~lauf** *m* race (*fig. mit der Zeit* against time). **~läufer(in** *f*) *m* runner.
'**wettmachen** *v/t* (*sep*, h) make up for.
'**Wett|rennen** *n a. fig.* race. **~rüsten** *n* arms race. **~streit** *m* contest.
wetzen ['vɛtsən] **I** *v/t* (h) sharpen, whet. **II** *v/i* (sn) F scoot.
Whisky ['vɪski] *m* (-s; -s) whisky.
wich [vɪç] *pret of* **weichen**.
wichsen ['vɪksən] (h) **I** *v/t* polish. **II** *v/i* V wank, jerk off.
Wichtel ['vɪçtəl] *m* (-s; -), '**Wichtelmännchen** *n* brownie, goblin.
wichtig ['vɪçtɪç] *adj* important (*für j-n* to s.o., *für et.* for s.th.): ~ *tun, sich ~ machen* be self-important; *Wichtigeres zu tun haben* have more important things to do; *das Wichtigste* the most important thing; *das Wichtigste zuerst!* first things first.
'**Wichtigkeit** *f* (-; *no pl*) importance.
'**Wichtigtuer** *m* F pompous ass.
Wichtigtue'rei *f* (-; *no pl*) F pomposity.
'**wichtigtuerisch** *adj* pompous.

Wicke ['vɪkə] *f* (-; -n) ❧ vetch, sweet pea.
Wickel ['vɪkəl] *m* (-s; -) 🎋 compress. **~kom‚mode** *f* (baby's) changing table.
wickeln ['vɪkəln] (h) **I** *v/t* **1.** (*um* [a]round) wind, tie, wrap: *et. in Papier* **~** wrap s.th. (up) in paper; → *Finger*. **2.** *ein Baby* **~** change a baby's nappies (*Am.* diapers). **II** *sich* **~** *um* wind (*or* coil) itself around; *sich in e-e Decke* **~** wrap o.s. up in a blanket.
Wickler ['vɪklər] *m* (-s; -) curler.
'Wicklung *f* (-; -en) ⚙ winding.
Widder ['vɪdər] *m* (-s; -) **1.** *zo.* ram. **2.** *astr.* (*er ist* [*ein*] **~** he is [an]) Aries.
wider ['vi:dər] *prep* against, contrary to: **~** *Erwarten* contrary to expectation(s); → *Für, Wille*. **wider'fahren** *v/i* (*irr, insep, no* -ge-, sn, → *fahren*) *j-m* **~** happen to s.o.; *j-m Gerechtigkeit* **~** *lassen* a) do justice to s.o., b) give s.o. his due.
'Widerhaken *m* (-s; -) barb.
'Widerhall *m* (-[e]s; -e) echo, *fig. a.* resonance: *k-n* **~** *finden* meet with no response. **'widerhallen** *v/i* (*sep*, h) (*von* with) echo, resound.
widerlegbar [-'le:kba:r] *adj* refutable.
wider'legen *v/t* (*insep, no* -ge-, h) refute.
Wider'legung *f* (-; -en) refutation.
'widerlich *adj* revolting, disgusting.
'widerna‚türlich *adj* perverse.
'widerrechtlich *adj* illegal, unlawful: **~** *betreten* trespass (up)on; *sich et.* **~** *aneignen* misappropriate s.th.
'Widerrede *f* (-; -n) contradiction(s), protest: *k-e* **~!** no argument!
'Widerruf *m* (-[e]s; -e) revocation, withdrawal: (*bis*) *auf* **~** until revoked.
wider'rufen *v/t* (*irr, insep, no* -ge-, h, → *rufen*) revoke, withdraw.
'Widersacher [-zaxər] *m* (-s; -) adversary, opponent.
'Widerschein *m* reflection.
wider'setzen: *sich* **~** (*insep, no* -ge-, h) put up resistance, (*dat*) oppose (*s.th., s.o.*). **wider'setzlich** *adj* recalcitrant.
'widersinnig *adj* absurd.
'widerspenstig [-'ʃpɛnstɪç] *adj* rebellious, unruly (*a. fig.* hair).
'Widerspenstigkeit *f* (-; *no pl*) rebelliousness, *a. fig.* unruliness.
'widerspiegeln (*sep*, h) **I** *v/t a. fig.* reflect. **II** *sich* **~** be reflected.
wider'sprechen *v/i* (*irr, insep, no* -ge-, h, → *sprechen*) contradict (*j-m* s.o., *sich*

o.s.), (*dat*) oppose (*suggestion etc*): *sich* (*or einander*) **~** be contradictory, conflict. **'Widerspruch** *m* (-[e]s; **~**e) a) contradiction (*in sich* in terms), b) protest, opposition: *im* **~** *zu* in contradiction to; *im* **~** *stehen zu* be inconsistent with, contradict; *auf* **~** *stoßen* meet with protest (*bei* from). **'widersprüchlich** [-'ʃpryçlɪç] *adj* contradictory, inconsistent, conflicting (*feelings*).
'Widerspruchsgeist *m* (-[e]s; *no pl*) spirit of contradiction.
'widerspruchslos *adj und adv* without contradiction (*or* protest).
'Widerstand *m* (-[e]s; **~**e) **1.** *no pl* (*gegen* to) resistance, opposition: **~** *leisten* offer resistance, fight back; *auf* (*heftigen*) **~** *stoßen* meet with (stiff) opposition; *den* **~** *aufgeben* give in; *den Weg des geringsten* **~***es wählen* take the line of least resistance. **2.** ⚡ resistor.
'Widerstands|bewegung *f pol.* resistance movement. **⍾fähig** *adj* resistant (*gegen* to), *a.* ⚙ robust. **~fähigkeit** *f* (-; *no pl*) resistance (*gegen* to), robustness. **~kämpfer(in** *f*) *m* resistance fighter. **~kraft** *f* (powers of) resistance.
'widerstandslos *adv* without resistance.
wider'stehen *v/i* (*irr, insep, no* -ge-, h → *stehen*) (*dat*) resist (*s.o., s.th.*).
wider'streben *v/i* (*insep, no* -ge-, h) be repugnant (*dat* to): *es widerstrebt mir zu inf* I hate to *inf*. **Wider'streben** *n* (-s) reluctance. **wider'strebend** *adv* reluctantly.
'Widerstreit *m* conflict. **'widerstreitend** *adj* conflicting (*feelings etc*).
'widerwärtig [-vɛrtɪç] *adj* repulsive, disgusting, F nasty.
'Widerwille *m* (-n; *no pl*) (*gegen* to) aversion (to), disgust (at). **'widerwillig** *adj* unwilling, reluctant.
widmen ['vɪtmən] (h) (*dat* to) **I** *v/t* **1.** dedicate. **2.** devote, give (*one's time etc*). **II** *sich* **~** devote o.s.; *sich ganz* **...** **~** give one's undivided attention to ...
widrig ['vi:drɪç] *adj* adverse.
widrigenfalls ['vi:drɪgən-] *adv* failing which, ⚖ in default of which.
wie [vi:] **I** *interrog adv* **1.** how: **~** *macht man das?* how is that done?; **~** *ist er* (*es*)? what is he (it) like?; **~** *nennt man das?* what do you call that?; **~** *sagten Sie?* (sorry,) what did you say?; **~** *wäre*

es mit ...? what about ...? **2. ~ schön!** how beautiful; **~ gut, daß er da war!** lucky for me *etc* that he was there; *und ~!* and how!, F you bet!; → *bitte* 3. **II** *conj* **3.** as, like: *stark ~ ein Bär* (as) strong as a bear; *ein Mann ~ er* a man like him; *dumm ~ er ist* fool that he is; *~ gesagt* as I said. **4. ~ (zum Beispiel), ~ etwa** such as. **5.** *time:* F as, when. **6.** *ich sah, ~ er weglief* I saw him running away; *ich hörte, ~ er es sagte* I heard him say so. **7. ~ (auch) immer** however, no matter how; **~ dem auch sei** be that as it may; **~ sie auch heißen mögen** whatever they are called.

Wiedehopf ['vi:dəhɔpf] *m* (-[e]s; -e) *zo.* hoopoe.

wieder ['vi:dər] *adv* again: **~ gesund** well again; **immer ~** again and again, time and again; **schon ~?** not again!; **ich bin gleich ~ da!** I'll be back in a minute!; **~ ist ein Tag vorbei!** another day's over.

Wieder|'annäherung *f pol.* rapprochement. **~'aufbau** *m* (-[e]s; *no pl*) **1.** reconstruction. **2.** recovery. **~'aufbereitung** *f* reprocessing. **~'aufbereitungsanlage** *f* reprocessing plant.

wieder|'aufführen *v/t* (*sep*, h) rerun (*film etc*). **~'aufleben** *v/i* (*sep*, sn) (*a. ~ lassen*) revive.

Wieder'aufnahme *f* (-; *no pl*) resumption. **Wieder'aufnahmeverfahren** *n* ⚖ a) new hearing, b) retrial.

wieder'aufnehmen *v/t* (*irr, sep*, -ge-, h, → *nehmen*) resume.

Wieder'aufrüstung *f* (-; *no pl*) rearmament.

wieder|'auftauchen *v/i* (*sep*, sn) re-emerge, ⚓ a. resurface, *fig.* reappear, turn up again. **~'auftreten** *v/i* (*irr, sep*, -ge-, sn, → *treten*) reappear.

Wieder'ausfuhr *f* re-exportation.

'Wiederbeginn *m* (-[e]s; *no pl*) recommencement, *of school etc:* reopening.

'wiederbekommen *v/t* (*irr, sep*, h, → *bekommen*) get *s.th.* back.

'wiederbeleben *v/t* (*sep*, h) resuscitate, *a. fig.* revive. **'Wiederbelebung** *f* (-; *no pl*) resuscitation, *fig.* revival.

'Wiederbelebungsversuch *m* attempt at resuscitation.

'wiederbeschaffen *v/t* (*sep*, h) replace.

'wiederbringen *v/t* (*irr, sep*, -ge-, h, → *bringen*) bring *s.o., s.th.* back, return.

wieder'einführen *v/t* (*sep*, h) **1.** reintroduce, revive. **2.** ✝ reimport. **Wieder'einführung** *f* (-; *no pl*) **1.** reintroduction, revival. **2.** ✝ reimportation.

Wieder'eingliederung *f* reintegration (*in acc* into), (*social etc*) rehabilitation.

wieder'einsetzen *v/t* (*sep*, h) reinstate (*in acc* in). **Wieder'einsetzung** *f* (-; *no pl*) reinstatement.

'Wiedereintritt *m* re-entry (*in acc* into).

'wiederentdecken *v/t* (*sep*, h) rediscover.

'Wiederergreifung *f* (-; *no pl*) recapture.

'wiedererkennen *v/t* (*irr, sep*, h, → *erkennen*) recognize: *nicht wiederzuerkennen* unrecognizable.

'wiedererlangen *v/t* (*sep*, h) recover, regain.

'wiedereröffnen *v/t* (*sep*, h) reopen. **'Wiedereröffnung** *f* reopening.

'wiederfinden *v/t* (*irr, sep*, -ge-, h, → *finden*) find again.

'Wiedergabe *f* (-; *no pl*) **1.** account. **2.** ♪ rendering, interpretation. **3.** reproduction (*a.* ⊕), ♪ playback. **~gerät** *n* playback unit. **~quali,tät** *f* fidelity of reproduction.

'wiedergeben *v/t* (*irr, sep*, -ge-, h, → *geben*) **1.** give *s.th.* back (*dat* to). **2.** a) describe, b) repeat, c) quote. **3.** ♪ render, interpret. **4.** reproduce (*a.* ⊕), ♪ *a.* play back.

'Wiedergeburt *f a. fig.* rebirth.

'wiedergewinnen *v/t* (*irr, sep*, h, → *gewinnen*) regain, recover (*a.* ⊕), ⊕ reclaim. **'Wiedergewinnung** *f* (-; *no pl*) recovery, ⊕ *a.* reclamation.

wieder'gutmachen *v/t* (*sep*, h) make up for, compensate for: *nicht wiedergutzumachen(d)* irreparable. **Wieder'gutmachung** *f* (-; -en) reparation.

'wiederhaben *v/t* (*irr, sep*, -ge-, h, → *haben*) F have *s.o., s.th.* back.

wieder'herstellen *v/t* (*sep*, h) restore, ⚕ *a.* cure, re-establish (*connections etc*). **Wieder'herstellung** *f* (-; -en) restoration, re-establishment, ⚕ recovery.

wieder'holbar *adj* repeatable. **wieder'holen** (*insep, no* -ge-, h) **I** *v/t a*) repeat, say (*or* do) *s.th.* (over) again, b) sum up, F recap. **II sich ~** a) repeat itself (*or* o.s.), b) recur. **wieder'holt** *adj* repeated. **Wieder'holung** *f* (-; -en) repetition, *radio, TV etc*: repeat, *TV, soccer etc*: replay.

Wieder'holungs|impfung *f* booster (shot). **~kurs** *m* refresher course. **~prüfung** *f* resit. **~spiel** *n sports*: replay. **~taste** *f* repeat key.

'Wiederhören: auf ~! goodbye(e)!

'wiederkäuen [-kɔyən] (*sep*, h) **I** *v/i zo.* ruminate. **II** *v/t fig.* rehash.

'Wiederkäuer *m* (-s; -) *zo.* ruminant.

'Wiederkehr [-ke:r] *f* (-; *no pl*) **1.** return. **2.** recurrence. **'wiederkehren** *v/i* (*sep*, sn) **1.** return, come back. **2.** recur: (*regelmäßig*) **~d** recurrent.

'wiederkommen *v/i* (*irr, sep*, -ge-, sn, → **kommen**) a) come again, b) come back.

'wiedersehen *v/t* (*irr, sep*, -ge-, h, → **sehen**) see *s.o., s.th.* again: **sich ~** meet again. **'Wiedersehen** *n* (-s; -) reunion: **~ mit London** London revisited: **auf ~!** goodbye(e)!, F so long!, bye!

wiederum ['vi:dərʊm] *adv* **1.** again. **2.** on the other hand.

'wiedervereinigen *v/t* (a. **sich ~**) (*sep*, h) reunite. **'Wiedervereinigung** *f* (-; -en) reunion, *pol. a.* reunification.

'Wieder|verheiratung *f* (-; -en) remarriage. **~verkäufer** *m* reseller. **~verkaufswert** *m* (-[e]s; *no pl*) resale value. **~verwendung** *f* (-; -en) reuse.

'wiederverwerten *v/t* (*sep*, h) recycle.

'Wiederverwertung *f* (-; -en) recycling.

'Wiederwahl *f* (-; *no pl*) re-election. **'wiederwählen** *v/t* (*sep*, h) re-elect.

'Wiederzulassung *f* (-; -en) **1.** readmission. **2.** *mot.* relicensing.

Wiege ['vi:gə] *f* (-; -n) *a. fig.* cradle.

wiegen¹ ['vi:gən] (h) **I** *v/t* rock, shake (*one's head*), sway (*one's hips*): **j-n in Sicherheit ~** lull *s.o.* into a false sense of security. **II sich ~** rock; **sich in den Hüften ~** sway one's hips; *fig.* **sich in Sicherheit ~** believe *o.s.* safe.

'wiegen² (wog, gewogen, h) **I** *v/t, v/i* weigh: *fig.* **schwer ~** carry (a lot of) weight. **II das ~** weigh *o.s.*

'wiegen³ *v/t* (h) *gastr.* chop, mince.

'Wiegenlied *n* lullaby.

wiehern ['vi:ərn] *v/i* (h) neigh: **~(d lachen)** heehaw.

Wiener¹ ['vi:nər] *f* (-; -) wiener(wurst).

'Wiener² *m* (-s; -), **'Wienerin** *f* (-; -nen), **'wienerisch** *adj* Viennese.

wienern ['vi:nərn] *v/t* (h) F polish.

wies [vi:s] *pret of* **weisen.**

Wiese ['vi:zə] *f* (-; -n) meadow.

Wiesel ['vi:zəl] *n* (-s; -) *zo.* weasel.

wieso [vi'zo:] → **warum.**

wieviel [vi'fi:l] *interrog adv* how much: **~(e)** how many. **'wievielmal** *adv* how many times, how often. **wie'vielt** *adj* **der (die, das) ~e** which; **zum ~en Male?** how many times?; **den ~en haben wir heute?** what's the date today?

wieweit [vi'vait] → **inwieweit.**

Wikinger ['vi:kiŋər] *m* (-s; -) Viking.

wild [vɪlt] *adj* **1.** wild (a. ⚥, *zo. or fig.*), *a.* savage (*dog, tribe, etc*): 🌱 **~es Fleisch** proud flesh; **~e Vermutungen** wild speculation; **~ wachsen** grow wild. **2.** violent, fierce, wild: **das ist halb so ~!** it's not all that bad. **3.** F *fig.* wild, mad: **wie ~ work** *etc* like mad; **j-n ~ machen** make *s.o.* mad; **~ werden** get mad, see red; **den ~en Mann spielen** go berserk. **4.** F **ganz ~ sein auf** (*acc*) be wild (*or* crazy) about. **5.** unauthorized (*camping etc*); → **Streik.**

Wild *n* (-[e]s; *no pl*) game, *gastr. a.* venison. **~bach** *m* torrent. **~bahn** *f* **in freier ~** in the wild. **~dieb** *m* poacher.

Wilde ['vɪldə] *m, f* (-n; -n) savage.

'Wildente *f zo.* wild duck.

Wilderer ['vɪldərər] *m* (-s; -) poacher.

wildern ['vɪldərn] *v/i* (h) poach.

'wild'fremd *adj* completely strange (*dat* to): **~er Mensch** complete stranger.

'Wildgans *f zo.* wild goose.

'Wildgehege *n* game preserve.

'Wildheit *f* (-; *no pl*) wildness (*a. fig.*), savagery, fury, *a.* unruliness.

'Wildhüter *m* (-s; -) gamekeeper.

'Wildkatze *f zo.* wild cat.

'wildlebend *adj* wild.

'Wildleder *n*, **'wildledern** *adj* suede.

'Wildnis *f* (-; -se) wilderness (*a. fig.*): **in der ~** in the wild.

'Wild|park *m* game park. **~sau** *f* wild sow. **~schwein** *n* wild boar. 2**wachsend** *adj* wild. **~wasser** *n* (-s; -) torrent, wildwater. **~wechsel** *m* run.

Wild'westfilm *m* western.

Wille ['vɪlə] *m* (-ns; *no pl*) will, *philos. a.* volition, *a.* intention: **böser ~** ill will; **guter ~** good will (*or* intention); **letzter ~** (last) will *and* testament; **aus freiem ~n** of one's own free will; **gegen m-n ~n** against my will; **j-m s-n**

~n lassen let s.o. have his (own) way; **ich kann Ihnen beim besten ~n nicht helfen** I can't help you, much as I should like to; **ich kann mich beim besten ~n nicht erinnern** I can't remember for the life of me; **wenn es nach ihrem ~n ginge** if she had her way; **sie mußte wider ~n lachen** she couldn't help laughing; → **durchsetzen¹** I. '**Willen** m → **Wille**.

willenlos adj weak, weak-willed: **j-s ~es Werkzeug sein** be s.o.'s slave.

willens adj **~ sein zu** inf be willing (or prepared) to inf.

'**Willens|akt** m act of volition. **~anstrengung** f effort of will. **~äußerung** f expression of one's will. **~erklärung** f 𝔱𝔥 declaration of intention. **~freiheit** f free will. **~kraft** f (-; no pl) **1.** willpower. **2.** strong will. **2schwach** adj weak, weak-willed. **2stark** adj strong-willed. **~stärke** f (-; no pl) strong will.

willentlich adv deliberately.

willfährig ['vɪlfɛːrɪç] adj compliant.

willig adj willing.

will'kommen adj welcome (dat to): **j-n ~ heißen** welcome s.o. **Will'kommen** n (-s; -) welcome, reception.

Willkür ['vɪlkyːr] f (-; no pl) arbitrariness: **j-s ~ ausgeliefert sein** be at s.o.'s mercy. **~akt** m arbitrary act. **~herrschaft** f (-; no pl) arbitrary rule, despotism.

'**willkürlich** adj **1.** arbitrary. **2.** random (selection etc). **3.** physiol. voluntary.

wimmeln ['vɪməln] v/i (h) **~ von** be teeming (F crawling) with.

wimmern ['vɪmərn] v/i (h) whimper.

Wimpel ['vɪmpəl] m (-s; -) pennant.

Wimper ['vɪmpər] f (-; -n) eyelash: **ohne mit der ~ zu zucken** without batting an eyelid.

'**Wimpernbürste** f eyelash brush.

'**Wimperntusche** f mascara.

Wind [vɪnt] m (-[e]s; -e) (**günstiger ~** fair) wind: fig. **ein frischer ~** a breath of fresh air; **gegen den ~** into the wind; **mit dem ~** down the wind; **bei ~ und Wetter** in rain or storm; fig. **~ bekommen von** get wind of; F **viel ~ machen** a) make a great fuss (**um** of, about, over), b) act big, talk big; **j-m den ~ aus den Segeln nehmen** take the wind out of s.o.'s sails; **in alle ~e zerstreut** scattered to the four winds; **in den ~ reden** waste one's breath; **in den ~ schlagen** cast to the winds; **wissen, woher der ~ weht** know how the wind blows; → **Mantel** 1.

'**Windbeutel** m gastr. cream puff.

Winde¹ ['vɪndə] f (-; -n) ⊕ winch, hoist.

'**Winde²** f (-; -n) ⊗ bindweed.

'**Windei** n wind egg.

Windel ['vɪndəl] f (-; -n) nappy, Am. diaper. '**windelweich** adj **j-n ~ schlagen** beat s.o. to a pulp.

winden ['vɪndən] (wand, gewunden, h) **I** v/t **1.** wind (**um** round). **2.** make, bind (wreath). **II** sich ~ **3.** wriggle, squirm: **sich vor Schmerzen ~** writhe with pain. **4.** wind its way (**durch** through). **5.** sich ~ um wind (or coil) itself round.

'**Windeseile** ['vɪndəs-] f in ~ at lightning speed, in no time; **sich mit ~ verbreiten** rumo(u)r etc: spread like wildfire.

'**windgeschützt** adj sheltered (from the wind).

'**Wind|hose** f meteor. whirlwind. **~hund** m **1.** zo. greyhound. **2.** F fig. loose fish.

'**windig** adj **1.** windy. **2.** F shady (fellow), fishy (business), lame (excuse etc).

'**Wind|jacke** f windcheater. **~ka,nal** m ⊕ wind tunnel. **~kraft** f (-; no pl) wind power. **~licht** n storm lantern. **~mühle** f windmill. **~pocken** pl 𝔰 chickenpox. **~richtung** f direction of the wind. **~rose** f compass card (or rose). **~sack** m wind sock. **~schatten** m ⚓ lee, ✈ sheltered zone, sports: slipstream. **2schlüpfig** [-ʃlʏpfɪç], **2schnittig** adj streamlined. **~schutzscheibe** f windscreen, Am. windshield. **~stärke** f wind force. **2still** adj calm. **~stille** f calm, a. lull. **~stoß** m gust (of wind). **~surfen** n (-s) windsurfing. **~surfer** m wind surfer.

Windung ['vɪndʊŋ] f (-; -en) winding, a. anat. convolution, bend (of river etc), whorl (of spiral, shell), ⊕ thread.

Wink [vɪŋk] m (-[e]s; -e) a) sign, fig. hint, tip, b) tip-off, warning: → **Zaunpfahl**.

Winkel ['vɪŋkəl] m (-s; -) **1.** A: angle: **im rechten ~** at right angles (**zu** to); → **tot**. **2.** corner. **3.** ✗ chevron. **4.** ⊕ a) square, b) knee, elbow. **~advo,kat** m contp. pettifogger, Am. F shyster. **~eisen** n ⊕ angle iron. **~funkti,on** f A goniometric function. **~hal,bierende** f (-n; -n) A bisector of an angle. **~maß** n ⊕ square.

~**messer** m (-s; -) & protractor, surv. goniometer. ~**zug** m F dodge, evasion.

winken ['vɪŋkən] (h) I v/i j-m ~ a) wave to s.o., b) reward etc: be in store for s.o.; *mit dem Taschentuch ~* wave one's handkerchief; *e-m Taxi ~* hail a taxi. II v/t *j-n zu sich ~* beckon s.o. (to come).

Winter ['vɪntər] m (-s; -) (*im ~* in) winter.

'**Winter...** winter (*coat, fashion, holiday, month, semester, etc*). ~**ausrüstung** f mot. winter equipment. 2**fest** adj winterproof, & hardy: ~ *machen* winterize. ~**garten** m conservatory. ~**getreide** n winter crop. ~**halbjahr** n winter.

'**winterlich** adj wintry.

'**Winter|pause** f winter break. ~**reifen** m mot. winter tyre (*Am.* tire). ~**schlaf** m zo. hibernation: ~ *halten* hibernate. ~**schlußverkauf** m winter sales. ~**sonnenwende** f winter solstice. ~**spiele** pl *Olympische ~* Winter Olympics. ~**sport** m winter sport(s). ~**sportler(in** f) m person doing winter sports.

Winzer ['vɪntsər] m (-s; -) wine grower.

winzig ['vɪntsɪç] adj tiny, minute.

Winzling ['vɪntslɪŋ] m (-s; -e) F mite.

Wipfel ['vɪpfəl] m (-s; -) (tree) top.

Wippe ['vɪpə] f (-; -n) seesaw, *Am.* teeter-totter. '**wippen** v/i (h) seesaw, rock, *skirt etc*: bob.

wir [viːr] pers pron we: ~ *beide (alle)* both (all) of us; ~ *drei* we three, the three of us.

Wirbel ['vɪrbəl] m (-s; -) **1.** whirl, eddy, vortex, turbulence. **2.** fig. a) turmoil, whirl, b) F fuss, to-do (*um* about): *e-n ziemlichen ~ verursachen* cause quite a stir. **3.** anat. vertebra. **4.** cowlick. **5.** (drum) roll. **6.** peg (*of violin*).

'**Wirbelknochen** m → **Wirbel** 3.

'**wirbellos** adj zo. invertebrate.

wirbeln ['vɪrbəln] v/i (sn) whirl, swirl.

'**Wirbelsäule** f spine, spinal column.

'**Wirbelsturm** m cyclone, tornado.

'**Wirbeltier** n vertebrate.

wirken ['vɪrkən] (h) I v/i **1.** take (*or* have) effect, be effective, work, act: ~ *auf* (*acc*) have a depressing etc effect on, affect, &, ◉ act on; ~ *gegen* be effective against; *stark ~d* potent, strong; *langsam ~d* slow-acting; *et. auf sich ~ lassen* take s.th. in; F *das wirkt immer!* it never fails (to work); *das hat gewirkt!* a) that did the trick, b) that hit

home. **2.** work (*an dat* at). **3.** seem, look: *jünger ~* look younger; *er wirkt schüchtern* he seems shy; *überzeugend ~* be convincing. II v/t **4.** → *bewirken, hinwirken, Wunder*. **5.** ◉ knit. '**Wirken** n (-s) **1.** activity, work. **2.** ⚒, ◉ action. '**Wirker** m (-s; -) ◉ knitter.

'**wirklich** I adj real, actual, true. II adv really, actually: ~? really?, is that so?

'**Wirklichkeit** f (-; no pl) (die rauhe ~ harsh) reality; *in ~* in reality, actually; ~ *werden* come true.

'**wirklichkeits|fremd** adj unrealistic, starry-eyed. ~**getreu** adj realistic, faithful (*copy etc*).

'**wirksam** adj effective: *sehr ~ a.* powerful, drastic; ~ *gegen* good for; ~ *werden* take effect, 𝕫𝕫 come into force.

'**Wirksamkeit** f (-; no pl) effectiveness.

'**Wirkstoff** m (-[e]s; -e) active substance.

'**Wirkung** f (-; -en) **1.** (*auf acc* on) a) effect, operation, b) impact: *mit ~ vom* with effect from, as from, as of; *mit sofortiger ~* as of now; ~ *erzielen* have an effect, a. s-e ~ *tun* work; s-e ~ *verfehlen* prove ineffective, have no effect; *Ursache und ~* cause and effect. **2.** phys. action. **3.** fig. appeal (*auf acc* to).

'**Wirkungs|bereich** m sphere of activity. ~**grad** m ◉ efficiency. ~**kraft** f (-; no pl) efficacy. ~**kreis** m sphere of activity.

'**wirkungslos** adj ineffective: ~ *bleiben* have no effect. '**Wirkungslosigkeit** f (-; no pl) ineffectiveness.

'**wirkungsvoll** adj effective.

'**Wirkungsweise** f (mode of) operation, function, ⚒ action, effect.

wirr [vɪr] adj **1.** dishevel(l)ed (*hair*), tangled (*growth*). **2.** fig. confused, muddleheaded (*person*), wild (*rumo[u]r etc*), incoherent (*speech*): ~*es Zeug reden* talk wild; *mir ist ganz ~ im Kopf* my head is spinning. '**Wirren** pl turmoil, confusion. '**Wirrkopf** m muddlehead.

Wirrwarr ['vɪrvar] m (-s; no pl) muddle, chaos, F jumble.

Wirsing ['vɪrzɪŋ] m (-s; no pl), ~**kohl** m (-[e]s; no pl) & savoy.

Wirt [vɪrt] m (-[e]s; -e) a) a. biol. host, b) landlord. '**Wirtin** f (-; -nen) a) hostess, b) landlady.

'**Wirtschaft** f (-; -en) **1.** ⚶, pol. a) economy, b) trade and industry. **2.** no pl a) management, b) housekeeping: *j-m die*

~ **führen** keep house for s.o. **3.** *no pl* F *contp.* mess. **4.** → *Wirtshaus.*

'**wirtschaften** *v/i* (h) **1.** manage (one's affairs): *sparsam* ~ economize, be economical (*mit* with); *schlecht* ~ mismanage. **2.** be busy.

'**Wirtschafterin** *f* (-; -nen) housekeeper.

'**wirtschaftlich** *adj* **1.** a) economic, b) financial, c) business ... **2.** economical, efficient: *ein* ~*es Auto* an economical car. **3.** profitable. '**Wirtschaftlichkeit** *f* (-; *no pl*) **1.** profitability, economic efficiency. **2.** economy.

'**Wirtschafts|abkommen** *n* economic (*or* trade) agreement. ~**berater** *m* economic adviser. ~**beziehungen** *pl* economic (*or* trade) relations. ~**führer** *m* leading industrialist. ~**geld** *n* (-[e]s; *no pl*) housekeeping money. ~**gemeinschaft** *f Europäische* ~ European Economic Community (*abbr. EEC*). ~**gipfel** *m* economic summit. ~**güter** *pl* economic goods. ~**hilfe** *f* economic aid. ~**jahr** *n* financial year. ~**kriminali,tät** *f* white-collar crime. ~**krise** *f* economic crisis. ~**macht** *f* economic power. ~**mi,nister** *m* minister for economic affairs. ~**mini,sterium** *n* economics ministry. ~**poli,tik** *f* economic policy. &**po,litisch** *adj* (politico-)economic. ~**prüfer** *m* chartered (*Am.* certified public) accountant. ~**re,form** *f* economic reform. ~**spio,nage** *f* industrial espionage. ~**sy,stem** *n* economic system. ~**teil** *m* business section. ~**uni,on** *f* economic union. ~**verband** *m* trade association. ~**wachstum** *n* economic growth. ~**wissenschaft** *f* economics. ~**wissenschaftler** *m* economist. ~**wunder** *n* economic miracle. ~**zweig** *m* branch of industry.

'**Wirtshaus** *n* inn, public house, F pub, *Am.* saloon.

'**Wirtsleute** *pl* landlord and landlady.

'**Wirtstier** *n biol.* host.

Wisch [vɪʃ] *m* (-es; -e) scrap of paper.

wischen ['vɪʃən] *v/t* (h) a) wipe (*sich den Mund* one's mouth), b) mop (up).

'**Wischer** *m* (-s; -) *mot.* wiper.

'**Wischlappen** *m*, '**Wischtuch** *n* cloth.

Wisent ['vi:zɛnt] *m* (-s; -e) *zo.* bison.

wispern ['vɪspərn] *v/t, v/i* (h) whisper.

'**Wißbegier(de)** *f* **1.** thirst for knowledge. **2.** curiosity. '**wißbegierig** *adj* **1.**

eager for knowledge. **2.** curious.

wissen ['vɪsən] *v/t, v/i* (wußte, gewußt, h) know (*von* about): *man kann nie* ~ you never know; *weder ein noch aus* ~ be at one's wits' end; *ich weiß nicht recht* I'm not so sure; *nicht, daß ich wüßte* not that I know of; *woher weißt du das?* how do you know (that)?; *was weiß ich!* how should I know?; *weißt du noch?* (do you) remember?; *ich weiß nicht mehr* I don't remember; *ich will davon nichts* ~ I don't want anything to do with it; *sie will von ihm nichts mehr* ~ she is through with him; → *Bescheid.*

'**Wissen** *n* (-s) knowledge, learning, F know-how: *ohne mein* ~ without my knowing; *m-s* ~*s* as far as I know; *nach bestem* ~ *und Gewissen* to the best of one's knowledge and belief; *wider besseres* ~ against one's better judgement.

'**wissend** *adj* knowing (*look etc*).

'**Wissenschaft** *f* (-; -en) science.

'**Wissenschaftler** *m* (-s; -) scientist.

'**wissenschaftlich** *adj* **1.** scientific. **2.** academic (*career, work, etc*).

'**Wissens|durst** *m* thirst for knowledge. ~**gebiet** *n* province, field of knowledge. ~**lücke** *f* gap in one's knowledge. ~**stand** *m* level of knowledge: *auf dem neuesten* ~ *sein* to be up to date.

'**wissenswert** *adj* worth knowing: *Wissenswertes* interesting facts.

'**wissentlich I** *adj* conscious, deliberate. **II** *adv* knowingly, deliberately.

wittern ['vɪtərn] *v/t* (h) scent, smell, *fig.* sense (*danger*), see (*chance*).

'**Witterung**¹ *f* (-; -en) *hunt.* scent.

'**Witterung**² *f* (-; -en) weather: *bei jeder* ~ in all weathers. '**witterungsbeständig** *adj* weatherproof. '**Witterungseinflüsse** *pl* influence of the weather.

Witwe ['vɪtvə] *f* (-; -n) widow.

'**Witwenrente** *f* widow's pension.

Witwer ['vɪtvər] *m* (-s; -) widower.

Witz [vɪts] *m* (-es; -e) **1.** joke, quip: ~*e machen* (*or reißen*) crack jokes; F *das ist der* ~ *an der Sache* a) that's the funny thing about it, b) that's the whole point; F *mach k-e* ~*e!* you're joking. **2.** *no pl* wit. '**Witzbold** [-bɔlt] *m* (-[e]s; -e) F joker. **Witze'lei** *f* (-; -en) silly jokes. **witzeln** ['vɪtsəln] *v/i* (h) joke (*über acc* about), quip. '**witzig** *adj* witty, funny: *a. iro.* **sehr ~!** very funny!, big joke! **'witzlos** *adj* **1.** unfunny. **2.** F pointless, (of) no use.

wo [vo:] I *interrog and rel adv* where. II *conj* **wo ... (doch)** when, F although. III F *indef adv* somewhere. IV F *int* **i wo, ach wo!** nonsense!, nothing of the kind! **wo'anders** *adv* somewhere else, anywhere else. **wo'bei** I *interrog adv* **~ bist du gerade?** what are you doing right now? II *rel adv* in doing so: **~ mir einfällt** which reminds me.

Woche ['vɔxə] *f* (-; -n) week: **in e-r ~** in a week('s time); **zweimal die ~** twice a week; **auf ~n hinaus** sold out *etc* for weeks (to come); **~ um ~** week after week; F **unter der ~** during the week.

'Wochenbett *n* (-[e]s; *no pl*) childbed.
'Wochenend... weekend (*edition etc*).
'Wochenende *n* (**am ~** at the) weekend.
'Wochenkarte *f* weekly season ticket.
'wochenlang I *adj* lasting several weeks: **nach ~em Warten** after weeks of waiting. II *adv* for weeks.
'Wochenlohn *m* weekly wages.
'Wochenschau *f* newsreel.
'Wochentag *m* weekday.
'wochentags *adv* on weekdays.
wöchentlich ['vœçəntlɪç] *adj* weekly: **einmal ~** once a week.
'Wochenzeitung *f* weekly (paper).
Wöchnerin ['vœçnərɪn] *f* (-; -nen) woman in childbed.

Wodka ['vɔtka] *m* (-s; -s) vodka.
wo'durch I *interrog adv* how. II *rel adv* by which, through which, whereby.
wo'für I *interrog adv* what for. II *rel adv* for which, which ... for.
wog [vo:k] *pret of* **wiegen²**.
Woge ['vo:gə] *f* (-; -n) wave, surge: **die ~n glätten** pour oil on troubled waters.
wo'gegen I *interrog adv* against what, what ... against. II *rel adv* against which, which ... against. III *conj* → **wohingegen**.
wo'her I *interrog and rel adv* where (...) from: → **wissen**. II *int* F **~ denn!** nonsense!
wo'hin *interrog and rel adv* where (... to).
wohin'gegen *conj* whereas.
wohl [vo:l] *adv* **1.** well: **sich ~ fühlen** a) feel fine, feel good, be happy, b) **bei j-m** feel at home with s.o.; **ich fühle mich nicht ~** I don't feel well; F *fig.* **mir ist**

nicht ~ dabei I don't feel happy about it; **~ oder übel** willy-nilly, whether you *etc* like it or not; → **bekommen** II. **2. sehr ~** very well; **ich bin mir dessen sehr ~ bewußt** I am well aware of that; **das kann man ~ sagen!** you can say that again. **3.** probably, I suppose: **das ist ~ möglich** that's quite possible; **ob er es ~ weiß?** I wonder if he knows (that); **~ kaum** hardly. **4. ~ 100 Leute** *etc* about 100 people *etc.* **Wohl** *n* (-[e]s; *no pl*) welfare, good, well-being: **auf j-s ~ trinken** drink to s.o.'s health; **zum ~!** to your health!, F cheers!
wohl'auf *adj* **~ sein** be well, be in good health.
'Wohlbefinden *n* (-s; *no pl*) well-being.
'wohl|behalten *adj* safe (and sound), *object:* safe, undamaged. **~bekannt** *adj* well-known, *b.s.* notorious.
'Wohlergehen *n* (-s; *no pl*) well-being.
'wohlerzogen *adj* well-behaved.
'Wohlfahrt *f* (-; *no pl*) welfare.
'Wohlfahrts|marke *f* charity stamp. **~organisati̱on** *f* charitable institution. **~staat** *m* welfare state.
'wohlgeformt *adj* well-shaped, shapely.
'Wohlgefühl *n* (-[e]s; *no pl*) sense of well-being.
'wohlgemeint *adj* well-meant.
'wohlgemerkt *int* mind you!
'wohlgenährt *adj* well-fed.
'wohlgesinnt *adj* well-meaning: **j-m ~ sein** be well disposed towards s.o.
'wohlhabend *adj* well-to-do, prosperous, affluent: **~ sein** be well off.
'wohlig *adj* pleasant, cosy.
'Wohlklang *m* (-[e]s; *no pl*) melodiousness. **'wohlklingend** *adj* melodious.
'wohlmeinend *adj* well-meaning.
'wohlriechend *adj* fragrant.
'wohlschmeckend *adj* tasty.
'Wohlsein: zum ~! F cheers!
'Wohlstand *m* (-[e]s; *no pl*) prosperity, affluence. **'Wohlstandsgesellschaft** *f* affluent society.
'Wohltat *f* (-; -en) **1.** good deed. **2.** *no pl* a) relief, b) blessing. **'Wohltäter(in** *f) m* benefactor (benefactress). **'wohltätig** *adj* charitable. **'Wohltätigkeit** *f* (-; *no pl*) charity. **'Wohltätigkeits...** charity (*or* benefit) (*ball, concert, match, etc*).
'wohltuend *adj* **1.** pleasant. **2.** soothing.
'wohltun *v/i* (*irr, sep, -ge-, h, → tun*) **j-m**

~ do s.o. good; *das tut wohl* that does you good.

'**wohlüberlegt** *adj* well-considered.
'**wohlverdient** *adj* well-deserved.
'**Wohlverhalten** *n* good behavio(u)r.
'**wohlweislich** [-vaislıç] *adv* wisely, for good reason: ~ *tun* be careful to do *s.th.*
'**Wohlwollen** *n* (-s; *no pl*) goodwill, favo(u)r. **wohlwollend** *adj* benevolent, kind: *e-r Sache ~ gegenüberstehen* take a favo(u)rable view of s.th.
'**Wohn|anlage** *f* housing area. **~bezirk** *m* residential district. **~block** *m* block of flats. **~einheit** *f* housing unit.
wohnen ['vo:nən] *v/i* (h) (*in dat* in, at, *bei* with) a) live, reside, b) stay.
'**Wohn|fläche** *f* living space. **~gebäude** *n* residential building. **~geld** *n* housing subsidy. **~gemeinschaft** *f* flat-sharing community: *in e-r ~ leben* share a flat with s.o. (*or* several other people).
'**wohnhaft** *adj* resident (*in dat* in, at).
'**Wohn|haus** *n* residential building. **~heim** *n* hostel, *Am.* rooming house. **~küche** *f* kitchen-cum-living-room.
'**wohnlich** *adj* comfortable, cosy.
'**Wohnmo,bil** *n* (-s; -e) camper.
'**Wohn|ort** *m* (place of) residence. **~raum** *m* 1. housing, accommodation. 2. → *Wohnfläche.* 3. → *Wohnzimmer.*
Wohn-'Schlafzimmer *n* bedsit(ter).
'**Wohnsiedlung** *f* housing estate.
'**Wohnsitz** *m* (place of) residence.
'**Wohnung** *f* (-; -en) flat, *Am.* apartment.
'**Wohnungsamt** *n* housing office.
'**Wohnungsbau** *m* (-[e]s; *no pl*) house building. **~mi,nister** *m* housing minister. **~pro,gramm** *n* housing scheme.
'**Wohnungsinhaber(in** *f*) *m* tenant.
'**wohnungslos** *adj* homeless.
'**Wohnungs|markt** *m* housing market. **~not** *f* (-; *no pl*) housing shortage. **~schlüssel** *m* key (to the flat). **~suche** *f* F flat-hunting. **~suchende** *m, f* (-n; -n) F flat-hunter. **~tür** *f* front door. **~wechsel** *m* change of residence.
'**Wohn|verhältnisse** *pl* housing conditions. **~viertel** *n* residential area. **~wagen** *m* caravan, *Am.* trailer. **~zimmer** *n* sitting (*or* living) room.
wölben ['vœlbən] *v/t* (*a.* sich ~) (h) arch: → *gewölbt.*
'**Wölbung** *f* (-; -en) 1. arch. 2. vault.
Wolf [vɔlf] *m* (-[e]s; ⸚e) 1. *zo.* wolf: *fig. mit*

den Wölfen heulen howl with the wolves; → *Schafpelz.* 2. mincer. 3. ✻ intertrigo: *sich e-n ~ laufen* get sore.
Wölfin ['vœlfɪn] *f* (-; -nen) *zo.* she-wolf.
Wolfram ['vɔlfram] *n* (-s; *no pl*) tungsten.
'**Wolfsmilch** *f* ✿ spurge.
'**Wolfsrachen** *m* ✻ cleft palate.
Wolke ['vɔlkə] *f* (-; -n) cloud: *fig. aus allen ~n fallen* be thunderstruck; *in den ~n schweben* have one's head in the clouds.
'**Wolken|bruch** *m* cloudburst. **~decke** *f* cloud cover. **~kratzer** *m* skyscraper.
'**wolkenlos** *adj* cloudless, clear.
'**Wolkenwand** *f* bank of clouds.
'**wolkig** *adj* cloudy (*a.* ✻, *phot. etc*), clouded.
'**Wolldecke** *f* wool(l)en blanket.
Wolle ['vɔlə] *f* (-; -n) wool: F *sich in die ~ kriegen* quarrel, (have a) fight (*mit* with).
'**wollen¹** *adj* wool(l)en.
'**wollen²** I *v/t, v/i* (wollte, gewollt, h) a) want, *a.* demand, b) be willing (*or* prepared) to, c) want to: *lieber ~* prefer; *ich will lieber* I'd rather; *et. unbedingt ~* insist on s.th.; *ich will nicht* I don't want to; *sie will, daß ich komme* she wants me to come; *was ~ Sie von mir?* what do you want?; *was willst du mit e-m Regenschirm?* what do you want an umbrella for?; *Verzeihung, das wollte ich nicht!* sorry, that was unintentional; *ob er will oder nicht* whether he likes it or not; *du weißt nicht, was du willst!* you don't know your own mind!; *mach, was du willst!* do what you like!; *du hast es ja so gewollt!* you asked for it!; *was (wann) du willst* whatever (whenever) you like; *wie du willst* as you like, suit yourself; *ich wollte, ich wäre (hätte) ...* I wish I were (had) ...; *F hier ist nichts zu ~* nothing doing; → *gewollt.* II *v/aux* (*pp* wollen) want: *et. haben ~* want (to have) s.th.; *et. tun ~* want (*or* be going) to do s.th.; *er will es nicht tun* he refuses to do it; *was ~ Sie damit sagen?* what do you mean (by that)?; *er will dich gesehen haben* he says he saw you; → *heißen¹ I etc.*
'**wollig** *adj* wool(l)y.
'**Woll|jacke** *f* cardigan. **~knäuel** *m, n* ball of wool. **~sachen** *pl* wool(l)ens.

~socken pl wool(l)en socks. **~stoff** m wool(l)en fabric, (broad)cloth.

wollte ['vɔltə] pret of **wollen²**.

Wollust ['vɔlʊst] f (-; no pl) voluptuousness, sensuality. **wollüstig** ['vɔlʏstiç] adj voluptuous, sensual.

'Wollwaren pl wool(l)ens.

wo'mit I interrog adv what (...) with: **~ kann ich dienen?** what can I do for you?; **~ hab' ich das verdient?** what did I do to deserve that? II rel adv with which. **~ ich nicht sagen will** by which I don't mean to say.

wo'möglich adv if possible, possibly.

wo'nach I interrog adv after what: **~ fragt er?** what is he asking about? II rel adv what, after (or according to) which.

Wonne ['vɔnə] f (-; -n) delight, bliss: **e-e wahre ~** a real treat; F **mit ~** with relish.

'**wonnig** adj lovely, sweet.

wor'an I interrog adv **~ denken Sie?** what are you thinking about?; **~ arbeitet er?** what is he working on (or at)?; **~ liegt es, daß?** how is it that?; **~ hast du ihn erkannt?** how did you recognize him?; **~ sieht man, welche (ob)?** how can you tell which (if)? II rel adv **ich weiß nicht, ~ ich bin** I don't know where I stand, **mit ihm** I don't know what to make of him; **~ ich dich erinnern möchte** what I want to remind you of; **~ man merkte, daß** which showed that.

wor'auf I interrog adv what: **~ wartest du noch?** what are you (still) waiting for? II rel adv **et., ~ ich bestehe** s.th. (which or that) I insist (up)on; **~ er sagte** upon which he said; **~ alle gingen** whereupon everybody left.

wor'aus I interrog adv **~ ist es (gemacht)?** what is it made of?; **~ schließt du das?** what makes you think that? II rel adv **~ zu entnehmen war, daß** from which we understood that.

wor'in I interrog adv **~ liegt der Unterschied?** what (or where) is the difference? II rel adv in which.

Wort [vɔrt] n (-[e]s; -e, ⁓er) **1.** (pl ⁓er) word. **2.** (pl -e) word, eccl. Word, Word, saying: **geflügelte ~e** familiar quotations; **in ~en** with sums: in letters; **~ für ~** word for word; **ein gutes ~ einlegen** put in a good word;

das ~ ergreifen (begin to) speak, parl. a. take the floor; **mir fehlen die ~e** words fail me; **das ~ führen** do the talking; **das große ~ führen** a) do all the talking, b) talk big; **das ~ hat Herr X** the word is with Mr. X; **das letzte ~** the last word (in dat on); **das letzte ~ haben** have the final say; **du willst (or mußt) immer das letzte ~ haben** you always have to have the last word; **kein ~ darüber!** not a word of it!; **kein ~ mehr!** not another word!; F **hast du ~e?** would you believe it?; **ein ~ gab das andere** one thing led to another; → **abschneiden** 1, **entziehen** 1. **3.** no pl word (of hono[u]r): **sein ~ geben (brechen, halten)** give (break, keep) one's word; → **Mann. 4. aufs ~ gehorchen (glauben)** obey (believe) implicitly; **j-n beim ~ nehmen** take s.o. at his word; **j-m ins ~ fallen** cut s.o. short; **in ~e fassen** put into words; **mit anderen ~en** in other words; **mit 'einem ~** in a word; **zu ~e kommen** have one's say; **nicht zu ~e kommen** not to get a word in edgeways.

'**Wortart** f ling. part of speech.

'**Wortbildung** f word formation.

'**wortbrüchig** adj **~ werden** break one's word.

Wörterbuch ['vœrtər-] n dictionary.

'**Wörterverzeichnis** n list of words, vocabulary.

'**Wort|führer** m spokesman. **~gefecht** n battle of words, argument.

'**wortgetreu** adj literal, word-for-word.

'**wortgewandt** adj eloquent.

'**wortkarg** adj taciturn.

Wortklauberei [-klaubə'raɪ] f (-; no pl) hairsplitting.

'**Wortlaut** m (-[e]s; no pl) wording, text: **der Brief hat folgenden ~** the letter runs as follows.

wörtlich ['vœrtliç] adj literal, word-to--word: **~e Rede** direct speech.

'**wortlos** adj wordless.

'**Wortmeldung** f request to speak.

'**wortreich** adj verbose, wordy.

'**Wortschatz** m (-es; no pl) vocabulary.

'**Wortschöpfung** f coinage, neologism.

'**Wortschwall** m torrent of words.

'**Wortspiel** n play on words, pun.

'**Wortstellung** f word order.

'**Wortwechsel** m argument, dispute.

'**wort'wörtlich** → **wörtlich**.

wor'über I *interrog adv* ~ **lachst du?** what are you laughing about (*or* at)? II *rel adv* et., ~ **ich sehr verärgert war** s.th. I was very angry about (*or* at); ~ **er ärgerlich war** which annoyed him.

wor'um I *interrog adv* ~ **handelt es sich?** what is it about? II *rel adv* et., ~ **ich dich bitten möchte** s.th (which *or* that) I want to ask you.

wor'unter I *interrog adv* what ... under. II *rel adv* et., ~ **ich mir nichts vorstellen kann** s.th. which doesn't mean anything to me; ~ **ich leide** what I suffer from (*or* under).

wo'von I *interrog adv* ~ **leben sie?** what do they live on?; ~ **sprecht ihr?** what are you talking about? II *rel adv* et., ~ **ich nur zu träumen wage** s.th. I can only dream about (*or* of).

wo'vor I *interrog adv* ~ **hast du Angst?** what are you afraid of? II *rel adv* ~ **du dich hüten mußt, ist** what you must be careful of is.

wo'zu I *interrog adv* **1.** ~ **hat er sich entschlossen?** what did he decide upon? **2.** why. II *rel adv* ~ **er bereit ist** what (*or* which) he is prepared to do.

Wrack [vrak] *n* (-[e]s; -s) *a. fig.* wreck.

wringen ['vrɪŋən] *v/t* (wrang, gewrungen, h) wring.

Wucher ['vu:xər] *m* (-s; *no pl*) usury.

'**Wucherer** *m* (-s; -) usurer.

'**Wuchermiete** *f* rack rent.

wuchern ['vu:xərn] *v/i* (h) **1.** 🌿 grow rampant, *a.* 🌿 proliferate, *fig. a.* be rampant. **2.** practi/se (*Am.* -ce) usury.

'**Wucherpreis** *m* exorbitant price.

'**Wucherung** *f* (-; -en) 🌿 a) excrescence, tumo(u)r, b) (tissue) proliferation.

'**Wucherzinsen** *pl* usurious interest.

wuchs [vu:ks] *pret of* **wachsen¹**.

Wuchs *m* (-es; *no pl*) **1.** growth. **2.** build, physique: **klein von** ~ of small build.

Wucht [vʊxt] *f* (-; *no pl*) force, *a.* impact: **mit voller** ~ with full force; F **das ist 'ne** ~**!** it's terrific! '**wuchten** *v/t* (h) **1.** heave. **2.** **Räder** ~ balance wheels.

'**wuchtig** *adj* heavy (*a. blow*), powerful.

'**Wühlarbeit** *f fig.* subversive activity.

wühlen ['vy:lən] (h) I *v/i* **1.** dig, *animal*: burrow, *pig*: root, grub: ~ **in** (*dat*) rummage in. **2.** *pol.* agitate. II **sich** ~ **in** (*acc*) burrow (o.s.) into.

'**Wühler** *m* (-s; -) *pol.* agitator.

'**Wühlmaus** *f zo.* vole.

'**Wühltisch** *m* ✝ rummage counter.

Wulst [vʊlst] *m* (-es; ⸚e) **1.** roll. **2.** pad. **3.** bulge. **4.** (*tyre*) bead.

'**wulstig** *adj* bulging, thick (*lips*).

wund [vʊnt] *adj* sore, raw: ~ **reiben** chafe; ~**e Stelle** sore; *fig.* ~**er Punkt** sore point; **sich die Füße** ~ **laufen** get sore feet, *fig.* run from pillar to post.

'**Wundbrand** *m* (-es; *no pl*) 🌿 gangrene.

Wunde ['vʊndə] *f* (-; -n) wound, cut, gash: *fig.* **alte** ~**n** wieder aufreißen open old sores; **die Zeit heilt alle** ~**n** time is a great healer.

Wunder ['vʊndər] *n* (-s; -) miracle, wonder: ~ **der Technik** engineering marvel; (**es ist**) **kein** ~(, **daß**) no wonder (that); ~ **tun,** ~ **wirken** perform miracles, *fig.* work wonders; **es grenzt an ein** ~ it borders on the miraculous; F **er wird sein blaues** ~ **erleben** he's in for a shock; **wie durch ein** ~ miraculously; **wunder wie** goodness knows how; **er glaubt wunder was er getan hat** he thinks he's done goodness knows what; → **Zeichen** 2.

'**wunderbar** *adj* **1.** miraculous. **2.** wonderful, marvel(l)ous.

'**wunderbarer'weise** *adv* miraculously.

'**Wunderding** *n* wonder.

'**Wunderdoktor** *m iro.* miracle doctor.

'**Wunderglaube** *m* belief in miracles.

wunder'hübsch *adj* lovely.

'**Wunderkerze** *f* sparkler.

'**Wunderkind** *n* child prodigy.

'**wunderlich** *adj* strange, peculiar.

'**Wundermittel** *n* wonder drug.

wundern ['vʊndərn] (h) I *v/t* surprise: **es wundert mich** I'm surprised. II **sich** ~ (**über** *acc* at) be surprised, wonder; **du wirst dich** ~**!** you'll be surprised!

wunder'schön *adj* very beautiful.

'**Wundertäter(in** *f*) *m* miracle worker.

'**wundervoll** → **wunderbar** 2.

'**Wunderwerk** *n fig.* wonder, marvel.

'**Wundfieber** *n* wound fever.

'**wundliegen: sich** ~ (*irr, sep*, -ge-, h, → **liegen**) get bedsores.

'**Wundmal** *n eccl.* stigma.

'**Wundschmerz** *m* traumatic pain.

'**Wundstarrkrampf** *m* 🌿 tetanus.

Wunsch [vʊnʃ] *m* (-[e]s; ⸚e) **1.** wish, desire, request: **auf j-s** ~ (**hin**) at s.o.'s request; *auf eigenen* ~ at one's own request; *auf allgemeinen* ~ by popular request; *(je) nach* ~ as desired; *es ging alles nach* ~ everything went as planned; *haben Sie noch e-n* ~*?* is there anything else I can do for you?; → *ablesen²* 3, *fromm* 1. *2. mit den besten Wünschen* with best wishes.

'**Wunschbild** n ideal.

'**Wunschdenken** n wishful thinking.

Wünschelrute ['vʏnʃəl-] f divining rod.

'**Wünschelrutengänger** [-gɛŋər] m (-s; -) diviner.

wünschen ['vʏnʃən] (h) I v/t wish; want: *sich et.* ~ wish (*or* long) for s.th.; *was* ~ *Sie?* what can I do for you?; *du darfst dir et.* ~ you can make a wish; *ich wünsche mir* I'd like to have; → *gewünscht.* II v/i *Sie* ~*?* what can I do for you?; *wie Sie* ~ as you wish (*or* like), *iro.* suit yourself; *viel zu* ~ *übriglassen* leave much to be desired.

'**wünschenswert** adj desirable.

'**wunschgemäß** adv as requested.

'**Wunsch|kind** n planned child. ~**kon-,zert** n request program(me Br.).

'**wunschlos** adv ~ *glücklich* perfectly happy.

'**Wunschtraum** m (*iro.* pipe) dream.

'**Wunschzettel** m list of presents.

wurde ['vʊrdə] *pret of* **werden**.

Würde ['vʏrdə] f (-; -n) dignity, a. hono(u)r, a. rank, a. title: *akademische* ~ academic degree; *unter aller* ~ beneath contempt; *unter m-r* ~ beneath my dignity. '**würdelos** adj undignified.

'**Würdenträger** m (-s; -) dignitary.

'**würdevoll** I adj dignified. II adv with dignity.

'**würdig** adj 1. dignified. 2. (gen of) worthy, deserving: *ein* ~*er Nachfolger* a worthy successor; *er ist dessen nicht* ~ he doesn't deserve it.

würdigen ['vʏrdɪgən] v/t (h) 1. appreciate, acknowledge, recognize. 2. *j-n k-s Blickes* ~ not to deign to look at s.o.

'**Würdigung** f (-; -en) appreciation, acknowledgement: *in* ~ *s-r Verdienste* in recognition of his merits.

Wurf [vʊrf] m (-[e]s; ⸚e) 1. throw: *fig. glücklicher* ~ lucky strike; *großer* ~ great success. 2. *zo.* litter.

'**Wurfdiszi,plin** f sports: throwing event.

Würfel ['vʏrfəl] m (-s; -) 1. cube. 2. dice:

die ~ *sind gefallen* the die is cast.

'**Würfelbecher** m (dice) shaker.

'**würfelförmig** adj cubic, cube-shaped.

würfeln ['vʏrfəln] (h) I v/i 1. play dice: *um et.* ~ throw dice for s.th. II v/t 2. throw. 3. *gastr.* dice.

'**Würfelspiel** n game of dice.

'**Würfelzucker** m lump (*or* cube) sugar.

'**Wurf|geschoß** n projectile. ~**kreis** m sports: (throwing) circle. ~**pfeil** m dart. ~**sendung(en** pl) f unaddressed advertising matter, *contp.* junk mail. ~**spieß** m javelin. ~**taube** f sports. clay pigeon.

'**Würgegriff** m *a. fig.* stranglehold.

würgen ['vʏrgən] (h) I v/t strangle, throttle, choke. II v/i a) choke, b) retch: ~ *an* (dat) choke on.

Wurm¹ [vʊrm] m (-[e]s; ⸚er) *zo.* worm (*a. fig.*), a. maggot: 🐛 *Würmer haben* suffer from worms; F *j-m die Würmer aus der Nase ziehen* drag it out of s.o.; *da ist der* ~ *drin* s.th. is wrong (with it).

Wurm² n (-[e]s; ⸚er), **Würmchen** ['vʏrmçən] n (-s; -) F (little) mite.

wurmen ['vʊrmən] v/t (h) *j-n* ~ gall (*or* get) s.o., rankle with s.o.

'**Wurm|fortsatz** m anat. (vermiform) appendix. ~**kur** f 🐛 deworming. ~**mittel** n 🐛 vermifuge.

'**wurmstichig** adj wormy, worm-eaten.

Wurst [vʊrst] f (-; ⸚e) sausage: F *es ist mir (völlig)* ~*!* I don't care (a damn)!; *jetzt geht's um die* ~ now or never.

Würstchen ['vʏrstçən] n (-s; -) 1. small sausage: *Frankfurter* ~ frankfurter; *Wiener* ~ wiener(wurst). 2. F nobody: *armes* ~ poor soul. ~**bude** f, ~**stand** m hot-dog stand.

wursteln ['vʊrstəln] v/i (h) F muddle along.

'**Wursthaut** f sausage skin.

'**Wurstigkeit** f (-; no pl) F couldn't-care-less attitude.

'**Wurstwaren** pl sausages.

Würze ['vʏrtsə] f (-; -n) 1. spice (a. fig.), seasoning, flavo(u)r. 2. wort.

Wurzel ['vʊrtsəl] f (-; -n) 1. root (a. fig., 🅐 a. radical: 🅐 *zweite (dritte)* ~ square (cubic) root; *die* ~ *(aus)* e-r *Zahl ziehen* extract the (square) root of a number; *a. fig.* ~*n schlagen* take root. 2. *dial.* carrot. ~**behandlung** f 🦷 root treatment. ~**gemüse** n root vegetables. ~**größe** f 🅐 radical quantity.

'wurzellos adj a. fig. rootless.
wurzeln ['vʊrtsəln] v/i (h) take root: fig. **~ in** (dat) be rooted in, have its roots in.
'Wurzelwerk n (-[e]s; no pl) roots.
'Wurzelzeichen n ⅋ radical sign.
'Wurzelziehen n (-s) ⅋ root extraction.
würzen ['vʏrtsən] v/t (h) a. fig. spice.
'würzig adj spicy, fig. fragrant (air).
'Würzkräuter pl (pot) herbs.
wusch [vuːʃ] pret of waschen.
wuschelig ['vʊʃəlɪç] adj F fuzzy.
wußte ['vʊstə] pret of wissen.
Wust [vuːst] m (-[e]s; no pl) 1. tangled mass. 2. trash. 3. jumble.
wüst [vyːst] adj 1. desert, waste. 2. a) wild, dissolute, b) rude, c) vile: **~ aussehen** look a real mess.
Wüste ['vyːstə] f (-; -n) desert, fig. a. waste: F fig. **j-n in die ~ schicken** give s.o. the boot.
'Wüsten... desert (sand, wind, etc).
'Wüstling m (-s; -e) libertine, rake.

Wut [vuːt] f (-; no pl) rage, fury: **e-e ~ bekommen** (F kriegen), **in ~ geraten** get furious (F mad), fly into a rage; **j-n in ~ bringen** enrage (or infuriate) s.o.; **vor ~ kochen** (or schäumen) seethe with rage, fume; **e-e ~ auf j-n haben** F be mad at s.o.; **s-e ~ an j-m auslassen** take it out on s.o.
'Wutanfall m fit (or outburst) of rage: **e-n ~ bekommen** blow one's top.
wüten ['vyːtən] v/i (h) rage (a. fig. storm, epidemic, etc): **~ gegen** rage at (or against); **~ unter** create havoc among.
'wütend adj 1. furious, F mad: **auf j-n ~ sein** be furious with (F mad at) s.o.; **über et. ~ sein** be furious at (F mad about) s.th.; **j-n ~ machen** infuriate (or enrage) s.o. 2. fig. raging (pain etc).
'wutentbrannt adj furious, infuriated.
'wutschäumend adj foaming with rage.
'Wutschrei m yell of rage.

X

X, x [ɪks] n (-; -) X, x: F **j-m ein X für ein U vormachen** fool s.o.; **ich habe x Leute gefragt** I've asked umpteen people.
'X-Achse f ⅋ x-axis.
Xanthippe [ksan'tɪpə] f (-; -n) F shrew, battle-axe(e).
'X-Beine pl knock-knees.
x-beinig ['ɪksbaɪnɪç] adj knock-kneed.
x-be'liebig adj F any (... you like): **jeder ~e** anybody, any Tom, Dick and Harry; **et. Ωes** anything (you like).

'X-Chromo,som n X chromosome.
Xenon ['kseːnɔn] n (-s; no pl) 🜛 xenon.
Xerographie [kseroɡra'fiː] f (-; no pl) print. xerography.
'x-fach adv ever so often.
x-förmig ['ɪksfœrmɪç] adj x-shaped.
'x-mal adv F umpteen times.
x-te ['ɪkstə] adj F **zum ~n Mal** for the umpteenth time.
Xylophon [ksylo'foːn] n (-s; -e) ♪ xylophone.

Y

Y, y ['ʏpsilɔn] n (-; -) Y, y.
'Y-Achse f ⅋ y-axis.
'Y-Chromo,som n Y chromosome.

Yen [jɛn] m (-[s]; -[s]) 🜊 yen.
Yoga ['joːɡa] m, n (-[s]; no pl) yoga.
Yogi ['joːɡi] m (-s; -s) yogi.

Z

Z, z [tsɛt] *n* (-; -) Z, z; → **A.**

Zack [tsak] F *auf ~ sein* (*bringen*) be on the ball (bring *s.o.*, *s.th.* up to scratch).

Zacke ['tsakə] *f* (-; -n) a) (sharp) point, jag, ✿ tooth, indentation, b) prong.

zacken ['tsakən] *v/t* (h) a) indent, jag, b) pink (*cloth, paper*), c) tooth.

'Zacken *m* (-s; -) *dial* → **Zacke:** F *er bricht sich k-n ~ aus der Krone, wenn er ihr hilft* it won't kill him to help her.

'Zackenschere *f* pinking shears.

'zackig *adj* **1.** a) indented, jagged, b) toothed. **2.** F *fig.* snappy.

zaghaft ['tsaːkhaft] *adj* timid, cautious.

zäh [tsɛː] *adj* **1.** tough (*meat*), viscous (*liquid*). **2.** *fig.* a) tough, tenacious, b) stubborn, c) slow, sluggish, slow-moving (*traffic*): *ein ~er Bursche* a tough fellow; *~ festhalten an* (*dat*) stick doggedly to. **'zähflüssig** *adj* **1.** viscous. **2.** *fig.* sluggish, slow-moving (*traffic*).

'Zähigkeit *f* (-; *no pl*) *fig.* toughness.

Zahl [tsaːl] *f* (-; -en) a) number (*a. ling.*), b) figure, c) numeral, cipher, d) digit: *genaue ~en* exact figures; *römische ~en* Roman numerals; *sechsstellige ~* six-digit number; *fig. in großer ~* in large numbers; *an ~ übertreffen* outnumber; → **rot.**

'zahlbar *adj* payable (*an acc* to, *bei* at, with): *~ nach Erhalt* payable (up)on receipt; → **Lieferung** 1.

'zählbar *adj* countable.

'zählebig [-leːbɪç] *adj* tough, tenacious.

'Zählebigkeit *f* (-; *no pl*) tenacity of life.

zahlen ['tsaːlən] *v/t*, *v/i* (h) pay: (*Herr Ober,*) *~, bitte!* the bill (*Am. check*), please!

zählen ['tsɛːlən] (h) **I** *v/t* count, *sports:* score: *s-e Tage sind gezählt* his days are numbered; *ich zähle ihn zu m-n Freunden* I count him as a friend. **II** *v/i* count (*bis zehn* up to ten): *fig. er* (*es*) *zählt nicht* he (it) doesn't count; *~ auf* (*acc*) count on; *~ zu* rank with, belong to (*the best etc*); *er zählt zu m-n Freunden* he is a friend (of mine); → **drei** I.

'Zahlen|angaben *pl* figures. **~folge** *f* order of numbers. **~gedächtnis** *n* memory for figures. **~lotto** *n* → **Lotto** 2.

'zahlenmäßig *adj* numerical: *j-m ~ überlegen sein* outnumber s.o.

'Zahlenschloß *n* combination lock.

Zahler ['tsaːlər] *m* (-s; -) payer.

Zähler ['tsɛːlər] *m* (-s; -) **1.** counter, ⚡ *a.* meter. **2.** Å numerator. **3.** *sports:* point.

'Zählerablesung *f* ⚡ meter reading.

'Zählerstand *m* ⚡ count.

'Zahlgrenze *f* fare stage.

'Zahlkarte *f* ✝ paying-in slip.

'zahllos *adj* countless, innumerable.

'Zahlmeister *m* **1.** ⚓ purser. **2.** ✗ paymaster.

'zahlreich *adj* a) numerous, many, b) large: *~ versammelt sein* be present in large numbers.

'Zahltag *m* payday.

'Zahlung *f* (-; -en) (*e-e ~ leisten* make a) payment: *et. in ~ geben* trade s.th. in; *et. in ~ nehmen* take s.th. in part exchange.

'Zählung *f* (-; -en) count, *a.* census.

'Zahlungs|abkommen *n* payments agreement. **~anweisung** *f* **1.** order to pay. **2.** money order. **~aufforderung** *f* request for payment. **~aufschub** *m* respite. **~auftrag** *m* of depositor: banker's order. **~bedingungen** *pl* terms of payment. **~bi,lanz** *f* balance of payments. **~einstellung** *f* suspension of payment. **~empfänger(in** *f*) *m* payee. **~erleichterungen** *pl* easy terms (for payment). **②fähig** *adj* able to pay, solvent. **~fähigkeit** *f* (-; *no pl*) ability to pay, solvency. **~frist** *f* term of payment. **②kräftig** *adj* F potent, wealthy. **~mittel** *n* a) means of payment, b) currency: *gesetzliches ~* legal tender. **②pflichtig** *adj* liable to pay. **~schwierigkeiten** *pl* financial difficulties. **~ter,min** *m* date of payment. **②unfähig** *adj* unable to pay, insolvent. **~unfähigkeit** *f* inability to pay, insolvency. **~verpflichtung** *f* liability (to pay): *s-n ~en pünktlich nachkommen* be punctual in one's payments. **~verzug** *m* default (of payment): *in ~ geraten* default. **~weise** *f* mode of payment. **~ziel** *n* date of payment.

'Zählwerk *n* counter.

'Zahlwort *n* (-[e]s; ⁻er) *ling.* numeral.

'Zahlzeichen n figure, numeral.

zahm [tsa:m] adj tame (a. fig.), domesticated, fig. tractable. **'zähmbar** adj tam(e)able. **zähmen** ['tsɛ:mən] v/t (h) **1.** a. fig. tame, domesticate. **2.** control, restrain (**sich** o.s.). **'Zahmheit** f (-; no pl) a. fig. tameness. **'Zähmung** f (-; no pl) taming (a. fig.), domestication.

Zahn [tsa:n] m (-[e]s; ⸚e) **1.** tooth (a. ☉), zo. a. fang, a. tusk: **Zähne bekommen** → **zahnen** I; humor. **die dritten Zähne** (a set of) false teeth; **der ~ der Zeit** the ravages of time; **bis an die Zähne bewaffnet** armed to the teeth; **sich e-n ~ ziehen lassen** have a tooth out; F fig. **sich an e-r Sache die Zähne ausbeißen** find s.th. too hard a nut to crack; **j-m auf den ~ fühlen** sound s.o. out; F **et. für den hohlen ~** precious little; → **fletschen, Haar, knirschen, putzen** I. **2.** F speed: **er hatte e-n ziemlichen ~ drauf** he was going at a terrific lick; **e-n ~ zulegen** step on it.

'Zahn|arzt m dentist, dental surgeon. **~arzthelferin** f dentist's assistant. **Ʒärztlich** adj dental. **~arztpraxis** f dental practice. **~behandlung** f dental treatment. **~belag** m plaque. **~bett** n anat. tooth socket. **~bürste** f toothbrush. **~creme** f toothpaste.

zähne|fletschend ['tsɛ:nə-] adj and adv snarling. **~klappernd** adj and adv with chattering teeth. **~knirschend** adv fig. gritting one's teeth.

zahnen ['tsa:nən] (h) **I** v/i teethe, cut one's teeth. **II** a. **zähnen** ['tsɛ:nən] v/t (h) ☉ tooth.

'Zahn|ersatz m dentures. **~fäule** f tooth decay, caries. **~fleisch** n gums: humor. **auf dem ~ gehen** be on one's last legs. **~fleischbluten** n bleeding of the gums. **~füllung** f filling. **~hals** m neck of a tooth. **~klinik** f dental clinic. **~kranz** m ☉ a) gear rim, b) sprocket (wheel). **~krone** f ⚒ crown. **~la,bor** n dental laboratory. **~laut** m dental (sound).

'zahnlos adj toothless.

'Zahn|lücke f gap (in one's teeth). **~medi,zin** f dentistry. **~medi,ziner** m **1.** dentist. **2.** dental student. **~nerv** m nerve of a tooth. **~pasta** f toothpaste. **~pflege** f dental hygiene. **~pro,these** f dentures.

'Zahnrad n ☉ gearwheel, toothed wheel.

~antrieb m gearwheel drive. **~bahn** f rack railway (Am. railroad). **~getriebe** n toothed gearing.

'Zahn|schmelz m (dental) enamel. **~schmerzen** pl (~ haben have [a]) toothache. **~schutz** m boxing: gumshield. **~seide** f dental floss. **~spange** f brace. **~stange** f ☉ rack. **~stein** m ⚒ tartar. **~stocher** m (-s; -) toothpick. **~stummel** m stump. **~technik** f dentistry. **~techniker** m dental technician. **~wechsel** m second dentition. **~weh** n → **Zahnschmerzen**. **~wurzel** f root of a tooth). **~ze,ment** m (dental) cement.

Zander ['tsandər] m (-s; -) zo. zander, pike-perch.

Zange ['tsaŋə] f (-; -n) pliers, tongs, a. zo. pincers, ⚒, zo. forceps: **e-e ~** a pair of tongs etc; F fig. **j-n in die ~ nehmen** put the screws on s.o.; **den würde ich nicht mit der ~ anfassen!** I wouldn't touch him with a bargepole.

Zank [tsaŋk] m (-[e]s; no pl) quarrel. **'Zankapfel** m (-s; no pl) bone of contention. **'zanken** v/i (h) **1.** (a. **sich ~**) quarrel (**über** acc about, **um** about, over). **2.** dial. (**mit j-m**) ~ scold (s.o.). **Zanke'rei** f (-; -en) bickering.

zänkisch ['tsɛŋkɪʃ] adj quarrelsome.

Zäpfchen ['tsɛpfçən] n (-s; -) **1.** anat. uvula. **2.** ⚒ suppository.

zapfen ['tsapfən] v/t (h) **1.** tap, draw (beer etc). **2.** ☉ mortise.

'Zapfen m (-s; -) **1.** ♀ cone. **2.** tap, spigot, Am. faucet. **3.** ☉ a) journal, b) pivot, c) tenon, d) peg.

'Zapfenstreich m ✕ tattoo.

'Zapfer m (-s; -) tapster.

'Zapf|hahn m **1.** tap, Am. faucet. **2.** → **~pi,stole** f mot. nozzle. **~säule** f mot. petrol (Am. gasoline) pump.

Zappe'lei f (-; no pl) F fidgets.

'zapp(e)lig adj F fidgety: **du machst mich ganz ~!** you give me the fidgets.

zappeln ['tsapəln] v/i (h) **1.** struggle, wriggle: F fig. **j-n ~ lassen** keep s.o. on tenterhooks. **2.** F fidget (**vor Aufregung** with excitement).

'Zappelphilipp [-filɪp] m (-s; -e) F fidget.

Zar [tsa:r] m (-en; -en) czar, tsar.

Zarge ['tsargə] f (-; -n) ☉ **1.** notch, groove. **2.** frame, case (of door etc).

Zarin ['tsa:rɪn] f (-; -nen) czarina, tsarina.

zart [tsart] *adj* tender (*meat etc, a. fig. age, love, etc*), delicate (*a. child, health, colo[u]r, etc*), frail (*a. fig.*), filmy (*fabric etc*), gentle (*touch etc*), soft (*skin etc*), a. sensitive: *das ~e Geschlecht* the gentle sex; *ein ~er Wink* a gentle hint; *nicht für ~e Ohren* not for tender (*or* sensitive) ears; (*nicht gerade*) *~ umgehen mit* handle *s.o.*, *s.th.* (none too) gently.

'zartbesaitet *adj* highly sensitive.

'zartbitter *adj* plain (*chocolate*).

'zartblau *adj* pale-blue.

'zartfühlend *adj* **1.** sensitive. **2.** tactful, discreet. **'Zartgefühl** *n* (-[e]s; *no pl*) **1.** delicacy (of feeling), sensitivity. **2.** tact.

'zartgliedrig *adj* delicate, gracile.

'Zartheit *f* (-; *no pl*) tenderness (*a. fig.*), delicacy, delicateness, fragility, softness, gentleness.

zärtlich ['tsɛːrtlɪç] *adj* tender, affectionate (*zu* with), caressing: *~e Mutter* fond mother. **'Zärtlichkeit** *f* (-; -en) **1.** *no pl* tenderness, affection, fondness. **2.** endearment, caress.

Zaster ['tsastər] *m* (-s; *no pl*) F dough.

Zäsur [tsɛ'zuːr] *f* (-; -en) **1.** *metr.*, ♪ c(a)esura, break. **2.** *fig.* turning point.

Zauber ['tsaʊbər] *m* (-s; *no pl*) **1.** (*wie durch ~* as if by) magic: F *contp. fauler ~* mumbo-jumbo. **2.** *fig.* charm, magic, spell. **3.** F *contp.* a) fuss, b) nonsense: *der ganze ~* the whole bag of tricks. **Zaube'rei** *f* (-; *no pl*) **1.** magic, witchcraft. **2.** conjuring trick. **'Zauberer** *m* (-s; -) **1.** magician, sorcerer, *a. fig.* wizard. **2.** → *Zauberkünstler.*

'Zauberformel *f* magic formula.

'zauberhaft *adj* charming, enchanting.

'Zauberin *f* (-; -nen) *a. fig.* sorceress.

'Zauber|kraft *f* magic power. **~kunst** *f* magic (art). **~künstler** *m* conjurer, magician. **~kunststück** *n* conjuring trick.

zaubern ['tsaʊbərn] (h) **I** *v/t* produce *s.th.* by magic, conjure up. **II** *v/i* a) perform magic, b) conjure, do conjuring tricks, c) *soccer etc*: put on a brilliant show: *ich kann doch nicht ~!* I can't perform miracles.

'Zauber|spruch *m* charm, spell. **~stab** *m* (magic) wand. **~trank** *m* magic potion. **~wort** *n* (-[e]s; -e) magic word.

'Zauderer *m* (-s; -) waverer.

zaudern ['tsaʊdərn] *v/i* (h) hesitate, waver: *ohne Zaudern* without hesitation.

Zaum [tsaʊm] *m* (-[e]s; ~e) (*a. fig. im ~e halten*) bridle.

zäumen ['tsɔymən] *v/t* (h) bridle

'Zaumzeug *n* headgear, bridle.

Zaun [tsaʊn] *m* (-[e]s; ~e) a) fence, b) hoarding: *vom ~ brechen* a) *e-n Streit* pick a quarrel, b) *e-n Krieg* start a war. **~gast** *m* onlooker. **~könig** *m zo.* wren. **~pfahl** *m* pale: F *ein Wink mit dem ~* a broad hint.

zausen ['tsaʊzən] *v/t* (h) ruffle, *a.* tousle.

Zebra ['tseːbra] *n* (-s; -s) *zo.* zebra.

'Zebrastreifen *m* zebra crossing.

Zeche¹ ['tsɛçə] *f* (-; -n) ✕ pit, (coal) mine, colliery.

Zeche² *f* (-; -n) bill, *Am.* check: *die ~ prellen* leave without paying; *fig. die ~ zahlen müssen* F have to pay the piper. **'Zechpreller** *m* (-s; -) bilk. **Zechprelle'rei** *f* (-; -en) bilking.

Zecke ['tsɛkə] *f* (-; -n) *zo.* tick.

Zeder ['tseːdər] *f* (-; -n) ♀ cedar.

'Zedernholz *n* cedar(wood).

Zeh [tseː] *m* (-s; -en) → *Zehe* **1. Zehe** ['tseːə] *f* (-; -n) **1.** *anat.*, *zo.* toe: *große (kleine)* ~ big (little) toe; *j-m auf die ~n treten a.* F *fig.* tread on *s.o.'s* toes. **2.** clove (of garlic).

'Zehen|nagel *m* toenail. **~san,dale** *f* flip-flop. **~spitze** *f* tip of one's toe: *auf (den) ~n* on tiptoe.

zehn [tseːn] *adj/zw.* **Zehn** *f* (-; -en) (number) ten. **'Zehneck** *n* (-[e]s; -e) decagon.

'Zehner¹ *m* (-s; -) **1.** ten. **2.** F → *Zehnpfennigstück, Zehnmarkschein.*

'Zehner² *f* (-; -) → *Zehnpfennig-(brief)marke.*

'Zehnerkarte *f* ten-trip ticket.

'Zehnerpackung *f* pack(et) of ten.

'Zehnerstelle *f* A tens digit.

'zehnfach *adj* and *adv* tenfold.

'Zehnfache *n* (-n) ten times the amount: *um das ~* increase *etc* tenfold.

Zehn'fingersy,stem *n* touch system.

'zehnjährig [-jɛːrɪç] *adj* **1.** ten-year-old: *ein ~er Junge* a. a boy of ten. **2.** *~es Jubiläum etc* ten-year (*or* tenth) anniversary *etc*. **3.** *nach ~er Abwesenheit etc* after an absence *etc* of ten years.

'Zehnkampf *m sports*: decathlon.

'Zehnkämpfer *m* decathlete.

'zehnmal *adv* ten times.

Zehn'markschein *m* ten-mark note (*Am.* bill), F tenner.

Zehn'pfennig|(brief)marke *f* ten-pfennig stamp. **~stück** *n* ten-pfennig piece.

zehnt *adj* tenth.

'zehn'tausend *adj* ten thousand: *fig.* **die oberen ♀** the upper ten (thousand); **♀e von ...** tens of thousands of ...

Zehntel ['tse:ntəl] *n* (-s; -) tenth.

'Zehntelse,kunde *f* tenth of a second.

zehntens ['tse:ntəns] *adv* tenthly.

zehren ['tse:rən] *v/i* (h) **1.** **~ von** live on (*a. fig. memories etc*); **von s-m Kapital ~** live off one's capital. **2.** **~ an** (*dat*) weaken, undermine; **an j-s Kräften ~** sap s.o.'s energy.

Zeichen ['tsaiçən] *n* (-s; -) **1.** a) sign, *a.* mark, *a.* characteristic, b) signal, c) symbol, *computer:* character: **chemisches ~** chemical symbol; **j-m ein ~ geben** give s.o. a sign (*or* signal), signal to s.o.; **er gab das ~ zum Aufbruch** he gave the sign to leave. **2.** *fig.* sign, *a.* mark, token, *a.* omen, *a.* symptom: **ein ~ für** (*or* **von**) a sign of; **zum ~ daß** as a proof that; **als** (*or* **zum**) **~ m-r Dankbarkeit** as a token of my gratitude; **es ist ein ~ der Zeit** it's a symptom of our times; **es geschehen noch ~ und Wunder** wonders never cease. **3.** punctuation mark. **4.** *astr.* sign: **im ~ des Löwen** under the sign of Leo; *fig.* **im ~ stehen von** (*or* **gen**) be marked by. **5.** reference (number): **✝ unser (Ihr) ~** our (your) reference. **6.** **✝** trademark.

'Zeichen|block *m* sketch pad. **~brett** *n* drawing board. **~dreieck** *n* set square. **~erklärung** *f* key (**für, zu** to), *on maps etc:* legend, *in textbooks etc:* signs and symbols. **~feder** *f* drawing pen. **~gerät** *n* computer: plotter. **~heft** *n* drawing book. **~kunst** *f* art. **~lehrer** *m* art teacher. **~pa,pier** *n* drawing paper. **~saal** *m* art room. **~setzung** *f* (-; *no pl*) punctuation. **~sprache** *f* (-; *no pl*) sign language. **~stift** *m* pencil, crayon. **~trickfilm** *m* (animated) cartoon. **~unterricht** *m* drawing lessons, *ped.* art.

zeichnen ['tsaiçnən] (h) **I** *v/t* **1.** draw (*a. fig.*), sketch, *a. fig.* delineate, design. **2.** mark: **er war von der Krankheit gezeichnet** the illness had left its mark (on him). **3.** sign (*letter etc*). **4.** **✝** subscribe (**für Aktien** *etc* for shares *etc*, **für e-n Fonds** to a fund). **II** *v/i* **5.** draw (**nach der Natur** from nature). **6.** sign:

ich zeichne ... I remain ...; **verantwortlich ~ für** be responsible for.

'Zeichner *m* (-s; -) **1.** drawer, draughtsman, *Am.* draftsman. **2.** **✝** subscriber (**gen** for, to). **'Zeichnerin** *f* (-; -nen) **1.** drawer, draughtswoman, *Am.* draftswoman. **2.** → **Zeichner** 2.

'zeichnerisch *adj* graphic: **~e Begabung haben, ~ begabt sein** have (a) talent for drawing.

'Zeichnung *f* (-; -en) **1.** a) drawing, **◎** *a.* design, diagram, b) sketch, c) illustration. **2. ♀,** *zo.* marking(s), patterning. **3.** **✝** subscription: **e-e Anleihe zur ~ auflegen** invite subscriptions for a loan.

'zeichnungsberechtigt *adj* authorized to sign, having signatory power.

'Zeigefinger *m* forefinger, index finger.

zeigen ['tsaigən] (h) **I** *v/t* show (*a. fig.*), *a.* present (*film etc*), *a. fig.* display, exhibit, *a.* indicate, *a.* demonstrate, point out: **j-m die Stadt ~** show s.o. (around) the town; **er will nur s-e Macht ~** he just wants to demonstrate his power; **großen Mut ~** display great courage; **F dem werd' ich's ~!** I'll show him. **II** *v/i* (**mit dem Finger**) **~ auf** (*acc*) point (one's finger) at; **nach Norden ~** point (to the) north; **die Uhr zeigte (auf) 12** the clock said twelve. **III sich ~** show (o.s.), appear, turn up; *fig.* **sie zeigte sich sehr großzügig** she was very generous; **sich von s-r besten Seite ~** present o.s. to best advantage; **er zeigte sich der Aufgabe nicht gewachsen** it became obvious that he wasn't equal to the task. **IV** *v/impers* turn out, prove: **es zeigte sich, daß er recht gehabt hatte** (**es richtig gewesen war**) he (it) turned out to have been right; **es wird sich ~, wer recht hat** we'll see who is right in the end.

'Zeiger *m* (-s; -) hand, **◎** *a.* index, pointer, needle (*of speedometer etc*).

'Zeigestock *m* pointer.

Zeile ['tsailə] *f* (-; -n) **1.** line: **j-m ein paar ~n schreiben** drop s.o. a line. **2.** row.

'Zeilen|abstand *m* **1.** spacing. **2.** *TV* line advance. **~anzeige** *f* computer: line display. **~drucker** *m* computer: line printer. **~eingabe** *f* computer: line entry. **~raster** *n* *TV* line-scanning picture pattern. **~schalter** *m* typewriter: line spacer. **~vorschub** *m* computer: line feed.

tent peg. **~plane** f tarpaulin. **~stadt** f tent city. **~stange** f tent pole.

Zement [tse'mɛnt] m (-[e]s; -e) cement.

zementieren [tsemɛn'tiːrən] v/t (h) cement (a. fig.), metall. carburize.

Ze'mentsack m cement bag.

Zenit [tse'niːt] m (-[e]s; no pl) astr. or fig. (**im ~** at the) zenith.

zensieren [tsɛn'ziːrən] v/t (h) **1.** ped. mark, Am. grade. **2.** censor. **Zensor** ['tsɛnzɔr] m (-s; -en [-'zoːrən]) censor.

Zensur [tsɛn'zuːr] f (-; -en) **1.** ped. mark, Am. grade: **gute ~en haben** a. have a good report. **2.** no pl censorship: **der ~ unterliegen** be censored.

Zensus ['tsɛnzus] m (-; -) census.

Zentimeter [tsɛnti'meːtər] m, n (-s; -) centimet/re (Am. -er).

Zentner ['tsɛntnər] m (-s; -) (metric) hundredweight (abbr. cwt.), centner (50 kg). **~last** f fig. heavy burden: **mir fiel e-e ~ vom Herzen** it was a great weight off my mind. **⚤schwer** adj fig. very heavy: **es liegt mir ~ auf der Seele** it weighs very heavily on my mind.

zentral [tsɛn'traːl] adj central: **~ gelegen sein** be centrally located; fig. **das ~e Problem** the crucial problem.

Zen'tralbank f (-; -en) central bank.

zen'tralbeheizt adj centrally heated.

Zentrale [tsɛn'traːlə] f (-; -n) **1.** central office, headquarters. **2.** telephone exchange, in firm: switchboard. **3.** ⊕ control room. **4.** fig. centre, Am. center.

Zen'tralheizung f central heating.

zentralisieren [tsɛntrali'ziːrən] v/t (h) centralize. **Zentrali'sierung** f (-; -en) centralization.

Zentralismus [tsɛntra'lismus] m (-; no pl) pol. centralism. **zentra'listisch** [-tɪʃ] adj centralist(ic).

Zen'tral|komi,tee n pol. central committee. **~nervensy,stem** n central nervous system. **~or,gan** n official party organ. **~verband** m ✝ etc central association. **~verriegelung** f mot. central locking (system).

zentrieren [tsɛn'triːrən] v/t (h) centre, Am. center.

zentrifugal [tsɛntrifu'gaːl] adj centrifugal. **Zentri'fugalkraft** f centrifugal force. **Zentrifuge** [tsɛntri'fuːgə] f (-; -n) centrifuge.

zentrisch ['tsɛntrɪʃ] adj centric(al).

Zentrum ['tsɛntrum] n (-s; -tren) centre, Am. center: **im ~ von New York** Am. a. (in) downtown New York; **sie stand im ~ des Interesses** she was the centre of interest.

Zepter ['tsɛptər] n (-s; -) sceptre, Am. scepter: humor. **das ~ schwingen** rule the roost.

zer'beißen v/t (irr, no -ge-, h, → beißen) bite to pieces, crunch.

zerbeult [-'bɔylt] adj battered.

zerbomben [-'bɔmbən] v/t (h) bomb.

zerbombt [-'bɔmpt] adj bomb-wrecked.

zer'brechen (irr, no -ge-, h, → brechen) **I** v/t break, crack, smash: → **Kopf** 2. **II** v/i break (fig. up): fig. **~ an** (dat) be crushed (or broken) by. **zerbrechlich** [-'brɛçlɪç] adj breakable, a. fig. frail, delicate, fragile: **Vorsicht, ~!** fragile, handle with care! **Zer'brechlichkeit** f (-; no pl) a. fig. fragility, frailness.

zer'bröckeln v/t (h), v/i (sn) crumble.

zer'drücken v/t (h) crush, a. mash (potatoes etc), a. crumple (clothes).

zerebral [tsere'braːl] adj cerebral.

Zeremonie [tseremo'niː] f (-; -n) ceremony. **zeremoniell** [tseremo'niɛl] adj ceremonial. **Zeremoni'ell** n (-s; -e) ceremonial, fig. a. ritual. **zeremoniös** [tseremo'niøːs] adj ceremonious.

Zer'fall m (-[e]s; no pl) disintegration, decay, a. fig. ruin, ☢ decomposition.

zer'fallen¹ v/i (irr, no -ge-, sn, → fallen) **1.** disintegrate (in acc, zu into), decay, ☢ decompose, building etc: crumble (a. fig. empire etc), fall to pieces. **2.** fig. **~ in** (acc) be divided into.

zer'fallen² adj **1.** decayed, in ruins. **2.** **mit j-m ~ sein** be at odds with s.o.; **mit sich und der Welt ~** disgusted with life. **Zer'falls|erscheinung** f sign of decay. **~pro,dukt** n nucl. decay product. **~reihe** f nucl. family, decay chain. **~zeit** f nucl. decay period (or time).

zer'fetzen v/t (h) tear s.th. (in)to pieces, shred, slash, mangle.

zerfleddern [-'flɛdərn] v/t (h) tatter.

zerfleischen [-'flaɪʃən] (h) **I** v/t mangle, tear s.o., s.th. to pieces: fig. **einander ~** tear each other apart. **II sich ~** fig. torment o.s.

zer'fließen v/i (irr, no -ge-, sn, → fließen) a) run, b) melt: **sie zerfloß vor Mitleid** she was melting with pity.

zer'fressen¹ v/t (irr, no -ge-, h, → **fressen**) **1.** moths: eat (holes into), mice etc: gnaw s.th. to pieces. **2.** 🦷, ◎ corrode.

zer'fressen² adj von Motten ~ motheaten; vom Rost ~ corroded; fig. vom Neid ~ eaten up with envy.

zerfurcht [-'furçt] adj a. fig. furrowed.

zer'gehen v/i (irr, no -ge-, sn, → **gehen**) dissolve, melt: auf der Zunge ~ melt in one's mouth.

zer'gliedern v/t (h) analy/se (Am. -ze), dissect, a. parse (sentence).

zer'hacken v/t (h) chop (a. 🎵), mince.

zer'hauen v/t (h) cut s.th. to pieces.

zer'kauen v/t (h) chew (well).

zerkleinern [-'klaɪnərn] v/t (h) reduce s.th. to small pieces, crush, cut s.th. up.

zerklüftet [-'klʏftət] adj jagged, rugged.

zer'knautschen v/t (h) F crumple.

zerknirscht [-'knɪrʃt] adj contrite: ~ sein feel remorse (über acc at).

Zer'knirschung f (-; no pl) contrition.

zer'knittern v/t (h), v/i (sn) crumple, crease.

zer'knüllen v/t (h) crumple up.

zer'kratzen v/t (h) scratch.

zer'krümeln v/t (h), v/i (sn) crumble.

zer'lassen v/t (irr, no -ge-, h, → **lassen**) melt (butter etc).

zer'laufen v/i (irr, no -ge-, sn, → **laufen**) butter etc: melt, colo[u]r: bleed.

zerlegbar [-'le:kba:r] adj dismountable, knock-down ...: ... ist ~ ... can be taken apart. **zer'legen** v/t (h) **1.** take s.th. apart, a. dismantle, knock down. **2.** cut s.th. up, dissect, carve (roast). **3.** 🜛 reduce, a. 🦷 decompose: 🜛 in Faktoren ~ factorize. **4.** → **zergliedern**.

zer'lesen adj well-thumbed (book etc).

zerlöchert [-'lœçərt] adj full of holes.

zerlumpt [-'lʊmpt] adj ragged, tattered.

zermalmen [-'malmən] v/t (h) crush.

zer'martern v/t (h) sich den Kopf ~ rack one's brain (über acc over).

zermürben [-'mʏrbən] v/t (h) wear s.o. down, ⚔ soften up: ~d trying.

Zer'mürbungskrieg m war of attrition.

zer'nagen v/t (h) gnaw s.th. to pieces.

zer'pflücken v/t (h) pick s.th. to pieces.

zer'platzen v/i (sn) burst, explode.

zer'quetschen v/t (h) crush (a. ◎), squash, mash: F **70 Mark und ein paar Zerquetschte** 70 marks and some.

'**Zerrbild** n a. fig. caricature, distorted picture, fig. a. travesty.

zer'reden v/t (h) flog s.th. to death.

zer'reiben v/t (irr, no -ge-, h, → **reiben**) crush, grind: et. zwischen den Fingern ~ rub s.th. between one's fingers.

zer'reißen (irr, no -ge-, h, → **reißen**) **I** v/t tear s.th. up, tear s.th. to pieces (or apart), rip up, break (thread, fetters, fig. ties etc): er zerriß sich die Hose er rissen he tore his pants; es zerriß ihr das Herz it broke her heart; F fig. in der Luft ~ a) tear s.o. limb from limb, b) tear s.o., s.th. to pieces. **II** v/i tear, chain, thread, etc: break, bag etc: burst. **III** sich (fast) ~ F fig. bend over backwards; ich kann mich doch nicht ~! I can't be in two places at once.

Zer'reiß|festigkeit f ◎ tear resistance. ~**probe** f **1.** ◎ tension test. **2.** ordeal.

zerren ['tsɛrən] (h) **I** v/t **1.** drag, haul: j-n hinter sich her ~ drag s.o. along; fig. et. an die Öffentlichkeit ~ drag s.th. into the limelight. **2.** 🦴 pull, strain (sich e-n Muskel a muscle). **II** v/i ~ an (dat) pull at, tug at; der Hund zerrte an der Leine the dog strained at its leash.

zer'rinnen v/i (irr, no -ge-, sn, → **rinnen**) melt away (a. fig. money etc), fig. dreams etc: fade, vanish, plans etc: come to nothing: wie gewonnen, so zerronnen easy come, easy go.

zerrissen [-'rɪsən] adj a. fig. torn: er ist innerlich ~ he is torn by inner conflicts. **Zer'rissenheit** f (-; no pl) fig. (innere) ~ inner conflicts.

'**Zerrung** f (-; -en) 🦴 strain.

zerrütten [-'rʏtən] v/t (h) ruin, wreck (a. health, marriage, etc), a. unhinge, derange (mind): ihre Nerven sind zerrüttet her nerves are shattered; zerrüttete Ehe (Familienverhältnisse) broken marriage (home).

Zer'rüttung f (-; -en) ruin, ruinous state: 🏛 (unheilbare) ~ der Ehe (irretrievable) breakdown of a marriage.

zer'sägen v/t (h) saw s.th. up.

zer'schellen v/i (sn) smash, be smashed to pieces, ✈ crash, ⚓ be wrecked.

zer'schießen v/t (irr, no -ge-, h, → **schießen**) bombard, batter.

zer'schlagen¹ (irr, no -ge-, h, → **schlagen**) **I** v/t smash (a. fig.), smash s.th. to pieces, shatter. **II** sich ~ hopes, plans,

'**Ziehung** f (-; -en) drawing, draw.
Ziel [tsi:l] n (-[e]s; -e) **1.** destination. **2.**
sports: finish(ing line): **als Erster
durchs ~ gehen** finish first; **sich ins ~
werfen** lunge into the tape. **3.** *esp.* ✕
mark, aim, *a.* target, *a. (tactical)* objective: **das ~ verfehlen** miss; **über das ~
hinausschießen** *a. fig.* overshoot the
mark. **4.** *fig.* aim, goal, end, objective,
target (*a.* ✝): **sein ~ erreichen** reach
one's goal, F get there; **(nicht) zum ~
führen** succeed (fail); **sich das ~ setzen
zu** *inf* aim to *inf*, aim at ger; **sein ~ aus
dem Auge verlieren (im Auge behal-
ten)** lose (keep) sight of one's goal.
'**Zielanflug** m approach run.
'**Zielband** n sports: tape.
'**zielbewußt** → **zielstrebig.**
'**Zieleinlauf** m sports: finish.
zielen ['tsi:lən] v/i (h) **(auf** acc at) (take)
aim, level, *fig.* be aimed: → **gezielt.**
'**Ziel|fernrohr** n telescopic sight. **~flug** m
homing. **~foto** n sports: photo of the
finish. **~gerade** f sports: home stretch.
₂**gerichtet** adj goal-directed. **~gruppe**
f target group. **~kamera** f photo-finish
camera. **~kurve** f sports: home bend.
~linie f sports: finishing line.
'**ziellos** adj aimless.
'**Ziel|richter** m sports: judge (at the fin-
ish). **~scheibe** f target, *fig. a.* butt: **~
des Spottes** laughing-stock.
'**Zielsetzung** f (-; -en) objective, target.
'**zielsicher** adj unerring.
'**Zielsprache** f target language.
'**Zielvorstellung** f objective.
'**zielstrebig** [-ʃtre:bɪç] adj purposeful,
single-minded, determined.
'**Zielstrebigkeit** f (-; no pl) determination, single-mindedness.
ziemlich ['tsi:mlɪç] **I** adj **1.** F considerable, quite a: **er wird mit ~er Sicherheit kommen** he's fairly certain to
come; **das ist e-e ~e Frechheit** that's
rather a cheek. **II** adv **2.** rather, quite: **~
gut** F pretty good; **~ ausführlich** in
some detail; **~ viel** quite a lot (of); **~
viele** quite a few; **ich bin ~ sicher** F I'm
pretty sure. **3.** almost, just about, F
pretty well: **ich bin so ~ fertig** I've more
or less finished; **so ~ alles** practically
everything; **es ist so ~ dasselbe** F it's
pretty much the same thing.
Zierde ['tsi:rdə] f (-; -n) **1.** **(zur ~** for)

decoration. **2.** *fig.* credit (*gen or* **für** to).
zieren ['tsi:rən] (h) **I** v/t adorn, decorate.
II sich **~** make a fuss, *woman*: play coy;
er zierte sich nicht lange he didn't
need much pressing; **komm, zier dich
nicht!** come on!
'**Zierfisch** m ornamental fish.
'**Ziergarten** m ornamental garden.
'**Zierleiste** f border (*a. print.*), ornamental mo(u)lding, *mot.* trim.
'**zierlich** adj **1.** delicate, dainty. **2.** graceful, gracile, *woman: a.* petite. '**Zierlich-
keit** f (-; no pl) delicateness, daintiness.
'**Zierpflanze** f ornamental plant.
Ziffer ['tsɪfər] f (-; -n) **1.** a) figure, number, b) digit: **in ~n** in figures. **2.** 𝕤𝕥
subparagraph, *in contract etc*: item.
'**Zifferblatt** n dial, face.
zig [tsɪç] adj F umpteen.
Zigarette [tsiga'retə] f (-; -n) cigarette,
Am. a. cigaret.
Ziga'retten|anzünder m mot. cigarette
lighter. **~auto,mat** m cigarette machine. **~e,tui** n cigarette case. **~marke** f
brand of cigarettes. **~packung** f cigarette packet (*Am.* pack). **~pause** f F
(**e-e ~ machen** have a) smoke. **~rau-
cher** m cigarette smoker. **~schachtel** f
cigarette packet (*Am.* pack). **~spitze** f
cigarette holder. **~stummel** m cigarette
end, stub, butt.
Zigarillo [tsiga'rɪlo] m (-s; -s) cigarillo.
Zigarre [tsi'garə] f (-; -n) cigar.
Zi'garrenabschneider m cigar cutter.
Zi'garrenstummel m cigar end, butt.
Zigeuner [tsi'gɔɪnər] m (-s; -), **Zi'geu-
nerin** f (-; -nen) gypsy, *Br. a.* gipsy.
Zi'geunerleben n *fig.* gypsy life.
zigst [tsɪçst] adj F umpteenth.
Zikade [tsi'ka:də] f (-; -n) zo. cicada.
Zimmer ['tsɪmər] n (-s; -) room. **~an,ten-
ne** f indoor aerial (*Am.* antenna). **~ein-
richtung** f **1.** furnishing, interior (decoration). **2.** furniture.
'**Zimmerhandwerk** n carpentry.
...zimm(e)rig [-tsɪm(ə)rɪç] ...-roomed.
'**Zimmer|kellner** m room waiter. **~laut-
stärke** f household noise level: **das
Radio auf ~ stellen** turn one's radio
down to moderate volume. **~mädchen**
n chambermaid.
'**Zimmermann** m (-[e]s; -leute) carpenter. '**zimmern** v/t (h) carpenter (*a. v/i*),
a. build (of wood), *fig.* shape.

'**Zimmer|nachweis** m accommodation office. **~pflanze** f indoor plant. **~re-ser,vierung** f room reservation(s). **~schlüssel** m room key. **~service** m room service. **~suche** f (auf ~ sein) be room-hunting. **~tempera,tur** f room temperature. **~the,ater** n small theat/re (Am. -er). **~vermittlung** f → **Zimmernachweis.**

zimperlich ['tsɪmpərlɪç] adj a) soft, over-sensitive, b) squeamish, c) prim, prissy: **sei nicht so ~!** don't be a softie!; F **nicht gerade ~, wenig ~** none too good, not exactly scrupulous (in one's methods).

'**Zimperlichkeit** f (-; no pl) a) softness, b) squeamishness, c) primness.

'**Zimt** [tsɪmt] m (-[e]s; -e) **1.** cinnamon. **2.** F contp. (**red k-n ~** don't talk: rubbish: **der ganze ~** the whole business.

Zink [tsɪŋk] n (-[e]s; no pl) zinc. **~blech** n a) sheet zinc, b) zinc plate.

Zinke ['tsɪŋkə] f (-; -n) **1.** prong. **2.** tooth (of comb). **'zinken** v/t (h) mark (cards).

'**Zinken** m (-s; -) **1.** → **Zinke. 2.** F conk.

Zinn [tsɪn] n (-[e]s; no pl) **1.** tin. **2.** pewter.

Zinne ['tsɪnə] f (-; -n) △ pinnacle, pl battlement.

'**Zinngeschirr** n pewter.

Zinnober [tsɪ'no:bər] m (-s; -) **1.** min. cinnabar. **2.** no pl F a) rubbish, b) fuss.

zin'noberrot adj vermilion.

Zins [tsɪns] m (-es; -en) interest: **~en tra-gen** (or **bringen**) bear interest; **ohne ~en** ex interest; **zu 4% ~en** at 4% interest; → **Zinseszins.**

'**zinsbringend** adj interest-bearing.

'**Zinseinnahme** f income from interest.

'**Zinsen|dienst** ['tsɪnzən-] m interest payment. **~last** f burden of interest.

'**Zinsertrag** m interest yield.

'**Zinseszins** m compound interest.

'**Zinsfuß** m (-es; ⸚e) interest rate.

'**zinsgünstig** adj low-interest.

'**Zinsgutschrift** f interest credited.

'**Zinsku,pon** m interest coupon.

'**zinslos** adj interest-free.

'**Zins|poli,tik** f interest rate policy. **~rechnung** f **1.** calculation of interest. **2.** interest account. **~satz** m interest rate. **~senkung** f lowering of interest rates. **~verlust** m loss of interest.

Zionismus [tsio'nɪsmʊs] m (-; no pl) Zionism. **Zionist** [-'nɪst] m (-en; -en), **zio'nistisch** adj Zionist.

Zipfel ['tsɪpfəl] m (-s; -) a) tip, point, b) end (of sausage etc), c) corner.

'**Zipfelmütze** f pointed cap.

Zirbeldrüse ['tsɪrbəl-] f pineal gland.

zirka ['tsɪrka] adv about, approximately.

'**Zirkapreis** m ♥ approximate price.

Zirkel ['tsɪrkəl] m (-s; -) **1.** (**ein ~** a pair of) compasses, dividers. **2.** a. fig. circle.

'**Zirkelkasten** m compasses case.

'**Zirkelschluß** m philos. vicious circle.

'**Zirkeltraining** n sports: circuit training.

Zirkulation [tsɪrkula'tsɪo:n] f (-; no pl) circulation. **zirkulieren** [tsɪrku'li:rən] v/i (sn) (a. ~ lassen) circulate.

Zirkumflex [tsɪrkʊm'flɛks] m (-es; -e) ling. circumflex (accent).

Zirkus ['tsɪrkʊs] m (-; -se) **1.** circus. **2.** no pl F fuss, carry-on.

zirpen ['tsɪrpən] v/t, v/i (h) chirp (a. fig.).

'**Zirpen** n (-s) chirp(ing).

Zirrhose [tsɪ'ro:zə] f (-; -n) ✚ cirrhosis.

Zirrus ['tsɪrʊs] m (-; -, Zirren), **~wolke** f cirrus (cloud).

zischeln ['tsɪʃəln] v/t, v/i (h) hiss.

zischen ['tsɪʃən] (h) **I** v/i **1.** hiss (a. fig.), fat: sizzle, bullet etc: whiz(z). **II** v/t **2.** hiss (words). **3.** F **e-n ~** knock one back.

'**Zischen** n (-s) **1.** hiss(ing), sizzle. **2.** hisses '**Zischlaut** m ling. sibilant.

ziselieren [tsizə'li:rən] v/t (h) chase.

Zisterne [tsɪs'tɛrnə] f (-; -n) cistern.

Zitadelle [tsita'dɛlə] f (-; -n) citadel.

Zitat [tsi'ta:t] n (-[e]s; -e) quotation.

Zither ['tsɪtər] f (-; -n) ♪ zither.

zitieren [tsi'ti:rən] v/t (h) **1.** cite, quote: **falsch ~** misquote. **2.** summon, cite.

Zitronat [tsitro'na:t] n (-[e]s; -e) candied lemon peel.

Zitrone [tsi'tro:nə] f (-; -n) lemon.

Zi'tronen|falter m zo. brimstone. **~limo,nade** f lemonade, Am. lemon soda. **~saft** m lemon juice. **~säure** f citric acid. **~schale** f lemon peel.

Zitrusfrucht ['tsi:trʊs-] f citrus fruit.

'**zitt(e)rig** adj shaky.

zittern ['tsɪtərn] v/i (h) (**vor** with) tremble, shake, quiver: **vor j-m ~** be terrified of s.o.; **~ um** tremble for; **mir ~ die Knie** my knees are shaking.

'**Zittern** n (-s) tremble, shake, vibration: fig. **mit ~ und Zagen** trembling; F **das große ~ kriegen** get the willies.

'**Zitterpappel** f ♠ (quaking) aspen.

Zitze ['tsɪtsə] f (-; -n) teat, dug.

Zivi ['tsi:vi] *m* (-s; -s) F → *Zivildienstleistende.*

zivil [tsi'vi:l] *adj* **1.** a) civil, b) civilian. **2.** *fig.* a) decent, b) reasonable (*price etc*).

Zi'vil *n* (-s; *no pl*) civilian dress, *a.* plain clothes: **in** ~ F *a.* in mufti; **Kriminalbeamter in** ~ plain-clothes policeman. ~**beruf** *m* civilian profession (*or* trade). ~**bevölkerung** *f* civilian population, *the* civilians. ~**cou,rage** *f* (-; *no pl*) courage of one's convictions.

Zi'vildienst *m* alternative (*or* community) service (*in lieu of military service*). ~**leistende** *m* (-n; -n) *conscientious objector doing community service.*

Zi'vil|**ehe** *f* civil marriage. ~**fahnder** *m* plain-clothes policeman. ~**fahndung** *f* plain-clothes search. ~**gericht** *n* civil court.

Zivilisation [tsiviliza'tsĭo:n] *f* (-; -en) civilization.

zivilisieren [tsivili'zi:rən] *v/t* (h) civilize.

Zivilist [tsivi'lɪst] *m* (-en; -en) civilian.

Zi'vil|**kammer** *f* ⚖ civil division. ~**klage** *f* ⚖ civil suit. ~**kleidung** *f* → *Zivil.* ~**luftfahrt** *f* civil aviation. ~**per,son** *f* civilian. ~**pro,zeß** *m* ⚖ civil action. ~**pro,zeßordnung** *f* code of civil procedure. ~**recht** *n* (-[e]s; *no pl*) civil law. **⚖rechtlich** *adj* (*adv* under) civil law. ~**schutz** *m* civil defen/ce (*Am.* -se). ~**stand** *m* *Swiss* civil (*or* marital) status. ~**trauung** *f* civil marriage.

Zloty ['zlɔti, 'slɔti] *m* (-s; -s) zloty.

Zobel ['tso:bəl] *m* (-s; -) **1.** *zo.* sable. **2.** *a.* '**Zobelfell** *n* sable-skin. **3.** *a.* '**Zobelpelz** sable (fur).

zocken ['tsɔkən] *v/i* (h) F gamble.

'**Zocker** *m* (-s; -) F gambler.

Zoff [tsɔf] *m* (-s; *no pl*) F trouble.

zog [tso:k] *pret of* **ziehen.**

'**zögerlich** *adj* → *zögernd.* **zögern** ['tsø:gərn] *v/i* (h) hesitate, waver: **ohne zu** ~ without hesitation; **er zögerte mit der Antwort** he was slow to answer; **sie zögerten mit der Entscheidung** they deferred their decision; **nicht** ~ **zu** *inf* lose no time in *ger.* '**Zögern** *n* (-s) hesitation. '**zögernd** *adj* hesitating, slow.

Zögling ['tsø:klɪŋ] *m* (-s; -e) pupil.

Zölibat [tsøli'ba:t] *n, eccl. m* (-[e]s; *no pl*) celibacy.

Zoll¹ [tsɔl] *m* (-[e]s; -) inch.

Zoll² *m* (-[e]s; ⸚e) **1.** (customs) duty. **2.** customs. ~**abfertigung** *f* customs clearance. ~**amt** *n* customs office. ~**beamte** *m* customs officer. ~**behörde** *f* customs authorities. ~**bestimmungen** *pl* customs regulations.

'**zollen** *v/t* (h) **Anerkennung** ~ pay tribute (*dat* to); **j-m Beifall** ~ applaud s.o.

'**Zoll**|**erklärung** *f* customs declaration. ~**fahnder** *m* customs investigator. ~**fahndung** *f* **1.** customs investigation. **2.** → ~**fahndungsstelle** *f* customs investigation office. ~**formali,täten** *pl* customs formalit/ies. **⚖frei** *adj and adv* duty-free. ~**freiheit** *f* (-; *no pl*) exemption from duty. ~**gebiet** *n* customs territory. ~**grenze** *f* customs frontier. ~**kon,trolle** *f* customs examination.

Zöllner ['tsœlnər] *m* (-s; -) **1.** customs officer. **2.** *bibl.* publican.

'**Zollpa,piere** *pl* customs documents.

'**zollpflichtig** *adj* liable to duty, dutiable.

'**Zollschranke** *f* customs barrier.

'**Zollstock** *m* ⚙ folding rule.

'**Zoll**|**ta,rif** *m* (customs) tariff. ~**uni,on** *f* customs union. ~**vergehen** *n* customs offen/ce (*Am.* -se). ~**wert** *m* dutiable (*or* customs) value.

Zone ['tso:nə] *f* (-; -n) **1.** zone. **2.** fare stage.

Zoo [tso:] *m* (-s; -s) zoo.

'**Zoobesucher(in** *f*) *m* visitor to the zoo.

'**Zoodi,rektor** *m* zoo director.

Zooge [tsoo'lo:gə] *m* (-n; -n), **Zoo'login** *f* (-; -nen) zoologist.

Zoologie [tsoolo'gi:] *f* (-; *no pl*) zoology.

zoologisch [tsoo'lo:gɪʃ] *adj* zoologic(al): ~**er Garten** zoological garden(s).

Zoomobjek,tiv ['zu:m-] *n* zoom lens.

Zopf [tsɔpf] *m* (-[e]s; ⸚e) **1.** plait, pigtail: F *alter* ~ antiquated custom. **2.** *gastr.* twist. ~**stil** *m art:* late rococo (style).

Zorn [tsɔrn] *m* (-[e]s; *no pl*) anger (**auf** *acc* at), rage, temper, fury: **in** ~ **geraten** become furious, fly into a rage; (**der**) ~ **packte ihn** he was seized with anger.

'**Zornausbruch** *m* fit of anger.

'**zornentbrannt** *adj* incensed, furious.

'**zornig** *adj* (**auf, über** *acc* at) angry, furious, F mad; → *a.* **wütend.**

'**Zornröte** *f* flush of anger.

'**Zote** ['tso:tə] *f* (-; -n) dirty joke: ~**n reißen** talk smut.

Zotte ['tsɔtə] *f* (-; -n) *zo.* tuft (of hair).

Zottel ['tsɔtəl] *f* (-; -n) F **1.** → *Zotte.* **2.**

straggly hair. **'zott(e)lig** *adj* F straggly, unkempt (*hair*). **'zottig** *adj* shaggy.

zu [tsuː] **I** *prep* **1.** a) at, b) to, towards: ~ **m-n Füßen** at my feet; ~ **m Friseur gehen** go to the hairdresser; **komm ~ mir!** come to me!; **sich ~ j-m setzen** sit with s.o.; ~ **Wasser und ~ Lande** on land and sea; **von Mann ~ Mann** between men. **2.** *time*: at, *occasion*: for: ~ **Ostern** at Easter; ~ **Beginn** at the beginning; **ein Geschenk ~m Geburtstag** a present for his *etc* birthday; → **bis 1. 3.** for: **Stoff ~ Kleid** material for a dress; **et. ~m Essen** s.th. to eat; **der Schlüssel ~m Schrank** the key to the cupboard; ~**m Preis von 100 Mark** at a price of 100 marks; **aus Liebe ~ j-m** out of love for s.o. **4.** as: ~**m Vergnügen** for fun; **j-n ~m Freund haben** have s.o. as a friend; **j-n ~m Präsidenten wählen** elect s.o. president. **5.** with: ~**m Essen Wein trinken** drink wine with one's dinner; **ich nehme k-n Zucker ~m Tee** I don't take sugar with (*or* in) my tea; **Lieder ~r Laute** songs to the lute. **6.** ~ **10 DM das Pfund** at ten marks the pound; **sie gewannen 7:5** they won 7 (to) 5; **wir sind ~ dritt** there are three of us; ~**m ersten Mal** for the first time; → **bis 3. 7.** in(to): **werden ~** turn into, *person*: a. become; ~ **Asche verbrennen** burn to ashes; **er hat ihn sich ~m Feind gemacht** he made him his enemy. **II** *adv* **8.** too: ~ **sehr** too much, overmuch; ~ **sehr betonen** overemphasize; ~ **dumm!** too bad!, what a nuisance! **9.** to, towards: **er ging dem Ausgang ~** he went towards the exit. **10.** shut, closed: (**mach die) Tür ~!** shut the door! **11.** F **immer ~!, nur ~!** go on! **III** *conj* **j-n bitten ~ kommen** ask s.o. to come; **ich habe ~ arbeiten** I have work to do; **du bist ~ beneiden** you are to be envied; **nicht ~ gebrauchen** useless; **ohne es ~ wissen** unknowingly. **IV** *adj* F a) glued, b) shut, closed, c) *fig*. bombed, sloshed.

zu'allererst *adv* first of all.

zu'allerletzt *adv* last of all.

'zubauen *v/t* (*sep*, h) **1.** build *area etc* up. **2.** block (*a.* view).

'Zubehör [-bəhøːr] *n* (-[e]s; -e) accessories: **mit allem ~** with all conveniences.

'Zubehörteil *n* fitting, accessory.

'zubeißen *v/i* (*irr, sep,* -ge-, h, → **beißen**) bite, *dog*: snap.

'zubekommen *v/t* (*irr, sep,* h, → **bekommen**) F **et. ~** get s.th. shut.

Zuber ['tsuːbər] *m* (-s; -) tub.

'zubereiten *v/t* (*sep*, h) prepare, make.

'Zubereitung *f* (-; -en) preparation.

'zubilligen *v/t* (*sep*, h) grant, concede, *a.* ⚖ allow (*all*: **j-m et.** s.o. s.th.).

'zubinden *v/t* (*irr, sep,* -ge-, h, → **binden**) tie (*or* bind) *s.th.* up.

'zubleiben *v/i* (*irr, sep,* -ge-, sn, → **bleiben**) F stay closed, stay shut.

'zublinzeln *v/i* (*sep*, h) **j-m ~** wink at s.o.

'zubringen *v/t* (*irr, sep,* -ge-, h, → **bringen**) spend, pass (*time*).

'Zubringer *m* (-s; -) → **Zubringerbus, -dienst, -linie, -straße.** ~**bus** *m* feeder bus. ~**dienst** *m* feeder service. ~**linie** *f* feeder line. ~**straße** *f* feeder (road).

Zucchino [tsuˈkiːno] *m* (-s; -ni) ⚘ courgette, *esp. Am.* zucchini.

Zucht [tsuxt] *f* (-; -en) **1.** breeding, rearing, raising, ⚘ cultivation, growing, culture (*of bees, bacteria, etc*). **2.** breed. **3.** *no pl* (*a.* ~ **und Ordnung**) discipline.

'Zuchtbuch *n* studbook.

'Zuchtbulle *m* breeding bull.

züchten ['tsʏçtən] *v/t* (h) breed (*a. fig.*), *a.* rear, raise (*animals*), *a.* cultivate, grow (*plants*), culture (*bacteria etc*).

'Züchter *m* (-s; -) breeder, *a.* grower.

'Zuchterfolg *m* breeding success.

'Zuchthaus *n* † prison; → *a.* **Gefängnis.**

'Zuchthengst *m* stud horse, stallion.

züchtigen ['tsʏçtɪgən] *v/t* (h) punish, flog. **'Züchtigung** *f* (-; -en) (*körperliche* ~ corporal) punishment.

'zuchtlos *adj* undisciplined. **'Zuchtlosigkeit** *f* (-; *no pl*) lack of discipline.

'Zucht|mittel *n* disciplinary measure. ~**perle** *f* cultured pearl. ~**stier** *m* breeding bull. ~**stute** *f* stock mare. ~**tier** *n* breeding animal, *pl a.* breeding stock.

'Züchtung *f* (-; -en) → **Zucht 1, 2.**

'Zuchtvieh *n* breeding cattle.

'Zuchtwahl *f biol*. selection.

zucken ['tsʊkəln] *v/i* (sn) F trundle (*mot. etc* chug) along.

zucken ['tsʊkən] *v/i* (h) **1.** jerk, twitch, move convulsively, wince: → **Achsel, Schulter, Wimper. 2.** *lightning etc*: flash, *flames*: flicker.

zücken ['tsʏkən] v/t (h) draw (knife etc), F pull out, produce (wallet etc).
Zucker ['tsʊkər] m (-s; -) **1.** sugar. **2.** ♣ (er hat ~ he is suffering from) diabetes. **~brot** n F **mit ~ und Peitsche** with a stick and a carrot. **~dose** f sugar bowl. **~erbse** f ♀ sugar pea. **~guß** m icing, frosting: **mit ~ überziehen** ice, frost. **~hut** m sugar loaf.
'zuck(e)rig adj sugary.
'zuckerkrank adj, **'Zuckerkranke** m, f diabetic. **'Zuckerkrankheit** f diabetes.
zuckern ['tsʊkərn] v/t (h) sugar.
'Zuckerrohr n (-[e]s; -e) sugar cane. **~rübe** f sugar beet. ♀**süß** adj (as) sweet as sugar, fig. honeyed, sugary. **~watte** f candy floss. **~zange** f sugar tongs.
'Zuckung f (-; -en) a) twitch(ing), jerk, b) convulsion, spasm.
'zudecken v/t (sep, h) cover (up): **sich ~** cover o.s. (up); F **j-n mit Arbeit ~** swamp s.o. with work.
zu'dem adv besides, moreover.
'zudrehen v/t (sep, h) **1.** turn off. **2.** j-m **den Rücken ~** turn one's back on s.o.
'zudringlich adj obtrusive, F pushy: **e-r Frau gegenüber ~ werden** F make a pass at a woman. **'Zudringlichkeit** f (-; -en) **1.** no pl obtrusiveness, F pushiness. **2.** advances, F pass.
'zudrücken v/t (sep, h) close, (press) shut: → **Auge** 1.
'zueilen v/i (sep, sn) rush up (**auf** acc to).
zuein'ander adv to each other, to one another: **Vertrauen ~ haben** trust each other. **~halten** v/i (irr, sep, -ge-, h, → **halten**) F stick together.
'zuerkennen v/t (irr, sep, h, → **erkennen**) (dat) award (to), confer (on).
zu'erst adv **1.** first: **wer ~ kommt, mahlt ~ first** come, first served. **2.** first (of all). **3.** at first, at the beginning. **4.** for the first time, first.
'Zufahrt f (-; -en) **1.** access. **2.** → **'Zufahrtsstraße** f access road.
'Zufall m (-[e]s; ⁻e) chance, accident, a. coincidence: **durch ~** by chance; **reiner ~** pure chance; **glücklicher ~** lucky coincidence, F fluke; **unglücklicher ~** bit of bad luck; **was für ein ~!** what a coincidence!; **wie es der ~ wollte** as luck would have it; **es ist kein ~, daß** it's no accident that; **et. dem ~ überlassen** leave it to chance.

'zufallen v/i (irr, sep, -ge-, sn, → **fallen**) **1.** eyes etc: close, door etc: slam (shut): **mir fallen die Augen zu** I can't keep my eyes open. **2.** j-m ~ inheritance etc: fall to s.o., prize etc: be awarded to s.o., task etc: be assigned to s.o.; fig. **ihm fällt alles nur so zu** everything comes quite naturally to him.
'zufällig I adj accidental, chance: **~es Zs.-treffen** a) chance encounter, b) coincidence; **jede Ähnlichkeit (mit ...) ist rein ~** any resemblance (to ...) is purely coincidental. **II** adv by chance, accidentally: **er war ~ zu Hause** he happened to be at home; **wir trafen uns ~** we met by chance; F **wir bumped into each other; ~ stoßen auf** (acc) chance (up)on; **rein ~** by sheer chance; **weißt du ~, wo er ist?** do you happen by any chance where he is? **'Zufälligkeit** f (-; -en) **1.** no pl coincidence, accidentalness. **2.** fortuity, contingency.
'Zufalls|auswahl f statistics: random selection. **~bekanntschaft** f chance acquaintance. **~treffer** m lucky (F fluke) hit, sports: a. lucky goal.
'zufassen v/i (sep, h) **1.** take hold of it, grasp it. **2.** F give a hand, help.
'zufliegen v/i (irr, sep, -ge-, sn, → **fliegen**) **1.** F door etc: slam (shut). **2.** ~ **auf** (acc) fly toward(s). **3.** j-m ~ a) bird: fly into s.o.'s home, b) come easily to s.o.
'zufließen v/i (irr, sep, -ge-, sn, → **fließen**) a. fig. flow into.
'Zuflucht f (-; -en) **1.** refuge, shelter: ~ **suchen (finden)** seek (find) refuge (**bei** with, fig. in). **2.** fig. (m-e letzte ~ my last) resort: **s-e ~ nehmen zu** resort to.
'Zufluchtsort m place of refuge, retreat.
'Zufluß m (-sses; ⁻sse) **1.** influx, inflow. **2.** a) inlet, b) tributary.
'zuflüstern v/t (sep, h) whisper (dat to).
zufolge [tsu'fɔlgə] prep (dat) according to, in accordance with (his request etc).
zu'frieden adj (**mit** with) a) content(ed), b) satisfied, pleased: **ein ~es Gesicht machen** look pleased; **~ Lächeln** contented smile; **mit wenig ~** easily satisfied; **sie ist nie ~** there is no pleasing her; iro. **bist du nun ~?** are you satisfied now?; **~ lächeln** smile contentedly.
zu'friedengeben: sich ~ (irr, sep, -ge-, h, → **geben**) content o.s. (**mit** with).

Zu'friedenheit f (-; no pl) contentment, (**zu m-r** etc ~ to my etc) satisfaction.

zu'friedenlassen v/t (irr, sep, -ge-, h, → **lassen**) leave s.o. alone (or in peace).

zu'friedenstellen v/t (sep, h) satisfy: **sie sind schwer zufriedenzustellen** they are hard to please.

zu'friedenstellend adj satisfactory.

'zufrieren v/i (irr, sep, -ge-, sn, → **frieren**) freeze up (or over).

'zufügen v/t (sep, h) 1. add (dat to). 2. **j-m e-n Schaden** ~ harm s.o.; **j-m e-e Niederlage** etc ~ inflict defeat etc on s.o.; **j-m (ein) Unrecht** ~ wrong s.o.

'Zufuhr f (-; -en) supply, meteor. influx: **die** ~ **abschneiden** cut off supplies.

'zuführen (sep, h) I v/t (dat to) carry, bring, lead, ⚙ feed, supply: **dem Körper Nahrung** ~ feed the body; **j-n s-r (gerechten) Strafe** ~ punish s.o. (as he deserves). II v/i **auf** ~ (acc) a. fig. lead to. **'Zuführung** f (-; -en) 1. no pl conveyance, feeding, delivery. 2. ⚡ lead.

Zug¹ [tsu:k] m (-[e]s; ⸚e) (**mit dem** ~ **fahren** go by) train: **im** ~ on the train; **wir brachten sie zum** ~ we saw her off at the station; F fig. **im falschen** ~ **sitzen** be on the wrong track; **der** ~ **ist abgefahren!** it's too late for that now!

Zug² m (-[e]s; ⸚e) 1. no pl draw(ing), pull(ing), traction. 2. ⚙ tension, tensible force. 3. no pl draught, Am. draft. 4. a) breath, b) gulp, F swig, c) drag, puff: **in 'einem** ~ a. fig. in one go; **in den letzten Zügen liegen** be breathing one's last, humor. object: be on its last legs; **et. in vollen Zügen genießen** enjoy s.th. to the full. 5. chess: move: **wer ist am** ~? who is to move?; ~ **um** ~ a) step by step, b) without delay, c) ✝ concurrently; **er kam nicht zum** ~(**e**) F he didn't get a look-in. 6. stroke (of pen etc), a. writing: fig. **in groben Zügen** in broad outline, roughly. 7. procession, column, ⚔ etc platoon: **endlose Züge von Flüchtlingen** an endless procession of refugees. 8. passage, migration (of birds), a. flight, movement (of clouds etc). 9. **im** ~**e** (gen) in the course of; **im besten** ~**e sein** be well under way, person: be going strong. 10. no pl F ~ **bringen in** (acc) bring a class, team, etc up to scratch; **da ist kein** ~ **drin** it's a slow show, they lack the real drive. 11.

⚙ flue. 12. groove, pl rifling. 13. ped. etc: stream.

Zug³ m (-[e]s; ⸚e) a) feature, b) line, look, c) characteristic, trait, b.s. streak, d) bent (zu for): **das war kein schöner** ~ **von ihr** that wasn't nice of her; **der** ~ **der Zeit** the trend of the times.

'Zugabe f (-; -n) 1. extra, bonus. 2. addition, ⚙ makeweight: 3. ♪ etc encore.

'Zugang m (-[e]s; ⸚e) 1. access (a. fig.), gate(way) (a. fig.), approach, access road: **ich finde k-n** ~ **zur modernen Musik** I'm unable to appreciate modern music. 2. in library etc: accession, in hospital etc: admission, at university etc: intake.

'zugänglich [-gɛŋlɪç] adj a. fig. accessible (für to), get-at-able, available: **et. (der Allgemeinheit)** ~ **machen** open s.th. (to the public); ~ **für** open to arguments etc; **er war für neue Methoden** ~ he was quite willing to try out new methods; **sie war k-n Vernunftgründen** ~ she wasn't amenable to reason.

'Zugänglichkeit f (-; no pl) (**für** to) accessibility, fig. a. amenability.

'Zugangsstraße f access road.

'Zugbrücke f drawbridge.

'zugeben v/t (irr, sep, -ge-, h, → **geben**) 1. add (dat to), ✝ give as an extra, F throw in, ♪ give s.th. as an encore. 2. admit, confess, a. grant, concede: **zugegeben, er hat recht, aber ...** I grant you he's right but ... 3. allow.

'zugegebener'maßen adv admittedly.

zu'gegen adj ~ **sein** be present (**bei** at).

'zugehen (irr, sep, -ge-, sn, → **gehen**) I v/i 1. ~ **auf** (acc) go up to, go (or walk) towards, head for; fig. **er geht auf die Achtzig zu** he's getting on for eighty; **dem Ende** ~ be drawing to a close; **man muß auf die Leute** ~ you have to talk to people (openly). 2. **j-m** ~ reach s.o.; **j-m et.** ~ **lassen** have s.th. sent to s.o. 3. F walk faster: **geh zu!** get a move on! 4. F **door, suitcase,** etc: shut. 5. ~ **zulaufen** 4. II v/impers 6. **es geht auf 8 Uhr zu** it's getting on for eight (o'clock); **es geht dem Winter zu** winter is drawing near (or is on its way). 7. happen, go: **wie geht es zu, daß?** how is it that?, F how come ...?; **bei ihnen geht's vielleicht hektisch zu!** things are pretty hectic with them; → **Ding** 2.

'**Zugehörigkeit** *f* (-; *no pl*) (**zu**) membership (in), affiliation (to, with).

'**zugeknöpft** *adj* F *fig.* reserved, silent.

'**Zügel** ['tsy:gəl] *m* (-s; -) rein: *fig.* **die ~** **(fest) in der Hand halten** have things (firmly) under control; **die ~ lockern** loosen the reins; **der Phantasie** *etc die* **~ schießen lassen** give free rein to one's imagination *etc*.

'**zügellos** *adj fig.* **1.** unrestrained. **2.** licentious. '**Zügellosigkeit** *f* (-; *no pl*) **1.** lack of restraint. **2.** licentiousness.

'**zügeln** ['tsy:gəln] *v/t* (h) **1.** rein (up). **2.** *fig.* curb, check, bridle.

'**Zugereiste** *m, f* (-n; -n) newcomer.

'**Zugeständnis** *n* (-ses; -se) concession (**an** *acc* to). '**zugestehen** *v/t* (*irr, sep*, h, → **gestehen**) **1.** (*dat* to) concede, grant. **2.** admit.

'**zugetan** *adj* (*dat*) **~ sein** be fond of.

'**Zugewinn** *m* (-[e]s; -e) gain(s).

'**Zugfeder** *f* ⚙ tension spring, *of watch*: main spring.

'**Zugfestigkeit** *f* (-; *no pl*) ⚙ tensile strength.

'**Zugführer** *m* **1.** 🚂 guard, *Am.* train conductor. **2.** ✗ platoon leader.

'**Zugfunk** *m* 🚂 train radio.

'**zugießen** *v/t* (*irr, sep,* -ge-, h, → **gießen**) add.

zugig ['tsu:gɪç] *adj* draughty, *Am.* drafty.

zügig ['tsy:gɪç] *adj* quick, speedy: **~ vorankommen** make rapid progress.

'**Zugkraft** *f* **1.** ⚙ tractive (*or* tensile) force. **2.** *fig.* attraction, appeal, *of person*: magnetism. '**zugkräftig** *adj fig.* powerful, catchy (*slogan*), crowd-pulling (*actor, film, etc*), *pol.* vote-getting (*candidate etc*): **~ sein** *a.* have appeal.

zu'gleich *adv* at the same time.

'**Zugluft** *f* (-; *no pl*) draught, *Am.* draft.

'**Zugmaˌschine** *f mot.* tractor.

'**Zugmittel** *n fig.* draw, attraction.

'**Zugnummer** *f fig.* draw(ing card).

'**Zugpferd** *n fig.* draw, *thea. etc* crowd-puller, *pol. a.* (great) vote-getter.

'**Zugpflaster** *m* 💊 blistering plaster.

'**zugreifen** *v/i* (*irr, sep,* -ge-, h, → **greifen**) **1.** → **zufassen**. **2.** help o.s.: *greifen Sie bitte zu!* please help yourself! **3.** *fig.* seize (*or* jump at) the opportunity: *du brauchst nur zuzugreifen!* you may have it for the asking. **4.** *fig.* intervene.

'**Zugriff** *m* (-[e]s; -e) **1.** intervention: *er entzog sich dem ~ der Polizei* he escaped the police. **2.** *computer*: access.

'**Zugriffszeit** *f computer*: access time.

zu'grunde *adv* **1.** **~ gehen** (**an** *dat*) a) perish (of), die (of), b) be ruined (by). **2.** (*dat*) **et. ~ legen** base s.th. on. **3.** (*dat*) **~ liegen** form the basis of, be based on. **4.** **~ richten** ruin, wreck.

'**Zugschaffner** *m* 🚂 train conductor.

'**Zugstück** *n thea. etc* draw, hit.

'**Zugteleˌfon** *n* telephone on the train.

'**Zugtier** *n* draught (*Am.* draft) animal.

'**zugucken** F → **zusehen**.

'**Zugunglück** *n* train accident.

zu'gunsten *prep* (*gen*) in favo(u)r of.

zu'gute *adv* **1.** *j-m* **et. ~ halten** a) give s.o. credit for s.th., b) pardon s.o. s.th.; *sie hielten ihm s-e Unerfahrenheit ~* they made allowances for his lack of experience. **2.** **~ kommen** (*dat*) a) go to, be for the benefit of, b) be of advantage to, stand *s.o.* in good stead. **3.** *sich* **et. ~** *halten* (*or* **tun**) *auf* (*acc*) pride o.s. on.

'**Zugverbindung** *f* train connection.

'**Zugverkehr** *m* train services.

'**Zugvogel** *m* bird of passage.

'**Zugzwang** *m fig. in* **~ geraten** be forced to make a move; *unter* **~ stehen** be under pressure to act.

'**zuhaben** *v/i* (*irr, sep,* -ge-, h, → **haben**) F be closed.

'**zuhalten** (*irr, sep,* -ge-, h, → **halten**) **I** *v/t* **1.** keep *s.th.* closed. **2.** put (*or* hold) one's hand(s) over (*one's eyes, ears*): *sich die Nase* **~** hold one's nose. **II** *v/i* **~** *auf* (*acc*) make for, head for.

Zuhälter ['tsu:hɛltər] *m* (-s; -) pimp.

Zuhälte'rei *f* (-; *no pl*) pimping.

Zuhause [tsu'haʊzə] *n* (-s; *no pl*) home.

Zu'hilfenahme *f unter* (*ohne*) **~ von** (*or gen*) with (without) the aid of.

zu'hinterst *adv* at the very end.

'**zuhören** *v/i* (*sep*, h) listen (*dat* to).

'**Zuhörer(in** *f) m* listener: *die Zuhörer a.* the audience. '**Zuhörerraum** *m* auditorium. '**Zuhörerschaft** *f* (-; *no pl*) audience, *radio: a.* listeners.

'**zujubeln** *v/i* (*sep*, h) (*dat*) cheer.

'**zuklappen** *v/t* (*sep*, h), *v/i* (sn) shut, close *s.th.* with a snap.

'**zukleben** *v/t* (*sep*, h) seal.

'**zuklinken** *v/t* (*sep*, h) latch.

'**zuknallen** *v/t* (*sep*, h) slam *s.th.* (shut).

'zuknöpfen *v/t* (*sep*, h) button (up); → **zugeknöpft**.

'zukommen *v/i* (*irr*, *sep*, -ge-, sn, → **kommen**) **1.** ~ *auf* (*acc*) approach, come up to; *fig*. *auf j-n* ~ be in store for s.o.; *adm*. *wir werden auf Sie* ~ we'll contact you; *die Sache auf sich* ~ *lassen* let the matter take its course, wait and see. **2.** *j-m et.* ~ *lassen* send (*or* give) s.o. s.th. **3.** *j-m* ~ a) befit s.o., b) be due to s.o.

Zukunft ['tsu:kʊnft] *f* (-; *no pl*) **1.** (*in* ~ in) future: *in naher* (*nächster*) ~ in the near (immediate) future; *in die* ~ *blicken* look ahead; *dieser Beruf hat k-e* ~ there is no future in this profession; F *das hat k-e* ~*!* that has no future; *abwarten, was die* ~ *bringt* wait and see what the future has in store for us. **2.** *ling*. future (tense). **'zukünftig I** *adj* future, *person*: *a*. prospective, *father etc* -to-be. **II** *adv* in (the) future.

'Zukunfts|aussichten *pl* future prospects. **2bezogen I** *adj* forward-looking. **II** *adv* with a view to the future. **~forscher** *m* futurologist. **~forschung** *f* futurology. **~glaube** *m* faith in the future. **~mu,sik** *f fig*. *das ist alles noch* ~ that's all still up in the air. **2orien,tiert** *adj* future-oriented. **~pläne** *pl* plans for the future. **2reich** *adj* with a great future, promising. **~ro,man** *m* science fiction novel.

'zukunft(s)weisend *adj* advanced.

'zulächeln *v/i* (*sep*, h) *j-m* ~ smile at s.o.

'Zulage *f* (-; -n) a) extra pay, additional allowance, b) bonus, c) rise, *Am*. raise.

'zulangen *v/i* (*sep*, h) **1.** F → *zugreifen* 2. **2.** → *zupacken*.

zu'lassen *v/t* (*irr*, *sep*, -ge-, h, → **lassen**) **1.** F leave *door etc* shut. **2.** admit s.o. (*zu* to), *adm*. license, *a*. register (*car etc*): *amtlich* ~ authorize; *staatlich* ~ register; *j-n als Rechtsanwalt* ~ call (*or* admit) s.o. to the bar. **3.** a) allow, permit, b) admit (of) (*doubt etc*).

'zulässig *adj* admissible, permissible, allowable: ~*e* (*Höchst*)*Belastung* maximum permissible (*or* safe) load; ~*e Höchstgeschwindigkeit* speed limit; *das ist* (*nicht*) ~ that is (not) allowed.

'Zulassung *f* (-; -en) **1.** *no pl* admission (*zu* to). **2.** *mot*. a) licen/ce (*Am*. -se), b) registration.

'Zulassungs|beschränkung *f* restriction on admissions. **~nummer** *f mot*. registration number. **~pa,piere** *pl* registration papers. **~prüfung** *f* entrance exam(ination). **~stelle** *f* registration office.

'Zulauf *m* (-[e]s; *no pl*) **1.** a) run (*of customers etc*), b) custom, c) approval: *großen* ~ *haben* be much sought after, *film etc*: be very popular, draw large crowds. **2.** ⊚ supply.

'zulaufen *v/i* (*irr*, *sep*, -ge-, sn, → **laufen**) **1.** ~ *auf* (*acc*) run up to. **2.** *j-m* ~ a) *animal*: stray to s.o., b) *customers etc*: flock to s.o.; *zugelaufener Hund* stray dog. **3.** flow in: ~ *lassen* add, run *hot water etc* in. **4.** *spitz* ~ taper to a point. **5.** F hurry: *lauf zu!* hurry up!

'zulegen (*sep*, h) **I** *v/t* **1.** F *sich ein Auto etc* ~ buy (*or* get) o.s. a car *etc*; *fig*. *er hat sich e-e Freundin* (*e-n Bart*) *zugelegt* he has got himself a girlfriend (he has grown a beard). **2.** add (*dat* to): → *Zahn* 2. **II** *v/i* **1.** a) put on weight, b) increase the pace, c) score gains.

zuleide [tsu'laɪdə] *adv j-m et.* ~ *tun* harm (*or* hurt) s.o.; → *Fliege* 1.

'zuleiten *v/t* (*sep*, h) **1.** ⊚ feed, supply, *a*. let in (*water*). **2.** pass *s.th*. on (*dat* to).

'Zuleitung *f* (-; -en) **1.** ⊚ supply (*or* feeding) pipe. **2.** ⚡ a) feeder, b) lead(-in).

zu'letzt *adv* **1.** last: *du kommst immer* ~ you are alway the last (to arrive); *ganz* ~ last of all. **2.** *bis* ~ to the (very) end. **3.** finally, in the end. **4.** last: *wann haben Sie ihn* ~ *gesehen?* when did you see him last? **5.** *nicht* ~ not least.

zu'liebe *adv mir et.* ~ for my *etc* sake.

'Zulieferer *m* (-s; -) supplier.

'Zulieferindu,strie *f* ancillary industry.

'zumachen (*sep*, h) F **I** *v/t* **1.** shut, close (*door etc*, *a*. *shop etc*), stop up (*hole*), button up, do up (*jacket etc*), put down (*umbrella*), seal (*envelope etc*): *ich habe kein Auge zugemacht* I didn't sleep a wink. **II** *v/i* **2.** *shop etc*: a) close, b) close down. **3.** hurry: *mach zu!* hurry up!

zu'mal I *conj* ~ (*da or weil*) particularly since. **II** *adv* particularly, above all.

'zumauern *v/t* (*sep*, h) wall up.

'zumessen *v/t* (*irr*, *sep*, -ge-, h, → **messen**) **1.** (*dat* to) apportion, allot. **2.** attach (*importance etc*).

zu'mindest *adv* at least.

zumute [tsu'muːtə] *adv* **wie ist dir ~?** how do you feel?; **mir ist jämmerlich ~** I feel miserable; **mir ist nicht nach Essen ~** I don't feel like eating; **mir ist bei dieser Sache gar nicht wohl ~** I don't feel at all happy about it.

zumuten ['tsuːmuːtən] *v/t (sep, h)* **j-m et. ~** expect s.th. of s.o; **sich zuviel ~** overdo things, F bite off more than one can chew.

'**Zumutung** *f* (-; -en) a) unreasonable demand, b) cheek: **das ist e-e ~!** that's asking a bit much!, *a.* what a nerve!

zu'nächst *adv* **1.** first (of all), above all. **2.** to begin with, in the first place. **3.** for the present, for the time being.

'**zunageln** *v/t (sep, h)* nail up.

'**zunähen** *v/t (sep, h)* sew up.

Zunahme ['tsuːnaːmə] *f* (-; -n) increase *(gen or an dat* in).

'**Zuname** *m* surname, last name.

'**Zündeinstellung** *f mot.* ignition timing.

zünden ['tsyndən] (h) **I** *v/i* **1.** *mot.* ignite. **2.** detonate. **3.** fire *(rocket etc)*. **II** *v/i* **4.** catch fire. **5.** ⚡, *mot.* ignite, fire. **6.** *fig.* arouse enthusiasm, idea *etc:* catch on.
'**zündend** *adj fig.* rousing *(speech)*.

Zunder ['tsʊndər] *m* (-s; -) **(brennen wie ~** burn like) tinder: F *fig.* **j-m ~ geben** give s.o. hell.

'**Zünder** *m* (-s; -) ⚙ fuse, *Am.* fuze, ⚡ igniter.

'**Zünd**|**funke** *m mot.* (ignition) spark. **~holz** *n*, **~kabel** *n* match. **~kabel** *n* *mot.* ignition cable. **~kerze** *f mot.* spark(ing) plug. **~punkt** *m* 🔥 ignition point. **~satz** *m* primer. **~schloß** *n mot.* ignition lock. **~schlüssel** *m mot.* ignition key. **~schnur** *f* fuse, *a.* slow match wick. **~spule** *f mot.* ignition coil. **~stoff** *m* (-[e]s; *no pl)* dynamite.

'**Zündung** *f* (-; -en) *mot.* ignition.

'**zunehmen** *(irr, sep, -ge-, h, → nehmen)* **I** *v/i* **1.** increase, grow: **an Wert ~** increase in value; **an Bedeutung ~** gain in importance. **2.** *moon:* wax. **3.** *(stark or sehr) ~* put on (a lot of) weight. **II** *v/t* **sie hat 10 Pfund zugenommen** she has put on *(or* gained) ten pounds.
'**zunehmend** **I** *adj* **1.** increasing, growing: **mit ~em Alter** as one gets older; **in ~em Maße** → II. **2.** waxing: **bei ~em Mond** when the moon is waxing. **II** *adv* increasingly, more and more.

'**zuneigen** *(sep, h)* **I** *v/i* **der Ansicht ~, daß** be inclined to think that. **II** **sich dem Ende ~** draw to a close.

'**Zuneigung** *f* (-; -en) affection *(für, zu* for).

Zunft [tsʊnft] *f* (-; ⸚e) *hist.* guild.

zünftig ['tsynftɪç] *adj* F proper, good.

Zunge ['tsʊŋə] *f* (-; -n) tongue: put one's **anstoßen** (have a) lisp; **sich auf die ~ beißen** bite one's tongue *(fig.* lips); *(j-m)* **die ~ herausstrecken** put one's tongue out (at s.o.); *fig.* **es lag mir auf der ~** I had it on the tip of my tongue; **sie hat e-e lose (scharfe) ~** she has a loose (sharp) tongue; → **zergehen**.

züngeln ['tsʏŋəln] *v/i* (h) *snake:* dart its tongue, *flames:* lick.

'**Zungen**|**belag** *m* 🔥 coat(ing) of the tongue. **~brecher** *m* F tongue twister. ⚡**fertig** *adj* glib. **~kuß** *m* French *(or* deep) kiss. **~laut** *m* lingual (sound). **~spitze** *f* tip of the tongue.

Zünglein ['tsʏŋlaɪn] *n fig.* **das ~ an der Waage sein** tip the scales.

zunichte [tsu'nɪçtə] *adv* **~ machen** ruin; **~ werden** come to nothing.

'**zunicken** *v/i (sep, h)* nod *(dat* to): **j-m freundlich ~** give s.o. a friendly nod.

zunutze [tsu'nʊtsə] *adv* **sich et. ~ machen** make (good) use of s.th., *a. b.s.* take advantage of s.th.

zu'oberst *adv* (right) at the top.

'**zuordnen** *v/t (sep, h) (dat)* assign (to) *(a.* 🅰), class (with).

'**zupacken** *v/i (sep, h)* work hard.

zupfen ['tsʊpfən] (h) **I** *v/t* pull, pick, *a.* ♪ pluck: **j-n am Ärmel ~** tug at s.o.'s sleeve. **II** *v/i* **~ an** *(dat)* pull at, tug at.

'**Zupfinstru**,**ment** *n* plucked instrument.

zuprosten ['tsuːproːstən] *v/i (sep, h)* raise one's glass *(dat* to).

'**zuraten** *v/i (irr, sep, -ge-, h, → raten)* **j-m ~, et. zu tun** advise s.o. to do s.th.; **auf mein** *etc* **Zuraten** on my *etc* advice.

'**zurechnen** *v/t (sep, h)* **1.** → **zuordnen**. **2.** add *(dat* to).

'**zurechnungsfähig** *adj* sane, of sound mind, ⚖ responsible. '**Zurechnungsfähigkeit** *f* (-; *no pl)* ⚖ (**verminderte ~** diminished) responsibility.

'**zu**'**rechtbasteln** *v/t (sep, h)* rig up.

zu'rechtbiegen *v/t (irr, sep, -ge-, h, → biegen)* **1.** bend *s.th.* into shape. **2.** F *fig.* straighten *s.o., s.th.* out.

zu'rechtfinden: *sich* ~ (*irr*, *sep*, -ge-, h, → *finden*) find one's way (around), *fig.* cope, manage: *findest du dich darin zurecht?* can you make sense of it all?

zu'rechtkommen *v/i* (*irr*, *sep*, -ge-, sn, → *kommen*) 1. arrive in time. 2. (*mit* with) manage, cope: *mit j-m* (*gut*) ~ get on (well) with s.o.

zu'rechtlegen *v/t* (*sep*, h) 1. lay *s.th.* ready, arrange. 2. *fig. sich et.* ~ work (*or* figure) out, have *excuse etc* ready.

zu'rechtmachen (*sep*, h) F I *v/t* get *s.th.* ready, prepare, make, *Am.* F *a.* fix (*salad etc*), make up (*bed*). II *sich* ~ a) do o.s. up, b) make up.

zu'rechtrücken *v/t* (*sep*, h) adjust, *a. fig.* put *s.th.* straight.

zu'rechtstutzen *v/t* (*sep*, h) *a. fig.* trim.

zu'rechtweisen *v/t* (*irr*, *sep*, -ge-, h, → *weisen*) rebuke, reprimand. **Zu'rechtweisung** *f* (-; -en) rebuke, reprimand.

'zureden *v/i* (*sep*, h) *j-m* ~(, *et. zu tun*) encourage (*or* persuade, urge) s.o. (to do s.th.); *auf j-n etc Zureden* upon her *etc* encouragement: *alles Zureden war umsonst* all persuasion was in vain.

'zureiten (*irr*, *sep*, -ge-, → *reiten*) I *v/t* (h) break in (*horse*). II *v/i* (sn) ~ *auf* (*acc*) ride up to.

'zurichten *v/t* (*sep*, h) 1. ⚙ a) finish, b) shape. 2. *print.* make ready. 3. *übel* ~ injure *s.o.* badly, batter (*s.o.*, *s.th.*).

'zuriegeln *v/t* (*sep*, h) bolt.

zürnen ['tsʏrnən] *v/i* (h) *j-m* ~ be angry with s.o.

Zur'schaustellung *f* (-; -en) exhibition, display, *fig. a.* parading.

zurück [tsu'rʏk] *adv* back: ~ *sein* a) be (*or* have come) back, b) F lag behind (*a. ped.*), *in one's development*: be retarded, be backward; *mit s-r Arbeit* ~ *sein* be behind (*or* in arrears) with one's work; *sports*: **5 Punkte** (**3 Meter** *etc*) ~ *liegen* be five points down (be three metres *etc*) behind.

Zu'rück *n* es gibt kein ~ (*mehr*) there's no turning back (now).

zu'rück|bekommen *v/t* (*irr*, *sep*, h, → *bekommen*) get *s.th.* back. ~**beordern** *v/t* (*sep*, h) order *s.o.* back. ~**beugen** *v/t* (*a. sich* ~) (*sep*, h) bend back. ~**bilden**: *sich* ~ (*sep*, h) recede, *biol.* regress. ~**bleiben** *v/i* (*irr*, *sep*, -ge-, sn, → *bleiben*) 1. stay (*or* be left) behind. 2. be

left. 3. lag behind (*a. ped.*), *sports*: a. drop back, *in one's development*: be retarded: *hinter den Erwartungen* ~ fall short of expectations. ~**blicken** *v/i* (*sep*, h) look back (*auf acc* at, *fig.* on). ~**bringen** *v/t* (*irr*, *sep*, -ge-, h, → *bringen*) bring (*or* take) s.o., s.th. back, return: *j-n ins Leben* ~ bring s.o. back to life. ~**da,tieren** *v/t* (*sep*, h) backdate. ~**denken** *v/i* (*irr*, *sep*, -ge-, h, → *denken*) (*an acc*) think back (to), recall (*s.o.*, *s.th.*). ~**drängen** *v/t* (*sep*, h) 1. push *s.o.* back. 2. *fig.* repress. ~**drehen** *v/t* (*sep*, h) turn (*or* put) back. ~**dürfen** *v/i* (*irr*, *sep*, -ge-, h, → *dürfen*) be allowed back. ~**eilen** *v/i* (*sep*, sn) hurry back. ~**erobern** *v/t* (*sep*, h) recapture, *fig.* win back. ~**erstatten** *v/t* (*sep*, h) refund, reimburse. ~**erwarten** *v/t* (*sep*, h) expect *s.o.* back. ~**fahren** (*irr*, *sep*, -ge-, → *fahren*) I *v/i* (sn) 1. drive (*or* travel, go) back, return. 2. *fig.* recoil (*vor dat* from). II *v/t* (h) drive *s.o.*, *s.th.* back. ~**fallen** *v/i* (*irr*, *sep*, -ge-, sn, → *fallen*) 1. fall back. 2. fall behind (*a. ped.*), *sports*: a. drop back (*auf den dritten Platz* to third place). 3. ~ *in* (*acc*) relapse (*or* fall back) into. 4. *fig.* ~ *auf* (*acc*) reflect on. ~**finden** *v/i* (*irr*, *sep*, -ge-, h, → *finden*) find one's way back (*zu* to). ~**fließen** *v/i* (*irr*, *sep*, -ge-, sn, → *fließen*) flow back. ~**fordern** *v/t* (*sep*, h) reclaim, demand *s.th.* back. ~**führen** *v/t* (*sep*, h) 1. lead *s.o.* back: (*in die Heimat*) ~ repatriate. 2. *fig.* (*auf acc* to) reduce, trace (*s.th.* back), attribute. ~**geben** *v/t* (*irr*, *sep*, -ge-, h, → *geben*) 1. give *s.th.* back, return. 2. *sports*: pass the *ball* back.

zu'rückgeblieben *adj fig.* retarded, backward.

zu'rückgehen *v/i* (*irr*, *sep*, -ge-, sn, → *gehen*) 1. go back, return, retreat: *fig. et.* ~ *lassen* send s.th. back, return s.th.; *bis ins 19. Jh.* ~ go back to the 19th century. 2. *fig.* go down (*a.* ♣), fall of, decrease: *das Geschäft geht zurück* business is falling off. 3. *fig.* ~ *auf* (*acc*) go back to, have its origin in.

zu'rückgezogen *adj* retired, secluded: ~ *leben* lead a secluded life.

zu'rückgreifen *v/i* (*irr*, *sep*, -ge-, h, → *greifen*) ~ *auf* (*acc*) fall back on.

zu'rückhalten (*irr*, *sep*, -ge-, h, → *halten*) I *v/t* 1. hold *s.o.*, *s.th.* back, with-

zurückhaltend 692

hold, *a.* suppress (*tears etc*). **II sich ~ 2.** restrain o.s.; **sich ~ mit** go easy on (*drinks etc*). **3.** be reserved, keep (o.s.) to o.s., *buyer*: hold back: **sich sehr ~** keep very much in the background. **III** *v/i ~ mit* keep back; *mit s-r Meinung ~* reserve judg(e)ment.

zu'rückhaltend *adj* a) reserved (*a.* ✝), b) guarded, cautious, c) reticent, d) unobtrusive: **~ sein mit** be sparing in (*or* with) *one's praise etc*; **er reagierte sehr ~** his reaction was very cool.

Zu'rückhaltung *f* (-; *no pl*) *fig.* a) reserve, b) caution, discretion.

zu'rück|holen *v/t* (*sep*, h) fetch *s.o.*, *s.th.* back. **~kehren** *v/i* (*sep*, sn) come back, return. **~kommen** *v/i* (*irr*, *sep*, -ge-, sn, → *kommen*) **1.** come back, return. **2.** ~ *auf* (*acc*) come back to, refer to (*letter etc*); *auf j-s Angebot* ~ take s.o. up on his offer. **~können** *v/i* (*irr*, *sep*, -ge-, h, → *können*) F be able to go back: *fig. jetzt kann ich nicht mehr zurück!* I can't go back on my word (*or* decision *etc*) now. **~lassen** *v/t* (*irr*, *sep*, -ge-, h, → *lassen*) **1.** leave *o.s.*, *s.th.* behind. **2.** F allow *s.o.* back. **~laufen** *v/i* (*irr*, *sep*, -ge-, sn, → *laufen*) run back. **~legen** (*sep*, h) **I** *v/t* **1. et.** (*an s-n Platz*) ~ put *s.th.* back (in its place). **2.** a) put *s.th.* aside, b) save, put by, lay aside (*money*): *können Sie mir den Mantel bis morgen* ~? would you keep the coat for me till tomorrow? **3.** cover, *a.* walk (*distance*): *zurückgelegte Strecke* distance covered, *mot. a.* mileage. **II sich ~** lie back. **~lehnen** *v/t* (*a. sich ~*) (*sep*, h) lean back. **~liegen** *v/i* (*irr*, *sep*, -ge-, h, → *liegen*) *das liegt zwei Jahre zurück* that was two years ago. **~melden: sich ~** (*sep*, h) report back (*bei* to). **~müssen** *v/i* (*irr*, *sep*, -ge-, h, → *müssen*) F have to go back.

Zu'rücknahme [-na:mə] *f* (-; *no pl*) taking back, ⚖ *a.* withdrawal, retraction.

zu'rück|nehmen *v/t* (*irr*, *sep*, -ge-, h, → *nehmen*) take *s.th.* back, withdraw (*troops etc*, ⚖ *action*), revoke (*statement*), cancel (*offer etc*). **~prallen** *v/i* (*sep*, sn) **1.** rebound. **2.** *fig.* (*vor dat* from) recoil, start back. **~rechnen** *v/i* (*sep*, h) reckon back. **~reichen** (*sep*, h) **I** *v/t* hand *s.th.* back, return. **II** *v/i* ~ *bis* go (*or* date) back to. **~reisen** *v/i* (*sep*, sn) trav-

el back, return. **~rufen** (*irr*, *sep*, -ge-, h, → *rufen*) **I** *v/t* call *s.o.* back (*a. teleph.*), recall (*a. defective cars etc*): *ins Gedächtnis* ~ recall. **II** *v/i* teleph. call back. **~schalten** *v/i* (*sep*, h) change (*Am.* shift) down. **~scheuen** *v/i* (*sep*, h) shrink (back) (*vor dat* from): *fig. er scheut vor nichts zurück* he sticks at nothing. **~schicken** *v/t* (*sep*, h) send *s.o.*, *s.th.* back, return. **~schlagen** (*irr*, *sep*, -ge-, h, → *schlagen*) **I** *v/t* **1.** hit *s.o.* back. **2.** repulse, beat off (*attack*, *enemy*). **3.** fold back (*cover etc*), turn down (*collar*). **4.** return (*ball*). **II** *v/i* **5.** hit back. **6.** *flames*: flare back. **~schrauben** *v/t* (*sep*, h) F *fig.* cut down, reduce, lower (*expectations etc*). **~schrecken** *v/i* (*sep*, sn) (*vor dat* from) recoil, start back: *fig. er schreckt vor nichts zurück* he sticks at nothing. **~sehnen: sich ~** (*sep*, h) long to be back.

zu'rücksetzen (*sep*, h) **I** *v/t* **1.** put *s.th.* back, back (up) (*car*). **2.** *fig. j-n ~* treat s.o. unfairly, slight s.o. **II** *v/i mot.* back (up). **Zu'rücksetzung** *f* (-; -en) *fig.* unfair treatment, slight.

zu'rück|spielen *v/t*, *v/i* (*sep*, h) pass (the ball) back. **~springen** *v/i* (*irr*, *sep*, -ge-, sn, → *springen*) **1.** jump back. **2.** △ recess. **~spulen** *v/t*, *v/i* (*sep*, h) rewind. **~stecken** (*sep*, h) **I** *v/t* put *s.th.* back. **II** *v/i* F *fig.* come down a peg. **~stehen** *v/i* (*irr*, *sep*, -ge-, h, → *stehen*) **1.** stand back. **2.** *fig.* a) take second place (*hinter j-m* behind s.o.), b) stand down (*or* aside). **~stellen** *v/t* (*sep*, h) **1.** put *s.th.* back. **2.** ✕ defer. **3.** postpone, defer. **4.** put *s.th.* aside (*or* last). **~stoßen** (*irr*, *sep*, -ge-, h, → *stoßen*) **I** *v/t* push *s.o.*, *s.th.* back. **II** *v/i mot.* back (up). **~stufen** *v/t* (*sep*, h) downgrade. **~treiben** *v/t* (*irr*, *sep*, -ge-, h, → *treiben*) drive *s.o.*, *s.th.* back. **~treten** *v/i* (*irr*, *sep*, -ge-, sn, → *treten*) **1.** a) step (*or* stand) back, b) recede. **2.** *government etc*: resign, step down: *von s-m Posten* ~ resign one's post; ~ *von* withdraw from, back out of (*a deal etc*). **3.** *fig.* be of secondary importance (*gegenüber* in comparison with). **~verfolgen** *v/t* (*sep*, h) *fig.* trace *s.th.* back (*zu* to). **~versetzen** *v/t* (*sep*, h) **1.** move *pupil* down, transfer *official* back. **2.** *fig.* take *s.o.* back (*in acc* to): *wir fühlten uns ins Mittelalter zurück-*

versetzt we felt to have stepped back into the Middle Ages. **~weichen** *v/i* (*irr, sep,* -ge-, sn, → *weichen*) **1.** step back, ✗ fall back. **2.** *fig.* ~ *vor* (*dat*) yield to, *a.* shrink back from.

zu'rückweisen *v/t* (*irr, sep,* -ge-, h, → *weisen*) **1.** refuse, reject, repudiate (*accusation etc*). **2.** *j-n* ~ turn s.o. back, refuse s.o. entry. **Zu'rückweisung** *f* (-; -en) refusal, rejection.

zu'rück|werfen *v/t* (*irr, sep,* -ge-, h, → *werfen*) **1.** throw *s.o., s.th.* back, *a.* reflect (*light*), *a.* reverberate (*sound*). **2.** *fig.* set *s.o.* back in one's development, work, *etc* (*um 10 Jahre* [by] ten years). **~wollen** *v/i* (*irr, sep,* -ge-, h, → *wollen*) F want to go back. **~zahlen** *v/t* (*sep,* h) *a. fig.* pay back, repay. **~ziehen** (*irr, sep,* -ge-, → *ziehen*) **I** *v/t* (h) pull (or draw) *s.o., s.th.* back, ✗ or *fig.* withdraw. **II** *sich* ~ (h) (*aus, von* from) retire, withdraw, ✗ *a.* retreat; *sich* ~ *von* ~ give up (*activity etc*); *sich von j-m* ~ dissociate o.s. from s.o.; *sich zur Beratung* ~ retire for deliberation. **III** *v/i* (sn) move back. **~zucken** *v/i* (*sep,* sn) flinch (*vor dat* at).

'Zuruf *m* (-[e]s; -e) a) shout, b) cheer; *durch* ~ by acclamation.

'zurufen *v/t* (*irr, sep,* -ge-, h, → *rufen*) *j-m et.* ~ shout s.th. to s.o.

Zusage ['tsu:za:gə] *f* (-; -n) **1.** promise, word. **2.** acceptance (*of invitation*). **3.** assent, consent. **'zusagen** (*sep,* h) **I** *v/t* **1.** promise (*sein Kommen* to come). **2.** F *j-m et. auf den Kopf* ~ tell s.o. s.th. to his face. **II** *v/i* **3.** accept an invitation, promise to come. **4.** agree. **5.** *j-m* ~ a) agree with s.o., b) be to s.o.'s liking.

zusammen [tsu'zamən] *adv* together, *a.* jointly; ~ *mit* together (*or* along) with; *alle* ~ all of them; *wir alle* ~ all of us; *alles* ~ all together, (all) in all; *wir haben* ~ *100 Mark* we have one hundred marks between us; *das macht* ~ ... that amounts to (*or* totals) ...

Zu'sammenarbeit *f* (-; *no pl*) cooperation, *a.* collaboration, *a.* teamwork: *in* ~ *mit* in cooperation with. **zu'sammenarbeiten** *v/i* (*sep,* h) (*mit* with) cooperate, collaborate, work together.

zu'sammen|ballen (*sep,* h) **I** *v/t* form into a ball. **II** *sich* ~ mass, gather. **~bauen** *v/t* (*sep,* h) ⚙ assemble. **~bei-**

ßen *v/t* (*irr, sep,* -ge-, h, → *beißen*) *a. fig. die Zähne* ~ clench one's teeth. **~bekommen** *v/t* (*irr, sep,* h, → *bekommen*) get s.th. together, raise (*money*). **~binden** *v/t* (*irr, sep,* -ge-, h, → *binden*) bind (or tie) *s.th.* together. **~brauen** *v/t* (*sep,* h) concoct (*a. fig.*): *fig. sich* ~ be brewing. **~brechen** *v/i* (*irr, sep,* -ge-, sn, → *brechen*) break down, collapse, *traffic:* come to a standstill. **~bringen** *v/t* (*irr, sep,* -ge-, h, → *bringen*) **1.** bring (or get) *s.o., s.th.* together, raise (*money*). **2.** F *fig.* manage, bring off, remember (*poem*).

Zu'sammenbruch *m* (-[e]s; ⸚e) breakdown, collapse.

zu'sammen|drängen *v/t* (*sep,* h) **1.** (*a. sich* ~) crowd (*or* huddle) together. **2.** *fig.* compress, condense. **~drücken** *v/t* (*sep,* h) compress. **~fahren** *v/i* (*irr, sep,* -ge-, sn, → *fahren*) **1.** ~ *zusammenstoßen*. **2.** *fig.* (give a) start (*bei* at). **~fallen** *v/i* (*irr, sep,* -ge-, sn, → *fallen*) **1.** fall in, collapse. **2.** coincide. **3.** waste away. **~falten** *v/t* (*sep,* h) fold up.

zu'sammenfassen *v/t* (*sep,* h) **1.** unite, combine: *in Gruppen* ~ group. **2.** (*a. v/i*) summarize, sum up. **zu'sammenfassend** *adj* summary: ~ *kann man sagen* to sum it up it can be said.

Zu'sammenfassung *f* (-; -en) **1.** combination. **2.** summary, résumé, synopsis.

zu'sammen|finden: *sich* ~ (*irr, sep,* -ge-, h, → *finden*) meet. **~fließen** *v/i* (*irr, sep,* -ge-, sn, → *fließen*) flow together, meet.

Zu'sammenfluß *m* confluence.

zu'sammen|fügen *v/t* (*sep,* h) join (together), ⚙ assemble. **~führen** *v/t* (*sep,* h) bring *persons* together: *wieder* ~ reunite. **~gehen** *v/i* (*irr, sep,* -ge-, sn, → *gehen*) *fig.* (*mit* with) go together, make common cause.

zu'sammengehören *v/i* (*sep,* h) belong together, *a.* be a pair. **zu'sammengehörig** *adj* belonging together, *a.* matching, *fig. a.* related. **Zu'sammengehörigkeit** *f* (-; *no pl*) unity, solidarity. **Zu'sammengehörigkeitsgefühl** *n* (-[e]s; *no pl*) feeling of solidarity.

zu'sammengesetzt *adj* ⚕ composite, *a. ling.* compound: ~ *sein aus* be composed of; *~es Wort* compound (word).

zu'sammengewürfelt adj (**bunt**) ~ motley: **~e Mannschaft** scratch team.

Zu'sammenhalt m (-[e]s; no pl) **1.** a. ☉ cohesion. **2.** fig. a) bond, b) team spirit. **zu'sammenhalten** (irr, sep, -ge-, h, → **halten**) **I** v/i hold (F stick) together. **II** v/t hold s.th., persons together.

Zu'sammenhang m (-[e]s; ~e) a) connection, b) context: **in diesem ~** in this connection; **et. in ~ bringen mit** connect s.th. with; **im ~ stehen mit** be connected with; **nicht im ~ stehen mit** have no connection with; **et. aus dem ~ reißen** divorce s.th. from its context. **zu'sammenhängen** v/i (irr, sep, -ge-, h, → **hängen**) fig. be connected (**mit** with): **wie hängt das zusammen?** how is that linked up? **zu'sammenhängend** adj coherent (thoughts, speech, etc), connected, related (questions etc). **zu'sammenhang(s)los** adj incoherent, disconnected.

zu'sammen|hauen v/t (sep, h) **1.** smash s.th. to pieces: F **j-n** ~ beat s.o. up. **2.** F fig. knock s.th. together. **~klappbar** adj folding, collapsible. **~klappen** (sep) **I** v/t (h) fold up, shut (knife etc). **II** v/i (sn) F fig. break down, collapse. **~kleben** v/t, v/i (sep, h) stick together. **~knüllen** v/t (sep, h) crumple up. **~kommen** v/i (irr, sep, -ge-, sn, → **kommen**) **1.** come (or get) together, meet, assemble. **2.** fig. combine: **heute kommt mal wieder alles zuammen!** it never rains but it pours! **3.** accumulate, mount up, money: be collected: F **da kommt ganz schön was zusammen** it comes to quite a lot in the end.

Zu'sammenkunft [-kʊnft] f (-; ~e) get-together, meeting, gathering.

zu'sammenlaufen v/i (irr, sep, -ge-, sn, → **laufen**) **1.** people: gather. **2.** roads etc: meet, converge. **3.** colo(u)rs: run. **zu'sammenleben I** v/i (sep, h) live together: **mit j-m** ~ live with s.o. **II** 2 n (-s) living together: **das 2 mit ...** life with ...

zu'sammenlegen (sep, h) **I** v/t **1.** fold up. **2.** put things in one place, put persons together (in one room). **3.** ✝ fuse, combine, centralize. **II** v/i club together (**für ein Geschenk** for a present).

Zu'sammenlegung f (-; -en) ✝ fusion.

zu'sammen|nehmen (irr, sep, -ge-, h, → **nehmen**) **I** v/t gather (up): **alles**

zusammengenommen all things considered; **ich mußte all m-n Mut** ~ I had to muster up all my courage. **II sich** ~ control o.s., pull o.s. together. **~pakken** v/t (sep, h) pack up. **~passen** (sep, h) **I** v/i harmonize (with each other), colo(u)rs etc: a. go well together, partners: a. be well matched: **sie passen nicht zusammen** they are mismatched. **II** v/t ☉ adjust, match. **~pferchen** v/t (sep, h) herd (fig. a. crowd) together.

Zu'sammenprall m (-[e]s; no pl) a. fig. collision, clash. **zu'sammenprallen** v/i (sep, sn) a. fig. collide, clash.

zu'sammen|pressen v/t (sep, h) compress. **~raffen** v/t (sep, h) **1.** gather up. **2.** fig. amass. **~rechnen** v/t (sep, h) add (or sum) s.th. up. **~reimen** v/t (sep, h) fig. **sich et. ~** work (or figure) s.th. out, put two and two together. **~reißen: sich ~** (irr, sep, -ge-, h, → **reißen**) F pull o.s. together. **~rollen** (sep, h) **I** v/t roll up. **II sich** ~ coil up, cat etc: curl up.

Zu'sammenrotten: sich ~ (sep, h) gang up, form a mob. **Zu'sammenrottung** f (-; -en) a) riot(ing), b) riotous mob, ⚖ riotous assembly.

zu'sammen|rücken (sep) **I** v/t (h) move things together (or closer). **II** v/i (sn) move up, make room. **~rufen** v/t (irr, sep, -ge-, h, → **rufen**) convene, call persons together. **~sacken** v/i (sep, sn) (**in sich**) ~ slump (down). **~scharen: sich** ~ (sep, h) flock together. **~scharren** v/t (sep, h) scrape s.th. together. **~schiebbar** adj telescopic, sliding. **~schieben** v/t (irr, sep, -ge-, h, → **schieben**) push things together, (**a. sich ~ lassen**) telescope. **~schlagen** (irr, sep, -ge-, → **schlagen**) **I** v/t (h) **1.** clap (hands), click (heels etc). **2.** F smash s.th. to pieces: **j-n** ~ beat s.o. up. **II** v/i (sn) ~ **über** (dat) close over, a. fig. engulf. **~schließen** (irr, sep, -ge-, h, → **schließen**) v/t **1.** lock (or chain) together. **2.** unite, ✝ merge. **II sich** ~ unite, join forces, team up, form an alliance.

Zu'sammenschluß m (-sses; ~sse) **1.** union (a. pol.), ✝ merger. **2.** alliance. **zu'sammen|schnüren** v/t (sep, h) tie s.th. up: **der Anblick schnürte ihr das Herz zusammen** the sight made her heart bleed. **~schrauben** v/t (sep, h) screw (or bolt) s.th. together. **~schrei-**

ben v/t (irr, sep, -ge-, h, → **schreiben**) **1.** write s.th. in one word: **wird das zusammengeschrieben?** is that one word? (2. contp. scribble. ~**schustern** v/t (sep, h) F contp. cobble together. ~**schweißen** v/t (sep, h) a. fig. weld.

Zu'sammensein n (-s) gathering, meeting, get-together.

zu'sammensetzen (sep, h) I v/t **1.** put s.th. together, ⊙ a. compose, a. 🠷, ling. compound. **2.** seat persons together. **II sich ~ 3.** sit together. **4.** get together. **5.** **sich ~ aus** consist of, be composed of.

Zu'sammensetzung f (-; -en) **1.** no pl composition (a. of court, team, etc), assembly. **2.** 🠷, ling. compound.

zu'sammensinken v/i (irr, sep, -ge-, sn, → **sinken**) collapse: **in sich ~** slump (down).

Zu'sammenspiel n (-[e]s; no pl) sports: teamwork.

zu'sammen|stauchen v/t (sep, h) F j-n ~ haul s.o. over the coals. ~**stecken** (sep, h) I v/t put things together. II v/i F **immer ~** be as thick as thieves. ~**stehen** v/i (irr, sep, h, → **stehen**) stand (F fig. stick) together.

zu'sammen|stellen v/t (sep, h) **1.** put things together. **2.** combine, draw up, compile, form (team etc), make up, form (team etc), arrange: **in e-r Liste ~** list; **ein Menü ~** compose a menu. **Zu'sammenstellung** f (-; -en) **1.** combination, arrangement. **2.** a) survey, synopsis, b) table, c) list.

Zu'sammenstoß m (-[e]s; ⁓e) **1.** mot. collision, crash. **2.** F fig. clash.

zu'sammen|stoßen v/i (irr, sep, sn, → **stoßen**) collide (**mit** with): **~ mit** a. run (or crash) into. ~**streichen** v/t (irr, sep, -ge-, h, → **streichen**) F shorten (text etc). ~**strömen** v/i (sep, sn) fig. flock together. ~**suchen** v/t (sep, h) gather, collect. ~**tragen** v/t (irr, sep, -ge-, h, → **tragen**) collect (a. fig.), fig. compile (facts etc). ~**treffen** I v/i (irr, sep, sn, → **treffen**) **1. mit** j-m meet s.o. **2.** coincide. **II** 2 n (-s) meeting, b.s. encounter. ~**treiben** v/t (irr, sep, -ge-, h, → **treiben**) round up. ~**treten** v/i (irr, sep, -ge-, sn, → **treten**) meet, parl. convene. ~**trommeln** v/t (sep, h) F call persons together. ~**tun: sich ~** (irr, sep, -ge-, h, → **tun**) (**mit** with) team up, join

forces. ~**wachsen** v/i (irr, sep, -ge-, sn, → **wachsen**) grow together. ~**wirken** I v/i (sep, h) factors etc: combine. **II** 2 n (-s) combination, interplay. ~**zählen** v/t (sep, h) add up, sum up. ~**ziehen** (irr, sep, -ge-, → **ziehen**) I v/t (h) **1.** pull s.th. together, a. 🠷 contract. **2.** concentrate, mass (troops). **II** v/i (sn) **3. mit** j-m move in (together) with s.o., go to live with s.o. **III** sich ~ (h) **4.** contract. **5.** storm etc: be brewing.

Zu'sammenziehung f (-; -en) **1.** contraction. **2.** 🠷 concentration.

zu'sammenzucken v/i (sep, sn) wince (**bei** at).

'**Zusatz** m (-es; ⁓e) a) addition, a. additive, admixture, b) addendum, 🠷🠷 rider. ~**abkommen** n supplementary agreement. ~**batte,rie** f 🠷 booster battery. ~**gerät** n ⊙ attachment.

'**zusätzlich** [-zetslıç] I adj a) additional, extra, b) supplementary, c) auxiliary. II adv in addition (**zu** to).

'**Zusatzversicherung** f supplementary insurance.

zuschanden [tsu'ʃandən] adv ~ **machen** ruin, destroy (a. hopes etc), thwart (plans etc); ~ **fahren** ruin, smash (up).

'**zuschanzen** v/t (sep, h) j m et. ~ linc s.o. up with s.th.

'**zuschauen** v/i → **zusehen**.

'**Zuschauer** m (-s; -) onlooker, sports, thea. etc spectator, TV viewer: **die ~** a. the audience. ~**raum** m auditorium. ~**reakti,on** f audience (TV viewer) response. ~**sport** m spectator sport.

'**zuschicken** v/t (sep, h) j-m et. ~ send (or mail, post) s.th. to s.o.

'**zuschieben** v/t (irr, sep, -ge-, h, → **schieben**) **1.** close, shut. **2.** j-m et. ~ push s.th. over to s.o.; **j-m die Schuld** (**Verantwortung**) ~ put (or shift) the blame (responsibility) on s.o.

'**zuschießen** (irr, sep, -ge-, → **schießen**) I v/t (h) F contribute (money). II v/i (sn) ~ **auf** (acc) rush towards, dart up to.

'**Zuschlag** m (-[e]s; ⁓e) **1.** a) extra charge, b) supplementary fare, c) extra pay. **2.** award: **er erhielt den ~** a) at an auction: the object went to him, b) 🠷 he was awarded the contract.

'**zuschlagen** (irr, sep, -ge-, h, → **schlagen**) I v/t **1.** slam door etc (shut), shut, close (book etc). **2.** j-m et. ~ at an auctoo much of a good thing; **was ~ ist, ist ~!** there's a limit to everything.

zu'vor *adv* **1.** (*kurz* ~ shortly) before: **am Tag** ~ the day before, (on) the previous day. **2.** first.

zu'vorkommen *v/i* (*irr, sep, -ge-, sn,* → **kommen**) (*dat*) anticipate, forestall, F *a.* beat *s.o.* to it. **zu'vorkommend** *adj* obliging, courteous. **Zu'vorkommenheit** *f* (-; *no pl*) obligingness, courtesy.

Zuwachs ['tsu:vaks] *m* (-es; *no pl*) **1.** (**an** *dat* in) increase, growth (*a.* ♥): F **auf ~ kaufen** buy *shoes etc* on the big side. **2.** F addition to the family, baby.

'zuwachsen *v/i* (*irr, sep, -ge-, sn,* → **wachsen¹**) **1.** become overgrown. **2.** ✿ heal up, close.

'Zuwachsrate *f* ♥ growth rate.

'Zuwanderer *m* (-s; -) immigrant.

'zuwandern *v/i* (*sep,* sn) immigrate.

'Zuwanderung *f* (-; -en) immigration.

zuwege [tsu've:gə] *adv* **1.** ~ **bringen** bring *s.th.* off, achieve, manage to do. **2.** F (**noch**) **gut ~ sein** be (still) very fit.

zu'weilen *adv* at times, occasionally.

'zuweisen *v/t* (*irr, sep, -ge-, h,* → **weisen**) assign (*dat* to).

'zuwenden *v/t* (*sep,* h, → **wenden²**) **I** *v/t* **1.** turn (*dat* towards): **j-m den Rücken ~** turn one's back on *s.o.*; **j-m das Gesicht ~** face *s.o.* **2.** **j-m et.** ~ give *s.o. s.th.* **II sich** ~ turn to, *fig. a.* devote o.s. to (*a task etc*). **'Zuwendung** *f* (-; -en) **1.** a) grant, b) allowance, c) donation. **2.** *no pl* love, (loving) care, attention.

zu'wenig *indef pron* a) too little, b) too few: **das ist** ~ that's not enough; **du schläfst** ~ you don't get enough sleep.

'zuwerfen *v/t* (*irr, sep, -ge-, h,* → **werfen**) **1.** slam *s.th.* (shut). **2.** (*dat* to) throw, toss: *fig.* **j-m e-n Blick ~** dart (*or* flash) *s.o.* a look; → **Kußhand.**

zu'wider *adj* **j-m ist ... ~** *s.o.* hates (*or* detests) ... **II** *prep* (*dat*) contrary to, against.

zu'widerhandeln *v/i* (*sep,* h) (*dat*) act against, act contrary to, violate, contravene (*law etc*). **Zu'widerhandelnde** *m, f* (-n; -n) ⚖ offender. **Zu'widerhandlung** *f* (-; -en) ⚖ (**gegen**) offen/ce (*Am.* -se) (against), contravention (of).

zu'widerlaufen *v/i* (*irr, sep, -ge-, sn,* → **laufen**) (*dat*) run counter to.

'zuwinken *v/i* (*sep,* h) **j-m ~** wave to *s.o.*

'zuzahlen *v/t* (*sep,* h) pay *s.th.* extra.

'zuzählen *v/t* (*sep,* h) **1.** add. **2.** (*dat*) count among.

'zuziehen (*irr, sep, -ge-,* → **ziehen**) **I** *v/t* (h) **1.** pull *noose etc* tight, tighten, draw (*curtains*). **2. sich et.** ~ a) catch (*disease etc*), suffer (*injury*), b) incur (*s.o.'s hatred etc*). **3.** → **hinzuziehen. II** *v/i* (sn) a) move in, b) settle (down). **'Zuzug** *m* (-[e]s; *no pl*) **1.** move. **2.** → **Zuwanderung.**

zuzüglich ['tsu:tsy:klıç] *prep* (*gen*) plus.

zwang [tsvaŋ] *pret of* **zwingen.**

Zwang *m* (-[e]s; ⸚e) compulsion (*a.* psych.), constraint, pressure, force: **ohne ~** without being forced to; **unter ~ handeln** ⚖ act under duress; **~ ausüben** exert pressure (**auf** *acc* on); **gesellschaftliche Zwänge** social constraints; **... ist ~ ...** is compulsory; *iro.* **tu dir k-n ~ an!** just go ahead!

zwängen ['tsvɛŋən] *v/t* (h) squeeze.

'zwanglos *adj* informal, casual, unconstrained, *a.* free and easy: **in ~er Folge erscheinen** *magazine etc*: appear at irregular intervals; **sich ~ unterhalten** talk at ease; **es geht bei ihnen sehr ~ zu** things are very informal with them. **'Zwanglosigkeit** *f* (-; *no pl*) informality, casualness.

'Zwangs|anleihe *f* compulsory loan. **~arbeit** *f* (-; *no pl*) forced labo(u)r. **~arbeiter(in** *f*) *m* forced labo(u)r convict. **~aufenthalt** *m* enforced stay, detention. **~bewirtschaftung** *f* (economic) control: **die ~ aufheben von** (*or gen*) decontrol. **~einweisung** *f* committal (*in acc* to). **2ernähren** *v/t* (h) forcefeed. **~ernährung** *f* force feeding. **~handlung** *f* compulsive act. **~herrschaft** *f* despotism, tyranny. **~jacke** *f* straitjacket. **~lage** *f* predicament.

'zwangsläufig *adj* inevitable: **er mußte ~ davon erfahren** he was bound to hear of it.

'Zwangs|maßnahme *f* coercive measure, *pol.* sanction. **~neu,rose** *f* obsessional neurosis. **~pause** *f* enforced break. **~räumung** *f* eviction. **~umsiedler(in** *f*) *m* displaced person. **2versteigern** *v/t* (*only inf and pp* zwangsversteigert, h) put *s.th.* up for compulsory auction. **~versteigerung** *f* compulsory auction. **~verwaltung** *f* sequestration. **~vollstreckung** *f* execution. **~vorstel-**

lung *f psych.* obsession: **von der ~ befallen, daß** obsessed with the idea that.

'**zwangsweise I** *adj* compulsory. **II** *adv* compulsorily, by force.

'**Zwangswirtschaft** *f* government control, controlled economy.

zwanzig ['tsvantsɪç] *adj* (~ *[Jahre alt] sein* be) twenty. '**Zwanzig** *f* (-; -en) twenty: *sie ist Mitte (der) ~* she is in her mid-twenties. **zwanziger** ['tsvantsɪɡər] *adj* **die goldenen ~ Jahre** the roaring twenties. '**zwanzigfach** *adj and adv* twentyfold. '**zwanzigjährig** [-jɛːrɪç] *adj* **1.** twenty-year-old, of twenty. **2.** twentieth (*jubilee etc*). '**Zwanzigjährige** [-jɛːrɪɡə] *m, f* (-n; -n) twenty-year--old (person): *die ~n* the twenty-year-olds. '**zwanzigst** *adj*, '**Zwanzigstel** *n* (-s; -) twentieth.

zwar [tsva:r] *adv* **1.** ~ ..., *aber* ... it is true ..., but; *es ist ~ verboten, aber ...* a. it may be forbidden, but ... **2.** *und ~* a) namely, b) in fact.

Zweck [tsvɛk] *m* (-[e]s; -e) **1.** purpose, object, aim, end, use: *zu diesem ~* a) for that purpose, b) to this end; *ein Mittel zum ~* a means to an end; *der ~ heiligt die Mittel* the end justifies the means; *s-n ~ erfüllen (verfehlen)* serve (defeat) its purpose; *für wohltätige ~e* for charity. **2.** point, use: *es hat k-n ~ zu warten* it's no use waiting; *es hat wenig ~, daß ich hingehe* there's little point in my going; *F das ist ja (gerade) der ~ der Übung!* that's the whole point (of the exercise).

'**Zweck|bau** *m* (-[e]s; -ten) functional building. **~bindung** *f* earmarking *of funds* for specific purposes. **~denken** *n* (-s) pragmatism.

'**zweckdienlich** *adj* relevant, useful: **~e Hinweise** relevant information.

'**zweckentfremden** *v/t (only inf and pp* zweckentfremdet, h) use *s.th.* for a purpose not intended, misappropriate.

'**zweckentsprechend** *adj* appropriate.

'**zweckfrei** *adj* nonutility.

'**zweckfremd** *adj* foreign to the purpose.

'**zweckgebunden** *adj* earmarked.

'**zweckgemäß** *adj* appropriate.

'**zwecklos** *adj* useless, pointless, futile: ~ *sein* a. be no use; *es ist ~, daß ich hingehe* there's no point in my going.

'**Zwecklosigkeit** *f* (-; *no pl*) uselessness, futility.

'**zweckmäßig** *adj* **1.** practical, functional. **2.** expedient, advisable.

'**Zweckmäßigkeit** *f* (-; *no pl*) **1.** practicality, functionality. **2.** advisability.

'**Zweck|opti,mismus** *m* calculated optimism. **~pessi,mismus** *m* calculated pessimism.

zwecks *prep* (*gen*) for the purpose of, with a view to.

'**Zwecksparen** *n* target saving.

'**zweckwidrig** *adj* inappropriate.

zwei [tsvai] *adj* **wir ~** we two, the two of us; *dazu gehören ~* it takes two. **Zwei** *f* (-; -en) **1.** (number) two. **2.** *ped.* (*mark, grade*) B.

'**zweiachsig** [-ʔaksɪç] *adj* **1.** ꢀ biaxial. **2.** *mot.* two-axle.

'**zwei,tomig** *adj* ꢀ diatomic.

'**zweibändig** [-bɛndɪç] *adj* two-volume.

'**Zweibeiner** [-bainər] *m* (-s; -) F man.

'**Zweibettzimmer** *n* twin-bedded room.

'**zweideutig** [-dɔytɪç] *adj* ambiguous, equivocal, *b.s.* suggestive, off-colo(u)r.

'**Zweideutigkeit** *f* (-; -en) **1.** *no pl* ambiguity, equivocality, *b.s.* suggestiveness. **2.** a) suggestive remark, b) risqué joke.

Zwei'drittelmehrheit *f* two thirds majority.

'**zweieiig** [-ʔaiç] *adj biol.* binovular: **~e Zwillinge** fraternal twins.

'**Zweier** *m* (-s; -) *rowing*: pair: **~ mit (Steuermann)** coxed pair.

'**Zweierbeziehung** *f* partnership.

'**Zweierbob** *m* (-s; -s) two-man bob.

'**zweierlei** *adj* two different (kinds of): *mit ~ Maß messen* apply double standards.

'**zweifach** *adj* double, *adv* a. doubly: *in ~er Ausfertigung* in duplicate.

Zweifa'milienhaus *n* two-family (*Am.* duplex) house.

'**zweifarbig** *adj* two-colo(u)red.

Zweifel ['tsvaifəl] *m* (-s; -) doubt (*an dat, wegen* about): *ohne ~* → *zweifellos*; *im ~ sein über* (*acc*) be doubtful (*or* in two minds) about; *ihm kamen ~* he was beginning to have doubts; *es bestehen berechtigte ~ an s-r Ehrlichkeit* there is good reason to doubt his honesty; *sie ließen k-n ~ daran, daß* they made it quite plain that.

'**zweifelhaft** *adj* doubtful, dubious,

questionable, F shady: **~es Vergnügen** dubious pleasure; **von ~em Wert** of debatable value (*or* merit); **es erscheint ~, ob** it seems doubtful whether.

'**zweifellos** *adv* undoubtedly, doubtless, without (a) doubt.

zweifeln ['tsvaɪfəln] *v/i* (h) doubt: **~ an** (*dat*) doubt (*or* question) *s.th.*; **daran ist nicht zu ~** there's no doubt about it. '**Zweifelsfall** *m* **im ~** in case of doubt.

'**Zweifler** ['tsvaɪflər] *m* (-s; -) doubter, sceptic, *Am.* skeptic. '**zweiflerisch** *adj* doubting, sceptical, *Am.* skeptical.

Zweig [tsvaɪk] *m* (-[e]s; -e) branch (*a. fig.*), twig: → **grün** I. **~betrieb** *m* branch. **~bü,ro** *n* branch (office).

'**zweigeschlechtig** *adj* ♀ bisexual.

'**zweigeteilt** *adj* divided in(to) two.

'**Zweiggeschäft** *n* branch.

'**zweigleisig** [-glaɪzɪç] *adj* **1.** 🚂 double-tracked. **2.** *fig.* two-track: **~ fahren** leave both one's options open.

'**Zweigniederlassung** *f* (**~ im Ausland** foreign) branch.

'**Zweigstelle** *f* branch (office).

'**zweihändig** [-hɛndɪç] *adj* two-handed, ♪ for two hands.

'**Zweihundert'jahrfeier** *f* bicentenary.

'**zweijährig** [-jɛːrɪç] *adj* **1.** two-year. **2.** two-year-old. '**Zweijährige** [-jɛːrɪgə] *m, f* (-n; -n) two-year-old (child).

'**Zweikampf** *m* duel.

'**Zweika,nal...** ♬ two-channel. **~ton** *m* *TV mit* ~ F with two language channels.

'**zweimal** *adv* twice: **das ließ sie sich nicht ~ sagen** she didn't wait to be told twice. '**zweimalig** *adj* (twice) repeated.

Zwei'markstück *n* two-mark piece.

'**zweimotorig** [-mo,toːrɪç] *adj* twin-engined.

Zweipar'teiensy,stem *n* two-party system.

'**zweiphasig** [-fa:zɪç] *adj* ⚡ two-phase.

'**zweipolig** [-po:lɪç] *adj* ⚡ two-pole, bipolar, two-pin (*plug*).

'**Zweirad** *n* (-[e]s; ~er) bicycle, F bike.

'**zweirädrig** [-rɛːdrɪç] *adj* two-wheeled.

'**Zweireiher** [-raɪər] *m* (-s; -) double--breasted suit. '**zweireihig** *adj* **1.** in two rows. **2.** double-breasted (*suit*).

'**zweischneidig** *adj a. fig.* double-edged.

'**zweiseitig** [-zaɪtɪç] *adj* **1.** bilateral. **2.** two-page (*letter*); double-page (*ad*).

'**zweisilbig** [-zɪlbɪç] *adj* two-syllable.

'**Zweisitzer** [-zɪtsər] *m* (-s; -) two-seater.

'**zweispaltig** [-ʃpaltɪç] *adj* two-column: **~ gedruckt** printed in two columns.

'**zweisprachig** [-ʃpraːxɪç] *adj* bilingual, *document etc* in two languages. '**Zweisprachigkeit** *f* (-; *no pl*) bilingualism.

'**zweispurig** [-ʃpuːrɪç] *adj* **1.** 🚂 double-tracked. **2.** two-lane (*road etc*).

Zwei'stärken|glas *n opt.* bifocal lens. **~brille** *f* (pair of) bifocals.

'**zweistellig** [-ʃtɛlɪç] *adj* two-digit (*number*), two-place (*decimal*).

'**zweistimmig** [-ʃtɪmɪç] *adj* ♪ for (*or* in) two voices.

'**zweistöckig** [-ʃtœkɪç] *adj* two-storeyed, *Am.* two-storied.

'**zweistrahlig** [-ʃtraːlɪç] *adj* ✈ twin-jet.

'**zweistufig** [-ʃtuːfɪç] *adj* ⊙ two-stage.

'**zweistündig** [-ʃtʏndɪç] *adj* two-hour, lasting two hours.

zweit *adj* second: **der ~e Band** volume two; **~er Mai** May 2nd, *Am.* May 2; **ein ~er Mozart** another Mozart; **jeder ~e** every other person; **zu ~** in twos, in pairs; **sie waren zu ~** there were two of them; **~er Klasse** *a. fig.* second-class; → **Geige, Hand, Ich, Wahl** 1.

'**Zweitakter** *m*, '**Zweitaktmotor** *m* two-stroke engine.

'**zweitältest** *adj*, **Zweitälteste** *m, f* (-n; -n) second eldest.

'**zwei'tausend** *adj* two thousand.

'**zweitbest** *adj*, '**Zweitbeste** *m, f* (-n; -n) second best.

'**Zweite** *m, f* (-n; -n) second: *sports:* **sie wurde ~ hinter ...** she came in second behind ..., she was runner-up to ...; *fig.* **wie kein Zweiter** like nobody else.

'**Zweiteiler** *m* (-s; -) F **1.** two-piece (suit). **2.** *film, TV* two-parter. '**zweiteilig** [-taɪlɪç] *adj* **1.** two-piece. **2.** in two parts.

'**zweitens** *adv* secondly.

'**Zweitfri,sur** *f* wig.

'**zweitgrößt** *adj* second largest.

'**zweithöchst** *adj* second highest.

'**zweitklassig** [-klasɪç] *adj* second-class, *contp.* second-rate.

'**zweitletzt** *adj* last but one.

'**zweitrangig** [-raŋɪç] *adj* secondary: **~ sein** be of secondary importance.

'**Zweitschlüssel** *m* spare key.

'**Zweitschrift** *f* (-; -en) duplicate.

'**Zweitstimme** *f pol.* second vote.

'**Zweitstudium** *n ein ~ beginnen* begin a second course of studies.

'**zweitürig** [-ty:rɪç] *adj mot.* two-door.

'**Zweitwagen** *m* second car.

'**Zweitwohnung** *f* second home.

Zwei'vierteltakt *m ♩* two-four time.

'**zweiwertig** [-ve:rtɪç] *adj ♠* bivalent.

'**zweiwöchig** [-vœçɪç] *adj* two-week.

'**zweizeilig** [-tsaɪlɪç] *adj* double-spaced: *~ schreiben* double-space.

Zwei'zimmerwohnung *f* two-room(ed) flat (*Am.* apartment).

Zwerchfell ['tsvɛrç-] *n* diaphragm. **~atmung** *f* abdominal breathing. **Ꝑerschütternd** *adj fig.* sidesplitting.

Zwerg [tsvɛrk] *m* (-[e]s; -e) dwarf, gnome, *fig. a.* midget.

'**zwergenhaft** *adj* dwarfish.

'**Zwergpudel** *m* miniature poodle.

'**Zwergwuchs** *m biol.*, *⚕* dwarfism, *♀* dwarf growth. '**zwergwüchsig** [-vy:ksɪç] *adj* dwarfish.

Zwetsch(g)e ['tsvɛtʃ(g)ə] *f* (-; -n) plum.

'**Zwetsch(g)en|baum** *m* plum tree. **~wasser** *n* (-s; ") plum brandy.

Zwickel ['tsvɪkəl] *m* (-s; -) **1.** gusset. **2.** △ spandrel.

zwicken ['tsvɪkən] *v/t, v/i* (h) pinch.

'**Zwickmühle** *f* F *fig.* (*in c-r ~ sein or sitzen* be on the horns of a) dilemma.

Zwieback ['tsvi:bak] *m* (-[e]s; -e) rusk.

Zwiebel ['tsvi:bəl] *f* (-; -n) **1.** onion. **2.** bulb.

'**Zwiebelkuchen** *m* onion gateau.

'**Zwiebelmuster** *n* onion pattern.

zwiebeln ['tsvi:bəln] *v/t* (h) F *j-n ~* give s.o. a hard time.

'**Zwiebel|ringe** *pl gastr.* onion rings. **~schale** *f* onion skin. **~suppe** *f* onion soup. **~turm** *m* △ onion spire.

Zwielicht ['tsvi:-] *n* (-[e]s; *no pl*) twilight: *fig. ins ~ geraten* lay o.s. open to suspicion. '**zwielichtig** [-lɪçtɪç] *adj fig.* dubious, F shady.

'**Zwiespalt** *m* (-[e]s; *rare* -e) conflict.

'**zwiespältig** [-ʃpɛltɪç] *adj* conflicting: *er ist ein ~er Mensch* he has a conflicting personality; *mein Eindruck war ~* I came away with mixed impressions.

Zwilling ['tsvɪlɪŋ] *m* (-s; -e) **1.** twin. **2.** *pl astr.* (*er ist [ein] ~* he is [a]) Gemini.

'**Zwillings|bruder** *m* twin brother. **~paar** *n* pair of twins. **~reifen** *m mot.*

dual (*or* double, twin) tyres (*Am.* tires). **~schwester** *f* twin sister.

Zwinge ['tsvɪŋə] *f* (-; -n) clamp, cramp.

zwingen ['tsvɪŋən] (zwang, gezwungen, h) **I** *v/t* force, compel: *j-n ~, et. zu tun a.* make s.o. do s.th.; *j-n zum Rücktritt ~* force s.o. to resign; *ich sehe mich gezwungen zu verkaufen* I find myself compelled to sell; → *a. gezwungen.* **II** *v/i ~ zu* necessitate; *die Lage zwingt zu e-r schnellen Entscheidung* the situation calls for a quick decision. **III** *sich ~* force o.s. (*et. zu tun* to do s.th.); *sie zwang sich zu e-m Lächeln* she forced a smile; *ich mußte mich dazu ~* it cost me an effort (to do that).

'**zwingend** *adj* compelling (*reason etc*), absolute, urgent (*necessity etc*), cogent, conclusive (*argument, evidence, etc*).

Zwinger ['tsvɪŋər] *m* (-s; -) kennel(s).

zwinkern ['tsvɪŋkərn] *v/i* (h) (*mit den Augen*) *~* a) blink, b) wink.

zwirbeln ['tsvɪrbəln] *v/t* (h) twist, twirl.

Zwirn [tsvɪrn] *m* (-[e]s; -e) twine, twist.

zwischen ['tsvɪʃən] *prep* (*dat, acc*) a) between, b) among.

'**Zwischenakt** *m*, **~mu,sik** *f* entr'acte.

'**Zwischen|aufenthalt** *m* stop(over). **~bemerkung** *f* interjection. **~bericht** *m* interim report. **~bescheid** *m* provisional reply. **~bi,lanz** *f* interim balance sheet: *fig. e-e ~ ziehen* take stock in between. **~blutung** *f ♀* bleeding between periods, intermenstrual bleeding. **~deck** *n ♣* between decks.

zwischen'durch *adv* a) in between, b) in the meantime, c) now and then.

'**Zwischen|ergebnis** *n* provisional result, *sports*: interim results (*or* score). **~fall** *m* incident: *ohne Zwischenfälle* without a hitch. **~finan,zierung** *f* intermediate financing, bridging. **~frage** *f* (interposed) question. **~gericht** *n gastr.* entrée. **~geschoß** *n △* mezzanine. **~glied** *n* link. **~größe** *f* intermediate size. **~händler** *m* intermediary. **~hoch** *n meteor.* ridge of high pressure. **~lagerung** *f nucl.* interim storage. **Ꝑlanden** *v/i* (*only inf and pp* zwischengelandet, sn) make an intermediate landing, stop. **~landung** *f* stop(over): *ohne ~* nonstop. **~lauf** *m sports*: intermediate heat. **~lösung** *f* interim solution. **~mahlzeit** *f* snack (between meals). **⊇menschlich** *adj* interpersonal: **~e Beziehungen** human relations. **~prüfung** *f* intermediate examination (*or* test). **~raum** *m* **1.** space, distance, ⊚ clearance, *a.* gap, *print.* spacing: **e-e Zeile ~ lassen** leave a space. **2.** interval. **~ruf** *m* interruption: **~e** heckling. **~rufer** *m* (-s; -) heckler. **~runde** *f* *sports*: intermediate round. **⊇schalten** *v/t* (*only inf and pp* zwischengeschaltet, h) ⚡ connect *s.th.* in series. **~schaltung** *f* ⚡ insertion. **~speicher** *m computer*: buffer store (*or* storage). **~spiel** *n* interlude. **~spurt** *m sports*: (sudden) spurt: **e-n ~ einlegen** put in a burst of speed. **⊇staatlich** *adj* **1.** international, intergovernmental. **2.** interstate. **~stadium** *n* intermediate stage. **~stand** *m* (-[e]s; *no pl*) *sports*: interim score. **~stati₀on** *f* stopover, (*a. place*) stop. **~stecker** *m* ⚡ adapter. **~stück** *n* ⊚ intermediary, ⚡ adapter. **~stufe** *f* intermediate stage. **~summe** *f* subtotal. **~text** *m* (inserted) caption. **~tief** *n meteor.* ridge of low pressure. **~töne** *pl fig.* overtones. **~urteil** *n* ⚖ interlocutory judg(e)ment. **~wand** *f* dividing wall, partition. **~zeit** *f* **1.** time in between: **in der ~** → **zwischenzeitlich. 2.** *sports*: intermediate time. **⊇zeitlich I** *adj* intermediate, interim. **II** *adv* meanwhile, (in the) meantime. **~zeugnis** *n* intermediate report.

Zwist [tsvɪst] *m* (-[e]s; -e), **'Zwistigkeit** *f* (-; -en) quarrel.

zwitschern ['tsvɪtʃərn] *v/t, v/i* (h) twitter, chirp: F **e-n ~** down one. **'Zwitschern** *n* (-s) twitter(ing), chirp(ing).

Zwitter ['tsvɪtər] *m* (-s; -) hermaphrodite.

zwo [tsvoː] F → **zwei.**

zwölf [tsvœlf] *adj* twelve: **um ~ (Uhr)** at twelve (o'clock), *a.* at noon, *a.* at midnight; *fig.* **fünf Minuten vor ~** at the eleventh hour.

Zwölf'fingerdarm *m anat.* duodenum. **~geschwür** *n* ☤ duodenal ulcer.

'Zwölfkampf *m gym.* twelve events.

'zwölfte *adj*, **'Zwölfte** *m, f* (-n; -n) twelfth.

'Zwölftonmu₊sik *f* twelve-tone music.

Zyankali [tsyaˈnkaːli] *n* (-s; *no pl*) 🜹 potassium cyanide.

zyklisch ['tsyklɪʃ] *adj* cyclic(al).

Zyklon [tsyˈkloːn] *m* (-s; -e) cyclone.

Zyklone [tsyˈkloːnə] *f* (-; -n) cyclone.

Zyklotron [tsyˈklotroːn] *n* (-s; -e) *phys.* cyclotron.

Zyklus ['tsyklʊs] *m* (-; Zyklen) **1.** cycle. **2.** series (*of lectures etc*).

Zylinder [tsiˈlɪndər] *m* (-s; -) **1.** top hat. **2.** 🜛, 🜛, *mot.* cylinder.

Zy'linderkopf *m mot.* cylinder head. **~dichtung** *f mot.* cylinder-head gasket. **~schraube** *f mot.* cylinder-head stud.

zylindrisch [tsiˈlɪndrɪʃ] *adj* cylindric(al).

Zyniker ['tsyːnikər] *m* (-s; -) cynic.

zynisch ['tsyːnɪʃ] *adj* cynical.

Zynismus [tsyˈnɪsmʊs] *m* (-; -men) cynicism.

Zypern ['tsyːpərn] *n* (-s) Cyprus.

Zyprer ['tsyːprər] *m* (-s; -), **'Zyprerin** *f* (-; -nen) Cypriote.

Zypresse [tsyˈprɛsə] *f* (-; -n) ♣ cypress.

zyprisch ['tsyːprɪʃ] *adj* Cyprian.

Zyste ['tsʏstə] *f* (-; -n) cyst.

Zystoskopie [tsʏstoskoˈpiː] *f* (-; -n) ☤ cystoscopy.

zytologisch [tsytoˈloːgɪʃ] *adj* cytologic(al). **Zytostatikum** [tsytoˈstaːtikʊm] *n* (-s; -ka) ☤ cytostatic agent.

German Abbreviations

A

AA *das Auswärtige Amt* Foreign Office; *Anonyme Alkoholiker* Alcoholics Anonymous

Abb. *Abbildung* ill(us)., illustration; fig., figure

Abf. *Abfahrt* dep., departure

Abk. *Abkürzung* abbr., abbreviation

ABM *Arbeitsbeschaffungsmaßnahme* job creation scheme

Abo *Abonnement* subscription

ABS *Antiblockiersystem* anti-lock braking system

Abs. *Absatz* par., paragraph; *Absender* sender

Abschn. *Abschnitt* section; ch., chapter

Abt. *Abteilung* dept, department

abzgl. *abzüglich* less, minus

a. D. *außer Dienst* retd, retired; *an der Donau* on the Danube

ADAC *Allgemeiner Deutscher Automobil-Club* General German Automobile Association

Adr. *Adresse* address

AG *Aktiengesellschaft* *Br.* PLC, Plc, plc, Ltd, public limited company, *Am.* (stock) corporation

AKW *Atomkraftwerk* nuclear power station *or* plant

allg. *allgemein* gen., general

a. M. *am Main* on the Main

am., amer(ik). *amerikanisch* Am., American

amtl. *amtlich* off., official

Anh. *Anhang* app., appendix

Ank. *Ankunft* arr., arrival

Anl. *Anlage(n)* encl., enclosure(s)

Anm. *Anmerkung* note

anschl. *anschließend* foll., following

AOK *Allgemeine Ortskrankenkasse* compulsory health insurance scheme

a. o. Prof. *außerordentlicher Professor* *Br.* senior lecturer; *Am.* associate professor

App. *Apparat* ext., extension; telephone

ARD *Arbeitsgemeinschaft der öffentlich-rechtlichen Rundfunkanstalten der Bundesrepublik Deutschland* Working Pool of the Broadcasting Corporations of the Federal Republic of Germany

a. Rh. *am Rhein* on the Rhine

Art. *Artikel* art., article

ASU *Abgassonderuntersuchung* exhaust emission test

Aufl. *Auflage* ed., edition

Ausg. *Ausgabe* ed., edition; copy

Az. *Aktenzeichen* file number

B

B *Bundesstraße* major road, federal highway

b. *bei* at; with; nr., near; c/o, care of

BAföG *Bundesausbildungsförderungsgesetz* student financial assistance scheme

BAT *Bundesangestelltentarif* salary scale for public employees

BBk *Deutsche Bundesbank* German Federal Bank

Bde. *Bände* vols, volumes

BE *Broteinheit* bread unit

beil. *beiliegend* encl., enclosed

BENELUX *Belgien, Niederlande, Luxemburg* Belgium, the Netherlands, and Luxembourg

bes. *besonders* esp., especially

Best.-Nr. *Bestellnummer* ord. no., order number

Betr. *Betreff, betrifft* ✝ re

betr. *betreffend, betreffs* conc., concerning; regarding

Bev. *Bevölkerung* pop., population

Bez. *Bezeichnung* mark; name, designation; *Bezirk* dist., district

BGB *Bürgerliches Gesetzbuch* Civil Code

BGH *Bundesgerichtshof* Federal Supreme Court

BGS *Bundesgrenzschutz* Federal Border Guard

Bhf. *Bahnhof* Sta., station

BLZ *Bankleitzahl* bank code

BND *Bundesnachrichtendienst* Federal Intelligence Service

Bq *Becquerel* Bq., Becquerel

BR *Bayerischer Rundfunk* Bavarian Broadcasting Corporation

BRD *Bundesrepublik Deutschland* FRG, Federal Republic of Germany

brit. *britisch* Br(it)., British

GMD *Generalmusikdirektor* (chief) musical director

GUS *Gemeinschaft Unabhängiger Staaten* CIS, Commonwealth of Independent States

H

ha *Hektar* hectare(s)

Hbf. *Hauptbahnhof* cent. sta., central station; main sta., main station

h. c. *honoris causa, ehrenhalber* hon., honorary

HGB *Handelsgesetzbuch* Commercial Code

hins. *hinsichtlich* with regard to, regarding, as to

Hj. *Halbjahr* half-year, six months

hl *Hektoliter* hl, hectolitre(s)

hl. *heilig* holy

HP *Halbpension* half board

hPa *Hektopascal* hPa, hectopascal

HR *Hessischer Rundfunk* Hessian Broadcasting Corporation

Hr(n). *Herr(n)* Mr

H(rs)g. *Herausgeber* ed., editor

h(rs)g. *herausgegeben* ed., edited

Hz *Hertz* Hz, hertz

Hzg. *Heizung* heating

I

i. *im, in* in (the)

i. A. *im Auftrag* p.p., per procurationem, by proxy

i. allg. *im allgemeinen* in general, gen., generally; on the whole

i. b. *im besonderen* in particular

IC *Intercity(-Zug)* inter-city (train)

ICE *Intercity-Expresszug* intercity express (train)

i. D. *im Dienst* on duty; *im Durchschnitt* on av., on average

i. e. *im einzelnen* in detail *or* particular; *id est, das heißt, das ist* i.e., that is

IFO *Institut für Wirtschaftsforschung* Institute for Economic Research

IG *Industriegewerkschaft* industrial union

i. H. *im Hause* on the premises

IHK *Industrie- und Handelskammer* Chamber of Industry and Commerce

i. J. *im Jahre* in (the year)

i. M. *im Monat* in (the month of) *May etc*

inf. *infolge* owing to; as a result of

Ing. *Ingenieur* eng., engineer

Inh. *Inhaber* prop., propr, proprietor; *Inhalt* cont., contents

inkl. *inklusive* incl., including, included; inclusive of

IOK *Internationales Olympisches Komitee* IOC, International Olympic Committee

IQ *Intelligenzquotient* IQ, intelligence quotient

i. R. *im Ruhestand* ret., retd, retired

IRK *Internationales Rotes Kreuz* IRC, International Red Cross

ISBN *Internationale Standardbuchnummer* ISBN, international standard book number

ital. *italienisch* It., Ital., Italian

i. Tr. *in der Trockenmasse percentage of fat* in dry matter

i. V. *in Vertretung* p.p., by proxy; *in Vorbereitung* in prep., in preparation

IWF *Internationaler Währungsfonds* IMF, International Monetary Fund

J

J *Joule* joule(s)

Jan. *Januar* Jan., January

jap. *japanisch* Jap., Japanese

JH *Jugendherberge* Y.H., youth hostel

Jh. *Jahrhundert* c, cent., century

jhrl. *jährlich* yearly, ann., annual(ly)

jr., jun. *junior* Jun., jun., Jnr, Jr, junior

jur. *juristisch* leg., legal

JVA *Justizvollzugsanstalt* prison

K

Kap. *Kapitel* ch(ap)., chapter

Kat *Katalysator* cat., catalytic converter, catalyst

kath. *katholisch* C(ath)., Catholic

KB *Kilobyte(s)* KB, kilobyte(s)

kcal *Kilokalorie(n)* kcal., kilocalorie(s), kilogram(me) calorie(s)

Kffr. *Kauffrau* businesswoman

Kfm. *Kaufmann* merchant; businessman; trader; dlr, dealer; agt, agent

kfm. *kaufmännisch* com(m)., commercial

Kfz *Kraftfahrzeug* motor verhicle

kg *Kilogramm* kg, kilogramme(s)

KG *Kommanditgesellschaft* limited partnership

kgl. *königlich* royal

kHz *Kilohertz* kHz, kilohertz

kJ *Kilojoule* kJ, kilojoule(s)

k.k. *kaiserlich-königlich* imperial and royal

KKW *Kernkraftwerk* nuclear power station *or* plant

Kl. *Klasse* cl., class

km *Kilometer* km, kilometre(s)

KP *Kommunistische Partei* CP, Communist Party

Kripo *Kriminalpolizei* CID, criminal investigation department

KSZE *Konferenz über Sicherheit und Zusammenarbeit in Europa hist.* CSCE, Conference on Security and Cooperation in Europe

Kto. *Konto* acct., a/c, account

KV *Köchelverzeichnis* K, Köchel catalogue

kW *Kilowatt* kW, kilowatt(s)

kWh *Kilowattstunde(n)* kilowatt-hour(s)

KZ *Konzentrationslager* concentration camp

L

l *Liter* litre(s)

l. *links* l., left

lat. *lateinisch* Lat., Latin

l. c. *loco citato, am angegebenen Ort* l.c., in the place cited

led. *ledig* single, unmarried

lfd. *laufend* current, running

lfde. Nr. *laufende Nummer* ser. no., serial number

Lf(r)g. *Lieferung* dely, delivery

LG *Landgericht* district court

Lkw, LKW *Lastkraftwagen* lorry, *esp. Am.* truck

log *Logarithmus* log, logarithm

LP *Langspielplatte* LP, long-playing record

LPG *landwirtschaftliche Produktionsgenossenschaft hist. DDR* collective farm

LSD *Lysergsäurediäthylamid* LSD, lysergic acid dieathylamide

lt. *laut* acc. to, according to; as per

ltd. *leitend* man., managing

Ltg. *Leitung* direction; mangt, management

luth. *lutherisch* Luth., Lutheran

LZB *Landeszentralbank* State Central Bank

M

m *Meter* m, metre(s)

MA *Mittelalter* MA, Middle Ages

M. A. *Magister Artium* MA, Master of Arts

MAD *Militärischer Abschirmdienst* Military Counter-Intelligence Service

Math. *Mathematik* math., mathematics

m. a. W. *mit anderen Worten* in other words

max. *maximal* max., maximum

MAZ *magnetische Bildaufzeichnung* VTR, video tape recording

MB *Megabyte* mb, megabyte

mbH *mit beschränkter Haftung* with limited liability

MdB *Mitglied des Bundestages* Member of the Bundestag

MdL *Mitglied des Landtages* Member of the Landtag

mdl. *mündlich* verbal, oral

m. E. *meines Erachtens* in my opinion

MEZ *mitteleuropäische Zeit* CET, Central European Time

MG *Maschinengewehr* MG, machine gun

mg *Milligramm* milligramme(s)

MHz *Megahertz* MHz, megahertz

Mi. *Mittwoch* Wed., Wednesday

Mill. *Million(en)* m, million

Min., min. *Minute(n)* min., minute(s)

min. *minimal* min., minimum

Mio. *Million(en)* m, million

Mitw. *Mitwirkung* assistance, participation, cooperation

mm *Millimeter* mm, millimetre(s)

Mo. *Montag* Mon., Monday

möbl. *möbliert* furn., furnished

mod. *modern* mod., modern

MP *Maschinenpistole* submachine gun

Mrd. *Milliarde(n)* bn, billion

MS, Ms. *Manuskript* MS, ms, manuscript

MS, m.s. *multiple Sklerose* multiple sclerosis

MT *Megatonne* megaton

MTA *medizinisch-technische Assistentin* medical laboratory assistant

mtl. *monatlich* monthly

m. ü. M. *Meter über (dem) Meer(esspiegel)* metres above sea level

mus. *musikalisch* mus., musical

m. W. *meines Wissens* as far as I know

MwSt., MWSt. *Mehrwertsteuer* VAT, value-added tax

N

N *Nord(en)* N, north

n. *nach* after

N(a)chf. *Nachfolger* successor

nachm. *nachmittags* p.m., pm, in the afternoon

näml. *nämlich* viz, i.e., namely, that is to say

NATO *Nordatlantikpakt-Organisation* NATO, North Atlantic Treaty Organization

NB *notabene* NB, note well

n. Br. *nördlicher Breite* N lat, northern latitude

n. Chr. *nach Christus* AD, anno domini

NDR *Norddeutscher Rundfunk* Northern German Broadcasting Corporation

n. J. *nächsten Jahres* of next year

nkr *norwegische Krone(n)* Nkr, Norwegian crown(s)

n. M. *nächsten Monats* of next month

N. N. *nomen nominandum* name hitherto unknown

NO *Nordost(en)* NE, northeast

No. *Nummer* No., no., number

NOK *Nationales Olympisches Komitee* National Olympic Committee

nördl. *nördlich* N, north, northern

norw. *norwegisch* Norw., Norwegian

Nov. *November* Nov., November

NPD *Nationaldemokratische Partei Deutschlands* National-Democratic Party of Germany

Nr. *Nummer* No., no., number

NS *Nachschrift* PS, postscript; *hist. Nationalsozialismus* National Socialism

NVA *Nationale Volksarmee* hist. *DDR*

NW *Nordwest(en)* NW, northwest

O

O *Ost(en)* E, east

o. *oben* above; *oder* or; *ohne* w/o, without

o. a. *oben angeführt* above(-mentioned)

o. ä. *oder ähnlich(e, -es etc)* or the like

ÖAMTC *Österreichischer Automobil-, Motorrad- und Touring-Club* Austrian Automobile, Motorcycling and Touring Association

OB *Oberbürgermeister* mayor

o. B. *ohne Befund ♪* results negative

Obb. *Oberbayern* Upper Bavaria

ÖBB *Österreichische Bundesbahnen* Austrian Federal Railways

od. *oder* or

offiz. *offiziell* off., official

OHG *offene Handelsgesellschaft* general partnership

OLG *Oberlandesgericht* Higher Regional Court

OP *Operationssaal* operating theatre (*Am.* room)

op. *Opus ♪* op., opus

o. Prof. *ordentlicher Professor* Prof., prof., (full) professor

ORF *Österreichischer Rundfunk* Austrian Broadcasting Corporation

Orig. *Original* orig., original

orth. *orthodox* Orth., Orthodox

österr. *österreichisch* Aus., Austrian

ÖTV *(Gewerkschaft) Öffentliche Dienste, Transport und Verkehr* the (German) Public Services and Transport Union

ÖVP *Österreichische Volkspartei* Austrian People's Party

P

p. A(dr). *per Adresse* c/o, care of

PC *Personalcomputer* PC, pc, personal computer

PCB *polychlorierte Biphenyle*

PDS *Partei des demokratischen Sozialismus* Party of Democratic Socialism

pers. *persönlich* pers., personal; personally, in person

Pf *Pfennig* pf., pfennig

Pfd. *Pfund* German pound(s)

PGiroA *Postgiroamt* postal giro office

PH *Pädagogische Hochschule* college of education, *Am.* teachers' college

soz. *sozial* social

span. *spanisch* Span., Spanish

SPD *Sozialdemokratische Partei Deutschlands* Social Democratic Party of Germany

spez. *speziell* special, particular

SPÖ *Sozialistische Partei Österreichs* Austrian Socialist Party

SR *Saarländischer Rundfunk* Broadcasting Corporation of the Saar

s. R. *siehe Rückseite* see over

SRG *Schweizerische Radio- und Fernsehgesellschaft* Swiss Broadcasting Corporation

SS *Sommersemester* summer semester *or* term

St. *Sankt* St., Saint; *Stück* pc(s)

Std. *Stunde(n)* h., hr(s), hour(s)

stdl. *stündlich* hourly, every hour

stellv. *stellvertretend* asst., assistant

StGB *Strafgesetzbuch* penal code

StPO *Strafprozeßordnung* Code of Criminal Procedure

Str. *Straße* St, Street; Rd, Road

stud. *studiosus, Student* student

StVO *Straßenverkehrsordnung* traffic regulations, *Br.* Highway Code

s. u. *siehe unten* see below

SW *Südwest(en)* SW, southwest

SWF *Südwestfunk* Southwest German Broadcasting Corporation

P *persönliche Identifikationsnummer, PIN, PIN-Nummer* PIN, personal identification number; PIN number

Pkt. *Punkt* pt, point

Pkw *PKW Personenkraftwagen* car

Pl. *Platz* Sq., Square; *Plural* Plural

PLO *Palästinensische Befreiungsorganisation* PLO, Palestine Liberation Organization

PLZ *Postleitzahl* postcode

pol. *polizeilich* police ...

poln. *polnisch* Pol., Polish

portug. *portugiesisch* Port., Portuguese

pp(a). *per Prokura* p.p., per procurationem, by proxy

PR *Public Relations, Öffentlichkeitsarbeit* PR, public relations

prakt. *praktisch* practical

Priv.-Doz. *Privatdozent(in)* lecturer

Prof. *Professor* Prof., Professor

PS *Pferdestärke(n)* HP, horse power; *Postskriptum* PS

Pta(s) *Peseta(s)* pta(s), peseta(s)

PTT *Post, Telefon, Telegraf, Schweizerische Post-, Telefon- und Telegrafenbetriebe* Swiss Postal, Telephone and Telegraph Services

PVC *Polyvinylchlorid* PVC, polyvinyl chloride

Q

qkm *Quadratkilometer* (*obs. for* sq. km), square kilometre(s)

qm *Quadratmeter* (*obs. for* sq. m), square metre(s)

Qual. *Qualität* qual., quality

R

r. *rechts* r., right

RA *Rechtsanwalt* lawyer; solicitor; bar., barrister; *Am.* attorney

RAF *Rote Armee-Fraktion* Red Army Fraction

RB *Radio Bremen* Broadcasting Corporation of Bremen

Rbl *Rubel* Rbl., rbl., r(o)uble

T

t *Tonne(n)* t, ton(s)

t(ä)gl. *täglich* daily, a *or* per day

Tb(c) *Tuberkulose* TB, tuberculosis

TEE *Trans-Europ-Express* Trans-European-Express

Tel. *Telefon* tel., (tele)phone

Telegr. *Telegramm* telegram

TH *Technische Hochschule* technology, technical university

TL *türkische Lira (pl Lire)* lira *(pl* lire *or* liras)

TU *Technische Universität* university

TÜV *Technischer Überwachungsverein* Technical Control Board

TV *Turnverein* gymnastics club; *Television* TV, television

...ifikationsnum- ...tification num-	**rd.** *rund* roughly
	Reg.-Bez. *Regierungsbezirk* administrative district
	Rel. *Religion* rel., religion
...ftwagen* (mo-	**Rep.** *Republik* Rep., Republic
	resp. *respektive* resp., respectively
, Plural pl.,	**RIAS** *Rundfunk im (ehemaligen) amerikanischen Sektor (von Berlin)* Radio in the (*former*) American Sector (*of Berlin*)
Befreiungsor- ...ine Liberation	**rk, r.-k.** *römisch-katholisch* RC, Roman Catholic
, Am. zip code	**RNS** *Ribonukleinsäure* RNA, ribonucleic acid
...h	**röm.** *römisch* Rom., Roman
...Port., Portu-	**RT** *Registertonne(n)* reg. t., register ton(s)
...er pro(c)., by	**russ.** *russisch* Russ., Russian

S

...ntlichkeitsar- ...s ...(ly)	**S** *Süd(en)* S, south; *Schilling* S., schilling
...n) unsalaried	**s** *Sekunde(n)* s, sec., second(s)
...fessor	**S.** *Seite* p., page
...hp, horse-	**s.** *siehe* v., vide, see
...postscript	**s. a.** *siehe auch* see also
...eseta(s)	**SB-** *Selbstbedienungs-* self-service ...
...af; Schweize- ...und Telegra- ...l, Telephone	**SBB** *Schweizerische Bundesbahnen* Swiss Federal Railways
	SC *Sportclub* sports club
	schwed. *schwedisch* Swedish
	schweiz. *schweizerisch* Swiss
...C, polyvinyl	**SDR** *Süddeutscher Rundfunk* Southern German Broadcasting Corporation
...bs. for km²* ...s)	**SED** *Sozialistische Einheitspartei Deutschlands hist. DDR* Socialist Unity Party of Germany
...r m²)* sq. m,	**Sek., sek.** *Sekunde(n)* s, sec., second(s)
...y	**sen.** *senior* Sen., sen., Snr, Sr, senior
	Sept. *September* Sept., September
	SFB *Sender Freies Berlin* Broadcasting Corporation of Free Berlin
	sFr., sfr *Schweizer Franken* SF, Sfr, Swiss Franc(s)
...Br. sol., solr,	**Sg.** *Singular* sing., singular
...m. att., atty,	**SJ** *Societate Jesu, Jesuit* Jesuit
	skr *schwedische Krone(n)* Kr, Skr, Swedish crown(s)
...Red Army	**sm** *Seemeile(n)* n. m., nautical mile(s)
...sting Corpo-	**SO** *Südost(en)* SE, southeast
	s.o. *siehe oben* see above
...le(s)	**sog.** *sogenannt(e, -es etc)* so-called

PIN *persönliche Identifikationsnummer* PIN, personal identification number, PIN number

Pkt. *Punkt* pt, point

Pkw, PKW *Personenkraftwagen* (motor)car

Pl. *Platz* Sq., Square; *Plural* pl., plural

PLO *Palästinensische Befreiungsorganisation* PLO, Palestine Liberation Organization

PLZ *Postleitzahl* postcode, *Am.* zip code

pol. *polizeilich* police ...

poln. *polnisch* Pol., Polish

port(ug). *portugiesisch* Port., Portuguese

pp(a). *per Prokura* p.p., per pro(c)., by proxy

PR *Public Relations, Öffentlichkeitsarbeit* PR, public relations

prakt. *praktisch* practical(ly)

Priv.-Doz. *Privatdozent(in)* unsalaried lecturer

Prof. *Professor* Prof., Professor

PS *Pferdestärke(n)* HP, hp, horsepower; *Postskriptum* PS, postscript

Pta(s) *Peseta(s)* pta(s), peseta(s)

PTT *Post, Telefon, Telegraf; Schweizerische Post-, Telefon- und Telegrafenbetriebe* Swiss Postal, Telephone and Telegraph Services

PVC *Polyvinylchlorid* PVC, polyvinyl chloride

Q

qkm *Quadratkilometer* (*obs. for* km²) sq. km, square kilometre(s)

qm *Quadratmeter* (*obs. for* m²) sq. m, square metre(s)

Qual. *Qualität* qual., quality

R

r. *rechts* r., right

RA *Rechtsanwalt* lawyer; *Br.* sol., solr, solicitor; bar., barrister; *Am.* att., atty, attorney

RAF *Rote Armee-Fraktion* Red Army Fraction

RB *Radio Bremen* Broadcasting Corporation of Bremen

Rbl *Rubel* Rbl., rbl., r(o)uble(s)

rd. *rund* roughly

Reg.-Bez. *Regierungsbezirk* administrative district

Rel. *Religion* rel., religion

Rep. *Republik* Rep., Republic

resp. *respektive* resp., respectively

RIAS *Rundfunk im* (*ehemaligen*) *amerikanischen Sektor* (*von Berlin*) Radio in the (*former*) American Sector (*of Berlin*)

rk, r.-k. *römisch-katholisch* RC, Roman Catholic

RNS *Ribonukleinsäure* RNA, ribonucleic acid

röm. *römisch* Rom., Roman

RT *Registertonne(n)* reg. t., register ton(s)

russ. *russisch* Russ., Russian

S

S *Süd(en)* S, south; *Schilling* S., schilling

s *Sekunde(n)* s, sec., second(s)

S. *Seite* p., page

s. *siehe* v., vide, see

s. a. *siehe auch* see also

SB- *Selbstbedienungs-* self-service ...

SBB *Schweizerische Bundesbahnen* Swiss Federal Railways

SC *Sportclub* sports club

schwed. *schwedisch* Swedish

schweiz. *schweizerisch* Swiss

SDR *Süddeutscher Rundfunk* Southern German Broadcasting Corporation

SED *Sozialistische Einheitspartei Deutschlands* hist. *DDR* Socialist Unity Party of Germany

Sek., sek. *Sekunde(n)* s., sec., second(s)

sen. *senior* Sen., sen., Snr, Sr, senior

Sept. *September* Sept., September

SFB *Sender Freies Berlin* Broadcasting Corporation of Free Berlin

sFr., sfr *Schweizer Franken* SF, Sfr, Swiss Franc(s)

Sg. *Singular* sing., singular

SJ *Societate Jesu, Jesuit* Jesuit

skr *schwedische Krone(n)* Kr, Skr, Swedish crown(s)

sm *Seemeile(n)* n. m., nautical mile(s)

SO *Südost(en)* SE, southeast

s.o. *siehe oben* see above

sog. *sogenannt(e, -es etc)* so-called

soz. *sozial* social

span. *spanisch* Span., Spanish

SPD *Sozialdemokratische Partei Deutschlands* Social Democratic Party of Germany

spez. *speziell* special, particular

SPÖ *Sozialistische Partei Österreichs* Austrian Socialist Party

SR *Saarländischer Rundfunk* Broadcasting Corporation of the Saarland

s. R. *siehe Rückseite* see overleaf

SRG *Schweizerische Radio- und Fernsehgesellschaft* Swiss Broadcasting Corporation

SS *Sommersemester* summer semester *or* term

St. *Sankt* St., Saint; *Stück* pc(s)., piece(s)

Std. *Stunde(n)* h., hr(s)., hour(s)

stdl. *stündlich* hourly, every hour

stellv. *stellvertretend* asst., assistant

StGB *Strafgesetzbuch* penal *or* criminal code

StPO *Strafprozeßordnung* Code of Criminal Procedure

Str. *Straße* St, Street; Rd, Road

stud. *studiosus, Student* student

StVO *Straßenverkehrsordnung* (road) traffic regulations, *Br.* Highway Code

s. u. *siehe unten* see below

SW *Südwest(en)* SW, southwest

SWF *Südwestfunk* Southwestern German Broadcasting Corporation

T

t *Tonne(n)* t, ton(s)

t(ä)gl. *täglich* daily, a *or* per day

Tb(c) *Tuberkulose* TB, tuberculosis

TEE *Trans-Europ-Express* TEE, Trans-European-Express

Tel. *Telefon* tel., (tele)phone

Telegr. *Telegramm* teleg., telegram

TH *Technische Hochschule* college of technology, technical university

TL *türkische Lira (pl Lire)* TL, Turkish lira (*pl* lire *or* liras)

TU *Technische Universität* technical university

TÜV *Technischer Überwachungsverein* Technical Control Board

TV *Turnverein* gymnastics club; *Television* TV, television

U

U *Unterseeboot* sub., submarine

u. *und* and

u. a. *und andere(s)* and others (other things); *unter anderem (anderen)* among other things, inter alia (among others)

u. ä. *und ähnliche(s)* and the like

U. (*or* **u.**) **A. w. g.** *um Antwort wird gebeten* RSVP, please reply

U-Bahn *Untergrundbahn* underground, *Am.* subway

u. d(er)gl. (m.) *und dergleichen (mehr)* and so on; and the like

u. d. M. *unter dem Meeresspiegel* below sea level

ü. d. M. *über dem Meeresspiegel* above sea level

u. E. *unseres Erachtens* in our opinion, as we see it

UFO, Ufo *unbekanntes Flugobjekt* UFO, unidentified flying object

U-Haft *Untersuchungshaft* custody, detention (pending trial)

UKW *Ultrakurzwelle* USW, ultrashort wave; FM, frequency modulation

U/min. *Umdrehungen pro Minute* r.p.m., revolutions per minute

U-Musik *Unterhaltungsmusik* light music

unbek. *unbekannt* unknown

unbez. *unbezahlt* unpaid

unehel. *unehelich* illegit., illegitimate

ung(ar). *ungarisch* Hung., Hungarian

ungebr. *ungebräuchlich* unusual

unverb. *unverbindlich* not binding

unverh. *unverheiratet* unm., unmarried, sgl., single

unvollst. *unvollständig* incomplete

unz. *unzählig* innumerable

urspr. *ursprünglich* orig., original(ly)

US(A) *Vereinigte Staaten (von Amerika)* US(A), United States (of America)

usw. *und so weiter* etc., and so on

u. U. *unter Umständen* poss., possibly; perh., perhaps; if need be

UV *Ultraviolett* UV, ultraviolet

u. W. *unseres Wissens* as far as we know

Ü-Wagen *Übertragungswagen* outside broadcast (OB) van *or* unit

V

V *Volt* V, volt(s)
V. *Vers* v., verse; l., line
v. von, vom of; from; by; **versus, gegen** v., vs., versus
VAE *Vereinigte Arabische Emirate* UAE, United Arab Emirates
VB *Verhandlungsbasis* o.n.o., or near-(est) offer
v. Chr. *vor Christus* BC, before Christ
v. D. *vom Dienst* on duty, in charge
VDE *Verein Deutscher Elektrotechniker* Association of German Electricians
VEB *volkseigener Betrieb* hist. DDR state-owned enterprise or company
Verf. *Verfasser* author
vergr. *vergriffen* out of print
verh. *verheiratet* mar., married
Verl. *Verlag* publishing house or company, publishers
Verw. *Verwaltung* admin, administration; mngmt, management
verw. *verwitwet* widowed
vgl. *vergleiche* cf., confer; cp., compare
v. H. *vom Hundert* pc, per cent, percent
VHS *Volkshochschule* adult education program(me); adult evening classes
v. J. *vorigen Jahres* of last year
v. l. n. r. *von links nach rechts* from left to right
v. M. *vorigen Monats* of last month
V-Mann *Vertrauensmann, Verbindungsmann* contact
Vollm. *Vollmacht* full power(s), auth., authority
vollst. *vollständig* complete(ly)
vorl. *vorläufig* temp., temporary
vorm. *vormittags* a.m., am, in the morning; *vormals* formerly
Vors. *Vorsitzende(r)* chairperson, chm., chairman, chw., chairwoman
VP *Vollpension* full board, board and lodging
VR *Volksrepublik* People's Republic
v. T. *vom Tausend* per thousand
VW *Volkswagen* VW, Volkswagen

W

W *West(en)* W, west; *Watt* W, watt(s)
WAA *Wiederaufbereitungsanlage* reprocessing plant

wbl. *weiblich* fem., female
WC *Wasserklosett* WC toilet
Wdh(lg). *Wiederholung* repetition; *TV etc* repeat
WDR *Westdeutscher Rundfunk* Western German Broadcasting Corporation
werkt. *werktags* (on) weekdays
westl. *westlich* west, western
WEU *Westeuropäische Union* WEU, Western European Union
WEZ *westeuropäische Zeit* GMT, Greenwich Mean Time
WG *Wohngemeinschaft* flat share; people sharing a flat (*esp. Am.* an apartment) *or.* a house
Whg. *Wohnung* flat, *esp. Am.* apt., apartment
wirtsch. *wirtschaftlich* econ., economic
wiss. *wissenschaftlich* academic
w. L. *westlicher Länge* W long., Western longitude
WM *Weltmeisterschaft* world championship; *soccer:* World Cup
wö. *wöchentlich* weekly, every week
WS *Wintersemester* winter semester or term
WSV *Winterschlußverkauf* winter sales
Wwe. *Witwe* widow
Wz. *Warenzeichen* TM, trademark; *Wasserzeichen* watermark

Z

Z. *Zeile* l., line; *Zahl* number
z. *zu, zum, zur* at; to
z. B. *zum Beispiel* e.g., for example, for instance
ZDF *Zweites Deutsches Fernsehen* Second Channel *or* Program(me) of German Television Broadcasting
zeitgen. *zeitgenössisch* contemporary
zeitl. *zeitlich* temporal, time ...
zeitw. *zeitweilig, zeitweise* occasionally, from time to time
ZH *Zentralheizung* centr. heat., central heating
z. H(d). *zu Händen* attn, attention (of)
Zi. *Zimmer* rm (no.), room (number); *Ziffer* fig., figure; No., no., number; ₝ subparagraph; *in contract etc:* item
ZK *Zentralkomitee* Central Committee
Zl *Zloty* Zl, zloty(s)
Zlg. *Zahlung* payment

ZOB *zentraler Omnibusbahnhof* bus *or* coach station

z. T. *zum Teil* partly

Ztg. *Zeitung* newspaper

Ztr. *Zentner* cwt, hundredweight(s)

Ztschr. *Zeitschrift* mag., magazine

Zub. *Zubehör* accessories, fittings

zul. *zulässig* permissible; ✪ safe

zur. *zurück* back

zus. *zusammen* tog., together

z(u)zgl. *zuzüglich* plus

Zwgst. *Zweigstelle* branch (office)

z. Z(t). *zur Zeit* at present

Alphabetical List of the German Irregular Verbs
Infinitive — Preterite — Past Participle

backen – backte (buk) – gebacken
bedingen – bedang – (bedingte) – bedungen (*conditional*: bedingt)
befehlen – befahl – befohlen
beginnen – begann – begonnen
beißen – biß – gebissen
bergen – barg – geborgen
bersten – barst – geborsten
bewegen – bewog – bewogen
biegen – bog – gebogen
bieten – bot – geboten
binden – band – gebunden
bitten – bat – gebeten
blasen – blies – geblasen
bleiben – blieb – geblieben
bleichen – blich – geblichen
braten – briet – gebraten
brauchen – brauchte – gebraucht (*v/aux* brauchen)
brechen – brach – gebrochen
brennen – brannte – gebrannt
bringen – brachte – gebracht
denken – dachte – gedacht
dreschen – drosch – gedroschen
dringen – drang – gedrungen
dürfen – durfte – gedürft (*v/aux* dürfen)
empfehlen – empfahl – empfohlen
erlöschen – erlosch – erloschen
erschrecken – erschrak – erschrocken
essen – aß – gegessen
fahren – fuhr – gefahren
fallen – fiel – gefallen
fangen – fing – gefangen
fechten – focht – gefochten
finden – fand – gefunden
flechten – flocht – geflochten
fliegen – flog – geflogen
fliehen – floh – geflohen
fließen – floß – geflossen
fressen – fraß – gefressen
frieren – fror – gefroren
gären – gor (*esp. fig.* gärte) – gegoren (*esp. fig.* gegärt)
gebären – gebar – geboren
geben – gab – gegeben
gedeihen – gedieh – gediehen
gehen – ging – gegangen
gelingen – gelang – gelungen
gelten – galt – gegolten
genesen – genas – genesen

genießen – genoß – genossen
geschehen – geschah – geschehen
gewinnen – gewann – gewonnen
gießen – goß – gegossen
gleichen – glich – geglichen
gleiten – glitt – geglitten
glimmen – glomm – geglommen
graben – grub – gegraben
greifen – griff – gegriffen
haben – hatte – gehabt
halten – hielt – gehalten
hängen – hing – gehangen
hauen – haute (hieb) – gehauen
heben – hob – gehoben
heißen – hieß – geheißen
helfen – half – geholfen
kennen – kannte – gekannt
klimmen – klomm – geklommen
klingen – klang – geklungen
kneifen – kniff – gekniffen
kommen – kam – gekommen
können – konnte – gekonnt (*v/aux* können)
kriechen – kroch – gekrochen
laden – lud – geladen
lassen – ließ – gelassen (*v/aux* lassen)
laufen – lief – gelaufen
leiden – litt – gelitten
leihen – lieh – geliehen
lesen – las – gelesen
liegen – lag – gelegen
lügen – log – gelogen
mahlen – mahlte – gemahlen
meiden – mied – gemieden
melken – melkte (molk) – gemolken (gemelkt)
messen – maß – gemessen
mißlingen – mißlang – mißlungen
mögen – mochte – gemocht (*v/aux* mögen)
müssen – mußte – gemußt (*v/aux* müssen)
nehmen – nahm – genommen
nennen – nannte – genannt
pfeifen – pfiff – gepfiffen
preisen – pries – gepriesen
quellen – quoll – gequollen
raten – riet – geraten
reiben – rieb – gerieben
reißen – riß – gerissen
reiten – ritt – geritten
rennen – rannte – gerannt

714

riechen – roch – gerochen
ringen – rang – gerungen
rinnen – rann – geronnen
rufen – rief – gerufen
salzen – salzte – gesalzen (gesalzt)
saufen – soff – gesoffen
saugen – sog – gesogen
schaffen – schuf – geschaffen
schallen – schallte (scholl) – geschallt
(*for* erschallen *a.* erschollen)
scheiden – schied – geschieden
scheinen – schien – geschienen
scheißen – schiß – geschissen
schelten – schalt – gescholten
scheren – schor – geschoren
schieben – schob – geschoben
schießen – schoß – geschossen
schinden – schindete – geschunden
schlafen – schlief – geschlafen
schlagen – schlug – geschlagen
schleichen – schlich – geschlichen
schleifen – schliff – geschliffen
schleißen – schliß – geschlissen
schließen – schloß – geschlossen
schlingen – schlang – geschlungen
schmeißen – schmiß – geschmissen
schmelzen – schmolz – geschmolzen
schnauben – schnob – geschnoben
schneiden – schnitt – geschnitten
schrecken – schrak – *obs.* geschrocken
schreiben – schrieb – geschrieben
schreien – schrie – geschrie(e)n
schreiten – schritt – geschritten
schweigen – schwieg – geschwiegen
schwellen – schwoll – geschwollen
schwimmen – schwamm – geschwommen
schwinden – schwand – geschwunden
schwingen – schwang – geschwungen
schwören – schwor – geschworen
sehen – sah – gesehen
sein – war – gewesen
senden – sandte – gesandt
sieden – sott – gesotten
singen – sang – gesungen
sinken – sank – gesunken
sinnen – sann – gesonnen
sitzen – saß – gesessen
sollen – sollte – gesollt (*v/aux* sollen)

spalten – spaltete – gespalten (gespaltet)
speien – spie – gespie(e)n
spinnen – spann – gesponnen
sprechen – sprach – gesprochen
sprießen – sproß – gesprossen
springen – sprang – gesprungen
stechen – stach – gestochen
stecken – steckte (stak) – gesteckt
stehen – stand – gestanden
stehlen – stahl – gestohlen
steigen – stieg – gestiegen
sterben – starb – gestorben
stieben – stob – gestoben
stinken – stank – gestunken
stoßen – stieß – gestoßen
streichen – strich – gestrichen
streiten – stritt – gestritten
tragen – trug – getragen
treffen – traf – getroffen
treiben – trieb – getrieben
treten – trat – getreten
triefen – triefte (troff) – getrieft
trinken – trank – getrunken
trügen – trog – getrogen
tun – tat – getan
verderben – verdarb – verdorben
verdrießen – verdroß – verdrossen
vergessen – vergaß – vergessen
verlieren – verlor – verloren
verschleißen – verschliß – verschlissen
verzeihen – verzieh – verziehen
wachsen – wuchs – gewachsen
wägen – wog (wägte) – gewogen (gewägt)
waschen – wusch – gewaschen
weben – wob – gewoben
weichen – wich – gewichen
weisen – wies – gewiesen
wenden – wandte – gewandt
werben – warb – geworben
werden – wurde – geworden (worden*)
werfen – warf – geworfen
wiegen – wog – gewogen
winden – wand – gewunden
wissen – wußte – gewußt
wollen – wollte – gewollt (*v/aux* wollen)
wringen – wrang – gewrungen
zeihen – zieh – geziehen
ziehen – zog – gezogen
zwingen – zwang – gezwungen

* only in connection with the past participles of other verbs, *e.g.*, **er ist gesehen worden** he has been seen.

States of the Federal Republic of Germany

Baden-Württemberg Baden-Württemberg
Bayern Bayern
Berlin Berlin
Brandenburg Brandenburg
Bremen Bremen
Hamburg Hamburg
Hessen Hessen
Mecklenburg-Vorpommern Mecklenburg-Western Pomerania
Niedersachsen Lower Saxony
Nordrhein-Westfalen North Rhine-Westphalia
Rheinland-Pfalz Rhineland-Palatinate
Saarland Saarland
Sachsen Saxony
Sachsen-Anhalt Saxony-Anhalt
Schleswig-Holstein Schleswig-Holstein
Thüringen Thuringia

States of the Republic of Austria

Burgenland Burgenland
Kärnten Carinthia
Niederösterreich Lower Austria
Oberösterreich Upper Austria
Salzburg Salzburg
Steiermark Styria
Tirol Tyrol
Vorarlberg Vorarlberg
Wien Vienna

Cantons of the Swiss Confederation

(Half cantons in brackets)

Aargau Aargau
Appenzell (Inner-Rhoden; Außer-Rhoden) Appenzell (Inner Rhodes; Outer Rhodes)
Basel Basel, Basle
Bern Bern, Berne
Freiburg, Fribourg Fribourg
Genf, Genève Geneva
Glarus Glarus
Graubünden Graubünden, Grisons
Jura Jura
Luzern Lucerne
Neuenburg, Neuchâtel Neuchâtel
St. Gallen St Gallen, St Gall
Schaffhausen Schaffhausen
Schwyz Schwyz
Solothurn Solothurn
Tessin, Ticino Ticino
Thurgau Thurgau
Unterwalden (Obwalden; Nidwalden) Unterwalden (Obwalden; Nidwalden)
Uri Uri
Waadt, Vaud Vaud
Wallis, Valais Valais, Wallis
Zug Zug
Zürich Zurich

716

Numerals
Cardinal Numbers

0 null *nought, zero*	41 einundvierzig *forty-one*
1 eins *one*	50 fünfzig *fifty*
2 zwei *two*	51 einundfünfzig *fifty-one*
3 drei *three*	60 sechzig *sixty*
4 vier *four*	61 einundsechzig *sixty-one*
5 fünf *five*	70 siebzig *seventy*
6 sechs *six*	71 einundsiebzig *seventy-one*
7 sieben *seven*	80 achtzig *eighty*
8 acht *eight*	81 einundachtzig *eighty-one*
9 neun *nine*	90 neunzig *ninety*
10 zehn *ten*	91 einundneunzig *ninety-one*
11 elf *eleven*	100 hundert *a (or one) hundred*
12 zwölf *twelve*	101 hundert(und)eins *a hundred and one*
13 dreizehn *thirteen*	200 zweihundert *two hundred*
14 vierzehn *fourteen*	300 dreihundert *three hundred*
15 fünfzehn *fifteen*	572 fünfhundert(und)zweiundsiebzig *five hundred and seventy-two*
16 sechzehn *sixteen*	1000 tausend *a (or one) thousand*
17 siebzehn *seventeen*	2000 zweitausend *two thousand*
18 achtzehn *eighteen*	1 000 000 eine Million *a (or one) million*
19 neunzehn *nineteen*	2 000 000 zwei Millionen *two million*
20 zwanzig *twenty*	1 000 000 000 eine Milliarde *a (or one) billion*
21 einundzwanzig *twenty-one*	
22 zweiundzwanzig *twenty-two*	
23 dreiundzwanzig *twenty-three*	
30 dreißig *thirty*	
31 einunddreißig *thirty-one*	
40 vierzig *forty*	

Ordinal Numbers

1. erste *first*	19. neunzehnte *nineteenth*
2. zweite *second*	20. zwanzigste *twentieth*
3. dritte *third*	21. einundzwanzigste *twenty-first*
4. vierte *fourth*	22. zweiundzwanzigste *twenty-second*
5. fünfte *fifth*	23. dreiundzwanzigste *twenty-third*
6. sechste *sixth*	30. dreißigste *thirtieth*
7. siebente *seventh*	31. einunddreißigste *thirty-first*
8. achte *eighth*	40. vierzigste *fortieth*
9. neunte *ninth*	41. einundvierzigste *forty-first*
10. zehnte *tenth*	50. fünfzigste *fiftieth*
11. elfte *eleventh*	51. einundfünfzigste *fifty-first*
12. zwölfte *twelfth*	60. sechzigste *sixtieth*
13. dreizehnte *thirteenth*	61. einundsechzigste *sixty-first*
14. vierzehnte *fourteenth*	70. siebzigste *seventieth*
15. fünfzehnte *fifteenth*	71. einundsiebzigste *seventy-first*
16. sechzehnte *sixteenth*	80. achtzigste *eightieth*
17. siebzehnte *seventeenth*	
18. achtzehnte *eighteenth*	

81. einundachtzigste *eighty-first*
90. neunzigste *ninetieth*
100. hundertste (*one*) *hundredth*
101. hundertunderste *hundred and first*
200. zweihundertste *two hundredth*
300. dreihundertste *three hundredth*

572. fünfhundertundzweiundsiebzigste *five hundred and seventy-second*
1000. tausendste (*one*) *thousandth*
2000. zweitausendste *two thousandth*
1 000 000. millionste *millionth*
2 000 000. zweimillionste *two millionth*

Fractions and other numerical values

$^1/_2$ ein halb *one* (or *a*) *half*
$1^1/_2$ anderthalb *one and a half*
$2^1/_2$ zweieinhalb *two and a half*
$^1/_2$ Meile *half a mile*
$^1/_3$ ein Drittel *one* (or *a*) *third*
$^2/_3$ zwei Drittel *two thirds*
$^1/_4$ ein Viertel *one* (or *a*) *fourth, one* (or *a*) *quarter*
$^3/_4$ drei Viertel *three fourths, three quarters*
$1^1/_4$ Stunden *one* (or *an*) *hour and a quarter*
$^1/_5$ ein Fünftel *one* (or *a*) *fifth*
$3^4/_5$ drei vier Fünftel *three and four fifths*
0,4 null Komma vier (*nought*) *point four* (0.4)
2,5 zwei Komma fünf *two point five* (2.5)

Einfach *single*
  zweifach *double*
  dreifach *treble, triple, threefold*
  vierfach *fourfold, quadruple*
  fünffach *fivefold etc*

Einmal *once*
  zweimal *twice*
  drei-, vier-, fünfmal *etc three, four, five times*
  zweimal soviel(e) *twice as much* (*many*)
  noch einmal *once more*

Erstens, zweitens, drittens *etc firstly, secondly, thirdly, in the first* (*second, third*) *place*

7 + 8 = 15 sieben plus (or und) acht ist fünfzehn *seven plus* (or *and*) *eight is fifteen*

10 − 3 = 7 zehn minus (or weniger) drei ist sieben *ten minus* (or *less*) *three is seven*

2 × 3 = 6 zweimal drei ist sechs *twice three is six*

20 : 5 = 4 zwanzig dividiert (or geteilt) durch fünf ist vier *twenty divided by five is four*

German Weights and Measures

I. Measure of length

1 mm *Millimeter* millimetre
= $1/1000$ metre
= 0.0010936 yards
= 0.0032809 feet
= 0.03937079 inches

1 cm *Zentimeter* centimetre
= $1/100$ metre
= 0.3937 inches

1 dm *Dezimeter* decimetre
= $1/10$ metre
= 3.9370 inches

1 m *Meter* metre
= 1.0936 yards
= 3.2809 feet
= 39.37079 inches

1 km *Kilometer* kilometre
= 1,000 metres
= 1,093.637 yards
= 3,280.8692 feet
= 39,370.79 inches
= 0.62138 British or Statute Miles

1 sm *Seemeile* nautical mile
= 1,852 metres

II. Surface measurements

1 mm² *Quadratmillimeter*
square millimetre
= $1/1000000$ square metre
= 0.000001196 square yards
= 0.0000107641 square feet
= 0.00155 square inches

1 cm² *Quadratzentimeter*
square centimetre
= $1/10000$ square metre

1 dm² *Quadratdezimeter*
square decimetre
= $1/100$ square metre

1 m² *Quadratmeter* square metre
= 1.19599 square yards
= 10.7641 square feet
= 1,550 square inches

1 a *Ar* are
= 100 square metres
= 119.5993 square yards
= 1,076.4103 square feet

1 ha *Hektar* hectare
= 100 ares
= 10,000 square metres
= 11,959.90 square yards
= 107,641.03 square feet
= 2.4711 acres

1 km² *Quadratkilometer*
square kilometre
= 100 hectares
= 1,000,000 square metres
= 247.11 acres
= 0.3861 square miles

III. Solid measures

1 cm³ *Kubikzentimeter*
cubic centimetre
= 1,000 cubic millimetres
= 0.061 cubic inches

1 dm³ *Kubikdezimeter*
cubic decimetre
= 1,000 cubic centimetres
= 61.0253 cubic inches

1 m³ *Kubikmeter*
1 rm *Raummeter* } cubic metre
1 fm *Festmeter*
= 1,000 cubic decimetres
= 1.3079 cubic yards
= 35.3156 cubic feet

1 RT *Registertonne*
register ton
= 2.832 m³
= 100 cubic feet

IV. Measure of Capacity

1 l *Liter* litre
= 10 decilitres
= 1.7607 pints (*Br.*)
= 7.0431 gills (*Br.*)
= 0.8804 quarts (*Br.*)
= 0.2201 gallons (*Br.*)
= 2.1134 pints (*Am.*)
= 8.4534 gills (*Am.*)
= 1.0567 quarts (*Am.*)
= 0.2642 gallons (*Am*).

1 hl *Hektoliter* hectolitre
= 100 litres
= 22.009 gallons (*Br.*)
= 2.751 bushels (*Br.*)
= 26.418 gallons (*Am.*)
= 2.84 bushels (*Am.*)

V. Weights

1 mg *Milligramm* milligram(me)
= $^{1}/_{1000}$ gram(me)
= 0.0154 grains

1 g *Gramm* gram(me)
= $^{1}/_{1000}$ kilogram(me)
= 15.4324 grains

1 Pfd *Pfund* pound (German)
= $^{1}/_{2}$ kilogram(me)
= 500 gram(me)s
= 1.1023 pounds (avdp.)
= 1.3396 pounds (troy)

1 kg *Kilogramm, Kilo*
kilogram(me)
= 1,000 gram(me)s
= 2.2046 pounds (avdp.)
= 2.6792 pounds (troy)

1 Ztr. *Zentner* centner
= 100 pounds (German)
= 50 kilogram(me)s
= 110.23 pounds (avdp.)
= 0.9842 British hundredweights
= 1.1023 U.S. hundredweights

1 dz *Doppelzentner*
= 100 kilogram(me)s
= 1.9684 British hundredweights
= 2.2046 U.S. hundredweights

1 t *Tonne* ton
= 1,000 kilogram(me)s
= 0.984 British tons
= 1.1023 U.S. tons

Phonetic Alphabet

	German	British English	American English	International	Civil Aviation (ICAO)
A	Anton	Andrew	Abel	Amsterdam	Alfa
Ä	Ärger	—	—	—	—
B	Berta	Benjamin	Baker	Baltimore	Bravo
C	Cäsar	Charlie	Charlie	Casablanca	Charlie
CH	Charlotte	—	—	—	—
D	Dora	David	Dog	Danemark	Delta
E	Emil	Edward	Easy	Edison	Echo
F	Friedrich	Frederick	Fox	Florida	Foxtrot
G	Gustav	George	George	Gallipoli	Golf
H	Heinrich	Harry	How	Havana	Hotel
I	Ida	Isaac	Item	Italia	India
J	Julius	Jack	Jig	Jerusalem	Juliett
K	Kaufmann	King	King	Kilogramme	Kilo
L	Ludwig	Lucy	Love	Liverpool	Lima
M	Martha	Mary	Mike	Madagaskar	Mike
N	Nordpol	Nellie	Nan	New York	November
O	Otto	Oliver	Oboe	Oslo	Oscar
Ö	Ökonom	—	—	—	—
P	Paula	Peter	Peter	Paris	Papa
Q	Quelle	Queenie	Queen	Québec	Quebec
R	Richard	Robert	Roger	Roma	Romeo
S	Samuel	Sugar	Sugar	Santiago	Sierra
Sch	Schule	—	—	—	—
T	Theodor	Tommy	Tare	Tripoli	Tango
U	Ulrich	Uncle	Uncle	Upsala	Uniform
Ü	Übermut	—	—	—	—
V	Viktor	Victor	Victor	Valencia	Victor
W	Wilhelm	William	William	Washington	Whiskey
X	Xanthippe	Xmas	X	Xanthippe	X-Ray
Y	Ypsilon	Yellow	Yoke	Yokohama	Yankee
Z	Zacharias	Zebra	Zebra	Zürich	Zulu

Second Part

English-German

by

Helmut Willmann

LANGENSCHEIDT

NEW YORK · BERLIN · MUNICH
VIENNA · ZURICH

Guide for the User

1. English Headwords.

1.1 The alphabetical order of the headwords has been observed throughout, including the irregular forms.

1.2 Centred dots or stress marks within a headword indicate syllabification,

> e.g. **cul·ti·vate ...** , **,cul·ti'va·tion**

1.3 In hyphenated compounds a hyphen coinciding with the end of a line is repeated at the beginning of the next.

1.4 The tilde (~, ~) represents the repetition of a headword.

1.4.1 In compounds the tilde in bold type (~) replaces the catchword,

> e.g. **af·ter ...** '~**·birth** (= afterbirth) ...

1.4.2 The simple tilde (~) replaces the headword immediately preceding (which itself may contain a tilde in bold type),

> e.g. **dis·tance ...** *at a* ~ = at a distance.
> **day ...** '~**·light ...** ~ *saving time* = daylight saving time.

1.5 When the initial letter changes from small to capital or vice versa, the usual tilde is replaced by ♀ or ♀,

> e.g. **state ...** ♀ *Department* = State Department.

2. Pronunciation.

2.1 The pronunciation of English headwords is given in square brackets by means of the symbols of the International Phonetic Association.

2.2 To save space the tilde (~) has been made use of in many places within the phonetic transcription. It replaces any part of the preceding complete transcription which remains unchanged,

> e.g. **gym·na·si·um** [dʒɪmˈneɪzjəm] ... **gym·nast** [ˈ~næst] ...

3. Subject Labels.
The field of knowledge from which an English headword or some of its meanings are taken is indicated by figurative or abbreviated labels or other labels written out in full. A figurative or abbreviated label placed immediately after the phonetic transcription of a headword refers to all translations. A label preceding an individual translation refers to this only.

4. Usage Label.
The indication of the level of usage by abbreviations such as F, *sl.* etc refers to the English headword. Wherever possible the same level of usage between headword and translation has been aimed at.

5. Grammatical References.

5.1 When the last element of a compound is a noun with an irregular plural, a reference such as (*irr man*) indicates that the plural form is given under the separate headword (in this case *man*):

> **fore·man** (*irr man*).

5.2 An adjective marked with □ takes the regular adverbial form, i.e. by affixing ...ly to the adjective or by changing ...le into ...ly or ...y into ...ily.

5.3 (~*ally*) means that an adverb is formed by affixing ...ally to the adjective.

5.4 When there is only one adverb for adjectives ending in both ...ic and ...ical, this is indicated in the following way:

ge·o·met·ric, ge·o·met·ri·cal □,
i.e. geometrically is the adverb of both adjectives.

6. Translations.

6.1 The direct and indirect objects of verbs are printed in italics before the translation. Where necessary the subject of an adjective or verb is indicated in italics and in brackets after the translation,

e.g. **a·ban·don** ... **2.** *Hoffnung etc* aufgeben, *Suche etc a.* einstellen ...
a·bate ... abklingen (*Begeisterung, Lärm, Schmerz etc*) ...
ab·ject ... bitter (*Armut etc*) ...

6.2 Prepositions governing an English catchword (verb, adjective, noun) are given in both languages,

e.g. **place** ... **10.** (*with*) *Auftrag* erteilen (*dat*), vergeben (an *acc*), *Bestellung* aufgeben (bei) ...
pose ... **3.** ... *Bedrohung, Gefahr etc* darstellen (*for, to* für) ...

6.3 Where a German preposition may govern the dative or the accusative case, the case is given in brackets,

e.g. **en·ter** ... eindringen in (*acc*) ...

7. Illustrative phrases and their translations follow the translation of the headword. When the translation can easily be gathered from the meanings of the separate words, it has occasionally been omitted, e.g.

gain ... **4.** zunehmen an (*dat*): ~ *speed* schneller werden, ...
a·board ... **1.** ♻, ✈ an Bord (*gen*): *go* ~; ...

A

A [eɪ] s: *from A to Z* F von A bis Z.

a [ə], *vor vokalischem Anlaut* **an** [ən] *adj od. Artikel* **1.** ein(e): *he is a doctor* er ist Arzt. **2.** der-, die-, dasselbe: *they are of an age* sie sind gleichaltrig. **3.** per, pro, je: *twice a week* zweimal wöchentlich *od.* in der Woche.

a·back [ə'bæk] *adv: taken ~* überrascht, verblüfft; bestürzt.

a·ban·don [ə'bændən] *v/t* **1.** *Frau etc* verlassen. **2.** *Hoffnung etc* aufgeben, *Suche etc* a. einstellen, (*Sport*) *Spiel* abbrechen.

a·base [ə'beɪs] *v/t* erniedrigen, demütigen. **a'base·ment** s Erniedrigung *f*, Demütigung *f*.

a·bashed [ə'bæʃt] *adj* beschämt, verlegen: *feel ~* sich schämen.

a·bate [ə'beɪt] *v/i* abklingen (*Begeisterung, Lärm, Schmerz etc*), (*a. Sturm etc*) sich legen.

ab·at·toir ['æbætwɑː] s Schlachthaus *n*, -hof *m*.

ab·bess ['æbes] s Äbtissin *f*. **ab·bey** ['æbɪ] s Abtei *f*. **ab·bot** ['æbət] s Abt *m*.

ab·bre·vi·ate [ə'briːvɪeɪt] *v/t* (ab-, ver)kürzen: *~d form* Kurzform *f*. **ab·bre·vi·a·tion** s (Ab-, Ver)Kürzung *f*.

ABC [ˌeɪbiː'siː] s **1.** Am. oft pl Abc *n*, Alphabet *n*: (*as*) *easy as ~* kinderleicht; *~ weapons* pl ✕ ABC-Waffen pl. **2.** *fig.* Abc *n*, Anfangsgründe pl.

ab·di·cate ['æbdɪkeɪt] **I** *v/i* abdanken. **II** *v/t Amt* niederlegen: *~ the throne* abdanken. **,ab·di'ca·tion** s Abdankung *f*.

ab·do·men ['æbdəmen] s anat. Unterleib *m*. **ab·dom·i·nal** [æb'dɒmɪnl] *adj* Unterleibs...

ab·duct [æb'dʌkt] *v/t* entführen. **ab·duc·tion** [æb'dʌkʃn] s Entführung *f*.

ab·er·ra·tion [ˌæbə'reɪʃn] s **1.** Abweichung *f, ast., biol., phys. a.* Aberration *f*. **2.** geistige Verwirrung.

a·bet [ə'bet] → *aid* 3.

a·bey·ance [ə'beɪəns] s: *fall into ~* außer Gebrauch kommen.

ab·hor [əb'hɔː] *v/t* verabscheuen.

ab·hor·rence [əb'hɒrəns] s Abscheu *m, f* (*of* vor *dat*). **ab'hor·rent** *adj* □ **1.** zuwider, verhaßt (*to dat*): *it is ~ to me* es widerstrebt mir zutiefst (*to do* zu tun). **2.** abstoßend.

a·bide [ə'baɪd] **I** *v/i: ~ by* sich halten an (*acc*); *Folgen* tragen. **II** *v/t* ertragen, aushalten: *I cannot ~ him* ich kann ihn nicht ausstehen.

a·bil·i·ty [ə'bɪlətɪ] s Fähigkeit *f: ~ to pay* Zahlungsfähigkeit; *to the best of one's ~* nach besten Kräften.

ab·ject ['æbdʒekt] *adj* □ **1.** bitter (*Armut etc*), (*a. Verzweiflung etc*) tiefst. **2.** demütig, unterwürfig.

ab·jure [əb'dʒʊə] *v/t* abschwören (*dat*).

a·blaze [ə'bleɪz] *adv u. adj* **1.** *be ~ in* Flammen stehen. **2.** *fig. be ~ with light* im Lichterglanz erstrahlen; *his eyes were ~ with anger* s-e Augen funkelten vor Zorn; *his face was ~ with excitement* sein Gesicht glühte vor Aufregung.

a·ble ['eɪbl] *adj* □ fähig, tüchtig, geschickt: *be ~ to* imstande *od.* in der Lage sein zu, können; *~ to pay* zahlungsfähig. **~·bod·ied** [ˌ~'bɒdɪd] *adj* körperlich leistungsfähig, kräftig: *~ seaman* ♪ Vollmatrose *m*.

ab·ne·ga·tion [ˌæbnɪ'geɪʃn] s Selbstverleugnung *f*.

ab·nor·mal [æb'nɔːml] *adj* □ anormal, *bsd.* ♪ abnorm.

a·board [ə'bɔːd] *adv u. prp* **1.** ♪, ✈ an Bord (*gen*): *go ~; all ~! ♪* alle Mann an Bord!; 🚌 alles einsteigen! **2.** in (*ein od. e-m Verkehrsmittel*): *~ a bus*.

a·bode [ə'bəʊd] s *a. place of ~* 🏠 Wohnsitz *m: of* (*od. with*) *no fixed ~* ohne festen Wohnsitz.

a·bol·ish [ə'bɒlɪʃ] *v/t* abschaffen, *Gesetz etc a.* aufheben. **a·bol·ish·ment, ab·o·li·tion** [ˌæbəʊ'lɪʃn] s Abschaffung *f*, Aufhebung *f*.

'A-bomb s Atombombe *f*.

a·bom·i·na·ble [ə'bɒmɪnəbl] *adj* □ abscheulich, scheußlich: *~ snowman*

Schneemensch *m.* **a·bom·i·nate** [⁓neɪt] *v/t* verabscheuen. **a,bom·i·na·tion** *s* 1. Abscheu *m, f* (**of** vor *dat*). 2. Scheußlichkeit *f.*

ab·o·rig·i·nal [,æbəˈrɪdʒənl] **I** *adj* □ eingeboren, einheimisch, Ur... **II** *s* Ureinwohner *m, pl a.* Urbevölkerung *f.* **,ab·o'rig·i·ne** [⁓dʒəni] → **aboriginal** II.

a·bort [əˈbɔːt] **I** *v/t* 1. *⚕ Schwangerschaft* abbrechen; *Kind* abtreiben. 2. *Raumflug etc* abbrechen. **II** *v/i* 3. e-e Fehlgeburt haben. 4. *fig.* fehlschlagen, scheitern. **a'bor·tion** *s* 1. *⚕* Fehlgeburt *f;* Schwangerschaftsabbruch *m,* Abtreibung *f:* **have an ~** abtreiben (lassen). 2. *fig.* Fehlschlag *m.* **a'bor·tive** [⁓tɪv] *adj* □ erfolglos, fehlgeschlagen: **prove ~** sich als Fehlschlag erweisen.

a·bound [əˈbaʊnd] *v/i* 1. reichlich vorhanden sein. 2. Überfluß haben, reich sein (**in** an *dat*). 3. voll sein, wimmeln (**with** von).

a·bout [əˈbaʊt] **I** *prp* 1. um (... herum). 2. herum in (*dat*): **wander ~ the streets** in den Straßen herumwandern. 3. bei, auf (*dat*), an (*dat*): **I had no money ~ me** ich hatte kein Geld bei mir. 4. um, gegen: **~ noon** um die Mittagszeit, gegen Mittag. 5. über (*acc*): **talk ~ business** über Geschäfte reden. 6. im Begriff, dabei: **he was ~ to go out** er wollte gerade weggehen. 7. F beschäftigt mit: **what are you ~?** was macht ihr da? **II** *adv* 8. herum, umher: **all ~** überall. 9. ungefähr, etwa: **it's ~ right** F es kommt so ungefähr hin. 10. **be (up and) ~** auf den Beinen sein. 11. in der Nähe, da: **there was no one ~.**

a·bove [əˈbʌv] **I** *prp* 1. über (*dat od. acc*), oberhalb. 2. über (*dat od. acc*), mehr als: **~ all** vor allem; **be ~ s.o.** j-m überlegen sein; **it is ~ me** es ist mir zu hoch. **II** *adv* 3. (dr)oben: **from ~** von oben. 4. darüber (hinaus). **III** *adj* 5. *a.* **~-mentioned** obig, obenerwähnt. **IV** *s* 6. *das* Obige, *das* Obenerwähnte. **a,bove'board** *adv u. adj* ehrlich, offen.

ab·rade [əˈbreɪd] *v/t* 1. abschaben, -reiben, *Reifen* abfahren. 2. *Haut etc* abschürfen.

ab·ra·sion [əˈbreɪʒn] *s* 1. Abschaben *n,* -reiben *n.* 2. (Haut)Abschürfung *f.* **ab'ra·sive** [⁓sɪv] *s* ⊚ Schleifmittel *n.*

ab·re·act [,æbrɪˈækt] *v/t psych.* abreagieren.

a·breast [əˈbrest] *adv:* **three ~** zu dritt nebeneinander; **keep ~ of** *fig.* Schritt halten mit; **keep ~ of the times** auf dem laufenden bleiben.

a·bridge [əˈbrɪdʒ] *v/t Buch, Rede etc* kürzen. **a'bridg(e)·ment** *s* 1. Kürzung *f.* 2. Kurzfassung *f.*

a·broad [əˈbrɔːd] *adv* 1. im *od.* ins Ausland: **from ~** aus dem Ausland; **trip ~** Auslandsreise *f.* 2. überall(hin): **spread ~** (sich) verbreiten; **a rumo(u)r is ~** es geht das Gerücht (um); **get ~** ruchbar werden.

ab·ro·gate ['æbrəʊɡeɪt] *v/t Vertrag etc* außer Kraft setzen, *Gesetz etc a.* aufheben. **,ab·ro'ga·tion** *s* Außerkraftsetzung *f,* Aufhebung *f.*

ab·rupt [əˈbrʌpt] *adj* □ 1. kurz (angebunden), schroff. 2. plötzlich, abrupt: **come to an ~ stop** plötzlich *od.* mit e-m Ruck anhalten.

ab·scess ['æbsɪs] *s* ⚕ Abszeß *m.*

ab·scond [əbˈskɒnd] *v/i.* sich heimlich davonmachen; flüchten (**from** vor *dat*).

ab·sence ['æbsəns] *s* 1. Abwesenheit *f:* **~ of mind** → **absent-mindedness.** 2. Fernbleiben *n* (**from** von). 3. (**of**) Fehlen *n* (*gen od.* von), Mangel *m* (an *dat*): **in the ~ of** in Ermangelung (*gen*).

ab·sent I *adj* ['æbsənt] 1. abwesend: **be ~** fehlen (**from school** in der Schule; **from work** am Arbeitsplatz). 2. fehlend. 3. a) (geistes)abwesend (*Blick etc*), b) → **absent-minded. II** *v/t* [æbˈsent] 4. **~ o.s.** (**from**) fernbleiben (*dat od.* von); sich entfernen (von, aus). **ab·sen·tee** [,æbsənˈtiː] *s* Abwesende *m, f:* **~ ballot** *bsd. Am.* Briefwahl *f;* **~ voter** *bsd. Am.* Briefwähler(in). **,ab·sen'tee·ism** *s* häufiges *od.* längeres (unentschuldigtes) Fehlen (*am Arbeitsplatz, in der Schule*).

,ab·sent-'mind·ed *adj* □ geistesabwesend, zerstreut. **,~-'mind·ed·ness** *s* Geistesabwesenheit *f,* Zerstreutheit *f.*

ab·so·lute ['æbsəluːt] *adj* □ absolut (*a.* ♈, *ling., phys.*): a) unumschränkt (*Herrscher*), b) vollkommen, völlig, c) ♋ rein, unvermischt. **,ab·so'lu·tion** *s* Lossprechung *f,* *eccl.* Absolution *f.* **'ab·so·lut·ism** *s phls., pol.* Absolutismus *m.*

ab·solve [əb'zɒlv] v/t frei-, lossprechen (**of** von *Sünde*); entbinden (**from** von *Verpflichtung* etc); eccl. die Absolution erteilen (*dat*).

ab·sorb [əb'sɔːb] v/t **1.** absorbieren, auf-, einsaugen, a. fig. *Wissen* etc aufnehmen. **2.** fig. ganz in Anspruch nehmen; fesseln: **~ed in** vertieft in (*acc*). **3.** *Stoß* etc dämpfen. **ab'sorb·ent** adj absorbierend: **~ cotton** ✿ *Am.* (Verband-)Watte f.

ab·stain [əb'steɪn] v/i sich enthalten (**from** gen): **~** (**from voting**) sich der Stimme enthalten.

ab·ste·mi·ous [æb'stiːmjəs] adj □ **1.** enthaltsam; mäßig. **2.** bescheiden, kärglich (*Mahlzeit*).

ab·sten·tion [əb'stenʃn] s: **~** (**from voting**) (Stimm)Enthaltung f.

ab·sti·nence ['æbstɪnəns] s Abstinenz f, Enthaltsamkeit f. **'ab·sti·nent** adj □ abstinent, enthaltsam.

ab·stract I adj □ **1.** abstrakt (a. ✿, paint. etc): a) theoretisch, b) schwerverständlich. II s [~] **2.** das Abstrakte: **in the ~** rein theoretisch (betrachtet), an u. für sich. **3.** a. **~ noun** ling. Abstraktum n, Begriffswort n. **4.** Auszug m, Abriß m. III v/t [æb'strækt] **5.** abstrahieren. **6.** entwenden. **7.** e-n Auszug machen von. **ab'stract·ed** adj □ fig. zerstreut. **ab·strac·tion** [æb'strækʃn] s **1.** Abstraktion f. **2.** Entwendung f. **3.** fig. Zerstreutheit f.

ab·struse [æb'struːs] adj □ abstrus, schwerverständlich.

ab·surd [əb'sɜːd] adj □ **1.** absurd, widersinnig. **2.** unsinnig, albern, lächerlich.

a·bun·dance [ə'bʌndəns] s (**of**) Überfluß m (an *dat*), Fülle f (von): **in ~** in Hülle u. Fülle. **a'bun·dant** adj □ **1.** reichlich (vorhanden). **2. ~ in** reich an (*dat*).

a·buse I s [ə'bjuːs] **1.** Mißbrauch m: **~ of drugs** Drogenmißbrauch. **2.** Beschimpfung pl: → **term** **3.** II v/t [~z] **3.** mißbrauchen. **4.** beschimpfen. **a'bu·sive** [~sɪv] adj □ beleidigend: **~ language** Beleidigungen pl, Beschimpfungen pl.

a·but [ə'bʌt] v/i (an)grenzen (**on** an acc). **a'but·ment** s △ Strebe-, Stützpfeiler m.

a·bys·mal [ə'bɪzml] adj □ miserabel. **a·byss** [ə'bɪs] s Abgrund m (a. fig.).

a·ca·cia [ə'keɪʃə] s ✿ Akazie f.

ac·a·dem·ic [ˌækə'demɪk] I adj (**~ally**) **1.** akademisch: a) Universitäts...: **~ freedom** akademische Freiheit; **~ year** Studienjahr n, b) (rein) theoretisch: **~ question** akademische Frage. **2.** gelehrt, wissenschaftlich. II s **3.** Universitätslehrer(in).

a·cad·e·my [ə'kædəmɪ] s Akademie f: **~ of music** Musikhochschule f.

ac·cede [æk'siːd] v/i (**to**) **1.** e-m *Vorschlag* etc beipflichten, zustimmen. **2.** *Amt* antreten, *Macht* übernehmen, *Thron* besteigen.

ac·cel·er·ate [ək'seləreɪt] I v/t beschleunigen. II v/i schneller werden, mot. a. Gas geben. **ac,cel·er'a·tion** s Beschleunigung f: **~ lane** mot. Beschleunigungsspur f, -streifen m. **ac'cel·er·a·tor** s mot. Gaspedal n.

ac·cent I s ['æksent] Akzent m: a) ling. Ton m, Betonung f, b) ling. Betonungs-, Tonzeichen n, c) Tonfall m, (lokale etc) Aussprache f) fig. Nachdruck m: **the ~ is on** der Akzent liegt auf (*dat*). II v/t [æk'sent] → **accentuate**.

ac·cen·tu·ate [æk'sentjʊeɪt] v/t akzentuieren, betonen (a. fig.). **ac,cen·tu-'a·tion** s Akzentuierung f, Betonung f.

ac·cept [ək'sept] v/t **1.** an-, entgegennehmen. **2.** j-n, etc. akzeptieren: a) et., ✝ *Wechsel* annehmen, b) et. hinnehmen, sich abfinden mit. **3.** *Verantwortung* etc auf sich nehmen. **4.** aufnehmen (**into** in acc). **ac'cept·a·ble** adj □ **1.** akzeptabel, annehmbar (**to** für). **2.** angenehm, willkommen. **ac'cept·ance** s **1.** Annahme f. **2.** Akzeptierung f; Hinnahme f: **win ~** Anerkennung finden. **3.** Aufnahme f. **4.** ✝ Akzept n. **ac'cept·ed** adj allgemein anerkannt, üblich.

ac·cess ['ækses] s **1.** Zugang m (**to** zu) (a. fig.): **~ road** Zufahrts- od. Zubringerstraße f. **2.** fig. Zutritt m (**to** bei, zu): **easy of ~** zugänglich (*Person*). **3.** Computer: Zugriff m (**to** auf acc).

ac·ces·sa·ry → **accessory**.

ac·ces·si·ble [ək'sesəbl] adj □ **1.** (leicht) zugänglich (**to** für od. dat) (a. fig.). **2.** um-, zugänglich (*Person*). **3.** empfänglich (**to** für). **ac·ces·sion** [æk'seʃn] s **1.** Antritt m (**to** e-s *Amts*): **~ to power** Machtübernahme f; **~ to the throne**

Thronbesteigung f. **2.** (Neu)Anschaffung f (to für). **3.** Zustimmung f (to zu).

ac·ces·so·ry [əkˈsesərɪ] s **1.** Zubehörteil n, (Mode) Accessoire n, pl a. Zubehör n. **2.** 🏛 Mitschuldige m, f (to an dat).

ac·ci·dence [ˈæksɪdəns] s ling. Formenlehre f.

ac·ci·dent [ˈæksɪdənt] s **1.** by ~ zufällig. **2.** Unfall m, Unglück(sfall m) n, (in Kernkraftwerk) Störfall m: have (od. meet with) an ~ e-n Unfall haben, verunglücken; be killed in an ~ bei e-m Unfall ums Leben kommen, tödlich verunglücken; ~ insurance Unfallversicherung f; ~-prone unfallgefährdet.

ac·ci·den·tal [ˌæksɪˈdentl] adj □ **1.** zufällig. **2.** versehentlich. **3.** Unfall...

ac·claim [əˈkleɪm] I v/t **1.** feiern (as als). **2.** ~ s.o. king j-n zum König ausrufen. II s **3.** hohes Lob.

ac·cla·ma·tion [ˌæklə'meɪʃn] s **1.** lauter Beifall. **2.** hohes Lob. **3.** by ~ pol. durch Zuruf od. Akklamation.

ac·cli·mate [əˈklaɪmət] → **acclimatize**.

ac·cli·ma·tion [ˌæklaɪˈmeɪʃn] → **acclimatization**.

ac·cli·ma·ti·za·tion [əˌklaɪmətaɪˈzeɪʃn] s Akklimatisierung f. **ac'cli·ma·tize** v/t u. v/i (to) (sich) akklimatisieren (an acc), (sich) eingewöhnen (in dat) (beide a. fig.).

ac·cliv·i·ty [əˈklɪvətɪ] s Steigung f.

ac·com·mo·date [əˈkɒmədeɪt] v/t **1.** (to) anpassen (dat od. an acc); in Einklang bringen (mit). **2.** j-m aushelfen (with mit). **3.** unterbringen. **4.** Platz haben für, fassen. **ac'com·mo·dat·ing** adj □ gefällig, entgegenkommend. **ac,com·mo'da·tion** s **1.** Anpassung f (to an acc). **2.** Gefälligkeit f. **3.** Am. mst pl Unterkunft f, -bringung f; Einrichtung(en pl) f: sanitary ~.

ac·com·pa·ni·ment [əˈkʌmpənɪmənt] s ♪ Begleitung f. **ac'com·pa·nist** s ♪ Begleiter(in). **ac'com·pa·ny** v/t begleiten (a. ♪).

ac·com·plice [əˈkʌmplɪs] s Komplice m.

ac·com·plish [əˈkʌmplɪʃ] v/t erreichen; leisten. **ac'com·plished** adj fähig, tüchtig. **ac'com·plish·ment** s Fähigkeit f, Fertigkeit f.

ac·cord [əˈkɔːd] I v/t **1.** gewähren, Empfang bestehen. II v/i **2.** übereinstimmen (with mit). III s **3.** Übereinstimmung f:

be in ~ → 2; with one ~ einstimmig. **4.** of one's own ~ aus freien Stücken, von selbst. **ac'cord·ance** s: in ~ with entsprechend (dat), gemäß (dat). **ac'cord·ing:** ~ to prp laut; nach. **ac'cord·ing·ly** adv **1.** (dem)entsprechend. **2.** also, folglich.

ac·cor·di·on [əˈkɔːdjən] s ♪ Akkordeon n, Ziehharmonika f.

ac·cost [əˈkɒst] v/t Frau (in eindeutiger Absicht) ansprechen; j-n anpöbeln.

ac·count [əˈkaʊnt] I v/t **1.** ansehen als, halten für. II v/i **2.** ~ (to s.o.) for (j-m) Rechenschaft ablegen über (acc). **3.** ~ for (sich) et. erklären, et. begründen: there's no ~ing for tastes über Geschmack läßt sich nicht streiten. **4.** ~ for der Grund sein für. III s **5.** ✝ Konto n (with bei): for ~ only nur zur Verrechnung; on one's own ~ fig. auf eigene Faust; auf eigene Gefahr; settle (od. square) ~s with fig. abrechnen mit. **6.** Rechenschaft(sbericht m) f: bring (od. call) to ~ zur Rechenschaft ziehen; give (an) ~ of Rechenschaft ablegen über (acc); give a good (bad) ~ of o.s. sich von s-r guten (schlechten) Seite zeigen; gut (schlecht) abschneiden. **7.** Bericht m, Darstellung f: by all ~s nach allem, was man hört; give an ~ of Bericht erstatten über (acc). **8.** of great (no) ~ von großer (ohne) Bedeutung; on ~ of um ... willen, wegen; on my ~ meinetwegen; on no ~ auf keinen Fall; leave out of ~ außer acht lassen; take into ~, take ~ of in Betracht ziehen, berücksichtigen. **9.** put (od. turn) to (good) ~ (aus)nutzen, Kapital schlagen aus. **ac'count·a·ble** adj verantwortlich (to dat; for für): hold s.o. ~ j-n verantwortlich machen. **ac'count·ant** s **1.** Buchhalter(in). **2.** Buchprüfer(in). **3.** Br. Steuerberater(in).

ac·cred·it [əˈkredɪt] v/t Botschafter etc akkreditieren (to bei).

ac·crue [əˈkruː] v/i **1.** erwachsen (to dat; from aus). **2.** anwachsen: ~d interest aufgelaufene Zinsen pl.

ac·cu·mu·late [əˈkjuːmjʊleɪt] v/t u. v/i (sich) ansammeln od. anhäufen. **ac,cu·mu'la·tion** s Anhäufung f, Ansammlung f. **ac'cu·mu·la·tor** s ⚡ Akkumulator m.

ac·cu·ra·cy [ˈækjʊrəsɪ] s Genauigkeit f.

ac·cu·rate [ˈ⌣rət] *adj* □ genau: *be* ~ genau gehen (*Uhr*).

ac·cu·sa·tion [ˌækjuːˈzeɪʃn] *s* **1.** ⚖ Anklage *f*: *bring an* ~ *(of murder) against* (Mord)Anklage erheben gegen. **2.** An-, Beschuldigung *f*. **3.** Vorwurf *m*.

ac·cu·sa·tive [əˈkjuːzətɪv] *s a.* ~ *case ling.* Akkusativ *m*, 4. Fall *m*.

ac·cuse [əˈkjuːz] *v/t* **1.** ⚖ anklagen (*of gen od.* wegen). **2.** beschuldigen (*of gen*): ~ *s.o. of doing s.th.* j-n beschuldigen, et. getan zu haben. **3.** ~ *s.o. of s.th.* j-m et. zum Vorwurf machen. **ac'cused:** *the* ~ ⚖ der *od.* die Angeklagte, die Angeklagten *pl.* **ac'cus·ing** *adj* □ anklagend, vorwurfsvoll.

ac·cus·tom [əˈkʌstəm] *v/t* gewöhnen (*to* an *acc*): *be* ~*ed to doing s.th.* (es) gewöhnt *od.* gewohnt sein, et. zu tun; *get* ~*ed to* sich gewöhnen an (*acc*). **ac'cus·tomed** *adj* gewohnt: ~ *seat* Stammplatz *m*.

ace [eɪs] **I** *s* **1.** As *n* (*Spielkarte; a.* Tennis *etc*); Eins *f* (*auf Würfeln*): *have an* ~ *in the hole (od. up one's sleeve) fig.* (noch) e-n Trumpf in der Hand haben. **2.** *he came within an* ~ *of losing* er hätte um ein Haar verloren. **3.** F As *n*, Kanone *f* (*at* in *dat*). **II** *adj* **4.** F ~ *skier* Spitzenskiläufer(in); ~ *reporter* Starreporter(in). ~ ≈ Spitze sein.

ac·e·tate [ˈæsɪteɪt] *s* 🜛 Acetat *n*. **a·ce·tic** [əˈsiːtɪk] *adj* essigsauer: ~ *acid* Essigsäure *f*. **a·cet·y·lene** [əˈsetɪliːn] *s* Acetylen *n*.

ache [eɪk] **I** *v/i* **1.** schmerzen, weh tun: *I am aching all over* mir tut alles weh. **2.** sich sehnen (*for* nach), darauf brennen (*to do* zu tun). **II** *s* **3.** *anhaltender* Schmerz: *he has* ~*s and pains all over* ihm tut alles weh.

a·chieve [əˈtʃiːv] *v/t* Ziel erreichen, *Erfolg* erzielen. **a'chieve·ment** *s* Leistung *f*: ~ *test* Leistungstest *n*.

A·chil·les| heel [əˈkɪliːz] *s fig.* Achillesferse *f*. ~ **ten·don** *s anat.* Achillessehne *f*.

ac·id [ˈæsɪd] **I** *adj* **1.** sauer: ~ *drops pl* saure Drops *pl*. **2.** *fig.* bissig. **3.** 🜛 säurehaltig, Säure...: ~ *rain* saurer Regen. **II** *s* **4.** 🜛 Säure *f*. **5.** *sl.* Acid *n* (*LSD*).

ac·knowl·edge [əkˈnɒlɪdʒ] *v/t* **1.** anerkennen. **2.** zugeben: ~ *having done*

s.th. zugeben, et. getan zu haben. **3.** *Brief, Empfang etc* bestätigen. **ac·'knowl·edg·e·ment** *s* **1.** Anerkennung *f*: *in* ~ *of* in Anerkennung (*gen*). **2.** (Empfangs)Bestätigung *f*.

ac·me [ˈækmɪ] *s fig.* Gipfel *m*, Höhepunkt *m*.

ac·ne [ˈæknɪ] *s* 🜪 Akne *f*.

a·corn [ˈeɪkɔːn] *s* 🜎 Eichel *f*.

a·cous·tic [əˈkuːstɪk] **I** *adj* (~*ally*) akustisch, Gehör...: ~ *nerve anat.* Gehörnerv *m*. **II** *s pl* Akustik *f* (*e-s Raums*).

ac·quaint [əˈkweɪnt] *v/t* bekannt *od.* vertraut machen (*with* mit): *be* ~*ed with* j-n, et. kennen; *we are* ~*ed* wir kennen uns; *become* ~*ed with* j-n, et. kennenlernen. **ac'quaint·ance** *s* **1.** Bekanntschaft *f* (*with* mit): *make s.o.'s* ~ j-n kennenlernen, j-s Bekanntschaft machen. **2.** Kenntnis *f* (*with* von *od.* gen). **3.** Bekannte *m*, *f*.

ac·qui·esce [ˌækwɪˈes] *v/i* (zögernd) einwilligen (*in* in *acc*).

ac·quire [əˈkwaɪə] *v/t* erwerben (*a. fig.*), sich *Wissen etc* aneignen.

ac·qui·si·tion [ˌækwɪˈzɪʃn] *s* **1.** Erwerb *m*. **2.** Anschaffung *f*, Errungenschaft *f*. **ac·quis·i·tive** [əˈkwɪzɪtɪv] *adj* □ habgierig. **ac'quis·i·tive·ness** *s* Habgier *f*.

ac·quit [əˈkwɪt] *v/t* **1.** ⚖ freisprechen (*of* von). **2.** ~ *o.s. well* s-e Sache gut machen. **ac'quit·tal** *s* ⚖ Freispruch *m*.

a·cre [ˈeɪkə] *s* Acre *m* (*4047 qm*).

ac·rid [ˈækrɪd] *adj* □ scharf, beißend (*beide a. fig.*).

ac·ri·mo·ni·ous [ˌækrɪməʊnjəs] *adj* □ *fig.* bitter; scharf, beißend; erbittert (geführt) (*Diskussion etc*). **ac·ri·mo·ny** [ˈækrɪmənɪ] *s fig.* Bitterkeit *f*; Schärfe *f*.

ac·ro·bat [ˈækrəbæt] *s* Akrobat(in). **ac·ro'bat·ic** [ˌ] *adj* (~*ally*) akrobatisch. **II** *s pl* (*a. sg konstruiert*) Akrobatik *f* (*a. fig.*): *mental* ~*s* Gedankenakrobatik.

a·cross [əˈkrɒs] **I** *prp* **1.** (quer) über (*acc*); (quer) durch, mitten durch: *run* ~ *the road* über die Straße laufen; *swim* ~ *a river* e-n Fluß durchschwimmen. **2.** jenseits (*gen*): *he lives* ~ *the street* er wohnt auf der gegenüberliegenden Straßenseite. **II** *adv* **3.** (quer) hinüber *od.* herüber; (quer) durch; im Durchmesser: *go* ~ hinübergehen; *saw* ~ durchsägen; *a lake three miles* ~ ein 3 Meilen breiter See. **4.** drüben, auf der anderen Seite. **5.** waag(e)recht (*in Kreuzworträtseln*).

a‚cross-the-'board *adj* linear (*Steuersenkung etc*).

act [ækt] **I** *s* **1.** (☓ *a.* Straf)Tat *f*, Handlung *f*, Akt *m*: **an ~ of God** höhere Gewalt; **catch in the (very) ~** auf frischer Tat ertappen; **catch s.o. in the ~ of doing s.th.** j-n (dabei) ertappen, als er et. tut. **2.** ☲ (*of Parliament, Am. of Congress*) Gesetz *n*. **3.** *thea.* Aufzug *m*, Akt *m*. **4.** (Programm)Nummer *f*; *fig.* F Tour *f*: **put on an ~** Theater spielen. **II** *v/t* **5.** *thea. etc* Rolle spielen, j-n *a.* darstellen, *Stück a.* aufführen: **~ the fool** *fig.* sich wie ein Narr benehmen; den Dummen spielen. **III** *v/i* **6.** (Theater) spielen, *fig.* Theater spielen. **7.** handeln, tätig sein: **~ as** amtieren *od.* fungieren *od.* dienen als; **~ for s.o.** j-n vertreten; **~ on** sich richten nach. **8.** sich verhalten *od.* benehmen (**towards** *j-m* gegenüber): **~ up** F Theater machen; angeben; verrückt spielen (*Gerät etc*). **9.** (ein)wirken (**on** auf *acc*). **'act·ing I** *adj* stellvertretend, amtierend, geschäftsführend. **II** *s thea. etc* Spiel *n*; Schauspielerei *f*.

ac·tion ['ækʃn] *s* **1.** Handlung *f* (*a. thea. etc*), Tat *f*: **man of ~** Mann *m* der Tat; **put into ~** in die Tat umsetzen; **take ~** handeln. **2.** *Film etc*: Action *f*: **~ film.** **3.** *bsd* ⊙ Funktionieren *n*: **~ of the heart** *physiol.* Herztätigkeit *f*. **4.** (Ein)Wirkung *f* (**on** auf *acc*). **5.** ☲ Klage *f*, Prozeß *m*: **bring an ~ against** verklagen. **6.** ⚔ Gefecht *n*, Einsatz *m*: **killed in ~** gefallen. **~-re·play** *s Sport, TV*: Br. (*bsd. Zeitlupen*)Wiederholung *f* (*e-r Spielszene*).

ac·ti·vate ['æktɪvet] *v/t* **1.** *Alarm etc* auslösen. **2.** *bsd.* 🗪 aktivieren.

ac·tive ['æktɪv] **I** *adj* □ **1.** *allg.* aktiv, (*Vulkan a.*) tätig, (*Phantasie*) lebhaft. **2.** *ling.* aktivisch: **~ voice → 3. II** *s* **3.** *ling.* Aktiv *n*, Tatform *f*. **ac'tiv·i·ty** *s* **1.** Aktivität *f*. **2.** *mst pl* Aktivität *f*, Betätigung *f*.

ac·tor ['æktə] *s* Schauspieler *m*. **ac·tress** ['æktrɪs] *s* Schauspielerin *f*.

ac·tu·al ['æktʃʊəl] *adj* wirklich, tatsächlich; eigentlich. **'ac·tu·al·ly** *adv* **1.** → **actual. 2.** sogar.

ac·tu·ate ['æktjoeit] *v/t*: **be ~d by** *fig.* getrieben werden von.

a·cu·men ['ækjʊmən] *s* Scharfsinn *m*.

ac·u·pres·sure ['ækjʊ‚preʃə] *s* 🌢 Akupressur *f*. **ac·u·punc·ture** ['ækjʊ‚pʌŋktʃə] 🌢 **I** *s* Akupunktur *f*. **II** *v/t* akupunktieren.

a·cute [ə'kjuːt] *adj* □ **1.** 🗛 spitz (*Winkel*). **2.** scharf (*Gehör etc*). **3.** scharfsinnig. **4.** akut (*Krankheit*). **5.** stark (*Schmerzen*), erheblich (*Mangel etc*).

ad [æd] F → **advertisement.**

Ad·am ['ædəm] *npr.*: **I don't know him from ~** ⸏ ich hab' keine Ahnung, wer er ist; **~'s apple** *anat.* Adamsapfel *m*.

ad·a·mant ['ædəmənt] *adj* unnachgiebig: **be ~ that s.o. should do s.th.** darauf bestehen, daß j-d et. tut.

a·dapt [ə'dæpt] **I** *v/t* **1.** anpassen (**to** *dat*): **~ o.s → 3. 2.** *Text* bearbeiten (**for** für). **II** *v/i* **3.** (**to**) sich anpassen (*dat*); sich gewöhnen (an *acc*). **a'dapt·a·ble** *adj* anpassungsfähig. **a·dap·ta·tion** [‚ædæp'teɪʃn] *s* **1.** Anpassung *f* (**to** an *acc*). **2.** Bearbeitung *f*. **a·dap·ter, a·dap·tor** [ə'dæptə] *s* ⚡ Adapter *m*.

add [æd] **I** *v/t* **1.** hinzuzählen, -rechnen (**to** zu). **2.** hinzufügen (**to** *dat od.* zu; **that** daß): → **fuel. 3. ~ up** (*od.* **together**) addieren, zs.-zählen. **4.** 🕈 *etc* aufschlagen (**to** auf *acc*): **~ 5% to the price. II** *v/i* **5. ~ to** hinzukommen *od.* beitragen zu, vermehren. **6. ~ up** 🗛 aufgehen, stimmen; *fig.* e-n Sinn ergeben. **7. ~ up to** sich belaufen auf (*acc*), betragen; *fig.* hinauslaufen auf (*acc*), bedeuten. **'ad·ded** *adj* zusätzlich.

ad·den·dum [ə'dendəm] *pl* **-da** [‚~də] *s* Zusatz *m*, Nachtrag *m*.

ad·der ['ædə] *s zo.* Natter *f*.

ad·dict ['ædɪkt] *s* (Drogen-, Fernseh- *etc*) Süchtige *m*, *f*, (*Fußball- etc*)Fanatiker *m*, (*Film- etc*)Narr *m*. **ad·dict·ed** [ə'dɪktɪd] *adj*: **be ~ to ...** ...süchtig sein. **ad'dic·tion** *s* Sucht *f*, (*Zustand a.*) Süchtigkeit *f*: **~ to alcohol** Alkoholsucht. **ad'dic·tive** *adj* suchterzeugend: **be ~** süchtig machen; **~ drug** Suchtmittel *n*.

add·ing ma·chine ['ædɪŋ] *s* Addier-, Additionsmaschine *f*.

ad·di·tion [ə'dɪʃn] *s* **1.** Hinzufügung *f*, Zusatz *m*: **in ~** noch dazu, außerdem; **~ to** außer (*dat*), zusätzlich zu. **2.** Vermehrung f (**to** gen): **an ~ to the family** Familienzuwachs m. **3.** ✻ Addition f: **~ sign** Pluszeichen n. **ad·di·tion·al** [~ʃənl] adj ⬜ zusätzlich, Zusatz...

ad·di·tive ['ædɪtɪv] s Zusatz m (a. ✿).

ad·dress [ə'dres] **I** v/t **1.** Worte etc richten (**to** an acc), j-n anreden od. ansprechen (**as** als), Brief etc adressieren (**to** an acc). **2.** e-e Ansprache halten an (acc). **II** s **3.** Anrede f. **4.** Ansprache f, Rede f. **5.** Adresse f, Anschrift f. **ad·dress·ee** [ædre'si:] s Adressat(in), Empfänger(in).

ad·duce [ə'dju:s] v/t Grund anführen, Beweis erbringen.

ad·e·noids ['ædɪnɔɪdz] s pl ♠ Polypen pl.

ad·ept ['ædept] **I** adj erfahren, geschickt (**at, in** in dat). **II** s Meister m, Experte m (**at, in** in dat).

ad·e·qua·cy ['ædɪkwəsɪ] s Angemessenheit f. **ad·e·quate** [~kwət] adj ⬜ **1.** angemessen (**to** dat). **2.** ausreichend: **be ~ for** reichen für.

ad·here [əd'hɪə] v/i **1.** (an)kleben, (-)haften (**to** an dat). **2.** fig. (**to**) festhalten (an dat), bleiben (bei). **ad'her·ence** s **1.** (An)Kleben n, (-)Haften n. **2.** fig. Festhalten n. **ad'her·ent** **I** adj (an)klebend, (-)haftend. **II** s Anhänger(in).

ad·he·sion [əd'hi:ʒn] s **1.** → **adherence**. **2.** phys., ✿ Adhäsion f, Haftvermögen n.

ad·he·sive [əd'hi:sɪv] **I** adj ⬜ (an)haftend, klebend, Haft..., Klebe(e)...: **~ plaster** Heftpflaster n; **~ tape** Klebstreifen m; Am. Heftpflaster n. **II** s Klebstoff m.

ad·ja·cent [ə'dʒeɪsənt] adj ⬜ **1.** angrenzend, -stoßend (**to** an acc). **2.** bsd. Å, ✿ Nachbar..., Neben...

ad·jec·ti·val [,ædʒek'taɪvl] adj ⬜ ling. adjektivisch. **ad·jec·tive** ['ædʒɪktɪv] s Adjektiv n, Eigenschaftswort n.

ad·join [ə'dʒɔɪn] **I** v/t (an)stoßen od. (-)grenzen an (acc). **II** v/i aneinandergrenzen, nebeneinander liegen. **ad'join·ing** adj angrenzend, -stoßend, Nachbar..., Neben...

ad·journ [ə'dʒɜːn] **I** v/t verschieben, -tagen (**till, until** auf acc; **for** um). **II** v/i sich vertagen. **ad'journ·ment** s Vertagung f, -schiebung f.

ad·judge [ə'dʒʌdʒ] v/t **1.** e-e Sache (gerichtlich) entscheiden; j-n für (schul-

dig etc) erklären. **2.** ⚖, Sport: zusprechen, -erkennen (**to** dat).

ad·ju·di·cate [ə'dʒu:dɪkeɪt] → **adjudge**.

ad·junct ['ædʒʌŋkt] s **1.** Zusatz m (**to** zu). **2.** ling. Attribut n, Beifügung f.

ad·ju·ra·tion [,ædʒuə'reɪʃn] s Beschwörung f. **ad·jure** [ə'dʒuə] v/t beschwören (**to do** zu tun).

ad·just [ə'dʒʌst] v/t **1.** (**to**) anpassen, -gleichen (dat od. an acc), abstimmen (auf acc). **2.** in Ordnung bringen, regeln. **3.** ✿ (ein)stellen, regulieren, Gewehr etc justieren, Uhr stellen. **ad'just·a·ble** ✿ ein-, verstellbar, regulierbar. **ad'just·ment** s **1.** Anpassung f, -gleichung f. **2.** Regelung f. **3.** ✿ Einstellung f, Regulierung f; Einstellvorrichtung f.

ad·ju·tant ['ædʒutənt] s ✕ Adjutant m.

ad·lib [,æd'lɪb] v/t u. v/i F improvisieren.

ad·man ['ædmæn] s (irr **man**) F **1.** Werbetexter m für Zeitungsanzeigen. **2.** Anzeigenvertreter m. **ad·mass** ['ædmæs] s F **1.** Konsumbeeinflussung f. **2.** werbungsmanipulierte Gesellschaft.

ad·min·is·ter [əd'mɪnɪstə] v/t **1.** verwalten, Amt etc ausüben. **2.** Arznei, Schlag verabreichen, Sakrament spenden, Tadel erteilen (**to** dat): **~ justice** Recht sprechen. **ad,min·is'tra·tion** s **1.** Verwaltung f Ausübung f. **2.** Verabreichung f, Spendung f, Erteilung f: **~ of justice** Rechtsprechung f. **3.** pol. bsd. Am. Regierung f, Amtsdauer f (e-s Präsidenten etc). **ad'min·is·tra·tive** [~trətɪv] adj Verwaltungs... **ad'min·is·tra·tor** [~treɪtə] s **1.** Verwalter m. **2.** Verwaltungsbeamte m.

ad·mi·ra·ble ['ædmərəbl] adj ⬜ bewundernswert, großartig.

ad·mi·ral ['ædmərəl] s Admiral m.

ad·mi·ra·tion [,ædmə'reɪʃn] s Bewunderung f (**for** für): **she was the ~ of all** sie wurde von allen bewundert.

ad·mire [əd'maɪə] v/t **1.** bewundern (**for** wegen). **2.** verehren. **ad'mir·er** s **1.** Bewunderer m. **2.** Verehrer(in).

ad·mis·si·ble [əd'mɪsəbl] adj zulässig, statthaft. **ad·mis·sion** [əd'mɪʃn] s **1.** Einlaß m (**to** ✿); Ein-, Zutritt m; Aufnahme f: **~free** Eintritt frei; **~ ticket** Eintrittskarte f. **2.** Eintritt(sgeld n) m. **3.** Zulassung f. **4.** Eingeständnis n: **by** (od. **on**) **his own ~** wie er selbst zugab; **~ of guilt** Schuld-

eingeständnis. **5.** Zugeständnis *n*. **6.** ⚙
(*Luft- etc*)Zufuhr *f*.

ad·mit [əd'mɪt] **I** *v/t* **1.** *j-n* einlassen. **2.**
(*into, to*) *j-n* aufnehmen (in *acc od. dat*),
zulassen (zu): → *bar* 9. **3.** zulassen,
gestatten. **4.** anerkennen, gelten lassen.
5. zugeben, (ein)gestehen: **~ doing s.th.**
zugeben, et. getan zu haben. **6.** zugeben, einräumen (*that* daß). **7.** Platz haben für, fassen. **8.** ⚙ einlassen, zuführen. **II** *v/i* **9. ~ of** → 3: **it ~s of no excuse**
es läßt sich nicht entschuldigen. **10. ~ to**
→ 5. **ad'mit·tance** *s* Ein-, Zutritt *m*: *no*
~ (*except on business*) Zutritt (für
Unbefugte) verboten. **ad'mit·ted·ly**
adv zugegeben(ermaßen).

ad·mix·ture [æd'mɪkstʃə] *s* Beimischung
f, Zusatz *m*.

ad·mon·ish [əd'mɒnɪʃ] *v/t* **1.** warnen (*of,
against* vor *dat*). **2.** ermahnen (*for* wegen). **ad·mo·ni·tion** [ˌædməʊ'nɪʃn] *s* **1.**
Warnung *f*. **2.** Ermahnung *f*.

a·do [ə'duː] *s* Getue *n*: *much ~ about
nothing* viel Lärm um nichts; *without
more* (*od. further*) *~* ohne weitere Umstände.

ad·o·les·cence [ˌædəʊ'lesns] *s* jugendliches Alter. **,ad·o'les·cent I** *adj*
jugendlich, heranwachsend. **II** *s* Jugendliche *m*, *f*.

a·dopt [ə'dɒpt] *v/t* **1.** adoptieren: **~ed
child** Adoptivkind *n*; **~ed country**
Wahlheimat *f*. **2.** *fig.* annehmen, sich
zu eigen machen, *Handlungsweise* wählen, *Haltung* einnehmen. **a'dop·tion** *s*
1. Adoption *f*: *give up for ~* zur Adoption freigeben. **2.** Annahme *f*. **a'dop·tive** *adj* Adoptiv...: *~ child* (*parents*)
~ country Wahlheimat *f*.

a·dor·a·ble [ə'dɔːrəbl] *adj* □ allerliebst,
entzückend. **ad·o·ra·tion** [ˌædə'reɪʃn] *s*
Anbetung *f*, Verehrung *f*. **a·dore**
[ə'dɔː] *v/t* anbeten, verehren (*beide a.
fig.*); F *et.* entzückend *od.* hinreißend
finden.

a·dorn [ə'dɔːn] *v/t* **1.** schmücken,
(ver)zieren (*beide a. fig.*). **2.** *fig.*
Glanz verleihen (*dat*). **a'dorn·ment** *s*
Schmuck *m*, Verzierung *f*.

a·dren·al·in(e) [ə'drenəlɪn] *s* **1.** 🐾, *physiol.* Adrenalin *n*. **2.** *fig.* Aufputschmittel *n*.

a·droit [ə'drɔɪt] *adj* □ geschickt, gewandt (*at, in* in *dat*). **a'droit·ness** *s*

s Geschicklichkeit *f*, Gewandtheit *f*.
ad·u·late ['ædjʊleɪt] *v/t* *j-m* schmeicheln. **,ad·u'la·tion** *s* Schmeichelei
f. **'ad·u·la·tor** *s* Schmeichler *m*.
'ad·u·la·to·ry *adj* schmeichlerisch.

a·dult ['ædʌlt] **I** *adj* **1.** erwachsen. **2.**
(nur) für Erwachsene (*Film etc*). **II** *s* **3.**
Erwachsene *m*, *f*: *~ education* Erwachsenenbildung *f*.

a·dul·ter·ate [ə'dʌltəreɪt] *v/t* *Nahrungsmittel* verfälschen, *Wein* panschen.
a,dul·ter'a·tion *s* Verfälschung *f*.
a·dul·ter·er [ə'dʌltərə] *s* Ehebrecher *m*.
a·dul·ter·ess *s* Ehebrecherin *f*.
a·dul·ter·ous *adj* □ ehebrecherisch.
a·dul·ter·y *s* Ehebruch *m*.

ad·um·brate ['ædʌmbreɪt] *v/t* vorausahnen lassen, hindeuten auf (*acc*).

ad·vance [əd'vɑːns] **I** *v/t* **1.** vorrücken,
-schieben, *Fuß* vorsetzen. **2.** *Zeitpunkt*
vorverlegen. **3.** *Argument etc* vorbringen, geltend machen. **4.** *Projekt etc* fördern. **5.** *j-n* befördern, *Stellung etc* verbessern. **6.** *Preis* erhöhen. **7.** *Wachstum
etc* beschleunigen. **8.** im voraus liefern;
Geld vorauszahlen, vorschießen. **II** *v/i*
9. vordringen, -rücken (*a. Zeit*). **10.**
zunehmen (*in an dat*): *~ in age* älter
werden. **11.** vorankommen, Fortschritte machen. **12.** *im Rang* aufrücken, befördert werden. **13.** (an)steigen
(*Preise*). **III** *s* **14.** Vorrücken *n*. **15.** Beförderung *f*, (*beruflicher etc*) Aufstieg.
16. Fortschritt *m*, Verbesserung *f*. **17.**
Vorsprung *m*: *in ~* vorn; im voraus; *in ~
of* vor (*dat*); *be in ~* e-n Vorsprung
haben (*of* vor *dat*); *paid in ~* vorausbezahlt. **18.** Vorschuß *m*, Vorauszahlung
f. **19.** (Preis)Erhöhung *f*. **IV** *adj* **20.**
Vor(aus)...: *~ booking* Vor(aus)bestellung *f*; *thea. etc* Vorverkauf *m*; *~ payment* Vorauszahlung *f*. **ad'vanced** *adj*
1. vorgerückt (*Alter, Stunde*): *be ~ in
years* in fortgeschrittenem Alter sein.
2. fortgeschritten: *~ English* Englisch
für Fortgeschrittene. **3.** fortschrittlich.
ad'vance·ment *s* Fortschritt *m*, Verbesserung *f*.

ad·van·tage [əd'vɑːntɪdʒ] *s* Vorteil *m* (*a.
Sport*): *to ~* günstig, vorteilhaft; *gain
an ~ over s.o.* sich *j-m* gegenüber e-n
Vorteil verschaffen; *have an ~ over
s.o.* *j-m* gegenüber im Vorteil sein;
have the ~ (*over s.o.*) (*j-m* gegenüber)

den Vorteil haben (*of being* zu sein); *take ~ of* j-n, et. ausnutzen; *~ law* (*od. rule*) Vorteilsregel *f*. **ad·van·ta·geous** [ˌædvənˈteɪdʒəs] *adj* □ vorteilhaft, günstig.

Ad·vent [ˈædvənt] *s eccl.* Advent *m*.

ad·ven·ture [ədˈventʃə] *s* Abenteuer *n*: *~ holiday* (*bsd. Am. vacation*) Abenteuerurlaub *m*; *~ playground Br.* Abenteuerspielplatz *m*. **ad·ven·tur·er** *s* Abenteurer *m*. **ad·ven·tur·ess** *s* Abenteu(r)erin *f*. **ad·ven·tur·ous** *adj* □ **1.** abenteuerlich. **2.** abenteuerlustig.

ad·verb [ˈædvɜːb] *s ling.* Adverb *n*, Umstandswort *n*. **ad·ver·bi·al** [ədˈvɜːbjəl] *adj* □ adverbial: *~ phrase* Adverbiale *n*, Adverbialbestimmung *f*.

ad·ver·sa·ry [ˈædvəsərɪ] *s* Gegner(in). **ad·verse** [ˈvɜːs] *adj* □ **1.** widrig. **2.** ungünstig, nachteilig (*to* für): *~ balance of trade* passive Handelsbilanz. **ad·ver·si·ty** [ədˈvɜːsətɪ] *s* **1.** Not *f*, Unglück *n*. **2.** Mißgeschick *n*.

ad·vert [ˈædvɜːt] *s Br.* F *für advertisement.*

ad·ver·tise [ˈædvətaɪz] **I** *v/t* **1.** ankündigen. **2.** Reklame machen für, werben für. **3.** *contp.* ausposaunen, an die große Glocke hängen. **II** *v/i* **4.** inserieren, annoncieren: *~ for* durch Inserat suchen. **5.** Reklame machen, Werbung treiben. **ad·ver·tise·ment** [ədˈvɜːtɪsmənt] *s* **1.** Inserat *n*, Annonce *f*. **2.** → *advertising* I. **ad·ver·tis·ing** **I** *s* Werbung *f*, Reklame *f*. **II** *adj* Werbe..., Reklame...: *~ agency* Werbeagentur *f*; *~ campaign* (*od. drive*) Werbekampagne *f*; *~ manager* Werbeleiter *m*; *~ medium* Werbeträger *m*.

ad·vice [ədˈvaɪs] *s* **1.** Rat(schlag) *m*; Ratschläge *pl*: *a piece* (*od. bit*) *of ~* ein Ratschlag; *at* (*od. on*) *s.o.'s ~* auf j-s Rat hin; *take my ~ and ...* hör auf mich u. ...; *take medical ~* e-n Arzt zu Rate ziehen. **2.** ✝ Avis *m, n*: *letter of ~* Benachrichtigungsschreiben *n*.

ad·vis·a·ble [ədˈvaɪzəbl] *adj* ratsam. **ad·vise** *v/t* **1.** j-m raten *od.* empfehlen (*to do* zu tun), j-n beraten: *~ against* j-m abraten von; *be well ~d* gut beraten sein, gut daran tun (*to do* zu tun). **2.** *et.* empfehlen, raten zu. **3.** ✝ avisieren (*s.o. of s.th.* j-m et.). **ad·vis·ed·ly** [ˈˌɪdlɪ] *adv* mit Überlegung. **ad·vis·er** *s*

Berater(in), Ratgeber(in). **ad·vi·so·ry** [ˈˌərɪ] *adj* beratend.

ad·vo·ca·cy [ˈædvəkəsɪ] *s* (*of*) Eintreten *n* (für), Befürwortung *f* (*gen*). **ad·vo·cate** **I** *s* [ˈˌkət] Verfechter *m*, Befürworter *m*. **II** *v/t* [ˈˌkeɪt] befürworten, eintreten für.

ae·gis [ˈiːdʒɪs] *s* Schirmherrschaft *f*: *under the ~ of.*

aer·ate [ˈeɪəreɪt] *v/t* **1.** lüften. **2.** mit Kohlensäure anreichern.

aer·i·al [ˈeərɪəl] **I** *adj* Luft...: *~ cableway* Seilschwebebahn *f*; *~ camera* Luftkamera *f*; *~ view* Luftbild *n*. **II** *s bsd. Br.* Antenne *f*.

aer·o·drome [ˈeərədrəum] *s Br.* Flugplatz *m*. **ˌaer·o·dyˈnam·ic** *phys.* **I** *adj* (*~ally*) aerodynamisch. **II** *s pl* (*sg konstruiert*) Aerodynamik *f*. **aer·o·gram** [ˈˌgræm] *s* **1.** Funkspruch *m*. **2.** Aerogramm *n*, Luftpostleichtbrief *m*. **ˌaer·o·ˈnau·ti·cal** *adj* aeronautisch: *~ engineering* Flugzeugbau *m*. **ˌaer·o·ˈnau·tics** *s* Aeronautik *f*, Luftfahrtkunde *f*. **ˈaer·o·plane** *s bsd. Br.* Flugzeug *n*. **ˈaer·o·space** **I** *s* **1.** Weltraum *m*. **II** *adj* **2.** Raumfahrt...: *~ industry* (*medicine*). **3.** (Welt)Raum...: *~ research* (*vehicle*).

aes·thete [ˈiːsθiːt] *s* Ästhet *m*. **aes·thet·ic**, **aes·thet·i·cal** [iːsˈθetɪk(l)] *adj* □ ästhetisch. **aes·thet·ics** *s pl* (*sg konstruiert*) Ästhetik *f*.

a·far [əˈfɑː] *adv*: *from ~* von weit her, aus weiter Ferne.

af·fa·bil·i·ty [ˌæfəˈbɪlətɪ] *s* Leutseligkeit *f*. **ˈaf·fa·ble** *adj* □ leutselig.

af·fair [əˈfeə] *s* **1.** Angelegenheit *f*, Sache *f*: → *foreign* 1. **2.** F Ding *n*. **3.** Affäre *f*: a) Ereignis *n*, b) Skandal *m*, c) Verhältnis *n*.

af·fect¹ [əˈfekt] *v/t* **1.** e-e Vorliebe haben für. **2.** vortäuschen: *he ~ed not to understand* er tat so, als ob er nicht verstehe.

af·fect² [ˈˌ] *v/t* **1.** beeinflussen, in Mitleidenschaft ziehen. **2.** ✿ angreifen, befallen. **3.** bewegen, rühren: *be deeply ~ed.*

af·fec·ta·tion [ˌæfekˈteɪʃn] *s* **1.** Vorliebe *f* (*of* für). **2.** Verstellung *f*.

af·fec·tion [əˈfekʃn] *s* **1.** *oft pl* Liebe *f*, Zuneigung *f* (*for, towards* zu); Gefühl *n*: *play on s.o.'s ~s* mit j-s Gefühlen spielen. **2.** Gemütsbewegung *f*. **af·'fec·tion·ate** [~k∫nət] *adj* □ liebevoll, herzlich: *yours ~ly* Dein Dich liebender (*Briefschluß*).

af·fi·da·vit [ˌæfɪ'deɪvɪt] *s* ✠ schriftliche eidliche Erklärung.

af·fil·i·ate [ə'fɪlɪeɪt] **I** *v/t* **1.** als Mitglied aufnehmen. **2.** angliedern (*to dat od.* an *acc*): *~d company* ✝ Tochtergesellschaft *f.* **II** *v/i* **3.** sich anschließen (*with dat od.* an *acc*). **af‚fil·i·'a·tion** *s* **1.** Aufnahme *f*. **2.** Angliederung *f*.

af·fin·i·ty [ə'fɪnətɪ] *s* **1.** Verschwägerung *f*. **2.** (geistige) Verwandtschaft. **3.** 🐘 Affinität *f.* **4.** Neigung *f* (*for, to* zu).

af·firm [ə'fɜːm] *v/t* **1.** versichern; beteuern. **2.** bekräftigen, ✠ *Urteil* bestätigen. **3.** ✠ an Eides Statt versichern. **af·fir·ma·tion** [ˌæfə'meɪ∫n] *s* **1.** Versicherung *f*; Beteuerung *f*. **2.** Bekräftigung *f*, Bestätigung *f*. **3.** ✠ Versicherung *f* an Eides Statt. **af·firm·a·tive** [ə'fɜːmətɪv] **I** *adj* bejahend, zustimmend. **II** *s*: *answer in the ~* bejahen.

af·fix *v/t* [ə'fɪks] **1.** (*to*) befestigen, anbringen (an *dat*), anheften, -kleben (an *acc*). **2.** (*to*) *Unterschrift* setzen (unter *acc*). **II** *s* ['æfɪks] **3.** *ling.* Affix *n*.

af·flict [ə'flɪkt] *v/t* plagen, heimsuchen: *~ed with* geplagt von, leidend an (*dat*). **af·'flic·tion** *s* **1.** Kummer *m*. **2.** Gebrechen *n*; *pl* Beschwerden *pl*: *~s of old age* Altersbeschwerden. **3.** Not *f*, Elend *n*.

af·flu·ence ['æflʊəns] *s* **1.** Überfluß *m*. **2.** Reichtum *m*, Wohlstand *m*. **'af·flu·ent** **I** *adj* □ wohlhabend, reich (*in* an *dat*): *~ society* Wohlstandsgesellschaft *f.* **II** *s* Nebenfluß *m*.

af·flux ['æflʌks] *s* Zufluß *m*.

af·ford [ə'fɔːd] *v/t* **1.** sich leisten: *we can't ~ it* wir können es uns nicht leisten. **2.** aufbringen, *Zeit* erübrigen. **3.** *Schutz etc* gewähren, bieten, *Freude* machen. **af·ford·a·ble** *adj* **1.** erschwinglich (*Preis*). **2.** finanziell möglich *od.* tragbar.

af·for·est [æ'fɒrɪst] *v/t* aufforsten. **af‚for·est·a·tion** *s* Aufforstung *f*.

af·front [ə'frʌnt] *v/t* beleidigen. **II** *s* Beleidigung *f*.

a·fi·cio·na·do [əˌfɪsjə'nɑːdəʊ] *pl* **-dos** *s* Fan *m*, Liebhaber *m*.

a·field [ə'fiːld] *adv* in der *od.* die Ferne.

a·fire [ə'faɪə] *adv u. adj* in Flammen: *be ~* in Flammen stehen; *fig.* glühen (*with* vor *dat*); *set ~* in Brand stecken, anzünden; *all ~ fig.* Feuer u. Flamme.

a·flame [ə'fleɪm] → *afire.*

a·float [ə'fləʊt] *adv u. adj* **1.** flott, schwimmend: *keep ~* (sich) über Wasser halten (*a. fig.*); *set ~* ⚓ flottmachen. **2.** in Umlauf (*Gerücht etc*): *set ~* in Umlauf bringen; *there is a rumo(u)r ~ that* es geht das Gerücht (um), daß. **3.** im Gange: *set ~* in Gang setzen. **4.** überschwemmt: *be ~* unter Wasser stehen.

a·foot [ə'fʊt] → *afloat* 3.

a‚fore'men·tioned [əˌfɔː-], **~said** [ə'fɔː~] *adj* obenerwähnt. **~thought** [ə'fɔː~] *adj:* → *malice.*

a·fraid [ə'freɪd] *adj:* *be ~ of* sich fürchten *od.* Angst haben vor (*dat*); *be ~ to do* sich fürchten *od.* scheuen zu tun; *I'm ~ I must go* leider muß ich jetzt gehen.

a·fresh [ə'fre∫] *adv* von neuem.

Af·ri·can ['æfrɪkən] **I** *adj* afrikanisch. **II** *s* Afrikaner(in).

af·ter ['ɑːftə] **I** *adj* **1.** nach-, hinterher, darauf: *for months ~* noch monatelang; *during the weeks ~* in den (nach)folgenden Wochen; *shortly ~* kurz danach. **II** *prp* **2.** hinter (*dat*) (... her), nach: *be ~* hersein hinter. **3.** *zeitlich* nach: *~ a week; day ~ day* Tag für Tag; *the month ~ next* der übernächste Monat; *~ all* schließlich, im Grunde; immerhin, dennoch; (also) doch. **4.** nach, gemäß: *named ~ his father* nach s-m Vater genannt. **III** *adj* **5.** später: *in ~ years.* **6.** ⚓ Achter... **IV** *cj* **7.** nachdem. **'~·birth** *s* ✿ Nachgeburt *f*. **'~·care** *s* **1.** ✿ Nachbehandlung *f*, -sorge *f*. **2.** ✠ Resozialisierungshilfe *f*. **'~·din·ner** *adj:* ~ *speech* Tischrede *f*; ~ *walk* Verdauungsspaziergang *m*. **'~·ef‚fect** *s* ✿ Nachwirkung *f* (*a. fig.*). **'~·glow** *s* Abendrot *n*. **'~·life** *s* **1.** Leben *n* nach dem Tode. **2.** (zu)künftiges Leben. **~·math** ['~·mæθ] *s* Folgen *pl*, Nachwirkungen *pl*. **‚~'noon** *I s* Nachmittag *m*: *in the ~* am Nachmittag; *this ~* heute nachmittag; *good ~!* guten Tag! **II** *adj* Nachmittags... **'~·play** *s* sexuelles Nachspiel.

af·ters ['ɑːftəz] *s pl* (*sg* konstruiert) *Br.* F

Nachtisch *m*: **for ~** als *od.* zum Nachtisch.

'af·ter|-sales ser·vice *s* Kundendienst *m*. **'~·taste** *s* Nachgeschmack *m* (*a. fig.*). **'~·thought** *s* nachträglicher Einfall. **'~·treat·ment** *s* ✵, ☢ Nachbehandlung *f*. **~·wards** ['~wədz] *adv* später, nachher, hinterher.

a·gain [ə'gen] *adv* **1.** wieder: **~ and ~** immer wieder; → **now** 1, **time** 4. **2.** schon wieder: *that fool ~!* **3.** außerdem, ferner. **4.** noch einmal: → **much** 1. **5.** and(e)rerseits.

a·gainst [ə'genst] *prp* **1.** gegen: **be ~ s.th.** gegen et. sein; e-r Sache zuwiderlaufen. **2.** gegenüber (*dat*): (**over**) **~ the town hall** gegenüber dem Rathaus; *my rights ~ the landlord* m-e Rechte gegenüber dem Vermieter. **3.** an (*dat od. acc*), gegen: **~ the wall.** **4.** *a.* **as ~** verglichen mit, im Vergleich zu.

a·gape [ə'geɪp] *adv u. adj* mit (vor Staunen *etc*) offenem Mund.

ag·ate ['ægət] *s min.* Achat *m*.

age [eɪdʒ] **I** *s* **1.** (Lebens)Alter *n*: **at the ~ of** im Alter von; *I have a daughter your ~* in Ihrem Alter; **when I was your ~** als ich so alt war wie du; *ten years of ~* zehn Jahre alt; *what is his ~?*, *what is he?* wie alt ist er?; **be your ~!** sei kein Kindskopf! **2.** Reife *f*: (**come**) **of ~** mündig *od.* volljährig (werden); **under ~** minderjährig, unmündig. **3.** vorgeschriebenes Alter (*für ein Amt etc*): **be over ~** die Altersgrenze überschritten haben. **4.** Zeit(alter *n*) *f*: **in our ~** in unserer Zeit. **5.** *a.* **old ~** (hohes) Alter: **~ before beauty!** *humor.* Alter vor Schönheit! **6.** *oft pl* F Ewigkeit *f*: *I haven't seen him for ~s* seit e-r Ewigkeit. **II** *v/t* **7.** alt machen (*Kleid etc*); um Jahre älter machen (*Sorgen etc*). **III** *v/i* **8.** alt werden, altern. **~ brack·et** → **age group.**

aged[1] [eɪdʒd] *adj* im Alter von ..., ...jährig, ... Jahre alt: **~ twenty.**

a·ged[2] ['eɪdʒɪd] *adj* alt, betagt, bejahrt.

age| group *s* Altersgruppe *f*, -klasse *f*. **'~·less** *adj* **1.** nicht alternd, ewig jung. **2.** zeitlos. **~ lim·it** *s* Altersgrenze *f*.

a·gen·cy ['eɪdʒənsɪ] *s* **1.** (*Handels-, Nachrichten- etc*)Agentur *f*; (Handels)Vertretung *f*. **2.** *bsd. Am.* Geschäfts-, Dienststelle *f*; Amt *n*, Behörde

f. **3.** Mittel *n*: **by** (*od.* **through**) **the ~ of** mit Hilfe von (*od.* gen).

a·gen·da [ə'dʒendə] *s* Tagesordnung *f*: **be on the ~** auf der Tagesordnung stehen.

a·gent ['eɪdʒənt] *s* **1.** *biol., phys. etc* Agens *n*, Wirkstoff *m*, Mittel *n*. **2.** ✝ Agent *m* (*a. pol.*), Vertreter *m*; (*Grundstücks- etc*)Makler *m*.

ag·glom·er·ate [ə'glɒməreɪt] *v/t u. v/i* (sich) zs.-ballen; (sich) (an)häufen. **ag,glom·er'a·tion** *s* Zs.-ballung *f*; Anhäufung *f*.

ag·glu·ti·nate [ə'glu:tɪneɪt] *v/t* **1.** zs.-kleben. **2.** *biol., ling.* agglutinieren. **ag,glu·ti'na·tion** *s* **1.** Zs.-kleben *n*. **2.** zs.-klebende Masse, Klumpen *m*. **3.** *biol., ling.* Agglutination *f*.

ag·gra·vate ['ægrəveɪt] *v/t* **1.** verschlimmern. **2.** F (ver)ärgern. **'ag·gra·vat·ing** *adj* **1.** verschlimmernd. **2.** F ärgerlich. **,ag·gra'va·tion** *s* **1.** Verschlimmerung *f*. **2.** F Ärger *m*.

ag·gre·gate I *adj* ['ægrɪgət] **1.** gesamt, Gesamt...: **~ amount** → 5. **II** *v/t* ['~geɪt] **2.** anhäufen, -sammeln. **3.** sich (insgesamt) belaufen auf (*acc*). **III** *s* ['~gət] **4.** Anhäufung *f*, -sammlung *f*. **5.** Gesamtbetrag *m*, -summe *f*: **in the ~** insgesamt, alles in allem. **6.** ☢ *etc* Aggregat *n*. **ag·gre·ga·tion** [,~'geɪʃn] *s* (An)Häufung *f*, Ansammlung *f*.

ag·gres·sion [ə'greʃn] *s* bsd. ✕ Angriff *m*, Aggression *f* (*a. psych.*). **ag·gres·sive** [ə'gresɪv] *adj* aggressiv. **ag'gres·sive·ness** *s* Aggressivität *f*. **ag'gres·sor** *s* bsd. ✕ Angreifer *m*.

ag·grieve [ə'gri:v] *v/t* **1.** betrüben, -drücken. **2.** kränken.

ag·gro ['ægrəʊ] *s Br. sl.* Aggressivität *f*.

a·ghast [ə'gɑ:st] *adj u. adj* entgeistert, entsetzt, bestürzt (**at** über *acc*).

ag·ile ['ædʒaɪl] *adj* ☐ beweglich, wendig: **have an ~ mind** geistig beweglich sein. **a·gil·i·ty** [ə'dʒɪlətɪ] *s* Beweglichkeit *f*, Wendigkeit *f*.

ag·i·tate ['ædʒɪteɪt] **I** *v/t* **1.** schütteln, (um)rühren. **2.** aufregen, -wühlen. **3.** aufwiegeln, -hetzen. **II** *v/i* **4.** agitieren, hetzen (**against** gegen); Propaganda machen (**for** für). **,ag·i'ta·tion** *s* **1.** Aufregung *f*. **2.** Agitation *f*. **'ag·i·ta·tor** *s* Agitator *m*, Hetzer *m*.

a·glow [ə'gləʊ] *adv u. adj* glühend.

a·go [ə'gəʊ] *adv* vor: *a year ~* vor e-m Jahr; *long ~* vor langer Zeit; *not long ~* (erst) vor kurzem.

a·gog [ə'gɒg] *adv u. adj* erpicht; gespannt (*for aut acc*): *all ~* ganz aus dem Häuschen; *be ~ to do s.th.* es kaum mehr erwarten können, et. zu tun.

ag·o·nize ['ægənaɪz] *v/i* **1.** mit dem Tode ringen. **2.** sich abquälen, verzweifelt ringen (*over* mit). '**ag·o·niz·ing** *adj* □ qualvoll. **ag·o·ny** ['ʌnɪ] *s* **1.** Qual *f*: *be in an ~ of doubt* von Zweifeln gequält werden; *~ aunt* F Kummerkastentante *f*; *~ column* F Scufzerspalte *f* (*Zeitung*). **2.** Todeskampf *m*.

a·grar·i·an [ə'greərɪən] *adj* landwirtschaftlich, Agrar...: *~ reform* Bodenreform *f*.

a·gree [ə'gri:] **I** *v/t* **1.** vereinbaren (*to do* zu tun; *that* daß): *~d!* einverstanden!, abgemacht!; *~ to differ* sich auf verschiedene Standpunkte einigen. **2.** *bsd. Br.* sich einigen auf (*acc*); *Streit* beilegen. **II** *v/i* **3.** (*on, about*) einig werden (über *acc*), sich einigen (auf *acc*), vereinbaren (*acc*). **4.** (*to*) zustimmen (*dat*), einverstanden sein (mit). **5.** sich einig sein, gleicher Meinung sein (*with* wie). **6.** (*with*) übereinstimmen (mit), entsprechen (*dat*). **7.** bekommen (*with dat*) (*Speise etc*). **a·gree·a·ble** [ə'grɪəbl] *adj* □ **1.** angenehm (*to dat od.* für): *agreeably surprised* angenehm überrascht. **2.** liebenswürdig. **3.** einverstanden (*to* mit). **a'gree·a·ble·ness** *s* Liebenswürdigkeit *f*; **a'greed** *adj*: *be ~* sich einig sein, gleicher Meinung sein. **a·gree·ment** [ə'gri:mənt] *s* **1.** Vereinbarung *f*; *bsd. pol.* Abkommen *n*; Einigung *f*: *come to an ~* sich einigen. **2.** Einigkeit *f*. **3.** Übereinstimmung *f*.

ag·ri·cul·tur·al [ˌægrɪ'kʌltʃərəl] *adj* □ landwirtschaftlich: *~ prices pl* Agrarpreise *pl.* **ag·ri·cul·ture** ['ʌtʃə] *s* Landwirtschaft *f*.

a·ground [ə'graʊnd] *adv u. adj* ⚓ gestrandet: *run ~* auflaufen, stranden; *Schiff* auf Grund setzen; *be ~* aufgelaufen sein; *fig.* auf dem trock(e)nen sitzen.

ah [ɑ:] *int* ah!, ach!

a·ha [ɑ:'hɑ:] **I** *int* aha! **II** *adj*: *~ experience psych.* Aha-Erlebnis *n*.

a·head [ə'hed] *adv u. adj* **1.** vorn, nach vorn zu. **2.** voraus, vorwärts: *~ of* vor (*dat*), voraus (*dat*).

a·hoy [ə'hɔɪ] *int* ⚓ ahoi!

aid [eɪd] **I** *v/t* **1.** unterstützen, *j-m* helfen (*in* bei). **2.** *Verdauung etc* fördern. **II** *v/i* **3.** *he was accused of ~ing and abetting* er wurde wegen Beihilfe angeklagt. **III** *s* **4.** Hilfe *f* (*to* für), Unterstützung *f*: *by* (*od. with*) (*the*) *~ of* mit Hilfe von (*od. gen*); *in ~ of* zugunsten von (*od. gen*); *come to s.o.'s ~* j-m zu Hilfe kommen. **5.** Hilfsmittel *n*, -gerät *n*.

AIDS [eɪdz] *s* ✴ AIDS *n* (*acquired immune deficiency syndrome*).

ail [eɪl] *v/i* kränklich sein, kränkeln (*beide a. fig. Wirtschaft etc*).

ai·ler·on ['eɪlərɒn] *s* ✈ Querruder *n*.

ail·ing ['eɪlɪŋ] *adj* kränkelnd, kränklich (*beide a. fig. Wirtschaft etc*). '**ail·ment** *s* Leiden *n*.

aim [eɪm] **I** *v/i* **1.** zielen (*at* auf *acc*, nach). **2.** beabsichtigen, bezwecken (*at* acc): *~ to do s.th.* vorhaben, et. zu tun. **3.** streben (*at* nach). **4.** abzielen, anspielen (*at* auf *acc*). **II** *v/t* **5.** *Waffe* richten (*at* auf *acc*). **6.** (*at*) *Bemerkung etc* richten (gegen); *Bestrebungen* richten (auf *acc*). **III** *s* **7.** Ziel *n*: *take ~ → 1*. **8.** *fig.* Ziel *n*; Absicht *f*. '**aim·less** *adj* □ ziellos.

ain't [eɪnt] F *für are not, am not, is not, have not, has not.*

air¹ [eə] **I** *s* **1.** Luft *f*: *by ~* auf dem Luftweg; *in the open ~* im Freien; *be in the ~* im Umlauf sein (*Gerücht etc*); in der Schwebe sein (*Frage etc*); *take the ~* frische Luft schöpfen; → *light*² 1, *thin* 1. **2.** *Rundfunk, TV:* Äther *m*: *on the ~* im Rundfunk od. Fernsehen; *be on the ~* senden (*Sender*); gesendet werden (*Programm*); im Rundfunk zu hören od. im Fernsehen zu sehen sein (*Person*). **3.** Miene *f*, Aussehen *n*: *an ~ of importance* e-e gewichtige Miene. **4.** *mst pl* Getue *n*: *~s and graces* affektiertes Getue; *put on ~s, give o.s. ~s* vornehm tun. **II** *v/t* **5.** *Wäsche* zum Trocknen aufhängen. **6.** *et.* an die Öffentlichkeit *od.* zur Sprache bringen.

air² [~] *s* ♪ Lied *n*, Melodie *f*.

air¦ **bag** *s mot.* Luftsack *m.* *~ base* *s* Luftstützpunkt *m.* *~ bath* *s* Luftbad *n.* '*~borne* *adj* **1.** in Flugzeug befördert: *~ radar* Bordradar *m, n*; *~ troops pl* ✕ Luftlandetruppen *pl.* **2.** *be ~* sich in der

Luft befinden, fliegen. ~ **brake** s ⊙ Druckluftbremse f. '**~bus** s ✈ Airbus m. ~ **car·go** s Luftfracht f. '**~con·di·tioned** adj mit Klimaanlage, klimatisiert. ~ **con·di·tion·ing** s 1. Klimatisierung f. **2.** Klimaanlage f. '**~cooled** adj luftgekühlt. '**~craft** s Flugzeug n; coll. Flugzeuge pl: ~ **car·rier** Flugzeugträger m. ~ **crash** s Flugzeugabsturz m. ~ **cush·ion** s Luftkissen n. '**~drop** v/t mit dem Fallschirm abwerfen; ✗ Fallschirmjäger etc absetzen. '**~field** s Flugplatz m. ~ **force** s Luftwaffe f. ~ **freight** s 1. Luftfracht f. **2.** Luftfrachtgebühr f. ~ **gun** s Luftgewehr n. ~ **host·ess** s Stewardeß f.

air·ing ['eərɪŋ] s 1. Lüftung f: give s.th. an ~ et. lüften; the room needs an ~ das Zimmer muß (durch)gelüftet werden. **2.** Spaziergang m: take an ~ frische Luft schöpfen. **3.** give s.th. an ~ → **air**[1] 7.

air| **jack·et** s Schwimmweste f. '**~less** adj 1. luftlos. **2.** stickig. ~ **let·ter** s Luftpost(leicht)brief m. '**~lift** s Luftbrücke f. '**~line** s Fluggesellschaft f. '**~lin·er** s Verkehrsflugzeug n. '**~mail** s Luftpost f. **II** v/t per Luftpost schicken. ~ **pas·sen·ger** s Fluggast m. ~ **pho·to·graph** s Luftbild n. ~ **pi·rate** s Luftpirat(in). '**~ plane** s Am. Flugzeug n. ~ **pock·et** s ✈ Luftloch n. ~ **pol·lu·tion** s Luftverschmutzung f. '**~port** s Flughafen m, -platz m. ~ **pres·sure** s Luftdruck m. '**~proof** adj luftdicht. ~ **pump** s Luftpumpe f. ~ **raid** s ✗ Luftangriff m. '**~raid** adj: ~ **precautions** pl Luftschutz m; ~ **shelter** Luftschutzbunker m, -raum m. ~ **shaft** s Luftschacht m. '**~ship** s Luftschiff n. '**~sick** adj luftkrank. '**~space** s Luftraum m. '**~strip** s (behelfsmäßige) Start- u. Landebahn. ~ **ter·mi·nal** s 1. Flughafenabfertigungsgebäude n. **2.** Br. Endstation f der Zubringerlinie zum u. vom Flughafen. ~ **tick·et** s Flugticket n, -schein m. '**~tight** adj 1. luftdicht. **2.** fig. hieb- u. stichfest (Argument etc). ~ **traf·fic** s Flug-, Luftverkehr m. '**~traf·fic** adj: ~ **control** Flugsicherung f; ~ **controller** Fluglotse m. '**~way** s ✈ Luftstraße f. '**~wor·thy** adj ✈ flugtüchtig.

air·y ['eərɪ] adj □ 1. Luft... **2.** luftig. **3.** graziös, anmutig. **4.** lebhaft, munter. **5.** verstiegen, überspannt. **6.** vornehmtuerisch. **7.** lässig, ungezwungen.

aisle [aɪl] s 1. △ Seitenschiff n. **2.** Gang m (zwischen Bänken etc).

a·jar [ə'dʒɑː] adv u. adj angelehnt (Tür etc).

a·kim·bo [ə'kɪmbəʊ] adv u. adj: **with arms** ~ die Arme in die Seite gestemmt.

a·kin [ə'kɪn] adj 1. verwandt (to mit). **2.** fig. verwandt, ähnlich (to dat): be ~ sich ähneln; ähneln (to dat).

al·a·bas·ter [ˌælə'bɑːstə] s Alabaster m.

a·lac·ri·ty [ə'lækrɪtɪ] s Bereitwilligkeit f, Eifer m.

a·larm [ə'lɑːm] **I** s 1. Alarm m: give (od. raise, sound) the ~ Alarm geben; fig. Alarm schlagen. **2.** Weckvorrichtung f (e-s Weckers): ~ (clock) Wecker m. **3.** Alarmvorrichtung f, -anlage f. **4.** Angst f, Unruhe f. **II** v/t **5.** alarmieren. **6.** ängstigen, beunruhigen. a'**larm·ist** s Bangemacher m.

a·las [ə'læs] int ach!, leider!

Al·ba·ni·an [æl'beɪnjən] **I** adj albanisch. **II** s Albanier(in).

al·ba·tross ['ælbətrɒs] s orn. Albatros m, Sturmvogel m.

al·bi·no [æl'biːnəʊ] pl -**nos** s biol. Albino m.

al·bum ['ælbəm] s Album n (a. Langspielplatte).

al·bu·men ['ælbjʊmɪn] s biol. Eiweiß m.

al·che·my ['ælkəmɪ] s hist. Alchimie f.

al·co·hol ['ælkəhɒl] s Alkohol m. ‚**al·co'hol·ic** [-'hɒlɪk] **I** adj (∼ally) alkoholisch. **II** s Alkoholiker(in): ♀s **Anonymous** die Anonymen Alkoholiker. '**al·co·hol·ism** s Alkoholismus m.

al·cove ['ælkəʊv] s 1. Alkoven m, Nische f. **2.** bsd. poet. (Garten)Laube f.

al·der ['ɔːldə] s ♀ Erle f.

al·der·man ['ɔːldəmən] s (irr man) Ratsherr m, Stadtrat m.

ale [eɪl] s Ale n (helles, obergäriges Bier).

a·lert [ə'lɜːt] **I** adj □ 1. auf der Hut (to vor dat), wachsam. **2.** munter, flink. **3.** aufgeweckt, (hell)wach: be ~ to sich e-r Sache bewußt sein. **II** s 4. ✗ (Alarm)Bereitschaft f: be on the ~ in Alarmbereitschaft sein; fig. auf der Hut sein. **5.** bsd. ✗ Alarm(signal n) m. **III** v/t **6.** alarmieren, ✗ a. in Alarmzustand versetzen. **7.** fig. aufrütteln: ~

alfresco

s.o. to s.th. j-m et. (deutlich) zum Bewußtsein bringen.

al·fres·co [æl'freskəʊ] *adj u. adv* im Freien: **~** *lunch;* *lunch* **~.**

al·ga ['ælgə] *pl* **-gae** ['~dʒiː] *s* ℞ Alge *f.*

al·ge·bra ['ældʒɪbrə] *s* ℞ Algebra *f.* **al·ge·bra·ic** [,~'breɪk] *adj* (**~ally**) algebraisch.

a·li·as ['eɪlɪəs] I *adv* alias. II *s* Deck-, ℞ *a.* Falschname *m.*

al·i·bi ['ælɪbaɪ] *s* ℞ Alibi *n, fig.* F *a.* Ausrede *f,* Entschuldigung *f: give s.o. an* **~** j-m ein Alibi geben.

al·ien ['eɪljən] I *adj* **1.** ausländisch. **2.** außerirdisch. **3.** *fig.* fremd (*to dat*): *that is* **~** *to his nature* das ist ihm wesensfremd. II *s* **4.** Ausländer(in). **5.** außerirdisches Wesen. **al·ien·ate** ['~eɪt] *v/t* **1.** ℞ veräußern. **2.** befremden; entfremden (*from dat*). **,al·ien·a·tion** *s* **1.** ℞ Veräußerung *f.* **2.** Entfremdung *f.*

a·light¹ ['əlaɪt] *adv u. adj* in Flammen: *be* **~** in Flammen stehen; *fig.* strahlen (*with* vor *dat*); *set* **~** in Brand stecken, anzünden.

a·light² [~] *v/i* (*a. irr*) **1.** (*from*) aussteigen (aus), absteigen (von *Fahrrad etc*), absitzen (von *Pferd*). **2.** (*on*) (sanft) fallen (auf *acc*) (*Schnee*), sich niederlassen (auf *dat od. acc*) (*Vogel*). **3.** ✈ niedergehen, landen (*a. allg.*): **~** *on one's feet* auf die Füße fallen.

a·lign [ə'laɪn] I *v/t* **1.** in e-e (gerade) Linie bringen, ⊙ (aus)fluchten. **2.** ausrichten (*with* nach). **3.** **~** *o.s. with fig.* sich anschließen (*dat od. an acc*). II *v/i* **4.** sich ausrichten (*with* nach). **a·lign·ment** *s* Ausrichtung *f: in* **~** *with* in 'einer Linie mit, *fig. a.* in Übereinstimmung mit.

a·like [ə'laɪk] I *adj* gleich; ähnlich (*to dat*). II *adv* gleich, ebenso, in gleicher Weise; ähnlich: *treat* **~** gleich behandeln.

al·i·men·ta·ry [,ælɪ'mentərɪ] *adj* **1.** Nahrungs... **2.** Ernährungs..., Speise...: **~** *canal* Verdauungskanal *m.*

al·i·mo·ny ['ælɪmənɪ] *s* ℞ Unterhalt(szahlung *f*) *m.*

a·live [ə'laɪv] *adj* **1.** lebend, lebendig, am Leben: *his grandparents are still* **~** leben noch; *be burnt* **~** bei lebendigem Leib verbrennen. **2.** in voller Kraft *od.* Wirksamkeit: *keep* **~** aufrechterhalten. **3.** lebendig, lebhaft: **~** *and kicking* F

gesund u. munter; *look* **~!** F mach fix! **4.** *be* **~** *to* sich e-r *Sache* bewußt sein. **5.** *be* **~** *with* wimmeln von.

al·ka·li ['ælkəlaɪ] *s* ℞ Alkali *n,* Laugensalz *n.* **al·ka·line** ['~laɪn] *adj* alkalisch.

all [ɔːl] I *adj* **1.** all, gesamt, ganz: **~** *day* (*long*) den ganzen Tag (hindurch); **~** *the time* die ganze Zeit. **2.** jeder, jede, jedes, alle *pl*: *at* **~** *hours* zu jeder Stunde. II *adv* **3.** ganz, gänzlich: **~** *the better* um so besser; **~** *in* F total fertig *od.* erledigt; **~** *over* überall; *that is John,* **~** *over* das ist typisch John; **~** *right* schon gut; in Ordnung; *it's* **~** *right for you to talk!* F du hast gut reden!; **~** *round* rings- *od.* rundherum; *it's* **~** *up with him* mit ihm ist's aus; → *there* **1.** III *pron* **4.** alles: **~** *in* **~** alles in allem; *or* *it* alles, das Ganze; **~** *of us* wir alle; → *above* **2,** *after* **3.** IV *s* **5.** *his* **~** sein Hab u. Gut; sein ein u. alles.

,all-A'mer·i·can *adj* **1.** rein *od.* typisch amerikanisch. **2.** die ganzen USA vertretend.

al·lay [ə'leɪ] *v/t* beschwichtigen; *Schmerzen etc* mildern, lindern.

al·le·ga·tion [,ælɪ'ɡeɪʃn] *s* Behauptung *f.* **al·lege** [ə'ledʒ] *v/t* behaupten. **al·'leged** *adj* angeblich.

al·le·giance [ə'liːdʒəns] *s* Treue *f,* Loyalität *f.*

al·le·gor·ic, al·le·gor·i·cal [,ælɪ'ɡɒrɪk(l)] *adj* □ allegorisch. **al·le·go·ry** ['~ɡərɪ] *s* Allegorie *f.*

al·le·lu·ia [,ælɪ'luːjə] *s* Halleluja *n.*

al·ler·gic [ə'lɜːdʒɪk] *adj* (**~ally**) allergisch (*to* gegen) (*a. fig.* F). **al·ler·gy** ['ælədʒɪ] *s* ☤ Allergie *f.*

al·le·vi·ate [ə'liːvɪeɪt] *v/t* mildern, lindern. **al,le·vi·a·tion** *s* Milderung *f,* Linderung *f.*

al·ley ['ælɪ] *s* **1.** Gasse *f:* → *blind alley.* **2.** *Bowling:* Bahn *f: that's down* (*od.* up) *my* **~** F das ist et. für mich.

All Fools' Day *s* der 1. April.

al·li·ance [ə'laɪəns] *s* **1.** Verbindung *f.* **2.** Bund *m,* Bündnis *n: form an* **~** ein Bündnis schließen. **3.** Verschwägerung *f; weitS.* Verwandtschaft *f.* **al·lied** [ə'laɪd; *attr.* 'ælaɪd] *adj* **1.** verbündet. **2.** *fig.* verwandt (*to dat*). **Al·lies** ['ælaɪz] *s pl hist.* die Alliierten *pl.*

al·li·ga·tor ['ælɪɡeɪtə] *s zo.* Alligator *m.*

,all-'in *adj* Gesamt..., Pauschal...

al·lit·er·a·tion [ə‚lɪtə'reɪʃn] s Alliteration f.

al·lo·cate ['æləʊkeɪt] v/t zuteilen, zuweisen (**to** dat). **‚al·lo'ca·tion** s Zuteilung f, Zuweisung f.

al·lop·a·thy [ə'lɒpəθɪ] s ✷ Allopathie f.

al·lot [ə'lɒt] v/t 1. zuteilen, zuweisen (**to** dat). 2. Geld etc bestimmen (**to, for** für). **al'lot·ment** s 1. Zuteilung f, Zuweisung f. 2. Parzelle f: ~ (**garden**) bsd. Br. Schrebergarten m.

‚all-'out adj F 1. total: ~ **effort** äußerste Anstrengung. 2. Am. kompromißlos, radikal.

al·low [ə'laʊ] I v/t 1. erlauben, gestatten; bewilligen, gewähren: **be** ~**ed to do s.th.** et. tun dürfen; **we are** ~**ed** ... uns stehen ... zu. 2. Summe geben. 3. zugeben; anerkennen, gelten lassen. II v/i 4. ~ **of** erlauben, gestatten: **it** ~**s of no excuse** es läßt sich nicht entschuldigen. 5. ~ **for** in Betracht ziehen, berücksichtigen (acc). **al'low·a·ble** adj □ erlaubt, zulässig. **al'low·ance** s 1. Erlaubnis f; Bewilligung f. 2. Anerkennung f. 3. Zuschuß m, Beihilfe f; Taschengeld n. 4. ✝ Nachlaß m, Rabatt m: ~ **for cash** Skonto n. 5. Toleranz f: **make** ~**(s) for** → **allow** 5. 6. ℞, ☉ Toleranz f.

al·loy ☉ I s ['ælɔɪ] Legierung f. II v/t [ə'lɔɪ] legieren.

'all-‚pur·pose adj Allzweck..., Universal... , **‚~'round** adj vielseitig, Allround...

All‖ Saints' Day s eccl. Allerheiligen n. ~ **Souls' Day** s eccl. Allerseelen n.

'all-‚time adj bisher unerreicht, beispiellos: ~ **high** Höchstleistung f, -stand m; ~ **low** Tiefststand m.

al·lude [ə'lu:d] v/i anspielen (**to** auf acc).

al·lure [ə'ljʊə] v/t 1. (an-, ver)locken. 2. anziehen, verzaubern. **al'lure·ment** s 1. Verlockung f. 2. Anziehungskraft f, Zauber m. **al'lur·ing** adj □ (ver)lockend, verführerisch.

al·lu·sion [ə'lu:ʒn] s Anspielung f (**to** auf acc).

al·lu·vi·al [ə'lu:vjəl] adj geol. angeschwemmt, Schwemm...

'all-‚weath·er adj Allwetter...

al·ly [ə'laɪ] I v/t verbinden, -einigen (**to, with** mit): ~ **o.s.** → II; → **allied.** II v/i sich vereinigen od. verbünden (**to, with** mit). III s ['ælaɪ] Verbündete m, f, Bundesgenosse m: → **Allies.**

al·ma·nac ['ɔ:lmənæk] s Almanach m, Kalender m.

al·might·y [ɔ:l'maɪtɪ] adj allmächtig: **the** ⁂ der Allmächtige.

al·mond ['ɑ:mənd] s ✿ Mandel f.

al·most ['ɔ:lməʊst] adv fast, beinahe.

alms [ɑ:mz] s 1. (mst pl konstruiert) Almosen n. 2. eccl. Kollekte f.

al·oe ['æləʊ] s ✿ Aloe f.

a·lone [ə'ləʊn] I adj allein: → **leave**¹ 2, **let**¹ 1. II adv allein, bloß, nur.

a·long [ə'lɒŋ] I prp 1. entlang (dat od. acc), längs (gen, a. dat), an (dat) ... vorbei: ~ **the river** od. den Fluß entlang, entlang dem Fluß. II adv 2. vorwärts, weiter: → **get along**, etc. 3. ~ **with** zs. mit: → **take along**, etc. 4. F da: **I'll be** ~ **shortly** ich bin gleich da. **a‚long'side** I adv 1. ⚓ längsseits. 2. Seite an Seite. II prp 3. neben (dat od. acc).

a·loof [ə'lu:f] I adv fern, abseits: **hold** (od. **keep**) (**o.s.**) ~, **stand** ~ sich fernhalten (**from** von), für sich bleiben. II adj reserviert, zurückhaltend.

a·loud [ə'laʊd] adv laut, mit lauter Stimme.

al·pha·bet ['ælfəbet] s Alphabet n. **‚al·pha'bet·ic, ‚al·pha'bet·i·cal** adj □ alphabetisch: **in** ~ **order** in alphabetischer Reihenfolge, alphabetisch (an)geordnet.

Al·pine ['ælpaɪn] adj 1. Alpen... 2. alpin, (Hoch)Gebirgs...

al·read·y [ɔ:l'redɪ] adv bereits, schon.

al·right [‚ɔ:l'raɪt] Br. F u. Am. für **all right** (→ **all** 3).

Al·sa·tian [æl'seɪʃən] I adj 1. elsässisch. II s 2. Elsässer(in). 3. a. ~ **dog** deutscher Schäferhund.

al·so ['ɔ:lsəʊ] adv auch, ebenfalls. **'‚~ran** s 1. Sport: Teilnehmer an e-m Rennen, der sich nicht plazieren kann: **she was an** ~ sie kam unter ,ferner liefen' ein. 2. F Versager m, Niete f.

al·tar ['ɔ:ltə] s eccl. Altar m. ~ **boy** s Ministrant m.

al·ter ['ɔ:ltə] I v/t (ver-, ab-, um)ändern. II v/i sich (ver)ändern. **'al·ter·a·ble** adj □ veränderlich. **‚al·ter'a·tion** s Änderung f (**to** an dat), Ver-, Ab-, Umänderung f.

al·ter·ca·tion [ˌɔːltəˈkeɪʃn] s heftige Auseinandersetzung.

al·ter·nate I adj [ɔːlˈtɜːnət] **1.** abwechselnd: **on ~ days** jeden zweiten Tag. **II** v/t [ˈɔːltəneɪt] **2.** abwechseln lassen. **3.** miteinander vertauschen. **4.** ⚡, ⚙ (periodisch) verändern. **III** v/i [ˈɔːltəneɪt] **5.** abwechseln. **al·ter·nate·ly** adv abwechselnd, wechselweise. **'al·ter·nat·ing** adj abwechselnd, Wechsel...: ~ **cur·rent** ⚡ Wechselstrom m. **al·ter·na·tion** [ˌɔːltəˈneɪʃn] s Abwechslung f, Wechsel m. **al·ter·na·tive** [ɔːlˈtɜːnətɪv] **I** adj **1.** alternativ, Ersatz...: ~ **airport** Ausweichflughafen m; ~ **society** alternative Gesellschaft. **2.** ander(er, e, es) (von zweien). **II** s **3.** Alternative f (to zu): **have no** (**other**) ~ keine andere Möglichkeit od. Wahl haben (**but to** als zu).

al·though [ɔːlˈðəʊ] cj obwohl, obgleich.

al·tim·e·ter [ˈæltɪmiːtə] s phys. Höhenmesser m.

al·ti·tude [ˈæltɪtjuːd] s ast., ✓, ⚹ Höhe f: **at an ~ of** in e-r Höhe von; ~ **of the sun** Sonnenstand m.

al·to [ˈæltəʊ] pl **-tos** ♪ Alt(stimme f) m; Altistin f.

al·to·geth·er [ˌɔːltəˈgeðə] **I** adv **1.** insgesamt. **2.** ganz (u. gar), völlig. **3.** im ganzen genommen. **II** s **4.** **in the ~** humor. im Adams- od. Evaskostüm.

al·tru·ism [ˈæltrʊɪzəm] s Altruismus m, Selbstlosigkeit f. **'al·tru·ist** s Altruist(in). **ˌal·tru'is·tic** adj (**~ally**) altruistisch, selbstlos.

al·u·min·i·um [ˌæljʊˈmɪnjəm], Am. **a·lu·mi·num** [əˈluːmənəm] s 🜕 Aluminium n.

a·lum·na [əˈlʌmnə] pl **-nae** [~niː] s Am. ehemalige Schülerin od. Studentin. **a'lum·nus** [~nəs] pl **-ni** [~naɪ] s Am. ehemaliger Schüler od. Student.

al·ways [ˈɔːlweɪz] adv immer, stets: **as ~** wie immer.

am [æm] ich bin.

a·mal·gam [əˈmælɡəm] s **1.** 🜕, ⚙ Amalgam n. **2.** fig. Mischung f. **a'mal·gam·ate** [~meɪt] v/t u. v/i **1.** 🜕, ⚙ (sich) amalgamieren, a. fig. (sich) vereinigen, verschmelzen. ✝ a. fusionieren. **a·ˌmal·gam'a·tion** s **1.** 🜕, ⚙ Amalgamieren n, a. fig. Vereinigung f, Verschmelzung f. **2.** fig. Zs.-schluß m, ✝ a. Fusion f.

a·mass [əˈmæs] v/t an-, aufhäufen.

am·a·teur [ˈæmətə] s Amateur m: a) (Kunst- etc)Liebhaber(in): ~ **painter** Sonntagsmaler(in), b) Amateursportler(in): ~ **boxer** Amateurboxer m, c) Nichtfachmann m, contp. Dilettant(in): ~ **detective** Amateurdetektiv m. **am·a·teur·ish** [ˌ~ˈtɜːrɪʃ] adj □ amateurhaft, dilettantisch.

a·maze [əˈmeɪz] v/t in (Er)Staunen setzen, verblüffen. **a'mazed** adj □ erstaunt, verblüfft (**at** über acc). **a'maze·ment** s (Er)Staunen n, Verblüffung f: **in ~** staunend, verblüfft; **to my ~** zu m-m Erstaunen, zu m-r Verblüffung. **a'maz·ing** adj □ erstaunlich, verblüffend.

Am·a·zon [ˈæməzən] s **1.** antiq. Amazone f. **2.** a. ⚢ fig. Amazone f, Mannweib n.

am·bas·sa·dor [æmˈbæsədə] s pol. Botschafter m (**to** in dat). **am'bas·sa·dress** [~drɪs] s Botschafterin f.

am·ber [ˈæmbə] **I** s **1.** min. Bernstein m. **2.** Br. Gelb(licht) n, gelbes Licht (Verkehrsampel): **at ~** bei Gelb; **the lights were at ~** die Ampel stand auf Gelb. **II** adj **3.** Bernstein... **4.** bernsteinfarben. **5.** **the lights were ~** Br. die Ampel stand auf Gelb.

am·bi·dex·trous [ˌæmbɪˈdekstrəs] adj □ **1.** beidhändig. **2.** fig. doppelzüngig, falsch.

am·bi·gu·i·ty [ˌæmbɪˈɡjuːətɪ] s Zweideutigkeit f (a. Äußerung), Mehr-, Vieldeutigkeit f. **am'big·u·ous** [~ɡjʊəs] adj □ zwei-, mehr-, vieldeutig.

am·bi·tion [æmˈbɪʃn] s Ehrgeiz m. **am'bi·tious** adj □ ehrgeizig (a. Plan etc): **be ~ to do s.th.** den Ehrgeiz haben, et. zu tun; **be ~ for s.o.** große Dinge mit j-m vorhaben.

am·biv·a·lent [æmˈbɪvələnt] adj bsd. psych. ambivalent, doppelwertig.

am·ble [ˈæmbl] **I** v/i **1.** im Paßgang gehen od. reiten. **2.** fig. schlendern. **II** s **3.** Paßgang m. **4.** fig. gemächlicher Gang.

am·bu·lance [ˈæmbjʊləns] s Kranken-, Sanitätswagen m.

am·bush [ˈæmbʊʃ] **I** s Hinterhalt m: **lay an ~** e-n Hinterhalt legen; **lie** (od. **wait**) **in ~** → III. **II** v/t aus dem Hinterhalt überfallen; auflauern (dat). **III** v/i im Hinterhalt liegen.

a·me·ba *Am.* → amoeba.

a·mel·io·rate [ə'mi:ljərent] **I** *v/t* verbessern, ✍ (a)meliorieren. **II** *v/i* besser werden. **a‚mel·io'ra·tion** *s* Verbesserung *f*, ✍ (A)Melioration *f*.

a·men [‚ɑ:'men] **I** *int* amen! **II** *s* Amen *n*.

a·me·na·ble [ə'mi:nəbl] *adj* □ **(to) 1.** zugänglich (*dat*). **2.** verantwortlich (*dat*); unterworfen (*dat*).

a·mend [ə'mend] *v/t* **1.** verbessern. **2.** *parl.* *Gesetz* abändern, ergänzen. **a'mend·ment** *s* **1.** Verbesserung *f*. **2.** *parl.* Abänderungs-, Ergänzungsantrag *m*; *Am.* Zusatzartikel *m* zur Verfassung. **a'mends** *s pl (mst sg konstruiert)* (Schaden)Ersatz *m*: **make ~** Schadenersatz leisten, es wiedergutmachen; **make ~ to s.o. for s.th.** j-n für et. entschädigen.

a·men·i·ty [ə'mi:nəti] *s* **1.** *oft pl* Liebenswürdigkeit *f*, Höflichkeit *f*: *his ~ of temper* sein angenehmes Wesen. **2.** schöne Lage (*e-s Hauses etc*); *oft pl* Annehmlichkeit(en *pl*) *f*; *pl* (natürliche) Vorzüge *pl od.* Reize *pl* (*e-r Person, e-s Ortes etc*).

A·mer·i·can [ə'merikən] **I** *adj* amerikanisch: ~ *Dream* der amerikanische Traum; ~ *Indian* (*bes.* nordamer.) Indianer(in). **II** *s* Amerikaner(in). **A'mer·i·can·ism** *s* Amerikanismus *m*. **A‚mer·i·can·i'za·tion** *s* Amerikanisierung *f*. **A'mer·i·can·ize** *v/t u. v/i* (sich) amerikanisieren.

am·e·thyst ['æmiθist] *s min.* Amethyst *m*.

a·mi·a·bil·i·ty [‚eimjə'biləti] *s* Liebenswürdigkeit *f*. **'a·mi·a·ble** *adj* □ liebenswürdig, freundlich.

am·i·ca·ble ['æmikəbl] *adj* freund(schaft)lich, friedlich, *a.* ⚖ gütlich. **'am·i·ca·bly** *adv* in Güte, gütlich: *part* ~ im guten auseinandergehen.

a·mid(st) [ə'mid(st)] *prp* inmitten (*gen*), (mitten) in *od.* unter (*dat od. acc*).

a·miss [ə'mis] *adj u. adv* verkehrt, falsch: *take ~* übelnehmen; *there is s.th. ~ with* et. stimmt nicht mit; *it would not be ~* es würde nicht schaden (*for s.o. to do s.th.* wenn j-d et. täte).

am·i·ty ['æməti] *s* Freundschaft *f*, gutes Einvernehmen.

am·me·ter ['æmitə] *s* ⚡ Amperemeter *n*.

am·mo·ni·a [ə'məʊnjə] *s* 🜍 Ammo-

niak *n*: *liquid ~* Salmiakgeist *m*.

am·mu·ni·tion [‚æmjʊ'niʃn] *s* ✕ Munition *f*: ~ *dump* Munitionslager *n*.

am·ne·sia [æm'ni:zjə] *s* ⚕ Amnesie *f*, Gedächtnisschwund *m*.

am·nes·ty ['æmnəsti] **I** *s* Amnestie *f*. **II** *v/t* amnestieren, begnadigen.

a·moe·ba [ə'mi:bə] *s zo.* Amöbe *f*.

a·mok [ə'mɒk] → amuck.

a·mong(st) [ə'mʌŋ(st)] *prp* (mitten) unter (*dat od. acc*), zwischen (*dat od. acc*), bei: *from* ~ aus ... hervor; *be* ~ gehören zu; ~ *other things* unter anderem; *they had two pounds* ~ *them* sie hatten zusammen zwei Pfund.

a·mor·al [‚ei'mɒrəl] *adj* □ amoralisch.

am·o·rous ['æmərəs] *adj* □ **1.** verliebt (*of* in *acc*). **2.** Liebes...: ~ *song*.

a·mor·phous [ə'mɔ:fəs] *adj* □ form-, gestaltlos.

am·or·ti·za·tion [ə‚mɔ:ti'zeiʃn] *s* Amortisation *f*, Tilgung *f*, Abschreibung *f*. **am'or·tize** [~taiz] *v/t* amortisieren: a) *Schuld* tilgen, b) *Anlagewerte* abschreiben.

a·mount [ə'maʊnt] **I** *v/i* **1. (to)** sich belaufen (auf *acc*), betragen (*acc*). **2.** *fig.* **(to)** hinauslaufen (auf *acc*), bedeuten (*acc*). **II** *s* **3.** Betrag *m*, Summe *f*; Höhe *f* (*e-r Summe*): *to the ~ of* in Höhe von; bis zum Betrag von. **4.** Menge *f*.

a·mour-pro·pre [‚æmʊə'prɒprə] *s* Eigenliebe *f*.

amp [æmp] F → ampere, amplifier.

am·pere ['æmpeə] *s* ⚡ Ampere *n*.

am·phet·a·mine [æm'fetəmi:n] *s* 🜿 Amphetamin *n*.

am·phib·i·an [æm'fibiən] **I** *adj* **1.** → amphibious. **II** *s* **2.** *zo.* Amphibie *f*, Lurch *m*. **3.** Amphibienfahrzeug *n*. **am'phib·i·ous** *adj* *zo.*, ✈ amphibisch, Amphibien...

am·phi·the·a·ter, *bsd. Br.* **am·phi·the·a·tre** ['æmfi‚θiətə] *s* Amphitheater *n*.

am·ple ['æmpl] *adj* □ **1.** weit, groß, geräumig. **2.** weitläufig, -gehend, ausführlich. **3.** reich(lich), beträchtlich. **4.** stattlich (*Figur etc*).

am·pli·fi·ca·tion [‚æmplifi'keiʃn] *s* **1.** Erweiterung *f*, Vergrößerung *f*, Ausdehnung *f*. **2.** nähere Ausführung *od.* Erläuterung; Weitschweifigkeit *f*. **3.** ⚡, *phys.* Verstärkung *f*. **am·pli·fi·er** ['~taiə] *s* ⚡, *phys.* Verstärker *m*.

'am·pli·fy I v/t **1.** erweitern, vergrößern, ausdehnen. **2.** näher ausführen od. erläutern. **3.** ⚡, phys. verstärken. **II** v/i **4.** sich weitläufig auslassen (*on* über acc). **am·pli·tude** ['ᴧtju:d] s **1.** Weite f, Umfang m (a. fig.). **2.** Fülle f, Reichtum m. **3.** ⚡, phys. Amplitude f, Schwingungsweite f.

am·poule ['æmpu:l] s ⚕ Ampulle f.

am·pu·tate ['æmpjʊteɪt] v/t ⚕ amputieren, abnehmen. **ˌam·pu'ta·tion** s Amputation f, Abnahme f.

a·muck [ə'mᴧk] adv: **run ~** Amok laufen.

am·u·let ['æmjʊlɪt] s Amulett n.

a·muse [ə'mju:z] v/t amüsieren; unterhalten; Spaß machen (dat): **be ~d** sich freuen (*at, by* über acc). **a'muse·ment** s Unterhaltung f; Zeitvertreib m: **for ~** zum Vergnügen; **~ arcade** Br. Spielsalon m; **~ park** Vergnügungspark m. **a'mus·ing** adj □ amüsant; unterhaltsam.

an [ən] → **a**.

a·nach·ro·nism [ə'nækrənɪzəm] s Anachronismus m.

an·a·con·da [ˌænə'kɒndə] s zo. Anakonda f, Riesenschlange f.

a·nae·mi·a [ə'ni:mjə] s bsd. Br. ⚕ Anämie f, Blutarmut f. **a'nae·mic** adj bsd. Br. anämisch; blutarm.

an·aes·the·si·a [ˌænɪs'θi:zjə] s bsd. Br. ⚕ Anästhesie f, Narkose f, Betäubung f. **an·aes·thet·ic** [ˌᴧ'θetɪk] **I** adj (**~ally**) betäubend, Narkose... **II** s Betäubungsmittel n. **an·aes·the·tist** [æ'ni:sθətɪst] s bsd. Br. Anästhesist m, Narkosearzt m. **an'aes·the·tize** v/t bsd. Br. betäuben, narkotisieren.

an·a·log·i·cal, an·a·log·i·cal [ˌænə'lɒdʒɪk(l)], **a·nal·o·gous** [ə'næləgəs] adj □ analog, entsprechend (*to, with* dat). **a'nal·o·gy** [ˌdʒɪ] s Analogie f, Entsprechung f: **on the ~ of, by ~ with** analog, gemäß, entsprechend (dat).

an·a·lyse ['ænəlaɪz] v/t analysieren: a) 🜂 etc zerlegen, b) gründlich untersuchen, c) ling. zergliedern, d) 🜍 auflösen. **a·nal·y·sis** [ə'næləsɪs] pl **-ses** [ᴧsi:z] s **1.** Analyse f, Zerlegung f, gründliche Untersuchung, Zergliederung f, Auflösung f. 🜂 Analysis f. **3.** Psychoanalyse f. **an·a·lyst** ['ænəlɪst] s **1.** Analytiker m: **public ~** (behördlicher) Lebensmittelchemiker. **2.** Psy-

choanalytiker m. **an·a·lyt·ic, an·a·lyt·i·cal** [ˌænə'lɪtɪk(l)] adj □ **1.** analytisch. **2.** psychoanalytisch.

an·ar·chic, an·ar·chi·cal [æ'nɑ:kɪk(l)] adj □ anarchisch. **an·arch·ism** ['ænəkɪzəm] s Anarchismus m. **'an·arch·ist I** s Anarchist(in). **II** adj anarchistisch. **'an·arch·y** s Anarchie f.

a·nath·e·ma [ə'næθəmə] s **1.** eccl. Bannfluch m, Kirchenbann m. **2. be an ~ to s.o.** fig. j-m verhaßt od. ein Greuel sein. **a'nath·e·ma·tize** v/t in den Bann tun, mit dem Kirchenbann belegen.

an·a·tom·i·cal [ˌænə'tɒmɪkl] adj □ anatomisch. **a·nat·o·mize** [ə'nætəmaɪz] v/t ⚕ sezieren, fig. a. zergliedern. **a'nat·o·my** s **1.** ⚕ Anatomie f. **2.** fig. Zergliederung f, Analyse f.

an·ces·tor ['ænsestə] s Vorfahr m, Ahn(herr) m: **~ cult** Ahnenkult m. **an·ces·tral** [ᴧ'sestrəl] adj angestammt, Ahnen...: **~ home** Stammsitz m. **an·ces·tress** ['ænsestrɪs] s Ahnfrau f, Ahne f. **'an·ces·try** s **1.** (bsd. vornehme) Abstammung. **2.** Vorfahren pl, Ahnen(reihe f) pl: **~ research** Ahnenforschung f.

an·chor ['æŋkə] **I** s **1.** ⚓ Anker m: **cast** (od. **drop**) **~** → 5a; **lie** (od. **ride**) **at ~** → 5b; **~ weigh** 3. **2.** Rundfunk, TV: Am. Moderator m, Moderatorin f (e-r Nachrichtensendung); Diskussionsleiter(in). **II** v/t **3.** ⚓, ⚓ verankern (a. fig.). **4.** Rundfunk, TV: Am. Nachrichtensendung moderieren; Diskussion leiten. **III** v/i **5.** ⚓ ankern: a) vor Anker gehen, b) vor Anker liegen. **'an·chor·age** s **1.** Ankerplatz m. **2.** a. **~ dues** pl Anker-, Liegegebühr f.

an·chor·man ['æŋkəmən] s (irr **man**), **'~·wom·an** s (irr **woman**) → **anchor** 2.

an·cho·vy ['æntʃəvɪ] s ichth. An(s)chovis f, Sardelle f.

an·cient ['eɪnʃənt] **I** adj **1.** alt, aus alter Zeit. **2.** uralt. **3.** altertümlich. **II** s **4. the ~s** pl die Alten pl (Griechen u. Römer).

an·cil·lar·y [æn'sɪlərɪ] adj untergeordnet (*to* dat), Zusatz..., Neben...: **~ industries** pl Zulieferbetriebe pl.

and [ænd] cj und: **better ~ better** immer besser; **thousands ~ thousands** Tausende u. aber Tausende; **there are books ~ books** es gibt gute u. schlechte Bücher; **for miles ~ miles** viele Meilen weit; *he ran ~ ran* er lief immer weiter; **bread ~ butter** Butterbrot *n*; *try ~ come* versuche zu kommen; → **nice** 4.

an·ec·do·tal [ˌænekˈdəʊtl] *adj* anekdotenhaft, anekdotisch. **an·ec·dote** [ˈænɪkdəʊt] *s* Anekdote *f*.

a·ne·mi·a, *etc Am.* → **anaemia**, *etc.*

an·e·mom·e·ter [ˌænɪˈmɒmɪtə] *s phys.* Windmesser *m*.

a·nem·o·ne [əˈnemənɪ] *s* ♣ Anemone *f*.

an·es·the·si·a, *etc Am.* → **anaesthesia**, *etc.*

a·new [əˈnjuː] *adv* 1. von neuem, noch einmal. 2. neu.

an·gel [ˈeɪndʒəl] *s* Engel *m* (*a. fig.*): *you are an ~* du bist ein Schatz. **an·gel·ic**, **an·gel·i·cal** [ænˈdʒelɪk(l)] *adj* □ engelhaft, Engels...

an·ger [ˈæŋɡə] **I** *s* Zorn *m*, Ärger *m*, Wut *f* (*at* über *acc*). **II** *v/t* erzürnen, (ver)ärgern.

an·gi·na (pec·to·ris) [ænˈdʒaɪnə (ˈpektərɪs)] *s* ♠ Angina *f* pectoris.

an·gle¹ [ˈæŋɡl] **I** *s* 1. *bsd.* ♠ Winkel *m*: *at an ~* schräg; *at right ~s* im rechten Winkel zu. 2. Ecke *f*. 3. *fig.* Standpunkt *m*. 4. *fig.* Seite *f*, Aspekt *m*. **II** *v/t* 5. ab-, umbiegen. 6. *Bericht etc* färben.

an·gle² [~] *v/i* angeln: *~ for* etwas aussein auf (*acc*); → **compliment** 1.

an·gle|-i·ron ○ Winkeleisen *n*. **'~park** *v/t u. v/i mot.* schräg parken.

an·gler [ˈæŋɡlə] *s* Angler(in).

An·gles [ˈæŋɡlz] *s pl hist.* Angeln *pl.*

An·gli·can [ˈæŋɡlɪkən] *eccl.* **I** *adj* anglikanisch. **II** *s* Anglikaner(in).

An·gli·cism [ˈæŋɡlɪsɪzəm] *s ling.* Anglizismus *m*.

Anglo|-A·mer·i·can [ˌæŋɡləʊəˈmerɪkən] **I** *s* Angloamerikaner(in). **II** *adj* angloamerikanisch. **,~'Sax·on I** *s* Angelsachse *m*. **II** *adj* angelsächsisch.

an·go·ra [æŋˈɡɔːrə] *s a. ~ cat zo.* Angorakatze *f*. **~ wool** *s* Angorawolle *f*.

an·gry [ˈæŋɡrɪ] *adj* □ (*at, about*) ärgerlich (auf, über *acc*), verärgert (über *acc*), böse (auf *j-n*, über *et.*; *with* mit *j-m*).

an·guish [ˈæŋɡwɪʃ] *s* Qual *f*, Pein *f*: *be in ~* Ängste ausstehen.

an·gu·lar [ˈæŋɡjʊlə] *adj* □ 1. wink(e)lig, Winkel...: *~ point* ♠ Scheitelpunkt *m*. 2. knochig. 3. *fig.* steif: a) linkisch, b) formell.

an·i·line [ˈænɪliːn] *s* ♠ Anilin *n*.

an·i·mal [ˈænɪml] **I** *s* Tier *n*. **II** *adj* animalisch, tierisch. **~ food** *s* 1. Fleischnahrung *f*. 2. Tierfutter *n*. **~ lov·er** *s* Tierfreund(in). **'~·lov·ing** *adj* tierliebend. **~ shel·ter** *s Am.* Tierheim *n*. **~ spir·its** *pl* Lebenskraft *f*, -geister *pl.*

an·i·mate I *v/t* [ˈænɪmeɪt] 1. beleben, mit Leben erfüllen. 2. anregen, aufmuntern. **II** *adj* [ˈ~mət] 3. belebt, lebend. 4. lebhaft, munter. **an·i·mat·ed** [ˈ~meɪtɪd] *adj* 1. lebendig: *~ cartoon* Zeichentrickfilm *m*. 2. → **animate** 4. **an·i·ma·tion** [ˌ~ˈmeɪʃn] *s* Lebhaftigkeit *f*, Munterkeit *f*.

an·i·mos·i·ty [ˌænɪˈmɒsətɪ] *s* Feindseligkeit *f* (*against, toward[s]* gegen[über]; *between* zwischen *dat*).

an·ise [ˈænɪs] *s* ♠ Anis *m*. **an·i·seed** [ˈ~siːd] *s* Anis(samen) *m*.

an·kle [ˈæŋkl] *s anat.* (Fuß)Knöchel *m*. **,~'deep** *adj* knöcheltief. **~ sock** *s Br.* Söckchen *n*.

an·klet [ˈæŋklɪt] *s* 1. Fußring *m*. 2. *Am.* Söckchen *n*.

an·nals [ˈænlz] *s pl* 1. Annalen *pl*, Jahrbücher *pl*. 2. (Jahres)Bericht *m*.

an·neal [əˈniːl] *v/t* 1. *metall.* ausglühen, *a. Kunststoffe* tempern. 2. *Keramik:* einbrennen. 3. *fig.* härten, stählen.

an·nex I *v/t* [əˈneks] 1. (*to*) beifügen (*dat*), anhängen (an *acc*). 2. *Gebiet* annektieren, sich einverleiben. **II** *s* [ˈæneks] 3. Anhang *m*, Zusatz *m*. 4. Anbau *m*, Nebengebäude *n*. **an·nex·a·tion** *s* Annektierung *f*, Einverleibung *f* (*to* in *acc*).

an·ni·hi·late [əˈnaɪəleɪt] *v/t* vernichten. **an·ni·hi·la·tion** *s* Vernichtung *f*.

an·ni·ver·sa·ry [ˌænɪˈvɜːsərɪ] *s* Jahrestag *m*.

an·no·tate [ˈænəʊteɪt] *v/t* mit Anmerkungen versehen, kommentieren. **an·no·ta·tion** *s* Anmerkung *f*; Kommentar *m*.

an·nounce [əˈnaʊns] *v/t* 1. ankündigen. 2. bekanntgeben, verkünden, *Geburt etc* anzeigen. 3. *Rundfunk, TV:* ansagen; *über Lautsprecher* durchsagen. **an·nounce·ment** *s* 1. Ankündigung *f*. 2. Bekanntgabe *f*, (*Geburts- etc*)Anzeige *f*. 3. *Rundfunk, TV:* Ansage *f*; (Lautsprecher)Durchsage *f*. **an·nounc·er** *s Rundfunk, TV:* Ansager(in).

an·noy [əˈnɔɪ] *v/t* **1.** ärgern: *be ~ed* sich ärgern (*at s.th.* über et.; *with s.o.* über j-n). **2.** belästigen, stören. **an'noy·ance** *s* **1.** Ärger *m.* **2.** Belästigung *f*, Störung *f.* **an'noy·ing** *adj* □ **1.** ärgerlich. **2.** lästig, störend.

an·nu·al [ˈænjʊəl] **I** *adj* □ **1.** jährlich, Jahres...: *~ ring* ❀ Jahresring *m.* **2.** *a.* ❀ einjährig. **II** *s* **3.** jährlich erscheinende Veröffentlichung. **4.** ❀ einjährige Pflanze.

an·nu·i·ty [əˈnjuːɪtɪ] *s* (Jahres-, Leib-) Rente *f.*

an·nul [əˈnʌl] *v/t* annullieren, *Gesetz, Ehe etc* aufheben, für ungültig erklären, *Vorschrift etc* abschaffen.

an·nu·lar [ˈænjʊlə] *adj* □ ringförmig, Ring...

an·nul·ment [əˈnʌlmənt] *s* Annullierung *f*, Aufhebung *f*, Ungültigkeitserklärung *f*, Abschaffung *f.*

An·nun·ci·a·tion (Day) [əˌnʌnsɪˈeɪʃn] *s eccl.* Mariä Verkündigung *f.*

an·ode [ˈænəʊd] *s* ⚡ Anode *f*, positiver Pol.

an·o·dyne [ˈænəʊdaɪn] *adj u. s* 💊 schmerzstillend(es Mittel).

a·noint [əˈnɔɪnt] *v/t bsd. eccl.* salben.

a·nom·a·lous [əˈnɒmələs] *adj* □ **1.** anomal. **2.** ungewöhnlich. **a'nom·a·ly** *s* Anomalie *f.*

an·o·nym·i·ty [ˌænəˈnɪmətɪ] *s* Anonymität *f.* **a·non·y·mous** [əˈnɒnɪməs] *adj* □ anonym.

a·no·rak [ˈænəræk] *s* Anorak *m.*

an·oth·er [əˈnʌðə] *adj u. pron* **1.** ein anderer, e-e andere, ein anderes: *~ thing* etwas anderes; *one after ~* e-r nach dem andern; → *one* 6. **2.** noch ein(er, e, es), ein zweiter *od.* weiterer, e-e zweite *od.* weitere, ein zweites *od.* weiteres: *~ ten years* noch *od.* weitere zehn Jahre; *tell me ~!* F das kannst du deiner Großmutter erzählen!

an·swer [ˈɑːnsə] **I** *s* **1.** Antwort *f* (*a. fig. Reaktion*) (*to* auf *acc*): *in ~ to* in Beantwortung (*gen*); auf (*acc*) hin; als Antwort auf. **2.** Lösung *f* (*to* e-s *Problems*). **II** *v/i* **3.** antworten (*to* auf *acc*): *~ back* freche Antworten geben; widersprechen; sich (*mit Worten etc*) verteidigen *od.* wehren. **4.** *~ to* → 10 u. 11. **5.** (*to s.o.*) sich (j-m gegenüber) verantworten, (j-m) Rechenschaft ablegen (*for*

für). **6.** verantwortlich sein, haften (*for* für). **7.** *~ to* hören auf (*e-n Namen*). **III** *v/t* **8.** *j-m* antworten: *~ s.o. back* j-m freche Antworten geben; j-m widersprechen; sich gegen j-n (*mit Worten etc*) verteidigen *od.* wehren. **9.** antworten auf (*acc*), beantworten. **10.** *fig.* reagieren auf (*acc*): a) eingehen auf: *~ the bell* (*od. door*) (*auf das Läuten od. Klopfen*) die Tür öffnen, aufmachen; *~ the telephone* ans Telefon gehen, b) ⚙ *dem Steuer etc* gehorchen, c) *e-m Befehl etc* Folge leisten, gehorchen, d) *Wunsch etc* erfüllen, *Gebet* erhören, e) sich auf *e-e Anzeige* hin melden *od.* bewerben. **11.** *e-r Beschreibung* entsprechen. **12.** sich *j-m* gegenüber verantworten, *j-m* Rechenschaft ablegen (*for* für). **'an·swer·a·ble** *adj* **1.** verantwortlich (*to dat; for* für). **2.** zu beantworten(d).

ant [ænt] *s zo.* Ameise *f.*

an·tag·o·nism [ænˈtægənɪzəm] *s* Feindschaft *f* (*between* zwischen *dat*). **an'tag·o·nist** *s* Feind(in). **an,tag·o·'nis·tic** *adj* (*~ally*) feindlich (*to* gegen). **an'tag·o·nize** *v/t* **1.** bekämpfen. **2.** sich *j-n* zum Feind machen.

ant·arc·tic [ænˈtɑːktɪk] **I** *adj* antarktisch: ♀ *Circle* südlicher Polarkreis. **II** *s* ♀ Antarktis *f.*

ant bear *s zo.* Ameisenbär *m.*

an·te·ced·ent [ˌæntɪˈsiːdənt] **I** *adj* **1.** (*to*) vorhergehend (*dat*), früher (als). **II** *s* **2.** *pl* Vorgeschichte *f*: *his ~s* sein Vorleben; s-e Abstammung. **3.** *ling.* Bezugswort *n.*

an·te·cham·ber [ˈæntɪˌtʃeɪmbə] *s* Vorzimmer *n.*

an·te·date [ˌæntɪˈdeɪt] *v/t Brief etc* zurückdatieren.

an·te·di·lu·vi·an [ˌæntɪdaɪˈluːvjən] *adj* vorsintflutlich (*a. fig.*).

an·te·lope [ˈæntɪləʊp] *s zo.* Antilope *f.*

an·te me·rid·i·em [ˌæntɪməˈrɪdɪəm] *adv* vormittags (*abbr. a.m.*): *3 a.m.* 3 Uhr morgens.

an·te·na·tal [ˌæntɪˈneɪtl] **I** *adj* □ vor der Geburt: *~ examination* Mutterschaftsvorsorgeuntersuchung *f*; *~ exercises* *pl* Schwangerschaftsgymnastik *f.* **II** *s* F Mutterschaftsvorsorgeuntersuchung.

an·ten·na [ænˈtenə] *s* **1.** *pl* **-nae** [~niː] *zo.* Fühler *m.* **2.** *pl* **-nas** *bsd. Am.* Antenne *f.*

an·te·ri·or [æn'tɪərɪə] *adj* **1.** (*to*) vorhergehend (*dat*), früher (als). **2.** vorder.

an·te·room ['æntɪrʊm] *s* Vorzimmer *n.*

an·them ['ænθəm] *s* Hymne *f.*

'ant·hill *s* Ameisenhaufen *m.*

an·thol·o·gy [æn'θɒlədʒɪ] *s* Anthologie *f*, (*bsd.* Gedicht)Sammlung *f.*

an·thra·cite ['ænθrəsaɪt] *s min.* Anthrazit *m*, Glanzkohle *f.*

an·thro·poid ['ænθrəʊpɔɪd] *zo.* **I** *adj* menschenähnlich. **II** *s* Menschenaffe *m.*

an·thro·po·log·i·cal [ˌænθrəpə'lɒdʒɪkl] *adj* □ anthropologisch. **an·thro·pol·o·gist** [ˌ~'pɒlədʒɪst] *s* Anthropologe *m.* **an·thro·pol·o·gy** [ˌ~'pɒlədʒɪ] *s* Anthropologie *f*, Menschenkunde *f.*

an·ti... ['æntɪ] *in Zssgn* Gegen..., gegen... eingestellt, anti..., Anti..., Anti...

ˌan·ti'air·craft *adj* ✕ Flugabwehr...: ~ *gun* Flakgeschütz *n.*

an·ti·bi·ot·ic [ˌæntɪbaɪ'ɒtɪk] *s* ✿ Antibiotikum *n.*

'an·ti·bod·y *s* ✿ Antikörper *m*, Abwehrstoff *m.*

'An·ti·christ *s eccl.* Antichrist *m.*

an·tic·i·pate [æn'tɪsɪpeɪt] *v/t* **1.** vorausschen, (-)ahnen. **2.** erwarten, erhoffen. **3.** vorwegnehmen. **4.** *j-m, e-m Wunsch etc* zuvorkommen. **5.** ✝ vor Fälligkeit bezahlen *od.* einlösen. **an·tic·i·pa·tion** *s* **1.** (Vor)Ahnung *f.* **2.** Erwartung *f*, Hoffnung *f*: *in* ~ *of* in Erwartung (*gen*). **3.** Vorwegnahme *f*: *in* ~ im voraus. **an·tic·i·pa·to·ry** [ˌ~peɪtərɪ] *adj* □ vorwegnehmend.

ˌan·ti'cler·i·cal *adj* □ antiklerikal, kirchenfeindlich.

ˌan·ti'cli·max *s* **1.** *rhet.* Antiklimax *f.* **2.** *fig.* enttäuschendes Abfallen; Enttäuschung *f.*

ˌan·ti'clock·wise *adj u. adv* entgegen dem *od.* gegen den Uhrzeigersinn.

ˌan·ti'cor·ro·sive *s* **1.** korrosionsverhütend: ~ *agent* Rostschutzmittel *n.* **2.** rostfest.

ˌan·ti'cy·clone *s meteor.* Hoch(druckgebiet) *n.*

ˌan·ti'daz·zle *adj* Blendschutz...: ~ *switch* Abblendschalter *m.*

an·ti·dote ['æntɪdəʊt] *s* Gegengift *n*, -mittel *n* (*a. fig.*) (*against, for, to* gegen).

ˌan·ti'fas·cist *s* **I** Antifaschist(in). **II** *adj* antifaschistisch.

'an·ti·freeze *s* Frostschutzmittel *n.*

'an·ti·he·ro *s* Antiheld *m.*

ˌan·ti'knock ✿, *mot.* **I** *adj* klopffest. **II** *s* Antiklopfmittel *n.*

an·tip·a·thy [æn'tɪpəθɪ] *s* Antipathie *f*, Abneigung *f* (*against, to, towards* gegen).

an·tip·o·des [æn'tɪpədiːz] *s pl* **1.** *die* diametral gegenüberliegenden Teile *pl* der Erde. **2.** (*a. sg konstruiert*) *das* (genaue) Gegenteil.

ˌan·ti·pol'lu·tion *adj* umweltschützend: ~ *device* Abgasentgiftungsanlage *f.*

an·ti·quar·i·an [ˌæntɪ'kweərɪən] **I** *adj* **1.** antiquarisch. **2.** ~ *bookseller* Antiquar *m*; ~ *bookshop* (*bsd. Am. bookstore*) Antiquariat *n.* **II** *s* **3.** → *antiquary* **1.** **an·ti·quar·y** ['~kwərɪ] *s* **1.** Altertumskenner(in), -forscher(in). **2.** Antiquitätensammler(in). -händler(in). **an·ti·quat·ed** ['~kweɪtɪd] *adj* antiquiert, veraltet.

an·tique [æn'tiːk] **I** *adj* **1.** antik, alt. **2.** F → *antiquated*. **II** *s* **3.** Antiquität *f*: ~ *dealer* Antiquitätenhändler(in); ~ *shop* (*bsd. Am. store*) Antiquitätenladen *m.* **an·tiq·ui·ty** [ˌ~'tɪkwətɪ] *s* **1.** Altertum *n.* **2.** *die* Antike. **3.** *pl* Altertümer *pl.*

ˌan·ti'rust *adj* Rostschutz...

ˌan·ti'Sem·ite *s* Antisemit(in). **ˌan·ti-'Se'mit·ic** *adj* antisemitisch. **an·ti-'Sem·i·tism** [ˌ~'semɪtɪzəm] *s* Antisemitismus *m.*

ˌan·ti'sep·tic ✿ **I** *adj* □ antiseptisch. **II** *s* Antiseptikum *n.*

ˌan·ti'so·cial *adj* **1.** asozial, gesellschaftsfeindlich. **2.** ungesellig.

an·tith·e·sis [æn'tɪθɪsɪs] *pl* -ses [ˌ~siːz] *s* Antithese *f*, Gegensatz *m.* **an·ti·thet·ic**, **an·ti·thet·i·cal** [ˌ~'θetɪk(l)] *adj* □ gegensätzlich.

ant·ler ['æntlə] *s* **1.** (Geweih)Sprosse *f.* **2.** *pl* Geweih *n.*

an·to·nym ['æntəʊnɪm] *s ling.* Antonym *n.*

a·nus ['eɪnəs] *s anat.* After *m.*

an·vil ['ænvɪl] *s* Amboß *m* (*a. anat.*).

anx·i·e·ty [æŋ'zaɪətɪ] *s* **1.** Angst *f*, Sorge *f* (*about, for* wegen, um). **2.** ✿, *psych.* Beklemmung *f*: ~ *dream* Angsttraum *m.* **3.** (starkes) Verlangen (*for* nach).

anx·ious ['æŋkʃəs] *adj* □ **1.** ängstlich; besorgt (*about, for* wegen, um). **2.** *fig.*

(*for, to inf*) begierig (auf *acc*, zu *inf*), (ängstlich) bedacht (auf *acc*, darauf zu *inf*), bestrebt (zu *inf*): *I am very ~ to see him* mir liegt (sehr) viel daran, ihn zu sehen.

an·y ['enɪ] **I** *adj* **1.** (*fragend, verneinend*) (irgend)ein(e), einige *pl*, etwas: *not ~* kein. **2.** (*bejahend*) jeder, jede, jedes (beliebige): *at ~ time* jederzeit; → *case²*, *rate* 2. **II** *adv* **3.** irgend(wie), (noch) etwas: *~ more?* noch (etwas) mehr? '*~₁bod·y* *pron* **1.** (irgend) jemand, irgendeine(r). **2.** jeder(mann): *~ who* jeder, der; wer; *hardly ~* kaum j-d, fast niemand; *not ~* niemand, keiner. '*~·how* *adv* **1.** irgendwie. **2.** jedenfalls. '*~·one* → *anybody*. '*~·thing* *pron* **1.** (irgend) etwas: *not ~* (gar *od.* überhaupt) nichts; *not for ~* um keinen Preis; *take ~ you like* nimm, was du willst. **2.** alles: *~ but* alles andere als. '*~·way* → *anyhow*. '*~·where* *adv* **1.** irgendwo(hin): *not ~* nirgendwo(hin); *hardly ~* fast nirgends. **2.** überall.

a·or·ta [eɪ'ɔːtə] *s anat.* Aorta *f*, Hauptschlagader *f*.

a·part [ə'pɑːt] *adv* **1.** einzeln, für sich: *live ~* getrennt leben; → *take apart, tell* 4. **2.** beiseite: → *joking* II.

a·part·heid [ə'pɑːtheɪt] *s pol.* Apartheid *f*.

a·part·ment [ə'pɑːtmənt] *s* **1.** *bsd. Am.* Wohnung *f*. **2.** *mst pl* Gemach *n*. *~ ho·tel* *s* Appartementhotel *n*. *~ house* *s Am.* Wohnhaus *n*.

ap·a·thet·ic [ˌæpə'θetɪk] *adj* (*~ally*) apathisch, teilnahmslos, gleichgültig. '**ap·a·thy** *s* Apathie *f*, Teilnahmslosigkeit *f*, Gleichgültigkeit *f* (*to* gegenüber).

ape [eɪp] **I** *s zo.* (*bsd. Menschen*)Affe *m*. **II** *v/t* nachäffen.

a·pe·ri·ent [ə'pɪərɪənt] *ℱ, pharm.* **I** *s* Abführmittel *n*. **II** *adj* abführend.

ap·er·ture ['æpəˌtjʊə] *s* **1.** Öffnung *f*. **2.** *phot.* Blende *f*.

a·pex ['eɪpeks] *pl* '**a·pex·es**, **ap·i·ces** ['eɪpɪsiːz] *s* **1.** (*Kegel-, Lungen- etc-*) Spitze *f*. **2.** *fig.* Gipfel *m*, Höhepunkt *m*.

aph·o·rism ['æfərɪzəm] *s* Aphorismus *m*.

ap·i·ces ['eɪpɪsiːz] *pl von* apex.

a·piece [ə'piːs] *adv* pro Stück; pro Kopf *od.* Person.

ap·ish ['eɪpɪʃ] *adj* □ äffisch.

a·poc·a·lypse [ə'pɒkəlɪps] *s* Enthüllung *f*, Offenbarung *f*.

a·pol·o·gize [ə'pɒlədʒaɪz] *v/i* sich entschuldigen (*for* wegen; *to* bei). **a'pol·o·gy** *s* **1.** Entschuldigung *f*: *in ~ for* zur *od.* als Entschuldigung für; *make* (*od. offer*) *s.o. an ~* sich bei j-m entschuldigen (*for* für). **2.** F minderwertiger Ersatz (*for* für): *an ~ for a meal* ein armseliges Essen.

ap·o·plec·tic [ˌæpəʊ'plektɪk] *adj*: *~ stroke* (*od. fit*) → *apoplexy*. **ap·o·plex·y** ['æpleksɪ] *s ℱ* Schlaganfall *m*, Gehirnschlag *m*.

a·pos·tle [ə'pɒsl] *s eccl.* Apostel *m*.

a·pos·tro·phe [ə'pɒstrəfɪ] *s ling.* Apostroph *m*, Auslassungszeichen *n*. **a·'pos·tro·phize** *v/t* apostrophieren.

ap·pal [ə'pɔːl] *v/t* erschrecken, entsetzen: *be ~led* entsetzt sein (*at* über *acc*). **ap'pal·ling** *adj* □ erschreckend, entsetzlich.

ap·pa·ra·tus [ˌæpə'reɪtəs] *pl* **-tus**, **-tus·es** *s* Apparat *m*, Gerät *n*, Vorrichtung *f*.

ap·par·el [ə'pærəl] *s* Kleidung *f*.

ap·par·ent [ə'pærənt] *adj* □ **1.** augenscheinlich, offenbar, -sichtlich: *be ~ from* hervorgehen aus; *with no ~ reason* ohne ersichtlichen Grund. **2.** anscheinend, scheinbar.

ap·pa·ri·tion [ˌæpə'rɪʃn] *s* Erscheinung *f*, Gespenst *n*, Geist *m*.

ap·peal [ə'piːl] **I** *v/i* **1.** *ℱℱ* Berufung *od.* Revision einlegen (*to* bei). *a. allg.* Einspruch erheben, Beschwerde einlegen (*against*, *ℱℱ mst from* gegen; *to* bei). **2.** appellieren, sich wenden (*to an acc*). **3.** sich berufen (*to* auf *acc*). **4.** (*to*) Anklang finden (bei), gefallen, zusagen (*dat*), reizen (*acc*). **5.** *~ to* j-n dringend bitten (*for* um). **II** *s* **6.** *ℱℱ* Berufung *f*, Revision *f*: *file* (*od. lodge*) *an ~* → 1. **7.** Appell *m* (*to* an *acc*). **8.** Berufung *f* (*to* auf *acc*). **9.** dringende Bitte (*to* an *acc*; *for* um). **10.** (*to*) Anziehung(skraft) *f*, Zugkraft *f*, Wirkung *f* (auf *acc*), Anklang *m* (bei). **ap'peal·ing** *adj* □ **1.** bittend, flehend. **2.** reizvoll, gefällig, ansprechend.

ap·pear [ə'pɪə] *v/i* **1.** erscheinen (*a. vor Gericht*), (*von Büchern etc a.*) herauskommen: *~ in public* sich in der Öffentlichkeit zeigen; *~ on television* im

Fernsehen auftreten. **2.** scheinen, aussehen, *j-m* vorkommen: *it ~s to me you are right* mir scheint; *he ~ed calm* er war äußerlich ruhig. **ap'pear·ance** *s* **1.** Erscheinen *n*: *public ~* Auftreten *n* in der Öffentlichkeit; *make an ~ on television* im Fernsehen auftreten. **2.** (äußere) Erscheinung, Aussehen *n*, *das* Äußere: *have an unhealthy ~* ungesund aussehen. **3.** *mst pl* (An)Schein *m*: *to all ~(s)* allem Anschein nach; *there is every ~ that* es hat ganz den Anschein, als ob; *~s are deceptive* der Schein trügt; *keep up (od. save) ~s* den Schein wahren.

ap·pease [ə'pi:z] *v/t* besänftigen, beschwichtigen; *Durst etc* stillen, *Neugier* befriedigen. **ap'pease·ment** *s* Besänftigung *f*, Beschwichtigung *f*: (*policy of*) *~* Beschwichtigungspolitik *f*.

ap·pend [ə'pend] *v/t* (**to**) **1.** befestigen, anbringen (*an dat*), anheften (*an acc*). **2.** bei-, hinzufügen (*dat*). **ap'pend·age** *s* Anhang *m*; Anhängsel *n*. **ap·pen·dec·to·my** [ˌæpen'dektəmɪ] *s* ✻ Blinddarmoperation *f*. **ap·pen·di·ci·tis** [əˌpendɪ'saɪtɪs] *s* ✻ Blinddarmentzündung *f*. **ap·pen·dix** [ə'pendɪks] *pl* **-dix·es, -di·ces** [ˌdɪsi:z] *s* **1.** Anhang *m* (*e-s Buchs*). **2.** (**vermiform**) *~ anat.* Wurmfortsatz *m*, Blinddarm *m*.

ap·per·tain [ˌæpə'teɪn] *v/i* gehören (*to* zu).

ap·pe·tite ['æpɪtaɪt] *s* **1.** Appetit *m* (*for* auf *acc*): *give s.o. an ~* j-m Appetit machen; *have an ~* Appetit haben; *take away (od. spoil) s.o.'s ~* j-m den Appetit nehmen *od.* verderben. **2.** (*for*) Verlangen *n* (nach), Lust *f* (zu). **ap·pe·tiz·er** ['ˌtaɪzə] *s* appetitanregendes Mittel *od.* Getränk *od.* Gericht. **'ap·pe·tiz·ing** *adj* □ appetitanregend; appetitlich, lecker (*beide a. fig.*).

ap·plaud [ə'plɔːd] *v/i u. v/t* applaudieren (*dat*), Beifall spenden (*dat*). **ap·plause** [ə'plɔːz] *s* Applaus *m*, Beifall *m*.

ap·ple ['æpl] *s* Apfel *m*: *~ of discord fig.* Zankapfel *m*; *the ~ of s.o.'s eye fig.* j-s Liebling. **'~·cart** *s* Apfelkarren *m*: *upset s.o.'s ~ fig.* j-s Pläne über den Haufen werfen. **'~·jack** *s Am.* Apfelschnaps *m*. **~ pie** *s* gedeckter Apfelkuchen. **'~·pie or·der** *s*: *in ~* F in Butter, in bester Ordnung. **'~·pol·ish** *v/i Am.* F

radfahren. *~ pol·ish·er* *s Am.* F Radfahrer *m*, Speichellecker *m*. **'~·sauce** *s* **1.** Apfelmus *n*. **2.** *Am. sl.* Schmus *m*; Quatsch *m*. *~ tree* *s* Apfelbaum *m*.

ap·pli·ance [ə'plaɪəns] *s* Gerät *n*; *engS.* (elektrisches) Haushaltsgerät.

ap·pli·ca·ble ['æplɪkəbl] *adj* □ (**to**) anwendbar (auf *acc*), passend (für): *be ~* (**to**) → *apply* 4; *not ~* (*in Formularen*) nicht zutreffend. **'ap·pli·cant** *s* Bewerber(in) (*for* um); Antragsteller(in). **ˌap·pli'ca·tion** *s* **1.** (**to**) Anwendung *f* (auf *acc*); Anwendbarkeit *f* (auf *acc*): *have no ~* (**to**) nicht zutreffen (auf *acc*), in keinem Zs.-hang stehen (mit). **2.** (*for*) Gesuch *n* (um), Antrag *m* (auf *acc*): *on ~* auf Ersuchen *od.* Verlangen *od.* Wunsch. **3.** Bewerbung *f* (*for* um): (**letter of**) *~* Bewerbungsschreiben *n*.

ap·plied [ə'plaɪd] *adj* angewandt: *~ linguistics* (**psychology,** *etc*).

ap·ply [ə'plaɪ] **I** *v/t* **1.** (**to**) auflegen, -tragen (auf *acc*), anbringen (an, auf *dat*). **2.** (**to**) verwenden (auf *acc*, für); anwenden (auf *acc*); betätigen: *~ the brakes* bremsen. **3.** *~ one's mind to* sich beschäftigen mit; *~ o.s. to* sich widmen (*dat*). **II** *v/i* **1.** (**to**) zutreffen (auf *acc*), gelten (für). **5.** (*for*) beantragen (*acc*), nachsuchen (um). **6.** sich bewerben (*for* um).

ap·point [ə'pɔɪnt] *v/t* **1.** ernennen *od.* berufen zu: *~ s.o. one's heir* j-n als Erben einsetzen. **2.** festsetzen, bestimmen. **3.** ausstatten, einrichten (**with** mit). **ap'point·ment** *s* **1.** Ernennung *f*, Berufung *f*. **2.** Amt *n*, Stellung *f*: *hold an ~* e-e Stelle innehaben. **3.** Festsetzung *f*, Bestimmung *f*. **4.** Verabredung *f*, (*geschäftlich, beim Arzt etc*) Termin *m*: *by ~* nach Verabredung; *make an ~* e-e Verabredung treffen, e-n Termin ausmachen; *~ book* Terminkalender *m*. **5.** *mst pl* Ausstattung *f*, Einrichtung *f*.

ap·por·tion [ə'pɔːʃn] *v/t* **1.** zuteilen (**to** dat). **2.** (proportional *od.* gerecht) verteilen; *Kosten* umlegen.

ap·po·site ['æpəʊzɪt] *adj* □ passend, angemessen, (*Antwort etc*) treffend.

ap·po·si·tion [ˌæpəʊ'zɪʃn] *s* Beifügung *f*, *ling. a.* Apposition *f*.

ap·prais·al [ə'preɪzl] *s* (Ab)Schätzung *f*, Taxierung *f*. **ap'praise** *v/t* (ab)schätzen, taxieren: *~d value* Schätzwert *m*.

ap·pre·ci·a·ble [ə'pri:ʃəbl] *adj* □ merklich, spürbar. **ap'pre·ci·ate** [~ʃıeıt] **I** *v/t* **1.** (hoch)schätzen, würdigen, zu schätzen *od.* zu würdigen wissen. **2.** Gefallen finden an (*dat*); Sinn haben für. **3.** dankbar sein für. **4.** (richtig) beurteilen *od.* einschätzen. **II** *v/i* **5.** im Wert steigen. **ap,pre·ci'a·tion** *s* **1.** Würdigung *f.* **2.** Sinn *m* (*of*, for für). **3.** Dankbarkeit *f* (*of* für). **4.** (richtige) Beurteilung. **ap·pre·ci·a·tive** [ə'pri:ʃjətıv] *adj* □ würdigend: *be* ~ *of* → *appreciate* I.

ap·pre·hend [,æprı'hend] *v/t* **1.** festnehmen, verhaften. **2.** *fig.* begreifen, erfassen. **3.** *fig.* (be)fürchten. **,ap·pre-'hen·sion** *s* **1.** Festnahme *f,* Verhaftung *f.* **2.** *fig.* Begreifen *n,* Erfassen *n;* Fassungskraft *f.* **3.** *fig.* Besorgnis *f,* oft *pl* Befürchtung *f.* **,ap·pre'hen·sive** *adj* □ besorgt (*for* um; *that* daß): *be* ~ Bedenken haben.

ap·pren·tice [ə'prentıs] **I** *s* Auszubildende *m, f,* Lehrling *m.* **II** *v/t* in die Lehre geben (*to* bei, zu): *be* ~*d to* in der Lehre sein bei. **ap'pren·tice·ship** *s* Lehrzeit *f;* Lehre *f.*

ap·pro ['æprəʊ] *s: on* ~ ✝ F zur Ansicht, zur Probe.

ap·proach [ə'prəʊtʃ] **I** *v/i* **1.** sich nähern, (heran)nahen. **II** *v/t* **2.** sich nähern (*dat*). **3.** *fig.* nahekommen (*dat*), (fast) erreichen. **4.** herangehen an (*acc*), *Aufgabe etc* anpacken. **5.** an *j-n* herantreten, sich an *j-n* wenden; *bsd. b.s.* sich an *j-n* heranmachen. **III** *s* **6.** (Heran)Nahen *n,* Annäherung *f* (*a. fig. to* an *acc*), ✈ Anflug *m.* **7.** Zugang *m:* ~ (*road*) Zufahrtsstraße *f.* **8.** *fig.* (*to*) erster Schritt (zu), (erster) Versuch (*gen*). **9.** Herantreten *n* (*to* an *acc*), *mst pl* Annäherungsversuch *m: make* ~*es to* → *approach* 5. **10.** Methode *f,* Verfahren *n;* Einstellung *f* (*to* zu); Behandlung *f* (*to* e-s *Themas etc*). **ap'proach·a·ble** *adj* zugänglich (*a. fig.*).

ap·pro·ba·tion [,æprəʊ'beıʃn] *s* (amtliche) Billigung, Genehmigung *f.*

ap·pro·pri·ate I *adj* [ə'prəʊprıət] **1.** (*to,* for) passend (zu), geeignet (für, zu). **II** *v/t* [~eıt] **2.** *bsd. parl.* Geld bewilligen, bereitstellen. **3.** sich *et.* aneignen. **ap,pro·pri'a·tion** [~prı'eıʃn] *s* **1.** Bewilligung *f,* Bereitstellung *f.* **2.** Aneignung *f.*

ap·prov·al [ə'pru:vl] *s* **1.** Billigung *f,* Genehmigung *f: on* ~ ✝ zur Ansicht, zur Probe. **2.** Anerkennung *f,* Beifall *m: meet with* ~ Beifall finden. **ap'prove I** *v/t* billigen, genehmigen. **II** *v/i* (*of*) billigen, genehmigen (*acc*), einverstanden sein (mit), zustimmen (*dat*).

ap·prox·i·mate I *adj* [ə'prɒksımət] □ annähernd, ungefähr: ~ *value* Näherungswert *m.* **II** *v/t* [~meıt] sich nähern (*dat*), (*e-m Wert etc*) nähern. **III** *v/i* [~meıt] sich nähern (*to* dat). **ap,prox·i'ma·tion** [~'meıʃn] *s* Annäherung *f* (*to* an *acc*).

ap·pur·te·nance [ə'pɜ:tınəns] *s mst pl* Zubehör *n,* Ausrüstung *f.*

a·pri·cot ['eıprıkɒt] *s* Aprikose *f.*

A·pril ['eıprəl] *s* April *m: in* ~ im April; *make an* ~ *fool of s.o.* j-n in den April schicken.

a·pron ['eıprən] *s* **1.** Schürze *f.* **2.** ✈ (Hallen)Vorfeld *n.* **3.** *thea.* Vorbühne *f.* ~ *strings pl* Schürzenbänder *pl: be tied to one's mother's* (*wife's*) ~ *fig.* an Mutters Schürzenzipfel hängen (unter dem Pantoffel stehen).

apt [æpt] *adj* □ **1.** passend, geeignet. **2.** treffend (*Bemerkung etc*). **3.** neigend, geneigt (*to do* zu tun): *he is* ~ *to believe it* er wird es wahrscheinlich glauben; ~ *to be overlooked* leicht zu übersehen. **4.** (*at*) geschickt (in *dat*), begabt (für). **ap·ti·tude** ['~tıtju:d] *s* **1.** (*for*) Begabung *f* (für), Geschick *n* (in *dat*): ~ *test* Eignungsprüfung *f.* **2.** Neigung *f,* Hang *m* (*for* zu). **3.** Auffassungsgabe *f.*

aq·ua·ma·rine [,ækwəmə'ri:n] *s* **1.** *min.* Aquamarin *m.* **2.** Aquamarinblau *n.*

aq·ua·plan·ing ['ækwə,pleınıŋ] *s mot.* Aquaplaning *n.*

aq·ua·relle [,ækwə'rel] *s* **1.** Aquarell *n.* **2.** Aquarellmalerei *f.* **,aq·ua'rel·list** *s* Aquarellmaler(in).

a·quar·i·um [ə'kweərıəm] *pl* **-i·ums, -i·a** [~ıə] *s* Aquarium *n.*

A·quar·i·us [ə'kweərıəs] *s ast.* Wassermann *m: be* (*an*) ~ Wassermann sein.

a·quat·ic [ə'kwætık] *adj* Wasser...: ~ *plants;* ~ *sports pl* Wassersport *m.*

aq·ue·duct ['ækwıdʌkt] *s* Aquädukt *m, n.*

a·que·ous ['eıkwıəs] *adj* wäßrig, wässerig.

aq·ui·cul·ture ['ækwıkʌltʃə] *s* Hydrokultur *f.*

aq·ui·line ['ækwɪlaɪn] adj Adler..., weitS. a. gebogen: ~ **nose** Adlernase f.

Ar·ab ['ærəb] **I** s **1.** Araber(in). **2.** zo. Araber m (Pferd). **II** adj **3.** arabisch.

ar·a·besque [,~'besk] s Arabeske f.

A·ra·bi·an [ə'reɪbjən] **I** adj arabisch: **The ~ Nights** Tausendundeine Nacht. **II** s → **Arab** I. **Ar·a·bic** ['ærəbɪk] **I** adj arabisch: ~ **numeral** arabische Ziffer. **II** s ling. Arabisch n.

ar·a·ble ['ærəbl] adj pflügbar, anbaufähig: ~ **land** Ackerland n.

ar·bi·ter ['ɑːbɪtə] s **1.** Schiedsrichter m. **2.** Gebieter m (of über acc): **be the ~ of fashion** die Mode bestimmen od. diktieren. **'ar·bi·trar·y** adj □ willkürlich: a) beliebig (a. ℞), b) eigenmächtig. **ar·bi·trate** ['~treɪt] **I** v/t (als Schiedsrichter) entscheiden, schlichten. **II** v/i als Schiedsrichter fungieren. **,ar·bi'tra·tion** s **1.** Schieds(gerichts)verfahren n. **2.** Schiedsspruch m; Schlichtung f: **court of ~** Schiedsgericht n.

ar·bo(u)r ['ɑːbə] s Laube f.

arc [ɑːk] s Bogen m, ℞ a. Arkus m, ½ a. Lichtbogen.

ar·cade [ɑː'keɪd] s Arkade f, Bogen-, Laubengang m.

arch¹ [ɑːtʃ] **I** s **1.** △ Bogen m. **2.** △ überwölbter Gang, Gewölbe n. **3.** Bogen m, Wölbung f: ~ **support** Senkfußeinlage f. **II** v/t **4.** a. ~ **over** überwölben. **5.** wölben, krümmen: ~ **one's back** e-n Buckel machen (bsd. Katze). **III** v/i **6.** sich wölben.

arch² [~] adj □ schalkhaft, schelmisch, spitzbübisch.

arch³ [~] adj Erz...

ar·chae·o·log·i·cal [,ɑːkɪə'lɒdʒɪkl] adj □ bsd. Br. archäologisch. **ar·chae·ol·o·gist** [,~'ɒlədʒɪst] s bsd. Br. Archäologe m. **,ar·chae'ol·o·gy** s bsd. Br. Archäologie f.

ar·cha·ic [ɑː'keɪɪk] adj (~ally) archaisch: a) altertümlich, b) ling. veraltet.

arch·an·gel ['ɑːk,eɪndʒəl] s Erzengel m. **,arch'bish·op** s Erzbischof m. **,arch-'bish·op·ric** [~rɪk] s Erzbistum n.

,arch'duch·ess s Erzherzogin f. **,arch-'duch·y** s Erzherzogtum n. **,arch'duke** s Erzherzog m.

ar·che·o·log·i·cal, etc Am. → **archaeological**, etc.

arch·er ['ɑːtʃə] s **1.** Bogenschütze m. **2.** ♀

ast. Schütze m: **be (an)** ♀ Schütze sein. **'arch·er·y** s Bogenschießen n.

ar·che·type ['ɑːkɪtaɪp] s Archetyp(us) m, Urform f.

ar·chi·pel·a·go [,ɑːkɪ'pelɪgəʊ] pl **-go(e)s** s Archipel m, Inselgruppe f.

ar·chi·tect ['ɑːkɪtekt] s **1.** Architekt(in). **2.** fig. Urheber(in), Schöpfer(in). **,archi'tec·tu·ral** [~tʃərəl] adj □ architektonisch, Bau..., baulich. **'ar·chi·tec-ture** s Architektur f, a. Baustil m.

ar·chive ['ɑːkaɪv] s mst pl Archiv n. **ar·chi·vist** ['ɑːkɪvɪst] s Archivar(in).

'arch·way s △ **1.** Bogengang m. **2.** Bogen m (über e-m Tor etc).

arc·tic ['ɑːktɪk] adj arktisch, nördlich, Polar...: ♀ **Circle** nördlicher Polarkreis; ♀ **Ocean** Nördliches Eismeer. **II** s Arktis f.

ar·dent ['ɑːdənt] adj □ fig. **1.** heiß, feurig, glühend. **2.** leidenschaftlich, heftig. **3.** eifrig, begeistert. **ar·do(u)r** ['ɑːdə] s **1.** Leidenschaft f, Glut f, Feuer n. **2.** Eifer m, Begeisterung f.

ar·du·ous ['ɑːdjʊəs] adj □ schwierig, mühsam, anstrengend.

are [ɑː] du bist, wir (od. sie od. Sie) sind, ihr seid.

a·re·a ['eərɪə] s **1.** (Boden-, Grund)Fläche f. **2.** Gebiet n (a. fig.), Gegend f: ~ **code** teleph. Am. Vorwahl(nummer) f. **3.** fig. Bereich m.

a·re·na [ə'riːnə] s Arena f, fig. a. Schauplatz m.

aren't [ɑːnt] F für **are not**.

Ar·gen·tine ['ɑːdʒəntaɪn], **Ar·gen·tin-e·an** [,~'tɪnɪən] **I** adj argentinisch. **II** s Argentinier(in).

ar·gu·a·ble ['ɑːgjʊəbl] adj □ **1.** zweifelhaft, fraglich. **2.** it is ~ that man kann durchaus die Meinung vertreten, daß. **ar·gue** ['ɑːgjuː] **I** v/i **1.** argumentieren: ~ **for** eintreten für; sprechen für (Sache); ~ **against** Einwände machen gegen; sprechen gegen (Sache). **2.** streiten (with mit; about über acc): **don't** ~! keine Widerrede! **II** v/t **3.** erörtern, diskutieren. **4.** behaupten (that daß). **5.** j-n überreden (into zu): ~ **s.o. out of s.th.** j-n von et. abbringen.

ar·gu·ment ['ɑːgjʊmənt] s **1.** Argument n. **2.** Erörterung f, Diskussion f. **3.** Streitfrage f. **4.** Wortwechsel m, Auseinandersetzung f. **ar·gu·men·ta·tion**

[ˌmenˈteɪʃn] s **1.** Argumentation f, Beweisführung f. **2.** → **argument** 2.

ar·gu·men·ta·tive [ˌˈmentətɪv] adj □ **1.** streitlustig. **2.** strittig, umstritten.

a·ri·a [ˈɑːrɪə] s ♪ Arie f.

ar·id [ˈærɪd] adj dürr, trocken (a. fig.).

a'rid·i·ty s Dürre f, Trockenheit f.

Ar·ies [ˈeəriːz] s ast. Widder m: **be (an) ~** Widder sein.

a·rise [əˈraɪz] v/i (irr) **1. (from, out of)** entstehen, hervorgehen (aus), herrühren, stammen (von). **2.** entstehen, sich erheben, auftauchen. **a·ris·en** [əˈrɪzn] pp von **arise.**

ar·is·to·cra·cy [ˌærɪˈstɒkrəsɪ] s Aristokratie f. **a·ris·to·crat** [ˈæristəkræt] s Aristokrat(in). **ˌa·ris·to'crat·ic, ˌa·ris·to·'crat·i·cal** adj □ aristokratisch.

a·rith·me·tic [əˈrɪθmətɪk] s Arithmetik f, Rechnen n.

ar·ith·met·ic, ar·ith·met·i·cal [ˌærɪθ-ˈmetɪk(l)] adj □ arithmetisch, Rechen...

ark [ɑːk] s: **Noah's ~** Bibl. die Arche Noah.

arm¹ [ɑːm] s **1.** Arm m (a. ⊕ u. fig.): **with open ~s** mit offenen Armen; **within ~'s reach** in Reichweite; **the ~ of the law** der Arm des Gesetzes; **keep s.o. at ~'s length** j-n vom Leibe halten; **take s.o. in one's ~s** j-n in die Arme nehmen. **2.** Fluß-, Meeresarm m. **3.** Ast m. **4.** Arm-, Seitenlehne f (e-s Stuhls etc). **5.** Ärmel m.

arm² [~] I s **1.** mst pl Waffe f (a. fig.): **up in ~s** kampfbereit; fig. in hellem Zorn **(about, over** wegen); **take up ~s** zu den Waffen greifen; **~s control** Rüstungskontrolle f; **~s dealer** Waffenhändler m; **~s race** Wettrüsten n, Rüstungswettlauf m. **2.** ✕ Waffen-, Truppengattung f. **3.** pl Wappen(schild) n. II v/t **4.** bewaffnen. **5.** ~ o.s. fig. sich wappnen **(with** mit).

ar·ma·da [ɑːˈmɑːdə] s (hist. ℃) Armada f.

ar·ma·ment [ˈɑːməmənt] s **1.** Kriegsstärke f. **2.** Bewaffnung f. **3.** Rüstung f: **~ race** Wettrüsten n, Rüstungswettlauf m. **ar·ma·ture** [ˈɑːˌtjʊə] s ⚡ Anker m.

'arm·chair s Lehnstuhl m: **~ politician** Stammtischpolitiker m.

armed [ɑːmd] adj bewaffnet **(to the teeth** bis an die Zähne): **~ conflict** bewaffnete Auseinandersetzung; **~ forces**

pl Streitkräfte pl; **~ robbery** bewaffneter Raubüberfall.

...-armed [ɑːmd] ...armig, mit ... Armen.

arm·ful [ɑːmfʊl] s Armvoll m.

ar·mi·stice [ˈɑːmɪstɪs] s Waffenstillstand m.

ar·mo·ri·al [ɑːˈmɔːrɪəl] adj Wappen...

ar·mour [ˈɑːmə] bsd. Br. I s **1.** Rüstung f, Panzer m (a. zo.). **2.** ✕ Panzer(fahrzeuge) pl; Panzertruppen pl. II v/t **3.** panzern: **~ed car** ✕ Panzerkampfwagen m; gepanzertes Fahrzeug (für Geldtransporte etc). **'~clad, '~plat·ed** adj bsd. Br. gepanzert, Panzer...

ar·mour·y [ˈɑːmərɪ] s bsd. Br. Waffenfabrik f.

'arm|·pit s Achselhöhle f. **'~rest** s Armlehne f.

ar·my [ˈɑːmɪ] s Armee f, Heer n (a. fig.): **be in the ~** beim Militär sein; **join the ~** Soldat werden.

a·ro·ma [əˈrəʊmə] s Aroma n. **ar·o·mat·ic** [ˌærəʊˈmætɪk] adj **(~ally)** aromatisch.

a·rose [əˈrəʊz] pret von **arise.**

a·round [əˈraʊnd] I adv **1.** (rings)herum, überall(hin), nach od. auf allen Seiten. **2.** umher, in (der Gegend) herum: **look ~** sich umsehen; zurückschauen. **3.** F in der Nähe, da. II prp **4.** um (... herum), rund um. **5.** in **(dat)** ... herum. **6.** F ungefähr, etwa. **7.** F (nahe) bei.

a·rouse [əˈraʊz] v/t **1.** (auf)wecken. **2.** fig. auf-, wachrütteln, **Gefühle etc** wachrufen, erregen.

ar·range [əˈreɪndʒ] I v/t **1.** (an)ordnen, aufstellen; **Angelegenheiten** ordnen, regeln. **2.** festsetzen, -legen. **3.** in die Wege leiten, arrangieren. **4.** verabreden, vereinbaren. **5.** Streit schlichten, beilegen. **6.** ♪ arrangieren, a. thea. etc bearbeiten. II v/i **7.** sich verständigen **(with** mit; **about** über acc). **8.** Vorkehrungen treffen **(for, about** für; **to** inf zu inf): **~ for s.th. to be there** dafür sorgen, daß et. da ist. **ar'range·ment** s **1.** (An)Ordnung f. **2.** Festsetzung f. **3.** Verabredung f, Vereinbarung f: **make an ~** e-e Verabredung treffen **(with** mit). **4.** Schlichtung f, Beilegung f. **5.** ♪ Arrangement n, a. thea. etc Bearbeitung f. **6.** pl Vorkehrungen pl: **make ~s** Vorkehrungen treffen.

ar·ray [ə'reɪ] **I** v/t **1.** *Truppen etc* aufstellen. **2.** (*o.s.* sich) kleiden, (heraus)putzen. **II** s **3.** ✗ Schlachtordnung f. **4.** *fig.* Phalanx f, (stattliche) Reihe. **5.** Kleidung f, Staat m.

ar·rear [ə'rɪə] s mst pl Rückstand m, -stände pl: **~s of rent** rückständige Miete; **~s of work** Arbeitsrückstände; **be in ~s** im Rückstand od. Verzug sein (**for, in** mit).

ar·rest [ə'rest] **I** s **1.** Verhaftung f, Festnahme f; Haft f: **be under ~** verhaftet sein; in Haft sein; → **warrant 2. II** v/t **2.** an-, aufhalten, hemmen. **3.** *Aufmerksamkeit etc* fesseln. **4.** verhaften, festnehmen.

ar·riv·al [ə'raɪvl] s **1.** Ankunft f: **'~s' pl** ,Ankunft' (*Fahrplan etc*). **2.** Erscheinen n, Auftauchen n. **3.** Ankömmling m: **new ~** Neuankömmling m, F a. Familienzuwachs m. **ar·rive** [ə'raɪv] v/i **1.** (an)kommen, eintreffen. **2.** erscheinen, auftauchen. **3.** *fig.* (**at**) erreichen (*acc*), kommen od. gelangen (zu).

ar·ro·gance ['ærəgəns] s Arroganz f, Überheblichkeit f. **'ar·ro·gant** adj □ arrogant, überheblich.

ar·row ['ærəʊ] s Pfeil m. '~**head** s Pfeilspitze f.

arse [ɑːs] s Br. V Arsch m (a. fig. contp.). '~**hole** s Br. V Arschloch n (a. fig. contp.).

ar·se·nal ['ɑːsənl] s **1.** Arsenal n (a. fig.). **2.** Waffen-, Munitionsfabrik f.

ar·se·nic ['ɑːsnɪk] s 🜍 Arsen n.

ar·son ['ɑːsn] s ⚖ Brandstiftung f.

art [ɑːt] **I** s **1.** (*bsd.* bildende) Kunst: **work of ~** Kunstwerk n; → **fine**¹ 1. **2.** Kunst(fertigkeit) f: **the ~ of cooking** die hohe Schule des Kochens; **~s and crafts** pl Kunstgewerbe n. **3.** pl univ. Geisteswissenschaften pl: **Faculty of ~s, Am. ~s Department** philosophische Fakultät; → **bachelor** 2, **master** 5. **4.** mst pl Kniff m, Trick m. **II** adj **5.** Kunst...: **~ critic; ~ gallery** Gemäldegalerie f.

ar·te·ri·al [ɑː'tɪərɪəl] adj **1.** anat. arteriell, Arterien... **2.** **~ road**, Am. a. **~ highway** Hauptverkehrsstraße f. **ar·te·ri·o·scle·ro·sis** [ɑː,tɪərɪəʊsklɪə-'rəʊsɪs] s 🖉 Arteriosklerose f, Arterienverkalkung f. **ar·ter·y** ['ɑːtərɪ] s **1.** anat. Arterie f, Schlagader f. **2.**

fig. (Haupt)Verkehrsader f.

ar·te·sian well [ɑː'tiːzjən] s Artesischer Brunnen m.

art·ful ['ɑːtfʊl] adj □ schlau, listig.

ar·thrit·ic [ɑː'θrɪtɪk] adj 🖉 arthritisch. **ar·thri·tis** [ɑː'θraɪtɪs] s Arthritis f, Gelenkentzündung f.

ar·ti·choke ['ɑːtɪtʃəʊk] s 🌿 Artischocke f.

ar·ti·cle ['ɑːtɪkl] **I** s **1.** (*Zeitungs- etc*)Artikel m. **2.** Artikel m, Gegenstand m. **3.** ling. Artikel m, Geschlechtswort n. **4.** Artikel m, Paragraph m, Abschnitt m (*e-s Gesetzes etc*); Punkt m, Klausel f (*e-s Vertrags etc*): **~s** pl **of apprenticeship** Lehrvertrag m; **~s** pl **of association** (Am. **incorporation**) Satzung f (*e-r Aktiengesellschaft*). **II** v/t **5.** in die Lehre geben (**to** bei, zu): **be ~d to** in der Lehre sein bei.

ar·tic·u·late I v/t [ɑː'tɪkjʊleɪt] **1.** artikulieren, deutlich (aus)sprechen. **2.** äußern; zur Sprache bringen. **3.** ⚙ durch Gelenke verbinden. **II** adj [~lət] □ **4.** deutlich ausgesprochen, verständlich (*Wörter etc*). **5.** fähig, sich klar auszudrücken. **ar'tic·u·lat·ed** [~leɪtɪd] adj ⚙ Gelenk...; **~ lorry** mot. Br. Sattelschlepper m. **ar,tic·u'la·tion** s **1.** Artikulation f, deutliche Aussprache. **2.** ⚙ Gelenk(verbindung f) n.

ar·ti·fice ['ɑːtɪfɪs] s **1.** List f. **2.** Kunstgriff m, Kniff m. **ar·ti·fi·cial** [~'fɪʃl] adj □ Kunst..., künstlich: **~ flower** (**insemination, respiration,** *etc*) künstliche Blume (Befruchtung, Beatmung *etc*); **~ person** juristische Person; **~ silk** Kunstseide f; **~ tears** pl falsche Tränen pl.

ar·til·ler·y [ɑː'tɪlərɪ] s Artillerie f. **ar'til·ler·y·man** [~mən] s (*irr man*) Artillerist m.

ar·ti·san [,ɑːtɪ'zæn] s (Kunst)Handwerker m.

art·ist ['ɑːtɪst] s **ar·tiste** [ɑː'tiːst] s Künstler(in), *weitS.* a. Könner(in). **ar·tis·tic, ar·tis·ti·cal** [ɑː'tɪstɪk(l)] adj □ **1.** künstlerisch, Künstler..., Kunst... **2.** kunstverständig.

art·less ['ɑːtlɪs] adj □ **1.** aufrichtig, arglos. **2.** naiv.

art·y ['ɑːtɪ] adj F künstlerisch aufgemacht. ,~**(-and)-'craft·y** adj F gewollt künstlerisch.

Ar·y·an ['ɛərɪən] **I** *adj* arisch. **II** *s* Arier(in).

as [æz] **I** *adv* 1. (eben-, gerade)so: *I ran ~ fast ~ I could* so schnell ich konnte; *just ~ good* ebenso gut; *twice ~ large* zweimal so groß; *~ well* ebenfalls, auch; → *much* 2. 2. wie (z. B.): *statesmen, ~ Churchill.* **II** *cj* 3. (so) wie: *~ follows* wie folgt; *~ requested* wunschgemäß; *~ ... ~* (eben)so ... wie; *(~) soft ~ butter* butterweich; *(~) happy ~ can be* überglücklich; *~ far ~ I know* soviel ich weiß; *~ it were* sozusagen, gleichsam; → *good* 5, *long*¹⁷, *soon, though* 3, *word* 1. 4. als, während: *~ he entered* als er eintrat, bei s-m Eintritt. 5. da, weil: *~ you are sorry, I'll forgive you.* 6. *~ for* (*od. to*) was an... (an)betrifft; *~ from* (*vor Zeitangaben*) von ... an, ab; → *against* 4, *per* 3, *yet* 2. **III** *pron* 7. was, wie: *~ he himself admits.* **IV** *prp* 8. als: *appear ~ Hamlet* als Hamlet auftreten.

as·bes·tos [æs'bestɒs] *s* Asbest *m.*

as·cend [ə'send] **I** *v/i* 1. (auf)steigen. 2. ansteigen. **II** *v/t* 3. *a. fig.* den Thron besteigen. **as'cend·an·cy** *s* Übergewicht *n*, Überlegenheit *f* (*over* über *acc*). **as'cend·ant I** *s* 1. *ast.* Aszendent *m*, Aufgangspunkt *m*: *in the ~ fig.* im Aufstieg *od.* Kommen. **II** *adj* 2. (auf)steigend. 3. überlegen (*over dat*). **as'cend·en·cy, as'cend·ent** → **ascendancy, ascendant.**

as·cen·sion [ə'senʃn] *s* 1. Aufsteigen *n.* 2. *the* ♀ *Christi Himmelfahrt f;* ♀ *Day* Himmelfahrtstag *m.*

as·cent [ə'sent] *s* 1. Aufstieg *m.* 2. Besteigung *f.* 3. Steigung *f,* Gefälle *n.*

as·cer·tain [,æsə'teɪn] *v/t* ermitteln, feststellen, in Erfahrung bringen. **,as·cer'tain·a·ble** *adj* feststellbar. **,as·cer'tain·ment** *s* Ermittlung *f,* Feststellung *f.*

as·cet·ic [ə'setɪk] **I** *adj* (*~ally*) asketisch. **II** *s* Asket(in). **as'cet·i·cism** [~tɪsɪzəm] *s* Askese *f.*

as·cor·bic ac·id [ə'skɔːbɪk] *s* ♣ Ascorbinsäure *f*, Vitamin *n* C.

as·crib·a·ble [ə'skraɪbəbl] *adj* zuzuschreiben(d). **as'cribe** *v/t* (*to*) 1. zurückführen (auf *acc*), zuschreiben (*dat*). 2. zuschreiben, beimessen (*dat*).

a·sep·tic [,eɪ'septɪk] *adj* (*~ally*) aseptisch, keimfrei.

a·sex·u·al [,eɪ'seksʊəl] *adj* □ *biol.* geschlechtslos.

ash¹ [æʃ] *s* 1. ♣ Esche *f.* 2. Eschenholz *n.*

ash² [~] *s* 1. *mst pl* Asche *f:* *burn to* (*od. lay in*) *~es* einäschern, niederbrennen. 2. *pl* Asche *f,* (sterbliche) Überreste *pl.*

a·shamed [ə'ʃeɪmd] *adj* beschämt: *be* (*od. feel*) *~ of* sich e-r *Sache od. j-s* schämen; *be ~ of o.s.* sich schämen; *be* (*od. feel*) *~ to do* (*of doing*) *s.th.* sich schämen, et. zu tun.

ash| bin, ~ can *s Am.* 1. Abfall-, Mülleimer *m.* 2. Abfall-, Mülltonne *f.*

ash·en¹ ['æʃn] *adj* eschen, aus Eschenholz.

ash·en² [~] *adj* 1. Aschen... 2. aschfarben. 3. aschgrau, -fahl.

a·shore [ə'ʃɔː] *adv u. adj* am *od.* ans Ufer: *go ~* an Land gehen.

'ash|·pan *s* Asche(n)kasten *m.* **'~·tray** *s* Aschenbecher *m.* ♀ **Wednes·day** *s* Aschermittwoch *m.*

ash·y ['æʃɪ] *adj* 1. Aschen... 2. mit Asche bedeckt. 3. → *ashen²* 3, → *ashen²* 2, 3.

A·sian ['eɪʃn], **A·si·at·ic** [,eɪʃɪ'ætɪk] **I** *adj* asiatisch. **II** *s* Asiat(in).

a·side [ə'saɪd] **I** *adv* 1. beiseite, auf die Seite: *step ~* zur Seite treten. 2. *~ from bsd. Am.* abgesehen von. **II** *s* 3. *thea.* Aparte *n.*

as·i·nine ['æsɪnaɪn] *adj* 1. Esels... 2. *fig.* eselhaft, dumm.

ask [ɑːsk] **I** *v/t* 1. *j-n* fragen. 2. *j-n* fragen nach, sich bei *j-m* nach *et.* erkundigen: *~ s.o. the way; ~ s.o. a question* j-m e-e Frage stellen, j-n *et.* fragen. 3. bitten um, *et.* erbitten: *~ advice;* → *favo(u)r* 4. 4. *j-n* bitten, fragen (*for* um): *~ s.o. for advice.* 5. einladen; bitten: *~ s.o. to dinner* j-n zum Essen einladen; *~ s.o. in* j-n hereinbitten; *~ s.o. out* j-n ausführen. 6. verlangen, fordern (*of* von): *~ a high price for s.th.; that is ~ing too much* das ist zuviel verlangt. **II** *v/i* 7. fragen, sich erkundigen (*for, about, after* nach): *~ for s.o. a.* j-n *od.* nach j-m verlangen, j-n zu sprechen wünschen; *~ around* herumfragen, sich umhören. 8. bitten (*for* um): *he ~ed for it* (*od. trouble*) F er wollte es ja so haben.

a·skance [ə'skæns] *adv:* *look ~ at s.o.* j-n von der Seite ansehen; *fig.* j-n schief *od.* mißtrauisch ansehen.

a·skew [ə'skjuː] *adv* 1. schief: *go ~ fig.*

schiefgehen. **2. look ~ at s.o.** j-n verächtlich ansehen.

ask·ing ['ɑːskɪŋ] *s* Fragen *n*, Bitten *n*: **to be had for the ~** umsonst *od.* leicht zu haben sein.

a·slant [ə'slɑːnt] **I** *adv u. adj* schräg, quer. **II** *prp* quer über (*acc*) *od.* durch.

a·sleep [ə'sliːp] *adv u. adj* schlafend, (*Fuß etc*) eingeschlafen: **be ~** schlafen; **drop** (*od. fall*) **~** einschlafen.

as·par·a·gus [ə'spærəgəs] *s* ♀ Spargel *m*: **~ tips** *pl* Spargelspitzen *pl.*

as·pect ['æspekt] *s* **1.** Aussehen *n*, Erscheinung *f*. **2.** Aspekt *m* (*a. ling.*), Seite *f*, Gesichtspunkt *m*. **3.** Beziehung *f*, Hinsicht *f*.

as·pen ['æspən] *s* ♀ Espe *f*: **tremble like an ~ leaf** wie Espenlaub zittern.

as·per·i·ty [æ'sperəti] *s* **1.** Rauheit *f* (*a. fig.*), Unebenheit *f*. **2.** *fig.* Schärfe *f*, Schroffheit *f*.

as·perse [ə'spɜːs] *v/t* verleumden. **as'per·sion** *s* Verleumdung *f*: **cast ~s on** verleumden.

as·phalt ['æsfælt] **I** *s* Asphalt *m*. **II** *v/t* asphaltieren.

as·phyx·i·a [əs'fɪksɪə] *s* ✲ Erstickung(stod *m*) *f* (*a. ling.*). **as'phyx·i·ate** [~eɪt] *v/t u. v/i* ersticken: **be ~d** ersticken. **as,phyx·i'a·tion** *s* Erstickung *f*.

as·pic ['æspɪk] *s* Aspik *m*, Gelee *n*.

as·pir·ant [ə'spaɪərənt] *s* (**to, after, for**) Bewerber(in) (um *acc*), Anwärter(in) (auf *acc*). **as·pi·ra·tion** [,æspə'reɪʃn] *s* Streben *n*, Bestrebung *f* (**for, after** nach). **as·pire** [ə'spaɪə] *v/i* streben, trachten (**to, after** nach): **~ to** (*od. after*) **s.th.** *a.* et. erstreben.

as·pi·rin ['æspərɪn] *s pharm.* Aspirin *n*.

as·pir·ing [ə'spaɪərɪŋ] *adj* □ **1.** ehrgeizig, strebsam. **2.** auf-, emporstrebend.

ass¹ [æs] *s zo.* Esel *m* (*a. fig.*): **make an ~ of o.s.** sich lächerlich machen *od.* blamieren.

ass² [~], **'~·hole** *Am.* ∨ → **arse, arse·hole.**

as·sail [ə'seɪl] *v/t* **1.** angreifen. **2.** *fig.* bestürmen (**with** mit *Fragen etc*): **~ed by fear** von Furcht gepackt. **3.** *Aufgabe etc* in Angriff nehmen. **as'sail·a·ble** *adj* angreifbar. **as'sail·ant** *s* Angreifer *m.*

as·sas·sin [ə'sæsɪn] *s* (*bsd.* politischer) Mörder, Attentäter *m.* **as'sas·si·nate**

[~neɪt] *v/t bsd. pol.* ermorden: **be ~d** e-m Attentat zum Opfer fallen. **as,sas·si'na·tion** *s* (**of**) (*bsd.* politischer) Mord, Ermordung *f* (*gen*), Attentat *n* (auf *acc*).

as·sault [ə'sɔːlt] **I** *s* **1.** Angriff *m* (**on** auf *acc*) (*a. fig.*). **2.** ✗ Sturm *m*: **take by ~** im Sturm nehmen, erstürmen. **3.** *a.* **~ and battery** 🕱 tätliche Beleidigung: **criminal** (*od. indecent*) **~** unzüchtige Handlung (*unter Gewaltandrohung od. -anwendung*). **II** *v/t* **4.** angreifen (*a. fig.*). **5.** ✗ stürmen. **6.** 🕱 tätlich beleidigen. **7.** *euphem.* vergewaltigen.

as·say [ə'seɪ] **I** *s* **1.** Prüfung *f*, Untersuchung *f*. **II** *v/t* **2.** Metall etc prüfen, untersuchen. **3.** *fig.* versuchen, probieren.

as·sem·blage [ə'semblɪdʒ] *s* **1.** Ansammlung *f*. **2.** Versammlung *f*. **3.** ⚙ Montage *f*. **as'sem·ble I** *v/t* **1.** versammeln. **2.** ⚙ montieren, zs.-setzen. **II** *v/i* **3.** sich versammeln. **as'sem·bler** *s* ⚙ Monteur *m.* **as'sem·bly** *s* **1.** Versammlung *f*. **2.** ⚙ Montage *f*: **~ line** Fließband *n*; **~ shop** Montagehalle *f*.

as·sent [ə'sent] **I** *v/i* (**to**) **1.** zustimmen, beipflichten (*dat*). **2.** billigen, genehmigen (*acc*). **II** *s* **3.** Zustimmung *f*, Beipflichtung *f*: **by common ~** mit allgemeiner Zustimmung. **4.** Billigung *f*, Genehmigung *f*.

as·sert [ə'sɜːt] *v/t* **1.** behaupten, erklären. **2.** *Anspruch etc* geltend machen, bestehen auf (*dat*). **3. ~ o.s.** sich behaupten *od.* durchsetzen; sich zu viel anmaßen. **as'ser·tion** *s* **1.** Behauptung *f*, Erklärung *f*: **make an ~** e-e Behauptung aufstellen. **2.** Geltendmachung *f*. **as'ser·tive** *adj* □ **1.** ausdrücklich. **2.** anmaßend.

as·sess [ə'ses] *v/t* **1.** *Geldstrafe etc* festsetzen. **2.** *Einkommen etc* (zur Steuer) veranlagen (**at** mit). **3.** *fig.* ab-, einschätzen, (be)werten. **as'sess·ment** *s* **1.** Festsetzung *f*. **2.** (Steuer)Veranlagung *f*. **3.** Steuer(betrag *m*) *f*. **4.** *fig.* Ab-, Einschätzung *f*, (Be)Wertung *f*: **what is your ~ of ...?** wie beurteilen Sie ... (*acc*)?

as·set ['æset] *s* **1.** ✝ Aktivposten *m*; *pl* Aktiva *pl*: **~s and liabilities** Aktiva u. Passiva. **2.** *pl* 🕱 Vermögen(smasse *f*) *n*; Konkursmasse *f*. **3.** *fig.* Vorzug *m*,

Plus *n*; Gewinn *m* (**to** für): **be a great ~** viel wert sein.

as·si·du·i·ty [ˌæsɪˈdjuːətɪ] *s* Fleiß *m*, Eifer *m*. **as·sid·u·ous** [əˈsɪdjʊəs] *adj* □ fleißig, eifrig.

as·sign [əˈsaɪn] *v/t* **1.** *Aufgabe etc* zu-, anweisen, zuteilen (**to** *dat*). **2.** (**to**) *j-n* bestimmen, einteilen (zu, für *e-e Aufgabe etc*), beauftragen (mit). **3.** *Zeitpunkt etc* bestimmen, festsetzen. **4.** *et.* zuschreiben (**to** *dat*). **5.** ⚖ abtreten, übertragen (**to** *dat*). **as·sign·ment** *s* **1.** Zu-, Anweisung *f* (**to** an *acc*). **2.** Bestimmung *f*, Festsetzung *f*. **3.** Aufgabe *f*, Arbeit *f* (*beide a. ped.*), Auftrag *m*. **4.** ⚖ Abtretung *f*, Übertragung *f* (**to** an *acc*).

as·sim·i·late [əˈsɪmɪleɪt] **I** *v/t* **1.** assimilieren: a) angleichen (*a. ling.*), anpassen (**to, with** *dat*, an *acc*), b) *biol.* (sich) *Nahrung* einverleiben, *v) sociol.* aufnehmen. **II** *v/i* **2.** sich angleichen *od.* anpassen (**to, with** *dat*). **3.** *biol., sociol.* sich assimilieren. **as·sim·i·la·tion** *s* **1.** Assimilierung *f*: a) Angleichung *f*, Anpassung *f* (**to** an *acc*), b) *biol.* Einverleibung *f*.

as·sist [əˈsɪst] **I** *v/t* **1.** *j-m* helfen, beistehen, *j-n* unterstützen: **~** *s.o.* **in doing s.th.** *j-m* (dabei) helfen, et. zu tun. **II** *v/i* **2.** mithelfen, Hilfe leisten (**in** bei). **3.** (**at**) beiwohnen (*dat*), teilnehmen (an *dat*). **as·sist·ance** *s* Hilfe *f*, Beistand *m*, Unterstützung *f*: **come to s.o.'s ~** *j-m* zu Hilfe kommen. **as·sist·ant I** *adj* **1.** stellvertretend: **~** *editor* Redaktionsassistent *m*; **~** *professor univ. Am.* (*etwa*) Lehrbeauftragte *m, f*. **II** *s* **2.** Assistent(in), Mitarbeiter(in). **3.** Angestellte *m, f*: (*shop*) **~** *Br.* Verkäufer(in).

as·so·ci·ate [əˈsəʊʃɪeɪt] **I** *v/t* **1.** vereinigen, -binden, zs.-schließen (**with** mit): **~** *o.s.* **with** *a.* sich *e-r Partei, j-s Ansichten etc* anschließen. **2.** *bsd. psych.* assoziieren, (gedanklich) verbinden (**with** mit). **II** *v/i* **3.** sich vereinigen *etc*, → **1. 4.** verkehren (**with** mit). **III** *adj* [~ʃɪət] **5.** verwandt (**with** mit). **6.** beigeordnet, Mit...: **~** *editor* Mitherausgeber *m*. **7.** außerordentlich (*Mitglied*). **IV** *s* [~ʃɪət] **8.** ⚖ Teilhaber *m*, Gesellschafter *m*. **9.** Gefährte *m*, Genosse *m*. **10.** außerordentliches Mitglied. **as·so·ci·a·tion** [əˌsəʊsɪˈeɪʃn] *s* **1.** Vereinigung *f*, -bindung *f*, Zs.-schluß *m*: **in ~ with** zusam-

men mit. **2.** Verein(igung *f*) *m*. **3.** ⚽ Genossenschaft *f*, (Handels)Gesellschaft *f*, Verband *m*: **~** *football Br.* Fußball *m*. **4.** Umgang *m*, Verkehr *m*. **5.** *psych.* (Ideen-, Gedanken)Assoziation *f*, Gedankenverbindung *f*.

as·sort·ed [əˈsɔːtɪd] *adj* **1.** sortiert, geordnet. **2.** zs.-gestellt, gemischt, verschiedenartig. **as·sort·ment** *s bsd.* ⚽ (**of**) Sortiment *n* (von), Auswahl *f* (an *dat*).

as·sume [əˈsjuːm] *v/t* **1.** annehmen, voraussetzen: *assuming that* angenommen *od.* vorausgesetzt, daß. **2.** *Amt, Verantwortung etc* übernehmen. **3.** *Eigenschaft, Gestalt etc* annehmen. **4.** sich *Recht etc* anmaßen. **as·sum·ing** *adj* □ anmaßend. **as·sump·tion** [əˈsʌmpʃn] *s* **1.** Annahme *f*, Voraussetzung *f*: **on the ~ that** in der Annahme *od.* unter der Voraussetzung, daß. **2.** Übernahme *f*. **3.** Anmaßung *f*. **4.** ♀ (*Day*) *eccl.* Mariä Himmelfahrt *f*.

as·sur·ance [əˈʃɔːrəns] *s* **1.** Ver-, Zusicherung *f*. **2.** *bsd. Br.* (Lebens)Versicherung *f*. **3.** Sicherheit *f*, Gewißheit *f*. **4.** Selbstsicherheit *f*; *b.s.* Dreistigkeit *f*.

as·sure [əˈʃɔː] *v/t* **1.** *j-m* versichern (*that* daß): **~** *s.o.* **of s.th.** *j-m* et. zusichern. **2.** sichern, sicherstellen, bürgen für. **3.** überzeugen (**of** von): **~** *o.s.* *a.* sich vergewissern (**of** *gen*). **4.** beruhigen. **5.** *bsd. Br.* Leben versichern: **~** *one's life with* *e-e* Lebensversicherung abschließen bei. **as·sured I** *adj* **1.** (**of**) überzeugt (von), sicher (*gen*): *you can rest ~ that* Sie können sicher sein *od.* sich darauf verlassen, daß. **2.** gesichert. **3.** selbstsicher; *b.s.* dreist. **II** *s* **4.** *bsd. Br.* Versicherte *m, f*. **as·sur·ed·ly** [~rɪdlɪ] *adv* ganz gewiß.

as·ter [ˈæstə] *s* ♣ Aster *f*.

as·ter·isk [ˈæstərɪsk] *s typ.* Sternchen *n*.

a·stern [əˈstɜːn] *adv* ♣ achtern.

asth·ma [ˈæsmə] *s* ♥ Asthma *n*. **asth·mat·ic** [~ˈmætɪk] **I** *adj* (*~ally*) asthmatisch: **~** *attack* Asthmaanfall *m*; **be ~** Asthma haben. **II** *s* Asthmatiker(in).

a·stig·ma·tism [əˈstɪgmətɪzəm] *s* ♣, *phys.* Astigmatismus *m*.

as·ton·ish [əˈstɒnɪʃ] *v/t* in Erstaunen setzen: **be ~ed** erstaunt *od.* überrascht sein (*at* über *acc*; *to inf* zu *inf*), sich wundern (*at* über *acc*). **as·ton·ish·ing**

attach

adj □ erstaunlich. **as'ton·ish·ment** *s* (Er)Staunen *n*, Verwunderung *f*: **to one's ~** zu s-r Verwunderung.

as·tound [ə'staund], **as'tound·ing** → **astonish, astonishing**.

a·stray [ə'streı] *adv*: **go ~** vom Weg abkommen; *fig.* auf Abwege geraten; **lead ~** *fig.* irreführen.

as·trin·gent [ə'strındʒənt] **I** *adj* □ **1.** ✝ adstringierend, zs.-ziehend. **2.** *fig.* streng, hart. **II** *s* **3.** ✝ Adstringens *n*.

as·trol·o·ger [ə'strɒlədʒə] *s* Astrologe *m*. **as·tro·log·i·cal** [,æstrə'lɒdʒıkl] *adj* □ astrologisch. **as·trol·o·gy** [ə'strɒlədʒı] *s* Astrologie *f*.

as·tro·naut ['æstrənɔːt] *s* Astronaut *m*. **'as·tro·naut·ess** *s* Astronautin *f*. **,as·tro'nau·tics** *s pl (mst sg konstruiert)* Raumfahrt *f*.

as·tron·o·mer [ə'strɒnəmə] *s* Astronom *m*. **as·tro·nom·i·cal** [,æstrə'nɒmıkl] *adj* □ astronomisch. **as·tron·o·my** [ə'strɒnəmı] *s* Astronomie *f*.

as·tute [ə'stjuːt] *adj* □ **1.** scharfsinnig. **2.** schlau, gerissen. **as'tute·ness** *s* **1.** Scharfsinn *m*. **2.** Schlauheit *f*.

a·sun·der [ə'sʌndə] *adv* auseinander, entzwei.

a·sy·lum [ə'saıləm] *s* **1.** Asyl *n*: a) Zufluchtsort *m*, b) *fig.* Zuflucht *f*. **2.** (politisches) Asyl: **ask for ~** um Asyl bitten *od.* nachsuchen; **give s.o. ~** j-m Asyl gewähren; **~ seeker** Asylant(in), Asylbewerber(in).

a·sym·met·ric [,eısı'metrık], **,a·sym'met·ri·cal** *adj* □ asymmetrisch, ungleichmäßig. **a·sym·me·try** [,eı'sımıtrı] *s* Asymmetrie *f*, Ungleichmäßigkeit *f*.

at [æt] *prp* **1.** (*Ort*) in (*dat*), an (*dat*), bei, auf (*dat*): **~ a ball** auf e-m Ball; **~ the baker's** beim Bäcker; **~ the door** an der Tür. **2.** (*Richtung*) auf (*acc*), nach, gegen, zu: **he threw a stone ~ the door** er warf e-n Stein gegen die Tür. **3.** (*Beschäftigung*) bei, beschäftigt mit, in (*dat*): **he is still ~ it** er ist noch dabei *od.* damit beschäftigt. **4.** (*Art u. Weise, Zustand*) in (*dat*) bei, zu, unter (*dat*): **~ all** überhaupt; **not ~ all** überhaupt *od.* gar nicht; **not ~ all!** F nichts zu danken!; **nothing ~ all** keinerlei Zweifel. **5.** (*Preis, Wert etc*) für, um: **~ 6 dollars**. **6.**

(*Zeit, Alter*) um, bei: **~ 21** mit 21 (Jahren); **~ 3 o'clock** um 3 Uhr; **~ his death** bei s-m Tod.

ate [et] *pret von* **eat**.

a·the·ism ['eıθıızəm] *s* Atheismus *m*. **'a·the·ist** *s* Atheist(in). **,a·the'is·tic**, **,a·the'is·ti·cal** *adj* □ atheistisch.

ath·lete ['æθliːt] *s* **1.** Athlet *m*: a) Sportler *m*, b) Kraftmensch *m*. **2.** *Br.* Leichtathlet *m*. **ath·let·ic** [æθ'letık] *adj* (**~ally**) **1.** athletisch: a) Sport...: **~ field** Sportplatz *m*, b) von athletischem Körperbau. **2.** *Br.* leichtathletisch. **II** *s pl* **3.** (*a. sg konstruiert*) Sport *m*. **4.** (*mst sg konstruiert*) *Br.* Leichtathletik *f*.

at-home [ət'həʊm] *s* zwangloser Empfang: **give an ~.**

a·thwart [ə'θwɔːt] **I** *adv* quer. **II** *prp* (quer) über (*acc*) *od.* durch.

At·lan·tic [ət'læntık] *adj* atlantisch.

at·las ['ætləs] *s* Atlas *m* (*Buch*).

at·mos·phere ['ætməˌsfıə] *s* Atmosphäre *f* (*a. fig.*). **at·mos·pher·ic** [,~'ferık] **I** *adj* (**~ally**) atmosphärisch. **II** *s pl* atmosphärische Störungen *pl.*

at·oll ['ætɒl] *s* Atoll *n*.

at·om ['ætəm] *s phys.* Atom *n* (*a. fig.*): **not an ~ of truth** kein Körnchen Wahrheit; **~ bomb** Atombombe *f*. **a·tom·ic** [ə'tɒmık] *adj* (**~ally**) atomar, Atom...: **~ age** Atomzeitalter *n*; **~ bomb** Atombombe *f*; **~ energy** Atomenergie *f*; **~ nucleus** Atomkern *m*; **~ pile** Atomreaktor *m*; **~ power** Atomkraft *f*; **~powered** mit Atomkraft betrieben, Atom...; **~ power plant** Atomkraftwerk *n*; **~ research** Atomforschung *f*; **~ waste** Atommüll *m*; **~ weight** Atomgewicht *n*. **at·om·ize** ['ætəʊmaız] *v/t* **1.** atomisieren. **2.** Flüssigkeit zerstäuben. **'at·om·iz·er** *s* Zerstäuber *m* (*Gerät*).

a·tone [ə'təʊn] *v/i*: **~ for** büßen für *et.*, *et.* sühnen. **a'tone·ment** *s* Buße *f*, Sühne *f*.

a·top [ə'tɒp] **I** *adv* oben(auf). **II** *prp a.* **~ of** (oben) auf (*dat*).

a·tro·cious [ə'trəʊʃəs] *adj* □ scheußlich, gräßlich (*beide a.* F). **a·troc·i·ty** [ə'trɒsətı] *s* **1.** Scheußlichkeit *f*, Gräßlichkeit *f*. **2.** Greueltat *f*.

at·ro·phy ['ætrəfı] ✝ **I** *s* Atrophie *f*, Verkümmerung *f* (*a. fig.*). **II** *v/i* verkümmern (*a. fig.*).

at·tach [ə'tætʃ] **I** *v/t* **1.** (**to**) befestigen, anbringen (an *dat*), anheften, ankleben (an *acc*). **2. (to)** *fig. Sinn etc* verbinden (*mit*); *Wert, Wichtigkeit etc* beimessen (*dat*); *magische Kräfte etc* zuschreiben (*dat*); *Bedingungen* knüpfen (an *acc*). **3.** *fig.* ~ **o.s.** sich anschließen (**to** *dat* od. an *acc*): **be ~ed to s.o.** an j-m hängen. **4.** *fig.* **(to)** zuteilen (*dat*), ✗ *a.* abkommandieren (zu). **5.** 🛇 *j-n* verhaften; *et.* beschlagnahmen; pfänden. **II** *v/i* **6. (to)** anhaften (*dat*), verknüpft od. verbunden sein mit.

at·ta·ché [ə'tæʃeɪ] *s* Attaché *m*: ~ **case** Aktentasche *f*, -koffer *m*.

at·tach·ment [ə'tætʃmənt] *s* **1.** Befestigung *f*. **2.** Anhängsel *n*, Beiwerk *n*; ⊘ Zusatzgerät *n*. **3.** *fig.* **(to)** Anhänglichkeit *f* (an *acc*); Bindung *f* (an *acc*). **4.** 🛇 Verhaftung *f*; Beschlagnahme *f*; Pfändung *f*.

at·tack [ə'tæk] **I** *v/t* **1.** (*a. v/i*) *allg.* angreifen. **2.** *fig. Arbeit etc* in Angriff nehmen, über *e-e Mahlzeit etc* herfallen. **II** *s* **3.** Angriff *m*. **4.** 🞄 Anfall *m*. **at'tack·er** *s* Angreifer *m*.

at·tain [ə'teɪn] *v/t* (*u. v/i* ~ **to**) *Ziel etc* erreichen, erlangen. **at'tain·a·ble** *adj* erreichbar. **at'tain·ment** *s* **1.** Erreichung *f*, Erlangung *f*. **2.** *pl* Kenntnisse *pl*, Fertigkeiten *pl*.

at·tempt [ə'tempt] **I** *v/t* **1.** versuchen (**to do, doing** zu tun): **~ed suicide** Selbstmordversuch *m*. **2.** sich machen *od.* wagen an (*acc*), in Angriff nehmen. **II** *v/i* **3.** Versuch *m* (**to do, doing** zu tun): **~ at explanation** Erklärungsversuch; **~s** *pl* **at resuscitation** 🞄 Wiederbelebungsversuche *pl*. **4.** Anschlag *m*: **an ~ on s.o.'s life** ein Mordanschlag *od.* Attentat auf j-n.

at·tend [ə'tend] **I** *v/t* **1.** *Kranke* pflegen; (ärztlich) behandeln. **2.** *fig.* begleiten: **~ed with** (*od. by*) verbunden mit. **3.** teilnehmen an (*dat*), *Schule, Versammlung etc* besuchen. **II** *v/i* **4. (to)** beachten (*acc*), achten auf (*acc*). **5. (to)** sich kümmern (um); erledigen (*acc*). **6.** ~ **to** *j-n* (*im Laden*) bedienen: **are you being ~ed to** werden Sie schon bedient? **7.** anwesend sein; erscheinen. **8.** ~ **on** *j-n* bedienen. **at'tend·ance** *s* **1.** Dienst *m*, Bereitschaft *f*: **physician in ~** diensthabender Arzt; **hours** *pl* **of ~** Dienststunden *pl*. **2.** Pflege *f* (**on** *gen*), Dienstlei-

stung *f*: **be in ~ on** → **attend** 1. **3.** Anwesenheit *f*, Erscheinen *n*: ~ **list** (*od.* **record**) Anwesenheitsliste *f*. **4.** Besucher *pl*, Teilnehmer *pl*; Besuch(erzahl *f*) *m*, Beteiligung *f*. **at'tend·ant I** *adj* **1.** begleitend. **2.** *fig.* verbunden (**on** mit): ~ **circumstances** *pl* Begleitumstände *pl*. **3.** anwesend. **II** *s* **4.** Begleiter(in). **5.** Aufseher(in). **6.** *pl* Dienerschaft *f*.

at·ten·tion [ə'tenʃn] *s* **1.** Aufmerksamkeit *f* (*a. fig.*): **attract** ~ Aufmerksamkeit erregen; **call** (*od.* **draw**) ~ **to** die Aufmerksamkeit lenken auf (*acc*), aufmerksam machen auf (*acc*); **pay** ~ **to** Beachtung schenken (*dat*), achtgeben auf (*acc*); **(for the)** ~ **of** zu Händen von (*od. gen*). **2. give (prompt)** ~ **to s.th.** et. (rasch) erledigen. **3.** ~! ✗ Achtung!; stillgestanden! **at'ten·tive** *adj* □ aufmerksam (**to** auf *acc*; *fig.* gegen).

at·ten·u·ate [ə'tenjoeɪt] *v/t* **1.** *bsd.* 🞄 verdünnen. **2.** *fig.* vermindern, (ab)schwächen.

at·test [ə'test] *v/t* **1.** beglaubigen, bescheinigen. **2.** zeugen von, bestätigen. **at·tes·ta·tion** [ˌæte'steɪʃn] *s* **1.** Beglaubigung *f*, Bescheinigung *f*. **2.** Zeugnis *n*.

at·tic ['ætɪk] *s* Dachgeschoß *n*; Dachstube *f*, -kammer *f*.

at·tire [ə'taɪə] *v/t* (be)kleiden. **II** *s* Kleidung *f*, Gewand *n*.

at·ti·tude ['ætɪtjuːd] *s* **1.** (Körper)Haltung *f*, Stellung *f*. **2.** *fig.* Haltung *f*: a) Verhalten *n*, b) Einstellung *f* (**to, toward[s]** zu, gegenüber): **what is your ~ to ...?** wie stehen Sie zu ...?

at·tor·ney [ə'tɜːnɪ] *s* 🛇 **1.** *bsd. Am.* ~ (**at law**) (Rechts)Anwalt *m*; ~ (**in fact**) Bevollmächtigte *m*. **2. (power of)** ~ Vollmacht *f*; ~ **gen·er·al** *pl* ~ **gen·er·al,** **gen·er·als** *s* 🛇 **1.** *Br.* erster Kronanwalt. **2.** *Am.* Justizminister *m*.

at·tract [ə'trækt] *v/t* **1.** *phys.* anziehen (*a. fig.*). **2.** *fig. j-n* anlocken, reizen, *j-s Interesse, Blicke etc* auf sich ziehen: **be ~ed to** sich hingezogen fühlen zu; → **attention** 1. **at'trac·tion** [~kʃn] *s* **1.** *phys.* Anziehung(skraft) *f*. **2.** *fig.* a) Anziehungskraft *f*, Reiz *m*: **have ~ little ~ for** wenig anziehend sein für, b) Attraktion *f*, *thea. etc* Zugnummer *f*. **at'trac·tive** *adj* □ **1.** *phys.* anziehend: ~ **force** (*od.* **power**) Anziehungskraft *f*. **2.** *fig.* attraktiv: a) anziehend, reizvoll,

b) einnehmend (*Äußeres etc*), c) zugkräftig (*Angebot etc*).

at·trib·ute I v/t [ə'trɪbjuːt] **1.** zuschreiben (**to** *dat*). **2.** zurückführen (**to** auf *acc*). **II** s ['ætrɪbjuːt] **3.** Attribut n (*a. ling.*): a) Eigenschaft f, Merkmal n, b) (Kenn)Zeichen n. **at·trib·u·tive** [ə'trɪb-jʊtɪv] *ling.* **I** *adj* □ attributiv. **II** s Attribut n.

at·tri·tion [ə'trɪʃn] s **1.** Abnutzung f, Verschleiß m (*beide a. fig.*). **2.** *fig.* Zermürbung f.

au·burn ['ɔːbən] *adj* kastanienbraun (*Haar*).

auc·tion ['ɔːkʃn] **I** s Auktion f, Versteigerung f: **sell** (**buy**) **by** (*Am.* **at**) ~ versteigern (ersteigern); **sale by** (*Am.* **at**) ~ **sale** Versteigerung f. **II** v/t mst ~ **off** versteigern. **auc·tion·eer** [ˌɔːkʃə'nɪə] s Auktionator m, Versteigerer m: ~**s** pl Auktionshaus n.

au·da·cious [ɔː'deɪʃəs] *adj* □ **1.** kühn, verwegen. **2.** dreist, unverfroren. **au·dac·i·ty** [ɔː'dæsətɪ] s **1.** Kühnheit f, Verwegenheit f. **2.** Dreistigkeit f, Unverfrorenheit f.

au·di·ble ['ɔːdəbl] *adj* □ hörbar, vernehmlich.

au·di·ence ['ɔːdjəns] s **1.** Audienz f (**of**, **with** bei). **2.** Publikum n: a) Zuhörer(schaft f) pl, b) Zuschauer pl, c) Besucher pl, d) Leser(kreis m) pl.

au·di·o|·phile ['ɔːdɪəʊfaɪl] s Hi-Fi-Fan m. **'~·typ·ist** s Phonotypistin f. **~·'vis·u·al I** *adj* □ audiovisuell: ~ **aids** ~ II. **II** s pl audiovisuelle Unterrichtsmittel pl.

au·dit ['ɔːdɪt] ✝ **I** s Buch-, Rechnungsprüfung f. **II** v/t prüfen.

au·di·tion [ɔː'dɪʃn] s **1.** *physiol.* Hörvermögen n, Gehör n. **2.** ♩, *thea.* Vorspiel(en) n; Vorsingen n; Vorsprechen n; Anhörprobe f. **II** v/t u. v/i **3.** ♩, *thea.* vorspielen *od.* vorsingen *od.* vorsprechen (lassen).

au·di·tor ['ɔːdɪtə] s **1.** ✝ Buch-, Rechnungsprüfer m. **2.** *univ. Am.* Gasthörer(in).

au·di·to·ri·um [ˌɔːdɪ'tɔːrɪəm] pl **-ri·ums**, **-ri·a** [~ə] s **1.** Auditorium n, Zuhörer-, Zuschauerraum m. **2.** *Am.* Vortragssaal m, Konzerthalle f.

aug·ment [ɔːg'ment] **I** v/t vermehren, steigern, *Gehalt etc* aufbessern. **II** v/i

sich vermehren, zunehmen. **‚aug·men·'ta·tion** s Vermehrung f, Zunahme f; Aufbesserung f.

au·gur ['ɔːgə] **I** v/t vorher-, weissagen. **II** v/i: ~ **well** (**ill**) ein gutes (schlechtes) Zeichen sein (**for** für). **au·gu·ry** ['ɔːgjʊrɪ] s Vorzeichen n.

Au·gust ['ɔːgəst] s August m: **in** ~ im August.

auld lang syne [ˌɔːldlæŋ'saɪn] *schott.* die gute alte Zeit.

aunt [ɑːnt] s Tante f.

au·pair [ˌəʊ'peə] *Br.* **I** s a. ~ **girl** Au-pair-Mädchen n. **II** *adv* als Au-pair-Mädchen: **work** ~. **III** v/i als Au-pair-Mädchen arbeiten.

au·ra ['ɔːrə] s *fig.* Aura f.

au·ral ['ɔːrəl] *adj* □ **1.** Ohren...: ~ **surgeon** Ohrenarzt m. **2.** akustisch, Hör...

au·re·ole ['ɔːrɪəʊl] s *ast.* Aureole f, Hof m.

au·ri·cle ['ɔːrɪkl] s *anat.* **1.** Ohrmuschel f. **2.** Herzvorhof m. **au·ric·u·lar** [ɔː'rɪk-jʊlə] *adj* Ohren...: ~ **confession** *eccl.* Ohrenbeichte f; ~ **witness** Ohrenzeuge m.

aus·cul·ta·tion [ˌɔːskəl'teɪʃn] s ♣ Abhorchen n.

aus·pic·es ['ɔːspɪsɪz] s pl: **under the** ~ **of** unter der Schirmherrschaft von (*od.* gen). **aus·pi·cious** [ɔː'spɪʃəs] *adj* □ **1.** günstig: a) vielversprechend, b) glücklich: **be** ~ unter e-m günstigen Stern stehen.

Aus·sie ['ɒzɪ] **I** s Australier(in). **II** *adj* australisch.

aus·tere [ɒ'stɪə] *adj* □ **1.** streng, ernst. **2.** enthaltsam; dürftig, karg. **3.** herb, rau, hart. **4.** nüchtern, schmucklos. **aus·ter·i·ty** [ɒ'sterətɪ] s **1.** Strenge f, Ernst m. **2.** Enthaltsamkeit f; Dürftigkeit f. **3.** Herbheit f, Rauheit f. **4.** Nüchternheit f, Schmucklosigkeit f. **II** *adj* **5.** ✝, *pol.* Spar...: ~ **budget**; ~ **program(me)**.

Aus·tra·lian [ɒ'streɪljən] **I** *adj* australisch. **II** s Australier(in).

Aus·tri·an ['ɒstrɪən] **I** *adj* österreichisch. **II** s Österreicher(in).

au·tar·kic [ɔː'tɑːkɪk] *adj* ✝ autark. **au·tar·ky** ['~kɪ] s Autarkie f.

au·then·tic [ɔː'θentɪk] *adj* (~**ally**) **1.** authentisch: a) echt, verbürgt, b) original, urschriftlich. **2.** ⚖ gültig, rechtskräftig. **au'then·ti·cate** [~keɪt] v/t **1.** beglaubigen. **2.** als echt erweisen, verbürgen. **au,then·ti'ca·tion** s Beglaubigung f. **,au·then'tic·i·ty** [~sətɪ] s **1.** Authentizität f, Echtheit f. **2.** ⚖ Gültigkeit f, Rechtskräftigkeit f.

au·thor ['ɔ:θə] s **1.** Urheber(in). **2.** Autor(in), Verfasser(in), a. allg. Schriftsteller(in). **'au·thor·ess** s Autorin f, Verfasserin f, a. allg. Schriftstellerin f. **au·thor·i·tar·i·an** [ɔ:,θɒrɪ'teərɪən] adj autoritär.

au'thor·i·ta·tive [~tətɪv] adj □ **1.** gebieterisch, herrisch. **2.** autoritativ, maßgebend, -geblich. **au'thor·i·ty** s **1.** Autorität f, (Amts)Gewalt f. **2.** Autorität f, Ansehen n (**with** bei), Einfluß m (**over** auf acc). **3.** Vollmacht f: **~ to sign** Unterschriftsvollmacht f; **without ~** unbefugt, unberechtigt. **4.** Quelle f, Beleg m: **on good ~** aus glaubwürdiger Quelle. **5.** Autorität f, Kapazität f (**on** in e-r Sache, auf e-m Gebiet). **6.** mst pl Behörde(n pl) f.

au·thor·i·za·tion [,ɔ:θəraɪ'zeɪʃn] s **1.** Ermächtigung f, Bevollmächtigung f, Befugnis f. **2.** Genehmigung f. **'au·thor·ize** v/t **1.** autorisieren, ermächtigen, bevollmächtigen: **~d to sign** unterschriftsbevollmächtigt. **2.** billigen, genehmigen.

au·thor·ship ['ɔ:θəʃɪp] s **1.** Urheberschaft f. **2.** Autorschaft f.

au·to ['ɔ:təʊ] pl **-tos** s Am. F Auto n.

au·to... ['ɔ:təʊ] auto..., selbst..., Auto..., Selbst...

'au·to,bi·o'graph·ic, 'au·to,bi·o'graph·i·cal adj □ autobiographisch. **,au·to·bi'og·ra·phy** s Autobiographie f.

au·to·cade ['ɔ:təʊkeɪd] Am. → **motorcade.**

'au·to,chang·er s Plattenwechsler m.

au·toc·ra·cy [ɔ:'tɒkrəsɪ] s pol. Autokratie f. **au·to·crat** ['ɔ:təʊkræt] s pol. Autokrat m: a) pol. diktatorischer Alleinherrscher, b) selbstherrlicher Mensch. **,au·to'crat·ic, ,au·to'crat·i·cal** adj □ autokratisch: a) pol. unumschränkt, b) selbstherrlich.

au·to·di·dact ['ɔ:təʊdɪ,dækt] s Autodidakt(in). **,au·to·di'dac·tic** adj autodidaktisch.

au·to·gen·ic [,ɔ:təʊ'dʒenɪk] adj ⚕ autogen: **~ training.**

au·to·graph ['ɔ:təɡrɑ:f] **I** s Autogramm

n: **sign ~s** Autogramme geben. **II** adj Autogramm...: **~ album (hunter, etc).** **III** v/t sein Autogramm schreiben in (acc) od. auf (acc), Buch etc signieren.

au·to·mat ['ɔ:təʊmæt] s **1.** bsd. Am. Automatenrestaurant n. **2.** (Verkaufs)Automat m. **au·to·mate** ['ɔ:təmeɪt] v/t automatisieren. **au·to·mat·ic** [,ɔ:tə'mætɪk] **I** adj (~ally) **1.** automatisch: **~ choke** mot. Startautomatik f. **II** s **2.** ⚙ Automat m. **3.** Selbstladepistole f, -gewehr n. **4.** Auto n mit Automatik. **au·to·ma·tion** [,ɔ:tə'meɪʃn] s **1.** Automation f. **2.** Automatisierung f. **au·tom·a·tize** [ɔ:'tɒmətaɪz] v/t automatisieren. **au'tom·a·ton** [~tən] pl **-ta** [~tə], **-tons** s Automat m, Roboter m (a. fig.).

au·to·mo·bile ['ɔ:təməʊbi:l] s Auto(mobil) n. **au·to·mo·tive** [,ɔ:tə'məʊtɪv] adj **1.** selbstfahrend, mit Eigenantrieb. **2.** Auto(mobil)..., Kraftfahrzeug...

au·ton·o·mous [ɔ:'tɒnəməs] adj autonom. **au'ton·o·my** s Autonomie f.

'au·to,pi·lot s ✈ Autopilot m, automatische Steuerungsanlage.

au·top·sy ['ɔ:təpsɪ] s ⚕ Autopsie f.

au·tumn ['ɔ:təm] **I** s Herbst m (a. fig.): **the ~ of life; in (the) ~** im Herbst. **II** adj Herbst... **au·tum·nal** [ɔ:'tʌmnəl] adj □ herbstlich, Herbst...

aux·il·ia·ry [ɔ:g'zɪljərɪ] **I** adj **1.** Hilfs..., ⚙ a. Zusatz...: **~ verb** → **II** s **2.** Helfer(in), Hilfskraft f. **3.** ling. Hilfsverb n, -zeitwort n.

a·vail [ə'veɪl] **I** v/t: **~ o.s. of** sich e-r Sache bedienen, sich et. zunutze machen. **II** v/i nützen. **III** s Nutzen m: **of no ~** nutzlos; **to no ~** vergeblich. **a,vail·a·'bil·i·ty** s Verfügbarkeit f. **a'vail·a·ble** adj □ **1.** verfügbar, vorhanden: **make ~** zur Verfügung stellen. **2.** ♦ lieferbar, vorrätig, erhältlich: **no longer ~** nicht mehr lieferbar, vergriffen; **~ prescription.** **3.** erreichbar, abkömmlich.

av·a·lanche ['ævəlɑ:ntʃ] s **1.** Lawine f. **2.** fig. Flut f: **an ~ of letters.**

av·a·rice ['ævərɪs] s Habsucht f, Habgier f. **,av·a·'ri·cious** adj □ habsüchtig, habgierig.

a·venge [ə'vendʒ] v/t rächen: **~ o.s., be ~d** sich rächen (**on** an dat; **for** für). **a'veng·er** s Rächer(in).

av·e·nue ['ævənju:] s **1.** Allee f. **2.** Hauptstraße f. **3.** fig. Weg m (**to** zu).

av·er·age ['ævərɪdʒ] **I** s **1.** Durchschnitt m: *be above (the)* ~ über dem Durchschnitt liegen; *be below (the)* ~ unter dem Durchschnitt liegen; *on (an od. the)* ~ durchschnittlich, im Durchschnitt. **2.** ⚓, 🚂 Havarie f, Seeschaden m. **II** adj **3.** durchschnittlich, Durchschnitts... **III** v/t **4.** a. ~ *out* den Durchschnitt ermitteln od. nehmen von (od. gen). **5.** ✝ anteil(s)mäßig aufteilen (*among* unter dat). **6.** durchschnittlich betragen od. haben od. leisten etc. **IV** v/i **7.** ~ *out at* → 6.

a·verse [ə'vɜːs] adj □ abgeneigt (*to*, bsd. Br. a. *from* dat). **a'ver·sion** s **1.** Abneigung f, Aversion f (*to*, *for*, *from* gegen). **2.** ... *is my* ... ... ist mir ein Greuel.

a·vert [ə'vɜːt] v/t abwenden (a. fig.).

a·vi·a·tion [ˌeɪvɪ'eɪʃn] s Luftfahrt f.

av·id ['ævɪd] adj □ gierig (*for*, a. *of* nach): ~ *for fame* ruhmsüchtig. **a·vid·i·ty** [ə'vɪdətɪ] s Gier f.

a·void [ə'vɔɪd] v/t (ver)meiden, ausweichen (dat), aus dem Wege gehen (dat), Pflicht etc umgehen, e-r Gefahr entgehen: ~ *s.o.* j-n meiden; ~ *doing s.th.* es vermeiden, et. zu tun. **a'void·a·ble** adj vermeidbar; **a'void·ance** s (Ver)Meiden n, Umgehung f: *in* ~ *of* um zu vermeiden.

av·oir·du·pois [ˌævədə'pɔɪz] s a. ~ *weight* ✝ Handelsgewicht n (= *16 Unzen*).

a·vow [ə'vaʊ] v/t bekennen, (ein)gestehen. **a'vow·al** s Bekenntnis n, (Ein)Geständnis n. **a'vowed** adj erklärt (*Gegner*, *Prinzip* etc). **a'vow·ed·ly** [~ɪdlɪ] adv eingestandenermaßen.

a·wait [ə'weɪt] v/t erwarten (a. fig.).

a·wake [ə'weɪk] **I** v/t (irr) **1.** (auf)wecken. **2.** fig. auf-, wachrütteln (*from* aus): ~ *s.o. to s.th.* j-m et. zum Bewußtsein bringen. **II** v/i (irr) **3.** auf-, erwachen. **4.** ~ *to s.th.* fig. sich e-r Sache bewußt werden. **III** adj **5.** wach: *wide* ~ hellwach, fig. a. aufgeweckt; *be* ~ *to s.th.* fig. sich e-r Sache bewußt sein. **a'wak·en** → awake 1–4. **a'wak·en·ing** s Erwachen n: *a rude* ~ fig. ein unsanftes od. böses Erwachen.

a·ward [ə'wɔːd] **I** v/t **1.** zuerkennen, zusprechen, *Preis* etc a. verleihen. **II** s **2.** Urteil n, bsd. Schiedsspruch m. **3.** Auszeichnung f, Preis m. **4.** (*Preis-* etc-)

Verleihung f. **5.** univ. Stipendium n.

a·ware [ə'weə] adj: *be* ~ *of s.th.* et. wissen od. kennen, sich e-r Sache bewußt sein; *become* ~ *of s.th.* et. merken; *make s.o.* ~ *of s.th.* j-m et. bewußt machen. **a'ware·ness** s Bewußtsein n, Kenntnis f.

a·way [ə'weɪ] **I** adv u. adj **1.** weg, fort (*from* von): *go* ~ weg-, fortgehen. **2.** (weit) entfernt od. weg: *six miles* ~ sechs Meilen entfernt. **3.** fort, abwesend, verreist: ~ *on business* geschäftlich unterwegs. **4.** d(a)rauflos, immer weiter (→ *Verben*). **II** adj **5.** Sport: Auswärts...: ~ *match.*

awe [ɔː] **I** s (Ehr)Furcht f, Scheu f: *hold s.o. in* ~ → II; *stand in* ~ *of* e-e (heilige) Scheu od. gewaltigen Respekt haben vor (dat). **II** v/t j-m (Ehr)Furcht od. großen Respekt einflößen. '~·in,spir·ing adj ehrfurchtgebietend.

awe·some ['ɔːsəm] adj □ **1.** furchteinflößend. **2.** ehrfurchtgebietend.

'**awe-struck** adj von Ehrfurcht ergriffen.

aw·ful ['ɔːfʊl] adj □ umgs. **1.** schrecklich (*beide a.* F). '**aw·ful·ly** adv F furchtbar, schrecklich: ~ *nice* furchtbar od. riesig nett; *thanks* ~! tausend Dank!

awk·ward ['ɔːkwəd] adj □ **1.** ungeschickt, unbeholfen, linkisch: *be* ~ *with* ungeschickt umgehen mit. **2.** verlegen (a. *Schweigen* etc): *feel* ~ verlegen sein. **3.** peinlich, unangenehm. **4.** unhandlich, sperrig. **5.** unangenehm, schwierig: *an* ~ *customer* F ein unangenehmer Zeitgenosse. **6.** ungünstig (*Zeitpunkt* etc).

awl [ɔːl] s ⚙ Ahle f, Pfriem m.

awn·ing ['ɔːnɪŋ] s **1.** Plane f. **2.** Markise f. **3.** ⚓ Sonnensegel n. **4.** Vorzelt n.

a·woke [ə'wəʊk] pret u. pp von awake. **a'wok·en** pp von awake.

a·wry [ə'raɪ] adv u. adj schief: *go* ~ fig. schiefgehen.

ax(e) [æks] **I** s Axt f, Beil n: *have an* ~ *to grind* fig. eigennützige Zwecke verfolgen; *get the* ~ F rausfliegen, entlassen werden. **II** v/t F *Ausgaben* etc rücksichtslos kürzen od. (zs-)streichen; *Beamte*, *Dienststellen* abbauen, *Leute* feuern, entlassen.

ax·es ['æksiːz] pl von axis.

ax·i·om ['æksɪəm] s Axiom n, Grundsatz m.

axis 760

ax·is ['æksɪs] *pl* **ax·es** ['ⁿsiːz] *s* & *etc* Achse *f* (*a. pol.*).
ax·le ['æksl] *s* ⊕ (Rad)Achse *f*, Welle *f*.
ay(e) [aɪ] *s parl.* Jastimme *f*: **the ⁿs**

have it die Mehrheit ist dafür.
a·zal·ea [ə'zeɪljə] *s* ♣ Azalee *f*.
az·ure ['æʒə] I *adj* himmelblau. II *s* Himmelblau *n*.

B

baa [baː] *v/i* blöken.
Bab·bitt ['bæbət] *s Am.* selbstzufriedener Spießer.
bab·ble ['bæbl] I *v/i* **1.** *a. v/t* stammeln. **2.** *a. v/t* plappern, schwatzen: ~ (*out*) ausplaudern. **3.** plätschern. II *s* **4.** Geplapper *n*, Geschwätz *n*. **5.** Geplätscher *n*.
babe [beɪb] *s* **1.** Baby *n*: → *innocent* b. **2.** *bsd. Am. sl.* Puppe *f* (*Mädchen*).
ba·bel ['beɪbl] *s* Wirrwarr *m*, Durcheinander *n*; Stimmengewirr *n*.
ba·boon [bə'buːn] *s zo.* Pavian *m*.
ba·by ['beɪbɪ] I *s* **1.** Baby *n*, Säugling *m*: *be left holding the ~* F der Dumme sein; *that's your ~ sl.* das ist dein Bier *od.* d-e Sache. **2.** Benjamin *m* (*der Familie etc*). **3.** Kindskopf *m*; Heulsuse *f*. **4.** *sl.* Puppe *f* (*Mädchen*); Schatz *m*, Liebling *m*. II *adj* **5.** Baby..., Säuglings... **6.** Klein... III *v/t* **7.** verhätscheln. ~ *boom* *s* Babyboom *m*. ~ *car* *s* Kleinwagen *m*. ~ *car·riage* *s Am.* Kinderwagen *m*.
ba·by·hood ['beɪbɪhʊd] *s* Säuglingsalter *n*. **'ba·by·ish** *adj* **1.** kindisch. **2.** kindlich.
'ba·by|-mind·er *s Br.* Tagesmutter *f*. **'~-sit** *v/i* (*irr sit*) babysitten. **'~-sit·ter** *s* Babysitter(in). **~ talk** *s* kindlich(tuend)es Gebabbel.
bach·e·lor ['bætʃələ] *s* **1.** Junggeselle *m*: ~ *girl* Junggesellin *f*. **2.** *univ.* Bakkalaureus *m*: ♀ *of Arts* (*Science*) Bakkalaureus der philosophischen Fakultät (der Naturwissenschaften). **bach·e·lor·ette** [ˌⁿ'ret] *s* Junggesellin *f*. **bach·e·lor·hood** ['ⁿhʊd] *s* **1.** Junggesellenstand *m*. **2.** *univ.* Bakkalaureat *n*.
ba·cil·lus [bə'sɪləs] *pl* **-li** [ˌⁿlaɪ] *s* ✻ Bazillus *m*.

back [bæk] I *s* **1.** *anat., zo.* Rücken *m*: *at the ~ of* hinter (*dat*); hinten in (*dat*); *be at the ~ of s.th. fig.* hinter et. stecken; *behind s.o.'s ~ fig.* hinter j-s Rücken; *to ~* Rücken an Rücken; *be on one's ~* bettlägerig sein; *break s.o's ~* j-m das Kreuz brechen (*a. fig.*); *break the ~ of s.th. fig.* das Schwierigste e-r Sache hinter sich bringen; *have one's ~ to the wall fig.* mit dem Rücken zur Wand stehen; *put* (*od. get*) *s.o.'s ~ up fig.* j-n auf die Palme bringen; *put one's ~ into s.th. fig.* sich in e-e Sache hineinknien; *turn one's ~ on* den Rücken zuwenden (*dat*); *fig.* den Rücken kehren (*dat*). **2.** Hinter-, Rückseite *f*, (*Buch-, Hand-etc*) Rücken *m*, (Rück)Lehne *f* (*e-s Stuhls*), linke Seite (*e-s Stoffs*). **3.** hinterer *od.* rückwärtiger Teil: ~ *of the head* Hinterkopf *m*; *in the ~ of the car* auf dem Rücksitz *od.* im Fond des Autos. **4.** Rückenteil *m* (*e-s Kleidungsstücks*): *have one's pullover on ~ to front* den Pullover verkehrt herum anhaben. **5.** *Sport*: Verteidiger *m*. II *adj* **6.** rückwärtig, Hinter...: ~ *entrance.* **7.** fern, abgelegen: ~ *country* Hinterland *n*. **8.** rückständig (*Zahlung*). **9.** alt, zurückliegend (*Zeitung etc*). III *adv* **10.** zurück, rückwärts: ~ *and forth* hin u. her, vor u. zurück; *move ~* zurückgehen. **11.** (wieder) zurück: *he is ~* (*again*) er ist wieder da. **12.** zurück, vorher: *20 years ~* vor 20 Jahren; ~ *in 1900* (noch *od.* schon) im Jahre 1900. **13.** F zurück, im Rückstand: *be ~ in one's rent* mit der Miete im Rückstand sein. IV *v/t* **14.** *a.* ~ *up* unterstützen, j-m den Rücken stärken, ♥ *Währung etc* stützen. **15.** *a.* ~ *up* zurückbewegen, rückwärts fahren *od.* laufen lassen: ~ *the car out of the* *garage* den Wagen rückwärts aus der Garage fahren. **16.** wetten *od.* setzen auf (*acc*). **V** *v/i* **17.** oft ~ *up* sich rückwärts bewegen, zurückgehen *od.* -fahren, *mot. a.* zurückstoßen: ~ *out* (*of*) rückwärts herausfahren (aus). **18.** ~ *out* (*of*) zurücktreten *od.* abspringen (von), aussteigen (aus).

'**back**|·**ache** *s* Rückenschmerzen *pl.* ~ **al·ley** *s Am.* finsteres Seitengäßchen. ,~'**bench·er** *s parl. Br.* Hinterbänkler *m.* '~**bite** *v/t* (*irr bite*) lästern über *j-n.* '~**bone** *s* Rückgrat *n* (*a. fig.*), Wirbelsäule *f*: *to the* ~ *fig.* bis auf die Knochen, durch u. durch. '~,**break·ing** *adj* zermürbend, mörderisch. '~**chat** *s* freche Antwort(en *pl*). ~**cloth** *s thea. bsd. Br.* Prospekt *m.* '~**date** *v/t* (zu)rückdatieren. ~ **door** *s* Hintertür *f*; *fig.* Hintertürchen *n.* '~**door** *adj* geheim, heimlich. '~**drop** *s thea.* Prospekt *m*: *be the* ~ *for fig.* den Hintergrund bilden (*gen*).

back·er ['bækə] *s* Unterstützer(in), Helfer(in); Geldgeber(in).

,**back**|'**fire** *I v/i* **1. ⚙** früh-, fehlzünden. **2.** *fig.* fehlschlagen, ins Auge gehen. **II** *s* **3. ⚙** Früh-, Fehlzündung *f.* ~ **for·ma·tion** *s ling.* Rückbildung *f.* '~**gam·mon** *s* Backgammon *n* (*Spiel*). '~**ground** *s* **1.** Hintergrund *m* (*a. fig.*): *against the* ~ *of* vor dem Hintergrund (*gen*); *keep in the* ~ im Hintergrund bleiben; ~ *music* musikalische Untermalung, Hintergrundsmusik *f.* **2.** *fig.* Hintergrund *m*, Umstände *pl*; Umwelt *f*, Milieu *n*; Werdegang *m*; Erfahrung *f*, Wissen *n*: ~ *information* Hintergrundinformationen *pl*; *educational* ~ Vorbildung *f.* '~**hand** *I s Sport*: Rückhand(schlag *m*) *f.* **II** *adj* → **backhanded.** '~,**hand·ed** *adj* **1.** *Sport*: Rückhand... **2.** indirekt (*Zensur etc*). **3.** unredlich (*Methode etc*). **4.** zweifelhaft (*Kompliment etc*).

back·ing ['bækɪŋ] *s* Unterstützung *f.*

'**back**|·**lash** *s* (heftige) Reaktion (*to* auf *acc*). '~**log** *s* (*Arbeits-, Auftrags-etc*)Rückstand *m*; Überhang *m* (*of* an *dat*): ~ *demand* Nachholbedarf *m.* ~ **num·ber** *s* **1.** alte Nummer (*e-r Zeitung etc*). **2.** F rückständige Person *od.* Sache. '~**pack** *s bsd. Am.* Rucksack *m.* '~,**pack·ing** *s bsd. Am.* Rucksacktou-

rismus *m.* ,~'**ped·al** *v/i* pret u. p ... -**aled,** *bsd. Br.* -**alled 1.** rückwärts treten (*Radfahrer*). **2.** *fig.* e-n Rückzieher machen. ~ **seat** *s* Rücksitz *m*: *take a* ~ F in den Hintergrund treten (*to* gegenüber). '~**seat driv·er** *s* F Besserwisser(in). ,~'**side** *s* **1.** Kehr-, Rückseite *f.* **2.** F Hintern *m.* ,~'**slide** *v/i* (*irr slide*) rückfällig werden. '~**stage** *adj u. adv thea.* hinter den Kulissen (*a. fig.*). '~**stair** → **backstairs** II. ,~'**stairs** *I s pl* **1.** Hintertreppe *f.* **II** *adj* **2.** ~ *gossip* (*od. talk*) (bösartige) Anspielungen *pl* (*about* auf *acc*). **3.** ~ *influence* Protektion *f.* ,~'**street** *s* Seitenstraße *f.* '~**street** heimlich: ~ *abortion* illegale Abtreibung; ~ *abortionist* Engelmacher(in). '~**stroke** *s* Rückenschwimmen *n.* ~ **talk** *s bsd. Am.* F freche Antwort(en *pl*). '~**track** *v/i* **1.** denselben Weg zurückgehen. **2.** *fig.* sich zurückziehen (*from* von), e-n Rückzieher machen; e-e Kehrtwendung machen. '~**up** *s* **1.** Unterstützung *f.* **2.** *mot. Am.* (Rück)Stau *m.* **3.** *fig.* Rückzieher *m* (*on* hinsichtlich). **4. ⚙** Ersatzgerät *n.*

back·ward ['bækwəd] **I** *adj* **1.** rückwärts gerichtet, Rückwärts...: ~ *flow* Rückfluß *m*; *a* ~ *glance* ein Blick zurück *od.* nach hinten. **2.** *in der Entwicklung etc* zurück(geblieben). **3.** rückständig: *be* ~ *in one's work* mit s-r Arbeit in Rückstand liegen. **II** *adv* **4.** rückwärts, zurück: ~ *and forward* hin u. her, vor u. zurück. **back·wards** ['~dz] → **backward** II.

'**back**|·**wash** *s* **1.** Rückströmung *f*, **⚓** *a.* Kielwasser *n.* **2.** *fig.* Aus-, Nachwirkung(en *pl*) *f.* '~,**wa·ter** *s* **1.** → **backwash** 1. **2.** Stauwasser *n.* **3.** *fig.* Ort *m od.* Zustand *m der* Rückständigkeit u. Stagnation. '~**woods** *s pl* **1.** unerschlossenes Waldgebiet. **2.** *contp.* Provinz *f.* '~,**woods·man** [-smən] *s* (*irr man*) *contp.* Hinterwäldler *m.* ,~'**yard** *s* **1.** *Br.* Hinterhof *m.* **2.** *Am.* Garten *m* hinter dem Haus.

ba·con ['beɪkən] *s* Frühstücks-, Schinkenspeck *m*: *bring home the* ~ F die Brötchen verdienen; Erfolg haben; *save one's* ~ *Br.* F mit heiler Haut davonkommen.

bac·te·ri·al [bæk'tɪərɪəl] *adj* □ bakteriell. **bac·te·ri·o·log·i·cal** [bæk,tɪərɪə-

'lɒdʒɪkl] *adj* □ bakteriologisch, Bakterien... **bac·te·ri·ol·o·gist** [ˌtɪərɪˈɒlədʒɪst] *s* Bakteriologe *m.* **bac·te·ri·um** [ˌrɪəm] *pl* **-ri·a** [ˌrɪə] *s* Bakterie *f.*

bad [bæd] **I** *adj comp* **worse** [wɜːs] *sup* **worst** [wɜːst] (□ → **badly**) **1.** *allg.* schlecht: a) fehler-, mangelhaft (*Qualität, Zustand etc*): *not* ~ nicht schlecht *od.* übel; ~ *trip sl.* Bad Trip *m* (*Drogenrausch mit Angstzuständen*), b) ungünstig (*Nachricht etc*), c) schädlich, ungesund (*for* für): ~ *for one's health* ungesund, d) verdorben (*Nahrungsmittel*): **go** ~ schlecht werden, verderben, e) angegriffen (*Gesundheit*), f) widerlich (*Geruch*), g) schwach (*at* in e-m Fach). **2.** böse: a) schlimm, schwer (*Verbrechen, Erkältung etc*), b) ungezogen (*Junge etc*). **3.** unanständig, unflätig, (*Wort a.*) häßlich: ~ *language* unanständige Ausdrücke *pl*; beleidigende Äußerungen *pl.* **4.** ungedeckt (*Scheck*), ungültig (*Münze etc*): ~ *debts pl* † zweifelhafte Forderungen *pl.* **5.** unangenehm, ärgerlich: *that's too* ~ das ist (doch) zu dumm. **6.** unwohl, krank: *she is* (*od. feels*) *very* ~ *today* es geht ihr heute sehr schlecht; *he felt* ~ *at* (*od. about*) *it* er war (sehr) deprimiert darüber. **II** *s* **7.** *das Schlechte:* **go from** ~ **to worse** immer schlimmer werden; **go to the** ~ auf die schiefe Bahn geraten; **be in the** ~ **with** F schlecht angeschrieben sein bei. **8.** † Defizit *n*: **be £ 100 to the** ~ ein Defizit *od.* e-n Verlust von 100 Pfund haben. **III** *adv* **9.** F → **badly.**

bade [bæd] *pret u. pp von* **bid.**

badge [bædʒ] *s* **1.** (⚔ Rang)Abzeichen *n.* **2.** *fig.* Kennzeichen *n.*

badg·er ['bædʒə] **I** *s zo.* Dachs *m.* **II** *v/t* plagen, *j-m* zusetzen (*for* wegen).

bad·ly ['bædlɪ] *adv* **1.** schlecht, schlimm: *he is* ~ *off* es geht ihm sehr schlecht; *do* ~ schlecht fahren (*in* bei, mit). **2.** dringend, sehr: ~ *needed* dringend nötig. **3.** schwer: ~ *wounded.*

bad·min·ton ['bædmɪntən] *s* Federball(spiel *n*) *m, Sport:* Badminton *n.*

bad-tem·pered *adj* schlechtgelaunt.

baf·fle ['bæfl] *v/t* **1.** verwirren, -blüffen: *be* ~*d a.* vor e-m Rätsel stehen. **2.** *Plan etc* durchkreuzen, vereiteln: *it* ~*s* (*all*) *description* es spottet jeder Beschreibung.

bag [bæg] **I** *s* **1.** Sack *m;* Beutel *m;* Tasche *f;* Tüte *f:* ~ *and baggage* mit Sack u. Pack; ~*s of* F jede Menge (*Geld etc*). **2.** *hunt.* (Jagd)Beute *f,* Strecke *f.* **3.** (*pair of*) ~*s pl bsd. Br.* F Hose *f.* **II** *v/t* **4.** in e-n Sack *etc* stecken; in Beutel verpacken *od.* abfüllen. **5.** *hunt.* zur Strecke bringen. **6.** F klauen, stehlen. **III** *v/i* **7.** *a.* ~ *out* sich bauschen.

bag·a·telle [ˌbægəˈtel] *s* Bagatelle *f.*

bag·gage ['bægɪdʒ] *s bsd. Am.* (Reise)Gepäck *n.* ~ **al·low·ance** *s* ✓ *bsd. Am.* Freigepäck *n.* ~ **car** *s* 🚃 *Am.* Gepäckwagen *m.* ~ **check** *s bsd. Am.* Gepäckschein *m.* ~ **in·sur·ance** *s bsd. Am.* Reisegepäckversicherung *f.* ~ **lock·er** *s bsd. Am.* Gepäckschließfach *n.* ~ **re·claim** *s* ✓ *bsd. Am.* Gepäckausgabe *f.*

bag·gy ['bægɪ] *adj* **1.** bauschig. **2.** ausgebeult (*Hose*).

'bag·pip·er *s* Dudelsackpfeifer *m.* '~**pipes** *s pl* ♪ Dudelsack *m.* '~**snatch·er** *s* Handtaschenräuber *m.*

bah [bɑː] *int contp.* bah!

bail[1] [beɪl] ⚖ **I** *s* **1.** Bürge (*n pl*) *m.* **2.** (Haft)Kaution *f,* Sicherheitsleistung *f:* *be out on* ~ gegen Kaution auf freiem Fuß sein; *go* (*od. stand*) ~ *for s.o.* für *j-n* Kaution stellen. **II** *v/t* **3.** *a. mst* ~ *out j-s* Freilassung gegen Kaution erwirken.

bail[2] [~] **I** *v/t mst* ~ *out* Wasser, *Boot etc* ausschöpfen. **II** *v/i:* ~ *out* ✓ aussteigen (*a. F fig. of* aus), (*mit dem Fallschirm*) abspringen.

bail[3] [~] *s* Henkel *m* (*e-s Eimers etc*).

bail·iff ['beɪlɪf] *s Br.* **1.** ⚖ Gerichtsvollzieher *m.* **2.** (Guts)Verwalter *m.*

bait [beɪt] **I** *s* **1.** Köder *m* (*a. fig.*): *rise to* (*od. swallow, take*) *the* ~ anbeißen (*a. fig.*). **II** *v/t* **2.** mit e-m Köder versehen. **3.** *fig.* ködern. **4.** *hunt.* (*mit Hunden*) hetzen. **5.** *fig.* quälen, peinigen.

bake [beɪk] **I** *v/t* **1.** backen: ~*d beans pl* Baked Beans *pl* (*in Tomatensoße gekochte Bohnen*); ~*d potatoes pl* ungeschälte, im Ofen gebackene Kartoffeln. **2.** dörren, härten; *Ziegel* brennen; *Lack* einbrennen. **II** *v/i* **3.** backen, *mst fig.* (*in der Sonne*) braten. **4.** zs.- *od.* festbacken. **'bak·er** *s* Bäcker *m:* *at the* ~*'s* beim Bäcker; ~*'s dozen* dreizehn. **'bak·er·y** *s* Bäckerei *f.* [**bak·ing-'hot** *adj* glühendheiß (*Tag etc*).

bak·ing pow·der s Backpulver n.
bal·ance ['bæləns] **I** s **1.** Waage f. **2.** Gleichgewicht n: a) Balance f, b) a. ~ **of mind** Fassung f: **in the ~** in der Schwebe; **hold the ~** fig. das Zünglein an der Waage bilden; **keep one's ~** das Gleichgewicht halten; fig. sich nicht aus der Fassung bringen lassen; **lose one's ~** das Gleichgewicht od. (fig.) die Fassung verlieren; **strike a ~ between ... and ...** fig. e-n Mittelweg finden zwischen (dat) ... u.; **throw s.o. off (his) ~** fig. j-n aus der Fassung bringen; ~ **of power** pol. Gleichgewicht der Kräfte. **3.** bsd. fig. **(to)** Gegengewicht n (zu), Ausgleich m (für). **4.** † Bilanz f; Saldo m, Guthaben n; Restbetrag m: ~ **of payments** Zahlungsbilanz; ~ **of trade** Handelsbilanz; **on ~** fig. alles in allem. **II** v/t **5.** fig. ab-, erwägen. **6. (o.s.)** sich im Gleichgewicht halten; balancieren. **7.** ins Gleichgewicht bringen, ausbalancieren. **8.** † Konten, Rechnungen ausgleichen, saldieren. **III** v/i **9.** sich im Gleichgewicht halten (a. fig.); balancieren. **10.** † sich ausgleichen. '**bal·anced** adj fig. ausgewogen, -geglichen.
bal·ance| sheet s † Bilanz f. ~ **wheel** s ◉ Unruh f (e-r Uhr).
bal·anc·ing ['bælənsıŋ] adj Balance..., Balancier...: ~ **act** Balanceakt m (a. fig.); ~ **pole** Balancierstange f.
bal·co·ny ['bælkənı] s Balkon m, thea. a. zweiter Rang.
bald [bɔːld] adj □ **1.** kahl: **go ~** e-e Glatze bekommen, kahl werden. **2.** (völlig) abgefahren (Reifen).
bal·der·dash ['bɔːldədæʃ] s Quatsch m, Unsinn m.
'**bald|·head** s Kahl-, Glatzkopf m; ,~'head·ed adj kahl-, glatzköpfig.
bale¹ [beıl] **I** s † Ballen m: **in ~s** ballenweise. **II** v/t in Ballen verpacken.
bale² [~] → **bail².**
balk [bɔːk] v/i **1.** stocken, stutzen. **2.** scheuen **(at** vor dat) (Pferd). **3.** sich sträuben (gegen); zurückschrecken (vor dat).
ball¹ [bɔːl] **I** s **1.** Ball m; Kugel f; Knäuel m, n: **be on the ~** F auf Draht sein; **the ~ is with you** (od. **in your court**) du bist an der Reihe od. am Zug; **have the ~ at one's feet** Br. s-e große Chance haben; **keep the ~ rolling** das Gespräch od. die

Sache in Gang halten; **play ~** F mitmachen, spuren; **set** (od. **start**) **the ~ rolling** den Stein ins Rollen bringen. **2.** anat. ~ **of the eye** Augapfel m; ~ **of the foot** Fußballen m; ~ **of the thumb** Handballen m. **3.** pl V Eier pl (Hoden). **II** v/t u. v/i **4.** (sich) zs.-ballen.
ball² [~] s Ball m (Tanzveranstaltung): **have a ~** bsd. Am. F sich köstlich amüsieren.
bal·lad ['bæləd] s Ballade f.
,**ball-and-'sock·et** adj: ~ **joint** anat., ◉ Kugelgelenk n.
bal·last ['bæləst] bsd. ✔, ⚓ **I** s Ballast m. **II** v/t mit Ballast beladen.
ball| bear·ing s ◉ Kugellager n. ~ **boy** s Sport: Balljunge f.
bal·let ['bæleı] s Ballett n. ~ **danc·er** s Balletttänzer(in).
bal·lis·tics [bə'lıstıks] s pl (meist sg konstruiert) ✗, phys. Ballistik f.
bal·loon [bə'luːn] **I** s **1.** (Frei-, Fessel-, Luft)Ballon m. **2.** Sprech-, Denkblase f. **II** v/i **3.** sich (auf)blähen. **bal'loon·ist** s Ballonfahrer(in).
bal·lot ['bælət] **I** s **1.** Stimmzettel m. **2.** Gesamtzahl f der abgegebenen Stimmen: **large ~** hohe Wahlbeteiligung. **3.** (bsd. geheime) Wahl od. Abstimmung: **have** (od. **hold, take**) **a ~** abstimmen **(on** über acc). **4.** Wahlgang m. **II** v/i **5.** (for) stimmen (für), (bsd. in geheimer Wahl) wählen (acc). ~ **box** s Wahlurne f. ~ **card,** ~ **pa·per** s Stimmzettel m.
'**ball|·point (pen)** s Kugelschreiber m. '**~·room** s Ball-, Tanzsaal m.
bal·ly·hoo [,bælı'huː] s F **1.** Wirbel m, Tamtam n, Getue n **(about** um). **2.** marktschreierische Reklame.
balm [bɑːm] s Balsam m (a. fig.). '**balm·y** adj □ **1.** balsamisch. **2.** lind, mild (Wetter). **3.** bsd. Am. sl. bekloppt, verrückt: **go ~** überschnappen.
ba·lo·ney → **boloney.**
bal·us·trade [,bælə'streıd] s Balustrade f.
bam·boo [bæm'buː] s Bambus m.
bam·boo·zle [bæm'buːzl] v/t F **1.** betrügen **(out of** um), übers Ohr hauen: ~ **s.o. into doing s.th.** j-n so einwickeln, daß er et. tut. **2.** irremachen, verwirren.
ban [bæn] **I** v/t **1.** verbieten: ~ **s.o. from speaking** j-m Rede- od. Sprechverbot erteilen. **2.** Sport: sperren. **II** s **3.** (amt-

liches) Verbot (**on** gen), Sperre f (a. Sport): **import** ~ Einfuhrverbot, -sperre.

ba·nal [bəˈnɑːl] adj □ banal, abgedroschen.

ba·nan·a [bəˈnɑːnə] s 1. ❦ Banane f. 2. sl. **be ~s** bekloppt od. verrückt sein; **go ~s** überschnappen. → **re·pub·lic** s Bananenrepublik f.

band[1] [bænd] I s 1. Schar f, Gruppe f; b.s. (bsd. Räuber)Bande f. 2. (Musik)Kapelle f, (Jazz-, Rock- etc)Band f: **big ~** Big Band. II v/i 3. mst ~ **together** sich zs.-tun, b.s. sich zs.-rotten.

band[2] [~] I s 1. Band n; Gurt m; (Hosenetc)Bund m; Bauchbinde f (e-r Zigarre); andersfarbiger od. -artiger Streifen. 2. Radio: (Frequenz)Band n. 3. Ring m. 4. ❂ Treibriemen m; Band n. II v/t 5. mit e-m Band zs.-binden.

'**band·age** [ˈbændɪdʒ] I s ⚕ Bandage f; Binde f; Verband m. II v/t bandagieren; verbinden.

'**band-aid** s Am. Heftpflaster n.

ban·dit [ˈbændɪt] s Bandit m.

'**band|,lead·er** s ♪ Bandleader m. '**~,mas·ter** s ♪ Kapellmeister m. '**~,wag·(g)on** s Wagen m mit e-r Musikkapelle: **climb** (od. **get, jump**) **on the ~** fig. zur erfolgreichen Partei umschwenken.

ban·dy[1] [ˈbændɪ] v/t 1. sich e-n Ball etc zuwerfen. 2. sich Geschichten etc erzählen. 3. sich Beleidigungen etc an den Kopf werfen, sich (gegenseitig) Komplimente, Vorwürfe machen: ~ **blows** sich schlagen; ~ **words** sich streiten. 4. a. ~ **about** (od. **around**) Gerücht etc in Umlauf setzen; weitererzählen: **he has his name bandied about** sein Name fällt dauernd (**in connection with** in Zs.-hang mit); b.s. er ist ins Gerede gekommen.

ban·dy[2] [~] adj 1. krumm, nach außen gebogen: ~ **legs** pl Säbelbeine pl, O-Beine pl. 2. → **bandy-legged**. '**~-legged** adj säbelbeinig, O-beinig.

bang [bæŋ] I s 1. heftiger od. schallender Schlag. 2. Bums m, Krach m, Knall m: **shut the door with a ~** zuknallen, zuknallen. 3. sl. Schuß m (Heroin etc). II v/t 4. knallen mit, Tür etc zuschlagen, zuknallen: ~ **one's fist on the table** mit der Faust auf den Tisch schlagen; ~ **one's head** sich den Kopf anschlagen

(**against, on** an dat); ~ **sense into s.o.** fig. j-m Vernunft einhämmern. 5. V bumsen. III v/i 6. knallen: a) krachen, b) zuschlagen (Tür etc), c) schießen: ~ **away** drauflosknallen; ~ **into** stoßen od. prallen gegen od. an (acc); fig. F zufällig treffen. 7. sl. sich e-n Schuß (Heroin etc) setzen od. drücken. 8. V bumsen. IV adv 9. mit lautem Knall: **go ~** explodieren. 10. peng; genau: ~ **in the eye** peng ins Auge. V int 11. peng!, bum(s)! '**bang·er** s Br. 1. Feuerwerks-, Knallkörper m. 2. F (alter) Klapperkasten (Auto). 3. F (Brat)Wurst f, Würstchen n.

'**bang-up** adj bsd. Am. F prima.

ban·ish [ˈbænɪʃ] v/t 1. verbannen (a. fig.), ausweisen (**from** aus). 2. Sorgen etc verscheuchen, -treiben. '**ban·ish·ment** s Verbannung f, Ausweisung f.

ban·is·ters [ˈbænɪstəz] s pl Treppengeländer n.

ban·jo [ˈbændʒəʊ] pl -**jo(e)s** s ♪ Banjo n.

bank[1] [bæŋk] I s 1. ❦ Bank f. 2. Bank f (bei Glücksspielen): **break** (**be** od. **keep**) **the ~** die Bank sprengen (halten). 3. (Blut-, Daten- etc)Bank f. II v/i 4. ein Bankkonto haben (**with** bei). 5. die Bank halten (bei Glücksspielen). 6. ~ **on** bauen od. sich verlassen auf (acc). III v/t 7. Geld bei e-r Bank einzahlen, auf die Bank bringen.

bank[2] [~] I s 1. (Erd)Wall m; Böschung f; Überhöhung f (e-r Straße etc in Kurven). 2. (Fluß- etc)Ufer n. 3. (Sand-)Bank f. 4. Zs.-ballung f: ~ **of clouds** Wolkenbank f; ~ **of snow** Schneewall m, -wächte f. II v/t 5. mit e-m Wall umgeben. 6. Straße etc (in der Kurve) überhöhen. 7. ~ **up** aufhäufen, zs.-ballen. III v/i 8. a. ~ **up** sich aufhäufen, sich zs.-ballen. 9. überhöht sein (Straße, Kurve).

bank·a·ble [ˈbæŋkəbl] adj fig. zuverlässig, verläßlich.

bank| ac·count s Bankkonto n. ~ **bill** Am. → **bank note**. '**~-book** s Sparbuch n. ~ **card** s Scheckkarte f. ~ **clerk** s Bankangestellte m, f.

bank·er [ˈbæŋkə] s 1. ❦ Bankier m. 2. Bankhalter m (bei Glücksspielen).

bank| hold-up s Banküberfall m. ~ **hol·i·day** s Br. Bankfeiertag m.

bank·ing ['bæŋkɪŋ] ✝ **I** s Bankwesen n. **II** adj Bank...: ~ **hours** pl Öffnungszeiten pl (e-r Bank).

bank| man·ag·er s Bankdirektor m. ~ **note** s Banknote f, Geldschein m. ~ **raid** s Banküberfall m, -raub m. ~ **raid·er** s Bankräuber m. ~ **rate** s ✝ Diskontsatz m. ~ **rob·ber** s Bankräuber m. ~ **rob·ber·y** s Bankraub m, -überfall m.

bank·rupt ['bæŋkrʌpt] ⚖ **I** s **1.** Konkurs-, Gemeinschuldner m: ~'s **estate** (od. **property**) Konkursmasse f. **2.** (betrügerischer) Bankrotteur. **II** adj **3.** bankrott: **go** ~ in Konkurs gehen, Bankrott machen; **declare o.s.** ~ Konkurs anmelden. **bank·rupt·cy** ['~rəptsɪ] s ⚖ Bankrott m, Konkurs m.

ban·ner ['bænə] s **1.** Standarte f; Banner n. **2.** Spruchband n, Transparent n. **3.** a. ~ **headline** Balkenüberschrift f, breite Schlagzeile. **II** adj **4.** Am. hervorragend.

banns [bænz] s pl eccl. Aufgebot n: **have one's** ~ **called** das Aufgebot bestellen.

ban·quet ['bæŋkwɪt] **I** s Bankett n, Festessen n. **II** v/i tafeln.

ban·tam·weight ['bæntəmweɪt] (Sport) **I** s Bantamgewicht(ler m) n. **II** adj Bantamgewichts...

ban·ter ['bæntə] **I** v/t u. v/i necken. **II** s Neckerei f.

bap·tism ['bæptɪzəm] s eccl. Taufe f. **bap·tis·mal** ['~tɪzml] adj Tauf...: ~ **font** Taufbecken n. **'Bap·tist** s Baptist(in). **bap·tize** ['~taɪz] v/t taufen.

bar [ba:] **I** s **1.** Stange f, Stab m: ~s **of** Gitter n; **behind** ~s fig. hinter Schloß u. Riegel. **2.** Riegel m. **3.** Schranke f, Sperre f; fig. Hindernis n (**to** für). **4.** Riegel m, Stange f: **a** ~ **of soap** ein Riegel od. Stück Seife; **a** ~ **of chocolate** ein Riegel (weitS. e-e Tafel) Schokolade. **5.** (Gold- etc)Barren m. **6.** (dicker) Strich. **7.** ♪ Taktstrich m; ein Takt m. **8.** ⚖ (Gerichts)Schranke f: **prisoner at the** ~ Angeklagte m,f. **9.** ⚖ Anwaltsberuf m; coll. Anwaltschaft f, Br. Stand m der **barristers: be admitted** (Br. **called**) **to the** ~ als Anwalt (Br. **barrister**) zugelassen werden; **read for the** ~ Br. Jura studieren. **10.** (Tor-, Quer-, Sprung)Latte f. **11.** Bar f; Lokal n, Imbißstube f; Bar f, Theke f. **II** v/t **12.**

verriegeln. **13.** a. ~ **up** vergittern. **14.** a. ~ **in** einsperren: ~ **out** aussperren. **15.** hemmen; (**from**) hindern (an dat), abhalten (von). **III** prp **16.** außer, abgesehen von: ~ **none** (alle) ohne Ausnahme.

barb [ba:b] s **1.** Widerhaken m; Stachel m. **2.** fig. Spitze f.

bar·bar·i·an [ba:'beərɪən] **I** s Barbar(in). **II** adj barbarisch. **bar·bar·ic** ['~bærɪk] adj (~**ally**) barbarisch. **bar·ba·rism** ['~bərɪzəm] s **1.** Barbarismus m, Sprachwidrigkeit f. **2.** Barbarei f. **bar·bar·i·ty** ['~'bærətɪ] s Barbarei f. **bar·ba·rize** ['~bəraɪz] v/t barbarisieren. **'bar·ba·rous** adj □ barbarisch.

bar·be·cue ['ba:bɪkju:] **I** v/t auf dem Rost od. am Spieß braten, grillen. **II** s Barbecue n: a) Grillfest n, b) Bratrost m, Grill m, c) auf dem Rost od. Grill gebratenes Fleisch.

barbed [ba:bd] adj **1.** mit Widerhaken od. Stacheln: ~ **wire** Stacheldraht m. **2.** fig. spitz (Bemerkung etc).

bar·ber ['ba:bə] s (Herren)Friseur m: ~**('s) shop** Friseurgeschäft n.

bar·bi·tu·rate [ba:'bɪtjʊrət] s ⚗ etc Barbiturat n.

bare [beə] **I** adj (□ → **barely**) **1.** nackt: a) entblößt: **on one's** ~ **feet** barfuß; **in one's** ~ **skin** nackt, b) kahl (Wand etc), c) fig. ungeschminkt: ~ **facts** pl nackte Tatsachen pl. **2.** fig. unverhüllt: ~ **nonsense** blanker Unsinn; **lay** ~ → II. **3.** ~ **of** arm an (dat); ohne, ...los. **4.** knapp (Mehrheit etc): **earn a** ~ **living** knapp das Nötigste zum Leben verdienen. **5.** bloß: **the** ~ **thought** allein od. schon der Gedanke. **II** v/t **6.** entblößen, weitS. Zähne zeigen. **7.** fig. enthüllen, bloßlegen. '~**back(ed)** adj u. adv ungesattelt, ohne Sattel. '~**faced** adj unverschämt, schamlos. '~**foot** , ~**'foot·ed** adj u. adv barfuß, -füßig. ~**'head·ed** adj u. adv barhäuptig.

bare·ly ['beəlɪ] adv **1.** kaum, knapp. **2.** ärmlich, spärlich.

bar·gain ['ba:gɪn] **I** s **1.** Handel m, Geschäft n (a. fig.): **it's a** ~**!** abgemacht!; **into the** ~ noch dazu, obendrein; **make the best of a bad** ~ sich so gut wie möglich aus der Affäre ziehen; **strike a** ~ vorteilhaft abschließen; → **drive** 12. **2.** vorteilhaftes Geschäft, Gelegenheitskauf m. **II** v/i **3.** handeln, feilschen (*for* um). **4.** verhandeln (*for* über *acc*): ∼ **on** vereinbaren (*acc*). **5.** (*for*) rechnen (mit), gefaßt sein (auf *acc*). **III** *v/t* **6.** aushandeln. ∼ **base·ment** *s* Niedrigpreisabteilung *f* im Tiefgeschoß (*e-s Kaufhauses*). ∼ **count·er** *s* Wühltisch *m*. ∼ **price** *s* Gelegenheits-, Sonderpreis *m*. ∼ **sale** *s* **1.** Verkauf *m* zu herabgesetzten Preisen. **2.** Ausverkauf *m*.

barge [baːdʒ] **I** *s* **1.** Last-, Schleppkahn *m*. **II** *v/i* **2.** sich schwerfällig bewegen. **3.** F (*into*) stoßen, prallen, bumsen (gegen, an *acc*). **4.** ∼ **in**(**to**) F hereinplatzen (in *acc*); sich einmischen (in *acc*).

bar·i·tone ['bærɪtəʊn] *s* ♩ Bariton *m*.

bark¹ [baːk] **I** *s* **1.** (Baum)Rinde *f*, Borke *f*. **II** *v/t* **2.** abrinden. **3.** sich *die Knie etc* auf-, abschürfen: ∼ *one's knees*.

bark² [∼] **I** *v/i* bellen (*a.* F husten): ∼ *at s.o.* j-n anbellen; *fig.* j-n anschnauzen; *∼ing dogs never bite* Hunde, die bellen, beißen nicht; ∼ *up the wrong tree* F auf dem Holzweg sein; an der falschen Adresse sein. **II** *s* Bellen (*a.* F Husten): *his ∼ is worse than his bite* er bellt nur(, aber beißt nicht).

'**bar·keep·er** *s* Barkeeper *m*: a) Barbesitzer *m*, b) Barmann *m*, -mixer *m*.

bar·ley ['baːlɪ] *s* ♣ Gerste *f*.

'**bar·maid** *s bsd. Br.* Bardame *f*. '**∼·man** ['∼mən] *s* (*irr man*) Barmann *m*, -keeper *m*, -mixer *m*.

barm·y ['baːmɪ] *adj sl.* bekloppt, verrückt: *go* ∼ überschnappen.

barn [baːn] *s* **1.** Scheune *f*. **2.** (Vieh)Stall *m*.

ba·rom·e·ter [bə'rɒmɪtə] *s* Barometer *n* (*a. fig.*).

bar·on ['bærən] *s* **1.** Baron *m*. **2.** (*Industrie- etc*)Baron *m*, Magnat *m*. '**bar·on·ess** *s* Baronin *f*. **bar·on·et** ['∼nɪt] *s* Baronet *m*.

ba·roque [bə'rɒk] **I** *adj* barock. **II** *s* Barock *n*, *m*.

bar·racks ['bærəks] *s pl* (*meist sg konstruiert*) **1.** Kaserne *f*. **2.** *contp.* Mietskaserne *f*.

bar·rage ['bæraːʒ] *s* **1.** (Stau)Damm *m*, Talsperre *f*. **2.** ✕ Sperrfeuer *n*. **3.** *fig.* Hagel *m*, Schwall *m*.

bar·rel ['bærəl] **I** *s* **1.** Faß *n*, (*Rohölmaß mst*) Barrel *n*: ∼*s* (*od. a* ∼) *of* F ein Haufen (*Geld etc*). **2.** (Gewehr)Lauf *m*, (Geschütz)Rohr *n*. **II** *v/t pret u. pp*

-reled, *bsd. Br.* -relled **3.** in Fässer füllen; ∼(*l*)*ed beer* Faßbier *n*. ∼ **or·gan** *s* ♩ Drehorgel *f*, Leierkasten *m*.

bar·ren ['bærən] *adj* □ **1.** unfruchtbar (*Lebewesen, Land etc*). **2.** geistig unproduktiv. **3.** ∼ *of* arm an (*dat*), ...los. **4.** nutzlos, ✝ tot (*Kapital*).

bar·rette [bæ'ret] *s Am.* Haarspange *f*.

bar·ri·cade [,bærɪ'keɪd] **I** *s* Barrikade *f*: *go to* (*od. mount*) *the* ∼*s fig.* auf die Barrikaden gehen *od.* steigen. **II** *v/t* verbarrikadieren.

bar·ri·er ['bærɪə] *s* **1.** Schranke *f*, Barriere *f*, Sperre *f*. **2.** Schlag-, Grenzbaum *m*. **3.** *phys.* (*Schall*)Grenze *f*. **4.** *fig.* Hindernis *n* (*to* für). ∼ **cream** *s* Schutzcreme *f*.

bar·ring ['baːrɪŋ] *prp* ausgenommen, abgesehen von: ∼ *a miracle* falls *od.* wenn kein Wunder geschieht.

bar·ris·ter ['bærɪstə] *s* ⚖ **1.** *Br.* Barrister *m* (*vor höheren Gerichten plädierender Anwalt*). **2.** *Am. allg.* Rechtsanwalt *m*.

bar·row ['bærəʊ] *s* (Hand-, Schub)Karre(n *m*) *f*.

'**bar·tend·er** *bsd. Am.* → **barman**.

bar·ter ['baːtə] **I** *v/t* (ein)tauschen (*against, for* gegen). **II** *v/i* verhandeln (*for* über *acc*). **III** *s* Tausch(handel *m*, -geschäft *n*) *m*.

ba·salt ['bæsɔːlt] *s geol.* Basalt *m*.

base¹ [beɪs] *adj* □ **1.** gemein, niederträchtig. **2.** minderwertig, (*Metall*) unedel.

base² [∼] **I** *s* **1.** *a. fig.* Basis *f*, Grundlage *f*, Fundament *n* (*a.* △). **2.** Grundstoff *m*, Hauptbestandteil *m*. **3.** *fig.* Ausgangspunkt *m*, -basis *f*. **4.** ✕ Standort *m*; Basis *f*, Stützpunkt *m*. **5.** *Baseball*: Mal *n*. **II** *v/t* **6.** stützen, gründen (*on* auf *acc*): *be* ∼*d on* beruhen *od.* basieren auf (*dat*).

'**base·ball** *s Sport*: Baseball(spiel *n*) *m*. '**∼·board** *s Am.* Fuß(boden)-, Scheuerleiste *f*. '**∼·less** *adj* □ grundlos. ∼ **line** *s* Grundlinie *f*.

base·ment ['beɪsmənt] *s* Kellergeschoß *n*.

base·ness ['beɪsnɪs] *s* **1.** Gemeinheit *f*, Niedertracht *f*. **2.** Minderwertigkeit *f*.

ba·ses ['beɪsiːz] *pl von* **basis**.

bash [bæʃ] F **I** *v/t* **1.** heftig schlagen, j-n verprügeln: ∼ *in* einschlagen. **II** *s* **2.** heftiger Schlag: *give s.o. a* ∼ (*on the*

battery

nose) j-m ein Ding (auf die Nase) verpassen. **3.** Versuch *m*: **have a ~ at s.th.** es mit et. probieren.

bash·ful ['bæʃfʊl] *adj* □ scheu, schüchtern.

bas·ic ['beisik] **I** *adj* grundlegend, Grund...: **~ fact** grundlegende Tatsache; **~ fee** (*law, salary, etc*) Grundgebühr *f* (-gesetz *n*, -gehalt *n* etc). **II** *s pl* Grundlagen *pl.* **'bas·i·cal·ly** *adv* **1.** im Grunde. **2.** im wesentlichen.

ba·sil·i·ca [bə'zilikə] *s* △ Basilika *f.*

ba·sin ['beisn] *s allg.* Becken *n* (*a. geol. etc*); *engS.* Schale *f*, Schüssel *f.*

ba·sis ['beisis] *pl* **-ses** ['~si:z] *s* **1.** ✗ Basis *f*, Stützpunkt *m.* **2.** *fig.* Basis *f*, Grundlage *f*: **on the ~ of** auf der Basis von (*od. gen*); **~ of discussion** Diskussionsgrundlage; **take as a ~** zugrunde legen.

bask [bɑːsk] *v/i* sich sonnen (*a. fig.*): **~ in the sun** sich im Sonnenbad nehmen.

bas·ket ['bɑːskit] *s* Korb *m.* '**~·ball** *s Sport:* Basketball(spiel *n*) *m.*

bass [beis] *s* ♪ Baß(stimme *f*) *m*; Bassist *m.*

bas·soon [bə'su:n] *s* ♪ Fagott *n.*

bas·tard ['bɑːstəd] **I** *s* **1.** Bastard *m* (*a. biol.*). **2.** *sl.* Scheißkerl *m*; *allg.* Kerl *m*: **poor ~** armes Schwein; **a ~ of a headache** verfluchte Kopfschmerzen *pl.* **II** *adj* **3.** unehelich. **4.** *biol.* Bastard...

baste¹ [beist] *v/t* Braten mit Fett begießen.

baste² [~] *v/t* verprügeln.

baste³ [~] *v/t* (an)heften.

bas·tion ['bæstiən] *s* ✗ Bastion *f.*

bat¹ [bæt] *s zo.* Fledermaus *f*: **(as) blind as a ~** stockblind; **have ~s in the belfry** F e-n Vogel haben.

bat² [~] **I** *s* **1.** *Baseball, Kricket:* Schlagholz *n*, Schläger *m*: **off one's own ~** *fig.* selbständig; auf eigene Faust. **2.** *Br.* F Tempo *n*: **at a fair ~** mit e-m ganz schönen Zahn. **3.** *Am. sl.* Sauferei *f*: **go on a ~** e-e Sauftour machen. **II** *v/i* **4.** *Baseball, Kricket:* am Schlagen sein.

bat³ [~] *v/t*: **without ~ting an eyelid** ohne mit der Wimper zu zucken.

batch [bætʃ] *s* Stapel *m*, Stoß *m.*

bat·ed ['beitid] *adj*: **with ~ breath** mit angehaltenem Atem, gespannt.

bath [bɑːθ] **I** *pl* **baths** ['~ðz] *s* **1.** (Wannen)Bad *n*: **have** (*od.* **take**) **a ~** ein Bad

nehmen, baden. **2.** Badewanne *f.* **3.** Bad(ezimmer) *n.* **4.** *mst pl* Bad *n*: a) Badeanstalt *f*, b) Badeort *m.* **5.** ♨, *phot.* Bad *n.* **II** *v/t* **6.** *Br.* Kind *etc* baden. **III** *v/i* **7.** *Br.* baden, ein Bad nehmen.

bathe [beið] **I** *v/t* **1.** *Wunde etc, bsd. Am. a. Kind etc* baden. **~d in sunlight** (**sweat, tears**) *fig.* sonnenüberflutet (schweißgebadet, tränenüberströmt). **II** *v/i* **3.** *bsd. Am.* baden, ein Bad nehmen. **4.** baden, schwimmen. **III** *s* **5.** Bad *n* (*im Freien*): **have** (*od.* **take**) **a ~** → 4.

bath·ing ['beiðiŋ] **I** *s* Baden *n.* **II** *adj* Bade...: **~ accident** (**cap, costume** *od.* **dress** *od.* **suit, trunks**) Badeunfall *m* (-mütze *f od.* -kappe *f*, -anzug *m*, -hose *f*).

'bath·robe *s* **1.** Bademantel *m.* **2.** *Am.* Morgen-, Schlafrock *m.* **~·room** *s* **1.** ['~rʊm] *s* **1.** Badezimmer *n.* **2.** *Am.* Toilette *f.* **~ tow·el** *s* Badetuch *n.* '**~·tub** *s* Badewanne *f.*

ba·tik [bə'ti:k] *s* Batik(druck) *m.*

ba·tiste [bæ'ti:st] *s* Batist *m.*

ba·ton ['bætən] *s* **1.** (Amts-, Kommando)Stab *m.* **2.** ♪ Taktstock *m.* **3.** *Leichtathletik:* (Staffel)Stab *m.* **4.** Schlagstock *m*, Gummiknüppel *m* (*der Polizei*).

bats·man ['bætsmən] *s* (*irr man*) *Kricket:* Schläger *m*, Schlagmann *m.*

bat·tal·ion [bə'tæljən] *s* ✗ Bataillon *n.*

bat·ten¹ ['bætn] **I** *s* Latte *f*, Leiste *f.* **II** *v/t*: **~ down the hatches** ♻ die Luken schalken; *fig.* alles dichtmachen.

bat·ten² [~] *v/i mst fig.* dick u. fett werden (**on** auf Kosten *gen*).

bat·ter¹ ['bætə] **I** *v/t* **1.** wiederholt heftig schlagen; *Frau, Kind etc* (wiederholt) mißhandeln: **~ down** (*od.* **in**) einschlagen; **~ed wives' refuge** Frauenhaus *n.* **2.** abnutzen. **3.** (arg) lädieren *od.* zerbeulen, *a. fig.* arg in Mitleidenschaft ziehen. **II** *v/i* **4.** wiederholt heftig schlagen *od.* stoßen (**against** gegen; **at** an *acc*): **~ (away) at the door** gegen die Tür hämmern. **III** *s* **5.** *gastr.* Eierkuchenteig *m.*

bat·ter² [~] *s Baseball, Kricket:* Schläger *m*, Schlagmann *m.*

bat·ter·y ['bætəri] *s* **1.** ⚡ Batterie *f.* **2.** Batterie *f*, Reihe *f*, Satz *m.* **3.** ✶ Legebatterie *f.* **4.** 🔨 Tätlichkeit *f*; Körper-

verletzung f. **~ hen** s ✐ Batteriehenne f.
'**~op·er·at·ed** adj batteriebetrieben,
Batterie...

bat·tle ['bætl] **I** s **1.** ✕ Schlacht f (of bei).
2. fig. Kampf m (for um). **II** v/i **3.** bsd.
fig. kämpfen: **~ for breath** um Atem
ringen. '**~ax(e)** s **1.** ✕ hist. Streitaxt f.
2. F alter Drachen. '**~field**, '**~ground**
s ✕ Schlachtfeld n: **~ country** kriegführendes Land. '**~ship** s Schlacht-
schiff n.

bat·tue [bæ'tu:] s Treibjagd f.

bat·ty ['bætɪ] adj sl. bekloppt, verrückt.

baulk → **balk**.

baux·ite ['bɔːksaɪt] s min. Bauxit m.

Ba·var·i·an [bə'veərɪən] **I** adj bay(e)-
risch. **II** s Bayer(in).

bawd·y ['bɔːdɪ] adj unflätig, obszön.

bawl [bɔːl] **I** v/i schreien, brüllen: **~ at
s.o.** j-n anbrüllen; **~ for help** um Hilfe
schreien. **II** v/t oft **~ out** (heraus)schrei-
en, (-)brüllen.

bay¹ [beɪ] s Bai f, Bucht f.

bay² [~] s △ Erker m.

bay³ [~] s ♀ Lorbeer(baum) m.

bay⁴ [~] **I** v/i bellen: **~ at s.o.** j-n anbellen;
fig. j-n anschreien. **II** s Gebell n: **be** (od.
stand) **at ~** gestellt sein (Wild); fig. in
die Enge getrieben sein; **bring to ~** Wild
stellen; fig. in die Enge treiben; **hold**
(od. **keep**) **at ~** j-n in Schach halten;
Krankheit etc von sich fernhalten; Feuer, Seuche etc unter Kontrolle halten.

bay·o·net ['beɪənɪt] s ✕ Bajonett n, Sei-
tengewehr n.

bay win·dow s **1.** Erkerfenster n. **2.** Am.
humor. Vorbau m (Bauch).

ba·zaar [bə'zɑː] s (a. Wohltätigkeits)Ba-
sar m.

be [bi:] (irr) **I** v/aux **1.** Zustand: sein: **he
is gone** er ist weg. **2.** Passiv: werden: **I
was cheated** ich wurde betrogen. **3.**
sollen, müssen, dürfen, können: **he is
to be pitied** er ist zu bedauern; **it is not
to be seen** es ist nicht zu sehen; **it was
not to be** es sollte nicht sein. **4.** Ver-
laufsform: **he is reading** er liest (gerade); **he was watching TV when the
telephone rang** er sah gerade fern, als
das Telefon läutete. **5.** nahe Zukunft: **I
am leaving tomorrow** ich reise morgen
ab; → **go** 27. **6.** Kopula: sein: **he is my
father. II** v/i **7.** sein, der Fall sein: **how
is it that ...?** wie kommt es, daß ...?; **it is**

I (F me) ich bin es. **8.** sein, bestehen: **to
be or not to be: that is the question**
Sein oder Nichtsein, das ist hier die
Frage. **9.** sein, stattfinden (Versammlung etc); gehen, fahren (Bus etc). **10.**
sein, sich befinden: **have you ever
been to London?** sind Sie schon einmal
in London gewesen?; **has anyone
been?** F ist j-d dagewesen? **11.** (beruflich) werden: **I'll be an engineer** ich
werde einmal Ingenieur. **12.** gehören:
this book is mine. 13. sein, stammen
(from aus). **14.** kosten: **how much are
these gloves?** **15.** dauern (Veranstaltung etc).

beach [bi:tʃ] **I** s Strand m: **on the ~** am
Strand. **II** v/t Schiff auf den Strand
setzen od. ziehen. **~ ball** s Wasserball
m. **~ bug·gy** s mot. Strandbuggy m. **~
tow·el** s Bade-, Strandlaken n. '**~wear**
s Strandkleidung f.

bea·con ['bi:kən] s **1.** Leucht-, Signal-
feuer n. **2.** → **Belisha beacon.**

bead [bi:d] **I** s **1.** (Glas-, Schweiß-, Tau-
etc)Perle f. pl eccl. Rosenkranz m:
say (od. **tell**) **one's ~s** den Rosenkranz
beten. **II** v/t **3.** mit Perlen besetzen. **III**
v/i **4.** perlen.

beak [bi:k] s **1.** orn. Schnabel m. **2.** ✆
Tülle f. **beaked** adj **1.** schnabelförmig.
2. vorspringend, spitz.

beak·er ['bi:kə] s Becher m.

beam [bi:m] **I** s **1.** Balken m. **2.** Strahl m,
⚡, phys. a. Bündel n: **~ of rays** Strahlen-
bündel; **~ of hope** Hoffnungsstrahl. **3.**
Peil-, Leit-, Richtstrahl m: **be off (the) ~**
↗, ⚓ vom Kurs abgekommen sein; F
auf dem Holzweg sein; **be on (the) ~** ↗,
⚓ auf Kurs sein; F auf dem richtigen
Weg sein. **4.** strahlendes Lächeln. **II** v/t
5. ausstrahlen (a. phys. u. Rundfunk,
TV). **III** v/i **6.** strahlen (a. fig. **with** vor
dat): **~ing with joy** freudestrahlend.
.~'ends s pl: **be on one's ~** fig. auf
dem letzten Loch pfeifen.

bean [bi:n] s **1.** ♀ Bohne f: **be full of ~s**
F aufgekratzt sein; voller Leben(skraft)
stecken; **spill the ~s** F alles ausplaudern. **2.** Am. sl. Birne f (Kopf).

bear¹ [beə] **I** s **1.** zo. Bär m. **2.** fig.
Brummbär m; Tolpatsch m. **3.** ♥ Bais-
sespekulant m. **II** v/i **4.** ♥ auf Baisse
spekulieren.

bear² [~] (irr) **I** v/t **1.** Last, a. fig. Datum,

Verantwortung, Verlust etc tragen: → **fruit** 2a, **interest** 6, **resemblance**, *etc*. **2.** zur Welt bringen, gebären. **3.** *Gefühl* hegen: → **grudge** 3. **4.** *Gehorsam etc* leisten: → **company** 1. **5.** ertragen, aushalten, -stehen: → **comparison** 1. **II** *v/i* **6.** tragen, halten (*Balken, Eis etc*). **7.** (**on**) sich beziehen (auf *acc*), betreffen (*acc*): → **pressure**. **8.** ~ (**to the**) **left** sich links halten.

Verbindungen mit Adverbien:

~ **a·way** *v/t* **1.** forttragen. **2.** *Sieg etc* davontragen. ~ **down I** *v/t* überwinden, -wältigen, *Widerstand* brechen. **II** *v/i* (**on**) sich (schnell) nähern (*dat*); sich stürzen (auf *acc*); *fig.* lasten (auf *dat*), bedrücken (*acc*); e-r *Sache* zu Leibe gehen. ~ **in** *v/t*: *it was borne in on him* es wurde ihm klar (*that* daß). ~ **out** *v/t* bekräftigen, bestätigen; *j-m* recht geben. ~ **up I** *v/t* **1.** ermutigen. **II** *v/i* **2.** (**against, under**) sich behaupten (gegen), (tapfer) ertragen (*acc*). **3.** *Br.* Mut fassen, (wieder) fröhlich werden: ~*!* Kopf hoch!

bear·a·ble ['beərəbl] *adj* □ erträglich.

beard [biəd] **I** *s* Bart *m*: *laugh in one's* ~ sich ins Fäustchen lachen. **II** *v/t*: ~ **the lion in his den** *fig.* sich in die Höhle des Löwen wagen. **'beard·ed** *adj* bärtig. **'beard·less** *adj* bartlos.

bear·er ['beərə] *s* **1.** Träger(in). **2.** Überbringer(in) (*a.* ✝ *e-s Schecks etc*). **3.** ✝ Inhaber(in) (*e-s Wertpapiers*).

bear·ing ['beəriŋ] *s* **1.** Ertragen *n*: *beyond* (*od. past*) ~ unerträglich. **2.** Betragen *n*, Verhalten *n*. **3.** (Körper)Haltung *f*. **4.** (**on**) Beziehung *f* (zu), Bezug *m* (auf *acc*). **5.** ✗, ⚓ Lage *f*, Position *f*; (*a.* Funk)Peilung *f*, *a. fig.* Orientierung *f*: *take one's* ~*s* e-e Peilung vornehmen; sich orientieren; *lose one's* ~(*s*) die Orientierung verlieren; *find* (*od. get*) *one's* ~*s* sich zurechtfinden. **6.** ☉ (Achsen-, Kugel- *etc*)Lager *n*.

bear·ish ['beəriʃ] *adj* **1.** bärenhaft. **2.** *fig.* brummig; tolpatschig. **3.** ✝ flau; Baisse...

bear| paw *s Am.* Radkralle *f*, Parkriegel *m*. **'~·skin** *s* Bärenfell *n*.

beast [bi:st] *s* **1.** (*a.* wildes) Tier: ~ *of burden* Lasttier; ~ *of prey* Raubtier. **2.** *fig.* Bestie *f*; F Biest *n*, Ekel *n*. **'beast·ly**

adj **1.** *fig.* tierisch. **2.** F ekelhaft, gemein; scheußlich.

beat [bi:t] **I** *s* **1.** (*Herz-, Trommel-etc*)Schlag *m*. **2.** ♪ Takt *m*; (*Jazz*) Beat *m*; Beat(musik *f*) *m*: *in* ~ im Takt; *out of* ~, *off* (*the*) ~ aus dem Takt. **3.** Runde *f*, Revier *n* (*e-s Schutzmanns etc*): *be on one's* ~ s-e *od.* die Runde machen; *that is out of my* ~ *fig.* das schlägt nicht in mein Fach. **II** *adj* **4.** F wie erschlagen, fix u. fertig. **5.** ♪ Beat...: ~ *group* (*music, etc*). **III** *v/t* (*irr*) **6.** schlagen, (ver)prügeln. **7.** a) schlagen; *Teppich etc* (aus)klopfen; *Metall* hämmern *od.* schmieden, b) → **beat up** 3. **8.** *Weg* treten, sich bahnen: ~ *it* F abhauen, verduften. **9.** *j-n* schlagen, besiegen (*at* in *dat*); *et.* übertreffen, -bieten: *that* ~*s all* (*od. everything*)*!* das ist doch die Höhe! **10.** verblüffen: *that* ~*s me* das ist mir zu hoch. **IV** *v/i* **11.** schlagen: ~ *at* (*od. on*) *the door* gegen die Tür hämmern.

Verbindungen mit Adverbien:

beat| back *v/t* Gegner zurückschlagen. ~ **down I** *v/t* **1.** *Aufstand etc* niederschlagen. **2.** *Preis* drücken, *a. j-n* herunterhandeln (*to* auf *acc*). **II** *v/i* **3.** herunterbrennen (**on** auf *acc*) (*Sonne*); herunter-, niederprasseln (**on** auf *acc*) (*Regen*). ~ **off** *v/t Angriff, Gegner* zurückschlagen. ~ **in** *v/t Tür* einschlagen. ~ **out** *v/t Feuer* ausschlagen. ~ **up** *v/t* **1.** aufrütteln (*a. fig.*). **2.** *j-n* zs.-schlagen. **3.** *Eier etc* (zu Schaum *od.* Schnee) schlagen.

beat·en ['bi:tn] **I** *pp von* **beat**. **II** *adj* **1.** ☉ gehämmert: ~ *gold* Blattgold *n*. **2.** vielbegangen (*Weg*): *off the* ~ *track* ungewohnt, ungewöhnlich. **'beat·er** *s* **1.** ☉ Stampfe *f*; Stößel *m*; Klopfer *m*. **2.** *gastr.* Schneebesen *m*. **'beat·ing** *s* Prügel *pl*; *fig.* Niederlage *f*: *give s.o. a sound* ~ j-m e-e tüchtige Tracht Prügel verabreichen; j-m e-e böse Schlappe zufügen.

beat·nik ['bi:tnik] *s* Beatnik *m*.

beau·ti·cian [bju:'tiʃn] *s* Kosmetiker(in).

beau·ti·ful ['bju:təful] *adj* □ schön: *the* ~ *people pl* die Schickeria.

beau·ti·fy ['bju:tifai] *v/t* verschönern.

beau·ty ['bju:ti] *s* **1.** Schönheit *f* (*a. Frau*). **2.** F das Schön(st)e. **3.** F Gedicht *n*, Prachtstück *n* (*of* von). ~ **com-pe·ti·tion**, ~**con·test** *s* Schönheitswett-bewerb *m*. ~ **farm** *s* Schönheitsfarm *f*. ~ **par·lo(u)r** *s* Schönheitssalon *m*. ~ **patch** → **beauty spot** 1. ~ **queen** *s* Schönheitskönigin *f*. ~ **sa·lon**, *Am*. ~ **shop** → **beauty parlo(u)r**. ~ **sleep** *s* F Schlaf *m* vor Mitternacht. ~ **spot** *s* 1. Schönheitspfläst erchen *n*. 2. schönes Fleckchen Erde.

bea·ver ['biːvə] *s zo*. Biber *m*.

be·came [bɪ'keɪm] *pret von* **become**.

be·cause [bɪ'kɒz] **I** *cj* weil, da. **II** *prp*: ~ **of** wegen (*gen*).

beck [bek] *s*: *be at s.o.'s ~ and call* j-m auf den leisesten Wink gehorchen, nach j-s Pfeife tanzen. **beck·on** ['~ən] *v/t* j-m (zu)winken, j-m ein Zeichen geben.

be·come [bɪ'kʌm] (*irr*) **I** *v/i* 1. werden: *what has become of him?* was ist aus ihm geworden? **II** *v/t* 2. sich ziemen für. 3. *j-m* stehen, passen zu.

be·com·ing *adj* □ 1. passend, kleidsam: *be very ~ to s.o.* j-m sehr gut stehen. 2. schicklich, geziemend.

bed [bed] **I** *s* 1. (*a. Fluß- etc*)Bett *n*: *go to ~* ins Bett gehen (*with* mit); *keep one's ~* das Bett hüten; *make the ~* das Bett machen; *as you make your ~ so you must lie on it* wie man sich bettet, so liegt man; *put to ~* ins Bett bringen; *take to one's ~* sich (krank) ins Bett legen; ~ *and breakfast* Zimmer *n* mit Frühstück. 2. (Garten)Beet *n*. 3. ⚙ Bett(ung *f*) *n*, Unterlage *f*. **II** *v/t* 4. ins Bett bringen. 5. ~ **out** auspflanzen, -setzen.

be·daub [bɪ'dɔːb] *v/t* beschmieren; ~*ed with clay* lehmbeschmiert.

'**bed**|**·bug** *s zo*. Wanze *f*. '~**clothes** *s pl* Bettwäsche *f*. '~**cov·er** *s* Bettdecke *f*.

bed·ding ['bedɪŋ] *s* Bettzeug *n*.

be·deck [bɪ'dek] *v/t* schmücken.

be·dev·il [bɪ'devl] *v/t pret u. pp* -**iled**, *bsd. Br.* -**illed** durcheinanderbringen, verwirren.

bed·lam ['bedləm] *s fig*. Tollhaus *n*.

bed| **lin·en** *s* Bettwäsche *f*. '~**pan** *s* Stechbecken *n*, Bettpfanne *f*, -schüs-sel *f*. '~**post** *s* Bettpfosten *m*: → **be-tween** 2.

be·drag·gled [bɪ'dræɡld] *adj* 1. durch-näßt; verdreckt. 2. *fig*. heruntergekom-

men (*Haus etc*); ungepflegt (*Erschei-nung etc*).

bed| **rest** *s* Bettruhe *f*. '~**rid·den** *adj* bettlägerig. '~**rock** *s geol*. Grund-, Muttergestein *n*: *get down to the ~ of a matter fig*. e-r Sache auf den Grund gehen. '~**room** ['~rʊm] *s* Schlafzimmer *n*: ~ **suburb** (*od. town*) Schlafstadt *f*. '~**side** *s*: *at the ~* am Bett; *have a good ~ manner* gut mit Kranken umgehen können; ~ **lamp** Nachttischlampe *f*; ~ **rug** Bettvorleger *m*; ~ **table** Nacht-tisch(chen *n*) *m*. '~**sit**, ,~'**sit·ter**, ,~'**sit·ting room** *s Br.* 1. möbliertes Zimmer. 2. Einzimmerapartment *n*. '~**sore** *s* ✚ wundgelegene Stelle: *get ~s* sich durch- *od*. wundliegen. '~**space** *s* Bettenzahl *f*, -kapazität *f* (*in Klinik, Hotel etc*). '~**spread** *s* Tagesdecke *f*. '~**stead** *s* Bettgestell *n*. '~**tick** *s* Inlett *n*. '~**time** *s* Schlafenszeit *n*: ~ *reading* Bettlektüre *f*; ~ *story* Gutenachtge-schichte *f*.

bee [biː] *s zo*. Biene *f*: (*as*) *busy as a ~* bienenfleißig; *have a ~ in one's bonnet* F e-n Fimmel *od*. Tick haben.

beech [biːtʃ] *s* ♣ Buche *f*. '~**nut** *s* Buch-ecker *f*.

beef [biːf] **I** *s* 1. Rindfleisch *n*. 2. F (Muskel)Kraft *f*. 3. *sl*. Meckerei *f*, Nörgelei *f*. **II** *v/i* 4. *sl*. meckern, nörgeln (*about* über *acc*). ~**bur·ger** ['~,bɜːɡə] *s gastr*. Hamburger *m*. '~**eat·er** *s Br.* Beefeater *m*, Tower-Wächter *m*. '~**steak** *s* Beef-steak *n*. ~ **tea** *s* (Rind)Fleischbrühe *f*, Bouillon *f*.

beef·y ['biːfɪ] *adj* F bullig.

'**bee·line** *s*: *make a ~ for* schnurstracks zu- *od*. losgehen auf (*acc*).

been [biːn] *pp von* **be**.

beer [bɪə] *s* Bier *n*: → *small* I. ~ **gar·den** *s* Biergarten *m*.

beer·y ['bɪərɪ] *adj* 1. bierselig. 2. nach Bier riechend: ~ *breath* Bierfahne *f*.

'**bees·wax** *s* Bienenwachs *n*.

beet [biːt] *s* ♣ Runkelrübe *f*, *Am. a.* rote Bete *od*. Rübe.

bee·tle ['biːtl] *s zo*. Käfer *m*.

be·fore [bɪ'fɔː] **I** *adv* 1. *räumlich*: vorn, voran: *go ~* vorangehen. 2. *zeitlich*: vorher, zuvor: *the year ~* das vorherge-hende Jahr. **II** *prp* 3. *räumlich*: vor (*acc od. dat*): ~ *my eyes* vor m-n Augen. 4. vor (*dat*), in Gegenwart von (*od. gen*): ~

witnesses vor Zeugen. **5.** *zeitlich:* vor (*dat*): *the week ~ last* vorletzte Woche; *~ long* in Kürze, bald. **6.** *Reihenfolge, Rang:* voraus, vor (*acc od. dat*): *be ~ the others* den anderen voraus sein. **III** *cj* **7.** bevor, ehe: *not ~* erst als *od.* wenn.

be'fore·hand *adv* **1.** zu'vor, (im) vor-aus: *know s.th. ~* et. im voraus wissen. **2.** zuvor, früher. **3.** zu früh, verfrüht.

be·friend [bɪ'frend] *v/t* **1.** *j-m* behilflich sein; sich *j-s* annehmen.

beg [beg] **I** *v/t* **1.** et. erbitten (*of s.o.* von *j-m*): *~ leave* (*of s.o.*) (*j-n*) um Erlaubnis bitten; → *pardon* **1. 2.** erbetteln, betteln um. **3.** *j-n* bitten (*to do* zu tun). **II** *v/i* **4.** betteln: *go ~ging* betteln gehen; *fig.* keinen Interessenten *od.* Abnehmer finden. **5.** (dringend) bitten (*for* um; *of s.o.* *j-n*). **6.** sich erlauben *od.* gestatten (*to do* zu tun).

be·gan [bɪ'ɡæn] *pret von* begin.

be·get [bɪ'ɡet] *v/t (irr)* **1.** *Kind* zeugen. **2.** *fig.* erzeugen.

beg·gar ['beɡə] **I** *s* **1.** Bettler(in). **2.** F *Kerl m:* *lucky ~* Glückspilz *m.* **II** *v/t* **3.** an den Bettelstab bringen. **4.** *~ description* sich nicht mit Worten beschreiben lassen; jeder Beschreibung spotten. **'beg·gar·ly** *adj* **1.** bettelarm. **2.** *fig.* armselig, kümmerlich. **'beg·gar·y** *s* Bettelarmut *f.*

be·gin [bɪ'ɡɪn] *v/t u. v/i (irr)* beginnen, anfangen: *to ~ with* zunächst (einmal); erstens (einmal); *~ on s.th.* et. in Angriff nehmen; *~ (on) a new bottle* e-e neue Flasche anbrechen. **be'gin·ner** *s* Anfänger(in): *~'s luck* Anfängerglück *n.* **be'gin·ning** *s* **1.** Beginn *m,* Anfang *m:* *at* (*od. in*) *the ~* am Anfang; *from the ~* (ganz) von Anfang an. **2.** *pl* (erste) Anfänge *pl.*

be·go·ni·a [bɪ'ɡəʊnjə] *s* ♣ Begonie *f.*

be·got [bɪ'ɡɒt] *pret von* beget. **be'got·ten** [~tn] *pp von* beget.

be·grudge [bɪ'ɡrʌdʒ] *v/t* **1.** *~ s.o. s.th.* *j-m* et. mißgönnen. **2.** *~ doing s.th.* et. nur widerwillig tun.

be·guile [bɪ'ɡaɪl] *v/t* **1.** betrügen (*of, out of* um), täuschen. **2.** verleiten (*into doing* zu tun). **3.** sich *die Zeit* (angenehm) vertreiben (*by, with* mit).

be·gun [bɪ'ɡʌn] *pp von* begin.

be·half [bɪ'hɑːf] *s:* *on* (*Am. a. in*) *~ of* zugunsten von (*od. gen*), für; im Na-

men *od.* Auftrag von (*od. gen*), für.

be·have [bɪ'heɪv] **I** *v/i* **1.** sich (gut) benehmen. **2.** sich verhalten *od.* benehmen (*to, towards* gegen, gegenüber). **3.** sich verhalten (*Sache*), arbeiten, funktionieren (*Maschine etc*). **II** *v/t* **4.** *~ o.s.* → 1: *~ yourself!* benimm dich!

be'hav·io(u)r [~jə] *s* Benehmen *n,* Betragen *n,* Verhalten *n:* *be on one's best ~* sich von s-r besten Seite zeigen; *put s.o. on his best ~* *j-m* einschärfen, sich gut zu benehmen; *~ pattern* *psych.* Verhaltensmuster *n.* **be'hav·io(u)r·al** *adj* *psych.* Verhaltens...: *~ disturbance* Verhaltensstörung *f.* **be'hav·io(u)r-·ism** *s* *psych.* Behaviorismus *m.*

be·head [bɪ'hed] *v/t* enthaupten.

be·hind [bɪ'haɪnd] **I** *prp* **1.** *räumlich u. zeitlich:* hinter (*acc od. dat*): *get s.th. ~ one* et. hinter sich bringen. **2.** *Reihenfolge, Rang:* hinter (*acc od. dat*): *be ~ s.o.* *j-m* nachstehen (*in in dat*). **II** *adv* **3.** hinten, dahinter: *walk ~* hinterhergehen. **4.** nach hinten: *look ~* zurückblicken. **III** *adj* **5.** im Rückstand *od.* Verzug (*in, with* mit). **IV** *s* **6.** F Hintern *m.* **be'hind·hand** *adv u. adj* **1.** im Rückstand *od.* Verzug (*with* mit). **2.** rückständig.

beige [beɪʒ] *adj* beige.

be·ing ['biːɪŋ] *s* **1.** (Da)Sein *n,* Existenz *f:* *in ~* existierend, wirklich (vorhanden); *call into ~* ins Leben rufen; *come into being* entstehen. **2.** *j-s* Wesen *n,* Natur *f.* **3.** (Lebe)Wesen *n,* Geschöpf *n.*

be·la·bo(u)r [bɪ'leɪbə] *v/t mit Worten* bearbeiten, *j-m* zusetzen.

be·lat·ed [bɪ'leɪtɪd] *adj* verspätet: *~ best wishes* nachträglich herzliche Glückwunsch.

belch [beltʃ] **I** *v/i* **1.** aufstoßen, rülpsen. **2.** quellen (*from* aus) (*Rauch etc*). **II** *v/t* **3.** *a. ~ out* (*od. forth*) *Feuer, Rauch etc* speien, *a. fig.* *Beleidigungen etc* ausstoßen. **III** *s* **4.** Aufstoßen *n,* Rülpsen *n;* Rülpser *m.* **5.** *fig.* (Rauch-, Flammen- *etc*)Stoß *m.* **6.** *fig.* Schwall *m* (*von Beleidigungen etc*).

bel·fry ['belfrɪ] *s* Glockenstuhl *m;* Glokkenturm *m:* → *bat¹.*

Bel·gian ['beldʒən] **I** *adj* belgisch. **II** *s* Belgier(in).

be·lie [bɪ'laɪ] *v/t* **1.** *j-n, et.* Lügen strafen. **2.** hinwegtäuschen über (*acc*). **3.** *Hoff-*

belief

772

nung *etc* enttäuschen, *e-r Sache* nicht entsprechen.

be·lief [bɪˈliːf] *s* **1.** Glaube *m* (*in* an *acc*): *beyond ~* unglaublich. **2.** Vertrauen *n* (*in* auf *e-e Sache*, zu *j-m*). **3.** Anschauung *f*, Überzeugung *f*: *to the best of my ~* nach bestem Wissen u. Gewissen.

be·liev·a·ble [bɪˈliːvəbl] *adj* **1.** glaubhaft. **2.** glaubwürdig.

be·lieve [bɪˈliːv] I *v/i* **1.** glauben (*in* an *acc*). **2.** (*in*) vertrauen (auf *acc*), Vertrauen haben (zu). **3.** viel halten (*in* von): *not to ~ in doing s.th.* nichts *od.* nicht viel davon halten, et. zu tun. II *v/t* **4.** glauben: *~ it or not!* od. Sie es glauben oder nicht!; *would you ~ it!* ist das denn die Möglichkeit!; *he is ~d to be rich* man hält ihn für reich; *→ reason* 1. **5.** glauben (*dat*). **be'liev·er** *s* Gläubige *m*, *f*: *be a great ~ in* fest glauben an (*acc*); viel halten von.

Be·li·sha bea·con [bɪˈliːʃə] *s Br.* Blinklicht *n* (*an Fußgängerüberwegen*).

be·lit·tle [bɪˈlɪtl] *v/t* **1.** herabsetzen, schmälern. **2.** verharmlosen, bagatellisieren.

bell [bel] I *s* **1.** Glocke *f*, Klingel *f*, Schelle *f*: *that rings a ~* F das kommt mir bekannt vor, das erinnert mich an et. **2.** Glockenzeichen *n*, Läuten *n*, Klingeln *n*: *→ answer* 10. **3.** *teleph.* Wecker *m*. **4.** Taucherglocke *f*. II *v/t* **5.** *~ the cat fig.* der Katze die Schelle umhängen. '*~boy* s bsd. Am. (Hotel)Page *m*. '*~flow·er* ♀ Glockenblume *f*. '*~hop* s Am. (Hotel)Page *m*.

bel·li·cose [ˈbelɪkəʊs] *adj* □ **1.** kriegslustig, kriegerisch. **2.** *→ belligerent* 3.

bel·lied [ˈbelɪd] *adj* bauchig.

bel·lig·er·ent [bɪˈlɪdʒərənt] I *adj* □ **1.** *→ bellicose* 1. **2.** kriegführend. **3.** *fig.* streitlustig, aggressiv. II *s* **4.** kriegführendes Land.

bel·low [ˈbeləʊ] I *v/i* **1.** brüllen (*with* vor *dat*). **2.** grölen. II *v/t* **3.** *a. ~ out* **3.** *Befehl etc* brüllen. **4.** *Lied etc* grölen. III *s* **5.** Brüllen *n*. **6.** Grölen *n*.

bel·lows [ˈbeləʊz] *s pl* (*a. sg konstruiert*) Blasebalg *m*.

bell∣ push *s* Klingelknopf *m*. '*~weth·er* s Leithammel *m* (*a. fig.*).

bel·ly [ˈbelɪ] I *s* **1.** Bauch *m* (*a. e-s Schiffs etc*). **2.** Magen *m*. II *v/i u. v/t* **3.** *a. ~ out* (an)schwellen (lassen). '*~ache* I *s* F

Bauchweh *n.* II *v/i sl.* meckern, nörgeln (*about* über *acc*). *~ but·ton* s F Bauchknöpfchen *n.* *~ danc·er* s Bauchtänzerin *f.*

bel·ly·ful [ˈbelɪfʊl] *s* F **1.** *have a ~ of* sich den Bauch vollschlagen mit. **2.** *have had a* (*od. one's*) *~ of* die Nase voll haben von.

bel·ly land·ing *s* ✈ Bauchlandung *f.*

be·long [bɪˈlɒŋ] *v/i* **1.** gehören (*to* dat). **2.** gehören (*to* zu; *in* in *acc*). **3.** angehören (*to dat*). **be'long·ings** *s pl* Habseligkeiten *pl*, Habe *f*; F Angehörige *pl.*

be·lov·ed [bɪˈlʌvd; -vɪd] I *adj* (innig) geliebt. II *s* Geliebte *m*, *f.*

be·low [bɪˈləʊ] I *adv* **1.** unten. **2.** hinunter, nach unten. II *prp* **3.** unter (*acc od. dat*), unterhalb (*gen*): *~ s.o.* unter j-s Rang, würde.

belt [belt] I *s* **1.** Gürtel *m*: *hit below the ~* (*Boxen*) tief schlagen, *j-m* e-n Tiefschlag versetzen; *→ tighten* 1. **2.** (Sicherheits)Gurt *m.* **3.** Gürtel *m*, Gebiet *n*, Zone *f.* **4.** ⚙ (Treib)Riemen *m.* II *v/t* **5.** *~ on* an-, umschnallen. **6.** *a. ~ out Lied etc* schmettern. III *v/i* **7.** *~ up mot. etc* sich anschnallen. **8.** *bsd. mot.* F rasen. **9.** *~ up! sl.* halt die Schnauze!

be·moan [bɪˈməʊn] *v/t* betrauern, beklagen.

be·mused [bɪˈmjuːzd] *adj* **1.** verwirrt. **2.** gedankenverloren.

bench [bentʃ] *s* **1.** (Sitz)Bank *f.* **2.** Werkbank *f*, -tisch *m.*

bend [bend] I *s* **1.** Biegung *f*, Krümmung *f*, (*e-r Straße a.*) Kurve *f*: *drive s.o. round the ~ Br.* F j-n verrückt machen. II *v/t* (*irr*) **2.** biegen, krümmen: *~ out of shape* verbiegen. **3.** *Kopf* neigen, *Knie* beugen. **4.** *Bogen*, *Feder etc* spannen. **5.** ⚖ *Recht* beugen. **6.** *Blicke*, *Gedanken etc* richten, *Anstrengungen etc* konzentrieren (*on*, *to* auf *acc*). III *v/i* (*irr*) **7.** sich biegen *od.* krümmen; e-e Biegung machen (*Fluß*), (*Straße a.*) e-e Kurve machen. **8.** *a. ~ down* sich bücken; sich nach unten biegen; sich verbeugen (*to*, *before* vor *dat*).

be·neath [bɪˈniːθ] I *adv* **1.** unten. **2.** darunter. II *prp* **3.** unter (*acc od. dat*), unterhalb (*gen*): *~ him* (*od. his dignity*) unter s-r Würde; *→ contempt* 1.

ben·e·dic·tion [ˌbenɪˈdɪkʃn] *s eccl.* **1.** Segen *m.* **2.** Segnung *f.*

best man

ben·e·fac·tion [ˌbenɪˈfækʃn] s 1. Wohltat f. 2. wohltätige Gabe. **ben·e·fac·tor** [ˈ⁓tə] s Wohltäter m. **ben·e·fac·tress** [ˈ⁓trɪs] s Wohltäterin f.

be·nef·i·cence [bɪˈnefɪsns] s Wohltätigkeit f. **be'nef·i·cent** adj □ wohltätig.

ben·e·fi·cial [ˌbenɪˈfɪʃl] adj □ (to) nützlich, zuträglich (dat), vorteilhaft, günstig (für).

ben·e·fit [ˈbenɪfɪt] I s 1. Vorteil m, Nutzen m, Gewinn m: be of ⁓ to nützen (dat); for the ⁓ of zugunsten (gen); derive (od. get) ⁓ (from) → 5; → reap. 2. (Arbeitslosen- etc)Unterstützung f; (Kranken- etc)Geld n; (Sozial-, Versicherungs- etc)Leistung f. 3. Wohltätigkeitsveranstaltung f. II v/t pret u. pp -ed, bsd. Am. -ted 4. nützen (dat), fördern (acc), im Interesse (gen) sein od. liegen. III v/i 5. (by, from) Vorteil haben (von, durch), Nutzen ziehen (aus).

be·nev·o·lence [bɪˈnevələns] s 1. Wohltätigkeit f. 2. Wohlwollen n. 3. Wohltat f. **be'nev·o·lent** adj □ 1. wohltätig. 2. wohlwollend.

be·nign [bɪˈnaɪn] adj □ 1. gütig, freundlich. 2. mild: ⁓ climate. 3. ✿ gutartig: ⁓ tumo(u)r.

bent [bent] I pret u. pp von **bend**. II adj 1. entschlossen (on doing zu tun); erpicht (on auf acc), darauf aus (on doing zu tun). III s 2. Neigung f, Hang m (for zu): to the top of one's ⁓ nach Herzenslust. 3. Veranlagung f: have a ⁓ for art künstlerisch veranlagt sein; ⁓ for languages Sprachbegabung f.

be·numbed [bɪˈnʌmd] adj 1. gefühllos, starr (with cold vor Kälte). 2. fig. gelähmt.

ben·zene [ˈbenziːn] s ✿ Benzol n.

ben·zine [ˈbenziːn] s ✿ Leichtbenzin n.

be·queath [bɪˈkwiːð] v/t hinterlassen, vermachen (s.th. to s.o. j-m et.). **be·quest** [bɪˈkwest] s Vermächtnis n.

be·rate [bɪˈreɪt] v/t ausschelten (about, for wegen).

be·reave [bɪˈriːv] v/t (a. irr) berauben (of gen): ⁓ s.o. of speech j-m die Sprache rauben; the ⁓d der od. die Hinterbliebene, die Hinterbliebenen pl. **be'reavement** s 1. schmerzlicher Verlust (durch Tod). 2. Trauerfall m.

be·reft [bɪˈreft] I pret u. pp von **bereave**. II adj mst fig. beraubt (of gen): ⁓ of all hope.

ber·ry [ˈberɪ] s ✿ Beere f.

ber·serk [bəˈzɜːk] adj: go ⁓ wild werden; Amok laufen.

berth [bɜːθ] s 1. ✧ Liege-, Ankerplatz m. 2. ✧ Koje f. 3. ⊞ (Schlafwagen)Bett n. 4. give a wide ⁓ to e-n großen Bogen machen um. 5. F Stellung f, Pöstchen n: he's got a good ⁓. II v/i 6. ✧ festmachen, anlegen.

be·seech [bɪˈsiːtʃ] v/t (a. irr) 1. j-n anflehen (for um; to do zu tun). 2. et. erflehen (of von). **be'seech·ing** adj flehend. **be'seech·ing·ly** adv flehentlich.

be·set·ting [bɪˈsetɪŋ] adj hartnäckig: ⁓ sin Gewohnheitslaster n.

be·side [bɪˈsaɪd] prp 1. neben (acc od. dat). 2. außerhalb: → point 11. 3. be ⁓ o.s. außer sich sein (with vor dat). **be'sides** [⁓dz] I adv außerdem. II prp außer, neben (dat).

be·siege [bɪˈsiːdʒ] v/t 1. ✕ belagern (a. fig.). 2. fig. bestürmen, bedrängen (with mit).

be·sought [bɪˈsɔːt] pret u. pp von **beseech**.

be·spec·ta·cled [bɪˈspektəkld] adj bebrillt.

be·spoke [bɪˈspəʊk] adj Br. Maß...: ⁓ tailor Maßschneider m.

best [best] I (sup von **good**) adj 1. best. 2. größt, meist: the ⁓ part of der größte Teil (gen). II (sup von **well²**) adv 3. am besten: the ⁓hated man der meistgehaßte Mann; as ⁓ they could so gut sie konnten; you had ⁓ go es wäre das beste, wenn Sie gingen. III s 4. der, die, das Beste: at ⁓ bestenfalls, höchstens; do one's ⁓ sein möglichstes tun; have (od. get) the ⁓ of übertreffen; F übers Ohr hauen; make the ⁓ of sich zufriedengeben mit; sich abfinden mit; voll ausnutzen; das Beste machen aus; all the ⁓! alles Gute!; → ability, belief 3, etc.

bes·tial [ˈbestjəl] adj □ tierisch, fig. a. bestialisch, viehisch. **bes·ti·al·i·ty** [ˌ⁓ˈælətɪ] s 1. Bestialität f (a. fig.). 2. Sodomie f.

be·stir [bɪˈstɜː] v/t: ⁓ o.s. to do s.th. sich dazu aufraffen, et. zu tun.

best man s (irr **man**) Freund des Bräuti

gams, der bei der Ausrichtung der Hochzeit e-e wichtige Rolle spielt.

be·stow [bɪˈstəʊ] *v/t Preis, Titel* verleihen (**on** *dat*). **be'stow·al** *s* Verleihung *f*.

best¦ sell·er *s* **1.** Bestseller *m*. **2.** Bestsellerautor *m*. '**~·,sell·ing** *adj:* **~ novel** Bestseller *m*; **~ author** Bestsellerautor *m*.

bet [bet] **I** *s* **1.** Wette *f*; Wetteinsatz *m*: **have** (*od.* **make**) **a ~** e-e Wette abschließen *od.* eingehen (**on** auf *acc*). **2.** *my* ~ *is that* ich würde sagen, daß; *it's a safe* ~ *that* es steht so gut wie fest, daß. **3.** *your best* ~ *is to take the car* F du nimmst am besten den Wagen. **II** *v/t* (*a. irr*) **4.** *Geld* wetten, setzen (**on** auf *acc*): *I'll* ~ *you £10 that* ich wette mit dir (um) 10 Pfund, daß; *you can* ~ *your boots* (*od.* **bottom dollar, shirt**) *that* F du kannst Gift darauf nehmen, daß. **5.** ~ (*s.o.*) *that fig.* (mit j-m) wetten, daß. **III** *v/i* (*a. irr*) **6.** wetten, setzen (**on** auf *acc*): *you ~!* F das kann man wohl sagen.

be·tray [bɪˈtreɪ] *v/t* verraten (*to dat od.* an *acc*) (*a. fig.*). **be'tray·al** *s* Verrat *m*.

bet·ter¹ [ˈbetə] **I** (*comp von* **good**) *adj* besser: *I am* ~ es geht mir (*gesundheitlich*) besser; *get* ~ besser werden; sich erholen. **II** *s* das Bessere: *for* ~ *for worse* in Freud u. Leid (*Trauformel*); *was auch (immer) geschieht*; *get the* ~ *of j-n* besiegen, ausstechen; *et*. überwinden. **III** (*comp von* **well²**) *adv* besser: ~ *off* besser daran; (*finanziell*) bessergestellt; *think* ~ *of it* es sich anders überlegen; *you had* ~ *go* es wäre besser, du gingest; *you had* ~ *not!* laß das lieber sein!; → *know* 6, *like²* I. **IV** *v/t* *Beziehungen, Rekord etc* verbessern: ~ *o.s.* sich (*finanziell*) verbessern; sich weiterbilden. **V** *v/i* besser werden.

bet·ter² [~] *s* Wetter(in).

bet·ter·ment [ˈbetəmənt] *s* **1.** (Ver)Besserung *f*. **2.** ♦ Wertsteigerung *f*, -zuwachs *m*.

bet·ting [ˈbetɪŋ] *s* Wetten *n*: ~ *office* (*Br. shop*) Wettbüro *n*.

be·tween [bɪˈtwiːn] **I** *prp* **1.** räumlich u. zeitlich: zwischen (*dat od. acc*): → *devil* 1, *stool* 1. **2.** unter (*dat od. acc*): ~ *you and me* (*and the bedpost od. gatepost od. lamppost* F) unter uns gesagt, im Vertrauen (gesagt); *we had ten pounds ~*

us wir hatten zusammen zehn Pfund. **II** *adv* **3.** dazwischen: *the space* ~ der Zwischenraum; *in* ~ dazwischen.

bev·el [ˈbevl] **I** *s* Schräge *f*, Abschrägung *f*. **II** *v/t pret u. pp* **-eled**, *bsd. Br.* **-elled** abschrägen. **III** *adj* abgeschrägt, schräg.

bev·er·age [ˈbevərɪdʒ] *s* Getränk *n*.

bev·y [ˈbevɪ] *s orn.* Schwarm *m*, Schar *f*.

be·wail [bɪˈweɪl] *v/t* beklagen.

be·ware [bɪˈweə] *v/i* sich hüten, sich in acht nehmen (**of** vor *dat*): ~ *of the dog!* Vorsicht, bissiger Hund!; ~ *of pickpockets!* vor Taschendieben wird gewarnt!

be·wil·der [bɪˈwɪldə] *v/t* irremachen, verwirren. **be'wil·der·ment** *s* Verwirrung *f*.

be·witch [bɪˈwɪtʃ] *v/t* bezaubern, behexen.

be·yond [bɪˈjɒnd] **I** *adv* **1.** darüber hinaus. **II** *prp* **2.** jenseits. **3.** über ... (*acc*) hinaus: *that is* ~ *me* F das ist mir zu hoch, das geht über m-n Verstand; → *belief* 1, *endurance* 1, *measure* 2, *word* 1, *etc.*

bi... [baɪ] zwei...

bi·an·nu·al [ˌbaɪˈænjʊəl] *adj* zweimal jährlich vorkommend *od.* erscheinend. **bi'an·nu·al·ly** *adv* zweimal im Jahr.

bi·as [ˈbaɪəs] *s* **1.** (*towards*) Neigung *f*, Hang *m* (zu); Vorliebe *f* (für). **2.** Vorurteil *n*, ⚖ Befangenheit *f*: *free from* ~ unvoreingenommen. **II** *adj od. adv* **3.** schräg. **III** *v/t pret u. pp* **-as(s)ed 4.** (*mst ungünstig*) beeinflussen, *j-n* einnehmen (*against* gegen). **'bi·as(s)ed** *adj* voreingenommen, ⚖ befangen.

bib [bɪb] *s* **1.** Lätzchen *n*. **2.** Schürzenlatz *m*.

Bi·ble [ˈbaɪbl] *s* Bibel *f*. **bib·li·cal** [ˈbɪblɪkl] *adj* □ biblisch, Bibel...

bib·li·o·graph·ic, bib·li·o·graph·i·cal [ˌbɪblɪəʊˈɡræfɪk(l)] *adj* □ bibliographisch. **bib·li·og·ra·phy** [ˌ~ˈɒɡrəfɪ] *s* Bibliographie *f*. **bib·li·o·phile** [ˈ~əʊfaɪl] *s* Bücherfreund *m*, Bibliophile *m*.

bi·car·bon·ate [ˌ~ ♠] *s* Bikarbonat *n*: ~ *of soda* Natriumbikarbonat.

bi·ceps [ˈbaɪseps] *pl* **-ceps(·es)** *s anat.* Bizeps *m*.

bick·er [ˈbɪkə] **I** *v/i* sich zanken *od.* streiten (*about, over* um). **II** *s* Zank *m*, Streit *m*. '**bick·er·ing** *s* Gezänk *n*.

bi·cy·cle ['baɪsɪkl] **I** *s* Fahrrad *n*. **II** *v/i* radfahren; mit dem Rad fahren.

bid [bɪd] **I** *s* **1.** ✝ Gebot *n* (*bei Versteigerungen*); ✝ Angebot *n* (*bei Ausschreibungen*); ✝ *Am.* Kostenvoranschlag *m*; *fig.* Bewerbung *f* (**for** um), Versuch *m* (**to do** zu tun): *highest* ~ Meistgebot *n*; *make a* ~ *for* sich bemühen um; ~ *for power* Griff *m* nach der Macht. **II** *v/t* (*irr*) **2.** ✝ *bei Versteigerungen* bieten. **3.** *j-m e-n guten Morgen etc* wünschen: ~ *s.o. good morning*; ~ *farewell* Lebewohl sagen. **III** *v/i* (*irr*) **4.** ✝ *bei Versteigerungen* bieten; ✝ *Am.* e-n Kostenvoranschlag machen; *fig.* sich bemühen (**for** um): ~ *for power* nach der Macht greifen. '**bid·den** *pp von* **bid**. '**bid·der** *s* ✝ Bieter *m* (*bei Versteigerungen*): *highest* ~ Meistbietende *m*, *f*. '**bid·ding** *s* ✝ Gebot *n* (*bei Versteigerungen*).

bide [baɪd] *v/t* (*a. irr*): ~ *one's time* den rechten Augenblick abwarten *od.* abpassen.

bi·en·ni·al [baɪ'enɪəl] *adj* □ **1.** zweijährlich. **2.** zweijährig.

bier [bɪə] *s* (Toten)Bahre *f*.

bi·fur·cate ['baɪfəkeɪt] **I** *v/i* sich gabeln. **II** *adj* gegabelt, gabelförmig. ‚**bi·fur·'ca·tion** *s* Gabelung *f*.

big [bɪg] **I** *adj* **1.** *allg.* groß: a) dick, stark: *the* ~*gest party* die stärkste Partei; *earn* ~ *money* F das große Geld verdienen, b) breit, weit: *the coat is too* ~ *for me* der Mantel ist mir zu groß; *get too* ~ *for one's boots* (*od. breeches, bsd. Am. pants*) F größenwahnsinnig werden, c) hoch: ~ *trees*, d) Mords...: ~ *rascal* Erzgauner *m*; ~ *eater* starker Esser, e) erwachsen, f) wichtig, bedeutend: → *shot* **3. 2.** ausgiebig, reichlich: ~ *meal*. **3.** F aufgeblasen, eingebildet: *have* ~ *ideas* große Rosinen im Kopf haben; ~ *talk* große Töne *pl*. **4.** *that's very* ~ *of you* das ist sehr großzügig *od.* nobel von Ihnen. **5.** *be* ~ *on* F stehen auf (*acc*). **II** *adv* **6.** F mächtig, mordsmäßig. **7.** F großspurig: *talk* ~ große Töne spucken.

big·a·mist ['bɪgəmɪst] *s* Bigamist(in). '**big·a·my** *s* Bigamie *f*, Doppelehe *f*.

big| bang *s Kosmologie*: Urknall *m*. '**~·cir·cu·'la·tion** *adj* auflagenstark (*Zeitung*). '**~·mouth** *s* F Großmaul *n*.

big·ness ['bɪgnɪs] *s* Größe *f*.

big·ot ['bɪgət] *s* **1.** selbstgerechte *od.* intolerante Person. **2.** Frömmler(in). '**big·ot·ed** *adj* **1.** selbstgerecht, intolerant. **2.** bigott, frömmlerisch. '**big·ot·ry** *s* **1.** Selbstgerechtigkeit *f*, Intoleranz *f*. **2.** Bigotterie *f*, Frömmelei *f*.

'**big·wig** *s* F großes *od.* hohes Tier.

bike [baɪk] **I** *s* Rad *n* (*Fahrrad*); Maschine *f* (*Motorrad*). **II** *v/i* radeln, Motorrad fahren; mit dem Motorrad fahren.

‚**bi·'lat·er·al** *adj* bilateral, zweiseitig.

bil·ber·ry ['bɪlbərɪ] *s* ❀ Blau-, Heidelbeere *f*.

bile [baɪl] *s* **1.** *physiol.* Galle *f*. **2.** *fig.* Gereiztheit *f*; Reizbarkeit *f*. '~·**stone** *s physiol.* Gallenstein *m*.

bilge [bɪldʒ] *s* **1.** ⚓ Kielraum *m*. **2.** F Quatsch *m*, Mist *m*.

bi·lin·gual *adj* □ zweisprachig.

bil·ious ['bɪljəs] *adj* □ **1.** ⚕ gallig; Gallen...: ~ *attack* Gallenkolik *f*. **2.** *fig.* gereizt; reizbar.

bill¹ [bɪl] **I** *s zo.* Schnabel *m*. **II** *v/i a.* ~ *and coo* (miteinander) turteln.

bill² [~] **I** *s* **1.** *pol.* (Gesetzes)Vorlage *f*, Gesetzentwurf *m*. **2.** ⚖ (An)Klageschrift *f*. **3.** *a.* ~ *of exchange* ✝ Wechsel *m*. **4.** Rechnung *f*: *waiter, the* ~, *please* (Herr) Ober, bitte zahlen! **5.** Liste *f*, Aufstellung *f*: ~ *of fare* Speise(n)karte *f*. **6.** Bescheinigung *f*: ~ *of delivery* ✝ Lieferschein *m*. **7.** Plakat *n*. **8.** *thea. etc* Programm(zettel *m*) *n*; *weitS.* Programm *n*: *be on the* ~ auftreten; → *top¹* **12. 9.** *Am.* Banknote *f*, (Geld)Schein *m*. **II** *v/t* **10.** *j-m e-e* Rechnung ausstellen *od.* schicken: ~ *s.o. for s.th.* j-m et. in Rechnung stellen. **11.** (durch Plakate) ankündigen *od.* bekanntgeben.

'**bill·board** *s bsd. Am.* **1.** Reklametafel *f*. **2.** *Film, TV*: Vorspann *m*.

bil·let ['bɪlɪt] **I** *s* **1.** ✕ (Privat)Quartier *n*. **2.** Unterkunft *f*. **II** *v/t* **3.** ✕ einquartieren (**with, on** bei). **4.** unterbringen. **III** *v/i* **5.** ✕ einquartiert sein. **6.** (*bsd.* vorübergehend) wohnen.

'**bill·fold** *s Am.* Scheintasche *f*; Brieftasche *f*.

bil·liard ['bɪljəd] **I** *s pl* (*mst sg konstruiert*) Billard(spiel) *n*. **II** *adj* Billard...: ~ *ball* (**table**); ~ *cue* Queue *f*.

bil·lion ['bɪljən] *s* **1.** Milliarde *f.* **2.** *Br. obs.* Billion *f.*

bil·low ['bɪləʊ] **I** *s* **1.** Woge *f.* **2.** *(Nebel-, Rauch)*Schwaden *m.* **II** *v/i* **3.** wogen. **4.** *a.* ~ *out* sich bauschen *od.* blähen *(Segel, Vorhänge etc).* **III** *v/t* **5.** bauschen, blähen. **'bil·low·y** *adj* **1.** wogend. **2.** in Schwaden ziehend. **3.** gebauscht, gebläht.

'bill|**,post·er**, **'~,stick·er** *s* Plakatkleber *m.*

bil·ly ['bɪlɪ] *s Am.* (Polizei)Knüppel *m.* ~ **goat** *s* Ziegenbock *m.*

,bil'month·ly *adj u. adv* zweimonatlich.

bin [bɪn] *s* Behälter *m.*

bi·na·ry ['baɪnərɪ] *adj* ⚕, ⚙ *etc* binär, Binär...

bind [baɪnd] **I** *v/t (irr)* **1.** binden *(to an acc):* ~ *together* zs.-binden; ~ *up* aneinander-, zs.-binden; *Wunde* verbinden. **2.** *Saum* einfassen. **3.** ⚕ *etc* (mit e-m Bindemittel) binden. **4.** *Buch* (ein)binden. **5.** *fig. (a. vertraglich)* binden, verpflichten *(to s.th.* zu et.; *to do* zu tun). **II** *v/i (irr)* **6.** ⚕ *etc* binden. **7.** fest *od.* hart werden. **8.** *fig.* binden(d sein). **III** *s* **9.** *be in a* ~ F in Schwulitäten sein. **'bind·er** *s* **1.** *(Buch- etc)*Binder(in). **2.** *(Akten- etc)*Deckel *m,* Umschlag *m.* **3.** ⚕ *etc* Bindemittel *n.* **'bind·ing I** *adj* □ **1.** *fig.* bindend, verbindlich (*on* für): *legally* ~ rechtsverbindlich; *not* ~ unverbindlich. **II** *s* **2.** (Buch)Einband *m.* **3.** Einfassung *f,* Borte *f.* **4.** *(Ski)*Bindung *f.* **5.** → *binder* 3.

binge [bɪndʒ] *s* F Sauf- *od.* Freßgelage *n: go (out) on a* ~ e-e Sauf- *od.* Freßtour machen; *go on a buying (od. shopping, spending)* ~ wie verrückt einkaufen.

bin·go ['bɪŋgəʊ] *s* Bingo *n (ein Glücksspiel).*

bin·oc·u·lars [bɪ'nɒkjʊləz] *s pl (a pair of* ein) Fernglas *n.*

bi·o·chem·i·cal [,baɪəʊ'kemɪkl] *adj* □ biochemisch. **,bi·o'chem·ist** *s* Biochemiker(in). **,bi·o'chem·is·try** *s* Biochemie *f.*

bi·o·graph·ic, bi·o·graph·i·cal [,baɪəʊ'græfɪk(l)] *adj* □ biographisch. **bi·og·ra·phy** [~'ɒgrəfɪ] *s* Biographie *f.*

bi·o·log·i·cal [,baɪəʊ'lɒdʒɪkl] *adj* □ biologisch. **bi·ol·o·gist** [~'ɒlədʒɪst] *s* Biologe *m.* **bi·ol·o·gy** *s* Biologie *f.*

bi·par·ti·san [,baɪpɑːtɪ'zæn] *adj pol.* Zweiparteien...

birch [bɜːtʃ] *s* ⚕ Birke *f.*

bird [bɜːd] *s* **1.** Vogel *m:* ~ *of passage* Zugvogel *(a. fig.);* ~ *of prey* Raubvogel; *a* ~ *in the hand is worth two in the bush* besser ein Spatz in der Hand als e-e Taube auf dem Dach; *tell a child about the* ~*s and the bees* ein Kind aufklären; *that's (strictly) for the* ~*s* F das ist für die Katz; das taugt nichts; *give s.o. the* ~ j-n auspfeifen *od.* ausbuhen; → *early* 4, *feather* I, *fly*¹ 2, *kill* 1. **2.** F Kerl *m: queer* ~ komischer Kauz. **'~cage** *s* Vogelkäfig *m.* **'~house** *s* Nistkasten *m.*

bird·ie ['bɜːdɪ] *s* Vögelchen *n.*

bird| **sanc·tu·a·ry** *s* Vogelschutzgebiet *n.* **'~seed** *s* Vogelfutter *n.* **'bird's-eye** *adj:* ~ *view* (Blick *m* aus der) Vogelschau; *fig.* allgemeiner Überblick *(of* über *acc);* ~ *perspective* Vogelperspektive *f.* ~ *nest* *s* Vogelnest *n.*

bird strike *s* ✈ Vogelschlag *m.*

bi·ro ['baɪərəʊ] *pl* **-ros** *(TM) s Br.* Kugelschreiber *m.*

birth [bɜːθ] *s* **1.** Geburt *f: at* ~ bei der Geburt; *from (od. since)* (*one's*) ~ von Geburt an; *give* ~ *to* gebären, zur Welt bringen; *fig.* hervorbringen, -rufen. **2.** Abstammung *f,* Herkunft *f: he's a man of (good)* ~ er stammt aus gutem Hause; *she's English by* ~ sie ist gebürtige Engländerin. **3.** Ursprung *m,* Entstehung *f.* ~ **cer·tif·i·cate** *s* Geburtsurkunde *f.* ~ **con·trol** *s* Geburtenregelung *f,* -kontrolle *f.* '~**day** I *s* Geburtstag *m: when is your* ~? wann hast du Geburtstag?; *happy* ~*!* alles Gute *od.* herzlichen Glückwunsch zum Geburtstag! **II** *adj* Geburtstags...: ~ *party (present, etc);* ~ *honours pl* Titelverleihungen *pl* anläßlich des Geburtstags des Königs *od.* der Königin; *in one's* ~ *suit* im Adams- *od.* Evaskostüm. **'~mark** *s* Muttermal *n.* **~pill** *s* 🕮 Antibabypille *f.* **'~place** *s* Geburtsort *m.* **'~rate** *s* Geburtenziffer *f: falling* ~ Geburtenrückgang *m.*

bis·cuit ['bɪskɪt] *s* **1.** *Br.* Keks *m, n.* **2.** *Am.* kleines weiches Brötchen.

bi·sect [baɪ'sekt] *v/t* **1.** in zwei Teile (zer)schneiden. **2.** ⚕ halbieren. **,bi'sec·tion** *s* ⚕ Halbierung *f.*

bi'sex·u·al adj □ bisexuell.

bish·op ['bɪʃəp] s **1.** eccl. Bischof m. **2.** Schach: Läufer m. **bish·op·ric** ['∼rɪk] s eccl. Bistum n.

bit[1] [bɪt] s **1.** Gebiß n (am Pferdezaum): *take the ∼ between one's teeth* durchgehen (Pferd); fig. störrisch werden; fig. sich reinknien. **2.** ⚙ Backe f, Maul n (e-r Zange etc); (Schlüssel)Bart m. **3.** Mundstück n (e-r Tabakspfeife etc).

bit[2] [∼] s **1.** Bissen m, Happen m. **2.** Stück(chen) n (a. fig.): *fall to ∼s* entzweigehen, zerbrechen; *a* ∼ ein bißchen; ziemlich; *not a* ∼ überhaupt nicht; *a ∼ of a coward* ziemlich feig; *a ∼ of a fool* ein bißchen dumm; *∼ by ∼* Stück für Stück, nach u. nach; *do one's ∼* s-e Pflicht (u. Schuldigkeit) tun; s-n Beitrag leisten. **3.** F Augenblick m, Moment m: *after a ∼* nach e-m Weilchen. **4.** F kleine Münze.

bit[3] [∼] s Computer: Bit n.

bit[4] [∼] pret von *bite*.

bitch [bɪtʃ] s **1.** zo. Hündin f. **2.** sl. Schlampe f; Miststück n: → *son* **1.**

bite [baɪt] **I** v/t (irr) **1.** beißen: ∼ *back* sich e-e Äußerung etc verkneifen; ∼ *off* abbeißen; ∼ *off more than one can chew* F sich zuviel zumuten; ∼ *the dust* (Am. a. *ground*) F ins Gras beißen; ∼ *one's nails* an den Nägeln kauen; fig. nervös sein; → *lip* **1**, *tongue* **1. 2.** beißen, stechen (Insekt). **II** v/i (irr) **3.** (zu)beißen: ∼ *into* (hinein)beißen in (acc). **4.** anbeißen (a. fig.), schnappen (*at* nach) (Fisch). **5.** beißen, stechen (Insekt). **6.** beißen (Rauch, Gewürz etc). **7.** fassen, greifen (Rad, Schraube etc). **8.** fig. beißend od. verletzend sein. **9.** sich (bsd. negativ) auswirken (Maßnahme). **III** s **10.** Biß m, (e-s Insekts a.) Stich m. **11.** Biß(wunde f) m. **12.** Bissen m, Happen m (a. weitS. Imbiß, Nahrung). **13.** Fassen n, Greifen n (von Rädern, Schrauben etc): *s.th. has lost its ∼* fig. et. greift od. zieht nicht mehr. **14.** Schärfe f (a. fig.).

bit·ing ['baɪtɪŋ] adj beißend (Rauch etc), schneidend (Wind, Kälte etc) (beide a. Worte etc).

bit·ten ['bɪtn] **I** pp von *bite*. **II** adj: *once ∼ twice shy* (ein) gebranntes Kind scheut das Feuer.

bit·ter ['bɪtə] **I** adj □ **1.** bitter (a. fig.): *to*

the ∼ end bis zum bitteren Ende; *weep ∼ly* bitterlich weinen. **2.** fig. scharf, heftig (Kritik etc). **3.** fig. erbittert (Feinde etc); verbittert (*about* wegen). **II** adv **4.** ∼ *cold* bitterkalt. **III** s **5.** Bitterkeit f. **6.** fig. das Bittere. **7.** Br. stark gehopftes (Faß)Bier. **8.** mst pl Magenbitter m.

bit·ter·ness ['bɪtənɪs] s **1.** Bitterkeit f (a. fig.). **2.** fig. Verbitterung f.

bi·tu·men ['bɪtjʊmən] s min. Bitumen n.

bi·tu·mi·nous [bɪ'tjuːmɪnəs] adj: ∼ *coal* Steinkohle f.

biz [bɪz] F für *business*.

bi·zarre [bɪ'zɑː] adj bizarr.

blab [blæb] **I** v/t **1.** oft ∼ *out* ausplaudern. **II** v/i **2.** schwatzen. **3.** fig. plaudern.

black [blæk] **I** adj **1.** allg. schwarz (a. fig.): ∼ *coffee*; ∼ *humo(u)r*; ∼ *man* Schwarze m; ∼ *in the face* dunkelrot im Gesicht (vor Aufregung etc); *beat s.o. ∼ and blue* j-n grün u. blau schlagen; *look ∼ at s.o., give s.o. a ∼ look* j-n (böse) anfunkeln; *he's not so (od. as) ∼ as he's painted* er ist besser als sein Ruf. **2.** ✝ bsd. Br. boykottiert. **II** s **3.** Schwarz n: *dressed in ∼* schwarz od. in Schwarz gekleidet; *be in (od. wear) ∼* Trauer tragen. **4.** oft ⓔ Schwarze m, f. **5.** *be in the ∼* ✝ mit Gewinn arbeiten; aus den roten Zahlen heraussein. **III** v/t **6.** → *blacken* **I. 7.** ✝ bsd. Br. boykottieren. **8.** ∼ *out* abdunkeln. **X** verdunkeln. **9.** ∼ *out* Nachrichten etc unterdrücken. **IV** v/i **10.** schwarz werden. **11.** ∼ *out* ein Blackout haben. **12.** ∼ *out* bewußtlos werden.

black| and white pl **black and whites** s **1.** *in* ∼ schwarz auf weiß, schriftlich. **2.** Schwarzweißbild n. **3.** *depict s.th. in ∼* fig. et. schwarzweißmalen. ˌ∼**-and- -'white** adj **1.** schriftlich. **2.** Schwarzweiß...: ∼ *television*; ∼ *depiction* Schwarzweißmalerei f. '∼**·ball** v/t stimmen gegen. '∼**·ber·ry** ['∼bərɪ] s ⚘ Brombeere f. '∼**·bird** s orn. Amsel f. '∼**·board** s (Schul-, Wand)Tafel f. ∼ **box** s ✈ F Flugschreiber m.

black·en ['blækən] **I** v/t **1.** schwarz machen, schwärzen. **2.** fig. ∼ *s.o.'s character* j-n verunglimpfen; ∼ *s.o.'s name* (od. *reputation*) j-n schlechtmachen. **II** v/i **3.** schwarz werden.

black| eye s blaues Auge, Veilchen n: *give s.o. a ∼* j-m ein blaues Auge schlagen. **~guard** ['blægɑːd] s Schuft m, Lump m. **~ ice** s Glatteis n.

black·ish ['blækɪʃ] adj schwärzlich.

'**black|·jack** s **1.** Siebzehnundvier n. **2.** bsd. Am. Totschläger m (Waffe). **~ lead** [led] s min. Graphit m. '**~leg** s bsd. Br. Streikbrecher m. '**~let·ter** day s schwarzer Tag, Unglückstag m. '**~list** I s schwarze Liste. II v/t auf die schwarze Liste setzen. **~ mag·ic** s Schwarze Magie. '**~mail** I s Erpressung f. II v/t j-n erpressen (**over** mit). '**~mail·er** s Erpresser(in). ♀ **Ma·ri·a** [mə'raɪə] s F grüne Minna. **~ mar·ket** s schwarzer Markt, Schwarzmarkt m. **~ mar·ket·eer** [ˌmɑːkə'tɪə] s Schwarzhändler(in). **~ mass** s Schwarze Messe.

black·ness ['blæknɪs] s Schwärze f.

'**black|·out** s **1.** ✕, ♫, ✈, thea. etc Blackout n, m. **2.** ✈ Ohnmacht f, Bewußtlosigkeit f. **3.** (bsd. Nachrichten)Sperre f: **draw a ~ over** e-e Nachrichtensperre verhängen über (acc). **~ pud·ding** s Blutwurst f. **~ sheep** s (irr **sheep**) fig. schwarzes Schaf.

blad·der ['blædə] s anat. Blase f.

blade [bleɪd] s **1.** ♣ Halm m: **~ of grass** Grashalm. **2.** ◎ Blatt n (e-r Säge, e-s Ruders etc). **3.** ◎ Flügel m (e-s Propellers); Schaufel f (e-r Turbine etc). **4.** ◎ Klinge f (e-s Messers etc).

blah [blɑː], a. **'blah'blah** s F Blabla n, Geschwafel n.

blame [bleɪm] I v/t **1.** tadeln (**for** wegen). **2. ~ s.o. for s.th., ~ s.th. on s.o.** j-n verantwortlich machen für et., j-m die Schuld geben an et.; **he is to ~ for it** er ist daran schuld; **he has only himself to ~** er hat es sich selbst zuzuschreiben. II s **3.** Tadel m. **4.** Schuld f, Verantwortung f: **lay** (od. **put, cast**) **the ~ on s.o.** j-m die Schuld geben; **bear** (od. **take**) **the ~** die Schuld auf sich nehmen. '**blame·less** adj ☐ **1.** untadelig. **2.** schuldlos (**of** an acc).

blanch [blɑːntʃ] I v/t **1.** bleichen. **2.** gastr. blanchieren. **3.** erbleichen lassen. II v/i **4.** erbleichen, bleich werden (**with** vor dat).

blanc·mange [blə'mɒndʒ] s Pudding m.

blan·dish ['blændɪʃ] v/t j-m schmeicheln, schöntun. '**blan·dish·ment** s mst pl Schmeichelei f.

blank [blæŋk] I adj ☐ **1.** leer, unbe-

schrieben: **leave ~** frei lassen. **2.** ✝, ⚏ Blanko...: **~ check** (Br. **cheque**) Blankoscheck m, Scheckformular n; **~ signature** Blankounterschrift f. **3.** inhaltslos, unausgefüllt (Leben etc); ausdruckslos (Gesicht etc). **4.** verdutzt, verblüfft; verständnislos. **5. ~ cartridge ~** 9. II s **6.** freier Raum, Lücke f. **7.** unbeschriebenes Blatt (a. fig.); Formular n, Vordruck m. **8.** Lotterie: Niete f: **draw a ~** e-e Niete ziehen, fig. a. kein Glück haben. **9.** ✕ Platzpatrone f.

blan·ket ['blæŋkɪt] I s (engS. Bett)Decke f: **~ of snow** (**clouds**) Schnee-(Wolken)decke; → **wet** 1. II v/t zudecken: **~ed in** (od. **with**) **fog** in Nebel eingehüllt. III adj umfassend, Gesamt..., Pauschal...

blare [bleə] I v/i schmettern (Trompete); brüllen, plärren (Radio etc). II s Schmettern n; Brüllen n, Plärren n.

blar·ney ['blɑːnɪ] I s Schmeichelei f. II v/t u. v/i (j-m) schmeicheln.

bla·sé ['blɑːzeɪ] adj gleichgültig.

blas·pheme [blæs'fiːm] I v/t **1.** Gott etc lästern. **2.** allg. schmähen. II v/i **3.** Gott lästern: **~ against →** I. **blas'phem·er** s (Gottes)Lästerer m. **blas·phe·mous** ['~fəməs] adj ☐ blasphemisch, (gottes)lästerlich. '**blas·phe·my** s **1.** Blasphemie f, (Gottes)Lästerung f. **2.** allg. Schmähung f.

blast [blɑːst] I s **1.** Windstoß m. **2.** (**at**) **full ~** ◎ u. fig. auf Hochtouren (laufen od. arbeiten). **3.** Explosion f, Detonation f; Druckwelle f. **4.** Sprengung f; Sprengladung f. II v/t **5.** sprengen. **6.** fig. zunichte machen, vereiteln. **7. ~ off** (**into space**) in den Weltraum schießen. **8.** sl. verfluchen: **~ed** verdammt, verflucht; **~ed idiot** Vollidiot m; **~ it** (**all**)! verdammt (nochmal)!; **~ him!** der Teufel soll ihn holen! **~ fur·nace** s ◎ Hochofen m. '**~off** s Start m (e-r Rakete).

bla·tant ['bleɪtənt] adj ☐ **1.** lärmend, laut. **2.** marktschreierisch; aufdringlich. **3.** offenkundig, eklatant.

blath·er ['blæðə] I v/i quatschen. II s Gequatsche n.

blaze [bleɪz] I s **1.** (lodernde) Flamme: **be in a ~** in hellen Flammen stehen. **2.** Glanz m (a. fig.): **~ of colo(u)rs** Farbenpracht f. **3.** fig. plötzlicher Ausbruch: **~ of anger** Wutanfall m. **4.** F **go to ~s!** scher dich zum Teufel!; **like ~s** wie verrückt; **what the ~s ...?** was zum Teufel ...? II v/i **5.** lodern: **~ up** aufflammen, -lodern, fig. a. entbrennen. **6.** a. fig. leuchten, glühen (**with** vor dat). III v/t **7.** a. ~ **abroad** verkünden, contp. ausposaunen. **'blaz·er** s Blazer m, Klub-, Sportjacke f. **'blaz·ing** adj **1.** glühend. **2.** auffällig, schreiend, (Farben a.) grell.

bla·zon ['bleizn] I s Wappen n. II v/t mst ~ **abroad** → **blaze** 7.

bleach [bli:tʃ] I v/t bleichen. II s Bleichmittel n.

bleak [bli:k] adj □ **1.** kahl, öde. **2.** ungeschützt, windig. **3.** fig. trost-, freudlos (Dasein etc), trüb, düster (Aussichten etc).

blear·y ['bliəri] adj **1.** verschwommen. **2.** trüb (Augen). **'~eyed** adj **1.** mit trüben Augen. **2.** fig. kurzsichtig.

bleat [bli:t] I v/i blöken (Schaf), meckern (Ziege). II v/t et. in weinerlichem Ton sagen. III s Blöken n, Meckern n.

bled [bled] pret u. pp von **bleed.**

bleed [bli:d] (irr) I v/i **1.** bluten: ~ **to death** verbluten. II v/t **2. ⚕** zur Ader lassen. **3.** F schröpfen: ~ **s.o. for s.th.** j-m et. abknöpfen. **4. ⚙** Bremsen entlüften. III s Blöken n, Meckern n. **'bleed·er** s **⚕** Bluter m: **~'s disease** Bluterkrankheit f. **'bleed·ing** I s **1.** Blutung f: ~ **of the nose** Nasenbluten n. **2. ⚕** Aderlaß m. II adj u. adv **3.** sl. verdammt, verflucht.

bleep [bli:p] I s **1.** Piepton m. **2.** F Piepser m (Funkrufempfänger). II v/i **3.** piepen. III v/t **4.** j-n anpiepsen. **'bleep·er** → **bleep** 2.

blem·ish ['blemiʃ] I v/t verunstalten; fig. beflecken. II s Fehler m, Mangel m; fig. Makel m.

blend [blend] I v/t **1.** vermengen, (ver-) mischen; e-e (Tee- etc)Mischung zs.-stellen aus, Wein verschneiden. II v/i **2.** (**with**) sich vermischen (mit), gut zusammen passen (zu). **3.** verschmelzen, ineinander übergehen (Farben, Klänge, Kulturen etc): ~ **into** sich vereinigen zu. III s **4.** Mischung f; Verschnitt m.

bless [bles] v/t (a. irr) **1.** segnen (a. fig.): **be ~ed with** gesegnet sein mit; ~ **me!**, ~ **my soul!** F du m-e Güte!; **(God)** ~ **you!** Gesundheit! **2.** ~ **o.s.** sich glücklich schätzen. **3.** ~ **him!** euphem. der Teufel soll ihn holen! **bless·ed** ['blesɪd] adj **1.** gesegnet, selig: **the ♀ Virgin** die heilige Jungfrau. **2.** euphem. verwünscht, verflixt: **not a ~ soul** keine Menschenseele. **'bless·ed·ness** s Seligkeit f. **'bless·ing** s Segen m (a. fig. to für): **it turned out to be a ~ in disguise** es stellte sich im nachhinein als Segen heraus.

blest [blest] pret u. pp von **bless.**

bleth·er ['bleðə] → **blather.**

blew [blu:] pret von **blow[1].**

blight [blait] I s **1. ♣** Mehltau m. **2.** fig. schädlicher Einfluß. II v/t **3.** fig. zunichte machen, zerstören. **'blight·er** s Br. F Kerl m: **lucky ~** Glückspilz m; **poor ~** armer Hund.

bli·mey ['blaimi] int bsd. Br. sl. Mensch Meier! (überrascht); verdammt!

blind [blaind] I adj **1.** blind (a. fig. **to** gegenüber; **with** vor dat): ~ **in one eye** auf e-m Auge blind; **turn a ~ eye** ein Auge zudrücken (**to** bei). **2.** unübersichtlich (Kurve etc). II adv **3.** ~ **drunk** F sternhagelvoll. III v/t **4.** blenden (a. fig.); blind machen (a. fig. **to** für, gegen). IV s **5.** Rolladen m; Rouleau n; bsd. Br. Markise f: **~ Venetian. ~ al·ley** s Sackgasse f (a. fig.): **lead up a ~** in e-e Sackgasse führen. ~ **flight** s **✈** Blindflug m. **'~fold** I adj mit verbundenen Augen. II adv fig. blindlings. III v/t j-m die Augen verbinden. IV s Augenbinde f. **,~man's 'buff** s Blindekuh(spiel n) f.

blind·ness ['blaindnɪs] s Blindheit f (a. fig.).

blind| spot s **1.** mot. toter Winkel (im Rückspiegel). **2.** fig. schwacher Punkt. **'~worm** s zo. Blindschleiche f.

blink [blɪŋk] I v/i **1.** blinzeln, zwinkern: ~ **at** a) j-m zublinzeln, b) fig. sich maßlos wundern über (acc), c) → **4. 2.** flimmern; blinken. II v/t **3.** ~ **one's eyes** (mit den Augen) zwinkern. **4.** a. ~ **away** fig. ignorieren. III s **4.** Blinzeln n. **'blink·er** s Blinklicht n; mot. Blinker m. **'blink·ing** adj u. adv Br. F verdammt.

bliss [blɪs] s (Glück)Seligkeit f. **bliss·ful** ['~fʊl] adj □ (glück)selig.

blis·ter ['blɪstə] I s **⚕, ⚙** Blase f. II v/t Blasen hervorrufen auf (dat). III v/i Blasen ziehen od. **⚙** werfen.

blith·er·ing ['blɪðərɪŋ] *adj Br.* F verdammt: ~ *idiot* Vollidiot *m.*

blitz [blɪts] ✕ **I** *s* **1.** heftiger Luftangriff. **2.** Blitzkrieg *m.* **II** *v/t* **3.** schwer bombardieren: ~*ed* zerbombt.

bliz·zard ['blɪzəd] *s* Blizzard *m*, Schneesturm *m.*

bloat·ed ['bləʊtɪd] *adj* aufgeblasen (*a. fig. Person*), aufgebläht (*a. fig. Budget etc*), aufgedunsen (*Gesicht etc*).

bloat·er ['bləʊtə] *s gastr.* Bückling *m.*

blob [blɒb] *s* Klecks *m.*

bloc [blɒk] *s* *pol.* Block *m.*

block [blɒk] **I** *s* **1.** (*a. Motor- etc*)Block *m*, Klotz *m*; Baustein *m*, (Bau)Klötzchen *n* (*für Kinder*). **2.** (*Schreib-, Notiz*)Block *m.* **3.** *bsd. Am.* (*Häuser*)Block *m*: ~ (*of flats*) *Br.* Wohnhaus *n.* **4.** *fig.* Block *m*, Gruppe *f.* **II** *v/t* **5.** *a.* ~ *up* (ab-, ver)sperren, blockieren, verstopfen. **6.** ✝ *Konto* sperren: ~*ed account* Sperrkonto *n.*

block·ade [blɒ'keɪd] **I** *s* Blockade *f.* **II** *v/t* blockieren.

'**block·head** *s* Dummkopf *m.* '~**house** *s* Blockhaus *n.* ~ **let·ters** *s pl* Blockschrift *f.*

bloke [bləʊk] *s bsd. Br.* F Kerl *m.*

blond [blɒnd] *adj* **1.** blond (*Haar*), hell (*Haut*). **2.** blond(haarig). **blonde** [blɒnd] **I** *s* Blondine *f.* **II** *adj* → **blond.**

blood [blʌd] *s* **1.** Blut *n* (*a. fig.*): *his ~ froze* das Blut erstarrte ihm in den Adern; *related by* ~ blutsverwandt; → *cold* 1, *sweat* 2. **2.** Geblüt *n*, Abstammung *f.* ~ **al·co·hol** *s* 🍶 Blutalkohol *m.* ,~**and-'thun·der** *adj*: ~ *novel* Reißer *m.* ~ **bank** *s* 🍶 Blutbank *f.* '~**bath** *s* Blutbad *n.* ~ **clot** *s* 🍶 Blutgerinnsel *n.* '~,**cur·dling** *adj* grauenhaft. ~ **do·nor** *s* 🍶 Blutspender(in). ~ **group** *s* Blutgruppe *f.* '~**hound** *s* Bluthund *m.*

blood·less ['blʌdlɪs] *adj* □ **1.** blutlos, -leer (*a. fig.*). **2.** unblutig (*Kampf etc*).

blood| or·ange *s* Blutorange *f.* ~ **poi·son·ing** *s* 🍶 Blutvergiftung *f.* ~ **pres·sure** *s* 🍶 Blutdruck *m.* ~ **pud·ding** *s* Blutwurst *f.* ~ **re·la·tion**, ~ **rel·a·tive** *s* Blutsverwandte *m*, *f.* ~ **re·venge** *s* Blutrache *f.* ~ **sam·ple** *s* 🍶 Blutprobe *f.* '~**shed** *s* Blutvergießen *n.* '~**shot** *adj* blutunterlaufen. '~**stained** *adj* blutbefleckt. '~,**suck·er** *s zo.* Blutsauger *m* (*a. fig.*). ~ **sug·ar** *s physiol.* Blutzucker *m.*

'~,**thirst·y** *adj* blutdürstig. ~ **trans·fu·sion** *s* 🍶 Bluttransfusion *f*, -übertragung *f.* ~ **ves·sel** *s anat.* Blutgefäß *n.*

blood·y ['blʌdɪ] **I** *adj* **1.** blutig. **2.** *Br. sl.* verdammt, verflucht: ~ *fool* Vollidiot *m*; *not a* ~ *soul* kein Schwanz. **II** *adv* **3.** *Br. sl.* → 2: ~ *awful* saumäßig.

bloom [bluːm] *s* → **blossom** I. **II** *v/i* blühen (*a. fig.*).

bloom·er ['bluːmə] *s bsd. Br.* F grober Fehler, Schnitzer *m.*

bloom·ing ['bluːmɪŋ] *adj* **1.** blühend (*a. fig.*). **2.** (*a. adv*) F verflixt.

blos·som ['blɒsəm] **I** *s* **1.** Blüte *f*: *be in full* ~ in voller Blüte stehen. **2.** *fig.* Blüte (-zeit) *f.* **II** *v/i* **3.** blühen (*a. fig.*): ~ (*out*) erblühen (*into* zu).

blot [blɒt] **I** *s* **1.** Klecks *m.* **2.** *fig.* Makel *m.* **II** *v/t* **3.** beklecksen. **4.** *fig.* beflecken. **5.** *Familie, Erinnerungen etc* auslöschen. **6.** mit *Löschpapier* (ab)löschen.

blotch [blɒtʃ] → **blot** 1–3.

blot·ter ['blɒtə] *s Am.* Kladde *f.*

blot·ting pa·per ['blɒtɪŋ] *s* Löschpapier *n.*

blot·to ['blɒtəʊ] *adj sl.* (stink)besoffen.

blouse [blaʊz] *s* Bluse *f.*

blow[1] [bləʊ] **I** *s* **1.** Blasen *n*, Wehen *n.* **2.** Luftzug *m.* **3.** Blasen *n*: ~ *on a whistle* Pfiff *m*; *give one's nose a* ~ sich schneuzen. **II** *v/i* (*irr*) **4.** blasen, wehen. **5.** ertönen (*Pfiff etc*). **6.** keuchen, schnaufen. **7.** explodieren; platzen (*Reifen*); ≸ durchbrennen (*Sicherung*). **III** *v/t* (*irr*) **8.** blasen, wehen. **9.** *Suppe etc* blasen, *Feuer* anfachen. **10.** (auf-, aus)blasen: ~ *bubbles* Seifenblasen machen; ~ *glass* Glas blasen; ~ *one's nose* sich schneuzen. **11.** ~ *one's lid* (*od. top, stack*) F an die Decke gehen. **12.** *sl. Geld* verpulvern (*on* für); *Chance* vergeben.

Verbindungen mit Adverbien:

blow| a·way *v/t* fort-, wegblasen. ~ **down** *v/t* um-, herunterwehen. ~ *in v/i* F hereinschneien (*Besucher*). ~ **off** → *blow away.* ~ **out I** *v/t* **1.** Licht etc ausblasen. **2.** ~ *one's brains* F sich e-e Kugel durch den Kopf jagen. ~ **up I** *v/t* **1.** (in die Luft) sprengen. **2.** aufblasen, -pumpen. **3.** *phot.* vergrößern; *fig.* aufbauschen (*Story etc*). ~ *in* anschnauzen. **II** *v/i* **5.** in die Luft fliegen; explodieren (*a. fig.* F): ~ *at* → 4. **6.** losbrechen (*Sturm etc*), ausbrechen (*Streit etc*).

blow² [~] *s* (*a.* Schicksals)Schlag *m*, Stoß *m*: **at one** (*od. a* [*single*]) ~ mit 'einem Schlag; **come to** ~**s** handgreiflich werden.

'**blow**·**dry** *v/t* **1.** *j-m die Haare* fönen: ~ **s.o.'s hair. 2.** *j-m* die Haare fönen: ~ **s.o.** ~ **dry·er** *s* Haartrockner *m*.

blow·er ['bləʊə] ⊙ Gebläse *n*.

'**blow**|·**fly** *s zo.* Schmeißfliege *f.* '~·**gun** ⊙ Spritzpistole *f.* '~·**lamp** ⊙ Lötlampe *f.*

blown [bləʊn] *pp von* **blow**¹.

'**blow**|·**out** *s mot.* Reifenpanne *f.* '~·**torch** ⊙ Lötlampe *f.* → **lamp 1. 2.** Explosion *f* (*a. fig.* F). **2.** F Krach *m*, Streit *m*. **3.** *phot.* Vergrößerung *f.*

blow·y ['bləʊɪ] *adj* windig.

blowz·y ['blaʊzɪ] *adj* schlampig (*bsd. Frau*).

blub·ber ['blʌbə] *v/i* flennen, plärren.

bludg·eon ['blʌdʒən] I *s* **1.** Knüppel *m.* II *v/t* **2.** niederknüppeln. **3.** ~ **s.o. into doing s.th.** *j-n* zwingen, et. zu tun.

blue [bluː] I *adj* **1.** blau: → **moon 1. 2.** F melancholisch, traurig. **3.** unanständig, schlüpfrig: ~ **jokes**; ~ **film** Pornofilm *m.* **4.** F schrecklich: ~ **fear** Heidenangst *f*; → **funk** I, **murder 1.** II *s* **5.** Blau *n*: **dressed in** ~ blau *od.* in Blau gekleidet; **out of the** ~ *fig.* aus heiterem Himmel. **6.** *pl* (*a. sg konstruiert*) F Melancholie *f*: **have** (*od. be in*) **the** ~**s** den Moralischen haben. **7.** → **blues.** III *v/t* **8.** blau färben. ~·**ber·ry** ['~bərɪ] *s* ♀ Blau-, Heidelbeere *f.* ~·**blood·ed** *adj* blaublütig, adlig. '~·**bot·tle** *s* **1.** *zo.* Schmeißfliege *f.* **2.** ♀ Kornblume *f.* ~ **jeans** *s pl* Blue jeans *pl.* ~·**pen·cil** *s* **1.** Blaustift *m.* **2.** *fig.* Rotstift *m*, Zensur *f.* ~·**pen·cil** *v/t pret u. pp* -**ciled**, *bsd. Br.* -**cilled** zensieren. '~·**print** I *s* **1.** *phot.* Blaupause *f.* **2.** *fig.* Plan *m*, Entwurf *m*: ~ **stage** Planungsstadium *n.* II *v/t* **3.** e-e Blaupause machen von. **4.** planen, entwerfen.

blues [bluːz] *s pl* **1.** → **blue 6. 2.** (*a. sg konstruiert*) ♪ Blues *m.*

'**blue**,**stock·ing** *s bsd. contp.* Blaustrumpf *m.*

bluff [blʌf] I *v/t u. v/i* bluffen. II *s* Bluff *m.* '**bluff·er** *s* Bluffer *m.*

blu·ish ['bluːɪʃ] *adj* bläulich.

blun·der ['blʌndə] I *s* **1.** (grober) Fehler. II *v/i* **2.** e-n (groben) Fehler machen. **3.** pfuschen, stümpern. **4.** stolpern, tappen (*into in acc*) (*beide a. fig.*). III *v/t* **5.** verpfuschen, verpatzen. '**blun·der·er** *s* Pfuscher *m*, Stümper *m.* '**blun·der·ing** *adj* stümperhaft.

blunt [blʌnt] I *adj* **1.** stumpf. **2.** *fig.* abgestumpft (*to* gegen). **3.** *fig.* ungehobelt. **4.** *fig.* offen, schonungslos. II *v/t* **5.** stumpf machen, abstumpfen (*a. fig. to* gegen). '**blunt·ly** *adv fig.* frei heraus: **to put it** ~ um es ganz offen zu sagen; **refuse** ~ glatt ablehnen.

blur [blɜː] I *v/t* **1.** verwischen: a) *Schrift etc* verschmieren, b) *a. fig.* undeutlich *od.* verschwommen machen. **2.** *phot.* verwackeln. **3.** *Sinne etc* trüben. II *v/i* **4.** verschwimmen (*a. Eindruck etc*). **5.** *fig.* sich verwischen (*Unterschiede etc*).

blurt [blɜːt] *v/t*: ~ **out** herausplatzen mit.

blush [blʌʃ] I *v/i* erröten, rot werden (*at* bei): ~ **for** (*od. with*) **shame** schamrot werden. II *s* Erröten *n*, (Scham)Röte *f.* '**blush·er** *s* Rouge *n.*

boar [bɔː] *s zo.* Eber *m*, (*Wildschwein*) Keiler *m.*

board [bɔːd] I *s* **1.** Brett *n*, Diele *f*, Planke *f.* **2.** (*Anschlag-, Schach- etc*)Brett *n*; (Wand)Tafel *f*: → **sweep 4. 3.** *pl thea.* Bretter *pl*, Bühne *f*: **tread** (*od. walk*) **the** ~**s** auf den Brettern stehen. **4.** Kost *f*, Verpflegung *f*: ~ **and lodging** Kost u. Logis, Wohnung u. Verpflegung. **5.** Ausschuß *m*, Kommission *f*; Amt *n*, Behörde *f*: ~ **of examiners** Prüfungskommission; ♀ **of Trade** *Br.* Handelsministerium *n*, *Am.* Handelskammer *f.* **6.** **on** ~ an Bord (*e-s Schiffs, Flugzeugs*); im Zug *od.* Bus; **on** ~ **(a) ship** an Bord e-s Schiffs; **go on** ~ an Bord gehen; einsteigen. **7.** Pappe *f*: (**bound**) **in** ~**s** kartoniert. II *v/t* **8.** dielen, täfeln, verschalen. **9.** an Bord (*e-s Schiffs od. Flugzeugs*) gehen, ⚓, ✈ entern; einsteigen in (*e-n Zug od. Bus*). '**board·er** *s* **1.** Kostgänger(in); Pensionsgast *m.* **2.** *Br.* Internatsschüler(in).

board game *s* Brettspiel *n.*

board·ing ['bɔːdɪŋ] *s* Dielenbelag *m*, Täfelung *f*, Verschalung *f.* ~ **card** *s* ✈ Bordkarte *f.* '~·**house** *s* Pension *f*, Fremdenheim *n.* ~·**pass** *s* ✈ Bordkarte *f.* ~ **school** *s* Internat *n*, Pensionat *n.*

board room s Sitzungssaal m.
boast [bəʊst] **I** s 1. Prahlerei f. 2. Stolz m
(*Gegenstand des Stolzes*). **II** v/i 3. prahlen (**of**, **about** mit). **III** v/t 4. sich des
Besitzes (*gen*) rühmen (können), aufzuweisen haben. **'boast·er** s Prahler(in).
boast·ful [~fʊl] adj □ prahlerisch.
boat [bəʊt] **I** s 1. Boot n; Schiff n: **be in
the same ~** fig. im selben Boot sitzen;
burn one's ~s (**behind one**) fig. alle
Brücken hinter sich abbrechen; **take to
the ~s** ♣ in die (Rettungs)Boote gehen;
→ **miss²** 1, **rock²** 2. **2.** (*bsd.* So-
ßen)Schüssel f. **II** v/i 3. Boot fahren: **go
~ing** e-e Bootsfahrt machen. **'~house**
s Bootshaus n.
boat·ing ['bəʊtɪŋ] s 1. Bootfahren n. 2.
Bootsfahrt f.
boat| race s Bootrennen n. **~·swain**
['bəʊsn] s ♣ Bootsmann m. **~ train** s
Zug m mit Schiffsanschluß.
bob [bɒb] **I** s 1. Knicks m. 2. Sport: Bob
m. **II** v/t 3. Haare etc kurz schneiden,
stutzen. **III** v/i 4. sich auf u. ab bewegen: **~ up** (plötzlich) auftauchen (a.
fig.). **5.** knicksen (**at**, **before**, **to** vor
dat).
bob·bin ['bɒbɪn] s Spule f (a. ⚡).
bob·by ['bɒbɪ] s Br. F Bobby m (*Polizist*). **~ pin** s bsd. Am. Haarklammer f,
-klemme f.
'bob|·sled, **'~·sleigh** s Sport: Bob m.
bode¹ [bəʊd] v/i: **~ ill** Unheil verkünden;
~ well Gutes versprechen.
bode² [~] pret von **bide**.
bod·ice ['bɒdɪs] s 1. Mieder n. 2. Oberteil n (e-s Kleids etc).
bod·i·ly ['bɒdɪlɪ] **I** adj 1. körperlich: **~
harm** (*od.* **injury**) ⚖ Körperverletzung
f; **~ needs** (*od.* **wants**) pl leibliche Bedürfnisse pl. **II** adv 2. leibhaftig. 3. als
Ganzes; geschlossen.
bod·y ['bɒdɪ] s 1. Körper m, Leib m,
engS. Rumpf m. 2. oft **dead ~** Leiche f.
3. ♣, ✈ Rumpf m; mot. Karosserie f.
4. Gesamtheit f: **in a ~** geschlossen, wie
ein Mann. **~ of laws** Gesetz(es)samm-
lung f. **5.** Körper(schaft f) m, Gruppe f,
Gremium n: → **diplomatic**, **governing**
2. **6.** fig. Kern m, das Wesentliche. **7.**
Hauptteil m, Text(teil) m (e-s Briefs
etc). **8.** phys. etc Körper m: → **celestial**, **heavenly**. **9.** fig. Körper m, Gehalt
m (*von Wein*), (Klang)Fülle f. **~**

build·ing s Bodybuilding n. **'~·guard** s
1. Leibwächter m. 2. Leibgarde f, -wa-
che f. **~ lan·guage** s Körpersprache f. **~
o·do(u)r** s (*bsd. unangenehmer*) Körpergeruch. **~ search** s Leibesvisitation
f. **'~·work** s mot. Karosserie f.
bog [bɒg] **I** s Sumpf m, Morast m (*beide
a. fig.*). **II** v/t: **~ down** fig. zum Stocken
bringen; **get ~ged** (**down**) → **III**. **III** v/i
sich festfahren, steckenbleiben (*beide a.
fig.*).
bo·gey → **bogy**.
bog·gle ['bɒgl] v/i fassungslos sein: **imagination** (*od.* **the mind**) **~s at the
thought** es wird e-m schwindlig bei dem
Gedanken.
bog·gy ['bɒgɪ] adj sumpfig, morastig.
bo·gie → **bogy**.
bo·gus ['bəʊgəs] adj 1. falsch, unecht.
Schwindel..., Schein...
bo·gy ['bəʊgɪ] s Kobold m; (Schreck-)
Gespenst n (a. fig.).
boil¹ [bɔɪl] s ✚ Geschwür n, Furunkel m,
n.
boil² [~] **I** s Kochen n, Sieden n: **bring to
the ~** zum Kochen bringen. **II** v/i kochen (a. fig. **with** vor dat), sieden: →
kettle, **pot** 1. **III** v/t kochen (lassen).
Verbindungen mit Adverbien:
boil| a·way **I** v/i 1. kochen, sieden. **2.**
verdampfen. 3. fig. abkühlen (*Interesse
etc*). **II** v/t 4. verdampfen lassen. **~
down I** v/t 1. einkochen lassen. **2.** fig.
zs.-fassen (**to a few sentences** in ein
paar Sätzen). **II** v/i 3. einkochen. **4. ~ to**
fig. hinauslaufen auf (*acc*). **~ o·ver** v/i
1. überkochen, -laufen. **2.** fig. vor Wut
kochen. **3.** fig. Situation etc: außer
Kontrolle geraten; sich auswachsen
(**into** zu).
boil·er ['bɔɪlə] s 1. ⚙ Dampfkessel m. 2.
Boiler m, Heißwasserspeicher m. **3.**
Suppenhuhn n. **~ suit** s Overall m.
boil·ing ['bɔɪlɪŋ] **I** adj siedend, kochend.
II adv: **~ hot** kochendheiß. **~ point** s
Siedepunkt m (a. fig.): **reach ~ den**
Siedepunkt erreichen.
bois·ter·ous ['bɔɪstərəs] adj □ 1. stürmisch (*Meer, Wetter etc*). 2. lärmend,
laut. 3. ausgelassen, wild (*Person, Party etc*).
bold [bəʊld] adj □ 1. kühn: a) mutig,
unerschrocken, b) gewagt, c) fortschrittlich. 2. dreist, frech: **make ~ to**

sich erdreisten *od.* es wagen zu. **3.** scharf hervortretend: *in ~ outline* in deutlichen Umrissen.

bole [bəʊl] *s* Baumstamm *m.*

bo·lo·ney [bə'ləʊnɪ] *s sl.* Quatsch *m.*

bol·ster ['bəʊlstə] I *s* **1.** Keilkissen *n;* Nackenrolle *f.* **2.** Polster *n,* Kissen *n,* Unterlage *f (a.* ☉*).* II *v/t* **3.** (aus)polstern. **4.** *mst ~ up fig.* unterstützen.

bolt¹ [bəʊlt] I *s* **1.** Bolzen *m: he has shot his ~ fig.* er hat sein Pulver verschossen. **2.** Blitz(strahl) *m: a ~ from the blue fig.* ein Blitz aus heiterem Himmel. **3.** ☉ Riegel *m.* **4.** ☉ (Schrauben)Bolzen, Schraube *f* (mit Mutter): *~ nut* Schraubenmutter *f.* **5.** plötzlicher Satz *od.* Sprung: *he made a ~ for the door* er machte e-n Satz zur Tür. II *adv* **6. ~ upright** bolzen-, kerzengerade. III *v/i* **7.** durchbrennen, ausreißen. **8.** durchgehen *(Pferd).* IV *v/t* **9.** ver-, zuriegeln. **10.** *oft ~ down* Essen hinunterschlingen, *Getränk* hinunterstürzen.

bolt² [~] *v/t Mehl* sieben.

bomb [bɒm] I *s* Bombe *f.* II *v/t* bombardieren: *~ed out* ausgebombt. *~ a·lert s* Bombenalarm *m.*

bom·bard [bɒm'bɑːd] *v/t* bombardieren *(a. fig. with* mit*).* **bom'bard·ment** *s* Bombardement *n,* Bombardierung *f.*

bom·bast ['bɒmbæst] *s* Bombast *m,* Schwulst *m.* **bom'bas·tic** *adj (~ally)* bombastisch, schwülstig.

bombed [bɒmd] *adj sl.* **1.** besoffen. **2.** high *(im Drogenrausch).*

bomb·er ['bɒmə] *s* **1.** ✈ Bomber *m.* **2.** Bombenleger *m.*

'**bomb|·proof** *adj* bombensicher: *~ shelter* → II. II *s* Bunker *m.* '*~·shell s: be a ~* wie e-e Bombe einschlagen. *~ threat s* Bombendrohung *f.*

bo·nan·za [bəʊ'nænzə] I *s fig.* Goldgrube *f.* II *adj* äußerst einträglich.

bond [bɒnd] I *s* **1.** *pl fig.* Bande *pl: the ~s of love.* **2.** Bund *m,* Verbindung *f.* **3.** ✝ Zollverschluß *m: in ~* unter Zollverschluß. **4.** ✝ Schuldverschreibung *f,* Obligation *f.* II *v/t* **5.** ✝ unter Zollverschluß legen: *~ed warehouse* Zollspeicher *m.* '*~·hold·er s* ✝ Obligationshaber *m.*

bone [bəʊn] I *s* **1.** Knochen *m, pl a.* Gebeine *pl: make no ~s about (od. of)* nicht viel Federlesens machen mit, *feel*

s.th. in one's ~s et. in den Knochen *od.* instinktiv spüren; *have a ~ to pick with s.o.* mit j-m ein Hühnchen zu rupfen haben; *chilled* (*od. frozen*) *to the ~* völlig durchgefroren; → *contention* 1. **2.** (Fisch)Gräte *f.* II *v/t* **3.** entbeinen; *Fisch* entgräten. III *v/i* **4.** *~ up on s.th.* F et. pauken *od.* büffeln. '*~'dry adj* knochentrocken. '*~·head s* F Holzkopf *m.* ,*~·'la·zy adj* stinkfaul. '*~·shak·er s* F Klapperkasten *m (Bus etc).*

bon·fire ['bɒn,faɪə] *s* **1.** Freudenfeuer *n.* **2.** Feuer *n* im Freien *(zum Unkrautverbrennen etc).*

bonk [bɒŋk] *v/t u. v/i sl.* bumsen.

bon·kers ['bɒŋkəz] *adj sl.* übergeschnappt: *go ~* überschnappen.

bon·net ['bɒnɪt] *s* **1.** ☉ (Schutz)Kappe *f,* Haube *f.* **2.** *mot. Br.* Motorhaube *f.*

bo·nus ['bəʊnəs] *s* **1.** ✝ Bonus *m,* Prämie *f.* **2.** Gratifikation *f.* **3.** ✝ *bsd. Br.* Extradividende *f.*

bon·y ['bəʊnɪ] *adj* **1.** (stark-, grob)knochig. **2.** voll(er) Knochen; voll(er) Gräten *(Fisch).* **3.** knochendürr.

boo [buː] I *int* buh! II *s* Buh(ruf *m*) *n.* III *v/i* buhen. IV *v/t* ausbuhen.

boob [buːb] *sl.* I *s* **1.** Blödmann *m,* Idiot *m.* **2.** *Br.* Schnitzer *m.* II *v/i* **3.** *Br.* e-n Schnitzer machen.

boo·by ['buːbɪ] *s* **1.** Trottel *m,* Dummkopf *m.* **2.** *Sport etc:* Letzte *m, f,* Schlechteste *m, f.* *~ hatch s Am. sl.* Klapsmühle *f.* *~ prize s Sport etc: Scherzpreis für den Letzten od. Schlechtesten.* *~ trap s* **1.** versteckte Sprengladung; *Auto etc,* in dem e-e Sprengladung versteckt ist. **2.** grober Scherz *(bsd. über halbgeöffneter Tür angebrachter Wassereimer).*

book [bʊk] I *s* **1.** Buch *n: the* ☢ die Bibel; *a closed ~ fig.* ein Buch mit sieben Siegeln *(to* für*); an open ~ fig.* ein offenes *od.* aufgeschlagenes Buch *(to* für*); be at one's ~s* über s-n Büchern sitzen; *speak (od. talk) like a ~* geschraubt *od.* gestelzt reden; → *suit* 5. **2.** ✝ Geschäftsbuch *n: be deep in s.o.'s ~s* bei j-m tief in der Kreide stehen. **3.** Liste *f,* Verzeichnis *n: be on the ~s* auf der *(Mitglieder- etc)*Liste stehen. **4.** Notizbuch *n,* -block *m;* (Schreib-, Schul)Heft *n: be in s.o.'s good (bad)~s* bei j-m gut (schlecht) angeschrieben sein. **5.**

Heft(chen) *n*: ~ *of stamps* (**tickets**) Marken-(Fahrschein)heft(chen); ~ *of matches* Streichholzbriefchen *n*. **II** *v/t* **6.** 🕆 (ver)buchen; *Auftrag* notieren. **7.** aufschreiben, *Sport*: a. verwarnen. **8.** verpflichten, engagieren. **9.** *Zimmer etc* bestellen, *Reise etc* buchen, (*Eintritts-, Fahrkarte* lösen: *~ed up* ausgebucht (*Künstler, Hotel, Veranstaltung*). **10.** *Gepäck* aufgeben (**to** nach). **III** *v/i* **11.** *Br. a.* ~ *up* e-e (Fahr- *etc*)Karte lösen (**to, for** nach): ~ *through* durchlösen (**to** bis, nach). **12.** sich (*für e-e Fahrt etc*) vormerken lassen, e-n Platz *etc* bestellen, buchen. **13.** ~ *in bsd. Br.* sich (*im Hotel*) eintragen: ~ *in at* absteigen in (*dat*).

book·a·ble ['bʊkəbl] *adj* im Vorverkauf erhältlich.

'**book|,bind·er** *s* Buchbinder *m*. '**~·case** *s* Bücherschrank *m*. ~ **club** *s* Buchgemeinschaft *f*. ~ **end** *s* Bücherstütze *f*.

book·ie ['bʊkɪ] *s* F Buchmacher *m*.

book·ing ['bʊkɪŋ] *s* Buchung *f*, (Vor)Bestellung *f*: *make a* (**firm**) ~ (fest) buchen. ~ **clerk** *s* Fahrkartenverkäufer *m*. ~ **of·fice** *s* **1.** (Fahrkarten)Schalter *m*. **2.** (*Theater- etc*)Kasse *f*, Vorverkaufsstelle *f*.

book·ish ['bʊkɪʃ] *adj* **1.** belesen. **2.** papieren (*Stil*).

'**book|,keep·er** *s* 🕆 Buchhalter(in). '**~·keep·ing** *s* 🕆 Buchhaltung *f*, -führung *f*. '**~·mak·er** *s* Buchmacher *m*. '**~·mark**, '**~·mark·er** *s* Lesezeichen *n*. **~·mo·bile** ['~məʊˌbiːl] *s Am.* Wanderbücherei *f*. '**~·sell·er** *s* Buchhändler(in). '**~·shop** *s* Buchhandlung *f*. '**~·stall** *s* **1.** Bücherstand *m*. **2.** *bsd. Br.* Zeitungskiosk *m*, -stand *m*. '**~·store** *s bsd. Am.* Buchhandlung *f*. '**~·worm** *s zo.* Bücherwurm *m* (*a. fig.*).

boom¹ [buːm] **I** *v/i* dröhnen (*Stimme etc*), donnern (*Geschütz etc*), brausen (*Wellen etc*). **II** *s* Dröhnen, Donner *n*, Brausen *n*.

boom² [~] *s* **1.** ⚓ Baum *m*, Spiere *f*. **2.** ⊙ (*Kran*)Ausleger *m*. **3.** *Film, TV*: (*Mikrophon*)Galgen *m*.

boom³ [~] 🕆 **I** *s* Boom *m*: a) Hochkonjunktur *f*, b) *Börse*: Hausse *f*, c) (plötzlicher) Aufschwung. **II** *v/i* e-n Boom erleben.

boom·er·ang ['buːməræŋ] **I** *s* Bumerang

m (*a. fig.*). **II** *v/i fig.* sich als Bumerang erweisen (**on** für).

boon [buːn] *s fig.* Segen *m* (**to** für).

boor [bʊə] *s* ungehobelter Kerl. **boor·ish** ['bʊərɪʃ] *adj* □ ungehobelt. '**boor·ish·ness** *s* ungehobeltes Benehmen *od.* Wesen.

boost [buːst] **I** *v/t* **1.** F *Preise* in die Höhe treiben. **2.** F Auftrieb geben (*dat*), *Produktion etc* ankurbeln, *Moral* heben. **3.** ⊙ *Druck* erhöhen; 🗲 *Spannung* verstärken. **II** *s* **4.** F Auftrieb *m*. **5.** ⊙ Erhöhung *f*; 🗲 Verstärkung *f*. '**boost·er** *s* **1.** *a.* ~ *shot* 🕭 Wiederholungsimpfung *f*. **2.** Zündstufe *f* (*e-r Rakete*): ~ *rocket* Startrakete *f*.

boot¹ [buːt] **I** *s* **1.** Stiefel *m*: *the ~ is on the other foot* (*od. leg*) der Fall liegt umgekehrt; ~ *bet* **4**, *lick* **1**. **2.** F (Fuß)Tritt *m*: *give s.o. a* ~ → **4**; *get the* ~ rausgeschmissen (*entlassen*) werden. **3.** *mot. Br.* Kofferraum *m*. **II** *v/t* **4.** F *j-m* e-n (Fuß)Tritt geben: ~ (**out**) rausschmeißen (*entlassen*).

boot² [~] *s*: *to* ~ obendrein, noch dazu.

'**boot·black** *s* Schuhputzer *m*.

booth [buːð] *s* **1.** (Markt-, Schau)Bude *f*, (Messe)Stand *m*. **2.** (Telefon)Zelle *f*; (Wahl)Kabine *f*, (-)zelle *f*.

'**boot|·lace** *s* Schnürsenkel *m*. '**~·lick** *v/t u. v/i* F (vor *j-m*) kriechen. '**~·lick·er** *s* F Kriecher *m*.

boots [buːts] *pl* **boots** *s Br.* Hausdiener *m* (*im Hotel*).

boo·ty ['buːtɪ] *s* (*fig. a.* Aus)Beute *f*.

booze [buːz] **I** *v/i* saufen. **II** *s* Zeug *n* (*alkoholisches Getränk*); Sauferei *f*; (*Br. a.* ~**up**) Saufgelage *n*; (*Br. a.* ~**up**) Besäufnis *n*. '**booz·er** *s* F **1.** Säufer(in). **2.** Kneipe *f*. '**booz·y** *adj* F versoffen.

bor·der ['bɔːdə] **I** *s* **1.** Rand *m*. **2.** Einfassung *f*, Saum *m*, Umrandung *f*. **3.** (Gebiets-, Landes)Grenze *f*: ~ *incident* Grenzzwischenfall *m*. **II** *v/t* **4.** einfassen. **5.** begrenzen, grenzen an (*acc*). **III** *v/i* **6.** grenzen (**on** an *acc*) (*a. fig.*). '**bor·der·er** *s* Grenzbewohner *m*.

'**bor·der|·land** *s* Grenzgebiet *n*. '**~·line** *s* **1.** Grenzlinie *f*. **2.** *fig.* Grenze *f*. **II** *adj* **3.** *fig.* Grenz...: ~ *case* Grenzfall *m*.

bore¹ [bɔː] **I** *s* Bohrung *f*: a) Bohrloch *n*, b) ⊙ Kaliber *n*. **II** *v/t* (*bsd.* aus)bohren. **III** *v/i* bohren (**for** nach).

bore² [~] **I** *s* **1.** langweilige Sache; *bsd.*

Br. lästige Sache. **2.** Langweiler *m; bsd. Br.* lästiger Kerl. **II** *v/t* **3.** j-n langweilen; *bsd. Br.* j-m lästig sein: *be ~d* sich langweilen; *be ~d stiff* F sich zu Tode langweilen.

bore³ [~] *pret von* **bear².**

bore·dom ['bɔːdəm] *s* **1.** Lang(e)weile *f.* **2.** Langweiligkeit *f.*

bor·er ['bɔːrə] *s* ⊚ Bohrer *m.*

bo·ric ac·id ['bɔːrɪk] *s* 🧪 Borsäure *f.*

bor·ing ['bɔːrɪŋ] *adj* langweilig.

born [bɔːn] **I** *pp von* **bear²** **2. II** *adj* geboren *(a. fig.):* **a ~ poet.**

borne [bɔːn] *pp von* **bear².**

bo·ron ['bɔːrɒn] *s* 🧪 Bor *n.*

bor·ough ['bʌrə] *s* **1.** *Br.* Stadt *f (mit Selbstverwaltung); (a. parliamentary ~)* Stadt *f od.* städtischer Wahlbezirk mit eigener Vertretung im Parlament; Stadtteil *m (von Groß-London).* **2.** *Am.* Stadtbezirk *m (in New York).*

bor·row ['bɒrəʊ] **I** *v/t* **1.** (sich) *et.* (aus)borgen, leihen *(from* von). **2.** *fig.* entlehnen *(from* von): *~ed word* Lehnwort *n.* **II** *v/i* **3.** 🕂 Kredit aufnehmen. **'bor·row·er** *s* **1.** Entleiher(in). **2.** 🕂 Kreditnehmer(in).

bosh [bɒʃ] *s* F Blödsinn *m,* Quatsch *m.*

bos·om ['buzəm] *s* **1.** Busen *(a. fig.):* **~ friend** Busenfreund(in). **2.** *fig.* Schoß *m:* **in the ~ of one's family.**

boss¹ [bɒs] *s* Buckel *m,* Knauf *m.*

boss² [~] F **I** *s* Boß *m,* Chef *m.* **II** *v/t:* **~ about** *(od. around)* herumkommandieren.

boss·y ['bɒsɪ] *adj* F herrisch.

bo·tan·i·cal [bə'tænɪkl] *adj* □ botanisch: **~ garden(s** *pl)* botanischer Garten. **bot·a·nist** ['bɒtənɪst] *s* Botaniker(in). **'bot·a·ny** *s* Botanik *f.*

botch [bɒtʃ] **I** *s* Pfusch(arbeit *f) m:* **make a ~ of →** II. **II** *v/t* verpfuschen. **III** *v/i* pfuschen. **'botch·er** *s* Pfuscher *m.*

both [bəʊθ] **I** *adj u. pron* beide(s): **~ my brothers** m-e beiden Brüder; **~ of them** alle beide; **~ sex** 1. **II** *adv od. cj:* **~ ... and** sowohl ... als (auch).

both·er ['bɒðə] **I** *s* Belästigung *f,* Störung *f.* **II** *v/t* belästigen, stören: **don't ~ me!** laß mich in Ruhe!; **I can't be ~ed** ich habe keine Lust **(to do** zu tun). **III** *v/i* (*about* sich) kümmern (um); sich aufregen (über *acc*).

bot·tle ['bɒtl] **I** *s* Flasche *f:* **→ hit** 7. **II** *v/t*

in Flaschen abfüllen: **~d beer** Flaschenbier *n;* **~ up** *Gefühle etc* unterdrücken; **~d-up** aufgestaut. **'~·neck** *s* **1.** Flaschenhals *m,* Engpaß *m (e-r Straße) (a. fig.).* **~·o·pen·er** *s* Flaschenöffner *m.* **~ post** *s* Flaschenpost *f.*

bot·tom ['bɒtəm] **I** *s* **1.** Boden *m (e-s Gefäßes etc),* Fuß *m (e-s Bergs etc),* Sohle *f (e-s Tals etc),* Unterseite *f:* **at the ~ of the street** am Ende der Straße; **from the ~ of one's heart** aus tiefstem Herzen; **~s up!** F ex! **2.** Boden *m,* Grund *m:* **~ of the sea** Meeresboden, -grund. **3.** Grund(lage *f) m:* **be at the ~ of** der Grund sein für, hinter *e-r Sache* stecken; **get to the ~ of s.th.** e-r Sache auf den Grund gehen *od.* kommen; **knock the ~ out of s.th.** et. gründlich widerlegen. **4.** (Stuhl)Sitz *m.* **5.** F Popo *m.* **II** *adj* **6.** unterst: **~ line** letzte Zeile; **→ bet** 4, **rung²**. **'bot·tom·less** *adj* □ *fig.* ungründlich; unerschöpflich.

bough [baʊ] *s* Ast *m,* Zweig *m.*

bought [bɔːt] *pret u. pp von* **buy.**

bouil·lon ['buːjɔ̃ːŋ] *s* Fleischbrühe *f,* Bouillon *f.*

bou·le·vard ['buːləvɑːd] *s* Boulevard *m.*

bounce [baʊns] **I** *s* **1.** Elastizität *f.* **2.** Sprung *m,* Satz *m.* **3.** F Schwung *m,* Schmiß *m.* **4.** F Rausschmiß *m (a. Entlassung):* **give s.o. the ~ → 6;** *get the ~* rausgeschmissen werden. **II** *v/t* **5.** Ball *etc* aufprallen *od.* aufspringen lassen. **6.** F j-n rausschmeißen *(a. entlassen).* **III** *v/i* **7.** aufprallen, -springen *(Ball etc):* **~ off** abprallen *(from etc).* **8.** federn, elastisch sein *(Gummi etc);* springen *(Ball).* **9.** a) springen, hüpfen *(over* über *acc),* b) stürmen, stürzen *(into* in *acc).* **10.** F platzen *(Scheck).* **'bounc·er** *s* F **1.** Rausschmeißer *m.* **2.** ungedeckter Scheck. **'bounc·ing** *adj* stramm *(Baby etc).*

bound¹ [baʊnd] **I** *pret u. pp von* **bind. II** *adj:* **be ~ to do s.th.** (zwangsläufig) et. tun müssen; **he was ~ to be late** er mußte ja zu spät kommen.

bound² [~] *adj* unterwegs *(for* nach): **where are you ~ for?** wohin reisen *od.* gehen Sie?

bound³ [~] *s mst pl* Grenze *f, fig. a.* Schranke *f:* **keep within ~s** in (vernünftigen) Grenzen halten; **beyond all ~s** maß-, grenzenlos; **the park is out of ~s**

(*to*) das Betreten des Parks ist (für *od.*
dat) verboten; *within the ~s of possi-*
bility im Bereich des Möglichen. **II** *v/t*
begrenzen.

bound⁴ [~] **I** *s* → **bounce** 2. **II** *v/i* →
bounce 7, 9 a.

bound·a·ry ['baʊndərɪ] *s* Grenze *f*.

boun·den ['baʊndən] *adj*: **my ~ duty**
meine Pflicht u. Schuldigkeit.

bound·less ['baʊndlɪs] *adj* □ grenzenlos (*a. fig.*).

boun·te·ous ['baʊntɪəs], **boun·ti·ful**
['~tɪfʊl] *adj* □ **1.** freigebig (*of* mit). **2.**
reichlich.

boun·ty ['baʊntɪ] *s* **1.** Freigebigkeit *f*. **2.**
großzügige Spende. **3.** Prämie *f*: a) Belohnung *f*, b) ✝ Zuschuß *m* (*on* auf *acc*,
für).

bou·quet [bʊ'keɪ] *s* Bukett *n*: a) (Blumen)Strauß *m*, b) Blume *f* (*von Wein*).

bour·bon ['bɜːbən] *s* Bourbon *m* (*amerikanischer Maiswhisky*).

bout [baʊt] *s* **1.** *fenc.* Gefecht *n*; (*Box-,
Ring*)Kampf *m*. **2.** ✽ Anfall *m*: ~ *of
rheumatism* Rheumaanfall.

bou·tique [bu:'ti:k] *s* Boutique *f*.

bo·vine ['baʊvaɪn] *adj* (*a. geistig*) träge,
schwerfällig.

bov·ver ['bɒvə] *Br. sl.* **I** *s* Straßenkämpfe
pl (*bsd. unter Rockerbanden*): ~ *boots pl*
*schwere Stiefel, mit denen Rocker auf-
einander eintreten*; ~ *boy* Rocker *m*. **II**
v/i sich Straßenkämpfe liefern (*with*
mit).

bow¹ [baʊ] **I** *s* Verbeugung *f*. **II** *v/t* beugen, *Kopf* neigen. **III** *v/i* sich verbeugen
(*to* vor *dat*): *have a ~ing acquaintance*
with s.o. j-n flüchtig kennen.

bow² [~] *s* ♣ Bug *m*.

bow³ [bəʊ] *s* **1.** (Schieß)Bogen *m*: →
string 3 a. **2.** ♪ (*Violin- etc*)Bogen *m*. **3.**
Knoten *m*, Schleife *f*.

bowd·ler·ize ['baʊdləraɪz] *v/t Text* von
anstößigen Stellen reinigen.

bow·el ['baʊəl] *s anat.* Darm *m*, *pl a.*
Eingeweide *pl*. ~ **move·ment** *s physiol.*
Stuhl(gang) *m*.

bowl¹ [bəʊl] *s* **1.** Schüssel *f*; (*Obst-
etc*)Schale *f*; (*Zucker*)Dose *f*; Napf *m*
(*für Tiere etc*). **2.** (*Wasch*)Becken *n*. **3.**
(*Pfeifen*)Kopf *m*.

bowl² [~] **I** *s* **1.** (*Bowling-, Kegel*)Kugel *f*.
2. Wurf *m*. **II** *v/t* **3.** ~ *over* umwerfen,
fig. a. j-m die Sprache verschlagen.

bow·legged ['bəʊlegd] *adj* O-beinig. ~
legs *s pl* O-Beine *pl*.

bowl·er ['bəʊlə] *s* **1.** Bowlingspieler(in);
Kegler(in). **2.** *a.* ~ *hat bsd. Br.* Bowler
m, Melone *f*.

bowl·ing ['bəʊlɪŋ] *s* Bowling *n*; Kegeln *n*.
~ **al·ley** *s* Bowling-, Kegelbahn *f*.

bow·man ['bəʊmən] *s* (*irr man*) Bogenschütze *m*. ~ **sprit** ['~sprɪt] *s* ♣ Bug-
spriet *n*. '**~·string** *s* Bogensehne *f*. ~ **tie**
s (Frack)Schleife *f*, Fliege *f*.

bow-wow **I** *int* [baʊ'waʊ] wauwau! **II** *s*
['baʊwaʊ] *Kindersprache:* Wauwau *m*
(*Hund*).

box¹ [bɒks] *s* **1.** Kasten *m*, Kiste *f*. **2.**
Schachtel *f*: ~ *of chocolates* Bonbon-
niere *f*. **3.** Büchse *f*, Dose *f*, Kästchen *n*.
4. Behälter *m*. **5.** ⊙ Gehäuse *n*. **6.** Briefkasten *m*; Postfach *n*. **7.** (Wahl)Urne *f*.
8. *Br.* (Telefon)Zelle *f*. **9.** → *Christmas
box.* **10.** → *box junction.* **11.** *thea. etc*
Loge *f*. **12.** ♔ Zeugenstand *m*; Geschworenenbank *f*. **13.** Box *f*: a) *Pfer-
destand*, b) *abgeteilter Einstellplatz in
e-r Großgarage.* **14.** → *box number.*
15. F Kasten *m* (*Fernseher*); Fernsehen
n: *on the ~* im Fernsehen. **II** *v/t* **16.** *oft ~
in* (*od. up*) in Schachteln *etc* packen,
ver-, einpacken; *parkendes Fahrzeug*
einklemmen. **17.** *oft ~ up* einschließen,
-sperren.

box² [~] **I** *s* **1.** ~ *on the ear* Ohrfeige *f*. **II**
v/t **2.** ~ *s.o.'s ears* j-n ohrfeigen. **3.**
Sport: boxen mit *od.* gegen. **III** *v/i* **4.**
boxen.

box·er ['bɒksə] *s Sport:* Boxer *m* (*a. zo.*).

box·ing ['bɒksɪŋ] *s* Boxen *n*, Boxsport *m*.
~ **bout** *s* Boxkampf *m*. **2 Day** *s Br.* der
2. Weihnachtsfeiertag. ~ **gloves** *pl*
Boxhandschuhe *pl*. ~ **match** *s* Boxkampf *m*.

box junc·tion *s Br.* gelbmarkierte Kreuzung, in die bei stehendem Verkehr nicht
eingefahren werden darf. ~ **num·ber** *s*
Chiffre(nummer) *f*. ~ **of·fice** *thea. etc*
1. Kasse *f*. **2.** *be a good* ~ ein Kassenerfolg *od.* -schlager sein. '**~·of·fice** *adj*: ~
success thea. etc Kassenerfolg *m*,
-schlager *m*.

boy [bɔɪ] *s* Junge *m* (*a.* F *Sohn*), Knabe *m*.

boy·cott ['bɔɪkɒt] **I** *v/t* boykottieren. **II** *s*
Boykott *m*.

'**boy·friend** *s* Freund *m* (*e-s Mädchens*).

boy·hood ['bɔɪhʊd] s Knabenjahre pl, Jugend(zeit) f.

boy·ish ['bɔɪɪʃ] adj □ **1.** jungenhaft: *his ~ laughter.* **2.** knabenhaft: *her ~ movements.* **3.** Jungen...: ~ *games.*

boy scout s Pfadfinder m.

bra [brɑː] s F BH m (*Büstenhalter*).

brace [breɪs] I s **1.** ⚙ Strebe f, △ a. Stützbalken m. **2.** pl Br. Hosenträger pl. **3.** mst pl ⚙ (Zahn)Klammer f, (-)Spange f. **4.** (pl **brace**) Paar n. II v/t **5.** ⚙ verstreben. **6.** fig. (a. v/i) erfrischen; kräftigen, stärken. **7.** ~ *o.s.* for fig. sich gefaßt machen auf (acc).

brace·let ['breɪslɪt] s Armband n.

brack·et ['brækɪt] I s **1.** ⚙ Träger m, Stütze f. **2.** ♈, typ. Klammer f: *in ~s;* **round (square)** ~s runde (eckige) Klammern. **3.** (*Alters-, Steuer*)Klasse f, (*Einkommens- etc*)Gruppe f, (-)Stufe f. II v/t **4.** einklammern.

brag [bræg] I s **1.** Prahlerei f. **2.** Prahler m. II v/i **3.** prahlen (about, of mit).

brag·gart ['brægət] I s Prahler m. II adj prahlerisch.

braid [breɪd] I v/t **1.** Haar, Bänder flechten. **2.** mit Litze od. Borte besetzen. II s **3.** Zopf m. **4.** Borde f, Litze f, bsd. ⚔ Tresse f.

braille [breɪl] s Blindenschrift f.

brain [breɪn] s **1.** anat. Gehirn n. **2.** oft pl fig. F Köpfchen n, Grips m, Verstand m: *cudgel (od. rack) one's ~s* sich das Hirn zermartern, sich den Kopf zerbrechen; → *blow out* 2. '**~case** s anat. Hirnschale f, Schädeldecke f. ~ **child** s (*irr child*) F Geistesprodukt n. ~ **death** s 🕱 Hirntod n. ~ **drain** s Brain-Drain m (*Abwanderung von Wissenschaftlern ins Ausland*). '**~fag** s geistige Erschöpfung.

brain·less ['breɪnlɪs] adj □ hirn-, geistlos.

'**brain**|·**pan** → braincase. '**~storm** s F **1.** *have a* ~ *Br.* geistig weggetreten sein. **2.** *Am.* a) hirnverbrannte Idee, b) → *brain wave.* '**~storm·ing** s Brainstorming n (*Sammeln von spontanen Einfällen zur Lösung e-s Problems*).

brains trust [breɪnz] s Br. **1.** Teilnehmer pl an e-r Podiumsdiskussion. **2.** → *brain trust.*

'**brain**|**teas·er** → brain twister. ~ **trust** s Am. Brain-Trust m (*bsd. politische*

od. wirtschaftliche Beratergruppe). ~ **twist·er** s F harte Nuß. '~**wash** v/t j-n e-r Gehirnwäsche unterziehen. '~**wash·ing** s Gehirnwäsche f. ~ **wave** s F Geistesblitz m, tolle Idee. '~**work·er** s Geistes-, Kopfarbeiter m.

brain·y ['breɪnɪ] adj F gescheit (a. Vorschlag etc).

braise [breɪz] v/t gastr. schmoren.

brake [breɪk] I s ⚙ Bremse f. II v/t u. v/i bremsen. ~ **flu·id** s Bremsflüssigkeit f. ~ **lin·ing** s Bremsbelag m. ~ **ped·al** s Bremspedal n.

brak·ing dis·tance ['breɪkɪŋ] s Bremsweg m.

bram·ble ['bræmbl] s ♣ bsd. Br. Brombeerstrauch m; Brombeere f.

branch [brɑːntʃ] I s **1.** Ast m, Zweig m. **2.** fig. Zweig m, Linie f (e-r Familie). **3.** fig. Zweig m, Sparte f (e-r Wissenschaft etc); ♈ Branche f. **4.** ♈ Filiale f. **5.** → **branch line** I. **6.** geogr. Arm m (e-s Gewässers); Am. Nebenfluß m. II v/i **7.** oft ~ **off** (od. **out**) sich verzweigen od. verästeln; abzweigen od. sich gabeln (*Straße etc*). ~ **line** s **1.** 🚂 Neben-, Zweiglinie f. **2.** Seitenlinie f (e-r Familie). ~ **man·ag·er** s ♈ Filialleiter m. ~ **of·fice** s ♈ Filiale f.

brand [brænd] I s **1.** ♈ (Handels-, Schutz)Marke f, Warenzeichen n; Markenname m; Sorte f, Klasse f (e-r Ware). **2.** fig. Sorte f, Art f. **3.** Brandmal n, -zeichen n. II v/t **4.** mit e-m Warenzeichen etc versehen: **~ed goods** pl Markenartikel pl. **5.** fig. unauslöschlich einprägen (on s.o.'s mind j-m).

bran·dish ['brændɪʃ] v/t (bsd. drohend) schwingen.

'**brand-'new** adj (funkel)nagelneu.

bran·dy ['brændɪ] s **1.** Weinbrand m, Kognak m, Brandy m. **2.** Obstwasser n: **plum** ~ Zwetschgenwasser n.

bran-new [‚bræn'njuː] → brand-new.

brash [bræʃ] adj □ **1.** ungestüm; draufgängerisch; unüberlegt; taktlos, unbezogen; frech, unverfroren. **2.** aufdringlich, laut (*Musik etc*); grell, schreiend (*Farben*).

brass [brɑːs] s **1.** Messing n. **2.** *the* ~ ♩ das Blech (*im Orchester*), die Blechbläser pl. **3.** Br. F Knete f (*Geld*). **4.** F Frechheit f, Unverschämtheit f. ~ **band** s Blaskapelle f.

bras·sière ['bræsɪə] s Büstenhalter m.

brass tacks s pl: **get down to ~** F zur Sache od. auf den Kern der Sache kommen.

bras·sy ['brɑːsɪ] adj □ **1.** messingartig od. -farben. **2.** blechern (Klang). **3.** F frech, unverschämt. **4.** unangenehm laut.

brat [bræt] s contp. Balg m, n, Gör n.

brave [breɪv] **I** adj □ tapfer, mutig. **II** v/t die Stirn bieten, trotzen (dat): **~ it out** es (tapfer) durchstehen. '**brav·er·y** s Tapferkeit f, Mut m.

bra·vo [ˌbrɑːˈvəʊ] **I** int bravo! **II** pl **-vos** s Bravo(ruf m) n.

brawl [brɔːl] **I** v/i **1.** e-e laute Auseinandersetzung haben. **2.** raufen, sich schlagen. **3.** tosen, rauschen (Fluß etc). **II** s **4.** laute Auseinandersetzung. **5.** Rauferei f, Schlägerei f. **6.** Tosen n, Rauschen n.

brawn [brɔːn] s **1.** Muskeln pl. **2.** Muskelkraft f. **3.** gastr. Br. (Schweine)Sülze f. '**brawn·y** adj muskulös.

bray [breɪ] **I** v/i **1.** schreien (Esel, a. Person): **~ at s.o.** j-n anschreien. **2.** schmettern (Trompete). **3.** lärmen, tosen (Verkehr etc). **II** s **4.** Schrei m. **5.** Schmettern n. **6.** Lärmen n, Tosen n.

bra·zen ['breɪzn] **I** adj □ **1.** Messing... **2.** metallisch (Klang). **3.** fig. unverschämt, unverfroren. **II** v/t **4.** **~ it out** sich mit großer Unverfrorenheit behaupten. '**~·faced** → **brazen** 3.

breach [briːtʃ] **I** s **1.** fig. Bruch m, Verletzung f: **~ of confidence** Vertrauensbruch; **~ of contract** ✍ Vertragsbruch; **~ of the peace** ✍ öffentliche Ruhestörung; → **duty** 1, **promise** 1. **2.** ✗ Bresche f (a. fig.): **fill (od. step into) the ~** in die Bresche springen (**for** für). **II** v/t **3.** ✗ e-e Bresche schlagen in (acc).

bread [bred] **I** s **1.** Brot n (a. Lebensunterhalt): **~ and butter** Butterbrot; **earn (od. make) one's ~** sein Brot verdienen; **know which side one's ~ is buttered (on)** F s-n Vorteil (er)kennen; **take the ~ out of s.o.'s mouth** j-n brotlos machen. **2.** sl. Knete f (Geld). **II** v/t **3.** gastr. panieren. '**~·bas·ket** s **1.** Brotkorb m. **2.** sl. Magen m. **~ bin** s Brotkasten m. **~ crumb** s Brotkrume f, -krümel m: **~s** pl Paniermehl n. '**~-crumb** → **bread** 3.

breadth [bretθ] s Breite f: **ten yards in**

~ 10 Yards breit; **what ~ is it?** wie breit ist es?

'**bread,win·ner** s Ernährer m, (Geld-)Verdiener m (e-r Familie).

break [breɪk] **I** s **1.** Bruch(stelle f) m. **2.** fig. Bruch m (**from, with** mit; **between** zwischen dat): **make a ~ from** brechen mit. **3.** Pause f, Unterbrechung f: **without a ~** ununterbrochen; **take a ~ for a cigarette** e-e Zigarettenpause machen. **4.** (plötzlicher) Wechsel, Umschwung m: **~ in the weather** Wetterumschlag m; **at ~ of day** bei Tagesanbruch. **5.** F **bad ~** Pech n; **lucky ~** Dusel m, Schwein n. **6.** F Chance f: **give s.o. a ~.** **II** v/t (irr break) **7.** (ab-, auf-, durch-, zer)brechen; Schallmauer durchbrechen: **~ one's arm** sich den Arm brechen; **~ s.o.'s resistance** j-s Widerstand brechen; → **heart** 1, **ice** 1. **8.** zerschlagen, -trümmern, kaputtmachen: → **bank¹** 2. **9.** ~ **s.o. of s.th.** j-m et. abgewöhnen. **10.** Speise, Ware, Geldschein anbrechen; Geldschein kleinmachen, wechseln. **11.** a) Tiere zähmen, abrichten, Pferd zureiten, a. j-n gewöhnen (**to** an acc), b) → **break in** 3 b, c. **12.** Gesetz, Vertrag etc brechen. **13.** ~ **the bad news gently to s.o.** j-m die schlechte Nachricht schonend beibringen. **14.** Code etc knacken, entschlüsseln. **III** v/i (irr) **15.** brechen (a. fig. Widerstand etc): **~ into** einbrechen in (ein Haus etc); **~ with** brechen mit (j-m, e-r Tradition etc). **16.** (zer)brechen, (-)reißen, kaputtgehen. **17.** umschlagen (Wetter); anbrechen (Tag). **18.** fig. ausbrechen (**into** in Tränen etc). Verbindungen mit Adverbien:

break| a·way I v/i **1.** ab-, losbrechen (**from** von). **II** v/i **2.** ab-, losbrechen (**from** von). **3.** fig. sich lossagen od. trennen (**from** von). **~ down I** v/t **1.** ein-, niederreißen, Haus abbrechen, abreißen. **2.** Maschine zerlegen. **3.** fig. aufgliedern, -schlüsseln. **II** v/i **4.** zs.-brechen (a. fig.). **5.** versagen (Maschine, Stimme etc), kaputtgehen, mot. e-e Panne haben. **6.** scheitern (Ehe, Verhandlungen etc). **~ in I** v/i **1.** einbrechen, -dringen; **~ on** bei j-m hereinplatzen; sich in e-e Unterhaltung ein mischen. **II** v/t **2.** einschlagen, Tür aufbrechen. **3.** a) → **break** 10 a, b) Auto etc einfahren, Schuhe einlaufen, c) j-n ein-

arbeiten, anlernen. **~ off I** v/t **1.** →
break away 1. 2. Rede, Verhandlungen
etc abbrechen, Verlobung (auf)lösen:
break it off sich entloben. **II** v/i **3.** →
break away 2. ~ out v/i ausbrechen
(Gefangener, Krieg etc): **~ in laughter
(tears)** in Gelächter (Tränen) ausbrechen; **he broke out in a cold sweat**
ihm brach der Angstschweiß aus. **~
through I** v/t **1.** durchbrechen. **II** v/i **2.**
durchbrechen, (Sonne a.) hervorkom-
men. **3.** fig. den Durchbruch schaffen.
~ up I v/t **1.** Straße, Eis etc aufbrechen.
2. Sitzung etc aufheben, Versammlung,
Haushalt etc auflösen. **II** v/i **3.** aufbrechen (Straße, Eis etc). **4.** aufgehoben
werden (Sitzung etc), sich auflösen
(Versammlung). **5.** zerbrechen, auseinandergehen (Ehe etc); sich trennen
(Ehepaar etc).
break·a·ble ['breɪkəbl] adj zerbrechlich.
'**break·age** s Bruch(stelle f) m.
'**break|·a·way** s Trennung f (**from** von).
'**~·down** s **1.** Zs.-bruch m (a. fig.): **nervous ~** Nervenzusammenbruch. **2.**
mot. Panne f: **~ service** Br. Pannen-,
Straßendienst m; **~ van** Br. Abschleppwagen m. '**~·fast** [breɪkfəst] **I** s Frühstück n: **have ~** → **II**; **~ television**
Frühstücksfernsehen n. **II** v/i frühstücken. '**~·in** s **1.** 🚓 Einbruch m. **2.**
Abrichten n, Einfahren n etc (→ **break**
10 a, **break in** 2 b, c). '**~·neck** adj halsbrecherisch (Geschwindigkeit). '**~·out** s
Ausbruch m (aus dem Gefängnis etc).
'**~·through** s ✕ Durchbruch m (a. fig.).
'**~·up** s Aufhebung f (e-r Sitzung etc),
Auflösung f (e-r Versammlung, e-s
Haushalts etc).
breast [brest] **I** s Brust f (a. gastr.): **make
a clean ~ of s.th.** sich et. von der Seele
reden. **II** v/t: **~ the tape** (Sport) das
Zielband durchreißen, weitS. durchs
Ziel gehen. '**~·bone** s anat. Brustbein n.
'**~·feed** v/t u. v/i (irr feed) stillen. '**~·pin**
s Brosche f, Ansteckbadel f. '**~·pock·et** s
Brusttasche f. '**~·stroke** s Sport: Brust-
schwimmen n.
breath [breθ] s **1.** Atem(zug) m: **bad ~**
Mundgeruch m; **in the same ~** im gleichen Atemzug; **under** (od. **below**)
one's ~ im Flüsterton, leise; **out of ~**
außer Atem sein; **get one's ~ back** wieder zu Atem kommen; **waste one's ~**

in den Wind reden. **2.** fig. Hauch m,
Spur f. **3.** a. **~ of air** Lufthauch m,
Lüftchen n.
breath·a·lys·er ['breθəlaɪzə] s mot. Al-
koholtestgerät n, Röhrchen n.
breathe [briːð] **I** v/i **1.** atmen: **~ in (out)**
ein-(aus)atmen. **II** v/t **2.** atmen: **~ in
(out)** ein-(aus)atmen; → **sigh II. 3.** flüstern, hauchen. '**breath·er** s F Atem-,
Verschnaufpause f: **have** (od. **take**) **a ~**
verschnaufen. '**breath·ing** s Atmen
n, Atmung f: **~ space** Atem-, Verschnaufpause f.
breath·less ['breθlɪs] adj □ atemlos (a.
fig.).
'**breath|,tak·ing** adj □ atemberaubend.
~ test s mot. Br. Alkoholtest m.
bred [bred] pret u. pp von **breed.**
breech·es ['brɪtʃɪz] s pl (**a pair of** e-e)
Kniebund-, Reithose f.
breed [briːd] **I** v/t (irr) **1.** Tiere, Pflanzen
züchten. **2.** fig. hervorrufen, verursachen. **II** v/i (irr) **3.** sich fortpflanzen od.
vermehren. **III** s **4.** Rasse f, Zucht f. **5.**
Art f, (Menschen)Schlag m. '**breed·er** s
1. Züchter(in). **2.** Zuchttier n. **3.** phys.
Brüter m: **~ reactor** Brutreaktor m.
'**breed·ing** s **1.** Fortpflanzung f. **2.**
Züchtung f, Zucht f. **3.** Ausbildung f,
Erziehung f. **4.** (gutes) Benehmen, (gute) Manieren pl.
breeze [briːz] **I** s Brise f. **II** v/i F schweben (Person): **~ in** hereingeweht kom-
men. '**breez·y** adj □ **1.** luftig, windig.
2. heiter, unbeschwert.
breth·ren ['breðrən] pl von **brother** 2.
bre·vi·ar·y [briˈviːjərɪ] s eccl. Brevier n.
brev·i·ty ['brevɪtɪ] s Kürze f.
brew [bruː] **I** v/t **1.** Bier brauen, Tee etc
a. zubereiten. **2.** fig. aushecken, -brü-
ten. **II** v/i **3.** fig. sich zs.-brauen, im
Anzug sein (Gewitter, Unheil). **III** s **4.**
Gebräu n. '**brew·er** s Brauer m.
'**brew·er·y** s Brauerei f.
brib·a·ble ['braɪbəbl] adj bestechlich.
bribe [braɪb] **I** v/t bestechen. **II** s Bestechungs-
geld n, -geschenk n: **accept** (od. **take**)
~s sich bestechen lassen. '**brib·er·y** s
Bestechung f: **~ open to ~** bestechlich.
bric-a-brac ['brɪkəbræk] s Nippsachen
pl.
brick [brɪk] **I** s **1.** Ziegel(stein) m, Back-
stein m: **drop a ~** Br. F ins Fettnäpfchen
treten. **2.** Br. Baustein m, (Bau)Klötz-

chen *n* (*für Kinder*): *box of ~s* Baukasten *m*. **3.** F Pfundskerl *m*, feiner Kerl. **II** *v/t* **4.** *~ up* (*od. in*) zumauern. '**~·lay·er** *s* Maurer *m*.

brid·al ['braɪdl] *adj* Braut...: *~ dress* Braut-, Hochzeitskleid *n*; *~ ceremony* Hochzeitsfeier *f*.

bride [braɪd] *s* Braut *f*: *give away the ~* die Braut zum Altar führen. '**~·groom** ['~grʊm] *s* Bräutigam *m*.

brides·maid ['braɪdzmeɪd] *s* Brautjungfer *f*.

bridge¹ [brɪdʒ] **I** *s* **1.** (♫ *a.* Kommando)Brücke *f*: *burn one's ~s* (*behind one*) *fig.* alle Brücken hinter sich abbrechen. **2.** *~ of the nose anat.* Nasenrücken *m*. **II** *v/t* **3.** e-e Brücke schlagen über (*acc*). **4.** *oft ~ over* ⚡ überbrücken (*a. fig.*).

bridge² [~] *s* Bridge *n* (*Kartenspiel*).

'**bridge·head** *s* ✕ Brückenkopf *m*.

bri·dle ['braɪdl] **I** *s* **1.** Zaum(zeug *n*) *m*; Zügel *m*. **II** *v/t* **2.** (auf)zäumen. **3.** zügeln, im Zaum halten (*beide a. fig.*). **III** *v/i* **4.** *oft ~ up* den Kopf zurückwerfen.

brief [briːf] **I** *adj* □ **1.** kurz: *be ~!* fasse dich kurz! **2.** kurz angebunden (*with* mit). **3.** knapp (*Bikini etc*). **II** *s* **4.** *in ~* kurz(um). **5.** ⚖ *Br.* schriftliche Beauftragung u. Information (*des Barristers durch den Solicitor*) zur Vertretung des Falles vor Gericht, *weitS.* Mandat *n*: *abandon* (*od. give up*) *one's ~* sein Mandat niederlegen; *hold a ~ for j-n od. j-s Sache* vor Gericht vertreten; *fig.* sich einsetzen für. **6.** *pl → briefs.* **II** *v/t* **7.** *j-n* instruieren, *j-m* genaue Anweisungen geben. **8.** ⚖ *Br. Barrister* mit der Vertretung des Falles betrauen; *Anwalt* über den Sachverhalt informieren. '**~·case** *s* Aktentasche *f*.

brief·ness ['briːfnɪs] *s* Kürze *f*.

briefs [briːfs] *s pl* (*a pair of* ein) Slip *m* (*kurze Unterhose*).

bri·gade [brɪ'geɪd] *s* ✕ Brigade *f*.

bright [braɪt] *adj* □ **1.** hell, glänzend, leuchtend, strahlend. **2.** heiter (*Wetter etc*). **3.** gescheit, hell. **4.** günstig, vielversprechend (*Aussichten*). '**bright·en I** *v/t oft ~ up* **1.** hell(er) machen, auferhellen (*a. fig.*). **2.** *j-n* fröhlich stimmen, aufheitern. **II** *v/i* **3.** *oft ~ up* sich aufhellen (*Gesicht, Wetter etc*), aufleuchten (*Augen*). '**bright·ness** *s* **1.**

Helligkeit *f* (*a. TV*), Glanz *m*. **2.** Heiterkeit *f*. **3.** Gescheitheit *f*.

bril·liance ['brɪljəns], '**bril·lian·cy** *s* **1.** Leuchten *n*, Glanz *m*, Helligkeit *f*. **2.** *fig.* Brillanz *f*. '**bril·liant I** *adj* □ **1.** leuchtend, glänzend, hell. **2.** *fig.* brillant. **II** *s* **3.** Brillant *m*.

brim [brɪm] **I** *s* **1.** Rand *m* (*bsd. e-s Gefäßes*); *full to the ~* randvoll. **2.** (Hut-) Krempe *f*. **II** *v/i* **3.** voll sein: *~ over* übervoll sein (*with* von) (*a. fig.*); überfließen (*with* von) (*a. fig.*). ,**brim'ful(l)** *adj* randvoll.

brine [braɪn] **I** *s* **1.** Sole *f*; Lake *f*. **2.** Salzwasser *n*. **II** *v/t* **3.** (ein)salzen.

bring [brɪŋ] *v/t* (*irr*) **1.** (mit-, her)bringen: *what ~s you here?* was führt Sie zu mir?; *→ bacon, home* 9, *light¹* 1e. **2.** *Gewinn etc* (ein)bringen. **3.** nach sich ziehen, bewirken. **4.** *j-n* dazu bringen *od.* bewegen (*to do* zu tun): *I can't ~ myself to do it* ich kann mich nicht dazu durchringen(, es zu tun).

Verbindungen mit Adverbien:

bring| a·bout *v/t* **1.** zustande bringen. **2.** bewirken, verursachen. *~ a·long* *v/t* mitbringen. *~ back* *v/t* **1.** zurückbringen. **2.** *Erinnerungen* wachrufen (*of* an *acc*); Erinnerungen wachrufen an (*acc*). **3.** *~ to life j-n* wieder zu(m) Bewußtsein bringen; (*a. ~ to health*) *j-n* wieder gesund machen. *~ down* *v/t* **1.** herunterbringen. **2.** *Regierung etc* zu Fall bringen, stürzen. **3.** *Preis etc* herabsetzen. **4.** *~ the house thea. etc* F stürmischen Beifall auslösen; Lachstürme entfesseln. *~ forth* *v/t* hervorbringen. *~ for·ward* *v/t* **1.** *Entschuldigung etc* vorbringen. **2.** ✝ *Betrag* übertragen. **3.** *Versammlung etc* vorverlegen (*to* auf *acc*); *Uhr* vorstellen (*one hour* um e-e Stunde). *~ in* *v/t* **1.** hereinbringen. **2.** *Kapital, Gesetzesvorlage etc* einbringen. **3.** *→ verdict. ~ off* *v/t* zustande bringen. *~ on* *v/t* **1.** *bsd. Krankheit* verursachen. **2.** in Gang bringen. *~ out* *v/t allg., a. Buch, Auto etc* herausbringen. *~ o·ver* *v/t* **1.** herüberbringen. **2.** *→ bring round* 3. *~ round* *v/t* **1.** hervorbeibringen. **2.** a) *Ohnmächtigen* wieder zu sich bringen, b) *Kranken* wieder auf die Beine bringen. **3.** *j-n* umstimmen, herumkriegen. *~ through* *v/t Kranken* durchbringen. *~ to → bring* *round* 2 a. ~ *up* v/t **1.** heraufbringen. **2.** *Kind* auf-, großziehen; erziehen: ~ *s.o. up to do s.th.* j-n dazu erziehen, et. zu tun. **3.** *et.* (er)brechen. **4.** zum Stillstand *od.* Halten bringen.

bring·er ['brɪŋə] s Überbringer(in).

brink [brɪŋk] s Rand m (*a. fig.*): *be on the ~ of war* am Rande e-s Krieges stehen; *bring s.o. to the ~ of ruin* j-n an den Rand des Ruins bringen. **~·man-ship** ['~mənʃɪp] s Politik f des äußersten Risikos.

brin·y ['braɪnɪ] adj salzig.

bri·quet(te) [brɪ'ket] s Brikett n.

brisk [brɪsk] adj □ **1.** flott. **2.** lebhaft, munter. **3.** frisch (*Luft etc*).

bris·ket ['brɪskɪt] s gastr. Brust(stück n) f.

bris·tle ['brɪsl] **I** s **1.** Borste f; (Bart)Stoppel f. **II** v/i **2.** a. ~ *up* sich sträuben. **3.** a. ~ *up* zornig werden. **4.** strotzen, wimmeln (*with* von). '**bris·tly** adj **1.** borstig; stopp(e)lig: ~ *beard* Stoppelbart m. **2.** fig. kratzbürstig.

Brit·ish ['brɪtɪʃ] **I** adj britisch. **II** s: *the ~ pl* die Briten pl. '**Brit·ish·er** s Am. Brite m, Britin f.

Brit·on ['brɪtn] s Brite m, Britin f.

brit·tle ['brɪtl] adj **1.** spröde, zerbrechlich. **2.** brüchig (*Metall etc*) (*a. fig.*).

broach [brəʊtʃ] v/t **1.** *Faß* anstechen. **2.** *Thema* anschneiden.

broad [brɔːd] adj (□ → *broadly*) **1.** breit. **2.** weit, ausgedehnt. **3.** → *daylight*. **4.** weitreichend, -gehend: *in the ~est sense* im weitesten Sinne. **5.** → *broad-minded*. **6.** derb; anstößig, schlüpfrig. **7.** klar, deutlich: → *hint* **1.** **8.** allgemein: *in ~ outline* in großen Zügen, in groben Umrissen. **9.** breit, stark (*Akzent*). '**~·cast I** v/t (*a. irr*) **1.** *Nachricht* verbreiten, *contp.* ausposaunen. **2.** im Rundfunk *od.* Fernsehen bringen; übertragen. **II** v/i (*a. irr*) **3.** im Rundfunk *od.* Fernsehen auftreten. **4.** senden. **III** s **5.** *Rundfunk, TV:* Sendung f; Übertragung f. '**~·cast·er** s Rundfunk-, Fernsehsprecher(in). '**~·cast·ing** s **1.** → *broadcast* **5. 2.** Sendebetrieb m. **3.** Rundfunk od. Fernsehen n. **II** adj **4.** Rundfunk..., Fernsehen...: ~ *station* Sender m.

broad·en ['brɔːdn] **I** v/t verbreitern: ~ *one's horizons* (*od. mind*) s-n Hori-

zont erweitern. **II** v/i a. ~ *out* sich verbreitern (*into* zu), sich erweitern (*a. fig.*).

broad| jump s Leichtathletik: Am. Weitsprung m. **~ jump·er** s Am. Weitspringer(in).

broad·ly ['brɔːdlɪ] adv **1.** a. ~ *speaking* allgemein (gesprochen). **2.** in großen Zügen.

,broad·|-'mind·ed adj □ großzügig, tolerant. '**~·side** s ♪ Breitseite f (*a. fig.*).

bro·cade [brəʊ'keɪd] s Brokat m.

bro·chure ['brəʊʃə] s Broschüre f.

brogue [brəʊg] s derber Straßenschuh.

broil¹ [brɔɪl] **I** v/t **1.** (auf dem Rost) braten, grillen. **2.** *get ~ed* vor Hitze fast umkommen. **II** v/i **3.** *be ~ing in the sun* in der Sonne schmoren. **4.** vor Wut kochen.

broil² [~] s laute Auseinandersetzung.

broil·ing ['brɔɪlɪŋ] **I** adj glühendheiß: *a ~ day.* **II** adv: ~ *hot* glühend heiß.

broke¹ [brəʊk] pret von *break*.

broke² [~] adj F pleite (*a. ♣*), abgebrannt: *go* ~ pleite gehen.

bro·ken ['brəʊkən] **I** pp von *break.* **II** adj **1.** zerbrochen, entzwei, kaputt. **2.** gebrochen (*a. fig.*): *a ~ leg* (*promise*, *etc*). **3.** unterbrochen, gestört: ~ *sleep.* **4.** (*seelisch od. körperlich*) gebrochen. **5.** zerrüttet: ~ *marriage*; ~ *health*; ~ *home* zerrüttete Familienverhältnisse pl. **6.** *ling.* gebrochen: *speak ~ English* gebrochen Englisch sprechen.

bro·ker ['brəʊkə] s **1.** ♣ Makler m. **2.** Vermittler m. '**bro·ker·age** s Maklergebühr f.

brol·ly ['brɒlɪ] s Br. F (Regen)Schirm m.

bro·mide ['brəʊmaɪd] s **1.** ♣ Bromid n. **2.** fig. Gemeinplatz m. **bro·mine** ['~miːn] s ♣ Brom n.

bron·chi ['brɒŋkaɪ] s pl anat. Bronchien pl. **bron·chi·al** ['~kjəl] adj anat., ♣ Bronchial... **bron·chi·tis** ['~kaɪtɪs] s ♣ Bronchitis f.

bronze [brɒnz] **I** s **1.** Bronze f. **II** adj **2.** bronzefarben. **3.** Bronze...: ♀ *Age* Bronzezeit f; ~ *medal* Bronzemedaille f; ~ *medal(l)ist* Bronzemedaillengewinner(in).

brooch [brəʊtʃ] s Brosche f.

brood [bruːd] **I** s Brut f (*a. fig. contp.*). **II** v/t ausbrüten (*a. fig.*). **III** v/i brüten (*a. fig. on, over, about* über *dat*). **IV** adj

Brut...: **~ hen**. **'brood·er** s Brutapparat
m, -kasten m.

brook [brʊk] s Bach m.

broom [bruːm] s Besen m: **a new ~
sweeps clean** neue Besen kehren gut.
'~stick s Besenstiel m.

broth [brɒθ] s (Kraft-, Fleisch)Brühe f.

broth·el [brɒθl] s Bordell n.

broth·er ['brʌðə] s 1. Bruder m: **~s** pl and
sisters pl Geschwister pl; **Smith ~s** †
Gebrüder Smith. **2.** eccl. pl **brethren**
Bruder m. **broth·er·hood** ['~hʊd] s
eccl. Bruderschaft f.

'broth·er-in-law pl **'broth·ers-in-law** s
Schwager m.

broth·er·ly ['brʌðəlɪ] adj brüderlich.

brought [brɔːt] pret u. pp von **bring**.

brow [braʊ] s 1. (Augen)Braue f. **2.** Stirn
f. **3.** Miene f, Gesichtsausdruck m.
'~beat v/t (irr beat) einschüchtern.

brown [braʊn] **I** adj braun: **~ bread**
Misch-; Vollkorn-; Schwarzbrot n; **~
coal** Braunkohle f; **~ paper** Packpapier
n; → **study** 1. **II** s Braun n: **dressed in ~**
braun od. in Braun gekleidet. **III** v/t
Haut etc bräunen, Fleisch etc (an)bräu-
nen. **IV** v/i braun werden. **brown·ie**
['~nɪ] s Heinzelmännchen n. **'brown·
ish** adj bräunlich.

browse [braʊz] v/i 1. grasen, weiden. **2.**
a. **~ around** sich umsehen: **~ through a
book** in e-m Buch schmökern od. blättern; **~ in** (od. **around) a shop** (bsd. Am.
store) sich (unverbindlich) in e-m Laden umsehen.

bruise [bruːz] **I** v/t 1. sich e-n Körperteil
quetschen; Früchte anstoßen. **II** v/i **2.**
e-e Quetschung od. e-n blauen Fleck
bekommen. **III** s **3.** Quetschung f,
blauer Fleck. **4.** Druckstelle f (auf
Früchten).

brunch [brʌntʃ] s F Brunch n (spätes
reichliches Frühstück).

bru·nette [bruː'net] **I** s Brünette f. **II** adj
brünett.

brunt [brʌnt] s: **bear the ~** fig. die
Hauptlast tragen.

brush¹ [brʌʃ] **I** s 1. Bürste f. **2.** Pinsel m:
→ **tar** II. **3. give s.th. a ~** et. ab- od. ausbürsten. **4.** ✕ Scharmützel n (a.
fig.): **have a ~ with** s.o. mit j-m aneinandergeraten. **II** v/t 5. bürsten: **brush
one's teeth** sich die Zähne putzen; **~
aside** (od. **away)** zur Seite schieben,

wegschieben; fig. (mit e-r Handbewegung) abtun, wegwischen; **~ away** (od.
off) wegbürsten; **~ down** abbürsten; **~
off** sl. j-n abwimmeln; j-m e-e Abfuhr
erteilen; **~ up** Kenntnisse aufpolieren,
-frischen. **6.** streifen, leicht berühren.
III v/i 7. **~ past** s.o. j-n streifen od.
leicht berühren; an j-m vorbeihuschen;
an j-m (gerade noch) vorbeikommen.

brush² [~], a. **'~wood** s Gestrüpp n, Unterholz n.

brusque [bruːsk] adj □ brüsk, barsch,
schroff.

Brus·sels sprouts [ˌbrʌsl'spraʊts] s pl ♀
Rosenkohl m.

bru·tal ['bruːtl] adj □ brutal. **bru·tal·i·ty**
[~'tælətɪ] s Brutalität f. **bru·tal·ize**
['~təlaɪz] v/t 1. brutalisieren. **2.** brutal
behandeln. **brute** [bruːt] **I** s 1. Vieh n,
fig. a. Untier n, Scheusal n. **II** adj **2.**
brutal: **~ force** (od. **strength)** rohe Gewalt. **3.** hirnlos, dumm. **'brut·ish** adj □
→ **brute** II.

bub·ble ['bʌbl] **I** s 1. (Luft- etc)Blase f: **~
bath** Schaumbad n; **~ gum** Bubble-gum
m, Ballon-, Knallkaugummi m. **2.** fig.
Seifenblase f. **II** v/i 3. sprudeln, brodeln
(kochendes Wasser etc); sprudeln, perlen (Sekt etc); in Blasen aufsteigen
(Gas): **~ over** übersprudeln (a. fig. **with**
vor dat). **'bub·bly I** adj 1. sprudelnd. **2.**
fig. temperamentvoll. **II** s 3. bsd. Br. F
Schampus m.

buck¹ [bʌk] **I** s 1. zo. Bock m, engS.
Rehbock, allg. Männchen n. **2. pass
the ~** F den Schwarzen Peter weitergeben; **pass the ~ to s.o.** F j-m den
Schwarzen Peter zuschieben. **II** v/i 3.
bocken (Pferd etc). **4. ~ up** F aufleben;
sich ranhalten: **~ up!** Kopf hoch! **III** v/t
5. ~ up F j-n aufmuntern; j-m Dampf
machen.

buck² [~] s Am. sl. Dollar m.

buck·et ['bʌkɪt] **I** s Eimer m, Kübel m:
kick the ~ F den Löffel weglegen (sterben). **II** v/t schöpfen: **~ out** ausschöpfen. **III** v/i: **it's** (od. **the rain's) ~ing**
(**down)** Br. F es gießt wie aus od. mit
Kübeln. **buck·et·ful** ['~fʊl] s ein Ei-
mer(voll) m.

buck·et seat s mot. Schalensitz m.

buck·le ['bʌkl] **I** s 1. Schnalle f, Spange f.
II v/t 2. a. **~ up** zu-, festschnallen: **~ on**
anschnallen. **III** v/i 3. **~ up** mot., ✈ sich

anschnallen. **4.** ~ **down** F sich dahinterklemmen: ~ **down to a task** sich hinter e-e Aufgabe klemmen.
'**buck·skin** s Wildleder n.
bud [bʌd] I s Knospe f: **be in** ~ knospen; **nip in the** ~ fig. im Keim ersticken. II v/i knospen: **~ding lawyer** angehender Jurist.
Bud·dhism ['bʊdɪzəm] s Buddhismus m. '**Bud·dhist** I s Buddhist m. II adj buddhistisch.
bud·dy ['bʌdɪ] s bsd. Am. F Kumpel m, Spezi m.
budge [bʌdʒ] mst neg I v/i sich (von der Stelle) rühren: ~ **from** fig. von et. abrücken. II v/t (vom Fleck) bewegen: ~ **from** fig. j-n abbringen von.
bud·ger·i·gar ['bʌdʒərɪgɑː] s orn. Wellensittich m.
budg·et ['bʌdʒɪt] s Budget n, Etat m: **for the low** ~ für den schmalen Geldbeutel; **~conscious** preisbewußt; **~(-priced)** preisgünstig. '**budg·et·a·ry** adj Budget..., Etat...
bud·gie ['bʌdʒɪ] F → **budgerigar**.
buff [bʌf] s F **1. in the** ~ im Adams- od. Evaskostüm. **2.** in Zssgn ...fan m; ...experte m.
buf·fa·lo ['bʌfələʊ] pl **-lo(e)s** s zo. Büffel m.
buff·er ['bʌfə] s ⊙ Stoßdämpfer m; Puffer m (a. fig.); Prellbock m (a. fig.). ~ **state** s pol. Pufferstaat m. ~ **zone** s ✗ Pufferzone f.
buf·fet¹ ['bʌfɪt] s **1.** (Faust)Schlag m; Ohrfeige f. II v/t **2.** j-m e-n (Faust-)Schlag versetzen; j-m e-e Ohrfeige geben. **3.** ankämpfen gegen.
buf·fet² s **1.** ['bʌfɪt] Büfett n, Anrichte f. **2.** ['bʊfeɪ] Büfett n, Theke f.
buf·foon [bə'fuːn] s Possenreißer m, Hanswurst m (a. fig. contp.).
bug [bʌg] s **1.** zo. Wanze f (a. F Minispion); bsd. Am. allg. Insekt n. **2.** F Bazillus m, fig. a. Fieber n: **he got bitten by** (od. **he's got) the** ~ ihn hat's gepackt. **3.** ⊙ F Defekt m, pl Mucken pl. II v/t **4.** Am. F j-n wütend machen; j-m auf den Wecker fallen. **5.** F Wanzen anbringen in (dat). '**~·bear** s (Schreck-) Gespenst n.
bug·ger ['bʌgə] V I s Scheißkerl m; allg. Kerl m: **poor** ~ armes Schwein. II v/t: ~ **up** versauen; **~ed up** im Arsch. III

v/i: ~ **off** Br. (mst imp) sich verpissen.
bug·gy¹ ['bʌgɪ] adj verwanzt.
bug·gy² [~] s mot. Buggy m (geländegängiges Freizeitauto).
bu·gle ['bjuːgl] s (Wald-, Jagd)Horn n; ✗ Signalhorn n: ~ **call** Hornsignal n. '**bu·gler** s Hornist m.
build [bɪld] I v/t (irr) **1.** bauen: a) errichten, b) herstellen: ~ **in(to)** einbauen (in acc). **2.** ~ **up** Gelände bebauen. **3.** ~ **up** Geschäft etc aufbauen: ~ **up a reputation** sich e-n Namen machen. **4.** ~ **up** j-n (in der Presse etc) aufbauen. **5.** ~ **one's hope on** s-e Hoffnung setzen auf (acc). II v/i (irr) **6.** bauen: **be** ~**ing** im Bau sein. **7.** fig. bauen (**on** auf acc). III s **8.** Körperbau m, Statur f. '**build·er** s **1.** Erbauer m. **2.** Bauunternehmer m. '**build·ing** I s **1.** Bauwesen n. **2.** Gebäude n, Bau(werk n) m. II adj **3.** Bau...: ~ **contractor → builder** 2; ~ **freeze** Baustopp m; ~ **industry** Baugewerbe n, -wirtschaft f; ~ **site** Baustelle f; ~ **society** Br. Bausparkasse f.
built [bɪlt] pret u. pp von **build**. '**~-'in** adj eingebaut, Einbau... '**~-'up** adj: ~ **area** bebautes Gelände od. Gebiet; (Verkehr) geschlossene Ortschaft.
bulb [bʌlb] s **1.** ♀ Knolle f, Zwiebel f. **2.** ⚡ Glühbirne f. '**bulb·ous** adj □ knollenförmig: ~ **nose** Knollennase f.
Bul·gar·i·an [bʌl'geərɪən] I s **1.** Bulgare m, Bulgarin f. **2.** ling. Bulgarisch n. II adj **3.** bulgarisch.
bulge [bʌldʒ] I s **1.** (Aus)Bauchung f, Ausbuchtung f. **2.** fig. (rapide) Zunahme. II v/i **3.** a. ~ **out** sich (aus)bauchen, hervorquellen (a. Augen). III v/t **4.** Backen aufblähen. **5.** Taschen etc vollstopfen (**with** mit).
bulk [bʌlk] s **1.** Umfang m, Größe f, Masse f. **2.** Großteil m, Mehrheit f. **3.** **in** ~ **♦** lose, unverpackt; en gros. '**bulk·y** adj **1.** massig. **2.** unhandlich, sperrig: ~ **refuse** (od. **waste**) Sperrmüll m.
bull [bʊl] I s **1.** zo. Bulle m, (Zucht)Stier m: **take the** ~ **by the horns** fig. den Stier bei den Hörnern packen; **like a** ~ **in a china shop** wie ein Elefant im Porzellanladen; → **shoot** 5a. **2.** ♦ Haussespekulant m. II v/i **3.** ♦ auf Hausse spekulieren. '**~·dog** s zo. Bulldogge f. '**~·doze** v/t **1.** planieren. **2.** F einschüchtern;

zwingen (*into doing* zu tun). '**~·doz·er** *s* ⊙ Bulldozer *m*, Planierraupe *f*.

bul·let ['bʊlɪt] *s* (Gewehr-, Pistolen)Kugel *f*.

bul·le·tin ['bʊlətɪn] *s* **1.** Bulletin *n*: a) Tagesbericht *m*, b) ⚕ Krankenbericht *m*, c) offizielle Bekanntmachung: **~ board** *Am*. Schwarzes Brett. **2.** Mitteilungsblatt *n*.

'**bul·let·proof** *adj* kugelsicher: **~ glass** Panzerglas *n*. **~ wound** *s* Schußwunde *f*, -verletzung *f*.

'**bull|·fight** *s* Stierkampf *m*. '**~·fight·er** *s* Stierkämpfer *m*.

bul·lion ['bʊljən] *s* (Gold-, Silber)Barren *m*.

bull·ish ['bʊlɪʃ] *adj* ✝ Hausse...

bull·ock ['bʊlək] *s* *zo*. Ochse *m*.

'**bull·ring** *s* Stierkampfarena *f*.

'**bull's-eye** *s* **1.** △, ⚓ Bullauge *n*. **2.** Zentrum *n*, *das* Schwarze (*e-r* Zielscheibe): **hit the ~** ins Schwarze treffen (*a*. *fig*.).

'**bull|·shit** *s* V Scheiß *m*: **talk ~** Scheiß reden. **~ ter·ri·er** *s zo*. Bullterrier *m*.

bul·ly ['bʊlɪ] **I** *s* brutaler *od*. tyrannischer Kerl. **II** *v/t* tyrannisieren, schikanieren: **~ about** (*od*. **around**) *j-n* herumkommandieren. **III** *adj u. int* F prima: **~ for you!** na und?; *iro*. gratuliere!

bul·wark ['bʊlwək] *s* Bollwerk *n*.

bum¹ [bʌm] *s bsd. Br*. F Hintern *m*.

bum² [~] *bsd. Am*. F **I** *s* **1.** Gammler *m*; Tippelbruder *m*. **2.** Schnorrer *m*, Nassauer *m*. **3.** Saukerl *m*. **II** *v/i* **4.** *mst* **~ about** (*od*. **around**) herumgammeln. **5.** schnorren, nassauern (*off* bei). **6.** tippeln (*through* durch). **III** *adj* **7.** mies; kaputt.

bum·ble·bee ['bʌmblbiː] *s zo*. Hummel *f*.

bump [bʌmp] **I** *v/t* **1.** (heftig) stoßen. **2.** mit *et*. rennen (*against* gegen), et. rammen, auf *ein* Auto auffahren. **3. ~ off** F umlegen (*umbringen*). **II** *v/i* **4.** (*against*, *into*) prallen, stoßen (gegen, an *acc*), zs.-stoßen (mit): **~ into** *fig*. *j-n* zufällig treffen. **5.** rumpeln, holpern (*Fahrzeug*). **III** *s* **6.** heftiger Ruck *od*. Stoß. **7.** Beule *f*. **8.** Unebenheit *f*.

bump·er¹ ['bʌmpə] **I** *s* et. Riesiges. **II** *adj* riesig: **~ crop** Rekordernte *f*.

bump·er² [~] *s* **1.** *mot*. Stoßstange *f*. **2.** 🚃 *etc Am*. Puffer *m*.

bump·er| car *s* (Auto)Skooter *m*. **~ stick·er** *s* Autoaufkleber *m*.

bump·kin ['bʌmpkɪn] *s a*. **country ~** *contp*. Bauer *m*, Provinzler *m*.

bump| start *s Br*. Anschieben *n*. '**~-start** *v/t Br. Auto* anschieben.

bump·tious ['bʌmpʃəs] *adj* □ F aufgeblasen, wichtigtuerisch.

bump·y ['bʌmpɪ] *adj* □ **1.** holp(e)rig, uneben. **2.** unruhig (*Flug*).

bun [bʌn] *s* **1.** süßes Brötchen: **she has a ~ in the oven** F bei ihr ist was unterwegs. **2.** (Haar)Knoten *m*.

bunch [bʌntʃ] **I** *s* **1.** Bündel *n*, Bund *n*: **~ of flowers** Blumenstrauß *m*; **~ of grapes** Weintraube *f*; **~ of keys** Schlüsselbund *m, n*. **2.** F Verein *m*, Haufen *m*. **II** *v/t* **3.** *a*. **~ up** bündeln. **III** *v/i* **4.** *oft* **~ up** (*od*. **together**) Grüppchen *od*. Haufen bilden.

bun·combe *bsd. Am*. → **bunkum**.

bun·dle ['bʌndl] **I** *s* **1.** Bündel *n*, Bund *n*. **2.** F (Energie-, Nerven- *etc*)Bündel *n*. **II** *v/t* **3.** *oft* **~ up** bündeln. **4.** stopfen (*into* in *acc*). **5.** *mst* **~ off** eilig *od*. ohne viel Federlesens fortschaffen. **III** *v/i* **6.** *mst* **~ off** sich packen *od*. eilig davonmachen.

bung [bʌŋ] **I** *s* **1.** a) Spund(zapfen) *m*, b) → **bunghole**. **II** *v/t* **2.** *Faß* verspunden. **3.** *mst* **~ up** F Öffnung *etc* verstopfen: **my nose is ~ed up** m-e Nase ist zu.

bun·ga·low ['bʌŋgələʊ] *s* Bungalow *m*.

'**bung·hole** *s* Spundloch *n*.

bun·gle ['bʌŋgl] **I** *v/i* pfuschen. **II** *v/t* verpfuschen. **III** *s* Pfusch(arbeit *f*) *m*. '**bun·gler** *s* Pfuscher(in). '**bun·gling** *adj* □ stümperhaft.

bunk¹ [bʌŋk] *s* ⚓ Koje *f*.

bunk² [~] *s* F → **bunkum**.

bunk³ [~] *s*: **do a ~** *Br*. F verduften, türmen.

bunk bed *s* Etagenbett *n*.

bunk·er ['bʌŋkə] *s* ⚓, ✕ Bunker *m*.

bun·kum ['bʌŋkəm] *s* Blödsinn *m*, Gewäsch *n*.

bun·ny ['bʌnɪ] *s* Häschen *n* (*a*. F *attraktives Mädchen*).

buoy [bɔɪ] **I** *s* **1.** ⚓ Boje *f*, Bake *f*. **2.** Rettungsring *m*. **II** *v/t* **3.** *mst* **~ up** *fig*. Auftrieb geben (*dat*).

buoy·an·cy ['bɔɪənsɪ] *s* **1.** *phys.* Schwimm-, Tragkraft *f*. **2.** ✈ Auftrieb *m*. **3.** *fig*. Spannkraft *f*; Schwung *m*.

'**buoy·ant** adj **1.** federnd (*Schritt*). **2.** schwungvoll.

bur [bɜː] s ♀ Klette f (a. fig.).

bur·den[^1] ['bɜːdn] I s Last f, fig. a. Bürde f: ~ *of proof* ⚖ Beweislast; *be a ~ to* (od. *on*) *s.o.* j-m zur Last fallen. II v/t belasten (a. fig.): ~ *s.o. with s.th.* j-m et. aufbürden.

bur·den[^2] [~] s **1.** Kehrreim m, Refrain m. **2.** Hauptgedanke m.

bur·den·some ['bɜːdnsəm] adj lästig, beschwerlich.

bu·reau ['bjʊərəʊ] pl -**reaus**, -**reaux** ['~rəʊz] s **1.** Br. Schreibtisch m, -pult n. Am. (bsd. Spiegel)Kommode f. **3.** Büro n. **4.** Auskunfts- od. Vermittlungsstelle f. **bu·reauc·ra·cy** [~'rɒkrəsɪ] s Bürokratie f. **bu·reau·crat** ['~kræt] s Bürokrat m. **,bu·reau'crat·ic** adj (~ally) bürokratisch. **bu·reauc·ra·tize** [~'rɒkrətaɪz] v/t bürokratisieren.

burg·er ['bɜːɡə] s gastr. bsd. Am. F Hamburger m.

bur·glar ['bɜːɡlə] s Einbrecher m: *we had ~s* bei uns wurde eingebrochen; ~ *alarm* Alarmanlage f. **bur·glar·ize** ['~raɪz] Am. → **burgle**.

'**bur·glar·proof** adj einbruch(s)sicher.

bur·gla·ry ['bɜːɡlərɪ] s Einbruch m.

bur·gle ['bɜːɡl] v/t u. v/i einbrechen (in acc od. aus): *he was ~d* bei ihm wurde eingebrochen.

bur·i·al ['berɪəl] s Begräbnis n, Beerdigung f. ~ **ground** s Friedhof m. ~ **place** s Grabstätte f. ~ **ser·vice** s Trauerfeier f.

bur·lesque [bɜː'lesk] I adj burlesk, possenhaft. II s Burleske f, Posse f.

bur·ly ['bɜːlɪ] adj stämmig.

burn [bɜːn] I s **1.** verbrannte Stelle. **2.** ✷ Verbrennung f, Brandwunde f. II v/i (a. irr) **3.** allg. brennen (*Feuer, Licht, Haus, Wunde etc*): ~ *down* ab-, niederbrennen. **4.** fig. brennen (*with* vor dat): ~*ing with anger* wutentbrannt; *be ~ing to do s.th.* darauf brennen, et. zu tun. **5.** ver-, anbrennen (*Speise etc*). III v/t (a. irr) **6.** verbrennen: ~ *down* ab-, niederbrennen; *his house was ~t* sein Haus brannte ab; *be ~t to death* verbrennen; → *boat* 1, *bridge* 1, *candle*. **7.** verbrennen, -sengen, *Speise* anbrennen (lassen): ~ *one's fingers* sich die Finger verbrennen (a. fig.); ~ *a hole in* ein

Loch brennen in (acc). **8.** *Ziegel, Porzellan etc* brennen. '**burn·er** s Brenner m (*Person u. Gerät*). '**burn·ing** adj brennend (a. fig.): *take a ~ interest in* brennend interessiert sein an (dat); ~ *sensation* ✷ Brennen n.

bur·nish ['bɜːnɪʃ] v/t polieren.

burnt [bɜːnt] I pret u. pp von **burn.** II adj: ~ *almonds* pl gebrannte Mandeln pl.

burp [bɜːp] F I v/i rülpsen, aufstoßen, (*Baby*) ein Bäuerchen machen. II s Rülpser m, Bäuerchen n.

burr → **bur.**

bur·row ['bʌrəʊ] I s (*Fuchs- etc*)Bau m. II v/i (*into*) sich eingraben (in acc); fig. sich vertiefen (in acc).

burst [bɜːst] I v/i (irr) **1.** bersten (*Eis etc*), (zer)platzen (*Luftballon etc*): ~ (*open*) aufplatzen (*Wunde etc*), aufspringen (*Tür etc*); → *seam* 1. **2.** explodieren. **3.** fig. ausbrechen (*into* in acc): ~ *into laughter* (*tears*) in Gelächter (Tränen) ausbrechen; ~ *into flame(s)* in Flammen aufgehen. **4.** ~ *out* fig. herausplatzen. **5.** ~ *with* zum Bersten voll sein von; fig. strotzen vor (dat) od. von; fig. platzen vor (dat). **6.** ~ *in* (*out*) herein-(hinaus)stürmen; ~ *into sight* (od. *view*) plötzlich sichtbar werden. II v/t (irr) **7.** (auf)sprengen, zum Platzen bringen: ~ *open* aufbrechen; *the car ~ a tire* (bsd. Br. *tyre*) ein Reifen am Wagen platzte. III s **8.** Bersten n, Platzen n. **9.** Explosion f. **10.** fig. Ausbruch m: ~ *of applause* Beifallssturm m; ~ *of laughter* Lachsalve f. **11.** a. ~ *of fire* Feuerstoß m, Salve f.

bur·y ['berɪ] v/t **1.** begraben: a) beerdigen, b) verschütten, c) *Streit etc* vergessen: ~ *o.s. in* sich vertiefen in (acc); *buried in thought(s)* gedankenversunken. **2.** ver-, eingraben, ♾, ⚙ in die Erde verlegen: ~ *hatchet.*

bus [bʌs] pl -(**s**)**es** s (Omni-, Auto)Bus m: → *miss*[^2] 1.

bush[^1] [bʊʃ] s **1.** Busch m, Strauch m: *beat about* (od. *around*) *the ~* fig. wie die Katze um den heißen Brei herumgehen, um die Sache herumreden. **2.** Gebüsch n. **3.** Busch m; Waldland n.

bush[^2] [~] s ⚙ Buchse f.

bush·el ['bʊʃl] s Bushel m, Scheffel m (*Br. 36, 37 l, Am. 35, 24 l*): → *light*[^1] 1d.

bush·y ['bʊʃɪ] adj □ buschig.

busi·ness ['bɪznɪs] s **1.** Geschäft n, Beruf m, Tätigkeit f: **on** ~ geschäftlich, beruflich. **2.** ✝ Geschäft(sgang m) n: **how is ~?** wie gehen die Geschäfte? **3.** ✝ Geschäft n, Unternehmen n. **4.** Arbeit f, Beschäftigung f: ~ **before pleasure** erst die Arbeit, dann das Vergnügen; → **mix** 2. **5.** Sache f, Aufgabe f: **make it one's ~ to do s.th.** es sich zur Aufgabe machen, et. zu tun. **6.** Angelegenheit f, Sache f: **get down to** ~ zur Sache kommen; **that's none of your** ~ das geht Sie nichts an; **send s.o. about his** ~ j-m heimleuchten; → **mean³** 1, **mind** 8. **7.** Anlaß m, Berechtigung f: **have no** ~ **doing** (od. **to do**) **s.th.** kein Recht haben, et. zu tun. **8.** Geschäft n (Notdurft): **do one's** ~ sein Geschäft erledigen od. machen. ~ **ad·dress** s Geschäftsadresse f. ~ **hours** s pl Geschäftsstunden pl, -zeit f: **after** ~ nach Geschäftsschluß. ~ **let·ter** s Geschäftsbrief m. '~·**like** adj sachlich, nüchtern. '~·**man** s (irr **man**) Geschäftsmann m. ~ **se·cret** s Betriebs-, Geschäftsgeheimnis n. ~ **trip** s Geschäftsreise f. '~·**wom·an** s (irr **woman**) Geschäftsfrau f. ~ **year** s ✝ Geschäftsjahr n.

bus·ker ['bʌskə] s Br. Straßenmusikant(in); -sänger(in).

bus|·man ['bʌsmən] s (irr **man**) (Omni)Busfahrer m: ~'s **holiday** Urlaub, der mit der üblichen Berufsarbeit verbracht wird. ~ **ser·vice** s Busverbindung f. ~ **stop** s Bushaltestelle f.

bust¹ [bʌst] I s Büste f.

bust² [~] I s I v/i (a. irr) **1.** kaputtgehen. **2.** pleite gehen. II v/t (a. irr) **3.** kaputtmachen. III s **4.** Pleite f, a. weitS. Reinfall m. **5.** Sauferei f; Sauftour f: **go on a** ~ e-e Sauftour machen. IV adj **6.** kaputt. **7.** pleite: **go** ~ → 2.

bus·tle ['bʌsl] I v/i **1.** a. ~ **about** (od. **around**) geschäftig hin u. her eilen. **2.** sich beeilen; eilen, hasten. **3. the streets were bustling with life** auf den Straßen herrschte geschäftiges Treiben. II v/t **4.** a. ~ **up** antreiben, hetzen. III s **5.** Geschäftigkeit f; geschäftiges Treiben. '**bus·tler** s geschäftiger Mensch. '**bus·tling** adj **1.** geschäftig. **2.** belebt (Straße etc).

bus·y ['bɪzɪ] I adj □ **1.** beschäftigt: **be** ~ **doing s.th.** damit beschäftigt sein, et.

zu tun. **2.** geschäftig, fleißig: **get** ~**!** an die Arbeit!; → **bee**. **3.** Straße etc: belebt; verkehrsreich. **4.** arbeitsreich (Tag etc). **5.** übereifrig, aufdringlich. **6.** teleph. bsd. Am. besetzt: ~ **signal** Besetztzeichen n. II v/t **7.** (o.s. sich) beschäftigen (**with** mit): ~ **o.s. doing s.th.** sich damit beschäftigen, et. zu tun. '~·**bod·y** s j-d, der sich in alles einmischt.

bus·y·ness ['bɪznɪs] s Geschäftigkeit f.

but [bʌt] I cj **1.** aber, jedoch: ~ **then** (**again**) and(e)rerseits. **2.** sondern: **not only ...** ~ **also** nicht nur ..., sondern auch. **3.** als, außer: ~ **for** ohne; ~ **for my parents** wenn m-e Eltern nicht (gewesen) wären. II prp **4.** außer: **nothing** ~ nichts als, nur; **the last** ~ **one** (**two**) der vorletzte (drittletzte); ~ **anything** 2. **5. all** ~ fast, beinahe. III s **6. no** ~s **about it** kein Aber; → **if** 4.

bu·tane ['bjuːteɪn] s ⚗ Butan n.

butch·er ['butʃə] I s **1.** Fleischer m, Metzger m: **at the** ~'s beim Fleischer. II v/t **2.** schlachten. **3.** abschlachten, niedermetzeln. '**butch·er·y** s **1.** Fleischer-, Metzgerhandwerk n. **2.** Gemetzel n.

but·ler ['bʌtlə] s Butler m.

butt¹ [bʌt] I s **1.** (Gewehr- etc)Kolben m. **2.** (Zigarren-, Zigaretten-, Kerzen-) Stummel m, (Zigaretten)Kippe f. **3.** fig. Zielscheibe f. **4.** Kopfstoß m; Stoß mit den Hörnern. II v/t **5.** j-m e-n Kopfstoß od. e-n Stoß mit den Hörnern versetzen. **6.** Zigarre, Zigarette ausdrücken. III v/i **7.** ~ **in** F sich einmischen: ~ **in on**, ~ **into** sich einmischen in (acc).

but·ter ['bʌtə] I s **1.** Butter f: **he looks as if** ~ **would not melt in his mouth** er sieht aus, als könnte er nicht bis drei zählen od. als könnte er kein Wässerchen trüben. II v/t **2.** mit Butter bestreichen. **3.** ~ **up** F j-m schöntun, j-m Honig ums Maul schmieren. ~ **dish** s Butterdose f, -schale f. '~·**fin·gered** adj F tolpatschig. '~·**fin·gers** pl -,**fin·gers** s F Tolpatsch m. '~·**fly** s **1.** zo. Schmetterling m: **have butterflies in one's stomach** F ein flaues Gefühl in der Magengegend haben. **2.** a. ~ **stroke** (Schwimmen) Schmetterlingsstil m. '~·**milk** s Buttermilch f.

but·tock ['bʌtək] s anat. Gesäßbacke f: ~s pl Gesäß n.

but·ton ['bʌtn] **I** s **1.** (Kleider-, a. Klingel- etc)Knopf m. **2.** (Ansteck)Plakette f, Abzeichen n. **3.** pl (sg konstruiert) bsd. Br. F Hotelpage m. **II** v/t **4.** mst ~ **up** zuknöpfen; ~ed **up** F zugeknöpft, zurückhaltend. **III** v/i **5.** hinten etc geknöpft werden. '~·hole s **1.** Knopfloch n. **2.** bsd. Br. Blume f im Knopfloch.
but·tress ['bʌtrɪs] **I** s **1.** △ Strebe-, Stützpfeiler m. **2.** fig. Stütze f. **II** v/t a. ~ **up 3.** stützen. **4.** fig. (unter)stützen.
bux·om ['bʌksəm] adj drall.
buy [baɪ] **I** s **1.** F Kauf m: a good ~. **II** v/t (irr) **2.** (ein)kaufen (of, from von; at bei): ~ s.th. from s.o. j-m et. abkaufen. **3.** Fahrkarte etc lösen. **4.** fig. Sieg etc erkaufen (with mit): dearly bought teuer erkauft. **5.** j-n kaufen, bestechen. **6.** bsd. Am. F et. glauben: I won't ~ that! das kauf' ich dir etc nicht ab!
Verbindungen mit Adverbien:
buy| back v/t zurückkaufen. ~ **in** v/i sich eindecken mit. ~ **off** → **buy** 5. ~ **out** v/t Teilhaber etc abfinden, auszahlen. ~ **up** v/t aufkaufen.
buy·er ['baɪə] s Käufer(in).
buzz [bʌz] **I** v/i summen, surren, schwirren: ~ **off** F (mst imp) abschwirren, abhauen; ~ **for** → **II** a. **II** v/t a) j-n mit dem Summer rufen, b) teleph. F j-n anrufen. **III** s **1.** Summen n, Surren n, Schwirren n: give s.o. a ~ → **II**.
buz·zard ['bʌzəd] s orn. Bussard m.
buzz·er ['bʌzə] s ⚡ Summer m.
'**buzz·word** s Modewort n.
by [baɪ] **I** prp **1.** örtlich: (nahe od. dicht) bei od. an (dat), neben (dat): side ~ side Seite an Seite. **2.** vorbei od. vorüber an (dat), an (dat) ... entlang. **3.** Verkehrsmittel: per, mit: → air¹ 1, etc. **4.** zeitlich: bis um od. spätestens: be here ~ **4.30** sei um 4 Uhr 30 hier; → now 1. **5.** Tageszeit: während, bei: → day 1, etc.

6. nach, ...weise: sold by the yard yardweise verkauft; → hour 1, etc. **7.** nach, gemäß: it is ten ~ my watch nach od. auf m-r Uhr ist es zehn. **8.** von: → nature 2, trade 4. **9.** Urheberschaft: von, durch: a play ~ Shaw ein Stück von Shaw; → oneself 1. **10.** mit Hilfe von, mit, durch: ~ listening durch Zuhören; → force 1, 3, 4. **11.** Größenverhältnisse: um: (too) short ~ an inch um e-n Zoll zu kurz. **12.** ☈ a) mal: **3 ~ 4**; the size is 9 feet ~ **6** die Größe ist 9 auf 6 (od. 9 × 6) Fuß; on: ~ **2**, b) durch: **6 ~ 2**; → **divide** 4, 6. **13.** an (dat), bei: → **root¹**, etc. **II** adv **14.** nahe: ~ and large im großen u. ganzen; ~ and ~ bald, demnächst; nach u. nach; → **close** 9, **hard** 13. **15.** vorbei, vorüber: → **go by**, etc. **16.** beiseite: → **put by**, etc.
by(e)... Neben..., Seiten...
bye [baɪ] s → **bye-bye** II.
bye-bye I s ['baɪbaɪ]: go to ~(s) in die Heia gehen; einschlafen. **II** int [ˌbaɪˈbaɪ] F Wiedersehen!, Tschüs!; teleph. Wiederhören!
'**by|-ef·fect** s Nebenwirkung f. '~·e·lec·tion s Nachwahl f. '~·gone I adj vergangen. **II** s: let ~s be ~s laß(t) das Vergangene ruhen. '~·law s bsd. Br. Ortsstatut n, städtische Verordnung. '~·name s Beiname m. '~·pass s **1.** Umleitung f, Umgehungsstraße f. **2.** ☈ Bypass m: ~ operation Bypassoperation f. '~·prod·uct s Nebenprodukt n (a. fig.). '~·road s Seiten-, Nebenstraße f. '~·stand·er s Umstehende m, f, Zuschauer(in). '~·street → **byroad**.
byte [baɪt] s Computer: Byte n, Binärwort n.
'**by|·way** → **byroad**. '~·word s Inbegriff m (for gen): be a ~ for stehen für, gleichbedeutend sein mit.

C

cab [kæb] *s* **1.** Taxi *n*, Taxe *f*. **2.** 🚂 Führerstand *m*; Fahrerhaus *n* (*e-s Lastkraftwagens*), (*a. e-s Krans*) Führerhaus *n*.

cab·a·ret ['kæbəreɪ] *s a.* ~ *show* Varietédarbietungen *pl* (*in e-m Restaurant od. Nachtklub*).

cab·bage ['kæbɪdʒ] *s* 🌿 Kohl *m*.

cab·bie, cab·by ['kæbɪ] *s bsd. Am.* F Taxifahrer(in).

'cab·driv·er *s bsd. Am.* Taxifahrer(in).

cab·in ['kæbɪn] *s* **1.** Häuschen *n*, Hütte *f*. **2.** ⚓ Kabine *f*, Kajüte *f*. **3.** ✈ Kabine *f* (*a. e-r Seilbahn etc*). ~ *class* *s* ⚓ Kabinen-, Kajütsklasse *f*. ~ *cruis·er* *s* ⚓ Kabinenkreuzer *m*.

cab·i·net ['kæbɪnɪt] *s* **1.** *oft* 2 *pol.* Kabinett *n*. **2.** Vitrine *f*. **3.** (*Büro-, Kartei-etc*)Schrank *m*. **4.** (*Radio- etc*)Gehäuse *n*.

ca·ble ['keɪbl] **I** *s* **1.** Kabel *n* (*a. ⚡*), (Draht)Seil *n*. **2.** → *cablegram*. **II** *v/t* **3.** *TV*: Gegend *etc* verkabeln. **4.** *j-m et.* telegrafieren; *j-n* telegrafisch benachrichtigen. **5.** *j-m* Geld telegrafisch an- *od.* überweisen. **III** *v/i* **6.** telegrafieren. ~ *ad·dress* *s* Telegrammadresse *f*. ~ *car* *s* Seilbahn: Kabine *f*; Wagen *m*.

ca·ble·gram ['keɪblɡræm] *s* (Übersee-) Telegramm *n*.

ca·ble tel·e·vi·sion *s* Kabelfernsehen *n*.

cab·man ['kæbmən] *s* (*irr man*) Taxifahrer *m*.

ca·boo·dle [kə'buːdl] *s*: *the whole* ~ F die ganze Chose.

ca·boose [kə'buːs] *s* ⚓ Kombüse *f*.

cab| rank, '~stand *s bsd. Am.* Taxistand *m*.

cache [kæʃ] **I** *s* Versteck *n*, geheimes Lager. **II** *v/t* verstecken.

cack·le ['kækl] **I** *v/i* gackern (*Huhn*), schnattern (*Gans*), *fig. a.* gackernd lachen. **II** *s* Gegacker *n*, Geschnatter *n*, *fig. a.* gackerndes Lachen.

ca·coph·o·ny [kæ'kɒfənɪ] *s* ♪ Kakophonie *f*, Mißklang *m*.

cac·tus ['kæktəs] *pl* **-ti** ['~taɪ], **-tus·es** *s* 🌿 Kaktus *m*.

ca·das·tre [kə'dæstə] *s* Grundbuch *n*.

ca·dav·er·ous [kə'dævərəs] *adj* ☐ leichenblaß.

cad·die ['kædɪ] *s* Golf: Caddie *m* (*Schlägerträger*).

cad·dy ['kædɪ] *s* (*bsd. Tee*)Büchse *f*, (-)Dose *f*.

ca·dence ['keɪdəns] *s* **1.** (Vers-, Sprech-) Rhythmus *m*. **2.** ♪ Kadenz *f*.

ca·det [kə'det] *s* **1.** ✕ Kadett *m*. **2.** (*Polizei- etc*)Schüler *m*: ~ *nurse* Schwesternschülerin *f*.

cadge [kædʒ] *v/t u. v/i* schnorren (*from* bei). **'cadg·er** *s* Schnorrer(in).

cad·mi·um ['kædmɪəm] *s* 🧪 Cadmium *n*.

ca·dre ['kɑːdə] *s* ✕, ✕, *pol.* Kader *m*.

Cae·sar·e·an, *a.* **c~** [siː'zeərɪən] **I** *adj:* ~ *section* → II. **II** *s* ✚ Kaiserschnitt *m*.

cae·su·ra [sɪ'zjʊərə] *s* Zäsur *f*.

ca·fé ['kæfeɪ] *s* **1.** Café *n*. **2.** Restaurant *n*. **3.** *Am.* Kneipe *f*; Nachtklub *m*.

caf·e·te·ri·a [,kæfɪ'tɪərɪə] *s* Cafeteria *f*, Selbstbedienungsrestaurant *n*, *a.* Kantine *f*, *univ.* Mensa *f*.

caf·feine ['kæfiːn] *s* 🧪 Koffein *n*.

cage [keɪdʒ] **I** *s* **1.** Käfig *m*. **2.** Kabine *f* (*e-s Aufzugs*); ⚒ Förderkorb *m*. **II** *v/t* **3.** in e-n Käfig sperren, einsperren.

cage·y ['keɪdʒɪ] *adj* ☐ F **1.** verschlossen. **2.** vorsichtig. **3.** *Am.* gerissen, schlau.

ca·jole [kə'dʒəʊl] *v/t* **1.** *j-m* schmeicheln. **2.** *j-n* beschwatzen (*into doing* zu tun); ~ *s.o. out of s.th.* *j-m* et. ausreden; ~ *s.th. out of s.o.* *j-m* et. abbetteln.

cake [keɪk] **I** *s* **1.** Kuchen *m*, Torte *f*: *go* (*od. sell*) *like hot* ~s weggehen wie die warmen Semmeln; *take the* ~ F den Vogel abschießen; *you can't have your* ~ *and eat it* du kannst nur eines von beiden tun *od.* haben; → *piece* **1**. **2.** Tafel *f* Schokolade, Riegel *m* Seife. **II** *v/i* **3.** klumpen.

ca·lam·i·tous [kə'læmɪtəs] *adj* ☐ verheerend, katastrophal. **ca·lam·i·ty** *s* **1.** Katastrophe *f*: *in the* ~ bei der Katastrophe; ~ *of nature* Naturkatastrophe; ~ *howler bsd. Am.* Schwarzseher(in), Panikmacher(in). **2.** Elend *n*, Misere *f*.

cal·cif·er·ous [kæl'sɪfərəs] *adj* kalkhal-

tig. **cal·ci·fy** ['ˈfaɪ] v/t u. v/i verkalken.
cal·ci·um ['ˈsɪəm] s ℞ Kalzium n.
cal·cu·la·ble ['kælkjʊləbl] adj □ **1.** berechen-, kalkulierbar: ~ **risk** kalkulierbares Risiko. **2.** verläßlich. **cal·cu·late** ['ˈleɪt] **I** v/t **1.** be-, ausrechnen: ~ **that** damit rechnen, daß. **2.** Preise, Entfernung etc kalkulieren, Chancen etc abwägen. **3.** Am. F vermuten, glauben (**that** daß). **II** v/i **4.** ~ **on** rechnen mit od. auf (acc), zählen od. sich verlassen auf (acc). **cal·cu·lat·ed** adj **1.** gewollt, beabsichtigt, (Indiskretion) gezielt, (Beleidigung) bewußt, (Risiko) kalkuliert. **2.** gedacht, bestimmt (**for** für; **to do** zu tun): **it was ~ to impress** es sollte Eindruck machen. '**cal·cu·lat·ing** adj □ **1.** (kühl) überlegend; berechnend. **2.** Rechen...: ~ **machine**. **cal·cu·la·tion** s **1.** Berechnung f (a. fig.), Ausrechnung f: **be out in one's** ~ sich verrechnet haben. **2.** Kalkulation f: ~ **of profits** ℞ Gewinnkalkulation. **3.** Überlegung f: **after much** ~ nach reiflicher Überlegung. '**cal·cu·la·tor** s Rechner m (Gerät). **cal·cu·lus** ['ˈləs] pl **-li** ['ˈlaɪ], **-lus·es** s ℞ Rechnungsart f, (Differential- etc)Rechnung f: ~ **of probabilities** Wahrscheinlichkeitsrechnung.

cal·en·dar ['kælɪndə] s **1.** (engS. Termin)Kalender m, fig. a. Zeitrechnung f. **2.** Liste f, Register m.

cal·ends ['kælɪndz] s pl: **on the Greek** ~ am St. Nimmerleinstag.

calf¹ [kɑːf] pl **calves** [kɑːvz] s **1.** Kalb n. **2.** Kalb(s)leder n.

calf² [ˈ~] pl **calves** [ˈ~] s anat. Wade f.

calf **love** s F jugendliche Schwärmerei. '**~·skin** → **calf¹ 2**.

cal·i·ber Am. → **calibre**. **cal·i·brate** ['kælɪbreɪt] v/t ⊛ kalibrieren, eichen. **cal·i·bre** ['ˈbə] s Kaliber n, fig. a. Format n (e-s Menschen).

call [kɔːl] **I** s **1.** Ruf m (**for** nach): ~ **for help** Hilferuf m; **within** ~ in Rufweite. **2.** teleph. Anruf m: **give s.o. a** ~ j-n anrufen; **make a** ~ telefonieren. **3.** (Lock)Ruf m (e-s Tiers). **4.** fig. Ruf m (der Natur etc). **5.** Berufung f (**to** auf e-n Lehrstuhl, an e-e Universität, in ein Amt). **6.** Aufruf m: **make a** ~ **for s.th.** zu et. aufrufen. **7.** thea. Herausruf m, Vorhang m. **8.** (kurzer) Besuch (**on**

s.o., **at s.o.'s** [house] bei j-m): **make** (od. **pay**) **a** ~ **on s.o.** j-n besuchen, j-m e-n Besuch abstatten. **9.** ✝ Zahlungsaufforderung f; Abruf m, Kündigung f (von Geldern). **II** v/t **10.** j-n (herbei)rufen, Arzt etc kommen lassen: → **attention 1, being** 1. **11.** zu e-m Streik etc aufrufen. **12.** Versammlung etc einberufen. **13.** j-n wecken. **14.** teleph. anrufen. **15.** j-n berufen (**to** → 5). **16.** j-n, et. nennen: **be ~ed** heißen; → **spade¹** 1. **17.** nennen, bezeichnen (als): **what do you ~ this?** wie nennt man od. heißt das? **18.** nennen, finden, halten für: **I ~ that stupid.** **19.** j-n et. schimpfen: **he ~ed me a fool.** **III** v/i **20.** rufen (a. fig. Pflicht etc): ~ **for** um Hilfe rufen; nach j-m, et. rufen; fig. erfordern. **21.** e-n (kurzen) Besuch machen (**on s.o., at s.o.'s** [house] bei j-m): **call on s.o.** j-n besuchen, j-m e-n Besuch abstatten; ~ **for** et. anfordern; ~ **for** et. abholen. **22.** ~ **on** sich wenden an (acc) (**for s.th.** um et., wegen e-r Sache); j-n bitten (**to do** zu tun). **23.** ~ **at** ⚓ anlegen in (dat), Hafen anlaufen; 🚋 halten in (dat); ✈ Flughafen anfliegen. **24.** anrufen, telefonieren.
Verbindungen mit Adverbien:
call a·way v/t **1.** wegrufen (**from** von). **2.** Gedanken etc ablenken (**from** von). ~ **back I** v/t **1.** a. teleph. zurückrufen. **2.** defekte Autos etc (in die Werkstatt) zurückrufen. **II** v/i **3.** a. teleph. zurückrufen. **4.** noch einmal vorbeikommen. ~ **down** v/t **1.** Segen etc herabflehen, -rufen. **2.** sich j-s Zorn zuziehen. **3.** Am. F zs.-stauchen (**for** wegen). ~ **forth** v/t hervorrufen, auslösen, Fähigkeiten etc wachrufen, wecken. ~ **in I** v/t **1.** hinein-, hereinrufen. **2.** Arzt etc (hin)zuziehen, zu Rate ziehen. **3.** Schulden einfordern, Forderungen etc einziehen. **II** v/i **4.** (kurz) vorbeischauen (**on s.o., at s.o.'s** [house] bei j-m). ~ **off** v/t **1.** j-n (von s-m Posten) abberufen. **2.** Streik etc absagen; abbrechen. ~ **out I** v/t **1.** ausrufen, Namen etc aufrufen. **2.** Polizei etc aufbieten; alarmieren. **3.** Fähigkeiten etc wachrufen, wecken. **4.** zum Streik aufrufen. **II** v/i **5.** rufen (**for** um Hilfe). ~ **o·ver** v/t Namen, Liste etc verlesen. ~ **up** v/t **1.** teleph. anrufen. **2.** Erinnerungen etc wachrufen, wecken. **3.** ✗ einberufen.

'**call**·**back** s Rückruf(aktion f) m. ~ **box** s Br. Telefonzelle f.

call·er ['kɔːlə] s **1.** Rufer(in). **2.** teleph. Anrufer(in). **3.** Besucher(in). **4.** Abholer(in).

call| girl s Callgirl n. '**~in** Am. → **phone-in**.

call·ing ['kɔːlɪŋ] s **1.** Beruf m: **what is his ~?** was ist er von Beruf? **2.** bsd. eccl. Berufung f: **have a ~ to do s.th.** sich berufen fühlen, et. zu tun. **~ card** s Am. Visitenkarte f.

cal·lis·then·ics [ˌkælɪs'θenɪks] s pl Gymnastik f, Freiübungen pl.

cal·los·i·ty [kæ'lɒsətɪ] s **1.** Schwiele f. **2.** fig. Gefühllosigkeit f. '**cal·lous** adj □ **1.** schwielig. **2.** fig. abgestumpft, gefühllos (**to** gegenüber).

'**call-up** s ✕ Einberufung f.

cal·lus ['kæləs] s Schwiele f.

calm [kɑːm] **I** s **1.** Stille f, Ruhe f (a. fig.): **the ~ before the storm**; ~ (of **mind**) Gelassenheit f, Gemütsruhe f. **2.** Windstille f. **II** adj □ **3.** still, ruhig. **4.** windstill. **5.** fig. ruhig, gelassen. **III** v/t **6.** oft ~ **down** beruhigen, besänftigen. **IV** v/i oft ~ **down 7.** sich beruhigen. **8.** sich legen (Sturm, Zorn etc).

cal·o·rie ['kælərɪ] s Kalorie f. '~·**con·scious** adj □ kalorienbewußt.

ca·lum·ni·ate [kə'lʌmnɪeɪt] v/t verleumden. **ca'lum·ni·a·tor** s Verleumder(in). **ca'lum·ni·ous** adj □ verleumderisch. **cal·um·ny** ['kæləmnɪ] s Verleumdung f.

calve [kɑːv] v/i kalben.

calves [kɑːvz] pl von **calf** ¹ u. ².

ca·lyp·so [kə'lɪpsəʊ] pl **-sos** s ♪ Calypso m.

cam [kæm] s ⊚ Nocken m.

cam·ber ['kæmbə] **I** v/t u. v/i **1.** (sich) wölben. **II** s **2.** (leichte) Wölbung. **3.** mot. Sturz m.

came [keɪm] pret von **come**.

cam·el ['kæml] s zo. Kamel n.

cam·el's| hair ['kæmlz] s Kamelhaar(stoff m) n. '~-**hair** adj Kamelhaar...

cam·er·a ['kæmərə] s **1.** (a. Film-, Fernseh)Kamera f, Fotoapparat m. **2.** in ~ ⚜ unter Ausschluß der Öffentlichkeit; fig. geheim. '~·**man** s (irr **man**) **1.** Kameramann m. **2.** Pressefotograf m. '~-**shy** adj kamerascheu.

cam·i·on ['kæmɪən] s Last(kraft)wagen m.

cam·o·mile ['kæməmaɪl] s ⚘ Kamille f: ~ **tea** Kamillentee m.

cam·ou·flage ['kæməflɑːʒ] **I** s ✕, zo. Tarnung f, fig. a. Verschleierung f. **II** v/t ✕ tarnen, fig. a. verschleiern.

camp¹ [kæmp] **I** s **1.** (Zelt- etc)Lager n (fig. a. Partei). ~ **bed** (Am. a. **cot**) Feldbett n; Campingliege f; ~ **chair** Klapp-, Campingstuhl m. **II** v/i **2.** sein Lager aufschlagen, kampieren. **3.** oft ~ **out** zelten, campen.

camp² [~] **F I** adj **1.** künstlich, gewollt; aufgemotzt, thea. etc a. überzogen. **2.** tuntenhaft. **II** v/i **3.** sich tuntenhaft benehmen. **III** v/t **4.** ~ **it up** a) → 3, b) die Sache aufmotzen, thea. etc a. überziehen.

cam·paign [kæm'peɪn] **I** s **1.** ✕ Feldzug m, fig. a. Kampagne f. **2.** pol. Wahlkampf m: ~ **pledge** (od. **promise**) Wahlversprechen n. **II** v/i **3.** ✕ an e-m Feldzug teilnehmen. **4.** fig. kämpfen (**for** für; **against** gegen). **cam'paign·er** s **1.** ✕ Feldzugteilnehmer m: **old** ~ Veteran m; fig. alter Praktikus. **2.** fig. Kämpfer m.

camp·er ['kæmpə] s **1.** Zeltler(in), Camper(in). **2.** Am. Wohnanhänger m, -wagen m; Wohnmobil n.

'**camp|·fire** s Lagerfeuer n. '~·**ground** s **1.** Lagerplatz m. **2.** Zelt-, Campingplatz m.

cam·phor ['kæmfə] s 🌰 Kampfer m: ~ **ball** Mottenkugel f.

camp·ing ['kæmpɪŋ] s Camping n, Zelten n: ~ **ground** (od. **site**) → **campground**.

'**camp·site** → **campground**.

cam·pus ['kæmpəs] s Campus m (Gesamtanlage e-r Universität, e-s College od. e-r Schule).

'**cam·shaft** s ⊚ Nockenwelle f.

can¹ [kæn] v/aux (irr) ich kann etc.

can² [~] **I** s **1.** (Blech)Kanne f: **have to carry the** ~ F den Kopf hinhalten müssen (**for** für). **2.** (Blech-, Konserven)Dose f, (-)Büchse f: ~ **opener** Dosen-, Büchsenöffner m. **3.** Kanister m. **4.** Am. Müll-, Abfalleimer m; Müll-, Abfalltonne f. **II** v/t **5.** einmachen, -dosen: → **canned** 1. **6.** F (auf Band etc) aufnehmen: → **canned** 2.

Ca·na·di·an [kəˈneɪdjən] **I** *adj* kanadisch. **II** *s* Kanadier(in).

ca·nal [kəˈnæl] *s* Kanal *m*, anat. a. Gang *m*, Röhre *f*. **ca·nal·i·za·tion** [ˌkænəlaɪˈzeɪʃn] *s* Kanalisation *f*, Kanalisierung *f*. **ˈca·nal·ize** *v/t* kanalisieren.

can·a·pé [ˈkænəpeɪ] *s gastr.* Appetit-, Cocktailhappen *m*.

ca·nard [kæˈnɑːd] *s* (Zeitungs)Ente *f*, Falschmeldung *f*.

ca·nar·y [kəˈneərɪ] *s* Kanarienvogel *m*.

can·cel [ˈkænsl] **I** *v/t pret u. pp* **-celed**, *bsd. Br.* **-celled** **1.** (durch-, aus)streichen. **2.** *Erlaubnis etc* widerrufen, *Beschluß etc* rückgängig machen, *Abonnement etc* kündigen, *Auftrag etc* stornieren. **3.** *Verabredung etc* absagen, *Veranstaltung etc* ausfallen lassen. **4.** *Briefmarke, Fahrschein* entwerten. **5.** *A* kürzen. **6.** *a.* ~ **out** ausgleichen, kompensieren. **II** *v/i* **7.** *A* sich kürzen lassen. **8.** *a.* ~ **out** sich (gegenseitig) aufheben. **can·cel·(l)a·tion** [ˌsəˈleɪʃn] *s* **1.** Streichung *f*. **2.** Widerrufung *f*, Rückgängigmachung *f*, Kündigung *f*, Stornierung *f*. **3.** Absage *f*. **4.** Entwertung *f*. **5.** *A* Kürzung *f*.

can·cer [ˈkænsə] **I** *s* **1.** ✻ Krebs *m*. **2.** *fig.* Krebsgeschwür *m*. **3.** ♋ *astr.* Krebs *m*. **II** *adj* **4.** Krebs...: ~ **cells** (**research**, *etc*). **ˈcan·cer·ous** *adj* ✻ krebsbefallen; Krebs...; krebsartig.

can·de·la·bra [ˌkændɪˈlɑːbrə] *s* **1.** *pl* **-bras** → **candelabrum**. **2.** *pl von* **candelabrum**. **ˌcan·de·la·brum** [ˌbrəm] *pl* **-bra** [ˌbrə], **-brums** *s* Kandelaber *m*, Armleuchter *m*.

can·did [ˈkændɪd] *adj* □ **1.** offen, aufrichtig. **2.** unvoreingenommen. **3.** *phot.* ungestellt: ~ **camera** versteckte Kamera; ~ **picture** Schnappschuß *m*.

can·di·da·cy [ˈkændɪdəsɪ] *s bsd. Am.* Kandidatur *f*, Bewerbung *f*, Anwartschaft *f* (**for** *auf acc*). **can·di·date** [ˈdət] *s* **1.** (**for**) Kandidat(in) (für), Anwärter(in) (auf *acc*), Bewerber(in) (um). **can·di·da·ture** [ˈtʃə] *bsd. Br.* → **candidacy**.

can·died [ˈkændɪd] *adj* **1.** kandiert. **2.** *fig.* honigsüß, schmeichlerisch.

can·dle [ˈkændl] *s* Kerze *f*: **burn the** ~ **at both ends** Raubbau mit s-r Gesundheit treiben; **not to be fit** (*od.* **able**) **to hold a** ~ **to** *j-m* nicht das Wasser reichen können; **the game is not worth the** ~

die Sache ist nicht der Mühe wert. **ˈ~·light** *s* Kerzenlicht *n*: **by** ~ bei Kerzenlicht; ~ **dinner** Essen *n* bei Kerzenlicht.

Can·dle·mas [ˈkændlməs] *s eccl.* (Mariä) Lichtmeß *f*.

ˈcan·dle·stick *s* Kerzenleuchter *m*, -ständer *m*.

can·do(u)r [ˈkændə] *s* **1.** Offenheit *f*, Aufrichtigkeit *f*. **2.** Unvoreingenommenheit *f*.

can·dy [ˈkændɪ] **I** *s* **1.** Kandis(zucker) *m*. **2.** *bsd. Am.* Süßigkeiten *pl*: (**hard**) ~ Bonbon *m, n*. **II** *v/t* **3.** kandieren. **ˈ~·floss** *s Br.* Zuckerwatte *f*.

cane [keɪn] **I** *s* **1.** Spazierstock *m*. **2.** (Rohr)Stock *m*. **3.** (*Bambus-, Zucker-, Schilf*)Rohr *n*. **II** *v/t* **4.** (mit dem Stock) züchtigen. ~ **sug·ar** *s* Rohrzucker *m*.

ca·nine [ˈkeɪnaɪn] *adj* **1.** Hunde..., Hunds... **2.** *contp.* hündisch: ~ **devotion** hündische Ergebenheit. **II** *s* **3.** *a.* ~ **tooth** Eckzahn *m*.

can·is·ter [ˈkænɪstə] *s* Blechbüchse *f*, -dose *f*.

can·ker [ˈkæŋkə] *s* **1.** ✻ Soor *m*; Lippengeschwür *n*. **2.** ❀ Baumkrebs *m*. **3.** *fig.* Krebsgeschwür *n*.

can·na·bis [ˈkænəbɪs] *s* Cannabis *m*: a) ❀ Hanf *m*, b) Haschisch *n*.

canned [kænd] *adj* **1.** Dosen..., Büchsen...: ~ **fruit** Obstkonserven *pl*; ~ **meat** Büchsenfleisch *n*. **2.** F ~ **music** Musik *f* aus der Konserve; ~ **program(me)** (*Rundfunk, TV*) Programmkonserve *f*. **3.** *sl.* blau, betrunken.

can·ni·bal [ˈkænɪbl] *s* Kannibale *m*, Menschenfresser *m*. **can·ni·bal·ism** [ˈbəlɪzəm] *s* Kannibalismus *m*. **ˌcan·ni·bal·is·tic** *adj* (**~ally**) kannibalisch. **ˈcan·ni·bal·ize** *v/t Auto etc* ausschlachten.

can·non [ˈkænən] *pl* **-nons** *s* ✕ (✔ Bord)Kanone *f*, (-)Geschütz *n*. **can·non·ade** [ˌneɪd] *s* ✕ Kanonade *f*. **ˈcan·non·ball** *s* Kanonenkugel *f*. ~ **fod·der** *s* Kanonenfutter *n*.

can·not [ˈkænɒt] kann *etc* nicht.

can·ny [ˈkænɪ] *adj* □ schlau, gerissen.

ca·noe [kəˈnuː] *s* Kanu *n*, Paddelboot *n*: **paddle one's own** ~ *fig.* auf eigenen Beinen *od.* Füßen stehen. **II** *v/i* paddeln.

can·on [ˈkænən] *s* **1.** Kanon *m* (*a. eccl.*),

Regel *f.* **2.** Grundsatz *m.* **3.** ♪ Kanon *m.*

can·on·i·za·tion [ˌnaɪˈzeɪʃn] *s eccl.* Heiligsprechung *f.* **'can·on·ize** *v/t* heiligsprechen.

can·on law *s* Kirchenrecht *n.*

ca·noo·dle [kəˈnuːdl] *v/i sl.* knutschen, schmusen (**with** mit).

can·o·py [ˈkænəpɪ] *s* **1.** Baldachin *m* (*a.* △). **2.** △ Vordach *n.* **3.** ✈ Kabinenhaube *f.*

cant¹ [kænt] **I** *s* **1.** Schrägung *f.* **2.** Neigung *f.* **II** *v/t* **3.** kanten, kippen: **~ over** umkippen. **4.** ⊙ abschrägen. **III** *v/i* **5.** *a.* **~ over** umkippen.

cant² [~] **I** *s* **1.** Jargon *m.* **2.** Kauderwelsch *n.* **3.** (leere) Phrase(n *pl.*) *f.* **II** *v/i* **4.** Jargon reden. **5.** Phrasen dreschen.

can't [kɑːnt] F → **cannot.**

can·tan·ker·ous [kænˈtæŋkərəs] *adj* □ giftig, streitsüchtig.

can·teen [kænˈtiːn] *s* **1.** *bsd. Br.* Kan'tine *f.* **2.** ✕ Feldflasche *f;* Kochgeschirr *n.* **3.** Erfrischungsstand *m.* **4.** Besteckkasten *m;* Besteck *n.*

can·ter [ˈkæntə] **I** *s* Kanter *m:* **win at a ~** *fig.* mühelos siegen. **II** *v/i* kantern.

can·ti·le·ver [ˈkæntɪliːvə] *s* **1.** △ Konsole *f.* **2.** ⊙ Ausleger *m.*

can·vas [ˈkænvəs] *s* **1.** Segeltuch *n.* **2.** Zeltleinwand *f.* **3.** *paint.* Leinwand *f.*

can·vass [ˈkænvəs] **I** *v/t* **1.** eingehend erörtern *od.* prüfen. **2.** *pol.* um *Stimmen* werben. **3.** † *Geschäftsbezirk* bereisen; *Aufträge* hereinholen, *Abonnenten, Inserate* sammeln. **II** *v/i* **4.** *pol.* e-n Wahlfeldzug veranstalten. **5.** † werben (**for** um, für); e-n Werbefeldzug durchführen. **III** *s* **6.** eingehende Erörterung *od.* Prüfung. **7.** *pol.* Wahlfeldzug *m.* **8.** † Werbefeldzug *m.* **'can·vass·er** *s* **1.** *pol.* Stimmenwerber *m.* **2.** † Handelsvertreter *m.*

can·yon [ˈkænjən] *s* Cañon *m.*

caou·tchouc [ˈkaʊtʃʊk] *s* Kautschuk *m.*

cap [kæp] **I** *s* **1.** Mütze *f,* Kappe *f,* Haube *f:* **~ in hand** demütig, unterwürfig; **set one's ~ at** (*od.* **for**) *s.o.* F j-n zu angeln suchen (*Frau*). **2.** ⊙ (Schutz-, Verschluß)Kappe *f,* (Abdeck-, Schutz-) Haube *f;* Deckel *m.* **II** *v/t* **3.** *Flasche etc* verschließen. **4.** krönen: a) oben liegen auf (*dat*), b) *fig.* abschließen. **5.** *fig.* übertreffen, -trumpfen: **~ everything** allem die Krone aufsetzen, alles über-

treffen; **to ~ it all** als Krönung des Ganzen.

ca·pa·bil·i·ty [ˌkeɪpəˈbɪlətɪ] *s* **1.** Fähigkeit *f* (**of** zu). **2.** *a. pl* Befähigung *f,* Begabung *f.* **ca·pa·ble** [ˈ~bl] *adj* □ **1.** fähig, tüchtig. **2.** fähig (**of** zu *od. gen:* **~ of doing** zu tun), imstande (**of doing** zu tun). **3.** **be ~ of s.th.** et. zulassen: **~ of being divided** teilbar.

ca·pa·cious [kəˈpeɪʃəs] *adj* □ **1.** geräumig (*Saal, Tasche etc*), groß (*Flasche, Topf etc*). **2.** aufnahmefähig (*Verstand*). **ca·pac·i·tate** [kəˈpæsɪteɪt] *v/t* befähigen. **ca'pac·i·tor** [~tə] *s* ⚡ Kondensator *m.* **ca'pac·i·ty I** *s* **1.** (Raum)Inhalt *m;* Fassungsvermögen *n,* Kapazität *f* (*a.* ⚡): **~** ganz voll, *thea. etc* ausverkauft; → **measure** 1. **2.** (*a.* ⚡, ⊙ Leistungs)Fähigkeit *f.* **3.** *fig.* Auffassungsgabe *f:* **that is beyond his ~** das ist zu hoch für ihn. **4.** Eigenschaft *f,* Stellung *f:* **in his ~ as** in s-r Eigenschaft als. **II** *adj* **5.** Höchst..., maximal. **6.** **~ audience** *thea. etc* ausverkauftes Haus.

cape¹ [keɪp] *s* Kap *n,* Vorgebirge *n.*

cape² [~] *s* Cape *n,* Umhang *m.*

ca·per¹ [ˈkeɪpə] *s* Kaper *f:* **~ sauce** Kapernsoße *f.*

ca·per² [~] **I** *s* Kapriole *f:* a) Freudensprung, Luftsprung *m:* **cut ~s** → II, b) übermütiger Streich. **II** *v/i* Freuden- *od.* Luftsprünge machen; herumtollen, -hüpfen.

cap·il·lar·y [kəˈpɪlərɪ] **I** *adj* haarförmig, -fein: **~ vessel** → II. **II** *s anat.* Kapillargefäß *n.*

cap·i·tal¹ [ˈkæpɪtl] *s* △ Kapitell *n.*

cap·i·tal² [~] **I** *s* **1.** Hauptstadt *f.* **2.** Großbuchstabe *m.* **3.** † Kapital *n:* **make ~ (out) of** → **capitalize** 3. **II** *adj* **4.** Kapital...: **~ crime** Kapitalverbrechen *n;* **~ error** Kapitalfehler *m;* **~ punishment** Todesstrafe *f.* **5.** Haupt..., wichtigst: **~ city** → 1. **6.** großartig: **a ~ fellow** ein Prachtkerl. **7.** **~ letter** → 2; **~ B** großes B.

cap·i·tal|as·sets *s pl* † Kapitalvermögen *n;* (*Bilanz*) Anlagevermögen *n.* **~ flight** *s* Kapitalflucht *f.* **~ goods** *s pl* Investitionsgüter *pl.* **'~-in,ten·sive** *adj* □ kapitalintensiv. **~ in·vest·ment** *s* Kapitalanlage *f.*

cap·i·tal·ism [ˈkæpɪtəlɪzəm] *s* Kapitalismus *m*. **'cap·i·tal·ist I** *s* Kapitalist *m*. **II** *adj* kapitalistisch. **,cap·i·tal'is·tic** *adj* (*∼ally*) kapitalistisch. **'cap·i·tal·ize I** *v/t* **1.** ✝ kapitalisieren. **2.** groß schreiben. **II** *v/i* **3.** *∼ on* Kapital schlagen aus.

cap·i·tal mar·ket *s* ✝ Kapitalmarkt *m*.

Cap·i·tol ['kæpɪtl] *s* Kapitol *n* (*Kongreßhaus in Washington*).

ca·pit·u·late [kə'pɪtʃʊleɪt] *v/i* ⚔ kapitulieren (**to** vor *dat*) (*a. fig.*). **ca,pit·u'la·tion** *s* Kapitulation *f*.

ca·price [kə'priːs] *s* **1.** Laune *f*. **2.** Launenhaftigkeit *f*. **ca·pri·cious** [kə'prɪʃəs] *adj* (*∼ly*) launisch, launenhaft, kapriziös.

Cap·ri·corn ['kæprɪkɔːn] *s ast.* Steinbock *m*.

cap·size [kæp'saɪz] **I** *v/i* kentern. **II** *v/t* zum Kentern bringen.

cap·sule ['kæpsjuːl] *s allg.* Kapsel *f*.

cap·tain ['kæptɪn] **I** *s* **1.** (An)Führer *m*: *∼ of industry* Industriekapitän *m*. **2.** ✕ Hauptmann *m*. **3.** ⚓ (✈ Flug)Kapitän *m*. **4.** *Sport:* (Mannschafts)Kapitän *m*, Mannschaftsführer *m*. **II** *v/t* **5.** Kapitän (*gen*) sein, *Schiff a.* befehligen.

cap·tion ['kæpʃn] *s* **1.** Überschrift *f*. **2.** Bildunterschrift *f*, -text *m*; (*Film*) Untertitel *m*.

cap·tious ['kæpʃəs] *adj* □ kritt(e)lig, spitzfindig.

cap·ti·vate ['kæptɪveɪt] *v/t fig.* gefangennehmen, fesseln. **'cap·tive I** *adj* gefangen (*a. fig.* **to** von), in Gefangenschaft: *hold ∼* gefangenhalten (*a. fig.*); *take ∼* gefangennehmen (*a. fig.*); *∼ balloon* Fesselballon *m*. **II** *s* Gefangene *m, f* (*a. fig.* **to, of** *gen*).

cap·ture ['kæptʃə] **I** *v/t* **1.** fangen, gefangennehmen. **2.** ✕ erobern (*a. fig.*); erbeuten. **3.** ⚓ kapern, aufbringen. **4.** *Stimmung* einfangen. **II** *s* **5.** Gefangennahme *f*. **6.** ✕ Eroberung *f* (*a. fig.*); Erbeutung *f*. **7.** ⚓ Kapern *n*, Aufbringen *n*; Beute *f*, Prise *f*.

car [kɑː] *s* **1.** Auto *n*, Wagen *m*: *by ∼* mit dem Auto. **2.** 🚋 *Am. allg.* Wagen *m*, Waggon *m*, *Br.* (*nur in Zssgn*) Personenwagen *m*: *→ dining car, etc.* **3.** (*Straßenbahn- etc*)Wagen *m*; Gondel *f* (*e-s Ballons etc*); Kabine *f* (*e-s Aufzugs*).

ca·rafe [kə'ræf] *s* Karaffe *f*.

car·a·mel ['kærəmel] *s* **1.** Karamel *m*. **2.** Karamelle *f* (*Bonbon*).

car·at ['kærət] *s* Karat *n*: *18-∼ gold* 18karätiges Gold.

car·a·van ['kærəvæn] *s* **1.** Karawane *f*. **2.** Wohnwagen *m* (*von Schaustellern etc*); *Br.* Caravan *m*, Wohnwagen *m*, -anhänger *m*: *∼ site* (*od. park*) Platz *m* für Wohnwagen. **'car·a·van·(n)er** *s Br.* Caravaner *m*.

car·a·way ['kærəweɪ] *s* 🌿 Kümmel *m* (*a. Gewürz*).

car·bide ['kɑːbaɪd] *s* 🜹 Karbid *n*.

car·bine ['kɑːbaɪn] *s* Karabiner *m*.

car·bo·hy·drate [,kɑːbəʊ'haɪdreɪt] *s* 🜹 Kohle(n)hydrat *n*.

car bomb *s* Autobombe *f*.

car·bon ['kɑːbən] *s* **1.** 🜹 Kohlenstoff *m*: *∼ dioxide* Kohlendioxyd *n*; *∼ monoxide* Kohlenmonoxyd *n*. **2.** a) a. *∼ paper* Kohlepapier *n*, b) *a. ∼ copy* Durchschlag *m*. **car·bon·ate** ['∼bənɪt] *s* 🜹 Karbonat *n*, kohlensaures Salz. **car·bon·at·ed** ['∼bəneɪtɪd] *adj* kohlensäurehaltig. **car·bon·ic** [∼'bɒnɪk] *adj* kohlenstoffhaltig: *∼ acid* Kohlensäure *f*. **'car·bon·ize** *v/t u. v/i* verkohlen.

car·bu·ret·(t)er, **car·bu·ret·(t)or** [,kɑːbə'retə] *s mot.* Vergaser *m*.

car·case, **car·cass** ['kɑːkəs] *s* **1.** Kadaver *m, contp.* Leiche *f*. **2.** *humor.* Leichnam *m* (*Körper*). **3.** Rumpf *m* (*e-s ausgeweideten Tiers*): *∼ meat* frisches (*Ggs. konserviertes*) Fleisch. **4.** Gerippe *n*, Skelett *n* (*e-s Schiffs etc*).

car| cem·e·ter·y *s* Autofriedhof *m*. *∼* **chase** *s* Verfolgungsjagd *f* im Auto.

car·ci·no·gen·ic [,kɑːsɪnəʊ'dʒenɪk] *adj* ⚕ karzinogen, krebserzeugend.

car·ci·no·ma [,∼'nəʊmə] *pl* **-ma·ta** [∼mətə], **-mas** *s* Karzinom *n*, Krebsgeschwulst *f*.

card [kɑːd] *s* **1.** (*Spiel-, Post-, Visitenetc*)Karte *f*: *house of ∼s* Kartenhaus *n* (*a. fig.*); *have a ∼ up one's sleeve fig.* (noch) e-n Trumpf in der Hand haben; *at ∼s* beim Kartenspiel; *→ stack* 6. **2.** *pl* (Arbeits)Papiere *pl*: *get one's ∼s* entlassen werden. **'∼·board** *s* Karton *m*, Pappe *f*: *∼ box* Pappschachtel *f*, -karton *m*. *∼* **game** *s* Kartenspiel *n*.

car·di·ac ['kɑːdiæk] **I** *adj* ⚕, *anat., physiol.* Herz...: *∼ arrest* Herzstillstand *m*; *∼ pacemaker* Herzschrittmacher *m*. **II** *s pharm.* Herzmittel *n*.

car·di·gan ['kɑːdɪgən] *s* Strickjacke *f*.

car·di·nal ['kɑːdɪnl] **I** adj ☐ **1.** hauptsächlich, Haupt...: ~ *number* → 4. **2.** scharlachrot. **II** s **3.** eccl. Kardinal m. **4.** Kardinal-, Grundzahl f.

'**card**|**sharp·er** s Falschspieler m. ~ **trick** s Kartenkunststück n.

care [keə] **I** s **1.** Kummer m, Sorge f: *be free from* ~(**s**) keine Sorgen haben. ~ *Sorgfalt* f, Vorsicht f: *have a* ~! Br. ┣ paß (doch) auf!; *take* ~ vorsichtig sein, aufpassen; sich Mühe geben; darauf achten, nicht vergessen (*to do* zu tun; *that* daß); *take* ~! F mach's gut! **3.** Obhut f, Fürsorge f, Betreuung f: ~ *and custody* ⚖ Sorgerecht n; *take* ~ *of* aufpassen auf (*acc.*). **4.** (*Körperetc*)Pflege f. **II** v/i u. v/t **5.** sich sorgen (*about* über *acc*, um): *I couldn't* ~ *less* das ist mir völlig egal. **6.** ~ *for* sorgen für, sich kümmern um, betreuen. **7.** (*for*) Interesse haben (an *dat*), (*j-n, et.*) gern mögen: *I don't* ~ *for* ich mache mir nichts aus. **8.** *I don't* ~ *if* ich habe nichts dagegen *od.* es macht mir nichts aus, wenn; *I don't* ~ *if I do!* F von mir aus!

ca·reer [kə'rɪə] s **1.** Karriere f, Laufbahn f: *enter upon a* ~ e-e Laufbahn einschlagen; *make a* ~ *for o.s.* Karriere machen. **2.** Beruf m: ~ *diplomat* Berufsdiplomat m; ~ *girl* (*od. woman*) Karrierefrau f. **ca·reer·ist** [kə'rɪərɪst] s Karrieremacher m.

'**care·free** sorgenfrei.

care·ful ['keəful] adj ☐ **1.** vorsichtig, achtsam: *be* ~! paß auf!, gib acht!; *be* ~ *to do* darauf achten *od.* nicht vergessen zu tun. **2.** sorgfältig, gründlich. **3.** sorgsam, bedacht (*of, for, about* auf *acc*): *be* ~ *with Br.* sparsam umgehen mit. '**care·ful·ness** s **1.** Vorsicht f. **2.** Sorgfalt f, Gründlichkeit f.

care·less ['keəlɪs] adj ☐ **1.** nachlässig. **2.** unüberlegt. **3.** *be* ~ *of* nicht achten auf (*acc*), unachtsam umgehen mit. **4.** unvorsichtig, leichtsinnig. **5.** sorglos. '**care·less·ness** s **1.** Nachlässigkeit f. **2.** Unüberlegtheit f. **3.** Unvorsichtigkeit f, Leichtsinn m. **4.** Sorglosigkeit f.

ca·ress [kə'res] **I** s Liebkosung f. **II** v/t liebkosen, streicheln.

'**care**|**tak·er** **I** s Hausmeister m; (Hausetc)Verwalter m. **II** adj Interims...: ~ *government* geschäftsführende Re-

gierung. '~·**worn** adj abgehärmt.

'**car**|**fare** s *Am.* Fahrgeld n (*für Bus etc*). ~ **fer·ry** s Autofähre f.

car·go ['kɑːgəʊ] **I** pl **-go(e)s** s Ladung f, Fracht f. **II** adj Fracht...; Transport...

car·i·ca·ture ['kærɪkə,tjʊə] **I** s Karikatur f (*a. fig.*). **II** v/t karikieren. '**car·i·ca·tur·ist** s Karikaturist m.

car·i·es ['keəriːz] s ⚕ Karies f: a) Knochenfraß m, b) Zahnfäule f.

car·il·lon ['kærɪljən] s (Turm)Glockenspiel n.

car·i·ous ['keəriəs] adj ⚕ kariös, von Karies befallen.

'**car**|**jack** ⊙ Wagenheber m. '~·**load** s **1.** Wagenladung f. **2.** 🚂 *Am.* Waggonladung f.

car·mine ['kɑːmaɪn] adj karminrot.

car·nage ['kɑːnɪdʒ] s Blutbad n, Gemetzel n.

car·nal ['kɑːnl] adj ☐ fleischlich, sinnlich.

car·na·tion [kɑː'neɪʃn] s ♣ Nelke f.

car·ni·val ['kɑːnɪvl] s **1.** Karneval m, Fasching m. **2.** Volksfest n.

car·ni·vore ['kɑːnɪvɔː] s zo., ♣ Fleischfresser m. **car·niv·o·rous** [~'nɪvərəs] adj ☐ fleischfressend.

car·ol ['kærəl] **I** s Weihnachtslied n. **II** v/i pret u. pp **-oled**, *bsd. Br.* **-olled** Weihnachtslieder singen.

ca·rot·id [kə'rɒtɪd] s anat. Halsschlagader f.

car·ou·sel [,kærə'sel] s *bsd. Am.* Karussell n.

car own·er s Autobesitzer(in).

carp¹ [kɑːp] s ichth. Karpfen m.

carp² [~] v/i (herum)nörgeln, (-)kritteln (*at* an *dat*).

'**car**|**park** s *bsd. Br.* **1.** Parkplatz m. **2.** Parkhaus n. ~ **pas·sen·ger** s Autoinsasse m.

car·pen·ter ['kɑːpəntə] **I** s Zimmermann m, (Bau)Tischler m: ~'*s bench* Hobelbank f. **II** v/t u. v/i zimmern.

car·pet ['kɑːpɪt] **I** s **1.** Teppich m (*a. fig.*): *sweep* (*od. brush*) *under the* ~ *Br. fig. et.* unter den Teppich kehren. **II** v/t **2.** mit e-m Teppich auslegen. **3.** *bsd. Br.* F *j-n* zs.-stauchen. '~·**bag** s Reisetasche f.

car·pet·ing ['kɑːpɪtɪŋ] s **1.** Teppichstoff m, -material n. **2.** coll. Teppiche pl.

car·pet| **square** s Teppichfliese f. ~

sweep·er s Teppichkehrmaschine f. ~
tile s Teppichfliese f.

car| pool s 1. Fahrbereitschaft f, Fuhr-
park m. 2. Fahrgemeinschaft f. '~**port**
s Einstellplatz m (im Freien).

car·riage ['kærɪdʒ] s 1. Wagen m, Kutsche f. 2. 🚂 Br. (Personen)Wagen m. 3.
Beförderung f, Transport m. 4. 🚢
Transport-, Beförderungskosten pl,
Fracht(gebühr) f: ~ **free** (od. **paid**)
frachtfrei. 5. ⚙ Wagen m (e-r Schreibmaschine etc); Schlitten m (e-r Werk-
zeugmaschine). 6. (Körper)Haltung f: ~
of head Kopfhaltung f. '~**way** s Fahrbahn f.

car·ri·er ['kærɪə] s 1. Überbringer m, Bote m. 2. Spediteur m. 3. 🦠 Keimträger
m, (Krankheits)Überträger m. 4. Ge-
päckträger m (am Fahrrad); mot.
Dachgepäckträger m. 5. Transportbe-
hälter m. 6. Flugzeugträger m. 7. →
carrier pigeon. ~ bag s Br. Einkaufsbeutel m, -tasche f. ~ **pi·geon** s Brief-
taube f.

car·ri·on ['kærɪən] I s Aas n. II adj aas-
fressend, Aas...

car·rot ['kærət] s 1. 🥕 Karotte f, Mohrrübe f. 2. F a) pl rotes Haar, b) Rotkopf
m. '**car·rot·y** adj 1. gelbrot. 2. rothaarig.

car·ry ['kærɪ] I v/t 1. tragen. 2. bringen,
tragen, befördern: → **coal.** 3. Nachricht etc (über)bringen; Bericht etc
bringen (Medien). 4. mitführen, mit od.
bei sich tragen: ~ **s.th. in one's head**
fig. et. im Kopf haben. 5. fig. (an sich
od. zum Inhalt) haben: ~ **conviction**
überzeugen(d sein od. klingen); ~
weight Gewicht od. Bedeutung haben
(**with** bei). 6. fig. nach sich ziehen, zur
Folge haben: ~ **interest** Zinsen tragen.
7. fig. treiben: ~ **s.th. too far** (od. **to
excess**) et. übertreiben od. zu weit treiben. 8. fig. erreichen, durchsetzen;
parl. Antrag etc durchbringen: **be carried** durchgehen. 9. a) → **carry off** 3, b)
siegreich hervorgehen aus (e-r Wahl
etc): → **day** 2. 10. Mineralien etc führen. 11. 🚢 Ware führen. II v/i 12. weit
tragen, reichen (Stimme, Schußwaffe
etc).
Verbindungen mit Adverbien:

car·ry| a·bout v/t herumtragen: ~ **with
one** mit sich herumtragen, Paß etc bei

sich haben. ~ **a·way** v/t 1. weg-, forttragen. 2. wegreißen (Sturm etc), (Flut etc
a.) wegspülen. 3. fig. mitreißen. ~
for·ward v/t 🚢 Summe, Saldo vor-,
übertragen. ~ **off** v/t 1. weg-, forttragen. 2. wegraffen (Krankheit). 3. Preis
etc erringen, gewinnen. ~ **on** I v/t 1.
fortführen, -setzen. 2. Geschäft betreiben. II v/i 3. weitermachen (**with** mit).
4. F e-e Szene machen (**about** wegen). ~
out v/t Plan etc aus-, durchführen,
Drohung wahrmachen. ~ **o·ver** →
carry forward. ~ **through** v/t aus-,
durchführen.

car·ry| all s bsd. Am. Reisetasche f.
'~**cot** s Br. (Baby)Tragetasche f. '~**on**
🚢 I s Bordcase n, m. II adj: ~ **baggage**
(bsd. Br. **luggage**) Bordgepäck n.
'~**out** → **takeaway.**

'**car| sick** adj: **she gets easily** ~ ihr wird
beim Autofahren leicht übel od.
schlecht. ~ **sick·ness** s Übelkeit f beim
Autofahren. ~ **stick·er** s Autoaufkle-
ber m.

cart [kɑːt] s 1. Karren m: **put the ~ before the horse** fig. das Pferd beim
Schwanz aufzäumen. 2. (Hand)Wagen
m.

car·tel [kɑː'tel] s 🚢 Kartell n.

car·ti·lage ['kɑːtɪlɪdʒ] s anat. Knorpel m.

'**cart·load** s Fuhre f.

car·tog·ra·pher [kɑː'tɒɡrəfə] s Karto-
graph(in). **car'tog·ra·phy** s Kartographie f.

car·ton ['kɑːtən] s (Papp)Karton m,
(-)Schachtel f; Tüte f (Milch); Stange f
(Zigaretten).

car·toon [kɑː'tuːn] s 1. Cartoon m, n,
Karikatur f. 2. Zeichentrickfilm m. 3.
Cartoon m, n, Bilderforsetzungsge-
schichte f. **car'toon·ist** s Cartoonist m,
Karikaturist m.

car·tridge ['kɑːtrɪdʒ] s 1. ✠ Patrone f. 2.
phot. (Film)Patrone f, (-)Kassette f. 3.
Tonabnehmer m (e-s Plattenspielers).
4. Patrone f (e-s Füllhalters). ~ **case** s
Patronenhülse f.

'**cart·wheel** s 1. Wagenrad n. 2. Sport:
Rad n: **turn ~s** radschlagen. 3. Am. F
Silberdollar m.

carve [kɑːv] v/t 1. (in) Holz schnitzen,
(in) Stein meißeln: ~ **out of stone** aus
Stein meißeln od. hauen; ~ **one's name
on a tree** s-n Namen in e-n Baum

schnitzen. **2.** (mit Schnitzereien) verzieren. **3.** *Fleisch etc* zerlegen, tranchieren. **'carv·er** s **1.** (Holz)Schnitzer m, Bildhauer m. **2.** Tranchiermesser n: (*pair of*) **~s** pl Tranchierbesteck n. **'carv·ing** s **1.** Schnitzen n, Meißeln n. **2.** Schnitzerei f. **3.** Tranchieren n: **~ knife** Tranchiermesser n.

car wash s **1.** Autowäsche f. **2.** Waschanlage f, -straße f.

cas·cade [kæ'skeɪd] s Kaskade f, (*bsd. mehrstufiger*) Wasserfall.

case¹ [keɪs] **I** s **1.** Kiste f, Kasten m. **2.** *allg.* Behälter m: a) Schachtel f, b) (*Brillen- etc*)Etui n, (-)Futteral n, c) (*Schreib- etc*)Mappe f, d) (*Kissen*)Bezug m, Überzug m. **3.** ⊕ Verkleidung f, Mantel m. **II** v/t **4.** in ein Futteral etc stecken. **5.** ⊕ verkleiden, ummanteln.

case² [~] s Fall m (a. ✍, ⚖): **it is a ~ of** es handelt sich um; **in any ~** auf jeden Fall, jedenfalls; **in no ~** auf keinen Fall, keinesfalls; **in ~ (that)** falls; **in ~ of** im Falle von (*od. gen*); **in ~ of need** nötigenfalls, im Notfall.

'case|·book s ✍ Patientenbuch n. **'~·hard·ened** adj fig. hartgesotten. **~ his·to·ry** s **1.** *bsd.* ✍ ⚖ Vorgeschichte f (*e-s Falls*). **2.** ✍ Krankengeschichte f.

case·ment ['keɪsmənt] s Fensterflügel m: **~ (window)** Flügelfenster n.

case stud·y s *sociol.* Fallstudie f.

cash [kæʃ] **I** s **1.** (Bar)Geld n. **2.** ✝ Barzahlung f, Kasse f: **for ~, ~ down** gegen bar od. Barzahlung; **in ~** bar; **~ in advance** gegen Vorauszahlung; **~ with order** zahlbar bei Bestellung; **be in (out of) ~** (nicht) bei Kasse sein; **short of ~** knapp bei Kasse; **→ delivery** 1. **II** v/t a. **~ in 3.** *Scheck etc* einlösen. **a.** Geld machen. **III** v/i **5. ~ in on** F profitieren von; ausnutzen. **~ and car·ry** s *econ.* Cash-and-carry-Geschäft n. **~ cheque** s ✝ Br. Barscheck m. **~ desk** s Kasse f (*im Warenhaus etc*). **~ dis·count** s ✝ Barzahlungsrabatt m. **~ dis·pens·er** s *bsd. Br.* Geldautomat m.

cash·ier [kæ'ʃɪə] s Kassierer(in): **~'s desk** (*od. office*) Kasse f.

cash·less ['kæʃlɪs] adj bargeldlos.

cash ma·chine s *bsd. Am.* Geldautomat m.

cash·mere [kæʃ'mɪə] s Kaschmir(wolle f) m.

cash| pay·ment s Barzahlung f. **~ price** s Bar(zahlungs)preis m. **~ vouch·er** s Kassenbeleg m, -zettel m.

cas·ing ['keɪsɪŋ] s **1.** → **case¹** 3. **2.** (*Fenster-, Tür*)Futter n. **3.** (*Wurst*)Haut f.

ca·si·no [kə'siːnəʊ] pl **-nos** s Kasino n.

cask [kɑːsk] s Faß n.

cas·ket ['kɑːskɪt] s **1.** Schatulle f, Kästchen n. **2.** *bsd. Am.* Sarg m.

cas·se·role ['kæsərəʊl] s Kasserolle f.

cas·sette [kə'set] s (*Film- etc*)Kassette f. **~ deck** s Kassettendeck n. **~ ra·di·o** s Radiorecorder m. **~ re·cord·er** s Kassettenrecorder m.

cas·sock ['kæsək] s *eccl.* Soutane f.

cast [kɑːst] **I** s **1.** Wurf m. **2.** *thea. etc* Besetzung f: a) Rollenverteilung f, b) Ensemble n. **3.** Schattierung f, Anflug m (*a. fig.*). **4.** ⊕ Guß(form f) m; Abdruck m. **5.** ✍ Gips(verband) m. **6.** Typ m, Gattung f. **II** v/t (*irr*) **7.** werfen: → **die²** 1, **doubt** 5, **light¹** 1, **spell³** 2. **8.** *Angel, Netz etc* auswerfen. **9.** *zo.* Haut, Gehörn abwerfen. **10.** *Stimmzettel, Stimme* abgeben: → **vote** 2. **11.** Blick werfen (**at, on** auf *acc*): Schatten etc werfen (**on** auf *acc*). **12.** ⊕ *Metall, Statue etc* gießen, formen. **13.** *thea. etc Stück etc* besetzen; *Rollen* verteilen (**to** an *acc*). **III** v/i (*irr*) **14.** sich werfen (*Holz*).

Verbindungen mit Adverbien:

cast| a·bout, ~ a·round v/i: **~ for** suchen (nach), *fig. a.* sich umsehen nach. **~ a·side** v/t **1.** *Möbel etc* ausrangieren, *Kleidung a.* ablegen. **2.** *Gewohnheit etc* ablegen, *Freund etc* fallenlassen. **~ a·way** v/t wegwerfen. **~ down** v/t **1.** entmutigen: **be ~** niedergeschlagen *od.* deprimiert sein. **2.** *Augen* niederschlagen. **~ off** v/t **1.** *Kleidung* ablegen, ausrangieren. **2.** *Freund etc* fallenlassen. **~ out** v/t verstoßen, vertreiben (*from* aus), *Dämonen etc* austreiben. **~ up** v/t **1.** *Augen* aufschlagen. **2.** zs.-zählen, ausrechnen.

'cast·a·way I s et. Ausrangiertes, *bsd.* abgelegtes Kleidungsstück. **II** adj ausrangiert (*Möbel etc*), (*Kleidung a.*) abgelegt.

caste [kɑːst] s **1.** Kaste f. **2.** gesellschaftliche Stellung, Ansehen n.

cas·ter → **castor**.

cas·ti·gate ['kæstɪgeɪt] v/t **1.** züchtigen.

2. scharf kritisieren. **,cas·ti'ga·tion** s **1.** Züchtigung f. **2.** scharfe Kritik (*of* an *dat*).

cast·ing ['kɑːstɪŋ] **I** s **1.** ⚙ Guß(stück n) m. **2.** → **cast** 2a. **II** adj **3.** Wurf... **4.** entscheidend (*Stimme*).

cast| i·ron s ⚙ Gußeisen n. **,~'i·ron** adj **1.** gußeisern. **2.** *fig.* eisern (*Wille, Konstitution*), hieb- u. stichfest (*Alibi*).

cas·tle ['kɑːsl] **I** s **1.** Burg f; Schloß n: **build ~s in the air** (*od.* **in Spain**) *fig.* Luftschlösser bauen. **2.** *Schach:* Turm m. **II** v/i **3.** *Schach:* rochieren.

cas·tling ['kɑːslɪŋ] s *Schach:* Rochade f.

,cast|·'off adj abgelegt, ausrangiert (*Kleidungsstück*). '**~off** s abgelegtes *od.* ausrangiertes Kleidungsstück.

cas·tor ['kɑːstə] s **1.** Laufrolle f. **2.** (*Salzetc*)Streuer m. **~ oil** s Rizinusöl n.

cas·trate [kæ'streɪt] v/t kastrieren. **cas'tra·tion** s Kastrierung f, Kastration f.

cast steel s ⚙ Gußstahl m.

cas·u·al ['kæʒʊəl] adj □ **1.** zufällig. **2.** gelegentlich: **~ customer** Laufkunde m; **~ labo(u)rer** Gelegenheitsarbeiter m. **3.** nachlässig (*Bemerkung*), flüchtig (*Blick*). **4.** lässig (*Art etc*). **5.** sportlich, salopp (*Kleidung*): **~ wear** Freizeitkleidung f.

cas·u·al·ty ['kæʒʊəltɪ] s **1.** Unfall m. **2.** Verunglückte m, f; ⚔ Verwundete m, Gefallene m: **casualties** pl Opfer pl (*e-r Katastrophe etc*), ⚔ mst Verluste pl. **3.** a. **~ ward** (*od.* **department**) Unfallstation f.

cat [kæt] s **1.** *zo.* Katze f: **let the ~ out of the bag** die Katze aus dem Sack lassen; **play ~ and mouse with** Katz u. Maus spielen mit; **it is raining ~s and dogs** es gießt in Strömen; **see which way the ~ jumps** sehen, wie der Hase läuft. **2.** *fig.* Katze f, falsches Frauenzimmer: **old ~** boshafte Hexe.

cat·a·comb ['kætəkuːm] s mst pl Katakombe f.

cat·a·logue, Am. a. **cat·a·log** ['kætəlɒg] **I** s **1.** Katalog m. **2.** (*univ. Am. Vorlesungs*)Verzeichnis n, (*Preis- etc*)Liste f. **II** v/t **3.** katalogisieren.

ca·tal·y·sis [kə'tæləsɪs] s 🧪 Katalyse f. **cat·a·lyst** ['kætəlɪst] s Katalysator m (a. *fig.*). **cat·a·lyt·ic** [,kætə'lɪtɪk] adj ka-

talytisch (a. *fig.*): **~ converter** mot. Katalysator m.

,cat-and-'dog adj: **lead a ~ life** wie Hund u. Katze leben.

cat·a·pult ['kætəpʌlt] **I** s Katapult n, m: **~ seat** ✈ Schleudersitz m. **II** v/t katapultieren.

cat·a·ract ['kætərækt] s **1.** Katarakt m, Wasserfall m. **2.** 🩺 grauer Star.

ca·tarrh [kə'tɑː] s 🩺 Katarrh m.

ca·tas·tro·phe [kə'tæstrəfɪ] s Katastrophe f. **cat·a·stroph·ic** [,kætə'strofɪk] adj (**~ally**) katastrophal.

cat| bur·glar s Fassadenkletterer m. '**~call I** s Buh(ruf m) n; Pfiff m. **II** v/i buhen; pfeifen. **III** v/t ausbuhen; -pfeifen.

catch [kætʃ] **I** s **1.** Fangen n. **2.** Fang m, Beute f (*beide a. fig.*). **3.** ⚙ Haken m (*a. fig.*), (*Tür*)Klinke f; Verschluß m (*e-r Brosche etc*). **II** v/t (irr) **4.** *allg.* fangen; Blick, Flüssigkeit auffangen, Tier etc (ein)fangen: → **sight 2.** **5.** kriegen, bekommen, erwischen. **6.** *j-n* einholen. **7.** erwischen, ertappen (**s.o. at s.th.** bei et.): **~ s.o. lying** j-n bei e-r Lüge ertappen; **~ me (doing that)!** Br. F denkste! → **nap** 1, **unawares. 8.** a. *fig.* packen, ergreifen, erfassen: → **hold 1. 9.** sich *e-e Krankheit etc* holen, sich *e-e Erkältung etc* zuziehen: **~ (a) cold** sich erkälten; **~ it** sl. sein Fett (ab)kriegen; → **fire 1. 10.** *fig.* **~ the ear** ans Ohr dringen; **~ the eye** ins Auge fallen; **~ s.o.'s eye** (*od.* **attention**) j-s Aufmerksamkeit auf sich lenken. **11.** verstehen, mitkriegen. **12.** *Gewohnheit, Aussprache* annehmen. **13.** hängenbleiben *od.* sich verfangen mit et. (**in** in *dat*): **my fingers were caught in the door** ich klemmte mir die Finger in der Tür. **III** v/i (irr) **14.** **~ at** greifen *od.* schnappen nach, *Gelegenheit* ergreifen. **15.** einschnappen, -rasten (*Schloß etc*); klemmen, festsitzen. **16.** sich verfangen, hängenbleiben (**on** an *dat*; **in** in *dat*). **17.** anspringen (*Motor*).

Verbindungen mit Adverbien:

catch| on v/i F **1. ~ to s.th.** et. kapieren. **2.** Anklang finden, einschlagen. **~ out** v/t ertappen; überführen. **~ up I** v/t **1.** Br. einholen (a. *bei der Arbeit*). **2.** **be caught up in** vertieft sein in (*acc*); verwickelt sein in (*acc*). **II** v/i **3.** aufholen:

Zeit. **~ heat·ing** s Zentralheizung f.

cen·tral·ize ['sentrəlaız] v/t u. v/i (sich) zentralisieren.

cen·tral‖ lock·ing s mot. Zentralverrieg(e)lung f. **~ nervous system** s physiol. Zentralnervensystem n. **~ reserve** s Br. Mittelstreifen m (e-r Autobahn). **~ sta·tion** s Hauptbahnhof m.

cen·tre ['sentə] **I** s **1.** Mitte f, a. fig. Zentrum n, Mittelpunkt m: **in** (od. **at**) **the ~** in der Mitte; **~ of gravity** phys. Schwerpunkt m; **be the ~ of interest** im Mittelpunkt des Interesses stehen. **2.** Fußball: Flanke f. **II** v/t **3.** fig. konzentrieren (**on** auf acc). **4.** ⊙ zentrieren. **III** v/i **5.** fig. sich konzentrieren (**in**, **on** auf acc), sich drehen (**round** um). **6.** Fußball: flanken. **~ for·ward** s Sport: Mittelstürmer(in).

cen·trif·u·gal [sen'trɪfjʊgl] adj □ phys. zentrifugal: **~ force** Flieh-, Zentrifugalkraft f. **cen·tri·fuge** ['-fjuːdʒ] s ⊙ Zentrifuge f.

cen·tu·ry ['sentʃʊrɪ] s Jahrhundert n.

ce·ram·ic [sɪ'ræmɪk] **I** adj **1.** keramisch. **II** s **2.** Keramik f, pl a. keramische Erzeugnisse pl. **3.** pl (mst sg konstruiert) Keramik f (Technik).

ce·re·al ['sɪərɪəl] **I** adj **1.** Getreide... **II** s **2.** Getreidepflanze f. **3.** Getreide n. **4.** Getreideflocken pl, Frühstückskost f (aus Getreide).

cer·e·bel·lum [ˌserɪ'beləm] s anat. Kleinhirn n.

cer·e·bral ['serɪbrəl] adj anat. Gehirn...: **~ death** ⚕ Hirntod m.

cer·e·brum ['serɪbrəm] s anat. Großhirn n.

cer·e·mo·ni·al [ˌserɪ'məʊnjəl] **I** adj □ **1.** zeremoniell, feierlich. **2. →** ceremonious 2, 3. **II** s **3.** Zeremoniell n. **cer·e·mo·ni·ous** adj □ **1.** feierlich. **2.** förmlich. **3.** rituell. **4.** umständlich.

cer·e·mo·ny ['serɪmənɪ] s **1.** Zeremonie f, Feier(lichkeit) f: **master of ceremonies** Zeremonienmeister m; thea. etc bsd. Am. Conférencier m. **2.** Förmlichkeit(en pl) f: **without ~** ohne Umstände; **→ stand on** 2.

cert [sɜːt] s Br. F sichere Sache: **it's a dead ~ that** es ist todsicher, daß.

cer·tain ['sɜːtn] adj **1.** sicher: a. (mst von Sachen) bestimmt: **it is ~ to happen** es wird mit Sicherheit geschehen; **for ~**

mit Sicherheit, b) (mst von Personen) überzeugt: **make ~ of** sich (gen) vergewissern; sich et. sichern; **make ~ (that)** dafür sorgen, daß, c) zuverlässig. **2.** (ganz) bestimmt: **a ~ day. 3.** gewiß: **a ~ Mr Brown; for ~ reasons** aus bestimmten Gründen. **'cer·tain·ly** adv **1.** sicher, bestimmt. **2.** Antwort: aber sicher, natürlich. **'cer·tain·ty** s Sicherheit f, Bestimmtheit f: **it is a ~ that** es ist sicher, daß.

cer·tif·i·cate I s [sə'tɪfɪkət] **1.** Bescheinigung f, Attest n: **~ of (good) conduct** Führungszeugnis n. **2.** ped. Zeugnis n. **3.** Gutachten n. **II** v/t [sə'tɪfɪkeɪt] **4.** et. bescheinigen. **5.** j-m e-e Bescheinigung od. ein Zeugnis geben: **~d** (amtlich) zugelassen; diplomiert. **cer·ti·fy** ['sɜːtɪfaɪ] v/t **1.** bescheinigen, attestieren: **this is to ~ that** hiermit wird bescheinigt, daß. **2.** beglaubigen. **3.** amtlich für geisteskrank erklären.

cer·ti·tude ['sɜːtɪtjuːd] s Sicherheit f, Bestimmtheit f.

ces·sa·tion [se'seɪʃn] s Aufhören n, Einstellung f.

ces·sion ['seʃn] s Abtretung f.

cess‖pit ['sespɪt], **'~·pool** s Senkgrube f.

chafe [tʃeɪf] **I** v/t **1.** warmreiben, frottieren. **2.** auf-, durchreiben, wund reiben. **3.** fig. ärgern, reizen. **II** v/i **4.** (sich durch)reiben, scheuern. **5.** fig. sich ärgern (**at, against** über acc).

chaff [tʃɑːf] s Spreu f: **→ wheat.**

cha·grin ['ʃægrɪn] **I** v/t verdrießen. **II** s Verdruß m.

chain [tʃeɪn] **I** s allg. Kette f (a. fig.): **~ of evidence** Beweiskette; **~ of mountains** Gebirgskette. **II** v/t (an)ketten (**to** an acc): **~ (up)** Hund an die Kette legen. **~ re·ac·tion** s phys. Kettenreaktion f (a. fig.). **~ smok·er** s Kettenraucher(in). **~ store** s Kettenladen m.

chair [tʃeə] **I** s **1.** (Am. F elektrischer) Stuhl, Sessel m: **on a ~** auf e-m Stuhl; **in a ~** in e-m Sessel; **take a ~** Platz nehmen. **2.** fig. Vorsitz m: **be in the ~** den Vorsitz führen. **3.** univ. Lehrstuhl m (**of** für). **II** v/t **4.** bestimmen. **5.** den Vorsitz führen bei: **~ed by** unter dem Vorsitz von (od. gen). **~ lift** s Sessellift m.

chair·man ['tʃeəmən] s (irr man) Vorsitzende m. **'chair·man·ship** s Vorsitz m: **under the ~ of** unter dem Vorsitz von (*od. gen*). '**chair,wom·an** *s* (*irr wom-an*) Vorsitzende *f*.

chal·ice ['tʃælɪs] *s eccl.* (Abendmahls-) Kelch *m*.

chalk [tʃɔːk] **I** *s* **1.** Kreide *f*: (**as**) **different** (*od. like*) **as ~ and cheese** verschieden wie Tag u. Nacht. **II** *v/t* **2.** mit Kreide markieren. **3. ~ out** *Plan etc* entwerfen, skizzieren.

chal·lenge ['tʃælɪndʒ] **I** *s* **1.** Herausforderung *f* (**to** *gen od.* an *acc*) (*a. fig.*): **~ cup** (*bsd. Sport*) Wanderpokal *m*. **2.** (schwieriger *od.* reizvolle) Aufgabe. **3.** ⚖ Ablehnung *f*. **II** *v/t* **4.** herausfordern. **5.** ⚖ *Geschworenen, Richter* ablehnen. **6.** *j-n* fordern *od.* reizen (*Aufgabe*). **7.** stark anzweifeln, in Frage stellen. **chal·leng·er** *s bsd. Sport:* Herausforderer *m.* '**chal·leng·ing** *adj* □ **1.** herausfordernd. **2.** schwierig; reizvoll (*Aufgabe*).

cham·ber ['tʃeɪmbə] *s* ⚙, *parl. etc* Kammer *f*: **~ of commerce** Handelskammer. '**~maid** *s* Zimmermädchen *n*. **~ mu·sic** *s* Kammermusik *f*. **~ pot** *s* Nachtgeschirr *n*, -topf *m*.

cha·me·le·on [kə'miːljən] *s zo.* Chamäleon *n*.

cham·fer ['tʃæmfə] **I** *s* **1.** △ Auskehlung *f*. **2.** ⚙ Abschrägung *f*. **II** *v/t* **3.** △ auskehlen. **4.** ⚙ abschrägen.

cham·ois ['ʃæmwɑː] *s* **1.** *zo.* Gemse *f*. **2.** *a.* **~ leather** [*mst* 'ʃæmɪ] Sämischleder *n*. **3.** Polier-, Fensterleder *n*.

champ¹ [tʃæmp] *v/i u. v/t* (heftig *od.* geräuschvoll) kauen: **~ at the bit** *fig.* ungeduldig sein, es kaum mehr erwarten können (**to do** zu tun).

champ² [~] F → **champion** 2.

cham·pagne [ʃæm'peɪn] *s* Champagner *m*; Sekt *m*.

cham·pi·on ['tʃæmpjən] **I** *s* **1.** Verfechter *m*, Fürsprecher *m* (**of** von *od.* gen). **2.** *Sport:* Meister *m*. **II** *v/t* **3.** verfechten, eintreten für. '**cham·pi·on·ship** *s Sport:* Meisterschaft *f*.

chance [tʃɑːns] **I** *s* **1.** Zufall *m*: **by ~** zufällig; **game of ~** Glücksspiel *n*. **2.** Möglichkeit *f*, Wahrscheinlichkeit *f*: **the ~s are that** es besteht Aussicht, daß. **3.** Chance *f*, (günstige) Gelegenheit; Aussicht *f* (**of** auf *acc*): **stand a ~** Aussichten *od.* e-e Chance haben. **4.** Risiko *n*: **take a ~** es darauf ankommen

lassen, es riskieren (**on** mit); **take no ~s** nichts riskieren (wollen). **II** *v/i* **5.** *I* **~d to meet her** ich traf sie zufällig. **6. ~ on** zufällig begegnen (*dat*) *od.* treffen (*acc*); zufällig stoßen auf (*acc*). **III** *v/t* **7.** riskieren: **~ missing him** es riskieren, ihn zu verfehlen; **~ it** F es darauf ankommen lassen. **IV** *adj* **8.** zufällig, Zufalls...

chan·cel·lor ['tʃɑːnsələ] *s pol.* Kanzler *m*: **C~ of the Exchequer** *Br.* Schatzkanzler *m*, Finanzminister *m*.

chanc·y ['tʃɑːnsɪ] *adj* F riskant.

chan·de·lier [,ʃændə'lɪə] *s* Kronleuchter *m*, Lüster *m*.

change [tʃeɪndʒ] **I** *v/t* **1.** (ver)ändern, verwandeln (**into** in *acc*): → **subject** 1. **2.** wechseln, (ver)tauschen: **~ one's shirt** ein anderes Hemd anziehen; **~ places with s.o.** mit j-m den Platz tauschen; **~ trains** (**planes**) umsteigen; → **hand** 1, **mind** 4. **3.** *Bettzeug etc* wechseln, *Bett* frisch beziehen, *Baby* wickeln. **4.** *Geld* (um)wechseln (**into** in *acc*). **5.** ⚙ *Teile* (aus)wechseln, *Öl* wechseln. **6.** *mot.*, ⚙ schalten: **~ over** umschalten; *Maschine, a. Industrie etc* umstellen (**to** auf *acc*); → **gear** 1. **II** *v/i* **7.** sich (ver)ändern, wechseln. **8.** sich verwandeln (**to, into** in *acc*). **9.** übergehen (**to** zu). **10.** sich umziehen (**for dinner** zum Abendessen). **11.** 🚂, ✈ umsteigen. **12.** wechseln, umspringen (**from ... to** von ... auf *acc*) (*Verkehrsampel*). **13.** *mot.*, ⚙ schalten: **~ up** (**down**) hinauf- (herunter)schalten; → **gear** 1. **III** *s* **14.** (Ver)Änderung *f*, Wechsel *m*, *weitS. a.* Umschwung *m*: **~ of air** Luftveränderung; **~ of life** *physiol.* Wechseljahre *pl*; **~ in weather** Witterungsumschlag *m*; → **scene** 1a. **15.** (Aus)Tausch *m*. **16.** *et.* Neues, Abwechslung *f*: **for a ~** zur Abwechslung. **17.** Wechselgeld *n*; Kleingeld *n*: **can you give me ~ for a pound?** können Sie mir auf ein Pfund herausgeben?; weitere *nur* ein Pfund wechseln?; → **small** I. '**change-a·ble** *adj* □ unbeständig: a) wankelmütig (*Person*), b) veränderlich (*Wetter*).

chan·nel ['tʃænl] *s* Kanal *m* (*a. fig.*), (*Rundfunk, TV a.*) Programm *n*: **switch ~s** umschalten; **through official ~s** auf dem Dienst- *od.* Instanzenweg.

chant [tʃɑːnt] **I** s 1. Gesang m. 2. Singsang m. 3. Sprechchor m. **II** v/t 4. singen. 5. herunterleiern. 6. in Sprechchören rufen.

cha·os ['keɪɒs] s Chaos n. **cha'ot·ic** adj (~ally) chaotisch.

chap¹ [tʃæp] **I** v/t Haut rissig machen. **II** v/i rissig werden, aufspringen. **III** s Riß m.

chap² [~] s F Bursche m, Kerl m.

chap·el ['tʃæpl] s Kapelle f.

chap·er·on ['ʃæpərəʊn] **I** s 1. Anstandsdame f. 2. Aufsichts-, Begleitperson f. **II** v/t 3. (als Anstandsdame) begleiten. 4. beaufsichtigen.

chap·fall·en ['tʃæpˌfɔːlən] adj niedergeschlagen, bedrückt.

chap·lain ['tʃæplɪn] s Kaplan m.

chapped [tʃæpt], **chap·py** ['tʃæpɪ] adj aufgesprungen, rissig.

chap·ter ['tʃæptə] s Kapitel n (a. fig.).

char¹ [tʃɑː] v/t u. v/i verkohlen.

char² [~] **I** s Br. F → **charwoman**. **II** v/i putzen: go out ~ring putzen gehen.

char·ac·ter ['kærəktə] **I** s 1. allg. Charakter m. 2. Ruf m, Leumund m. 3. Eigenschaft f, Stellung f: in one's ~ as in s-r Eigenschaft als. 4. Figur f, Gestalt f (e-s Romans etc), pl a. Charaktere pl. 5. Schriftzeichen n, Buchstabe m. **II** adj 6. Charakter...: ~ actor (study, etc); ~ assassination Rufmord m. ˌchar·ac·ter'is·tic **I** adj (~ally) charakteristisch (of für). **II** s charakteristisches Merkmal. 'char·ac·ter·ize v/t charakterisieren.

char·coal ['tʃɑːkəʊl] s Holzkohle f.

charge [tʃɑːdʒ] **I** v/t 1. Gewehr etc laden, Batterie etc (auf)laden. 2. beauftragen (with mit): ~ s.o. to be careful j-m einschärfen, vorsichtig zu sein. 3. (with) j-m (et.) zur Last legen od. vorwerfen, a. ⚖ j-n (e-r Sache) beschuldigen od. anklagen. 4. (with) ✝ j-n belasten (mit e-m Betrag), j-m (et.) in Rechnung stellen. 5. berechnen, verlangen, fordern (for für). 6. ✕ angreifen; stürmen. **II** v/i 7. ~ at losgehen auf (acc). **III** s 8. Ladung f (e-s Gewehrs etc). 9. Preis m; Forderung f; Gebühr f; a. pl Unkosten pl, Spesen pl: free of ~ kostenlos, gratis. 10. Beschuldigung f, a. ⚖ Anklage(punkt m) f: be on a ~ of murder unter Mordanklage stehen. 11. Verant-

wortung f: the person in ~ der od. die Verantwortliche; be in ~ of verantwortlich sein für, leiten (acc); be in (od. under) s.o.'s ~ von j-m betreut werden; take ~ of die Leitung od. Aufsicht (gen) übernehmen. 12. Schützling m, Mündel m, n; j-m anvertraute Sache. ~ ac·count s ✝ 1. Kundenkreditkonto n. 2. Abzahlungskonto n (bei Teilzahlungen).

char·gé d'af·faires [ˌʃɑːʒeɪdæˈfeə] pl **char·gés d'af·faires** [ˌ~ʒeɪz~] s Geschäftsträger m.

charg·er ['tʃɑːdʒə] s ⚡ Ladegerät n.

char·is·ma [kəˈrɪzmə] s Charisma n, Ausstrahlung(skraft) f. **char·is·mat·ic** [ˌkærɪzˈmætɪk] adj charismatisch.

char·i·ta·ble ['tʃærətəbl] adj □ 1. wohltätig, karitativ. 2. gütig, nachsichtig (to gegenüber). **char·i·ty** ['~tɪ] s 1. Nächstenliebe f. 2. Wohltätigkeit f. 3. Güte f, Nachsicht f. 4. Almosen n, milde Gabe.

char·la·tan ['ʃɑːlətən] s Scharlatan m. 'char·la·tan·ry s Scharlatanerie f.

char·ley horse ['tʃɑːlɪ] s Am. F Muskelkater m.

charm [tʃɑːm] **I** s 1. Charme m, Zauber m. 2. Zauber(formel f; -mittel n) m. 3. Talisman m, Amulett n. **II** v/t 4. bezaubern, entzücken: 5. verzaubern, Schlangen beschwören: ~ away wegzaubern, Sorgen etc zerstreuen. 'charm·er s 1. Zauberer m, Zauberin f. 2. reizvolles Geschöpf (Frau); Charmeur m. 'charm·ing adj □ charmant, bezaubernd.

chart [tʃɑːt] **I** s 1. (See-, Himmels-, Wetter)Karte f. 2. Diagramm n, Schaubild n, Kurve(nblatt n) f. 3. pl Charts pl, Hitliste(n pl) f. **II** v/t 4. auf e-r Karte etc einzeichnen od. verzeichnen.

char·ter ['tʃɑːtə] **I** s 1. Urkunde f. 2. Konzession f. 3. pol. Charta f. 4. Chartern n. **II** v/t 5. konzessionieren. 6. chartern: ~ed Charter... ~ flight s Charterflug m.

'char·wom·an s (irr woman) Putzfrau f, Raumpflegerin f.

char·y ['tʃeərɪ] adj □ 1. vorsichtig (in, of in dat, bei). 2. sparsam, zurückhaltend (of mit).

chase¹ [tʃeɪs] **I** v/t 1. jagen, Jagd machen auf, (a. fig. e-m Traum etc) nachjagen;

F *e-m Mädchen etc* nachlaufen. **2.** *hunt.* hetzen, jagen: **~ up** (*od.* **down**) *mst fig.* aufstöbern. **3.** *a.* **~ away** verjagen, -treiben. **II** *v/i* **4. ~ after s.o.** j-m nachjagen. **5.** F rasen, rennen. **III** *s* **6.** *hunt.* (Hetz-) Jagd *f*, *fig. a.* Verfolgung(sjagd) *f*: **give ~ to** verfolgen (*acc*), nachjagen (*dat*).

chase² [~] *v/t* ziselieren.

chas-er¹ ['tʃeɪsə] *s* Jäger *m*, Verfolger *m*.

chas-er² [~] *s* Ziseleur *m*.

chasm ['kæzəm] *s* **1.** Kluft *f*, Abgrund *m* (*a. fig.*). **2.** Schlucht *f*, Klamm *f*. **3.** Riß *m*, Spalte *f*. **4.** *fig.* Lücke *f*.

chas-sis ['ʃæsɪ] *pl* **-sis** ['~sɪz] *s* ✔, *mot.* Chassis *n*, Fahrgestell *n*.

chaste [tʃeɪst] *adj* □ **1.** keusch, züchtig. **2.** bescheiden, schlicht (*Mahl etc*).

chas-ten ['tʃeɪsn] *v/t* **1.** züchtigen. **2.** *fig.* läutern. **3.** *fig.* ernüchtern, nachdenklich stimmen.

chas-tise [tʃæ'staɪz] *v/t* **1.** züchtigen. **2.** *fig.* geißeln, scharf tadeln.

chas-ti-ty ['tʃæstətɪ] *s* **1.** Keuschheit *f*. **2.** Schlichtheit *f*.

chat [tʃæt] **I** *v/i* plaudern. **II** *v/t* **~ up** Br. F einreden auf (*acc*); sich ranmachen an (*ein Mädchen etc*), anquatschen. **III** *s* Plauderei *f*: **have a ~** plaudern.

chat show *s* Br. Talk-Show *f*.

chat-tels ['tʃætlz] *s pl* ⚖ bewegliches Eigentum: **→ good** 3.

chat-ter ['tʃætə] **I** *v/i* **1.** schnattern, schwatzen, plappern. **2.** klappern. **II** *s* **3.** Geschnatter *n*, Geplapper *n*. **4.** Klappern *n*. **'~box** *s* Plaudertasche *f*, Plappermaul *n*.

chat-ty ['tʃætɪ] *adj* □ **1.** geschwätzig, gesprächig. **2.** *fig.* wortreich, ausführlich; im Plauderton (geschrieben).

chauf-feur ['ʃəʊfə] **I** *s* Chauffeur *m*, Fahrer *m*. **II** *v/t* chauffieren, fahren: **~ed** mit Chauffeur.

chau-vi ['ʃəʊvɪ] *s* F Chauvi *m*. **'chau-vin-ism** *s* Chauvinismus *m*: **male ~** männlicher Chauvinismus. **'chau-vin-ist** *s* Chauvinist *m*: **male ~** männlicher Chauvinist; **male ~ pig** F a) *contp.* Chauvinschwein *n*, b) *humor.* Chauvi *m*. **,chau-vin'ist-ic** *adj* (**~ally**) chauvinistisch.

cheap [tʃiːp] **I** *adj* □ **1.** billig, Billig... **2.** billig, minderwertig. **3.** schäbig, gemein: **feel ~** sich schäbig vorkommen. **II** *adv* **4.** billig: **buy s.th. ~**. **III** *s* **5.** *on*

the **~** billig. **'cheap-en** *v/t u. v/i* (sich) verbilligen. **'cheap-ness** *s* Billigkeit *f*. **'cheap-skate** *s* F Knicker *m*, Geizkragen *m*.

cheat [tʃiːt] **I** *s* **1.** Betrüger(in), Schwindler(in). **2.** Betrug *m*, Schwindel *m*. **II** *v/t* **3.** betrügen (*of, out of* um). **III** *v/i* **4.** betrügen, schwindeln. **5. ~ on** F *s-e Frau etc* betrügen. **'cheat-ing** *adj*: **~ pack** Mogelpackung *f*.

check [tʃek] **I** *s* **1.** Schach(stellung *f*) *n*: **give ~** Schach bieten; **hold** (*od.* **keep**) **in ~** *fig.* in Schach halten. **2.** Hemmnis *n*, Hindernis *n* (*on* für). **3.** Einhalt *m*: **give a ~ to** Einhalt gebieten (*dat*). **4.** Kontrolle *f*, Überprüfung *f*: **keep a ~ on** unter Kontrolle halten (*acc*). **5.** *Am.* Häkchen *n* (*auf Liste etc*). **6.** ✝ *Am.* Scheck *m* (*for* über *acc*). **7.** *bsd. Am.* Kassenzettel *m*, Rechnung *f*. **8.** Kontrollabschnitt *m*, -schein *m*. **9.** *bsd. Am.* Garderobenmarke *f*; Gepäckschein *m*. **10.** Schachbrett-, Karomuster *n*; Karo *n*, Viereck *n*; karierter Stoff. **11.** *Poker etc*: Spielmarke *f*: **pass** (*od.* **hand**) **in one's ~s** *Am.* F den Löffel weglegen (*sterben*). **II** *v/t* **12.** Schach bieten (*dat*). **13.** hemmen, hindern. **14.** ⚙ drosseln, bremsen (*a. fig.*). **15.** zurückhalten, zügeln: **~ o.s.** sich beherrschen. **16.** checken, kontrollieren, überprüfen (*for auf acc hin*). **17.** *Am. auf Liste etc* abhaken. **18.** *bsd. Am.* (zur Aufbewahrung *od.* in der Garderobe) abgeben; (*als Reisegepäck*) aufgeben. **19.** *a.* **~ out** *Am.* Geld mittels Scheck abheben. **III** *v/i* **20.** (plötzlich) innehalten, stutzen. **21.** *Am.* e-n Scheck ausstellen (*for* über *acc*). *Verbindungen mit Adverbien:*

check| **back** *v/i* rückfragen (*with* bei). **~ in** *v/i* **1.** sich (*in e-m Hotel*) anmelden. **2.** einstempeln. **3.** ✔ (*a. v/t*) einchecken. **~ off → check** 17. **~ out I** *v/i* **1. →** *check* 19. **2.** sich erkundigen nach, sich informieren über (*acc*). **II** *v/i* **3.** *aus e-m Hotel* abreisen. **4.** ausstempeln. **~ up** *v/i*: **~ on** *et.* nachprüfen, *et.*, *j-n* überprüfen.

'check|-back *s* Rückfrage *f*. **'~book** *s* *Am.* Scheckbuch *n*, -heft *n*. **~ card** *s* *Am.* Scheckkarte *f*.

checked [tʃekt] *adj* kariert: **~ pattern** Karomuster *n*.

check-er¹ ['tʃekə] *s* **1.** *Am.* a) (Dame)Stein *m*, b) *pl* (*sg konstruiert*) Dame(spiel) *n*) *f*. **2.** Karomuster *n*.

check·er² [~] *s bsd. Am.* **1.** Kassiererin *f* (*bsd. im Supermarkt*). **2.** Garderobenfrau *f*. **3.** 🚉 Angestellte *m*, *f* in e-r Gepäckaufbewahrung.

'**check·er·board** *s Am.* Schach-, Damebrett *n*.

ohcck·crcd ['tʃckəd] *adj* **1.** kariert. **2.** bunt (*a. fig.*). **3.** *fig.* wechselvoll, bewegt (*Geschichte etc*).

'**check·in** *s* **1.** Anmeldung *f* (*in e-m Hotel*). **2.** Einstempeln *n*. **3.** *fig.* Einchecken *n*: ~ *counter* Abfertigungsschalter *m*.

check·ing ac·count ['tʃekɪŋ] *s* 🇹 *Am.* Girokonto *n*.

check| list *s* Check-, Kontrolliste *f*. '**~·mate** I *s* (Schach)Matt *n*, Mattstellung *f*. II *v/t* (schach)matt setzen (*a. fig.*). '**~·out** *s* **1.** Abreise *f* (*aus e-m Hotel*): ~ (*time*) Zeit, zu der ein Hotelzimmer geräumt sein muß. **2.** Ausstempeln *n*. **3.** *a.* ~ *counter* Kasse *f* (*bsd. im Supermarkt*): ~ *point* s Kontrollpunkt *m* (*an der Grenze*). '**~·room** *s bsd. Am.* **1.** 🚉 Gepäckaufbewahrung(sstelle) *f*. **2.** Garderobe(nraum *m*) *f* '**~·up** *s* **1.** Überprüfung *f*. **2.** 🩺 Check-up *m*, Vorsorgeuntersuchung *f*.

cheek [tʃiːk] I *s* **1.** Backe *f* (*a.* ⚙), Wange *f*: *be ~ by jowl* Tuchfühlung haben (*with* mit) (*a. fig.*). **2.** *F* Frechheit *f*. II *v/t* **3.** F frech sein zu. '**~·bone** *s* Backenknochen *m*.

cheek·y ['tʃiːkɪ] *adj* □ F frech (*to* zu).

cheep [tʃiːp] I *v/i u. v/t* piepsen. II *s* Piepsen *n*; Pieps(er) *m* (*a. fig.*).

cheer [tʃɪə] I *s* **1.** Beifall(sruf *m*), Hoch(ruf *m*) *n*: *give three ~s for s.o.* j-n dreimal hochleben lassen. **2.** Auf-, Ermunterung *f*, Aufheiterung *f*: *words pl of ~* aufmunternde Worte *pl*; *~s!* → *cheerio*. **3.** (gute) Laune: *be of good ~* guter Laune *od.* Dinge sein. II *v/t* **4.** Beifall spenden (*dat*), hochleben lassen. **5.** *a.* ~ *on* anspornen, anfeuern. **6.** *a.* ~ *up* auf-, ermuntern, aufheitern. III *v/i* **7.** Beifall spenden, jubeln. **8.** *mst* ~ *up* Mut fassen, (wieder) fröhlich werden: ~ *up!* Kopf hoch!, laß den Kopf nicht hängen! **cheer·ful** ['~fʊl] *adj* □ **1.** fröhlich (*a. Lied etc*), vergnügt. **2.** freundlich (*Raum, Wetter etc*).

cheer·i·o [,tʃɪərɪ'əʊ] *int bsd. Br.* F **1.** mach's gut!, tschüs! **2.** prost!

'**cheer,lead·er** *s Sport:* Einpeitscher *m*.

cheer·less ['tʃɪəlɪs] *adj* □ **1.** freudlos. **2.** unfreundlich (*Raum, Wetter etc*). '**cheer·y** *adj* □ fröhlich, vergnügt.

cheese [tʃiːz] *s* Käse *m*: *say ~!* *phot.* bitte recht freundlich!; *hard ~! sl.* Künstlerpech!; *the ~ sl.* genau das Richtige. '**~·cake** *s* **1.** *ein* Käsekuchen *m*. **2.** *sl.* Zurschaustellung *f* weiblicher Reize (*bsd. auf Fotografien*). '**~,par·ing** *s* Knauserei *f*. II *adj* knaus(e)rig. '**~ spread** *s* Streichkäse *m*.

chees·y ['tʃiːzɪ] *adj* käsig.

chef [ʃef] *s* Küchenchef *m*.

chem·i·cal ['kemɪkl] I *adj* □ chemisch: ~ *fiber* (*bsd. Br. fibre*) Chemie-, Kunstfaser *f*; ~ *warfare* chemische Kriegsführung. II *s* Chemikalie *f*.

chem·ist ['kemɪst] *s* **1.** Chemiker(in). **2.** *Br.* Apotheker(in); Drogist(in): *~'s shop* Apotheke *f*; Drogerie *f*. '**chem·is·try** *s* Chemie *f*.

chem·o·ther·a·py [,kiːməʊ'θerəpɪ] *s* 🩺 Chemotherapie *f*.

cheque [tʃek] *s* 🇹 *Br.* Scheck *m*. ~ **ac·count** *s* 🇹 *Br.* Girokonto *n*. '**~·book** *s Br.* Scheckbuch *n*, -heft *n*. '**~ card** *s* Scheckkarte *f*.

cheq·uer, cheq·uer·board, cheq·uered *bsd. Br.* → *checker¹, checkerboard, checkered.*

cher·ish ['tʃerɪʃ] *v/t* **1.** j-s Andenken in Ehren halten. **2.** *Gefühle* hegen. **3.** festhalten an (*dat*).

che·root [ʃə'ruːt] *s* Stumpen *m* (*Zigarre ohne Spitzen*).

cher·ry ['tʃerɪ] I *s* **1.** 🌸 Kirsche *f*. II *adj* kirschrot. ~ **bran·dy** *s* Cherry Brandy *m*, Kirschlikör *m*.

cher·ub ['tʃerəb] *pl* **-ubs**, **-u·bim** ['~əbɪm] *s* **1.** Cherub *m*, Engel *m*. **2.** geflügelter Engelskopf.

chess [tʃes] *s* Schach(spiel) *n*. '**~·board** *s* Schachbrett *n*. '**~·man** *s* (*irr man*), **piece** *s* Schachfigur *f*.

chest [tʃest] *s* **1.** Kiste *f*, Kasten *m*; Truhe *f*: ~ *of drawers*) Kommode *f*. **2.** *anat.* Brust(kasten *m*) *f*: *get s.th. off one's* ~ F sich etc. von der Seele reden.

chest·nut ['tʃesnʌt] I *s* **1.** 🌰 Kastanie *f*: *pull the ~s out of the fire (for s.o.) fig.* (für j-n) die Kastanien aus dem Feuer holen. **2.** F alte *od.* olle Kamelle, alter Witz. **II** *adj* **3.** kastanienbraun.

chest·y ['tʃestɪ] *adj* F **1.** mit viel Holz vor der Hütte (*vollbusig*). **2.** tiefsitzend (*Husten*).

chev·ron ['ʃevrən] *s* ✕ Winkel *m* (*Rangabzeichen*).

chew [tʃuː] **I** *v/t* **1.** (zer)kauen: **~ one's nails** an den Nägeln kauen; → **cud** 1, **fat** 3. **II** *v/i* **2.** kauen: **~ on** herumkauen auf (*dat*). **3.** nachsinnen, grübeln (*on, over* über *acc*).

chew·ing gum ['tʃuːɪŋ] *s* Kaugummi *m, n.*

chic [ʃiːk] **I** *s* Schick *m*, Eleganz *f.* **II** *adj* schick, elegant.

chick [tʃɪk] *s* **1.** Küken *n*, junger Vogel. **2.** F Kleine(s) (*Kind; oft Anrede*). **3.** *sl.* Biene *f*, Puppe *f* (*Mädchen*).

chick·en ['tʃɪkɪn] **I** *s* **1.** Küken *n* (*a.* F *junge Person*), Hühnchen *n*, Hähnchen *n*: **she's no ~** F sie ist (auch) nicht mehr die Jüngste. **2.** Huhn *n*. **3.** F Feigling *m.* **II** *adj* **4.** F feig. **III** *v/i* **5. ~ out** F kneifen (*of, on* vor *dat*). **~-broth** *s* Hühnerbrühe *f.* **~ farm·er** *s* Geflügelzüchter *m.* **~ feed** *s* **1.** Hühnerfutter *n.* **2.** *sl. contp.* ein paar Pfennige *pl, a.* Hungerlohn *m.* **'~-heart·ed**, **'~-liv·ered** *adj* furchtsam, feig. **~ pox** *s* 🩺 Windpocken *pl.*

chic·o·ry ['tʃɪkərɪ] *s* 🌿 Chicorée *f, a. m.*

chief [tʃiːf] **I** *s* **1.** (Ober)Haupt *n*, (An)Führer *m*, Chef *m*: **~ of the department** Abteilungsleiter *m*; **~ of state** Staatschef, -oberhaupt. **2.** Häuptling *m*: **~ of the tribe** Stammeshäuptling. **II** *adj* **3.** erst, oberst, Ober..., Haupt...: **~ designer** Chefkonstrukteur *m.* **4.** hauptsächlich, wichtigst. '**chief·ly** *adv* hauptsächlich, vor allem.

chif·fon ['ʃɪfɒn] *s* Chiffon *m.*

chil·blain ['tʃɪlbleɪn] *s* Frostbeule *f.*

child [tʃaɪld] *pl* **chil·dren** ['tʃɪldrən] *s* Kind *n*: **from a ~** von Kindheit an; **be a good ~!** sei artig *od.* brav!; **that's ~'s play** *fig.* das ist ein Kinderspiel. '**~-bed** *s*: **be in ~** im Wochenbett liegen; **~ fever** 🩺 Kindbettfieber *n.* **~ ben·e·fit** *s* Br. Kindergeld *n.* '**~-birth** *s* Geburt *f*, Niederkunft *f*, Entbindung *f.*

child·hood ['tʃaɪldhʊd] *s* Kindheit *f*: **from ~** von Kindheit an; → **second** 1 . **child·ish** ['tʃaɪldɪʃ] *adj* □ **1.** kindlich. **2.** kindisch.

child·less ['tʃaɪldlɪs] *adj* kinderlos.

'**child·like** *adj* kindlich. **~ mind·er** *s* Tagesmutter *f.* **~ prod·i·gy** *s* Wunderkind *n.* '**~-proof** *adj* kindersicher: **~ lock** *mot.* Kindersicherung *f.*

chil·dren ['tʃɪldrən] *pl von* **child**: **~'s clin·ic** Kinderklinik *f.*

chil·e ['tʃɪlɪ] *s*, **'chil·i** *pl* **-ies** *s* 🌿 Chili *m* (*a. Cayennepfeffer*): **~ sauce** Chili(soße *f*) *m.*

chill [tʃɪl] **I** *s* **1.** Kältegefühl *n*, Frösteln *n.* **2.** Kälte *f*, Kühle *f* (*beide a. fig.*): **take the ~ off** *et.* leicht anwärmen. **3.** Erkältung *f*: **catch a ~** sich erkälten. **4.** *fig.* gedrückte Stimmung: **cast** (*od.* **put**) **a ~ on** (*od.* **over**) → **II** *adj* **5.** kalt, frostig, kühl (*alle a. fig.*). **III** *v/i* **6.** abkühlen. **IV** *v/t* **7.** j-n frösteln lassen; abkühlen (lassen), *Lebensmittel etc* kühlen: **~ed meat** Kühlfleisch *n.* **8.** *fig.* abkühlen, dämpfen; entmutigen.

chil·li *pl* **-lies** → **chill**

chil·ly ['tʃɪlɪ] *adj* → **chill** 5: **feel ~** frösteln.

chime [tʃaɪm] **I** *s* **1.** *oft pl* Glockenspiel *n*, (Glocken)Geläute *n.* **2.** (Glocken-) Schlag *m.* **II** *v/i* **3.** läuten; ertönen; schlagen (*Uhr*). **4.** *fig.* harmonieren, übereinstimmen (*with* mit): **~ in** (ins Gespräch) einmischen, einfallen (*a.* ♪); **~ in with** zustimmen, beipflichten (*dat*); übereinstimmen mit. **III** *v/t* **5.** *Glocken* läuten; *die Stunde* schlagen.

chim·ney ['tʃɪmnɪ] *s* Schornstein *m*, Kamin *m.* '**~-piece** *s* Kaminsims *m, n.* **~ sweep** *s* Schornsteinfeger(in), Kaminkehrer(in).

chim·pan·zee [ˌtʃɪmpænˈziː] *s zo.* Schimpanse *m.*

chin [tʃɪn] **I** *s* Kinn *n*: **(keep your) ~ up!** F Kopf hoch!, halt die Ohren steif! **II** *v/t*: **~ o.s.** (*up*), **~ the bar** e-n Klimmzug machen. **III** *v/i Am.* F schwatzen, plappern.

chi·na ['tʃaɪnə] *s* **1.** Porzellan *n.* **2.** (Porzellan)Geschirr *n.* **2-man** ['~mən] *s* (*irr man*) *mst contp.* Chinese *m.* '**2-town** *s* Chinesenviertel *n.* '**~-ware** *s* Porzellan(waren *pl*) *n.*

Chi·nese [ˌtʃaɪˈniːz] **I** *s* **1.** Chinese *m*, Chinesin *f*: **the ~ pl** die Chinesen *pl.* **2.** *ling.* Chinesisch *n.* **II** *adj* **3.** chinesisch.

chink¹ [tʃɪŋk] *s* Riß *m*, Ritze *f*, Spalt *m*, Spalte *f.*

chug [tʃʌg] **I** s Tuckern n (des Motors). **II** v/i tuckern(d fahren).

chum [tʃʌm] F **I** s Kumpel m: *be great ~s* dicke Freunde sein. **II** v/i: *~ up with s.o.* enge Freundschaft mit j-m schließen.

chump [tʃʌmp] s **1.** Holzklotz m. **2.** dikkes Ende (e-r Hammelkeule etc). **3.** F Trottel m. **4.** Br. sl. Birne f (Kopf): *be off one's ~* e-n Vogel haben.

chunk [tʃʌŋk] s F (Holz)Klotz m; (dikkes) Stück: *a ~ of bread* ein Runken. **'chunk·y** adj F klobig, klotzig.

church [tʃɜːtʃ] **I** s Kirche f: *at (od. in) ~* in der Kirche; *go to ~* in die Kirche gehen. **II** adj Kirchen..., kirchlich. **'~-go·er** s Kirchgänger(in). **~ wed·ding** s kirchliche Trauung. **'~-yard** s Kirch-, Friedhof m.

churl [tʃɜːl] s **1.** Flegel m. **2.** Geizhals m. **'churl·ish** adj □ **1.** flegelhaft. **2.** geizig.

churn [tʃɜːn] **I** s **1.** Butterfaß n, -maschine f. **2.** Br. Milchkanne f. **II** v/t **3.** zu Butter verarbeiten. **4.** a. *~ up* Flüssigkeiten heftig schütteln, Wellen aufwühlen, peitschen. **III** v/i **5.** buttern. **6.** sich heftig bewegen.

chute [ʃuːt] s **1.** Stromschnelle f. **2.** Rutsche f (a. ⊙), Rutschbahn f. **3.** Müllschlucker m. **4.** F Fallschirm m.

chut·ney [ˈtʃʌtnɪ] s gastr. Chutney n (scharf gewürzte Paste aus Früchten).

ci·ce·ro·ne [ˌtʃɪtʃəˈrəʊnɪ] pl **-ni** [~niː], **-nes** s Cicerone m, Fremdenführer m.

ci·der [ˈsaɪdə] s (Am. hard~) Apfelwein m: (sweet) ~ Am. Apfelmost m, -saft m.

ci·gar [sɪˈgɑː] s Zigarre f. **~ cut·ter** s Zigarrenabschneider m.

cig·a·rette, Am. a. **cig·a·ret** [ˌsɪgəˈret] s Zigarette f. **~ case** s Zigarettenetui n. **~ end** s Zigarettenstummel m. **~ hold·er** s Zigarettenspitze f. **~ pa·per** s Zigarettenpapier n.

cig·a·ril·lo [ˌsɪgəˈrɪləʊ] pl **-los** s Zigarillo m, n.

ci·gar light·er s mot. Zigarren-, Zigarettenanzünder m.

cinch [sɪntʃ] s sl. todsichere Sache; Kinderspiel n.

cin·der [ˈsɪndə] s **1.** Schlacke f: *burnt to a ~* verkohlt, verbrannt. **2.** pl Asche f. **Cin·der·el·la** [ˌsɪndəˈrelə] s Aschenbrödel n, -puttel m (a. fig.).

cin·der track s Sport: Aschenbahn f.

cin·e·cam·er·a [ˈsɪnɪˌkæmərə] s (Schmal)Filmkamera f. **'cin·e·film** s Schmalfilm m.

cin·e·ma [ˈsɪnəmə] s **1.** bsd. Br. Kino n. **2.** Film(kunst f) m: *~-go·er* s bsd. Br. Kinobesucher(in).

cin·na·mon [ˈsɪnəmən] s Zimt m.

ci·pher [ˈsaɪfə] **I** s **1.** ℵ Null f (Ziffer). **2.** (arabische) Ziffer, Zahl f. **3.** fig. Null f (Person); Nichts n (Sache). **4.** Chiffre f: *in ~* chiffriert. **5.** fig. Schlüssel m (zu e-r Geheimschrift). **II** v/t **6.** chiffrieren, verschlüsseln.

cir·cle [ˈsɜːkl] **I** s **1.** (a. Familien-, Freundes- etc)Kreis m: *go (od. run) round in ~s* fig. sich im Kreis bewegen; → **vicious circle. 2.** thea. Rang m: *upper ~* zweiter Rang; → **dress circle. 3.** fig. Kreislauf m, Zyklus m. **II** v/t **4.** umringen. **5.** umkreisen. **6.** umzingeln. **7.** einringeln. **III** v/i **8.** kreisen (a. ✈), die Runde machen (a. Pokal etc).

cir·cuit [ˈsɜːkɪt] s **1.** Umfang m, Umkreis m. **2.** Runde f, Rundreise f, -flug m: *make (od. do) the (od. a) ~ of* die Runde od. e-e Rundreise machen in (dat). **3.** ⚡ Strom-, Schaltkreis m; Schaltung f, Schaltsystem n: → **closed 1, integrate Ia, short circuit. II** v/t **4.** umkreisen. **~ break·er** s ⚡ Unterbrecher m (a. mot.). **~ di·a·gram** s ⚡ Schaltplan m.

cir·cuit train·ing s Sport: Zirkel-, Circuittraining n.

cir·cu·i·tous [səˈkjuːɪtəs] adj □ **1.** gewunden (Flußlauf etc). **2.** fig. weitschweifig, umständlich.

cir·cu·lar [ˈsɜːkjʊlə] **I** adj □ **1.** (kreis)rund, kreisförmig. **2.** Kreis..., Rund...: *~ letter* → 4a; *~ saw* ⊙ Kreissäge f. **3.** → **circuitous 2. II** s **4.** a) Rundschreiben n, -brief m, b) Umlauf m, c) (Post)Wurfsendung f.

cir·cu·late [ˈsɜːkjʊleɪt] **I** v/i zirkulieren: a) kreisen, b) im Umlauf sein, kursieren (Geld, Nachricht etc). **II** v/t in Umlauf setzen (a. fig.), zirkulieren lassen. **'cir·cu·lat·ing** adj zirkulierend, kursierend: *~ library* Leihbücherei f. **ˌcir·cu·ˈla·tion** s **1.** (physiol. a. Blut)Kreislauf m, Zirkulation f. **2.** ✝ Umlauf m: *bring (od. put) into ~* in Umlauf setzen (a. fig.); *withdraw from ~* aus dem Verkehr ziehen; *out of ~* außer Kurs (ge-

819   claim

setzt). **3.** Auflage *f* (*e-r Zeitung etc*).
,cir·cu·la·to·ry *adj* ♥, physiol. (Blut-)
Kreislauf...: **~** *collapse* Kreislaufkol-
laps *m*; **~** *disturbances* *pl* Kreislaufstö-
rungen *pl*; **~** *system* Kreislauf *m*.
cir·cum·cise ['sɜ:kəmsaɪz] *v/t* ♥, eccl.
beschneiden. **cir·cum·ci·sion** [ˌ~'sɪʒn] *s*
Beschneidung *f*.
cir·cum·fer·ence [sə'kʌmfərəns] *s* A
Umfang *m*.
cir·cum·lo·cu·tion [ˌsɜ:kəmlə'kju:ʃn] *s* **1.**
Umschreibung *f*. **2.** Umschweife *pl*;
Weitschweifigkeit *f*.
cir·cum·nav·i·gate [ˌsɜ:kəm'nævɪgeɪt]
v/t umschiffen, umsegeln. **'cir·cum-**
,nav·i'ga·tion *s* Umschiffung *f*, Um-
seg(e)lung *f*: **~** *of the globe* Weltumseg-
lung.
cir·cum·scribe ['sɜ:kəmskraɪb] *v/t* **1.** begrenzen, einschränken. **2.** umschreiben
(*a.* A); definieren. **cir·cum·scrip·tion**
[ˌ~'skrɪpʃn] *s* **1.** Be-
grenzung *f*, Einschränkung *f*. **2.** Umschreibung *f*. **3.** Umschrift *f* (*e-r Münze*
etc).
cir·cum·spect ['sɜ:kəmspekt] *adj* □ **1.**
umsichtig. **2.** vorsichtig. **cir·cum-**
spec·tion [ˌ~'spekʃn] *s* **1.** Umsicht *f*. **2.**
Vorsicht *f*.
cir·cum·stance ['sɜ:kəmstəns] *s* **1.** Umstand *m*. **2.** meist *pl* (Sach)Lage *f*, Umstände *pl*: **in** (*od. under*) **no** ~s unter
keinen Umständen, auf keinen Fall; **in**
(*od. under*) **the** ~s unter diesen Umständen. **3.** *pl* Verhältnisse *pl*: **live in**
easy ~s in gesicherten Verhältnissen
leben. **cir·cum·stan·tial** [ˌ~'stænʃl] *adj*
□ **1.** umstandsbedingt. **2.** ausführlich.
3. umständlich. **4.** **~** *evidence* ♦♦ Indi-
zienbeweis *m*. **5.** nebensächlich.
cir·cus ['sɜ:kəs] *s* **1.** Zirkus *m*. **2.** *Br.*
runder, von Häusern umschlossener
Platz.
cir·rho·sis [sɪ'rəʊsɪs] *s* ♥ Zirrhose *f*.
cir·rus ['sɪrəs] *pl* **-ri** [ˌ~raɪ] *s* meteor. Zir-
rus-, Federwolke *f*.
cis·sy → *sissy.*
cis·tern ['sɪstən] *s* **1.** Wasserbehälter *m*,
(*in Toilette*) Spülkasten *m*. **2.** Zisterne *f*.
cit·a·del ['sɪtədəl] *s* ✕ Zitadelle *f*.
ci·ta·tion [saɪ'teɪʃn] *s* **1.** Zitieren *n*; Zitat
n. **2.** ♦♦ Vorladung *f*. **3.** ✕ lobende
Erwähnung *f*.

cite [saɪt] *v/t* **1.** zitieren. **2.** ♦♦ vorladen.
3. ✕ lobend erwähnen.
cit·i·zen ['sɪtɪzn] *s* **1.** Bürger(in). **2.** Städ-
ter(in). **3.** Staatsangehörige *m, f.*
'cit·i·zen·ship *s* Staatsangehörigkeit *f*.
cit·ric ac·id ['sɪtrɪk] *s* ♠ Zitronensäure *f*.
cit·rus ['sɪtrəs] *s* ♣ Zitrusgewächs *n*. **~**
fruit *s* Zitrusfrucht *f*.
cit·y ['sɪtɪ] *s* (Groß)Stadt *f*: **the** ♀ die
(Londoner) City. **~ cen·tre** *s Br.* Innenstadt *f*, City *f*. **~ fa·thers** *s pl* Stadtväter
pl. **~ hall** *s* Rathaus *n*. **~ plan·ning** *s*
Stadtplanung *f*. **~ state** *s* Stadtstaat *m*.
civ·ic ['sɪvɪk] **I** *adj* (~*ally*) **1.** → civil **2. 2.**
städtisch, Stadt... **II** *s pl* (*sg konstruiert*)
Staatsbürgerkunde *f*.
civ·il ['sɪvl] *adj* □ **1.** staatlich, Staats... **2.**
(*a.* staats)bürgerlich, Bürger... **3.** zivil,
Zivil... (*Ggs. militärisch, kirchlich etc*):
~ *aviation* Zivilluftfahrt *f*; **~** *marriage*
standesamtliche Traung. **4.** höflich. **5.**
♦♦ zivilrechtlich: **~** *case* (*od. suit*) Zivil-
prozeß *m*. **~ en·gi·neer** *s* Bauingenieur
m.
ci·vil·ian [sɪ'vɪljən] **I** *s* Zivilist *m*. **II** *adj*
zivil, Zivil...
civ·i·li·za·tion [ˌsɪvɪlaɪ'zeɪʃn] *s* Zivilisation *f*, Kultur *f*: *disease of* ~ ♥ Zivili-
sationskrankheit *f*. **'civ·i·lize** *v/t* zivilisieren: ~*d nations* *pl* Kulturvölker *pl*.
civ·il law *s* **1.** römisches Recht. **2.** Zivil-
recht *n*, bürgerliches Recht. **~ rights** *s*
pl bürgerliche Ehrenrechte *pl*,
(Staats)Bürgerrechte *pl*: **~** *activist* Bür-
gerrechtler(in); **~** *movement* Bürgerrechtsbewegung *f*. **~ ser·vant** *s* Staats-
beamte *m*. **~ ser·vice** *s* Staatsdienst *m*.
~ war *s* Bürgerkrieg *m*.
clack [klæk] **I** *v/i* **1.** klappern. **2.** plappern. **II** *s* **3.** Klappern *n*. **4.** Geplapper *n*.
clad [klæd] **I** *pret u. pp von* **clothe**. **II** *adj*
gekleidet.
claim [kleɪm] **I** *v/t* **1.** verlangen, *a. Todes-*
opfer etc fordern: **~** *back* zurückfor-
dern. **2.** in Anspruch nehmen, (er)for-
dern. **3.** behaupten (*s.th.* et.; *that* daß);
(von sich) behaupten (*to be* zu sein),
Anspruch erheben auf (*acc*); aufweisen
(können), haben; sich bekennen zu
(*e-m Terroranschlag etc*). **II** *s* **4.** Forderung *f* (*on, against* gegen): *make a* ~
e-e Forderung erheben. **5.** Anrecht *n*
(*to* auf *acc*): **~** *for damages* Schadener-

satzanspruch *m.* **6.** Behauptung *f.*
'claim·ant *s* **1.** Antragsteller(in): *right-
ful* ~ Anspruchsberechtigte *m, f.* **2.** An-
wärter(in) (*to* auf *acc*).
clair·voy·ance [kleə'vɔɪəns] *s* Hellsehen
n. **clair'voy·ant I** *adj* hellseherisch. **II** *s*
Hellseher(in).
clam [klæm] *s zo.* eßbare Muschel: *hard*
(*od. round*) ~ Venusmuschel.
clam·ber ['klæmbə] **I** *v/i* (mühsam) klettern. **II** *v/t* erklettern.
clam·my ['klæmɪ] *adj* □ feuchtkalt,
klamm.
clam·or·ous ['klæmərəs] *adj* □ **1.** lärmend. **2.** *fig.* lautstark (*Forderungen
etc*) **'clam·o(u)r I** *s* **1.** Lärm *m,* Geschrei *n.* **2.** *fig.* lautstarker Protest
(*against* gegen), *fordernder* Schrei (*for*
nach). **II** *v/i* **3.** lärmen, schreien. **4.** *fig.*
lautstark protestieren (*against* gegen),
lautstark verlangen (*for* nach).
clamp [klæmp] **I** *s* ⊕ Klemme *f,* Klammer *f.* **II** *v/t* festklemmen, mit Klammern befestigen. **III** *v/i:* ~ *down* F
scharf vorgehen (*on* gegen).
clan [klæn] *s* **1.** Clan *m:* a) *schott.* Stamm
m, b) *allg.* Sippe *f,* Geschlecht *n.* **2.**
Gruppe *f, bsd. contp.* Clique *f.*
clan·des·tine [klæn'destɪn] *adj* □ heimlich, verstohlen.
clang [klæŋ] **I** *v/i* klingen, klirren. **II** *v/t*
erklingen lassen. **III** *s* Klang *m,* Geklirr
n. **'clang·er** *s: drop a* ~ *Br.* F ins Fettnäpfchen treten. **clang·or·ous** ['klæŋ-
gərəs] *adj* □ klirrend.
clang·o(u)r ['klæŋə] → **clang** III.
clank [klæŋk] **I** *v/i u. v/t* klirren *od.* rasseln (mit). **II** *s* Geklirr *n,* Gerassel *n.*
clap¹ [klæp] **I** *s* **1.** (*a.* Hände-, Beifall)Klatschen *n.* **2.** Klaps *m.* **3.** Krachen *n:* ~ *of thunder* Donnerschlag *m.*
II *v/t* **4.** zs.-schlagen: ~ *one's hands* in
die Hände klatschen. **5.** *j-m* Beifall
klatschen, applaudieren, *a. et.* beklat-
schen. **6.** *j-m* auf die Schulter *etc* klopfen. **III** *v/i* **7.** klatschen. **8.** (Beifall)
klatschen, applaudieren.
clap² [~] *s* ♂ *sl.* Tripper *m.*
clap·per ['klæpə] *s* **1.** Klöppel *m* (*e-r
Glocke*). **2.** Klapper *f.*
'clap·trap *s* F **1.** Effekthascherei *f.* **2.**
Gewäsch *n.*
clar·et ['klærət] *s* roter Bordeaux(wein);
allg. Rotwein *m.*

clar·i·fi·ca·tion [ˌklærɪfɪ'keɪʃn] *s* **1.**
(Auf)Klärung *f,* Klarstellung *f.* **2.** ⊕
(Abwasser)Klärung *f,* Abklärung *f:* ~
plant Kläranlage *f.* **clar·i·fy** ['~faɪ] **I** *v/t*
1. (auf)klären, klarstellen. **2.** ⊕
(ab)klären. **II** *v/i* **3.** sich (auf)klären,
klar werden. **4.** sich (ab)klären.
clar·i·net [ˌklærə'net] *s* ♪ Klarinette *f.*
ˌclar·i'net·(t)ist *s* Klarinettist *m.*
clar·i·ty ['klærətɪ] *s* Klarheit *f.*
clash [klæʃ] **I** *v/i* **1.** prallen, stoßen (*into*
gegen), (*a. feindlich*) zs.-prallen, -sto-
ßen (*with* mit). **2.** *fig.* (*with*) kollidieren:
a) im Widerspruch stehen (zu), unver-
einbar sein (mit), b) (zeitlich) zs.-fallen
(mit). **3.** nicht zs.-passen (*with* mit),
(*Farben a.*) sich beißen. **II** *s* **4.** (*a. feindlicher*) Zs.-prall *od.* -stoß, Kollision *f*
(*a. fig.*): ~ *of interests* Interessenkolli-
sion. **5.** *fig.* Widerspruch *m.* **6.** (zeitli-
ches) Zs.-fallen.
clasp [klɑːsp] **I** *v/t* **1.** ein-, zuhaken, zu-
festschnallen. **2.** ergreifen, umklam-
mern: ~ *s.o.'s hand* j-m die Hand drük-
ken; j-s Hand umklammern; ~ *one's
hands* die Hände falten. **II** *s* **3.** Haken
m, Schnalle *f;* Schloß *n,* Schließe *f* (*e-r
Handtasche etc*). **4.** Umklammerung *f:*
by ~ *of hands* durch Händedruck *od.*
Handschlag. ~ *knife s* (*irr knife*)
Klapp-, Taschenmesser *n.*
class [klɑːs] **I** *s* **1.** Klasse *f* (*a.* 🐎, *biol.
etc*). **2.** (Wert-, Güte)Klasse *f; engS.* F
Klasse *f* (*Erstklassigkeit*): *in the same
~ with* gleichwertig mit; *in a ~ by o.s.*
(*od. of one's own*) e-e Klasse für sich;
have ~ F (große) Klasse sein. **3.** gesell-
schaftlicher Rang, soziale Stellung;
(Gesellschafts)Klasse *f,* (Bevölke-
rungs)Schicht *f.* **4.** *ped.* (Schul)Klasse *f;*
(Unterrichts)Stunde *f:* *attend* ~*es* am
Unterricht teilnehmen. **II** *v/t* **5.** klassifizieren: ~ *with* gleichstellen mit; ~ *as*
ansehen *od.* betrachten als. ~ **con·flict** *s*
Klassenkonflikt *m.* **'~ˌcon·scious** *adj*
klassenbewußt. ~ **dis·tinc·tion** *s* Klas-
senunterschied *m.* '~ˌfel·low *s* Klassen-
kamerad(in), Mitschüler(in). ~ **ha·tred**
s Klassenhaß *m.* ~ **hour** *s ped.* Unter-
richtsstunde *f.*
clas·sic ['klæsɪk] **I** *adj* (~*ally*) **1.** klassisch, vollendet: ~ *example* klassisches
Beispiel. **2.** klassisch: a) *das klassische
Altertum betreffend,* b) *die klassische*

Literatur etc betreffend. **3.** klassisch: a) herkömmlich, b) typisch, c) zeitlos. **II** *s* **4.** Klassiker *m* (*Person u. Werk*). **5.** *pl* Altphilologie *f*. **clas·si·cal** ['∼kl] *adj* □ **1.** → **classic** I. **2.** klassisch: a) humanistisch (gebildet), b) *die klassische Kunst od. Literatur betreffend:* ∼ **education** humanistische Bildung; **the** ∼ **languages** die alten Sprachen; ∼ **scholar** Altphilologe *m*. **3.** klassisch (*Musik*).

clas·si·fi·ca·tion [,klæsıfı'keıʃn] *s* Klassifikation *f*, Klassifizierung *f*. **clas·si·fied** ['∼faıd] *adj* **1.** klassifiziert: ∼ **ad(vertisement)** Kleinanzeige *f*; ∼ **directory** Branchenverzeichnis *n*. **2.** ⚔, *pol.* geheim. **clas·si·fy** ['∼faı] *v/t* **1.** klassifizieren. **2.** ⚔, *pol.* für geheim erklären.

class|·less ['klɑːslıs] *adj* klassenlos (*Gesellschaft*). **'∼·mate** → **classfellow**. **∼·room** ['∼rʊm] *s* Klassenzimmer *n*. ∼ **strug·gle,** ∼ **war** *s* Klassenkampf *m*. **class·y** ['klɑːsı] *adj* F Klasse, Klasse...

clat·ter ['klætə] **I** *v/i* **1.** klappern, rasseln. **2.** poltern: ∼ **about** (*od. around*) herumtrampeln. **II** *v/t* **3.** klappern *od.* rasseln mit. **III** *s* **4.** Geklapper *n*, Gerassel *n*.

clause [klɔːz] *s* **1.** *ling.* Satz(teil) *m*. **2.** ⚖ Klausel *f*; Abschnitt *m*, Absatz *m*.

claus·tro·pho·bi·a [,klɔːstrə'fəʊbjə] *s* ⚕ Klaustrophobie *f*, Platzangst *f*.

clav·i·cle ['klævıkl] *s anat.* Schlüsselbein *n*.

claw [klɔː] **I** *s* **1.** Klaue *f*, Kralle *f* (*beide a.* ⚙ *u. fig.*), Schere *f* (*e-s Krebses etc*). **II** *v/t* **2.** zerkratzen. **3.** umkrallen, packen. **III** *v/i* **4.** kratzen. **5.** reißen, zerren (*at an dat*). **6.** greifen (*at, for* nach).

clay [kleı] *s* Ton *m*, Lehm *m*: ∼ **pigeon** (*Sport*) Ton-, Wurftaube *f*. **clay·ey** ['∼ı] *adj* Ton..., Lehm...

clean [kliːn] **I** *adj* □ **1.** rein, sauber: → **breast** I, **heel²** 1, **sweep** 1. **2.** sauber, frisch (gewaschen). **3.** unvermischt, rein. **4.** makellos (*a. fig.*): ∼ **record** tadellose Vergangenheit. **5.** anständig, sauber: ∼ **living!** bleib sauber! **6.** glatt (*Schnitt, Bruch*). **7.** *sl.* clean (*nicht mehr drogenabhängig*). **8.** *sl.* sauber (*unbewaffnet*). **II** *adv* **9.** rein, sauber: **sweep** ∼ rein ausfegen; → **broom.** **10.** völlig, total. **III** *v/t* **11.** reinigen, säubern, putzen: ∼ **down** (*od. up*) gründlich reini-

gen. ∼**·cut** *adj* klar (umrissen), deutlich.

clean·er ['kliːnə] *s* **1.** *pl* Reinigung(sanstalt) *f*: **take to the** ∼**s** zur Reinigung bringen; F *j-n* ausnehmen. **2.** Rein(e)-machefrau *f*, (*Fenster- etc*)Putzer *m*. **'clean·ing I** *s*: **do the** ∼ saubermachen, putzen. **II** *adj* Reinigungs...: ∼ **cloth;** ∼ **woman** (*od. lady*) Rein(e)machefrau *f*.

clean·li·ness ['klenlınıs] *s* Reinlichkeit *f*. **'clean·ly** *adj* reinlich: a) sauber, b) sauberkeitsliebend.

clean·ness ['kliːnnıs] *s* Reinheit *f*, Sauberkeit *f*.

cleanse [klenz] *v/t* reinigen, säubern, reinwaschen (*from, of* von) (*alle a. fig.*). **'cleans·er** *s* Reinigungsmittel *n*. **,clean·'shav·en** *adj* glattrasiert.

clear [klıə] *adj* (□ → *clearly*) **1.** klar, hell. **2.** klar, heiter (*Wetter etc*). **3.** klar, rein, hell (*Stimme etc*). **4.** klar, verständlich, deutlich: **make s.th.** ∼ (**to s.o.**) (j-m) et. klarmachen; **make o.s.** ∼ sich klar ausdrücken, sich verständlich machen. **5.** klar, unvermischt: ∼ **soup** *gastr.* klare Suppe. **6.** deutlich, scharf (*Foto, Umrisse etc*). **7.** klar, offensichtlich: **a** ∼ **win** ein klarer Sieg; **for no** ∼ **reason** ohne ersichtlichen Grund. **8.** klar: a) sicher, b) in Ordnung. **9.** frei (*of* von) (*a. fig.*): ∼ **of snow** (*debt*) schneefrei (schuldenfrei); **a** ∼ **conscience** ein reines Gewissen. **10.** ✝ Netto..., Rein...: ∼ **gain** (*od. profit*) Reingewinn *m*. **II** *adv* **11.** hell, klar. **12.** klar, deutlich: **speak** ∼. **13.** los, weg (*of* von): **keep** (*od. steer*) ∼ **of** sich fernhalten von, meiden; **get** ∼ **of** loskommen von; **stand** ∼ **of** Tür etc freihalten. **III** *v/t* **14.** *oft* ∼ **away** wegräumen (*from* von), *Geschirr* abräumen. **15.** *Straße etc* freimachen, *Saal etc* räumen. **16.** reinigen, säubern: ∼ **one's throat** sich räuspern. **17.** frei-, lossprechen (*of* von), *Gewissen* entlasten, *Namen* reinwaschen. **18.** *Verbrechen etc* (auf)klären. **IV** *v/i* **19.** klar *od.* hell werden. **20.** aufklaren (*Wetter*). **21.** *oft* ∼ **away** sich verziehen (*Nebel etc*). **'clear·ance** *s* Räumung *f*: ∼ **sale** Räumungs-, Ausverkauf *m*. **,clear·|-'cut** *adj* **1.** scharfgeschnitten. **2.** *fig.* klar, deutlich. **,∼·'head·ed** *adj* klardenkend, intelligent.

clear·ly ['klıəlı] *adv* **1.** klar, deutlich. **2.**

offensichtlich. **'clear·ness** s **1.** Klarheit f. **2.** Reinheit f. **3.** Schärfe f.

cleav·age ['kliːvɪdʒ] s **1.** Spaltung f. **2.** Spalt m.

cleave [kliːv] (mst irr) v/t **1.** (zer)spalten. **2.** Luft, Wasser etc durchschneiden. **3.** Weg bahnen.

clef [klef] s ♪ (Noten)Schlüssel m.

cleft [kleft] **I** pret u. pp von **cleave.** **II** s **1.** Spalt m, Spalte f. **2.** fig. Kluft f. ~ **pal·ate** s ✵ Wolfsrachen m. ~ **stick** s: **be in a** ~ in der Klemme sitzen od. stecken.

clem·en·cy ['klemənsɪ] s Milde f, Nachsicht f. **'clem·ent** adj □ mild (a. Wetter), nachsichtig.

clench [klentʃ] v/t **1.** zs.-pressen, Faust ballen, Zähne zs.-beißen. **2.** fest packen od. anfassen.

cler·gy ['klɜːdʒɪ] s eccl. Klerus m, die Geistlichen pl. **~·man** ['~mən] s (irr **man**) Geistlicher m.

cler·i·cal ['klerɪkl] adj □ **1.** klerikal, geistlich. **2.** Schreib..., Büro...: ~ **error** Schreibfehler m; ~ **work** Büroarbeit f.

clerk [klɑːk] s **1.** Schriftführer m, Sekretär m. **2.** (Büro- etc)Angestellte m, f, (Bank- etc)Beamte m, (-)Beamtin f. **3.** Am. Verkäufer(in).

clev·er ['klevə] adj □ **1.** clever: a) geschickt, gewandt (at in dat), b) gerissen, raffiniert (a. Gerät etc): ~ **dick** bsd. Br. sl. Schlaumeier m. **2.** gescheit: a) clever, klug, b) geistreich (Bemerkung etc). **3.** begabt (at in dat, für). **'clev·er·ness** s **1.** Cleverness f. **2.** Gescheitheit f.

cli·ché ['kliːʃeɪ] s Klischee n, Gemeinplatz m.

click [klɪk] **I** s **1.** Klicken n. **2.** Einschnappen n. **3.** ✿ Sperrklinke f, -vorrichtung f. **4.** Schnalzer m. **II** v/i **5.** klicken. **6.** mit der Zunge schnalzen. **7.** zu-, einschnappen: ~ **shut** ins Schloß fallen. **8.** F einschlagen, Erfolg haben (**with** bei). **9.** F sofort Gefallen aneinander finden; sich sofort ineinander verknallen. **III** v/t **10.** klicken od. einschnappen lassen: ~ **one's heels** die Hacken zs.-schlagen. **11.** ~ **glasses** anstoßen. **12.** mit der Zunge schnalzen.

cli·ent ['klaɪənt] s **1.** ⚖ Klient(in), Mandant(in). **2.** Kunde m, Kundin f. **cli·en·tele** [ˌkliːɑːn'tel] s **1.** ⚖ Klientel f, Klienten pl. **2.** Kundschaft f, Kunden pl.

cliff [klɪf] s **1.** Klippe f, Felsen m. **2.** steiler Abhang. **'~ˌhang·er** s **1.** spannender Fortsetzungsroman (der immer im spannendsten Moment aufhört); (Rundfunk, TV) spannender Mehrteiler. **2.** fig. spannende Sache.

cli·mac·ter·ic [klaɪˈmæktərɪk] s physiol. Wechseljahre pl.

cli·mate ['klaɪmɪt] s Klima n, fig. a. Atmosphäre f. **cli·mat·ic** [~ˈmætɪk] adj (~ally) klimatisch, Klima...

cli·max ['klaɪmæks] **I** s Höhepunkt m, physiol. a. Orgasmus m. **II** v/t auf den Höhepunkt bringen. **III** v/i den Höhepunkt erreichen.

climb [klaɪm] **I** s **1.** Aufstieg m, Besteigung f. **2.** Berg-, Klettertour f. **II** v/i **3.** klettern: ~ **up** (**down**) **a tree** auf e-n Baum klettern (von e-m Baum herunterklettern). **4.** (auf-, empor)steigen. **III** v/t **6.** er-, besteigen, erklettern, klettern auf (acc).

clinch [klɪntʃ] **I** v/t **1.** Spiel etc entscheiden: **that ~ed it** damit war die Sache entschieden. **2.** ✿ sicher befestigen; (ver)nieten. **3.** Boxen: umklammern. **II** v/i **4.** Boxen: clinchen. **III** s **5.** ✿ Vernietung f. **6.** Boxen: Clinch m (a. sl. Umarmung f).

cling [klɪŋ] v/i (irr) **1.** kleben, haften (**to** an dat): ~ **together** zs.-halten (a. fig.). **2.** a. fig. (**to**) hängen (an dat), anhaften (dat). **3.** a. fig. (**to**) sich klammern (an acc), festhalten (an dat). **4.** sich (an-)schmiegen (**to** an acc). ~ **film** s Frischhaltefolie f.

clin·ic ['klɪnɪk] s Klinik f. **clin·i·cal** [ˈ~kl] adj □ klinisch: ~ **death;** ~ **thermometer** Fieberthermometer n.

clink[1] [klɪŋk] **I** v/i klingen, klirren. **II** v/t klingen od. klirren lassen: ~ **glasses** anstoßen. **III** s Klingen n, Klirren n.

clink[2] [~] s sl. Kittchen n: **in** ~ im Knast.

clip[1] [klɪp] **I** v/t **1.** (be)schneiden, stutzen (a. fig.). **2.** fig. kürzen, beschneiden. **3.** a. ~ **off** abschneiden. **4.** aus der Zeitung ausschneiden. **5.** Haare schneiden. **6.** Schaf etc scheren. **7.** Fahrschein etc lochen. **8.** Silben verschlucken. **9.** F j-m e-n Schlag versetzen. **10.** sl. j-n erleichtern (**for** um Geld); j-n neppen. **II** s **11.** Haarschnitt m. **12.** Schur f.

clip[2] [~] **I** v/t a. ~ **on** anklammern. **II** s (Heft-, Büro- etc)Klammer f.

clip joint s sl. Nepplokal n.

clip·pers ['klɪpəz] s pl, a. **pair of ~** (*Nagel- etc*)Schere f, Haarschneidemaschine f.

'**clip·ping** s **1.** bsd. Am. (Zeitungs)Ausschnitt m. **2.** pl Schnitzel pl, Abfälle pl.

clique [kli:k] s Clique f, Klüngel m.

clit·o·ris ['klɪtərɪs] s anat. Kitzler m.

cloak [kləʊk] **I** s (loser) Mantel, Umhang m: **under the ~ of** fig. unter dem Deckmantel der *Freundschaft etc*, im Schutz der *Dunkelheit etc*. **II** v/t fig. bemänteln, verhüllen. **~-room** ['~rʊm] s **1.** Garderobe f: **~ attendant** Garderobenfrau f; **~ ticket** (bsd. Am. **check**) Garderobenmarke f, -zettel m. **2.** Br. Toilette f.

clob·ber¹ ['klɒbə] s Br. sl. Klamotten pl; Plunder m, Kram m.

clob·ber² [~] v/t sl. **1.** zs.-schlagen. **2.** Sport: überfahren (hoch besiegen).

clock [klɒk] **I** s **1.** (Wand-, Turm-, Stand)Uhr f: (a)**round the ~** rund um die Uhr, 24 Stunden (lang); **five o'~** 5 Uhr; **put** (od. **turn**) **the ~ back** fig. das Rad der Zeit zurückdrehen. **2.** F Kontroll-, Stoppuhr f; Fahrpreisanzeiger m (Taxi). **3.** bsd. Sport: (ab)stoppen: **~** (**up**) Zeit erreichen (**for** über e-e Distanz). **III** v/i **4.** **~ in** (**out**) einstempeln (ausstempeln). **~ card** s Steckkarte f. '**~face** s Zifferblatt n. **~ ra·di·o** s Radiowecker m. '**~wise** adj u. adv im Uhrzeigersinn. '**~work** s Uhrwerk n: **like ~** wie am Schnürchen, wie geschmiert.

clod [klɒd] s **1.** (Erd)Klumpen m. **2.** Trottel m.

clog [klɒg] **I** s **1.** (Holz)Klotz m. **2.** fig. Hemmschuh m, Klotz m am Bein. **3.** Holzschuh m. **II** v/t **4.** (be)hindern, hemmen. **5.** a. **~ up** verstopfen. **III** v/i **6.** sich verstopfen.

clois·ter ['klɔɪstə] s **1.** Kloster n. **2.** △ Kreuzgang m.

close¹ [kləʊs] **I** adj □ **1.** geschlossen. **2.** verschlossen, verschwiegen. **3.** eng(anliegend). **4.** nah: **~ fight** Handgemenge n, weitS. zähes Ringen; **~ to tears** den Tränen nahe. **5.** eng (Freund); nah (Verwandter). **6.** knapp (Sieg etc): → **shave** 5. **7.** gespannt (Aufmerksamkeit). **8.** gründlich (Untersuchung etc). **II** adv **9.** eng, nahe, dicht: **~ by**

ganz in der Nähe; nahe od. dicht bei; **~ at hand** nahe bevorstehend; **come ~ to** fast ... sein; → **wind¹** 1. **III** s [kləʊz] **10.** Abschluß m: **come** (od. **draw**) **to a ~** sich dem Ende nähern. **IV** v/t [kləʊz] **11.** (ab-, ver-, zu)schließen, zumachen. **12.** Betrieb etc schließen; Straße etc sperren (**to** für). **13.** beenden, beschließen. **V** v/i [kləʊz] **14.** sich schließen (a. Wunde etc). **15.** geschlossen werden. **16.** schließen, zumachen. **17.** enden, aufhören, zu Ende gehen. **18.** schließen (**with the words** mit den Worten). **19.** sich verringern (Abstand etc).

Verbindungen mit Adverbien:

close| v/t **1.** Geschäft etc schließen, Betrieb stillegen. **II** v/i **2.** schließen, stillgelegt werden. **3.** fig. scharf vorgehen (**on** gegen). **~ in** v/i **1.** sich heranarbeiten (**on** an acc). **2.** kürzer werden (Tage). **3.** hereinbrechen (Dunkelheit, Nacht). **~ up** **I** v/t **1.** → close 11, 12. **2.** abschließen, beenden. **II** v/i **3.** → **close down** 2. **4.** aufschließen, -rücken (**on** zu).

closed [kləʊzd] adj **1.** geschlossen: **behind ~ doors** hinter verschlossenen Türen; **~ circuit** ⚡ geschlossener Stromkreis; → **book** 1. **2.** gesperrt (**to** für). '**close-down** s Schließung f, Stillegung f. **closed shop** s ↑ gewerkschaftspflichtiger Betrieb. ,**close|'fist·ed** adj geizig. ,**~·'fit·ting** adj enganliegend. '**~·knit** adj fig. engverbunden.

close·ness ['kləʊsnɪs] s **1.** Nähe f. **2.** Knappheit f. **3.** Gründlichkeit f.

close sea·son s hunt. Schonzeit f.

clos·et ['klɒzɪt] s **1.** (Wand-, Einbau)Schrank m. **2.** Kasett n.

'**close-up** s phot., Film: Nah-, Großaufnahme f.

clos·ing| date ['kləʊzɪŋ] s letzter Termin (**for** für). **~ time** s Laden-, Geschäftsschluß m; Ende n der Schalterstunden; Polizeistunde f.

clo·sure ['kləʊʒə] s **1.** Schließung f (e-s Betriebs etc). **2.** ⚙ Verschluß m. **3.** Schluß m, Beendigung f (e-r Debatte etc).

clot [klɒt] **I** s **1.** Klumpen m, Klümpchen n: **~ of blood** 🩸 Blutgerinnsel n. **2.** Br. F Trottel m. **II** v/i **3.** gerinnen. **4.** Klumpen bilden.

cloth [klɒθ] *s* **1.** Tuch *n*, Stoff *m*. **2.** Tuch *n*, Lappen *m*.

clothe [kləʊð] *v/t* (*a. irr*) **1.** (an-, be)kleiden. **2.** einkleiden. **3.** *fig.* umhüllen, einhüllen.

clothes [kləʊðz] *s pl* **1.** Kleider *pl*, Kleidung *f*: *change one's ~* sich umziehen. **2.** (*a.* Bett)Wäsche *f*. **~ bas·ket** *s* Wäschekorb *m*. **~ brush** *s* Kleiderbürste *f*. **~ hang·er** *s* Kleiderbügel *m*. '**~horse** *s* Wäscheständer *m*. '**~line** *s* Wäscheleine *f*. **~ peg** *s Br.*, '**~pin** *s Am.* Wäscheklammer *f*. **~ tree** *s* Garderoben-, Kleiderständer *m*.

cloth·ing ['kləʊðɪŋ] *s* Kleidung *f*: *~ indus·try* Bekleidungsindustrie *f*.

cloud [klaʊd] **I** *s* **1.** Wolke *f*: *~ of dust* Staubwolke; *have one's head in the ~s fig.* in höheren Regionen schweben; in Gedanken vertieft sein; *be on ~ nine* F im siebten Himmel schweben. **2.** *fig.* Schatten *m*: *cast a ~ on* e-n Schatten werfen auf (*acc*). **II** *v/t* **3.** be-, umwölken. **4.** *fig.* verdunkeln, trüben. **III** *v/i a. ~ over* **5.** sich bewölken. **6.** *fig.* sich trüben. **~ bank** *s* Wolkenbank *f*. '**~burst** *s* Wolkenbruch *m*. **~cuck·oo-land** *s* Wolkenkuckucksheim *n*.

cloud·less ['klaʊdlɪs] *adj* □ **1.** wolkenlos. **2.** *fig.* ungetrübt. '**cloud·y** *adj* □ **1.** wolkig, bewölkt. **2.** *fig.* nebelhaft, unklar.

clout [klaʊt] F **I** *s* **1.** Schlag *m*: *give s.o. a ~* j-m e-e runterhauen. **2.** *bsd. pol. Am.* Einfluß *m* (*with* auf *acc*). **II** *v/t* **3.** schlagen: *~ s.o. one* j-m e-e runterhauen.

clove[1] [kləʊv] *s* (Gewürz)Nelke *f*.

clove[2] [~] *s*: *~ of garlic* Knoblauchzehe *f*.

clove[3] [~] *pret von* **cleave**.

clo·ven ['kləʊvn] *pp von* **cleave**: *show the ~ foot* (*od.* **hoof**) *fig.* sein wahres Gesicht zeigen.

clo·ver ['kləʊvə] *s* ♣ Klee *m*: *be* (*od.* **live**) *in ~* wie Gott in Frankreich leben. '**~leaf** *s* (*irr* **leaf**) **1.** Kleeblatt *n*. **2.** *a. ~ intersection mot.* Kleeblatt *n*.

clown [klaʊn] **I** *s* Clown *m* (*a. fig.*). **II** *v/i a. ~ about* (*od.* **around**) herumkaspern. '**clown·ish** *adj* □ clownisch.

club [klʌb] **I** *s* **1.** Keule *f*, Knüppel *m*. *Sport:* Schlagholz *n*; (*Golf*)Schläger *m*. **3.** Klub *m*, Verein *m*: *join the ~!* *bsd. Br.* F du auch? **4.** Spielkarten: a) *pl*

Kreuz *n*, Eichel *f* (*Farbe*), b) Kreuz(karte *f*) *f*. **II** *v/t* **5.** einknüppeln auf (*acc*), (nieder)knüppeln. **6.** sich teilen in (*acc*); *Geld* zs.-legen. **III** *v/i* **7.** *mst ~ together* sich zs.-tun: a) e-n Verein *etc* bilden, b) (Geld) zs.-legen. **~ chair** *s* Klubsessel *m*. ,**~'foot** *s* (*irr* **foot**) ❦ Klumpfuß *m*. '**~house** *s* Klub-, Vereinshaus *n*.

cluck [klʌk] *v/i* gackern; glucken.

clue [klu:] **I** *s* **1.** (*to*) Hinweis *m* (auf *acc*), Anhaltspunkt *m* (für), Fingerzeig *m*. **2.** Schlüssel *m* (*to* zu e-m Rätsel *etc*): *I haven't a ~* F ich hab' keinen Schimmer. **II** *v/t* **3.** *~ in* j-m e-n Hinweis geben. **4.** *~ up* informieren (*on, about* über *acc*): *all ~d up* vollkommen im Bild.

clump [klʌmp] **I** *s* **1.** (*Baum-, Häuser*)Gruppe *f*. **2.** (*Holz*)Klotz *m*; (*Erdetc*)Klumpen *m*. **II** *v/i* **3.** trampeln: *~ about* (*od.* **around**) herumtrampeln. **4.** sich zs.-ballen. **II** *v/t* **5.** zs.-ballen, anhäufen.

clum·si·ness ['klʌmzɪnɪs] *s* Plumpheit *f*. '**clum·sy** *adj* □ plump: a) ungeschickt, unbeholfen, b) schwerfällig, c) taktlos, d) unförmig.

clung [klʌŋ] *pret u. pp von* **cling**.

clus·ter ['klʌstə] **I** *s* **1.** ♣ Büschel *n*, Traube *f*. **2.** Haufen *m*, Schwarm *m*, Gruppe *f*. **II** *v/i* **3.** e-e Gruppe (*od.* Gruppen bilden, sich versammeln *od.* drängen (*round* um).

clutch [klʌtʃ] **I** *v/t* **1.** packen, (er)greifen. **2.** umklammern. **II** *v/i* **3.** (gierig) greifen (*at* nach): *~ at a straw* **2.** *fig.* **3. 4.** (gieriger) Griff. **5.** *zo.* Klaue *f*, Kralle *f* (*beide a. fig.*): *in s.o.'s ~es* in j-s Klauen *od.* Gewalt. **6.** ❂ Kupplung *f*: *~ disk* Kupplungsscheibe *f*; *~ facing* (*od.* **lining**) Kupplungsbelag *m*; *~ pedal* Kupplungspedal *n*.

clut·ter ['klʌtə] **I** *v/t* **1.** *a. ~ up* (unordentlich) vollstopfen. **2.** durcheinanderwerfen, herumstreuen. **II** *s* **3.** Wirrwarr *m*, Durcheinander *n*. **4.** Unordnung *f*: *in a ~* in Unordnung.

coach [kəʊtʃ] **I** *s* **1.** Kutsche *f*. **2.** ❦ *Br.* (Personen)Wagen *m*. **3.** *Br.* Reisebus *m*. **4.** Nachhilfe-, Hauslehrer *m*. **5.** *Sport:* Trainer *m*. **II** *v/t* **6.** Nachhilfeunterricht geben: *~ s.o. in s.th.* j-m et. einpauken. **7.** *Sport:* trainieren. **~man**

cocoa

['∼mən] *s* (*irr* **man**) Kutscher *m.* '∼**work** *s mot.* Karosserie *f.*

co·ag·u·late [kəʊˈægjʊleɪt] *v/i u. v/t* gerinnen (lassen). **co**,**ag·u·la·tion** *s* Gerinnung *f.*

coal [kəʊl] *s* Kohle *f, engS.* Steinkohle *f:* **carry** (*od.* **take**) ∼**s to Newcastle** *fig.* Eulen nach Athen tragen; **haul** (*od.* **drag**) **s.o. over the** ∼**s** *fig.* j-m die Hölle heiß machen.

co·a·li·tion [ˌkəʊəˈlɪʃn] I *s* **1.** *pol.* Koalition *f:* **form a** ∼ e-e Koalition eingehen *od.* bilden, koalieren. **2.** Bündnis *n,* Zs.-schluß *m.* II *adj* **3.** *pol.* Koalitions...

coal| **mine,** '∼**pit** *s* Kohlenbergwerk *n,* -grube *f,* -zeche *f.* ∼ **pow·er sta·tion** *s* Kohlekraftwerk *n.*

coarse [kɔːs] *adj* □ grob: a) rauh, b) grobkörnig, c) *fig.* ungenau, d) *fig.* derb, ungehobelt.

coast [kəʊst] I *s* **1.** Küste *f:* **the** ∼ **is clear** *fig.* die Luft ist rein. II *v/i* **2.** ♻ die Küste entlangfahren. **3.** im Leerlauf (*Auto*) *od.* im Freilauf (*Fahrrad*) fahren. **coast·al** ['∼tl] *adj* Küsten... '**coast·er** *s* **1.** *Am.* Berg-u.-Tal-Bahn *f* (*im Vergnügungspark*). **2.** *bes. Am.* Untersatz *m* (*für Gläser etc*).

coast guard *s Br.* Küsten(zoll)wache *f.*

coat [kəʊt] I *s* **1.** Jacke *f,* Jackett *n.* **2.** Mantel *m:* **turn one's** ∼ *fig.* sein Mäntelchen nach dem Wind hängen. **3.** *zo.* Pelz *m,* Fell *n.* **4.** (*Farb- etc*) Überzug *m,* Anstrich *m,* Schicht *f.* II *v/t* **5.** (an)streichen, überstreichen, -ziehen, beschichten. **6.** bedecken, umhüllen, umgeben (**with** mit). '**coat·ed** *adj* **1.** mit ... überzogen *od.* beschichtet: **sugar-**∼ mit Zuckerüberzug; ∼ **tablet** Dragée *n.* **2.** ♻ belegt (*Zunge*).

coat| **hang·er** *s* Kleiderbügel *m.* ∼ **hook** *s* Kleiderhaken *m.*

coat·ing ['kəʊtɪŋ] *s* **1.** Mantelstoff *m.* **2.** → **coat** 4.

coat of arms *s* Wappen(schild *m, n*) *n.*

coax [kəʊks] *v/t* überreden, beschwatzen (**to do, into doing** zu tun): ∼ **s.th. out of** (*od.* **from**) **s.o.** j-m et. abschwatzen.

cob [kɒb] *s* Maiskolben *m.*

co·balt [kəʊˈbɔːlt] *s min.* Kobalt *n:* ∼ (*blue*) Kobaltblau *n.*

cob·ble¹ ['kɒbl] I *s* Kopfstein *m.* ∼**s** *pl* Kopfsteinpflaster *n.* II *v/t* mit Kopf-

steinen pflastern: ∼**d street** Straße *f* mit Kopfsteinpflaster.

cob·ble² [∼] *v/t* **1.** *Schuhe* flicken. **2.** *a.* ∼ **up** zs.-pfuschen, zs.-schustern. **cob·bler** ['kɒblə] *s* **1.** (Flick)Schuster *m.* **2.** Pfuscher *m.*

'**cob·ble·stone** *s* Kopfstein *m:* ∼ **pavement** Kopfsteinpflaster *n.*

co·bra ['kəʊbrə] *s zo.* Kobra *f.*

'**cob·web** *s* Spinn(en)webe *f,* Spinnennetz *n.*

co·cain(e) [kəʊˈkeɪn] *s* ♻ Kokain *n.*

cock [kɒk] I *s* **1.** *orn.* Hahn *m.* **2.** Männchen *n,* Hahn *m* (*von Vögeln*). **3.** Wetterhahn *m.* **4.** ∼ **of the walk** (*od.* **roost**) *oft contp.* der Größte. **5.** ⊙ (*Absperr-, Gewehr- etc*)Hahn *m.* **6.** V Schwanz *m* (*Penis*). II *v/t* **7.** aufrichten: ∼ **one's ears** die Ohren spitzen; ∼ **one's hat** den Hut schief aufsetzen; → **snook.**

Cock·aigne [kɒˈkeɪn] *s* Schlaraffenland *n.*

,**cock-and-'bull sto·ry** *s* F Ammenmärchen *n.*

cock·a·too [ˌkɒkəˈtuː] *s orn.* Kakadu *m.*

'**cock**,**chaf·er** *s zo.* Maikäfer *m.*

cocked hat [kɒkt] *s* Dreispitz *m:* **knock** (*od.* **beat**) **into a** ∼ *sl.* j-n, et. weit in den Schatten stellen; *Plan etc* völlig über den Haufen werfen.

cock·er¹ ['kɒkə] → **cocker spaniel.**

cock·er² [∼] *v/t* verhätscheln, verwöhnen: ∼ **up** aufpäppeln.

cock·er span·iel *s zo.* Cockerspaniel *m.*

'**cock**|**-eyed** *adj* F **1.** schielend: **be** ∼ schielen. **2.** blau (*betrunken*). '∼**fight,** '∼,**fight·ing** *s* Hahnenkampf *m.*

cock·ney ['kɒknɪ] *s* **1.** Cockney *m,* waschechter Londoner. **2.** Cockney(dialekt *m*) *n.* '**cock·ney·ism** *s* Cockneyausdruck *m.*

'**cock**|**-pit** *s* **1.** ✈, ♻ Cockpit *n* (*a. e-s Rennwagens*). **2.** Hahnenkampfplatz *m.* '∼**roach** *s zo.* (Küchen)Schabe *f.* ,∼'**sure** *adj* □ **1.** vollkommen überzeugt (**of, about** von), ganz sicher. **2.** übertrieben selbstsicher. '∼**tail** *s* Cocktail *m.*

cock·y ['kɒkɪ] *adj* □ F großspurig, anmaßend.

co·co ['kəʊkəʊ] *s pl* **-cos** *s* ♻ Kokospalme *f;* Kokosnuß *f.* II *adj* Kokos...: ∼ **matting** Kokosmatte *f.*

co·coa ['kəʊkəʊ] *s* Kakao(pulver *n*) *m.*

co·co·nut ['kəʊkənʌt] s Kokosnuß f. ~ **palm** s ⚕ Kokospalme f.

co·coon [kə'ku:n] s zo. Kokon m, Puppe f (der Seidenraupe).

cod [kɒd] s ichth. Kabeljau m, Dorsch m.

cod·dle ['kɒdl] v/t verhätscheln, verzärteln: ~ **up** aufpäppeln.

code [kəʊd] **I** s **1.** Kodex m: a) ᚦᚦ Gesetzbuch n, b) Regeln pl: ~ **of hono(u)r** Ehrenkodex; → **moral** 4. **2.** (Telegramm)Schlüssel m. **3.** Code m; Chiffre f; Code m, Schlüssel m: ~ **number** Code-, Kennziffer f; ~ **word** Code-, Schlüsselwort n. **II** v/t **4.** verschlüsseln, chiffrieren.

'cod·fish → **cod**.

cod·i·fy ['kəʊdɪfaɪ] v/t ᚦᚦ kodifizieren.

'cod-,liv·er oil s Lebertran m.

co·ed [,kəʊ'ed] ped. **F I** s **1.** Am. Studentin f od. Schülerin f e-r gemischten Schule. **2.** Br. gemischte Schule. **II** adj **3.** gemischt.

co·ed·u·ca·tion [,kəʊedjʊ'keɪʃn] s ped. Gemeinschaftserziehung f. **,co·ed·u·'ca·tion·al** [~ʃənl] adj: ~ **school** gemischte Schule; ~ **teaching** → **coeducation**.

co·ef·fi·cient [,kəʊɪ'fɪʃnt] s ➤, phys. Koeffizient m.

co·erce [kəʊ'ɜːs] v/t **1.** zwingen (**into** zu). **2.** erzwingen. **co·er·cion** [~ʃn] s Zwang m: **by** ~ → **coercively. co·er·cive** [~sɪv] adj **1.** Zwangs..., zwingend: ~ **measure** Zwangsmaßnahme f. **2.** überzeugend, zwingend (**Gründe** etc). **co·er·cive·ly** adv durch Zwang, zwangsweise.

co·ex·ist [,kəʊɪg'zɪst] v/i gleichzeitig od. nebeneinander bestehen od. leben. **,co·ex·'ist·ence** s Koexistenz f: **peace-ful** ~ pol. friedliche Koexistenz. **,co·ex·'ist·ent** adj gleichzeitig od. nebeneinander bestehend.

cof·fee ['kɒfɪ] s Kaffee m. ~ **bar** s Br. Café n; Imbißstube f. ~ **bean** s Kaffeebohne f. ~ **break** s Kaffeepause f. ~ **cup** s Kaffeetasse f. ~ **grind·er** s Kaffeemühle f. ~ **grounds** s pl Kaffeesatz m. **'~house** s Kaffeehaus n, Café n. ~ **ma·chine** s Kaffeeautomat m. **'~,mak·er** s Kaffeemaschine f. ~ **mill** s Kaffeemühle f. **'~pot** s Kaffeekanne f. ~ **set** s Kaffeeservice n. ~ **shop** Am. → **coffee bar.** ~ **ta·ble** s Couchtisch m.

cof·fin ['kɒfɪn] s Sarg m.

cog [kɒg] s ☼ (Rad)Zahn m; Zahnrad n: **be just a ~ in the machine** (od. **wheel**) fig. nur ein Rädchen im Getriebe sein.

co·gent ['kəʊdʒənt] adj □ zwingend, überzeugend (**Gründe** etc).

cogged [kɒgd] adj ☼ gezahnt.

cog·i·tate ['kɒdʒɪteɪt] **I** v/t nachdenken über (acc). **II** v/i (nach)denken: ~ **on** (od. **about**) → **I**.

cog·nate ['kɒgneɪt] adj **1.** (bluts)verwandt (**with** mit). **2.** fig. (art)verwandt (**with** mit).

cog·ni·tion [kɒg'nɪʃn] s Erkenntnis f.

cog·ni·zance ['kɒgnɪzəns] s **1.** Kenntnis f: **have** (**take**) ~ **of s.th.** von et. Kenntnis haben (nehmen). **2.** ᚦᚦ Zuständigkeit f: **have** ~ **over** zuständig sein für (a. weitS.). **'cog·ni·zant** adj unterrichtet (**of** über acc od. von): **be** ~ **of s.th.** a. von et. Kenntnis haben.

cog·no·men [kɒg'nəʊmen] pl **-mens,** **-nom·i·na** [~'nɒmɪnə] s **1.** Familien-, Zuname m. **2.** Spitz-, Beiname m.

'cog·wheel s ☼ Zahnrad n.

co·hab·it [kəʊ'hæbɪt] v/i (**unverheiratet**) zs.-leben. **,co·hab·i'ta·tion** s Zs.-leben n.

co·here [kəʊ'hɪə] v/i zs.-hängen (a. fig.). **co·'her·ence, co·'her·en·cy** s **1.** Zs.-halt m (a. fig.). **2.** phys. Kohärenz f. **3.** fig. Zs.-hang m. **co·'her·ent** adj □ **1.** zs.-hängend (a. fig.). **2.** phys. kohärent.

co·he·sion [kəʊ'hi:ʒn] s **1.** Zs.-halt m (a. fig.). **2.** phys. Kohäsion f. **co·'he·sive** adj □ **1.** (fest) zs.-haltend (a. fig.). **2.** phys. Kohäsions..., Binde...

coil [kɔɪl] **I** v/t **1.** a. ~ **up** aufrollen, (auf)wickeln. **2.** ⚡ wickeln. **II** v/i **3.** a. ~ **up** sich zs.-rollen. **III** s **4.** Spirale f (a.☼ u. 🌢). **5.** Rolle f, Spule f.

coin [kɔɪn] **I** s Münze f: **pay s.o. back in his own** (od. **in the same**) ~ fig. es j-m mit od. in gleicher Münze heimzahlen; **the other side of the** ~ fig. die Kehrseite der Medaille. **II** v/t Münzen, fig. Wort etc prägen: ~ **money** F Geld wie Heu verdienen. **'coin·age** s **1.** Prägen n. **2.** coll. Münzen pl. **3.** fig. Prägung f (e-s Worts etc); Neuprägung f (Wort etc).

'coin-box tel·e·phone s Münzfernsprecher m.

co·in·cide [,kəʊɪn'saɪd] v/i **1.** örtlich od. zeitlich zs.-treffen, -fallen (**with** mit). **2.**

übereinstimmen, sich decken (**with** mit). **co'in·ci·dence** [~ʁɪdəns] *s* **1.** Zs.-treffen *n*, -fallen *n*. **2.** zufälliges Zs.-treffen, Zufall *m*: **by mere ~** rein zufällig. **co'in·ci·dent** *adj* ☐ **1.** zs.-fallend, -treffend. **2.** übereinstimmend, sich deckend. **co**ˌ**in·ci'den·tal** *adj* ☐ **1.** → **coincident** 2. **2.** zufällig.

coin-op ['kɔɪnɒp] *s* F **1.** Waschsalon *m*. **2.** Münztankstelle *f*. **'~-**ˌ**op·er·at·ed** *adj* mit Münzbetrieb, Münz...

coke¹ [kəʊk] **I** *s* Koks *m*. **II** *v/t u. v/i* verkoken.

coke² [~] *s sl.* Koks *m* (*Kokain*).

co·la ['kəʊlə] *pl von* **colon¹**.

col·an·der ['kʌləndə] *s* Sieb *n*, Seiher *m*. **II** *v/t* durchseihen, (durch)sieben.

cold [kəʊld] **I** *adj* ☐ **1.** kalt: (**as**) **~ as ice** eiskalt; **I feel** (*od. am*) **~** mir ist kalt, ich friere; **in ~ blood** kaltblütig; **~ snap** Kälteeinbruch *m*; **get ~ feet** F kalte Füße (*Angst*) bekommen; → **shoulder** 1, **sweat, water** 1. **2.** *fig.* kalt, kühl: a) frostig, unfreundlich (*Empfang etc*), b) nüchtern, sachlich: **the ~ facts** die nackten Tatsachen; c) ruhig, gelassen: **it left me ~** es ließ mich kalt. **3.** (gefühls)kalt, frigid. **II** *s* **4.** Kälte *f*: **be left out in the ~** *fig.* kaltgestellt sein, ignoriert werden. **5.** 🟥 Erkältung *f*: (**common**) **~, ~** (**in the head**) Schnupfen *m*; → **catch** 9. **'~-**'**blood·ed** *adj* ☐ **1.** *zo.* kaltblütig (*a. fig.*). **2.** F kälteempfindlich: **be ~** *a.* leicht frieren. **'~-**'**heart·ed** *adj* ☐ kalt-, hartherzig.

cold·ish ['kəʊldɪʃ] *adj* ziemlich kalt. **'cold·ness** *s* Kälte *f* (*a. fig.*).

coldǀ **room** *s* Kühlraum *m*. **'~-'shoul·der** *v/t* F *j-m* die kalte Schulter zeigen, *j-n* kühl *od.* abweisend behandeln. **~ 'stor·age** *s* Kühlraumlagerung *f*: **put into ~** *fig.* auf Eis legen. **~ 'tur·key** *s sl.* radikale Entziehungskur: **go ~** *s-e* radikale Entziehungskur machen. **~ 'war** *s pol.* kalter Krieg. **~ 'wave** *s* **1.** *meteor.* Kältewelle *f*. **2.** Kaltwelle *f* (*Frisur*).

cole·slaw ['kəʊlslɔː] *s* Krautsalat *m*.

col·ic ['kɒlɪk] *s* 🟥 Kolik *f*.

col·lab·o·rate [kə'læbəreɪt] *v/i* **1.** zs.-arbeiten (**with** mit; **in, on** bei), mitarbeiten. **2.** *pol.* kollaborieren. **col**ˌ**lab·o'ra·tion** *s* **1.** Zs.-arbeit *f*: **in ~ with** gemeinsam mit. **2.** *pol.* Kollaboration *f*. **col'lab·o·ra·tor** *s* **1.** Mitar-

beiter(in). **2.** *pol.* Kollaborateur *m*.

col·lage ['kɒlɑːʒ] *s Kunst:* Collage *f*.

col·lapse [kə'læps] **I** *v/i* **1.** zs.-brechen, einfallen, -stürzen. **2.** *fig.* zs.-brechen, scheitern. **3.** moralisch *od.* physisch zs.-brechen. **4.** 🟥 e-n Kollaps erleiden. **5.** zs.-legbar sein, sich zs.-klappen lassen. **II** *v/t* **6.** zum Einsturz bringen. **7.** zs.-legen, -klappen. **III** *s* **8.** Einsturz *m*. **9.** *fig.* Zs.-bruch *m*. **10.** 🟥 Kollaps *m*: **nervous ~** Nervenzusammenbruch *m*. **col'laps·i·ble** *adj* zs.-klappbar, Klapp...: **~ chair**.

col·lar ['kɒlə] **I** *s* **1.** Kragen *m*. **2.** (*Hundeetc*)Halsband *n*. **3.** Hals-, Amts-, Ordenskette *f*. **4.** Kollier *n*: **~ of pearls** Perlenkollier. **II** *v/t* **5.** *j-n* beim Kragen packen. **6.** F *j-n* schnappen, verhaften, festnehmen; sich *et.* schnappen; sich *et.* unter den Nagel reißen. **'~-bone** *s anat.* Schlüsselbein *n*.

col·lat·er·al [kɒ'lætərəl] *adj* ☐ **1.** seitlich, Seiten... **2.** parallel (laufend). **3.** begleitend, Neben...: **~ circumstances** *pl* Begleit-, Nebenumstände *pl*.

col·league ['kɒliːg] *s* **1.** Kollege *m*, Kollegin *f*.

col·lect [kə'lekt] **I** *v/t* **1.** Briefmarken etc sammeln. **2.** (ein)sammeln. **3.** auflesen, -sammeln. **4.** *Fakten etc* sammeln, zs.-tragen. **5.** *j-n, et.* abholen. **6.** *Geld etc* (ein)kassieren. **7.** *Gedanken etc* sammeln: **~ o.s.** sich sammeln *od.* fassen. **8.** versammeln. **II** *v/i* **9.** sich (ver)sammeln. **10.** sich ansammeln. **III** *adj* **11.** *Am.* Nachnahme...: **~ call** *teleph.* R-Gespräch *n*. **IV** *adv* **12.** *a.* **~ on delivery** *Am.* per Nachnahme: **call ~** *teleph.* ein R-Gespräch führen. **col'lect·ed** *adj* ☐ **1.** gesammelt: **~ works**. **2.** *fig.* gefaßt. **col'lec·tion** *s* **1.** (Ein)Sammeln *n*. **2.** (*Briefmarkenetc*)Sammlung *f*. **3.** Kollekte *f*, (Geld-) Sammlung *f*. **4.** 🟥 Inkasso *n*. **5.** (*Muster*)Kollektion *f*. **6.** Abholung *f*. **7.** *fig.* Fassung *f*, Gefaßtheit *f*. **col'lec·tive** *adj* **1.** gesammelt, zs.-gefaßt. **2.** kollektiv: **~ agreement** 🟥 Tarifabkommen *n*; **~ bargaining** 🟥 Tarifverhandlungen *pl*; **~ noun** Sammelbegriff *m*. **col'lec·tive·ly** *adv* gemeinsam, gemeinschaftlich. **col'lec·tor** *s* **1.** Sammler(in): **~'s item** Sammlerstück *s*. **2.** Kassierer *m*. **3.** 🗲 Stromabnehmer *m*.

col·lege ['kɒlɪdʒ] s **1.** College n: ~ **of education** Br. pädagogische Hochschule. **2.** Akademie f. **3.** Kollegium n (a. eccl.). **col·le·gi·ate** [kə'li:dʒɪət] adj College..., akademisch: ~ **dictionary** Schulwörterbuch n.

col·lide [kə'laɪd] v/i (**with**) kollidieren (mit): a) zs.-stoßen (mit) (a. fig.), b) fig. im Widerspruch stehen (zu).

col·lie ['kɒlɪ] s zo. Collie m (langhaariger schottischer Schäferhund).

col·li·sion [kə'lɪʒn] s **1.** Kollision f, Zs.-stoß m (beide a. fig.): **be on a ~ course** auf Kollisionskurs sein. **2.** fig. Widerspruch m: **bring s.o. into ~ with the law** j-n mit dem Gesetz in Konflikt bringen.

col·lo·qui·al [kə'ləʊkwɪəl] adj □ umgangssprachlich: ~ **English** Umgangsenglisch n. **col·lo·qui·al·ism** s Ausdruck m der Umgangssprache.

col·lu·sion [kə'lu:ʒn] s **1.** geheimes Einverständnis. **2.** Verdunk(e)lung f: **risk** (od. **danger**) **of ~** Verdunklungsgefahr f.

col·ly·wob·bles ['kɒlɪ,wɒblz] s pl (a. sg konstruiert): **have the ~** F ein flaues Gefühl in der Magengegend haben.

co·lon¹ ['kəʊlən] pl **-lons, -la** [~lə] s anat. Dickdarm m.

co·lon² [~] s ling. Doppelpunkt m.

colo·nel ['kɜ:nl] s ✕ Oberst m.

co·lo·ni·al [kə'ləʊnjəl] adj □ kolonial, Kolonial...: ~ **masters** pl Kolonialherren pl. **co·lo·ni·al·ism** s pol. Kolonialismus m. **co·lo·nist** ['kɒlənɪst] s Kolonist(in), (An)Siedler(in). **co·lo·ni·za·tion** [,kɒlənaɪ'zeɪʃn] s Kolonisation f, Besiedlung f. **col·o·nize** I v/t **1.** kolonisieren, besiedeln. **2.** ansiedeln. II v/i **3.** sich ansiedeln. **4.** e-e Kolonie bilden.

col·on·nade [,kɒlə'neɪd] s △ Säulengang m, Kolonnade f.

col·o·ny ['kɒlənɪ] s (a. Ausländer-, Künstler- etc)Kolonie f.

col·or, etc Am. → **colour,** etc.

Col·o·ra·do bee·tle [,kɒlə'rɑ:dəʊ] s zo. Kartoffelkäfer m.

co·los·sal [kə'lɒsl] adj □ kolossal, riesig, Riesen... (alle a. fig. F).

co·los·sus [~sɒs] pl **-si** [~saɪ], **-sus·es** s Koloß m.

col·our ['kʌlə] bsd. Br. I s **1.** Farbe f: **what ~ is ...?** welche Farbe hat ...?; **to**

paint in bright (**glowing, gloomy**) **~s** et. in rosigen (glühenden, düsteren) Farben schildern; **local ~** fig. Lokalkolorit m. **2.** (a. gesunde) Gesichtsfarbe: **lose** (**all**) **~** (ganz) blaß werden. **3.** (bsd. dunkle) Hautfarbe: **people** pl **of ~** Farbige pl. **4.** fig. Färbung f, Ton m. **5.** pl ✕ Fahne f: **call to the ~s** einberufen; **pass** (**fail**) **an examination with flying ~s** e-e Prüfung mit Glanz u. Gloria bestehen (mit Pauken u. Trompeten durch e-e Prüfung fallen). **6.** pl ⚓ Flagge f: **sail under false ~s** unter falscher Flagge segeln (a. fig.); **show one's true ~s** fig. sein wahres Gesicht zeigen; Farbe bekennen. II v/t **7.** färben (a. fig.), kolorieren. III v/i **8.** sich (ver)färben. **9.** a. ~ **up** erröten, rot werden (**with** vor dat). **~·bar** s Rassenschranke f. **'~·blind** adj ✿ farbenblind.

col·oured ['kʌləd] adj bsd. Br. **1.** farbig, bunt (beide a. fig.): ~ **pencil** Bunt-, Farbstift m. **2.** farbig: **a ~ man** ein Farbiger. **3.** fig. gefärbt.

'col·our·fast adj bsd. Br. farbecht. ~ **film** s phot. Farbfilm m.

col·our·ful ['kʌləfʊl] adj □ bsd. Br. **1.** farbenfreudig, -prächtig. **2.** fig. farbig, bunt. **'col·our·ing** I s **1.** Färbung f (a. fig.), Farbgebung f. **2.** Gesichtsfarbe f. II adj **3.** Farb...: ~ **matter** Farbstoff m; ~ **book** Malbuch n.

'col·our·in,ten·sive adj □ bsd. Br. farbintensiv.

col·our·less ['kʌləlɪs] adj □ bsd. Br. **1.** farblos (a. fig.). **2.** fig. neutral, unparteiisch.

col·our| line s bsd. Br. Rassenschranke f. ~ **or·gan** s Lichtorgel f. ~ **prob·lem** s Rassenproblem n. ~ **set** s Farbfernseher m. ~ **sup·ple·ment** s Farbbeilage f (e-r Zeitung). ~ **tel·e·vi·sion** s Farbfernsehen n.

colt [kəʊlt] s **1.** Fohlen n. **2.** fig. Grünschnabel m.

col·umn ['kɒləm] s **1.** △ (a. Rauch-, Wasser- etc)Säule f. **2.** typ. Spalte f: **in double ~s** zweispaltig. **3.** Zeitung: Kolumne f. **4.** △, ✕ Kolonne f. **co·lum·nar** [kə'lʌmnə] adj **1.** säulenartig, -förmig. **2.** Säulen... **col·um·nist** ['kɒləmnɪst] s Kolumnist(in).

co·ma ['kəʊmə] s ✚ Koma n: **be in a ~** im Koma liegen.

comb [kəʊm] **I** s **1.** Kamm m (a. des Hahns, e-r Welle etc.). **II** v/t **2.** kämmen: ~ one's hair (od. o.s.) sich kämmen. **3.** fig. Gegend durchkämmen. **4.** mst ~ out fig. sieben, sichten; aussondern, -suchen.

com·bat ['kɒmbæt] **I** v/t bekämpfen, kämpfen gegen (beide a. fig.). **II** v/i kämpfen (with mit) (a. fig.). **III** s Kampf m, ✗ a. Gefecht n. **IV** adj Kampf...

com·bi·na·tion [,kɒmbɪ'neɪʃn] s **1.** Verbindung f (a. 🜚), Kombination f: ~ lock Kombinationsschloß n. **2.** 🜋 Konzern m; Kartell n, Ring m. **3.** Zs.-schluß m, Bündnis n. **com·bine** [kəm'baɪn] **I** v/t **1.** verbinden (a. 🜚), kombinieren: ~ business with pleasure das Nützliche mit dem Angenehmen verbinden. **2.** in sich vereinigen. **II** v/i **3.** sich verbinden (a. 🜚). **4.** zs.-wirken: everything ~d against him alles verschwor sich gegen ihn. **III** s ['kɒmbaɪn] **5.** Verbindung f. **6.** pol. Interessengemeinschaft f; 🜋 a. Verband m; Konzern m; Kartell n. **com·bined** [kəm~] adj gemeinsam, gemeinschaftlich.

com·bus·ti·ble [kəm'bʌstəbl] **I** adj □ **1.** brennbar, (leicht)entzündlich. **2.** fig. leichterregbar. **II** s **3.** Brennstoff m, -material n. **com·bus·tion** [~'bʌstʃən] s Verbrennung f (a. biol., 🜚): ~ engine ⚙ Verbrennungsmotor m.

come [kʌm] **I** v/i (irr) **1.** kommen (a. sl. e-n Orgasmus haben): s.o. is coming es kommt j-d; he came to see us er besuchte uns. **2.** (dran)kommen, an die Reihe kommen. **3.** kommen, erscheinen: ~ and go kommen u. gehen; erscheinen u. verschwinden. **4.** kommen, gelangen (to zu). **5.** kommen, abstammen (of, from von). **6.** kommen, herrühren (of von). **7.** kommen, geschehen, sich ereignen: what may (od. will) kommemöge, was da wolle; how ~s it that ...?, F how ~ that ...? wie kommt es, daß ...? **8.** sich erweisen: it ~s expensive es kommt teuer. **9.** vor inf: dahin od. dazu kommen: ~ to know s.o. j-n kennenlernen; ~ to know s.th. et. erfahren; I have ~ to believe that ich bin zu der Überzeugung gekommen, daß. **10.** bsd. vor adj: werden: ~ true sich bewahrheiten od. erfüllen, eintreffen. **11.** to ~ (als adj) zukünftig, kommend: for

all time to ~ für alle Zukunft. **II** v/t (irr) **12.** F sich aufspielen als, j-n, et. spielen. **III** int **13.** na!, komm!: ~, ~! nicht so wild!, immer langsam!; na komm schon!, nun geht's!

Verbindungen mit Präpositionen:

come| a·cross v/i zufällig treffen od. finden od. sehen, stoßen auf (acc). ~ **at** v/i **1.** erreichen, bekommen, Wahrheit etc herausfinden. **2.** losgehen auf (acc). ~ **for** v/i **1.** et. abholen kommen, kommen wegen. **2.** losgehen auf (acc). ~ **in·to** v/i **1.** kommen in (acc). **2.** ~ a fortune ein Vermögen erben; → fashion 1, own 5, use 5. ~ **near** v/i **1.** fig. nahekommen (dat). **2.** ~ doing s.th. et. beinahe tun. ~ **off** v/i **1.** herunterfallen von. **2.** ~ it! F hör schon auf damit! ~ **on** → come upon. ~ **o·ver** v/i überkommen, befallen: what has ~ you? was ist mit dir los? ~ **through** v/i Krankheit etc überstehen, -leben. ~ **to** v/i **1.** j-m (bsd. durch Erbschaft) zufallen. **2.** when it comes to paying wenn es ans Bezahlen geht. **3.** sich belaufen auf (acc). ~ **un·der** v/i **1.** unter ein Gesetz etc fallen. **2.** geraten unter (acc). ~ **up·on** v/i **1.** → come over. **2.** → come across.

Verbindungen mit Adverbien:

come| a·bout v/i geschehen, passieren. ~ **a·cross** v/i **1.** herüberkommen. **2.** verstanden werden; an-, rüberkommen (Rede etc). **3.** F damit herausrücken: ~ with mit Informationen herausrücken; Geld herausrücken. ~ **a·long** v/i **1.** mitkommen, -gehen: ~! F dalli! **2.** kommen, sich ergeben (Chance etc). ~ **a·part** v/i auseinanderfallen. ~ **a·way** v/i sich lösen, ab-, losgehen (Knopf etc). ~ **back** v/i **1.** zurückkommen: ~ to s.th. auf e-e Sache zurückkommen; it came back to him es fiel ihm wieder ein. **2.** wieder in Mode kommen. **3.** ein Comeback feiern. ~ **by** v/i vorbeikommen (Besucher). ~ **down** v/i **1.** herunterkommen, (Regen, Schnee) fallen. **2.** (ein)stürzen, (ein)fallen. **3.** fig. herunterkommen (Person): she has ~ quite a bit sie ist ganz schön tief gesunken. **4.** überliefert werden. **5.** F sinken (Preise); billiger werden (Ware). **6.** ~ on sich stürzen auf (acc); j-m aufs Dach steigen. **7.** ~ with F Geld herausrücken. **8.** ~ with erkranken an (dat). **9.** ~ to hinauslaufen auf (*acc*). **~ for·ward** *v/i* sich (freiwillig) melden, sich anbieten. **~ home** *v/i* **1.** nach Hause kommen, heimkommen. **2. ~ to s.o.** j-m schmerzlich bewußt werden. **~ in** *v/i* **1.** hereinkommen: **~!** herein!; (*Funk*) (bitte) kommen! **2.** eingehen, -treffen (*Nachricht etc*), *Sport*, ♣ einkommen, ♐ einlaufen: **~ second** den zweiten Platz belegen. **3.** aufkommen, in Mode kommen. **4.** an die Macht kommen. **5.** sich als *nützlich etc* erweisen: → **handy** 4. **6.** Berücksichtigung finden: *where do I* **~?** wo bleibe ich? **7. ~ for** *Bewunderung etc* erregen, auf *Kritik etc* stoßen. **8. ~ on** mitmachen bei, sich beteiligen an (*dat*). **~ off** *v/i* **1. → come away.** **2.** herunterfallen. **3.** auslaufen (*Stück*), enden (*Ausstellung*). **4.** ♐ stattfinden, über die Bühne gehen. **5.** ♐ abschneiden; erfolgreich verlaufen, glücken. **~ on** *v/i* **1.** herankommen: **~!** komm (mit)!; komm her!; los!; ♐ na, na! **2.** an die Reihe kommen. **3.** *thea.* auftreten; aufgeführt werden. **~ out** *v/i* **1.** herauskommen. **2.** *a.* **~ on strike** *bsd. Br.* streiken. **3.** herauskommen: a) erscheinen (*Buch etc*), b) an den Tag kommen (*Wahrheit etc*). **4.** ausgehen (*Haare, Farbe*), herausgehen (*Fleck etc*). **5.** ausbrechen (*Ausschlag*): **~ in a rash** e-n Ausschlag bekommen. **6.** *phot. etc gut etc* werden (*Bild*); *gut etc* herauskommen (*in dat*). **7. ~ with** ♐ mit der *Wahrheit etc* herausrücken; *Flüche etc* vom Stapel lassen. **8. ~ against** (**for**) sich aussprechen gegen (für). **~ o·ver** → **come across** 1, 2. **~ round** *v/i* **1.** vorbeikommen (**to** bei). **2.** wieder zu sich kommen; sich erholen. **~ through** *v/i* durchkommen (*Funkspruch, Patient etc*). **~ to** → **come round** 2. **~ up** *v/i* **1.** heraufkommen. **2.** herankommen: **~ to s.o.** auf j-n zukommen. **3.** ⚖ zur Verhandlung kommen. **4.** *a.* **~ for discussion** zur Sprache kommen. **5. ~ for** zur *Abstimmung, Entscheidung* kommen. **6.** aufkommen, Mode werden. **7. ~ to** reichen bis an (*acc*) *od.* zu; erreichen (*acc*); *fig.* heranreichen an (*acc*): → **expectation**. **8.** *his supper came up again* das Abendessen kam ihm wieder hoch. **9. ~ with** daherkommen mit, auftischen, präsentieren.

come|·at·a·ble [ˌkʌmˈætəbl] *adj* F erreichbar, zugänglich. **'~·back** s Comeback n: *stage* (*od.* *make*) *a* **~** ein Comeback feiern.

co·me·di·an [kəˈmiːdjən] *s* **1.** Komödienschauspieler *m*; Komiker *m* (*a. contp.*). **2.** Spaßvogel *m*, Witzbold *m* (*beide a. contp.*).

'come·down *s fig.* **1.** Niedergang *m*, Abstieg *m*. **2.** F Enttäuschung *f*.

com·e·dy [ˈkɒmədɪ] *s* **1.** Komödie *f* (*a. fig.*), Lustspiel *n*. **2.** Komik *f*.

come·ly [ˈkʌmlɪ] *adj* attraktiv, schön.

com·er [ˈkʌmə] *s* Ankömmling *m*.

com·et [ˈkɒmɪt] *s ast.* Komet *m*.

com·fort [ˈkʌmfət] **I** *v/t* **1.** trösten. **2.** beruhigen. **II** *s* **3.** Trost *m*: *cold* **~** ein schwacher Trost. **4.** Behaglichkeit *f*: *to live in* **~** sorgenfrei leben. **5.** *a. pl* Komfort *m*: *with every modern* **~** (*od.* *all modern* **~s**) mit allem Komfort; **~ sta·tion** *Am.* öffentliche Bedürfnisanstalt. **'com·fort·a·ble** *adj* □ **1.** komfortabel, bequem, behaglich: *make o.s.* **~** es sich bequem machen; *are you* **~?** haben Sie es bequem?, sitzen *od.* liegen *etc* Sie bequem?; *feel* **~** sich wohl fühlen. **2.** bequem, sorgenfrei (*Leben etc*). **3.** ausreichend, recht gut (*Einkommen etc*): *to be* **~** (*od.* *comfortably off*) einigermaßen wohlhabend sein. **'com·fort·er** *s* **1.** Tröster *m*. **2.** *bsd. Br.* Wollschal *m*. **3.** *Am.* Steppdecke *f*. **4.** *bsd. Br.* Schnuller *m*. **'com·fort·ing** *adj* tröstlich. **'com·fort·less** *adj* **1.** unbequem. **2.** trostlos.

com·fy [ˈkʌmfɪ] F → **comfortable** 1.

com·ic [ˈkɒmɪk] **I** *adj* (**~ally**) **1.** Komödien..., Lustspiel...: **~** *actor* Komödienschauspieler *m*; Komiker *m*; **~** *opera* ♪ komische Oper; **~** *tragedy* Tragikomödie *f* (*a. fig.*). **2.** komisch, humoristisch: **~** *paper* Witzblatt *n*; **~** *strips* *pl* Comics *pl*. **3.** → *comical* 1. **II** *s* **1.** → *comedian* 1. **2.** F Witzblatt *n*: **~s** *pl* Comics *pl*. **'com·i·cal** *adj* □ **1.** komisch, ulkig, spaßig. **2.** F komisch, sonderbar.

com·ing [ˈkʌmɪŋ] **I** *adj* kommend: a) zukünftig: *the* **~** *man* der kommende Mann, b) nächst: **~** *week* nächste Woche. **II** *s* Kommen *n*, Ankunft *f*: *the* **~s** *and goings* das Kommen u. Gehen.

com·ma [ˈkɒmə] *s* Komma *n*, Beistrich *m*.

com·mand [kəˈmɑːnd] **I** *v/t* **1.** befehlen

(**s.o. to do** j-m zu tun). **2.** fordern, verlangen: ~ **silence** sich Ruhe erbitten. **3.** ✕ kommandieren, befehligen. **4.** *Gefühle, Lage etc* beherrschen. **5.** *Vertrauen etc* einflößen: ~ (**s.o.'s**) **admiration** (j-m) Bewunderung abnötigen; ~ **respect** Achtung gebieten. **6.** zur Verfügung haben, verfügen über (*acc*). **II** *v/i* **7.** befehlen. **8.** ✕ das Kommando führen, den Befehl haben. **III** *s* **9.** Befehl *m*: **at s.o.'s** ~ auf j-s Befehl. **10.** Verfügung *f*: **be at s.o.'s** ~ j-m zur Verfügung stehen; **have a** ~ → 6. **11.** Beherrschung *f* (*e-r Sprache etc*): **have** ~ **of** *Fremdsprache etc* beherrschen; *his* ~ **of English** s-e Englischkenntnisse *pl*. **12.** ✕ Kommando *n*: a) (Ober)Befehl *m*: **be in** ~ → 8; ~ **module** (*Raumfahrt*) Kommandokapsel *f*, b) Befehl *m*. **com·man·dant** [ˌkɒmənˈdænt] *s* ✕ Kommandant *m*. **com·mand·er** [kəˈmɑːndə] *s* ✕ Kommandeur *m*, Befehlshaber *m*; Kommandant *m*: ~ **in chief** Oberbefehlshaber *m*. **com'mand·ing** *adj* □ **1.** ✕ kommandierend, befehlshabend. **2.** herrisch, gebieterisch. **3.** *die Gegend* beherrschend. weit (*Aussicht*). **com'mand·ment** *s* Gebot *n*, Vorschrift *f*: **the Ten** 2*s Bibl.* die Zehn Gebote. **com·man·do** [ˌﹸdəʊ] *pl* **-do(e)s** *s* ✕ Kommando *n*: ~ **squad** Kommandotrupp *m*.

com·mem·o·rate [kəˈmeməreɪt] *v/t* **1.** erinnern an (*acc*). **2.** (ehrend) gedenken (*gen*). **com,mem·o'ra·tion** *s* Gedenk-, Gedächtnisfeier *f*: **in** ~ **of** zum Gedenken *od*. Gedächtnis an (*acc*). **com'mem·o·ra·tive** [ˌﹸrətɪv] *adj* **1. be** ~ **of** erinnern an (*acc*). **2.** Gedenk-, Gedächtnis..., Erinnerungs...: ~ **issue** Gedenkausgabe *f* (*Briefmarken etc*); ~ **plaque** Gedenktafel *f*.

com·mence [kəˈmens] *v/i u. v/t* anfangen, beginnen (**to do, doing** zu tun). **com'mence·ment** *s* Anfang *m*, Beginn *m*.

com·mend [kəˈmend] *v/t* **1.** empfehlen. **2.** loben (**on** wegen). **3.** anvertrauen (**to** *dat*). **com'mend·a·ble** *adj* □ **1.** empfehlenswert. **2.** lobenswert, löblich. **com·men·da·tion** [ˌkɒmenˈdeɪʃn] *s* **1.** Empfehlung *f*. **2.** Lob *n*. **com'men·da·to·ry** [ˌﹸdətərɪ] *adj* **1.** Empfehlungs...: ~ **letter** Empfehlungsbrief *m*,

-schreiben *n*. **2.** lobend, anerkennend.

com·men·su·ra·ble [kəˈmenʃərəbl] *adj* □ vergleichbar (**to, with** mit). **com·'men·su·rate** [ˌﹸrət] *adj* (**to, with**) im Einklang stehend (mit), entsprechend *od*. angemessen (*dat*).

com·ment [ˈkɒment] **I** *s* (**on**) Kommentar *m* (zu): a) Bemerkung *f* (zu): **no** ~! kein Kommentar!, b) Anmerkung *f* (zu). **II** *v/i*: ~ **on** e-n Kommentar abgeben zu, *et.* kommentieren. **III** *v/t* bemerken (**that** daß). **com·men·ta·tor** [ˈﹸməntertə] *s* Kommentator *m*.

com·merce [ˈkɒmɜːs] *s* Handel *m*. **com·mer·cial** [kəˈmɜːʃl] **I** *adj* □ **1.** Geschäfts..., Handels...: ~ **attaché** Handelsattaché *m*; ~ **correspondence** Geschäfts-, Handelskorrespondenz *f*; ~ **letter** Geschäftsbrief *m*; ~ **travel(l)er** Handlungsreisende *m*. **2.** kaufmännisch (*Qualität etc*). **3.** *Rundfunk, TV:* Werbe..., Reklame...: ~ **broadcasting** Werbefunk *m*; kommerzieller Rundfunk; ~ **television** Werbefernsehen *n*; kommerzielles Fernsehen. **4.** kommerziell: a) auf finanziellen Gewinn abzielend, b) finanziell. **II** *s* *Rundfunk, TV:* Werbespot *m*; von e-m Sponsor finanzierte Sendung. **com'mer·cial·ize** [ˌﹸʃəlaɪz] *v/t* kommerzialisieren, vermarkten.

com·mie [ˈkɒmɪ] *s* F Kommunist(in).

com·mis·er·ate [kəˈmɪzəreɪt] *v/t* (*u. v/i* ~ **with**) bemitleiden. **com,mis·er'a·tion** *s* Mitleid *n*.

com·mis·sion [kəˈmɪʃn] **I** *s* **1.** Auftrag *m*. **2.** Kommission *f*, Ausschuß *m*: **be on the** ~ Mitglied der Kommission sein. **3.** ✝ a) Kommission *f*: **on** ~ in Kommission, b) Provision *f*: **on** ~ gegen Provision; **on a** ~ **basis** auf Provisionsbasis. **4.** Begehung *f*, Verübung *f* (*e-s Verbrechens etc*). **II** *v/t* **5.** beauftragen. **6.** *et.* in Auftrag geben: ~**ed work** Auftragsarbeit *f*. **com·mis·sion·aire** [kəˌmɪʃəˈneə] *s bsd. Br.* (livrierter) Portier (*Theater, Hotel etc*). **com'mis·sion·er** [ˌﹸʃnə] *s* Beauftragte *m*.

com·mit [kəˈmɪt] *v/t* **1.** anvertrauen, übergeben (**to** *dat*): ~ **to paper** zu Papier bringen. **2.** ✝️ einweisen (**to** in *acc*). **3.** *Verbrechen etc* begehen, verüben. **4.** (**to**) verpflichten (zu), festlegen (auf *acc*): ~**ted** engagiert (*Schriftsteller etc*).

com'mit·ment *s* 1. Übergabe *f*. 2. → **committal** 2. 3. Begehung *f*, Verübung *f*. 4. Verpflichtung *f*, Festlegung *f*, (*a. politisches etc*) Engagement: *without any* ~ ganz unverbindlich. **com'mit·tal** [~tl] *s* 1. → **commitment** 1, 3, 4. 2. ☆☆ Einweisung *f*. **com'mit·tee** [~tɪ] *s* Komitee *n*, Ausschuß *m*: *be* (*od. sit*) *on a* ~ in e-m Ausschuß sein.

com·mode [kə'məʊd] *s* (Wasch)Kommode *f*. **com'mo·di·ous** [~djəs] *adj* □ geräumig.

com·mod·i·ty [kə'mɒdətɪ] *s* ✝ Ware *f*, (Handels)Artikel *m*. ~ **ex·change** *s* Warenbörse *f*.

com·mo·dore ['kɒmədɔː] *s* ⚓ Kommodore *m*.

com·mon ['kɒmən] I *adj* (□ → *commonly*) 1. gemeinsam (*a.* A), gemeinschaftlich: ~ *to all* allen gemeinsam; ~ *room* Gemeinschaftsraum *m*; → *cause* 3, *denominator*. 2. allgemein: *by* ~ *consent* mit allgemeiner Zustimmung. 3. allgemein (bekannt), alltäglich: *it is* ~ *knowledge* (*usage*) es ist allgemein bekannt (üblich); ~ *name* häufiger Name; ~ *sight* alltäglicher *od.* vertrauter Anblick. 4. *bsd. biol.* gemein: ~ *or garden* F Feld-Wald-u.-Wiesen-...; → *cold* 5. 5. gewöhnlich, ohne Rang: *the* ~ *people* *pl* das einfache Volk; ~ *soldier* einfacher Soldat. II *s* 6. Gemeinsamkeit *f*: *in* ~ gemeinsam (*with* mit). 7. *das* Gewöhnliche: *out of the* ~ außergewöhnlich, -ordentlich. 8. → *commons*.

'com·mon·er *s* Bürger(liche) *m*.

com·mon **law** *s* 1. *Br.* Gewohnheitsrecht *n*. 2. *das* anglo-amerikanische Rechtssystem.

com·mon·ly ['kɒmənlɪ] *adv* gewöhnlich, im allgemeinen.

Com·mon| Mar·ket *s* Gemeinsamer Markt. **'2·place** I *s* 1. Gemeinplatz *m*. 2. alltägliche Sache. II *adj* 3. alltäglich, abgedroschen. ~ **Prayer** *s eccl.* anglikanische Liturgie.

com·mons ['kɒmənz] *s pl* 1. *the* 2 *parl. Br.* das Unterhaus. 2. *be kept on small* ~ auf schmale Kost gesetzt sein.

com·mon| **sense** *s* gesunder Menschenverstand. '~wealth *s*: *the* 2 (*of Nations*) das Commonwealth.

com·mo·tion [kə'məʊʃn] *s* 1. Aufregung *f*. 2. Aufruhr *m*, Tumult *m*.

com·mu·nal ['kɒmjʊnl] *adj* □ 1. Gemeinde..., Kommunal... 2. gemeinschaftlich: ~ *aerial* (*bsd. Am.* **antenna**) TV Gemeinschaftsantenne *f*.

com·mune¹ [kə'mjuːn] *v/i* 1. sich (vertraulich) unterhalten (*with* mit): ~ *with o.s.* mit sich zu Rate gehen. 2. *bsd. Am.* → **communicate** 6.

com·mune² ['kɒmjuːn] *s* Gemeinde *f*, Kommune *f* (*a. sociol.*).

com·mu·ni·ca·ble [kə'mjuːnɪkəbl] *adj* □ 1. mitteilbar. 2. ☆ übertragbar. **com'mu·ni·cate** [~keɪt] I *v/t* 1. mitteilen (*to* dat). 2. ☆, *phys.* übertragen (*to auf acc*) (*a. fig.*). II *v/i* 3. kommunizieren, besprechen, in Verbindung stehen (*with* mit). 4. sich in Verbindung setzen (*with* mit). 5. miteinander (durch e-e Tür *etc*) verbunden sein: *communicating door* Verbindungstür *f*. 6. *eccl.* das Abendmahl empfangen, kommunizieren. **com,mu·ni'ca·tion** *s* 1. Mitteilung *f* (*to an acc*): ~ *cord* 🚆 *Br.* Notbremse *f*. 2. Übertragung *f*: ~ *of power phys.* Kraftübertragung. 3. Verbindung *f*: *be in* ~ *with* in Verbindung stehen mit. 4. *pl bsd.* ✕ Fernmeldewesen *n*: ~*s satellite* Nachrichtensatellit *m*; ~ *system* Fernmeldenetz *n*. **com'mu·ni·ca·tive** [~kətɪv] *adj* □ mitteilsam, gesprächig, kommunikativ.

com·mun·ion [kə'mjuːnjən] *s* 1. (*eccl.* Religions)Gemeinschaft *f*. 2. 2 *eccl.* Abendmahl *n*, Kommunion *f*: *go to* ~ zum Abendmahl gehen; ~ *cup* Abendmahlskelch *m*.

com·mu·ni·qué [kə'mjuːnɪkeɪ] *s* Kommuniqué *n*.

com·mu·nism ['kɒmjʊnɪzəm] *s* Kommunismus *m*. **'com·mu·nist** I *s* Kommunist(in). II *adj* kommunistisch. **,com·mu'nis·tic** *adj* (~*ally*) kommunistisch.

com·mu·ni·ty [kə'mjuːnətɪ] *s* 1. Gemeinschaft *f*: ~ *of heirs* Erbengemeinschaft; ~ *singing* gemeinsames Singen; ~ *spirit* Gemeinschaftsgeist *m*. 2. Gemeinde *f*. 3. Gemeinsamkeit *f*, gemeinsamer Besitz: ~ *of goods* (*od. property*) Gütergemeinschaft *f*. ~ **cen·ter**, *bsd. Br.* ~ **cen·tre** *s* Gemeinschaftszentrum *n*. ~ **home** *s Br.* Erziehungsheim *n*.

com·mut·a·ble [kə'mjuːtəbl] *adj* umwandelbar. **com·mu·ta·tion** [,kɒmjuː-

compère

'tei∫n] *s* **1.** Umwandlung *f.* **2.** Ablösung *f;* Ablöse(summe) *f.* **3.** ⅍ (Straf)Umwandlung *f.* **4.** 🚇, *etc* Pendeln *n:* **~ ticket** *Am.* Dauer-, Zeitkarte *f.* **com-mute** [kə'mju:t] **I** *v/t* **1.** eintauschen (*for* für). **2.** ⅍ *Strafe* umwandeln (*to, into* in *acc*). **3.** *Verpflichtung etc* umwandeln (*into* in *acc*), ablösen (*for, into* durch). **II** *v/i* **4.** 🚇, *etc* pendeln. **com'mut-er** *s* a) *Am.* Zeitkarteninhaber(in,) b) Pendler(in): **~ train** Pendler-, Nahverkehrszug *m.*

com-pact [kəm'pækt] **I** *adj* □ **1.** kompakt: **~ cassette** Kompaktkassette *f.* **2.** eng, klein (*Wohnung etc*). **3.** gedrungen (*Gestalt*). **4.** knapp, gedrängt (*Stil etc*). **II** *v/t* **5.** zs.-drängen, fest miteinander verbinden. **III** *s* ['kɒmpækt] **6.** kompakte Masse. **7.** Puderdose *f.* **com'pact-ness** *s* **1.** Kompaktheit *f.* **2.** Knappheit *f,* Gedrängtheit *f.*

com-pan-ion [kəm'pænjən] *s* **1.** Begleiter(in) (*a. fig.*). **2.** Kamerad(in), Genosse *m,* Genossin *f.* **3.** Gesellschafterin *f.* **4.** Gegenstück *n,* Pendant *n.* **5.** Handbuch *n,* Leitfaden *m.* **com'pan-ion-a-ble** *adj* □ umgänglich, gesellig. **com'pan-ion-ship** *s* Begleitung *f,* Gesellschaft *f.*

com-pa-ny ['kʌmpənɪ] *s* **1.** Gesellschaft *f:* **in ~** (*with*) in Gesellschaft *f;* Begleitung (*gen od.* von); **be in good ~** sich in guter Gesellschaft befinden; **keep** (*od.* **bear**) **s.o. ~** *j-m* Gesellschaft leisten; **part ~** (*with*) sich trennen (von); *fig.* anderer Meinung sein (als) (*on* in *dat*). **2.** Gesellschaft *f;* Besuch *m,* Gäste *pl:* **be fond of ~** die Geselligkeit lieben; **present ~ excepted!** Anwesende ausgenommen! **3.** Gesellschaft *f,* Umgang *m:* **keep good ~** guten Umgang pflegen; **keep ~ with** verkehren mit. **4.** ✝ Gesellschaft *f,* Firma *f:* **~ car** Firmenwagen *m;* **~ pension** Betriebsrente *f.* **5.** ✕ Kompanie *f.* **6.** *thea.* Truppe *f.*

com-pa-ra-ble ['kɒmpərəbl] *adj* □ vergleichbar (*with, to* mit). **com-par-a-tive** [kəm'pærətɪv] **I** *adj* □ **1.** vergleichend. **2.** verhältnismäßig, relativ. **3.** ~ **degree** → **4.** **II** *s* **4.** *ling.* Komparativ *m.* **com'par-a-tive-ly** *adv* verhältnismäßig: a) vergleichsweise, b) ziemlich. **com-pare** [.'peə] **I** *v/t* **1.** vergleichen (*with, to* mit): **~d with** (*od.* **to**) im Ver-

gleich zu, gegenüber (*dat*). **2.** vergleichen, gleichsetzen, -stellen: *not to be ~d with* (*od.* **to**) nicht zu vergleichen mit. **3.** *ling.* steigern. **II** *v/i* **4.** sich vergleichen (lassen): **~ favo(u)rably with** den Vergleich mit ... nicht zu scheuen brauchen. **III** *s* **5. beyond** (*od. past, without*) **~** unvergleichlich. **com-par-i-son** [.'pærɪsn] *s* **1.** Vergleich *m:* **by ~** vergleichsweise; **in ~ with** im Vergleich mit *od.* zu; **bear** (*od.* **stand**) **~ with** e-n Vergleich aushalten mit; **without ~, beyond** (*all*) **~** unvergleichlich. **2.** *ling.* Steigerung *f.*

com-part-ment [kəm'pɑ:tmənt] *s* **1.** Fach *n.* **2.** 🚇 Abteil *n.*

com-pass ['kʌmpəs] *s* **1.** Kompaß *m.* **2.** *pl, a.* **pair of ~es** Zirkel *m.*

com-pas-sion [kəm'pæ∫n] *s* Mitleid *n,* -gefühl *n:* **have** (*od.* **take**) **~ on** (*od.* **for**) Mitleid mit *j-m* haben. **com'pas-sion-ate** [.∫ənət] *adj* □ mitleidsvoll, -fühlend.

com-pat-i-ble [kəm'pætəbl] *adj* □ **1.** vereinbar (*with* mit), miteinander vereinbar. **2.** verträglich: **be ~** (*with*) sich vertragen (mit), passen (zu), zs.-passen.

com-pa-tri-ot [kəm'pætrɪət] *s* Landsmann *m,* -männin *f.*

com-pel [kəm'pel] *v/t* **1.** zwingen: **be ~led to do** (*od. into doing*) s.th. gezwungen sein, et. zu tun, et. tun müssen. **2.** *et.* erzwingen. **3.** *a. Bewunderung etc* abnötigen (*from dat*).

com-pen-di-um [kəm'pendɪəm] *pl* -**ums**, -**a** [.ə] *s* **1.** Kompendium *n,* Handbuch *n.* **2.** Zs.-fassung *f,* Abriß *m.*

com-pen-sate ['kɒmpenseɪt] **I** *v/t* **1.** kompensieren (*a. psych.*), ausgleichen. **2.** *j-n* entschädigen (*for* für); et. ersetzen, vergüten, für et. Ersatz leisten (*to dat*). **3.** *Am. j-n* bezahlen, entlohnen. **II** *v/i* **4.** Ersatz leisten (*for* für). **5.** **~ for** → **1.** **com-pen-sa-tion** *s* **1.** Kompensation *f,* Ausgleich *m:* **in ~ for** als Ausgleich für. **2.** (Schaden)Ersatz *m,* Entschädigung *f;* Vergütung *f:* **pay ~** Schadenersatz leisten; **as** (*od. by way of*) **~** als Ersatz. **3.** *Am.* Bezahlung *f,* Gehalt *n,* Lohn *m.* **4.** *psych.* Kompensation *f,* Ersatzhandlung *f.*

com-père, com-pere ['kɒmpeə] *bsd. Br.* **I** *s* Conférencier *m,* Ansager(in). **II** *v/t* konferieren, ansagen. **III** *v/i* koncompete	834

ferieren, als Conférencier fungieren.
com·pete [kəmˈpiːt] v/i **1.** sich (mit)bewerben (**for** um). **2.** ✝ u. weitS. konkurrieren (**with** mit). **3.** wetteifern, sich messen (**with** mit). **4.** Sport: (am Wettkampf) teilnehmen; a. weitS. kämpfen (**for** um; **against** gegen).
com·pe·tence, com·pe·ten·cy [ˈkɒmpɪtəns(ɪ)] s **1.** Fähigkeit f, Tüchtigkeit f. **2.** ⚖ Zuständigkeit f, Kompetenz f (beide a. weitS.); Zulässigkeit f. **'com·pe·tent** adj □ **1.** fähig (**to do** zu tun), tüchtig. **2.** fach-, sachkundig. **3.** gut(gemacht), gekonnt. **4.** ⚖ zuständig, kompetent (beide a. weitS.); zulässig (Beweise, Zeuge).
com·pe·ti·tion [ˌkɒmpɪˈtɪʃn] s **1.** allg. Wettbewerb m (**for** um). **2.** Konkurrenz f: a) ✝ Wettbewerb m, Konkurrenzkampf m: **unfair** ~ unlauterer Wettbewerb, b) ✝ Konkurrenzfirma f, -firmen pl, c) weitS. Gegner pl, Rivalen pl. **3.** Preisausschreiben n. **com·pet·i-tive** [kəmˈpetətɪv] adj □ **1.** konkurrierend. **2.** Wettbewerbs..., Konkurrenz..., ✝ a. konkurrenzfähig. **com'pet·i·tor** [~tɪtə] s **1.** Mitbewerber(in) (**for** um). **2.** bsd. ✝ Konkurrent(in). **3.** bsd. Sport: Teilnehmer(in).
com·pi·la·tion [ˌkɒmpɪˈleɪʃn] s Kompilation f (a. Werk). **com·pile** [kəmˈpaɪl] v/t Verzeichnis etc kompilieren, zs.stellen, Material zs.-tragen. **com'pil·er** s Kompilator m.
com·pla·cence, com·pla·cen·cy [kəmˈpleɪsns(ɪ)] s Selbstzufriedenheit f, -gefälligkeit f. **com'pla·cent** adj □ selbstzufrieden, -gefällig.
com·plain [kəmˈpleɪn] v/i **1.** sich beklagen od. beschweren (**of, about** über acc; **to** bei): **~ing letter** Beschwerdebrief m. **2.** klagen (**of** über acc). **3.** ✝ reklamieren: **~ about** et. reklamieren od. beanstanden. **com'plaint** s **1.** Klage f, Beschwerde f: **make** (od. **lodge**) **a ~** (**about** ~ **complain** 1; ~ **book** Beschwerdebuch n. **2.** ✝ Reklamation f, Beanstandung f. **3.** ⚕ Leiden n, pl a. Beschwerden pl.
com·plai·sance [kəmˈpleɪzəns] s Gefälligkeit f, Entgegenkommen n. **com'plai·sant** adj □ gefällig, entgegenkommend.
com·ple·ment I s [ˈkɒmplɪmənt] **1.** (**to**

gen) Ergänzung f (a. ling.); Vervollkommnung f. **2.** Ergänzungsstück n. II v/t [ˈ~mənt] **3.** ergänzen; vervollkommnen. **com·ple·men·ta·ry** [ˌ~ˈmentərɪ] adj □ (sich) ergänzend: **be ~ to s.th.** et. ergänzen; ~ **colo(u)rs** pl Komplementärfarben pl.
com·plete [kəmˈpliːt] I adj □ **1.** komplett, vollständig. **2.** vollzählig, komplett. **3.** beendet, vollendet. II v/t **4.** vervollständigen. **5.** vollenden, abschließen. **6.** fig. vollenden, vollkommen machen. **7.** Formular ausfüllen. **com'plete·ness** s Vollständigkeit f. **com'ple·tion** s **1.** Vervollständigung f. **2.** Vollendung f: **bring to ~** zum Abschluß bringen. **3.** Ausfüllung f.
com·plex [ˈkɒmpleks] I adj □ **1.** zs.-gesetzt (a. ling.). **2.** komplex, vielschichtig. II s **3.** Komplex m, das Ganze. **4.** (Gebäude- etc)Komplex m. **5.** psych. Komplex m.
com·plex·ion [kəmˈplekʃn] s **1.** Gesichtsfarbe f, Teint m. **2.** fig. Aussehen n, Anstrich m. **3.** fig. Couleur f, (politische) Richtung.
com·plex·i·ty [kəmˈpleksətɪ] s **1.** Komplexität f, Vielschichtigkeit f. **2.** et. Komplexes.
com·pli·ance [kəmˈplaɪəns] s **1.** (**with**) Einwilligung f (in acc); Befolgung f (gen): **in ~ with e-r Vorschrift etc gemäß. **2.** Willfährigkeit f. **com'pli·ant** adj □ willfährig.
com·pli·cate [ˈkɒmplɪkeɪt] v/t komplizieren. **'com·pli·cat·ed** adj □ kompliziert. **com·pli·ca·tion** s **1.** Komplikation f (a. ⚕). **2.** Kompliziertheit f.
com·plic·i·ty [kəmˈplɪsətɪ] s Mitschuld f, Mittäterschaft f (**in** an dat): ~ **in murder** ⚖ Beihilfe f zum Mord.
com·pli·ment I s [ˈkɒmplɪmənt] **1.** Kompliment n: **angle** (od. **fish**) **for ~s** nach Komplimenten fischen; **pay s.o. a ~** j-m ein Kompliment machen. **2.** Empfehlung f, Gruß m: **with the ~s of the season** mit den besten Wünschen zum Fest. II v/t [ˈ~mənt] **3.** j-m ein Kompliment od. Komplimente machen (**on** wegen). **com·pli·men·ta·ry** [ˌ~ˈmentərɪ] adj □ **1.** höflich, Höflichkeits...: ~ **close** Gruß-, Schlußformel f (in Briefen). **2.** Ehren..., Frei..., Gratis...: ~ **ticket** Ehren-, Freikarte f.

com·ply [kəmˈplaɪ] *v/i* (**with**) einwilligen (**in** *acc*); (*e-m Wunsch od. Befehl*) nachkommen *od.* Folge leisten, erfüllen (*acc*); (*e-e Abmachung*) befolgen, einhalten: **~ with the law** sich an die Gesetze halten.

com·po·nent [kəmˈpəʊnənt] **I** *adj* Teil...: **~ part** Bestandteil *m*. **II** *s* (Bestand)Teil *m*, *a.* ⚛, *phys.* Komponente *f*.

com·pose [kəmˈpəʊz] **I** *v/t* **1.** zs.-setzen *od.* -stellen: **be ~d of** bestehen *od.* sich zs.-setzen aus. **2.** *Satz etc* bilden. **3.** *Gedicht etc* verfassen. **4.** ♪ komponieren. **5.** *Gemälde etc* entwerfen. **6.** *typ.* (ab)setzen. **7.** besänftigen: **~ o.s.** sich beruhigen *od.* fassen. **8.** *Streit etc* beilegen, schlichten. **9.** *Gedanken* sammeln. **II** *v/i* **10.** ♪ komponieren. **com·posed** *adj*, **com·pos·ed·ly** [~zɪdlɪ] *adv* ruhig, gelassen. **com·pos·er** *s* **1.** ♪ Komponist *m*. **2.** Verfasser(in). **com·po·site** [ˈkɒmpəzɪt] *adj* zs.-gesetzt. **com·po·'si·tion** *s* **1.** Zs.-setzung *f*. **2.** Verfassen *n*. **3.** Schrift(stück) *f* *n*. **4.** *ped.* Aufsatz *m*. **5.** Komposition *f*: a) Musikstück *n*, b) (künstlerische) Anordnung *od.* Gestaltung, Aufbau *m*. **6.** Beschaffenheit *f*, Art *f* **7.** *typ.* Setzen *n*, Satz *m*. **com·pos·i·tor** [kəmˈpɒzɪtə] *s* (Schrift)Setzer *m*. **com·post** [ˈkɒmpɒst] **I** *s* Kompost *m*: **~ heap** Komposthaufen *m*. **II** *v/t* kompostieren. **com·po·sure** [kəmˈpəʊʒə] *s* (Gemüts)Ruhe *f*, Fassung *f*, Gelassenheit *f*.

com·pote [ˈkɒmpɒt] *s* Kompott *n*.

com·pound¹ [kəmˈpaʊnd] **I** *v/t* **1.** zs.-setzen, (ver)mischen. **2.** zs.-setzen *od.* -stellen. **3.** *Streit* beilegen; *Sache* gütlich *od.* durch Vergleich regeln. **II** *v/i* **4.** sich vergleichen *od.* einigen (**with** mit; **for** über *acc*). **III** *adj* [ˈkɒmpaʊnd] **5.** zs.-gesetzt: **~ interest** ♣ Zinseszinsen *pl*; **~ word** → 11. **6.** ⚚ kompliziert (*Bruch*). **7.** ⚡, ⚙ Verbund... **IV** *s* [ˈkɒmpaʊnd] **8.** Zs.-setzung *f*, Mischung *f*. **9.** Mischung *f*, Masse *f* ⚛. **10.** ⚡ Verbindung *f*. **11.** *ling.* Kompositum *n*, zs.-gesetztes Wort.

com·pound² [ˈkɒmpaʊnd] *s* **1.** Lager *n*. **2.** Gefängnishof *m*. **3.** (Tier)Gehege *n*.

com·pre·hend [ˌkɒmprɪˈhend] *v/t* **1.** umfassen, einschließen. **2.** begreifen, verstehen. **com·pre·hen·si·ble** *adj* begreiflich, verständlich. **com·pre·hen-**

si·bly *adv* verständlicherweise. **com·pre·hen·sion** *s* **1.** Begriffsvermögen *n*, Verstand *m*: **past ~** unfaßbar, unfaßlich. **2.** (*of*) Begreifen *n* (*gen*), Verständnis *n* (für). **com·pre·hen·sive I** *adj* □ **1.** umfassend: **~ school** → 3. **2.** Begriffs...: **~ faculty** Fassungskraft *f*, Begriffsvermögen *n*. **II** *s* **3.** *Br.* Gesamtschule *f*.

com·press I *v/t* [kəmˈpres] **1.** zs.-drücken, -pressen, *phys.,* ⚙ komprimieren (*a. fig.*), verdichten: **~ed air** Preß-, Druckluft *f*. **II** *s* [ˈkɒmpres] ✚ Kompresse *f*. **com·pres·sion** [kəmˈpreʃn] *s* **1.** Zs.-drücken *n*, -pressen *n*. **2.** *phys.,* ⚙ Druck *m*; Kompression *f*, Verdichtung *f*. **com·pres·sor** [~sə] *s* ⚙ Kompressor *m*.

com·prise [kəmˈpraɪz] *v/t* **1.** einschließen, umfassen. **2.** bestehen *od.* sich zs.-setzen aus.

com·pro·mise [ˈkɒmprəmaɪz] **I** *s* **1.** Kompromiß *m*: **make a ~** e-n Kompromiß schließen; **~ formula** Kompromißformel *f*; **~ settlement** (*od. solution*) Kompromißlösung *f*. **II** *v/t* **2.** *Ruf, Leben etc* gefährden, aufs Spiel setzen. **3.** bloßstellen, kompromittieren. **III** *v/i* **4.** e-n Kompromiß schließen (*a. fig. contp.*) Kompromisse schließen.

com·pul·sion [kəmˈpʌlʃn] *s* Zwang *m* (*a. psych.*): **under ~** unter Zwang, zwangsweise. **com·pul·sive** [~sɪv] *adj* □ **1.** zwingend, Zwangs... **2.** *psych.* zwanghaft. **com·pul·so·ry** [~sərɪ] *adj* □ **1.** zwangsweise: **~ auction** Zwangsversteigerung *f*; **~ measures** *pl* Zwangsmaßnahmen *pl*. **2.** obligatorisch, Pflicht...: **~ education** allgemeine Schulpflicht; **~ military service** allgemeine Wehrpflicht; **~ subject** *ped. univ.* Pflichtfach *n*.

com·punc·tion [kəmˈpʌŋkʃn] *s* Gewissensbisse *pl*; Reue *f*; Bedenken *pl*: **without ~** *a.* bedenkenlos.

com·pu·ta·tion [ˌkɒmpjuːˈteɪʃn] *s* **1.** Berechnung *f*. **2.** Schätzung *f*. **com·pute** [kəmˈpjuːt] *v/t* **1.** berechnen. **2.** schätzen, veranschlagen (**at** *auf acc*). **com·put·er** *s* Computer *m*: **~ centre** (*Am.* **center**) Rechenzentrum *n*; **~-controlled** computergesteuert; **~ language** Computersprache *f*; **~ science** Informatik *f*. **com·put·er·ize** [~təraɪz] **I** *v/t*

Werk etc computerisieren, auf Computer umstellen; *System etc* mit e-m Computer durchführen; computerisieren, mit Hilfe e-s Computers errechnen *od.* zs.-stellen. **II** *v/i* sich auf Computer umstellen.

com·rade ['kɒmreɪd] *s* **1.** Kamerad *m*, Gefährte *m*. **2.** *pol.* (Partei)Genosse *m*. **'com·rade·ship** *s* Kameradschaft *f*.

con¹ [kɒn] **I** *s* **1.** Nein-Stimme *f*. **2.** Gegenargument *n*: → **pro¹**. **II** *adv* **3.** F dagegen: *be ~*.

con² [~] *sl.* **I** *adj* betrügerisch: *~ man* Betrüger *m*; Hochstapler *m*; *~ game* aufgelegter Schwindel; Hochstapelei *f*. **II** *v/t* betrügen (*out of* um), reinlegen.

con·cat·e·nate [kɒn'kætɪneɪt] *v/t* verknüpfen. **con,cat·e·na·tion** *s* **1.** Verkettung *f*. **2.** Kette *f*, Reihe *f*.

con·cave ['kɒŋkeɪv] *adj* □ konkav, hohl: *~ mirror* Hohlspiegel *m*.

con·ceal [kən'siːl] *v/t* **1.** (*from* vor *dat*) verbergen: a) verstecken, b) geheimhalten, c) verschweigen, verheimlichen. **con'ceal·ment** *s* **1.** Verbergung *f*, Geheimhaltung *f*, Verheimlichung *f*. **2.** Verborgenheit *f*: *stay in ~* sich verborgen halten.

con·cede [kən'siːd] *v/t* zugestehen, einräumen: a) gewähren, bewilligen, b) anerkennen (*a. that* daß). **con'ced·ed·ly** *adv* zugestandenermaßen.

con·ceit [kən'siːt] *s* Einbildung *f*, Dünkel *m*: *be full of ~* völlig von sich eingenommen sein. **con'ceit·ed** *adj* □ eingebildet, dünkelhaft.

con·ceiv·a·ble [kən'siːvəbl] *adj* □ denk-, vorstellbar: *the best plan ~* der denkbar beste Plan. **con'ceive** **I** *v/t* **1.** *biol.* Kind empfangen. **2.** begreifen. **3.** sich *et.* vorstellen *od.* denken, sich e-n Begriff *od.* e-e Vorstellung machen von. **4.** ersinnen, ausdenken. **II** *v/i* **5.** *biol.* empfangen, schwanger werden (*Mensch*); aufnehmen, trächtig werden (*Tier*). **6.** *~ of* → 3.

con·cen·trate ['kɒnsəntreɪt] **I** *v/t* konzentrieren: a) zs.-ziehen, -ballen, massieren, b) *Gedanken etc* richten (*on* auf *acc*), c) 🜂 anreichern. **II** *v/i* sich konzentrieren. **III** *s* Konzentrat *n*. ,con·cen'tra·tion *s* Konzentration *f*: a) Zs.-ziehung *f*, -ballung *f*, Massierung *f*: *~ camp* Konzentrationslager *n*, b) ge-

spannte Aufmerksamkeit: *power of ~* Konzentrationsfähigkeit *f*, c) 🜂 Anreicherung *f*.

con·cen·tric [kən'sentrɪk] *adj* (*~ally*) konzentrisch.

con·cept ['kɒnsept] *s* **1.** *phls.* Begriff *m*. **2.** Gedanke *m*, Auffassung *f*. **con·cep·tion** [kən'sepʃn] *s* **1.** *biol.* Empfängnis *f*. **2.** Begreifen *n*; Begriffsvermögen *n*; Begriff *m*, Vorstellung *f* (*of* von); Konzeption *f*, Idee *f*. **3.** Entwurf *m*, Konzept *n*. **con'cep·tu·al** [~tʃʊəl] *adj* begrifflich, Begriffs...

con·cern [kən'sɜːn] **I** *v/t* **1.** angehen: a) betreffen, b) von Wichtigkeit *od.* Interesse sein für. **2.** beunruhigen. **3.** *~ o.s. with* sich beschäftigen *od.* befassen mit. **II** *s* **4.** Angelegenheit *f*, Sache *f*: *that is no ~ of mine* das geht mich nichts an. **5.** ✝ Geschäft *n*, Unternehmen *n*. **6.** Unruhe *f*, Sorge *f* (*at, about, for* wegen, um). **7.** Wichtigkeit *f*: *a matter of national ~* ein nationales Anliegen. **8.** Beziehung *f* (*with* zu): *have no ~ with* nichts zu tun haben mit. **9.** (*at, about, for, in, with*) Teilnahme *f* (an *dat*), Rücksicht *f* (auf *acc*), Anteil *m* (an *dat*), Interesse *n* (für). **10.** F Ding *n*, Geschichte *f*. **con'cerned** *adj* **1.** betroffen, betreffend. **2.** (*in*) beteiligt, interessiert (an *dat*); verwickelt (in *acc*). **3.** (*with, in*) befaßt, beschäftigt (mit); handelnd (von). **4.** (*about, at, for*) besorgt (um), beunruhigt (wegen). **con'cern·ing** *prp* betreffend, hinsichtlich, was ... (an)betrifft.

con·cert *s* **1.** ['kɒnsət] ♪ Konzert *n*: *~ hall* Konzertsaal *m*; *~ pianist* Konzertpianist(in). **2.** ['kɒnsɜːt] *in ~ with* in Übereinstimmung *od.* gemeinsam mit. **con·cert·ed** [kən'sɜːtɪd] *adj* gemeinsam: *~ action* gemeinsames Vorgehen; ✝, *pol.* konzertierte Aktion. **con·cer·to** [kən'tʃeətəʊ] *pl* **-tos**, **-ti** [~tɪ] *s* ♪ (Solo)Konzert *n* (*mit Orchesterbegleitung*): *piano ~* Klavierkonzert.

con·ces·sion [kən'seʃn] *s* **1.** Konzession *f*, Zugeständnis *n*. **2.** Genehmigung *f*, Bewilligung *f*; (amtliche *od.* staatliche) Konzession.

con·cil·i·ate [kən'sɪlɪeɪt] *v/t* **1.** aus-, versöhnen, versöhnlich stimmen. **2.** *Gunst etc* gewinnen. **3.** in Einklang bringen. **con,cil·i'a·tion** *s* Aus-, Versöhnung *f*: *~*

committee Schlichtungsausschuß *m.*

con·cil·i·a·tor *s* Schlichter *m,* Vermittler *m.* **con'cil·i·a·to·ry** [~ətərɪ] *adj* □ versöhnlich, vermittelnd.

con·cise [kənˈsaɪs] *adj* □ kurz, knapp, prägnant. **con'cise·ness** *s* Kürze *f,* Prägnanz *f.*

con·clave [ˈkɒŋkleɪv] *s eccl.* Konklave *n.*

con·clude [kənˈkluːd] **I** *v/t* **1.** beenden, (be-, ab)schließen (*with* mit): *to be* ~*d* Schluß folgt. **2.** *Vertrag etc* abschließen. **3.** *et.* folgern, schließen (*from* aus): ~ *that* zu dem Schluß kommen, daß. **II** *v/i* **4.** enden, schließen (*with* mit). **con'clud·ing** *adj* abschließend, Schluß...

con·clu·sion [kənˈkluːʒn] *s* **1.** (Ab-)Schluß *m,* Ende *n:* *bring to a* ~ zum Abschluß bringen; *in* ~ zum Schluß. **2.** Abschluß *m* (*e-s Vertrags etc*). **3.** (Schluß)Folgerung *f:* *come to* (*od. arrive at*) *the* ~ *that* zu dem Schluß kommen, daß; *draw a* ~ e-n Schluß ziehen; *jump at* (*od. to*) ~*s, leap to* ~*s, rush at* ~*s* voreilig(e) Schlüsse ziehen. **con'clu·sive** [~sɪv] *adj* □ **1.** → *concluding.* **2.** schlüssig (*Beweis*).

con·coct [kənˈkɒkt] *v/t* **1.** (zs.-)brauen. **2.** *fig.* aushecken, -brüten. **con'coc·tion** *s* **1.** (Zs.-)Brauen *n.* **2.** Gebräu *n* (*a. contp.*). **3.** *fig.* Ausbrüten *n,* -hecken *n.* **4.** *fig.* Erfindung *f.*

con·course [ˈkɒŋkɔːs] *s* **1.** Zs.-treffen *n;* Zs.-fluß *m.* **2.** (Menschen)Auflauf *m,* (-)Menge *f.* **3.** freier Platz (*für Versammlungen etc*); *Am.* Bahnhofshalle *f.*

con·crete **I** *v/t* **1.** [kənˈkriːt] konkretisieren. **2.** [ˈkɒŋkriːt] betonieren: ~ *over* zubetonieren. **II** *adj* [ˈkɒŋkriːt] □ **3.** konkret (*a. ling., ♪ etc*). **4.** betoniert, Beton...: ~ *jungle* Betonwüste *f;* ~ *mix·er* Betonmischmaschine *f;* ~ *pile* Betonklotz *m,* -silo *m.* **III** *s* [ˈkɒŋkriːt] **5.** Beton *m.*

con·cu·bine [ˈkɒŋkjʊbaɪn] *s* Nebenfrau *f.*

con·cur [kənˈkɜː] *v/i* **1.** zs.-fallen, -treffen. **2.** zs.-wirken. **3.** übereinstimmen (*with* mit; *in* in *dat*): ~ *with s.o. a.* j-m beipflichten. **con·cur·rence** [~ˈkʌrəns] *s* **1.** Zs.-treffen *n.* **2.** Zs.-wirken *n.* **3.** Übereinstimmung *f.* **con'cur·rent** *adj* □ **1.** zs.-treffend. **2.** zs.-wirkend. **3.** übereinstimmend.

con·cuss [kənˈkʌs] *v/t* erschüttern: *be* ~*ed* ♂ e-e Gehirnerschütterung erleiden. **con'cus·sion** [~ʃn] *s* Erschütterung *f:* ~ (*of the brain*) ♂ Gehirnerschütterung.

con·demn [kənˈdem] *v/t* **1.** verdammen, verurteilen. **2.** ⚖ verurteilen (*to death* zum Tode): ~*ed cell* Todeszelle *f.* **3.** für unbrauchbar *od.* unbewohnbar *od.* gesundheitsschädlich erklären. **4.** *Kranken* aufgeben. **con·dem·na·tion** [ˌkɒndemˈneɪʃn] *s* Verdammung *f,* Verurteilung *f* (*a.* ⚖).

con·den·sa·tion [ˌkɒndenˈseɪʃn] *s* **1.** *phys.* Kondensation *f* (*a.* 🔬), Verflüssigung *f;* Kondensat *n,* Kondenswasser *n:* ~ *trail* ✈ Kondensstreifen *m.* **2.** Zs.-fassung *f.* **con·dense** [kənˈdens] **I** *v/t* **1.** *phys.* Gase, Dämpfe kondensieren, verflüssigen. **2.** 🔬 *Milch etc* eindicken, konzentrieren: ~*d milk* Kondensmilch *f.* **3.** *fig.* zs.-fassen, gedrängt darstellen. **II** *v/i* **4.** *phys.* kondensieren, sich verflüssigen. **con'dens·er** *s phys.* Kondensator *m* (*a.* ⚡), Verflüssiger *m.*

con·de·scend [ˌkɒndɪˈsend] *v/i* **1.** sich herablassen (*to do* zu tun; *to* zu). **2.** herablassend *od.* gönnerhaft sein (*to* gegen, zu). **con·de·scend·ing** *adj* □ herablassend, gönnerhaft.

con·di·ment [ˈkɒndɪmənt] *s* Gewürz *n,* Würze *f.*

con·di·tion [kənˈdɪʃn] **I** *s* **1.** Bedingung *f:* *on* ~ *that* unter der Bedingung *od.* vorausgesetzt, daß; *on no* ~ unter keinen Umständen, keinesfalls; *make s.th. a* ~ et. zur Bedingung machen. **2.** Verfassung *f:* a) Zustand *m,* Beschaffenheit *f,* b) (körperlicher *od.* Gesundheits)Zustand *m,* (*Sport*) Form *f:* *out of* ~ in schlechter Verfassung, in schlechtem Zustand; *the* ~ *of her health* ihr Gesundheitszustand. **3.** *pl* Bedingungen *pl,* Verhältnisse *pl:* *living* ~*s* Lebensbedingungen, -verhältnisse; *weather* ~*s* Witterungs-, Wetterverhältnisse. **II** *v/t* **4.** zur Bedingung machen, die Bedingung stellen (*that* daß). **5.** *j-n* programmieren (*to, for* auf *acc*). **con'di·tion·al** [~ʃənl] *adj* □ **1.** (*on*) bedingt (durch), abhängig (von): *be* ~ *on* abhängen von; *make* ~ *on* abhängig machen von. **2.** *ling.* Konditional...: ~ *clause* (*od. sentence*) Konditional-, Bedingungssatz

conditioned

838

m. **con'di·tioned** [-ʃnd] *adj* **1.** (*on*) bedingt (durch), abhängig (von): *be ~ on* abhängen von; *~ response* (*od. reflex*) *psych.* bedingter Reflex. **2.** beschaffen, geartet.

con·dole [kən'dəʊl] *v/i* sein Beileid ausdrücken, kondolieren (*with s.o. on s.th.* j-m zu et.). **con'do·lence** *s* Beileid *n*: *please accept my ~s* mein herzliches *od.* aufrichtiges Beileid; *register of ~* Kondolenzliste *f*.

con·dom ['kɒndəm] *s* Kondom *n, m*, Präservativ *n*.

con·do·min·i·um [ˌkɒndə'mɪnɪəm] *s Am.* Eigentumswohnanlage *f*: *~* (*apartment*) Eigentumswohnung *f*.

con·done [kən'dəʊn] *v/t* **1.** verzeihen, vergeben: *she ~d his infidelity* sie verzieh ihm s-e Untreue. **2.** wettmachen, wiedergutmachen.

con·duce [kən'djuːs] *v/i* (*to, toward*[*s*]) beitragen (zu), dienlich *od.* förderlich sein, dienen (*dat*). **con'du·cive** *adj* dienlich, förderlich (*to dat*).

con·duct I *s* ['kɒndʌkt] **1.** Führung *f*, Leitung *f*. **2.** Betragen *n*, Verhalten *n*: → *certificate* **1. II** *v/t* [kən'dʌkt] **3.** führen, geleiten: *~ed tour* Führung *f* (*of* durch). **4.** Prozeß, Verhandlungen etc führen, Geschäft *a.* betreiben, leiten. **5.** ♪ leiten, dirigieren. **6.** → *o.s.* sich betragen *od.* verhalten. **7.** *phys.* leiten. **con'duct·i·ble** [kən'dʌktəbl], **con'duc·tive** *adj phys.* leitfähig. **con'duc·tor** *s* **1.** Führer *m*, Leiter *m*. **2.** (*Bus-, Straßenbahn*)Schaffner *m*; *Am.* Zugbegleiter *m.* **3.** ♪ Dirigent *m*. **4.** *phys.* Leiter *m*; ⚡ *a.* Blitzableiter *m*. **con'duc·tress** *s* Schaffnerin *f*.

cone [kəʊn] *s* **1.** ♣ *u. fig.* Kegel *m.* **2.** ♀ (*Tannen- etc*)Zapfen *m.* **3.** kegelförmiger Gegenstand, *z. B.* a) Waffeltüte *f* (*für Speiseeis*), b) Pylon(e *f*) *m*, Leitkegel *m.* **II** *v/t* **4.** *~ off* mit Leitkegeln absperren.

con·fec·tion [kən'fekʃn] *s* Konfekt *n*. **con'fec·tion·er** *s* Konditor *m*. **con'fec·tion·er·y** *s* **1.** Süßwaren *pl.* **2.** Süßwarengeschäft *n*; Konditorei *f*.

con·fed·er·a·cy [kən'fedərəsɪ] *s* **1.** (Staaten)Bund *m.* **2.** Komplott *n*, Verschwörung *f.* **con'fed·er·ate** [~rət] **I** *adj* verbündet (*with* mit), Bundes... **II** *s* Verbündete *m*, Bundesgenosse *m.* **III** *v/t u.*

v/i [~reɪt] (sich) verbünden *od.* zs.-schließen. **con,fed·er'a·tion** *s* **1.** Bündnis *n.* **2.** (Staaten)Bund *m*.

con·fer [kən'fɜː] **I** *v/t Titel etc* verleihen (*on dat*). **II** *v/i* sich beraten (*with* mit). **con'fer·ence** ['kɒnfərəns] *s* Konferenz *f*: a) Tagung *f*, b) Besprechung *f*: *be in ~* in e-r Besprechung sein.

con·fess [kən'fes] **I** *v/t* **1.** bekennen, (ein)gestehen. **2.** zugeben (*a. that* daß). **3.** *eccl.* beichten; *j-m* die Beichte abnehmen. **II** *v/i* **4.** (*to*) (ein)gestehen (*acc*), sich schuldig bekennen (*gen od. an acc*), sich bekennen (zu): *~ to doing s.th.* (ein)gestehen, et. getan zu haben; *he has ~ed* ⚓ er hat gestanden, er ist geständig. **5.** *eccl.* beichten (*to dat*). **con'fessed** *adj* erklärt. **con'fess·ed·ly** [~ɪdlɪ] *adv* zugestandener-, eingestandenermaßen. **con'fes·sion** [~ʃn] *s* **1.** Geständnis *n* (*a.* ⚓): *make a full ~* ein volles Geständnis ablegen. **2.** *eccl.* Beichte *f*: *go to ~* zur Beichte gehen; → *auricular.* **3.** *eccl.* Konfession *f*: a) Glaubensbekenntnis *n*, b) Glaubensgemeinschaft *f*. **con'fes·sion·al** [~ʃənl] **I** *adj* **1.** konfessionell, Konfessions... **2.** Beicht... **II** *s* **3.** Beichtstuhl *m*: *secret of the ~* Beichtgeheimnis *n*. **con'fes·sor** [~sə] *s eccl.* Beichtvater *m*.

con·fet·ti [kən'fetɪ] *s pl* (*sg konstruiert*) Konfetti *n*.

con·fi·dant [ˌkɒnfɪ'dænt] *s* Vertraute *m*. **con·fi·dante** [ˌ~'dænt] *s* Vertraute *f*.

con·fide [kən'faɪd] **I** *v/i* **1.** sich anvertrauen (*in dat*). **2.** vertrauen (*in dat od.* auf *acc*). **II** *v/t* **3.** *~ s.th. to s.o.* j-m et. anvertrauen.

con·fi·dence ['kɒnfɪdəns] *s* **1.** (*in*) Vertrauen *n* (auf *acc*, zu), Zutrauen *n* (zu): *have ~ in* Vertrauen haben zu; *take s.o. into one's ~* j-n ins Vertrauen ziehen; *in ~* → *confidentially;* → *strict.* **2.** *a.* ~ *in o.s.* Selbstvertrauen *n.* **3.** *a.* ~ *in o.s.* vertrauliche Mitteilung, *pl a.* Vertraulichkeiten *pl.* ~ *game Am.* → *confidence trick.* ~ *man s* (*irr man*) Betrüger *m*; Hochstapler *m.* ~ *trick s* aufgelegter Schwindel; Hochstapelei *f.* ~ *trick·ster* → *confidence man.*

con·fi·dent ['kɒnfɪdənt] *adj* □ **1.** (*of; that*) überzeugt (von; daß), sicher (*gen*; daß). **2.** *a.* ~ *in o.s.* selbstsicher. **con·fi·den·tial** [ˌ~'denʃl] *adj* **1.** vertrau-

lich, geheim. **2.** vertraut, Vertrauens...:
~ clerk ✝ Prokurist(in). **,con'fi'den-
tial·ly** [~ʃəlɪ] *adv* vertraulich, im Vertrauen.

con·fine I *s* ['kɒnfaɪn] **1.** *mst pl* Grenze *f*,
Grenzgebiet *n*, *fig.* Rand *m*, Schwelle *f*.
II *v/t* [kən'faɪn] **1.** begrenzen, be-, einschränken (**to** auf *acc*). **2.** einschließen,
einsperren: **~d to bed** ans Bett gefesselt.
4. be ~d (of) niederkommen (mit), entbunden werden (von). **con'fine·ment** *s*
1. Be-, Einschränkung *f*. **2.** Haft *f*: **solitary ~** Einzelhaft. **3.** Niederkunft *f*,
Entbindung *f*.

con·firm [kən'fɜːm] *v/t* **1.** bestätigen. **2.**
Entschluß bekräftigen; bestärken
(**in** in *dat*). **3.** *eccl.* konfirmieren; firmen. **con·fir·ma·tion** [,kɒnfə'meɪʃn] *s*
1. Bestätigung *f*. **2.** Bekräftigung *f*; Bestärkung *f*. **3.** *eccl.* Konfirmation *f*; Firmung *f*. **con'firmed** *adj* **1.** fest (*Gewohnheit etc*). **2.** erklärt, überzeugt: **~
bachelor** eingefleischter Junggeselle.

con·fis·cate ['kɒnfɪskeɪt] *v/t* beschlagnahmen, konfiszieren. **,con·fis'ca·tion**
s Beschlagnahme *f*, Konfiszierung *f*.

con·flict I *s* ['kɒnflɪkt] *s* Konflikt *m*: a)
Zs.-stoß *m*: **→ armed**, b) Widerstreit
m: **come into ~ with** in Konflikt geraten mit; **~ of interests** Interessenkon-
flikt *m*, -kollision *f*. **II** *v/i* [kən'flɪkt]
(**with**) kollidieren (mit), im Widerspruch *od.* Gegensatz stehen (zu).
con'flict·ing *adj* widersprüchlich.

con·form [kən'fɔːm] **I** *v/t* **1.** anpassen (**to**
dat od. an *acc*). **2.** in Einklang bringen
(**to** mit). **II** *v/i* **3.** sich anpassen (**to** *dat*).
4. übereinstimmen (**to** mit). **con'form-
i·ty** *s* **1.** Übereinstimmung *f*: **be in ~**
übereinstimmen (**with** mit); **in ~ with** in
Übereinstimmung mit, gemäß (*dat*). **2.**
Anpassung *f* (**to** an *acc*).

con·found [kən'faʊnd] *v/t* **1.** verwechseln, durcheinanderbringen (**with** mit).
2. verwirren, durcheinanderbringen. **3.
~ it!** verdammt! **con'found·ed** *adj* □ **F**
verdammt.

con·front [kən'frʌnt] *v/t* **1.** (*oft feindlich*)
gegenübertreten, -stehen (*dat*): **be ~ed
with** *Schwierigkeiten etc* gegenüberstehen, sich gegenübersehen (*dat*). **2.**
sich *e-r Gefahr etc* stellen. **3.** *a.* ⚕ (mit)
konfrontieren (mit), gegenüberstellen
(*dat*): **~ s.o. with s.th.** j-m et. entge-

genhalten. **con·fron·ta·tion** [,kɒnfrʌn-
'teɪʃn] *s* Konfrontation *f* (*a. pol. etc*).

con·fuse [kən'fjuːz] *v/t* **1.** verwechseln,
durcheinanderbringen (**with** mit). **2.**
verwirren: a) in Unordnung bringen,
b) aus der Fassung bringen, verlegen
machen. **con'fused** *adj* **1.** verwirrt: a)
konfus, verworren, wirr, b) verlegen,
bestürzt. **2.** undeutlich, verworren.
con'fu·sion [~ʒn] *s* **1.** Verwechs(e)lung
f: **~ of names** Namensverwechslung. **2.**
Verwirrung *f*: a) Durcheinander *n*:
cause ~ Verwirrung stiften *od.* anrichten; **throw everything into ~** alles
durcheinanderbringen, b) Verlegenheit
f, Bestürzung *f*: **in ~ →** **confused** 1b;
put to ~ in Verlegenheit bringen.

con·fu·ta·tion [,kɒnfjuː'teɪʃn] *s* Widerlegung *f*. **con·fute** [kən'fjuːt] *v/t* widerlegen.

con·geal [kən'dʒiːl] *v/t u. v/i* gefrieren
od. gerinnen *od.* erstarren (lassen).

con·gen·ial [kən'dʒiːnjəl] *adj* □ **1.** gleichartig, (geistes)verwandt (**with** mit *od.*
dat). **2.** sympathisch, angenehm (**to**
dat): **be ~ to s.o.** j-m zusagen. **3.** zuträglich (**to** *dat od.* für): **~ to one's health**
gesund.

con·gen·i·tal [kən'dʒenɪtl] *adj* angeboren: **~ defect** Geburtsfehler *m*. **con-
'gen·i·tal·ly** [~təlɪ] *adv* **1.** von Geburt
(an). **2.** von Natur (aus).

con·gest·ed [kən'dʒestɪd] *adj* **1.** verstopft: **~ streets**. **2.** überfüllt (**with**
von): **~ area** übervölkertes Gebiet,
Ballungsgebiet *n*. **con'ges·tion** *s* **1.** Anhäufung *f*: **~ of population** Übervölkerung *f*; **~ of traffic** Verkehrsstockung *f*,
-stauung *f*, -stau *m*. **2.** ⚕ Blutandrang
m (*of the brain* zum Gehirn).

con·glom·er·ate I *v/t u. v/i* [kən-
'glɒməreɪt] (sich) zs.-ballen (**to** zu). **II**
adj [~rət] *fig.* zs.-gewürfelt. **III** *s* [~rət]
Konglomerat *n*, zs.-gewürfelte Masse,
Gemisch *n*. **con,glom·er'a·tion →**
conglomerate III.

con·grats [kən'græts] *int bsd. Br.* **F** gratuliere!

con·grat·u·late [kən'grætʃʊleɪt] *v/t* j-m
gratulieren, j-n beglückwünschen (**on**
zu). **con,grat·u'la·tion** *s* Gratulation *f*,
Glückwunsch *m*: **~s!** ich gratuliere!,
herzlichen Glückwunsch! **con'grat·u-
la·tor** *s* Gratulant(in). **con'grat·u·la-**

to·ry [‿lətəri] *adj* Glückwunsch...: *~ telegram.*

con·gre·gate [‘kɔŋgrɪgeɪt] *v/t u. v/i* (sich) versammeln. **‚con·gre'ga·tion** *s* **1.** Versammlung *f.* **2.** (Kirchen)Gemeinde *f.* **‚con·gre'ga·tion·al** [‿ʃənl] *adj eccl.* Gemeinde...

con·gress [‘kɔŋgres] *s* **1.** Kongreß *m,* Tagung *f.* **2.** ♀ *pol. Am.* der Kongreß. **♀·man** [‘‿mən] *s (irr man),* '♀‚wom·an *s (irr woman) pol. Am.* Mitglied *n* des Repräsentantenhauses.

con·gru·ence [‘kɔŋgrʊəns] *s* **1.** Übereinstimmung *f.* **2.** ♈ Kongruenz *f (a. fig.).* **'con·gru·ent** *adj* □ **1.** übereinstimmend **(to, with** mit). **2.** ♈ kongruent *(a. fig.).* **con·gru·i·ty** [‿’gruːətɪ] → **congruence. con·gru·ous** [‘‿grʊəs] → **congruent.**

con·ic, con·i·cal [‘kɔnɪk(l)] *adj* □ konisch, kegelförmig: *conic section* ♈ Kegelschnitt *m.*

co·ni·fer [‘kɔnɪfə] *s* ♣ Nadelbaum *m.* **co·nif·er·ous** [kəʊ’nɪfərəs] *adj* zapfentragend; Nadel...: *~ tree.*

con·jec·tur·al [kən’dʒektʃərəl] *adj* □ mutmaßlich. **con'jec·ture I** *s* Vermutung *f,* Mutmaßung *f: be reduced to ~* auf Vermutungen angewiesen sein. **II** *v/t* vermuten, mutmaßen. **III** *v/i* Vermutungen anstellen, mutmaßen **(of, about** über *acc).*

con·ju·gal [‘kɔndʒʊgl] *adj* □ ehelich: *~ life* Eheleben *n.* **con·ju·gate** [‘‿geɪt] *ling.* **I** *v/t* konjugieren, beugen. **II** *v/i* konjugiert *od.* gebeugt werden. **‚con·ju'ga·tion** *s ling.* Konjugation *f,* Beugung *f.*

con·junc·tion [kən’dʒʌŋkʃn] *s* **1.** Verbindung *f: in ~ with* in Verbindung *od.* zusammen mit. **2.** Zs.-treffen *n (von Ereignissen etc).* **3.** *ling.* Konjunktion *f,* Bindewort *n.* **con'junc·ti·va** [‚kɔn·dʒʌŋk’taɪvə] *pl* **-vas, -vae** [‿viː] *s anat.* Bindehaut *f.* **con·junc·ti·vi·tis** [kən‚dʒʌŋktɪ’vaɪtɪs] *s* ♨ Bindehautentzündung *f.*

con·jure [‘kʌndʒə] **I** *v/t* **1.** [kən’dʒʊə] beschwören **(to do** zu tun). **2.** *Teufel etc* beschwören, anrufen: *~ up* heraufbeschwören *(a. fig.).* **3.** *~ away* wegzaubern; *~ up* hervorzaubern *(a. fig.).* **II** *v/i* **4.** zaubern. **'con·jur·er** *s* **1.** Zauberer *m.* **2.** Zauberkünstler *m.* **'con·jur·ing**

trick *s* Zauberkunststück *n,* -trick *m.* **'con·jur·or** → *conjurer.*

conk¹ [kɔŋk] *s sl.* Riecher *m (Nase);* Birne *f (Kopf).*

conk² [‿] *v/i sl. mst → out* **1.** streiken, den Geist aufgeben *(Fernseher etc),* absterben *(Motor).* **2.** a) umkippen *(ohnmächtig werden),* b) *vor Erschöpfung etc* zs.-klappen, c) *a. → off* einpennen. **3.** den Löffel weglegen *(sterben).*

con·nect [kə’nekt] **I** *v/t* **1.** verbinden **(with** mit) *(a. fig.).* **2.** *fig.* in Zs.-hang *od.* Verbindung bringen **(with** mit). **3.** ⚙ **(to)** verbinden (mit), *Wagen etc* anhängen, ankuppeln (an *acc).* **4.** ⚡ ⊙ anschließen (an *acc),* zuschalten *(dat).* **5.** *teleph.* verbinden **(to, with** mit): *s.o. further* j-n weiterverbinden. **II** *v/i* **6.** ⟐ *etc* Anschluß haben **(with** an *acc).* **con'nect·ed** *adj* **1.** verbunden. **2.** (logisch) zs.-hängend. **3.** verwandt: *~ by marriage* verschwägert: *be well ~* einflußreiche Verwandte *od.* gute Beziehungen haben. **4. (with)** verwickelt (in *acc),* beteiligt (an *dat).* **con'nect·ing** *adj* Verbindungs...: *~ door;* ⟐ *flight* Anschlußflug *m;* ⟐ *train* Anschlußzug *m.*

con'nec·tion *s* **1.** Verbindung *f.* **2.** *allg.* Verbindung *f,* Anschluß *m (a. ⟐, ⊙, teleph. etc).* **3.** Zs.-hang *m: in this ~* in diesem Zs.-hang; *in ~ with* in Zs.-hang mit; mit Bezug auf *(acc).* **4.** *pl geschäftliche, gute etc* Beziehungen *od.* Verbindungen *pl;* Bekannten-, Kundenkreis *m.* **con'nec·tive I** *adj* □ verbindend: *~ tissue anat.* Bindegewebe *f;* *~ word* →II. **II** *s ling.* Bindewort *n.*

con·nex·ion *bsd. Br.* → *connection.*

con·nois·seur [‚kɔnə’sɜː] *s (Wein- etc)* Kenner *m.*

con·no·ta·tion [‚kɔnəʊ’teɪʃn] *s* Nebenbedeutung *f.* **con·note** [kə’nəʊt] *v/t* (zugleich) bedeuten.

con·quer [‘kɔŋkə] *v/t* **1.** erobern *(a. fig.).* **2.** besiegen, *fig. a.* bezwingen. **'con·quer·or** *s* Eroberer *m.*

con·quest [‘kɔŋkwest] *s* **1.** Eroberung *f (a. fig. Person): make a ~ of s.o.* j-n erobern. **2.** Besiegung *f, fig. a.* Bezwingung *f.*

con·san·guin·e·ous [‚kɔnsæŋ’gwɪnɪəs] *adj* blutsverwandt. **‚con·san'guin·i·ty** *s* Blutsverwandtschaft *f.*

con·science [‘kɔnʃəns] *s* Gewissen *n:* *a*

good (*guilty*) ~ ein gutes (schlechtes) Gewissen; *for ~'s sake* um das Gewissen zu beruhigen; *act on ~* nach s-m Gewissen handeln, s-m Gewissen folgen; *have s.th. on one's ~* Gewissensbisse *od.* ein schlechtes Gewissen haben wegen et.

con·sci·en·tious [ˌkɒnʃɪ'enʃəs] *adj* □ 1. gewissenhaft. 2. Gewissens...: **~ objector** Kriegs-, Wehrdienstverweigerer *m* (*aus Gewissensgründen*). **ˌcon·sci'en·tious·ness** *s* Gewissenhaftigkeit *f*.

con·scious ['kɒnʃəs] *adj* □ 1. bei Bewußtsein. 2. **be ~ of** sich bewußt sein (*gen*), sich im klaren sein über (*acc*). 3. bewußt, absichtlich. **'con·scious·ness** *s* Bewußtsein *n*: **lose ~** das Bewußtsein verlieren; **regain ~** wieder zu sich kommen; **~-expanding** bewußtseinserweiternd.

con·script ✕ **I** *v/t* [kən'skrɪpt] 1. einziehen, -berufen. **II** *s* ['kɒnskrɪpt] 2. Wehr(dienst)pflichtige *m*. 3. Einberufene *m*. **con·scrip·tion** [kən'skrɪpʃn] *s* 1. Einziehung *f*, -berufung *f*. 2. Wehrpflicht *f*.

con·se·crate ['kɒnsɪkreɪt] *v/t* 1. *eccl.* weihen. 2. weihen, widmen (*to dat*). **ˌcon·se'cra·tion** *s* 1. *eccl.* Weihe *f*, Weihung *f*. 2. Hingabe *f* (*to* an *acc*).

con·sec·u·tive [kən'sekjʊtɪv] *adj* 1. aufeinanderfolgend: *for two ~ days* zwei Tage hintereinander. 2. (fort)laufend (*Nummer*). 3. **~ clause** *ling.* Konsekutiv-, Folgesatz *m*. **con'sec·u·tive·ly** *adv* 1. nach-, hintereinander. 2. (fort)laufend.

con·sen·sus [kən'sensəs] *s a.* **~ of opinion** (allgemein) übereinstimmende Meinung, (allgemeine) Übereinstimmung.

con·sent [kən'sent] **I** *v/i* 1. (*to*) zustimmen (*dat*), einwilligen (in *acc*). 2. sich bereit erklären (*to do* zu tun). **II** *s* 3. (*to*) Zustimmung *f* (zu), Einwilligung *f* (in *acc*): *with the ~ of* mit Zustimmung von (*od. gen*); *with one ~* einstimmig, -mütig.

con·se·quence ['kɒnsɪkwəns] *s* 1. Folge *f*, Konsequenz *f*: *in ~* folglich, daher; *in* (*od. as a*) *~ of* infolge von (*od. gen*); *take the ~s* die Folgen tragen; *with the ~ that* mit dem Ergebnis, daß. 2. Folgerung *f*, Schluß *m*. 3. Bedeutung *f*,

Wichtigkeit *f*: *of* (*no*) *~* von (ohne) Bedeutung, (un)bedeutend, (un)wichtig (*to* für); *a person of great ~* e-e bedeutende *od.* einflußreiche Persönlichkeit. **'con·se·quent** *adj* (*on*) folgend (*dat od.* auf *acc*); sich ergebend (aus). **'con·se·quent·ly** *adv* folglich, daher.

con·ser·va·tion [ˌkɒnsə'veɪʃn] *s* 1. Erhaltung *f*, Bewahrung *f*. 2. Natur- *od.* Umweltschutz *m*: **~ area** Naturschutzgebiet *n*. 3. Konservieren *n*, Haltbarmachen *n*. **ˌcon·ser'va·tion·ist** *s* Natur- *od.* Umweltschützer(in). **con·serv·a·tive** [kən'sɜːvətɪv] **I** *adj* □ 1. konservativ (*pol. mst* Ⓐ). 2. vorsichtig (*Schätzung etc*). **II** *s* 3. *mst* Ⓐ Konservative *m*, *f*. 4. konservativer Mensch. **con·ser·va·toire** [~twɑː] *s* Konservatorium *n*, Musik(hoch)schule *f*. **con'serv·a·to·ry** [~trɪ] *s* 1. Treib-, Gewächshaus *n*, *bsd.* Wintergarten *m*. 2. → *conservatoire*. **con'serve** **I** *v/t* 1. erhalten, bewahren. 2. konservieren, haltbar machen, *Obst etc* einmachen. **II** *s* 3. *mst pl* Eingemachte *n*.

con·sid·er [kən'sɪdə] **I** *v/t* 1. nachdenken über (*acc*). 2. betrachten *od.* ansehen als, halten für: **~ s.th.** (**to be**) **a mistake**; **be ~ed rich** als reich gelten. 3. sich überlegen, erwägen (*doing* zu tun). 4. berücksichtigen, in Betracht ziehen. 5. Rücksicht nehmen auf (*acc*), denken an (*acc*). 6. finden, meinen, denken (*that* daß). **II** *v/i* 7. nachdenken, überlegen (*beide a. Person*). **con'sid·er·a·ble** *adj* □ 1. beachtlich, beträchtlich. 2. bedeutend, wichtig (*beide a. Person*). **con'sid·er·ate** [~rət] *adj* □ aufmerksam, rücksichtsvoll (*to, toward*[s] gegen): *be ~ of* Rücksicht nehmen auf (*acc*). **con·sid·er'a·tion** [~'reɪʃn] *s* 1. Erwägung *f*, Überlegung *f*: *take into ~* in Erwägung *od.* Betracht ziehen; *leave out of ~* ausklammern; *on* (*od. under*) *no ~* unter keinen Umständen. 2. Berücksichtigung *f*: *in ~ of* in Anbetracht (*gen*). 3. Rücksicht(nahme) *f* (*for, of* auf *acc*): *lack of ~* Rücksichtslosigkeit *f*. 4. (zu berücksichtigender) Grund: *money is no ~* Geld spielt keine Rolle. **con'sid·er·ing** *prp* in Anbetracht (*gen*). **II** *cj*: **~ that** in Anbetracht der Tatsache, daß. **III** *adv* F alles in allem.

con·sign [kən'saɪn] *v/t* 1. übergeben (**to**

dat). **2.** ✝ *Waren* übersenden, zusenden (*to dat*). **con·sig·nee** [ˌkɒnsaɪˈniː] *s* ✝ Empfänger *m*. **con·sign·er** [kənˈsaɪnə] → *consignor*. **con'sign·ment** *s* ✝ **1.** Übersendung *f*, Zusendung *f*: ~ *note* Frachtbrief *m*. **2.** (Waren)Sendung *f*. **con'sign·or** *s* ✝ Übersender *m*.

con·sist [kənˈsɪst] *v/i* **1.** ~ *of* bestehen *od.* sich zs.-setzen aus. **2.** ~ *in* bestehen in (*dat*). **con'sist·ence, con'sist·en·cy** *s* **1.** Konsistenz *f*, Beschaffenheit *f*, (Grad *m* der) Festigkeit *f od.* Dichtigkeit *f*. **2.** *fig.* Konsequenz *f*, Folgerichtigkeit *f*. **3.** *fig.* Übereinstimmung *f*, Einklang *m*. **con'sist·ent** *adj* □ **1.** konsistent, fest, dicht. **2.** *fig.* konsequent, folgerichtig. **3.** *fig.* übereinstimmend, vereinbar, in Einklang stehend (**with** mit). **4.** *fig.* beständig (*Leistung etc*).

con·so·la·tion [ˌkɒnsəˈleɪʃn] *s* Trost *m*: ~ *goal* (*Sport*) Ehrentor *n*; ~ *prize* Trostpreis *m*. **con·sol·a·to·ry** [kənˈsɒlətərɪ] *adj* tröstend, tröstlich.

con·sole¹ [ˈkɒnsəʊl] *s* **1.** Konsole *f*: ~ *table* Konsoltischchen *n*. **2.** (Fernseh-, Musik)Truhe *f*, (Radio)Schrank *m*. **3.** ♪ Schalt-, Steuerpult *n*.

con·sole² [kənˈsəʊl] *v/t* trösten: ~ *s.o. for s.th.* j-n über et. hinwegtrösten.

con·sol·i·date [kənˈsɒlɪdeɪt] **I** *v/t* **1.** (ver)stärken, festigen (*beide a. fig.*). **2.** ✕ *Truppen* zs.-ziehen. **3.** ♦ *Gesellschaften* zs.-schließen, -legen. **4.** ⊙ verdichten. **II** *v/i* **5.** ✝ sich zs.-schließen. **6.** ⊙ sich verdichten. **con·sol·i'da·tion** *s* **1.** (Ver)Stärkung *f*, Festigung *f*. **2.** ✕ Zs.-ziehung *f*. **3.** ✝ Zs.-legung *f*; Zs.-schluß *m*. **4.** ⊙ Verdichtung *f*.

con·som·mé [kənˈsɒmeɪ] *s* Consommé *f* (*klare Kraftbrühe*).

con·so·nant [ˈkɒnsənənt] **I** *adj* □ **1.** gleichlautend. **2.** übereinstimmend (**with** mit). **II** *s* **3.** *ling.* Konsonant *m*.

con·sort [ˈkɒnsɔːt] *s* Gemahl(in): *prince* ~ Prinzgemahl. **con'sor·ti·um** [~tjəm] *pl* **-ti·a** [~ə] *s* ✝ Konsortium *n*: ~ *of banks* Bankenkonsortium.

con·spic·u·ous [kənˈspɪkjʊəs] *adj* □ **1.** deutlich sichtbar: *be* ~ *a.* in die Augen fallen. **2.** auffallend, -fällig: *make o.s.* ~ sich auffällig benehmen, auffallen. **3.** bemerkenswert (*for* wegen): *be* ~ *by one's absence* durch Abwesenheit

glänzen; *render o.s.* ~ sich hervortun.

con·spir·a·cy [kənˈspɪrəsɪ] *s* Verschwörung *f*. **con'spir·a·tor** *s* Verschwörer *m*. **con·spire** [~ˈspaɪə] *v/i* **1.** sich verschwören (**against** gegen) (*a. fig.*). **2.** *fig.* zs.-wirken.

con·sta·ble [ˈkʌnstəbl] *s bsd. Br.* Polizist *m*, Wachtmeister *m*. **con·stab·u·lar·y** [kənˈstæbjʊlərɪ] *s bsd Br.* Polizei *f* (*e-s Bezirks*).

con·stan·cy [ˈkɒnstənsɪ] *s* **1.** Konstanz *f*, Beständigkeit *f*. **2.** Bestand *m*, Dauer *f*. **3.** *fig.* Standhaftigkeit *f*. **'con·stant** **I** *adj* □ **1.** konstant (*a. phys., ⋏ etc*), beständig, gleichbleibend. **2.** (be)ständig, (an)dauernd: ~ *rain* anhaltender Regen. **3.** *fig.* standhaft, beharrlich. **II** *s* **4.** *phys., ⋏* Konstante *f*.

con·stel·la·tion [ˌkɒnstəˈleɪʃn] *s ast.* Konstellation *f* (*a. fig.*), Sternbild *n*.

con·ster·na·tion [ˌkɒnstəˈneɪʃn] *s* Bestürzung *f*: *in* ~ konsterniert, bestürzt; *to my* ~ zu m-r Bestürzung.

con·sti·pate [ˈkɒnstɪpeɪt] *v/t* ✽ verstopfen: *be* ~*d* an Verstopfung leiden. **con·sti'pa·tion** *s* Verstopfung *f*.

con·stit·u·en·cy [kənˈstɪtjʊənsɪ] *s* **1.** Wählerschaft *f*. **2.** Wahlbezirk *m*, -kreis *m*. **con'stit·u·ent I** *adj* □ **1.** e-n (Bestand)Teil bildend: ~ *part* → **4. 2.** *pol.* Wähler-, Wahl...: ~ *body* Wählerschaft *f*. **3.** ~ *assembly* verfassunggebende Versammlung. **II** *s* **4.** (wesentlicher) Bestandteil. **5.** *pol.* Wähler(in).

con·sti·tute [ˈkɒnstɪtjuːt] *v/t* **1.** ernennen, einsetzen: ~ *s.o. a judge* j-n als Richter einsetzen *od.* zum Richter ernennen. **2.** *Gesetz* erlassen, in Kraft setzen. **3.** einrichten, gründen, *Ausschuß etc* einsetzen. **4.** ausmachen, bilden, darstellen. **con·sti'tu·tion** *s* **1.** Zs.-setzung *f*, (Auf)Bau *m*. **2.** Konstitution *f*, körperliche Veranlagung. **3.** Natur *f*, Wesen *n*: *by* ~ von Natur (aus). **4.** Einrichtung *f*, Gründung *f*, Einsetzung *f*. **5.** *pol.* Verfassung *f*. **con·sti'tu·tion·al I** *adj* □ **1.** ✽ konstitutionell, anlagebedingt. **2.** *pol.* a) verfassungsgemäß, Verfassungs...: → *monarchy*, b) rechtsstaatlich: ~ *state* Rechtsstaat *m*. **II** *s* **3.** F Gesundheitsspaziergang *m*.

con·strain [kənˈstreɪn] *v/t* **1.** j-n zwingen, nötigen: *feel* ~*ed to do s.th.* sich ge-

zwungen fühlen, et. zu tun. **2.** *et.* er-
zwingen. **con'straint** [~'streint] *s*
Zwang *m*, Nötigung *f*: *under* ~ unter
Zwang, gezwungen.

con·struct [kən'strʌkt] *v/t* **1.** errichten,
bauen. **2.** ⊙ konstruieren (*a. ling.*, ℞),
bauen. **3.** *fig.* gestalten, ausarbeiten.
con'struc·tion [~kʃn] *s* **1.** Errichtung *f*,
Konstruktion *f* (*a.* ⊙, ℞, *ling.*): *under* ~
im Bau (befindlich): ~ *industry* Baugewerbe *n*, -wirtschaft *f*; ~ *site* Baustelle *f*.
2. Bauweise *f*: *steel* ~ Stahlkonstruk-
tion *f*. **3.** Bau(werk *n*) *m.* **4.** *fig.* Aufbau
m, Gestaltung *f*. **con'struc·tion·al**
[~ʃənl] *adj* Konstruktions..., baulich.
con'struc·tive *adj* □ **1.** konstruktiv (*a.*
Kritik), schöpferisch. **2.** → **constructional.** **con'struc·tor** *s* Erbauer *m*;
Konstrukteur *m*.

con·strue [kən'stru:] *v/t ling.* konstruieren.

con·sul ['kɒnsəl] *s* Konsul *m*: ~ *general*
Generalkonsul *m*. **con·su·lar** ['~sjolə]
adj Konsulats..., Konsular..., konsula-
risch. **con·su·late** ['~lət] *s* Konsulat *n*
(*a. Gebäude*): ~ *general* Generalkon-
sulat.

con·sult [kən'sʌlt] **I** *v/t* **1.** um Rat fragen,
zu Rate ziehen, konsultieren (*about*
wegen). **2.** in *e-m Buch* nachschlagen
od. -sehen. **3.** berücksichtigen. **II** *v/i* **4.**
(sich) beraten (*about* über *acc*).
con'sult·ant *s* **1.** (fachmännischer) Berater. **2.** ♣ Facharzt; Facharzt *m* (*an e-m Krankenhaus*).
con·sul·ta·tion [,kɒnsəl'teiʃn] *s* Bera-
tung *f*, Konsultation *f*: *on* ~ *with* nach
Rücksprache mit; ~ *hour* Sprechstunde
f. **con'sult·ing** *adj* beratend: ~ *room*
Sprechzimmer *n*.

con·sume [kən'sju:m] *v/t* **1.** zerstören,
vernichten: *be* ~*d by fire* ein Raub der
Flammen werden. **2.** *fig.* verzehren: *be*
~*d with hatred* von Haß verzehrt werden. **3.** auf-, verzehren. **4.** auf-, verbrauchen, konsumieren. **5.** verschwenden, -geuden (*on* für). **6.** *Aufmerksamkeit etc* in Anspruch nehmen. **con-
'sum·er** *s* Verbraucher(in), Konsu-
ment(in): ~ *goods pl* Konsumgüter *pl*;
~ *protection* Verbraucherschutz *m*.

con·sum·mate I *v/t* ['kɒnsəmeit] **1.** vollenden; *Ehe* vollziehen. **2.** vollkommen
machen. **II** *adj* [kən'sʌmɪt] **3.** vollendet,

vollkommen. **con·sum·ma·tion** [,kɒn-
sə'meiʃn] *s* Vollendung *f*; Vollziehung *f*.

con·sump·tion [kən'sʌmpʃn] *s* **1.** Verbrauch *m* (*of* an *dat*), ♣ *a.* Konsum *m*.
2. Verzehr *m*: (*un*)*fit for human* ~ für
den menschlichen Verzehr (un)ge-
eignet.

con·tact ['kɒntækt] **I** *s* **1.** Kontakt *m* (*a.*
⚡ *u. fig.*), Berührung *f*: *make* ~*s* Verbindungen anknüpfen *od.* herstellen;
business ~*s pl* Geschäftsverbindungen
pl; ~ *lens* Haftlinse *f*, -schale *f*, Kon-
taktlinse *f*, -schale *f*. **2.** ⚡ Kontaktper-
son *f*. **3.** *a.* ~ *man* Verbindungs-, Kon-
taktmann *m*. **II** *v/t* **4.** Kontakt aufnehmen mit, sich in Verbindung setzen
mit.

con·ta·gion [kən'teidʒən] *s* ♣ Ansteckung *f* (*durch Berührung*); ansteckende
Krankheit. **con'ta·gious** *adj* □ ♣ ansteckend (*a. fig.*).

con·tain [kən'tein] *v/t* **1.** enthalten. **2.**
aufnehmen, fassen. **3.** *fig.* zügeln, zurückhalten: ~ *o.s.* (an) sich halten, sich
beherrschen. **con'tain·er** *s* **1.** Behälter
m, (*Benzin- etc*)Kanister *m*. **2.** ♣ Container *m*: ~ *ship* Containerschiff *n*.
con'tain·er·ize *v/t* **1.** auf Container betrieb umstellen. **2.** in Containern transportieren.

con·tam·i·nate [kən'tæmineit] *v/t* **1.** verunreinigen. **2.** infizieren, vergiften (*beide a. fig.*), (*a.* radioaktiv) verseuchen.
con·tam·i·na·tion *s* **1.** Verunreinigung
f. **2.** Infizierung *f*, Vergiftung *f* (*beide a.
fig.*), (*a.* radioaktiv) Verseuchung.

con·tem·plate ['kɒntempleit] **I** *v/t* **1.**
(nachdenklich) betrachten. **2.** nachdenken über (*acc*). **3.** erwägen, beabsichtigen (*doing* zu tun). **4.** erwarten,
rechnen mit. **II** *v/i* **5.** nachdenken (*a-
bout, on* über *acc*). **con·tem·pla·tion** *s*
1. (nachdenkliche) Betrachtung. **2.**
Nachdenken *n*. Erwägung *f*: *be in* ~
erwogen werden. **con'tem·pla·tive**
adj □ nachdenklich.

con·tem·po·ra·ne·ous [kən,tempə'rei-
njəs] *adj* □ gleichzeitig: *be* ~ *with* zeitlich zs.-fallen mit. **con'tem·po·ra·ry I**
adj □ **1.** zeitgenössisch. **2.** → *contem-
poraneous.* **3.** gleichalt(e)rig. **II** *s* **4.**
Zeitgenosse *m*, -genossin *f*. **5.** Altersgenosse *m*, -genossin *f*.

lieren über (*acc*); **lose ~ of o.s.** die (Selbst)Beherrschung verlieren. **8.** Aufsicht *f*, Kontrolle *f* (*of, over* über *acc*): **be in ~ of** et. leiten od. unter sich haben; **be under s.o.'s ~** j-m unterstehen od. unterstellt sein. **9.** Leitung *f*, Verwaltung *f*. **10.** *mst pl* ⚙ Steuerung *f*, Steuervorrichtung *f*; Kontroll-, Betätigungshebel *m*. **be at the ~s** *fig.* das Sagen haben; **an den (Schalt)Hebeln der Macht sitzen. 11.** ⚡, ⚙ Reg(e)lung *f*, Regulierung *f*; Regler *m*. **~ cen·tre** (*Am.* **cen·ter**) *s* Kontrollzentrum *n*. **~ desk** *s* **1.** ⚡ Schaltpult *n*. **2.** *Rundfunk, TV:* Regiepult *n*.

con·trol·la·ble [kən'trəʊləbl] *adj* **1.** kontrollierbar. **2.** ⚡, ⚙ steuer-, regel-, regulierbar. **con·trol·ler** *s* **1.** Kontrolleur *m*, Aufseher *m*. **2.** ✈ Controller *m* (*Fachmann für Kostenrechnung u. -planung*).

con·trol| **le·ver** *s* **1.** ⚙ Schalthebel *m*. **2.** → **control stick. ~ room** *s* *Rundfunk, TV:* Regieraum *m*. **~ stick** *s* ✈ Steuerknüppel *m*. **~ tow·er** *s* ✈ Kontrollturm *m*, Tower *m*.

con·tro·ver·sial [ˌkɒntrə'vɜːʃl] *adj* □ **1.** strittig, umstritten. **2.** polemisch. **3.** streitsüchtig. **con·tro·ver·sy** [ˈ~sɪ] *s* **1.** Kontroverse *f*, Streit *m*; Disput *m*, Wortwechsel *m*; attr. strittig. **2.** *a.* **point in ~** Streitfrage *f*, -punkt *m*.

con·tuse [kən'tjuːz] *v/t* ✚ sich et. quetschen. **con·tu·sion** [ˈ~ʒn] *s* Quetschung *f*.

co·nun·drum [kə'nʌndrəm] *s* Scherzfrage *f*, (Scherz)Rätsel *n*.

con·ur·ba·tion [ˌkɒnɜː'beɪʃn] *s* Ballungsraum *m*, -zentrum *n*.

con·va·lesce [ˌkɒnvə'les] *v/i* gesund werden. **con·va·les·cence** *s* Rekonvaleszenz *f*, Genesung *f*. **con·va·les·cent** I *adj* rekonvaleszent, genesend. II *s* Rekonvaleszent(in), Genesende *m, f*.

con·vene [kən'viːn] I *v/i* zs.-kommen, sich versammeln. II *v/t* sich versammeln, zs.-rufen, *Versammlung* einberufen.

con·ven·ience [kən'viːnjəns] *s* **1.** Annehmlichkeit *f*, Bequemlichkeit *f*: **all** (**modern**) **~s** aller Komfort; **at your ~** wenn es Ihnen gerade paßt; **at your earliest ~** so bald wie möglich. **2.** *bsd. Br.* Toilette *f*. **con·ven·ient** *adj* □ **1.** bequem, praktisch. **2.** günstig, passend: **be ~ for s.o.** j-m passen.

con·vent ['kɒnvənt] *s* (*bsd.* Nonnen)Kloster *n*.

con·ven·tion [kən'venʃn] *s* **1.** Zs.-kunft *f*, Tagung *f*, Versammlung *f*. **2.** a) *pol. Am.* Parteiversammlung *f*, -tag *m*, b) Kongreß *m*: **~ centre** (*Am.* **center**) Kongreßzentrum *n*. **3.** *bilaterales* Abkommen; *multilaterales* Übereinkommen, Konvention *f*. **4.** (gesellschaftliche) Konvention, Sitte *f*. **con·ven·tion·al** [ˈ~ʃənl] *adj* □ **1.** konventionell, herkömmlich (*beide a.* ✗). **2.** *contp.* schablonenhaft, unoriginell. **3.** konventionell, förmlich.

con·verge [kən'vɜːdʒ] *v/i* zs.-laufen (*Straßen, Flüsse*), ✈ konvergieren (*a. fig.*), *fig.* sich annähern. **con·ver·gence**, **con·ver·gen·cy** *s* **1.** Zs.-laufen *n*. **2.** ✈ Konvergenz *f* (*a. fig.*). **con·ver·gent** *adj* ✈ konvergent, *fig. a.* sich annähernd.

con·ver·sa·tion [ˌkɒnvə'seɪʃn] *s* Konversation *f*, Unterhaltung *f*, Gespräch *n*: **in ~** with im Gespräch mit; **get into ~ with s.o.** mit j-m ins Gespräch kommen; **make ~** Konversation machen. **con·ver·sa·tion·al** [ˈ~ʃənl] *adj* □ **1.** gesprächig. **2.** Unterhaltungs..., Gesprächs...: **~ English** Umgangsenglisch *n*; ~ tone Plauderton *m*. **con·ver·sa·tion·al·ly** [ˈ~nəlɪ] *adv* im Plauderton.

con·verse [kən'vɜːs] *v/i* sich unterhalten (*with* mit; *on, about* über *acc*).

con·ver·sion [kən'vɜːʃn] *s* **1.** Um-, Wandlung *f* (*into, to* in *acc*). **2.** △, ⚙ Umbau *m* (*into* zu). **3.** ⚙, *a.* ✚ Umstellung *f* (*to* auf *acc*). **4.** ✈ Umrechnung *f* (*into, to* in *acc*): **~ table** Umrechnungstabelle *f*. **5.** Bekehrung *f*, *eccl. a.* Konversion *f*, Übertritt *m* (*a. pol. etc*) (**to** zu).

con·vert I *v/t* [kən'vɜːt] **1.** *allg., a.* 🥀 um-, verwandeln (*into, to* in *acc*). **2.** △, ⚙ umbauen (*into* zu). **3.** ⚙, *a.* ✚ umstellen (*to* auf *acc*). **4.** ✈ umrechnen (*into, to* in *acc*). **5.** *eccl. etc* bekehren (**to** zu). II *v/i* [kən'vɜːt] **6.** sich umwandeln *od.* verwandeln (*into, to* in *acc*). **7.** sich bekehren, *eccl. a.* konvertieren, übertreten (*a. pol. etc*) (**to** zu). III *s* ['kɒnvɜːt] **8.** Bekehrte *m, f*, *eccl. a.* Konvertit(in). **con·vert·i·ble** I *adj* □ **1.** um-, verwandelbar. **2.** ✈ umrechenbar. II *s* **3.** *mot.* Kabriolett *n*.

copartner

con·vex [kɒnˈveks] *adj* □ konvex: **~ mirror** Konvex-, Wölbspiegel *m*.

con·vey [kənˈveɪ] *v/t* **1.** *Waren etc* befördern, transportieren (*beide a.* ☺). **2.** *Grüße etc* überbringen, -mitteln. **3.** *Ideen etc* mitteilen, vermitteln, *Meinung, Sinn* ausdrücken. **con'vey·ance** *s* **1.** Beförderung *f*, Transport *m*. **2.** Transport-, Verkehrsmittel *n*. **3.** Überbringung *f*, -mittlung *f*. **4.** Mitteilung *f*, Vermittlung *f*. **con'vey·er, con'vey·or** *s a.* **~ belt** ☺ Förderband *n*.

con·vict I *v/t* [kənˈvɪkt] **1.** ⚖ (*of*) überführen, für schuldig erklären (*gen*); verurteilen (wegen). **2.** überzeugen (**of** von). **II** *s* [ˈkɒnvɪkt] **1.** Verurteilte *m, f*. **4.** Strafgefangene *m, f*, Sträfling *m*. **con'vic·tion** *s* **1.** ⚖ Überführung *f*, Schuldspruch *m*; Verurteilung *f*: **~ previous** 1. **2.** Überzeugung *f*: **~ from** aus Überzeugung; → **carry** 5.

con·vince [kənˈvɪns] *v/t* überzeugen (**of** von; **that** daß). **con'vinc·ing** *adj* □ überzeugend: **~ proof** schlagender Beweis.

con·voy [ˈkɒnvɔɪ] **I** *s* **1.** Geleit *n*, Begleitung *f*. **2.** Konvoi *m*: a) ⚔, *a. allg.* (Wagen)Kolonne *f*, b) ♣ Geleitzug *m*. **II** *v/t* Geleitschutz geben (*dat*).

con·vulse [kənˈvʌls] **I** *v/t* **1.** in Zuckungen versetzen: **be ~d with** → 4. **2.** *Muskeln etc* krampfhaft zs.-ziehen: **~d features** *pl* verzerrte Züge *pl*. **3.** in Lachkrämpfe versetzen. **II** *v/i* **4. ~ with** sich krümmen vor (*Lachen, Schmerzen etc*). **con'vul·sion** *s* **1.** *bsd.* ⚕ Krampf *m*, Zuckung *f*: **nervous ~s** *pl* nervöse Zuckungen *pl*. **2.** *pl* Lachkrampf *m*: **they were in ~s** sie krümmten sich vor Lachen. **con'vul·sive** *adj* □ krampfhaft.

coo [kuː] **I** *v/i* gurren (*a. fig.*). **II** *s* Gurren *n*.

cook [kʊk] **I** *s* **1.** Koch *m*, Köchin *f*: **too many ~s spoil the broth** viele Köche verderben den Brei. **II** *v/t* **2.** kochen. **3.** *a.* **~ up** F *Geschichte etc* erfinden, sich ausdenken. **4.** F *Rechnung etc* frisieren. **III** *v/i* **5.** kochen. **6.** kochen, gekocht werden: **what's ~ing?** F was ist los? '**~·book** *s bsd. Am.* Kochbuch *n*.

cook·er [ˈkʊkə] *s* Kocher *m*, Kochgerät *n*; *Br.* Herd *m*: **~ hood** *Br.* Abzugshaube *f*. '**cook·er·y** *s* Kochen *n*, Kochkunst *f*: **~ book** *bsd. Br.* Kochbuch *n*.

cook·ie [ˈ~ɪ] *s Am.* (süßer) Keks, Plätzchen *n*. '**cook·ing I** *s* **1.** Kochen *n*. **2.** Küche *f*, Art *f* zu kochen: **Italian ~** die italienische Küche. **II** *adj* **3.** Koch... '**cook·y** → **cookie**.

cool [kuːl] **I** *adj* □ **1.** kühl, frisch: **get ~** sich abkühlen. **2.** *fig.* kühl: a) gelassen, kalt(blütig): **keep ~** e-n kühlen Kopf behalten, sich nicht aufregen; → **cucumber**, b) gleichgültig, c) abweisend. **3.** F glatt: **a ~ thousand pounds** glatte *od.* die Kleinigkeit von tausend Pfund. **4.** *bsd. Am.* F klasse, prima. **II** *s* **5.** Kühle *f*, Frische *f* (*der Luft*). **6.** F (Selbst)Beherrschung *f*: **blow** (*od.* **lose**) **one's ~** hochgehen; **keep one's ~** ruhig bleiben. **III** *v/t* **7.** (ab)kühlen, abkühlen lassen: **~ it!** F immer mit der Ruhe!; reg dich ab! **IV** *v/i* **8.** kühl werden, sich abkühlen: **~ down** F sich abregen. **~ bag** *s* Kühltasche *f*. **~ box** *s* Kühlbox *f*.

cool·er [ˈkuːlə] *s* **1.** (*Wein- etc*) Kühler *m*. **2.** *sl.* Kittchen *n*.

cool·head·ed *adj* □ besonnen.

cool·ing [ˈkuːlɪŋ] *adj* □ **1.** (ab)kühlend. **2.** ☺ Kühl... '**cool·ness** *s* **1.** Kühle *f* (*a. fig.*). **2.** Kaltblütigkeit *f*.

co-op [ˈkəʊɒp] *s* F Co-op *m* (*Genossenschaft u. Laden*).

co·op·er·ate [kəʊˈɒpəreɪt] *v/i* **1.** zs.-arbeiten (**with** mit; **in** bei; **to, toward[s]** zu e-m Zweck). **2.** (**in**) mitwirken (an *dat*), helfen, behilflich sein (bei). **co,op·er'a·tion** *s* **1.** Zs.-arbeit *f*. **2.** Mitwirkung *f*, Hilfe *f*. **co'op·er·a·tive** [~rətɪv] **I** *adj* □ **1.** zs.-arbeitend. **2.** mitwirkend. **3.** kooperativ, hilfsbereit. **4.** ♣ Gemeinschafts...; Genossenschafts...: **~ society** → 5; **~ store** → 6. **II** *s* **5.** Co-op *m*: a) Genossenschaft *f*, b) Konsumverein *m*. **6.** Co-op *m*, Konsumladen *m*.

co·or·di·nate I *v/t* [kəʊˈɔːdɪneɪt] koordinieren, bei-, gleichordnen, aufeinander abstimmen. **II** *adj* [~dnət] □ koordiniert, bei-, gleichgeordnet. **III** *s* [~dnət] ⚛ Koordinate *f*. **co,or·di'na·tion** *s* Koordinierung *f*, Koordination *f*, Bei-, Gleichordnung *f*, Abstimmung *f*.

cop [kɒp] *sl.* **I** *v/t* **1.** erwischen (**at** bei): **~ it** sein Fett (ab)kriegen; → **packet** 3. **II** *s* **2. no great ~, not much ~** *Br.* nicht so toll. **3.** Bulle *m* (*Polizist*).

co·part·ner [ˌkəʊˈpɑːtnə] *s* Teilhaber *m*,

Mitinhaber *m*. ‚**co'part·ner·ship** *s* **1.** Teilhaberschaft *f*. **2.** *Br.* Gewinn- *od*. Mitbeteiligung *f* (**of labour** der Arbeitnehmer).

cope [kəʊp] *v/i* (**with**) gewachsen sein (*dat*), fertig werden (mit).

cop·i·er ['kɒpɪə] *s* Kopiergerät *n*, Kopierer *m*.

co·pi·lot ['kəʊ‚paɪlət] *s* ✈ Kopilot *m*.

co·pi·ous ['kəʊpjəs] *adj* □ **1.** reich(lich), ausgiebig. **2.** wortreich, weitschweifig. **3.** produktiv (*Schriftsteller etc*).

cop·per¹ ['kɒpə] **I** *s* **1.** *min*. Kupfer *n*. **2.** Kupfermünze *f*: **~s** *pl* Kupfergeld *n*. **II** *adj* **3.** kupfern, Kupfer... **4.** kupferrot.

cop·per² [~] *s sl.* Bulle *m* (*Polizist*).

cop·per| ore *s min.* Kupfererz *n*. '**~plate** *s* Kupferstich(platte *f*) *m*: **like ~** wie gestochen (*Schrift*). '**~smith** *s* Kupferschmied *m*.

cop·u·la ['kɒpjʊlə] *s ling.* Kopula *f*. **cop·u·late** ['~leɪt] *v/i* kopulieren: a) koitieren, b) *zo.* sich paaren. ‚**cop·u'la·tion** *s* Kopulation *f*: a) Koitus *m*, b) Paarung *f*.

cop·y ['kɒpɪ] **I** *s* **1.** Kopie *f*, Abschrift *f*: **fair** (*od.* **clean**) **~** Reinschrift *f*; **rough** (*od.* **foul**) **~** Rohentwurf *m*, Konzept *n*. **2.** Durchschlag *m*, -schrift *f*. **3.** *phot.* Abzug *m*. **4.** Nachbildung *f*, Kopie *f*. **5.** *typ.* (Satz)Vorlage *f*. **6.** Exemplar *n* (*e-s Buchs etc*). **7.** (Werbe-, Zeitungs*etc*)Text *m*. **II** *v/t* **8.** abschreiben (**off, from** von), e-e Kopie anfertigen von, (*Kassette etc*) überspielen. **9.** durch-, abpausen; kopieren. **10.** *phot.* e-n Abzug machen von. **11.** nachbilden. **12.** kopieren, nachmachen, -machen. **III** *v/i* **13.** abschreiben (**from** von). '**~cat** F **I** *s* (*bsd.* sklavischer *od.* gedankenloser) Nachahmer. **II** *v/t* (*bsd.* sklavisch *od.* gedankenlos) nachahmen *od.* -machen. **~ ed·i·tor** *s* Zeitungsredakteur(in); Lektor(in).

cop·y·ing| ma·chine ['kɒpɪɪŋ] *s* Kopiergerät *n*. **~ pa·per** *s* Kopierpapier *n*.

'**cop·y|‚read·er** *Am.* → **copy editor**. '**~right** ⚖ **I** *s* Urheberrecht *n*, Copyright *n* (**in, on, of, for** für, von). **II** *v/t* das Urheberrecht erwerben für *od.* von; urheberrechtlich schützen. **III** *adj* urheberrechtlich geschützt. '**~‚writ·er** *s* Werbetexter *m*.

cor·al ['kɒrəl] **I** *s* **1.** *zo.* Koralle *f*. **II**

adj **2.** Korallen... **3.** korallenrot.

cord [kɔːd] **I** *s* **1.** Schnur *f* (*a.* ✗), Kordel *f*, Strick *m*. **2.** gerippter Stoff, *bsd.* Kordsamt *m*. **II** *v/t* **3.** festbinden; verschnüren.

cor·dial ['kɔːdjəl] **I** *adj* □ **1.** herzlich. **2.** ✦ belebend, stärkend. **II** *s* **3.** ✦ Stärkungsmittel *n*. **4.** Fruchtsaftgetränk *n*. **5.** Likör *m*. **cor·dial·i·ty** [‚kɔːdɪˈælətɪ] *s* Herzlichkeit *f*.

cor·don ['kɔːdn] **I** *s* Kordon *m*, Posten- *od.* Absperrkette *f*. **II** *v/t a.* **~ off** (mit Posten *od.* Seilen) absperren *od.* abriegeln.

cor·du·roy ['kɔːdərɔɪ] *s* **1.** Kordsamt *m*. **2.** *pl, a.* **pair of ~s** Kord(samt)hose *f*.

core [kɔː] **I** *s* **1.** ✤ Kerngehäuse *n*; Kern *m*. **2.** *fig.* Kern *m*, *das* Innerste: **to the ~** bis ins Innerste; durch u. durch. **II** *v/t* **3.** *Obst* entkernen. **~ time** *s* Kernzeit *f*.

cork [kɔːk] **I** *s* **1.** Kork *m*. **2.** Korken *m*, Pfropfen *m*. **II** *v/t* **3.** *oft* **~ up** zu-, verkorken.

'**cork·screw** *s* Korkenzieher *m*.

corn¹ [kɔːn] **I** *s* **1.** Korn *n*, Getreide *n*: *bsd.* a) *Br.* Weizen *m*, b) *schott.*, *ir.* Hafer *m*. **2.** *a.* **Indian ~** *Am.* Mais *m*. **II** *v/t* **3.** pökeln: **~ed beef** Corned beef *n*, gepökeltes Rindfleisch.

corn² [~] *s* ✦ Hühnerauge *n*: **tread on s.o.'s ~s** *fig.* j-m auf die Hühneraugen treten.

corn| bread *s Am.* Maisbrot *n*. '**~cob** *s Am.* Maiskolben *m*.

cor·ne·a ['kɔːnɪə] *pl* **-as, -ae** [~iː] *s* Hornhaut *f* (*des Auges*).

cor·ner ['kɔːnə] **I** *s* **1.** Ecke *f*, *bsd. mot.* Kurve *f*: **take a ~** → 5; **turn the ~** um die Ecke biegen; **he's turned the ~** *fig.* er ist über den Berg. **2.** Winkel *m*, Ecke *f*: **~ of the mouth** Mundwinkel; **look at s.o. from the ~ of one's eye** j-n aus den Augenwinkeln (heraus) ansehen; **drive** (*od.* **force, put**) **into a ~** → 4; **be in a tight ~** in der Klemme sein *od.* sitzen *od.* stecken. **3.** *Fußball:* Eckball *m*, Ecke *f*. **II** *v/t* **4.** in die Enge treiben. **III** *v/i* **5.** *mot.* e-e Kurve nehmen: **~ well** gut in der Kurve liegen, e-e gute Kurvenlage haben. **IV** *adj* **6.** Eck...: **~ house**; **~ seat** Eckplatz *m*. '**cor·nered** *adj in Zssgn* ...eckig.

cor·ner| kick *s Fußball:* Eckstoß *m*.

'**~·stone** s **1.** △ Eckstein m; Grundstein m. **2.** fig. Eckpfeiler m.

'**corn·field** s **1.** Br. Korn-, Getreidefeld n. **2.** Am. Maisfeld n. '**~·flakes** s pl Corn-flakes pl. '**~·flow·er** s ✿ Kornblume f.

Cor·nish ['kɔːnɪʃ] adj kornisch, aus Cornwall.

corn pop·py s ✿ Klatschmohn m.

corn·y ['kɔːnɪ] adj sl. sentimental, schmalzig; kitschig; abgedroschen: **a ~ joke** ein Witz mit Bart.

cor·o·nar·y ['kɒrənərɪ] adj anat. Koronar...: **~ vessel** (Herz)Kranzgefäß n.

cor·o·na·tion [ˌkɒrə'neɪʃn] s Krönung(sfeier) f.

cor·o·ner ['kɒrənə] s ⚖ Coroner m (richterlicher Beamter zur Untersuchung der Todesursache in Fällen gewaltsamen od. unnatürlichen Todes): **~'s inquest** gerichtliches Verfahren zur Untersuchung der Todesursache.

cor·po·ral¹ ['kɔːpərəl] s ✕ Unteroffizier m.

cor·po·ral² [~] adj □ körperlich, leiblich: **~ punishment** körperliche Züchtigung.

cor·po·rate ['kɔːpərət] adj □ **1.** a) ⚖ körperschaftlich, Körperschafts...: **~ body** → **corporation** 1, b) ✝ Am. Gesellschafts..., Firmen...: **~ planning** Unternehmensplanung f. **2.** gemeinsam, kollektiv. **cor·po·ra·tion** [ˌkɔːpə'reɪʃn] s **1.** ⚖ Körperschaft f, juristische Person: **~ tax** Körperschaftsteuer f. **2.** a. **stock ~** ✝ Am. Kapital- od. Aktiengesellschaft f. **3.** Br. Innung f. **4.** Br. Stadtverwaltung f. **5.** F Schmerbauch m.

corps [kɔː] pl **corps** [~z] s **1.** ✕ Korps n, Truppe f. **2.** Korps m: → **diplomatic**.

corpse [kɔːps] s Leichnam m, Leiche f.

cor·pu·lence, **cor·pu·len·cy** ['kɔːpjʊləns(ɪ)] s Beleibtheit f, Korpulenz f. '**cor·pu·lent** adj □ beleibt, korpulent.

Cor·pus Chris·ti [ˌkɔːpəs'krɪstɪ] s eccl. Fronleichnam(sfest n) m.

cor·ral [kɒ'rɑːl] bsd. Am. I s **1.** Pferch m. **II** v/t **2.** in e-n Pferch treiben. **3.** fig. einpferchen, -sperren. **4.** F sich ein. schnappen.

cor·rect [kə'rekt] **I** v/t **1.** korrigieren, verbessern, berichtigen: **I stand ~ed** ich nehme alles zurück. **2.** Mängel etc

abstellen. **3.** zurechtweisen, tadeln; (be)strafen (**for** wegen). **II** adj **4.** korrekt: a) richtig: **be ~** stimmen; recht haben, b) einwandfrei (Benehmen). **cor·rec·tion** s **1.** Korrektur f, Verbesserung f, Berichtigung f. **2.** Zurechtweisung f, Tadel m; Bestrafung f. **cor·rec·tive** adj □ korrigierend, verbessernd, berichtigend. **cor·rect·ness** s Korrektheit f, Richtigkeit f.

cor·re·late ['kɒrəleɪt] **I** v/t **1.** in Wechselbeziehung bringen (**with** mit). **2.** in Übereinstimmung bringen (**with** mit), aufeinander abstimmen. **II** v/i **3.** in Wechselbeziehung stehen (**with** mit), sich aufeinander beziehen. **4.** übereinstimmen (**with** mit). **cor·re·la·tion** s **1.** Wechselbeziehung f. **2.** Übereinstimmung f.

cor·re·spond [ˌkɒrɪ'spɒnd] v/i **1.** (**to**, **with**) entsprechen (dat), übereinstimmen (mit). **2.** (**to**) entsprechen (dat), das Gegenstück sein (von). **3.** korrespondieren, in Briefwechsel stehen (**with** mit). **cor·re·spond·ence** s **1.** Entsprechung f, Übereinstimmung f. **2.** Korrespondenz f: a) Briefwechsel m: **be in ~** (**with**) → **correspond** 3; **~ course** Fernkurs m; **~ school** Fernlehrinstitut n; Briefe pl. **cor·re·spond·ent I** s **1.** Briefpartner(in): **be a good** (**bad**) **~** fleißig schreiben (schreibfaul sein). **2.** ✝ (auswärtiger) Geschäftsfreund. **3.** Korrespondent(in), Berichterstatter(in) (e-r Zeitung etc): **foreign ~** Auslandskorrespondent(in). **II** adj □ **4.** entsprechend, gemäß (**to** dat). '**cor·re·'spond·ing** → **correspondent** 4.

cor·ri·dor ['kɒrɪdɔː] s Korridor m, Gang m. **~ train** s D-Zug m.

cor·rode [kə'rəʊd] **I** v/t **1.** 🜋, ⚙ korrodieren, an-, zerfressen, angreifen. **2.** fig. zerfressen, untergraben. **II** v/i **3.** korrodieren. **4.** rosten: **~d** rostig. **cor·ro·sion** [~ʒn] s **1.** 🜋, ⚙ Korrosion f. **2.** Rostfraß m, -bildung f. **3.** fig. Untergrabung f. **cor·ro·sive** [~sɪv] adj □ **1.** 🜋, ⚙ korrodierend, Korrosions... **2.** fig. nagend, quälend.

cor·ru·gat·ed ['kɒrʊgeɪtɪd] adj gewellt: **~ cardboard** Wellpappe f; **~ iron** (od. **sheet**) Wellblech n.

cor·rupt [kə'rʌpt] **I** adj □ **1.** (moralisch) verdorben. **2.** unredlich, unlauter. **3.**

korrupt: a) bestechlich, b) Bestechungs... **II** v/t **4.** (moralisch) verderben. **5.** korrumpieren, bestechen. **III** v/i **6.** (moralisch) verderben, -kommen.

cor·rupt·i·ble → **corrupt** 3a. **cor'rup·tion** s **1.** Verdorbenheit f. **2.** Unredlichkeit f, Unlauterkeit f. **3.** Korruption f: a) Bestechlichkeit f, b) Bestechung f. **cor'rup·tive** adj verderblich (Einfluß etc).

cor·set ['kɔ:sit] s a. pl Korsett n.

cosh [kɒʃ] s Br. F Totschläger m (Waffe).

co·sig·na·to·ry [ˌkəʊ'sɪɡnətəri] s Mitunterzeichner(in).

co·sine ['kəʊsaɪn] s A Kosinus m.

co·si·ness ['kəʊzɪnɪs] s Behaglichkeit f, Gemütlichkeit f.

cos·met·ic [kɒz'metɪk] **I** adj (~ally) kosmetisch (a. fig.): ~ surgery Schönheitschirurgie f. **II** s kosmetisches Mittel. **cos·me·ti·cian** [ˌkɒzmə'tɪʃn] s Kosmetiker(in).

cos·mic ['kɒzmɪk] adj □ kosmisch.

cos·mo·naut ['kɒzmənɔ:t] s (Welt-)Raumfahrer m, Kosmonaut m.

cos·mo·pol·i·tan [ˌkɒzmə'pɒlɪtən] **I** adj kosmopolitisch, weltbürgerlich, weitS. weltoffen. **II** s Kosmopolit(in), Weltbürger(in).

cos·mos ['kɒzmɒs] s Kosmos m, Weltall n.

cost [kɒst] **I** s **1.** Kosten pl, Aufwand m: ~ of living Lebenshaltungskosten. **2.** Kosten pl, Schaden m: at s.o.'s ~ auf j-s Kosten; at the ~ of his health auf Kosten s-r Gesundheit. **3.** Opfer n, Preis m: at all ~s, at any ~ um jeden Preis; at a heavy ~ unter schweren Opfern. **4.** † (Selbst-, Gestehungs)Kosten pl: ~ abatement Kostendämpfung f; ~ increase Kostensteigerung f; ~ inflation Kosteninflation f; ~ price Selbstkostenpreis m; at ~ zum Selbstkostenpreis. **5.** pl ⚖ (Gerichts-, Prozeß)Kosten pl: with ~s kostenpflichtig. **II** v/t (irr) **6.** Preis kosten: it ~ me one pound es kostete mich ein Pfund. **7.** kosten, bringen um: it ~ him his life es kostete ihn das Leben. **8.** et. Unangenehmes verursachen: it ~ me a lot of trouble es verursachte mir od. kostete mich große Mühe. **9.** pret u. pp 'cost·ed † den Preis od. die Kosten kalkulieren von

(od. gen). **III** v/i (irr) **10.** it ~ him dearly bsd. fig. es kam ihm teuer zu stehen.

co·star ['kəʊstɑ:] **I** v/t: the film ~red X X spielte in dem Film e-e der Hauptrollen. **II** v/i: ~ with die Hauptrolle spielen neben (dat).

'cost|-,con·scious adj □ kostenbewußt. **'~,cov·er·ing** adj □ kostendeckend.

cos·ter(·mon·ger) ['kɒstə(ˌmʌŋɡə)] s Br. Straßenhändler(in) für Obst, Gemüse etc.

cost es·ti·mate s Kostenvoranschlag m.

cost·ly ['kɒstlɪ] adj **1.** kostspielig, teuer. **2.** teuer erkauft (Sieg etc). **3.** prächtig.

,cost-of-'liv·ing| al·low·ance, ~ bo·nus s † Teuerungszulage f. ~ in·dex s (a. irr index) † Lebenshaltungs(kosten)index m.

cos·tume ['kɒstjuːm] s **1.** Kostüm n, Kleidung f, Tracht f. **2.** thea. etc Kostüm n: ~ ball Kostümball m; ~ de·signer Kostümbildner(in); ~ jew·el(le)ry Modeschmuck m.

co·sy ['kəʊzɪ] **I** adj □ behaglich, gemütlich. **II** s Wärmer m: → egg cosy, tea cosy.

cot [kɒt] s **1.** Feldbett n. **2.** Br. Kinderbett(chen) n.

cot·tage ['kɒtɪdʒ] s **1.** Cottage n, (kleines) Landhaus. **2.** Am. Ferienhaus n, -häuschen n. **3.** Am. Wohngebäude n, (e-s Krankenhauses etc) Einzelgebäude n, (e-s Hotels) Dependance f. ~ cheese s Hüttenkäse m. ~ in·dus·try s Heimgewerbe n, -industrie f.

cot·ton ['kɒtn] **I** s **1.** Baumwolle f: → absorbent. **II** adj **2.** baumwollen, Baumwoll... **III** v/i **3.** Am. F (with) gut auskommen (mit); sich anfreunden (mit). **4.** F ~ to et. sich anfreunden mit (e-r Idee etc); ~ on to et. kapieren. ~ pad s Wattestäbchen n. ~ wool s Br. (Verband)Watte f.

couch [kaʊtʃ] **I** s Couch f, Liege(sofa n) f. **II** v/t abfassen, formulieren; Gedanken etc in Worte fassen, ausdrücken.

cou·chette [kuː'ʃet] s 🚆 Platz m (im Liegewagen).

cough [kɒf] **I** s **1.** Husten m: have a ~ Husten haben; give a (slight) ~ hüsteln, sich räuspern. **2.** Husten n. **3.** mot. Stottern n. **II** v/i **4.** husten. **5.** mot. stottern, husten (Motor). **III** v/t **6.** mst

~ *out*, ~ *up* aushusten: ~ *up blood* Blut husten. **7.** ~ *up* sl. herausrücken mit *(der Wahrheit etc)*; *Geld* herausrücken, ausspucken. ~ *drop s* Hustenbonbon *m, n*.

cough·ing bout ['kɒfɪŋ] *s* Hustenanfall *m*.

cough| loz·enge → *cough drop.* ~ **syr·up** *s* Hustensaft *m*, -sirup *m*.

could [kʊd] *v/aux* **1.** *pret von* **can¹. 2.** konditional, vermutend *od. fragend*: *that* ~ *be right* das könnte stimmen.

couldn't ['kʊdnt] F *für* **could not.**

coun·cil ['kaʊnsl] *s* **1.** Rat(sversammlung *f*) *m*: *be in* ~ zu Rate sitzen; *family* ~ Familienrat. **2.** Rat *m (Körperschaft)*; *eng S.* Gemeinderat *m*: *Ω of Europe* Europarat; *municipal* ~ Stadtrat. ~ **es·tate** *s Br.* soziale Wohnsiedlung *(e-r Gemeinde).* ~ **house** *s Br.* gemeindeeigenes Wohnhaus *(mit niedrigen Mieten).*

coun·cil·(l)or ['kaʊnsələ] *s* Ratsmitglied *n*, Stadtrat *m*, -rätin *f*.

coun·sel ['kaʊnsl] I *s* **1.** Rat(schlag) *m*: *take* ~ *of s.o.* von j-m (e-n) Rat annehmen. **2.** Beratung *f*: *hold (od. take)* ~ *with* sich beraten mit; sich Rat holen bei. **3.** ⚖ *Am.* Rechtsberater *m*, -beistand *m*; *Br.* (Rechts)Anwalt *m*: ~ *for the defence* Verteidiger *m*; ~ *for the prosecution* Anklagevertreter *m*. II *v/t pret u. pp* **-seled,** *bsd. Br.* **-selled 4.** *j-m* raten, j-m e-n Rat geben *od.* erteilen: ~ *s.o. against* j-m abraten von. **5.** zu *et.* raten: ~ *s.th. to s.o.* j-m et. raten III *v/i* **6.** ~ *against* abraten von. **'coun·sel·(l)or** *s (Berufs- etc)* Berater(in).

count¹ ['kaʊnt] I *s* **1.** Zählen *n*, (Ab-, Auf-, Aus)Zählung *f*: *keep* ~ *of et.* genau zählen; *fig.* die Übersicht behalten über *(acc)*; *lose* ~ sich verzählen; *fig.* die Übersicht verlieren *(of* über *acc)*; *by this* ~ nach dieser Zählung *od.* Berechnung. **2.** Endzahl *f*, Ergebnis *n*. **3.** ⚖ Anklagepunkt *m*: *on all* ~*s* in allen Anklagepunkten; *fig.* in jeder Hinsicht. **4.** *leave out of* ~ unberücksichtigt lassen; *take no* ~ *of* nicht berücksichtigen. II *v/t* **5.** (ab-, auf-, aus-, zs.-)zählen, *Wechselgeld* nachzählen. **6.** aus-, berechnen. **7.** zählen bis: ~ *ten*. **8.** (mit)zählen, mit einrechnen: *(not)* ~*ing*

the persons present die Anwesenden (nicht) mitgerechnet; *without (od. not)* ~*ing* abgesehen von. **9.** halten für, betrachten als, zählen *(among* zu): ~ *o.s. lucky (od. fortunate)* sich glücklich schätzen. III *v/i* **10.** zählen *(fig. among* zu): ~ *up to ten* bis 10 zählen; ~*ing from today* von heute an (gerechnet). **11.** *(on)* zählen, sich verlassen (auf *acc*), sicher rechnen (mit). **12.** zählen: a) von Wert sein, ins Gewicht fallen, b) gelten: ~ *for much* viel gelten *od.* wert sein; ~ *against* sprechen gegen; sich nachteilig auswirken auf *(acc)*.
Verbindungen mit Adverbien:
count| down *v/t* **1.** *Geld* hinzuzählen. **2.** den Countdown durchführen mit *u. weitS.* letzte (Start)Vorbereitungen treffen für. ~ *in v/t* → **count¹** 8: *count me in!* ich bin dabei!, ich mache mit! ~ *off v/t u. v/i bsd.* ✕ abzählen. ~ *out v/t* **1.** *Münzen etc* (langsam) abzählen. **2.** ausschließen, unberücksichtigt lassen: *count me out!* ohne mich! **3.** *Boxen, Kinderspiel:* auszählen. ~ *o·ver v/t* nachzählen. ~ *up v/t* zs.-zählen.

count² [~] *s nichtbritischer* Graf.

count·a·ble ['kaʊntəbl] *adj* zählbar *(a. ling.).*

'count·down *s* Countdown *m, n, a. weitS.* letzte (Start)Vorbereitungen *pl.*

coun·te·nance ['kaʊntənəns] I *s* **1.** Gesichtsausdruck *m*, Miene *f*: *change one's* ~ s-n Gesichtsausdruck ändern. **2.** Fassung *f*, Haltung *f*: *in* ~ gefaßt; *keep one's* ~ die Fassung bewahren; *put s.o. out of* ~ j-n aus der Fassung bringen.

count·er¹ ['kaʊntə] I *s* **1.** Ladentisch *m*: *under the* ~ unter dem Ladentisch *verkaufen etc*; *fig.* unter der Hand, heimlich. **2.** Theke *f*. **3.** *(Bank-, Post)*Schalter *m*. II *adj* **4.** rezeptfrei *(Medikament).*

count·er² [~] *s* **1.** ⊙ Zähler *m*. **2.** Spielmarke *f*, Jeton *m*.

coun·ter³ [~] I *adv* **1.** in entgegengesetzter Richtung. **2.** ~ *to fig.* wider *(acc)*, zuwider *(dat)*, entgegen *(dat)*: *run* ~ *to* zuwiderlaufen *(dat)*. II *adj* **3.** Gegen..., entgegengesetzt. III *v/t* **4.** entgegenwirken *(dat)*. IV *v/i* **5.** *bsd. Sport:* kontern.

coun·ter... ['kaʊntə] *in Zssgn* Gegen...
coun·ter·act *v/t* **1.** entgegenwirken

(*dat*). **2.** *Wirkung* kompensieren, neutralisieren. ˌcoun·terˈacˈtive *adj* □ entgegenwirkend, Gegen...

'coun·terˌar·gu·ment *s* Gegenargument *n*.

'coun·terˌatˈtack *s* Gegenangriff *m*.

coun·terˈbal·ance *fig.* **I** *s* ['kaʊntəˌbæləns] Gegengewicht *n* (**to** zu). **II** *v/t* [ˌ∼ˈbæləns] ein Gegengewicht bilden zu, ausgleichen.

'coun·terˈblast *s* heftige Reaktion.

'coun·terˈcharge *s* **1.** ⚖️ Gegenklage *f*. **2.** ✕ Gegenangriff *m*.

'coun·terˈcheck *s* **1.** Gegen-, Nachprüfung *f*. **II** *v/t* gegen-, nachprüfen.

'coun·terˈclaim *s* ✝, ⚖️ Gegenanspruch *m*, -forderung *f*.

ˌcoun·terˈclockˈwise *Am.* → **anticlockwise**.

'coun·terˌdem·onˈstra·tion *s* Gegendemonstration *f*.

ˌcoun·terˈes·piˈoˈnage *s* Spionageabwehr *f*.

'coun·terˈexˌamˈple *s* Gegenbeispiel *n*.

coun·terˈfeit ['kaʊntəfɪt] **I** *adj* **1.** falsch: a) gefälscht: ∼ *money* Falschgeld *n*, b) vorgetäuscht. **II** *s* **2.** Fälschung *f*. **III** *v/t* **3.** *Geld, Unterschrift etc* fälschen. **4.** *vortäuschen, simulieren.

'coun·terˈfoil *s* bsd. *Br.* (Kontroll)Abschnitt *m*.

'coun·terˌinˌtel·liˈgence *s* Spionageabwehr(dienst *m*) *f*.

coun·terˈmand [ˌkaʊntəˈmɑːnd] **I** *v/t* **1.** *Befehl etc* widerrufen, rückgängig machen, ✝ *Auftrag* stornieren: **until** ∼*ed* bis auf Widerruf. **2.** *Ware* abbestellen. **II** *s* **3.** Widerrufung *f*, ✝ Stornierung *f*.

'coun·terˌmeas·ure *s* Gegenmaßnahme *f*.

'coun·terˈmove *s* Gegenzug *m*.

'coun·terˈofˌfen·sive *s* ✕ Gegenoffensive *f*.

'coun·terˌofˈfer *s* Gegenangebot *n*.

'coun·terˌor·der *s* bsd. ✕ Gegenbefehl *m*.

'coun·terˈpane *s* Tagesdecke *f*.

'coun·terˈpart *s* **1.** Gegenstück *n* (**to** zu). **2.** Pendant *n*, genaue Entsprechung. **3.** Ebenbild *n* (*Person*).

'coun·terˈpoint *s* ♪ Kontrapunkt *m*.

'coun·terˈpoise *s* Gegengewicht *n* (**to** zu) (*a. fig.*).

ˌcoun·terˈproˈducˈtive *adj* kontrapro-

duktiv: **be** ∼ nicht zum gewünschten Ziel führen, das Gegenteil bewirken.

'coun·terˈproˌpos·al *s* Gegenvorschlag *m*.

'coun·terˌrev·oˈlu·tion *s* pol. Konter-, Gegenrevolution *f*.

'coun·terˈsign *v/t* gegenzeichnen.

'coun·terˈweight *s* Gegengewicht *n* (**to** zu) (*a. fig.*).

count·ess ['kaʊntɪs] *s* Gräfin *f*.

count·less ['kaʊntlɪs] *adj* zahllos, unzählig.

coun·try ['kʌntrɪ] *s* **1.** Gegend *f*, Landschaft *f*: **flat** ∼ Flachland *n*. **2.** Land *n*, Staat *m*: **in this** ∼ hierzulande; ∼ **of birth** Geburtsland. **3.** Land *n* (*Ggs. Stadt*): **in the** ∼ auf dem Lande. **II** *adj* **4.** ländlich, Land... ∼ **home**, ∼ **house** *s* **1.** Landhaus *n*. **2.** Landsitz *m*. ∼**ˈman** ['∼mən] *s* (*irr man*) **1.** Landsmann *m*. **2.** Landbewohner *m*; Bauer *m*. ∼ **muˈsic** *s* Country-music *f*. ∼ **road** *s* Landstraße *f*. ∼ **seat** *s* Landsitz *m*. '∼**side** *s* **1.** Landstrich *m*, (ländliche) Gegend. **2.** Landschaft *f*. ˌ∼ˈ**wide** *adj* landesweit. ∼**ˈwomˈan** *s* (*irr woman*) **1.** Landsmännin *f*. **2.** Landbewohnerin *f*; Bäuerin *f*.

coun·ty ['kaʊntɪ] *s* **1.** *Br.* Grafschaft *f*. **2.** *Am.* (Land)Kreis *m* (*einzelstaatlicher Verwaltungsbezirk*).

coup [kuː] *s* **1.** Coup *m*: **make** (*od.* **pull off**) **a** ∼ e-n Coup landen. **2.** Staatsstreich *m*, Putsch *m*. ∼ **dˈéˈtat** [ˌkuːdeɪˈtɑː] *pl* **coups dˈéˈtat** [ˌkuːzˈ∼] → **coup** 2.

cou·pé ['kuːpeɪ] *s mot.* Coupé *n*.

cou·ple ['kʌpl] *s* **1.** Paar *n*: **a** ∼ *of* zwei; **f** ein paar; **in** ∼**s** paarweise. **2.** (*Ehe-, Liebes- etc*)Paar *n*. **II** *v/t* **3.** (zs.-)koppeln, verbinden (*a. fig.* **with** mit). **4.** ⚡ koppeln: ∼ **back** rückkoppeln; ∼ **out** auskoppeln.

cou·pon ['kuːpɒn] *s* **1.** Gutschein *m*, Bon *m*; Berechtigungsschein *m*. **2.** Kupon *m*, Bestellzettel *m* (*in Zeitungsinseraten etc*). **3.** *Br.* Tippzettel *m* (*Fußballtoto*).

cour·age ['kʌrɪdʒ] *s* Mut *m*, Tapferkeit *f*: **lose** ∼ den Mut verlieren; **muster up** (*od.* **pluck up**, **take**) ∼ Mut *od.* sich ein Herz fassen. cou·ra·geous [kəˈreɪdʒəs] *adj* □ mutig, tapfer.

cour·gette [ˌkɔːˈʒet] *s* 🌿 *Br.* Zucchini *f*.

cour·i·er ['kʊrɪə] *s* **1.** Eilbote *m*, (*a. diplomatischer*) Kurier *m*. **2.** Reiseleiter *m*.

course [kɔːs] *s* **1.** ✈, ⚓ Kurs *m* (*a. fig.*): *change one's* ~ s-n Kurs ändern; ~ *correction* Kurskorrektur *f*. **2.** *Sport:* (*Renn*)Bahn *f*, (-)Strecke *f*, (*Golf*)Platz *m*. **3.** (*zeitlicher, natürlicher*) (Ver-)Lauf: *in the* ~ *of* im (Ver)Lauf (*gen*); *in the* ~ *of time* im Laufe der Zeit; *of* ~ natürlich, selbstverständlich; *the* ~ *of events* der Gang der Ereignisse, der Lauf der Dinge; *take* (*od. run*) *its* ~ s-n Lauf nehmen; → *due* 6, *matter* 3. **4.** Gang *m* (*Speisen*): *a four-~ meal* e-e Mahlzeit mit 4 Gängen. **5.** Zyklus *m*, Reihe *f*: ~ *of lectures* Vortragsreihe. **6.** Kurs *m*, Lehrgang *m*: *English* ~ Englischkurs; ~ *of study* univ. Kurs; Lehrplan *m*.

court [kɔːt] **I** *s* **1.** Hof *m*: *in the* ~ auf dem Hof. **2.** *Sport:* (*Tennis- etc*)Platz *m*; (*Spiel*)Feld *n*. **3.** (*fürstlicher etc*) Hof: *at* ~ bei Hofe. **4.** *pay* (*one's*) ~ *to* a) → 6, b) *j-m* s-e Aufwartung machen. **5.** ⚖ Gericht *n*: *in* ~ vor Gericht; *bring into* ~ vor Gericht bringen; *come to* ~ vor Gericht *od.* zur Verhandlung kommen; *go to* ~ vor Gericht gehen; *out of* ~ außergerichtlich; → *arbitration* 2. **II** *v/t* **6.** *e-r Dame* den Hof machen. **7.** ~ *death* mit s-m Leben spielen; ~ *disaster* das Schicksal herausfordern. **III** *v/i* **8.** miteinander gehen: *~ing couple* Liebespaar *n*. ~ *card* *s* Kartenspiel: Bild(karte *f*) *n*.

cour·te·ous ['kɜːtjəs] *adj* □ höflich, liebenswürdig.

cour·te·sy ['kɜːtɪsɪ] *s* **1.** Höflichkeit *f*, Liebenswürdigkeit *f*: *by* ~ aus Höflichkeit; ~ *light* *mot.* Innenbeleuchtung *f*. ~ *visit* Höflichkeits-, Anstandsbesuch *m*. **2.** Gefälligkeit *f*: *by* ~ aus Gefälligkeit; *by* ~ *of* mit freundlicher Genehmigung von (*od. gen*).

'**court·house** *s* Gerichtsgebäude *n*. ~ **mar·tial** *pl* **court mar·tials, courts mar·tial** *s* Kriegsgericht *n*. ~-'**mar·tial** *v/t pret u. pp* **-'mar·tialed,** *bsd. Br.* **-'mar·tialled** vor ein Kriegsgericht stellen. ~ **or·der** *s* ⚖ Gerichtsbeschluß *m*, richterliche Verfügung. '~-**room** *s* Gerichtssaal *m*. '~-**yard** → *court* 1.

cous·in ['kʌzn] *s* Cousin *m*, Vetter *m*; Cousine *f*.

cov·er ['kʌvə] **I** *s* **1.** (*weitS. a.* Schnee-, Wolken- *etc*)Decke *f*. **2.** Deckel *m*. **3.** (*Buch*)Deckel *m*, Einband *m*; Umschlag-, Titelseite *f*; (Schutz)Umschlag *m*: *from* ~ *to* ~ von der ersten bis zur letzten Seite. **4.** Hülle *f*, Futteral *n*. **5.** Überzug *m*, Bezug *m*. **6.** Abdeck-, ⚙ Schutzhaube *f*. **7.** Briefumschlag *m*: *under separate* ~ mit getrennter Post; *under plain* ~ in neutralem Umschlag. **8.** ✕ *u. allg.* Deckung *f* (*from* vor *dat*): *take* ~ in Deckung gehen. **9.** Schutz *m* (*from* vor *dat*): *get under* ~ sich unterstellen; *under* (*the*) ~ *of night* im Schutze der Nacht. **10.** *fig.* Tarnung *f*: *under* ~ *of* unter dem Deckmantel (*gen*). **11.** Gedeck *n* (*bei Tisch*). **12.** ✝ a) Deckung *f*, Sicherheit *f*, b) → *coverage* 2. **II** *v/t* **13.** be-, zudecken (*with* mit), *Dach* decken: *~ed with* voll von; *~ed court* (*Sport*) Hallenplatz *m*. **14.** *Fläche* bedecken, sich über *e-e Fläche, a. e-n Zeitraum* erstrecken. **15.** *Seite etc* vollschreiben. **16.** einwickeln, -schlagen (*in, with* in *acc*). **17.** verbergen (*a. fig.*): ~ (*up*) *fig.* verheimlichen, -tuschen. **18.** decken, schützen (*from, against* vor *dat,* gegen) (*beide a.* ✕ *u. fig.*): ~ *o.s. fig.* sich absichern. **19.** ✝ ab)decken; versichern. **20.** *Thema* erschöpfend behandeln. **21.** *Presse, Rundfunk etc:* berichten über (*acc*). **22.** *Strecke* zurücklegen. **23.** *Sport:* Gegenspieler decken. **24.** *j-n* beschatten. **25.** *zo.* decken. ~ **ad·dress** *s* Deckadresse *f*.

cov·er·age ['kʌvərɪdʒ] *s* **1.** erschöpfende Behandlung (*e-s Themas*). **2.** ✝ Versicherungsschutz *m*, (Schadens)Deckung *f*. **3.** *Presse, Rundfunk etc:* Berichterstattung *f* (*of* über *acc*).

cov·er| charge *s* pro Gedeck berechneter Betrag. ~ **girl** *s* Covergirl *n*, Titelblattmädchen *n*.

cov·er·ing ['kʌvərɪŋ] *s* **1.** → *cover* 4. **2.** (*Fußboden*)Belag *m*. ~ **let·ter** *s* Begleitbrief *m*, -schreiben *n*.

cov·er·let ['kʌvəlɪt] *s* Tagesdecke *f*.

cov·er sto·ry *s* Titelgeschichte *f*.

cov·ert ['kʌvət] *adj* □ heimlich, verborgen.

'**cov·er-up** *s* Vertuschung *f* (*for gen*).

cow[1] [kaʊ] *s* Kuh *f* (*a. fig. contp.*): *till the* ~*s come home* F bis in alle Ewigkeit.

cow[2] [~] *v/t* einschüchtern.

cow·ard ['kaʊəd] *s* Feigling *m*. **cow-**

ard·ice ['~dɪs] s Feigheit f. '**cow·ard·ly** adj feig.

'**cow·boy** s Cowboy m.

cow·er ['kaʊə] v/i **1.** kauern, (zs.-gekauert) hocken. **2.** a. ~ **down** sich dukken.

'**cow·hide** s **1.** Kuhhaut f. **2.** Rind(s)leder n. '~**house** s Kuhstall m.

cowl [kaʊl] s **1.** Mönchskutte f. **2.** Kapuze f. **3.** Schornsteinkappe f.

'**cow·pat** s Kuhfladen m. '~**pox** s ♂ Kuh-, Impfpocken pl. '~**shed** s Kuhstall m. '~**skin** → **cowhide**. '~**slip** s ♀ **1.** Br. Schlüsselblume f. **2.** Am. Sumpfdotterblume f.

cox [kɒks] → **coxswain**. **~swain** ['kɒksn] **I** s **1.** Rudern: Steuermann m. **2.** Boot(s)führer m. **II** v/t u. v/i **3.** steuern.

coy [kɔɪ] adj □ **1.** schüchtern, scheu. **2.** neckisch-verschämt.

co·zi·ness, co·zy Am. → **cosiness, cosy.**

crab[1] [kræb] s **1.** zo. Krabbe f; Taschenkrebs m: **catch a ~** (Rudern) e-n Krebs fangen. **2.** ⚙ Winde f; Laufkatze f. **3.** → **crab louse.**

crab[2] [~] **I** s **1.** Nörgler(in); Nörgelei f. **II** v/i **2.** nörgeln. **III** v/t **3.** (herum)nörgeln an (dat). **4.** Am. verpatzen.

crab-bed ['kræbɪd] adj □ **1.** mürrisch, verdrießlich. **2.** verworren, unklar. **3.** unleserlich. '**crab·by** → **crabbed** 1.

crab louse s (irr **louse**) zo. Filzlaus f.

crack [kræk] **I** s **1.** Krach m, Knall m: **at the ~ of dawn** im Morgengrauen, in aller Frühe; **in a ~** f im Nu; **give s.o. a fair ~ of the whip** F j-m e-e faire Chance geben. **2.** F (heftiger) Schlag: **give s.o. a ~ on the head** j-m eins auf den Kopf geben. **3.** Sprung m, Riß m. **4.** Spalt(e f) m, Ritz(e f) m: **be open a ~** e-n Spalt (breit) offenstehen. **5.** F Knacks m (geistiger Defekt). **6.** sl. Versuch m: **have a ~ at s.th., give s.th. a ~** es (einmal) mit et. versuchen. **7.** sl. a) Witz m: **make ~s about** Witze machen über (acc), b) Seitenhieb m, Stichelei f. **8.** Br. F Crack m, As n (bsd. Sportler). **II** adj **9.** F erstklassig, großartig: **~ shot** Meisterschütze m. **III** v/i **10.** krachen, knallen. **11.** (zer)springen, (-)platzen, rissig werden, e-n Sprung od. Sprünge bekommen. **12.** überschnappen (Stimme). **13.** fig.

(F ~ **up**) zs.-brechen. **14.** **get ~ing** F loslegen. **15.** ~ **down on** F scharf vorgehen gegen, durchgreifen bei. **IV** v/t **16.** knallen mit (Peitsche), knacken mit (Fingern): → **joke** 1. **17.** zerbrechen, Ei aufschlagen, e-r Flasche den Hals brechen. **18.** e-n Sprung machen in (dat); sich e-e Rippe etc anbrechen. **19.** F a) schlagen, hauen: ~ **s.o. over the head** j-m eins auf den Kopf geben, b) einschlagen, zerschlagen. **20.** Nuß, F Code, Safe etc knacken. **21.** ~ **up** F hochjubeln. '~**brained** adj F verrückt. '~**down** s F (on) scharfes Vorgehen (gegen), Durchgreifen n (bei).

cracked [krækt] adj **1.** gesprungen, rissig: **be ~** e-n Sprung haben. **2.** F verrückt.

crack·er ['krækə] s **1.** Cracker m, Kräkker m: a) ungesüßtes, keksartiges Kleingebäck, b) Schwärmer m, Frosch m (Feuerwerkskörper), c) Knallbonbon m, n. **2.** pl Nußknacker m. **crack·ers** ['~əz] adj Br. F übergeschnappt: **go ~** überschnappen.

'**crack·jaw I** adj zungenbrecherisch. **II** s Zungenbrecher m.

crack·le ['krækl] **I** v/i knistern, prasseln, knattern. **II** s Knistern n, Prasseln n, Knattern n.

'**crack·pot** F **I** s Verrückte m, Spinner m. **II** adj verrückt. '~**up** s fig. F Zs.-bruch m.

crack·y ['krækɪ] → **cracked.**

cra·dle ['kreɪdl] **I** s **1.** Wiege f (a. fig.): **from the ~ to the grave** von der Wiege bis zur Bahre; **from the ~** von Kindheit od. von Kindesbeinen an. **2.** teleph. Gabel f: **put the receiver in the ~** den Hörer auf die Gabel legen. **II** v/t **3.** wiegen, schaukeln: ~ **to sleep** in den Schlaf wiegen. **4.** (zärtlich) halten. **5.** teleph. Hörer auflegen.

craft [krɑːft] s **1.** (Hand- od. Kunst)Fertigkeit f, Geschicklichkeit f: → **art** 2. **2.** Gewerbe n, Beruf m, Handwerk n. **3.** → **craftiness. 4.** Boot(e pl) n, Schiff(e pl) n; Flugzeug(e pl) n. '**craft·i·ness** s Schlauheit f, Verschlagenheit f, List f.

crafts·man ['krɑːftsmən] s (irr **man**) Handwerker m. '**crafts·man·ship** s Kunstfertigkeit f, handwerkliches Können.

craft·y ['krɑːfti] *adj* □ schlau, verschlagen, listig.

crag [kræg] *s* Felsenspitze *f*, Klippe *f*. **crag·ged** ['krægɪd] *adj Am.*, **'crag·gy** *adj* **1.** felsig, schroff. **2.** runz(e)lig, zerfurcht (*Gesicht*); knorrig, rauh (*Person*).

cram [kræm] **I** *v/t* **1.** vollstopfen, *a. fig.* vollpacken (**with** mit). **2.** (hinein)stopfen, (-)zwängen (**into** in *acc*). **3.** F a) mit *j-m* pauken (**for**: büffeln, b) *mst* ~ **up** ein *Fach* pauken, büffeln. **II** *v/i* **4.** sich vollstopfen. **5.** F pauken, büffeln (**for** für): ~ **up on** → 3b. **III** *s* **6.** F Pauken *n*, Büffeln *n*: ~ **course** Paukkurs *m*. **,~'full** *adj* vollgestopft (**of** mit), zum Bersten voll.

cram·mer ['kræmə] *s* F **1.** Paukstudio *n*. **2.** Einpauker *m*. **3.** Paukbuch *n*. **4** *j-d*, *der für e-e Prüfung paukt*.

cramp[1] [kræmp] *s* 🏥 Krampf *m*.

cramp[2] [~] **I** *s* **1.** ⚙ Krampe *f*, Klammer *f*. **II** *v/t* **2.** ⚙ ankrampen, anklammern. **3.** *a.* ~ **up** einzwängen, -engen: *be* ~*ed for space* (*od. room*) (zu) wenig Platz haben, räumlich beschränkt sein.

cran·ber·ry ['krænbərɪ] *s* 🌿 Preiselbeere *f*.

crane [kreɪn] **I** *s* **1.** *orn.* Kranich *m*. **2.** ⚙ Kran *m*. **II** *v/t* **3.** ~ *one's neck* sich den Hals verrenken (**for** nach), e-n langen Hals machen, den Hals recken. **III** *v/i* **4.** *a.* ~ **forward** den Hals recken. ~ **driv·er** *s* Kranführer *m*.

crank [kræŋk] **I** *s* **1.** ⚙ Kurbel *f*. **2.** F wunderlicher Kauz, Spinner *m*; *Am.* Miesepeter *m*. **3.** F fixe Idee, Marotte *f*. **II** *v/t* **4.** *oft* ~ **up** ankurbeln. **'~·shaft** *s* ⚙ Kurbelwelle *f*.

crank·y ['kræŋkɪ] *adj* □ F **1.** verschroben, wunderlich. **2.** *Am.* reizbar, schlechtgelaunt. **3.** wack(e)lig, unsicher, baufällig.

cran·nied ['krænɪd] *adj* rissig. **'cran·ny** *s* Riß *m*, Ritze *f*, Spalt *m*: → *nook*.

crape [kreɪp] *s* **1.** Krepp *m*. **2.** Trauerflor *m*.

crash [kræʃ] **I** *v/t* **1.** zertrümmern, -schmettern. **2.** F uneingeladen kommen zu, hineinplatzen in (*acc*): ~ *a par·ty;* ~ *the gate* → *gate-crash.* **II** *v/i* **3.** (krachend) zerbersten, zs.-krachen. **4.** krachend einstürzen, zs.-krachen. **5.** *bsd.* ✈ zs.-brechen. **6.** krachen (**against, into** gegen):

~ *open* krachend auffliegen (*Tür*). **7.** stürmen, platzen: ~ *in(to the room)* hereinplatzen. **8.** *mot.* zs.-stoßen, verunglücken; ✈ abstürzen. **III** *s* **9.** Krach(en) *m* **10.** *bsd.* ✝ Zs.-bruch *m*, (Börsen)Krach *m*. **11.** *mot.* Unfall *m*, Zs.-stoß *m*; ✈ Absturz *m*. ~ *bar·ri·er* *s Br.* Leitplanke *f*. ~ *course* *s* Schnell-, Intensivkurs *m*. ~ *di·et* *s* radikale Schlankheitskur. ~ *hel·met* *s* Sturzhelm *m*.

crash·ing ['kræʃɪŋ] *adj* F fürchterlich.

'crash|-land *v/i* ✈ Bruch *od.* e-e Bruchlandung machen, bruchlanden. ~ *land·ing* *s* ✈ Bruchlandung *f*. ~ *pro·gram(me)* *s* Sofortprogramm *n*. ~ *test* *s mot.* Crashtest *m*.

crass [kræs] *adj* □ **1.** grob, kraß (*Fehler etc*). **2.** derb, unfein (*Benehmen etc*).

crate [kreɪt] *s* **1.** (Latten)Kiste *f*. **2.** (Bieretc)Kasten *m*. **3.** *sl.* Kiste *f* (*Auto, Flugzeug*).

cra·ter ['kreɪtə] *s* **1.** *geol.* Krater *m*: ~ *lake* Kratersee *m*. **2.** (Bomben-, Granat)Trichter *m*.

cra·vat [krə'væt] *s* Halstuch *n*.

crave [kreɪv] **I** *v/t* **1.** *et.* ersehnen. **2.** (inständig) bitten *od.* flehen um. **II** *v/i* **3.** sich sehnen (**for, after** nach). **4.** ~ *for* → 2. **'crav·ing** *s* Sehnsucht *f* (**for** nach).

crawl [krɔːl] **I** *v/i* **1.** kriechen: a) krabbeln, b) *fig.* sich dahinschleppen (*Zeit etc*), c) im Schneckentempo gehen *od.* fahren, d) F unterwürfig sein: ~ *to s.o.* vor *j-m* kriechen. **2.** wimmeln (**with** von). **3.** kribbeln: *the sight made her flesh* ~ bei dem Anblick bekam sie e-e Gänsehaut. **4.** *Schwimmen:* kraulen. **II** *s* **5.** Kriechen *n*: *go at a* ~ → 1c. **6.** *Schwimmen:* Kraul(en) *n*, Kraulstil *m*. **'crawl·er** *s* **1.** Kriechtier *n*. **2.** *Br.* Kriecher(in). **3.** *Schwimmen:* Krauler(in).

cray·fish ['kreɪfɪʃ] *s zo.* **1.** Flußkrebs *m*. **2.** Languste *f*.

cray·on ['kreɪən] **I** *s* **1.** Zeichenkreide *f*. **2.** Zeichen-, Bunt-, Pastellstift *m*: *blue* ~ Blaustift. **3.** Kreide-, Pastellzeichnung *f*. **II** *v/t* **4.** mit Kreide *etc* zeichnen.

craze [kreɪz] *s* Manie *f*, Verrücktheit *f*: *be the* ~ große Mode sein; *the latest* ~ der letzte Schrei. **'cra·zi·ness** *s* Verrücktheit *f*. **'cra·zy** *adj* □ **1.** *a. fig.*

verrückt, wahnsinnig (*with* vor *dat*): *drive s.o.* ~ j-n wahnsinnig machen; ~ **bone** *Am.* Musikantenknochen *m.* **2** F (*about*) hingerissen (von), vernarrt in (*acc*); versessen, scharf (auf *acc*), wild, verrückt (nach): *be a* ~ *to do s.th.* darauf versessen sein, et. zu tun.

creak [kriːk] **I** *v/i* knarren (*Treppe etc*), quietschen (*Bremsen etc*). **II** *s* Knarren *n*, Quietschen *n*. **'creak·y** *adj* knarrend, quietschend.

cream [kriːm] **I** *s* **1.** Rahm *m*, Sahne *f*. **2.** Creme(speise) *f*. **3.** (*Haut-, Schuh-etc*)Creme *f*. **4.** *fig.* Creme *f*, Auslese *f*, Elite *f*: *the* ~ *of the* ~ die Crème de la crème. **II** *v/t* **5.** den Rahm abschöpfen von (*a. fig.*). **6.** zu Schaum schlagen; schaumig rühren. **7.** sich *das Gesicht etc* eincremen: ~ *one's face*. **III** *adj* **8.** creme(farben). ~ **cheese** *s* Rahm-, Vollfettkäse *m.* **'~·col·o(u)red** → **cream** 8. ~ **puff** *s* Windbeutel *m.*

crease [kriːs] **I** *s* **1.** Falte *f*. **2.** Bügelfalte *f*. **3.** Knick *m, a.* Eselsohr *n*. **II** *v/t* **4.** falten, knicken. **5.** Falten bügeln in (*e-e Hose*). **6.** zerknittern. **III** *v/i* **7.** knittern. **'~·proof, '~·re,sist·ant** *adj* knitterfrei, -fest.

cre·ate [kriːˈeɪt] *v/t* **1.** (er)schaffen. **2.** ins Leben rufen, *Arbeitsplätze* schaffen; hervorrufen, verursachen. **3.** *thea. etc, Mode:* kreieren. **4.** *j-n* machen *od.* ernennen zu. **cre·a·tion** *s* **1.** (Er)Schaffung *f*. **2.** Hervorrufung *f*, Verursachung *f*. **3.** the ⌖ *eccl.* die Schöpfung. **4.** *thea. etc, Mode:* Kreierung *f*. **5.** (Kunst-, Mode)Schöpfung *f*, (*Mode a.*) Kreation *f*. **6.** Ernennung *f*. **cre·a·tive** *adj* □ schöpferisch, kreativ. **cre·a·tor** *s* Schöpfer *m*, Urheber *m*: *the* ⌖ *eccl.* der Schöpfer.

crea·ture [ˈkriːtʃə] *s* **1.** Geschöpf *n*, (Lebe)Wesen *n*, Kreatur *f*: *dumb* ~ stumme Kreatur; *good* ~ gute Haut; *lovely* ~ süßes Geschöpf; *poor (silly)* ~ armes (dummes) Ding; ~ *of habit* Gewohnheitstier *n*. **2.** Produkt *n*: ~ *of the imagination* Phantasieprodukt. ~ **com·forts** *s pl* leibliches Wohl.

crèche [kreɪʃ] *s* **1.** (Kinder)Krippe *f*. **2.** *Am.* (Weihnachts)Krippe *f*.

cre·dence [ˈkriːdəns] *s*: *give* (*od. attach*) ~ *to* Glauben schenken (*dat*).

cre·den·tials [krɪˈdenʃlz] *s pl* **1.** Beglau-

bigungs- *od.* Empfehlungsschreiben *n*. **2.** (Leumunds)Zeugnis *n*. **3.** Ausweis(papiere *pl*) *m*.

cred·i·bil·i·ty [ˌkredəˈbɪlətɪ] *s* Glaubwürdigkeit *f*. **'cred·i·ble** *adj* □ glaubwürdig.

cred·it [ˈkredɪt] **I** *s* **1.** Glaube(n) *m*: *give* ~ *to* Glauben schenken (*dat*). **2.** Ansehen *n*, Achtung *f*: *be in high* ~ *with* in hohem Ansehen stehen bei. **3.** Ehre *f*: *be a* ~ *to s.o., be a* ~ *to s.o.'s* ~, *do s.o.* ~ j-m Ehre machen *od.* einbringen; *to his* ~ *it must be said* zu s-r Ehre muß man sagen; ~ *where* ~ *is due* Ehre, wem Ehre gebührt. **4.** Anerkennung *f*, Lob *n*: *get* ~ *for* Anerkennung finden für; *that's very much to his* ~ das ist sehr anerkennenswert *od.* verdienstvoll von ihm. **5.** Verdienst *n*: *give s.o.* (*the*) ~ *for* j-m *et.* hoch anrechnen; j-m *et.* zutrauen; j-m *et.* zuschreiben. **6.** ⌖ Kredit *m*: *on* ~ auf Kredit; *give s.o.* ~ *for £1,000* j-m e-n Kredit von 1000 Pfund geben; ~ *card* Kreditkarte *f*. **7.** ⌖ Guthaben *n*. Kredit(seite *f*) *n*, Haben *n*: *your* ~ Saldo zu Ihren Gunsten; *enter* (*od. place, put*) *a sum to s.o.'s* ~ j-m e-n Betrag gutschreiben. **II** *v/t* **8.** Glauben schenken (*dat*), glauben (*dat*). **9.** ~ *s.o. with* j-m *et.* zutrauen; j-m *et.* zuschreiben. **10.** ⌖ *Betrag* zuschreiben (*to s.o.* j-m). **'cred·it·a·ble** *adj* □ (*to*) ehrenvoll (für), anerkennenswert (von). **'cred·i·tor** *s* ⌖ Gläubiger *m*. **'cred·it,wor·thy** *adj* ⌖ kreditwürdig.

cre·du·li·ty [krɪˈdjuːlətɪ] *s* Leichtgläubigkeit *f*. **cred·u·lous** [ˈkredjʊləs] *adj* □ leichtgläubig.

creed [kriːd] *s* **1.** *eccl.* Glaubensbekenntnis *n*; Glaube *m*, Konfession *f*. **2.** *fig.* Überzeugung *f*, Weltanschauung *f*.

creek [kriːk] *s* **1.** *Am.* Bach *m*. **2.** *bsd. Br.* kleine Bucht. **3.** *be up the* ~ F in der Klemme sein *od.* sitzen *od.* stecken.

creep [kriːp] **I** *v/i* (*irr*) **1.** kriechen: a) krabbeln, b) *fig.* sich dahinschleppen (*Zeit etc*), c) im Schneckentempo gehen *od.* fahren, d) unterwürfig sein. **2.** schleichen: ~ *in* (sich) hinein- *od.* hereinschleichen; *fig.* sich einschleichen (*Fehler etc*). **3.** kribbeln: *the sight made her flesh* ~ bei dem Anblick bekam sie e-e Gänsehaut. **II** *s* **4.** Kriechen *n*, Schleichen *n*: *go at a* ~ → 1c. **5.** the

sight gave her the **~s** F bei dem Anblick bekam sie e-e Gänsehaut. **6.** F Kriecher(in). **'creep·er** s **1.** Kriechtier n. **2.** Kriech- od. Kletterpflanze f. **'creep·ing** adj □ kriechend: **~ inflation** ✝ schleichende Inflation. **'creep·y** adj grus(e)lig.

cre·mate [krɪˈmeɪt] v/t bsd. Leichen verbrennen, einäschern. **creˈma·tion** s Verbrennung f, Einäscherung f, Feuerbestattung f. **crem·a·to·ri·um** [ˌkremə-ˈtɔːrɪəm] pl **-ums, -a** [~ə], bsd. Am. **cre·ma·to·ry** [ˈ~tərɪ] s Krematorium n.

crept [krept] pret u. pp von **creep**.

cres·cent [ˈkresnt] s Halbmond m, Mondsichel f.

cress [kres] s ♣ Kresse f.

crest [krest] s **1.** orn. Büschel n, Haube f; Kamm m. **2.** zo. Mähne f. **3.** Bergrücken m, Kamm m. **4.** (Wellen)Kamm m: **be riding (along) on the ~ of a wave** fig. im Augenblick ganz oben schwimmen. **5.** fig. Gipfel m, Scheitelpunkt m: **at the ~ of his fame** auf dem Gipfel s-s Ruhms. **'~ˌfall·en** adj fig. niedergeschlagen, geknickt.

cre·tin [ˈkretɪn] s ♣ Kretin m (a. fig. contp.).

cre·vasse [krɪˈvæs] s **1.** tiefer Spalt od. Riß. **2.** Gletscherspalte f.

crev·ice [ˈkrevɪs] s Riß m, Spalt m, (Fels)Spalte f.

crew¹ [kruː] s **1.** (Arbeits)Gruppe f, (Bauetc)Trupp m, (Arbeiter)Kolonne f. **2.** ✈ (Bedienungs)Mannschaft f. **3.** ✔, ⚓ Besatzung f; ⚓ engS. Mannschaft f (a. Sport).

crew² [~] pret von **crow²**.

crew cut s Bürstenschnitt m.

crib [krɪb] s **1.** F Kinderbettchen n. **2.** (Futter)Krippe f. **3.** bsd. Br. (Weihnachts)Krippe f. **4.** F kleiner Diebstahl; Anleihe f, Plagiat n. **5.** ped. F Eselsbrücke f, Klatsche f; Spickzettel m. **II** v/t u. v/i **6.** F klauen (a. fig. plagiieren). **7.** ped. F abschreiben, spicken (**off, from** von).

crick [krɪk] s: **a ~ in one's neck** ein steifer Hals.

crick·et¹ [ˈkrɪkɪt] s zo. Grille f.

crick·et² [~] (Sport) **I** s Kricket n: **not ~** F nicht fair. **II** v/i Kricket spielen. **'crick·et·er** s Kricketspieler m.

cri·er [ˈkraɪə] s Schreier m, Schreihals m.

crime [kraɪm] s **1.** Verbrechen n, coll. a. pl: **~ prevention** Verbrechensverhütung f; **~ syndicate** Verbrechersyndikat n; **~ wave** Welle f von Verbrechen. **2.** → **criminality. 3.** F Verbrechen n; Jammer m, Zumutung f.

crim·i·nal [ˈkrɪmɪnl] **I** adj **1.** kriminell, verbrecherisch (beide a. fig. F): **~ act** Straftat f, strafbare Handlung; **~ association** kriminelle Vereinigung; → **record¹ 2.** strafrechtlich, Straf..., Kriminal...: **~ code** Strafgesetzbuch n; **~ law** Strafrecht n; **~ proceedings** pl Strafprozeß m, -verfahren n. **II** s **3.** Verbrecher(in), Kriminelle m, f. **crim·i·nal·i·ty** [ˌ~ˈnælɪtɪ] s Kriminalität f, Verbrechertum n. **crim·i·nol·o·gy** [ˌ~ˈnɒlədʒɪ] s Kriminologie f.

crimp [krɪmp] v/t **1.** kräuseln. **2.** falteln, fälteln. **3.** Haar wellen, locken.

crim·son [ˈkrɪmzn] adj **1.** karmin-, karmesinrot. **2.** puterrot (**from** vor dat).

cringe [krɪndʒ] v/i **1.** sich ducken od. (zs.-)krümmen: **~ at** zurückschrecken vor (dat). **2.** fig. kriechen, katzbuckeln (**to** vor dat). **'cring·ing** adj □ kriecherisch, unterwürfig.

crin·kle [ˈkrɪŋkl] **I** v/i **1.** Falten werfen. **2.** knittern. **3.** rascheln, knistern. **II** v/t **4.** zerknittern. **III** s **5.** Falte f, (im Gesicht) Fältchen n.

crip·ple [ˈkrɪpl] **I** s Krüppel m (a. fig.). **II** v/t zum Krüppel machen; lähmen, fig. a. lahmlegen.

cri·sis [ˈkraɪsɪs] pl **-ses** [~siːz] s Krise f (a. thea., ♣): **economic ~** Wirtschaftskrise; **~ of confidence** Vertrauenskrise; **~ staff** Krisenstab m.

crisp [krɪsp] **I** adj □ **1.** knusp(e)rig (Gebäck etc). **2.** kraus (Haar). **3.** frisch, knackig, fest (Gemüse). **4.** forsch, schneidig (Benehmen etc). **5.** klar (Stil etc). **6.** scharf, frisch (Luft etc). **II** s **7.** pl bsd. Br. (Kartoffel)Chips pl. **III** v/t **8.** knusp(e)rig backen od. braten. **IV** v/i **9.** knusp(e)rig werden.

criss·cross [ˈkrɪskrɒs] **I** adj kreuzweise, Kreuz... **II** adv kreuzweise, kreuz u. quer. **III** s Gewirr n. **IV** v/t kreuz u. quer ziehen durch. **V** v/i kreuz u. quer (ver)laufen.

cri·te·ri·on [kraɪˈtɪərɪən] pl **-ri·a** [~ə], **-ri·ons** s Kriterium n: a) Maßstab m, b) (Unterscheidungs)Merkmal n.

crit·ic ['krɪtɪk] s Kritiker(in): a) Beurteiler(in), b) Rezensent(in), c) Krittler(in). **crit·i·cal** ['ˌkl] adj □ kritisch: a) anspruchsvoll, b) mißbilligend, tadelnd (*of acc*): *be ~ of* et. auszusetzen haben an (*dat*), kritisch gegenüberstehen (*dat*), kritisieren (*acc*), c) entscheidend (*Augenblick etc*), d) gefährlich, bedenklich (*Situation etc*): *he is in* (a) *~ condition ♂* kritisieren ein Zustand ist kritisch. **crit·i·cism** ['ˌsɪzəm] s Kritik f: a) kritische Beurteilung, b) Tadel m, Vorwurf m: *open to ~* anfechtbar; *above ~* über jede Kritik *od.* jeden Tadel erhaben, c) → *critique* a. **crit·i·cize** ['ˌsaɪz] v/t kritisieren: a) kritisch beurteilen, b) Kritik üben an (*dat*), bekritteln, tadeln: *~ s.o. for doing s.th.* j-n kritisieren, weil er et. getan hat, c) besprechen, rezensieren. **cri·tique** [krɪˈtiːk] s Kritik f: a) Rezension f, Besprechung f, b) kritische Untersuchung.

croak [krəʊk] I v/i **1.** quaken (*Frosch*); krächzen (*Rabe etc, a. Mensch*). **2.** sl. abkratzen. II s **3.** Quaken n; Krächzen n.

cro·chet ['krəʊʃeɪ] I s a. *~ work* Häkelarbeit f, Häkelei f: *~ hook* Häkelnadel f. II v/t u. v/i häkeln.

crock¹ [krɒk] s irdener Topf *od.* Krug. **crock²** [~] s sl. Wrack n (*Person od. Sache*); Klapperkasten m (*Auto*).

crock·er·y ['krɒkərɪ] s Steingut n, Töpferware f.

croc·o·dile ['krɒkədaɪl] s zo. Krokodil n. *~ tears* f/pl Krokodilstränen pl.

cro·cus ['krəʊkəs] s ♀ Krokus m.

crook [krʊk] I s **1.** Haken m. **2.** Krümmung f, Biegung f: *~ of one's arm* Armbeuge f. **3.** F Gauner m; Gaunerei f: *on the ~* auf betrügerische Weise. II v/t u. v/i **4.** (sich) krümmen *od.* biegen. **crook·ed** ['ˌɪd] adj □ **1.** gekrümmt, gebogen, krumm. **2.** F betrügerisch.

croon [kruːn] v/t u. v/i **1.** schmachtend singen. **2.** leise singen *od.* summen. **'croon·er** s Schnulzensänger(in).

crop [krɒp] I s **1.** Ernte f: *~ failure* Mißernte. **2.** *fig.* Ertrag m, Ausbeute f (*of* an *dat*); große Menge, Masse f. **3.** kurzer Haarschnitt; kurzgeschnittenes Haar. II v/t **4.** stutzen, beschneiden. **5.** *Haar* kurz scheren. III v/i **6.** *mst ~ up* (*od. out*) *fig.* plötzlich auftauchen *od.*

eintreten. **'crop·per** s F **1.** schwerer Sturz: *come a ~* schwer stürzen. **2.** Mißerfolg m, Fehlschlag m: *come a ~* Schiffbruch erleiden.

cro·quet ['krəʊkeɪ] s Sport: Krocket n.

cross [krɒs] I s **1.** *eccl.* Kreuz n: *the ♀* das Kreuz (Christi), das Kruzifix. **2.** Kreuz(zeichen) n: *make the sign of the ~* sich bekreuzigen; *mark with a ~* ankreuzen. **3.** *fig.* Kreuz n, Leiden n: *bear* (*od. carry*) *one's ~* sein Kreuz tragen. **4.** Querstrich m. **5.** *biol.* Kreuzung(sprodukt n) f. **6.** *fig.* Mittel-, Zwischending n. II v/t **7.** das Kreuzzeichen machen auf (*acc*) *od.* über (*dat*): *~ o.s.* sich bekreuzigen. **8.** *fig.* kreuzen: *~ one's arms* die Arme kreuzen *od.* verschränken; *fig.* die Hände in den Schoß legen; *~ one's legs* die Beine kreuzen *od.* über(einander)schlagen; → *finger* I, *sword*. **9.** *Grenze, Meer, Straße etc* überqueren: *~ s.o.'s path* j-m in die Quere kommen. **10.** kreuzen, schneiden. **11.** sich kreuzen mit (*Brief*). **12.** ankreuzen. **13.** *oft ~ off* (*od. out*) aus-, durchstreichen: *~ off* abschreiben (*as* als). **14.** *Plan etc* durchkreuzen, vereiteln. **15.** *biol.* kreuzen. III v/i **16.** sich kreuzen (a. Briefe) *od.* schneiden. **17.** *oft ~ over* (*to*) hinübergehen, -fahren (nach), übersetzen (nach). **18.** *biol.* sich kreuzen (lassen). IV *adj* **19.** schräg, Schräg... **20.** (*to*) entgegengesetzt (*dat*), im Widerspruch (zu). **21.** F böse (*with* auf *acc*, mit), mürrisch. **'~·bar** s Sport: Tor-, Querlatte f. **'~·beam** s ⊙ Querträger m, -balken m. **'~·bones** s pl → *skull*. **'~·breed** *biol.* I s Mischling m, Kreuzung f. II v/t (irr *breed*) kreuzen. **'~·check** I v/t von verschiedenen Gesichtspunkten aus überprüfen. II s Überprüfung f von verschiedenen Gesichtspunkten aus. **'~·coun·try** *adj* Querfeldein..., Gelände..., *mot. a.* geländegängig: *~ skiing* Skilanglauf m. **'~·cur·rent** s Gegenströmung f (*a. fig.*). **'~·dress·ing** s Transvestismus m.

crossed [krɒst] *adj* gekreuzt: *~ cheque* ♀ Br. Verrechnungsscheck m.

'cross-ex·am·i'na·tion s ⚖ Kreuzverhör n. **'~-ex·am·ine** v/t ⚖ ins Kreuzverhör nehmen. **'~-eyed** *adj* schielend: *be ~* schielen. **'~·fire** s ⚔ Kreuzfeuer n (*a. fig.*). **'~·grained** *adj* **1.** quergefasert.

2. *fig.* widerspenstig (*a. Sache*); kratzbürstig.

cross·ing ['krɒsɪŋ] *s* 1. Überquerung *f*: ~ **point** Grenzübergang *m*. 2. ♣ Überfahrt *f*: **rough** ~ stürmische Überfahrt. 3. (*Straßen-* etc)Kreuzung *f*. 4. Straßenübergang *m*; *Br.* Fußgängerüberweg *m*: → **grade** 4, **level** 5. 5. *biol.* Kreuzung *f*.

cross-legged *adj u. adv* mit gekreuzten *od.* über(einander)geschlagenen Beinen, (*am Boden a.*) im Schneidersitz.

cross·ness ['krɒsnɪs] *s* F Mürrischkeit *f*, schlechte Laune.

cross|·patch *s* F Brummbär *m*. **~·pur·pos·es** *s pl*: **talk at ~** aneinander vorbeireden. **~ ref·er·ence** *s* Kreuz-, Querverweis *m*. **'~·road** *s* 1. *Am*. Quer*od*. Seitenstraße *f*. 2. *pl* (*mst sg konstruiert*) (Straßen)Kreuzung *f*; *fig*. Scheideweg *m*. **~ sec·tion** *s* ♠, ⊙ *u. fig.* Querschnitt *m* (**of** durch). **'~·walk** *s Am.* Fußgängerüberweg *m*. **'~·ways**, **'~·wise** *adv* quer, kreuzweise. **'~·word** (*puz·zle*) *s* Kreuzworträtsel *n*.

crotch [krɒtʃ] *s* 1. Gab(e)lung *f*. 2. Schritt *m* (*der Hose od. des Körpers*).

crotch·et ['krɒtʃɪt] *s* 1. ♪ *bsd. Br.* Viertelnote *f*. 2. *fig.* Grille *f*, Marotte *f*. **'crotch·et·y** *adj* 1. grillenhaft. 2. F mürrisch.

crouch [kraʊtʃ] I *v/i* 1. *a.* ~ **down** sich bücken *od.* ducken. 2. hocken; kauern. II *s* 3. Hocke *f*: **in a ~** gebückt; in der Hocke.

crou·pi·er ['kru:pɪə] *s* Croupier *m*.

crow¹ [krəʊ] *s* 1. *orn.* Krähe *f*: **as the ~ flies** (in der) Luftlinie; **eat ~** *bsd.Am.* F zu Kreuze kriechen; **have a ~ to pluck** (*od. pull, pick*) **with** F ein Hühnchen zu rupfen haben mit. 2. → **crowbar**.

crow² [~] I *v/i pret* **crowed** *u.* (*für* 1) **crew** [kru:], *pp* **crowed** 1. krähen (*Hahn*). 2. (*fröhlich*) krähen. 3. jubeln, frohlocken (**over** über *acc*). 4. protzen, prahlen (**over, about** mit). II *s* 5. Krähen *n*. 6. Jubel(schrei) *m*.

'crow·bar *s* ⊙ Brecheisen *n*, -stange *f*.

crowd [kraʊd] I *s* 1. dichte (Menschen)Menge, Masse *f*: **~s pl of people** Menschenmassen *pl*. 2. **the ~** die Masse, das (gemeine) Volk: **one of the ~** ein Mann aus dem Volk; **follow** (*od. move*

with) **the ~** mit der Masse gehen. 3. F Gesellschaft *f*, Haufen *m*, Verein *m*. 4. Ansammlung *f*, Haufen *m*. II *v/i* 5. (zs.-)strömen, sich drängen (**into** in *acc*; **round** um). III *v/t* 6. *Straßen etc* bevölkern. 7. sich drängen in (*acc od. dat*) *od*. um. 8. zs.-drängen, -pressen. 9. hineinpressen, -stopfen (**into** in *acc*). 10. vollstopfen (**with** mit). '**crowd·ed** *adj* 1. (**with**) überfüllt (mit), voll (von): ~ **street** stark befahrene *od*. verkehrsreiche Straße. 2. (zs.-)gedrängt. 3. *fig.* voll ausgefüllt, ereignisreich.

crowd| pull·er *s* Zuschauermagnet *m*. **~ scene** *s* Film, TV: Massenszene *f*.

crown [kraʊn] I *s* 1. Krone *f* (*a. fig.*), (*Sport a.*) (Meister)Titel *m*: **the ☽** die Krone, der König, die Königin. 2. Krone *f* (*Währung*). 3. Zahnmedizin: Krone *f*. 4. *fig.* Krönung *f*, Höhepunkt *m*. II *v/t* 5. *j-n* krönen (**king** zum König): **~ed heads** *pl* gekrönte Häupter *pl*. 6. *fig.* krönen: a) ehren, auszeichnen, b) schmücken, zieren, c) den Höhepunkt bilden von (*od. gen*): **~ all** allem die Krone aufsetzen (*a. iro.*); **to ~ it all** zu allem Überfluß *od*. Unglück, d) erfolgreich abschließen: **~ed with success** von Erfolg gekrönt. 7. Zahn überkronen. **~ col·o·ny** *s Br.* Kronkolonie *f*.

crown·ing ['kraʊnɪŋ] I *adj fig.* krönend. II *s* Krönung *f* (*a. fig.*).

crown| jew·els *s pl* Kronjuwelen *pl*. **~ prince** *s* Kronprinz *m* (*a. fig.*). **~ prin·cess** *s* Kronprinzessin *f*. **~ wit·ness** *s* ⚖ *Br.* Belastungszeuge *m*.

'crow's|-feet *s pl* Krähenfüße *pl*, Fältchen *pl*. **~ nest** *s* ♣ Krähennest *n*.

cru·ces ['kru:si:z] *pl von* **crux**.

cru·cial ['kru:ʃl] *adj* □ kritisch, entscheidend (**to, for** für): ~ **point** springender Punkt.

cru·ci·fix ['kru:sɪfɪks] *s* Kruzifix *n*. **cru·ci·fix·ion** [~'fɪkʃn] *s* Kreuzigung *f*. **cru·ci·fy** ['~faɪ] *v/t* kreuzigen.

crude [kru:d] *adj* □ 1. roh, unver-, unbearbeitet: ~ **oil** Rohöl *n*. 2. *fig.* roh, grob. 3. *fig.* nackt, ungeschminkt. '**crude·ness, cru·di·ty** ['~dɪtɪ] *s* Roheit (*a. fig.*).

cru·el [krʊəl] *adj* □ 1. grausam (**to** zu, gegen). 2. unmenschlich, unbarmherzig. 3. schrecklich, mörderisch. '**cru-**

cul·tur·al [ˈkʌltʃərəl] *adj* □ kulturell, Kultur...

cul·ture [ˈkʌltʃə] *s* **1.** → *cultivation* 1, 2. **2.** (*Tier*)Züchtung *f*, (-)Zucht *f*. **3.** *biol.* Kultur *f*. **4.** Kultur *f*: a) (Geistes)Bildung *f*, b) Kultiviertheit *f*. **5.** Kultur *f*: a) Kulturkreis *m*, b) Kulturform *f*, -stufe *f*. '**cul·tured** *adj* **1.** gezüchtet: **~ pearl** Zuchtperle *f*. **2.** kultiviert, gebildet.

cum·ber·some [ˈkʌmbəsəm] *adj* □ **1.** lästig, hinderlich. **2.** klobig, unhandlich, sperrig.

cu·mu·la·tive [ˈkjuːmjʊlətɪv] *adj* □ **1.** sich (an)häufend, anwachsend. **2.** ✝ kumulativ. **cu·mu·lus** [ˈ~ləs] *pl* **-li** [ˈ~laɪ] *s* Haufenwolke *f*.

cun·ning [ˈkʌnɪŋ] **I** *adj* □ **1.** klug, geschickt; schlau; listig, gerissen. **2.** *Am.* F niedlich, süß; drollig. **II** *s* **3.** Klugheit *f*, Geschicktheit *f*; Schlauheit *f*, List(igkeit) *f*, Gerissenheit *f*.

cunt [kʌnt] *s* V Fotze *f* (*Vagina*).

cup [kʌp] **I** *s* **1.** Tasse *f*: *that's not my ~ of tea Br.* F das ist nicht mein Fall. **2.** *Sport:* Cup *m*, Pokal *m*: **~ final** Pokalendspiel *n*; **~ tie** Pokalspiel *n*, -paarung *f*; **~ winner** Pokalsieger *m*. **3.** (*Wein*-*etc*)Becher *m*: **be fond of the ~** gern trinken. **4.** *eccl.* Kelch *m*, *fig. a.* Becher *m*. **5.** ⚘ Blüten-, Fruchtbecher *m*. **II** *v/t* **6.** *Hand* hohl machen: **~ped hand** hohle Hand. **~·board** [ˈkʌbəd] *s* (Geschirr-, Speise-, *bsd. Br. a.* Kleider-, Wäsche-)Schrank *m*: **~ bed** Schrankbett *n*. **~·ful** [ˈ~fʊl] *s* **~s** Tasse(voll).

cu·po·la [ˈkjuːpələ] *s* △ Kuppel *f*.

cup·pa, cup·per [ˈkʌpə] *s Br.* F Tasse *f* Tee.

cur [kɜː] *s* **1.** Köter *m*. **2.** *fig.* (Schweine)Hund *m*.

cur·a·ble [ˈkjʊərəbl] *adj* heilbar.

curb [kɜːb] *s* **1.** Kandare *f*. **2.** *bsd. Am.* Bord-, Randstein *m*. **II** *v/t* **3.** *Pferd* an die Kandare nehmen. **4.** *fig.* zügeln, im Zaum halten. **~·stone** → *curb* 2.

curd [kɜːd] *s oft pl* geronnene *od.* dicke Milch, Quark *m*.

cur·dle [ˈkɜːdl] **I** *v/t Milch* gerinnen lassen: **~ s.o.'s blood** j-m das Blut in den Adern erstarren lassen. **II** *v/i* gerinnen, dick werden (*Milch*): **the sight made my blood ~** bei den Anblick erstarrte mir das Blut in den Adern.

cure [kjʊə] **I** *s* **1.** ✚ Kur *f*, Heilverfahren

n (**for** gegen): **under ~** in Behandlung. **2.** ✚ Heilung *f*: *past ~* unheilbar krank (*Person*); unheilbar (*Krankheit*); *fig.* hoffnungslos (*Lage etc*). **3.** ✚ (Heil-)Mittel *n* (**for** gegen) (*a. fig.*). **II** *v/t* **4.** ✚ j-n heilen, kurieren, *fig. a.* abbringen (*of* von); ✚ *Krankheit* heilen; *fig. Mißstände etc* abstellen. **5.** haltbar machen: a) räuchern, b) trocknen, c) einpökeln, -salzen. **III** *v/i* **6.** ✚ Heilung bringen, heilen. '**~·all** *s* Allheilmittel *n*.

cur·few [ˈkɜːfjuː] *s* ✗ Ausgangsverbot *n*, -sperre *f*.

cu·ri·o [ˈkjʊərɪəʊ] *pl* **-os** → *curiosity* 2a, c. **cu·ri·os·i·ty** [ˌ~ˈɒsətɪ] *s* **1.** Neugier *f*; Wißbegierde *f*. **2.** Kuriosität *f*: a) Rarität *f*, b) Sehenswürdigkeit *f*, c) Kuriosum *n*. '**cu·ri·ous** *adj* □ **1.** neugierig; wißbegierig: *I am ~ to know if* ich möchte gern wissen, ob. **2.** kurios, seltsam: **~ly enough** merkwürdigerweise. **3.** F komisch, wunderlich.

curl [kɜːl] **I** *v/t* **1.** *Haar etc* locken; kräuseln. **II** *v/i* **2.** sich locken *od.* kräuseln: **~ up** in Ringen hochsteigen (*Rauch*); sich zs.-rollen; **~ up on the sofa** es sich auf dem Sofa gemütlich machen. **3.** *Sport:* Curling spielen. **III** *s* **4.** Locke *f*. **5.** (Rauch)Ring *m*. '**curl·er** *s* **1.** *Sport:* Curlingspieler(in). **2.** Lockenwickel *m*, -wickler *m*. '**curl·ing** *s Sport:* Curling *n*: **~ stone** Curlingstein *m*. '**curl·y** *adj* gelockt, lockig; gekräuselt, kraus.

cur·rant [ˈkʌrənt] *s* **1.** Korinthe *f*. **2.** ⚘ Johannisbeere *f*.

cur·ren·cy [ˈkʌrənsɪ] *s* **1.** Umlauf *m*: **give ~ to** *Gerücht etc* in Umlauf setzen. **2.** ✚ Währung *f*; Zahlungsmittel *pl*: **foreign ~** Devisen *pl*; **~ reform** Währungsreform *f*. **3.** ✚, ✚ Laufzeit *f*. '**cur·rent I** *adj* □ **1.** laufend (*Monat, Ausgaben etc*): **~ account** ✚ Girokonto *n*. **2.** gegenwärtig, augenblicklich, aktuell: **~ events** *pl* Tagesereignisse *pl*. **3.** üblich, gebräuchlich: **not in ~ use** nicht allgemein üblich. **II** *s* **4.** Strömung *f*, Strom *m* (*beide a. fig.*): **against the ~** gegen den Strom; **~ of air** Luftstrom, -zug *m*. **5.** ≠ Strom *m*: **~ meter** Stromzähler *m*.

cur·ric·u·lum [kəˈrɪkjələm] *pl* **-la** [ˌ~lə], **-lums** *s* Lehr-, Studienplan *m*. **~ vi·tae** [ˈviːtaɪ] *pl* **-la -** *s* Lebenslauf *m*.

cur·ry¹ [ˈkʌrɪ] **I** *s* Curry *m, n*. **II** *v/t* mit

Curry zubereiten: **curried** Curry...

cur·ry² [~] v/t **1.** *Pferd* striegeln. **2.** *Leder* zurichten. **3.** ~ **favo(u)r with** s.o., ~ **s.o.'s favo(u)r** sich bei j-m lieb Kind machen (wollen).

curse [kɜːs] **I** s **1.** Fluch m: **there is a** ~ **on the house, the house is under a** ~ auf dem Haus lastet od. liegt ein Fluch. **2.** Fluch(wort n) m, Verwünschung f. **3.** Fluch m, Unglück n (**to** für). **II** v/t **4.** verfluchen: a) mit e-m Fluch belegen, b) verwünschen, fluchen auf (acc) od. über (acc). **5. be ~d with** bestraft od. geplagt sein mit. **curs·ed** ['~sɪd] adj □ verflucht, F a. verdammt.

cur·so·ry ['kɜːsərɪ] adj □ flüchtig, oberflächlich.

curt [kɜːt] adj □ **1.** kurz(gefaßt), knapp. **2.** (**with**) barsch, schroff (gegen), kurz angebunden (zu).

cur·tail [kɜːˈteɪl] v/t **1.** (ab-, ver)kürzen. **2.** beschneiden, stutzen. **3.** fig. *Ausgaben etc* kürzen, *Rechte etc* beschneiden, einschränken. **cur·tail·ment** s **1.** (Ab-, Ver)Kürzung f. **2.** fig. Beschneidung f, Einschränkung f.

cur·tain ['kɜːtn] **I** s **1.** Vorhang m (a. thea. u. fig.), Gardine f: **draw the** ~**s** die Vorhänge auf- od. zuziehen; **the** ~ **rises** (**falls**) der Vorhang geht auf (fällt); **lift the** ~ den Schleier lüften. **2.** thea. Hervorruf m: **get** (od. **take**) **ten** ~**s** zehn Vorhänge haben. **II** v/t **3.** mit Vorhängen versehen: ~ **off** mit Vorhängen abteilen od. abschließen. ~ **call** → **curtain** 1. ~ **lec·ture** s Gardinenpredigt f. ~ **rais·er** s **1.** thea. kurzes Vorspiel. **2.** fig. Vorspiel n, Ouvertüre f (**to** zu).

curt·s(e)y ['kɜːtsɪ] **I** s Knicks m: **drop a** ~ (**to**) → **II. II** v/i e-n Knicks machen, knicksen (**to** vor dat).

cur·va·ture ['kɜːvətʃə] s Krümmung f: ~ **of the earth** Erdkrümmung f.

curve [kɜːv] **I** s Kurve f (a. A): a) Krümmung f, Biegung f, b) (Straßen)Kurve f, (-)Biegung f, c) Rundung f (pl F a. e-r Frau). **II** v/t u. v/i (sich) krümmen od. biegen.

cush·ion ['kʊʃn] **I** s **1.** Kissen n, Polster n (a. fig.). **2.** ✪ Puffer m, Dämpfer m. **II** v/t **3.** polstern (a. fig.). **4.** Stoß, Fall etc dämpfen, a. fig. abmildern. **5.** ✪ abfedern.

cush·y ['kʊʃɪ] adj F gemütlich, ruhig (Job etc).

cuss [kʌs] s F **1.** Fluch m. **2.** Kerl m: **queer** ~ komischer Kauz.

cus·tard ['kʌstəd] s Vanillesoße f.

cus·to·di·an [kʌˈstəʊdjən] s **1.** Aufseher m, Wächter m. **2.** (Haus- etc)Verwalter m. **3.** ⚖ (Vermögens)Verwalter m. **cus·to·dy** ['~tədɪ] s **1.** Obhut f, Schutz m: **in** s.o.'s ~ in j-s Obhut. **2.** Aufsicht f (**of** über acc). **3.** ⚖ (a. Untersuchungs)Haft f: **take into** ~ verhaften; → **remand** I. 4. ⚖ Sorgerecht n.

cus·tom ['kʌstəm] **I** s **1.** Brauch m, Gewohnheit f, Sitte f, pl a. Brauchtum n. **2.** ⚖ Gewohnheitsrecht n. **3.** † Kundschaft f: a) Kunden pl, b) Kundesein n: **get** s.o.'s ~ j-n als Kunden gewinnen; **have withdrawn one's** ~ **from** nicht mehr (ein)kaufen bei. **4.** pl Zoll m: ~**s clearance** Zollabfertigung f; ~**s examination** (od. **inspection**) Zollkontrolle f; ~**s officer** (od. **official**) Zollbeamte m. **II** adj **5.** → **custom-made.** **'cus·tom·ar·y** adj □ üblich, gebräuchlich. **'cus·tom·er** s **1.** Kunde m, Kundin f. **2.** F Kerl m, Kunde m: → **queer** 1.

cus·tom-'made adj bsd. Am. maßgefertigt, Maß...

cut [kʌt] **I** s **1.** Schnitt m; Schnittwunde f. **2.** Haarschnitt m. **3.** Schnitte f, Stück n (bsd. Fleisch): **cold** ~**s** pl bsd. Am. Aufschnitt m. **4.** F Anteil m (**of, in** an dat). **5.** (Zu)Schnitt m (von Kleidung). **6.** Schnitt m, Schliff m (von Edelsteinen). **7.** Kürzung f, Senkung f: ~ **in salary** Gehaltskürzung f. **8.** Kartenspiel: Abheben n; abgehobene Karte(n pl). **II** adj **9.** ge-, beschnitten: ~ **flowers** pl Schnittblumen pl. **III** v/t (irr) **10.** (ab-, be-, durch-, zer)schneiden: ~ **one's finger** sich in den Finger schneiden; ~ **to pieces** zerstückeln; ~ **one's teeth** Zähne bekommen, zahnen; ~ **one's teeth in** (od. **on**) s.th. fig. s-e ersten Erfahrungen mit. sammeln; → **throat.** 11. Gras mähen, Bäume fällen, Holz hacken. **12.** Hecke etc (be)schneiden, stutzen: ~ s.o.'s **hair** j-m die Haare schneiden. **13.** Kleid etc zuschneiden, et. zurechtschneiden; Stein behauen, Glas, Edelsteine schleifen. **14.** mot. Kurve schneiden. **15.** a) Löhne etc kürzen, *Text etc* a. zs.-streichen (**to** auf *acc*), b) *Film* schneiden. **16.** *Preise* herabsetzen, senken. **17.** (*auf Tonband*) mitschneiden. **18.** *fig. j-m* weh tun, *j-n* kränken. **19.** F *j-n* schneiden: ~ **dead** völlig ignorieren. **20.** *ped. univ.* F *Stunde etc* schwänzen. **21.** *Karten* abheben. **22.** *Tennis etc: Ball* (an)schneiden. **23.** F *Gewinne* teilen. **IV** *v/i* (*irr*) **24.** schneiden (**in**, **into** in *acc*): ~ **into** *Kuchen etc* abschneiden; einschneiden in (*acc*) (*a. fig.*); ~ **into** s.o.'s **time** j-n Zeit kosten; ~ **into** s.o.'s **savings** an j-s Ersparnisse reißen; ~ **into** a **conversation** sich in ein Gespräch einmischen; *it* ~s **both ways** es ist ein zweischneidiges Schwert. **25.** einschneiden (*Kragen etc*). **26.** sich schneiden lassen. **27.** *fig.* weh tun, kränken. **28.** F abhauen. **29.** *Kartenspiel:* abheben. **30.** F die Gewinne teilen.

Verbindungen mit Adverbien:

cut| back I *v/t* **1.** *Hecke etc* beschneiden, stutzen. **2.** → **cut** 15a. **II** *v/i* **3.** *bsd. Am.* (zu)rückblenden (**to** auf *acc*) (*Film, Roman etc*). **4.** ~ **on** et. einschränken. ~ **down I** *v/t* **1.** *Bäume* fällen, *Wald* abholzen. **2.** zurechtschneiden, -stutzen (*a. fig.*): → **size** 2. **3.** *j-n* herunterhandeln (**by** um; **to** auf *acc*). **II** *v/i* **5.** → **cut back** 4. ~ **in I** *v/t* **1.** F *j-n* beteiligen (**on** an *dat*). **II** *v/i* **2.** sich einmischen. **3.** ~ **on s.o.** *mot.* j-n schneiden. ~ **off** *v/t* **1.** abschneiden. **2.** *Strom etc* absperren, abdrehen, *Verbindung, Versorgung, Weg etc* abschneiden: *he had his electricity* ~ ihm wurde der Strom gesperrt. **3.** *teleph. Teilnehmer* trennen. ~ **out I** *v/t* **1.** (her)ausschneiden. **2.** *Kleid etc* zuschneiden. **3.** *be* ~ *for* wie geschaffen sein für. **4.** *Rivalen* ausstechen, verdrängen. **5.** *cut it out!* F hör auf (damit)! **6.** F *j-n* betrügen (**of** um ~*s-n Anteil*). **II** *v/i* **7.** *mot.* aussetzen. ~ **un-der** *v/t* ✝ *j-n* unterbieten. ~ **up** *v/t* **1.** zerschneiden. **2.** F verreißen.

'**cut**·**a**·**way I** *adj* Schnitt...: ~ **model.** **II** *s* *a.* ~ **coat** Cut(away) *m.* '~·**back** *s* **1.** Kürzung *f*, Zs.-streichung *f*. **2.** *Film etc: bsd. Am.* Rückblende *f.*

cute [kjuːt] *adj* □ F **1.** schlau, clever. **2.** niedlich, süß.

cut·ler·y ['kʌtləri] *s* (Tisch-, Eß)Besteck *n.*

cut·let ['kʌtlit] *s* **1.** Schnitzel *n.* **2.** Hacksteak *n.*

'**cut**|**·out** *s* **1.** Ausschnitt *m.* **2.** Ausschneidefigur *f.* '~·'**price** *adj* Br., '~·'**rate** *Am.* ✝ ermäßigt, herabgesetzt: ~ **offer** Billigangebot *n.*

cut·ter ['kʌtə] *s* **1.** Zuschneider *m*; (*Glas-, Diamant*)Schleifer *m.* **2.** ⚙ Schneidemaschine *f*, -werkzeug *n.* **3.** *Film:* Cutter(in). **4.** ⚓ Kutter *m.*

'**cut·throat I** *s* Mörder *m*; (professioneller) Killer. **II** *adj* mörderisch, *fig.* a. halsabschneiderisch: ~ **price** Wucherpreis *m.*

cut·ting ['kʌtin] **I** *s* **1.** (Ab-, Aus-, Be-, Zu)Schneiden *n.* **2.** *bsd. Br.* (Zeitungs)Ausschnitt *m.* **3.** *pl* (*Hobel- etc*)Späne *pl*; Abfälle *pl*, Schnitzel *pl.* **II** *adj* **4.** schneidend (*a. fig. Schmerz, Wind*), Schneid(e)-..., Schnitt...: ~ **blow-pipe** (*od. torch*) ⚙ Schneidbrenner *m*; ~ **edge** Schneide *f*; ~ **nippers** *pl* Kneifzange *f.*

cy·a·nide ['saɪənaɪd] *s*: ~ **of potash** 🜊 Zyankali *n.*

cy·ber·net·ics [,saɪbə'netɪks] *s pl* (*als Sg konstruiert*) Kybernetik *f.*

cyc·la·men ['sɪkləmən] *s* 🌺 Alpenveilchen *n.*

cy·cle ['saɪkl] **I** *s* **1.** Zyklus *m*, Kreis(lauf) *m.* **2.** (*Gedicht-, Lieder*)Zyklus *m.* **3.** a) Fahrrad *n*: ~ **lane** (*od. path*) Rad(fahr)weg *m*; ~ **race** (*Sport*) Radrennen *n*, b) Motorrad *n.* **4.** ⚙ Arbeitsgang *m*; Takt *m*: *four-*~ *engine* Viertaktmotor *m.* **5.** ⚡, *phys.* (Schwingungs)Periode *f.* **II** *v/i* **6.** radfahren, radeln. '**cy·cler** *Am.* → **cyclist.**

'**cy·cle·way** *s* Rad(fahr)weg *m.*

cy·clic, cy·cli·cal ['saɪklɪk(l)] *adj* □ **1.** zyklisch. **2.** ✝ konjunkturbedingt, Konjunktur-... **cy·cling** ['saɪklɪŋ] *s* **1.** Radfahren *n*: ~ **tour** Radtour *f.* **2.** Radrennsport *m.* '**cy·clist** *s* Rad- *od.* Motorradfahrer(in).

cy·clone ['saɪkləʊn] *s* Zyklon *m*, Wirbelsturm *m.*

cyl·in·der ['sɪlɪndə] *s* 𝒜 Zylinder *m*, ⚙ *a.* Walze *f*, Trommel *f.* **cy·lin·dri·cal** [~'drɪkl] *adj* □ 𝒜 zylindrisch, Zylinder-..., ⚙ *a.* walzenförmig.

cyn·ic ['sɪnɪk] **I** *s* Zyniker *m.* **II** *adj* (~**ally**)

damn

zynisch. **cyn·i·cal** ['~kl] → **cynic** II.
cyn·i·cism ['~sızəm] s Zynismus m, a.
zynische Bemerkung.
cy·press ['saıprəs] s ♀ Zypresse f.
Cyp·ri·ot ['sıprıət], **Cyp·ri·ote** ['~əʊt] I s
Zyprer(in). II adj zyprisch.
cyst [sıst] s ✚ Zyste f.

czar [zɑ:] s hist. Zar m.
Czech [tʃek] I s 1. Tscheche m, Tschechin f. 2. ling. Tschechisch n. II adj 3.
tschechisch.
Czech·o·slo·vak [ˌtʃekəʊ'sləʊvæk] I s
Tschechoslowake m, -slowakin f. II adj
tschechoslowakisch.

D

'd F für had, should, would.
dab¹ [dæb] I v/t 1. antippen. 2. be-, abtupfen (**with** mit). 3. Farbe etc (leicht)
auftragen (**on** auf acc). II s 4. Klecks m,
Spritzer m.
dab² [~] s a. ~ **hand** bsd. Br. F Könner m:
be a ~ **at** et. aus dem Effeff können; ~ **at**
tennis Tennisas m.
dab·ble ['dæbl] I v/t 1. bespritzen. II v/i
2. plan(t)schen. 3. ~ **at** (od. **in**) fig. sich
oberflächlich od. aus Liebhaberei od.
dilettantisch beschäftigen mit: ~ **in pol-**
itics ein bißchen in der Politik mitmischen.
dachs·hund ['dækshʊnd] s zo. Dackel
m.
dad [dæd] s F Vati m, Papa m.
dad·dy ['dædı] → **dad**. ~ **long·legs** pl
-dy -legs s zo. F 1. Schnake f. 2. Am.
Weberknecht m.
daf·fo·dil ['dæfədıl] s ♀ gelbe Narzisse,
Osterglocke f.
daft [dɑ:ft] adj □ F 1. doof, dämlich. 2.
be ~ **about** verrückt sein nach.
dag·ger ['dægə] s Dolch m: **be at** ~s
drawn auf Kriegsfuß stehen (**with** mit);
look ~s **at** s.o. j-n mit Blicken durchbohren.
da·go ['deıgəʊ] pl **-go(e)s** s Schimpfwort
für Italiener, Spanier u. Portugiesen.
dahl·ia ['deıljə] s ♀ Dahlie f.
dai·ly ['deılı] I adj 1. täglich (a adv),
Tage(s)....: ~ **help** → 3; ~ **newspaper**
→ 3; ~ **press** Tagespresse f; → **dozen**.
2. alltäglich: **be a** ~ **occurrence** an der
Tagesordnung sein. II s 3. Tageszei-
tung f. 4. Br. Putzfrau f (die jeden Tag
kommt).

dain·ty ['deıntı] I adj 1. zierlich, niedlich,
reizend. 2. wählerisch, verwöhnt (bsd.
im Essen). 3. schmackhaft, lecker. II s
4. Leckerbissen m (a. fig.).
dair·y ['deərı] s 1. Molkerei f. 2. Milch-
geschäft n. ~ **prod·uce** s Molkereipro-
dukte pl.
da·is ['deıɪs] s Podium n.
dai·sy ['deızı] s ♀ Gänseblümchen n:
push up the daisies sl. sich die Radieschen von unten ansehen od. betrachten.
dal·ly ['dælı] I v/i 1. schäkern: ~ **with** a.
spielen mit (j-s Gefühlen). 2. spielen,
liebäugeln (**with** mit e-r Idee etc) 3. a. ~
about (od. **around**) herumtrödeln,
bummeln. II v/t 4. ~ **away** Zeit vertrödeln; Gelegenheit verspielen.
dam [dæm] I s 1. (Stau)Damm m, Talsperre f. 2. Stausee m. II v/t 3. a. ~ **up**
stauen, ab-, eindämmen; Gefühle aufstauen: ~ **back** Tränen zurückhalten.
dam·age ['dæmıdʒ] I s 1. Schaden m (**to**
an dat). 2. pl ✠ Schadenersatz m: **sue**
for ~s auf Schadenersatz verklagen. 3.
what's the ~? F was kostet es? II v/t 4.
beschädigen. 5. j-m, j-s Ruf etc schaden.
dam·ask ['dæməsk] s Damast m.
dame [deım] s 1. ♀ Br. Ordens- od. Adelstitel. 2. bsd. Am. sl. Weib n.
damn [dæm] I v/t 1. eccl. u. weitS. verdammen. 2 verurteilen. 3. verwerfen,
ablehnen. 4. F ~ **it!**, ~ **me!** verflucht!,
verdammt!; ~ **you!** der Teufel soll dich
holen!; **I'll be** ~**ed if I do that** ich denk'
ja gar nicht daran, das zu tun. II s 5. F
I don't care a ~ das ist mir völlig egal;

not worth a ~ keinen Pfifferling wert.
III *int* **6.** F verflucht!, verdammt! **IV**
adj u. adv **7.** → **damned** 2, 4.
dam'na·tion I *s* Verdammung *f; eccl.*
Verdammnis *f.* **II** *int* → **damn** 6.
damned [dæmd] **I** *adj* **1.** verdammt:
the ~ pl eccl. die Verdammten *pl.* **2.**
verflucht, verdammt: *~ fool* Vollidiot
m. **3.** F *Bekräftigung: a ~ sight better*
viel besser. **II** *adv* **4.** F verdammt: *~*
cold. **5.** F *Bekräftigung: he ~ well*
ought to know it das müßte er wahrhaf-
tig wissen.
Dam·o·cles ['dæməkli:z]: *sword of ~*
Damoklesschwert *n; hang over s.o.*
like a sword of ~ über j-m wie ein
Damoklesschwert hängen.
damp [dæmp] **I** *adj* □ **1.** feucht, (*Raum*
etc a.) klamm: *~ squib Br.* F Pleite *f*,
Reinfall *m.* **II** *s* **2.** Feuchtigkeit *f: ~ in*
the air Luftfeuchtigkeit. **3.** *fig.* Dämpfer *m: cast* (*od. strike*) *a ~ on* (*od. over*)
et. dämpfen *od.* lähmen. **III** *v/t* **4.** an-,
befeuchten. **5.** *Begeisterung etc* dämpfen; *j-n* entmutigen. **'damp·en** →
damp III. **'damp·er** *s fig.* Dämpfer *m:*
cast (*od. put, strike*) *a ~ on et.* dämpfen
od. lähmen. **'damp·ness** *s* Feuchtigkeit *f.*
dance [dɑ:ns] **I** *v/i* **1.** tanzen: *~ to* (*od.*
after) *s.o.'s pipe* (*od. tune, whistle*) *fig.*
nach j-s Pfeife tanzen. **2.** tanzen, hüpfen (*with, for* vor *dat*). **II** *v/t* **3.** *Tanz*
tanzen: *~ attendance on s.o. fig.* um
j-n scharwenzeln. **III** *s* **4.** Tanz *m: lead*
s.o. a (*pretty*) *~ Br.* j-n zum Narren
halten. **5.** Tanz(veranstaltung *f*) *m.* **IV**
adj **6.** Tanz...: *~ music.* **'danc·ing I** *s*
Tanzen *n.* **II** *adj* Tanz...: *~ lesson*
Tanzstunde *f, pl a.* Tanzunterricht *m; ~*
master Tanzlehrer *m; ~ partner* Tanz-
partner(in); *~ school* Tanzschule *f.*
dan·de·li·on ['dændɪlaɪən] *s* ♀ Löwen-
zahn *m.*
dan·der ['dændə] *s* F: *get s.o.'s ~ up* j-n
auf die Palme bringen; *get one's ~ up*
auf die Palme gehen.
dan·druff ['dændrʌf] *s* (Kopf-, Haar-)
Schuppen *pl.*
dan·dy ['dændɪ] **I** *s* Dandy *m.* **II** *adj* F
prima.
Dane [deɪn] *s* Däne *m*, Dänin *f.*
dan·ger ['deɪndʒə] **I** *s* Gefahr *f* (*to* für): *~*
of infection ✻ Infektionsgefahr; *be in ~*

of one's life in Lebensgefahr sein *od.*
schweben; *without ~* gefahrlos. **II** *adj*
Gefahr...: *~ area* (*od. zone*) Gefahren-
zone *f*, -bereich *m; ~ money* (*od. pay*)
Gefahrenzulage *f.* **'dan·ger·ous** *adj* □
gefährlich (*to, for* für).
dan·gle ['dæŋgl] **I** *v/i* baumeln: *keep*
s.o. dangling F j-n im unklaren lassen.
II *v/t* baumeln lassen: *~ s.th. before*
s.o. fig. j-m et. (verlockend) in Aussicht
stellen, j-m mit et. winken.
Dan·ish ['deɪnɪʃ] **I** *adj* **1.** dänisch. **II** *s* **2.**
ling. Dänisch *n.* **3.** *the ~ pl* die Dänen
pl.
dank [dæŋk] *adj* □ (*unangenehm*) feucht,
naß(kalt).
dap·per ['dæpə] *adj* □ **1.** adrett, elegant.
2. flink, (*a. Benehmen*) gewandt.
dap·ple ['dæpl] **I** *v/t* sprenkeln.
dare [deə] **I** *v/i* es wagen, sich (ge)trau-
en: *who ~s wins* wer wagt, gewinnt;
how ~ you! untersteh dich!; was fällt
dir ein!; *how ~ you say that?* wie können Sie das sagen?; *don't* (*you*) *~* (*to*)
touch it! rühr es ja nicht an!; *I ~ say* ich
glaube wohl; allerdings. **II** *v/t et.* wagen, riskieren. **'~,dev·il** *s* Draufgänger
m.
dar·ing ['deərɪŋ] **I** *adj* **1.** wagemutig,
kühn. **2.** gewagt, verwegen (*beide a.*
fig.). **3.** unverschämt, dreist. **II** *s* **4.** Wa-
gemut *m*, Kühnheit *f.*
dark [dɑ:k] **I** *adj* □ **1.** dunkel, finster. **2.**
dunkel (*Farbe*). **3.** *fig.* düster, trüb
(*Aussichten etc*): *the ~ side of things*
die Schattenseite der Dinge; *one's ~est*
hour s-e schwärzeste Stunde. **4.** *fig.* düster, finster (*Blick etc*). **5.** finster, böse
(*Gedanken etc*). **6.** *fig.* geheim(nisvoll),
verborgen: *keep s.th. ~ et.* geheimhal-
ten. **II** *s* **7.** Dunkel(heit *f*) *n*, Finsternis
f: in the ~ im Dunkel(n); *after ~* nach
Einbruch der Dunkelheit. **8.** *fig. das*
Ungewisse *od.* Dunkle: *be in the ~* im
dunkeln tappen; *keep s.o. in the ~* j-n
im ungewissen lassen (*about* über *acc*).
♀ **Ag·es** *s pl das* (frühe *od.* finstere)
Mittelalter. ♀ **Con·ti·nent** *s der* dunkle
Erdteil, Afrika *n.*
dark·en ['dɑ:kən] *v/t* **1.** verdunkeln,
-düstern (*beide a. fig.*). **2.** dunkel *od.*
dunkler färben. **II** *v/i* **3.** dunkel werden,
sich verdunkeln. **4.** *fig.* sich verdüstern.
dark horse *s* **1.** *Sport:* unbekannte Grö-

ße (*Person*). **2.** *pol. Am.* unbeschriebenes Blatt.

dark·ness ['dɑːknɪs] *s* Dunkelheit *f*, Finsternis *f*: *be in complete* ~ völlig dunkel sein.

'dark·room *s phot.* Dunkelkammer *f*. **'~skinned** *adj* dunkelhäutig.

dar·ling ['dɑːlɪŋ] **I** *s* Liebling *m*. **II** *adj* reizend, goldig.

darn¹ [dɑːn] → *damn* 4–6.

darn² [~] *v/t* stopfen.

darned [dɑːnd] → *damned* 2–5.

dart [dɑːt] **I** *s* **1.** (Wurf)Pfeil *m*. **2.** Satz *m*, Sprung *m*: *make a* ~ *for* losstürzen auf (*acc*). **3.** *pl* (*sg konstruiert*) Darts *n* (*Wurfpfeilspiel*). **II** *v/t* **4.** Speer werfen, schleudern, *Pfeil* schießen: *a look at s.o.* j-m e-n Blick zuwerfen. **III** *v/i* **5.** sausen, flitzen: ~ *at* losstürzen auf (*acc*). **6.** zucken, schnellen (*Schlange, Zunge etc*), huschen (*Augen, Blick*). **'~·board** *s* Dartsscheibe *f*.

dash [dæʃ] **I** *v/t* **1.** schleudern, schmettern: ~ *to pieces* zerschmettern. **2.** ~ *down* (*od. off*) *Getränk* hinunterstürzen; *Aufsatz, Zeichnung etc* schnell hinhauen. **3.** *Hoffnungen etc* zerstören, zunichte machen; *j-n* deprimieren. **II** *v/i* **4.** stürmen: ~ *off* davonstürzen. **III** *s* **5.** Schlag *m*: *at one* ~ mit 'einem Schlag (*a. fig.*). **6.** Schuß *m* (*Rum etc*), Prise *f* (*Salz etc*). **7.** *fig.* Anflug *m* (*of* von); Stich *m* (*of green* ins Grüne). **8.** Gedankenstrich *m*. **9.** *make a* ~ *at* (*od. for*) losstürzen auf (*acc*). **10.** Schwung *m*, Schmiß *m*, Elan *m*. **11.** *Leichtathletik*: Sprint *m*, Kurzstreckenlauf *m*; **'~·board** *s mot.* Armaturen-, ✈ *a.* Instrumentenbrett *n*.

dash·ing ['dæʃɪŋ] *adj* □ schneidig, forsch.

da·ta ['deɪtə] *s pl* **1.** (*oft sg konstruiert*) (*a. technische*) Daten *pl od.* Angaben *pl*: ~ *protection* Datenschutz *m*. **2.** *Computer*: Daten *pl*: ~ *bank* Datenbank *f*; ~ *processing* Datenverarbeitung *f*; ~ *transmission* Datenübertragung *f*; ~ *typist* Datentypistin *f*.

date¹ [deɪt] *s* ❦ Dattel *f*.

date² [~] **I** *s* **1.** Datum *n*: a) Tag *m*: *what is the ~ today?* der Wievielte ist heute?, welches Datum haben wir heute?, b) Zeit(punkt *m*) *f*: *of recent* ~ neu(eren Datums), c) Datumsangabe *f*, d) ✝, 🗓

Tag *m*, Termin *m*: ~ *of delivery* Liefertermin; ~ *of maturity* Fälligkeitstag. **2.** heutiges Datum, heutiger Tag: *to* ~ bis heute; *out of* ~ veraltet, unmodern; *go out of* ~ veralten; (*up*) *to* ~ zeitgemäß, modern, auf dem laufenden; *bring up to* ~ auf den neuesten Stand bringen, modernisieren. **3.** Verabredung *f*, Rendezvous *n*: *have a* ~ *with s.o.* mit j-m verabredet sein; *make a* ~ sich verabreden. **4.** (Verabredungs)Partner(in): *who is your* ~? mit wem bist du verabredet? **II** *v/t* **5.** datieren. **6.** sich verabreden mit; gehen mit. **III** *v/i* **7.** ~ *back to* a) *a.* ~ *from* stammen aus, entstanden sein in (*dat*), b) bis in *e-e Zeit* zurückreichen, auf *e-e Zeit* zurückgehen. **8.** veralten. **'dat·ed** *adj* **1.** datiert. **2.** veraltet, überholt. **'date·less** *adj* **1.** undatiert. **2.** zeitlos.

date| line *s geogr.* Datumsgrenze *f*. **~ stamp** *s* Datums-, *a.* Poststempel *m*.

da·tive ['deɪtɪv] *s a.* ~ *case ling.* Dativ *m*, 3. Fall.

daub [dɔːb] **I** *v/t* **1.** be-, verschmieren: *~ed with oil* ölverschmiert. **2.** schmieren (*on* auf *acc*). **3.** *contp. Bild* zs.-klecksen. **II** *s* **4.** *paint. contp.* (Farb-) Kleckserei *f*.

daugh·ter ['dɔːtə] *s* Tochter *f*: ~ (*company*) ✝ Tochter(gesellschaft) *f*. **'~-in--law** *pl* **'daugh·ters-in-law** *s* Schwiegertochter *f*.

daunt [dɔːnt] *v/t* **1.** einschüchtern, erschrecken. **2.** entmutigen. **'daunt·less** *adj* □ unerschrocken.

dav·en·port ['dævnpɔːt] *s* **1.** kleiner Schreibtisch. **2.** *Am.* (*bsd.* Bett)Couch *f*.

daw·dle ['dɔːdl] **I** *v/i* (herum)trödeln, (-)bummeln. **II** *v/t oft* ~ *away Zeit* vertrödeln. **'daw·dler** *s* Trödler(in), Bummler(in).

dawn [dɔːn] **I** *v/i* **1.** dämmern (*Morgen, Tag*). **2.** ~ *on fig.* j-m dämmern, klarwerden. **3.** *fig.* sich zu entwickeln beginnen, erwachen. **II** *s* **4.** (Morgen)Dämmerung *f*: *at* ~ bei Tagesanbruch. **5.** *fig.* Beginn *m*.

day [deɪ] *s* **1.** Tag *m* (*Ggs. Nacht*): *by* ~ bei Tag(e). **2.** Tag *m* (*Zeitraum*): ~ *after* ~ Tag für Tag; *the* ~ *after tomorrow, Am.* ~ *after tomorrow* übermorgen; ~ *in, ~ out* tagaus, tagein; *let's call it a ~!*

F Feierabend!, Schluß für heute!; **carry** (*od.* **win**) **the ~** den Sieg davontragen. **3.** (*bestimmter, festgesetzter*) Tag: **~ of delivery** Liefertermin *m.* **4.** *oft pl* (Lebens)Zeit *f*, Zeiten *pl*, Tage *pl*: **in my young ~s** in m-n Jugendtagen; **in those ~s** damals. **5.** *oft pl* (*best* (*des Lebens*), Glanzzeit *f*: **he has had his ~** s-e beste Zeit ist vorüber; **those were the ~s!** das waren noch Zeiten! '**~•break** *s* Tagesanbruch *m*: **at ~** bei Tagesanbruch. '**~•dream I** *s* Tag-, Wachtraum *m*. **II** *v/i* (*a. irr dream*) (mit offenen Augen) träumen. '**~•dream•er** *s* Träumer(in). '**~•light** *s* Tageslicht *n*: **by** (*od.* **in**) **~** bei Tag(eslicht); **in broad ~** am hellichten Tag; **beat** (*od.* **knock**) **the** (**living**) **~s out of s.o.** F j-n fürchterlich verdreschen; **~ saving time** Sommerzeit *f*. **~ nurs•er•y** *s* Tagesheim *n*, -stätte *f*. **~ re•turn** (**tick•et**) → **day ticket. ~ shift** *s* Tagschicht *f*: **be** (*od.* **work**) **on ~** Tagschicht haben. **~ tick•et** *s Br.* Tagesrückfahrkarte *f*. '**~•time** *s*: **in the ~** bei Tag(e). '**~-to-'day** *adj* (tag)täglich.

day| trip *s* Tagesausflug *m*. **~ trip•per** *s* Tagesausflügler(in).

daze [deɪz] **I** *v/t* benommen machen. **II** *s* Benommenheit *f*: **in a ~** benommen.

daz•zle ['dæzl] **I** *v/t* **1.** blenden (*a. fig.*). **II** *s* **2.** Blenden *n*: **in a ~** geblendet. **3.** blendender Glanz.

dea•con ['diːkən] *s eccl.* Diakon *m.* **dea•con•ess** [͵~'nes] *f* Diakonisse *f*.

dead [ded] **I** *adj* (□ → **deadly** II) **1.** tot, gestorben: **shoot ~** erschießen; → **body** 2. *a. fig.* tot: a) leblos: **~ matter** tote Materie, b) ausgestorben: **~ language** tote Sprache, c) überlebt (*Brauch etc*). **3.** gefühllos, abgestorben (*Finger etc*). **4.** *fig.* (**to**) unempfänglich (für); gleichgültig, abgestumpft (gegen). **5.** *bsd.* ✝ flau. **6.** tot (*Kapital, Wissen etc*). **7.** ⚡ tot, stromlos. **8.** erloschen (*Vulkan, Gefühle etc*). **9.** matt, stumpf (*Farben, Blick etc*). **10.** völlig, total: **~ certainty** absolute Gewißheit; **~ silence** Totenstille *f*; → **cert, earnest** 4, **loss** 1a. **II** *s* **11.** **the ~** *pl* die Toten *pl*. **12.** **in the ~ of night** mitten in der Nacht; **in the ~ of winter** im tiefsten Winter. **III** *adv* **13.** völlig, total: **be ~ asleep** im tiefsten Schlaf liegen; **~ drunk** sinnlos betrunken; **~ slow!** *mot.* Schritt fahren!; **~**

straight schnurgerade; **~ tired** todmüde; → **set** 8. **14.** plötzlich, abrupt: **stop ~** (**in one's tracks**) plötzlich *od.* abrupt stehenbleiben. **15.** genau, direkt: **~ against** genau gegenüber von (*od. dat*). '͵~-'beat *adj* F todmüde, völlig kaputt. **~ cen•tre** (*Am.* **cen•ter**) *s* genaue Mitte.

dead•en ['dedn] *v/t* **1.** *Geräusch* abdämpfen, *a. Schlag etc* (ab)schwächen. **2.** *Schmerz* stillen; *Gefühl* abtöten, abstumpfen (**to** gegen).

dead| end *s* Sackgasse *f* (*a. fig.*): **come to a ~** in e-e Sackgasse geraten. '**~-end** *adj* **1. ~ street** Sackgasse *f*. **2.** ohne Aufstiegschancen (*Stellung*). **~ heat** *s Sport:* totes Rennen. '**~-line** *s* **1.** letzter (Ablieferungs)Termin, Anzeigen-, Redaktionsschluß *m*: **~ pressure** Termindruck *m*; **meet the ~** den Termin einhalten. **2.** Stichtag *m*. '**~-lock I** *s* völliger Stillstand, toter Punkt: **come to a ~** (*od.* **reach**) **a ~** → **II**. **II** *v/i* sich festfahren, an e-m toten Punkt anlangen (*Verhandlungen etc*). '**~-locked** *adj* festgefahren.

dead•ly ['dedlɪ] **I** *adj* **1.** tödlich; Tod...: **~ enemy** Todfeind *m*; **~ fight** mörderischer Kampf; **~ sin** Todsünde *f*. **2.** totenähnlich: **~ pallor** Leichen-, Todesblässe *f*. **3.** F schrecklich, äußerst. **II** *adv* **4.** totenähnlich: **~ pale** leichen-, totenblaß. **5.** F schrecklich, äußerst: **be ~ afraid of** e-e Sterbensangst haben vor (*dat*); **~ dull** sterbenslangweilig; **~ tired** todmüde.

dead| march *s* ♪ Trauermarsch *m*. **~ pan** *s* F ausdrucksloses Gesicht. '͵~'pan *adj* F **1.** ausdruckslos (*Gesicht*); mit ausdruckslosem Gesicht (*Person*). **2.** trocken (*Humor*).

deaf [def] **I** *adj* □ **1.** taub (*a. fig.* **to** gegen): **~ and dumb** taubstumm; **~ in one ear** auf einem Ohr taub; → **ear¹** 1. **2.** schwerhörig. **II** *s* **3. the ~** *pl* die Tauben *pl*. **~ aid** *s* Hörgerät *n*. '͵~-and-'dumb *adj* **1.** taubstumm. **2.** Taubstummen...: **~ language.**

deaf•en ['defn] *v/t* taub machen. '**deaf•en•ing** *adj* ohrenbetäubend.

'͵deaf-'mute **I** *adj* taubstumm. **II** *s* Taubstumme *m*, *f*.

deaf•ness ['defnɪs] *s* **1.** Taubheit *f* (*a. fig.* **to** gegen). **2.** Schwerhörigkeit *f*.

deal¹ [di:l] **I** v/i (irr) **1.** ~ **with** sich befassen od. beschäftigen mit; handeln von, et. behandeln od. zum Thema haben; et. erledigen, mit et., j-m fertig werden. **2.** ~ **with** ♥ Handel treiben od. Geschäfte machen mit. **3.** ~ **in** ♥ handeln od. Handel treiben mit: ~ **in paper** Papier führen. **4.** sl. dealen (mit Drogen handeln). **5.** Kartenspiel: geben. **II** v/t **6.** oft ~ **out** et. aus-, verteilen, Karten a. geben. **III** s **7.** F Handlungsweise f, Verfahren n. **8.** F Geschäft n, Handel m: **it's a ~!** abgemacht!; → **raw 6. 9.** Abkommen n: **make a ~** ein Abkommen treffen. **10.** Kartenspiel: Geben n: **it is my ~** ich muß geben.

deal² [~] s Menge f: **a great ~** sehr viel; **a good ~** e-e ganze Menge, ziemlich viel; **a ~ worse** F viel schlechter.

deal·er ['di:lə] s **1.** Händler(in): ~ **in antiques** Antiquitätenhändler. **2.** sl. Dealer m (Drogenhändler). **3.** Kartenspiel: Geber(in). **'deal·ing** s **1.** mst pl Umgang m, Beziehungen pl: **have ~s with** zu tun haben mit. **2.** ♥ Handel m (**in** in dat, mit).

dealt [delt] pret u. pp von **deal¹**.

dean [di:n] s eccl., univ. Dekan m.

dear [diə] **I** adj **1.** lieb, teuer (**to** dat): **2 Sir**, (in Briefen) Sehr geehrter Herr (Name); **run for ~ life** um sein Leben rennen. **2.** teuer, kostspielig. **II** adv **3.** teuer: **it cost him ~** es kam ihn od. ihn teuer zu stehen. **III** s **4.** Liebste m, f, Schatz m: **there's a ~** sei (so) lieb. **IV** int **5.** (oh) ~!, ~ **me!** du liebe Zeit!, ach je! **'dear·ly** adv **1.** innig, herzlich. **2.** teuer: → **buy 4.** **'dear·ness** s hoher Preis.

dearth [dɜ:θ] s Mangel m (**of** an dat).

death [deθ] s **1.** Tod m: **to ~** zu Tode; (**as**) **sure as ~** todsicher; **catch one's ~** sich den Tod holen (engS. durch Erkältung); **put to ~** hinrichten. **2.** Todesfall m. ~ **ag·o·ny** s Todeskampf m. **'~·bed** s Sterbebett n. **'~·blow** s fig. Todesstoß m (**to** für). ~ **cell** s Todeszelle f. ~ **du·ty** s Br. Erbschaftsteuer f.

death·less ['deθləs] adj □ unsterblich (Ruhm etc). **'death·like** adj totenähnlich: ~ **pallor** Leichen-, Todesblässe f; ~ **stillness** Totenstille f. **'death·ly** → **deadly:** ~ **silence** eisiges Schweigen; ~ **stillness** Totenstille f.

death| mask s Totenmaske f. ~ **pen·al·ty** s Todesstrafe f. ~ **rate** s Sterblichkeitsziffer f.

'death's-head s Totenkopf m (Symbol).

death| threat s Morddrohung f. ~ **toll** s Zahl f der Toten: **the ~ on the roads** die Zahl der Verkehrstoten. ~ **trap** s Todesfalle f. ~ **war·rant** s **1.** ♯♯ Hinrichtungsbefehl m. **2.** fig. Todesurteil n (**of** für): **sign one's ~** sein (eigenes) Todesurteil unterschreiben.

de·ba·cle [deɪ'bɑ:kl] s Debakel n, Zs.-bruch m.

de·bar [dɪ'bɑ:] v/t j-n ausschließen (**from** von).

de·base [dɪ'beɪs] v/t **1.** entwürdigen. **2.** im Wert mindern; Wert mindern.

de·bat·a·ble [dɪ'beɪtəbl] adj strittig, umstritten. **de·bate I** v/i **1.** debattieren, diskutieren (**on, about** über acc). **II** v/t **2.** et. debattieren, diskutieren. **3.** et. erwägen, sich et. überlegen. **III** s **4.** Debatte f, Diskussion f: **be under ~** zur Debatte stehen.

de·bauch [dɪ'bɔ:tʃ] **I** v/t sittlich verderben. **II** s Ausschweifung f, Orgie f. **de'bauch·er·y** [~tʃərɪ] s Ausschweifung f.

de·ben·ture [dɪ'bentʃə] s **1.** Schuldschein m. **2.** ♯ a) Br. a. ~ **bond** Obligation f, Schuldverschreibung f, b) Br. Pfandbrief m.

de·bil·i·tate [dɪ'bɪlɪteɪt] v/t schwächen, entkräften. **de·bil·i'ta·tion** s Schwächung f, Entkräftung f. **de'bil·i·ty** s Schwäche f, Kraftlosigkeit f.

deb·it ['debɪt] ♥ **I** s **1.** Soll n: ~ **and credit** Soll u. Haben n. **2.** Belastung f: **to the ~ of** zu Lasten von (od. gen); **charge** (od. **place**) **a sum to s.o.'s ~** j-s Konto mit e-r Summe belasten; ~ **entry** Lastschrift f. **II** v/t **3.** j-n, Konto belasten (**with** mit): ~ **£ 100 against s.o.** (**'s account**) j-n (j-s Konto) mit £ 100 belasten.

de·bouch [dɪ'baʊtʃ] v/i sich ergießen, (ein)münden (**into** in acc) (Fluß).

de·brief [,di:'bri:f] v/t sich informieren lassen von (e-m Piloten, Diplomaten etc).

de·bris ['deɪbri:] s Trümmer pl, Schutt m.

debt [det] s Schuld f: ~ **of hono(u)r** Ehrenschuld f; **be in ~** Schulden haben, ver-

schuldet sein; *be in ~ to s.o. for £100*
j-m £100 schulden; *be in s.o.'s ~* in j-s
Schuld stehen; *be out of ~* schuldenfrei
sein. **'debt·or** *s* Schuldner *m*.

de·bug [ˌdiːˈbʌg] *v/t* **1.** entwanzen (*a.* F
von Minispionen befreien). **2.** ⊛ F Fehler *od.* Fehler *e-r Maschine* beheben; (*Computer*)
Programm austesten.

de·bu·reau·cra·tize [ˌdiːbjʊəˈrɒkrətaɪz]
v/t entbürokratisieren.

de·but [ˈdeɪbjuː] *s* Debüt *n*: *make one's
~* sein Debüt geben.

deb·u·tant [ˈdebjuːtãːŋ] *s* Debütant
m. **deb·u·tante** [ˈ~tɑːnt] *s* Debütan-
tin *f*.

dec·ade [ˈdekeɪd] *s* Jahrzehnt *n*.

de·ca·dence [ˈdekədəns] *s* Dekadenz *f*.
'de·ca·dent *adj* dekadent.

de·caf·fein·at·ed [diːˈkæfɪneɪtɪd] *adj*
koffeinfrei (*Kaffee*).

de·cal [ˈdiːkæl] *s bsd. Am.* Abziehbild *n*.

de·camp [dɪˈkæmp] *v/i* F sich aus dem
Staub machen.

de·cant [dɪˈkænt] *v/t* **1.** dekantieren. **2.**
ab-, umfüllen. **de'cant·er** *s* Karaffe *f*.

de·cap·i·tate [dɪˈkæpɪteɪt] *v/t* enthaupten, köpfen. **de,cap·i'ta·tion** *s* Ent-
hauptung *f*.

de·car·tel·i·za·tion [ˈdiːˌkɑːtəlaɪˈzeɪʃn] *s*
♱ Entkartellisierung *f*, Entflechtung *f*.
de'car·tel·ize *v/t* entkartellisieren,
entflechten.

de·cath·lete [dɪˈkæθliːt] *s Leichtathletik*:
Zehnkämpfer *m*. **de'cath·lon** [ˌ~lɒn] *s*
Zehnkampf *m*.

de·cay [dɪˈkeɪ] I *v/i* **1.** zerfallen (*a. phys.*),
vermodern. **2.** verfaulen, -wesen; ka-
riös *od.* schlecht werden (*Zahn*). **3.** abnehmen, schwinden, schwach *od.*
kraftlos werden. **4.** zugrunde gehen. **5.**
geol. verwittern. II *s* **6.** Zerfall *m* (*a.
phys.*). **7.** Verfaulen *n*. **8.** *geol.* Verwitterung *f*.

de·cease [dɪˈsiːs] *s* Ableben *n*. **de-
'ceased** I *adj* verstorben. II *s*: *the ~* der
od. die Verstorbene, die Verstorbenen
pl.

de·ceit [dɪˈsiːt] *s* Betrug *m*, Täuschung *f*.
de'ceit·ful *adj* □ **1.** betrügerisch. **2.**
falsch, hinterlistig.

de·ceive [dɪˈsiːv] I *v/t* täuschen (*Person*),
(*Sache a.*) trügen: *be ~d* sich täuschen
(lassen); *be ~d in s.o.* sich in j-m täuschen; *~ o.s.* sich et. vormachen. II *v/i*

täuschen, trügen (*Sache*). **de'ceiv·er** *s*
Betrüger(in).

de·cel·er·ate [ˌdiːˈseləreɪt] I *v/t* verlang-
samen; die Geschwindigkeit herabset-
zen von (*od. gen.*). II *v/i* sich verlangsa-
men; s-e Geschwindigkeit verringern.

De·cem·ber [dɪˈsembə] *s* Dezember *m*:
in ~ im Dezember.

de·cen·cy [ˈdiːsnsɪ] *s* Anstand *m, pl a.*
Anstandsformen *pl*: *for ~'s sake* anstandshalber. **'de·cent** *adj* □ **1.** anständig. **2.** passabel, annehmbar. **3.** F
salonfähig (angezogen).

de·cen·tral·i·za·tion [diːˌsentrəlaɪˈzeɪʃn]
s Dezentralisierung *f*. **de'cen·tral·ize**
v/t dezentralisieren.

de·cep·tion [dɪˈsepʃn] *s* Täuschung *f*.
de'cep·tive *adj* □ täuschend, trügerisch: *be ~* → *deceive* II; → *appearance* **3**.

de·cide [dɪˈsaɪd] I *v/t* **1.** *et.* entscheiden;
et. bestimmen. **2.** *~ s.o. to do s.th.* j-n
veranlassen *od.* dazu bringen, et. zu
tun. II *v/i* **3.** beschließen, sich entscheiden *od.* entschließen (*to do, on doing*
zu tun; *against doing* nicht zu tun): *~
in favo(u)r of* (*od. on*) (*against*) sich
entscheiden für (gegen). **4.** entscheiden,
den Ausschlag geben. **de'cid·ed** *adj* □
entschieden, entschlossen. **de'cid·ing**
adj entscheidend, ausschlaggebend.

de·cid·u·ous [dɪˈsɪdjʊəs] *adj*: *~ tree*
Laubbaum *m*.

dec·i·mal [ˈdesɪml] I *adj* □ **1.** dezimal,
Dezimal...: *go ~* das Dezimalsystem
einführen; *~ fraction* → **2**; *~ point*
Komma *n* (*in GB u. USA Punkt*) vor
der ersten Dezimalstelle; *~ system*
Dezimalsystem *n*. II *s* **2.** Dezimalbruch
m. **3.** Dezimalzahl *f*. **dec·i·mal·ize**
[ˈ~məlaɪz] *v/t* auf das Dezimalsystem
umstellen.

dec·i·mate [ˈdesɪmeɪt] *v/t* dezimieren.

de·ci·pher [dɪˈsaɪfə] *v/t* entziffern.

de·ci·sion [dɪˈsɪʒn] *s* **1.** Entscheidung *f*:
make (*od. take*) *a ~* e-e Entscheidung
treffen (*on, over* über *acc*). **2.** Entschluß *m*: *arrive at* (*od. come to*) *a ~* zu
e-m Entschluß kommen. **3.** Entschluß-
kraft *f*, Entschlossenheit *f*. **de·ci·sive**
[dɪˈsaɪsɪv] *adj* □ **1.** → *deciding*: *be ~ of
et.* entscheiden. **2.** → *decided*.

deck [dek] I *s* **1.** ♻ Deck *n*: *on ~* an Deck;
bsd. Am. F auf dem Posten. **2.**

Stock(werk *n*) *m*, (*e-s Busses a.*) Deck *n*. **3.** *bsd. Am.* Spiel *n*, Pack *m* (Spiel)Karten. **II** *v/t* **4.** *oft ~ out* herausputzen; schmücken. ~ **chair** *s* Liegestuhl *m*.

de·claim [dɪ'kleɪm] *v/i* **1.** deklamieren, (*v/t a.*) vortragen. **2.** eifern, wettern (*against* gegen).

dec·la·ra·tion [ˌdeklə'reɪʃn] *s* **1.** Erklärung *f*: a) Aussage *f*: **make a ~** e-e Erklärung abgeben; ~ *of intent* Absichtserklärung; b) Verkündung *f*: ~ *of independence* Unabhängigkeitserklärung; ~ *of war* Kriegserklärung. **2.** (Zoll)Deklaration *f*, Zollerklärung *f*. **de·clare** [dɪ'kleə] **I** *v/t* **1.** erklären, verkünden: ~ *open* für eröffnet erklären; *s.o. the winner* j-n zum Sieger erklären; → *war*. **2.** deklarieren: *have you anything to ~?* haben Sie et. zu verzollen? **II** *v/i* **3.** sich erklären *od.* entscheiden (*for* für; *against* gegen). **de'clared** *adj* erklärt.

de·clen·sion [dɪ'klenʃn] *s ling.* Deklination *f*.

de·cline [dɪ'klaɪn] **I** *v/i* **1.** sich neigen *od.* senken. **2.** zur Neige *od.* zu Ende gehen. **3.** abnehmen, zurückgehen; fallen, sinken (*Preise*); verfallen. **4.** (höflich) ablehnen. **II** *v/t* **5.** (höflich) ablehnen: ~ *doing* (*od.* to *do*) es ablehnen zu tun. **6.** *ling.* deklinieren. **III** *s* **7.** Neigung *f*, Senkung *f*. **8.** Neige *f*: *be on the ~* zur Neige gehen; im Niedergang begriffen sein, sinken. **9.** Abnahme *f*, Rückgang *m*: ~ *of* (*od.* *in*) *strength* Kräfteverfall *m*; ~ *in value* Wertminderung *f*.

de·cliv·i·tous [dɪ'klɪvɪtəs] *adj* abschüssig. **de'cliv·i·ty** [~vəti] *s* **1.** Abschüssigkeit *f*. **2.** (Ab)Hang *m*.

de·clutch [ˌdiː'klʌtʃ] *v/i mot.* auskuppeln.

de·code [ˌdiː'kəʊd] *v/t* entschlüsseln.

de·colle·tage [ˌdeɪkɒl'tɑːʒ], **dé'colle·té** [~teɪ] *s* Dekolleté *n*.

de·com·pose [ˌdiːkəm'pəʊz] **I** *v/t* **1.** 🔬, *phys.* zerlegen, spalten. **2.** zersetzen. **II** *v/i* **3.** sich auflösen, zerfallen (*into* in *acc*). **4.** sich zersetzen. **de·com·po·si·tion** [ˌdiːkɒmpə'zɪʃn] *s* **1.** 🔬, *phys.* Zerlegung *f*, Spaltung *f*. **2.** Zersetzung *f*, Zerfall *m*.

de·con·tam·i·nate [ˌdiːkən'tæmɪneɪt] *v/t* entgasen, -seuchen, -strahlen. **'de·con-**

‚tam·i·na·tion *s* Entgasung *f*, -seuchung *f*, -strahlung *f*.

de·con·trol [ˌdiːkən'trəʊl] ✝ **I** *v/t* freigeben, die Zwangsbewirtschaftung aufheben von (*od. gen*). **II** *s* Freigabe *f*, Aufhebung *f* der Zwangsbewirtschaftung.

dé·cor, de·cor ['deɪkɔː] *s* **1.** Ausstattung *f* (*e-s Raums*). **2.** *thea.* Dekor *m*, *n*, Ausstattung *f*, Dekoration *f*.

dec·o·rate ['dekəreɪt] *v/t* **1.** schmücken, verzieren; ausschmücken, dekorieren. **2.** tapezieren; (an)streichen. **3.** dekorieren, (*mit Orden etc*) auszeichnen. **II** *s* Orden *m*, Ehrenzeichen *n*. **dec·o·ra·tive** ['dekərətɪv] *adj* dekorativ, Schmuck...: ~ *plant* Zierpflanze *f*. **dec·o·ra·tor** ['~reɪtə] *s* **1.** Dekorateur *m*: → *interior* 1. **2.** Maler *m* u. Tapezierer *m*.

dec·o·rous ['dekərəs] *adj* □ anständig, schicklich. **de·co·rum** [dɪ'kɔːrəm] *s* Anstand *m*, Schicklichkeit *f*.

de·coy **I** *s* ['diːkɔɪ] Lockvogel *m*, *fig. a.* Köder *m*. **II** *v/t* [dɪ'kɔɪ] (an)locken, ködern; *fig. a.* verleiten (*into* zu).

de·crease **I** *v/i* [diː'kriːs] abnehmen, sich vermindern *od.* verringern: ~ *in length* kürzer werden. **II** *v/t* vermindern, -ringern, herabsetzen. **III** *s* ['diːkriːs] Abnahme *f*, Verminderung *f*, -ringerung *f*: *be on the ~* → I; ~ *in value* Wertminderung *f*.

de·cree [dɪ'kriː] **I** *s* **1.** Dekret *n*, Erlaß *m*, Verfügung *f*. **2.** ⚖ Entscheid *m*, Urteil *n*. **II** *v/t* **3.** verfügen. ~ **ni·si** ['naɪsaɪ] *s* ⚖ vorläufiges Scheidungsurteil.

de·crep·it [dɪ'krepɪt] *adj* altersschwach (*Person, Auto etc*).

de·cry [dɪ'kraɪ] *v/t* schlecht-, heruntermachen, herabsetzen.

ded·i·cate ['dedɪkeɪt] *v/t* **1.** Buch, Leben, Zeit etc widmen (*to* dat). **2.** *Am.* feierlich eröffnen *od.* einweihen. **'ded·i·cat·ed** *adj* treusorgend (*Vater etc*), einsatzfreudig (*Angestellter etc*), engagiert (*Verfechter etc*). **‚ded·i'ca·tion** *s* **1.** Widmung *f*. **2.** Hingabe *f*. **3.** *Am.* feierliche Eröffnung *od.* Einweihung.

de·duce [dɪ'djuːs] *v/t* **1.** folgern, schließen (*from* aus). **2.** ab-, herleiten (*from* von).

de·duct [dɪˈdʌkt] *v/t* (*from*) *Betrag* a) abziehen (von): *after ~ing charges, charges ~ed* nach Abzug der Kosten, b) einbehalten (von), c) (*von der Steuer*) absetzen. **de'duct·i·ble** *adj* (*steuerlich*) absetzbar. **de'duc·tion** *s* **1.** Abzug *m*; Einbehaltung *f*; Absetzung *f*. **2.** ✝ Nachlaß *m*. **3.** (Schluß)Folgerung *f*, Schluß *m*.

deed [diːd] *s* **1.** Tat *f*: *do a good ~* e-e gute Tat vollbringen; → *will*[1] 1, *word* 1. **2.** Helden-, Großtat *f*. **3.** ✍ (Übertragungs)Urkunde *f*.

dee·jay [ˈdiːdʒeɪ] *s* F Diskjockey *m*.

deem [diːm] *v/t* halten *od.* erachten für, betrachten als.

deep [diːp] **I** *adj* ☐ **1.** tief (*a. fig.*): *~ breath* tiefer Atemzug; *~ disappointment* schwere *od.* bittere Enttäuschung; *~ly disappointed* schwer *od.* bitter enttäuscht; *~ poverty* tiefste Armut; *~ silence* tiefes *od.* völliges Schweigen; *~ sleep* tiefer Schlaf, Tiefschlaf *m*; *~ voice* tiefe *od.* dunkle Stimme; *in ~ water(s)* in Schwierigkeiten. **2.** schwerverständlich, schwierig: *that is too ~ for me* das ist mir zu hoch. **II** *adv* **3.** tief (*a. fig.*): *~ into the night* (bis) tief in die Nacht (hinein); *~ in thought* tief in Gedanken (versunken); *~ in winter* im tiefen Winter; → *water* 2. **III** *s* **4.** Tiefe *f*. **5.** *in the ~ of night* mitten in der Nacht; *in the ~ of winter* im tiefen Winter. **'deep·en** *v/t u. v/i* (sich) vertiefen, *fig. a.* (sich) steigern *od.* verstärken.

'deep|-felt *adj* tiefempfunden. **,~-'freeze I** *s* Tiefkühl-, Gefriergerät *n*. **II** *adj* Tiefkühl..., Gefrier...: *~ cabinet* Tiefkühl-, Gefriertruhe *f*. **III** *v/t* (*mst irr freeze*) tiefkühlen, einfrieren: *deep-frozen food* Tiefkühlkost *f*. **~ freez·er** → *deep-freeze* 1. **,~-'fry** *v/t* fritieren. **~ fry·er**, **'~-fry·ing pan** *s* Friteuse *f*.

deep·ness [ˈdiːpnɪs] *s* Tiefe *f* (*a. fig.*). **,deep|-'root·ed** *adj* tief verwurzelt (*a. fig.*). **,~-'sea** *adj* Tiefsee...: *~ fishing* Hochseefischerei *f*. **,~-'seat·ed** *adj fig.* tiefsitzend. **'~-set** *adj* tiefliegend (*Augen*).

deer [dɪə] *pl* **deer(s)** *s zo.* Hirsch *m*; Reh *n*.

de·es·ca·late [ˌdiːˈeskəleɪt] **I** *v/t* **1.** *Krieg etc* deeskalieren. **2.** *Erwartungen etc* herunterschrauben. **II** *v/i* **3.** deeskalieren. **,de·es·ca'la·tion** *s* Deeskalation *f*.

de·face [dɪˈfeɪs] *v/t* **1.** entstellen, verunstalten. **2.** aus-, durchstreichen, unleserlich machen.

def·a·ma·tion [ˌdefəˈmeɪʃn] *s* Verleumdung *f*, Diffamierung *f*. **de·fam·a·to·ry** [dɪˈfæmətərɪ] *adj* ☐ verleumderisch, diffamierend. **de·fame** [dɪˈfeɪm] *v/t* verleumden, diffamieren.

de·fault [dɪˈfɔːlt] **I** *s* **1.** Unterlassung *f*, (Pflicht)Versäumnis *n*. **2.** ✝ Nichterfüllung *f*, Verzug *m*: *be in ~* in Verzug sein (*od.* mit). **3.** ✍ Nichterscheinen *n* vor Gericht: *judg(e)ment by ~* Versäumnisurteil *n*. **4.** *Sport*: Nichtantreten *n*. **5.** *in ~ of* in Ermangelung von (*od. gen*), mangels (*gen*). **II** *v/i* **6.** s-n Verpflichtungen nicht nachkommen, ✝ *a.* im Verzug sein: *~ on s.th.* mit et. in Rückstand sein. **7.** ✍ nicht vor Gericht erscheinen. **8.** *Sport*: nicht antreten. **III** *v/t* **9.** *e-r Verpflichtung* nicht nachkommen, in Verzug geraten mit.

de·feat [dɪˈfiːt] **I** *v/t* **1.** *Gegner* besiegen, schlagen. **2.** *Hoffnung, Plan etc* vereiteln, zunichte machen. **II** *s* **3.** Besiegung *f*. **4.** Niederlage *f*: *admit ~* sich geschlagen geben. **5.** Vereit(e)lung *f*.

de·fect I *s* [ˈdiːfekt] **1.** Defekt *m*, Fehler *m*: *~ in character* Charakterfehler; *~ of vision* Sehfehler. **2.** Mangel *m* (*of an dat*): *~ of memory* Gedächtnisschwäche *f*. **II** *v/i* [dɪˈfekt] **3.** abtrünnig werden (*from dat*); übergehen, -laufen (*to* zu). **de'fec·tion** *s* Überlaufen *n*. **de'fec·tive** *adj* ☐ **1.** mangelhaft, unzulänglich: *he is ~ in* es mangelt ihm an (*dat*). **2.** schadhaft, defekt: *mentally ~* schwachsinnig. **de'fec·tor** *s* Überläufer *m*.

de·fence [dɪˈfens] *s Br.* Verteidigung *f* (*a. ⚔, ✍, Sport*), Schutz *m*: *in ~ of* zur Verteidigung *od.* zum Schutz von (*od. gen*); *come to s.o.'s ~* j-m zu Hilfe kommen; → *counsel* 3, *witness* 1. **de'fence·less** *adj* ☐ schutz-, wehrlos.

de·fend [dɪˈfend] *v/t* **1.** (*from, against*) verteidigen (gegen), schützen (vor *dat*, gegen). **2.** *Meinung etc* verteidigen, rechtfertigen. **de'fend·ant** *s* ✍ Beklagte *m*, *f*; Angeklagte *m*, *f*.

de'fend·er s **1.** Verteidiger(in). **2.** *Sport:* Abwehrspieler(in).

de·fense, *etc Am.* → **defence,** *etc.*

de'fen·sive I *adj* defensiv, Verteidigungs..., Abwehr... **II** s Defensive f: **on the ~** in der Defensive.

de·fer¹ [dɪ'fɜ:] v/t **1.** auf-, verschieben (**to** auf *acc*). **2.** hinausschieben, verzögern. **3.** ✕ *Am.* (vom Wehrdienst) zurückstellen.

de·fer² [~] v/i sich fügen (**to** *dat*). **def·er·ence** ['defərəns] s **1.** Ehrerbietung f, (Hoch)Achtung f: **in** (*od.* **out of**) **~ to** aus Achtung vor (*dat*). **2.** Rücksicht(nahme) f: **in** (*od.* **out of**) **~ to** mit *od.* aus Rücksicht auf (*acc*). **def·er·en·tial** [~'renʃl] *adj* □ **1.** ehrerbietig. **2.** rücksichtsvoll.

de·fer·ment [dɪ'fɜ:mənt] s **1.** Aufschub m, Verschiebung f. **2.** ✕ *Am.* Zurückstellung f (*vom Wehrdienst*).

de·fi·ance [dɪ'faɪəns] s **1.** Trotz m: **in ~ of** ungeachtet, trotz (*gen*), *e-m Gebot etc* zuwider, *j-m* zum Trotz. **2.** Herausforderung f. **de'fi·ant** *adj* □ **1.** trotzig. **2.** herausfordernd.

de·fi·cien·cy [dɪ'fɪʃnsɪ] s **1.** (**of**) Mangel m (an *dat*), Fehlen n (von): **~ of blood** Blutarmut f; **~ disease** ✚ Mangelkrankheit f. **2.** → **deficit. de'fi·cient** *adj* □ unzureichend, mangelhaft, ungenügend: **be ~ in** Mangel leiden an (*dat*); **he is ~ in** ihm fehlt es an (*dat*).

def·i·cit ['defɪsɪt] s Defizit n, Fehlbetrag m.

de·file [dɪ'faɪl] v/t beschmutzen, besudeln (*beide a. fig.*).

de·fine [dɪ'faɪn] v/t **1.** definieren: a) *Wort etc* erklären, b) *Begriff etc* bestimmen. **2.** abgrenzen. **3.** ~ **itself against** sich scharf *od.* deutlich abheben von *od.* gegen. **def·i·nite** ['defɪnɪt] *adj* **1.** bestimmt (*a. ling.*). **2.** endgültig, definitiv. **'def·i·nite·ly** *adv* ~ **definite:** ~ **not!** ganz bestimmt nicht! **,def·i'ni·tion** s Definition f: a) Erklärung f, b) Bestimmung f. **de·fin·i·tive** [dɪ'fɪnɪtɪv] *adj* □ **1.** → **definite** 2. **2.** maßgeblich.

de·flate [dɪ'fleɪt] v/t **1.** (die) Luft ablassen aus. **2.** ✝ deflationieren. **de'fla·tion** s ✝ Deflation f.

de·flect [dɪ'flekt] **I** v/t ablenken (**from** von). **II** v/i abweichen (**from** von) (*a.*

fig.). **de'flec·tion** s **1.** Ablenkung f. **2.** Abweichung f.

de·fo·li·ate [,di:'fəʊlɪeɪt] v/t entblättern, -lauben.

de·for·est [,di:'fɒrɪst] v/t abholzen.

de·form [dɪ'fɔ:m] v/t **1.** deformieren, verformen (*beide a. phys.*, ⚙). **2.** verunstalten, entstellen: **~ed by anger** wutverzerrt (*Gesicht*). **de·for·ma·tion** [,di:fɔ:'meɪʃn] s **1.** Deformierung f, Verformung f. **2.** Verunstaltung f, Entstellung f. **de·form·i·ty** [dɪ'fɔ:mətɪ] s **1.** Entstelltheit f. **2.** Mißbildung f.

de·fraud [dɪ'frɔ:d] v/t betrügen (**of** um).

de·fray [dɪ'freɪ] v/t *Kosten* tragen, bestreiten.

de·frost [,di:'frɒst] **I** v/t von Eis befreien, *Windschutzscheibe etc* entfrosten, *Kühlschrank etc* abtauen, *Tiefkühlkost etc* auftauen. **II** v/i ab-, auftauen.

deft [deft] *adj* □ gewandt, geschickt.

de·fuse [,di:'fju:z] v/t *Bombe, Lage etc* entschärfen.

de·fy [dɪ'faɪ] v/t **1.** trotzen (*dat*); sich widersetzen (*dat*): **~ description** unbeschreiblich sein, jeder Beschreibung spotten. **2.** herausfordern.

de·gen·er·ate I v/i [dɪ'dʒenəreɪt] degenerieren, entarten (**into** zu). **II** *adj* [~rət] degeneriert, entartet. **de,gen·er'a·tion** [~'reɪʃn] s Degeneration f, Entartung f.

deg·ra·da·tion [,degrə'deɪʃn] s **1.** Degradierung f. **2.** Erniedrigung f. **de·grade** [dɪ'greɪd] v/t **1.** degradieren. **2.** erniedrigen (**into, to** zu).

de·gree [dɪ'gri:] s **1.** Grad m, Stufe f: **by ~s** allmählich, nach u. nach; **by slow ~s** ganz allmählich; **to some** (*od.* **a certain**) **~** ziemlich, bis zu e-m gewissen Grade; **to a high ~** in hohem Maße; **~ of comparison** *ling.* Steigerungsstufe f; **~ of priority** Dringlichkeitsstufe f. **2.** ⚕, ⚙, *ast., geogr. etc* Grad m: **~ of latitude** (**longitude**) Breiten-(Längen)grad. **3.** *univ.* Grad m: **take one's ~** e-n akademischen Grad erwerben; **~ doctor** 2.

de·hu·man·ize [,di:'hju:mənaɪz] v/t entmenschlichen.

de·hy·drate [,di:'haɪdreɪt] v/t das Wasser entziehen (*dat*): **~d vegetables** pl Trockengemüse n.

de·ice [,di:'aɪs] v/t enteisen.

deign [deɪn] **I** v/i sich herablassen, geruhen (**to do** zu tun). **II** v/t sich herablassen zu.

de·i·ty ['di:ɪtɪ] s Gottheit f.

de·ject·ed [dɪ'dʒektɪd] adj □ niedergeschlagen.

de·jec·tion s Niedergeschlagenheit f.

de·lay [dɪ'leɪ] **I** v/t **1.** a) ver-, auf-, hinausschieben: ~ **doing s.th.** es verschieben, et. zu tun, b) verzögern, -schleppen: **be ~ed** sich verzögern. **2.** aufhalten: **be ~ed (for two hours)** 🐾, etc (zwei Stunden) Verspätung haben. **II** v/i **3.** zögern. **4.** Zeit zu gewinnen suchen. **III** s **5.** Verschiebung f, Aufschub m; Verzögerung f, Verschleppung f: **without ~** unverzüglich. **6.** 🐾, etc Verspätung f. **de·lay·ing** adj: ~ **tactics** pl Hinhalte-, Verzögerungstaktik f.

de·lec·ta·ble [dɪ'lektəbl] adj □ köstlich (bsd. Speise). **de·lec·ta·tion** [ˌdi:lek-'teɪʃn] s Vergnügen n: **for the ~** zum Ergötzen (gen).

del·e·gate **I** s ['delɪgət] **1.** Delegierte m, f, bevollmächtigter Vertreter. **II** v/t ['~geɪt] **2.** abordnen, delegieren. **3.** Vollmachten etc übertragen (**to** dat). **del·e·ga·tion** [ˌ~'geɪʃn] s **1.** Übertragung f. **2.** Abordnung f, Delegation f.

de·lete [dɪ'li:t] v/t (aus)streichen. **II** v/i: ~ **where inapplicable** Nichtzutreffendes bitte streichen. **de·le·tion** [dɪ'li:ʃn] s Streichung f.

de·lib·er·ate **I** adj [dɪ'lɪbərət] □ **1.** überlegt. **2.** bewußt, absichtlich, vorsätzlich. **3.** bedächtig, besonnen. **II** v/t [~reɪt] **4.** überlegen, erwägen. **III** v/i [~reɪt] **5.** nachdenken (**on** über acc), überlegen. **6.** beratschlagen, sich beraten (**on** über acc). **de·lib·er·a·tion** [~'reɪʃn] s **1.** Überlegung f. **2.** Beratung f. **3.** Bedächtigkeit f.

del·i·ca·cy ['delɪkəsɪ] s **1.** Zartheit f. **2.** Fein-, Zartgefühl n, Takt m. **3.** Empfindlichkeit f. **4. of great ~** sehr heikel. **5.** Delikatesse f, Leckerbissen m.

del·i·cate ['~kət] adj □ **1.** zart: a) fein (Farben etc), b) zierlich (Figur etc), c) zerbrechlich: **of** (od. **in**) ~ **health** von zarter Gesundheit, d) sanft, leise: ~ **hint** zarter Wink. **2.** delikat, heikel (Frage etc). **3.** fein, empfindlich (Instrument etc). **4.** feinfühlig, zartfühlend, taktvoll. **5.** delikat, schmackhaft. **del·i·ca·tes·sen** [ˌdelɪkə'tesn] s pl **1.** Deli-

katessen pl, Feinkost f. **2.** (sg konstruiert) Feinkostgeschäft n.

de·li·cious [dɪ'lɪʃəs] adj □ köstlich.

de·light [dɪ'laɪt] **I** s Vergnügen n, Entzücken n: **to my ~** zu m-r Freude; **take ~ in** → **III**. **II** v/t erfreuen, entzücken. **III** v/i: ~ **in** (große) Freude haben an (dat), sich ein Vergnügen machen aus. **de·light·ful** [~fʊl] adj □ entzückend, herrlich.

de·lim·it [di:'lɪmɪt], **de·lim·i·tate** [~teɪt] v/t abgrenzen.

de·lin·e·ate [dɪ'lɪnɪeɪt] v/t **1.** skizzieren, entwerfen. **2.** beschreiben, schildern.

de·lin·quen·cy [dɪ'lɪŋkwənsɪ] s Kriminalität f: → **juvenile** I. **de·lin·quent** **I** adj straffällig. **II** s Delinquent(in), Straffällige m, f: → **juvenile** I.

de·lir·i·ous [dɪ'lɪrɪəs] adj □ **1.** 🐾 im Delirium, phantasierend. **2.** fig. rasend (**with** vor dat): ~ **with joy** in e-m Freudentaumel; **~ly happy** vor Glück außer sich. **de·lir·i·um** [~əm] pl **-i·ums**, **-i·a** [~ɪə] s **1.** 🐾 Delirium n: ~ **tremens** ['tri:menz] Delirium tremens, Säuferwahn(sinn) m. **2.** fig. Taumel m: ~ **of joy** Freudentaumel.

de·liv·er [dɪ'lɪvə] v/t **1.** a. ~ **up** (od. **over**) übergeben, ausliefern: ~ **o.s. up to s.o.** sich j-m stellen od. ergeben. **2.** Waren liefern; Brief etc zustellen; Nachricht etc bestellen. **3.** Rede etc halten (**to** vor dat). **4.** befreien, erlösen (**from** von, aus). **5. be ~ed of** entbinden: **be ~ed of** entbunden werden von. **de·liv·er·y** s **1.** ✝ Lieferung f: **on** ~ bei Lieferung od. Empfang; **cash** (Am. **collect**) **on** ~ per Nachnahme; ~ **note** Lieferschein m. **2.** ✆ Zustellung f: ~ **charge** Zustellgebühr f. **3.** Halten n (e-r Rede); Vortrag(sweise) f) m. **4.** 🐾 Entbindung f: ~ **room** Kreißsaal m.

de·louse [ˌdi:'laʊs] v/t entlausen.

del·ta ['deltə] s (Fluß)Delta n.

de·lude [dɪ'lu:d] v/t **1.** täuschen, irreführen: ~ **o.s.** sich et. vormachen. **2.** verleiten (**into** zu).

del·uge ['delju:dʒ] **I** s **1.** Überschwemmung f: **the** ♀ Bibl. die Sintflut. **2.** fig. Flut f, (Un)Menge f. **II** v/t **3.** überschwemmen, -fluten (beide a. fig. with mit).

de·lu·sion [dɪ'lu:ʒn] s **1.** Täuschung f, Irreführung f. **2.** Wahn m (a. psych.):

be under the ~ that in dem Wahn leben, daß; *~s pl of grandeur* Größenwahn. **de·lu·sive** [~sɪv] *adj* □ **1.** täuschend, irreführend. **2.** Wahn...

de luxe [də'lʌks] *adj* Luxus..., De-Luxe-...

delve [delv] *v/i* angestrengt suchen *(for* nach): *~ into* sich vertiefen in *(acc)*; erforschen.

dem·a·gog·ic [ˌdemə'gɒgɪk] *adj* (*~ally*) demagogisch. **dem·a·gogue** ['~gɒg] *s* Demagoge *m.* **'dem·a·gog·y** *s* Demagogie *f.*

de·mand [dɪ'mɑːnd] **I** *v/t* **1.** fordern, verlangen *(of, from* von). **2.** *(fordernd)* fragen nach. **3.** *fig.* erfordern, verlangen. **II** *v/i* **4.** Forderung *f (for* nach): *on ~* auf Verlangen; *make ~s on s.o.* Forderungen an j-n stellen. **5.** *(on)* Anforderung *f (an acc)*, Beanspruchung *f (gen): make great ~s on* stark in Anspruch nehmen *(acc)*, große Anforderungen stellen an *(acc)*. **6.** ✝ *u. allg. (for)* Nachfrage *f (nach)*, Bedarf *m (an dat): be in great ~* sehr gefragt sein. **de'mand·ing** *adj* anspruchsvoll.

de·mar·cate ['diːmɑːkeɪt] *v/t* abgrenzen *(from* gegen, von) *(a. fig.).* **de·mar·'ca·tion** *s* Abgrenzung *f: ~ line* Grenz-, *pol.* Demarkationslinie *f; dividing line* Trennungslinie *f*, -strich *m.*

dem·i... [demɪ] *in Zssgn* Halb..., halb... **'dem·i·god** *s* Halbgott *m (a. fig.).* **'dem·i·john** *s* große Korbflasche.

de·mil·i·ta·rize [ˌdiː'mɪlɪtəraɪz] *v/t* entmilitarisieren.

de·mist [ˌdiː'mɪst] *v/t Windschutzscheibe* freimachen. **de'mist·er** *s mot.* Gebläse *n.*

dem·o ['deməʊ] *pl* **-os** *s* F Demo *f (Demonstration).*

de·mo·bi·lize [ˌdiː'məʊbɪlaɪz] *v/t* demobilisieren.

de·moc·ra·cy [dɪ'mɒkrəsɪ] *s* Demokratie *f.* **dem·o·crat,** *pol. Am.* ♀ ['deməkræt] *s* Demokrat(in). **dem·o·'crat·ic,** *pol. Am.* ♀ *adj (~ally)* demokratisch.

de·mog·ra·phy [diː'mɒgrəfɪ] *s* Demographie *f.*

de·mol·ish [dɪ'mɒlɪʃ] *v/t* **1.** ab-, ein-, niederreißen, abbrechen. **2.** *fig.* zerstören. **3.** F *Essen* verdrücken. **dem·o·li·tion** [ˌdemə'lɪʃn] *s* **1.** Niederreißen *n*, Abbruch *m.* **2.** *fig.* Zerstörung *f.*

de·mon ['diːmən] *s* **1.** Dämon *m.* **2.** *~ for work* Arbeitsfanatiker *m.* **de·mo·ni·ac** [dɪ'məʊnɪæk], **de·mon·ic** [diː'mɒnɪk] *adj (~ally)* dämonisch.

dem·on·strate ['demənstreɪt] **I** *v/t* **1.** demonstrieren: a) beweisen, b) darlegen, veranschaulichen, zeigen. **2.** *Auto etc* vorführen. **II** *v/i* **3.** *pol. etc* demonstrieren. **dem·on·'stra·tion** *s* **1.** Demonstrierung *f*, Veranschaulichung *f.* **2.** Vorführung *f: ~ car* Vorführwagen *m.* **3.** Demonstration *f*, Kundgebung *f.* **de·mon·stra·tive** [dɪ'mɒnstrətɪv] *adj* □ **1.** anschaulich: *be ~ of → demonstrate* 1. 2. *be ~* s-e Gefühle (offen) zeigen. **3.** demonstrativ, betont. **4.** *~ pronoun ling.* Demonstrativpronomen *n*, hinweisendes Fürwort. **dem·on·stra·tor** ['demənstreɪtə] *s* **1.** Vorführer(in), Propagandist(in). **2.** Demonstrant(in).

de·mor·al·ize [dɪ'mɒrəlaɪz] *v/t* demoralisieren.

de·mo·ti·vate [ˌdiː'məʊtɪveɪt] *v/t* demotivieren.

den [den] *s* **1.** *zo.* Höhle *f (a. fig.): ~ of vice* Lasterhöhle. **2.** F Bude *f.*

de·na·tion·al·ize [ˌdiː'næʃnəlaɪz] *v/t* ✝ reprivatisieren, entstaatlichen.

de·na·ture [ˌdiː'neɪtʃə] *v/t* ♋ denaturieren.

de·ni·al [dɪ'naɪəl] *s* **1.** Ablehnung *f.* **2.** (Ab)Leugnung *f: official ~* Dementi *n.*

den·im ['denɪm] *s* **1.** Köper *m.* **2.** *pl* Jeans *pl.*

de·nom·i·nate [dɪ'nɒmɪneɪt] *v/t* nennen, bezeichnen als. **de·nom·i·na·tion** *s* **1.** Bezeichnung *f.* **2.** *eccl.* Konfession *f*, Bekenntnis *n.* **3.** ✝ Nennwert *m.* **de·nom·i·'na·tion·al** [~'neɪʃənl] *adj* □ konfessionell, Konfessions... **de'nom·i·na·tor** *s* ♉ Nenner *m: common ~* gemeinsamer Nenner *(a. fig.); reduce to a common ~* auf e-n gemeinsamen Nenner bringen.

de·note [dɪ'nəʊt] *v/t* **1.** bedeuten, anzeigen. **2.** kenn-, bezeichnen.

de·nounce [dɪ'naʊns] *v/t* **1.** (öffentlich) anprangern. **2.** j-n anzeigen, *contp.* denunzieren *(to* bei). **3.** *Vertrag* kündigen.

dense [dens] *adj* □ **1.** *allg.* dicht: *~ly populated* dichtbevölkert. **2.** *fig.* beschränkt, begriffsstutzig. **'dense·ness**

s **1.** → *density.* **2.** *fig.* Beschränktheit *f,* Begriffsstutzigkeit *f.* '**den·si·ty** *s* Dichte *f,* Dichtheit *f:* ~ *of population* Bevölkerungsdichte; ~ *of traffic* Verkehrsdichte.

dent [dent] **I** *s* Beule *f,* Delle *f,* Einbeulung *f: make a ~ in fig.* ein Loch reißen in (*Ersparnisse etc*); *j-s Ruf etc* schaden, *j-s Stolz etc* verletzen. **II** *v/t* ein-, verbeulen.

den·tal ['dentl] *adj* **1.** Zahn...: ~ *hygiene* Zahnpflege *f;* ~ *plaque* Zahnbelag *m;* ~ *surgeon* → *dentist;* ~ *treatment* Zahnbehandlung *f.* **2.** Zahnarzt...: ~ *assistant* Zahnarzthelferin *f.* '**den·tist** *s* Zahnarzt *m,* -ärztin *f.* '**den·tist·ry** *s* Zahnmedizin *f.* **den·ture** ['~tʃə] *s mst pl* (Zahn)Prothese *f.*

de·nude [dɪ'njuːd] *v/t* (*of*) entblößen (von *od. gen*); *fig.* berauben (*gen*).

de·nun·ci·a·tion [dɪ,nʌnsɪ'eɪʃn] *s* **1.** (öffentliche) Anprangerung. **2.** Anzeige *f, contp.* Denunziation *f.* **3.** Kündigung *f* (*of e-s Vertrags*).

de·ny [dɪ'naɪ] *v/t* **1.** ab-, bestreiten, dementieren, (ab)leugnen: *it cannot be denied, there is no ~ing (the fact)* es läßt sich nicht bestreiten, es ist nicht zu leugnen (*that* daß). **2.** *Bitte etc* ablehnen, *j-m et.* abschlagen, verweigern. **3.** *Glauben, j-n etc* verleugnen.

de·o·dor·ant [diː'əʊdərənt] **I** *s* De(s)odorant *n,* Deo *n.* **II** *adj* de(s)odorierend. **de·o·dor·ize** *v/t* de(s)odorieren.

de·part [dɪ'pɑːt] *v/i* **1.** abreisen, abfahren (*for* nach). **2.** 🚂, *etc* abfahren, ✈ abfliegen. **3.** abweichen (*from* von e-r *Regel, der Wahrheit etc*). **de'part·ed** **I** *adj* verstorben. **II** *s: the ~* der *od.* die Verstorbene, die Verstorbenen *pl.* **de·'part·ment** *s* **1.** Fach *n,* Gebiet *n.* **2.** Abteilung *f, univ. a.* Fachbereich *m:* ~ *store* Kauf-, Warenhaus *n.* **3.** *pol.* Ministerium *n:* ♀ *of Defense Am.* Verteidigungsministerium; ♀ *of the Interior Am.* Innenministerium; ♀ *of State Am.* Außenministerium. **de·part·men·tal** [,diːpɑːt'mentl] *adj* Abteilungs... **de·par·ture** [dɪ'pɑːtʃə] *s* **1.** Abreise *f.* **2.** 🚂, *etc* Abfahrt *f,* ✈ Abflug *m:* ~*s pl* ,Abfahrt' (*Fahrplan etc*); ~ *lounge* Abflughalle *f.* **3.** Abweichen *n.*

de·pend [dɪ'pend] *v/i* **1.** sich verlassen (*on* auf *acc*). **2.** (*on*) abhängen, abhän-

gig sein (von): a) angewiesen sein (auf *acc*), b) ankommen (auf *acc*): *that ~s* das kommt darauf an, je nachdem; ~*ing on whether* je nachdem, ob. **de'pend·a·ble** *adj* □ verläßlich, zuverlässig. **de·pen·dance** *Am.* → *dependence.* **de'pen·dant** **I** *s* (Familien)Angehörige *m, f.* **II** *adj Am.* → *dependent* **I.** **de'pen·dence** *s* **1.** Vertrauen *n* (*on* auf *acc*). **2.** (*on*) Abhängigkeit *f* (von), Angewiesensein *n* (auf *acc*). **de'pen·dent** **I** *adj* (*on*) abhängig (von): a) angewiesen (auf *acc*), b) bedingt (durch): ~ *on weather* wetter-, witterungsbedingt. **II** *s bsd. Am.* → *dependant* **I.**

de·pict [dɪ'pɪkt] *v/t* **1.** (bildlich) darstellen. **2.** schildern, beschreiben.

de·pil·a·to·ry [dɪ'pɪlətərɪ] *s* Enthaarungsmittel *n.*

de·plete [dɪ'pliːt] *v/t* **1.** leeren. **2.** *fig.* Raubbau treiben mit, *Kräfte, Vorräte etc* erschöpfen, *Bestand etc* dezimieren.

de·plor·a·ble [dɪ'plɔːrəbl] *adj* □ **1.** bedauerlich, bedauerns-, beklagenswert. **2.** erbärmlich, kläglich. **de'plore** *v/t* bedauern, beklagen.

de·ploy [dɪ'plɔɪ] *v/t* **1.** ✕ *u. allg.* verteilen, einsetzen. **2.** ✕ *Truppen* stationieren, *Raketen etc a.* aufstellen.

de·pop·u·late [,diː'pɒpjʊleɪt] *v/t u. v/i* (sich) entvölkern.

de·port [dɪ'pɔːt] *v/t* **1.** des Landes verweisen, ausweisen, *Ausländer a.* abschieben. **2.** deportieren. **de·por·ta·tion** [,diːpɔː'teɪʃn] *s* **1.** Ausweisung *f,* Abschiebung *f.* **2.** Deportation *f.*

de·pose [dɪ'pəʊz] **I** *v/t* **1.** *j-n* absetzen: ~ *s.o. from office* j-n s-s Amtes entheben. **2.** ⚖ eidlich bezeugen *od.* erklären. **II** *v/i* **3.** ~ *to* → **2.**

de·pos·it [dɪ'pɒzɪt] **I** *v/t* **1.** absetzen, abstellen. **2.** ⚙, *geol.* ablagern, absetzen. **3.** deponieren, hinterlegen. **4.** ✝ *Betrag* anzahlen. **II** *v/i* **5.** ⚙ sich absetzen *od.* ablagern. **III** *s* **6.** ⚙ Ablagerung *f, geol. a.* (*Erz- etc*)Lager *n.* **7.** Deponierung *f,* Hinterlegung *f.* **8.** ✝ Anzahlung *f: make (od. pay) a ~* e-e Anzahlung leisten (*on* für). ~ *ac·count s bsd. Br.* Sparkonto *n.*

dep·o·si·tion [,depə'zɪʃn] *s* **1.** Absetzung *f.* **2.** ⚙, *geol.* Ablagerung *f.* **3.** ⚖ eidliche Aussage.

de·pot s 1. ['depəʊ] Depot n (a. ✕, ⚔). 2. ['diːpəʊ] Am. Bahnhof m.

de·prave [dɪ'preɪv] v/t moralisch verderben. **de·prav·i·ty** [dɪ'prævətɪ] s Verderbtheit f.

dep·re·cate ['deprɪkeɪt] v/t 1. mißbilligen. 2. → **depreciate** 2. '**dep·re·cat·ing** adj □ 1. mißbilligend. 2. entschuldigend. **dep·re·ca·tion** s Mißbilligung f. **dep·re·ca·to·ry** ['ᴗkətərɪ] → **deprecating**.

de·pre·ci·ate [dɪ'priːʃɪeɪt] I v/t 1. geringschätzen, verachten. 2. herabsetzen, herunterwürdigen. 3. im Preis od. Wert herabsetzen; Währung abwerten. II v/i 4. an Wert verlieren. **de'pre·ci·at·ing** adj □ geringschätzig, verächtlich. **de.pre·ci'a·tion** s 1. Geringschätzung f, Verachtung f. 2. Herabsetzung f. 3. ⚓ Wertminderung f; Abwertung f.

dep·re·da·tion [ˌdeprɪ'deɪʃn] s Verwüstung f.

de·press [dɪ'pres] v/t 1. Pedal, Taste etc (nieder)drücken. 2. j-n deprimieren, bedrücken. 3. Preis, Stimmung etc drücken. **de'press·ant** s ⚕ Beruhigungsmittel n. **de'pressed** adj 1. deprimiert, niedergeschlagen, bedrückt. 2. gedrückt. 3. ⚓ flau (Markt etc), notleidend (Industrie). 4. ~ **area** Notstandsgebiet n. **de·pres·sion** [dɪ'preʃn] s 1. Depression f, Niedergeschlagenheit f. 2. Senkung f, Vertiefung f; geol. Landsenke f. 3. ⚓ Depression f, Flaute f. 4. meteor. Tief(druckgebiet) n.

dep·ri·va·tion [ˌdeprɪ'veɪʃn] s 1. Beraubung f, Entzug m. 2. (empfindlicher) Verlust. **de·prive** [dɪ'praɪv] v/t (of s.th.) j-n od. et. (e-r Sache) berauben, j-m (et.) entziehen od. nehmen: be ~d of s.th. et. entbehren (müssen). **de'prived** adj benachteiligt.

depth [depθ] I s Tiefe f (a. fig.): at a ~ of in e-r Tiefe von; five feet in ~ fünf Fuß tief; in ~ bis in alle Einzelheiten, eingehend; in the ~(s) of winter im tiefsten Winter; be out of one's ~ nicht mehr stehen können; fig. ratlos od. unsicher sein, schwimmen; get out of one's ~ den Boden unter den Füßen verlieren (a. fig.); ~ (of field od. focus) phot. Tiefenschärfe f. II adj psych. etc Tiefen...: ~ psychology.

dep·u·tize ['depjʊtaɪz] I v/t (als Vertre-

ter) ernennen. II v/i: ~ for j-n vertreten. '**dep·u·ty** I s 1. (Stell)Vertreter(in f) m. 2. parl. Abgeordnete(r) m, f. 3. a. ~ **sheriff** Am. Hilfssheriff m. II adj 4. stellvertretend, Vize-.

de·rail [dɪ'reɪl] I v/t entgleisen lassen: be ~ed → II. II v/i entgleisen.

de·range [dɪ'reɪndʒ] v/t in Unordnung bringen, durcheinanderbringen. **de'ranged** adj 1. in Unordnung, durcheinander. 2. a. **mentally** ~ geistesgestört. **de'range·ment** s 1. Unordnung f. 2. a. **mental** ~ Geistesgestörtheit f.

der·by ['dɑːbɪ] s 1. Sport: Derby n: → local 1. 2. a. ~ **hat** Am. Bowler m, Melone f.

der·e·lict ['derəlɪkt] adj heruntergekommen, baufällig.

de·ride [dɪ'raɪd] v/t verhöhnen, -spotten. **de·ri·sion** [dɪ'rɪʒn] s Hohn m, Spott m. **de·ri·sive** [dɪ'raɪsɪv] adj □, **de'ri·so·ry** [ᴗsərɪ] adj □ 1. höhnisch, spöttisch: ~ laughter Hohngelächter n. 2. fig. lächerlich.

der·i·va·tion [ˌderɪ'veɪʃn] s 1. Ab-, Herleitung f. 2. Herkunft f, Abstammung f. **de·riv·a·tive** [dɪ'rɪvətɪv] I adj □ abgeleitet. II s et. Ab- od. Hergeleitetes, a. ling. Ableitung f. **de·rive** [dɪ'raɪv] I v/t 1. herleiten (from von): be ~d (from), ~ itself (from) → 4. 2. Nutzen ziehen, Gewinn schöpfen (from aus): ~ pleasure from Freude finden od. haben an (dat). 3. ling., 🜊, etc ableiten. II v/i 4. (from) abstammen (von); sich ab- od. herleiten (von).

der·ma·tol·o·gist [ˌdɜːmə'tɒlədʒɪst] s Dermatologe m, Hautarzt m. **der·ma'tol·o·gy** s Dermatologie f.

de·rog·a·to·ry [dɪ'rɒgətərɪ] adj □ 1. (from, to) nachteilig (für), abträglich (dat). 2. abfällig, geringschätzig.

der·rick ['derɪk] s 1. Derrick-, Mastenkran m. 2. Bohrturm m.

de·scale [ˌdiː'skeɪl] v/t Boiler etc entkalken.

de·scend [dɪ'send] I v/i 1. herunter-, hinuntersteigen, -gehen, -kommen, -fahren, -fallen. 2. ✈ niedergehen; (mit dem Fallschirm) abspringen. 3. abfallen (Straße etc). 4. abstammen, herkommen (from von j-m, aus e-r Familie). 5. (to) übergehen, sich vererben (auf acc), zufallen (dat). 6. (on) herfal-

len (über *acc*), sich stürzen (auf *acc*), *a.
fig.* überfallen (*acc*) (*Besuch etc*). **7.** *ast.*
sinken. **II** *v/t* **8.** Treppe etc herunter-,
hinuntersteigen, -gehen. **9. be ~ed
(from)** → **4. de'scend·ant** *s* Nachkomme *m*, Abkömmling *m*.

de·scent [dɪ'sent] *s* **1.** Herunter-, Hinuntersteigen *n*, -gehen *n*, -fahren *n*. **2.** ✈
Niedergehen *n*; (Fallschirm)Absprung
m. **3.** Abfallen *n*, Gefälle *n*. **4.** Abstammung *f*, Herkunft *f*: *of French* ~ fran-
zösischer Herkunft. **5.** Vererbung *f* (*to
auf acc*). **6.** Überfall *m* (*on auf acc*) (*a.
fig.*).

de·scribe [dɪ'skraɪb] *v/t* **1.** beschreiben,
schildern (*s.th. to s.o.* j-m et.). **2.** bezeichnen (*as* als).

de·scrip·tion [dɪ'skrɪpʃn] *s* **1.** Beschreibung *f* (*a.* ⊛), Schilderung *f*: *beyond ~*
unbeschreiblich; → *beggar* 4. **2.** Art *f*,
Sorte *f*. **de·scrip·tive** *adj* □ **1.** be-
schreibend. **2.** anschaulich.

des·e·crate ['desɪkreɪt] *v/t* entweihen.

de·seg·re·gate [ˌdiː'segrɪgeɪt] *v/t* die
Rassentrennung aufheben in (*dat*).
ˌde·seg·re'ga·tion *s* Aufhebung *f* der
Rassentrennung (*of* in *dat*).

de·sen·si·tize [ˌdiː'sensɪtaɪz] *v/t* 🐟 unempfindlich *od.* immun machen (*to* gegen).

de·sert¹ [dɪ'zɜːt] *v/t* verlassen, im Stich
lassen; 🔩 *Ehegatten* (böswillig) verlassen. **II** *v/i* ✕ desertieren.

de·sert² [~] *s* *mst pl* verdienter Lohn (*a.
iro. Strafe*).

des·ert³ ['dezət] **I** *s* Wüste *f*. **II** *adj*
Wüsten...

de·sert·ed [dɪ'zɜːtɪd] *adj* **1.** verlassen,
unbewohnt (*Insel etc*), (wie) ausgestorben, menschenleer (*Straßen etc*). **2.** verlassen, einsam (*Person*). **de'sert·er** *s* ✕
Deserteur *m*. **de'ser·tion** *s* **1.** (*a.* 🔩
böswilliges) Verlassen. **2.** ✕ Desertion
f, Fahnenflucht *f*.

de·serve [dɪ'zɜːv] *v/t* verdienen, verdient
haben. **de'serv·ed·ly** [~ɪdlɪ] *adv* ver-
dientermaßen. **de'serv·ing** *adj* verdienstvoll.

des·ic·cat·ed ['desɪkeɪtɪd] *adj*: ~ *fruit*
Dörrobst *n*; ~ *milk* Trockenmilch *f*.

de·sign [dɪ'zaɪn] **I** *v/t* **1.** entwerfen, ⊛
konstruieren. **2.** gestalten, anlegen. **3.**
ausdenken, ersinnen. **4.** bestimmen,
vorsehen (*for* für; *as* als): *~ed to do*

s.th. dafür bestimmt, et. zu tun. **II** *v/i*
5. Entwürfe machen (*for* für). **III** *s* **6.**
Design *n*, Entwurf *m*, (⊛ Konstruk-
tions)Zeichnung *f*. **7.** Design *n*, Muster
n. **8.** Gestaltung *f*. **9.** (*a.* böse) Absicht:
by ~ mit Absicht; *have* ~s *on* (*od.
against*) et. im Schilde führen gegen, *a.
humor.* e-n Anschlag vorhaben auf
(*acc*).

des·ig·nate ['dezɪgneɪt] **I** *v/t* **1.** et. bestimmen, festlegen. **2.** j-n bezeichnen,
bestimmen (*to, for* für ein Amt etc, zu
e-m Amtsträger etc). **3.** et. bestimmen,
vorsehen (*for* für). **II** *adj* **4.** *nachgestellt:* designiert.

des·ig·nat·ed·ly [dɪ'zaɪnɪdlɪ] *adv* absichtlich. **de'sign·er** *s* Designer(in); ⊛
Konstrukteur *m*; (*Mode*)Schöpfer(in).

de·sir·a·ble [dɪ'zaɪərəbl] *adj* □ **1.** wünschenswert, erwünscht. **2.** begehrens-
wert. **de·sire** [dɪ'zaɪə] **I** *v/t* **1.** wünschen: *if ~d* auf Wunsch; *leave much
(nothing) to be ~d* viel (nichts) zu wünschen übriglassen. **2.** begehren. **II** *s* **3.**
Wunsch *m*: *at his* ~ auf s-n Wunsch. **4.**
Verlangen *n*, Begierde *f* (*for* nach): ~ *for
knowledge* Wissensdurst *m*. **de·sir·
ous** [dɪ'zaɪərəs] *adj*: *be* ~ *to know s.th.*
et. (sehr) gern wissen wollen.

de·sist [dɪ'zɪst] *v/i* Abstand nehmen
(*from* von).

desk [desk] **I** *s* **1.** Schreibtisch *m*. **2.**
(*Schreib-, Noten- etc*)Pult *n*. **3.** Kasse *f*
(*im Restaurant etc*). **4.** Empfang *m*, Rezeption *f* (*im Hotel*): → *clerk* 4*m*. Emp-
fangschef *m*, -dame *f*. **II** *adj* **5.** Schreibtisch...; Büro... '~top *adj*: ~ *computer*
Tischcomputer *m*.

des·o·late ['desələt] *adj* □ **1.** einsam,
verlassen. **2.** trostlos. **des·o·la·tion**
[~'leɪʃn] *s* **1.** Einsamkeit *f*, Verlassenheit *f*. **2.** Trostlosigkeit *f*.

de·spair [dɪ'speə] **I** *v/i* verzweifeln (*of* an
dat). **II** *s* Verzweiflung *f* (*at* über *acc*): *a
look of* ~ ein verzweifelter Blick; *drive
s.o. to* ~, *be the* ~ *of s.o.* j-n zur Verzweiflung bringen. **de'spair·ing** *adj* □
verzweifelt.

des·patch → *dispatch*.

des·per·ate ['despərət] *adj* □ **1.** verzweifelt (*Mensch, Anstrengung, Lage
etc*): ~ *deed* Verzweiflungstat *f*; *be* ~
for s.th. et. dringend nötig haben; *be* ~
to do s.th. et. unbedingt tun wollen; →

strait. **2.** F hoffnungslos, schrecklich.
des·per·a·tion [͵ˌespəˈreɪʃn] s Verzweiflung f: **in ~** verzweifelt; **drive s.o. to ~** j-n zur Verzweiflung bringen.
des·pi·ca·ble [dɪˈspɪkəbl] adj □ verachtenswert, verabscheuungswürdig.
de·spise [dɪˈspaɪz] v/t verachten, *Speise etc a.* verschmähen: **not to be ~d** nicht zu verachten.
de·spite [dɪˈspaɪt] prp trotz (gen od. dat).
de·spond·ent [dɪˈspɒndənt] adj □ mutlos, verzagt.
des·pot [ˈdespɒt] s Despot m. **des·pot·ic** adj (**~ally**) despotisch. **des·pot·ism** [ˈ~pətɪzəm] s Despotismus m.
des·sert [dɪˈzɜːt] **I** s Dessert n, Nachtisch m. **II** adj Dessert...: **~ wine.** **des·'sert-spoon** s Dessertlöffel m.
des·ti·na·tion [͵ˌdestɪˈneɪʃn] s **1.** Bestimmungsort m; Reiseziel n: **country of ~** Bestimmungsland n. **2.** Bestimmung f, (End)Zweck m, Ziel n. **des·tine** [ˈ~tɪn] v/t bestimmen, vorsehen (**for** für): **~d for** unterwegs nach (Schiff etc); **be ~d to** (inf) dazu bestimmt od. dafür vorgesehen sein zu (inf); **he was ~d to** (inf) er sollte (früh sterben etc). **des·ti·ny** s Schicksal n: **he met his ~** sein Schicksal ereilte ihn.
des·ti·tute [ˈdestɪtjuːt] adj **1.** mittellos, (völlig) verarmt. **2.** (**of**) bar (gen), ohne (acc). **͵des·ti·'tu·tion** s **1.** Mittellosigkeit f, (völlige) Armut. **2.** (völliger) Mangel (**of** an dat).
de·stroy [dɪˈstrɔɪ] v/t **1.** zerstören, *a. Insekten etc* vernichten. **2.** *Tier* töten, einschläfern. **3.** j-n, j-s Ruf, Gesundheit etc ruinieren, Hoffnungen etc zunichte machen, zerstören. **de·stroy·er** s **1.** Zerstörer(in), Vernichter(in). **2.** ⚓, ✕ Zerstörer m.
de·struc·tion [dɪˈstrʌkʃn] s **1.** Zerstörung f, Vernichtung f. **2.** Tötung f, Einschläferung f. **de·'struc·tive** adj □ **1.** zerstörend, vernichtend. **2.** schädlich, verderblich: **~ to health** gesundheitsschädlich. **3.** destruktiv (Kritik). **de·'struc·tive·ness** s zerstörende od. vernichtende Wirkung.
des·ul·to·ry [ˈdesəltərɪ] adj □ **1.** unzusammenhängend. **2.** oberflächlich.
de·tach [dɪˈtætʃ] v/t (ab-, los)trennen, (los)lösen, *a.* ☉ abnehmen (**from** von). **de·'tached** adj □ **1.** (ab)getrennt: **be-**

come ~ sich (los)lösen. **2.** einzeln, frei-, alleinstehend: **~ house** Einzelhaus n. **3.** separat, gesondert. **4.** fig. unvoreingenommen; uninteressiert (**about** an dat): distanziert. **de·'tach·ment** s **1.** (Ab-)Trennung f, (Los)Lösung f. **2.** fig. Unvoreingenommenheit f; Distanz f.
de·tail [ˈdiːteɪl] **I** s **1.** Detail n, Einzelheit f: **~s** pl Näheres n; (**down) to the smallest ~** bis ins kleinste Detail; **in ~** ausführlich, in allen Einzelheiten; **go into ~** ins einzelne gehen, auf Einzelheiten eingehen. **II** v/t **2.** ausführlich berichten; einzeln aufzählen od. -führen. **3.** ✕ abkommandieren (**for** zu). **'de·tailed** adj detailliert, ausführlich, eingehend.
de·tain [dɪˈteɪn] v/t **1.** j-n aufhalten. **2.** a. **~ in custody** ⚖️ in (Untersuchungs-) Haft behalten. **3.** ped. nachsitzen lassen.
de·tect [dɪˈtekt] v/t **1.** entdecken, (heraus)finden, ermitteln. **2.** wahrnehmen. **3.** Verbrechen etc aufdecken. **de·'tec·tion** s **1.** Entdeckung f, Ermittlung f. **2.** Wahrnehmung f. **3.** Aufdeckung f. **de·'tec·tive** [~tɪv] **I** adj Detektiv...: **~ story** (od. **novel**) Kriminalroman m. **II** s Detektiv m, Kriminalbeamte m. **de·'tec·tor** s ⚡ Detektor m.
dé·tente [deɪˈtɑ̃ːnt] s pol. Entspannung f.
de·ten·tion [dɪˈtenʃn] s **1.** ⚖️ Haft f: **~ (pending trial)** Untersuchungshaft. **2.** ped. Nachsitzen n: **keep in ~** → detain 3.
de·ter [dɪˈtɜː] v/t abschrecken (**from** von).
de·ter·gent [dɪˈtɜːdʒənt] s Reinigungs-, Wasch-, Geschirrspülmittel n.
de·te·ri·o·rate [dɪˈtɪərɪəreɪt] **I** v/i sich verschlechtern, schlechter werden, (Material) verderben. **II** v/t verschlechtern. **de͵te·ri·o·'ra·tion** s Verschlechterung f.
de·ter·mi·na·ble [dɪˈtɜːmɪnəbl] adj □ bestimmbar. **de·'ter·mi·nant** **I** adj **1.** bestimmend, entscheidend. **II** s **2.** entscheidender Faktor (**in** für). **3.** biol., A Determinante f. **de·'ter·mi·nate** [~nət] adj □ bestimmt, festgelegt. **de͵ter·mi·'na·tion** [~ˈneɪʃn] s **1.** Entschluß m. **2.** Bestimmung f, Festsetzung f. **3.** Feststellung f, Ermittlung f. **4.** Bestimmtheit f, Entschlossenheit f. **de·'ter·mine** **I** v/t **1.** Streitfrage etc ent-

scheiden. **2.** *et.* beschließen (*a.* **to do** zu tun), *Zeitpunkt etc* bestimmen, festsetzen. **3.** feststellen, ermitteln, bestimmen. **4.** *j-n* bestimmen, veranlassen (**to do** zu tun). **II** *v/i* **5.** (**on**) sich entscheiden (für), sich entschließen (zu). **de-'ter·mined** *adj* □ entschlossen.

de·ter·rence [dɪ'terəns] *s* Abschreckung *f.* **de·ter·rent I** *adj* abschreckend, Abschreckungs... **II** *s* Abschreckungsmittel *n* (**to** für).

de·test [dɪ'test] *v/t* verabscheuen, hassen: **~ having to do s.th.** es hassen, et. tun zu müssen. **de·'test·a·ble** *adj* □ abscheulich. **,de·tes·'ta·tion** [,diː~] *s* (**of**) Verabscheuung *f* (*gen*), Abscheu *m* (vor *dat*, gegen).

de·throne [dɪ'θrəʊn] *v/t* entthronen (*a. fig.*).

det·o·nate ['detəneɪt] **I** *v/t* zünden. **II** *v/i* detonieren, explodieren. **,det·o·'na·tion** *s* Detonation *f,* Explosion *f;* Zündung *f.* **'det·o·na·tor** *s* Zünd-, Sprengkapsel *f.*

de·tour ['diː,tʊə] **I** *s* **1.** Umweg *m:* **make a ~** → **3. 2.** Umleitung *f.* **II** *v/i* **3.** e-n Umweg machen. **III** *v/t* **4.** e-n Umweg machen um. **5.** *Verkehr etc* umleiten.

de·tract [dɪ'trækt] **I** *v/t Aufmerksamkeit etc* ablenken (**from** von). **II** *v/i* (**from**) Abbruch tun (*dat*), herabsetzen, schmälern (*acc*).

det·ri·ment ['detrɪmənt] *s* Nachteil *m,* Schaden *m* (**to** für): **to the ~ of** zum Nachteil *od.* Schaden (*gen*). **det·ri·men·tal** [,~'mentl] *adj* □ nachteilig, schädlich (**to** für).

de·tri·tus [dɪ'traɪtəs] *s geol.* Geröll *n,* Schutt *m.*

deuce [djuːs] *s* **1.** *Kartenspiel, Würfeln:* Zwei *f.* **2.** *Tennis:* Einstand *m.* **3.** F Teufel *m:* **who (what) the ~?** wer (was) zum Teufel?

de·val·u·ate [,diː'væljʊeɪt] *v/t* ✝ abwerten (**against** gegenüber). **,de·val·u·'a·tion** *s* Abwertung *f.* **,de·'val·ue** [,~juː] → **devaluate**.

dev·as·tate ['devəsteɪt] *v/t* verwüsten, -nichten. **'dev·as·tat·ing** *adj* □ **1.** verheerend, vernichtend (*a. Kritik etc*). **2.** F toll, phantastisch. **3.** F umwerfend (*Humor etc*). **,dev·as·'ta·tion** *s* Verwüstung *f.*

de·vel·op [dɪ'veləp] **I** *v/t* **1.** *phot. u. fig.*

allg. entwickeln. **2.** *Krankheit, Fieber* bekommen. **3.** *Naturschätze, Bauland* erschließen, *Altstadt etc* sanieren. **II** *v/i* **4.** sich entwickeln (**from** aus; **into** zu). **de·'vel·op·er** *s* **1.** *phot.* Entwickler *m* (*a. Flüssigkeit*). **2.** *late* **~** *bsd. ped.* Spätentwickler *m.* **3.** (Stadt)Planer *m.* **de·'vel·op·ing** *adj* Entwicklungs...: **~ country.** **de·'vel·op·ment** *s* **1.** Entwicklung *f:* **~ aid** ✝ Entwicklungshilfe *f;* **~ country** ✝ Entwicklungsland *n.* **2.** Erschließung *f,* Sanierung *f.*

de·vi·ate ['diːvɪeɪt] *v/i* abweichen (**from** von). **,de·vi·'a·tion** *s* Abweichung *f.* **,de·vi·'a·tion·ist** [,~ʃənɪst] *s pol.* Abweichler(in).

de·vice [dɪ'vaɪs] *s* **1.** Vorrichtung *f,* Gerät *n.* **2.** Einfall *m;* Kunstgriff *m,* Trick *m:* **leave s.o. to his own ~s** j-n sich selbst überlassen.

dev·il ['devl] **I** *s* **1.** Teufel *m:* **poor ~** armer Teufel *od.* Schlucker; **be between the ~ and the deep blue sea** sich zwischen zwei Feuern befinden, in e-r bösen Zwickmühle sein *od.* sitzen; **like the ~** F wie der Teufel, wie verrückt; **go to the ~** F vor die Hunde gehen; **go to the ~!** scher dich zum Teufel!; **speak (od. talk) of the ~** wenn man vom Teufel spricht!; **who (what) the ~?** F wer (was) zum Teufel? **2.** *a.* **~ of a fellow** F Teufelskerl *m.* **II** *v/t pret u. pp* **-iled,** *bsd. Br.* **-illed 3.** F schikanieren, piesacken. **'dev·il·ish** *adj* □ **1.** teuflisch. **2.** (*a. adv*) F verteufelt, höllisch.

,dev·il-may-'care *adj* leichtsinnig.

dev·il·ry ['devlrɪ] *s* **1.** Teufelei *f.* **2.** Übermut *m.*

de·vi·ous ['diːvjəs] *adj* □ **1.** abwegig, falsch. **2.** gewunden (*a. fig.*): **~ route** Umweg *m.* **3.** verschlagen, unaufrichtig: **by ~ means** auf krummen Wegen.

de·vise [dɪ'vaɪz] *v/t* (sich) ausdenken, ersinnen.

de·void [dɪ'vɔɪd] *adj:* **~ of** ohne (*acc*), bar (*gen*), ...los.

dev·o·lu·tion [,diːvə'luːʃn] *s* **1.** Übertragung *f.* **2.** *pol.* Dezentralisierung *f.* **de·volve** [dɪ'vɒlv] **I** *v/t Rechte etc* übertragen (**on** *dat od.* auf *acc*). **II** *v/i* (**on, to**) übergehen (auf *acc*), zufallen (*dat*).

de·vote [dɪ'vəʊt] *v/t Zeit etc* widmen (**to** *dat*): **~ o.s. to** sich *j-m* widmen, sich e-r

Sache widmen *od.* verschreiben. **de·'vot·ed** *adj* □ hingebungsvoll: a) aufopfernd, b) anhänglich, c) eifrig, begeistert. **dev·o·tee** [ˌdevəʊˈtiː] *s* begeisterter Anhänger; glühender Verehrer *od.* Verfechter. **de·vo·tion** [dɪˈvəʊʃn] *s* **1.** Hingabe *f:* a) Aufopferung *f,* b) Anhänglichkeit *f.* **2.** Frömmigkeit *f: ~s pl* Gebet *n,* Andacht *f.*

de·vour [dɪˈvaʊə] *v/t* **1.** Essen, *fig. Buch etc* verschlingen. **2.** *fig. j-n* verzehren (*Leidenschaft etc*).

de·vout [dɪˈvaʊt] *adj* □ **1.** fromm. **2.** innig. **3.** herzlich.

dew [djuː] *s* Tau *m.* **1.** *~·drop s* **1.** Tautropfen *m.* **2.** *Br. humor.* Nasentropfen *m.* **dew·y** [ˈdjuːɪ] *adj* □ taufeucht, *a. fig.* taufrisch. *'~·eyed adj* blauäugig, naiv.

dex·ter·i·ty [dekˈsterətɪ] *s* Gewandtheit *f,* Geschicklichkeit *f.* **dex·ter·ous** ['~stərəs] *adj* □ gewandt, geschickt.

dex·trose [ˈdekstrəʊs] *s* Traubenzucker *m.*

dex·trous [ˈdekstrəs] → **dexterous**.

di·a·be·tes [ˌdaɪəˈbiːtiːz] *s* ♀ Diabetes *m,* Zuckerkrankheit *f: suffer from ~* Zucker haben. **di·a·bet·ic** [ˌ~ˈbetɪk] **I** *adj* diabetisch: a) zuckerkrank, b) Diabetes...: *~ chocolate* Diabetikerschokolade *f.* **II** *s* Diabetiker(in).

di·a·bol·ic, di·a·bol·i·cal [ˌdaɪəˈbɒlɪk(l)] *adj* □ **1.** diabolisch, teuflisch. **2.** F scheußlich, widerlich.

di·a·dem [ˈdaɪədem] *s* Diadem *n.*

di·ag·nose [ˈdaɪəgnəʊz] *v/t* ♀ diagnostizieren (*as* als) (*a. fig.*). **,di·ag'no·sis** [ˌ~sɪs] *pl* **-ses** [ˌ~siːz] *s* Diagnose *f* (*a. fig.*): *give* (*od. make*) *a ~* e-e Diagnose stellen.

di·ag·o·nal [daɪˈægənl] **I** *adj* □ diagonal. **II** *s* ♀ Diagonale *f.*

di·a·gram [ˈdaɪəgræm] *s* Diagramm *n,* graphische Darstellung.

di·al [ˈdaɪəl] **I** *s* **1.** *a. ~ plate* Zifferblatt *n* (*Uhr*). **2.** *a. ~ plate* ⊙ Skala *f,* Skalenscheibe *f.* **3.** *teleph.* Wählscheibe *f.* **4.** *Br. sl.* Visage *f* (*Gesicht*). **II** *v/t pret u. pp* **-aled,** *bsd. Br.* **-alled 5.** *teleph. Nummer* wählen, *Stadt* anwählen. **III** *v/i* **6.** *teleph.* wählen: *~ direct* durchwählen (*to* nach).

di·a·lect [ˈdaɪəlekt] *s* Dialekt *m,* Mundart *f.* **,di·a'lec·tal** *adj* □ Dialekt..., mundartlich.

di·al·ling| code [ˈdaɪəlɪŋ] *s teleph. Br.* Vorwahl(nummer) *f.* **~ tone** *s teleph. Br.* Wählton *m,* -zeichen *n.*

di·a·logue, *Am. a.* **di·a·log** [ˈdaɪəlɒg] *s* Dialog *m.*

di·al tone *Am.* → **dialling tone**.

di·am·e·ter [daɪˈæmɪtə] *s* Durchmesser *m: be ... in ~* e-n Durchmesser von ... haben.

di·a·met·ri·cal [ˌdaɪəˈmetrɪkl] *adj* □ **1.** diametrisch. **2.** *fig.* diametral, genau entgegengesetzt.

di·a·mond [ˈdaɪəmənd] *s* **1.** *min.* Diamant *m:* → **rough 4. 2.** ♀ Raute *f,* Rhombus *m.* **3.** *Kartenspiel:* a) *pl* Karo *n* (*Farbe*), b) Karo(karte *f*) *n. ~·cut·ter s* Diamantschleifer *m. ~ wed·ding s* diamantene Hochzeit.

di·a·per [ˈdaɪəpə] *s Am.* Windel *f.*

di·a·phragm [ˈdaɪəfræm] *s* **1.** *anat.* Zwerchfell *n.* **2.** *teleph. etc* Membran(e) *f.* **3.** *opt. phot.* Blende *f.*

di·ar·rh(o)e·a [ˌdaɪəˈrɪə] *s* ♀ Durchfall *m.*

di·a·ry [ˈdaɪərɪ] *s* **1.** Tagebuch *n.* **2.** Notizbuch *n,* Taschenkalender *m.* **3.** Terminkalender *m.*

dice [daɪs] **I** *s* **1.** *pl von* **die². 2.** *pl* **dice** → **die². II** *v/t* **3.** *gastr.* in Würfel schneiden. **4.** mit *j-m* würfeln *od.* knobeln (*for* um). **III** *v/i* **5.** würfeln, knobeln (*for* um): *~ with death* mit s-m Leben spielen. *~ cup s* Würfel-, Knobelbecher *m.*

dic·ey [ˈdaɪsɪ] *adj* F prekär, heikel (*Situation etc*).

dick [dɪk] *s* **1.** *bsd. Br. sl.* Kerl *m:* → **clever 1. 2.** *bsd. Am. sl.* Schnüffler *m* (*Detektiv*).

dick·ens [ˈdɪkɪnz] *s* F Teufel *m: who* (*what*) *the ~?* wer (was) zum Teufel?

dick·er [ˈdɪkə] *v/i* feilschen, schachern (*with* mit; *for* um).

dick·(e)y [ˈdɪkɪ] *adj* F schwach (*Herz*), wack(e)lig (*Leiter etc*).

dic·tate [dɪkˈteɪt] **I** *v/t* (*to dat*) **1.** *Brief etc* diktieren. **2.** diktieren: a) vorschreiben, b) aufzwingen. **II** *v/i* **3.** *~ to s.o.* j-m Vorschriften machen. **III** *s* [ˈdɪkteɪt] **4.** Gebot *n,* Diktat *n.* **dic'ta·tion** *s* Diktat *n.* **dic'ta·tor** *s* Diktator *m.* **dic·ta·to·ri·al** [ˌ~təˈtɔːrɪəl] *adj* □ diktatorisch. **dic·'ta·tor·ship** *s* Diktatur *f.*

dic·tion [ˈdɪkʃn] *s* Diktion *f,* Ausdrucksweise *f,* Sprache *f.*

dic·tion·ar·y ['dɪkʃənrɪ] s Wörterbuch n.

did [dɪd] pret von **do**.

di·dac·tic [dɪ'dæktɪk] adj (**~ally**) didaktisch.

did·dle ['dɪdl] v/t F betrügen (**out of** um), übers Ohr hauen.

didn't ['dɪdnt] F = **did not**.

die¹ [daɪ] I v/i (pres p dying) **1.** sterben (**of** an dat): **~ of hunger** (**thirst**) verhungern (verdursten); **never say ~!** nur nicht nach- od. aufgeben! **2.** eingehen (Pflanze, Tier), verenden (Tier). **3. be dying** (**for; to do**) sich sehnen (nach; danach, zu tun), brennen (auf acc; darauf, zu tun). II v/t **4.** e-s Todes sterben: → **natural** 1, **violent** 2.

Verbindungen mit Adverbien:

die| a·way v/i sich legen (Wind), verhallen, -klingen (Ton). **~ down** v/i **1.** → **die away**. **2.** sich legen (Aufregung etc). **~ out** v/i aussterben (a. fig.).

die² [~] s Würfel m (a. gastr. etc): **the ~ is cast** fig. die Würfel sind gefallen.

die·sel ['di:zl] I s Diesel m (Motor, Fahrzeug, Kraftstoff). II adj Diesel...

di·et ['daɪət] I s **1.** Nahrung f, Ernährung f, Kost f. **2.** ♣ Diät f: **be** (**put**) **on a ~** auf Diät gesetzt sein, diät leben (müssen). II v/t **3.** j-n auf Diät setzen: **~ o.s.** → **4.** II v/i **4.** Diät halten, diät leben.

dif·fer ['dɪfə] v/i **1.** sich unterscheiden, verschieden sein (**from** von). **2.** auseinandergehen (Meinungen). **3.** (**from, with**) nicht übereinstimmen (mit), anderer Meinung sein (als): → **agree** 1. **4.** sich nicht einig sein (**on, about, over** über acc). **dif·fer·ence** ['dɪfrəns] s **1.** Unterschied m: a) Unterscheidung f: **make no ~ between** keinen Unterschied machen zwischen (dat); **make no ~** nichts ausmachen (**to** dat), b) Verschiedenheit f: **~ of opinion** Meinungsverschiedenheit, c) Differenz f (a. ♣): → **in price**, **price ~** Preisunterschied; → **split** 2. **2.** Differenz f, Meinungsverschiedenheit f. **3.** Besonderheit f: **with a ~** (von) ganz besonderer Art, mit Pfiff. **'dif·fer·ent** adj ☐ **1.** verschieden(artig). **2.** (**from**) verschieden (von), anders (als): **he is ~** er ist anders. **dif·fer·en·tial** [ˌdɪfə'renʃl] I adj ☐ **1.** unterschiedlich. **2.** ♣, ⚙, etc Differential...: **~ calculus** Differentialrechnung f; **~**

gear → 4. II s 3. ♣ Differential n. **4.** ⚙ Differential-, Ausgleichsgetriebe n. **dif·fer·en·ti·ate** [~ʃɪeɪt] I v/t **1.** unterscheiden (**from** von); voneinander unterscheiden. II v/i **2.** sich unterscheiden (**from** von). **3.** differenzieren, unterscheiden (**between** zwischen dat). **dif·fer·en·ti·a·tion** s Differenzierung f, Unterscheidung f.

dif·fi·cult ['dɪfɪkəlt] adj schwierig (a. Person), schwer: **it was quite ~ for me to** inf es fiel mir schwer, zu inf. **'dif·fi·cul·ty** s **1.** Schwierigkeit f: a) Mühe f, Plage f: **with ~** mühsam, (nur) schwer; **have ~** (**in**) **doing s.th.** Mühe haben, et. zu tun, b) schwierige Sache, c) Hindernis n, Widerstand m: **make** (od. **raise**) **difficulties** Schwierigkeiten machen. **2.** mst pl (a. Geld)Schwierigkeiten pl, Verlegenheit f.

dif·fi·dence ['dɪfɪdəns] s Schüchternheit f, Mangel m an Selbstvertrauen. **'dif·fi·dent** adj ☐ schüchtern, ohne Selbstvertrauen: **be ~ about doing s.th.** et. nur zögernd od. zaghaft tun.

dif·fuse I v/t u. v/i [dɪ'fju:z] **1.** bsd. fig. (sich) verbreiten: **a widely ~d opinion** e-e weitverbreitete Meinung. **2.** ♣, phys. (sich) zerstreuen. II adj [~s] **3.** diffus: a) weitschweifig, langatmig (Stil, Autor), b) unklar, ungeordnet (Gedanken etc), c) ♣, phys. zerstreut: **~ light** diffuses Licht, Streulicht n. **dif·fu·sion** [~ʒn] s bsd. fig. Verbreitung f. **2.** ♣, phys. (Zer)Streuung f.

dig [dɪg] I s **1.** Puff m, Stoß m: **~ in the ribs** Rippenstoß m. **2.** fig. (Seiten)Hieb m (**at** auf acc). **3.** pl Br. F Bude f. II v/t (irr) **4.** Loch etc graben: **~** (**up**) umgraben; **~** (**up** od. **out**) ausgraben (a. fig.); → **grave²**. **5.** j-m e-n Stoß geben: **~ s.o. in the ribs** j-m e-n Rippenstoß geben. **6.** F kapieren. **7.** F stehen od. abfahren auf (acc). III v/i **8.** (**for**) graben (nach); fig. forschen (nach). **9.** **~ in(to)** F reinhauen (in e-n Kuchen etc). **10.** Br. F s-e Bude haben, wohnen.

di·gest [dɪ'dʒest] I v/t verdauen (a. fig.). II v/i sich verdauen lassen: **~ well** leicht verdaulich sein. III s ['daɪdʒest] (**of**) Auslese f (a. Zeitschrift), Auswahl f (aus); Abriß m (der, fig.). **di·gest·i·ble** [dɪ'dʒestəbl] adj verdaulich. **di'ges·tion** s Verdauung f (a. fig.). **di'ges·tive**

I *adj* □ **1.** verdauungsfördernd. **2.** Verdauungs...: **~ system** Verdauungs-
apparat *m*; **~ tract** Verdauungstrakt *m*.
II *s* **3.** ♂ verdauungsförderndes Mittel.

dig·ger ['dɪɡə] *s* **1.** (*bsd.* Gold)Gräber *m*;
Erdarbeiter *m*. **2.** Grabgerät *n*, -ma-
schine *f*.

dig·it ['dɪdʒɪt] *s* **1.** *anat. zo.* Finger *m*,
Zehe *f*. **2.** ♐ Ziffer *f*; Stelle *f*. **dig·i·tal**
['~tl] *adj* **1.** Finger...: **~ telephone**
Tastentelefon *n*. **2.** Digital...: **~ clock**
(*watch*), **~ computer** Digitalrechner *m*.

dig·ni·fied ['dɪɡnɪfaɪd] *adj* würdevoll,
würdig. **dig·ni·fy** ['~faɪ] *v/t* Würde verleihen (*dat*).

dig·ni·tar·y ['dɪɡnɪtərɪ] *s* Würdenträ-
ger(in). **'dig·ni·ty** *s* **1.** Rang *m*, (hohe)
Stellung. **2.** Würde *f*: → **beneath** 3.

di·gress [daɪ'ɡres] *v/i* abschweifen (*from*
von; *into* in *acc*). **di'gres·sion** *s* Ab-
schweifung *f*.

dike¹ [daɪk] **I** *s* **1.** Deich *m*, Damm *m*. **2.**
Graben *m*. **II** *v/t* **3.** eindämmen, -dei-
chen.

dike² [~] *s sl.* Lesbe *f* (*Lesbierin*).

di·lap·i·dat·ed [dɪ'læpɪdeɪtɪd] *adj* verfallen, baufällig (*Haus etc*), klapp(e)rig
(*Auto etc*).

di·late [daɪ'leɪt] **I** *v/t u. v/i* (sich) ausdehnen *od.* (-)weiten *od.* erweitern: **with ~d
eyes** mit aufgerissenen Augen; **his
eyes ~d with terror** s-e Augen weiteten
sich vor Entsetzen. **II** *v/i*: **~ on** *fig.* sich
(ausführlich) verbreiten *od.* auslassen
über (*acc*).

dil·a·to·ry ['dɪlətərɪ] *adj* □ **1.** verzö-
gernd, hinhaltend: **~ tactics** *pl* Verzö-
gerungs-, Verschleppungs-, Hinhaltetaktik *f*. **2.** langsam: **be ~ in doing s.th.**
sich mit et. Zeit lassen.

di·lem·ma [dɪ'lemə] *s* Dilemma *n*, Klemme *f*: **be on the horns of a ~** in e-r
Zwickmühle sein *od.* sitzen.

dil·et·tante [,dɪlɪ'tæntɪ] *mst contr.* **I** *pl* **-ti**
[~tiː], **-tes** Dilettant(in). **II** *adj* dilettantisch.

dil·i·gence ['dɪlɪdʒəns] *s* **1.** Fleiß *m*. **2.**
Sorgfalt *f*. **'dil·i·gent** *adj* □ **1.** fleißig. **2.**
sorgfältig, gewissenhaft.

dill [dɪl] *s* ♣ Dill *m*.

dil·ly·dal·ly ['dɪlɪdælɪ] *v/i* F (herum)trö-
deln.

di·lute [daɪ'ljuːt] **I** *v/t* **1.** verdünnen. **2.**
fig. verwässern, abschwächen. **II** *adj* **3.**

verdünnt. **4.** *fig.* verwässert, abge-
schwächt. **di'lu·tion** *s* **1.** Verdünnung *f*.
2. *fig.* Verwässerung *f*, Abschwächung
f.

dim [dɪm] **I** *adj* □ **1.** (halb)dunkel, düster
(*a. fig.*): → **view** 4. **2.** undeutlich, verschwommen, schwach. **3.** schwach,
trüb (*Licht*): **~ly lit** schwacherleuchtet.
4. matt (*Farbe*). **5.** *fig.* schwer von Begriff. **II** *v/t* **6.** verdunkeln, -düstern. **7.**
trüben (*a. fig.*). **8.** *a.* **~ out** Licht abblenden: **~ the headlights** *mot. Am.* abblenden. **III** *v/i* **9.** sich verdunkeln *od.* -dü-
stern. **10.** undeutlich werden. **11.** sich
trüben (*a. fig.*).

dime [daɪm] *s Am.* Zehncentstück *n*: **~
novel** Groschenroman *m*.

di·men·sion [dɪ'menʃn] *s* Dimension *f*
(*a. fig.*): a) Ausdehnung *f*, Maß *n*, Abmessung *f*, b) *pl oft* fig. Ausmaß *n*,
Umfang *m*. **di'men·sion·al** [~ʃənl] *adj*
□ *in Zssgn*: ...dimensional.

di·min·ish [dɪ'mɪnɪʃ] *v/t u. v/i* (sich) vermindern *od.* verringern: **~ in numbers**
weniger werden; **~ in value** an Wert
verlieren. **dim·i·nu·tion** [,dɪmɪ'njuːʃn] *s*
Verminderung *f*, Verringerung *f*. **di-
'min·u·tive** [~juːtɪv] **I** *adj* **1.** klein, winzig. **2.** *ling.* Diminutiv..., Verkleine-
rungs... **II** *s* **3.** *ling.* Diminutiv *n*, Ver-
kleinerungsform *f od.* -silbe *f*.

dim·mer ['dɪmə] *s* **1.** Dimmer *m* (*Hellig-
keitsregler*). **2.** *pl mot. Am.* Abblend-
od. Standlicht *n*. **'dim·ness** *s* **1.** Dunkelheit *f*, Düsterkeit *f*. **2.** Undeutlich-
keit *f*. **3.** Mattheit *f*.

dim·ple ['dɪmpl] *s* Grübchen *n*.

din [dɪn] **I** *s* Lärm *m*, Getöse *n*: **kick up**
(*od.* **make**) **a ~** Krach machen. **II** *v/t*: **~
s.th. into s.o.** j-m et. einhämmern. **III**
v/i lärmen, (*Motoren etc*) dröhnen (*in
s.o.'s ears* j-m in den Ohren).

dine [daɪn] **I** *v/i* speisen, essen (*off, on
acc*): **~ in** (*out*) zu Hause (auswärts)
essen. **II** *v/t* bewirten. **'din·er** *s* **1.** Spei-
sende *m, f*. **2.** Gast *m* (*im Restaurant*).
3. ♛ Speisewagen *m*. **4.** *Am.* Eß-, Spei-
selokal *n*. **di·nette** [daɪ'net] *s* Eßecke
f.

din·ghy ['dɪŋɡɪ] *s* **1.** ♕ Ding(h)i *n*; Beiboot *n*. **2.** Schlauchboot *n*.

din·gy ['dɪndʒɪ] *adj* □ schmutzig,
schmudd(e)lig.

din·ing| car ['daɪnɪŋ] *s* ♛ Speisewagen

m. **~ room** *s* Speise-, Eßzimmer *n.* **~ ta·ble** *s* Eßtisch *m.*

dink·y ['dɪŋkɪ] *adj* F **1.** *Br.* niedlich. **2.** *Am.* klein, unbedeutend.

din·ner ['dɪnə] *s* **1.** (Mittag-, Abend-) Essen *n* (*Hauptmahlzeit*): *after ~* nach dem Essen, nach Tisch; *at ~* bei Tisch. **2.** Diner *n*, Festessen *n*: *at a ~* auf *od.* bei e-m Diner. **~ coat** *s bsd. Am.*, **~ jack·et** *s* Smoking *m.* **~ par·ty** *s* Diner *n*, Abendgesellschaft *f.* **~ ser·vice**, **~ set** *s* Speiseservice *n*, Tafelgeschirr *n.* **~ ta·ble** *s* Eßtisch *m.* '**~·time** *s* Essens-, Tischzeit *f.*

di·no·saur ['daɪnəʊsɔː] *s zo.* Dinosaurier *m.*

di·o·cese ['daɪəsɪs] *s eccl.* Diözese *f.*

di·ode ['daɪəʊd] *s ⚡* Diode *f.*

di·ox·ide [daɪ'ɒksaɪd] *s 🜛* Dioxyd *n.*

dip [dɪp] **I** *v/t* **1.** (ein)tauchen (*in, into* in *acc*): *~ one's hand into one's pocket* in die Tasche greifen. **2.** *~ the headlights mot. bsd. Br.* abblenden. **II** *v/i* **3.** unter-, eintauchen. **4.** *~ into* a) sich flüchtig befassen mit, e-n Blick werfen in (*ein Buch etc*), b) Reserven etc angreifen: *~ into one's pocket* (*od. purse*) *fig.* tief in die Tasche greifen. **III** *s* **5.** (Unter-, Ein)Tauchen *n.* **6.** kurzes Bad: *have a ~* mal schnell ins Wasser springen.

diph·the·ri·a [dɪf'θɪərɪə] *s ⚕* Diphtherie *f.*

diph·thong ['dɪfθɒŋ] Diphthong *m*, Doppelvokal *m.*

di·plo·ma [dɪ'pləʊmə] *s* Diplom *n.*

di·plo·ma·cy [dɪ'pləʊməsɪ] *s pol.* Diplomatie *f* (*a. fig.*). **dip·lo·mat** ['dɪpləmæt] *s* Diplomat *m.* '**dip·lo·mat·ic** *adj* (*~ally*) diplomatisch: *~ corps* (*a. body*) diplomatisches Korps; *~ relations pl* diplomatische Beziehungen *pl.*

'**dip·stick** *s* (*Öl- etc*)Meßstab *m.*

dire ['daɪə] *adj* **1.** gräßlich, schrecklich. **2.** äußerst, höchst: *be in ~ need of s.th.* et. ganz dringend brauchen; *~ strait.*

di·rect [dɪ'rekt] **I** *v/t* **1.** *Aufmerksamkeit etc* richten, lenken (*to, toward*[s] auf *acc*): *~ away j-n, et.* ablenken (*from* von). **2.** *Betrieb etc* führen, leiten; Regie führen bei (*e-m Film od. Stück*): *~ed by* unter der Regie von. **3.** *Worte* richten, *Brief etc* adressieren, richten (*to* an *acc*). **4.** anweisen, beauftragen, *j-m* Anweisung geben (*to do* zu tun).

5. anordnen, verfügen: *~ s.th. to be done* anordnen, daß et. geschieht. **6.** (*to*) *j-m* den Weg zeigen (zu, nach); *fig. j-n* verweisen (an *acc*). **II** *adj* □ **7.** direkt, gerade. **8.** direkt, unmittelbar: *~ current ⚡* Gleichstrom *m*; *~ flight* Direktflug *m*; *~ train* durchgehender Zug. **9.** direkt, genau: *the ~ contrary* das genaue Gegenteil. **10.** *ling.* *~ speech* (*bsd. Am. discourse*) direkte Rede; *~ object* direktes Objekt, Akkusativobjekt *n.* **III** *adv* **11.** direkt, unmittelbar: *→ dial* 6. **di·rec·tion** *s* **1.** Richtung *f*: *in the ~ of* in Richtung auf (*acc*) *od.* nach; *from* (*in*) *all ~s* aus (nach) allen Richtungen *od.* Seiten; *sense of ~* Orts-, Orientierungssinn *m*; *~ indicator mot.* (Fahrt)Richtungsanzeiger *m*, Blinker *m.* **2.** Führung *f*, Leitung *f*; (*Film etc*) Regie *f.* **3.** Anweisung *f*, Anleitung *f*: *~s pl for use* Gebrauchsanweisung. **4.** Anweisung *f*, Anordnung *f*: *by* (*od. at*) *~ of* auf Anweisung von (*od. gen*). **di·rec·tion·al** [*~ʃənl*] *adj* **1.** Richtungs... **2.** *⚡* Peil...; Richt...: *~ aerial* (*bsd. Am. antenna*) Richtantenne *f.* **di·rec·tive** *s* Direktive *f*, Anweisung *f.* **di·rec·tor** *s* **1.** Direktor *m* (*a. 🜊*), Leiter *m*: *~'s secretary* Chefsekretärin *f*; *~-general* Generaldirektor. **2.** *Film etc*: Regisseur *m.* **di·rec·to·rate** [*~rət*] *s* **1.** Direktorat *n*, Direktor-, Direktorenposten *m.* **2.** Direktorium *n.* **di·rec·tor·ship** *s* → **directorate** 1. **di·rec·to·ry** *s* Adreßbuch *n*; Telefonbuch *n*; Branchenverzeichnis *n.* **di·rec·tress** *s* Direktorin *f*, Leiterin *f.*

dirt [dɜːt] *s* Schmutz *m* (*a. fig.*), Dreck *m*: *fling* (*od. throw*) *~ at s.o. fig. j-n* mit Schmutz bewerfen; *treat s.o. like ~ j-n* wie (den letzten) Dreck behandeln. '**,~·cheap** *adj u. adv* F spottbillig. **~ road** *s Am.* unbefestigte Straße.

dirt·y ['dɜːtɪ] **I** *adj* □ **1.** schmutzig (*a. fig.*), dreckig: *~ look* böser Blick; *~ mind* schmutzige Gedanken *pl*; schmutzige Phantasie; *~ word* Reizwort *n*; *~ work* Dreck(s)arbeit *f* (*a. fig.*); *→ linen* 2. **2.** gemein, niederträchtig: *→ trick* 1. **3.** schlecht, *bsd. ♣* stürmisch (*Wetter*). **II** *v/t* **4.** beschmutzen (*a. fig.*): *~ one's hands* sich die Hände schmutzig machen (*a. fig.*). **III** *v/i* **5.** schmutzig werden, schmutzen.

dis·a·bil·i·ty [ˌdɪsəˈbɪlətɪ] s **1.** Unvermögen n, Unfähigkeit f. **2.** Arbeits-, Erwerbsunfähigkeit f, Invalidität f: **~ benefit** Invaliditätsrente f. **3.** ⚕ Gebrechen n.

dis·a·ble [dɪsˈeɪbl] v/t **1.** unfähig machen, außerstand setzen (**from doing** zu tun). **2.** unbrauchbar od. untauglich machen (**for** für, zu). **3.** arbeits- od. erwerbsunfähig machen. **dis'a·bled** adj **1.** arbeits-, erwerbsunfähig, invalid. **2.** kriegsversehrt. **3.** (körperlich od. geistig) behindert. **dis'a·ble·ment** s **1.** → **disability** 2. **2.** (körperliche od. geistige) Behinderung.

dis·ad·van·tage [ˌdɪsədˈvɑːntɪdʒ] **I** s Nachteil m (**to** für): **to s.o.'s ~** zu j-s Nachteil od. Schaden; **be at a ~** im Nachteil od. benachteiligt sein; **put at a ~** od. **sell at a ~** mit Verlust verkaufen. **II** v/t benachteiligen. **dis·ad·van·ta·geous** [ˌ~ædvɑːnˈteɪdʒəs] adj □ nachteilig, ungünstig, unvorteilhaft (**to** für).

dis·af·fect·ed [ˌdɪsəˈfektɪd] adj □ unzufrieden (**to, toward[s]** mit), verdrossen. **ˌdis·af'fec·tion** s Unzufriedenheit f, (a. Staats)Verdrossenheit f.

dis·a·gree [ˌdɪsəˈɡriː] v/i **1.** (**with**) nicht übereinstimmen (mit), im Widerspruch stehen (zu). **2.** (**with**) anderer Meinung sein (als), nicht zustimmen (dat). **3.** (sich) streiten (**on, about** über acc). **4.** nicht einverstanden sein (**with** mit). **5.** nicht bekommen (**with** dat) (Essen). **dis·a·gree·a·ble** [ˌ~ˈɡrɪəbl] adj □ unangenehm. **ˌdis·a'gree·ment** s **1.** Unstimmigkeit f, Verschiedenheit f: **be in ~ (with)** → **disagree** 1. **2.** Widerspruch m (**between** zwischen dat). **3.** Meinungsverschiedenheit f (**over, on** über acc).

dis·al·low [ˌdɪsəˈlaʊ] v/t nicht anerkennen, nicht gelten lassen.

dis·ap·pear [ˌdɪsəˈpɪə] v/i verschwinden (**from** von, aus): → **thin** 1. **ˌdis·ap'pear·ance** s Verschwinden n.

dis·ap·point [ˌdɪsəˈpɔɪnt] v/t j-n enttäuschen, j-s Hoffnungen etc a. zunichte machen: **be ~ed** enttäuscht sein (**in, at** s.th. von, über acc; **in, with** s.o. von). **ˌdis·ap'point·ment** s Enttäuschung f.

dis·ap·prov·al [ˌdɪsəˈpruːvl] s (**of**) Mißbilligung f (gen), Mißfallen n (über

acc): **in ~** mißbilligend. **ˌdis·ap'prove I** v/t mißbilligen. **II** v/i dagegen sein: **~ of** → I.

dis·arm [dɪsˈɑːm] **I** v/t entwaffnen (a. fig.). **II** v/i ✕, pol. abrüsten. **dis'ar·ma·ment** s **1.** Entwaffnung f. **2.** ✕, pol. Abrüstung f. **dis'arm·ing** adj □ fig. entwaffnend.

dis·ar·range [ˌdɪsəˈreɪndʒ] v/t in Unordnung bringen, durcheinanderbringen (beide a. fig.).

dis·ar·ray [ˌdɪsəˈreɪ] **I** v/t in Unordnung bringen (a. fig.). **II** s Unordnung f (a. fig.).

dis·as·sem·ble [ˌdɪsəˈsembl] v/t auseinandernehmen, zerlegen, demontieren. **ˌdis·as'sem·bly** s **1.** Zerlegung f, Demontage f. **2.** zerlegter Zustand.

dis·as·ter [dɪˈzɑːstə] s **1.** Unglück n (**to** für). **2.** Unglück n, Katastrophe f: **~ area** Katastrophengebiet n. **dis'as·trous** adj □ katastrophal, verheerend.

dis·be·lief [ˌdɪsbɪˈliːf] s **1.** Unglaube m. **2.** Zweifel m (**in** an dat). **dis·be·lieve** [ˌ~ˈliːv] **I** v/t nicht glauben, bezweifeln; j-m nicht glauben. **II** v/i nicht glauben (**in** an dat). **ˌdis·be'liev·er** s Ungläubige m, f (a. eccl.).

dis·bur·den [dɪsˈbɜːdn] v/t entlasten (**of, from** von): **~ one's mind** sein Herz ausschütten od. erleichtern.

dis·burse [dɪsˈbɜːs] v/t **1.** Geld aus(be)zahlen. **2.** Geld auslegen, verauslagen.

disc, etc → **disk,** etc.

dis·card I v/t [dɪˈskɑːd] **1.** Spielkarten ablegen, Kleidung etc a. ausrangieren, Gewohnheit etc a. aufgeben. **2.** Freund etc fallenlassen. **II** s [ˈdɪskɑːd] **3.** abgelegte Karte(n pl). **4.** et. Abgelegtes.

dis·cern [dɪˈsɜːn] v/t wahrnehmen, erkennen. **dis'cern·ing** adj □ scharfsichtig, kritisch (urteilend). **dis'cern·ment** s **1.** Wahrnehmen n, Erkennen n. **2.** Scharfblick m.

dis·charge [dɪsˈtʃɑːdʒ] **I** v/t **1.** ausladen: a) Schiff etc entladen, b) Ladung löschen, c) Passagiere ausschiffen. **2.** Gewehr, Geschoß etc abfeuern, abschießen. **3. ~ itself** → 9. **4.** ausströmen, -stoßen, ⚕, physiol. absondern: **~ matter** eitern. **5.** Angestellten, Patienten, Strafgefangene etc entlassen (**from** aus). **6.** ⚖ freisprechen (**of** von). **7.** befreien, entbinden (**of, from** von; **from**

doing s.th. davon, et. zu tun). **8.** *Verpflichtungen etc* erfüllen, nachkommen (*dat*). **II** *v/i* **9.** sich ergießen, münden (*into* in *acc*). **10.** 🎇 eitern. **11.** ⚡ sich entladen. **III** *s* ['ˌtʃɑːdʒ] **12.** Entladung *f*; Löschung *f*. **13.** Abfeuern *n*. **14.** 🎇, *physiol.* Absonderung *f*. **15.** Entlassung *f*. **16.** 🏛 Freisprechung *f*. **17.** Befreiung *f*, Entbindung *f*. **18.** Erfüllung *f*.

dis·ci ['dɪskaɪ] *pl von* **discus.**

dis·ci·ple [dɪ'saɪpl] *s Bibl.* Jünger *m*, *fig. a.* Schüler *m*.

dis·ci·pli·na·ry ['dɪsɪplɪnərɪ] *adj* disziplinarisch, Disziplinar... '**dis·ci·pline I** *s* **1.** Disziplin *f*: *keep* ~ Disziplin halten. **2.** Disziplin *f*, Wissenschaftszweig *m*. **II** *v/t* **3.** disziplinieren, an Disziplin gewöhnen: *badly ~d* disziplinlos, undiszipliniert.

dis·claim [dɪs'kleɪm] *v/t* **1.** ab-, bestreiten. **2.** jede Verantwortung ablehnen für; *Verantwortung ablehnen*. **3.** widerrufen, dementieren. **4.** 🏛 verzichten *od.* keinen Anspruch erheben auf (*acc*), *Erbschaft* ausschlagen. **dis'claim·er** *s* **1.** Widerruf *m*, Dementi *n*. **2.** (*of*) Verzicht *m* (auf *acc*), Ausschlagung *f* (*gen*).

dis·close [dɪs'kləʊz] *v/t* **1.** bekanntgeben, -machen. **2.** enthüllen, aufdecken. **3.** zeigen, verraten. **dis'clo·sure** [~ʒə] *s* **1.** Bekanntgabe *f*. **2.** Enthüllung *f*.

dis·co ['dɪskəʊ] *pl* -**cos** *s* F Disko *f* (*Diskothek*).

dis·col·o(u)r [dɪs'kʌlə] *v/t u. v/i* (sich) verfärben.

dis·com·fit [dɪs'kʌmfɪt] *v/t* aus der Fassung bringen, verwirren; in Verlegenheit bringen. **dis'com·fi·ture** [~tʃə] *s* Verwirrung *f*; Verlegenheit *f*.

dis·com·fort [dɪs'kʌmfət] *s* **1.** Unannehmlichkeit *f*, Verdruß *m*. **2.** Unbehagen *n*.

dis·con·cert [ˌdɪskən'sɜːt] *v/t* **1.** aus der Fassung bringen, verwirren. **2.** beunruhigen.

dis·con·nect [ˌdɪskə'nekt] *v/t* **1.** trennen (*from* von) (*a. teleph. Teilnehmer*). **2.** ⚡ *Gerät, Stecker etc* ausstecken. **3.** *Gas, Strom, Telefon* abstellen: *we have been ~ed* uns ist das Gas *etc* abgestellt worden. ,**dis·con'nect·ed** *adj* □ zs.-hang(s)los.

dis·con·so·late [dɪs'kɒnsəlǝt] *adj* □ untröstlich (*about, at* über *acc*).

dis·con·tent [ˌdɪskən'tent] **I** *adj* → **discontented. II** *s* Unzufriedenheit *f*. ,**dis·con'tent·ed** *adj* □ unzufrieden (*with* mit).

dis·con·tin·ue [ˌdɪskən'tɪnjuː] *v/t* **1.** unterbrechen. **2.** einstellen (*a.* 🏛); *Gewohnheit etc* aufgeben; *Beziehungen* abbrechen; *Zeitung etc* abbestellen. **3.** aufhören (*doing* zu tun). ,**dis·con-'tin·u·ous** [~jʊəs] *adj* □ **1.** unterbrochen. **2.** zs.-hang(s)los.

dis·cord ['dɪskɔːd] *s* **1.** Uneinigkeit *f*. **2.** Zwietracht *f*, Zwist *m*: → **apple. 3.** ♪ Mißklang *m* (*a. fig.*), Dissonanz *f*. **dis'cord·ant** *adj* □ **1.** sich widersprechend. **2.** ♪ mißtönend (*a. weitS. u. fig.*).

dis·co·theque ['dɪskəʊtek] *s* Diskothek *f*.

dis·count ['dɪskaʊnt] **I** *s* **1.** † Preisnachlaß *m*, Rabatt *m*, Skonto *m*, *n* (*on* auf *acc*). **2.** † Diskont *m*: ~ (*rate*) Diskontsatz *m*. **3.** † Abzug *m* (*vom Nominalwert*): *at a* ~ unter Pari; *fig.* nicht geschätzt *od.* gefragt; *sell at a* ~ mit Verlust verkaufen. **II** *v/t* **4.** † abziehen, abrechnen; e-n Abzug gewähren auf (*acc*). **5.** † *Wechsel* diskontieren. **6.** *Geschichte etc* mit Vorsicht *od.* Vorbehalt aufnehmen.

dis·cour·age [dɪs'kʌrɪdʒ] *v/t* **1.** entmutigen. **2.** abschrecken, abhalten, *j-m* abraten (*from* von). **dis'cour·age·ment** *s* **1.** Entmutigung *f*. **2.** Abschreckung *f*.

dis·course I *s* ['dɪskɔːs] **1.** Unterhaltung *f*, Gespräch *n*. **2.** Vortrag *m*. **II** *v/i* [dɪ'skɔːs] **3.** sich unterhalten (*on* über *acc*). **4.** e-n Vortrag halten (*on* über *acc*).

dis·cour·te·ous [dɪs'kɜːtjəs] *adj* □ unhöflich. **dis'cour·te·sy** [~tɪsɪ] *s* Unhöflichkeit *f*.

dis·cov·er [dɪ'skʌvə] *v/t* entdecken, *fig. a.* ausfindig machen, (heraus)finden. **dis'cov·er·er** *s* Entdecker(in). **dis'cov·er·y** *s* Entdeckung *f*.

dis·cred·it [dɪs'kredɪt] **I** *v/t* **1.** in Verruf *od.* Mißkredit bringen (*with* bei). **2.** anzweifeln, keinen Glauben schenken (*dat*). **II** *s* **3.** Mißkredit *m*: *bring into* ~, *bring* ~ *on* → 1. **4.** Zweifel *m*.

dis·creet [dɪ'skriːt] *adj* □ **1.** umsichtig, besonnen. **2.** diskret: a) taktvoll, b) verschwiegen, c) dezent, unaufdringlich.

dis·crep·an·cy [dɪˈskrepənsɪ] *s* Diskrepanz *f*, Widerspruch *m*.

dis·crete [dɪˈskriːt] *adj* □ getrennt, einzeln.

dis·cre·tion [dɪˈskreʃn] *s* **1.** Ermessen *n*, Gutdünken *n*: *at* ~ nach Belieben; *it is at* (*od.* *within*) *your* ~ es steht Ihnen frei; *leave s.th. to s.o.'s* ~ j-m et. anheimstellen. **2.** Umsicht *f*, Besonnenheit *f*. **3.** Diskretion *f*.

dis·crim·i·nate [dɪˈskrɪmɪneɪt] **I** *v/i* (scharf) unterscheiden, e-n Unterschied machen (*between* zwischen *dat*): ~ *between* unterschiedlich behandeln (*acc*); ~ *against* j-n benachteiligen, diskriminieren. **II** *v/t* (scharf) unterscheiden (*from* von). **dis'crim·i·nat·ing** *adj* □ scharfsinnig, urteilsfähig. **dis,crim·i'na·tion** *s* **1.** unterschiedliche Behandlung; Diskriminierung *f*: ~ *against s.o.* Benachteiligung *f* e-r Person. **2.** Scharfsinn *m*, Urteilsfähigkeit *f*. **dis'crim·i·na·tive** [~nətɪv], **dis'crim·i·na·to·ry** [~nətərɪ] *adj* diskriminierend.

dis·cur·sive [dɪˈskɜːsɪv] *adj* □ weitschweifig.

dis·cus [ˈdɪskəs] *pl* **-cus·es, -ci** [ˈ~kaɪ] *s Leichtathletik:* a) Diskus *m*: ~ *throw* → b; ~ *thrower* Diskuswerfer(in), b) Diskuswerfen *n*.

dis·cuss [dɪˈskʌs] *v/t* diskutieren, besprechen, erörtern. **dis'cus·sion** *s* Diskussion *f*, Besprechung *f*, Erörterung *f*: *be under* ~ zur Diskussion stehen; *matter for* ~ Diskussionsgegenstand *m*.

dis·dain [dɪsˈdeɪn] **I** *v/t* verachten, geringschätzen. **II** *s* Verachtung *f*, Geringschätzung *f*. **dis'dain·ful** [~fʊl] *adj* □ verächtlich, geringschätzig: *be* ~ *of* (*od.* *toward*[*s*]) → *disdain* I.

dis·ease [dɪˈziːz] *s* Krankheit *f* (*a. fig.*). **dis'eased** *adj* krank.

dis·em·bark [ˌdɪsɪmˈbɑːk] **I** *v/t* ✈, ⚓ *Passagiere* von Bord gehen lassen, ⚓ *a.* ausschiffen, *Waren* ausladen. **II** *v/i* ✈, ⚓ von Bord gehen, ⚓ *a.* sich ausschiffen. **dis·em·bar'ka·tion** [~em~] *s* Ausschiffung *f*, -ladung *f*.

dis·en·chant [ˌdɪsɪnˈtʃɑːnt] *v/t* desillusionieren, ernüchtern.

dis·en·gage [ˌdɪsɪnˈgeɪdʒ] **I** *v/t* **1.** los-, freimachen, befreien (*from* von). **2.** ⚙ loskuppeln: ~ *the clutch* auskuppeln; ~ *the gears* in den Leergang schalten. **II**

v/i **3.** sich freimachen, loskommen (*from* von). **dis·en'gaged** *adj* **1.** frei, unbeschäftigt. **2.** ungebunden. **dis·en'gage·ment** *s* **1.** Befreiung *f*. **2.** Ungebundenheit *f*. **3.** Muße(stunden *pl*) *f*.

dis·en·tan·gle [ˌdɪsɪnˈtæŋgl] **I** *v/t* **1.** entwirren, -flechten (*beide a. fig.*). **2.** befreien (*from* von, aus). **II** *v/i* **3.** sich befreien.

dis·e·qui·lib·ri·um [ˌdɪsekwɪˈlɪbrɪəm] *s bsd.* ♱ Ungleichgewicht *n*.

dis·fa·vo(u)r [ˌdɪsˈfeɪvə] *s* **1.** Mißbilligung *f*, -fallen *n*. **2.** Ungnade *f*: *be in* (*fall into*) ~ in Ungnade stehen (fallen) (*with* bei).

dis·fig·ure [dɪsˈfɪgə] *v/t* entstellen, verunstalten (*with* durch).

dis·gorge [dɪsˈgɔːdʒ] **I** *v/t* **1.** *Essen* ausspeien, *Lava* speien. **2.** (widerwillig) wieder herausgeben. **II** *v/i* **3.** sich ergießen, fließen (*into* in *acc*).

dis·grace [dɪsˈgreɪs] **I** *s* **1.** Schande *f* (*to* für): *bring* ~ *on* → 3. **2.** → *disfavo(u)r* 2. **II** *v/t* **3.** Schande bringen über (*acc*). **dis'grace·ful** [~fʊl] *adj* □ schändlich.

dis·grun·tled [dɪsˈgrʌntld] *adj* verärgert, -stimmt (*at* über *acc*).

dis·guise [dɪsˈgaɪz] **I** *v/t* **1.** (*o.s.* sich) verkleiden *od.* maskieren (*as* als). **2.** *Handschrift, Stimme* verstellen. **3.** *Absichten, Fakten etc* verschleiern, *Gefühle etc* verbergen. **II** *s* **4.** Verkleidung *f*: *in* ~ verkleidet, maskiert; *fig.* verkappt; *in the* ~ *of* verkleidet als; → *blessing*. **5.** Verstellung *f*. **6.** Verschleierung *f*: *make no* ~ *of* kein Hehl machen aus.

dis·gust [dɪsˈgʌst] **I** *v/t* **1.** anekeln, anwidern: *be* ~*ed with* (*od.* *at, by*) Ekel empfinden über (*acc*). **2.** empören, entrüsten: *be* ~*ed with* empört *od.* entrüstet sein über (*acc*). **II** *s* **3.** Ekel *m* (*at, for* vor *dat*). **dis'gust·ing** *adj* □ ekelhaft, widerlich.

dish [dɪʃ] **I** *s* **1.** flache Schüssel; (Servier)Platte *f*; *pl* Geschirr *n*: *wash* (*od.* *do*) *the* ~*es* abspülen. **2.** Gericht *n*, Speise *f*. **II** *v/t* **3.** *oft* ~ *up* *Speisen* anrichten; auftragen. **4.** *oft* ~ *up* F *Geschichte etc* auftischen. **5.** ~ *out* F austeilen.

dis·har·mo·ny [ˌdɪsˈhɑːmənɪ] *s* Disharmonie *f*.

'dish·cloth *s* Geschirrtuch *n*.

dis·heart·en [dɪsˈhɑːtn] *v/t* entmutigen.

di·shev·el(l)ed [dɪˈʃevld] *adj* 1. zerzaust (*Haar*). 2. unordentlich, ungepflegt.

dis·hon·est [dɪsˈɒnɪst] *adj* □ unehrlich, unredlich. **dis·hon·es·ty** *s* Unredlichkeit *f*: a) Unehrlichkeit *f*, b) unredliche Handlung.

dis·hon·o·u·r [dɪsˈɒnə] **I** *s* 1. Unehre *f*, Schande *f* (*to* für). **II** *v/t* 2. entehren. 3. ✝ *Wechsel etc* nicht honorieren *od.* einlösen. **dis·hon·o·u·r·a·ble** *adj* □ schändlich, unehrenhaft.

'dish|·rag *s Br.*, ~ **tow·el** *s bsd. Am.* Geschirrtuch *n.* '~ˌwash·er *s* 1. Tellerwäscher(in), Spüler(in). 2. Geschirrspülmaschine *f*, -spüler *m.* '~ˌwa·ter *s* Abwasch-, Spülwasser *n.*

dish·y [ˈdɪʃɪ] *adj bsd. Br.* F dufte, toll (*Person*).

dis·il·lu·sion [ˌdɪsɪˈluːʒn] **I** *s* Ernüchterung *f*, Desillusion *f*. **II** *v/t* ernüchtern, desillusionieren. **ˌdis·il·lu·sion·ment** → *disillusion* I.

dis·in·cli·na·tion [ˌdɪsɪnklɪˈneɪʃn] *s* Abneigung *f* (**for** gegen; **to do** zu tun). **dis·in·clined** [ˌ~ˈklaɪnd] *adj* abgeneigt.

dis·in·fect [ˌdɪsɪnˈfekt] *v/t* desinfizieren. **ˌdis·in·fect·ant** *s* Desinfektionsmittel *n.* **ˌdis·in·fec·tion** *s* Desinfektion *f*, Desinfizierung *f*.

dis·in·gen·u·ous [ˌdɪsɪnˈdʒenjʊəs] *adj* □ unaufrichtig.

dis·in·her·it [ˌdɪsɪnˈherɪt] *v/t* enterben.

dis·in·te·grate [dɪsˈɪntɪgreɪt] **I** *v/t* 1. auflösen, *fig. a.* zersetzen. **II** *v/i* 2. sich auflösen (*a. fig.*). 3. ver-, zerfallen (*a. fig.*). 4. *geol.* verwittern. **disˌin·te·graˈtion** *s* 1. Auflösung *f.* 2. Zerfall *m.* 3. *geol.* Verwitterung *f.*

dis·in·ter·est·ed [dɪsˈɪntrəstɪd] *adj* □ 1. uneigennützig. 2. objektiv. 3. un-, desinteressiert (**in** an *dat*).

dis·joint·ed [dɪsˈdʒɔɪntɪd] *adj* □ zs.-hang(s)los.

disk [dɪsk] *s* 1. *allg.* Scheibe *f.* 2. (Schall)Platte *f.* ~ **brake** *s* ⊕ Scheibenbremse *f.*

disk·ette [dɪˈsket] *s Computer:* Diskette *f.*

disk jock·ey *s* Diskjockey *m.*

dis·like [dɪsˈlaɪk] **I** *v/t* nicht leiden können, nicht mögen: ~ **doing s.th.** et. nicht gern *od.* nicht ungern tun; **get o.s. ~d** sich unbeliebt machen. **II** *s* Abneigung *f*, Widerwille *m* (**of**, **for** gegen).

take a ~ to e-e Abneigung fassen gegen.

dis·lo·cate [ˈdɪsləʊkeɪt] *v/t* 1. verrücken. 2. ✻ sich *den Arm etc* ver- *od.* ausrenken. **ˌdis·loˈca·tion** *s* 1. Verrückung *f.* 2. ✻ Verrenkung *f*; Dislokation *f.*

dis·loy·al [ˌdɪsˈlɔɪəl] *adj* □ (**to**) untreu (*dat*), treulos (gegen). **ˌdis·loyˈal·ty** *s* Untreue *f*, Treulosigkeit *f.*

dis·mal [ˈdɪzməl] **I** *adj* □ düster, trüb, trostlos, bedrückend. **II** *s:* **be in the ~s** F Trübsal blasen.

dis·man·tle [dɪsˈmæntl] *v/t* 1. demontieren, abbauen; *Gebäude* abbrechen; ⚓ abwracken. 2. zerlegen, auseinandernehmen.

dis·may [dɪsˈmeɪ] **I** *v/t* erschrecken, bestürzen. **II** *s* Schreck(en) *m*, Bestürzung *f*: **in** (*od.* **with**) ~ bestürzt; **to one's** ~ zu s-r Bestürzung.

dis·mem·ber [dɪsˈmembə] *v/t* 1. zerstückeln; *bsd.* ✻ zergliedern. 2. *Land etc* zersplittern, aufteilen.

dis·miss [dɪsˈmɪs] *v/t* 1. entlassen, gehen lassen. 2. entlassen (**from** aus *e-m Amt etc*). 3. *Thema etc* fallenlassen; *Frage etc* abtun (**as** als). 4. *a.* ⚖ abweisen. **dis'miss·al** *s* 1. Entlassung *f.* 2. *a.* ⚖ Abweisung *f.*

dis·mount [ˌdɪsˈmaʊnt] *v/i* 1. absteigen, absitzen (**from** von). **II** *v/t* 2. *Reiter* abwerfen. 3. abmontieren.

dis·o·be·di·ence [ˌdɪsəˈbiːdjəns] *s* Ungehorsam *m.* **ˌdis·o·be·di·ent** *adj* □ ungehorsam (**to** gegen[über]). **dis·o·bey** [ˌ~ˈbeɪ] **I** *v/t* 1. *j-m* nicht gehorchen. 2. *Gesetz etc* nicht befolgen, mißachten. **II** *v/i* 3. nicht gehorchen, ungehorsam sein.

dis·o·blige [ˌdɪsəˈblaɪdʒ] *v/t* ungefällig sein gegen. **ˌdis·o·bligˈing** *adj* □ ungefällig, unfreundlich.

dis·or·der [dɪsˈɔːdə] **I** *s* 1. Unordnung *f*, Durcheinander *n:* **in** ~ durcheinander; **throw into** ~ → 4. 2. Aufruhr *m*, Unruhen *pl.* 3. ✻ Störung *f*: **mental** ~ Geistesstörung. **II** *v/t* 4. in Unordnung bringen, durcheinanderbringen. **dis'or·dered** *adj* 1. unordentlich, durcheinander. 2. ✻ gestört. **dis'or·der·ly** *adj* 1. unordentlich. 2. schlampig, (*a. Leben etc*) liederlich. 3. ⚖ ordnungswidrig.

dis·or·gan·ize [dɪsˈɔːgənaɪz] → *disorder* 4.

dis·own [dɪsˈəʊn] v/t **1.** nichts zu tun haben wollen mit, ablehnen. **2.** ableugnen.

dis·par·age [dɪˈspærɪdʒ] v/t **1.** herabsetzen, verächtlich machen. **2.** verachten, geringschätzen. **dis'par·age·ment** s **1.** Herabsetzung f, Verächtlichmachung f. **2.** Verachtung f, Geringschätzung f. **dis'par·ag·ing** adj □ herabsetzend, verächtlich, geringschätzig.

dis·pa·rate [ˈdɪspərət] adj □ ungleich(artig), (grund)verschieden. **dis·par·i·ty** [dɪˈspærətɪ] s Verschiedenheit f: **~ in** (od. **of) age** (zu großer) Altersunterschied.

dis·pas·sion·ate [dɪsˈpæʃnət] adj □ leidenschaftslos, kühl, sachlich.

dis·patch [dɪˈspætʃ] I v/t **1.** (ab)senden, (ab)schicken, Telegramm aufgeben. **2.** rasch erledigen. **3.** ins Jenseits befördern, töten. **4.** F wegputzen, schnell aufessen. II s **5.** Absendung f, Versand m: **~ by rail** Bahnversand. **6.** rasche Erledigung. **7.** Tötung f. **~ box, ~ case** s bsd. Br. Aktenkoffer m.

dis·pel [dɪˈspel] v/t Menge etc, a. fig. Befürchtungen etc zerstreuen, Nebel zerteilen.

dis·pen·sa·ble [dɪˈspensəbl] adj □ entbehrlich. **dis'pen·sa·ry** s Werks-, Krankenhausapotheke f. **dis·pen·sa·tion** [ˌdɪspenˈseɪʃn] s **1.** Aus-, Verteilung f. **2.** Zuteilung f, Gabe f. **3.** (göttliche) Fügung. **4.** Verzicht m (**with** auf acc).

dis·pense [dɪˈspens] I v/t **1.** aus-, verteilen; Sakrament spenden: **~ justice** Recht sprechen. **2.** Arzneien dispensieren, zubereiten u. abgeben. **3.** erlassen, entbinden (**from** von). II v/i **4.** **~ with** verzichten auf (acc); überflüssig machen (acc). **dis'pens·er** s **1.** Aus-, Verteiler m. **2.** ☼ Spender m, (für Klebestreifen etc a.) Abroller m, (Briefmarken- etc)Automat m. **dis'pens·ing** adj: **~ chemist** Br. Apotheker m.

dis·per·sal [dɪˈspɜːsl] s **1.** Zerstreuung f (a. fig.). **2.** Verbreitung f. **dis'perse** I v/t **1.** verstreuen (**over** über acc). **2.** → **dispel**. **3.** Nachrichten etc verbreiten. **4.** ☀, phys. dispergieren, zerstreuen. II v/i **5.** sich zerstreuen (Menge). **6.** sich verteilen. **dis'per·sion** s **1.** → **dispersal**. **2.** ☀, phys. Dispersion f, (Zer-)Streuung f.

dis·pir·it·ed [dɪˈspɪrɪtɪd] adj mutlos, niedergeschlagen.

dis·place [dɪsˈpleɪs] v/t **1.** versetzen, -rücken, -schieben. **2.** verdrängen (a. ♕, phys., Sport). **3.** j-n ablösen (**as** als). **4.** j-n verschleppen: **~d person** Verschleppte m, f, Zwangsumsiedler(in). **dis'place·ment** s **1.** Versetzung f, -schiebung f. **2.** Verdrängung f. **3.** Ablösung f. **4.** Verschleppung f.

dis·play [dɪˈspleɪ] I v/t **1.** Aktivität etc zeigen, entfalten, an den Tag legen. **2.** Waren auslegen, -stellen. **3.** zur Schau stellen, verschwenderisch. II s **4.** Entfaltung f. **5.** Ausstellung f: **be on ~** ausgestellt sein. **6.** Display n: a) (Sichtbild)Anzeige f, b) a. **~ unit** Sichtbildgerät n. III adj **7.** Ausstellungs..., Schau...: **~ cabinet** (od. **case**) Schaukasten m, Vitrine f; **~ window** Auslage(n)-, Schaufenster n.

dis·please [dɪsˈpliːz] v/t j-m mißfallen: **be ~d at** (od. **with**) unzufrieden sein mit. **2.** j-n ärgern, verstimmen. **dis'pleas·ing** adj □ unangenehm. **dis'pleas·ure** [~ˈpleʒə] s Mißfallen n (**at** über acc).

dis·pos·a·ble [dɪˈspəʊsəbl] adj **1.** (frei) verfügbar. **2.** Einweg..., Wegwerf... **dis'pos·al** s **1.** Erledigung f. **2.** Beseitigung f. **3.** Übergabe f, -tragung f: **~ (by sale)** Veräußerung f, Verkauf m. **4.** Verfügung(srecht n) f (**of** über acc): **be at s.o.'s ~** j-m zur Verfügung stehen; **place** (od. **put**) **s.th. at s.o.'s ~** j-m et. zur Verfügung stellen; **have the ~ of** verfügen (können) über (acc). **dis'pose** I v/t **1.** anordnen, aufstellen. **2.** geneigt machen, bewegen (**to** zu; **to do** zu tun). II v/i **3.** **~ of** (frei) verfügen über (acc); (endgültig) erledigen; wegschaffen, beseitigen; verkaufen, veräußern; übergeben, -tragen. **dis'posed** adj **1.** **be well ~ to** (od. **ward[s]**) j-n wohlgesinnt sein, j-m wohlwollen; **e-m** Plan etc wohlwollend gegenüberstehen; → **ill-disposed**. **2.** geneigt (**to do** zu tun): **feel ~ to do s.th.** et. tun wollen. **dis·po·si·tion** [ˌdɪspəˈzɪʃn] s **1.** Disposition f, Veranlagung f; Art f. **2.** Neigung f, Hang m (**to** zu); ✚ Anfälligkeit f (**to** für): **have a ~ to** neigen zu; anfällig sein für. **3.** → **disposal** 4.

dis·pos·sess [ˌdɪspəˈzes] v/t enteignen.

disproportionate

dis·pro·por·tion·ate [ˌdɪsprə'pɔːʃnət] *adj* □ unverhältnismäßig (groß *od.* klein); unangemessen; übertrieben: *be ~ to* in keinem Verhältnis stehen zu.
dis·prove [ˌdɪs'pruːv] *v/t* widerlegen.
dis·pu·ta·ble [dɪ'spjuːtəbl] *adj* □ strittig.
ˌdis·pu'ta·tion *s* 1. Disput *m.* 2. Disputation *f.* **ˌdis·pu'ta·tious** *adj* □ streitsüchtig. **dis'pute** I *v/i* 1. streiten (*on, about* über *acc*). II *v/t* 2. streiten über (*acc*). 3. in Zweifel ziehen, bezweifeln: *~d* umstritten. 4. kämpfen um. 5. (an)kämpfen gegen. III *s* 6. Disput *m*: *in* (*od. under*) *~* umstritten; *beyond* (*od. past, without*) *~* fraglos, unbestritten.
dis·qual·i·fi·ca·tion [dɪsˌkwɒlɪfɪ'keɪʃn] *s* 1. Disqualifikation *f*, Disqualifizierung *f.* 2. Untauglichkeit *f* (*for* für). **dis'qual·i·fy** *v/t* 1. disqualifizieren. 2. untauglich machen (*for* für). 3. für untauglich erklären.
dis·qui·et [dɪs'kwaɪət] I *v/t* beunruhigen. II *s* Unruhe *f*, Besorgnis *f.* **dis'qui·et·ing** *adj* □ beunruhigend, besorgniserregend.
dis·re·gard [ˌdɪsrɪ'gɑːd] I *v/t* 1. nicht beachten, ignorieren. 2. mißachten. II *s* 3. Nichtbeachtung *f*, Ignorierung *f* (*of, for* gen). 4. Mißachtung *f* (*of, for* gen).
dis·re·pair [ˌdɪsrɪ'peə] *s* Baufälligkeit *f*: *be in* (*a state of*) *~* baufällig sein; *fall into* *~* baufällig werden.
dis·rep·u·ta·ble [dɪs'repjʊtəbl] *adj* □ verrufen. **dis·re·pute** [ˌ~rɪ'pjuːt] *s* schlechter Ruf: *be in* *~* verrufen sein; *bring* (*fall, sink*) *into* *~* in Verruf bringen (kommen).
dis·re·spect [ˌdɪsrɪ'spekt] *s* Respektlosigkeit *f.* **ˌdis·re'spect·ful** [ˌ~fʊl] *adj* □ respektlos (*to* gegenüber).
dis·rupt [dɪs'rʌpt] *v/t* 1. auseinanderreißen, (zer)spalten. 2. *Gespräch, Verkehr etc* unterbrechen. 3. *Land etc* zerrütten; *Koalition etc* sprengen. **dis'rup·tion** *s* 1. Spaltung *f.* 2. Unterbrechung *f.* 3. Zerrüttung *f*; Sprengung *f.*
dis·sat·is·fac·tion [ˈdɪsˌsætɪs'fækʃn] *s* Unzufriedenheit *f.* **ˈdis·sat·is·fac·to·ry** [ˌ~tərɪ] *adj* □ unbefriedigend (*to* für). **ˌdis'sat·is·fied** [ˌ~faɪd] *adj* unzufrieden (*at, with* mit).
dis·sect [dɪ'sekt] *v/t* 1. 𝕖 sezieren. 2. *fig.* zergliedern.

dis·sem·ble [dɪ'sembl] *v/t* verbergen, -hehlen, sich *et.* nicht anmerken lassen.
dis·sem·i·nate [dɪ'semɪneɪt] *v/t* 1. ausstreuen. 2. *fig.* verbreiten. **dis·sem·i'na·tion** *s* 1. Ausstreuung *f.* 2. *fig.* Verbreitung *f.*
dis·sen·sion [dɪ'senʃn] *s* Meinungsverschiedenheit(en *pl*) *f.*
dis·sent [dɪ'sent] I *v/i* 1. (*from*) anderer Meinung sein (als), nicht übereinstimmen (mit). 2. *eccl.* von der Staatskirche abweichen. II *s* 3. Meinungsverschiedenheit *f.* **dis'sent·er** *s* 1. Andersdenkende *m*, *f.* 2. *eccl.* Dissident *m*; Dissenter *m.*
dis·ser·ta·tion [ˌdɪsə'teɪʃn] *s* 1. (wissenschaftliche) Abhandlung. 2. *univ.* Diplomarbeit *f.*
dis·ser·vice [ˌdɪs'sɜːvɪs] *s*: *do s.o. a ~* j-m e-n schlechten Dienst erweisen.
dis·si·dent ['dɪsɪdənt] I *adj* 1. (*from*) andersdenkend (als), abweichend (von). II *s* 2. Andersdenkende *m*, *f.* 3. *eccl.* Dissident(in), *pol. a.* Regime-, Systemkritiker(in).
dis·sim·i·lar [ˌdɪ'sɪmɪlə] *adj* □ (*to, from*) verschieden (von), unähnlich (*dat*). **dis·sim·i·lar·i·ty** [ˌ~'lærəti] *s* Verschiedenheit *f*, Unähnlichkeit *f.*
dis·sim·u·late [dɪ'sɪmjʊleɪt] → **dissemble.**
dis·si·pate ['dɪsɪpeɪt] I *v/t* 1. zerstreuen (*a. fig.*); *Nebel* zerteilen. 2. *Kräfte* verzetteln, -geuden; *Vermögen etc* durchbringen, verschwenden. II *v/i* 3. sich zerstreuen (*a. fig.*); sich zerteilen. **ˈdis·si·pat·ed** *adj* □ ausschweifend: a) zügellos (*Leben*), b) leichtlebig (*Person*). **ˌdis·si'pa·tion** *s* 1. Zerstreuung *f* (*a. fig.*); Zerteilung *f.* 2. Vergeudung *f.* 3. Ausschweifung *f*: *a life of ~* ein ausschweifendes *od.* zügelloses Leben.
dis·so·ci·ate [dɪ'səʊʃɪeɪt] *v/t* 1. trennen (*from* von). 2. *~ o.s.* sich distanzieren, abrücken (*from* von). **dis·so·ci·a·tion** [ˌ~sɪ'eɪʃn] *s* Trennung *f.*
dis·so·lute ['dɪsəluːt] → **dissipated.**
dis·so·lu·tion [ˌdɪsə'luːʃn] *s* 1. Auflösung *f* (*a. fig.*). 2. 𝕤𝕥 Annullierung *f*, Aufhebung *f.*
dis·solve [dɪ'zɒlv] I *v/t* 1. auflösen (*a. fig.*): *~ in the mouth* Tablette im Mund zergehen lassen; *~d in tears* in Tränen aufgelöst. 2. 𝕤𝕥 annullieren,

aufheben. **II** v/i **3.** sich auflösen (a. fig.): ~ *in the mouth* im Mund zergehen; ~ *in(to) tears* in Tränen zerfließen.

dis·so·nance ['dɪsənəns] s Dissonanz f: a) ♪ Mißklang m (a. fig.), b) fig. Unstimmigkeit f. **'dis·so·nant** adj □ **1.** ♪ dissonant. **2.** mißtönend. **3.** fig. unstimmig.

dis·suade [dɪ'sweɪd] v/t **1.** j-m abraten (*from* von; *from doing* [davon,] et. zu tun). **2.** abbringen (*from* von; *from doing* davon, et. zu tun). **3.** abraten von.

dis·tance ['dɪstəns] **I** s **1.** Entfernung f: *at a* ~ in einiger Entfernung; von weitem, von fern; *from a* ~ aus einiger Entfernung; *keep one's* ~ Abstand halten (*from* von); fig. Distanz wahren. **2.** Ferne f: *from* (*in*) *the* ~ aus (in) der Ferne. **3.** Strecke: a) Entfernung f: *go the* ~ fig. durchhalten, über die Runden kommen, b) Sport: Distanz f: ~ *runner* (*Leichtathletik*) Langstreckenläufer(in), Langstreckler(in). **4.** (a. zeitlicher) Abstand m: *at this* ~ *of time* nach all dieser Zeit. **II** v/t **5.** überholen, (weit) hinter sich lassen, (Sport a.) distanzieren. **6.** fig. überflügeln, -treffen. **7.** ~ *o.s.* sich distanzieren (*from* von). **'dis·tant** adj □ **1.** entfernt (a. fig.). **2.** fern (a. zeitlich), Fern...: ~ *heating* Fernheizung f. **3.** (weit) voneinander entfernt. **4.** fig. distanziert.

dis·taste [ˌdɪs'teɪst] s **1.** Ekel m (*for* vor dat). **2.** fig. Widerwille m, Abneigung f (*for* gegen). **dis·'taste·ful** [ˌ~fʊl] adj □ **1.** ekelerregend. **2.** fig. unangenehm: *be* ~ *to* j-m zuwider sein.

dis·tend [dɪ'stend] **I** v/t **1.** (aus)dehnen. **2.** Bauch etc aufblähen. **II** v/i **3.** sich (aus)dehnen. **4.** sich aufblähen. **5.** sich weiten (*with* vor dat) (*Augen*).

dis·til, til·til [dɪ'stɪl] v/t **1.** 🜃 destillieren: ~ *out* herausdestillieren (*from* aus) (a. fig.). **2.** Branntwein brennen (*from* aus). **dis·til·la·tion** [ˌ~'leɪʃn] s **1.** 🜃 Destillation f. **2.** 🜃 Destillat n. **3.** Brennen n. **dis·'til·er·y** s (Branntwein)Brennerei f.

dis·tinct [dɪ'stɪŋkt] adj □ **1.** verschieden (*from* von): *as* ~ *from* im Unterschied zu. **2.** ausgeprägt, klar, deutlich. **dis·'tinc·tion** s **1.** Unterscheidung f. **2.** Unterschied m: *in* ~ *from* im

zu; *draw* (*od. make*) *a* ~ *between* e-n Unterschied machen zwischen (dat). **3.** Auszeichnung f, Ehrung f. **4.** (hoher) Rang: *of* ~ von Rang (u. Namen). **dis·'tinc·tive** adj □ **1.** Unterscheidungs... **2.** kennzeichnend (*of* für): → *mark²* 3.

dis·tin·guish [dɪ'stɪŋgwɪʃ] **I** v/t **1.** unterscheiden (*from* von), auseinanderhalten. **2.** wahrnehmen, erkennen. **3.** kennzeichnen: *~ing mark* Kennzeichen n. **4.** ~ *o.s.* sich auszeichnen (a. iro.). **II** v/i **5.** unterscheiden, e-n Unterschied machen (*between* zwischen dat). **dis·'tin·guished** adj **1.** hervorragend, ausgezeichnet. **2.** vornehm.

dis·tort [dɪ'stɔːt] v/t **1.** verdrehen. **2.** Gesicht etc verzerren: *~ed with* (*od. by*) *pain* schmerzverzerrt. **3.** Tatsachen etc verdrehen, entstellen, verzerren. **dis·'tor·tion** s **1.** Verdrehung f. **2.** Verzerrung f. **3.** Entstellung f.

dis·tract [dɪ'strækt] v/t Aufmerksamkeit, Person etc ablenken (*from* von). **dis·'tract·ed** adj □ **1.** beunruhigt, besorgt. **2.** (*with, by*) außer sich (vor dat); wahnsinnig (vor dat). **dis·'trac·tion** s **1.** Ablenkung f. **2.** oft pl Zerstreuung f, Ablenkung f. **3.** Wahnsinn m: *drive s.o. to* ~ j-n zur Raserei od. zum Wahnsinn treiben.

dis·traught [dɪ'strɔːt] → **distracted**.

dis·tress [dɪ'stres] **I** s **1.** Leid n, Kummer m, Sorge f. **2.** Not f, Elend n. **3.** Notlage f, -stand m. **4.** ♘ Seenot f: *in* ~ in Seenot; ~ *call* SOS-Ruf m. **II** v/t **1.** mit Sorge erfüllen. **dis·'tressed** adj **1.** besorgt (*about* um). **2.** notleidend: ~ *area* Br. Notstandsgebiet n. **dis·'tress·ing** adj □ besorgniserregend.

dis·trib·ute [dɪ'strɪbjuːt] v/t **1.** ver-, austeilen (*among* unter dat od. acc; *to* an acc). **2.** zuteilen (*to* dat). **3.** ✝ Waren vertreiben, absetzen; Filme verleihen; Dividende, Gewinn ausschütten. **dis·tri·'bu·tion** s **1.** Ver-, Austeilung f: ~ *of seats* parl. Sitzverteilung f. **2.** Zuteilung f; Gabe f, Spende f. **3.** ✝ Vertrieb m, Absatz m; Verleih m; Ausschüttung f. **dis·'trib·u·tor** s **1.** Verteiler m (a. ⚙). **2.** ✝ Großhändler m; Generalvertreter m; pl (Film)Verleih m.

dis·trict ['dɪstrɪkt] s **1.** Distrikt m, (Verwaltungs)Bezirk m, Kreis m. **2.** (Stadt-)

Bezirk *m*, (-)Viertel *n*. **3.** Gegend *f*, Gebiet *n*.

dis·trust [dɪsˈtrʌst] **I** *s* Mißtrauen *n*: **with ~** mißtrauisch. **II** *v/t* mißtrauen (*dat*). **dis'trust·ful** [~fʊl] *adj* □ mißtrauisch (*of* gegen).

dis·turb [dɪˈstɜːb] *v/t u. v/i allg.* stören. **dis'turb·ance** *s* **1.** Störung *f* (*a.* ☉ *etc*). **2.** *politische etc* Unruhe; Ruhestörung *f*: *cause* (*od.* *create*) *a ~* für Unruhe sorgen; ruhestörenden Lärm machen. **dis'turb·er** *s* **1.** Störer(in), Störenfried *m*. **2.** Unruhestifter(in).

dis·u·nite [ˌdɪsjuːˈnaɪt] *v/t u. v/i* (sich) trennen *od.* entzweien. **ˌdis·u·ni·ty** [~nətɪ] *s* Uneinigkeit *f*, Zwietracht *f*.

dis·use [ˌdɪsˈjuːs] *s*: *fall into ~* ungebräuchlich werden. **ˌdis'used** [~zd] *adj* nicht mehr benutzt (*Maschine etc*), stillgelegt (*Bergwerk etc*), leerstehend (*Haus*).

ditch [dɪtʃ] **I** *s* **1.** Graben *m*. **II** *v/t* **2.** Gräben ziehen durch *od.* in (*dat*). **3.** *Fahrzeug* in den Straßengraben fahren. **4.** *sl. Wagen etc* stehenlassen; *j-m* entwischen; *dem Freund etc* den Laufpaß geben; *et.* wegschmeißen; *Am. die Schule* schwänzen.

dith·er [ˈdɪðə] **I** *v/i* **1.** (*bsd.* vor Kälte) zittern. **2.** schwanken, sich nicht entscheiden können (*between* zwischen *dat*). **3.** aufgeregt sein. **II** *s* **4.** Schwanken *n*. **5.** Aufregung *f*: *throw into a ~* in Aufregung versetzen; *be all of a ~, be in a ~, bsd. Br.* F *have the ~s* aufgeregt sein.

di·ur·nal [daɪˈɜːnl] *adj* □ täglich (wiederkehrend).

di·va·gate [ˈdaɪvəgeɪt] *v/i* abschweifen (*from* von), nicht bei der Sache bleiben.

di·van [dɪˈvæn] *s* Diwan *m*: *~* (*bed*) Bettcouch *f*.

dive [daɪv] **I** *v/i* **1.** tauchen (*for* nach; *into* in *acc*). **2.** (unter)tauchen (*a. U-Boot*). **3.** e-n Hecht- *od.* Kopfsprung machen; (*Wasserspringen*) springen; (*bsd. Sport*) sich werfen, hechten (*for the ball* nach dem Ball): *~ for cover* sich in Deckung werfen. **4.** ✓ e-n Sturzflug machen. **II** *s* **5.** (Unter)Tauchen *n*, ⚓ *a.* Unterwasser-, Tauchfahrt *f*. **6.** Kopfsprung *m*, Hechtsprung *m* (*a. des Tormanns etc*); (*Wasserspringen*) Sprung *m*: *make a ~ for* hechten nach; *make a*

~ for cover sich in Deckung werfen. **7.** ✓ Sturzflug *m*. **8.** F Spelunke *f*. **'div·er** *s* **1.** Taucher(in). **2.** *Sport:* Wasserspringer(in).

di·verge [daɪˈvɜːdʒ] *v/i* **1.** divergieren (*a.* ⅍, *phys.*), auseinandergehen, -laufen. **2.** abweichen (*from* von); voneinander abweichen. **di'ver·gent** *adj* □ **1.** divergierend (*a.* ⅍, *phys.*). **2.** abweichend (*from* von).

di·verse [daɪˈvɜːs] *adj* □ verschieden, ungleich, andersartig. **di·ver·si·fi·ca·tion** [~fɪˈkeɪʃn] *s* **1.** abwechslungsreiche Gestaltung. **2.** *a. ~ of risk* Risikoverteilung *f*. **3.** ✝ Diversifikation *f*, Diversifizierung *f*. **di'ver·si·fy** [~faɪ] *v/t* **1.** abwechslungsreich gestalten. **2.** *Risiko* verteilen. **3.** ✝ *Unternehmen* diversifizieren. **di'ver·sion** [~ʃn] *s* **1.** Ablenkung *f*. **2.** Zerstreuung *f*, Zeitvertreib *m*. **3.** *Br.* (Verkehrs)Umleitung *f*. **di'ver·si·ty** [~sətɪ] *s* Verschiedenheit *f*, Ungleichheit *f*. **di'vert** *v/t* **1.** ablenken, abwenden (*from* von), lenken (*to* auf *acc*). **2.** *Br. Verkehr* umleiten. **3.** zerstreuen, unterhalten (*with* mit, durch).

di·vide [dɪˈvaɪd] **I** *v/t* **1.** teilen (*s.th. with s.o.* et. mit j-m): *~ in halves* halbieren. **2.** (zer)teilen, spalten, *fig. a.* entzweien: *opinion is ~d* die Meinungen sind geteilt (*on* über *acc*). **3.** ver-, austeilen (*among, between* unter *dat od. acc*). **4.** ⅍ dividieren, teilen (*by* durch): *20 ~d by 5 is 4* 20 (geteilt) durch 5 ist 4; *~ 5 into 20* 20 durch 5 teilen. **II** *v/i* **5.** sich aufteilen, zerfallen (*into* in *acc*). **6.** ⅍ sich dividieren *od.* teilen lassen (*by* durch). **div·i·dend** [ˈdɪvɪdend] *s* **1.** ⅍ Dividend *m*. **2.** ✝ Dividende *f*. **di·vid·ers** [dɪˈvaɪdəz] *s pl, a. pair of ~* Stechzirkel *m*. **di·vid·ing** *adj* Trennungs...

div·i·na·tion [ˌdɪvɪˈneɪʃn] *s* Weissagung *f*. **di·vine** [dɪˈvaɪn] **I** *adj* □ **1.** göttlich (*a. fig.* F), Gottes-. **II** *v/t* **2.** weissagen. **3.** mit der Wünschelrute suchen (nach). **di'vin·er** *s* **1.** Wahrsager(in). **2.** (Wünschel)Rutengänger(in).

div·ing [ˈdaɪvɪŋ] *s* **1.** Tauchen *n*. **2.** *Sport:* Wasserspringen *n*. **~ bell** *s* Taucherglocke *f*. **~ board** *s* Sprungbrett *n*. **~ hel·met** *s* Taucherhelm *m*. **~ suit** *s* Taucheranzug *m*. **~ tow·er** *s* Sprungturm *m*.

di·vin·ing rod [dı'vaınıŋ] *s* Wünschelrute *f*.

di·vin·i·ty [dı'vınətı] *s* **1.** Göttlichkeit *f*. **2.** Gottheit *f*. **3.** Theologie *f*.

di·vis·i·ble [dı'vızəbl] *adj* □ teilbar (**by** durch). **di'vi·sion** [~ʒn] *s* **1.** (Ver-, Aus)Teilung *f*, Zerteilung *f*. *A* Arbeitsteilung. **2.** Zerteilung *f*, Spaltung *f*, *fig. a.* Entzweiung *f*. **3.** *A* Division *f*: ~ **sign** Teilungszeichen *n*. **4.** *parl. Br.* (Abstimmung *f* durch) Hammelsprung *m*. **5.** Abteilung *f*. **6.** ✕ Division *f*. **7.** *Sport*: Liga *f*. **di'vi·sor** [dı'vaızə] *s* *A* Divisor *m*, Teiler *m*.

di·vorce [dı'vɔːs] **I** *s* **1.** ⚖ (Ehe)Scheidung *f*: **get** (*od.* **obtain**) **a** ~ geschieden werden, sich scheiden lassen (**from** von). **2.** *fig.* (völlige) Trennung (**from** von; **between** zwischen *dat*). **II** *v/t* **3.** ⚖ *j-n*, *Ehe* scheiden: ~ **s.o.** j-s Ehe scheiden; **he has** ~**d his wife** er hat sich (von s-r Frau) scheiden lassen. **4.** *fig.* (völlig) trennen (**from** von).

diz·zi·ness ['dızınıs] *s* Schwindel(anfall) *m*. **'diz·zy I** *adj* □ **1.** schwind(e)lig. **2.** schwindelnd, schwindelerregend; schwindelnd hoch. **II** *v/t* **3.** schwind(e)lig machen.

do¹ [duː] (*irr*) **I** *v/t* **1.** tun, machen; ausführen, *Arbeiten* verrichten; anfertigen, herstellen: ~ **one's best** sein Bestes tun, sich alle Mühe geben. **2.** *j-m etc.* tun, zufügen, erweisen: → **disservice**, **favo(u)r** 4, *etc.* **3.** *Speisen* zubereiten. **4.** *Zimmer* aufräumen, machen. **5.** (her)richten: → **face** 1, **hair**. **6.** zurücklegen, schaffen: **the car does 100 m.p.h.** der Wagen fährt 160 km/h. **7.** F besichtigen, die Sehenswürdigkeiten besichtigen von (*od. gen.*). **8.** F betrügen (**out of** um), übers Ohr hauen. **9.** F *Strafe* abbrummen: → **time** 1. **II** *v/i* **10.** handeln, sich verhalten. **11.** weiter-, vorankommen: ~ **well** gut abschneiden (**in** bei, in *dat*); s-e Sache gut machen. **12.** sich befinden: ~ **well** gesund sein, in guten Verhältnissen leben; sich gut erholen; **how** ~ **you** ~? guten Tag! (*bei Vorstellung*). **13.** genügen, reichen (**for** für). **III** *v/t u. v/i* **14.** (*Ersatzverb zur Vermeidung von Wiederholungen; mst unübersetzt*) **you know it as well as I** ~ du weißt es so gut wie ich; **I take a bath. So** ~ **I** Ich nehme ein Bad. Ich auch; **he**

works hard, doesn't he? er arbeitet viel, nicht wahr?; **Did he buy it? He did** Kaufte er es? Ja(wohl); **He sold his car. Did he?** Er verkaufte sein Auto. Wirklich?, So? **IV** *v/aux* **15.** *in Fragesätzen:* ~ **you know him?** kennst du ihn? **16.** *in verneinten Sätzen:* **I** ~ **not believe it** ich glaube es nicht. **17.** *zur Verstärkung:* **I did like it** mir gefiel es wirklich.

Verbindungen mit Präpositionen:

do| **by** *v/i* behandeln, handeln an (*dat*). ~ **for** *v/i* **1.** erledigen, ruinieren. **2.** *j-m* den Haushalt führen; putzen bei. **3.** → **do¹** 13. ~ **with** *v/t u. v/i* **1.** **I can't do anything with him** (**it**) ich kann nichts mit ihm (damit) anfangen; **I won't have anything to** ~ **it** ich will nichts damit zu tun *od.* schaffen haben; **it has nothing to** ~ **you** es hat nichts mit dir zu tun. **2.** auskommen *od.* sich begnügen mit. **3.** F **he could** ~ **the money** er kann das Geld (sehr gut) brauchen; **I could** ~ **a glass of beer** ich könnte ein Glas Bier vertragen. ~ **with·out** *v/i* **1.** auskommen *od.* sich behelfen ohne. **2.** verzichten auf (*acc*).

Verbindungen mit Adverbien:

do| **a·way with** *v/i* **1.** beseitigen: a) wegschaffen, b) abschaffen. **2.** *Geld* durchbringen. **3.** umbringen, töten. ~ **down** *v/t Br.* F **1.** heruntermachen, schlechtmachen. **2.** → **do in** 2. ~ **in** *v/t* F **1.** erledigen: a) erschöpfen: **I'm done in** ich bin geschafft, b) zugrunde richten, ruinieren, c) um die Ecke bringen, umbringen. **2.** reinlegen, übers Ohr hauen. ~ **up** *v/t* **1.** zs.-schnüren; *Päckchen etc* zurechtmachen, verschnüren; einpakken; *Kleid, Reißverschluß etc* zumachen: **do s.o. up** j-m das Kleid *etc* zumachen. **2.** **do o.s. up** sich zurechtmachen.

do² [~] *pl* **dos, do's** [duːz] *s* **1.** *sl.* Schwindel *m*, Gaunerei *f*. **2.** **fair** ~**s!** F sei nicht unfair!; gleiches Recht für alle. **3.** ~**s and don'ts** F Gebote u. Verbote, (Spiel)Regeln.

doc [dɒk] F → **doctor** 1.

doc·ile ['dəʊsaıl] *adj* □ **1.** fügsam, gefügig. **2.** gelehrig. **do·cil·i·ty** [~'sılətı] *s* **1.** Fügsamkeit *f*. **2.** Gelehrigkeit *f*.

dock¹ [dɒk] **I** *s* **1.** Dock *n*. **2.** Hafenbekken *n*, Anlegeplatz *m*. **3.** Kai *m*, Pier *m*.

dock 894

4. *pl* Docks *pl*, Hafenanlagen *pl*. **II** *v/t*
5. *Schiff* (ein)docken. **6.** *Raumschiffe*
koppeln. **III** *v/i* **7.** docken. **8.** im Hafen
od. am Kai anlegen. **9.** andocken
(*Raumschiff*).

dock² [~] *v/t* **1.** *Schwanz* stutzen; *e-m Tier*
den Schwanz stutzen. **2.** *j-s Lohn etc*
kürzen: **~ £5 off** (*od. from*) **s.o.'s
wages** j-s Lohn um 5 Pfund kürzen.

dock³ [~] *s* **⁂** Anklagebank *f*: **be in the ~**
auf der Anklagebank sitzen.

dock·er ['dɒkə] *s* Dock-, Hafenarbeiter
m, Schauermann *m*.

'dock·yard *s* Werft *f*.

doc·tor ['dɒktə] **I** *s* **1.** Doktor *m*, Arzt *m*,
Ärztin *f*, (*Anrede*) Herr (Frau) Doktor:
be under the ~ F in Behandlung sein
(**for** wegen); **~'s certificate** ärztliches
Attest. **2.** *univ.* Doktor *m*: **⁂ of Divinity**
(**Laws, Medicine**) Doktor der Theolo-
gie (Rechte, Medizin); **~'s degree**
Doktortitel *m*; **take one's ~'s degree**
promovieren. **II** *v/t* **3.** (ärztlich) behandeln, verarzten. **4.** zs.-flicken, (notdürftig) ausbessern. **5.** *a.* **~ up** F Wein etc
(ver)panschen, *Abrechnung etc* frisieren. **'doc·tor·al** *adj*: **~ thesis → thesis**
2. **doc·tor·ate** ['~rət] *s* Doktorwürde *f*,
-titel *m*.

doc·tri·naire [ˌdɒktrɪ'neə] *adj* doktrinär.

doc·trine ['~trɪn] *s* Doktrin *f*: a) Lehre
f, b) *bsd. od.* Grundsatz *m*: **party ~**
Parteiprogramm *n*.

doc·u·ment I *s* ['dɒkjʊmənt] Dokument
n: a) Urkunde *f*, b) amtliches Schriftstück, *pl* Akten *pl*. **II** *v/t* ['~ment] dokumentieren, dokumentarisch *od.* urkundlich belegen. **doc·u·men·ta·ry**
[ˌ~'mentəri] **I** *adj* ☐ **1.** dokumentarisch,
urkundlich. **2.** Dokumentar...: **~ film
→ 3; ~ novel** Tatsachenroman *m*. **II** *s* **3.**
Dokumentar-, Tatsachenfilm *m*. **doc·
u·men'ta·tion** *s* Dokumentation *f*.

dod·der ['dɒdə] *v/i* F **1.** (*bsd. vor Altersschwäche*) zittern. **2.** wack(e)lig gehen.
'dod·der·er *s* F Tattergreis *m*. **'dod·
der·ing, 'dod·der·y** *adj* F tatterig.

dodge [dɒdʒ] **I** *v/i* **1.** (rasch) zur Seite
springen, ausweichen. **2.** Ausflüchte
machen; sich drücken. **II** *v/t* **3.** ausweichen (*dat*). **4.** sich drücken vor (*dat*). **III**
s **5.** Sprung *m* zur Seite. **6.** Kniff *m*,
Trick *m*. **dodg·em (car)** ['dɒdʒəm] *s*
(Auto)Skooter *m*. **'dodg·er** *s* **1.** gerie-

bener Kerl. **2.** Gauner *m*, Schwindler
m. **3.** Drückeberger *m*. **'dodg·y** *adj* F **1.**
verschlagen, gerieben. **2.** *Br.* unsicher:
a) wack(e)lig, b) riskant.

doe [dəʊ] *s zo.* (Reh)Geiß *f*.

do·er ['du:ə] *s* Tatmensch *m*, Macher *m*.

does [dʌz] *er, sie, es* tut (→ **do¹**).

'doe·skin *s* Rehleder *n*.

doesn't ['dʌznt] F = **does not** (→ **do¹**).

dog [dɒg] **I** *s* **1.** Hund *m*; *engS.* Rüde *m*:
~ in the manger j-d, der anderen et.
mißgönnt, womit er selbst gar nichts anfangen kann; **~ does not eat ~** e-e Krähe
hackt der anderen kein Auge aus; **go
to the ~s** vor die Hunde gehen; **lead a
~'s life** ein Hundeleben führen; **let
sleeping ~s lie** schlafende Hunde soll
man nicht wecken. **2.** *contp.* Schuft *m*:
dirty ~ Mistkerl *m*. **3.** F Kerl *m*: **lazy ~**
fauler Hund; **lucky ~** Glückspilz *m*. **4.**
the ~s *pl Br.* F das Windhundrennen. **II**
v/t **5.** *j-n* verfolgen (*a. Pech etc*). **~·
bis·cuit** *s* Hundekuchen *m*. **ˌ~'cheap**
adj u. adv spottbillig. **~ col·lar** *s* **1.**
Hundehalsband *n*. **2.** F steifer, hoher
Kragen (*e-s Geistlichen*). **~ days** *s pl*
Hundstage *pl*. **'~ˌear** *s* Eselsohr *n* (*in
Buch etc*). **'~ˌeared** *adj* mit Eselohren.

dog·ged ['dɒgɪd] *adj* ☐ verbissen, hartnäckig.

dog·gie ['dɒgɪ] → **doggy. 'dog·gish** *adj*
☐ **1.** hundeartig, Hunde... **2.** bissig;
mürrisch. **dog·go** ['dɒgəʊ] *adv*: **lie ~** *sl.*
sich mäuschenstill verhalten; sich versteckt halten. **'dog·gy** *s* Hündchen *n*,
(*Kindersprache*) Wauwau *m*: **~ bag**
Beutel für Essensreste, *die aus e-m
Restaurant mit nach Hause genommen
werden*.

dog·ma ['dɒgmə] *pl* **-mas, -ma·ta**
['ˌ~mətə] *s* Dogma *n*, Glaubens- *od.*
Grund- *od.* (*contp.* starrer) Lehrsatz.
dog·mat·ic [~'mætɪk] *adj* (**~ally**) dogmatisch.

ˌdog|·'poor *adj* F bettelarm. **ˌ~·'tired** *adj*
hundemüde.

doi·ly ['dɔɪlɪ] *s* (Zier)Deckchen *n*.

do·ing ['du:ɪŋ] *s* **1.** Tun *n*: **it was your ~**
du hast es getan, das war dein Werk. **2.**
pl Taten *pl*, Tätigkeit *f*, Begebenheiten
pl, Vorfälle *pl*; Treiben *n*. **3.** *pl* (*sg konstruiert*) *Br.* F Dingsbums *n*.

ˌdo-it-your'self I *s* Heimwerken *n*. **II** *adj*
Heimwerker...: **~ kit** Heimwerkeraus-

rüstung *f*; Bausatz *m* (*für Radio etc*); ~ *movement* Do-it-yourself-Bewegung *f*. ˌdo-it-your'self-er *s* Heimwerker *m*.

dol·drums ['dɒldrəmz] *s pl*: **be in the ~** deprimiert *od*. niedergeschlagen sein, Trübsal blasen.

dole [dəʊl] **I** *s* **1.** milde Gabe. **2.** *a*. ~ *money Br*. F Stempelgeld *n*: **be** (*od*. **go**) **on the** ~ stempeln gehen. **II** *v/t* **3.** ~ *out* sparsam *od*. austeilen.

dole·ful ['dəʊlfʊl] *adj* □ traurig, (*Gesicht etc a*.) trübselig.

doll [dɒl] **I** *s* Puppe *f* (*a*. F *hübsches, aber dummes Mädchen*): ~**'s house** *Br*. F Puppenhaus *n*; ~**'s pram** *bsd. Br*. F Puppenwagen *m*. **II** *v/t*: ~ **o.s. up** → III. **III** *v/i*: ~ **up** F sich feinmachen, sich in Schale werfen.

dol·lar ['dɒlə] *s* Dollar *m*.

doll| bug·gy *s Am*. F, ~ **car·riage** *s Am*. Puppenwagen *m*. '~**house** *s Am*. Puppenhaus *n*.

dol·lop ['dɒləp] *s* F **1.** Klumpen *m*. **2.** Schlag *m* (*Essensportion*); *Am*. Schuß *m* (*Alkohol etc, a. fig. Ironie etc*).

doll·y ['dɒlɪ] *s* **1.** *Kindersprache:* Püppchen *n*. **2.** *Film, TV:* Kamerawagen *m*. **3.** *a*. ~ *bird bsd. Br*. F Püppchen *n* (*hübsches, aber dummes Mädchen*).

dol·phin ['dɒlfɪn] *s zo*. Delphin *m*.

dolt [dəʊlt] *s* Dummkopf *m*, Tölpel *m*.

do·main [dəʊ'meɪn] *s* Domäne *f*, *fig. a*. Gebiet *n*, Bereich *m*.

dome [dəʊm] *s* △ Kuppel *f*.

do·mes·tic [dəʊ'mestɪk] **I** *adj* (~*ally*) **1.** häuslich, Haus(halts)...: ~ *appliance* Haushaltsgerät *n*; ~ *science ped.* Hauswirtschaftslehre *f*; ~ *servant* (*od*. *help*) → 6. **2.** häuslich (veranlagt). **3.** Haus...: ~ *animal*. **4.** inländisch, Inlands...: ~ *flight* Inlandsflug *m*; ~ *products* → 7; ~ *trade* Binnenhandel *m*. **5.** inner, Innen..., innenpolitisch: ~ *policy* Innenpolitik *f*. **II** *s* **6.** Hausangestellte *m, f, pl a*. (Dienst)Personal *n*. **7.** *pl* ✝ Landesprodukte *pl*, inländische Erzeugnisse *pl*. **do'mes·ti·cate** [~keɪt] *v/t* **1.** an häusliches Leben gewöhnen. **2.** *Tier* zähmen.

dom·i·cile ['dɒmɪsaɪl] **I** *s* **1.** (♟ ständiger) Wohnsitz. **2.** ✝ Sitz *m* (*e-r Gesellschaft*); Zahlungsort *m* (*für e-n Wechsel*). **II** *v/t* **3.** ansässig *od*. wohnhaft machen. **4.** ✝ *Wechsel* domizilieren.

'**dom·i·ciled** *adj* ansässig, wohnhaft.

dom·i·nance ['dɒmɪnəns] *s* **1.** (Vor-) Herrschaft *f*. **2.** Macht *f*, Einfluß *m*. '**dom·i·nant I** *adj* □ **1.** dominierend, (vor)herrschend. **2.** beherrschend: a) bestimmend, tonangebend, b) emporragend, weithin sichtbar. **II** *s* **3.** ♪ Dominante *f*. '**dom·i·nate** [~neɪt] **I** *v/t* beherrschen (*a. fig.*): a) herrschen über (*acc*), b) emporragen über (*acc*), c) dominieren *od*. (vor)herrschen in (*dat*). **II** *v/i* dominieren, vorherrschen: ~ *over* herrschen über (*acc*). ˌdom·i'na·tion *s* (Vor)Herrschaft *f*. **dom·i·neer** [~'nɪə] *v/i* **1.** (*over*) despotisch herrschen (über *acc*). **2.** anmaßend sein *od*. auftreten. ˌdom·i'neer·ing *adj* □ **1.** tyrannisch, despotisch. **2.** anmaßend.

do·min·ion [dəʊ'mɪnjən] *s* **1.** (Ober)Herrschaft *f*; Regierungsgewalt *f*. **2.** (Herrschafts)Gebiet *n*. **3.** *oft* ♀ *obs*. Dominion *n* (*im Commonwealth*).

dom·i·no ['dɒmɪnəʊ] *pl* **-no(e)s** *s* a) *pl* (*mst sg konstruiert*) Domino(spiel) *n*, b) Dominostein *m*.

don [dɒn] *v/t et*. anziehen, *Hut* aufsetzen.

do·nate [dəʊ'neɪt] *v/t* schenken (*a*. ♟), *a*. *Blut etc* spenden (**to** *s.o.* j-m). **do'na·tion** *s* Schenkung *f*, Spende *f*.

done [dʌn] **I** *pp von* **do¹**. **II** *adj* **1.** getan: **it isn't** ~ (*od*. **the** ~ **thing**) so et. tut man nicht, das gehört sich nicht. **2.** erledigt: **get** *s.th.* ~ erledigen (lassen). **3.** *gastr.* gar: **well** ~ durchgebraten. **4.** F fertig: **have** ~ **with** fertig sein mit (*a. fig.*); nichts mehr zu tun haben wollen mit; nicht mehr brauchen. **5.** ~! abgemacht!

don·key ['dɒŋkɪ] *s zo*. Esel *m* (*a. fig. contp.*): ~**'s years** *Br*. F e-e Ewigkeit. '~**work** *s* F Dreck(s)arbeit *f*.

do·nor ['dəʊnə] *s* Schenker(in) (*a*. ♟), (*a. Blut- etc*)Spender(in): ~('**s**) **card** Organspenderausweis *m*.

don't [dəʊnt] F **I** = **do not** (→ **do¹**). **II** *s pl* → **do²** 3.

doo·dle ['du:dl] **I** *s* Gekritzel *n*, gedankenlos hingekritzelte Figur(en *pl*). **II** *v/i* Männchen malen.

doom [du:m] *s* **1** Schicksal *n*, Geschick *n*, Verhängnis *n*: **he met his** ~ sein Schicksal ereilte ihn. **II** *v/t* verurteilen, verdammen (*beide a. fig.*): ~**ed to failure** (*od*. **to fail**) zum Scheitern verurteilt.

dooms·day ['du:mzdeɪ] s Jüngstes Gericht, Jüngster Tag.

door [dɔ:] s **1.** Tür f: *from* ~ *to* ~ von Haus zu Haus; *out of* ~*s* ins Freie, hinaus; im Freien, draußen; *two* ~*s down the street* zwei Häuser weiter; *bang* (*od. close, shut*) *the* ~ *on* j-n abweisen; *et.* unmöglich m⟨achⁿⁿe⟩n; *lay s.th. at s.o.'s* ~ j-m et. zur Last legen; *show s.o. the* ~ j-m die Tür weisen. **2.** Tor n, Pforte f (*to* zu) (*beide a. fig.*). '~**·bell** s Türklingel f, -glocke f: *ring the* ~ (an der Tür) klingeln *od.* läuten. ~ **chain** s Sicherheitskette f. '~**·frame** s Türrahmen m. ~ **han·dle** s Türgriff m, -klinke f. '~**·keep·er** s Pförtner m. '~**·knock·er** s Türklopfer m. '~**·man** s (*irr man*) (livrierter) Portier. ~ **mat** s (Fuß)Abtreter m. '~**·plate** s Türschild n. '~**·post** s Türpfosten m. '~**·step** s Türstufe f: *at* (*od. on*) *s.o.'s* ~ vor j-s Tür (*a. fig.*). ~**·to·**'~ *adj* von Haus zu Haus; *Verkauf* an der Haustür: ~ *collection* Haussammlung f; ~ *salesman* Hausierer m; Vertreter m. '~**·way** s **1.** Türöffnung f. **2.** *fig.* Weg m (*to* zu). '~**·yard** s Am. Vorgarten m.

dope [dəʊp] s **1.** F Stoff m (*Rauschgift*). **2.** a) *Sport:* Dopingmittel n, b) Betäubungsmittel n. **3.** *sl.* Trottel m. **4.** *sl.* a) *oft inside* ~ (vertrauliche) Informationen *pl*, Geheimtip(s *pl*) m, b) *allg.* Information(en *pl*) f, Material n. **II** *v/t* **5.** F j-m Stoff geben. **6.** a) *Sport:* dopen, b) *Getränk etc* präparieren, ein Betäubungsmittel untermischen (*dat*). ~ **ad·dict,** '~**·fiend** s F Rauschgiftsüchtige m, f. ~ **test** s *Sport:* Dopingkontrolle f. **dop·ey** ['dəʊpɪ] *adj* F **1.** benommen, benebelt. **2.** dämlich, doof.

dorm [dɔ:m] F → *dormitory*.

dor·mant ['dɔ:mənt] *adj* **1.** schlafend. **2.** *fig.* ruhend, (*a. fig.*) untätig. **3.** *fig.* schlummernd, verborgen, latent: *lie* ~ schlummern.

dor·mer ['dɔ:mə] s a) (Dach)Gaupe f, (-)Gaube f, b) *a.* ~ *window* stehendes Dachfenster.

dor·mi·to·ry ['dɔ:mətrɪ] s **1.** Schlafsaal m. **2.** (*bsd.* Studenten)Wohnheim n. ~ **sub·urb,** ~ **town** s Schlafstadt f.

dor·sal ['dɔ:sl] *adj* Rücken...: ~ *fin* Rückenflosse f.

dos·age ['dəʊsɪdʒ] s **1.** Dosierung f. **2.**

→ *dose* 1. **dose** [dəʊs] **I** s **1.** ⚕ Dosis f (*a. fig.*). **II** *v/t* **2.** *Arznei etc* dosieren. **3.** j-m Arznei geben.

doss [dɒs] *bsd. Br. sl.* **I** s **1.** Schlafplatz m. **2.** Schlaf m. **3.** Penne f. **II** *v/i* **4.** *oft* ~ *down* pennen. '**doss·er** s *bsd. Br. sl.* **1.** Pennbruder m. **2.** Penne f.

'**doss-house** s *bsd. Br. sl.* Penne f,

dos·si·er ['dɒsɪeɪ] s Dossier n, Akten *pl*: *keep a* ~ *on* ein Dossier angelegt haben über (*acc*).

dot [dɒt] **I** s **1.** Punkt m, Pünktchen n; Tupfen m: *on the* ~ F auf die Sekunde pünktlich; *at 8 o'clock on the* ~ F Punkt 8 Uhr; → *year*. **II** *v/t* **2.** punktieren, pünkteln: *sign on the* ~*ted line* unterschreiben; (formell *od.* bedingungslos) zustimmen. **3.** sprenkeln, übersäen (*with* mit).

dot·age ['dəʊtɪdʒ] s **1.** Senilität f: *be in one's* ~ kindisch *od.* senil sein. **2.** Vernarrtheit f (*on* in *acc*). **dote** [dəʊt] *v/i* vernarrt sein (*on* in *acc*). '**dot·ing** *adj* □ **1.** vernarrt (*on* in *acc*). **2.** kindisch, senil.

dou·ble ['dʌbl] **I** *adj* □ **1.** doppelt, Doppel..., zweifach: ~ *bottom* doppelter Boden; ~ *murder* Doppelmord m. **2.** Doppel..., verdoppelt, verstärkt: ~ *beer* Starkbier n. **3.** Doppel... (*für 2 bestimmt*): ~ *bed* Doppelbett n; ~ *room* Doppel-, Zweibettzimmer n. **4.** zweideutig. **II** *adv* **5.** doppelt: ~ *as long* noch einmal so lang. **6.** doppelt, zweifach: *play* (*at*) ~ *or quit(s)* alles riskieren *od.* aufs Spiel setzen; *see* ~ doppelt sehen. **III** s **7.** *das* Doppelte *od.* Zweifache. **8.** Doppel m, Duplikat n. **9.** Doppelgänger(in). **10.** *Film, TV:* Double n. **11.** *mst pl Tennis etc:* Doppel n: *a* ~*s match* ein Doppel; *men's* ~*s* Herrendoppel. **IV** *v/t* **12.** verdoppeln. **13.** *oft* ~ *up Papier etc* knüllen, falten, *Bettdecke etc* um-, zurückschlagen; zs.-falten, -legen. **14.** ⚓ umsegeln, umschiffen. **15.** *Film, TV:* j-n doubeln. **V** *v/i* **16.** sich verdoppeln. **17.** sich (zs.-)falten (lassen): ~ *up with* sich krümmen vor (*dat*). **18.** plötzlich kehrtmachen; e-n Haken schlagen. '~**·bar·rel(l)ed** *adj* **1.** doppelläufig: ~ *gun* Doppelflinte f, Zwilling m. **2.** zweideutig. ~ '~*name* Doppelname m. **3.** zweideutig. ~ *bend* s S-Kurve f. ~**·'breast·ed** *adj* zweireihig (*Anzug*).

~ check s genaue Nachprüfung. ,~'**check** v/t u. v/i genau nachprüfen. ~ **chin** s Doppelkinn n. **~ cross** s F doppeltes od. falsches Spiel. ,~'**cross** v/t F ein doppeltes od. falsches Spiel treiben mit. ,~'**deal·er** s Betrüger m. ,~'**deal·ing** I adj betrügerisch. II s Betrug m. ,~'**deck·er** s 1. Doppeldecker m (Autobus, Flugzeug etc). **2.** F Etagenbett n; Doppelsandwich n. **~ Dutch** s F Kauderwelsch n. ,~'**edged** adj **1.** zweischneidig (a. fig.). **2.** fig. zweideutig. '~**faced** adj heuchlerisch, unaufrichtig. **~ fea·ture** s Doppelprogramm n (2 Spielfilme in jeder Vorstellung). **~ life** s (irr life) Doppelleben n. ,~'**park** v/t u. v/i mot. in zweiter Reihe parken. ,~'**quick** I s → **double time** 1. II adj: **~ time** → III. III adv F im Eiltempo, fix. **~ stand·ard** s: **apply ~s** mit zweierlei Maß messen. **~ talk** s hinhaltendes od. nichtssagendes Gerede; doppelzüngiges Gerede; Augen(aus)wischerei f. **~ time** s **1.** ⚔ Am. Schnellschritt m: **in ~** F im Eiltempo, fix. **2.** doppelter Lohn (für Feiertagsarbeit etc).

doubt [daʊt] I v/i **1.** zweifeln (**of** an e-r Sache). **2.** Bedenken haben. II v/t **3.** bezweifeln (a. **that** daß), anzweifeln. **4.** mißtrauen (dat). III s **5.** Zweifel m (**of** an dat; **about** hinsichtlich): **no** (od. **without, beyond**) **~** zweifellos, fraglos; **be in ~** Zweifel haben (**about** an dat); ungewiß sein; unschlüssig sein; **cast** (od. **throw**) **~ on** et. in Zweifel ziehen; **if** (od. **when**) **in ~** im Zweifelsfall; **leave no ~s about** keinen Zweifel lassen an (dat). '**doubt·er** s Zweifler(in). **doubt·ful** ['~fʊl] adj □ **1.** allg. zweifelhaft. **2. be ~ of** (od. **about**) zweifeln an (dat), im Zweifel sein über (acc). '**doubt·less** adv zweifellos, sicherlich.

dough [dəʊ] s **1.** Teig m. **2.** bsd. Am. sl. Kohlen pl (Geld). **~nut** s Krapfen m, Berliner (Pfannkuchen).

dough·y ['dəʊɪ] adj **1.** teigig. **2.** fig. teigig, wächsern (Gesicht).

dour [dʊə] adj **1.** mürrisch. **2.** hart, streng. **3.** hartnäckig, halsstarrig.

douse [daʊs] v/t **1.** ins Wasser tauchen, eintauchen; Wäsche etc einweichen; Wasser schütten über (acc). **2.** F Licht ausmachen.

dove [dʌv] s **1.** orn. Taube f: **~ of peace** fig. Friedenstaube f. **2.** pol. Taube f (gemäßigter Politiker).

dow·dy ['daʊdɪ] adj □ nachlässig gekleidet; unelegant; unmodern.

dow·el ['daʊəl] s ⊙ Dübel m.

down[1] [daʊn] I adv **1.** nach unten, her-, hinunter, abwärts, (in Kreuzworträtseln) senkrecht. **2. go ~ to the country** (von London) aufs Land fahren. **3. ~ with ...!** nieder mit ...! **4.** (dr)unten: **~ there** dort unten; **~ under** F in od. nach Australien od. Neuseeland (→ **down under**). **5.** untergegangen (Sonne etc). **6.** gefallen (Thermometer etc): **~ by 10 degrees** um 10 Grad gefallen. **7.** niedergeschlagen, down: → **mouth** 1. **8.** bettlägerig: **~ with influenza** mit Grippe im Bett liegen. **9. they were 2 points** (**goals**) **~** (Sport) sie lagen 2 Punkte (Tore) zurück. II adj **10.** nach unten (gerichtet), Abwärts... **11.** von London abfahrend od. kommend: **~ platform** Abfahrtsbahnsteig m (in London). III prp **12.** her-, hinunter: **~ the river** flußabwärts. IV s **13. have a ~ on** F j-n auf dem Kieker haben. V v/t **14.** zu Fall bringen (a. Sport u. fig.). **15.** niederlegen: **~ tools** die Arbeit niederlegen. **16.** Flugzeug abschießen. **17.** F Getränk runterkippen.

down[2] [~] s **1.** orn. Daunen pl: **~ quilt** Daunendecke f. **2.** (a. Bart)Flaum m.

'**down|·cast** adj niedergeschlagen: a) gesenkt (Blick), b) deprimiert. '**~·fall** s **1.** fig. Sturz m. **2.** starker Regenguß, Platzregen m, a. starker Schneefall. '**~·grade** v/t **1.** niedriger einstufen. **2.** degradieren. ,~'**heart·ed** adj □ niedergeschlagen, entmutigt. ,~'**hill** I adv **1.** abwärts, bergab (beide a. fig.), den Berg hinunter: **he is going ~** es geht bergab mit ihm; **the rest was ~** (**all the way**) alles andere ging wie von selbst. II adj **2.** abschüssig. **3.** Skisport: Abfahrts...: **~ race** Abfahrtslauf m. **~ pay·ment** s **1.** Barzahlung f. **2.** Anzahlung f. '**~·pour** s Platzregen m. ,~'**right** adj u. adv völlig, absolut, ausgesprochen: **a ~ lie** e-e glatte Lüge. ,~'**stairs** I adv **1.** die Treppe her- od. hinunter, nach unten. **2.** unten, in e-m unteren Stockwerk. **3.** e-e Treppe tiefer. II adj ['~steəz] **4.** im unteren Stockwerk (gelegen), unter. ,~'**stream** adv flußab(wärts). **,~to-'earth** adj realistisch. **~town** Am. **I** adv [,~'taʊn] im od. ins Geschäftsviertel. **II** adj ['~taʊn] im Geschäftsviertel (gelegen od. tätig): **in ~ Los Angeles** in der Innenstadt von Los Angeles. **III** s ['~taʊn] Geschäftsviertel n, Innenstadt f, City f. **'~,trod-den** adj unterdrückt. **~ un-der** s F Australien n; Neuseeland n.

down·ward ['daʊnwəd] **I** adv **1.** nach unten: **face ~** mit dem Gesicht nach unten. **2.** fig. abwärts, bergab: **he went ~ in life** es ging bergab mit ihm. **3.** from **... ~** (zeitlich) von ... ab, seit. **II** adj **4.** Abwärts..., (Preise) sinkend. **down-wards** ['~wədz] → **downward** I.

down·y ['daʊnɪ] adj **1.** Daunen... **2.** flaumig.

dow·ry ['daʊərɪ] s Mitgift f, Aussteuer f.

dowse¹ → **douse**.

dowse² [daʊz] v/i mit der Wünschelrute (Wasser etc) suchen. **'dows·er** s (Wünschel)Rutengänger m. **'dows·ing rod** s Wünschelrute f.

doy·en [dɔɪ'en] s **1.** Rangälteste m. **2.** Doyen m. **3.** Nestor m.

doze [daʊz] v/i dösen, ein Nickerchen machen od. halten: **~ off** einnicken, -dösen. **II** s Nickerchen n: **have a ~** → I.

doz·en ['dʌzn] s Dutzend n: **~s of times** F x-mal; **do one's daily ~** Früh- od. Morgengymnastik machen; **talk nineteen** (od. **twenty, forty**) **to the ~** Br. wie ein Wasserfall reden; → **baker.**

doz·y ['daʊzɪ] adj □ **1.** schläfrig, verschlafen, dösig. **2.** Br. F schwer von Begriff.

drab [dræb] adj **1.** graubraun. **2.** fig. trist: a) grau (Stadt etc), b) düster (Farben etc), c) langweilig (Abend etc), d) freudlos (Dasein etc).

Dra·co·ni·an [drə'kəʊnjən] adj drakonisch.

draft [drɑːft] **I** s **1.** Entwurf m. **2.** (Luftetc)Zug m: **feel the draught** Br. F den Wind im Gesicht spüren. **3.** **make a ~ on** Geld abheben von; fig. in Anspruch nehmen. **4.** † Tratte f, Wechsel m. **5.** ✕ Am. Einberufung f, Einziehung f. **6.** → **draught** I. **II** v/t **7.** entwerfen, Schriftstück aufsetzen. **8.** ✕ Am. einziehen (**into** zu), einberufen.

drafts·man ['drɑːftsmən] s (irr **man**) **1.** j-d, der et. entwirft od. aufsetzt.

2. ⚙ (Konstruktions)Zeichner m.

draft·y ['drɑːftɪ] adj zugig.

drag [dræg] **I** s **1.** Schleppen n, Zerren n. **2.** Hemmschuh m (a. fig. on für). **3.** F a) et. Langweiliges od. Lästiges: **be a ~** langweilig sein; **what a ~!** so ein Mist!, b) Langweiler m; lästiger Kerl. **4.** Am. F Einfluß m: **use one's ~** s-e Beziehungen spielen lassen. **5.** F Zug m (**at, on** an e-r Zigarette etc): **give me a ~** laß mich mal ziehen. **6.** F (von Männern, bsd. von Transvestiten, getragene) Frauenkleidung. **II** v/t **7.** schleppen, zerren, schleifen, ziehen: → **mire, mud** 2. **8.** ~ **one's feet** a) schlurfen, b) a. ~ **one's heels** fig. sich Zeit lassen (**over, in, about** mit, bei). **9.** fig. hineinziehen (**into** in acc). **10.** F j-n langweilen; j-m lästig sein. **III** v/i **11.** (am Boden) schleppen od. schleifen. **12.** → **drag behind.** **13.** zerren (**at** an dat). **14.** F ziehen (**at, on** an e-r Zigarette etc).

Verbindungen mit Adverbien:

drag a·long I v/t wegschleppen, -zerren. **II** v/i sich dahinschleppen. **~ a·way** v/t → **drag along** I: **drag o.s. away from** fig. sich losreißen von. **~ be·hind** v/i zurückbleiben, nachhinken. **~ down** v/t **1.** herunter-, hinunterziehen; fig. in den Schmutz ziehen. **2.** fig. zermürben (Krankheit etc); entmutigen. **~ in** v/t **1.** herein-, hineinziehen. **2.** fig. (mit) hineinziehen. **~ off** v/t → **drag along** I: **drag s.o. off to a party** F j-n auf e-e Party schleppen. **~ on** **I** v/t weiterschleppen. **II** v/i fig. sich dahinschleppen; sich in die Länge ziehen: **the speech dragged on for two hours** die Rede zog sich über zwei Stunden hin. **~ out** v/t **1.** heraus-, hinausziehen. **2.** fig. hinausziehen, in die Länge ziehen. **~ up** v/t **1.** hochziehen. **2.** F Kind lieblos aufziehen. **3.** F Skandal etc ausgraben.

dra·gée [dræ'ʒeɪ] s Dragée n (a. pharm.).

'drag|·lift s Schlepplift m. **'~·net** s **1.** Schleppnetz n: **~ operation** Schleppnetzfahndung f. **2.** fig. Netz n (der Polizei etc).

drag·on ['drægən] s Drache m. **'~·fly** s zo. Libelle f.

drain [dreɪn] **I** v/t **1.** a. ~ **off** (od. **away**) Flüssigkeit abfließen lassen: ~ **off** abtropfen lassen; Gemüse abgießen. **2.** ⚡ Eiter etc drainieren. **3.** austrinken, leeren: → **dreg** 1. **4.** *Land* entwässern. **5.** *Gebäude etc* kanalisieren. **6.** *j-n, Vorräte etc* erschöpfen. **II** *v/i* **7.** ~ **off** (*od. away*) abfließen, ablaufen. **8.** leerlaufen. **9.** abtropfen. **10.** *a.* ~ *away fig.* dahinschwinden . **III** *s* **11.** → **drainage** 1–3. **12.** Abzugskanal *m*, Entwässerungsgraben *m*. **13.** *pl* Kanalisation *f*. **14.** *fig.* Abfluß *m*. **15.** *fig.* Belastung *f* (**on** *gen*). **'drain·age** *s* **1.** Ableitung *f*. **2.** Abfließen *n*, Ablaufen *n*. **3.** Entwässerung *f*. **4.** Kanalisation *f*. **5.** ⚓ Drainage *f*.

'drain·pipe *s* **1.** Abflußrohr *n*: ~ **trousers** → 3. **2.** Fallrohr *n* (*der Dachrinne*). **3.** *pl, a.* **pair of** ~**s** F Röhrenhose(n *pl*) *f*.

drake [dreɪk] *s orn.* Enterich *m*, Erpel *m*.

dram [dræm] *s* F Schluck *m* (*Alkohol*): **be fond of a** ~ gern einen trinken.

dra·ma ['drɑːmə] *s* Drama *n* (*a. fig.*): ~ **critic** Theaterkritiker(in); ~ **school** Schauspielschule *f*. **dra·mat·ic** [drə'mætɪk] **I** *adj* (~**ally**) **1.** dramatisch (*a.* ♪ *u. fig.*), Schauspiel..., Theater...: ~ **critic** Theaterkritiker(in). **2.** *fig.* dramatisch (*Beispiel, Veränderungen etc*); aufsehenerregend (*Rede etc*). **II** *s pl* **3.** (*a. sg konstruiert*) Dramaturgie *f*. **4.** theatralisches Getue.

dram·a·tis per·so·nae [ˌdrɑːmətɪspɜː'səʊnaɪ] *s pl* Personen *pl* der Handlung.

dram·a·tist ['dræmətɪst] *s* Dramatiker *m*. **dram·a·tize** ['~taɪz] *v/t* dramatisieren: a) für die Bühne bearbeiten, b) *fig.* aufbauschen, (*a. v/i*) übertreiben.

drank [dræŋk] *pret von* **drink**.

drape [dreɪp] *v/t* **1.** drapieren (**with** mit): a) (mit Stoff) behängen, b) in (dekorative) Falten legen. **2.** *Mantel etc* hängen (**over** über *acc*). **'drap·er** *s Br.* Textilkaufmann *m*. **'drap·er·y** *s* **1.** Textilien *pl.* **2.** *bsd. Am.* Vorhänge *pl*, Vorhangstoffe *pl*.

dras·tic ['dræstɪk] *adj* (~**ally**) drastisch.

draught [drɑːft] **I** *s* **1.** Zug *m*, Schluck *m*: **at a** ~ in einem Zug. **2.** **beer on** ~, ~ **beer** Bier *n* vom Faß, Faßbier. **3.** *Br.* a) *pl* (*sg konstruiert*) Dame(spiel *n*) *f*, b) → **draughtsman** 1. **4.** a) *bsd. Br. für* **draft** 2, b) *selten bsd. Br. für* **draft** 1, 4. **II** *v/t* **5.** *selten bsd. Br. für* **draft** 7. **'~board** *s Br.* Damebrett *n*.

draughts·man *s* (*irr* **man**) **1.** ['drɑːfts-

mæn] *Br.* Damestein *m.* **2.** ['drɑːftsmən] *selten bsd. Br. für* **draftsman**.

draught·y ['drɑːftɪ] *bsd. Br. für* **drafty**.

draw [drɔː] **I** *s* **1.** Ziehen *n*; Zug *m* (*a. an der Pfeife etc*). **2.** Ziehung *f*, Verlosung *f*. **3.** *fig.* Zugkraft *f*. **4.** *fig.* Attraktion *f* (*a. Person*), Zugstück *n.* **5.** *Sport:* Unentschieden *n:* **end in a** ~ unentschieden ausgehen. **II** *v/t* (*irr*) **6.** *Waffe, Zahn etc, fig. Schluß etc* ziehen; *Vorhänge* auf- *od.* zuziehen; *Bogen* spannen: ~ *s.o.* **into** *fig.* j-n hineinziehen in (*acc*). **7.** bringen (**on** *über acc*): ~ *s.o.'s* **anger on·o·s.** sich j-s Zorn zuziehen. **8.** *Atem* holen: ~ **a sigh** aufseufzen. **9.** *Tee* ziehen lassen. **10.** auslosen. **11.** *fig.* anziehen: **feel** ~**n to(ward[s])** sich zu j-m hingezogen fühlen. **12.** *Linie, Grenze etc, fig. Vergleich etc* ziehen. **13.** zeichnen. **14.** *Schriftstück* abfassen, aufsetzen; *Scheck* ausstellen, *Wechsel a.* ziehen (**on** auf *acc*). **15.** *Geld* abheben (**from** von); *Rente etc* beziehen. **16.** entlocken (**from** *dat*): ~ **applause** Beifall hervorrufen; ~ (**information from**) *s.o.* j-n aushorchen. **17.** entnehmen (**from** *dat*): ~ **consolation from** Trost schöpfen aus; ~ **inspiration from** sich Anregung holen von *od.* durch. **III** *v/i* (*irr*) **18.** ziehen (*a. Tee, Kamin etc*). **19.** (**to**) sich nähern (*dat*), herankommen (an *acc*): → **end** 9. **20.** (**on**) in Anspruch nehmen (*acc*), Gebrauch machen (*von*), (*Vorräte etc*) angreifen. **21.** *Sport:* unentschieden kämpfen *od.* spielen (**with** gegen), sich unentschieden trennen. **22.** losen (**for** um).

Verbindungen mit Adverbien:

draw| a·part I *v/t* auseinanderziehen. **II** *v/i* sich entfernen (**from** von), sich voneinander entfernen, *fig. a.* sich auseinanderleben. ~ **a·side** *v/t* j-n beiseite nehmen. ~ **a·way I** *v/t* **1.** wegziehen. **2.** *j-s Aufmerksamkeit* ablenken. **II** *v/i* **3.** sich entfernen, (*Sport*) sich lösen (**from** von). ~ **down** *v/t* **1.** herabziehen, *Jalousien* herunterlassen. **2.** → **draw** 7. ~ **In I** *v/t* **1.** *Luft* einziehen. **2.** *fig.* j-n (mit) hineinziehen. **II** *v/i* **3.** einfahren (*Zug*), vorfahren (*Wagen etc*). **4.** zu Ende gehen (*Tag*); abnehmen, kürzer werden (*Tage*). ~ **off** *v/t Handschuhe etc* ausziehen. ~ **on** *v/t Handschuhe etc* anziehen. ~ **out I** *v/t* **1.** herausziehen. **2.** *fig. Aus-*

sage *etc* herausholen (*of, from* aus); *j-n* aushorchen. **3.** *fig.* hinausziehen, in die Länge ziehen. **II** *v/i* **4.** länger werden (*Tage*). **~ up I** *v/t* **1.** aufrichten. **2.** *Schriftstück* abfassen, aufsetzen. **II** *v/i* **3.** (an)halten (*Wagen etc*). **4.** vorfahren (**to** vor *dat*).

'**draw**|**·back** *s* Nachteil *m* (**to** für). '**~·bridge** *s* Zugbrücke *f*.

draw·ee [drɔːˈiː] *s* ✝ Bezogene *m*.

draw·er [*1, 2*: drɔː; *3, 4*: ˈdrɔːə] *s* **1.** Schublade *f*, -fach *n*. **2.** *pl, a. pair of* **~s** Unterhose *f*. **3.** Zeichner *m*. **4.** ✝ Aussteller *m*.

draw·ing [ˈdrɔːɪŋ] *s* **1.** Zeichnen *n*. **2.** Zeichnung *f*. **~ block** *s* Zeichenblock *m*. **~ board** *s* Reiß-, Zeichenbrett *n*: **go back to the ~** *fig.* noch einmal von vorne anfangen. **~ pin** *s Br.* Reißzwecke *f*, -nagel *m*. **~ room** *s* Gesellschaftszimmer *n*, Salon *m*.

drawl [drɔːl] **I** *v/t u. v/i* gedehnt *od.* schleppend sprechen. **II** *s* gedehntes Sprechen.

drawn [drɔːn] **I** *pp von* **draw. II** *adj Sport:* unentschieden: **~ game** Unentschieden *n*.

dread [dred] **I** *v/t et., j-n* sehr fürchten, sich fürchten (**to do, doing** zu tun), (große) Angst haben *od.* sich fürchten vor (*dat*). **II** *s* (große) Angst, Furcht *f* (**of** vor *dat*). **dread·ful** [ˈ~fʊl] *adj* ☐ furchtbar, schrecklich (*beide a. fig.* F). **II** *s →* **penny dreadful.**

dream [driːm] **I** *s* **1.** Traum *m*: **have a ~ about** träumen von; **pleasant ~s!** träum was Schönes! **2.** *fig.* Traum *m*: a) Wunschtraum *m*: **that's beyond my wildest ~s** das übertrifft m-e kühnsten Träume, b) Ideal *n*: **a ~ of a hat** ein Gedicht von e-m Hut; **a perfect ~** traumhaft schön. **II** *v/i* (*a. irr*) **3.** träumen (**of, about** von) (*a. fig.*): **~ of doing s.th.** davon träumen, et. zu tun; daran denken, et. zu tun. **III** *v/t* (*a. irr*) **4.** träumen (*a. fig.*): **~ away** verträumen; **~ up** F sich ausdenken *od.* einfallen lassen. '**dream·er** *s* Träumer(in) (*a. fig.*).

dream read·er *s* Traumdeuter(in).

dreamt [dremt] *pret u. pp von* **dream.**

dream·y [ˈdriːmɪ] *adj* ☐ **1.** verträumt (*a. Augen*), träumerisch. **2.** dunkel, verschwommen (*Erinnerung*). **3.** zum Träumen: **~ music.**

drear·y [ˈdrɪərɪ] *adj* ☐ **1.** trübselig (*Ort etc*). **2.** trüb (*Tag etc*). **3.** langweilig (*Person, Arbeit etc*).

dredge¹ [dredʒ] ⊗ **I** *s* Bagger *m*. **II** *v/t* ausbaggern.

dredge² [~] *v/t* **1.** bestreuen (**with** mit). **2.** *Mehl etc* streuen (**over** über *acc*).

dredg·er¹ [ˈdredʒə] *s* ⊗ Bagger *m*.

dredg·er² [~] *s* Streubüchse *f*, Streuer *m*.

dreg [dreg] *s mst pl* **1.** (Boden)Satz *m*: **drain to the ~s** bis auf den letzten Tropfen *od.* bis zur Neige leeren. **2.** *fig.* Abschaum *m*.

drench [drentʃ] *v/t* durchnässen: **~ed in tears** in Tränen aufgelöst; → **skin** 1.

dress [dres] **I** *s* **1.** Kleidung *f*. **2.** (Damen)Kleid *n*. **II** *v/t* **3.** an-, bekleiden, anziehen; **~ o.s., get ~ed** sich anziehen; → **kill** 9. **4.** einkleiden. **5.** schmücken, dekorieren. **6.** zurechtmachen, (her-) richten, *bsd.* Speisen zubereiten; *Salat* anmachen; *Haar* frisieren. **7.** ✾ *Wunde etc* verbinden. **III** *v/i* **8.** sich anziehen: **~ well (badly)** *weitS.* sich geschmackvoll (geschmacklos) kleiden.

Verbindungen mit Adverbien:

dress| **down I** *v/t* F *j-m* e-e Standpauke halten, *j-m* aufs Dach steigen. **II** *v/i* sich unauffällig kleiden. **~ up I** *v/t* **1.** feinmachen; herausputzen. **2.** *Fakten etc* verpacken (**in** in *acc*); beschönigen; ausschmücken (**with** mit). **II** *v/i* **3.** sich feinmachen; sich herausputzen. **4.** sich kostümieren *od.* verkleiden (**as** als).

dress| **cir·cle** *s thea. etc* erster Rang. **~ coat** *s* Frack *m*.

dress·er [ˈdresə] *s* **1.** *thea.* Garderobiere *f*. **2. be a fashionable ~** immer modisch gekleidet sein. **3.** Küchen-, Geschirrschrank *m*. **4.** → **dressing table.**

dress·ing [ˈdresɪŋ] *s* **1.** Ankleiden *n*. **2.** Zubereitung *f*. **3.** Dressing *n* (*Salatsoße*). **4.** ✾ Verband *m*. **~ down** *s* F Standpauke *f*: **give** *s.o.* **a ~** → **dress down** I; **get a ~** eins aufs Dach bekommen. **~ gown** *s* Morgenmantel *m*, (*für Damen a.*) Morgenrock *m*. **~ room** *s* Ankleidezimmer *n*; (Künstler)Garderobe *f*; (*Sport*) (Umkleide)Kabine *f*. **~ ta·ble** *s* Toilettentisch *m*, Frisierkommode *f*.

'**dress**|**mak·er** *s* (*bsd.* Damen)Schneider(in). **~ re·hears·al** *s thea.* Generalprobe *f* (*a. fig.*); Kostümprobe *f*. **~ shirt** *s* Frackhemd *n*. **~ suit** *s* Abend-, Gesellschaftsanzug *m*.

dress·y ['dresɪ] *adj* □ F **1.** geschniegelt, aufgetakelt. **2.** elegant, schick.

drew [dru:] *pret von* **draw.**

drib·ble ['drɪbl] I *v/i* **1.** tröpfeln: **~ away** *fig.* allmählich zu Ende gehen (*Geld etc*). **2.** sabbern, geifern. **3.** *Sport:* dribbeln: **~ past** *j-n* umdribbeln. II *v/t* **4.** tröpfeln lassen, träufeln. III *s* **5.** → **drib(b)let. 6.** *Sport:* Dribbling *n*.

drib·(b)let ['drɪblɪt] *s* kleine Menge *od.* Summe: **in** (*od.* **by**) **~s** in kleinen Mengen *od.* Raten.

dribs and drabs [drɪbz] *s pl:* **in ~** F kleckerweise.

dried [draɪd] *adj* Dörr..., getrocknet: **~ fruit** Dörrobst *n*; **~ milk** Trockenmilch *f*.   Trockner *m*.⎫

dri·er ['draɪə] *s* Trockenapparat *m*.⎰

drift [drɪft] I *s* **1.** Treiben *n*; *fig.* (Sich-)Treibenlassen *n*, Ziellosigkeit *f*. **2.** ✓, ♣ Abtrift *f*. **3.** *fig.* Strömung *f*, Tendenz *f*; Absicht *f*; Gedankengang *m*. **4.** (*Schnee*)Verwehung *f*, (*Schnee-, Sand-*) Wehe *f*. II *v/i* **5.** getrieben werden, treiben (*a. fig.* **into** in e-n Krieg *etc*): **let things ~** den Dingen ihren Lauf lassen. **6.** *fig.* sich (willenlos) treiben lassen. **7.** sich häufen (*Sand, Schnee*). III *v/t* **8.** (dahin)treiben. **'drift·er** *s* ziellos herumwandernder Mensch.

drift| ice *s* Treibeis *n*. **'~·wood** *s* Treibholz *n*.

drill¹ [drɪl] I *s* **1.** ◎ Bohrer *m*. **2.** ✗ Drill *m* (*a. fig.*); Exerzieren *n*. II *v/t* **3.** Loch bohren (*in* in *acc*). **4.** ✗ drillen (*a. fig. in* in *dat*). **5. ~ s.th. into s.o.** *j-m et.* eindrillen *od.* einpauken. III *v/i* **6.** bohren (*for* nach).

drill² [~] *s* Drillich *m*.

drink [drɪŋk] I *s* **1.** Getränk *n*; *coll.* Getränke *pl*. **2.** das Trinken, der Alkohol: **take to ~** sich das Trinken angewöhnen. **3.** Schluck *m*. II *v/t* (*irr*) **4.** trinken, (*Tier a.*) saufen: **~ away** Geld *etc* vertrinken; *Sorgen etc* im Alkohol ertränken; **~ down** *j-n* unter den Tisch trinken; **~ in** *fig.* (gierig) in sich aufnehmen, verschlingen; **~ off** (*od.* **up**) austrinken; → **table. 5.** trinken *od.* anstoßen auf (*acc*): → **health** 3. III *v/i* (*irr*) **6.** trinken, *weitS. a.* (ein) Trinker sein, (*Tier a.*) saufen: **~ off** (*od.* **up**) austrinken. **7.**

trinken, anstoßen (**to** auf *acc*): **~ to s.o.** *j-m* zuprosten *od.* zutrinken; → *health* 3. **'drink·a·ble** *adj* trinkbar, Trink... **'drink·er** *s* **1.** Trinkende *m, f*. **2.** Trinker(in).

drink·ing ['drɪŋkɪŋ] I *s* Trinken *n*. II *adj* Trink...: **~ song** (**water**, *etc*); **~ straw** Trinkhalm *m*.

drip [drɪp] I *v/i* **1.** tropfen (*a. Hahn etc*), tröpfeln. **2.** triefen (**with** von, vor *dat*) (*a. fig.*). II *v/t* **3.** tropfen *od.* tröpfeln lassen. **4. ~ sweat** vor Schweiß triefen. III *s* **5.** → **dripping** 1. **6.** ⚕ Tropf(infusion *f*) *m*: **be on the ~** am Tropf hängen. **7.** F Nulpe *f*; Flasche *f*. **,~·'dry** *adj* bügelfrei. II *v/t* tropfnaß aufhängen.

drip·ping ['drɪpɪŋ] I *s* **1.** Tropfen *n* (*a. Geräusch*), Tröpfeln *n*. **2.** (abtropfendes) Bratenfett. II *adj* **3.** tropfend (*a. Hahn etc*), tröpfelnd. **4.** triefend (**with** von, vor *dat*) (*a. fig.*). **5.** triefend (naß), tropf-, triefnaß. III *adv* **6. ~ wet** → 5.

drive [draɪv] I *s* **1.** Fahrt *f*; *engS.* Aus-, Spazierfahrt *f*: **an hour's ~** e-e Autostunde. **2.** Fahrweg *m*; Zufahrt(sstraße) *f*; (*private*) Auffahrt *f*. **3.** *Golf, Tennis:* Drive *m*, Treibschlag *m*. **4.** *fig.* Kampagne *f*, Feldzug *m*. **5.** *fig.* Schwung *m*, Elan *m*. **6.** *psych.* Trieb *m*. **7.** ◎ Antrieb *m*. **8.** *mot.* (*Links- etc*) Steuerung *f*. II *v/t* (*irr*) **9.** treiben (*a. fig.*); Nagel *etc* schlagen, Pfahl rammen (**into** in *acc*): **~ s.th. into s.o.** *j-m et.* einbleuen; → **bend** 1, **corner** 2, **home** 9, **wall** 1, *etc*. **10.** *j-n* veranlassen (**to,** *into* zu; **to do** zu tun), dazu bringen (**to do** zu tun): **driven by hunger** vom Hunger getrieben. **11.** *Auto etc* lenken, steuern, fahren; (*im Auto etc*) fahren, befördern, bringen (**to** nach). **12.** ◎ (an)treiben. **13.** zielbewußt durchführen: **~ a hard bargain** hart verhandeln; überzogene Forderungen stellen. III *v/i* (*irr*) **14.** treiben, getrieben werden. **15.** jagen, stürmen. **16.** (*Auto*) fahren: **~ into a wall** gegen e-e Mauer fahren. **17.** *fig.* abzielen (**at** auf *acc*): **what is he driving at?** worauf will er hinaus?

Verbindungen mit Adverbien:

drive| a·way *v/t a. fig.* Sorgen *etc* vertreiben, -jagen; *Bedenken etc* zerstreuen. **~ in** *v/t* Nagel *etc* einschlagen, Pfahl einrammen. **~ up** I *v/t* Preise *etc* in die Höhe treiben. **II** *v/i* (*to*) vorfahren (vor *dat*); heranfahren (an *acc*).

'drive-in *adj* Auto...: ~ *cinema* (*Am. motion-picture theater*) → IIa; ~ *restaurant* → IIb; ~ *window* → IIc. **II** *s* a) Autokino *n*, Drive-in-Kino *n*, b) Drive-in-Restaurant *n*, c) Autoschalter *m*, Drive-in-Schalter *m* (*e-r Bank*).

driv·el ['drɪvl] **I** *v/i pret u. pp* **-eled,** *bsd. Br.* **-elled 1.** sabbern, geifern. **2.** faseln. **II** *s* **3.** Geifer *m*. **4.** Gefasel *n*.

driv·en ['drɪvn] *pp von* **drive.**

driv·er ['draɪvə] *s* (*Auto- etc*)Fahrer *m*; (*Kran- etc, Br. Lokomotiv*)Führer *m*; ~*'s cab s* Führerhaus *n* (*e-s Lastwagens od. Krans*), 🚂 *Br.* Führerstand *m*. ~*'s li·cense s Am.* Führerschein *m*.

'drive-way *s* Zufahrt(sstraße) *f*; (private) Auffahrt.

driv·ing ['draɪvɪŋ] **I** *adj* **1.** (an)treibend: ~ *force* treibende Kraft. **2.** ⚙ Treib..., Antriebs... **II** *s* **3.** Autofahren *n*. **4.** *mot.* Fahrweise *f*, -stil *m*. ~ **in·struc·tor** *s* Fahrlehrer(in). ~ **les·son** *s* Fahrstunde *f*: *take* ~*s* Fahrunterricht nehmen, den Führerschein machen. ~ **li·cence** *s Br.* Führerschein *m*. ~ **mir·ror** *s mot.* Rückspiegel *m*. ~ **school** *s* Fahrschule *f*. ~ **test** *s* Fahrprüfung *f*: *take one's* ~ die Fahrprüfung *od.* den Führerschein machen.

driz·zle ['drɪzl] **I** *v/impers* nieseln. **II** *s* Sprüh-, Nieselregen *m*.

droll [drəʊl] *adj* ☐ drollig, spaßig.

drom·e·dar·y ['drɒmədərɪ] *s zo.* Dromedar *n*.

drone¹ [drəʊn] *s zo.* Drohne *f*, *fig. a.* Schmarotzer *m*.

drone² [~] **I** *v/i* brummen, summen. **II** *v/t* her(unter)leiern. **III** *s* Brummen *n*, Summen *n*.

drool [druːl] **I** *v/i* **1.** → **drivel** I. **2.** ~ *over* (*od. about*) sich begeistern für, verrückt sein in (*acc*). **II** *s* **3.** → **drivel** II.

droop [druːp] **I** *v/i* **1.** (schlaff) herabhängen *od.* -sinken. **2.** ermatten, erschlaffen (*from, with* vor *dat*). **3.** sinken (*Mut etc*), erlahmen (*Interesse etc*). **4.** den Kopf hängenlassen (*a. Blume*). **II** *v/t* **5.** (schlaff) herabhängen lassen. **6.** *Kopf* hängenlassen. **III** *s* **7.** Herabhängen *n*.

drop [drɒp] **I** *s* **1.** Tropfen *m*: *a* ~ *in the bucket* (*od. ocean*) *fig.* ein Tropfen auf

den heißen Stein; *empty to the last* ~ bis auf den letzten Tropfen leeren; *he has had a* ~ *too much* er hat e-n über den Durst getrunken. **2.** Bonbon *m*, *n*: *fruit* ~ Drops *m*. **3.** Fall(tiefe *f*) *m*: *a* ~ *of ten yards* ein Fall aus 10 Yards Höhe. **4.** *fig.* (Ab)Fall *m*, Sturz *m*: ~ *in prices* 🡇 Preissturz; ~ *in* (*ahem*) *temperature* Temperatursturz, -abfall. **5.** Falltür *f*. **6.** *bsd. Am.* (*Brief- etc*)Einwurf *m*. **II** *v/i* **7.** (herab)tropfen, herabtröpfeln. **8.** (herunter)fallen. *let s.th.* ~ et. fallen lassen. **9.** sinken, fallen (*beide a. Preise etc*): ~ *into a chair* sich in e-n Sessel fallen lassen. **10.** a) (ohnmächtig) zu Boden sinken, umfallen: *be fit* (*od. ready*) *to* ~ (*with fatigue*) zum Umfallen müde sein, b) *a.* ~ *dead* tot umfallen: ~ *dead!* *sl.* geh zum Teufel! **11.** leiser werden (*Stimme*); sich legen (*Wind*). **III** *v/t* **12.** tropfen *od.* tröpfeln lassen. **13.** fallen lassen: *everything* ~ *s* alles liegen- u. stehenlassen. **14.** (hinein)werfen (*into* in *acc*). **15.** *Bemerkung* fallenlassen: ~ *s.o. a line* (*od. note*) j-m ein paar Zeilen schreiben. **16.** *j-n*, *Absicht etc* fallenlassen. **17.** *Tätigkeit* aufgeben, aufhören mit: ~ *it!* hör auf damit! **18.** *Last, a. Passagiere* absetzen. **19.** *Buchstaben etc* auslassen: → **H** 1. **20.** *Sport:* *Punkt etc* abgeben (*to* gegen). **21.** *Augen, a. Stimme* senken (*to a whisper* zu e-m Flüstern).

Verbindungen mit Adverbien:

drop| a·way *v/i* immer weniger werden. ~ **back,** ~ **be·hind** *v/i* **1.** zurückfallen. **2.** sich zurückfallen lassen. ~ **in** *v/i* **1.** hereinkommen (*a. fig. Aufträge etc*). **2.** (kurz) hereinschauen (*on* bei). ~ **off** *v/i* **1.** zurückgehen (*Umsatz etc*), nachlassen (*Interesse etc*). **2.** einschlafen; -nicken. **II** *v/t* **3.** → **drop** 18. ~ **out** *v/i* **1.** aussteigen (*of* aus Politik *etc*). **2.** die Schule *od.* das Studium abbrechen.

drop·let ['drɒplɪt] *s* Tröpfchen *n*.

'drop-out *s* **1.** Aussteiger *m* (*aus der Gesellschaft*). **2.** (Schul-, Studien)Abbrecher *m*.

drop·pings ['drɒpɪŋz] *s pl* (Tier)Kot *m*.

drop·sy ['drɒpsɪ] *s* 🔬 Wassersucht *f*.

drought [draʊt] *s* Trockenheit *f*, Dürre(periode) *f*.

drove¹ [drəʊv] *pret von* **drive.**

drove² [~] *s* Schar *f* (*Menschen*): *in* ~*s* in

dub

(großen *od.* hellen) Scharen, scharen-weise.

drown [draʊn] **I** *v/i* **1.** ertrinken. **II** *v/t* **2.** ertränken: *be drowned* → 1; ~ *one's sorrows* s-e Sorgen im Alkohol ertränken. **3.** überschwemmen: *be ~ed in tears* in Tränen schwimmen *od.* zerfließen. **4.** *a.* ~ *out bsd.* Stimme übertönen.

drowse [draʊz] **I** *v/i* **1.** dösen: ~ *off* eindösen. **II** *v/t* **2.** schläfrig machen. **3.** ~ *away* Zeit verdösen. **III** *s* **4.** Dösen *n.* '**drows·y** *adj* □ **1.** schläfrig; verschlafen. **2.** einschläfernd. **3.** *fig.* verschlafen, -träumt.

drudge [drʌdʒ] **I** *s* **1.** *fig.* Kuli *m*, Last-, Packesel *m*; Arbeitstier *n*. **2.** → *drudgery*. **II** *v/i* **3.** sich (ab)placken *od.* (ab)schinden. '**drudg·er·y** *s* (stumpfsinnige) Plackerei *od.* Schinderei.

drug [drʌg] **I** *s* **1.** Arzneimittel *n*, Medikament *n*. **2.** Droge *f* (*a. fig.*), Rauschgift *n*: *be on* (*off*) ~*s* rauschgift- *od.* drogensüchtig (clean) sein. **3.** Betäubungsmittel *n* (*a. fig.*). **4.** ~ *on* (*Am. a. in*) *the market* † schwerverkäufliche Ware, (*im Laden a.*) Ladenhüter *m*. **II** *v/t* **5.** j-m Medikamente geben. **6.** j-n unter Drogen setzen. **7.** ein Betäubungsmittel beimischen (*dat*). **8.** betäuben (*a. fig.*): ~*ged with sleep* schlaftrunken. ~ **a·buse** *s* **1.** Drogenmißbrauch *m*. **2.** Medikamentenmißbrauch *m*. ~ **ad·dict** *s* **1.** Drogen-, Rauschgiftsüchtige *m, f*. **2.** Medikamentensüchtige *m, f*. '~**ad,dict·ed** *adj* **1.** drogen-, rauschgiftsüchtig. **2.** medikamentensüchtig. ~ **ad·dic·tion** *s* **1.** Drogen-, Rauschgiftsucht *f*. **2.** Medikamentensucht *f*. ~ **clin·ic** *s* Drogenklinik *f*. ~ **deal·er** *s* Drogen-, Rauschgifthändler *m*. ~ **de·pend·ence** *s* **1.** Drogenabhängigkeit *f*. **2.** Medikamentenabhängigkeit *f*.

drug·gist [ˈdrʌgɪst] *s Am.* Inhaber(in) e-s Drugstores.

'**drug∣push·er** *s* F Pusher *m* (*Rauschgifthändler*). ~ **scene** *s* Drogenszene *f*.

drug·ster [ˈdrʌgstə] → *drug addict* 1.

'**drug·store** *s Am.* Drugstore *m*.

drum [drʌm] **I** *s* **1.** ♪ Trommel *f* (*a.* ⚙): ~*s* *pl* Schlagzeug *n*. **2.** Trommeln *n* (*a. weitS. des Regens etc*). **3.** *anat.* Mittelohr *n*; Trommelfell *n*. **II** *v/t* **4.** *Rhythmus* trommeln: ~ *s.th. into s.o.* *fig.* j-m

et. einhämmern. **5.** trommeln auf (*acc*); trommeln mit (*on* auf *acc*). **6.** ~ *up* Hilfe zs.-trommeln, (Kunden etc.)werben; *Aufträge etc* hereinholen; sich *et.* ausdenken. **III** *v/i* **7.** trommeln (*at* an *acc*; *on* auf *acc*). '~**beat** *s* Trommelschlag *m*. ~ **brake** *s* ⚙ Trommelbremse *f*. '~**fire** *s* Trommelfeuer *n* (*a. fig.*). '~**head** *s* ♪, *a. anat.* Trommelfell *n*.

drum·mer [ˈdrʌmə] *s* ♪ Trommler *m*; Schlagzeuger *m*.

'**drum·stick** *s* **1.** Trommelstock *m*, -schlegel *m*. **2.** Unterschenkel *m* (*von zubereitetem Geflügel*).

drunk [drʌŋk] **I** *pp von* **drink. II** *adj pred* **1.** betrunken: *get* ~ sich betrinken; (*as*) ~ *as a lord* F total blau. **2.** *fig.* berauscht (*with* von): ~ *with joy* freudetrunken. **III** *s* **3.** a) Betrunkene *m, f*, b) → *drunkard*. **drunk·ard** [ˈ-əd] *s* (Gewohnheits)Trinker(in), Säufer(in). '**drunk·en** *adj attr* **1.** betrunken: *a* ~ *man* ein Betrunkener; ~ *driving* Trunkenheit *f* am Steuer; → *stupor*. **2.** Sauf...: ~ *party*. '**drunk·en·ness** *s* **1.** Betrunkenheit *f*. **2.** Trunksucht *f*.

dry [draɪ] **I** *adj* □ **1.** *allg.* trocken (*a. fig. Humor etc*): *rub* ~ trockenreiben. **2.** F durstig. **3.** durstig machend (*Arbeit*). **4.** trocken (*ohne Aufstrich*). **5.** trocken, langweilig: (*as*) ~ *as dust* F stinklangweilig. **6.** trocken, herb (*Wein etc*). **7.** F trocken, weg vom Alkohol. **II** *v/t* **8.** trocknen. **9.** ~ *o.s.* (*one's hands*) sich (sich die Hände) abtrocknen (*on* an *dat*). **10.** *oft* ~ *up* Geschirr abtrocknen. **11.** *Obst etc* dörren. **III** *v/i* **12.** trocknen, trocken werden. **13.** ~ *up* ein-, aus-, vertrocknen; F die Klappe halten; F steckenbleiben (*Schauspieler etc*). ~ **bat·ter·y** *s* ⚡ Trockenbatterie *f*. ~ **cell** *s* ⚡ Trockenelement *n*. ~ **clean** *v/t* chemisch reinigen. ~ **clean·er('s)** *s* chemische Reinigung(sanstalt). ~ **clean·ing** *s* chemische Reinigung.

dry·er → **drier.**

dry∣ goods *s pl* † Textilien *pl*. ~ **ice** *s* 🝆 Trockeneis *n*.

dry·ness [ˈdraɪnɪs] *s* Trockenheit *f*.

dry nurse *s* Säuglingsschwester *f*.

du·al [ˈdjuːəl] *adj* □ doppelt, zweifach: ~ *carriageway* *mot. Br.* Schnellstraße *f*.

dub¹ [dʌb] *v/t* nennen, j-m den (Spitz-) Namen ... geben.

dub² [~] v/t Film synchronisieren.

du·bi·ous ['dju:bjəs] adj □ **1.** zweifelhaft: a) unklar, zweideutig, b) ungewiß, unbestimmt, c) fragwürdig, dubios: ~ *pleasure* zweifelhaftes Vergnügen, d) unzuverlässig. **2.** unschlüssig, schwankend; unsicher, im Zweifel (*of*, *about* über *acc*).

du·cal ['dju:kl] adj □ herzoglich, Herzogs...

duch·ess ['dʌtʃɪs] s Herzogin f.

duch·y ['dʌtʃɪ] s Herzogtum n.

duck¹ [dʌk] s **1.** orn. Ente f: *look like a dying* ~ (*in a thunderstorm*) F dumm aus der Wäsche schauen. **2.** Br. F Schatz m.

duck² [~] **I** v/i **1.** (rasch) (unter)tauchen. **2.** a. fig. sich ducken (*to* vor *dat*). **3.** ~ *out* F verduften; fig. sich drücken (*of* vor *dat*). **II** v/t **4.** (unter)tauchen. **5.** *Kopf* ducken, einziehen. **6.** F sich drücken vor (*dat*).

duct [dʌkt] s **1.** ◉ Röhre f, Rohr n, Leitung f. **2.** anat. Gang m, Kanal m.

duc·tile ['dʌktaɪl] adj □ **1.** phys., ◉ dehn-, streckbar. **2.** fig. fügsam.

dud [dʌd] s F **1.** ✗ Blindgänger m (a. fig.). **2.** Niete f, Versager m. **3.** ungedeckter Scheck.

dude [dju:d] s Am. F **1.** Dandy m. **2.** Stadtmensch m.

due [dju:] **I** adj (□ → *duly*) **1.** ✝ fällig: *fall* (*od. become*) ~ fällig werden; *when* ~ bei Fälligkeit; ~ *date* Fälligkeitstermin m. **2.** *zeitlich* fällig: *the train is* ~ *at* ... der Zug soll um ... ankommen. **3.** *be* ~ *to* zuzuschreiben sein (*dat*), zurückzuführen sein auf (*acc*): *it is* ~ *to him* es ist ihm zu verdanken. **4.** gebührend, geziemend: *be* ~ *to s.o.* j-m gebühren *od.* zukommen; → *credit* 3, *hono(u)r* 4. **5.** gebührend, angemessen: *after* ~ *consideration* nach reiflicher Überlegung. **6.** passend, richtig: *in* ~ *course* zur rechten *od.* gegebenen Zeit; *in* ~ *time* rechtzeitig, termingerecht; *in* ~ *form* ordnungsgemäß, vorschriftsmäßig. **7.** ~ *to* wegen (*gen*), infolge *od.* auf Grund (*gen od.* von). **II** s **8.** *das* Gebührende: *give s.o. his* ~ j-m Gerechtigkeit widerfahren lassen. **9.** pl Gebühren pl.

du·el ['dju:əl] **I** s Duell n (a. fig.). **II** v/i pret u. pp **-eled**, bsd. Br. **-elled** sich duellieren.

du·et [dju:'et] s ♩ **1.** Duett n. **2.** Duo n.

duff·er ['dʌfə] s F (alter) Trottel.

dug [dʌg] pret u. pp von **dig**. '~·out s **1.** ✗ Unterstand m. **2.** Einbaum m.

du·i ['dju:i:] pl von **duo**.

duke [dju:k] s Herzog m.

dull [dʌl] **I** adj □ **1.** schwer von Begriff, dumm. **2.** schwerfällig, träge. **3.** teilnahmslos. **4.** langweilig, fad(e). **5.** ✝ flau, schleppend. **6.** stumpf (*Klinge etc*). **7.** matt, glanzlos (*Augen, Farbe*). **8.** dumpf (*Klang, Schmerz etc*). **II** v/t **9.** abstumpfen. **10.** (ab)schwächen. **11.** mildern, dämpfen. **12.** *Schmerz* betäuben. **dull·ard** ['~əd] s Dummkopf m. **'dul(l)·ness** s **1.** Dummheit f. **2.** Trägheit f. **3.** Teilnahmslosigkeit f. **4.** Langweiligkeit f. **5.** ✝ Flaute f. **6.** Stumpfheit f. **7.** Mattheit f. **8.** Dumpfheit f.

du·ly ['dju:lɪ] adv **1.** ordnungsgemäß. **2.** rechtzeitig.

dumb [dʌm] adj □ **1.** stumm (*a. fig.*): *strike s.o.* ~ j-m die Sprache verschlagen *od.* rauben; (*struck*) ~ sprachlos (*with* vor *dat*); *the* ~ *masses* pl die stumme Masse. **2.** bsd. Am. F doof, dumm. '~·bell s **1.** Sport: Hantel f. **2.** bsd. Am. sl. Trottel m. ~'found v/t verblüffen. ~'found·ed adj verblüfft, sprachlos. ~ show s Pantomime f. ,~'wait·er s **1.** stummer Diener, Serviertisch m. **2.** Speiseaufzug m.

dum·found, etc → **dumbfound**, etc.

dum·my ['dʌmɪ] **I** s **1.** Attrappe f, ⊕ Leer-, Schaupackung f. **2.** Kleider-, Schaufensterpuppe f. **3.** ✝, ⚖ Strohmann m. **4.** Br. Schnuller m. **II** adj **5.** Schein...

dump [dʌmp] **I** v/t **1.** (hin)plumpsen *od.* (-)fallen lassen, hinwerfen. **2.** *Schutt etc* auskippen, abladen; *Karren etc* (um-) kippen, entladen. **3.** ✝ zu Dumpingpreisen verkaufen. **II** v/i **4.** plumpsen. **5.** (s-n) Schutt abladen. **III** s **6.** a) Schutt-, Abfallhaufen m, b) (Schutt-, Müll)Abladeplatz m, Müllkippe f, -halde f. '**dump·er** (**truck**) s mot. Dumper m, Kipper m. '**dump·ing** s **1.** (Schutt)Abladen n: ~ *ground* → **dump** 6b. **2.** ✝ Dumping n.

dump·ling ['dʌmplɪŋ] s **1.** Knödel m, Kloß m. **2.** F Dickerchen n.

dumps [dʌmps] s pl: (**down**) *in the* ~ F down, niedergeschlagen.

dump truck → *dumper* (*truck*).

dun [dʌn] *v/t bsd. Schuldner* mahnen.

dune [dju:n] *s* Düne *f*. ~ **bug·gy** *s mot.* Strandbuggy *m*.

dung [dʌŋ] *s* Mist *m*, Dung *m*.

dun·ga·rees [ˌdʌŋɡəˈriːz] *s pl* Arbeitsanzug *m*: (**pair of**) ~ Arbeitshose *f*.

dun·geon [ˈdʌndʒən] *s* Verlies *n*.

'**dung·hill** *s* Misthaufen *m*.

dunk [dʌŋk] *v/t Brot etc* eintunken, stippen.

du·o [ˈdjuːəʊ] *pl* -**os**, **du·i** [ˈ⌣iː] → *duet*.

du·o·de·num [ˌdjuːəʊˈdiːnəm] *pl* -**na** [⌣nə], -**nums** *s anat.* Zwölffingerdarm *m*.

dupe [dju:p] **I** *s* Betrogene *m*, *f*. **II** *v/t* betrügen.

du·plex [ˈdjuːpleks] **I** *adj* doppelt, Doppel..., zweifach: ~ **apartment** → IIa; ~ **house** → IIb. **II** *s Am.* a) Maison(n)ette *f*, b) Doppel-, Zweifamilienhaus *n*.

du·pli·cate [ˈdjuːplɪkət] **I** *adj* 1. doppelt, Doppel..., zweifach. 2. genau gleich *od.* entsprechend: ~ **key** → 5. **II** *s* 3. Duplikat *n*, Ab-, Zweitschrift *f*, Kopie *f*: *in* ~ in zweifacher Ausfertigung. 4. (genau gleiches) Seitenstück, Kopie *f*. 5. Zweit- *od.* Nachschlüssel *m*. **III** *v/t* [ˈ⌣keɪt] 6. ein Duplikat anfertigen von, kopieren, vervielfältigen. 7. *Experiment etc* (beliebig) wiederholen. **du·pli·ca·tor** [ˈ⌣keɪtə] *s* Vervielfältigungsapparat *m*.

du·ra·bil·i·ty [ˌdjʊərəˈbɪlətɪ] *s* a) Haltbarkeit *f*, b) Dauerhaftigkeit *f*. '**du·ra·ble I** *adj* □ a) haltbar, ✝ langlebig: ~ **goods** → II, b) dauerhaft. **II** *s pl* ✝ Gebrauchsgüter *pl*. **du·ra·tion** [⌣ˈreɪʃn] *s* Dauer *f*: *for the* ~ *of* für die Dauer von (*od. gen*).

du·ress [djʊəˈres] *s* Zwang *m* (*a.* ⚖).

du·ring [ˈdjʊərɪŋ] *prp* während.

dusk [dʌsk] *s* (Abend)Dämmerung *f*: *at* ~ bei Einbruch der Dunkelheit. '**dusk·y** *adj* □ dämmerig, düster (*a. fig.*).

dust [dʌst] **I** *s* 1. Staub *m*: *throw* (*od. cast*) ~ *in s.o.'s eyes fig.* j-m Sand in die Augen streuen; *raise a* ~ a) e-e Staubwolke aufwirbeln, b) *a. kick up a* ~ *fig.* viel Staub aufwirbeln; *the* ~ *has settled* die Aufregung hat sich gelegt, die Wogen haben sich geglättet; → *bite* 1, *kiss* 2. **I** *v/t* 2. abstauben. 3. bestreuen, bestäuben. **III** *v/i* 4. Staub wischen. 5. staubig werden, verstauben. '~**bin** *s Br.* Abfall-, Mülleimer *m*; Abfall-, Mülltonne *f*: ~ **man** Müllmann *m*. '~**cart** *s Br.* Müllwagen *m*. ~ **cov·er** *s* Schutzumschlag *m*.

dust·er [ˈdʌstə] *s* Staubtuch *n*.

dust| **jack·et** → *dust cover*. ~**man** [ˈ⌣mən] *s* (*irr man*) *Br.* Müllmann *m*. ~**storm** *s* Staubsturm *m*. ~ **trap** *s* Staubfänger *m*. '~**up** *s* F 1. Krach *m*. 2. handgreifliche Auseinandersetzung.

dust·y [ˈdʌstɪ] *adj* staubig: *not so* ~ *Br.* F gar nicht so übel.

Dutch [dʌtʃ] **I** *adj* 1. holländisch, niederländisch. **II** *adv* 2. *go* ~ getrennte Kasse machen. **III** *s* 3. *ling.* Holländisch *n*, Niederländisch *n*. 4. *the* ~ *pl* die Holländer *pl*, die Niederländer *pl*. ~ **courage** *s* F angetrunkener Mut. ~**man** [ˈ⌣mən] *s* (*irr man*) Holländer *m*, Niederländer *m*. '~**wom·an** *s* (*irr woman*) Holländerin *f*, Niederländerin *f*.

du·te·ous [ˈdjuːtjəs] *adj* → *dutiful*. **du·ti·a·ble** [ˈ⌣tjəbl] *adj* zollpflichtig. **du·ti·ful** [ˈ⌣tɪfʊl] *adj* □ pflichtgetreu, -bewußt.

du·ty [ˈdjuːtɪ] *s* 1. Pflicht *f*: a) Schuldigkeit *f* (*to, toward*[*s*] gegen[über]), b) Aufgabe *f*: *do one's* ~ s-e Pflicht tun; *breach of* ~ Pflichtverletzung *f*. 2. Dienst *m*: *be on* ~ Dienst haben, im Dienst sein; *be off* ~ nicht im Dienst sein, dienstfrei haben; *do* ~ *for* benutzt werden *od.* dienen als; *j-n* vertreten. 3. ✝ Zoll *m*. **II** *adj* 4. ~ **call** Höflichkeits-, Pflichtbesuch *m*. 5. ~ **chemist** *Br.* dienstbereite Apotheke; ~ **doctor** Bereitschaftsarzt *m*; ~ **officer** ✗ Offizier *m* vom Dienst; ~ **roster** Dienstplan *m*. '~**free I** *adj u. adv* zollfrei: ~ **shop** Duty-free-Shop *m*. **II** *s pl* F zollfreie Ware(n *pl*).

dwarf [dwɔ:f] **I** *pl* **dwarfs**, **dwarves** [⌣vz] *s* Zwerg(in) (*a. fig.*). **II** *adj* zwergenhaft, *bsd.* ♀, *zo.* Zwerg... **III** *v/t* klein erscheinen lassen; *fig.* in den Schatten stellen. '**dwarf·ish** *adj* □ zwergenhaft.

dwarves [dwɔ:vz] *pl von* dwarf.

dwell [dwel] *v/i* (*mst irr*) 1. wohnen, leben. 2. ~ *on (up)g.* (im Geiste) verweilen bei. '**dwell·er** *s mst in Zssgn* Bewohner(in). '**dwell·ing** *s* Wohnung *f*: ~ **house** Wohnhaus *n*.

dwelt [dwelt] *pret u. pp von* dwell.

dwin·dle ['dwɪndl] *v/i* abnehmen, schwinden.

dye [daɪ] **I** *s* **1.** Farbstoff *m.* **2.** Färbung *f*: *of the deepest* (*od. blackest*) ~ *fig.* von der übelsten Sorte. **II** *v/t* **3.** färben.

‚dyed-in-the-'wool *adj* eingefleischt, ... durch u. durch.

'dye·works *s pl* (*oft sg konstruiert*) Färberei *f.*

dy·ing ['daɪɪŋ] *adj* **1.** sterbend: *be* ~ im Sterben liegen. **2.** Sterbe...: ~ *hour* Todesstunde *f*; ~ *wish* letzter Wunsch.

dyke → *dike*[1] *u.* [2].

dy·nam·ic [daɪ'næmɪk] **I** *adj* (*~ally*) dynamisch (*a. fig.*). **II** *s pl* (*sg konstruiert*) Dynamik *f* (*a. fig.*).

dy·na·mite ['daɪnəmaɪt] **I** *s* Dynamit *n.* **II** *v/t* (*mit Dynamit*) sprengen.

dy·na·mo ['daɪnəməʊ] *pl* **-mos** *s ⚡* Dynamo *m.*

dy·nas·ty ['dɪnəstɪ] *s* Dynastie *f.*

dys·en·ter·y ['dɪsntrɪ] *s ⚕* Ruhr *f.*

dys·func·tion [dɪs'fʌŋkʃn] *s ⚕* Funktionsstörung *f.*

E

each [iːtʃ] **I** *adj* jede(r, -s): ~ *one* jede(r) einzelne. **II** *pron*: ~ *of us* jede(r) von uns; ~ *other* einander, sich. **III** *adv* je, pro Person *od.* Stück.

ea·ger ['iːgə] *adj* □ **1.** eifrig: ~ *beaver* F Übereifrige *m, f.* **2.** (*for*) begierig (nach), erpicht, gespannt (auf *acc*): *be* ~ *to do s.th.* darauf brennen, et. zu tun. **3.** gespannt (*Aufmerksamkeit, Blick etc*). **'ea·ger·ness** *s* **1.** Eifer *m.* **2.** Begierde *f.*

ea·gle ['iːgl] *s orn.* Adler *m.*

ear[1] [ɪə] *s* **1.** *anat.* Ohr *n*: *be all* ~*s* ganz Ohr sein; *be up to the* (*od. one's*) ~*s in debt* (*work*) bis über die Ohren in Schulden (Arbeit) sitzen *od.* stecken; *fall on deaf* ~*s* auf taube Ohren stoßen; *have* (*od. keep*) *an* (*od. one's*) ~ *to the ground* die Ohren offenhalten; *turn a deaf* ~ *to* die Ohren verschließen vor (*dat*); → *flea, prick* 7, *thick* 1, *wet* 1. **2.** *fig.* Gehör *n,* Ohr *n*: *play by* ~ nach dem Gehör spielen; *fig.* improvisieren.

ear[2] [~] *s* (Getreide)Ähre *f.*

ear·ache ['ɪəreɪk] *s* Ohrenschmerzen *pl.* **~·drum** ['ɪədrʌm] *s anat.* Trommelfell *n.*

earl [ɜːl] *s* britischer Graf.

'ear·lobe *s anat.* Ohrläppchen *n.*

ear·ly ['ɜːlɪ] **I** *adv* **1.** früh(zeitig): *as* ~ *as May* schon im Mai. **2.** bald: *as* ~ *as possible* so bald wie möglich. **3.** zu früh; früher. **II** *adj* **4.** früh(zeitig): ~

riser, humor. ~ *bird* Frühaufsteher(in); *the* ~ *bird catches the worm* Morgenstunde hat Gold im Munde; *Thursday is* ~ *closing* an Donnerstag schließen die Geschäfte früher; *in his* ~ *days* in s-r Jugend; *at an* ~ *hour* zu früher Stunde; ~ *warning system* ✕ Frühwarnsystem *n; at the* (*very*) *earliest* (aller-)frühestens; → *convenience* 1. **5.** vorzeitig: *his* ~ *death* sein früher Tod. **6.** zu früh: *be* ~ zu früh (daran) sein. **7.** anfänglich, Früh...: ~ *Christian* frühchristlich. **8.** baldig.

'ear·mark I *s* **1.** Ohrmarke *f* (*e-s Haustiers*). **2.** *fig.* Kennzeichen *n.* **II** *v/t* **3.** kennzeichnen. **4.** *bsd.* ✝ bestimmen, vorsehen (*for* für): ~*ed* zweckbestimmt, -gebunden (*Mittel*). **'~·muff** *s* Ohrenschützer *m.*

earn [ɜːn] *v/t* **1.** Geld *etc* verdienen: → *living* 6. **2.** *Zinsen etc* einbringen. **3.** *fig. j-m et.* einbringen, -tragen.

ear·nest ['ɜːnɪst] **I** *adj* □ **1.** ernst. **2.** ernst-, gewissenhaft. **3.** ernstlich. **II** *s* **4.** *in* ~ im Ernst; *in good* (*od. dead, perfect*) ~ in vollem Ernst; *are you in* ~? ist das dein Ernst?; *be in* ~ *about* es ernst meinen mit.

earn·ings ['ɜːnɪŋz] *s pl* Verdienst *m,* Einkommen *n.*

'ear·phones *s pl, a. pair of* ~ Kopfhörer *m.* **'~·piece** *s teleph.* Hörmuschel *f.* **'~·‚pierc·ing** → *earsplitting.* **'~·plug** *s*

Wattepfropf m. '**~ring** s Ohrring m.
'**~shot** s: **within** (**out of**) ~ in (außer)
Hörweite. '**~split·ting** adj ohrenbetäubend.

earth [ɜ:θ] **I** s **1.** Erde f: a) a. 2 Erdball m,
b) Welt f: **on** ~ auf Erden; **what** (**why**)
on ~? warum (was) in aller Welt? **2.**
Erde f, (Erd)Boden m: **come back** (**od.
down**) **to** ~ fig. auf den Boden der
Wirklichkeit zurückkehren. **3.** (Fuchsetc)Bau m. **4.** ⚡ bsd. Br. Erde f, Erdung
f: ~ **cable** Massekabel n. **II** v/t ⚡ bsd.
Br. erden. '**earth·en** adj irden. '**earthen·ware** s Steingut(geschirr) n.
'**earth·ly** adj **1.** irdisch, weltlich. **2.** F
there's no ~ **reason** es gibt nicht den
geringsten Grund; **of no** ~ **use** völlig
unnütz; **not to have an** ~ (**chance**)
nicht die geringste Chance haben.

'**earth|·quake** s Erdbeben n. '**~quake·proof** adj erdbebensicher. '**~shak·ing**,
'**~shat·ter·ing** adj fig. welterschütternd. ~ **sta·tion** s Raumfahrt: Bodenstation f. ~ **trem·or** s leichtes Erdbeben. '**~worm** s zo. Regenwurm m.

earth·y ['ɜ:θɪ] adj **1.** erdig, Erd... **2.** weltlich od. materiell (eingestellt). **3.** derb
(Humor etc).

'**ear|·wax** s physiol. Ohrenschmalz n.
'**~wig** s zo. Ohrwurm m. '**~wit·ness** s
Ohrenzeuge m.

ease [i:z] **I** s **1.** Bequemlichkeit f, Behaglichkeit f. **2.** a. ~ **of mind** (Gemüts)Ruhe f, Ausgeglichenheit f: **at**
(**one's**) ~ ruhig, entspannt; unbefangen; **be** (od. **feel**) **at** ~ sich wohl fühlen;
ill at ~ unruhig; befangen; **be** (od. **feel**)
ill at ~ sich (in s-r Haut) nicht wohl
fühlen. **3.** Sorglosigkeit f: **live at** ~ in
guten Verhältnissen leben. **4.** Leichtigkeit f, Mühelosigkeit f: **with** ~ leicht,
mühelos. **5.** Erleichterung f, Befreiung
f: **give s.o.** ~ j-m Erleichterung verschaffen. **II** v/t **6.** erleichtern, beruhigen: ~ **one's mind** sich erleichtern. **7.**
Schmerzen lindern. **III** v/i **8.** mst ~ **off**
(od. **up**) nachlassen, sich abschwächen;
sich entspannen (Lage); (bei der Arbeit) kürzertreten; weniger streng sein
(**on** zu).

ea·sel ['i:zl] s paint. Staffelei f.

eas·i·ly ['i:zɪlɪ] adv **1.** leicht, mühelos. **2.**
ohne Zweifel; mit Abstand, bei weitem.

east [i:st] **I** s **1.** Osten m: **in the** ~ **of** im
Osten von (od. gen); **to the** ~ **of** → **5.** **2.**
a. 2 Osten, östlicher Landesteil: **the** 2
Br. Ostengland n; Am. die Oststaaten
pl; pol. der Osten; der Orient. **II** adj **3.**
Ost..., östlich. **III** adv **4.** ostwärts, nach
Osten. **5.** ~ **of** östlich von (od. gen).
'**~-bound** adj nach Osten gehend od.
fahrend.

East·er ['i:stə] s Ostern n od. pl, Osterfest n: **at** ~ zu Ostern; **happy** ~ frohe
Ostern! **II** adj Oster...: ~ **egg** Osterei n;
(od. **Day**) Ostersonntag m.

east·er·ly ['i:stəlɪ] **I** adj östlich, Ost... **II**
adv von od. nach Osten. **east·ern**
['i:stən] adj östlich, Ost... '**east·ern·er** s
1. Bewohner(in) des Ostens (e-s Landes). **2.** Am. Oststaatler(in). **east·ern·most** ['~məʊst] adj östlichst.

east·ward ['i:stwəd] adj u. adv östlich,
ostwärts, nach Osten: **in a** ~ **direction**
in östlicher Richtung, Richtung Osten.
east·wards ['~z] adv → **eastward**.

eas·y ['i:zɪ] **I** adj (□ → **easily**) **1.** leicht,
mühelos: **it is** ~ **for him to talk** er hat gut
reden. **2.** leicht, einfach (**for** für): ~
money leichtverdientes Geld. **3.** bequem, angenehm: **live in** ~ **circumstances**, F **be in** ~ **street** in guten Verhältnissen leben. **4.** gemächlich, gemütlich
(Tempo, Spaziergang etc): → **stage** 2.
5. günstig, erträglich, (Strafe) leicht:
on ~ **terms** auf Raten. **6.** leichtfertig;
locker, frei (Moral etc). **7.** ungezwungen, natürlich: **be free and** ~ sich ganz
ungezwungen benehmen. **II** adv **8.**
leicht, bequem: **go** ~, **take it** ~ sich Zeit
lassen; sich nicht aufregen; **take it** ~!
immer mit der Ruhe!; keine Bange!; **go**
~ **on** j-n, et. sachte anfassen; schonend
od. sparsam umgehen mit; **easier said
than done** leichter gesagt als getan; ~
come, ~ **go** wie gewonnen, so zerronnen. ~ **chair** s Sessel m. '**~·go·ing** adj **1.**
gelassen. **2.** unbeschwert.

eat [i:t] **I** s **1.** pl F Fressalien pl. **II** v/t (irr)
2. essen (Mensch), fressen (Tier): ~
one's words alles(, was man gesagt
hat,) zurücknehmen; **what's** ~**ing him?**
F was hat er denn?; ~ **up** aufessen, -fressen; Reserven etc völlig aufbrauchen;
be ~**en up with** fig. sich verzehren vor
(dat), zerfressen werden von; → **cake**
1, **dog** 1, **hat**, **humble** Ia. **3.** zerfressen:
~**en by worms** wurmstichig. **4.** Loch

fressen (**into** in *acc*). **III** *v/i* (*irr*) **5.** essen (*Mensch*), fressen (*Tier*): **~ out** auswärts essen, essen gehen. **6. ~ into** sich (hin)einfressen in (*acc*); *Reserven etc* angreifen. **'eat·a·ble I** *adj* eß-, genießbar. **II** *s pl* Eßwaren *pl*. **eat·en** ['iːtn] *pp von* **eat. 'eat·er** *s* Esser(in) (*Mensch*), Fresser *m* (*Tier*): → **big** 1d, **small** I. **'eat·ing I** *s* Essen *n*. **II** *adj* Eß...: ~ **apple** Eß-, Speiseapfel *m*.

eau de Co·logne [ˌəʊdəkə'ləʊn] *s* Kölnischwasser *n*.

eaves [iːvz] *s pl* Traufe *f*. **'~drop** *v/i* (heimlich) lauschen *od.* horchen: ~ **on** belauschen. **'~drop·per** *s* Lauscher(in), Horcher(in).

ebb [eb] **I** *s* **1.** *a.* ~ **tide** Ebbe *f*. **2.** *fig.* Tiefstand *m*: **be at a low** ~ auf e-m Tiefpunkt angelangt sein. **II** *v/i* **3.** zurückgehen (*a. fig.*). **4.** *a.* ~ **away** *fig.* abnehmen, verebben.

eb·on·y ['ebənɪ] *s* Ebenholz *n*.

e·bul·li·ent [ɪ'bʌljənt] *adj* □ *fig.* sprudelnd, überschäumend (**with** von); überschwenglich.

ec·cen·tric [ɪk'sentrɪk] **I** *adj* (**~ally**) ⚭, ◎ exzentrisch, *fig. a.* überspannt. **II** *s* Exzentriker(in). **ec·cen·tric·i·ty** [ˌeksen-'trɪsətɪ] *s* ⚭, ◎ Exzentrizität *f*, *fig. a.* Überspanntheit *f*.

ec·cle·si·as·ti·cal [ɪˌkliːzɪ'æstɪkl] *adj* □ kirchlich: ~ **law** Kirchenrecht *n*.

ech·e·lon ['eʃəlɒn] ⚓, ✕ **I** *s* Staffelung *f*: **in ~** staffelförmig. **II** *v/t* staffeln.

ech·o ['ekəʊ] **I** *pl* **-oes** *s* **1.** Echo *n*, Widerhall *m* (*beide a. fig.*). **II** *v/i* **2.** widerhallen (**with** von). **3.** nach-, widerhallen, zurückgeworfen werden (*Ton*). **III** *v/t* **4.** *a.* ~ **back** Ton zurückwerfen. **5.** *Worte* nachbeten; *fig.* **j-m** alles nachbeten. ~ **sound·er** *s* ⚓ Echolot *n*.

é·clat ['eɪklɑː] *s* **1.** durchschlagender Erfolg. **2.** (allgemeiner) Beifall.

e·clipse [ɪ'klɪps] **I** *s* **1.** *ast.* (Sonnen-, Mond)Finsternis *f*. **2.** *fig.* Niedergang *m*: **be in ~** im Sinken sein; in der Versenkung verschwunden sein. **II** *v/t* **3.** *ast.* verfinstern. **4.** *fig.* in den Schatten stellen: **be ~d by** verblassen neben (*dat*).

e·co·cide ['iːkəʊsaɪd] *s* Umweltzerstörung *f*. **e·co·cri·sis** ['iːkəʊˌkraɪsɪs] *s* (*irr* **crisis**) Umweltkrise *f*.

e·co·log·i·cal [ˌiːkə'lɒdʒɪkl] *adj* □ ökologisch, Umwelt...: ~ **balance** ökologisches Gleichgewicht; **~ly beneficial** (**harmful**) umweltfreundlich (umweltfeindlich). **e·col·o·gist** [iː'kɒlədʒɪst] *s* Ökologe *m*. **e·col·o·gy** *s* Ökologie *f*.

e·co·nom·ic [ˌiːkə'nɒmɪk] **I** *adj* (**~ally**) **1.** (staats-, volks)wirtschaftlich, Wirtschafts...: ~ **aid** Wirtschaftshilfe *f*. **2.** rentabel, wirtschaftlich. **II** *s pl* (*sg konstruiert*) **3.** Volkswirtschaft(slehre) *f*. **e·co·nom·i·cal** [~kl] *adj* □ **1.** wirtschaftlich, sparsam, (*Person a.*) haushälterisch: **be ~ with** → **economize** I. **2.** Spar... **3.** → **economic** I. **e·con·o·mist** [ɪ'kɒnəmɪst] *s* Volkswirt(schaftler) *m*. **e·con·o·mize** I *v/t* sparsam umgehen *od.* wirtschaften mit, haushalten mit. **II** *v/i* sparsam wirtschaften: ~ **on** → I. **e·con·o·my** I *s* **1.** Wirtschaftlichkeit *f*, Sparsamkeit *f*. **2.** Sparmaßnahme *f*; Einsparung *f*. **3.** Wirtschaft(ssystem *n*) *f*. **II** *adj* **4.** Spar...: ~ **class** ✈ Economyklasse *f*; ~ **drive** Sparmaßnahmen *pl*; ~ **price** günstiger *od.* niedriger Preis.

e·co·sys·tem ['iːkəʊˌsɪstəm] *s* Ökosystem *n*.

ec·sta·size ['ekstəsaɪz] **I** *v/t* in Ekstase versetzen. **II** *v/i* in Ekstase geraten. **'ec·sta·sy** *s* Ekstase *f*: **be in an ~** außer sich sein (**of** vor *dat*); **in an ~ of joy** in e-m Freudentaumel; **go into ecstasies over** in Verzückung geraten über (*acc*). **ec·stat·ic** [ɪk'stætɪk] *adj* (**~ally**) ekstatisch, verzückt.

e·cu·men·i·cal [ˌiːkjuː'menɪkl] *adj* □ ökumenisch.

ec·ze·ma ['eksɪmə] *s* ✿ Ekzem *n*.

ed·dy ['edɪ] **I** *s* Wirbel *m*, Strudel *m*. **II** *v/i* wirbeln.

edge [edʒ] **I** *s* **1.** Schneide *f*; Schärfe *f*: **have no ~** stumpf sein, nicht schneiden; **take the ~ off** Klinge stumpf machen; *fig.* e-r Sache die Schärfe nehmen. **2.** Ecke *f*, scharfe Kante. **3.** (äußerster) Rand, Saum *m*; **on the ~ of** *fig.* kurz vor (*dat*); **be on the ~ of despair** am Rande der Verzweiflung sein; **be on the ~ of doing s.th.** im Begriff sein zu, kurz vor dem Tun stehen. **4.** Kante *f*, Schmalseite *f*: **set (up) on ~** hochkant stellen; **on ~** nervös; gereizt; **set s.o.'s teeth on ~** j-n nervös machen. **5.** F Vorteil *m*: **give s.o. an ~** j-m e-n Vorteil verschaffen; **have the ~ on s.o.**

j-m über sein. **II** v/t **6.** schärfen. **7.** umsäumen, einfassen. **8.** schieben, drängen: **~ on** antreiben, drängen III v/i **9.** sich schieben od. drängen. **edged** adj **1.** scharf. **2.** in Zssgn ...schneidig; ...kantig.

'edge|·ways, ~·wise ['⌣waɪz] adv hochkant: **I could hardly get a word in ~** fig. ich bin kaum zu Wort gekommen.

edg·y ['edʒɪ] adj □ nervös; gereizt.

ed·i·ble ['edɪbl] **I** adj eß-, genießbar: **~ oil** Speiseöl n. **II** s pl Eßwaren pl.

e·dict ['iːdɪkt] s Erlaß m, hist. Edikt n.

ed·i·fice ['edɪfɪs] s Gebäude n (a. fig.).

ed·i·fy ['⌣faɪ] v/t fig. erbauen. **'ed·i·fy·ing** adj □ erbaulich.

ed·it ['edɪt] v/t **1.** Texte etc a) herausgeben, b) redigieren. **2.** Film schneiden. **3.** Zeitung etc als Herausgeber leiten.

e·di·tion [ɪ'dɪʃn] s **1.** Ausgabe f: **first ~** Erstausgabe f; **morning ~** Morgenausgabe (Zeitung). **2.** Auflage f. **ed·i·tor** ['edɪtə] s **1.** a. **~ in chief** Herausgeber(in) (e-s Buchs etc). **2.** Zeitung: a) a. **~ in chief** Chefredakteur(in): → **letter** 2, b) Redakteur(in): **the ~s** pl die Redaktion. **3.** Film, TV: Cutter(in). **ed·i·to·ri·al** [‿'tɔːrɪəl] **I** adj □ redaktionell, Redaktions...: → **department** Redaktion f; → **staff** 1. **II** s Leitartikel m.

ed·u·cate ['edʒʊkeɪt] v/t **1.** erziehen, (aus)bilden: **he was ~d at** er besuchte die (Hoch)Schule in (dat). **2.** weitS. (to) erziehen (zu); gewöhnen (an acc). **'ed·u·cat·ed** adj **1.** gebildet. **2. ~ guess** mehr als e-e bloße Vermutung. **,ed·u·'ca·tion** s **1.** Erziehung f, (Aus)Bildung f: → **compulsory** 2, **university** II. **2.** Bildung(sstand m) f: → **general** 2. **3.** Bildungs-, Schulwesen n. **4.** Pädagogik f. **,ed·u·'ca·tion·al** [‿ʃənl] adj □ **1.** a) pädagogisch, Unterrichts...: → **film** Lehrfilm m; **~ television** Schulfernsehen n, b) lehrreich (Erfahrung etc), c) pädagogisch wertvoll (Spielzeug). **2.** Bildungs...: → **level** (od. **standard**) Bildungsniveau n.

eel [iːl] s ichth. Aal m: **(as) slippery as an ~** fig. aalglatt.

ee·rie, ee·ry ['ɪərɪ] adj □ unheimlich, (Schrei etc) schaurig.

ef·face [ɪ'feɪs] v/t wegwischen, -reiben, a. fig. (aus)löschen.

---

ef·fect [ɪ'fekt] **I** s **1.** Wirkung f (**on** auf acc): a) Erfolg m: **of no ~, without ~** erfolg-, wirkungslos, b) Auswirkung f, c) Effekt m, Eindruck m: **have an ~ on** wirken auf (acc), e-n Eindruck hinterlassen bei. **2.** Inhalt m, Sinn m: **a letter to the ~ that** ein Brief des Inhalts, daß; **inform s.o. to that ~** j-n entsprechend informieren. **3.** (Rechts)Wirksamkeit f, (-)Kraft f: **be ~ in** in Kraft sein; **take ~, come** (od. **go**) **into ~** in Kraft treten; **with ~ from** mit Wirkung vom. **4. carry into ~, give ~ to** verwirklichen, ausführen; **in ~** in Wirklichkeit, tatsächlich. **5.** ⊕ (Nutz)Leistung f. **6.** pl † Effekten pl; Vermögen(swerte pl) n. **II** v/t **7.** bewirken. **8.** ausführen, tätigen. **ef'fec·tive** adj □ **1.** wirksam, erfolgreich. **2.** eindrucks-, wirkungs-, effektvoll. **3.** (rechts)wirksam, rechtskräftig: **be ~ in** Kraft sein; **become ~ in** Kraft treten; **~ from** (od. **as of**) mit Wirkung vom. **4.** tatsächlich, effektiv: **~ salary** Effektivgehalt n. **ef'fec·tive·ness** s Wirksamkeit f. **ef'fec·tu·al** [‿tʃʊəl] adj □ **1.** wirksam. **2. → effective** 3. **ef'fec·tu·ate** [‿tʃʊeɪt] v/t bewirken.

ef·fem·i·nate [ɪ'femɪnət] adj □ **1.** weibisch, unmännlich. **2.** verweichlicht, weichlich.

ef·fer·vesce [ˌefə'ves] v/i **1.** sprudeln, schäumen, moussieren. **2.** fig. (über-)sprudeln, überschäumen (**with** vor dat). **,ef·fer·'ves·cent** [‿snt] adj □ **1.** sprudelnd, schäumend, moussierend: **~ powder** Brausepulver n. **2.** fig. (über-)sprudelnd, überschäumend.

ef·fi·ca·cious [ˌefɪ'keɪʃəs] adj □ wirksam. **ef·fi·ca·cy** ['efɪkəsɪ] s Wirksamkeit f.

ef·fi·cien·cy [ɪ'fɪʃənsɪ] s Effizienz f: a) Tüchtigkeit f, (Leistungs)Fähigkeit f: **~ rating** Leistungsbewertung f; → **principle** 1, b) rationelle Arbeitsweise, Wirtschaftlichkeit f: **~ expert** † Rationalisierungsfachmann m. **ef'fi·cient** adj □ effizient: a) tüchtig, (leistungs-)fähig, b) rationell, wirtschaftlich.

ef·fi·gy ['efɪdʒɪ] s **1.** Steinplastik f; Bildnis n (auf e-r Münze). **2.** Puppe od. bildhafte Darstellung e-r verhaßten Person: **burn (hang) s.o. in ~** j-n symbolisch verbrennen (hängen).

ef·fort ['efət] s Anstrengung f: a) Bemühung *f*, b) Mühe *f*: **make an ~** sich bemühen *od.* anstrengen; **make every ~** sich alle Mühe geben; **spare no ~** keine Mühe scheuen; **without ~** mühelos; **~ of will** Willensanstrengung. **'ef·fort·less** *adj* □ mühelos.

ef·fron·ter·y [ɪ'frʌntərɪ] *s* Frechheit *f*, Unverschämtheit *f* **have the ~** die Unverschämtheit haben *od.* besitzen (**to do** zu tun).

ef·fu·sive [ɪ'fjuːsɪv] *adj* □ überschwenglich.

egg¹ [eg] *s* Ei *n*: **in the ~** *fig.* im Anfangsstadium, im Entstehen; **(as) sure as ~s is** (*od.* **are**) **~s** F so sicher wie das Amen in der Kirche, todsicher; → **like¹** 4.

egg² [~] *v/t mst* **~ on** anstacheln, antreiben.

'egg|.beat·er *s* Schneebesen *m.* **~ co·sy** (*Am.* **co·zy**) *s* Eierwärmer *m.* **'~cup** *s* Eierbecher *m.* **'~head** *s* F Eierkopf *m* (*Intellektueller*). **'~shaped** *adj* eiförmig. **'~shell** *s* Eierschale *f.* **~ tim·er** *s* Eieruhr *f.* **~ whisk** *s* Schneebesen *m.* **~ white** *s* Eiweiß *n*.

e·go ['egəʊ] *pl* **-gos** *s phls., psych.* Ich *n*, Ego *n*; *weitS.* Selbst(wert)gefühl *n*: **boost s.o.'s ~, give s.o. an ~ boost** F *j*-s Selbstgefühl (an)heben. **e·go·cen·tric** [ˌ~'sentrɪk] **I** *adj* (**~ally**) egozentrisch. **II** *s* Egozentriker(in). **'e·go·ism** *s* Egoismus *m.* **'e·go·ist** *s* Egoist(in). **ˌe·go·is·tic, ˌe·go·is·ti·cal** [~kl] *adj* □ egoistisch. **e·go·tism** ['~tɪzəm] *s* **1.** Egotismus *m*, Geltungsbedürfnis *n*, Selbstgefälligkeit *f.* **2.** → **egoism**. **'e·go·tist** *s* **1.** Egotist(in). **2.** → **egoist**. **ˌe·go·tis·tic, ˌe·go·tis·ti·cal** [~kl] *adj* □ **1.** egotistisch, geltungsbedürftig, selbstgefällig. **2.** → **egoistic**.

e·go trip *s* F Egotrip *m* (*Akt geistiger Selbstbefriedigung*): **be off on an ~** auf e-m Egotrip sein.

E·gyp·tian [ɪ'dʒɪpʃn] **I** *adj* ägyptisch. **II** *s* Ägypter(in).

ei·der ['aɪdə] *s* **1.** → **eider duck**. **2.** → **eiderdown** 1. **'~down** *s* **1.** *coll.* Eiderdaunen *pl.* **2.** Daunendecke *f.* **~ duck** *s* *orn.* Eiderente *f.*

eight [eɪt] **I** *adj* **1.** acht: **~hour day** Achtstundentag *m.* **II** *s* **2.** Acht *f*: **~ of hearts** Herzacht. **3.** *Rudern:* Achter *m* (*Boot, Mannschaft*). **eight·een** [ˌeɪ'tiːn] *adj* achtzehn. **ˌeight'eenth** [~θ] *adj* acht-

zehnt. **eight·fold** ['~fəʊld] **I** *adj* achtfach. **II** *adv* achtfach, um das Achtfache: **increase ~** (sich) verachtfachen.

eighth [eɪtθ] **I** *adj* **1.** achte(r, -s). **II** *s* **2.** der, die, das Achte: **the ~ of May** der 8. Mai. **3.** Achtel *n.* **'eighth·ly** *adv* achtens.

eight·i·eth ['~ɪəθ] *adj* achtzigst.

'eight-time *adj* achtmalig.

eight·y ['eɪtɪ] **I** *adj* achtzig. **II** *s* Achtzig *f*: **be in one's eighties** in den Achtzigern sein; **in the eighties** in den achtziger Jahren (*e-s Jahrhunderts*).

ei·ther ['aɪðə] **I** *adj* **1.** jede(r, -s) (*von zweien*): **on ~ side** auf beiden Seiten. **2.** irgendein (*von zweien*): **~ way** auf die e-e *od.* die andere Art. **II** *pron* **3.** irgendein (*von zweien*): **I haven't seen ~** ich habe beide nicht gesehen, ich habe keinen (von beiden) gesehen. **4.** beides: **~ is possible. III** *cj* **5.** ~ ... **or** entweder ... oder. **6.** *neg.:* ~ ... **or** weder ... noch: **it isn't enough ~ for you or for me** es reicht weder für mich noch für dich. **IV** *adj* **7. not ~** auch nicht.

e·jac·u·late [ɪ'dʒækjʊleɪt] **I** *v/t* **1.** *physiol.* Samen ausstoßen. **2.** *Worte etc* aus-, hervorstoßen. **II** *v/i* **3.** *physiol.* ejakulieren, e-n Samenerguß haben. **e·jac·u·la·tion** *s* **1.** *physiol.* Ejakulation *f*, Samenerguß *m.* **2.** Ausruf *m*; Stoßseufzer *m.*

e·ject [ɪ'dʒekt] **I** *v/t* **1.** (**from**) *j*-n hinauswerfen (aus); vertreiben (aus, von). **2.** entlassen, entfernen (**from** aus *e-m Amt*). **3.** ✪ ausstoßen, -werfen. **II** *v/i* **4.** ✈ den Schleudersitz betätigen. **e'jec·tion** *s* **1.** Vertreibung *f.* Entfernung *f.* **3.** ✪ Ausstoßen *n*, -werfen *n*: **~ seat** ✈ Schleudersitz *m.* **e'jec·tor** *s* ✪ Auswerfer *m*: **~ seat** ✈ Schleudersitz *m.*

eke [iːk] *v/t*: **~ out** Flüssigkeit, Vorräte *etc* strecken; *Einkommen* aufbessern (**with** mit): **~ out a living** sich (mühsam) durchschlagen.

e·lab·o·rate I *adj* [ɪ'læbərət] **1.** sorgfältig *od.* kunstvoll gearbeitet *od.* ausgeführt. **2.** (wohl)durchdacht. **3.** umständlich. **II** *v/t* [~reɪt] **4.** sorgfältig ausarbeiten. **5.** *Theorie etc* entwickeln. **III** *v/i* [~reɪt] **6.** nähere Angaben machen: **~ on** näher eingehen auf (*acc*).

e·lapse [ɪ'læps] *v/i* vergehen, -streichen (*Zeit*), ablaufen (*Frist*).

e·las·tic [ɪ'læstɪk] **I** *adj* (~*ally*) **1.** *allg.* elastisch (*a. fig.*): ~ *conscience* weites Gewissen; ~ *word* dehnbarer Begriff. **2.** Gummi...: ~ *band* Gummiring *m*, -band *n*, (Dichtungs)Gummi *m*; ~ *stocking* Gummistrumpf *m*. **II** *s* **3.** *bsd. Am.* Gummiring *m*, -band *n*, (Dichtungs)Gummi *m*. **e·las·tic·i·ty** [,elæ'stɪsətɪ] *s allg.* Elastizität *f* (*a. fig.*).

e·lat·ed [ɪ'leɪtɪd] *adj* □ begeistert (*at* von), in Hochstimmung. **e·la·tion** *s* Begeisterung *f*, Hochstimmung *f*.

el·bow ['elbəʊ] **I** *s* **1.** Ell(en)bogen *m*: *at one's* ~ in Reichweite; *bsd. fig.* an s-r Seite; *out at* ~*(s)* schäbig, abgetragen (*Kleidung*); schäbig gekleidet; *Am.* knapp bei Kasse. **2.** (scharfe) Biegung *od.* Krümmung. **3.** (Rohr)Krümmer *m*, Kniestück *n*. **II** *v/t* **4.** *mit den Ellbogen* stoßen, drängen (*a. fig.*): ~ *out* hinausdrängen; ~ *one's way through* sich e-n Weg bahnen durch. ~ *grease s humor.* **1.** Armschmalz *n* (*Kraft*). **2.** Schufterei *f*. ~*room* ['~rʊm] *s* **1.** Ellbogenfreiheit *f*. **2.** *fig.* Bewegungsfreiheit *f*, Spielraum *m*.

eld·er¹ ['eldə] **I** *adj* **1.** älter (*Bruder, Schwester etc*). **2.** ~ *statesman* Staatsmann im Ruhestand, der die politischen Führer inoffiziell berät; *weitS.* großer alter Mann (*e-r Berufsgruppe etc*). **II** *s* **3.** *my* ~ Leute, die älter sind als ich.

el·der² [~] *s* ♀ Holunder *m*. '~,**ber·ry** *s* Holunderbeere *f*.

eld·er·ly ['eldəlɪ] *adj* ältlich, älter.

eld·est ['eldɪst] *adj* ältest (*Bruder, Schwester etc*).

e·lect [ɪ'lekt] **I** *v/t j-n* wählen ([*as, to be*] *president* zum Präsidenten). **II** *adj* (*nachgestellt*) designiert, zukünftig. **e'lec·tion** *s* Wahl *f*: → *stand for* 4. **II** *adj* Wahl...: ~ *campaign* Wahlkampf *m*. **e,lec·tion'eer** [~ʃə'nɪə] *v/i* Wahlkampf betreiben: ~ *for* Wahlpropaganda treiben für. **e,lec·tion'eer·ing** *s* Wahlkampf *m*; -propaganda *f*. **e'lec·tive I** *adj* **1.** gewählt, Wahl... **2.** wahlberechtigt. **3.** *ped., univ. bsd. Am.* fakultativ: ~ *subject* → 4. **II** *s* **4.** *ped. univ. bsd. Am.* Wahlfach *n*. **e'lec·tor** *s* Wähler(in); *Am.* Wahlmann *m*. **e'lec·tor·al** *adj* Wähler..., Wahl...: ~ *college Am.* Wahlmänner *pl*. **e'lec·tor·ate** [~tərət] *s* Wähler(schaft *f*) *pl*.

e·lec·tric [ɪ'lektrɪk] *adj* (~*ally*) **1.** a) elektrisch: ~ *chair* elektrischer Stuhl; ~ *cushion* Heizkissen *n*; ~ *shock* Stromschlag *m*; ⚡ *etc* Elektroschock *m*; ~ *torch bsd. Br.* Taschenlampe *f*, b) Elektro..., c) Elektrizitäts..., d) elektrotechnisch. **2.** *fig.* elektrisierend (*Wirkung etc*); spannungsgeladen (*Atmosphäre*). **e'lec·tri·cal** [~kl] *adj* □ → *electric*: ~ *engineer* Elektroingenieur *m*; -techniker *m*; ~ *engineering* Elektrotechnik *f*.

e·lec·tri·cian [,ɪlek'trɪʃn] *s* Elektrotechniker *m*, Elektriker *m*. **e·lec'tric·i·ty** [~sətɪ] *s* Elektrizität *f*; Strom *m*. **e'lec·tri·fy** [~faɪ] *v/t* **1.** elektrisieren (*a. fig.*). **2.** elektrifizieren.

e·lec·tro·car·di·o·gram [ɪ,lektrəʊ'kɑːdɪəʊgræm] *s* ⚕ Elektrokardiogramm *n*.

e·lec·tro·cute [ɪ'lektrəkjuːt] *v/t* **1.** auf dem elektrischen Stuhl hinrichten. **2.** *be* ~*d* e-n tödlichen Stromschlag erhalten. **e,lec·tro·cu·tion** *s* Hinrichtung *f* auf dem elektrischen Stuhl.

e·lec·trode [ɪ'lektrəʊd] *s* ⚡ Elektrode *f*.

e·lec·tron [ɪ'lektrɒn] *phys.* **I** *s* Elektron *n*. **II** *adj* Elektronen...: ~ *microscope*. **e·lec'tron·ic I** *adj* (~*ally*) elektronisch: ~ *data processing* elektronische Datenverarbeitung; ~ *flash phot.* Elektronenblitz *m*. **II** *s pl* (*sg konstruiert*) Elektronik *f*.

e·lec·tro·plate [ɪ'lektrəʊpleɪt] *v/t* galvanisieren. **e,lec·tro'ther·a·py** *s* ⚕ Elektrotherapie *f*.

el·e·gance ['elɪgəns] *s* Eleganz *f*. **'el·e·gant** *adj* □ elegant.

el·e·ment ['elɪmənt] *s* **1.** *allg.* Element *n*. **2.** *pl* Anfangsgründe *pl*. **3.** grundlegender Umstand, wesentlicher Faktor: ~ *of uncertainty* Unsicherheitsfaktor *m*; ~ *of surprise* Überraschungselement *n*. **4.** *fig.* Körnchen *n*, Fünkchen *n* (*Wahrheit etc*). **5.** (Lebens)Element *n*: *be in one's* ~ in s-m Element sein; *be out of one's* ~ sich fehl am Platz fühlen. **6.** *pl* Elemente *pl*, Naturkräfte *pl*. **el·e·men·tal** [,~'mentl] *adj* □ **1.** elementar: a) ursprünglich, natürlich, b) urgewaltig, c) wesentlich, grundlegend. **2.** Elementar..., Ur... **3.** → *elementary* 2, 3. **,el·e·men·ta·ry** *adj* □ **1.** → *elemental* 1, 2. **2.** elementar, Einführungs...: ~ *school Am.* Grundschule *f*. **3.** 🔥, 🜨, *phys.* Elementar...: **~ particle** Elementarteilchen *n.*

el·e·phant ['elɪfənt] *s zo.* Elefant *m.*

el·e·phan·tine [,~'fæntaɪn] *adj* **1.** elefantenartig: **an ~ memory** ein Gedächtnis wie ein Elefant. **2.** plump, schwerfällig.

el·e·vate ['elɪveɪt] *v/t* **1.** (hoch-, auf)heben. **2.** *j-n* erheben (**to peerage** in den Adelsstand), befördern (**to** zu). **'el·e·vat·ed** *adj* **1.** erhöht: **~ railway** (*Am.* **railroad**) Hochbahn *f.* **2.** gehoben (*Position, Stil etc*), erhaben (*Gedanken*). **3.** übersteigert (*Meinung etc*). **,el·e·va·tion** *s* **1.** (Boden)Erhebung *f*, (An-) Höhe *f*. **2.** Erhebung *f*, Beförderung *f*. **3.** △, *A* Aufriß *m.* **'el·e·va·tor** *s Am.* Aufzug *m*, Fahrstuhl *m*: **~ shaft** Aufzugschacht *m.*

e·lev·en [ɪ'levn] **I** *adj* elf. **II** *s* Elf *f* (*a. Sport*). **e'lev·en·ses** [~zɪz] *s pl Br. F* zweites Frühstück. **e'lev·enth** [~θ] *adj* elft: **at the ~ hour** *fig.* in letzter Minute.

elf *pl* **elves** [elvz] *s* **1.** Elf *m*, Elfe *f.* **2.** Kobold *m.* **'elf·ish** *adj* □ **1.** elfenhaft. **2.** koboldhaft, schelmisch.

e·lic·it [ɪ'lɪsɪt] *v/t* **1.** (**from**) *et.* entlocken (*dat*); *Wahrheit etc* herausholen, -locken (aus). **2.** *Applaus, Gelächter etc* hervorrufen.

el·i·gi·bil·i·ty [,elɪdʒə'bɪlətɪ] *s* **1.** Eignung *f.* **2.** Berechtigung *f.* **3.** Wählbarkeit *f.* **'el·i·gi·ble** *adj* □ (**for**) in Frage kommend (für): a) geeignet, annehmbar (für): **~ bachelor** begehrter Junggeselle, b) berechtigt, befähigt (zu), qualifiziert (für): **be ~ for** Anspruch haben auf (*acc*), **~ to vote** wahlberechtigt, c) teilnahmeberechtigt (an *dat*), (*Sport a.*) start- *od.* spielberechtigt (für), d) wählbar (für).

e·lim·i·nate [ɪ'lɪmɪneɪt] *v/t* **1.** beseitigen, entfernen, eliminieren (**from** aus). **2.** ⚗, *physiol.* ausscheiden. **3.** *Gegner* ausschalten: **be ~d** (*Sport*) ausscheiden. **e,lim·i'na·tion** *s* **1.** Beseitigung *f*, Eliminierung *f.* **2.** ⚗, *physiol.* Ausscheidung *f* (*a. Sport*): **~ contest** Ausscheidungswettbewerb *m.* **3.** Ausschaltung *f.*

e·lite, *Br. a.* **é·lite** [eɪ'li:t] *s* Elite *f.*

e·lix·ir [ɪ'lɪksə] *s* Elixier *n.*

elk [elk] *s zo.* Elch *m.*

el·lipse [ɪ'lɪps] *s A* Ellipse *f.* **el'lip·sis**

[~sɪs] *pl* **-ses** [~si:z] *s ling.* Ellipse *f.* **el'lip·tic**, **el'lip·ti·cal** [~kl] *adj* □ *A*, *ling.* elliptisch.

elm [elm] *s* ♣ Ulme *f*, Rüster *f.*

el·o·cu·tion [,elə'kju:ʃn] *s* **1.** Vortrag(sweise *f*) *m.* **2.** Vortrags-, Redekunst *f.* **3.** Sprechtechnik *f.*

e·lon·gate ['i:lɒŋgeɪt] *v/t* (*u. v/i* sich) verlängern. **,e·lon'ga·tion** *s* Verlängerung *f.*

e·lope [ɪ'ləʊp] *v/i* **1.** (mit s-m *od.* s-r Geliebten) ausreißen *od.* durchbrennen. **2.** sich davonmachen.

el·o·quence ['eləkwəns] *s* Beredsamkeit *f*, Redegewandtheit *f.* **'el·o·quent** *adj* □ beredt, redegewandt.

else [els] *adv* **1.** (*in Fragen u. Verneinungen*) sonst, weiter, außerdem: **anything ~?** sonst noch etwas?; **what ~ can we do?** was können wir sonst noch tun?; **no one ~** sonst *od.* weiter niemand. **2.** ander: **that's s.th. ~** das ist et. anderes; **everybody ~** alle anderen; **s.o. ~** j-d anders. **3.** *mst* **or ~** sonst, andernfalls. **,~'where** *adv* **1.** sonst-, anderswo. **2.** anderswohin.

e·lu·ci·date [ɪ'lu:sɪdeɪt] *v/t* Text, Gründe etc erklären, erläutern; Geheimnis etc aufklären.

e·lu·sive [ɪ'lu:sɪv] *adj* □ **1.** schwerfaßbar (*Dieb etc*), ausweichend (*Antwort*). **2.** schwer(er)faßbar *od.* -bestimmbar. **3.** unzuverlässig, schlecht (*Gedächtnis*).

elves [elvz] *pl von* **elf.**

e·ma·ci·at·ed [ɪ'meɪʃɪeɪtɪd] *adj* abgemagert, ausgemergelt.

em·a·nate ['eməneɪt] **I** *v/i* **1.** ausströmen (*Gas etc*), ausstrahlen (*Licht*) (**from** von). **2.** stammen, ausgehen (**from** von). **II** *v/t* **3.** ausströmen, -strahlen (*beide a. fig.*).

e·man·ci·pate [ɪ'mænsɪpeɪt] *v/t* emanzipieren, selbständig *od.* unabhängig machen (**from** von). **e'man·ci·pat·ed** *adj* emanzipiert (*Frau etc*), mündig (*Bürger*). **e,man·ci'pa·tion** *s* Emanzipation *f.*

em·balm [ɪm'ba:m] *v/t* (ein)balsamieren.

em·bank [ɪm'bæŋk] *v/t* eindämmen, -deichen. **em'bank·ment** *s* **1.** Eindämmung *f*, -deichung *f.* **2.** (Erd)Damm *m.* **3.** (Bahn-, Straßen)Damm *m.*

em·bar·go [em'ba:gəʊ] **I** *pl* **-goes** *s* **1.** ⚓ Embargo *n*: **lay** (*od.* **place, put**) **an ~ on**

→ 3. **2. ✝** a) Handelssperre *f*, -verbot *n*, b) *a. allg.* Sperre *f*, Verbot *n* (**on** auf *dat od. acc*): **~ on imports** Einfuhrsperre. **II** *v/t* **3.** ein Embargo verhängen über (*acc*).

em·bark [ɪm'bɑːk] **I** *v/t* **1.** ✓, ♨ *Passagiere* an Bord nehmen, ♨ *a.* einschiffen, *Waren a.* verladen (**for** nach). **II** *v/i* **2.** ✓, ♨ an Bord gehen, ♨ *a.* sich einschiffen (**for** nach). **3.** anfangen, unternehmen (**on** *acc*). **em·bar·ka·tion** [ˌembɑː'keɪʃn] *s* Einschiffung *f*, Verladung *f*.

em·bar·rass [ɪm'bærəs] *v/t* in (*a.* Geld)Verlegenheit bringen, verlegen machen. **em'bar·rassed** *adj* **1.** verlegen. **2.** in Geldverlegenheit. **em'bar·rass·ing** *adj* □ unangenehm, peinlich (**to** *dat*). **em'bar·rass·ment** *s* (*a.* Geld)Verlegenheit *f*: **be an ~ to** *j-n* in Verlegenheit bringen; *j-m* peinlich sein.

em·bas·sy ['embəsɪ] *s pol.* Botschaft *f*.

em·bed [ɪm'bed] *v/t* **1.** (ein)betten (**in in** *acc*): **~ded in concrete** einbetonieren. **2.** verankern (**in** *acc od. dat*) (*a. fig.*).

em·bel·lish [ɪm'belɪʃ] *v/t* **1.** verschöne(r)n, (aus)schmücken. **2.** *Erzählung etc* ausschmücken, *Wahrheit* beschönigen.

em·ber ['embə] *s* **1.** glühendes Stück Holz *od.* Kohle. **2.** *pl* Glut(asche) *f*.

em·bez·zle [ɪm'bezl] *v/t* veruntreuen, unterschlagen. **em'bez·zle·ment** *s* Veruntreuung *f*, Unterschlagung *f*. **em'bez·zler** *s* Veruntreuer(in).

em·bit·ter [ɪm'bɪtə] *v/t* **1.** *j-n* verbittern. **2.** *Lage etc* (noch) verschlimmern.

em·blem ['embləm] *s* **1.** Emblem *n*, Symbol *n*: **national ~** Hoheitszeichen *n*. **2.** Kennzeichen *n*.

em·bod·y [ɪm'bɒdɪ] *v/t* **1.** verkörpern: a) konkrete Form geben (*dat*), b) personifizieren. **2.** umfassen, (in sich) vereinigen: **be embodied in** enthalten *od.* vereinigt sein in (*dat*).

em·bo·lism ['embəlɪzəm] *s* ♨ Embolie *f*.

em·brace [ɪm'breɪs] **I** *v/t* **1.** umarmen. **2.** *fig.* einschließen, umfassen. **3.** *Beruf, Gelegenheit* ergreifen; *Angebot, Religion etc* annehmen. **II** *v/i* **4.** sich umarmen. **III** *s* **5.** Umarmung *f*.

em·broi·der [ɪm'brɔɪdə] **I** *v/t* **1.** *Muster* sticken; *Stoff* besticken. **2.** *Bericht etc* ausschmücken. **II** *v/i* **3.** sticken.

em·broi·der·y *s* **1.** Sticken *n*: **~ needle** Sticknadel *f*. **2.** Stickerei(arbeit) *f*: **do ~** sticken. **3.** *fig.* Ausschmückung *f*.

em·bry·o ['embrɪəʊ] *pl* **-os** *s biol.* Embryo *m*: **in ~** *fig.* im Entstehen *od.* Werden. **em·bry·on·ic** [ˌ~'ɒnɪk] *adj* **1.** *biol.* embryonal. **2.** *fig.* (noch) unentwickelt.

em·cee [ˌem'siː] *bsd. Am.* F **I** *s* Conférencier *m*. **II** *v/t u. v/i* als Conférencier leiten (fungieren).

e·mend [ɪ'mend] *v/t bsd. Texte* verbessern, korrigieren.

em·er·ald ['emərəld] **I** *s min.* Smaragd *m*. **II** *adj* smaragdgrün.

e·merge [ɪ'mɜːdʒ] *v/i* **1.** auftauchen (*a. fig.*). **2.** hervorkommen (**from behind** hinter *den Wolken etc*). **3.** sich herausstellen *od.* ergeben (*Tatsache*). **e·mer·gence** [iː'm~] *s* Auftauchen *n* (*a. fig.*).

e·mer·gen·cy [ɪ'mɜːdʒənsɪ] *s* plötzliche Notlage, kritische Lage: **in an ~, in case of ~** im Ernst- *od.* Notfall; **state of ~** Notstand *m*, *pol. a.* Ausnahmezustand *m*. **~ call** *s teleph.* Notruf *m*. **~ door, ~ ex·it** *s* Notausgang *m*. **~ land·ing** *s* ✓ Notlandung *f*: **make an ~** notlanden. **~ meet·ing** *s* Dringlichkeitssitzung *f*. **~ num·ber** *s teleph.* Notruf(nummer *f*) *m*. **~ op·er·a·tion** *s* ♨ Notoperation *f*. **~ ra·tion** *s* eiserne Ration. **~ stop** *s mot.* Vollbremsung *f*: **do** (*od.* **make**) **an ~** e-e Vollbremsung machen.

e·mer·gent [iː'mɜːdʒənt] *adj* □ **1.** auftauchend (*a. fig.*). **2.** *fig.* (jung u.) aufstrebend: **~ countries** *pl* Schwellenländer *pl*.

em·er·y ['emərɪ] *adj* Schmirgel...: **~ paper**.

e·met·ic [ɪ'metɪk] *s* Brechmittel *n*.

em·i·grant ['emɪɡrənt] *s* Auswanderer *m*, *bsd. pol.* Emigrant(in). **em·i·grate** ['~ɡreɪt] *v/i* auswandern, *bsd. pol.* emigrieren (**from** aus, von; **to** nach). **em·i·gra·tion** *s* Auswanderung *f*, *bsd. pol.* Emigration *f*.

em·i·nence ['emɪnəns] *s* **1.** (An)Höhe *f*. **2.** Berühmtheit *f*: **reach** (*od.* **win**) **~** Bedeutung erlangen (**as** als). **3.** *eccl.* Eminenz *f*. **'em·i·nent** *adj* **1.** hervorragend, berühmt. **2.** bedeutend. **3.** überragend, außergewöhnlich. **'em·i·nent·ly** *adv* in hohem Maße, überaus.

e·mis·sion [ɪˈmɪʃn] s **1.** Ausstoß m, -strahlung f, Aus-, Verströmen n. **2.** ✝ Ausgabe f, Emission f.

e·mit [ɪˈmɪt] v/t **1.** Lava, Rauch ausstoßen, Licht, Wärme ausstrahlen, Gas, Wärme aus-, verströmen. **2.** Ton, Meinung von sich geben; Schrei, Fluch etc ausstoßen. **3.** Banknoten ausgeben, Wertpapiere a. emittieren.

e·mo·tion [ɪˈməʊʃn] s **1.** Emotion f, Gefühl n. **2.** Erregung f. **3.** Rührung f, Ergriffenheit f. **e·mo·tion·al** [~ʃənl] adj □ **1.** emotional, emotionell: a) gefühlsmäßig, -bedingt, b) gefühlsbetont, empfindsam, c) Gemüts..., seelisch: ~ balance inneres od. seelisches Gleichgewicht. **2.** gefühlvoll, rührselig. **e·mo·tion·al·ize** [~ʃənlaɪz] v/t emotionalisieren. **e·mo·tion·less** adj gefühllos. **e·mo·tive** [~tɪv] adj **1.** gefühlvoll. **2.** gefühlsbetont: ~ term (od. word) emotionsgeladenes Wort; Reizwort n.

em·pa·thy [ˈempəθɪ] s Einfühlung(svermögen n) f: feel ~ for sich hineinversetzen in (acc).

em·per·or [ˈempərə] s Kaiser m.

em·pha·sis [ˈemfəsɪs] pl **-ses** [~siːz] s ling. Betonung f, fig. a. Schwerpunkt m; Nachdruck m: lay (od. place, put) ~ on → emphasize; with ~ nachdrücklich, mit Nachdruck. **em·pha·size** [~saɪz] v/t (nachdrücklich) betonen, Nachdruck legen auf (acc), hervorheben, unterstreichen. **em·phat·ic** [ɪmˈfætɪk] adj (~ally) nachdrücklich; eindringlich.

em·pire [ˈempaɪə] s **1.** Reich n, Imperium n (beide a. ✝ u. fig.). **2.** Kaiserreich n.

em·pir·i·cal [emˈpɪrɪkl] adj □ empirisch, Erfahrungs...

em·ploy [ɪmˈplɔɪ] **I** v/t **1.** j-n beschäftigen (as als); an-, einstellen. **2.** Gewalt etc anwenden, gebrauchen. **3.** (in) Energie etc widmen (dat), Zeit verbringen (mit): be ~ed in doing s.th. damit beschäftigt sein, et. zu tun. **II** s **4.** Dienst(e pl) m, Beschäftigung(sverhältnis n) f: in s.o.'s ~ bei j-m beschäftigt. **em·ploy·ee** [ˌemplɔɪˈiː] s Arbeitnehmer(in), Angestellte m, f, Arbeiter(in): the ~ pl die Belegschaft. **em·ploy·er** [ɪmˈplɔɪə] s Arbeitgeber(in); Unternehmer(in). **em·ploy·ment** s **1.** Beschäftigung f,

Arbeit f, (An)Stellung f: full ~ Vollbeschäftigung; ~ agency Stellenvermittlung(sbüro n) f; ~ contract Arbeitsvertrag m; ~ market Arbeits-, Stellenmarkt m; ~ office Br. Arbeitsamt n. **2.** An-, Einstellung f.

em·pow·er [ɪmˈpaʊə] v/t bevollmächtigen, ermächtigen (to do zu tun).

em·press [ˈemprɪs] s Kaiserin f.

emp·ti·ness [ˈemptɪnɪs] s Leere f (a. fig.). **'emp·ty I** adj □ **1.** allg. leer (a. fig. Versprechungen, Worte etc), (Haus etc a.) leerstehend: feel ~ sich (innerlich) leer fühlen; F Kohldampf schieben; stand ~ leerstehen; ~ of ohne; ~ of meaning nichtssagend; → stomach 1. **II** v/t leeren (into in acc), Fach etc a. ausräumen, Glas etc a. austrinken. **3.** Haus etc räumen. **III** v/i **4.** sich leeren. **5.** sich ergießen, münden (into in acc). **IV** s **6.** pl Leergut n. **~'hand·ed** adj mit leeren Händen, unverrichteterdinge.

em·u·late [ˈemjʊleɪt] v/t **1.** wetteifern mit. **2.** nacheifern (dat), es gleichtun wollen (dat).

e·mul·sion [ɪˈmʌlʃn] s ✿, etc Emulsion f.

en·a·ble [ɪˈneɪbl] v/t **1.** j-n berechtigen, ermächtigen (to do zu tun). **2.** j-n befähigen, es j-m möglich machen (to do zu tun). **3.** et. möglich machen, ermöglichen: ~ s.th. to be done es ermöglichen, daß et. getan wird.

en·act [ɪˈnækt] v/t **1.** ⚖ Gesetz erlassen; verfügen, -ordnen. **2.** thea. ein Stück aufführen; Person, Rolle darstellen, spielen. **en'act·ment** s Verfügung f, -ordnung f.

en·am·el [ɪˈnæml] **I** s **1.** Email(le f) n. **2.** Glasur f. **3.** anat. Zahnschmelz m. **II** v/t pret u. pp **-eled**, bsd. Br. **-elled 4.** emaillieren. **5.** glasieren.

en·am·o·u(r) [ɪˈnæmə] v/t: be ~ed of (od. with) verliebt sein in (acc); fig. gefesselt od. verzaubert sein von.

en·case [ɪnˈkeɪs] v/t: ~d in gehüllt in (acc), umhüllt von.

en·chant [ɪnˈtʃɑːnt] v/t **1.** verzaubern. **2.** fig. bezaubern, entzücken: be ~ed entzückt sein (by, with von). **en'chant·er** s Zauberer m. **en'chant·ing** adj □ bezaubernd, entzückend. **en'chant·ment** s **1.** Verzauberung f. **2.** Zauber m (a.

fig.). **3.** Zauberei *f*. **en'chant·ress** *s* **1.** Zauberin *f*. **2.** *fig.* bezaubernde Frau.

en·ci·pher [ın'saıfə] → **encode**.

en·cir·cle [ın'sɜ:kl] *v/t* **1.** umgeben: *~d by* (*od.* **with**) umgeben von. **2.** umfassen. **3.** einkreisen, umzingeln, ✗ *a.* einkesseln. **en'cir·cle·ment** *s* Einkreisung *f*, Umzing(e)lung *f*, ✗ *a.* Einkesselung *f*.

en·close [ın'kləuz] *v/t* **1.** (*in*) einschließen (in *acc od.* dat), umgeben (mit). **2.** umringen. **3.** *mit der Hand etc* umfassen. **4.** beilegen, -fügen (*in*, **with** *dat*): *~d please find* in der Anlage erhalten Sie. **en'clo·sure** [~ʒə] *s* Anlage *f* (*zu e-m Brief etc*).

en·code [en'kəud] *v/t Text* verschlüsseln, chiffrieren.

en·com·pass [ın'kʌmpəs] *v/t* **1.** umgeben (mit). **2.** *fig.* umfassen.

en·core **I** *int* [ɒŋ'kɔ:]: **1.** da capo!; Zugabe! **II** *s* ['ɒŋkɔ:] **2.** Dakapo(ruf *m*) *m*. **3.** Wiederholung *f* (*e-r Arie etc*); Zugabe *f*. **III** *v/t* ['ɒŋkɔ:] **4.** die Wiederholung (*gen*) verlangen *od.* erzwingen; von *j-m* e-e Zugabe verlangen *od.* erzwingen.

en·coun·ter [ın'kauntə] **I** *v/t* **1.** *j-m*, *e-r Sache* begegnen, *j-n* treffen, auf *j-n*, *Widerstand etc* stoßen. **2.** mit *j-m* (*feindlich*) zs.-treffen. **II** *v/i* **3.** sich begegnen *od.* treffen. **III** *s* **4.** Begegnung *f* (*of*, **with** mit). **5.** *feindlicher* Zs.-stoß *m*.

en·cour·age [ın'kʌrıdʒ] *v/t* **1.** *j-n* ermutigen, ermuntern (**to** zu), *j-m* Mut machen. **2.** *j-n* unterstützen, bestärken (**in** *in* dat). **3.** *et.* fördern, unterstützen. **en'cour·age·ment** *s* **1.** Ermutigung *f*, Ermunterung *f*. **2.** Unterstützung *f*, Bestärkung *f*. **3.** Förderung *f*.

en·croach [ın'krəutʃ] *v/i* **1.** (*on*) eingreifen (in *j-s Besitz od. Recht*), unberechtigt eindringen (in *acc*), sich Übergriffe leisten (in, *auf acc*). **2.** über Gebühr in Anspruch nehmen, mißbrauchen (**on** *acc*). **en'croach·ment** *s* Ein-, Übergriff *m*.

en·crust → **incrust**.

en·cum·ber [ın'kʌmbə] *v/t Grundstück etc* belasten: *~ed with mortgages* hypothekarisch belastet. **en'cum·brance** *s* Belastung *f*.

en·cy·clo·p(a)e·di·a [en,saıkləu'pi:djə] *s*

Enzyklopädie *f*. **en·cy·clo'p(a)e·dic** *adj* (*~ally*) enzyklopädisch.

end [end] **I** *v/t* **1.** beenden, zu Ende bringen *od.* führen. **2.** a) *a.* **~ up** *et.* ab-, beschließen (**with** mit), b) *den Rest s-r Tage* zu-, verbringen, *s-e Tage* beschließen. **II** *v/i* **3.** enden, aufhören. **4.** *a.* **~ up** enden, ausgehen: *~ happily* gut ausgehen; *~ in disaster* (*od.* **a fiasco**) mit e-m Fiasko enden; *~ up* a) enden, landen (**in prison** im Gefängnis), b) enden (**as** als). **III** *s* **6.** (*örtlich*) Ende *n*: *go off* (**at**) *the deep ~* F hochgehen, wütend werden; *make* (**both**) *~s meet* durchkommen, finanziell über die Runden kommen. **7.** (*oberes od.* unteres) Ende, Rest *m*: *~ to ~* → **thick** 1, **thin** 1. **8.** (*zeitlich*) Ende *n*: *in the ~* am Ende, schließlich; *at the ~ of May* Ende Mai; *without ~* unaufhörlich; *come* (*od.* **draw**) *to an ~* zu Ende gehen; *make an ~ of*, *put an ~ to* e-r Sache ein Ende setzen. **9.** Tod *m*, Ende *n*. **10.** *oft pl* Absicht *f*, (End)Zweck *m*, Ziel *n*: *the ~ justifies* (*od.* **sanctifies**) *the means* der Zweck heiligt die Mittel; *to this ~* zu diesem Zweck; *to no ~* vergebens.

en·dan·ger [ın'deındʒə] *v/t* gefährden.

end con·sum·er *s* ✝ End-, Letztverbraucher *m*.

en·dear·ing [ın'dıərıŋ] *adj* □ **1.** gewinnend (*Lächeln etc*). **2.** liebenswert (*Eigenschaft etc*). **en'dear·ment** *s*: (**term of**) *~* Kosename *m*, -wort *n*; *words pl of ~*, *~s pl* liebe *od.* zärtliche Worte *pl*.

en·deav·o(u)r [ın'devə] **I** *v/t* bemühen *od.* bestrebt sein (**to do** zu tun). **II** *s* Bemühung *f*, Bestrebung *f*: *make every ~* sich nach Kräften bemühen.

end·ing ['endıŋ] *s* **1.** Ende *n*, Schluß *m*: *happy ~* Happy-End *n*. **2.** *ling.* Endung *f*.

en·dive ['endıv] *s* ♣ (Winter)Endivie *f*.

end·less ['endlıs] *adj* □ *allg.* endlos.

en·dorse [ın'dɔ:s] *v/t* **1.** *Erklärung etc* vermerken (**on** auf dat); *bsd. Br.* e-e Strafe vermerken auf (*e-m Führerschein*). **2.** ✝ *Scheck etc* indossieren, girieren. **3.** *Plan etc* billigen. **en·dor·see** [ˌendɔ:'si:] *s* ✝ Indossat *m*. **en·dorse·ment** *s* **1.** Vermerk *m*; *bsd. Br.* Strafvermerk *m* (*auf e-m Führerschein*). **2.** ✝ Indossament *n*,

Giro n. **3.** Billigung f. **en'dors·er** s †
Indossant m.

en·dow [ɪn'daʊ] v/t **1.** e-e Stiftung machen (dat). **2.** et. stiften: ~ **s.o. with s.th.**
j-m et. stiften. **3.** fig. ausstatten (**with**
mit). **en'dow·ment** s **1.** Stiftung f. **2.**
Begabung f, Talent n.

end prod·uct s **1.** †, ⚙ Endprodukt n.
2. fig. (End)Produkt n.

en·dur·a·ble [ɪn'djʊərəbl] adj □ erträglich. **en'dur·ance** s **1.** Standhaftigkeit f, Ausdauer f; Aushalten n, Ertragen n: **beyond** (od. **past**) ~ unerträglich. **2.** ⚙ Dauerleistung f. **II** adj **3.**
Dauer...: ~ **test** ⚙ Belastungsprobe f.
en'dure I v/t **1.** andauern, Bestand haben. **2.** durchhalten. **II** v/t **3.** aushalten,
ertragen, erdulden. **4.** neg. ausstehen,
leiden.

end us·er → **end consumer.**

en·e·ma ['enɪmə] pl **-mas, -ma·ta**
[~mətə] s ✴ Klistier n, Einlauf m: **give
s.o. an** ~ j-m e-n Einlauf machen.

en·e·my ['enəmɪ] **I** s ✕ Feind m, weitS.
a. Gegner m (**of, to** gen): ~ **to reform**
Reformgegner; **make a** ~ **of s.o.** sich
j-n zum Feind machen. **II** adj feindlich,
Feind(es)...

en·er·get·ic [ˌenə'dʒetɪk] adj (~**ally**)
energisch. **'en·er·gy** s Energie f (a.
phys.): ~**saving** energiesparend.

en·er·vate ['enəːveɪt] v/t entkräften,
schwächen (a. fig.); entnerven.

en·fee·ble [ɪn'fiːbl] v/t entkräften,
schwächen (a. fig.).

en·fold [ɪn'fəʊld] v/t **1.** einhüllen (**in** in
acc), umhüllen (**with** mit) (beide a. fig.).
2. umfassen: ~ **s.o. in one's arms** j-n in
die Arme schließen.

en·force [ɪn'fɔːs] v/t **1.** Argument, †, ⚖
Forderung geltend machen; e-r Sache
Geltung verschaffen, Gesetz etc durchführen; Urteil vollstrecken. **2.** durchsetzen, erzwingen: ~ **s.th. on s.o.** et.
von j-m erzwingen; j-m et. aufzwingen.
en'force·ment s **1.** †, ⚖ Geltendmachung f; ⚖ Vollstreckung f. **2.** Durchsetzung f, Erzwingung f.

en·fran·chise [ɪn'fræntʃaɪz] v/t das
Wahlrecht verleihen (dat).

en·gage [ɪn'geɪdʒ] **I** v/t **1.** (o.s. sich)
verpflichten (**to do** zu tun). **2.** become
(od. **get**) ~**d** sich verloben (**to** mit). **3.** j-n
ein-, anstellen, Künstler etc engagieren

(**as** als). **4.** fig. j-n in Anspruch nehmen,
j-s Aufmerksamkeit a. auf sich ziehen.
5. ⚙ einrasten lassen, Kupplung etc einrücken, Gang einlegen. **II** v/i **6.** sich
verpflichten (**to do** zu tun). **7.** ~ **in** sich
einlassen auf (acc) od. in (acc); sich
beschäftigen mit. **8.** ⚙ einrasten.
en'gaged adj **1.** a. ~ **to be married**
verlobt: ~ **to** verlobt mit. **2.** beschäftigt
(**in, on** mit): be ~ **in** doing s.th. damit
beschäftigt sein, et. zu tun. **3.** in Anspruch genommen: **my time is fully** ~
ich bin zeitlich voll ausgelastet. **4.**
teleph. Br. besetzt: ~**tone** Besetztton m,
-zeichen n. **en'gage·ment** s **1.** Verpflichtung f: **without** ~ unverbindlich,
† a. freibleibend. **2.** Verabredung f:
have an ~ verabredet sein. **3.** Verlobung f (**to** mit): ~ **ring** Verlobungsring
m. **4.** (An)Stellung f, thea. etc Engagement n. **en'ga·ging** adj □ einnehmend
(Wesen etc), gewinnend (Lächeln etc).

en·gen·der [ɪn'dʒendə] v/t Neid etc erzeugen, hervorrufen (**in** bei).

en·gine ['endʒɪn] s **1.** Motor m. **2.** 🚂
Lokomotive f. ~ **block** s Motorblock
m. ~ **driv·er** s 🚂 Lokomotivführer m.

en·gi·neer [ˌendʒɪ'nɪə] **I** s **1.** Ingenieur
m; Techniker m; Mechaniker m. **2.** 🚂
Am. Lokomotivführer m. **II** v/t **3.** fig.
(geschickt) in die Wege leiten, organisieren. **en·gi·neer·ing** s allg. Technik
f, engS. Ingenieurwesen n, (a. **mechanical** ~) Maschinen- u. Gerätebau m.

En·glish ['ɪŋglɪʃ] **I** adj **1.** englisch. **II** s **2.**
the ~ pl die Engländer pl. **3.** ling. Englisch n; **in** ~ auf englisch; **in plain** ~
unverblümt; auf gut deutsch; **Queen's**
(od. **King's**) ~ hochsprachliches Englisch. ~**man** ['~mən] s (irr **man**) Engländer m. '~**wom·an** s (irr **woman**)
Engländerin f.

en·grave [ɪn'greɪv] v/t (**on** (in Metall,
Stein etc) (ein)gravieren, (-)meißeln, (in
Holz) einschnitzen: **it is** ~**d on** (od. **in**)
his memory (od. **mind**) es hat sich ihm
tief od. unauslöschlich eingeprägt. **en-
'grav·er** s Graveur m: ~ **on copper**
Kupferstecher m. **en'grav·ing** s **1.**
Gravieren n. **2.** Gravierung f, (Kupfer-,
Stahl)Stich m, (Holz)Schnitt m.

en·gross [ɪn'grəʊs] v/t j-s Aufmerksamkeit in Anspruch nehmen, Macht,
Unterhaltung etc an sich reißen.

en·grossed adj (**in**) (voll) in Anspruch genommen (von), vertieft, versunken (in acc).

en·gulf [ɪn'gʌlf] v/t verschlingen (a. fig.).

en·hance [ɪn'hɑːns] v/t Wert etc erhöhen, steigern, heben.

e·nig·ma [ɪ'nɪɡmə] s fig. Rätsel n. **en·ig·mat·ic** [ˌenɪɡ'mætɪk] adj (**~ally**) rätselhaft.

en·joy [ɪn'dʒɔɪ] v/t **1.** Vergnügen od. Gefallen finden od. Freude haben an (dat): **~ doing s.th.** daran Vergnügen finden, et. zu tun; **I ~ dancing** ich tanze gern, Tanzen macht mir Spaß; **did you ~ the play?** hat dir das Stück gefallen?; **~ o.s.** sich amüsieren od. unterhalten; **~ yourself!** viel Spaß! **2.** genießen, sich et. schmecken lassen. **3.** sich e-s Besitzes erfreuen, j-s Vertrauen etc genießen: **~ good health** sich e-r guten Gesundheit erfreuen. **en·joy·a·ble** adj □ angenehm, erfreulich. **en·joy·ment** s **1.** Vergnügen n, Freude f (**of** an dat). **2.** Genuß m: **be in the ~ of** → enjoy 3.

en·large [ɪn'lɑːdʒ] **I** v/t **1.** vergrößern (a. phot.), Kenntnisse etc a. erweitern, Einfluß etc a. ausdehnen. **II** v/i **2.** sich vergrößern od. erweitern od. ausdehnen. **3.** sich verbreiten od. (weitläufig) auslassen (**on** über acc). **en·large·ment** s Vergrößerung f (a. phot.).

en·light·en [ɪn'laɪtn] v/t aufklären, belehren (**on, as to** über acc). **en·light·en·ment** s Aufklärung f.

en·list [ɪn'lɪst] **I** v/t **1.** Soldaten anwerben, Rekruten einstellen. **2.** fig. heranziehen, j-s Dienste in Anspruch nehmen. **II** v/i **3.** ✗ Soldat werden, sich (freiwillig) melden (**to** zu). **4.** (**in**) mitwirken (bei), sich beteiligen (an dat).

en·liv·en [ɪn'laɪvn] v/t beleben, in Schwung bringen.

en·mesh [ɪn'meʃ] v/t: **be ~ed in one's own lies** sich in s-n eigenen Lügen verstrickt od. verfangen haben.

en·mi·ty ['enmətɪ] s Feindschaft f: **be at ~ with** verfeindet sein mit.

e·nor·mous [ɪ'nɔːməs] adj □ enorm, ungeheuer, gewaltig.

e·nough [ɪ'nʌf] **I** adj ausreichend, genug: **be ~** (aus)reichen, genügen. **II** s: **I have had ~, thank you** danke, ich bin satt!; **~ of that!** genug davon!, Schluß damit! **III** adv genug, genügend: **be kind** (od.

good) **~ to do this for me** sei so freundlich od. gut u. erledige das für mich; **curiously** (od. **strangely**) **~** merkwürdigerweise.

en·quire, en·quir·y → inquire, inquiry.

en·rage [ɪn'reɪdʒ] v/t wütend machen. **en·raged** adj wütend, aufgebracht (**at, by** über acc).

en·rap·ture [ɪn'ræptʃə] v/t hinreißen, entzücken. **en·rap·tured** adj hingerissen, entzückt (**at, by** von).

en·rich [ɪn'rɪtʃ] v/t **1.** bereichern (a. fig.). **2.** 🔧, etc anreichern.

en·rol(l) [ɪn'rəʊl] **I** v/t **1.** j-n, j-s Namen einschreiben, -tragen (**in** in dat od. acc), univ. j-n immatrikulieren: **~ o.s.** → 3. **2.** j-n aufnehmen (**in** in e-n Verein etc): **~ o.s. in** → 4. **II** v/i **3.** sich einschreiben (lassen), univ. sich immatrikulieren: **~ for a course** e-n Kurs belegen. **4. ~ in** beitreten (dat). **en·rol(l)·ment** s **1.** Einschreibung f, -tragung f, univ. Immatrikulation f. **2.** (Gesamt)Zahl f der Eingetragenen od. univ. Immatrikulierten.

en route [ãː'ruːt] adv unterwegs (**for** nach).

en·sem·ble [ãː'sãːmbl] s **1.** das Ganze, Gesamteindruck m. **2.** ♪, thea., Mode: Ensemble n.

en·sign ['ensaɪn] s ⚓ (bsd. National-) Flagge f.

en·slave [ɪn'sleɪv] v/t zum Sklaven machen (a. fig.), versklaven.

en·snare [ɪn'sneə] v/t **1.** in e-r Schlinge fangen (a. fig.). bestricken, umgarnen.

en·sue [ɪn'sjuː] v/i **1.** (darauf-, nach)folgen: **the ensuing years** die (darauf)folgenden Jahre. **2.** folgen, sich ergeben (**from** aus).

en·sure [ɪn'ʃɔː] v/t **1.** (**against, from**) sichern (vor dat, gegen), schützen (vor dat). **2.** sicherstellen, garantieren (**s.th.** et.; **that** daß; **s.o. being** daß j-d ist). **3.** sorgen für et.: **~ that** dafür sorgen, daß.

en·tail [ɪn'teɪl] v/t mit sich bringen, zur Folge haben, nach sich ziehen, Kosten etc verursachen, erfordern.

en·tan·gle [ɪn'tæŋɡl] v/t **1.** Haare, Garn etc verwirren, -filzen. **2.** (**o.s.** sich) verwickeln, -heddern (**in** in dat). **3.** fig. verwickeln, -stricken (**in** in acc).

en·ter ['entə] v/t **1.** (hinein-, herein)gehen, (-)kommen, (-)treten in (acc), eintreten, -steigen in (acc), betreten; ein-

reisen in (*acc*); ♆, ⛴ einlaufen, -fahren in (*acc*); eindringen in (*acc*): *it ~ed my mind* es kam mir in den Sinn. **2.** *fig.* eintreten in (*acc*), beitreten (*dat*). **3.** *Namen etc* eintragen, -schreiben, j-n aufnehmen, zulassen: *~ one's name* (*od.* **o.s.**) → 7a. **4.** *Sport*: melden, nennen (*for* für): *~ o.s.* → 7b. **5.** *Vorschlag etc* einreichen, -bringen: *~ a protest* Protest erheben *od.* einlegen. **II** *v/i* **6.** eintreten, herein-, hineinkommen, -gehen; *thea.* auftreten: ⚥ *Hamlet* Hamlet tritt auf. **7.** a) sich eintragen *od.* -schreiben *od.* anmelden (*for* für), b) (*Sport*) melden, nennen (*for* für).
Verbindungen mit Präpositionen:
en·ter| in·to *v/i* **1.** → enter 1, 2. **2.** anfangen, beginnen; sich einlassen auf (*acc*); eingehen auf (*acc*): *~ into correspondence with* in Briefwechsel treten mit. **3.** *Verpflichtung, Partnerschaft etc* eingehen. *~ on v/i* **1.** *Thema* anschneiden; sich in *ein Gespräch etc* einlassen. **2.** *Amt, Erbschaft* antreten; *Laufbahn* einschlagen; in *ein neues Stadium etc* treten.
en·ter·i·tis [ˌentəˈraɪtɪs] *s* 🔬 Darmkatarrh *m.*
en·ter·prise [ˈentəpraɪz] *s* **1.** Unternehmen *n*, -nehmung *f.* **2.** ♣ Unternehmen *n*, Betrieb *m*; Unternehmertum *n.* **3.** Unternehmungsgeist *m.* '**en·ter·pris·ing** *adj* □ unternehmungslustig.
en·ter·tain [ˌentəˈteɪn] *v/t* **1.** (angenehm) unterhalten. **2.** bewirten. **3.** *Furcht, Hoffnung etc* hegen. **4.** *Vorschlag etc* in Betracht *od.* Erwägung ziehen: *~ an idea* sich mit e-m Gedanken tragen. ˌ**en·ter·tain·er** *s* Entertainer(in). ˌ**en·ter·tain·ing** *adj* □ unterhaltend, -haltsam. ˌ**en·ter·tain·ment** *s* **1.** Unterhaltung *f*: *much* (*od. greatly*) *to his ~* sehr zu s-r Belustigung. **2.** (*öffentliche*) Unterhaltung, (*professionell dargeboten a.*) Entertainment *n*: *~ industry* Unterhaltungsindustrie *f*; *~ tax* Vergnügungssteuer *f.*
en·thral(l) [ɪnˈθrɔːl] *v/t* *fig.* bezaubern, fesseln.
en·thuse [ɪnˈθjuːz] *v/i* F (*about, over*) begeistert sein (von), schwärmen (von, für).
en·thu·si·asm [ɪnˈθjuːzɪæzəm] *s* Enthusiasmus *m*, Begeisterung *f* (*for* für;

about über *acc*). **en'thu·si·ast** [ˌæst] *s* Enthusiast(in). **en,thu·si'as·tic** *adj* (*~ally*) begeistert (*about, over* von), enthusiastisch.
en·tice [ɪnˈtaɪs] *v/t* **1.** locken (*into* in *acc*): *~ away* weglocken (*from* von); ☞ abwerben; *~ s.o.'s girlfriend away* j-m die Freundin abspenstig machen. **2.** verlocken, -leiten, -führen (*into* zu *et.*): *~ s.o. to do* (*od. into doing*) *s.th.* j-n dazu verleiten, et. zu tun. **en'tice·ment** *s* **1.** (Ver)Lockung *f*, (An)Reiz *m.* **2.** Verführung *f*, -leitung *f.* **en'tic·ing** *adj* □ verlockend, -führerisch.
en·tire [ɪnˈtaɪə] *adj* **1.** ganz: a) vollzählig, -ständig, b) gesamt, Gesamt..., c) unversehrt, unbeschädigt. **2.** *fig.* voll, uneingeschränkt (*Vertrauen etc*): *be in ~ agreement with* voll u. ganz *od.* völlig übereinstimmen mit. **en'tire·ly** *adv* völlig, gänzlich. **en'tire·ty** *s*: *in its ~* in s-r Gesamtheit, als (ein) Ganzes.
en·ti·tle [ɪnˈtaɪtl] *v/t* **1.** *Buch etc* betiteln: *~d* ... mit dem Titel ... **2.** j-n berechtigen (*to* zu): *be ~d to* ein Anrecht *od.* (e-n) Anspruch haben auf (*acc*); *be ~d to do s.th.* (dazu) berechtigt sein *od.* das Recht haben, et. zu tun; *~d to vote* wahl-, stimmberechtigt.
en·ti·ty [ˈentətɪ] *s* **1.** Einheit *f.* **2.** ⚖ Rechtspersönlichkeit *f*: *legal ~* juristische Person.
en·trails [ˈentreɪlz] *s pl anat.* Eingeweide *pl.*
en·trance¹ [ˈentrəns] *s* **1.** Eintreten *n*, -tritt *m*; ♆, ⛴ Einlaufen *n*, -fahrt *f.* **2.** Ein-, Zugang *m* (*to* zu); Zufahrt *f*: *~ hall* (Eingangs-, Vor)Halle *f*, (Haus-)Flur *m.* **3.** *fig.* Antritt *m* (*on an inheritance* e-r Erbschaft): *~ on an office* Amtsantritt *m.* **4.** Einlaß *m*, Ein-, Zutritt *m*: *~ fee* Eintritt(sgeld *n*); Aufnahmegebühr *f*; *no ~!* Zutritt verboten! **5.** *thea.* Auftritt *m*: *make one's ~* auftreten.
en·trance² [ɪnˈtrɑːns] *v/t* entzücken, hinreißen: *~d* entzückt, hingerissen (*at, by* von).
en·trant [ˈentrənt] *s* **1.** (Berufs)Anfänger(in) (*to* in *dat*). **2.** neues Mitglied. **3.** *Sport*: Teilnehmer(in) (*a. allg. an e-m Wettbewerb*).
en·treat [ɪnˈtriːt] *v/t* **1.** inständig *od.* dringend bitten, anflehen (*for* um). **2.**

et. erflehen (**of** von). **en'treat·ing** *adj* □ flehentlich. **en'treat·y** *s* dringende Bitte: **at s.o.'s ~** auf j-s Bitte (hin).

en·trée ['ɒntreɪ] *s* **1.** *bsd. fig.* Zutritt *m* (**into** zu). **2.** *gastr.* Zwischen-, *Am.* Hauptgericht *n.*

en·trench [ɪn'trentʃ] *v/t* ⚔ (**o.s.** sich) verschanzen (**behind** hinter *dat*) (*a. fig.*). **en'trenched** *adj fig.* eingewurzelt.

en·tre·pre·neur [ˌɒntrəprə'nɜː] *s* ✝ Unternehmer *m.*

en·trust [ɪn'trʌst] *v/t* **1.** *et.* anvertrauen (**to s.o.** j-m). **2.** *j-n* betrauen (**with** mit).

en·try ['entrɪ] *s* **1.** → *entrance*[1] **1. 2.** Einreise *f*, Zuzug *m*: **~ visa** Einreisevisum *n.* **3.** → *entrance*[1] **1. 2.** Beitritt *m* (**into** zu). **5.** Einlaß *m*, Zutritt *m*: **gain** (*od.* **obtain**) **~** Einlaß finden; **force an ~ into**, **make a forcible ~ into** gewaltsam eindringen in (*acc*); **no ~!** Zutritt verboten. **6.** Zu-, Eingang(stür *f*) *m*, Einfahrt(stor *n*) *f*; (Eingangs-, Vor)Halle *f*, (Haus)Flur *m.* **7.** Eintrag(ung *f*) *m*, ✝ *a.* Buchung *f*; Stichwort *n* (*im Lexikon etc*). **8.** *Sport:* a) Nennung *f*, Meldung *f*, b) → *entrant* **3.** '**~phone** *s* Türsprechanlage *f.*

en·twine [ɪn'twaɪn] *v/t* winden, schlingen ([a]**round** um), umwinden (**with** mit).

e·nu·mer·ate [ɪ'njuːməreɪt] *v/t* aufzählen. **e·nu·mer'a·tion** *s* Aufzählung *f.*

e·nun·ci·ate [ɪ'nʌnsɪeɪt] **I** *v/t* **1.** ausdrükken, -sprechen. **2.** formulieren. **3.** (*bsd.* deutlich) aussprechen. **II** *v/i* **4. ~ clearly** e-e deutliche Aussprache haben, deutlich sprechen.

en·vel·op [ɪn'veləp] *v/t* **1.** einschlagen, -wickeln, (ein)hüllen (**in** in *acc*). **2.** *fig.* ver-, einhüllen: **~ed in mystery** geheimnisumhüllt. **en·ve·lope** ['envələup] *s* **1.** Hülle *f*, Umschlag *m.* **2.** Briefumschlag *m*, Kuvert *n.*

en·vi·a·ble ['envɪəbl] *adj* □ beneidenswert. **'en·vi·er** *s* Neider(in). **'en·vi·ous** *adj* □ neidisch (**of** auf *acc*).

en·vi·ron·ment [ɪn'vaɪərənmənt] *s* **1.** Umgebung *f*, *sociol. a.* Milieu *n.* **2.** Umwelt *f*. **en·vi·ron'men·tal** [~'mentl] *adj* □ **1.** *sociol.* Milieu... **2.** Umwelt...: **~ pollution** Umweltverschmutzung *f*; **~ protection** Umweltschutz *m*; **~ly beneficial** (**harmful**) umweltfreundlich

(-feindlich). **en·vi·ron·men·tal·ist** [~'təlɪst] *s* Umweltschützer(in). **en'vi·rons** *s pl* Umgebung *f* (*e-s Ortes etc*).

en·vis·age [ɪn'vɪzɪdʒ] *v/t* **1.** gedenken (**doing** zu tun), in Aussicht nehmen, ins Auge fassen. **2.** sich *et.* vorstellen.

en·vi·sion [ɪn'vɪʒn] *v/t* → *envisage* **2.**

en·voy ['envɔɪ] *s* **1.** *pol.* Gesandte *m.* **2.** Abgesandte *m*, Bevollmächtigte *m.*

en·vy ['envɪ] **I** *s* **1.** Neid *m* (**of** auf *acc*). **2.** Gegenstand *m* des Neides: **his car is the ~ of everybody** alle beneiden ihn um s-n Wagen. **II** *v/t* **3.** *j-n* beneiden (**s.th.** um etwas).

en·zyme ['enzaɪm] *s Biochemie:* Enzym *n.*

e·phem·er·al [ɪ'femərəl] *adj* □ flüchtig, kurzlebig.

ep·ic ['epɪk] **I** *adj* (**~ally**) **1.** episch. **2.** heldenhaft. **II** *s* **3.** Epos *n.*

ep·i·cure ['epɪˌkjʊə] *s* **1.** Epikureer *m*, Genußmensch *m.* **2.** Feinschmecker *m.*

ep·i·dem·ic [ˌepɪ'demɪk] ⚕ **I** *adj* (**~ally**) epidemisch (*a. fig.*). **II** *s* Epidemie *f*, Seuche *f* (*beide a. fig.*).

ep·i·der·mis [ˌepɪ'dɜːmɪs] *s anat.* Oberhaut *f.*

ep·i·gram ['epɪgræm] *s* Epigramm *n.*

ep·i·lep·sy ['epɪlepsɪ] *s* ⚕ Epilepsie *f*. **ep·i·lep·tic** [~'leptɪk] *adj* (**~ally**) epileptisch: **~ fit** epileptischer Anfall. **II** *s* Epileptiker(in).

ep·i·logue ['epɪlɒg] *s* Epilog *m*: a) Nachwort *n* (*e-s Buchs etc*), b) *fig.* Nachspiel *n*, Ausklang *m.*

E·piph·a·ny [ɪ'pɪfənɪ] *s eccl.* Dreikönigsfest *n.*

ep·is·co·pal [ɪ'pɪskəpl] *adj* □ bischöflich, Bischofs... **e'pis·co·pate** [~'kəʊpət] *s* Episkopat *m*, Bistum *n.*

ep·i·sode ['epɪsəʊd] *s* **1.** Episode *f.* **2.** *Rundfunk, TV etc:* Folge *f.* **ep·i·sod·ic** [~'sɒdɪk] *adj* (**~ally**) episodisch, episodenhaft.

ep·is·tle [ɪ'pɪsl] *s eccl.* Epistel *f.*

ep·i·taph ['epɪtɑːf] *s* Grabschrift *f.*

ep·i·thet ['epɪθet] *s* **1.** Beiwort *n*, Attribut *n.* **2.** Beiname *m.*

e·pit·o·me [ɪ'pɪtəmɪ] *s* **1.** Auszug *m*, Abriß *m*; kurze Darstellung: **in ~** auszugsweise; in gedrängter Form. **2.** *fig.* Verkörperung *f*, Inbegriff *m.* **e'pit·o·mize** *v/t* verkörpern.

ep·och ['iːpɒk] *s* Epoche *f.* '**~·ˌmak·ing** *adj* epochemachend.

eq·ua·bil·i·ty [ˌekwə'bɪlətɪ] *s* **1.** Gleichförmigkeit *f.* **2.** Ausgeglichenheit *f,* Gleichmut *m.* '**eq·ua·ble** *adj* □ **1.** gleich(förmig). **2.** ausgeglichen (*a. Klima*), gleichmütig.

e·qual ['iːkwəl] **I** *adj* (□ → **equally**) **1.** gleich: **be ~ to** gleichen, gleich sein (*dat*); entsprechen, gleichkommen (*dat*); **~ opportunities** *pl* Chancengleichheit *f*; **~ rights** *pl* **for women** Gleichberechtigung *f* der Frau; **~ in size, of ~ size** (von) gleicher Größe, gleich groß. **2. be ~ to** e-r Aufgabe *etc* gewachsen sein. **3.** ebenbürtig (*to dat*), gleichwertig: **be on ~ terms** (**with**) auf gleicher Stufe stehen (mit); gleichberechtigt sein (*dat*). **II** *s* **4.** Gleichgestellte *m, f:* **your ~s** *pl* deinesgleichen; **~s** *pl* **in age** Altersgenossen *pl*; **he has no** (*od.* **is without**) **~** er hat nicht *od.* sucht seinesgleichen. **III** *v/t* **5.** (*dat*) gleichen, gleichkommen (**in** an *dat*). **6.** *Sport:* Rekord einstellen. **e·qual·i·ty** [ɪ'kwɒlətɪ] *s* Gleichheit *f:* **~ (of rights)** Gleichberechtigung *f*; **~ of opportunity** (*od.* **opportunities**) Chancengleichheit. **e·qual·i·za·tion** [ˌiːkwəlaɪ'zeɪʃn] *s* Gleichstellung *f.* '**e·qual·ize** **I** *v/t* **1.** gleichmachen, -setzen, -stellen. **2.** ausgleichen. **II** *v/i* **3.** *Sport:* ausgleichen. '**e·qual·iz·er** *s Sport:* Ausgleich(stor *n*) *m.* '**e·qual·ly** *adv* gleich (*groß etc*).

e·qua·nim·i·ty [ˌekwə'nɪmətɪ] *s* Ausgeglichenheit *f,* Gleichmut *m.*

e·quate [ɪ'kweɪt] *v/t* **1.** gleichsetzen, -stellen (**to, with** *dat*). **2.** als gleich(wertig) ansehen *od.* behandeln. **e·qua·tion** [~ʒn] *s* **1.** Å Gleichung *f.* **2.** Gleichsetzung *f,* -stellung *f.* **e·qua·tor** [~tə] *s* Äquator *m.* **e·qua·to·ri·al** [ˌekwə'tɔːrɪəl] *adj* äquatorial, Äquator...

e·ques·tri·an [ɪ'kwestrɪən] **I** *adj* Reit(er)...: **~ sports** *pl* Reit-, Pferdesport *m*; **~ statue** Reiterstatue *f*; -standbild *n.* **II** *s* (*a.* Kunst)Reiter(in).

e·qui·dis·tant [ˌiːkwɪ'dɪstənt] *adj* □ gleich weit entfernt. **e·qui·lat·er·al** [ˌ~'lætərəl] *adj* □ *bsd.* Å gleichseitig.

e·qui·lib·ri·um [ˌiːkwɪ'lɪbrɪəm] *pl* **-ri·ums, -ri·a** [~rɪə] *s* Gleichgewicht *n* (*a. fig.*).

e·qui·nox ['iːkwɪnɒks] *s* Tagundnachtgleiche *f.*

e·quip [ɪ'kwɪp] *v/t* **1.** ausrüsten, -statten (**with** mit), *Krankenhaus etc* einrichten. **2.** *fig. j-m* das (geistige *od.* nötige) Rüstzeug geben (**for** für): **be well ~ped for** das nötige Rüstzeug haben für. **e'quip·ment** *s* **1.** a) Ausrüstung *f,* -stattung *f,* b) *mst pl* Ausrüstung(sgegenstände *pl*) *f,* c) ⊕ Einrichtung *f,* Maschine(n *pl*) *f.* **2.** *fig.* (geistiges *od.* nötiges) Rüstzeug.

e·qui·poise ['ekwɪpɔɪz] **I** *s* **1.** Gleichgewicht *n* (*a. fig.*). **2.** *mst fig.* Gegengewicht *n* (**to** zu). **II** *v/t* **3.** im Gleichgewicht halten (*a. fig.*). **4.** *mst fig.* ein Gegengewicht bilden zu.

eq·ui·ta·ble ['ekwɪtəbl] *adj* □ gerecht, (recht u.) billig. **eq·ui·ty** ['ekwətɪ] *s* **1.** Gerechtigkeit *f,* Billigkeit *f.* **2.** *a.* **~ law** ⁑ (*ungeschriebenes*) Billigkeitsrecht.

e·quiv·a·lence [ɪ'kwɪvələns] *s* Gleichwertigkeit *f,* ⚛ *etc a.* Äquivalenz *f.* **e'quiv·a·lent** **I** *adj* □ **1.** gleichbedeutend (**to** mit). **2.** gleichwertig, ⚛ *etc a.* äquivalent: **be ~ to** gleichkommen, entsprechen (*dat*). **II** *s* **3.** (**of**) Äquivalent *n* (für), (genaue) Entsprechung (zu).

e·quiv·o·cal [ɪ'kwɪvəkl] *adj* □ **1.** zweideutig, doppelsinnig. **2.** unbestimmt, ungewiß, fraglich. **3.** fragwürdig.

e·ra ['ɪərə] *s* Ära *f,* Zeitalter *n.*

e·rad·i·cate [ɪ'rædɪkeɪt] *v/t* ausrotten (*a. fig.*). **e·rad·i·ca·tion** *s* Ausrottung *f.*

e·rase [ɪ'reɪz] *v/t* **1.** *Schrift etc* ausstreichen, -radieren, löschen (**from** von); *Tonband(aufnahme) etc,* ped. *Am. a. Tafel* löschen. **2.** *fig.* (aus)löschen (**from** aus). **e'ras·er** *s* Radiergummi *m*; ped. *Am.* Tafelwischer *m.* **e'ra·sure** [~ʒə] *s* **1.** Ausradieren *n*; Löschen *n.* **2.** ausradierte *od.* gelöschte Stelle.

e·rect [ɪ'rekt] **I** *v/t* **1.** aufrichten. **2.** *Gebäude etc* errichten; *Maschine etc* aufstellen. **II** *adj* □ **3.** aufgerichtet, aufrecht: **with head ~** erhobenen Hauptes. **4.** *physiol.* erigiert. **e'rec·tion** *s* **1.** Errichtung *f*; Aufstellung *f.* **2.** Bau *m,* Gebäude *n.* **3.** *physiol.* Erektion *f.*

er·e·mite ['erɪmaɪt] *s* Eremit *m,* Einsiedler *m.*

er·mine ['ɜːmɪn] *s zo.* Hermelin *n.*

e·rode [ɪ'rəʊd] *v/t* **1.** an-, zer-, wegfressen. **2.** *geol.* erodieren. **3.** *fig.* aushöhlen, untergraben.

e·rog·e·nous [ɪˈrɒdʒɪnəs] *adj physiol.* erogen: ~ **zone.**

e·ro·sion [ɪˈrəʊʒn] *s* **1.** *geol.* Erosion *f.* **2.** *fig.* Aushöhlung *f.*

e·rot·ic [ɪˈrɒtɪk] *adj* (~**ally**) erotisch. **e·rot·i·cism** [~sɪzəm], *bsd. Am.* **er·o·tism** [ˈerətɪzəm] *s* Erotik *f.*

err [ɜː] *v/i* (sich) irren: **to ~ is human** Irren ist menschlich.

er·rand [ˈerənd] *s* Botengang *m,* Besorgung *f:* **go on** (*od.* **run**) **an ~** e-n Botengang *od.* e-e Besorgung machen. **~ boy** *s* Laufbursche *m.*

er·ra·ta [eˈrɑːtə] *pl von* **erratum.**

er·rat·ic [ɪˈrætɪk] *adj* (~**ally**) sprunghaft, unberechenbar.

er·ra·tum [eˈrɑːtəm] *pl* **-ta** [~tə] *s* **1.** Druckfehler *m.* **2.** *pl* Errata *pl,* Druckfehlerverzeichnis *n.*

er·ro·ne·ous [ɪˈrəʊnjəs] *adj* irrig, falsch: ~ **belief** Irrglaube(n) *m.* **er·ro·ne·ous·ly** *adv* irrtümlicher-, fälschlicherweise.

er·ror [ˈerə] *s* Irrtum *m,* Fehler *m,* Versehen *n:* **in ~** irrtümlicherweise; **be in ~** im Irrtum sein, sich im Irrtum befinden; ~ **of judg(e)ment** falsche Beurteilung; ~**s excepted** † Irrtümer vorbehalten.

e·rupt [ɪˈrʌpt] *v/i* ausbrechen (*Ausschlag, Streit, Vulkan etc*): ~ **in** (*od.* **with**) **anger** e-n Wutanfall bekommen. **e·rup·tion** *s* **1.** Ausbruch *m:* **angry ~** Wutausbruch. **2.** ℋ Ausschlag *m.*

es·ca·late [ˈeskəleɪt] **I** *v/t* **1.** Krieg etc eskalieren. **2.** *Erwartungen etc* höherschrauben. **II** *v/i* **3.** eskalieren. **4.** steigen, in die Höhe gehen (*Preise etc*). **,es·ca·la·tion** *s* Eskalation *f.* **'es·ca·la·tor** *s* Rolltreppe *f.*

es·ca·lope [ˈeskæləp] *s gastr.* (*bsd. Wiener*) Schnitzel *n.*

es·ca·pade [ˌeskəˈpeɪd] *s* Eskapade *f.*

es·cape [ɪˈskeɪp] **I** *v/t* **1.** *j-m* entfliehen, -kommen; *e-r Sache* entgehen: **I cannot ~ the impression that** ich kann mich des Eindrucks nicht erwehren, daß; → **notice** 1. **2.** *fig. j-m* entgehen, übersehen *od.* nicht verstanden werden von. **3.** *dem Gedächtnis* entfallen: **his name ~s me** sein Name ist mir entfallen. **4.** *j-m* entschlüpfen, -fahren (*Fluch etc*). **II** *v/i* **5.** (ent)fliehen, entkommen (**from** aus, *dat*). **6.** sich retten (**from** vor *dat*),

davonkommen (**with a fright** mit dem Schrecken; **with one's life** mit dem Leben). **7.** ausfließen (*Flüssigkeit*); entweichen, ausströmen (**from** aus) (*Gas etc*). **III** *s* **8.** Entkommen *n,* Flucht *f:* **have a narrow** (*od.* **near**) ~ mit knapper Not davonkommen *od.* entkommen; **that was a narrow ~!** das war knapp! **9.** Entweichen *n,* Ausströmen *n.* ~ **chute** *s* ✈ Notrutsche *f.*

es·cort **I** *s* [ˈeskɔːt] **1.** ✕ Eskorte *f,* Begleitmannschaft *f.* **2.** ✈, ⚓ Geleit- (schutz) *m*) *n*; ⚓ Geleitschiff *n.* **3.** Geleit *n,* Schutz *m*; Gefolge *n,* Begleitung *f*; Begleiter(in). **II** *v/t* [ɪˈskɔːt] **4.** ✕ eskortieren. **5.** ✈, ⚓ *j-m* Geleitschutz geben. **6.** geleiten; begleiten.

Es·ki·mo [ˈeskɪməʊ] *pl* **-mos** *s* Eskimo *m.*

e·soph·a·gus *Am.* → **oesophagus.**

es·o·ter·ic [ˌesəˈterɪk] *adj* (~**ally**) esoterisch.

es·pe·cial [ɪˈspeʃl] *adj* besonder. **es·pe·cial·ly** [~ʃəlɪ] *adv* besonders, hauptsächlich.

Es·pe·ran·to [ˌespəˈræntəʊ] *s* Esperanto *n.*

es·pi·o·nage [ˈespɪənɑːʒ] *s* Spionage *f.*

es·pla·nade [ˌespləˈneɪd] *s* **1.** (*bsd.* Strand-, Ufer)Promenade *f.* **2.** Esplanade *f.*

es·pres·so [eˈspresəʊ] *pl* **-sos** *s* **1.** Espresso *m.* **2.** Espressomaschine *f.* ~ **bar** *s* Espresso *n.*

Es·quire [ɪˈskwaɪə] *s:* **John Smith, Esq.** *bsd. Br.* (*auf Briefen*) Herrn John Smith.

es·say [ˈeseɪ] *s* Essay *m, n, a. ped.* Aufsatz *m.* **'es·say·ist** *s* Essayist(in).

es·sence [ˈesns] *s* **1.** *das* Wesen(tliche), Kern *m* (*e-r Sache*): **in ~** im wesentlichen. **2.** Essenz *f,* Extrakt *m.*

es·sen·tial [ɪˈsenʃl] **I** *adj* (□ → **essentially**) **1.** wesentlich: a) grundlegend, b) unentbehrlich, unbedingt erforderlich (**to** für): ~ (**to life**) lebensnotwendig, -wichtig. **2.** ℛ ätherisch: ~ **oil.** **II** *s mst pl* **3.** *das* Wesentliche, Hauptsache *f.* **4.** (wesentliche) Voraussetzung (**to** für). **es·sen·tial·ly** [~ʃəlɪ] *adv* im wesentlichen.

es·tab·lish [ɪˈstæblɪʃ] *v/t* **1.** ein-, errichten, *Konto* eröffnen, *Gesetz etc* einführen, erlassen, *Rekord, Theorie* aufstellen, *Ausschuß etc* bilden, einsetzen, *Verbindung* herstellen, *diplomatische Beziehungen etc* aufnehmen. **2. ~ o.s.** ✝ sich (*a. beruflich*) etablieren *od.* niederlassen. **3.** *Ruhm etc* begründen: **~ one's reputation as** sich e-n Namen machen als. **4.** *Ansicht, Forderung etc* durchsetzen, *Ordnung* schaffen. **5.** be-, nachweisen. **es'tab·lished** *adj* **1.** bestehend. **2.** feststehend, unzweifelhaft. **3.** ⚜ *Church* Staatskirche *f*. **es'tab·lish·ment** *s* **1.** Ein-, Errichtung *f*, Einführung *f*, Aufstellung *f*, Bildung *f*, Herstellung *f*, Aufnahme *f*. **2. the** ⚜ das Establishment. **3.** ✝ Unternehmen *n*, Firma *f*; Niederlassung *f*. **4.** Anstalt *f*, (öffentliches) Institut.

es·tate [ı'steıt] *s* **1.** *sociol.* Stand *m*. **2.** ⚜ Besitz(tum *n*) *m*; (Erb-, Konkurs)Masse *f*, Nachlaß *m*; → **real** 3. **3.** Landsitz *m*, Gut *n*. **4.** *Br.* (Wohn)Siedlung *f*; Industriegebiet *n*. **~ a·gent** *s Br.* **1.** Grundstücksverwalter *m*. **2.** Grundstücks-, Immobilienmakler *m*. **~ car** *s Br.* Kombiwagen *m*.

es·teem [ı'sti:m] **I** *v/t* **1.** achten, (hoch)schätzen. **2.** erachten *od.* ansehen als, *et.* halten für. **II** *s* **3.** Achtung *f* (**for, of** vor *dat*): **hold in (high) ~** → 1.

es·thete, *etc. Am.* → **aesthete,** *etc.*

es·ti·ma·ble ['estıməbl] *adj* □ **1.** achtens-, schätzenswert. **2.** (ab)schätzbar.

es·ti·mate ['estımeıt] **I** *v/t* **1.** (ab-, ein)schätzen, veranschlagen (**at** *auf acc*): **~d value** Schätzwert *m*; **an ~d 200 people** schätzungsweise 200 Leute. **2.** beurteilen, bewerten. **II** *v/i* **3.** schätzen. **~** e-n Kostenvoranschlag machen (**for** für). **III** *s* ['~mət] **5.** Schätzung *f*, Veranschlagung *f*, Kostenvoranschlag *m*: **rough ~** grober Überschlag; **at a rough ~** grob geschätzt. **6.** Beurteilung *f*, Bewertung *f*. **es·ti·ma·tion** [~'meıʃn] *s* **1.** Meinung *f*: **in my ~** nach m-r Ansicht. **2.** Achtung *f*, Wertschätzung *f*.

es·trange [ı'streındʒ] *v/t* j-n entfremden (**from** *dat*): **become ~d** sich entfremden (**from** *dat*); sich auseinanderleben. **es'trange·ment** *s* Entfremdung *f*.

es·tro·gen *Am.* → **oestrogen.**

es·tu·ar·y ['estjʊərı] *s* **1.** (*den Gezeiten ausgesetzte*) Flußmündung *f*. **2.** Meeresbucht *f*, -arm *m*.

---

et cet·er·a [ıt'setərə] et cetera, und so weiter.

etch [etʃ] *v/t* **1.** ätzen. **2.** in Kupfer stechen; radieren: **be ~ed on (od. in) s.o.'s memory** sich j-s Gedächtnis (unauslöschlich) eingeprägt haben. **'etch·ing** *s* Kupferstich *m*; Radierung *f*.

e·ter·nal [ı'tɜ:nl] *adj* □ **1.** ewig. **2.** ewig, unaufhörlich. **e'ter·nal·ize** [~nəlaız] *v/t* verewigen. **e·ter·ni·ty** *s* Ewigkeit *f* (*a. fig.*).

e·ther ['i:θə] *s* ♠ Äther *m*. **e·the·re·al** [ı'θıərıəl] *adj* ätherisch (*a. fig.*).

eth·i·cal ['eθıkl] *adj* □ **1.** ethisch. **2.** *pharm.* rezeptpflichtig. **'eth·ics** *s pl* **1.** (*sg konstruiert*) Ethik *f*. **2.** (*Berufs-etc*)Ethos *n*.

eth·nic ['eθnık] *adj* (**~ally**) ethnisch: **~ group** Volksgruppe *f*.

eth·yl ['eθıl] *s* ♠ Äthyl *n*.

et·i·quette ['etıket] *s* Etikette *f*, Anstands-, Verhaltensregeln *pl*.

et·y·mo·log·i·cal [ˌetımə'lɒdʒıkl] *adj* □ etymologisch. **et·y·mol·o·gy** [~'mɒlədʒı] *s* Etymologie *f*.

eu·ca·lyp·tus [ˌju:kə'lıptəs] *pl* **-ti** [~taı], **-tus·es** *s* ⚘ Eukalyptus *m*.

eu·lo·gy ['ju:lədʒı] *s* **1.** Lob(preisung *f*) *n*. **2.** Lobrede *f*, -schrift *f* (**on** auf *acc*).

eu·nuch ['ju:nək] *s* Eunuch *m*.

eu·phe·mism ['ju:fəmızəm] *s* Euphemismus *m*. **eu·phe·mis·tic** *adj* (**~ally**) euphemistisch, beschönigend, verhüllend.

eu·phor·i·a [ju:'fɔ:rıə] *s* Euphorie *f*. **eu·phor·ic** [~'fɒrık] *adj* (**~ally**) euphorisch.

Eu·ro·cheque ['jʊərəʊtʃek] *s Br.* Eurocheque *m*.

Eu·ro·pe·an [ˌjʊərə'pi:ən] **I** *adj* europäisch: **~ (Economic) Community** Europäische (Wirtschafts)Gemeinschaft; **~ champion** (*Sport*) Europameister(in); **~ championship** (*Sport*) Europameisterschaft *f*. **II** *s* Europäer(in).

Eu·ro·vi·sion ['jʊərəʊˌvıʒn] *TV I s* Eurovision *f*. **II** *adj* Eurovisions...

eu·tha·na·si·a [ˌju:θə'neızjə] *s* Sterbehilfe *f*: **active (passive) ~.**

e·vac·u·ate [ı'vækjʊeıt] *v/t* Personen evakuieren; *Gebiet etc* evakuieren, *a. Haus etc* räumen. **e·vac·u·a·tion**

Evakuierung f; Räumung f. **e,vac-u'ee** [~ju:'i:] s Evakuierte m, f.

e·vade [ɪ'veɪd] v/t **1.** e-m Schlag etc ausweichen. **2.** sich e-r Pflicht etc entziehen, et. umgehen, vermeiden, Steuern hinterziehen: ~ (*answering*) *a question* e-r Frage ausweichen.

e·val·u·ate [ɪ'væljʊeɪt] v/t **1.** Wert etc schätzen, Schaden etc festsetzen (*at* auf acc). **2.** abschätzen, bewerten. **e,val-u'a·tion** s **1.** Schätzung f, Festsetzung f. **2.** Abschätzung f, Bewertung f.

e·vap·o·rate [ɪ'væpəreɪt] **I** v/t **1.** verdampfen od. verdunsten lassen. **2.** eindampfen. **~d milk** Kondensmilch f. **II** v/i **3.** verdampfen, verdunsten. **4.** fig. sich verflüchtigen, verfliegen. **e,vap-o'ra·tion** s Verdampfung f, Verdunstung f.

e·va·sion [ɪ'veɪʒn] s **1.** Umgehung f, Vermeidung f, (Steuer)Hinterziehung f. **2.** Ausflucht f, Ausrede f. **e·va·sive** [~sɪv] adj □ **1.** ausweichend (Antwort): **be ~** ausweichen. **2.** schwer feststell- od. faßbar.

eve [i:v] s **1.** mst ☿ Vorabend m, -tag m (e-s Festes). **2.** fig. Vorabend m: **on the ~ of** am Vorabend von (od. gen), kurz od. unmittelbar vor (dat).

e·ven¹ [ˈiːvn] adv **1.** sogar, selbst: **not ~** he nicht einmal er; **~ if** selbst wenn; **~ though** obwohl; **~ as a child he was …** schon als Kind war er … **2.** noch: **~ better** (sogar) noch besser.

e·ven² [~] **I** adj **1.** eben, flach, gerade. **2.** auf od. in gleicher Höhe (*with* mit). **3.** waag(e)recht. **4.** fig. ausgeglichen: **of an ~ temper** ausgeglichen; **~ voice** ruhige Stimme. **5.** gleichmäßig (Atmen etc). **6.** ✝ ausgeglichen (a. Sport): **be ~ with** quitt sein mit (a. fig.). **7.** gleich, identisch. **8.** gerade (Zahl). **II** v/t **9.** a. **~ out** (ein)ebnen, glätten; ausgleichen; (gleichmäßig) verteilen. **10.** **~ up** Rechnung aus-, begleichen: **~ things up** sich revanchieren. **III** v/i **11.** a. **~ out** eben werden (Gelände); sich ausgleichen; sich (gleichmäßig) verteilen.

eve·ning [ˈiːvnɪŋ] s Abend m: **in the ~** abends, am Abend; **on the ~ of** am Abend (gen); **last (this, tomorrow) ~** gestern (heute, morgen) abend. **~ class·es** s pl ped. Abendunterricht m. **~ dress** s **1.** Abendkleid n. **2.** Frack m;

Smoking m. **~ pa·per** s Abendzeitung f. **~ star** s ast. Abendstern m.

e·ven·ness [ˈiːvnnɪs] s **1.** Ausgeglichenheit f. **2.** Gleichmäßigkeit f.

e·vent [ɪ'vent] s **1.** Fall m: **at all ~s** auf alle Fälle; **in any ~** in jedem Fall; **in the ~ of** im Falle (gen). **2.** Ereignis n: **before the ~** vorher, im voraus; **after the ~** hinterher, im nachhinein. **3.** Sport: Disziplin f; Wettbewerb m.

e·ven-'tem·pered adj ausgeglichen.

e·vent·ful [ɪ'ventfʊl] adj □ ereignisreich.

e·ven·tu·al·i·ty [ɪ,ventʃʊ'æləti] s Möglichkeit f, Eventualität f. **e'ven·tu·al·ly** [~əlɪ] adv schließlich.

ev·er [ˈevə] adv **1.** immer (wieder), ständig: **~ after(wards)** (od. since) seit der Zeit, seitdem; **Yours ~, …** Viele Grüße, Dein(e) od. Ihr(e) … (Briefschluß); → **forever.** **2.** immer (vor comp): **~ larger.** **3.** je(mals): **have you ~ been to London?** bist du schon einmal in London gewesen?; **hardly** (od. **seldom if**) **~** fast nie. **4.** ~ **so** bsd. Br. F sehr, noch so: **~ so simpdd** ganz einfach; **~ so many** unendlich viele; **thank yge ~ so much** tausend Dank! **5.** F denn, überhaupt: **what's ch does he want?** was will er denn überhaupt? **'~·green** s **1.** ♣ immergrüne Pflanze. **2.** ♪ Evergreen m, n. **,~·'last·ing** adj □ **1.** ewig. **2.** fig. unaufhörlich. **3.** unverwüstlich, unbegrenzt haltbar. **,~·'more** adj: (for) ~ für immer.

ev·er·y [ˈevrɪ] adj: **1.** jede(r, -s): **~ day** jeden Tag, alle Tage; → **now** 1, **other** 4, **second¹** 1. **2.** jede(r, -s) (einzelne od. erdenkliche): **her ~ wish** jeder ihrer od. alle ihre Wünsche; **~ bit as much** F ganz genau so viel; **have ~ reason** allen Grund haben. **'~·bo·dy** ~ **everyone.** **'~·day** adj **1.** (all)täglich. **2.** Alltags... **3.** gewöhnlich, Durchschnitts... **'~·one** pron jeder(mann): **in ~'s mouth** in aller Munde; **to ~'s amazement** zum allgemeinen Erstaunen. **'~·thing** pron **1.** alles (that was). **2.** F die Hauptsache, alles (to für). **3. and ~** F und so. **'~·where** adv überall(hin): **~ he goes** wo er auch hingeht.

ev·i·dence [ˈevɪdəns] s **1.** ⚖ Beweis(stück n, -material n) m, Beweise pl: **for lack of ~** mangels Beweisen. **2.** ⚖ (Zeugen)Aussage f: **give ~** aussagen (for für; against gegen); **give ~ of**

aussage über (acc); fig. zeugen von; **turn queen's** (od. **king's,** Am. **state's**) ~ als Kronzeuge auftreten. **3.** (An)Zeichen n, Spur f (**of** von od. gen).

ev·i·dent adj □ augenscheinlich, offensichtlich.

e·vil [ˈiːvl] **I** adj □ übel, böse, schlimm: ~ **day** Unglückstag m; ~ **eye** der böse Blick. **II** s Übel n, das Böse; **do** ~ Böses tun; **the lesser** ~ das kleinere Übel. **~·'do·er** s Übeltäter(in). **~·'mind·ed** adj □ bösartig.

e·voc·a·tive [ɪˈvɒkətɪv] adj: **be** ~ **of** erinnern an (acc).

e·voke [ɪˈvəʊk] v/t **1.** Geister beschwören, herbeirufen. **2.** Bewunderung etc hervorrufen; Erinnerungen wachrufen, wecken.

ev·o·lu·tion [ˌiːvəˈluːʃn] s **1.** Entfaltung f, -wicklung f: **the** ~ **of events** die Entwicklung (der Dinge). **2.** biol. Evolution f.

e·volve [ɪˈvɒlv] v/t u. v/i (sich) entfalten od. -wickeln (**into** zu).

ex¹ [eks] prp ✝ ab: ~ **works** ab Werk.

ex² [~] s F Verflossene m, f.

ex- [eks] in Zssgn: Ex..., ehemalig.

ex·ac·er·bate [ɪɡˈzæsəbeɪt] v/t **1.** j-n verärgern. **2.** Krankheit, Schmerzen verschlimmern, Situation verschärfen.

ex·act [ɪɡˈzækt] **I** adj (□ → **exactly**) **1.** exakt, genau. **2.** genau, tatsächlich. **3.** methodisch, gewissenhaft (Person). **II** v/t **4.** Gehorsam, Geld etc fordern, verlangen (**from** von). **5.** Zahlung eintreiben, -fordern (**from** von). **ex'act·ing** adj □ **1.** streng, genau. **2.** aufreibend, anstrengend. **3.** anspruchsvoll: **be** ~ hohe Anforderungen stellen. **ex'act·i·tude** [~tɪtjuːd] → **exactness**. **ex'act·ly** adv **1.** → **exact. 2.** als Antwort: ganz recht, genau: **not** ~ nicht ganz od. direkt. **3.** wo, wann etc eigentlich. **ex'act·ness** s **1.** Exaktheit f, Genauigkeit f. **2.** Gewissenhaftigkeit f.

ex·ag·ger·ate [ɪɡˈzædʒəreɪt] v/t u. v/i übertreiben. **ex,ag·ger·a·tion** s Übertreibung f.

ex·alt [ɪɡˈzɔːlt] v/t **1.** im Rang etc erheben, erhöhen (**to** zu). **2.** (lob)preisen: ~ **to the skies** in den Himmel heben. **ex·al·ta·tion** [ˌeɡzɔːlˈteɪʃn] s **1.** Erhebung f, Erhöhung f. **2.** Begeisterung f: **fill with** ~ in Begeisterung versetzen.

ex·alt·ed [ɪɡˈzɔːltɪd] adj **1.** hoch (Rang, Ideal etc). **2.** begeistert. **3.** F übertrieben hoch (Meinung etc).

ex·am [ɪɡˈzæm] F → **examination** 2.

ex·am·i·na·tion [ɪɡˌzæmɪˈneɪʃn] s **1.** Untersuchung f (a. ✍), Prüfung f: **on** ~ bei näherer Prüfung; **be under** ~ untersucht od. geprüft werden. **2.** ped. etc Prüfung f, bsd. univ. Examen n: ~**paper** schriftliche Prüfung; Prüfungsarbeit f. **3.** 🏛 Vernehmung f; Verhör n. **ex·'am·ine** v/t **1.** untersuchen (a. ✍), prüfen (**for** auf acc). **2.** ped. etc prüfen (**in** in dat; **on** über acc). **3.** 🏛 vernehmen; verhören. **ex,am·i'nee** s ped. etc Prüfling m, (Prüfungs-, bsd. univ. Examens)Kandidat(in). **ex'am·in·er** s ped. etc Prüfer(in).

ex·am·ple [ɪɡˈzɑːmpl] s **1.** Beispiel n (**of** für): **for** ~ zum Beispiel; without ~ beispiellos. **2.** Vorbild n, Beispiel n: **set a good** ~ ein gutes Beispiel geben, mit gutem Beispiel vorangehen; **take** ~ **by,** **take as an** ~ sich ein Beispiel nehmen an (dat); → **hold up** 2. **3.** (warnendes) Beispiel: **make an** ~ (**of s.o.**) (an j-m) ein Exempel statuieren; **let this be an** ~ **to you** laß dir das ein e Warnung sein.

ex·as·per·ate [ɪɡˈzæspəreɪt] v/t aufbringen (**against** gegen), wütend machen. **ex·'as·per·at·ed** adj wütend, aufgebracht (**at, by** über acc). **ex,as·per'a·tion** s Wut f: **in** ~ wütend, aufgebracht.

ex·ca·vate [ˈekskəveɪt] v/t **1.** aushöhlen. **2.** ausgraben, -baggern. **,ex·ca'va·tion** s **1.** Aushöhlung f. **2.** Ausgrabung f. **'ex·ca·va·tor** s Bagger m.

ex·ceed [ɪkˈsiːd] v/t **1.** Tempolimit etc überschreiten. **2.** hinausgehen über (acc): ~ **the limit** den Rahmen sprengen. **3.** et., j-n übertreffen (**in** an dat). **ex'ceed·ing·ly** adv überaus, äußerst: ~ **kind** überfreundlich.

ex·cel [ɪkˈsel] **I** v/t übertreffen (**o.s.** sich selbst). **II** v/i sich auszeichnen od. hervortun (**in, at** in dat; **as** als). **ex·cel·lence** [ˈeksələns] s **1.** Vorzüglichkeit f. **2.** pl Vorzüge pl. **'Ex·cel·len·cy** s Exzellenz f (Titel). **'ex·cel·lent** adj □ ausgezeichnet, hervorragend, vorzüglich.

ex·cept [ɪkˈsept] **I** v/t **1.** ausnehmen, -schließen (**from** von): **present company** ~**ed** Anwesende ausgenommen; **no-**

body **~ed** ohne Ausnahme. **2.** sich *et.* vorbehalten: → **error. II** *prp* **3.** ausgenommen, außer, mit Ausnahme von (*od. gen*): **~ for** abgesehen von, bis auf (*acc*). **III** *cj* **4.** außer: **~ that** außer, daß. **ex'cept·ing** *prp* → **except 3. ex'ception** *s* **1.** Ausnahme *f* (**to the rule** von der Regel): **by way of ~** ausnahmsweise; **without ~** ohne Ausnahme, ausnahmslos; **make an ~** (**in s.o.'s case**) (bei j-m *od.* in j-s Fall) e-e Ausnahme machen. **2.** Einwand *m* (**to** gegen): **take ~ to** Einwendungen machen gegen; Anstoß nehmen an (*dat*). **ex'cep·tion·al** [~ʃənl] *adj* **1.** Ausnahme..., Sonder... **2.** außer-, ungewöhnlich. **ex'cep·tion·al·ly** [~ʃnəli] *adv* **1.** außergewöhnlich. **2.** ausnahmsweise.

ex·cerpt ['eksɜːpt] *s* Exzerpt *n*, Auszug *m* (**from** aus).

ex·cess [ik'ses] **I** *s* **1.** Übermaß *n*, -fluß *m* (**of** an *dat*): **in ~ of** mehr als, über (*acc*) (... hinaus); **to ~** übermäßig; → **carry** 7. **2.** *pl* Exzesse *pl*: a) Ausschweifungen *pl*, b) Ausschreitungen *pl.* **3.** Überschuß *m.* **II** *adj* **4.** überschüssig, Über...: **~ baggage** (*bsd. Br.* **luggage**) ✔ Übergepäck *n*; **~ fare** (Fahrpreis)Zuschlag *m*; **~ postage** Nachporto *n*, -gebühr *f*. **ex'cess·ive** *adj* □ übermäßig, -trieben.

ex·change [iks'tʃeɪndʒ] **I** *v/t* **1.** (**for**) aus-, umtauschen (gegen), vertauschen (mit). **2.** eintauschen, *Geld a.* (um-)wechseln (**for** gegen). **3.** *Blicke, die Plätze etc* tauschen, *Blicke wechseln, Gedanken, Gefangene etc* austauschen: **~ blows** aufeinander einschlagen; **~ words** e-n Wortwechsel haben. **4.** ⊗ auswechseln. **II** *s* **5.** (Aus-, Um)Tausch *m*: **in ~** als Ersatz, dafür; **in ~ for** (im Austausch) gegen, (als Entgelt) für; **~ of letters** Brief-, Schriftwechsel *m*; **~ of shots** Schußwechsel *m*; **~ of views** Gedanken-, Meinungsaustausch. **6.** ♰ (Um)Wechseln: **rate of ~, ~ rate** Wechselkurs *m*; → **bill**² 3, **foreign** 1. **7.** ♰ Börse *f.* **8.** *a.* **~ office** Wechselstube *f.* **9.** (Fernsprech)Amt *n*, Vermittlung *f.* **ex'change·a·ble** *adj* **1.** aus-, umtauschbar (**for** gegen). **2.** Tausch...

Ex·cheq·uer [iks'tʃekə] *s Br.* Finanzministerium *n*: → **chancellor.**

ex·cit·a·ble [ik'saɪtəbl] *adj* reizbar,

(leicht) erregbar. **ex·cite** *v/t* **1.** *j-n* er-, aufregen: **get ~d** sich aufregen (**over** über *acc*). **2.** *j-n* (an-, auf)reizen, aufstacheln. **3.** *Interesse etc* erregen, (er-)wecken, *Appetit, Phantasie* anregen. **ex'cit·ed** *adj* □ erregt, aufgeregt. **ex'cite·ment** *s* Er-, Aufregung *f.* **ex'cit·ing** *adj* □ er-, aufregend, spannend.

ex·claim [ik'skleɪm] **I** *v/i* (auf)schreien. **II** *v/t et.* (aus)rufen.

ex·cla·ma·tion [,eksklə'meɪʃn] *s* Ausruf *m*, (Auf)Schrei *m*: **~ of pain** Schmerzensschrei; **~ mark** (*Am. a.* **point**) Ausrufe-, Ausrufungszeichen *n.*

ex·clude [ik'skluːd] *v/t j-n, Möglichkeit etc* ausschließen (**from** von, aus). **ex'clud·ing** *prp* ausgenommen, nicht inbegriffen.

ex·clu·sion [ik'skluːʒn] *s* Ausschluß *m* (**from** von, aus): **to the ~ of** unter Ausschluß von (*od. gen*). **ex'clu·sive I** *adj* □ **1.** ausschließend: **~ of** ausschließlich, abgesehen von, ohne; **be ~ of s.th.** et. ausschließen; **be mutually ~** einander ausschließen. **2.** ausschließlich, Allein...; Exklusiv... **3.** exklusiv. **II** *s* **4.** Exklusivbericht *m.*

ex·com·mu·ni·cate [,ekskə'mjuːnɪkeɪt] *v/t eccl.* exkommunizieren. **'ex·com·mu·ni·ca·tion** *s* Exkommunikation *f.*

ex·cre·ment ['ekskrɪmənt] *s* Kot *m*, Exkremente *pl.*

ex·crete [ik'skriːt] *v/t* absondern, ausscheiden. **ex'cre·tion** *s* Absonderung *f*, Ausscheidung *f.*

ex·cru·ci·at·ing [ik'skruːʃɪeɪtɪŋ] *adj* □ qualvoll (**to** für).

ex·cur·sion [ik'skɜːʃn] *s* Ausflug *m*, *fig. a.* Abstecher *m* (**into politics** in die Politik): **go on an ~** e-n Ausflug machen. **ex'cur·sion·ist** *s* Ausflügler(in).

ex·cus·a·ble [ik'skjuːzəbl] *adj* □ entschuldbar, verzeihlich. **ex·cuse I** *v/t* [ik'skjuːz] **1.** *j-n*, *et.* entschuldigen, *j-m*, *et.* verzeihen: **~ me** entschuldigen Sie!, Verzeihung!; **~ me for being late, ~ my being late** entschuldige mein Zuspätkommen; **~ o.s.** sich entschuldigen. **2.** für *et.* e-e Entschuldigung finden: **I cannot ~ his conduct** ich kann sein Verhalten nicht gutheißen. **3.** **~ s.o. from s.th.** j-n von et. befreien, j-m et. erlassen: **he begs to be ~d** er läßt sich entschuldigen. **II** *s* [ɪkˈskjuːs] **4.** Entschuldigung *f*: *offer* (*od.* **make**) *an* ~ sich entschuldigen; *in* ~ *of* als Entschuldigung für. **5.** Entschuldigung(sgrund *m*) *f*, Rechtfertigung *f*: *without* (*good*) ~ unentschuldigt. **6.** Ausrede *f*, -flucht *f*.

ex·di·rec·to·ry [ˌeksdɪˈrektərɪ] *adj*: ~ *number* *teleph. Br.* Geheimnummer *f*.

ex·e·cute [ˈeksɪkjuːt] *v/t* **1.** *Auftrag, Plan etc* aus-, durchführen, *Vertrag* erfüllen. **2.** ♪ vortragen, spielen. **3.** ⚖️ *Urteil* vollziehen, -strecken; *j-n* hinrichten (*for* wegen). ,**ex·e'cu·tion** *s* **1.** Aus-, Durchführung *f*, Erfüllung *f*: *carry* (*od.* *put*) *into* ~ *execute* 1. **2.** ♪ Vortrag *m*, Spiel *n*. **3.** ⚖️ Vollziehung *f*, -strekkung *f*; Hinrichtung *f*. ,**ex·e'cu·tion·er** *s* Henker *m*, Scharfrichter *m*.

ex·ec·u·tive [ɪgˈzekjʊtɪv] **I** *adj* □ **1.** ausübend, vollziehend, *pol.* Exekutiv...: ~*power* (*od.* **authority**) → **3**. **2.** ✝ geschäftsführend, leitend: ~ *board* Vorstand *m*; ~ *post* (*od.* **position**) leitende Stellung; ~ *staff* leitende Angestellte *pl.* **II** *s* **3.** *pol.* Exekutive *f*. **4.** *a.* **senior** ~ ✝ leitender Angestellter.

ex·em·pla·ry [ɪgˈzemplərɪ] *adj* □ **1.** exemplarisch: a) beispiel-, musterhaft, b) warnend, abschreckend. **2.** typisch, Muster...

ex·em·pli·fy [ɪgˈzemplɪfaɪ] *v/t* veranschaulichen: a) durch Beispiele erläutern, b) als Beispiel dienen für.

ex·empt [ɪgˈzempt] **I** *v/t* *j-n* befreien (*from* von *Steuern, Verpflichtungen etc*), freistellen (*from military service* vom Wehrdienst): ~*ed amount* ✝ (Steuer)Freibetrag *m*. **II** *adj* befreit, ausgenommen (*from* von): ~ *from taxation* steuerfrei. **ex'emp·tion** *s* Befreiung *f*, Freistellung *f*: ~ *from taxes* Steuerfreiheit *f*.

ex·er·cise [ˈeksəsaɪz] **I** *s* **1.** Ausübung *f*, Geltendmachung *f*. **2.** (*körperliche od. geistige*) Übung, (körperliche) Bewegung: *do one's* ~*s* Gymnastik machen; *take* ~ sich Bewegung machen; ~ *bicycle* Zimmerfahrrad *n*; ~ *therapy* ✝ Bewegungstherapie *f*. **3.** *mst pl* ✕ Übung *f*, Manöver *n*. **4.** Übung(sarbeit) *f*, Schulaufgabe *f*: ~ *book* Übungs-, Schreibheft *n*. **5.** ♪ Übung(sstück *n*) *f*. **II** *v/t* **6.** *Amt, Recht, Macht etc* ausüben, *Einfluß, Macht etc* geltend machen. **7.** *Körper, Geist* üben, trainieren. **8.** *Geduld etc* üben. **III** *v/i* **9.** sich Bewegung machen. **10.** *Sport etc*: üben, trainieren. **11.** ✕ exerzieren. **'ex·er·cis·er** *s* Trainingsgerät *n*.

ex·ert [ɪgˈzɜːt] *v/t* **1.** *Druck, Einfluß etc* ausüben (*on* auf *acc*), *Autorität* geltend machen. **2.** ~ *o.s.* sich bemühen (*for* um; *to do* zu tun), sich anstrengen. **ex'er·tion** *s* **1.** Ausübung *f*, Geltendmachung *f*. **2.** Anstrengung *f*.

ex·e·unt [ˈeksɪʌnt] *thea.* Bühnenanweisung: (sie gehen) ab: ~ *omnes* alle ab.

ex·ha·la·tion [ˌekshəˈleɪʃn] *s* **1.** Ausatmen *n*. **2.** Verströmen *n*. **3.** Hauch, Rauch *m*. **ex·hale** [ˌ'heɪl] *v/t* **1.** (*a. v/i*) ausatmen. **2.** *Gas, Geruch etc* verströmen, *Rauch* ausstoßen.

ex·haust [ɪgˈzɔːst] **I** *v/t* erschöpfen: a) *Vorräte* ver-, aufbrauchen, b) *j-n* ermüden, entkräften, c) *j-s Kräfte* strapazieren: ~ *s.o.'s patience* j-s Geduld erschöpfen, d) *Thema* erschöpfend abd. behandeln: ~ *all possibilities* alle Möglichkeiten ausschöpfen. **II** *s* ⊕ *a.* ~ *fumes pl* Auspuff-, Abgase *pl*, b) Auspuff *m*: ~ *pipe* Auspuffrohr *n*. **ex'haust·ed** *adj* **1.** verbraucht, erschöpft, aufgebraucht (*Vorräte*), vergriffen (*Auflage*). **2.** erschöpft, entkräftet. **ex'haust·ing** *adj* erschöpfend, strapaziös. **ex'haus·tion** *s* Erschöpfung *f*: a) völliger Verbrauch, b) Entkräftung *f*. **ex'haus·tive** *adj* □ *fig.* erschöpfend.

ex·hib·it [ɪgˈzɪbɪt] **I** *v/t* **1.** *Bilder etc* ausstellen. **2.** *fig.* zeigen, an den Tag legen; zur Schau stellen. **II** *v/i* **3.** ausstellen (*at a fair* auf *e-r* Messe). **III** *s* **4.** Ausstellungsstück *n*, Exponat *n*. **5.** ⚖️ Beweisstück *n*. **ex·hi·bi·tion** [ˌeksɪˈbɪʃn] *s* **1.** Ausstellung *f*: *be on* ~ *od* of *s.th.* zu sehen sein; *make an* ~ *of o.s.* sich lächerlich *od.* zum Gespött machen. **2.** *fig.* Zurschaustellung *f*. **3.** *univ. Br.* Stipendium *f*. ,**ex·hi'bi·tion·ism** *s psych. u. fig.* Exhibitionismus *m*. ,**ex·hi'bi·tion·ist** *psych. u. fig.* I *s* Exhibitionist *m*. **II** *adj* exhibitionistisch. **ex·hib·i·tor** [ɪgˈzɪbɪtə] *s* Aussteller *m*.

ex·hort [ɪgˈzɔːt] *v/t* ermahnen (*to* zu; *to do* zu tun). **ex·hor·ta·tion** [ˌegzɔːˈteɪʃn] *s* Ermahnung *f*.

ex·hu·ma·tion [,ekshju:'meɪʃn] *s* Exhumierung *f*. **ex'hume** *v/t Leiche* exhumieren.

ex·i·gence, ex·i·gen·cy ['eksɪdʒəns(-ɪ)] *s* **1.** Dringlichkeit *f*. **2.** Not(lage) *f*. **3.** *mst pl* Erfordernis *n*. **'ex·i·gent** *adj* **1.** dringend, drängend. **2.** anspruchsvoll.

ex·ig·u·ous [eg'zɪgjʊəs] *adj* □ dürftig.

ex·ile ['eksaɪl] **I** *s* **1.** Exil *n*; Verbannung *f*: *go into* ~ ins Exil gehen; *live in* ~ im Exil *od*. in der Verbannung leben; *send into* ~ → **3**; *government in* ~ Exilregierung *f*. **2.** im Exil Lebende *m, f*; Verbannte *m, f*. **II** *v/t* **3.** ins Exil schicken; verbannen (*from* aus), in die Verbannung schicken.

ex·ist [ɪg'zɪst] *v/i* **1.** existieren, vorkommen: *do such things* ~? gibt es so etwas?; *right to* ~ Existenzberechtigung *f*. **2.** existieren, leben (*on* von). **3.** existieren, bestehen. **ex'ist·ence** *s* **1.** Existenz *f*, Vorkommen *n*: *call into* ~ ins Leben rufen; *come into* ~ entstehen; *be in* ~ → *exist* 3; *remain in* ~ weiterbestehen. **2.** Existenz *f*, Leben *n*, Dasein *n*. **3.** Existenz *f*, Bestand *m*. **ex'ist·ent** *adj* **1.** existierend, bestehend, vorhanden. **2.** gegenwärtig, augenblicklich. **ex·is-ten·tial·ism** [,egzɪ'stenʃəlɪzəm] *s phls.* Existentialismus *m*.

ex·it ['eksɪt] **I** *s* **1.** Ausgang *m*. **2.** *thea.* Abgang *m*. **3.** (Autobahn)Ausfahrt *f*. **4.** Ausreise *f*: ~ *visa* Ausreisevisum *n*. **II** *v/i* **5.** *thea. Bühnenanweisung*: (er, sie, es geht) ab: ~ *Macbeth* Macbeth ab.

ex·o·dus ['eksədəs] *s* Ab-, Auswanderung *f*: *rural* ~ Landflucht *f*.

ex·on·er·ate [ɪg'zɒnəreɪt] *v/t* **1.** *Angeklagten etc* entlasten (*from* von). **2.** *j-n* befreien, entbinden (*from* von *e-r Pflicht etc*). **ex,on·er'a·tion** *s* **1.** Entlastung *f*. **2.** Befreiung *f*, Entbindung *f*.

ex·or·bi·tance [ɪg'zɔːbɪtəns] *s* Unverschämtheit *f*, Maßlosigkeit *f*. **ex·or'bi·tant** *adj* □ unverschämt: a) astronomisch: ~ *price* Phantasiepreis *m*, b) übertrieben, maßlos (*Forderung etc*).

ex·or·cism ['eksɔːsɪzəm] *s* Exorzismus *m*, Geisterbeschwörung *f*, Teufelsaustreibung *f*. **'ex·or·cist** *s* Exorzist *m*, Geisterbeschwörer *m*, Teufelsaustreiber *m*. **ex·or·cize** ['~saɪz] *v/t* **1.** *böse Geister* austreiben, beschwören. **2.** *j-n, e-n Ort* von bösen Geistern be-

freien, *j-m* den Teufel austreiben.

ex·ot·ic [ɪg'zɒtɪk] *adj* (~*ally*) exotisch (*a. fig.*).

ex·pand [ɪk'spænd] **I** *v/t* **1.** ausbreiten, -spannen. **2.** ✞, *phys. etc, a. fig.* ausdehnen, -weiten, erweitern. **II** *v/i* **3.** ✞, *phys. etc, a. fig.* sich ausdehnen *od.* erweitern. **4.** expandieren. **4.** *fig.* (*vor Stolz etc*) aufblühen; aus sich herausgehen. **5.** *fig.* sich auslassen *od.* verbreiten (*on* über *acc*). **ex'pand·er** *s Sport*: Expander *m*. **ex'panse** [~'spæns] *s* weite Fläche, Weite *f*. **ex'pan·sion** *s* **1.** Ausbreitung *f*. **2.** ✞, *phys. etc, a. fig.* Ausdehnung *f*, -weitung *f*, Erweiterung *f*; *pol.* Expansion *f*. **ex'pan·sive** *adj* □ **1.** ausdehnungsfähig. **2.** ausgedehnt, weit. **3.** *fig.* mitteilsam.

ex·pa·tri·ate [eks'pætrɪeɪt] **I** *v/t* ausbürgern. **II** *adj* [~ət] ausgebürgert. **III** *s* [~ət] Ausgebürgerte *m, f*. **ex,pa·tri'a·tion** *s* Ausbürgerung *f*.

ex·pect [ɪk'spekt] **I** *v/t* **1.** *j-n, et.* erwarten: ~ *s.o. to do s.th.* erwarten, daß j-d et. tut; ~ *s.th. of* (*od. from*) *s.o.* et. von j-m erwarten. **2.** F vermuten, glauben: *I* ~ *so* ich nehme es an. **II** *v/i* **3.** *be* ~*ing* F in anderen Umständen sein. **ex'pec·tan·cy** *s* Erwartung *f*: *look of* ~ erwartungsvoller Blick. **ex'pec·tant** *adj* □ **1.** ~ *mother* werdende Mutter. **2.** erwartungsvoll. **ex·pec·ta·tion** [,ekspek'teɪʃn] *s* Erwartung *f*: *in* ~ *of* in Erwartung (*gen*); *beyond* (*all*) ~(*s*) über Erwarten; *against all* (*od. contrary to* [*all*]) ~(*s*) wider Erwarten; *come up to* ~*s* den Erwartungen entsprechen; *fall short of s.o.'s* ~*s* hinter j-s Erwartungen zurückbleiben; ~ *of life* Lebenserwartung.

ex·pe·di·ence, ex·pe·di·en·cy [ɪk'spiːdjəns(ɪ)] *s* **1.** Zweckdienlichkeit *f*, Nützlichkeit *f*. **2.** Eigennutz *m*. **ex'pe·di·ent I** *adj* **1.** ratsam, angebracht. **2.** zweckdienlich, -mäßig, nützlich. **3.** eigennützig. **II** *s* **4.** (Hilfs)Mittel *n*, (Not)Behelf *m*. **ex'pe·di·ent·ly** *adv* zweckmäßigerweise.

ex·pe·dite ['ekspɪdaɪt] *v/t* beschleunigen. **ex·pe·di·tion** [~'dɪʃn] *s* **1.** Expedition *f*: *on an* ~ auf e-r Expedition. **2.** Eile *f*, Schnelligkeit *f*. **,ex·pe'di·tious** *adj* □ schnell, rasch, prompt.

ex·pel [ɪk'spel] *v/t* (*from*) **1.** vertreiben

(aus). **2.** ausweisen (aus), verweisen (*des Landes*). **3.** ausschließen (aus, von).

ex·pen·di·ture [ɪkˈspendɪtʃə] *s* **1.** Aufwand *m*, Verbrauch *m* (*of* an *dat*). **2.** Ausgaben *pl*, (Kosten)Aufwand *m*.

ex·pense [ɪkˈspens] *s* **1.** → *expenditure* 2: *at s.o.'s* ~ auf j-s Kosten (*a. fig.*); *spare no* ~ keine Kosten scheuen. **2.** *pl* Unkosten *pl*, Spesen *pl*: *travel(l)ing* ~*s* Reisespesen; ~ *account* Spesenkonto *n*. **ex·pen·sive** *adj* □ teuer, kostspielig.

ex·pe·ri·ence [ɪkˈspɪərɪəns] **I** *s* **1.** Erfahrung *f*: a) (Lebens)Praxis *f*: *by* (*od. from*) ~ aus Erfahrung; *in my* ~ nach m-r Erfahrung, b) Fach-, Sachkenntnis *f*; Routine *f*. **2.** Erlebnis *n*. **II** *v/t* **3.** erfahren: a) kennenlernen, b) erleben, c) *Schmerzen, Verluste etc* erleiden, *et.* durchmachen, *Vergnügen etc* empfinden. **ex·pe·ri·enced** *adj* erfahren, routiniert.

ex·per·i·ment **I** *s* [ɪkˈsperɪmənt] Experiment *n*, Versuch *m* (*on* an *dat*; *with* mit): ~ *on animals* Tierversuch. **II** *v/i* [~ment] experimentieren, Versuche anstellen (*on* an *dat*; *with* mit). **ex·per·i·men·tal** [ek͵sperɪˈmentl] *adj* □ experimentell, Versuchs...: ~ *animal* Versuchstier *n*. **ex͵per·i·men·ta·tion** *s* Experimentieren *n*. **ex·per·i·ment·er** *s* Experimentator *m*.

ex·pert [ˈekspɜːt] **I** *adj* **1.** (*at, in* in *dat*) erfahren; geschickt: *be* ~ *at* Erfahrung haben in. **2.** fachmännisch, fach-, sachkundig: ~ *knowledge* Fach-, Sachkenntnis *f*; ~ *opinion* Gutachten *n*. **II** *s* **3.** (*at, in* in *dat*; *on* auf dem Gebiet *gen*) Fachmann *m*, Experte *m*; Sachverständige *m*, Gutachter *m*: ~ *on disarmament* Abrüstungsexperte. **ex·per·tise** [͵~ˈtiːz] *s* **1.** Expertise *f*, Gutachten *n*. **2.** Fach-, Sachkenntnis *f*.

ex·pi·ate [ˈekspɪeɪt] *v/t* sühnen, (ab)büßen. **͵ex·pi·ˈa·tion** *s* Sühne *f*, Buße *f*.

ex·pi·ra·tion [͵ekspɪˈreɪʃn] *s* **1.** Ablauf *m*, Erlöschen *n*, Ende *n*: *at* (*od. on*) *the* ~ *of* nach Ablauf (*gen*). **2.** Verfall *m*: ~ *date* Verfallstag *m*, -datum *n*. **3.** † Fälligwerden *n*. **ex·pire** [ɪkˈspaɪə] *v/i* **1.** ablaufen (*Frist, Paß etc*), erlöschen (*Konzession, Patent etc*), enden. **2.** ungültig werden, verfallen. **3.** † fällig werden. **ex·pi·ry** → *expiration* 1.

ex·plain [ɪkˈspleɪn] *v/t* erklären: a) erläutern (*s.th. to s.o.* j-m et.), b) begründen, rechtfertigen: ~ *s.th. away* e-e einleuchtende Erklärung für et. finden; sich aus et. herausreden; ~ *o.s.* sich erklären; sich rechtfertigen.

ex·pla·na·tion [͵ekspləˈneɪʃn] *s* Erklärung *f* (*for, of* für *od. gen*): a) Erläuterung *f*: *in* ~ *of* als Erklärung für, b) Begründung *f*, Rechtfertigung *f*. **ex·plan·a·to·ry** [ɪkˈsplænətərɪ] *adj* □ erklärend, erläuternd.

ex·ple·tive [ɪkˈspliːtɪv] *s* **1.** *ling.* Füllwort *n*. **2.** Fluch *m*; Kraftausdruck *m*.

ex·pli·ca·ble [ɪkˈsplɪkəbl] *adj* erklärbar, erklärlich.

ex·plic·it [ɪkˈsplɪsɪt] *adj* □ **1.** ausdrücklich, deutlich. **2.** ausführlich. **3.** offen, deutlich (*about, on* in bezug auf *acc*): (*sexually*) ~ freizügig (*Film etc*).

ex·plode [ɪkˈspləʊd] **I** *v/t* **1.** zur Explosion bringen; (in die Luft) sprengen. **2.** *Gerüchten etc* den Boden entziehen, *Theorie etc* widerlegen, *Mythos etc* zerstören. **II** *v/i* **3.** explodieren; in die Luft fliegen. **4.** *fig.* ausbrechen (*into, with* in *acc*), platzen (*with, in* vor *dat*). **5.** *fig.* sprunghaft ansteigen, sich explosionsartig vermehren (*bsd. Bevölkerung*).

ex·ploit I *s* [ˈeksplɔɪt] **1.** (Helden)Tat *f, z. T.* Großtat *f*, große Leistung. **II** *v/t* [ɪkˈsplɔɪt] **3.** *et.* auswerten, *Patent etc* (*kommerziell*) verwerten, *Erzvorkommen etc* ausbeuten, abbauen; *b.s.* j-n, *et.* ausbeuten. **͵ex·ploi·ˈta·tion** [͵eks~] *s* Auswertung *f*, Verwertung *f*, Ausbeutung *f*, Abbau *m*.

ex·plo·ra·tion [͵ekspləˈreɪʃn] *s* **1.** Erforschung *f*. **2.** Untersuchung *f*. **ex·plor·a·to·ry** [ekˈsplɔrətərɪ] *adj* Forschungs...: ~ *talks pl* Sondierungsgespräche *pl*. **ex·plore** [ɪkˈsplɔː] *v/t* **1.** *Land* erforschen. **2.** erforschen, untersuchen, sondieren. **ex·plor·er** *s* Forscher(in), Forschungsreisende *m, f*.

ex·plo·sion [ɪkˈspləʊʒn] *s* **1.** Explosion *f*; Sprengung *f*. **2.** *fig.* Widerlegung *f*, Zerstörung *f*. **3.** *fig.* Ausbruch *m*: ~ *of loud laughter* Lachsalve *f*. **4.** *fig.* sprunghafter Anstieg, (Bevölkerungs)Explosion *f*. **ex·plo·sive** [~sɪv] **I** *adj* □ **1.** explosiv (*a. fig.*), Spreng...: ~ *problem* brisantes Problem. **2.** *fig.* aufbrausend (*Temperament*). **II** *s* **3.** Sprengstoff *m*.

ex·po·nent [ık'spəʊnənt] s **1.** ♈ Exponent m, Hochzahl f. **2.** Vertreter(in); Verfechter(in).

ex·port I v/t u. v/i [ık'spɔːt] **1.** exportieren, ausführen: ~ing country Ausfuhrland n; ~ing firm Exportfirma f. **II** s ['ekspɔːt] **2.** Export m, Ausfuhr f. **3.** pl (Gesamt)Export m, (-)Ausfuhr f; Exportgüter pl, Ausfuhrware f. **III** adj ['eks~] **4.** Export..., Ausfuhr...: ~ trade Exportgeschäft n, Ausfuhrhandel m. **ex'port·er** [ık'sp~] s Exporteur m.

ex·pose [ık'spəʊz] v/t **1.** Kind aussetzen. **2.** Waren ausstellen (for sale zum Verkauf). **3.** ~ to fig. dem Wetter, e-r Gefahr etc aussetzen, der Lächerlichkeit etc preisgeben: ~ o.s. sich exponieren; ~ o.s. to ridicule sich zum Gespött (der Leute) machen. **4.** fig. j-n bloßstellen; j-n entlarven, Spion a. enttarnen; et. aufdecken, entlarven, enthüllen. **5.** entblößen. **6.** phot. belichten. **ex'posed** adj ungeschützt (Haus, Lage etc), (a. fig. Stellung etc) exponiert.

ex·po·si·tion [ˌekspəʊ'zıʃn] s **1.** Ausstellung f. **2.** Exposition f (e-s Dramas). **ex·po·sure** [ık'spəʊʒə] s **1.** (Kindes-) Aussetzung f. **2.** fig. Aussetzen n, Preisgabe f (to dat). **3.** fig. Ausgesetztsein n (to dat): die of ~ an Unterkühlung sterben. **4.** Bloßstellung f; Entlarvung f, Enttarnung f; Aufdeckung f, Enthüllung f. **5.** Entblößung f. **6.** ungeschützte od. exponierte Lage. **7.** phot. a) Belichtung f: ~ meter Belichtungsmesser m, b) Aufnahme f. **8.** Lage f (e-s Gebäudes): southern ~ Südlage.

ex·pound [ık'spaʊnd] v/t erklären, erläutern, Theorie etc entwickeln (to s.o. j-m).

ex·press [ık'spres] **I** v/t **1.** ausdrücken, äußern: ~ the hope that der Hoffnung Ausdruck geben, daß; ~ o.s. sich äußern; sich ausdrücken. **2.** bezeichnen, bedeuten. **3.** Br. durch Eilboten od. als Eilgut schicken. **II** adj □ **4.** ausdrücklich. **5.** Expreß..., Schnell...: ~ letter Br. Eilbrief m; ~ train → 9. **III** adv **6.** eigens. **7.** Br. durch Eilboten, als Eilgut. **IV** s **8.** Br. Eilbote m; -beförderung f. **9.** D-Zug m, Schnellzug m. **ex·pres·sion** [ık'spreʃn] s **1.** Ausdruck m, Äußerung f: find ~ in sich ausdrücken od. äußern in (dat); give ~ to e-r Sache Ausdruck

verleihen; **beyond** (od. past) ~ unsagbar. **2.** Ausdruck m, Redensart f. **3.** (Gesichts)Ausdruck m. **4.** Ausdruck(skraft f) m. **ex·pres·sion·ism** s Kunst: Expressionismus m. **ex·pres·sion·ist** (Kunst) **I** s Expressionist(in). **II** adj expressionistisch. **ex·pres·sion·less** adj ausdruckslos. **ex·pres·sive** adj □ **1.** be ~ of et. ausdrücken. **2.** ausdrucksvoll. **ex·press·way** s bsd Am. Schnellstraße f.

ex·pro·pri·ate [eks'prəʊprıeıt] v/t ♈ enteignen. **ex·pro·pri·a·tion** s Enteignung f.

ex·pul·sion [ık'spʌlʃn] s (from) **1.** Vertreibung f (aus). **2.** Ausweisung f (aus). **3.** Ausschluß m (aus, von).

ex·qui·site ['ekskwızıt] adj □ **1.** exquisit, köstlich, erlesen. **2.** gepflegt, erlesen (Wein etc). **3.** äußerst fein (Gehör etc). **4.** heftig (Schmerz), groß (Vergnügen).

ex·ser·vice·man [ˌeks'sɜːvısmən] s (irr man) ✕ bsd. Br. Veteran m.

ex·tant [ek'stænt] adj noch vorhanden od. bestehend.

ex·tem·po·ra·ne·ous [ekˌstempə'reınjəs], **ex·tem·po·rar·y** [ık'stempərərı] adj □ improvisiert, aus dem Stegreif, Stegreif... **ex·tem·po·re** [ek'stempərı] adj u. adv improvisiert, aus dem Stegreif. **ex·tem·po·rize** [ık'stempəraız] v/t aus dem Stegreif darbieten od. vortragen, (a. v/i) improvisieren.

ex·tend [ık'stend] **I** v/t **1.** (aus)dehnen, (-)weiten. **2.** Betrieb etc vergrößern, erweitern, ausbauen. **3.** Hand etc ausstrecken. **4.** Besuch, Macht, Vorsprung etc ausdehnen (to auf acc), Frist, Paß etc verlängern, ✝ a. prolongieren, Angebot etc aufrechterhalten. **5.** ~ o.s. sich völlig ausgeben. **II** v/i **6.** sich ausdehnen od. erstrecken (over über acc; to bis zu); hinausgehen (beyond über acc).

ex·ten·sion [ık'stenʃn] s **1.** Ausdehnung f (a. fig.: to auf acc). **2.** Vergrößerung f, Erweiterung f. **3.** (Frist)Verlängerung f, ✝ a. Prolongation f. **4.** △ Erweiterung f, Anbau m. **5.** teleph. Nebenanschluß m, Apparat m. ~ ca·ble f ⚡ bsd. Br. Verlängerungsschnur f. ~ cord Am. → extension cable. **lad·der** s Ausziehleiter f. ~ lead → extension cable.

ex·ten·sive [ık'stensıv] adj □ **1.** ausgedehnt (a. fig.). **2.** fig. umfassend; eingehend; beträchtlich.

ex·tent [ɪkˈstent] s **1.** Ausdehnung f. **2.** fig. Umfang m, (Aus)Maß n, Grad m: **to a large ~** in hohem Maße, weitgehend; **to some** (od. **a certain**) **~** bis zu e-m gewissen Grade; **to such an ~ that** so sehr, daß.

ex·ten·u·ate [ɪkˈstenjʊeɪt] v/t abschwächen, mildern: **extenuating circumstances** pl ﹩ﬔ mildernde Umstände pl. **ex,ten·u·a·tion** s Abschwächung f, Milderung f.

ex·te·ri·or [ɪkˈstɪərɪə] **I** adj □ **1.** äußer, Außen... **II** s **2.** das Äußere: a) Außenseite f, b) äußere Erscheinung (e-r Person). **3.** Film, TV: Außenaufnahme f.

ex·ter·mi·nate [ɪkˈstɜːmɪneɪt] v/t ausrotten (a. fig.), vernichten, Ungeziefer, Unkraut etc a. vertilgen. **ex,ter·mi·na·tion** s Ausrottung f, Vernichtung f, Vertilgung f.

ex·ter·nal [ɪkˈstɜːnl] **I** adj □ äußer, äußerlich, Außen...: **for ~ use ℱ** zum äußerlichen Gebrauch; **~ to** außerhalb (gen). **II** s pl Äußerlichkeiten pl.

ex·ter·ri·to·ri·al [ˈeksˌterɪˈtɔːrɪəl] adj □ exterritorial.

ex·tinct [ɪkˈstɪŋkt] adj **1.** erloschen (Vulkan) (a. fig.). **2.** ausgestorben (Pflanze, Tier etc), untergegangen (Reich etc): **become ~** aussterben. **ex·tinc·tion** s **1.** Erlöschen n. **2.** Aussterben n, Untergang m.

ex·tin·guish [ɪkˈstɪŋgwɪʃ] v/t **1.** Feuer, Licht (aus)löschen, Zigarette ausmachen. **2.** Leben, Gefühl auslöschen, ersticken, Hoffnungen, Pläne etc zunichte machen. **3.** Schuld tilgen. **ex·tin·guish·er** s (Feuer)Löscher m.

ex·tol [ɪkˈstəʊl] v/t (lob)preisen, rühmen: → **sky.**

ex·tort [ɪkˈstɔːt] v/t Geld, Geständnis etc erpressen (**from** von). **ex·tor·tion** s **1.** Erpressung f. **2.** Wucher m. **ex·tor·tion·ate** [~ʃnət] adj □ **1.** erpresserisch. **2.** Wucher...: **~ price. ex·tor·tion·er, ex·tor·tion·ist** s **1.** Erpresser m. **2.** Wucherer m.

ex·tra [ˈekstrə] **I** adj **1.** zusätzlich, Extra..., Sonder...: **be ~** gesondert berechnet werden; **~ charge** Zuschlag m; **~ charges** pl Nebenkosten pl; **~ pay** Zulage f; **if you pay an ~ two pounds**

wenn Sie noch zwei Pfund dazulegen. **2.** besonder. **II** adv **3.** extra, besonders: **charge ~ for** et. gesondert berechnen. **III** s **4.** Sonderleistung f; bsd. mot. Extra n, pl a. Sonderausstattung f; Zuschlag m: **be an ~** gesondert berechnet werden. **5.** Extrablatt n, -ausgabe f. **6.** Film: Statist(in).

ex·tract I v/t [ɪkˈstrækt] **1.** herausziehen, -holen (**from** aus). **2.** Zahn, ℱ Wurzel ziehen. **3.** fig. (**from**) Geld, Geständnis etc herausholen (aus), entlocken (dat). **II** s [ˈekstrækt] **4.** ℥, gastr. Extrakt m, (**from** aus e-m Buch etc a.) Auszug m. **ex·trac·tion** s **1.** ℱ, ℱ Ziehen n. **2.** Herkunft f, Abstammung f.

ex·tra·cur·ric·u·lar [ˌekstrəkəˈrɪkjələ] adj **1.** ped. univ. außerhalb des Stunden- od. Lehrplans. **2.** außerplanmäßig.

ex·tra·dite [ˈekstrədaɪt] v/t Verbrecher ausliefern. **ex·tra·di·tion** [~ˈdɪʃn] s Auslieferung f.

,ex·tra·mar·i·tal adj außerehelich.

ex·tra·ne·ous [ɪkˈstreɪnjəs] adj **1.** fremd (**to** dat): **~ to reality** realitätsfremd. **2.** nicht dazugehörig: **be ~ to** nicht gehören zu.

ex·traor·di·nar·y [ɪkˈstrɔːdnrɪ] adj □ **1.** außerordentlich, -gewöhnlich. **2.** ungewöhnlich, seltsam.

,ex·tra|ˈsen·so·ry adj: **~ perception** außersinnliche Wahrnehmung. **,~·ter-ˈres·tri·al** adj außerirdisch. **'~,ter·ri·to·ri·al** adj □ exterritorial. **~ time** s Sport: Verlängerung f: **after ~** nach Verlängerung; **the game went into ~** das Spiel ging in die Verlängerung.

ex·trav·a·gance [ɪkˈstrævəgəns] s **1.** Verschwendung(ssucht) f. **2.** Übertriebenheit f, Extravaganz f. **3.** Ausschweifung f, Zügellosigkeit f. **ex·trav·a·gant** adj □ **1.** verschwenderisch. **2.** übertrieben, -spannt, extravagant. **3.** ausschweifend, zügellos.

ex·treme [ɪkˈstriːm] **I** adj (□ → **extremely**). **1.** äußerst, extrem. **2.** äußerst, höchst: **~ necessity** zwingende Notwendigkeit f; **~ penalty** Höchststrafe f. **3.** extrem, radikal. **II** s **4.** äußerstes Ende: **at the other ~** am entgegengesetzten Ende. **5.** das Äußerste, Extrem n: **in the ~** extrem, höchst; **go to ~s** vor nichts zurückschrecken. **ex·treme·ly**

adv äußerst, höchst. **ex'trem·ism** *s bsd.*
pol. Extre'mismus *m.* **ex'trem·ist** *bsd.*
pol. **I** *s* Extremist(in). **II** *adj* extremi-
stisch. **ex·trem·i·ty** [ɪk'stremətɪ] *s* **1.**
äußerstes Ende. **2.** *das* Äußerste: *drive*
s.o. to extremities j-n bis zum Äußersten treiben. **3.** *be reduced to extrem-*
ities in größter Not sein. **4.** *mst od*
Gliedmaße *f,* Extremität *f.*

ex·tri·cate ['ekstrɪkeɪt] *v/t (from)* herausziehen (aus), befreien (aus, von).

ex·tro·vert ['ekstrəʊvɜːt] *adj psych.*
extra-, extrovertiert.

ex·u·ber·ance [ɪg'zjuːbərəns] *s* **1.** *(of)*
Fülle *f* (von *od. gen*), Reichtum *m* (an
dat). **2.** *fig.* Überschwang *m.* **ex'u·ber-**
ant *adj* □ **1.** üppig, (über)reich. **2.** *fig.*
überschwenglich; (-)sprudelnd.

ex·ude [ɪg'zjuːd] *v/t* **1.** ausschwitzen, absondern. **2.** *Duft, Charme etc* verströmen.

ex·ult [ɪg'zʌlt] *v/i* frohlocken, jubeln *(at,*
over, in über *acc*). **ex'ult·ant** *adj* □
frohlockend, jubelnd. **ex·ul·ta·tion**
[ˌegzʌl'teɪʃn] *s* Frohlocken *n,* Jubel *m.*

eye [aɪ] **I** *s* **1.** Auge *n: before (od. under)*
s.o.'s ~s vor j-s Augen; *all ~s* gespannt
warten *etc*; *be up to the ~s in work* bis
über die Ohren in Arbeit sitzen *od.*
stecken; *cry one's ~s out* sich die Au-

gen ausweinen; → *peel* I, *skin* 5. **2.** *fig.*
Blick *m,* Auge(nmerk) *n: have an ~ for*
Sinn *od.* ein (offenes) Auge *od.* e-n
Blick haben *für*; → *catch* 10. **3.** *fig.*
Ansicht *f: in my ~s* in m-n Augen, m-r
Ansicht nach. **4.** *(Nadel)*Öhr *n;* Öse *f.* **5.**
✿ Auge *n.* **II** *v/t* **6.** betrachten; mustern.
'**~·ball** *s anat.* Augapfel *m.* '**~·black** *s*
Wimperntusche *f.* '**~·brow** *s* (Augen-)
Braue *f: raise one's ~s (od. an ~)* die
Stirn runzeln *(at* über *acc*). '**~·catch·er**
s Blickfang *m.* **~ con·tact** *s* Blickkon-
takt *m.* '**~·ful** *s: get an ~* F was zu
sehen bekommen. '**~·glass·es** *s pl, a.*
pair of ~ bsd. Am. Brille *f.* '**~·lash** *s*
Augenwimper *f.* **~ lev·el** *s: on ~* in
Augenhöhe. '**~·lid** *s* Augenlid *n:* →
bat³. **~ lin·er** *s* Eyeliner *m.* **~ o·pen·er**
s: be an ~ to (od. for) s.o. F j-m die
Augen öffnen. **~ shad·ow** *s* Lidschatten *m.* '**~·shot** *s* Sicht-, Sehweite *f:*
(with)in (beyond, out of) ~ in (außer)
Sichtweite. '**~·sight** *s* Sehkraft *f: good*
(poor) ~ gute (schlechte) Augen *pl.*
'**~·sore** *s et.* Unschönes, Schandfleck
m. '**~·strain** *s* Überanstrengung *f* der
Augen. ˌ**~·wit·ness** **I** *s* Augenzeuge *m*
(to gen): **~** *account* Augenzeugenbe-
richt *m.* **II** *v/t* Augenzeuge sein *od.* werden von *(od. gen).*

F

fa·ble ['feɪbl] *s* **1.** Fabel *f;* Sage *f.* **2.** *fig.*
Märchen *n.* **fa·bled** ['~bld] *adj* sagen-
haft *(a. fig.).*

fab·ric ['fæbrɪk] *s* **1.** Gewebe *n,* Stoff *m.*
2. *fig.* Gefüge *n,* Struktur *f.* **fab·ri·cate**
['~keɪt] *v/t* **1.** fabrizieren *(a. fig.),* herstellen. **2.** *fig.* erfinden. ˌ**fab·ri'ca·tion** *s*
1. Fabrikation *f,* Herstellung *f.* **2.** *fig.*
Erfindung *f,* Märchen *n.*

fab·u·lous ['fæbjʊləs] *adj* □ sagenhaft
(a. fig.).

fa·çade, fa·cade [fə'sɑːd] *s* ⌂ Fassade
f (a. fig.).

face [feɪs] **I** *s* **1.** Gesicht *n: in (the) ~ of*
angesichts; trotz; *~ to ~ with* Auge in

Auge mit; *do (up) one's ~* sich schminken; *say s.th. to s.o.'s ~* j-m et. ins
Gesicht sagen; → *stare* II. **2.** Gesicht(s-
ausdruck) *n,* Miene *f: make (od. pull)*
a ~ ein Gesicht machen *od.* schneiden;
have the ~ to inf die Stirn haben *od.* so
unverfroren sein zu *inf*; → *straight* 1. **3.**
das Äußere: *on the ~ of it* oberflächlich
(betrachtet). **4.** Ansehen *n: save one's*
~ das Gesicht wahren; *lose ~* das Gesicht verlieren. **5.** Bildseite *f (e-r Spiel-*
karte). **6.** Zifferblatt *n.* **7.** → *façade.* **II**
v/t **8.** ansehen, *j-m* ins Gesicht sehen. **9.**
gegenüberstehen, -liegen, -sitzen *(dat)*;
nach *Osten etc* blicken *od.* liegen

(*Raum etc*). **10.** *j-m, e-r Sache* mutig entgegentreten *od.* begegnen, sich stellen: → **music** 1. **11.** *oft* **be ~d with** sich *e-r Gefahr etc* gegenübersehen, gegenüberstehen: **be ~d with ruin** vor dem Ruin stehen. **III** *v/i* **12.** sich wenden: ~ **about** kehrtmachen; ~ **away** sich abwenden. **13.** blicken, liegen (**to, toward[s]** nach; **south** nach Süden). **14.** ~ **up to** → 10. ~ **card** *s* Kartenspiel: Bild(karte) *f* n. '~cloth *s* Waschlappen *m*. ~ **cream** *s* Gesichtscreme *f*. '~,lift(·ing) *s* Facelifting *n*, Gesichtsstraffung *f*: **have a ~** sich das Gesicht liften lassen.

fa·ce·tious [fə'si:ʃəs] *adj* □ witzig, spaßig.

face val·ue *s* ✝ Nenn-, Nominalwert *m*: **take s.th. at (its)** ~ (*at its*) *fig.* et. unbesehen glauben; et. für bare Münze nehmen.

fa·cial ['feɪʃl] *adj* Gesichts...

fa·cil·i·tate [fə'sɪlɪteɪt] *v/t* erleichtern.

fa·cil·i·ty *s* **1.** Leichtigkeit *f*. **2.** (günstige) Gelegenheit, Möglichkeit *f* (**for** für). **3.** *pl* Einrichtungen *pl*, Anlagen *pl*. **4.** *pl* Erleichterungen *pl*, Vergünstigungen *pl*.

fac·sim·i·le [fæk'sɪmɪlɪ] *s* Faksimile *n*.

fact [fækt] *s* Tatsache *f*, Faktum *n*: **be founded on** ~ auf Tatsachen beruhen; **know s.th. for a** ~ et. (ganz) sicher wissen; **tell s.o. the ~s of life** j-n (*sexuell*) aufklären; → **matter** 3. '~,find·ing *adj* Untersuchungs...

fac·tion ['fækʃn] *s bsd. pol.* Splittergruppe *f*.

fac·ti·tious [fæk'tɪʃəs] *adj* □ künstlich, (*Freundlichkeit etc a.*) gekünstelt.

fac·tor ['fæktə] *s* Faktor *m*.

fac·to·ry ['fæktərɪ] *s* Fabrik *f*. ~ **hand**, ~ **work·er** *s* Fabrikarbeiter(in).

fac·to·tum [fæk'təʊtəm] *s* Faktotum *n*, Mädchen *n* für alles.

fac·tu·al ['fæktʃʊəl] *adj* □ **1.** Tatsachen...: ~ **report.** **2.** sachlich.

fac·ul·ty ['fæklti] *s* **1.** Fähigkeit *f*, Vermögen *n*: ~ **of hearing** Hörvermögen; (**mental**) **faculties** *pl* Geisteskräfte *pl*; **be in possession of one's faculties** im (Voll)Besitz s-r Kräfte sein. **2.** Gabe *f*, Talent *n*. **3.** *univ.* Fakultät *f*.

fad [fæd] *s* Mode(erscheinung, -torheit) *f*; (vorübergehende) Laune.

fade [feɪd] **I** *v/i* **1.** (ver)welken. **2.** ver-schießen, -blassen (*Farbe etc*). **3.** *a.* ~ **away** sich auflösen (*Menge*), ✻ immer schwächer werden (*Person*), verklingen (*Lied etc*), verblassen (*Erinnerung*), verrauchen (*Zorn etc*), zerrinnen (*Hoffnungen*). **4.** *Radio*: schwinden (*Ton, Sender*). **5.** nachlassen (*Bremsen*), (*Sportler u.*) abbauen. **6.** *a.* ~ **out** (*Film, Rundfunk, TV*) aus- *od.* abgeblendet werden (*Ton, Bild*): ~ **in** (*od.* **up**) auf- *od.* eingeblendet werden. **II** *v/t* **7.** (ver)welken lassen. **8.** *Farbe etc* ausbleichen. **9.** *a.* ~ **out** *Ton, Bild* aus- *od.* abblenden: ~ **in** (*od.* **up**) auf- *od.* einblenden. '**fad·ed** *adj* verwelkt, welk.

fae·ces ['fi:si:z] *s pl* Fäkalien *pl*, Kot *m*.

fag[1] [fæg] *s* F Glimmstengel *m*.

fag[2] [~] **F I** *v/i* sich abarbeiten *od.* (ab)schuften (**at** mit). **II** *v/t a.* ~ **out** ermüden, fertigmachen. **III** *s* Schinderei *f*.

fag[3] [~] → **faggot**[2].

fag end *s* **1.** letzter *od.* schäbiger Rest. **2.** *Br.* F Kippe *f* (*Zigarettenstummel*).

fag·got[1], *bsd. Am.* **fag·ot** ['fægət] *s gastr.* Frikadelle *f* (*bsd. aus Schweineleber*).

fag·got[2] [~] *s bsd. Am. sl.* Schwule *m*. '**fag·got·y** *adj bsd. Am. sl.* schwul.

Fahr·en·heit ['færənhaɪt]: **10°** ~ zehn Grad Fahrenheit.

fail [feɪl] **I** *v/i* **1.** versagen (*a. Stimme, Motor etc*); keinen Erfolg haben; *ped.* durchfallen (**in** in *dat*); ✻ Bankrott machen: **he ~ed in his attempt** sein Versuch schlug fehl. **2.** mißlingen, fehlschlagen, scheitern: **if everything else ~s** wenn alle Stricke reißen. **3.** nachlassen, schwinden (*Kräfte etc*); ausgehen, zu Ende gehen (*Vorräte etc*); abnehmen, schwächer werden (*Sehkraft etc*). **4.** ~ **to** *inf* es unterlassen *od.* versäumen zu *inf*: ~ **to do s.th.** *a.* et. nicht tun; **I ~ to see** ich sehe nicht ein. **II** *v/t* **5.** *j-m* versagen: **his courage ~ed him** ihm sank der Mut; **words ~ me** mir fehlen die Worte (**to** *inf* zu *inf*). **6.** *j-n* im Stich lassen. **7.** *ped. j-n* durchfallen lassen; durchfallen in (*e-r Prüfung*). **III** *s* **8.** **without** ~ mit Sicherheit, ganz bestimmt.

'**fail·ing** *prp* in Ermang(e)lung (*gen*): ~ **this** andernfalls.

'**fail-safe** *adj* störungs-, *a. fig.* pannensicher.

fail·ure ['feɪljə] s 1. Versagen n. 2. Unterlassung f, Versäumnis f: **~ to pay** Nichtzahlung f. 3. Fehlschlag(en n) m, Mißerfolg m. 4. ped. Durchfallen n (in in dat). 5. ✝ Bankrott m. 6. Versager m (Person, Sache).

faint [feɪnt] **I** adj □ schwach, matt (Person, Farbe etc; a. fig.): **I haven't a ~est idea** ich habe nicht die leiseste Ahnung. **II** s Ohnmacht f: **in a ~** ohnmächtig. **III** v/i ohnmächtig werden, in Ohnmacht fallen (**with, from** vor dat). ˌ~'heart·ed adj □ zaghaft, furchtsam.

fair¹ [feə] **I** adj (□ → **fairly**) 1. schön, hübsch: → **sex** 1. 2. hell (Haut, Haar, Teint), blond (Haar), zart (Teint, Haut); hellhäutig. 3. klar, heiter (Himmel), schön, trocken (Wetter, Tag). 4. sauber: → **copy** 1. 5. reell (Chance). 6. gerecht, fair: → **play** 2. **II** adv 7. anständig, fair: **play ~** fair spielen, a. fig. sich an die Spielregeln halten. 8. direkt, genau: **~ in the face** mitten ins Gesicht.

fair² [~] s 1. Jahrmarkt m; Volksfest n. 2. Messe f. '**~·ground** s 1. Rummelplatz m. 2. Messegelände n.

fair·ly ['feəlɪ] adv 1. gerecht(erweise). 2. ziemlich. '**fair·ness** s Gerechtigkeit f, Anständigkeit f, Fairneß f: **in ~ to him** um ihm Gerechtigkeit widerfahren zu lassen.

'**fair·way** s 1. ♣ Fahrwasser n, -rinne f. 2. Golf: Fairway n. '**~·weath·er** adj: **~ friend** Freund m nur in guten Zeiten.

fair·y ['feərɪ] s 1. Fee f. 2. sl. Schwule m. **~ sto·ry**, **~ tale** s Märchen n (a. fig.).

faith [feɪθ] s 1. (in) Glaube(n) m (an acc) (a. eccl.), Vertrauen n (auf acc, zu): **have ~ in** ... an et. glauben, e-r Sache an et. glauben; zu j-m Vertrauen haben. 2. Redlichkeit f: **in good ~** in gutem Glauben, gutgläubig (beide a. ✝). **~·ful** ['~fʊl] adj □ 1. treu (**to** dat): **Yours ~ly** Hochachtungsvoll (Briefschluß). 2. wahrheits- od. wortgetreu. 3. eccl. gläubig.

faith heal·ing s Gesundbeten n.

faith·less ['feɪθlɪs] adj □ 1. treulos (**to** gegenüber). 2. eccl. ungläubig.

fake [feɪk] **I** v/t 1. a. **~ up** Bilanz etc frisieren, Paß etc fälschen. 2. Interesse etc vortäuschen, Krankheit a. simulieren. **II** s 4. Fälschung f. 5.

Schwindel m. 6. Schwindler m; Simulant m.

fa·kir ['feɪˌkɪə] s Fakir m.

fal·con ['fɔːlkən] s orn. Falke m.

fall [fɔːl] **I** s 1. Fall m, Sturz m: **have a (bad od. heavy) ~** (schwer) stürzen. 2. bsd. Am. Herbst m: **in (the) ~** im Herbst. 3. (Regen-, Schnee)Fall m. 4. fig. Fallen n, Sinken n: **~ in temperature** Temperatursturz m. 5. Gefälle n (des Geländes). 6. Fall m (e-r Stadt etc). 7. Einbruch m (der Nacht etc). 8. mst pl Wasserfall m. **II** v/i (irr) 9. (um-, herunter-, hinunter)fallen; (ab)stürzen; (ab)fallen (Blätter): **he fell to his death** er stürzte tödlich ab. 10. a. **~ apart** zerfallen. 11. fig. fallen: a) (im Krieg) umkommen, b) erobert werden (Stadt), c) gestürzt werden (Regierung). 12. fig. fallen, sinken (Preise, Temperatur etc): **his face fell** er machte ein langes Gesicht. 13. abfallen (Gelände etc). 14. hereinbrechen (Nacht etc). 15. krank, fällig etc werden.

Verbindungen mit Präpositionen:

fall **be·hind** v/i zurückbleiben hinter (dat), zurückfallen hinter (acc) (beide a. fig.). **~ down** v/i die Treppe etc hinunterfallen. **~ for** v/i 1. hereinfallen auf (acc). 2. F sich verknallen in (acc). **~ in·to** v/i 1. kommen od. geraten in (acc): **~ difficulties;** → **line¹** 11, **trap** 1. 2. sich et. angewöhnen: **~ a habit** e-e Gewohnheit annehmen. 3. fallen in (ein Gebiet od. Fach). **~ on** v/i 1. fallen auf (acc) (a. zeitlich): **his glance fell on me; Christmas falls on a Monday this year;** → **ear¹** 1. 2. herfallen über (acc). 3. j-m zufallen (**to do** zu tun). **~ out of** v/i sich et. abgewöhnen: **~ a habit** e-e Gewohnheit ablegen. **~ o·ver** v/i: **~ o.s. to do s.th.** F sich fast umbringen, et. zu tun. **~ to** v/i 1. beginnen mit: **~ doing s.th.** sich daranmachen, et. zu tun. 2. → **fall on** 3. **~ un·der** v/i unter ein Gesetz etc fallen.

Verbindungen mit Adverbien:

fall **a·bout** v/i: **~ (laughing od. with laughter)** F sich (vor Lachen) kugeln. **a·way** → **fall off. ~ back** v/i 1. zurückweichen. 2. **~ on** zurückgreifen auf (acc). **~ be·hind** v/i zurückbleiben, -fallen (beide a. fig.): **~ with (od. on)** in Rückstand od. Verzug geraten mit. **~**

down v/i **1.** umfallen, einstürzen. **2.** F **(on)** enttäuschen, versagen (bei); Pech haben (mit). **~ in** v/i **1.** einfallen, -stürzen. **2. ~ with** beipflichten, zustimmen (*dat*); sich anpassen (*dat*); entsprechen (*dat*). **~ off** v/i **1.** zurückgehen (*Geschäfte, Zuschauerzahlen etc*), nachlassen (*Begeisterung etc*). **2. (from)** abfallen (von), abtrünnig werden (*dat*). **~ out** v/i **1.** *gut etc* ausfallen, -gehen. **2.** sich ereignen, geschehen. **3.** (sich) streiten (**with** mit; **over** über *acc*). **~ o·ver** v/i hinfallen (*Person*), umfallen (*Vase etc*): **~ backwards to do s.th.** F sich fast umbringen, et. zu tun. **~ through** v/i **1.** durchfallen (*a. fig.*). **2.** mißglücken, ins Wasser fallen. **~ to** v/i reinhauen, (tüchtig) zugreifen (*beim Essen*).

fal·la·cious [fəˈleɪʃəs] *adj* □ **1.** trügerisch, irreführend. **2.** irrig, falsch.

fal·la·cy [ˈfæləsɪ] s Trugschluß *m*, Irrtum *m*.

fall·en [ˈfɔːlən] I *pp von* **fall**. II *adj* gefallen (*a. Mädchen*).

fall guy s *bsd. Am.* F **1.** Opfer *n* (*e-s Betrügers*); Gimpel *m* (*leichtgläubiger Mensch*). **2.** Sündenbock *m*.

fal·li·ble [ˈfæləbl] *adj* □ fehlbar.

fall·ing star [ˈfɔːlɪŋ] s Sternschnuppe *f*.

ˈfall·out Fallout *m*, radioaktiver Niederschlag.

fal·low [ˈfæləʊ] *adj* ✓ brach(liegend) (*a. fig.*): **lie ~** brachliegen.

false [fɔːls] I *adj* □ *allg.* falsch: **~ alarm** falscher *od.* blinder Alarm (*a. fig.*); **~ bottom** doppelter Boden; **~ key** Dietrich *m*, Nachschlüssel *m*; **~ teeth** *pl* (*künstliches*) Gebiß; → **pretence** 2. II *adv*: **play s.o. ~** ein falsches Spiel mit j-m treiben. **false·hood** [ˈhʊd] s **1.** Unwahrheit *f*. **2.** Falschheit *f*. **ˈfalse·ness** s *allg.* Falschheit *f*.

fal·si·fi·ca·tion [ˌfɔːlsɪfɪˈkeɪʃn] s (Ver-)Fälschung *f*. **fal·si·fy** [ˈfaɪ] v/t **1.** fälschen. **2.** verfälschen, falsch darstellen *od.* wiedergeben. **3.** widerlegen. **fal·si·ty** [ˈ-ətɪ] → **falsehood**.

fal·ter [ˈfɔːltə] I v/i schwanken (*a:* taumeln, b) zögern, zaudern, c) stocken (*a. Stimme*). II v/t et. stammeln.

fame [feɪm] s Ruhm *m*. **famed** *adj* berühmt (**for** für, wegen).

fa·mil·iar [fəˈmɪljə] I *adj* □ **1.** vertraut, bekannt, geläufig (**to** *dat*): **a ~ sight** ein gewohnter Anblick. **2.** vertraut, bekannt (**with** mit): **be ~ with** a. sich auskennen in (*dat*); **make o.s. ~ with** sich vertraut machen mit. **3.** a) vertraulich, ungezwungen (*Ton etc*), b) plump-vertraulich, aufdringlich. **4.** vertraut, eng (*Freund etc*): **be on ~ terms with** auf vertrautem Fuß stehen mit. II s **5.** Vertraute *m, f*. **fa·mil·i·ar·i·ty** [ˌlɪˈærətɪ] s **1.** Vertrautheit *f*. **2.** a) Vertraulichkeit *f*, b) *oft pl* plumpe Vertraulichkeit, Aufdringlichkeit *f*. **fa·mil·iar·ize** [ˌjəraɪz] v/t vertraut *od.* bekannt machen (**with** mit).

fam·i·ly [ˈfæmlɪ] I s Familie *f, fig.* Herkunft *f*: **a ~ of good** → vierköpfige Familie; **of good ~** aus gutem Haus; → **run** 11. II *adj* Familien...: **~ allowance** Kindergeld *n*; **~ doctor** Hausarzt *m*; **~ man** Familienvater *m*; häuslicher Mensch; **~ name** → **surname**; **~ planning** Familienplanung *f*; **~ problems** *pl* familiäre Probleme *pl*; **~ tree** Stammbaum *m*.

fam·ine [ˈfæmɪn] s Hungersnot *f*.

fa·mous [ˈfeɪməs] *adj* □ berühmt (**for** wegen, für).

fan¹ [fæn] I s **1.** Fächer *m*. **2.** Ventilator *m*: **~ belt** ✪ Keilriemen *m*. II v/t **3.** j-m Luft zufächeln. **4.** anfachen, *fig. a.* entfachen, -flammen. III v/i **5.** *oft* **~ out** sich fächerförmig ausbreiten; ausschwärmen.

fan² [ˌ] s (*Sport- etc*)Fan *m*: **~ club** Fanklub *m*; **~ mail** Verehrerpost *f*.

fa·nat·ic [fəˈnætɪk] I s Fanatiker(in). II *adj* (**~ally**) fanatisch. **fa·nat·i·cism** [ˌsɪzəm] s Fanatismus *m*.

fan·ci·er [ˈfænsɪə] s (Tier-, Blumen- etc)Liebhaber(in). *od.* (-)Züchter(in).

fan·ci·ful [ˈfænsɪfʊl] *adj* □ **1.** phantasiereich. **2.** phantastisch, wirklichkeitsfremd.

fan·cy [ˈfænsɪ] I s **1.** Phantasie *f*; Einbildung *f*: → **tickle** I. **2.** Idee *f*, plötzlicher Einfall. **3.** Laune *f*, Grille *f*. **4.** (*for*) Neigung *f* (zu), Vorliebe *f* (für), Gefallen *n* (an *dat*): **have a ~ for** gern haben; Lust haben auf (*acc*); **take a ~ to** (*od.* **for**) Gefallen finden an (*dat*), sympathisch finden. II *adj* **5.** Phantasie..., phantastisch: **~ name** Phantasiename *m*; **~ price** Liebhaberpreis *m*. **6.** phantasie-, kunstvoll. III v/t **7.** sich j-n, et.

vorstellen: **~** *that!* stell dir vor!, denk nur!; sieh mal einer an! **8.** annehmen, glauben. **9. ~ o.s.** sich einbilden (*to be* zu sein), sich halten ([*as*] für): **~ o.s.** (*very important*) sich sehr wichtig vorkommen. **10.** gern haben *od.* mögen. **11.** Lust haben (auf *acc*; *doing* zu tun). **12.** *Tiere, Pflanzen* (aus Liebhaberei) züchten. **~ ball** *s* Kostümfest *n*, Maskenball *m*. **~ dress** *s* (Masken)Kostüm *n*. **'~-dress** *adj*: **~ ball → fancy ball.** **,~·'free** *adj* frei u. ungebunden. **~ goods** *s pl* **1.** Modeartikel *pl*. **2.** kleine Geschenkartikel *pl*; Nippes *pl*.

fan·fare ['fænfeə] *s* **1.** ♩ Fanfare *f*, Tusch *m*. **2.** *fig. contp.* Trara *n*, Tamtam *n*.

fang [fæŋ] *s* Reiß-, Fangzahn *m*, Fang *m* (*e-s Raubtiers etc*), Hauer *m* (*e-s Ebers*), Giftzahn *m* (*e-r Schlange*).

fan·ta·sia [fæn'teɪzjə] *s* ♩ Fantasie *f*. **fan·tas·tic** [~'tæstɪk] *adj* (**~ally**) phantastisch: a) unwirklich, b) absurd, c) F toll. **fan·ta·sy** ['fæntəsɪ] *s* Phantasie *f*: a) Einbildungskraft *f*, b) Phantasievorstellung *f*, c) Tag-, Wachtraum *m*.

far [fɑː] **I** *adj* **1.** fern, (weit)entfernt, weit: **→ cry** 1. **2.** (*vom Sprecher aus*) entfernter: **at the ~ end** am anderen Ende. **II** *adv* **3.** fern, weit: **~ away** (*od.* **off**) weit weg *od.* entfernt; **as ~ as** soweit *od.* soviel (wie); bis (nach); **so ~ so good** so weit, so gut. **4.** *fig.* (*from*) weit entfernt (von), alles andere (als): **~ from completed** noch längst nicht fertig. **5. ~ into** weit *od.* tief in (*acc*): **~ into the night** bis spät *od.* tief in die Nacht (hinein). **6.** *a.* **by ~** weit(aus), bei weitem, wesentlich. **'~·a·way** → **far** 1.

farce [fɑːs] *s thea.* Farce *f* (*a. fig.*), Posse *f*, Schwank *m*. **far·ci·cal** ['~sɪkl] *adj* □ **1.** farcen-, possenhaft. **2.** *fig.* absurd, lächerlich.

fare [feə] **I** *s* **1.** Fahrpreis *m*, -geld *n*; Flugpreis *m*: *what's the ~?* was kostet die Fahrt *od.* der Flug?; *any more ~s, please?* noch j-d zugestiegen?; → **dodger** (*od.* **evader**) Schwarzfahrer(in); → **stage** *Br.* Fahrpreiszone *f*, Teilstrecke *f*. **2.** Fahrgast *m* (*bsd. e-s Taxis*). **3.** Kost *f* (*a. fig.*), Nahrung *f*. **II** *v/i* **4.** (er)gehen: *how did you ~?* wie ist es dir ergangen?; *he ~d ill, it ~d ill with him* es erging ihm schlecht. **~well I** *int* leb(t)

wohl. **II** *s* Lebewohl *n*, Abschied(sgruß) *m*: *make one's ~s* sich verabschieden. **III** *adj* Abschieds...

,far-'fetched *adj fig.* weithergeholt, an den Haaren herbeigezogen.

farm [fɑːm] **I** *s* **1.** (*a. Geflügel- etc*)Farm *f*, Bauernhof *m*. **II** *v/t* **2.** *Land* bebauen, bewirtschaften. **3.** *Geflügel etc* züchten. **4. ~ out** ⊹ *Arbeit* vergeben (*to* an *acc*). **III** *v/i* **5.** Landwirtschaft betreiben. **'farm·er** *s* **1.** Bauer *m*, Landwirt *m*, Farmer *m*. **2.** (*Geflügel- etc*)Züchter *m*. **'farm·house** *s* Bauernhaus *n*. **'farm·ing** ['fɑːmɪŋ] *s* **1.** Landwirtschaft *f*. **2.** (*Geflügel- etc*)Zucht *f*.

,far·|·'off → **far** 1. **,~·'out** *adj sl.* **1.** toll, super. **2.** exzentrisch. **,~·'reach·ing** *adj* weitreichend, *fig. a.* folgenschwer. **,~·'see·ing** *adj fig.* weitblickend, umsichtig. **,~·'sight·ed** *adj* **1.** → **farseeing. 2.** ❦ weitsichtig.

fart [fɑːt] ∨ **I** *s* **1.** Furz *m*. **2.** *fig.* Arschloch *n*. **II** *v/i* **3.** furzen.

far·ther ['fɑːðə] **I** *adj* **1.** *comp von* **far. 2.** weiter weg liegend, entfernter. **3.** → **further** 5. **II** *adv* **4.** weiter: *so far and no ~* bis hierher u. nicht weiter. **5.** → **further** 2, 3. **far·thest** ['~ðɪst] **I** *adj* **1.** *sup von* **far. 2.** weitest, entferntest. **3.** → **furthest** 2. **II** *adv* **4.** am weitesten *od.* entferntesten. **5.** → **further** 4.

fas·ci·nate ['fæsɪneɪt] *v/t* faszinieren. **,fas·ci·na·tion** *s* Faszination *f*.

fas·cism, *oft* ♀ ['fæʃɪzəm] *s pl.* Faschismus *m*. **'fas·cist**, *a.* ♀ **I** *s* Faschist(in). **II** *adj* faschistisch.

fash·ion ['fæʃn] **I** *s* **1.** Mode *f*: *come into ~* in Mode kommen, modern werden; *go out of ~* aus der Mode kommen, unmodern werden; **~ parade** (*od.* **show**) Mode(n)schau *f*. **2.** Art *f* u. Weise *f*, Stil *m*: *after* (*od. in*) *a ~* schlecht u. recht, so lala. **II** *v/t* **3.** formen, gestalten. **'fash·ion·a·ble** *adj* □ **1.** modisch, elegant. **2.** a) in Mode: *be very ~* große Mode sein (*to do* zu tun), b) Mode...: **~ complaint** Modekrankheit *f*.

fast¹ [fɑːst] **I** *adj* **1.** schnell: **~ train** Schnell-, D-Zug *m*; *my watch is* (*ten minutes*) **~** m-e Uhr geht (10 Minuten) vor. **2.** *phot.* hochempfindlich (*Film*); lichtstark (*Objektiv*). **II** *adv* **3.** schnell.

fast² [~] **I** *adj* **1.** fest: *make ~* festmachen; **~ friends** *pl* unzertrennliche Freunde *pl.* **2.** widerstandsfähig (**to** gegen): ~ **colo(u)r** (wasch)echte Farbe; ~ **to light** lichtecht. **II** *adv* **3.** fest: *be* ~ *asleep* fest *od.* tief schlafen; *play* ~ *and loose with* Schindluder treiben mit.

fast³ [~] **I** *v/t* **1.** fasten. **II** *s* **2.** Fasten. **3.** Fastenzeit *f:* ~ (*day*) Fastentag *m.*

'fast|**back** *s mot.* (Wagen *m* mit) Fließheck *n.* ~ **breed·er,** ,~'**breed·er re·ac·tor** *s phys.* schneller Brüter.

fas·ten ['fɑːsn] **I** *v/t* **1.** befestigen, festmachen (**to, on** an *acc*): → *seat belt.* **2.** *a.* ~ *up* (ab-, ver)schließen, *Jacke etc* zuknöpfen, *Paket etc* zu-, verschnüren: ~ *s.o. down to* F j-n festnageln auf (*acc*). **3.** ~ *on fig.* Blick, Aufmerksamkeit *etc* richten auf (*acc*); j-m e-e Straftat *etc* in die Schuhe schieben, anhängen. **II** *v/i* **4.** sich festmachen *od.* schließen lassen.

'fas·ten·er *s* Verschluß *m.*

'fast-food re·stau·rant Schnellimbiß *m,* -gaststätte *f.*

fas·tid·i·ous [fəˈstɪdɪəs] *adj* □ anspruchsvoll, wählerisch, heikel (**about** in *dat*).

fast·ness ['fɑːstnɪs] *s* Widerstandsfähigkeit *f* (**to** gegen), Echtheit *f* (*von Farben*).

fat [fæt] **I** *adj* □ **1.** dick (*a. fig. Bankkonto etc*), *contp.* fett. **2.** fett(ig), fetthaltig. **II** *s* **3.** Fett *n: the* ~ *is in the fire* der Teufel ist los; *chew the* ~ F quatschen, plaudern; *live on* (*od. off*) *the* ~ *of the land* in Saus u. Braus *od.* wie Gott in Frankreich leben.

fa·tal [ˈfeɪtl] *adj* □ **1.** tödlich. **2.** fatal, verhängnisvoll (**to** für). **fa·tal·ism** [ˈ~təlɪzəm] *s* Fatalismus *m.* **'fa·tal·ist** *s* Fatalist(in). ,**fa·tal'is·tic** *adj* (**~ally**) fatalistisch. **fa·tal·i·ty** [fəˈtælətɪ] *s* **1.** Verhängnis *n.* **2.** tödlicher Unfall; (Todes)Opfer *n.*

fate [feɪt] *s* **1.** Schicksal *n: he met his* ~ das Schicksal ereilte ihn; (*as*) *sure as* ~ *is* ~ garantiert, mit Sicherheit; → *tempt* 2. **2.** Verhängnis *n,* Verderben *n.* **'fat·ed** *adj* **1.** *he was* ~ *to inf* es war ihm (vom Schicksal) bestimmt zu *inf.* **2.** → *fateful* 2. **fate·ful** [ˈ~fʊl] *adj* □ **1.** verhängnisvoll. **2.** schicksalhaft, Schicksals...

fa·ther [ˈfɑːðə] **I** *s* **1.** Vater *m, fig. a.* Begründer *m: like* ~ *like son* der Apfel fällt nicht weit vom Stamm; *2's Day*

Vatertag *m.* **2.** *pl* Ahnen *pl,* Vorfahren *pl,* Väter *pl.* **3.** *eccl. a)* Pater *m, b) the Holy* 2 der Heilige Vater. **II** *v/t* **4.** *et.* ins Leben rufen. **5.** ~ *s.th. on s.o.* j-m die Schuld für et. zuschreiben. 2 **Christmas** *s bsd. Br.* der Weihnachtsmann. ~ **fig·ure** *s psych.* Vaterfigur *f.*

fa·ther·hood [ˈfɑːðəhʊd] *s* Vaterschaft *f.* **'fa·ther**|**-in-law** *pl* **'fa·thers-in-law** *s* Schwiegervater *m.* '~**land** *s* Vaterland *n.*

fa·ther·less [ˈfɑːðəlɪs] *adj* vaterlos. **'fa·ther·ly** *adj* väterlich.

fath·om [ˈfæðəm] *v/t* ♣ ausloten, *fig. a.* ergründen. **'fath·om·less** *adj* □ unergründlich (*a. fig.*).

fa·tigue [fəˈtiːg] **I** *s* **1.** Ermüdung *f* (*a.* ☺). **2.** *pl* Strapazen *pl.* **II** *v/t u. v/i* **3.** ermüden (*a.* ☺).

fat·less [ˈfætlɪs] *adj* fettlos. **'fat·ness** *s* Dicke *f, contp.* Fettheit *f.* **fat·ten** [ˈ~tn] **I** *v/t* **1.** *a.* ~ *up* dick *od. contp.* fett machen. **2.** *Tier, Vieh* f. *a.* j-n mästen. **II** *v/i* **3.** dick *od. contp.* fett werden. **'fat·ty** *I adj* fettig, Fett... **II** *s* F Dickerchen *n.*

fa·tu·i·ty [fəˈtjuːətɪ] *s* Albernheit *f.* **fat·u·ous** [ˈfætjʊəs] *adj* □ albern.

fau·cet [ˈfɔːsɪt] *s Am.* (Wasser)Hahn *m.*

fault [fɔːlt] *s* **1.** Schuld *f,* Verschulden *n: it is my* ~ es ist m-e Schuld; *be at* ~ schuld sein. **2.** Fehler *m* (*a. Tennis etc*): *find* ~ *with* et. auszusetzen haben an (*dat*); *be at* ~ sich irren. **3.** ☺ Defekt *m.* '~**find·er** *s* Nörgler(in), Kritt(e)ler(in). '~**find·ing** *I s* Nörgelei *f,* Krittelei *f.* **II** *adj* nörglerisch, kritt(e)lig.

fault·less [ˈfɔːltlɪs] *adj* □ fehlerfrei, -los. **'fault·y** *adj* □ fehlerhaft, ☺ *a.* defekt, (*Argumentation etc a.*) falsch.

fau·na [ˈfɔːnə] *pl* -**nas,** -**nae** [ˈ~niː] *s* Fauna *f,* Tierwelt *f.*

fa·vo(u)r [ˈfeɪvə] **I** *v/t* **1.** begünstigen: a) favorisieren, bevorzugen, b) günstig sein für, fördern, c) unterstützen, für et. sein. **2.** *bsd. Sport:* favorisieren, zum Favoriten erklären. **II** *s* **3.** Gunst *f,* Wohlwollen *n: in* ~ *of* zugunsten von (*od. gen*); *in my* ~ zu m-n Gunsten; *be in* ~ *of* für et. sein; *be in* (*out of*) *s.o.'s* ~, *be in* (*out of*) ~ *with s.o.* bei j-m gut (schlecht) angeschrieben sein. **4.** Gefallen *m,* Gefälligkeit *f: ask s.o. a* ~ (*od. a* ~ *of s.o.*) j-n um e-n Gefallen bitten; *do s.o. a* ~ j-m e-n Gefallen tun. **'fa-**

vo(u)r·a·ble *adj* □ günstig: a) vorteilhaft (**to, for** für), b) positiv, zustimmend (*Antwort etc*). **'fa·vo(u)red** *adj* **1.** begünstigt. **2.** bevorzugt, Lieblings... **3.** *bsd. Sport*: favorisiert. **fa·vo(u)r·ite** ['~rɪt] **I** *s* **1.** Liebling *m*, *contp.* Günstling *m*. **2.** *bsd. Sport*: Favorit(in). **II** *adj* **3.** Lieblings...: **~** *dish* Lieblingsgericht *n*, Leibspeise *f*. **'fa·vo(u)r·it·ism** *s* Günstlings-, Vetternwirtschaft *f*.

fawn [fɔːn] *v/i*: **~** *on fig.* katzbuckeln vor (*dat*). **'fawn·ing** *adj* □ kriecherisch.

fax [fæks] *v/t* faxen.

fear [fɪə] **I** *s* **1.** Furcht *f*, Angst *f* (**of** vor *dat*; *that* daß): **for ~** *that* aus Furcht, daß; *be in* **~** (*of s.o.*) sich (vor j-m) fürchten, (vor j-m) Angst haben. **2.** Befürchtung, Sorge *f*: **for ~** *of hurting him* um ihn nicht zu verletzen. **3.** Ehrfurcht *f* (**of** vor *dat*): **~** *of God* Gottesfurcht *f*. **II** *v/t* **4.** fürchten, sich fürchten *od.* Angst haben vor (*dat*). **5.** *das Schlimmste etc* (be)fürchten. **6.** *Gott* fürchten. **III** *v/i* **7.** **~** *for* fürchten um. **'fear·ful** ['~fʊl] *adj* □ **1.** furchtbar, fürchterlich (*beide a. fig.* F). **2.** *be* **~** in (großer) Sorge sein, sich ängstigen (**of, for** um; *that* daß). **3.** furchtsam, angsterfüllt: *be* **~** *of* **~** *fear* 4. **'fear·less** *adj* □ furchtlos: *be* **~** *of* sich nicht fürchten *od.* keine Angst haben vor (*dat*).

fea·si·bil·i·ty [ˌfiːzə'bɪlətɪ] *s* Machbarkeit *f*, Durchführbarkeit *f*. **'fea·si·ble** *adj* □ machbar, (*Plan etc*) durchführbar.

feast [fiːst] **I** *s* **1.** *eccl.* Fest *n*, Feiertag *m*. **2.** Festessen *n*, -mahl *n*. **3.** *fig.* (Hoch-)Genuß *m*: **~** *for the eyes* Augenweide *f*. **II** *v/t* **4.** festlich bewirten (**on** mit). **5.** ergötzen (**on** mit): **~** *one's eyes* **on** s-e Augen weiden an (*dat*). **III** *v/i* **6.** sich gütlich tun (**on** an *dat*). **7.** sich weiden (**on** an *dat*).

feat [fiːt] *s* **1.** Helden-, Großtat *f*. **2.** Kunst-, Meisterstück *n*; Kraftakt *m*. **3.** (*technische etc*) Großtat, große Leistung.

feath·er ['feðə] **I** *s* Feder *f*, *pl* Gefieder *n*: *birds of a* **~** Leute vom gleichen Schlag; *birds of a* **~** *flock together* gleich u. gleich gesellt sich gern; *that is a* **~** *in his cap* darauf kann er stolz sein; → *light²* 1. **II** *v/t* mit Federn polstern *od.* schmücken, *Pfeil* fiedern: **~** *one's nest fig.* sein(e) Schäfchen ins trockene

bringen. **~** *bed* *s* Matratze *f* mit Federod. Daunenfüllung. **'~·bed** *v/t* *j-n* verhätscheln. **'~·brained** *adj* **1.** hohlköpfig. **2.** leichtsinnig. **'~·weight** **I** *s* **1.** *Sport*: Federgewicht(ler *m*) *n*. **2.** Leichtgewicht *n* (*Person*). **II** *adj* **3.** *Sport*: Federgewichts... **4.** leichtgewichtig.

fea·ture ['fiːtʃə] **I** *s* **1.** (Gesichts)Zug *m*. **2.** Merkmal *n*, Charakteristikum *n*. **3.** (Haupt)Attraktion *f*. **4.** a) *a.* **~** *program(me)* (*Rundfunk, TV*) Feature *n*, b) *a.* **~** *article* (*od. story*) (*Zeitung*) Feature *n*, c) *a.* **~** *film* Feature *n*, Haupt-, Spielfilm *m*. **II** *v/t* **5.** als (Haupt-)Attraktion zeigen *od.* bringen, groß herausbringen *od.* -stellen. **6.** in der Hauptrolle zeigen: *a film featuring X* ein Film mit X in der Hauptrolle. **7.** sich auszeichnen durch.

fe·brile ['fiːbraɪl] *adj* 🔥 fieb(e)rig, fieberhaft, Fieber...

Feb·ru·ar·y ['februəri] *s* Februar *m*: **in ~** im Februar.

fe·ces *bsd. Am.* → *faeces*.

fed [fed] *pret u. pp von* **feed**.

fed·er·al [fed] *adj* *pol.* Bundes...: ♀ *Bureau of Investigation* Am. Bundeskriminalpolizei *f*. **'fed·er·al·ism,** *mst* '♀ *s pol.* Föderalismus *m*. **'fed·er·al·ist** **I** *adj* föderalistisch. **II** *s mst* '♀ Föderalist *m*. **fed·er'a·tion** *s* **1.** *pol.* Bundesstaat *m*; Föderation *f*, Staatenbund *m*. **2.** (*Sport- etc*)Verband *m*.

fee [fiː] *s* (*Anwalts- etc*)Honorar *n*, (*Mitglieds- etc*)Beitrag *m*, (*Eintritts- etc*)Geld *n*, (*Aufnahme- etc*)Gebühr *f*.

fee·ble ['fiːbl] *adj* □ schwach (*a. fig.*). **,~·'mind·ed** *adj* □ schwachsinnig, geistesschwach.

fee·ble·ness ['fiːblnɪs] *s* Schwäche *f*.

feed [fiːd] **I** *v/t* (*irr*) **1.** *Tier, Kind* füttern (**on, with** mit): *be fed up with* F die Nase voll haben von, *et.* satt haben. **2.** *Familie etc* ernähren, unterhalten. **3.** ☉ *Maschine* speisen, beschicken, *a. j-n* versorgen (**with** mit): **~** *s.th. into a computer* et. in e-n Computer eingeben *od.* einspeisen. **4.** **~** *back* a) ⚡, *Kybernetik*: rückkoppeln, b) *Informationen etc* zurückleiten (**to** an *acc*). **5.** *Gefühl* nähren. **II** *v/i* (*irr*) **6.** fressen (*Tier*); F futtern (*Mensch*). **7.** sich ernähren, leben (**on** von). **III** *s* **8.** Füttern *n*, Fütterung *f*. **9.** F Mahlzeit *f*. **'~·back** *s* **1.** ⚡,

Kybernetik: Feedback *n*, Rückkopp(e)-
lung *f.* **2.** a) *Rundfunk, TV*: Feedback *n*,
b) Zurückleitung *f (von Informationen)*
(**to** an *acc*).
feed·er ['fi:də] *s* **1.** *a heavy ~* ein starker
Fresser (*Tier*) *od.* F Esser (*Mensch*). **2.**
→ *feeding bottle*. **3.** *Br.* Lätzchen *n.* ~
road *s* Zubringerstraße *f.*
feed·ing ['fi:dɪŋ] *s* Füttern *n*, Fütterung
f. ~ **bot·tle** *s* (Säuglings-, Saug)Flasche
f.
feel [fi:l] **I** *v/t (irr)* **1.** (an-, be)fühlen:
one's way sich tasten (*through* durch).
2. fühlen, (ver)spüren: *make itself felt*
spürbar werden, sich bemerkbar machen. **3.** *Freude etc* empfinden. **4.** a)
finden, glauben (*that* daß), b) halten
für: *I ~ it (to be) my duty* ich halte es für
m-e Pflicht. **II** *v/i (irr)* **5.** fühlen
(*whether, if* ob; *how* wie): ~ *for* tasten
nach. **6.** sich fühlen: ~ *ill*; ~ *up to s.th.*
sich e-r Sache gewachsen fühlen; ~ *like*
(*doing*) *s.th.* Lust haben zu e-r *od.* auf
e-e Sache (et. zu tun); → *cold* 1, *warm*
1. **7.** *how do you ~ about it?* was meinst
du dazu? **8.** sich *weich etc* anfühlen. **III**
s **9.** *klebriges etc* Gefühl. **10.** *be soft to
the ~,* *have a soft ~* sich weich anfüh-
len. **'feel·er** *s zo.* Fühler *m (a. fig.)*: *put
out ~s (od. a ~)* s-e Fühler ausstrecken.
'feel·ing *s* Gefühl *n*: a) Gefühlssinn *m*,
b) (Gefühls)Eindruck *m*: *have a ~ that*
das Gefühl haben, daß, c) Empfindung
f: ~*s pl of guilt* Schuldgefühle *pl*, d)
Feingefühl *n*: *have a ~ for* Gefühl haben für.
feet [fi:t] *pl von* **foot.**
feign [feɪn] **I** *v/t Interesse etc* vortäuschen, *Krankheit a.* simulieren: ~ *death
(od. to be dead)* sich totstellen. **II** *v/i*
sich verstellen, simulieren.
feint [feɪnt] *s Sport*: Finte *f (a. fig.)*.
fell¹ [fel] *pret von* **fall.**
fell² [~] *v/t* **1.** *Baum* fällen. **2.** *Gegner etc*
fällen, niederstrecken.
fel·loe ['feləʊ] *s* ⊕ Felge *f.*
fel·low ['feləʊ] **I** *s* **1.** Gefährte *m*, Gefähr-
tin *f*, Genosse *m*, Genossin *f*, Kame-
rad(in). **2.** Mitmensch *m*, Zeitgenosse
m. **3.** F Kerl *m*: *old ~* alter Knabe; *a ~*
man. **II** *adj* **4.** Mit...: ~ *being* Mitmensch *m*; ~ *citizen* Mitbürger *m*; ~
countryman Landsmann *m*; ~ *feeling*
Mitgefühl *n*; Zs.-gehörigkeitsgefühl *n*;

~ *student* Studienkollege *m*, Kommilitone *m*; ~ *travel(l)er* Mitreisende *m*;
pol. Mitläufer *m*. **'fel·low·ship** *s* **1.** Kameradschaft *f.* **2.** Gesellschaft *f*, Gruppe *f.*
felt¹ [felt] *pret u. pp von* **feel.**
felt² [~] **I** *s* Filz *m.* **II** *adj* Filz... ~ *tip*,
'~-tip(ped) pen *s* Filzschreiber *m*, -stift
m.
fe·male ['fi:meɪl] **I** *s* **1.** *contp.* Weib(s-
bild) *n*. **2.** *zo.* Weibchen *n.* **II** *adj* **3.**
weiblich: ~ *dog* Hündin *f*; ~ *screw*
Schraubenmutter *f*. **4.** Frauen...
fem·i·nine ['femɪnɪn] *adj* □ **1.** weiblich
(*a. ling.*), Frauen... **2.** fraulich. **3.** weibisch, feminin. ,**fem·i·nin·i·ty** *s* **1.**
Weiblichkeit *f.* **2.** Fraulichkeit *f.* **3.** wei-
bische *od.* feminine Art. **'fem·i·nism** *s*
Feminismus *m*, Frauenrechtsbewe-
gung *f.* **'fem·i·nist I** *s* Feminist(in),
Frauenrechtler(in). **II** *adj* femini-
stisch.
fe·mur ['fi:mə] *pl* **-murs, fem·o·ra**
['femərə] *s anat.* Oberschenkel(knochen) *m.*
fen [fen] *s* Fenn *n*, Sumpf-, Marschland
n.
fence [fens] **I** *s* **1.** Zaun *m*: *sit on the ~*
sich neutral verhalten; unentschlossen
sein. **2.** *sl.* Hehler *m*. **II** *v/t* **3.** *a.* ~ *in*
einzäunen: ~ *off* abzäunen. **III** *v/i* **4.**
Sport: fechten. **'fenc·er** *s Sport*: Fech-
ter(in). **'fenc·ing** *s* **1.** Zaun *m*, Einzäunung *f.* **2.** *Sport*: Fechten *n.* **3.** *sl.* Heh-
lerei *f.* **II** *adj* **4.** *Sport*: Fecht...: ~
master Fechtmeister *m.*
fend [fend] **I** *v/t oft* ~ *off Angreifer, Fragen etc* abwehren. **II** *v/i*: ~ *for o.s.* für
sich selbst sorgen. **'fend·er** *s mot. Am.*
Kotflügel *m.*
fen·nel ['fenl] *s* ♣ Fenchel *m.*
fer·ment [fə'ment] **I** *v/t* **1.** ⚗ in Gärung
bringen (*a. fig.*), gären lassen, vergä-
ren; *fig.* in Wallung bringen. **II** *v/i* **2.** ⚗
gären, in Gärung sein (*beide a. fig.*). **III**
s ['fɜ:ment] **3.** ⚗ Gärstoff *m*, Ferment
n. **4.** a) ⚗ Gärung *f (a. fig.)*, b) *fig.*
innere Unruhe, Aufruhr *m*. **fer·men·
ta·tion** [,fɜ:men'teɪʃn] *s* **1.** ⚗ Gärung *f
(a. fig.)*, Gärungsprozeß *m*. **2.** →
ferment 4b.
fern [fɜ:n] *s* ♣ Farn(kraut *n*) *m.*
fe·ro·cious [fə'rəʊʃəs] *adj* □ **1.** wild
(*Tier etc*). **2.** wild, grimmig (*Blick etc*),

grausam (*Strafe etc*), heftig, scharf (*Auseinandersetzung*).

fer·ret ['ferɪt] **I** *s zo.* Frettchen *n.* **II** *v/t mst* ~ **out** *et.* aufspüren, -stöbern, *Wahrheit* herausfinden, hinter *ein Geheimnis* kommen. **III** *v/i mst* ~ **about** (*od.* **around**) herumstöbern (**among** in *dat*; **for** nach).

fer·rous ['ferəs] *adj* eisenhaltig, Eisen...

fer·ry ['ferɪ] **I** *s* **1.** Fähre *f*, Fährschiff *n*, -boot *n.* **2.** Fährdienst *m*, -betrieb *m.* **II** *v/t* **3.** (in e-r Fähre) übersetzen. '~**boat** → **ferry** 1. '~**man** ['~mən] *s* (*irr man*) Fährmann *m.* ~ **ser·vice** → **ferry** *f.*

fer·tile ['fɜːtaɪl] *adj* □ fruchtbar, *fig. a.* produktiv, schöpferisch. **fer·til·i·ty** [fə'tɪlətɪ] *s* Fruchtbarkeit *f*, *fig. a.* Produktivität *f.* **fer·til·i·za·tion** [ˌfɜːtɪlaɪ'zeɪʃn] *s* **1.** Befruchtung *f* (*a. fig.*). **2.** Düngung *f.* **fer·til·ize** *v/t* **1.** befruchten (*a. fig.*). **2.** düngen. '**fer·til·iz·er** *s* (*bsd. Kunst*)Dünger *m.*

fer·vent ['fɜːvənt], **fer·vid** ['~vɪd] *adj* □ glühend, leidenschaftlich (*Haß, Verehrer etc*), inbrünstig (*Gebet, Verlangen etc*). '**fer·vo(u)r** *s* Leidenschaft *f*, Inbrunst *f.*

fes·ter ['festə] *v/i* **1.** eitern. **2.** ~ *in s.o.'s mind* an j-m nagen *od.* fressen.

fes·ti·val ['festəvl] *s* **1.** Fest(tag *m*) *n.* **2.** Festival *n*, Festspiele *pl.* **fes·tive** ['~tɪv] *adj* □ festlich, Fest...: ~ **season** Fest-, *bsd.* Weihnachtszeit *f.* **fes·tiv·i·ty** *s oft pl* Festlichkeit *f.*

fes·toon [fe'stuːn] **I** *s* Girlande *f.* **II** *v/t* mit Girlanden schmücken.

fetch [fetʃ] *v/t* **1.** (herbei)holen, (her)bringen (**go and**) ~ **a doctor** e-n Arzt holen. **2.** *Seufzer etc* ausstoßen. **3.** *Preis etc* erzielen, einbringen. **4.** *f j-m e-n Schlag od. Tritt* versetzen: ~ *s.o. one* j-m e-e langen *od.* kleben. '**fetch·ing** *adj* F bezaubernd: a) reizend, entzückend (*Kleid etc*), b) gewinnend, einnehmend (*Lächeln etc*).

fet·id ['fetɪd] *adj* □ stinkend.

fe·tish ['fetɪʃ] *s* Fetisch *m* (*a. psych.*). '**fe·tish·ism** *s* Fetischismus *m.* '**fe·tish·ist** *s* Fetischist(in).

fet·ter ['fetə] **I** *s* **1.** Fußfessel *f.* **2.** *pl fig.* Fesseln *pl.* **II** *v/t* **3.** *j-m* Fußfesseln anlegen. **4.** *fig.* fesseln.

fet·tle ['fetl] *s*: **in fine** (*od.* **good**) ~ (gut) in Form.

fe·tus ['fiːtəs] *s* # Fötus *m.*

feud [fjuːd] **I** *s* Fehde *f* (*a. fig.*): **be at** ~ (**with**) → **II. II** *v/i* sich befehden, in Fehde liegen (**with** mit) (*beide a. fig.*).

feu·dal ['fjuːdl] *adj* ~ Feudal..., Lehns... **feu·dal·ism** ['~dəlɪzəm] *s* Feudalismus *m*, Feudal-, Lehnssystem *n.*

fe·ver ['fiːvə] *s* # Fieber *n* (*a. fig.*): **have a** ~ Fieber haben; ~ **blister** Fieberbläschen *n*; ~ **heat** Fieberhitze *f*; *fig.* fieberhafte Auf- *od.* Erregung; **be in a** ~ (**of excitement**) in fieberhafter Aufregung sein, vor Aufregung fiebern. '**fe·ver·ish** *adj* □ **1.** # a) fieberkrank: **be** ~ Fieber haben, b) fieb(e)rig, Fieber...: ~ **cold** fiebrige Erkältung. **2.** *fig.* fieberhaft: **be** ~ **with excitement** vor Aufregung fiebern.

few [fjuː] *adj u. pron* **1.** wenige: **some** ~ einige wenige. **2. a** ~ einige, ein paar: **a good** ~, **quite a** ~ ziemlich viele, e-e ganze Menge; **every** ~ **days** alle paar Tage.

fi·an·cé [fɪ'ãːnseɪ] *s* Verlobte *m.* **fi·an·cée** [fɪ'ãːnseɪ] *s* Verlobte *f.*

fi·as·co [fɪ'æskəʊ] *pl* **-cos** *s* Fiasko *n.*

fib [fɪb] **I** *s* Flunkerei *f*, Schwindelei *f.* **II** *v/i* flunkern, schwindeln. '**fib·ber** *s* F Flunkerer *m*, Schwindler *m.*

fi·ber, *bsd. Br.* **fi·bre** ['faɪbə] *s* **1.** *biol.,* ⊚ Faser *f.* **2.** *fig.* Charakter *m*; Kraft *f*: **moral** ~ Charakterstärke *f.* '~**glass** *s* ⊚ Fiberglas *n.*

fib·u·la ['fɪbjʊlə] *s anat.* Wadenbein *n.*

fick·le ['fɪkl] *adj* launenhaft, launisch, unbeständig (*Wetter*), (*Person a.*) wankelmütig.

fic·tion ['fɪkʃn] *s* **1.** (freie) Erfindung, Fiktion *f.* **2.** *coll.* Prosa-, Romanliteratur *f.* **fic·tion·al** ['~ʃənl] *adj* erdichtet, erfunden.

fic·ti·tious [fɪk'tɪʃəs] *adj* □ (frei) erfunden, fiktiv.

fid·dle ['fɪdl] **F I** *s* **1.** ♪ Fiedel *f*, Geige *f*: **play first** (**second**) ~ *fig.* die erste (zweite) Geige spielen; (**as**) **fit as a** ~ kerngesund. **II** *v/i* **2.** a. ~ **away** fiedeln, geigen. **3.** ~ **about** (*od.* **around**) herumtrödeln. **4.** a. ~ **about** (*od.* **around**) (**with**) herumfummeln (an *dat*), spielen (mit). **III** *v/t* **5.** fiedeln. **6.** *Br.* frisieren, manipulieren. '**fid·dler** *s* **1.** Geiger *m.* **2.** *Br.* Schwindler *m*, Betrüger *m.* '**fid·dling** *adj* F läppisch, geringfügig.

fi·del·i·ty [fɪˈdelətɪ] *s* **1.** Treue *f* (*to* gegenüber, zu). **2.** Genauigkeit *f* (*a. e-r Übersetzung*). **3.** ♪ Klangtreue *f*.

fidg·et [ˈfɪdʒɪt] I *s* **1.** *oft pl* nervöse Unruhe, Zappelei *f*: **give s.o. the ~s** → 3; **have the ~s** → 4. **2.** Zappelphilipp *m*. II *v/t* **3.** *j-n* nervös *od.* zapp(e)lig machen. III *v/i* **4.** (herum)zappeln, unruhig *od.* nervös sein. **ˈfidg·et·y** *adj* zapp(e)lig, nervös.

fi·du·ci·ar·y [fɪˈdjuːʃjərɪ] ⚖ I *s* Treuhänder *m*. II *adj* treuhänderisch, Treuhand...

field [fiːld] I *s* **1.** ✗ Feld *n* (*a.* ♞, *phys. etc*): **in the ~** auf dem Feld; **~ of vision** Blick-, Gesichtsfeld; *fig.* Gesichtskreis *m*, Horizont *m*. **2.** *fig.* Bereich *m*, (Fach-, Sach)Gebiet *n*: **in his ~** auf s-m Gebiet, in s-m Fach; **~ of application** Anwendungsbereich. **3.** *Sport:* Spielfeld *n*, -fläche *f*; Feld *n* (*Läufer etc*). II *v/t* **4.** *Sport:* Spieler aufs Feld schicken, bringen; *Kandidaten etc* ins Rennen schicken. **~ day** *s:* **have a ~** riesigen Spaß haben (*with* mit); s-n großen Tag haben. **~ e·vents** *s pl Leichtathletik:* Sprung- u. Wurfdisziplinen *pl.* **~ glass·es** *s pl, a.* **pair of ~** Feldstecher *m.* **~ hock·ey** *s Sport:* bsd. *Am.* (Feld)Hockey *n.* **~ mar·shal** *s* ✗ Feldmarschall *m.* **ˈ~work** *s* **1.** praktische (wissenschaftliche) Arbeit, (*Archäologie etc a.*) Arbeit *f* im Gelände. **2.** *Markt-, Meinungsforschung:* Feldarbeit *f.* **~ work·er** *s Markt-, Meinungsforschung:* Befrager(in), Interviewer(in).

fiend [fiːnd] *s* **1.** Satan *m*, Teufel *m*, *fig. a.* Unhold *m.* **2.** F (*Frischluft- etc*)Fanatiker *m.* **ˈfiend·ish** *adj* □ **1.** teuflisch, unmenschlich. **2.** F verteufelt, höllisch.

fierce [fɪəs] *adj* □ **1.** wild (*Tier etc*). **2.** böse, grimmig (*Gesicht etc*), wild (*Blick, Haß etc*). **3.** scharf (*Rede, Wettbewerb etc*); heftig (*Angriff, Schmerz etc*). **ˈfierce·ness** *s* **1.** Wildheit *f.* **2.** Schärfe *f*; Heftigkeit *f.*

fi·er·y [ˈfaɪərɪ] *adj* □ **1.** brennend, glühend. **2.** feurig, hitzig (*Person, Temperament*). **3.** feurig, scharf (*Gewürz etc*). **4.** leidenschaftlich (*Rede, Affäre etc*).

fif·teen [ˌfɪfˈtiːn] *adj* fünfzehn. **ˌfif·teenth** [-θ] *adj* fünfzehnt. **fifth** [fɪfθ] I *adj* **1.** fünft: **~ column** *pol.* Fünfte Kolonne; **~**

wheel *fig.* fünftes Rad am Wagen. II *s* **2.** *der, die, das* Fünfte: **the ~ of May** der 5. Mai. **3.** Fünftel *n.* **ˈfifth·ly** *adv* fünftens. **fif·ti·eth** [ˈ~ɪəθ] *adj* fünfzigst.

fif·ty [ˈfɪftɪ] I *adj* fünfzig. II *s* Fünfzig *f*: **be in one's fifties** in den Fünfzigern sein; **in the fifties** in den fünfziger Jahren (*e-s Jahrhunderts*). **ˌ~·ˈfif·ty** *adj u. adv* F fifty-fifty: **go ~ (with)** halbe-halbe machen (mit).

fig [fɪg] *s* ♠ Feige *f*: **I don't care a ~** F das ist mir völlig egal.

fight [faɪt] I *s* **1.** Kampf *m* (*for* um; **against** gegen) (*a. fig.*): **put up a good ~** sich tapfer schlagen. **2.** a) *Boxen:* Kampf *m*, b) *Rauferei f*, Schlägerei *f*: **have a ~ (with)** → 7. **3.** Kampf(es)lust *f*: **show ~** sich zur Wehr setzen. II *v/t* (*irr*) **4.** *j-n, et.* bekämpfen. **5.** kämpfen gegen *od.* mit: **~ back** (*od.* **down**) *Enttäuschung, Tränen etc* unterdrücken; **~ off** *j-n, et.* abwehren. III *v/i* (*irr*) **6.** kämpfen (*for* um; **against** gegen): **~ back** sich zur Wehr setzen *od.* wehren, zurückschlagen; → **shy** 2. **7.** sich raufen *od.* schlagen (*with* mit), prügeln (*with* mit). **ˈfight·er** *s* **1.** Kämpfer *m.* **2.** *Sport:* Boxer *m.* **3.** Schläger *m*, Raufbold *m.* **4.** *a.* **~ plane** ✈, ✗ Jagdflugzeug *n.* **ˈfight·ing** I *s* Kampf *m*, Kämpfe *pl.* II *adj* Kampf...: **~ chance** reelle Chance (*wenn man sich anstrengt*); **~ spirit** Kampfgeist *m.*

fig·ment [ˈfɪgmənt] *s oft* **~ of the imagination** reine Erfindung.

fig tree *s* Feigenbaum *m.*

fig·u·ra·tive [ˈfɪgərətɪv] *adj* □ bildlich, übertragen.

fig·ure [ˈfɪgə] I *s* **1.** Zahl *f*, Ziffer *f*: **run into three ~s** in die Hunderte gehen; **five-~ income** fünfstelliges Einkommen. **2.** Summe *f*, Preis *m*: **at a high (low) ~** teuer (billig). **3.** Figur *f* (*a. Sport etc*), Gestalt *f.* **4.** *fig.* Figur *f*, Persönlichkeit *f*: **~ of fun** komische Figur, *contp.* Witzfigur; **cut** (*od.* **make**) **a poor ~** e-e traurige Figur abgeben. **5.** *a.* **~ of speech** (Rede-, Sprach)Figur *f.* II *v/t* **6.** *oft* **~ to o.s.** sich *et.* vorstellen *od.* ausmalen. **7.** *a.* **~ out** F ausrechnen; ausknobeln, rauskriegen; kapieren. **8.** *Am.* F meinen, glauben. III *v/i* **9.** erscheinen, auftauchen, vorkommen. **10.** *~ on* bsd. *Am.* F rechnen mit; sich verlassen auf (*acc*). '**~head** *s* ⚓ Galionsfigur *f*, *fig. a.* Aushängeschild *n*. **~ skat·ing** *s* Sport: Eiskunstlauf *m*.

filch [fɪltʃ] *v/t* klauen, stibitzen.

file¹ [faɪl] **I** *s* **1.** (Akten- *etc*)Ordner *m*. **2.** a) Akte *f*: *keep (od. have) a ~ on* e-e Akte führen über (*acc*); **~ number** Aktenzeichen *n*, b) Akten *pl*, Ablage *f*: *on ~* bei den Akten. **3.** Reihe *f*: → *Indian file, single file*. **II** *v/t* **4.** *a. ~ away* Briefe *etc* ablegen, zu den Akten nehmen. **5.** *Antrag etc* einreichen, *Forderung* anmelden.

file² [~] **I** *s* **1.** ⚙ Feile *f*. **II** *v/t* **2.** (zu)feilen, *sich die Nägel* feilen: *~ away (od. down)* abfeilen. **3.** *fig. Stil etc* (zurecht)feilen.

fil·i·al [ˈfɪljəl] *adj* Kindes...

fil·i·bus·ter [ˈfɪlɪbʌstə] *parl. bsd. Am.* **I** *s* Obstruktion *f*; Obstruktionspolitiker *m*. **II** *v/i* Obstruktion treiben.

fil·i·gree [ˈfɪlɪɡriː] *s* Filigran(arbeit *f*) *n*.

fil·ing cab·i·net [ˈfaɪlɪŋ] *s* Aktenschrank *m*.

fil·ings [ˈfaɪlɪŋz] *s pl* Feilspäne *pl*.

fill [fɪl] **I** *s* **1.** *eat one's ~* sich satt essen; *have had one's ~ of* von *et.*, *j-m* genug haben, *et.*, *j-n* satt haben. **2.** Füllung *f*. **II** *v/t* **3.** (an-, aus-, voll)füllen; *Pfeife* stopfen; *Zahn* füllen, plombieren. **4.** erfüllen (*with* mit) (*a. fig.*): *~ed with envy* neiderfüllt. **5.** *Posten*, *Amt* besetzen; ausfüllen, bekleiden: *~ s.o.'s place* j-s Stelle einnehmen, j-n ersetzen. **6.** *Auftrag, Bestellung* ausführen; *Rezept* ausfertigen. **III** *v/i* **7.** sich füllen. *Verbindungen mit Adverbien:*

fill| **in I** *v/t* **1.** *Loch* auf-, ausfüllen. **2.** *Br. Formulare etc* ausfüllen. **3.** *Namen etc* einsetzen; *Fehlendes* ergänzen. **4.** *F j-n* informieren (*on* über *acc*). **II** *v/i* **5.** einspringen (*for* für). **~ out** *v/t* **1.** *bsd. Am.* → *fill in* 1, 2. **2.** *Bericht etc* abrunden. **II** *v/i* **3.** fülliger werden (*Figur*), (*Person a.*) zunehmen, (*Gesicht etc*) runder *od.* voller werden. **~ up** *v/t* **1.** vollfüllen. **2.** → *fill in* 1, 2. **II** *v/i* **3.** → *fill* 7.

fill·er [ˈfɪlə] *s* **1.** Trichter *m*. **2.** Zeitungswesen *etc*: Füller *m*, Füllsel *n*. **3.** *ling.* Füllwort *n*.

fil·let [ˈfɪlɪt] *s gastr.* Filet *n*. **~ steak** *s* Filetsteak *n*.

fill·ing [ˈfɪlɪŋ] **I** *s* **1.** Füllung *f*, Füllmasse *f*. **2.** *Zahnmedizin:* Füllung *f*, Plombe *f*.

II *adj* **3.** sättigend. **~ sta·tion** *s* Tankstelle *f*.

fil·lip [ˈfɪlɪp] *s* **1.** Schnalzer *m*, Schnipser *m* (*mit den Fingern*). **2.** *fig.* Ansporn *m*, Auftrieb *m*.

film [fɪlm] **I** *s* **1.** Film *m* (*a. phot.*). **2.** (hauch)dünne Schicht, Film *m*; (Plastik)Folie *f*. **II** *adj* **3.** Film... **III** *v/t* **4.** *Roman etc* verfilmen; *Szene etc* filmen.

fil·ter [ˈfɪltə] **I** *s* **1.** Filter *m*, ⊙ *etc mst n*. **II** *v/t* **2.** filtern. **III** *v/i* **3.** durchsickern (*through* durch). **4.** **~ out** grüppchenweise *od.* e-r nach dem anderen herauskommen (*of* aus). **5.** **~ out** (*od. through*) *fig.* durchsickern (*Nachricht etc*). **6.** *mot.* die Spur wechseln; sich einordnen (*to the- left* links). **~ tip** *s* **1.** Filter *m*. **2.** Filterzigarette *f*. '**~-tipped** *adj* Filter... : **~ cigarette.**

filth [fɪlθ] *s* **1.** Schmutz *m* (*a. fig.*), Dreck *m*. **2.** unflätige Sprache *od.* Ausdrücke *pl*. '**filth·y** *adj* □ **1.** schmutzig (*a. fig.*), dreckig. **2.** *fig.* unflätig. **3.** *bsd. Br.* F ekelhaft, scheußlich: **~ weather** Sauwetter *n*.

fin [fɪn] *s* **1.** *ichth.* Flosse *f*. **2.** Schwimmflosse *f*.

fi·nal [ˈfaɪnl] **I** *adj* (□ → *finally*) **1.** letzt; End..., Schluß...: **~ examination** (Ab-)Schlußprüfung *f*; **~ whistle** (Sport) Schluß-, Abpfiff *m*. **2.** endgültig. **II** *s* **3.** Sport: Finale *n*. **4.** *mst pl bsd. univ.* (Ab)Schlußexamen *n*, -prüfung *f*. **5.** F Spätausgabe *f* (e-r *Zeitung*). **fi·na·le** [fɪˈnɑːlɪ] *s ♪, thea.* Finale *n*. **fi·nal·ist** [ˈfaɪnəlɪst] *s* Sport: Finalist(in). **fi·nal·i·ty** [~ˈnælətɪ] *s* **1.** Endgültigkeit *f*. **2.** Entschiedenheit *f*. **fi·nal·ize** [ˈfaɪnəlaɪz] *v/t* **1.** be-, vollenden, abschließen. **2.** endgültige Form geben (*dat*). '**fi·nal·ly** *adv* **1.** endlich, schließlich, zuletzt. **2.** zum (Ab)Schluß. **3.** endgültig.

fi·nance [faɪˈnæns] **I** *s* **1.** Finanz(wesen *n*) *f*: **~ company** Finanzierungsgesellschaft *f*. **2.** *pl* Finanzen *pl*. **II** *v/t* **3.** finanzieren. **fi·nan·cial** [~ʃl] *adj* □ finanziell, Finanz..., Geld...: **~ year** *Br.* Geschäftsjahr *n*. **fi·nan·cier** [~sɪə] *s* Finanzier *m*.

finch [fɪntʃ] *s orn.* Fink *m*.

find [faɪnd] **I** *s* Fund *m*. **II** *v/t* (*irr*) **1.** *allg.* finden. **2.** bemerken, feststellen, (heraus)finden. **4.** ⚖ für *schuldig* erklären *od.* befinden. **5.** **~ out** *et.* heraus-

finden; *j-n* ertappen; *j-n, et.* durchschauen. **III** *v/i* (*irr*) **6.** ~ **out** es herausfinden. **7.** ~ **against** (**for**) **the defendant**
⚖ den Angeklagten verurteilen (frei-
sprechen). **'find·er** *s* Finder(in): ~**'s re-**
ward Finderlohn *m.* **'find·ing** *s* **1.** *mst*
pl Befund *m* (*a.* ♣). **2.** ⚖ Feststellung *f*
(*des Gerichts*), (*der Geschworenen a.*)
Spruch *m.*

fine¹ [faın] **I** *adj* □ **1.** *allg.* fein: ~ **arts** *pl*
die schönen Künste *pl;* **one** ~ **day** e-s
schönen Tages. **2.** großartig, ausgezeichnet. **3.** F fein, schön: **that's all**
very ~ **but** das ist ja alles gut u. schön,
aber. **II** *adv* **4.** F sehr gut, bestens: **that**
will suit me ~ das paßt mir ausgezeichnet.

fine² [~] **I** *s* Geldstrafe *f,* Bußgeld *n.* **II** *v/t*
mit e-r Geldstrafe belegen, zu e-r Geld-
strafe verurteilen: **he was** ~**d £ 50** er
mußte 50 Pfund Strafe bezahlen, er
wurde zu e-r Geldstrafe von 50 Pfund
verurteilt.

fine·ness *s allg.* Feinheit *f.*
fi·nesse [fı'nes] *s* **1.** Finesse *f.* **2.** Raffinesse *f,* Schlauheit *f.*
fin·ger ['fıŋgə] **I** *s* Finger *m:* **first** (**sec-**
ond, third) ~ Zeige- (Mittel-, Ring)fin-
ger; **fourth** (*od.* **little**) ~ kleiner Finger;
have a (*od.* **one's**) ~ **in the pie** die
Hand im Spiel haben; **keep one's** ~**s**
crossed for s.o. *j-m* die Daumen drük-
ken *od.* halten; **not to lift** (*od.* **raise,**
stir) **a** ~ keinen Finger rühren; → **burn**
7, **twist** 2. **II** *v/t* betasten, befühlen;
herumfingern an (*dat*), spielen mit. **III**
v/i herumfingern (**at** an *dat*), spielen
(**with** mit). ~ **al·pha·bet** *s* Fingeralpha-
bet *n.* '**~·mark** *s* Fingerabdruck *m*
(*Schmutzfleck*). '**~·nail** *s* Fingernagel
m. '**~·print I** *s* Fingerabdruck *m:* **take**
s.o.'s ~**s** → **II.** **II** *v/t* *j-m* Fingerabdrük-
ke abnehmen, von *j-m* Fingerabdrücke
abnehmen, von *j-m* Fingerabdrücke
machen. '**~·tip** *s* Fingerspitze *f:* **have at**
one's ~**s** *Kenntnisse* parat haben; *et.*
aus dem Effeff beherrschen.

fin·ick·y ['fınıkı] *adj* **1.** pedantisch. **2.**
wählerisch (**about** in *dat*). **3.** geziert,
affektiert.

fin·ish ['fınıʃ] **I** *v/t* **1.** beenden, aufhören
mit: ~ **reading** aufhören zu lesen. **2.** *a.*
~ **off** vollenden, zu Ende führen, erledigen, *Buch etc* auslesen. **3.** *a.* ~ **off** (*od.*

up) *Vorräte* aufbrauchen; aufessen,
austrinken. **4.** *a.* ~ **off** *j-n* erledigen, fertigmachen. **5.** *a.* ~ **off** (*od.* **up**) vervollkommnen, den letzten Schliff geben
(*dat*). **II** *v/i* **6.** *a.* ~ **off** (*od.* **up**) enden,
aufhören (**with** mit): **have you** ~**ed?**
bist du fertig? **7.** enden, zu Ende gehen.
8. ~ **with** mit *j-m, et.* Schluß machen, *et.*
aufgeben: **I am** ~**ed with him** ich bin
mit ihm fertig. **9.** ~ **third** (*Sport*) Dritter
werden; *allg.* als dritter fertig sein. **III** *s*
10. Ende *n,* Schluß *m.* **11.** *Sport:* Endspurt *m,* Finish *n;* Ziel *n.* **12.** Vollendung *f;* letzter Schliff. **'fin·ished** *adj* **1.**
beendet, fertig: ~ **goods** (*od.* **products**)
pl Fertigwaren *pl.* **2.** *fig.* vollendet,
vollkommen. **'fin·ish·ing** *adj* abschließend: ~ **line** (*Sport*) Ziellinie *f;* →
touch 4.

fink [fıŋk] *s bsd. Am. sl.* **1.** Streikbrecher
m. **2.** Spitzel *m.*

Finn [fın] *s* Finne *m,* Finnin *f.* **'Finn·ish I**
adj finnisch. **II** *s ling.* Finnisch *n.*

fiord [fjɔːd] *s geogr.* Fjord *m.*

fir [fɜː] *s* ♣ Tanne *f;* Fichte *f.* ~ **cone** *s*
Tannenzapfen *m.*

fire [faıə] **I** *s* **1.** Feuer *n* (*a.* ✕ *u. fig.*),
Brand *m:* **be on** ~ in Flammen stehen,
brennen; **come under** ~ unter Beschuß
geraten (*a. fig.*); **catch** (*od.* **take**) ~
Feuer fangen, in Brand geraten; **play**
with ~ *fig.* mit dem Feuer spielen; **set**
on ~, **set** ~ **to** → 2; → **chestnut** 1,
Thames. **II** *v/t* **2.** anzünden, in Brand
stecken. **3.** *Kessel* heizen, *Ofen* (be)feu-
ern, beheizen. **4.** *j-n, j-s Gefühle* entflammen, *j-s Phantasie* beflügeln. **5.** *a.*
~ **off** *Schußwaffe* abfeuern, abschießen;
Schuß (ab)feuern, abgeben (**at,** on *auf*
acc). **6.** F feuern, rausschmeißen. **III** *v/i*
7. feuern, schießen (**at** auf *acc*). **8.** zünden (*Motor*). ~ **a·larm** *s* **1.** Feueralarm
m. **2.** Feuermelder *m.* '**~·arm** *s* Feuer-,
Schußwaffe *f.* '**~·ball** *s* Feuerball *m.* ~
bri·gade *s Br.* Feuerwehr *f.* '**~·bug** *s*
Feuerteufel *m.* ~ **de·part·ment** *s Am.*
Feuerwehr *f.* '**~·eat·er** *s* **1.** Feuer-
schlucker *m,* -fresser *m.* **2.** *fig.* aggressi-
ver Mensch. ~ **en·gine** *s* Löschfahr-
zeug *n.* ~ **es·cape** *s* **1.** Feuerleiter *f,*
-treppe *f.* **2.** *Br.* Feuerwehrleiter *f.* ~
ex·tin·guish·er *s* Feuerlöscher *m.* ~
fight·er *s* Feuerwehrmann *m.* ~ **house**
s Am. Feuerwache *f.* ~ **hy·drant** *s Br.*

Hydrant *m*. **~man** [*'~mæn*] *s* (*irr* **man**)
1. Feuerwehrmann *m, pl a.* Löschtrupp
m. **2.** Heizer *m*. **'~place** *s* (offener)
Kamin. **'~plug** *s Am.* Hydrant *m*. **~**
pre·ven·tion *s* Brandverhütung *f*.
'~proof *adj* feuerfest, -sicher. **~ rais·er**
s Br. Brandstifter(in). **~ rais·ing** *s Br.*
Brandstiftung *f*. **~ ser·vice** *s Br.* Feuerwehr *f*. **'~side** *s* **1.** (offener) Kamin: **by**
the ~ am Kamin. **2.** *fig.* häuslicher
Herd, Daheim *n*. **~ sta·tion** *s* Feuerwache *f*. **'~wa·ter** *s F* Feuerwasser *n*.
'~wood *s* Brennholz *n*. **'~work** *s* **1.**
Feuerwerkskörper *m*. **2.** *pl* Feuerwerk
n (*a. fig.: a. sg* konstruiert).

fir·ing [*'faɪərɪŋ*] *s* **1.** Heizen *n*. **2.**
(Ab)Feuern *n*, (Ab)Schießen *n*. **~ line** *s*
✕ Feuer-, Frontlinie *f*: **be in** (*Am.* **on**)
the ~ *fig.* an vorderster Front stehen; in
der Schußlinie stehen. **~ par·ty,** **~**
squad *s* Exekutionskommando *n*.

firm[1] [fɜːm] **I** *adj* (□ → **firstly**) **1.** fest: a) hart, *gastr.*
steif, b) standhaft, c) sicher (*Beweise*
etc), d) *bsd.* ✝, ⚖ bindend. **II** *adv*:
stand ~ *fig.* festbleiben, hart bleiben.

firm[2] [~] *s* Firma *f*.

fir·ma·ment [*'fɜːməmənt*] *s* Firmament *n*.

firm·ness [*'fɜːmnɪs*] *s* Festigkeit *f*.

first [fɜːst] **I** *adj* (□ → **firstly**) **1.** erst: **at ~**
hand zu erster Hand; → **offender,**
place 6, **sight** 3, **thing**, **view** 1. **2.**
erst, best: → **fiddle** 1. **II** *adv* **3.** zuerst:
go ~ vorangehen. **4.** (zu)erst (einmal).
5. als erst(er, e, es), an erster Stelle:
~ come, ~ served wer zuerst kommt,
mahlt zuerst; **~ of all** vor allen Dingen,
zu allererst. **III** *s* **6.** der, die, das Erste
od. (*fig.*) Beste: **the ~ of May** der 1. Mai;
at ~ (zu)erst, anfangs; **from the** (*very*) **~**
von (allem) Anfang an. **7.** *mot.* erster
Gang. **~ aid** *s* Erste Hilfe: **give** (*od.*
render) **s.o. ~** j-m Erste Hilfe leisten.
,~'aid *adj*: **~ box** (*od.* **kit**) Ver-
band(s)kasten *m*; **~ post** (*od.* **station**)
Unfallstation *f*. **,~'born** *adj* erstgeboren. **~'class I** *adj* **1.** erstklassig, -ran-
gig. **2.** 🚂 *etc* erster Klasse. **II** *adv* **3.** 🚂
etc erste(r) Klasse. **'~day cov·er** *s*
Philatelie: Ersttagsbrief *m*. **,~de'gree**
adj Verbrennungen ersten Grades. **,~-**
'hand *adj u. adv* aus erster Hand.

first·ly [*'fɜːstlɪ*] *adv* erstens.

first name *s* Vorname *m*: **what is his ~?**

wie heißt er mit Vornamen? **~ night** *s*
Premiere *f*, Uraufführung *f*. **,~'rate** →
first-class 1. **'~time** *adj*: **~ voter** Erst-
wähler(in).

firth [fɜːθ] *s* Meeresarm *m*, Förde *f*.

fis·cal [*'fɪskl*] *adj* □ fiskalisch, Finanz...:
~ year *Am.* Geschäftsjahr *n*.

fish [fɪʃ] **I** *pl* **fish,** (*bsd. Fischarten*)
'fish·es *s* **1.** Fisch *m*: **drink like a ~** F
saufen wie ein Loch; **have other ~ to**
fry F Wichtigeres zu tun haben; **queer**
~ F komischer Kauz; → **kettle. 2.** **♋**es *pl*
ast. Fische *pl*. **II** *v/t* **3.** fischen, angeln.
4. *fig.* fischen (*from, out of* aus): **~ out**
herausholen. **III** *v/i* **5.** fischen (*a. fig.:*
for nach), angeln: → **trouble** 4. **~ and**
chips *s Br.* paniertes Fischfilet mit
Pommes frites. **~ ball** *s gastr.* Fischfri-
kadelle *f*. **'~bone** *s* Gräte *f*. **~ cake** *s*
fish ball.

fish·er·man [*'fɪʃəmən*] *s* (*irr* **man**) Fischer *m*, Angler *m*.

fish·er·y [*'fɪʃərɪ*] *s* **1.** Fischerei *f*, Fisch-
fang *m*. **2.** Fischgründe *pl*, Fanggebiet *n*.

fish fin·ger *s gastr. Br.* Fischstäbchen *n*.
'~hook *s* Angelhaken *m*.

fish·ing [*'fɪʃɪŋ*] *s* **1.** Fischen *n*, Angeln *n*.
2. → **fishery** 1. **~ boat** *s* Fischerboot *n*.
~ grounds *s pl* → **fishery** 2. **~ line** *s*
Angelschnur *f*. **~ net** *s* Fisch(er)netz *n*.
~ rod *s* Angelrute *f*. **~ tack·le** *s* Angel-
gerät(e *pl*) *n*. **~ vil·lage** *s* Fischerdorf *n*.

'fish mon·ger *s bsd. Br.* Fischhänd-
ler(in). **~ stick** *Am.* → **fish finger**.

fis·sile [*'fɪsaɪl*] *adj* spaltbar. **fis·sion**
[*'fɪʃn*] *s* **1.** Spaltung *f* (*a. fig.*). **2.** *biol.*
(Zell)Teilung *f*. **fis·sure** [*'fɪʃə*] *s* Spalt(e
f) *m*, Riß *m* (*a. fig.*), Ritz(e *f*) *m*.

fist [fɪst] *s* Faust *f*.

fis·tu·la [*'fɪstjʊlə*] *pl* **-las, -lae** [*'~liː*] *s* 🩺
Fistel *f*.

fit[1] [fɪt] **I** *adj* □ **1.** passend, geeignet;
fähig, tauglich: **~ for service** *bsd.* ✕
dienstfähig, (-)tauglich; **~ to drink**
trinkbar; **~ to eat** eß-, genießbar; **~ to**
drive fahrtüchtig; → **consumption** 2,
drop 10a. **2.** angemessen, angebracht:
see (*od.* **think**) **~** es für richtig *od.* angebracht halten (**to do** zu tun). **3.** schicklich, geziemend. **4.** fit, (gut) in Form:
keep ~ sich fit halten; → **fiddle** 1. **II** *s* **5.**
Paßform *f*, Sitz *m*: **be a perfect ~** genau
passen, tadellos sitzen; **be a tight ~** sehr

für). '**flat·ter·y** s Schmeichelei(en pl) f:
→ **obtain** I.

flat·u·lence ['flætjʊləns] s ✷ Blähung(en
pl) f: **cause** (od. **produce**) ~ blähen.

flaunt [flɔːnt] v/t zur Schau stellen, protzen mit.

flau·tist ['flɔːtɪst] s ♪ Flötist(in).

fla·vo(u)r ['fleɪvə] I s 1. Geschmack m,
Aroma n. 2. fig. Beigeschmack m. II v/t
3. würzen (a. fig.). '**fla·vo(u)r·ing** s
Würze f, Aroma n (beide a. fig.).

flaw [flɔː] s 1. (⊙ Material-, ☆ Form-)
Fehler m, ⊙ a. Defekt m. 2. fig. schwache Stelle. '**flaw·less** adj □ einwandfrei, tadellos.

flax [flæks] s ✿ Flachs m. '**flax·en** adj 1.
Flachs... 2. flachsen, flachsfarben.

flay [fleɪ] v/t Tier abhäuten: ~ s.o. alive F
kein gutes Haar an j-m lassen, j-m gehörig v-e Meinung sagen.

flea [fliː] s zo. Floh m: **send s.o. away
with a ~ in his ear** F j-m heimleuchten.
'~**bite** s 1. Flohbiß m. 2. fig. Bagatelle
f. ~ **cir·cus** s Flohzirkus m. ~ **mar·ket** s
Flohmarkt m.

fled [fled] pret u. pp von **flee**.

fledged [fledʒd] adj flügge. **fledg(e)·ling**
['~lɪŋ] s 1. eben flügge gewordener Vogel. 2. fig. Grünschnabel m.

flee [fliː] v/i (irr) I v/i fliehen, flüchten (from
vor dat; aus). II v/t fliehen vor (dat) od.
aus.

fleece [fliːs] I s 1. Vlies n, bsd. Schaffell
n. II v/t 2. Schaf etc scheren. 3. F j-n
schröpfen (of um), ausnehmen.

fleet[1] [fliːt] s 1. ⚓ Flotte f. 2. ~ **of cars**
Wagenpark m.

fleet[2] [~] adj □ schnell, flink.

fleet·ing ['fliːtɪŋ] adj □ flüchtig, vergänglich.

Fleet Street s das Londoner Pressevier-
tel; fig. die (Londoner) Presse.

flesh [fleʃ] s 1. Fleisch n: **put on** ~ zunehmen; **lose** ~ abmagern, abnehmen; →
creep 3. 2. Körper m, Leib m: **my own
~ and blood** mein eigen Fleisch u. Blut;
in the ~ leibhaftig, höchstpersönlich; in
natura, in Wirklichkeit. 3. (Frucht-)
Fleisch n. '~**col·o(u)red** adj fleischfarben. '~**eat·ing** adj ✿, zo. fleischfressend. ~ **wound** s ✷ Fleischwunde f.

flew [fluː] pret von **fly**[1].

flex [fleks] I v/t bsd. anat. biegen, beugen.
II s ⚡ bsd. Br. (Anschluß-, Verlänge-

rungs)Kabel n, (-)Schnur f. '**flex·i·
ble** adj □ flexibel: a) elastisch, b) fig.
anpassungsfähig, beweglich.

flex·i·time ['fleksɪtaɪm] s Br. gleitende
Arbeitszeit: **be on** ~ gleitende Arbeitszeit haben.

flick [flɪk] I s 1. Klaps m. 2. Knall m,
Schnalzer m. 3. Schnipser m. II v/t 4.
j-m e-n Klaps geben. 5. schnalzen mit
(Fingern), (mit Peitsche a.) knallen mit.
6. schnippen, schnipsen: ~ away (od.
off) wegschnippen.

flick·er ['flɪkə] I s 1. Flackern n. 2. TV
Flimmern n. II v/i 3. flackern. 4. flimmern (Fernsehbild).

flick knife s (irr knife) Br. Schnappmesser n.

flight[1] [flaɪt] s 1. (a. Gedanken- etc)Flug
m: **in** ~ im Flug. 2. Schwarm m (Vögel):
in the first ~ fig. in vorderster Front. 3.
a. ~ **of stairs** Treppe f.

flight[2] [~] s Flucht f: **in his** ~ auf s-r
Flucht; **put to** ~ in die Flucht schlagen;
take (to) ~ die Flucht ergreifen; ~ **of
capital** ✝ Kapitalflucht.

flight| en·gi·neer s Bordingenieur m.
~ **re·cord·er** s Flug(daten)schreiber
m.

flight·y ['flaɪtɪ] adj □ flatterhaft.

flim·sy ['flɪmzɪ] I adj □ 1. dünn, zart. 2.
fig. fadenscheinig (Ausrede). II s
Durchschlagpapier n.

flinch [flɪntʃ] v/i 1. zurückschrecken
(from, at vor dat). 2. (zurück)zucken,
zs.-fahren: **without** ~**ing** ohne mit den
Wimper zu zucken.

fling [flɪŋ] I s 1. Wurf m: (at) **full** ~ mit
voller Wucht. 2. **have one's** (od. **a**) ~
sich austoben. 3. F Versuch m: **have**
(od. **take**) **a** ~ **at** es versuchen od. probieren mit. II v/t (irr) 4. werfen, schleudern (at nach): ~ **open** (to) Tür etc
aufreißen (zuschlagen); ~ **away** wegwerfen; ~ **o.s.** sich stürzen (at s.o. auf
j-n; **into s.th.** in od. auf e-e Sache).

flint [flɪnt] s Feuerstein m.

flip [flɪp] I v/t 1. → **flick** 6. 2. a. ~ **over**
Pfannkuchen, Schallplatte etc wenden,
umdrehen. II v/i 3. a. ~ **out** bsd. Am. sl.
ausflippen, durchdrehen (for, over
bei). III s/t 4. Schnipser m. 5. Flip m
(Getränk). '~**flop** s Zehensandale f.

flip·pant ['flɪpənt] adj □ respektlos,
schnodd(e)rig.

flip·per ['flɪpə] s **1.** zo. Flosse f. **2.** Schwimmflosse f.

flip side s B-Seite f (e-r Single).

flirt [flɜːt] **I** v/i flirten, fig. a. spielen, liebäugeln (with mit). **II** s: be a ~ gern flirten. **flir'ta·tion** s Flirt m, fig. a. Spielen n, Liebäugeln n. **flir'ta·tious** adj □ kokett.

flit [flɪt] v/i flitzen, huschen.

float [fləʊt] **I** v/i **1.** (auf dem Wasser) schwimmen, (im Wasser) treiben. **2.** ♻ flott sein od. werden. **3.** schweben, ziehen. **4.** a. ♈ in Umlauf sein. **II** v/t **5.** schwimmen od. treiben lassen. **6.** ♻ flottmachen. **7.** ♈ Wertpapiere etc in Umlauf bringen; Anleihe auflegen; Gesellschaft gründen. **8.** ♈ Währung floaten, den Wechselkurs (gen) freigeben. **9.** Gerücht etc in Umlauf setzen. **III** s **10.** flacher Plattformwagen, bsd. Festwagen m. '**float·er** s pol. Wechselwähler(in). '**float·ing I** adj **1.** treibend, schwimmend: ~ **ice** Treibeis n. **2.** ♈ umlaufend (Geld etc); frei konvertierbar (Währung). **3.** ~ **voter** → **floater**.

flock [flɒk] **I** s **1.** Herde f (bsd. Schafe od. Ziegen), Schwarm m (Vögel). **2.** Menge f, Haufen m: come in ~s in (hellen) Scharen herbeiströmen. **3.** eccl. Herde f, Gemeinde f. **II** v/i **4.** fig. strömen: ~ **together** zs.-strömen.

floe [fləʊ] s **1.** Treibeis n. **2.** Eisscholle f.

flog [flɒg] v/t **1.** prügeln, schlagen: ~ a **dead horse** fig. offene Türen einrennen; s-e Zeit verschwenden. **2.** auspeitschen. **3.** Br. F verkloppen, -scheuern. '**flog·ging** s **1.** Tracht f Prügel. **2.** ⚖ Prügelstrafe f.

flood [flʌd] **I** s **1.** a. ~ **tide** Flut f. **2.** Überschwemmung f (a. fig.), Hochwasser n. **3.** fig. Flut f, Strom m, Schwall m: ~ **of tears** Tränenstrom m. **II** v/t **4.** überschwemmen, -fluten (beide a. fig. mit). **5.** unter Wasser setzen. **6.** Fluß etc anschwellen od. über die Ufer treten lassen. **III** v/i **7.** fluten, strömen, sich ergießen (alle a. fig.). **8.** anschwellen; über die Ufer treten. '~·light **I** s Scheinwerfer-, Flutlicht n: by ~ unter Flutlicht. **II** v/t (irr light¹) (mit Scheinwerfern) beleuchten od. anstrahlen: **floodlit match** (Sport) Flutlichtspiel n.

floor [flɔː] **I** s **1.** (Fuß)Boden m: → **wipe** **II**. **2.** Tanzfläche f: take the ~ auf die

Tanzfläche gehen. **3.** Stock(werk n) m, Geschoß n. **4.** parl. Sitzungs-, Plenarsaal m: take the ~ das Wort ergreifen. **II** v/t **5.** e-n (Fuß)Boden legen in (dat). **6.** zu Boden schlagen (Boxen a.) auf die Bretter schicken. **7.** F a) j-n umhauen, j-m die Sprache verschlagen, b) j-n schaffen (Problem etc). '~·board s Diele f. ~ **ex·er·cis·es** s pl Sport: Bodenturnen n. '**floor·ing** ['flɔːrɪŋ] s (Fuß)Bodenbelag m. **floor| lamp** s Stehlampe f. ~ **lead·er** s parl. Am. Fraktionsführer m. ~ **show** s Varietévorstellung f (in Nachtclub etc). ~ **wait·er** s Etagenkellner m. ~ **vase** s Bodenvase f.

floo·zy ['fluːzɪ] s sl. Flittchen n.

flop [flɒp] **I** v/i **1.** plumpsen; sich plumpsen lassen (into in acc). **2.** F durchfallen (Prüfling, Theaterstück etc), allg. e-e Pleite od. ein Reinfall sein. **II** s **3.** Plumps m. **4.** F a) thea. etc Flop m, Durchfall m, b) Reinfall m, Pleite f, c) Versager m. '**flop·py** adj □ **1.** schlaff, schlott(e)rig. **2.** ~ **disk** (Computer) Diskette f.

flo·ra ['flɔːrə] pl -ras, -rae ['-riː] s ♣ Flora f, Pflanzenwelt f. '**flo·ral** adj Blumen..., Blüten...: ~ **pattern** Blumenmuster n.

flor·id ['flɒrɪd] adj □ **1.** blühend (Gesichtsfarbe, Gesundheit). **2.** blumig (Stil).

flo·rist ['flɒrɪst] s **1.** Blumenhändler(in). **2.** Blumenzüchter(in).

flot·sam ['flɒtsəm] s a. ~ **and jetsam** ♻ Treibgut n: ~ **and jetsam** Strandgut n (a. fig.), Wrackgut n.

flounce [flaʊns] v/i erregt stürmen od. stürzen.

floun·der¹ ['flaʊndə] s ichth. Flunder f.

floun·der² [~] v/i **1.** zappeln; strampeln. **2.** fig. sich verhaspeln, ins Schwimmen kommen.

flour ['flaʊə] **I** s Mehl n. **II** v/t mit Mehl bestreuen.

flour·ish ['flʌrɪʃ] **I** v/i **1.** gedeihen, fig. a. blühen, florieren. **2.** auf der Höhe s-r Macht od. s-s Ruhms stehen; s-e Blütezeit haben. **II** v/t **3.** Fahne etc schwenken. **III** s **4.** ♪ Tusch m. **5.** Schnörkel m.

flout [flaʊt] v/t Befehl etc mißachten.

flow [fləʊ] **I** v/i **1.** fließen, strömen (beide a. fig.): ~ **freely** in Strömen fließen

2. Zuneigung *f* (**of** zu). **3.** Vorliebe *f* (**for** für).

font [font] *s eccl.* Taufstein *m*, -becken *n*.

food [fuːd] *s* **1.** Nahrung *f* (*a. fig.*), Essen *n*, Verpflegung *f*: **~ for thought** (*od. reflection*) Stoff *m* zum Nachdenken. **2.** Nahrungs-, Lebensmittel *pl.* **~ poi·son·ing** *s ✗* Lebensmittelvergiftung *f*. **'~stuff** → **food** 2.

fool [fuːl] **I** *s* **1.** Narr *m*, Närrin *f*, Dummkopf *m*: **make a ~ of** → 2; **make a ~ of o.s.** sich lächerlich machen; **I am a ~ to him** gegen ihn bin ich ein Waisenknabe. **II** *v/t* **2.** zum Narren halten. **3.** betrügen (**out of** um); verleiten (**into doing** zu tun). **4. ~ away** Zeit, Geld *etc* vergeuden. **III** *v/i* **5.** *a.* **~ about** (*od. around*) Unsinn machen, herumalbern. **6.** *oft* **~ about** (*od. around*) spielen (**with** mit); sich herumtreiben; herumtrödeln. **'fool·er·y** *s* Torheit *f*.

'fool·har·dy *adj* □ tollkühn, verwegen.

fool·ish ['fuːlɪʃ] *adj* □ dumm, töricht.

'fool·proof *adj* **1.** ⚙ betriebssicher. **2.** todsicher (*Plan etc*). **3.** narren-, idiotensicher (*Gerät etc*).

foot [fut] **I** *pl* **feet** [fiːt] *s* **1.** Fuß *m*: **on ~** zu Fuß; **be on ~** im Gange sein; **set on ~** in die Wege leiten, in Gang bringen; **be on one's feet (again)** (wieder) auf den Beinen sein; **put one's ~ in it** ins Fettnäpfchen treten; → **sweep** 6. **2.** (*pl a.* **foot**) Fuß *m* (= 0,3048 m). **3.** Fuß *m* (*e-s Berges, Strumpfes etc*), Fußende *n* (*e-s Bettes etc*): **at the ~ of** am Fuß (*gen*), unten an (*dat*). **II** *v/t* **4. ~ it** F zu Fuß gehen. **5.** Rechnung bezahlen. **~-and-'mouth dis·ease** *s vet.* Maulu. Klauenseuche *f*. **'~ball** (*Sport*) **I** *s* **1.** *Br.* Fußball(spiel *n*) *m*; *Am.* Football(spiel *n*) *m*. **2.** *Br.* Fußball *m*; *Am.* Football-Ball *m*. **II** *adj* **3.** *Br.* Fußball...; *Am.* Football...: **~ pools** *pl* Fußballtoto *n*, *m*. **'~bridge** *s* Fußgängerbrücke *f*. **'~fall** *s* Schritt *m*, Tritt *m* (*Geräusch*). **'~hills** *s pl* Vorgebirge *n*. **'~hold** *s* Stand *m*: **safe ~** fester Stand, sicherer Halt; **gain** (*od. get*) **a ~** *fig.* (festen) Fuß fassen (**in** in *dat*; **as** als).

foot·ing ['futɪŋ] *s* **1.** Stand *m*: **lose** (*od. miss*) **one's ~** den Halt verlieren. **2.** *fig.* Basis *f*, Grundlage *f*: **place on a** (*od. the same*) **~** gleichstellen (**with** *dat*); **be**

on a friendly ~ auf freundschaftlichem Fuße stehen (**with** mit).

'foot·lights *s pl thea.* **1.** Rampenlicht(er *pl*) *n.* **2.** *fig.* die Bühne, das Theater.

foot·ling ['fuːtlɪŋ] *adj* F läppisch (*Sache*), (*a. Person*) albern.

'foot·loose *adj* frei, ungebunden: **~ and fancy-free** frei u. ungebunden. **'~note I** *s* Fußnote *f* (**to** zu). **II** *v/t* mit Fußnoten versehen. **~ path** *s Am.* Fußgänger(in). **'~path** *s* **1.** (Fuß)Pfad *m*, (-)Weg *m.* **2.** *bsd. Br.* Bürgersteig *m*. **'~print** *s* Fußabdruck *m*.

foot·sie ['futsɪ] *s*: **play ~** F füßeln (**with** mit).

'foot·slog *v/i* F latschen. **'~sore** *adj* fußwund, *bsd.* ✗ fußkrank. **~ spray** *s* Fußspray *m*, *n.* **'~step** *s* **1.** Tritt *m*, Schritt *m.* **2.** Fußstapfe *f*: **follow in s.o.'s ~s** *fig.* in j-s Fußstapfen treten. **'~wear** *s* Schuhwerk *n.* **'~work** *s Sport*: Beinarbeit *f*.

for [fɔː] **I** *prp* **1.** für: a) zugunsten von: **a gift ~ him** ein Geschenk für ihn, b) (mit der Absicht) zu: **come ~ dinner** zum Essen kommen, c) (*passend od. geeignet*) für; (*bestimmt*) für, zu: **tools** *pl* **~ cutting** Schneidewerkzeuge *pl*; **the right man ~ the job** der richtige Mann für diesen Posten, d) (*als Belohnung od. Entgelt*) für, e) (*als Strafe etc*) wegen, f) in Anbetracht (*gen*), im Hinblick auf (*acc*): **he is tall ~ his age** er ist groß für sein Alter, g) (*Begabung, Neigung*) für, (*Hang*) zu, h) (*zeitlich*) auf (*acc*), für die Dauer von, seit: **~ hours** stundenlang; **he has been here ~ a week** er ist schon seit e-r Woche hier, i) an Stelle von (*od. gen*), (an)statt; in Vertretung *od. im* Namen von (*od. gen*). **2.** (*Wunsch, Ziel*) nach, auf (*acc*). **3.** (*Mittel*) gegen. **4.** dank, wegen: **if it wasn't ~ him** wenn er nicht wäre, ohne ihn. **5.** (*Strecke*) weit: **run ~ a mile** e-e Meile (weit) laufen. **6.** nach: **the train ~ London. 7.** trotz: **~ all that** trotz alledem. **8.** was ... betrifft: **~ me** was mich betrifft *od.* anbelangt; **~ all I know** soviel ich weiß. **9.** *nach adj u. vor inf*: **it is impossible ~ me to come** ich kann unmöglich kommen. **10.** *mit s od. pron u. inf*: **it is time ~ you to go home** es ist Zeit für dich heimzugehen; **it is ~ you to decide** die Entscheidung liegt bei Ihnen. **II** *cj* **11.** denn, weil.

fo·ra ['fɔːrə] *pl von* **forum.**

for·ay ['fɔreɪ] *s* **1.** Beute-, Raubzug *m.* **2.** *bsd.* ✕ Ein-, Überfall *m.*

for·bad(e) [fə'bæd] *pret von* **forbid.**

for·bear → **forebear.**

for·bid [fə'bɪd] (*irr*) **I** *v/t* **1.** verbieten, untersagen: ~ *s.o. the house* j-m das Haus verbieten. **2.** ausschließen, unmöglich machen. **II** *v/i* **3.** *God* (*od. heaven*) ~*!* Gott behüte *od.* bewahre! **for'bid·den** [ˌdn] *pp von* **forbid. for'bid·ding** *adj* □ **1.** abstoßend, abschreckend. **2.** bedrohlich.

force [fɔːs] **I** *s* **1.** Stärke *f*, Kraft *f*, Wucht *f* (*a. fig.*): ~ *of gravity phys.* Schwerkraft; *by* ~ *of* Kraft, vermittels; *by* ~ *of arms* mit Waffengewalt; *join* ~*s* sich zs.-tun (*with* mit). **2.** *fig.* Kraft *f*: ~*s pl of nature* Naturkräfte *pl*, -gewalten *pl*. **3.** Gewalt *f*: *by* ~ gewaltsam. **4.** Zwang *m* (*a.* ✝): *by* ~ zwangsweise. **5.** (Rechts)Kraft *f*, (-)Gültigkeit *f*: *come* (*put*) *into* ~ in Kraft treten (setzen). **6.** Einfluß *m*, Wirkung *f*: ~ *of habit* Macht *f* der Gewohnheit. **7.** *pl, a. armed* ~*s* ✕ Streitkräfte *pl.* **II** *v/t* **8.** *j-n* zwingen, nötigen (*to do* zu tun). **9.** *et.* erzwingen, durchsetzen. **10.** zwängen, drängen: ~ *one's way* sich (durch)drängen (*through* durch). **11.** ~ *s.th. on s.o.* j-m et. aufzwingen *od.* -drängen; ~ *o.s. on s.o.* sich j-m aufdrängen; → *throat.* **12.** *a.* ~ *up* Preise in die Höhe treiben. **13.** *Tempo* beschleunigen, forcieren. **14.** *a.* ~ *open* Tür etc aufbrechen. **forced** *adj* **1.** erzwungen, Zwangs...: ~ *landing* ✈ Notlandung *f.* **2.** gezwungen, gequält. **forc·ed·ly** ['ˌɪdlɪ] *adv* **1.** → **forced** 2. **2.** gezwungenermaßen.

'force-feed *v/t* (*irr feed*) zwangsernähren.

force·ful ['fɔːsfʊl] *adj* □ **1.** energisch, kraftvoll (*Person*). **2.** eindrucksvoll, -dringlich (*Rede etc*). **3.** zwingend, überzeugend (*Argument etc*).

for·ceps ['fɔːseps] *pl* **-ceps, -ci·pes** ['ˌsɪpiːz] *s* **1.** *f*, *z.* Zange *f*: ~ *delivery* Zangengeburt *f.* **2.** Pinzette *f.*

for·ci·ble ['fɔːsəbl] *adj* □ **1.** gewaltsam; zwangsweise. **2.** → **forceful.**

ford [fɔːd] **I** *s* Furt *f.* **II** *v/t* durchwaten.

fore [fɔː] **I** *adj* **1.** vorder, Vorder... *od.* früher. **II** *adv* **3.** ⚓ vorn. **III** *s* **4.** Vor-

derteil *m*, -seite *f*, Front *f*: *come to the* ~ *fig.* sich hervortun. **'~arm** *s* Unterarm *m.* **'~bear** *s mst pl* Vorfahr *m*, Ahn *m.* **~'bode** *v/t* **1.** *Schlimmes* ahnen, voraussehen. **2.** ein (böses) Vorzeichen *od.* Omen sein für. **~'bod·ing** *s* **1.** (*böse*) (Vor)Ahnung. **2.** (böses) Vorzeichen *od.* Omen. **'~cast** **I** *v/t pret u. pp* **-cast(·ed) 1.** voraussagen, vorhersehen. **2.** *Wetter etc* vorhersagen. **II** *s* **3.** Voraussage *f.* **4.** (Wetter)Vorhersage *f.* **'~fa·ther** *s* Ahn *m*, Vorfahr *m.* **'~fin·ger** *s* Zeigefinger *m.* **'~front** *s* vorderste Reihe (*a. fig.*). **~'go** *v/t u. v/i* (*irr go*) vorangehen (*dat*), (*zeitlich a.*) vorhergehen (*dat*). **'~gone** *adj:* ~ *conclusion* ausgemachte Sache; *be a* ~ *conclusion a.* von vornherein feststehen. **'~ground** *s* Vordergrund *m* (*a. fig.*). **'~hand** (*Sport*) **I** *s* Vorhand(schlag *m*) *f.* **II** *adj* Vorhand... **~head** ['fɒrɪd] *s* Stirn *f.*

for·eign ['fɒrən] *adj* **1.** fremd, ausländisch, Auslands...: ~ *affairs pl* Außenpolitik *f*, auswärtige Angelegenheiten *pl*; ~ *currency* (*od. exchange*) ✝ Devisen *pl*; ~ *language* Fremdsprache *f*; ☑ *Office pol. Br.* Außenministerium *n*; ~ *policy* Außenpolitik *f*; ☑ *Secretary pol. Br.* Außenminister *m*; ~ *trade* Außenhandel *m*; ~ *word* Fremdwort *n*; ~ *worker* Gastarbeiter *m*; → *correspondent* 3. **2.** fremd (*to dat*): *this is* ~ *to his nature* das ist ihm wesensfremd; ~ *body* (*od. matter*) ✈ Fremdkörper *m.* **'for·eign·er** *s* Ausländer(in).

fore·knowl·edge *s* Vorherwissen *n*, vorherige Kenntnis. **~·man** ['ˌmən] *s* (*irr man*) **1.** Vorarbeiter *m*, (*am Bau*) Polier *m.* **2.** ⚖ Obmann *m* (*der Geschworenen*). **'~·most** *adj* **1.** vorderst, erst. **2.** *fig.* herausragendst. **II** *adv* **3.** zuerst. **~·name** *s* Vorname *m.*

fo·ren·sic [fə'rensɪk] *adj* Gerichts...: ~ *medicine.*

'fore·play *s* (*sexuelles*) Vorspiel. **'~·run·ner** *s fig.* **1.** Vorläufer *m.* **2.** Vorbote *m*; (*erstes*) Anzeichen *n.* **~'see** *v/t* (*irr see*) vorher-, voraussehen. **~'see·a·ble** *adj: in the* ~ *future* in absehbarer Zeit. **~'shad·ow** *v/t* ahnen lassen, andeuten. **'~·sight** *s* Weitblick *m*; (*weise*) Voraussicht. **'~·skin** *s anat.* Vorhaut *f.*

for·est ['fɔrɪst] s (a. fig. Antennen-etc)Wald m; Forst m.

fore·stall [fɔː'stɔːl] v/t **1.** j-m, e-r Sache zuvorkommen. **2.** Einwand etc vorwegnehmen.

for·est·er ['fɔrɪstə] s Förster m. **'for·est·ry** s Forstwirtschaft f.

'fore|·taste s Vorgeschmack m (of von). **~'tell** v/t (irr tell) vorher-, voraussagen: ~ s.o.'s future j-m die Zukunft vorhersagen.

for·ev·er, Br. a. **for ev·er** [fə'revə] adv **1.** für od. auf immer. **2.** ständig, (an)dauernd.

fore|'warn v/t vorher warnen (of vor dat). **~'wom·an** s (irr woman) Vorarbeiterin f. **'~·word** s Vorwort n (to zu).

for·feit ['fɔːfɪt] I s pl (sg konstruiert) Pfänderspiel n: **play ~s** ein Pfänderspiel machen. II v/t verwirken, verlustig gehen (gen); einbüßen. III adj verwirkt, verfallen. **for·fei·ture** ['~tʃə] s Verlust m; Einbuße f.

forge¹ [fɔːdʒ] v/t fälschen.

forge² [~] v/i mst ~ ahead sich (mühsam) vorankämpfen: ~ ahead fig. allmählich Fortschritte machen.

forg·er ['fɔːdʒə] s Fälscher m. **'forg·er·y** s Fälschen n; Fälschung f: ~ of a document ᵗᵗ Urkundenfälschung.

for·get [fə'get] (irr) I v/t **1.** allg. vergessen: **I ~ his name** sein Name fällt mir im Moment nicht ein. **2.** ~ o.s. sich vergessen; (nur) an andere denken. II v/i **3.** a. ~ about it es vergessen. **for'get·ful** [~fʊl] adj □ vergeßlich.

for'get-me-not s ♀ Vergißmeinnicht n.

for·give [fə'gɪv] v/t (irr give) **1.** j-m et. verzeihen, -geben. **2.** j-m e-e Schuld etc erlassen. **for'giv·ing** adj □ **1.** versöhnlich. **2.** verzeihend.

for·go [fɔː'gəʊ] v/t (irr go) verzichten auf (acc).

for·got [fə'gɒt] pret u. pp von **forget**. **for'got·ten** [~tn] pp von **forget**.

fork [fɔːk] I s **1.** Gabel f. **2.** Gab(e)lung f, Abzweigung f. II v/t **3.** ~ out (od. up) F Geld herausrücken, lockermachen. III v/i **4.** sich gabeln (Fluß, Straße a.) abzweigen. **forked** adj gegabelt, (Zunge) gespalten.

'fork·lift (truck) s ☺ Gabel-, Hubstapler m.

for·lorn [fə'lɔːn] adj **1.** verlassen, einsam.

2. verzweifelt (Versuch): ~ hope aussichtsloses od. verzweifeltes Unternehmen.

form [fɔːm] I s **1.** Form f, Gestalt f: **take ~** Form od. Gestalt annehmen (a. fig.); **in the ~ of** in Form von (od. gen); **in tablet ~** in Tablettenform. **2.** ☺ Form f, Schablone f. **3.** Form f, Art f: ~ **of government** Regierungsform; → **due** 6. **4.** a. **printed ~** Formular n, Vordruck m: **~·letter** Schemabrief m. **5.** Form f (a. ling.), Fassung f (e-s Textes etc). **6.** **good (bad) ~** guter (schlechter) Ton: **it is good (bad) ~** es gehört sich (nicht). **7.** Formalität f: → **matter** 3. **8.** Verfassung f: **in (out of, off one's) ~** (nicht) in Form. **9.** bsd. Br. (Schul)Klasse f: ~ **master (mistress)** Klassenlehrer(in). II v/t **10.** formen, gestalten (into zu; **after, on** nach), Regierung etc bilden, Gesellschaft gründen. **11.** Charakter etc formen, bilden. **12.** sich e-e Meinung bilden. III v/i **13.** Form od. Gestalt annehmen (a. fig.).

for·mal ['fɔːml] adj (□ → **formally**) **1.** förmlich, formell: ~ **call** Höflichkeitsbesuch m; ~ **dress** Gesellschaftskleidung f. **2.** formal, formell: ~ **defect** ᵗᵗ Formfehler m. **for·mal·ism** ['~məlɪzəm] s Formalismus m. **for·mal·i·ty** [~'mælətɪ] s **1.** Förmlichkeit f. **2.** Formalität f, Formsache f. **for·mal·ize** ['~məlaɪz] v/t **1.** formalisieren. **2.** e-e feste Form geben (dat). **'for·mal·ly** adv formell, in aller Form.

for·mat ['fɔːmæt] s typ. Aufmachung f; Format n.

for·ma·tion [fɔː'meɪʃn] s **1.** Formung f, Gestaltung f. **2.** ✈, ✕, geol., Sport: Formation f. **form·a·tive** ['~mətɪv] adj formend, gestaltend: ~ **years** pl Entwicklungsjahre pl.

for·mer ['fɔːmə] adj **1.** früher, vorig; ehemalig: **in ~ times** früher. **2.** ersterwähnt, -genannt: **the ~, the latter** ersterer, letzterer. **'for·mer·ly** adv früher, ehemals.

for·mi·da·ble ['fɔːmɪdəbl] adj □ **1.** furchterregend. **2.** gefährlich (Gegner etc), gewaltig, riesig (Schulden etc), schwierig (Frage etc).

form·less ['fɔːmlɪs] adj □ formlos.

for·mu·la ['fɔːmjʊlə] pl **-las, -lae** ['~liː] s **1.** ♀, mot. etc Formel f (a. fig.). **2.**

foundation

pharm. Rezept *n* (*zur Anfertigung*).
for·mu·late ['_lert] *v/t* formulieren.
for·mu·la·tion *s* Formulierung *f*.

for·sake [fə'seɪk] *v/t* (*irr*) **1.** *j-n* verlassen, im Stich lassen. **2.** *et.* aufgeben. **for-'sak·en** *pp von* **forsake. for·sook** [fə'sʊk] *pret von* **forsake.**

for·swear [fɔː'sweə] *v/t* (*irr* swear) **1.** unter Eid verneinen. **2.** abschwören (*dat*). **3. ~ o.s.** e-n Meineid leisten.

fort [fɔːt] *s* ✕ Fort *n*: **hold the ~** *fig.* die Stellung halten.

for·te ['fɔːteɪ] *s j-s* Stärke *f*, starke Seite.

forth [fɔːθ] *adv* **1.** weiter, fort: **and so ~** und so weiter. **2.** (her)vor. **~'com·ing** *adj* **1.** bevorstehend, kommend. **2.** in Kürze erscheinend (*Buch*) *od.* anlaufend (*Film*).

for·ti·eth ['fɔːtɪəθ] *adj* vierzigst.

for·ti·fi·ca·tion [ˌfɔːtɪfɪ'keɪʃn] *s* **1.** ✕ Befestigung *f*: **~s** *pl* Festungswerk *n*. **2.** Verstärkung *f*; Anreicherung *f*. **3.** *fig.* Untermauerung *f*. **for·ti·fy** ['~faɪ] *v/t* **1.** ✕ befestigen. **2.** *Wein etc* verstärken; *Nahrungsmittel* anreichern. **3.** *Theorie etc* untermauern (**with** mit).

for·ti·tude ['fɔːtɪtjuːd] *s* (innere) Kraft *od.* Stärke.

fort·night ['fɔːtnaɪt] *s bsd. Br.* vierzehn Tage: **in a ~** in 14 Tagen. **'fort·night·ly** *bsd. Br.* **I** *adj* vierzehntägig, halbmonatlich. **II** *adv* vierzehntäglich, alle 14 Tage.

for·tress ['fɔːtrɪs] *s* ✕ Festung *f*.

for·tu·i·tous [fɔː'tjuːɪtəs] *adj* □ zufällig.

for·tu·nate ['fɔːtʃnət] *adj* glücklich: **be ~** Glück haben; **be ~ in having s.th., be ~ enough to have s.th.** das Glück haben, et. zu besitzen. **'for·tu·nate·ly** *adv* glücklicherweise, zum Glück: **~ for me** zu m-m Glück.

for·tune ['fɔːtʃuːn] *s* **1.** Vermögen *n*: **come into a ~** ein Vermögen erben; **make a ~** ein Vermögen verdienen; **marry a ~** e-e gute Partie machen, reich heiraten. **2.** (glücklicher) Zufall, Glück(sfall *m* *n*). **3.** Geschick *n*, Schicksal *n*: **good ~** Glück *n*; **bad** (*od.* **ill**) **~** Unglück *n*; **tell ~s** wahrsagen; **read s.o.'s ~** j-m die Karten legen; j-m aus der Hand lesen. **4.** *oft* ♀ Fortuna *f*, das Glück, die Glücksgöttin. **~ hunt·er** ['~tʃən] *s* Mitgiftjäger *m*. **~ tell·er** ['~tʃən] *s* Wahrsager(in).

for·ty ['fɔːtɪ] **I** *adj* vierzig: **have ~ winks** F ein Nickerchen machen. **II** *s* Vierzig *f*: **be in one's forties** in den Vierzigern sein; **in the forties** in den vierziger Jahren (*e-s Jahrhunderts*).

fo·rum ['fɔːrəm] *pl* **-rums, -ra** ['~rə] *s* Forum *n* (*a. fig.*).

for·ward ['fɔːwəd] **I** *adv* **1.** nach vorn, vorwärts. **II** *adj* □ **2.** Vorwärts...: **~ planning** Vorausplanung *f*. **3.** fortschrittlich. **4.** vorlaut, dreist. **III** *s* **5.** *Sport*: Stürmer *m*: **~ line** Sturmreihe *f*. **IV** *v/t* **6.** fördern, begünstigen. **7.** (ver)senden, schicken; befördern; *Brief etc* nachsenden. **'for·ward·er** *s* Spediteur *m*.

'for·ward·ing *s* Versand *m*; Beförderung *f*; Nachsendung *f*: **~ address** Nachsendeadresse *f*; **~ agent** Spediteur *m*.

'for·ward·look·ing *adj* vorausschauend, fortschrittlich.

for·wards ['fɔːwədz] → **forward I.**

fos·sil ['fɒsl] *geol.* **I** *s* Fossil *n* (*a. fig.* F), Versteinerung *f*. **II** *adj* fossil (*a. fig.* F), versteinert.

fos·ter ['fɒstə] **I** *v/t* **1.** *Kind* in Pflege haben *od.* nehmen; *bsd. Br.* in Pflege geben (**with** bei). **2.** *Gefühle, Plan etc* hegen. **II** *adj* **3.** Pflege...: **~ mother.**

fought [fɔːt] *pret u. pp von* **fight.**

foul [faʊl] **I** *adj* □ **1.** stinkend, widerlich. **2.** verpestet, schlecht (*Luft*); verdorben, faul (*Lebensmittel etc*). **3.** schmutzig, verschmutzt. **4.** schlecht, stürmisch (*Wetter*). **5.** *fig.* schmutzig, zotig. **6.** *Sport*: regelwidrig. **II** *adv* **7.** **fall ~ of** ♣ kollidieren mit, *a. fig.* zs.-stoßen mit: **fall ~ of the law** mit dem Gesetz in Konflikt geraten. **III** *s* **8.** *Sport*: Foul *n*: **commit a ~** an ein Foul begehen an (*dat*). **IV** *v/t* **9.** *a.* **~ up** beschmutzen (*a. fig.*), verschmutzen: **~ one's (own) nest** das eigene Nest beschmutzen. **10.** *Sport*: foulen. **11.** **~ up** F verpatzen, -sauen. **~·mouthed** ['~maʊðd] *adj* unflätig.

found¹ [faʊnd] *pret u. pp von* **find.**

found² [~] *v/t* **1.** (be)gründen, *Schule etc* stiften. **2.** gründen, stützen (**on** auf *acc*): **be ~ed on** sich gründen auf (*acc*), beruhen auf (*dat*).

found³ [~] *v/t* ✿ gießen.

foun·da·tion [faʊn'deɪʃn] *s* **1.** △ Fundament *n*: **lay the ~(s) of** *fig.* den

Grund(stock) legen zu. **2.** Gründung *f.*
3. Stiftung *f.* **4.** Grundlage *f*, Basis *f.* ~
stone *s* **1.** △ Grundstein *m (a. fig.).* **2.**
→ *foundation* 4.

found·er¹ ['faʊndə] *s* (Be)Gründer(in),
Stifter(in): ~ *member* Gründungsmit-
glied *n.*

found·er² [~] *s* ⊕ Gießer *m.*

found·er³ *v/i* scheitern, *(Koalition etc a.)*
zerbrechen, *(Ehe etc a.)* in die Brüche
gehen.

found·ry ['faʊndrı] *s* ⊕ Gießerei *f.*

foun·tain ['faʊntın] *s* **1.** Quelle *f (a. fig.).*
2. Fontäne *f:* a) *(Wasser- etc)*Strahl *m*,
b) Springbrunnen *m.* **3.** Trinkbrunnen
m. ~ **pen** *s* Füll(feder)halter *m.*

four [fɔː] **I** *adj* **1.** vier. **II** *s* **2.** Vier *f:* ~ *of
hearts* Herzvier; *on all* ~*s* auf allen
vieren. **3.** Rudern: Vierer *m.* **four·fold**
['~fəʊld] **I** *adj* vierfach. **II** *adv* vierfach,
um das Vierfache: *increase* ~ (sich)
vervierfachen.

,four|-'hand·ed *adj* □ ♪ vierhändig.
'**~-leaf clo·ver** *s* ♣ vierblätt(e)riges
Kleeblatt. '**~-legged** *adj* vierbeinig.
'**~,let·ter word** *s* unanständiges Wort.
~ **star** *s mot.* Br. F Super *n (Benzin).*
'**~-star** *adj:* ~ *petrol mot.* Br. Superbenzin *n.*

four·teen [,fɔː'tiːn] *adj* vierzehn. **,four-
'teenth** [~θ] *adj* vierzehnt. **fourth** [fɔːθ]
I *adj* **1.** viert. **II** *s* **2.** der, die, das Vierte:
the ~ *of May* der 4. Mai. **3.** Viertel *n.*
'**fourth·ly** *adv* viertens.

'**four-time** *adj* viermalig.

fowl [faʊl] *s coll.* Geflügel *n.*

fox [fɒks] **I** *s* **1.** *zo.* Fuchs *m.* **2.** *oft sly old*
~ gerissener *od.* verschlagener Kerl. **II**
v/t **3.** verblüffen. **4.** täuschen, reinlegen. ~ **hunt(·ing)** *s* Fuchsjagd *f.* ~ **ter-
ri·er** *s zo.* Foxterrier *m.* '**~-trot** *s* ♪ Foxtrott *m.*

fox·y ['fɒksı] *adj* □ gerissen, verschlagen.

foy·er ['fɔıeı] *s* Foyer *n.*

fra·cas ['fræka:] *pl* **-cas** [-ka:z], *Am.*
-cas·es ['freıkəsız] *s* Aufruhr *m*, Tumult *m.*

frac·tion ['frækʃn] *s* **1.** ♣ Bruch *m:* ~ *bar
(od. line, stroke)* Bruchstrich *m.* **2.**
Bruchteil *m.* **frac·tion·al** ['~ʃənl] *adj* □
1. ♣ Bruch... **2.** *fig.* minimal, geringfügig.

frac·tious ['frækʃəs] *adj* □ mürrisch,
reizbar.

frac·ture ['fræktʃə] **I** *s* Bruch *m*, ♣ *a.*
Fraktur *f.* **II** *v/t* (zer)brechen: ~ *one's
arm* sich den Arm brechen; **~d skull** ♣
Schädelbruch *m;* **speak ~d English** *fig.*
gebrochen Englisch sprechen. **III** *v/i*
(zer)brechen.

frag·ile ['frædʒaıl] *adj* □ **1.** zerbrechlich
(a. fig.). **2.** schwach, zart *(Gesundheit);*
gebrechlich *(Person).* **fra·gil·i·ty** [frə-
'dʒılətı] *s* **1.** Zerbrechlichkeit *f.* **2.**
Zartheit *f;* Gebrechlichkeit *f.*

frag·ment ['frægmənt] *s* **1.** literarisches
etc Fragment. **2.** Bruchstück *n*, -teil *m.*
'**frag·men·ta·ry** *adj* □ fragmentarisch,
bruchstückhaft.

fra·grance ['freıgrəns] *s* Wohlgeruch *m*,
Duft *m.* '**fra·grant** *adj* □ wohlriechend, duftend.

frail [freıl] *adj* □ zart, schwach *(Gesundheit, Stimme etc);* gebrechlich *(Person);*
(charakterlich od. moralisch) schwach.
'**frail·ty** *s* Zartheit *f;* Gebrechlichkeit *f;*
Schwäche *f.*

frame [freım] **I** *s* **1.** *(Bilder- etc)*Rahmen
m. **2.** *(Brillen- etc)*Gestell *n.* **3.** *fig.* Rahmen *m: within the ~ of* im Rahmen
(gen). **4.** *bsd.* ~ *of mind* (Gemüts)Ver-
fassung *f*, (-)Zustand *m.* **II** *v/t* **5.** *Bild
etc* (ein)rahmen; *fig.* umrahmen. **6.**
Plan schmieden, *Politik etc* abstecken.
7. *a.* ~ *up Sache* drehen, schaukeln,
Spiel (vorher) absprechen; *j-m* et. anhängen. **III** *v/i* **8.** sich entwickeln. '**~-up**
s F **1.** Komplott *n*, Intrige *f.* **2.** abgekartetes Spiel, Schwindel *m.* '**~-work** →
frame 3.

franc [fræŋk] *s* Franc *m;* Franken *m.*

fran·chise ['fræntʃaız] *s* **1.** *pol.* Wahlrecht *n.* **2.** ♣ *bsd. Am.* Konzession *f.*

Fran·co- ['fræŋkəʊ] *in Zssgn* französisch, franko...

frank [fræŋk] **I** *adj* □ offen(herzig), aufrichtig, frei(mütig): *to be* ~, *~ly
(speaking)* offen gestanden *od.* gesagt;
be ~ *with s.o.* ehrlich zu j-m sein. **II** *v/t*
♥ frankieren, *(maschinell a.)* freistem-
peln: **~ing machine** Frankiermaschine
f, Freistempler *m.*

frank·furt·er ['fræŋkfɜ:tə] *s* Frankfurter
(Würstchen *n*) *f.*

frank·in·cense ['fræŋkın,sens] *s* Weihrauch *m.*

frank·ness ['fræŋknıs] *s* Offenheit *f*,
Freimütigkeit *f.*

fran·tic ['fræntɪk] *adj* (**~ally**) **1.** außer sich, rasend (**with** vor *dat*). **2.** verzweifelt. **3.** hektisch.

fra·ter·nal [frə'tɜːnl] *adj* □ brüderlich.

fra'ter·ni·ty *s* **1.** Brüderlichkeit *f*. **2.** Vereinigung *f*, Zunft *f*: **the medical ~** die Ärzteschaft. **3.** *Am.* (Studenten-) Verbindung *f*.

frat·er·ni·za·tion [,frætənaɪ'zeɪʃn] *s* Verbrüderung *f*. **'frat·er·nize** *v/i* sich verbrüdern.

fraud [frɔːd] *s* **1.** 🏛 Betrug *m* (**on** an *dat*); arglistige Täuschung: **obtain by ~** sich et. erschleichen. **2.** Schwindel *m* (*a. Sache*). **3.** F Betrüger *m*, Schwindler *m*.

fraud·u·lence ['~jʊləns] *s* Betrügerei *f*. **'fraud·u·lent** *adj* □ betrügerisch.

fray¹ [freɪ] **I** *v/t a.* **~ out** ausfransen, durchscheuern: **~ed nerves** *pl* verschlissene *od.* strapazierte Nerven *pl*. **II** *v/i a.* **~ out** ausfransen, sich durchscheuern.

fray² [~] *s* Rauferei *f*, Schlägerei *f*.

freak [friːk] **I** *s* **1.** Mißgeburt *f*, Monstrosität *f*. **2.** Grille *f*, Laune *f*. **3.** *sl.* ...freak *m*, ...fanatiker *m*. **4.** *sl.* Freak *m*, irrer Typ. **II** *v/i* **5.** *a.* **~ out** *sl. allg.* ausflippen (**for, over**) bein.

freck·le ['frekl] *s* Sommersprosse *f*. **'freck·led** ['~ld] *adj* sommersprossig.

free [friː] **I** *adj* □ **1.** frei: a) unabhängig, b) selbständig, c) ungebunden, d) ungehindert, e) uneingeschränkt, f) in Freiheit (befindlich): **he is ~ to go** es steht ihm frei zu gehen; **give s.o. a ~ hand** j-m freie Hand lassen; **→ set** 13, **will¹** 1. **2.** frei: a) unbeschäftigt, b) ohne Verpflichtungen, c) unbesetzt. **3.** frei (*nicht wörtlich od. an Regeln gebunden*): **~ translation**; **~ skating** (*Eis-, Rollkunstlauf*) Kür(laufen *n*) *f*. **4.** (**from, of**) frei (von), ohne (*acc*): **~ from error** fehlerfrei. **5.** frei, befreit (**from, of** von): **~ from pain** schmerzfrei; **~ of debt** schuldenfrei; **→ charge** 9. **6.** ungezwungen, natürlich; **→ easy** 7. **7.** offen(herzig), freimütig; unverblümt; dreist; plump-vertraulich: **make ~ with** sich Freiheiten herausnehmen gegen *j-n*; sich (ungeniert) gütlich tun an *e-r Sache*. **8.** frei, kostenlos, unentgeltlich: **~ copy** Freiexemplar *n*; **for ~** F umsonst. **9.** freigebig: **be ~ with** großzügig sein *od.* umgehen mit. **II** *adv* **10.** *allg.* frei. **III** *v/t* **11.** befreien

(**from** von, aus) (*a. fig.*). **12.** freilassen.

free·bee, free·bie ['friːbiː] *s sl. et.*, **was es gratis gibt**, z. B. Freikarte *f*.

'free,boot·er *s* Freibeuter *m*.

free·dom ['friːdəm] *s* **1.** Freiheit *f*: **~ of the press** Pressefreiheit. **2.** Freisein *n*: **~ from pain** Schmerzfreiheit *f*.

free| en·ter·prise *s* freies Unternehmertum. **~ fall** *s* ✈, *phys.* freier Fall. **,~-'hand·ed** *adj* □ freigebig, großzügig. **~ kick** *s* Fußball: Freistoß *m*: (**in**)**direct ~**. **'~·lance I** *s* Freiberufler *m*, Freischaffende *m*; freier Mitarbeiter. **II** *adj* frei(beruflich tätig), freischaffend. **III** *adv* freiberuflich: **work ~ → IV. IV** *v/i* freiberuflich arbeiten (**for** für). **'~·lanc·er → freelance** I. **'~·load** *v/i Am.* F schnorren (**off, of** bei), nassauern. **'~·load·er** *s Am.* F Schnorrer *m*, Nassauer *m*. **~ mar·ket e·con·o·my** *s* freie Marktwirtschaft. **~ port** *s* Freihafen *m*. **,~-'spo·ken** *adj* □ freimütig, offen. **~ state** *s* Freistaat *m*. **'~·style** (*Sport*) **I** *s* Freistil *m*. **II** *adj* Freistil... **~ trade** *s* Freihandel *m*. **,~-'trade a·re·a** *s* Freihandelszone *f*.

freeze [friːz] **I** *v/i* (*irr*) **1.** *impers* frieren: **it is freezing hard** es herrscht starker Frost. **2.** frieren: **~ to death** erfrieren; **I am freezing** mir ist eiskalt. **3.** (ge)frieren, zu Eis werden; **→ blood** 1. **4.** *a.* **~ up** (*od.* **over**) zufrieren (*See etc*), vereisen (*Windschutzscheibe etc*); **~** (**up**) einfrieren (*Türschloß etc*); **~ to** fest- *od.* anfrieren an (*dat*). **5.** *fig.* erstarren. **II** *v/t* (*irr*) **6.** zum Gefrieren bringen. **7.** *Fleisch etc* einfrieren, tiefkühlen. **8.** ✈ vereisen. **9.** ✈ *Preise etc, pol. diplomatische Beziehungen* einfrieren. **III** *s* **10.** Frost(periode *f*) *m*. **11.** ✈, *pol.* Einfrieren *n*: **~ on wages** Lohnstopp *m*.

'freez·er *s* a) Tiefkühl-, Gefriergerät *n*, b) Gefrierfach *n* (*e-s Kühlschranks*).

'freez·ing *adj* **1.** Gefrier..., Kälte...: **~ compartment → freezer** b; **~ point** Gefrierpunkt *m*. **2.** eisig kalt, eiskalt.

freight [freɪt] **I** *s* **1.** Fracht(gebühr) *f*. **2.** ⚓ (*Am. a.* ✈, *mot.*) Fracht *f*, Ladung *f*. **II** *v/t* **3.** Schiff, *Am. a. Güterwagen etc* befrachten, beladen. **4.** *Güter* verfrachten. **~ car** *s* 🚃 *Am.* Güterwagen *m*.

freight·er ['freɪtə] *s* Frachter *m*, Frachtschiff *n*; Transportflugzeug *n*.

freight train *s Am.* Güterzug *m*.

French [frentʃ] **I** adj **1.** französisch: ~ beans pl ⚕ bsd. Br. grüne Bohnen pl; ~ fried potatoes, F ~ fries pl bsd. Am. Pommes frites pl; ~ kiss Zungenkuß m; take ~ leave sich (auf) französisch empfehlen; ~ letter Br. F Pariser m (Kondom); ~ window(s pl) Terrassen-, Balkontür f. **II** s **2.** the ~ pl die Franzosen pl. **3.** ling. Französisch n: in ~ auf französisch. ~'man s (irr man) Franzose m. '~,wom·an s (irr woman) Französin f.

fre·net·ic [frə'netɪk] adj (~ally) **1.** a) ausgelassen, b) → frenzied 2. **2.** → frenzied 3.

fren·zied ['frenzɪd] adj **1.** außer sich, rasend (with vor dat). **2.** frenetisch (Geschrei etc), (Beifall a.) rasend. **3.** wild, hektisch. 'fren·zy s **1.** helle Aufregung. **2.** wildes od. hektisches Treiben. **3.** Wahnsinn m, Raserei f.

fre·quen·cy ['fri:kwənsɪ] s **1.** Häufigkeit f. **2.** ⚡, phys. Frequenz f. **fre·quent I** adj ['fri:kwənt] häufig. **II** v/t [frɪ'kwent] häufig besuchen.

fres·co ['freskəʊ] pl -co(e)s s Fresko(gemälde) n.

fresh [freʃ] **I** adj □ **1.** allg. frisch: ~ butter ungesalzene Butter; ~ meat Frischfleisch n; ~ shirt sauberes Hemd. **2.** neu: → ground² 1, start 9. **3.** grün, unerfahren: be ~ to noch keine Erfahrung haben in (dat). **4.** F frech (with zu): don't get ~ with me! werd bloß nicht pampig! **II** adv **5.** frisch: ~ from the oven ofenfrisch; ~ from the press druckfrisch; ~-laid eggs pl frisch gelegte Eier pl. 'fresh·en **I** v/t **1.** mst ~ up erfrischen: ~ o.s. (up) sich frisch machen. **2.** ~ s.o. (up) j-n nachgießen od. -schenken. **II** v/i mst ~ up **3.** sich frisch machen. **4.** auffrischen (Wind). 'fresh·er Br. F → freshman.

fresh·man ['freʃmən] s (irr man) Student(in) im ersten Jahr.

fresh·ness ['freʃnɪs] s Frische f.

fret [fret] **I** v/t **1.** j-m Sorgen machen. **2.** j-n ärgern, reizen. **3.** abscheuern, abnutzen; reiben od. scheuern an (dat): ~ s.o.'s nerves an j-s Nerven zerren. **II** v/i **4.** sich Sorgen machen (about, at, for, over wegen). **5.** sich ärgern (about, at, for, over über acc): ~ and fume vor Wut schäumen. **6.** sich abscheuern od.

abnutzen. **III** s **7.** be in a ~ → 4, 5. **fret·ful** ['~fʊl] adj □ verärgert, gereizt.

Freud·i·an ['frɔɪdɪən] adj Freudsch: ~ slip Freudsche Fehlleistung.

fri·a·ble ['fraɪəbl] adj bröck(e)lig, krümelig.

fric·as·see ['frɪkəsiː] s gastr. Frikassee n: ~ of chicken Hühnerfrikassee.

fric·tion ['frɪkʃn] s **1.** ⚙, phys. Reibung f. **2.** fig. Reiberei(en pl) f. **fric·tion·al** ['~ʃənl] adj ⚙, phys. Reibungs...

Fri·day ['fraɪdɪ] s Freitag m: on ~ (am) Freitag; on ~s freitags.

fridge [frɪdʒ] s bsd. Br. F Kühlschrank m. ,~-'freez·er s bsd. Br. F Kühl- u. Gefrierkombination f.

friend [frend] s **1.** Freund(in): be ~s with j-m befreundet sein mit; make ~s with sich anfreunden mit; make ~s again sich wieder vertragen. **2.** Bekannte m, f. **'friend·li·ness** s Freundlichkeit f. **'friend·ly I** adj **1.** freundlich (a. fig. Zimmer etc). **2.** freundschaftlich: ~ game (od. match) (Sport) Freundschaftsspiel n; → term 5. **3.** befreundet (with mit). **II** s **4.** Sport: F Freundschaftsspiel n. **'friend·ship** s Freundschaft f.

frieze [friːz] s △ Fries m.

frig·ate ['frɪgət] s ⚓ Fregatte f.

frige → fridge.

fright [fraɪt] s **1.** Schreck(en) m: get (od. have) a ~ e-n Schreck bekommen, erschrecken; get off with a ~ mit dem Schrecken davonkommen; give s.o. a ~ j-m e-n Schrecken einjagen, j-n erschrecken. **2.** look a ~ zum Abschießen aussehen. **'fright·en I** v/t **1.** j-n erschrecken (to death zu Tode); j-m Angst einjagen: be ~ed erschrecken (at, by, of vor dat); Angst haben (of vor dat). **2.** mst ~ away (od. off) vertreiben, -scheuchen. **II** v/i **3.** ~ easily leicht erschrecken, schreckhaft sein. **fright·ful** ['~fʊl] adj □ schrecklich, fürchterlich (beide a. F).

frig·id ['frɪdʒɪd] adj □ **1.** kalt, frostig, eisig (alle a. fig.). **2.** psych. frigid. **fri'gid·i·ty** s **1.** Kälte f, Frostigkeit f (beide a. fig.). **2.** psych. Frigidität f.

frill [frɪl] s **1.** Krause f, Rüsche f. **2.** pl Verzierungen pl, Kinkerlitzchen pl.

fringe [frɪndʒ] s **1.** Franse f, Besatz m. **2.** Rand m, Einfassung f, Umrandung *f.* **II** *v/t* **3.** mit Fransen besetzen. **4.** umsäumen. **~ ben·e·fits** *s pl* ✝ (Gehalts-, Lohn)Nebenleistungen *pl.* **~ group** *s sociol.* Randgruppe *f.*

frisk [frɪsk] **I** *v/i* herumtollen. **II** *v/t* F *j-n* filzen, durchsuchen. **'frisk·y** *adj* □ **1.** lebhaft, munter. **2.** ausgelassen.

frit·ter ['frɪtə] *v/t mst* **~ away** Geld, *Gelegenheit* vertun, *Zeit a.* vertrödeln, *Geld, Kräfte* vergeuden.

fri·vol·i·ty [frɪ'vɒlɪtɪ] *s* Frivolität *f:* a) Leichtsinnigkeit *f*, -fertigkeit *f*, Oberflächlichkeit *f*, b) leichtfertige Rede *od.* Handlung. **friv·o·lous** ['~ələs] *adj* □ **1.** frivol, leichtfertig, -sinnig. **2.** nicht ernst zu nehmen(d).

friz·zy ['frɪzɪ] *adj* gekräuselt, kraus: **~ hair** Kraushaar *n.*

fro [frəʊ] *adv:* → **to.**

frock [frɒk] *s* **1.** (Mönchs)Kutte *f.* **2.** (Kinder-, Arbeits)Kittel *m.* **3.** Kleid *n.*

frog [frɒg] *s zo.* Frosch *m:* **have a ~ in the** (*od.* **one's**) **throat** *fig.* e-n Frosch im Hals haben. **~·man** ['~mən] *s* (*irr* **man**) Froschmann *m*, ✕ *a.* Kampfschwimmer *m.*

frol·ic ['frɒlɪk] *v/i pret u. pp* **-icked** *a.* **~ about** (*od.* **around**) herumtollen, -tollen. **frol·ic·some** ['~səm] *adj* □ ausgelassen, übermütig.

from [frɒm] *prep* **1.** von, aus, von ... aus *od.* her: **he took it ~ me** er nahm es mir weg; **~ what he said** nach dem, was er sagte. **2.** von (... an), seit: **~ 2 to 4 o'clock** von 2 bis 4 Uhr; **~ day to day** von Tag zu Tag. **3.** von ... an: **~ £5 von** 5 Pfund an (aufwärts). **4.** (weg *od.* entfernt) von. **5.** von (*Wandlung*): **~ dishwasher to millionaire** vom Tellerwäscher zum Millionär. **6.** von (*Unterscheidung*): **he does not know black ~ white** er kann Schwarz u. Weiß nicht auseinanderhalten. **7.** von (*Geben etc*): **a letter ~ his son. 8.** aus, vor (*dat*), an (*dat*) (*Grund*): **he died ~ fatigue** er starb vor Erschöpfung.

front [frʌnt] **I** *s* **1.** *allg.* Voder-, Stirnseite *f*, Front *f:* **at the ~** auf der Vorderseite, vorn. **2.** △ (Vorder)Front *f*, Fassade *f* (*a. fig.* F). **3.** ✕ Front *f:* **to the ~** an die Front; **on all ~s** an allen Fronten (*a. fig.*). **4.** Vordergrund *m:* **in ~** an der *od.* die Spitze, vorn; **in ~ of** vor (*dat*); **to the**

~ nach vorn. 5. *fig.* Bereich *m*, Sektor *m:* **on the educational ~** auf dem Erziehungssektor. **6.** *fig.* Frechheit *f*, Unverschämtheit *f:* **have the ~ to do s.th.** die Stirn haben, et. zu tun. **7.** *meteor.* Front *f.* **II** *adj* **8.** Front..., Vorder...: **~ entrance** Vordereingang *m;* **~** vorder(st)e Reihe; **~ tooth** Vorderzahn *m.* **III** *v/t* **9.** gegenüberstehen, -liegen: **the windows ~ the street** der Garten geht auf die Straße (hinaus). **IV** *v/i* **10. ~ on** (*od.* **to, toward**[**s**]) → 9. **'front·age** *s* △ (Vorder)Front *f.* **'fron·tal** *adj* **1.** Frontal... **2.** *anat.*, ⚙ Stirn...

,front|'bench·er *s parl. Br.* führendes Fraktionsmitglied. **~ door** *s* Haus-, Vordertür *f:* **by** (*od.* **through**) **the ~** *fig.* direkt, ohne Umschweife; legal.

fron·tier ['frʌn,tɪə] **I** *s* Grenze *f* (*a. fig.*). **II** *adj* Grenz...: **~ town.**

front| line *s* ✕ Front(linie) *f:* **be in the ~** an vorderster Front stehen (*a. fig.*). **~ page** *s* erste Seite, Titelseite *f* (*e-r Zeitung*): **hit the ~s** Schlagzeilen machen. **'~-page** *adj* wichtig, aktuell: **~ news. ~ pas·sen·ger** *s mot.* Beifahrer(in). **'~- ,pas·sen·ger seat** *s mot.* Beifahrersitz *m.* **~ rank** *s:* **be in the ~** *fig.* zur Spitze gehören *od.* zählen. **'~-seat pas·sen·ger** *s mot.* Beifahrer(in). **'~-wheel drive** *s* ⚙ Vorderrad-, Frontantrieb *m.*

frost [frɒst] **I** *s* **1.** Frost *m.* **2.** Reif *m.* **II** *v/t* **3.** mit Reif überziehen. **4.** ⚙ *Glas* mattieren: **~ed glass** Matt-, Milchglas *n.* **5.** *gastr. bsd. Am.* glasieren, mit Zuckerguß überziehen; mit (Puder)Zucker bestreuen. **'~bite** *s* Erfrierung *f.* **'~- ,bit·ten** [~tn] *adj* erfroren.

frost·ing ['frɒstɪŋ] *s gastr. bsd. Am.* Zuckerguß *m*, Glasur *f.* **'frost·y** *adj* □ **1.** eisig, frostig (*beide a. fig.*). **2.** mit Reif bedeckt. **3.** (eis)grau: **~ hair.**

froth [frɒθ] **I** *s* Schaum *m.* **II** *v/t a.* **~ up** zum Schäumen bringen; zu Schaum schlagen. **III** *v/i* schäumen. **'froth·y** *adj* □ **1.** schaumig; schäumend. **2.** *fig.* seicht.

frown [fraʊn] **I** *v/i* die Stirn runzeln (**at** über *acc*) (*a. fig.*): **~ on** et. mißbilligen. **II** *s* Stirnrunzeln *n:* **with a ~** stirnrunzelnd.

frowst [fraʊst] *s bsd. Br.* F Mief *m:* **there's a ~ in here** hier mieft es.

'frowst·y adj bsd. Br. F miefig, vermieft.

frowz·y ['frauzɪ] adj **1.** schlampig, ungepflegt. **2.** muffig.

froze [frəʊz] pret von **freeze.** **'fro·zen** I pp von **freeze.** II adj Gefrier...: ~ **meat;** ~ **food** Tiefkühlkost f.

fru·gal ['fru:gl] adj □ **1.** sparsam: a) haushälterisch (**of** mit, in dat), b) wirtschaftlich (**Auto** etc). **2.** genügsam, bescheiden. **3.** einfach, bescheiden (**Mahlzeit**).

fruit [fru:t] s **1.** Frucht f. **2.** coll. a) Früchte pl: **bear** ~ Früchte tragen (a. fig.), b) Obst n. **3.** mst pl fig. Früchte pl. **'~cake** s englischer Kuchen. ~ **cock·tail** s Frucht-, Früchtecocktail m.

fruit·er·er ['fru:tərə] s bsd. Br. Obsthändler m. **fruit·ful** ['~fʊl] adj □ **1.** fruchtbar (a. fig.). **2.** fig. erfolgreich.

fru·i·tion [fru:'ɪʃn] s: **bring to** ~ verwirklichen; **come to** ~ sich verwirklichen; Früchte tragen.

fruit knife s (irr **knife**) Obstmesser n. **fruit·less** ['fru:tlɪs] adj □ **1.** unfruchtbar. **2.** fig. frucht-, erfolglos.

fruit| ma·chine s Br. (Geld)Spielautomat m. ~ **sal·ad** s Obstsalat m. ~ **tree** s Obstbaum m.

fruit·y ['fru:tɪ] adj **1.** fruchtartig. **2.** fruchtig (**Wein**). **3.** Br. F saftig, gepfeffert (**Witz** etc). **4.** Am. F schmalzig: ~ **song** Schnulze f.

frump [frʌmp] s: **old** ~ alte Schachtel.

frus·trate [frʌ'streɪt] v/t **1.** Plan etc vereiteln, durchkreuzen; Hoffnungen zunichte machen. **2.** j-n frustrieren. **frus·'tra·tion** s **1.** Vereit(e)lung f, Durchkreuzung f. **2.** Frustration f (a. psych.).

fry¹ [fraɪ] v/t u. v/i braten: **fried eggs** pl Spiegeleier pl; **fried potatoes** pl Bratkartoffeln pl.

fry² [~] s: **small** ~ ein kleiner Fisch, kleine Fische pl (**Person**[en]).

fry·ing pan ['fraɪɪŋ] s Bratpfanne f: **jump** (od. **leap**) **out of the** ~ **into the fire** fig. vom Regen in die Traufe kommen.

fuck [fʌk] v/t u. v/i V ficken, vögeln: ~ **off!** verpiß dich! **'fuck·ing** adj V Scheiß..., verflucht.

fud·dled ['fʌdld] adj F **1.** benebelt. **2.** verwirrt, durcheinander.

fuel [fjʊəl] s Brennstoff m: a) Heiz-, Brennmaterial n, b) mot. etc Treib-,

Kraftstoff m: ~ **ga(u)ge** Benzinuhr f; ~ **injection engine** Einspritzmotor m; **add** ~ **to the fire** (od. **flames**) fig. Öl ins Feuer gießen.

fug [fʌg], **'fug·gy** → **frowst, frowsty.**

fu·gi·tive ['fju:dʒətɪv] I s a) Flüchtige m, b) pol. etc Flüchtling m, c) Ausreißer m. II adj flüchtig: a) entflohen, b) fig. vergänglich.

ful·fil, Am. a. **ful·fill** [fʊl'fɪl] v/t Bedingung, Versprechen etc erfüllen, Befehl etc ausführen: ~ **o.s.** sich (selbst) verwirklichen; **be fulfilled** sich erfüllen. **ful·'fil(l)·ment** s Erfüllung f, Ausführung f.

full [fʊl] I adj (□ → **fully**) **1.** allg. voll: ~ **of** voll von, voller; → **stomach** 1. **2.** voll, ganz: **a** ~ **hour** e-e volle od. geschlagene Stunde. **3.** voll (**Gesicht**), vollschlank (**Figur**). **4.** voll, besetzt: ~ (**up**) (voll) besetzt (**Bus** etc); **house** ~! thea. ausverkauft! **5.** fig. (ganz) erfüllt (**of** von): ~ **of o.s.** (ganz) von sich eingenommen. **6.** reichlich (**Mahlzeit**). **7.** voll, unbeschränkt: ~ **power** Vollmacht f; **have** ~ **power to do s.th.** bevollmächtigt sein, et. zu tun. **8.** voll(berechtigt): ~ **member** Vollmitglied m. **9.** a. ~ **up** F voll, satt. II adv **10.** völlig, ganz: **know** ~ **well that** ganz genau wissen, daß. **11.** ~ **out** mit Vollgas fahren, auf Hochtouren arbeiten. III s **12.** **in** ~ vollständig, ganz: **spell** (od. **write**) **in** ~ ausschreiben; **to the** ~ vollständig, bis ins letzte od. kleinste.

full| age s: **of** ~ ⚤ mündig, volljährig. **'~back** s Fußball: (Außen)Verteidiger m. **~'blood·ed** adj **1.** vollblütig, Vollblut... (**beide** a. fig.). **2.** eindringlich (**Argument** etc). **~'blown** adj **1.** ⚘ ganz aufgeblüht. **2.** voll entwickelt, ausgereift (**Idee** etc). **3.** ausgemacht (**Skandal** etc). **~'fledged** bsd. Am. → **fully fledged.** **~'grown** adj ausgewachsen. **~'length** adj **1.** in voller Größe, lebensgroß. **2.** abendfüllend (**Film**); ausgewachsen (**Roman**). ~ **moon** s Vollmond m: **at** ~ bei Vollmond.

full·ness ['fʊlnɪs] s (♪ Klang)Fülle f: **feeling of** ~ Völlegefühl n.

'full|-page adj ganzseitig. **'~-scale** adj **1.** in Originalgröße, im Maßstab 1:1. **2.** fig. großangelegt, Groß... ~ **stop** s ling. Punkt m. **'~-time I** adj ganztägig,

Ganztags... **II** *adv* ganztags: **work ~**.

ful·ly ['fʊlɪ] *adv* voll, völlig, ganz: **~ automatic** vollautomatisch; **~ two hours** volle *od.* geschlagene zwei Stunden. **~ fledged** *adj* **1.** flügge (*Vogel*). **2.** *fig.* richtig.

ful·mi·nate ['fʌlmɪneɪt] *v/i* donnern, wettern (**against, at** gegen).

ful·ness *bsd. Am.* → **fullness**.

ful·some ['fʊlsəm] *adj* □ übertrieben; überschwenglich (*Lob etc*).

fum·ble ['fʌmbl] **I** *v/i a.* **~ about** (*od. around*) herumtappen, -tasten; (herum)fummeln (**at** an *dat*); ungeschickt umgehen (**with** mit); tastend suchen (**for, after** nach): **~ in one's pockets** in s-n Taschen (herum)wühlen; **~ for words** nach Worten suchen. **II** *v/t* verpatzen. **'fum·bler** *s* Patzer(in).

fume [fjuːm] **I** *s* **1.** *oft pl* Dampf *m*, Rauch *m.* **II** *v/i* **2.** dampfen, rauchen. **3.** *fig.* wütend *od.* aufgebracht sein (**at** über *acc*).

fu·mi·gate ['fjuːmɪgeɪt] *v/t* ausräuchern.

fun [fʌn] *s* Spaß *m*: **for ~** aus *od.* zum Spaß; **in ~** im *od.* zum Scherz; **make ~ of** sich lustig machen über (*acc*); → **poke** 4.

func·tion ['fʌŋkʃn] **I** *s* **1.** *allg.* Funktion *f*: **out of ~** ⊙ außer Betrieb. **II** *v/i* **2. ~ as** tätig sein *od.* fungieren als; dienen als (*Sache*). **3.** ⊙ *etc* funktionieren. **'func·tion·al** *adj* □ **1.** *allg.* funktionell, Funktions...: **~ disorder** 🗲 Funktionsstörung *f*. **2.** zweckbetont, -mäßig, praktisch. **'func·tion·ar·y** *s bsd. pol.* Funktionär *m*.

fund [fʌnd] *s* **1.** ✝ Kapital *n*, Vermögen *n*; Fonds *m*. **2.** *pl* ✝ (Geld)Mittel *pl*: **no ~s** (*Scheck*) keine Deckung; **be in** (**out of**) **~s** (nicht) bei Kasse sein, zahlungs(un)fähig sein. **3.** *fig.* Vorrat *m* (**of** an *dat*).

fun·da·men·tal [ˌfʌndə'mentl] **I** *adj* (□ → **fundamentally**) **1.** grundlegend, wesentlich, fundamental (**to** für). **2.** grundsätzlich, elementar. **3.** Grund..., Fundamental...: **~ research** Grundlagenforschung *f*. **II** *s* **4.** Grundlage *f*, -prinzip *n*, -begriff *m*. **fun·da'men·tal·ly** *adv* im Grunde, im wesentlichen.

fu·ner·al ['fjuːnərəl] *s* Begräbnis *n*, Beerdigung *f*: **that's your ~** F das ist dein Problem. **II** *adj* Begräbnis...: **~ march**

♪ Trauermarsch *m*; **~ parlo(u)r** Leichenhalle *f*; **~ service** Trauergottesdienst *m*.

'fun·fair *s bsd. Br.* Vergnügungspark *m*, Rummelplatz *m*.

fun·gus ['fʌŋgəs] *pl* **-gi** ['~gaɪ], **-gus·es** *s* 🗲 Pilz *m*, Schwamm *m*.

fu·nic·u·lar (**rail·way**) [fjuː'nɪkjʊlə] *s* (Draht)Seilbahn *f*.

funk [fʌŋk] F **I** *s* Schiß *m*, Bammel *m*: **be in a blue ~ of** e-n mächtigen Schiß *od.* Bammel haben vor (*dat*). **II** *v/t* kneifen *od.* sich drücken vor (*dat*).

fun·nel ['fʌnl] *s* **1.** Trichter *m*. **2.** 🏴, 🚂 Schornstein *m*.

fun·nies ['fʌnɪz] *s pl bsd. Am.* F *Zeitung*: Comics *pl*; Comic-Teil *m*.

fun·ny ['fʌnɪ] *adj* □ komisch: a) spaßig, lustig, b) sonderbar, merkwürdig. **~ bone** *s anat.* Musikantenknochen *m*.

fur [fɜː] *s* **1.** Pelz *m*, Fell *n*: **make the ~ fly** *fig.* Stunk machen (*Person*), (*die Sache*) für helle Aufregung sorgen. **2.** a) Pelzfutter *n*, -besatz *m*: **~ collar** Pelzkragen *m*, b) a. **~ coat** Pelzmantel *m*.

fur·bish ['fɜːbɪʃ] *v/t* **1.** polieren, blank reiben. **2.** *oft* **~ up** herrichten, *Gebäude etc a.* renovieren; *fig. Kenntnisse* auffrischen.

fu·ri·ous ['fjʊərɪəs] *adj* □ **1.** wütend, zornig (**with** *s.o.* auf, über *acc*; **at** *s.th.* über *acc*). **2.** wild, heftig (*Kampf etc*).

furl [fɜːl] *v/t Fahne, Transparent etc* auf-, einrollen, *Schirm* zs.-rollen.

fur·nace ['fɜːnɪs] *s* ⊙ (Schmelz-, Hoch-) Ofen *m*.

fur·nish ['fɜːnɪʃ] *v/t* **1.** versorgen, ausrüsten, -statten (**with** mit): **~ s.o. with s.th.** *a.* j-n mit et. beliefern. **2.** *Informationen etc* liefern: **~ proof** den Beweis liefern *od.* erbringen. **3.** *Wohnung etc* einrichten, möblieren: **~ed room** möbliertes Zimmer; → **furnish·ings** *s pl*. **'fur·nish·ings** *s pl* Einrichtung *f*, Mobiliar *n*.

fur·ni·ture ['fɜːnɪtʃə] *s* Möbel *pl*: **piece of ~** Möbelstück *n*; → **stick**[1] 4.

furred [fɜːd] *adj* **1.** Pelz... **2.** mit Pelz besetzt. **3.** 🗲 belegt (*Zunge*).

fur·row ['fʌrəʊ] **I** *s* **1.** (Acker)Furche *f*. **2.** Runzel *f*, Furche *f*. **II** *v/t* **3.** *Land* furchen; *Wasser* durchfurchen. **4.** *Gesicht, Stirn* furchen, runzeln.

fur·ther ['fɜːðə] **I** *adv* **1.** *comp von* **far**. **2.** *fig.* mehr, weiter. **3.** *fig.* ferner, weiterhin. **4.** → **farther 4. II** adj **5.** fig. weiter: **~ education** Br. Fort-, Weiterbildung f; **anything ~?** (sonst) noch etwas? **6.** → **farther 2. III** v/t **7.** fördern, unterstützen. ,**fur·ther'more** → **further 3.** '**further·most** adj fig. äußerst. **fur·thest** ['~ðɪst] **I** adj **1.** sup von **far. 2.** fig. weitest, meist: **at (the)** ~ höchstens. **3.** → **farthest 2. II** adv **4.** fig. am weitesten, am meisten. **5.** → **farthest 4.**

fur·tive ['fɜːtɪv] adj □ heimlich, (Blick a.) verstohlen.

fu·ry ['fjʊərɪ] s Wut f, Zorn m: **for** ~ vor lauter Wut; **fly into a** ~ wütend od. zornig werden.

fuse [fjuːz] **I** s **1.** Zünder m. **2.** ≠ Sicherung f: **~ box** Sicherungskasten m. **II** v/t **3.** phys., ⊛ schmelzen. **4.** fig. verschmelzen, ✝, pol. a. fusionieren. **III** v/i **5.** ⊛ schmelzen. **6.** fig. verschmelzen, ✝, pol. a. fusionieren.

fu·se·lage ['fjuːzəlɑːʒ] s (Flugzeug-)Rumpf m.

fu·sion ['fjuːʒn] s **1.** phys., ⊛ Schmelzen n. **2.** biol., opt., phys. Fusion f: **~ bomb** Wasserstoffbombe f. **3.** fig. Verschmelzung f, ✝, pol. a. Fusion f.

fuss [fʌs] **I** s **1.** (unnötige) Aufregung:

get into a ~ → **3. 2.** Wirbel m, Theater n: **make a** ~ → **4. II** v/i **3.** sich (unnötig) aufregen (**about** über acc): **don't** ~! nur keine Aufregung. **4.** viel Wirbel machen (**about, over** um). **5.** ~ **about** (od. **around**) herumfuhrwerken. '**~,budg·et** s Am. F, '**~,pot** s F Kleinlichkeitskrämer m. **fuss·y** ['fʌsɪ] adj □ **1.** (unnötig) aufgeregt. **2.** kleinlich, pedantisch. **3.** heikel, wählerisch (**about** in dat).

fust·y ['fʌstɪ] adj □ **1.** mod(e)rig, muffig. **2.** fig. verstaubt, -altet; rückständig.

fu·tile ['fjuːtaɪl] adj □ **1.** nutzlos, vergeblich. **2.** unbedeutend, geringfügig. **fu·til·i·ty** [~'tɪlətɪ] s **1.** Nutzlosigkeit f. **2.** Geringfügigkeit f.

fu·ture ['fjuːtʃə] **I** s **1.** Zukunft f: **in** ~ in Zukunft. **2.** ling. Futur n, Zukunft f. **II** adj **3.** (zu)künftig, Zukunfts... **4.** ling. futurisch: ~ **perfect** Futurum n exaktum, zweites Futur; ~ **tense** → 2.

fuze bsd. Am. → **fuse.**

fuzz¹ [fʌz] s feiner Flaum.

fuzz² [~] s sl. Bulle m (Polizist): **the** ~ coll. die Bullen.

fuzz·y ['fʌzɪ] adj □ **1.** flaumig. **2.** kraus, wuschelig. **3.** unscharf, verschwommen.

G

gab [gæb] s F Gequassel n, Gequatsche n: **have the gift of the** ~ (Am. **of** ~) ein flottes Mundwerk haben.

gab·ble ['gæbl] **I** v/i **1.** a. ~ **away** brabbeln. **2.** schnattern (Gänse). **II** v/t **3.** Gebet etc herunterleiern, -rasseln. **4.** et. brabbeln. **III** s **5.** Gebrabbel n. **6.** Geschnatter n.

gab·er·dine [,gæbə'diːn] s Gabardine m.

ga·ble ['geɪbl] s Giebel m: ~ **window** Giebelfenster n. '**ga·bled** adj Giebel...

gad [gæd] v/i: ~ **about** (od. **around**) (viel) unterwegs sein (in dat); (viel) herumkommen (in dat); sich herumtreiben (in dat).

gadg·et ['gædʒɪt] s ⊛ F Apparat m, Gerät n; oft contp. technische Spielerei.

Gael·ic ['geɪlɪk] **I** s ling. Gälisch n. **II** adj gälisch: ~ **coffee** Irish coffee m.

gaff [gæf] s sl.: **blow the** ~ alles verraten, plaudern; **blow the** ~ **on s.th.** et. ausplaudern.

gaffe [gæf] s Fauxpas m, bsd. taktlose Bemerkung.

gag [gæg] **I** v/t **1.** knebeln (a. fig.). **2.** fig. mundtot machen. **II** s **3.** Knebel m (a. fig.). **4.** F Gag m.

ga·ga ['gɑːgɑː] adj sl. verkalkt, -trottelt; plemplem.

gage Am. → **gauge.**

gag·gle ['gægl] **I** v/i **1.** schnattern (Gänse) (a. fig.). **II** s **2.** Geschnatter n (a. fig.). **3.** Gänseherde f; F schnatternde Schar.

gai·e·ty ['geɪətɪ] s **1.** Fröhlichkeit f. **2.** oft pl Vergnügung f.

gain [geɪn] **I** v/t **1.** Zeit, j-s Vertrauen etc gewinnen: → ground², upper I. **2.** erreichen, erwerben, Erfahrungen sammeln: → advantage. **3.** j-m et. einbringen, -tragen. **4.** zunehmen an (dat): ~ speed schneller werden; he ~ed 10 pounds er nahm 10 Pfund zu; → weight I. **5.** vorgehen (um) (Uhr). **II** v/i **6.** Einfluß od. Boden gewinnen. **7.** zunehmen (in an dat). **8.** vorgehen (by two minutes zwei Minuten) (Uhr). **III** s **9.** Gewinn (to für) (a. ✝). **10.** Zunahme f (in an dat): ~ in weight Gewichtszunahme. **gain·ful** ['feɪl] adj □ einträglich, gewinnbringend: ~ employment Erwerbstätigkeit f; ~ly employed erwerbstätig. '**gain·ings** s pl Gewinn(e pl) m.

gait [geɪt] s **1.** Gang(art f) m. **2.** Gangart f (des Pferdes).

gal [gæl] s F Mädchen n.

ga·la ['gɑːlə] **I** adj **1.** festlich, Gala... **II** s **2.** Festlichkeit f. **3.** Gala(veranstaltung) f.

ga·lac·tic [gə'læktɪk] adj ast. Milchstraßen..., galaktisch.

gal·ax·y ['gæləksɪ] s ast. Milchstraße f.

gale [geɪl] s Sturm m (a. fig. F): a ~ of laughter e-e Lachsalve, stürmisches Gelächter.

gall¹ [gɔːl] **I** s **1.** wund geriebene od. gescheuerte Stelle. **II** v/t **2.** wund reiben od. scheuern. **3.** fig. (ver)ärgern.

gall² [~] s **1.** Bitterkeit f, Erbitterung f. **2.** F Frechheit f.

gal·lant ['gælənt] adj □ **1.** tapfer. **2.** prächtig, stattlich. **3.** galant. '**gal·lant·ry** s **1.** Tapferkeit f. **2.** Galanterie f.

gall blad·der s anat. Gallenblase f.

gal·ler·y ['gælərɪ] s **1.** △ Galerie f, Empore f (in Kirchen). **2.** thea. Galerie f (a. Publikum): play to the ~ für die Galerie spielen (a. weitS.). **3.** (Gemälde- etc-) Galerie f.

gal·ley ['gælɪ] s **1.** ♣ hist. Galeere f. **2.** ♣ Kombüse f.

Gal·li·cism ['gælɪsɪzəm] s ling. Gallizismus m.

gal·lon ['gælən] s Gallone f (GB: 4,55 l, USA: 3,79 l).

gal·lop ['gæləp] **I** v/i galoppieren (a. Pferd), (im) Galopp reiten: ~ing infla-

---

tion ✝ galoppierende Inflation. **II** s Galopp m: at a ~ im Galopp.

gal·lows ['gæləʊz] pl -lows·es, -lows s Galgen m. ~ **bird** s F Galgenvogel m. ~ **hu·mo(u)r** s Galgenhumor m.

'**gall·stone** s ♣ Gallenstein m.

Gal·lup poll ['gæləp] s Meinungsumfrage f.

ga·lore [gə'lɔː] adv F in rauhen Mengen: money ~ Geld in rauhen Mengen.

ga·lumph [gə'lʌmf] v/i F stampfen, stapfen.

gal·va·nize ['gælvənaɪz] v/t **1.** ⊙ galvanisieren. **2.** fig. elektrisieren.

gam·ble ['gæmbl] **I** v/i (um Geld) spielen: ~ with s.th. fig. mit et. spielen, et. aufs Spiel setzen. **II** v/t mst ~ away verspielen (a. fig.). **III** s Hasardspiel n (a. fig.), Glücksspiel n. '**gam·bler** s **1.** (Glücks)Spieler m. **2.** fig. Hasardeur m. '**gam·bling** adj Spiel...: ~ casino; ~ den Spielhölle f.

gam·bol ['gæmbl] **I** v/i pret u. pp -boled, bsd.Br. -bolled (herum)tanzen, (-)hüpfen, Freuden- od. Luftsprünge machen. **II** s Freuden-, Luftsprung m.

game [geɪm] **I** s **1.** (Karten-, Ball- etc-) Spiel n: play the ~ sich an die Spielregeln halten (a. fig.); → chance 1, skill 1. **2.** (einzelnes) Spiel: a ~ of chess e-e Partie Schach. **3.** fig. Spiel n, Plan m: the ~ is up das Spiel ist aus; play a double ~ ein doppeltes Spiel treiben; beat s.o. at his own ~ j-n mit s-n eigenen Waffen schlagen. **4.** F Branche f: be in the advertising ~ in Werbung machen. **5.** pl ped. Sport m. **6.** Wild(bret) n. **II** adj □ **7.** mutig. **8.** a) aufgelegt (for zu): be ~ to do s.th. dazu aufgelegt sein, et. zu tun, b) bereit (for zu; to do zu tun). '~,**keep·er** s bsd. Br. Wildhüter m. ~ **park** s Wildpark m. ~ **pre·serve** s Wildgehege n.

gam·ma rays ['gæmə] s pl phys. Gammastrahlen pl.

gam·mon ['gæmən] s schwachgepökelter od. -geräucherter Schinken.

gamp [gæmp] s Br. F (bsd. großer) Regenschirm.

gam·ut ['gæmət] s **1.** ♪ Tonleiter f. **2.** fig. Skala f.

gan·der ['gændə] s Gänserich m.

gang [gæŋ] **I** s **1.** (Arbeiter)Kolonne f, (-)Trupp m. **2.** Gang f, Bande f. **3.** Cli-

que f (a. contp.). **4.** contp. Horde f. **II** v/i
5. mst ~ **up** sich zs.-tun, bsd. contp. sich
zs.-rotten: ~ **up against** (od. **on**) sich
verbünden od. verschwören gegen.

gan·grene ['gæŋgriːn] s ✦ Brand m.

gang·ster ['gæŋstə] s Gangster m, Verbrecher m.

'**gang·way** s **1.** Durchgang m, Passage f.
2. ⚓, ✈ Gangway f. **3.** Br. thea etc
(Zwischen)Gang m.

gaol [dʒeil], etc bsd. Br. → **jail**, etc.

gap [gæp] s **1.** Lücke f (a. fig.): **fill in a ~
in one's education** e-e Bildungslücke
schließen. **2.** fig. Kluft f.

gape [geip] **I** v/i **1.** den Mund aufreißen
(vor Staunen etc). **2.** (mit offenem
Mund) gaffen od. glotzen: ~ **at s.o.** j-n
angaffen od. anglotzen. **II** s **3.** Gaffen
n, Glotzen n. **4.** gähnender Abgrund.
'**gap·ing** adj □ **1.** gaffend, glotzend. **2.**
klaffend (Wunde), gähnend (Abgrund).

ga·rage ['gærɑːʒ] **I** s **1.** Garage f. **2.**
Reparaturwerkstätte f (u. Tankstelle
f). **II** v/t **3.** Auto in die Garage fahren.

gar·bage ['gɑːbɪdʒ] s **1.** bsd. Am. Abfall
m, Müll m: ~ **can** Abfall-, Mülleimer
m; Abfall-, Mülltonne f; ~ **chute** Müllschlucker m; ~ **collection** Müllabfuhr
f; ~ **collector** (od. **man**) Müllmann m; ~
truck Müllwagen m. **2.** fig. Schund m;
Unfug m.

gar·ble ['gɑːbl] v/t Text etc durcheinanderbringen; (durch Auslassungen etc)
verfälschen.

gar·den ['gɑːdn] **I** s **1.** Garten m. **2.** oft pl
Garten(anlagen pl) m: → **botanical**,
zoological. II adj **3.** Garten...: ~ **center**
(bsd. Br. **centre**) Gartencenter n; ~ **city**
Br. Gartenstadt f; ~ **party** Gartenfest n,
-party f; **lead s.o. up the ~ path** j-n
hinters Licht führen; ~ **suburb** Br. Gartenvorstadt f. **III** v/i **4.** im Garten arbeiten. '**gar·den·er** s Gärtner(in).
'**gar·den·ing** s Gartenarbeit f.

gar·gan·tu·an [gɑːˈgæntjʊən] adj riesig,
gewaltig.

gar·gle ['gɑːgl] **I** v/t **1.** gurgeln mit. **II** v/i
2. gurgeln (with mit). **III** s **3.** Gurgeln n:
have a ~ gurgeln. **4.** Gurgelmittel n.

gar·ish ['geərɪʃ] adj □ grell (Licht), (Farben a.) schreiend, (Parfüm) aufdringlich.

gar·land ['gɑːlənd] **I** s Girlande f, (a.

Sieges)Kranz m. **II** v/t bekränzen.

gar·lic ['gɑːlɪk] s ♣ Knoblauch m.

gar·ment ['gɑːmənt] s Kleidungsstück n,
pl a. Kleidung f.

gar·net ['gɑːnɪt] s min. Granat m.

gar·nish ['gɑːnɪʃ] **I** v/t **1.** (**with** mit)
schmücken, verzieren; fig. ausschmükken. **2.** gastr. garnieren (**with** mit). **II** s
3. Verzierung f; fig. Ausschmückung f.
4. gastr. Garnierung f.

gar·ret ['gærət] s Dachkammer f.

gar·ri·son ['gærɪsn] ✕ **I** s **1.** Garnison f:
~ **town** Garnison(s)stadt f. **II** v/t **2.** Ort
mit e-r Garnison belegen. **3.** Truppen in
Garnison legen.

gar·ru·li·ty [gæˈruːlətɪ] s Geschwätzigkeit f. **gar·ru·lous** ['gærələs] adj □ geschwätzig.

gar·ter ['gɑːtə] s Strumpfband n; Sokkenhalter m; Am. Strumpfhalter m,
Straps m.

gas [gæs] **I** pl ~**(·es)es 1.** Gas n. **2.** F a) Am.
Benzin n, Sprit m, b) **step on the ~** Gas
geben, auf die Tube drücken (beide a.
fig.). **3.** F Gewäsch n, Blech n. **II** v/t **4.**
vergasen: **be ~sed** a. e-e Gasvergiftung
erleiden. **III** v/i **5.** F faseln. '~**·bag** s F
Quatscher(in). ~ **cham·ber** s Gaskammer f. ~ **cook·er** s Gasherd m.

gas·e·ous ['gæsjəs] adj **1.** gasförmig. **2.**
Gas...

gas ex·plo·sion s Gasexplosion f.

gash [gæʃ] **I** s klaffende Wunde, tiefer
Riß od. Schnitt. **II** v/t j-m e-e klaffende
Wunde beibringen, Haut aufreißen
-schlitzen.

gas heat·ing s Gasheizung f.

gas·ket ['gæskɪt] s ⊙ Dichtung(smanschette) f.

'**gas·|man** s (irr **man**) Gasmann m, -ableser m. ~ **mask** s Gasmaske f. ~ **me·ter**
s Gasuhr f, -zähler m.

gas·o·lene, **gas·o·line** ['gæsəʊliːn] s
Am. Benzin n: ~ **attendant** Tankwart
m; ~ **bomb** Molotowcocktail m; ~ **station** Tankstelle f.

gasp [gɑːsp] **I** v/i **1.** keuchen, schwer
atmen: ~ **for breath** nach Luft schnappen. **2.** den Atem anhalten (**with**, **in** vor
dat): **make s.o. ~** j-m den Atem nehmen od. verschlagen. **II** v/t **3.** mst ~ **out**
Worte keuchen, (keuchend) hervorstoßen. **III** s **4.** Keuchen n, schweres Atmen: **be at one's last ~** in den letzten

Zügen liegen; **to the last** ~ bis zum letzten Atemzug.

gas| sta·tion s Am. F Tankstelle f. ~ **stove** s Gasofen m, -herd m.

gas·sy ['gæsɪ] adj **1.** gasartig. **2.** kohlensäurehaltig. **3.** F geschwätzig.

gas·tric ['gæstrɪk] adj ♠, physiol. Magen...: ~ **acid** Magensäure f; ~ **ulcer** Magengeschwür n. **gas·tri·tis** [gæ-'straɪtɪs] s ♠ Gastritis f, Magenschleimhautentzündung f.

gas·tro·nom·ic [͵gæstrə'nɒmɪk] adj (~**ally**) gastronomisch, feinschmeckerisch. **gas·tron·o·my** [~'strɒnəmɪ] s **1.** Gastronomie f (feine Kochkunst). **2.** fig. Küche f: **the Italian** ~

'**gas·works** s pl (mst sg konstruiert) Gaswerk n.

gate [geɪt] s **1.** Tor n (a. Skisport), Pforte f. **2.** fig. Tor n, Zugang m (**to** zu). **3.** 🚇 Sperre f, Schranke f; ✈ Flugsteig m. **4.** Sport: a) Zuschauer(zahl f) pl, b) (Gesamt)Einnahmen pl. '~**crash** v/i u. v/t F uneingeladen kommen (zu); sich ohne zu bezahlen hineinschmuggeln (in acc). '~**house** s Pförtnerhaus n. '~͵**keep·er** s **1.** Pförtner m. **2.** Bahn-, Schrankenwärter m. '~**leg(ged) ta-ble** s Klapptisch m. ~**man** ['~mən] s (irr man) bsd. Am. → gatekeeper. ~**mon·ey** → gate 4b. '~**post** s Torpfosten m: → **between** 2. '~**way** s **1.** Torweg m, Einfahrt f. **2.** → gate 2.

gath·er ['gæðə] I v/t **1.** Reichtümer, Erfahrungen etc sammeln, Informationen einholen, -ziehen. **2.** Personen versammeln. **3.** erwerben, gewinnen: ~ **dust** verstauben; ~ **speed** schneller werden. **4.** a. ~ **up** auflesen, (vom Boden) aufheben. **5.** Blumen etc pflücken. **6.** fig. folgen, schließen (**from** aus). II v/i **7.** sich (ver)sammeln od. scharen (**round s.o.** um j-n). **8.** sich (an)sammeln. '**gath·er·ing** s (Menschen)Ansammlung f; Versammlung f, Zs.-kunft f.

gauche [gəʊʃ] adj □ **1.** linkisch. **2.** taktlos.

gaud·y ['gɔːdɪ] adj □ auffällig bunt, (Farben) grell, schreiend, (Einrichtung etc) protzig.

gauge [geɪdʒ] v/t **1.** (ab-, aus)messen. **2.** ⊕ eichen. **3.** fig. (ab)schätzen, beurteilen. II s **4.** ⊕ Eichmaß n. **5.** fig. Maßstab m, Norm f (**of** für). **6.** ⊕ Meß-

gerät n, Lehre f. **7.** ⊕ Stärke f, Dicke f (bsd. von Blech od. Draht). **8.** 🚇 Spur(weite) f.

gaunt [gɔːnt] adj □ hager; ausgemergelt, -gezehrt.

gaunt·let¹ ['gɔːntlɪt] s fig. Fehdehandschuh m: **fling** (od. **throw**) **down the** ~ (**to s.o.**) (j-m) den Fehdehandschuh hinwerfen, (j-n) herausfordern; **pick** (od. **take**) **up the** ~ den Fehdehandschuh aufnehmen, die Herausforderung annehmen.

gaunt·let² [~] s: **run the** ~ Spießruten laufen (a. fig.).

gauze [gɔːz] s Gaze f, ♠ a. (Verband[s])Mull m: ~ **bandage** Mullbinde f. '**gauz·y** adj □ gazeartig, hauchdünn.

gave [geɪv] pret von **give**.

gav·el ['gævl] s Hammer m (e-s Auktionators, Vorsitzenden etc).

gawk [gɔːk] v/i glotzen: ~ **at** glotzen auf (acc), anglotzen.

gay [geɪ] I adj □ **1.** lustig, fröhlich. **2.** bunt, (farben)prächtig; fröhlich, lebhaft (Farben). **3.** lebenslustig. **4.** F schwul (homosexuell); Schwulen... II s **5.** F Schwule m.

gaze [geɪz] I v/i starren: ~ **at** starren auf (acc), anstarren. II s starrer Blick, Starren n.

ga·zette [gə'zet] s Br. Amtsblatt n, Staatsanzeiger m.

gear [gɪə] I s **1.** mot. a) Gang m: **change** (bsd. Am. **shift**) ~(**s**) schalten; **change** (bsd. Am. **shift**) **into second** ~ den zweiten Gang einlegen, in den zweiten Gang schalten, b) pl Getriebe n. **2.** Vorrichtung f, Gerät n. **3.** F Kleidung f, Aufzug m. II v/t **4.** ~ **up** (**down**) fig. steigern (drosseln). **5.** fig. (**to, for**) anpassen (dat od. an acc), abstimmen (auf acc). '~**box** s mot. Getriebe n. ~ **change** s mot. Br. (Gang)Schaltung f. ~ **le·ver** s mot. Br. Schalthebel m. '~**shift** s mot. Am. **1.** (Gang)Schaltung f. **2.** a. ~ **lever** Schalthebel m. '~**wheel** s ⊕ Getriebe-, Zahnrad n.

gee [dʒiː] int Am. F na so was!, Mann!

geese [giːs] pl von **goose.**

Gei·ger count·er ['gaɪgə] s phys. Geigerzähler m.

gei·sha ['geɪʃə] pl -**sha(s)** s Geisha f.

gel·a·tin ['dʒelətɪn], **gel·a·tine** [͵~'tiːn] s **1.** Gelatine f. **2.** Gallerte f. **ge·lat·i-**

nous [dʒə'læɪnəs] *adj* □ gallertartig.

geld [geld] *v/t* (*a. irr*) Tier, *bsd.* Hengst kastrieren, verschneiden. **'geld·ing** *s* kastriertes Tier, *bsd.* Wallach *m*.

gelt [gelt] *pret u. pp von* **geld.**

gem [dʒem] *s* **1.** Edelstein *m.* **2.** *fig.* Perle *f*, Juwel *n* (*beide a. Person*), Prachtstück *n*.

Gem·i·ni ['dʒemɪnaɪ] *s pl* (*mst sg konstruiert*) *ast.* Zwillinge *pl*.

gen·der ['dʒendə] *s ling.* Genus *n*, Geschlecht *n*: **what ~ is ...?** welches Genus hat ...? '**~,bend·er** *s sl.* Transvestit *m*.

gene [dʒiːn] *s biol.* Gen *n*, Erbfaktor *m*.

gen·e·a·log·i·cal [,dʒiːnjə'lɒdʒɪkl] *adj* □ genealogisch: **~ tree** Stammbaum *m.* **gen·e·al·o·gy** [,dʒiːnɪ'ælədʒɪ] *s* Genealogie *f*.

gen·er·a ['dʒenərə] *pl von* **genus.**

gen·er·al ['dʒenərəl] **I** *adj* (□ → **generally**) **1.** allgemein (gebräuchlich *od.* verbreitet), üblich, gängig: **as a ~ rule** meistens, üblicherweise. **2.** allgemein, generell: **~ education** (*od.* **knowledge**) Allgemeinbildung *f*; **the ~ public** die breite Öffentlichkeit; **~ term** Allgemeinbegriff *m.* **3.** allgemein (*nicht spezialisiert*): **the ~ reader** der Durchschnittsleser. **4.** allgemein (gehalten); ungefähr: **a ~ idea** e-e ungefähre Vorstellung. **5.** Haupt..., General...: **~ manager** Generaldirektor *m.* **II** *s* **6.** ✕ General *m.* **7. in ~** im allgemeinen, im großen u. ganzen. **~ e·lec·tion** *s* Parlamentswahlen *pl*.

gen·er·al·i·ty [,dʒenə'rælətɪ] *s* **1.** *mst pl* allgemeine Redensart, Gemeinplatz *m.* **2.** Allgemeingültigkeit *f*.

gen·er·al·ize ['dʒenərəlaɪz] *v/t* verallgemeinern.

gen·er·al·ly ['dʒenərəlɪ] *adv a.* **~ speaking** im allgemeinen, allgemein.

gen·er·al| prac·ti·tion·er *s* praktischer Arzt. **~ staff** *s* ✕ Generalstab *m.* **~ strike** *s* ✝ Generalstreik *m.*

gen·er·ate ['dʒenəreɪt] *v/t* **1.** *Elektrizität etc* erzeugen. **2.** *biol.* zeugen. **3.** *fig.* bewirken, erzeugen, verursachen. ,**gen·er'a·tion** *s* **1.** Generation *f* (*a.* ◎ *etc*). **2.** Erzeugung *f*. **3.** *biol.* Zeugung *f*, Fortpflanzung *f*. ,**gen·er'a·tion·al** [~ʃənl] *adj* Generations...: **~ conflict** (*od.* **clash**) Generationskonflikt *m.* **gen·er·a·tive** ['~rətɪv] *adj biol.* Zeu-

gungs..., Fortpflanzungs...: **~ power** Zeugungskraft *f*. **gen·er·a·tor** ['~reɪtə] *s* ⚡ Generator *m*.

ge·ner·ic [dʒɪ'nerɪk] *adj*: **~ term** (*od.* **name**) *biol.* Gattungsname *m*; *allg.* Oberbegriff *m*.

gen·er·os·i·ty [,dʒenə'rɒsətɪ] *s* Großzügigkeit *f*, Freigebigkeit *f*. **'gen·er·ous** *adj* □ **1.** großzügig, freigebig. **2.** reichlich, üppig.

gen·e·sis ['dʒenəsɪs] *pl* **-e·ses** ['~siːz] *s* Entstehung *f*.

ge·net·ic [dʒɪ'netɪk] **I** *adj* (**~ally**) genetisch: **~ engineering** Gentechnologie *f*; **~ factor** Erbfaktor *m.* **II** *s pl* (*sg konstruiert*) Genetik *f*, Vererbungslehre *f*.

ge·ni·al ['dʒiːnjəl] *adj* □ freundlich (*a. fig.* Klima *etc*). **ge·ni·al·i·ty** [,~nɪ'ælətɪ] *s* Freundlichkeit *f*.

gen·i·tals ['dʒenɪtlz] *s pl* Genitalien *pl*, Geschlechtsteile *pl*.

gen·i·tive ['dʒenɪtɪv] *s a.* **~ case** *ling.* Genitiv *m*, zweiter Fall.

gen·ius ['dʒiːnjəs] *s* **1.** Genie *n*: a) genialer Mensch, b) Genialität *f*. **2.** (natürliche) Begabung: **have a ~ for languages** sprachbegabt sein.

gen·o·cide ['dʒenəʊsaɪd] *s* Völkermord *m*.

genre ['ʒɑ̃ːŋrə] *s* Genre *n*, Gattung *f*. **~ paint·ing** *s* Genremalerei *f*.

gent [dʒent] *s* **1.** F *od. humor. für* **gentleman: ~s' hairdresser** Herrenfriseur *m.* **2.** *pl* (*sg konstruiert*) *Br.* F Herrenklo *n.*

gen·teel [dʒen'tiːl] *adj* □ **1.** vornehm. **2.** vornehm tuend, affektiert.

gen·tle ['dʒentl] *adj* □ **1.** freundlich. **2.** sanft, zart: **~ hint** zarter Wink; → **sex** 1. '**~·folk(s)** *s pl* vornehme *od.* feine Leute *pl*.

gen·tle·man ['dʒentlmən] *s* (*irr* **man**) **1.** Gentleman *m*: **~'s** (*od.* **gentlemen's**) **agreement** Gentleman's *od.* Gentlemen's Agreement *n.* **2.** Herr *m*: **gentlemen** (*Anrede*) m-e Herren; (*in Briefen*) Sehr geehrte Herren. '**gen·tleman·like**, '**gen·tle·man·ly** *adj* gentlemanlike.

gen·tle·ness ['dʒentlnɪs] *s* **1.** Freundlichkeit *f*, Liebenswürdigkeit *f*. **2.** Sanftheit *f*, Zartheit *f*.

gen·try ['dʒentrɪ] *s* **1.** Oberschicht *f*. **2.** *Br.* niederer Adel.

gen·u·ine ['dʒenjʊɪn] *adj* □ **1.** echt: a)

authentisch (*Unterschrift etc*), b) ernsthaft (*Angebot etc*), c) aufrichtig (*Mitgefühl etc*). **2.** natürlich, ungekünstelt (*Lachen, Person*).

ge·nus ['dʒiːnəs] *pl* **gen·er·a** ['dʒenərə] *s* ♘, zo. Gattung *f*.

ge·og·ra·pher [dʒɪˈɒɡrəfə] *s* Geograph(in). **ge·o·graph·ic**, **ge·o·graph·i·cal** [ˌ~ɡræfɪk(l)] *adj* □ geographisch. **ge·og·ra·phy** [~ˈɒɡrəfɪ] *s* Geographie *f*, Erdkunde *f*.

ge·o·log·ic, **ge·o·log·i·cal** [ˌdʒɪəʊˈlɒdʒɪk(l)] *adj* □ geologisch. **ge·ol·o·gist** [~ˈɒlədʒɪst] *s* Geologe *m*. **ge·ol·o·gy** [~ˈɒlədʒɪ] *s* Geologie *f*.

ge·o·met·ric, **ge·o·met·ri·cal** [ˌdʒɪəʊˈmetrɪk(l)] *adj* □ geometrisch. **ge·om·e·try** [~ˈɒmətrɪ] *s* Geometrie *f*.

ge·ra·ni·um [dʒɪˈreɪnjəm] *s* ♘ Geranie *f*.

ger·i·at·rics [ˌdʒerɪˈætrɪks] *s pl* (*sg konstruiert*) ♣ Geriatrie *f*, Altersheilkunde *f*.

germ [dʒɜːm] *s* **1.** *biol.*, ♘ Keim *m* (*a. fig.*): **in** ~ im Keim, im Werden. **2.** ♣ Bazillus *m*, Bakterie *f*, (Krankheits)Erreger *m*.

Ger·man ['dʒɜːmən] **I** *adj* **1.** deutsch: ~ **measles** *pl* (*sg konstruiert*) ♣ Röteln *pl*. **II** *s* **2.** Deutsche *m*, *f*. **3.** *ling.* Deutsch *n*: **in** ~ auf deutsch.

ger·mane [dʒɜːˈmeɪn] *adj*: ~ **to** gehörig zu, betreffend (*acc*).

Ger·man·ic [dʒɜːˈmænɪk] *adj* germanisch. **Ger·man·ism** ['~mənɪzəm] *s ling.* Germanismus *m*.

'germ-free *adj* ♣ keimfrei.

ger·mi·nate ['dʒɜːmɪneɪt] *v/i u. v/t* keimen (lassen) (*a. fig.*).

germ war·fare *s* ✗ bakteriologische Kriegführung.

ger·on·tol·o·gy [ˌdʒerɒnˈtɒlədʒɪ] *s* ♣ Gerontologie *f*, Alternsforschung *f*.

ger·und ['dʒerənd] *s ling.* Gerundium *n*.

ges·ta·tion [dʒeˈsteɪʃn] *s* Schwangerschaft *f*; *zo.* Trächtigkeit *f*: ~ **period** Trag(e)zeit *f*.

ges·tic·u·late [dʒeˈstɪkjʊleɪt] *v/i* gestikulieren. **ges·tic·u·la·tion** *s* Gestikulation *f*.

ges·ture ['dʒestʃə] *s* Geste *f* (*a. fig.*), Gebärde *f*.

get [get] (*irr*) **I** *v/t* **1.** bekommen, erhalten. **2.** sich *et.* verschaffen *od.* besorgen: ~ **s.th. for s.o.** j-m et. besorgen:

3. erringen, erwerben, sich *Wissen etc* aneignen. **4.** erwischen; (*a. telefonisch*) erreichen. **5.** holen. **6.** schaffen, bringen. **7.** machen: ~ **s.th. ready** et. fertigmachen. **8.** (*mit pp*) lassen: ~ **one's hair cut** sich die Haare schneiden lassen. **9.** *j-n* dazu bringen (**to** zu tun): ~ **s.o. to speak** j-n zum Sprechen bringen. **10.** ~ **going** Maschine etc, *fig.* Verhandlungen etc in Gang bringen; *fig.* Schwung bringen in (*acc*). **11. have got** haben: **have got to** müssen. **12.** F kapieren, (*a. akustisch*) verstehen: **don't** ~ **me wrong** versteh mich nicht falsch. **II** *v/i* **13.** kommen, gelangen: ~ **home** nach Hause kommen. **14.** dahin kommen (**to** do zu tun): ~ **to know s.th.** et. erfahren *od.* kennenlernen. **15.** (*mit pp od. adj*) werden: ~ **tired** müde werden, ermüden. **16.** beginnen, anfangen (**doing** zu tun): ~ **going** in Gang kommen (*Maschine etc, fig. Verhandlungen etc*); *fig.* in Schwung kommen.

Verbindungen mit Präpositionen:

get| at *v/i* **1.** herankommen an (*acc*), erreichen. **2.** an *j-n* herankommen, *j-m* beikommen. **3. what is he getting at?** worauf will er hinaus? ~ **off** *v/i* absteigen von; aussteigen aus. ~ **o·ver** *v/i* hinwegkommen über (*acc*), *fig. a.* sich erholen von. ~ **through** *v/i* **1.** kommen durch (*e-e Prüfung etc*). **2.** Geld durchbringen. ~ **to** *v/i* **1.** kommen nach, erreichen. **2.** ~ **talking about** zu sprechen kommen auf (*acc*).

Verbindungen mit Adverbien:

get| a·bout *v/i* **1.** herumkommen. **2.** sich herumsprechen *od.* verbreiten (*Gerücht etc*). ~ **a·cross I** *v/t* **1.** verständlich machen; *Idee etc* an den Mann bringen. **II** *v/i* **2.** ankommen; sich verständlich machen. **3.** ankommen, einschlagen; klarwerden (**to s.o.** j-m). ~ **a·long** *v/i* **1.** vorwärts-, weiterkommen (*a. fig.*). **2.** auskommen, sich vertragen (**with** mit *j-m*). **3.** zurechtkommen (**with** mit *et.*). ~ **a·round** *v/i* **1.** → **get about**. **2.** → **get round II.** ~ **a·way** *v/i* **1.** loskommen, sich losmachen. **2.** entkommen, -wischen. ~ **with** davonkommen mit. ~ **back I** *v/t* **1.** zurückbekommen: **get one's own back** F sich rächen; **get one's own back on s.o.** → 3; → **breath** 1. **II** *v/i* **2.** zurückkommen. **3.** ~ **at s.o.** F sich an j-m rächen, es j-m heimzahlen. **~ be·hind** v/i in Rückstand kommen (**with** mit). **~ by** v/i **1.** aus-, durchkommen (**on** mit). **2.** gerade noch annehmbar sein (*Arbeit etc*), gerade noch ausreichen (*Kenntnisse*). **~ down I** v/t **1.** *Essen etc* runterkriegen. **II** v/i **2.** aus-, absteigen. **3. ~ to** sich machen an (*acc*). → **brass tacks, business** 6. **~ in I** v/t **1.** *Bemerkung etc* anbringen. **2.** *Spezialisten etc* (hin)zuziehen. **II** v/i **3.** hinein-, hereinkommen. **4.** einsteigen. **5. ~ on** F mitmachen bei. **~ off** v/i **1.** (**from**) absteigen (von), aussteigen (aus). **2.** davonkommen (**with** mit). **~ on** v/i **1.** vorwärts-, vorankommen (*a. fig.*): *he is getting on for sixty* er geht auf die Sechzig zu; *it is getting on for 5 o'clock* es geht auf 5 Uhr (zu). **2.** → **get along** 2, 3. **~ out I** v/t **1.** herausbekommen (*a. fig.*). **2.** *Worte etc* herausbringen. **II** v/i **3.** aussteigen. *a.fig.* durchsickern, herauskommen (*Geheimnis etc*). **~ o·ver** v/t hinter sich bringen. **~ round I** v/t j-n herumkriegen. **II** v/i **2.** dazu kommen (*to doing* zu tun). **~ through I** v/t **1.** durchbringen, -bekommen (*a. fig.*). **2.** → **get over.** **II** v/i **3.** durchkommen (*a. fig.*). **~ to·geth·er I** v/t **1.** *Menschen etc* zs.-bringen. **2.** zs.-tragen. **II** v/i **3.** zs.-kommen. **~ up I** v/t **1.** j-n herausputzen. **2.** *Buch etc* ausstatten, *Waren* (hübsch) aufmachen. **II** v/i **3.** aufstehen, (*von e-m Stuhl etc a.*) sich erheben.

get|-at-a·ble [get'ætəbl] *adj* F **1.** erreichbar (*Ort, Sache*). **2.** zugänglich (*Ort, Person*). **'~-a·way** s Flucht f: **~ car** Fluchtauto n. **'~to·geth·er** s F (zwanglose) Zs.-kunft: **have a ~** sich treffen, zs.-kommen. **'~-up** s F Aufmachung f: a) Ausstattung f, b) Aufzug m (*Kleidung*).

gey·ser s **1.** ['gaɪzə] Geysir m. **2.** ['giːzə] Br. Durchlauferhitzer m.

ghast·ly ['gɑːstlɪ] I *adj* **1.** gräßlich, entsetzlich (*beide a. fig.* F). **2.** gespenstisch. **II** *adv* **3. ~ pale** totenblaß.

gher·kin ['gɜːkɪn] s Gewürz-, Essiggurke f.

ghet·to ['getəʊ] *pl* **-to(e)s** s G(h)etto n. **~ blast·er** s s/. Ghetto-Blaster m (*tragbarer Stereo-Kassettenrecorder*). **~ dwell·er** s G(h)ettobewohner(in).

ghost [gəʊst] s **1.** Geist m, Gespenst n. **2.**

give up the **~** den Geist aufgeben. **3.** *fig.* Spur f. **'ghost·ly** *adj* geister-, gespensterhaft.

ghost| sto·ry s Geister-, Gespenstergeschichte f. **~ town** s Geisterstadt f. **~ train** s Geisterbahn f: *go on the* **~** Geisterbahn fahren. **~ writ·er** s Ghostwriter m.

gi·ant ['dʒaɪənt] I s Riese m. II *adj* riesig: **~ slalom** (*Skisport*) Riesenslalom m.

gib·ber ['dʒɪbə] v/i schnattern (*Affen, Personen*). **gib·ber·ish** ['~rɪʃ] s Geschnatter n.

gibe [dʒaɪb] I v/i: **~ at** (*od. about*) spotten über (*acc*), verhöhnen, -spotten. **II** s höhnische Bemerkung.

gib·lets ['dʒɪblɪts] s pl Innereien pl (*vom Geflügel*).

gid·di·ness ['gɪdɪnɪs] s **1.** Schwindel(gefühl n) m. **2.** *fig.* Leichtsinn m. **'gid·dy** *adj* □ **1. I am** (*od. feel*) **~** mir ist schwind(e)lig. **2.** schwindelerregend (*a. fig.*). **3.** *fig.* leichtsinnig.

gift [gɪft] I s **1.** Geschenk n: **I wouldn't have it as a ~** das möchte ich nicht (mal) geschenkt; *at £10 it's a* **~** für 10 Pfund ist es geschenkt. **2.** *fig.* Begabung f, Talent n (**for,** of für): **~ for languages** Sprachtalent; → **gab. II** *adj* **3.** geschenkt, Geschenk...: **don't look a ~ horse in the mouth** e-m geschenkten Gaul schaut man nicht ins Maul. **'gift·ed** *adj* begabt, talentiert.

gi·gan·tic [dʒaɪˈgæntɪk] *adj* (**~ally**) gigantisch, riesig.

gig·gle ['gɪgl] I v/i kichern. II s Gekicher n.

gild [gɪld] v/t (*a. irr*) **1.** vergolden. **2.** *fig.* versüßen; beschönigen: → **pill** 1.

gill [gɪl] s **1.** *ichth.* Kieme f. **2. ❦** Lamelle f.

gilt [gɪlt] I *pret u. pp von* **gild. II** s Vergoldung f: *take the* **~ off the gingerbread** *fig.* der Sache den Reiz nehmen. **~-edged** *adj* **1.** mit Goldschnitt. **2. ~ securities** pl ✝ mündelsichere (Wert-)Papiere pl.

gim-crack ['dʒɪmkræk] *adj* **1.** wertlos; kitschig. **2.** wack(e)lig.

gim·mick ['gɪmɪk] s F **1.** → **gadget. 2.** (*bsd.* Reklame)Trick m, (-)Dreh m.

gin [dʒɪn] s Gin m.

gin·ger ['dʒɪndʒə] I s **1.** Ingwer m. **2.** F Schmiß m, Schwung m. **II** *adj* **3.** rötlich- *od.* gelblichbraun. **III** *v/t* **4.** mit Ingwer würzen. **5.** *mst* ~ **up** F *j-n* aufmöbeln, -muntern; *et.* ankurbeln, in Schwung bringen. ~ **ale** *s* Ginger-ale *n.* ~ **beer** *s* Ginger-beer *n,* Ingwerbier *n.* '~**bread** *s* Leb-, Pfefferkuchen *m* (*mit Ingwergeschmack*): → **gilt** II.

gin·ger·ly ['dʒɪndʒəlɪ] *adj u. adv* **1.** behutsam, vorsichtig. **2.** zimperlich.

gin·gi·vi·tis [ˌdʒɪndʒɪ'vaɪtɪs] *s* ✠ Zahnfleischentzündung *f.*

gip·sy ['dʒɪpsɪ] *s* Zigeuner(in).

gi·raffe [dʒɪ'rɑːf] *pl* -'**raffes,** *bsd.* coll. -'**raffe** *s zo.* Giraffe *f.*

gird·er ['gɜːdə] *s* ⊙ Balken *m,* Träger *m.*

gir·dle ['gɜːdl] *s* **1.** Gürtel *m,* Gurt *m.* **2.** Hüfthalter *m,* -gürtel *m.*

girl [gɜːl] *s* **1.** Mädchen *n.* **2.** (Dienst-) Mädchen *n.* '~**friend** *s* Freundin *f* (*e-s Jungen*). ~ **guide** *s Br.* Pfadfinderin *f.*

girl·hood ['gɜːlhʊd] *s* Mädchenjahre *pl,* Jugend(zeit) *f.*

girl·ish ['gɜːlɪʃ] *adj* □ **1.** mädchenhaft. **2.** Mädchen...: ~ **games.**

girl scout *s Am.* Pfadfinderin *f.*

gi·ro ['dʒaɪərəʊ] *s Br.* Postgirodienst *m:* ~ **account** Postgirokonto *n;* ~ **cheque** Postscheck *m.*

girth [gɜːθ] *s* **1.** (*a.* Körper)Umfang *m.* **2.** (Sattel-, Pack)Gurt *m.*

gist [dʒɪst] *s* das Wesentliche, Kern *m.*

give [gɪv] (*irr*) **I** *v/t* **1.** geben; schenken; *Blut etc* spenden; *j-m* geben, reichen: ~ *s.o.* one's hand j-m die Hand geben. **3.** *Auskunft, Rat etc* geben, erteilen. **4.** *sein Wort* geben. **5.** *Aufmerksamkeit etc* widmen (**to** *dat*): → **attention** 2. **6.** *sein Leben* hingeben, opfern (**for** für). **7.** geben, gewähren: ~ *s.o. until* j-m bis ... Zeit geben *od.* lassen (**to** *do* tun). **8.** *Befehl, Auftrag etc* geben, erteilen. **9.** *Hilfe* gewähren, leisten, *Schutz* bieten. **10.** *Grüße etc* übermitteln: → **him my love** bestelle ihm herzliche Grüße von mir. **11.** *j-m e-n Schlag etc* geben, versetzen. **12.** *j-m e-n Blick* zuwerfen. *Lebenszeichen etc* von sich geben: ~ *a cry* (*od.* **shout**) e-n Schrei ausstoßen, aufschreien; ~ *a laugh* auflachen. **14.** *Grund etc* (an)geben. **15.** *Konzert etc* geben, veranstalten, *Theaterstück etc* geben, aufführen, *Vortrag* halten. **16.** *Schmerzen etc* bereiten, verursachen.

17. *j-m zu tun etc* geben: *I was* ~*n to understand* man gab mir zu verstehen. **II** *v/i* **18.** geben, spenden (**to** *dat*). **19.** nachgeben (*a.* Preise). **20.** *what* ~*s?* *sl.* was gibt's? **21.** führen (**into** in *acc;* **on**[to] auf *acc,* nach) (*Straße etc*); gehen (**on**[to] nach) (*Fenster etc*). *Verbindungen mit Adverbien:*

give| **a·way** *v/t* **1.** her-, weggeben; verschenken: → **bride.** **2.** *j-n, et.* verraten. **3.** *Chance etc* vertun. ~ **back** *v/t* **1.** zurückgeben (*a.* fig.), *Blick* erwidern. **2.** *Schall* zurückwerfen; *Licht etc* reflektieren. ~ **in I** *v/t* **1.** *Gesuch etc* einreichen, *Prüfungsarbeit etc* abgeben. **II** *v/i* **2.** (**to**) nachgeben (*dat*); sich anschließen (*dat*). **3.** aufgeben, sich geschlagen geben. ~ **off** *v/t* *Geruch* verbreiten, ausströmen, *Rauch etc* ausstoßen, *Gas, Wärme etc* aus-, verströmen. ~ **out I** *v/t* **1.** aus-, verteilen. **2.** bekanntgeben. **3.** *give o.s. out to be s.th.* sich als et. ausgeben. **4.** → **give off. II** *v/i* **5.** zu Ende gehen (*Kräfte, Vorräte*). **6.** versagen (*Maschine, Nieren etc*). ~ **o·ver I** *v/t* **1.** übergeben (**to** *dat*). **2.** et. aufgeben: ~ *doing s.th.* aufhören, et. zu tun. **3.** *give o.s. over to* sich hingeben (*dat*). **II** *v/i* **4.** aufhören. ~ **up I** *v/t* **1.** aufgeben, aufhören mit: ~ *smoking* das Rauchen aufgeben. **2.** *Plan, Patienten etc* aufgeben: → **adoption** 1. **3.** *j-n* ausliefern: *give o.s. up* sich stellen (**to** *dat*). **4.** (**to**) *Posten etc* abgeben, abtreten (an *acc*); *Sitzplatz etc* freimachen (für). **5.** *give o.s. up to* sich hingeben (*dat*); sich widmen (*dat*). **II** *v/i* **6.** → **give in** 3. **7.** resignieren.

ˌ**give**|-**and**-ˈ**take** *s* **1.** beiderseitiges Entgegenkommen *od.* Nachgeben, Kompromiß(bereitschaft *f*) *m.* **2.** Meinungs-, Gedankenaustausch *m.* '~**a·way** I *s bsd. Am.* → Werbegeschenk *n.* **II** *adj:* ~ **price** Schleuderpreis *m.*

giv·en ['gɪvn] **I** *pp von* **give. II** *adj* **1.** gegeben: ~ *name bsd. Am.* → **first name;** *at the* ~ *time* zur festgesetzten Zeit; *within a* ~ *time* innerhalb e-r bestimmten Zeit. **2.** *be* ~ *to* neigen zu: *be* ~ *to doing s.th.* die (An)Gewohnheit haben, et. zu tun. **3.** vorausgesetzt. **4.** in Anbetracht (*gen*): ~ *that* in Anbetracht der Tatsache, daß. '**giv·er** *s* Geber(in), Spender(in).

gla·cé ['glæseɪ] adj 1. glasiert; kandiert. 2. Glacé...

gla·cial ['gleɪsjəl] adj □ 1. eiszeitlich: ~ **epoch** (od. **era**) Eiszeit f. 2. eisig (a. fig.). **gla·cier** ['glæsjə] s Gletscher m.

glad [glæd] adj (□ → **gladly**) 1. froh, erfreut (**of, about, at** über acc): **be** ~ **of** sich freuen über; **I am** ~ **to hear** es freut mich zu hören; **I am** ~ **to go** ich gehe gern. 2. freudig, froh, erfreulich. **glad·den** ['~dn] v/t erfreuen.

glad·i·a·tor ['glædɪeɪtə] s hist. Gladiator m.

glad·i·o·lus [ˌglædɪ'əʊləs] pl **-li** [~laɪ], **-lus·es** s ♀ Gladiole f.

glad·ly ['glædlɪ] adv mit Freuden, gern. **'glad·ness** s Freude f.

glam·or·ize ['glæmərɑɪz] v/t verherrlichen, glorifizieren. **'glam·or·ous** adj □ bezaubernd (schön). **glam·our** ['~mə] s Zauber m, (contp. falscher) Glanz: ~**girl** Glamourgirl n, Film-, Reklameschönheit f.

glance [glɑːns] I v/i 1. e-n (schnellen) Blick werfen, (rasch od. flüchtig) blikken (**at** auf acc): ~ **over** (od. **through**) a **letter** e-n Brief überfliegen; ~ **at a problem** ein Problem streifen. 2. ~ **off** abprallen (von) (Kugel etc), abgleiten (von) (Messer etc). II s 3. (schneller od. flüchtiger) Blick (**at** auf acc): **at** a ~ auf 'einen Blick; **at first** ~ auf den ersten Blick; **take a** ~ **at** → 1; → **steal** 1.

gland [glænd] s anat. Drüse f. **glan·du·lar** ['~djʊlə] adj Drüsen...

glare [gleə] I v/i 1. grell scheinen (Sonne etc), grell leuchten (Scheinwerfer etc). 2. wütend starren: ~ **at s.o.** j-n wütend anstarren, j-n anfunkeln. II s 3. greller Schein, grelles Leuchten. 4. wütender od. funkelnder Blick. **glar·ing** ['~rɪŋ] adj □ 1. grell. 2. grell, schreiend (Farben). 3. eklatant, kraß (Fehler, Unterschied etc), (himmel)schreiend (Unrecht etc). 4. wütend, funkelnd (Blick).

glass [glɑːs] I s 1. Glas n. 2. coll. Glas(waren pl) n. 3. (Trink)Glas n; Glas(gefäß) n. 4. (Fern-, Opern)Glas. 5. pl, a. **pair of** ~**es** Brille f. II adj 6. Glas...: ~ **eye.** ~ **blow·er** s Glasbläser m. ~ **case** s Glaskasten m, Vitrine f.

glass·ful ['glɑːsfʊl] s ein Glasvoll n. **'glass|·house** s 1. bsd. Br. Gewächs-, Glas-, Treibhaus n. 2. **people who live**

in ~**s should not throw stones** wer (selbst) im Glashaus sitzt, soll nicht mit Steinen werfen. '~**ware** s Glaswaren pl.

glass·y ['glɑːsɪ] adj □ 1. gläsern. 2. glasig (Augen).

glau·co·ma [glɔː'kəʊmə] s ♀ grüner Star.

glaze [gleɪz] I v/t 1. verglasen: ~ **in** einglasen; ~**d veranda** Glasveranda f. 2. ☼, a. gastr. glasieren: ~**d tile** Kachel f. II v/i 3. a. ~ **over** glasig werden (Augen). **gla·zier** ['~jə] s Glaser m. **'glaz·ing** s 1. Verglasung f. 2. ☼, a. gastr. Glasur f.

gleam [gliːm] I s schwacher Schein, Schimmer m (a. fig.): ~ **of hope** Hoffnungsschimmer. II v/i scheinen, schimmern.

glean [gliːn] v/t fig. sammeln, zs.-tragen; herausfinden, in Erfahrung bringen: ~ **from** schließen od. entnehmen aus. **'glean·ings** s pl das Gesammelte.

glee [gliː] s 1. Freude f. 2. Schadenfreude f.

glee·ful ['~fʊl] adj □ 1. fröhlich. 2. schadenfroh.

glib [glɪb] adj □ 1. schlagfertig (a. Antwort etc). 2. oberflächlich.

glide [glaɪd] I v/i 1. gleiten. 2. ✈ gleiten, e-n Gleitflug machen; segelfliegen. II s 3. Gleiten n. 4. ✈ Gleitflug m. **'glid·er** s ✈ a) Segelflugzeug n, b) a. ~ **pilot** Segelflieger(in). **'glid·ing** s ✈ Segelfliegen n.

glim·mer ['glɪmə] I v/i 1. glimmen. 2. schimmern. II s 3. Glimmen n. 4. Schimmer m (a. fig.): ~ **of hope** Hoffnungsschimmer.

glimpse [glɪmps] I s flüchtiger Blick: **catch** (od. **get**) a ~ **of** → III. II v/i flüchtig blicken (**at** auf acc). III v/t (nur) flüchtig zu sehen bekommen.

glint [glɪnt] I v/i glänzen, glitzern. II s Glanz m, Glitzern n.

glis·ten ['glɪsn] v/i → **glint.**

glit·ter ['glɪtə] I v/i 1. glitzern, funkeln, glänzen: **all that** ~**s is not gold, all is not gold that** ~**s** es ist nicht alles Gold, was glänzt. II s 2. Glitzern n, Funkeln n, Glanz m. 3. fig. Glanz m, Pracht f. **'glit·ter·ing** adj □ 1. glitzernd, funkelnd, glänzend. 2. fig. glänzend, prächtig.

gloat [gləʊt] *v/i* (**over, at**) sich weiden (an *dat*): a) verzückt betrachten (*acc*), b) sich hämisch *od.* diebisch freuen (über *acc*). **'gloat·ing** *adj* □ hämisch, schadenfroh.

glob·al ['gləʊbl] *adj* □ global: a) weltumspannend, Welt..., b) umfassend, Gesamt...

globe [gləʊb] *s* **1.** Kugel *f.* **2.** Erde *f,* Erdball *m,* -kugel *f.* **3.** *geogr.* Globus *m.* **'~₁trot·ter** *s* Globetrotter(in), Weltenbummler(in).

glob·u·lar ['glɒbjʊlə] *adj* □ kugelförmig: **~ lightning** Kugelblitz *m.* **glob·ule** ['~ju:l] *s* **1.** Kügelchen *n.* **2.** Tröpfchen *n.*

gloom [glu:m] *s* **1.** Düsterkeit *f.* **2.** *fig.* düstere *od.* gedrückte Stimmung: **throw a ~ over** e-n Schatten werfen auf (*acc*). **'gloom·y** *adj* □ **1.** düster (*a. fig.*). **2.** hoffnungslos: **feel ~ about the future** schwarzsehen.

glo·ri·fi·ca·tion [ˌglɔ:rɪfɪ'keɪʃn] *s* **1.** Verherrlichung *f.* **2.** *eccl.* Lobpreisung *f.* **glo·ri·fied** ['~faɪd] *adj* F besser. **glo·ri·fy** ['~faɪ] *v/t* **1.** verherrlichen, glorifizieren. **2.** *eccl.* lobpreisen. **3.** F aufmotzen. **'glo·ri·ous** *adj* □ **1.** ruhm-, glorreich. **2.** herrlich, prächtig. **3.** *iro.* schön, großartig.

glo·ry ['glɔ:rɪ] **I** *s* **1.** Ruhm *m.* **2.** Zier(de) *f,* Stolz *m.* **3.** Herrlichkeit *f,* Glanz *m.* **II** *v/i* **4.** sich freuen, glücklich sein (*in* über *acc*). **5.** sich sonnen (*in* in *dat*). **~ hole** *s* F Rumpelkammer *f.*

gloss¹ [glɒs] *s* Glosse *f,* Erläuterung *f,* Anmerkung *f.*

gloss² [~] **I** *s* **1.** Glanz *m.* **2.** *fig.* (äußerer) Glanz. **II** *v/t* **3.** *mst* **~ over** beschönigen; vertuschen.

glos·sa·ry ['glɒsərɪ] *s* Glossar *n.*

gloss·y ['glɒsɪ] **I** *adj* □ glänzend: **be ~** glänzen; **~ magazine** Hochglanzmagazin *n.* **II** *s* F Hochglanzmagazin *n.*

glove [glʌv] *s* Handschuh *m:* **fit (s.o.) like a ~** (j-m) wie angegossen passen; *fig.* (zu j-m *od.* auf j-n) ganz genau passen. **~ box, ~ com·part·ment** *s mot.* Handschuhfach *n.* **~ pup·pet** *s* Handpuppe *f.*

glow [gləʊ] **I** *v/i* glühen (*a. fig.* **with** vor *dat*). **II** *s* Glühen *n,* Glut *f* (*beide a. fig.*).

glow·er ['glaʊə] *v/i* finster blicken: **~ at**

s.o. j-n finster anblicken. **'glow·er·ing** *adj* □ finster.

'glow·worm *s zo.* Glühwürmchen *n.*

glu·cose ['glu:kəʊs] *s* 🜋 Glukose *f,* Traubenzucker *m.*

glue [glu:] **I** *s* Leim *m;* Klebstoff *m.* **II** *v/t* leimen, kleben (**on** auf *acc;* **to** an *acc*): **be ~d to** *fig.* kleben an (*dat*). **'glue·y** *adj* klebrig.

glum [glʌm] *adj* □ bedrückt, niedergeschlagen.

glut [glʌt] **I** *v/t* **1.** übersättigen (*a. fig.*): **~ o.s. with** (*od.* **on**) sich übersessen mit *od.* an (*dat*). **2.** † *Markt* überschwemmen. **II** *s* **3.** † Schwemme *f.*

glu·ti·nous ['glu:tɪnəs] *adj* □ klebrig.

glut·ton ['glʌtn] *s* **1.** Vielfraß *m.* **2.** *fig.* Unersättliche *m, f:* **~ for books** Leseratte *f,* Bücherwurm *m;* **~ for work** Arbeitstier *n.* **'glut·ton·ous** *adj* □ gefräßig, unersättlich (*a. fig.*). **'glut·ton·y** *s* Gefräßigkeit *f,* Unersättlichkeit *f* (*a. fig.*).

glyc·er·in(e) [ˈglɪsərɪn/'~ri:n] *s* 🜋 Glyzerin *f.*

G-man ['dʒi:mæn] *s* (*irr* **man**) G-man *m,* FBI-Agent *m.*

gnarled [nɑ:ld] *adj* **1.** knorrig. **2.** schwielig (*Hände*).

gnash [næʃ] *v/t:* **~ one's teeth** mit den Zähnen knirschen.

gnat [næt] *s zo. Br.* (Stech)Mücke *f.*

gnaw [nɔ:] (*a. irr*) **I** *v/t* **1.** *Loch etc* nagen (**into** in *acc*). **2.** nagen an (*dat*) (*a. fig.*). **II** *v/i* **3.** nagen (**at** an *dat*) (*a. fig.*).

gnome [nəʊm] *s* Gnom *m,* Zwerg *m* (*beide a. contp. Mensch*).

go [gəʊ] **I** *s pl* **goes 1.** F Schwung *m,* Schmiß *m.* **2. be all the ~** F große Mode sein. **3. it's a ~!** F abgemacht! **4.** F Versuch *m:* **have a ~ at s.th.** *et.* probieren; **at one ~** auf 'einen Schlag, auf Anhieb. **II** *v/i* (*irr*) **5.** gehen, fahren, reisen (**to** nach): **~ on foot** zu Fuß gehen; **~ by plane** (*od.* **air**) mit dem Flugzeug reisen. **6.** (fort)gehen: **I must be ~ing** ich muß gehen *od.* weg. **7.** anfangen: **~!** (*Sport*) los! **8.** gehen, führen (**to** nach) (*Straße etc*). **9.** sich erstrecken, gehen (**to** bis). **10.** verkehren, fahren (*Bus etc*). **11.** *fig.* gehen: **let it ~ at that** laß es dabei bewenden. **12.** gehen, passen (**into** in *acc*). **13.** (**to**) gehen (an *acc*) (*Preis etc*), zufallen (*dat*) (*Erbe*). **14.** 😊

gehen, laufen, funktionieren (*alle a. fig.*): *keep* (*set*) *s.th. ~ing* et. in Gang halten (bringen); → *get* 10, 16. **15.** werden: *~ cold; ~ blind* erblinden. **16.** (*with*) gehen (mit), sich anschließen (an *acc*): → *tide* 2. **17.** sich halten (*by, on* an *acc*), gehen, sich richten (*on* nach): *~ing by her clothes* ihrer Kleidung nach (zu urteilen). **18.** kursieren, im Umlauf sein (*Gerücht etc*): *the story ~es* es heißt, man erzählt sich. **19.** vergehen, -streichen: *one minute to ~* noch eine Minute. **20.** gelten (for für): it *~es without saying* es versteht sich von selbst. **21.** verkauft werden (*at, for* für): → *cake* 1. **22.** dazu beitragen *od.* dienen (*to do* zu tun): *it ~es to show* dies zeigt, daran erkennt man. **23.** ausgehen, -fallen (*Entscheidung etc*). **24.** (*with*) harmonieren (mit), passen (zu). **25.** lauten (*Worte etc*). **26.** sterben. **27.** (*im pres p mit inf*) zum Ausdruck e-r Zukunft, *bsd.* a) e-r Absicht, b) et. *Unabänderlichen*: *it is ~ing to rain* es gibt Regen; *she is ~ing to have a baby* sie bekommt ein Kind; *I am ~ing to tell him* ich werde *od.* will es ihm sagen. **28.** (*mit ger*) gehen: *he went ~ing swimming* schwimmen. **29.** (daran)gehen (*to do* zu tun): *he went to find her* er ging sie suchen; *she went to see him* sie besuchte ihn. **III** *v/t* (*irr*) **30.** *Weg, Strecke etc* gehen: *~ it alone* F es ganz allein machen.
Verbindungen mit Präpositionen:
go| a·bout *v/i* in Angriff nehmen, sich machen an (*acc*). **~ af·ter** *v/i* **1.** nachlaufen (*dat*). **2.** sich bemühen um. **~ a·gainst** *v/i* **1.** *j-m* widerstreben. **2.** e-m Verbot *etc* zuwiderhandeln, sich widersetzen (*dat*). **~ at** *v/i* **1.** losgehen auf (*acc*). **2.** → *go about*. **~ be·tween** *v/i* vermitteln zwischen (*dat*). **~ be·yond** *v/i fig.* überschreiten, hinausgehen über (*acc*). **~ by** → *go* 17. **~ for** *v/i* **1.** holen (gehen). **2.** *Spaziergang etc* machen. **3.** a) gelten als *od.* für, b) → *go* 20. **~ in·to** *v/i* **1.** in *die Politik etc* gehen. **2.** geraten in (*acc*). **3.** (genau) untersuchen *od.* prüfen. **~ off** *v/i* aufgeben: *have gone off j-n, et.* nicht mehr mögen. **~ on** *v/i* **1.** → *go* 17. **2.** → *strike* 1. **~ o·ver** *v/i* **1.** → *go into* 3. **2.** → *go through* 1. **~ through** *v/i* **1.** durchgehen, -nehmen,

-sprechen. **2.** → *go into* 3. **3.** erleiden, durchmachen; erleben. **~ with** *v/i* **1.** begleiten. **2.** mit *e-m Mädchen etc* gehen. **3.** → *go* 24. **~ with·out** *v/i* **1.** auskommen *od.* sich behelfen ohne. **2.** verzichten auf (*acc*).
Verbindungen mit Adverbien:
go| a·bout *v/i* **1.** herumgehen, -fahren, -reisen. **2.** a) → *go* 18, b) umgehen (*Grippe etc*). **~ a·head** *v/i* **1.** voran-, vorausgehen (*of s.o. j-m*): *~! fig.* nur zu!; *~ with fig.* weitermachen *od.* fortfahren mit. **2.** vorankommen (*Person, Arbeit*). **~ a·long** *v/i* **1.** weitergehen. **2.** *fig.* weitermachen, fortfahren. **3. ~ with** einverstanden sein mit; *j-m* beipflichten. **~ a·round** *v/i* **1.** → *go about*. **2.** → *go round*. **~ back** *v/i* **1.** zurückgehen. **2.** (*to*) *fig.* zurückgehen (auf *acc*), zurückreichen (bis). **3. ~ on** *fig. j-n* im Stich lassen; *sein Wort etc* nicht halten; *Entscheidung* rückgängig machen. **~ by** *v/i* vorbeigehen (*a. Chance etc*); vergehen (*Zeit*). **~ down** *v/i* **1.** hinuntergehen. **2.** untergehen, sinken (*Schiff, Sonne etc*). **3.** → *go back* 2. **4.** (hinunter)rutschen (*Essen*). **5.** *fig.* (*with*) Anklang finden, ankommen (bei); geschluckt werden (von). **6.** zurückgehen, sinken, fallen (*Fieber, Preise etc*), billiger werden. **7. ~ in history** in die Geschichte eingehen. **8.** sich im Niedergang befinden. **~ in** *v/i* **1.** hineingehen. **2.** verschwinden (*Sonne etc*). **3. ~ for** sich befassen mit, betreiben, *Sport* treiben; mitmachen (bei); sich beteiligen an (*dat*), *Prüfung* machen; sich einsetzen für; sich begeistern für. **~ off** *v/i* **1.** fort-, weggehen. **2.** losgehen (*Gewehr etc*). **3.** verfallen, geraten (*in, into* in *acc*): *~ in a fit* e-n Anfall bekommen. **4.** nachlassen (*Schmerz etc*). **5.** gut *etc* verlaufen. **6.** verderben (*Nahrungsmittel*). **~ on** *v/i* **1.** weitergehen, -fahren. **2.** angehen (*Licht etc*). **3.** weitermachen, fortfahren (*doing* zu tun; *with* mit): *~ talking* weiterreden; *he went on to say* darauf sagte er. **4.** weitergehen (*Verhältnisse etc*). **5.** vor sich gehen, passieren, vorgehen. **6.** *it is going on for 5 o'clock* es geht auf 5 Uhr zu; *he is going on for 60* er geht auf die Sechzig zu. **~ out** *v/i* **1.** hinausgehen. **2.** ausgehen. **3.** ausgehen, erlöschen (*Licht, Feuer*). **4.** in den Streik

treten, streiken: → **strike** 1. **~ o·ver** v/i
1. hinübergehen (**to** zu). **2.** fig. übergehen (**into** in acc). **3.** fig. übergehen,
-treten (**from** von; **to** zu). **~ round** v/i 1.
herumgehen (a. fig.). **2.** (für alle)
(aus)reichen: **there are enough chairs
to ~** es sind genügend Stühle da. **~
through** v/i **1.** durchgehen, angenommen werden (**Antrag**). **2. ~ with** durchführen, zu Ende führen. **~ to·geth·er**
v/i **1.** zs.-passen (**Farben etc**). **2.** F miteinander gehen (**Liebespaar**). **~ up** v/i **1.**
hinaufgehen. **2.** steigen (**Fieber etc**),
(**Preise** a.) anziehen. **3. ~ in flames**
in Flammen aufgehen; **~ in smoke** in
Rauch aufgehen (u. Flammen). fig. in
Rauch aufgehen, sich in Rauch auflösen.

goad [gəʊd] v/t a. **~ on** anstacheln (**to do
s.th., into doing s.th.** dazu, et. zu tun).

'go-a·head F I adj mit Unternehmungsgeist od. Initiative. II s: **get the ~** grünes
Licht bekommen (**for** für).

goal [gəʊl] s **1.** Ziel n (a. fig.). **2.** Sport:
(a. erzieltes) Tor: **keep ~** im Tor stehen,
das Tor hüten. **~ a·re·a** s Sport: Tor-
raum m. **'~,get·ter** s Torjäger(in).

goal·ie [gəʊlɪ] F → **goalkeeper.**

'goal,keep·er s Sport: Torwart m,
-mann m, -frau f, -hüter(in). **~ kick** s
Fußball: Abstoß m. **~ line** s Sport: Tor-
linie f. **~ post** s Sport: Torpfosten m.

goat [gəʊt] s zo. Ziege f: **act** (od. **play**)
the (**giddy**) **~** fig. herumalbern, -kas-
pern; **get s.o.'s ~** F j-n auf die Palme
bringen. **goat·ee** s Spitzbart m.

gob·ble [ˈgɒbl] v/t mst **~ up** verschlingen
(a. fig. **Buch** etc), hinunterschlingen.

'go-be,tween s Vermittler(in): **act as a
~** vermitteln.

gob·lin [ˈgɒblɪn] s Kobold m.

go-by [ˈgəʊbaɪ] s: **give s.o. the ~** F j-n
schneiden od. ignorieren.

'go-cart s **1.** bsd. Am. Laufstuhl m (**für
Kinder**). **2.** bes. Am. Sportwagen m (**für
Kinder**). **3.** Sport: Go-Kart m.

god [gɒd] s **1.** Gott m, Gottheit f. **2.** ♀
eccl. Gott m: **so help me** ♀! so wahr mir
Gott helfe!; **thank** ♀ Gott sei Dank; →
act 1, **bless** 1, **forbid** 3, **sake, willing**
1. **'~·child** s (irr **child**) Patenkind n.

god·dess [ˈgɒdɪs] s Göttin f (a. fig.).

'god|,fa·ther s Pate m: **stand ~ to** Pate
stehen bei (a. fig.). **'♀-,fear·ing** adj got-

tesfürchtig. **'~·for,sak·en** adj contp.
gottverlassen. **'~·less** adj □ gottlos.
'~·like adj gottähnlich, göttergleich.

god·ly [ˈgɒdlɪ] adj fromm.

'god|,moth·er s Patin f. **'~,par·ent** s
Pate m, Patin f. **'~·send** s Geschenk n
des Himmels.

,go-'get·ter s F Draufgänger m.

gog·gle [ˈgɒgl] I v/i glotzen: **~ at s.o.** j-n
anglotzen. II s pl, a. **pair of ~s** Schutzbrille f. **'~·box** s Br. F Glotze f, Glotzki-
ste f (**Fernseher**).

go·ing [ˈgəʊɪŋ] I s **1.** Boden-, Straßenzu-
stand m, (**Pferderennsport**) Geläuf n;
Tempo n. II adj **2. ~ concern** gutgehen-
des Geschäft. **3. ~, ~, gone!** (bei Versteigerungen) zum ersten, zum zweiten,
zum dritten! **'go·ings-'on** s pl mst b.s.
Treiben n, Vorgänge pl: **there were
strange ~** es passierten merkwürdige
Dinge.

goi·ter, bsd. Br. **goi·tre** [ˈgɔɪtə] s ✱
Kropf m.

go-kart [ˈgəʊkɑːt] s Sport: Go-Kart
m.

gold [gəʊld] I s Gold n: → **glitter** 1. II adj
golden, Gold... **~ dig·ger** s **1.** Goldgrä-
ber m. **2.** F Frau, die nur hinter dem Geld
der Männer her ist.

gold·en [ˈgəʊldən] adj **1.** mst fig. golden:
~ days pl glückliche Tage pl; **~ opportunity** einmalige Möglichkeit; **~ wedding**
goldene Hochzeit. **2.** golden, goldgelb:
~ hamster zo. Goldhamster m.

'gold|fish s Goldfisch m. **~ med·al** s
Goldmedaille f. **~ med·al·(l)ist** s Gold-
medaillengewinner(in). **~ mine** s Goldgrube f (a. fig.), -mine f, -bergwerk n.
,~·'plat·ed adj vergoldet. **'~·smith** s
Goldschmied(in).

golf [gɒlf] (**Sport**) I s Golf(spiel) n. II v/i
Golf spielen. **~ ball** s **1.** Sport: Golfball
m. **2.** ⚙ Kugel-, Schreibkopf m (**der
Schreibmaschine**). **~ club** s (**Sport**) **1.**
Golfschläger m. **2.** Golfclub m. **~
course** s Sport: Golfplatz m.

golf·er [ˈgɒlfə] s Sport: Golfer(in), Golf-
spieler(in).

golf links s pl (a. sg konstruiert) Sport:
Golfplatz m.

Go·li·ath [gəʊˈlaɪəθ] s fig. Goliath m.

gon·do·la [ˈgɒndələ] s Gondel f.

gone [gɒn] I pp von **go.** II adj **1.** fort,
weg. **2.** F verknallt (**on** in acc). **3. she's**

six months ~ F sie ist im 6. Monat (*schwanger*).

gong [gɒŋ] *s* Gong *m*.

gon·or·rh(o)e·a [ˌgɒnəˈrɪə] *s* ♂ Tripper *m*.

goo [guː] *s* F **1.** Papp *m*, klebriges Zeug. **2.** Schmalz *m*, sentimentales Zeug.

good [gʊd] **I** *s* **1.** Nutzen *m*, Wert *m*: *for one's own* ~ zu s-m eigenen Vorteil; *what ~ is it?* wozu soll das gut sein?; *it is no* ~ *trying* es hat keinen Sinn od. Zweck, es zu versuchen. **2.** *das Gute*, Gutes *n*: *do s.o.* ~ j-m Gutes tun; j-m guttun; *be up to no* ~ nichts Gutes im Schilde führen. **3.** *pl* bewegliches Vermögen: ~*s and chattels* Hab *u* Gut *n*; F Siebensachen *pl*. **4.** *pl* ♦ Güter *pl*, Ware(n *pl*) *f*: ~*s lift* Br. Lastenaufzug *m*; ~*s train* Br. Güterzug *m*. **II** *adj* **5.** *allg.* gut: *as* ~ *as* so gut wie, praktisch; *have a* ~ *time* es (sich) (gut) amüsieren; es sich gutgehen lassen. **6.** gut, lieb: *be so* ~ *as to fetch it* sei so gut u. hol es; → *enough* III. **7.** gut, geeignet: ~ *for colds* gut gegen *od.* für Erkältungen; ~ *for one's health* gesund. **8.** gut, richtig: *in* ~ *time* zur rechten Zeit, (gerade) rechtzeitig; *all in* ~ *time* alles zu s-r Zeit. **9.** gut, reichlich: *a* ~ *hour* e-e gute Stunde; *a* ~ *many* ziemlich viele. **10.** (*vor adj*) verstärkend: *a* ~ *long time* sehr lange (*Zeit*); ~ *and ...* F ganz schön, mordsmäßig; ~ *and tired* F hundemüde. **11.** gut, triftig (*Grund*). **12.** gut, tüchtig (*at* in *dat*). ~'*by(e)* **I** *s* Abschiedsgruß *m*: *wish s.o.* ~, *say* ~ *to s.o.* j-m auf Wiedersehen sagen, sich von j-m verabschieden. **II** *adj* Abschieds...: ~ *kiss*. **III** *int* auf Wiedersehen!, *teleph.* auf Wiederhören! '~*-for-*ˌnoth·ing [*adj*] nichtsnutzig. **II** *s* Taugenichts *m*, Nichtsnutz *m*. ♀ **Fri·day** *s eccl.* Karfreitag *m*. ˌ~·'hu·mo(u)red *adj* □ gutgelaunt. **2.** gutmütig. ˌ~·'look·ing *adj* gutaussehend. ˌ~·'na·tured *adj* □ gutmütig.

good·ness [ˈgʊdnɪs] *s* **1.** Güte *f*. **2.** *thank* ~ Gott sei Dank; (*my*) ~!, ~ *gracious!* du m-e Güte!, du lieber Himmel!; → *sake*.

ˌ**good**-l-'tem·pered *adj* □ gutmütig. ˌ~·'**will** *s* **1.** gute Absicht, guter Wille: ~ *tour bsd. pol.* Goodwillreise *f*, -tour *f*. **2.** Goodwill *m*: a) guter Ruf (*e-r Instituti-*

on etc), b) ♦ ideeller Firmen- *od.* Geschäftswert.

good·y [ˈgʊdɪ] **I** *s* F **1.** Bonbon *m*, *pl*: *goodies pl* Süßigkeiten *pl*. **2.** *Film, TV etc*: Gute *m*, Held *m*. **3.** Tugendbold *m*. **II** *adj* **4.** F (betont) tugendhaft. **III** *int* **5.** *bsd. Kindersprache*: prima! '~-ˌ**good·y** → *goody* 3, 4.

goo·ey [ˈguːɪ] *adj* F **1.** pappig, klebrig. **2.** schmalzig, sentimental: ~ *song* Schnulze *f*.

goof [guːf] F **I** *s* **1.** Schnitzer *m*. **2.** Trottel *m*. **II** *v/t* **3.** *oft* ~ *up* vermasseln. **III** *v/i* **4.** Mist bauen. '**goof·y** *adj* F **1.** vertrottelt. **2.** *Br.* vorstehend (*Zähne*).

goose [guːs] *pl* **geese** [giːs] *s* **1.** *orn.* Gans *f*: *all his geese are swans* bei ihm ist immer alles besser als bei anderen; *cook s.o.'s* ~ F j-m alles kaputtmachen. **2.** *fig.* (dumme) Gans. ~'**ber·ry** [ˈgʊzbərɪ] *s* **1.** ♣ Stachelbeere *f*. **2.** *play* ~ *bsd. Br.* das fünfte Rad am Wagen sein. ~ **flesh** *s*, ~ **pim·ples** *s pl* Gänsehaut *f*.

goos·(e)y [ˈguːsɪ] *adj* **1.** *get* ~ e-e Gänsehaut bekommen. **2.** dumm.

Gor·di·an [ˈgɔːdjən] *adj*: *cut the* ~ *knot fig.* den gordischen Knoten durchhauen.

gore [gɔː] *s* Zwickel *m*, Keil *m*.

gorge [gɔːdʒ] **I** *s* **1.** enge Schlucht. **2.** *it makes my* ~ *rise, my* ~ *rises at it* mir wird übel davon *od.* dabei; mir kommt die Galle dabei hoch. **II** *v/i* schwelgen: ~ *on* (*od.* *with*) → **5.** **III** *v/t* **4.** gierig verschlingen. **5.** ~ *o.s. on* (*od.* *with*) sich vollstopfen mit.

gor·geous [ˈgɔːdʒəs] *adj* □ **1.** prächtig, prachtvoll (*beide a. fig.* F). **2.** F großartig, wunderbar.

go·ril·la [gəˈrɪlə] *s zo.* Gorilla *m* (*a. fig.* F *Leibwächter*).

gor·mand·ize [ˈgɔːməndaɪz] *v/i* schlemmen. '**gor·mand·iz·er** *s* Schlemmer(in).

gor·y [ˈgɔːrɪ] *adj* □ blutrünstig.

gosh [gɒʃ] *int* F Mensch!, Mann!

ˌ**go·'slow** *s* ♀ *Br.* Bummelstreik *m*.

gos·pel, *mst* ♀ [ˈgɒspl] *s* Evangelium *n* (*a. fig.*): *gospel truth* reine Wahrheit.

gos·sa·mer [ˈgɒsəmə] *s* **1.** Altweibersommer *m*. **2.** feine Gaze.

gos·sip [ˈgɒsɪp] **I** *s* **1.** Klatsch *m*, Tratsch *m*: ~ *column* Klatschspalte *f*. **2.** Plauderei *f*, Schwatz *m*: **have a ~** → 5. **3.** Klatschbase *f*, -maul *n*. **II** *v/i* **4.** klatschen, tratschen. **5.** plaudern, schwatzen (**with** mit; **about** über *acc*).

got [gɒt] *pret u. pp von* **get.**

Goth·ic ['gɒθɪk] **I** *adj* (**~ally**) **1.** gotisch. **2. ~** *novel* Schauerroman *m*. **II** *s* **3.** △ Gotik *f*.

got·ten ['gɒtn] *Am. pp von* **get.**

gou·lash ['guːlæʃ] *s gastr.* Gulasch *n*.

gourd [guəd] *s* ♀ Kürbis *m*.

gour·mand ['guəmənd] *s* Schlemmer *m*.

gour·met ['guəmeɪ] *s* Feinschmecker *m*.

gout [gaʊt] *s* ♂ Gicht *f*.

gov·ern ['gʌvn] **I** *v/t* **1.** regieren (*a. ling.*). **2.** leiten, verwalten. **3.** *fig.* bestimmen, regeln: *be* **~ed by** sich leiten lassen von. **4.** *fig.* zügeln, beherrschen: **~ o.s.** (*od.* **one's temper**) sich beherrschen. **II** *v/i* **5.** regieren. **'gov·ern·ing** *adj* **1.** regierend, Regierungs... **2.** leitend, Vorstands...: **~ body** Leitung *f*, Direktion *f*, Vorstand *m*. **3.** *fig.* leitend, bestimmend: **~ idea** Leitgedanke *m*. **'gov·ern·ment** *s* **1.** *oft* ♀ Regierung *f*: **~ spokesman** Regierungssprecher *m*; → **exile** 1. **2.** Regierung(sform) *f*. **3.** Leitung *f*, Verwaltung *f*. **4.** Staat *m*: **~ monopoly** Staatsmonopol *n*. **gov·ern·men·tal** [~'mentl] *adj* **1.** Regierungs... **2.** Staats..., staatlich. **gov·er·nor** ['gʌvənə] *s* **1.** Gouverneur *m*. **2.** Direktor *m*, Leiter *m*. **3.** F *der* Alte: a) alter Herr (*Vater*), b) Chef *m* (*a. Anrede*).

gown [gaʊn] *s* **1.** *mst in Zssgn* Kleid *n*. **2.** ♂♀, *eccl.*, *univ.* Talar *m*, Robe *f*.

grab [græb] **I** *v/t* **1.** (hastig *od.* gierig) ergreifen, packen. **2.** *fig.* an sich reißen; *Gelegenheit* beim Schopf ergreifen. **3.** F *Zuhörer etc* packen, fesseln. **II** *v/i* **4. ~ at** (gierig *od.* hastig) greifen nach, schnappen nach. **III** *s* **5.** (hastiger *od.* gieriger) Griff: **make a ~ at** → 1, 4. **6. be up for ~s** F (für jeden) zu haben *od.* zu gewinnen sein.

grace [greɪs] **I** *s* **1.** Anmut *f*, Grazie *f*. **2.** Anstand *m*. **3.** *mst pl* gute Eigenschaft: → **saving** 3. **4.** Gunst *f*, Wohlwollen *n*: **be in s.o.'s good** (**bad**) **~s** in j-s Gunst stehen (bei j-m in Ungnade sein). **5.** (*a. göttliche*) Gnade, Barmherzigkeit *f*. **6.** Tischgebet *n*: **say ~** das Tischgebet sprechen. **II** *v/t* **7.** zieren, schmücken.

8. (be)ehren. **grace·ful** ['greɪsfʊl] *adj* □ **1.** anmutig, graziös. **2.** würde-, taktvoll. **'grace·less** *adj* □ ungraziös.

gra·cious ['greɪʃəs] **I** *adj* □ **1.** wohlwollend. **2.** gnädig, barmherzig (*Gott*). **II** *int* **3.** *good* **~!**, **~ me!** du m-e Güte!, lieber Himmel!

gra·da·tion [grə'deɪʃn] *s* Abstufung *f*.

grade [greɪd] **I** *s* **1.** Grad *m*, Stufe *f*. **2.** ✕ *bsd. Am.* (Dienst)Grad *m*. **3.** ♂ Qualität *f*, Handelsklasse *f*. **4.** *bsd. Am.* Steigung *f*, Gefälle *n*: **make the ~** *fig.* es schaffen, Erfolg haben; **~ crossing** schienengleicher (Bahn)Übergang *m*. *ped. Am.* Klasse *f*; Note *f*, Zensur *f*. **II** *v/t* **6.** sortieren, einteilen. **7.** abstufen, staffeln. **~ school** *s Am.* Grundschule *f*.

gra·di·ent ['greɪdjənt] *s* Steigung *f*, Gefälle *n*.

grad·u·al ['grædʒʊəl] *adj* □ allmählich, stufen-, schrittweise: **~ly** *a.* nach u. nach.

grad·u·ate I *s* ['grædʒʊət] **1.** *univ.* Hochschulabsolvent(in), Akademiker(in); Graduierte *m*, *f*, *pl. Am.* Schulabgänger(in). **II** *adj* ['grædʒʊət] **3.** *univ.* Akademiker...; graduiert. **III** *v/i* ['~jʊeɪt] **4.** *univ.* graduieren. **5.** *ped. Am.* die Abschlußprüfung bestehen (**from** an *dat*): **~ from** *a.* Schule absolvieren. **IV** *v/t* ['~jʊeɪt] **6.** → **grade** 7. **grad·u·a·tion** [ˌgrædʒʊ'eɪʃn] *s* **1.** Abstufung *f*, Staffelung *f*. **2.** *univ.* Graduierung *f*. **3.** *ped. Am.* Absolvieren *f* (*e-r Schule*).

graf·fi·ti [grə'fiːtɪ] *s pl* Wandschmierereien *pl*.

graft¹ [grɑːft] ♂ **I** *s* Transplantat *n*. **II** *v/t* *Gewebe* verpflanzen, transplantieren.

graft² [~] F **I** *s* **1.** *hard* **~** Schufterei *f*. **2.** *bsd. Am.* Schmiergelder *pl*. **II** *v/i* **3. ~** *hard* schuften. **II** *Am.* Schmiergelder zahlen.

grain [greɪn] *s* **1.** ♀ (Samen-, *bsd.* Getreide)Korn *n*. **2.** *coll.* Getreide *n*, Korn *n*. **3.** (*Sand- etc*)Körnchen *n*, (-)Korn *n*: → **salt** 1. **4.** *fig.* Spur *f*: **not a ~ of hope** kein Funke Hoffnung. **5.** Maserung *f* (*vom Holz*): **it goes** (*od.* **is**) **against the ~** (**with** [*od.* **for**] **me**) *fig.* es geht mir gegen den Strich.

gram [græm] *s* Gramm *n*.

gram·mar ['græmə] *s* **1.** Grammatik *f*: **bad ~** grammatisch falsch; **~** (**book**) Grammatik. **gram·mat·i·cal** [grə'mætɪkl] *adj* □ grammatisch, Grammatik...

gramme [græm] *s bsd. Br.* Gramm *n.*

gram·o·phone ['græməfəʊn] *s Br.* Plattenspieler *m.*

grand [grænd] **I** *adj* □ **1.** großartig, grandios, prächtig. **2.** groß, bedeutend, wichtig. **3.** Haupt...: **~ prize; ~ total** Gesamt-, Endsumme *f.* **4.** ⊢ großartig, glänzend. **II** *s* **5.** ♪ Flügel *m.* **6.** *pl* **grand** *Am. sl.* Riese *m ($ 1000).*

gran·dad → **granddad.**

grand·child ['græntʃaɪld] *s* (*irr* **child**) Enkelkind *n.* '**~·dad** *s* F Opa *m* (*a. alter Mann*), Großpapa *m.* '**~·daugh·ter** *s* Enkelin *f.*

gran·deur ['grændʒə] *s* **1.** Pracht *f.* **2.** Größe *f,* Wichtigkeit *f.*

'**grand·fa·ther** *s* Großvater *m:* **~('s) clock** Standuhr *f.*

gran·dil·o·quent [græn'dɪləkwənt] *adj* □ **1.** schwülstig, hochtrabend. **2.** großsprecherisch.

gran·di·ose ['grændɪəʊs] *adj* □ großartig, grandios.

grand·ma ['grænmɑː] *s* F Oma *f,* Großmama *f.* '**~·moth·er** *s* Großmutter *f.* '**~·pa** *s* F Opa *m,* Großpapa *m.* '**~·par·ents** *s pl* Großeltern *pl.* '**~·son** *s* Enkel *m.* **~·stand** ['grænd~] *s Sport:* Haupttribüne *f.*

gran·ite ['grænɪt] *s geol.* Granit *m.*

gran·ny ['grænɪ] *s* F Oma *f.*

grant [grɑːnt] **I** *v/t* **1.** bewilligen, gewähren. **2.** *Erlaubnis etc* geben, erteilen. **3.** *Bitte etc* erfüllen, *a.* ☇ *e-m Antrag etc* stattgeben. **4.** ☇ (*bsd.* formell) übertragen, übereignen. **5.** zugeben, zugestehen: **I ~ you that** ich gebe zu, daß; **take s.th. for ~ed** et. als erwiesen *od.* gegeben ansehen; et. als selbstverständlich betrachten *od.* hinnehmen. **II** *s* **6.** Bewilligung *f,* Gewährung *f.* **7.** Stipendium *n.* **8.** ☇ Übertragung *f,* Übereignung *f.*

gran·u·lar ['grænjʊlə] *adj* gekörnt, körnig, granuliert. **gran·u·lat·ed** ['~leɪtɪd] *adj* = **granular: ~ sugar** Kristallzucker *m.* **gran·ule** ['~juːl] *s* Körnchen *n.*

grape [greɪp] *s* Weintraube *f,* -beere *f.* '**~·fruit** *s* ♀ Grapefruit *f,* Pampelmuse *f.* **~ juice** *s* Traubensaft *m.* **~ sug·ar** *s* Traubenzucker *m.* **~ vine** *s* ♀ Weinstock *m.* **2. I heard on the ~ that** F mir ist zu Ohren gekommen, daß.

graph [græf] *s* **1.** Diagramm *n,* Schaubild *n,* graphische Darstellung. **2.** *bsd.* A Kurve *f:* **~ paper** Millimeterpapier *n.* **II** *v/t* **3.** graphisch darstellen. '**graph·ic** *adj* (**~ally**) **1.** anschaulich, plastisch. **2.** graphisch: **~ artist** Graphiker(in); **~ arts** *pl* Graphik *f.*

graph·ite ['græfaɪt] *s min.* Graphit *m.*

graph·ol·o·gist [græ'fɒlədʒɪst] *s* Graphologe *m.* **graph'ol·o·gy** *s* Graphologie *f.*

grap·ple ['græpl] *v/i:* **~ with** kämpfen mit, *fig. a.* sich herumschlagen mit.

grasp [grɑːsp] **I** *v/t* **1.** packen, (er)greifen, *Gelegenheit* ergreifen; an sich reißen. **2.** *fig.* verstehen, begreifen. **II** *v/i* **3.** zugreifen, zupacken: **~ at** greifen nach (*a. fig.*). **III** *s* **4.** Griff *m.* **5.** Reichweite *f* (*a. fig.*). **6.** *fig.* Verständnis *n:* **be beyond s.o.'s ~** über j-s Verstand gehen.

grass [grɑːs] *s* **1.** ♀ Gras *n:* **hear the ~ grow** *fig.* das Gras wachsen hören; **not let the ~ grow under one's feet** *fig.* keine Zeit verschwenden. **2.** Rasen *m:* **keep off the ~** Betreten des Rasens verboten! **3.** *sl.* Gras(s) *n* (*Marihuana*). **4.** *Br. sl.* Spitzel *m.* **II** *v/i* **5.** grasen, weiden. **6.** *Br. sl.* singen (*to* bei): **~ on** j-n verpfeifen. **~ blade** *s* Grashalm *m.* '**~·hop·per** *s zo.* Heuschrecke *f,* Grashüpfer *m.* **~ roots** *s pl* (*a. sg konstruiert*) **1.** *fig.* Wurzel *f:* **attack a problem at the ~** ein Problem an der Wurzel packen. **2.** *pol.* Basis *f* (*e-r Partei*). **~ snake** *s zo.* Ringelnatter *f.* **~ wid·ow** *s* Strohwitwe *f.* **~ wid·ow·er** *s* Strohwitwer *m.*

grass·y ['grɑːsɪ] *adj* grasbedeckt, Gras...

grate¹ [greɪt] **I** *s* **1.** Gitter *n.* **2.** (Feuer)Rost *m.* **II** *v/t* **3.** vergittern.

grate² [~] **I** *v/t* **1.** *Käse etc* reiben, *Gemüse etc a.* raspeln. **2.** knirschen *od.* kratzen *od.* quietschen mit. **3.** *et.* krächzen(d sagen). **II** *v/i* **4.** knirschen; kratzen; quietschen. **5.** *fig.* weh tun (**on s.o.** j-m): **~ on s.o.'s ears** j-m in den Ohren weh tun.

grate·ful ['greɪtfʊl] *adj* □ dankbar (**to s.o. for s.th.** j-m für et.).

grat·er ['greɪtə] *s* Reibe *f,* Reibeisen *n,* Raspel *f.*

grat·i·fi·ca·tion [ˌgrætɪfɪ'keɪʃn] *s* **1.** Befriedigung *f,* Genugtuung *f* (**at** über *acc*). **2.** Freude *f,* Genuß *m.* **grat·i·fy**

['~faɪ] v/t **1.** j-n, *Verlangen etc* befriedigen. **2.** erfreuen: *be gratified* sich freuen (*at* über *acc*); *I am gratified to hear* ich höre mit Befriedigung *od.* Genugtuung. '**grat·i·fy·ing** *adj* □ erfreulich (*to* für).

grat·ing ['greɪtɪŋ] s Gitter(werk) n.

gra·tis ['greɪtɪs] I *adv* gratis, umsonst. II *adj* unentgeltlich, Gratis...

grat·i·tude ['grætɪtjuːd] s Dankbarkeit f: *in ~ for* aus Dankbarkeit für.

gra·tu·i·tous [grə'tjuːɪtəs] *adj* □ **1.** → *gratis* II. **2.** freiwillig. **3.** grundlos, unbegründet. **gra'tu·i·ty** s **1.** Zuwendung f, Gratifikation f. **2.** Trinkgeld n.

grave[1] [greɪv] *adj* □ ernst (*Angelegenheit, Stimme, Zustand etc*).

grave[2] [~] s Grab n: *dig one's own ~* sich sein eigenes Grab schaufeln; *turn (over) in one's ~* sich im Grab (her)umdrehen. '~**dig·ger** s Totengräber m (*a. fig.*).

grav·el ['grævl] I s Kies m. II v/t pret u. pp **-eled**, *bsd. Br* **-elled** mit Kies bestreuen: ~(*l*)*ed path* Kiesweg m. ~ **pit** s Kiesgrube f.

'**grave**·**stone** s Grabstein m. '~**yard** s Friedhof m.

grav·i·tate ['grævɪteɪt] v/i: ~ *toward*(s) sich hingezogen fühlen zu, neigen zu. ,**grav·i'ta·tion** s phys. Gravitation f. ,**grav·i'ta·tion·al** *adj* phys. Gravitations...: ~ *force* Schwerkraft f; ~ *pull* Anziehungskraft f.

grav·i·ty ['grævətɪ] s **1.** Ernst m. **2.** phys. Gravitation f, Schwerkraft f: → *centre* 1, *force* 1, *specific* 1.

gra·vy ['greɪvɪ] s **1.** Braten-, Fleischsaft m. **2.** (Braten)Soße f. ~ **boat** s Soßenschüssel f.

gray, *etc Am.* → **grey**, *etc.*

graze[1] [greɪz] v/i weiden, grasen.

graze[2] [~] I v/t **1.** streifen. **2.** ✶ sich *das Knie etc* (ab-, auf)schürfen *od.* (auf)schrammen. II s **3.** ✶ Abschürfung f, Schramme f. **4.** a. *grazing shot* Streifschuß m.

grease I s [griːs] **1.** (*zerlassenes*) Fett. **2.** ⚙ Schmierfett m, Schmiere f. II v/t [griːz] **3.** (ein)fetten, ⚙ (ab)schmieren: *like ~d lightning* F wie ein geölter Blitz; → *palm*[1] 1. **greas·y** ['griːzɪ] *adj* □ fett(ig).

great [greɪt] *adj* (□ → *greatly*) **1.** groß,

beträchtlich: *a ~ many* sehr viele. **2.** groß, bedeutend, wichtig. **3.** ausgezeichnet, großartig. **4.** F *be ~ at* gut *od.* groß sein in (*dat*); *be ~ on* sich begeistern für. **5.** F großartig, herrlich. ,~'**grand**·**child** s (*irr child*) Urenkel(in). ,~'**grand**,**daugh·ter** s Urenkelin f. ,~'**grand**,**fa·ther** s Urgroßvater m. ,~'**grand**,**moth·er** s Urgroßmutter f. ,~'**grand**,**par·ents** s pl Urgroßeltern pl. ,~'**grand**·**son** s Urenkel m.

'**great·ly** ['greɪtlɪ] *adv* sehr, überaus. '**great·ness** s Größe f, Bedeutung f.

greed [griːd] s **1.** Gier f (*for* nach): ~ *for power* Machtgier. **2.** Habgier f, -sucht f. **3.** Gefräßigkeit f. '**greed·i·ness** s **1.** Gierigkeit f. **2.** Habgier f. **3.** Gefräßigkeit f. '**greed·y** *adj* □ **1.** gierig (*for* auf *acc*, nach): ~ *for power* machtgierig. **2.** habgierig, -süchtig. **3.** gefräßig.

Greek [griːk] I s **1.** Grieche m, Griechin f. **2.** ling. Griechisch n: *that's ~ to me* fig. das sind für mich böhmische Dörfer. II *adj* **3.** griechisch.

green [griːn] I *adj* □ **1.** grün: *have ~ fingers* fig. e-e grüne Hand haben; *the lights are ~* die Ampel steht auf Grün; *give s.o. the ~ light* fig. j-m grünes Licht geben (*to*, *for*); ~ *with envy* grün *od.* gelb vor Neid. **2.** fig. grün, unerfahren. II s **3.** Grün n: *dressed in ~* grün *od.* in Grün gekleidet; *at ~* bei Grün; *the lights are at ~* die Ampel steht auf Grün. **4.** pl grünes Gemüse. '~,**gro·cer** s bsd. Br. Obst- u. Gemüsehändler m. '~**horn** s F Grünschnabel m; Neuling m. '~**house** s Gewächs-, Treibhaus n.

green·ish ['griːnɪʃ] *adj* grünlich.

Green·wich (Mean) Time ['grenɪdʒ] s Greenwicher Zeit f.

greet [griːt] v/t **1.** grüßen. **2.** begrüßen, empfangen. **3.** *Nachricht etc* aufnehmen. '**greet·ing** s **1.** Gruß m, Begrüßung f. **2.** pl Grüße pl; Glückwünsche pl: ~**s card** Glückwunschkarte f. **3.** Am. Anrede f (*im Brief*).

gre·gar·i·ous [grɪ'geərɪəs] *adj* □ **1.** gesellig. **2.** zo. in Herden lebend, Herden...

gre·nade [grə'neɪd] s ✕ (*Hand-, Gewehr*)Granate f.

grew [gruː] pret von *grow*.

grey [greɪ] *bsd. Br.* I *adj* □ **1.** grau: ~

area Grauzone *f;* ~ *eminence* graue Eminenz; ~ *matter anat.* graue Substanz; F Grips *m.* **2.** grau(haarig), ergraut. **3.** *fig.* trüb, düster, grau: ~ *prospects pl* trübe Aussichten *pl.* **II** *s* **4.** Grau *n: dressed in* ~ grau *od.* in Grau gekleidet. **III** *v/i* **5.** grau werden, ergrauen: ~*ing* angegraut, grsumeliert *(Haare).* '~**haired** *adj* grauhaarig. '~**hound** *s zo.* Windhund *m.*

grey·ish ['greɪʃ] *adj* grau-, gräulich.

grid [grɪd] *s* **1.** Gitter *n,* (Eisen)Rost *m.* **2.** *⚡ etc* Versorgungsnetz *n.* **3.** *geogr.* Gitter(netz) *n (auf Karten).* **4.** Bratrost *m.*

grid-dle ['grɪdl] *s* (rundes) Backblech.

'**grid,i·ron** *s* Bratrost *m.*

grief [griːf] *s* Gram *m,* Kummer *m: come to* ~ zu Schaden kommen; fehlschlagen, scheitern.

griev·ance ['griːvns] *s* **1.** Beschwerde(grund *m) f;* Mißstand *m.* **2.** *nurse a* ~ *against* s-n Groll hegen gegen. **grieve** **I** *v/t* betrüben, bekümmern. **II** *v/i* bekümmert sein, sich grämen (*at, about, over* über *acc,* wegen): ~ *for* trauern um. '**griev·ous** *adj* □ **1.** schmerzlich, bitter. **2.** schwer, schlimm *(Fehler, Verlust etc):* ~ *bodily harm ⚕ Br.* schwere Körperverletzung.

grill [grɪl] **I** *s* **1.** Grill *m.* **2.** Grillen *n.* **3.** Gegrillte *n: a* ~ *of meat* gegrilltes Fleisch. **4.** Grillroom *m.* **II** *v/t* **5.** grillen. **6.** ~ *o.s.* → **9. 7.** F *j-n* in die Mangel nehmen *(bsd. Polizei):* ~ *s.o. about* j-n ausquetschen über *(acc).* **III** *v/i* **8.** gegrillt werden. **9.** sich *(in der Sonne)* grillen (lassen).

grille [grɪl] *s* **1.** (Schalter-, Sprech)Gitter *n.* **2.** *mot.* (Kühler)Grill *m.*

grill-room ['~ruːm] *s* Grillroom *m.*

grim [grɪm] *adj* □ **1.** grimmig. **2.** erbittert, verbissen. **3.** hart, unerbittlich. **4.** grausig.

gri·mace [grɪ'meɪs] **I** *s* Grimasse *f.* **II** *v/i* e-e Grimasse *od.* Grimassen schneiden.

grime [graɪm] **I** *s* (dicker) Schmutz *od.* Ruß. **II** *v/t* beschmutzen. '**grim·y** *adj* □ schmutzig, rußig.

grin [grɪn] **I** *v/i* grinsen: ~ *at s.o.* j-n angrinsen; ~ *and bear it* gute Miene zum bösen Spiel machen. **II** *s* Grinsen *n.*

grind [graɪnd] **I** *v/t (irr)* **1.** Messer etc schleifen: → *ax(e)* 1. **2.** *a.* ~ *down*

(zer)mahlen, zerreiben, -kleinern. **3.** *Kaffee etc* mahlen; *Fleisch* durchdrehen. **4.** ~ *one's teeth* mit den Zähnen knirschen. **II** *v/i (irr)* **5.** knirschen. **6.** F schuften; pauken, büffeln *(für).* **III** *s* **7.** Knirschen. **8.** F Schufterei *f;* Pauken *n,* Büffeln *n.* '**grind·er** *s* **1.** (*Messeretc*)Schleifer *m.* **2.** *(Kaffee etc)*Mühle *f;* *(Fleisch)*Wolf *m.* **3.** *anat.* Backenzahn *m.*

'**grind·stone** *s* Schleifstein *m: keep* (*od. have*) *one's nose to the* ~ *fig.* schuften.

grip [grɪp] **I** *s* **1.** Griff *m: come (od. get) to* ~*s with* aneinandergeraten mit; *fig.* sich auseinandersetzen mit. **2.** *fig.* Herrschaft *f,* Gewalt *f: have (od. keep) a* ~ *on et.* in der Gewalt haben, *Zuhörer etc* fesseln. **3.** (Hand)Griff *m (e-s Koffers etc).* **II** *v/t (Am. a. irr)* **4.** ergreifen, packen. **5.** *fig. j-n* packen *(Furcht etc),* *Zuhörer etc* fesseln.

gripe [graɪp] **I** *v/t* **1.** *Am.* F ärgern. **II** *v/i* **2.** Bauchschmerzen haben. **3.** F *(about)* meckern (über *acc*), nörgeln (an *dat,* über *acc*): ~ *at j-n* anmeckern. **III** *s* **4.** *mst pl* Bauchschmerzen *pl.*

grip·ping ['grɪpɪŋ] *adj* □ packend, fesselnd.

gript [grɪpt] *Am. pret u. pp von* **grip.**

gris·ly ['grɪzlɪ] *adj* gräßlich, schrecklich.

grist [grɪst] *s* Mahlgut *n: all is* ~ *that comes to his mill fig.* er weiß aus allem Kapital zu schlagen.

gris·tle ['grɪsl] *s* Knorpel *m.* '**gris·tly** *adj* knorp(e)lig.

grit [grɪt] **I** *s* **1.** (grober) Sand, Kies *m.* **2.** Streusand *m.* **3.** *fig.* Mut *m.* **II** *v/t* **4.** *Straße etc* sanden, streuen. **5.** ~ *one's teeth* die Zähne zs.-beißen (*a. fig.*).

griz·zle ['grɪzl] *v/i Br.* F **1.** quengeln. **2.** sich beklagen *(about* über *acc).*

griz·zly ['grɪzlɪ] **I** *adj* grau(haarig). **II** *s a.* ~ *bear zo.* Grizzly(bär) *m.*

groan [grəʊn] **I** *v/i* **1.** stöhnen, ächzen (*with* vor *dat;* *fig. under* unter *dat*). **2.** ächzen, knarren (*under* unter *dat*) *(Fußboden etc).* **II** *s* **3.** Stöhnen *n,* Ächzen *n.*

groats [grəʊts] *s pl* Hafergrütze *f.*

gro·cer ['grəʊsə] *s* Lebensmittelhändler *m.* '**gro·cer·y** *s* **1.** Lebensmittelgeschäft *n.* **2.** *pl* Lebensmittel *pl.*

grog [grɒg] *s* Grog *m.*

grog·gy ['grɒgɪ] *adj* F **1.** groggy (*a. Boxen*). **2.** wacklig (*Tisch etc*).

groin [grɔɪn] *s anat.* Leiste(ngegend) *f*.

groom [gru:m] **I** *s* **1.** Pferdepfleger *m*, Stallbursche *m*. **2.** Bräutigam *m*. **II** *v/t* **3.** *Pferde* versorgen, pflegen. **4.** *Person, Kleidung* pflegen.

groove [gru:v] **I** *s* **1.** Rinne *f*, Furche *f*. **2.** ⊚ Rille *f* (*a. e-r Schallplatte*), Nut *f*. **3.** *fig.* ausgefahrenes Gleis. **II** *v/t* ⊚ rillen, nuten.

grope [grəʊp] **I** *v/i* tasten (*for* nach): ~ *about* (*od. around*) herumtappen, -tasten; ~ *in the dark fig.* im dunkeln tappen. **II** *v/t*: ~ *one's way* sich vorwärtstasten.

gross [grəʊs] **I** *adj* □ **1.** Brutto...: ~ *national product* Bruttosozialprodukt *n*. **2.** schwer, grob (*Fehler etc*), schreiend (*Ungerechtigkeit*), stark, maßlos (*Übertreibung*): ~ *negligence* ⁂ grobe Fahrlässigkeit. **3.** unfein, derb. **4.** dick, feist. **II** *s* **5.** *das Ganze*: *in (the)* ~ im ganzen. **6.** *pl* **gross** Gros *n* (*12 Dutzend*). **III** *v/t* *brutto* verdienen *od.* einnehmen.

gro·tesque [grəʊ'tesk] *adj* □ grotesk.

grot·to ['grɒtəʊ] *pl* **-to(e)s** *s* Grotte *f*.

grouch [graʊtʃ] F **I** *v/i* (*about*) nörgeln (an *dat*, über *acc*), meckern (über *acc*). **II** *s* Nörgler(in). **'grouch·y** *adj* □ F nörglerisch.

ground¹ [graʊnd] **I** *pret u. pp von* **grind**. **II** *adj* gemahlen (*Kaffee etc*): ~ *meat* Hackfleisch *n*.

ground² [~] **I** *s* **1.** (Erd)Boden *m*, Erde *f* (*a. fig.*): *on German* ~ auf deutschem Boden; *gain* ~ (an) Boden gewinnen, *fig. a.* um sich fassen. **3.** Grundbesitz *m*. **4.** *oft pl Sport*: Platz *m*. **5.** *fig.* Standpunkt *m*: *hold* (*od. stand*) *one's* ~ sich *od.* s-n Standpunkt behaupten. **6.** *fig.* (Beweg)Grund *m*: *on the* ~(*s*) *of* auf Grund von (*od. gen*); *on* ~*s of age* aus Altersgründen; *on the* ~(*s*) *that* mit der Begründung, daß. **7.** *pl* (Boden)Satz *m*. **8.** ⚡ *Am.* Erde *f*, Erdung *f*. **II** *v/t* **9.** *fig.* gründen, stützen (*on, in* auf *acc*): ~*ed*

in fact auf Tatsachen beruhend. **10.** ⚓ Startverbot erteilen (*dat*). **11.** ⚡ *Am.* erden. **III** *v/i* **12.** ⚓ auflaufen.

'ground|-,break·ing *adj* bahnbrechend, wegweisend. ~ **ca·ble** *s* ⚡ *Am.* Massekabel *n*. ~ **crew** *s* ⚓ Bodenpersonal *n*. ~ **floor** *s* Erdgeschoß *n*. ~ **fog** *s* Bodennebel *m*. ~ **frost** *s* Bodenfrost *m*.

ground·less ['graʊndlɪs] *adj* □ grundlos, unbegründet.

'ground|-nut *s* ♀ Erdnuß *f*. ~ **plan** *s* △ Grundriß *m*. ~ **staff** *s* ⚓ *Br.* Bodenpersonal *n*. ~ **sta·tion** *s Raumfahrt*: Bodenstation *f*. ~ **wa·ter** *s* Grundwasser *n*. **'~-,wa·ter lev·el** *s* Grundwasserspiegel *m*. **'~-work** *s* △ Fundament *n* (*a. fig.*).

group [gru:p] **I** *s* **1.** Gruppe *f*: ~ *of islands* Inselgruppe. **2.** ✝ Gruppe *f*, Konzern *m*. **II** *v/t* **3.** eingruppieren (*into* in *acc*). **4.** zu e-r Gruppe zs.-stellen. **III** *v/i* **5.** sich gruppieren. ~ **dy·nam·ics** *s pl* (*sg konstruiert*) *Sozialpsychologie*: Gruppendynamik *f*. ~ **sex** *s* Gruppensex *m*. ~ **ther·a·py** *s* ⚕, *psych.* Gruppentherapie *f*.

grouse [graʊs] → **grouch** I.

grove [grəʊv] *s* Wäldchen *n*, Gehölz *n*.

grov·el ['grɒvl] *v/i pret u. pp* **-eled**, *bsd. Br.* **-elled**: ~ *before* (*od. to*) *s.o. fig.* vor j-m kriechen. **'grov·el·(l)er** *s* Kriecher *m*. **'grov·el·(l)ing** *adj* □ kriecherisch.

grow [grəʊ] (*irr*) **I** *v/i* **1.** wachsen: ~ *up* auf-, heranwachsen; ~ *out of* a) herauswachsen aus (*e-m Kleidungsstück*), b) *e-r Angewohnheit etc* entwachsen. **2.** *fig.* zunehmen (*in* an *dat*), anwachsen. **3.** *fig.* (*bsd.* allmählich) werden: ~ *less* sich vermindern. **II** *v/t* **4.** *Gemüse etc* anbauen, anpflanzen, *Blumen etc* züchten. **5.** ~ *a beard* sich e-n Bart wachsen lassen. **'grow·er** *s* Pflanzer *m*, Züchter *m*, *in Zssgn* ...bauer *m*.

growl [graʊl] **I** *v/i* **1.** knurren (*Hund*), brummen (*Bär*) (*beide a. Person*): ~ *at* j-n anknurren. **2.** (g)rollen (*Donner*). **II** *v/t* **3.** *oft* ~ *out Worte* knurren, brummen. **III** *s* **4.** Knurren *n*, Brummen *n*. **5.** (G)Rollen *n*.

grown [grəʊn] *pp von* **grow**. **'~-up** **I** *adj* [*a.* ~'ʌp] **1.** erwachsen. **2.** (nur) für Erwachsene; Erwachsenen... **II** *s* **3.** Erwachsene *m, f*.

growth [grəʊθ] *s* **1.** Wachsen *n*, Wachstum *n*. **2.** Wuchs *m*, Größe *f*. **3.** *fig.*

Zunahme f, Anwachsen n (**in** gen). **4.** Anbau m. **5.** ✿ Gewächs n, Wucherung f. **~ in·dus·try** s ✝ Wachstumsindustrie f. **~ rate** s ✝ Wachstumsrate f.

grub [grʌb] **I** v/i **1.** graben. **2.** stöbern, wühlen (**among, in** in dat; **for** nach). **II** v/t **3.** oft **~ up** (od. **out**) ausgraben, fig. a. aufstöbern. **III** s **4.** zo. Made f, Larve f. **5.** sl. Futter n (Essen).

'grub·by adj schmudd(e)lig, schmutzig.

grudge [grʌdʒ] **I** v/t **1.** mißgönnen (**s.o. s.th.** j-m et.). **2.** **~ doing s.th.** et. nur widerwillig od. ungern tun. **II** s **3.** Groll m: **bear s.o. a ~** e-n Groll auf j-n haben. **'grudg·ing** adj □ **1.** mißgünstig. **2.** widerwillig.

gru·el [ˈgruəl] s Haferschleim m. **'gru·el·(l)ing** adj fig. aufreibend, zermürbend.

grue·some [ˈgruːsəm] adj □ grausig, schauerlich.

gruff [grʌf] adj □ **1.** schroff, barsch. **2.** rauh (Stimme).

grum·ble [ˈgrʌmbl] **I** v/i **1.** murren (**at, about, over** über acc). **2.** → **growl** 2. **II** v/t **3.** oft **~ out** et. murren. **III** s **4.** Murren. **5.** → **growl** 5.

grump·y [ˈgrʌmpɪ] adj □ mißmutig, mürrisch.

grunt [grʌnt] **I** v/i **1.** grunzen (Schwein, a. Person). **2.** murren, brummen (**at** über acc). **II** v/t **3.** oft **~ out** et. grunzen, murren, brummen. **III** s **4.** Grunzen n.

guar·an·tee [ˌgærənˈtiː] **I** s **1.** Garantie f (**on** auf acc, für): **the watch is still under ~** auf der Uhr ist noch Garantie; **~ (card)** Garantiekarte f, -schein m. **2.** Kaution f, Sicherheit f. **3.** Bürge m, Bürgin f, Garant(in). **II** v/t **4.** (sich ver)bürgen für, Garantie leisten für. **5.** garantieren. **guar·an·tor** [ˌ~ˈtɔː] → **guarantee** 3.

guard [gɑːd] **I** v/t **1.** bewachen, wachen über (acc); behüten, beschützen (**against, from** vor dat): **a closely ~ed secret** ein streng gehütetes Geheimnis. **2.** bewachen, beaufsichtigen. **II** v/i **3.** sich hüten od. in acht nehmen od. schützen (**against** vor dat). **III** s **4.** Wache f, (Wach)Posten m, Wächter m; Aufseher m, Wärter m. **5.** Wache f, Bewachung f: **be on ~** Wache stehen; **keep ~ over** et. bewachen. **6.** 🚂 Br. Schaffner m; Am. Bahnwärter m. **7.**

Garde f: **~ of hono(u)r** Ehrengarde. **8.** fig. Wachsamkeit f: **be on (off) one's ~** (nicht) auf der Hut sein (**against** vor dat). **9.** Boxen etc: Deckung f. **~ dog** s Wachhund m. **~ du·ty** s Wachdienst m: **be on ~** Wache haben.

guard·ed [ˈgɑːdɪd] adj □ vorsichtig, zurückhaltend, (Optimismus) verhalten, gedämpft.

guard·i·an [ˈgɑːdjən] s **1.** Hüter m, Wächter m: **~ angel** Schutzengel m. **2.** ⚖ Vormund m. **'guard·i·an·ship** s ⚖ Vormundschaft f (**of** über acc, für): **be (place) under ~** unter Vormundschaft stehen (stellen).

'guard·rail s **1.** Handlauf m. **2.** mot. Leitplanke f. **~ rope** s Absperrseil n.

'guards·man [ˈgɑːdzmən] s (irr **man**) ✕ Gardist m.

gue(r)·ril·la [gəˈrɪlə] s ✕ Guerilla m: **~ war(fare)** Guerillakrieg m.

guess [ges] **I** v/t **1.** schätzen (**at** auf acc). **2.** (er)raten. **3.** ahnen, vermuten. **4.** bsd. Am. F glauben, meinen, annehmen. **II** v/i **5.** schätzen (**at s.th.** et.). **6.** raten: **~ing game** Ratespiel n. **III** s **7.** Schätzung f, Vermutung f: **at a ~** schätzungsweise; **I'll give you three ~es** dreimal darfst du raten; → **educated** 2, **rough** 5, **wild** 5. **'~·work** s (reine) Vermutung(en pl).

guest [gest] **I** s Gast m. **II** adj a) Gast...: **~ speaker** Gastredner m, b) Gäste...: **~ list.** '**~·house** s **1.** Gästehaus n. **2.** Pension f, Fremdenheim n. **~ room** s Gast-, Gäste-, Fremdenzimmer n.

guf·faw [gʌˈfɔː] **I** s schallendes Gelächter. **II** v/i schallend lachen.

guid·ance [ˈgaɪdns] s **1.** Leitung f, Führung f. **2.** Anleitung f, Unterweisung f: **for your ~** zu Ihrer Orientierung. **3.** (Berufs-, Ehe- etc)Beratung f.

guide [gaɪd] **I** v/t **1.** j-n führen, j-m den Weg zeigen. **2.** fig. lenken, leiten. **3.** et., a. j-n bestimmen: **be ~d by** sich leiten lassen von. **4.** anleiten. **II** s **5.** (Reise-, Berg- etc)Führer m. **6.** (Reise- etc)Führer m (**to** durch, von) (Buch): **~ to London** London-Führer. **7.** (to) Leitfaden m (gen), Einführung f (in acc), Handbuch n (gen). '**~·book** → **guide** 7.

guid·ed [ˈgaɪdɪd] adj **1.** **~ tour** Führung f (**of** durch). **2.** ✕, ⊗ (fern)gelenkt, (-)gesteuert: **~ missile** Lenkflugkörper m.

guide| dog s Blindenhund m. '**~lines** s pl Richtlinien pl (**on** gen).

guid·ing ['gaɪdɪŋ] adj leitend: ~**principle** Leitprinzip n.

guild [gɪld] s **1.** hist. Gilde f, Zunft f. **2.** Vereinigung f, Gesellschaft f.

guile [gaɪl] s Arglist f, Tücke f. **guile·ful** ['~fʊl] adj □ arglistig, tückisch. '**guile·less** adj □ arglos.

guil·lo·tine [ˌgɪlə'tiːn] **I** s Guillotine f, Fallbeil n. **II** v/t durch die Guillotine od. mit dem Fallbeil hinrichten.

guilt [gɪlt] s Schuld f: ~**complex** Schuldkomplex m. '**guilt·less** adj □ schuldlos, unschuldig (**of** an dat). '**guilt·y** adj □ **1.** schuldig (**of** gen): → **plea** 2, **plead** 2. **2.** schuldbewußt: a ~**conscience** ein schlechtes Gewissen (**about** wegen).

guin·ea pig ['gɪnɪ] s **1.** zo. Meerschweinchen n. **2.** fig. Versuchskaninchen n.

guise [gaɪz] s: **in the** ~ **of** als ... (verkleidet); **under** (od. **in the** ~ **of** fig. in der Maske (gen), unter dem Deckmantel (gen).

gui·tar [gɪ'tɑː] s ♪ Gitarre f. **gui'tar·ist** s Gitarrist(in).

gulch [gʌlʃ] s bsd. Am. (Berg)Schlucht f.

gulf [gʌlf] s **1.** Golf m, Meerbusen m. **2.** Abgrund m (a. fig.). **3.** fig. Kluft f.

gull [gʌl] s orn. Möwe f.

gul·let ['gʌlɪt] s **1.** anat. Speiseröhre f. **2.** Gurgel f, Kehle f.

gul·li·ble ['gʌləbl] adj □ leichtgläubig.

gul·ly ['gʌlɪ] s **1.** (Wasser)Rinne f. **2.** ⊕ Gully m: ~ (**drain**) Abzugskanal m.

gulp [gʌlp] **I** v/t **1.** oft ~**down** Getränk hinunterstürzen, Speise hinunterschlingen. **2.** oft ~**back** Tränen etc hinunterschlucken, unterdrücken. **II** s **3.** (großer) Schluck: **at one** ~ auf 'einen Zug.

gum¹ [gʌm] s oft pl anat. Zahnfleisch n.

gum² [gʌm] **I** s **1.** Gummi m, n, Kautschuk m. **2.** Klebstoff m, bsd. Gummilösung f. **II** v/t **3.** gummieren. **4.** (an-, ver)kleben. '**gum·my** adj klebrig.

gump·tion ['gʌmpʃn] s F **1.** Grips m. **2.** Mumm m, Schneid m.

gun [gʌn] **I** s **1.** ⚔ Geschütz n, Kanone f: **stand** (od. **stick**) **to one's** ~**s** F festbleiben, nicht nachgeben. **2.** Gewehr n; Pistole f, Revolver m. **3.** Sport: Startpistole f; Startschuß m: → **jump** 9. **4.** Tankstelle: Zapfpistole f. **II** v/t **5.** a. ~**to**

death erschießen: ~**down** niederschießen. ~ **bat·tle** s Feuergefecht n, Schießerei f, Schußwechsel m. '**~fight** → **gun battle.** ~ **li·cence** (Am. **li·cense**) s Waffenschein m. ~**man** ['~mən] s (irr **man**) **1.** Bewaffnete r m. **2.** Revolverheld m. '**~point** s: **at** ~ mit vorgehaltener Waffe, mit Waffengewalt. '**~pow·der** s Schießpulver n. '**~run·ner** s Waffenschmuggler m. '**~run·ning** s Waffenschmuggel m. '**~shot** s **1.** Schuß m. **2.** a. ~ **wound** Schußwunde f, -verletzung f. **3.** Schußweite f: **within** (**out of**) ~ in (außer) Schußweite.

gur·gle ['gɜːgl] **I** v/i gurgeln: a) gluckern (Wasser), b) glucksen (**with** vor dat) (Person, Stimme). **II** s Gurgeln n, Glukkern n, Glucksen n.

gu·ru ['gʊruː] s Guru m.

gush [gʌʃ] **I** v/i **1.** strömen, schießen (**from** aus). **2.** F schwärmen (**over** von). **II** s **3.** Schwall m, Strom m (beide a. fig.). **4.** F Schwärmerei f. '**gush·er** s **1.** F Schwärmer(in). **2.** Springquelle f (Erdöl). '**gush·ing**, '**gush·y** adj □ F schwärmerisch.

gus·set ['gʌsɪt] s Schneiderei: Zwickel m, Keil m.

gust [gʌst] s **1.** Windstoß m, Bö f. **2.** fig. (Gefühls)Ausbruch m: ~**of anger** Wutanfall m.

gus·to ['gʌstəʊ] s Begeisterung f, Genuß m.

gus·ty ['gʌstɪ] adj □ **1.** böig. **2.** stürmisch (a. fig.).

gut [gʌt] **I** s **1.** pl bsd. zo. Eingeweide pl, Gedärme pl: **hate s.o.'s** ~**s** F j-n hassen wie die Pest. **2.** anat. Darm m. **3.** oft pl F Bauch m. **4.** pl F Mumm m, Schneid m. **II** v/t **5.** ausweiden, -nehmen. '**gut·less** adj F ohne Mumm od. Schneid. '**guts·y** adj F **1.** mutig. **2.** verfressen.

gut·ter ['gʌtə] **I** s **1.** Gosse f (a. fig.), Rinnstein m. **2.** Dachrinne f. **II** v/i **3.** tropfen (Kerze). ~ **press** s Skandal-, Sensationspresse f. '**~snipe** s Gassenkind n.

gut·tur·al ['gʌtərəl] **I** adj □ Kehl..., guttural (beide a. ling.), kehlig. **II** s ling. Guttural m, Kehllaut m.

guy [gaɪ] s F Kerl m, Typ m.

guz·zle ['gʌzl] v/t **1.** (a. v/i) saufen; fressen. **2.** oft ~**away** Geld verprassen, bsd. versaufen.

gym [dʒɪm] F → **gymnasium**; **gymnastic**: ~ **shoes** pl Turnschuhe pl.

gym·na·si·um [dʒɪm'neɪzjəm] pl **-si-ums, -si·a** [~zɪə] s Turn-, Sporthalle f.

gym·nast ['~næst] s Turner(in). **gym-'nas·tic** I adj (~ally) **1.** turnerisch, Turn..., gymnastisch, Gymnastik... II s **2.** pl (sg konstruiert) Turnen n, Gymnastik f. **3.** *mental* ~s pl Gehirnakrobatik f.

gyn·(a)e·co·log·i·cal [ˌɡaɪnəkə'lɒdʒɪkl] adj □ ⚕ gynäkologisch. **gyn·(a)e-**

col·o·gist [ˌ~'kɒlədʒɪst] s Gynäkologe m, Gynäkologin f, Frauenarzt m, -ärztin f. **gyn·(a)e'col·o·gy** s Gynäkologie f.

gyp [dʒɪp] sl. I v/t u. v/i **1.** bescheißen. II s **2.** Gauner(in). **3.** Beschiß m.

gyp·sum ['dʒɪpsəm] s min. Gips m.

gyp·sy bsd. Am. → **gipsy**.

gy·rate [ˌdʒaɪə'reɪt] v/i kreisen, sich (im Kreis) drehen. **gy'ra·tion** s Kreisbewegung f, Drehung f. **gy·ra·to·ry** ['~rətərɪ] adj kreisend, sich (im Kreis) drehend.

H

H [eɪtʃ] pl **H's** ['eɪtʃɪz] s **1.** drop one's H's das H nicht aussprechen (Zeichen der Unbildung). **2.** sl. H [eɪtʃ] n (Heroin).

ha [hɑː] int ha!, ah!

ha·be·as cor·pus [ˌheɪbjəs'kɔːpəs] s a. **writ of ~** ⚖️ gerichtliche Anordnung e-s Haftprüfungstermins.

hab·er·dash·er ['hæbədæʃə] s **1.** Br. Kurzwarenhändler m. **2.** Am. Herrenausstatter m. **'hab·er·dash·er·y** s **1.** Br. Kurzwarengeschäft n; Kurzwaren pl. **2.** Am. Herrenmodengeschäft n; Herrenbekleidung f.

hab·it ['hæbɪt] s **1.** (An)Gewohnheit f: out of (od. by) ~ aus Gewohnheit; get into (out of) a ~ e-e Gewohnheit annehmen (ablegen); get into (out of) the ~ of smoking sich das Rauchen angewöhnen (abgewöhnen); be in the ~ of doing s.th. die (An)Gewohnheit haben, et. zu tun. **2.** oft ~ of mind Geistesverfassung f. **3.** (bsd. Ordens)Tracht f.

hab·it·a·ble ['hæbɪtəbl] adj □ bewohnbar.

hab·it·tat ['hæbɪtæt] s ⚘, zo. Standort m, Heimat f.

ha·bit·u·al [hə'bɪtʃʊəl] adj □ **1.** gewohnheitsmäßig, Gewohnheits...: ~ criminal Gewohnheitsverbrecher m. **2.** gewohnt, ständig: be ~ly late ständig zu spät kommen. **ha'bit·u·ate** [~eɪt] v/t (o.s. sich) gewöhnen (to an acc): ~ o.s. to doing s.th. sich daran gewöhnen, et. zu tun.

hack¹ [hæk] I v/t **1.** (zer)hacken: ~ to pieces (od. bits) in Stücke hacken; fig. Ruf etc zerstören. II v/i **2.** a. ~ away einhauen (auf acc). **3.** trocken u. stoßweise husten: ~ing cough → **5.** III s **4.** Hieb m. **5.** trockener, stoßweiser Husten.

hack² [~] Am. F I s **1.** Taxi n. II v/i **2.** in e-m Taxi fahren. **3.** ein Taxi fahren.

hack·ie ['hækiː] s Am. F Taxifahrer(in).

hack·le ['hækl] s: get s.o.'s ~ up j-n wütend machen.

hack·neyed ['hæknɪd] adj abgedroschen.

had [hæd] pret u. pp von **have**.

had·dock ['hædək] pl **-docks**, bsd. coll. **-dock** s ichth. Schellfisch m.

hae·mo·glo·bin [ˌhiːməʊ'ɡləʊbɪn] s physiol. bsd. Br. Hämoglobin n.

hae·mo·phile ['hiːməʊfaɪl] s ⚕ bsd. Br. Bluter m. **hae·mo·phil·i·a** [ˌ~'fɪlɪə] s bsd. Br. Bluterkrankheit f.

haem·or·rhage ['hemərɪdʒ] s ⚕ bsd. Br. Blutung f. **haem·or·rhoids** ['~rɔɪdz] s pl ⚕ bsd. Br. Hämorrhoiden pl.

haft [hɑːft] s Griff m, Heft n (bsd. e-r Stichwaffe), Stiel m (e-r Axt).

hag [hæg] s häßliches altes Weib, Hexe f.

hag·gard ['hæɡəd] adj □ **1.** wild (Blick). **2.** abgehärmt; abgespannt; abgezehrt, hager.

hag·gle ['hæɡl] v/i feilschen, handeln, schachern (about, over um).

hail¹ [heɪl] **I** s **1.** Hagel m (a. fig. von Flüchen, Fragen etc): ~ of bullets Geschoßhagel. **II** v/i **2.** impers hageln. **3.** ~ down fig. niederhageln, -prasseln (on auf acc).

hail² [~] **I** v/t **1.** j-m zujubeln. **2.** j-n, Taxi etc herbeirufen od. -winken. **3.** fig. et. begrüßen. **II** s **4.** (Zu)Ruf m: within ~ in Rufweite.

'hail·stone s Hagelkorn n, (Hagel-)Schloße f. **'~·storm** s Hagelschauer m.

hair [heə] s **1.** (einzelnes) Haar; coll. Haar n, Haare pl: **to a ~** aufs Haar, haargenau; **do one's ~** sich die Haare richten, sich frisieren; **keep your ~ on!** F reg dich ab!; **let one's ~ down** sich ungezwungen benehmen; aus sich herausgehen; **split ~s** Haarspalterei treiben; **tear one's ~ (out)** sich die Haare raufen; **without turning a ~** ohne mit der Wimper zu zucken. **~·breadth** ['~bretθ] s: **by a ~** um Haaresbreite; **have a ~ escape** mit knapper Not entkommen. **'~·brush** s Haarbürste f. **'~·cut** s Haarschnitt m: **have a ~** sich die Haare schneiden lassen. **'~·do** pl **-dos** s F Frisur f. **'~·dress·er** s Friseur m (für Frau f. **'~·dress·ing** s Frisieren n: **~ salon** Friseur-, Frisiersalon m. **'~·dri·er** s Haartrockner m.

haired [heəd] adj **1.** behaart. **2.** in Zssgn ...haarig. **'hair·less** adj unbehaart, kahl.

'hair·line s **1.** Haaransatz m. **2.** a. ~ crack ⊗ Haarriß m. **'~·piece** s Haarteil n (für Frauen), Toupet n (für Männer). **'~·pin** s **1.** Haarnadel f. **2.** a. ~ bend Haarnadelkurve f. **'~·rais·ing** adj haarsträubend. **~ re·stor·er** s Haarwuchsmittel n. **~ slide** s Br. Haarspange f. **'~·split·ting** **I** s Haarspalterei f. **II** adj haarspalterisch. **~ spray** s Haarspray m, n. **'~·style** s Frisur f. **~ styl·ist** s Hair-Stylist(in).

hair·y ['heərɪ] adj **1.** haarig, behaart. **2.** F haarig, schwierig; gefährlich.

hale [heɪl] adj gesund, kräftig, rüstig: ~ and hearty gesund u. munter.

half [hɑːf] **I** adj **1.** halb: ~ a mile e-e halbe Meile; **two pounds and a ~**, two and a ~ pounds zweieinhalb Pfund; in od. mit 5. **II** adv **2.** halb, zur Hälfte: ~ as long halb so lang; ~ past two halb drei. **3.** halb(wegs), fast, nahezu: ~ dead halb-

tot; **not ~ bad** F gar nicht übel; **I ~ suspect** ich vermute fast. **III** pl **halves** [hɑːvz] s **4.** Hälfte f: **cut in(to) halves** (od. in ~) halbieren; **go halves with s.o.** in (od. on) s.th. et. mit j-m teilen. **5.** Sport: a) (Spiel)Hälfte f, Halbzeit f, b) (a. ~ of the field Spielfeld)Hälfte f. **,~·'baked** adj F nicht durchdacht, unausgegoren (Plan etc); grün (Person). **'~·breed** s Mischling m, Halbblut n. **~·broth·er** s Halbbruder m. **~·caste** ['~kɑːst] → **half-breed**. **~ face** s paint., phot. Profil n. **,~·'heart·ed** adj ☐ halbherzig. **,~·'mast** s: **fly at ~** a) a. put at ~ auf halbmast setzen, b) auf halbmast wehen. **~ meas·ure** s Halbheit f, halbe Sache. **~ moon** s Halbmond m. **~·pen·ny** ['heɪpnɪ] s **1.** pl **half·pence** ['heɪpəns] halber Penny. **2.** pl **'half·pen·nies** Halbpennystück n. **,~·'price** adj u. adv zum halben Preis. **,~·'seas o·ver** s F blau, betrunken. **~·sis·ter** s Halbschwester f. **'~·tim·ber(ed)** adj △ Fachwerk... **~ time** s Sport: Halbzeit f (Pause): **at ~** bei od. zur Halbzeit. **,~·'time** **I** adj **1.** Halbtags...: **~ job.** **2.** Sport: Halbzeit...: **~ interval** Halbzeitpause f, **~ score** Halbzeitstand m. **II** adv **3.** halbtags: **work ~.** **'~·'truth** s Halbwahrheit f. **,~·'way** **I** adj **1.** auf halbem Weg od. in der Mitte (liegend). **2.** fig. halb, teilweise: **~ measure** → **half measure**. **II** adv **3.** auf halbem Weg, in der Mitte: **meet s.o. ~** bsd. fig. j-m auf halbem Weg entgegenkommen. **4.** teilweise, halb(wegs). **'~·wit** s Schwachkopf m, Trottel m. **,~·'year·ly** adj u. adv halbjährlich.

hal·i·but ['hælɪbət] pl **-buts**, bsd. coll. **-but** s ichth. Heilbutt m.

hal·i·to·sis [,hælɪ'təʊsɪs] s übler Mundgeruch.

hall [hɔːl] s **1.** Halle f, Saal m. **2.** Diele f, Flur m. **3.** univ. a) ~ of residence Studentenheim n, b) Speisesaal m.

hal·le·lu·jah [,hælɪ'luːjə] **I** s Halleluja n. **II** int halleluja!

'hall·mark **I** s **1.** Br. Feingehaltsstempel m. **2.** fig. (Kenn)Zeichen n, Merkmal n. **II** v/t **3.** Br. Gold, Silber stempeln. **4.** fig. kennzeichnen.

hal·lo bsd. Br. → **hello**.

hal·low ['hæləʊ] v/t heiligen.

hall| por·ter s bsd. Br. Hausdiener m (im Hotel). '**~stand** s Garderoben-, Kleiderständer m; (Flur)Garderobe f.

hal·lu·ci·nate [həˈluːsɪneɪt] v/i halluzinieren. **hal,lu·ci'na·tion** s Halluzination f.

ha·lo [ˈheɪləʊ] pl **-lo(e)s** s **1.** Heiligenschein m. **2.** ast. Hof m.

hal·o·gen [ˈhælədʒən] s 🜓 Halogen n.

halt [hɔːlt] **I** s Halt m: bring to a ~ → II; come to a ~ → III. **II** v/t anhalten, a. fig. zum Stehen od. Stillstand bringen. **III** v/i anhalten, a. fig. zum Stehen od. Stillstand kommen.

hal·ter [ˈhɔːltə] s **1.** Halfter m, n. **2.** Strick m, Strang m (zum Hängen).

halve [hɑːv] v/t halbieren. **halves** [~z] pl von **half**.

ham [hæm] s **1.** Schinken m: ~ and eggs Schinken mit (Spiegel)Ei. **2.** a. ~ actor F Schmierenkomödiant m. **3.** F Funkamateur m, Amateurfunker m.

ham·burg·er [ˈhæmbɜːgə] s gastr. Hamburger m.

,**ham|-'fist·ed** adj bsd. Br. F, '**~-,hand -ed** adj F tolpatschig, ungeschickt.

ham·let [ˈhæmlɪt] s Weiler m, Dörfchen n.

ham·mer [ˈhæmə] **I** s **1.** Hammer m: come (od. go) under the ~ unter den Hammer kommen; go at it ~ and tongs F sich mächtig ins Zeug legen; (sich) streiten, daß die Fetzen fliegen. **2.** Leichtathletik: Hammer m: ~ throw Hammerwerfen n; ~ thrower Hammerwerfer m. **II** v/t **3.** hämmern: ~ in einhämmern; ~ s.th. into s.o.'s head fig. j-m et. einhämmern od. -bleuen. **III** v/i **4.** hämmern (a. Puls etc): ~ at einhämmern auf (acc).

ham·mock [ˈhæmək] s Hängematte f.

ham·per¹ [ˈhæmpə] v/t (be)hindern.

ham·per² [~] s **1.** (Deckel)Korb m. **2.** Geschenk-, Freßkorb m. **3.** Am. Wäschekorb m.

ham·ster [ˈhæmstə] s zo. Hamster m.

'**ham·string I** s anat. Kniesehne f. **II** v/t (irr string) fig. vereiteln; lähmen.

hand [hænd] **I** s **1.** Hand f: at ~ in Reichweite; nahe (bevorstehend); bei der od. zur Hand; by ~ mit der Hand, manuell; ~s down spielend, mühelos (gewinnen etc); ~s off! Hände weg!; ~s up! Hände hoch!; be ~ in glove (with) ein Herz u.

e-e Seele sein (mit); unter 'einer Decke stecken (mit); change ~s den Besitzer wechseln; give (od. lend) a (helping) ~ mit zugreifen, j-m helfen (with bei); have a ~ in s-e Hand im Spiel haben bei, beteiligt sein an (dat); hold ~s Händchen halten; not to lift (od. raise) a .. keinen Finger rühren; live from .. to mouth von der Hand in den Mund leben; shake ~s with j-m die Hand schütteln od. geben; → tie 7a. **2.** oft pl Hand f, Macht f, Gewalt f: be entirely in s.o.'s ~s ganz in j-s Hand sein; fall into s.o.'s ~s j-m in die Hände fallen. **3.** pl Hände pl, Obhut f: in good ~s. **4.** Seite f: on the right ~ rechts; on the one ~ ..., on the other ~ fig. einerseits ..., andererseits. **5.** oft in Zssgn Arbeiter m. **6.** Fachmann m, Routinier m: an old ~ ein alter Praktikus od. Hase; be a good ~ at sehr geschickt od. geübt sein in (dat). **7.** Hand f, Quelle f: at first ~ aus erster Hand. **8.** Handschrift f. **9.** Unterschrift f: set one's ~ to s-e Unterschrift setzen unter (acc), unterschreiben. **10.** Applaus m, Beifall m: get a big ~ stürmischen Beifall bekommen. **11.** (Uhr)Zeiger m. **12.** Kartenspiel: Spieler m; Blatt n, Karten pl: show one's ~ fig. s-e Karten aufdecken. **II** v/t **13.** aushändigen, (über)geben, (-)reichen.

Verbindungen mit Adverbien:

hand| a·round v/t herumreichen, herumgeben lassen. ~ **back** v/t zurückgeben. ~ **down** v/t **1.** hinunter-, herunterreichen, -langen (from von; to dat). **2.** (to) Tradition etc weitergeben (an acc), Bräuche etc überliefern (dat). ~ **in** v/t **1.** hinein-, hereinreichen, -langen (to dat). **2.** Prüfungsarbeit etc abgeben, Gesuch etc einreichen (to bei): → check 11. ~ **on** v/t **1.** weiterreichen, -geben (to dat, an acc). **2.** → hand down 2. ~ **out** v/t **1.** aus-, verteilen (to an acc). **2.** Ratschläge, Komplimente etc verteilen. ~ **o·ver** v/t (to dat) **1.** übergeben. **2.** geben, aushändigen. ~ **round** → hand around. ~ **up** v/t hinauf-, heraufreichen, -langen (to dat).

'**hand|·bag** s Handtasche f. ~ **bag·gage** s bsd. Am. Handgepäck n. '**~·bill** s Handzettel m, Flugblatt n. '**~·book** s **1.** Handbuch n. **2.** Reiseführer m (of durch, von): a ~ of London ein London-Führer. **~ brake** s ⊚ Handbremse f. **~breadth** ['~bretθ] s Handbreit f. **'~-carved** adj handgeschnitzt. **~ cream** s Handcreme f. **'~cuff** s mst pl Handschelle f. **II** v/t j-m Handschellen anlegen: **~ed** in Handschellen.

hand·ful ['hændfʊl] s **1.** e-e Handvoll (a. fig. Personen). **2.** F Plage f (Person, Sache), Nervensäge f.

hand gre·nade s ✕ Handgranate f.

hand·i·cap ['hændɪkæp] **I** s Handikap s: a) Vorgabe(rennen n, -spiel n) f, b) fig. Behinderung f, Nachteil m (**to** für): → **mental** 1, **physical** 1. **II** v/t behindern, benachteiligen: → **mentally** 1, **physically**.

hand·i·craft ['hændɪkrɑft] s **1.** Handfertigkeit f. **2.** (bsd. Kunst)Handwerk n. **'hand·i,crafts·man** [~mən] s (irr man) (bsd. Kunst)Handwerker m.

hand·i·work ['hændɪwɜːk] s **1.** Handarbeit f. **2.** fig. Werk n.

hand·ker·chief ['hæŋkətʃɪf] s Taschentuch n.

han·dle ['hændl] **I** s **1.** (Hand)Griff m; Stiel m; Henkel m; Klinke f, Drücker m: **fly off the ~** F hochgehen, wütend werden. **2.** fig. Handhabe f (**against** gegen). **II** v/t **3.** anfassen, berühren. **4.** hantieren od. umgehen mit, Maschine bedienen. **5.** Thema etc behandeln; et. erledigen, durchführen; mit et., j-m fertigwerden. **6.** j-n behandeln, umgehen mit: → **kid glove**, **III** v/i **7.** **glass** – **with care!** Vorsicht, Glas! **'~bar** s mst pl Lenkstange f.

hand| lug·gage s Handgepäck n. **'~-made** adj handgearbeitet. **'~-op-er·at·ed** adj handbedient, Hand... **'~out** s **1.** Almosen n, milde Gabe. **2.** Prospekt m, Hand-, Werbezettel m. **3.** Handout n (für Pressevertreter etc). **'~rail** s Handlauf m. **'~set** s teleph. Hörer m. **'~shake** s Händedruck m: **give s.o. a firm ~** j-m kräftig die Hand schütteln.

hand·some ['hænsəm] adj □ **1.** gutaussehend (bsd. Mann). **2.** beträchtlich, ansehnlich (Summe etc). **3.** großzügig, nobel.

'hand·stand s Handstand m: **do a ~** e-n Handstand machen. **'~-to-'mouth** adj: **lead a ~ existence** von der Hand in den Mund leben. **'~work** s Handarbeit

f. **'~,writ·ing** s (Hand)Schrift f. **'~,writ-ten** adj handgeschrieben.

hand·y ['hændɪ] adj □ **1.** zur od. bei der Hand: **keep s.th. ~** et. griffbereit aufbewahren. **2.** geschickt, gewandt. **3.** handlich, praktisch. **4.** nützlich: **come in ~** sich als nützlich erweisen; (sehr) gelegen kommen. **'~·man** s (irr man) Mädchen n für alles, Faktotum n.

hang [hæŋ] **I** s **1.** Sitz m (e-s Kleids etc). **2.** **get the ~ of s.th.** F et. rauskriegen od. kapieren. **II** v/t (irr) **3.** (auf)hängen; Tür etc einhängen: **~ on a hook** an n Haken hängen. **4.** pret u. pp **hanged** j-n (auf)hängen: **~ o.s.** sich erhängen. **5.** Kopf hängen lassen od. senken. **6.** behängen (**with** mit). **7.** Tapeten ankleben. **III** v/i (irr) **8.** hängen (**by, on** an dat): **~ by a thread** fig. an e-m (dünnen od. seidenen) Faden hängen; **~ over** fig. hängen od. schweben über (dat). **9.** **~ about** (od. **around**) herumlungern od. sich herumtreiben (in dat).

Verbindungen mit Adverbien:

hang| a·bout, **~ a·round** v/i herumlungern, sich herumtreiben. **~ back** v/i zögern (**from doing** zu tun). **~ down** v/i hinunter-, herunterhängen (**from** von). **~ on** v/i **1.** (**to**) sich klammern (an acc) (a. fig.), festhalten (acc). **2.** warten; teleph. am Apparat bleiben. **3.** nicht nachlassen (Krankheit etc). **~ out I** v/t **1.** (hin-, her)aushängen, Wäsche (draußen) aufhängen. **II** v/i **2.** heraushängen. **3.** aushängen, ausgehängt sein. **~ o·ver I** v/i andauern, existieren (**from** seit). **II** v/t: **be hung over** F e-n Kater haben. **~ to·geth·er** v/i **1.** zs.-halten (Personen). **2.** e-n (logischen) Zs.-hang haben, zs.-hängen. **~ up I** v/t **1.** aufhängen. **2.** aufschieben. **3.** **be hung up on** F e-n Komplex haben wegen; besessen sein von. **II** v/i **4.** teleph. einhängen, auflegen.

hang·ar ['hæŋə] s Hangar m, Flugzeughalle f.

hang·er ['hæŋə] s Kleiderbügel m; Schlaufe f, Aufhänger m.

hang| glid·er s (Sport) **1.** (Flug)Drachen m. **2.** Drachenflieger(in). **~ glid·ing** s Drachenfliegen n.

hang·ing ['hæŋɪŋ] **I** adj Hänge...: **~ bridge**. **II** s mst pl Wandbehang m.

hang·man ['hæŋmən] s (irr man) Hen-

ker *m.* '~**nail** *s ✵* Nied-, Neidnagel *m.*
'~‚**o·ver** *s* 1. Überbleibsel *n*, -rest *m.* 2.
F Katzenjammer *m*, Kater *m* (*beide a.*
fig.). '~‚**up** *s* F 1. Komplex *m.* 2. Problem *n*, Schwierigkeit *f.*

han·ker ['hæŋkə] *v/i* sich sehnen, Verlangen haben (*after, for* nach): ~ *to do*
s.th. sich danach sehnen, et. zu tun.
'**han·ker·ing** *s* Sehnsucht *f*, Verlangen *n.*

han·kie, han·ky ['hæŋkɪ] *s* F Taschentuch *n.*

han·ky-pan·ky [‚hæŋkɪ'pæŋkɪ] *s* F 1.
Hokuspokus *m*, fauler Zauber. 2.
Techtelmechtel *n.*

hap·haz·ard [‚hæp'hæzəd] *adj* □ *u. adv*
plan-, wahllos, *adv a.* aufs Geratewohl.

hap·pen ['hæpən] *v/i* 1. geschehen, sich
ereignen, passieren: *it will not ~ again*
es wird nicht wieder vorkommen. 2.
zufällig geschehen, sich zufällig ergeben: *it ~ed that* es traf *od.* ergab sich,
daß. 3. *if you ... to see it* wenn du es
zufällig siehst *od.* sehen solltest; *it ~ed*
to be cold zufällig war es kalt. 4. ~ *to*
geschehen *od.* passieren mit (*od. dat*),
zustoßen (*dat*), werden aus. 5. ~ *on*
zufällig begegnen (*dat*) *od.* treffen
(*acc*); zufällig stoßen auf (*acc*). **hap-
pen·ing** ['hæpnɪŋ] *s* 1. Ereignis *n.*
2. *Kunst:* Happening *n.*

hap·pi·ly ['hæpɪlɪ] *adv* 1. glücklich. 2.
glücklicherweise, zum Glück. '**hap·pi-
ness** *s* Glück *n.*

hap·py ['hæpɪ] *adj* (□ → **happily**) 1. *allg.*
glücklich (*at, about* über *acc*; *with* mit):
I am ~ to see you es freut mich (sehr),
Sie zu sehen; → *birthday* I, *Easter* I,
new year 1. 2. F beschwipst. 3. *in*
Zssgn: a) ...begeistert: → *trigger-happy*, b) F ...süchtig. ‚~·**go-'luck·y** *adj*
unbekümmert, sorglos. ~ *hour s* F *Zeit,*
in der in Pubs etc alkoholische Getränke
verbilligt ausgeschenkt werden.

har·ass ['hærəs] *v/t* 1. ständig belästigen
(*with* mit). 2. aufreiben, zermürben. 3.
schikanieren.

har·bin·ger ['hɑːbɪndʒə] *fig.* I *s* Vorläufer *m*; Vorbote *m*; (erstes) Anzeichen.
II *v/t* ankündigen.

har·bo(u)r ['hɑːbə] I *s* 1. Hafen *m.* 2.
Zufluchtsort *m*, Unterschlupf *m.* II *v/t*
3. j-m Zuflucht *od.* Unterschlupf gewähren. 4. *Gedanken, Groll etc* hegen.

---

hard [hɑːd] I *adj* 1. *allg.* hart. 2. schwer,
schwierig: ~ *work* harte Arbeit; ~ *to*
believe kaum zu glauben; ~ *to please*
schwer zufriedenzustellen; ~ *to imagine* schwer vorstellbar. 3. heftig, stark:
a ~ blow ein harter Schlag, *fig. a.* ein
schwerer Schlag. 4. hart (*Winter*), (*a.*
Frost) streng, (*Klima*) rauh. 5. hart,
streng: *be ~ on s.o.* j-n hart *od.* ungerecht behandeln; j-m hart zusetzen. 6.
hart, drückend: ~ *times pl* schwere Zeiten *pl*; *it is ~ on him* es ist hart für ihn,
es trifft ihn schwer. 7. hart, nüchtern:
the ~ facts pl die nackten Tatsachen *pl.*
8. hart (*Droge*), (*Getränk a.*) stark. 9. ~
of hearing schwerhörig. 10. ~ *up* f in
(Geld)Schwierigkeiten; in Verlegenheit
(*for* um). II *adv* 11. hart, fest: *frozen ~*
hartgefroren. 12. hart, schwer: *work ~;*
brake ~ scharf bremsen; *think* ~ scharf
nachdenken; *try* ~ sich große Mühe geben. 13. nahe, dicht: ~ *by* ganz in der
Nähe. '~·**back** *s* gebundene Ausgabe.
‚~·'**boiled** *adj* 1. hart(gekocht) (*Ei*). 2.
fig. hart, unsentimental; nüchtern,
sachlich. ~ *core s* harter Kern (*e-r Bande etc*). '~-**core** *adj* 1. zum harten Kern
gehörend. 2. hart (*Pornographie*).
'~‚**cov·er** → **hardback**. '~‚**earned** *adj*
hartverdient.

hard·en ['hɑːdn] I *v/t* 1. härten (*a. ✵*),
hart machen. 2. *fig.* hart machen, abstumpfen (*to* gegen): ~*ed* verstockt, abgebrüht. 3. *fig.* abhärten (*to* gegen). II
v/i 4. erhärten (*a. ✵*), hart werden. 5.
fig. hart werden, abstumpfen (*to* gegen). 6. *fig.* sich abhärten (*to* gegen). 7.
⚕ anziehen (*Preise*).

‚**hard**|'**head·ed** *adj* nüchtern, reali-
stisch. ‚~'**heart·ed** *adj* □ hartherzig. ~
line s bsd. pol. harter Kurs: *follow*
(*od. adopt*) *a* ~ e-n harten Kurs einschlagen. *pl bsd. Br.* Pech *n* (*on* für).

hard·ly ['hɑːdlɪ] *adv* 1. kaum, fast nicht:
~ *ever* fast nie. 2. (wohl) kaum, schwerlich. 3. (*zeitlich*) kaum. '**hard·ness** *s* 1.
Härte *f* (*a. fig.*). 2. Schwierigkeit *f.*
'**hard·ship** *s* 1. Not *f*, Elend *n.* 2. Härte
f: ~ *case* Härtefall *m.*

hard| **shoul·der** *s mot. Br.* Standspur *f.*
'~·**top** *s mot.* Hardtop *n*, *m* (*a. Wagen*).
'~·**ware** *s* 1. Metall-, Eisenwaren *pl*;
Haushaltswaren *pl.* 2. *Computer:*
Hardware *f.* ‚~'**wear·ing** *adj* Br. stra-

pazierfähig. ,~·'**work·ing** *adj* fleißig, arbeitsam.

har·dy ['hɑːdɪ] *adj* □ **1.** zäh, ausdauernd, robust; abgehärtet. **2.** ♀ winterfest.

hare [heə] *s zo.* Hase *m*: (**as**) **mad as a March ~** F total verrückt; **play ~ and hounds** e-e Schnitzeljagd machen. '**~·bell** *s* ♀ Glockenblume *f*. '**~·brained** *adj* verrückt. ,~'**lip** *s* ✸ Hasenscharte *f*.

ha·rem ['hɑːriːm] *s* Harem *m* (*a. fig. humor.*).

harm [hɑːm] **I** *s* Schaden *m*: **there is no ~ in doing s.th.** es kann nicht(s) schaden, et. zu tun; **there is no ~ in trying** ein Versuch kann nicht schaden; **come to ~** zu Schaden kommen; **do s.o. ~** j-m schaden *od.* et. antun; → **bodily** 1, **mean³** 1. **II** *v/t* j-n verletzen (*a. fig.*), j-m, j-s Ruf *etc* schaden. **harm·ful** ['∼fʊl] *adj* □ schädlich (**to** für): **~ to one's health** gesundheitsschädlich. '**harm·less** *adj* □ *allg.* harmlos.

har·mon·ic [hɑː'mɒnɪk] *adj* (**∼ally**) harmonisch. **har·mon·i·ca** [∼kə] *s* ♪ Mundharmonika *f*. **har·mo·ni·ous** [∼'məʊnjəs] *adj* □ harmonisch. **har·mo·ni·um** [∼'məʊnjəm] *s* ♪ Harmonium *n*. **har·mo·nize** ['∼mənaɪz] **I** *v/i* harmonieren, zs.-passen, in Einklang sein (**with** mit). **II** *v/t* harmonisieren, in Einklang bringen (**with** mit). **har·mo·ny** ['∼mənɪ] *s* ♪ Harmonie *f*, *fig. a.* Einklang *m*, Eintracht *f*.

har·ness ['hɑːnɪs] **I** *s* **1.** (*Pferde- etc*)Geschirr *n*: **die in ~** *fig.* in den Sielen sterben. **2.** *mot.* (Sicherheits)Gurt *m*. **II** *v/t* **3.** Pferd *etc* anschirren; anspannen (**to** an *acc*).

harp [hɑːp] **I** *s* **1.** ♪ Harfe *f*. **II** *v/i* **2.** Harfe spielen. **3.** *fig.* (**on, on about**) herumreiten (auf *dat*), dauernd reden (von). '**harp·er**, '**harp·ist** *s* Harfenist(in).

har·poon [hɑː'puːn] **I** *s* Harpune *f*. **II** *v/t* harpunieren.

harp·si·chord ['hɑːpsɪkɔːd] *s* ♪ Cembalo *n*.

har·row ['hærəʊ] **I** *s* **1.** ✎ Egge *f*. **II** *v/t* **2.** ✎ eggen. **3.** *fig.* quälen, peinigen.

harsh [hɑːʃ] *adj* □ rauh (*Stoff, Stimme*), grell (*Farbe*); barsch, schroff (*Art etc*); streng (*Disziplin etc*), hart (*Worte etc*).

har·um-scar·um [ˌheərəm'skeərəm] *adj* unbesonnen, leichtsinnig.

har·vest ['hɑːvɪst] **I** *s* Ernte *f*: a) Erntezeit *f*, b) Ernten *n*, c) (Ernte)Ertrag *m*. **II** *v/t* ernten, *fig. a.* einheimsen. **~ fes·ti·val** *s* Erntedankfest *n*.

has [hæz] *er, sie, es hat.* '**~-been** *s* F **1.** *et.* Überholtes. **2.** j-d, der den Höhepunkt s-r Karriere überschritten hat. **3.** *pl* alte Zeiten *pl*.

hash¹ [hæʃ] **I** *v/t* **1.** *a.* **~ up** Fleisch zerhacken, -kleinern. **2.** *a.* **~ up** *fig.* durcheinanderbringen; verpfuschen. **II** *s* **3.** *gastr.* Haschee *n*. **4.** *fig.* Aufgewärmtes. **5. make a ~ of** → 2.

hash² [∼] *s* F Hasch *n* (*Haschisch*).

hash·ish ['hæʃɪʃ] *s* Haschisch *n*.

has·sle ['hæsl] F **I** *s* **1.** Krach *m*, (*a.* handgreifliche) Auseinandersetzung. **2.** Mühe *f*: **it was quite a ~** es war ganz schön mühsam (**doing, to do** zu tun). **II** *v/i* **3.** Krach *od.* e-e (handgreifliche) Auseinandersetzung haben.

haste [heɪst] *s* Hast *f*, Eile *f*: **make ~** sich beeilen; **more ~, less speed** eile mit Weile. **has·ten** ['heɪsn] **I** *v/t* j-n antreiben; *et.* beschleunigen. **II** *v/i* (**sich** be)eilen, hasten. **hast·y** ['heɪstɪ] *adj* □ **1.** eilig, hastig (*Abreise*) überstürzt. **2.** voreilig, -schnell, übereilt.

hat [hæt] *s* Hut *m*: **I'll eat my ~ if ...** F ich fresse e-n Besen, wenn ...; **talk through one's ~** F dummes Zeug reden; **~s off!** Hut ab!, alle Achtung! (**to** vor *dat*); → **cocked hat, old** 1.

hatch¹ [hætʃ] *s* **1.** ✈, ⚓ Luke *f*, *allg. a.* Boden(luke *f*, -öffnung *f*. **2.** Durchreiche *f*.

hatch² [∼] **I** *v/t* **1.** *a.* **~ out** Eier, Junge ausbrüten. **2.** *a.* **~ out** (*od.* **up**) Racheplan *etc* ausbrüten, -hecken; Programm *etc* entwickeln. **II** *v/i* **3.** brüten. **4.** *a.* **~ out** (*aus dem Ei*) ausschlüpfen. **III** *s* **5.** Brut *f*.

hatch³ [∼] *v/t* schraffieren.

'**hatch·back** *s mot.* (Wagen *m* mit) Hecktür *f*.

hatch·et ['hætʃɪt] *s* Beil *n*: **bury** (**take up**) **the ~** *fig.* das Kriegsbeil begraben (ausgraben).

hate [heɪt] **I** *v/t* **1.** hassen: **~d** verhaßt. **2.** nicht ausstehen können: → **gut** 1. **3.** nicht wollen *od.* mögen: **~ doing** (*od.* **to do**) **s.th.** et. (nur) äußerst ungern tun.

II s 4. Haß m (*of, for* auf *acc,* gegen): *full of ~* haßerfüllt. **5.** *et.* Verhaßtes: *... is my pet ~* F ... kann ich auf den Tod nicht ausstehen *od.* leiden.

ha·tred ['heɪtrɪd] → **hate** 4.

hat·ter ['hætə] s Hutmacher m: *(as) mad as a ~* total verrückt.

hat trick s *Sport:* Hattrick m.

haugh·ty ['hɔːtɪ] *adj* □ hochmütig, überheblich.

haul [hɔːl] **I** s **1.** Ziehen n, Zerren n; kräftiger Zug. **2.** Fischzug m, *fig. a.* Fang m, Beute f: *make a big ~* e-n guten Fang machen. **3.** a) Beförderung f, Transport m, b) Transportweg m. **II** v/t **4.** ziehen, zerren: *~ down* Flagge etc ein-, niederholen; *~ up* F sich j-n vorknöpfen; j-n schleppen (*before* vor acc); → *coal.* **5.** befördern, transportieren. **III** v/i **6.** *~ away* ziehen, zerren (*at, on* an *dat*). **'haul·age** s → **haul** 3a. **'haul·er,** *bsd. Br.* **haul·i·er** ['~jə] s Transportunternehmer m.

haulm [hɔːm] s Halm m, Stengel m.

haunch [hɔːntʃ] s *gastr.* Lendenstück n, Keule f: *~ of beef* Rindslende f.

haunt [hɔːnt] **I** v/t **1.** spuken *od.* umgehen in (*dat*): *this room is ~ed* in diesem Zimmer spukt es; *~ed castle* Spukschloß n. **2.** *fig.* a) verfolgen, quälen: *~ed look* gehetzter Blick, b) j-m nicht mehr aus dem Kopf gehen, j-n nicht mehr loslassen. **3.** häufig besuchen. **II** s **4.** häufig besuchter Ort. **'haunt·ing** *adj* □ **1.** quälend. **2.** unvergeßlich: *~ melo·dy* (*od. tune*) Ohrwurm m.

have [hæv] **I** v/t (*irr*) **1.** *allg.* haben: *~ on Kleidungsstück* anhaben, *Hut* aufhaben; → *get* 11. **2.** haben, erleben. **3.** *Kind* bekommen; *zo. Junge* werfen. **4.** behalten: *may I ~ it?* **5.** *Gefühle, Verdacht etc* haben, hegen. **6.** erhalten, bekommen: *~ back* zurückbekommen. **7.** essen, trinken: → *breakfast* I, *etc.* **8.** haben, machen: → *down* I, *try* 1, *walk* 1, *wash* 1. **9.** *a. ~ on* F j-n reinlegen. **10.** *~ on et.* vorhaben. **11.** *vor inf:* müssen: *I ~ to go now;* → *get* 11. **12.** *mit Objekt u. pp:* lassen: *I had a suit made* ich ließ mir e-n Anzug machen. **13.** *mit Objekt u. inf:* veranlassen: *I had him sit down* ich ließ ihn Platz nehmen. **14.** *I had rather go than stay* ich möchte lieber gehen als bleiben; *you had best*

go du tätest am besten daran zu gehen. **II** v/aux (*irr*) **15.** haben, (*bei vielen v/i*) sein: *I have come* ich bin gekommen. **III** s **16.** *the ~s and the ~-nots* die Begüterten u. die Habenichtse.

ha·ven ['heɪvn] s **1.** *mst fig.* (sicherer) Hafen. **2.** *fig.* Zufluchtsort m.

'have-not s *mst pl* Habenichts m: → **have** 16.

hav·oc ['hævək] s Verwüstung f, Zerstörung f: *cause ~* schwere Zerstörungen *od.* (*a. fig.*) ein Chaos verursachen; *play ~ with, make ~ of* verwüsten, zerstören; *fig.* verheerend wirken auf (*acc*).

haw [hɔː] v/i → *hem²* II, *hum* 2.

hawk¹ [hɔːk] s *orn.* Falke m (*a. pol.*), Habicht m.

hawk² [~] v/t **1.** hausieren mit; auf der Straße verkaufen. **2.** *a. ~ about* (*od. around*) *Gerücht etc* verbreiten. **'hawk·er** s Hausierer(in); Straßenhändler(in).

haw·ser ['hɔːzə] s ♨ Kabeltau n, Trosse f.

haw·thorn ['hɔːθɔːn] s ♣ Weißdorn m.

hay [heɪ] s Heu n: *make ~ while the sun shines fig.* das Eisen schmieden, solange es heiß ist; *hit the ~ sl.* sich in die Falle od. Klappe hauen. **~ fe·ver** s ♨ Heuschnupfen m. **'~·wire** *adj* F kaputt (*Gerät*); (völlig) durcheinander (*Pläne etc*); übergeschnappt (*Person*): *go ~* kaputtgehen; (völlig) durcheinandergeraten; überschnappen.

haz·ard ['hæzəd] **I** s **1.** Gefahr f, Risiko n: *at all ~s* unter allen Umständen; *at the ~ of one's life* unter Lebensgefahr, unter Einsatz s-s Lebens; *~ to health* Gesundheitsrisiko; *~ warning lights pl mot.* Warnblinkanlage f. **2.** Zufall m: *by ~* durch Zufall, zufällig. **II** v/t **3.** riskieren: a) aufs Spiel setzen, b) (zu sagen) wagen, sich e-e *Bemerkung etc* erlauben. **'haz·ard·ous** *adj* □ gewagt, gefährlich, riskant.

haze [heɪz] s **1.** Dunst(schleier) m. *fig.* Nebel m, Schleier m.

ha·zel ['heɪzl] *adj* □ (hasel)nußbraun. **'~·nut** s ♣ Haselnuß f.

ha·zy ['heɪzɪ] *adj* □ **1.** dunstig, diesig. **2.** *fig.* verschwommen, nebelhaft (*Vorstellung etc*): *be rather ~ about* nur e-e ziemlich verschwommene *od.* vage Vorstellung haben von

'H-bomb s ✕ H-Bombe f, Wasserstoffbombe f.

he [hi:] **I** pron er: ~ **who** wer; derjenige, welcher. **II** s Er m: a) Junge m, Mann m, b) zo. Männchen n. **III** adj in Zssgn zo. ...männchen n: ~**goat** Ziegenbock m.

head [hed] **I** v/t **1.** anführen, an der Spitze stehen von (od. gen). **2.** voran-, vorausgehen (dat). **3.** (an)führen, leiten: ~ed by unter der Leitung von. **4.** Fußball: köpfen. **II** v/i **5.** (for) gehen, fahren (nach); sich bewegen (auf acc ... zu), lossteuern, -gehen (auf acc); ♻ Kurs halten (auf acc). **III** adj **6.** Kopf... **7.** Chef..., Haupt..., Ober...: ~ **cook** Chefkoch m; ~ **nurse** Oberschwester f. **IV** s **8.** Kopf m: **above** (od. **over**) s.o.'s ~ zu hoch für j-n; **from** ~ **to foot** von Kopf bis Fuß; ~ **over heels** kopfüber (die Treppe hinunterstürzen); bis über beide Ohren (verliebt sein); **be** ~ **over heels in debt** bis über die Ohren in Schulden stecken; **bury one's** ~ **in the sand** den Kopf in den Sand stecken; **cry one's** ~ **off** F sich die Augen ausweinen; **go to s.o.'s** ~ j-m in den Kopf od. zu Kopf steigen (Alkohol, Erfolg etc); **keep one's** ~ **above water** sich über Wasser halten (a. fig.); **lose one's** ~ den Kopf od. die Nerven verlieren; → **snap** 5. **9.** (Ober)Haupt n: ~ **of the family** Familienvorstand m, -oberhaupt; ~ **of state** Staatsoberhaupt; ~ **crown** 5. **10.** (An)Führer m, Leiter m: ~ **of government** Regierungschef m. **11.** Spitze f, führende Stellung: **at the** ~ **of** an der Spitze (gen). **12.** Kopf(ende n) m (e-s Bettes etc); Kopf m (e-s Briefs, Nagels etc). **13.** Kopf m, (einzelne) Person: **one pound a** ~ ein Pfund pro Kopf od. Person. **14.** pl Vorderseite f (e-r Münze): ~s **or tails?** Wappen od. Zahl?; **I cannot make** ~ **or tail of it** ich kann daraus nicht schlau werden. **15.** ♻ (Salat- etc)Kopf m. **16.** Schaum(krone f) m (vom Bier etc). **17.** Quelle f (e-s Flusses). **18.** Überschrift f, Titelkopf m. **19.** in Zssgn F ...süchtige m, f. '~**ache** s Kopfschmerz(en pl) m, -weh n: **be a bit of a** ~ **for s.o.**, **give s.o. a** ~ F j-m Kopfschmerzen od. Sorgen machen. '~**band** s Kopf-, Stirnband n.

head·er ['hedə] s **1.** Kopfsprung m. **2.** Fußball: Kopfball m.

,**head**|'**first** → **headlong.** '~,**hunt·er** s Kopfjäger m.

head·ing ['hedɪŋ] s **1.** Überschrift f, Titel(zeile f) m. **2.** Thema n, (Gesprächs)Punkt m.

'**head**|**lamp** → **headlight.** ~**land** ['~lənd] s Landspitze f, -zunge f. '~**light** s mot. etc Scheinwerfer m: ~ **flasher** Lichthupe f. '~**line** s **1.** Schlagzeile f: **hit the** ~s Schlagzeilen machen. **2.** Überschrift f. '~**long** **I** adv **1.** kopfüber, mit dem Kopf voran. **2.** fig. a) Hals über Kopf, b) ungestüm, stürmisch. **II** adj **3.** mit dem Kopf voran. **4.** fig. a) voreilig, -schnell, b) → 2b. ,~'**mas·ter** s ped. (Di)Rektor m. ,~'**mis·tress** s ped. (Di)Rektorin f. ~**of·fice** s Hauptbüro n, -sitz m, Zentrale f. ,~'**on** adj **1.** frontal (a. adv), Frontal... **2.** fig. direkt (Art etc). '~**phones** s pl Kopfhörer m. '~**quar·ters** s pl (oft sg konstruiert) **1.** ✕ Hauptquartier n. **2.** (Polizei)Präsidium n. **3.** → **head office.** ~**rest** s Kopfstütze f. '~**set** s Kopfhörer m. '~**shrink·er** s sl. Psychiater m. ~ **start** s Sport: Vorsprung m (a. fig.): **have a** ~ **on** (od. **over**) **s.o.** j-m gegenüber im Vorteil sein. '~**strong** adj eigensinnig, halsstarrig. ~**voice** s ♪ Kopfstimme f. ,~'**wait·er** s Oberkellner m. '~**way** s: **make** ~ (**with**) (gut) vorankommen (mit), Fortschritte machen (bei). ~ **wind** s ✈, ♻ Gegenwind m. '~**work** s geistige Arbeit.

head·y ['hedɪ] adj □ **1.** → **headlong** 4a. **2.** berauschend (a. fig.).

heal [hi:l] **I** v/t heilen (of von) (a. fig.). **II** v/i oft ~ **up** (od. **over**) (zu)heilen. '**heal·ing** **I** s Heilung f. **II** adj heilsam (a. fig.), heilend: ~ **process** Heil(ungs)prozeß m.

health [helθ] s **1.** Gesundheit f: ~ **certificate** ärztliches Attest; ~ **club** Fitneßclub m; ~ **food** Reform- od. Biokost f; **on** ~ **grounds** aus gesundheitlichen Gründen; ~ **hazard** Gesundheitsrisiko n; ~**insurance** Krankenversicherung f; ~ **resort** Kurort m; ~ **service** Gesundheitsdienst m. **2.** a. **state of** ~ Gesundheitszustand m: **in good** (**poor**) ~ gesund, bei guter Gesundheit (kränklich, bei schlechter Gesundheit). **3.** Gesundheit *f*, Wohl *n*: **drink (to)** (*od.* **propose**) **s.o.'s** ~ auf j-s Wohl trinken; **your (very good)** ~! auf Ihr Wohl! **'health·y** *adj* □ **1.** *allg.* gesund (*a. fig.*). **2.** F gesund, kräftig (*Appetit*).

heap [hiːp] **I** *s* **1.** Haufen *m*: **in ~s** haufenweise. **2.** F Haufen *m*, Menge *f*: **~s of time** e-e Menge Zeit; **~s of times** unzählige Male; **~s better** sehr viel besser. **II** *v/t* **3.** häufen: **~ up** auf-, *fig. a.* anhäufen. **4.** *fig.* überhäufen (**with** mit).

hear [hiə] (*irr*) **I** *v/t* **1.** hören: **I ~d him laugh(ing)** ich hörte ihn lachen; **make o.s. ~d** sich Gehör verschaffen. **2.** *et.* hören, erfahren (**about,** *of* von, über *acc*). **3.** *j-n* anhören, *j-m* zuhören: ~ **s.o. out** j-n ausreden lassen. **4.** (an)hören, sich *et.* anhören. **5.** *Bitte etc* erhören. **6.** *Schüler, Gelerntes* abhören. **7.** 🏛 verhören, -nehmen; *Fall* verhandeln. **II** *v/i* **8.** hören: ~ **say** sagen hören; **he would not ~ of it** er wollte davon nichts hören *od.* wissen; **~! ~!** bravo!, sehr richtig!, *iro.* hört, hört! **9.** hören, erfahren (**about,** *of* von). **heard** [hɜːd] *pret u. pp von* **hear. 'hear·ing** *s* **1.** Hören *n*: **within (out of)** ~ in (außer) Hörweite; ~ **aid** Hörgerät *n*. **2.** Gehör(sinn *m*) *n*: ~ **hard** 9. **3.** *gain* (*od.* *get*) **a** ~ sich Gehör verschaffen. **4.** 🏛 Verhör *n*, Vernehmung *f*; Verhandlung *f*. **5.** *bsd. pol.* Hearing *n*, Anhörung *f*.

·'hear·say *s: by* ~ vom Hörensagen.

hearse [hɜːs] *s* Leichenwagen *m*.

heart [hɑːt] *s* **1.** *anat.* Herz *n* (*a. fig.* Gemüt, *Mitgefühl, Empfindungen etc*): *by* ~ auswendig; **to one's ~'s content** nach Herzenslust; **with all one's** (*od.* **one's whole**) ~ von ganzem Herzen; **break s.o.'s** ~ j-m das Herz brechen; **cry** (*od.* **sob**) **one's** ~ **out** sich die Augen ausweinen; **have no** ~ kein Herz haben, herzlos sein; **my** ~ **sank** ich wurde deprimiert; **take s.th. to** ~ sich et. zu Herzen nehmen; → **bottom** 1, **stone** 1. **2.** *fig.* Kern *m*. **3.** *Kartenspiel:* a) *pl* Herz *n* (*Farbe*), b) Herz(karte *f*) *n*. **'·~·ache** *s* Kummer *m*, Gram *m*. **~ at·tack** *s* 🏛 Herzanfall *m*; Herzinfarkt *m*. **'·~·beat** *s* *physiol.* Herzschlag *m*. **'·~·break·ing** *adj* □ herzzerreißend. **'·~·burn** *s* 🏛 Sodbrennen *n*. ~ **con·di·tion** *s* 🏛 Herzleiden *n*.

heart·en [ˈhɑːtn] *v/t* ermutigen.

heart| fail·ure *s* 🏛 Herzversagen *n*. **'·~·felt** *adj* tiefempfunden, aufrichtig.

hearth [hɑːθ] *s* **1.** Kamin *m*. **2.** *a.* ~ **and home** *fig.* häuslicher Herd, Heim *n*.

heart·i·ly [ˈhɑːtɪlɪ] *adv* **1.** herzlich, von Herzen. **2.** herzhaft.

heart·less [ˈhɑːtlɪs] *adj* □ herzlos.

,heart·'lung ma·chine *s* 🏛 Herz-Lungen-Maschine *f*. ~ **pace·mak·er** *s* 🏛 Herzschrittmacher *m*. **'·~,rend·ing** *adj* □ herzzerreißend. **,~·to-** ~ *adj* aufrichtig, offen. ~ **trans·plant** *s* 🏛 Herzverpflanzung *f*.

heart·y [ˈhɑːtɪ] *adj* (□ → **heartily**) **1.** herzlich. **2.** → **hale**. **3.** herzhaft, kräftig (*Appetit, Mahlzeit etc*).

heat [hiːt] **I** *s* **1.** *allg.* Hitze *f*; *a. phys.* Wärme *f*. **2.** *fig.* Ungestüm *n*; Eifer *m*: **in the ~ of the moment** im Eifer *od.* in der Hitze des Gefechts; **in the ~ of passion** 🏛 im Affekt. **3.** *Sport:* (Einzel)Lauf *m*: (**preliminary**) ~ Vorlauf. **4. the** ~ *Am. coll.* F die Bullen *pl* (*Polizei*). **5.** *zo.* Läufigkeit *f*: **in** ~ läufig. **II** *v/t* **6.** *a.* ~ **up** erhitzen, *Speisen a.* aufwärmen. **7.** heizen. **8.** ~ **up** *Diskussion etc* anheizen. **III** *v/i* **9.** sich erhitzen (*a. fig.*). **'heat·ed** *adj* **1.** geheizt. **2.** erhitzt, *fig. a.* erregt, hitzig. **'heat·er** *s* Heizgerät *n*, -körper *m*.

heath [hiːθ] *s* **1.** *bsd. Br.* Heide(land *n*) *f*. **2.** 🌿 a) Erika *f*, b) → **heather**.

hea·then [ˈhiːðn] **I** *s* **1.** Heide *m*, Heidin *f*: **the** ~ *coll.* die Heiden *pl*. **2.** Barbar *m*. **II** *adj* **3.** heidnisch, Heiden... **4.** unzivilisiert, barbarisch. **hea·then·ish** [ˈ~ənɪʃ] → **heathen** II.

heath·er [ˈheðə] *s* 🌿 Heidekraut *n*.

heat·ing [ˈhiːtɪŋ] **I** *s* Heizung *f*. **II** *adj* Heiz...: ~ **pad** Heizkissen *n*.

heat| light·ning *s* Wetterleuchten *n*. **'·~·proof** *adj* hitzebeständig, -fest. ~ **rash** *s* 🏛 Hitzeausschlag *m*. **'·~·re,sist·ant** → **heatproof. '·~·stroke** *s* 🏛 Hitzschlag *m*. ~ **wave** *s* Hitzewelle *f*.

heave [hiːv] **I** *s* **1.** Hochziehen *n*, -winden *n*. **2.** F Wurf *m*. **3.** Wogen *n*: ~ **of the sea** ⚓ Seegang *m*. **II** *v/t* (*bsd.* ⚓ *irr*) **4.** (hoch)stemmen, (-)hieven. **5.** hochziehen, -winden, *Anker* lichten. **6.** F schmeißen, werfen. **7.** *Seufzer etc* ausstoßen: → **sigh** II. **8.** F auskotzen. **III** *v/i* (*bsd.* ⚓ *irr*) **9.** sich heben u. senken, wogen. **10.** F würgen, Brechreiz haben:

~ (*up*) kotzen. **11. ~ to** ⚓ beidrehen.

heav·en ['hevn] *s* **1.** Himmel(reich *n*) *m*: *move ~ and earth fig.* Himmel u. Hölle in Bewegung setzen; *in the seventh ~* (*of delight*) *fig.* im sieb(en)ten Himmel; *thank ~!* Gott sei Dank!; *what in ~ ...?* was in aller Welt ...?; → *forbid* 3, *sake*, *stink* 1. **2.** ♀ Himmel *m*, Gott *m*. '**heav·en·ly** *adj* himmlisch (*a. fig.*): *~ body ast.* Himmelskörper *m*.

heav·i·ly ['hevɪlɪ] *adv* schwer (*a. fig.*): *~ armed* schwerbewaffnet; *suffer ~* schwere (finanzielle) Verluste erleiden.

heav·y ['hevɪ] **I** *adj* (□ → *heavily*) **1.** *allg.* schwer. **2.** schwer (*Sturz, Verluste etc*), stark (*Regen, Trinker, Verkehr etc*), wuchtig (*Schlag*), hoch (*Geldstrafe, Steuern etc*): *~ current* ⚡ Starkstrom *m*. **3.** schwer (*Wein etc*), (*Nahrung a.*) schwerverdaulich: *~ beer* Starkbier *n*. **4.** drückend, lastend (*Stille etc*). **5.** (*with*) (schwer)beladen (mit); *fig.* überladen, voll (von): *~ with meaning* bedeutungsvoll, -schwer. **6.** begriffsstutzig, dumm. **7.** benommen (*with* von): *~ with sleep* schlaftrunken. **8. with a ~ heart** schweren Herzens. **II** *adv* **9. hang ~** dahinschleichen (*Zeit*); *lie ~ on s.o.* schwer auf j-m lasten. **,~·'du·ty** *adj* **1.** ⚙ Hochleistungs... **2.** strapazierfähig. '**~·weight** (*Sport*) **I** *s* Schwergewicht(ler *m*) *n*. **II** *adj* Schwergewichts...

heck·le ['hekl] *v/t* Redner durch Zwischenrufe *od.* -fragen aus dem Konzept bringen *od.* in die Enge treiben. '**heck·ler** *s* Zwischenrufer *m*.

hec·tic ['hektɪk] *adj* (*~ally*) hektisch (*a.* 🩺).

hec·to·li·ter, *bsd. Br.* **hec·to·li·tre** ['hektəʊ,liːtə] *s* Hektoliter *m, n*.

he'd [hiːd] F *für* he had; he would.

hedge [hedʒ] **I** *s* **1.** Hecke *f*. **2.** *fig.* (Ab)Sicherung *f* (*against* gegen). **II** *v/t* **3.** *a. ~ in* (*od. round*) mit e-r Hecke einfassen: *~ off* mit e-r Hecke abgrenzen *od.* abtrennen. **4.** *fig.* (ab)sichern (*against* gegen). **III** *v/i* **5.** *fig.* ausweichen, sich nicht festlegen (wollen). '**~·hog** *s zo.* Igel *m; Am.* Stachelschwein *n*.

heed [hiːd] **I** *v/t* beachten, Beachtung schenken (*dat*). **II** *s*: *give* (*od. pay*) *~ to*, *take ~ of* → I. **heed·ful** ['~fʊl] *adj* □ achtsam: *be ~ of* → *heed* I. '**heed·less**

adj □ achtlos, unachtsam: *be ~ of* nicht beachten, keine Beachtung schenken (*dat*), *Warnung etc* in den Wind schlagen.

hee-haw [,hiː'hɔː] **I** *s* **1.** Iah *n* (*Eselsschrei*). **2.** *fig.* wieherndes Gelächter, Gewieher *n.* **II** *v/i* **3.** iahen. **4.** *fig.* wiehernd lachen, wiehern.

heel¹ [hiːl] *v/i* ⚓ sich auf die Seite legen, krängen.

heel² [~] **I** *s* **1.** *anat.* Ferse *f* (*a. vom Strumpf etc*); Absatz *m*, Hacken *m* (*vom Schuh*): *down at ~* a) mit schiefen Absätzen b) *a. out at ~s fig.* heruntergekommen (*Hotel etc*), (*Person a.*) abgerissen; *on the ~s of* unmittelbar auf (*acc*), gleich nach; *follow s.o.'s ~s*, *follow s.o. at* (*od. on*) *his ~s* j-m auf den Fersen folgen, sich j-m an die Fersen heften; *show a clean pair of ~s, take to one's ~s* die Beine in die Hand *od.* unter den Arm nehmen. **II** *v/t* **2.** Absätze machen auf (*acc*). **3.** *Fußball:* Ball mit dem Absatz kicken.

heft·y ['heftɪ] *adj* □ **1.** schwer. **2.** kräftig, stämmig. **3.** F mächtig, gewaltig (*Schlag etc*), stattlich (*Mehrheit etc*), saftig (*Preise etc*).

he·gem·o·ny [hɪ'geməni] *s bsd. pol.* Hegemonie *f*.

height [haɪt] *s* **1.** Höhe *f*: *10 feet in ~* 10 Fuß hoch. **2.** (Körper)Größe *f*: *what is your ~?* wie groß sind Sie? **3.** Anhöhe *f*, Erhebung *f*. **4.** *fig.* Höhe(punkt *m*) *f*, Gipfel *m*: *at the ~ of one's fame* auf der Höhe s-s Ruhms; *at the ~ of summer* im Hochsommer. '**height·en I** *v/t* **1.** erhöhen (*a. fig.*). **2.** *fig.* vergrößern, steigern. **II** *v/i* **3.** *fig.* sich erhöhen, (an)steigen, zunehmen.

hei·nous ['heɪnəs] *adj* □ abscheulich, scheußlich.

heir [eə] *s* ⚖ Erbe *m* (*to, of gen*): *~ to the throne* Thronerbe *m*, -folger *m*; → *universal* 1. **heir·ess** ['~rɪs] *s* Erbin *f*.

held [held] *pret u. pp von* **hold**.

hel·i·cop·ter ['helɪkɒptə] *s* Hubschrauber *m*.

hel·i·port ['helɪpɔːt] *s* Hubschrauberlandeplatz *m*.

he·li·um ['hiːljəm] *s* 🧪 Helium *n*.

hell [hel] *s* Hölle *f* (*a. fig.*): *like ~* F wie verrückt *arbeiten etc*; *a ~ of a noise* F ein Höllenlärm; *what the ~ ...?* F was zum Teufel ...?; *give s.o.* ~ F j-m die Hölle heiß machen; *go to* ~*!* F scher dich zum Teufel!; *raise* ~ F e-n Mordskrach schlagen; *suffer* ~ *on earth* die Hölle auf Erden haben.

he'll [hi:l] F *für he will.*

,hell'bent *adj* F ganz versessen, wie wild (*on, for* auf *acc*). '~•**cat** *s* Xanthippe *f*.

hell•ish ['helɪʃ] *adj* □ **1.** höllisch (*a. fig.* F). **2.** F verteufelt, scheußlich.

hel•lo [hə'ləʊ] **I** *int* **1.** hallo!, (*überrascht a.*) nanu! **II** *pl* **-los** *s* **2.** Hallo *n*. **3.** Gruß *m*: *say* ~ (*to s.o.*) (j-m) guten Tag sagen.

helm [helm] *s* ⚓ Ruder *n* (*a. fig.*), Steuer *n*: *be at the* ~ am Ruder *od.* an der Macht (*sein*); *take the* ~ das Ruder übernehmen.

helms•man ['helmzmən] *s* (*irr man*) ⚓ Steuermann *m* (*a. fig.*).

help [help] **I** *s* **1.** Hilfe *f*: *come to s.o.'s* ~ j-m zu Hilfe kommen. **2.** Abhilfe *f*. **3.** (*bsd.* Haus)Angestellte *f*. **II** *v/t* **4.** j-m helfen *od.* behilflich sein (*in* [*od.* with] bei): ~ *s.o. out* j-m aushelfen (*with* mit); → *god.* **5.** ~ *s.o. to s.th.* j-m zu et. verhelfen; ~ *o.s.* sich bedienen, zugreifen. **6.** *mit can: I cannot* ~ *it* ich kann es nicht ändern; ich kann nichts dafür; *it cannot be* ~*ed* da kann man nichts machen, es ist nicht zu ändern; *I could not* ~ *laughing* ich mußte einfach lachen. **III** *v/i* **7.** helfen: ~ *out* aushelfen (*with* mit). **'help•er** *s* Helfer(in). **help•ful** ['_fʊl] *adj* □ **1.** hilfsbereit. **2.** hilfreich. **'help•ing** F *adj* hilfreich: → *hand* 1. **II** *s* Portion *f* (*Essen*): *have* (*od. take*) *a second* ~ sich nachnehmen. **'help•less** *adj* □ hilflos.

hel•ter-skel•ter [,heltə'skeltə] **I** *adv* holterdiepolter, Hals über Kopf. **II** *adj* hastig, überstürzt. **III** *s* (*wildes*) Durcheinander, (wilde) Hast.

hem¹ [hem] **I** *s* **1.** Saum *m*. **2.** Rand *m*, Einfassung *f*. **II** *v/t* **3.** *Kleid etc* (ein)säumen. **4.** ~ *in* a) ~ *about* (*od. around*) umranden, einfassen, b) ⚔ einschließen, c) *fig.* einengen.

hem² [~] **I** *int* h(e)m! **II** *v/i* sich (*verlegen*) räuspern: ~ *and haw* herumdrucksen, nicht recht mit der Sprache herauswollen.

'he-man *s* (*irr man*) F He-man *m* (*bsd. männlich wirkender Mann*).

hem•i•sphere ['hemɪˌsfɪə] *s geogr.* Halbkugel *f*, Hemisphäre *f*.

'hem•line *s* Saum *m*: ~*s are going up again* die Kleider werden wieder kürzer.

he-mo-glo-bin, hem-or-rhoids *etc bsd. Am.* → **haemoglobin, haemorrhoids** *etc.*

hemp [hemp] *s* Hanf *m*.

hen [hen] *s orn.* **1.** Henne *f*, Huhn *n*. **2.** (*Vogel*)Weibchen *n*.

hence [hens] *adv* **1.** *a week* ~ in e-r Woche. **2.** folglich, daher, deshalb. **3.** hieraus, daraus: ~ *it follows that* daraus folgt, daß. **,~'forth**, **,~'for•ward(s)** *adv* von nun an, fortan.

hench•man ['hentʃmən] *s* (*irr man*) *bsd. pol.* Anhänger *m*; *contp.* Handlanger *m*.

hen| par•ty *s* F Damengesellschaft *f*, Kaffeeklatsch *m*. '~•**pecked** *adj* unter dem Pantoffel stehend: ~ *husband* Pantoffelheld *m*.

hep [hep] → *hip⁴*.

hep•a•ti•tis [,hepə'taɪtɪs] *s* 🛠 Leberentzündung *f*.

her [hɜ:] *I personal pron* **1.** sie (*acc von she*): *I know* ~. **2.** ihr (*dat von she*): *I gave* ~ *the book.* **3.** F sie (*nom*): *he's younger than* ~; *it's* ~ sie ist es. **II** *possessive pron* **4.** ihr(e). **III** *reflex pron* **5.** sich: *she looked about* ~ sie sah sich um.

her•ald ['herəld] **I** *s* **1.** *hist.* Herold *m*. **2.** *fig.* Vorbote *m*. **II** *v/t* **3.** ankündigen (*a. fig.*). **he•ral•dic** [he'rældɪk] *adj* (~*ally*) heraldisch, Wappen... **her•ald•ry** ['herəldrɪ] *s* Heraldik *f*, Wappenkunde *f*.

herb [hɜ:b] *s* 🌿 Kraut *n*; *engS.* Heilkraut; Gewürz-, Küchenkraut. **herb•al** ['_bl] *adj* Kräuter..., Pflanzen... **her•bar•i•um** [~'beəriəm] *s* Herbarium *n*. **her•biv•o•rous** [~'bɪvərəs] *adj* □ *zo.* pflanzenfressend.

herd [hɜ:d] **I** *s* **1.** Herde *f*, (*wildlebender Tiere a.*) Rudel *n* (*a. von Menschen*). **2.** *contp.* Herde *f*, Masse *f* (*Menschen*): *the* (*common od. vulgar*) ~ die große *od.* breite Masse. **II** *v/i* **3.** *a.* ~ *together* in Herden leben; sich zs.-drängen (*a. Menschen*). **4.** sich zs.-tun (*with* mit). **III** *v/t* **5.** Vieh hüten. **6.** Vieh, *a. Menschen* treiben: ~ *together* zs.-treiben. **'herd•er** *s bsd. Am.* Hirt *m*.

herd in·stinct *s* zo. Herdeninstinkt *m*, (*a. bei Menschen*) Herdentrieb *m*.

herds·man ['hɜ:dzmən] *s* (*irr* man) *bsd. Br.* Hirt *m*.

here [hɪə] *adv* hier; (hier)her: **come ~** komm her; **~ and there** hier u. da, da u. dort; hierhin u. dorthin; **~'s to you!** auf dein Wohl!; **~ you** (*od.* **we**) **are!** hier (bitte)! (*da hast du es*). '**~·a.bouts** *adv* hier herum, in dieser Gegend. **,~'af·ter** I *adv* 1. nachstehend, im folgenden. 2. künftig, in Zukunft. II *s* 3. Jenseits *n*. **,~'by** *adv* hiermit.

he·red·i·ta·ry [hɪ'redɪtərɪ] *adj* □ 1. (ver)erblich, Erb...: **~ disease** Erbkrankheit *f*. 2. fig. althergebracht, Erb...: **~ enemy** Erbfeind *m*.

,here'in *adv* hierin. **,~'of** *adv* hiervon.

her·e·sy ['herəsɪ] *s* Ketzerei *f*.

her·e·tic ['herətɪk] *s* Ketzer(in). **he·ret·i·cal** [hɪ'retɪkl] *adj* □ ketzerisch.

,here|·up'on *adv* hierauf, darauf(hin). **,~'with** *adv* hiermit.

her·it·a·ble ['herɪtəbl] *adj* □ erblich, vererbbar. **'her·it·age** *s* Erbe *n*.

her·maph·ro·dite [hɜ:'mæfrədaɪt] *s* biol. Zwitter *m*.

her·met·ic [hɜ:'metɪk] *adj* (**~ally**) hermetisch, ⚙ luftdicht: **~ally sealed** luftdicht verschlossen.

her·mit ['hɜ:mɪt] *s* Einsiedler *m* (*a. fig.*), Eremit *m*. '**her·mit·age** *s* Einsiedelei *f*.

her·ni·a ['hɜ:njə] *s* 𝔰 Bruch *m*.

he·ro ['hɪərəʊ] *pl* **-roes** *s* Held *m*, thea. etc *a.* Hauptperson *f*. **he·ro·ic** [hɪ'rəʊɪk] *adj* (**~ally**) 1. heroisch, heldenhaft, Helden... 2. hochtrabend, bombastisch (*Sprache, Stil*).

her·o·in ['herəʊɪn] *s* Heroin *n*.

her·o·ine ['herəʊɪn] *s* Heldin *f*, thea. etc *a.* Hauptperson *f*. '**her·o·ism** *s* Heldentum *n*.

her·on ['herən] *s* orn. Reiher *m*.

her·pes ['hɜ:pi:z] *s* 𝔰 Herpes *m*.

her·ring ['herɪŋ] *pl* **-rings**, *bsd. coll.* **-ring** *s* ichth. Hering *m*. '**~·bone** *s a.* **~ design** (*od.* **pattern**) Fischgrätenmuster *n*.

hers [hɜ:z] *possessive pron*: **it is ~** es gehört ihr; **a friend of ~** e-e Freundin von ihr; **my mother and ~** m-e u. ihre Mutter.

her'self *pron* 1. *verstärkend*: sie (*nom od. acc*) selbst, ihr (*dat*) selbst: **she did it ~,**

she ~ did it sie hat es selbst getan. 2. *reflex* sich: **she killed ~.** 3. sich (selbst): **she wants it for ~.**

he's [hi:z] F *für* **he is**; **he has**.

hes·i·tate ['hezɪteɪt] *v/i* 1. zögern, zaudern, Bedenken haben (**to do** zu tun), unschlüssig sein (**over** hinsichtlich). 2. (*beim Sprechen*) stocken. **,hes·i'ta·tion** *s* 1. Zögern *n*, Zaudern *n*, Unschlüssigkeit *f*: **without** (**any**) **~** ohne zu zögern. 2. Stocken *n*.

het·er·o·dox ['hetərədɒks] *adj* heterodox, anders-, irrgläubig. **het·er·o·ge·ne·ous** [,~'dʒi:njəs] *adj* □ heterogen, ungleichartig, verschiedenartig. **,het·er·o'sex·u·al** I *adj* □ heterosexuell. II *s* Heterosexuelle *m*, *f*.

het¹ [het] *adj*: **be ~ up** F aufgeregt *od.* nervös sein (**about** wegen).

het² [~] F I *adj* hetero (*heterosexuell*). II *s* Hetero *m*, *f*.

hew [hju:] *v/t* (*a. irr*) 1. hauen, hacken: **~ down** umhauen; **~ off** abhauen; **~ up** zerhauen, -hacken. 2. Steine etc behauen. **hewn** [hju:n] *pp von* **hew**.

hex·a·gon ['heksəgən] *s* Sechseck *n*. **hex·ag·o·nal** [~'sægənl] *adj* □ sechseckig.

hey [heɪ] *int* 1. → **presto**. 2. he!

hey·day ['heɪdeɪ] *s a.* Höhepunkt *m*, Gipfel *m*: **in the ~ of one's power** auf dem Gipfel der Macht, b) Blüte(zeit) *f*: **in one's ~** in s-r Glanzzeit.

hi [haɪ] *int* F hallo!

hi·ber·nate ['haɪbəneɪt] *v/i* überwintern: a) zo. Winterschlaf halten, b) den Winter verbringen. **,hi·ber'na·tion** *s* Überwinterung *f*, Winterschlaf *m*.

hi·bis·cus [hɪ'bɪskəs] *s* ⚘ Hibiskus *m*, Eibisch *m*.

hic·cough, hic·cup ['hɪkʌp] I *s* 1. **have** (**the**) **~s** e-n Schluckauf haben. 2. *fig.* Panne *f*. II *v/i* 3. hicksen.

hick [hɪk] *bsd. Am.* F I *s* Bauer *m*, Provinzler *m*. II *adj* Bauern..., provinziell: **~ town** (Provinz)Nest *n*, (Bauern-)Kaff *n*.

hick·o·ry ['hɪkərɪ] *s* 1. ⚘ Hickory(baum) *m*. 2. Hickory(holz) *n*.

hid [hɪd] *pret u. pp von* **hide²**. '**hid·den** I *pp von* **hide²**. II *adj* □ geheim, verborgen.

hide¹ [haɪd] I *s* 1. Haut *f*, Fell *n* (*beide a. fig.*): **save one's own ~** die eigene Haut retten; *tan s.o.'s* ~ F j-m das Fell gerben. **II** *v/t* **2.** abhäuten. **3.** F verprügeln.

hide² [~] (*irr*) **I** *v/t* (*from*) verbergen (vor *dat*): a) verstecken (vor *dat*), b) verheimlichen (*dat od.* vor *dat*), c) verhüllen, -decken. **II** *v/i a.* ~ *out* (*bsd. Am. up*) sich verbergen *od.* verstecken. ,~**-and-'seek** *s* Versteckspiel *n*: *play* ~ Versteck spielen. '~**a·way** *s* **1.** Versteck *n.* **2.** Zufluchtsort *m.*

hid·e·ous ['hɪdɪəs] *adj* □ abscheulich, scheußlich.

'**hide-out** *s* Versteck *n.*

hid·ing¹ ['haɪdɪŋ] *s* F Tracht *f* Prügel.

hid·ing² [~] *s a.* ~ *place* Versteck *n*: *be in* ~ sich versteckt halten; *go into* ~ untertauchen.

hi·er·arch·y ['haɪərɑːkɪ] *s* Hierarchie *f.*

hi·er·o·glyph ['haɪərəʊglɪf] → *hieroglyphic* 1, 3. **hi·er·o·'glyph·ic** *s* **1.** Hieroglyphe *f.* **2.** *pl* (*mst sg konstruiert*) Hieroglyphenschrift *f.* **3.** *pl humor.* Hieroglyphen *pl*, unleserliches Gekritzel.

hi·fi ['haɪfaɪ] F **I** *s* **1.** Hi-Fi *n.* **2.** Hi-Fi-Anlage *f*; -Gerät *n.* **II** *adj* **3.** Hi-Fi-...

hig·gle·dy-pig·gle·dy [,hɪgldɪ'pɪgldɪ] F **I** *adv* drunter u. drüber, (wie Kraut u. Rüben) durcheinander. **II** *adj* kunterbunt.

high [haɪ] **I** *adj* (□ → *highly*) **1.** *allg.* hoch; *engS. a.* hochgelegen: → *horse.* **2.** hoch (*Geschwindigkeit, Preise etc*), groß (*Hoffnungen, Lob etc*). **3.** (*rang·od. stellungsmäßig*) hoch: ~ *society* High-Society *f.* **4.** fortgeschritten (*Zeit*): ~ *season* Hochsaison *f*; ~ *summer* Hochsommer *m*; *it is* ~ *time* es ist höchste Zeit. **5.** hoch, erstklassig (*Qualität etc*). **6.** a) gehoben: → *spirit* 4, b) F blau (*betrunken*), c) F high. **7.** F scharf (*on auf acc*). **II** *adv* **8.** hoch: *aim* ~ *fig.* sich hohe Ziele setzen *od.* stecken; *search* ~ *and low* überall suchen. **9.** hoch, mit hohem Einsatz (*spielen*). **III** *s* **10.** (An)Höhe *f*: *on* ~ hoch oben, droben; im Himmel. **11.** *meteor.* Hoch *n.* **12.** *fig.* Höchststand *m.* **13.** *am.* F High-School *f.* ~ *al·tar* *s* Hochaltar *m.* ,~·**'al·ti·tude** *adj* Höhen... ~ *and dry adj*: *leave s.o.* ~ j-n im Stich lassen. ~ *and might·y adj* F anmaßend, arrogant. '~**ball** *s Am.* Highball *m* (*Whiskycocktail*). ~ *beam* *s mot. Am.* Fern-

licht *n.* '~**brow** *oft contp.* **I** *s* Intellektuelle *m, f.* **II** *adj* (betont) intellektuell. '~**chair** *s* (Kinder)Hochstuhl *m.* �858 **Church** *s* anglikanische Hochkirche. ,~**·cir·cu·la·tion** *adj* auflagenstark. ,~**·class** *adj* erstklassig. ,~**·du·ty** *adj* ☼ Hochleistungs... ~ **fi·del·i·ty** *s* High-Fidelity *f.* ,~**·fi·del·i·ty** *adj* High-Fidelity-... '~**flown** *adj* **1.** bombastisch, hochtrabend (*Worte etc*). **2.** (allzu) hochgesteckt (*Ziele etc*), (allzu) hochfliegend (*Pläne etc*). ,~**·grade** *adj* **1.** hochwertig. **2.** *a.* ☼ erstklassig. ~ '**hand·ed** *adj* □ anmaßend, willkürlich. ,~**·'heeled** *adj* hochhackig (*Schuhe*). ~ *jump* *s* Leichtathletik: Hochsprung *m.* ~ *jump·er* *s* Hochspringer(in). ,~**·'lev·el** *adj* hoch (*a. fig.*): ~ *talks* *pl* Gespräche *pl* auf höherer Ebene. '~**light** **I** *s* Höhe-, Glanzpunkt *m*; *pl* Querschnitt *m* (*of* durch *e-e Oper etc*). **II** *v/t* hervorheben.

high·ly ['haɪlɪ] *adv* **1.** *fig.* hoch: ~ *gifted* hochbegabt; ~ *interesting* hochinteressant; ~ *paid* hochbezahlt; teuer bezahlt. **2.** lobend, anerkennend: *think* ~ *of* viel halten von.

High| Mass *s eccl.* Hochamt *n.* �858 ~'**necked** *adj* hochgeschlossen (*Kleid*).

high·ness ['haɪnɪs] *s* **1.** *mst fig.* Höhe *f.* **2.** �858 Hoheit *f* (*Titel*).

,**high|·'pow·er(ed)** *adj* **1.** ☼ Hochleistungs... **2.** *fig.* dynamisch, energisch. ,~**'pres·sure** *adj* ☼, *meteor.* Hochdruck... ~ *priest* *s eccl.* Hohepriester *m* (*a. fig.*). ,~**·'qual·i·ty** *adj* hochwertig. '~**·rank·ing** *adj* hochrangig: ~ *officer* ✗ hoher Offizier. '~**rise** *s* Hochhaus *n.* ~ *school* *s Am.* High-School *f.* ,~**·'sea** *adj* Hochsee... '~**·sound·ing** *adj* hochtönend, -trabend. ~ *street* *s* Hauptstraße *f.* ~ *tea* *s Br.* frühes Abendessen. ~**·tech** [,~'tek] *adj* F High-Tech-... ~ *tech·nol·o·gy* *s* Hochtechnologie *f.* ~ *ten·sion* *s* ⚡ Hochspannung *f.* ,~**·'ten·sion** *adj* ⚡ Hochspannungs... ~ *trea·son* *s* Hochverrat *m.* ~ *wa·ter* *s* Hochwasser *n.* '~**way** *s* Highway *m*, Haupt(verkehrs)straße *f*: ~ *code* *Br.* Straßenverkehrsordnung *f.*

hi·jack ['haɪdʒæk] **I** *v/t* **1.** entführen. **2.** *j-n, Geldtransport etc* überfallen. **II** *s* **3.** (Flugzeug)Entführung *f.* **4.** Überfall *m.* '**hi·jack·er** *s* **1.** (Flugzeug)Entführer *m*. **2.** Räuber *m*. **'hi·jack·ing** → **hijack** II.

hike [haɪk] I *v/i* wandern. II *s* Wanderung *f*: **go on a ~** e-e Wanderung machen. **'hik·er** *s* Wanderer *m*.

hi·lar·i·ous [hɪ'leərɪəs] *adj* □ **1.** vergnügt, ausgelassen, übermütig. **2.** lustig (*Geschichte etc*). **hi·lar·i·ty** [hɪ'lærətɪ] *s* Vergnügtheit *f*, Ausgelassenheit *f*, Übermütigkeit *f*.

hill [hɪl] *s* Hügel *m*, Anhöhe *f*: (*as*) **old as the ~s** uralt, (*Person a.*) steinalt; **be over the ~** F s-e besten Jahre *od.* s-e beste Zeit hinter sich haben; *bsd.* ⚓ über den Berg sein. **'~bil·ly** *s Am. mst contp.* Hillbilly *m*, Hinterwäldler *m*.

hill·ock ['hɪlək] *s* kleiner Hügel.

hill·side *s* (Ab)Hang *m*. **~top** *s* Hügelspitze *f*. **~ walk** *s* Bergwanderung *f*.

hilt [hɪlt] *s* Heft *n*, Griff *m* (*Schwert*, *Dolch*): (**up**) **to the ~** bis ans Heft; *fig.* durch u. durch, ganz u. gar.

him [hɪm] I *personal pron* **1.** ihn (*acc von* **he**): *I know ~.* **2.** ihm (*dat von* **he**): *I gave ~ the book.* **3.** F er (*nom*): *she's younger than ~; it's ~* cı ist es. II *reflex pron* **4.** sich: *he looked about ~* er sah sich um.

him·self *pron* **1.** *verstärkend:* er *od.* ihm *od.* ihn selbst: *he did it ~*, *he ~ did it* er hat es selbst getan. **2.** *reflex von* **he**: *he killed ~*. **3.** sich (selbst): *he wants it for ~*

hind [haɪnd] *adj* hinter, Hinter...: **~ wheel** Hinterrad *n*.

hind·er ['hɪndə] *v/t* **1.** *j-n, et.* aufhalten (**in** bei); behindern. **2.** (**from**) hindern (an *dat*), abhalten (von).

hind·most ['haɪndməʊst] *sup von* **hind**.

hind·quar·ters *s pl* Hinterhand *f* (*vom Pferd*); Hinterteil *n*.

hin·drance ['hɪndrəns] *s* **1.** Behinderung *f*: **be a ~ to** → **hinder** 1. **2.** Hindernis *n* (**to** für).

'hind·sight *s*: **with ~** im nachhinein (betrachtet).

Hin·du [ˌhɪn'duː] *eccl.* I *s* Hindu *m*. II *adj* Hindu... **'Hin·du·ism** *s* Hinduismus *m*.

hinge [hɪndʒ] I *s* **1.** ⊕ Scharnier *n*, (Tür)Angel *f*. **2.** *fig.* Angelpunkt *m*. II *v/t* **3.** Tür etc einhängen. III *v/i* **4.** (**on**) *fig.* abhängen (von), ankommen (auf *acc*); sich drehen (um).

hint [hɪnt] I *s* **1.** Wink *m*, Andeutung *f*:

drop a ~ e-e Andeutung machen; *broad ~* Wink mit dem Zaunpfahl. **2.** Fingerzeig *m*, Tip *m* (**on** für). **3.** Anspielung *f* (**at** auf *acc*). **4.** Anflug *m*, Spur *f* (**of** von). II *v/t* **5.** andeuten. III *v/i* **6.** (**at**) andeuten (*acc*); anspielen (auf *acc*).

hin·ter·land ['hɪntəlænd] *s* **1.** Hinterland *n*. **2.** Umland *n*.

hip¹ [hɪp] *s anat.* Hüfte *f*.

hip² [~] *s* ♀ Hagebutte *f*.

hip³ [~] *int*: **~, ~, hurrah!** hipp, hipp, hurra!

hip⁴ [~] *adj sl.* **1.** **be ~** alles mitmachen, was gerade in ist. **2.** **be ~** auf dem laufenden sein (**of** über).

'hip|·bath *s* Sitzbad *n*. **'~·bone** *s anat.* Hüftbein *n*, -knochen *m*. **~ flask** *s* Taschenflasche *f*, Flachmann *m*. **~ joint** *s anat.* Hüftgelenk *n*.

hip·pie ['hɪpɪ] *s* Hippie *m*.

hip pock·et *s* Gesäßtasche *f*.

hip·po·pot·a·mus [ˌhɪpə'pɒtəməs] *pl* **-mus·es, -mi** [~maɪ] *s zo.* Fluß-, Nilpferd *n*.

hip·py → **hippie**.

hire ['haɪə] I *v/t* **1.** Auto etc mieten, Flugzeug etc chartern: **~d car** Leih-, Mietwagen *m*; **~d plane** Charterflugzeug *n*. **2.** *a.* **~ on** *j-n* ein-, anstellen, ⚓ (an)heuern; *j-n* engagieren; *bsd. b.s.* anheuern: **~d killer** gekaufter Mörder, Killer *m*. **3.** *mst* **~ out** vermieten. II *s* **4.** Miete *f*: **~ company** Verleih(firma *f*) *m*; **on ~** mietweise; **for ~** zu vermieten; (*Taxi*) frei. **5.** Lohn *m*, Entgelt *n*. **~ pur·chase** *s*: **on ~** *bsd. Br.* auf Abzahlung *od.* Raten.

his [hɪz] *possessive pron*: **it is ~** es gehört ihm; **a friend of ~** ein Freund von ihm; **my mother and ~** m-e u. s-e Mutter.

hiss [hɪs] I *v/i* **1.** zischen, (*Katze*) fauchen: **~ at** → 2. II *v/t* **2.** auszischen. **3.** *et.* zische(l)n. III *s* **4.** Zischen *n*, Fauchen *n*.

his·to·ri·an [hɪ'stɔːrɪən] *s* Historiker *m*.

his·tor·ic [hɪ'stɒrɪk] *adj* (**~ally**) **1.** historisch, geschichtlich (berühmt *od.* bedeutsam). **2.** → **historical**. **his·tor·i·cal** [~kl] *adj* □ **1.** → **historic** 1. **2.** historisch: a) geschichtlich (belegt *od.* überliefert), b) Geschichts..., c) geschichtlich(en Inhalts): **~ novel** historischer Roman. **his·to·ry** ['~tərɪ] *s* **1.** Geschichte *f*: *contemporary* ~ Zeitgeschichte; ~ *of art* Kunstgeschichte; *go down in* ~ in die Geschichte eingehen; *make* ~ Geschichte machen. **2.** (Entwicklungs-)Geschichte *f*, Werdegang *m*. **3.** *allg.*, *a.* 🏵 Vorgeschichte *f*: → *case history*.

hit [hɪt] **I** *s* **1.** Hieb *m* (*a. fig. at* gegen), Schlag *m*: *that was a* ~ *at me* das ging gegen mich. **2.** Treffer *m* (*a. Sport u. fig.*): *make* (*od. score*) *a* ~ e-n Treffer erzielen; *fig.* gut ankommen (*with* bei). **3.** Hit *m* (*Buch, Schlager etc*): *it was a big* ~ es hat groß eingeschlagen. **4.** *sl.* Schuß *m* (*Drogeninjektion*): *give o.s. a* ~ sich e-n Schuß setzen *od.* drücken. **5.** *bsd. Am. sl.* (*von e-m hit man ausgeführter*) Mord. **II** *v/t* (*irr*) **6.** schlagen. **7.** *a. fig. seelisch, finanziell etc*) treffen: ~ *the nail on the head fig.* den Nagel auf den Kopf treffen; ~ *the bottle* F saufen; ~ *hay, road, sack*[1] **3. 8.** *mot. etc* j-n, *et.* anfahren, *et.* rammen: ~ *one's head against* (*od. on*) sich den Kopf anschlagen an (*dat*), mit dem Kopf stoßen gegen. **9.** *et.* erreichen, schaffen: ~ *front page, headline* **1. 10.** *bsd. fig.* stoßen auf (*acc*), finden. **11.** *a.* ~ *up bsd. Am.* F anhauen, anpumpen (*for* um). **12.** F ankommen in (*dat*), erreichen. **13.** *bsd. Am. sl.* j-n umlegen (*hit man*). **III** *v/i* (*irr*) **14.** treffen. **15.** schlagen (*at* nach). **16.** stoßen, schlagen (*against* gegen; *on* auf *acc*). **17.** ~ *on* → **10**.
Verbindungen mit Adverbien:
hit| back *v/i* zurückschlagen (*a. fig.*). ~ **off** *v/t*: *hit it off* F sich gut vertragen (*with* mit). ~ **out** *v/i* **1.** um sich schlagen: ~ *at s.o.* auf j-n einschlagen. **2.** *fig.* her-, losziehen (*at, against* über *acc*).
,hit-and-'run *adj*: ~ *accident* Unfall *m* mit Fahrerflucht; ~ *driver* (unfall-)flüchtiger Fahrer.

hitch [hɪtʃ] **I** *s* **1.** Ruck *m*, Zug *m*. **2.** Schwierigkeit *f*, Haken *m*: *without a* ~ glatt, reibungslos. **3.** *get a* ~ F im Auto mitgenommen werden. **II** *v/t* **4.** rücken, ziehen: ~ *up* hochziehen. **5.** befestigen, festhaken (*to* an *acc*): *get ~ed* F heiraten. **6.** ~ *a ride* → **3**. **III** *v/i* **7.** sich festhaken, hängenbleiben (*on* an *dat*). **8.** F → *hitchhike*.
'hitch·er F → *hitchhiker*.
'hitch|·hike *v/i* per Anhalter fahren,

trampen. '~**,hik·er** *s* Anhalter(in), Tramper(in).

hith·er ['hɪðə] *adv* hierher. ~**'to** *adv* bisher, bis jetzt.

hit| list *s*: *be on the* ~ *bsd. Am. sl.* auf der Abschußliste stehen (*a. fig.*). ~ **man** *s* (*irr man*) *bsd. Am. sl.* Killer *m* (*e-s Verbrechersyndikats*). ~ **or miss** *adv* aufs Geratewohl, auf gut Glück. ~ **pa·rade** *s* Hitparade *f*. ~ **song** *s* Hit *m*.

hive [haɪv] **I** *s* **1.** Bienenkorb *m*, -stock *m*. **2.** Bienenvolk *n*; *fig.* Schwarm *m* (*Menschen*). **II** *v/i* **3.** ~ *off fig.* abschwenken (*from* von); sich selbständig machen; *bsd. Br.* F sich aus dem Staub machen. **4.** sich zs.-drängen.
hives [haɪvz] *s pl* (*a. sg konstruiert*) 🏵 Nesselausschlag *m*.

hoard [hɔːd] **I** *s* Vorrat *m* (*of* an *dat*). **II** *v/t a.* ~ *up* horten, hamstern. **III** *v/i* hamstern, sich Vorräte anlegen.
hoard·ing ['hɔːdɪŋ] *s* **1.** Bau-, Bretterzaun *m*. **2.** *Br.* Reklametafel *f*.
hoar-frost [,hɔː'frɒst] *s* (Rauh)Reif *m*.
hoarse [hɔːs] *adj* □ heiser. **'hoarse-ness** *s* Heiserkeit *f*.
hoar·y ['hɔːrɪ] *adj* □ **1.** weiß(grau). **2.** (alters)grau.
hoax [həʊks] **I** *s* **1.** (Zeitungs)Ente *f*. **2.** Streich *m*, (übler) Scherz: *play a* ~ *on s.o.* j-m e-n Streich spielen, sich mit j-m e-n Scherz erlauben. **II** *v/t* **3.** j-m e-n Bären aufbinden.

hob·ble ['hɒbl] *v/i* hinken, humpeln.
hob·by ['hɒbɪ] *s* Hobby *n*, Steckenpferd *n*. ~ **room** *s* Hobbyraum *m*.
hob·gob·lin ['hɒbˌgɒblɪn] *s* Kobold *m*.
hob·nob ['hɒbnɒb] *v/i* freundschaftlich verkehren, auf du u. du sein (*with* mit).
ho·bo ['həʊbəʊ] *s* Am. Landstreicher *m*, Tippelbruder *m*.
Hob·son's choice ['hɒbsnz] *s*: *it was (a case of)* ~ es gab nur 'eine Möglichkeit; *he had to take* ~ es blieb ihm keine andere Wahl.

hock[1] [hɒk] *s* weißer Rheinwein.
hock[2] [~] *bsd. Am.* F **I** *s*: *be in* ~ versetzt sein; Schulden haben (*to* bei); im Kittchen sein *od.* sitzen; *put into* ~ → **II. II** *v/t* versetzen, ins Leihhaus tragen.
hock·ey ['hɒkɪ] *s Sport*: *bsd. Br.* Hockey *n*; *bsd. Am.* Eishockey *n*.
ho·cus-po·cus [,həʊkəs'pəʊkəs] *s* Hokuspokus *m*, fauler Zauber.

hodge·podge ['hɒdʒpɒdʒ] → *hotch-potch.*

hoe [həʊ] **I** *s* Hacke *f.* **II** *v/t* Boden hak-ken: ~ *(up) Unkraut* aushacken.

hog [hɒg] **I** *s* **1.** (Haus-, Schlacht-)Schwein *n*: **go the whole ~** F aufs Ganze gehen. **2.** F rücksichtsloser Kerl; gieriger *od.* gefräßiger Kerl; Schmutzfink *m*, Ferkel *n.* **II** *v/t* **3.** F rücksichtslos an sich reißen: ~ *the road* mot. die ganze Straße für sich brauchen; rücksichtslos fahren.

Hog·ma·nay ['hɒgməneɪ] *s schott.* Silvester(abend *m*) *m, n.*

'hog·wash *s* **1.** Schweinefutter *n.* **2.** *fig.* Spülwasser *n (dünner Kaffee etc).* **3.** *fig.* Gewäsch *n*, Geschwätz *n.*

hoi pol·loi [ˌhɔɪˈpɒlɔɪ] *s contp.* breite Masse, Pöbel *m.*

hoist [hɔɪst] **I** *v/t* **1.** hochziehen; *Flagge, Segel* hissen. **II** *s* **2.** Hochziehen *n.* **3.** ⚙ (Lasten)Aufzug *m.*

hoi·ty-toi·ty [ˌhɔɪtɪˈtɔɪtɪ] *adj* hochnäsig, eingebildet.

hold [həʊld] **I** *s* **1.** Griff *m (a. Ringen)*, Halt *m*: **catch** (*od.* **get, take**) *~ of s.th.* et. ergreifen *od.* zu fassen bekommen; **get ~ of s.o.** j-n erwischen; **keep ~ of** festhalten; **let go one's ~ of s.th.** et. loslassen. **2.** Halt *m*, Stütze *f*: **lose one's ~** den Halt verlieren. **3.** (*on, over, of*) Gewalt *f*, Macht *f* (über *acc*), Einfluß *m* (auf *acc*): **have a (firm) ~ on s.o.** j-n in s-r Gewalt haben, j-n beherrschen; **lose ~ of o.s.** die Fassung verlieren. **II** *v/t (irr)* **4.** (fest)halten. **5.** sich *die Nase, die Ohren* zuhalten: ~ *one's nose* (**ears**). **6.** *Gewicht etc* tragen, (aus)halten. **7.** (*in e-m Zustand*) halten: ~ *o.s. erect* sich geradehalten; ~ *(o.s.)* ready (sich) bereithalten. **8.** zurück-, abhalten (*from* von): ~ *s.o. from doing s.th.* j-n davon abhalten, et. zu tun; **there was no ~ing him** er war nicht zu halten. **9.** *Wahlen, Pressekonferenz etc* abhalten; *Fest etc* veranstalten. **10.** ✕ *u. fig. Stellung* halten, behaupten: ~ *one's own* (**with**) sich behaupten (gegen), bestehen (neben). **11.** *Aktien, Rechte etc* besitzen; *Amt etc* bekleiden. **12.** *Platz etc* (inne)haben; *Rekord* halten; *Titel* führen. **13.** fassen: a) enthalten, b) Platz bieten für. **14.** *Bewunderung, Sympathie etc* hegen, haben (*for* für).

15. der Ansicht sein (*that* daß). **16.** halten für: *I ~ him to be a liar* ich halte ihn für e-n Lügner. **17.** halten: ~ *responsible* verantwortlich machen; → *contempt* 1, *esteem* 3. **18.** *bsd.* ⚖ entscheiden (*that* daß). **19.** *Publikum, j-s Aufmerksamkeit* fesseln. **20.** ~ *s.th. against s.o.* j-m et. vorhalten. vorwerfen; j-m et. übelnehmen *od.* nachtragen. **III** *v/i (irr)* **21.** halten, nicht (zer)reißen *od.* (zer)brechen. **22.** (sich) festhalten (*by, to* an *dat*). **23.** *a. ~ good* (weiterhin) gelten, gültig sein *od.* bleiben. **24.** anhalten, andauern.

Verbindungen mit Adverbien:

hold| back I *v/t* **1.** zurückhalten. **2.** → **hold in I. 3.** *fig.* zurückhalten mit, verschweigen. **II** *v/i* **4.** *fig.* sich zurückhalten. **5.** nicht mit der Sprache herausrücken. ~ **down** *v/t* **1.** niederhalten, *fig. a.* unterdrücken. **2.** F *Posten* haben; sich in *e-r Stellung etc* halten. ~ **in I** *v/t* **1.** zügeln, zurückhalten: *hold o.s. in* a) → **II**, b) den Bauch einziehen. **II** *v/i* sich zurückhalten *od.* beherrschen. ~ **off I** *v/t* **1.** ab-, fernhalten, abwehren. **2.** et. aufschieben, *j-n* hinhalten. **II** *v/i* **3.** sich fernhalten (*from* von). **4.** zögern; warten (*from* mit). **5.** ausbleiben (*Regen etc*). ~ **on** *v/i* **1.** festhalten (*to* an *dat*) (*a. fig.*). **2.** sich festhalten (*to* an *dat*). **3.** aus-, durchhalten. **4.** andauern, anhalten. **5.** *teleph.* am Apparat bleiben. ~ **out I** *v/t* **1.** *Hand etc* ausstrecken: *hold s.th. out to s.o.* j-m et. hinhalten. **II** *v/i* **2.** reichen (*Vorräte*). **3.** aus-, durchhalten. ~ **o·ver** *v/t* **1.** *Sitzung, Entscheidung etc* vertagen, -schieben (*till, until* auf *acc*). **2.** *Film etc* verlängern (*for* um). ~ **to·geth·er** *v/t u. v/i* zs.-halten (*a. fig.*). ~ **up I** *v/t* **1.** hochhalten. **2.** *fig.* hinstellen (*as an example* als Beispiel). **3.** *j-n et.* aufhalten; *et.* verzögern: *be held up* sich verzögern. **4.** *j-n, Bank etc* überfallen. **II** *v/i* **5.** sich halten (*Preise, Wetter etc*).

'hold·all *s bsd. Br.* Reisetasche *f.*

hold·er ['həʊldə] *s* **1.** *oft in Zssgn* Halter *m*, ⚙ *a.* Halte-*f.* **2.** Inhaber(in).

'hold·ing *s oft pl* Besitz *m (an Effekten etc)*: ~ *company* ✝ Holding-, Dachgesellschaft *f.*

'hold·up *s* (bewaffneter) (Raub)Überfall.

hole [həʊl] **I** s **1.** Loch n: *be in a ~* F in der Klemme sein *od.* sitzen *od.* stecken; *make a ~ in fig.* ein Loch reißen in (*Vorräte*); *pick* (*od. knock*) *~s in fig.* an e-r *Sache* herumkritteln, *Argument etc* zerpflücken; *j-m* am Zeug flicken. **2.** Höhle f, Bau m (*e-s Tiers*), Loch n (*e-r Maus*). **3.** F a) *a. ~ in the wall* Loch n, (*Bruch*)Bude f, b) Kaff n, Nest n. **II** v/t **4.** ein Loch *od.* Löcher machen in (*acc*); durchlöchern. **5.** *Golf:* Ball einlochen. **III** v/i **6.** *oft ~ out* (*Golf*) einlochen.

hol·i·day [ˈhɒlədeɪ] **I** s **1.** Feiertag m: → *public* 3b. **2.** freier Tag: *take a ~* (sich) e-n Tag frei nehmen. **3.** *mst pl bsd.Br.* Ferien pl, Urlaub m: *be on ~* im Urlaub sein, Urlaub machen. **II** adj **4.** bsd. Br. Ferien..., Urlaubs... **III** v/i **5.** bsd. Br. Urlaub machen , die Ferien verbringen. **~·mak·er** [ˈ~dɪ͵~] s bsd. Br. Urlauber(in).

hol·ler [ˈhɒlə] v/i u. v/t F schreien, brüllen: *~ for help* um Hilfe schreien; *~ at j-n* anbrüllen.

hol·low [ˈhɒləʊ] **I** s **1.** (Aus)Höhlung f, Hohlraum m: *~ of the hand* hohle Hand. **II** adj □ **2.** hohl: *beat s.o. ~* Br. F j-n haushoch schlagen; *feel ~* Hunger haben. **3.** hohl, dumpf (*Klang, Stimme*). **4.** fig. hohl, leer; falsch, unaufrichtig: → *ring²* 2, 6. **5.** hohl: a) eingefallen (*Wangen*), b) tiefliegend (*Augen*). **III** adv **6.** hohl: *ring ~ fig.* hohl klingen (*Versprechen etc*), unglaubwürdig klingen (*Protest etc*). **IV** v/t **7.** *oft ~ out* aushöhlen.

hol·ly [ˈhɒlɪ] s ♀ Stechpalme f.

hol·o·caust [ˈhɒləkɔːst] s Massenvernichtung f, -sterben n, (bsd. Brand)Katastrophe f: *the* ♀ *hist.* der Holocaust.

hol·ster [ˈhəʊlstə] s (Pistolen)Halfter f, n.

ho·ly [ˈhəʊlɪ] adj heilig, (*Hostie etc*) geweiht. ♀ *Ghost* s eccl. der Heilige Geist. ♀ *Scrip·ture* s eccl. die Heilige Schrift. ♀ *Spir·it* → *Holy Ghost.* ~ *ter·ror* s F Nervensäge f. ♀ *Thurs·day* s eccl. Gründonnerstag m. ~ *wa·ter* s eccl. Weihwasser n. ♀ *Week* s eccl. Karwoche f.

hom·age [ˈhɒmɪdʒ] s Huldigung f, Reverenz f: *do* (*od. pay*) *~ to s.o.* j-m huldigen, j-m (die *od.* s-e) Reverenz erweisen *od.* bezeigen.

home [həʊm] **I** s **1.** Heim n: a) Haus n, (*eigene*) Wohnung f, b) Zuhause n, Daheim n, c) Elternhaus n: *at ~* zu Hause, daheim (*beide a. Sport*); *at ~ in* fig. zu Hause in (*dat*), bewandert in (*dat*); *make o.s. at ~* es sich bequem machen; *away from ~* abwesend, verreist, (*bsd. Sport*) auswärts; *his ~ is in London* er ist in London zu Hause. **2.** Heimat f (*u. fig.*): *at ~ and abroad* im In- u. Ausland. **3.** Heim n: *~ for the aged* Alters-, Altenheim n. **II** adj **4.** häuslich, Heim...: *~ address* Privatanschrift f; *~ life* häusliches Leben, Familienleben n. **5.** inländisch, Inlands...: *~ affairs* pl innere Angelegenheiten pl, Innenpolitik f; *~ mar·ket* ♠ Inlands-, Binnenmarkt m; *~ trade* ♠ Binnenhandel m. **6.** Heimat...: *~ town.* **7.** Sport: Heim...: *~ match.* **III** adv **8.** heim, nach Hause: *way ~* Heimweg m; *that's nothing to write ~ about* F das ist nichts Besonderes; → *come home.* **9.** zu Hause, daheim. **10.** fig. ins Ziel: *bring* (*od. drive*) *s.th. ~ to s.o.* j-m et. klarmachen; *the thrust went ~* der Hieb saß. **'~·com·ing** s Heimkehr f. **~ com·pu·ter** s Heimcomputer m. **'~·grown** adj selbstangebaut (*Obst*), (*Gemüse a.*) selbstgezogen. **'~·land** s Heimatland n.

home·less [ˈhəʊmlɪs] adj **1.** heimatlos. **2.** obdachlos: *be left ~* heimatlos werden. **'home·like** adj wie zu Hause, gemütlich. **'home·ly** adj **1.** einfach (*Mahlzeit, Leute*). **2.** Am. unscheinbar, reizlos.

͵home'made adj haus-, selbstgemacht, Hausmacher...

homeo... → **homoeo...**

Home| Of·fice s Br. Innenministerium n. ♀ *rule* s pol. Selbstverwaltung f. ~ *Sec·re·tar·y* s Br. Innenminister m. **'♀·sick** adj: *be ~* Heimweh haben. **'♀·sick·ness** s Heimweh n. **'♀·spun** adj schlicht, einfach. ♀ *truth* s unangenehme Wahrheit.

home·ward [ˈhəʊmwəd] **I** adv heimwärts, nach Hause. **II** adj Heim..., Rück... **'~·wards** → *homeward* I.

'home|·work s **1.** ♠ Heimarbeit f. **2.** ped. Hausaufgabe(n pl) f: *do one's ~* s-e Hausaufgaben machen (a. fig.). **'~·work·er** s ♠ Heimarbeiter (-in).

hop

hom·i·cide ['hɒmɪsaɪd] s ⚖ Mord m; Totschlag m.

ho·mo ['həʊməʊ] pl **-mos** F Homo m (Homosexuelle).

ho·moe·o·path ['həʊmjəʊpæθ] s ✚ Homöopath(in). ,**ho·moe·o·'path·ic** adj (∼ally) homöopathisch. **ho·moe·op·a·thy** [,həʊmɪ'ɒpəθɪ] s Homöopathie f.

ho·mo·ge·ne·ous [,hɒməʊ'dʒiːnjəs] adj □ homogen, gleichartig. **ho·mog·e·nize** [hɒ'mɒdʒənaɪz] v/t homogenisieren.

hom·o·graph ['hɒməʊgrɑːf] s ling. Homograph n. **hom·o·nym** ['∼nɪm] s ling. Homonym n. **hom·o·phone** ['∼fəʊn] s ling. Homophon n.

ho·mo·sex·u·al [,hɒməʊ'seksʊəl] I adj □ homosexuell. II s Homosexuelle m, f. **ho·mo·sex·u·al·i·ty** [,∼ʃʊ'ælətɪ] s Homosexualität f.

hom·y ['həʊmɪ] adj F gemütlich, behaglich.

hon·est ['ɒnɪst] adj ehrlich: a) redlich, b) aufrichtig. '**hon·est·ly** I adv → **honest.** II int F ganz bestimmt!, ehrlich! '**hon·es·ty** s Ehrlichkeit f: a) Redlichkeit f, b) Aufrichtigkeit f.

hon·ey ['hʌnɪ] s 1. Honig m: **(as) sweet as** ∼ honigsüß (a. fig.). 2. bsd. Am. F Liebling m, Schatz m. '**∼·bee** s Honigbiene f. '**∼·dew** s Honigtau m: ∼ **melon** Honigmelone f.

hon·eyed ['hʌnɪd] adj honigsüß (a. fig.).

'**hon·ey·moon** I s Flitterwochen pl: ∼ **(trip)** Hochzeitsreise f. II v/i in den Flitterwochen sein, s-e Flitterwochen verbringen; s-e Flitterwochen machen, auf Hochzeitsreise sein. '**∼·moon·er** s Flitterwöchner m; Hochzeitsreisende m, f.

honk [hɒŋk] mot. I s Hupsignal n. II v/i hupen.

hon·or, etc Am. → **honour**, etc.

hon·or·ar·y ['ɒnərərɪ] adj 1. Ehren... 2. ehrenamtlich.

hon·our ['ɒnə] bsd. Br. I v/t 1. ehren. 2. ehren, auszeichnen: ∼ **s.o. with** j-m et. verleihen; j-n beehren mit. 3. ✝ Scheck etc honorieren, einlösen. II s 4. Ehre f: **(sense of)** ∼ Ehrgefühl n; ∼ **to whom** ∼ **is due** Ehre, wem Ehre gebührt; **guest of** ∼ Ehrengast m; **do s.o.** ∼ j-m zur Ehre gereichen, j-m Ehre machen; → **debt.** 5. Ehrung f, Ehre(n pl) f: **in s.o.'s** ∼ zu

j-s Ehren, j-m zu Ehren. 6. **Your** ⚖ bsd. ⚖ Euer Gnaden. '**hon·our·a·ble** adj □ bsd. Br. 1. achtbar, ehrenwert. 2. ehrenvoll, -haft. 3. ⚖ der, die Ehrenwerte (Titel).

hood [hʊd] s 1. Kapuze f. 2. mot. Br. Verdeck n; Am. (Motor)Haube f. 3. ⚙ (Schutz)Haube f.

hood·lum ['huːdləm] s F 1. Rowdy m; Schläger m. 2. Ganove m; Gangster m.

'**hood·wink** v/t hinters Licht führen.

hoo·ey ['huːɪ] s bsd. Am. sl. Krampf m, Quatsch m.

hoof [huːf] pl **hoofs, hooves** [huːvz] s zo. Huf m.

hook [hʊk] I s 1. Haken m: **by** ∼ **or (by) crook** unter allen Umständen, mit allen Mitteln; **on one's own** ∼ F auf eigene Faust. 2. Angelhaken m: ∼, **line and sinker** F voll (u. ganz); **be on the** ∼ F in der Patsche sein od. sitzen od. stecken. 3. Boxen: Haken m. II v/t 4. an-, ein-, fest-, zuhaken. 5. angeln (a. fig. F): ∼ **a husband** sich e-n Mann angeln. 6. ∼ **it** F Leine ziehen, verschwinden. III v/i 7. sich (zu)haken lassen. **hooked** [hʊkt] adj 1. hakenförmig, Haken... 2. mit (e-m) Haken (versehen). 3. F süchtig **(on** nach) (a. fig.): ∼ **on TV** fernsehsüchtig. '**hook·er** s Am. sl. Nutte f. '**hook·y** s: **play** ∼ bsd. Am. F (die Schule) schwänzen.

hoo·li·gan ['huːlɪgən] s Rowdy m. '**hoo·li·gan·ism** s Rowdytum n.

hoop [huːp] s allg. Reif(en) m: **put through the** ∼**(s)** fig. durch die Mangel drehen, in die Mangel nehmen.

hoo·ray [hʊ'reɪ] → **hurah.**

hoot [huːt] I v/i 1. **(höhnisch)** johlen: ∼ **at s.o.** j-n verhöhnen. 2. bsd. Br. heulen (Fabriksirene etc); mot. hupen. II v/t 3. auszischen, -pfeifen: ∼ **down** niederschreien. III s 4. **(höhnischer, johlender)** Schrei: **I don't care a** ∼ **(od. two** ∼**s)** F das ist mir völlig egal. 5. bsd. Br. Heulen n; mot. Hupen n. '**hoot·er** s bsd. Br. Sirene f; mot. Hupe f.

Hoo·ver ['huːvə] TM I s Staubsauger m. II v/t mst ⚐ (staub)saugen, Teppich etc a. absaugen: ∼ **up** aufsaugen. III v/i mst ⚐ (staub)saugen.

hooves [huːvz] pl von **hoof.**

hop¹ [hɒp] I s ♣ Hopfen m. II v/t Bier hopfen.

hop² [~] **I** v/i **1.** hüpfen: ~ off Br. F abschwirren. **2.** F schwofen, tanzen. **II** v/t **3.** hüpfen über (acc): ~ it F abschwirren. **4.** F keep s.o. on the ~ F j-n in Trab halten. **5.** F Schwof m, Tanz(veranstaltung f) m.

hope [həʊp] **I** s Hoffnung f (of auf acc): past (od. beyond) (all) ~ hoffnungs-, aussichtslos; in the ~ auf gut Glück; in der Hoffnung (of getting zu bekommen); no ~ of success keine Aussicht auf Erfolg; ~s pl of victory Siegeshoffnungen pl. **II** v/i hoffen (for auf acc): ~ for the best das Beste hoffen; I ~ so hoffentlich; I ~ not hoffentlich nicht. **III** v/t hoffen (that daß). **hope-ful** ['~fʊl] adj hoffnungsvoll: be ~ that hoffen, daß. **'hope·ful·ly** adv **1.** → hopeful. **2.** hoffentlich. **'hope·less** adj □ hoffnungslos.

hop·ping ['hɒpɪŋ] adv: be ~ mad F e-e Stinkwut (im Bauch) haben.

horde [hɔːd] s Horde f, (wilder) Haufen.

ho·ri·zon [hə'raɪzn] s Horizont m: appear on the ~ am Horizont auftauchen, fig. a. sich abzeichnen; → broaden I. **hor·i·zon·tal** [,hɒrɪ'zɒntl] **I** adj □ horizontal, waag(e)recht: ~ bar (Turnen) Reck n; ~ line → II. **II** s ⚓ Horizontale f, Waag(e)rechte f.

hor·mone ['hɔːməʊn] s biol. Hormon n.

horn [hɔːn] s **1.** zo. Horn n, pl a. Geweih n: show one's ~s fig. die Krallen zeigen; → bull **1**, dilemma. **2.** zo. Fühler m, Fühlhorn n. **3.** (Pulver-, Trink)Horn n: ~ of plenty Füllhorn. **4.** Horn n (Substanz). **5.** ♪ Horn n. **6.** mot. Hupe f. **II** v/i **7.** ~ in sl. sich eindrängen od. einmischen (on in acc).

hor·net ['hɔːnɪt] s zo. Hornisse f: stir up a ~'s nest fig. in ein Wespennest stechen.

'horn-rimmed adj: ~ spectacles pl Hornbrille f.

horn·y ['hɔːnɪ] adj **1.** hornig, schwielig. **2.** aus Horn, Horn...

hor·o·scope ['hɒrəskəʊp] s Horoskop n: cast a ~ ein Horoskop stellen.

hor·ren·dous [hɒ'rendəs] → horrific.

hor·ri·ble ['hɒrəbl] adj □ schrecklich, furchtbar, scheußlich (alle a. fig. F). **hor·rid** ['hɒrɪd] → horrible. **hor·rif·ic** [hɒ'rɪfɪk] adj (~ally) schrecklich, entsetzlich. **hor·ri·fy** ['~faɪ] v/t entsetzen:

be horrified at (od. by) entsetzt sein über (acc); ~ing → horrible.

hor·ror ['hɒrə] **I** s **1.** Entsetzen n: to one's ~ zu s-m Entsetzen; in ~ entsetzt. **2.** Abscheu m, Horror m (of vor dat). **3.** Schrecken m, Greuel m. **4.** F Greuel m (Person od. Sache). **II** adj **5.** Horror...: ~ film. '~·strick·en, '~·struck adj von Entsetzen gepackt.

horse [hɔːs] s Pferd n (a. Turnen): back the wrong ~ fig. aufs falsche Pferd setzen; eat like a ~ wie ein Scheunendrescher essen; get (od. come) off one's high ~ fig. von s-m hohen Roß herunterkommen; a ~ of another (od. a different) colo(u)r fig. et. (ganz) anderes; (straight od. right) from the ~'s mouth F aus erster Hand; → cart 1, dark horse, flog 1, gift 3. '~·back adv: on ~ zu Pferd; go on ~ reiten. ~·chest·nut s ♣ Roßkastanie f. '~·hair s Roßhaar n. '~·laugh s wieherndes Gelächter. ~·man ['~mən] s (irr man) (geübter) Reiter. ~ op·er·a s F Western m (Film). '~·pow·er s phys. Pferdestärke f. ~ race s Sport: Pferderennen n. '~·rad·ish s ♣ Meerrettich m. ~ sense s gesunder Menschenverstand. ~·shoe ['hɔːʃuː] s Hufeisen n. ~ trad·ing s bsd. pol. F Kuhhandel m. '~·wom·an s (irr woman) (geübte) Reiterin.

hor·ti·cul·tur·al [,hɔːtɪ'kʌltʃərəl] adj Garten(bau)...: ~ show Gartenschau f. **'hor·ti·cul·ture** s Gartenbau m.

ho·san·na [həʊ'zænə] **I** int hos(i)anna! **II** s Hos(i)anna n.

hose¹ [həʊz] s (pl konstruiert) Strümpfe pl, Strumpfwaren pl.

hose² [~] **I** s Schlauch m. **II** v/t spritzen: ~ down abspritzen.

ho·sier·y ['həʊzɪərɪ] s coll. Strumpfwaren pl.

hos·pice ['hɒspɪs] s Sterbeklinik f.

hos·pi·ta·ble [hɒ'spɪtəbl] adj □ gast(freund)lich (Person); gastlich, gastfrei (Haus etc.).

hos·pi·tal ['hɒspɪtl] s Krankenhaus n, Klinik f: in (Am. in the) ~ im Krankenhaus.

hos·pi·tal·i·ty [,hɒspɪ'tælətɪ] s Gastfreundschaft f, Gastlichkeit f.

hos·pi·tal·ize ['hɒspɪtlaɪz] v/t ins Krankenhaus einliefern od. einweisen.

host¹ [həʊst] **I** s **1.** Gastgeber m. **2.** biol.

Wirt *m* (*Tier od. Pflanze*). **3.** *Rundfunk, TV:* Talkmaster *m*; Showmaster *m*; Moderator *m*. **II** *v/t* **4.** *Rundfunk, TV: Sendung* moderieren.

host² [~] *s* Menge *f*, Masse *f*: **a ~ of questions** e-e Unmenge Fragen.

Host³ [~] *s eccl.* Hostie *f*.

hos·tage ['hɒstɪdʒ] *s* Geisel *f*: **take s.o. ~** j-n als Geisel nehmen.

hos·tel ['hɒstl] *s* **1.** *mst youth ~* Jugendherberge *f*. **2.** *bsd. Br.* (*Studenten-, Arbeiter- etc*)Wohnheim *n*.

host·ess ['həʊstɪs] *s* **1.** Gastgeberin *f*. **2.** Hosteß *f* (*Betreuerin auf Messen etc*). **3.** ✈ Hosteß *f*, Stewardeß *f*. **4.** Animier-, Tischdame *f*.

hos·tile ['hɒstaɪl] *adj* □ **1.** feindlich, Feind(es)... **2.** (*to*) feindselig (gegen), feindlich gesinnt (*dat*): **~ to foreigners** ausländerfeindlich. **hos·til·i·ty** [hɒ'stɪlətɪ] *s* **1.** Feindschaft *f*, Feindseligkeit *f*: **~ to foreigners** Ausländerfeindlichkeit *f*. **2.** *pl* ✕ Feindseligkeiten *pl*.

hot [hɒt] **I** *adj* □ **1.** *allg.* heiß (*a. fig.*): **I am ~** mir ist heiß; **I went ~ and cold** es überlief mich heiß u. kalt; **~ favo(u)rite** F (*bsd. Sport*) heißer *od.* hoher Favorit; **~ music** *sl.* heiße Musik; **~ tip** heißer Tip; **be in ~ water** F in Schwulitäten sein. **2.** warm, heiß (*Speisen*): **~ meal** warme Mahlzeit; **~ potato.** **3.** scharf (*gewürzt*). **4. be ~ for** (*od. on*) F brennen *od.* scharf sein auf (*acc*). **5.** ganz neu *od.* frisch: **~ from the press** frisch aus der Presse (*Nachrichten*), soeben erschienen (*Buch etc*); **~ scent** (*od. trail*) *hunt.* warme *od.* frische Fährte *od.* Spur (*a. fig.*). **6.** F toll, großartig (*Nachrichten*) sensationell. **7.** F heiß (*gestohlen, geschmuggelt etc*). **II** *adv* **8.** *fig.:* **give it s.o. ~** (*and strong*) F j-m gründlich einheizen; → **track** 1, **trail** 7. **III** *v/t* **9.** *mst* **~ up** *bsd. Br.* heiß machen, *Speisen a.* warm machen, aufwärmen. **10. ~ up** *fig.* F an-, aufheizen; Schwung bringen in (*acc*); *Auto, Motor* frisieren. **IV** *v/i* **11. ~ up** F sich verschärfen; schwungvoller werden. **~ air** *s* **1.** ⊙ Heißluft *f*. **2.** F heiße Luft, leeres Geschwätz *n*. '**~·air** *adj* ⊙ Heißluft... '**~·bed** *s* **1.** ✈ Mist-, Frühbeet *n*. **2.** *fig.* Brutstätte *f*. '**~·blood·ed** *adj* heißblütig.

hotch·potch ['hɒtʃpɒtʃ] *s* **1.** *gastr.* Eintopf *m, bsd.* Gemüsesuppe *f* mit Fleisch. **2.** *fig.* Mischmasch *m*, Durcheinander *n*.

hot dog *s* Hot dog *n, m*.

ho·tel [həʊ'tel] **I** *s* Hotel *n*. **II** *adj* Hotel... **ho·tel·ier** [həʊ'telɪeɪ], **ho'tel‚keep·er** *s* Hotelier *m*.

'**hot·foot** F **I** *adv* schleunigst, schnell. **II** *v/i u. v/t:* **~** (**it**) rennen. '**~·head** *s* Hitzkopf *m*. ‚**~'head·ed** *adj* □ hitzköpfig. '**~·house** *s* Treib-, Gewächshaus *n*. '**~·line** *s bsd. pol.* heißer Draht. **~ pants** *s pl* Hot pants *pl*, heiße Höschen *pl*. '**~·plate** *s* **1.** Koch-, Heizplatte *f*. **2.** Warmhalteplatte *f*. **~ rod** *s bsd. Am. sl.* frisierter Wagen. **~ spot** *s* **1.** *bsd. pol.* Unruhe-, Krisenherd *m*. **2.** *bsd. Am.* F Nachtklub *m.* Amüsierbetrieb, in dem et. los ist. ‚**~'wa·ter** *adj* Heißwasser...: **~ bottle** Wärmflasche *f*.

hound [haʊnd] **I** *s* **1.** Jagdhund *m*. **2.** *contp.* Hund *m*, gemeiner Kerl. **II** *v/t* **3.** (*bsd. mit Hunden, a. fig. j-n*) jagen, verfolgen.

hour ['aʊə] *s* **1.** Stunde *f*: **by the ~** stundenweise; **for ~s** (**and ~s**) stundenlang; **on the ~** (immer) zur vollen Stunde; **24 ~s a day** Tag u. Nacht. **2.** (*Tages*)Zeit *f*, Stunde *f*: **at all ~s** zu jeder Zeit, jederzeit; **at what ~?** um wieviel Uhr?; → **early** 4, **eleventh** 1, **late** 1, **small** I. **3.** Zeitpunkt *m*, Stunde *f*. **4.** Stunde *f, Tag m*: **the man of the ~** der Mann des Tages. **5.** *pl* (*Arbeits*)Zeit *f*, (*Geschäfts*)Stunden *pl*: **after ~s** nach Geschäftsschluß; nach der Polizeistunde; nach der Arbeit; *fig.* zu spät. **~ hand** *s* Stundenzeiger *m*.

hour·ly ['aʊəlɪ] *adj u. adv* stündlich.

house I *s* [haʊs] *pl* **hous·es** ['haʊzɪz] **1.** Haus *n* (*a. ✞, parl., thea.*): → **bring down** 4, **card** 1. **2.** Haus(halt *m*) *n*: **keep ~** den Haushalt führen (**for s.o.** j-m); **put** (*od.* **set**) **one's ~ in order** *fig.* s-e Angelegenheiten in Ordnung bringen. **3.** Haus *n*, Geschlecht *n*: **the ♀ of Hanover** das Haus Hannover. **II** *v/t* [haʊz] **4.** unterbringen; beherbergen (*a. fig. enthalten*). **~ a·gent** *s Br.* Häusermakler *m*. **~ ar·rest** *s* Hausarrest *m*: **be under ~** unter Hausarrest stehen. '**~·boat** *s* Hausboot *n*. '**~·bound** *adj fig.* ans Haus gefesselt. '**~‚break·er** *s* Einbrecher *m*. '**~‚break·ing** *s* Einbruch *m*. '**~‚bro·ken** *adj Am.* stubenrein (*Hund* *etc,* F *a. Witz etc*). '**~clean** *v/i* Hausputz machen. '**~clean·ing** *s* Hausputz *m.* '**~coat** *s* Morgenrock *m,* -mantel *m.* '**~fly** *s zo.* Stubenfliege *f.*

house·hold ['haʊshəʊld] **I** *s* **1.** Haushalt *m.* **II** *adj* **2.** Haushalts..., häuslich: ~ *remedy* Hausmittel *n.* **3.** ~ *name* (*od word*) (fester *od.* geläufiger) Begriff. '**house·hold·er** *s* Haushaltsvorstand *m.*

'**house|-hunt** *v/i* auf Haussuche sein: *go ~ing* auf Haussuche gehen. '**~keep·er** *s* Haushälterin *f,* Wirtschafterin *f.* '**~keep·ing** *s* Haushaltung *f,* Haushaltsführung *f:* ~ (*money*) Haushalts-, Wirtschaftsgeld *n.* '**~maid** *s* Hausangestellte *f,* -mädchen *n.* **2 of Com·mons** *s parl.* Unterhaus *n* (*GB*). **2 of Lords** *s parl.* Oberhaus *n* (*GB*). **2 of Rep·re·sent·a·tives** *s parl.* Repräsentantenhaus *n* (*USA*). '**~proud** *adj* übertrieben ordentlich (*Hausfrau*). ~ *rules s pl* Hausordnung *f.* ~ *search s* 룛 Haussuchung *f.* '**~to-'~** *adj* von Haus zu Haus: ~ *collection* Haussammlung *f;* ~ *salesman* Hausierer *m;* Vertreter *m.* '**~top** *s* Dach *n:* **cry** (*od.* **proclaim**, **shout**) *from the ~s et.* öffentlich verkünden, *et. Vertrauliches* an die große Glocke hängen. '**~trained** *adj bsd.* Br. stubenrein (*Hund etc*). '**~warm·ing** (**par·ty**) *s* Einzugsparty *f* (*im neuen Haus*). '**~wife** *s* (*irr wife*) Hausfrau *f.* '**~work** *s* Hausarbeit *f.*

hous·ing ['haʊzɪŋ] *s* **1.** Wohnung *f:* ~ *development bsd. Am.,* ~ *estate Br.* Wohnsiedlung *f;* ~ *market* Wohnungsmarkt *m;* ~ *shortage* Wohnungsnot *f.* **2.** *coll.* Häuser *pl.* **3.** Wohnen *n:* ~ *con·ditions pl* Wohnverhältnisse *pl.*

hove [həʊv] *pret u. pp von* **heave**.

hov·el ['hɒvl] *s contp.* Bruchbude *f,* Loch *n.*

hov·er ['hɒvə] *v/i* **1.** schweben (*a. fig. between* zwischen *Leben u. Tod etc*). **2.** sich herumtreiben (*about* in der Nähe von). **3.** *fig.* schwanken (*between* zwischen *dat*). '**~craft** *pl* -**craft** *s* Luftkissenfahrzeug *n.*

how [haʊ] *adv* **1.** *fragend:* wie: ~ *are you?* wie geht es dir?; ~ *is your toothache?* was machen da-e Zahnschmerzen?; ~ *about ...?* wie steht *od.* wäre es mit ...?; ~ *do you know?* woher wissen Sie das?; ~ *much?* wieviel?; ~ *many?*

wieviel?, wie viele?; → *be* 7, *come* 7, *do¹* 12. **2.** *ausrufend u. relativ:* wie: ~ *absurd!* wie absurd!; *he knows ~ to ride* er kann reiten; *I know ~ to do it* ich weiß, wie man es macht; *and ~! F* u. ob! ~'**ev·er I** *adv* wie auch (immer): ~ *it* (*may*) *be* wie dem auch sei; ~ *you do it* wie du es auch machst. **II** *cj* jedoch.

howl [haʊl] **I** *v/i* **1.** heulen (*Wölfe, Wind etc*). **2.** brüllen, schreien (*in agony* vor Schmerzen; *with laughter* vor Lachen). **II** *v/t* **3.** brüllen, schreien: ~ *down j-n* niederschreien, -brüllen. **III** *s* **4.** Heulen *n.* '**howl·er** *s* F grober Schnitzer. '**howl·ing** *adj* **1.** heulend. **2.** F Mords...: ~ *success* Bombenerfolg *m.*

hub [hʌb] *s* **1.** ◉ (Rad)Nabe *f.* **2.** *fig.* Mittel-, Angelpunkt *m.*

hub·bub ['hʌbʌb] *s* **1.** Stimmengewirr *n.* **2.** Tumult *m.*

'**hub·cap** *s mot.* Radkappe *f.*

huck·le·ber·ry ['hʌklbərɪ] *s* ♀ Amer. Heidelbeere *f.*

huck·ster ['hʌkstə] → **hawker**.

hud·dle ['hʌdl] **I** *v/t* **1.** *mst* ~ *together* (*od. up*) zs.-werfen, auf e-n Haufen werfen; zs.-drängen: ~ *s.th. into bsd. Br.* et. stopfen in (*acc*). **II** *v/i* **2.** (sich) kauern: ~ *up* sich zs.-kauern. **3.** *mst* ~ *together* (*od. up*) sich zs.-drängen. **4.** ~ (*up*) *against* (*od. to*) sich kuscheln *od.* schmiegen an (*acc*). **III** *s* **5.** (wirrer) Haufen; Wirrwarr *m,* Durcheinander *n.* **6.** *go into a* ~ F die Köpfe zs.-stecken; sich beraten (*with* mit).

hue¹ [hjuː] *s* **1.** Farbe *f.* **2.** (Farb)Ton *m,* Tönung *f, a. fig.* Färbung *f,* Schattierung *f.*

hue² [~] *s:* *raise a* ~ *and cry against* lautstark protestieren gegen.

huff [hʌf] **I** *v/i* keuchen, schnaufen. **II** *s:* *be in a* ~ muffeln; *go into a* ~ muff(e)lig werden. '**huff·y** *adj* □ **1.** muff(e)lig. **2.** übelnehmerisch.

hug [hʌg] **I** *v/t* **1.** umarmen, (*a. ~ to one*) an sich drücken. **2.** *fig.* (zäh) festhalten an (*dat*). **II** *v/i* **3.** sich umarmen. **III** *s* **4.** Umarmung *f: give s.o. a* ~ j-n umarmen.

huge [hjuːdʒ] *adj* riesig, riesengroß (*beide a. fig.*). '**huge·ly** *adv* ungeheuer, gewaltig. '**huge·ness** *s* ungeheure *od.* gewaltige Größe.

hulk [hʌlk] *s* Koloß *m*: a) *Gebilde von gewaltigem Ausmaß*, b) klotziges *od.* sperriges *od.* unhandliches Ding, c) ungeschlachter Kerl, schwerfälliger Riese. **'hulk·ing**, **'hulk·y** *adj* **1.** klotzig, sperrig, unhandlich. **2.** ungeschlacht, schwerfällig.

hull¹ [hʌl] **I** *s* ♆ Schale *f*, Hülse *f*. **II** *v/t* schälen, enthülsen.

hull² [~] *s* ♆ Rumpf *m*.

hul·la·ba·lo·o [ˌhʌləbə'luː] *s* Lärm *m*, Getöse *n*.

hul·lo → **hello.**

hum [hʌm] **I** *v/i* **1.** *allg.* summen: *my head is ~ming* mir brummt der Kopf; *~ (with activity)* F voller Leben *od.* Aktivität sein. **2.** *~ and haw* herumdrucksen, nicht recht mit der Sprache herauswollen. **II** *v/t* **3.** *Lied* summen. **III** *s* **4.** Summen *n*.

hu·man ['hjuːmən] **I** *adj* (□ → *human·ly*) **1.** menschlich, Menschen...: *~ being* Mensch *m*; *~ chain* Menschenkette *f*; *~ dignity* Menschenwürde *f*; *~ medicine* Humanmedizin *f*; *~ race* Menschengeschlecht *n*; *~ rights* *pl* Menschenrechte *pl*; → **err. II** *s* Mensch *m*. **hu·mane** [hjuː'meɪn] *adj* □ **1.** human, menschlich. **2.** humanistisch. **hu·man·ism** ['hjuːmənɪzəm] *s* Humanismus *m*. **'hu·man·ist** *s* Humanist(in). **ˌhu·man·'is·tic** *adj* (*~ally*) humanistisch. **hu·man·i·tar·i·an** [hjuːˌmænɪ'teərɪən] *adj* humanitär, menschenfreundlich. **hu-'man·i·ty** *s* **1.** die Menschheit. **2.** Humanität *f*, Menschlichkeit *f*. **3.** *pl* Altphilologie *f*; Geisteswissenschaften *pl*. **hu·man·ize** ['hjuːmənaɪz] *v/t* **1.** humanisieren, humaner *od.* menschenwürdiger gestalten. **2.** vermenschlichen, personifizieren. **hu·man·kind** [ˌ~'kaɪnd] → **humanity** 1. **'hu·man·ly** *adv*: *do everything ~ possible* alles menschenmögliche *od.* sein menschenmöglichstes tun.

hum·ble ['hʌmbl] **I** *adj* □ bescheiden: a) demütig: *in my ~ opinion* m-r unmaßgeblichen Meinung nach; *eat ~ pie fig.* klein beigeben; *~ self*, b) anspruchslos, einfach, c) niedrig: *of ~ birth* von niederer Geburt. **II** *v/t* demütigen, erniedrigen. **'hum·ble·ness** *s* Bescheidenheit *f*, Demut *f*.

hum·bug ['hʌmbʌg] *s* **1.** Humbug *m*: a)

Schwindel *m*, Betrug *m*, b) Unsinn *m*, dummes Zeug. **2.** *Br.* Pfefferminzbonbon *m*, *n*.

hum·ding·er [ˌhʌm'dɪŋə] *s bsd. Am.* F **1.** Mordskerl *m*. **2.** tolles Ding.

hum·drum ['hʌmdrʌm] **I** *adj* **1.** eintönig, langweilig. **II** *s* **2.** Eintönigkeit *f*, Langweiligkeit *f*. **3.** eintönige *od.* langweilige Arbeit; Langweiler *m*.

hu·mid ['hjuːmɪd] *adj* □ feucht. **hu-'mid·i·fi·er** [ˌ~dɪfaɪə] *s* ⊙ (Luft)Befeuchter *m*. **hu'mid·i·fy** [ˌ~faɪ] *v/t* befeuchten. **hu'mid·i·ty** *s* Feuchtigkeit *f*: *~ of the air* Luftfeuchtigkeit *f*.

hu·mil·i·ate [hjuː'mɪlɪeɪt] *v/t* demütigen, erniedrigen. **hu·mil·i·a·tion** *s* Demütigung *f*, Erniedrigung *f*.

hum·ming·bird ['hʌmɪŋbɜːd] *s orn.* Kolibri *m*.

hum·mock ['hʌmək] *s* Hügel *m*.

hu·mor *Am.* → **humour.**

hu·mor·ist ['hjuːmərɪst] *s* **1.** Humorist(in). **2.** Spaßvogel *m*. **ˌhu·mor'is·tic** *adj* (*~ally*) humoristisch.

hu·mor·ous ['hjuːmərəs] *adj* □ humorvoll, humorig.

hu·mour ['hjuːmə] *bsd. Br.* **I** *s* **1.** Humor *m*: (*a. good*) *sense of ~* (Sinn *m* für) Humor. **2.** Komik *f*, das Komische. **3.** (Gemüts)Verfassung *f*: *in a good (bad) ~* (bei) guter (schlechter) Laune; *out of ~* schlecht gelaunt. **II** *v/t* **4.** *j-m* s-n Willen tun *od.* lassen; *j-n*, *et.* hinnehmen. **'hu·mour·less** *adj bsd. Br.* humorlos.

hump [hʌmp] **I** *s* **1.** Buckel *m*, (*e-s Kamels*) Höcker *m*. **2.** (kleiner) Hügel: *be over the ~ fig.* über den Berg sein. **II** *v/t* **3.** *~ one's back* e-n Buckel machen. **4.** *bsd. Br.* F auf den Rücken *od.* die Schulter nehmen; tragen. **'~·back** *s* **1.** Buckel *m*. **2.** Buck(e)lige *m*, *f*. **'~·backed** *adj* buck(e)lig.

humph [hʌmf] *int* hm!

Hun [hʌn] *s* **1.** *hist.* Hunne *m*. **2.** F *contp.* Deutsche *m*.

hu·mus ['hjuːməs] *s* Humus *m*.

hunch [hʌntʃ] **I** *s* **1.** → **hump** 1. **2.** dickes Stück. **3.** (Vor)Ahnung *f*: *have a ~ that* das Gefühl *od.* den Verdacht haben, daß. **II** *v/t* **4.** → **hump** 3: *~ one's shoulders* die Schultern hochziehen. **'~·back** → **humpback.** '**~·backed** → **humpbacked.**

hun·dred ['hʌndrəd] **I** *adj* **1.** hundert: *a (one)* ~ (ein)hundert. **II** *s* **2.** Hundert *n*: *~s of times* hundertmal; *~s pl of thousands* Hunderttausende *pl.* **3.** ⚓ Hunderter *m.* **hun·dred·fold** ['~fəʊld] **I** *adj u. adv* hundertfach. **II** *s das* Hundertfache. **hun·dredth** ['~tθ] **I** *adj* **1.** hundertst. **II** *s* **2.** der, die, das Hundertste. **3.** Hundertstel *n*: *a* ~ *of a second* e-e Hundertstelsekunde.

hung [hʌŋ] *pret u. pp von* **hang.**

Hun·gar·i·an [hʌŋ'geərɪən] **I** *adj* **1.** ungarisch. **II** *s* **2.** Ungar(in). **3.** *ling.* Ungarisch *n.*

hun·ger ['hʌŋgə] **I** *s* Hunger *m* (*a. fig. for, after* nach). ~ *for knowledge* Wissensdurst *m.* **II** *v/i fig.* hungern (*for, after* nach). ~ *strike s* Hungerstreik *m*: *go on* (*a*) ~ in den Hungerstreik treten.

hun·gry ['hʌŋgrɪ] *adj* □ hungrig (*a. fig. for* nach): *be* (*od. feel*) (*very*) ~ (sehr) hungrig sein, (großen) Hunger haben; *go* ~ hungern; ~ *for knowledge* wissensdurstig.

hunk [hʌŋk] *s* großes Stück.

hunt [hʌnt] **I** *s* **1.** Jagd *f*, Jagen *n.* **2.** *fig.* Jagd *f*: a) Verfolgung *f*, b) Suche *f* (*for, after* nach): *be on the* ~ *for* auf der Jagd sein nach. **II** *v/t* **3.** (*a. fig. j-n*) jagen, Jagd machen auf (*acc*): ~ *down* erlegen, zur Strecke bringen (*a. fig.*); *~ed look* gehetzter Blick. **4.** verfolgen. **5.** ~ *away* (*od. off*) wegjagen, vertreiben. **6.** ~ *out* (*od. up*) heraussuchen; aufstöbern, -spüren. **III** *v/i* **7.** jagen: *go ~ing* auf die Jagd gehen; ~ *for* Jagd machen auf (*acc*) (*a. fig.*). **8.** suchen (*for, after* nach). **'hunt·er** *s* Jäger *m* (*a. fig.*). **'hunt·ing I** *s* Jagen *n*, Jagd *f.* **II** *adj* Jagd...: ~ *licence* (*Am. license*) Jagdschein *m*; ~ *season* Jagdzeit *f.*

hur·dle ['hɜːdl] *s* Hürde *f* (*a. Leichtathletik u. fig.*): ~ *race* Hürdenlauf *m.* **'hur·dler** *m* Leichtathletik: Hürdenläufer(in).

hur·dy-gur·dy ['hɜːdɪ,gɜːdɪ] *s* Leierkasten *m.*

hurl [hɜːl] *v/t* schleudern: ~ *down* zu Boden schleudern; ~ *o.s.* sich stürzen (*on, at* auf *acc*); ~ *abuse at s.o.* j-m Beleidigungen ins Gesicht schleudern.

hurl·y-burl·y ['hɜːlɪ,bɜːlɪ] *s* Tumult *m*, Aufruhr *m.*

hur·rah [hʊ'rɑː], **hur·ray** [hʊ'reɪ] **I** *int* hurra! **II** *s* Hurra(ruf *m*) *n.*

hur·ri·cane ['hʌrɪkən] *s* Hurrikan *m*, Wirbelsturm *m*; Orkan *m*, *fig. a.* Sturm *m*: *rise to a* ~ zum Orkan anschwellen.

hur·ried ['hʌrɪd] *adj* □ eilig, hastig, übereilt.

hur·ry ['hʌrɪ] **I** *s* **1.** Hast *f*, Eile *f*: *be in a* ~ es eilig haben (*to do* zu tun), in Eile sein; *be in no* ~ es nicht eilig haben (*do s.th. in a* ~ et. eilig *od.* hastig tun); *there is no* ~ es eilt nicht. **2.** Hetze *f.* **II** *v/t* **3.** schnell *od.* eilig befördern *od.* bringen. **4.** *oft* ~ *up* j-n antreiben, hetzen; *et.* beschleunigen. **III** *v/i* **5.** eilen, hasten: ~ (*up*) sich beeilen; ~ *up!* (mach) schnell!

hurt [hɜːt] (*irr*) **I** *v/t* **1.** (*a. fig. j-n, j-s Gefühle etc*) verletzen: ~ *one's knee* sich das *od.* am Knie verletzen; *feel* ~ gekränkt sein; → *fly².* **2.** schmerzen, *j-m* weh tun (*beide a. fig.*). **3.** schaden (*dat*). **II** *v/i* **4.** schmerzen, weh tun (*beide a. fig.*). **hurt·ful** ['~fʊl] *adj* □ **1.** verletzend. **2.** schmerzlich. **3.** schädlich (*to* für).

hus·band ['hʌzbənd] **I** *s* (Ehe)Mann *m*, Gatte *m.* **II** *v/t* haushalten *od.* sparsam umgehen mit. **'hus·band·ry** *s* Landwirtschaft *f.*

hush [hʌʃ] **I** *int* **1.** still!, pst! **II** *v/t* **2.** zum Schweigen bringen. **3.** *mst* ~ *up* vertuschen. **III** *v/i* **4.** still werden, verstummen. **IV** *s* **5.** Stille *f*, Schweigen *n*: ~ *money* Schweigegeld *n.*

husk [hʌsk] **I** *s* ♀ Hülse *f*, Schale *f*, Schote *f.* **II** *v/t* enthülsen, schälen.

husk·y¹ ['hʌskɪ] *adj* □ **1.** heiser, rauh (*Stimme*). **2.** F stämmig, kräftig.

hus·ky² [~] *s zo.* Husky *m*, Eskimohund *m.*

hus·sy ['hʌsɪ] *s* **1.** Fratz *m*, Göre *f.* **2.** Flittchen *n.*

hus·tle ['hʌsl] **I** *v/t* **1.** stoßen, drängen; (an)rempeln. **2.** hetzen, (an)treiben; drängen (*into doing* zu tun). **3.** (*in aller Eile*) *wohin* bringen *od.* schicken. **4.** sich beeilen mit. **5.** *bsd. Am.* F ergattern; (sich) *et.* erganuern. **II** *v/i* **6.** sich drängen. **7.** hasten, hetzen. **8.** sich beeilen. **III** *s* **9.** *mst* ~ *and bustle* Gedränge *n*; Gehetze *n*; Betrieb *m*, Wirbel *m.* **'hus·tler** *s bsd. Am.* F Nutte *f.*

hut [hʌt] *s* Hütte *f.*

hy·a·cinth ['haɪəsɪnθ] s ♣ Hyazinthe f.
hy·ae·na → *hyena.*
hy·brid ['haɪbrɪd] s biol. Hybride f, m, Kreuzung f.
hy·dran·gea [haɪ'dreɪndʒə] s ♣ Hortensie f.
hy·drant ['haɪdrənt] s Hydrant m.
hy·drate ['haɪdreɪt] s 🜍 Hydrat n.
hy·drau·lic [haɪ'drɔːlɪk] I adj (~ally) phys., ⚙ hydraulisch. II s pl (sg konstruiert) phys. Hydraulik f.
hy·dro... ['haɪdrəʊ] Wasser...
,**hy·dro**|'**car·bon** s 🜍 Kohlenwasserstoff m. ,~'**chlo·ric** adj: ~ **acid** 🜍 Salzsäure f. ,~·e'**lec·tric** adj: ~ **power station** Wasserkraftwerk n. '~·foil s Tragflächen-, Tragflügelboot n.
hy·dro·gen ['haɪdrədʒən] s 🜍 Wasserstoff m: ~ **bomb** ⚔ Wasserstoffbombe f.
,**hy·dro**|'**pho·bi·a** s 1. psych. Hydrophobie f. 2. vet. Tollwut f. '~·plane s Wasserflugzeug n.
hy·e·na [haɪ'iːnə] s zo. Hyäne f (a. fig.).
hy·giene ['haɪdʒiːn] s Hygiene f, Gesundheitspflege f. **hy·gien·ic** adj (~ally) hygienisch.
hy·grom·e·ter [haɪ'grɒmɪtə] s Hygrometer n, Luftfeuchtigkeitsmesser m.
hymn [hɪm] s Kirchenlied n, Choral m. **hym·nal** ['~nəl], '**hymn·book** s Gesangbuch n.
hy·per... ['haɪpə] hyper..., übermäßig.
hy·per·bo·la [haɪ'pɜːbələ] pl -**las**, -**lae** [~iː] s ⅄ Hyperbel f. **hy·per·bo·le** [~lɪ] s rhet. Hyperbel f, Übertreibung f.
hy·per·bol·ic [,haɪpə'bɒlɪk] adj (~ally) ⅄ hyperbolisch, rhet. a. übertreibend.
,**hy·per**|'**crit·i·cal** adj □ hyperkritisch. '~,**mar·ket** s Br. Groß-, Verbraucher-

,~'**sen·si·tive** adj □ hypersensibel, a. 🜍 überempfindlich (**to** gegen). ~'**ten·sion** s 🜍 erhöhter Blutdruck.
hy·phen ['haɪfn] s 1. Bindestrich m. 2. Trennungszeichen n. **hy·phen·ate** ['~fəneɪt] v/t 1. mit Bindestrich schreiben. 2. trennen.
hyp·no·sis [hɪp'nəʊsɪs] pl -**ses** [~siːz] s Hypnose f. **hyp·not·ic** [~'nɒtɪk] adj (~ally) hypnotisch. **hyp·no·tist** ['~nətɪst] s Hypnotiseur m. **hyp·no·tize** ['~taɪz] v/t hypnotisieren.
hy·po... ['haɪpəʊ] Unter..., Sub...
hy·po·chon·dri·a [,haɪpəʊ'kɒndrɪə] s Hypochondrie f. ,**hy·po·chon·dri·ac** [~drɪæk] I adj □ hypochondrisch. II s Hypochonder m.
hy·poc·ri·sy [hɪ'pɒkrəsɪ] s Heuchelei f. **hyp·o·crite** ['hɪpəkrɪt] s Heuchler(in). ,**hyp·o'crit·i·cal** adj □ heuchlerisch.
hy·po·der·mic [,haɪpəʊ'dɜːmɪk] ✽ I adj (~ally) subkutan, unter od. die Haut: ~ **injection** → II. II s subkutane Injektion od. Einspritzung.
,**hy·po'ten·sion** s 🜍 zu niedriger Blutdruck.
hy·pot·e·nuse [haɪ'pɒtənjuːz] s ⅄ Hypotenuse f.
hy·po·ther·mi·a [,haɪpəʊ'θɜːmɪə] s 🜍 Unterkühlung f.
hy·poth·e·sis [haɪ'pɒθɪsɪs] pl -**ses** [~siːz] s Hypothese f. **hy·po·thet·i·cal** [,~pəʊ'θetɪkl] adj □ hypothetisch.
hys·te·ri·a [hɪ'stɪərɪə] s Hysterie f. **hys·ter·ic** [hɪ'sterɪk] I s 1. Hysteriker(in). 2. pl (mst sg konstruiert) hysterischer Anfall: **go** (**off**) **into** ~**s** hysterisch werden. II adj 3. → *hysterical.* **hys'ter·i·cal** adj □ hysterisch.

I

I [aɪ] pron ich: *it is* ~ ich bin es.
i·bex ['aɪbeks] pl '**i·bex·es**, **ib·i·ces** ['ɪbɪsiːz] s zo. Steinbock m.
ice [aɪs] I s 1. **be** (**skating**) **on thin** ~ fig. sich auf gefährlichem Boden bewegen;

break the ~ fig. das Eis brechen; *cut no* ~ (**with**) F keinen Eindruck machen (auf acc), nicht ziehen (bei); *put on* ~ kalt stellen; fig. F auf Eis legen. 2. a) Am. Fruchteis n, b) Br. → **ice cream.**

3. → **icing. II** v/t **4.** gefrieren lassen. **5.** Getränk etc mit od. in Eis kühlen. **6.** gastr. glasieren. **III** v/i **7.** gefrieren. **8.** mst ~ **up** (od. **over**) zufrieren; vereisen. **9.** ~ **out** auftauen (Gewässer). ♀ **Age** s geol. Eiszeit f. ~ **ax(e)** s Eispickel m. ~ **bag** s ♣ Eisbeutel m. ~**berg** ['~bɜːg] s Eisberg m (a. flg. Person): **the tip of the** ~ die Spitze des Eisberges (a. fig.). '~**bound** adj eingefroren (Schiff); zugefroren (Hafen). '~**box** s **1.** Eisfach n (e-s Kühlschranks). **2.** Am. Eis-, Kühlschrank m. '~**break·er** s ♣ Eisbrecher m. ~ **buck·et** s Eiskübel m. ~**'cold** adj eiskalt. ~ **cream** s (Speise)Eis n, Eiscreme f: **chocolate** ~ Schokoladeneis. '~**cream** adj Eis...: ~ **parlo(u)r** Eisdiele f. ~ **cube** s Eiswürfel m.

iced [aɪst] adj **1.** eisgekühlt. **2.** gefroren. **3.** gastr. glasiert, mit Zuckerguß.

ice| **floe** → **floe.** ~ **hock·ey** s Sport: Eishockey n.

Ice·land·er ['aɪsləndə] s Isländer(in). **Ice·lan·dic** [~'lændɪk] **I** adj isländisch. **II** s ling. Isländisch n.

ice| **lol·ly** s Br. Eis n am Stiel. '~**man** s (irr man) Am. Eismann m, -verkäufer m. ~**pack** s **1.** Packeis n. **2.** ♣ Eisbeutel m. ~ **pail** s Eiskübel m. ~ **rink** s (Kunst)Eisbahn f. ~ **wa·ter** s Eiswasser n.

ich·thy·ol·o·gy [ˌɪkθɪˈɒlədʒɪ] s Fischkunde f.

i·ci·cle ['aɪsɪkl] s Eiszapfen m.

i·ci·ness ['aɪsɪnɪs] s eisige Kälte (a. fig.).

ic·ing ['aɪsɪŋ] s gastr. Glasur f, Zuckerguß m.

i·con ['aɪkɒn] s Ikone f.

i·cy ['aɪsɪ] adj eisig (a. fig.).

I'd [aɪd] F für **I had; I would.**

i·de·a [aɪˈdɪə] s **1.** Idee f, Vorstellung f, Begriff m: **form an** ~ **of** sich et. vorstellen, sich e-n Begriff machen von; **have no** ~ keine Ahnung haben; **put** ~**s into s.o.'s head** j-m Flausen in den Kopf setzen. **2.** Absicht f, Gedanke m, Idee f: **the** ~ **is** ... der Zweck der Sache ist, ...; es geht darum, ...; **the** ~ **entered my mind** mir kam der Gedanke. **3. I have an** ~ **that** ich habe so das Gefühl, daß; es kommt mir vor, als ob.

i·de·al [aɪˈdɪəl] **I** adj (□ ~ **ideally**) **1.** ideal. **2.** ideell. **II** s **3.** Ideal n.

i·de·al·ism s Idealismus m. **i·de·al·ist** s

Idealist(in). **i**ˌ**de·al'is·tic** adj (~**ally**) idealistisch. **i'de·al·ize** v/t u. v/i idealisieren. **i'de·al·ly** adv **1.** → **ideal** I. **2.** im Idealfall.

i·den·ti·cal [aɪˈdentɪkl] adj □ identisch (**to, with** mit): ~ **twins** pl eineiige Zwillinge pl.

i·den·ti·fi·ca·tion [aɪˌdentɪfɪˈkeɪʃn] s **1.** Identifizierung f: ~ **card** (Personal-)Ausweis m; ~ **papers** pl Ausweispapiere pl; ~ **parade** ♣♣ Br. Gegenüberstellung f. **2.** Ausweis m, Legitimation f: **he didn't have any** ~ er konnte sich nicht ausweisen. **i'den·ti·fy** [~faɪ] **I** v/t **1.** identifizieren, gleichsetzen (**with** mit): ~ **o.s. with** → **4. 2.** identifizieren, erkennen (**as** als). **3.** ~ **o.s.** sich ausweisen od. legitimieren. **II** v/i **4.** ~ **with** sich identifizieren mit.

i·den·ti·kit (**pic·ture**) [aɪˈdentɪkɪt] s ♣♣ Br. Phantombild n.

i·den·ti·ty [aɪˈdentətɪ] s Identität f: a) (völlige) Gleichheit, b) Persönlichkeit f: **prove one's** ~ → **identify** 3; **loss of** ~ Identitätsverlust m; ~ **mistaken 2.** ~ **card** s (Personal)Ausweis m. ~ **cri·sis** s (irr **crisis**) Identitätskrise f. ~ **pa·rade** ♣♣ Gegenüberstellung f.

i·de·o·log·i·cal [ˌaɪdɪəˈlɒdʒɪkl] adj □ ideologisch. **i·de·ol·o·gy** [~'ɒlədʒɪ] s Ideologie f.

id·i·o·cy ['ɪdɪəsɪ] s ♣ Idiotie f, contp. a. Blödheit f.

id·i·om ['ɪdɪəm] s ling. Idiom n, idiomatischer Ausdruck, Redewendung f. **id·i·o·mat·ic** [~'mætɪk] adj (~**ally**) idiomatisch.

id·i·ot ['ɪdɪət] s ♣ Idiot m, contp. a. Trottel m. **id·i·ot·ic** [~'ɒtɪk] adj (~**ally**) adj ♣ idiotisch, contp. a. vertrottelt.

i·dle ['aɪdl] **I** adj □ **1.** untätig, müßig. **2.** ruhig, still: ~ **hours** pl Mußestunden pl. **3.** faul, träge. **4.** ◎ stillstehend, außer Betrieb; leer laufend, im Leerlauf: **run** ~ → **8. 5.** nutz-, sinn-, zwecklos; vergeblich. **6.** leer, hohl: ~ **gossip** (od. **talk**) leeres Geschwätz. **II** v/i **7.** faulenzen: ~ **about** (od. **around**) herumtrödeln. **8.** ◎ leer laufen. **III** v/t **9.** mst ~ **away** Zeit vertrödeln. **'i·dler** s Müßiggänger(in).

i·dol ['aɪdl] s Idol n (a. fig.); Gottesstatue f, Götterbild n; contp. Götze(nbild n) m: **make an** ~ **of** → **idolize** b. **i·dol·a·trous** [aɪˈdɒlətrəs] adj □ **1.**

contp. Götzen... **2.** fig. abgöttisch. **i·dol·a·try** s **1.** Anbetung e-r kultisch verehrten Figur od. e-s Götterbildes; contp. Götzenanbetung f, -dienst m. **2.** fig. Vergötterung f. **i·dol·ize** ['aɪdəlaɪz] v/t a) abgöttisch verehren, vergöttern, b) idolisieren, zum Idol machen.

i·dyll ['ɪdɪl] s Idyll n. **i·dyl·lic** [ɪ'dɪlɪk] adj (_ally) idyllisch.

if [ɪf] **I** cj **1.** wenn, falls: ~ I were you wenn ich du wäre; as ~ als wenn od. ob; ~ so gegebenenfalls; wenn ja. **2.** wenn auch, aber. **3.** indirekt fragend: ob: try ~ you can do it; and ~! F u. ob! **II** s **4.** Wenn n: without ~s and buts ohne Wenn u. Aber.

ig·loo ['ɪɡluː] s Iglu m, n.

ig·nite [ɪɡ'naɪt] **I** v/t **1.** an-, entzünden. **2.** fig. entzünden, -flammen. **II** v/i **3.** sich entzünden. **4.** mot., ⊕ zünden. **ig·ni·tion** [ɪɡ'nɪʃn] **I** s **1.** An-, Entzünden n. **2.** mot., ⊕ Zündung f. **II** adj **3.** mot., ⊕ Zünd...: ~ key; ~ coil Zündspule f.

ig·no·min·i·ous [ˌɪɡnəʊ'mɪnɪəs] adj □ schändlich, schimpflich. **ig·no·min·y** ['ɪɡnəmɪnɪ] s **1.** Schande f. **2.** Schändlichkeit f.

ig·no·ra·mus [ˌɪɡnə'reɪməs] s Ignorant (-in). **'ig·no·rance** s **1.** Unkenntnis f (of gen), Unwissenheit f: from (od. through) ~ aus Unwissenheit. **2.** contp. Ignoranz f. **'ig·no·rant** adj **1.** be ~ of s.th. et. nicht wissen od. kennen, nichts wissen von et. **2.** contp. ignorant; ungebildet. **'ig·no·rant·ly** adv unwissentlich. **ig·nore** [ɪɡ'nɔː] v/t ignorieren, nicht beachten, keine Notiz nehmen von.

ill [ɪl] **I** adj **1.** pred krank: be taken (od. fall) ~ erkranken (with an dat), krank werden. **2.** schlecht, schlimm: ~ fortune 3, luck 1, etc. **II** adv **3.** schlecht: speak (think) ~ of j-m schlecht sprechen (denken) von; → ease 2. **III** s **4.** a) oft pl Übel n, b) et. Übles.

I'll [aɪl] F für I will.

ill·-ad'vised adj **1.** schlecht beraten. **2.** unbesonnen, unklug. **ˌ~·'bred** adj **1.** schlechterzogen. **2.** ungezogen. **ˌ~·dis-'posed** adj übelgesinnt: be ~ to (-ward[s]) j-m übel gesinnt sein, j-m übelwollen; e-m Plan etc ablehnend gegenüberstehen.

il·le·gal [ɪ'liːɡl] adj □ unerlaubt, verbo-

ten; illegal, gesetzwidrig, ungesetzlich: ~ parking Falschparken n. **il·le·gal·i·ty** [ˌɪliː'ɡælɪtɪ] s Gesetzwidrigkeit f: a) Illegalität f, b) gesetzwidrige Handlung.

il·leg·i·ble [ɪ'ledʒəbl] adj □ unleserlich.

il·le·git·i·mate [ˌɪlɪ'dʒɪtɪmət] adj □ **1.** gesetzwidrig, ungesetzlich. **2.** nicht-, unehelich.

ˌill·-'fat·ed adj unglücklich, Unglücks... **ˌ~·'fa·vo(u)red** adj □ unschön. **ˌ~·'hu·mo(u)red** adj schlecht-, übelgelaunt.

il·lib·er·al [ɪ'lɪbərəl] adj □ **1.** knaus(e)rig. **2.** engstirnig. **3.** pol. illiberal.

il·lic·it [ɪ'lɪsɪt] adj □ unerlaubt, verboten: ~ trade Schwarzhandel m.

il·lit·er·a·cy [ɪ'lɪtərəsɪ] s **1.** Unbildung f. **2.** Analphabetentum n. **il·lit·er·ate** [~rət] **I** adj □ **1.** ungebildet. **2.** analphabetisch. **II** s **3.** Ungebildete m, f. **4.** Analphabet(in).

ˌill·-'judged → ill-advised 2. **ˌ~·'mannered** adj □ ungehobelt, ungezogen. **ˌ~·'matched** adj schlecht zs.-passend. **ˌ~·'na·tured** adj **1.** unfreundlich. **2.** → ill-tempered.

ill·ness ['ɪlnɪs] s Krankheit f.

il·log·i·cal [ɪ'lɒdʒɪkl] adj □ unlogisch.

ˌill·-'tem·pered adj schlechtgelaunt, übellaunig. **ˌ~·'timed** adj ungelegen, unpassend.

il·lu·mi·nate [ɪ'luːmɪneɪt] v/t **1.** be-, erleuchten, erhellen. **2.** illuminieren, festlich beleuchten. **3.** fig. et. aufhellen, erläutern; j-n erleuchten. **il·lu·mi'na·tion** s **1.** Beleuchtung f. **2.** Illumination f, Festbeleuchtung f. **3.** fig. Erläuterung f; Erleuchtung f.

il·lu·sion [ɪ'luːʒn] s Illusion f: a) Sinnestäuschung f: → optical, b) Einbildung f: be under the ~ that sich einbilden, daß; have no ~s sich keine Illusionen machen (about über acc). **il'lu·sive** [~sɪv], **il'lu·so·ry** [~sərɪ] adj □ illusorisch.

il·lus·trate ['ɪləstreɪt] v/t illustrieren: a) erläutern, veranschaulichen, b) bebildern. **ˌil·lus'tra·tion** s Illustration f: a) Erläuterung f, Veranschaulichung f: in ~ zur Erläuterung von (od. gen); by way of ~ als Beispiel, b) Bebilderung f, c) Bild n, Abbildung f. **il·lus·tra·tive** ['ɪləstrətɪv] adj □ illustrativ, erläuternd, veranschaulichend. **il·lus·tra·tor** ['ɪləstreɪtə] s Illustrator m.

il·lus·tri·ous [ɪˈlʌstrɪəs] *adj* □ berühmt.

I'm [aɪm] F *für* **I am.**

im·age [ˈɪmɪdʒ] *s* **1.** Bild *n* (*a. TV etc*). **2.** Ab-, Ebenbild *n*: *he is the very ~ of his father* er ist s-m Vater wie aus dem Gesicht geschnitten, er ist ganz der Vater; → *spitting*. **3.** Image *n*. **4.** bildlicher Ausdruck, Metapher *f*: *speak in ~s* in Bildern sprechen.

im·ag·i·na·ble [ˈɪmædʒɪnəbl] *adj* □ vorstellbar: *the greatest difficulty ~* die denkbar größte Schwierigkeit. **im'ag·i·na·ry** *adj* imaginär (*a. Ⱥ*), eingebildet. **im,ag·i'na·tion** [ˌ~ˈneɪʃn] *s* **1.** Phantasie *f*. **2.** Vorstellung *f*, Einbildung *f*: *pure ~* reine Einbildung. **im'ag·i·na·tive** [ˌ~ətɪv] *adj* □ **1.** phantasie-, einfallsreich. **2.** phantasievoll. **im'ag·ine** I *v/t* **1.** sich *j-n, et.* vorstellen: *I ~ him as a tall man* ich stelle ihn mir groß vor; *can you ~ him becoming famous?* kannst du dir vorstellen, daß er einmal berühmt wird? **2.** sich *et.* einbilden: *don't ~ that* bilde dir nur nicht ein, daß. **II** *v/i* **3.** *just ~! iro.* stell dir vor!, denk dir nur!

im·bal·ance [ˌɪmˈbæləns] *s* **1.** Unausgewogenheit *f*, Unausgeglichenheit *f*. **2.** *pol. etc* Ungleichgewicht *n*.

im·be·cile [ˈɪmbɪsiːl] I *adj* idiotisch, vertrottelt. **II** *s* Idiot *m*, Trottel *m*. **im·be·cil·i·ty** [ˌ~ˈsɪlətɪ] *s* Idiotie *f*, Blödheit *f*.

im·bibe [ɪmˈbaɪb] *v/t* **1.** *Feuchtigkeit etc* aufsaugen. **2.** *Wissen etc* einsaugen, in sich aufnehmen.

im·bue [ɪmˈbjuː] *v/t fig.* erfüllen (*with* mit): *~d with hatred* haßerfüllt.

im·i·tate [ˈɪmɪteɪt] *v/t* **1.** nachahmen, -machen, imitieren. **2.** fälschen. **,im·i·'ta·tion** I *s* **1.** Nachahmung *f*, Imitation *f*: *in ~ of* nach dem Muster von (*od. gen*). **2.** Fälschung *f*. **II** *adj* **3.** unecht, künstlich: *~ leather* Kunstleder *n*. **im·i·ta·tive** [ˈ~ətɪv] *adj* □ nachahmend, imitierend: *be ~ of → imitate* 1. **im·i·ta·tor** [ˈ~teɪtə] *s* Nachahmer *m*, Imitator *m*.

im·mac·u·late [ɪˈmækjʊlət] *adj* □ **1.** *fig.* unbefleckt, makellos. **2.** tadel-, fehlerlos.

im·ma·nent [ˈɪmənənt] *adj* innewohnend (*in dat*).

im·ma·te·ri·al [ˌɪməˈtɪərɪəl] *adj* □ **1.** unkörperlich, unstofflich. **2.** unwesentlich, unerheblich (*to* für).

im·ma·ture [ˌɪməˈtjʊə] *adj* □ unreif, unausgereift (*beide a. fig.*). **,im·ma'tu·ri·ty** *s* Unreife *f*.

im·meas·ur·a·ble [ɪˈmeʒərəbl] *adj* □ unermeßlich, grenzenlos.

im·me·di·ate [ɪˈmiːdjət] *adj* **1.** (*räumlich, zeitlich*) unmittelbar: *in the ~ vicinity* in unmittelbarer Nähe, in der nächsten Umgebung; *in the ~ future* in nächster Zukunft. **2.** sofortig, umgehend. **3.** nächst (*Verwandtschaft*): *my ~ family* m-e nächsten Angehörigen *pl*. **im'me·di·ate·ly** *adv* **1.** unmittelbar, direkt. **2.** sofort, umgehend.

im·me·mo·ri·al [ˌɪmɪˈmɔːrɪəl] *adj*: *from* (*od. since*) *time ~* seit undenklichen Zeiten.

im·mense [ɪˈmens] *adj* □ riesig, *fig. a.* enorm, immens. **im'men·si·ty** *s* Riesigkeit *f*.

im·merse [ɪˈmɜːs] *v/t* **1.** (ein)tauchen (*in* in *acc*). **2.** *~ o.s. in fig.* sich vertiefen in (*acc*): *~d in* vertieft in; *~d in thought* gedankenversunken. **im'mer·sion** *s* **1.** Eintauchen *n*: *~ heater* Tauchsieder *m*. **2.** *fig.* Versunkenheit *f*, Vertiefung *f*.

im·mi·grant [ˈɪmɪɡrənt] *s* Einwanderer *m*, Einwanderin *f*, Immigrant(in). **im·mi·grate** [ˈ~ɡreɪt] *v/i* einwandern, immigrieren (*into* in *acc*). **,im·mi'gra·tion** *s* Einwanderung *f*, Immigration *f*.

im·mi·nence [ˈɪmɪnəns] *s* nahes Bevorstehen. **'im·mi·nent** *adj* □ **1.** nahe bevorstehend: *his ~ death* sein naher Tod. **2.** drohend (*Gefahr etc*).

im·mo·bile [ɪˈməʊbaɪl] *adj* unbeweglich. **im·mo·bil·i·ty** [ˌ~ˈbɪlətɪ] *s* Unbeweglichkeit *f*. **im'mo·bi·lize** [ˌ~bɪlaɪz] *v/t* unbeweglich machen; *ℬ* ruhigstellen: *~d* bewegungsunfähig.

im·mod·er·ate [ɪˈmɒdərət] *adj* □ unmäßig, maßlos.

im·mod·est [ɪˈmɒdɪst] *adj* □ **1.** unbescheiden. **2.** schamlos.

im·mo·late [ˈɪməʊleɪt] *v/t* opfern (*a. fig.*).

im·mor·al [ɪˈmɒrəl] *adj* □ unmoralisch, unsittlich.

im·mor·tal [ɪˈmɔːtl] *adj* □ unsterblich, *fig. a.* unvergänglich. **im·mor·tal·i·ty** [ˌ~ˈtælətɪ] *s* Unsterblichkeit *f*, *fig. a.* Unvergänglichkeit *f*. **im'mor·tal·ize** [ˌ~təlaɪz] *v/t* unsterblich machen, verewigen.

impermeable

im·mov·a·ble [ɪˈmuːvəbl] *adj* □ **1.** unbeweglich. **2.** *fig.* fest, unerschütterlich; hart, unnachgiebig. **3.** (*zeitlich*) unveränderlich: **~ feast** *eccl.* unbeweglicher Feiertag.

im·mune [ɪˈmjuːn] *adj* **1.** ~ *u. fig.* (**against, from, to**) immun (gegen), unempfänglich (für). **2.** geschützt, gefeit (**against, from, to** gegen). **3.** befreit, ausgenommen (**from** von). **im·mu·ni·ty** *s* ~, ~ *u. fig.* Immunität *f*: **diplomatic ~**. **im·mu·nize** [ˈ~naɪz] *v/t* immunisieren, immun machen (**against** gegen) (*a. fig.*).

im·mu·ta·ble [ɪˈmjuːtəbl] *adj* □ unveränderlich.

imp [ɪmp] *s* **1.** Kobold *m*. **2.** F Racker *m*.

im·pact [ˈɪmpækt] *s* **1.** Zs-, Anprall *m*; Aufprall *m*; ⚔ Auf-, Einschlag *m*. **2.** *fig.* (Ein)Wirkung *f*, (starker) Einfluß (**on** auf *acc*).

im·pair [ɪmˈpeə] *v/t* beeinträchtigen.

im·pale [ɪmˈpeɪl] *v/t* aufspießen (**on** auf *acc*), durchbohren.

im·pal·pa·ble [ɪmˈpælpəbl] *adj* □ **1.** unfühlbar. **2.** äußerst fein. **3.** *fig.* kaum (er)faßbar *od.* greifbar.

im·part [ɪmˈpaːt] *v/t* (**to** *dat*) **1.** *Eigenschaft etc* verleihen. **2.** mitteilen; *Kenntnisse etc* vermitteln.

im·par·tial [ɪmˈpaːʃl] *adj* □ unparteiisch, unvoreingenommen. **im·par·ti·al·i·ty** [ˌ~ʃɪˈælətɪ] *s* Unparteilichkeit *f*, Unvoreingenommenheit *f*.

im·pass·a·ble [ɪmˈpaːsəbl] *adj* □ **1.** unpassierbar. **2.** *bsd. fig.* unüberwindbar (*Hindernis etc*).

im·passe [ˈæmpaːs] *s fig.* Sackgasse *f*: **reach an ~** in e-e Sackgasse geraten.

im·pas·sioned [ɪmˈpæʃnd] *adj* leidenschaftlich.

im·pas·sive [ɪmˈpæsɪv] *adj* □ **1.** teilnahmslos; ungerührt. **2.** gelassen.

im·pa·tience [ɪmˈpeɪʃns] *s* **1.** Ungeduld *f*. **2.** Unduldsamkeit *f*. **im·pa·tient** *adj* □ **1.** ungeduldig: **be ~ with** keine Geduld haben mit. **2.** **be ~ for** *et.* nicht erwarten können; **be ~ to do s.th.** es nicht erwarten können, et. zu tun. **3.** unduldsam (**of** gegenüber).

im·peach [ɪmˈpiːtʃ] *v/t* **1.** ⚖ anklagen (**for, of, with** gen); *Am. bsd.* Präsidenten unter Amtsanklage stellen. **2.** ⚖ anfechten. **3.** in Frage stellen, in Zweifel ziehen. **im·peach·ment** *s* **1.** ⚖ Anklage *f*; *Am.* Impeachment *n*. **2.** ⚖ Anfechtung *f*. **3.** Infragestellung *f*.

im·pec·ca·ble [ɪmˈpekəbl] *adj* □ untadelig, einwandfrei.

im·pede [ɪmˈpiːd] *v/t* **1.** *j-n, et.* (be)hindern: **~ s.o.'s doing s.th.** j-n daran hindern, et. zu tun. **2.** *et.* erschweren.

im·ped·i·ment [ɪmˈpedɪmənt] *s* **1.** Behinderung *f*. **2.** Hindernis *n* (**to** für). **3.** ⚔ (*bsd.* angeborener) Fehler: → **speech** 1.

im·pel [ɪmˈpel] *v/t* **1.** antreiben (*a. fig.*). **2.** zwingen: **I felt ~led** ich sah mich gezwungen *od.* fühlte mich genötigt (**to do** zu tun).

im·pend·ing [ɪmˈpendɪŋ] *adj* **1.** nahe bevorstehend: **his ~ death** sein naher Tod. **2.** drohend (*Gefahr etc*).

im·pen·e·tra·ble [ɪmˈpenɪtrəbl] *adj* □ **1.** undurchdringlich (**by** für) (*a. fig.*). **2.** *fig.* unergründlich, unerforschlich.

im·pen·i·tent [ɪmˈpenɪtənt] *adj* □ verstockt; *eccl.* unbußfertig.

im·per·a·tive [ɪmˈperətɪv] **I** *adj* □ **1.** gebieterisch. **2.** unumgänglich, unbedingt erforderlich. **3.** *ling.* Imperativ..., Befehls...: **~ mood** → **4. II** *s* **4.** *ling.* Imperativ *m*, Befehlsform *f*.

im·per·cep·ti·ble [ˌɪmpəˈseptəbl] *adj* □ **1.** nicht wahrnehmbar, unmerklich. **2.** verschwindend klein.

im·per·fect [ɪmˈpɜːfɪkt] **I** *adj* □ **1.** unvollkommen: a) unvollständig, b) mangel-, fehlerhaft. **2.** **~ tense** → **3. II** *s* **3.** *ling.* Imperfekt *n*, unvollendete Vergangenheit. **im·per·fec·tion** [ˌ~pəˈfekʃn] *s* **1.** Unvollkommenheit *f*. **2.** Mangel *m*, Fehler *m*.

im·pe·ri·al [ɪmˈpɪərɪəl] *adj* □ **1.** kaiserlich, Kaiser... **2.** *Br.* gesetzlich (*Maße u. Gewichte*). **im·pe·ri·al·ism** *s pol.* Imperialismus *m*. **im·pe·ri·al·ist** *s* Imperialist *m*. **II** *adj* imperialistisch. **im·pe·ri·al·is·tic** *adj* (**~ally**) imperialistisch.

im·per·il [ɪmˈperəl] *v/t* gefährden.

im·pe·ri·ous [ɪmˈpɪərɪəs] *adj* □ **1.** gebieterisch. **2.** dringend: **~ necessity** zwingende Notwendigkeit.

im·per·ish·a·ble [ɪmˈperɪʃəbl] *adj* □ **1.** unverderblich. **2.** *fig.* unvergänglich.

im·per·ma·nent [ˌɪmˈpɜːmənənt] *adj* □ vorübergehend, nicht von Dauer.

im·per·me·a·ble [ɪmˈpɜːmjəbl] *adj* □

undurchlässig (**to** für): **~ to water** wasserdicht.

im·per·son·al [ɪmˈpɜːsnl] *adj* □ unpersönlich (*a. ling.*).

im·per·son·ate [ɪmˈpɜːsəneɪt] *v/t* 1. *thea. etc* verkörpern, darstellen. 2. *j-n* imitieren, nachahmen.

im·per·ti·nence [ɪmˈpɜːtɪnəns] *s* 1. Unverschämtheit *f*, Frechheit *f*. 2. Belanglosigkeit *f*. **im·per·ti·nent** *adj* □ 1. unverschämt, frech. 2. belanglos (**to** für).

im·per·turb·a·ble [ˌɪmpəˈtɜːbəbl] *adj* □ unerschütterlich.

im·per·vi·ous [ɪmˈpɜːvjəs] *adj* □ 1. → **impermeable**. 2. *fig.* unzugänglich (**to** für *od. dat*).

im·pet·u·ous [ɪmˈpetjʊəs] *adj* □ 1. heftig, ungestüm. 2. impulsiv. 3. übereilt, vorschnell.

im·pe·tus [ˈɪmpɪtəs] *s* 1. *phys.* Triebkraft *f*, Schwung *m* (*a. fig.*). 2. *fig.* Antrieb *m*, Impuls *m*: **give an ~ to** Auftrieb *od.* Schwung verleihen (*dat*).

im·pi·e·ty [ɪmˈpaɪətɪ] *s* 1. Gottlosigkeit *f*. 2. (**to** gegenüber) Pietätlosigkeit *f*; Respektlosigkeit *f*.

im·pinge [ɪmˈpɪndʒ] *v/i* 1. auftreffen (**on** auf *acc*). 2. *fig.* (**on**) sich auswirken (auf *acc*), beeinflussen (*acc*).

im·pi·ous [ˈɪmpɪəs] *adj* □ 1. gottlos. 2. (**to** gegenüber) pietätlos; respektlos.

imp·ish [ˈɪmpɪʃ] *adj* □ schelmisch, spitzbübisch.

im·plac·a·ble [ɪmˈplækəbl] *adj* □ unversöhnlich, unnachgiebig.

im·plant I *v/t* [ɪmˈplɑːnt] 1. ⚕ implantieren, einpflanzen (**in, into** *dat*). 2. *fig.* einprägen (**in, into** *dat*): **deeply ~ed hatred** tiefverwurzelter Haß. II *s* [ˈɪmplɑːnt] 3. ⚕ Implantat *n*.

im·plau·si·ble [ˌɪmˈplɔːzəbl] *adj* □ unglaubwürdig.

im·ple·ment I *s* [ˈɪmplɪmənt] Werkzeug *n* (*a. fig.*), Gerät *n*. II *v/t* [ˈ~ment] aus-, durchführen. **im·ple·men·ta·tion** [ˌ~menˈteɪʃn] *s* Aus-, Durchführung *f*.

im·pli·cate [ˈɪmplɪkeɪt] *v/t* 1. *j-n* verwikkeln, hineinziehen (**in** *in acc*). 2. → **imply** 1, 3. ,**im·pli·ca·tion** *s* 1. Verwicklung *f*. 2. Folgerung *f*. 3. Folge *f*, Auswirkung *f*. 4. Andeutung *f*.

im·plic·it [ɪmˈplɪsɪt] *adj* 1. → **implied**. 2. vorbehalt-, bedingungslos: **~ faith (obedience)** blinder Glaube (Gehor-

sam). **im·plic·it·ly** *adv* 1. stillschweigend. 2. → **implicit** 2.

im·plied [ɪmˈplaɪd] *adj* impliziert, (stillschweigend *od.* mit) inbegriffen.

im·plode [ɪmˈpləʊd] *v/i phys.* implodieren.

im·plore [ɪmˈplɔː] *v/t* 1. *j-n* anflehen. 2. *et* erflehen, flehen um.

im·plo·sion [ɪmˈpləʊʒn] *s phys.* Implosion *f*.

im·ply [ɪmˈplaɪ] *v/t* 1. implizieren, (sinngemäß *od.* stillschweigend) beinhalten. 2. andeuten, zu verstehen geben. 3. mit sich bringen, zur Folge haben.

im·po·lite [ˌɪmpəˈlaɪt] *adj* □ unhöflich.

im·pol·i·tic [ɪmˈpɒlɪtɪk] *adj* □ undiplomatisch, unklug.

im·pon·der·a·ble [ɪmˈpɒndərəbl] I *adj* unwägbar. II *s pl* Imponderabilien *pl*, Unwägbarkeiten *pl*.

im·port I *v/t u. v/i* [ɪmˈpɔːt] 1. importieren, einführen: **~ing country** Einfuhrland *n*; **~ing firm** Importfirma *f*. II *s* [ˈɪmpɔːt] 2. Import *m*, Einfuhr *f*. 3. *pl* (Gesamt)Import *m*, (-)Einfuhr *f*; Importgüter *pl*, Einfuhrware *f*. III *adj* [ˈɪmpɔːt] 4. Import..., Einfuhr...: **~ trade** Importgeschäft *n*, Einfuhrhandel *m*.

im·por·tance [ɪmˈpɔːtns] *s* Bedeutung *f*: a) Wichtigkeit *f*: **attach ~ to** Bedeutung beimessen (*dat*); **be of no ~** unwichtig *od.* belanglos sein (**to** für), b) Ansehen *n*, Gewicht *n*: **a person of ~** e-e gewichtige Persönlichkeit. **im·por·tant** *adj* □ bedeutend: a) wichtig, von Belang (**to** für), b) angesehen, gewichtig.

im·port·er [ɪmˈpɔːtə] *s* Importeur *m*.

im·por·tu·nate [ɪmˈpɔːtjʊnət] *adj* □ lästig, zu-, aufdringlich. **im·por·tune** [ˌ~tjuːn] *v/t* belästigen, dauernd (*bsd.* mit Bitten) behelligen.

im·pose [ɪmˈpəʊz] I *v/t* 1. (**on**) *et.* auferlegen, -bürden (*dat*); *Strafe* verhängen (gegen). 2. (**on**) a) *et.* aufdrängen, -zwingen (*dat*): **~ o.s. o.s.** *od.* **one's presence) on s.o.** sich j-m aufdrängen; **one's will on s.o.** j-m s-n Willen aufzwingen, b) *et.* (*mit Gewalt*) einführen *od.* durchsetzen (bei). II *v/i* 3. ausnutzen, *b.s. a.* mißbrauchen (**on** *acc*). 4. (**on** *dat*) sich aufdrängen; zur Last fallen. **im·pos·ing** *adj* □ imponierend, imposant. **im·po·si·tion** [ˌɪmpəˈzɪʃn] *s*

1. Auferlegung *f*, -bürdung *f*; Verhängung *f*. **2.** Auflage *f*, Pflicht *f*. **3.** Abgabe *f*, Steuer *f*. **4.** Ausnutzung *f*, *b.s. a.* Mißbrauch *m* (**on** gen).

im·pos·si·bil·i·ty [ɪmˌpɒsə'bɪlətɪ] *s* Unmöglichkeit *f*. **im'pos·si·ble** *adj* unmöglich (*a. F unglaublich, unerträglich etc*): **it is ~ for me to come** ich kann unmöglich kommen. **im'pos·si·bly** *adv* unglaublich.

im·post·er, im·post·or [ɪm'pɒstə] *s* Betrüger(in), *bsd.* Hochstapler(in).

im·po·tence ['ɪmpətəns] *s* **1.** Unvermögen *n*, Unfähigkeit *f*; Hilflosigkeit *f*, Ohnmacht *f*. **2.** ✱ Impotenz *f*. **'im·po·tent** *adj* □ **1.** unfähig (**in doing, to do** zu tun); hilflos, ohnmächtig. **2.** ✱ impotent.

im·pov·er·ish [ɪm'pɒvərɪʃ] *v/t* arm machen: **be ~ed** verarmen; verarmt sein.

im·prac·ti·ca·ble [ɪm'præktɪkəbl] *adj* □ **1.** undurchführbar. **2.** unpassierbar (*Straße etc*).

im·prac·ti·cal [ɪm'præktɪkl] *adj* □ **1.** unpraktisch (*Person*). **2.** undurchführbar.

im·preg·nate ['ɪmpregneɪt] *v/t* **1.** *biol.* schwängern; befruchten (*a. fig.*). **2.** ✿, ⊚ imprägnieren, tränken. **3.** *fig.* durchdringen, erfüllen (**with** mit).

im·pre·sa·ri·o [ˌɪmprɪ'sɑːrɪəʊ] *pl* **-os** *s* Impresario *m*, Theater-, Konzertagent *m*.

im·press I *v/t* [ɪm'pres] **1.** beeindrucken, Eindruck machen auf (*acc*), imponieren (*dat*). **2.** (auf)drücken (**on** auf *acc*), (ein)drücken (**in, into** in *acc*). II *s* ['ɪmpres] **3.** Ab-, Eindruck *m*. **im'pres·sion** [~ʃn] *s* **1.** Eindruck *m* (**of** von): **give s.o. a wrong ~** bei j-m e-n falschen Eindruck erwecken; **make a good (bad) ~** e-n guten (schlechten) Eindruck machen. **2.** Eindruck *m*, Vermutung *f*: **I have an** (*od.* **the**) **~** (*od.* **I am under the ~) that** ich habe den Eindruck, daß; **under the ~ that** in der Annahme, daß. **3.** Abdruck *m* (*a.* ✱). **4.** *typ.* (*bsd.* unveränderte) Auflage, Nachdruck *m*. **im'pres·sion·a·ble** *adj* leicht zu beeinflussen(d). **im'pres·sion·ism** *s* Impressionismus *m*. **im'pres·sion·ist** I *s* Impressionist(in). II *adj* impressionistisch. **im,pres·sion·'is·tic** [~ʃə'n~] *adj* (**~ally**) impressioni-

stisch. **im'pres·sive** [~sɪv] *adj* □ eindrucksvoll.

im·print I *s* ['ɪmprɪnt] **1.** Ab-, Eindruck *m*. **2.** *fig.* Stempel *m*, Gepräge *n*. **3.** *typ.* Impressum *n*. II *v/t* [ɪm'prɪnt] **4.** (auf-) drücken (**on** auf *acc*). **5.** ~ **s.th. on** (*od.* **in**) **s.o.'s memory** j-m et. ins Gedächtnis einprägen.

im·pris·on [ɪm'prɪzn] *v/t* ⚖ inhaftieren, *a. weitS.* einsperren. **im'pris·on·ment** *s* a) Freiheitsstrafe *f*, Gefängnis(strafe *f*) *n*, Haft *f*: **he was given 10 years ~** er wurde zu e-r zehnjährigen Freiheitsstrafe verurteilt, b) Inhaftierung *f*.

im·prob·a·bil·i·ty [ɪmˌprɒbə'bɪlətɪ] *s* Unwahrscheinlichkeit *f*. **im'prob·a·ble** *adj* □ unwahrscheinlich.

im·promp·tu [ɪm'prɒmptjuː] I *s* ♪ Impromptu *n*. II *adj u. adv* aus dem Stegreif, Stegreif...

im·prop·er [ɪm'prɒpə] *adj* □ **1.** ungeeignet, unpassend. **2.** unanständig, unschicklich. **3.** unrichtig. **4.** ₳ unecht (*Bruch*). **im·pro·pri·e·ty** [ˌɪmprə'praɪətɪ] *s* **1.** Unschicklichkeit *f*. **2.** Unrichtigkeit *f*.

im·prove [ɪm'pruːv] I *v/t* **1.** verbessern. **2.** *Wert etc* erhöhen, steigern. II *v/i* **3.** sich (ver)bessern, besser werden, Fortschritte machen (*a. Patient*), sich erholen (*gesundheitlich od.* ✚ *Preise etc*): **he is improving** (**in health**) es geht ihm besser; **~ in strength** kräftiger werden. **im'prove·ment** *s* **1.** (Ver)Besserung *f* (**in** gen, **on** gegenüber, im Vergleich zu): **~ in the weather** Wetterbesserung. **2.** Erhöung *f*, Steigerung *f*.

im·prov·i·dent [ɪm'prɒvɪdənt] *adj* □ **1.** sorglos: **be ~ of** nicht vorsorgen für. **2.** verschwenderisch.

im·pro·vi·sa·tion [ˌɪmprəvaɪ'zeɪʃn] *s* Improvisation *f*. **im·pro·vise** ['~vaɪz] *v/t u. v/i* improvisieren.

im·pru·dence [ɪm'pruːdəns] *s* **1.** Unklugheit *f*. **2.** Unvorsichtigkeit *f*. **im'pru·dent** *adj* □ **1.** unklug. **2.** unvorsichtig.

im·pu·dence ['ɪmpjʊdəns] *s* Unverschämtheit *f*. **'im·pu·dent** *adj* □ unverschämt.

im·pugn [ɪm'pjuːn] *v/t* bestreiten; anfechten.

im·pulse ['ɪmpʌls] *s* **1.** *phys.*, ✱, ⚡ *etc* Impuls *m*. **2.** *fig.* Impuls *m*: a) Anstoß *m*, Anreiz *m*, b) plötzliche Regung *od.* Eingebung: **act on ~** impulsiv *od.* spontan handeln; **on the ~ of the moment, on ~** e-r plötzlichen Eingebung folgend. **im'pul·sion** *s* **1.** Triebkraft *f (a. fig.).* **2.** *psych.* Zwang *m.* **im'pul·sive** *adj* □ *fig.* impulsiv.

im·pu·ni·ty [ɪm'pjuːnətɪ] *s* Straflosigkeit *f*: **with ~** straflos.

im·pure [ɪm'pjʊə] *adj* □ **1.** unrein (*a. eccl.*), unsauber. **2.** *fig.* schlecht, unmoralisch. **im'pur·i·ty** *s* **1.** Unreinheit *f.* **2.** *fig.* Schlechtheit *f.*

im·pu·ta·tion [ˌɪmpjuː'teɪʃn] *s* Bezichtigung *f.* **im'pute** *v/t* zuschreiben (*to dat*): a) beimessen, b) anlasten: **~ s.th. to s.o.** j-n e-r Sache bezichtigen.

in [ɪn] **I** *prp* **1.** *räumlich:* a) (*wo?*) in (*dat*), an (*dat*), auf (*dat*): **~ London** in London; → **country** 3, **field** 1, **sky, street,** *etc,* b) (*wohin?*) in (*acc*): **put it ~ your pocket** steck es in die Tasche. **2.** *zeitlich:* in (*dat*), an (*dat*): **~ 1988** 1988; **~ two hours** in zwei Stunden; → **April, beginning** 1, **evening,** *etc.* **3.** *Zustand, Beschaffenheit, Art u. Weise:* in (*dat*), auf (*acc*), mit: → **brief** 4, **cash** 2, **English** 3, *etc.* **4.** *Tätigkeit, Beschäftigung:* in (*dat*), bei, auf (*dat*): **~ crossing the river** beim Überqueren des Flusses; → **accident** 2, **search** 4. **5.** bei (*Schriftstellern*): **~ Shakespeare.** **6.** *Richtung:* in (*acc, dat*), auf (*acc*), zu: → **confidence** 1, *etc.* **7.** *Zweck:* in (*dat*), zu, als: → **answer** 1, **defence,** *etc.* **8.** *Grund:* in (*dat*), aus, zu: → **honour** 5, **sport,** *etc.* **9.** *Hinsicht, Beziehung:* in (*dat*), an (*dat*): **the latest thing ~** das Neueste auf dem Gebiet (*gen*); → **equal** 1, **number** 3, *etc.* **10.** nach, gemäß: → **opinion** 1, **probability,** *etc.* **11.** *Material:* in (*dat*), aus, mit: → **black** 3, **oil** 3, *etc.* **12.** *Zahl, Betrag:* in (*dat*), von, aus, zu: **five ~ all** insgesamt *od.* im ganzen fünf; **one ~ ten Americans** einer von zehn Amerikanern; → **all** 4, **two,** *etc.* **II** *adv* **13.** (dr)innen: **be ~ for s.th.** *et.* zu erwarten haben; **be ~ on** eingeweiht sein in (*acc*); beteiligt sein an (*dat*); **know ~ and out** in- u. auswendig kennen. **14.** hinein; herein: → **come in** 1, *etc.* **15.** da, (an)gekommen. **16.** da, zu Hause. **17.** *pol.* an der Macht, an der Regierung. **III** *adj* **18. ~**

party *pol.* Regierungspartei *f.* **19. ~ restaurant** Restaurant, das gerade in ist. **IV** *s* **20. know the ~s and outs of** in- u. auswendig kennen.

in·a·bil·i·ty [ˌɪnə'bɪlətɪ] *s* Unfähigkeit *f,* Unvermögen *n*: **~ to pay** ✝ Zahlungsunfähigkeit.

in·ac·ces·si·ble [ˌɪnæk'sesəbl] *adj* □ unzugänglich (**to** für *od. dat*) (*a. fig.*).

in·ac·cu·ra·cy [ɪn'ækjʊrəsɪ] *s* Ungenauigkeit *f.* **in'ac·cu·rate** [~rət] *adj* □ ungenau: **be ~** falsch gehen (*Uhr*).

in·ac·tion [ɪn'ækʃn] *s* **1.** Untätigkeit *f.* **2.** Trägheit *f,* Faulheit *f.*

in·ac·tive [ɪn'æktɪv] *adj* □ **1.** untätig. **2.** träge (*a. phys.*), faul. **3.** ✝ lustlos, flau. **in·ac'tiv·i·ty** *s* **1.** → **inaction.** **2.** ✝ Lustlosigkeit *f,* Flauheit *f.*

in·ad·e·quate [ɪn'ædɪkwət] *adj* □ **1.** unzulänglich, ungenügend: **be ~ for** nicht reichen für. **2.** unangemessen (**to** *dat*): **feel ~ to the occasion** sich der Situation nicht gewachsen fühlen.

in·ad·mis·si·ble [ˌɪnəd'mɪsəbl] *adj* □ unzulässig, unstatthaft.

in·ad·vert·ent [ˌɪnəd'vɜːtənt] *adj* □ unabsichtlich, versehentlich: **~ly** *a.* aus Versehen.

in·ad·vis·a·ble [ˌɪnəd'vaɪzəbl] *adj* nicht ratsam *od.* empfehlenswert.

in·al·ien·a·ble [ɪn'eɪljənəbl] *adj* □ unveräußerlich.

in·ane [ɪ'neɪn] *adj* □ geistlos, albern.

in·an·i·mate [ɪn'ænɪmət] *adj* □ **1.** leblos, unbelebt. **2.** *fig.* schwunglos, langweilig.

in·ap·pli·ca·ble [ɪn'æplɪkəbl] *adj* □ nicht anwendbar *od.* zutreffend (**to** auf *acc*): → **delete** II.

in·ap·pre·ci·a·ble [ˌɪnə'priːʃəbl] *adj* □ unmerklich.

in·ap·pro·pri·ate [ˌɪnə'prəʊprɪət] *adj* □ unpassend, ungeeignet (**to, for** für).

in·apt [ɪn'æpt] *adj* □ **1.** unpassend, ungeeignet. **2.** ungeschickt. **3.** unfähig, außerstande (**to do** zu tun). **in'apt·i·tude** [~tɪtjuːd] *s* **1.** Ungeschicktheit *f.* **2.** Unfähigkeit *f.*

in·ar·tic·u·late [ˌɪnɑː'tɪkjʊlət] *adj* □ **1.** undeutlich (ausgesprochen), unverständlich. **2.** (unfähig(, deutlich) zu sprechen. **3.** unfähig, sich klar auszudrücken. **4.** sprachlos (**with** vor *dat*).

in·as·much as [ˌɪnəzˈmʌtʃ] *cj* da (ja), weil.

in·at·ten·tion [ˌɪnəˈtenʃn] *s* Unaufmerksamkeit *f*. **ˌin·atˈten·tive** [~tɪv] *adj* □ unaufmerksam (**to** gegen).

in·au·di·ble [ɪnˈɔːdəbl] *adj* □ unhörbar.

in·au·gu·ral [ɪˈnɔːgjʊrəl] **I** *adj* Einweihungs..., Eröffnungs...: **~ speech** → II. **II** *s* Antrittsrede *f*. **inˈau·gu·rate** [~reɪt] *v/t* **1.** *j-n* (feierlich) (in sein Amt) einführen *od.* einsetzen. **2.** einweihen, eröffnen. **3.** *Ära etc* einleiten. **inˌau·guˈra·tion** *s* **1.** (feierliche) Amtseinsetzung *od.* -einführung: **2 Day** *pol. Am.* Tag *m* des Amtsantritts des Präsidenten (*20. Januar*). **2.** Einweihung *f*, Eröffnung *f*. **3.** Beginn *m*.

in·aus·pi·cious [ˌɪnɔːˈspɪʃəs] *adj* □ ungünstig: **be ~** unter e-m ungünstigen Stern stehen.

in·board [ˈɪnbɔːd] ♣ **I** *adj* **1.** Innenbord...: **~ motor.** *Am.* **2.** binnenbords. **III** *s* **3.** Innenbordmotor *m*. **4.** Innenborder *m* (*Boot*).

in·born [ˌɪnˈbɔːn] *adj* angeboren.

in·bred [ˌɪnˈbred] *adj* **1.** angeboren. **2.** durch Inzucht erzeugt. **in·breed·ing** [ˈɪnˌbriːdɪŋ] *s* Inzucht *f* (*a. fig.*).

in·cal·cu·la·ble [ɪnˈkælkjʊləbl] *adj* □ **1.** unberechenbar (*a. Person etc*). **2.** unermeßlich.

in·can·des·cent [ˌɪnkænˈdesnt] *adj* □ **1.** (weiß)glühend: **~ lamp** Glühlampe *f*. **2.** *fig.* leuchtend, strahlend.

in·can·ta·tion [ˌɪnkænˈteɪʃn] *s* **1.** Beschwörung *f*. **2.** Zauberformel *f*, -spruch *m*.

in·ca·pa·bil·i·ty [ɪnˌkeɪpəˈbɪlətɪ] *s* Unfähigkeit *f*. **inˈca·pa·ble** *adj* □ **1.** unfähig (**of** zu *od.* gen; **of doing** zu tun), nicht imstande (**of doing** zu tun). **2.** nicht zulassend (**of** acc): **a problem ~ of solution** ein unlösbares Problem; **~ of being misunderstood** unmißverständlich.

in·ca·pac·i·tate [ˌɪnkəˈpæsɪteɪt] *v/t* **1.** unfähig *od.* untauglich machen (**for s.th.** für et.; **for** [*od.* **from**] **doing** zu tun). **2.** ♣♣ für rechts- *od.* geschäftsunfähig erklären. **ˌin·caˈpac·i·tat·ed** *adj* **1.** *a.* **~ for work** arbeits- *od.* erwerbsunfähig. **2.** *körperlich, geistig* behindert. **3.** *a. legally* **~** rechts-, geschäftsunfähig. **ˌin·caˈpac·i·ty** [~ətɪ] *s* **1.** Unfähigkeit *f*, Untauglichkeit *f*: **~ for work** Arbeits-

od. Erwerbsunfähigkeit *f*. **2.** *a.* **legal ~** Rechts-, Geschäftsunfähigkeit *f*.

in·car·cer·ate [ɪnˈkɑːsəreɪt] *v/t* einkerkern.

in·car·nate [ɪnˈkɑːneɪt] *adj* a) leibhaftig, *ein Teufel etc* in Menschengestalt, b) personifiziert, *die Unschuld etc* in Person. **ˌin·carˈna·tion** *s* Verkörperung *f*, Inbegriff *m*.

in·cen·di·ar·y [ɪnˈsendjərɪ] **I** *adj* **1.** Brand...: **~ bomb. 2.** *fig.* aufwiegelnd: **~ speech** Hetzrede *f*. **II** *s* **3.** Brandstifter(in). **4.** *fig.* Aufwiegler(in).

in·cense[1] [ˈɪnsens] **I** *s* Weihrauch *m*. **II** *v/t* beweihräuchern.

in·cense[2] [ɪnˈsens] *v/t* erzürnen, erbosen: **~d** zornig (**at** über *acc*).

in·cen·tive [ɪnˈsentɪv] *s* Ansporn *m*, Anreiz *m* (**to** zu): **~ to buy** Kaufanreiz.

in·cer·ti·tude [ɪnˈsɜːtɪtjuːd] *s* Unsicherheit *f*, Ungewißheit *f*.

in·ces·sant [ɪnˈsesnt] *adj* □ unaufhörlich, unablässig.

in·cest [ˈɪnsest] *s* Blutschande *f*, Inzest *m*.

inch [ɪntʃ] **I** *s* Inch *m*, Zoll *m* (*a. fig.*): **by ~es, ~ by ~** Zentimeter um Zentimeter; *fig.* allmählich, ganz langsam; **every ~** *fig.* jeder Zoll, *ein Gentleman etc* vom Scheitel bis zur Sohle; **come within an ~ of death** beinahe *od.* um Haaresbreite sterben. **II** *v/t u. v/i* (sich) zentimeterweise *od.* sehr langsam bewegen.

in·ci·dence [ˈɪnsɪdəns] *s* **1.** Auftreten *n*, Vorkommen *n*, Häufigkeit *f*: **have a high ~** häufig vorkommen. **ˈin·ci·dent** **I** *adj* verbunden (**to** mit). **II** *s* Vorfall *m*, Ereignis *n*, *a. pol.* Zwischenfall *m*: **full of ~s** ereignisreich. **in·ci·den·tal** [ˌ~ˈdentl] *adj* □ **1.** nebensächlich, Neben...: **~ earnings** *pl* Nebenverdienst *m*. **2.** beiläufig. **3.** gelegentlich. **4.** zufällig. **II** *s* **5.** Nebensächlichkeit *f*. **6.** *pl* ♣ Nebenausgaben *pl*. **ˌin·ci·denˈtal·ly** [~tlɪ] *adv* nebenbei bemerkt, übrigens.

in·cin·er·ate [ɪnˈsɪnəreɪt] *v/t u. v/i* verbrennen. **inˈcin·er·a·tor** *s* Verbrennungsofen *m od.* -anlage *f*.

in·cise [ɪnˈsaɪz] *v/t* **1.** ein-, aufschneiden (*a. ♣*). **2.** *Muster etc* einritzen, -schnitzen, -kerben (**on** in *acc*): **~ s.th. with a pattern** ein Muster in et. einritzen *od.* -schnitzen *od.* -kerben. **in·ci·sion** [~ˈsɪʒn] *s* (Ein)Schnitt *m* (*a. ♣*). **in·ci·sive**

[ˌ∪ˈsaɪsɪv] *adj* □ **1.** (ein)schneidend. **2.** *fig.* scharf (*Verstand, Ton etc*). **3.** *fig.* prägnant, treffend. **in·ci·sor** [ɪnˈsaɪzə] *s anat.* Schneidezahn *m.*

in·cite [ɪnˈsaɪt] *v/t* **1.** aufwiegeln, -hetzen, ⚖ anstiften (**to** zu). **2.** *Zorn etc* erregen. **in'cite·ment** *s* Aufwieg(e)lung *f,* -hetzung *f,* ⚖ Anstiftung *f.*

in·ci·vil·i·ty [ˌɪnsɪˈvɪlətɪ] *s* Unhöflichkeit *f* (*a. Bemerkung etc*).

in·clem·ent [ɪnˈklemənt] *adj* □ **1.** rauh, unfreundlich (*Klima*). **2.** hart, unerbittlich.

in·cli·na·tion [ˌɪnklɪˈneɪʃn] *s* **1.** Neigung *f, fig. a.* Hang *m.* **2.** *fig.* Zuneigung *f* (**for** zu). **3.** Gefälle *n.* **in·cline** [ˌ∪ˈklaɪn] **I** *v/i* **1.** sich neigen (**to, toward[s]** nach). **2.** *fig.* neigen (**to, toward[s]** zu): ~ **to do s.th.** dazu neigen, et. zu tun. **II** *v/t* **3.** *Kopf etc* neigen. **4.** *fig.* veranlassen, bewegen (**to** zu; **to do** zu tun). **III** *s* **5.** Gefälle *n.* **6.** (Ab)Hang *m.* **in'clined** *adj* geneigt (*a. fig.*): **be ~ to do s.th.** dazu neigen, et. zu tun; **~ plane** 𝔸, *phys.* schiefe Ebene.

in·close, in·clo·sure → **enclose, enclosure.**

in·clude [ɪnˈkluːd] *v/t* **1.** einschließen, -beziehen, -rechnen (**in** *acc*): **tax ~d** einschließlich *od.* inklusive Steuer. **2.** erfassen, aufnehmen: **be ~d on the list** auf der Liste stehen. **in'clud·ing** *prp* einschließlich.

in·clu·sion [ɪnˈkluːʒn] *s* Einschluß *m,* Einbeziehung *f* (**in** *acc*). **in'clu·sive** [ˌ∪sɪv] *adj* □ **1.** einschließlich, inklusive (**of** *gen*): **be ~ of** einschließen (*acc*). **2.** Pauschal...: ~ **price.**

in·cog·ni·to [ˌɪnkɒɡˈniːtəʊ] **I** *adv* inkognito. **II** *pl* **-tos** *s* Inkognito *n:* **preserve (disclose, reveal) one's ~** sein Inkognito wahren (lüften).

in·co·her·ent [ˌɪnkəʊˈhɪərənt] *adj* □ (logisch) unzusammenhängend.

in·come [ˈɪŋkʌm] *s* Einkommen *n* (**from** aus): **live within (beyond) one's ~** s-n Verhältnissen entsprechend (über s-e Verhältnisse) leben. **~ brack·et, ~ group** *s* Einkommensgruppe *f.* **~ tax** *s* Einkommensteuer *f.*

in·com·ing [ˈɪnˌkʌmɪŋ] *adj* **1.** hereinkommend. **2.** ankommend (*Telefongespräch etc*), nachfolgend, neu (*Mieter, Regierung etc*). **3.** ✝ eingehend, -lau-

fend: ~ **orders** *pl* Auftragseingänge *pl;* ~ **mail** Posteingang *m.*

in·com·men·su·ra·ble [ˌɪnkəˈmenʃərəbl] *adj* □ **1.** nicht vergleichbar (**with** mit). **2.** unangemessen, unverhältnismäßig. **in·com'men·su·rate** [ˌ∪rət] *adj* □ **1.** unangemessen, nicht entsprechend (**with, to** *dat*). **2.** → **incommensurable.**

in·com·mu·ni·ca·tive [ˌɪnkəˈmjuːnɪkətɪv] *adj* □ nicht mitteilsam, verschlossen.

in·com·pa·ra·ble [ɪnˈkɒmpərəbl] *adj* □ **1.** unvergleichlich. **2.** unvergleichbar (**with, to** mit).

in·com·pat·i·ble [ˌɪnkəmˈpætəbl] *adj* □ **1.** unvereinbar. **2.** unverträglich, 🖋 *a.* inkompatibel: **be ~ (with)** sich nicht vertragen (mit), nicht zs.-passen (mit).

in·com·pe·tence, in·com·pe·ten·cy [ɪnˈkɒmpɪtəns(ɪ)] *s* **1.** Unfähigkeit *f.* **2.** ⚖ *a. weitS.* Nichtzuständigkeit *f,* Inkompetenz *f.* **in'com·pe·tent** *adj* □ **1.** unfähig (**to do** zu tun). **2.** ⚖ *a. weitS.* unzuständig, inkompetent.

in·com·plete [ˌɪnkəmˈpliːt] *adj* □ **1.** unvollständig. **2.** unvollzählig. **3.** unvollkommen.

in·com·pre·hen·si·ble [ɪnˌkɒmprɪˈhensəbl] *adj* unbegreiflich, unfaßbar, unverständlich. **in·com·pre'hen·si·bly** *adv* unverständlicherweise. **in·com·pre'hen·sion** *s* Unverständnis *n* (**of** für).

in·con·ceiv·a·ble [ˌɪnkənˈsiːvəbl] *adj* □ **1.** unbegreiflich, unfaßbar. **2.** undenkbar, unvorstellbar (**to** für): **it is ~ to me that** ich kann mir nicht vorstellen, daß.

in·con·clu·sive [ˌɪnkənˈkluːsɪv] *adj* □ **1.** nicht überzeugend *od.* schlüssig. **2.** ergebnis-, erfolglos.

in·con·gru·i·ty [ˌɪnkɒŋˈɡruːətɪ] *s* **1.** Nichtübereinstimmung *f.* **2.** Unvereinbarkeit *f.* **in·con·gru·ous** [ˌ∪ɡrʊəs] *adj* □ **1.** nicht übereinstimmend (**to, with** mit). **2.** unvereinbar (**to, with** mit).

in·con·se·quent [ɪnˈkɒnsɪkwənt] *adj* □ **1.** inkonsequent, unlogisch. **2.** belanglos.

in·con·sid·er·a·ble [ˌɪnkənˈsɪdərəbl] *adj* □ **1.** gering(fügig). **2.** unbedeutend, unwichtig (*a. Person*).

in·con·sid·er·ate [ˌɪnkənˈsɪdərət] *adj* □ **1.** rücksichtslos (**to, toward[s]** gegen).

2. unbesonnen, (*Handlung a.*) un-überlegt.

in·con·sist·ent [ˌɪnkən'sɪstənt] *adj* □ **1.** inkonsequent. **2.** unvereinbar (**with** mit). **3.** widersprüchlich.

in·con·sol·a·ble [ˌɪnkən'səʊləbl] *adj* □ untröstlich.

in·con·spic·u·ous [ˌɪnkən'spɪkjʊəs] *adj* □ unauffällig.

in·con·stant [ɪn'kɒnstənt] *adj* □ **1.** unbeständig. **2.** wankelmütig.

in·con·test·a·ble [ˌɪnkən'testəbl] *adj* □ unanfechtbar.

in·con·ti·nent [ɪn'kɒntɪnənt] *adj* □ **1.** (*bsd. sexuell*) unmäßig, zügellos. **2.** unaufhörlich.

in·con·tro·vert·i·ble [ˌɪnkɒntrə'vɜːtəbl] *adj* □ **1.** unbestreitbar, unstreitig. **2.** unanfechtbar.

in·con·ven·ience [ˌɪnkən'viːnjəns] **I** *s* **1.** Unbequemlichkeit *f*. **2.** Ungelegenheit *f*; Unannehmlichkeit *f*: *put to* ~ → 4. **II** *v/t* **3.** *j-m* lästig sein *od.* zur Last fallen. **4.** *j-m* Ungelegenheiten bereiten *od.* Umstände machen. ˌin·con'ven·ient *adj* □ **1.** unbequem (**to** für). **2.** ungelegen, lästig (**to** für): *at an* ~ *time* ungelegen.

in·con·vin·ci·ble [ˌɪnkən'vɪnsəbl] *adj* nicht zu überzeugen(d).

in·cor·po·rate [ɪn'kɔːpəreɪt] **I** *v/t* **1.** vereinigen, zs.-schließen. **2.** *Staatsgebiet* eingliedern; *Ort* eingemeinden. **3.** ✝, ⚖ als (*Am.* Aktien)Gesellschaft eintragen (lassen): *~d company Am.* Aktiengesellschaft *f*; *~d society* eingetragener Verein. **4.** in sich schließen, enthalten. **II** *v/i* **5.** sich zs.-schließen (**with** mit). **in·cor·po'ra·tion** *s* **1.** Vereinigung *f*, Zs.-schluß *m*. **2.** Eingliederung *f*; Eingemeindung *f*. **3.** ✝, ⚖ Eintragung *f* als (*Am.* Aktien)Gesellschaft: → **article** 4.

in·cor·rect [ˌɪnkə'rekt] *adj* □ inkorrekt: a) unrichtig, b) ungehörig.

in·cor·ri·gi·ble [ɪn'kɒrɪdʒəbl] *adj* □ unverbesserlich.

in·cor·rupt·i·ble [ˌɪnkə'rʌptəbl] *adj* □ **1.** unbestechlich. **2.** unverderblich (*Speisen*).

in·crease [ɪn'kriːs] **I** *v/i* zunehmen, (an)wachsen, (*Preise*) steigen, anziehen: ~ *in price* (*value*) teurer (wertvoller) werden; → **threefold** II, **fourfold** II,

etc. **II** *v/t* vergrößern, -mehren, erhöhen: → **threefold** II, **fourfold** II, *etc.* **III** *s* ['ɪnkriːs] Vergrößerung *f*, -mehrung *f*, Erhöhung *f*, Zunahme *f*, (An)Wachsen *n*: *be on the* ~ zunehmen; ~ *in population* Bevölkerungszunahme, -zuwachs *m*; ~ *in value* Wertsteigerung *f*, -zuwachs *m*. **in'creas·ing·ly** *adv* immer mehr: ~ *clear* immer klarer.

in·cred·i·ble [ɪn'kredəbl] *adj* □ **1.** unglaublich (*a.* F *unerhört etc*). **2.** unglaubwürdig.

in·cred·u·lous [ɪn'kredjʊləs] *adj* □ ungläubig: *be* ~ *of s.th.* e-r Sache skeptisch gegenüberstehen.

in·cre·ment ['ɪnkrɪmənt] *s* (✝ Gewinn)Zuwachs *m*, Zunahme *f*.

in·crim·i·nate [ɪn'krɪmɪneɪt] *v/t* belasten. **in'crim·i·nat·ing**, **in'crim·i·na·to·ry** [~nətərɪ] *adj* belastend, Belastungs...

in·crust [ɪn'krʌst] *v/i* **1.** sich ver- od. überkrusten. **2.** e-e Kruste bilden.

in·cu·ba·tor ['ɪnkjʊbeɪtə] *s* ✝ Brutkasten *m*.

in·cul·cate ['ɪnkʌlkeɪt] *v/t*: ~ *s.th. in*(*to*) (*od.* **on**) *s.o.*, ~ *s.o. with s.th.* j-m et. einschärfen.

in·cur [ɪn'kɜː] *v/t* sich et. zuziehen, auf sich laden: ~ *debts* Schulden machen; ~ *losses* Verluste erleiden.

in·cur·a·ble [ɪn'kjʊərəbl] *adj* □ ✝ unheilbar, *fig. a.* unverbesserlich.

in·cur·sion [ɪn'kɜːʃn] *s* **1.** (feindlicher) Einfall: *make an* ~ *on* einfallen in (*acc, dat*). **2.** Eindringen *n* (**into** in *acc*) (*a. fig.*).

in·debt·ed [ɪn'detɪd] *adj* **1.** verschuldet (**to** bei): *be* ~ *to s.o.* a. bei j-m Schulden haben, j-m Geld schulden. **2.** (zu Dank) verpflichtet (**to** *s.o.* j-m): *I am greatly* ~ *to you for* ich bin Ihnen zu großem Dank verpflichtet für, ich stehe tief in Ihrer Schuld wegen. **in'debt·ed·ness** *s* **1.** Verschuldung *f*. **2.** Dankesschuld *f* (**to** gegenüber).

in·de·cen·cy [ɪn'diːsnsɪ] *s* **1.** Unanständigkeit *f*, Anstößigkeit *f*, ⚖ Unzucht *f* (**with children** mit Kindern). **2.** Zote *f*. **3.** Unschicklichkeit *f*. **in'de·cent** *adj* □ **1.** unanständig, anstößig, ⚖ unzüchtig: → **assault** 3. **2.** unschicklich, ungehörig. **3.** ungebührlich: ~ *haste* unziemliche Hast.

in·de·ci·pher·a·ble [ˌɪndɪ'saɪfərəbl] *adj*

☐ nicht zu entziffern(d), unentzifferbar.

in·de·ci·sion [ˌɪndɪˈsɪʒn] s Unentschlossenheit f, Unschlüssigkeit f. **in·de·ci·sive** [ˌˈsaɪsɪv] adj ☐ **1.** nicht entscheidend; noch nicht entschieden, unentschieden. **2.** unentschlossen, unschlüssig. **3.** unbestimmt, ungewiß.

in·dec·o·rous [ɪnˈdekərəs] adj ☐ unschicklich, ungehörig.

in·deed [ɪnˈdiːd] I adv **1.** in der Tat, tatsächlich, wirklich: *thank you very much* ~ vielen herzlichen Dank. **2.** *fragend*: wirklich?, tatsächlich?: *I saw him yesterday. did you* ~? tatsächlich? **3.** allerdings, freilich; zwar. II int **4.** ach wirklich?, was Sie nicht sagen!

in·de·fat·i·ga·ble [ˌɪndɪˈfætɪgəbl] adj ☐ unermüdlich.

in·de·fen·si·ble [ˌɪndɪˈfensəbl] adj ☐ **1.** ✕ unhaltbar (a. fig.). **2.** nicht zu rechtfertigen(d), unentschuldbar.

in·de·fin·a·ble [ˌɪndɪˈfaɪnəbl] adj ☐ unbestimmbar, undefinierbar.

in·def·i·nite [ɪnˈdefɪnət] adj ☐ **1.** unbestimmt (a. ling.): ~ **article**; ~ **pronoun** Indefinitivpronomen n, unbestimmtes Fürwort. **2.** unbegrenzt, unbeschränkt: ~*ly* a. auf unbestimmte Zeit.

in·del·i·ble [ɪnˈdelǝbl] adj ☐ unauslöschlich (a. fig.): ~ **ink** Zeichen-, Kopiertinte f; ~ **pencil** Tintenstift m.

in·del·i·cate [ɪnˈdelɪkǝt] adj ☐ **1.** taktlos. **2.** unanständig, anstößig. **3.** unfein, grob.

in·dem·ni·fy [ɪnˈdemnɪfaɪ] v/t **1.** entschädigen, j-m Schadenersatz leisten (**for** für). **2.** absichern (**from, against** gegen). **in·dem·ni·ty** s **1.** Entschädigung f. **2.** Absicherung f.

in·dent I v/t [ɪnˈdent] **1.** (ein)kerben, auszacken. **2.** *Zeile* einrücken, -ziehen. II s ['ɪndent] **3.** Kerbe f, Auszackung f. **4.** Einrückung f, -zug m.

in·de·pend·ence [ˌɪndɪˈpendǝns] s Unabhängigkeit f (**from, of** von) (a. pol.), Selbständigkeit f: ♀ *Day Am.* Unabhängigkeitstag m (4. Juli). **,in·de·'pend·ent** adj ☐ **1.** unabhängig (**of** von) (a. pol.), selbständig. **2.** finanziell unabhängig: *be* ~ auf eigenen Füßen stehen. **3.** *parl.* partei-, fraktionslos.

,in-'depth adj tiefschürfend, gründlich.

in·de·scrib·a·ble [ˌɪndɪˈskraɪbǝbl] adj ☐ unbeschreiblich.

in·de·struct·i·ble [ˌɪndɪˈstrʌktǝbl] adj ☐ unzerstörbar.

in·de·ter·mi·na·ble [ˌɪndɪˈtɜːmɪnǝbl] adj ☐ unbestimmbar. **,in·de·'ter·mi·nate** [ˌˈnǝt] adj ☐ **1.** unbestimmt (a. A). **2.** ungewiß, unsicher.

in·dex [ˈɪndeks] I pl **'in·dex·es, in·di·ces** [ˈˈdɪsiːz] s **1.** Index m, (Stichwortetc)Verzeichnis n, (Sach)Register n. **2.** a. ~ **file** Kartei f. **3.** ✝ Index m. **4.** A Exponent m; Index m, Kennziffer f. **5.** fig. (**of, to**) (An)Zeichen n (von od. für od. gen); Hinweis m (auf acc); Gradmesser m (für od. gen): *be an* ~ **of** (od. **to**) a. et. aufzeigen, hinweisen od. -deuten auf (acc). II v/t **6.** in ein Verzeichnis aufführen. **7.** karteimäßig erfassen. ~ **card** s Karteikarte f. ~ **fin·ger** s Zeigefinger m. **,~-'linked** adj ✝ indexgebunden, Index...

In·di·an [ˈɪndjǝn] I adj **1.** indisch. **2.** indianisch, Indianer... II s **3.** Inder(in). **4.** Indianer(in). ~ **club** s *Sport*: Keule f. ~ **corn** s Mais m. ~ **file** I s: *in* ~ → II. II adv im Gänsemarsch. ~ **sum·mer** s Altweiber-, Nachsommer m.

In·di·a rub·ber [ˈɪndjǝ] s **1.** Kautschuk m, Gummi m, n. **2.** Radiergummi m.

in·di·cate [ˈɪndɪkeɪt] v/t **1.** deuten od. zeigen auf (acc). **2.** fig. hinweisen od. -deuten auf (acc); zu erkennen od. verstehen geben: *everything* ~*s that* alles deutet darauf hin, daß. **3.** *be* ~*d* angebracht od. angezeigt sein. **4.** ◉ anzeigen. **,in·di·'ca·tion** s **1.** (**of**) (An)Zeichen n (für); Hinweis m (auf acc); Andeutung f (gen): *there is every* ~ *that* alles deutet darauf hin, daß. **2.** ✚ Indikation f. **3.** ◉ Anzeige f. **in·dic·a·tive** [ɪnˈdɪkǝtɪv] I adj ☐ **1.** *be* ~ **of** → *indicate* **2.** **2.** ling. indikativisch: ~ **mood** → **3.** II s **3.** ling. Indikativ m. **in·di·ca·tor** [ˈˈkeɪtǝ] s **1.** Statistik etc: Indikator m. **2.** ◉ Anzeiger m. **3.** mot. Blinker m.

in·di·ces [ˈɪndɪsiːz] pl von **index**.

in·dict [ɪnˈdaɪt] v/t ✝✝ anklagen (**for** wegen). **in·dict·ment** s **1.** Anklage f. **2.** a. **bill of** ~ Anklageschrift f.

in·dif·fer·ence [ɪnˈdɪfrǝns] s **1.** Gleichgültigkeit f, Indifferenz f. **2.** Mittelmäßigkeit f. **in·dif·fer·ent** adj ☐ **1.** gleichgültig, indifferent (**to** gegen[über]): *he* *is* ~ *to it* es ist ihm gleichgültig. **2.** mittelmäßig.

in·dig·e·nous [ɪnˈdɪdʒɪnəs] *adj* □ **1.** einheimisch (*to* in *dat*) (a. ♀, *zo.*). **2.** *fig.* angeboren (*to* dat).

in·di·gest·i·ble [ˌɪndɪˈdʒestəbl] *adj* □ un-, schwerverdaulich (a. *fig.*). ˌin·diˈges·tion *s* Magenverstimmung *f*, verdorbener Magen.

in·dig·nant [ɪnˈdɪɡnənt] *adj* □ entrüstet, empört (*at s.th.*, *with s.o.* über *acc*). ˌin·digˈna·tion *s* Entrüstung *f*, Empörung *f*: *to my* ~ zu m-r Entrüstung.

in·di·rect [ˌɪndɪˈrekt] *adj* □ *allg.* indirekt: *by* ~ *means fig.* auf Umwegen; ~ *object ling.* Dativobjekt *n*; ~ *speech* (*bsd. Am. discourse*) *ling.* indirekte Rede.

in·dis·cern·i·ble [ˌɪndɪˈsɜːnəbl] *adj* □ nicht wahrnehmbar, unmerklich.

in·dis·creet [ˌɪndɪˈskriːt] *adj* □ **1.** unbesonnen, unbedacht. **2.** indiskret. **in·dis·cre·tion** [ˌ~ˈskreʃn] *s* **1.** Unbesonnenheit *f.* **2.** Indiskretion *f.*

in·dis·crim·i·nate [ˌɪndɪˈskrɪmɪnət] *adj* □ **1.** nicht wählerisch; urteils-, kritiklos. **2.** wahl-, unterschiedslos; ungeordnet.

in·dis·pen·sa·ble [ˌɪndɪˈspensəbl] *adj* □ unentbehrlich (a. Person), unerläßlich (*to* für).

in·dis·posed [ˌɪndɪˈspəʊzd] *adj* **1.** indisponiert, unpäßlich. **2.** abgeneigt (*for* dat; *to do* zu tun): *be* ~ *to do s.th. a.* et. nicht tun wollen. **in·dis·po·si·tion** [ˌɪndɪspəˈzɪʃn] *s* **1.** Unpäßlichkeit *f.* **2.** Abgeneigtheit *f* (*for* gegenüber; *to do* zu tun).

in·dis·pu·ta·ble [ˌɪndɪˈspjuːtəbl] *adj* □ unstrittig, unstreitig.

in·dis·so·lu·ble [ˌɪndɪˈsɒljʊbl] *adj* □ **1.** unlöslich. **2.** *fig.* unauflösbar.

in·dis·tinct [ˌɪndɪˈstɪŋkt] *adj* □ **1.** undeutlich; unscharf. **2.** verschwommen (*Erinnerung etc*).

in·dis·tin·guish·a·ble [ˌɪndɪˈstɪŋɡwɪʃəbl] *adj* □ nicht zu unterscheiden(d) (*from* von).

in·di·vid·u·al [ˌɪndɪˈvɪdʒʊəl] **I** *adj* (□ → *individually*) **1.** individuell, einzeln, Einzel...: ~ *case* Einzelfall *m*; ~ *traffic* Individualverkehr *m.* **2.** individuell, persönlich (*Stil etc*). **II** *s* **3.** Individuum *n* (a. *contp.*), Einzelne *m*, *f.* ˌin·di-

'vid·u·al·ism *s* Individualismus *m.* ˌin·diˈvid·u·a·list **I** *s* Individualist(in). **II** *adj* individualistisch. ˈin·diˌvid·u·alˈis·tic *adj* (*~ally*) individualistisch. ˈin·diˌvid·u·alˈi·ty [ˌ~ˈælətɪ] *s* Individualität *f.* ˌin·diˈvid·u·al·ize [ˌ~əlaɪz] *v/t* **1.** individualisieren. **2.** individuell gestalten. ˌin·diˈvid·u·al·ly *adv* **1.** individuell. **2.** einzeln, jede(r, -s) für sich.

in·di·vis·i·ble [ˌɪndɪˈvɪzəbl] *adj* □ unteilbar.

in·doc·tri·nate [ɪnˈdɒktrɪneɪt] *v/t* **1.** *contp. bsd. pol.* indoktrinieren. **2.** unterweisen, schulen (*in* in dat). **in·doc·tri·na·tion** *s* **1.** Indoktrination *f.* **2.** Unterweisung *f*, Schulung *f.*

in·do·lence [ˈɪndələns] *s* Trägheit *f.* ˈin·do·lent *adj* □ träg; träg machend (*Hitze etc*).

in·dom·i·ta·ble [ɪnˈdɒmɪtəbl] *adj* □ **1.** unbezähmbar, nicht unterzukriegen(d). **2.** unbeugsam.

in·door [ˈɪndɔː] *adj* Haus..., Zimmer..., (*Sport*) Hallen...: ~ *aerial* (*bsd. Am. antenna*) Zimmerantenne *f*; ~ *dress* Hauskleid *n*; ~ *plant* Zimmerpflanze *f*; ~ *shot phot.* Innenaufnahme *f*; ~ *swimming pool* Hallenbad *n.* ˈin·doors *adv* **1.** im Haus, drinnen. **2.** ins Haus (hinein). **3.** *Sport:* in der Halle.

in·du·bi·ta·ble [ɪnˈdjuːbɪtəbl] *adj* □ unzweifelhaft, *adv a.* zweifel-, fraglos.

in·duce [ɪnˈdjuːs] *v/t* **1.** j-n veranlassen, bewegen (*to do* zu tun). **2.** herbeiführen, verursachen, auslösen: ~ *labo(u)r* ♀ die Geburt einleiten. **3.** *⚡ etc* induzieren: *~d current* Induktionsstrom *m.* **in·duce·ment** *s* Veranlassung *f*; Anreiz *m*: ~ *to buy* Kaufanreiz.

in·duc·tion [ɪnˈdʌkʃn] *s* **1.** Herbeiführung *f*, Auslösung *f.* **2.** *⚡ etc* Induktion *f.*

in·dulge [ɪnˈdʌldʒ] **I** *v/t* **1.** nachsichtig sein gegen: ~ *o.s. in s.th.* → **4. 2.** Kinder verwöhnen. **3.** e-r Neigung *etc* nachgeben, frönen. **II** *v/i* **4.** ~ *in s.th.* sich et. gönnen *od.* leisten. **5.** (*in*) schwelgen (in dat), frönen (dat). **in·dul·gence** *s* **1.** Nachsicht *f.* **2.** Verwöhnung *f.* **3.** Schwelgen *n* (*in* in dat). **4.** Luxus *m*; Genuß *m.* **in·dul·gent** *adj* □ nachsichtig (*to* gegen).

in·dus·tri·al [ɪnˈdʌstrɪəl] *adj* □ **1.** industriell, Industrie...: ~ *action Br.* Arbeitskampf *m*; ~ *disease* Berufskrankheit *f*; ~ *espionage* Industrie-, Werkspionage *f*. **2.** industrialisiert, Industrie... **3.** Betriebs...: ~ *management* Betriebsführung *f*. **4.** industriell erzeugt, Industrie...: ~ *products pl* gewerbliche Erzeugnisse *pl*. **in·dus·tri·al·ist** *s* Industrielle *m*, *f*. **in·dus·tri·al·ize** *v/t* industrialisieren.

in·dus·tri·ous [ɪn'dʌstrɪəs] *adj* □ fleißig.

in·dus·try ['ɪndəstrɪ] *s* **1.** Industrie *f*; Industrie(zweig *m*) *f*: *steel* ~ Stahlindustrie. **2.** Fleiß *m*.

in·ed·i·ble [ɪn'edəbl] *adj* ungenießbar.

in·ef·fa·ble [ɪn'efəbl] *adj* □ unbeschreiblich, unsagbar.

in·ef·face·a·ble [ˌɪnɪ'feɪsəbl] *adj* □ **1.** unlöschbar. **2.** *fig.* unauslöschlich.

in·ef·fec·tive [ˌɪnɪ'fektɪv], **in·ef·fec·tu·al** [ˌ~'fektʃʊəl] *adj* □ **1.** unwirksam, wirkungslos. **2.** unfähig, untauglich.

in·ef·fi·cient [ˌɪnɪ'fɪʃnt] *adj* □ ineffizient: a) untüchtig, b) unrationell, unwirtschaftlich.

in·el·e·gant [ɪn'elɪɡənt] *adj* □ unelegant.

in·el·i·gi·ble [ɪn'elɪdʒəbl] *adj* □ **(for)** nicht in Frage kommend (für): a) ungeeignet, unannehmbar (für), b) nicht berechtigt *od.* befähigt (zu): *be* ~ *for* keinen Anspruch haben auf (*acc*), c) nicht teilnahmeberechtigt (an *dat*), (*Sport a.*) nicht start- *od.* spielberechtigt (für).

in·ept [ɪ'nept] *adj* □ **1.** unpassend. **2.** ungeschickt, unbeholfen; unfähig.

in·e·qual·i·ty [ˌɪnɪ'kwɒlətɪ] *s* Ungleichheit *f*, Verschiedenheit *f*.

in·eq·ui·ta·ble [ɪn'ekwɪtəbl] *adj* □ ungerecht. **in'eq·ui·ty** [~wətɪ] *s* Ungerechtigkeit *f*.

in·e·rad·i·ca·ble [ˌɪnɪ'rædɪkəbl] *adj* □ unausrottbar (*a. fig.*).

in·ert [ɪ'nɜːt] *adj* □ *phys.* träg (*a. fig.*). **in·er·tia** [ɪ'nɜːʃə] *s* Trägheit *f*.

in·es·cap·a·ble [ˌɪnɪ'skeɪpəbl] *adj* □ unvermeidlich: a) unabwendbar, b) unweigerlich.

in·es·sen·tial [ˌɪnɪ'senʃl] **I** *adj* unwesentlich. **II** *s et.* Unwesentliches, Nebensache *f*.

in·es·ti·ma·ble [ɪn'estɪməbl] *adj* □ unschätzbar.

in·ev·i·ta·ble [ɪn'evɪtəbl] **I** *adj* □ unvermeidlich. **II** *s das* Unvermeidliche.

in·ex·act [ˌɪnɪɡ'zækt] *adj* □ ungenau.

in·ex·cus·a·ble [ˌɪnɪk'skjuːzəbl] *adj* □ unverzeihlich, unentschuldbar.

in·ex·haust·i·ble [ˌɪnɪɡ'zɔːstəbl] *adj* □ unerschöpflich (*Thema etc*).

in·ex·o·ra·ble [ɪn'eksərəbl] *adj* □ unerbittlich.

in·ex·pe·di·ent [ˌɪnɪk'spiːdjənt] *adj* □ **1.** nicht ratsam, unangebracht. **2.** unzweckmäßig.

in·ex·pen·sive [ˌɪnɪk'spensɪv] *adj* □ billig, nicht teuer.

in·ex·pe·ri·ence [ˌɪnɪk'spɪərɪəns] *s* Unerfahrenheit *f*. **in·ex·pe·ri·enced** *adj* unerfahren.

in·ex·pert [ɪn'eksp3ːt] *adj* □ **1.** unerfahren (*at, in* in *dat*). **2.** unfachmännisch. **3.** ungeschickt, unbeholfen (*at, in* in *dat*).

in·ex·pli·ca·ble [ˌɪnɪk'splɪkəbl] *adj* □ unerklärlich.

in·ex·press·i·ble [ˌɪnɪk'spresəbl] *adj* □ unaussprechlich, unsäglich.

in·ex·tin·guish·able [ˌɪnɪk'stɪŋwɪʃəbl] *adj* □ **1.** unlöschbar. **2.** *fig.* unauslöschlich.

in·ex·tri·ca·ble [ɪn'ekstrɪkəbl] *adj* □ **1.** unentwirrbar (*a. fig.*). **2.** *fig.* ausweglos.

in·fal·li·bil·i·ty [ɪnˌfælə'bɪlətɪ] *s* Unfehlbarkeit *f* (*a. eccl.*). **in·fal·li·ble** *adj* unfehlbar. **in'fal·li·bly** *adv* **1.** unfehlbar. **2.** F todsicher, ganz bestimmt.

in·fa·mous ['ɪnfəməs] *adj* □ **1.** verrufen, berüchtigt (*for* wegen). **2.** infam, niederträchtig. **'in·fa·my** *s* **1.** Verrufenheit *f*. **2.** Infamie *f*: a) Niedertracht *f*, b) niederträchtige Handlung.

in·fan·cy ['ɪnfənsɪ] *s* frühe Kindheit, *bsd.* Säuglingsalter *n*: *be still in its* ~ *fig.* noch in den Anfängen *od.* Kinderschuhen stecken. **'in·fant I** *s* Säugling *m*; kleines Kind. **II** *adj* Säuglings...: ~ *mortality* Säuglingssterblichkeit *f*; ~ *prodigy* Wunderkind *n*.

in·fan·ti·cide [ɪn'fæntɪsaɪd] *s* **1.** Kind(es)tötung *f*. **2.** Kind(es)-, Kindermörder(in).

in·fan·tile ['ɪnfəntaɪl] *adj* **1.** infantil, kindisch. **2.** kindlich. **3.** Kinder..., Kindes...

in·fan·try ['ɪnfəntrɪ] *s* ✕ Infanterie *f*. **~·man** ['~mən] *s* (*irr man*) Infanterist *m*.

in·farct [ɪnˈfɑːkt] s ✝ Infarkt m.

in·fat·u·at·ed [ɪnˈfætjʊeɪtɪd] adj vernarrt (**with** in acc).

in·fect [ɪnˈfekt] v/t **1.** ✝ infizieren, anstecken (**with** mit; **by** durch): **become** ~**ed** sich anstecken. **2.** Luft verpesten; fig. Atmosphäre vergiften. **3.** fig. anstecken (**with** mit). **in'fec·tion** s **1.** ✝ Infektion f, Ansteckung f. **2.** Verpestung f; fig. Vergiftung f. **in'fec·tious** adj □ **1.** ✝ ansteckend (a. fig. Lachen etc), infektiös: ~ **disease** Infektionskrankheit f; **be** ~ fig. anstecken.

in·fe·lic·i·tous [ˌɪnfɪˈlɪsɪtəs] adj □ unglücklich (a. fig. Ausdruck etc).

in·fer [ɪnˈfɜː] v/t schließen, folgern (**from** aus). **in·fer·ence** [ˈɪnfərəns] s (Schluß-) Folgerung f, (Rück)Schluß m.

in·fe·ri·or [ɪnˈfɪərɪə] I adj **1.** (**to**) untergeordnet (dat), niedriger (als): **be** ~ **to s.o.** j-m untergeordnet sein; j-m unterlegen sein. **2.** weniger wert (als). **3.** minderwertig, mittelmäßig. **II** s **4.** Untergebene m, f. **in·fe·ri·or·i·ty** [ˌ~ˈɒrətɪ] s **1.** Unterlegenheit f. **2.** Minderwertigkeit f, Mittelmäßigkeit f: ~ **complex** psych. Minderwertigkeitskomplex m.

in·fer·nal [ɪnˈfɜːnl] adj □ **1.** höllisch, Höllen..., infernalisch. **2.** teuflisch. **in'fer·no** [ˌ~nəʊ] pl -nos s Inferno n, Hölle f.

in·fer·tile [ɪnˈfɜːtaɪl] adj unfruchtbar. **in·fer·til·i·ty** [ˌɪnfəˈtɪlətɪ] s Unfruchtbarkeit f.

in·fest [ɪnˈfest] v/t **1.** verseuchen, befallen (Parasiten etc): ~**ed with lice** verlaust. **2.** fig. überschwemmen, -laufen: **be** ~**ed with** wimmeln von.

in·fi·del [ˈɪnfɪdəl] eccl. I s Ungläubige m, f. **II** adj ungläubig. **in·fi·del·i·ty** [ˌ~ˈdelətɪ] s **1.** eccl. Ungläubigkeit f. **2.** (bsd. eheliche) Untreue f.

in·fight·ing [ˈɪnˌfaɪtɪŋ] s **1.** Boxen: Infight m, Nahkampf m. **2.** (partei- etc)interne Kämpfe pl od. Streitereien pl.

in·fil·trate [ˈɪnfɪltreɪt] I v/t **1.** einsickern in (acc). **2.** einschleusen, -schmuggeln (**into** in acc). **3.** pol. unterwandern. **II** v/i **4.** einsickern (**into** in acc). **in·fil'tra·tion** s **1.** Einsickern n. **2.** pol. Unterwanderung f.

in·fi·nite [ˈɪnfɪnɪt] adj □ **1.** unendlich (a. Å), grenzenlos (beide a. fig.). **2.** gewaltig, ungeheuer. **in·fi·ni·tes·i·mal** [ˌ~nɪ-

'tesɪml] adj □ **1.** unendlich klein. **2.** Å infinitesimal: ~ **calculus** Infinitesimalrechnung f. **in'fin·i·tive** [ˌ~ɒtɪv] s ling. Infinitiv m. **in'fin·i·ty** s **1.** Unendlichkeit f, Grenzenlosigkeit f (beide a. fig.). **2.** unendliche Menge od. Größe (a. Å): **an** ~ **of people** unendlich viele Leute.

in·firm [ɪnˈfɜːm] adj □ **1.** schwach, gebrechlich. **2.** fig. schwach. **in'fir·ma·ry** s **1.** Krankenhaus n. **2.** Krankenzimmer n, -stube f (in Internat etc). **in'fir·mi·ty** s Schwäche f, Gebrechlichkeit f; Gebrechen n.

in·flame [ɪnˈfleɪm] I v/t **1.** entzünden (a. ✝): **become** ~**d** → **3. 2.** fig. Gefühle etc entfachen, -flammen; j-n entflammen, erregen: ~**d with rage** wutentbrannt. **II** v/i **3.** sich entzünden (a. ✝). **4.** fig. entbrennen (**with** vor dat); in Wut geraten.

in·flam·ma·ble [ɪnˈflæməbl] adj □ **1.** brennbar, leichtentzündlich; feuergefährlich. **2.** fig. reizbar, leichterregbar. **in·flam·ma·tion** [ˌɪnfləˈmeɪʃn] s ✝ Entzündung f. **in·flam·ma·to·ry** [ɪnˈflæmətərɪ] adj **1.** ✝ entzündlich, Entzündungs... **2.** fig. aufrührerisch, Hetz...

in·flate [ɪnˈfleɪt] v/t aufblasen, Reifen etc aufpumpen. **in'flat·ed** adj **1.** aufgeblasen: ~ **with pride** fig. stolzgeschwellt. **2.** fig. schwülstig, bombastisch. **in'fla·tion** [ˌ~ʃn] s **1.** Aufblasen n, -pumpen n. **2.** ✝ Inflation f: ~ **creeping, gallop** I, **runaway** 3. **in'fla·tion·ar·y** adj ✝ Inflations..., inflationär.

in·flect [ɪnˈflekt] v/t **1.** beugen. **2.** ling. flektieren, beugen. **in'flec·tion** s **1.** Beugung f. **2.** ling. Flexion f, Beugung f.

in·flex·i·ble [ɪnˈfleksəbl] adj □ inflexibel: a) unbiegsam, b) fig. unbeweglich.

in·flex·ion bsd. Br. → **inflection.**

in·flict [ɪnˈflɪkt] v/t (**on**) **1.** Leid, Schaden etc zufügen (dat), Niederlage, Wunde etc beibringen (dat); Strafe auferlegen (dat), verhängen (über acc). **2.** aufbürden (dat): ~ **o.s. on s.o.** sich j-m aufdrängen. **in'flic·tion** s **1.** Zufügung f; Auferlegung f. **2.** Plage f, Last f.

'in·flight adj ✈ **1.** Bord...: ~ **fare** Bordverpflegung f. **2.** während des Flugs.

in·flow [ˈɪnfləʊ] → **influx.**

in·flu·ence [ˈɪnfluəns] I s **1.** Einfluß m (**on, over** auf acc; **with** bei): **be under s.o.'s** ~ unter j-s Einfluß stehen; **under the** ~

of drink (*od. alcohol*) unter Alkoholeinfluß; **under the ~** F alkoholisiert. **II** *v/t* beeinflussen. **in·flu·en·tial** [ˌ~'enʃl] *adj* □ einflußreich.

in·flu·en·za [ˌɪnflʊ'enzə] *s* 𝔐 Grippe *f*.

in·flux ['ɪnflʌks] *s* Zustrom *m* (*a. fig.*), († *Kapital- etc*)Zufluß *m*: **~ of visitors** Besucherstrom *m*.

in·fo ['ɪnfəʊ] F → *information*.

in·form [ɪn'fɔ:m] **I** *v/t* (*of, about*) benachrichtigen, unterrichten (von), informieren (über *acc*): **keep s.o. ~ed** j-n auf dem laufenden halten; **~ s.o. that** j-n davon in Kenntnis setzen, daß. **II** *v/i*: **~ against** (*od. on*) **s.o.** j-n anzeigen; *b.s.* j-n denunzieren.

in·for·mal [ɪn'fɔ:ml] *adj* □ **1.** formlos, 𝔱𝔱 *a.* formfrei. **2.** zwanglos, ungezwungen. **3.** inoffiziell.

in·form·ant [ɪn'fɔ:mənt] *s* **1.** Informant *m*, Gewährsmann *m*. **2.** → *informer*.

in·for·mat·ics [ɪnfə'mætɪks] *s pl* (*sg konstruiert*) Informatik *f*.

in·for·ma·tion [ˌɪnfə'meɪʃn] *s* **1.** Benachrichtigung *f*, Unterrichtung *f*; Nachricht *f*, Mitteilung *f*, Bescheid *m*. **2.** Auskünfte *pl*, Auskunft *f*, Information *f*: **for your ~** zu Ihrer Information *od.* Kenntnisnahme. **3.** *coll.* Nachrichten *pl*, Informationen *pl*: **bit** (*od. piece*) **of ~** Nachricht *f*, Information *f*. **4.** *coll.* Erkundigungen *pl*: **gather ~** Erkundigungen einziehen. **in·form·a·tive** [ɪn'fɔ:mətɪv] *adj* □ informativ, aufschlußreich. **in'form·er** *s* **1.** Denunziant(in). **2.** Spitzel *m*.

in·fra|dig [ˌɪnfrə'dɪg] *adj*: **it is ~ for him** F es ist unter s-r Würde (**to do** zu tun). **'~red** *adj phys.* infrarot. **'~struc·ture** *s* Infrastruktur *f*.

in·fre·quent [ɪn'fri:kwənt] *adj* □ **1.** selten. **2.** spärlich.

in·fringe [ɪn'frɪndʒ] *v/t u. v/i* (**~ on**) Gesetz, Vertrag *etc* brechen, verletzen, verstoßen gegen. **in'fringe·ment** *s* Verletzung *f*; Verstoß *m* (*of* gegen).

in·fu·ri·ate [ɪn'fjʊərɪeɪt] *v/t* wütend machen.

in·fuse [ɪn'fju:z] *v/t* **1.** *Tee etc* aufgießen; ziehen lassen. **2.** *fig. Mut etc* einflößen (*into* dat); *j-n* erfüllen (**with** mit). **in'fu·sion** [-ʒn] *s* **1.** 𝔐 Infusion *f*. **2.** Aufguß *m*. **3.** *fig.* Einflößung *f*.

in·gen·ious [ɪn'dʒi:njəs] *adj* □ genial: a) erfinderisch, einfallsreich, b) sinnreich, raffiniert. **in·ge·nu·i·ty** [ˌɪndʒɪ'nju:ətɪ] *s* Genialität *f*, Einfallsreichtum *m*.

in·gen·u·ous [ɪn'dʒenjʊəs] *adj* □ **1.** offen(herzig), aufrichtig. **2.** naiv, kindlich-unbefangen.

in·gle·nook ['ɪŋglnʊk] *s Br.* Kaminecke *f*.

in·glo·ri·ous [ɪn'glɔ:rɪəs] *adj* □ unrühmlich, schmählich.

in·go·ing ['ɪn,gəʊɪŋ] *adj* **1.** nachfolgend, neu (*Mieter etc*). **2. ~ mail** Posteingang *m*.

in·got ['ɪŋgət] *s* (*Gold- etc*)Barren *m*: **~ of gold.**

in·gra·ti·ate [ɪn'greɪʃɪeɪt] *v/t*: **~ o.s. with s.o.** sich bei j-m einschmeicheln.

in·grat·i·tude [ɪn'grætɪtju:d] *s* Undank (-barkeit *f*) *m*.

in·gre·di·ent [ɪn'gri:djənt] *s* **1.** Bestandteil *m* (*a. fig.*). **2.** *gastr.* Zutat *f*.

in·hab·it [ɪn'hæbɪt] *v/t* bewohnen. **in-'hab·it·a·ble** *adj* bewohnbar. **in'hab·it·ant** *s* Einwohner(in) (*e-s Orts, Landes*), Bewohner(in) (*bsd. e-s Hauses*).

in·hale [ɪn'heɪl] **I** *v/t* **1.** einatmen, 𝔐 *a.* inhalieren. **II** *v/i* **2.** einatmen. **3.** inhalieren, Lungenzüge machen.

in·har·mo·ni·ous [ˌɪnhɑ:'məʊnjəs] *adj* □ unharmonisch.

in·here [ɪn'hɪə] *v/i* innewohnen (**in** dat). **in'her·ent** *adj* innewohnend.

in·her·it [ɪn'herɪt] *v/t* erben (**from** von) (*a. fig.*). **in'her·i·tance** *s* Erbe *n* (*a. fig.*).

in·hib·it [ɪn'hɪbɪt] *v/t* **1.** hemmen (*a. psych.*), (ver)hindern. **2.** *j-n* hindern (**from** an *dat*): **~ s.o. from doing s.th.** j-n daran hindern, et. zu tun. **in·hi·bi·tion** [ˌɪnhɪ'bɪʃn] *s psych.* Hemmung *f*.

in·hos·pi·ta·ble [ˌɪnhɒ'spɪtəbl] *adj* □ wenig gastfreundlich; ungastlich.

in·hu·man [ɪn'hju:mən] *adj* □ inhuman, unmenschlich. **in·hu·man·i·ty** [ˌ~'mænətɪ] *s* Unmenschlichkeit *f*.

in·im·i·cal [ɪ'nɪmɪkl] *adj* □ **1.** feindselig (**to** gegen). **2.** (**to**) nachteilig (für), abträglich (*dat*).

in·im·i·ta·ble [ɪ'nɪmɪtəbl] *adj* □ unnachahmlich.

in·iq·ui·tous [ɪ'nɪkwɪtəs] *adj* □ **1.** ungerecht. **2.** schändlich. **in'iq·ui·ty** *s* **1.** Ungerechtigkeit f. **2.** Schändlichkeit f; Schandtat f.

in·i·tial [ɪˈnɪʃl] **I** adj anfänglich, Anfangs... **II** s Initiale f, (großer) Anfangsbuchstabe. **III** v/t pret u. pp **-tialed**, bsd. Br. **-tialled** abzeichnen, pol. paraphieren. **in·i·tial·ly** [~ʃəlɪ] adv anfänglich, am Anfang. **in·i·ti·ate I** v/t [ɪˈnɪʃɪeɪt] **1.** einleiten, ins Leben rufen. **2.** j-n einführen (*into* in acc): a) einweihen, b) aufnehmen, c) einarbeiten. **II** s [~ʃɪət] **3.** Eingeweihte m, f. **in·i·ti·a·tion** s **1.** Einleitung f. **2.** Einführung f: a) Einweihung f, b) Aufnahme f, c) Einarbeitung f. **in·i·ti·a·tive** [~ətɪv] s Initiative f: *take the* ~ die Initiative ergreifen; *on one's own* ~ aus eigenem Antrieb. **in·i·ti·a·tor** [~eɪtə] s Initiator m, Urheber m.

in·ject [ɪnˈdʒekt] v/t ✱ injizieren, einspritzen (a. ⊙): ~ *s.th. into s.o.*, ~ *s.o. with s.th.* et. spritzen; fig. j-m et. einflößen. **in·jec·tion** s ✱ Injektion f: a) Einspritzung f (a. ⊙), Spritze f, b) eingespritztes Medikament.

in·ju·di·cious [ˌɪndʒuːˈdɪʃəs] adj ☐ unklug, unvernünftig.

in·junc·tion [ɪnˈdʒʌŋkʃn] s **1.** ⚖ gerichtliches Verbot: (*interim*) ~ einstweilige Verfügung. **2.** ausdrücklicher Befehl.

in·jure [ˈɪndʒə] v/t **1.** verletzen: ~ *one's leg* sich am Bein verletzen. **2.** fig. kränken, verletzen. **3.** fig. schaden (dat), schädigen. **in·ju·ri·ous** [ɪnˈdʒʊərɪəs] adj ☐ (*to*) schädlich (für), abträglich (dat): *be* ~ (*to*) a. schaden (dat). **in·ju·ry** [ˈɪndʒərɪ] s **1.** ✱ Verletzung f (*to* an dat): ~ *to the head* Kopfverletzung f, -wunde f. **2.** fig. Kränkung f, Verletzung f (*to* gen).

in·jus·tice [ɪnˈdʒʌstɪs] s Unrecht n, Ungerechtigkeit f: *do s.o. an* ~ j-m unrecht tun; *suffer an* ~ ungerecht behandelt werden.

ink [ɪŋk] s **1.** Tinte f. **2.** Tusche f. **3.** typ. (Drucker)Schwärze f.

ink·ling [ˈɪŋklɪŋ] s **1.** Andeutung f, Wink m. **2.** dunkle Ahnung: *give s.o. an* ~ *of* (*od. as to*) j-m e-e ungefähre Vorstellung geben von.

'ink·pad s Stempelkissen n. ~ **stain** s Tintenklecks m, -fleck m.

ink·y [ˈɪŋkɪ] adj **1.** tinten-, pechschwarz. **2.** tintig, voller Tinte.

in·land I adj [ˈɪnlənd] **1.** binnenländisch, Binnen... **2.** inländisch, einheimisch: 2 *Revenue* Br. F Finanzamt n. **II** adv [ɪnˈlænd] **3.** landeinwärts.

in·laws [ˈɪnlɔːz] s pl angeheiratete Verwandte pl, engS. Schwiegereltern pl.

in·lay I v/t (irr *lay*) [ˌɪnˈleɪ] **1.** einlegen (*with* mit): *inlaid work* → 3. **2.** parkettieren: *inlaid floor* Parkett(fußboden m) n. **II** s [ˈɪnleɪ] **3.** Einlegearbeit f.

in·let [ˈɪnlet] s **1.** Eingang m. Einlaß m (a. ⊙). **3.** schmale Bucht; Meeresarm m.

in·mate [ˈɪnmeɪt] s Insasse m, Insassin f (*e-r Anstalt, e-s Gefängnisses etc*).

in·most [ˈɪnməʊst] adj innerst, fig. a. tiefst, geheimst.

inn [ɪn] s **1.** Gasthaus n, -hof m. **2.** Wirtshaus n.

in·nards [ˈɪnədz] s pl F Eingeweide pl: *his* ~ *were rumbling* es rumorte in s-m Bauch.

in·nate [ˌɪˈneɪt] adj angeboren (*in* dat).

in·ner [ˈɪnə] adj **1.** inner, Innen...: ~ *door* Innentür f; ~ *life* Innen-, Seelenleben n; ~ *man* Seele f; Geist m; humor. Magen m. **2.** fig. tiefer, verborgen (*Sinn etc*). **in·ner·most** [ˈ~məʊst] → **inmost**.

'inn·keep·er s (Gast)Wirt(in).

in·no·cence [ˈɪnəsəns] s Unschuld f: a) Schuldlosigkeit f, b) Unberührtheit f: *lose one's* ~ s-e Unschuld verlieren, c) Harmlosigkeit f, d) Arglosigkeit f, Naivität f. **in·no·cent** [~snt] adj ☐ unschuldig: a) schuldlos (*of* an dat), b) sittlich rein, (*Mädchen a.*) unberührt: (*as*) ~ *as a newborn babe* so unschuldig wie ein neugeborenes Kind, c) harmlos: ~ *air* Unschuldsmiene f, d) arglos, naiv.

in·noc·u·ous [ɪˈnɒkjʊəs] adj ☐ unschädlich, harmlos.

in·no·vate [ˈɪnəʊveɪt] v/i Neuerungen einführen (*on, in* bei, in dat). **in·no·va·tion** s Neuerung f.

in·nu·en·do [ˌɪnjuːˈendəʊ] pl **-do(e)s** s (*about, at*) versteckte Andeutung (über acc) od. Anspielung (auf acc).

in·nu·mer·a·ble [ɪˈnjuːmərəbl] adj ☐ unzählig, zahllos.

in·oc·u·late [ɪˈnɒkjʊleɪt] v/t ✱ impfen (*against* gegen): ~ *s.o. with s.th.* fig. j-m et. einimpfen. **in·oc·u·la·tion** s ✱ Impfung f.

in·o·dor·ous [ɪnˈəʊdərəs] adj geruchlos.

in·of·fen·sive [ˌɪnəˈfensɪv] *adj* □ harmlos.

in·op·er·a·ble [ɪnˈɒpərəbl] *adj* **1.** undurchführbar. **2.** ✗ inoperabel.

in·op·er·a·tive [ɪnˈɒpərətɪv] *adj* unwirksam: a) wirkungslos, b) ✗✗ ungültig.

in·op·por·tune [ɪnˈɒpətjuːn] *adj* □ ungünstig, unpassend.

in·or·di·nate [ɪnˈɔːdɪnət] *adj* □ un-, übermäßig, *(Forderung etc a.)* überzogen.

in·or·gan·ic [ˌɪnɔːˈɡænɪk] *adj* (**~ally**) **1.** unorganisch. **2.** 🜚 anorganisch.

in·pa·tient [ˈɪnˌpeɪʃnt] *s* stationärer Patient: **~ treatment** stationäre Behandlung.

in·put [ˈɪnpʊt] *s* Input *m*: a) ✝ eingesetzte Produktionsmittel *pl*, b) ⚡ Eingangsleistung *f*, c) 🖥 eingespeiste Menge, d) *Computer:* (Daten)Eingabe *f*.

in·quest [ˈɪnkwest] *s* ✗✗ gerichtliche Untersuchung: → **coroner.**

in·qui·e·tude [ɪnˈkwaɪətjuːd] *s* Unruhe *f*, Besorgnis *f*.

in·quire [ɪnˈkwaɪə] **I** *v/t* **1. ~ s.th. (of s.o.)** sich (bei j-m) nach et. erkundigen. **II** *v/i* **2.** (nach)fragen, sich erkundigen (*of s.o.* bei j-m; *after, for* nach; *about* wegen): **~ within** Näheres im Hause (zu erfragen). **3. ~ into** et. untersuchen, prüfen. **in·quir·y** *s* **1.** Erkundigung *f*, (An-, Nach)Frage *f*: **on ~** auf An- *od.* Nachfrage; **make inquiries** Erkundigungen einziehen (**of s.o.** bei j-m; **about, after** über *acc*, wegen). **2.** Untersuchung *f*, Prüfung *f* (**of, into** gen), Nachforschung *f*, Ermittlung *f*, Recherche *f*. **3.** *pl* 🕾 *etc* Auskunft *f* (*Büro, Schalter*).

in·qui·si·tion [ˌɪnkwɪˈzɪʃn] *s* **1.** (*a.* gerichtliche *od.* amtliche) Untersuchung (**into** gen). **2.** ♀ *eccl. hist.* Inquisition *f*. **in·quis·i·tive** [ɪnˈkwɪzətɪv] *adj* □ **1.** wißbegierig. **2.** neugierig.

in·quo·rate [ɪnˈkwɔːrət] *adj* beschlußunfähig.

in·road [ˈɪnrəʊd] *s bsd. pl* **1.** *bsd.* ✗ Einfall *m* (**in, into, on** *in acc*). **2.** *fig.* (**in, into, on**) Eingriff *m* (**in** *acc*), Übergriff *m* (auf *acc*). **3.** *a.* **heavy ~** *fig.* übermäßige Inanspruchnahme (**in, into, on** *gen*): **make ~s on s.o.'s free time** j-s Freizeit stark einschränken; **make ~s**

into s.o.'s savings ein großes Loch in j-s Ersparnisse reißen.

in·rush [ˈɪnrʌʃ] *s* **1.** (Her)Einströmen *n*. **2.** *fig.* Flut *f*, (Zu)Strom *m*: **~ of tourists** Touristenstrom.

in·sa·lu·bri·ous [ˌɪnsəˈluːbrɪəs] *adj* □ ungesund.

in·sane [ɪnˈseɪn] *adj* □ wahn-, irrsinnig, ✗ *a.* geisteskrank.

in·san·i·tar·y [ɪnˈsænɪtərɪ] *adj* unhygienisch, gesundheitsschädlich.

in·san·i·ty [ɪnˈsænətɪ] *s* Wahn-, Irrsinn *m*, ✗ *a.* Geisteskrankheit *f*.

in·sa·ti·a·ble [ɪnˈseɪʃəbl] *adj* □ unersättlich (*Person*), unstillbar (*Durst etc*) (*beide a. fig.*).

in·scrip·tion [ɪnˈskrɪpʃn] *s* **1.** In- *od.* Aufschrift *f*. **2.** (persönliche) Widmung.

in·scru·ta·ble [ɪnˈskruːtəbl] *adj* □ unerforschlich, unergründlich.

in·sect [ˈɪnsekt] *s zo.* Insekt *n*: **~ spray** Insektenspray *n*. **in·sec·ti·cide** [ˌɪntɪsaɪd] *s* Insektizid *n*, Insektenvernichtungsmittel *n*.

in·se·cure [ˌɪnsɪˈkjʊə] *adj* □ **1.** ungesichert, nicht fest. **2.** *fig.* unsicher. **in·se·cu·ri·ty** [~rətɪ] *s* Unsicherheit *f*.

in·sem·i·nate [ɪnˈsemɪneɪt] *v/t biol.* befruchten, *zo. a.* besamen. **in·sem·i·'na·tion** *s* Befruchtung *f*, Besamung *f*.

in·sen·si·ble [ɪnˈsensəbl] *adj* □ **1.** unempfindlich (**to** gegen): **~ to pain** schmerzunempfindlich. **2.** bewußtlos. **3.** *fig.* (**of, to**) unempfänglich (für), gleichgültig (gegen). **4.** unmerklich. **in·sen·si·tive** [ɪnˈsensətɪv] *adj* □ **1.** *a. phys.*, 🜚 unempfindlich (**to** gegen): **~ to light** lichtunempfindlich. **2.** → **insensible** 1, 3.

in·sep·a·ra·ble [ɪnˈsepərəbl] *adj* □ **1.** untrennbar (*a. ling.*). **2.** unzertrennlich (**from** von).

in·sert I *v/t* **1.** einfügen, -setzen, -schieben, *Instrument etc* einführen, *Schlüssel etc* (hinein)stecken, *Münze etc* einwerfen (**in, into** *in acc*). **2. ~ an advertisement in(to) a newspaper** e-e Anzeige in e-e Zeitung setzen, in e-r Zeitung inserieren. **II** *s* [ˈɪnsɜːt] **1.** *od.* **insertion** 2-4. **in·ser·tion** *s* **1.** Einsetzen *n*, Einführung *f*, Einwurf *m*. **2.** Einsatz(stück *n*) *m*. **3.** Anzeige *f*, Inserat *n*. **4.** (Zeitungs)Beilage *f*, (Buch)Einlage *f*.

in·shore [ˌɪnˈʃɔː] *adj* an *od.* nahe der

Küste: ~ *fishing* Küstenfischerei *f*.

in·side I *s* [ˌɪnˈsaɪd] **1.** Innenseite *f*; *das* Innere: *on the* ~ innen; *from the* ~ von innen; *turn* ~ *out* umdrehen, umstülpen; *fig.* (völlig) umkrempeln; *know* ~ *out* in- u. auswendig kennen. **II** *adj* [ˈɪnsaɪd] **2.** inner, Innen...: ~ *lane* (*Sport*) Innenbahn *f*; *mot. Br.* äußere Fahrspur; *overtake s.o. on the* ~ *lane* (*in GB etc*) j-n links überholen, (*in Deutschland etc*) j-n rechts überholen. **3.** ~ *information* (F *stuff*) Insiderinformationen *pl*, interne *od.* vertrauliche Informationen *pl*. **III** *adv* [ˌɪnˈsaɪd] **4.** im Inner(e)n, (dr)innen. **5.** hinein, herein. **6.** ~ *of* a) *zeitlich:* innerhalb (*gen*), b) *Am.* → 7. **IV** *prp* [ˌɪnˈsaɪd] **7.** innerhalb, im Inner(e)n (*gen*): ~ *the house* im Hause. **ˌin·ˈsid·er** *s* Insider(in), Eingeweihte *m*, *f*.

in·sid·i·ous [ɪnˈsɪdɪəs] *adj* □ hinterhältig, heimtückisch.

in·sight [ˈɪnsaɪt] *s* **1.** (*into*) Einblick *m* (*in acc*); Verständnis *n* (für). **2.** Einsicht *f*.

in·sig·ni·a [ɪnˈsɪgnɪə] *pl* -**a**(**s**) *s* **1.** Insignie *f*, Amts-, Ehrenzeichen *n*. **2.** ✕ Abzeichen *n*.

in·sig·nif·i·cant [ˌɪnsɪgˈnɪfɪkənt] *adj* □ **1.** bedeutungslos. **2.** geringfügig, unerheblich (*Betrag*). **3.** unbedeutend (*Person*).

in·sin·cere [ˌɪnsɪnˈsɪə] *adj* □ unaufrichtig, falsch.

in·sin·u·ate [ɪnˈsɪnjʊeɪt] *v/t* andeuten, anspielen auf (*acc*): *are you insinuating that ...?* wollen Sie damit sagen, daß ...? **in,sin·u'a·tion** *s* (*about*) Anspielung *f* (auf *acc*), Andeutung *f* (über *acc*): *by* ~ andeutungsweise.

in·sip·id [ɪnˈsɪpɪd] *adj* □ fad (*a. fig.*).

in·sist [ɪnˈsɪst] **I** *v/i* **1.** darauf bestehen: ~ *on* bestehen auf (*dat*), verlangen (*acc*); ~ *on doing sth.* darauf bestehen, et. zu tun; et. unbedingt tun wollen. **2.** (*on*) beharren (auf *dat*), bleiben bei. **3.** (*on*) Gewicht legen (auf *acc*), (nachdrücklich) betonen (*acc*). **II** *v/t* **4.** darauf bestehen (*that* daß). **5.** darauf beharren, dabei bleiben (*that* daß). **in'sist·ence** *s* **1.** Bestehen *n*, Beharren *n* (*on* auf *dat*). **2.** Betonung *f* (*on gen*): *with great* ~ mit großem Nachdruck. **3.** Beharrlichkeit *f*, Hartnäckigkeit *f*. **in'sist·ent** *adj* □ **1.** beharrlich, hartnäckig: *be* ~ (*on*) →

insist I; *be* ~ *that* darauf bestehen, daß. **2.** eindringlich, nachdrücklich.

ˌin·so'far *adv:* ~ *as* soweit.

in·sole [ˈɪnsəʊl] *s* **1.** Brandsohle *f*. **2.** Einlegesohle *f*.

in·so·lence [ˈɪnsələns] *s* Unverschämtheit *f*, Frechheit *f*. **ˈin·so·lent** *adj* □ unverschämt, frech.

in·sol·u·ble [ɪnˈsɒljʊbl] *adj* □ **1.** ☈ un(auf)löslich. **2.** *fig.* unlösbar.

in·sol·ven·cy [ɪnˈsɒlvənsɪ] *s* ✝ Zahlungsunfähigkeit *f*, Insolvenz *f*. **in'sol·vent** *adj* zahlungsunfähig, insolvent.

in·som·ni·a [ɪnˈsɒmnɪə] *s* Schlaflosigkeit *f*.

ˌin·so'much *adv:* ~ *that* dermaßen *od.* so sehr, daß.

in·spect [ɪnˈspekt] *v/t* **1.** untersuchen, prüfen (*for* auf *acc*). **2.** besichtigen, inspizieren. **in'spec·tion** *s* **1.** Untersuchung *f*, Prüfung *f*: *on* ~ bei näherer Prüfung; *for* ~ ✝ zur Ansicht. **2.** Besichtigung *f*, Inspektion *f*. **in'spec·tor** *s* **1.** Inspektor *m*, Aufsichtsbeamte *m*, Kontrolleur *m* (*a.* ⚙ *etc*). **2.** *police* ~ *Br.* Polizeiinspektor *m*, -kommissar *m*.

in·spi·ra·tion [ˌɪnspəˈreɪʃn] *s* Inspiration *f*: a) (*eccl.* göttliche) Eingebung, (plötzlicher) Einfall *m*, b) Anregung *f*: *be s.o.'s* ~, *be an* ~ *to* (*od.* for) *s.o.* j-n inspirieren. **in·spire** [ɪnˈspaɪə] *v/t* **1.** inspirieren, anregen (*to* zu; *to do* zu tun). **2.** *Gefühl etc* erwecken, auslösen (*in* in *dat*). **3.** erfüllen (*with* mit).

in·sta·bil·i·ty [ˌɪnstəˈbɪlətɪ] *s* **1.** mangelnde Festigkeit *od.* Stabilität. **2.** *bsd.* ✕, ⚙ Instabilität *f*. **3.** *fig.* Unbeständigkeit *f*. **4.** (*emotional*) ~ *fig.* Labilität *f*.

in·stall [ɪnˈstɔːl] *v/t* **1.** ⚙ installieren: a) *Bad etc* einbauen, b) *Leitung etc* legen, c) *Telefon etc* anschließen. **2.** j-n einsetzen (*interim president* als Interimspräsidenten). **in·stal·la·tion** [ˌɪnstəˈleɪʃn] *s* **1.** ⚙ Installation *f*, Einbau *m*, Anschluß *m*. **2.** ⚙ Anlage *f*, Einrichtung *f*. **3.** (Amts)Einsetzung *f*.

in·stall·ment, *bsd. Br.* **in·stal·ment** [ɪnˈstɔːlmənt] *s* **1.** ✝ Rate *f*: *by* (*od.* in) ~**s** in Raten, ratenweise; *first* ~ Anzahlung *f* (*toward*[s] auf *acc*); *monthly* ~ Monatsrate; *buy on* (*od.* by) *the* ~ *plan Am.* auf Raten kaufen. **2.** (Teil)Lieferung *f* (*e-s Buchs etc*). **3.** a) Fortsetzung *f*: *novel by* (*od.* in) ~**s** Fortsetzungsroman *m*, b) *Rundfunk, TV:* Folge *f*.

in·stance ['ɪnstəns] *s* **1.** (*einzelner*) Fall: *in this* ~ in diesem (besonderen) Fall. **2.** Beispiel *n: for* ~ zum Beispiel; *as an* ~ *of* als Beispiel für. **3.** *at s.o.'s* ~ auf j-s Veranlassung (hin), auf j-s Betreiben *od.* Drängen. **4.** 🗲 Instanz *f: in the last* ~ in letzter Instanz, *fig.* letztlich; *in the first* ~ *fig.* in erster Linie; zuerst.

in·stant ['ɪnstənt] **I** *s* **1.** Moment *n*, Augenblick *m: in an* ~, *on the* ~ sofort, augenblicklich; *at this* ~ in diesem Augenblick. **II** *adj* (□ → *instantly*) **2.** sofortig, augenblicklich: ~ *camera* phot. Sofortbildkamera *f*; ~ *coffee* Pulverkaffee *m*; ~ *meal* Fertig-, Schnellgericht *n*. **3.** *the 10th* ~ ✝ der 10. dieses Monats. **4.** dringend: *be in* ~ *need of et.* dringend brauchen.

in·stan·ta·ne·ous [͵ɪnstən'teɪnjəs] *adj* sofortig, augenblicklich: *his death was* ~ er war auf der Stelle tot. **͵in·stan'ta·ne·ous·ly** *adv* sofort, auf der Stelle.

in·stant·ly ['ɪnstəntlɪ] *adv* sofort, augenblicklich.

in·stead [ɪn'sted] *adv* **1.** ~ *of* an Stelle von (*od. gen*), (an)statt (*gen*): ~ *of me* an m-r Stelle; ~ *of going* (an)statt zu gehen. **2.** statt dessen, dafür.

in·step ['ɪnstep] *s anat.* Rist *m*, Spann *m*.

in·sti·gate ['ɪnstɪgeɪt] *v/t* **1.** j-n aufhetzen, *a.* 🗲 anstiften (*to* zu; *to do* zu tun). **2.** *et. Böses* anstiften, anzetteln; *et.* in Gang setzen, in die Wege leiten. **͵in·sti'ga·tion** *s* **1.** Aufhetzung *f*, Anstiftung *f*. **2.** *at s.o.'s* ~ → *instance* 3.

in·stil(l) [ɪn'stɪl] *v/t* **1.** einträufeln (*into dat*). **2.** *fig.* einflößen (*into dat*).

in·stinct ['ɪnstɪŋkt] *s* Instinkt *m: by* (*od. from*) ~ instinktiv; ~ *for self-preservation* Selbsterhaltungstrieb *m*. **in'stinc·tive** *adj* □ instinktiv.

in·sti·tute ['ɪnstɪtjuːt] **I** *v/t* **1.** gründen, ins Leben rufen. **2.** in Gang setzen, in die Wege leiten. **II** *s* **3.** Institut *n*. **͵in·sti·'tu·tion** *s* **1.** Institution *f*, Einrichtung *f* (*beide a. sociol.*); Institut *n*; Anstalt *f*. **2.** Sitte *f*, Brauch *m*. **3.** Gründung *f*. **͵in·sti'tu·tion·al** [~ʃənl] *adj* **1.** Instituts...; Anstalts... **2.** *bsd. contp.* Einheits... **͵in·sti'tu·tion·al·ize** *v/t* **1.** institutionalisieren. **2.** in e-e Anstalt einweisen.

in·struct [ɪn'strʌkt] *v/t* **1.** (*in in dat*) un-

terrichten; ausbilden, schulen. **2.** informieren, unterrichten. **3.** instruieren, anweisen, beauftragen (*to do* zu tun). **in'struc·tion** *s* **1.** Unterricht *m*; Ausbildung *f*, Schulung *f*. **2.** Informierung *f*, Unterrichtung *f*. **3.** Instruktion *f*, Anweisung *f*, (*Computer*) Befehl *m: according to* ~*s* auftragsgemäß; vorschriftsmäßig; ~*s pl for use* Gebrauchsanweisung, -anleitung *f*. **in'struc·tive** *adj* □ instruktiv, lehrreich. **in'struc·tor** *s* Lehrer *m*; Ausbilder *m*. **in'struc·tress** *s* Lehrerin *f*.

in·stru·ment ['ɪnstrʊmənt] **I** *s* **1.** ⚙ Instrument *n* (*a.* ♪): a) Werkzeug *n*: ~ *of torture* Foltergerät *n*, -instrument, -werkzeug, b) (*bsd.* Meß)Gerät *n*. **2.** ♪ Instrument *n*. **3.** ✝, 🗲 Dokument *n*, Urkunde *f*. **4.** *fig.* Werkzeug *n*: a) (Hilfs)Mittel *n*, Instrument *n*, b) Handlanger(in). **II** *v/t* **5.** ♪ instrumentieren. **in·stru·men·tal** [͵ɪnstrʊ'mentl] *adj* □ **1.** ⚙ Instrumenten... **2.** ♪ Instrumental...: ~ *music.* **3.** behilflich, förderlich: *be* ~ *in* beitragen zu.

in·sub·or·di·nate [͵ɪnsəb'bɔːdnət] *adj* □ aufsässig.

in·sub·stan·tial [͵ɪnsəb'stænʃl] *adj* □ **1.** unkörperlich. **2.** unwirklich. **3.** wenig *od.* nicht gehaltvoll (*Essen etc*). **4.** nicht *od.* wenig stichhaltig (*Argument etc*); gegenstandslos (*Befürchtung etc*).

in·suf·fer·a·ble [ɪn'sʌfərəbl] *adj* □ unerträglich, unausstehlich.

in·suf·fi·cien·cy [͵ɪnsə'fɪʃnsɪ] *s* **1.** Unzulänglichkeit *f*. **2.** Untauglich-, Unfähigkeit *f*. **3.** ♥ Insuffizienz *f*. **͵in·suf'fi·cient** *adj* □ **1.** unzulänglich, ungenügend. **2.** untauglich, unfähig (*to do* zu tun).

in·su·lar ['ɪnsjʊlə] *adj* □ **1.** Insel... **2.** *fig.* engstirnig.

in·su·late ['ɪnsjʊleɪt] *v/t* ⚡, ⚙ isolieren (*a. fig. from* von): *insulating tape* Br. Isolierband *n*. **͵in·su·la·tion** *s* Isolierung *f*.

in·su·lin ['ɪnsjʊlɪn] *s* ♥ Insulin *n*.

in·sult *v/t* [ɪn'sʌlt] beleidigen. **II** *s* ['ɪnsʌlt] Beleidigung *f* (*to* für *od. gen*).

in·su·per·a·ble [ɪn'suːpərəbl] *adj* □ unüberwindlich (*a. fig.*).

in·sup·port·a·ble [͵ɪnsə'pɔːtəbl] *adj* □ unerträglich, unausstehlich.

in·sur·ance [ɪn'ʃɔːrəns] *s* **1.** ✝ Versicherung *f*: **~ agent** Versicherungsvertreter *m*; **~ company** Versicherungs(gesellschaft *f*); **~ policy** Versicherungspolice *f*, -schein *m*. **2.** ✝ Versicherungssumme *f*; -prämie *f*. **3.** *fig.* (Ab)Sicherung *f* (**against** gegen). **in'sure** *v/t* ✝ versichern (**against** gegen; **for** mit e-r Summe). **in'sured** *s* Versicherte *m*, *f*, Versicherungsnehmer(in). **in'sur·er** *s* Versicherer *m*, Versicherungsträger *m*: **~s** *pl* Versicherung(sgesellschaft) *f*.

in·sur·mount·a·ble [ˌɪnsəˈmaʊntəbl] *adj* □ *fig.* unüberwindlich.

in·sur·rec·tion [ˌɪnsəˈrekʃn] *s* Aufstand *m*, Revolte *f*.

in·sus·cep·ti·ble [ˌɪnsəˈseptəbl] *adj* □ **1.** unempfindlich (**to** gegen): **~ to pain** schmerzunempfindlich. **2.** unempfänglich (**to** für).

in·tact [ɪnˈtækt] *adj* intakt: a) unversehrt, unbeschädigt, b) ganz, vollständig.

in·take [ˈɪnteɪk] *s* **1.** ⚙ Einlaß(öffnung *f*) *m*. **2.** (*Nahrungs- etc*)Aufnahme *f*. **3.** aufgenommene Menge, Zufuhr *f*; (Neu)Aufnahme(n *pl*) *f*, (Neu)Zugänge *pl*.

in·tan·gi·ble [ɪnˈtændʒəbl] *adj* □ **1.** nicht greifbar. **2.** *fig.* unbestimmt, vage.

in·te·ger [ˈɪntɪdʒə] *s* A ganze Zahl.

in·te·gral [ˈɪntɪɡrəl] *adj* □ **1.** integral (*Bestandteil etc*). **2.** ganz, vollständig. **3.** A Integral...: **~ calculus** Integralrechnung *f*.

in·te·grate [ˈɪntɪɡreɪt] **I** *v/t* integrieren: a) zs.-schließen (**into** zu): **~d circuit** ⚡ integrierter Schaltkreis, b) eingliedern (**into** in acc), c) einbeziehen, einbauen (**into, with** in acc). **II** *v/i* sich integrieren (→ Ia, b); sich einbeziehen *od.* einbauen lassen. **in·te'gra·tion** *s* Integration *f*, Integrierung *f*.

in·teg·ri·ty [ɪnˈteɡrətɪ] *s* **1.** Integrität *f*. **2.** Vollständigkeit *f*; Einheit *f*.

in·tel·lect [ˈɪntəlekt] *s* Intellekt *m*, Verstand *m*. **in·tel'lec·tu·al** [ˌ~tjʊəl] **I** *adj* □ intellektuell: a) geistig, Geistes...: **~ property** *f*, b) verstandesbetont. **II** *s* Intellektuelle *m*, *f*.

in·tel·li·gence [ɪnˈtelɪdʒəns] *s* **1.** Intelligenz *f*: **~ quotient** Intelligenzquotient *m*; **~ test** Intelligenztest *m*. **2.** nachrichtendienstliche Informationen *pl*. **3.** a. **~ service** Nachrichten-, Geheimdienst *m*. **in·tel·li·gent** *adj* □ **1.** intelligent. **2.**

vernünftig. **in,tel·li·gent·si·a** [ˌ~ˈdʒentsɪə] *s* (*pl konstruiert*) *coll.* die Intelligenz, die Intellektuellen *pl*.

in·tel·li·gi·ble [ɪnˈtelɪdʒəbl] *adj* □ verständlich (**to** für *od. dat*).

in·tem·per·ate [ɪnˈtempərət] *adj* □ unmäßig.

in·tend [ɪnˈtend] *v/t* **1.** beabsichtigen, vorhaben (*s.th.* et.; *doing, to do* zu tun): **was this ~ed?** war das Absicht? **2.** bestimmen (**for** für, zu): **it was ~ed for you** es war für dich (bestimmt *od.* gedacht). **3.** sagen wollen, meinen (**by** mit). **4.** bedeuten, sein wollen: **it was ~ed for** (*od.* **as, to be**) **a compliment** es sollte ein Kompliment sein. **in'tend·ed I** *adj* **1.** beabsichtigt. **2.** absichtlich. **3.** **her ~ husband** F ihr Zukünftiger. **II** *s* **4.** F Zukünftige *m*, *f*.

in·tense [ɪnˈtens] *adj* □ intensiv: a) stark, heftig: **~ heat** starke Hitze, b) hell, grell (*Licht*), c) satt (*Farben*), d) durchdringend (*Geräusch, Geruch*), e) angestrengt, f) sehnlich, dringend. **in'tense·ness** *s* Intensität *f*.

in·ten·si·fi·ca·tion [ɪnˌtensɪfɪˈkeɪʃn] *s* Verstärkung *f*, Intensivierung *f*. **in'ten·si·fy** [ˌ~faɪ] *v/t* (*a. v/i* sich) verstärken, intensivieren.

in·ten·sive [ɪnˈtensɪv] *adj* □ intensiv: a) → **intense**, b) gründlich, erschöpfend: **~ course** Intensivkurs *m*; **be in** (*od.* **at**) **the ~ care unit** ⚕ auf der Intensivstation liegen.

in·tent [ɪnˈtent] **I** *s* **1.** Absicht *f*, Vorsatz *m* (*a.* ⚖): **with ~** absichtlich, mit Absicht, *bsd.* ⚖ vorsätzlich. **II** *adj* □ **2.** **be ~ on doing s.th.** fest entschlossen sein, et. zu tun; et. unbedingt tun wollen. **3.** aufmerksam, gespannt (*Blick etc*). **in'ten·tion** *s* Absicht *f*, Vorsatz *m* (*of doing, to do* zu tun): **with the best** (*of*) **~s** in bester Absicht; **good ~s** *pl* gute Vorsätze *pl*. **in'ten·tion·al** [ˌ~ʃənl] *adj* absichtlich, *bsd.* ⚖ vorsätzlich: **~ly** *a.* mit Absicht.

in·ter... [ˈɪntə] Zwischen...; Wechsel...

in·ter'act *v/i* aufeinander (ein)wirken. **in·ter'ac·tion** *s* Wechselwirkung *f*.

in·ter'breed *v/t u. v/i* (*irr* **breed**) *biol.* (sich) kreuzen.

in·ter·ca·lar·y [ɪnˈtɜːkələrɪ] *adj* Schalt...: **~ day**; **~ year**.

in·ter·cede [ˌɪntəˈsiːd] *v/i* sich verwenden *od.* einsetzen (**with** bei; *for, on be-half of* für).

in·ter·cept [ˌintəˈsept] *v/t* Brief, Boten, Funkspruch *etc* abfangen. **ˌin·terˈcep·tion** *s* Abfangen *n.* **ˌin·terˈcep·tor** *s a.* ~ **plane** ✈, ✕ Abfangjäger *m.*

in·ter·ces·sion [ˌintəˈseʃn] *s* Fürsprache *f.*

in·ter·change I *v/t* [ˌ~ˈtʃ~] **1.** gegen- *od.* untereinander austauschen, auswechseln. **2.** Geschenke, Meinungen *etc* austauschen, Briefe wechseln (**with** mit). II *s* [ˈ~tʃ~] **3.** Austausch *m:* ~ **of ideas** Gedankenaustausch. **4.** *mot.* Autobahnkreuz *n.* **5.** *a.* ~ **station** Umsteig(e)bahnhof *m,* -station *f.*

ˌin·terˈcit·y 🚄 *Br.* Intercity *m:* ~ **train** Intercityzug *m.*

in·ter·com [ˈintəkɒm] *s* (Gegen-, Haus-, ⚓, ✈) Bord)Sprechanlage *f.*

ˌin·terˈcom·mu·ni·cate *v/i* **1.** miteinander in Verbindung stehen. **2.** miteinander (durch e-e Tür *etc*) verbunden sein.

ˈin·terˌcon·ti·nen·tal *adj* interkontinental, Interkontinental...: ~ **ballistic missile** ✕ Interkontinentalrakete *f.*

ˈin·terˈcourse *s* **1.** Verkehr *m,* Umgang *m* (**with** mit): **commercial** ~ Geschäfts-, Handelsverkehr. **2.** (Geschlechts)Verkehr *m.*

ˈin·terˌde·nomˈi·naˈtion·al *adj* interkonfessionell, konfessionsübergreifend.

ˌin·ter·deˈpend·ence *s* gegenseitige Abhängigkeit. **ˌin·ter·deˈpen·dent** *adj* voneinander abhängig.

in·ter·dict I *s* [ˈintədikt] (amtliches) Verbot. II *v/t* [ˌintəˈdikt] (amtlich) verbieten.

in·ter·est [ˈintrəst] I *s* **1.** Interesse *n* (**in** an *dat,* für): **take** (*od.* **have**) **an** ~ **in** sich interessieren für. **2.** Reiz *m,* Interesse *n:* **be of** ~ (**to**) reizvoll sein (für), interessieren (*acc*). **3.** Wichtigkeit *f,* Bedeutung *f:* **of great** (**little**) ~ von großer Wichtigkeit (von geringer Bedeutung). **4.** *bsd.* 🕇 Beteiligung *f,* Anteil *m* (**in** an *dat*): **have an** ~ **in s.th.** an *od.* bei et. beteiligt sein. **5.** Interesse *n,* Vorteil *m,* Nutzen *m:* **be in** (*od.* **to**) **s.o.'s** ~ in j-s Interesse liegen; **in your** (**own**) ~ zu Ihrem (eigenen) Vorteil. **6.** 🕇 Zins(en *pl*) *m:* **bear** (*od.* **carry**) ~ Zinsen tragen, sich verzinsen (**at 4 %** mit 4 %); ~ **rate, rate of** ~

Zinssatz *m.* II *v/t* **7.** interessieren (**in** für). **ˈin·ter·est·ed** *adj* interessiert (**in** an *dat*): **be** ~ **in** sich interessieren für. **ˈin·ter·est·ing** *adj* □ interessant.

ˈin·ter·face *s* ⚡ Schnittstelle *f,* (*Computer a.*) Nahtstelle *f.*

in·ter·fere [ˌintəˈfiə] *v/i* **1.** (**in** *acc*) eingreifen; sich einmischen. **2.** ~ **with** *j-n,* et. stören, behindern; sich zu schaffen machen an (*dat*). **ˌin·terˈfer·ence** *s* **1.** Eingriff *m;* Einmischung *f.* **2.** Störung *f,* Behinderung *f* (**with** *gen*).

in·ter·im [ˈintərim] I *s:* **in the** ~ in der Zwischenzeit, inzwischen. II *adj* Interims..., Zwischen...: ~ **aid** Überbrückungshilfe *f;* ~ **government** Interims-, Übergangsregierung *f;* ~ **report** Zwischenbericht *m.*

in·te·ri·or [inˈtiəriə] I *adj* **1.** inner..., Innen...: ~ **decorator** a) Innenausstatter(in), b) *a.* ~ **designer** Innenarchitekt(in). **2.** binnenländisch, Binnen...; inländisch, Inlands... II *s* **3.** *oft pl das* Innere. **4.** Innenraum *m,* -seite *f.* **5.** *phot.* Innenaufnahme *f,* (*Film, TV a.*) Studioaufnahme *f.* **6.** Binnenland *n,* das Innere. **7.** *pol.* innere Angelegenheiten *pl:* → **department** 3.

in·ter·ject [ˌintəˈdʒekt] *v/t* Bemerkung *etc* dazwischen-, einwerfen. **ˌin·terˈjec·tion** *s ling.* Interjektion *f.*

ˌin·terˈlace I *v/t* **1.** verflechten, -schlingen, *a. fig.* verweben. **2.** durchflechten (**with** mit) (*a. fig.*). II *v/i* **3.** sich verflechten.

in·ter·loc·u·tor [ˌintəˈlɒkjutə] *s* Gesprächspartner *m.*

in·ter·lop·er [ˈintələupə] *s* Eindringling *m.*

in·ter·lude [ˈintəluːd] *s* **1.** (*kurze*) Zeit, Periode *f.* **2.** Unterbrechung *f* (**in** *gen*). **3.** *thea.,* ♪ Zwischenspiel *n,* Intermezzo *n* (*beide a. fig.*).

ˌin·terˈmar·riage *s* **1.** Mischehe *f.* **2.** Heirat *f* innerhalb der Familie *od.* zwischen Blutsverwandten. **ˌin·terˈmar·ry** *v/i* **1.** e-e Mischehe eingehen; untereinander heiraten. **2.** innerhalb der Familie heiraten.

in·ter·me·di·ar·y [ˌintəˈmiːdjəri] I *adj* **1.** → **intermediate**. **2.** vermittelnd. II *s* **3.** Vermittler(in), Mittelsmann *m.* **4.** 🕇 Zwischenhändler *m.* **ˌin·terˈme·di·ate** [~djət] *adj* □ **1.** Zwischen... **2.**

ped. für fortgeschrittene Anfänger.

in·ter·mez·zo [ˌɪntəˈmetsəʊ] pl **-zi** [ˌtsiː], **-zos** s ♪ Intermezzo n, Zwischenspiel n.

in·ter·mi·na·ble [ɪnˈtɜːmɪnəbl] adj ☐ endlos.

ˌin·terˈmin·gle v/t u. v/i (sich) vermischen.

ˌin·terˈmis·sion s Pause f (a. thea. etc), Unterbrechung f: **without ~** pausenlos.

in·ter·mit·tent [ˌɪntəˈmɪtənt] adj ☐ mit Unterbrechungen, periodisch (auftretend), ✷ etc intermittierend: **~ fever** ✷ Wechselfieber n.

in·tern [ɪnˈtɜːn] v/t internieren.

in·ter·nal [ɪnˈtɜːnl] adj ☐ **1.** inner, Innen...: **~ injury** (**medicine**) innere Verletzung (Medizin); **he was bleeding ~ly** er hatte innere Blutungen. **2.** ✷, pharm. innerlich anzuwenden(d). **3.** einheimisch, Inlands...: **~ trade** Binnenhandel m. **4.** pol. innenpolitisch, Innen...: **~ affairs** pl innere Angelegenheiten pl. **5.** (✝ a. betriebs)intern.

in·ter·nal-com·bus·tion en·gine s ⚙ Verbrennungsmotor m.

in·ter·nal·ize [ɪnˈtɜːnəlaɪz] v/t verinnerlichen.

ˌin·ter·naˈtion·al I adj ☐ **1.** international: **~ law** Völkerrecht n; ⚖ **Monetary Fund** Internationaler Währungsfonds; **~ reply coupon** ✉ internationaler Antwortschein. **2.** Auslands...: **~ call** teleph. Auslandsgespräch n; **~ flight** Auslandsflug m. **II** s **3.** Sport: Internationale m, f, Nationalspieler(in); Länderkampf m, -spiel n. **ˌin·ter·ˈnation·al·ize** v/t internationalisieren.

in·tern·ee [ˌɪntɜːˈniː] s Internierte m, f.

in·tern·ist [ɪnˈtɜːnɪst] s ✷ Internist(in).

in·tern·ment [ɪnˈtɜːnmənt] s Internierung f: **~ camp** Internierungslager n.

ˈin·ter·phone → **intercom**.

ˌin·terˈplan·e·ta·ry adj interplanetar(isch).

ˈin·ter·play s Wechselspiel n.

in·ter·pret [ɪnˈtɜːprɪt] I v/t **1.** auslegen, interpretieren (**as** als). **2.** dolmetschen. **3.** Daten etc auswerten. **II** v/i **4.** dolmetschen (**for s.o.** j-m). **in·ter·pre·ˈta·tion** s **1.** Auslegung f, Interpretation f. **2.** Dolmetschen n. **3.** Auswertung f. **in·ˈter·pret·er** s Dolmetscher(in).

in·ter·re·lat·ed adj in Wechselbezie-

hung stehend, zs.-hängend. **ˌin·ter·reˈla·tion** s Wechselbeziehung f.

in·ter·ro·gate [ɪnˈterəʊgeɪt] v/t verhören, -nehmen. **in·ter·roˈga·tion** s **1.** Verhör n, Vernehmung f. **2.** Frage f (a. ling.): **~ mark** (od. **point**) Fragezeichen n. **in·ter·rog·a·tive** [ˌɪntəˈrɒgətɪv] adj ☐ **1.** fragend. **2.** ling. Interrogativ..., Frage...: **~ pronoun** Interrogativpronomen n, Fragefürwort n. **in·ter·rog·a·to·ry** [ˌtərɪ] adj fragend.

in·ter·rupt [ˌɪntəˈrʌpt] I v/t unterbrechen (a. ✎), j-m ins Wort fallen. **II** v/i **don't ~!** unterbrich mich etc nicht! **in·ter·ˈrupt·ed·ly** adv mit Unterbrechungen. **ˌin·terˈrupt·er** s ✎ Unterbrecher m. **ˌin·terˈrup·tion** s Unterbrechung f: **without ~** ununterbrochen.

in·ter·sect [ˌɪntəˈsekt] I v/t (durch)schneiden, (-)kreuzen. **II** v/i sich schneiden od. kreuzen. **ˌin·terˈsec·tion** s **1.** ➤ Schnitt m: (**point of**) **~** Schnittpunkt m. **2.** (Straßen)Kreuzung f.

in·ter·sperse [ˌɪntəˈspɜːs] v/t **1.** einstreuen. **2.** durchsetzen (**with** mit).

ˈin·ter·state adj Am. zwischenstaatlich: **~ highway** (zwei od. mehrere Bundesstaaten verbindende) Autobahn.

in·ter·stice [ɪnˈtɜːstɪs] s **1.** Zwischenraum m. **2.** Lücke f, Spalt m.

ˌin·terˈtwine, ˌin·terˈtwist v/t u. v/i (sich) verflechten od. verschlingen.

ˌin·terˈur·ban adj zwischen mehreren Städten (bestehend od. verkehrend): **~ traffic** Überlandverkehr m.

in·ter·val [ˈɪntəvl] s **1.** (zeitlicher od. räumlicher) Abstand, (zeitlich a.) Intervall n: **at regular ~s** in regelmäßigen Abständen. **2.** Br. Pause f (a. thea. etc), Unterbrechung f: **~ signal** (Rundfunk, TV) Pausenzeichen n. **3.** ♪, ➤ Intervall n.

in·ter·vene [ˌɪntəˈviːn] v/i **1.** eingreifen, -schreiten, bsd. ✕, pol. intervenieren. **2.** (zeitlich) dazwischenliegen. **3.** sich inzwischen ereignen; dazwischenkommen: **if nothing ~s** wenn nichts dazwischenkommt. **in·ter·ven·tion** [ˌˈven·ʃn] s Eingreifen n, -schreiten n, Intervention f.

in·ter·view [ˈɪntəvjuː] I s **1.** Interview n: **give s.o. an ~.** **2.** Einstellungsgespräch n. **II** v/t **3.** interviewen. **4.** ein Einstellungsgespräch führen mit. **in·ter·view-**

ee [∼ˈiː] s Interviewte m, f. **'in·ter·**
‚view·er s Interviewer(in).

‚in·ter'weave v/t (irr **weave**) **1.** (miteinander) verweben od. verflechten (a.
fig.). **2.** vermengen, -mischen (**with** mit)
(beide a. fig.).

in·tes·tate [ɪnˈtesteɪt] adj: **die ∼ sⁱⁱₐ** ohne
Hinterlassung e-s Testaments sterben.

in·tes·tine [ɪnˈtestɪn] s anat. Darm m: **∼s**
pl Gedärme pl; **large ∼** Dickdarm;
small ∼ Dünndarm.

in·ti·ma·cy [ˈɪntɪməsɪ] s Intimität f: a)
Vertrautheit f, b) (a. contp. plumpe)
Vertraulichkeit, c) intime (sexuelle) Be-
ziehungen pl, d) Gemütlichkeit f.

in·ti·mate¹ [ˈɪntɪmət] adj □ intim: a) vertraut, eng (Freund etc), b) vertraulich
(Mitteilung etc), contp. a. plump-vertraulich, c) in sexuellen Beziehungen
stehend (**with** mit), d) anheimelnd, gemütlich (Atmosphäre etc), e) innerst
(Wünsche etc), f) gründlich, genau
(Kenntnisse etc): **be on ∼ terms (with)**
auf vertrautem Fuße stehen (mit); intime Beziehungen haben (zu).

in·ti·mate² [ˈɪntɪmeɪt] v/t **1.** andeuten: **∼**
to s.o. that j-m zu verstehen geben,
daß. **2.** ankündigen; mitteilen. **‚in·ti·**
'ma·tion s **1.** Andeutung f. **2.** Ankündigung f; Mitteilung f.

in·tim·i·date [ɪnˈtɪmɪdeɪt] v/t einschüchtern: **∼ s.o. into doing s.th.** j-n nötigen,
et. zu tun. **in‚tim·i'da·tion** s Einschüchterung f.

in·to [ˈɪntʊ] prp **1.** in (acc), in (acc) ...
hinein. **2.** gegen: **∼ crash** 6, etc. **3.**
Zustandsänderung: zu: **make water ∼**
ice. 4. A in (acc): → **divide** 4. **5. be ∼** F
stehen auf (acc).

in·tol·er·a·ble [ɪnˈtɒlərəbl] adj □ unerträglich. **in'tol·er·ance** s Intoleranz f.
in'tol·er·ant adj □ intolerant (**of** gegenüber): **be ∼ of s.th.** et. nicht dulden
od. tolerieren.

in·to·na·tion [‚ɪntəʊˈneɪʃn] s **1.** ling. Intonation f, Satzmelodie f. **2.** Tonfall m. **3.**
♪ Intonation f. **in'tone** v/t ♪ intonieren: a) Lied etc anstimmen, b) Ton angeben.

in·tox·i·cant [ɪnˈtɒksɪkənt] **I** adj berauschend (a. fig.). **II** s Rauschmittel n,
bsd. berauschendes Getränk. **in'tox·**
i·cate [∼keɪt] v/t berauschen (a. fig.).
in‚tox·i'ca·tion s Rausch m (a. fig.).

in·trac·ta·ble [ɪnˈtræktəbl] adj □ **1.** eigensinnig. **2.** hartnäckig (Krankheit,
Problem etc).

in·tran·si·gent [ɪnˈtrænsɪdʒənt] adj □
unnachgiebig.

in·tran·si·tive [ɪnˈtrænsətɪv] adj □ ling.
intransitiv.

in·tra·ve·nous [‚ɪntrəˈviːnəs] adj □
anat., ✣ intravenös.

in·trep·id [ɪnˈtrepɪd] adj □ unerschrok-
ken.

in·tri·ca·cy [ˈɪntrɪkəsɪ] s **1.** Kompliziertheit f. **2.** Verworrenheit f. **in'tri·cate**
[∼kət] adj □ **1.** verwickelt, kompliziert. **2.** verworren.

in·trigue [ɪnˈtriːg] **I** v/t faszinieren; interessieren; neugierig machen. **II** v/i intrigieren (**against** gegen). **III** s Intrige f.
in'tri·guer s Intrigant(in). **in'tri·guing**
adj □ **1.** faszinierend; interessant. **2.**
intrigant.

in·trin·sic [ɪnˈtrɪnsɪk] adj **1.** inner. **2.** wesentlich.

in·tro·duce [‚ɪntrəˈdjuːs] v/t **1.** neue Methode etc einführen. **2.** (**to**) j-n bekannt
machen (mit), vorstellen (dat). **3.** (**to**)
j-n einführen (in ein Fach etc), bekannt
machen (mit). **4.** Redner, Programm
etc ankündigen. **5.** Gedanken, Gesetzesvorlage etc einbringen (**into** in acc).
6. (**into** in acc) einfügen; (hinein)stek-
ken, einführen. **in·tro·duc·tion** [∼ˈdʌk-
ʃn] s **1.** Einführung f. **2.** Vorstellung f.
3. Einleitung f, Vorwort n. **4.** Leitfaden
m (**to** gen). **5.** Einbringung f. **‚in·tro·**
'duc·to·ry [∼tərɪ] adj **1.** Einführungs...:
∼ price. **2.** einleitend, Einleitungs...

in·tro·spec·tion [‚ɪntrəʊˈspekʃn] s Selbst-
beobachtung f. **‚in·tro'spec·tive** [∼tɪv]
adj □ introspektiv.

in·tro·vert [ˈɪntrəʊvɜːt] adj psych. introvertiert.

in·trude [ɪnˈtruːd] **I** v/t **1. ∼ o.s.** → **3. 2.**
aufdrängen (**s.th. on s.o.** j-m et.; **o.s.**
on s.o. sich j-m). **II** v/i **3.** sich eindrängen (**into** in acc) (a. fig.). **4.** sich aufdrängen (**on** dat). **5.** stören (**on s.o.** j-n).
in'trud·er s **1.** Eindringling m. **2.** Störenfried m.

in·tru·sion [ɪnˈtruːʒn] s Störung f (**on**
gen). **in'tru·sive** [∼sɪv] adj □ aufdringlich.

in·tu·i·tion [‚ɪntjuːˈɪʃn] s Intuition f.
in'tu·i·tive [∼tɪv] adj □ intuitiv.

invitation

in·un·date ['ɪnʌndeɪt] *v/t* überschwemmen, -fluten (*beide a. fig.*). ‚**in·un'da·tion** *s* Überschwemmung *f*, -flutung *f*.

in·ure [ɪ'njʊə] *v/t* (*to*) abhärten (gegen), *fig. a.* gewöhnen (an *acc*).

in·vade [ɪn'veɪd] *v/t* **1.** einfallen *od.* eindringen in (*acc*), ✕ *a.* einmarschieren in (*acc*). **2.** sich ausbreiten über (*acc*) *od.* in (*dat*), erfüllen. **3.** *fig.* überlaufen, -schwemmen. **4.** *j-s* Privatsphäre *etc* verletzen, in *j-s* Rechte eingreifen. **in'vad·er** *s* **1.** Eindringling *m*. **2.** *pl* ✕ Invasoren *pl*.

in·va·lid¹ ['ɪnvəlɪd] **I** *adj* **1.** krank, gebrechlich; invalid, arbeits-, erwerbsunfähig; kriegsbeschädigt. **2.** Kranken... **II** *s* **3.** Kranke *m, f*, Gebrechliche *m, f*; Invalide *m*, Arbeits-, Erwerbsunfähige *m, f*; Pflegefall *m*. **III** *v/t* ['ɪnvəliːd] **4.** zum Invaliden machen.

in·val·id² [ɪn'vælɪd] *adj* □ (rechts)ungültig, unwirksam. **in'val·i·date** [‿deɪt] *v/t* für ungültig erklären. **in‚val·i'da·tion** *s* Ungültigkeitserklärung *f*.

in·va·lid·i·ty¹ [ˌɪnvə'lɪdətɪ] *s* Invalidität *f*, Arbeits-, Erwerbsunfähigkeit *f*.

in·va·lid·i·ty² [‿] *s* (Rechts)Ungültigkeit *f*.

in·val·u·a·ble [ɪn'væljʊəbl] *adj* □ unschätzbar, von unschätzbarem Wert (*beide a. fig.*): *be ~ to s.o.* für j-n von unschätzbarem Wert sein.

in·var·i·a·ble [ɪn'veərɪəbl] *adj* □ unveränderlich, gleichbleibend.

in·va·sion [ɪn'veɪʒn] *s* **1.** (*of*) Einfall *m* (in *acc*), Eindringen *n* (in *acc*), ✕ *a.* Invasion *f* (*gen*), Einmarsch *m* (in *acc*): *~ of tourists* Touristeninvasion. **2.** *fig.* (*of*) Verletzung *f* (*gen*), Eingriff *m* (in *acc*).

in·vec·tive [ɪn'vektɪv] *s* Beschimpfung(en *pl*) *f*, Schmähung(en *pl*) *f*.

in·veigh [ɪn'veɪ] *v/i* (*against*) schimpfen (über *od.* auf *acc*), herziehen (über *acc*).

in·vei·gle [ɪn'veɪgl] *v/t* verleiten, -führen (*into* zu; *into doing s.th.* dazu, et. zu tun).

in·vent [ɪn'vent] *v/t* erfinden, *et. Unwahres a.* erdichten. **in'ven·tion** *s* Erfindung *f*. **in'ven·tive** [‿tɪv] *adj* □ **1.** erfinderisch. **2.** einfallsreich. **in'ven·tor** *s* Erfinder(in).

in·ven·to·ry ['ɪnvəntrɪ] 🕇 **I** *s* **1.** Inventar *n*: a) Bestandsliste *f*: *make* (*od. take*) *an ~ of* → 3, b) (Waren-, Lager)Be-

stand *m*. **2.** Inventur *f*. **II** *v/t* **3.** e-e Bestandsliste machen von.

in·verse [ˌɪn'vɜːs] *adj* □ umgekehrt: *in ~ order* in umgekehrter Reihenfolge. **in'ver·sion** *s* **1.** Umkehrung *f*. **2.** 🕇, *ling. etc* Inversion *f*.

in·vert [ɪn'vɜːt] *v/t* **1.** umkehren: *~ed commas pl bsd. Br.* Anführungszeichen *pl*. **2.** umwenden, umstülpen: *~ s.th. over et.* stülpen über (*acc*).

in·ver·te·brate [ɪn'vɜːtɪbreɪt] *zo.* **I** *adj* wirbellos. **II** *s* wirbelloses Tier.

in·vest [ɪn'vest] **I** *v/t* **1.** 🕇 (*in*) investieren (in *acc od. dat*), anlegen (in *dat*). **2.** *~ s.o. with* j-n *et.* verleihen; j-n mit *Befugnissen etc* ausstatten. **II** *v/i* **3.** 🕇 *a* in *a*) 🕇 investieren in (*acc od. dat*), sein Geld anlegen in (*dat*), b) F sich *et.* kaufen *od.* zulegen.

in·ves·ti·gate [ɪn'vestɪgeɪt] **I** *v/t Verbrechen etc* untersuchen, Ermittlungen *od.* Nachforschungen anstellen über (*acc*), *Fall* recherchieren, *j-n*, *Anspruch etc* überprüfen, *e-r Beschwerde etc* nachgehen, *Gebiet etc* (*wissenschaftlich*) erforschen. **II** *v/i* ermitteln, recherchieren, Ermittlungen *od.* Nachforschungen anstellen (*into* über *acc*): *investigating committee* Untersuchungsausschuß *m*. **in‚ves·ti'ga·tion** *s* Untersuchung *f* (*into*, *of* gen), Nachforschung *f*, Recherche *f*, Überprüfung *f*: *be under ~* untersucht werden.

in·vest·ment [ɪn'vestmənt] *s* 🕇 Investition *f*, (Kapital)Anlage *f*; Anlagekapital *n*: *~ adviser* (*od. consultant*) Anlageberater(in); *~ trust* Kapitalanlagegesellschaft *f*. **in'ves·tor** *s* Investor *m*, Kapitalanleger *m*.

in·vet·er·ate [ɪn'vetərət] *adj* □ **1.** eingewurzelt, unausrottbar. **2.** 🖋 hartnäckig; chronisch. **3.** eingefleischt, unverbesserlich.

in·vid·i·ous [ɪn'vɪdɪəs] *adj* □ gehässig, boshaft.

in·vig·or·ate [ɪn'vɪgəreɪt] *v/t* stärken, kräftigen; beleben, anregen; er-, aufmuntern.

in·vin·ci·ble [ɪn'vɪnsəbl] *adj* □ **1.** ✕, *Sport:* unbesiegbar. **2.** *fig.* unüberwindlich.

in·vis·i·ble [ɪn'vɪzəbl] *adj* □ unsichtbar (*to* für).

in·vi·ta·tion [ˌɪnvɪ'teɪʃn] *s* **1.** Einladung *f*

(*to* an *acc*; zu): *at the ~ of* auf Einladung von (*od. gen*). **2.** (höfliche) Aufforderung, Ersuchen *n*. **3.** Herausforderung *f*: *be an ~ for* → *invite* 4. **in·vite** *v/t* **1.** einladen (*to dinner* zum Essen). **2.** (höflich) auffordern, ersuchen (*to do* zu tun). **3.** bitten *od.* ersuchen um, erbitten. **4.** herausfordern (zu), einladen zu.

in·vo·ca·tion [ˌɪnvəʊˈkeɪʃn] *s* **1.** Anrufung *f* (*to gen*). **2.** Beschwörung *f*.

in·voice [ˈɪnvɔɪs] † **I** *s* (Waren)Rechnung *f*, Faktura *f*. **II** *v/t* fakturieren, in Rechnung stellen.

in·voke [ɪnˈvəʊk] *v/t* **1.** flehen um, erflehen. **2.** *Gott etc* anrufen. **3.** *Geist* beschwören.

in·vol·un·tar·y [ɪnˈvɒləntərɪ] *adj* □ **1.** unfreiwillig. **2.** unabsichtlich. **3.** unwillkürlich.

in·volve [ɪnˈvɒlv] *v/t* **1.** a) *j-n* verwickeln, hineinziehen (*in* in *acc*): *~d in an accident* in e-n Unfall verwickelt, b) *j-n, et.* angehen, betreffen: *the persons ~d* die Betroffenen. **2.** *be ~d* zu tun haben (*with* mit). **3.** zur Folge haben, nach sich ziehen; verbunden sein mit; erfordern, nötig machen. **in·volved** *adj* kompliziert; verworren.

in·vul·ner·a·ble [ɪnˈvʌlnərəbl] *adj* □ **1.** unverwundbar (*a. fig.*). **2.** *fig.* unanfechtbar, hieb- u. stichfest.

in·ward [ˈɪnwəd] **I** *adv* **1.** einwärts, nach innen. **2.** → *inwardly* 1, 2. **II** *adj* **3.** innerlich, inner (*beide a. fig.*), Innen... **'in·ward·ly** *adv* **1.** innerlich, im Inner(e)n (*beide a. fig.*). **2.** *fig.* im stillen, insgeheim. **3.** → *inward* 1. **in·wards** [ˈ∼z] → *inward* I.

i·o·dine [ˈaɪəʊdiːn] *s* 🜍 Jod *n*.

i·on [ˈaɪən] *s* 🜍, *phys.* Ion *n*. **i·on·ic** [aɪˈɒnɪk] *adj* Ionen...

i·o·ta [aɪˈəʊtə] *s fig.* Jota *n*: *not an ~ of truth* kein Körnchen Wahrheit.

IOU [ˌaɪəʊˈjuː] *s* Schuldschein *m* (= *I owe you*).

i·ras·ci·ble [ɪˈræsəbl] *adj* □ jähzornig, reizbar.

i·rate [aɪˈreɪt] *adj* zornig, wütend.

ir·i·des [ˈaɪrɪdiːz] *pl von* **iris**.

ir·i·des·cent [ˌɪrɪˈdesnt] *adj* □ (*in den Regenbogenfarben*) schillernd.

i·ris [ˈaɪərɪs] *pl* **'i·ris·es**, **ir·i·des** [ˈaɪrɪdiːz] *s* **1.** *anat.* Iris *f*, Regenbogen-

haut *f*. **2.** ♀ Iris *f*, Schwertlilie *f*.

I·rish [ˈaɪərɪʃ] **I** *adj* **1.** irisch: *~ coffee* Irish Coffee *m*. **II** *s* **2.** *the ~ pl* die Iren *pl*. **3.** *ling.* Irisch *n*. **'∼·man** [ˈ∼mən] *s* (*irr* **man**) Ire *m*. **'∼·wom·an** *s* (*irr* **woman**) Irin *f*.

irk [ɜːk] *v/t* **1.** ärgern, verdrießen. **2.** ermüden, langweilen. **irk·some** [ˈɜːksəm] *adj* □ **1.** ärgerlich, verdrießlich. **2.** ermüdend, langweilig.

i·ron [ˈaɪən] **I** *s* **1.** Eisen *n*: *have several ~s in the fire fig.* mehrere Eisen im Feuer haben; *strike while the ~ is hot fig.* das Eisen schmieden, solange es heiß ist; *will of ~* eiserner Wille. **2.** Bügeleisen *n*. **II** *adj* **3.** eisern (*a. fig.*), Eisen...: ⚥ *Curtain pol.* Eiserner Vorhang; *~ lung* ♥ eiserne Lunge; *~ ore min.* Eisenerz *n*. **III** *v/t* **4.** bügeln: *~ out* ausbügeln; *fig. Meinungsverschiedenheiten etc* aus der Welt schaffen, beseitigen.

i·ron·ic, **i·ron·i·cal** [aɪˈrɒnɪk(l)] *adj* □ ironisch.

i·ron·ing board [ˈaɪənɪŋ] *s* Bügelbrett *n*.

'i·ron·work *s* **1.** Eisenbeschläge *pl*. **2.** *pl* (*oft sg konstruiert*) Eisenhütte *f*.

i·ro·ny [ˈaɪərənɪ] *s* Ironie *f*: *~ of fate* Ironie des Schicksals.

ir·ra·tion·al [ɪˈræʃənl] *adj* □ **1.** irrational, unvernünftig. **2.** Ⱥ irrational.

ir·rec·og·niz·a·ble [ɪˈrekəgnaɪzəbl] *adj* □ nicht zu erkennen(d) *od.* wiederzuerkennen(d), unkenntlich.

ir·rec·on·cil·a·ble [ɪˈrekənsaɪləbl] *adj* □ **1.** unvereinbar (*with* mit). **2.** unversöhnlich.

ir·re·cov·er·a·ble [ˌɪrɪˈkʌvərəbl] *adj* □ nicht wiedergutzumachen(d), unersetzlich, -bar (*Verlust etc*).

ir·re·deem·a·ble [ˌɪrɪˈdiːməbl] *adj* □ **1.** † unkündbar (*Obligation etc*). **2.** nicht wiedergutzumachen(d) (*Verlust etc*).

ir·ref·u·ta·ble [ɪˈrefjʊtəbl] *adj* □ unwiderlegbar.

ir·reg·u·lar [ɪˈregjʊlə] *adj* □ **1.** unregelmäßig (*a. ling.*). **2.** regel- *od.* vorschriftswidrig. **ir·reg·u·lar·i·ty** [∼ˈlærətɪ] *s* **1.** Unregelmäßigkeit *f*. **2.** Regel- *od.* Vorschriftswidrigkeit *f*.

ir·rel·e·vance, **ir·rel·e·van·cy** [ɪˈreləvəns(ɪ)] *s* Irrelevanz *f*, Unerheblichkeit *f*, Belanglosigkeit *f*. **ir·rel·e·vant** *adj* □ irrelevant, unerheblich, belanglos (*to* für).

ir·re·me·di·a·ble [ˌɪrɪˈmiːdjəbl] *adj* □ nicht behebbar *od.* abstellbar.

ir·re·mis·si·ble [ˌɪrɪˈmɪsəbl] *adj* □ unverzeihlich.

ir·re·mov·a·ble [ˌɪrɪˈmuːvəbl] *adj* □ unabsetzbar.

ir·rep·a·ra·ble [ɪˈrepərəbl] *adj* □ irreparabel, nicht wieder gutzumachen(d).

ir·re·place·a·ble [ˌɪrɪˈpleɪsəbl] *adj* □ unersetzlich, -bar.

ir·re·press·i·ble [ˌɪrɪˈpresəbl] *adj* □ un(be)zähmbar.

ir·re·proach·a·ble [ˌɪrɪˈprəʊtʃəbl] *adj* □ untadelig, tadellos.

ir·re·sist·i·ble [ˌɪrɪˈzɪstəbl] *adj* □ unwiderstehlich.

ir·res·o·lute [ɪˈrezəluːt] *adj* □ unentschlossen, unschlüssig.

ir·re·spec·tive [ˌɪrɪˈspektɪv] *adj* □: **~ of** ohne Rücksicht auf (*acc*).

ir·re·spon·si·ble [ˌɪrɪˈspɒnsəbl] *adj* □ **1.** verantwortungslos: a) unzuverlässig, b) unverantwortlich. **2.** ᚗᚗ unzurechnungsfähig; nicht haftbar (**for** für).

ir·re·triev·a·ble [ˌɪrɪˈtriːvəbl] *adj* □ unersetzlich, -bar.

ir·rev·er·ence [ɪˈrevərəns] *s* Respektlosigkeit *f.* **ir·rev·er·ent** *adj* □ respektlos.

ir·re·vers·i·ble [ˌɪrɪˈvɜːsəbl] → *irrevocable.*

ir·rev·o·ca·ble [ɪˈrevəkəbl] *adj* □ unwiderruflich, unumstößlich.

ir·ri·gate [ˈɪrɪgeɪt] *v/t* **1.** ✗ bewässern. **2.** ✗ *Wunde etc* ausspülen. **ˌir·riˈga·tion** *s* **1.** ✗ Bewässerung *f*: **~ ditch** Bewässerungsgraben *m.* **2.** ✗ Ausspülung *f.*

ir·ri·ta·ble [ˈɪrɪtəbl] *adj* □ reizbar. **ir·ri·tate** [ˈ~teɪt] *v/t* reizen, (ver)ärgern: **~d at** (**by, with**) verärgert *od.* ärgerlich über (*acc*). **ˈir·ri·tat·ing** *adj* □ ärgerlich. **ˌir·riˈta·tion** *s* Verärgerung *f*; Ärger *m* (**at** über *acc*).

is [ɪz] *er, sie, es* ist.

Is·lam [ˈɪzlɑːm] *s* Islam *m.* **Is·lam·ic** [ɪzˈlæmɪk] *adj* islamisch.

is·land [ˈaɪlənd] *s* **1.** Insel *f.* **2.** Verkehrsinsel *f.* **ˈis·land·er** *s* Inselbewohner(in).

isn't [ˈɪznt] F *für* **is not.**

i·so·late [ˈaɪsəleɪt] *v/t* **1.** a. ✗ isolieren, absondern (**from** von). **2.** ⚗ isolieren. **3.** *fig.* a) isoliert *od.* einzeln betrachten, b) trennen (**from** von). **ˈi·so·lat·ed** *adj* **1.** isoliert, abgesondert. **2.**

einzeln, vereinzelt: **~ case** Einzelfall *m.* **3.** abgeschieden. **ˌi·soˈla·tion** *s* **1.** Isolierung *f*, Absonderung *f*: **~ ward** ⚕ Isolierstation *f.* **2.** **consider in ~** → *isolate* 3a. **3.** Abgeschiedenheit *f*: **live in ~** zurückgezogen leben.

i·so·met·rics [ˌaɪsəʊˈmetrɪks] *s pl* (*a. sg konstruiert*) Isometrik *f.*

i·sos·ce·les [aɪˈsɒsɪliːz] *adj* ⚓ gleichschenk(e)lig (*Dreieck*).

i·so·tope [ˈaɪsəʊtəʊp] *s phys.* Isotop *n.*

Is·rae·li [ɪzˈreɪlɪ] **I** *adj* israelisch. **II** *s* Israeli *m, f.*

is·sue [ˈɪʃuː] **I** *s* **1.** Ausgabe *f*, Erlaß *m.* **2.** ✝ Ausgabe *f*, Emission *f*, Begebung *f*, Auflegung *f*, Ausstellung *f.* **3.** Ausgabe *f* (*e-r Zeitung etc*). **4.** Streitfrage *f*, -punkt *m*: **be at ~** zur Debatte stehen; **point at ~** strittige Frage. **5.** Ausgang *m*, Ergebnis *n*: **bring to an ~** zur Entscheidung bringen; **force an ~** e-e Entscheidung erzwingen. **6.** ᚗᚗ Nachkommen(schaft *f*) *pl*: **die without ~** kinderlos sterben. **II** *v/t* **7.** *Befehle etc* ausgeben, a. ᚗᚗ *Haftbefehl* erlassen. **8.** ✝ *Banknoten, Wertpapiere etc* ausgeben, *Anleihe* begeben, auflegen, *Dokument, Wechsel etc* ausstellen. **9.** *Zeitung etc* herausgeben. **10.** *bsd.* ✗ *Munition etc* ausgeben. **III** *v/i* **11.** heraus-, hervorkommen. **12.** herausfließen, -strömen. **13.** herrühren (**from** von).

isth·mus [ˈɪsməs] *pl* **-mus·es, -mi** [ˈ~maɪ] *s* Landenge *f*, Isthmus *m.*

it [ɪt] *pron* **1.** es (*nom od. acc*). **2.** *auf schon Genanntes bezogen*: es, er, ihn, sie. **3.** *unpersönliches od. grammatisches Subjekt*: es: **~ is raining; oh, ~ was you** oh, Sie waren es *od.* das. **4.** *unbestimmtes Objekt* (*oft unübersetzt*) es: → *foot* 4, *etc.* **5.** *verstärkend*: **~ is to him that you should turn** an ihn solltest du dich wenden.

I·tal·ian [ɪˈtæljən] **I** *adj* **1.** italienisch. **II** *s* **2.** Italiener(in). **3.** *ling.* Italienisch *n.*

i·tal·ic [ɪˈtælɪk] *typ.* **I** *adj* kursiv. **II** *s oft pl* Kursivschrift *f*: **in ~s** kursiv. **iˈtal·i·cize** [ˈ~saɪz] *v/t* kursiv drucken.

itch [ɪtʃ] **I** *s* **1.** Jucken *n*, Juckreiz *m.* **2.** ⚕ Krätze *f.* **3.** *fig.* Verlangen *n* (**for** nach): **have** (*od.* **feel**) **an ~ to do s.th.** große Lust haben *od.* darauf brennen, et. zu tun. **II** *v/i* **4.** jucken, (*Pullover etc* a.) kratzen. **5.** *fig.* F **be ~ing for s.th.** et.

unbedingt (haben) wollen; *he's ~ing to try it* es reizt *od.* juckt ihn, es zu versuchen. **III** *v/t* **6.** *j-n* jucken, kratzen. **'itch•y** *adj* juckend; kratzend: → **palm¹** 1.

i•tem ['aɪtəm] *s* **1.** Punkt *m* (*der Tagesordnung etc*), (*Bilanz- etc*)Posten *m.* **2.** (Waren)Artikel *m; weitS* Gegenstand *m,* Ding *m.* **3.** (*Presse-, Zeitungs*)Notiz *f,* (*a. Rundfunk, TV*) Nachricht *f,* Meldung *f.* **i•tem•ize** ['~maɪz] *v/t* Rechnungsposten einzeln aufführen, *a.* Rechnung spezifizieren, *Kosten etc* aufgliedern.

i•tin•er•ant [ɪ'tɪnərənt] *adj* □ (*beruflich*) reisend, Reise..., Wander... **i•tin•er•ar•y** [aɪ'tɪnərərɪ] *s* **1.** Reiseweg *m,* -route *f;* Reiseplan *m.* **2.** Reiseführer *m* (*Buch*). **i•tin•er•ate**

[ɪ'tɪnəreɪt] *v/i* (herum)reisen.

it'll ['ɪtl] F *für* **it will.**

its [ɪts] *pron* sein, s-e, ihr, ihre.

it's [ɪts] F *für* **it is; it has.**

it•self [ɪt'self] *pron* **1.** *reflex* sich. **2.** sich selbst. **3.** *verstärkend:* selbst: *by ~* (für sich) allein; von allein *od.* selbst.

it•sy-bit•sy [ˌɪtsɪ'bɪtsɪ] *adj* F klitzeklein, winzig.

I've [aɪv] F *für* **I have.**

i•vo•ry ['aɪvərɪ] **I** *s* **1.** Elfenbein *n.* **2.** *pl sl.* (*bsd.* Klavier)Tasten *pl: tickle the ivories* (auf dem Klavier) klimpern. **II** *adj* **3.** elfenbeinern, Elfenbein...: *live in an ~ tower fig.* in e-m Elfenbeinturm leben *od.* sitzen.

i•vy ['aɪvɪ] *s* ⚘ Efeu *m:* ♀ *League* Eliteuniversitäten im Osten der USA.

J

jab [dʒæb] **I** *v/t* **1.** (hinein)stechen, (-)stoßen (*into* in *acc*). **II** *v/t* **2.** stechen, stoßen (*at* nach; *with* mit). **III** *s* **3.** Stich *m,* Stoß *m.* **4.** *Boxen:* Jab *m.* **5.** 💉 F Spritze *f.*

jab•ber ['dʒæbə] **I** *v/t a. ~ out* (daher)plappern, *Gebet etc* herunterrasseln. **II** *v/i a. ~ away* plappern, schwatzen. **III** *s* Geplapper *n,* Geschwätz *n.*

jack [dʒæk] **I** *s* **1.** ♀ F *für John: before you could say* ♀ *Robinson* im Nu, im Handumdrehen; *every man ~* jeder, alle. **2.** *Kartenspiel:* Bube *m:* **~ of hearts** Herzbube *m.* **3.** ⚙ Hebevorrichtung *f:* (*car*) *~* Wagenheber *m.* **II** *v/t* **4.** hochheben, *Auto* aufbocken.

jack•al ['dʒækɔ:l] *s zo.* Schakal *m.*

'jack•ass *s* **1.** (männlicher) Esel. **2.** *fig.* Esel *m,* Dummkopf *m.* **'~•boot** *s* **1.** Stulp(en)stiefel *m.* **2.** Wasserstiefel *m.* **~•daw** ['~dɔ:] *s orn.* Dohle *f.*

jack•et ['dʒækɪt] *s* **1.** Jacke *f,* Jackett *n.* **2.** ⚙ Mantel *m.* **3.** (Schutz)Umschlag *m,* (*Buch-, Am. a. Schallplatten*)Hülle *f.* **4.** Schale *f: potatoes pl* (*boiled*) *in their*

~s, ~ potatoes pl Pellkartoffeln *pl.* *~ crown s* ⚙ Jacketkrone *f.*

'jack|•ham•mer *s* ⚙ Preßlufthammer *m.* **'~-in-the-box** *pl* **'~-in-the-ˌbox•es,** **'~-s-in-the-box** *s* Schachtelmännchen *n,* -teufel *m.* **'~•knife** *s* (*irr knife*) Klappmesser *n.* **,~-of-'all-trades** *s a. contp.* Hansdampf *m* in allen Gassen. **'~•pot** *s* *Poker etc:* Jackpot *m: hit the ~* F den Jackpot gewinnen; *fig.* das große Los ziehen (*with* mit).

jade [dʒeɪd] *s min.* Jade *m, f.*

jad•ed ['dʒeɪdɪd] *adj* **1.** erschöpft, ermattet. **2.** abgestumpft, übersättigt. **3.** schal, reizlos geworden.

jag [dʒæg] **I** *s* **1.** Zacke *f.* **2.** Loch *n,* Riß *m.* **II** *v/t* **3.** auszacken. **4.** ein Loch reißen in (*acc*). **jag•ged** ['~gɪd], **'jag•gy** *adj* □ **1.** (aus)gezackt, zackig. **2.** zerklüftet (*Steilküste etc*).

jag•uar ['dʒægjʊə] *s zo.* Jaguar *m.*

jail [dʒeɪl] **I** *s* Gefängnis *n: in ~* im Gefängnis; *put in ~* → **II. II** *v/t* einsperren. **'~•bird** *s* F Knastbruder *m,* Knacki *m.* **'~•break** *s* Ausbruch *m* (aus dem Gefängnis). **'~•break•er** *s* Ausbrecher *m*

jail·er ['dʒeɪlə] *s* Gefängniswärter *m*, -aufseher *m*.

ja·lop·(p)y [dʒə'lɒpɪ] *s* F alte Kiste *od.* Mühle (*Auto, Flugzeug*).

jam¹ [dʒæm] *s* Marmelade *f*.

jam² [~] I *v/t* **1.** (hinein)pressen, (-)quetschen, (-)zwängen, *Menschen a.* (-)pferchen (*into* in *acc*): ~ *in* hineinpressen *etc.* **2.** (ein)klemmen, (-)quetschen: ~ *med his finger* (*od.* *got his finger* ~*med*) *in the door* er quetschte sich den Finger in der Tür; *be* ~*med in* eingekeilt sein (*between* zwischen *dat*). **3.** *a.* ~ *up* blockieren, verstopfen. **4.** *a.* ~ *up* (*Funk etc*) *Empfang* (*durch Störsender*) stören. **5.** ~ *on the brakes mot.* voll auf die Bremse treten. II *v/i* **6.** sich (hinein)drängen *od.* (-)quetschen *od.* (-)zwängen (*into* in *acc*): ~ *in* sich hineindrängen *etc.* **7.** ⚙ sich verklemmen, (*Bremsen*) blockieren; Ladehemmung haben (*Pistole etc*). III *s* **8.** Gedränge *n*. **9.** Verstopfung *f*: → *traffic jam.* **10.** ⚙ Verklemmung *f*, Blockierung *f*; Ladehemmung *f*. **11.** F Klemme *f*: *be in a* ~ in der Klemme sein *od.* sitzen *od.* stecken.

Ja·mai·ca (rum) [dʒə'meɪkə] *s* Jamaikarum *m*.

jamb [dʒæm] *s* (Tür-, Fenster)Pfosten *m*.

jam·bo·ree [ˌdʒæmbə'riː] *s* **1.** Jamboree *n*, (internationales) Pfadfindertreffen. **2.** große (Partei- *etc*)Veranstaltung. **3.** F ausgelassene Feier.

jam·my ['dʒæmɪ] *adj Br. sl.* **1.** (kinder)leicht. **2.** Glücks...: ~ *fellow* Glückspilz *m*.

jam-'packed *adj* F vollgestopft (*with* mit), (*Stadion etc*) bis auf den letzten Platz besetzt.

jan·gle ['dʒæŋgl] I *v/i* klimpern (*Münzen etc*), klirren, rasseln (*Ketten etc*). II *v/t* klimpern *od.* klirren mit. III *s* Klimpern *n*, Klirren *n*.

jan·i·tor ['dʒænɪtə] *s* **1.** Pförtner *m*. **2.** *bsd. Am.* Hausmeister *m*.

Jan·u·ar·y ['dʒænjʊərɪ] *s* Januar *m*: *in* ~ im Januar.

Jap [dʒæp] *s* F Japs *m* (*Japaner*).

Jap·a·nese [ˌdʒæpə'niːz] I *s* **1.** *pl* -**nese** Japaner(in). **2.** *ling.* Japanisch *n*. II *adj* **3.** japanisch.

jar¹ [dʒɑː] *s* **1.** (irdenes *od.* gläsernes) Gefäß, Krug *m*. **2.** (Marmelade-,

Einmach)Glas *n*. **3.** *Br.* F Glas *n* Bier.

jar² [~] I *v/i* **1.** kratzen, kreischen, quietschen (*on* auf *dat*). **2.** sich beißen (*Farben*); sich widersprechen (*Meinungen etc*); ♪ dissonieren: ~*ring tone* Mißton *m* (*a. fig.*). **3.** ~ *on* weh tun (*dat*) (*Farbe, Geräusch etc*), *Auge etc* beleidigen. **4.** wackeln: ~ *loose* sich lockern. II *v/t* **5.** kratzen *od.* quietschen mit. **6.** erschüttern, *fig. a.* er-, aufregen. **7.** → **3.** III *s* **8.** Kratzen *n etc* (→ **1.**). **9.** Erschütterung *f* (*a. fig.*); Stoß *m*. **10.** ♪ Mißklang *m*, Dissonanz *f* (*beide a. fig.*).

jar·gon ['dʒɑːgən] *s* Jargon *m*.

jas·min(e) ['dʒæsmɪn] *s* ♣ Jasmin *m*.

jas·per ['dʒæspə] *s min.* Jaspis *m*.

jaun·dice ['dʒɔːndɪs] *s* **1.** ⚕ Gelbsucht *f*. **2.** *fig.* Neid *m*, Eifersucht *f*. **'jaun·diced** *adj* **1.** ⚕ gelbsüchtig. **2.** *fig.* neidisch, eifersüchtig.

jaunt [dʒɔːnt] I *v/i* e-n Ausflug *od.* e-e Spritztour machen. II *s* Ausflug *m*, *mot.* Spritztour *f*: *go for* (*od. on*) *a* ~ → I.

jaun·ty ['dʒɔːntɪ] *adj* □ **1.** fesch, flott (*Hut etc*). **2.** unbeschwert, unbekümmert (*Einstellung, Person*). **3.** flott, schwungvoll (*Melodie*).

jave·lin ['dʒævlɪn] *s* Leichtathletik: Speer *m*: ~ *throw* Speerwerfen *n*; ~ *thrower* Speerwerfer(in).

jaw [dʒɔː] I *s* **1.** *anat.* Kiefer *m*: *lower* ~ Unterkiefer *m*; *upper* ~ Oberkiefer *m*. **2.** *mst pl* Mund *m*; *zo.* Rachen *m* (*a. fig.*), Maul *n*. **3.** ⚙ (Klemm)Backe *f*, Klaue *f*. **4.** F Geschwätz *n*. II *v/i* **5.** F schwatzen. '~**·bone** *s anat.* Kieferknochen *m*. '~**·break·er** *s* F Zungenbrecher *m*.

jay [dʒeɪ] *s orn.* Eichelhäher *m*. '~**·walk·er** *s* unachtsamer Fußgänger *m*.

jazz [dʒæz] I *s* **1.** ♪ Jazz *m*. **2.** *and all that* ~ F u. so ein Zeug(s). II *adj* **3.** ♪ Jazz... III *v/t* **4.** *oft* ~ *up* ♪ verjazzen. **5.** *mst* ~ *up* F Schmiß *od.* Schwung bringen in (*acc*); *j-n, et.* aufmöbeln. '**jaz·zy** *adj* □ **1.** jazzartig. **2.** F knallig (*Farben*), (*a. Kleidung etc*) poppig.

jeal·ous ['dʒeləs] *adj* □ **1.** eifersüchtig (*of* auf *acc*). **2.** neidisch (*of* auf *acc*): *be* ~ *of s.o.'s success* j-m sein Erfolg mißgönnen. **3.** eifersüchtig besorgt (*of* um). '**jeal·ous·y** *s* **1.** Eifersucht *f*; *pl* Eifersüchteleien *pl*. **2.** Neid *m*.

jeans [dʒiːnz] *s pl* Jeans *pl*.

jeep [dʒiːp] *s mot.* Jeep *m*.

jeer [dʒɪə] **I** v/i (at) höhnische Bemerkungen machen (über acc); höhnisch lachen (über acc): ~ at → a. **II.** **II** v/t verhöhnen. **III** s höhnische Bemerkung; Hohngelächter n. '**jeer·ing** adj □ höhnisch: ~ laughter Hohngelächter n.

Je·ho·va's Wit·ness [dʒɪˈhəʊvəz] s eccl. Zeuge m Jehovas.

jell [dʒel] **I** v/i **1.** gelieren. **2.** fig. Gestalt annehmen. **II** v/t **3.** gelieren lassen, zum Gelieren bringen.

jel·lied ['dʒelɪd] adj in Aspik od. Sülze.

jel·ly ['dʒelɪ] **I** s Gallert(e f) n; Gelee n; Aspik n, Sülze f; Götterspeise f. **II** v/i → jell I. **III** v/t → jell II. ~ **ba·by** s Br. Gummibärchen n. '~**fish** s **1.** zo. Qualle f. **2.** fig. F Waschlappen m.

jem·my ['dʒemɪ] Br. **I** s Brech-, Stemmeisen n. **II** v/t a. ~ **open** aufbrechen, -stemmen.

jeop·ard·ize ['dʒepədaɪz] v/t j-n, et. gefährden, in Gefahr bringen, et. in Frage stellen. '**jeop·ard·y** s Gefahr f: put (od. förmlich) in ~ → jeopardize.

jerk [dʒɜːk] **I** s **1.** Ruck m; Sprung m, Satz m: by ~s sprung-, ruckweise; give a ~ rucken, e-n Satz machen (Auto etc), zs.-zucken (Person). **2.** 🐾 Zuckung f; (bsd. Knie)Reflex m. **3.** Am. sl. Trottel m. **II** v/t **4.** ruckartig ziehen an (dat): ~ o.s. free sich losreißen. **III** v/i **5.** sich ruckartig od. ruckweise bewegen: ~ to a stop ruckweise od. mit e-n Ruck stehenbleiben. **6.** (zs.-)zucken. '**jerk·y** adj □ **1.** ruckartig, (Bewegungen) fahrig; stoß-, ruckweise. **2.** Am. sl. blöd.

jer·ry ['dʒerɪ] s Br. F Pott m (Nachttopf). '~**built** adj schlampig gebaut: ~ house Bruchbude f.

jer·sey ['dʒɜːzɪ] s **1.** Pullover m. **2.** Sport: Trikot n. **3.** Jersey m (Stoff).

jest [dʒest] **I** s Spaß m: in ~ im od. zum Scherz. **II** v/i spaßen: ~ with (s-n) Spaß treiben mit. '**jest·er** s **1.** Spaßvogel m. **2.** hist. (Hof)Narr m. '**jest·ing** adj spaßend; spaßhaft. '**jest·ing·ly** adv im od. zum Scherz.

Jes·u·it ['dʒezjʊɪt] s eccl. Jesuit m. ˌJes·u·it·ic, ˌJes·u·it·i·cal adj □ jesuitisch, Jesuiten...

jet [dʒet] **I** s **1.** (Feuer-, Wasseretc)Strahl m. **2.** ⊙ Düse f. **3.** ✈ Jet m. **II** v/i **4.** (heraus-, hervor)schießen

(from aus). **5.** ✈ jetten. ~ **age** s Düsenzeitalter n. ~ **en·gine** s Strahlmotor m, -triebwerk n. ~ **fight·er** s ✈, ✕ Düsenjäger m. ~ **lag** s Störung des gewohnten Alltagsrhythmus durch die Zeitverschiebung bei Langstreckenflügen. '~**lin·er** s Jetliner m, Düsenverkehrsflugzeug n. ~ **plane** s Düsenflugzeug n. '~**pro·pelled** adj bsd. ✈ mit Düsen- od. Strahlantrieb. ~ **pro·pul·sion** s bsd. ✈ Düsen-, Strahlantrieb m.

jet·sam ['dʒetsəm] s ⚓ **1.** Seewurfgut n. **2.** Strandgut n: → flotsam.

jet| set s Jet-set m. '~ˌset·ter** s Angehörige m, f des Jet-set.

jet·ti·son ['dʒetɪsn] v/t **1.** ⚓ über Bord werfen (a. fig.). **2.** ✈ (im Notwurf) abwerfen, Treibstoff ablassen. **3.** ausgebrannte Raketenstufe absprengen.

jet·ty ['dʒetɪ] s ⚓ **1.** Hafendamm m, Mole f. **2.** Strombrecher m (an Brücken).

Jew [dʒuː] s Jude m, Jüdin f.

jew·el ['dʒuːəl] **I** s **1.** Juwel n (a. fig.), Edelstein m: ~ box Schmuckkassette f. **2.** ⊙ Stein m (e-r Uhr). **II** v/t pret u. pp -eled, bsd. Br. -elled **3.** mit Juwelen schmücken od. besetzen. '**jew·el·(l)er** s Juwelier m. '**jew·el·ry**, bsd. Br. **jew·el·le·ry** ['~əlrɪ] s Juwelen pl, weitS. Schmuck m: piece of ~ Schmuckstück n.

Jew·ish ['dʒuːɪʃ] adj jüdisch, Juden...

jib¹ [dʒɪb] s **1.** ⚓ Klüver m. **2.** ⊙ Ausleger m (e-s Krans).

jib² [~] v/i **1.** scheuen, bocken (at vor dat). **2.** fig. störrisch od. bockig sein: ~ at sich sträuben gegen; streiken bei.

jif·fy ['dʒɪfɪ] s F Augenblick m: in a ~ im Nu, im Handumdrehen.

jig·gered ['dʒɪgəd] adj F **1.** I'm ~ if der Teufel soll mich holen, wenn. **2.** be ~ Br. baff od. platt sein: well, I'm ~! da bin ich aber baff!

jig·gle ['dʒɪgl] **I** v/t wackeln mit; schütteln; rütteln an (dat). **II** v/i wackeln, -drehen.

jig·saw (puz·zle) ['dʒɪgsɔː] s Puzzle (-spiel) n.

jilt [dʒɪlt] v/t Mädchen sitzenlassen (for wegen e-s anderen Mädchens); e-m Liebhaber, e-m Mädchen den Laufpaß geben.

jim-jams ['dʒɪmdʒæmz] s pl F **1.** Säuferwahn m. **2.** → jitter I.

jim·my ['dʒɪmɪ] *Am.* → **jemmy.**

jin·gle ['dʒɪŋgl] **I** *v/i* klimpern (*Münzen etc*), bimmeln (*Glöckchen etc*). **II** *v/t* klimpern mit, bimmeln lassen. **III** *s* Klimpern *n*, Bimmeln *n*.

jin·go ['dʒɪŋgəʊ] *pl* **-goes** *s* Chauvinist(in). **'jin·go·ism** *s* Chauvinismus *m*. **ˌjin·go·is·tic** *adj* (**~ally**) chauvinistisch.

jinks [dʒɪŋks] *s pl*: **high ~** Ausgelassenheit *f*; **they were having high ~** bei ihnen ging es hoch her.

jinx [dʒɪŋks] F **I** *s* **1.** Unglücksbringer *m*. **2.** Unglück *n*: **put a ~ on →** 3. **II** *v/t* **3.** Unglück bringen (*dat*); verhexen.

jit·ter ['dʒɪtə] F **I** *s*: **the ~s** *pl* Bammel *m*, e-e Heidenangst (*about* od *at*): **have the ~s →** II. **II** *v/i* Bammel od. e-e Heidenangst haben; furchtbar nervös sein. **'jit·ter·y** *adj* F furchtbar nervös.

jiu·jit·su [dʒuːˈdʒɪtsuː] → **jujitsu.**

job¹ [dʒɒb] **I** *s* **1.** (einzelne) Arbeit: **make a good (bad) ~ of s.th.** et. gut (schlecht) machen; → **odd** 5. **2.** *a.* **~ work** Akkordarbeit *f*: **by the ~** im Akkord. **3.** Stellung *f*, Tätigkeit *f*, Arbeit *f*, Job *m*, Arbeitsplatz *m*: **~ creation** Arbeits(platz)beschaffung *f*; **~ description** Arbeits(platz)beschreibung *f*; **computers are ~ killers** Computer vernichten Arbeitsplätze; **know one's ~** s-e Sache verstehen. **4.** Sache *f*: a) Aufgabe *f*, Pflicht *f*, b) Geschmack *m*: **this is not everybody's ~** das ist nicht jedermanns Sache, das sagt nicht jedem. **5.** F Sache *f*, Angelegenheit *f*: **make the best of a bad ~** gute Miene zum bösen Spiel machen; **das Beste daraus machen. 6.** F Ding *n*, krumme Sache: **pull a ~** ein Ding drehen. **II** *v/i* **7.** Gelegenheitsarbeiten machen, jobben. **8.** (im) Akkord arbeiten. **III** *v/t* **9.** *a.* **~ out** Arbeit in Auftrag geben; im Akkord vergeben.

Job² [dʒəʊb] *npr Bibl.* Hiob *m*: **have the patience of ~,** be (**as**) **patient as ~** e-e Engelsgeduld haben; **~'s comforter** *j-d, der durch s-n Trost alles nur noch schlimmer macht.*

job·ber ['dʒɒbə] *s* **1.** Gelegenheitsarbeiter *m*, Jobber *m*. **2.** Akkordarbeiter *m*. **3.** *Börse*: *Br.* Jobber *m*.

'job·hunt *v/i* auf Arbeitssuche sein: **go ~ing** auf Arbeitssuche gehen.

jock·ey ['dʒɒkɪ] **I** *s* **1.** *Pferderennsport*: Jockey *m*. **II** *v/t* **2.** Pferd (*als Jockey*)

reiten. **3.** manövrieren (*a. fig.*): **~ out of** *j-n* hinausbugsieren aus (*e-r Stellung etc*); *j-n* betrügen um. **III** *v/i* **4.** **~ for** rangeln um (*a. fig.*): **~ for position** (*Sport etc, a. fig.*) sich e-e günstige (Ausgangs)Position zu verschaffen suchen.

jo·cose [dʒəʊˈkəʊs], **joc·u·lar** ['dʒɒkjʊlə] *adj* □ **1.** ausgelassen (*Person*). **2.** witzig, spaßig (*Bemerkung etc*).

jog [dʒɒg] **I** *v/t* **1.** stoßen an (*acc*) od. gegen, *j-n* anstoßen, stupsen: **~ s.o.'s memory** *fig.* j-s Gedächtnis nachhelfen. **II** *v/i* **2.** trotten (*Person, Tier*), zuckeln (*Bus etc*); (*Sport*) joggen. **III** *s* **3.** Stoß *m*, Stups *m*. **4.** Trott *m*; (*Sport*) Trimmtrab *m*. **'jog·ger** *s Sport*: Jogger(in). **'jog·ging** *s Sport*: Joggen *n*, Jogging *n*.

jog·gle ['dʒɒgl] *v/t* (leicht) schütteln, rütteln an (*dat*).

jog|trot *s* gemächlicher Trab, Trott *m* (*a. fig.*). **'~-trot** *v/i* gemächlich traben (*bsd. Pferd*), trotten (*Person, Tier*).

John [dʒɒn] *s Am.* F Klo *n*: **in the ~** auf dem *od.* im Klo. ♀ **Bull** *s* England *n*, die Engländer *pl*; ein typischer Engländer. ♀ **Han·cock** ['hæŋkɒk] *s Am.* F Friedrich Wilhelm *m* (*Unterschrift*).

join [dʒɔɪn] **I** *v/t* **1.** *et.* verbinden, -einigen, zs.-fügen (**to** mit): **~ hands** die Hände falten; sich die Hand *od.* die Hände reichen; *fig.* sich zs.-tun (**with** mit). **2.** *Personen* vereinigen, zs.-bringen (**with, to** mit). **3.** sich anschließen (*dat od.* an *acc*), stoßen *od.* sich gesellen zu: **I'll ~ you later** ich komme später nach. **4.** eintreten in (*e-e Firma, e-n Verein etc*). **5.** teilnehmen *od.* sich beteiligen an (*dat*), mitmachen bei. **6.** einmünden in (*acc*) (*Fluß, Straße*). **II** *v/i* **7.** sich vereinigen. verbinden (**with** mit). **8.** **~ in** a) teilnehmen, sich beteiligen, mitmachen, b) → 5. **9.** zs.-kommen (*Straßen*), (*Flüsse a.*) zs.-fließen. **'join·er** *s* Tischler *m*, Schreiner *m*: **~'s bench** Hobelbank *f*. **'join·er·y** *s* **1.** Tischler-, Schreinerhandwerk *n*. **2.** Tischler-, Schreinerarbeit *f*.

joint [dʒɔɪnt] **I** *s* **1.** Verbindung(sstelle) *f*, *bsd.* a) (Löt)Naht *f*, Nahtstelle *f*, b) *anat.,* ☉ Gelenk *n*: **out of ~** ausgerenkt, *fig.* aus den Fugen; **put out of ~** sich *et.* ausrenken; → **nose** 1. **2.** *gastr.*

Braten(stück *n*) *m*. **3.** *sl*. Laden *m*, Bude *f* (*Lokal, Firma etc*): → **clip joint. 4.** *sl*. Joint *m* (*Haschisch- od. Marihuanazigarette*). **II** *adj* □ **5.** gemeinsam, gemeinschaftlich: **take ~ action** gemeinsam vorgehen; **~ venture** ✝ Gemeinschaftsunternehmen *n*. ˌ~·'**stock com·pa·ny** *s* **1.** *Br.* Kapital- *od.* Aktiengesellschaft *f*. **2.** *Am.* Offene Handelsgesellschaft auf Aktien.

joist [dʒɔɪst] *s* △ **1.** Deckenträger *m*, -balken *m*. **2.** I-Träger *m*.

joke [dʒəʊk] **I** *s* **1.** Witz *m*: **crack ~s** Witze reißen. **2.** a) Scherz *m*, Spaß *m*: **in** (*od.* **for a**) ~ im *od.* zum Spaß; **that's going beyond a ~** das ist kein Spaß mehr, das ist nicht mehr lustig; **he can't take a ~** er versteht keinen Spaß, b) *mst* **practical ~** Streich *m*: **play a ~ on** s.o. j-m e-n Streich spielen. **II** *v/i* **3.** scherzen, Witze *od.* Spaß machen: **I'm not joking** ich meine das ernst; **you must be joking, are you joking?** das ist doch nicht dein Ernst! '**jok·er** *s* **1.** Spaßvogel *m*, Witzbold *m*. **2.** Joker *m* (*Spielkarte*). **3.** *sl.* Typ *m*, Kerl *m*. '**jok·ing I** *adj* □ scherzhaft, spaßend: **~ly** a. im Spaß. **II** *s* Witze *pl*: **~ apart** Scherz *od.* Spaß beiseite.

jol·li·fi·ca·tion [ˌdʒɒlɪfɪ'keɪʃn] *s* ✝ (feucht)fröhliches Fest, Festivität *f*.

jol·ly¹ ['dʒɒlɪ] **I** *adj* □ **1.** lustig, fröhlich, vergnügt. **2.** F angeheitert: **be ~** e-n Schwips haben. **II** *adv* **3.** *Br.* F ganz schön, ziemlich: **a ~ good fellow** ein prima Kerl.

jol·ly² [~], **~ boat** *s* ✈ Jolle *f*.

Jol·ly Rog·er [ˌdʒɒlɪ'rɒdʒə] *s* Totenkopf-, Piratenflagge *f*.

jolt [dʒəʊlt] **I** *v/t* **1.** e-n Ruck *od.* Stoß geben (*dat*); *Passagiere* durchrütteln, -schütteln. **2.** *fig. j-m* e-n Schock versetzen; *j-n* auf- *od.* wachrütteln: **~ s.o. out of a.** j-n reißen aus. **II** *v/i* **3.** e-n Ruck machen; rütteln, holpern (*Fahrzeug*). **III** *s* **4.** Ruck *m*, Stoß *m*. **5.** *fig.* Schock *m*: **give s.o. a ~** j-m e-n Schock versetzen.

josh [dʒɒʃ] *v/t Am.* F *j-n* aufziehen, veräppeln.

joss stick [dʒɒs] *s* Räucherstäbchen *n*.

jos·tle ['dʒɒsl] **I** *v/t* **1.** anrempeln. **2.** dränge(l)n: **~ one's way through** sich (durch)drängen durch. **II** *v/i* **3.** ~

against rempeln gegen, anrempeln (*acc*). **4.** (sich) dränge(l)n.

jot [dʒɒt] **I** *s fig.* Spur *f*: **not a ~ of truth** kein Funke *od.* Körnchen Wahrheit. **II** *v/t mst* **~ down** sich *et.* notieren. '**jot·ter** *s* Notizbuch *n*, -block *m*. '**jot·ting** *s mst pl* Notiz *f*.

joule [dʒuːl] *s phys.* Joule *n*.

jour·nal ['dʒɜːnl] *s* **1.** Journal *n*, Zeitschrift *f*. **2.** Tagebuch *n*. **3.** *Buchhaltung:* Journal *n*: **cash ~** Kassenbuch *n*. **4.** ✈ Logbuch *n*. **jour·nal·ese** [ˌ~nə'liːz] *s* Zeitungsstil *m*, Tagesreisen *pl*. '**jour·nal·ism** *s* Journalismus *m*. '**jour·nal·ist** *s* Journalist(in). ˌ**jour·nal·'is·tic** *adj* (**~ally**) journalistisch.

jour·ney ['dʒɜːnɪ] *s* **1.** Reise *f*: **go on a ~** verreisen. **2.** Reise *f*, Entfernung *f*: **a two days' ~** zwei Tagesreisen (**to** nach). **~·man** ['~mən] *s* (*irr man*) Geselle *m*: **~ tailor** Schneidergeselle.

jo·vi·al ['dʒəʊvjəl] *adj* □ lustig, fröhlich, vergnügt. **jo·vi·al·i·ty** [ˌ~vɪ'ælətɪ] *s* Lustigkeit *f*, Fröhlichkeit *f*.

jowl [dʒaʊl] *s* **1.** (Unter)Kiefer *m*. **2.** Wange *f*, Backe *f*; Hängebacke *f*: → **cheek** 1.

joy [dʒɔɪ] *s* **1.** Freude *f* (**at** über *acc*; **in** *dat*): **for ~** vor Freude *weinen etc*; **tears** *pl* **of ~** Freudentränen *pl*; **to s.o.'s ~** zu j-s Freude. **2.** *Br.* F Erfolg *m*: **I didn't have any ~** ich hatte kein Glück. '**joy·ful** ['~fʊl] *adj* □ **1.** freudig, erfreut: **be ~** sich freuen, froh sein. **2.** erfreulich, freudig (*Ereignis etc*). '**joy·less** *adj* □ **1.** freudlos. **2.** unerfreulich. '**joy·ous** → **joyful.**

joy·ride *s* F Spritztour *f* (*bsd. in e-m gestohlenen Wagen*): **go on a ~** e-e Spritztour machen. **~ stick** *s* F **1.** ✈ Steuerknüppel *m*. **2.** *Computer:* Joystick *m*.

ju·bi·lant ['dʒuːbɪlənt] *adj* □ **1.** überglücklich. **2.** jubelnd: **~ shout** Jubelschrei *m*. **ju·bi·late** ['~leɪt] *v/i* jubilieren, jubeln. **ju·bi·la·tion** *s* Jubel *m*. **ju·bi·lee** ['~liː] *s* Jubiläum *n*.

judge [dʒʌdʒ] **I** *s* **1.** ⚖ Richter *m*: → **sober** I. **2.** Schiedsrichter *m*; Preisrichter *m*; (*Sport a.*) Kampfrichter *m*, (*Boxen*) Punktrichter *m*. **3.** Kenner *m*: **a (good) ~ of wine** ein Weinkenner. **II** *v/t* **4.** ⚖ *Fall* verhandeln; die Verhandlung führen gegen. **5.** *Wettbewerbsteil-*

nehmer, Leistungen etc beurteilen (**on** nach); als Schiedsrichter (*etc*, → 2) fungieren bei. **6.** entscheiden (**s.th.** et; *that* daß). **7.** beurteilen, einschätzen (**by** nach). **III** *v/i* **8.** als Schiedsrichter (*etc*, → 2) fungieren (**at** bei). **9.** urteilen (**of** über *acc*): *judging by his words* s-n Worten nach zu urteilen.

judg(e)·ment ['dʒʌdʒmənt] *s* **1.** ⚖ Urteil *n*. **2.** Urteilsvermögen *n*: *against* (*one's*) *better* ~ wider bessere Einsicht. **3.** Meinung *f*, Ansicht *f*, Urteil *n* (**on** über *acc*): *in my* ~ m-s Erachtens; *form a* (*final*) ~ *on* sich ein (abschließendes *od.* endgültiges) Urteil bilden über. **4.** göttliche(r) (Straf)Gericht: *the Last* ♋ das Jüngste Gericht; *Day of* ♋, ♋ *Day* Jüngster Tag.

ju·di·ca·ture ['dʒu:dɪkətʃə] *s* ⚖ **1.** Rechtsprechung *f*, Rechtspflege *f*. **2.** Gerichtswesen *n*. **3.** → *judiciary* 1.

ju·di·cial [dʒu:'dɪʃl] *adj* □ **1.** ⚖ gerichtlich, Gerichts...: ~ *error* Justizirrtum *m*; ~ *murder* Justizmord *m*. **2.** ⚖ richterlich. **3.** kritisch.

ju·di·ci·a·ry [dʒu:'dɪʃərɪ] ⚖ **I** *adj* **1.** → *judicial* 1, 2. **II** *s* **2.** → *judicature* 2. **3.** *coll.* Richter(schaft *f*) *pl*.

ju·di·cious [dʒu:'dɪʃəs] *adj* □ **1.** vernünftig, umsichtig. **2.** wohlüberlegt.

ju·do ['dʒu:dəʊ] *s Sport:* Judo *n*. **ju·do·ka** ['·ka:] *s* Judoka *m*.

jug [dʒʌɡ] **I** *s* **1.** Krug *m*; *bsd. Br.* Kanne *f*; Kännchen *n*. **2.** *sl.* Knast *m* (*Gefängnis*). **II** *v/t* **3.** *sl.* einlochen.

jug·ger·naut ['dʒʌɡənɔ:t] *s* **1.** *mot. Br.* Schwerlastzug *m*. **2.** *fig.* Moloch *m*.

jug·gins ['dʒʌɡɪnz] *s bsd. Br.* F Trottel *m*.

jug·gle ['dʒʌɡl] **I** *v/t* **1.** jonglieren (mit). **2.** *fig.* jonglieren mit (*Fakten, Worten etc*); *Fakten, Worte etc* verdrehen; *Konten etc* fälschen, frisieren. **II** *v/i* **3.** jonglieren. **4.** ~ *with* → 2. '**jug·gler** *s* **1.** Jongleur *m*. **2.** ~ *of words* Wortverdreher *m*. **3.** Schwindler *m*.

Ju·go·slav → *Yugoslav.*

juice [dʒu:s] **I** *s* **1.** Saft *m*: *let s.o. stew in his own* ~ F j-n im eigenen Saft schmoren lassen. **2.** *sl.* ⚡ Saft *m*; *mot.* Sprit *m*. **II** *v/t* **3.** entsaften. '**juic·y** *adj* □ **1.** saftig. **2.** F knackig (*Mädchen*); saftig (*Gewinn etc*); lukrativ (*Vertrag etc*); pikant (*Einzelheiten etc*).

ju·jit·su [dʒu:'dʒɪtsu:] *s Sport:* Jiu-Jitsu *n*.

juke·box ['dʒu:kbɒks] *s* Jukebox *f*, Musikautomat *m*.

Ju·ly [dʒu:'laɪ] *s* Juli *m*: *in* ~ im Juli.

jum·ble ['dʒʌmbl] **I** *v/t a.* ~ *together* (*od. up*) *Sachen* durcheinanderwerfen; *Fakten etc* durcheinanderbringen. **II** *s* Durcheinander *n*. ~ *sale* *s Br.* Wohltätigkeitsbasar *m*.

jum·bo ['dʒʌmbəʊ] **I** *pl* **-bos** *s* **1.** Koloß *m* (*Sache, Person*). **2.** ✈ Jumbo *m*. **II** *adj* **3.** riesig, Riesen...: ~ *jet* ✈ Jumbo-Jet *m*. '**~-sized** → *jumbo* 3.

jump [dʒʌmp] **I** *s* **1.** Sprung *m*: *make* (*od. take*) *a* ~ e-n Sprung machen; *have the* ~ *on s.o.* F j-m vorausein. **2.** *Sport:* (*Hoch-, Ski- etc*)Sprung *m*. **3.** *give a* ~ → 6; *it gives me the* ~*s* F es macht mich ganz nervös *od.* unruhig; *have the* ~*s* F ganz nervös *od.* aufgeregt sein. **II** *v/i* **4.** springen: ~ *at fig.* sich stürzen auf (*acc*); ~ *off* abspringen (**von**); ~ *out of one's skin fig.* aus der Haut fahren; ~ *to one's feet* aufspringen; → *conclusion* 3. **5.** hüpfen, springen: ~ *for joy* Freudensprünge machen. **6.** zs.-zucken, auf-, zs.-fahren (**at** bei). **7.** *fig.* abrupt übergehen, überspringen, -wechseln (**to** zu). **III** *v/t* **8.** springen über (*acc*). **9.** *fig.* überspringen, auslassen: ~ *the gun* (*Sport*) e-n Fehlstart verursachen; *fig.* voreilig sein *od.* handeln; ~ *the line* (*bsd. Br. Queue*) sich vordränge(l)n (*beim Schlangestehen u. fig.*); *mot.* aus e-r Kolonne ausscheren u. überholen; → *light*[1] 3. **10.** (her-aus)springen aus: → *rail*[1] 3, *track* 3.

jump·er[1] ['dʒʌmpə] *s Sport:* (*Hoch-etc*)Springer(in).

jump·er[2] [~] *s* **1.** *bsd. Br.* Pullover *m*. **2.** *Am.* Trägerrock *m*, -kleid *n*.

jump·er ca·bles *s pl Am.* → *jump leads.*

jump| **leads** [li:dz] *s pl Br. mot.* Starthilfekabel *n*. ~ *rope* *s Am.* Spring-, Sprungseil *n*. ~ *seat* *s* Klapp-, Notsitz *m*. ~ *suit* *s* Overall *m*.

jump·y ['dʒʌmpɪ] *adj* □ nervös; schreckhaft.

junc·tion ['dʒʌŋkʃn] *s* **1.** Verbindung *f*, -einigung *f*. **2.** 🚆 Knotenpunkt *m*. **3.** (Straßen)Kreuzung *f*, (-)Einmündung *f*.

junc·ture ['dʒʌŋktʃə] *s*: *at this* ~ in die-

sem Augenblick, zu diesem Zeitpunkt.
June [dʒuːn] *s* Juni *m*: **in ~** im Juni.

jun·gle ['dʒʌŋgl] *s* Dschungel *m* (*a. fig.*).

jun·ior ['dʒuːnjə] **I** *adj* **1.** junior. **2.** (*to*) jünger (als); untergeordnet (*dat*): **~ partner** ✝ Junior(partner) *m*; → **management** 2. **3.** *ped.* **~ high (school)** *Am.* die unteren Klassen der High-School; **~ school** *Br.* Grundschule *f* (*für Kinder von 7–11*). **4.** *Sport:* Junioren... **II** *s* **5.** Jüngere *m, f*: **he is my ~ by two years, he is two years my ~** er ist 2 Jahre jünger als ich. **6.** *Sport:* Junior(in).

ju·ni·per ['dʒuːnɪpə] *s* ♣ Wacholder *m*.

junk¹ [dʒʌŋk] *s* ♣ Dschunke *f*.

junk² [~] **I** *s* **1.** Trödel *m*; Altmaterial *n*; Schrott *m*. **2.** Gerümpel *n*, Abfall *m* **3.** *contp.* Schund *m*, Mist *m*. **4.** *sl.* Stoff *m*, *bsd.* Heroin *n*. **II** *v/t* **5.** *et.* unbrauchbar Gewordenes ausrangieren, *Auto etc* verschrotten.

jun·ket ['dʒʌŋkɪt] *s* (Sahne)Quark *m*; Dickmilch *f*.

junk food *s* Junk-food *m* (*kalorienreiche Nahrung von geringem Nährwert*).

junk·ie ['dʒʌŋkɪ] *s sl.* Junkie *m* (*Rauschgiftsüchtiger*), *bsd.* H-Fixer *m*.

'junk·yard *s* Schuttabladeplatz *m*; Schrottplatz *m*.

jun·ta ['dʒʌntə] *s pol.* Junta *f*.

ju·rid·i·cal [,dʒʊə'rɪdɪkl] *adj* □ **1.** gerichtlich, Gerichts... **2.** juristisch, Rechts...

ju·ris·dic·tion [,dʒʊərɪs'dɪkʃn] *s* Gerichtsbarkeit *f*; (*örtliche u. sachliche*) Zuständigkeit (*of, over* für): **come** (*od. fall*) **under** (*od. within*) **the ~ of** unter die Zuständigkeit fallen von (*od. gen*); **have ~ over** zuständig sein für.

ju·ris·pru·dence [,dʒʊərɪs'pruːdəns] *s* Rechtswissenschaft *f*.

ju·rist ['dʒʊərɪst] *s* **1.** Jurist *m*, Rechtsgelehrte *m*. **2.** *Br.* Rechtsstudent *m*. **3.** *Am.* Rechtsanwalt *m*.

ju·ror ['dʒʊərə] *s* **1.** ⚖ Geschworene *m, f*. **2.** Preisrichter(in).

ju·ry ['dʒʊərɪ] *s* **1.** ⚖ die Geschworenen *pl*: → **trial** 1. **2.** Jury *f*, Preis-, (*Sport a.*)

Kampfgericht *n*. **~ box** *s* ⚖ Geschworenenbank *f*. **~·man** ['~mən] *s* (*irr* **man**) ⚖ Geschworene *m*. **'~·wom·an** *s* (*irr* **woman**) Geschworene *f*.

just [dʒʌst] **I** *adj* (□ → **justly**) **1.** gerecht (*to* gegen). **2.** gerecht, angemessen: **it was only ~** es war nur recht u. billig. **3.** rechtmäßig (*Anspruch etc*); berechtigt, gerechtfertigt (*Zorn etc*). **II** *adv* **4.** gerade, (so)eben: → **now** 3. **5.** gerade, genau, eben: **~ as** gerade als; **that is ~ like you** das sieht dir ähnlich; → **well¹** 1. **6.** gerade (noch), ganz knapp. **7.** nur, lediglich, bloß: → **moment** 1, *etc* **8. ~ about** ungefähr, etwa; gerade noch.

jus·tice ['dʒʌstɪs] *s* **1.** Gerechtigkeit *f* (*to* gegen): **do ~ to** gerecht werden (*dat*); *et.* richtig würdigen. **2.** ⚖ Gerechtigkeit *f*, Recht *n*: **do ~** der Gerechtigkeit Genüge tun; **bring to ~** vor den Richter bringen; → **administer** 2. **3.** ⚖ Richter *m*: **~ of the peace** Friedensrichter.

jus·ti·fi·a·ble ['dʒʌstɪfaɪəbl] *adj* zu rechtfertigen(d), berechtigt, vertretbar. **'jus·ti·fi·a·bly** *adv* berechtigterweise, mit gutem Grund, mit Recht.

jus·ti·fi·ca·tion [,dʒʌstɪfɪ'keɪʃn] *s* Rechtfertigung *f*: **in ~ of** zur Rechtfertigung von (*od. gen*).

jus·ti·fy ['dʒʌstɪfaɪ] *v/t* rechtfertigen (**before, to** vor *dat*, gegenüber): **be justified in doing s.th.** et. mit gutem Recht tun; berechtigt sein, et. zu tun.

just·ly ['dʒʌstlɪ] *adv* mit *od.* zu Recht.

jut [dʒʌt] *v/i a.* **~ out** vorspringen; herausragen.

jute [dʒuːt] *s* Jute(faser) *f*.

ju·ve·nile ['dʒuːvənaɪl] **I** *adj* jugendlich; Jugend...: **~ court** Jugendgericht *n*; **~ delinquency** Jugendkriminalität *f*; **~ delinquent** (*od. offender*) straffälliger Jugendlicher. **II** *s* Jugendliche *m, f*.

jux·ta·pose [,dʒʌkstə'pəʊz] *v/t* nebeneinanderstellen (*a. fig.*). **jux·ta·po·si·tion** [,~pə'zɪʃn] *s* **1.** Nebeneinanderstellung *f*. **2.** Nebeneinanderstehen *n*: **be in ~** nebeneinanderstehen.

K

kale [keɪl] s **1.** ♀ Grün-, Braunkohl m. **2.** Am. sl. Kies m (Geld).

ka·lei·do·scope [kə'laɪdəskəʊp] s Kaleidoskop n (a. fig.).

kan·ga·roo [,kæŋgə'ruː] s zo. Känguruh n.

ka·put [kæ'pʊt] adj pred F kaputt.

kar·at bsd. Am. → **carat**.

ka·ra·te [kə'rɑːtɪ] s Karate n: ~ **chop** Karateschlag m.

kar·ma ['kɑːmə] s Buddhismus, Hinduismus: Karma(n) n.

ka·yak ['kaɪæk] s Kajak m, n (a. Sport).

keck [kek] v/i bsd. Am. **1.** würgen (beim Erbrechen). **2.** fig. sich ekeln (at vor dat).

keel [kiːl] ⚓ I s Kiel m: **on an even ~** fig. gleichmäßig, ruhig. II v/i mst **~ over** (od. **up**) umschlagen, kentern.

keen [kiːn] adj □ **1.** scharf (geschliffen). **2.** schneidend (Kälte), scharf (Wind). **3.** scharf (Sinne, Verstand etc). **4.** ♥ scharf (Wettbewerb); lebhaft, stark (Nachfrage). **5.** heftig, stark (Gefühl): **~ interest** starkes od. lebhaftes Interesse. **6.** begeistert, leidenschaftlich (Schwimmer etc). **7.** versessen, scharf (on, about auf acc): **be ~ on** a. begeistert sein von; **be ~ on doing** (od. **to do**) **s.th.** et. unbedingt tun wollen.

keep [kiːp] I s **1.** (Lebens)Unterhalt m. **2.** for **~s** F für immer, endgültig: **it's yours for ~s** du kannst od. darfst es behalten. II v/t (irr) **3.** (be)halten. **4.** j-n, et. lassen, (in e-m bestimmten Zustand) (er)halten: **~ closed** Tür etc geschlossen halten; **~ s.th. a secret** et. geheimhalten (from vor dat); → **wait** 1, etc. **5.** (im Besitz) behalten: **~ the change** der Rest (des Geldes) ist für Sie; **~ your seat, please** bitte behalten Sie Platz. **6.** j-n aufhalten: **don't let me ~ you** laß dich nicht aufhalten. **7.** aufheben, -bewahren: **can you ~ a secret?** kannst du schweigen? **8.** Beziehungen etc unterhalten (with zu). **9.** Ware führen. **10.** Laden etc haben, betreiben. **11.** Versprechen, Wort halten. **12.** Bett, Haus, Zimmer hüten. **13.** ernähren, er-, unterhalten: **have a family to ~** e-e Fami-

lie ernähren müssen. **14.** Tiere halten; sich ein Auto etc halten. III v/i (irr) **15.** bleiben: **~ in sight** in Sicht(weite) bleiben; **~ still** stillhalten. **16.** sich halten, (in e-m bestimmten Zustand) bleiben: **~ friends** (weiterhin) Freunde bleiben. **17.** mit ger weiter...: **~ smiling!** immer nur lächeln!; **~ (on) trying** es weiterversuchen, es immer wieder versuchen.

Verbindungen mit Präpositionen:

keep| at v/i **1.** weitermachen mit. **2.** j-m zusetzen (to do zu tun). **~ from** I v/t **1.** abhalten von: **keep s.o. from doing s.th.** j-n davon abhalten, et. zu tun. **2.** bewahren vor (dat). **3.** j-m et. vorenthalten, verschweigen. II v/i **4.** vermeiden (acc): **~ doing s.th.** es vermeiden od. sich davor hüten, et. zu tun; **I could hardly ~ laughing** ich konnte mir kaum das Lachen verkneifen. **~ off** v/t u. v/i (sich) fernhalten von: **keep your hands off it!** Hände weg (davon)!; → **grass** 2. **~ on** v/i leben od. sich ernähren von. **~ to** I v/t **1.** bleiben in (dat): → **left²** 3, **right** 9. **2.** fig. festhalten an (dat), bleiben bei. II v/t **3. keep s.th. to a** (od. **the**) **minimum** et. auf ein Minimum beschränken. **4. keep s.th. to o.s.** et. für sich behalten.

Verbindungen mit Adverbien:

keep| a·way v/t u. v/i (sich) fernhalten (from von). **~ back** v/t **1.** zurückhalten: **keep s.o. back from doing s.th.** j-n davon abhalten od. daran hindern, et. zu tun. **2.** fig. zurückhalten: a) Lohn etc einbehalten, b) Tränen etc unterdrücken, c) et. verschweigen. **~ down** I v/t **1.** Kopf etc unten behalten. **2.** Kosten etc niedrig halten. **3.** unter Kontrolle halten, Volk, Gefühle etc a. unterdrücken. **4.** Nahrung etc bei sich behalten. II v/i **5.** unten bleiben; sich geduckt halten. **~ in** I v/t **1.** nicht heraus- od. hinauslassen; ped. nachsitzen lassen. **2.** Atem anhalten. **3.** Gefühle zurückhalten, unterdrücken. II v/i **4.** drin bleiben, nicht herauskommen. **5.** ~ **with** sich mit j-m gut stellen. **~ off** v/t u. v/i (sich) fernhalten: **keep your hands off!** Hände weg!; **~!** Berühren verboten!; Betreten verboten! **~ on I** v/t **1.** *Kleidungsstück* anbehalten, anlassen, *Hut* aufbehalten: → *shirt*. **2.** *Licht* brennen lassen, anlassen. **II** v/i **3.** a) weitermachen, b) nicht lockerlassen, c) → *keep* 17. **4. ~ at** → *keep at* 2. **~ out I** v/t **1.** (*of*) nicht hinein- *od.* hereinlassen (in *acc*), fern-, abhalten (von). **2.** *fig.* heraushalten (*of* aus). **II** v/i **3.** draußen bleiben: *~!* Zutritt verboten! **4.** *fig.* sich heraushalten (*of* aus): **~ of sight** sich nicht blicken lassen. **~ to·geth·er I** v/t *Dinge, fig. Mannschaft etc* zs.-halten. **II** v/i zs.-bleiben (*a. fig. Mannschaft etc*), zs.-halten (*a. fig. Freunde etc*). **~ up I** v/t **1.** oben halten, hochhalten: → *chin* 1. **2.** *fig.* aufrechterhalten, *Brauch etc* a. weiterpflegen, *Tempo* halten, *Preise etc* (hoch)halten, *Mut* nicht sinken lassen: → *appearance* 3. **3.** in gutem Zustand *od.* in Ordnung halten. **II** v/i **4.** oben bleiben. **5.** *fig.* sich halten, (*Preise etc a.*) sich behaupten; andauern, nicht nachlassen. **6. ~ with** a) Schritt halten mit (*a. fig.*): **~ with the Joneses** es den Nachbarn gleichtun (wollen); → *time* 1, b) sich auf dem laufenden halten über (*acc*), c) in Kontakt bleiben mit.

keep·er ['ki:pə] s **1.** Wächter *m*, Aufseher *m*. **2.** *mst in Zssgn* Inhaber *m*, Besitzer *m*; Halter *m*, Züchter *m*. **3.** Betreuer *m*, Verwalter *m*.

keep-'fresh bag s Frischhaltebeutel *m*.

keep·ing ['ki:pɪŋ] s **1.** Verwahrung *f*: *put in s.o.'s* ~ *j-n* in *j-s* Obhut geben; *j-m et.* zur Aufbewahrung geben. **2. be in (out of)** ~ **with** (nicht) übereinstimmen mit; (nicht) passen zu; (nicht) entsprechen (*dat*).

keep·sake ['ki:pseɪk] s (*Geschenk zum*) Andenken *n*: *as* (*od. for*) **a** ~ als *od.* zum Andenken.

keg [keg] s Fäßchen *n*.

ken [ken] s: *this is beyond* (*od. outside*) *my* ~ das entzieht sich m-r Kenntnis; das ist mir zu hoch.

ken·nel ['kenl] s **1.** Hundehütte *f*. **2.** *oft pl* (*sg konstruiert*) Hundezwinger *m*; Hundeheim *n*.

kept [kept] *pret u. pp von* **keep**.

kerb [kɜːb], **'~·stone** s *Br.* Bord-, Randstein *m*.

ker·chief ['kɜːtʃɪf] s Hals-, Kopftuch *n*.

ker·nel ['kɜːnl] s **1.** Kern *m* (*a. fig.*).

2. (*Hafer-, Mais- etc*)Korn *n*.

ker·o·sene ['kerəsiːn] s 🜊 Kerosin *n*.

ketch·up ['ketʃəp] s Ketchup *m, n.*

ket·tle ['ketl] s Kessel *m*: **a pretty** (*od. fine*) ~ **of fish** *iro.* e-e schöne Bescherung; *that's a different* ~ **of fish** das ist et. ganz anderes; *keep the* ~ **boiling** sich über Wasser halten; die Sache in Schwung halten.

key [kiː] I s **1.** Schlüssel *m* (*a. fig.* fig. to zu). **2.** Taste *f* (*e-s Klaviers, e-r Schreibmaschine etc*). **3.** ♪ Tonart *f*: **major** (**minor**) ~ Dur *n* (Moll *n*); **off** (*od. out of*) ~ falsch singen *etc*. **II** adj **4.** Schlüssel... (*a. fig.*). **III** v/t **5.** ♪ stimmen. **6.** ~ **in** (*Computer*) *Daten* eintasten, -tippen. **7.** ~ (**up**) **to**, ~ **in with** *j-n* abstimmen auf (*acc*). **8.** ~ **up** *j-n* in nervöse Spannung versetzen: *~ed up* nervös, aufgeregt (*about* wegen). '**~·board** s **1.** Tastatur *f* (*e-s Klaviers, e-r Schreibmaschine etc*): ~ **instrument** Tasteninstrument *n*. **2.** Schlüsselbrett *n*. '**~·hole** s Schlüsselloch *n*. '**~·man** s (*irr man*) **1.** Schlüsselfigur *f*. **2.** Mann *m* in e-r Schlüsselstellung. '**~·note** s **1.** ♪ Grundton *m*. **2.** *fig.* Grund-, Leitgedanke *m*: ~ **address** (*od. speech*) *pol.* programmatische Rede. '**~·phone** s *Br.* Tastentelefon *n*. **~ sig·na·ture** s ♪ Vorzeichen *n u. pl*. '**~·stone** s **1.** △ Schlußstein *m*. **2.** *fig.* Grundpfeiler *m*.

khak·i ['kɑːkɪ] I s **1.** Khaki *n* (*Farbe*). **2.** Khaki *n* (*Stoff*); *mst pl* Khakiuniform *f*. **II** adj **3.** Khaki...: a) khakifarben, b) aus Khaki.

kib·itz·er ['kɪbɪtsə] s F **1.** Kiebitz *m*. **2.** *fig.* Besserwisser *m*.

kick [kɪk] I s **1.** (Fuß)Tritt *m*, Stoß *m*: *give s.o. a* ~ *j-m* e-n Tritt geben *od.* versetzen; *get the* ~ F (raus)fliegen (*entlassen werden*). **2.** Fußball: Schuß *m*. **3.** *Schwimmen:* Beinschlag *m*. **4.** F Schwung *m*: *give s.th. a* ~ et. in Schwung bringen. **5.** F *for* ~*s* zum Spaß; *he gets a* ~ *out of it* es macht ihm e-n Riesenspaß. **II** v/t **6.** (mit dem Fuß) stoßen, treten, e-n Tritt geben *od.* versetzen (*dat*): *I could have* ~*ed myself* ich hätte mich ohrfeigen *od.* mir in den Hintern beißen können; → *bucket* I. **7.** loskommen von (*e-r Droge, Gewohnheit etc*). **III** v/i **8.** (mit dem Fuß) stoßen, treten (*at* nach); strampeln; aus-

schlagen (*Pferd etc*): → **trace²**. **9. ~ about** (*od.* **around**) F sich herumtreiben in (*dat*). **10.** F meutern, rebellieren (**against, at** gegen).
Verbindungen mit Adverbien:
kick| a·bout, ~ a·round F **I** v/t **1.** j-n herumkommandieren. **2.** j-n, *et.* herumstoßen, -schubsen. **II** v/i **3.** sich herumtreiben. **~ back** v/i **1.** zurücktreten. **2.** *fig.* unangenehme Folgen haben (**at** für); zurückschlagen. **~ in 1.** Tür eintreten. **2.** *Am.* F *et.* beisteuern (**for** zu). **~ off** I v/i **1.** *Fußball:* anstoßen. **2.** F anfangen. **II** v/t **3.** *et.* wegtreten, *Schuhe* wegschleudern. **~ out I** v/i um sich treten; losschlagen (*Pferd etc*). **II** v/t F j-n rausschmeißen (**of** aus) (*a. fig.*). **~ o·ver** v/t mit dem Fuß umstoßen. **~ up** v/t mit dem Fuß hochschleudern, *Staub* aufwirbeln: → **din** I, **dust** 1, **row³** I, *etc.*
'kick|·back s unangenehme Folge(n *pl*). **'~·off** s *Fußball:* Anstoß m. **'~·out** s F Rausschmiß m (*a. fig.*). **'~·start·er** s *es Motorrads*.
kid¹ [kɪd] s **1.** Zicklein n, Kitz n. **2.** *a.* **~ leather** Ziegen-, Glacéleder n. **3.** F a) Kind n: **my ~ brother** mein kleiner Bruder, b) *bsd. Am.* Jugendliche m, f.
kid² [~] F **I** v/t j-n auf den Arm nehmen. **II** v/i albern; Spaß machen; schwindeln: *he was only ~ding* er hat nur Spaß gemacht, er hat es nicht ernst gemeint; *no ~ding?* im Ernst?, ehrlich?
kid glove s Glacéhandschuh m: *handle s.o. with ~s fig.* j-n mit Samt- *od.* Glacéhandschuhen anfassen.
kid·nap ['kɪdnæp] v/t pret u. pp **-naped**, *bsd. Br.* **-napped** kidnappen, entführen. **'kid·nap·(p)er** s Kidnapper m, Entführer m. **'kid·nap·(p)ing** s Kidnapping n, Entführung f.
kid·ney ['kɪdnɪ] s **1.** *anat.* Niere f. **2.** *fig.* Art f, Schlag m. **~ bean** s ♀ Weiße Bohne. **~ ma·chine** s ♀ künstliche Niere: *put on a ~* j-n an e-e künstliche Niere anschließen. **~ stone** s ♣ Nierenstein m. **~ trans·plant** s ♣ Nierenverpflanzung f.
kill [kɪl] **I** v/t **1.** töten, umbringen, ermorden: **~ two birds with one stone** *fig.* zwei Fliegen mit 'einer Klappe schlagen; **be ~ed** a. ums Leben kommen, umkommen; → **accident** 2, **action** 6. **2.**

Tier schlachten. **3.** (fast) umbringen: *my feet are ~ing me* m-e Füße bringen mich (noch) um. **4.** *a.* **~ off** *Knospen, Rost etc* vernichten. **5.** *Gefühle* (ab)töten, ersticken; *Schmerzen* stillen. **6.** *Zeit* totschlagen. **7.** F *Flasche etc* vernichten, austrinken. **II** v/i **8.** töten. **9.** *dressed to ~* F todschick gekleidet, *contp.* aufgedonnert. **'kill·er** s **1.** Mörder m, (*kaltblütiger, professioneller*) Killer m. **2.** *bsd. in Zssgn* Vertilgungs-*od.* Vernichtungsmittel n. **II** adj **3.** tödlich: **~ whale** zo. Schwert-, Mordwal m. **'kill·ing** adj □ **1.** tödlich. **2.** vernichtend (*a. fig. Blick*), mörderisch (*a. fig. Tempo etc*). **3.** F umwerfend, hinreißend.
'kill·joy s Spielverderber(in), Miesmacher(in).
kiln [kɪln] s Brenn- *od.* Trockenofen m.
ki·lo ['kiːləʊ] pl **-los** s Kilo n.
ki·lo|·gram(me) ['kɪləʊɡræm] s Kilogramm n. **'~·me·ter,** *bsd. Br.* **'~·me·tre** s Kilometer m. **'~·watt** s ✓ Kilowatt n.
kilt [kɪlt] s Kilt m, Schottenrock m.
ki·mo·no [kɪ'məʊnəʊ] pl **-nos** s Kimono m.
kin [kɪn] s coll. (*pl konstruiert*) Blutsverwandtschaft f, Verwandte pl: *be of no ~ to* nicht verwandt sein mit; → **next** 5.
kind¹ [kaɪnd] s **1.** Art f, Sorte f: *all ~s of* alle möglichen, allerlei; *nothing of the ~* nichts dergleichen. **2.** Art f, Wesen n: *different in ~* der Art *od.* dem Wesen nach verschieden. **3. ~ of** F ein bißchen, irgendwie: *I've ~ of promised* ich habe es halb u. halb versprochen. **4.** *in ~* in Naturalien *zahlen*.
kind² [~] adj (□ → **kindly** II) **1.** freundlich, liebenswürdig, nett (**to** zu): **~ to animals** tierlieb; *would you be so ~ as to do this for me?* sei so gut *od.* freundlich u. erledige das für mich, erledige das doch bitte für mich; → **enough** III. **2.** herzlich: → **regard** 4.
kin·der·gar·ten ['kɪndəˌɡaːtn] s Kindergarten m: **~ teacher** Kindergärtnerin f.
,kind'heart·ed adj □ gütig, gutherzig.
kin·dle ['kɪndl] **I** v/t **1.** an-, entzünden. **2.** *Haß etc* entfachen, -flammen, *Interesse etc* wecken. **II** v/i **3.** sich entzünden, Feuer fangen. **4.** *fig.* entbrennen, -flammen.
kin·dling ['kɪndlɪŋ] s Anzündmaterial n.

kind·ly ['kaɪndlɪ] **I** adj **1.** freundlich, liebenswürdig. **II** adv **2.** → **kind²** 1. **3.** freundlicher-, liebenswürdiger-, netterweise: ~ **tell me** sagen Sie mir bitte. **4. take ~ to** sich mit et. an- od. befreunden.

kind·ness ['kaɪndnɪs] s **1.** Freundlichkeit f, Liebenswürdigkeit f. **2.** Gefälligkeit f: **do s.o. a ~** j-m e-e Gefälligkeit erweisen.

kin·dred ['kɪndrɪd] **I** s **1.** (Bluts)Verwandtschaft f. **2.** coll. (pl konstruiert) Verwandte pl, Verwandtschaft f. **II** adj **3.** (bluts)verwandt. **4.** fig. verwandt, ähnlich.

ki·net·ic [kɪ'netɪk] phys. **I** adj (~ally) kinetisch. **II** s pl (sg konstruiert) Kinetik f.

king [kɪŋ] s **1.** König m (a. Schach u. Kartenspiel): ~ **of hearts** Herzkönig; → **English** 3, **evidence** 2. **2.** Damespiel: Dame f. '**king·dom** s **1.** Königreich n. **2.** a. ♀ eccl. Reich n (Gottes). **3.** fig. Reich n: **animal (mineral, vegetable** od. **plant)** ~ Tier-(Mineral-, Pflanzen)reich. '**king·ly** adj königlich. '**king|·pin** s F wichtigster Mann; Dreh- u. Angelpunkt m. '**~-size(d)** adj Riesen...: ~ **cigarettes** pl King-size-Zigaretten pl.

kink [kɪŋk] s **1.** Knick m (in Draht etc). **2.** fig. Spleen m, Tick m. **3.** **have a ~ in one's back (neck)** e-n steifen Rücken (Hals) haben. '**kink·y** adj **1.** kraus (Haar). **2.** fig. spleenig. **3.** F abartig, pervers.

kins·folk ['kɪnzfəʊk] s pl Verwandtschaft f, (Bluts)Verwandte pl.

kin·ship ['kɪnʃɪp] s (Bluts)Verwandtschaft f.

kins·man ['kɪnzmən] s (irr **man**) (Bluts)Verwandte m. '**kins,wom·an** s (irr **woman**) (Bluts)Verwandte f.

ki·osk ['ki:ɒsk] s **1.** Kiosk m. **2.** Br. Telefonzelle f.

kip [kɪp] sl. **I** s **1.** Schlaf m: **have a ~** pennen. **2.** Schlafstelle f. **II** v/i **3.** pennen. **4.** ~ **down** sich hinhauen.

kip·per ['kɪpə] s Kipper m (Räucherhering).

kiss [kɪs] **I** s **1.** Kuß m: ~ **of life** Br. Mund-zu-Mund-Beatmung f. **II** v/t **2.** küssen: ~ **s.o. good night** j-m e-n Gutenachtkuß geben; ~ **the dust** F ins Gras beißen. **3.** leicht berühren. **III** v/i **4.** sich küssen. **5.** sich leicht berühren. '**kiss·er** s sl. Schnauze f, Fresse f; Visage f. '**kiss·proof** adj kußecht.

kit [kɪt] **I** s **1.** (Reise-, Reit- etc)Ausrüstung f, (-)Sachen pl. **2.** ✗ Montur f; Gepäck n. **3.** Arbeitsgerät n, Werkzeug(e pl) n; Werkzeugtasche f, -kasten m. **4.** Baukasten m; Bastelsatz m. **5.** a. ~ **press** ~ Pressemappe f. **II** v/t **6.** oft ~ **out** (od. **up**) ausstatten (**with** mit). ~ **bag** s **1.** ✗ Kleider-, Seesack m. **2.** Reisetasche f.

kitch·en ['kɪtʃɪn] **I** s Küche f. **II** adj Küchen...: ~ **knife (table,** etc); ~ **garden** (Obst- u.) Gemüsegarten m; ~ **help** Küchenhilfe f; ~ **sink** Ausguß m, Spüle f; **with everything but the ~ sink** humor. mit Sack u. Pack. **kitch·en·et(te)** [,~-'net] s Kochnische f.

kite [kaɪt] s Drachen m: **fly a ~** e-n Drachen od. fig. e-n Versuchsballon steigen lassen.

kith [kɪθ] s: **with ~ and kin** mit Kind u. Kegel.

kit·ten ['kɪtn] s Kätzchen n: **have ~s** Br. F Zustände kriegen. '**kit·ten·ish** adj **1.** (kindlich) verspielt od. ausgelassen. **2.** kokett.

kit·ty ['kɪtɪ] s Kätzchen n.

ki·wi ['ki:wi:] **I** s **1.** orn. Kiwi m. **2.** ✿ Kiwi f. **3.** mst ♀ F Neuseeländer(in). **II** adj **4.** mst ♀ F neuseeländisch.

klax·on ['klæksn] s mot. Hupe f.

klep·to·ma·ni·a [,kleptəʊ'meɪnjə] s psych. Kleptomanie f. ,**klep·to'ma·ni·ac** [~nɪæk] s Kleptomane m, -manin f.

knack [næk] s **1.** Kniff m, Trick m: **get the ~ of doing s.th.** dahinterkommen od. herausbekommen, wie man et. tut; **have the ~ of s.th.** den Dreh von od. bei et. heraushaben. **2.** Geschick n: **have the** (od. **a**) ~ **of doing s.th.** Geschick od. das Talent haben, et. zu tun.

knack·er ['nækə] s Br. **1.** Abdecker m: ~'**s yard** Abdeckerei f. **2.** Abbruchunternehmer m. '**knack·ered** adj Br. F geschlaucht, kaputt. '**knack·er·y** s Br. Abdeckerei f.

knag [næg] s Knorren m.

knap·sack ['næpsæk] s **1.** ✗ Tornister m. **2.** Rucksack m.

knave [neɪv] s **1.** obs. Schurke m. **2.** Kar-

tenspiel: Bube *m*: **~ of hearts** Herzbube *m*.

knead [ni:d] *v/t* Teig etc (durch)kneten, Muskeln *a.* massieren.

knee [ni:] *s* **1.** Knie *n*: **on one's ~s** kniefällig, auf Knien; **bring s.o. to his ~s** j-n auf *od.* in die Knie zwingen; **go (down)** *(od.* **fall) on one's ~s to** niederknien vor *(dat)*, *fig. a.* in die Knie gehen vor *(dat)*. **2.** ⚙ Knie(stück) *n*; (Rohr)Krümmer *m.* **~ bend** *s* Kniebeuge *f.* '**~·cap** *s anat.* Kniescheibe *f.* **~'deep, ~'high** *adj* knietief, -hoch. **~ joint** *s anat.*, ⚙ Kniegelenk *n.*

kneel [ni:l] *v/i* (*mst irr*) **1.** *a.* **~ down** (sich) hinknien, niederknien **(to** vor *dat)*. **2.** knien, auf den Knien liegen **(before** vor *dat)*.

'**knee·pad** *s* Knieschützer *m.* '**~·pan** → **kneecap.** '**~·room** *s* ✈, *mot.* Kniefreiheit *f.*

knelt [nelt] *pret u. pp von* **kneel.**

knew [nju:] *pret von* **know.**

knick·er·bock·ers ['nɪkəbɒkəz] *s pl, a.* **pair of ~** Knickerbocker *pl.*

knick·ers ['nɪkəz] *s pl, a.* **pair of ~ 1.** → **knickerbockers. 2.** *bsd. Br.* (Damen)Schlüpfer *m*: **get one's ~ in a twist** F, *oft humor.* sich ins Hemd machen.

knick-knack ['nɪknæk] *s* **1.** Nippsache *f.* **2.** billiges Schmuckstück. **3.** Spielerei *f*, Schnickschnack *m.*

knife [naɪf] **I** *pl* **knives** [naɪvz] *s* Messer *n*: **before you can say ~** *bsd. Br.* im Nu, im Handumdrehen; **to the ~** bis aufs Messer, bis zum Äußersten; **have one's ~ into s.o.** j-n auf dem Kieker haben; **go under the ~** ✂ unters Messer kommen. **II** *v/t* mit e-m Messer stechen *od.* verletzen: **~ (to death)** erstechen. **~ blade** *s* Messerklinge *f.* **~ edge** *s* Messerschneide *f*: **be balanced on a ~** *fig.* auf des Messers Schneide stehen. **~ point** *s* Messerspitze *f*: **at ~** mit vorgehaltenem Messer.

knight [naɪt] **I** *s* **1.** *hist.* Ritter *m* (*Br. a. Adelsstufe*). **2.** Schach: Springer *m*, Pferd *n.* **II** *v/t* **3.** zum Ritter schlagen. '**knight·ly** *adj u. adv* ritterlich.

knit [nɪt] **I** *v/t* (*a. irr*) **1.** stricken. **2.** *a.* **~ together** zs.-fügen, verbinden (*a. fig.*). **3.** *fig.* verknüpfen. **4.** *Stirn* runzeln; *Augenbrauen* zs.-ziehen. **II** *v/i* **5.** stricken. '**knit·ting I** *s* **1.** Stricken *n.* **2.**

Strickarbeit *f*, -zeug *n.* **II** *adj* **3.** Strick...: **~ needle.**

'**knit·wear** *s* Strickwaren *pl.*

knives [naɪvz] *pl von* **knife.**

knob [nɒb] *s* **1.** (runder) Kniff, Knauf *m.* **2.** Beule *f*, Höcker *m.* **3.** *bsd. Br.* Stück(chen) *n* (*Zucker etc*).

knock [nɒk] **I** *s* **1.** Schlag *m*, Stoß *m.* **2.** Klopfen *n* (*a. mot.*): **there is a ~** (*at* [*Am. on*] *the door*) es klopft. **II** *v/t* **3.** schlagen, stoßen: **~ one's head against** sich den Kopf anschlagen an (*dat*); **~ one's head against a brick wall** *fig.* mit dem Kopf gegen die Wand rennen. **III** *v/i* **4.** schlagen, klopfen: **~ at** (*Am. on*) *the door* an die Tür klopfen. **5.** schlagen, prallen, stoßen (**against, into** gegen; **on** auf *acc*). **6.** ⚙ klopfen (*Motor, Brennstoff*). **7.** **~ about** (*od.* **around**) F sich herumtreiben in (*dat*); herumliegen in (*dat*) (*Gegenstand*).

Verbindungen mit Adverbien:

knock| a·bout, ~ a·round I *v/t* **1.** herumstoßen. **II** *v/i* **2.** F sich herumtreiben: **~ with** *a.* gehen mit (*e-m Mädchen etc*). **3.** F herumliegen (*Gegenstand*). **~ back** *v/t* **1.** *Stuhl* zurückstoßen. **2.** *bsd. Br.* F *Getränk* runterkippen. **~ down** *v/t* **1.** a) umstoßen, umwerfen, b) niederschlagen, c) an-, umfahren; überfahren, d) F umhauen, sprachlos machen. **2.** *Gebäude etc* abreißen, abbrechen. **3.** (**to** auf *acc*; **£2** um 2 Pfund) j-n, *Preis* herunterhandeln; mit dem *Preis* heruntergehen. **4.** **knock s.th. down to s.o.** (*Auktion*) j-m et. zuschlagen (**at, for** für). **~ in** *v/t Nagel* einschlagen. **~ off I** *v/t* **1.** herunter-, abschlagen. **2.** F aufhören mit: **knock it off!** hör auf (damit!); **~ work(ing)** → 6b. **3.** F *Arbeit* erledigen. **4.** F j-n umlegen. **5.** F *Essen* wegputzen. **II** *v/i* **6.** F a) allg. aufhören, b) Feierabend *od.* Schluß machen. **~ out** *v/t* **1.** herausschlagen, -klopfen (**of** aus), *Pfeife* ausklopfen. → **bottom** 3. **2.** a) bewußtlos schlagen, b) Boxen: k.o. schlagen, ausknocken, c) betäuben (*Droge etc*), d) F umhauen (*sprachlos machen, hinreißen*). **~ to·geth·er** *v/t* **1.** (*a. v/i*) aneinanderstoßen, -schlagen. **2.** F *et.* schnell zs.-zimmern, *Essen etc* (her)zaubern. **~ o·ver** *v/t* **1.** umwerfen, umstoßen. **2.** überfahren. **~ up I** *v/t* **1.** hochschlagen, in die Höhe schlagen. **2.**

Br. F herausklopfen, (*durch Klopfen*) wecken. **3.** *Br.* F *Geld* verdienen. **4.** *sl. Mädchen* anbumsen. **II** *v/i* **5.** *Tennis etc*: sich einschlagen *od.* einspielen.

'knock·a·bout *adj* **1.** strapazierfähig (*Kleidung etc*). **2.** *thea. etc* Klamauk...: ~ *comedy* Klamaukstück *n*. **'~·down I** *adj* **1.** niederschmetternd (*a. fig.*). **2.** ~ *price* Schleuderpreis *m*: *at a* ~ spottbillig. **II** *s* **3.** *Boxen*: Niederschlag *m*.

knock·er ['nɒkə] *s* **1.** (Tür)Klopfer *m*. **2.** *pl sl.* Titten *pl*.

,knock·'kneed *adj* X-beinig: *be* ~ X-Beine haben. **,~·'knees** *s pl* X-Beine *pl*. **'~·out I** *s* **1.** *Boxen*: K.o. *m*: *win by a* ~ durch K.o. gewinnen. **2.** F tolle Person *od.* Sache; Attraktion *f*; Bombenerfolg *m*. **II** *adj* **3.** *Boxen*: K.-o.-...: ~ *system* K.-o.-System *n*. **'~·up** *s Tennis etc*: Einschlagen *n*, -spielen *n*.

knoll [nəʊl] *s* Hügel *m*.

knot [nɒt] **I** *s* **1.** Knoten *m*: *make* (*od. tie*) *a* ~ e-n Knoten machen; *tie s.o.* (*up*) *in* ~*s* F j-n völlig durcheinanderbringen. **2.** Astknoten *m*, Knorren *m*. **3.** ♣ Knoten *m*, Seemeile *f*. **4.** *fig.* Knoten *m*, Schwierigkeit *f*: *cut the* ~ den Knoten durchhauen. **II** *v/t* **5.** (*od.* tie) machen in (*acc*). **6.** (ver)knoten, (-)knüpfen. **III** *v/i* **7.** sich verknoten. **'knot·ty** *adj* **1.** knotig. **2.** knorrig (*Holz*). **3.** *fig.* verwickelt, kompliziert.

know [nəʊ] **I** *v/t* (*irr*) **1.** *allg.* wissen. **2.** können: ~ *how to do s.th.* et. tun können. **3.** kennen: a) sich auskennen in (*dat*), b) vertraut sein mit, c) bekannt sein mit. **4.** erfahren, erleben: *he has* ~*n better days* er hat schon bessere Tage gesehen. **5.** (wieder)erkennen (*by* an *dat*); unterscheiden (können) (*from* von): ~ *apart* auseinanderhalten. **II** *v/i*

(*irr*) **6.** wissen (*of* von, um), Bescheid wissen (*about* über *acc*): *you never* ~ man kann nie wissen; ~ *better than to do s.th.* sich davor hüten, et. zu tun. **III** *s* **7.** *be in the* ~ Bescheid wissen. **'~·all** *s* Besserwisser *m*. **'~·how** *s* Know-how *n* (*a.* ✝): *industrial* ~ praktische Betriebserfahrung.

know·ing ['nəʊɪŋ] *adj* **1.** klug, gescheit. **2.** schlau, durchtrieben. **3.** verständnisvoll, wissend (*Blick*). **'know·ing·ly** *adv* **1.** → *knowing*. **2.** wissentlich, bewußt, absichtlich.

knowl·edge ['nɒlɪdʒ] *s* **1.** Kenntnis *f*: *bring s.th. to s.o.'s* ~ j-n von et. in Kenntnis setzen; *it has come to my* ~ ich habe erfahren (*that* daß); (*not*) *to my* ~ m-s Wissens (nicht); *without my* ~ ohne mein Wissen. **2.** Wissen *n*, Kenntnisse *pl*: *have a good* ~ *of* viel verstehen von, sich gut auskennen in (*dat*).

known [nəʊn] **I** *pp von know*. **II** *adj* bekannt (*as* als; *for* für; *to s.o.* j-m): ~ *to the police* polizeibekannt; *make* ~ bekanntmachen; *make o.s.* ~ *to s.o.* sich j-m vorstellen.

knuck·le ['nʌkl] **I** *s* **1.** *anat.* (Finger)Knöchel *m*: → *rap*[1] 1, 3. **2.** (*Kalbs-, Schweins*)Haxe *f*, (-)Hachse *f*: *near the* ~ F reichlich gewagt (*Witz etc*). **II** *v/i* **3.** ~ *down* sich anstrengen *od.* dahinterklemmen: ~ *down to work* sich an die Arbeit machen, sich hinter die Arbeit klemmen. **4.** ~ *under* sich unterwerfen *od.* beugen (*to dat*), klein beigeben. **'~·dust·er** *s* Schlagring *m*.

kook [ku:k] *s Am.* F Spinner *m*.

Ko·ran [kɒ'rɑ:n] *s eccl.* Koran *m*.

kraut [kraʊt] *s sl. contp.* Deutsche *m, f*.

Krem·lin ['kremlɪn] *npr* Kreml *m*.

L

lab [læb] *s* F Labor *n*.

la·bel ['leɪbl] **I** *s* **1.** Etikett *n*, (Klebe-, Anhänge)Zettel *m*, (-)Schild(chen) *n*. **II** *v/t pret u. pp* **-beled**, *bsd. Br.* **-belled**

2. etikettieren, beschriften. **3.** als ... bezeichnen, zu ... stempeln: *be* ~(*l*)*ed a criminal* zum Verbrecher gestempelt werden.

la·bi·al ['leɪbjəl] *s ling.* Lippen-, Labiallaut *m.*

la·bor ['leɪbə] *Am.* **I** → labour, *etc.* **II** *adj* **1.** Gewerkschafts... **2.** ~ **union** Gewerkschaft *f.*

la·bor·a·to·ry [lə'bɒrətərɪ] *s* Labor(atorium) *n:* ~ **assistant** Laborant(in).

la·bo·ri·ous [lə'bɔːrɪəs] *adj* □ **1.** mühsam. **2.** schwerfällig (*Stil*). **3.** arbeitsam, fleißig.

la·bour ['leɪbə] *bsd. Br.* **I** *s* **1.** (schwere) Arbeit. **2.** Mühe *f*, Plage *f: lost* ~ vergebliche Mühe. **3.** ⚓ Arbeiterschaft *f*; Arbeiter *pl*, Arbeitskräfte *pl.* **4.** ⚓ *pol.* die Labour Party (*Großbritanniens etc*). **5.** ⚓ *When pl:* **be in** ~ in den Wehen liegen. **II** *v/i* **6.** (schwer) arbeiten (*at an dat*), sich bemühen (*for* um), sich anstrengen (*od.* abmühen (*to do* zu tun). **7.** *a.* ~ **along** sich mühsam fortbewegen: ~ **through** sich kämpfen durch (*Schlamm, Buch etc*). **8.** (*under*) zu leiden haben (unter *dat*), zu kämpfen haben (mit); befangen sein (in *dat*). **9.** ⚓ in den Wehen liegen. **III** *v/t* **10.** ausführlich *od.* umständlich behandeln, breitwalzen. **IV** *adj* **11.** Arbeits...; Arbeiter... **12.** ⚓ *pol.* Labour...: ~ **Party** Labour Party *f.* '**la·bour·er** *s bsd. Br.* (*bsd.* Hilfs)Arbeiter *m.*

'**la·bour|-in,ten·sive** *adj* □ *bsd. Br.* arbeitsintensiv. '**~·,sav·ing** *adj bsd. Br.* arbeitssparend.

lab·y·rinth ['læbərɪnθ] *s* Labyrinth *n*, *fig. a.* Gewirr *n.*

lace [leɪs] **I** *s* **1.** *Textilwesen:* Spitze *f.* **2.** Litze *f*, Tresse *f*, Borte *f.* **3.** Schnürband *n*, -senkel *m.* **4.** Schuß *m* Alkohol (*in Getränken*): **with a ~ of rum** mit e-m Schuß Rum. **II** *v/t* **5.** *a.* ~ **up** (zu-, zs.-)schnüren. **6.** mit Spitzen *od.* Litzen besetzen. **7.** ~ **one's tea with rum** sich e-n Schuß Rum in den Tee geben; ~ *s.o.'s beer with vodka* j-m heimlich Wodka ins Bier schütten; *tea ~d with rum* Tee *m* mit e-m Schuß Rum. **III** *v/i* **8.** ~ **into** *s.o.* F über j-n herfallen (*a. mit Worten*).

lac·er·ate ['læsəreɪt] *v/t Gesicht etc* aufreißen; zerschneiden; zerkratzen. ,**lac·er·a·tion** *s* Riß-; Schnitt-, Kratzwunde *f.*

lach·ry·mal ['lækrɪml] *adj* **1.** Tränen...: ~ **gland** *anat.* Tränendrüse *f.* **2.** → lach-

rymose 1, 2. lach·ry·mose ['lækrɪməʊs] *adj* □ **1.** tränenreich. **2.** weinerlich. **3.** traurig, ergreifend.

lack [læk] **I** *s* **1.** Mangel *m* (*of* an *dat*): ~ **of sleep** fehlender Schlaf; **for** (*od.* **through**) ~ **of time** aus Zeitmangel. **II** *v/t* **2.** nicht haben, Mangel haben *od.* leiden an (*dat*): **we** ~ **coal** es fehlt uns an Kohle. **3.** es fehlen lassen an (*dat*). **III** *v/i* **4.** *a.* **be** ~**ing** fehlen, b) ~ **in** Mangel haben *od.* leiden an (*dat*): **he is** ~**ing in courage** ihm fehlt der Mut. **5.** ~ **for nothing** von allem genug haben: **he** ~**s for nothing** es fehlt ihm an nichts.

lack·a·dai·si·cal [,lækə'deɪzɪkl] *adj* □ **1.** lustlos. **2.** nachlässig (*about* in *dat*).

lack·ey ['lækɪ] *s* Lakai *m* (*a. fig. contp.*).

lack·ing ['lækɪŋ] *adj* **1.** **be found** ~ sich nicht bewähren. **2.** *Br.* F beschränkt, dumm.

'**lack|,lus·ter** *adj Am.*, '**~,lus·tre** *adj bsd. Br.* glanzlos, matt.

la·con·ic [lə'kɒnɪk] *adj* (~**ally**) **1.** lakonisch. **2.** wortkarg.

lac·quer ['lækə] **I** *s* **1.** (Farb)Lack *m.* **2.** (Haar)Festiger *m.* **II** *v/t* **3.** lackieren.

la·crosse [lə'krɒs] *s Sport:* Lacrosse *n* (*Ballspiel*).

lad [læd] *s* **1.** junger Kerl *od.* Bursche. **2.** **a bit of a** ~ *Br.* F ein ziemlicher Draufgänger.

lad·der ['lædə] **I** *s* **1.** Leiter *f* (*a. fig.*). **2.** *bsd. Br.* Laufmasche *f.* **II** *v/i* **3.** *bsd. Br.* Laufmaschen bekommen. '**~·proof** *adj* maschenfest.

lad·en ['leɪdn] *adj* **1.** (schwer) beladen (**with** mit). **2.** *fig.* bedrückt (**with** von): ~ **with guilt** schuldbeladen.

la-di-da [,lɑːdɪ'dɑː] *adj* F affektiert, affig.

la·dies' choice → Damenwahl *f.* ~ **man** *s* (*irr man*) Frauenheld *m.* ~ **room** *s* Damentoilette *f.*

la·dle ['leɪdl] **I** *s* **1.** Schöpflöffel *m*, -kelle *f.* **2.** ⚙ Schaufel *f* (*e-s Baggers etc*). **II** *v/t* **3.** *a.* ~ **out** (aus)schöpfen. **4.** *a.* ~ **out** austeilen (*a. fig.*).

la·dy ['leɪdɪ] **I** *s* **1.** Dame *f: ladies and gentlemen* m-e Damen u. Herren. **2.** ⚓ Lady *f* (*Titel*). **3.** *Our* ⚓ *eccl.* Unsere Liebe Frau, die Mutter Gottes. **4.** **Ladies** *pl* (*sg konstruiert*) Damentoilette *f.* **II** *adj* **5.** weiblich: ~ **doctor** Ärztin *f.* '**~·bird**, *Am. a.* '**~·bug** *s zo.* Marienkäfer *m.* ,**~·in·'wait·ing** *pl* ,**la·dies-in·**

-**'wait·ing** s Hofdame f. **'~‚kill·er** s F Ladykiller m, Herzensbrecher m. **'~-like** adj damenhaft.
la·dy's man → *ladies' man.*

lag¹ [læg] **I** v/i **1.** mst ~ *behind* zurückbleiben, nicht mitkommen (*beide a.* fig.): ~ *behind s.o.* hinter j-m zurückbleiben. **2.** mst ~ *behind* sich verzögern.
II s **3.** → *time lag.*

lag² [~] v/t ⊕ verschalen; isolieren, ummanteln.

la·ger ['lɑːɡə] s Lagerbier n.

la·goon [lə'ɡuːn] s Lagune f.

laid [leɪd] pret u. pp von *lay¹.*

lain [leɪn] pp von *lie².*

lair [leə] s **1.** zo. Lager n; Bau m; Höhle f. **2.** Versteck n.

la·i·ty ['leɪətɪ] s Laien pl.

lake [leɪk] s See m. ~ **dwell·ings** s pl Pfahlbauten pl.

lam [læm] sl. **I** v/t verdreschen, -möbeln. **II** v/i: ~ *into s.o.* auf j-n eindreschen; über j-n herfallen (a. mit Worten).

la·ma ['lɑːmə] s eccl. Lama m.

lamb [læm] **I** s **1.** Lamm n: (*as*) *gentle* (od. *meek*) *as a* ~ lammfromm. **2.** Lamm n: a) gastr. Lammfleisch n: ~ *chop* Lammkotelett n, b) → *lambskin.*
II v/i **3.** lammen.

lam·baste [læm'beɪst] v/t sl. **1.** → *lam* I. **2.** fig. herunterputzen, zs.-stauchen.

'lamb|·like adj lammfromm. **'~·skin** s **1.** Lammfell n. **2.** Schafleder n.

lamb's wool s Lambswool f, Lammwolle f.

lame [leɪm] adj □ **1.** a) lahm: *walk ~ly* hinken, (*Tier a.*) lahmen, b) gelähmt. **2.** fig. lahm: a) faul (*Ausrede*), b) schwach (*Argument*), c) matt, schwach (*Anstrengungen*). **II** v/t **3.** lähmen (a. fig.). ~ **duck** s F **1.** Niete f, Versager m (a. Sache). **2.** pol. Am. nicht wiedergewähltes Kongreßmitglied bis zum Ablauf s-r Amtszeit.

la·mel·la [lə'melə] pl -**lae** [~liː], -**las** s Lamelle f.

lame·ness ['leɪmnɪs] s Lahmheit f (a. fig.).

la·ment [lə'ment] **I** v/i **1.** jammern, (weh)klagen, contp. lamentieren (*for, over* um). **2.** trauern (*for, over* um). **II** v/t **3.** beklagen: a) bejammern, bedauern, b) betrauern. **III** s **4.** Jammer m, (Weh)Klage f. **5.** Klagelied n.

lam·en·ta·ble ['læməntəbl] adj □ **1.** beklagenswert, bedauerlich. **2.** contp. erbärmlich, kläglich. **lam·en·ta·tion** [‚~men'teɪʃn] s **1.** (Weh)Klage f. **2.** contp. Lamento n, Lamentieren n.

lam·i·nat·ed ['læmɪneɪtɪd] adj ⊕ laminiert, geschichtet: ~ *glass* Verbundglas n.

lamp [læmp] s Lampe f, (Straßen)Laterne f.

lam·poon [læm'puːn] **I** s Spott-, Schmähschrift f. **II** v/t (*schriftlich*) verspotten.

'lamp-post s Laternenpfahl m: → *between* 2.

'lamp-shade s Lampenschirm m.

lance [lɑːns] **I** s Lanze f. **II** v/t ✶ Geschwür etc (mit e-r Lanzette) öffnen.

lan·cet ['lɑːnsɪt] s **1.** ✶ Lanzette f. **2.** △ a) a. ~ *arch* Spitzbogen m, b) a. ~ *window* Spitzbogenfenster n.

land [lænd] **I** s **1.** Land n (Ggs. Wasser, Luft): *by* ~ auf dem Landweg; *by* ~ *and sea* zu Wasser u. zu Lande; *see* (od. *find out*) *how the* ~ *lies* fig. die Lage peilen; sich e-n Überblick verschaffen. **2.** Land n, Boden m: *ploughed* ~ Ackerland. **3.** Land n, Staat m. a. fig. Land n, Reich n: → *milk* I. **II** v/i **5.** ✈ landen, ⚓ a. anlegen. **6.** oft ~ *up* landen, (an)kommen: ~ *up in prison* im Gefängnis landen. **III** v/t **7.** Personen, Güter, Flugzeug landen, Güter ausladen, ⚓ a. löschen. **8.** j-n bringen: ~ *o.s.* (od. *be ~ed*) *in trouble* in Schwierigkeiten geraten od. kommen. **9.** F Schlag, Treffer landen, anbringen: *he ~ed him one* er knallte ihm eine. **10.** F j-n, et. kriegen, erwischen, Preis ergattern. **11.** ~ *s.o. s.th.* F j-m et. einbringen.

land·ed ['lændɪd] adj Land..., Grund...: ~ *property* Land-, Grundbesitz m.

land forc·es s pl ✕ Landstreitkräfte pl.

land·ing ['lændɪŋ] s **1.** ✈ Landung f, Landen n, ⚓ a. Anlegen n. **2.** (Treppen)Absatz m. ~ **ap·proach** s ✈ Landeanflug m. ~ **field** s ✈ Landeplatz m. ~ **gear** s ✈ Fahrgestell n, -werk n. ~ **per·mit** s ✈ Landeerlaubnis f.

'land|·la·dy s (Haus-, Gast-, Pensions)Wirtin f. **~·lord** ['læn~] s **1.** Grundeigentümer m, -besitzer m. **2.** (Haus-, Gast-, Pensions)Wirt m. **~·lub·ber** ['lænd‚~] s ⚓ Landratte f. **'~·mark** s

1. Grenzstein *m*, -zeichen *n*. **2.** ♣ Landmarke *f*, Seezeichen *n*. **3.** Wahrzeichen *n* (*e-r Stadt etc*). **4.** *fig*. Mark-, Meilenstein *m*. **~ of·fice** *s Am*. Grundbuchamt *n*. '**~,own·er** *s* Grundbesitzer(in), -eigentümer(in). **~ reg·is·ter** *s Br*. Grundbuch *n*. **~ reg·is·try** *s Br*. Grundbuchamt *n*. **~scape** ['lænskeɪp] *s* Landschaft *f* (*a*. *paint*.): **~ architect** Landschaftsarchitekt *m*; **~ gardener** Landschaftsgärtner *m*; **~painter** Landschaftsmaler *m*. '**~slide** *s* **1.** Erdrutsch *m*. **2.** *a*. **~ victory** (*od*. **win**) *pol*. überwältigender Wahlsieg.

land·ward(s) ['lændwəd(z)] *adv* land(ein)wärts.

lane [leɪn] *s* **1.** (Feld)Weg *m*. **2.** Gasse *f*: a) Sträßchen *n*, b) Durchgang *m* (*zwischen Menschenreihen etc*): **form a ~** Spalier stehen, e-e Gasse bilden. **3.** Schneise *f*. **4.** ♣ Fahrrinne *f*. **5.** ✈ Flugschneise *f*. **6.** *mot*. (Fahr)Spur *f*: **change ~s** die Spur wechseln; **get in ~** sich einordnen. **7.** *Sport*: (*einzelne*) Bahn.

lan·guage ['læŋgwɪdʒ] *s* **1.** Sprache *f*. **2.** Sprache *f*, Ausdrucks-, Redeweise *f*: → **bad 3, strong 7**. **3.** (Fach)Sprache *f*. **~ course** *s* Sprachkurs *m*. **~ la·bo·ra·to·ry** *s* Sprachlabor *n*. **~ school** *s* Sprachenschule *f*.

lan·guid ['læŋgwɪd] *adj* □ **1.** schwach, matt. **2.** *fig*. lau, interesselos.

lan·guish ['læŋgwɪʃ] *v/i* **1.** ermatten, erschlaffen. **2.** erlahmen (*Interesse etc*). **3.** sich sehnen, schmachten (**for** nach). '**lan·guish·ing** *adj* □ sehnsüchtig, schmachtend (*Blick etc*).

lan·guor ['læŋgə] *s* **1.** Schwachheit *f*, Mattigkeit *f*. **2.** *fig*. Lauheit *f*, Interesselosigkeit *f*. **3.** einschläfernde Schwüle. '**lan·guor·ous** *adj* □ **1.** → **languid**. **2.** einschläfernd schwül.

lank [læŋk] *adj* □ **1.** hager, mager. **2.** glatt (*Haar*). '**lank·y** *adj* □ schlaksig.

lan·tern ['læntən] *s* Laterne *f*.

lap¹ [læp] *s* Schoß *m* (*a*. *fig*.): **drop** (*od*. **fall**) **into s.o.'s ~** j-m in den Schoß fallen.

lap² [~] **I** *v/t* **1.** wickeln ([a]round um). **2.** einschlagen, -wickeln (**in** in *acc*). **3.** hinausragen über (*acc*). **4.** *Sport*: überrunden. **II** *v/i* **5.** überstehen, hinausragen (**over** über *acc*). **6.** sich überlappen. **III**

s **7.** *Sport*: Runde *f*: **~ of hono(u)r** Ehrenrunde *f*.

lap³ [~] **I** *v/t* **1.** (sch)lecken: **~ up** a) auf(sch)lecken, b) *fig*. F fressen, schlucken (*kritiklos glauben*), c) *fig*. F Komplimente *etc* gierig aufnehmen. **II** *v/i* **2.** plätschern (**against** gegen, an *acc*). **3.** (sch)lecken: **take a ~ at** (sch)lecken an (*dat*). **4.** Plätschern *n*.

lap belt *s* ✈, *mot*. Beckengurt *m*.

la·pel [lə'pel] *s* Aufschlag *m*, Revers *n*, *m*.

lapse [læps] **I** *s* **1.** Versehen *n*, (kleiner) Fehler *m*. Irrtum. **2.** Vergehen *n*, Entgleisung *f*. **3.** Zeitspanne *f*. **4.** ⚖ Verfall *m*, Erlöschen *n*. **II** *v/i* **5.** vergehen, -streichen (*Zeit*); ablaufen (*Frist*). **6.** verfallen, -sinken (**into** in *acc*). **7.** ⚖ verfallen, erlöschen (*Anspruch etc*).

lar·ce·ny ['lɑːsənɪ] *s* ⚖ Diebstahl *m*: **grand** (**petty**) **~** schwerer (einfacher) Diebstahl.

larch [lɑːtʃ] *s* ♣ Lärche *f*.

lard [lɑːd] *s* **1.** Schweinefett *n*, -schmalz *n*. **II** *v/t* **2.** einfetten. **3.** *Fleisch* spicken: **~ing needle** (*od*. **pin**) Spicknadel *f*. **4.** *fig*. spicken, (aus)schmücken (**with** mit).

lard·er ['lɑːdə] *s* **1.** Speisekammer *f*. **2.** Speiseschrank *m*.

large [lɑːdʒ] *adj* (□ → **largely**) **1.** *allg*. groß: (**as**) **~ as life** in voller Lebensgröße; **~r than life** überlebensgroß. **2.** groß (*Familie etc*), (*Einkommen etc a*.) beträchtlich, (*Mahlzeit*) ausgiebig, reichlich. **3.** umfassend, weitgehend (*Vollmachten etc*). **4.** Groß...: **~ consumer** Großverbraucher *m*. **5.** F großspurig. **II** *adv* **6.** **talk ~** F große Töne spucken. **III** *s* **7.** **at ~** a) in Freiheit, auf freiem Fuß: **set at ~** auf freien Fuß setzen, b) (sehr) ausführlich, c) in der Gesamtheit: **the nation at ~** die ganze Nation.

'**large·ly** *adv* **1.** großen-, größtenteils. **2.** allgemein.

,**large-'mind·ed** *adj* □ aufgeschlossen, tolerant.

large·ness ['lɑːdʒnɪs] *s* **1.** Größe *f*. **2.** F Großspurigkeit *f*.

'**large-scale** *adj* groß(angelegt), Groß...: **~ experiment** Großversuch *m*.

lar·gess(e) [lɑː'dʒes] *s* Freigebigkeit *f*, Großzügigkeit *f*.

lar·go ['lɑːgəʊ] *pl* **-gos** *s* ♪ Largo *n*.

lar·i·at ['lærɪət] s bsd. Am. Lasso n, m.

lark¹ [lɑːk] s orn. Lerche f.

lark² [~] F I s Jux m, Ulk m: **for a ~** zum Spaß, aus Jux. II v/i mst **~ about** (od. **around**) Blödsinn machen, herumalbern.

lark·spur ['lɑːkspɜː] s ♀ Rittersporn m.

lar·va ['lɑːvə] pl **-vae** ['~viː] s zo. Larve f.

lar·yn·gi·tis [,lærɪn'dʒaɪtɪs] s ✻ Kehlkopfentzündung f. **lar·ynx** ['lærɪŋks] pl **la·ryn·ges** [lə'rɪndʒiːz], **'lar·ynx·es** s anat. Kehlkopf m.

las·civ·i·ous [lə'sɪvɪəs] adj □ 1. geil, lüstern. 2. lasziv, schlüpfrig.

la·ser ['leɪzə] s phys. Laser m. **~ beam** s Laserstrahl m.

lash¹ [læʃ] I s 1. Peitschenschnur f. 2. Peitschenhieb m. 3. fig. (Peitschen-)Hieb m (**at** gegen). 4. Peitschen n (a. fig.). 5. (Augen)Wimper f. II v/t 6. (aus)peitschen. 7. fig. a) peitschen, b) peitschen an (acc) od. gegen. 8. peitschen mit: **~ its tail** mit dem Schwanz um sich schlagen. 9. fig. aufpeitschen (**into** zu): **~ o.s. into a fury** sich in Wut hineinsteigern. 10. fig. geißeln, vom Leder ziehen gegen. III v/i 11. **~ against** → 7b; **~ down** niederprasseln (Regen). 12. schlagen (**at** nach): **~ about** (od. **around**) (wild) um sich schlagen; **~ into** a) einschlagen auf (acc), b) fig. j-n zs.-stauchen; **~ out** (wild) um sich schlagen; ausschlagen (Pferd); **~ out at** a) einschlagen auf (acc), b) a. **~ out against** → 10.

lash² [~] v/t 1. a. **~ down** fest(binden (**to**, **on** an dat). 2. ✿ (fest)zurren.

lash·ing ['læʃɪŋ] s 1. Auspeitschung f. 2. pl bsd. Br. F e-e Unmenge (**of** von, an dat): **~s of** (od. **to**) **drink** jede Menge zu trinken.

lass [læs], **lass·ie** ['læsɪ] s 1. Mädchen n. 2. Freundin f, Schatz m.

las·si·tude ['læsɪtjuːd] s Mattigkeit f, Abgespanntheit f.

las·so [læ'suː] I s pl **-so(e)s** s Lasso n, m. II v/t mit e-m Lasso (ein)fangen.

last¹ [lɑːst] I adj □ (□ → **lastly**) 1. letzt: **at a ~ hour** spät (a. fig.), zu später Stunde; **~ but one** vorletzt; **~ but two** drittletzt. 2. letzt, vorig: **~ Monday** (am) letzten od. vorigen Montag; **~ night** gestern abend; letzte Nacht. 3. letzt (allein übrigbleibend): **my ~ hope**. 4. letzt (am wenigsten erwartet od. geeignet): **the ~**

thing I would do das letzte, was ich tun würde. II adv 5. zuletzt, an letzter Stelle: **he came ~** er kam als letzter; **~ but not least** nicht zuletzt, nicht zu vergessen. 6. zuletzt, zum letzten Mal. 7. in Zssgn: **~-mentioned** letztgenannt, -erwähnt. III s 8. **at ~** endlich, schließlich, zuletzt. 9. der, die, das Letzte: **tho ~ to arrive** der letzte, der ankam; **to the ~** bis zum äußersten; bis zum Ende od. Schluß.

last² I v/i 1. (an-, fort)dauern. 2. a. **~ out** durch-, aushalten. 3. (sich) halten. 4. a. **~ out** (aus)reichen (Geld etc). II v/t 5. j-m reichen (Geld etc). 6. mst **~ out** überdauern, -leben.

last³ [~] s Leisten m: **stick to one's ~** fig. bei s-m Leisten bleiben.

'last-ditch adj allerletzt: **~ attempt** a. letzter verzweifelter Versuch.

last·ing ['lɑːstɪŋ] adj □ 1. dauerhaft: a) andauernd, beständig: **~ peace** dauerhafter Friede; **~ effect** anhaltende Wirkung; **~ memories** pl bleibende Erinnerungen pl, b) haltbar. 2. nachhaltig (Eindruck etc).

last·ly ['lɑːstlɪ] adv zuletzt, zum Schluß.

latch [lætʃ] I s 1. Schnappriegel m. 2. Schnappschloß n. II v/t 3. ein-, zuklinken. III v/i 4. einschnappen. 5. **~ on** F kapieren: **~ on to** (od. **onto**) **s.th.** et. kapieren. '**~·key** s Haus-, Wohnungsschlüssel m: **~ child** (→ **kid**) Schlüsselkind n.

late [leɪt] I adj (□ → **lately**) 1. spät: **at a ~ hour** spät (a. fig.), zu später Stunde; **~ shift** ✝ Spätschicht f; **it's getting ~** es ist schon spät. 2. vorgerückt, Spät...: **~ summer** Spätsommer m. 3. verspätet: **be ~** zu spät kommen (**for dinner** zum Essen), sich verspäten; Verspätung haben (Zug etc). 4. **the latest fashion** die neueste Mode. 5. letzt, früher, ehemalig; verstorben. II adv 6. spät: **as ~ as last year** erst od. noch letztes Jahr; **see you ~** auf bald, bis später; **~ on** später; **→ sleep** II. 7. zu spät: **the train came ~** der Zug hatte Verspätung. '**~·com·er** s Zuspätkommende m, f; Zuspätgekommene m, f.

late·ly ['leɪtlɪ] adv 1. vor kurzem, kürzlich. 2. in letzter Zeit, neuerdings. '**late·ness** s 1. späte Zeit: **the ~ of his arrival**

s-e späte Ankunft. **2.** Verspätung *f*, Zuspätkommen *n*.

la·tent ['leɪtənt] *adj* □ latent (*a.* ✿ *etc*), verborgen.

lat·er·al ['lætərəl] *adj* seitlich, Seiten... **'lat·er·al·ly** *adv* **1.** seitlich, seitwärts. **2.** von der Seite.

la·test ['leɪtɪst] **I** *adj u. adv sup von* **late**. **II** *s* **at the ~** spätestens.

lath [lɑːθ] *s* **1.** Latte *f*, Leiste *f*: **(as) thin as a ~** spindeldürr. **2.** *coll.* Latten *pl*, Leisten *pl*.

lathe [leɪð] *s* ✿ Drehbank *f*.

lath·er ['lɑːðə] **I** *s* **1.** (Seifen)Schaum *m*. **2. get in a ~**, **work o.s. up into a ~** F außer sich geraten (**over** wegen). **II** *v/t* **3.** einseifen. **4.** F verprügeln. **III** *v/i* **5.** schäumen.

Lat·in ['lætɪn] *ling.* **I** *adj* lateinisch. **II** *s* Latein(isch) *n*. **~ A·mer·i·can** **I** *adj* lateinamerikanisch. **II** *s* Lateinamerikaner(in).

Lat·in·ism ['lætɪnɪzəm] *s ling.* Latinismus *m*.

lat·i·tude ['lætɪtjuːd] *s* **1.** *geogr.* Breite *f*: **in these ~s** in diesen Breiten *od.* Gegenden; → **degree** 2, **parallel** 3. **2.** *fig.* Spielraum *m*, (Bewegungs)Freiheit *f*.

la·trine [lə'triːn] *s* Latrine *f*.

lat·ter ['lætə] *adj* **1.** letzterwähnt, -genannt (*von zweien*): → **former** 2. **2.** letzt, später: **the ~ half of June** die zweite Junihälfte.

lat·tice ['lætɪs] **I** *s* Gitter(werk) *n*. **II** *v/t* vergittern.

laud·a·ble ['lɔːdəbl] *adj* □ löblich, lobenswert. **laud·a·to·ry** ['_dətərɪ] *adj* lobend: **~ speech** Lobrede *f*, Laudatio *f*.

laugh [lɑːf] **I** *s* Lachen *n*, Gelächter *n*: **with a ~** lachend; **have a good ~** herzlich lachen; **have the last ~** am Ende recht haben. **II** *v/i* lachen (**at** über *acc*): **~ at s.o.** *a.* j-n auslachen; **~ to o.s.** in sich hineinlachen; **~ out** auf- *od.* herauslachen; → **beard**, **sleeve** 1. **III** *v/t*: **~ away** (*od.* **off**) *et.* lachend *od.* mit e-m Scherz abtun. **'laugh·a·ble** *adj* □ lächerlich, lachhaft. **'laugh·er** *s* Lacher *m*.

laugh·ing ['lɑːfɪŋ] **I** *s* **1.** Lachen *n*, Gelächter *n*. **II** *adj* □ **2.** lachend. **3.** lustig: **it is no ~ matter** es ist nicht(s) zum Lachen. **~ gas** *s* 🜊 Lachgas *n*. **'~stock** *s* Zielscheibe *f* des Spotts: **make s.o.**

the ~ of j-n zum Gespött (*gen*) machen.

laugh·ter ['lɑːftə] *s* Lachen *n*, Gelächter *n*.

launch¹ [lɔːntʃ] **I** *v/t* **1.** *Boot* zu Wasser lassen; *Schiff* vom Stapel lassen: **be ~ed** vom Stapel laufen. **2.** *Geschoß*, *Torpedo* abschießen, *Rakete*, *Raumfahrzeug a.* starten. **3.** *Rede*, *Kritik etc* vom Stapel lassen; *Drohungen etc* ausstoßen. **4.** *Projekt etc* in Gang setzen, starten. **5. ~ o.s. on a task** (**into work**) sich an e-e Aufgabe (in die Arbeit) stürzen. **II** *v/i* **6. ~ out** *fig.* sich stürzen (**into** *in acc*). **III** *s* **7.** ⚓ Stapellauf *m*. **8.** Abschuß *m*, Start *m*.

launch² [~] *s* ⚓ Barkasse *f*.

launch·ing ['lɔːntʃɪŋ] → **launch** III. **~ pad** *s* Abschußrampe *f*. **~ site** *s* Abschußbasis *f*.

laun·der ['lɔːndə] **I** *v/t Wäsche* waschen (u. bügeln). **II** *v/i* sich waschen (lassen). **laun·der·ette** [~'ret] *s* Waschsalon *m*.

laun·dro·mat ['lɔːndrəmæt] *s bsd. Am.* Waschsalon *m*.

laun·dry ['lɔːndrɪ] *s* **1.** Wäscherei *f*. **2.** Wäsche *f*. **~ bas·ket** *s* Wäschekorb *m*.

lau·rel ['lɒrəl] *s* **1.** ♣ Lorbeer(baum) *m*. **2.** Lorbeerkranz *m*. **3. rest on one's ~s** *fig.* (sich) auf s-n Lorbeeren ausruhen.

lav [læv] *s* F Klo *n*: **in the ~** auf dem *od.* im Klo.

la·va ['lɑːvə] *s* Lava *f*.

lav·a·to·ry ['lævətərɪ] *s* **1.** Waschraum *m*. **2.** Toilette *f*, Klosett *n*: **in the ~** in *od.* auf der Toilette. **~ at·tend·ant** *s* Toilettenfrau *f*. **~ pa·per** *s Br.* Toiletten-, Klosettpapier *n*.

lav·en·der ['lævəndə] *s* ♣ Lavendel *m*.

lav·ish ['lævɪʃ] **I** *adj* □ **1.** sehr freigebig, verschwenderisch (**of** mit; **in** *in dat*): **be ~ of** *a.* verschwenderisch umgehen mit. **2.** überschwenglich (*Lob etc*), großzügig (*Geschenk etc*), luxuriös, aufwendig (*Einrichtung etc*). **3.** verschwenden: **~ s.th. on s.o.** j-n mit et. überhäufen.

law [lɔː] *s* **1.** (*objektives*) Recht, Gesetz(e *pl*) *n*: **contrary to ~**, **against the ~** gesetz-, rechtswidrig; **under German ~** nach deutschem Recht; **~ and order** Recht *od.* Ruhe u. Ordnung. **2.** (*einzelnes*) Gesetz. **3.** Recht *n*: a) Rechtssystem *n*, b) (*einzelnes*) Rechtsgebiet: → **international** 1. **4.** Rechtswissenschaft f, Jura pl: **read** (od. **study**) ~ Jura studieren. **5.** Gericht n, Rechtsweg m: **at** ~ vor Gericht; **go to** ~ vor Gericht gehen, prozessieren; **go to** ~ **with** j-n verklagen, belangen. **6.** F Bullen pl (Polizei); Bulle m (Polizist). **7.** allg. Gesetz n, Vorschrift f. **8.** a) a. ~ **of nature, natural** ~ Naturgesetz n, b) (wissenschaftliches) Gesetz, c) (Lehr)Satz m. **'~a,bid·ing** adj gesetzestreu. **'~**‚**break·er** s Gesetzesübertreter(in), Rechtsbrecher(in). **~ court** s Gerichtshof m.

law·ful ['lɔːfʊl] adj □ **1.** gesetzlich, legal. **2.** rechtmäßig, legitim. **3.** gesetzlich anerkannt, rechtsgültig. **'law·less** adj □ **1.** gesetzlos. **2.** rechts-, gesetzwidrig. **3.** zügellos.

lawn [lɔːn] s Rasen m. **~ chair** s Am. Liegestuhl m. **~ mow·er** s Rasenmäher m.

'law·suit s ♦ (Zivil)Prozeß m, Verfahren n.

law·yer ['lɔːjə] s **1.** (Rechts)Anwalt m. **2.** Jurist m.

lax [læks] adj □ **1.** schlaff, lose, locker. **2.** fig. lax, lasch (Einstellung etc), locker (Sitten etc). **3.** fig. unklar, verschwommen (Vorstellung etc). **lax·a·tive** ['~ətɪv] s pharm. mildes Abführmittel. **'lax·i·ty, 'lax·ness** s **1.** Schlaffheit f. **2.** Laxheit f, Laschheit f.

lay¹ [leɪ] (irr) I v/t **1.** legen, Teppich verlegen. **2.** Eier legen. **3.** fig. Hinterhalt etc legen, Hoffnungen etc setzen (**on** auf acc). **4.** (her)richten, Tisch decken. **5.** be-, auslegen (**with** mit). **6.** (before) vorlegen (dat), bringen (vor dat). **7.** Anspruch etc geltend machen. **8.** Schuld etc zuschreiben, zur Last legen (**to** dat). II v/i **9.** (Eier) legen. **10.** ~ **about one** → **lay about!**; ~ **into** s.o. über j-n herfallen (a. mit Worten). **11.** ~ **off** F j-n, etc. in Ruhe lassen; aufhören mit: **~ off it!** hör auf (damit)!

Verbindungen mit Adverbien:

lay| a·bout v/i (wild) um sich schlagen (**with** mit). **~ a·side** v/t **1.** beiseite legen, weglegen. **2.** Gewohnheit etc ablegen, aufgeben. **3.** (für die Zukunft) beiseite od. auf die Seite legen, zurücklegen. **~ a·way** v/t **1.** → **lay aside 3. 2.** angezahlte Ware zurücklegen. **~ down** v/t **1.** hinlegen. **2.** Amt, Waffen etc niederle-

gen. **3.** sein Leben hingeben, opfern. **4.** planen, entwerfen; Straße etc anlegen. **5.** Grundsatz etc aufstellen, Regeln etc festlegen, -setzen, Bedingungen (in e-m Vertrag) niederlegen, verankern. **~ in** v/t sich eindecken mit; einlagern. **~ off** I v/t **1.** Arbeiter (bsd. vorübergehend) entlassen. **2.** Arbeit einstellen. **3.** F aufhören mit: **~ smoking** a. das Rauchen aufgeben. II v/i **4.** F Feierabend machen; Ferien machen, ausspannen; aufhören; e-e Pause machen. **~ on** v/t **1.** Farbe etc auftragen: **lay it on** F dick auftragen; → **thick 6, trowel. 2.** Br. Gas etc installieren. **3.** Br. Busse etc einsetzen. **~ o·pen** v/t **1.** bloß-, freilegen. **2.** fig. offen darlegen; aufdecken, enthüllen. **~ out** v/t **1.** ausbreiten, -legen. **2.** ausstellen. **3.** Toten aufbahren. **4.** planen, entwerfen. **5.** typ. aufmachen, das Layout (gen) machen. **6.** lay o.s. out F sich mächtig anstrengen. **~ o·ver** Am. I v/i Zwischenstation machen. II v/t verschieben, -tagen (until auf acc, bis). **~ to** v/i ♦ beidrehen. **~ up** v/t **1.** anhäufen, (an)sammeln; ~ **trouble for o.s.** sich Schwierigkeiten einbrocken od. einhandeln. **2.** be laid up das Bett hüten müssen, bettlägerig sein: **be laid up with influenza** mit Grippe im Bett liegen.

lay² [~] pret von **lie²**.

lay³ [~] adj Laien...: a) eccl. weltlich: ~ **preacher** Laienprediger m, b) laienhaft, nicht fachmännisch.

'lay·a·bout s bsd. Br. F Faulenzer m, Tagedieb m. **'~‚a‚way** s angezahlte u. zurückgelegte Ware. **'~-by** s mot. Br. Park-, Rastplatz m (Autobahn), Parkbucht f (Landstraße).

lay·er ['leɪə] I s **1.** Schicht f (a. geol.), Lage f: **in ~s** schicht-, lagenweise. **2.** in Zssgn ...leger m. **3.** ✓, ♣ Ableger m. II v/t **4.** schicht- od. lagenweise anordnen, schichten.

lay·ette [leɪ'et] s Babyausstattung f.

lay·man ['leɪmən] s (irr man) Laie m. **'~-off** s **1.** (bsd. vorübergehende) Entlassung. **2.** F Pause f. **'~out** s **1.** Grundriß m, Lageplan m. **2.** typ. Layout n. **'~‚o·ver** s Am. Zwischenstation f.

laze [leɪz] v/t mst ~ **away** Zeit vertrödeln. **'la·zi·ness** s Faulheit f; Trägheit f.

la·zy ['leɪzɪ] *adj* □ **1.** faul; träg. **2.** träg, langsam. '**~,bones** *s pl* (*sg konstruiert*) F Faulpelz *m*.

lead¹ [led] **I** *s* **1.** ♘ Blei *n*. **2.** ♻ Senkblei *n*, Lot *n*. **3.** (Bleistift)Mine *f*. **4.** Blei *n*, Kugeln *pl*. **II** *v/t* **5.** verbleien: **~ed** verbleit, (*Benzin a.*) bleihaltig. **6.** mit Blei beschweren.

lead² [li:d] **I** *s* **1.** Führung *f*: a) Leitung *f*: **under s.o.'s ~** b) führende Stelle, Spitze *f*: **be in the ~** an der Spitze stehen, führend sein, (*Sport etc*) in Führung liegen, führen; **take the ~** die Führung übernehmen, sich an die Spitze setzen (**from** vor *dat*) (*beide a. Sport*). **2.** Vorsprung *m* (**over** vor *dat*) (*a. Sport*). **3.** Vorbild *n*, Beispiel *n*: **follow s.o.'s ~** j-s Beispiel folgen; **give s.o. a ~** j-m ein gutes Beispiel geben. **4.** Hinweis *m*, Wink *m*; Anhaltspunkt *m*. **5.** *thea. etc* Hauptrolle *f*; Hauptdarsteller(in). **6.** (Hunde)Leine *f*: **keep on the ~** an der Leine führen (*a.* halten). **II** *adj* **7.** Leit..., Führungs...: **~ guitarist** ♩ Leadgitarrist *m*. **III** *v/t* (*irr*) **8.** führen: **~ the way** vorangehen; → **garden** 3, **nose** 1. **9.** führen, bringen (*a. Straße etc*). **10.** dazu bringen, veranlassen (**to do** zu tun). **11.** (an)führen, leiten. **12.** *Leben* führen. **IV** *v/i* (*irr*) **13.** führen: a) vorangehen, b) die erste Stelle einnehmen, c) (*Sport*) an der Spitze od. in Führung liegen. **14.** führen (*Straße etc*): **~ to** *fig.* führen zu.

Verbindungen mit Adverbien:

lead| a·stray *v/t fig.* irreführen; verführen. **~ a·way** *v/t* **1.** wegführen, *Verhafteten etc* abführen. **2.** *fig.* abbringen (**from** von). **~ off** *v/t* **1.** → **lead away. 2.** einleiten, beginnen (**with** mit). **II** *v/i* **3.** anfangen, beginnen. **~ on** *v/t* j-m etc. vor- od. weismachen: **lead s.o. on to think that** j-n glauben machen, daß. **~ up** *v/i fig.* (**to**) (allmählich) führen (zu); hinauswollen (auf *acc*).

lead-en ['ledn] *adj* □ bleiern: a) Blei..., b) bleigrau, c) *fig.* schwer: **~ limbs** *pl* bleischwere Glieder *pl*; **~ sleep** bleierner Schlaf.

lead-er ['li:də] *s* **1.** Führer(in). **2.** (An)Führer *m*, (Delegations-, Oppositions- *etc*)Führer *m*. **3.** ♩ *a.) bsd. Am.* Leiter *m*, Dirigent *m*, b) *bsd. Br.* Konzertmeister *m*, c) (*Band*)Leader *m*. **4.**

bsd. Br. Leitartikel *m*. **5.** *Sport etc:* Spitzenreiter *m*. **6.** ⚓ Zug-, Lockartikel *m*. '**lead-er-ship** *s* **1.** Führung *f*, Leitung *f*. **2.** *a.* **~ qualities** *pl* Führungsqualitäten *pl*.

lead-free ['led~] *adj* bleifrei (*Benzin*).

lead-ing ['li:dɪŋ] *adj* **1.** führend: a) Leit..., leitend, b) Haupt..., erst. **2.** erst. **~ ar·ti·cle** → **leader** 4. **~ la·dy** *s thea. etc* Hauptdarstellerin *f*. **~ light** *s* führende *od.* wichtige Persönlichkeit. **~ man** *s* (*irr man*) *thea. etc* Hauptdarsteller *m*. **~ ques·tion** *s* Suggestivfrage *f*. **~ strings** *s pl Am.* Gängelband *n* (*a. fig.*): **keep s.o. in ~** j-n am Gängelband führen *od.* haben *od.* halten.

leaf [li:f] **I** *pl* **leaves** [li:vz] *s* **1.** ♣ Blatt *n*: **come into ~** ausschlagen. **2.** Blatt *n* (*Buch*): **take a ~ out of s.o.'s book** *fig.* sich an j-m ein Beispiel nehmen; **turn over a new ~** *fig.* ein neues Leben beginnen. **3.** (Fenster-, Tür)Flügel *m*; (*Tisch*)Klappe *f*; Ausziehplatte *f* (*e-s Tisches*): **pull out the leaves** den Tisch ausziehen. **II** *v/t* **4.** *dm.* durchblättern. **III** *v/i* **5.** **~ through** durchblättern.

leaf-let ['li:flɪt] *s* Flugblatt *n*, Hand-, Reklamezettel *m*; Prospekt *m*.

league [li:g] *s* **1.** Liga *f*, Bund *m*. **2.** Bündnis *n*, Bund *m*: **be in ~ with** gemeinsame Sache machen mit. **3.** *Sport:* Liga *f*: **~ game** Punktspiel *n*.

leak [li:k] **I** *s* **1.** a) ♻ Leck *n* (*a. in Tank etc*): **spring a ~** ein Leck bekommen, b) undichte Stelle (*a. fig.*). **2.** Auslaufen *n*; *fig.* Durchsickern *n*. **II** *v/i* **3.** lecken, leck sein. **4.** tropfen (*Wasserhahn*). **5.** **~ out** auslaufen, -treten; *fig.* durchsickern. **III** *v/t* **6.** *fig.* durchsickern lassen. '**leak-age** [~ɪdʒ] *s* → **leak** 2. **2.** ⚓ Leckage *f.* '**leak-y** *adj* leck, undicht (*a. fig.*).

lean¹ [li:n] **I** *adj* □ mager (*a.* ◉ *u. fig.*). **II** *s das* Magere (*des Fleisches*).

lean² [~] **I** *v/i* (*bsd. Br. a. irr*) **1.** sich neigen, schief sein *od.* stehen. **2.** sich beugen (**over** über *acc*): **~ back** sich zurücklehnen; **~ forward** sich vorbeugen; **~ over backward(s)** F sich fast umbringen (**to do** zu tun). **3.** (*against*) sich lehnen (an *acc*, gegen); lehnen (an *dat*). **4.** (**on**) sich stützen (auf *acc*); *fig.* sich verlassen (auf *acc*). **5.** **~ to(ward[s])** *fig.* (hin)neigen *od.* tendieren zu. **II** *v/t* (*bsd. Br. a. irr*) **6.** lehnen (*against* an *acc*, gegen). **III** *s* 7. Neigung *f*. '**lean·ing** I *adj* schräg, schief. **II** *s fig.* Neigung *f*, Tendenz *f* (**to**, **to-ward[s]** zu).

leant [lent] *bsd. Br. pret u. pp von* **lean²**.

leap [li:p] **I** *v/i* (*a. irr*) springen: ~ **at** *fig.* sich stürzen auf (*ein Angebot etc*); ~ **for joy** Freudensprünge machen; ~ **(in)to fame** schlagartig berühmt werden; ~ **out** ins Auge springen (**to s.o.** j-m); ~ **up** aufspringen; *fig.* sprunghaft anwachsen; → **conclusion** 3. **II** *v/t* (*a. irr*) überspringen (*a. fig.*), springen über (*acc*). **III** *s* Sprung *m* (*a. fig.*): **take a** ~ e-n Sprung machen; **by** (*od.* **in**) ~**s and bounds** *fig.* sprunghaft. **IV** *adj* Schalt...: ~ **year**. '**~frog** I *s* Bockspringen. **II** *v/i* bockspringen.

leapt [lept] *pret u. pp von* **leap**.

learn [lɜ:n] (*a. irr*) **I** *v/t* **1.** (er)lernen: ~ **(how) to swim** schwimmen lernen. **2.** (**from**) erfahren, hören (von); ersehen, entnehmen (aus *e-m Brief etc*). **II** *v/i* **3.** lernen. **4.** hören, erfahren (**about**, **of** von). **learn·ed** ['-nid] *adj* gelehrt (*Mensch*), (*Abhandlung etc a.*) wissenschaftlich. '**learn·er** *s* **1.** Anfänger(in). **2.** Lernende *m*, *f*: **be a fast** (**slow**) ~ schnell (langsam) lernen. **learnt** [lɜ:nt] *pret u. pp von* **learn**.

lease [li:s] **I** *s* **1.** Pacht-, Mietvertrag *m*. **2.** Verpachtung *f*, Vermietung *f* (**to an** *acc*); Pacht *f*, Miete *f*: **put out to** (**let out on**) ~ → 4; **take on** ~ → 5. **3.** Pacht-, Mietzeit *f*. **II** *v/t* **4.** ~ **out** verpachten, -mieten (**to an** *acc*). **5.** pachten, mieten; leasen.

leash [li:ʃ] *s* (Hunde)Leine *f*: **keep on the** ~ an der Leine halten *od.* führen; **keep** (*od.* **hold**) **in** ~ *fig.* im Zaum halten; → **strain** 5.

least [li:st] **I** *adj* (*sup von* **little**) **1.** geringst, mindest, wenigst: → **resistance** 1. **2.** geringst, unbedeutendst: **at the** ~ **thing** bei der geringsten Kleinigkeit. **II** *s* **3.** *das* Mindeste, *das* Wenigste: **at** ~ wenigstens, zumindest; **at** (**the**) ~ mindestens; **not in the** ~ nicht im geringsten *od.* mindesten; **to say the** ~ (**of it**) gelinde gesagt. **III** *adv* **4.** am wenigsten: ~ **of all** am allerwenigsten.

leath·er ['leðə] **I** *s* Leder *n* (*a. humor.* Haut; *a. Sport:* Ball): → **tough** 1. **II** *v/t*

F versohlen. '**~neck** *s* ✕ *Am. sl.* Ledernacken *m*.

leath·er·y ['leðəri] *adj* lederartig, zäh.

leave¹ [li:v] (*irr*) **I** *v/t* **1.** verlassen: a) von *j-m*, *e-m Ort etc* fort-, weggehen, b) abreisen, abfahren *etc* von, c) von *der Schule* abgehen, d) *j-n*, *et.* im Stich lassen, *et.* aufgeben: **she left him for another man** sie verließ ihn wegen e-s anderen Mannes. **2.** lassen: ~ **alone** allein lassen; *j-n*, *et.* in Ruhe lassen; ~ **it at that** es dabei belassen *od.* (bewenden) lassen; ~ **s.o. to himself** j-n sich selbst überlassen; → **cold** 4, **lurch²**. **3.** übriglassen: **be left** übrigbleiben *od.* übrig sein. **4.** *Narbe etc* zurücklassen, *Nachricht, Spur etc* hinterlassen. **5.** hängen-, liegen-, stehenlassen, vergessen. **6.** überlassen, anheimstellen (**to s.o.** j-m). **7.** vermachen, -erben. **II** *v/i* **8.** (fort-, weg)gehen, abreisen, abfahren (**for** nach). **9.** gehen (*die Stellung aufgeben*).

Verbindungen mit Adverbien:

leave | **be·hind** *v/t* **1.** zurücklassen. **2.** → **leave¹** 4, 5. **3.** *Gegner etc* hinter sich lassen (*a. fig.*). ~ **on** *v/t* *Radio etc* anlassen, *Kleidungsstück a.* anbehalten. ~ **out** *v/t* **1.** draußen lassen. **2.** aus-, weglassen (**of** von, bei). ~ **o·ver** *v/t Br.* **1.** → **leave¹** 3. **2.** verschieben (**until** auf *acc*, bis).

leave² [~] *s* **1.** Erlaubnis *f*, Genehmigung *f*: **ask** ~ **of s.o.**, **ask s.o.'s** ~ j-n um Erlaubnis bitten. **2.** Urlaub *m*: **on** ~ auf Urlaub. **3.** Abschied *m*: **take** (**one's**) ~ Abschied nehmen (**of** von).

leav·en ['levn] **I** *s* **1.** Sauerteig *m*; Treibmittel *n*. **II** *v/t* **2.** *Teig* säuern; (auf)gehen lassen. **3.** *fig.* auflockern (**with** mit, durch).

leaves [li:vz] *pl von* **leaf**.

leav·ing ['li:vɪŋ] **1.** *mst pl* Überbleibsel *n*, Rest *m*. **2.** *pl* Abfall *m*.

lech·er ['letʃə] *s* Lüstling *m*. '**lech·er·ous** *adj* □ geil, lüstern. '**lech·er·y** *s* Geilheit *f*, Lüsternheit *f*.

lec·ture ['lektʃə] **I** *s* **1.** (**on** über *acc*; **to** vor *dat*) Vortrag *m*; *univ.* Vorlesung *f*: ~ **hall** (*od.* **theater**, *bsd. Br.* **theatre**) Hörsaal *m*. **2.** Strafpredigt *f*: **give** (*od.* **read**) **s.o. a** ~ → 4. **II** *v/i* **3.** (**on** über *acc*; **to** vor *dat*) e-n Vortrag *od.* Vorträge halten; *univ.* e-e Vorlesung *od.* Vorlesungen halten. **III** v/t **4.** j-m e-e Straf-predigt halten. **'lec·tur·er** s **1.** Vortragende m, f. **2.** univ. Dozent(in).

led [led] pret u. pp von **lead²**.

ledge [ledʒ] s Leiste f, Sims m, n.

ledg·er ['ledʒə] s ✝ Hauptbuch n.

lee [liː] s ♣ Lee(seite) f.

leech [liːtʃ] s **1.** zo. Blutegel m. **2.** fig. Klette f; Blutsauger m.

leek [liːk] s ♣ Lauch m, Porree m.

leer [lɪə] **I** s höhnisches od. boshaftes od. anzügliches Grinsen; lüsterner Seitenblick. **II** v/i höhnisch od. boshaft od. anzüglich grinsen; lüstern schielen (**at** nach).

lees [liːz] s pl Bodensatz m.

lee·ward ['liːwəd] adv ♣ leewärts.

'lee·way s **1.** ✈, ♣ Abtrift f. **2.** fig. Rückstand m, Zeitverlust m: **make up ~** (den Rückstand od. Zeitverlust) aufholen. **3.** fig. Spielraum m.

left¹ [left] pret u. pp von **leave¹**.

left² [∼] **I** adj **1.** link, Links... **II** s **2.** die Linke, linke Seite: **on** (od. **at, to**) **the ~** (**of**) links (von), linker Hand (von); **on our ~** zu unserer Linken; **the second turning to** (od. **on**) **the ~** die zweite Querstraße links; **keep to the ~** sich links halten; mot. links fahren. **3. the ~** pol. die Linke. **III** adv **4.** links (of von): **turn ~** (sich) nach links wenden; mot. links abbiegen. **'~-hand** adj **1.** link: **~ bend** Linkskurve f. **2.** ⚙ linksgängig, -läufig: **~ drive** Linkssteuerung f. **~·'hand·ed** adj □ **1.** linkshändig: **be ~** Linkshänder(in) sein. **2.** linkisch, ungeschickt. **3.** zweifelhaft, fragwürdig (Kompliment etc). **~·'hand·er** s Linkshänder(in).

left·ist ['leftɪst] adj pol. linksgerichtet, -stehend.

,left|-'lug·gage lock·er s 🚉 Br. (Gepäck)Schließfach n. **~·'lug·gage of-fice** s 🚉 Br. Gepäckaufbewahrung(sstelle) f. **'~·o·ver** s mst pl Überbleibsel n, Rest m.

'left-wing adj pol. dem linken Flügel angehörend, links...

leg [leg] **I** s **1.** (a. Hosen-, Stuhl- etc)Bein n: **be on one's last ~** auf dem letzten Loch pfeifen; **give s.o. a ~ up** j-m (hin)aufhelfen; fig. j-m unter die Arme greifen; **pull s.o.'s ~** F j-n auf den Arm nehmen; **stretch one's ~s** sich die Bei-

ne vertreten; → **shake** 7. **2.** (Hammel-etc)Keule f: **~ of mutton.** 3. ⚓ Kathete f, Schenkel m (e-s Dreiecks). **4.** Etappe f, Abschnitt m (e-r Reise etc). **II** v/i **5.** mst **~ it** F zu Fuß gehen.

leg·a·cy ['legəsɪ] s ⚖ Vermächtnis n, fig. a. Erbe n.

le·gal ['liːgl] adj □ **1.** gesetzlich, rechtlich: **~ holiday** Am. gesetzlicher Feiertag; → **tender²** 4. **2.** legal, gesetzmäßig, rechtsgültig. **3.** Rechts..., juristisch: **~ adviser** Rechtsberater m; **~ aid** Prozeßkostenhilfe f. **4.** gerichtlich: **take ~ action** (od. **steps**) **against s.o.** gerichtlich gegen j-n vorgehen. **le·gal·i·ty** [liːˈgælətɪ] s Legalität f. **le·gal·i·za·tion** [ˌliːgəlaɪˈzeɪʃn] s Legalisierung f. **'le·gal·ize** v/t legalisieren.

le·ga·tion [lɪˈgeɪʃn] s Gesandtschaft f.

leg·end ['ledʒənd] s **1.** Legende f (a. fig.), Sage f. **2.** Legende f: a) erläuternder Text, Bildunterschrift f, b) Zeichenerklärung f (auf Karten etc), c) Inschrift f (auf Münzen etc).

leg·er·de·main [ˌledʒədəˈmeɪn] s **1.** Taschenspielerei f (a. fig.). **2.** Schwindel m.

leg·gy ['legɪ] adj langbeinig.

leg·i·ble ['ledʒəbl] adj □ leserlich, lesbar.

le·gion ['liːdʒən] s Legion f. **'le·gion-ar·y** s Legionär m.

leg·is·late ['ledʒɪsleɪt] v/i Gesetze erlassen. **,leg·is·la·tion** s Gesetzgebung f. **leg·is·la·tive** ['∼lətɪv] **I** adj □ **1.** gesetzgebend, legislativ: **~ assembly** gesetzgebende Versammlung; **~ body** → 3b; **~ power** → 3a. **2.** gesetzgeberisch, Legislatur...: **~ period** Legislaturperiode f. **II** s **3.** Legislative f: a) gesetzgebende Gewalt, b) gesetzgebende Körperschaft. **leg·is·la·tor** ['∼leɪtə] s Gesetzgeber m. **leg·is·la·ture** ['∼leɪtʃə] → **legislative** 3b.

le·git·i·ma·cy [lɪˈdʒɪtɪməsɪ] s Legitimität f: a) Gesetzmäßigkeit f, Gesetzlichkeit f, b) Rechtmäßigkeit f, Berechtigung f, c) Ehelichkeit f. **le·git·i·mate** [∼mət] adj □ legitim: a) gesetzmäßig, gesetzlich, b) rechtmäßig, berechtigt, c) ehelich. **le·git·i·mize** v/t legitimieren.

leg·room ['legrʊm] s ✈, mot. Beinfreiheit f.

leg·ume ['legjuːm] s ♣ Hülsenfrucht f.

lei·sure ['leʒə] **I** s freie Zeit: **at ~** mit Muße, in (aller) Ruhe; frei, unbeschäftigt; **at your ~** wenn es Ihnen (gerade) paßt, bei Gelegenheit. **II** adj Freizeit...: **~ activities** pl Freizeitgestaltung f; **~ facilities** pl Freizeiteinrichtungen pl; **~ hours** or Mußestunden pl; **~ occupation** Freizeitbeschäftigung f; **~ time** Freizeit f; **~ wear** Freizeitkleidung f. **'lei·sure·ly** adj u. adv gemächlich, gemütlich.

lem·on ['lemən] **I** s **1.** Zitrone f. **2.** sl. Niete f (Sache, Person). **II** adj **3.** Zitronen...: **~ juice; ~ soda** Am. Zitronenlimonade f; **~ squash** Br. Getränk aus Zitronenkonzentrat u. Wasser; **~ squeezer** Zitronenpresse f. **4.** zitronengelb.

lend [lend] v/t (irr) **1.** (ver-, aus)leihen. **2.** fig. Nachdruck, Würde etc verleihen (**to** dat). **3.** fig. leihen, gewähren: **~ o.s. to s.th.** sich zu et. hergeben; **~ itself to s.th.** sich für od. zu et. eignen; **~ hand** 1. **'lend·er** s Aus-, Verleiher(in). **'lend·ing** adj: **~ library** Leihbücherei f.

length [leŋθ] s **1.** Länge f: a) Dimension: **two feet in ~** 2 Fuß lang; **what ~ is it?** wie lang ist es?), b) Strecke f: **go to great ~s** sich sehr bemühen, c) Umfang m (e-s Buchs etc), d) Dauer f: **at ~** a) ausführlich; **at full ~** in allen Einzelheiten. **2.** Bahn f (Stoff etc). **3.** Sport: Länge f (Vorsprung). **'length·en** **I** v/t verlängern, länger machen, Kleidungsstück a. auslassen. **II** v/i sich verlängern, länger werden. **'length·ways, length·wise** ['~waɪz] adv der Länge nach, längs. **'length·y** adj □ ermüdend lang, langatmig.

le·ni·ence, le·ni·en·cy ['liːnjəns(ɪ)] s Milde f, Nachsicht f. **'le·ni·ent** adj □ mild, nachsichtig (**to, toward[s]** gegenüber).

lens [lenz] s **1.** anat., phot., phys. Linse f: **~ aperture** phot. Blende f. **2.** phot., phys. Objektiv n. **3.** (einzelnes) Glas (e-r Brille).

lent¹ [lent] pret u. pp von **lend**.

Lent² [~] s Fastenzeit f.

len·til ['lentɪl] s ♀ Linse f.

Leo ['liːəʊ] s ast. Löwe m.

leop·ard ['lepəd] s zo. Leopard m.

le·o·tard ['liːəʊtɑːd] s **1.** Trikot n. **2.** Gymnastikanzug m.

les·bi·an ['lezbɪən] **I** adj lesbisch. **II** s Lesbierin f.

lese maj·es·ty [ˌliːzˈmædʒɪstɪ] s **1.** Majestätsbeleidigung f (a. fig.). **2.** Hochverrat m.

le·sion ['liːʒn] s Verletzung f, Wunde f.

less [les] **I** adv (comp von **little**) weniger: **~ and ~** immer weniger; **the ~ so as** (dies) um so weniger, als. **II** adj (comp von **little**) geringer, kleiner, weniger: **in ~ time** in kürzerer Zeit; **no ~ a man than** kein geringerer als. **III** s weniger, e-e kleinere Menge od. Zahl: **little ~ than** so gut wie, schon fast; **no ~ than** nicht weniger als. **IV** prp weniger, minus, abzüglich.

less·en ['lesn] **I** v/i **1.** sich vermindern od. verringern, abnehmen. **II** v/t **2.** vermindern, verringern. **3.** fig. herabsetzen, schmälern; bagatellisieren.

less·er ['lesə] adj kleiner, geringer: → **evil** 2.

les·son ['lesn] s **1.** Lektion f (a. fig.): → **teach** 2. **2.** (Lehr-, Unterrichts)Stunde f; pl Unterricht m, Stunden pl: **give ~s** Unterricht erteilen, unterrichten; **take ~s from** Stunden od. Unterricht nehmen bei. **3.** fig. Lehre f: **this was a ~ to me** das war mir e-e Lehre.

lest [lest] cj **1.** (mst mit folgendem **should**) daß od. damit nicht: **he ran away ~ he should be seen** er lief weg, um nicht gesehen zu werden. **2.** (nach Ausdrücken des Befürchtens) daß.

let¹ [let] (irr) **I** v/t **1.** lassen: **~ alone** et. seinlassen; j-n, et. in Ruhe lassen; geschweige denn, ganz zu schweigen von; **~ s.th. go** et. loslassen; **~ o.s. go** sich gehenlassen; aus sich herausgehen; **~ it go at that** laß es dabei bewenden; **~'s go** gehen wir!; **~ s.o. know** j-n wissen lassen, j-m Bescheid geben; **~ in** (her-, hin)einlassen (in acc); j-n einweihen in (ein Geheimnis). **2.** bsd. Br. vermieten, -pachten (**to** an acc; **for** auf ein Jahr etc): **"to ~"** „zu vermieten". **II** v/i **3.** **~ go** loslassen (**of s.th.** et.). **4.** **~ into** über j-n herfallen.

Verbindungen mit Adverbien:

let| by v/t vorbeilassen. **~ down** v/t **1.** hinunter-, herunterlassen: → **hair** 2. im Stich lassen; enttäuschen. **~ in** v/t **1.** (her-, hin)einlassen. **2.** Stück etc einlassen, -setzen. **3.** j-n einweihen (**on** in ein

Geheimnis). **4. let o.s. in for s.th.** sich et. einbrocken, sich auf et. einlassen. ~ **off** v/t **1.** *Feuerwerk* abbrennen, *Gewehr etc* abfeuern. **2.** *Gas etc* ablassen: → **steam** 1. ~ **on** F I v/i **1.** sich et. anmerken lassen (**about** von). II v/t **2.** zugeben (*that* daß). **3.** vorgeben. ~ **out** I v/t **1.** heraus-, hinauslassen (**of** aus): *let the air out of* die Luft lassen aus. **2.** *Kleidungsstück* auslassen. **3.** *Schrei etc* ausstoßen. **4.** *Geheimnis* ausplaudern, verraten. **5.** → **let**¹ 1. II v/i **6.** herfallen (*at* über *acc*) (*a. mit Worten*). ~ **through** v/t durchlassen. ~ **up** v/i F nachlassen; aufhören.

let² [~] s *Tennis:* Netzaufschlag m: *~!* Netz!

'let-down s Enttäuschung f.

le·thal ['li:θl] *adj* □ tödlich; *Todes...*

le·thar·gic [ləˈθɑːdʒɪk] *adj* (**~ally**) lethargisch, teilnahmslos. **leth·ar·gy** ['leθədʒɪ] s Lethargie f, Teilnahmslosigkeit f.

let's [lets] F *für* **let us.**

let·ter ['letə] s I s **1.** Buchstabe m: *to the ~* wortwörtlich, buchstäblich; *fig.* peinlich genau. **2.** Brief m, Schreiben n (*to* an *acc*): *by ~* brieflich; ~ *of application* Bewerbungsschreiben; ~ *of complaint* Beschwerdebrief; ~ *to the editor* Leserbrief. **3.** *typ.* Letter f, Type f. **4.** *pl* (*a. sg konstruiert*) (schöne) Literatur; Bildung f. II v/t **5.** beschriften. ~ **bomb** s Briefbombe f. ~ **box** s *bsd. Br.* Briefkasten m. **~·file** s Briefordner m. '**~·head** s (gedruckter) Briefkopf m. ~ **o·pen·er** s Brieföffner m. ~ **pa·per** s Briefpapier n. ~ **scales** s pl Briefwaage f. '**~·weight** s Briefbeschwerer m.

let·tuce ['letɪs] s ♣ (*bsd.* Kopf)Salat m.

'let-up s F Nachlassen n; Aufhören n.

leu·co·cyte ['lu:kəʊsaɪt] s ♣ Leukozyt m, weißes Blutkörperchen.

leu·k(a)e·mi·a [luːˈkiːmɪə] s ♣ Leukämie f.

lev·el ['levl] s I s **1.** ☉ Libelle f, Wasserwaage f. **2.** Ebene f (*a. fig.*), ebene Fläche: *at government* ~ auf Regierungsebene. **3.** Höhe f (*a. geogr.*), (*Wasser etc*)Spiegel m, (-)Stand m, (-)Pegel m; *fig.* (*a. geistiges*) Niveau, Stand m, Stufe f: ~ *of sound* Geräuschpegel, Tonstärke f; *be on a ~ with* auf gleicher Höhe sein mit; genauso hoch sein wie;

fig. auf dem gleichen Niveau *od.* auf der gleichen Stufe stehen wie. II *adj* □ **4.** eben (*Straße etc*): *a ~ teaspoon* ein gestrichener Teelöffel(voll). **5.** gleich (*a. fig.*): ~ *crossing Br.* schienengleicher (Bahn)Übergang; *be ~ on points* (*Sport*) punktgleich sein; *be ~ with* auf gleicher Höhe sein mit; genauso hoch sein wie; *fig.* auf dem gleichen Niveau *od.* auf der gleichen Stufe stehen wie; *draw ~* (*Sport*) ausgleichen; *draw ~ with* j-n einholen; *make ~ with the ground* → 9b. **6.** a) gleichmäßig: ~ *stress ling.* schwebende Betonung, b) ausgeglichen (*Rennen etc*). **7. do one's ~ best** sein möglichstes tun. **8. have (keep) a ~ head** e-n kühlen Kopf haben (bewahren), sich nicht aus der Ruhe bringen lassen; *give s.o. a ~ look* j-n ruhig *od.* fest anschauen. III v/t *pret u. pp* **-eled,** *bsd. Br.* **-elled 9.** a) (ein)ebnen, planieren, b) a. ~ *to* (*od. with*) *the ground* dem Erdboden gleichmachen. **10.** *fig.* gleichmachen, nivellieren; *Unterschiede* beseitigen, ausgleichen. *Verbindungen mit Adverbien:*

lev·el| down v/t *Preise, Löhne etc* drücken, herabsetzen. ~ **off** I v/t → **level** 9a, 10. **2.** *Flugzeug* abfangen. II v/i **3.** flach werden *od.* auslaufen (*Gelände etc*). ~ **up** *fig.* sich stabilisieren *od.* einpendeln (*at* bei). ~ **out** I v/t → **level** 10. **2.** → **level off** 2. II v/i **3.** → **level off** II. ~ **up** v/t *Preise, Löhne etc* hinaufschrauben.

‚lev·el-'head·ed *adj* □ vernünftig.

le·ver ['liːvə] s I s **1.** *phys.,* ☉ Hebel m. **2.** Brechstange f. **3.** Anker m (*e-r Uhr*). **4.** *fig.* Druckmittel n. II v/t **5.** ~ **out** (**of**) herausstemmen (aus); *fig.* j-n verdrängen (aus).

lev·i·ty ['levətɪ] s Leichtfertigkeit f.

lev·y ['levɪ] I s **1.** † Erhebung f. **2.** † Steuer f, Abgabe f. **3.** ✕ Aushebung f. II v/t **4.** *Steuern etc* a) erheben, b) (**on**) legen (auf *acc*), auferlegen (*dat*). **5.** ✕ *Truppen* ausheben.

lewd [ljuːd] *adj* □ **1.** geil, lüstern. **2.** unanständig, obszön. **'lewd·ness** s **1.** Geilheit f, Lüsternheit f. **2.** Unanständigkeit f, Obszönität f.

lex·i·cog·ra·pher [ˌleksɪˈkɒɡrəfə] s Lexikograph(in). **lex·i·co·graph·ic** [ˌleksɪkəʊˈɡræfɪk] *adj* (**~ally**) lexikographisch.

lex·i·cog·ra·phy [ˌ~'kɒɡrəfɪ] s Lexikographie f.

li·a·bil·i·ty [ˌlaɪə'bɪlətɪ] s 1. ✝, ⚖ Verpflichtung f, Verbindlichkeit f; Haftung f, Haftpflicht f: ~ insurance
Haftpflichtversicherung f; → limit 4. 2.
pl ✝ Passiva pl. 3. allg. Verantwortung
f, Verantwortlichkeit f. 4. ~ to penalty
Strafbarkeit f; ~ to taxation Steuer-
pflicht f. 5. (to) Hang m, Neigung f
(zu), Anfälligkeit f (für).

li·a·ble ['laɪəbl] adj 1. ✝, ⚖ haftbar,
-pflichtig (for für): be ~ for a. haften
für. 2. unterworfen (to s.th. e-r Sache):
be ~ to s.th. a. e-r Sache unterliegen; ~
to penalty strafbar; ~ to taxation
steuerpflichtig. 3. be ~ to neigen zu,
anfällig sein für. 4. be ~ to do s.th. et.
gern od. leicht tun; et. wahrscheinlich
tun: he is ~ to come er kommt wahrscheinlich; that is ~ to happen das
kann durchaus od. leicht passieren.

li·aise [lɪ'eɪz] v/i 1. Verbindung aufnehmen (with mit). 2. sich verbünden (with
mit). 3. zs.-arbeiten (with mit). li-ai-
-son [lɪ'eɪzɒn] s 1. Verbindung f: ~ man
Verbindungsmann m. 2. Bündnis n. 3.
Zs.-arbeit f. 4. Liaison f, (Liebes)Ver-
hältnis n.

li·ar ['laɪə] s Lügner(in).

li·bel ['laɪbl] ⚖ I s (schriftliche) Verleumdung od. Beleidigung (of, on gen).
II v/t pret u. pp -beled, bsd. Br. -belled
(schriftlich) verleumden od. beleidigen.
'li·bel·(l)ous adj □ verleumderisch.

lib·er·al ['lɪbərəl] I adj □ 1. liberal, aufgeschlossen. 2. mst ☉ pol. liberal. 3.
großzügig: a) freigebig (of mit), b)
reichlich (bemessen): ~ gift großzügiges
Geschenk. 4. ~ arts pl Geisteswissenschaften pl. II s 5. mst ☉ pol. Liberale m,
f. 'lib·er·al·ism s Liberalismus m. lib-
er·al·i·ty [ˌ~'rælətɪ] s 1. Liberalität
f. 2. Großzügigkeit f. lib·er·al·ize
['lɪbərəlaɪz] v/t liberalisieren.

lib·er·ate ['lɪbəreɪt] v/t 1. befreien (from
von, aus) (a. fig.); Sklaven etc freilassen. 2. Gase etc, fig. Kräfte etc freisetzen: be ~d a. frei werden. ˌlib·er'a·tion
s 1. Befreiung f; Freilassung f. 2. Freisetzung f.

lib·er·tine ['lɪbətiːn] s Wüstling m.

lib·er·ty ['lɪbətɪ] s 1. Freiheit f: a) persönliche etc Freiheit f: religious ~ Reli-

gionsfreiheit; ~ of the press Pressefreiheit; ~ of speech Redefreiheit; at ~ frei,
in Freiheit, auf freiem Fuß, b) freie
Wahl, Erlaubnis f: be at ~ to do s.th. et.
tun dürfen, c) mst pl Privileg n, Vorrecht n. 2. Dreistigkeit f, (plumpe) Vertraulichkeit f: take liberties with sich
Freiheiten gegen j-n herausnehmen;
willkürlich mit et. umgehen.

li·bid·i·nous [lɪ'bɪdɪnəs] adj □ libidinös,
triebhaft. **li·bi·do** [lɪ'biːdəʊ] s Libido f,
Geschlechtstrieb m.

Li·bra ['laɪbrə] s ast. Waage f.

li·brar·i·an [laɪ'breərɪən] s Bibliothe-
kar(in). **li·brar·y** ['~brərɪ] s 1. Bibliothek f: a) öffentliche Bücherei: ~ ticket
Leseausweis m, b) private Bücher-
sammlung, c) Bibliothekszimmer n. 2.
(Bild-, Zeitungs)Archiv n: ~ picture Ar-
chivbild n.

li·bret·tist [lɪ'bretɪst] s Librettist m, Text-
dichter m. **li·bret·to** [~təʊ] pl -tos, -ti
[~tɪ] s Libretto n: a) Textbuch n, b)
(Opern- etc)Text m.

lice [laɪs] pl von louse 1.

li·cence ['laɪsəns] I s 1. Lizenz f, Konzession f, behördliche Genehmigung;
(Führer-, Jagd-, Waffen- etc)Schein m:
~ number mot. Kennzeichen n. 2. dichterische Freiheit f. 3. Zügellosigkeit f. II
v/t 4. Am. → license 1.

li·cense ['laɪsəns] I v/t 1. lizensieren,
konzessionieren, behördlich genehmigen: fully ~d mit voller Schankkonzes-
sion. 2. j-m e-e Lizenz od. Konzession
erteilen; (es) j-m (offiziell) erlauben (to
do zu tun). II s 3. Am. → licence I: ~
plate mot. Nummern-, Kennzeichenschild n.

li·cen·tious [laɪ'senʃəs] adj □ ausschweifend, zügellos.

li·chen ['laɪkən] s 1. ♀ Flechte f. 2. ♨
Knötchenflechte f.

lick [lɪk] I v/t 1. (ab)lecken: ~ up (out)
auf-(aus)lecken; ~ s.o.'s boots fig. vor
j-m kriechen; ~ one's lips sich die Lippen lecken (a. fig.). 2. F verprügeln,
-dreschen; übertreffen: this ~s me das
geht über m-n Horizont. II v/i 3. lecken
(at an dat). III s 4. Lecken n: give s.th.
a ~ an etwas lecken. 5. F Tempo n: at
full ~ mit voller Geschwindigkeit.
'lick·ing s F Prügel pl, Dresche f.

lic·o·rice ['lɪkərɪs] s ♀ Lakritze f.

lid [lɪd] s **1.** Deckel m: *put the ~ on* Br. F *e-r Sache* die Krone aufsetzen; *e-r Sache* ein Ende machen. **2.** (Augen-)Lid n.

li-do ['liːdəʊ] pl **-dos** s Br. Frei- od. Strandbad n.

lie¹ [laɪ] I s Lüge f: *tell ~s* (od. *a ~*) lügen; *give the ~ to et.*, *j-n* Lügen strafen; → *white lie*. II v/i lügen: *~ to s.o.* j-n belügen.

lie² [~] I s **1.** Lage f (a. fig.): *the ~ of the land* fig. Br. die Lage (der Dinge). II v/i (irr) **2.** liegen: a) *allg. im Bett, im Hinterhalt etc* liegen; *ausgebreitet, tot etc* daliegen, b) begraben sein, ruhen, c) gelegen sein, sich befinden: *the town ~s on a river* die Stadt liegt e-m Fluß; *~ second* (Sport etc) an zweiter Stelle liegen, d) begründet liegen (*in* in dat). **3.** a) *~ heavy on s.o.'s stomach* j-m schwer im Magen liegen, b) fig. lasten (*on* auf *der Seele etc*). **4.** fig. stecken (*behind* hinter dat).

Verbindungen mit Adverbien:

lie| a·bout v/i herumliegen. **~ a·head** v/i: *what lies ahead of us* was vor uns liegt, was uns bevorsteht. **~ a·round** → *lie about.* **~ back** v/i sich zurücklegen od. -lehnen; *fig.* sich ausruhen. **~ down** v/i: **1.** sich hin- od. niederlegen: *~ on* sich legen auf (acc). **2.** *take lying down Beleidigung etc* widerspruchslos hinnehmen, sich *e-e Beleidigung etc* gefallen lassen. **~ in** v/i Br. (*morgens*) lang im Bett bleiben. **~ low** v/i sich verstecken od. versteckt halten; sich ruhig verhalten. **~ o·ver** v/i liegenbleiben, unerledigt bleiben; aufgeschoben od. zurückgestellt werden. **~ up** v/i: **1.** das Bett od. das Zimmer hüten (müssen). **2.** nicht benutzt werden, (*Maschine etc*) außer Betrieb sein.

'lie-a-bed s Langschläfer(in).

lie de·tec·tor s Lügendetektor m.

'lie|-down s F Schläfchen n: *have a ~* ein Schläfchen machen; sich (kurz) hinlegen. **'~-in** s: *have* (od. *take*) *a ~* F → *lie in*.

lieu [ljuː] s: *in ~* statt dessen; *in ~ of* an Stelle von (*od. gen*), (an)statt (gen); → *oath* 1.

lieu·ten·ant [lef'tenənt] s ✕ a) Leutnant m, b) Br. (Am. first *~*) Oberleutnant m.

life [laɪf] pl **lives** [laɪvz] s **1.** Leben n: a)

organisches Leben, b) Lebenskraft f, c) Lebewesen pl, d) Menschenleben n: *they lost their lives* sie kamen ums Leben; *a matter of ~ and death* e-e lebenswichtige Angelegenheit; *early in ~* in jungen Jahren; *late in ~* in vorgerücktem Alter, e) Lebenszeit f, -dauer f: *all his ~* sein ganzes Leben lang; *for ~* fürs (ganze) Leben, für den Rest s-s Lebens; *bsd.* ⚖, *pol.* lebenslänglich, auf Lebenszeit, f) menschliches Tun u. Treiben, g) Lebensweise f, -wandel m, h) Schwung m: *full of ~* voller Leben. **2.** ⚖ Laufzeit f (*e-s Wechsels, Vertrags etc*); ✝ Haltbarkeit f, Lagerfähigkeit f. **3.** ⚖ F lebenslängliche Freiheitsstrafe: *he is doing ~* er sitzt lebenslänglich; *he got ~* er bekam lebenslänglich. **~ an·nu·i·ty** s Leibrente f. **~ as·sur·ance** s bsd. Br. Lebensversicherung f. **'~-boat** s ⚓ Rettungsboot n. **~ buoy** s ⚓ Rettungsring m. **~ ex·pect·an·cy** s Lebenserwartung f. **'~-guard** s Rettungsschwimmer m; Bademeister m. **~ im·pris·on·ment** s ⚖ lebenslängliche Freiheitsstrafe. **~ in·sur·ance** s Lebensversicherung f. **~ jack·et** s ⚓ Rettungs-, Schwimmweste f.

life-less ['laɪflɪs] adj □ **1.** leblos: a) tot, b) unbelebt. **2.** fig. matt, schwunglos.

'life|-like adj lebensecht, naturgetreu. **'~-line** s **1.** ⚓ Rettungsleine f. **2.** fig. Rettungsanker m. **3.** Lebenslinie f (*in der Hand*). **'~-long** adj lebenslang. **~ mem·ber** s Mitglied n auf Lebenszeit. **~ peer** s Peer m auf Lebenszeit. **~ pre·serv·er** s **1.** ⚓ Am. Rettungs-, Schwimmweste f; Rettungsgürtel m. **2.** bsd. Br. Totschläger m (*Waffe*).

lif·er ['laɪfə] s ⚖ F Lebenslängliche m, f.

life| raft s ⚓ Rettungsfloß n. **'~-sav·er** s **1.** Lebensretter m. **2.** → *lifeguard.* **3.** F rettender Engel; Rettung f. **'~-sav·ing** adj lebensrettend. **~ sen·tence** s ⚖ lebenslängliche Freiheitsstrafe. **'~-size(d)** adj lebensgroß, in Lebensgröße. **'~-time** I s Lebenszeit f: *once in a ~* sehr selten, einmal im Leben; *during* (od. *in*) *s.o.'s ~* zu j-s Lebzeiten od. Zeit; in j-s Leben. II adj auf Lebenszeit, lebenslang: *~ post* Lebensstellung f. **'~-work** s Lebenswerk n.

lift [lɪft] I s **1.** (Hoch-, Auf)Heben n. **2.** ⚙ Hub(höhe f) m. **3.** Luftbrücke f. **4.** ✈, *phys.* Auftrieb *m, fig. a.* Aufschwung *m: give s.o. a ~ →* 10. **5.** *give s.o. a ~* j-n (im Auto) mitnehmen; *get a ~ from s.o.* von j-m mitgenommen werden; → *thumb* II. **6.** *bsd. Br.* Lift *m,* Aufzug *m,* Fahrstuhl *m.* **7.** *(Ski- etc)*Lift *m.* **8.** ☆ Lift *m, n,* Lifting *n: have a ~* sich liften lassen. **II** *v/t* **9.** *a. ~ up* (hoch , auf)heben; *Stimme etc* erheben: *~ one's eyes* aufschauen, -blicken; *→ finger* I, *hand* 1. **10.** *a. ~ up* j-m aufmuntern, j-m Auftrieb *od.* Aufschwung geben. **11.** F klauen (*a.* plagiieren). **12.** *Gesicht etc* liften, straffen. **13.** *Embargo, Verbot etc* aufheben. **III** *v/i* **14.** sich heben, steigen (*a. Nebel*): *~ off* starten (*Rakete*); abheben (*Flugzeug*). **15.** sich (hoch)heben lassen. '*~boy s bsd. Br.* Liftboy *m.* '*~man s* [~ (*ir irr man*) *bsd. Br.* Fahrstuhlführer *m.* '*~off s* Start *m (e-r Rakete)*; Abheben *n (e-s Flugzeugs).*

lig·a·ment ['lɪɡəmənt] *s anat.* Band *n.*

lig·a·ture ['lɪɡətʃə] *s typ., ♪* Ligatur *f.*

light¹ [laɪt] **I** *s* **1.** Licht *n:* a) Helligkeit *f: stand (od. be)* in *s.o.'s ~* j-m im Licht (*fig.* im Weg) stehen, b) Beleuchtung *f: in subdued ~* bei gedämpftem Licht, c) Schein *m: by the ~ of a candle* bei Kerzenschein, d) Lichtquelle *f: hide one's ~ under a bushel* sein Licht unter den Scheffel stellen, e) Sonnen-, Tageslicht *n: bring (come) to ~ fig.* ans Licht bringen (kommen); *see the ~ (of day)* das Licht der Welt erblicken; *fig.* herauskommen, auf den Markt kommen; *fig.* bekannt *od.* veröffentlicht werden, f) *fig.* Aspekt *m: in the ~ of* unter dem Aspekt *od.* in Anbetracht (*gen*), g) *fig.* Erleuchtung *f: cast (od. shed, throw) ~ on* Licht auf e-e Sache werfen; zur Lösung *od.* Aufklärung e-r Sache beitragen; *I see the ~* mir geht ein Licht auf. **2.** *mot.* Scheinwerfer *m.* **3.** *Br. mst pl* (Verkehrs)Ampel *f: jump (od. shoot)* the *~s* bei Rot über die Kreuzung fahren; *→ amber* 2, 5, *green* 1, 3, *red* 1, 3, *yellow* 3. **4.** Feuer *n (zum Anzünden), bsd.* Streichholz *n: have you got a ~?* haben Sie Feuer? **5.** *a. shining ~ fig.* Leuchte *f,* großes Licht (*Person*): *→ leading light.* **II** *adj* **6.** hell, licht: *~ red* Hellrot *n.* **III** *v/t (a. irr)* **7.** *a. ~ up* anzünden: *~ a cigarette* sich e-e Zigarette anzünden. **8.** be-, erleuchten,

erhellen: *~ up* hell beleuchten. **9.** j-m leuchten. **IV** *v/i (a. irr)* **10.** *a. ~ up* entzünden. **11.** *mst ~ up fig.* aufleuchten (*Augen etc*). **12.** *~ up* Licht machen; *mot.* die Scheinwerfer einschalten; F sich e-e (*Zigarette etc*) anzünden.

light² [~] **I** *adj* (□ *→ lightly*) **1.** *allg.* leicht (*z. B. Last; Kleidung; Mahlzeit, Wein, Schlaf; Fehler, Strafe*): (*as*) *~ as air* (*od. a feather*) federleicht; *~ current ♭* Schwachstrom *m; no ~ matter* keine Kleinigkeit; *~ metal* Leichtmetall *n; ~ reading* Unterhaltungslektüre *f; make ~ of* auf die leichte Schulter nehmen; verharmlosen, bagatellisieren. **2.** locker (*Erde, Schnee*), leicht gebacken (*Brot etc*). **3.** *Sport:* Halb...: *~ heavyweight* Halb-, Leichtschwergewicht(ler *m*) *n.* **II** *adv* **4.** *travel ~* mit leichtem Gepäck reisen.

light bar·ri·er *s ♭* Lichtschranke *f.* ~ **bulb** *s ♭* Glühbirne *f.*

light·en¹ ['laɪtn] **I** *v/i* **1.** sich aufhellen, hell(er) werden. **2.** *impers* blitzen. **II** *v/t* **3.** (*a.* blitzartig) erhellen.

light·en² [~] **I** *v/t* **1.** leichter machen, erleichtern (*beide a. fig.*): *~ s.o.'s heart* j-m das Herz leichter machen. **2.** j-n aufheitern. **II** *v/i* **3.** leichter werden: *her heart ~ed fig.* ihr wurde leichter ums Herz.

light·er ['laɪtə] *s* **1.** Anzünder *m* (*a. Gerät*). **2.** Feuerzeug *n.*

'**light|-,fin·gered** *adj* **1.** fingerfertig, geschickt. **2.** langfing(e)rig, diebisch. '*~-,foot·ed adj* □ leichtfüßig. '*~-,head-ed adj* □ **1.** leichtsinnig, -fertig. **2.** *feel ~* (leicht) benommen sein; wie auf Wolken schweben. '*~-,heart·ed adj* □ unbeschwert. '*~·house s* Leuchtturm *m.*

light·ing ['laɪtɪŋ] *s* Beleuchtung *f.*

light·ly ['laɪtlɪ] *adv* **1.** leicht. **2.** wenig: *eat ~.* **3.** leichthin. **4.** geringschätzig.

light-'mind·ed *adj* □ leichtfertig, -sinnig; unbeständig, flatterhaft.

light·ness¹ ['laɪtnɪs] *s* Helligkeit *f.*

light·ness² [~] *s* **1.** Leichtheit *f,* Leichtigkeit *f (a. fig.).* **2.** Lockerheit *f.*

light·ning ['laɪtnɪŋ] **I** *s* Blitz *m:* (*as*) *quick as ~,* blitzartig; *struck by ~* vom Blitz getroffen; *like ~* wie der Blitz; → *flash* 1, *grease* 3, *streak* 1, *stroke* 2. **II** *adj* blitzschnell, Blitz...: *with ~ speed* mit

Blitzesschnelle. **~ con·duc·tor, ~ rod** *s*
⚡ Blitzableiter *m*.

light| pen *s Computer:* Lichtstift *m.*
'~·proof *adj* lichtundurchlässig.

lights [laɪts] *s pl zo.* Lunge *f.*

'light|·ship *s* ⚓ Feuer-, Leuchtschiff *n.*
'~·weight I *adj* leicht(gewichtig). **II** *s
Sport:* Leichtgewicht(ler *m*) *n.* **~ year** *s
ast.* Lichtjahr *n.*

lig·ne·ous ['lɪgnɪəs] *adj* holzig, holzartig,
Holz...

lik·a·ble ['laɪkəbl] *adj* liebenswert, -würdig, sympathisch.

like¹ [laɪk] **I** *adj u. prp* **1.** gleich (*dat*), wie
(*a. adv*): *a man ~ you* ein Mann wie du;
what is he ~? wie ist er?; *what does it
look ~?* wie sieht es aus?; → *feel* 6. **2.**
ähnlich (*dat*), bezeichnend für: *that is
just ~ him!* das sieht ihm ähnlich. **3.**
gleich (*Menge etc*): *in ~ manner* auf
gleiche Weise; gleichermaßen. **4.** ähnlich: *they are (as) ~ as two eggs* sie
gleichen sich wie ein Ei dem anderen. **5.**
ähnlich, gleich-, derartig. **II** *s* **6.** *der,
die, das* gleiche: *his ~* seinesgleichen;
the ~ dergleichen; *the ~s pl of me* F
meinesgleichen, Leute *pl* wie ich.

like² [~] **I** *v/t* gern haben, mögen: *I ~ it* es
gefällt mir; *I ~ him* ich kann ihn gut
leiden; *how do you ~ it?* wie gefällt es
dir?, wie findest du es?; *what do you ~
better?* was hast du lieber?; *~ doing*
(*bsd. Am. a.* **to do**) *s.th.* et. gern tun; *I should* (*od. would*) *~
to know* ich möchte gern wissen. **II** *v/i*
wollen: (*just*) *as you ~* (ganz) wie du
willst; *do as you ~* mach, was du willst;
if you ~ wenn du willst. **III** *s* Neigung *f*,
Vorliebe *f*: *~s pl and dislikes pl* Neigungen *pl* u. Abneigungen *pl*.

like·a·ble → **likable**.

like·li·hood ['laɪklɪhʊd] *s* Wahrscheinlichkeit *f*: *in all ~* aller Wahrscheinlichkeit nach, höchstwahrscheinlich. **'like·ly I** *adj* **1.** wahrscheinlich, voraussichtlich: *he is (not) ~ to come* er kommt
wahrscheinlich (es ist unwahrscheinlich, daß er kommt). **2.** glaubhaft: *a ~
story! iro.* das soll glauben, wer mag! **3.**
in Frage kommend, geeignet. **II** *adv* **4.**
wahrscheinlich: *most ~* höchstwahrscheinlich; *(as) ~ as not* (sehr) wahrscheinlich; *not ~!* F wohl kaum!

,like-'mind·ed *adj* □ gleichgesinnt.

lik·en ['laɪkən] *v/t* vergleichen (*to* mit).

like·ness ['laɪknɪs] *s* **1.** Ähnlichkeit *f*
(*between* zwischen *dat*; *to* mit). **2.** Abbild *n* (*of* gen).

like·wise ['laɪkwaɪz] *adv* desgleichen,
ebenso.

lik·ing ['laɪkɪŋ] *s* Vorliebe *f* (*for* für): *this
is not* (*to*) *my ~* das ist nicht nach m-m
Geschmack.

li·lac ['laɪlək] **I** *s* ♀ Flieder *m.* **II** *adj*
lila(farben).

Lil·li·pu·tian [,lɪlɪ'pju:ʃn] **I** *adj* winzig,
zwergenhaft; Liliput..., Klein(st)... **II** *s*
Liliputaner(in).

li·lo ['laɪləʊ] *pl* **-los** *s Br.* F Luftmatratze *f.*

lilt [lɪlt] *s* flotter Rhythmus; flotte *od.*
schwungvolle Melodie.

lil·y ['lɪlɪ] *s* ♀ Lilie *f*: *~ of the valley*
Maiglöckchen *n.* **,~·'liv·ered** *adj* feig.

limb [lɪm] *s* **1.** (*Körper*)Glied *n*, *pl a* (*-es*)
Gliedmaßen *pl.* **2.** Hauptast *m* (*e-s
Baums*): *be out on a ~* F in e-r gefährlichen Lage sein; *Br.* allein (da)stehen.

lim·ber ['lɪmbə] **I** *adj* **1.** biegsam, geschmeidig. **2.** beweglich, gelenkig. **II** *v/t*
3. *mst ~ up* biegsam *od.* geschmeidig
machen, *Muskeln etc.* auflockern: *~ o.s.
up* → **4. III** *v/i* **4.** *mst ~ up* sich auflockern, Lockerungsübungen machen.

lime¹ [laɪm] **I** *s* 🦌 Kalk *m.* **II** *v/t* kalken.

lime² [~] *s* ♀ Linde *f.*

lime³ [~] *s* ♀ Limonelle *f* (*Baum*); Limone
f, Limonelle *f* (*Frucht*).

lime·light *s*: *be in the ~* im Rampenlicht
od. im Licht der Öffentlichkeit stehen.

lim·er·ick ['lɪmərɪk] *s* Limerick *m.*

'lime|·stone *s geol.* Kalkstein *m.* **'~-
-wash I** *v/t* kalken, weißen, tünchen. **II**
s (Kalk)Tünche *f.*

lim·it ['lɪmɪt] **I** *s* **1.** *fig.* Grenze *f*, Beschränkung *f*, (*Zeit- etc*)Limit *n*: *to the
~* bis zum Äußersten (*od.* Letzten; *within ~s* in (gewissen) Grenzen; *there is
a ~ to everything* alles hat s-e Grenzen;
off ~s Zutritt verboten (*to* für); *that's
the ~!* F das ist (doch) die Höhe! **2.** ⚹,
⚙ Grenzwert *m.* **3.** ♱ Limit *n*, Preisgrenze *f.* **II** *v/t* **4.** beschränken, begrenzen (*to* auf *acc*); *Auflage, Preise etc*
limitieren: *~ed in time* befristet; *~ed
(liability) company* ♱ Aktiengesellschaft *f.* **,lim·i'ta·tion** *s* **1.** *fig.* Grenze *f*: *know one's (own) ~s* s-e Grenzen

kennen. **2.** Begrenzung *f*, Beschränkung *f*: **~ of liability** ⚖ Haftungsbeschränkung. **3.** ⚖ Verjährung *f*: **~ (period)** Verjährungsfrist *f*.

lim·ou·sine ['lɪməziːn] *s mot.* **1.** *Br.* Luxuslimousine *f*. **2.** *Am.* Kleinbus *m*.

limp¹ [lɪmp] **I** *v/i* hinken (*a. fig. Vers etc*), humpeln. **II** *s* Hinken *n*: **walk with a ~** hinken, humpeln.

limp² [~] *adj* schlaff, schlapp: **go ~** erschlaffen.

lim·pet ['lɪmpɪt] *s zo.* Napfschnecke *f*: **hold on** (*od.* **hang on, cling**) **to s.o. like a ~** *fig.* wie e-e Klette an j-m hängen.

lim·pid ['lɪmpɪd] *adj* □ klar (*a. fig. Stil etc*), durchsichtig.

lim·y ['laɪmɪ] *adj* kalkig, Kalk...

lin·age ['laɪnɪdʒ] *s* **1.** Zeilenzahl *f*. **2.** Zeilenhonorar *n*.

linch·pin ['lɪntʃpɪn] *s* **1.** ⚙ Achsnagel *m*. **2.** *fig.* Stütze *f*.

lin·den ['lɪndən] *s* ♣ Linde *f*.

line¹ [laɪn] **I** *s* **1.** Linie *f* (*a. Sport*), Strich *m*: → **toe** II. **2.** a) (*Hand- etc*)Linie *f*, b) Falte *f*, Runzel *f*: **~s of worry** Sorgenfalten *pl*, c) Zug *m* (*im Gesicht*). **3.** Zeile *f* (*a. TV*): **read between the ~s** *fig.* zwischen den Zeilen lesen; → **line** 15. **4.** *pl thea. etc* Rolle *f*, Text *m*. **5.** *pl* (*mst sg konstruiert*) *bsd. Br.* F Trauschein *m*. **6.** Linie *f*, Richtung *f*: **~ of sight** Blickrichtung. **7.** *pl* Grundsätze *pl*, Richtlinien *pl*: **along these ~s** nach diesen Grundsätzen; folgendermaßen. **8.** Art *f* u. Weise *f*, Methode *f*: **~ of thought** Auffassung *f*; Gedankengang *m*; **take a strong ~** energisch auftreten *od.* werden (**with s.o.** gegenüber j-m). **9.** Grenze *f* (*a. fig.*), Grenzlinie *f*: **draw the ~** die Grenze ziehen, haltmachen (**at** bei). **10.** Reihe *f*, Kette *f*; *bsd. Am.* (Menschen-, *a.* Auto)Schlange *f*: **stand in ~** anstehen, Schlange stehen (**for** um, nach); **drive in ~** *mot.* Kolonne fahren. **11.** Reihe *f*, Linie *f*: **be in** (**out of**) **~** *fig.* (nicht) übereinstimmen (**with** mit); **bring** (*od.* **get**) **into ~** *fig.* in Einklang bringen (**with** mit); auf Vordermann bringen; **fall into ~** sich einordnen; *fig.* sich anschließen (**with** *dat*); **keep s.o. in ~** *fig.* j-n bei der Stange halten. **12.** (Abstammungs)Linie *f*: **in the direct ~** in direkter Linie. **13.** Fach *n*, Gebiet *n*: **~ (of business)** Branche *f*; **that's not in**

my ~ das schlägt nicht in mein Fach; das liegt mir nicht. **14.** (*Verkehrs-, Eisenbahn- etc*)Linie *f*, Strecke *f*, Route *f*, engS. 🚃 Gleis *n*: **the end of the ~** *fig.* das (bittere) Ende. **15.** (*Flug- etc*)Gesellschaft *f*. **16.** *bsd. teleph.* Leitung *f*: **the ~ is busy** (*Br.* **engaged**) die Leitung ist besetzt; **hold the ~** bleiben Sie am Apparat; → **hot line. 17.** ⚙ (Rohr)Leitung *f*. **18.** ✕ a) Linie: **behind the enemy ~s** hinter den feindlichen Linien, b) Front *f*: **all along the ~, down the ~** *fig.* auf der ganzen Linie. **19.** *geogr.* Längen- *od.* Breitenkreis *m*: **the** 2 der Äquator. **20.** Leine *f*; Schnur *f*; *bsd.* II *v/i* **21.** → **line up** I. **III** *v/t* **22.** lini(i)eren. **23.** zeichnen; skizzieren. **24.** *Gesicht* (zer)furchen. **25.** *Straße etc* säumen.

Verbindungen mit Adverbien:

line| off *v/t* abgrenzen. **~ up I** *v/i* **1.** sich in e-r Reihe *od.* Linie aufstellen, (*Sport*) sich aufstellen. **2.** *bsd. Am.* sich anstellen (**for** um, nach). **II** *v/t* **3.** in e-r Reihe *od.* Linie aufstellen. **4.** F auf die Beine stellen, organisieren.

line² [~] *v/t* **1.** *Kleid etc* füttern. **2.** *bsd.* ⚙ auskleiden, -schlagen (**with** mit), *Bremsen, Kupplung* belegen. **3.** (an)füllen: **~ one's pocket(s)** (*od.* **purse**) sich bereichern.

lin·e·age¹ ['lɪnɪɪdʒ] *s* **1.** geradlinige Abstammung. **2.** Stammbaum *m*. **3.** Geschlecht *n*.

lin·e·age² → **linage**.

lin·e·al ['lɪnɪəl] *adj* □ geradlinig, direkt (*Nachkomme etc*).

lin·e·a·ment ['lɪnɪəmənt] *s mst pl* (Gesichts)Zug *m*.

lin·e·ar ['lɪnɪə] *adj* □ **1.** ⅍, ⚙ *etc* linear. **2.** Längen...

lin·en ['lɪnɪn] **I** *s* **1.** Leinen *n*. **2.** (*Bett-, Unter- etc*)Wäsche *f*: **wash one's dirty ~ in public** *fig.* s-e schmutzige Wäsche in der Öffentlichkeit waschen. **II** *adj* **3.** Leinen... **~ bas·ket** *s bsd. Br.* Wäschekorb *m*.

lin·er ['laɪnə] *s* **1.** ♦ Linienschiff *n*. **2.** ✈ Verkehrsflugzeug *n*. **3.** → **eye liner**.

lines·man ['laɪnzmən] *s* (*irr man*) *Sport:* Linienrichter *m*. **~·wom·an** *s* (*irr woman*) Linienrichterin *f*.

'line-up *s* **1.** *Sport:* Aufstellung *f*. **2.** *bsd. Am.* (Menschen)Schlange *f*.

lin·ger ['lɪŋgə] v/i **1.** verweilen, sich aufhalten (*beide a. fig.* **over, on** bei e-m *Thema etc*): **~ on** noch dableiben; nachklingen (*Ton*); *fig.* fortleben, -bestehen (*Tradition etc*). **2.** *fig.* (zurück)bleiben (*Verdacht etc*). **3.** trödeln: **~ about** (*od.* **around**) herumtrödeln. **'lin·ger·ing** *adj* □ **1.** nachklingend. **2.** schleichend (*Krankheit*).

lin·go ['lɪŋgəʊ] *pl* **-goes** *s* F **1.** Kauderwelsch *n*. **2.** (*Fach*)Jargon *m*.

lin·gual ['lɪŋgwəl] *adj* Zungen...

lin·guist ['lɪŋgwɪst] *s* **1.** Linguist(in), Sprachwissenschaftler(in). **2.** Sprachkundige *m, f*: **be a good ~** (sehr) sprachbegabt sein. **lin'guis·tic** I *adj* (**~ally**) **1.** linguistisch, sprachwissenschaftlich. **2.** Sprach(en)... II *s pl* (*mst sg konstruiert*) **3.** Linguistik *f*, Sprachwissenschaft *f*.

lin·i·ment ['lɪnɪmənt] *s* 🞋 Einreibemittel *n*.

lin·ing ['laɪnɪŋ] *s* **1.** Futter(stoff *m*) *n*. **2.** *bsd.* ⚙ Auskleidung *f*, (*Brems-, Kupplungs*)Belag *m*.

link [lɪŋk] I *s* **1.** (Ketten)Glied *n*; *fig.* Glied *n* (*in e-r Kette von Ereignissen etc*); Bindeglied *n*; Verbindung *f*, Zs.-hang *m*. **2.** Manschettenknopf *m*. II *v/t* **3.** *a.* **~ up** verketten, -binden (**to, with** mit): **~ arms** sich unter- *od.* einhaken (**with** bei). **4.** *a.* **~ up** *fig.* in Verbindung *od.* Zs.-hang bringen (**with** mit), e-n Zs.-hang herstellen zwischen (*dat*). III *v/i* **5.** *a.* **~ up** sich verketten *od.* verbinden (**to, with** mit). **6.** *a.* **~ up** *fig.* sich zs.-fügen.

links [lɪŋks] → *golf links*.

'link-up *s* Verbindung *f*, Zs.-hang *m*.

li·no·le·um [lɪ'nəʊljəm] *s* Linoleum *n*.

lin·seed ['lɪnsiːd] *s* 🞋 Leinsamen *m*: **~ oil** *s* Leinöl *n*.

lin·tel ['lɪntl] *s* 🔺 Oberschwelle *f*, (*Tür-, Fenster*)Sturz *m*.

li·on ['laɪən] *s* **1.** *zo.* Löwe *m* (*a. ast.* 2): **go into the ~'s den** *fig.* sich in die Höhle des Löwen wagen; **the ~'s share** der Löwenanteil; → **beard** II. **2.** *fig.* Größe *f*, Berühmtheit *f* (*Person*). **li·on·ess** ['~es] *s* Löwin *f*.

lip [lɪp] *s* **1.** *anat.* Lippe *f*: **lower (upper) ~** Unter-(Ober)lippe; **keep a stiff upper ~** *fig.* Haltung bewahren; sich nichts anmerken lassen; **bite one's ~** *fig.* sich

auf die Lippen beißen; → **smack²** 2. **2.** F Unverschämtheit *f*: **none of your ~!** sei nicht so unverschämt *od.* frech! **3.** Rand *m* (*e-r Wunde, e-s Kraters etc*). **'~-read** *v/t u.* *v/i* (*irr* **read**) von den Lippen ablesen. **~ ser·vice** *s* Lippenbekenntnis *n*. **'~-stick** *s* Lippenstift *m*: **put on ~** sich die Lippen schminken.

liq·ue·fy ['lɪkwɪfaɪ] *v/t u.* *v/i* **1.** (sich) verflüssigen. **2.** schmelzen.

li·queur [lɪ'kjʊə] *s* Likör *m*.

liq·uid ['lɪkwɪd] I *adj* □ **1.** flüssig. **2.** Flüssigkeits...: **~ measure** Flüssigkeitsmaß *n*. **3.** 🞋 liquid, flüssig. II *s* **4.** Flüssigkeit *f*.

liq·ui·date ['lɪkwɪdeɪt] *v/t* **1.** 🞋 liquidieren: a) *Gesellschaft* auflösen, b) *Sachwerte etc* realisieren, zu Geld machen, c) *Schulden etc* tilgen. **2.** *fig.* j-n liquidieren, beseitigen. **liq·ui'da·tion** *s* **1.** 🞋 Liquidation *f*: a) Auflösung *f*, b) Realisierung *f*, c) Tilgung *f*. **2.** *fig.* Liquidierung *f*, Beseitigung *f*.

li·quid·i·ty [lɪ'kwɪdətɪ] *s* **1.** flüssiger Zustand. **2.** 🞋 Liquidität *f*, Flüssigkeit *f*.

liq·ui·dize ['lɪkwɪdaɪz] *v/t* **1.** (*v/i* sich) verflüssigen. **2.** *Küche* zerkleinern *od.* pürieren. **'liq·ui·diz·er** *s* Mixer *m*, Mixgerät *n*.

liq·uor ['lɪkə] *s* a) *Br.* alkoholische Getränke *pl*, Alkohol *m*: **hard ~** → b, b) *Am.* Schnaps *m*, Spirituosen *pl*: **~ cabinet** Hausbar *f*.

liq·uo·rice → *licorice*.

li·ra ['lɪərə] *pl* **-re** ['~rɪ], **-ras** *s* Lira *f*.

lisp [lɪsp] I *v/i* lispeln (*a. v/t*), mit der Zunge anstoßen. II *s* Lispeln *n*: **speak with a ~** → I.

list¹ [lɪst] I *s* **1.** Liste *f*, Verzeichnis *n*: **be on the ~** auf der Liste stehen; **~ price** Listenpreis *m*. II *v/t* **2.** (in e-r Liste) verzeichnen, erfassen, registrieren: **~ed building** *Br.* Gebäude *n* unter Denkmalschutz. **3.** in e-e Liste eintragen.

list² [~] ⚓ I *s* Schlagseite *f*. II *v/i* Schlagseite haben *od.* bekommen.

lis·ten ['lɪsn] *v/i* **1.** hören, horchen (*to auf acc*): **~ to** a) j-m zuhören, j-n anhören: **~!** hör mal!, b) auf j-n, j-s Rat hören, c) *e-m Rat etc* folgen; → **reason** 3. **2.** **~ in** Radio hören: **~ in to a concert** sich ein Konzert im Radio anhören. **'lis·ten·er** *s* **1.** Horcher(in). **2.** Zuhörer(in): **be a**

good ~ (gut) zuhören können. **3.** *Radio:* Hörer(in).

list·less ['lɪstlɪs] *adj* ~ lust-, teilnahmslos.

lit [lɪt] *pret u. pp von* **light¹**.

lit·a·ny ['lɪtənɪ] *s eccl.* Litanei *f (a. fig.).*

li·ter *Am.* → **litre.**

lit·er·a·cy ['lɪtərəsɪ] *s* **1.** Fähigkeit *f* zu lesen u. zu schreiben. **2.** (literarische) Bildung, Belesenheit.

lit·er·al ['lɪtərəl] *adj* □ **1.** wörtlich (*Übersetzung etc*): **take s.th. ~ly** et. wörtlich nehmen. **2.** genau, wahrheitsgetreu. **3.** nüchtern, trocken, prosaisch. **4.** wörtlich, eigentlich (*Bedeutung e-s Worts etc*). **5.** buchstäblich: **he did ~ly nothing.**

lit·er·a·ry ['lɪtərərɪ] *adj* □ **1.** literarisch, Literatur...: ~ **critic** Literaturkritiker(in); ~ **history** Literaturgeschichte *f.* **2.** gewählt, hochgestochen (*Ausdruck etc*).

lit·er·ate ['lɪtərət] *adj* □ **1.** *be ~* lesen u. schreiben können. **2.** (literarisch) gebildet, belesen. **lit·er·a·ture** ['~ətʃə] *s* **1.** Literatur *f.* **2.** F Informationsmaterial *n.*

lith·o·graph ['lɪθəʊgrɑːf] *s* Lithographie *f,* Steindruck *m.*

lit·i·gant ['lɪtɪgənt] ⚖ **I** *adj* streitend, prozeßführend. **II** *s* Prozeßführende *m, f,* streitende Partei. **lit·i·gate** ['~geɪt] *v/i (u. v/t)* prozessieren *od.* streiten (um). ‚**lit·i'ga·tion** *s* Rechtsstreit *m,* Prozeß *m.*

li·to·tes ['laɪtəʊtiːz] *s rhet.* Litotes *f.*

li·tre ['liːtə] *s bsd. Br.* Liter *m, a. n.*

lit·ter ['lɪtə] **I** *s* **1.** (herumliegender) Abfall. **2.** Streu *f (für Tiere),* (*a. für Pflanzen*) Stroh *n.* **3.** *zo.* Wurf *m.* **4.** Trage *f;* Sänfte *f.* **II** *v/t* **5.** Abfall herumliegen lassen in (*dat*) *od.* auf (*dat*) (*Park etc* verschandeln (**with** mit). **6.** *mst* ~ **down** Streu legen für; *Stall* einstreuen. **7.** *Pflanzen mit Stroh abdecken.* **8.** *zo.* Junge werfen. **III** *v/i* **9.** *zo.* (Junge) werfen. ~ **bas·ket,** '~**bin** *s* Abfallkorb *m.* '~**bug** *s bsd. Am.* F, ~ **lout** *s bsd. Br.* F *j-d, der Straßen etc mit Abfall verschandelt.*

lit·tle ['lɪtl] **I** *adj* **1.** klein (*Kind etc*): **the ~ ones** *pl* die Kleinen *pl;* → **finger** I. **2.** kurz (*Strecke od. Zeit*). **3.** wenig (*Hoffnung etc*): **a ~ jam** ein wenig *od.* ein

bißchen Marmelade. **4.** klein, gering(fügig). **II** *adv* **5.** wenig, kaum: **think ~ of** wenig halten von; **for as ~ as £10** für nur 10 Pfund. **6.** wenig, selten: **I see him very ~.** **III** *s* **7.** Kleinigkeit *f, das* wenige, *das* bißchen: **a ~** ein wenig, ein bißchen; ~ **by ~** (ganz) allmählich, nach u. nach. **8.** *in ~* im kleinen, in kleinem Maßstab.

lit·ur·gy ['lɪtədʒɪ] *s eccl.* Liturgie *f.*

liv·a·ble ['lɪvəbl] *adj* **1.** wohnlich, bewohnbar. **2.** lebenswert (*Leben*). **3.** *a.* ~ **with** erträglich (*Schmerzen etc*): **not ~** (**with**) unerträglich. **4.** ~ **with** umgänglich (*Person*).

live¹ [lɪv] **I** *v/i* leben: a) am Leben sein, b) am Leben bleiben: ~ **through the night** die Nacht überleben; **you ~ and learn** man lernt nie aus; ~ **on** *bsd. fig.* weiter-, fortleben, c) sich ernähren (**on** von): **he ~s on his wife** er lebt auf Kosten *od.* von (den Einkünften) s-r Frau, d) ein *ehrliches etc* Leben führen: ~ **honestly;** ~ **up to** s-n *Grundsätzen etc* gemäß leben, *s-m Ruf etc* gerecht werden, *den Erwartungen etc* entsprechen, e) wohnen (**with** bei): ~ **with** zs.-leben mit; ~ **together** zs.-leben, f) das Leben genießen: ~ **and let** ~ leben u. leben lassen. **II** *v/t ein bestimmtes Leben* führen.

live² [laɪv] **I** *adj* **1.** lebend, lebendig: ~ **weight** Lebendgewicht *n;* **a real ~ lord** F ein richtiger *od.* echter Lord. **2.** aktuell (*Frage etc*). **3.** scharf (*Munition etc*). **4.** ⚡ stromführend: ~ **wire** F Energiebündel *n.* **5.** *Rundfunk, TV:* Direkt..., Original..., Live-... **II** *adv* **6.** direkt, original, live.

live·a·ble → **livable.**

live·li·hood ['laɪvlɪhʊd] *s* Lebensunterhalt *m:* **earn** (*od.* **gain, make**) **a** (*od.* **one's**) ~ s-n Lebensunterhalt verdienen.

live·li·ness ['laɪvlɪnɪs] *s* **1.** Lebhaftigkeit *f.* **2.** Lebendigkeit *f.* '**live·ly** *adj* □ **1.** lebhaft (*Interesse, Person, Phantasie etc*). **2.** lebendig (*Schilderung etc*). **3.** aufregend (*Zeiten*): **make it** (*od.* **things**) ~ **for s.o., give s.o. a ~ time** j-m (kräftig) einheizen. **4.** schnell, flott (*Tempo etc*).

liv·en ['laɪvn] *mst* ~ **up** **I** *v/t* beleben, Leben bringen in (*acc*). **II** *v/i* in Schwung kommen.

1061   local

liv·er¹ ['lɪvə] s anat. Leber f (a. gastr.).

liv·er² [~] s: *be a fast* ~ ein flottes Leben führen; *loose* ~ liederlicher Mensch.

liv·er·ied ['lɪvərɪd] adj livriert.

liv·er·ish ['lɪvərɪʃ] adj **1.** *be* ~ F es mit der Leber haben. **2.** mürrisch.

liv·er | sau·sage s Leberwurst f. ~ *spot* s Leberfleck m. ~*wurst* ['~wɜ:st] s bsd. Am. Leberwurst f.

liv·er·y ['lɪvərɪ] s Livree f: *in* ~ in Livree.

lives [laɪvz] pl von *life*.

live·stock ['laɪvstɒk] s Vieh(bestand m) n.

liv·id ['lɪvɪd] adj □ **1.** blau, bläulich (verfärbt). **2.** bleifarben, graublau. **3.** fahl, aschgrau, bleich (*with* vor dat). **4.** F fuchsteufelswild.

liv·ing ['lɪvɪŋ] **I** adj **1.** lebend (a. Sprache): *while* ~ bei od. zu Lebzeiten; *within* ~ *memory* seit Menschengedenken; → *daylight*. **2.** Lebens...: ~ *conditions* pl Lebensbedingungen pl. **II** s **3.** *the* ~ pl die Lebenden pl. **4.** das Leben: → *cost* **1. 5.** Leben(sweise f) n: *loose* ~ lockerer Lebenswandel; → *clean* **5. 6.** Lebensunterhalt m: *earn* (od. *gain*, *get*, *make*) *a* ~ s-n Lebensunterhalt verdienen (*as* als; *out of* durch, mit). ~ *room* s Wohnzimmer n. ~ *space* s Wohnfläche f, -raum m.

liz·ard ['lɪzəd] s zo. Eidechse f.

lla·ma ['lɑ:mə] s zo. Lama n.

load [ləʊd] **I** s **1.** Last f, fig. a. Bürde f: *his decision took a* ~ *off my mind* bei s-r Entscheidung fiel mir ein Stein vom Herzen. **2.** Ladung f (a. e-r Schußwaffe): *get a* ~ *of* F sich et. ansehen od. anhören; et. zu sehen od. zu hören bekommen; *get a* ~ *of this!* F hör od. schau dir das mal an! **3.** pl F (of) Massen pl (von Geld etc), e-e Unmasse (Leute etc): *there were* ~*s to eat* es gab massenhaft zu essen. **4.** ⚡, ⚙ Belastung f. **II** v/t **5.** a. ~ *up* Fahrzeug etc beladen (*with* mit). **6.** Gegenstand etc laden (*into* in acc; *onto* auf acc), Güter verladen. **7.** Schußwaffe laden: ~ *the camera* e-n Film (in die Kamera) einlegen. **8.** j-n überhäufen (*with* mit Arbeit, Vorwürfen etc). **9.** beschweren, schwerer machen, engS. Würfel einseitig beschweren, präparieren. **III** v/i **10.** mst ~ *up* (auf-, ein)laden. **11.** (das Gewehr etc) laden, phot. e-n Film einlegen.

'load·ed adj **1.** be-, geladen etc, → *load* **II. 2.** ~ *question* Fang- od. Suggestivfrage f; ~ *word* emotionsgeladenes Wort; vorbelastetes Wort; Reizwort n. **3.** F stinkreich: *be* ~ a. Geld wie Heu haben.

loaf¹ [ləʊf] pl **loaves** [ləʊvz] s **1.** Laib m (Brot); weitS. Brot n. **2.** a. *meat* ~ gastr. Hackbraten m. **3.** *use one's* ~ Br. sl. sein Hirn anstrengen, (nach)denken.

loaf² [~] **I** v/i **1.** a. *about* (od. *around*) herumlungern. ~ *about* (od. *around*) *the streets* auf den Straßen herumlungern. **2.** faulenzen. **II** v/t **3.** ~ *away* Zeit verbummeln. **'loaf·er** s F **1.** Müßiggänger(in). **2.** Faulenzer(in). **3.** bsd. Am. leichter Slipper.

loam [ləʊm] s Lehm m. **'loam·y** adj lehmig, Lehm...

loan [ləʊn] **I** s **1.** (Ver)Leihen n: *on* ~ leihweise; *a book on* ~ ein geliehenes Buch; *may I have the* ~ *of ...?* darf ich (mir) ... (aus)leihen? **2.** ✝ Anleihe f (a. fig.): *take up a* ~ e-e Anleihe aufnehmen (*on* auf acc). **3.** ✝ Darlehen n, Kredit m. **4.** Leihgabe f (für e-e Ausstellung). **II** v/t **5.** bsd. Am. (*to*) (aus)leihen (dat), ver-, ausleihen (an acc). ~ *shark* s F Kredithai m. '~*word* s ling. Lehnwort n.

loath [ləʊθ] adj: *be* ~ *to do s.th.* et. nur (sehr) ungern od. widerwillig tun.

loathe [ləʊð] v/t verabscheuen, hassen: ~ *doing s.th.* es hassen, et. zu tun. '**loath·ing** s Abscheu m. '**loath·some** ['~səm] adj □ widerlich, abscheulich.

loaves [ləʊvz] pl von *loaf¹*.

lob [lɒb] (bsd. Tennis) **I** s Lob m. **II** v/t a) ~ *a ball* → III, b) Gegner überlobben. **III** v/i lobben, e-n Lob spielen od. schlagen.

lob·by ['lɒbɪ] **I** s **1.** Vor-, Eingangshalle f; Wandelhalle f; thea. Foyer n. **2.** pol. Lobby f, Interessengruppe f, -verband m. **II** v/t **3.** a. ~ *through* Gesetzesvorlage mit Hilfe e-r Lobby durchbringen. **4.** Abgeordnete beeinflussen. '**lob·by·ist** s Lobbyist m.

lobe [ləʊb] s ♀, anat. Lappen m: ~ (*of the ear*) Ohrläppchen n.

lob·ster ['lɒbstə] s zo. Hummer m: (*as*) *red as a* ~ krebsrot.

lo·cal ['ləʊkl] **I** adj □ **1.** lokal, örtlich: ~ *call* teleph. Ortsgespräch n; ~ *derby*

(*Sport*) Lokalderby *n*; ~ **elections** *pl* Kommunalwahlen *pl*; ~ **hero** (*bsd. Sport*) Lokalmatador *m*; ~ **news** Lokalnachrichten *pl*; ~ **time** Ortszeit *f*; ~ **traffic** Lokal-, Orts-, Nahverkehr *m*; → **colour** 1. **2.** Orts..., ansässig, hiesig. **3.** lokal, örtlich (beschränkt): ~ **an(a)es-thesia** örtliche Betäubung; ~ **custom** ortsüblicher Brauch. **II** *s* **4.** *mst pl* Ortsansässige *m, f*, Einheimische *m, f*. **5.** *Br.* F (nächstgelegene) Kneipe, *bsd.* Stammkneipe *f*.

lo·cale [ləʊ'kɑːl] *s* Schauplatz *m*, Szene *f*.

lo·cal·i·ty [ləʊ'kælətɪ] *s* **1.** a) Örtlichkeit *f*, Ort *m*: **sense of** ~ Ortssinn *m*, b) Gegend *f*. **2.** (*örtliche*) Lage.

lo·cal·ize ['ləʊkəlaɪz] *v/t* lokalisieren (**to** auf *acc*).

lo·cate [ləʊ'keɪt] **I** *v/t* **1.** ausfindig machen, aufspüren; ♣ *etc* orten; ✗ *Ziel* ausmachen; *Büro etc* errichten. **3.** (*an e-m bestimmten Ort*) an- *od.* unterbringen; (*an e-n Ort*) verlegen: **be** ~**d** gelegen sein, liegen, sich befinden. **II** *v/i* **4.** *Am.* sich niederlassen. **lo'ca·tion** *s* **1.** Ausfindigmachen *n*; ♣ *etc* Ortung *f*; ✗ Ausmachen *n*. **2.** Stelle *f*, Platz *m*; Lage *f*, Standort *m*. **3.** *Film, TV:* Gelände *n* für Außenaufnahmen: ~ **shooting**, **shooting on** ~ Außenaufnahmen *pl*.

loch [lɒx] *s schott.* **1.** See *m*. **2.** Bucht *f*.

lock¹ [lɒk] **I** *s* **1.** (*Tür-, Gewehr- etc*) Schloß *n*: **under** ~ **and key** hinter Schloß u. Riegel; unter Verschluß; ~, **stock and barrel** *fig.* mit allem Drum u. Dran; mit Stumpf u. Stiel; mit Sack u. Pack. **2.** Verschluß *m*; Sperrvorrichtung *f*. **3.** Schleuse(nkammer) *f*. **II** *v/t* **4.** *a.* ~ **up** zu-, verschließen, zu-, versperren. **5.** *a.* ~ **up** einschließen, (ein)sperren (*in, into* in *acc*): ~ **away** wegschließen; ~ **out** ausschließen (*a.* ✝). **6.** umschlingen, umfassen, *in die Arme* schließen. **7.** ⊙ sperren. **III** *v/i* **8.** schließen: ~ **up** abschließen. **9.** *a.* ~ **up** abschließbar sein. **10.** *mot. etc* blockieren (*Räder*).

lock² [⌣] *s* (*Haar*)Locke *f*, (-)Strähne *f*.

lock·er ['lɒkə] *s* **1.** Schließfach *n*. **2.** Spind *m, n*.

lock·et ['lɒkɪt] *s* Medaillon *n*.

'lock·jaw *s* ✤ **1.** Kiefersperre *f*. **2.** Wundstarrkrampf *m*. ~ **keep·er** *s* Schleusenwärter *m*. **'~·out** *s* ✝ Aus-

sperrung *f*. **'~·up** *s* **1.** Arrestzelle *f*; F Kittchen *n*. **2.** *bsd. Br.* (Einzel)Garage *f*.

lo·co ['ləʊkəʊ] *bes. Am. sl.* verrückt (*a. Ideen etc*).

lo·co·mo·tion [ˌləʊkə'məʊʃn] *s* Fortbewegungs... **'lo·co·mo·tive** [⌐ɪv] **I** *adj* Fortbewegungs... **II** *s* 🛢 Lokomotive *f*.

lo·cust ['ləʊkəst] *s zo.* Heuschrecke *f*.

lo·cu·tion [ləʊ'kjuːʃn] *s* **1.** Ausdrucks-, Redeweise *f*. **2.** Redewendung *f*, Ausdruck *m*.

lodge [lɒdʒ] **I** *s* **1.** Sommer-, Gartenhaus *n*; (*Jagd- etc*)Hütte *f*; Gärtner-, Pförtnerhaus *n*. **2.** Portier-, Pförtnerloge *f*. **II** *v/i* **3.** logieren, (*bsd.* vorübergehend *od.* in Untermiete) wohnen. **4.** übernachten. **5.** stecken(bleiben) (*Kugel, Bissen etc*). **II** *v/t* **6.** aufnehmen, beherbergen, (für die Nacht) unterbringen. **7.** *Antrag, Beschwerde etc* einreichen, *Anzeige* erstatten, *Berufung, Protest* einlegen (**with** bei). **lodg·er** *s* Untermieter(in): **take** ~**s** Zimmer vermieten. **'lodg·ing** *s* **1.** Wohnen *n*. **2.** *a. pl* Unterkunft *f*: **night's** ~, ~ **for the night** Nachtquartier *n*; ~ **house** Fremdenheim *n*, Pension *f*; → **board** 4. **3.** *pl* möbliertes Zimmer: **live in** ~**s** möbliert wohnen.

loft [lɒft] *s* **1.** Dachboden *m*; Speicher *m*. **2.** △ Empore *f*, (*Orgel*)Chor *m*. **'loft·y** *adj* □ **1.** hoch(ragend). **2.** hochfliegend (*Pläne etc*), hochgesteckt (*Ziele etc*), erhaben (*Gedanken, Stil etc*). **3.** stolz, hochmütig.

log [lɒg] **I** *s* **1.** (Holz)Klotz *m*; (*gefällter*) Baumstamm; (*großes*) (Holz)Scheit: → **sleep** II. **2.** → **logbook**. **II** *v/t* **3.** *a.* ~ **up** in das Logbuch *etc* eintragen; *allg.* *Ereignisse etc* aufzeichnen, festhalten.

log·a·rithm ['lɒgərɪðəm] *s* A̧ Logarithmus *m*.

'log·book *s* **1.** ♣ Logbuch *n*. **2.** ✈ Flugbuch *n*. **3.** *mot.* Bord-, Fahrtenbuch *n*. **4.** *mot. Br.* Kraftfahrzeugbrief *m*. ~ **cab·in** *s* Blockhaus *n*, -hütte *f*.

log·ger·heads ['lɒgəhedz] *s pl*: **be at** ~ Streit haben (**with** mit), sich in den Haaren liegen.

log·ic ['lɒdʒɪk] *s phls. u. allg.* Logik *f*. **'log·i·cal** *adj* □ logisch.

lo·gis·tics [ləʊ'dʒɪstɪks] *s pl* (*oft sg konstruiert*) ✗, ✝ Logistik *f*.

loin [lɔɪn] *s* **1.** *mst pl anat.* Lende *f*. **2.**

gastr. Lende(nstück *n*) *f.* '**~·cloth** *s* Lendenschurz *m.*

loi·ter ['lɔɪtə] **I** *v/i* **1.** bummeln: a) schlendern, b) trödeln. **2.** *a.* **~ about** (*od.* **around**) herumlungern. **II** *v/t* **3.** **~ away** *Zeit* vertrödeln. '**loi·ter·er** *s* Bummler(in).

loll [lɒl] **I** *v/i* **1.** sich rekeln *od.* räkeln: **~ about** (*od.* **around**) herumlümmeln. **2.** **~ out** heraushängen (*Zunge*). **II** *v/t* **3.** **~ out** *Zunge* heraushängen lassen.

lol·li·pop ['lɒlɪpɒp] *s* **1.** Lutscher *m.* **2.** *Br.* Eis *n* am Stiel. **~ man** *s* (*irr* **man**) *Br.* F (*etwa*) Schülerlotse *m.* **~ wom·an** *s* (*irr* **woman**) *Br.* F (*etwa*) Schülerlotsin *f.*

lol·lop ['lɒləp] *v/i* hoppeln (*Hase, Fahrzeug*), latschen (*Person*).

lol·ly ['lɒlɪ] *s* **1.** F → **lollipop** 1. **2.** → **lollipop** 2. **3.** *Br. sl.* Kies *n* (*Geld*).

Lon·don·er ['lʌndənə] *s* Londoner(in).

lone [ləʊn] *adj* **1.** einzeln: **play a ~ hand** *fig.* e-n Alleingang machen; → **wolf** 1. **2.** alleinstehend, einzeln (*Haus etc*). **'lone·li·ness** ['~lɪnɪs] *s* Einsamkeit *f.* **'lone·ly** *adj* einsam. **'lon·er** *s* Einzelgänger *m* (*a. zo.*). **'lone·some** ['~səm] *adj* □ *bsd. Am.* einsam.

long¹ [lɒŋ] **I** *adj* **1.** *allg.* lang (*a. fig.*): → **run** 1. **2.** weit, lang (*Weg*), weit (*Entfernung*). **3.** zu lang: **the coat is ~ on him** der Mantel ist ihm zu lang. **4.** weitreichend (*Gedanken*), gut (*Gedächtnis*). **5.** ♥ langfristig. **6. be ~ on** F e-e Menge ... haben. **II** *adv* **7.** lang(e): **~ dead** schon lange tot; **as** (*od.* **so**) **~ as** solange wie; vorausgesetzt, daß; falls; **~ after** lange danach; **as ~ ago as 1900** schon 1900; **so ~!** F bis dann!; → **ago, all** 1. **III** *s* **8.** (e-e) lange Zeit: **at** (**the**) **~est** längstens; **for ~** lange (Zeit); **take ~** (**to do s.th.**) lange brauchen(, um et. zu tun); → **before** 5.

long² [~] *v/i* sich sehnen (**for** nach): **~ to do s.th.** sich danach sehnen, et. zu tun.

long·'dis·tance *adj* **1.** Fern...: **~ call** *teleph.* Ferngespräch *n*; **~ driver** Fernfahrer *m.* **2.** ✔, *Sport:* Langstrecken... **~ drink** *s* Longdrink *m.* **,~'haired** *adj* langhaarig.

long·ing ['lɒŋɪŋ] **I** *adj* □ sehnsüchtig. **II** *s* Sehnsucht *f* (**for** nach).

long·ish ['lɒŋɪʃ] *adj* **1.** ziemlich lang. **2.** länglich.

lon·gi·tude ['lɒndʒɪtjuːd] *s geogr.* Länge *f*: → **degree** 2.

long johns *s pl* F lange Unterhose. **~ jump** *s Leichtathletik: bsd. Br.* Weitsprung *m.* **~ jump·er** *s Leichtathletik: bsd. Br.* Weitspringer(in). **,~'lived** *adj* **1.** langlebig. **2.** dauerhaft. **'~,play·ing rec·ord** *s* Langspielplatte *f.* **,~'range** *adj* **1.** ✕, ✔ Fern...; Langstrecken... **2.** langfristig. **~'shore·man** ['~mən] *s* (*irr* **man**) *bsd. Am.* Dock-, Hafenarbeiter *m.* **~ shot** *s* **1.** *Sport:* Weitschuß *m.* **2.** *fig.* riskante Angelegenheit. **3.** **not by a ~** *fig.* bei weitem nicht, nicht im entferntesten. **,~'sight·ed** *adj* □ ✻ weitsichtig, *fig. a.* weitblickend. **,~'standing** *adj* seit langer Zeit bestehend, alt. **'~·term** *adj* langfristig: **~ memory** Langzeitgedächtnis *n.* **'~·time** → **long-standing. ~ wave** *s* ⚡, *phys.* Langwelle *f.* **'~·wave** *adj* ⚡, *phys.* Langwellen... **'~·wind·ed** [,~'wɪndɪd] *adj* □ **1.** ausdauernd (*Person*). **2.** langatmig, weitschweifig (*Erzählung etc*), (*a. Person*) umständlich.

loo [luː] *s bsd. Br.* F Klo *n*: **in the ~** auf dem *od.* im Klo; **~ attendant** Klofrau *f*; **~ paper** Klopapier *n.*

look [lʊk] **I** *s* **1.** Blick *m* (**at** auf *acc*): **cast** (*od.* **throw**) **a ~ at** e-n Blick werfen auf; **give s.o. an angry ~** j-m e-n wütenden Blick zuwerfen, j-n wütend ansehen; **have a ~ at s.th.** (sich) et. ansehen; **have a ~ round** sich umschauen in (*dat*). *Miene f,* (Gesichts)Ausdruck *m*: **the ~ on his face** sein Gesichtsausdruck. **3.** *oft pl* Aussehen *n*: **have the ~ of** aussehen wie. **II** *v/i* **4.** schauen: **don't ~!** nicht hersehen!; **~ who is coming!** schau (mal), wer da kommt. **5.** (nach-)schauen, nachsehen. **6.** ausschauen, -sehen (*beide a. fig.*): **~ well on s.o.** j-m stehen (*Hut etc*); **it ~s like snow(ing)** es sieht nach Schnee aus. **7.** liegen *od.* (hinaus)gehen nach: **my room ~s north. III** *v/t* **8.** j-m (*in die Augen etc*) sehen *od.* schauen *od.* blicken: **~ s.o. in the eyes. 9.** aussehen wie: **she does not ~ her age** man sieht ihr ihr Alter nicht an; **~ an idiot** *fig.* wie ein Idiot dastehen. **10.** durch Blicke ausdrücken: **~ one's surprise** überrascht blicken *od.* dreinschauen; → **dagger.**

Verbindungen mit Präpositionen:

look| a·bout → **look around**. ~ **af·ter** *v/i* **1.** nachblicken, -schauen, -sehen (*dat*). **2.** aufpassen auf (*acc*), sich kümmern um. ~ **a·round** *v/i* **1.** sich umschauen *od.* umsehen in (*dat*). **2.** ~ **one** sich umsehen *od.* umblicken. ~ **at** *v/i* **1.** ansehen, anschauen, betrachten: ~ **one's watch** auf die Uhr schauen; **to ~ him** wenn man ihn (so) ansieht. **2.** sich *et.* anschauen, *et.* prüfen. ~ **for** *v/i* suchen (nach). ~ **in·to** *v/i* **1.** (hinein-) schauen *od.* (-)sehen in (*acc*): ~ **the mirror** in den Spiegel schauen; ~ **s.o.'s eyes** j-m in die Augen schauen. **2.** untersuchen, prüfen. ~ **on** *v/i* ansehen, betrachten (**as** als). ~ **on·to** *v/i* (hinaus)gehen auf (*acc*) *od.* nach: **my room looks onto the garden.** ~ **o·ver** *v/i* **1.** schauen *od.* blicken über (*acc*). **2.** (sich) *et.* (flüchtig) ansehen *od.* anschauen, *et.* (flüchtig) überprüfen. ~ **round** → **look around.** ~ **through** *v/i* **1.** blicken durch. **2.** (hin)durchsehen *od.* (-)durchschauen durch. **3.** *fig. j-n, et.* durchschauen. **4.** *et.* (flüchtig) durchsehen *od.* -schauen. ~ **to** *v/i* **1.** achten *od.* achtgeben auf (*acc*): ~ **it that** sorge dafür, daß; sieh zu, daß. **2.** ~ **s.o. to do s.th.** von j-m erwarten, daß er et. tut: **I ~ you to help me** (*od.* **for help**) ich erwarte Hilfe von dir. ~ **to·ward(s)** → **look** 7.

Verbindungen mit Adverbien:

look| a·bout → **look around.** ~ **a·head** *v/i* **1.** nach vorne sehen *od.* blicken *od.* schauen. **2.** *fig.* vorausschauen (**two years** um zwei Jahre). ~ **a·round** *v/i* sich umblicken *od.* -sehen *od.* -schauen (**for** nach). ~ **a·way** *v/i* wegblicken, -sehen, -schauen. ~ **back** *v/i* **1.** sich umsehen. **2.** *a. fig.* zurückblicken, -schauen (**on, to** auf *acc*). ~ **down** *v/i* **1.** hinunterblicken, -sehen, -schauen, herunterblicken, -sehen, -schauen (**on** auf *acc*): ~ **on** *fig.* a) herabschauen auf (*acc*), b) → **look onto. 2.** zu Boden blicken. ~ **for·ward** *v/i* sich freuen (**to** auf *acc*): ~ **to doing s.th.** sich darauf freuen, et. zu tun. ~ **in** *v/i* **1.** hineinsehen, -schauen, hereinsehen, -schauen. **2.** e-n kurzen Besuch machen, vorbeischauen (**on** auf *acc*) zu j-m zusehen, zuschauen. ~ **out** *v/i* **1.** hinausblicken, -sehen, -schauen, herausblicken, -sehen, -schauen (**of**

zu): ~ **of the window** aus dem Fenster blicken. **2.** (**for**) aufpassen (auf *acc*), auf der Hut sein (vor *dat*): ~**!** paß auf!, Vorsicht! **3.** Ausschau halten (**for** nach). **4.** ~ **on** (*od.* **over**) → **look onto.** **II** *v/t* **5.** *bsd. Br. et.* heraussuchen; sich *et.* aussuchen: **look s.th. out for s.o.** j-m et. aussuchen. ~ **o·ver** *v/t* (sich) *et.* (flüchtig) ansehen *od.* anschauen, *et.* (flüchtig) (über)prüfen. ~ **round** → **look around.** ~ **through** *v/i* **1.** (flüchtig) durchsehen *od.* -schauen. ~ **up** **I** *v/i* **1.** hinaufblicken, -sehen, -schauen, heraufblicken, -sehen, -schauen. **2.** *fig.* sich bessern, aufwärtsgehen. ~ **up to** *v/i* aufblicken, -sehen, -schauen (**from** von; *fig. to* zu). **II** *v/t* **3.** *Wort etc* nachschlagen (*in in dat*). **4.** **look s.o. up and down** j-n von oben bis unten mustern.

'look·a,like *s* **1.** Doppelgänger(in). **2.** (genaues) Gegenstück.

look·er ['lʊkə] *s:* **she's a real ~** F sie sieht einfach klasse aus. **,~·'on** *pl* **,look·ers-'on** *s* Zuschauer(in).

'look-in *s* **1.** kurzer Besuch. **2.** F (Erfolgs- *etc*)Chance *f:* **I don't get a ~** ich hab' keine Chance.

look·ing glass ['lʊkɪŋ] *s* Spiegel *m*.

'look|-out *s* **1.** be on the ~ (for) → **look out** 3. **2.** Wache *f*, Beobachtungsposten *m:* **act as ~** Schmiere stehen. **3.** a) *bsd.* ✕ Beobachtungsstand *m:* ~ **tower** Wachturm *m*, b) ♣ Krähennest *n*. **4.** F Angelegenheit *f*, Sache *f:* **'~·,o·ver** *s:* **give s.th. a ~** → **look over** (*adv*). **'~through** *s:* **give s.th. a ~** → **look through** (*adv*).

loom¹ [luːm] *s* Webstuhl *m*.

loom² [~] *v/i* **1.** *a.* ~ **up** undeutlich *od.* drohend sichtbar werden; *fig.* bedrohlich näherrücken. **2.** *a.* ~ **up** (drohend) aufragen: ~ **large** *fig.* sich auftürmen (*Schwierigkeiten etc*); e-e große Rolle spielen.

loon·y ['luːnɪ] *sl.* **I** *adj* bekloppt, verrückt. **II** *s* Verrückte *m, f.* ~ **bin** *s sl.* Klapsmühle *f*.

loop [luːp] **I** *s* **1.** Schlinge *f*, Schleife *f*. **2.** Schleife *f*, Windung *f* (*e-s Flusses etc*). **3.** Schlaufe *f*; Öse *f*. **4.** ✔ Looping *m*, *a. n.* **II** *v/t* **5.** *Schnur etc* schlingen ([*a*]*round* um). **6.** ~ **the** ~ ✔ loopen, e-n Looping fliegen *od.* ausführen. **III** *v/i* **7.** sich schlingen ([*a*]*round* um). **8.** → 6. **'~·hole** *s* **1.** ✕ Schießscharte *f*. **2.** *fig.*

Schlupfloch *n*, Hintertürchen *n*: ~ *in the law, legal* ~ Gesetzeslücke *f*.

loose [luːs] **I** *adj* □ 1. los(e), locker; frei, nicht angebunden *od.* eingesperrt: **break** ~ sich losreißen (*from* von); **come** (*od.* **get**) ~ abgehen (*Knopf etc*), sich lockern (*Schraube etc*), sich ablösen, abblättern (*Farbe etc*); **let** ~ *Hund* von der Leine lassen, *a. Flüche etc* loslassen, *s-m Ärger etc* Luft machen, freien Lauf lassen; ~ **connection** ⚡ Wackelkontakt *m*; → **screw** 1. 2. a) lose (*Haar, Geldscheine etc*): ~ **money** Kleingeld *n*, Münzen *pl*, b) offen, lose, unverpackt (*Ware*). 3. lose sitzend, weit (*Kleidungsstück*). 4. *fig.* lose (*Abmachung, Zs.-hang etc*); frei, ungenau (*Übersetzung etc*); unkonzentriert, nachlässig (*Spielweise etc*); unkontrolliert: **have a** ~ **tongue** den Mund nicht halten können. 5. locker (*Moral, Lebenswandel etc*): → **liver²**, **living** 5. **II** *s* 6. **be on the** ~ a) auf freiem Fuß sein, b) *a.* **go on the** ~ F auf den Putz hauen. '~,**fit·ting** → **loose** 3. '~-**leaf** *adj* Loseblatt...: ~ **binder** Schnellhefter *m*.

loos·en [luːsn] **I** *v/t* 1. *Knoten, Fesseln etc, a.* 🌿 *Husten, fig. Zunge* lösen: ~ **s.o.'s tongue** j-m die Zunge lösen. 2. *Schraube, Griff etc, a. fig. Disziplin etc* lockern: ~ **one's hold of** et. loslassen. 3. *a.* ~ **up** *Muskeln etc, a. fig. j-n* auflockern. **II** *v/i* 4. sich lösen *od.* lockern. 5. ~ **up** (*bsd. Sport*) sich auflockern.

loot [luːt] **I** *s* (Kriegs-, Diebes)Beute *f*. **II** *v/t u. v/i* plündern.

lop [lɒp] *v/t* 1. *Baum etc* beschneiden, (zu)stutzen. 2. *oft* ~ **off** abhauen, abhacken. '~**·sid·ed** *adj* 1. schief, nach 'einer Seite hängend, ⚓ mit Schlagseite. 2. *fig.* einseitig.

lo·qua·cious [ləʊˈkweɪʃəs] *adj* □ geschwätzig, redselig.

lord [lɔːd] **I** *s* 1. Herr *m*, Gebieter *m* (*of* über *acc*). 2. *fig.* Magnat *m*. 3. ℞ *a.* ℞ **God** Gott *m* (der Herr): ℞ (*only*) **knows where ...** Gott *od.* der Himmel weiß, wo ...; b) *a.* **our** ℞ (Christus *m*) der Herr: ℞'s **Prayer** Vaterunser *n*; ℞'s **Supper** (heiliges) Abendmahl. 4. *Br.* Lord *m*: the ℞s das Oberhaus; → **drunk** 1. **II** *v/t* 5. ~ **it** den Herren spielen (*over s.o.* j-m gegenüber). ℞ **Chan·cel·lor** *s*

Br. Lordkanzler *m*. ℞ **May·or** *s Br.* Oberbürgermeister *m*.

lor·ry [ˈlɒrɪ] *s Br.* Last(kraft)wagen *m*, Lastauto *m*.

lose [luːz] (*irr*) **I** *v/t* 1. *Sache, Interesse etc* verlieren, *Geld, Stellung etc a.* einbüßen: ~ **o.s.** sich verirren; ~ **10 pounds** 10 Pfund abnehmen; → **life** 1d, **sight** 2, *etc*. 2. *Spiel, Prozeß etc* verlieren. 3. *Zug etc, fig. Chance etc* versäumen, -passen. 4. *Gelerntes* vergessen. 5. *5 Minuten etc* nachgehen (*Uhr*). 6. *Gewohnheit, Krankheit etc* loswerden, *Verfolger a.* abschütteln. 7. ~ **s.o. s.th.** j-n et. kosten, j-n um et. bringen. **II** *v/i* 8. *a.* ~ **out** (*to*) verlieren (gegen), unterliegen (*dat*). 9. *a.* ~ **out** verlieren, draufzahlen (*on* bei). 10. nachgehen (*Uhr*). '**los·er** *s* Verlierer(in): **good** (**bad**) ~, **be a bad** ~ *a.* nicht verlieren können; **be a born** ~ der geborene Verlierer sein. '**los·ing** *adj* 1. verlustbringend, Verlust... 2. verloren, aussichtslos: **fight a battle** *fig.* auf verlorenem Posten stehen.

loss [lɒs] *s* 1. Verlust *m*: a) Einbuße *f*: ~ **of blood** (**memory, time**) Blut-(Gedächtnis-, Zeit)verlust; **dead** ~ Totalverlust; *fig.* hoffnungsloser Fall (*Person*); **sell s.th. at a** ~ et. mit Verlust verkaufen; **work at a** ~ mit Verlust arbeiten; → **identity**, b) Schaden *m*, c) *verlorene Sache od. Person*, d) Abnahme *f*, Schwund *m*: ~ **in weight** Gewichtsverlust, -abnahme. 2. *pl* ✕ Verluste *pl*, Ausfälle *pl*. 3. **be at a** ~ in Verlegenheit sein (**for** um): **be at a** ~ **for words** keine Worte finden.

lost [lɒst] **I** *pret u. pp von* **lose**. **II** *adj* 1. verloren: ~ **cause** *fig.* aussichtslose Sache; **be a** ~ **cause** *a.* aussichtslos sein. 2. verloren(gegangen): **be** ~ verlorengehen (*a. fig. Arbeitsplätze etc*); **give up for** (*od.* **as**) ~ verloren geben; → **property** 1. 3. verirrt: **be** ~ sich verirrt haben, sich nicht mehr zurechtfinden (*a. fig.*); **get** ~ sich verirren; **get** ~! F hau ab! 4. **be** ~ **on s.o.** keinen Eindruck auf j-n machen, j-n kaltlassen. 5. ~ **in** vertieft *od.* versunken in (*acc*): ~ **in thought** in Gedanken versunken, *bsd. adv a.* gedankenversunken, -verloren. ˌ**~-and-'found** (**of·fice**) *s Am.* Fundbüro *n*.

lot [lɒt] *s* **1.** Los *n*: **cast** (*od.* **draw**) **~s** losen (*for* um); *the* **~** *fell on* (*od.* *to*) *me* das Los fiel auf mich. **2.** Los *n*, Schicksal *n*. **3.** Anteil *m*. **4.** Parzelle *f*; Grundstück *n*. **5.** ✝ Partie *f*, Posten *m*. **6.** Gruppe *f*, Gesellschaft *f*: *the whole* **~** a) die ganze Gesellschaft, b) → 7. **7.** *the* **~** alles, das Ganze. **8.** F Menge *f*, Haufen *m*: *a* **~** *of*, **~s** *of* viel, e-e Menge; *a* **~** (*od.* **~s**) *better* (sehr) viel besser. **9.** *a bad* **~** F ein mieser Typ; ein mieses Pack.
loth → *loath*.
lo·tion ['ləʊʃn] *s* Lotion *f*, (Haut-, Rasier)Wasser *n*.
lot·ter·y ['lɒtərɪ] *s* **1.** Lotterie *f*: **~** *ticket* Lotterielos *n*. **2.** *fig.* Glückssache *f*, Lotteriespiel *n*.
lo·tus ['ləʊtəs] *s* ♣ Lotos(blume *f*) *m*.
loud [laʊd] *adj* □ **1.** (*a. adv*) laut. **2.** *fig.* grell, schreiend (*Farben*), auffallend (*Kleidung, Benehmen*). '**~mouth** *s* F Großmaul *n*. '**~speak·er** *s* Lautsprecher *m*.
lounge [laʊndʒ] **I** *s* **1.** Wohnzimmer *n*. **2.** Gesellschaftsraum *m*, Salon *m* (*es Hotels, Schiffs*). **3.** Foyer *n* (*es Theaters*). **4.** Wartehalle *f* (*es Flughafens*). **5.** Br. vornehmeren u. teueren *Lokals*. **II** *v/i* **6.** → *loll* 1. **III** *v/t* **7.** *mst* **~** *away* Zeit vertrödeln, -bummeln. **~** *bar* → *lounge* 5. **~** *chair* *s* Klubsessel *m*. **~** *suit* *s* bsd. Br. Straßenanzug *m*.
lour, lour·ing → *lower*[1], *lowering*.
louse I *s* [laʊs] **1.** *pl* **lice** [laɪs] *zo.* Laus *f*. **2.** *pl* '**lous·es** *sl.* Scheißkerl *m*. **II** *v/t* [laʊz] **3.** **~** *up sl.* versauen, -murksen.
lous·y ['laʊzɪ] *adj* □ **1.** verlaust. **2.** *sl.* fies, hundsgemein; lausig, mies. **3.** *be* **~** *with sl.* wimmeln von; strotzen vor (*dat*) *od.* von: *be* **~** *with money* vor Geld stinken.
lout [laʊt] *s* Flegel *m*, Rüpel *m*. '**lout·ish** *adj* □ flegel-, rüpelhaft.
lov·a·ble ['lʌvəbl] *adj* □ liebenswert, reizend.
love [lʌv] **I** *s* **1.** Liebe *f* (*of, for, to toward*[*s*] zu): **~** herzliche Grüße (*Briefschluß*); *be in* **~** verliebt sein (*with* in *acc*); *fall in* **~** sich verlieben (*with* in *acc*); *not for* **~** *or money* nicht für Geld u. gute Worte; um nichts in der Welt; *make* **~** sich (*körperlich*) lieben; *make* **~** *to s.o.* j-n (*körperlich*) lieben; *there is no* **~** *lost between them* sie können

sich nicht leiden; **~** *of adventure* Abenteuerlust *f*; **~** *of one's country* Vaterlandsliebe; → *give* 10. **2.** F a) (*Anrede, oft unübersetzt*) Schatz, b) Schatz *m*: *he's a real* **~** er ist ein richtiger Schatz; *a* **~** *of a car* ein süßer Wagen. **3.** *bsd. Tennis*: null. **II** *v/t* **4.** *j-n* (*a. körperlich*) lieben, liebhaben. **5.** *et.* lieben, gerne mögen: **~** *doing* (*bsd. Am. a. to do*) **s.th.** et. gern tun.
love·a·ble → *lovable*.
love| af·fair *s* (Liebes)Affäre *f*, (-)Verhältnis *n*. **~** *bite* *s* F Knutschfleck *m*. **~** *du·et* ♪ Liebesduett *n*. **~hate** (*re·la·tion·ship*) *s* Haßliebe *f*.
love·less ['lʌvlɪs] *adj* □ **1.** lieblos, ungeliebt.
love| let·ter *s* Liebesbrief *m*. **~** *life* *s* (*irr life*) Liebesleben *n*.
love·ly ['lʌvlɪ] *adj* □ **1.** (wunder)schön. **2.** nett, reizend. **3.** F prima, großartig.
love|mak·ing *s* **1.** (*körperliche*) Liebe. **2.** Liebeskunst *f*. **~** *match* *s* Liebesheirat *f*. **~** *po·em* *s* Liebesgedicht *n*.
lov·er ['lʌvə] *s* **1.** Liebhaber *m*, Geliebte *m*; Geliebte *f*. **2.** *pl* Liebende *pl*, Liebespaar *n*: *they are* **~s** sie lieben sich. **3.** (*Musik- etc*)Liebhaber(in), (-)Freund (-in): **~** *of music, music* **~**.
love| scene *s* *thea. etc* Liebesszene *f*. '**~sick** *adj* liebeskrank: *be* **~** Liebeskummer haben. **~** *song* *s* Liebeslied *n*. **~** *sto·ry* *s* Liebesgeschichte *f*, (*bsd. rührselige a.*) Love-Story *f*.
lov·ing ['lʌvɪŋ] *adj* □ liebevoll, zärtlich: *your* **~** *father* Dein Dich liebender Vater (*Briefschluß*).
low[1] [ləʊ] **I** *adj u. adv* **1.** *allg.* niedrig (*a. fig. Löhne etc*): **~** *in fat* fettarm; → *lie low, profile* 1. **2.** tief (*a. fig.*): *a* **~** *bow* e-e tiefe Verbeugung; **~** *shot* (*Sport*) Flachschuß *m*; *the sun is* **~** die Sonne steht tief; *sunk thus* **~** *fig.* so tief gesunken. **3.** tiefgelegen. **4.** knapp (*Vorrat etc*): *get* (*od. run*) **~** knapp werden, zur Neige gehen; *we are getting* (*od. running*) **~** *on money* uns geht allmählich das Geld aus; **~** *on funds* knapp bei Kasse. **5.** schwach (*a. Puls*); niedergeschlagen, deprimiert: *feel* **~** in gedrückter Stimmung sein; sich elend fühlen; → *spirit* 4. **6.** gering(schätzig): → *opinion* 2. **7.** ordinär, vulgär (*Ausdruck etc*); gemein, niederträchtig (*Trick etc*):

feel ~ sich gemein vorkommen. **8.** tief (*Ton etc*); leise (*Ton, Stimme etc*): *in a* ~ *voice* leise. II *s* **9.** *meteor.* Tief *n.* **10.** *fig.* Tief(punkt *m*, -stand *m*) *n*: *be at a new* ~ e-n neuen Tiefpunkt erreicht haben.

low² [~] I *v/i* brüllen, muhen (*Rind*). II *s* Brüllen *n*, Muhen *n*.

,**low**|'**bred** *adj* ungebildet, gewöhnlich. '~**brow I** *s* geistig Anspruchslose *m, f,* Unbedarfte *m, f.* II *adj* geistig anspruchslos, unbedarft. ,~'**cal·o·rie** *adj* kalorienarm. ~ **com·e·dy** *s* Posse *f,* (derber) Schwank. '~**cost** *adj* kostengünstig. '~**down** *adj* F fies, hundsgemein. '~**down** *s* F: *give s.o. the* ~ j-n aufklären (*on* über *acc*); *get the* ~ aufgeklärt werden (*on* über *acc*).

low·er¹ ['lauə] *v/i* **1.** finster *od.* drohend blicken: ~ *at s.o.* j-n finster *od.* drohend ansehen. **2.** sich auftürmen (*Wolken*); sich mit schwarzen Wolken überziehen (*Himmel*).

low·er² ['ləuə] I *v/t* **1.** niedriger machen. **2.** *Augen, Preis, Stimme etc* senken. **3.** *fig.* erniedrigen: ~ *o.s.* sich herablassen. **4.** herunter-, herablassen, *Fahne, Segel* niederholen, streichen. II *v/i* **5.** niedriger werden. **6.** *fig.* sinken, fallen.

low·er³ ['ləuə] I *comp. von* **low¹**. II *adj* **1.** niedriger (*a. fig.*). **2.** unter, Unter...: *the* ~ *class*(*es pl*) sociol. die Unterschicht; ~ *court* ⚖ untergeordnetes Gericht; ~ *deck* ⚓ Unterdeck *n*; → *jaw* 1, *lip* 1.

low·est ['ləuɪst] I *sup von* **low¹**. II *adj* **1.** niedrigst (*a. fig.*): ~ *bid* ✝ Mindestgebot *n*. **2.** unterst. III *s* **3.** *at the* ~ wenigstens, mindestens.

'**low**|**-fat** *adj* fettarm. ,~'**in·come** *adj* einkommensschwach. ,~'**key(ed)** *adj* **1.** gedämpft (*Farbe*), (*Ton a.*) leise. **2.** zurückhaltend (*Empfang etc*). ~**land** ['~lənd] *s* Tief-, Flachland *n*. ♀ **Mass** *s eccl.* Stille Messe. ,~'**necked** *adj* tief ausgeschnitten, mit tiefem Ausschnitt (*Kleid*). ,~'**noise** *adj* rauscharm (*Tonband etc*). ,~'**pres·sure** *adj*: ~ *area* Tiefdruckgebiet *n*. '~**rise** *s* Flachbau *m*. ~ **sea·son** *s* Vor- *od.* Nachsaison *f.* ~**shoe** *s* Halbschuh *m*. ,~'**spir·it·ed** *adj* □ niedergeschlagen, deprimiert.

loy·al ['lɔɪəl] *adj* □ **1.** loyal (*to* gegenüber). **2.** (ge)treu (*to dat*). '**loy·al·ty** *s* Loyalität *f* (*to* zu).

loz·enge ['lɒzɪndʒ] *s* **1.** ♦ Raute *f,*

Rhombus *m.* **2.** *pharm.* Pastille *f,* Tablette *f.*

lub·ber ['lʌbə] *s* Flegel *m*, Rüpel *m*; Trottel *m*; Tolpatsch *m*.

lu·bri·cant ['luːbrɪkənt] *s* ⚙ Schmiermittel *n.* **lu·bri·cate** ['~keɪt] *v/t* schmieren. ,**lu·bri·ca·tion** *s* Schmieren *n.*

lu·cid ['luːsɪd] *adj* □ klar (*Auskunft, Gedanke, Verstand etc*); hell, (*geistig*) klar: ~ *interval* (*od. moment*) bsd. *psych.* heller *od.* lichter Augenblick.

luck [lʌk] *s* **1.** Schicksal *n*, Zufall *m*: *as* ~ *would have it* wie es der Zufall wollte, (un)glücklicherweise; *bad* (*od. hard, ill*) ~ Pech *n* (*on* für), Unglück *n*; *good* ~ Glück *n*; *good* ~ *!* viel Glück! **2.** Glück *n*: *for* ~ als Glücksbringer; *be in* (*out of*) ~ (kein) Glück haben; *try one's* ~ sein Glück versuchen. '**luck·i·ly** *adv* zum Glück, glücklicherweise: ~ *for me* zu m-m Glück. '**luck·less** *adj* □ glück-, erfolglos. '**luck·y** *adj* (□ → *luckily*) **1.** Glücks..., glücklich: *be* (*very*) ~ (großes) Glück haben; ~ *day* Glückstag *m*; ~ *fellow* Glückspilz *m*. **2.** glückbringend, Glücks...: *be* ~ Glück bringen; ~ *penny* Glückspfennig *m*; → *star* 1.

lu·cra·tive ['luːkrətɪv] *adj* □ einträglich, lukrativ.

lu·cre ['luːkə] *s*: *filthy* ~ oft humor. schnöder Mammon.

lu·di·crous ['luːdɪkrəs] *adj* □ lächerlich, absurd.

lu·do ['luːdəʊ] *s Br* Mensch, ärgere dich nicht *n* (*Spiel*).

lug [lʌg] *v/t* zerren, schleifen; schleppen.

lug·gage ['lʌgɪdʒ] *s* (Reise)Gepäck *n.* ~ **al·low·ance** ✈ Freigepäck *n.* ~ **com·part·ment** *s mot. Br.* Kofferraum *m.* ~ **in·sur·ance** *s* Reisegepäckversicherung *f.* ~ **lock·er** *s* Gepäckschließfach *n.* ~ **re·claim** *s* ✈ Gepäckausgabe *f.*

luke·warm [,luːk'wɔːm] *adj* □ lau(-warm) (*a. fig. Zustimmung etc*), (*Unterstützung etc a.*) halbherzig, (*Applaus etc*) lau, mäßig.

lull [lʌl] I *v/t* **1.** *mst* ~ *to sleep* einlullen. **2.** *fig. j-n* beruhigen, beschwichtigen, *j-s Argwohn* zerstreuen: ~ *s.o. into* (*a false sense of*) *security* j-n in Sicherheit wiegen (*v/i* **3.** sich legen, nachlassen (*Sturm*). III *s* **4.** (Ruhe)Pause *f* (*in in dat*): ~ (*in the wind*) Flaute *f*; *the* ~

before the storm die Stille vor dem Sturm (a. fig.).

lull·a·by ['lʌləbaɪ] s Wiegenlied n.

lum·ba·go [lʌm'beɪgəʊ] s ⚕ Hexenschuß m.

lum·ber¹ ['lʌmbə] I s 1. bsd. Am. Bau-, Nutzholz n. 2. Gerümpel n. II v/t 3. a. ~ up Zimmer etc vollstopfen, a. Erzählung etc überladen (**with** mit). 4. ~ **s.o. with s.th.** Br. F j-m et. aufhängen od. aufhalsen.

lum·ber² [~] v/i sich (dahin)schleppen, schwerfällig gehen; (dahin)rumpeln (Wagen).

'lum·ber|·jack s bsd. Am. Holzfäller m, -arbeiter m. ~ **mill** s bsd. Am. Sägewerk n. ~ **room** s Rumpelkammer f.

lu·mi·nar·y ['lu:mɪnərɪ] s fig. Leuchte f.

lu·mi·nos·i·ty [ˌluːmɪ'nɒsətɪ] s 1. Lichtkraft f; ast., phys. Lichtstärke f, Helligkeit f. 2. fig. Brillanz f. **'lu·mi·nous** adj □ 1. leuchtend: ~ **paint** Leuchtfarbe f. 2. fig. intelligent, brillant; klar, einleuchtend.

lump¹ [lʌmp] I s 1. Klumpen m: **have a ~ in one's** (od. **the**) **throat** fig. e-n Kloß im Hals haben. 2. Schwellung f, Beule f; ⚕ Geschwulst f, (in der Brust) Knoten m. 3. Stück n Zucker etc. 4. fig. Gesamtheit f, Masse f: **in the ~** in Bausch u. Bogen, pauschal; im großen u. ganzen. 5. F Klotz m (ungeschlachter, dummer Mensch). II adj 6. Stück...: ~ **sugar** Würfelzucker m. 7. Pauschal... III v/t 8. oft ~ **together** zs.-ballen; fig. zs.-werfen, in 'einen Topf werfen (**with** mit). IV v/i 9. Klumpen bilden, klumpen.

lump² [~] v/t: ~ **it** F sich damit abfinden.

lu·na·cy ['lu:nəsɪ] s ⚕ Wahnsinn m (a. fig.).

lu·nar ['lu:nə] adj Mond...: ~ **eclipse** ast. Mondfinsternis f; ~ **landing** Mondlandung f; ~ **module** Mond(lande)fähre f.

lu·na·tic ['lu:nətɪk] I adj a) ⚕ wahnsinnig, geistesgestört: ~ **asylum** contp. Irrenanstalt f, b) fig. verrückt. II s a) ⚕ Wahnsinnige m, f, Geistesgestörte m, f, b) fig. Verrückte m, f.

lunch [lʌntʃ] I s Mittagessen n: **have ~** → II; ~ **hour** a) a. ~ **break** Mittagspause f, b) → **lunchtime**. II v/i (zu) Mittag essen: ~ **out** auswärts od. im Restaurant zu Mittag essen.

lunch·eon| meat ['lʌntʃən] s Frühstücksfleisch n. ~ **vouch·er** s Essen(s)-bon m.

'lunch·time s Mittagszeit f: **at ~** zur Mittagszeit; ~ **train** Mittagszug m.

lung [lʌŋ] s anat. Lungenflügel m: ~**s** pl Lunge f.

lunge [lʌndʒ] I s a) bsd. fenc. Ausfall m, b) Sprung m vorwärts, Satz m: **make a ~** → II. II v/i a) a. ~ **out** bsd. fenc. e-n Ausfall machen, b) a. ~ **out** e-n Sprung vorwärts od. e-n Satz machen, c) sich stürzen (**at** auf acc).

lurch¹ [lɜːtʃ] I s 1. Taumeln n, Torkeln n. 2. ⚓ Schlingern n. 3. Ruck m: **give a ~** → 6. II v/i 4. taumeln, torkeln. 5. ⚓ schlingern. 6. rucken, e-n Ruck machen.

lurch² [~] s: **leave in the ~** im Stich lassen.

lure [lʊə] I s 1. Köder m (**to** für) (a. fig.). 2. fig. Lockung f, Reiz m. II v/t 3. (an)locken, ködern (beide a. fig.): ~ **away** weglocken; ~ **into** locken in (acc); verlocken od. -führen zu.

lu·rid ['lʊərɪd] adj □ 1. fahl, gespenstisch (Beleuchtung etc). 2. grell (Farben). 3. gräßlich, grausig etc.

lurk [lɜːk] v/i 1. lauern (a. fig.): ~ **for s.o.** j-m auflauern. 2. schleichen: ~ **about** (od. **around**) herumschleichen.

lus·cious ['lʌʃəs] adj □ 1. köstlich, lecker; süß (u. saftig). 2. sinnlich (Lippen etc), üppig (Figur, Frau etc), knackig (Mädchen).

lush [lʌʃ] adj □ saftig (Gras etc), üppig (Vegetation).

lust [lʌst] I s 1. sinnliche Begierde. 2. Gier f (**of**, **for** nach): ~ **for power** Machtgier. II v/i 3. gieren (**for**, **after** nach).

lus·ter Am. → **lustre**.

lust·ful ['lʌstfʊl] adj □ lüstern.

lus·tre ['lʌstə] s bsd. Br. 1. Glanz m (a. fig.). 2. Lüster m, Kronleuchter m.

lus·trous ['lʌstrəs] adj □ 1. glänzend (a. fig.). 2. fig. illuster.

lust·y ['lʌstɪ] adj □ 1. kräftig, robust. 2. tatkräftig.

lute¹ [lu:t] s ♪ Laute f.

lute² [~] I s Kitt m. II v/t (ver)kitten.

lux·ate ['lʌkseɪt] v/t ⚕ sich die Schulter etc aus- od. verrenken: **he ~d his left**

shoulder. **lux'a·tion** *s* Luxation *f*, Aus-, Verrenkung *f*.

lux·u·ri·ant [lʌɡˈʒʊərɪənt] *adj* □ **1.** üppig (*Vegetation*) (*a. fig.*). **2.** *fig.* (über)reich, verschwenderisch, (*Phantasie*) blühend. **lux'u·ri·ate** [⁓eɪt] *v/i* schwelgen (*in* in *dat*). **lux'u·ri·ous** *adj* □ **1.** luxuriös, Luxus... **2.** verschwenderisch, genußsüchtig. **lux·u·ry** [ˈlʌkʃərɪ] **I** *s* **1.** *allg.* Luxus *m*. **2.** Luxusartikel *m*. **II** *adj* **3.** Luxus..., der Luxusklasse.

lye [laɪ] *s* 🜍 Lauge *f*.

ly·ing [ˈlaɪɪŋ] **I** *pres p von* **lie¹**. **II** *adj* lügnerisch, verlogen.

lymph [lɪmf] *s physiol.* Lymphe *f*. ~ **gland,** ~ **node** *s anat.* Lymphknoten *m*.

lynch [lɪntʃ] *v/t* lynchen. ~ **law** *s* Lynchjustiz *f*.

lynx [lɪŋks] *s zo.* Luchs *m*. '~**-eyed** *adj fig.* mit Augen wie ein Luchs.

lyr·ic [ˈlɪrɪk] **I** *adj* (~**ally**) **1.** lyrisch (*a. fig. gefühlvoll*). **II** *s* **2.** lyrisches Gedicht: ~**s** *pl* Lyrik *f*. **3.** *pl* (Lied)Text *m*. **lyr·i·cal** *adj* □ **1.** → *lyric* 1. **2.** schwärmerisch: *get* ~ ins Schwärmen geraten. **lyr·i·cist** [ˈ⁓sɪst] *s* **1.** Lyriker(in). **2.** Texter(in), Textdichter(in).

M

ma [mɑː] *s* F Mama *f*, Mutti *f*.

ma'am [mæm] F → *madam*.

mac [mæk] F → *mackintosh*.

ma·ca·bre [məˈkɑːbrə] *adj* □ makaber.

mac·(c)a·ro·ni [ˌmækəˈrəʊnɪ] *s pl* (*sg konstruiert*) Makkaroni *pl*.

mace¹ [meɪs] *s* Amtsstab *m*.

mace² [⁓] *s* Muskatblüte *f*.

Mach [mæk] *s*: *fly at* ~ *two* ✈, *phys.* mit e-r Geschwindigkeit von zwei Mach fliegen.

ma·che·te [məˈtʃetɪ] *s* Machete *f*, Buschmesser *n*.

ma·chine [məˈʃiːn] **I** *s* **1.** Maschine *f* (F *a. Flugzeug, Motorrad etc*). **2.** Apparat *m*; Automat *m*. **3.** *pol.* (*Partei- etc*)Apparat *m*. **II** *v/t* **4.** maschinell herstellen. ~ **gun** *s* Maschinengewehr *n*.

ma'chine|-read·a·ble *adj* maschinell hergestellt. ~**,read·a·ble** *adj* maschinell lesbar, maschinenlesbar.

ma·chin·er·y [məˈʃiːnərɪ] *s* **1.** Maschinen *pl*; Maschinerie *f*. **2.** *fig.* a) Maschinerie *f*, Räderwerk *n*, b) → *machine* 3.

ma·chine| tool *s* ⚙ Werkzeugmaschine *f*. ~ **trans·la·tion** *s* maschinelle Übersetzung.

ma·chin·ist [məˈʃiːnɪst] *s* **1.** Maschinenschlosser *m*. **2.** Maschinist *m*.

ma·chis·mo [məˈtʃɪzməʊ] *s* Machismo *m*, Männlichkeitswahn *m*. **ma·cho** [ˈmætʃəʊ] *pl* **-chos** *s* Macho *m*.

mack·er·el [ˈmækrəl] *pl* **-el** *s ichth.* Makrele *f*.

mack·in·tosh [ˈmækɪntɒʃ] *s bsd. Br.* Regenmantel *m*.

mac·ro·cosm [ˈmækrəʊkɒzəm] *s* Makrokosmos *m*, Weltall *n*.

mad [mæd] *adj* (□ ~ly *madly*) **1.** wahnsinnig, verrückt (*beide a. fig.*): *go* ~ verrückt werden; *drive s.o.* ~ j-n verrückt machen; *like* ~ wie verrückt. **2.** (*after, about, for, on*) wild, versessen (auf *acc*), verrückt (nach), vernarrt (in *acc*): ~ *about soccer* fußballverrückt. **3.** F außer sich, verrückt (*with* vor *dat*). **4.** *bsd. Am.* F wütend (*at, about* über *acc, auf acc*). **5.** wild (geworden) (*Stier etc*). **6.** *vet.* tollwütig.

mad·am [ˈmædəm] *s* gnädige Frau (*Anrede, oft unübersetzt*).

'mad·cap I *s* verrückter Kerl. **II** *adj* verrückt.

mad·den [ˈmædn] *v/t* verrückt machen (*a. fig.*). **'mad·den·ing** *adj* □ unerträglich: *it is* ~ es ist zum Verrücktwerden.

made [meɪd] **I** *pret u. pp von* **make**. **II** *adj*: *a* ~ *man* ein gemachter Mann. **~-to-'meas·ure** *adj* **1.** nach Maß angefertigt, Maß...: ~ *suit* maßgeschneiderter Anzug, Maßanzug *m*. **~-to-'or·der** *adj* **1.** → *made-to-measure*. **2.** *fig.*

maßgeschneidert, nach Maß. '**~up** *adj*
1. (frei) erfunden. **2.** geschminkt.

'**mad·house** *s* Irrenhaus *n*, *fig. a.* Tollhaus *n*.

mad·ly ['mædlɪ] *adv* **1.** wie verrückt. **2.** F wahnsinnig, schrecklich.

mad·man ['mædmən] *s* (*irr man*) Verrückte *m*.

mad·ness ['mædnɪs] *s* **1.** Wahnsinn *m* (*a. fig.*): **sheer ~** heller *od.* blanker Wahnsinn. **2.** *bsd. Am.* F Wut *f*.

'**mad,wom·an** *s* (*irr woman*) Verrückte *f*.

mael·strom ['meɪlstrɒm] *s* Strudel *m*, Sog *m* (*beide a. fig.*).

Ma·fi·a ['mæfɪə] *s* Mafia *f* (*a. fig.*).
ma·fi·o·so [,~'əʊsəʊ] *pl* **-sos**, **-si** [,~sɪ] *s* Mafioso *m* (*a. fig.*).

mag [mæg] F → *magazine* 3.

mag·a·zine [,mægə'zi:n] *s* **1.** Magazin *n* (*e-r Feuerwaffe, e-s Fotoapparats*). **2.** Magazin *n*, Lagerhaus *n*. **3.** Magazin *n*, Zeitschrift *f*. **~ rack** *s* Zeitungsständer *m*.

mag·got ['mægət] *s zo.* Made *f*. '**mag·got·y** *adj* madig.

Ma·gi ['meɪdʒaɪ] *s pl*: **the** (**three**) **~** die (drei) Weisen aus dem Morgenland, die Heiligen Drei Könige.

mag·ic ['mædʒɪk] **I** *s* **1.** Magie *f*, Zauberei *f*: **as if by ~, like ~** wie durch Zauberei. **2.** Zauber(kraft *f*) *m*, magische Kraft (*a. fig.*). **II** *adj* (*~ally*) **3.** magisch, Zauber...: **~ carpet** fliegender Teppich; **~ eye** ⚡ magisches Auge; **~ trick** Zaubertrick *m*, -kunststück *n*; **~ wand** Zauberstab *m*. **4.** zauberhaft. **ma·gi·cian** [mə'dʒɪʃn] *s* **1.** Magier *m*, Zauberer *m*. **2.** Zauberkünstler *m*.

mag·is·trate ['mædʒɪstreɪt] *s* ⚖ Richter *m* (*an e-m* **magistrates' court**): **~s' court** *Br.*, **~'s court** *Am.* erstinstanzliches Gericht für Straf- *u.* Zivilsachen *niederer Ordnung*.

mag·na·nim·i·ty [,mægnə'nɪmətɪ] *s* Großmut *f*. **mag·nan·i·mous** [~'nænɪməs] *adj* □ großmütig.

mag·nate ['mægneɪt] *s* Magnat *m*.

mag·ne·sia [mæg'ni:ʃə] *s* 🜨 Magnesia *f*. **mag·ne·si·um** [~'ni:zɪəm] *s* 🜨 Magnesium *n*.

mag·net ['mægnɪt] *s* Magnet *m* (*a. fig.*). **mag·net·ic** [~'netɪk] *adj* (*~ally*) **1.** magnetisch, Magnet...: **~ field** *phys.* Ma-

gnetfeld *n*; **~ pole** *phys.* magnetischer Pol, Magnetpol *m*. **2.** *fig.* magnetisch, faszinierend. **mag·net·ism** ['~nɪtɪzəm] *s* **1.** *phys.* Magnetismus *m*. **2.** *fig.* Anziehungskraft *f*. '**mag·ne·tize** *v/t* **1.** magnetisieren. **2.** *fig.* anziehen, fesseln.

mag·nif·i·cence [mæg'nɪfɪsns] *s* Großartigkeit *f*, Herrlichkeit *f*. **mag'nif·i·cent** *adj* □ großartig, prächtig, herrlich (*alle a. fig.*).

mag·ni·fy ['mægnɪfaɪ] *v/t* **1.** (*a. v/i*) vergrößern: **~ing glass** Vergrößerungsglas *n*, Lupe *f*. **2.** *fig.* aufbauschen.

mag·ni·tude ['mægnɪtju:d] *s* Größenordnung *f*, *fig. a.* Ausmaß *n*, Schwere *f*: **of the first ~** von äußerster Wichtigkeit.

mag·no·lia [mæg'nəʊljə] *s* 🌹 Magnolie *f*.

mag·pie ['mægpaɪ] *s* **1.** *orn.* Elster *f*. **2.** *fig.* Schwätzer(in). **3.** *Br. fig.* sammelwütiger Mensch.

ma·hog·a·ny [mə'hɒgənɪ] *s* Mahagoni(holz) *n*.

maid [meɪd] *s* **1.** *old* ~ alte Jungfer; **~ of hono(u)r** Hofdame *f*; *Am.* (erste) Brautjungfer. **2.** (Dienst)Mädchen *n*, Hausangestellte *f*: **~ of all work** *bsd. fig.* Mädchen für alles.

maid·en ['meɪdn] *adj* **1.** **~ name** Mädchenname *m* (*e-r Frau*). **2.** unverheiratet. **3.** Jungfern...: **~ flight** ✈ Jungfernflug *m*; **~ speech** *parl.* Jungfernrede *f*; **~ voyage** ⚓ Jungfernfahrt *f*.

mail [meɪl] **I** *s* Post(sendung) *f*: **by ~** *bsd. Am.* mit der Post; → **incoming** 3, **outgoing** 2. **II** *v/t bsd. Am.* aufgeben, *Brief* einwerfen; (zu)schicken (**to** *dat*). '**~·box** *s bsd. Am.* Briefkasten *m*. **~ car·ri·er** *s bsd. Am.*, '**~·man** *s* (*irr man*) *bsd. Am.* Postbote *m*, Briefträger *m*. '**~·,or·der** *adj*: **~ catalog(ue)** Versandhauskatalog *m*; **~ firm** (*od.* **house**) Versandhaus *n*.

maim [meɪm] *v/t* verstümmeln (*a. fig. Text*).

main [meɪn] **I** *adj* (□ → **mainly**) **1.** Haupt..., wichtigst: **~ clause** *ling.* Hauptsatz *m*; **~ office** Hauptbüro *n*, Zentrale *f*; **~ reason** Hauptgrund *m*; **~ thing** Hauptsache *f*. **II** *s* **2.** *mst pl* Haupt(gas-, -wasser)leitung *f*; (Strom-)Netz *n*: **~s cable** Netzkabel *n*. **3.** *in* (*Am. a.* **for**) **the ~** hauptsächlich, in der Hauptsache. '**~·land** ['~lənd] *s* Festland *n*.

make

main·ly ['meɪnlɪ] *adv* hauptsächlich, vorwiegend.

'main·spring *s fig.* (Haupt)Triebfeder *f.* **'~·stay** *s fig.* Hauptstütze *f.*

main·tain [meɪn'teɪn] *v/t* **1.** *Zustand* (aufrecht)erhalten, beibehalten, (be-) wahren; ✝ *Preis* halten. **2.** instand halten, pflegen, ⚙ *a.* warten. **3.** (*in e-m bestimmten Zustand*) lassen. **4.** *Familie etc* unterhalten, versorgen. **5.** behaupten (**that** daß; **to** *inf* zu *inf*). **6.** *Meinung, Recht etc* verfechten; auf e-r Forderung bestehen: ~ **one's ground** *bsd. fig.* sich behaupten.

main·te·nance ['meɪntənəns] *s* **1.** (Aufrecht)Erhaltung *f*, Beibehaltung *f*. **2.** Instandhaltung *f*, Pflege *f*, ⚙ *a.* Wartung *f*: **~-free** wartungsfrei. **3.** Unterhalt *m*: ~ **grant** Unterhaltszuschuß *m*.

mai·son·(n)ette [ˌmeɪzə'net] *s* **1.** Maison(n)ette *f*. **2.** Einliegerwohnung *f*.

maize [meɪz] *s* ♫ *bsd. Br.* Mais *m*.

ma·jes·tic [mə'dʒestɪk] *adj* (**~ally**) majestätisch. **maj·es·ty** ['mædʒəstɪ] *s* Majestät *f* (*a. fig.*): **His** (**Her**) ♑ Seine (Ihre) Majestät.

ma·jor ['meɪdʒə] **I** *s* **1.** ✖ Major *m*. **2.** *univ. Am.* Hauptfach *n*. **3.** ⚖ Volljährige *m*, *f*: **become a ~** volljährig werden. **4.** ♪ Dur *n*. **II** *adj* **5.** größer, *fig. a.* bedeutend, wichtig. **6.** ⚖ volljährig. **III** *v/i* **7.** ~ **in** *univ. Am.* als *od.* im Hauptfach studieren. **ma·jor·i·ty** [mə'dʒɒrətɪ] *s* **1.** Mehrheit *f*: **by a large ~** mit großer Mehrheit; **in the ~ of cases** in der Mehrzahl der Fälle; ~ **of votes** Stimmenmehrheit; **be in the** (*od.* **a**) ~ in der Mehrzahl sein; ~ **decision** Mehrheitsbeschluß *m*. **2.** ⚖ Volljährigkeit *f*: **reach one's ~** volljährig werden.

make [meɪk] **I** *s* **1.** Machart *f*, Ausführung *f*; Erzeugnis *n*, Fabrikat *n*, Produkt *n*. **II** *v/t* (*irr*) **2.** *allg. z. B. Reise, Versuch* machen: ~ **a speech** e-e Rede halten. **3.** machen: a) anfertigen, herstellen, erzeugen (**from, of, out of** von, aus), b) verarbeiten, formen (**to, into** in *acc*, zu), c) *Tee etc* zubereiten. **4.** (er)schaffen: **he is made for this job** er ist für diese Arbeit wie geschaffen. **5.** ergeben, bilden. **6.** verursachen: a) *Geräusch, Schwierigkeiten etc* machen, b) bewirken, mit sich bringen. **7.** machen *od.* ernennen zu: ~ **s.o.** (**a**) **gen-**

eral j-n zum General ernennen. **8.** *mit adj, pp etc*: machen: ~ **angry** zornig machen, erzürnen. **9.** sich erweisen als (*Person*): **he would ~ a good teacher** er würde e-n guten Lehrer abgeben. **10.** *mit inf*: j-n lassen, veranlassen *od.* bringen zu: ~ **s.o. wait** j-n warten lassen; ~ **s.o. talk** j-n zum Sprechen bringen; ~ **s.th. do, ~ do with s.th.** mit et. auskommen, sich mit et. behelfen. **11.** ~ **much of** viel Wesens machen von; viel halten von. **12.** sich e-e Vorstellung machen von, halten für: **what do you ~ of it?** was halten Sie davon? **13.** schätzen auf (*acc*). **14.** sich *Vermögen etc* erwerben, *Geld, Profit* machen, *Gewinn* erzielen. **15.** schaffen: a) *Strecke* zurücklegen, b) *Geschwindigkeit* erreichen, machen. **16.** F *Zug* erwischen: ~ **it** es schaffen. **17.** sich belaufen auf (*acc*), ergeben: **two and two ~ four** 2 u. 2 macht *od.* ist 4. **III** *v/i* (*irr*) **18.** ~ **as if** (*od.* **as though**) so tun als ob *od.* als wenn: ~ **believe** (**that; to do**) vorgeben (daß; zu tun).

Verbindungen mit Präpositionen:

make| *at v/i* losgehen *od.* sich stürzen auf (*acc*). ~ **for** *v/i* **1.** zugehen *od.* lossteuern auf (*acc*); sich aufmachen nach; sich stürzen auf (*acc*). **2.** förderlich sein, dienen (*dat*), beitragen zu.

Verbindungen mit Adverbien:

make| **a·way** *v/i* sich davonmachen (**with** mit). ~ **off** → **make away.** ~ **out I** *v/t* **1.** *Scheck etc* ausstellen; *Urkunde etc* ausfertigen; *Liste etc* aufstellen. **2.** ausmachen, erkennen. **3.** aus j-m, e-r Sache klug werden. **4.** **make s.o. out to be bad** (**a liar**) j-n als schlecht (als Lügner) hinstellen. **II** *v/i* **5.** *bsd. Am.* auskommen (**with** mit j-m). **6.** *bsd. Am.* F *gut etc* zurechtkommen. ~ **o·ver** *v/t* **1.** *Eigentum* übertragen (**to** *dat*). **2.** umarbeiten; umbauen (**into** zu). ~ **up I** *v/t* **1.** bilden: **be made up of** bestehen *od.* sich zs.-setzen aus. **2.** *Schriftstück etc* abfassen, aufsetzen, *Liste etc* anfertigen, *Tabelle* aufstellen, *Arznei, Bericht etc* zs.-stellen. **3.** sich *e-e Geschichte etc* ausdenken, *a. b.s.* erfinden. **4.** *Paket etc* (ver)packen, (-)schnüren. **5.** → **mind** 5. **6.** *Versäumtes* nachholen, wettmachen. **7. make it up** sich versöhnen *od.* wieder vertragen (**with** mit). **II** *v/i* **8.** sich schminken. **9.** ~

for wiedergutmachen, wettmachen. **10.** → 7. **11.** ~ **to s.o.** F j-m schöntun; sich an j-n heranmachen.

'**make-be‚lieve** *adj* Phantasie..., Schein...: ~ *world*.

mak·er ['meɪkə] *s* **1.** ✝ Hersteller *m*, Erzeuger *m*. **2.** *the* ♀ *eccl.* der Schöpfer.

'**make‚shift I** *s* Notbehelf *m*. **II** *adj* behelfsmäßig, provisorisch, Behelfs... '~**up** *s* **1.** Make-up *n*: *without* ~ *a.* ungeschminkt. **2.** Aufmachung *f*, (Ver)Kleidung *f*. **3.** *Film etc*: Maske *f*. **4.** Zs.-setzung *f*.

mak·ing ['meɪkɪŋ] *s* **1.** Erzeugung *f*, Herstellung *f*, Fabrikation *f*: *be in the* ~ im Werden *od.* Kommen sein; noch in Arbeit sein. **2.** *have the* ~*s of* das Zeug haben zu.

mal·ad·just·ed [ˌmælə'dʒʌstɪd] *adj psych.* nicht angepaßt, milieugestört.

mal·ad·min·is·tra·tion ['mælədˌmɪnɪ'streɪʃn] *s* schlechte Verwaltung.

mal·a·droit [ˌmælə'drɔɪt] *adj* □ **1.** ungeschickt. **2.** taktlos.

ma·laise [mæ'leɪz] *s* **1.** Unpäßlichkeit *f*, Unwohlsein *n*. **2.** *fig.* Unbehagen *n*.

ma·lar·i·a [mə'leərɪə] *s* ✿ Malaria *f*.

mal·con·tent ['mælkən‚tent] **I** *adj* unzufrieden. **II** *s* Unzufriedene *m*, *f*.

male [meɪl] **I** *adj* männlich: ~ *choir* Männerchor *m*; ~ *cousin* Vetter *m*; ~ *model* Dressman *m*; ~ *nurse* (Kranken)Pfleger *m*; ~ *prostitute* Strichjunge *m*; → *chauvinism, chauvinist*. **II** *s* Mann *m*; *zo.* Männchen *n*.

mal·e·dic·tion [ˌmælɪ'dɪkʃn] *s* Fluch *m*, Verwünschung *f*.

ma·lev·o·lence [mə'levələns] *s* Böswilligkeit *f*. **ma'lev·o·lent** *adj* □ übelwollend (*to dat*), böswillig.

mal·for·ma·tion [ˌmælfɔː'meɪʃn] *s bsd. ✿* Mißbildung *f*.

mal·func·tion [ˌmæl'fʌŋkʃn] **I** *s* **1.** ✿ Funktionsstörung *f*. **2.** ⚙ schlechtes Funktionieren *od.* Arbeiten; Versagen *n*. **II** *v/i* **3.** ⚙ schlecht funktionieren *od.* arbeiten; versagen.

mal·ice ['mælɪs] *s* **1.** Böswilligkeit *f*. **2.** Groll *m*: *bear s.o.* ~ e-n Groll auf j-n haben *od.* gegen j-n hegen, j-m grollen. **3.** ⚖ böse Absicht, Vorsatz *m*: *with* ~ *(aforethought)* vorsätzlich.

ma·li·cious [mə'lɪʃəs] *adj* □ **1.** böswillig, ⚖ *a.* vorsätzlich. **2.** arglistig.

ma·lig·nant [mə'lɪgnənt] *adj* □ **1.** bösartig (*a.* ✿), böswillig. **2.** arglistig.

ma·lin·ger [mə'lɪŋgə] *v/i* sich krank stellen, simulieren. **ma'lin·ger·er** *s* Simulant(in).

mall [mɔːl] *s* **1.** Allee *f*. **2.** *Am.* Einkaufszentrum *n*.

mal·le·a·ble ['mælɪəbl] *adj* **1.** ⚙ verformbar. **2.** *fig.* formbar.

mal·let ['mælɪt] *s* Holzhammer *m*, Schlegel *m*.

mal·low ['mæləʊ] *s* 🌸 Malve *f*.

mal·nu·tri·tion [ˌmælnjuː'trɪʃn] *s* **1.** Unterernährung *f*. **2.** Fehlernährung *f*.

mal·o·dor·ous [mæl'əʊdərəs] *adj* □ übelriechend.

mal·prac·tice [ˌmæl'præktɪs] *s* Vernachlässigung *f* der beruflichen Sorgfalt; (ärztlicher) Kunstfehler.

malt [mɔːlt] **I** *s* Malz *n*. **II** *v/t* mälzen.

Mal·tese [ˌmɔːl'tiːz] **I** *s* Malteser(in): *the* ~ *pl* die Malteser *pl*. **II** *adj* maltesisch: ~ *cross* Malteserkreuz *n*.

mal·treat [ˌmæl'triːt] *v/t* **1.** schlecht behandeln. **2.** mißhandeln. '**mal'treat·ment** *s* **1.** schlechte Behandlung. **2.** Mißhandlung *f*.

mam·mal ['mæml] *s zo.* Säugetier *n*.

mam·mon ['mæmən] *s* Mammon *m*.

mam·moth ['mæməθ] **I** *s zo.* Mammut *n*. **II** *adj* Mammut..., Riesen...

man [mæn] **I** *pl* **men** [men] *s* **1.** Mensch *m*. **2.** *oft* ♀ *coll.* der Mensch, die Menschen *pl*. **3.** Mann *m*: *the* ~ *in* (*Am. a. on*) *the street* der Mann auf der Straße; ~ *of straw fig.* Strohmann *m*; *be one's own* ~ sein eigener Herr sein. **4.** *weitS.* Mann *m*, Person *f*; jemand; man: *every* ~ jeder(mann); *no* ~ niemand; ~ *by* ~ Mann für Mann; *to a* ~ bis auf den letzten Mann; → *jack* 1. **5.** (*Dame*)Stein *m*, (*Schach*)Figur *f*. **II** *v/t* **6.** (*Raum*)*Schiff etc* bemannen.

man·age ['mænɪdʒ] **I** *v/t* **1.** *Betrieb etc* leiten, führen. **2.** *Künstler, Sportler etc* managen. **3.** *et.* zustande bringen, bewerkstelligen; es fertigbringen (*to do* tun). **4.** umgehen (können) mit (*Werkzeug, Tieren etc*); mit *j-m, et.* fertig werden, *j-n* zu nehmen wissen. **5.** F *Arbeit, Essen etc* bewältigen, schaffen. **II** *v/i* **6.** auskommen (*with* mit; *without* ohne). **7.** F es schaffen, zurechtkommen; es einrichten *od.* ermöglichen. '**man·age-**

a·ble *adj* □ **1.** lenk-, fügsam. **2.** handlich. **'man·age·ment** *s* **1.** (*Haus- etc*)Verwaltung *f*. **2.** ✝ Management *n*, Unternehmensführung *f*: *junior* (*middle, top*) ~ untere (mittlere, obere) Führungskräfte *pl*; ~ **consultant** Betriebs-, Unternehmensberater *m*. **3.** ✝ Geschäftsleitung *f*, Direktion *f*: *under new* ~ unter neuer Leitung, (*Geschäft etc*) neu eröffnet. **'man·ag·er** *s* **1.** (*Haus- etc*)Verwalter *m*. **2.** ✝ Manager *m*; Führungskraft *f*; Geschäftsführer *m*, Leiter *m*, Direktor *m*. **3.** Manager *m* (*e-s Schauspielers etc*). **4.** *be a good* ~ gut *od.* sparsam wirtschaften können. **5.** *Fußball:* (Chef)Trainer *m*. **man·ag·er·ess** [ˌ~'res] *s* **1.** (*Haus- etc*)Verwalterin *f*. **2.** ✝ Managerin *f*; Geschäftsführerin *f*, Leiterin *f*, Direktorin *f*. **3.** Managerin *f* (*e-s Schauspielers etc*). **man·a·ger·i·al** [ˌ~ə'dʒɪərɪəl] *adj* ✝ geschäftsführend, leitend: ~ *position* leitende Stellung; ~ *staff* leitende Angestellte *pl*. **man·ag·ing** [ˈ~dʒɪŋ] *adj* ✝ geschäftsführend, leitend: ~ *dIrector* Generaldirektor *m*, leitender Direktor.

man·da·rin(e) ['mændərɪn] *s* ♀ Mandarine *f*.

man·date ['mændeɪt] *s* **1.** ⚖️ Mandat *n*, (Prozeß)Vollmacht *f*. **2.** *parl.* Mandat *n*, Auftrag *m*. **man·da·to·ry** ['~dətərɪ] *adj* □ obligatorisch, zwingend, verbindlich.

man·di·ble ['mændɪbl] *s anat.* Unterkiefer(knochen) *m*.

man·do·lin ['mændəlɪn], **man·do·line** [ˌ~'liːn] *s* ♪ Mandoline *f*.

mane [meɪn] *s* Mähne *f* (*a. fig. e-s Menschen*).

'man·ˌeat·er *s* **1.** Menschenfresser *m*. **2.** menschenfressendes Tier. **3.** F männermordendes Wesen (*Frau*).

ma·neu·ver, *etc Am.* → **manoeuvre**, *etc.*

man·ga·nese ['mæŋgəniːz] *s* 🜍 Mangan *n*.

mange [meɪndʒ] *s vet.* Räude *f*.

man·ger ['meɪndʒə] *s* Krippe *f*, Futtertrog *m*: → *dog* 1.

man·gle¹ ['mæŋgl] **I** *s* (Wäsche)Mangel *f*. **II** *v/t* mangeln.

man·gle² [ˌ~] *v/t* **1.** zerfleischen, -reißen, -fetzen. **2.** *fig.* Text verstümmeln.

man·go ['mæŋgəʊ] *pl* **-go(e)s** *s* ♀ **1.**

Mango(frucht, -pflaume) *f*. **2.** Mangobaum *m*.

man·gy ['meɪndʒɪ] *adj* □ **1.** *vet.* räudig. **2.** *fig.* schmutzig, eklig. **3.** *fig.* schäbig, heruntergekommen.

'man·ˌhan·dle *v/t* **1.** mißhandeln. **2.** mit Menschenkraft bewegen. **'~·hole** *s* Kanal-, Einsteigeschacht *m*: ~ *cover* Schachtdeckel *m*.

man·hood ['mænhʊd] *s* **1.** Mannesalter *n*: *reach* ~ ins Mannesalter kommen. **2.** *euphem.* Manneskraft *f*.

'man·ˌhour *s* Arbeitsstunde *f*. **'~·hunt** *s* (Groß)Fahndung *f*.

ma·ni·a ['meɪnjə] *s* **1.** 🩺 Manie *f*, Wahn(sinn) *m*: → *persuasion* 1. **2.** *fig.* (*for*) Sucht *f* (nach), Leidenschaft *f* (für), Manie *f*, Fimmel *m*: *collector's* ~ Sammelwut *f*, -leidenschaft *f*; *for cleanliness* Sauberkeitsfimmel *m*; *have a* ~ *for* verrückt sein nach. **ma·ni·ac** ['~nɪæk] **I** *s* **1.** 🩺 Wahnsinnige *m, f*, Verrückte *m, f*. **2.** *fig.* (*Sportetc*)Fanatiker(in): *car* ~ Autonarr *m*. **II** *adj* (~*ally*) 🩺 wahnsinnig, verrückt.

man·ic-de·pres·sive [ˌmænɪkdɪ'presɪv] *psych.* **I** *adj* manisch-depressiv. **II** *s* Manisch-Depressive *m, f*: *be a* ~ manisch-depressiv sein.

man·i·cure ['mænɪˌkjʊə] **I** *s* Maniküre *f*. **II** *v/t* maniküren.

man·i·fest ['mænɪfest] **I** *adj* □ offenkundig, augenscheinlich. **II** *v/t* offenbaren, manifestieren. **III** *s* ✈ *bsd. Am.* Passagierliste *f* od. ↗. **man·i·fes'ta·tion** *s* **1.** Offenbarung *f*, Manifestation *f*. **2.** Anzeichen *n*, Symptom *n*. **man·i'fes·to** [ˌ~təʊ] *pl* **-to(e)s** *s* Manifest *n*.

man·i·fold ['mænɪfəʊld] *adj* □ **1.** mannigfaltig, vielfältig. **2.** ⚙ Mehr-, Vielfach...; Kombinations... **II** *s* **3.** ⚙ Verteiler *m*. **III** *v/t* **4.** vervielfältigen.

ma·nip·u·late [mə'nɪpjʊleɪt] *v/t* **1.** *j-n, Preise etc* manipulieren. **2.** ⚙ bedienen, betätigen. **3.** *Konten etc* frisieren. **ma·ˌnip·uˈla·tion** *s* **1.** Manipulation *f*. **2.** ⚙ Bedienung *f*, Betätigung *f*. **3.** Frisieren *n*. **ma'nip·u·la·tor** *s* Manipulator *m* (*a. Zauberkünstler*).

man·kind [mæn'kaɪnd] *s* die Menschheit, die Menschen *pl*. **'man·ly** *adj* männlich; Männer...

'man-made *adj* vom Menschen geschaffen *od.* verursacht; künstlich: ~ *fibers* *(bsd. Br. **fibres**) pl* Kunst-, Chemiefasern *pl.*

man·ne·quin ['mænıkın] *s* **1.** Mannequin *n.* **2.** Kleider- *od.* Schaufensterpuppe *f.*

man·ner ['mænə] *s* **1.** Art *f* (u. Weise *f*): *in this* ~ auf diese Art *od.* Weise, so; *in such a* ~ (*that*) so *od.* derart (daß); *adverb of* ~ Umstandswort *n* der Art u. Weise, Modaladverb *n*; *in a* ~ *of speaking* sozusagen. **2.** Betragen *n*, Auftreten *n*: *it's just his* ~ das ist so s-e Art. **3.** *pl* Benehmen *n*, Umgangsformen *pl*, Manieren *pl*: *it is bad* ~*s* es gehört *od.* schickt sich nicht (*to do* zu tun). **4.** *pl* Sitten *pl* (u. Gebräuche *pl*). **'man·ner·ism** *s* **1.** *paint. etc* Manierismus *m.* **2.** Manieriertheit *f.* **3.** manierierte Wendung (*in Rede etc*).

ma·noeu·vra·ble [məˈnuːvrəbl] *adj bsd. Br.* manövrierfähig; lenk-, steuerbar; *weitS.* wendig (*Fahrzeug*). **ma'noeu·vre** [~və] I *s* **1.** *a. pl* ♣, ✕ Manöver *n*: *be on* ~*s* im Manöver sein; *room for* ~ *fig.* Handlungsspielraum *m.* **2** *fig.* Manöver *n*, Schachzug *m*, List *f.* II *v/t* **3.** ♣, ✕ manövrieren (*a. fig.*). III *v/t* **4.** manövrieren (*a. fig.*): ~ *s.o. into s.th.* j-n in et. hineinmanövrieren.

man·or ['mænə] *s Br.* (Land)Gut *n*: ~ (*house*) Herrenhaus *n.*

'man·pow·er *s* **1.** menschliche Arbeitskraft *od.* -leistung. **2.** (verfügbare) Arbeitskräfte *pl*: ~ *shortage* Arbeitskräftemangel *m.*

'man·ser·vant *pl* **'men·ser·vants** *s* Diener *m.*

man·sion ['mænʃn] *s* **1.** herrschaftliches Wohnhaus. **2.** *pl bsd. Br.* (großes) Mietshaus.

'man·slaugh·ter *s* 𝔱𝔱 Totschlag *m.*

man·tel·piece ['mæntl~] *s*, **'~·shelf** *s* (*irr shelf*) Kaminsims *m.*

man|-to-'man *adj* von Mann zu Mann. **'~·trap** *s* Fußangel *f.*

man·u·al ['mænjʊəl] I *adj* □ **1.** Hand..., manuell: ~ *work* körperliche Arbeit; ~ *worker* (Hand)Arbeiter(in). **2.** handschriftlich. II *s* **3.** Handbuch *n*, Leitfaden *m.*

man·u·fac·ture [,mænjʊˈfæktʃə] I *s* **1.** Fertigung *f*, Erzeugung *f*, Herstellung *f*: *year of* ~ Herstellungs-, Baujahr *n.* **2.** Erzeugnis *n*, Fabrikat *n.* II *v/t* **3.** erzeu-

gen, herstellen. **4.** verarbeiten (*into* zu). **5.** *fig. Ausrede etc* erfinden. **,man·u·'fac·tur·er** *s* Hersteller *m*, Erzeuger *m.* **,man·u·'fac·tur·ing** *adj* Herstellungs...: ~ *cost* Herstellungskosten *pl.*

ma·nure [məˈnjʊə] I *s* (*bsd. natürlicher*) Dünger. II *v/t* düngen.

man·u·script ['mænjʊskrıpt] *s* Manuskript *n.*

man·y ['menı] I *adj* **1.** viel(e): ~ *times* oft; *as* ~ *as forty* nicht weniger als vierzig; *we had one chair too* ~ wir hatten e-n Stuhl zuviel. **2.** ~ *a* manch (ein): ~ *a time* so manches Mal. II *s* **3.** viele: ~ *of us* viele von uns; *a good* ~ ziemlich viel(e); *a great* ~ sehr viele. **,~·'sid·ed** *adj* **1.** vielseitig (*a. fig.*). **2.** *fig.* vielschichtig (*Problem etc*).

map [mæp] I *s* **1.** (Land- *etc*)Karte *f*; (Stadt- *etc*)Plan *m*: *be off the* ~ F hinter dem Mond liegen; *put on the* ~ F *Stadt etc* bekannt machen. II *v/t* **2.** e-e Karte machen von, *Gebiet* kartographisch erfassen; in e-e Karte eintragen. **3.** *mst* ~ *out fig.* (bis in die Einzelheiten) (vor-aus)planen.

ma·ple ['meıpl] *s* 𝄞 Ahorn *m.*

mar [mɑː] *v/t* **1.** beschädigen; verunstalten. **2.** *fig. Pläne etc* stören, beeinträchtigen; *Spaß etc* verderben.

mar·a·thon ['mærəθn] (*Leichtathletik*) I *s a.* ~ *race* Marathonlauf *m.* II *adj* Marathon..., *fig. a.* Dauer...

ma·raud [məˈrɔːd] I *v/i* plündern. II *v/t* (aus)plündern. **ma'raud·er** *s* Plünderer *m.*

mar·ble ['mɑːbl] I *s* **1.** Marmor *m.* **2.** a) Murmel *f*, b) *pl* (*sg konstruiert*) Murmelspiel *n*: *play* ~*s* (mit) Murmeln spielen. II *adj* **3.** marmorn (*a. fig.*).

March[1] [mɑːtʃ] *s* März *m*: *in* ~ im März.

march[2] [~] I *v/i* **1.** ✕ *etc* marschieren: ~ *off* abrücken; ~ *past* (*s.o.*) (an j-m) vorbeiziehen *od.* -marschieren; *time is ~ing on* es ist schon spät; → *time* **1.** II *v/t* **2.** *Strecke* marschieren, zurücklegen. **3.** ~ *s.o. off* j-n abführen. III *s* **4.** ✕ Marsch *m* (*a. ♪*); *allg.* (Fuß)Marsch *m.* **5.** Marsch(strecke *f*) *m*: *a day's* ~ ein Tage(s)marsch; *steal a* ~ *on s.o. fig.* j-m zuvorkommen. **6.** *fig.* (Ab)Lauf *m*, (Fort)Gang *m.*

march·ing or·ders ['mɑːtʃıŋ] *s pl* ✕ Marschbefehl *m*: *get one's* ~ *fig.* F den

Laufpaß bekommen (*von Firma od. Freundin*); (*Sport*) vom Platz fliegen.
mare [meə] *s* zo. Stute *f*: **~'s nest** fig. Windei *m*, *a*. (Zeitungs)Ente *f*.
mar·ga·rine [‚mɑːdʒəˈriːn] *s*, **marge** [mɑːdʒ] *s Br.* F Margarine *f*.
mar·gin [ˈmɑːdʒɪn] *s* **1.** Rand *m* (*a. fig.*). **2.** (Seiten)Rand *m*: **in the ~** am Rand. **3.** Grenze *f* (*a. fig.*): **~ of income** Einkommensgrenze. **4.** fig. Spielraum *m*: **allow** (*od.* **leave**) **a ~ for** Spielraum lassen für. **5.** † (Gewinn-, Verdienst-) Spanne *f*. **6.** Sport: Abstand *m*, (*a.* Punkt)Vorsprung *m*: **by a wide ~** mit großem Vorsprung. **mar·gin·al** [ˈ~nl] *adj* **1.** Rand...: **~ note** Randbemerkung *f*. **2.** Grenz... (*a. fig.*). **3.** fig. geringfügig. **mar·gin·al·ly** [ˈ~əlɪ] *adv* fig. **1.** geringfügig. **2.** (nur) am Rand.
mar·gue·rite [‚mɑːɡəˈriːt] *s* ♀ **1.** Gänseblümchen *n*. **2.** Margerite *f*.
mar·i·hua·na, **mar·i·jua·na** [‚mærɪˈjuːɑːnə] *s* Marihuana *f*.
ma·ri·nade [‚mærɪˈneɪd] *s* Marinade *f*. **mar·i·nate** [ˈ~neɪt] *v/t* marinieren.
ma·rine [məˈriːn] **I** *adj* **1.** a) See...: **~ chart** Seekarte *f*, b) Meeres...: **~ animal**. **II** *s* **2.** Marine *f*. **3.** ✕ Marineinfanterist *m*: **tell that to the ~s!** F das kannst du deiner Großmutter erzählen!
mar·i·o·nette [‚mærɪəˈnet] *s* Marionette *f*: **~ play** Puppenspiel *n*.
mar·i·tal [ˈmærɪtl] *adj* □ ehelich, Ehe...: **~ duties** *pl* (**rights** *pl*) eheliche Pflichten *pl* (Rechte *pl*); **~ status** Familienstand *m*.
mar·i·time [ˈmærɪtaɪm] *adj* **1.** See...: **~ blockade** Seeblockade *f*. **2.** seefahrend. **3.** Küsten...
mar·jo·ram [ˈmɑːdʒərəm] *s* ♀ Majoran *m*.
mark¹ [mɑːk] *s* (deutsche) Mark.
mark² [~] **I** *s* **1.** Markierung *f*, bsd. ⊙ Marke *f*. **2.** fig. Zeichen *n*: **~ of confidence** Vertrauensbeweis *m*; **~ of respect** Zeichen der Hochachtung. **3.** (Kenn)Zeichen *n*, Merkmal *n*: **distinctive ~** Kennzeichen. **4.** Narbe *f* (*a.* ⊙); Kerbe *f*, Einschnitt *m*. **5.** Ziel *n* (*a. fig.*): **hit the ~** (das Ziel) treffen; fig. ins Schwarze treffen; **miss the ~** das Ziel verfehlen, danebenschießen (*a. fig.*); **be off** (**wide of**) **the ~** (weit) danebenschießen; fig. sich (gewaltig) irren; (weit)

danebenliegen (Schätzung etc). **6.** fig. Norm *f*: **be up to the ~** den Anforderungen gewachsen sein (Person) *od.* genügen (Leistungen etc); gesundheitlich auf der Höhe sein. **7.** a) (Fuß-, Brems- etc)Spur *f* (*a. fig.*): **leave one's ~ on** s-n Stempel aufdrücken (dat); bei *j-m* s-e Spuren hinterlassen, b) Fleck *m*. **8.** † (Fabrik-, Waren)Zeichen *n*, (Schutz-, Handels)Marke *f*. **9.** ped. Note *f* (a. Sport), Zensur *f*: **get** (*od.* **obtain**) **full ~s** die beste Note bekommen, die höchste Punktzahl erreichen. **10.** a) Fußball: Elfmeterpunkt *m*, b) Laufsport: Startlinie *f*: **on your ~s!** auf die Plätze!; **be quick** (**slow**) **off the ~** e-n guten (schlechten) Start haben; fig. schnell (langsam) schalten *od.* reagieren. **II** *v/t* **11.** markieren, anzeichnen, *a.* fig. kennzeichnen; Wäsche zeichnen; Waren auszeichnen; Preis festsetzen; Temperatur etc anzeigen; fig. ein Zeichen sein für: **to ~ the occasion** zur Feier des Tages, aus diesem Anlaß; **~ time** ✕ auf der Stelle treten (*a. fig.*); fig. abwarten. **12.** Spuren hinterlassen auf (dat); fig. *j-n* zeichnen (Krankheit etc). **13.** bestimmen (**for** für). **14.** ped. benoten, zensieren, (Sport) bewerten. **15.** Sport: Gegenspieler decken, markieren. **III** *v/i* **16.** ~ **easily** leicht schmutzen.
Verbindungen mit Adverbien:
mark| down *v/t* **1.** † (im Preis) herunter-, herabsetzen. **2.** bestimmen, vormerken (**for** für). **~ off** *v/t* **1.** abgrenzen, abstecken. **2.** (auf e-r Liste) abhaken. **~ out** *v/t* **1.** → mark² 13. **2.** abgrenzen, markieren. **~ up** *v/t* † (im Preis) hinauf-, heraufsetzen.
'**mark-down** *s* † Preissenkung *f* (**of** um).
marked [mɑːkt] *adj* deutlich, merklich, ausgeprägt. **mark·ed·ly** [ˈ~kɪdlɪ] *adv* deutlich, ausgesprochen.
mark·er [ˈmɑːkə] *s* **1.** Markierstift *m*. **2.** Lesezeichen *n*. **3.** Sport: Bewacher(in).
mar·ket [ˈmɑːkɪt] † **I** *s* **1.** Markt *m*: a) Handel: **be on the ~** auf dem Markt *od.* im Handel sein; **put** (*od.* **place**) **on the ~** auf den Markt *od.* in den Handel bringen; zum Verkauf anbieten, b) Handelszweig, c) Marktplatz *m*: **in the ~** auf dem Markt, auf d) Wochen-, Jahrmarkt *m*, e) Absatzgebiet: **hold the ~** den Markt beherrschen, f) Absatz *m*, Verkauf *m*:

meet with a ready ~ schnellen Absatz finden; *there is no* ~ *for* ... lassen sich nicht absetzen. **2.** *Am.* (Lebensmittel)Geschäft *n*, Laden *m*. **II** *v/t* **3.** auf den Markt *od.* in den Handel bringen. **4.** vertreiben. **III** *adj* **5.** Markt... ~ **a·nal·y·sis** *s* (*irr analysis*) Marktanalyse *f*. ~ **e·con·o·my** *s· free* (*social*) freie (soziale) Marktwirtschaft.

mar·ket·ing ['mɑːkɪtɪŋ] *s* ✝ Marketing *n*: ~ *research* Absatzforschung *f*.

mar·ket| place *s* Marktplatz *m*. ~ **re·search** *s* Marktforschung *f*.

mark·ing ['mɑːkɪŋ] *s* **1.** Markierung *f*, *a. fig.* Kennzeichnung *f*. **2.** *zo.* Musterung *f*, Zeichnung *f*. **3.** *ped.* Benotung *f*, Zensierung *f*, (*Sport*) Bewertung *f*. **4.** *Sport*: Deckung *f*.

marks·man ['mɑːksmən] *s* (*irr man*) guter Schütze.

'mark·up *s* ✝ Preiserhöhung *f* (*of* um).

mar·ma·lade ['mɑːməleɪd] *s* (*bsd.* Orangen)Marmelade *f*.

mar·mot ['mɑːmət] *s zo.* Murmeltier *n*.

ma·roon [mə'ruːn] *adj* kastanienbraun.

mar·quee [mɑː'kiː] *s* großes Zelt.

mar·riage ['mærɪdʒ] *s* **1.** Heirat *f*, Vermählung *f*, Hochzeit *f* (*to* mit). **2.** Ehe *f*: *by* ~ angeheiratet; *related by* ~ verschwägert. ~ **bu·reau** *s* (*a. irr bureau*) Heiratsinstitut *n*. ~ **cer·tif·i·cate** *s* Trauschein *m*. ~ **guid·ance cen·ter** (*bsd. Br.* **cen·tre**) *s* Eheberatungsstelle *f*. ~ **lines** *s pl* (*mst sg konstruiert*) *bsd. Br.* Trauschein *m*.

mar·ried ['mærɪd] *adj* verheiratet, ehelich, Ehe...: ~ *couple* Ehepaar *n*; ~ *life* Eheleben *n*.

mar·row ['mærəʊ] *s* **1.** *anat.* (Knochen)Mark *n*: *be frozen to the* ~ völlig durchgefroren sein. **2.** *fig.* Mark *n*, Kern *m*, *das* Innerste.

mar·ry ['mærɪ] **I** *v/t* **1.** heiraten: *be married* verheiratet sein (*to* mit); heiraten. **2.** *a.* ~ *off Tochter etc* verheiraten (*to an acc*, mit). **3.** *Paar* trauen. **II** *v/i* **4.** heiraten: ~ *into* einheiraten in (*acc*).

Mars [mɑːz] *s ast.* Mars *m*.

marsh [mɑːʃ] *s* Sumpf(land *n*) *m*, Marsch *f*.

mar·shal ['mɑːʃl] **I** *s* **1.** ✕ Marschall *m*. **2.** *Am.* Bezirkspolizeichef *m*. **II** *v/t pret u. pp* **-shaled**, *bsd. Br.* **-shalled 3.** (an)ordnen, arrangieren.

marsh·y ['mɑːʃɪ] *adj* sumpfig, Sumpf...

mar·ten ['mɑːtɪn] *s zo.* Marder *m*.

mar·tial ['mɑːʃl] *adj* ☐ **1.** kriegerisch. **2.** Kriegs..., Militär...: ~ *law* Kriegsrecht *n*. **3.** ~ *arts pl* asiatische Kampfsportarten *pl*.

Mar·tian ['mɑːʃn] *s* Marsmensch *m*, -bewohner(in).

mar·ti·ni [mɑː'tiːnɪ] *s* Martini *m* (*Cocktail*).

Mar·tin·mas ['mɑːtɪnməs] *s* Martinstag *m* (*11. November*).

mar·tyr ['mɑːtə] **I** *s* **1.** Märtyrer(in): *make a* ~ *of o.s.* sich (auf)opfern; *iro.* den Märtyrer spielen. **II** *v/t* **2.** zum Märtyrer machen. **3.** zu Tode martern. **'mar·tyr·dom** *s* Martyrium *n* (*a. fig.*).

mar·vel ['mɑːvl] **I** *s* Wunder *n* (*of* an *dat*): *work* (*od. do*) ~*s* Wunder wirken. **II** *v/i pret u. pp* **-veled**, *bsd. Br.* **-velled** sich wundern, staunen (*at* über *acc*).

mar·vel·(l)ous ['mɑːvələs] *adj* ☐ **1.** erstaunlich, wunderbar. **2.** F fabelhaft, phantastisch.

Marx·ism ['mɑːksɪzəm] *s* Marxismus *m*. **'Marx·ist** **I** *s* Marxist(in). **II** *adj* marxistisch.

mar·zi·pan [ˌmɑːzɪ'pæn] *s* Marzipan *n*, *m*.

mas·ca·ra [mæ'skɑːrə] *s* Wimperntusche *f*.

mas·cot ['mæskət] *s* Maskottchen *n*: a) Glücksbringer(in), b) Talisman *m*.

mas·cu·line ['mæskjʊlɪn] *adj* ☐ **1.** männlich (*a. ling.*), Männer... **2.** unfraulich, maskulin.

mash [mæʃ] **I** *s* **1.** breiige Masse, Brei *m*. **2.** *Br.* F Kartoffelbrei *m*. **II** *v/t* **3.** zerdrücken, -quetschen: ~*ed potatoes pl* Kartoffelbrei *m*.

mask [mɑːsk] **I** *s* **1.** *allg.* Maske *f* (*a. fig.*): *throw off the* ~ die Maske fallen lassen, sein wahres Gesicht zeigen. **II** *v/t* **2.** maskieren: ~*ed ball* Maskenball *m*. **3.** *fig.* verschleiern: ~*ed advertising* ✝ Schleichwerbung *f*.

mas·o·chism ['mæsəʊkɪzəm] *s psych.* Masochismus *m*. **'mas·o·chist** *s* Masochist(in). **ˌmas·o·chis·tic** (~*ally*) masochistisch.

ma·son ['meɪsn] *s* **1.** Steinmetz *m*. **2.** *oft* ⊈ Freimaurer *m*.

mas·quer·ade [ˌmæskə'reɪd] *s* Maskerade *f* (*a. fig.*).

mass¹ [mæs] *s eccl.* Messe *f:* **go to ~** zur Messe gehen.

mass² [~] **I** *s* **1.** *allg.* Masse *f (a. phys.):* **a ~ of errors** e-e (Un)Menge Fehler; **~es** *pl* **of ice** Eismassen *pl;* **the ~es** *pl* die (breite) Masse. **2.** Mehrzahl *f,* überwiegender Teil. **II** *v/t u. v/i* **3.** (sich) (an)sammeln *od.* (an)häufen. **III** *adj* **4.** Massen...: **~ demonstration,** *etc.*

mas·sa·cre ['mæsəkə] **I** *s* Massaker *n.* **II** *v/t* niedermetzeln.

mas·sage ['mæsɑːʒ] **I** *s* Massage *f.* **II** *v/t* massieren.

mas·seur [mæ'sɜː] *s* Masseur *m.* **mas·seuse** [~'sɜːz] *s* Masseurin *f,* Masseuse *f.*

mas·sive ['mæsɪv] *adj □ allg.* massiv *(a. fig.):* **on a ~ scale** in ganz großem Rahmen.

mass| me·di·a *s pl (a. sg konstruiert)* Massenmedien *pl.* **~·pro·duce** *v/t* serienmäßig herstellen. **~ pro·duc·tion** *s* Massen-, Serienproduktion *f.*

mast¹ [mɑːst] *s ⚓ (a. Antennen- etc)* Mast *m.*

mast² [~] *s* Mast(futter *n*) *f.*

mas·ter ['mɑːstə] **I** *s* **1.** Meister *m,* Herr *m:* **be ~ of s.th.** et. *(a. e-e Sprache etc)* beherrschen; **be ~ of the situation** Herr der Lage sein; **be one's own ~** sein eigener Herr sein; **find one's ~** s-n Meister finden *(in s.o.* in j-m). **2.** (dazu passende Sache *od.* Person, Gegenstück *n.* **3.** *paint. etc* Meister *m:* **an old ~** ein alter Meister. **5.** *univ.* Magister *m:* ♀ **of Arts** Magister Artium *od.* der Geisteswissenschaften; ♀ **of Science** Magister der Naturwissenschaften. **6. → ceremony** 1. **II** *v/t* **7.** Herr sein über *(acc), a.* Sprache *etc* beherrschen. **8.** Aufgabe, Schwierigkeit *etc* meistern, Temperament *etc* zügeln. **III** *adj* **9.** meisterhaft, -lich, Meister... **10.** Haupt... **~ cop·y** *s* Originalkopie *f (a. e-s Films etc).*

mas·ter·ful ['mɑːstəful] *adj □* **1.** herrisch, gebieterisch. **2. → master** 9.

mas·ter| fuse *s ⚡* Hauptsicherung *f.* **~ key** *s* Hauptschlüssel *m.*

mas·ter·ly ['mɑːstəli] *→ master* 9.

'mas·ter|-mind *s* **1.** überragender Geist, Genie *n.* **2.** (führender) Kopf: **be the ~ behind** stecken hinter *(dat).* **II** *v/t*

3. der Kopf *(gen)* sein, stecken hinter *(dat).* **'~·piece** *s* **1.** Haupt-, Meisterwerk *n.* **2.** Meisterstück *n.* **~ plan** *s* Gesamtplan *m.* **'~·stroke** *s* Meisterstück *n,* -leistung *f.*

mas·ter·y ['mɑːstəri] *s* **1.** Herrschaft *f,* Gewalt *f (of, over* über *acc):* **gain the ~ over** die Oberhand gewinnen über. **2.** Beherrschung *f (e-r Sprache etc).*

mas·ti·cate ['mæstɪkeɪt] *v/t* (zer)kauen. **mas·ti·ca·tion** *s* (Zer)Kauen *n.*

mas·tiff ['mæstɪf] *s zo.* Bulldogge *f.*

mas·tur·bate ['mæstəbeɪt] *v/i* masturbieren, onanieren. **mas·tur·ba·tion** *s* Masturbation *f,* Onanie *f.*

mat¹ [mæt] **I** *s* **1.** Matte *f (a. Ringen etc).* **2.** Untersetzer *m,* -satz *m.* **3.** Vorleger *m,* Abtreter *m.* **4.** verfilzte Masse. **II** *v/i* **5.** sich verfilzen.

mat² [~] **I** *adj* matt *(a. phot.),* mattiert. **II** *v/t* mattieren.

match¹ [mætʃ] *s* Streich-, Zündholz *n.*

match² [~] **I** *s* **1.** der, die, das gleiche *od.* Ebenbürtige: **his ~** seinesgleichen; sein Ebenbild; j-d, der es mit ihm aufnehmen kann; **be a (no) ~ for s.o.** j-m (nicht) gewachsen sein; **find (od. meet) one's ~** s-n Meister finden *(in s.o.* in j-m). **2.** (dazu) passende Sache *od.* Person, Gegenstück *n.* **3.** (zs.-passendes) Paar, Gespann *n (a. fig.):* **they are an excellent ~** sie passen ausgezeichnet zueinander. **4.** *(Fußball etc)*Spiel *n,* *(Box- etc)*Kampf *m.* **5.** Heirat *f;* gute Partie *(Person).* **II** *v/t* **6.** j-m, e-r Sache ebenbürtig *od.* gewachsen sein, gleichkommen: **no one can ~ her in cooking** niemand kann so gut kochen wie sie; **... cannot be ~ed** ... ist unerreicht *od.* nicht zu übertreffen. **7.** j-m, e-r Sache *(a. farblich etc)* entsprechen, passen zu. **8.** j-n, et. vergleichen *(with* mit): **~ one's strength against s.o.('s)** s-e Kräfte mit j-m messen. **III** *v/i* **9.** zs.-passen, übereinstimmen *(with* mit), entsprechen *(to* dat).

'match·box *s* Streich-, Zündholzschachtel *f.*

'match·ing ['mætʃɪŋ] *adj* (dazu) passend. **'match·less** *adj □* unvergleichlich, einzigartig.

'match|,mak·er *s* **1.** Ehestifter(in). **2.** *b.s.* Kuppler(in). **~ point** *s* Tennis *etc:* Matchball *m.*

mate¹ [meɪt] → *checkmate.*

mate² [~] I *s* 1. (Arbeits)Kamerad *m*, (-)Kollege *m*; (*Anrede*) Kamerad!, Kumpel! 2. *zo., bsd. orn.* Männchen *n od.* Weibchen *n.* 3. ⚓ Maat *m.* II *v/t* 4. *Tiere* paaren. III *v/i* 5. *zo.* sich paaren.

ma·te·ri·al [məˈtɪərɪəl] I *adj* □ 1. materiell, physisch; Material... *: ~ damage* Sachschaden *m; ~ defect* Materialfehler *m.* 2. materiell: a) leiblich (*Wohlergehen*), b) wirtschaftlich: *~ wealth* materieller Wohlstand. 3. wesentlich, ausschlaggebend (*to* für); *~* erheblich, relevant. II *s* 4. Material *n*, Stoff *m* (*beide a. fig. for* zu *e-m Buch etc*). **ma·'te·ri·al·ism** *s* Materialismus *m.* **ma·'te·ri·al·ist** *s* Materialist(in). **ma,te·ri·al·'is·tic** *adj* (*~ally*) materialistisch. **ma·'te·ri·al·ize** I *v/t* 1. *et.* verwirklichen. II *v/i* 2. sich verwirklichen. 3. erscheinen, sich materialisieren (*Geist*).

ma·ter·nal [məˈtɜːnl] *adj* □ 1. mütterlich, Mutter... 2. *Großvater etc* mütterlicherseits.

ma·ter·ni·ty [məˈtɜːnətɪ] I *s* Mutterschaft *f.* II *adj:* *~ allowance* (*od. benefit*) Mutterschaftsbeihilfe *f; ~ dress* Umstandskleid *n; ~ leave* Mutterschaftsurlaub *m; ~ ward* Entbindungsstation *f.*

mat·ey [ˈmeɪtɪ] *adj* kameradschaftlich: *be ~ with s.o.* mit j-m auf du u. du stehen.

math [mæθ] *s Am.* F Mathe *f.*

math·e·mat·i·cal [ˌmæθəˈmætɪkl] *adj* □ mathematisch; Mathematik... **math·e·ma·ti·cian** [ˌmæθəˈmɪʃn] *s* Mathematiker(in). **math·e·mat·ics** [ˌ~ˈmætɪks] *s pl* (*mst sg konstruiert*) Mathematik *f.*

maths [mæθs] *s pl* (*mst sg konstruiert*) *Br.* F Mathe *f.*

mat·i·née [ˈmætɪneɪ] *s thea.* Nachmittagsvorstellung *f.*

mat·ing [ˈmeɪtɪŋ] *s zo.* Paarung *f; ~ season* Paarungszeit *f.*

ma·tri·arch·y [ˈmeɪtrɪɑːkɪ] *s sociol.* Matriarchat *n.*

ma·tri·ces [ˈmeɪtrɪsiːz] *pl von* **matrix.**

ma·tric·u·late I *v/t u. v/i* [məˈtrɪkjʊleɪt] (sich) immatrikulieren. II *s* [ˌ~lət] Immatrikulierte *m, f.* **ma,tric·u·'la·tion** *s* Immatrikulation *f.*

mat·ri·mo·ni·al [ˌmætrɪˈməʊnjəl] *adj* □ ehelich, Ehe...: *~ agency* Heiratsinsti-

tut *n.* **mat·ri·mo·ny** [ˈ~mənɪ] *s* Ehe(-stand *m*) *f.*

ma·trix [ˈmeɪtrɪks] *pl* **ma·tri·ces** [ˈ~trɪsiːz], **'ma·trix·es** *s* 1. ☉ Matrize *f.* 2. ℞ Matrix *f.*

ma·tron [ˈmeɪtrən] *s* 1. Matrone *f.* 2. *Br.* Oberschwester *f*, Oberin *f.* **'ma·tron·ly** *adj* matronenhaft.

mat·ter [ˈmætə] I *s* 1. Materie *f* (*a. phys.*), Substanz *f*, Stoff *m.* 2. ⚕ Eiter *m.* 3. Sache *f*, Angelegenheit *f: this is an entirely different ~* das ist et. ganz anderes; *a ~ of course* e-e Selbstverständlichkeit; *as a ~ of course* selbstverständlich, natürlich; *a ~ of fact* e-e Tatsache; *as a ~ of fact* tatsächlich, eigentlich; *a ~ of form* e-e Formsache; *as a ~ of form* der Form halber; *a ~ of taste* (e-e) Geschmackssache; *a ~ of time* e-e Frage der Zeit; *it is a ~ of life and death* es geht um Leben u. Tod; *~ laughing* 3. 4. *pl* die Sache, die Dinge *pl: to make ~s worse* was die Sache noch schlimmer macht; *as ~s stand* wie die Dinge liegen. 5. *what's the ~ (with him)?* was ist los (mit ihm)?; *it's no ~ whether* es spielt keine Rolle, ob; *no ~ what he says* ganz gleich, was er sagt; *no ~ who* gleichgültig, wer. II *v/i* 6. von Bedeutung sein (*to* für): *it doesn't ~* es macht nichts; *it hardly ~s to me* es macht mir nicht viel aus; *it little ~s* es spielt kaum e-e Rolle. 7. ⚕ eitern. ˌ~-of-'course *adj* selbstverständlich, natürlich. ˌ~-of-'fact *adj* sachlich, nüchtern.

mat·tress [ˈmætrɪs] *s* Matratze *f.*

ma·ture [məˈtjʊə] I *adj* □ 1. *allg.* reif (*a. fig.*). 2. *fig.* ausgereift (*Pläne etc*): *after ~ reflection* nach reiflicher Überlegung. 3. ♦ fällig (*Wechsel etc*). II *v/t* 4. reifen lassen (*a. fig.*). III *v/i* 5. (heran)reifen (*into* zu), reif werden (*beide a. fig.*). 6. ♦ fällig werden. **ma·'tur·i·ty** 1. Reife *f* (*a. fig.*). 2. ♦ Fälligkeit *f.*

maud·lin [ˈmɔːdlɪn] *adj* 1. weinerlich (*Stimme*). 2. rührselig.

maul [mɔːl] *v/t* 1. *j-n, et.* übel zurichten. 2. *fig.* herunter-, verreißen (*Kritiker*).

Maun·dy Thurs·day [ˈmɔːndɪ] *s* Gründonnerstag *m.*

mau·so·le·um [ˌmɔːsəˈlɪəm] *pl* **-le·ums, -le·a** [ˌ~ˈlɪə] *s* Mausoleum *n.*

mauve [məʊv] *adj* malvenfarbig, mauve.

mav·er·ick [ˈmævərɪk] *s pol.* (abtrünniger) Einzelgänger; *allg.* Außenseiter *m*.

mawk·ish ['mɔ:kɪʃ] *adj* □ **1.** (unangenehm) süßlich. **2.** *fig.* rührselig, süßlich.

max·im ['mæksɪm] *s* Maxime *f*, Grundsatz *m*.

max·i·ma ['mæksɪmə] *pl von* **maximum.**
max·i·mal ['ml] *adj* □ → **maximum** II. **'max·i·mize** *v/t* ↑, ⊚ maximieren.
max·i·mum ['mɔm] **I** *pl* **-ma** ['mə], **-mums** *s* Maximum *n*. **II** *adj* maximal, Maximal..., Höchst...: ~ **(permissible) speed** (zulässige) Höchstgeschwindigkeit.

May¹ [meɪ] *s* Mai *m*: **in** ~ im Mai.

may² [~] *v/aux* (*irr*) **1.** *Möglichkeit, Gelegenheit:* ich kann, du kannst *etc*, ich mag, du magst *etc*: **it** ~ **happen any time** es kann jederzeit geschehen; **it might happen** es könnte geschehen; **you** ~ **be right** du magst recht haben, vielleicht hast du recht. **2.** *Erlaubnis:* ich kann, du kannst *etc*, ich darf, du darfst *etc*. **3. you** ~ **well say so** du hast gut reden; **we might as well go** da könnten wir (auch) ebensogut gehen. **4.** *ungewisse Frage:* **how old** ~ **she be?** wie alt mag sie wohl sein? **5.** *Aufforderung:* **you might help me** du könntest mir (eigentlich) helfen.

may·be ['meɪbi:] *adv* vielleicht.

May bee·tle, ~ **bug** *s zo.* Maikäfer *m*. ~ **Day** *s* der 1. Mai. **'2-day** *int* ↗, ⚓ Mayday! (*internationaler Funknotruf*).

may·hem ['meɪhem] *s* **1.** ⚖ *bsd. Am.* schwere Körperverletzung. **2.** *fig.* Chaos *n*: **cause** (*od.* **create**) ~ ein Chaos auslösen.

may·on·naise [ˌmeɪə'neɪz] *s* Mayonnaise *f*.

may·or [meə] *s* Bürgermeister *m*.

'may·pole *s* Maibaum *m*.

maze [meɪz] *s* **1.** Irrgarten *m*, Labyrinth *n* (*a. fig.*): ~ **of streets** Straßengewirr *n*; **be in a** ~ verwirrt sein.

me [mi:] **I** *personal pron* **1.** mich (*acc von* **I**): **he knows** ~. **2.** mir (*dat von* **I**): **he gave** ~ **the book. 3.** F ich (*nom*): **he's younger than** ~; **it's** ~ ich bin's. **II** *reflex pron* **4.** mich: **I looked about** ~ ich sah mich um.

mead·ow ['medəʊ] *s* Wiese *f*, Weide *f*: **in the** ~ auf der Wiese *od.* Weide.

mea·ger *Am.*, **mea·gre** *bsd. Br.* ['mi:gə]

adj □ **1.** mager, dürr, (*Gesicht*) hager. **2.** *fig.* dürftig, kärglich: ~ **attendance** spärlicher Besuch.

meal¹ [mi:l] *s* Mahl(zeit *f*) *n*, Essen *n*: ~**s pl on wheels** Essen auf Rädern.

meal² [~] *s* Schrotmehl *n*.

'meal·time *s* Essenszeit *f*.

meal·y [mi:lɪ] *adj* mehlig. ~**mouthed** [ˌmaʊðd] *adj* schönfärberisch, heuchlerisch (*Person*), (*Äußerung etc a.*) verschlüsselt.

mean¹ [mi:n] *adj* □ **1.** gemein, niederträchtig. **2.** schäbig, geizig. **3.** F (*charakterlich*) schäbig: **feel** ~ sich schäbig *od.* gemein vorkommen (*about* wegen).

mean² [~] **I** *adj* **1.** mittler, Mittel..., durchschnittlich, Durchschnitts... **II** *s* **2.** Mitte *f*, Mittel(weg *m*) *n*, Durchschnitt *m*. **3.** *pl* (*a. sg singular*) Mittel *n od. pl*, Weg *m*: **by all** ~**s** auf alle Fälle, unbedingt; **by no** ~**s** keineswegs, auf keinen Fall; **by** ~**s of** mittels, durch, mit; **find the** ~**s** Mittel u. Wege finden; **a** ~**s of communication** ein Kommunikationsmittel; → **end** 10. **4.** *pl* Mittel *pl*, Vermögen *n*: **live within** (*beyond*) **one's** ~**s** s-n Verhältnissen entsprechend (über s-e Verhältnisse) leben.

mean³ [~] (*irr*) **I** *v/t* **1.** beabsichtigen, vorhaben: ~ **to do s.th.** et. tun wollen; **I** ~ **it** es ist mir Ernst damit; ~ **business** es ernst meinen; ~ **no harm** es nicht böse meinen; **no harm** ~**t!** nichts für ungut! **2. be** ~**t for** bestimmt sein für, (*Bemerkung etc*) gemünzt sein auf (*acc*). **3.** meinen, sagen wollen: **what do you** ~ **by this?** was wollen Sie damit sagen?; was verstehen Sie darunter? **4.** *e-e Menge Arbeit etc* bedeuten. **5.** bedeuten, heißen (*Wort etc*): **does this** ~ **anything to you?** ist Ihnen das ein Begriff?, sagt Ihnen das et.? **II** *v/i* **6.** ~ **well** (*ill*) **by** (*od.* **to**) **s.o.** j-m wohlgesinnt (übel gesinnt) sein. **7.** ~ **everything** (*little*) **to s.o.** j-m alles (wenig) bedeuten.

me·an·der [mɪ'ændə] *v/i* sich winden *od.* schlängeln.

mean·ing ['mi:nɪŋ] **I** *s* **1.** Sinn *m*, Bedeutung *f*: **full of** ~. **3.** *do you get* (*od.* **take**) *my* ~? verstehst du, was ich meine? **2.** Sinn *m*, Inhalt *m*: **give one's life a new** ~ s-m Leben e-n neuen Sinn geben. **II** *adj* □ **3.** bedeutungsvoll, bedeutsam (*Blick etc*). **mean·ing·ful**

['⁓fʊl] *adj* □ **1.** bedeutungsvoll (*Blick, Ereignis etc*). **2.** sinnvoll (*Arbeit etc*). **'mean·ing·less** *adj* □ sinnlos.

mean·ness ['mi:nnɪs] *s* **1.** Gemeinheit *f*, Niederträchtigkeit *f*. **2.** Schäbigkeit *f*, Geiz *m*.

meant [ment] *pret u. pp von* **mean³**.

,mean|'time I *adv* inzwischen, unterdessen, in der Zwischenzeit. II *s*: *in the* ⁓ → I. ⁓'**while** → **meantime** I.

mea·sles ['mi:zlz] *s pl* (*mst sg konstruiert*) ⚕ Masern *pl*: → **German** 1.

meas·ur·a·ble ['meʒərəbl] *adj* □ **1.** meßbar. **2.** merklich.

meas·ure ['meʒə] I *s* **1.** Maß(einheit *f*) *n*: ⁓ *of capacity* Hohlmaß; ⁓ *of length* Längenmaß. **2.** *fig.* (richtiges *od.* vernünftiges) Maß, Ausmaß *n*: *set* ⁓*s to* Grenzen setzen (*dat*); *know no* ⁓ kein Maß kennen; *beyond* (*all*) ⁓ über alle Maßen, grenzenlos; *in a great* (*od. large*) ⁓ in großem Maße; großenteils; *in some* ⁓, *in a* (*certain*) ⁓ bis zu e-m gewissen Grade. **3.** Maß *n*, Meßgerät *n*: *weigh with two* ⁓*s fig.* mit zweierlei Maß messen. **4.** ♪ Takt *m*. **5.** *Metrik:* Versmaß *n*. **6.** Maßnahme *f*: *take* ⁓*s* Maßnahmen treffen *od.* ergreifen. II *v/t* **7.** (ver)messen, ab-, ausmessen: ⁓ *s.o.* j-m Maß nehmen (*for* für); ⁓ *one's length* *fig.* der Länge nach hinfallen. **8.** *fig.* messen (*by* an *dat*). **9.** *fig.* vergleichen, messen (*against, with* mit): ⁓ *one's strength with* s-e Kräfte messen mit. III *v/i* **10.** messen, groß sein: *it* ⁓*s 7 inches* es mißt 7 Zoll, ist 7 Zoll lang. **'meas·ure·ment** *s* **1.** (Ver)Messung *f*. **2.** Maß *n; pl a.* Abmessungen *pl*: *take s.o.'s* ⁓*s* j-m Maß nehmen (*for* für). **'meas·ur·ing** *adj* Meß...: ⁓ *instrument* Meßgerät *n*.

meat [mi:t] *s* **1.** Fleisch *n*: *cold* ⁓ kalter Braten. **2.** *fig.* Substanz *f*, Gehalt *m*. '⁓·**ball** *s* Fleischklößchen *n*.

me·chan·ic [mɪ'kænɪk] *s* Mechaniker *m*. **me'chan·i·cal** *adj* □ mechanisch (*a. fig.*): ⁓ *engineering* Maschinenbau *m*; ⁓ *pencil Am.* Drehbleistift *m*.

mech·a·nism ['mekənɪzəm] *s* Mechanismus *m* (*a. fig.*). **'mech·a·nize** *v/t* mechanisieren.

med·al ['medl] *s* **1.** Medaille *f*. **2.** Orden *m*. **med·al·ist** *Am.* → **medallist**. **me·dal·lion** [mɪ'dæljən] *s* Medaillon *n*.

med·al·list ['medlɪst] *s bsd. Br.* Medaillengewinner(in).

med·dle ['medl] *v/i* sich einmischen (*with, in* in *acc*). **med·dle·some** ['⁓səm] *adj* aufdringlich.

me·di·a ['mi:djə] I *pl von* **medium**. II *s pl* (*a. sg konstruiert*) Medien *pl*: ⁓ *event* Medienereignis *s*; ⁓*shy* medienscheu.

me·di·ae·val → **medieval**.

me·di·ate ['mi:dɪeɪt] I *v/i* vermitteln (*between* zwischen *dat*). II *v/t* (durch Vermittlung) zustande bringen *od.* beilegen. **,me·di'a·tion** *s* Vermittlung *f*. **'me·di·a·tor** *s* Vermittler *m*.

med·ic ['medɪk] → **medico**.

med·i·cal ['medɪkl] I *adj* □ **1.** medizinisch, ärztlich, Kranken...: ⁓ *certificate* ärztliches Attest; ⁓ *examination* ärztliche Untersuchung; *on* ⁓ *grounds* aus gesundheitlichen Gründen; ⁓ *student* Medizinstudent(in). **2.** internistisch: ⁓ *ward* innere Abteilung (*e-r Klinik*). II *s* **3.** F ärztliche Untersuchung.

me·dic·a·ment [mə'dɪkəmənt] *s* Medikament *n*.

med·i·cate ['medɪkeɪt] *v/t* medizinisch *od.* medikamentös behandeln. **,med·i·'ca·tion** *s* medizinische *od.* medikamentöse Behandlung.

me·dic·i·nal [mə'dɪsɪnl] *adj* □ heilkräftig, Heil...: ⁓ *herbs pl* Heilkräuter *pl*.

med·i·cine ['medsɪn] *s* **1.** Medizin *f*, Arznei *f*: *give s.o. a dose* (*od. taste*) *of his own* ⁓ *fig.* es j-m in *od.* mit gleicher Münze heimzahlen. **2.** Medizin *f*, Heilkunde *f*; innere Medizin. ⁓ *ball s Sport:* Medizinball *m*. ⁓ *chest s* Hausapotheke *f*. ⁓ *man s* (*irr man*) Medizinmann *m*.

med·i·co ['medɪkəʊ] *pl* **-cos** *s* F Mediziner *m* (*Arzt u. Student*).

me·di·e·val [,medɪ'i:vl] *adj* □ mittelalterlich.

me·di·o·cre [,mi:dɪ'əʊkə] *adj* mittelmäßig. **me·di·oc·ri·ty** [,⁓'ɒkrətɪ] *s* Mittelmäßigkeit *f*.

med·i·tate ['medɪteɪt] I *v/i* (*on*) nachdenken (über *acc*), grübeln (über *acc, dat*), *a. engS.* meditieren (über *acc*). II *v/t* erwägen: ⁓ *revenge* auf Rache sinnen. **,med·i'ta·tion** *s* Nachdenken *n*, Grübeln *n; engS.* Meditation *f*.

me·di·um ['mi:djəm] I *pl* **-di·a** ['⁓djə],

-di·ums s **1.** _fig._ Mitte f, Mittelweg m. **2.** _biol. etc_ Medium n, Träger m. **3.** ☿ (_a. künstlerisches etc_) Medium n, Mittel n: → **advertising** II. **4.** _Hypnose, Parapsychologie_: Medium n. **II** _adj_ **5.** mittler, Mittel..., _a._ mittelmäßig. **6.** _gastr._ englisch (_Steak_). '**~-priced** _adj_ der mittleren Preislage. '**~-range** _adj_: ~ **missile** ✕ Mittelstreckenrakete f. '**~-size(d)** _adj_ mittelgroß: ~ **car** _mot._ Mittelklassewagen m. '**~-term** _adj_ mittelfristig (_Planung etc_). ~ **wave** ⚡ Mittelwelle f: **on** ~ auf Mittelwelle.

med·ley ['medlɪ] s **1.** Gemisch n, _contp._ Mischmasch m, Durcheinander n. **2.** ♩ Medley n, Potpourri n.

meek [miːk] _adj_ □ **1.** sanft(mütig). **2.** bescheiden, _contp._ unterwürfig: **be** ~ **and mild** sich alles gefallen lassen. '**meek·ness** s **1.** Sanftmut f. **2.** Bescheidenheit f; _contp._ Unterwürfigkeit f.

meet [miːt] (_irr_) **I** _v/t_ **1.** begegnen (_dat_); treffen, sich treffen mit. **2.** _j-n_ kennenlernen: **when I first met him** als ich s-e Bekanntschaft machte; **pleased to ~ you** F sehr erfreut(, Sie kennenzulernen). **3.** _j-n_ abholen (**at the station** von der Bahn). **4.** → **halfway** 3. **5.** (_feindlich_) zs.-treffen mit, (_Sport a._) treffen auf (_acc_): → **fate** 1. **6.** _fig._ entgegentreten (_dat_). **7.** münden in (_acc_) (_Straße acc_); stoßen _od._ treffen auf (_acc_): **there is more to it than ~s the eye** da steckt mehr dahinter. **8.** _j-s Wünschen_ entgegenkommen, entsprechen, _e-r Forderung, Verpflichtung_ nachkommen, _Unkosten_ bestreiten, decken. **II** _v/i_ **9.** zs.-kommen, -treten. **10.** sich begegnen, sich (_a. verabredungsgemäß_) treffen: ~ **again** sich wiedersehen; **our eyes met** unsere Blicke trafen sich. **11.** (_feindlich_) zs.-stoßen, (_Sport_) aufeinandertreffen. **12.** sich kennenlernen: **we have met before** wir kennen uns schon. **13.** sich vereinigen (_Straßen etc_); sich berühren (_a. Interessen etc_). **14.** genau zs.-passen, sich decken: → **end** 6. **15.** ~ **with** zs.-treffen mit; sich treffen mit; erleben, erleiden: ~ **with an accident** e-n Unfall erleiden, verunglücken; ~ **with a refusal** auf Ablehnung stoßen; → **approval** 2.

meet·ing ['miːtɪŋ] s **1.** Begegnung f, Zs.-treffen n, -kunft f. **2.** Versammlung f, Konferenz f, Tagung f: **at a** ~ auf e-r Versammlung; ~ **of members** Mitgliederversammlung. **3.** _Sport:_ Veranstaltung f. ~ **place** s **1.** Tagungs-, Versammlungsort m. **2.** Treffpunkt m.

meg·a·lo·ma·ni·a [ˌmeɡələʊˈmeɪnjə] s Größenwahn m. ˌ**meg·a·lo'ma·ni·ac** [~nɪæk] _adj_ größenwahnsinnig.

meg·a·phone ['meɡəfəʊn] s Megaphon f.

mel·an·chol·y ['melənkəlɪ] **I** s **1.** Melancholie f, Schwermut f. **II** _adj_ **2.** melancholisch, schwermütig. **3.** traurig, schmerzlich (_Pflicht etc_).

mel·low ['meləʊ] **I** _adj_ □ **1.** reif, weich (_Obst_). **2.** ausgereift, lieblich (_Wein_). **3.** sanft, mild (_Licht_), zart (_Farbton_). **4.** _fig._ gereift, abgeklärt (_Person_). **5.** angeheitert, beschwipst. **II** _v/t_ **6.** reifen lassen (_a. fig._). **III** _v/i_ **7.** reifen (_a. fig._).

me·lo·di·ous [mɪˈləʊdjəs] _adj_ □ melodisch, melodiös.

mel·o·dra·ma ['meləʊˌdrɑːmə] s Melodrama(n) n (_a. fig._). ˌ**mel·o·dra·mat·ic** [~drəˈmætɪk] _adj_ (**~ally**) melodramatisch.

mel·o·dy ['melədɪ] s Melodie f.

melt [melt] (_a. irr_) **I** _v/i_ **1.** (zer)schmelzen, sich auflösen: ~ **in the mouth** auf der Zunge zergehen; ~ **away** _fig._ sich auflösen (_Menge_); dahinschmelzen (_Geld_); → **into tears** _fig._ in Tränen zerfließen; → **butter** 1. **2.** verschmelzen (_Farben, Ränder etc_): ~ **into** übergehen in (_acc_). **II** _v/t_ **3.** schmelzen, _Butter_ zerlassen: ~ **down** einschmelzen. **4.** _fig. j-s Herz_ erweichen.

melt·ing ['meltɪŋ] _adj_ weich, angenehm (_Stimme_). ~ **fur·nace** ⊕ Schmelzofen m. ~ **point** s _phys._ Schmelzpunkt m. ~ **pot** s Schmelztiegel m (_a. fig._).

mem·ber ['membə] s **1.** Mitglied n, Angehörige m, f: ~ **of the family** Familienmitglied; ♀ **of Parliament** _Br._ Unterhausabgeordnete m, f; ♀ **of Congress** _Am._ Mitglied des Repräsentantenhauses; **~s only** (Zutritt) nur für Mitglieder; **~-country** Mitgliedsland n. **2.** _anat._ Glied(maße f) n; (männliches) Glied. '**mem·ber·ship** s **1.** (**of**) Mitgliedschaft f (bei), Zugehörigkeit f (zu): ~ **card** Mitgliedsausweis m; ~ **fee** Mitgliedsbeitrag m. **2.** Mitgliederzahl f: **have**

a ~ of 200 200 Mitglieder haben.

mem·brane ['membreɪn] *s* Membran(e) *f.*

mem·o ['meməʊ] *pl* **-os** *s* F Memo *n* (→ **memorandum** 1).

mem·oirs ['memwɑːz] *s pl* Memoiren *pl.*

mem·o·ra·ble ['memərəbl] *adj* □ **1.** denkwürdig. **2.** einprägsam. **3.** unvergeßlich.

mem·o·ran·dum [ˌmemə'rændəm] *pl* **-da** [~də], **-dums** *s* **1.** (*a.* Akten)Vermerk *m,* (-)Notiz *f; (geschäftliche)* Kurzmitteilung. **2.** *pol.* Memorandum *n,* Denkschrift *f.*

me·mo·ri·al [mə'mɔːrɪəl] **I** *adj* **1.** Gedenk..., Gedächtnis...: ♀ *Day Am.* Gedenktag *m* für die Gefallenen (*30. Mai*); ~ *service* Gedenkgottesdienst *m.* **II** *s* **2.** Denk-, Ehrenmal *n,* Gedenkstätte *f* (*to* für). **3.** Gedenkfeier *f* (*to* für). **4.** *mst pl* Erinnerung *f: childhood memories* Kindheitserinnerungen. **5.** *Computer:* Speicher *m.*

mem·o·rize ['meməraɪz] *v/t* auswendig lernen, sich einprägen.

mem·o·ry ['meməri] *s* **1.** Gedächtnis *n: from* (*od. by*) ~ aus dem Gedächtnis, auswendig; ~ *for names* Namensgedächtnis; *to the best of my* ~ soweit ich mich erinnern kann; *call to* ~ sich *et.* ins Gedächtnis zurückrufen; → *sieve* I. **2.** Andenken *n,* Erinnerung *f* (*of* an *acc*): *in* ~ *of* zum Andenken an. **3.** *mst pl* Erinnerung *f: childhood memories* Kindheitserinnerungen. **4.** *Computer:* Speicher *m.*

men [men] *pl von* **man**: ~*'s magazine* Herrenmagazin *n;* ~*'s room Am.* Herrentoilette *f.*

men·ace ['menəs] **I** *v/t* bedrohen. **II** *s* Drohung *f;* Bedrohung *f* (*to gen*).

mend [mend] **I** *v/t* **1.** ausbessern, reparieren, flicken, *Strümpfe etc* flicken; *fig. Freundschaft etc* kitten. **2.** (ver)bessern: ~ *one's ways* sich bessern. **II** *v/i* **3.** sich bessern (*a. Person*). **4.** *be* ~ *ing* auf dem Weg der Besserung sein. **III** *s* **5.** Besserung *f: be on the* ~ → 4. **6.** ausgebesserte Stelle.

men·da·cious [men'deɪʃəs] *adj* □ lügnerisch, verlogen. **men·dac·i·ty** [~'dæsətɪ] *s* Verlogenheit *f.*

me·ni·al ['miːnjəl] *adj* □ untergeordnet, niedrig (*Arbeit*).

men·in·gi·tis [ˌmenɪn'dʒaɪtɪs] *s* ✠ Hirnhautentzündung *f.*

men·o·pause ['menəʊpɔːz] *s physiol.*

Wechseljahre *pl: go through the* ~ in den Wechseljahren sein.

men·stru·ate ['menstrʊeɪt] *v/i physiol.* menstruieren. **,men·stru·a·tion** *s* Menstruation *f.*

men·tal ['mentl] *adj* (□ → **mentally**) **1.** geistig, Geistes...: ~ *arithmetic* Kopfrechnen *n;* ~ *deficiency* (*od. derangement*) Geistesstörung *f;* ~ *disease* (*od. illness*) Geisteskrankheit *f;* ~ *handicap* geistige Behinderung; ~ *hospital* psychiatrische Klinik, Nervenheilanstalt *f; make a* ~ *note of s.th.* sich *et.* (vor)merken; ~ *state* Geisteszustand *m.* **2.** seelisch, psychisch: ~ *cruelty* ✠ seelische Grausamkeit. **men·tal·i·ty** [~'tælətɪ] *s* Mentalität *f.* **men·tal·ly** ['~təlɪ] *adv* **1.** geistig, geistes...: ~ *deficient* (*od. deranged*) geistesgestört; ~ *handicapped* geistig behindert; ~ *ill* geisteskrank. **2.** im Geist, in Gedanken.

men·thol ['menθɒl] *s* ✿ Menthol *n.*

men·tion ['menʃn] **I** *s* Erwähnung *f: get* (*od. be given*) *a* ~ erwähnt werden. **II** *v/t* erwähnen (*to* gegenüber); *don't* ~ *it!* bitte (sehr)!, gern geschehen!; *not to* ~ ganz abgesehen *od.* zu schweigen von; nicht zu vergessen; → *worth* I.

men·u ['menjuː] *s* Speise(n)karte *f.*

mer·can·tile ['mɜːkəntaɪl] *adj* Handels...: ~ *law* Handelsrecht *n.*

mer·ce·nar·y ['mɜːsɪnərɪ] *s* ✗ Söldner *m.*

mer·chan·dise ['mɜːtʃəndaɪz] *s* Ware(n *pl*) *f.*

mer·chant ['mɜːtʃənt] **I** *s* (Groß)Händler *m,* (Groß)Kaufmann *m.* **II** *adj* Handels...: → *ship.*

mer·ci·ful ['mɜːsɪfʊl] *adj* □ (*to*) barmherzig (gegen), gnädig (*dat*). '**mer·ci·less** *adj* □ unbarmherzig, erbarmungslos.

mer·cu·ri·al [mɜː'kjʊərɪəl] *adj* □ **1.** Quecksilber... **2.** *fig.* quecksilb(e)rig, quicklebendig; sprunghaft.

mer·cu·ry ['mɜːkjʊrɪ] *s* **1.** ♀ *ast., myth.* Merkur *m.* **2.** ✿ Quecksilber *n.*

mer·cy ['mɜːsɪ] *s* **1.** Barmherzigkeit *f,* Erbarmen *n,* Gnade *f: without* ~ → *merciless; be at s.o.'s* ~ j-m (auf) Gedeih u. Verderb) ausgeliefert sein; *have* ~ *on* Mitleid *od.* Erbarmen haben mit. **2.** (wahres) Glück, (wahrer) Segen. ~ *kill·ing* *s* Sterbehilfe *f.*

mere [mɪə] *adj* bloß, nichts als: *a* ~ *ex-*

cuse nur e-e Ausrede; **~ imagination** bloße od. reine Einbildung. **'mere·ly** adv bloß, nur, lediglich.

merge [mɜːdʒ] **I** v/i **1.** (**in, into**) verschmelzen (mit), aufgehen (in dat.). **2.** zs.-laufen (Straßen etc). **3.** ✝ fusionieren. **II** v/t **4.** verschmelzen (**in, into** mit). **5.** ✝ fusionieren. **'merg·er** s ✝ Fusion f.

me·rid·i·an [mə'rɪdɪən] s **1.** geogr. Meridian m, Längenkreis m. **2.** ast. Kulminationspunkt m; fig. Gipfel m, Zenit m, Höhepunkt m.

mer·it ['merɪt] **I** s **1.** Verdienst n: **a man of ~** ein verdienter od. verdienstvoller Mann. **2.** Wert m; Vorzug m: **work of ~** bedeutendes Werk; **of artistic ~** von künstlerischem Wert. **II** v/t **3.** Lohn, Strafe etc verdienen. **mer·i·toc·ra·cy** [ˌ~'tɒkrəsɪ] s Leistungsgesellschaft f.

mer·maid ['mɜːmeɪd] s Meerjungfrau f, Nixe f.

mer·ri·ment ['merɪmənt] s **1.** Fröhlichkeit f, Lustigkeit f, Ausgelassenheit f. **2.** Gelächter n, Heiterkeit f.

mer·ry ['merɪ] adj □ **1.** lustig (a. Streich etc), fröhlich, ausgelassen: **~ Christmas!** fröhliche od. frohe Weihnachten! **2.** F beschwipst, angeheitert: **get ~** sich e-n anludeln.

mesh [meʃ] **I** s **1.** Masche f. **2.** mst pl fig. Netz n, Schlingen pl: **~ of lies** Lügennetz, -gespinst n; **be caught in the ~es of the law** sich in den Schlingen des Gesetzes verfangen (haben). **II** v/t **3.** in e-m Netz fangen. **III** v/i **4.** ineinandergreifen (Zahnräder; a. fig.). **5.** fig. passen (**with** zu), zs.-passen.

mess [mes] **I** s **1.** Unordnung f, a. fig. Durcheinander n; Schmutz m; fig. Patsche f, Klemme f: **in a ~** in Unordnung; schmutzig; **be in a nice ~** ganz schön in der Klemme sein od. sitzen od. stecken; **make a ~ of →** 3. **2.** ✗ Messe f: **officers' ~** Offiziersmesse, -kasino n. **II** v/t **3.** a. **~ up** in Unordnung bringen, a. fig. durcheinanderbringen; schmutzig machen; fig. verpfuschen; Pläne etc über den Haufen werfen. **III** v/i **4.** **~ about** (od. **around**) herumspielen, b.s. a. herumbasteln (**with** an dat).

mes·sage ['mesɪdʒ] s **1.** Mitteilung f, Nachricht f: **can I give him a ~?** kann ich ihm et. ausrichten?; **leave a ~ (for**

s.o.) (j-m) e-e Nachricht hinterlassen; **can I take a ~?** kann ich et. ausrichten?; **get the ~** F kapieren. **2.** fig. Anliegen n (e-s Künstlers etc); Aussage f (e-s Romans etc).

mes·sen·ger ['mesɪndʒə] s **1.** Bote m: **by ~** durch Boten. **2.** fig. (Vor)Bote m. **~ boy** s Laufbursche m, Botenjunge m.

Mes·si·ah [mɪ'saɪə] s eccl. der Messias.

'mess·up s Durcheinander n (a. fig.).

mess·y ['mesɪ] adj □ **1.** schmutzig (a. fig.). **2.** fig. verfahren.

met [met] pret u. pp von **meet**.

met·a·bol·ic [ˌmetə'bɒlɪk] adj physiol. Stoffwechsel... **me·tab·o·lism** [me'tæbəlɪzəm] s physiol. Stoffwechsel m.

met·al ['metl] **I** s Metall n. **II** adj → **metallic** 1. **me·tal·lic** [mɪ'tælɪk] adj (**~ally**) **1.** metallen, Metall... **2.** metallisch (glänzend od. klingend). **met·al·lur·gy** [me'tælədʒɪ] s Metallurgie f, Hüttenkunde f.

'met·al-ˌpro·cess·ing adj metallverarbeitend.

met·a·mor·pho·sis [ˌmetə'mɔːfəsɪs] pl **-ses** [ˌ~siːz] s Metamorphose f, Verwandlung f.

met·a·phor ['metəfə] s Metapher f. **met·a·phor·i·cal** [ˌ~'fɒrɪkl] adj □ metaphorisch, bildlich.

met·a·phys·i·cal [ˌmetə'fɪzɪkl] adj □ **1.** phls. metaphysisch. **2.** übersinnlich. **met·a·phys·ics** s pl (sg konstruiert) phls. Metaphysik f.

me·tas·ta·sis [mə'tæstəsɪs] pl **-ses** [ˌ~siːz] s ⚕ Metastase f; Metastasenbildung f.

me·te·or ['miːtɪɔː] s ast. Meteor m. **me·te·or·ic** [ˌmiːtɪ'ɒrɪk] adj (**~ally**) **1.** ast. meteorisch, Meteor... **2.** fig. kometenhaft (Aufstieg etc). **me·te·or·ite** ['miːtɪəraɪt] s ast. Meteorit m.

me·te·or·o·log·i·cal [ˌmiːtɪərə'lɒdʒɪkl] adj □ meteorologisch, Wetter..., Witterungs...: **~ office** Wetteramt n. **me·te·or·ol·o·gist** [ˌ~'rɒlədʒɪst] s Meteorologe m. **me·te·or·ol·o·gy** [ˌ~dʒɪ] s Meteorologie f.

me·ter¹ ['miːtə] Am. → **metre**.

me·ter² [ˌ~] s ⚙ Meßgerät n, Zähler m: **~ maid** bsd. Am. F Politesse f; **~ reader** Gas- od. Stromableser m.

meth·od ['meθəd] s **1.** Methode f, Verfahren n: **the ~ of doing s.th.** die Art u. Weise, et. zu tun. **2.** Methode f, System *n*, Planmäßigkeit *f*: **work with ~** methodisch arbeiten. **me·thod·i·cal** [mɪˈθɒdɪkl] *adj* □ methodisch, systematisch, planmäßig.

meth·yl [ˈmeθɪl] *s* 🔧 Methyl *n*: **~ alcohol** Methylalkohol *m*.

me·tic·u·lous [mɪˈtɪkjʊləs] *adj* □ peinlich genau, akribisch.

me·tre [ˈmiːtə] *s bsd. Br.* **1.** Meter *m*, *n*. **2.** Versmaß *n*.

met·ric [ˈmetrɪk] **I** *adj* (**~ally**) metrisch: **~ system** metrisches (Maß- u. Gewichts)System. **II** *s pl (sg konstruiert)* Metrik *f*, Verslehre *f*.

me·trop·o·lis [mɪˈtrɒpəlɪs] *s* Metropole *f*, Hauptstadt *f*. **met·ro·pol·i·tan** [ˌmetrəˈpɒlɪtən] **I** *adj* ... der Hauptstadt. **II** *s* Bewohner(in) der Hauptstadt.

met·tle [ˈmetl] *s* Mut *m*; Eifer *m*, Feuer *n*: **put s.o. on his ~** j-n zur Aufbietung all s-r Kräfte zwingen. **met·tle·some** [ˈ~səm] *adj* mutig; eifrig, feurig.

mew [mjuː] *v/i* miauen.

Mex·i·can [ˈmeksɪkən] **I** *adj* mexikanisch. **II** *s* Mexikaner(in).

mez·za·nine [ˈmetsəniːn] *s* △ Zwischen-, Halbgeschoß *n*.

mi·aow [miːˈaʊ] *v/i* miauen.

mice [maɪs] *pl von* **mouse**.

mick·ey [ˈmɪkɪ] *s*: **take the ~ out of s.o.** *bsd. Br.* F j-n auf den Arm nehmen.

mi·cro... [ˈmaɪkrəʊ] *in Zssgn* Mikro..., (sehr) klein.

mi·crobe [ˈmaɪkrəʊb] *s biol.* Mikrobe *f*.

ˈmi·cro|·chip *s* ⚡ Mikrochip *m*. **ˈ~·com·put·er** *s* Mikrocomputer *m*. **~·fiche** [ˈ~fiːʃ] *s* Mikrofiche *m*. **ˈ~·film** **I** *s* Mikrofilm *m*. **II** *v/t* auf Mikrofilm aufnehmen. **ˌ~·ˈor·gan·ism** *s biol.* Mikroorganismus *m*.

mi·cro·phone [ˈmaɪkrəfəʊn] *s* Mikrophon *f*: **at the ~** am Mikrophon.

mi·cro·scope [ˈmaɪkrəskəʊp] **I** *s* Mikroskop *n*. **II** *v/t* mikroskopisch untersuchen. **mi·cro·scop·ic** [ˌ~ˈskɒpɪk] *adj* (**~ally**) **1.** mikroskopisch. **2.** mikroskopisch klein.

mi·cro·wave [ˈmaɪkrəweɪv] *s* ⚡ Mikrowelle *f*: **~ oven** Mikrowellenherd *m*.

mid [mɪd] *adj attr. od. in Zssgn* mittler..., Mittel...: **in ~April** Mitte April; **be in one's ~-forties** Mitte vierzig sein. **ˌ~·ˈair** *s*: **in ~** in der Luft; **~ collision** Zs.-stoß *m* in der Luft. **ˈ~·day** **I** *s* Mit-

tag *m*. **II** *adj* mittägig, Mittag(s)...

mid·dle [ˈmɪdl] **I** *adj* **1.** mittler, Mittel...: **~ classes** *pl* Mittelstand *m*; **~ ear** *anat.* Mittelohr *n*; **~ finger** Mittelfinger *m*; **~ name** zweiter Vorname; → **management** 2. **II** *s* **2.** Mitte *f*: **in the ~** in der Mitte; **in the ~ of** in der Mitte (*gen*), mitten in (*dat*); **in the ~ of July** Mitte Juli; **in the ~ of the street** mitten auf der Straße. **3.** Taille *f*. **4.** mittlerer Teil, Mittelstück *n*. **~ age** *s* mittleres Alter: **be in ~** mittleren Alters sein. ♀ **Ag·es** *s pl das* Mittelalter *n*. ♀ **~·ˈdis·tance** *adj Sport:* Mittelstrecken... ♀ **East** *s geogr. der* Nahe Osten. **~·man** *s (irr man) s* **1.** Mittelsmann *m*. **2.** ✝ Zwischenhändler *m*. **ˌ~·of-the-ˈroad** *adj bsd. pol.* gemäßigt. **ˈ~·weight** *s Sport:* Mittelgewicht(ler *m*) *n*.

mid·dling [ˈmɪdlɪŋ] **I** *adj von* mittlerer Größe *od.* Güte, mittelmäßig (*a. contp.*): **how are you? fair to ~** so einigermaßen, mittelprächtig. **II** *adv* F leidlich, einigermaßen.

ˌmidˈfield *s bsd. Fußball:* Mittelfeld *n*: **in ~** im Mittelfeld; **~ man** (*od.* **player**) Mittelfeldspieler *m*.

midge [mɪdʒ] *s zo.* Mücke *f*.

midg·et [ˈmɪdʒɪt] **I** *s* Zwerg *m*, Knirps *m*. **II** *adj* Zwerg..., Miniatur..., Kleinst...

mid·land [ˈmɪdlənd] *s*: **the ~s** *pl* Mittelengland *n*. **ˈ~·life cri·sis** *s (irr crisis) psych.* Midlife-crisis *f*. **ˈ~·night** **I** *s* Mitternacht *f*: **at ~** um Mitternacht. **II** *adj* Mitternachts...: **~ sun**; **burn the ~ oil** bis spät in die Nacht arbeiten *od.* aufbleiben. **ˈ~·point** *s*: **be at ~** die Hälfte hinter sich haben. **ˈ~·sum·mer** **I** *s* **1.** Hochsommer *m*. **2.** *ast.* Sommersonnenwende *f*. **II** *adj* **3.** hochsommerlich, Hochsommer... **ˌ~·ˈway** *adj a. fig.* auf halbem Weg (**between** zwischen *dat*). **ˈ~·wife** *s (irr wife)* Hebamme *f*. **ˌ~·ˈwin·ter** *s* **1.** Mitte *f* des Winters. **2.** *ast.* Wintersonnenwende *f*.

might¹ [maɪt] *s*: **with ~ and main** mit aller Kraft *od.* Gewalt.

might² [~] *pret von* **may²**.

might·y [ˈmaɪtɪ] **I** *adj* □ mächtig, gewaltig (*beide a. fig.*). **II** *adv* F ungeheuer: **~ easy** kinderleicht; **~ fine** prima.

mi·graine [ˈmiːgreɪn] *s* ✚ Migräne *f*.

mi·grant [ˈmaɪgrənt] → **migratory**.

mi·grate [maɪˈgreɪt] *v/i* (ab-, aus)wandern, (*a. orn.* fort)ziehen. **mi·gra·tion** *s* **1.** Wanderung *f* (*a.* 🐦, *zo.*). **2.** Abwandern *n*, Fortziehen *n*. **mi·gra·to·ry** [ˈ~grətəri] *adj* Wander..., Zug...: **~ bird** Zugvogel *m*; **~ worker** Wanderarbeiter *m*.

mike [maɪk] *s* F Mikro *n* (*Mikrophon*).

mild [maɪld] *adj* □ mild (*Strafe, Wein, Wetter etc*), (*Licht etc a.*) sanft, (*Fieber, Zigarre etc a.*) leicht: **to put it ~ly** gelinde gesagt; **that's putting it ~ly** das ist gar kein Ausdruck.

mil·dew [ˈmɪldjuː] **I** *s* **1.** 🌿 Mehltau *m*. **2.** Schimmel *m*, Moder *m*. **II** *v/i* **3.** schimm(e)lig *od.* mod(e)rig werden.

mild·ness [ˈmaɪldnɪs] *s* Milde *f*.

mile [maɪl] *s* Meile *f*: **~s apart** meilenweit auseinander; *fig.* himmelweit (voneinander) entfernt; **~s better** F wesentlich besser; **for ~s** meilenweit; **it sticks out a ~** F wie ein Blinder; **talk a ~ a minute** F wie ein Maschinengewehr *od.* Wasserfall reden.

mile·age [ˈmaɪlɪdʒ] *s* **1.** zurückgelegte Meilenzahl *od.* Fahrtstrecke, Meilenstand *m*: **~ indicator** (*od.* **recorder**) *mot.* Meilenzähler *m*. **2.** *a.* **~ allowance** Meilengeld *n*.

mile·om·e·ter [maɪˈlɒmɪtə] *s mot.* Meilenzähler *m*.

ˈmile·stone *s* Meilenstein *m* (*a. fig.*).

mil·i·tant [ˈmɪlɪtənt] **I** *adj* □ **1.** kriegführend. **2.** militant. **II** *s* **3.** militante Person, militantes Mitglied. **mil·i·ta·rism** [ˈ~tərɪzəm] *s* Militarismus *m*. **ˈmil·i·ta·rist** *s* Militarist *m*. **ˌmil·i·ta·ˈris·tic** *adj* (**~ally**) militaristisch. **ˈmil·i·tar·y** **I** *adj* □ militärisch, Militär...: **~ academy** Militärakademie *f*; **of ~ age** in wehrpflichtigem Alter; **~ cemetery** Soldatenfriedhof *m*; **~ dictatorship** Militärdiktatur *f*; **~ government** Militärregierung *f*; **~ police** Militärpolizei *f*; **do one's ~ service** s-n Militärdienst ableisten. **II** *s* (*pl konstruiert*): **the ~** das Militär.

mi·li·tia [mɪˈlɪʃə] *s* Miliz *f*, Bürgerwehr *f*. **mi·li·tia·man** [~mən] *s* (*irr man*) Milizsoldat *m*.

milk [mɪlk] **I** *s* Milch *f* (*a.* 🌿, 🐄): **land of ~ and honey** *fig.* Schlaraffenland *n*; **it's no use crying over spilt ~** geschehen ist geschehen. **II** *v/t* melken (*a. fig.*). **III** *v/i*

Milch geben. **~ bar** *s* Milchbar *f*. **~ choc·o·late** *s* Vollmilchschokolade *f*. **~ float** *s Br.* Milchwagen *m*. **~ glass** *s* Milchglas *n*. **~·man** [ˈ~mən] *s* (*irr man*) Milchmann *m*. **~ pow·der** *s* Milchpulver *n*, Trockenmilch *f*. **~ shake** *s* Milchshake *m*. **~·sop** *s* Weichling *m*, Muttersöhnchen *n*. **~ tooth** *s* (*irr tooth*) Milchzahn *m*.

milk·y [ˈmɪlkɪ] *adj* □ **1.** milchig. **2.** mit (viel) Milch (*Kaffee etc*). ♀ **Way** *s ast.* Milchstraße *f*.

mill [mɪl] **I** *s* **1.** *allg.* Mühle *f*: **go through the ~** *fig.* e-e harte Schule durchmachen; **put s.o. through the ~** *fig.* j-n hart rannehmen. **2.** Fabrik *f*, Werk *n*: → **rolling mill, spinning mill. II** *v/t* **3.** *Korn etc* mahlen. **4.** ⚙ *allg.* verarbeiten. **III** *v/i* **5.** *a.* **~ about** (*od.* **around**) herumlaufen: **~ing crowd** wogende Menge, (Menschen)Gewühl *n*.

mil·len·ni·um [mɪˈleniəm] *pl* **-ums, -a** [~ə] *s* Jahrtausend *n*.

mil·le·pede [ˈmɪlipiːd] *s zo.* Tausendfüßer *m*.

mill·er [ˈmɪlə] *s* Müller *m*.

mil·li·gram(me) [ˈmɪlɪgræm] *s* Milligramm *n*.

mil·li·me·ter *Am.*, **mil·li·me·tre** *bsd. Br.* [ˈmɪlɪˌmiːtə] *s* Millimeter *m*, *n*.

mil·lion [ˈmɪljən] *s* Million *f*: **feel like a ~ dollars** F sich ganz prächtig fühlen. **mil·lion·aire** [ˌ~ˈneə] *s* Millionär(in).

ˈmill·pond *s* Mühlteich *m*: (**as**) **smooth as a ~** spiegelglatt (*Meer etc*). **ˈ~·stone** *s* Mühlstein *m*: **be a ~ round s.o.'s neck** *fig.* j-m ein Klotz am Bein sein.

mime [maɪm] **I** *s* **1.** Pantomime *f*. **2.** Pantomime *m*. **II** *v/t* **3.** (panto)mimisch darstellen. **4.** mimen, nachahmen. **III** *v/i* **5.** *TV etc* Playback singen *od.* spielen. **ˈmim·ic·ry** *s* **1.** Nachahmung *f*. **2.** *zo.* Mimikry *f*.

mim·ing [ˈmaɪmɪŋ] *s TV etc* Playback *n*.

mim·ic [ˈmɪmɪk] **I** *adj* **1.** mimisch. **2.** nachgeahmt, Schein... **II** *s* **3.** Nachahmer *m*, Imitator *m*. **III** *v/t pret u. pp* **-icked 4.** nachahmen (*a. biol.*).

mi·mo·sa [mɪˈməʊzə] *s* ♀ Mimose *f*.

min·a·ret [ˈmɪnəret] *s* △ Minarett *n*.

mince [mɪns] **I** *v/t* zerhacken, (zer-)schneiden: **~ meat** Fleisch durchdrehen, Hackfleisch machen; **~d meat** Hackfleisch *n*; **not to ~ matters** (*od.*

one's words) *fig.* kein Blatt vor den Mund nehmen. **II** *v/i* geziert *od.* affektiert sprechen; tänzeln, trippeln. **III** *s bsd. Br.* Hackfleisch *n.* '**~meat** *s* **1.** Hackfleisch *n:* **make ~ of** *fig.* aus *j-m* Hackfleisch machen; *Argument etc* (in der Luft) zerreißen. **2.** Pastetenfüllung *f.* **~ pie** *s* gefüllte Pastete.

minc·er ['mɪnsə] *s* Fleischwolf *m.* '**minc·ing** *adj* □ **1. ~ machine** Fleischwolf *m.* **2.** geziert, affektiert; tänzelnd, trippelnd.

mind [maɪnd] **I** *s* **1.** Sinn *m*, Gemüt *n*, Herz *n:* **have s.th. on one's ~** et. auf dem Herzen haben. **2.** Verstand *m*, Geist *m:* **before one's ~'s eye** vor s-m geistigen Auge; **be out of one's ~** nicht (recht) bei Sinnen sein; **enter s.o.'s ~** j-m in den Sinn kommen; **lose one's ~** den Verstand verlieren; **put s.th. out of one's ~** sich et. aus dem Kopf schlagen; **read s.o.'s ~** j-s Gedanken lesen; **~ presence.** **3.** Kopf *m*, Geist *m* (*Person*). **4.** Ansicht *f*, Meinung *f:* **to my ~** m-r Ansicht nach, m-s Erachtens; **change one's ~** es sich anders überlegen, s-e Meinung ändern; **give s.o. a piece of one's ~** j-m gründlich die Meinung sagen; **speak one's ~ (to s.o.)** (j-m) s-e Meinung sagen. **5.** Neigung *f*, Lust *f*, Absicht *f:* **have s.th. in ~** et. im Sinn haben; **have a good (half a) ~ to do s.th.** gute (nicht übel) Lust haben, et. zu tun; **make up one's ~** sich entschließen, e-n Entschluß fassen; zu der Überzeugung kommen (**that** daß), sich klarwerden (**about** über *acc*). **6.** Erinnerung *f*, Gedächtnis *n:* **bear** (*od.* **keep**) **in ~** (immer) denken an *acc*, et. nicht vergessen; → **stick²** 7. **II** *v/t* **7.** achtgeben auf (*acc*): **~ the step!** Vorsicht, Stufe!; *in* **~ (you)** wohlgemerkt; allerdings; **never ~!** macht nichts!, ist schon gut! **11.** et. dagegen haben: *I don't* **~** meinetwegen, von mir aus

(*gern*). '**~-**,**bend·ing** *adj* F (nahezu) unfaßbar *od.* unverständlich. '**~-**,**blow-ing,** '**~-**,**bog·gling** *adj* F irr(e).

mind·ed ['maɪndɪd] *adj in Zssgn* ...gesinnt; *religiös, technisch etc* veranlagt; ...begeistert. '**mind·er** *s* Aufseher *m*; Aufpasser *m.*

'**mind-ex,pand·ing** *adj* bewußtseinserweiternd.

mind·ful ['maɪndfʊl] *adj* □ **1.** aufmerksam, achtsam: **be ~ of** achten auf (*acc*). **2.** eingedenk (**of** *gen*): **be ~ of** denken an (*acc*), bedenken. '**mind·less** *adj* □ **1.** (**of**) unbekümmert (um), ohne Rücksicht (auf *acc*). **2.** gedankenlos, blind.

mind read·er *s* Gedankenleser(in).

mine¹ [maɪn] *possessive pron:* **it is ~** es gehört mir; **a friend of ~** ein Freund von mir; **his mother and ~** s-e u. m-e Mutter.

mine² [~] **I** *v/i* **1.** schürfen, graben (**for** nach). **II** *v/t* **2.** *Erz, Kohle* abbauen, gewinnen. **3.** ⚓, ✕ verminen. **4.** *fig.* untergraben, -minieren. **III** *s* **5.** Bergwerk *n*, Zeche *f*, Grube *f*. **6.** ⚓, ✕ Mine *f.* **7.** *fig.* Fundgrube *f* (**of** an *dat*): **he is a ~ of information** er ist e-e gute *od.* reiche Informationsquelle. **~ de·tec·tor** *s* ✕ Minensuchgerät *n.*

min·er ['maɪnə] *s* Bergmann *m*, Kumpel *m.*

min·er·al ['mɪnərəl] **I** *s* **1.** Mineral *n.* **2.** *mst pl Br.* Mineralwasser *n.* **3.** Mineral...: **~ oil; ~ water; ~ coal** Steinkohle *f;* **~ resources** *pl* Bodenschätze *pl.*

min·er·al·og·i·cal [,mɪnərə'lɒdʒɪkl] *adj* □ mineralogisch. **min·er·al·o·gist** [,~'rælədʒɪst] *s* Mineraloge *m.* ,**min·er-'al·o·gy** [~dʒɪ] *s* Mineralogie *f.*

min·gle ['mɪŋgl] **I** *v/i* **1.** sich (ver)mischen (**with** mit). **2.** sich (ein)mischen (**in** in *acc*); sich mischen (**among, with** unter *acc*). **II** *v/t* **3.** (ver)mischen (**with** mit).

min·i... ['mɪnɪ] *in Zssgn* Mini...

min·i·a·ture ['mɪnətʃə] **I** *s* **1.** Miniatur(gemälde *n*) *f.* **2.** *fig.* Miniaturausgabe *f:* **in ~** en miniature, im kleinen. **II** *adj* **3.** Miniatur...

'**min·i·bus** *s* Kleinbus *m.* '**~dress** *s* Minikleid *n.*

min·im ['mɪnɪm] *s* ♩ halbe Note.

min·i·ma ['mɪnɪmə] *pl von* **minimum.**

min·i·mal ['⁓ml] *adj* □ **1.** minimal. **2.** → *minimum* II. **'min·i·mize** *v/t* **1.** auf ein Minimum herabsetzen, möglichst gering halten. **2.** bagatellisieren, herunterspielen. **min·i·mum** ['⁓məm] **I** *pl* **-ma** ['⁓mə] *s* Minimum *n*: *with a ⁓ of* mit e-m Minimum an (*dat*); → *keep to* 3. **II** *adj* Minimal..., Mindest...

min·ing ['maɪnɪŋ] **I** *s* Bergbau *m*. **II** *adj* Bergwerks..., Berg(bau)...: *⁓ disaster* Grubenunglück *n*.

'min·i·skirt *s* Minirock *m*.

min·is·ter ['mɪnɪstə] **I** *s* **1.** *eccl.* Geistliche *m*, Pfarrer *m*. **2.** *pol. bsd. Br.* Minister *m*: **♀** *of Defence* Verteidigungsminister. **II** *v/i* **3.** *⁓ to s.o.* sich um j-n kümmern, für j-n sorgen. **min·is·te·ri·al** [⁓'stɪərɪəl] *adj* □ **1.** *eccl.* geistlich. **2.** *pol. bsd. Br.* ministeriell, Minister...

min·is·tra·tion [ˌmɪnɪ'streɪʃn] *s mst pl* Dienst *m* (**to** an *dat*).

min·is·try ['mɪnɪstrɪ] *s* **1.** *eccl.* geistliches Amt. **2.** *pol. bsd. Br.* Ministerium *n*: **♀** *of Defence* Verteidigungsministerium.

mink [mɪŋk] *s zo.* Nerz *m*.

mi·nor ['maɪnə] **I** *s* **1.** *univ. Am.* Nebenfach *n*. **2.** ⚖ Minderjährige *m, f.* **3.** ♩ Moll *n*. **II** *adj* **4.** kleiner, *fig. a.* unbedeutend, unwichtig. **5.** ⚖ minderjährig. **III** *v/i* **6.** *⁓ in univ. Am.* als *od.* im Nebenfach studieren. **mi·nor·i·ty** [maɪ-'nɒrətɪ] *s* **1.** Minderheit *f*: *be in the* (*od. a*) *⁓* in der Minderheit sein; *⁓ government pol.* Minderheitsregierung *f*. **2.** ⚖ Minderjährigkeit *f*.

mint¹ [mɪnt] *s* **1.** ♣ Minze *f*: *⁓ sauce* Minzsoße *f*. **2.** Pfefferminz *n* (*Bonbon*).

mint² [⁓] **I** *s* **1.** Münze *f*, Münzanstalt *f*. **2.** *a ⁓* (*of money*) F ein Heidengeld. **II** *adj* **3.** ungebraucht (*Münze*), postfrisch (*Briefmarke*): *in ⁓ condition* in einwandfreiem *od.* tadellosem Zustand. **III** *v/t* **4.** Geld, *a. fig. Wort etc* prägen.

min·u·et [ˌmɪnjʊ'et] *s* ♩ Menuett *n*.

mi·nus ['maɪnəs] **I** *prp* ♣ minus, weniger. **2.** F ohne. **II** *adj* **3.** Minus...: *⁓ amount* → 5a; *⁓ sign* → 4. **III** *s* **4.** Minus(zeichen) *n*. **5.** Minus *n*: a) Fehlbetrag *m*, b) Nachteil *m*, c) Mangel *m* (*of an dat*).

min·ute¹ ['mɪnɪt] **I** *s* **1.** Minute *f*: *to the ⁓* auf die Minute (genau); *I won't be a ⁓* ich bin gleich wieder da; ich bin gleich fertig; *ten-⁓* zehnminütig; → *silence* I.

2. Augenblick *m*: *at the last ⁓* in letzter Minute; *in a ⁓* sofort; *just a ⁓!* Moment mal! **3.** *pl* (Sitzungs)Protokoll *n*: *keep the ⁓s* das Protokoll führen. **II** *v/t* **4.** protokollieren.

mi·nute² [maɪ'njuːt] *adj* □ **1.** winzig. **2.** peinlich genau, minuziös.

min·ute| hand *s* Minutenzeiger *m* (*e-r Uhr*). **⁓ steak** *s gastr.* Minutensteak *n*.

minx [mɪŋks] *s* (kleines) Biest.

mir·a·cle ['mɪrəkl] *s* Wunder *n* (*a. fig. of* an *dat*): *as if by* (*a*) *⁓* wie durch ein Wunder; *work* (*perform*) *⁓s* Wunder tun (vollbringen). **mi·rac·u·lous** [mɪ'rækjʊləs] *adj* □ (*a. fig.*), Wunder... **mi'rac·u·lous·ly** *adv* wie durch ein Wunder.

mi·rage ['mɪrɑːʒ] *s* **1.** *phys.* Luftspieg(e)lung *f*, Fata Morgana *f* (*a. fig.*). **2.** *fig.* Illusion *f*.

mire [maɪə] *s* Schlamm *m*: *drag through the ⁓ fig.* in den Schmutz ziehen.

mir·ror ['mɪrə] **I** *s* **1.** Spiegel *m*: *hold up the ⁓ to s.o. fig.* j-m den Spiegel vorhalten. **2.** *fig.* Spiegel(bild *n*) *m*. **II** *v/t* **3.** (wider)spiegeln (*a. fig.*): *be ⁓ed* sich spiegeln (*in in dat*); sich widerbar (*a. fig.*). **⁓ im·age** *s* Spiegelbild *n*. **'⁓-in‚vert·ed** *adj* seitenverkehrt. **⁓ writ·ing** *s* Spiegelschrift *f*.

mirth [mɜːθ] *s* **1.** Fröhlichkeit *f*, Heiterkeit *f*, Freude *f*. **mirth·ful** ['⁓fʊl] *adj* □ fröhlich, heiter, lustig. **'mirth·less** *adj* □ freudlos.

mis... [mɪs] *in Zssgn* miß..., falsch.

mis·ad·ven·ture *s* **1.** Unfall *m*, Unglück(sfall *m*) *n*. **2.** Mißgeschick *n*: *he's had a ⁓* ihm ist ein Mißgeschick passiert.

mis·an·thrope ['mɪsənθrəʊp] *s* Menschenfeind(in), -hasser(in). **mis·an·throp·ic** [⁓'θrɒpɪk] *adj* (*⁓ally*) menschenfeindlich. **mis·an·thro·py** [mɪ-'sænθrəpɪ] *s* Menschenfeindlichkeit *f*, -haß *m*.

mis·ap·ply *v/t* **1.** falsch verwenden. **2.** → *misappropriate* 1.

'mis·ap·pre'hend *v/t* mißverstehen. **'mis·ap·pre'hen·sion** *s* Mißverständnis *n*: *be* (*od. labo[u]r*) *under a ⁓* sich in e-m Irrtum befinden.

mis·ap·pro·pri·ate *v/t* **1.** unterschlagen, veruntreuen. **2.** zweckentfremden. **'mis·ap‚pro·pri'a·tion** *s* **1.** Unterschlagung f, Veruntreuung f. **2.** Zweckentfremdung f.

ˌmis·be'have v/i sich schlecht benehmen, sich danebenbenehmen, (Kind) ungezogen sein. ˌmis·be'hav·io(u)r s schlechtes Benehmen, Ungezogenheit f.

ˌmis'cal·cu·late I v/t falsch berechnen, sich verrechnen in (dat). II v/i sich verrechnen od. verkalkulieren. 'mis,calcu'la·tion s Rechenfehler m, Fehlkalkulation f.

ˌmis'car·riage s 1. Fehlschlag(en n) m, Mißlingen n: ~ of justice ⚖ Fehlurteil n, Justizirrtum m. 2. ⚕ Fehlgeburt f. ˌmis'car·ry v/i 1. fehlschlagen, mißlingen. 2. ⚕ e-e Fehlgeburt haben.

ˌmis·cel·la·ne·ous [ˌmɪsə'leɪnjəs] adj □ ge-, vermischt; verschiedenartig. **mis·cel·la·ny** [mɪ'selənɪ] s 1. Gemisch n. 2. Sammlung f, Sammelband m.

ˌmis'chance s: by ~ durch e-n unglücklichen Zufall.

mis·chief ['mɪstʃɪf] s 1. Unheil n, Schaden m: do ~ Unheil od. Schaden anrichten; **make** ~ Unfrieden stiften (between zwischen dat); **mean** ~ Böses im Schilde führen. **2.** Unfug m, Dummheiten pl: **be up to** ~ et. aushecken. **3.** Übermut m, Ausgelassenheit f: **be full of** ~ immer zu Dummheiten aufgelegt sein. **'~,mak·er** s Unruhestifter(in).

mis·chie·vous ['mɪstʃɪvəs] adj □ 1. boshaft, mutwillig. 2. schelmisch.

ˌmis·con'ceive v/t falsch auffassen, mißverstehen. ˌmis·con'cep·tion s Mißverständnis n.

ˌmis·con'duct I v/t [ˌmɪskən'dʌkt] 1. schlecht führen. 2. ~ o.s. sich schlecht benehmen. II s [ˌmɪs'kɒndʌkt] 3. schlechte Führung. **4.** schlechtes Benehmen. **5.** Verfehlung f.

ˌmis·con'struc·tion s Mißdeutung f, falsche Auslegung. ˌmis·con'strue v/t mißdeuten, falsch auslegen.

ˌmis'count I v/t falsch (aus)zählen. II v/i sich verzählen.

ˌmis'deal v/t u. v/i (irr deal): ~ (the cards) (Kartenspiel) sich vergeben.

ˌmis'deed s Missetat f.

ˌmis·de·mean·o(u)r [ˌmɪsdɪ'miːnə] ⚖ Vergehen n.

ˌmis·di'rect v/t 1. j-n, et. fehl-, irreleiten (a. fig.), j-m den falschen Weg zeigen. **2.** Brief etc falsch adressieren.

mi·ser ['maɪzə] s Geizhals m.

mis·er·a·ble ['mɪzərəbl] adj □ 1. jämmerlich, erbärmlich, kläglich, contp. a. miserabel. **2.** traurig, unglücklich.

mis·er·ly ['maɪzəlɪ] adj geizig.

mis·er·y ['mɪzərɪ] s 1. Elend n, Not f. 2. Trübsal f, Jammer m.

ˌmis'fire I v/i 1. versagen (Schußwaffe). **2.** mot. fehlzünden, aussetzen. **3.** fig. danebengehen (Witz etc), fehlschlagen (Plan etc). II s 4. mot. Fehlzündung f.

'mis'fit s 1. schlechtsitzendes Kleidungsstück. **2.** Außenseiter(in).

ˌmis'for·tune s 1. schweres Schicksal, Unglück n. 2. Unglücksfall m; Mißgeschick n.

ˌmis'giv·ing s Befürchtung f, Zweifel m.

ˌmis'gov·ern v/t schlecht regieren od. verwalten.

ˌmis'guid·ed adj irrig (Entscheidung etc), unangebracht (Optimismus etc).

ˌmis'han·dle v/t 1. et. schlecht behandeln od. handhaben. 2. fig. falsch anpacken.

mis·hap ['mɪshæp] s 1. Unglück(sfall m) n; Mißgeschick n: **he's had a** ~ ihm ist ein Mißgeschick passiert; **without** ~ ohne Zwischenfälle.

ˌmis'hear (irr hear) I v/t falsch hören. II v/i sich verhören.

mish·mash ['mɪʃmæʃ] s Mischmasch m.

ˌmis·in'form v/t j-n falsch informieren (about über acc). ˌmis·in·for'ma·tion s Fehlinformation f.

ˌmis·in'ter·pret v/t mißdeuten, falsch auffassen od. auslegen. 'mis·in,ter·pre'ta·tion s Mißdeutung f, falsche Auslegung.

ˌmis'judge v/t 1. falsch beurteilen, verkennen. 2. falsch einschätzen.

ˌmis'lay v/t (irr lay) et. verlegen.

ˌmis'lead v/t (irr lead) 1. irreführen, täuschen: **be misled** sich täuschen lassen. 2. verführen, -leiten (into doing zu tun).

ˌmis'man·age v/t schlecht verwalten od. führen. ˌmis'man·age·ment s Mißwirtschaft f.

mis·no·mer [ˌmɪs'nəʊmə] s falsche Benennung od. Bezeichnung.

mi·sog·a·mist [mɪ'sɒgəmɪst] s Ehefeind m.

mi·sog·y·nist [mɪ'sɒdʒɪnɪst] s Frauenfeind m.

ˌmisˈplace v/t **1.** et. verlegen. **2.** et. an e-e falsche Stelle legen od. setzen: **~d** fig. unangebracht, deplaziert.

misˈprint I v/t [ˌmisˈprint] verdrucken. **II** s [ˈmisprint] Druckfehler m.

ˌmisproˈnounce v/t falsch aussprechen. **ˈmisproˌnunciˈaˈtion** s falsche Aussprache.

ˌmisquoˈtaˈtion s falsches Zitat. **ˌmisˈquote** v/t falsch zitieren.

ˌmisˈread v/t (irr read) **1.** falsch lesen. **2.** mißdeuten.

ˈmisˌrepreˈsent v/t **1.** falsch darstellen. **2.** entstellen, verdrehen. **ˈmisˌrepreˈsenˈtaˈtion** s **1.** falsche Darstellung. **2.** Entstellung f, Verdrehung f.

miss¹ [mis] s **1.** ℚ (mit folgendem Namen) Fräulein n: ℚ Smith; ℚ America Miß f Amerika. **2.** (ohne folgenden Namen) Fräulein n (Anrede für Lehrerinnen, Kellnerinnen etc).

miss² [~] I v/t **1.** Chance, Zug etc verpassen, Beruf, Ziel etc verfehlen, sich et. entgehen lassen: **~ the boat** (od. bus) F den Anschluß od. e-e Chance verpassen; **~ doing s.th.** versäumen, et. zu tun. **2.** a. **~ out** auslassen, übergehen, -springen. **3.** überhören; übersehen; nicht bemerken; nicht verstehen od. begreifen. **4.** vermissen: **we ~ her very much** sie fehlt uns sehr. **II** v/i **5.** nicht treffen: a) danebenschlagen etc, b) danebengehen (Schuß etc). **6.** mißglücken, -lingen. **7.** **~ out on** et. verpassen; et. weglassen od. nicht berücksichtigen. **III** s **8.** Fehlschuß m, -wurf m etc. **9.** Verpassen n, Verfehlen n: → **near** 9.

ˌmisˈshapen adj mißgebildet, ungestalt.

misˈsile [ˈmisail] s **1.** (Wurf)Geschoß n. **2.** ✗ Rakete f: **~ base** (od. site) Raketen(abschuß)basis f.

missˈing [ˈmisin̩] adj **1.** fehlend: **be ~** fehlen; verschwunden od. weg sein. **2.** (✗ a. **~ in action**) vermißt: **be ~** vermißt sein od. werden.

misˈsion [ˈmiʃn̩] s **1.** (Militär- etc)Mission f. **2.** bsd. pol. Auftrag m, Mission f. **3.** eccl. Mission f. **4.** (innere) Berufung: **~ in life** Lebensaufgabe f; **sense of ~** Sendungsbewußtsein n. **5.** ✓, ✗ Einsatz m.

ˌmisˈspell v/t (a. irr spell) falsch schreiben. **ˌmisˈspellˈing** s Rechtschreibfehler m.

ˌmisˈstate v/t falsch angeben. **ˌmisˈstateˈment** s falsche Angabe.

mist [mist] **I** s **1.** (feiner) Nebel. **2.** fig. Nebel m, Schleier m: **see things through a ~** alles wie durch e-n Schleier sehen; **through a ~ of tears** durch e-n Tränenschleier. **3.** Beschlag m (auf Glas). **II** v/i **4.** a. **~ up** (od. over) (sich) beschlagen (Glas).

misˈtakˈaˈble [miˈsteikəbl] adj **1.** leicht zu verwechseln(d). **2.** mißverständlich.

misˈtake I v/t (irr take) **1.** verwechseln (for mit); verkennen, sich irren in (dat). **2.** falsch verstehen, mißverstehen. **II** s **3.** Irrtum m, Versehen n, Fehler m: **by ~** irrtümlich, aus Versehen; **make a ~** einen Fehler machen; sich irren. **4.** (Rechen- etc)Fehler m. **misˈtakˈen** I pp von **mistake. II** adj **1.** be **~** sich irren: **be ~ in s.o.** sich in j-m täuschen; **unless I am very much ~** wenn mich nicht alles täuscht. **2.** irrig, falsch (Meinung etc), unangebracht (Freundlichkeit etc): **a case of ~ identity** e-e (Personen)Verwechslung.

ˌmisˈtime v/t e-n schlechten Zeitpunkt wählen für.

misˈtleˈtoe [ˈmisltəu] s ♣ **1.** Mistel f. **2.** Mistelzweig m.

ˌmisˈtransˈlate v/t falsch übersetzen. **ˌmisˈtransˈlaˈtion** s Übersetzungsfehler m.

misˈtress [ˈmistris] s **1.** Herrin f (a. fig.). **2.** bsd. Br. Lehrerin f. **3.** Mätresse f, Geliebte f.

ˌmisˈtrust I s Mißtrauen n (of gegen). **II** v/t mißtrauen (dat). **misˈtrustˈful** [~ful] adj □ mißtrauisch (of gegen).

mistˈy [ˈmisti] adj □ **1.** (leicht) neb(e)lig. **2.** fig. unklar, verschwommen (Vorstellung etc): **have only ~ memories of s.th.** sich nur schwach od. undeutlich an et. erinnern können. **3.** beschlagen (Glas).

ˌmisˌunˈderˈstand v/t (irr stand) **1.** mißverstehen: **don't ~ me** versteh mich nicht falsch. **2.** j-n nicht verstehen: **his wife ~s him.** **ˌmisˌunˈderˈstandˈing** s Mißverständnis n, weitS. a. Meinungsverschiedenheit f, Differenz f.

misˈuse I s [ˌmisˈjuːs] **1.** Mißbrauch m: **~ of power** Machtmißbrauch m. **2.** falscher

Gebrauch. **II** *v/t* [ˌˈjuːz] **3.** mißbrauchen. **4.** falsch *od.* zu unrechten Zwecken gebrauchen.

mite¹ [maɪt] *s zo.* Milbe *f*.

mite² [ˌ] *s* **1** kleines Ding, Würmchen *n*. **2.** *a ~* F ein bißchen.

mit·i·gate [ˈmɪtɪgeɪt] *v/t Schmerzen etc* lindern, *Strafe etc* mildern, *Zorn etc* besänftigen: **mitigating circumstances** *pl* 🏛 mildernde Umstände *pl*. ˌmit·iˈga·tion *s* Linderung *f*, Milderung *f*, Besänftigung *f*.

mitt [mɪt] *s* **1.** Halbhandschuh *m*. **2.** *Baseball:* Fanghandschuh *m*. **3.** → **mitten** 1. **4.** *sl.* Flosse *f*, Pfote *f* (*Hand*). **5.** *sl.* Boxhandschuh *m*.

mit·ten [ˈmɪtn] *s* **1.** Fausthandschuh *m*, Fäustling *m*. **2.** → **mitt** 5.

mix [mɪks] **I** *v/t* **1.** (ver)mischen, vermengen (**with** mit), *Cocktail etc* mixen, *Teig* anrühren: *~ into* mischen in (*acc*), beimischen (*dat*): *~ up* zs.-, durcheinandermischen; gründlich mischen; (völlig) durcheinanderbringen; verwechseln (**with** mit); *be ~ed up* verwickelt sein *od.* werden (**in** in *acc*); (*geistig*) ganz durcheinander sein. **2.** *fig.* verbinden: *~ business with pleasure* das Angenehme mit dem Nützlichen verbinden. **II** *v/i* **3.** sich (ver)mischen. **4.** sich mischen lassen. **5.** *~* **well** kontaktfreudig sein: *~ well with s.o.* gut mit j-m auskommen. **6.** verkehren (**with** mit; **in** in *dat*). **III** *s* **7.** (*a. Back- etc*)Mischung *f*. **8.** F Durcheinander *n*. **mixed** [mɪkst] *adj* gemischt (*a. fig. Gefühle etc*); vermischt, Misch...: *~ blessing* zweifelhaftes Vergnügen; *~ double(s* pl) (*Tennis etc*) gemischtes Doppel, Mixed *n*; *a ~ doubles match* ein gemischtes Doppel; *~ grill* Mixed grill *m*; *~ pickles* *pl* Mixed Pickles *pl*, Mixpickles *pl*. **'mix·er** *s* **1.** Mixer *m* (*a. Küchengerät*). **2.** 🔌 Mischmaschine *f*. **3.** *TV etc* Mischpult *n*. **4.** *be a good (bad) ~* F kontaktfreudig (-arm) sein. **mix·ture** [ˈmɪkstʃə] *s* Mischung *f*, *a.* 🜍 Gemisch *n* (**of** ... **and** aus ... u.): *~ of teas* Teemischung.

'mix-up *s* F **1.** Durcheinander *n*. **2.** Verwechslung *f*. **3.** Handgemenge *n*.

mne·mon·ic [niːˈmɒnɪk] *s* Gedächtnishilfe *f*, -stütze *f*.

mo [məʊ] *pl* **mos** *s* F Moment *m*, Augenblick *m*.

moan [məʊn] **I** *v/i* stöhnen, ächzen. **II** *s* Stöhnen *n*, Ächzen *n*.

moat [məʊt] *s* (Burg-, Stadt)Graben *m*.

mob [mɒb] **I** *s* **1.** Mob *m*. **2.** Pöbel *m*, Gesindel *n*. **3.** *sl.* (Verbrecher)Bande *f*. **II** *v/t* **1.** herfallen über (*acc*); *Filmstar etc* bedrängen, belagern.

mo·bile [ˈməʊbaɪl] *adj allg.* beweglich, 🔌 *a.* fahrbar, ✕ *a.* motorisiert: *~ home* Wohnwagen *m*; *~ library* Wander-, Autobücherei *f*. **mo·bil·i·ty** [ˌˈbɪlətɪ] *s* Beweglichkeit *f*. **mo·bi·li·za·tion** [ˌməʊbɪlaɪˈzeɪʃn] *s* Mobilisierung *f*, ✕ *a.* Mobilmachung *f*. **'mo·bi·lize** **I** *v/t* mobilisieren, ✕ *a.* mobil machen. **II** *v/i* ✕ mobil machen.

moc·ca·sin [ˈmɒkəsɪn] *s* Mokassin *m*.

mo·cha [ˈmɒkə] *s* Mokka *m*.

mock [mɒk] **I** *v/t* **1.** verspotten, lächerlich machen. **2.** nachäffen. **II** *v/i* **3.** sich lustig machen, spotten (**at** über *acc*). **III** *adj* **4.** nachgemacht, Schein... **'mock·er** *s* **1.** Spötter(in). **2.** Nachäffer(in). **'mock·er·y** *s* **1.** Spott *m*, Hohn *m*: *hold up to ~* j-n lächerlich machen; *et. ins Lächerliche ziehen*. **2.** *fig.* Hohn *m* (**of** auf *acc*). **3.** Gespött *n*: *make a ~ of* zum Gespött (der Leute) machen; *ad absurdum führen*. **'mock·ing** *adj* □ spöttisch.

'mock-up *s* Modell *n* (in natürlicher Größe), Attrappe *f*.

mod·al [ˈməʊdl] **I** *adj* □ *ling. etc* modal: *~ auxiliary* modales Hilfsverb. **II** *s ling.* F modales Hilfsverb. **mo·dal·i·ty** [ˌˈdælətɪ] *s* Modalität *f*.

mode [məʊd] *s* **1.** (Art *f* u.) Weise *f*: *~ of address* Anrede *f*; *~ of life* Lebensweise. **2.** *ling.* Modus *m*, Aussageweise *f*.

mod·el [ˈmɒdl] **I** *s* **1.** Muster *n*, Vorbild *n* (**for** für): *after (od. on) the ~ of* nach dem Muster von (*od. gen*); *he is a ~ of self-control* er ist ein Muster an Selbstbeherrschung. **2.** (*fig.* Denk)Modell *n*. **3.** Muster *n*, Vorlage *f*. **4.** *paint. etc* Modell *n*. **5.** *Mode:* Mannequin *n*. **6.** 🔌 Modell *n*, Typ(e) *f* (*n*). **II** *adj* **7.** vorbildlich, musterhaft: *~ husband* Mustergatte *m*. **8.** Modell...: *~ builder* Modellbauer *m*. **III** *v/t pret u. pp* *-eled, bsd. Br.* **-elled** **9.** modellieren. **10.** *fig.* formen (*after, on* nach [dem Vorbild gen]): **~ o.s. on** sich j-n zum Vorbild nehmen. **11.** *Kleider etc* vorführen. **IV** v/i **12.** Modell stehen *od.* sitzen (*for dat*). **13.** als Mannequin *od.* Dressman arbeiten.

mod·er·ate ['mɒdərət] **I** *adj* □ **1.** mäßig: a) gemäßigt (*a. pol.*), maßvoll, b) mittelmäßig, c) gering: **~ly successful** mäßig erfolgreich, d) vernünftig, angemessen: **~ demands** *pl* maßvolle Forderungen *pl.* **2.** mild (*Strafe, Winter etc*). **II** *s* **3.** *bsd. pol.* Gemäßigte *m, f.* **III** v/t ['~reɪt] **4.** mäßigen: **~ one's language** sich mäßigen. **mod·er·a·tion** ['~'reɪʃn] *s* Mäßigung *f:* **in ~** in *od.* mit Maßen, maßvoll.

mod·ern ['mɒdən] *adj* □ modern. **'mod·ern·ize** v/t modernisieren.

mod·est ['mɒdɪst] *adj* □ bescheiden: a) zurückhaltend, b) anspruchslos, c) maßvoll, vernünftig. **'mod·es·ty** *s* Bescheidenheit *f:* a) Zurückhaltung *f: in all ~* bei aller Bescheidenheit, b) Anspruchslosigkeit *f.*

mod·i·cum ['mɒdɪkəm] *s* kleine Menge: **a ~ of sense** ein Funke Verstand.

mod·i·fi·a·ble ['mɒdɪfaɪəbl] *adj* modifizierbar. **mod·i·fi·ca·tion** [~fɪ'keɪʃn] *s* Modifikation *f*, (Ab-, Ver)Änderung *f.* **mod·i·fy** ['~faɪ] v/t **1.** (ab-, ver)ändern, modifizieren. **2.** *ling.* näher bestimmen.

mod·u·lar ['mɒdjʊlə] *adj* ⊕ Modul...

mod·u·late ['mɒdjʊleɪt] v/t u. v/i ♪ etc modulieren. **,mod·u·la·tion** *s* Modulation *f.*

mod·ule ['mɒdjuːl] *s* **1.** ⊕ Modul *n, ∮ a.* Baustein *m.* **2.** *Raumfahrt:* (*Kommando- etc*)Kapsel *f.*

mo·hair ['məʊheə] *s* Mohair *m.*

Mo·ham·med·an [məʊ'hæmɪdən] **I** *adj* mohammedanisch. **II** *s* Mohammedaner(in).

moist [mɔɪst] *adj* □ feucht (**with** von): **~ with tears** tränenfeucht. **moisten** ['mɔɪsn] **I** v/t an-, befeuchten. **II** v/i feucht werden. **mois·ture** ['~tʃə] *s* Feuchtigkeit *f.* **mois·tur·iz·er** ['~tʃəraɪzə] *s* ⊕ Luftbefeuchter *m.*

mo·lar ['məʊlə] **I** *adj:* **~ tooth** → **II. II** *s* Backenzahn *m.*

mo·las·ses [məʊ'læsɪz] *s pl Am.* Sirup *m.*

mold, etc *Am.* → **mould**, etc.

mole¹ [məʊl] *s zo.* Maulwurf *m* (F *a. Spionage*).

mole² [~] *s* Muttermal *n*, Leberfleck *m.*

mole³ [~] *s* Mole *f*, Hafendamm *m.*

mo·lec·u·lar [məʊ'lekjʊlə] *s* ⚛, *phys.* Molekular... **mol·e·cule** ['mɒlɪkjuːl] *s* Molekül *n.*

'mole·hill *s* Maulwurfshügel *m:* → **mountain** I.

mo·lest [məʊ'lest] v/t (*a. unsittlich*) belästigen. **mo·les·ta·tion** [,~le'steɪʃn] *s* Belästigung *f.*

moll [mɒl] *s sl.* **1.** Gangsterbraut *f.* **2.** Nutte *f.*

mol·li·fy ['mɒlɪfaɪ] v/t besänftigen, beschwichtigen.

mol·lusc, mol·lusk ['mɒləsk] *s zo.* Molluske *f*, Weichtier *n.*

mol·ly·cod·dle ['mɒlɪˌkɒdl] **I** *s* Weichling *m.* **II** v/t verhätscheln.

Mol·o·tov cock·tail ['mɒlətɒf] *s* Molotowcocktail *m.*

mol·ten ['məʊltən] *pp von* **melt.**

mom [mɒm] *s bsd. Am.* F Mami *f*, Mutti *f.* **,~-and-'pop store** *s Am.* F Tante-Emma-Laden *m.*

mo·ment ['məʊmənt] *s* **1.** Moment *m*, Augenblick *m:* **at the ~** im Augenblick; **at the last ~** im letzten Augenblick; (**not**) **for a ~** (k)einen Augenblick (lang); **just a ~!** a) a. **wait a ~!** Moment mal!, b) Augenblick!; **the ~ of truth** die Stunde der Wahrheit. **2.** Bedeutung *f*, Belang *m* (**to** für): **of great** (**little**) **~** von großer (geringer) Bedeutung; **of no ~** bedeutungs-, belanglos. **3.** *phys.* Moment *n:* **~ of inertia** Trägheitsmoment. **mo·men·tar·i·ly** ['~tərəli] *adv* **1.** momentan, e-n Augenblick (lang). **2.** jeden Augenblick. **'mo·men·tar·y** *adj* momentan. **mo·men·tous** [~'mentəs] *adj* □ bedeutsam, folgenschwer. **mo·men·tum** [~təm] *s* **1.** *phys.* Moment *n*, Impuls *m.* **2.** Wucht *f*, Schwung *m:* **gather** (*od.* **gain**) **~** in Fahrt kommen; *fig. a.* an Boden gewinnen (*Bewegung etc*); **lose ~** an Schwung verlieren (*a. fig.*).

mon·arch ['mɒnək] *s* Monarch(in), Herrscher(in). **mo·nar·chic** [mɒ'nɑːkɪk] *adj* (**~ally**) **1.** monarchisch. **2.** monarchistisch. **mon·arch·ism** ['mɒnəkɪzəm] *s* Monarchismus *m.* **'mon·arch·ist I** *s* Monarchist(in). **II** *adj* monarchistisch. **'mon·arch·y** *s* Monarchie f: *constitutional* ~ konstitutionelle Monarchie.

mon·as·ter·y ['mɒnəstərɪ] s (Mönchs-) Kloster n. **mo·nas·tic** [mə'næstɪk] adj (**~ally**) **1.** klösterlich, Kloster... **2.** mönchisch, Mönchs...

Mon·day ['mʌndɪ] s Montag m: *on ~* (am) Montag; *on ~s* montags.

mon·e·tar·y ['mʌnɪtərɪ] adj □ **1.** Währungs...: → *reform.* **2.** Geld..., finanziell.

mon·ey ['mʌnɪ] s Geld n: *be out of ~* kein Geld (mehr) haben; *be in the ~* F reich od. vermögend sein; *be short of ~* knapp bei Kasse sein; *I'll bet you any ~ that* F ich wette mit dir um jeden Betrag, daß; *get one's money's worth* et. für sein Geld bekommen; *have ~ to burn* F Geld wie Heu haben; *for ~ reasons* aus finanziellen Gründen; → *roll* 7. '*~·bags* s pl (sg konstruiert) F Geldsack m (reiche Person). ~ *box* s Sparbüchse f. '*~·chang·er* s **1.** (Geld-) Wechsler m. **2.** bsd. Am. Wechselautomat m.

mon·eyed ['mʌnɪd] adj wohlhabend, vermögend.

'**mon·ey·,lend·er** s Geldverleiher m. '*~·,mak·er* s **1.** guter Geschäftsmann. **2.** gutes Geschäft, einträgliche Sache. ~ *or·der* s Post- od. Zahlungsanweisung f. ~ *spin·ner* F bsd. Br. → *money-maker* 2.

mon·ger ['mʌŋgə] s in Zssgn **1.** ...händler m. **2.** fig. contp. → *scandalmonger, scaremonger, etc.*

mon·go·li·an [mɒŋ'gəʊljən] adj ✱ mongoloid.

mon·gol·ism ['mɒŋgəlɪzəm] s ✱ Mongolismus m. '**mon·gol·oid** adj ✱ mongoloid.

mon·grel ['mʌŋgrəl] s biol. Bastard m, bsd. Promenadenmischung f.

mon·i·tor ['mɒnɪtə] I s **1.** Monitor m: a) Abhörgerät n, b) Kontrollgerät n, -schirm m. II v/t **2.** abhören. **3.** überwachen.

monk [mʌŋk] s Mönch m.

mon·key ['mʌŋkɪ] I s **1.** zo. Affe m: *make a ~ (out) of s.o.* F j-n zum Deppen machen. **2.** (kleiner) Schlingel. II v/i **3.** ~ *about (od. around)* herumalbern. **4.** a. ~ *about (od. around)* (with) F herumspielen (mit), herumpfuschen an (dat). ~ *busi·ness* s F **1.** krumme Tour. **2.**

Blödsinn m, Unfug m. ~ *wrench* s ⊙ Engländer m: *throw a ~ into s.th.* Am. F et. behindern od. beeinträchtigen.

mon·o ['mɒnəʊ] I pl -os s F Mono n. **2.** F Monogerät n od. -schallplatte f. II adj **3.** Mono...

mon·o... [~] in Zssgn ein..., mono...

mon·o·cle ['mɒnəkl] s Monokel n.

mo·nog·a·mous [mɒ'nɒgəməs] adj □ monogam(isch). **mo'nog·a·my** s Monogamie f, Einehe f.

mon·o·gram ['mɒnəgræm] s Monogramm n.

mon·o·lith ['mɒnəʊlɪθ] s Monolith m. ˌ**mon·o'lith·ic** adj (**~ally**) **1.** monolithisch (a. fig.). **2.** fig. gigantisch.

mon·o·logue ['mɒnəlɒg] s Monolog m, Selbstgespräch n.

mo·nop·o·lize [mə'nɒpəlaɪz] v/t **1.** ♦ monopolisieren. **2.** fig. a) an sich reißen, Unterhaltung a. ganz allein bestreiten, b) j-n, et. mit Beschlag belegen. **mo'nop·o·ly** ♦ Monopol n (of auf acc) (a. fig.).

ˌ**mon·o·'syl·lab·ic** adj (**~ally**) ling. einsilbig (a. fig. Antworten etc).

mo·not·o·nous [mə'nɒtnəs] adj □ monoton, eintönig, fig. a. einförmig. **mo'not·o·ny** [~tnɪ] s Monotonie f, Eintönigkeit f, fig. a. Einförmigkeit f, (ewiges) Einerlei.

mon·ox·ide [mɒ'nɒksaɪd] s 🧪 Monoxyd n.

mon·soon [ˌmɒn'suːn] s Monsun m.

mon·ster ['mɒnstə] I s **1.** Monster n, Ungeheuer n (beide a. fig.). **2.** Monstrum n (a. fig.). II adj **3.** Riesen..., Monster...: ~ *film* Monsterfilm m.

mon·strance ['mɒnstrəns] s eccl. Monstranz f.

mon·stros·i·ty [mɒn'strɒsətɪ] s **1.** Ungeheuerlichkeit f. **2.** → *monster* 2. **mon·strous** ['~strəs] adj □ monströs: a) ungeheuer, riesig, b) unförmig, ungestalt, c) fig. ungeheuerlich, scheußlich.

month [mʌnθ] s Monat m: *we haven't seen each other in a ~ of Sundays* F wir haben uns schon seit einer Ewigkeit nicht mehr gesehen. '**month·ly** I adj **1.** (a. adv) monatlich. **2.** Monats...: ~ *sea·son ticket* Monatskarte f. II s **3.** Monatsschrift f.

mon·u·ment ['mɒnjʊmənt] s a. fig. Mo-

nument n, Denkmal n (**to** für od. gen).
mon·u·men·tal [ˌ~ˈmentl] adj □ **1.** monumental (a. fig.). **2.** F kolossal: ~ **stupidity** Riesendummheit f.
moo [muː] **I** v/i muhen. **II** s Muhen n.
mood[1] [muːd] s ling. Modus m.
mood[2] [~] s **1.** Stimmung f, Laune f: **be in a good (bad)** ~ gute (schlechte) Laune haben, gut (schlecht) aufgelegt sein; **be in the (in no)** ~ **to do** (nicht) dazu aufgelegt sein zu tun, (keine) Lust haben zu tun; **be in the** ~ **for** aufgelegt sein zu; **I am in no laughing** ~ od. **for laughing**) mir ist nicht nach od. zum Lachen zumute. **2. be in a** ~ schlechte Laune haben, schlecht aufgelegt sein; **he is in one of his** ~**s again** er hat wieder einmal schlechte Laune.
mood·y [ˈmuːdɪ] adj □ **1.** launisch, launenhaft. **2.** schlechtgelaunt.
moon [muːn] **I** s Mond m: **there is a (no)** ~ der Mond scheint (nicht); **be over the** ~ F überglücklich sein (**about, at** über acc); **cry for the** ~ nach et. Unmöglichem verlangen; **promise s.o. the** ~ j-m das Blaue vom Himmel (herunter)versprechen; **once in a blue** ~ F alle Jubeljahre (einmal). **II** v/i: ~ **about** od. **around**) herumtrödeln; ziellos herumstreichen. **III** v/t: ~ **away** Zeit vertrödeln, -träumen. '~·**beam** s Mondstrahl m. '~·**light** **I** s Mondlicht n, -schein m: ~ **walk** Mondscheinspaziergang m. **II** v/i F schwarzarbeiten. '~·**light·er** s F Schwarzarbeiter(in). '~·**lit** adj mondhell: ~ **night** Mondnacht f. '~·**shine** s **1.** Mondschein m. **2.** F Unsinn m, Quatsch m.
moon·y [ˈmuːnɪ] adj □ F verträumt.
moor[1] [mɔː] s (Hoch)Moor n.
moor[2] [~] v/t ♣ vertäuen, festmachen.
moo·rings [ˈmɔːrɪŋz] s pl ♣ **1.** Vertäuung f. **2.** Liegeplatz m.
moose [muːs] pl **moose** s zo. Elch m.
moot [muːt] adj strittig (Punkt): ~ **question** Streitfrage f.
mop [mɒp] **I** s **1.** Mop m. **2.** (Haar)Wust m. **II** v/t **3.** wischen: ~ **up** aufwischen; ~ **one's face** sich das Gesicht (ab)wischen. **4.** Blut etc abtupfen (**from** von).
mope [məʊp] v/i den Kopf hängen lassen: ~ **about** (od. **around**) mit e-r Leichenbittermiene herumlaufen.
mo·ped [ˈməʊped] s Br. Moped n.

mo·raine [mɒˈreɪn] s geol. Moräne f.
mor·al [ˈmɒrəl] **I** adj □ **1.** moralisch: a) sittlich, b) geistig, innerlich: ~ **obligation** moralische Verpflichtung; ~ **support** moralische Unterstützung; ~ **victory** moralischer Sieg, c) sittenstreng, tugendhaft. **2.** Moral..., Sitten...: ~ **theology** Moraltheologie f. **II** s **3.** Moral f (e-r Geschichte etc): **draw the** ~ **from** die Lehre ziehen aus. **4.** pl Moral f, Sitten pl: **code of** ~**s** Sittenkodex m. **mo·rale** [mɒˈrɑːl] s Moral f, Stimmung f: **raise (lower) the** ~ die Moral heben (senken). **mor·al·ist** [ˈmɒrəlɪst] s Moralist(in). **mo·ral·i·ty** [məˈrælətɪ] s **1.** Moral f, Tugend(haftigkeit) f. **2.** Ethik f, Moral f. **mor·al·ize** [ˈmɒrəlaɪz] v/i moralisieren (**about, on** über acc).
mor·a·to·ri·um [ˌmɒrəˈtɔːrɪəm] pl **-ri·a** [ˌ~rɪə], **-ri·ums** s ✝, ✕, pol. Moratorium n.
mor·bid [ˈmɔːbɪd] adj □ **1.** morbid, krankhaft (beide a. fig.). **2.** gräßlich, grauenerregend. **3.** trübsinnig, pessimistisch. **mor'bid·i·ty** s **1.** Morbidität f, Krankhaftigkeit f (beide a. fig.). **2.** Trübsinn m; Pessimismus m.
mor·dant [ˈmɔːdənt] adj □ fig. ätzend, beißend.
more [mɔː] **I** adj **1.** mehr: **they are** ~ **than we are** sie sind zahlreicher als wir. **2.** mehr, noch (mehr): **some** ~ **tea** noch et. Tee; **two** ~ **miles** noch zwei Meilen. **II** adv **3.** mehr: ~ **and** ~ immer mehr; ~ **and** ~ **difficult** immer schwieriger; ~ **or less** mehr od. weniger; ungefähr; **the** ~ ... **so because** um so mehr, da. **4.** zur Bildung des comp: ~ **important** wichtiger; ~ **often** öfter. **5.** noch: ~ **once** noch einmal. **III** s **2.** Mehr n (**of** an dat). **7.** **some** ~ noch et. (mehr); **a little** ~ et. mehr; **what** ~ **do you want?** was willst du denn noch?
mo·rel [mɒˈrel] s ♀ Morchel f.
mo·rel·lo [mɒˈreləʊ] pl **-los** s a. ~ **cherry** ♀ Morelle f.
more·o·ver [mɔːˈrəʊvə] adv außerdem, überdies, weiter, ferner.
morgue [mɔːg] s **1.** Leichenschauhaus n. **2.** F Archiv n (e-s Zeitungsverlags etc).
Mor·mon [ˈmɔːmən] **I** s Mormone m, Mormonin f. **II** adj mormonisch.
morn·ing [ˈmɔːnɪŋ] **I** s Morgen m; Vor-

mittag *m*: *in the* ~ morgens, am Morgen; vormittags, am Vormittag; *early in the* ~ frühmorgens, früh am Morgen; *this* ~ heute morgen *od.* vormittag; *tomorrow* ~ morgen früh *od.* vormittag. **II** *adj* Morgen...; Vormittags...; Früh... ~ **coat** *s* Cut(away) *m*. ~ **pa·per** *s* Morgenzeitung *f.* ~ **star** *s ast.* Morgenstern *m.*

mo·rose [məˈrəʊs] *adj* □ mürrisch, verdrießlich.

mor·pheme [ˈmɔːfiːm] *s ling.* Morphem *n.*

mor·phi·a [ˈmɔːfjə], **mor·phine** [ˈmɔːfiːn] *s* Morphium *n.*

mor·pho·log·i·cal [ˌmɔːfəˈlɒdʒɪkl] *adj* □ *biol., ling.* morphologisch. **mor·phol·o·gy** [~ˈfɒlədʒɪ] *s* Morphologie *f.*

Morse code [mɔːs] *s* Morsealphabet *n.*

mor·sel [ˈmɔːsl] *s* **1.** Bissen *m*, Happen *m.* **2.** *a* ~ *of* ein bißchen: *a* ~ *of sense* ein Funke Verstand.

mor·tal [ˈmɔːtl] **I** *adj* □ **1.** sterblich. **2.** tödlich (*to* für). **3.** Tod(es)...: ~ *fear* Todesangst *f*; ~ *hour* Todesstunde *f*; ~ *sin* Todsünde *f.* **4.** auf Leben u. Tod: ~ *enemy* Todfeind *m*; ~ *hatred* tödlicher Haß. **5.** *F of no* ~ *use* absolut zwecklos; *every* ~ *thing* alles menschenmögliche; *I'm in a* ~ *hurry* ich hab's furchtbar eilig. **6.** *F* ewig (lang): *three* ~ *hours pl* drei endlose Stunden *pl.* **II** *s* **7.** Sterbliche *m*, *f*: *an ordinary* ~ ein gewöhnlicher Sterblicher. **mor·tal·i·ty** [~ˈtælətɪ] *s* **1.** Sterblichkeit *f.* **2.** *a.* ~ *rate* Sterblichkeit(sziffer) *f.*

mor·tar¹ [ˈmɔːtə] *s* **1.** Mörser *m.* **2.** ✕ Granatwerfer *m.*

mor·tar² [~] *s* Mörtel *m.*

mort·gage [ˈmɔːgɪdʒ] **I** *s* Hypothek *f*: *raise a* ~ e-e Hypothek aufnehmen (*on* auf *acc*). **II** *v/t* mit e-r Hypothek belasten, e-e Hypothek aufnehmen auf (*acc*).

mor·ti·cian [mɔːˈtɪʃn] *s Am.* Leichenbestatter *m.*

mor·ti·fi·ca·tion [ˌmɔːtɪfɪˈkeɪʃn] *s* **1.** Demütigung *f*, Kränkung *f.* **2.** Ärger *m*, Verdruß *m*: *to one's* ~ zu s-m Verdruß. **3.** Kasteiung *f.* **4.** Abtötung *f.* **5.** ✸ Absterben *n.* **mor·ti·fy** [~ˈfaɪ] **I** *v/t* **1.** demütigen, kränken. **2.** ärgern, verdrießen. **3.** *Fleisch etc* kasteien. **4.** Lei-

denschaften abtöten. **II** *v/i* **5.** ✸ absterben (*Gewebe*).

mor·tu·ar·y [ˈmɔːtʃʊərɪ] **I** *s* Leichenhalle *f.* **II** *adj* Begräbnis..., Leichen...

mo·sa·ic [məʊˈzeɪɪk] *s* Mosaik *n.*

Mos·lem [ˈmɒzləm] **I** *s* Moslem *m.* **II** *adj* moslemisch.

mosque [mɒsk] *s* Moschee *f.*

mos·qui·to [məˈskiːtəʊ] *pl* **-to(e)s** *s zo.* Moskito *m*; *allg.* Stechmücke *f.* ~ **net** *s* Moskitonetz *n.*

moss [mɒs] *s* Moos *n.* **'moss·y** *adj* moosig, bemoost.

most [məʊst] **I** *adj* **1.** meist, größt: *the* ~ *part* größten-, meistenteils. **2.** (*vor e-m* *s im pl*, *mst ohne Artikel*) die meisten: ~ *people* die meisten Leute. **II** *s* **3.** das meiste, *das* Höchste: *at* (*the*) ~ höchstens, bestenfalls; *make the* ~ *of et.* nach Kräften ausnützen, das Beste herausholen aus. **4.** das meiste, der größte Teil: *he spent* ~ *of his time there* er verbrachte die meiste Zeit dort. **5.** die meisten *pl*: *better than* ~ besser als die meisten; ~ *of my friends* die meisten m-r Freunde. **III** *adv* **6.** am meisten: ~ *of all* am allermeisten. **7.** *zur Bildung des sup*: *the* ~ *important point* der wichtigste Punkt. **8.** (*vor adj*) höchst, äußerst: ~ *agreeable* äußerst angenehm; *he is* ~ *likely to come* er kommt höchstwahrscheinlich. **'most·ly** *adv* **1.** größtenteils. **2.** meist(ens).

MOT [ˌeməʊˈtiː] *s Br.* a) *a.* ~ *test* (*etwa*) TÜV-Prüfung *f*: *my car has failed* (*od. hasn't got through*) *its* (*od. the*) ~ mein Wagen ist nicht durch den TÜV gekommen, b) *a.* ~ *certificate* (*etwa*) TÜV-Bescheinigung *f.*

mo·tel [məʊˈtel] *s* Motel *n.*

moth [mɒθ] *s zo.* **1.** Nachtfalter *m.* **2.** Motte *f.* '~**ball** *s* Mottenkugel *f*: *put in* ~**s** einmotten (*a. fig.*). '~**,eat·en** *adj* **1.** mottenzerfressen. **2.** *fig.* veraltet.

moth·er [ˈmʌðə] *s* Mutter *f* (*a. fig.*): ℒ**'s Day** Muttertag *m*; ~**'s milk** Muttermilch *f*; *a* ~ *of four* e-e Mutter von vier Kindern. **II** *v/t* bemuttern. ~ **ship.** **III** *v/t* bemuttern. ~ **coun·try** *s* **1.** Mutterland *n.* **2.** Vater-, Heimatland *n.*

moth·er·hood [ˈmʌðəhʊd] *s* Mutterschaft *f.*

'moth·er·in·law *pl* **'moth·ers·in·law** *s* Schwiegermutter *f*: ~ *joke* Schwiegermutterwitz *m.* '**~·land** → *mother country.*

moth·er·less ['mʌðəlɪs] *adj* mutterlos. '**moth·er·ly** *adj* mütterlich.

,**moth·er|-of-'pearl** *s* Perlmutter *f*, *n*, Perlmutt *n*. ,**~-to-'be** *pl* ,**moth·ers-to-'be** *s* werdende Mutter. **~ tongue** *s* Muttersprache *f*. **~ wit** *s* Mutterwitz *m*.

mo·tif [məʊ'tiːf] *s Kunst:* Motiv *n*.

mo·tion ['məʊʃn] **I** *s* **1.** Bewegung *f* (*a. phys. etc*): **be in ~** in Gang sein (*a. fig.*), in Bewegung sein; *put* (*od.* **set**) *in ~* in Gang bringen (*a. fig.*), in Bewegung setzen; *go through the ~s of doing s.th.* *fig.* et. mechanisch *od.* pro forma tun. **2.** Bewegung *f*, Geste *f*, Wink *m*: **~ of the head** Kopfbewegung; *make a ~ with one's hand* e-e Handbewegung machen. **3.** *parl. etc* Antrag *m*: **on the ~ of** auf Antrag von (*od. gen*). **II** *v/i* **4.** winken (*with* mit; *to, at* dat). **III** *v/t* **5.** *j-n durch e-n Wink auffordern, j-m ein Zeichen geben (to do zu tun): ~ s.o. into the room* j-n ins Zimmer winken. '**mo·tion·less** *adj* □ bewegungs-, regungslos.

motion| pic·ture *s Am.* Film *m*. **~ ther·a·py** *s* Bewegungstherapie *f*.

mo·ti·vate ['məʊtɪveɪt] *v/t* motivieren, anspornen. ,**mo·ti·va·tion** *s* Motivation *f*, Ansporn *m*, Antrieb *m*.

mo·tive ['məʊtɪv] **I** *s* Motiv *n*, Beweggrund *m* (*for* zu). **II** *adj* treibend (*a. fig.*): **~ power** Antriebskraft *f*, *bsd. fig.* Triebkraft *f*.

mot·ley ['mɒtlɪ] *adj* (kunter)bunt (*a. fig.*).

mo·tor ['məʊtə] **I** *s* **1.** Motor *m*, *fig. a.* treibende Kraft. **II** *adj* **2.** Motor... **3.** *physiol.* motorisch, Bewegungs...: **~ nerve.** '**~·bike** *s* F Motorrad *n*. '**~·boat** *s* Motorboot *n*. '**~·cade** [-keɪd] *s* Auto-, Wagenkolonne *f*. '**~·car** *s* Kraftfahrzeug *n*. **~ car·a·van** *s Br.* Wohnmobil *n*. '**~·cy·cle** *s* Motorrad *n*. '**~·cy·clist** *s* Motorradfahrer(in).

mo·tor·ing ['məʊtərɪŋ] **I** *s* Autofahren *n*: *school of ~* Fahrschule *f*. **II** *adj* Verkehrs..., Auto... '**mo·tor·ist** *s* Autofahrer(in).

mo·tor·i·za·tion [,məʊtəraɪ'zeɪʃn] *s* Motorisierung *f*. '**mo·tor·ize** *v/t* motorisieren.

mo·tor| scoot·er *s* Motorroller *m*. '**~·way** *s Br.* Autobahn *f*.

mot·tled ['mɒtld] *adj* gesprenkelt.

mot·to ['mɒtəʊ] *pl* **-to(e)s** *s* Motto *n*.

mould¹ [məʊld] *bsd. Br.* **I** *s* **1.** ⚙ (Gieß-, Guß-, Press)Form *f*: *be cast* (*od.* **made**) *in the same* (*a different*) *~ fig.* aus demselben (e-m anderen) Holz geschnitzt sein. **II** *v/t* **2.** ⚙ gießen. **3.** formen (*a. fig. Charakter etc*), bilden (*out of* aus), gestalten (*on* nach dem Muster *gen*); formen (*into* zu).

mould² [~] *s bsd. Br.* Schimmel *m*; Moder *m*.

mould·er ['məʊldə] *v/i a.* **~ away** *bsd. Br.* vermodern; zerfallen.

mould·y ['məʊldɪ] *adj bsd. Br.* **1.** a) verschimmelt, schimm(e)lig: *get* (*od.* **go**) *~* (ver)schimmeln, b) mod(e)rig: *~ smell* Modergeruch *m*. **2.** *sl.* schäbig (*Person, Summe etc*).

mound [maʊnd] *s* Erdwall *m*, -hügel *m*: **~ of work** *fig.* Berg *m* Arbeit.

mount¹ [maʊnt] **I** *v/t* **1.** Pferd *etc, fig.* Thron besteigen; *Treppen* hinaufgehen. **~ one's bicycle** auf sein Fahrrad steigen. **2.** *Kind etc* setzen (*on* auf *ein Pferd etc*). **3.** errichten, *a. Maschine* aufstellen. **4.** anbringen, befestigen; *Bild etc* aufkleben; *Edelstein* fassen. **II** *v/i* **5.** aufsitzen (*Reiter*). **6.** steigen, *fig. a.* (an)wachsen. **7.** *oft* **~ up** *fig.* sich belaufen (*to* auf *acc*). **III** *s* **8.** Gestell *n*; Fassung *f*. **9.** Reittier *n*.

Mount² [~] *s in Eigennamen:* a) Berg *m*: **~ Sinai,** b) Mount *m*: **~ Everest.**

moun·tain ['maʊntɪn] **I** *s* Berg *m* (*a. fig.*), *pl a.* Gebirge *n*: *in the ~s* im Gebirge; *make a ~ out of a molehill* aus e-r Mücke e-n Elefanten machen. **II** *adj* Berg..., Gebirgs... **~ chain** *s* Berg-, Gebirgskette *f*. **~ crys·tal** *s min.* Bergkristall *m*.

moun·tain·eer [,maʊntɪ'nɪə] *s* Bergsteiger(in). ,**moun·tain·eer·ing** *s* Bergsteigen *n*. '**moun·tain·ous** *adj* □ **1.** bergig, gebirgig. **2.** *fig.* riesig, (*Wellen a.*) haushoch.

mountain range *s* Gebirgszug *m*.

mount·ed ['maʊntɪd] *adj* beritten: **~ po·lice.**

mourn [mɔːn] **I** *v/i* **1.** trauern (*at, over* über *acc*; *for, over* um). **2.** Trauer(kleidung) tragen. **II** *v/t* **3.** betrauern, trau-

ern um. **'mourn·er** *s* Trauernde *m, f.*
mourn·ful [ˈ⁓fʊl] *adj* □ traurig.
'mourn·ing *s* **1.** Trauer *f:* **⁓ band** Trauerband *n,* -flor *m.* **2.** Trauer(kleidung)
f: **go into ⁓** Trauerkleidung anlegen.
mouse [maʊs] *pl* **mice** [maɪs] *s* **1.** *zo.*
Maus *f.* **2.** *fig.* schüchterne *od.* ängstliche Person. **'⁓·hole** *s* Mauseloch *n.*
'⁓·trap *s* Mausefalle *f.*
mous·tache [məˈstɑːʃ] *s* Schnurrbart *m.*
mous·y [ˈmaʊsɪ] *adj* □ **1.** mausgrau. **2.**
schüchtern; ängstlich.
mouth I *s* [maʊθ] *pl* **mouths** [maʊðz] **1.**
Mund *m:* **down in the ⁓** F deprimiert;
keep one's ⁓ shut F den Mund halten;
take the words out of s.o.'s ⁓ j-m das
Wort aus dem Mund nehmen; → **stop**
12, **word** 1. **2.** *zo.* Maul *n,* Schnauze *f:*
→ **horse. 3.** Mündung *f* (*e-s Flusses
etc*); Öffnung *f* (*e-r Flasche etc*), Ein-,
Ausfahrt *f* (*e-s Hafens etc*). II *v/t*
[maʊð] **4.** *Worte* (*unhörbar*) mit den
Lippen formen. **mouth·ful** [ˈ⁓fʊl] *s* **1.**
ein Mundvoll *m,* Bissen *m.* **2.** *fig.* Bandwurm *m,* ellenlanges Wort; Zungenbrecher *m.*

mouth|·or·gan *s* ♩ Mundharmonika *f.*
'⁓·piece *s* **1.** Mundstück *n* (*e-s Blasinstruments, e-r Pfeife etc*). **2.** *fig.* Sprachrohr *n* (*a. Person*). **'⁓-to-'⁓ res·pi·ra·tion** *s* ⚕ Mund-zu-Mund-Beatmung *f.*
'⁓·wash *s* ♩ Mundwasser *n.* **'⁓·wa·ter·ing** *adj* appetitlich, lecker.
mov·a·ble [ˈmuːvəbl] I *adj* □ beweglich
(*a. eccl.,* ⚖); transportierbar. II *s pl*
⚖ Mobilien *pl,* bewegliches Vermögen.
move [muːv] I *v/t* **1.** (von der Stelle)
bewegen, rücken; transportieren; *Körperteil* bewegen, rühren: **⁓ one's car**
s-n Wagen wegfahren; → **heaven** 1. **2.**
a) *Wohnsitz etc* verlegen (**to** nach): **⁓
house** umziehen, b) *Angestellten etc*
versetzen (**to** nach). **3. ⁓ on** vorwärtstreiben; *j-n* auffordern weiterzugehen.
4. *fig.* bewegen, rühren: **be ⁓d to tears**
zu Tränen gerührt sein. **5.** bewegen,
veranlassen (**to** zu): **feel ⁓d to say s.th.**
sich veranlaßt fühlen, et. zu sagen. **6.**
Schach etc: ziehen *od.* e-n Zug machen
mit. **7.** *parl. etc* beantragen (*a.* **that**
daß). II *v/i* **8.** sich bewegen *od.* rühren;
fig. sich ändern (*Ansichten etc*): **begin
to ⁓, ⁓ off** sich in Bewegung setzen; **⁓ on**
weitergehen; → **time** 1. **9.** umziehen: **⁓**

to *a.* ziehen nach; **⁓ in** (**out, away**) ein-
(aus-, weg)ziehen. **10.** handeln, et. unternehmen. **11.** (**in** *in guter Gesellschaft
etc*) verkehren (*a.* **with** mit), sich bewegen. **12.** *Schach etc:* e-n Zug machen,
ziehen. III *s* **13.** Bewegung *f:* **on the ⁓** in
Bewegung; auf den Beinen; **get a ⁓ on!**
Γ Tempo!, mach(t) schon! **14.** Umzug
m. **15.** a) *Schach etc:* Zug *m:* **it is your ⁓**
Sie sind am Zug, b) *fig.* Schritt *m:* **a
clever ⁓** ein kluger Schachzug; **make
the first ⁓** den ersten Schritt tun. **16.**
Sport: Kombination *f;* Spielzug *m.*
'move·ment *s* **1.** Bewegung *f* (*a. fig.*):
without ⁓ bewegungslos. **2.** ♩ Satz *m.*
mov·ie [ˈmuːvɪ] *bsd. Am.* F I *s* **1.** Film *m.*
2. Kino *n.* **3. go to the ⁓s** ins Kino
gehen. II *adj* **4.** Film..., Kino...: **⁓ camera** Filmkamera *f;* **⁓ star** Filmstar *m.*
mov·ing [ˈmuːvɪŋ] *adj* □ **1.** beweglich,
sich bewegend, (*Verkehr*) fließend: **⁓
staircase** Rolltreppe *f.* **2.** *fig.* bewegend, rührend.
mow [məʊ] *v/t u. v/i* (*a. irr*) mähen: **⁓
down** niedermähen (*a. fig.*). **'mow·er** *s*
a) Mähmaschine *f,* b) Rasenmäher *m.*
mown *pp von* **mow.**
much [mʌtʃ] I *adj* **1.** viel: **as ⁓ again**
noch einmal soviel. II *adv* **2.** sehr: **⁓ to
my regret** sehr zu m-m Bedauern; **⁓ to
my surprise** zu m-r großen Überraschung; **I thought as ⁓** das habe ich mir
gedacht. **3.** (*in Zssgn*) viel...: **⁓·admired**
vielbewundert. **4.** (*vor comp*) viel: **⁓
better. 5.** fast, mehr *od.* weniger: **⁓ the
same.** III *s* **6.** große Sache: **nothing ⁓**
nichts Besonderes; **think ⁓ of** viel halten
von; **he is not ⁓ of a dancer** er ist kein
großer *od.* berühmter Tänzer; → **make**
11.
muck [mʌk] I *s* **1.** Mist *m,* Dung *m.* **2.**
Kot *m,* → Dreck *m,* Schmutz *m.* **3. make
a ⁓ of** → 6b. II *v/t* **4.** düngen. **5. ⁓ out**
ausmisten. **6.** *oft* **⁓ up** a) schmutzig
machen, b) *bsd. Br.* F verpfuschen,
-masseln. III *v/i* **7.** *mst* **⁓ about** (*od.
around*) *bsd. Br.* F a) herumgammeln,
b) herumpfuschen (**with** *an dat*), c) herumalbern. **'⁓·heap, '⁓·hill** *s* Misthafen *m.* **'⁓·rake** *v/i* Skandale aufdecken;
im Schmutz wühlen.
muck·y [ˈmʌkɪ] *adj* □ schmutzig, drekkig.
mu·cous [ˈmjuːkəs] *adj* schleimig: **⁓**

membrane *anat.* Schleimhaut f. **mu-cus** ['kəs] s Schleim m.

mud [mʌd] s **1.** Schlamm m, Matsch m. **2.** Schmutz m (a. fig.): *drag through the ~ fig.* in den Schmutz ziehen *od.* zerren; *sling* (*od. throw*) *~ at s.o. fig.* j-n mit Schmutz bewerfen.

mud·dle ['mʌdl] **I** s Durcheinander n, Unordnung f; Verwirrung f: *be in a ~* durcheinander sein (*Dinge*), (*Person a.*) konfus sein; *get in(to) a ~* durcheinandergeraten (*Dinge*); konfus werden (*Person*); *make a ~ of →* IIa. **II** v/t durcheinanderbringen: a) in Unordnung bringen, b) konfus machen, c) verwechseln (*with* mit). **III** v/i: *~ through* sich durchwursteln. '**~·head·ed** *adj* wirr(köpfig), konfus.

mud·dy ['mʌdi] *adj* □ **1.** schlammig, trüb. **2.** schmutzig. **3.** *fig.* wirr; unklar, verschwommen.

'**mud·guard** s mot. Kotflügel m; Schutzblech n (*e-s Fahrrads*). **~ pack** s ✿ Fango-, Schlammpackung f. '**~·sling·er** s Verleumder(in). '**~·sling-ing** s Verleumdung f.

muf·fin ['mʌfɪn] s Muffin n: a) *Br.* Hefeteigsemmel f, b) *Am. kleine süße Semmel.*

muf·fle ['mʌfl] v/t **1.** *oft ~ up* einhüllen, -wickeln. **2.** *Ton etc* dämpfen: *~d voices pl* gedämpfte Stimmen pl. '**muf·fler** s **1.** dicker Schal. **2.** *mot. Am.* Auspufftopf m.

muf·ti ['mʌfti] s: *in ~* in Zivil.

mug [mʌg] **I** s **1.** Krug m; Becher m; große Tasse. **2.** sl. Visage f (*Gesicht*): Fresse f (*Mund*). **II** v/t F **3.** (*bsd. auf der Straße*) überfallen u. ausrauben. **4.** a. **~ up** *Br. etc* büffeln. **III** v/i **5.** *Br.* F büffeln. '**mug·ger** s F (*bsd. Straßen*)Räuber m. '**mug·ging** s F Raubüberfall m, *bsd.* Straßenraub m.

mug·gy ['mʌgi] *adj* □ schwül.

mule¹ [mjuːl] s zo. Maultier n; Maulesel m: (*as*) *stubborn* (*od. obstinate*) *as a ~* (so) störrisch wie ein Maulesel.

mule² [~] s Pantoffel m.

mul·ish ['mjuːlɪʃ] *adj* □ störrisch, stur.

mull¹ [mʌl] s (✿ Verband[s])Mull m.

mull² [~] v/i u. v/t: *~ over s.th.*, *~ s.th. over* nachdenken *od.* -grübeln über (*acc*).

mulled [mʌld] *adj*: *~ wine* Glühwein m.

mul·ti... ['mʌlti] *in Zssgn* viel..., mehr..., Mehr..., Multi...

mul·ti·far·i·ous [ˌmʌltiˈfeərɪəs] *adj* □ mannigfaltig, vielfältig.

mul·ti·lat·er·al *adj* □ **1.** vielseitig. **2.** *pol.* multilateral, mehrseitig. ˌ**mul·ti·'lin·gual** *adj* mehrsprachig. ˌ**mul·ti·mil·lion·aire** s Multimillionär m. ˌ**mul·ti·'na·tion·al** ✟ **I** *adj* multinational (*Konzern*). **II** s F Multi m.

mul·ti·ple ['mʌltɪpl] **I** *adj* □ **1.** viel-, mehrfach: *~ sclerosis* ✿ multiple Sklerose. **2.** mannigfaltig, vielfältig. **3.** ⚡, ⊙ Mehr(fach)..., Vielfach... **II** s **4.** *das* Vielfache (a. Ⱥ).

mul·ti·pli·ca·tion [ˌmʌltɪplɪˈkeɪʃn] s **1.** Vermehrung f (a. biol.). **2.** Ⱥ Multiplikation f: *~ sign* Mal-, Multiplikationszeichen n; *~ table* Einmaleins n. **mul·ti·plic·i·ty** [ˌ~ˈplɪsəti] s **1.** Vielfalt f. **2.** Vielzahl f. **mul·ti·pli·er** ['~plaɪə] s Ⱥ Multiplikator m. **mul·ti·ply** ['~plaɪ] **I** v/t **1.** vermehren, -vielfachen. **2.** Ⱥ multiplizieren, malnehmen (*by* mit): *6 multiplied by 5 is 30* 6 mal 5 ist 30. **II** v/i **3.** sich vermehren (a. biol.), sich vervielfachen.

ˌ**mul·ti·'pur·pose** *adj* Mehrzweck... ˌ**mul·ti·sto·r(e)y** *adj* vielstöckig: *~ car park* Park(hoch)haus n.

mul·ti·tude ['mʌltɪtjuːd] s **1.** große Zahl, Vielzahl f: *for a ~ of reasons* aus vielerlei Gründen. **2.** *the ~(s pl)* die Masse. **mul·ti·tu·di·nous** [ˌ~ˈtjuːdɪnəs] *adj* □ zahlreich.

mum¹ [mʌm] **I** *int*: *~'s the word* Mund halten!, kein Wort darüber! **II** *adj*: *keep ~* nichts verraten (*about, on* von), den Mund halten.

mum² [~] s *bsd. Br.* F Mami f, Mutti f.

mum·ble ['mʌmbl] v/t u. v/i (vor sich hin) murmeln.

mum·bo jum·bo [ˌmʌmbəʊˈdʒʌmbəʊ] s **1.** Hokuspokus m, fauler Zauber. **2.** Kauderwelsch n.

mum·mi·fi·ca·tion [ˌmʌmɪfɪˈkeɪʃn] s Mumifizierung f. **mum·mi·fy** ['~faɪ] **I** v/t mumifizieren. **II** v/i vertrocknen.

mum·my¹ ['mʌmi] s Mumie f.

mum·my² [~] → **mum.**

mumps [mʌmps] s pl (*sg konstruiert*) ✿ Mumps m, Ziegenpeter m.

munch [mʌntʃ] v/t u. v/i mampfen: *~ away at et.* mampfen.

mun·dane [ˌmʌnˈdeɪn] *adj* □ **1.** weltlich. **2.** alltäglich, profan; prosaisch, sachlich-nüchtern.

mu·nic·i·pal [mjuːˈnɪsɪpl] *adj* □ städtisch, Stadt..., kommunal, Gemeinde...: **~ council** Stadt-, Gemeinderat *m*; **~ elections** *pl* Kommunalwahlen *pl*. **mu·nic·i·pal·i·ty** [ˌ~ˈpælətɪ] *s* **1.** Gemeinde *f*. **2.** Kommunalbehörde *f*, -verwaltung *f*.

mu·ral [ˈmjʊərəl] **I** *adj* Mauer..., Wand...: **~ painting** → **II**. **II** *s* Wandgemälde *n*.

mur·der [ˈmɜːdə] **I** *s* **1.** (*of*) Mord *m* (an *dat*), Ermordung *f* (*gen*): **cry** (*od.* **scream**) **blue ~** F zetermordio schreien; **get away with ~** F sich alles erlauben können. **II** *adj* **2.** Mord...: **~ trial** Mordprozeß *m*; **~ victim** Mordopfer *n*; **~ weapon** Mordwaffe *f*. **III** *v/t* **3.** ermorden. **4.** *fig.* verschandeln, verhunzen. **'mur·der·er** *s* Mörder *m*. **'mur·der·ess** *s* Mörderin *f*. **'mur·der·ous** *adj* □ mörderisch (*a. fig.*).

murk·y [ˈmɜːkɪ] *adj* □ dunkel, finster (*beide a. fig.*).

mur·mur [ˈmɜːmə] **I** *s* **1.** Murmeln *n*. **2.** Murren *n*: **without a ~** ohne zu murren. **II** *v/i* **3.** murmeln. **4.** murren (*at, against* gegen). **III** *v/t* **5.** *et.* murmeln.

mus·cle [ˈmʌsl] **I** *s* *anat.* Muskel *m*: **not to move a ~** *fig.* nicht mit der Wimper zucken. **II** *v/i*: **~ in on** *fig.* F sich eindrängen in (*acc*). **'~·man** *s* (*irr man*) Muskelmann *m*, -paket *n*.

mus·cu·lar [ˈmʌskjʊlə] *adj* □ **1.** Muskel...: **~ atrophy** ♣ Muskelschwund *m*. **2.** muskulös.

muse [mjuːz] *v/i* (nach)sinnen, (-)grübeln (*on, over* über *acc*).

mu·se·um [mjuːˈzɪəm] *s* Museum *n*.

mush [mʌʃ] *s* **1.** Brei *m*, Mus *n*. **2.** *Am.* Maisbrei *m*.

mush·room [ˈmʌʃrʊm] **I** *s* **1.** ♣ (eßbarer) Pilz, *engS.* Champignon *m*. **II** *adj* **2.** Pilz...; pilzförmig: **~ cloud** Atompilz *m*. **III** *v/i* **3.** Pilze sammeln: **go ~ing** in die Pilze gehen. **4.** *oft* **~ up** *fig.* wie Pilze aus dem Boden schießen.

mush·y [ˈmʌʃɪ] *adj* □ **1.** breiig, weich. **2.** F rührselig.

mu·sic [ˈmjuːzɪk] *s* **1.** Musik *f*: **that's ~ to my ears** das ist Musik in m-n Ohren; **face the ~** F dafür geradestehen; **put**

(*od.* **set**) **to ~** vertonen. **2.** Noten *pl*. **'mu·si·cal I** *adj* □ **1.** Musik...: **~ instrument.** **2.** musikalisch. **II** *s* **3.** Musical *n*.

mu·sic| book *s* Notenheft *n*, -buch *n*. **~ cen·tre** (*Am.* **cen·ter**) *s* Kompaktanlage *f*. **~ hall** *s bsd. Br.* Varieté(theater) *n*.

mu·si·cian [mjuːˈzɪʃn] *s* Musiker(in).

mu·sic| pa·per *s* Notenpapier *n*. **~ stand** *s* Notenständer *m*. **~ stool** *s* Klavierstuhl *m*.

muss [mʌs] *Am.* F **I** *s* Durcheinander *n*, Verhau *m*. **II** *v/t oft* **~ up** durcheinanderbringen, *Haar* zerwühlen.

mus·sel [ˈmʌsl] *s* (Mies)Muschel *f*.

must[1] [mʌst] **I** *v/aux ich muß, du mußt etc*: **you ~ not smoke here** du darfst hier nicht rauchen. **II** *s* Muß *n*: **this book is a(n absolute) ~** dieses Buch muß man (unbedingt) gelesen haben.

must[2] [~] *s* Most *m*.

mus·tache *Am.* → **moustache**.

mus·tang [ˈmʌstæŋ] *s zo.* Mustang *m*.

mus·tard [ˈmʌstəd] *s* Senf *m*.

mus·ter [ˈmʌstə] **I** *v/t* **1.** ✗ (zum Appell) antreten lassen; *allg.* zs.-rufen, versammeln. **2.** *j-n, et.* aufbieten. **3.** *a.* **~ up** *fig. s-e Kraft etc* aufbieten: → **courage**. **II** *v/i* **4.** ✗ (zum Appell) antreten; *allg.* sich versammeln. **III** *s* **5.** ✗ (Antreten *n zum*) Appell: **pass ~** *fig.* durchgehen (**with** bei); ganz passabel sein, den Anforderungen genügen.

mustn't [ˈmʌsnt] F *für* **must not**.

mus·ty [ˈmʌstɪ] *adj* □ **1.** muffig. **2.** mod(e)rig.

mu·ta·tion [mjuːˈteɪʃn] *s* **1.** (Ver)Änderung *f*. **2.** Umwandlung *f*. **3.** *biol.* Mutation *f*.

mute [mjuːt] **I** *adj* □ **1.** stumm (*a. ling.*), *weitS. a.* sprachlos. **II** *s* **2.** Stumme *m, f*. **3.** ♪ Dämpfer *m*. **II** *v/t* **4.** ♪ dämpfen.

mu·ti·late [ˈmjuːtɪleɪt] *v/t* verstümmeln (*a. fig.*). **ˌmu·ti·laˈtion** *s* Verstümm(e)lung *f*.

mu·ti·neer [ˌmjuːtɪˈnɪə] *s* Meuterer *m*. **II** *v/i* meutern. **'mu·ti·nous** *adj* □ **1.** meuternd. **2.** meuterisch. **'mu·ti·ny** *s* Meuterei *f*. **II** *v/i* meutern.

mut·ter [ˈmʌtə] **I** *v/i* **1.** murmeln: **~ (away) to o.s.** vor sich hin murmeln. **2.** murren (*about* über *acc*). **II** *v/t* **3.** murmeln. **III** *s* **4.** Murmeln *n*. **5.** Murren *n*.

mut·ton [ˈmʌtn] *s* Hammelfleisch *n*: (*as*)

dead as ~ F mausetot. **~ chop** s Hammelkotelett n. **,~'chops** s pl Koteletten pl.

mu·tu·al ['mjuːtʃʊəl] adj □ **1.** gegen-, wechselseitig: **be** ~ auf Gegenseitigkeit beruhen; **by** ~ **consent** (od. **agreement**) in gegenseitigem Einvernehmen. **2.** gemeinsam.

muz·zle ['mʌzl] **I** s **1.** zo. Maul n, Schnauze f. **2.** Maulkorb m (a. fig.). **3.** Mündung f (e-r Feuerwaffe). **II** v/t **4.** e-n Maulkorb anlegen (dat), fig. a. mundtot machen.

my [maɪ] possessive pron mein(e).

my·o·pi·a [maɪˈəʊpjə] s ⚕ Kurzsichtigkeit f (a. fig.). **my·op·ic** [~ˈɒpɪk] adj (~ally) ⚕ kurzsichtig (a. fig.).

myr·i·ad ['mɪrɪəd] **I** s Myriade f, fig. a. Unzahl f: **a** ~ **of** → **II**. **II** adj: **a** ~ unzählige, zahllose.

myrrh [mɜː] s ⚘ Myrrhe f.

myr·tle ['mɜːtl] s ⚘ Myrte f.

my·self [maɪˈself] pron **1.** verstärkend: ich, mich od. mir selbst: **I did it** ~, **I** ~ **did it** ich habe es selbst getan. **2.** reflex mich: **I cut** ~. **3.** mich (selbst): **I want it for** ~.

mys·te·ri·ous [mɪˈstɪərɪəs] adj mysteriös: a) geheimnisvoll: **be very** ~ **about** ein großes Geheimnis machen aus, b) rätsel-, schleierhaft, unerklärlich. **mys·'te·ri·ous·ly** adv auf mysteriöse Weise, unter mysteriösen Umständen.

mys·ter·y ['mɪstərɪ] s **1.** Geheimnis n, Rätsel n (**to** für od. dat): **it is a** (**complete**) ~ **to me** es ist mir (völlig) schleierhaft; **make a** ~ **of** ein Geheimnis machen aus; **wrapped in** ~ in geheimnisvolles Dunkel gehüllt. **2.** eccl. Mysterium n.

mys·tic ['mɪstɪk] **I** adj (~ally) mystisch. **II** s Mystiker(in). **'mys·ti·cal** → **mystic** I. **mys·ti·cism** ['~sɪzəm] s Mystizismus m; Mystik f.

mys·ti·fy ['mɪstɪfaɪ] v/t verwirren, vor ein Rätsel stellen: **be mystified** vor e-m Rätsel stehen.

myth [mɪθ] s Mythos m, Mythus m, fig. a. Märchen n. **myth·i·cal** ['mɪθɪkl] adj □ mythisch, sagenhaft, fig. a. erdichtet.

myth·o·log·i·cal [ˌmɪθəˈlɒdʒɪkl] adj □ mythologisch. **my·thol·o·gy** [mɪˈθɒlədʒɪ] s Mythologie f.

N

nab [næb] v/t F **1.** schnappen, erwischen. **2.** sich et. schnappen.

na·bob ['neɪbɒb] s Nabob m, Krösus m.

na·dir ['neɪdɪə] s **1.** ast. Nadir m, Fußpunkt m. **2.** fig. Tief-, Nullpunkt m: **reach its** ~ den Nullpunkt erreichen.

nag [næg] **I** v/t **1.** herumnörgeln an (dat). **2.** ~ **s.o. for s.th.** j-m wegen et. in den Ohren liegen; ~ **s.o. into doing s.th.** j-m so lange zusetzen, bis er et. tut; ~ **s.o. to do s.th.** j-m zusetzen, damit er et. tut. **II** v/i **3.** nörgeln: ~ **at** → 1. **III** s **4.** Nörgler(in). **'nag·ger** s Nörgler(in). **'nag·ging I** s **1.** Nörgelei f. **II** adj □ **2.** nörgelnd. **3.** fig. nagend, bohrend (Schmerzen etc).

nail [neɪl] **I** s **1.** (Finger-, Zehen)Nagel m. **2.** ⚙ Nagel m: (**as**) **hard as** ~**s** a) a. (**as**)

tough as ~**s** von eiserner Gesundheit, b) eisern, unerbittlich; → **hit** 7. **II** v/t **3.** (an)nageln (**on** auf acc; **to** an acc): ~**ed to the spot** fig. wie angenagelt; ~ **down** ver-, zunageln; fig. j-n festnageln (**to** auf acc). ~ **bed** s anat. Nagelbett n. ~ **brush** s Nagelbürste f. ~ **file** s Nagelfeile f. ~ **pol·ish** s Nagellack m. ~ **scis·sors** s pl, a. **pair of** ~ Nagelschere f. ~ **var·nish** s bsd. Br. Nagellack m.

na·ive, na·ïve [naɪˈiːv] adj □ naiv (a. Kunst). **na·ive·ty** s Naivität f.

na·ked ['neɪkɪd] adj □ allg. nackt (a. fig. Wahrheit etc), (Wand etc a.) kahl: **with the** ~ **eye** mit bloßem Auge. **'na·ked·ness** s Nacktheit f.

nam·by·pam·by [ˌnæmbɪˈpæmbɪ] **I** adj **1.** sentimental. **2.** verweichlicht. **II**

s **3.** Mutterkind *n*, -söhnchen *n*.

name [neɪm] **I** *v/t* **1.** (be)nennen (*after*, *Am. a. for* nach): *~d* genannt, namens. **2.** beim Namen nennen. **3.** nennen, erwähnen. **4.** ernennen zu; nominieren, vorschlagen (*for* für); wählen zu; benennen, bekanntgeben. **5.** *Datum etc* festsetzen, bestimmen. **II** *s* **6.** Name *m*: *what is your ~?* wie heißen Sie?; *by ~* mit Namen, namentlich; dem Namen nach; *in the ~ of* im Namen *des Gesetzes etc*; auf *j-s* Namen *bestellen etc*; *put one's ~ down for* sich anmelden für; sich vormerken lassen für. **7.** Name *m*, Bezeichnung *f*. **8.** Schimpfname *m*: *call s.o. ~s* j-n beschimpfen *od.* verspotten. **9.** Name *m*, Ruf *m*: *get a bad ~* in Verruf kommen; *have a bad ~* in schlechtem Ruf stehen. **10.** (berühmter) Name, (guter) Ruf: *a man of ~* ein Mann von Ruf; *have a ~ for being ...* im Rufe stehen, ... zu sein; *make a ~ for o.s.* sich e-n Namen machen (*as* als). *~ day s* Namenstag *m*. **'~-,drop-per** *s* F *j-d, der dadurch Eindruck schindet, daß er ständig (angeblich) prominente Bekannte erwähnt*.

name-less ['neɪmlɪs] *adj* □ **1.** namenlos, unbekannt. **2.** ungenannt, unerwähnt. **3.** *fig.* namenlos, unbeschreiblich; unaussprechlich.

name-ly ['neɪmlɪ] *adv* nämlich.

name| plate *s* Namensschild *n*. **'~-sake** *s* Namensvetter *m*, -schwester *f*. *~ tag s* (*am Revers etc getragenes*) Namensschild.

nan-ny ['nænɪ] *s bsd. Br.* **1.** Kindermädchen *n*. **2.** Oma *f*, Omi *f*. *~ goat s* Geiß *f*, Ziege *f*.

nap [næp] **I** *v/i* ein Schläfchen *od.* Nikkerchen machen: *catch s.o. ~ping* j-n überrumpeln *od.* -raschen. **II** *s* Schläfchen *n*, Nickerchen *n*: *have (od. take) a ~ → I*.

na-palm ['neɪpɑːm] *s* Napalm *n*: *~ bomb* ✕ Napalmbombe *f*.

nape [neɪp] *s mst ~ of the neck* Genick *n*.

nap-kin ['næpkɪn] *s* **1.** Serviette *f*: *~ ring* Serviettenring *m*. **2.** *bsd. Br.* Windel *f*.

nap-py ['næpɪ] *s bsd. Br.* F Windel *f*.

nar-cis-si [nɑːˈsɪsaɪ] *pl von* **narcissus**.

nar-cis-sism [nɑːˈsɪsɪzəm] *s psych.* Narzißmus *m*. **'nar-cis-sist** *s* Narzißt(in). **,nar-cis'sis-tic** *adj* (*~ally*) narzißtisch.

nar-cis-sus [nɑːˈsɪsəs] *pl* -'cis-sus-es, -'cis-si [~saɪ] *s* ♀ Narzisse *f*.

nar-co-sis [nɑːˈkəʊsɪs] *pl* -ses [~siːz] *s* ✚ Narkose *f*.

nar-cot-ic [nɑːˈkɒtɪk] **I** *adj* (*~ally*) **1.** narkotisch, betäubend, einschläfernd (*a. fig.*). **2.** Rauschgift...: *~ addiction* Rauschgiftsucht *f*. **II** *s* **3.** Narkotikum *n*, Betäubungsmittel *n*. **4.** *oft pl* Rauschgift *n*.

nark [nɑːk] *Br. sl.* **I** *s* (Polizei)Spitzel *m*. **II** *v/t* ärgern.

nar-rate [nəˈreɪt] *v/t* **1.** erzählen. **2.** berichten, schildern. **nar'ra-tion** *s* Erzählung *f*. **nar-ra-tive** ['nærətɪv] **I** *s* **1.** Erzählung *f*. **2.** Bericht *m*, Schilderung *f*. **II** *adj* **3.** erzählend: *~ perspective* Erzählperspektive *f*. **4.** Erzählungs...

nar-row ['nærəʊ] **I** *adj* (□ → *a.* **narrowly**) **1.** eng, schmal. **2.** eng (*a. fig.*), (*räumlich*) beschränkt: *in the ~est sense* im engsten Sinne. **3.** zs.-gekniffen (*Augen*). **4.** *fig.* eingeschränkt, beschränkt. **5.** *fig.* knapp, dürftig (*Einkommen etc*). **6.** *fig.* knapp (*Mehrheit, Sieg etc*): *by a ~ margin* knapp, mit knappem Vorsprung; *win by a ~ majority* knapp gewinnen; → *escape* 8, *squeak* 6. **7.** *fig.* gründlich, eingehend (*Untersuchung etc*). **II** *v/i* **8.** enger *od.* schmäler werden, sich verengen ([*in*]*to* zu): *his eyes ~ed to slits* s-e Augen wurden zu Schlitzen. **9.** *fig.* knapp(er) werden, zs.-schrumpfen (*to auf acc*). **10.** *fig.* sich annähern (*Standpunkte etc*). **III** *v/t* **11.** enger *od.* schmäler machen, verenge(r)n, *Augen* zs.-kneifen. **12.** *a. ~ down fig.* be-, einschränken (*to auf acc*); eingrenzen. **'nar-row-ly** *adv* mit knapper Not: *he ~ escaped death* er ist gerade noch mit dem Leben davongekommen; *he ~ escaped drowning* er wäre beinahe *od.* um ein Haar ertrunken.

na-sal ['neɪzl] **I** *adj* □ **1.** *anat.* Nasen...: *~ bone* Nasenbein *n*. **2.** a) näselnd (*Stimme*): → *twang*, b) *ling.* nasal, Nasal... **II** *s* **3.** *ling.* Nasal(laut) *m*.

nas-ty ['nɑːstɪ] **I** *adj* □ **1.** ekelhaft, eklig, widerlich (*Geschmack etc*); abscheulich (*Verbrechen, Wetter etc*). **2.** schmutzig, zotig (*Buch etc*). **3.** bös, schlimm (*Unfall etc*). **4.** a) häßlich (*Charakter, Benehmen etc*), b) gemein, fies (*Person*,

Trick etc), c) übelgelaunt: **turn ~** unangenehm werden. **II** *s* **5.** *Br.* F *pornographische od. gewaltverherrlichende Videokassette.*

na·tal ['neɪtl] *adj* Geburts...

na·tion ['neɪʃn] *s* Nation *f*: a) Volk *n*, b) Staat *m*.

na·tion·al ['næʃənl] **I** *adj* □ **1.** national, National..., Landes..., Volks...: ~ **anthem** Nationalhymne *f*; ~ **championship** (*Sport*) Landesmeisterschaft *f*; ~ **currency** ✝ Landeswährung *f*; ♀ **Guard** *Am.* Nationalgarde *f*; ~ **language** Landessprache *f*; ~ **park** Nationalpark *m*; ~ **team** (*Sport*) Nationalmannschaft *f*. **2.** staatlich, öffentlich, Staats...: ♀ **Health Service** *Br.* Staatlicher Gesundheitsdienst. **3.** landesweit (*Streik etc*), überregional (*Sender, Zeitung etc*); inländisch: ~ **call** *teleph.* Inlandsgespräch *n*. **II** *s* **4.** Staatsangehörige *m, f*. **na·tion·al·ism** ['næʃnəlɪzəm] *s* Nationalismus *m*. **'na·tion·al·ist I** *s* Nationalist(in). **II** *adj* nationalistisch. ˌna·tion·al·ist·lic *adj* (~ally) nationalistisch. **na·tion·al·i·ty** [ˌnæʃə'næləti] *s* Nationalität *f*, Staatsangehörigkeit *f*: **have French ~** die französische Staatsangehörigkeit besitzen *od.* haben. **na·tion·al·i·za·tion** [ˌnæʃnəlaɪ'zeɪʃn] *s* ✝ Verstaatlichung *f*. **'na·tion·al·ize** *v/t* ✝ verstaatlichen.

'na·tion·wide *adj u. adv* landesweit.

na·tive ['neɪtɪv] **I** *adj* □ **1.** eingeboren, Eingeborenen... **2.** einheimisch, inländisch, Landes... **3.** heimatlich, Heimat...: ~ **country** Heimat *f*, Vaterland *n*; ~ **language** Muttersprache *f*; ~ **speaker** Muttersprachler(in); ~ **speaker of English** englischer Muttersprachler; ~ **town** Heimat-, Vaterstadt *f*. **II** *s* **4.** Eingeborene *m, f*. **5.** Einheimische *m, f*: **a ~ of London** ein gebürtiger Londoner; **are you a ~ here?** sind Sie von hier?

na·tiv·i·ty [nə'tɪvəti] *s* die Geburt Christi (*a. Kunst*): ~ **play** Krippenspiel *n*.

nat·ter ['nætə] *bsd. Br.* F **I** *v/i a.* ~ **away** schwatzen, plaudern. **II** *s* Schwatz *m*, Plausch *m*: **have a ~** e-n Schwatz *od.* Plausch halten.

nat·u·ral ['nætʃrəl] **I** *adj* (□ → **naturally**) **1.** natürlich, Natur...: ~ **blonde** echte Blondine; **die a ~ death** e-s natürlichen

Todes sterben; ~ **disaster** Naturkatastrophe *f*; ~ **gas** Erdgas *n*; ~ **resources** *pl* Naturschätze *pl*; ~ **science** Naturwissenschaft *f*; ~ **scientist** Naturwissenschaftler(in). **2.** naturgemäß, -bedingt. **3.** angeboren, eigen (**to** *dat*): ~ **talent** natürliche Begabung. **4.** natürlich, selbstverständlich. **5.** natürlich, ungekünstelt (*Benehmen etc*). **6.** naturgetreu, natürlich wirkend. **7.** Natur..., Roh..., (*Lebensmittel*) naturbelassen. **8.** leiblich (*Eltern etc*). **II** *s* **9.** ♪ Auflösungszeichen *n*. **10.** F Naturtalent *n* (*Person*). **'nat·u·ral·ism** *s* Naturalismus *m*. **'nat·u·ral·ist** *s* Naturalist(in). **II** *adj* naturalistisch. ˌnat·u·ral·is·tic *adj* (~ally) naturalistisch. **nat·u·ral·i·za·tion** [ˌnætʃrəlaɪ'zeɪʃn] *s* Naturalisierung *f*, Einbürgerung *f*. **'nat·u·ral·ize** *v/t* **1.** naturalisieren, einbürgern: **become ~d** *fig.* sich einbürgern (*Wort etc*). **2.** ♀, *zo.* heimisch machen: **become ~d** heimisch werden. **'nat·u·ral·ly** *adv* **1.** *a. int* natürlich. **2.** von Natur (aus). **3.** instinktiv, spontan: **learning comes ~ to him** das Lernen fällt ihm leicht. **4.** auf natürlichem Wege.

na·ture ['neɪtʃə] *s* **1.** *allg.* Natur *f*: **back to ~** zurück zur Natur. **2.** Natur *f*, Wesen *n*, Veranlagung *f*: **by ~** von Natur (aus); **it is (in) her ~** es liegt in ihrem Wesen; → **alien** 3, **second¹** 1. **3.** Art *f*, Sorte *f*: **of a grave ~** ernster Natur. **4.** (natürliche) Beschaffenheit.

naught·y ['nɔːtɪ] *adj* □ **1.** ungezogen, unartig. **2.** unanständig (*Witz etc*).

nau·se·a ['nɔːsjə] *s* Übelkeit *f*, Brechreiz *m*. **nau·se·ate** ['~sɪeɪt] *v/t* Übelkeit erregen in (*dat*); *fig.* anwidern.

nau·ti·cal ['nɔːtɪkl] *adj* □ nautisch, See(fahrts)...: ~ **mile** Seemeile *f*.

na·val ['neɪvl] *adj* **1.** Flotten..., Marine...: ~ **base** Flottenstützpunkt *m*; ~ **officer** Marineoffizier *m*; ~ **power** Seemacht *f*; ~ **review** Flottenparade *f*. **2.** See..., Schiffs...: ~ **battle** Seeschlacht *f*.

nave [neɪv] *s* △ Mittel-, Hauptschiff *n*.

na·vel ['neɪvl] *s* *anat.* Nabel *m*, *fig. a.* Mittelpunkt *m*. ~ **or·ange** *s* Navelorange *f*.

nav·i·ga·ble ['nævɪgəbl] *adj* ⚓ schiffbar. **nav·i·gate** ['~geɪt] *v/t* **1.** ⚓ befahren; durchfahren. **2.** ✈, ⚓ steuern, lenken. ˌnav·i·ga·tion *s* **1.** Schifffahrt *f*, Seefahrt *f*. **2.** ✓, ⚓ Navigation *f*. **'navi·ga·tor** *s* ✓, ⚓ Navigator *m*.

nav·vy ['nævɪ] *s* Erd- *od*. Bauarbeiter *m*.

na·vy ['neɪvɪ] *s* **1.** (Kriegs)Marine *f*. **2.** Kriegsflotte *f*. **~ blue** *s* Marineblau *n*.

nay [neɪ] *s parl*. Gegen-, Neinstimme *f*: **the ~s have it** die Mehrheit ist dagegen.

near [nɪə] **I** *adv* **1.** *a*. **~ at hand** nahe, (ganz) in der Nähe. **2.** *a*. **~ at hand** nahe (bevorstehend) (*Zeitpunkt etc*). **3.** nahezu, beinahe, fast: **~ impossible; she came ~ to tears** sie war den Tränen nahe; **~ nowhere** 1. **II** *adj* (□ *→ nearly*) **4.** nahe(gelegen): ♀ *East geogr. der* Nahe Osten. **5.** kurz, nahe (*Weg*). **6.** nahe (*Zukunft etc*). **7.** nahe (verwandt): **the ~est relations** *pl* die nächsten Verwandten *pl*. **8.** eng (befreundet): **a ~ friend** ein guter *od*. enger Freund. **9.** knapp: **~ miss** ✓ Beinahezusammenstoß *m*; **be a ~ miss** knapp scheitern; **that was a ~ thing** F das hätte ins Auge gehen können, das ist gerade noch einmal gutgegangen. **10.** genau, wörtlich (*Übersetzung etc*). **III** *prp* **11.** nahe (*dat*), in der Nähe von (*od. gen*): **~ here** nicht weit von hier; hier in der Nähe. **IV** *v/t u. v/i* **12.** sich nähern, näherkommen (*dat*): **be ~ing completion** der Vollendung entgegengehen. **~·by I** *adv* [,nɪə'baɪ] in der Nähe. **II** *adj* ['nɪəbaɪ] nahe(gelegen).

near·ly ['nɪəlɪ] *adv* **1.** beinahe, fast. **2.** annähernd: **not ~** bei weitem nicht, nicht annähernd.

,near|'sight·ed *adj* □ ♀ kurzsichtig. **~'sight·ed·ness** *s* Kurzsichtigkeit *f*.

neat [niːt] *adj* □ **1.** sauber: a) ordentlich, reinlich: **keep ~** *et*. sauberhalten, b) übersichtlich, c) geschickt: **a ~ solution** e-e saubere *od*. elegante Lösung. **2.** pur: **drink one's whisky ~; two ~ whiskies** zwei Whisky pur.

neb·u·lous ['nebjʊləs] *adj* □ *fig*. verschwommen, nebelhaft.

nec·es·sar·i·ly ['nesəsərəlɪ] *adv* **1.** notwendigerweise. **2. not ~** nicht unbedingt. **'nec·es·sar·y I** *adj* **1.** notwendig, nötig, erforderlich (*to, for* für): **it is ~ for me to do it** ich muß es tun; **a ~ evil** ein notwendiges Übel; **if ~** nötigenfalls. **2.** unvermeidlich, zwangsläufig, notwendig (*Konsequenz etc*). **II** *s* **3. necessaries** *pl of life* Lebensbedürfnisse *pl*.

ne·ces·si·tate [nɪ'sesɪteɪt] *v/t et*. notwendig *od*. erforderlich machen, erfordern: **~ doing s.th.** es notwendig machen, et. zu tun. **ne'ces·si·ty** *s* **1.** Notwendigkeit *f*: **of** (*od. by*) **~** notgedrungen; **be under the ~ of doing s.th.** gezwungen sein, et. zu tun. **2.** (dringendes) Bedürfnis: **necessities** *pl of life* lebensnotwendiger Bedarf; **be a ~ of life** lebensnotwendig sein. **3.** Not *f*: **~ is the mother of invention** Not macht erfinderisch; **in case of ~** im Notfall; *→ virtue* 2.

neck [nek] **I** *s* **1.** Hals *m* (*a. e-r Flasche etc*): **be ~ and ~** Kopf an Kopf liegen (*a. fig*.); **be up to one's ~ in debt** bis an den Hals in Schulden stecken; **it is ~ or nothing** es geht um alles *od*. nichts; **risk one's ~** Kopf u. Kragen riskieren; **save one's ~** den Kopf aus der Schlinge ziehen; **stick out one's ~** einiges riskieren. **2.** Genick *n*: **break one's ~** sich das Genick brechen; **get it in the ~** F eins aufs Dach bekommen. **3.** *→ neckline*. **4.** *gastr*. Halsstück *n* (*of lamb* vom Lamm). **II** *v/i* **5.** F knutschen, schmusen. **~·and·'~** *adj*: **~ race** Kopf-an-Kopf-Rennen *n* (*a. fig*.).

neck·lace ['neklɪs] *s* Halskette *f*.

neck·let ['~lɪt] *s* Halskettchen *n*.

'neck|·line *s* Ausschnitt *m* (*e-s Kleids etc*): **with a low** (*od. plunging*) **~** tief ausgeschnitten. **~·tie** *s Am*. Krawatte *f*, Schlips *m*.

nec·tar ['nektə] *s* ♀ Nektar *m*.

née, nee [neɪ] *adj bei Frauennamen*: geborene.

need [niːd] **I** *s* **1.** (**of, for**) (dringendes) Bedürfnis (nach), Bedarf *m* (an *dat*): **in ~ of help** hilfs-, hilfebedürftig; **in ~ of repair** reparaturbedürftig; **be in ~ of s.th.** et. dringend brauchen. **2.** Mangel *m* (**of, for** an *dat*). **3.** dringende Notwendigkeit: **there is no ~ for you to come** du brauchst nicht zu kommen. **4.** Not(lage) *f*: **if ~ be** nötigen-, notfalls. **5.** Armut *f*, Not *f*: **in ~ in** Not. **6.** *pl* Bedürfnisse *pl*, Erfordernisse *pl*. **II** *v/t* **7.** benötigen, brauchen: **your hair ~s cutting** du mußt dir wieder einmal die Haare schneiden lassen. **8.** erfordern. **III** *v/aux* **9.** brauchen, müssen: **she ~ not do it** sie braucht es nicht zu tun; **you ~ not have come** du hättest nicht zu kommen brauchen.

nee·dle ['ni:dl] **I** s **1.** allg. Nadel f, ⊙ a. Zeiger m: **a ~ in a haystack** fig. e-e Stecknadel im Heuhaufen. **II** v/t **2.** F j-n aufziehen, hänseln (**about** wegen). **3. ~ one's way through** sich (durch-)schlängeln durch.

need·less ['ni:dlıs] adj unnötig, überflüssig: **~ to say** selbstverständlich, natürlich. **'need·less·ly** adv unnötig(erweise).

'nee·dle·work s Hand-, Nadelarbeit f: **do ~** handarbeiten; **~ magazine** Handarbeitsheft n.

neg [neg] s phot. F Negativ n.

ne·gate [nı'geıt] v/t **1.** verneinen. **2.** Wirkung etc neutralisieren, aufheben. **ne·ga·tion** s **1.** Verneinung f. **2.** Neutralisierung f, Aufhebung f.

neg·a·tive ['neɡətıv] **I** adj □ **1.** negativ (a. ⚡, ℞, ⚓ etc): a) verneinend: **he was ~** ⚓ sein Befund war negativ; **~ pole** ⚡ Minuspol m; **~ sign** Minuszeichen n, negatives Vorzeichen n; b) abschlägig, ablehnend. **II** s **2.** Verneinung f (a. ling.): **answer in the ~** verneinen; **his answer was in the ~** s-e Antwort fiel negativ aus. **3.** abschlägige Antwort. **4.** negative Eigenschaft. **5.** phot. Negativ n.

ne·glect [nı'glekt] **I** v/t **1.** vernachlässigen: **~ed** ungepflegt (Erscheinung etc), verwahrlost (Kind etc). **2.** es versäumen od. unterlassen (**doing, to do** zu tun). **II** s **3.** Vernachlässigung f: **be in a state of ~** vernachlässigt od. verwahrlost sein. **4.** Versäumnis n, Unterlassung f: **~ of duty** Pflichtversäumnis n. **ne·glect·ful** [~ful] → **negligent** 1.

neg·li·gee, neg·li·gé(e) ['neglıʒeı] s Negligé n.

neg·li·gence ['neglıdʒəns] s **1.** Nachlässigkeit f, Unachtsamkeit f: **dress with ~** sich nachlässig kleiden. **2.** ⚖ Fahrlässigkeit f. **'neg·li·gent** adj □ **1.** nachlässig, unachtsam: **be ~ of** j-n, et. vernachlässigen, et. außer acht lassen. **2.** ⚖ fahrlässig. **3.** lässig, salopp.

neg·li·gi·ble ['neglıdʒəbl] adj □ **1.** nebensächlich, unwesentlich. **2.** geringfügig, unbedeutend, nicht der Rede wert.

ne·go·ti·a·ble [nı'gəʊʃjəbl] adj □ **1.** ⚓ verkäuflich; übertragbar, begebbar. **2.** passier-, befahrbar (Straße etc).

ne·go·ti·ate [nı'gəʊʃıeıt] **I** v/i **1.** verhandeln (**with** mit; **for, about, on** über acc): **negotiating skills** pl Verhandlungsgeschick n; **negotiating table** Verhandlungstisch m. **II** v/t **2.** Vertrag etc aushandeln (**with** mit). **3.** verhandeln über (acc). **4.** ⚓ verkaufen; Wechsel begeben. **5.** Straße etc passieren, Hindernis etc überwinden, Steigung etc schaffen; Musikstück etc meistern. **ne·go·ti·a·tion** s **1.** Verhandlung f: **by way of ~** auf dem Verhandlungsweg; **it is still under ~** darüber wird noch verhandelt. **2.** Aushandeln n. **3.** ⚓ Verkauf m; Begebung f. **4.** Passieren n, Überwindung f.

Ne·gress ['ni:grıs] s Negerin f. **Ne·gro** ['~grəʊ] pl **-groes** s Neger m.

neigh [neı] **I** v/i wiehern. **II** s Wiehern n.

neigh·bo(u)r ['neıbə] **I** s Nachbar(in): **~ at table** Tischnachbar(in). **II** v/t (a. v/i **~ on**) (an)grenzen an (acc). **neigh·bo(u)r·hood** ['~hʊd] s **1.** Nachbarschaft f, coll. a. Nachbarn pl: **in the ~ of** in der Umgebung od. Gegend von (od. gen); fig. um (... herum). **2.** Gegend f, Viertel n. **'neigh·bo(u)r·ing** adj benachbart, angrenzend; Nachbar... **'neigh·bo(u)r·ly** adj **1.** (gut)nachbarlich. **2.** Nachbarschafts...: **~ help**.

nei·ther ['naıðə] **I** adj u. pron **1.** kein (von beiden): **~ of you** keiner von euch (beiden). **II** cj **2. ~ ... nor** weder ... noch. **3.** auch nicht: **he does not know, ~ do I** er weiß es nicht, u. ich auch nicht.

ne·ol·o·gism [ni:'ɒlədʒızəm] s ling. Neologismus m, Neuwort n.

ne·on ['ni:ɒn] s 🜇 Neon n: **~ lamp** Neonlampe f; **~ sign** Neon-, Leuchtreklame f.

neph·ew ['nevju:] s Neffe m.

ne·phri·tis [nı'fraıtıs] s ⚕ Nierenentzündung f.

nep·o·tism ['nepətızəm] s Vetternwirtschaft f.

nerve [nɜ:v] **I** s **1.** Nerv m: **get on s.o.'s ~s** j-m auf die Nerven gehen od. fallen; **get ~s** F Nerven bekommen; **have ~s of iron (steel)** eiserne Nerven (Nerven aus Stahl) haben; **hit (od. touch) a ~** e-n wunden Punkt treffen; **bag (od. bundle) of ~s** F Nervenbündel n. **2.** fig. Stärke f, Energie f; Mut m; Selbstbeherrschung f; F Frechheit f: **have the ~ to do s.th.** den Nerv haben, et. zu tun; **lose one's ~** den Mut od. die Nerven

verlieren. **II** v/t **3.** ~ **o.s.** sich moralisch
od. seelisch vorbereiten (**for** auf acc). ~
cell s Nervenzelle f. ~ **cen·tre** (Am.
cen·ter) s **1.** Nervenzentrum n. **2.** fig.
Schaltzentrale f.

nerve·less ['nɜːvlɪs] adj □ **1.** kraft-,
energielos; mutlos. **2.** ohne Nerven,
kaltblütig. '**nerve-ˌrack·ing** adj ner-
venaufreibend.

nerv·ous ['nɜːvəs] adj □ **1.** Nerven...,
nervös: ~ **system** Nervensystem n; →
breakdown 1, **collapse** 10. **2.** nervös:
make s.o. ~ j-n nervös machen (**with**
mit). '**nerv·ous·ness** s Nervosität f.

nerv·y ['nɜːvɪ] adj □ F **1.** Br. nervös,
ängstlich. **2.** Am. frech, unverfroren.

nest [nest] **I** s **1.** orn., zo. Nest n: →
feather II, **foul** 9. **2.** fig. Brutstätte f. **3.**
Serie f, Satz m (ineinanderpassender
Dinge). **II** v/i **4.** nisten. **~·egg** s **1.** Nestei
n. **2.** fig. Spar-, Notgroschen m.

nes·tle ['nesl] **I** v/i **1.** a. ~ **down** sich
behaglich niederlassen, es sich bequem
machen (**in** in dat). **2.** sich schmiegen
od. kuscheln (**against, to** an acc). **II** v/t
3. schmiegen, kuscheln (**against, to** an
acc).

net¹ [net] **I** s **1.** Netz n (a. fig.): ~ **curtain**
Store m. **II** v/t **2.** mit e-m Netz fangen.
3. fig. einfangen. **4.** mit e-m Netz abdecken.

net² [~] † **I** adj **1.** netto, Netto..., Rein...
II v/t **2.** netto einbringen. **3.** netto verdienen od. einnehmen.

net·ting ['netɪŋ] s Netz(werk) n, Geflecht n.

net·tle ['netl] **I** s ♀ Nessel f: **grasp the** ~
fig. den Stier bei den Hörnern packen.
II v/t ärgern, reizen (**with** mit). ~ **rash** s
♯ Nesselausschlag m.

'**net·work** s **1.** Netz(werk) n, Geflecht n.
2. fig. (Händler-, Straßen- etc)Netz n:
social ~ soziales Netz. **3.** Rundfunk,
TV: Sendernetz n.

neu·ral·gia [ˌnjʊəˈrældʒə] s ♯ Neuralgie
f. ˌ**neu·ral·gic** adj (~**ally**) neuralgisch.

neu·ri·tis [ˌnjʊəˈraɪtɪs] s ♯ Nervenent-
zündung f.

neu·ro·log·i·cal [ˌnjʊərəˈlɒdʒɪkl] adj ♯
neurologisch. **neu·rol·o·gist** [~ˈrɒl-
ədʒɪst] s Neurologe m, Nervenarzt m.
ˌ**neu·rol·o·gy** s Neurologie f.

neu·ro·sis [ˌnjʊəˈrəʊsɪs] pl **-ses** [~siːz] s
♯ Neurose f. **neu·rot·ic** [~ˈrɒtɪk] **I** adj

(~**ally**) neurotisch (a. contp.). **II** s Neu-
rotiker(in).

neu·ter ['njuːtə] **I** adj **1.** ling. neutral,
sächlich. **2.** biol. geschlechtslos, unge-
schlechtlich. **II** s **3.** ling. Neutrum n. **III**
v/t **4.** zo. kastrieren.

neu·tral ['njuːtrəl] **I** adj □ **1.** allg. neutral. **II** s **2.** Neutrale m, f. **3.** mot. Leer-
laufstellung f: **the car is in** ~ es ist kein
Gang eingelegt; **put the car in** ~ den
Gang herausnehmen. **neu·tral·i·ty**
[~ˈtrælətɪ] s Neutralität f. **neu·tral·i·za·
tion** [ˌ~trəlaɪˈzeɪʃn] s Neutralisierung f,
a. 🜊 Neutralisation f. '**neu·tral·ize**
v/t neutralisieren: ~ **each other** sich
gegenseitig aufheben.

neu·tron ['njuːtrɒn] s phys. Neutron n: ~
bomb ✕ Neutronenbombe f.

nev·er ['nevə] adv **1.** nie(mals): → **die¹** 1.
2. durchaus nicht, ganz u. gar nicht: →
mind 10. '**~-ˌend·ing** adj endlos, nicht
enden wollend. ˌ**~'nev·er** s: **buy s.th.
on the** ~ Br. F et. auf Pump od. Stottern
kaufen.

ˌ**nev·er·the'less** adv nichtsdestoweniger, dennoch, trotzdem.

new [njuː] adj (□ → **newly**) allg. neu:
nothing ~ nichts Neues; **this is not** ~ **to
me** das ist mir nichts Neues; **be** ~ **to
s.o.** j-m neu od. ungewohnt sein; **be** ~
to s.th. (noch) nicht vertraut sein mit
et.; **feel a** ~ **man** sich wie neugeboren
fühlen; ~ **moon** Neumond m; ~ **publi-
cations** pl Neuerscheinungen pl; ~
snow Neuschnee m; ♀ **Testament** das
Neue Testament; ♀ **World** die Neue
Welt; → **broom, leaf** 2. '**~-born** adj
neugeboren. '**~-ˌcom·er** s **1.** Neuankömmling m. **2.** Neuling m (**to** auf e-m
Gebiet). '**~-fan·gled** ['~ˌfæŋgld] adj
contp. neumodisch.

new·ly ['njuːlɪ] adv **1.** kürzlich, jüngst: ~
married jungverheiratet, -vermählt. **2.**
neu: ~ **arranged furniture** umgestellte
Möbel pl; ~ **raised hope** neuerweckte
Hoffnung. '**~·weds** s pl die Jungverhei-
rateten pl od. -vermählten pl.

news [njuːz] s pl (sg konstruiert) Neuig-
keit(en pl) f, Nachricht(en pl) f: **a bit**
(od. **piece**) **of** ~ e-e Neuigkeit od. Nachricht; **at this** ~ bei dieser Nachricht;
what's the ~**?** was gibt es Neues?; **this
is** ~ **to me** das ist mir (ganz) neu; **have** ~
from s.o. Nachricht von j-m haben; **I**

haven't had any ~ from her for two months ich habe schon seit zwei Monaten nichts mehr von ihr gehört; **I heard it on the ~** ich hörte es in den Nachrichten. ~ **a·gen·cy** s Nachrichtenagentur f. '~**a·gent** s Zeitungshändler(in). ~ **black·out** s Nachrichtensperre f: **order a ~ on** e-e Nachrichtensperre verhängen über (*acc*). '~**boy** s Zeitungsjunge m. '~**cast** s *Rundfunk, TV:* Nachrichtensendung f. '~**cast·er** s *Rundfunk, TV:* Nachrichtensprecher(in). ~ **con·fer·ence** → **press conference.** ~ **deal·er** s *Am.* Zeitungshändler(in). ~ **flash** s *Rundfunk, TV:* Kurzmeldung f. '~**let·ter** s Rundschreiben n, Mitteilungsblatt n. ~ **mag·a·zine** s Nachrichtenmagazin n. ~**pa·per** s ['njuːs,peɪpə] s Zeitung f: ~ **publisher** Zeitungsverleger(in); ~ **rack** Zeitungsständer m. '~**read·er** *Br.* → **newscaster.** '~**stand** s Zeitungskiosk m, -stand m. ~ **ven·dor** s Zeitungsverkäufer(in).

new| year s *oft* **New Year** das neue Jahr: **happy New Year!** gutes neues Jahr!, Prosit Neujahr! ♀ **Year's Day** s Neujahr(stag m) n. ♀ **Year's Eve** s Silvester(abend m) m, n.

next [nekst] **I** adj **1.** allg. nächst: **(the) ~ day** am nächsten Tag; ~ **door** nebenan, im nächsten Raum od. Haus; **be ~ door to** fig. grenzen an (*acc*); ~ **month** nächsten Monat; ~ **time** das nächste Mal; ~ **but one** übernächst; ~ **to** gleich neben (*dat. od. acc*); gleich nach (*Rang, Reihenfolge*); beinahe, fast *unmöglich etc*, so gut wie *nichts etc*, praktisch *zwecklos etc*. **II** adv **2.** als nächste(r, -s): **you will be ~** du wirst der nächste sein. **3.** demnächst, das nächste Mal. **4.** dann, darauf. **III** s **5.** der, die, das nächste: **the ~ of kin** pl of kin die nächsten Angehörigen pl od. Verwandten pl. ~-**door** adj u. adv (von) nebenan: **we are ~ neighbo(u)rs** wir wohnen Tür an Tür.

NHS [‚eneɪtʃ'es] *Br.* **I** s Staatlicher Gesundheitsdienst: **get s.th. on the ~** et. auf Krankenschein od. Rezept bekommen. **II** adj a) Kassen...: ~ **glasses, etc** Behandlung etc auf Krankenschein: ~ **treatment.**

nib·ble ['nɪbl] **I** v/t **1.** knabbern an (*dat*). **2.** *Loch etc* knabbern, nagen (**in** in *acc*). **II** v/i **3.** knabbern (**at** an *dat*): ~ **at one's**

food im Essen herumstochern. **III** s **4.** Knabbern n.

nice [naɪs] adj **1.** fein (*Unterschied etc*). **2.** fein, lecker (*Speise etc*). **3.** nett, freundlich (**to** zu j-m). **4.** nett, hübsch, schön: ~ **and warm** schön warm; → **mess** 1. '**nice·ly** adv **1.** gut, fein: **that will do ~** das genügt vollauf; das paßt ausgezeichnet; **she is doing ~** es geht ihr gut od. besser, sie macht gute Fortschritte. **2.** genau, sorgfältig. **ni·ce·ty** ['~sətɪ] s **1.** Feinheit f. **2.** peinliche Genauigkeit: **to a ~** peinlich od. äußerst genau. **3.** pl feine Unterschiede pl, Feinheiten pl.

niche [nɪtʃ] s **1.** Nische f. **2.** fig. Platz m, wo man hingehört: **he has finally found his ~ in life** er hat endlich s-n Platz im Leben gefunden.

nick [nɪk] s **1.** Kerbe f, Einkerbung f. **2. in the ~ of time** gerade noch rechtzeitig, im letzten Moment. **3.** *Br.* F Kittchen n: **in the ~** im Kittchen. **4.** *Br.* F Zustand m: **in good ~** F gut in Schuß sein. **II** v/t **5.** a) (ein)kerben: ~ **o.s. while shaving** sich beim Rasieren schneiden, b) *j-n* streifen (*Kugel*). **6.** *Br.* F klauen. **7.** *Br.* F *j-n* schnappen. **8.** ~ **s.o. (for) $ 100** *Am.* F j-m 100 Dollar abknöpfen.

nick·el ['nɪkl] **I** s **1.** 🜍, min. Nickel n. **2.** *Am.* Fünfcentstück n. **II** v/t pret u. pp **-eled,** bsd. Br. **-elled 3.** vernickeln. '~**plate** v/t vernickeln.

nick·name ['nɪkneɪm] **I** s Spitzname m. **II** v/t j-m den Spitznamen ... geben.

nic·o·tine ['nɪkətiːn] s Nikotin n.

niece [niːs] s Nichte f.

niff [nɪf] s *Br.* F Gestank m. '**niff·y** adj *Br.* F stinkend: **be ~** stinken.

nif·ty ['nɪftɪ] adj □ F **1.** flott, fesch (*Kleidung, Person*). **2.** praktisch (*Gerät*).

nig·gard ['nɪgəd] s Knicker(in), Geizhals m. '**nig·gard·ly** adj **1.** geizig, knick(e)rig. **2.** schäbig, kümmerlich.

nig·gle ['nɪgl] v/i **1.** herumnörgeln (**a·bout, over** an *dat*). **2.** ~ **at** fig. nagen an (*dat*), plagen quälen.

night [naɪt] s **1.** Nacht f: **at** (od. **by, in the**) ~ in der od. bei Nacht, nachts; ~ **and day** Tag u. Nacht; **have a good** (**bad**) ~ gut (schlecht) schlafen; **make a ~ of it** bis zum Morgen feiern, durchmachen; **stay the ~** übernachten (**at** in *dat*; **s.o.'s** bei j-m). **2.** Abend m: **last ~** gestern abend; **the ~ before last** vorgestern nacht; *on the ~ of May 5th* am Abend des 5. Mai. **3.** Nacht *f*, Dunkelheit *f*. **~ bird** *s* **1.** *orn.* Nachtvogel *m*. **2.** *fig.* Nachtmensch *m*; Nachtschwärmer *m*. '**~blind** *adj* ✻ nachtblind. **~ blindness** *s* ✻ Nachtblindheit *f*. '**~cap** *s* Schlummertrunk *m*. '**~club** *s* Nachtklub *m*, -lokal *n*. '**~dress** *s* Nachthemd *n*. '**~fall** *s*: *at ~* bei Einbruch der Dunkelheit. '**~flight** *s* Nachtflug *m*. '**~gown** *s* Nachthemd *n*.

night·ie ['naɪtɪ] *s* F Nachthemd *n*.

night·in·gale ['naɪtɪŋgeɪl] *s orn.* Nachtigall *f*.

night life *s* Nachtleben *n*.

night·ly ['naɪtlɪ] **I** *adj* (all)nächtlich; (all)abendlich. **II** *adv* jede Nacht; jeden Abend.

night·mare ['naɪtmeə] *s* Alptraum *m* (*a. fig.*).

night| nurse *s* Nachtschwester *f*. **~ owl** *s* F Nachteule *f*, -mensch *m*; Nachtschwärmer *m*. **~ por·ter** *s* Nachtportier *m*. **~ school** *s* Abendschule *f*. **~ shift** *s* Nachtschicht *f*: *be* (*od. work*) *on ~* Nachtschicht haben. '**~shirt** *s* Nachthemd *n*. '**~spot** F → *nightclub*. '**~stick** *s Am.* Gummiknüppel *m*, Schlagstock *m* (*der Polizei*). '**~time** *s*: *in the* (*od. at*) *~* zur Nachtzeit, nachts. **~ watch** *s* Nachtwache *f*. **~ watch·man** *s* (*irr man*) Nachtwächter *m*.

ni·hil·ism ['naɪlɪzəm] *s* Nihilismus *m*. '**ni·hil·ist I** *s* Nihilist(in). **II** *adj* nihilistisch. ,**ni·hil'is·tic** *adj* (*~ally*) nihilistisch.

nil [nɪl] *s*: *our team won three to ~* (*od. by three goals to ~*) (*3-0*) unsere Mannschaft gewann drei zu null (3 : 0).

nim·bi ['nɪmbaɪ] *pl von* **nimbus**.

nim·ble ['nɪmbl] *adj* ☐ **1.** flink, gewandt. **2.** *fig.* geistig beweglich: *~ mind* beweglicher Geist.

nim·bus ['nɪmbəs] *pl* **-bi** ['~baɪ], **-bus·es** *s* Nimbus *m*, Heiligenschein *m*.

nin·com·poop ['nɪŋkəmpuːp] *s* Einfaltspinsel *m*, Trottel *m*.

nine [naɪn] **I** *adj* neun: *~ times out of ten* in neun von zehn Fällen, fast immer; → *wonder* 5. **II** *s* Neun *f*: *~ of hearts* Herzneun; *be dressed* (*up*) *to the ~s* F in Schale sein. **nine·fold** ['~fəʊld] **I** *adj* neunfach. **II** *adv* neunfach, um das Neunfache: *increase ~* (sich) verneun-

fachen. **nine·teen** [,~'tiːn] *adj* neunzehn: → *dozen*. ,**nine'teenth** [~θ] *adj* neunzehnt. **nine·ti·eth** ['~tɪɪθ] *adj* neunzigst. '**nine·time** *adj* neunmalig. **nine·ty** ['naɪntɪ] **I** *adj* neunzig. **II** *s* Neunzig *f*: *be in one's nineties* in den Neunzigern sein; *in the nineties* in den neunziger Jahren (*e-s Jahrhunderts*).

nin·ny ['nɪnɪ] *s* F Dussel *m*, Dummkopf *m*.

ninth [naɪnθ] **I** *adj* **1.** neunt. **II** *s* **2.** *der*, *die*, *das* Neunte: *the ~ of May* der 9. Mai. **3.** Neuntel *n*. '**ninth·ly** *adv* neuntens.

nip[1] [nɪp] **I** *v/t* **1.** kneifen, zwicken: *~ off* abzwicken; *~ one's finger in the door* sich den Finger in der Tür einzwicken. **2.** *Pflanzen* schädigen (*Frost etc*): → *bud* I. **II** *v/i* **3.** *fig.* flitzen, sausen: *~ in mot.* einscheren. **III** *s* **4.** *there's a ~ in the air today* heute ist es ganz schön kalt. **5.** Kniff *m*.

nip[2] [~] *s* Schlückchen *n* (*Whisky etc*).

nip·pers ['nɪpəz] *s pl*, *a.* **pair of ~** (Kneif)Zange *f*.

nip·ple ['nɪpl] *s* **1.** *anat.* Brustwarze *f*. **2.** (Gummi)Sauger *m* (*e-r Saugflasche*). **3.** ⚙ (Schmier)Nippel *m*.

nip·py ['nɪpɪ] *adj* **1.** frisch, kühl, kalt. **2.** *be ~ bsd. Br.* F sich beeilen.

nit[1] [nɪt] *s zo.* Nisse *f*, Niß *f*.

ni·ter *Am.* → **nitre**.

'**nit**|**,pick·er** *s* F pingeliger *od.* kleinlicher Mensch. '**~,pick·ing** *adj* F pingelig, kleinlich.

ni·trate ['naɪtreɪt] *s* 🜍 Nitrat *n*.

ni·tre ['naɪtə] *s bsd. Br.* 🜍 Salpeter *m*.

ni·tric ac·id ['naɪtrɪk] *s* 🜍 Salpetersäure *f*.

ni·tro·gen ['naɪtrədʒən] *s* 🜍 Stickstoff *m*. **ni·trog·e·nous** [~'trɒdʒɪnɪs] *adj* stickstoffhaltig.

ni·tro·glyc·er·in(e) [,naɪtrəʊ'glɪsəriːn] *s* 🜍 Nitroglyzerin *n*.

nit·ty-grit·ty [,nɪtɪ'grɪtɪ] *s*: *go down* (*od. come*) *to the ~* sl. zur Sache kommen.

nit·wit ['nɪtwɪt] *s* Schwachkopf *m*.

no [nəʊ] **I** *adv* **1.** nein: *say ~* to nein sagen zu. **2.** *beim comp*: um nichts, nicht: *they ~ longer live here* sie wohnen nicht mehr hier; *~ longer ago than yesterday* erst gestern. **II** *adj* **3.** kein: *~ one* keiner, niemand; *in ~ time* im Nu ohne Handumdrehen. **4.** *vor ger*: → *deny* 1.

please 4. **III** *pl* **noes** *s* 5. Nein *n*: *a clear* ~ ein klares Nein (**to** auf *acc*) **6.** *parl.* Gegen-, Neinstimme *f*: **the** *~es* **have it** der Antrag ist abgelehnt.

No-bel prize [nəʊbel] *s* Nobelpreis *m*: *Nobel peace prize* Friedensnobelpreis; ~ *winner* Nobelpreisträger(in).

no-bil-i-ty [nəʊ'bɪlətɪ] *s* 1. (Hoch)Adel *m*. 2. *fig.* Adel *m*.

no-ble ['nəʊbl] *adj* □ 1. adlig, von Adel. 2. *fig.* edel, nobel. 3. prächtig, stattlich (*Gebäude etc*). 4. Edel...: ~ *metal*. **~·man** ['~mən] *s* (*irr man*) (hoher) Adliger. **'~·wom·an** *s* (*irr woman*) (hohe) Adlige.

no-bod-y ['nəʊbədɪ] **I** *pron* keiner, niemand. **II** *s fig.* Niemand *m*, Null *f*.

noc-tur-nal [nɒk'tɜːnl] *adj* □ nächtlich, Nacht...

nod [nɒd] **I** *v/i* 1. nicken: ~ *at* (*od. to*) *s.o.* j-m zunicken; *have a ~ding acquaintance with s.o.* j-n flüchtig kennen. **2.** ~ *off* einnicken. **II** *v/t* 3. ~ *one's head* mit dem Kopf nicken. **III** *s* 4. Nicken *n*: *give a* ~ nicken; *give s.o. a* ~ j-m zunicken.

node [nəʊd] *s* Knoten *m* (*a.* ♣).

nod-ule ['nɒdjuːl] *s* ♀, ♣ Knötchen *n*.

noise [nɔɪz] **I** *s* 1. Krach *m*, Lärm *m*: *not to make any* ~ keinen Krach machen; *make a lot of* ~ *about s.th.* *fig.* viel Tamtam um et. machen. 2. Geräusch *n*: *what's that* ~? was ist das für ein Geräusch? 3. *Radio etc*: Rauschen *n*. **II** *v/t* 4. ~ *about* (*od. abroad, around*) Gerücht *etc* verbreiten: *it is being ~d about that* man erzählt sich, daß. **'noise·less** *adj* □ geräuschlos.

nois-y ['nɔɪzɪ] *adj* □ laut.

no-mad ['nəʊmæd] *s* Nomade *m*, Nomadin *f*. **no'mad·ic** *adj* (*~ally*) nomadisch, Nomaden...

'no-man's-land *s* Niemandsland *n* (*a. fig.*).

no-men-cla-ture [nəʊ'menklətʃə] *s* 1. Nomenklatur *f*. 2. (Fach)Terminologie *f*.

nom-i-nal ['nɒmɪnl] *adj* □ 1. nominal, nominell (*beide a.* ✝): ~ *income* Nominaleinkommen *n*; ~ *value* Nominalwert *m*. 2. *ling.* nominal, Nominal...

nom-i-nate ['nɒmɪneɪt] *v/t* 1. ernennen (zu), einsetzen (in *acc*): *be ~d* (*as od. to be*) ... als ... eingesetzt werden. **2.**

(*for*) nominieren (für), vorschlagen (als), als Kandidaten aufstellen (für).

nom-i-na-tion *s* 1. Ernennung *f*, Einsetzung *f*. 2. Nominierung *f*: *place s.o.'s name in* ~ j-n vorschlagen.

nom-i-na-tive ['nɒmɪnətɪv] *s a.* ~ *case ling.* Nominativ *m*, erster Fall.

non... [nɒn] nicht..., Nicht..., un...

,non-ac'cept-ance *s* Annahmeverweigerung *f*, Nichtannahme *f*.

,non-ag'gres-sion pact *s pol.* Nichtangriffspakt *m*.

,non-al-co'hol-ic *adj* alkoholfrei.

,non-a'ligned *adj pol.* blockfrei.

,non-ap'pear-ance *s* Nichterscheinen *n* (*vor Gericht etc*).

,non-at'tend-ance *s* Nichtteilnahme *f*.

nonce word [nɒns] *s ling.* Ad-hoc-Bildung *f*.

non-cha-lance ['nɒnʃələns] *s* Nonchalance *f*, Lässigkeit *f*, Unbekümmertheit *f*. **'non-cha-lant** *adj* □ nonchalant, lässig, unbekümmert.

,non-com'mis-sioned *adj*: ~ *officer* ✕ Unteroffizier *m*.

,non-com'mit-tal [*~*tl] *adj* □ zurückhaltend, (*Antwort etc*) unverbindlich: *be* ~ sich nicht festlegen wollen.

,non-com'pli-ance *s* (*with*) Zuwiderhandlung *f* (gegen), Nichtbefolgung *f* (*gen*).

non com·pos men·tis [,nɒn'kɒmpəs'mentɪs] *adj* ⚖ unzurechnungsfähig.

,non-con'form-ist **I** *s* Nonkonformist (-in). **II** *adj* nonkonformistisch. **,non-con'form-i-ty** *s* mangelnde Übereinstimmung (*with mit*).

non-de-script ['nɒndɪskrɪpt] *adj* unbestimmbar; unauffällig.

none [nʌn] **I** *pron u. s* (*mst pl konstruiert*) kein, niemand: ~ *of them are* (*od. is*) *here* keiner von ihnen ist hier; ~ *of your tricks!* laß diese Späße!; ~ *but* niemand *od.* nichts außer, nur; → *business* 6. **II** *adv* in keiner Weise, nicht im geringsten: ~ *too high* keineswegs zu hoch; ~ *too soon* kein bißchen zu früh.

non-en-ti-ty [nɒ'nentətɪ] *s contp.* Null *f* (*Person*).

,non-es'sen-tial *adj* unwesentlich (**to** für).

,none-the'less *adv* nichtsdestoweniger, dennoch, trotzdem.

,non-e'vent *s* F Reinfall *m*, Pleite *f*.

ˌnon·ex'ist·ence *s* Nichtvorhandensein *n*, Fehlen *n*. ˌnon·ex'ist·ent *adj* nicht existierend.

ˌnon'fic·tion *s* Sachbücher *pl.*

ˌnon·ful'fil(l)·ment *s* Nichterfüllung *f*.

ˌnon·in·ter'fer·ence, ˌnon·in·ter'ven·tion *s pol.* Nichteinmischung *f*.

ˌnon'i·ron *adj* bügelfrei.

ˌnon·mem·ber *s* Nichtmitglied *n*.

ˌnon·ob'serv·ance *s* Nichtbefolgung *f*, -beachtung *f*.

ˌno-'non·sense *adj* nüchtern, sachlich, (*Warnung*) unmißverständlich.

ˌnon·par·ti·san *adj* **1.** *pol.* überparteilich. **2.** unparteiisch.

ˌnon'pay·ment *s bsd.* † Nicht(be)zahlung *f*.

ˌnon'plus *v/t pret u. pp* -'plused, *bsd. Br.* -'plussed verblüffen.

ˌnon·pol'lut·ing *adj* umweltfreundlich.

ˌnon'prof·it *adj Am.*, ˌnon-'prof·it-ˌmak·ing *adj* gemeinnützig.

ˌnon·pro·lif·er'a·tion *s pol.* Nichtweitergabe *f* von Atomwaffen. ~ **treaty** Atomsperrvertrag *m*.

ˌnon·res·i·dent **I** *adj* **1.** nicht (orts)ansässig. **2.** nicht im Hause wohnend. **II** *s* **3.** Nichtansässige *m*, *f*. **4.** nicht im Hause Wohnende *m*, *f*.

ˌnon·re'turn·a·ble *adj* Einweg...: ~ **bottle.**

non·sense ['nɒnsəns] *s* Unsinn *m*, dummes Zeug: **make (a) ~ of** ad absurdum führen; illusorisch machen; **stand no ~** sich nichts gefallen lassen, nicht mit sich spaßen lassen. non·sen·si·cal [ˌ'sensɪkl] *adj* □ unsinnig.

ˌnon'smok·er *s* **1.** Nichtraucher(in). **2.** 🚂 *Br.* Nichtraucherwagen *m*. ˌnon-'smok·ing *adj*: ~ **compartment** 🚂 Nichtraucher(abteil *n*) *m*.

ˌnon'stan·dard *adj ling.* nicht hochsprachlich.

ˌnon'start·er *s*: **be a ~** keine *od.* kaum e-e Chance haben (*Person, Sache*).

ˌnon'stick *adj* mit Antihaftbeschichtung (*Pfanne etc*).

ˌnon'stop **I** *adj* durchgehend (*Zug etc*), ohne Unterbrechung (*Reise etc*), ohne Zwischenlandung (*Flug*): ~ **flight** *a.* Nonstopflug *m*. **II** *adv* nonstop, ohne Unterbrechung *od.* Zwischenlandung: **talk ~** ununterbrochen reden.

ˌnon'un·ion *adj* † nicht organisiert.

ˌnon'vi·o·lence *s* Gewaltlosigkeit *f*. ˌnon'vi·o·lent *adj* □ gewaltlos.

noo·dle ['nuːdl] *s* Nudel *f*: ~ **soup** Nudelsuppe *f*.

nook [nʊk] *s* Winkel *m*, Ecke *f*: **search for s.th. in every ~ and cranny** nach et. in jedem Winkel *od.* in allen Ecken suchen.

noon [nuːn] **I** *s* Mittag(szeit *f*) *m*: **at ~** am *od.* zu Mittag, engl*S.* um 12 Uhr (mittags). **II** *adj* mittägig, Mittags...

noose [nuːs] *s* Schlinge *f*: **put one's head in(to) the ~** *fig.* den Kopf in die Schlinge stecken.

nope [nəʊp] *adv* F nein.

nor [nɔː] *cj* **1.** → **neither 2.** **2.** auch nicht: **he does not know, ~ do I** er weiß es nicht, u. ich auch nicht.

norm [nɔːm] *s* Norm *f*. nor·mal ['ˌml] **I** *adj* (□ → *normally*) normal, Normal... **II** *s* Normalzustand *m*: **be back to ~** sich normalisiert haben, wieder normal sein; **go back** (*od.* **return**) **to ~** sich normalisieren; **be above** (**below**) **~** über (unter) dem Durchschnitt *od.* Normalwert liegen. nor·mal·ize ['ˌməlaız] **I** *v/t* **1.** normalisieren. **2.** normen, vereinheitlichen. **II** *v/i* **3.** sich normalisieren. nor·mal·ly ['ˌməlɪ] *adv* normalerweise, (für) gewöhnlich.

Nor·man ['nɔːmən] **I** *s hist.* Normanne *m*, Normannin *f*. **II** *adj* normannisch.

nor·ma·tive ['nɔːmətɪv] *adj* □ normativ.

north [nɔːθ] **I** *s* **1.** Norden *m*: **in the ~ of** im Norden von (*od. gen*): **to the ~ of** → **5. 2.** *a.* ♀ Norden *m*, nördlicher Landesteil: **the** ♀ *Br.* Nordengland *n*; *Am.* die Nordstaaten *pl.* **II** *adj* **3.** Nord..., nördlich: ♀ **Pole** Nordpol *m*; ♀ **Star** *ast.* Polarstern *m*. **III** *adv* **4.** nordwärts, nach Norden. **5.** ~ **of** nördlich von (*od. gen*). '~·bound *adj* nach Norden gehend *od.* fahrend. ˌ~'east **I** *s* Nordosten *m*. **II** *adj* nordöstlich, Nordost... **III** *adv* nordöstlich, nach Nordosten.

north·er·ly ['nɔːðəlɪ] **I** *adj* nördlich, Nord... **II** *adv* von *od.* nach Norden.

north·ern ['nɔːðn] *adj* nördlich, Nord... north·ern·er ['ˌðənə] *s* **1.** Bewohner(in) des Nordens (*e-s Landes*). **2.** ♀ *Am.* Nordstaatler(in). north·ern·most ['ˌðnməʊst] *adj* nördlichst. north·ward ['ˌwəd] *adj u. adv* nördlich, nordwärts, nach Norden: **in a ~ direction** in nördlicher Richtung, Richtung Norden. **'north·wards** *adv* → **northward.** **ˌnorth'west I** *s* Nordwesten *m*. **II** *adj* nordwestlich, Nordwest... **III** *adv* nordwestlich, nach Nordwesten.

Nor·we·gian [nɔː'wiːdʒən] **I** *adj* **1.** norwegisch. **II** *s* **2.** Norweger(in). **3.** *ling.* Norwegisch *n*.

nose [nəʊz] **I** *s* **1.** Nase *f*: *bite* (*od.* **snap**) *s.o.'s* ~ *off* j-n anschnauzen; *cut off one's* ~ *to spite one's face* sich ins eigene Fleisch schneiden; *follow one's* ~ immer der Nase nach gehen; *lead s.o. by the* ~ j-n unter s-r Fuchtel haben; *look down one's* ~ *at* die Nase rümpfen über (*acc*), auf *j-n, et.* herabblicken; *poke* (*od.* **put, stick, thrust**) *one's* ~ *into* s-e Nase stecken in (*acc*); *put s.o.'s* ~ *out of joint* j-n ausstechen; j-n vor den Kopf stoßen; *under s.o.'s* (**very**) ~ direkt vor j-s Nase; *vor j-s Augen*; → **grindstone, pick** 7, **rub** 3. **2.** *fig.* Nase *f*, Riecher *m* (*for* für). **3.** *bsd.* ⊙ Nase *f*, Vorsprung *m*; ⚓ Bug *m*; ✈ Nase *f*. **II** *v/t* **4.** *Auto etc* vorsichtig fahren. **5.** ~ *out* riechen. **III** *v/i* **6.** *a.* ~ *about* (*od.* **around**) *fig.* herumschnüffeln (*in dat*) (*for* nach). **'~·bleed** *s* Nasenbluten *n*: *have a* ~ Nasenbluten haben. **~ dive** *s* ✈ Sturzflug *m*. **'~·dive** *v/i* **1.** ✈ e-n Sturzflug machen. **2.** F purzeln (*Preise etc*). ~ *drops* *s pl* 💊 Nasentropfen *pl*. **'~·gay** *s* Sträußchen *n*. **'~·ˌpick·ing** *s* Nasenbohren *n*.

nosh [nɒʃ] *sl.* **I** *s* **1.** *bsd. Br.* Essen *n*: *have a* ~ (et.) essen; *have a quick* ~ schnell et. essen. **2.** *Am.* Bissen *m*, Happen *m*: *have a* ~ e-n Happen essen. **II** *v/i* **3.** *bsd. Br.* essen. **4.** *Am.* e-n Bissen *od.* Happen essen.

nos·tal·gia [nɒ'stældʒə] *s* Nostalgie *f*; *weitS.* Sehnsucht *f* (*for* nach). **nos·'tal·gic** [~dʒɪk] *adj* (~ally) nostalgisch.

nos·tril ['nɒstrəl] *s* Nasenloch *n*, *bsd. zo.* Nüster *f*.

nos·trum ['nɒstrəm] *s* Allheilmittel *n*, Patentrezept *n*.

nos·y ['nəʊzɪ] *adj* □ F neugierig: ~ *parker bsd. Br.* neugierige Person, Schnüffler(in).

not [nɒt] *adv* **1.** nicht: ~ *that* nicht, daß; *it is wrong, is it* ~ (F *isn't it?*) es ist falsch, nicht wahr?; → *yet* 2. **2.** ~ *a* kein(e).

no·ta·ble ['nəʊtəbl] **I** *adj* **1.** beachtens-, bemerkenswert. **2.** beträchtlich (*Unterschied etc*). **3.** angesehen, bedeutend. **II** *s* **4.** bedeutende *od.* prominente Persönlichkeit. **'no·ta·bly** *adv* besonders, vor allem.

no·ta·ry ['nəʊtərɪ] *s mst* ~ *public* Notar *m*.

no·ta·tion [nəʊ'teɪʃn] *s* ♪ Notenschrift *f*.

notch [nɒtʃ] **I** *s* **1.** Kerbe *f*. **2.** *Am.* Engpaß *m*. **3.** *fig.* Grad *m*: *be a* ~ *above* e-e Klasse besser sein als. **II** *v/t* **4.** (ein)kerben. **5.** *oft* ~ *up* F *Sieg, Einnahmen etc* erzielen: ~ *s.o. s.th.* j-m et. einbringen.

note [nəʊt] **I** *s* **1.** Bedeutung *f*: *man of* ~ bedeutender Mann. **2.** *take* ~ *of s.th.* von et. Notiz *od.* et. zur Kenntnis nehmen; *et.* beachten. **3** *mst pl* Notiz *f*, Aufzeichnung *f*: *make a* ~ *of s.th.* sich et. notieren *od.* vormerken; *take* ~s (*of*) sich Notizen machen (über *acc*); *speak without* ~s frei sprechen; → *mental* 1. **4.** (diplomatische) Note. **5.** Briefchen *n*, Zettel *m*. **6.** Anmerkung *f*; Vermerk *m*, Notiz *f*. **7.** Banknote *f*, Geldschein *m*. **8.** ♪ Note *f*. **9.** *fig.* Ton(art *f*) *m*: *strike the right* (*a false*) ~ den richtigen Ton treffen (sich im Ton vergreifen). **II** *v/t* **10.** (besonders) beachten *od.* achten auf (*acc*). **11.** bemerken. **12.** *oft* ~ *down* (sich) *et.* aufschreiben *od.* notieren. **'~·book** *s* Notizbuch *n*.

not·ed ['nəʊtɪd] *adj* bekannt, berühmt (*for* wegen).

'note·ˌpa·per *s* Briefpapier *n*. **'~·ˌwor·thy** *adj* □ bemerkenswert.

noth·ing ['nʌθɪŋ] **I** *pron* nichts (*of* von): *as if* ~ *had happened* als ob nichts passiert sei; ~ *doing* F das kommt nicht in Frage; nichts zu machen; ~ *much* nicht (sehr) viel, nichts Bedeutendes; *that's* ~ *to* das ist nichts gegen *od.* im Vergleich zu; *that's* ~ *to me* das bedeutet mir nichts; *there is* ~ *like* es geht nichts über (*acc*); *there is* ~ *to* (*od.* **in**) *it* da ist nichts dran; an der Sache ist nichts dran; *I can make* ~ *of* ich kann nichts anfangen mit, ich werde nicht schlau aus; *to say* ~ *of* ganz zu schweigen von; *think* ~ *of* nichts halten von; sich nichts machen aus; → *but* 4. **II** *s* Nichts *n*: *for* ~ umsonst; *end in* ~ sich in nichts auflösen. **III** *adv* durchaus nicht, keineswegs: ~ *like complete* alles andere als *od.* längst nicht vollständig.

no·tice ['nəʊtɪs] **I** *s* **1.** Beachtung *f*, Wahrnehmung *f*: **bring s.th. to s.o.'s ~** j-m et. zur Kenntnis bringen; **escape ~** unbemerkt bleiben; **escape s.o.'s ~** j-m *od.* j-s Aufmerksamkeit entgehen; **take (no) ~ of** (keine) Notiz nehmen von, (nicht) beachten. **2.** Ankündigung *f*, Bekanntgabe *f*, Mitteilung *f*: **give s.o. ~ of s.th.** j-n von et. benachrichtigen. **3.** Kündigung(sfrist) *f*: **give s.o. (his) ~ (for Easter)** j-m (zu Ostern) kündigen; **give the company one's ~** kündigen; **at short ~** kurzfristig; **till** (*od.* **until**) **further ~** bis auf weiteres; **without ~** fristlos. **4.** bemerken: **~ s.o. do(ing) s.th.** bemerken, daß j-d et. tut. **5.** (besonders) beachten *od.* achten auf (*acc*). **III** *v/i* **6.** es bemerken. **'no·tice·a·ble** *adj* □ **1.** erkennbar, wahrnehmbar. **2.** bemerkenswert, beachtlich.

notice board *s bsd. Br.* Anschlagtafel *f*, Schwarzes Brett.

no·ti·fi·a·ble ['nəʊtɪfaɪəbl] *adj* meldepflichtig (*bsd. Krankheit*). **no·ti·fi·ca·tion** [ˌ~fɪ'keɪʃn] *s* Meldung *f*, Mitteilung *f*, Benachrichtigung *f*. **no·ti·fy** ['~faɪ] *v/t* **1.** melden, mitteilen (**s.th. to s.o.** j-m et.). **2.** j-n benachrichtigen (*of* von, *that* daß).

no·tion ['nəʊʃn] *s* **1.** Begriff *m* (*a. ⅀, phls.*), Vorstellung *f*: **not to have the faintest** (*od.* **vaguest**) **~ of** nicht die leiseste Ahnung haben von. **2.** Idee *f*: **take** (**have**) **a ~ to do s.th.** Lust bekommen (haben), et. zu tun. **no·tion·al** ['~ʃənl] *adj* □ fiktiv, angenommen.

no·to·ri·e·ty [ˌnəʊtə'raɪətɪ] *s* traurige Berühmtheit. **no·to·ri·ous** [~'tɔːrɪəs] *adj* □ berüchtigt (*for* für).

not·with·stand·ing [ˌnɒtwɪθ'stændɪŋ] **I** *prp* ungeachtet, trotz. **II** *adv* nichtsdestoweniger, dennoch.

nou·gat ['nuːgɑː] *s* (*etwa*) Türkischer Honig.

nought [nɔːt] *s*: **bring** (**come**) **to ~** zunichte machen (werden).

noun [naʊn] *s ling.* Substantiv *n*, Hauptwort *n*.

nour·ish ['nʌrɪʃ] *v/t* **1.** (er)nähren (*of* von). **2.** *Gefühl* nähren, hegen. **'nour·ish·ing** *adj* □ nahrhaft. **'nour·ish·ment** *s* **1.** Ernährung *f*. **2.** Nahrung *f*:

take ~ Nahrung zu sich nehmen.

nov·el ['nɒvl] **I** *adj* (ganz) neu(artig). **II** *s* Roman *m*. **nov·el·ette** [ˌnɒvə'let] *s* Kurzroman *m*; *contp. bsd. Br.* Groschenroman *m*. **'nov·el·ist** *s* Romanschriftsteller(in). **no·vel·la** [nəʊ'velə] *pl* **-las, -le** [~liː] *s* Novelle *f*. **nov·el·ty** ['nɒvltɪ] *s* **1.** Neuheit *f*: a) *das Neue, weitS. der* Reiz des Neuen, b) *et.* Neues. **2.** *pl* (billige) Neuheiten *pl*.

No·vem·ber [nəʊ'vembə] *s* November *m*: **in ~** im November.

nov·ice ['nɒvɪs] *s* **1.** *eccl.* Novize *m*, Novizin *f*. **2.** Anfänger(in), Neuling *m* (**at** auf e-m Gebiet).

now [naʊ] **I** *adv* **1.** nun, jetzt: **~ and again, (every) ~ and then** von Zeit zu Zeit, dann u. wann; **by ~** mittlerweile, inzwischen; **from ~ (on)** von jetzt an; *up* **to ~** bis jetzt. **2.** sofort. **3.** *just* **~** gerade eben. **II** *cj* **4.** *a.* **~ that** nun da, jetzt wo.

now·a·days ['naʊədeɪz] *adv* heutzutage.

no·where ['nəʊweə] *adv* **1.** nirgends, nirgendwo: **have ~ to live** kein Zuhause haben; **~ near** bei weitem nicht, auch nicht annähernd. **2.** nirgendwohin: **get ~ (fast)** überhaupt nicht weiterkommen, überhaupt keine Fortschritte machen; **this will get us ~** damit *od.* so kommen wir auch nicht weiter, das bringt uns auch nicht weiter.

nox·ious ['nɒkʃəs] *adj* □ schädlich (**to** für): **~ substance** Schadstoff *m*.

noz·zle ['nɒzl] *s ⊛* Schnauze *f*; Stutzen *m*; Düse *f*; Zapfpistole *f*.

nu·ance ['njuːɑːns] *s* Nuance *f*.

nub [nʌb] *s* springender Punkt.

nu·cle·ar ['njuːklɪə] *adj* **1.** *biol. etc* Kern... **2.** *phys.* Kern-, Atom...: **~ energy** Atom-, Kernenergie *f*; **~ fission** Kernspaltung *f*; **~-free** atomwaffenfrei; **~ fusion** Kernfusion *f*, -verschmelzung *f*; **~ physics** *pl* (*sg konstruiert*) Kernphysik *f*; **~ power** Atom-, Kernkraft *f*; *pol.* Atommacht *f*; **~ power plant** Atom-, Kernkraftwerk *n*; **~ reactor** Atom-, Kernreaktor *m*; **~ scientist** Atomwissenschaftler *m*; **~ test** Atomtest *m*; **~ war(fare)** Atomkrieg(führung *f*) *m*; **~ warhead** Atomsprengkopf *m*; **~ weapons** *pl* Atom-, Kernwaffen *pl*. **3.** *a.* **~-powered** atomgetrieben: **~ submarine** Atom-U-Boot *n*. **nu·cle·us** ['~klɪəs] *pl* **-cle·i** [~aɪ] *s* **1.** (*Atom-,*

Zell- etc)Kern *m*. **2.** *fig.* Kern *m*.

nude [nju:d] **I** *adj* **1.** nackt: ~ **beach** Nacktbadestrand *m*, FKK-Strand *m*; ~ **model** Aktmodell *n*; ~ **photograph** Aktaufnahme *f*; ~ **swimming** Nacktbaden *n*. **II** *s* **2.** *Kunst:* Akt *m*. **3.** *in the* ~ nackt.

nudge [nʌdʒ] **I** *v/t* j-n anstoßen, stupsen. **II** *s* Stups *m*.

nud-ism ['nju:dɪzəm] *s* Nudismus *m*, Freikörper-, Nacktkultur *f*. **'nud-ist** *s* Nudist(in), Anhänger(in) der Freikörperkultur, FKK-Anhänger(in): ~ **beach** Nacktbadestrand *m*, FKK-Strand *m*.

nug-get ['nʌɡɪt] *s* Nugget *n*: ~**s** *pl of information fig.* bruchstückhafte Information(en *pl*).

nui-sance ['nju:sns] *s* **1.** Plage *f*, Belästigung *f*, Mißstand *m*: *what a* ~*!* wie ärgerlich!; *public* ~ ⚖ öffentliches Ärgernis (*a. fig.*). **2.** Landplage *f*, Nervensäge *f*, Quälgeist *m*: *be a* ~ *to s.o.* j-m lästig fallen, j-n nerven; *make a* ~ *of o.s* den Leuten *od.* j-m auf die Nerven gehen *od.* fallen.

nukes [nju:ks] *s pl bsd. Am.* F Atom-, Kernwaffen *pl*.

null [nʌl] *adj*: ~ *and void bsd.* ⚖ null u. nichtig. **nul-li-fy** ['nʌlɪfaɪ] *v/t* **1.** *bsd.* ⚖ für null u. nichtig erklären. **2.** aufheben.

numb [nʌm] **I** *adj* □ **1.** starr (*with* vor *Kälte etc*), taub (*empfindungslos*). **2.** *fig.* wie betäubt (*with* vor *Schmerz etc*). **II** *v/t* **3.** starr *od.* taub machen. **4.** *fig.* betäuben.

num-ber ['nʌmbə] **I** *s* **1.** Zahl *f*; Ziffer *f*: *be good at* ~*s* gut rechnen können. **2.** (*Haus-, Telefon- etc*)Nummer *f*: *be* ~ *one fig.* die Nummer Eins sein; *look after* (*od. take care of*) ~ *one* F (vor allem) an sich selbst denken; *have s.o.'s* ~ F j-n durchschaut haben; *his* ~ *is* (*od. has come*) *up* F jetzt ist er dran. **3.** (An)Zahl *f*: *a* (*great*) ~ *of people* mehrere (sehr viele) Leute; *five in* ~ fünf an der Zahl; ~*s of times* zu wiederholten Malen; *in large* ~*s* in großen Mengen, in großer Zahl. **4.** Nummer *f*, Ausgabe *f* (*e-r Zeitschrift etc*): → *back number.* **5.** *thea. etc* (Programm)Nummer *f*; ♪ Nummer *f*, Stück *n*. **II** *v/t* **6.** *his days are* ~*ed* s-e Tage sind gezählt.

7. numerieren. **8.** ~ *s.o.* *among* (*od.* *with*) *fig.* j-n zählen *od.* rechnen zu. **9.** sich belaufen auf (*acc*). **III** *v/i* **10.** ~ *in* sich belaufen auf (*acc*). **11.** ~ *among* (*od. with*) *fig.* zählen zu. **'num-ber-ing** *s* Numerierung *f*. **'num-ber-less** *adj* unzählig, zahllos.

'num-ber-plate *s mot. Br.* Nummern-, Kennzeichenschild *n*.

numb-ness ['nʌmnɪs] *s* **1.** Starr-, Taubheit *f*. **2.** *fig.* Betäubung *f*.

nu-mer-al ['nju:mərəl] *s* **1.** Ziffer *f*. **2.** *ling.* Zahlwort *n*.

nu-mer-i-cal [nju:'merɪkl] *adj* □ numerisch: a) Zahlen..., b) zahlenmäßig.

nu-mer-ous ['nju:mərəs] *adj* □ zahlreich.

nu-mis-mat-ics [ˌnju:mɪz'mætɪks] *s pl* (*sg konstruiert*) Numismatik *f*, Münzkunde *f*.

num-skull ['nʌmskʌl] *s* F Dummkopf *m*.

nun [nʌn] *s eccl.* Nonne *f*.

nun-ci-o ['nʌnsɪəʊ] *pl* **-os** *s eccl.* Nuntius *m*.

nun-ner-y ['nʌnərɪ] *s* Nonnenkloster *n*.

nup-tial ['nʌpʃl] **I** *adj* Hochzeits... **II** *s pl* Trauung *f*.

nurse [nɜːs] **I** *s* **1.** (Kranken)Schwester *f*: → *male* **I. 2.** Kindermädchen *n*. **II** *v/t* **3.** *Baby* säugen, stillen, *e-m Baby* die Brust geben. **4.** *Kranke* pflegen: ~ *s.o.* *back to health* j-n gesund pflegen. **5.** *Krankheit* auskurieren. **6.** *Stimme etc* schonen. **7.** *fig. Gefühl* hegen, nähren. **III** *v/i* **8.** stillen (*Mutter*). **9.** die Brust nehmen, trinken (*Baby*). **10.** als Krankenschwester *od.* als Krankenpfleger arbeiten. **'~-maid** → *nurse* **1.**

nurs-er-y ['nɜːsərɪ] *s* **1.** Tagesheim *n*, -stätte *f*. **2.** Pflanz-, Baumschule *f*. **3.** Kinderzimmer *n*. **~ rhyme** *s* Kinderreim *m*, -vers *m*. **~ school** *s* Kindergarten *m*: ~ *teacher* Kindergärtnerin *f*.

nurs-ing ['nɜːsɪŋ] *s* **1.** Stillen *n*. **2.** Krankenpflege *f*. **~ bot-tle** *s bsd. Am.* Saugflasche *f*. **~ home** *s* **1.** Pflegeheim *n*. **2.** *bsd. Br.* Privatklinik *f*.

nut [nʌt] *s* **1.** ♦ Nuß *f*: *a hard* (*od. tough*) ~ *to crack fig.* e-e harte Nuß. **2.** ⚙ (Schrauben)Mutter *f*. **3.** F Birne *f* (*Kopf*): *be* (*go*) *off one's* ~ (anfangen zu) spinnen. **4.** *pl* V Eier *pl* (*Hoden*). **'~-crack-er** *s a. pl* Nußknacker *m*: *a* (*pair of*) ~**(s)** ein Nußknacker. **'~-**

house s bsd. Br. sl. Klapsmühle f.

nut·meg ['nʌtmeg] s ✿ Muskatnuß f.

nu·tri·ent ['nju:trɪənt] **I** adj nahrhaft. **II** s Nährstoff m.

nu·tri·tion [nju:'trɪʃn] s Ernährung f. **nu'tri·tious** adj □ nahrhaft.

nuts [nʌts] adj F: **be ~** spinnen; **be ~ about** (od. **on**) verrückt sein nach, wild od. scharf sein auf (acc).

'nut·shell s ✿ Nußschale f: (**to put it**) in a

~ fig. kurz gesagt, mit 'einem Wort.

nut·ty ['nʌtɪ] adj **1.** Nuß... **2.** F verrückt (a. Idee etc): **be ~** spinnen; **be ~ about** (od. **on**) verrückt sein nach, wild od. scharf sein auf (acc).

ny·lon ['naɪlɒn] s Nylon n.

nymph [nɪmf] s Nymphe f.

nym·pho·ma·ni·ac [ˌnɪmfəʊ'meɪnɪæk] **I** adj nymphoman, mannstoll. **II** s Nymphomanin f.

O

O [əʊ] pl **O's, Os** s Null f (Ziffer, a. teleph.).

oaf [əʊf] s Lümmel m, Flegel m. **'oaf·ish** adj □ lümmel-, flegelhaft.

oak [əʊk] s ✿ Eiche f. **oak·en** ['~ən] adj eichen, Eichen...

oar [ɔ:] s Ruder n, Riemen m: **put** (od. **shove, stick**) **one's ~s in** F sich einmischen, s-n Senf dazugeben; **rest on one's ~s** fig. ausspannen.

oars·|man ['ɔːzmən] s (irr man) Sport: Ruderer m. **'~wom·an** s (irr woman) Sport: Ruderin f.

o·a·sis [əʊ'eɪsɪs] pl **-ses** [~si:z] s Oase f (a. fig.).

oath [əʊθ] pl **oaths** [əʊðz] s **1.** Eid m, Schwur m: **~ of office** Amts-, Diensteid; **on** (od. **under**) **~** unter Eid, eidlich; **be on** (od. **under**) **~** unter Eid stehen; **swear** (od. **take**) **an ~** e-n Eid leisten od. ablegen, schwören (**on, to** auf acc); **in lieu of an ~** an Eides Statt. **2.** Fluch m.

oat·meal ['əʊtmi:l] s Hafermehl n, -grütze f.

oats [əʊts] s pl ✿ Hafer m: **he feels his ~** F ihn sticht der Hafer; **be off one's ~** F keinen Appetit haben; **he's gone off his ~** F ihm ist der Appetit vergangen; **sow one's wild ~** sich die Hörner abstoßen.

ob·du·ra·cy ['ɒbdjʊrəsɪ] s Starrsinn m, Verstocktheit f. **ob·du·rate** ['~rət] adj □ starrsinnig, verstockt.

o·be·di·ence [ə'bi:djəns] s Gehorsam m (**to** gegen[über]), Folgsamkeit f. **o'be·**

di·ent adj □ gehorsam (**to** dat), folgsam: **be ~ to s.o.** a. j-m folgen.

ob·e·lisk ['ɒbəlɪsk] s Obelisk m.

o·bese [əʊ'bi:s] adj fettleibig. **o'bes·i·ty** s Fettleibigkeit f.

o·bey [ə'beɪ] **I** v/t **1.** j-m gehorchen, folgen. **2.** Befehl etc befolgen. **II** v/i **3.** gehorchen, folgen.

ob·fus·cate ['ɒbfʌskeɪt] v/t fig. **1.** verwirren. **2.** vernebeln.

o·bit·u·ar·y [ə'bɪtjʊərɪ] s **1.** Nachruf m. **2.** a. **~ notice** Todesanzeige f.

ob·ject¹ [əb'dʒekt] **I** v/t **1.** einwenden (**that** daß). **II** v/i **2.** Einspruch erheben (**to** gegen). **3.** et. dagegen haben: **if you don't ~** wenn du nichts dagegen hast; **~ to s.th.** et. beanstanden; **do you ~ to my smoking?** haben Sie et. dagegen, wenn ich rauche?

ob·ject² ['ɒbdʒɪkt] s **1.** Objekt n, Gegenstand m (a. fig. des Mitleids etc): **money (is) no ~** Geld od. der Preis spielt keine Rolle. **2.** Ziel n, Zweck m, Absicht f: **with the ~ of doing s.th.** mit der Absicht, et. zu tun. **3.** ling. Objekt n.

ob·jec·tion [əb'dʒekʃn] s Einspruch m (a. ⚖), Einwand m (**to** gegen); Abneigung f (**to** gegen): **if you have no ~s** wenn du nichts dagegen hast; **I have no ~ to him** ich habe nichts an ihm auszusetzen; **raise an ~ to s.th.** gegen et. e-n Einwand erheben. **ob'jec·tion·a·ble** adj □ **1.** unangenehm. **2.** anstößig.

ob·jec·tive [əb'dʒektɪv] **I** adj □ **1.** objektiv, sachlich. **2.** objektiv, tatsächlich. **II** *s* **3.** *opt.* Objektiv *n.* **4.** Ziel *n.* **ob·jec·tiv·i·ty** [ˌɒbdʒekˈtɪvətɪ] *s* Objektivität *f.*

'ob·ject les·son *s* **1.** *ped.* Anschauungsunterricht *m.* **2.** *fig.* Parade-, Schulbeispiel *n* (*in* für).

ob·jec·tor [əbˈdʒektə] *s* Gegner(in) (**to** *gen*): → **conscientious** 2.

ob·li·gate [ˈɒblɪgeɪt] *v/t:* **feel** ~**d to do s.th.** sich verpflichtet fühlen, et. zu tun. **ˌob·li·ga·tion** *s* Verpflichtung *f:* ~ **to buy** Kaufzwang *m; without* ~ unverbindlich; **be under an** ~ **to do s.th.** verpflichtet sein, et. zu tun. **ob·lig·a·to·ry** [əˈblɪɡətərɪ] *adj* □ verpflichtend, verbindlich, obligatorisch (**on** für): **attendance is** ~ Anwesenheit ist Pflicht.

o·blige [əˈblaɪdʒ] *v/t* **1.** nötigen, zwingen: **be** ~**d to do s.th.** *a.* et. tun müssen. **2.** *fig.* (*a.* zu Dank) verpflichten: **feel** ~**d to do s.th.** sich verpflichtet fühlen, et. zu tun; (*I am*) **much** ~**d (to you)** ich bin Ihnen sehr zu Dank verpflichtet, besten Dank; **would you** ~ **me by** (*ger*)? wären Sie so freundlich, zu (*inf*)? **3.** *j-m* gefällig sein, *j-m* e-n Gefallen tun. **o·blig·ing** *adj* □ entgegenkommend, gefällig.

ob·lique [əˈbliːk] *adj* □ **1.** *bsd.* ☒ schief, schiefwink(e)lig, schräg: **at an** ~ **angle to** im spitzen Winkel zu. **2.** *fig.* indirekt.

ob·lit·er·ate [əˈblɪtəreɪt] *v/t* **1.** unkenntlich *od.* unleserlich machen. **2.** vernichten, völlig zerstören. **3.** *Sonne etc* verdecken. **ob·ˌlit·er·a·tion** *s* **1.** Unkenntlichmachung *f.* **2.** Vernichtung *f.*

o·bliv·i·on [əˈblɪvɪən] *s:* **fall** (*od.* **sink**) **into** ~ in Vergessenheit geraten. **o·bliv·i·ous** *adj:* **be** ~ **to** (*od.* **of**) **s.th.** sich e-r Sache nicht bewußt sein; et. nicht bemerken *od.* wahrnehmen.

ob·long [ˈɒblɒŋ] **I** *adj* rechteckig. **II** *s* Rechteck *n.*

ob·nox·ious [əbˈnɒkʃəs] *adj* □ widerwärtig, widerlich.

o·boe [ˈəʊbəʊ] *s* ♩ Oboe *f.* **'o·bo·ist** *s* Oboist(in).

ob·scene [əbˈsiːn] *adj* □ obszön, unanständig, unzüchtig. **ob·scen·i·ty** [əbˈsenətɪ] *s* Obszönität *f* (*a. Wort etc*), Unanständigkeit *f*, Unzüchtigkeit *f.*

ob·scure [əbˈskjʊə] **I** *adj* □ **1.** a) dunkel, unklar, (*Motive etc a.*) undurchsichtig:

for some ~ **reason** aus e-m unerfindlichen Grund, b) unbestimmt, undeutlich (*Gefühl*). **2.** obskur, unbekannt, unbedeutend. **II** *v/t* **3.** *Sonne etc* verdecken. **4.** nicht klarmachen. **ob·scu·ri·ty** *s* **1.** Unklarheit *f.* **2.** Unbekanntheit *f.*

ob·se·quies [ˈɒbsɪkwɪz] *s* Trauerfeierlichkeit(en *pl*) *f.*

ob·se·qui·ous [əbˈsiːkwɪəs] *adj* □ unterwürfig. **ob·ˈse·qui·ous·ness** *s* Unterwürfigkeit *f.*

ob·serv·a·ble [əbˈzɜːvəbl] *adj* □ wahrnehmbar, merklich. **ob·ˈserv·ance** *s* Beachtung *f*, Befolgung *f*, Einhaltung *f.* **ob·ˈserv·ant** *adj* □ aufmerksam, achtsam. **ob·ser·va·tion** [ˌɒbsəˈveɪʃn] *s* **1.** Beobachtung *f*, Überwachung *f:* **keep s.o. under** ~ j-n beobachten (lassen). **2.** Bemerkung *f* (**on** über *acc*). **ob·ser·va·to·ry** [əbˈzɜːvətrɪ] *s* Observatorium *n.* **ob·ˈserve** *v/t* **1.** beobachten: a) überwachen, b) studieren, c) bemerken: **he was** ~**d entering the house** er wurde beim Betreten des Hauses beobachtet. **2.** *Vorschrift etc* beachten, befolgen, einhalten; *Fest* feiern, begehen. **3.** bemerken, äußern (**that** daß). **ob·ˈserv·er** *s* Beobachter(in). **ob·ˈserv·ing** → **observant**.

ob·sess [əbˈses] *v/t:* **be** ~**ed by** (*od.* **with**) besessen sein von. **ob·ses·sion** [əbˈseʃn] *s* **1.** Besessenheit *f:* **have an** ~ **with** → **obsess**. **2.** fixe Idee, *psych.* Zwangsvorstellung *f.* **ob·ses·sion·al** [~ʃnl] *adj* □ *psych.* zwanghaft: ~ **neurosis** Zwangsneurose *f.*

ob·so·les·cent [ˌɒbsəʊˈlesnt] *adj* □ veraltend: **be** ~ veralten. **ob·so·lete** [ˈɒbsəliːt] *adj* □ veraltet.

ob·sta·cle [ˈɒbstəkl] *s* Hindernis *n* (**to** für) (*a. fig.*): **be an** ~ **to s.th.** et. behindern, e-r Sache im Weg stehen; **put** ~**s in s.o.'s way** j-m Steine in den Weg legen. ~ **race** *s Sport:* Hindernisrennen *n.*

ob·ste·tri·cian [ˌɒbstəˈtrɪʃn] *s* ☞ Geburtshelfer(in). **ob·stet·rics** [ɒbˈstetrɪks] *s pl* (*mst sg konstruiert*) Geburtshilfe *f.*

ob·sti·na·cy [ˈɒbstɪnəsɪ] *s* Hartnäckigkeit *f* (*a. fig.*), Halsstarrigkeit *f.* **ob·sti·nate** [ˈɒbstənət] *adj* □ hartnäckig (*a. fig.*), halsstarrig.

obstreperous

1114

ob·strep·er·ous [əb'strepərəs] *adj* □ **1.** lärmend. **2.** aufsässig.

ob·struct [əb'strʌkt] *v/t* **1.** *Straße etc* blockieren, versperren, *a. Röhre, Arterie etc* verstopfen. **2.** *Aussicht etc* versperren, die Sicht versperren auf (*acc*): **~ s.o.'s view** j-m die Sicht nehmen. **3.** *Straßenverkehr, fig. Fortschritt etc* behindern, aufhalten, *Gesetzesvorlage etc* blockieren, sich *e-m Plan etc* in den Weg stellen. **ob'struc·tion** *s* **1.** Blockierung *f*, Versperrung *f*, Verstopfung *f*. **2.** Behinderung *f*. **3.** *pol.* Obstruktion *f*. **ob'struc·tion·ism** [~ʃənɪzəm] *s pol.* Obstruktionspolitik *f*. **ob'struc·tive** [~tɪv] *adj* □ hinderlich (**to** für): **be ~ to s.th.** *a.* et. behindern.

ob·tain [əb'teɪn] **I** *v/t* erhalten, bekommen, sich *et.* verschaffen: **~ by flattery** sich *et.* erschmeicheln; **~ s.th. for s.o.** j-m et. beschaffen *od.* besorgen. **II** *v/i* bestehen; Geltung haben. **ob'tain·a·ble** *adj* erhältlich: **no longer ~** nicht mehr lieferbar, vergriffen.

ob·trude [əb'truːd] **I** *v/t* aufdrängen (**on** *dat*): **~ o.s.** → **II. II** *v/i* sich aufdrängen (**on** *dat*). **ob'tru·sive** [~sɪv] *adj* □ aufdringlich.

ob·tuse [əb'tjuːs] *adj* □ **1.** ⅋ stumpf (*Winkel*). **2.** *fig.* begriffsstutzig, beschränkt.

ob·vi·ous ['ɒbvɪəs] *adj* □ offensichtlich, klar, einleuchtend: **it is** (**very**) **~ that** es liegt (klar) auf der Hand, daß.

oc·ca·sion [ə'keɪʒn] **I** *s* **1.** (günstige) Gelegenheit, richtiger Zeitpunkt (**for** für): **take the ~ to do s.th.** die Gelegenheit ergreifen, et. zu tun. **2.** (besondere) Gelegenheit, Anlaß *m*: **on this ~** bei dieser Gelegenheit; **on the ~ of** anläßlich (*gen*); **for the ~** eigens zu diesem Zweck *od.* Anlaß. **3.** (*bsd.* festliches) Ereignis: **to celebrate the ~** zur Feier des Tages; **rise to the ~** sich der Lage gewachsen zeigen; → **mark²** 11. **4.** Anlaß *m*, Anstoß *m*: **give ~ to** Anlaß *od.* den Anstoß geben zu. **5.** Grund *m*, Veranlassung *f* (**for** zu). **II** *v/t* **6.** veranlassen, verursachen. **oc'ca·sion·al** [~ʒənl] *adj* gelegentlich, Gelegenheits...; vereinzelt: **smoke an ~ cigarette** gelegentlich *od.* hin u. wieder e-e Zigarette rauchen. **oc'ca·sion·al·ly** [~ʒnəlɪ] *adv* gelegentlich, hin u. wieder.

Oc·ci·dent ['ɒksɪdənt] *s der* Westen, *poet. das* Abendland. **oc·ci·den·tal** [~'dentl] *adj* □ abendländisch, westlich.

oc·cult [ɒ'kʌlt] **I** *adj* □ okkult: a) geheimnisvoll, verborgen, b) übersinnlich, c) geheim, Geheim... **II** *s: the ~ das* Okkulte. **oc·cult·ism** ['ɒkəltɪzəm] *s* Okkultismus *m*.

oc·cu·pant ['ɒkjʊpənt] *s* **1.** Bewohner(in): **the ~s** *pl* **of the house** die Hausbewohner *pl.* **2.** Insasse *m*, Insassin *f*: **the ~s** *pl* **of the car** die Autoinsassen *pl.* **oc·cu·pa·tion** *s* **1.** Besitznahme *f*, -ergreifung *f*. **2.** ✕, *pol.* Besetzung *f*: **~ troops** *pl* Besatzungstruppen *pl.* **3.** Beschäftigung *f*. **4.** Beruf *m*: **by ~** von Beruf. **oc·cu·pa·tion·al** [~ʃənl] *adj* **1.** Berufs...: **~ accident** Arbeitsunfall *m*; **~ disease** Berufskrankheit *f*; **~ hazard** Berufsrisiko *n*. **2.** Beschäftigungs...: **~ therapy.** **oc·cu·pi·er** ['~paɪə] → **occupant** 1. **oc·cu·py** ['~paɪ] *v/t* **1.** in Besitz nehmen, Besitz ergreifen von; ✕, *pol.* besetzen. **2.** *be occupied* bewohnt sein; besetzt sein (*Platz*). **3.** *Amt* bekleiden, innehaben. **4.** *Raum* einnehmen; *Zeit* in Anspruch nehmen. **5.** j-n beschäftigen: **~ o.s. with** (*od.* **in**) **s.th.** sich mit et. beschäftigen.

oc·cur [ə'kɜː] *v/i* **1.** sich ereignen, vorkommen. **2.** vorkommen (**in** bei *Shakespeare etc*). **3.** zustoßen (**to** *dat*). **4.** einfallen, in den Sinn kommen (**to** *dat*): **it ~red to me that** es fiel mir ein *od.* mir kam der Gedanke, daß. **oc·cur·rence** [ə'kʌrəns] *s* **1.** Vorkommen *n.* **2.** Ereignis *n*, Vorfall *m*, Vorkommnis *n*: **be an everyday ~** et. (ganz) Alltägliches sein.

o·cean ['əʊʃn] *s* **1.** Ozean *m*, Meer *n*: **~ climate** Meeres-, Seeklima *n*; **~ liner** Ozeandampfer *m.* **2.** **~s** *pl* **of** F e-e Unmenge von. **'~·go·ing** *adj* hochseetüchtig, Hochsee...

o·cher *Am.*, **o·chre** *bsd. Br.* ['əʊkə] **I** *s min.* Ocker *m*, *n.* **II** *adj* ockerfarben, -gelb.

o·clock [ə'klɒk] *adv* ... Uhr: **five ~.**

oc·ta·gon ['ɒktəgən] *s* Achteck *n.* **oc·tag·o·nal** [ɒk'tægənl] *adj* □ achteckig.

oc·tane ['ɒkteɪn] *s* 🜂 Oktan *n*: **~ number** (*od. rating*) Oktanzahl *f*.

oc·tave ['ɒktɪv] *s* ♪ Oktave *f*.

Oc·to·ber [ɒkˈtəʊbə] *s* Oktober *m*: *in ~* im Oktober.

oc·to·pus [ˈɒktəpəs] *pl* **-pus·es, -pi** [~paɪ] *s zo.* Krake *m*.

oc·u·lar [ˈɒkjʊlə] *adj* Augen... '**oc·u·list** *s* Augenarzt *m*.

odd [ɒd] *adj* (□ → *oddly*) **1.** sonderbar, seltsam, merkwürdig. **2.** *nach Zahlen:* **50 ~** (*et.*) über 50, einige 50. **3.** ungerade (*Zahl*). **4.** Einzel..., einzeln (*Schuh etc*). **5.** gelegentlich, Gelegenheits...: **~ jobs** *pl* Gelegenheitsarbeiten *pl.* '**~·ball** *s bsd. Am.* F komischer Kauz.

odd·i·ty [ˈɒdɪtɪ] *s* **1.** Merkwürdigkeit *f.* **2.** komische Person *od.* Sache.

ˌodd-'job man *s* (*irr man*) Mädchen *n* für alles.

odd·ly [ˈɒdlɪ] *adv* **1.** → **odd** 1. **2.** *a.* **~ enough** seltsamer-, merkwürdigerweise.

odds [ɒdz] *s pl* **1.** (Gewinn)Chancen *pl:* **the ~ are 10 to 1** die Chancen stehen 10 zu 1; **the ~ are that he will come** er kommt wahrscheinlich; **the ~ are in our favo(u)r** (*od.* **on us**) (**against us**) unsere Chancen stehen gut (schlecht); **against all ~** wider Erwarten, entgegen allen Erwartungen; → **stack** 6. **2.** *be at* ~ uneins sein (**with** mit): **be at ~ with** *a.* im Widerspruch stehen zu. **3.** *it makes no ~ Br.* es spielt keine Rolle, es macht keinen Unterschied. **4.** **~ and ends** Krimskrams *m.* ˌ**~-'on** *adj* aussichtsreich (*Kandidat etc*), hoch, klar (*Favorit*): **it's ~ that he will come** er kommt höchstwahrscheinlich.

o·di·ous [ˈəʊdjəs] *adj* □ **1.** abscheulich. **2.** widerlich, ekelhaft.

o·dom·e·ter [əʊˈdɒmɪtə] *s mot. Am.* Meilenzähler *m.*

o·dor, *etc Am.* → **odour,** *etc.*

o·dor·if·er·ous [ˌəʊdəˈrɪfərəs] *adj* □ duftend.

o·dour [ˈəʊdə] *s bsd. Br.* **1.** Geruch *m, bsd.* Duft *m.* **2.** *be in bad ~ with fig.* schlecht angeschrieben sein bei. '**o·dour·less** *adj bsd. Br.* geruchlos.

od·ys·sey [ˈɒdɪsɪ] *s* Odyssee *f.*

oec·u·men·i·cal → **ecumenical.**

oe·de·ma [iːˈdiːmə] *pl* **-ma·ta** [~mətə] *s* ✠ Ödem *n.*

Oe·di·pus com·plex [ˈiːdɪpəs] *s psych.* Ödipuskomplex *m.*

oe·soph·a·gus [ɪˈsɒfəgəs] *pl* **-gi** [~gaɪ],

-gus·es *s anat. bsd. Br.* Speiseröhre *f.*

oes·tro·gen [ˈiːstrəʊdʒən] *s biol. bsd. Br.* Östrogen *n.*

of [ɒv] *prp* **1.** *allg.* von. **2.** *zur Bezeichnung des Genitivs:* **the tail ~ the dog** der Schwanz des Hundes. **3.** *Ort:* bei: **the Battle ~ Hastings** die Schlacht bei Hastings. **4.** *Entfernung, Trennung, Befreiung:* a) von: **south ~ London** südlich von London; → **cure** 4, *etc*, b) *gen:* → **rob,** *etc*, c) um: → **cheat** 3, *etc*. **5.** *Herkunft:* von, aus: **Mr X ~ London** Mr X aus London; → **family** I, *etc*. **6.** *Eigenschaft:* von, mit: **a man ~ courage** ein mutiger Mann, ein Mann mit Mut; → **importance,** *etc*. **7.** *Stoff:* aus, von: **a dress ~ silk** ein Kleid aus Seide, ein Seidenkleid; (**made**) **~ steel** aus Stahl (hergestellt). **8.** *Urheberschaft, Art u. Weise:* von: **the works ~ Shakespeare;** **it was clever ~ him.** **9.** *Ursache, Grund:* a) an (*dat*): → **die** 1, *etc*, b) auf (*acc*): → **proud** 1, *etc*, c) vor (*dat*): → **afraid,** *etc*, d) nach: → **smell** 2, *etc*. **10.** *Thema:* an (*acc*): → **think** 6, *etc*. **11.** *Apposition, unübersetzt:* a) **the city ~ London** die Stadt London; **the month ~ April** der Monat April, b) *Maß:* **a glass ~ wine** ein Glas Wein; **a piece ~ meat** ein Stück Fleisch. **12.** *Zeit:* a) von: **your letter ~ March 3rd** Ihr Schreiben vom 3. März, b) *Am.* vor: **ten** (**minutes**) **~ three.**

off [ɒf] **I** *adv* **1.** fort(...), weg(...): **be ~** (*Sport*) gestartet sein; **I must be ~** ich muß gehen *od.* weg; **~ with you!** fort mit dir!; → **go off** 1, *etc*. **2.** ab(...): → **cut off, hat,** *etc*. **3.** weg, entfernt: **three miles ~. 4. ~ and on** ab u. zu, hin u. wieder. **5.** **5 %** ~ ✠ **5 %** Nachlaß; → **take off** 5. **6.** aus(...), aus-, abgeschaltet: → **switch** 5, 6, *etc*. **7.** *be* **~** ausfallen, nicht stattfinden: **their engagement is ~** sie haben ihre Verlobung gelöst. **8.** aus(gegangen), alle. **9.** **she is ~ today** sie hat heute ihren freien Tag; **give s.o. the afternoon ~** j-m den Nachmittag freigeben; **take a day ~** sich e-n Tag frei nehmen. **10.** nicht mehr frisch, verdorben (*Nahrungsmittel*): → **go off** 6. **11.** **well** (**badly**) **~** gut (schlecht) d(a)ran *od.* gestellt *od.* situiert: **how are you ~ for ...?** wie sieht es bei dir mit ... aus? **II** *prp* **12.** weg von, von (... *weg od.* ab *od.*

herunter): **jump ~ the bus** vom Bus abspringen; → **get off, grass** 2, *etc.* **13.** abseits von (*od. gen*), von ... weg: **a street ~ Piccadilly** e-e Seitenstraße von Piccadilly. **14.** *be ~ duty* nicht im Dienst sein, dienstfrei haben. **15.** *be ~ s.th.* et. nicht mehr mögen; von et. kuriert sein: → **drug** 2. **16.** ♫ vor *der Küste etc.* **III** *adj* **17.** (arbeits-, dienst)frei. **18.** schlecht (*Tag etc*): **this is an ~ day for me** heute geht mir alles schief, das ist heut nicht mein Tag; **an ~ year for fruit** ein schlechtes Obstjahr. **19.** *on the ~ chance* auf gut Glück; in der Hoffnung (*of getting* zu bekommen); **~ season** Nebensaison *f.*

of·fal ['ɒfl] *s gastr.* Innereien *pl.*

'off·beat *adj* F ausgefallen, unkonventionell. **~·'col·o(u)r** *adj* **1.** *be* (*od. feel*) ~ sich nicht wohl fühlen. **2.** gewagt (*Witz etc*).

of·fence [ə'fens] *s* **1.** *allg.* Vergehen *n*, Verstoß *m* (*against* gegen). **2.** ‡‡ Straftat *f*; Vergehen *n*. **3.** Beleidigung *f*, Kränkung *f*: *give* (*od. cause*) ~ Anstoß *od.* Ärgernis erregen (*to* bei); *take* ~ Anstoß nehmen (*at* an *dat*); *be quick* (*od. swift*) *to take* ~ schnell beleidigt sein; *no* ~ (*meant od. intended*) nichts für ungut!; *no* ~ (*taken*) (es) ist schon gut! **4.** *Am.* → **offense**.

of·fend [ə'fend] **I** *v/t* beleidigen, kränken: *be ~ed at* (*od. by*) sich beleidigt fühlen durch. **II** *v/i* verstoßen (*against* gegen). **of'fend·er** *s* (Übel-, Misse)Täter(in): *first ~* ‡‡ nicht Vorbestrafte *m*, *f*, Ersttäter(in).

of·fense *Am.* → **offence.**

of·fen·sive [ə'fensɪv] **I** *adj* □ **1.** beleidigend, anstößig: *get ~* ausfallend werden. **2.** widerlich (*Geruch etc*). **3.** ✕, *Sport*: Angriffs..., Offensiv... **II** *s* **4.** *allg.* Offensive *f*: *take the ~* die Offensive ergreifen.

of·fer ['ɒfə] **I** *v/t* **1.** anbieten: → **resistance** 1. 2. a) ✝ *Ware* anbieten (*for sale* zum Verkauf), offerieren, b) ✝ *Preis, Summe* bieten, c) *Preis, Belohnung* aussetzen. **3.** *Entschuldigung etc* vorbringen, *Vorschlag* machen. **4.** sich bereit erklären (*to do* zu tun): ~ *to help* s-e Hilfe anbieten. **II** *v/i* **5.** es *od.* sich anbieten. **III** *s* **6.** Angebot *n*: *make s.o. an ~ of s.th.* j-m et. anbieten; *his ~ of help*

sein Angebot zu helfen, s-e angebotene Hilfe. **7.** ✝ (An)Gebot *n*, Offerte *f* (*of* über *acc*): *on ~* zu verkaufen; im Angebot; *or near ~* Verhandlungsbasis.

,off'hand **I** *adv* **1.** auf Anhieb, so ohne weiteres. **II** *adj* **2.** improvisiert, Stegreif... **3.** lässig (*Art etc*), hingeworfen (*Bemerkung*).

of·fice ['ɒfɪs] *s* **1.** Büro *n*, (*e-r Institution*) Geschäftsstelle *f*, (*Anwalts*)Kanzlei *f*: *at the ~* im Büro. **2.** *mst* ♀ *bsd. Br.* Ministerium *n*: → **foreign** 1, **Home Office.** **3.** (*bsd.* öffentliches) Amt, Posten *m*: *be in* (*out of*) ~ (nicht mehr) im Amt sein; (nicht mehr) an der Macht sein. ~ **block** *s* Bürogebäude *n.* ~ **boy** *s* Bürogehilfe *m.* ~ **cli·mate** *s* Betriebsklima *n.* ~ **girl** *s* Bürogehilfin *f.* **'~·hold·er** *s* Amtsinhaber(in). ~ **hours** *s pl* Dienstzeit *f*; Geschäfts-, Öffnungszeiten *pl.*

of·fi·cer ['ɒfɪsə] *s* **1.** ✕ Offizier *m.* **2.** (*Polizei- etc*)Beamte *m.*

of·fi·cial [ə'fɪʃl] **I** *adj* □ **1.** offiziell, amtlich, dienstlich: ~ *duties* *pl* Amtspflichten *pl*; ~ *language* Amtssprache *f*; ~ *secret* Amts-, Dienstgeheimnis *n*; ~ *trip* Dienstreise *f*; → **channel, residence** 1. **II** *s* **2.** Beamte *m*, Beamtin *f.* **3.** (*Gewerkschafts- etc*)Funktionär (-in). **of'fi·cial·dom** *s* Beamtentum *n*, *die* Beamten *pl.* **of,fi·cial'ese** [~ʃə'liːz] *s* Amtsenglisch *n*, Behördensprache *f.*

of·fi·cious [ə'fɪʃəs] *adj* □ übereifrig, übertrieben diensteifrig.

off·ing ['ɒfɪŋ] *s*: *be in the ~* sich abzeichnen, in Sicht sein.

'off·|·li·cence *s Br.* Wein- u. Spirituosenhandlung *f.* **'~·peak** *adj*: ~ *electricity* Nachtstrom *m*; ~ *hours* *pl* verkehrsschwache Stunden *pl.* **'~·put·ting** *adj Br.* F unangenehm, störend; unsympathisch (*Person, Wesen*). **~·set I** *s* ['ɒfset] **1.** Ausgleich *m*: *as an ~* als Ausgleich (*to* für). **2.** *typ.* Offsetdruck *m.* **II** *v/t* [ɒf'set] (*irr set*) **3.** ausgleichen. **'~·shoot** *s* ⚘ Ableger *m* (*a. fig.*), Sprößling *m.* **'~·shore I** *adv* vor der Küste. **II** *adj* küstennah: ~ *boring* Off-shore-Bohrung *f*; ~ *fishing* Küstenfischerei *f.* **'~·side I** *adj u. adv Sport*: abseits: *be ~* abseits *od.* im Abseits stehen; ~ *position* Abseitsposition *f*, -stellung *f*; ~ *trap* Abseitsfalle *f.* **'~·spring** *s* **1.** Nachkomme(schaft *f*) *pl.* **2.** *pl* **offspring**

Abkömmling *m*, Nachkomme *m*.
~-the-'rec·ord *adj u. adv* nicht für die Öffentlichkeit bestimmt, inoffiziell.

of·ten ['ofn] *adv* oft(mals), häufig: *more ~* öfters; *as ~ as* jedesmal wenn; *as ~ as (od. more ~ than) not* sehr oft; *ever so ~* öfters, von Zeit zu Zeit.

o·gle ['əʊgl] *v/t (a. v/i: ~ at)* j-m (schöne) Augen machen; *contp.* begaffen.

oh [əʊ] *int.* oh!: → *dear* 5, *yes* I.

ohm [əʊm] *s ⚡* Ohm *n*.

oil [ɔɪl] I *s* 1. Öl *n*: *pour ~ on troubled waters fig.* Öl auf die Wogen gießen; → *midnight* II. 2. (Erd)Öl *n*: *strike ~* auf Öl stoßen; *fig.* Glück *od.* Erfolg haben, *a.* fündig werden. 3. Ölfarbe *f*: *paint in ~s* in Öl malen. II *v/t* 4. (ein)ölen, schmieren: *~ the wheels fig.* für e-n reibungslosen Ablauf sorgen; → *palm*¹ 1. *~ change s mot.* Ölwechsel *m*: *do an ~* e-n Ölwechsel machen. *~ col·o(u)r s* Ölfarbe *f*. *~ cri·sis s (irr crisis)* Ölkrise *f*. *~ dip·stick s mot.* Ölmeßstab *m*. '~·field *s* Ölfeld *n*. '~·fired *adj*: *~ central heating* Ölzentralheizung *f*. *~ lamp s* Öl-, Petroleumlampe *f*. *~ lev·el s mot.* Ölstand *m*. *~ paint s* Ölfarbe *f*. *~ paint·ing s* 1. Ölmalerei *f*. 2. Ölgemälde *n*: *she's no ~* F sie ist keine strahlende Schönheit. '~·pro·duc·ing coun·try *s* Ölförderland *n*. *~ rig s* (Öl)Bohrinsel *f*. *~ sheik(h) s* Ölscheich *m*. *~ slick s* Ölteppich *m*. *~ tank·er s* (Öl)Tanker *m*. *~ well s* Ölquelle *f*.

oil·y ['ɔɪlɪ] *adj* 1. ölig. 2. *fig.* schleimig.

oint·ment ['ɔɪntmənt] *s* Salbe *f*.

OK, o·kay [əʊ'keɪ] F I *adj u. int* okay(!), o.k.(!), in Ordnung(!). II *v/t* genehmigen, e-r Sache zustimmen. III *s* Okay *n*, O.K. *n*, Genehmigung *f*, Zustimmung *f*.

old [əʊld] I *adj* 1. *allg.* alt: *grow ~* alt werden, altern; *I'm getting ~!* ich werde alt!; *ten years ~* zehn Jahre alt; *a ten-year-~ boy* ein zehnjähriger Junge; *~ boy Br.* ehemaliger Schüler, Ehemalige *m*; *~ girl Br.* ehemalige Schülerin, Ehemalige *f*; *be ~ hat* F ein alter Hut sein; *the (od. his) ~ lady (od. woman)* F s-e Alte; s-e alte Dame; *the (od. her) ~ man* F ihr Alter; ihr alter Herr; *~ people's home* Alten-, Altersheim *n*; *of the ~ school Gentleman etc* der alten Schule; 2 *Testament* das Alte

Testament; *~ wives' tale* Ammenmärchen *n*; 2 *World* die Alte Welt; → *flame* 1, *hand* 6, *maid* 1. 2. *sl. (verstärkend) have a fine ~ time* sich köstlich amüsieren; *I can use any ~ thing* ich hab' für alles Verwendung; *come any ~ time* komm, wann es dir gerade paßt. II *s* 3. *the ~ pl* die Alten *pl.* *~ age s* (hohes) Alter: *in one's ~* im Alter; *die of (od. from) ~* an Altersschwäche sterben. '~-age *adj* Alters...: *~ pension* Rente *f*, Pension *f*; *~ pensioner* Rentner(in), Pensionär(in). '~·es·'tab·lished *adj* alteingesessen *(Firma etc)*, alt *(Brauch etc)*. '~·'fash·ioned *adj* 1. altmodisch. 2. *Br.* F mißbilligend *(Blick etc)*. '~· 'maid·ish *adj* □ altjüngferlich.

old·ster ['əʊldstə] *s* F ältere Person.

old-'tim·er *s* F 1. alter Hase. 2. *bsd. Am.* → *oldster*.

o·le·an·der [ˌəʊlɪ'ændə] *s* ⚘ Oleander *m*.

ol·fac·to·ry [ɒl'fæktərɪ] *adj* Geruchs...

ol·i·garch·y ['ɒlɪgɑːkɪ] *s* Oligarchie *f*.

ol·ive ['ɒlɪv] I *s* 1. *a. ~ tree* Oliven-, Ölbaum *m*. 2. Olive *f*: *~ oil* Olivenöl *n*. II *adj* 3. olivgrün.

O·lym·pi·ad [əʊ'lɪmpɪæd] *s* Olympiade *f*. **O·lym·pic** I *adj* olympisch: *~ champion* Olympiasieger(in); *~ Games* → II; *Summer (Winter) ~ Games pl* Olympische Sommer-(Winter)spiele *pl*. II *s pl* Olympische Spiele *pl*.

om·buds·man ['ɒmbʊdzmən] *s (irr man)* *s pol.* Ombudsmann *m*.

om·e·lett *Am.*, **om·e·lette** *s bsd. Br.* ['ɒmlɪt] Omelett *n*.

o·men ['əʊmen] *s* Omen *n*, Vorzeichen *n*.

om·i·nous ['ɒmɪnəs] *adj* □ ominös, unheilvoll: *that's ~* das läßt nichts Gutes ahnen.

o·mis·sion [ə'mɪʃn] *s* 1. Aus-, Weglassung *f*. 2. Unterlassung *f*, Versäumnis *n*: *sin of ~* Unterlassungssünde *f*.

o·mit [ə'mɪt] *v/t* 1. aus-, weglassen *(from aus)*. 2. *~ doing (od. to do) s.th.* versäumen *od.* es unterlassen, et. zu tun.

om·ni·bus ['ɒmnɪbəs] *s* Sammelband *m*.

om·nis·ci·ent [ɒm'nɪsɪənt] *adj* □ allwissend.

on [ɒn] I *prp* 1. auf *(acc od. dat)*. 2. getragen von: auf *(dat)*, an *(dat)*, in *(dat)*: *find s.th. ~ s.o.* et. bei j-m finden; *have you got some money ~ you?* hast du Geld bei dir?; → *foot* 1, *etc.* 3. *fest-*

gemacht od. sehr nahe: an (*dat*): **the dog is ~ the chain;** **~ the Thames. 4.** *Richtung, Ziel:* auf (*acc*) ... (hin), an (*acc*): **drop s.th. ~ the floor** et. zu Boden fallen lassen; **hang s.th. ~ a peg** et. an e-n Haken hängen; → **board 6**, *etc.* **5.** *fig. auf der Grundlage von:* auf (*acc*) ... (hin): **~ this theory** nach dieser Theorie; → **condition 1**, *etc.* **6.** *aufeinanderfolgend:* auf (*acc*), über (*acc*): **loss ~ loss** Verlust auf *od.* über Verlust; **be ~ one's second glass** beim zweiten Glas sein. **7.** (*gehörig*) zu, (*beschäftigt*) bei: **be ~ a committee** zu e-m Ausschuß gehören. **8.** *Zustand:* in (*dat*), auf (*dat*): **be ~ Medikament etc** ständig nehmen; *b.s.* ...süchtig sein; **~** ...süchtig sein; → **duty 2**, *etc.* **9.** *gerichtet:* auf (*acc*): **a joke ~ s.o.** ein Spaß auf j-s Kosten; **the next round is ~ me** F die nächste Runde geht auf m-e Rechnung. **10.** *Thema:* über (*acc*): **talk ~ a subject. 11.** *Zeitpunkt:* an (*dat*): **~ June 3rd** am 3. Juni; **~ the morning of July 1st** am Morgen des 1. Juli. **II** *adv* **12.** an..., auf...: → **put on 1, keep on 1**, *etc.* **13.** weiter(...): **and so ~** u. so weiter; **~ and ~** immer weiter; **~ and off** ab u. zu, hin u. wieder; **from that day ~** von dem Tage an. **III** *adj* **14.** **be ~** a) vor sich gehen: **what's ~?** was ist los?, b) an sein (*Licht, Radio etc*), c) *thea.* gegeben werden (*Stück*), laufen (*Film*), (*Rundfunk, TV*) gesendet werden. **15. be always ~ at s.o.** F j-m dauernd in den Ohren liegen (*about* wegen).

once [wʌns] **I** *adv* **1.** einmal: **~ again** (*od. more*) noch einmal; **~ or twice** ein paarmal; **~ in a while** ab u. zu, hin u. wieder; **~ and for all** ein für allemal; **not ~** kein einziges Mal; → **lifetime** I, **moon** I. **2.** einmal, einst: **~ upon a time there was** es war einmal. **II** *s* **3.** **the ~** einmal, ein einziges Mal; **this ~** dieses 'eine Mal. **4. at ~** a) auf einmal, gleichzeitig, b) sofort: **all at ~** mit 'einem Mal. **III** *cj* **5.** sobald *od.* wenn (einmal).

'~-o•ver *s*: **give s.th. the** (*od. a*) **~** F et. kurz mustern.

on•com•ing ['ɒnˌkʌmɪŋ] *adj* entgegenkommend: **~ traffic** Gegenverkehr *m*.

one [wʌn] **I** *adj* **1.** ein(e): **~ hundred** u. **thousand 1. 2.** *betont:* einzig: **they were all of ~ mind** sie waren alle 'einer

Meinung; **his ~ thought** sein einziger Gedanke; **my ~ and only hope** m-e einzige Hoffnung; **the ~ and only ...** der einzigartige *od.* unvergleichliche ... **3.** ein gewisser, e-e gewisse, ein gewisses: **~ day** e-s Tages; **~ John Smith** ein gewisser John Smith. **II** *s* **4.** Eins *f*, eins: **at ~** um eins; **be ~ up on s.o.** j-m voraus sein; → **number 2. 5.** *der, die, das einzelne:* **~ by ~,** **~ after the other** e-r nach dem andern; **I for ~** ich zum Beispiel; → **another 1. III** *pron* **6.** ein(e): **the ~ who** der(jenige), welcher; **~ another** sich (gegenseitig), einander. **7.** *Stützwort, mst unübersetzt:* **the little ~s** die Kleinen; **a red pencil and a blue ~** ein roter Bleistift u. ein blauer. **8.** man. **9.** **~'s** sein: **break ~ leg** sich das Bein brechen. **,~-'armed** *adj:* **~ bandit** F einarmiger Bandit. **,~-'eyed** *adj* einäugig. **,~-'hand•ed** *adj u. adv* einhändig. **,~-'horse** *adj* einspännig: **~ town** F Nest *n*, Kaff *n*. **,~-'legged** *adj* einbeinig. **'~-man** *adj* Einmann...: **~ band** Einmannkapelle *f*; **~ play** *thea.* Einpersonenstück *n*; **~ show** One-man-Show *f*. **'~-night** *adj:* **~ stand** *thea. etc* einmaliges Gastspiel. **'~-piece** *adj* einteilig.

on•er•ous ['ɒnərəs] *adj* □ lästig, beschwerlich (**to** für).

one'self *pron* **1.** *reflex.* sich (selbst *od.* selber): (**all**) **by ~** ganz allein; **cut ~** sich schneiden. **2.** sich selbst *od.* selber. **3.** man selbst *od.* selber: **be ~** sich normal *od.* natürlich benehmen; sich geben; **not to be ~** nicht auf der Höhe sein; nicht ganz bei Verstand sein; **be ~ again** wieder ganz der alte sein.

,one|-'sid•ed *adj* □ einseitig (*a. fig.*). **'~-time** *adj* ehemalig, früher. **'~-track** *adj* 🚂 eingleisig: **have a ~ mind** *fig.* immer nur dasselbe im Kopf haben. **'~-way** *adj* **1.** Einbahn...: **~ street. 2. ~ ticket** *Am.* einfache Fahrkarte, ✈ einfaches Ticket. **3.** *fig.* einseitig.

'on,go•ing *adj* laufend (*Verhandlungen etc*).

on•ion ['ʌnjən] *s* 🌿 Zwiebel *f*: **know one's ~s** F sein Geschäft verstehen.

'on,look•er *s* Zuschauer(in).

on•ly ['əʊnlɪ] **I** *adj* **1.** einzig: **~ child** Einzelkind *n*; → **but 2. 2.** nur, bloß: **if ~ he would leave!** wenn er doch nur endlich ginge!; → **but 2. 3.** erst: **~ yes-**

terday; **~ just** eben erst, gerade. **III** *cj* **4.** nur, bloß.

'on|·rush *s* Ansturm *m*. **'~·set** *s* Einbruch *m*, Beginn *m* (*des Winters*); Ausbruch *m* (*e-r Krankheit*). **~·slaught** ['~slɔːt] *s* (heftiger) Angriff (*a. fig.*). **ı~·the-'job** *adj* praktisch (*Ausbildung*).

on·to ['ɒntʊ] *prp* **1.** auf (*acc*). **2. be ~ s.o.** F j-m auf die Schliche gekommen sein.

on·ward(s) ['ɒnwəd(z)] *adv* vorwärts, weiter: **from today ~** von heute an.

oo·dles ['uːdlz] *s pl* F: **~ of money** Geld wie Heu; **~ of time** jede Menge *od*. massenhaft Zeit.

ooze [uːz] **I** *v/i* (ein-, durch)sickern, (-)dringen (*a. Licht, Geräusch etc*): **~ away** versickern; *fig.* schwinden (*Mut etc*); **~ out** aussickern; entweichen (*Luft, Gas*); *fig.* durchsickern (*Geheimnis etc*). **II** *v/t* absondern; *fig.* Charme ausstrahlen, Optimismus, gute Laune *etc a*. verströmen; von *Sarkasmus etc* triefen.

o·pal ['əʊpl] *s min*. Opal *m*.

o·paque [əʊ'peɪk] *adj* □ **1.** undurchsichtig. **2.** *fig.* unverständlich.

o·pen ['əʊpən] **I** *adj* □ **1.** *allg.* offen (*Buch, Fenster, Flasche etc*): **the door is ~** die Tür ist *od*. steht offen; **hold the door ~ for s.o.** j-m die Tür aufhalten; **keep one's eyes ~** *fig.* die Augen offenhalten; → **arm**¹ **1**, **book** 1. **2.** (*Gelände, Meer*), frei (*Feld*): → **air**¹ **1**. **3.** geöffnet, offen (*Laden etc*). **4.** *fig.* offen (für), öffentlich: **~ letter** offener Brief; **~ tournament** → **13**. **5.** *fig.* zugänglich, aufgeschlossen (**to** für *od*. dat). **6.** *fig.* ausgesetzt, unterworfen (**to** dat): **~ to question** anfechtbar; **that is ~ to argument** darüber läßt sich streiten. **7.** *fig.* offen, unentschieden (*Frage etc*). **8.** *fig.* a) offen, freimütig: **be ~ with s.o.** offen mit j-m reden, b) offen(kundig), unverhüllt: **~ secret** offenes Geheimnis. **9. ~ cheque** ✝ *Br.* Barscheck *m*. **10. ~ season** Jagdzeit *f*. **11.** *ling.* offen (*Vokal*). **III** *s* **12. in the ~** im Freien: **bring into the ~** *fig.* an die Öffentlichkeit bringen; **come into the ~** Farbe bekennen; an die Öffentlichkeit treten (**with** mit). **13.** *Golf, Tennis*: offenes Turnier. **III** *v/t* **14.** *allg.* öffnen, aufmachen, *Buch etc a*. aufschlagen. **15.** *Debatte, Feuer, Konto etc* eröffnen, neuen

Markt etc erschließen: **~ to traffic** Straße *etc* dem Verkehr übergeben. **16.** *fig.* Gefühle, Gedanken enthüllen: **~ o.s. to s.o.** sich j-m mitteilen. **IV** *v/i* **17.** sich öffnen, aufgehen. **18.** öffnen, aufmachen (*Laden etc*). **19.** führen, gehen (**onto** auf *acc* [... hinaus]) (*Tür, Fenster*). **20.** anfangen, beginnen; anlaufen (*Film*).

Verbindungen mit Adverbien:

o·pen| out I *v/t* ausbreiten, *Stadtplan etc* auseinanderfalten. **II** *v/i* auftauen, mitteilsam werden. **~ up I** *v/t* **1.** aufmachen, *neuen Markt etc* erschließen, *Möglichkeiten etc* eröffnen. **II** *v/i* **3.** aufmachen, -schließen. **4.** *fig.* a) loslegen (**with** mit), b) → **open out II**.

ı·o·pen|-'air *adj* im Freien: **~ festival** Open-air-Festival *n*; **~ swimming pool** Freibad *n*; **~ theater** (*bsd. Br. theatre*) Freilichttheater *n*. **ı~-'end·ed** *adj* zeitlich unbegrenzt: **~ discussion** Open-end-Diskussion *f*.

o·pen·er ['əʊpnə] *s* **1.** (*Dosen-, Flaschen*)Öffner *m*. **2.** *Am*. Eröffnungsnummer *f* (*e-r Show etc*).

ı·o·pen|-'eyed *adj* mit großen Augen, staunend. **ı~-'hand·ed** *adj* □ freigebig.

o·pen·ing ['əʊpnɪŋ] **I** *s* **1.** Öffnung *f*. **2.** ✝ freie Stelle. **3.** Eröffnung *f* (*e-r Debatte, des Feuers, e-s Kontos etc*), Erschließung *f* (*e-s neuen Markts etc*). **II** *adj* **4.** Eröffnungs...: **~ ceremony**; **~ night** *thea.* Eröffnungsvorstellung *f*. **5.** Öffnungs...: **~ time**; **~ time is at ...** das Geschäft *etc* ist ab ... geöffnet.

ı·o·pen|-'mind·ed *adj* □ aufgeschlossen. **ı~-'mouthed** *adj* mit offenem Mund. **ı~-'plan** *adj*: **~ office** Großraumbüro *n*. **~ shop** *s* ✝ Betrieb, *der auch Nichtgewerkschaftsmitglieder beschäftigt*. ♀ **U·ni·ver·si·ty** *s Br.* Fern(seh)universität *f* (*deren Kurse a. ohne entsprechenden Schulabschluß belegt werden können*).

op·er·a¹ ['ɒpərə] *s* ♪ Oper *f*: **go to the ~** in die Oper gehen.

op·er·a² [~] *pl von* **opus**.

op·er·a·ble ['ɒpərəbl] *adj* □ **1.** durchführbar. **2.** ⚙ betriebsfähig. **3.** ✚ operabel, operierbar.

op·er·a| glass·es *s pl, a.* **pair of ~**

(*Sport*) vom Platz stellen; **~ out** hinausweisen. **15.** ✍ *j-m et.* verordnen: **~ s.o. to (stay in) bed** j-m Bettruhe verordnen. **16.** ♱ bestellen (*a. im Restaurant*). **17.** *fig.* ordnen, in Ordnung bringen: **~ed life** geordnetes Leben. **III** *v/i* **18.** bestellen (*im Restaurant*): **are you ready to ~?** haben Sie schon gewählt? **'or·der·ly I** *adj* **1.** ordentlich, geordnet. **2.** *fig.* gesittet, friedlich (*Menge etc*). **II** *s* **3.** ✍ Hilfspfleger *m.* **4.** ✗ (Offiziers)Bursche *m.*

or·di·nal (num·ber) ['ɔ:dɪnl] *s* ♉ Ordnungszahl *f.*

or·di·nar·i·ly ['ɔ:dnrəlɪ] *adv* **1.** normalerweise, gewöhnlich. **2.** wie gewöhnlich *od.* üblich, normal.

or·di·nar·y ['ɔ:dnrɪ] **I** *adj* **1.** üblich, gewöhnlich, normal: **in the ~ way** *od.* **dinarily** 1. **2.** alltäglich, mittelmäßig, Durchschnitts... **3.** ordentlich (*Gericht, Mitglied*). **II** *s* **4. out of the ~** ungewöhnlich, unüblich: **nothing out of the ~** nichts Ungewöhnliches.

ore [ɔ:] *s min.* Erz *n.*

or·gan ['ɔ:gən] *s* **1.** *anat.* Organ *n:* **~s pl of speech** Sprechwerkzeuge *pl.* **2.** *fig.* Organ *n:* a) Werkzeug *n,* Instrument *n,* b) Sprachrohr *n:* **party ~** Parteiorgan. **3.** ♪ Orgel *f.* **~ grind·er** *s* Leierkastenmann *m.*

or·gan·ic [ɔ:'gænɪk] *adj* (**~ally**) organisch (*a. fig.*): **~ chemistry** organische Chemie. **or·gan·ism** ['ɔ:gənɪzəm] *s biol.* Organismus *m* (*a. fig.*).

or·gan·ist ['ɔ:gənɪst] *s* ♪ Organist(in).

or·gan·i·za·tion [,ɔ:gənaɪ'zeɪʃn] *s allg.* Organisation *f.* **,or·gan·i·za·tion·al** *adj* ♉ organisatorisch, Organisations... **'or·gan·ize I** *v/t allg.* organisieren: **~d crime** das organisierte Verbrechen; **~d tour** Gesellschaftsreise *f.* **II** *v/i* sich (gewerkschaftlich) organisieren. **'or·gan·iz·er** *s* Organisator(in).

or·gasm ['ɔ:gæzəm] *s physiol.* Orgasmus *m.*

or·gy ['ɔ:dʒɪ] *s* Orgie *f* (*a. fig.*).

o·ri·ent I *s* ['ɔ:rɪənt] ♉ *der* Orient, *poet. das* Morgenland. **II** *v/t* ['~ent] *fig. et.* ausrichten (**toward[s]** auf *acc*): **~ o.s.** sich orientieren (**by** an *dat,* nach) (*a. fig.*); **~ o.s. to a new situation** sich auf e-e neue Situation einstellen. **o·ri·en·tal** [,~'entl] **I** *adj* ♉ orientalisch, *poet.*

morgenländisch: **~ carpet** (*od.* **rug**) Orientteppich *m.* **II** *s* Orientale *m,* Orientalin *f.* **o·ri·en·tate** ['~entert] → **orient** II. **,o·ri·en·ta·tion** *s* Orientierung *f, fig. a.* Ausrichtung *f.*

or·i·fice ['ɒrɪfɪs] *s bsd. anat.* Öffnung *f.*

or·i·gin ['ɒrɪdʒɪn] *s* Ursprung *m,* Abstammung *f,* Herkunft *f:* **country of ~** Ursprungsland *n;* **have its ~ in** zurückgehen auf (*acc*); (her)stammen von *od.* aus.

o·rig·i·nal [ə'rɪdʒənl] **I** *adj* (□ → **originally**) **1.** Original..., Ur...: **~ text** *od.* Originaltext *m.* **2.** originell. **II** *s* **3.** Original *n:* **in the ~** im Original *od.* Urtext. **4.** Original *n* (*Person*). **o,rig·i'nal·i·ty** [,~'nælətɪ] *s* Originalität *f.* **o'rig·i·nal·ly** [,~nəlɪ] *adv* **1.** ursprünglich. **2.** originell.

o·rig·i·nate [ə'rɪdʒəneɪt] **I** *v/i* **1.** (**from**) zurückgehen (auf *acc*), (her)stammen (von *od.* aus). **2.** ausgehen (**from, with** von *j-m*). **II** *v/t* **3.** schaffen, ins Leben rufen. **o'rig·i·na·tor** *s* Urheber(in).

or·na·ment I *s* ['ɔ:nəmənt] **1.** Ornament(e *pl*) *n,* Verzierung(en *pl*) *f,* Schmuck *m.* **2.** *fig.* Zier(de) *f* (**to** für *od. gen*). **II** *v/t* ['~ment] **3.** verzieren, schmücken (**with** mit). **or·na·men·tal** [,~'mentl] *adj* □ dekorativ, schmückend, Zier...: **~ plant** Zierpflanze *f.* **,or·na·men'ta·tion** [,~men~] *s* Ausschmückung *f,* Verzierung *f.*

or·nate [ɔ:'neɪt] *adj* □ **1.** reichverziert *od.* -geschmückt. **2.** *fig.* überladen (*Stil etc*).

or·ni·thol·o·gist [,ɔ:nɪ'θɒlədʒɪst] *s* Ornithologe *m,* Ornithologin *f.* **,or·ni'thol·o·gy** *s* Ornithologie *f,* Vogelkunde *f.*

or·phan ['ɔ:fn] **I** *s* Waise(nkind *n*) *f.* **II** *adj* Waisen... **III** *v/t:* **be ~ed** verwaisen, Waise werden. **or·phan·age** ['ɔ:fənɪdʒ] *s* Waisenhaus *n.*

or·tho·dox ['ɔ:θədɒks] *adj* □ *eccl. u. allg.* orthodox: **2 Church** griechisch-orthodoxe Kirche.

or·tho·graph·ic, or·tho·graph·i·cal [,ɔ:θəʊ'græfɪk(l)] *adj* □ orthographisch. **or·thog·ra·phy** [ɔ:'θɒgrəfɪ] *s* Orthographie *f,* Rechtschreibung *f.*

or·tho·pae·dic *bsd. Br.,* **or·tho·pe·dic** *Am.* [,ɔ:θəʊ'pi:dɪk] ✍ **I** *adj* (**~ally**) orthopädisch. **II** *s pl* (*oft sg konstruiert*)

Orthopädie f. ‚**or·tho'p(a)e·dist** s Orthopäde m, Orthopädin f.

Os·car ['ɒskə] s Oscar m (amerikanischer Filmpreis).

os·cil·late ['ɒsɪleɪt] v/i **1.** bsd. phys. oszillieren, schwingen. **2.** fig. schwanken (**between** zwischen dat). ‚**os·cil'la·tion** s **1.** bsd. phys. Oszillation f, Schwingung f. **2.** fig. Schwanken n.

os·si·fy ['ɒsɪfaɪ] v/t u. v/i verknöchern (a. fig.).

os·ten·si·ble [ɒ'stensəbl] adj □ **1.** scheinbar. **2.** an-, vorgeblich.

os·ten·ta·tion [ˌɒsten'teɪʃn] s **1.** (protzige) Zurschaustellung. **2.** Protzerei f, Prahlerei f. ‚**os·ten'ta·tious** adj □ **1.** protzend, prahlerisch: **be ~ about s.th.** mit et. protzen od. prahlen. **2.** ostentativ, demonstrativ.

os·tra·cism ['ɒstrəsɪzəm] s Ächtung f. **os·tra·cize** ['ɒstrəsaɪz] v/t ächten.

os·trich ['ɒstrɪtʃ] s orn. Strauß m.

oth·er ['ʌðə] **I** adj **1.** ander. **2.** vor s im pl: andere, übrige: **the ~ guests. 3.** ander, weiter, sonstig: **the ~ two** die anderen beiden, die beiden anderen; **any ~ questions?** sonst noch Fragen? **4.** zweit (nur in): **every ~** jeder (jede, jedes) zweite; **every ~ day** jeden zweiten Tag, alle zwei Tage. **5. the ~ day** neulich, kürzlich; **the ~ night** neulich abend. **II** pron **6.** ander: **the ~** der (die, das) andere; **the two ~s** die anderen beiden, die beiden anderen; → **each** II. **III** adv **7.** anders (**than** als). **oth·er·wise** ['~waɪz] adv **1.** a. cj sonst, andernfalls. **2.** sonst, im übrigen. **3.** anderweitig: **be ~ engaged** anderweitig beschäftigt sein; **unless you are ~ engaged** wenn Sie nichts anderes vorhaben. **4.** anders (**than** als): **think ~** anderer Meinung sein; **X, ~ (called)** Y X, auch Y genannt; **or ~** od. sonst irgendwie: **or not.**

ot·ter ['ɒtə] s zo. Otter m.

ought [ɔːt] v/aux ich sollte, du solltest etc: **he ~ to do it** er sollte es (eigentlich) tun.

ounce [aʊns] s **1.** Unze f. **2.** fig. Körnchen n (Wahrheit), Funke m (Verstand).

our ['aʊə] possessive pron unser: ♀ **Father** eccl. Vaterunser n. **ours** ['aʊəz] possessive pron: **it is ~** es gehört uns; **a friend of ~** ein Freund von uns; **their children and ~** ihre Kinder u. unsere. **our-**

selves [ˌ~'selvz] pron **1.** verstärkend: wir od. uns selbst: **we did it ~, we ~ did it** wir haben es selbst getan. **2.** reflex uns: **we cut ~. 3.** uns (selbst): **we want it for ~.**

oust [aʊst] v/t fig. verdrängen (**from** aus).

out [aʊt] **I** adv **1.** hinaus(...), heraus(...); aus(...): **way ~** Ausgang m; **on the way ~** beim Hinausgehen; **have a tooth ~** e-n Zahn gezogen bekommen. **2.** außen, draußen. **3.** nicht zu Hause, ausgegangen. **4.** be ~, → **come out** 2, **go out** 4. **5.** ins Freie; draußen, im Freien. **6.** (aus dem Gefängnis etc) entlassen. **7.** heraus: a) erschienen (Buch etc), b) enthüllt (Geheimnis): **~ with it!** F heraus damit!, heraus mit der Sprache! **8.** pol. nicht (mehr) im Amt od. an der Macht. **9.** aus der Mode, out. **10.** weit u. breit: **~ and away** bei weitem. **11.** aus, vorbei; vorüber: **before the week is ~** vor Ende der Woche. **12.** aus, erloschen: → **go out** 3. **13.** aus(verkauft). **14. be ~ for** aussein auf (acc): **be ~ to do s.th.** darauf aussein, et. zu tun. **15. ~ of** a) aus (... heraus); zu ... hinaus, b) aus, von: **two ~ of three Americans** zwei von drei Amerikanern, c) außer Reichweite etc, d) außer Atem, Übung etc: **be ~ of** ... nicht mehr haben; **we are ~ of oil** uns ist das Öl ausgegangen, e) aus der Mode etc, f) außerhalb von (od. gen), g) um et. betrügen, h) aus Bosheit, Mitleid etc. **II** prp **16.** → 15a. ‚**~-and-'out** adj absolut, ausgesprochen: **an ~ lie** e-e faustdicke Lüge. ‚**~'bal·ance** v/t überwiegen. ‚**~'bid** v/t (irr bid) überbieten. '**~board** ♪ **I** adj **1.** Außenbord...: **~ motor. II** adv **2.** außenbords. **III** s **3.** Außenbordmotor m. **4.** Außenborder m (Boot). '**~break** s Ausbruch m: **~ of anger** Zornausbruch; **at the ~ of war** bei Kriegsausbruch. '**~build·ing** s Nebengebäude n. '**~burst** s (Zorn- etc)Ausbruch m. '**~cast I** adj ausgestoßen, verstoßen. **II** s Ausgestoßene m, f, Verstoßene m, f. '**~class** v/t weit überlegen sein (dat), (Sport a.) deklassieren. '**~come** s Ergebnis n, Resultat n: **what was the ~ of the talks?** was ist bei den Gesprächen herausgekommen? '**~cry** s fig. Aufschrei m, Schrei m der Entrü-

od. veranschlagen. **2.** *fig.* überschätzen, überbewerten. **~·ex'pose** *v/t phot.* überbelichten. **~·'flow I** *v/i* **1.** überlaufen, -fließen, (*Fluß etc*) über die Ufer treten: **full to ~ing** zum Überlaufen voll; (*Raum*) überfüllt. **2.** überquellen (**with** von) (*a. fig.*). **II** *v/t* **3. ~ its banks** über die Ufer treten. **III** *s* [*'~fləʊ*] **4.** Überlaufen *n*, -fließen *n*. **5.** ☼ Überlauf *m*: **~ valve** Überlaufventil *n*. **6.** Überschuß *m* (**of** an *dat*): **~ of population** Bevölkerungsüberschuß. **~·'grown** *adj* **1.** überwachsen, -wuchert (**with** von). **2.** übergroß, (*Junge etc*) hoch aufgeschossen. **~·haul I** *v/t* [*~·'hɔ:l*] **1.** ☼ überholen, (*Fahrzeug*) generalüberholen. **2.** *fig. Pläne etc* überprüfen. **3.** *j-n, Fahrzeug etc* überholen **II** *s* [*'~hɔ:l*] **4.** ☼ Überholung *f*: **complete ~** Generalüberholung. **5.** *fig.* Überprüfung *f*. **'~·head I** *adj* **1.** oberirdisch, Frei..., Hoch...: **~ line** ⚡ Oberleitung *f*; **~ projector** Overhead-, Tageslichtprojektor *m*. **2.** allgemein: **~ costs** (*od.* **expenses**) *pl* → **3.** § **4. ~** (*s pl Br.*) *Am.* ⛵ laufende (Geschäfts)Kosten *pl*. **5.** *Tennis:* Überkopfball *m*. **III** *adv* [*~·'hed*] **6.** (dr)oben; über uns. **~·'hear** *v/t* (*irr hear*) zufällig hören. **~·'heat** *v/t Motor* überhitzen, *Raum* überheizen. **II** *v/i* ☼ heißlaufen. **~·in'dulge I** *v/t* **1.** zu nachsichtig behandeln, *j-m* zuviel durchgehen lassen. **2.** *e-r Leidenschaft etc* übermäßig frönen. **II** *v/i* **3.** *in television* zuviel fernsehen. **~·joyed** [*~·'dʒɔɪd*] *adj* überglücklich. **'~·kill** *s* ✗ Overkill *n*. **~·land I** *adv* [*~·'lænd*] über Land, auf dem Landweg. **II** *adj* [*'~·lænd*] (Über-)Land... **~·'lap** *v/i* **1.** (sich) überlappen. **2.** *fig.* sich überschneiden, überlappen. **~·'load** *v/t* überlasten (*a. ⚡*), -laden.

o·ver·ly [*'əʊvəli*] *adv* übermäßig, allzu: **he wasn't ~ enthusiastic** s-e Begeisterung hielt sich in Grenzen.

,o·ver·'manned *adj* (personell) überbesetzt. **~·'much I** *adj* (all)zuviel. **II** *adv* übermäßig: **I don't like him ~** ich mag ihn nicht besonders. **~·'night I** *adv* über Nacht (*a. fig.*): **stay ~** über Nacht bleiben; **stay ~ with s.o.** (*od.* **at s.o.'s place**) bei j-m übernachten. **II** *adj*

Nacht...: **~ bag** Reisetasche *f*; **~ stay** (*od.* **stop**) Übernachtung *f*. **'~·pass** *s bsd. Am.* (Straßen-, Eisenbahn)Überführung *f*. **~·'pay** *v/t* (*irr pay*) **1.** zu teuer bezahlen, zuviel bezahlen für. **2.** *j-m* zuviel zahlen, *j-n* überbezahlen. **~·'play** *v/t* **1.** a) → **overact** I, b) hochspielen. **2. ~ one's hand** sich überreizen *od.* übernehmen. **~·'pop·u·lat·ed** *adj* überbevölkert. **~·'pop·u·'la·tion** *s* Übervölkerung *f*. **2.** Überbevölkerung *f*. **~·'pow·er** *v/t* überwältigen, -mannen (*beide a. fig.*): **~ing** *fig.* überwältigend, (*Geruch*) aufdringlich, penetrant. **~·'rate** *v/t* überbewerten (*a. Sport*), -schätzen. **~·'reach** *v/t* **1.** sich übernehmen. **2.** *Pferd:* übergreifen. **~·re'act** *v/i* überreagieren, überzogen reagieren (**to** auf *acc*). **~·re'ac·tion** *s* Überreaktion *f*, überzogene Reaktion. **~·'ride** *v/t* (*irr ride*) sich hinwegsetzen über (*acc*). **~·'rid·ing** *adj* vordringlich, -rangig: **his ~ concern was** es ging ihm vor allem darum (**to do** zu tun). **~·'rule** *v/t* *Entscheidung etc* aufheben, *Einspruch etc* abweisen. **~·'run** (*irr run*) **I** *v/t* **1. be ~ with** überlaufen sein von. **2.** 🚂 *Signal* überfahren. **II** *v/i* **3.** länger dauern als vorgesehen. **~·'seas I** *adv* nach *od.* in Übersee. **II** *adj* überseeisch, Übersee..., aus Übersee. **~·'see** *v/t* (*irr see*) beaufsichtigen, überwachen. **~·'se·er** [*'~·sɪə*] *s* Aufseher(in). **~·'shad·ow** *v/t fig.* **1.** in den Schatten stellen. **2.** überschatten, e-n Schatten werfen auf (*acc*). **~·'shoot** *v/t* (*irr shoot*) hinausschießen über (*ein Ziel*) (*a. fig.*). '**~·sight** *s* Versehen *n*: **by** (*od.* **through an**) **~** aus Versehen. **'~·sim·pli·fy** *v/t* (zu) grob vereinfachen, vergröbern. **~·'size(d)** *adj* übergroß, mit Übergröße. **~·'sleep** *v/i* (*irr sleep*) verschlafen. **~·'staffed** *adj* (personell) überbesetzt. **~·'state** *v/t* übertreiben, übertrieben darstellen. **~·'state·ment** *s* Übertreibung *f*. **~·'stay** *v/t* länger bleiben als: → **welcome** 6. **~·'step** *v/t fig.* überschreiten. **~·'take** *v/t* (*irr take*) **1.** einholen (*a. fig.*). **2.** (*a. v/i*) *bsd. Br.* überholen. **3.** *fig.* überraschen. **~·'tax** *v/t* **1.** zu hoch besteuern. **2.** überbeanspruchen, *Geduld etc* strapazieren: **~ one's strength** (*od.* **o.s.**) sich übernehmen. **~·'throw I** *v/t* [*~·'θrəʊ*] (*irr throw*) **1.** *Regierung etc* stürzen. **2.** besiegen. **II** s ['ˌθrəʊ] **3.** Sturz m. **4.** Niederlage f. **'ˌtime I** s **1.** ♀ a) Überstunden pl: **be on** (od. **do**) ~ Überstunden machen, b) a. ~ **pay** Überstundenlohn m. **2.** Sport: Am. Verlängerung f: **after** ~ nach Verlängerung; **the game went into** ~ das Spiel ging in die Verlängerung. **II** adv **3. work** ~ ♀ Überstunden machen.

o·ver·ture ['əʊvəˌtjʊə] s ♪ Ouvertüre f (**to** zu).

ˌo·ver'turn I v/t **1.** umwerfen, -stoßen, -kippen. **2.** fig. Regierung etc stürzen. **II** v/i **3.** umkippen, ♻ kentern. **'ˌview** s fig. Überblick m (**of** über acc). **ˌweight I** s ['ˌweɪt] Übergewicht n (a. fig.). **II** adj ['ˌweɪt] übergewichtig (Person), zu schwer (**by** um) (Gegenstand): **be** ~ **by five kilos, be five kilos** ~ fünf Kilo Übergewicht haben. **ˌwhelm** [ˌ'welm] v/t **1.** überwältigen (a. fig.). **2.** fig. überhäufen, -schütten (**with** mit). **ˌwhelm·ing** adj überwältigend: **ˌly** mit überwältigender Mehrheit. **ˌwork I** v/t überstrapazieren (a. fig.), überanstrengen: **ed** a. gestreßt; ~ **o.s.** → II. **II** v/i sich überarbeiten.

o·vi·duct ['əʊvɪdʌkt] s anat. Eileiter m.

o·vip·a·rous [əʊ'vɪpərəs] adj □ zo. eierlegend.

o·vu·la·tion [ˌɒvjʊ'leɪʃn] s biol. Eisprung m.

o·vum ['əʊvəm] pl **o·va** ['əʊvə] s biol. Ei(zelle f) n.

owe [əʊ] v/t **1.** j-m et. schulden, schuldig sein (**for** für). **2.** bei j-m Schulden haben, j-m Geld schulden. **3.** et. verdanken, zu verdanken haben.

ow·ing ['əʊɪŋ] adj **1.** unbezahlt: **how**

much **is still** ~ **to you?** wieviel bekommst du noch?; **there is still £1,000** ~ es stehen noch 1000 Pfund aus. **2.** ~ **to** infolge, wegen.

owl [aʊl] s orn. Eule f. **'owl·ish** adj □ eulenhaft (Aussehen etc).

own [əʊn] **I** v/t **1.** besitzen: **who ˌs this car?** wem gehört dieser Wagen? **2.** zugeben, (ein)gestehen (**that** daß). **II** v/i **3.** ~ **up** es zugeben: ~ (**up**) **to s.th.** et. zugeben od. (ein)gestehen; ~ (**up**) **to doing s.th.** zugeben od. (ein)gestehen, et. getan zu haben. **III** adj **4.** eigen: ~ **goal** (Sport) Eigentor n (a. fig.). **IV** s **5. my** ~ mein Eigentum: **a car of one's** ~ ein eigenes Auto; **on one's** ~ allein; **come into one's** ~ zur Geltung kommen; → **get back** 1, **hold** 10.

own·er ['əʊnə] s Eigentümer(in), Besitzer(in). **ˌown·er'oc·cu·pied** adj eigengenutzt (Haus, Wohnung).

own·er·ship ['əʊnəʃɪp] s Besitz m.

ox [ɒks] pl **ox·en** ['ˌn] s zo. Ochse m.

Ox·bridge ['ɒksbrɪdʒ] s (die Universitäten) Oxford u. Cambridge pl.

ox·en ['ɒksn] pl von **ox**.

ox·ide ['ɒksaɪd] s ♠ Oxyd n. **ox·i·dize** ['ɒksɪdaɪz] v/t u. v/i oxydieren.

'ox·tail s Ochsenschwanz m: ~ **soup**.

ox·y·gen ['ɒksɪdʒən] s ♠ Sauerstoff m. ~ **mask** s ♣ Sauerstoffmaske f. ~ **tent** s ♣ Sauerstoffzelt n.

oys·ter ['ɔɪstə] s zo. Auster f. ~ **bed** s Austernbank f.

o·zone ['əʊzəʊn] s ♠ Ozon n. **lay·er,** ~ **shield** s Ozonschicht f (der Atmosphäre).

P

P [piː] s: **mind one's p's and q's** F sich anständig aufführen.

pace [peɪs] **I** s **1.** Tempo n (a. fig.), Geschwindigkeit f: **at a (very) slow** ~ (ganz) langsam; **keep** ~ **with** Schritt halten od. mitkommen mit (a. fig.); **keep** ~ **with the times** mit der Zeit

gehen; **set the** ~ das Tempo angeben (a. fig.), (Sport) das Tempo machen. **2.** Schritt m. **3.** Gangart f (e-s Pferdes): **put s.o. through his ˌs** fig. j-n auf Herz u. Nieren prüfen; **show one's ˌs** fig. zeigen, was man kann. **II** v/t **4.** Sport: j-m Schrittmacherdienste leisten. **5.** a. ~

m: **grease** (*od.* **oil**) **s.o.'s ~** F j-n schmieren (**with** mit); **have an itching** (*od.* **itchy**) **~** F e-e offene Hand haben (*bestechlich sein*); **have** (*od.* **hold**) **s.o. in the ~ of one's hand** j-n völlig in der Hand *od.* in s-r Gewalt haben. **II** *v/t* **2.** *et.* in der Hand verschwinden lassen (*Zauberkünstler*). **3.** F **~ s.th. off as** et. an den Mann bringen als; **~ s.th. off on(to) s.o.** j-m et. andrehen; **~ s.o. off with s.th.** j-m et. andrehen; j-n mit et. abspeisen.

palm² [~] *s* ♀ Palme *f*.

palm·ist ['pɑ:mɪst] *s* Handleser(in).

'**palm·is·try** *s* Handlesekunst *f*.

Palm| Sun·day *s eccl.* Palmsonntag *m*. ♀ **tree** *s* ♀ Palme *f*.

pal·pa·ble ['pælpəbl] *adj* □ **1.** fühl-, greif-, tastbar. **2.** *fig.* augenfällig, deutlich; offensichtlich.

pal·pi·tate ['pælpɪteɪt] *v/i* **1.** klopfen, pochen (*Herz*). **2.** zittern (**with** vor *dat*). ‚**pal·pi'ta·tion** *s. a. pl* Herzklopfen *n*.

pal·sy ['pɔ:lzɪ] *s ♀* Lähmung *f*.

pal·try ['pɔ:ltrɪ] *adj* □ armselig, schäbig: **a ~ £10** lumpige 10 Pfund.

pam·per ['pæmpə] *v/t* verwöhnen, *Kind a.* verhätscheln.

pam·phlet ['pæmflɪt] *s* **1.** Broschüre *f*, Druckschrift *f*. **2.** Flugblatt *n*, -schrift *f*.

pan¹ [pæn] **I** *s* **1.** Pfanne *f*, Topf *m*. **2.** (Waag)Schale *f*. **3.** *bsd. Br.* (Klosett)Schüssel *f*. **II** *v/t* **4.** F *Theaterstück etc* verreißen. **III** *v/i* **5. ~ out** F klappen: **~ out well** hinhauen.

pan² [~] **I** *s* (Kamera)Schwenk *m*. **II** *v/t Filmkamera* schwenken. **III** *v/i* schwenken.

pan·a·ce·a [‚pænə'sɪə] *s* Allheilmittel *n*, *fig. a.* Patentrezept *n*.

‚**Pan-A'mer·i·can** *adj* panamerikanisch.

'**pan·cake** *s* Pfannkuchen *m*.

pan·cre·as ['pæŋkrɪəs] *s anat.* Bauchspeicheldrüse *f*.

pan·da ['pændə] *s zo.* Panda *m*. ♀ **car** *s Br.* (Funk)Streifenwagen *m*.

pan·de·mo·ni·um [‚pændɪ'məʊnjəm] *s* Chaos *n*, Tumult *m*.

pan·der ['pændə] *v/i:* **~ to** e-m *Laster etc* Vorschub leisten, *j-s Bedürfnisse etc* befriedigen.

pane [peɪn] *s* (*Fenster*)Scheibe *f*.

pan·el ['pænl] **I** *s* **1.** Tafel *f*, Platte *f*; (vertieftes) Feld. **2.** ⚡, ☉ (Schalt-, Kon-

troll- *etc*)Tafel *f*. **3.** ⚖ Liste *f* der Geschworenen. **4.** Diskussionsteilnehmer *pl*, -runde *f*; Rateteam *n*. **II** *v/t pret u. pp* **-eled,** *bsd. Br.* **-elled 5.** täfeln. **~ dis·cus·sion** *s* Podiumsdiskussion *f*. **~ game** *s* Rundfunk, *TV:* Ratespiel *n*.

pan·el·(l)ing ['pænlɪŋ] *s* Täfelung *f*. **pan·el·(l)ist** ['~əlɪst] *s* Diskussionsteilnehmer(in).

pang [pæŋ] *s* stechender Schmerz: **~s** *pl* **of hunger** nagender Hunger; **feel a ~ of conscience** Gewissensbisse haben.

pan·ic ['pænɪk] *adj* **1.** panisch: **~ buying** Angstkäufe *pl*; **be at ~ stations** rotieren; **push the ~ button** F panisch reagieren. **II** *s* **2.** Panik *f*: **be in a ~** in Panik sein; **get into a ~** → **5**; **throw into a ~** → **4**. **3. be a ~** *Am.* F zum Totlachen sein. **III** *v/t pret u. pp* **-icked 4.** in Panik versetzen, e-e Panik auslösen unter (*dat*). **IV** *v/i* **5.** in Panik geraten: **don't ~!** nur keine Panik! **'pan·ick·y** *adj* F **1.** überängstlich. **2. get ~** → **panic** 5.

'**pan·ic-‚strick·en** *adj* von panischem Schrecken erfaßt *od.* ergriffen.

pan·o·ra·ma [‚pænə'rɑ:mə] *s* **1.** Panorama *n*. **2.** *fig.* (allgemeiner) Überblick (**of** über *acc*). **pan·o·ram·ic** [‚pænə'ræmɪk] *adj* (**~ally**) panoramisch, Panorama...: **~ view** a) Rundblick *m* (**of** über *acc*), b) → **panorama** 2.

pan·sy ['pænzɪ] *s* **1.** ♀ Stiefmütterchen *n*. **2.** F Weichling *m*.

pant [pænt] **I** *v/i* **1.** keuchen: **~ for breath** nach Luft schnappen. **2. be ~ing** *fig.* lechzen (**after, for** nach; **to do s.th.** danach, et. zu tun). **II** *v/t* **3. ~ out** *Worte* (hervor)keuchen. **III** *s* **4.** Atemstoß *m*.

pan·the·ism ['pænθiɪzəm] *s* Pantheismus *m*. '**pan·the·ist I** *s* Pantheist(in). **II** *adj* pantheistisch. ‚**pan·the'is·tic** *adj* (**~ally**) pantheistisch.

pan·ther ['pænθə] *s zo.* Panther *m*.

pant·ies ['pæntɪz] *s pl, a. pair of ~* Höschen *n* (*für Kinder*), (*für Damen a.*) Schlüpfer *m*, Slip *m*.

pan·to·mime ['pæntəmaɪm] *s* **1.** *Br.* Weihnachtsspiel *n* (*für Kinder*). **2.** *thea.* Pantomime *f*.

pan·try ['pæntrɪ] *s* Speise-, Vorratskammer *f*.

pants [pænts] *s pl, a. pair of ~* **1.** *Br.* Unterhose *f*. **2.** *bsd. Am.* Hose *f*: **catch s.o. with his ~ down** F j-n überrumpeln; *talk the ～ off s.o.* F j-m ein Loch *od.* Löcher in den Bauch reden; → *wear* 3.

pant·suit ['pæntsu:t] *s bsd. Am.* Hosenanzug *m.*

pan·ty hose ['pæntɪ] *s bsd. Am.* Strumpfhose *f.*

pap [pæp] *s* Brei *m.*

pa·pal ['peɪpl] *adj* □ päpstlich.

pa·per ['peɪpə] **I** *s* **1.** Papier *n*: *on ～ fig.* auf dem Papier. **2.** Tapete *f.* **3.** Zeitung *f*: *be in the ～s* in der Zeitung stehen. **4.** *pl (Ausweis)*Papiere *pl*; Akten *pl*, Unterlagen *pl.* **5.** *ped.* Arbeit *f, univ.* Klausur(arbeit) *f.* **6.** Referat *n*: *give (od. read) a ～* ein Referat halten, referieren (*to* vor *dat; on* über *acc*). **II** *v/t* **7.** tapezieren. **8.** *～ over (od. up) fig.* Differenzen *etc* (notdürftig) übertünchen. **'～back** *s* Taschenbuch *n*: *in ～* als Taschenbuch. **～ bag** *s* (Papier-) Tüte *f.* **'～boy** *s* Zeitungsjunge *m.* **～ chase** *s* Schnitzeljagd *f.* **～ clip** *s* Büro-, Heftklammer *f.* **～ cup** *s* Pappbecher *m.* **～ hand·ker·chief** *s* Papiertaschentuch *n.* **'～hang·er** *s* Tapezierer(in). **～ knife** (*irr knife*) *s* Brieföffner *m.* **～ mon·ey** *s* Papiergeld *n.* **～ plate** *s* Pappteller *m.* **'～thin** *adj* hauchdünn (*a. fig.*), papierdünn. **～ ti·ger** *s fig.* Papiertiger *m,* (*Person a.*) Gummilöwe *m.* **'～weight** *s* **1.** Briefbeschwerer *m.* **2.** *Sport:* Papiergewicht(ler *m*) *n.* **'～work** *s* Schreibarbeit *f.*

pa·pier-mâ·ché [,pæpjeɪ'mæʃeɪ] *s* Pappmaché *n.*

pap·ri·ka ['pæprɪkə] *s* Paprika *m.*

pa·py·rus [pə'paɪərəs] *pl* **-ri** [～raɪ], **-rus·es** *s* **1.** ♀ Papyrus(staude *f*) *m.* **2.** *antiq.* Papyrus(rolle *f*) *m.*

par [pɑː] **I** *s* **1.** ♥ Nennwert *m*: *at ～* zum Nennwert, al pari. **2.** *be on a ～* auf gleicher Stufe stehen (*with* wie): *be on a ～ with a.* j-m ebenbürtig sein; *I'm feeling below (od. under) ～ today* F ich fühle mich heute nicht (ganz) auf dem Posten. **3.** *Golf:* Par *n*: *that's ～ for the course* F das ist ganz normal (*for* für). **II** *adj* **4.** ～ *value* ♥ Nennwert *m.*

par·a·ble ['pærəbl] *s* Parabel *f,* Gleichnis *n.*

pa·rab·o·la [pə'ræbələ] *s* ⅍ Parabel *f.* **par·a·bol·ic** [,pærə'bɒlɪk] *adj* (～*ally*) **1.** ⅍ parabolisch, Parabel... **2.** ～ *mirror* ⊙ Parabolspiegel *m.*

par·a·chute ['pærəʃuːt] **I** *s* Fallschirm *m*: *～ jump* Fallschirmabsprung *m.* **II** *v/t* mit dem Fallschirm absetzen *od.* abwerfen. **III** *v/i* (mit dem Fallschirm) abspringen. **'par·a·chut·ist** *s* Fallschirmspringer(in); ✗ Fallschirmjäger *m.*

pa·rade [pə'reɪd] **I** *s* **1.** Umzug *m, bsd.* ✗ Parade *f*: *be on ～* e-e Parade abhalten. **2.** *fig.* Zurschaustellung *f*: *make a ～ of* → **4. II** *v/t* **3.** stolzieren durch. **4.** *fig.* zur Schau stellen. **III** *v/i* **5.** ziehen (*through* durch), *bsd.* ✗ paradieren. **5.** stolzieren (*through* durch). **～ ground** *s* ✗ Exerzierplatz *m.*

par·a·digm ['pærədaɪm] *s* **1.** Musterbeispiel *n* (*of* für). **2.** *ling.* Paradigma *n.*

par·a·dise *eccl. mst* **2** ['pærədaɪs] *s* Paradies *n* (*a. fig.*).

par·a·dox ['pærədɒks] *s* Paradox(on) *n.* **par·a·dox·i·cal** *adj* □ paradox. **～*ly* (*enough*)** paradoxerweise.

par·af·fin ['pærəfɪn] *s* **1.** *Br.* Petroleum *n.* **2.** *a.* ～ *wax* Paraffin *n.*

par·a·gon ['pærəgən] *s* Muster *n* (*of* an *dat*): ～ *of virtue bsd. iro.* Ausbund *m* an Tugend.

par·a·graph ['pærəgrɑːf] *s* **1.** Absatz *m,* Abschnitt *m.* **2.** (Zeitungs)Notiz *f.*

par·a·keet ['pærəkiːt] *s orn.* Sittich *m.*

par·al·lel ['pærəlel] **I** *adj* **1.** parallel (*to, with* zu) (*a. fig.*): ～ *bars pl (Turnen)* Barren *m.* **II** *s* **2.** ⅍ Parallele *f* (*to, with* zu) (*a. fig.*): *without ～* ohne Parallele, ohnegleichen; *draw a ～ between* e-e Parallele ziehen zwischen (*dat*); *have close ～s* e-e starke Ähnlichkeit haben (*with* mit). **3.** *a.* ～ *of latitude geogr.* Breitenkreis *m.* **III** *v/t pret u. pp* **-leled,** *Br. a.* **-lelled 4.** gleichkommen (*dat*), entsprechen (*dat*). **'par·al·lel·ism** *s* **1.** Parallelität *f* (*a. fig.*). **2.** *ling.* Parallelismus *m.* **,par·al·'lel·o·gram** [～əʊgræm] *s* ⅍ Parallelogramm *n.*

par·a·lyse ['pærəlaɪz] *v/t bsd. Br.* ⅋ lähmen, *fig. a.* lahmlegen, zum Erliegen bringen: ～*d* *mit fig.* starr *od.* wie gelähmt vor (*dat*). **pa·ral·y·sis** [pə'rælɪsɪs] *pl* **-ses** [～siːz] *s* ⅋ Lähmung *f, fig. a.* Lahmlegung *f.* **par·a·lyt·ic** [,pærə'lɪtɪk] **I** *adj* (～*ally*) **1.** ⅋ Lähmungs...; gelähmt. **2.** *Br.* F sternhagelsein; *for no ~ reason* aus keinem besonderen Grund. **2. be very ~ about** (*od. over*) es sehr genau nehmen mit, großen Wert legen auf (*acc*); sehr heikel *od.* wählerisch sein in (*dat*). **II** *s* **3.** Einzelheit *f*: *~s pl* nähere Umstände *pl od.* Angaben *pl*; *in ~* insbesondere; *in every ~, in all ~* in allen Einzelheiten; *enter* (*od. go*) *into ~s* ins einzelne gehen; *further ~s from* Näheres bei. **4.** *pl* Personalien *pl*. **par·tic·u·lar·ize** *v/t* spezifizieren, einzeln aufführen. **par·tic·u·lar·ly** *adv* besonders: *not ~ a.* nicht sonderlich.

part·ing ['pɑːtɪŋ] **I** *adj* **1.** Abschieds...: *~ kiss.* **II** *s* **2.** Abschied *m*. **3.** *bsd. Br.* (Haar)Scheitel *m*.

par·ti·san [ˌpɑːtɪˈzæn] **I** *s* **1.** Parteigänger(in). **2.** ✕ Partisan(in). **II** *adj* **3.** parteiisch. **4.** ✕ Partisanen...

par·ti·tion [pɑːˈtɪʃn] **I** *s* **1.** Teilung *f*. **2.** *a. ~ wall* Trennwand *f*. **II** *v/t* **3.** *Land etc* teilen: *~ off* abteilen, abtrennen.

part·ly ['pɑːtlɪ] → **partially.**

part·ner ['pɑːtnə] **I** *s* **1.** *allg.* Partner(in). **2.** ✝ Gesellschafter(in), Partner(in), Teilhaber(in). **II** *v/t* **3.** *j-n* zum Partner haben, *j-s* Partner sein. **4.** *oft ~ up* (als Partner) zs.-bringen (*with* mit). **III** *v/i* **5.** *oft ~ up* sich (als Partner) zs.-tun (*with* mit). **'part·ner·ship** *s* **1.** Partnerschaft *f*: *go into ~* sich (als Partner) zs.-tun (*with* mit). **2.** ✝ Personen-, Personalgesellschaft *f*: *general od. ordinary) ~* offene Handelsgesellschaft; *limited* (*Am. special*) *~* Kommanditgesellschaft *f*.

par·tridge ['pɑːtrɪdʒ] *s orn.* Rebhuhn *n*.

part-time *adj* Teilzeit..., Halbtags...: *~ worker* Teilzeitbeschäftigte *m, f*, Halbtagskraft *f*. **II** *adv* halbtags.

par·ty ['pɑːtɪ] *s* **1.** *pol.* Partei *f*: *within the ~* innerparteilich, parteiintern. **2.** Gesellschaft, Gruppe *f*: *we were a ~ of three* wir waren zu dritt. **3.** (*Rettungs- etc*)Mannschaft *f*, ✕ Kommando *n*, Trupp *m*. **4.** Gesellschaft *f*, Party *f*: *give a ~*. **5.** ✝ (*Prozeß-, Vertrags*)Partei *f*: *a third ~* ein Dritter. Teilnehmer(in), Beteiligte *m, f*: *be a ~ to* beteiligt sein an (*dat*), *et.* mitmachen. **7.** F Person *f*, Kerl *m*. *~ line s* **1.** *teleph.* Gemeinschaftsanschluß *m*. **2.** *pol.* Parteilinie *f*: *follow the ~* linientreu sein.

par·ve·nu ['pɑːvənjuː] *s* Emporkömmling *m*, Parvenu *m*.

pass [pɑːs] **I** *s* **1.** (*Gebirgs*)Paß *m*. **2.** Passierschein *m*: *free ~* (Dauer)Freikarte *f*, ☗ *etc* (Dauer)Freifahrkarte *f*, -schein *m*. **3.** *get a ~ in physics ped.* die Physikprüfung bestehen. **4.** *things have come to such a ~ that* die Dinge haben sich derart zugespitzt, daß. **5.** *Sport:* Paß *m*, Zuspiel *n*. **6.** *make a ~ at* F Annäherungsversuche machen bei. **II** *v/t* **7.** vorbeigehen, -fahren an (*dat*). **8.** überholen. **9.** *Prüfung* bestehen; *Prüfling* durchkommen lassen. **10.** *fig.* hinausgehen über (*acc*), übersteigen, -treffen: *~ s.o.'s comprehension* (*od. understanding*) über *j-s* Verstand *od.* Horizont gehen. **11.** *~ one's hand over* (sich) mit der Hand fahren über (*acc*). **12.** *j-m et.* reichen, geben, *et.* weitergeben: → *buck* **2**. **13.** *Sport:* Ball abspielen, passen (*to* zu). **14.** *Gesetz* verabschieden. **15.** *Zeit* ver-, zubringen: *~ the time reading* sich die Zeit mit Lesen vertreiben. **16.** *Urteil* abgeben, fällen, ⚖ *a.* sprechen (*on* über *acc*). **III** *v/i* **17.** vorbeigehen, -fahren (*by* an *dat*): *let s.o. ~* j-n vorbeilassen. **18.** (*to*) übergehen (auf *acc*), fallen (an *acc*). **19.** vergehen (*Schmerz etc*), (*Zeit a.*) verstreichen. **20.** durchkommen, (die Prüfung) bestehen. **21.** (*as, for*) gelten (als), gehalten *od.* angesehen werden (für). **22.** durchgehen, unbeanstandet bleiben: *let s.th. ~* et. durchgehen lassen. **23.** *Sport:* (den Ball) abspielen *od.* passen (*to* zu). **24.** *Kartenspiel:* passen (*a. fig.*): *I ~ on that* da muß ich passen. **25.** *~ over s.th.* et. übergehen *od.* ignorieren (*in silence* stillschweigend).

Verbindungen mit Adverbien:

pass | **a·way** *v/i* **1.** → **pass 15**. **II** *v/i* **2.** → **pass 19**. **3.** verscheiden, sterben. **~ by I** *v/i* **1.** vorbeigehen, -fahren. **2.** → **pass 19**. **II** *v/t* **3.** übergehen. **~ down** *v/t* (*to*) *Tradition etc* weitergeben (*dat od.* an *acc*), *Bräuche etc* überliefern (*dat*). **~ off I** *v/t* **1.** *et.* ausgeben (*as* als). **II** *v/i* **2.** *gut etc* vorübergehen, verlaufen. **3.** vergehen (*Schmerz etc.*). **~ on I** *v/i* **1.** weitergehen (*to* zu *dat etc*) (*a. fig.*); *Krankheit* übertragen. **II** *v/i* **2.** übergehen (*to* zu *e-m anderen Thema etc*). **3.** → **pass away 3**. **~ o·ver**

pass by 3. **~ round I** v/t herumreichen, *Gerücht etc* in Umlauf setzen: **be passed round** a. die Runde machen. **II** v/i herumgereicht werden, a. *fig.* die Runde machen, *fig.* in Umlauf sein. **~ up** v/t sich *e-e Chance etc* entgehen lassen.

pass·a·ble ['pɑ:səbl] adj □ **1.** passierbar, befahrbar. **2.** *fig.* passabel.

pas·sage ['pæsɪdʒ] s **1.** Durchfahrt f, -reise f: → **bird** 1. **2.** Passage f, (Durch-, Verbindungs)Gang m. **3.** (See-, Flug-) Reise f: → **rough** 2. **4.** *with the* **~ of time** mit der Zeit. **5.** Verabschiedung f (*e-s Gesetzes*). **6.** Passage f, Stelle f (*e-s Texts*). '**~way** → **passage** 2.

pas·sen·ger ['pæsɪndʒə] s Passagier m, Fahr-, Fluggast m, (*Auto- etc*)Insasse m. **~ train** s Personenzug m.

pass·er·'by pl **pass·ers·'by** s Passant(in).

pass·ing ['pɑ:sɪŋ] **I** s **1.** *with the* **~ of time** mit der Zeit. **2.** → **passage** 5. **3.** *in* **~** beiläufig, nebenbei. **II** adj **4.** flüchtig (*Blick, Gedanke etc*).

pas·sion ['pæʃn] s **1.** Leidenschaft f, *weitS. a.* Passion f: **be a ~ with s.o.** e-e Leidenschaft bei j-m sein, j-s Leidenschaft sein; **have a ~ for s.th.** e-e Leidenschaft für et. haben; **~s ran high** die Erregung schlug hohe Wellen; → **heat** 2. **4. fly into a ~** e-n Wutanfall bekommen. **3.** ♀ *eccl.* Passion f: ♀ **play** Passionsspiel n. **pas·sion·ate** ['~ʃənət] adj □ leidenschaftlich.

pas·sive ['pæsɪv] **I** adj □ **1.** passiv: **~ resistance** passiver Widerstand; **~ smoking** passives Rauchen, Passivrauchen n; **~ vocabulary** passiver Wortschatz. **2.** *ling.* passivisch: **~ voice** → **3.** **II** s **3.** *ling.* Passiv n, Leideform f. **pas'siv·i·ty** s Passivität f.

'**pass·key** s Hauptschlüssel m.

Pass·o·ver ['pɑ:sˌəʊvə] s *eccl.* Passah n.

pass·port ['pɑ:spɔ:t] s **1.** (Reise)Paß m: **hold a British ~** e-n britischen Paß haben; **~ picture** Paßbild n. **2.** *fig.* Schlüssel m (*to* zu).

'**pass·word** s Kennwort n, Parole f.

past [pɑ:st] **I** adj **1.** vergangen: **be ~** vorüber od. vorbei sein; **for some time ~** seit einiger Zeit; **learn from ~ mistakes** aus Fehlern in der Vergangenheit lernen. **2.** *ling.* **~ participle** Partizip

n Perfekt, Mittelwort n der Vergangenheit; **~ perfect** Plusquamperfekt n, Vorvergangenheit f; **~ tense** Vergangenheit f, Präteritum n. **3.** früher, ehemalig. **II** s **4.** Vergangenheit f (*a. ling.*): **in the ~** in der Vergangenheit, früher. **III** adv **5.** vorbei, vorüber: **run ~** vorbeilaufen. **IV** prp **6.** *Zeit*: nach, über (*acc*): **half ~ seven** halb acht; **she is ~ forty** sie ist über vierzig. **7.** an ... (*dat*) vorbei od. vorüber. **8.** über ... (*acc*) hinaus: **I'm ~ caring** das kümmert mich nicht mehr; **be ~ it** F es nicht mehr bringen; **I wouldn't put it ~ him** F das traue ich ihm glatt od. ohne weiteres zu; → **cure** 2, **hope** 1, *etc*.

pas·ta ['pæstə] s Teigwaren pl.

paste [peɪst] **I** s **1.** (Fisch-, Zahn- etc)Paste f. **2.** Kleister m. **3.** Am. → **pastry**. **II** v/t **4.** kleben (**to**, an acc): **~ up** ankleben. '**~board** s Karton m, Pappe f.

pas·tel s [pæˈstel] **1.** Pastellstift m. **2.** Pastell(zeichnung f) n. **3.** Pastellfarbe f, -ton m. **II** adj ['pæstl] **4.** Pastell... **5.** pastellfarben.

pas·teur·ize ['pɑ:stʃəraɪz] v/t pasteurisieren, keimfrei machen.

pas·time ['pɑ:staɪm] s Zeitvertreib m, Freizeitbeschäftigung f: **as a ~** zum Zeitvertreib.

pas·tor ['pɑ:stə] s Pastor m, Pfarrer m. '**pas·to·ral I** adj □ **1.** pastoral, ländlich, idyllisch. **2.** pastoral, seelsorgerisch: **~ letter** → **4**. **II** s **3.** ♪ Pastorale n, f. **4.** *eccl.* Hirtenbrief m.

pas·try ['peɪstrɪ] s **1.** (Blätter-, Mürbeetc)Teig m. **2.** Br. oft pl (Fein)Gebäck n.

pas·ture ['pɑ:stʃə] **I** s Weide(land n) f. **II** v/t weiden (lassen). **III** v/i grasen, weiden.

past·y¹ ['peɪstɪ] adj blaß, käsig.

past·y² ['pæstɪ] s bsd. Br. (Fleisch)Pastete f.

pat¹ [pæt] **I** s **1.** Klaps m: **give s.o.** (**o.s.**) **a ~ on the back** fig. F j-m (sich selbst) auf die Schulter klopfen. **2.** Portion f (*bsd. Butter*). **3.** (Kuh)Fladen m. **4.** Trappeln n. **II** v/t **5.** tätscheln; abtupfen (**with** mit): **~ s.o. on the head** (**shoulder**) j-m den Kopf tätscheln (auf die Schulter klopfen); **~ s.o.** (**o.s.**) **on the back** fig. F j-m (sich selbst) auf die Schulter klopfen; **~ down** *Haar etc* an-,

pat   **1136**

festdrücken, *Erde etc* festklopfen. **III**
v/i **6.** trappeln.

pat² [~] **I** *adv* **1. have** (*od.* **know**) *s.th.*
(*off*) ~ et. aus dem Effeff *od.* wie am
Schnürchen können. **2.** wie aus der Pistole geschossen: *answer* ~; *the answer came* ~. **II** *adj* **3.** glatt (*Antwort
etc*).

patch [pætʃ] **I** *s* **1.** Fleck *m*; Flicken *m*:
~*es pl of mist* Nebelschwaden *pl*; *in* ~*es*
fig. stellenweise; *not to be a* ~ *on Br.* F
nichts sein gegen. **2.** Beet *n.* **3.** *go
through a bad* (*difficult*) ~ e-e Pechsträhne haben (e-e schwierige Zeit
durchmachen). **II** *v/t* **4.** flicken: ~ *up*
zs.-flicken (*a. fig.*); *fig.* Streit beilegen;
~ *things up* sich zs.-raufen. ~ **pock·et** *s*
aufgesetzte Tasche. '~**work** *s* Patch-
work *n:* ~ *blanket* Flickendecke *f.*

patch·y ['pætʃɪ] *adj* □ **1.** fleckig. **2.** *fig.*
lückenhaft; unterschiedlich.

pat·ent ['peɪtənt] **I** *adj* □ **1.** offenkundig,
-sichtlich. **2.** patentiert; Patent...: ~ *office* Patentamt *n.* **3.** *Br.* F patent (*Methode etc*). **II** *s* **4.** Patent *n: protected by*
~ patentrechtlich geschützt; *take out a*
~ *on* → 5. **III** *v/t* **5.** *et.* patentieren
lassen. ~ **leath·er** *s* Lackleder *n.*

pa·ter·nal [pə'tɜːnl] *adj* □ **1.** väterlich,
Vater... **2.** *Großvater etc* väterlicherseits.

pa·ter·ni·ty [pə'tɜːnətɪ] *s* Vaterschaft *f:* ~
suit ♊ Vaterschaftsprozeß *m.*

path [pɑːθ] *pl* **paths** [pɑːðz] *s* **1.** Weg *m*
(*a. fig. to* zu), Pfad *m: stand in s.o.'s* ~
j-m im Weg stehen; → *cross* 9. **2.** *phys.,*
☉ Bahn *f.*

pa·thet·ic [pə'θetɪk] *adj* (~*ally*) **1.** mitleiderregend: ~ *sight* Bild *n* des Jam-
mers. **2.** *Br.* kläglich (*Versuch etc*), erbärmlich, miserabel (*Leistung etc*).

path·o·log·i·cal [ˌpæθə'lɒdʒɪkl] *adj* □
pathologisch, krankhaft. **pa·thol·o-
-gist** [pə'θɒlədʒɪst] *s* Pathologe *m.*
pa·thol·o·gy *s* Pathologie *f.*

pa·thos ['peɪθɒs] *s das* Mitleiderregende.

'**path·way** → **path** 1.

pa·tience ['peɪʃns] *s* **1.** Geduld *f: lose
one's* ~ die Geduld verlieren (*with* mit);
→ *saint* 1. **2.** *bsd. Br.* Patience *f* (*Kartenspiel*): *play* ~ Patiencen *od.* e-e Patience legen. '**pa·tient I** *adj* □ geduldig
(*with* mit). **II** *s* Patient(in).

pat·i·na ['pætɪnə] *s* Patina *f.*

pa·ti·o ['pætɪəʊ] *pl* **-os** *s* **1.** Patio *m*,
Innenhof *m.* **2.** Veranda *f*, Terrasse
f.

pa·tri·arch ['peɪtrɪɑːk] *s* Patriarch *m.*
pa·tri·ar·chal [~kl] *adj* □ patriarchalisch. **pa·tri·arch·ate** ['~kɪt] *s* Patriar-
chat *n.*

pa·tri·ot ['pætrɪət] *s* Patriot(in). **pa·tri-
ot·ic** [ˌ~'ɒtɪk] *adj* (~*ally*) patriotisch.
pa·tri·ot·ism ['~ətɪzəm] *s* Patriotismus *m.*

pa·trol [pə'trəʊl] **I** *s* **1.** ✕ Patrouille *f*
(*Polizei*)Streife *f.* **2.** Patrouille *f*, Streife
f, Runde *f: on* ~ auf Patrouille *od.* Streife; ~ *car* (Funk)Streifenwagen *m*; ~
wagon Am. (Polizei)Gefangenenwa-
gen *m.* **II** *v/t* **3.** abpatrouillieren (*Soldaten*), auf Streife sein in (*dat*) (*Polizist*),
s-e Runde machen in (*dat*) (*Wach-
mann*). **pa·trol·man** *s* (*irr man*) **1.** *Am.*
Streifenpolizist *m.* **2.** *Br.* motorisierter
Pannenhelfer.

pa·tron ['peɪtrən] *s* **1.** Schirmherr *m.* **2.**
Gönner *m*, Förderer *m.* **3.** (Stamm-)
Kunde *m*; Stammgast *m.* **pa·tron·age**
['pætrənɪdʒ] *s* **1.** Schirmherrschaft *f:
under the* ~ *of* unter der Schirmherrschaft von (*od. gen*). **2.** Förderung *f.*
pa·tron·ess ['peɪtrənɪs] *s* **1.** Schirmher-
rin *f.* **2.** Gönnerin *f*, Förderin *f.* **pa-
tron·ize** ['pætrənaɪz] *v/t* **1.** fördern. **2.**
(Stamm)Kunde *od.* Stammgast sein in
(*dat*). **3.** gönnerhaft *od.* herablassend
behandeln. '**pa·tron·iz·ing** *adj* □ gönnerhaft, herablassend.

pa·tron saint *s* Schutzheilige *m*, *f.*

pat·ter¹ ['pætə] *v/i* **1.** prasseln (*Regen
etc*). **2.** trappeln. **II** *s* **3.** Prasseln *n.* **4.**
Trappeln *n.*

pat·ter² [~] *s* **1.** Sprüche *pl* (*e-s Vertreters
etc*). **2.** Jargon *m: thieves'* ~ Gaunersprache *f.*

pat·tern ['pætən] **I** *s* **1.** (*a. Schnitt-,
Strick*)Muster *n*; *fig.* Muster *n*, Vorbild
n. **2.** ♱ Muster *n*, (Waren)Probe *f.* **3.**
(*Stoff- etc*)Muster *n.* **4.** *fig.* Muster *n*,
Schema *n: follow its usual* ~ nach dem
üblichen Schema *od.* wie üblich verlau-
fen. **II** *v/t* **5.** mustern. **6.** bilden, gestalten (*after, on* nach): ~ *o.s. on s.o.*
j-n zum Vorbild nehmen.

paunch [pɔːntʃ] *s* (dicker) Bauch, Wanst
m. '**paunch·y** *adj* dickbäuchig.

pau·per ['pɔːpə] *s* Arme *m*, *f.*

pearl

pause [pɔːz] **I** s Pause f: **without a ~** ohne Pause. **II** v/i innehalten.

pave [peɪv] v/t pflastern: **~ the way for** fig. den Weg ebnen (dat). **'pave·ment** s **1.** (Straßen)Pflaster n. **2.** Br. Bürger-, Gehsteig m: **~ artist** Pflastermaler(in); **~ café** Straßencafé n. **3.** Am. Fahrbahn f.

pa·vil·ion [pə'vɪljən] s Pavillon m.

pav·ing stone ['peɪvɪŋ] s Pflasterstein m.

paw [pɔː] **I** s **1.** Pfote f (a. F Hand), Tatze f. **II** v/t **2.** Boden scharren, scharren an (der Tür etc). **3.** F betatschen. **III** v/i **4.** scharren (**at** an dat).

pawn¹ [pɔːn] s **1.** Schach: Bauer m. **2.** fig. Schachfigur f.

pawn² [\~] **I** s: **be in ~** verpfändet od. versetzt sein. **II** v/t verpfänden, versetzen. **'~·brok·er** s Pfandleiher m. **'~-shop** s Leih-, Pfandhaus n. **~ tick·et** s Pfandschein m.

pay [peɪ] **I** s **1.** Bezahlung f, Gehalt n, Lohn m. **II** v/t (irr) **2.** Betrag zahlen, entrichten, Rechnung (be)zahlen, begleichen: **~ into** einzahlen auf (ein Konto). **3.** j-n bezahlen. **4.** fig. Aufmerksamkeit schenken, Besuch abstatten, Kompliment machen: → **attention** 1, etc. **III** v/i (irr) **5.** zahlen: **~ for** et. bezahlen (a. fig.); **he had to ~ dearly for it** es kam ihn teuer zu stehen, er mußte teuer dafür bezahlen. **6.** fig. sich lohnen, sich bezahlt machen.

Verbindungen mit Adverbien:

pay| back → **repay:** → **coin** I. **~ in** v/t einzahlen. **~ off I** v/t **1.** j-n auszahlen. **2.** et. ab(be)zahlen, tilgen. **II** v/i **3.** → **pay** 6. **~ out** v/t ausgeben, bezahlen (**for** für). **~ up I** v/t j-n, et. voll od. sofort bezahlen. **II** v/i zahlen.

pay·a·ble ['peɪəbl] adj zahlbar, fällig: **be ~ to** ausgestellt sein auf (acc).

pay| bed s Br. Privatbett n (in Klinik). **'~·day** s Zahltag m. **~ en·ve·lope** s Am. Lohntüte f.

pay·ing ['peɪɪŋ] adj **1.** **~ guest** zahlender Gast. **2.** lohnend, rentabel. **,~·'in slip** s Einzahlungsschein m.

pay·ment ['peɪmənt] s (Be)Zahlung f: **in ~ of** als Bezahlung für; **on ~ of** gegen Zahlung von (od. gen).

'pay|·off s F Pointe f. **~ pack·et** s Br. Lohntüte f. **~ phone** s Münzfernspre-

cher m. **~ rise** s Lohn-, Gehaltserhöhung f. **'~·roll** s Lohnliste f: **be on s.o.'s ~** bei j-m beschäftigt sein. **~ slip** s Lohn-, Gehaltsstreifen m. **~ sta·tion** s Am. Münzfernsprecher m.

pea [piː] s **♀** Erbse f: **they are (as) like as two ~s (in a pod)** sie gleichen sich wie ein Ei dem anderen.

peace [piːs] **I** s **1.** Friede(n) m: **the two countries are at ~** zwischen den beiden Ländern herrscht Frieden; **make one's ~ with** sich aus- od. versöhnen mit. **2.** ⚖ öffentliche Ruhe u. Ordnung: **keep the ~** die öffentliche Ordnung aufrechterhalten; → **breach** 1. **3.** Ruhe f: **~ of mind** Seelenfrieden m; **in ~ and quiet** in Ruhe u. Frieden. **II** adj **4.** Friedens...: **~ conference** Friedenskonferenz f; **~ movement** Friedensbewegung f; **~ pipe** Friedenspfeife f; **~ treaty** Friedensvertrag m. **'peace·a·ble** adj □ friedlich (Diskussion etc), (Person a.) friedfertig. **peace·ful** ['~fʊl] adj □ friedlich.

'peace|·,lov·ing adj friedliebend. **'~-time I** s Friedenszeiten pl. **II** adj in Friedenszeiten.

peach [piːtʃ] s **1.** **♀** Pfirsich m; Pfirsichbaum m. **2.** F prima od. klasse Person od. Sache: **a ~ of a girl** ein süßes Mädchen; **a ~ of a hat** ein Gedicht von e-m Hut.

pea·cock ['piːkɒk] s orn. Pfau m: **(as) proud as a ~** stolz wie ein Pfau.

peak [piːk] **I** s **1.** Spitze f, (e-s Bergs a.) Gipfel m. **2.** Schirm m (e-r Mütze). **3.** fig. Höhepunkt m, Höchststand m: **be at its ~** am höchsten sein. **II** v/i **4.** e-n Höchststand erreichen. **III** adj **5.** Höchst..., Spitzen...: **~ hours** pl Hauptverkehrs-, Stoßzeit f; ⚡ Hauptbelastungszeit f. **peaked** [piːkt] adj: **~ cap** Schirmmütze f (nur mit Schirm), kränklich. **'peak·y** adj F blaß, kränklich.

peal [piːl] **I** s **1.** (Glocken)Läuten n. **2.** (Donner)Schlag m: **~s pl of laughter** schallendes od. dröhnendes Gelächter. **II** v/i a. **~ out 3.** läuten. **4.** krachen (Donner).

'pea·nut s **♀** Erdnuß f: **~s pl** F lächerliche Summe. **~ but·ter** s Erdnußbutter f.

pear [peə] s **♀** a) Birne f, b) a. **~ tree** Birnbaum m.

pearl [pɜːl] s **1.** Perle f. **2.** Perlmutter f,

n, Perlmutt *n*. **II** *adj* **3**. Perlen... **4**. Perlmutt(er)...

peas·ant ['peznt] *s* **1**. Kleinbauer *m*. **2**. *fig*. F Bauer *m*.

pea-soup·er [ˌpiːˈsuːpə] *s* F Waschküche *f* (*dicker, gelber Nebel*).

peat [piːt] *s* Torf *m*: *cut* (*od. dig*) *~* Torf stechen.

peb·ble ['pebl] *s* Kiesel(stein) *m*: *you are not the only ~ on the beach* F ich *etc* kann auch ohne dich auskommen. **'peb·bly** *adj* Kiesel...: → *beach*.

pec·ca·dil·lo [ˌpekəˈdɪləʊ] *pl* **-lo(e)s** *s* **1**. kleine Sünde. **2**. Kavaliersdelikt *n*.

peck [pek] **I** *v/t* **1**. picken. **2**. F *j-m* e-n flüchtigen Kuß geben (*on auf acc*). **II** *v/i* **3**. picken, hacken (*at* nach): *~ at one's food* im Essen herumstochern. **III** *s* **4**. F flüchtiger Kuß. **'peck·er** *s* **1**. *Am. sl.* Schwanz *m* (*Penis*). **2**. *keep one's ~ up* F die Ohren steifhalten. **'peck·ing** *adj*: *~ order orn.* Hackordnung *f* (*a. fig.*).

pec·to·ral ['pektərəl] *adj* Brust...

pe·cu·li·ar [pɪˈkjuːljə] *adj* (□ → *peculiarly*) **1**. eigen(tümlich) (*to dat*): *be ~ to a.* typisch sein für. **2**. eigenartig, seltsam. **pe¸cu·li·ar·i·ty** [ˌlɪˈærətɪ] *s* **1**. Eigenheit *f*, Eigentümlichkeit *f*: *be a ~ of a.* typisch sein für. **2**. Eigenartigkeit *f*, Seltsamkeit *f*. **pe'cu·li·ar·ly** *adv* **1**. → *peculiar* **2**. besonders.

pe·cu·ni·ar·y [pɪˈkjuːnjərɪ] *adj* geldlich, Geld...: *~ difficulties pl* finanzielle Schwierigkeiten *pl*.

ped·a·gog·ic, ped·a·gog·i·cal [ˌpedəˈgɒdʒɪk(l)] *adj* □ → *pedagogical*. **'ped·a·gogue** ['~gɒg] *s contp.* Schulmeister (-in), Pedant(in). **ped·a·go·gy** ['~gɒdʒɪ] *s* Pädagogik *f*.

ped·al ['pedl] **I** *s* **1**. Pedal *n*. **II** *v/i pret u. pp* **-aled**, *bsd. Br.* **-alled 2**. das Pedal treten. **3**. (mit dem Rad) fahren, strampeln. *~ bin s* Treteimer *m*. *~ boat s* Tretboot *n*.

ped·ant ['pedənt] *s* Pedant(in). **pe·dan·tic** [pɪˈdæntɪk] *adj* (*~ally*) pedantisch (*about* wenn es um ... geht). **ped·ant·ry** ['pedəntrɪ] *s* Pedanterie *f*.

ped·dle ['pedl] *v/t* hausieren (gehen) mit (*a. fig.*): *~ drugs* mit Drogen handeln. **'ped·dler** *s* **1**. Drogenhändler(in). **2**. *Am.* → *pedlar*.

ped·es·tal ['pedɪstl] *s* Sockel *m*: *place*

(*od. put, set*) *s.o. on a ~ fig.* j-n aufs Podest erheben; *knock s.o. off his ~fig.* j-n von s-m Sockel stoßen.

pe·des·tri·an [pɪˈdestrɪən] **I** *adj* **1**. Fußgänger...: *~ crossing Br.* Fußgängerüberweg *m*; *~ precinct* (*od. zone*) Fußgängerzone *f*. **2**. *fig.* prosaisch, trocken; phantasielos. **II** *s* **3**. Fußgänger(in).

pe·di·a·tri·cian, pe·di·a·trics *Am.* → *paediatrician, paediatrics*.

ped·i·cure ['pedɪˌkjʊə] *s* Pediküre *f*.

ped·i·gree ['pedɪgriː] **I** *s* **1**. Stammbaum *m*. **2**. Ab-, Herkunft *f*. **II** *adj* **3**. *zo.* reinrassig.

ped·lar ['pedlə] *s* Hausierer(in).

pee [piː] F **I** *v/i* pinkeln. **II** *s*: *have* (*go for*) *a ~* pinkeln (gehen).

peek [piːk] **I** *v/i* kurz *od.* verstohlen gucken (*at auf acc*). **II** *s*: *have* (*od. take*) *a ~ at* e-n kurzen *od.* verstohlenen Blick werfen auf (*acc*).

peel [piːl] **I** *v/t* Kartoffeln *etc* schälen: *~* (*off*) *Tapete etc* abziehen, ablösen; *Kleider* abstreifen; *keep one's eyes ~ed* F die Augen offenhalten. **II** *v/i a. ~ off* sich lösen (*Tapete etc*), abblättern (*Farbe etc*), sich schälen (*Haut*). **III** *s* Schale *f*. **'peel·er** *s* (*Kartoffel- etc*)Schäler *m*. **'peel·ings** *s pl* (*Kartoffel- etc*)Schalen *pl*.

peep¹ [piːp] **I** *v/i* **1**. piep(s)en. **II** *s* **2**. Piep(s)en *n*. **3**. F Piepser *m* (*Ton*).

peep² [~] **I** *v/i* **1**. → *peek* **I**. **2**. *mst ~ out* vorschauen (*from under* unter *dat*). **II** *s* **3**. → *peek* **II**. **'peep·er** *s mst pl* F Gucker *m* (*Auge*).

'peep·hole *s* Guckloch *n*, (*in Tür*) Spion *m*.

Peep·ing Tom ['piːpɪŋ] *s* Spanner *m*, Voyeur *m*.

peep show *s* Peep-Show *f*.

peer¹ [pɪə] *v/i* angestrengt schauen, spähen: *~ at s.o.* j-n anstarren.

peer² [~] *s* **1**. *Br.* Peer *m*. **2**. Gleichgestellte *m,f*, Ebenbürtige *m,f*, Altersgenosse *m*, -genossin *f*: *one's ~s pl* seinesgleichen. **'peer·age** *s Br.* Peerage *f*: *raise to the ~* in den Adelsstand erheben. **'peer·ess** *s Br.* Peereß *f*. **'peer·less** *adj* □ unvergleichlich, einzigartig.

peeved [piːvd] *adj* F sauer (*about, at* über *acc*).

pee·vish ['piːvɪʃ] *adj* □ gereizt; reizbar.

peg [peg] **I** s **1.** Pflock m; (Holz)Nagel m, (-)Stift m; (Zelt)Hering m: *be a square ~ in a round hole* fig. am falschen Platz sein; *take s.o. down a ~ (or two)* F j-m e-n Dämpfer aufsetzen. **2.** (Kleider-) Haken m: *off the ~* von der Stange (Anzug). **3.** Br. (Wäsche)Klammer f. **II** v/t **4.** anpflocken. **5.** a. *~out* (od. up) Br. Wäsche (an der Leine) anklammern. **6.** ✝ Preise etc stützen, halten. **III** v/i **7.** *~ away* at F dranbleiben an (e-r Arbeit). **8.** *~ out* bsd. Br. F den Löffel weglegen (sterben).

pe·jo·ra·tive [pɪˈdʒɒrətɪv] adj □ pejorativ, abschätzig, herabsetzend.

Pe·kin·ese [ˌpiːkɪˈniːz] pl **-ese** s zo. Pekinese m.

pel·i·can [ˈpelɪkən] s orn. Pelikan m. *~ cross·ing* s Br. Ampelübergang m.

pel·let [ˈpelɪt] s **1.** Kügelchen n. **2.** Schrotkorn n.

pelt¹ [pelt] s Fell m, Pelz m.

pelt² [~] **I** v/t **1.** bewerfen, a. fig. bombardieren (with mit). **II** v/i **2.** *it is ~ing (down), it is ~ing with rain* es gießt in Strömen. **3.** stürmen, stürzen. **III** s **4.** (at) *full ~* mit voller Geschwindigkeit.

pel·vic [ˈpelvɪk] adj anat., ✻ Becken...: *~ fin* ichth. Bauchflosse f.

pel·vis [ˈpelvɪs] pl **-ves** [ˈ~viːz] s anat. Becken n.

pen¹ [pen] s (Schreib)Feder f; Füller m; Kugelschreiber m.

pen² [~] **I** s **1.** Pferch m, (Schaf)Hürde f. **2.** (Lauf)Gitter n, (-)Stall m. **II** v/t (a. irr) a. *~in* (od. up) **3.** Tiere einpferchen. **4.** Personen zs.-pferchen.

pe·nal [ˈpiːnl] adj □ **1.** Straf...: *~ code* Strafgesetzbuch n; *~ colony* Strafkolonie f; *~ law* Strafrecht n; *~ reform* Strafrechtsreform f. **2.** strafbar: *~ act* strafbare Handlung. **pe·nal·ize** [ˈpiːnəlaɪz] v/t **1.** bestrafen, weitS. a. benachteiligen. **2.** et. unter Strafe stellen. **pen·al·ty** [ˈpenltɪ] s **1.** Strafe f: *pay the ~ for s.th.* et. bezahlen od. büßen (with mit). **2.** Nachteil m. **3.** Fußball: Elfmeter m: *~ area* (od. box) Strafraum m; *~ kick* Strafstoß m.

pen·ance [ˈpenəns] s eccl. Buße f: *do ~* Buße tun (for für).

pen-and-ink draw·ing s Federzeichnung f.

pence [pens] pl von **penny**.

pen·chant [ˈpɑ̃ːŋʃɑ̃ːŋ] s (for) Neigung f, Hang m (zu), Vorliebe f (für).

pen·cil [ˈpensl] **I** s **1.** Bleistift m. **2.** ⅄, phys. (Strahlen- etc)Bündel m. **II** v/t pret u. pp **-ciled,** bsd. Br. **-cilled 3.** mit Bleistift markieren od. schreiben od. zeichnen. **4.** Augenbrauen etc nachziehen. *~ case* s Federmäppchen n. *~ sharp·en·er* s (Bleistift)Spitzer m.

pen·dant [ˈpendənt] s Anhänger m (Schmuckstück).

pen·dent [ˈpendənt] adj **1.** Hänge...: *~ lamp.* **2.** überhängend (Felsen etc).

pend·ing [ˈpendɪŋ] **I** adj **1.** bsd. ⚖ schwebend, anhängig. **2.** bevorstehend. **II** prp **3.** bis zu.

pen·du·lum [ˈpendjʊləm] s Pendel n (a. fig.).

pen·e·trate [ˈpenɪtreɪt] **I** v/t eindringen in (acc) (a. fig.); durchdringen, dringen durch. **II** v/i eindringen (into in acc) (a. fig.); durchdringen: *~ through a.* dringen durch. **'pen·e·trat·ing** adj □ **1.** durchdringend; (Verstand) scharf. **2.** scharfsinnig. **ˌpen·e·ˈtra·tion** s **1.** Ein-, Durchdringen n. **2.** Scharfsinn m.

pen friend s Brieffreund(in).

pen·guin [ˈpeŋgwɪn] s orn. Pinguin m.

pen·i·cil·lin [ˌpenɪˈsɪlɪn] s ✻ Penicillin n.

pen·in·su·la [pəˈnɪnsjʊlə] s Halbinsel f. **pen·in·su·lar** adj Halbinsel...; halbinselförmig.

pe·nis [ˈpiːnɪs] pl **-nis·es, -nes** [ˈ~niːz] s anat. Penis m.

pen·i·tence [ˈpenɪtəns] s Buße f: a) eccl. Bußfertigkeit f, b) Reue f. **'pen·i·tent, pen·i·ten·tial** [ˌ~ˈtenʃl] adj □ a) eccl. bußfertig, b) reuig. **pen·i·ten·tia·ry** [ˌ~ˈtenʃərɪ] s Am. (Staats)Gefängnis n.

'pen·knife s (irr knife) Taschenmesser n. *~ name* s Schriftstellername m.

pen·nant [ˈpenənt] s Wimpel m.

pen·ni·less [ˈpenɪlɪs] adj □ (völlig) mittellos: *be ~ a.* keinen Pfennig Geld haben.

pen·ny [ˈpenɪ] pl **-nies,** coll. **pence** [pens] s Br. Penny m: *in for a ~, in for a pound* wer A sagt, muß auch B sagen; *a pretty ~* F ein hübsches Sümmchen; *count (the) pennies* jeden Pfennig umdrehen; *the ~('s) dropped* F der Groschen ist gefallen; *spend a ~* F mal verschwinden. *~ dread·ful* pl **-fuls** s Br. F Groschenroman m. *~ pinch·er* s F

Pfennigfuchser(in). '~,**pinch·ing** *adj* F knick(e)rig.

pen pal F → **pen friend**.

pen·sion ['penʃn] **I** *s* Rente *f*, Pension *f*: ~ *scheme* Rentenversicherung *f*. **II** *v/t*: ~ *off j-n* pensionieren, in den Ruhestand versetzen; *fig.* F *Maschine etc* ausrangieren. '**pen·sion·a·ble** *adj*: *of* ~ *age* im Renten- *od.* Pensionsalter. **pen·sion·er** ['~ʃənə] *s* Rentner(in), Pensionär(in).

pen·sive ['pensɪv] *adj* □ **1.** nachdenklich. **2.** trübsinnig.

pent [pent] *pret u. pp von* **pen²**.

pen·ta·gon ['pentəgən] *s* Fünfeck *n*: *the* ♀ das Pentagon. **pen·tag·o·nal** [~'tægənl] *adj* □ fünfeckig.

pen·tath·lete [pen'tæθliːt] *s Sport:* Fünfkämpfer(in). **pen'tath·lon** [~lɒn] *s* Fünfkampf *m*.

Pen·te·cost ['pentɪkɒst] *s eccl.* Pfingsten *n, a. pl.*

pent·house ['penthaʊs] *s* Penthouse *n*, -haus *n*.

,**pent·up** *adj* an-, aufgestaut (*Gefühle*).

pe·nul·ti·mate [pe'nʌltɪmət] *adj* vorletzt.

pe·o·ny ['pɪəni] *s* ♀ Pfingstrose *f*.

peo·ple ['piːpl] **I** *s* **1.** (*pl konstruiert*) die Menschen *pl*, die Leute *pl*; Leute *pl*, Personen *pl*: *my* ~ F m-e Angehörigen *pl od.* Leute. **2.** (*pl konstruiert*) man: ~ *say that* man sagt, daß. **3.** (*pl konstruiert*) *the* ~ a) das (*gemeine*) Volk: *a man of the* (*common*) ~ ein Mann des Volks, b) die Bürger *pl od.* Wähler *pl*, die Bevölkerung: ~*'s front* Volksfront *f*; ~*'s republic* Volksrepublik *f*. **4.** Volk *n*, Nation *f*. **II** *v/t* **5.** besiedeln, bevölkern (*with* mit).

pep [pep] F **I** *s* Pep *m*, Schwung *m*. **II** *v/t*: ~ *up j-n* aufmöbeln: ~ *things up* Schwung in den Laden bringen.

pep·per ['pepə] **I** *s* Pfeffer *m*; Paprikaschote *f*. **II** *v/t* pfeffern, *fig. a.* spicken (*with* mit). '~·*box* Am. → *pepper pot*. '~·*corn s* Pfefferkorn *n*. ~ *mill s* Pfeffermühle *f*. '~·*mint s* **1.** ♀ Pfefferminze *f*. **2.** Pfefferminz *n* (*Bonbon*). **3.** Pfefferminz... ~ *pot s* Pfefferstreuer *m*.

pep·per·y ['pepəri] *adj* □ **1.** pfeff(e)rig. **2.** *fig.* hitzig (*Person*).

pep| pill *s* F Aufputschpille *f*. ~ *talk s* F aufmunternde Worte *pl*: *give s.o. a* ~

j-m ein paar aufmunternde Worte sagen.

pep·tic ['peptɪk] *adj*: ~ *ulcer* ♪ Magengeschwür *n*.

per [pɜː] *prp* **1.** per, durch. **2.** pro, je. **3.** *mst* **as** ~ laut, gemäß.

per·am·bu·la·tor [pə'ræmbjʊleɪtə] *s bsd. Br.* Kinderwagen *m*.

per cap·i·ta [pə'kæpɪtə] **I** *adj* Pro-Kopf-... **II** *adv* pro Kopf.

per·ceive [pə'siːv] *v/t* **1.** wahrnehmen. **2.** begreifen, erkennen.

per cent *Br.*, **per·cent** *bsd. Am.* [pə'sent] **I** *adj u. adv* ...prozentig. **II** *s* Prozent *n*.

per'cent·age *s* **1.** Prozentsatz *m*; Teil *m*: *what* ~ *of* ...? wieviel Prozent von ...?; *in* ~ *terms* prozentual (ausgedrückt). **2.** *there's no* ~ *in doing s.th.* F es bringt nichts, et. zu tun.

per·cep·ti·ble [pə'septəbl] *adj* □ wahrnehmbar, merklich. **per'cep·tion** *s* **1.** Wahrnehmung *f*. **2.** Auffassung(sgabe) *f*. **per'cep·tive** *adj* □ scharfsinnig.

perch¹ [pɜːtʃ] *s ichth.* Flußbarsch *m*.

perch² [~] **I** *s* **1.** (Sitz)Stange *f* (*für Vögel*): *knock s.o. off his* ~ F j-n von s-m Sockel stoßen. **2.** F hochgelegener Platz *od.* Standort. **II** *v/i* **3.** (*on*) sich niederlassen (auf *acc, dat*), sich setzen (auf *acc*) (*Vogel*). **4.** F hocken (*on dat*). **III** *v/t* **5.** ~ *o.s.* F sich hocken (*on* auf *acc*).

per·co·late ['pɜːkəleɪt] **I** *v/t Kaffee* filtern, *weitS.* kochen, machen. **II** *v/i* durchsickern (*a. fig.*), (*Kaffee*) durchlaufen '**per·co·la·tor** *s* Kaffeemaschine *f*.

per·cus·sion [pə'kʌʃn] **I** *s* **1.** Schlag *m*, Stoß *m*; Erschütterung *f*. **2.** ♪ Schlagzeug *n*. **II** *adj* **3.** ~ *instrument* Schlaginstrument *n*; ~ *section* → **2**. **per'cus·sion·ist** *s* Schlagzeuger *m*.

per·emp·to·ry [pə'remptəri] *adj* □ **1.** gebieterisch, herrisch. **2.** kategorisch (*Befehl etc*).

per·en·ni·al [pə'renjəl] *adj* □ **1.** ewig, immerwährend. **2.** ♀ mehrjährig.

per·fect ['pɜːfɪkt] **I** *adj* □ **1.** perfekt: a) vollkommen, vollendet: ~ *crime* perfektes Verbrechen, b) fehler-, makellos. **2.** gänzlich, vollständig: ~ *fool* ausgemachter Narr; ~ *nonsense* kompletter Unsinn; ~ *strangers pl* wildfremde Leute *pl*. **3.** ~ *tense* → **4**. **II** *s* **4.** *ling.*

Perfekt *n*: → *future* 4, *past* 2, *present* 3. **III** *v/t* [pə'fekt] **5.** vervollkommnen, perfektionieren. **per·fec·tion** [pə'fekʃn] *s* **1.** Vervollkommnung *f*, Vollendung *f*. **2.** Vollkommenheit *f*, Perfektion *f*: *bring to ~* vervollkommnen; *to ~* vollkommen, perfekt. **per'fec·tion·ism** *s* Perfektionismus *m*. **per'fec·tion·ist** **I** Perfektionist(in). **II** *adj* perfektionistisch.

per·fid·i·ous [pə'fidiəs] *adj* □ treulos, verräterisch. **per·fi·dy** ['pɜːfidi] *s* Treulosigkeit *f*.

per·fo·rate ['pɜːfəreit] *v/t* **1.** durchbohren, -löchern. **2.** perforieren, lochen. **‚per·fo'ra·tion** *s* **1.** Durchbohrung *f*, -löcherung *f*. **2.** Perforation *f*.

per·form [pə'fɔːm] **I** *v/t* **1.** *Arbeit, Dienst etc* verrichten, *Pflicht, a. Vertrag* erfüllen, ✽ *Operation* durchführen. **2.** *Theaterstück etc* aufführen, spielen, *a. Konzert* geben, *Musikstück, Lied etc* vortragen, *Kunststück etc* vorführen, *Rolle* spielen. **II** *v/i* **3.** *~ well* (*bsd. Sport*) e-e gute Leistung zeigen; *ped. aut* abschneiden. **4.** ✿ funktionieren, arbeiten (*Maschine etc*). **5.** *thea. etc* e-e Vorstellung geben, auftreten, spielen. **per'form·ance** *s* **1.** Verrichtung *f*, Erfüllung *f*, Durchführung *f*. **2.** ♪, *thea.* Aufführung *f*, Vorstellung *f*, Vortrag *m*. **3.** Leistung *f* (*a.* ✿): *~ principle sociol.* Leistungsprinzip *n*. **per'form·er** *s* Darsteller(in), Künstler(in). **per'form·ing** *adj* dressiert (*Tier*).

per·fume I *s* ['pɜːfjuːm] **1.** Duft *m*. **2.** Parfüm *n*. **II** *v/t* [pə'fjuːm] **3.** parfümieren.

per·func·to·ry [pə'fʌŋktəri] *adj* □ flüchtig (*Blick etc*), (*a. Person*) oberflächlich.

per·haps [pə'hæps] *adv* vielleicht.

per·il ['perəl] *s* Gefahr *f*: *be in ~ of one's life* sich in Lebensgefahr befinden; *at one's ~* auf eigene Gefahr. **'per·il·ous** *adj* □ gefährlich.

pe·ri·od ['piəriəd] **I** *s* **1.** Periode *f*, Zeit (-dauer *f*, -raum *m*, -spanne *f*) *f*, Frist *f*: *for a ~ of* für die Dauer von. **2.** Zeit(alter *n*) *f*, Epoche *f*. **3.** *physiol.* Periode *f*. **4.** *ped.* (Unterrichts)Stunde *f*. **5.** *ling. bsd. Am.* Punkt *m*. **6.** zeitgenössisch, historisch, Stil...: *~ furniture* Stilmöbel *pl*. **pe·ri·od·ic** [‚~'ɒdik] *adj*

(*~ally*) periodisch, regelmäßig wiederkehrend. **‚pe·ri'od·i·cal I** *adj* → *periodic*. **II** *s* Zeitschrift *f*.

pe·riph·er·y [pə'rifəri] *s* Peripherie *f*, *a. fig.* Rand *m*: *on the ~ of the town* am Stadtrand.

per·i·scope ['periskəup] *s* Periskop *n*, Sehrohr *n*.

per·ish ['periʃ] **I** *v/i* **1.** umkommen: *be ~ing* (*with cold*) F vor Kälte umkommen. **2.** brüchig werden, verschleißen (*Material*), schlecht werden, verderben (*Lebensmittel*). **II** *v/t* **3.** *be ~ed* (*with cold*) F ganz durchgefroren sein. **'per·ish·a·ble** *adj* leichtverderblich. **'per·ish·ing** *bsd. Br.* F **I** *adj* saukalt. **II** *adv*: *~ly cold* → I.

per·i·to·ni·tis [‚peritəu'naitis] *s* ✽ Bauchfellentzündung *f*.

per·jure ['pɜːdʒə] *v/t*: *~ o.s.* e-n Meineid leisten. **'per·ju·ry** *s* Meineid *m*: *commit ~ →* *perjure*.

perk¹ [pɜːk] F **I** *v/t* → *percolate* I. **II** *v/i* durchlaufen (*Kaffee*).

perk² [‚~] F **I** *v/t*: *~ up* j-n aufmöbeln. **II** *v/i*: *~ up* aufleben, neuen Schwung bekommen.

perk³ [‚~] F → *perquisite*.

perk·y ['pɜːki] *adj* □ F **1.** munter, lebhaft. **2.** keck, selbstbewußt.

perm [pɜːm] F **I** *s* Dauerwelle *f*: *give s.o. a ~* → II. **II** *v/t*: *~ s.o.'s hair* j-m e-e Dauerwelle machen.

per·ma·nence ['pɜːmənəns], **'per·ma·nen·cy** *s* Beständigkeit *f*, Dauerhaftigkeit *f*. **'per·ma·nent I** *adj* □ beständig, dauerhaft, Dauer...: *~ address* ständiger Wohnsitz; *~ wave* Dauerwelle *f*. **II** *s Am.* Dauerwelle *f*.

per·me·a·ble ['pɜːmjəbl] *adj* □ durchlässig (*to* für). **per·me·ate** ['~mieit] **I** *v/t* durchdringen (*a. fig.*). **II** *v/i* dringen (*into* in *acc*; *through* durch).

per·mis·si·ble [pə'misəbl] *adj* □ zulässig, statthaft, erlaubt. **per·mis·sion** [pə'miʃn] *s* Erlaubnis *f*: *by ~ of* mit Genehmigung (*gen*); *without ~* uncrlaubt, unbefugt; *ask s.o.'s ~, ask s.o. for ~* j-n um Erlaubnis bitten; *give s.o. ~ to do s.th.* j-m die Erlaubnis geben *od.* j-m erlauben, et. zu tun. **per'mis·sive** [‚~siv] *adj* □ (*a.*; (sexuell) freizügig: *~ society* tabufreie Gesellschaft.

per·mit I *v/t* **1.** *et.* erlauben, gestatten: *not ~ted a.* verboten; *~ s.o. to do s.th.* j-m erlauben, et. zu tun. **II** *v/i* **2.** es erlauben *od.* gestatten: *weather ~ting* wenn es das Wetter erlaubt. **3.** *~ of et.* zulassen. **III** *s* ['pɜ:mɪt] **4.** Genehmigung *f.*

per·ni·cious [pə'nɪʃəs] *adj* □ schädlich, verderblich.

per·nick·et·y [pə'nɪkətɪ] *adj* F **1.** pingelig, pedantisch. **2.** kitz(e)lig (*Angelegenheit etc*).

per·pen·dic·u·lar [,pɜ:pən'dɪkjʊlə] **I** *adj* □ senkrecht, rechtwink(e)lig (*to* zu). **II** *s* Senkrechte *f.*

per·pe·trate ['pɜ:pɪtreɪt] *v/t Verbrechen etc* begehen, verüben; *humor. Buch etc* verbrechen. **'per·pe·tra·tor** *s* Täter(in).

per·pet·u·al [pə'petʃʊəl] *adj* □ fortwährend, ständig, ewig. **per'pet·u·ate** [~eɪt] *v/t* verewigen. **per·pe·tu·i·ty** [,pɜ:pɪ'tju:ətɪ] *s*: *in ~* auf ewig, für immer.

per·plex [pə'pleks] *v/t* verwirren, verblüffen; *~ed a.* perplex. **per'plex·i·ty** *s* Verwirrung *f*, Verblüffung *f.*

per·qui·site ['pɜ:kwɪzɪt] *s mst pl* Vergünstigung *f.*

per·se·cute ['pɜ:sɪkju:t] *v/t* **1.** *bsd. pol., eccl.* verfolgen. **2.** belästigen. **per·se·'cu·tion** *s* **1.** Verfolgung *f*: *~ complex* (*od. mania*) *psych.* Verfolgungswahn *m.* **2.** Belästigung *f.*

per·se·ver·ance [,pɜ:sɪ'vɪərəns] *s* Ausdauer *f*, Beharrlichkeit *f.* **per·se·vere** [~'vɪə] *v/i* beharrlich weitermachen (*at, in, with* mit). **per·se'ver·ing** *adj* □ ausdauernd, beharrlich.

Per·sian ['pɜ:ʃn] **I** *adj* **1.** persisch: *~ carpet* Perser(teppich) *m.* **II** *s* **2.** Perser(in). **3.** *ling.* Persisch *n.*

per·sist [pə'sɪst] *v/i* **1.** *~ in doing s.th.* et. unbedingt tun wollen; darauf bestehen, et. zu tun; et. auch *od.* noch weiterhin tun. **2.** *~ with* hartnäckig *od.* unbeirrt fortfahren mit. **3.** anhalten, fortdauern. **per'sist·ence** *s* **1.** Hartnäckigkeit *f*, Unbeirrtheit *f.* **2.** Fortdauer *f.* **per'sist·ent** *adj* □ **1.** unbeirrt (*Person*), (*a. Gerücht etc*) hartnäckig. **2.** anhaltend, fortdauernd.

per·snick·e·ty [pə'snɪkətɪ] *Am.* → **pernickety.**

per·son ['pɜ:sn] *s* Person *f* (*a. ling.*), Mensch *m*: *in ~* persönlich. **'per·son-**

a·ble *adj* von sympathischem *od.* angenehmem Äußeren. **'per·son·age** *s* (bedeutende *od.* prominente) Persönlichkeit. **'per·son·al** *adj* □ **1.** persönlich, Personal...: *~ column* (*Zeitung*) Persönliches *n; ~ computer* Personal Computer *m*, Personalcomputer *m; ~ file* Personalakte *f; ~ pronoun ling.* Personalpronomen *n*, persönliches Fürwort. **2.** persönlich, privat (*Angelegenheit etc*). **3.** äußer, körperlich: *~ hygiene* Körperpflege *f.* **4.** persönlich, anzüglich (*Bemerkung etc*): *get ~* persönlich werden. **per·son·al·i·ty** [,pɜ:sə'nælətɪ] *s* **1.** Persönlichkeit *f* (*a. e-s Menschen*): *~ cult* Personenkult *m.* **2.** *pl* persönliche *od.* anzügliche Bemerkungen *pl*, Persönliches *n.* **per·son·i·fi·ca·tion** [pə,sɒnɪfɪ'keɪʃn] *s* Personifizierung *f*: *be the ~ of avarice* die Habgier in Person sein. **per'son·i·fy** [~faɪ] *v/t* personifizieren: *be avarice personified* die Habgier in Person sein. **per·son·nel** [,pɜ:sə'nel] *s* **1.** Personal *n*, Belegschaft *f*: *~ manager* Personalchef *m.* **2.** die Personalabteilung.

per·spec·tive [pə'spektɪv] *s* Perspektive *f* (*a. fig.*): *in ~* perspektivisch richtig; *fig.* in *od.* aus der richtigen Perspektive; *the houses are out of ~* bei den Häusern stimmt die Perspektive nicht.

per·spex ['pɜ:speks] (*TM*) *s Br.* Plexiglas *n.*

per·spi·ra·tion [,pɜ:spə'reɪʃn] *s* **1.** Transpirieren *n*, Schwitzen *n.* **2.** Schweiß *m.* **per·spire** [pə'spaɪə] *v/i* transpirieren, schwitzen.

per·suade [pə'sweɪd] *v/t* **1.** *j-n* überreden (*into doing, to do* zu tun); *~ s.o. out of s.th.* j-m et. ausreden. **2.** *j-n* überzeugen (*of* von; *that* [davon,] daß).

per·sua·sion [pə'sweɪʒn] *s* **1.** Überredung *f.* **2.** *a. powers pl of ~* Überredungskunst *f.* **3.** Überzeugung *f*: *be of the ~ that* der Überzeugung sein, daß. **per'sua·sive** [~sɪv] *adj* □ überzeugend.

pert [pɜ:t] *adj* □ keck (*a. Hut etc*), keß.

per·tain [pə'teɪn] *v/i*: *~ to s.th.* et. betreffen; zu et. gehören.

per·ti·na·cious [,pɜ:tɪ'neɪʃəs] *adj* □ **1.** hartnäckig, zäh. **2.** beharrlich.

per·ti·nent ['pɜ:tɪnənt] *adj* □ relevant (*to* für); sachdienlich.

pert·ness ['pɜːtnɪs] *s* Keckheit *f*, Keßheit *f*.

per·turb [pə'tɜːb] *v/t* beunruhigen.

pe·ruse [pə'ruːz] *v/t* sorgfältig durchlesen.

per·vade [pə'veɪd] *v/t* durchdringen, erfüllen. **per'va·sive** [‿sɪv] *adj* □ weitverbreitet.

per·verse [pə'vɜːs] *adj* □ **1.** eigensinnig, querköpfig. **2.** pervers, widernatürlich. **per'ver·sion** *s* **1.** Pervertierung *f*; Verdrehung *f*, Entstellung *f*. **2.** Perversion *f*. **per'ver·si·ty** *s* **1.** Eigensinn *m*, Querköpfigkeit *f*. **2.** Perversität *f*.

per·vert I *v/t* [pə'vɜːt] pervertieren; verdrehen, entstellen: ~ *the course of justice* das Recht beugen. **II** *s* ['pɜːvɜːt] perverser Mensch.

pes·ky ['peskɪ] *adj* □ *bsd. Am.* F lästig.

pes·sa·ry ['pesərɪ] *s* ⚕ Pessar *n*.

pes·si·mism ['pesɪmɪzəm] *s* Pessimismus *m*. **'pes·si·mist** *s* Pessimist(in). **,pes·si'mis·tic** *adj* (~ally) pessimistisch.

pest [pest] *s* **1.** Schädling *m*: ~ **oontrol** Schädlingsbekämpfung *f*. **2.** F Nervensäge *f*; Plage *f*. **'pes·ter** *v/t* F *j-m* belästigen (*with* mit), *j-m* keine Ruhe lassen (*for* wegen), *j-n* drängeln (*to do* zu tun): ~ *s.o. into doing s.th.* j-n so lange quälen, bis er et. tut.

pest·i·cide ['pestɪsaɪd] *s* Schädlingsbekämpfungsmittel *n*.

pet [pet] **I** *s* **1.** Heimtier *n*. **2.** a) *oft contp.* Liebling *m*, b) Schatz *m*. **II** *adj* **3.** Lieblings...: ~ *name* Kosename *m*; → *hate* 5. **4.** Tier...: ~ *food* Tiernahrung *f*; ~ *shop* Tierhandlung *f*, Zoogeschäft *n*, -handlung *f*. **III** *v/t* **5.** streicheln. **IV** *v/i* **6.** F Petting machen.

pet·al ['petl] *s* ♣ Blütenblatt *n*.

pe·ter ['piːtə] *v/i*: ~ *out* versickern (*Bach etc*), allmählich zu Ende gehen (*Vorräte etc*), versanden (*Unterhaltung etc*), sich verlieren (*Erinnerung etc*), sich totlaufen (*Verhandlungen*).

pe·tite [pə'tiːt] *adj* zierlich (*Frau*).

pe·ti·tion [pə'tɪʃn] **I** *s* Eingabe *f*, Gesuch *n*, (schriftlicher) Antrag: ~ *for divorce* ⚖ Scheidungsklage *f*. **II** *v/t* ersuchen (*for* um; *to do* zu tun). **III** *v/i* einkommen, nachsuchen (*for* um): ~ *for divorce* ⚖ die Scheidung einreichen. **pe'ti·tion·er** *s* Antragsteller(in), ⚖

Kläger(in) (*im Scheidungsprozeß*).

pet·ri·fy ['petrɪfaɪ] **I** *v/t*: *petrified with horror* vor Entsetzen wie versteinert, starr *od.* wie gelähmt vor Entsetzen; *be petrified of* panische Angst haben vor (*dat*). **II** *v/i* versteinern, *fig. a.* sich versteinern.

pet·rol ['petrəl] *Br.* **I** *s* Benzin *n*. **II** *adj* Benzin...: ~ *bomb* Molotowcocktail *m*; ~ *coupon* Benzingutschein *m*; ~ *pump* Benzinpumpe *f*; Tank-, Zapfsäule *f*; ~ *station* Tankstelle *f*.

pe·tro·le·um [pə'trəʊljəm] *s* Erdöl *n*.

pet·ti·coat ['petɪkəʊt] *s* Unterrock *m*.

pet·ti·fog·ging ['petɪfogɪŋ] *adj* **1.** kleinlich, pedantisch. **2.** belanglos, unwichtig.

pet·ting ['petɪŋ] *s* F Petting *f*.

pet·tish ['petɪʃ] *adj* □: *be* ~ sich wegen jeder Kleinigkeit aufregen; *don't be so* ~*!* sei doch nicht so kindisch.

pet·ty ['petɪ] *adj* □ **1.** belanglos, unbedeutend, (*Vergehen*) geringfügig: ~ *cash* Portokasse *f*. **2.** engstirnig.

pet·u·lant ['petjolənt] → *pettish*.

pew [pjuː] *s* **1.** (Kirchen)Bank *f*. **2.** *Br.* F (Sitz)Platz *m*: *take a* ~ sich setzen.

pew·ter ['pjuːtə] *s* **1.** Zinn *n*. **2.** *a.* ~ *ware coll.* Zinn(geschirr) *n*.

pha·lanx ['fælæŋks] *pl* **-lanx·es, -lan·ges** [fæ'lændʒiːz] *s* **1.** Phalanx *f*. **2.** *anat.* Finger- *od.* Zehenglied *n*.

phal·li ['fælaɪ] *pl von* **phallus.**

phal·lic ['fælɪk] *adj* phallisch: ~ *symbol* Phallussymbol *n*.

phal·lus ['fæləs] *pl* **-li** ['‿laɪ] *s* Phallus *m*.

phan·tom ['fæntəm] **I** *s* **1.** Phantom *n*, Trugbild *n*. **2.** Geist *m* (*e-s Verstorbenen*). **II** *adj* **3.** ~ (*limb*) *pain* Phantomschmerz *m*; ~ *pregnancy* Scheinschwangerschaft *f*.

phar·i·sa·ic [,færɪ'seɪɪk] *adj* (~ally) pharisäerhaft, pharisäisch. **phar·i·see** ['‿siː] *s* Pharisäer(in).

phar·ma·ceu·ti·cal [,fɑːmə'sjuːtɪkl] *adj* □ pharmazeutisch. **,phar·ma'ceu·tics** *s pl* (*sg konstruiert*) → *pharmacy* 1.

phar·ma·cist ['‿sɪst] *s* **1.** Pharmazeut(in). **2.** Apotheker(in). **'phar·ma·cy** *s* **1.** Pharmazeutik *f*, Pharmazie *f*. **2.** Apotheke *f*.

pha·ryn·ges [fə'rɪndʒiːz] *pl von* **pharynx.**

phar·yn·gi·tis [,færɪn'dʒaɪtɪs] *s* ⚕ Rachenkatarrh *m*.

phar·ynx ['færɪŋks] *pl* **'phar·ynx·es, pha·ryn·ges** [fə'rɪndʒiːz] *s anat.* Rachen *m*.

phase [feɪz] **I** *s* **1.** *allg.* Phase *f*. *~s pl of the moon* Mondphasen *pl*. **II** *v/t* **2.** schritt- *od.* stufenweise planen *od.* durchführen· *~d* schritt-, stufenweise; *~ in* schritt- *od.* stufenweise einführen; *~ out* auslaufen lassen.

pheas·ant ['feznt] *s orn.* Fasan *m*.

phe·nom·e·na [fə'nɒmɪnə] *pl von phenomenon*. **phe'nom·e·nal** [*~nl*] *adj* □ phänomenal. **phe'nom·e·non** [*~nən*] *pl* **-na** [*~nə*] *s allg.* Phänomen *n*.

phew [fjuː] *int* puh!

phi·al ['faɪəl] *s* (*bsd.* Arznei)Fläschchen *n*.

phil·an·throp·ic [ˌfɪlən'θrɒpɪk] *adj* (*~ally*) philanthropisch, menschenfreundlich. **phi·lan·thro·pist** [fɪ'lænθrəpɪst] *s* Philanthrop(in), Menschenfreund(in). **phi'lan·thro·py** *s* Philanthropie *f*, Menschenfreundlichkeit *f*.

phil·a·tel·ic [ˌfɪlə'telɪk] *adj* (*~ally*) philatelistisch. **phi'lat·e·list** [fɪ'lætəlɪst] *s* Philatelist(in). **phi'lat·e·ly** *s* Philatelie *f*.

phil·har·mon·ic [ˌfɪlɑː'mɒnɪk] *adj* philharmonisch.

phi·lis·tine ['fɪlɪstaɪn] *s* Spießer *m*, Banause *m*.

phil·o·log·i·cal [ˌfɪlə'lɒdʒɪkl] *adj* □ philologisch. **phi·lol·o·gist** [fɪ'lɒlədʒɪst] *s* Philologe *m*, -login *f*. **phi'lol·o·gy** *s* Philologie *f*.

phi·los·o·pher [fɪ'lɒsəfə] *s* Philosoph (-in). **phil·o·soph·i·cal** [ˌfɪlə'sɒfɪkl] *adj* □ philosophisch, *fig. a.* abgeklärt, gelassen. **phi·los·o·phize** [fɪ'lɒsəfaɪz] *v/i* philosophieren (*about, on* über *acc*). **phi'los·o·phy** *s* Philosophie *f*, *fig. a.* (Welt)Anschauung *f*.

phle·bi·tis [flɪ'baɪtɪs] *s* ✷ Venenentzündung *f*.

phlegm [flem] *s* **1.** *physiol.* Schleim *m*. **2.** *fig.* Phlegma *n*. **phleg·mat·ic** [fleg'mætɪk] *adj* (*~ally*) phlegmatisch.

pho·bi·a ['fəʊbjə] *s psych.* Phobie *f*, krankhafte Angst (*about* vor *dat*).

phone [fəʊn] **I** *s* **1.** Telefon *n*: *by ~* telefonisch; *be on the ~* Telefon(anschluß) haben; am Telefon sein. **2.** Hörer *m*. **II** *v/i* **3.** telefonieren, anrufen: *~ back* zurückrufen. **III** *v/t* **4.** *a. ~ up* anrufen: *~ back* zurückrufen; *~ s.th. to s.o.* j-m et.

telefonisch durchgeben. **IV** *adj* **5.** Telefon...: *~ book* Telefonbuch *n*; *~ booth* (*Br. box*) Telefonzelle *f*; *~ call* Anruf *m*, Gespräch *n*; *~ number* Telefonnummer *f*. **'~-in** *s Rundfunk, TV: Br.* Sendung *f* mit telefonischer Zuhörer- *od.* Zuschauerbeteiligung.

pho·neme ['fəʊniːm] *s ling.* Phonem *n*.

pho·net·ic [fəʊ'netɪk] **I** *adj* (*~ally*) phonetisch: *~ character* (*od.* symbol) Lautzeichen *n*; *~ transcription* Lautschrift *f*. **II** *s pl* (*mst sg* konstruiert) Phonetik *f*.

pho·n(e)y ['fəʊnɪ] F **I** *adj* □ **1.** falsch: a) gefälscht (*Geld, Paß etc*), b) unecht (*Schmuck, Gefühle etc*), c) erfunden (*Geschichte etc*), faul (*Sache, Entschuldigung etc*), Schein..., Schwindel...(-*firma etc*), d) verlogen (*Moral etc*). **II** *s* **2.** Fälschung *f*. **3.** Schwindler(in).

phos·phate ['fɒsfeɪt] *s* 🜋 Phosphat *n*.

phos·pho·res·cent [ˌfɒsfə'resnt] *adj* □ phosphoreszierend.

phos·pho·rus ['fɒsfərəs] *s* 🜋 Phosphor *m*.

pho·to ['fəʊtəʊ] *pl* **-tos** *s* F Foto *n*, Bild *n*: *in the ~* auf dem Foto; *take a ~* ein Foto machen (*of* von); *~ album* Fotoalbum *n*; *~ safari* Fotosafari *f*. **'~-cell** *s* ⚡ Photozelle *f*. **'~·cop·i·er** *s* Fotokopierer *m*, -kopiergerät *n*. **'~·cop·y I** *s* Fotokopie *f*: *make* (*od.* take) *a ~ of* e-e Fotokopie machen von. **II** *v/t* fotokopieren. **~ fin·ish** *s Sport:* Fotofinish *n*.

pho·to·gen·ic [ˌfəʊtəʊ'dʒenɪk] *adj* (*~ally*) fotogen.

pho·to·graph ['fəʊtəgrɑːf] **I** *s* Fotografie *f*, Aufnahme *f*: *in the ~* auf der Fotografie; *take a ~* e-e Aufnahme machen (*of* von). **II** *v/t* fotografieren. **III** *v/i* sich *gut etc* fotografieren (lassen). **pho·tog·ra·pher** [fə'tɒgrəfə] *s* Fotograf(in). **pho·to·graph·ic** [ˌfəʊtə'græfɪk] *adj* (*~ally*) fotografisch: *~ memory* fotografisches Gedächtnis; *~ studio* Fotostudio *n*. **pho·tog·ra·phy** [fə'tɒgrəfɪ] *s* Fotografie *f* (*Verfahren etc*).

pho·to'sen·si·tive *adj* lichtempfindlich. **~·syn·the·sis** *s biol.* Photosynthese *f*.

phras·al ['freɪzl] *adj*: *~ verb ling.* Verb in Verbindung mit e-m Adverb u./*od.* e-r Präposition.

phrase [freɪz] **I** *s* **1.** *ling.* Phrase *f*, Satzteil *m*. **2.** (Rede)Wendung *f*, Redensart *f*. **3.** *contp*. Phrase *f*: **empty ~s** *pl* leere Phrasen *pl*. **II** *v/t* **4.** ausdrücken, formulieren. '**~·book** *s* Sprachführer *m*.

phra·se·ol·o·gy [ˌfreɪzɪˈɒlədʒɪ] *s* Ausdrucksweise *f*, Sprache *f*; Jargon *m*.

phut [fʌt] *adv*: **go ~** F kaputtgehen (*a. fig. Ehe etc*); *fig*. platzen (*Pläne etc*).

phys·i·cal [ˈfɪzɪkl] **I** *adj* (□ → **physically**) **1.** physisch, körperlich: **~ education** (*od. training*) *ped*. Leibeserziehung *f*, Sport *m*; **~ examination** → 3; **~ handicap** Körperbehinderung *f*; **~ jerks** *pl Br*. F Gymnastik *f*; **~ strength** Körperkraft *f*. **2.** physikalisch. **II** *s* **3.** ärztliche Untersuchung. **phys·i·cal·ly** [ˈ~kəlɪ] *adv* → **physical**: **~ handicapped** körperbehindert; **~ impossible** F völlig unmöglich. **phy·si·cian** [fɪˈzɪʃn] *s* Arzt *m*, Ärztin *f*. **phys·i·cist** [ˈ~sɪst] *s* Physiker(in). **phys·ics** [ˈfɪzɪks] *s pl* (*mst sg konstruiert*) Physik *f*.

phys·i·og·no·my [ˌfɪzɪˈɒnəmɪ] *s* Physiognomie *f*, Gesichtsausdruck *m*.

phys·i·o·log·i·cal [ˌfɪzɪəˈlɒdʒɪkl] *adj* □ physiologisch. **phys·i·ol·o·gy** [ˌ~ˈɒlə-dʒɪ] *s* Physiologie *f*.

phys·i·o·ther·a·py [ˌfɪzɪəʊˈθerəpɪ] *s* Physiotherapie *f*.

phy·sique [fɪˈziːk] *s* Körperbau *m*, Statur *f*.

pi·an·ist [ˈpɪənɪst] *s* Pianist(in).

pi·an·o [pɪˈænəʊ] *pl* **-os** *f* Klavier *n*.

pick [pɪk] **I** *s* **1.** (Spitz)Hacke *f*, Pickel *m*. **2.** (*Zahn*)Stocher *m*. **3.** (*Aus*)Wahl *f*: **have one's ~ of** auswählen können aus; **take one's ~** sich et. aussuchen; **the ~ of the bunch** das (Aller)Beste, das Beste vom Besten. **II** *v/t* **4.** (auf)hakken, (-)picken → **hole** 1. **5.** *Körner* aufpicken; auflesen, (auf)sammeln; *Blumen, Obst* pflücken. **6.** *Knochen* abnagen; *Am. Hühner etc* rupfen: **~ a bone** 1. **7.** **~ one's nose** in der Nase bohren, popeln; **~ one's teeth** in den Zähnen (herum)stochern. **8.** *Schloß* mit e-m Dietrich *etc* öffnen, knacken. **9.** *Streit* vom Zaun brechen (**with** mit). **10.** (aus)wählen, aussuchen: **~ one's way** (*od. steps*) sich s-n Weg suchen, mit vorsichtigen Schritten gehen (**through** durch); **~ a winner** fig. das Große Los ziehen; **~ one's words** s-e Worte genau wählen. **11.** zerpflücken,

-reißen: → **piece** 1. **III** *v/i* **12.** **~ and choose** wählerisch sein; sich bei der Auswahl Zeit lassen.

Verbindungen mit Präpositionen:

pick| at *v/i* **1.** **~ one's food** im Essen herumstochern. **2.** herumnörgeln an (*dat*); herumhacken auf (*dat*). **~ on** *v/i* **1.** → **pick at** 2. **2.** *j-n* (*für et. Unangenehmes*) aussuchen.

Verbindungen mit Adverbien:

pick| out *v/t* **1.** (sich) *et.* auswählen. **2.** ausmachen, erkennen. **~ up I** *v/t* **1.** aufheben, -lesen: **pick o.s. up** sich aufrappeln (*a. fig.*); → **gauntlet¹, thread** 1. **2.** F *Passagiere* aufnehmen; *j-n* abholen. **3.** F *Mädchen* aufgabeln, -lesen; *Anhalter* mitnehmen; sich *e-e Krankheit* holen *od.* einfangen. **4.** *Funkspruch etc* auffangen. **5.** *Kenntnisse, Informationen etc* aufschnappen. **6.** zunehmen an (*dat*): **~ speed** schneller werden. **II** *v/i* **7.** sich (wieder) erholen (*a. ♥*). **8.** stärker werden (*Wind etc*).

pick·a·back [ˈpɪkəbæk] **I** *adv* huckepack: **carry s.o. ~** → II. **II** *s*: **give s.o. a ~** *j-n* huckepack tragen.

'**pick·ax(e)** → **pick** 1.

pick·er [ˈpɪkə] *s* Pflücker(in).

pick·et [ˈpɪkɪt] **I** *s* **1.** Pfahl *m*. **2.** Streikposten *m*: **~ line** Streikpostenkette *f*. **II** *v/t* **3.** Streikposten aufstellen vor (*dat*), durch Streikposten blockieren. **III** *v/i* **4.** Streikposten stehen.

pick·ings [ˈpɪkɪŋz] *s pl* Ausbeute *f*: **there are easy ~ in this job** bei diesem Job kann man leicht ein paar Mark (dazu)verdienen.

pick·le [ˈpɪkl] **I** *s* **1.** Salzlake *f*; Essigsoße *f*. **2.** a) *Am*. Essig-, Gewürzgurke *f*, b) *mst pl* Pickles *pl*: → **mixed. 3. be in a** (**pretty**) **~** F (ganz schön) in der Patsche sein *od.* stecken. **II** *v/t* **4.** *gastr*. einlegen. '**pick·led** *adj* **1.** eingelegt. **2.** F blau (*betrunken*).

'**pick|·lock** *s* **1.** Einbrecher *m*. **2.** Dietrich *m*. '**~·me-up** *s* F Muntermacher *m*, Anregungsmittel *n*. '**~·pock·et** *s* Taschendieb(in). '**~·up** *s* **1.** Tonabnehmer *m*, Pick-up *m* (*am Plattenspieler*): **~ arm** Tonarm *m*. **2.** a. **~ truck** kleiner Lieferwagen, Kleintransporter *m*. **3.** F (Zufalls)Bekanntschaft *f*. **4.** *mot*. F Beschleunigung(svermögen *n*) *f*: **have good ~** gut beschleunigen).

pick·y ['pɪkɪ] *adj* □ F heikel, wählerisch: *be a very ~ eater* im Essen sehr heikel sein.

pic·nic ['pɪknɪk] **I** *s* Picknick *n*: *go on* (*od. for*) *a ~ in the country* zum Picknick aufs Land fahren; *have a ~* Picknick machen; *it's no ~* F es ist kein Honiglecken (*doing* zu tun). **II** *v/i pret* u. *pp* **-nicked** picknicken.

pic·to·ri·al [pɪk'tɔːrɪəl] **I** *adj* □ **1.** bebildert, illustriert: *~ report* Bildbericht *m*. **2.** bildhaft (*Sprache etc*). **II** *s* **3.** Illustrierte *f*.

pic·ture ['pɪktʃə] **I** *s* **1.** Bild *n* (*a. TV*): a) Abbildung *f*, Illustration *f*: *in the ~* auf dem Bild, b) Gemälde *n*: (*as*) *pretty as a ~* sehr hübsch; *be a ~* e-e Pracht *od.* ein Gedicht sein; *be the ~ of health* aussehen wie das blühende Leben; *his face was a ~* du hättest sein Gesicht sehen sollen; → *paint* 1, c) *phot.* Aufnahme *f*: *take a ~* e-e Aufnahme machen (*of* von), d) *fig.* Vorstellung *f*: *be in* (*out of*) *the ~* (nicht) im Bild sein; *put in the ~* ins Bild setzen; *get the ~?* F kapiert? **2.** a) Film *m*, b) *pl bsd. Br.* Kino *n*: *go to the ~s* ins Kino gehen. **II** *v/t* **3.** darstellen, malen. **4.** *fig. sich j-n, et.* vorstellen (*as* als). **~ book** *s* Bilderbuch *n*. **~ card** *s* Kartenspiel: Bild(karte *f*) *n*. **~ de·fi·ni·tion** *s phot., TV* Bildschärfe *f*. **~ frame** *s* Bilderrahmen *m*. **~ gal·ler·y** *s* Gemäldegalerie *f*. **~ post·card** *s* Ansichtskarte *f*. **~ tube** *s TV* Bildröhre *f*.

pic·tur·esque [ˌpɪktʃə'resk] *adj* □ malerisch.

pid·dle ['pɪdl] F **I** *v/i* pinkeln, (*Kind*) Pipi machen. **II** *v/t:* **~ away** *Zeit* vertrödeln. **'pid·dling** *adj* F unwichtig.

pidg·in Eng·lish ['pɪdʒɪn] *s* Pidgin-Englis(c)h *n*.

pie [paɪ] *s gastr.* Pie *f*: a) (*Fleisch- etc*)Pastete *f*, b) (*mst gedeckter*) (*Apfel- etc*)Kuchen: (*as*) *easy as ~* F kinderleicht; → *finger* I, *humble* I.

piece [piːs] **I** *s* **1.** Stück *n*: *~ of cake* Stück Kuchen; *fig.* F Kinderspiel *n*; *a ~* das Stück; *by ~* Stück für Stück; *by the ~* stückweise; *in ~s* entzwei, kaputt; (*all*) *in one ~* F ganz, unbeschädigt; heil, unverletzt; *break* (*od. fall*) *to ~s* zerbrechen, entzweigehen; *go to ~s* F zs.-brechen (*Person*); *pull* (*od. pick, tear*) *to ~s*

in Stücke reißen; *fig. Äußerung etc* zerpflücken; → *advice* 1, *furniture*, *mind* 4, *news*. **2.** Teil *n* (*e-r Maschine etc*): *take to ~s* auseinandernehmen, zerlegen. **3.** Teil *m* (*e-s Services etc*): *a 30-~ service* ein 30teiliges Service. **4.** (*Geld*)Stück *n*, Münze *f*. **5.** (*Schach*) Figur *f*; (*Dame etc*) Stein *m*. **6.** (*Zeitungs*)Artikel *m*. **II** *v/t* **7.** *~ together* zs.-stücke(l)n; *fig.* zs.-fügen. **'~meal I** *adv* **1.** schrittweise. **II** *adj* **2.** schrittweise. **3.** unsystematisch. **'~work** *s* Akkordarbeit *f*: *be on* (*od. do*) *~* im Akkord arbeiten.

pie-'eyed *adj* F blau (*betrunken*).

pier [pɪə] *s* **1.** Pier *m*, ♣ *a. f*, Landungsbrücke *f*, -steg *m*. **2.** (*Brücken- etc*)Pfeiler *m*.

pierce [pɪəs] *v/t* **1.** durchbohren, -stoßen: *~ s.o.'s ears* j-m die Ohren durchstechen. **2.** *fig.* durchdringen: *a cry ~d the silence* ein Schrei zerriß die Stille. **'pierc·ing** *adj* □ durchdringend, (*Kälte etc a.*) schneidend, (*Blick, Schmerz etc a.*) stechend, (*Schrei a.*) gellend.

pi·e·ty ['paɪətɪ] *s* Frömmigkeit *f*.

pif·fle ['pɪfl] *s* F Quatsch *m*. **'pif·fling** *adj* F albern.

pig [pɪg] *s* **1.** Schwein *n*: *buy a ~ in a poke fig.* die Katze im Sack kaufen; *make a ~'s ear of s.th. Br. sl.* et. vermasseln. **2.** F *contp.* Schwein *n*; Freßsack *m*. **3.** *sl.* Bulle *m* (*Polizist*).

pi·geon ['pɪdʒɪn] *s orn.* Taube *f*: *that's not my ~ fig.* F das ist nicht mein Bier. **'~hole I** *s* **1.** (Ablege)Fach *n*: *put in ~s* → 3. **II** *v/t* **2.** (in Fächern) ablegen. **3.** *fig.* einordnen, klassifizieren. **4.** *fig.* zurückstellen. **'~toed** *adv:* *walk ~* über den großen Onkel gehen.

pig·gish ['pɪgɪʃ] *adj* □ schweinisch; gefräßig.

pig·gy ['pɪgɪ] **I** *s* **1.** *Kindersprache:* Schweinchen *n*. **II** *adj* **2.** Schweins...: *~ eyes*. **3.** gefräßig (*bsd. Kind*). **'~back** → *pickaback*. **~ bank** *s* Sparschwein *n*. **pig,head·ed** *adj* □ dickköpfig, stur. **~ i·ron** *s* Roheisen *n*.

pig·let ['pɪglɪt] *s* Ferkel *n*, Schweinchen *n*.

pig·ment ['pɪgmənt] *s* Pigment *n*.

pig·my → **pygmy.**

'pig·pen *bsd. Am.* → **pigsty. '~skin** *s* Schweinsleder *n*. **'~sty** *s* Schweinestall *m, fig. a.* Saustall *m.* '**~tail** *s* Zopf *m.*

pike¹ [paɪk] *pl* **pikes,** *bsd. coll.* **pike** *s ichth.* Hecht *m.*

pike² [~] *s* ✕ *hist.* Pike *f,* Spieß *m.*

pike³ [~] → **turnpike.**

'**pike-staff** *s:* **(as) plain as a ~** deutlich sichtbar; *fig.* sonnenklar.

pile¹ [paɪl] **I** *s* **1.** Stapel *m,* Stoß *m.* **2.** Scheiterhaufen *m.* **3.** Gebäude(komplex *m) n.* **4.** (*Atom*)Reaktor *m.* **5. ~** (*od.* **a ~**) **of ...** F einen Haufen ..., e-e *od.* jede Menge ... **6. a ~ (of money)** F e-e Menge Geld: **make a (od. one's) ~ (from)** e-e Menge Geld machen (bei), sich gesundstoßen (an *dat,* mit). **II** *v/t* **7. a. ~ up** (an-, auf)häufen, (auf)stapeln: **~ it on** F dick auftragen. **8.** laden, aufhäufen (**on, onto** auf *acc*); überhäufen, -laden (**with** mit). **III** *v/i* **9.** *mst* **~ up** sich (auf *od.* an)häufen, sich ansammeln (*beide a. fig.*). **10.** F (sich) drängen (**into** in *acc*): **~ in** (sich) hinein- *od.* hereindrängen. **11. ~ up** *mot.* F aufeinander auffahren.

pile² [~] *s* Pfahl *m.*

piles [paɪlz] *s pl* ✚ Hämorrhoiden *pl.*

'**pile-up** *s mot.* F Massenkarambolage *f.*

pil-fer ['pɪlfə] *v/t u. v/i* stehlen, klauen. '**pil-fer-er** *s* Dieb(in).

pil-grim ['pɪlɡrɪm] *s* Pilger(in), Wallfahrer(in): **the ✚ Fathers** *pl hist.* die Pilgerväter *pl.* '**pil-grim-age** *s* Pilger-, Wallfahrt *f:* **go on** (*od.* **make**) **a ~** e-e Pilgerod. Wallfahrt machen. **II** *v/i* pilgern, wallfahr(t)en.

pill [pɪl] *s* **1.** Pille *f,* Tablette *f:* **a bitter ~ (for s.o.) to swallow** *fig.* e-e bittere Pille (für j-n); **gild** (*od.* **sugar, sweeten**) **the ~** *fig.* die bittere Pille versüßen. **2. the ~** F die (*Antibaby*)Pille: **be on the ~** die Pille nehmen.

pil-lage ['pɪlɪdʒ] **I** *v/t u. v/i* plündern. **II** *s* Plünderung *f.*

pil-lar ['pɪlə] *s* Pfeiler *m;* Säule *f (a. fig.):* **from ~ to post** *fig.* von Pontius zu Pilatus. **~ box** *s Br.* Briefkasten *m.*

pil-lion ['pɪljən] **I** *s mot.* Sozius(sitz) *m.* **II** *adv:* **ride ~** auf dem Sozius(sitz) (mit-) fahren. **~ pas-sen-ger** *s* Soziusfahrer(in).

pil-lo-ry ['pɪlərɪ] **I** *s hist.* Pranger *m:* **be in the ~** am Pranger stehen. **II** *v/t hist.* an den Pranger stellen; *fig.* anprangern.

pil-low ['pɪləʊ] **I** *s* (Kopf)Kissen *n.* **II** *v/t*

bsd. Kopf betten (**on** auf *acc*). '**~case** *s* (Kopf)Kissenbezug *m.* **~ fight** *s* Kissenschlacht *f.* **~ slip** → **pillowcase. ~ talk** *s* Bettgeflüster *m.*

pi-lot ['paɪlət] **I** *s* **1.** ✈ Pilot(in): **~'s licence** (*Am.* **license**) Flug-, Pilotenschein *m.* **2.** ⚓ Lotse *m,* Lotsin *f.* **II** *v/t* **3.** ✈ steuern, fliegen. **4.** ⚓ lotsen, *fig. a.* führen, leiten. **III** *adj* **5.** Versuchs..., Probe...: **~ film** *TV* Pilotfilm *m;* **~ scheme** Versuchs-, Pilotprojekt *n;* **~ study** Pilot-, Leitstudie *f.* **6. ~ lamp** Kontrollampe *f.*

pimp [pɪmp] **I** *s* Zuhälter *m.* **II** *v/i* von Zuhälterei leben: **~ for s.o.** j-s Zuhälter sein.

pim-ple ['pɪmpl] *s* Pickel *m,* Pustel *f.* '**pim-pled** *adj* pick(e)lig.

pin [pɪn] **I** *s* **1.** (Steck)Nadel *f.* **2.** (*Haar-, Krawatten- etc*)Nadel *f.* **3.** *bsd. Am.* Brosche *f;* (Ansteck)Nadel *f.* **4.** ◎ Bolzen *m,* Stift *m;* ✄ Nagel *m.* **5.** (*Reiß*)Nagel *m,* (-)Zwecke *f.* **6.** *Am.* (*Wäsche*)Klammer *f.* **7.** *pl* Gestell *n* (*Beine*). **8.** *Bowling:* Kegel *m.* **II** *v/t* **9. a. ~ up** (**to, on**) heften, stecken (an *acc*), festmachen, befestigen (an *dat*): **~ s.th. on s.o.** *fig.* j-m et. in die Schuhe schieben; j-m et. anhängen; **~ one's hopes on** s-e Hoffnung setzen auf (*acc*). **10. ~ down** zu Boden drücken; *fig. j-n* festlegen, -nageln (**to** auf *acc*).

pin-a-fore ['pɪnəfɔː] *s* **1.** Schürze *f.* **2.** *a.* **~ dress** Trägerkleid *n,* Kleiderrock *m.*

'**pin-ball** *s* Flippern *n:* **play ~** flippern. **~ ma-chine** *s* Flipper *m.*

pin-cers ['pɪnsəz] *s pl, a.* **pair of ~** Kneifzange *f.*

pinch [pɪntʃ] **I** *v/t* **1.** kneifen, zwicken: **~ s.o.'s** (*od.* **s.o. on the**) **arm** j-n in den Arm zwicken; **~ one's fingers in the door** sich die Finger in der Tür (ein)klemmen. **2. be ~ed for money** (**time**) knapp bei Kasse sein (wenig Zeit haben). **3.** F klauen. **4.** F *j-n* hopsnehmen (**for wegen**). **II** *v/i* **5.** drücken (*Schuh*): → **shoe** 1. **6. ~ and scrape** (*od.* **save**) *fig.* sich sehr einschränken, sich nichts gönnen. **III** *s* **7.** Kneifen *n,* Zwicken *n:* **give s.o. a ~** j-n kneifen *od.* zwicken. **8.** Prise *f* (*Salz etc*): → **salt** 1. **9.** *fig.* Not(lage) *f:* **at** (*Am.* **in**) **a ~** zur Not, notfalls; **feel the ~** die schlechte Lage zu spüren bekommen.

'pin,cush·ion s Nadelkissen n.

pine¹ [paɪn] s ♣ Kiefer f.

pine² [~] v/i 1. sich sehnen (for nach). 2. mst ~ away vor Gram vergehen.

'pine|ˌap·ple s ♣ Ananas f. ~ tree → pine¹.

ping-pong ['pɪŋpɒŋ] s F Pingpong n (Tischtennis).

'pin·head s 1. Stecknadelkopf m. 2. F Dummkopf m.

pin·ion ['pɪnjən] s ⊙ Ritzel n.

pink [pɪŋk] I s 1. ♣ Nelke f. 2. Rosa n. 3. be in the ~ vor Gesundheit strotzen. II adj 4. rosa: see ~ elephants weiße Mäuse sehen; → tickle I. 5. pol. rot angehaucht.

'pin|ˌpoint I s 1. Nadelspitze f. 2. (winziger) Punkt: ~ of light Lichtpunkt m. II v/t 3. genau zeigen. 4. fig. genau bestimmen od. bestimmen. III adj 5. (haar)genau. '~prick s 1. Nadelstich m. 2. fig. Stichelei f. '~stripe(d) adj: ~ suit Nadelstreifenanzug m.

pint [paɪnt] s 1. Pint n. 2. Br. F Halbe f (Bier): meet for a ~ sich auf ein Bier treffen.

pin|ˌta·ble s Flipper m. '~up s 1. a. ~girl Pin-up-Girl n. 2. Pin-up-Foto n.

pi·o·neer [ˌpaɪə'nɪə] I s Pionier m, fig. a. Bahnbrecher m, Wegbereiter m. II v/i u. v/t fig. den Weg bahnen (für), Pionierarbeit leisten (für).

pi·ous ['paɪəs] adj □ fromm: ~ hope frommer Wunsch.

pip¹ [pɪp] s: give s.o. the ~ Br. F j-m auf die Nerven gehen, j-n nerven.

pip² [~] s 1. (Apfel- etc)Kern m. 2. Auge n (auf Spielkarten), Punkt m (auf Würfeln etc). 3. ✕ bsd. Br. F Stern m (Rangabzeichen). 4. Ton m (e-s Zeitzeichens etc).

pip³ [~] v/t Br. F knapp besiegen od. schlagen: ~ s.o. at the post (Sport) j-n im Ziel abfangen; fig. j-m um Haaresbreite zuvorkommen.

pipe [paɪp] I s 1. ⊙ Rohr n, Röhre f. 2. (Tabaks)Pfeife f. 3. (Orgel)Pfeife f. 4. pl Dudelsack m. II v/t 5. (durch Rohre od. Kabel) leiten: ~d music contp. Musikberies(e)lung f; ~d water Leitungswasser n. 6. Torte etc spritzen. III v/i 7. F ~ down die Luft anhalten, den Mund halten; ~ up loslegen (Sänger, Band etc); den Mund aufmachen, losreden. ~

clean·er s Pfeifenreiniger m. ~ dream s Hirngespinst n, Luftschloß n. '~line s Rohrleitung f, (für Erdöl, Erdgas) Pipeline f: in the ~ fig. in Vorbereitung (Pläne etc), im Kommen (Entwicklung etc), im Anrollen (Aktion etc).

pip·er ['paɪpə] s Dudelsackpfeifer m: pay the ~ fig. für die Kosten aufkommen.

pipe smok·er s Pfeifenraucher m.

pip·ing ['paɪpɪŋ] I s 1. Rohrleitung f, -netz n. 2. gastr. Spritzguß m. II adv 3. ~ hot kochendheiß.

'pip·squeak s F contp. Würstchen n (Person).

pi·quant ['piːkənt] adj □ pikant (a. fig.).

pique [piːk] I v/t kränken, verletzen: be ~d pikiert sein (at über acc). II s: in a fit of ~ gekränkt, verletzt, pikiert.

pi·ra·cy ['paɪərəsɪ] s 1. Seeräuberei f, Piraterie f. 2. Raubdruck m; Raubpressung f. pi·rate ['~rət] I s 1. Pirat m, Seeräuber m. II adj 2. Piraten-..., Seeräuber-...: ~ ship. 3. ~ copy Raubkopie f; ~ edition Raubdruck m; ~ record Raubpressung f; ~ (radio) station Piraten-, Schwarzsender m. III v/t 4. unerlaubt kopieren od. nachdrucken od. nachpressen: ~d copy (edition, record) → 3.

pir·ou·ette [ˌpɪrʊ'et] s Pirouette f: do a ~ e-e Pirouette drehen.

Pis·ces ['paɪsiːz] s pl (sg konstruiert) ast. Fische pl: be a ~ Fisch sein.

piss [pɪs] V I v/i 1. pissen: it is ~ing down bsd. Br. es schifft. 2. ~ off! verpiß dich! II v/t 3. anpissen, pissen in (acc). 4. ~ off ankotzen: be ~ed off with die Schnauze voll haben von. III s 5. Pisse f: take the ~ out of s.o. j-n verarschen. 6. Pissen n: have (go for) a ~ pissen (gehen).

pissed adj V 1. Br. blau (betrunken). 2. Am. (stock)sauer (at auf acc).

pis·ta·chi·o [pɪ'stɑːʃɪəʊ] pl -os ♣ Pistazie f.

pis·til ['pɪstɪl] s ♣ Stempel m.

pis·tol ['pɪstl] s Pistole f.

pis·ton ['pɪstən] s ⊙ Kolben m. ~ ring s Kolbenring m. ~ rod s Kolbenstange f. ~ stroke s Kolbenhub m.

pit¹ [pɪt] I s 1. Grube f: ~ of the stomach anat. Magengrube. 2. Grube f, Zeche f: ~ closure Zechenstillegung f; ~ disas-ter Grubenunglück n. 3. thea. a) bsd.

Br. Parkett *n*, b) (*Orchester*)Graben *m*. **4.** *mst pl Motorsport:* Box *f:* ~ **stop** Boxenstopp *m*. **5.** (*bsd. Pocken*)Narbe *f*. **II** *v/t* **6.** **~ted with smallpox** pockennarbig. **7.** ~ **one's wits** (**strength**) **against** sich (geistig) (s-e Kräfte) messen *an* (*dat*).

pit² [~] *Am.* → **stone** 2, 6.

pitch¹ [pɪtʃ] *s* Pech *n:* (**as**) **black as ~** → **pitch-black**.

pitch² [~] **I** *v/t* **1.** *Lager, Zelt etc* aufschlagen. **2.** werfen, schleudern. **II** *v/i* **3.** stürzen, fallen. **4.** ♪ stampfen. **5.** sich neigen (*Dach etc*). **6.** **~ in** F sich ins Zeug legen; kräftig zulangen (*beim Essen*); zu Hilfe kommen, aushelfen (**with** mit). **III** *s* **7.** *Sport: Br.* (Spiel)Feld *n*. **8.** ♪ Tonhöhe *f*. **9.** *fig.* Grad *m*, Stufe *f*. **10.** *bsd. Br.* (Verkaufs)Stand *m:* **queer s.o.'s ~** *fig.* F j-m die Tour vermasseln, j-m e-n Strich durch die Rechnung machen. **11.** ♪ Stampfen *n*. **12.** Neigung *f* (*e-s Dachs etc*). **13.** → **sales pitch**.

,**pitch**|-'**black**, **~-'dark** *adj* pechschwarz; stockdunkel.

pitch·er¹ [ˈpɪtʃə] *s Baseball:* Werfer *m*.

pitch·er² [~] *s* Krug *m*.

'**pitch·fork I** *s* **1.** Heugabel *f*. **II** *v/t* **2.** Heu gabeln. **3.** *fig. j-n* (*unversehens od. gegen s-n Willen*) (hinein)drängen (**into** in *acc*).

'**pit·fall** *s fig.* Falle *f*, Fallstrick *m*.

pith [pɪθ] *s* **1.** ♀ Mark *n*. **2.** weiße Haut (*e-r Orange etc*). **3.** *fig.* Kern *m*. ~ **hel·met** *s* Tropenhelm *m*.

'**pith·y** [ˈpɪθɪ] *adj* □ markig, prägnant.

pit·i·a·ble [ˈpɪtɪəbl] → **pitiful**. **pit·i·ful** [ˈ~fʊl] *adj* □ **1.** mitleiderregend (*Anblick etc*), bemitleidenswert (*Person, Zustand etc*). **2.** erbärmlich, jämmerlich, kläglich. '**pit·i·less** *adj* □ unbarmherzig, mitleid(s)los.

'**pit·man** [ˈpɪtmən] *s* (*irr man*) Bergmann *m*.

'**pit·tance** [ˈpɪtəns] *s* Hungerlohn *m*.

pi·tu·i·tar·y [pɪˈtjʊɪtərɪ] *s anat.* Hirnanhang(drüse *f*) *m*.

pit·y [ˈpɪtɪ] **I** *s* **1.** Mitleid *n:* **out of ~** aus Mitleid; **feel ~ for, have ~ on** Mitleid haben mit; **take ~ on** Mitleid bekommen mit. **2.** *it is a* (**great**) **~** es ist (sehr) schade; *it is a thousand pities* es ist jammerschade; **what a ~!** wie schade! **II** *v/t* **3.** bemitleiden, bedauern: *I ~ him*

er tut mir leid. '**pit·y·ing** *adj* □ mitleid(s)voll, mitleidig.

piv·ot [ˈpɪvət] **I** *s* **1.** ⊙ Drehzapfen *m*. **2.** *fig.* Dreh- u. Angelpunkt *m*. **II** *v/i* **3.** sich drehen: **~ on** *fig.* abhängen von. **piv·ot·al** [ˈ~tl] *adj fig.* zentral: **~ position** Schlüsselstellung *f*.

pix·ie, pix·y [ˈpɪksɪ] *s* Elf(e *f*) *m*; Kobold *m*.

piz·za [ˈpiːtsə] *s* Pizza *f*. **piz·ze·ri·a** [ˌpiːtsəˈriːə] *s* Pizzeria *f*.

pla·card [ˈplækɑːd] **I** *s* **1.** Plakat *n*; Transparent *n*. **II** *v/t* **2.** mit Plakaten bekleben. **3.** Plakatwerbung machen für.

pla·cate [pləˈkeɪt] *v/t* beschwichtigen, besänftigen.

place [pleɪs] **I** *s* **1.** Ort *f*, Stelle *f*, Platz *m:* **from ~ to ~** von Ort zu Ort; **in ~** stellenweise; **in ~ of** an Stelle von (*od. gen*); **~** an s-m (richtigen) Platz; **out of ~** nicht an s-m (richtigen) Platz; fehl am Platz; unangebracht; *if I were in your ~ I would ...* an Ihrer Stelle würde ich ...; *put o.s. in s.o.'s ~* sich in j-s Lage versetzen; *put s.o. back in his ~* j-n in die *od.* s-e Schranken verweisen; *take ~* stattfinden; *take s.o.'s ~* j-s Stelle einnehmen. **2.** Ort *m*, Stätte *f:* **~ of birth** Geburtsort; **~ of work** Arbeitsstätte. **3.** Haus *n*, Wohnung *f:* **at his ~** bei ihm (zu Hause). **4.** Wohnort *m*, Ort(schaft *f*) *m:* **in this ~** hier. **5.** Stelle *f* (*in e-m Buch etc*): **lose one's ~** die Stelle verblättern; die Zeile verlieren. **6.** *Reihenfolge:* Platz *m*, Stelle *f:* **in the first ~** erstens; in erster Linie; überhaupt (erst). **7.** *Sport:* Platz *m:* **in third ~** auf dem dritten Platz. **8.** (*Arbeits-, Lehr-*) Stelle *f*; Platz *m* (*in e-m Heim etc*); (*Studien- etc*)Platz *m*. **II** *v/t* **9.** stellen, setzen, legen: **~ in** in e-e Lage etc versetzen. **10.** (**with**) *Auftrag* erteilen (*dat*), vergeben (*an acc*), *Bestellung* aufgeben (**bei**). **11.** *I can't ~ him* ich weiß nicht, wo ich ihn unterbringen *od.* wohin ich ihn tun soll (*woher ich ihn kenne*). **12.** **be ~d** (*Sport*) sich placieren (**third** an dritter Stelle), placiert sein.

pla·ce·bo [pləˈsiːbəʊ] *pl* **-bo(e)s** *s* ♣ Placebo *n*.

place| card *s* Tischkarte *f*. **~ mat** *s* Set *n*, *m*, Platzdeckchen *n*. **~ name** *s* Ortsname *m*. **~ set·ting** *s* Gedeck *n*.

plac·id ['plæsɪd] *adj* □ **1.** ruhig, gelassen. **2.** ruhig, friedlich.

pla·gia·rism ['pleɪdʒərɪzəm] *s* Plagiat *n.* '**pla·gia·rist** *s* Plagiator(in). '**pla·gia·rize** *v/t u. v/i* plagiieren (**from** von).

plague [pleɪɡ] **I** *s* **1.** ✻ Seuche *f*; Pest *f*. **2.** (*Insekten- etc*)Plage *f*: ~ *of insects.* **II** *v/t* **3.** plagen (**with** mit): *be* ~*d by* geplagt werden von.

plaice [pleɪs] *pl* **plaice** *s ichth.* Scholle *f.*

plaid [plæd] *s* Plaid *n.*

plain [pleɪn] **I** *adj* □ **1.** einfach, schlicht: ~ *clothes pl* Zivil(kleidung *f*) *n*; *in* ~ *clothes* in Zivil; ~ *chocolate* zartbittere Schokolade; ~ *cooking* gutbürgerliche Küche. **2.** unscheinbar, reizlos. **3.** klar (u. deutlich), unmißverständlich: *the* ~ *truth* die nackte Wahrheit; *make s.th.* ~ et. klarstellen; *make s.th.* ~ *to s.o.* j-m et. klarmachen. **4.** offen (u. ehrlich): *be* ~ *with s.o.* j-m gegenüber offen sein. **5.** ausgesprochen, rein, völlig: ~ *nonsense* barer Unsinn. **II** *adv* **6.** F (ganz) einfach. **III** *s* **7.** Ebene *f*, Flachland *n.* '~**-clothes** *adj* in Zivil.

plain·ness ['pleɪnnɪs] *s* **1.** Einfachheit *f*, Schlichtheit *f*. **2.** Unscheinbarkeit *f*. **3.** Klarheit *f*. **4.** Offenheit *f.*

‚**plain·'spo·ken** *adj* offen, freimütig: *be* ~ *a.* sagen, was man denkt.

plain·tiff ['pleɪntɪf] *s* ✻✻ Kläger(in). **plain·tive** ['~tɪv] *adj* □ klagend, kläglich; (*Lied etc*) schwermütig.

plait [plæt] **I** *s* Zopf *m.* **II** *v/t* flechten.

plan [plæn] **I** *s* **1.** (*Arbeits- etc*)Plan *m*: *according to* ~ planmäßig, -gemäß; *make* ~*s* (*for the future*) (Zukunfts)Pläne machen. **2.** Plan *m*, Absicht *f*: *change one's* ~*s* umdisponieren. **3.** (*Stadt-, Sitz- etc*)Plan *m.* **4.** ☉ Grundriß *m.* **II** *v/t* **5.** planen: ~*ned economy* Planwirtschaft *f.* **6.** planen, beabsichtigen (*to do* zu tun). **III** *v/i* **7.** planen: ~ *ahead* vorausplanen; ~ *for* (*od. on*) einplanen, rechnen mit. **8.** ~ *on doing s.th.* planen *od.* beabsichtigen, et. zu tun.

plane¹ [pleɪn] **I** *adj* **1.** eben (*a.* ✻); ☉ plan, Plan... **II** *s* **2.** ✻ Ebene *f*: → *inclined.* **3.** *fig.* Ebene *f*, Stufe *f*: *on the same* ~ as auf dem gleichen Niveau wie. **4.** Hobel *m.* **III** *v/t* **5.** hobeln: ~ *down* abhobeln.

plane² [~] *s* Flugzeug *n*: *by* ~ mit dem Flugzeug; *go by* ~ fliegen.

plan·et ['plænɪt] *s ast.* Planet *m.*

plan·e·tar·i·um [ˌplænɪ'teərɪəm] *pl* **-i·ums**, **-i·a** [~ɪə] *s* Planetarium. **plan·e·tar·y** ['~tərɪ] *adj* planetarisch, Planeten...

plank [plæŋk] *s* **1.** Planke *f*, Bohle *f*, Brett *n*: (*as*) *thick as two* (*short*) ~*s Br.* F strohdumm. **2.** *pol.* Schwerpunkt *m* (*e-s Parteiprogramms*). '**plank·ing** *s* Planken *pl.*

plank·ton ['plæŋktən] *s zo.* Plankton *n.*

plant [plɑːnt] **I** *s* **1.** Pflanze *f*: ~ *louse zo.* Blattlaus *f.* **2.** Werk *n*, Betrieb *m.* **II** *v/t* **3.** (an-, ein)pflanzen; *Land* bepflanzen (*with* mit). **4.** *Garten etc* anlegen. **5.** *Polizisten etc* aufstellen, postieren; *Bombe* legen. **6.** *Fuß etc* setzen (*on* auf *acc*); *Messer etc* stoßen (*into* in *acc*): ~ *a kiss on s.o.'s lips* j-m e-n Kuß auf die Lippen drücken. **7.** ~ *s.th. on s.o.* F j-m et. (*Belastendes*) unterschieben *od.* -jubeln. **plan·ta·tion** [plæn'teɪʃn] *s* **1.** Plantage *f*, Pflanzung *f.* **2.** Schonung *f.* **plant·er** ['plɑːntə] *s* **1.** Plantagenbesitzer(in), Pflanzer(in). **2.** Pflanzmaschine *f.* **3.** Übertopf *m.*

plaque [plɑːk] *s* **1.** Gedenktafel *f.* **2.** ✻ (*Zahn*)Belag *m.*

plas·ma ['plæzmə] *s* Plasma *n.*

plas·ter ['plɑːstə] **I** *s* **1.** ✻ Pflaster *n.* **2.** (Ver)Putz *m.* **3.** *a.* ~ *of Paris* Gips *m*: *have one's arm in* ~ ✻ den Arm in Gips haben; *put in* ~ ✻ eingipsen; ~ *cast* Gipsabguß *m*, -modell *n*; ✻ Gipsverband *m.* **II** *v/t* **4.** verputzen; (ver-)gipsen; ~ *over fig.* übertünchen. **5.** bekleben (*with* mit); *Plakate etc* kleben (*on* an *od.* auf *acc*). '**plas·tered** *adj sl.* blau (*betrunken*): *get* ~ sich vollaufen lassen.

plas·tic ['plæstɪk] **I** *adj* (~*ally*) **1.** plastisch: ~ *surgery* ✻ plastische Chirurgie. **2.** plastisch, formbar: ~ *bomb* Plastikbombe *f.* **3.** Plastik..., Kunststoff...: ~ *bag* Plastikbeutel *m*, -tüte *f*; ~ *bullet* Plastikgeschoß *n*; ~ *film* Kunststofffolie *f*; ~ *money* → **5.** **II** *s* **4.** Plastik *n*, Kunststoff *m.* **5.** Kreditkarten *pl*, Plastikgeld *n.* '**plas·tics I** *s pl* Kunststoffe *pl.* **II** *adj* Plastik..., Kunststoff...: ~ *film* Kunststofffolie *f*; ~ *industry* Kunststoffindustrie *f.*

plate [pleɪt] **I** s **1.** Teller m; **hand s.o. s.th. on a** ~ F j-m et. auf dem Tablett servieren; **have a lot on one's** ~ viel am Hals haben. **2.** Platte f. **3.** (Namens-, Tür- etc)Schild n. **4.** (Bild)Tafel f (in e-m Buch etc). **5.** Gegenstände pl aus Edelmetall. **6.** Doublé n, Dublee n. **II** v/t **7.** panzern. **8.** d(o)ublieren, plattieren: ~d with gold vergoldet.

pla·teau [ˈplætəʊ] pl **-teaux, -teaus** [ˈ-təʊz] s Plateau n, Hochebene f.

plate·ful [ˈpleɪtfʊl] pl **-fuls** s ein Teller(voll) m.

plate rack s Geschirrständer m.

plat·form [ˈplætfɔːm] s **1.** Plattform f; Podium n, Tribüne f. **2.** 🚉 Bahnsteig m. **3.** pol. Plattform f.

plat·i·num [ˈplætɪnəm] s chem. Platin n.

plat·i·tude [ˈplætɪtjuːd] s Platitüde f, Plattheit f.

pla·ton·ic [pləˈtɒnɪk] adj (~ally) platonisch: ~ love.

pla·toon [pləˈtuːn] s ✕ Zug m.

plat·ter [ˈplætə] s Servierplatte f.

plau·si·ble [ˈplɔːzəbl] adj □ **1.** plausibel, glaubhaft. **2.** geschickt (Lügner).

play [pleɪ] **I** s **1.** Spiel n: **at** ~ beim Spiel(en), spielend (Kinder etc); **be at** ~ spielen; **in (out of)** ~ im Spiel (im Aus) (Ball). **2.** Spiel(weise f) n: **fair** ~ (Sport) Fair play n, Fairneß f (beide a. fig.). **3.** fig. Spiel n: **bring into** ~ ins Spiel bringen, Routine etc aufbieten; **come into** ~ ins Spiel kommen. **4.** fig. Spiel(erei f) n: ~ **on words** Wortspiel; **in** ~ im Scherz. **5.** thea. Schauspiel n, (Theater)Stück n. **6.** ⚙ Spiel n; fig. Spielraum m: **allow (od. give) full (od. free)** ~ **to** freien Lauf lassen (dat). **II** v/i **7.** spielen (a. Sport, thea. etc): ~ **at** Karten, Indianer etc spielen; fig. sich nur so nebenbei beschäftigen mit; ~ **for money** um Geld spielen; ~ **for time** Zeit zu gewinnen suchen; (Sport) auf Zeit spielen; ~ **with** spielen mit (a. fig.); ~ **safe** F auf Nummer Sicher gehen. **III** v/t **8.** Karten, Rolle, Stück etc spielen, (Sport) Spiel austragen: ~ **(s.th. on) the piano** (et. auf dem) Klavier spielen; ~ **it safe** F auf Nummer Sicher gehen; → **trick** f, etc. **9.** Sport: spielen gegen: ~ **s.o. at chess** gegen j-n Schach spielen. **10.** Karte ausspielen: → **trump¹** I. **11.** thea. etc spielen od. Vorstellungen geben in (dat).

Verbindungen mit Adverbien:

play| back v/t Tonband etc abspielen: **play s.th. back to s.o.** j-m et. vorspielen. ~ **down** v/t herunterspielen, bagatellisieren. ~ **off** I v/t j-n ausspielen (**against** gegen). II v/i Sport: ein Entscheidungsspiel austragen (**for** um). ~ **up** I v/i **1.** Br. F verrückt spielen, Schwierigkeiten machen (Auto, Bein etc). **2.** ~ **to** j-m schöntun. **3.** hochspielen, aufbauschen. **4.** Br. F j-n auf die Palme bringen; j-m Schwierigkeiten machen (Bein etc).

play·a·ble [ˈpleɪəbl] adj Sport: bespielbar (Platz).

'play|·act v/i contp. schauspielern. **'~back** s Wiedergabe f, Abspielen n. **'~boy** s Playboy m.

play·er [ˈpleɪə] s **1.** ♪, Sport: Spieler(in). **2.** (Platten)Spieler m.

'play·fel·low → **playmate**.

play·ful [ˈpleɪfʊl] adj □ **1.** verspielt. **2.** schelmisch, neckisch.

'play|·go·er s Theaterbesucher(in). **'~ground** s **1.** Schulhof m. **2.** Spielplatz m. **3.** fig. Tummelplatz m. ~ **group** s bsd. Br. Spielgruppe f. **'~house** s **1.** Schauspielhaus n. **2.** Spielhaus n.

play·ing| card [ˈpleɪɪŋ] s Spielkarte f. ~ **field** s Sportplatz m.

'play|·mak·er s Sport: Spielmacher(in). **'~mate** s Spielkamerad(in). **'~off** s Sport: Entscheidungsspiel n. **'~pen** s Laufgitter n, -stall m. **~room** [ˈ-rʊm] s Spielzimmer n. **'~school** → **play group.** **'~thing** s Spielzeug n (a. fig.): **~s** pl Spielsachen pl, -zeug n. **'~time** s ped. große Pause. **~wright** [ˈ-raɪt] s Dramatiker(in).

plea [pliː] s **1.** (dringende) Bitte, Gesuch n (**for** um): **make a** ~ **for mercy** um Gnade bitten. **2.** ⚖ **enter a** ~ **of (not) guilty** sich schuldig bekennen (s-e Unschuld erklären); **make a** ~ **of s.th.** et. geltend machen.

plead [pliːd] (bsd. schott. u. Am. irr) **I** v/i **1.** (dringend) bitten (**for** um): ~ **with s.o.** j-n bitten (**to do** zu tun). **2.** ⚖ ~ **guilty** sich schuldig bekennen (**to doing s.th.** et. getan zu haben); ~ **not guilty** s-e Unschuld erklären. **3.** ⚖ u. allg. zu s-r Verteidigung od. Entschuldigung anführen, geltend machen. **4.** ~ **s.o.'s**

case 🔀 j-n vertreten; *allg.* sich für j-n einsetzen.

pleas·ant ['pleznt] *adj* □ **1.** angenehm, (*Nachricht etc a.*) erfreulich: → *dream* 1. **2.** freundlich.

please [pli:z] **I** *v/i* **1.** gefallen. **2.** *as you ~* wie Sie wünschen; *if you ~* wenn ich bitten darf, *iro. a.* gefälligst. **II** *v/t* **3.** *j-m* gefallen *od.* zusagen, *j-n* erfreuen: *be ~d about* (*od. at*) sich freuen über (*acc*); *I am ~d with it* es gefällt mir; *I am ~d to hear* es freut mich zu hören. **4.** zufriedenstellen: (*only*) *to ~ you* (nur) dir zuliebe; *there is no pleasing him, you can't ~ him* man kann es ihm nicht recht machen; *~ o.s.* tun, was man will; *~ yourself!* mach, was du willst!; *be ~d with* zufrieden sein mit; → *hard* 2. **III** *int* **5.** bitte. **'pleas·ing** *adj* □ angenehm.

pleas·ur·a·ble ['pleʒərəbl] *adj* □ angenehm.

pleas·ure ['pleʒə] *s* **1.** Vergnügen *n*: *for ~* zum Vergnügen; *with ~* mit Vergnügen; *give s.o. ~* j-m Vergnügen *od.* Freude *od.* Spaß machen; *have the ~ of doing s.th.* das Vergnügen haben, et. zu tun; *take ~ in* Vergnügen *od.* Freude finden an (*dat*); *he takes no ~ in it* es macht ihm keinen Spaß. **2.** *at* (*one's*) ~ nach Belieben.

pleat [pli:t] *s* Falte *f*. **'pleat·ed** *adj*: ~ *skirt* Faltenrock *m*.

pleb [pleb] *s* F *contp.* Prolet(in).

ple·be·ian [plɪ'bi:ən] *contp.* **I** *adj* proletenhaft. **II** *s* Prolet(in).

pleb·i·scite ['plebɪsɪt] *s* Volksabstimmung *f*, -entscheid *m*.

pled [pled] *bsd. schott. u. Am.* pret *u.* pp von *plead*.

pledge [pledʒ] **I** *s* **1.** Pfand *n*: *as a ~* als Pfand. **2.** *fig.* Unterpfand *n*: *as a ~ of* zum Zeichen (*gen*). **3.** Versprechen *n*, Zusicherung *f*: *make a* (*firm*) ~ (fest) versprechen *od.* zusichern (*to do* zu tun). **II** *v/t* **4.** verpfänden: ~ *one's word fig.* sein (Ehren)Wort geben. **5.** versprechen, zusichern (*to do* zu tun, *that* daß). **6.** ~ *s.o. to s.th.* j-n zu et. verpflichten, j-m et. auferlegen; ~ *o.s.* sich verpflichten (*to do* zu tun).

ple·na·ry ['pli:nərɪ] *adj* **1.** ~ *session* Plenarsitzung *f*, Vollversammlung *f*. **2.** ~ *powers pl* unbeschränkte Vollmacht.

plen·i·po·ten·ti·a·ry [ˌplenɪpəʊ'tenʃərɪ] **I**

s **1.** (General)Bevollmächtigte *m*, *f*. **II** *adj* **2.** (general)bevollmächtigt. **3.** ~ *powers pl* Generalvollmacht *f*.

plen·ti·ful ['plentɪful] *adj* □ reichlich.

plen·ty ['plentɪ] **I** *s* **1.** Überfluß *m*: *live in ~* im Überfluß leben; *... in ~* ...im Überfluß, ... in Hülle u. Fülle; → *horn* 3. **2.** e-e Menge: *that is ~* das ist reichlich; *there are ~ more* es gibt noch viel mehr; ~ *of ...* e-e Menge ..., viel(e) ... **II** *adv* **3.** F ganz schön.

ple·o·nasm ['plɪəʊnæzəm] *s ling.* Pleonasmus *m*. **ple·o·nas·tic** [ˌ~'næstɪk] *adj* (*~ally*) pleonastisch.

pleu·ri·sy ['plʊərəsɪ] *s ✻* Brustfell-, Rippenfellentzündung *f*.

pli·a·ble ['plaɪəbl], **pli·ant** ['~ənt] *adj* □ **1.** biegsam. **2.** *fig.* flexibel. **3.** *fig.* leicht beeinflußbar.

pli·ers ['plaɪəz] *s pl*, *a. pair of ~* Beißzange *f*.

plight [plaɪt] *s* Not(lage) *f*.

plim·soll ['plɪmsəl] *s Br.* Turnschuh *m*.

plod [plɒd] *v/i* **1.** trotten. **2.** *mst* ~ *away fig.* sich abmühen *od.* abplagen (*at* mit), schuften. **'plod·der** *s fig.* Arbeitstier *n*.

plonk [plɒŋk] *v/t* F schmeißen, knallen: ~ *down* hinschmeißen.

plop [plɒp] F **I** *v/i* plumpsen, (*ins Wasser*) platschen: ~ *into a chair* sich in e-n Sessel plumpsen lassen. **II** *s* Plumps *m*, Platsch *m*.

plot [plɒt] *s* **1.** Grundstück *n*; Parzelle *f*; Beet *n*. **2.** △ *bsd. Am.* Grundriß *m*. **3.** Handlung *f* (*e-s Films etc*). **4.** Komplott *n*, Verschwörung *f*. **II** *v/i* **5.** sich verschwören (*against* gegen). **III** *v/t* **6.** aushecken, planen. **7.** (*in e-e Karte etc*) einzeichnen. **'plot·ter** *s* Verschwörer(in).

plough [plaʊ] **I** *s* Pflug *m*. **II** *v/t a.* ~ *up* (um)pflügen: ~ *back* Gewinne reinvestieren (*into* in *acc*). **III** *v/i* pflügen: ~ *through* sich e-n Weg bahnen durch; ♣ sich pflügen durch; ~ *through a book* F ein Buch durchackern.

plow *Am.* → *plough*.

ploy [plɔɪ] *s* Masche *f*, Tour *f*.

pluck [plʌk] **I** *s* **1.** Ruck *m*. **2.** Innereien *pl. fig.* Mut *m*. **II** *v/t* **4.** *Geflügel* rupfen. **5.** *mst* ~ *out* ausreißen, -rupfen, -zupfen: → *courage*. **III** *v/i* **6.** zupfen (*at an dat*): ~ *at s.o.'s sleeve* j-n am

Ärmel zupfen. '**pluck·y** *adj* □ mutig.

plug [plʌg] **I** *s* **1.** Stöpsel *m*. **2.** ⚡ Stecker *m*; Steckdose *f*. **3.** *mot.* (*Zünd*)Kerze *f*. **II** *v/t* **4.** *a.* ~ *up* zustöpseln; zu-, verstopfen. **5.** ~ *in* ⚡ einstecken, einstecken. **III** *v/i* **6.** ~ *away at* F sich abschuften mit. '**~·hole** *s* Abfluß(loch *n*) *m*.

plum [plʌm] *s* **1.** Pflaume *f*; Zwetsch(g)e *f*. **2.** *fig.* F a) Rosine *f*, b) *a.* ~ *job* Bombenjob *m*.

plum·age ['pluːmɪdʒ] *s* Gefieder *n*.

plumb [plʌm] **I** *s* **1.** (Blei)Lot *n*, Senklot *n*: *out of* ~ aus dem Lot, nicht senkrecht. **II** *adj* **2.** lot-, senkrecht. **III** *adv* F **3.** (haar)genau. **4.** *bsd. Am.* komplett, total. **IV** *v/t* **5.** ⚓ ausloten, *fig. a.* ergründen. **6.** ~ *in bsd. Br. Waschmaschine etc* anschließen. '**plumb·er** *s* Installateur *m*. '**plumb·ing** *s* **1.** Installateurarbeit *f*. **2.** Rohre *pl*, Rohrleitungen *pl*.

plumb| **line** *s* **1.** ⚓ Lotschnur *f*, -leine *f*. **2.** → **plumb rule. ~ rule** *s* △ Setzlatte *f*, Richtscheit *n*.

plume [pluːm] **I** *s* **1.** (Schmuck)Feder *f*; Federbusch *m*. **2.** (*Rauch*)Fahne *f*. **II** *v/t* **3.** *a. its feathers* sich die Federn putzen.

plum·my ['plʌmɪ] *adj* **1.** affektiert (*Stimme*). **2.** F prima, toll: ~ *job* Bombenjob *m*.

plump¹ [plʌmp] **I** *adj* drall, mollig, rund(lich). **II** *v/t*: ~ *up* Kissen aufschütteln.

plump² [~] **I** *v/i* **1.** *mst* ~ *down* fallen, plumpsen (*on* auf *acc*): ~ *down into a chair* sich in e-n Sessel fallen lassen. **2.** ~ *for bsd. Br.* sich entscheiden für. **II** *v/t* **3.** fallen *od.* plumpsen lassen (*on* auf *acc*).

plum pud·ding *s* Plumpudding *m*.

plun·der ['plʌndə] **I** *v/t* **1.** (aus)plündern. **2.** *et.* rauben. **II** *v/i* **3.** plündern. **III** *s* **4.** Plünderung *f*. **5.** Beute *f*. '**plun·der·er** *s* Plünderer *m*.

plunge [plʌndʒ] **I** *v/t* **1.** ~ *a knife into s.o.'s back* j-m ein Messer in den Rükken stoßen. **2.** ~ *into* in Schulden, e-n Krieg *etc* stürzen: *be ~d into darkness* in Dunkel gehüllt sein. **II** *v/i* **3.** ~ *into* ins Zimmer *etc* stürzen; sich ins Wasser, in *e-e* Tätigkeit, in Schulden *etc* stürzen. **4.** stürzen (*Preise, Kurse*). **5.** ⚓ stampfen. **II** *s* **6.** (Kopf)Sprung *m*: *take the* ~ *fig.* den Sprung *od.* den ent-

scheidenden Schritt wagen. '**plung·ing** *adj* tief (*Ausschnitt*): *with a* ~ *neckline* tief ausgeschnitten.

plu·per·fect [,pluː'pɜːfɪkt] *s a.* ~ *tense* *ling.* Plusquamperfekt *n*, Vorvergangenheit *f*.

plu·ral ['plʊərəl] *ling.* **I** *adj* Plural..., Mehrzahl... **II** *s* Plural *m*, Mehrzahl *f*. '**plu·ral·ism** *s* *sociol.* Pluralismus *m*. ,**plu·ral'is·tic** *adj* (~*ally*) pluralistisch.

plus [plʌs] **I** *prp* **1.** ₳ plus, und, *bsd.* ✝ zuzüglich. **II** *adj* **2.** Plus...: ~ *sign* → **3.** **III** *s* **3.** Plus(zeichen) *n*. **4.** *fig.* Plus *n*, Vorteil *m*.

plush [plʌʃ] **I** *s* **1.** Plüsch *m*. **II** *adj* **2.** Plüsch... **3.** F feudal: ~ *restaurant* Nobelrestaurant *n*. nium *n*.⚓

plu·to·ni·um [pluː'təʊnɪəm] *s* 🜍 Pluto-

ply¹ [plaɪ] **I** *v/i* **1.** verkehren (*between* zwischen *dat*). **II** *v/t* **2.** verkehren auf (*dat*), befahren. **3.** *fig.* j-n überhäufen (*with* mit Fragen).

ply² [~] *s* Lage *f*, Schicht *f*. '**~·wood** *s* Sperrholz *n*.

pneu·mat·ic [nju:'mætɪk] *adj* (~*ally*) pneumatisch, Luft...; ⊕ Druck-, Preßluft...: ~ *brake* Druckluftbremse *f*; ~ *drill* Preßluftbohrer *m*; ~ *hammer* Preßlufthammer *m*.

pneu·mo·ni·a [nju:'məʊnjə] *s* 🜍 Lungenentzündung *f*.

poach¹ [pəʊtʃ] **I** *v/t* **1.** wildern. **2.** *Arbeitskräfte* abwerben (*from dat*). **II** *v/i* **3.** wildern.

poach² [~] *v/t* Eier pochieren: ~*ed eggs* *pl a.* verlorene Eier *pl*.

poach·er ['pəʊtʃə] *s* Wilderer *m*.

PO Box [,piː'əʊ] *s* Postfach *n*.

pock [pɒk] *s* 🜍 **1.** Pocke *f*, Blatter *f*. **2.** → **pockmark. pocked. pocked** → **pockmarked.**

pock·et ['pɒkɪt] **I** *s* **1.** (*Hosen- etc*)Tasche *f*: *with nothing in one's* ~ *except* mit nichts in der Tasche als; *have in one's* ~ *fig.* j-n, *et.* in der Tasche haben. **2.** *fig.* Geldbeutel *m*: *pay for s.th. out of one's own* ~ *et.* aus eigener Tasche bezahlen; *to suit every* ~ für jeden Geldbeutel. **3.** (*Nebel*)Bank *f*; (*Widerstands- etc*)Nest *n*. **4.** Billard: Loch *n*; ✈ (*Luft*)Loch *n*. **II** *adj* **5.** Taschen...: ~ *calculator* Taschenrechner *m*; ~ *edition* Taschenausgabe *f*; ~ *money* Taschengeld *n*. **III** *v/t* **6.** einstecken, in die Tasche stecken; *fig.* in die eigene Tasche stecken. **7.**

Billard: einlochen. '**~·book** *s* **1.** Notizbuch *n*. **2.** *Am.* Brieftasche *f*. '**~·knife** *s* (*irr* **knife**) Taschenmesser *n*.

'**pock**|**·mark** *s* Pockennarbe *f*. '**~·marked** *adj* pockennarbig; *fig.* übersät (*with* mit).

pod [pɒd] **I** *s* ♀ Hülse *f*, Schote *f*, **II** *v/t* aus-, enthülsen.

po·di·um ['pəʊdɪəm] *pl* **-di·ums, -di·a** ['~dɪə] *s* Podium *n*, Podest *n*.

po·em ['pəʊɪm] *s* Gedicht *n*.

po·et ['pəʊɪt] *s* Dichter *m*. '**po·et·ess** Dichterin *f*. **po·et·ic** [~'etɪk] *adj* (*~ally*) dichterisch: ~ *justice fig.* ausgleichende Gerechtigkeit; ~ *licence* (*Am.* **license**) dichterische Freiheit. **po·et·i·cal** → **poetic**. **po·et·ry** ['pəʊɪtrɪ] *s* Dichtung *f*; Gedichte *pl*.

poign·ant ['pɔɪnjənt] *adj* □ **1.** schmerzlich (*Erinnerungen etc*). **2.** scharf (*Verstand*).

point [pɔɪnt] **I** *s* **1.** (*Messer-, Nadel- etc-*)Spitze *f*. **2.** *geogr.* Landspitze *f*. **3.** *ling. Am.* Punkt *m*. **4.** *four* ~ *three* (*4.3*) 4,3. **5.** Punkt *m* (*a.* ♟). Grad *m* (*e-r Skala*): ~ *of contact* Berührungspunkt (*a. fig.*); ~ *of intersection* Schnittpunkt; → *freezing* 1, *etc*. **6.** Punkt *m*, Stelle *f*, Ort *m*: *up to a* ~ *fig.* bis zu e-m gewissen Punkt *od.* Grad; ~ *of view fig.* Gesichts-, Standpunkt. **7.** ⚡ *Br.* Steckdose *f*. **8.** *Sport etc*: Punkt *m*: *win on* ~*s* nach Punkten gewinnen; *winner on* ~*s* Punktsieger *m*. **9.** *a.* ~ *of time* Zeitpunkt *m*, Augenblick *m*: *be on the* ~ *of doing s.th.* im Begriff sein, et. zu tun. **10.** Punkt *m* (*e-r Tagesordnung etc*), (*Einzel-, Teil-*)Frage *f*: ~ *of interest* interessante Einzelheit. **11.** Kernpunkt *m*, -frage *f*, springender Punkt: *be* (*beside*) *the* ~ (nicht) zur Sache gehören; *come to the* ~ zur Sache kommen; *keep* (*od.* *stick*) *to the* ~ bei der Sache bleiben; *make a* ~ *of doing s.th.* Wert darauf legen, et. zu tun; *get* (*od.* *see, take*) *s.o.'s* ~ verstehen, was j-d meint; *miss the* ~ nicht verstehen, worum es geht; *that's not the* ~ darum geht es nicht; *that's the* (*whole*) ~ genau (das ist es)! **12.** Ziel *n*, Absicht *f*: *carry* (*od.* *gain*) *one's* ~ sich *od.* s-e Absicht durchsetzen. **13.** Sinn *m*, Zweck *m*: *what's the* ~? wozu?; *what's the* ~ *of* (*od.* *in*) *waiting?* was hat es für e-n Sinn

zu warten?; *there's no* ~ *in that* das hat keinen Zweck. **14.** (hervorstechende) Eigenschaft, (Vor)Zug *m*: *strong* (*weak*) ~ starke (schwache) Seite; *it has its* ~*s* es hat s-e Vorzüge. **II** *v/t* **15.** (an-, zu)spitzen. **16.** *Waffe etc* richten (*at* auf *acc*): ~ *one's finger at s.o.* (mit dem Finger) auf j-n deuten *od.* zeigen. **17.** zeigen: ~ *the way* den Weg weisen (*a. fig.*); ~ *out* zeigen; *fig.* hinweisen *od.* aufmerksam machen auf (*acc*); ~ *out to s.o. that* j-n darauf aufmerksam machen, daß. **III** *v/i* **18.** (mit dem Finger) deuten *od.* zeigen (*at, to* auf *acc*): ~ *to* nach e-r *Richtung* weisen *od.* liegen (*Haus etc*); *fig.* hinweisen *od.* -deuten auf (*acc*). ~*'blank adj u. adv* **1.** *a.* *at* ~ *range* aus kürzester Entfernung. **2.** *fig.* unverblümt.

point·ed ['pɔɪntɪd] *adj* □ **1.** spitz: ~ *arch* △ Spitzbogen *m*. **2.** *fig.* scharf (*Bemerkung etc*). **3.** *fig.* ostentativ. '**point·er** *s* **1.** Zeiger *m* (*e-s Meßgeräts*). **2.** Zeigestock *m*. **3.** F Fingerzeig *m*, Tip *m*. '**point·less** *adj* □ sinn-, zwecklos.

poise [pɔɪz] **I** *s* **1.** (Körper)Haltung *f*. **2.** *fig.* Gelassenheit *f*; (Selbst)Sicherheit *f*. **II** *v/t* **3.** balancieren: *be* ~*d fig.* schweben (*between* zwischen *dat*). **poised** *adj* gelassen; (selbst)sicher.

poi·son ['pɔɪzn] **I** *s* Gift *n* (*to* für) (*a. fig.*): *hate like* ~ wie die Pest hassen; *what's your* ~? F was willst du trinken? **II** *v/t* vergiften (*a. fig.*). **III** *adj* Gift...: ~ *gas*; ~ *fang zo.* Giftzahn *m*. '**poi·son·ing** *s* Vergiftung *f*. '**poi·son·ous** *adj* □ giftig (*a. fig.*), Gift...

poke [pəʊk] **I** *v/t* **1.** j-n (an)stoßen: ~ *s.o. in the ribs* j-m e-n Rippenstoß geben. **2.** *a.* ~ *up Feuer* schüren. **3.** *den Kopf etc* strecken: → *nose* 1. **4.** ~ *fun at* sich lustig machen über (*acc*). **II** *v/i* **5.** ~ *about* (*od.* *around*) (herum)stöbern, (-)wühlen (*in* in *dat*). **III** *s* **6.** Stoß *m*: ~ *in the ribs* Rippenstoß.

pok·er¹ ['pəʊkə] *s* Feuerhaken *m*.

po·ker² [~] *s* Poker(spiel) *n*. ~ *face s* Pokergesicht *n*, Pokerface *n*.

pok·y ['pəʊkɪ] *adj* winzig (*Zimmer etc*).

po·lar ['pəʊlə] *adj* □ polar (*a. fig.*), Polar...: ~ *bear zo.* Eisbär *m*; ~ *circle geogr.* Polarkreis *m*. '**po·lar·ize** *v/t* (*a. phys.* polarisieren *f*.)

Pole¹ [pəʊl] *s* Pole *m*, Polin *f*.

pole² [~] *s geogr.*, *⚡, etc* Pol *m*: *they are* **~s** *apart fig.* zwischen ihnen liegen Welten.

pole³ [~] *s* Pfosten *m*; (*Fahnen-, Leitungs*)Mast *m*; (*Bohnen- etc*)Stange *f*; (*Leichtathletik*) (Sprung)Stab *m*. '**~cat** *s zo.* Iltis *m*.

po·lem·ic [pə'lemɪk] **I** *adj* (**~ally**) **1.** polemisch. **II** *s* **2.** *a. pl* (*sg konstruiert*) Polemik *f*. **3.** polemische Äußerung. **po·'lem·i·cal** → *polemic* **1.**

pole star *s ast.* Polarstern *m*.

pole vault *s Leichtathletik:* Stabhochsprung *m.* **~ 'vault·er** *s* Stabhochspringer *m.*

po·lice [pə'liːs] **I** *s* (*pl konstruiert*) Polizei *f.* **II** *v/t* (polizeilich) überwachen. **III** *adj* polizeilich, Polizei...: **~ constable** → *constable*; **~ force** Polizei *f*; **~ officer** Polizeibeamte(r *m*; **~ protection** Polizeischutz *m*; **~ record** Strafregister *n*; *have a* **~ record** vorbestraft sein; **~ state** Polizeistaat *m*; **~ station** Polizeirevier *n*, -wache *f*. **po'lice·man** [~mən] *s* (*irr man*) Polizist *m.* **po·lice,wom·an** *s* (*irr woman*) Polizistin *f.*

pol·i·cy¹ [pɒləsɪ] *s* **1.** Verfahren(sweise *f*) *n*, Taktik *f*, Politik *f*: *it is our* **~** es ist unser Grundsatz (*to do* zu tun). **2.** (*Außen-, Wirtschafts- etc*)Politik *f*. **3.** Klugheit *f*: *be good* (*bad*) **~** (un)klug od. (un)vernünftig sein.

pol·i·cy² [~] *s* (*Versicherungs*)Police *f*: *take out a* **~** e-e Versicherung abschließen.

po·li·o [pəʊlɪəʊ] *s ⚡ F* Polio *f.* **po·li·o·my·e·li·tis** [~maɪə'laɪtɪs] *s ⚡* (spinale) Kinderlähmung.

Pol·ish¹ [pəʊlɪʃ] **I** *adj* polnisch. **II** *s ling.* Polnisch *n.*

pol·ish² [pɒlɪʃ] **I** *v/t* **1.** polieren, ⚙ *etc a.* (ab)schleifen, *Fußboden* bohnern: **~ off** F *Arbeit* wegschaffen; *Essen* wegputzen; **~ up** aufpolieren (*a. fig.*). **II** *s* **2.** Politur *f*, Glanz *m*. **3.** (*Möbel*)Politur *f*; (*Schuh*)Creme *f*; Bohnerwachs *n*; (*Nagel*)Lack *m*. **4.** *fig.* Schliff *m*. '**pol·ished** *adj* **1.** poliert, glänzend. **2.** *fig.* geschliffen; brillant.

po·lite [pə'laɪt] *adj □* höflich: *to be* **~** aus Höflichkeit. **po'lite·ness** *s* Höflichkeit *f.*

po·lit·i·cal [pə'lɪtɪkl] *adj □* politisch: **~ economy** Volkswirtschaft *f*; **~ science**

Politologie *f*; **~ scientist** Politologe *m*, -login *f*. **po·'lit·i·cian** [ˌpɒlɪ'tɪʃn] *s* Politiker(in). **po·lit·i·cize** [pə'lɪtɪsaɪz] *v/t* politisieren. **pol·i·tics** [pɒlɪtɪks] *s pl* (*mst sg konstruiert*) Politik *f*: *what are his* **~?** wo steht er politisch?; *go into* **~** in die Politik gehen; *talk* **~** über Politik reden, politisieren.

pol·ka [pɒlkə] *s ♪* Polka *f.* '**~dot** *adj* gepunktet, getupft (*Kleid etc*).

poll [pəʊl] **I** *s* **1.** (*Meinungs*)Umfrage *f*. **2.** *a. pl* Stimmabgabe *f*, Wahl *f*: *be defeated at the* **~s** e-e Wahlniederlage erleiden; *go to the* **~s** zur Wahl gehen. **3.** Wahlbeteiligung *f*. **II** *v/t* **4.** befragen: *65 % of those* **~ed** 65 % der Befragten. **5.** *Stimmen* erhalten, auf sich vereinigen.

pol·len [pɒlən] *s ♣* Pollen *m*, Blütenstaub *m.*

poll·ing [pəʊlɪŋ] **I** *s* → *poll* 2, 3. **II** *adj* Wahl...: **~ booth** Wahlkabine *f*, -zelle *f*; **~ day** Wahltag *m*; **~ place** Am., **~ station** *bsd. Br* Wahllokal *n.*

poll·ster [pəʊlstə] *s* Meinungsforscher(-in).

pol·lut·ant [pə'luːtənt] *s* Schadstoff *m.*

pol·lute [pə'luːt] *v/t* **1.** *Umwelt* verschmutzen, *Flüsse etc a.* verunreinigen. **2.** (*moralisch*) verderben. **pol'lut·er** *s* (*Umwelt*)Verschmutzer(in). **pol'lu·tion** *s* (*Umwelt*)Verschmutzung *f*, Verunreinigung *f.*

po·lo [pəʊləʊ] *s Sport:* Polo *n.* **~ neck** *s* Rollkragen(pullover) *m.* '**~neck** *adj* Rollkragen... **~ shirt** *s* Polohemd *n.*

pol·yg·a·mist [pə'lɪɡəmɪst] *s* Polygamist *m.* **po'lyg·a·mous** *adj □* polygam (*a. ♣, zo.*). **po'lyg·a·my** *s* Polygamie *f* (*a. ♣, zo.*).

pol·y·glot [pɒlɪɡlɒt] *adj* polyglott, viel-, mehrsprachig.

pol·y·gon [pɒlɪɡən] *s A* Vieleck *n.*

pol·yp [pɒlɪp] *s ♣, zo.* Polyp *m.*

pol·y·syl·lab·ic [ˌpɒlɪsɪ'læbɪk] *adj* (**~ally**) *ling.* viel-, mehrsilbig. **pol·y·syl·la·ble** [~ˌsɪləbl] *s* vielsilbiges Wort.

pol·y·tech·nic [ˌpɒlɪ'teknɪk] *s* (*etwa*) Technische Hochschule.

pol·y·va·lent [ˌpɒlɪ'veɪlənt] *adj 🜊* mehrwertig.

po·made [pə'meɪd] *s* Pomade *f.*

pome·gran·ate [pɒmɪˌɡrænɪt] *s ♣* Granatapfel *m.*

pom·mel ['pʌml] s **1.** (*Sattel- etc*)Knopf
m. **2.** *Turnen*: (*Pferd*)Pausche f: **~ horse**
Seitpferd n.

pomp [pɒmp] s Pomp m. **'pomp·ous** adj
☐ **1.** aufgeblasen, wichtigtuerisch. **2.**
bombastisch, schwülstig (*Sprache*).

ponce [pɒns] s *Br. sl* **1.** Zuhälter m. **2.**
Tunte f.

pond [pɒnd] s Teich m, Weiher m.

pon·der ['pɒndə] I v/i nachdenken (**on**,
over über *acc*). II v/t überlegen, nachdenken über (*acc*): **~ doing s.th.** erwägen, et. zu tun. **'pon·der·ous** adj ☐ **1.**
massig, schwer. **2.** *fig.* schwerfällig.

pong [pɒŋ] *Br.* F I s Gestank m. II v/i
stinken. **'pong·y** adj *Br.* F stinkend,
stinkig.

pon·toon [pɒn'tu:n] s Ponton m. **~
bridge** s Ponton-, Schiffsbrücke f.

po·ny ['pəʊnɪ] s zo. Pony n. **'~·tail** s Pfer-
deschwanz m (*Frisur*).

poo·dle ['pu:dl] s zo. Pudel m.

poof [pu:f] s *Br. sl.* Schwule m.

pooh [pu:] int pah! **,pooh-'pooh** v/t geringschätzig abtun.

pool¹ [pu:l] s **1.** Teich m, Tümpel m.
2. Pfütze f, (*Blut- etc*)Lache f. **3.**
(*Schwimm*)Becken n, (*Swimming-*)
Pool m.

pool² [~] I s **1.** (gemeinsame) Kasse,
(*Kartenspiel a.*) Pot m. **2.** pl *Br.* (*Fußball*)Toto n, m: **win (on) the ~s** im Toto
gewinnen; **win on the ~s** Totogewinn
m. **3.** *Am.* Poolbillard n: **shoot ~** Poolbillard spielen. **4.** ✝ *bsd. Am.* Pool m,
Kartell n. **5.** (*Arbeits-, Fahr*)Gemein-
schaft f; (*Mitarbeiter- etc*)Stab m;
(*Fuhr*)Park m; (*Schreib*)Pool m. II v/t
6. *Geld etc* zs.-legen; *fig. Kräfte etc* vereinen.

poop [pu:p] s ♨ **1.** Heck n. **2.** a. **~ deck**
(erhöhtes) Achter- *od.* Hinterdeck.

pooped (out) [pu:pt] adj *Am.* F erledigt,
kaputt.

poor [pɔː] I adj (☐ → **poorly** II) **1.** arm,
mittellos. **2.** arm, bedauernswert. **3.** *fig.*
arm (**in** an *dat*); dürftig, mangelhaft,
schwach: **~ consolation** ein schwacher
Trost; → **health 2.** II s **4. the ~** pl die
Armen pl. **'poor·ly** I adj **1.** F unpäßlich,
kränklich. II adv **2.** ärmlich: **he is ~
off** es geht ihm schlecht. **3.** *fig.* dürftig, mangelhaft, schwach: **~ gifted**
schwachbegabt; **~ paid** schlechtbe-

zahlt; **be ~ off for** knapp sein an (*dat*);
do ~ in schlecht abschneiden bei; **think
~ of** nicht viel halten von. **'poor·ness** s
1. Armut f. **2.** *fig.* Dürftigkeit f, Mang-
gelhaftigkeit f.

pop¹ [pɒp] I v/i **1.** knallen. **2.** (zer)plat-
zen: **~ open** aufplatzen, -springen. **3.** F
hallern, schießen (**at** auf *acc*). **4.** F
sau-
sen: **~ in** auf e-n Sprung vorbeikommen; **~ off** den Löffel weglegen (*sterben*); **~ up** (plötzlich) auftauchen (*a.
fig.*). II v/t **5.** zerknallen. **6.** F (schnell)
stecken: **~ on** Hut aufstülpen. **7. he's
~ped the question** F er hat ihr e-n (Heirats)Antrag gemacht. III s **8.** Knall m.
9. F Limo f.

pop² [~] I s Pop m. II adj a) Schlager...: **~
singer**; **~ song** Schlager m, b) Pop...: **~
concert** (**group**, **singer**, *etc*).

pop³ [~] s *bsd. Am.* Papa m, Vati m.

'pop·corn s Popcorn n, Puffmais m.

pope [pəʊp] s *eccl.* Papst m: **~'s nose**
F Bürzel m.

'pop|-eyed adj F glotzäugig. **'~·gun** s
Spielzeuggewehr n, -pistole f.

pop·lar ['pɒplə] s ♣ Pappel f.

pop·lin ['pɒplɪn] s Popelin m.

pop·per ['pɒpə] s *bsd. Br.* F Druckknopf m.

pop·py ['pɒpɪ] s ♣ Mohn m. **'~·cock** s F
Quatsch m.

pop·u·lar ['pɒpjʊlə] adj (☐ → **popular-
ly**) **1.** populär, beliebt: **make o.s. ~ with**
sich bei j-m beliebt machen. **2.** weitverbreitet. **3.** populär, volkstümlich; allge-
mein- *od.* leichtverständlich: **~ etymology** ling. Volksetymologie f; **~ music**
volkstümliche Musik; **~ press** Boulevardpresse f. **4.** volkstümlich (*Preise*):
~ edition Volksausgabe f. **5.** *bsd. pol.*
Volks...: **~ front** Volksfront f. **pop·u-
lar·i·ty** [,~'lærətɪ] s Popularität f: a) Be-
liebtheit f, b) Volkstümlichkeit f.
pop·u·lar·ize ['~ləraɪz] v/t **1.** populär machen. **2.** allgemeinverständlich
darstellen. **'pop·u·lar·ly** adv allgemein.

pop·u·late ['pɒpjʊleɪt] v/t bevölkern, besiedeln. **,pop·u·'la·tion** s **1.** Bevölkerung f; Einwohnerschaft f: **~ density**
Bevölkerungsdichte f; **~ explosion** Be-
völkerungsexplosion f. **2.** (Gesamt)Be-
stand m (an Tieren etc).

pop·u·lous ['pɒpjʊləs] adj ☐ dichtbesie-

delt, -bevölkert, (*Stadt*) einwohner-
stark.
por·ce·lain ['pɔːsəlɪn] *s* Porzellan *n*.
porch [pɔːtʃ] *s* **1.** überdachter Vorbau,
Vordach *n*, (e-r *Kirche etc*) Portal *n*. **2.**
Am. Veranda *f*.
por·cu·pine ['pɔːkjʊpaɪn] *s zo.* Stachelschwein *n*.
pore[1] [pɔː] *s* Pore *f*.
pore[2] [~] *v/i:* ~ **over** vertieft sein in (*acc*),
über *s-n* Büchern *etc* hocken.
pork [pɔːk] *s* Schweinefleisch *n*. ~ **chop** *s*
Schweinekotelett *n*. ~ **cut·let** *s* Schwei-
neschnitzel *n*.
pork·y ['pɔːkɪ] *adj* F fett, dick.
porn [pɔːn] → *porno*.
por·no ['pɔːnəʊ] **I** *pl* -**nos** *s* **1.** Porno *m*.
2. Porno(film) *m*. **II** *adj* **3.** Porno...
por·no·graph·ic [,pɔːnəʊ'græfɪk] *adj*
(~*ally*) pornographisch. **por·nog·ra·**
phy [~'nɒɡrəfɪ] *s* Pornographie *f*.
po·rous ['pɔːrəs] *adj* □ porös.
por·poise ['pɔːpəs] *s zo.* Tümmler *m*.
por·ridge ['pɒrɪdʒ] *s* Porridge *n*, *m*, Haferbrei *m*.
port[1] [pɔːt] *s* **1.** Hafen *m*: **come into** ~
einlaufen; **leave** ~ auslaufen; **any** ~ **in a**
storm *fig.* in der Not frißt der Teufel
Fliegen; ~ **of call** Anlaufhafen *m*. **2.** *a.* ~
city Hafenstadt *f*.
port[2] [~] *s* ✒, ⚓ Backbord *n*.
port[3] [~] *s* Portwein *m*.
port·a·ble ['pɔːtəbl] **I** *adj* tragbar: ~ **ra-**
dio (*set*) → IIa; ~ **television set** → IIb;
~ **typewriter** → IIc. **II** *s* a) Kofferradio
n, b) Portable *n*, tragbares Fernsehgerät, c) Koffer-, Reiseschreibmaschine *f*.
por·tal ['pɔːtl] *s* Portal *n*.
por·tend [pɔː'tend] *v/t* bedeuten, ankündigen.
por·ter[1] ['pɔːtə] *s* a) Pförtner *m*: ~*'s* **lodge**
Pförtnerloge *f*, b) *bsd. Br.* Portier *m*.
por·ter[2] [~] *s* **1.** (Gepäck)Träger *m*. **2.** 🚂
Am. Schlafwagenschaffner(in).
'**por·ter·house** (**steak**) *s* Porterhouse-
steak *n*.
port·fo·li·o [,pɔːt'fəʊljəʊ] *pl* -**os** *s* **1.** (Ak-
ten-, Dokumenten)Mappe *f*. **2.** *pol.*
Portefeuille *n*, Geschäftsbereich *m*.
'**port·hole** *s* ⚓ Bullauge *n*.
por·ti·co ['pɔːtɪkəʊ] *pl* -**co(e)s** *s* Säulen-
halle *f*.
por·tion ['pɔːʃn] **I** *s* **1.** Teil *m*. **2.** Anteil *m*
(*of* an *dat*). **3.** Portion *f* (*Essen*). **II** *v/t* **4.**

~ **out** auf-, verteilen (**among, between**
unter *acc*).
port·ly ['pɔːtlɪ] *adj* beleibt, korpulent.
port·man·teau word [,pɔːt'mæntəʊ] *s*
ling. Kurzwort *n*.
por·trait ['pɔːtreɪt] *s paint.* Porträt *n*,
phot. a. Porträtaufnahme *f*: ~ **painter**
Porträtmaler(in). '**por·trait·ist** *s* Por-
trätist(in), Porträtmaler(in) *od.* -foto-
graf(in). **por·trai·ture** ['~trɪtʃə] *s* Por-
trätmalerei *f od.* -fotografie *f*.
por·tray [pɔː'treɪ] *v/t* **1.** porträtieren. **2.**
fig. schildern, darstellen (**as** als). **3.**
thea. etc darstellen, verkörpern. **por-**
'**tray·al** *s* **1.** Schilderung *f*, Darstellung
f. **2.** *thea. etc* Verkörperung *f*.
Por·tu·guese [pɔːtʃʊ'giːz] **I** *adj* **1.** portugiesisch. **II** *s* **2.** Portugiese *m*, Portu-
giesin *f*: **the** ~ *pl* die Portugiesen *pl*. **3.**
ling. Portugiesisch *n*.
pose [pəʊz] **I** *s* **1.** Pose *f* (*a. fig.*), Positur
f. **II** *v/t* **2.** aufstellen, in Positur stellen
od. setzen. **3.** *fig. Problem, Frage* aufwerfen, *Bedrohung, Gefahr etc* darstel-
len (**for, to** für). **III** *v/i* **4.** sich aufstellen,
sich in Positur stellen *od.* setzen. **5.**
paint. Modell stehen *od.* sitzen (**for**
dat); als (Maler- *od.* Foto)Modell arbeiten. **6.** sich ausgeben (**as** als). **posed**
adj gestellt (*Aufnahme*). '**pos·er** *s* **1.** F
harte Nuß. **2.** Wichtigtuer(in).
posh [pɒʃ] *adj* F piekfein, feudal: ~ **hotel**
Nobelhotel *n*.
po·si·tion [pə'zɪʃn] **I** *s* **1.** Position *f*, Lage
f, Standort *m*: ~ **of the sun** *ast.* Sonnenstand *m*; **in** (**out of**) ~ an der richtigen (falschen) Stelle. **2.** (*Körper*)Stel-
lung *f*, Position *f*. **3.** Stelle *f*, Stellung *f*
(**with, in** bei). **4.** a) Position *f* (*in e-m*
Beruf, Wettbewerb etc), (Rang)Stel-
lung *f*: **be in third** ~ in dritter Position
od. auf dem dritten Platz liegen, b) (gesellschaftliche *od.* soziale) Stellung:
people *pl* **of** ~ Leute *pl* von Rang. **5.** *fig.*
Lage *f*, Situation *f*: **be in a** ~ **to do s.th.**
in der Lage sein, et. zu tun. **6.** *fig.*
(Sach)Lage *f*, Stand *m* (der Dinge): **le-**
gal ~ Rechtslage *f*. **7.** *fig.* Einstellung *f*
(**on** zu): **what is your** ~ **on ...?** wie
stehen Sie zu ...?; **take the** ~ **that** den
Standpunkt vertreten, daß. **II** *v/t* **8.**
(auf)stellen; *Polizisten etc* postieren.
pos·i·tive ['pɒzətɪv] **I** *adj* □ **1.** *allg.* positiv: **he was** ~ 🩺 sein Befund war posi-

tiv; **~ pole** ⚡ Pluspol *m.* **2.** ausdrücklich (*Befehl etc*), definitiv, fest (*Versprechen etc*). **3.** sicher, eindeutig (*Beweis etc*). **4.** greifbar, konkret; konstruktiv. **5. be ~** sicher sein (*that* daß); **be ~ about** sich sicher sein (*gen*). **6.** F ausgesprochen, absolut. **II** *s* **7.** *phot.* Positiv *n.* **8.** *ling.* Positiv *m.*

pos·sess [pə'zes] *v/t* **1.** besitzen (*a. fig.*). **2.** *fig.* beherrschen (*Gedanke, Gefühl etc*): **~ed with** (*od. by*) beherrscht *od.* erfüllt von; besessen von; *like a man* **~ed** wie ein Besessener. **pos·ses·sion** [pə'zeʃn] *s* **1.** Besitz *m*: **be in s.o.'s ~** in j-s Besitz sein; **be in** (*od. have*) **~ of** im Besitz sein von (*od. gen*); **come** (*od. get*) **into ~ of** in den Besitz gelangen von (*od. gen*); **take ~ of** Besitz ergreifen von, in Besitz nehmen. **2.** Besitz(tum) *n m.* **3.** *fig.* Besessenheit *f.* **pos·ses·sive** [~sɪv] *adj* □ **1.** besitzgierig; (*Mutter etc*) besitzergreifend. **2.** *ling.* **~ case** Genitiv *m*, zweiter Fall; **~ adjective** attributives Possessivpronomen (*z. B.* **my** *car*); **~ pronoun** substantivisches Possessivpronomen (*z. B. it is* **mine**). **pos'ses·sor** *s* Besitzer(in).

pos·si·bil·i·ty [ˌpɒsɪ'bɪlətɪ] *s* Möglichkeit *f* (**of** *of doing* zu tun). **'pos·si·ble** *adj* möglich: **do everything ~** alles tun, was e-m möglich ist; **make s.th. ~ for s.o.** j-m et. möglich machen *od.* ermöglichen; **if ~** falls möglich. **'pos·si·bly** *adv* **1.** möglicherweise, vielleicht. **2.** *when I* **~ can** wenn ich irgend kann; *I can't* **~ do this** ich kann das unmöglich tun; *how can I* **~ do it?** wie kann ich es nur *od.* bloß machen?

pos·sum ['pɒsəm] F → **opossum**: *play* **~** sich tot- *od.* schlafend *od.* dumm stellen.

post¹ [pəʊst] **I** *s* **1.** (*Tür-, Tor-, Ziel-etc*)Pfosten *m*, (*Laternen*)Pfahl *m*, (*Telegrafen- etc*)Mast *m*: → **pip³. II** *v/t* **2.** *a.* **~ up** Plakat etc anschlagen, ankleben. **3.** et. durch Aushang bekanntgeben: **~ (as) missing** 💀, ⚓ als vermißt melden.

post² [~] **I** *s* **1.** ✗ Posten *m*; Standort *m*, Garnison *f.* **2.** Posten *m*, Platz *m*: *at one's* **~** auf s-m Posten. **3.** Posten *m*, Stelle *f.* **II** *v/t* **4.** Polizisten etc aufstellen, postieren. **5.** *bsd. Br.* versetzen, ✗ abkommandieren (**to** nach).

post³ [~] **I** *s* **1.** *bsd. Br.* Post *f*: **by ~** mit der *od.* per Post; **has the ~ been yet?** ist die Post schon da? **II** *v/t* **2.** *bsd. Br.* aufgeben; einwerfen; mit der Post (zu)senden. **3. keep s.o. ~ed** j-n auf dem laufenden halten.

post·age ['pəʊstɪdʒ] *s* Porto *n*: **what is the ~ for a letter to ...?** wieviel kostet ein Brief nach ...? **~ stamp** *s* Postwertzeichen *n*, Briefmarke *f.*

post·al ['pəʊstl] *I adj* postalisch, Post...: **~ card** *Am.* Postkarte *f*; **~ charges** *pl* Postgebühren *pl.* **II** *s Am.* F Postkarte *f.*

'post|·box *s bsd. Br.* Briefkasten *m.* **'~·card** *s* Postkarte *f.* **'~·code** *s Br.* Postleitzahl *f.*

post·er ['pəʊstə] *s* Plakat *n*; Poster *m, n.*

poste res·tante [ˌpəʊst'resta:nt] *bsd. Br.* **I** *s* Abteilung *f* für postlagernde Sendungen. **II** *adv* postlagernd.

pos·te·ri·or [pɒ'stɪərɪə] *s humor.* Allerwerteste *m.*

pos·ter·i·ty [pɒ'sterətɪ] *s* die Nachwelt.

post|·'free *adj u. adv bsd. Br.* portofrei. **~ horn** *s hist.* Posthorn *n.*

post·hu·mous ['pɒstjʊməs] *adj* □ post(h)um.

pos·til·(l)ion [pə'stɪljən] *s hist.* Postillion *m.*

post·man ['pəʊstmən] *s (irr* **man)** *bsd. Br.* Briefträger *m*, Postbote *m.* **'~·mark** **I** *s* Poststempel *m.* **II** *v/t* (ab)stempeln: **be ~ed London** in London abgestempelt sein. **'~·mas·ter** *s* Postamtsvorsteher *m*: ♀ **General** Postminister *m.*

post| me·rid·i·em [ˌpəʊstmə'rɪdɪəm] *adv* nachmittags (*abbr. p.m.*): **3 p.m.** 15 Uhr. **~·mor·tem** [ˌ~'mɔ:tem] *s a.* **~ examination** Autopsie *f*, Obduktion *f.*

post| of·fice *s* Post(amt *n*) *f*: **~ box** Postfach *n.* **,~'paid** → **post-free**.

post·pone [ˌpəʊst'pəʊn] *v/t* verschieben (**to** *auf acc*), aufschieben (**to** *auf acc*; **till, until** bis): **he ~ed seeing his doctor** er verschob s-n Arztbesuch. **,post'pone·ment** *s* Verschiebung *f*, Aufschub *m.*

post·script ['pəʊsskrɪpt] *s* **1.** Postskript(um) *n*, Nachschrift *f.* **2.** Nachbemerkung *f* (*zu e-r Rede etc*).

pos·tu·late I *v/t* ['pɒstjʊleɪt] postulieren, (als gegeben) voraussetzen. **II** *s* ['~lət] Postulat *n*, Voraussetzung *f.*

pos·ture ['pɒstʃə] **I** *s* **1.** (Körper)Haltung *f*; Positur *f*, Stellung *f*. **2.** *fig.* Haltung *f* (*on* in *dat*, zu). **II** *v/i* **3.** sich in Positur stellen *od.* setzen. **4.** *fig.* sich aufspielen.

post-war [͵pəʊst'wɔː] *adj* Nachkriegs...

pot [pɒt] **I** *s* **1.** (Blumen-, Koch- *etc*)Topf *m*: **big ~** F großes *od.* hohes Tier; **a ~ of money** F e-e Menge Geld; **he's got ~s of money** F er hat Geld wie Heu; **go to ~** F auf den Hund kommen (*Person etc*); immer schlechter werden (*Sprachkenntnisse etc*); ins Wasser fallen (*Pläne etc*); **keep the ~ boiling** *fig.* sich über Wasser halten; die Sache in Schwung halten. **2.** (Kaffee-, Tee)Kanne *f*; Kännchen *n*, Portion *f* (*Tee etc*). **3.** *Sport:* Pokal *m*. **4.** *Poker:* Pot *m*, Kasse *f*. **5.** F → **potbelly**. **6.** *sl.* Pot *n* (*Marihuana*). **II** *v/t* **7.** *Pflanze* eintopfen: **~ted plant** Topfpflanze *f*. **8.** *Fleisch* einmachen, *Fisch* einlegen. **9.** *Billard:* Br. einlochen. **10.** F *Kind* aufs Töpfchen.

po-ta-ble ['pəʊtəbl] *adj* trinkbar, Trink...

po-tas-si-um [pə'tæsɪəm] *s* 🜨 Kalium *n*. **~ cy-a-nide** *s* Zyankali *n*.

po-ta-to [pə'teɪtəʊ] *pl* **-toes** *s* Kartoffel *f*: **hot ~** F heißes Eisen. **~ bee-tle**, *bsd. Am.* **~ bug** *s zo.* Kartoffelkäfer *m.* **~ chips** *s pl Am.*, **~ crisps** *s pl Br.* Kartoffelchips *pl*. **~ sal-ad** *s* Kartoffelsalat *m.*

'pot|bel-ly *s* Schmerbauch *m*. **'~boil-er** *s contp.* rein kommerzielle Arbeit (*Buch etc*).

po-ten-cy ['pəʊtənsɪ] *s* **1.** Stärke *f*; Wirksamkeit *f*, Wirkung *f*. **2.** *physiol.* Potenz *f*. **'po-tent** *adj* □ **1.** stark (*Medikament etc*). **2.** *fig.* überzeugend, zwingend (*Argument etc*). **3.** *physiol.* potent. **po-ten-tate** ['~teɪt] *s* Potentat *m.* **po-ten-tial** [~'tenʃl] **I** *adj* **1.** potentiell, möglich. **II** *s* **2.** Potential *n*, Leistungsfähigkeit *f*: **have the ~ to be a top manager** das Zeug zu e-m Spitzenmanager haben. **3.** ⚡ Spannung *f*. **po-ten-tial-ly** [~'tenʃəlɪ] *adv* potentiell, möglicherweise.

'pot|hole *s mot.* Schlagloch *n*. **'~holed** *adj* voller Schlaglöcher.

po-tion ['pəʊʃn] *s* Trank *m.*

͵pot'luck *s:* **take ~** mit dem vorliebnehmen, was es gerade (*zu essen*) gibt; *fig.* es probieren. **~ plant** *s* Topfpflanze *f*.

pot-pour-ri [͵pəʊ'pʊərɪ] *s* ♪ Potpourri *n*, *fig. a.* Allerlei *n*, Kunterbunt *n*.

pot-ter¹ ['pɒtə] *v/i* **1.** schlendern. **2.** *a.* **~ about** (*od. around*) herumwerkeln, -hantieren.

pot-ter² [~] *s* Töpfer(in): **~'s wheel** Töpferscheibe *f*. **'pot-ter-y** *s* **1.** Töpferei *f*. **2.** Töpferware(n *pl*) *f*.

pot-ty¹ ['pɒtɪ] *adj bsd. Br.* F verrückt (*about* nach).

pot-ty² [~] *s* Töpfchen *n*. **'~-trained** *adj* sauber.

pouch [paʊtʃ] *s* Beutel *m* (*a. zo.*); *anat.* (Tränen)Sack *m*; *zo.* (Backen)Tasche *f*.

poul-tice ['pəʊltɪs] *s* 🌿 (warmer) (Senf- *etc*)Umschlag *od.* (-)Wickel.

poul-try ['pəʊltrɪ] *s* Geflügel *n*.

pounce [paʊns] **I** *v/i* sich stürzen (*on* auf *acc*) (*a. fig.*). **II** *s* Sprung *m*, Satz *m*.

pound¹ [paʊnd] *s* Pfund *n* (*Gewichts- u. Währungseinheit*): **by the ~** pfundweise; **five-~ note** Fünfpfundschein *m.*

pound² [~] *s* **1.** Tierheim *n*. **2.** Abstellplatz *m* für (polizeilich) abgeschleppte Fahrzeuge.

pound³ [~] **I** *v/t* **1.** zerstoßen, -stampfen (*to* zu). **2.** trommeln *od.* hämmern auf (*acc*) *od.* an (*acc*) *od.* gegen. **II** *v/i* **3.** hämmern (*with vor dat*) (*Herz*): **~ at** (*od. on*) → **2. 4.** stampfen.

pour [pɔː] **I** *v/t* **1.** gießen, schütten: **~ s.th. on o.s.** sich mit et. übergießen; **~ s.o. a cup of tea** j-m e-e Tasse Tee eingießen; **~ out** ausgießen-, -schütten; *Getränke* eingießen, -schenken; *fig.* Sorgen *etc* ausbreiten (*to* vor *dat*), *Herz* ausschütten (*to dat*). **II** *v/i* **2.** strömen (*a. fig.*). **3.** **it is ~ing down** (*od. ~ing with rain*) es gießt in Strömen; **in the ~ing rain** im strömenden Regen.

pout [paʊt] **I** *v/i* e-n Schmollmund machen *od.* ziehen; schmollen. **II** *v/t* Lippen schürzen. **III** *s* Schmollmund *m*; Schmollen *n*: **with a ~** schmollend; **be in a ~, have the ~s** schmollen.

pov-er-ty ['pɒvətɪ] *s* Armut *f* (*a. fig. of* an *dat*): **~ of ideas** Ideenarmut. **~ line** *s* Armutsgrenze *f*. **'~-strick-en** *adj* arm, notleidend.

pow-der ['paʊdə] **I** *s* **1.** (Back-, Schieß- *etc*)Pulver *n*. **2.** (Gesichts- *etc*)Puder *m.* **II** *v/t* **3.** pulverisieren: **~ed milk** Milchpulver *n*, Trockenmilch *f*; **~ed sugar** *Am.* Puderzucker *m.* **4.** *Baby etc* (ein-)

pudern, sich *die Nase etc* pudern: ~ **one's nose** *a. euphem.* mal verschwinden. ~ **keg** *s fig.* Pulverfaß *n.* ~ **puff** *s* Puderquaste *f.* ~ **room** *s* Damentoilette *f.*

pow·der·y ['paʊdərɪ] *adj* **1.** pulv(e)rig: ~ **snow** Pulverschnee *m.* **2.** (ein)gepudert.

pow·er ['paʊə] **I** *s* **1.** Kraft *f*, Macht *f*, Vermögen *n*: *do all in one's* ~ alles tun, was in s-r Macht steht; *it was out of* (*od. not* [*with*]*in, beyond*) *his* ~ es stand nicht in s-r Macht (*to do* zu tun). **2.** Kraft *f*, Energie *f*; *weitS.* Wucht *f*, Gewalt *f.* **3.** *mst pl* hypnotische *etc* Kräfte *pl*, geistige *etc* Fähigkeiten *pl*, (*Denk-, Konzentrations- etc*)Vermögen *n.* **4.** Macht *f*, Gewalt *f* (*over* über *acc*): *be in* ~ *pol.* an der Macht sein; *be in s.o.'s* ~ in j-s Gewalt sein; *come into* ~ *pol.* an die Macht kommen. **5.** *pol.* Gewalt *f* (*als Staatsfunktion*): → *separation* 2. **6.** *pol.*, *tž etc* (Amts)Gewalt *f*; Befugnis *f*: *give* (*have*) *full* ~*s* Vollmacht geben (haben); → *attorney* 2. **7.** *mst pl pol.* Macht *f* (*Staat*). **8.** Macht(faktor *m*) *f*, einflußreiche Stelle *od.* Person: *the* ~*s pl that be* F die *pl* da oben. **9.** *A* Potenz *f*: *raise to the third* ~ in die dritte Potenz erheben. **10.** *ℰ* Strom *m.* **II** *v/t* **11.** *☉* antreiben. '~**-as,sist·ed** *adj mot.* Servo... '~**-boat** *s* Rennboot *n.* ~ **brake** *s mot.* Servobremse *f.*

pow·er·ful ['paʊəfʊl] *adj* □ **1.** stark (*a. fig.*), kräftig. **2.** mächtig, einflußreich. '**pow·er·less** *adj* □ **1.** kraftlos. **2.** machtlos: *be* ~ *to do s.th.* nicht in der Lage sein, et. zu tun; *be* ~ *to prevent s.th.* nichts tun können, um et. zu verhindern.

pow·er| pack *s ℰ* Netzteil *n.* ~ **plant** → **power station.** ~ **point** *s ℰ Br.* Steckdose *f.* ~ **sta·tion** *s* Kraft-, Elektrizitätswerk *n.* ~ **steer·ing** *s mot.* Servolenkung *f.*

pow·wow ['paʊwaʊ] *s* F Besprechung *f.*

pox [pɒks] *s ♂* F Syph *f* (*Syphilis*).

prac·ti·ca·ble ['præktɪkəbl] *adj* □ **1.** durchführbar. **2.** passierbar (*Straße etc*).

prac·ti·cal ['præktɪkl] *adj* **1.** *allg.* praktisch: → *purpose* 1. **2.** praktisch denkend *od.* veranlagt. **3.** ~ *joke* Streich *m*: *play a* ~ *joke on s.o.* j-m e-n Streich

spielen. **prac·ti·cal·ly** ['~klɪ] *adv* praktisch, so gut wie.

prac·tice ['præktɪs] **I** *s* **1.** Praxis *f*: *in* ~ in der Praxis; *put in*(*to*) ~ in die Praxis umsetzen. **2.** Übung *f*: *in* (*out of*) ~ in (aus) der Übung; *keep in* ~ in der Übung bleiben; ~ *makes perfect* Übung macht den Meister. **3.** (*Arzt-etc*)Praxis *f.* **4.** Brauch *m*, Gewohnheit *f*: ~*s pl contp.* Praktiken *pl*; *it is common* ~ es ist allgemein üblich; *make it a* ~ es sich zur Gewohnheit machen (*to do* zu tun). **II** *adj* **5.** Übungs..., Probe... **III** *v/t u. v/i* **6.** *Am.* → *practise.*

prac·tise ['præktɪs] *bsd. Br.* **I** *v/t* **1.** *als Beruf* ausüben: ~ *law* (*medicine*) als Anwalt (Arzt) praktizieren. **2.** (ein)üben. **3.** *Grundsätze etc* praktizieren, *Geduld etc* üben. **II** *v/i* **4.** (*als Anwalt od. Arzt*) praktizieren: *practising Catholic* praktizierender Katholik. **5.** üben. **'prac·tised** *adj* **1.** geübt (*at, in* in *dat*): *be* ~ *at doing s.th.* darin geübt sein, et. zu tun. **2.** eingeübt, *contp. a.* gekünstelt.

prac·ti·tion·er [præk'tɪʃnə] *s*: *medical* ~ → **general practitioner.**

prag·mat·ic [præg'mætɪk] *adj* (~*ally*) pragmatisch. **prag·ma·tist** ['~mətɪst] *s* Pragmatiker(in).

prai·rie ['preərɪ] *s* Prärie *f.* ~ **schoon·er** *s hist. Am.* Planwagen *m.*

praise [preɪz] **I** *v/t* loben (*for* wegen): → *sky.* **II** *s* Lob *n.* '~**,wor·thy** *adj* □ lobenswert, löblich.

pram [præm] *s bsd. Br.* F Kinderwagen *m.*

prance [prɑːns] *v/i* **1.** tänzeln (*Pferd, Person*). **2.** stolzieren.

prank [præŋk] *s* Streich *m*: *play a* ~ *on s.o.* j-m e-n Streich spielen.

prate [preɪt] *v/i* schwafeln (*about, of* von).

prat·tle ['prætl] *v/i a.* ~ *on* plappern (*about* von).

prawn [prɔːn] *s zo.* Garnele *f.*

pray [preɪ] *v/i* beten (*to* zu; *for* für, um).

prayer [preə] *s* **1.** Gebet *n*: ~ *book* Gebetbuch *n*; ~ *mat* (*od. rug*) Gebetteppich *m.* **2.** *oft pl* Andacht *f.*

preach [priːtʃ] **I** *v/i* predigen (*to* zu, *dat*): ~ *to the converted fig.* offene Türen einrennen; ~ *at* (*od. to*) *s.o. fig.* j-m e-e Predigt halten (*about* wegen). **II** *v/t* predigen (*a. fig.*); *Predigt* halten. **'preach·er** *s* Prediger(in).

pre·am·ble [priː'æmbl] *s* Einleitung *f*, 🏛 Präambel *f* (**to** zu).

pre·ar·range [ˌpriːəˈreɪndʒ] *v/t* vorher abmachen *od.* vereinbaren.

pre·car·i·ous [prɪˈkeərɪəs] *adj* □ prekär, unsicher.

pre·cau·tion [prɪˈkɔːʃn] *s* Vorkehrung *f*, Vorsichtsmaßnahme *f* (**against** gegen): **as a ~** zur Vorsicht, vorsichtshalber. **pre'cau·tion·ar·y** *adj* vorbeugend, Vorsichts...

pre·cede [ˌpriːˈsiːd] *v/t* **1.** voraus-, vorangehen (*dat*). **2.** (den) Vorrang haben vor (*dat*). **3. ~ s.th. with** (*od.* **by**) **s.th.** et. mit et. einleiten, et. e-r Sache vorausschicken. **prec·e·dence** ['presɪdəns] *s* Vorrang *m*: **have** (*od.* **take**) **~ over →** **precede** 2; **give ~ to** (den) Vorrang geben (*dat*). **prec·e·dent** ['presɪdənt] *s* 🏛 Präzedenzfall *m* (*a. fig.*): **without ~** ohne Beispiel, noch nie dagewesen; **set a ~** e-n Präzedenzfall schaffen.

pre·cept ['priːsept] *s* Regel *f*, Richtlinie *f*.

pre·cinct ['priːsɪŋkt] *s* **1.** *pl* Gelände *n*; Umgebung *f*. **2.** (*Fußgänger*)Zone *f*, (*Einkaufs*)Viertel *n*. **3.** *Am.* (*Polizei*)Revier *m*; (*Wahl*)Bezirk *m*.

pre·cious ['preʃəs] **I** *adj* □ **1.** kostbar, wertvoll (*beide a. fig.*). **2.** Edel...: **~ stone**; **~ metals. II** *adv* **3. ~ little** F herzlich wenig.

prec·i·pice ['presɪpɪs] *s* Abgrund *m* (*a. fig.*).

pre·cip·i·tate [prɪˈsɪpɪteɪt] **I** *v/t* **1.** (hinunter-, herunter)schleudern; *fig.* stürzen (**into** in *acc*). **2.** *fig. Ereignis* beschleunigen. **3.** 🧪 ausfällen. **II** *v/i* **4.** 🧪 ausfallen. **III** *adj* [~tət] **5.** überstürzt. **IV** *s* **6.** 🧪 Niederschlag *m*. **pre·cip·i'ta·tion** *s* **1.** Überstürzung *f*. **2.** *meteor.* Niederschlag *m*. **3.** 🧪 Ausfällung *f*. **pre'cip·i·tous** *adj* □ **1.** steil (abfallend). **2.** *fig.* überstürzt.

pré·cis ['preɪsiː] **I** *pl* **-cis** [~siːz] *s* Zs.-fassung *f*. **II** *v/t* zs.-fassen.

pre·cise [prɪˈsaɪs] *adj* **1.** genau, präzis: **to be ~** genau gesagt. **2.** gewissenhaft. **pre'cise·ly** *adv* **1. ~ precise. 2. ~!** genau! **pre·ci·sion** [~ˈsɪʒn] **I** *s* Genauigkeit *f*, *a.* ⚙ Präzision *f*. **II** *adj* ⚙ Präzi-

sions..., Fein...: **~ instrument** Präzisionsinstrument *n*.

pre·clude [prɪˈkluːd] *v/t* **1.** et. ausschließen. **2. ~ s.o. from doing s.th.** j-n (daran) hindern, et. zu tun.

pre·co·cious [prɪˈkəʊʃəs] *adj* □ frühreif. **pre'co·cious·ness, pre·coc·i·ty** [~ˈkɒsətɪ] *s* Frühreife *f*.

pre·con·ceived [ˌpriːkənˈsiːvd] *adj* vorgefaßt. **pre·con·cep·tion** [~ˈsepʃn] *s* vorgefaßte Meinung (**about** über *acc*).

pre·con·di·tion [ˌpriːkənˈdɪʃn] *s* Vorausbedingung *f*, Voraussetzung *f*.

pre·cook [ˌpriːˈkʊk] *v/t* vorkochen.

pre·cur·sor [ˌpriːˈkɜːsə] *s* (**of, to** *gen*) **1.** Vorläufer *m*. **2.** Vorbote *m*.

pred·a·to·ry ['predətərɪ] *adj* räuberisch: **~ animal** Raubtier *n*.

pre·de·ces·sor ['priːdɪsesə] *s* Vorgänger(in): **~ in office** Amtsvorgänger(in).

pre·des·ti·na·tion [priːˌdestɪˈneɪʃn] *s* *eccl. u. weitS.* Prädestination *f*, Vorherbestimmung *f*. **pre·des·tined** *adj* prädestiniert, vorherbestimmt (**to** für, zu): **be ~ to failure** (*od.* **fail**) von vornherein) zum Scheitern verurteilt sein; **he was ~ to do s.th.** es war ihm vorherbestimmt, et. zu tun.

pre·de·ter·mine [ˌpriːdɪˈtɜːmɪn] *v/t* **1.** vorherbestimmen. **2. → prearrange.**

pre·dic·a·ment [prɪˈdɪkəmənt] *s* mißliche Lage, Zwangslage *f*.

pred·i·cate ['predɪkət] *s ling.* Prädikat *n*, Satzaussage *f*. **pred·i·ca·tive** [prɪˈdɪkətɪv] *adj* □ prädikativ.

pre·dict [prɪˈdɪkt] *v/t* vorher-, voraussagen. **pre'dic·tion** *s* Vorher-, Voraussage *f*: **against all ~s** entgegen allen Voraussagen.

pre·di·lec·tion [ˌpriːdɪˈlekʃn] *s* Vorliebe *f* (**for** für).

pre·dis·pose [ˌpriːdɪˈspəʊz] *v/t* **1.** geneigt machen, einnehmen (**in favo[u]r of** für). **2.** *bsd.* 🩺 anfällig machen (**to** für). **'pre·dis·po·si·tion** [~pəˈzɪʃn] *s* (**to**) Neigung *f* (zu), *bsd.* 🩺 *a.* Anfälligkeit *f* (für).

pre·dom·i·nant [prɪˈdɒmɪnənt] *adj* □ (vor)herrschend, überwiegend. **pre·dom·i·nate** [~neɪt] *v/i* **1.** vorherrschen, -wiegen, überwiegen. **2.** überlegen sein;

die Oberhand *od.* das Übergewicht haben (*over* über *acc*).

pre·em·i·nent [ˌpriːˈemɪnənt] *adj* □ hervor-, überragend.

pre·emp·tive [ˌpriːˈemptɪv] *adj* **1.** *~ right* Vorkaufsrecht *n.* **2.** *~ strike* ✕ Präventivschlag *m.*

preen [priːn] *v/t* sich, *das Gefieder putzen* (*Vogel*): *~ o.s.* sich herrichten (*Person*).

pre·fab [ˈpriːfæb] *s* F Fertighaus *n.* ˌpre·ˈfab·ri·cate [ˌ~rɪkeɪt] *v/t* vorfabrizieren, -fertigen: *~d house* Fertighaus *n.*

pref·ace [ˈprefɪs] **I** *s* Vorwort *n* (*to* zu). **II** *v/t* *Rede, Buch etc* einleiten (*with* mit).

pre·fer [prɪˈfɜː] *v/t* vorziehen (*to* *dat*), lieber mögen (*als*), bevorzugen: *I ~ meat to fish* Fleisch ist mir lieber als Fisch; *~ listening to talking* lieber zuhören als reden; *I'd ~ to stay at home* ich bliebe lieber zu Hause; *I'd ~ you not to go* es wäre mir lieber, wenn du nicht gingst. **pref·er·a·ble** [ˈprefərəbl] *adj*: *be ~* (*to*) vorzuziehen sein (*dat*), besser sein (als). **'pref·er·a·bly** *adv* vorzugsweise, lieber, am liebsten. **'pref·er·ence** *s* **1.** Bevorzugung *f*, Vorzug *m*: *give s.o. ~* (*over*) j-m den Vorzug geben (gegenüber); *what is your ~?* was möchtest du lieber? **2.** Vorliebe *f* (*for* für). **pref·er·en·tial** [ˌ~ˈrenʃl] *adj* □ bevorzugt, Vorzugs...

pre·fix I *s* [ˈpriːfɪks] **1.** *ling.* Präfix *n*, Vorsilbe *f*. **II** *v/t* [ˌpriːˈfɪks] **2.** *ling.* *e-m Wort* e-e Vorsilbe voranstellen. **3.** *Bemerkung etc* voranstellen (*to* *dat*).

preg·nan·cy [ˈpregnənsɪ] *s* Schwangerschaft *f*; *zo.* Trächtigkeit *f*: *~ test* Schwangerschaftstest *m.* **'preg·nant** *adj* □ schwanger; *zo.* trächtig: *she's four months ~* sie ist im vierten Monat schwanger; *~ with meaning fig.* bedeutungsschwer, -voll.

pre·heat [ˌpriːˈhiːt] *v/t* Bratröhre vorheizen.

pre·his·tor·ic [ˌpriːhɪˈstɒrɪk] *adj* (*~ally*) prähistorisch, vorgeschichtlich.

pre·judge [ˌpriːˈdʒʌdʒ] *v/t* j-n vorverurteilen: *~ the issue* sich vorschnell e-e Meinung bilden.

prej·u·dice [ˈpredʒʊdɪs] **I** *s* **1.** Vorurteil *n*, Voreingenommenheit *f*, *bsd.* ✖ Befangenheit *f*: *have a ~ against* Vorurteile haben *od.* voreingenommen sein

gegen. **2.** *to the ~ of* zum Nachteil *od.* Schaden (*gen*); *without ~ to bsd.* ✖ unbeschadet. **II** *v/t* **3.** einnehmen (*in favo[u]r of* für; *against* gegen): *~d* (vor)eingenommen, *bsd.* ✖ befangen. **4.** schaden (*dat*), beeinträchtigen. **prej·u·di·cial** [ˌ~ˈdɪʃl] *adj* □ (*to*) abträglich (*dat*), schädlich (für): *be ~ to → prejudice* 4; *~ to health* gesundheitsschädlich.

pre·lim·i·nar·y [prɪˈlɪmɪnərɪ] **I** *adj* Vor...: *~ discussion* Vorbesprechung *f*; *~ measures pl* vorbereitende Maßnahmen *pl*; *~ round* (*Sport*) Vorrunde *f*. **II** *s pl* Vorbereitungen *pl*, vorbereitende Maßnahmen *pl*.

prel·ude [ˈpreljuːd] *s* ♪ Vorspiel *n* (*to* zu) (*a. fig.*); Präludium *n.*

pre·mar·i·tal [ˌpriːˈmærɪtl] *adj* □ vorehelich.

pre·ma·ture [ˈpremətjʊə] *adj* □ **1.** vorzeitig, verfrüht: *be four weeks ~* vier Wochen zu früh auf die Welt kommen; *~ baby* Frühgeburt *f*. **2.** *fig.* voreilig.

pre·med·i·tat·ed [ˌpriːˈmedɪteɪtɪd] *adj* vorsätzlich. **pre·med·i·ta·tion** *s* Vorsatz *m*: *with ~* vorsätzlich.

pre·mi·er [ˈpremjə] *s* Premier(minister) *m.*

prem·i·ere, prem·i·ère [ˈpremɪeə] **I** *s* Premiere *f*, Ur-, Erstaufführung *f*. **II** *v/t* ur-, erstaufführen.

prem·is·es [ˈpremɪsɪz] *s pl* Gelände *n*, Grundstück *n*; Räumlichkeiten *pl*, (*Geschäfts*)Räume *pl*: *on the ~* an Ort u. Stelle, im Haus *od.* Lokal.

pre·mi·um [ˈpriːmjəm] *s* **1.** Prämie *f*, Bonus *m*: *be at a ~ fig.* hoch im Kurs stehen; *put a ~ on fig.* sehr viel Wert legen auf (*acc*); fördern. **2.** *mot. Am.* F Super *n.* **~ gas·o·line** *s mot. Am.* Superbenzin *n.*

pre·mo·ni·tion [ˌpreməˈnɪʃn] *s* (böse) Vorahnung.

pre·na·tal [ˌpriːˈneɪtl] → **antenatal**.

pre·oc·cu·pa·tion [priːˌɒkjʊˈpeɪʃn] *s* Beschäftigung *f* (*with* mit): *he's got so many ~s that* er hat so viele Dinge im Kopf, daß. **pre·ˈoc·cu·pied** [~paɪd] *adj* gedankenverloren, geistesabwesend. **pre·ˈoc·cu·py** [~paɪ] *v/t* (stark) beschäftigen.

pre·or·dain [ˌpriːɔːˈdeɪn] *v/t* vorherbestimmen: *his success was ~ed, he*

presentation

was ~ed to succeed sein Erfolg war ihm vorherbestimmt.

prep [prep] *s Br.* F Hausaufgabe(n *pl*) *f*: *do one's ~* s-e Hausaufgaben machen.

pre·paid [ˌpriːˈpeɪd] *adj* 🏵 frankiert, freigemacht: *~ envelope* Freiumschlag *m*.

prep·a·ra·tion [ˌprepəˈreɪʃn] *s* **1.** Vorbereitung *f (for* auf *acc*, für): *be in ~* in Vorbereitung sein; *make ~s* Vorbereitungen treffen. **2.** Zubereitung *f.* **3.** 🏵, 🏵 Präparat *n*.

pre·par·a·to·ry [prɪˈpærətərɪ] *adj* □ **1.** vorbereitend, Vor(bereitungs)... **2.** *~ to* vor *(dat)*: *~ to doing s.th.* bevor od. ehe man et. tut. *~ school s Br. private Vorbereitungsschule auf das College; Am. private Vorbereitungsschule auf die High-School.*

pre·pare [prɪˈpeə] I *v/t* **1.** Fest, Rede etc vorbereiten; *j-n (a. seelisch)* vorbereiten *(for* auf *acc*): *~ o.s.* für et. gefaßt machen auf. **2.** anfertigen; Speise etc zubereiten. II *v/i* **3.** *~ for* sich vorbereiten auf *(acc)*; Vorbereitungen treffen für; sich gefaßt machen auf *(acc)*. **pre'pared** *adj* **1.** vorbereitet *(Erklärung etc)*. **2.** bereit, gewillt *(to do* zu tun). **3.** gefaßt, vorbereitet *(for* auf *acc*; *to do* darauf, zu tun). **pre'pared·ness** *s* Bereitschaft *f*.

pre·pon·der·ance [prɪˈpɒndərəns] *s fig.* Übergewicht *n.* **pre'pon·der·ant** *adj* □ überwiegend: *be ~ → preponderate.* **pre'pon·der·ate** [ˌ~reɪt] *v/i* überwiegen; überlegen sein *(over dat)*.

prep·o·si·tion [ˌprepəˈzɪʃn] *s ling.* Präposition *f*, Verhältniswort *n*.

pre·pos·sess [ˌpriːpəˈzes] *v/t*: *be ~ed by* eingenommen sein von. **ˌpre·pos'sess·ing** *adj* □ einnehmend.

pre·pos·ter·ous [prɪˈpɒstərəs] *adj* □ **1.** absurd. **2.** lächerlich, lachhaft.

prep school F → *preparatory school.*

pre·puce [ˈpriːpjuːs] *s anat.* Vorhaut *f*.

pre·re·cord·ed [ˌpriːrɪˈkɔːdɪd] *adj* bespielt *(Musik-, Videokassette)*.

pre·req·ui·site [ˌpriːˈrekwɪzɪt] *s* Vorbedingung *f*, Voraussetzung *f (for, of, to* für).

pre·rog·a·tive [prɪˈrɒgətɪv] *s* Vorrecht *n*.

Pres·by·te·ri·an [ˌprezbɪˈtɪərɪən] I *adj* presbyterianisch. II *s* Presbyterianer (-in).

pre·school [ˌpriːˈskuːl] *adj* vorschulisch:

of ~ age im Vorschulalter; *~ child* Vorschulkind *n.*

pre·scribe [prɪˈskraɪb] *v/t* **1.** et. vorschreiben. **2.** 🏵 *j-m* et. verschreiben, -ordnen *(for* gegen).

pre·scrip·tion [prɪˈskrɪpʃn] *s* **1.** Vorschrift *f.* **2.** 🏵 verordnete Medizin; Rezept *n: available only on ~* rezeptpflichtig. *~ charge s* Rezeptgebühr *f.*

pres·ence [ˈprezns] *s* Gegenwart *f*, Anwesenheit *f: in the ~ of* in Gegenwart od. in Anwesenheit od. im Beisein von *(od. gen)*, vor *Zeugen; make one's ~ felt n.* sich bemerkbar od. sich aufmerksam machen; *~ of mind* Geistesgegenwart *f.*

pres·ent¹ [ˈpreznt] I *adj* (□ → *present·ly*) **1.** anwesend *(at* bei); vorhanden: → *company* 2. **2.** gegenwärtig, jetzig, derzeitig: *at the ~ moment* zum gegenwärtigen Zeitpunkt; *in the ~ case* im vorliegenden Fall. **3.** *ling. ~ participle* Partizip *n* Präsens, Mittelwort *n* der Gegenwart; *~ perfect* Perfekt *n*, zweite Vergangenheit; *~ tense* Präsens *n*, Gegenwart *f.* II *s* **4.** Gegenwart *f, ling. a.* Präsens *n: at ~* gegenwärtig, zur Zeit; *for the ~* vorerst, -läufig, einstweilen.

pre·sent² [prɪˈzent] *v/t* **1.** präsentieren *(to dat)*: a) (über)reichen, (-)bringen, (-)geben: *~ s.th. to s.o.*, *~ s.o. with s.th.* a. j-m et. schenken, überbringen, -legen, unterbreiten, c) zeigen, vorführen, *thea.* etc aufführen, d) schildern, darstellen, e) *j-n, Produkt etc* vorstellen, f) *Programm etc* moderieren. **2.** Sicht, Ziel, Möglichkeit etc bieten, Schwierigkeit etc darstellen, bieten: *if the chance ~s itself* wenn sich die Chance bietet; *this ~s no problem (to him)* das ist kein Problem (für ihn). **3.** *~ o.s.* sich einfinden *(Person)*; *~ itself* sich einstellen *(Gedanke etc)*.

pres·ent³ [ˈpreznt] *s* Geschenk *n: make s.o. a ~ of s.th.* j-m et. schenken *(a. fig.)*.

pre·sent·a·ble [prɪˈzentəbl] *adj* □ vorzeigbar *(Person)*: *be ~* sich sehen lassen können *(a. Sache); make o.s. ~* sich zurechtmachen.

pres·en·ta·tion [ˌprezənˈteɪʃn] *s* Präsentation *f*: a) Überreichung *f*, -gabe *f*, b) Unterbreitung *f*, c) Vorführung *f*, *thea.* etc Aufführung *f*, d) Schilderung *f*,

Darstellung *f,* e) Vorstellung *f,* f) *Rundfunk, TV:* Moderation *f.*

pres·ent-'day *adj* heutig, gegenwärtig.

pre·sent·er [prɪ'zentə] *s* Rundfunk, *TV: Br.* Moderator(in).

pre·sen·ti·ment [prɪ'zentɪmənt] *s* (böse) Vorahnung.

pres·ent·ly ['prezntlɪ] *adv* **1.** ın Kürze, bald. **2.** *bsd. Am.* gegenwärtig, derzeit.

pres·er·va·tion [,prezə'veɪʃn] *s* **1.** Bewahrung *f;* Erhaltung *f: in a good state of ~* gut erhalten; *there is a ~ order on this building bsd. Br.* dieses Gebäude steht unter Denkmalschutz. **2.** Konservierung *f.* **pre·serv·a·tive** [prɪ'zɜːvətɪv] *s* Konservierungsmittel *n.*

pre·serve [prɪ'zɜːv] **I** *v/t* **1.** bewahren, (be)schützen (*from* vor *dat*). **2.** bewahren, erhalten. **3.** konservieren, *Obst etc* einmachen, -kochen. **II** *s* **4.** *mst pl* Eingemachte *n: strawberry ~s* eingemachte Erdbeeren *pl.* **5.** (*Jagd*)Revier *n.* **6.** *fig.* Revier *n,* Ressort *n.*

pre·side [prɪ'zaɪd] *v/i* den Vorsitz führen *od.* haben (*at, over* bei): *~ at a meeting a.* e-e Versammlung leiten.

pres·i·den·cy ['prezɪdənsɪ] *s pol.* Präsidentschaft *f;* Amtszeit *f* (*e-s Präsidenten*). **'pres·i·dent** *s* **1.** Präsident(in) (*a. pol.*). **2.** Vorsitzende *m, f.* **3.** *univ. bsd. Am.* Rektor(in). **pres·i·den·tial** [,~'denʃl] *adj pol.* Präsidenten..., Präsidentschafts...

press [pres] **I** *v/t* **1.** drücken, pressen: *~ s.o.'s hand* j-m die Hand drücken. **2.** drücken auf (*e-n Knopf etc*), *Pedal etc* niederdrücken. **3.** *Frucht* (aus)pressen. **4.** *Schallplatte* pressen. **5.** bügeln; *Blumen* pressen. **6.** (*zurück- etc*)drängen: *~ back.* **7.** *j-n* (be)drängen (*to do* zu tun): *be ~ed for time* unter Zeitdruck stehen, in Zeitnot sein. **8.** *~ s.th. on s.o.* j-m et. aufdrängen *od.* -nötigen. **9.** bestehen auf (*dat*): *~ the point* darauf bestehen; *home Forderung etc* durchsetzen; *Vorteil* ausnützen. **II** *v/i* **10.** drücken. **11.** drängen (*Zeit etc*): *~ for* drängen auf (*acc*). **12.** (sich) (*vorwärts- etc*)drängen: *~ forward, ~ on* (*od. ahead*) *fig.* weitermachen (*with* mit). **III** *s* **13.** (*Frucht etc*)Presse *f;* Spanner *m* (*für Tennisschläger etc*). **14.** (*Druck*)Presse *f: be in (the) ~* in Druck sein; *go to ~* in Druck gehen. **15.** *give s.th. a ~* et.

drücken. **16.** Presse *f: have a good (bad) ~* e-e gute (schlechte) Presse haben. *~ a·gen·cy s* Presseagentur *f.* *~ box s* Pressetribüne *f: in the ~* auf der Pressetribüne. *~ card s* Presseausweis *m.* *~ clip·ping s bsd. Am.* Zeitungsausschnitt *m.* *~ con·fer·ence s* Pressekonferenz *f: at a ~* auf e-r Pressekonferenz. *~ cut·ting s bsd. Br.* Zeitungsausschnitt *m.* *~ gal·ler·y s parl.* Pressetribüne *f: in the ~* auf der Pressetribüne.

press·ing ['presɪŋ] *adj* □ **1.** dringend. **2.** eindringlich.

press| pho·tog·ra·pher *s* Pressefotograf(in). *~ stud s bsd. Br.* Druckknopf *m.* *'~-up s* Liegestütz *m: do a ~* e-n Liegestütz machen.

pres·sure ['preʃə] **I** *s phys.,* ⚙, *etc* Druck *m: under ~ fig.* unter Druck; *bring ~ to bear on, put ~ on fig.* Druck ausüben auf (*acc*); *work at high ~ fig.* mit Hochdruck arbeiten. **II** *v/t bsd. Am.* → *pressurize* 2. *~ cab·in s* ✈ Druck(ausgleichs)kabine *f.* *~ cook·er s* Schnellkochtopf *m.* *~ group s pol.* Interessengruppe *f.* *'~-,sen·si·tive adj* □ 🖋 *etc* druckempfindlich.

pres·sur·ize ['preʃəraɪz] *v/t* **1.** *~d cabin* → *pressure cabin.* **2.** *fig. bsd. Br.* j-n unter Druck setzen (*to do s.th.* damit er et. tut): *~ s.o. into doing sth.* j-n so lange unter Druck setzen, bis er et. tut.

pres·tige [pre'stiːʒ] *s* Prestige *n,* Ansehen *n.* **pres·tig·ious** [pre'stɪdʒəs] *adj* □ renommiert.

pres·to ['prestəʊ] *adv: hey ~* Hokuspokus (Fidibus).

pre·sum·a·ble [prɪ'zjuːməbl] *adj* □ vermutlich. **pre'sume** **I** *v/t* **1.** annehmen, vermuten. **2.** sich erdreisten *od.* anmaßen (*to do* zu tun). **II** *v/i* **3.** → 1. **4.** anmaßend *od.* aufdringlich sein: *~ on et.* ausnützen *od.* mißbrauchen. **pre'sum·ing** *adj* □ anmaßend.

pre·sump·tion [prɪ'zʌmpʃn] *s* **1.** Annahme *f,* Vermutung *f.* **2.** Anmaßung *f.* **pre'sump·tu·ous** [~tʃʊəs] *adj* □ anmaßend.

pre·sup·pose [,priːsə'pəʊz] *v/t* voraussetzen (*that* daß). **pre·sup·po·si·tion** [,~sʌpə'zɪʃn] *s* Voraussetzung *f.*

pre·tence [prɪ'tens] *s* **1.** Heuchelei *f,* Verstellung *f: his friendliness is only ~* s-e Freundlichkeit ist nur gespielt;

make a ~ *of doing s.th.* so tun, als tue man et. **2. *under false*** ~*s* unter falschen Voraussetzungen. **3.** Anspruch *m* (*to* auf *acc*): *make no* ~ *to* keinen Anspruch erheben auf. **pre·tend** [prɪ'tend] **I** *v/t* **1.** vorgeben, -schützen, -täuschen; ~ *sleep* (*od. to be asleep*) sich schlafend stellen. **2.** behaupten (*to do* zu tun). **II** *v/i* **3.** sich verstellen: *he's only* ~*ing* er tut nur so. **4.** Anspruch erheben (*to* auf *acc*). **pre'tend·ed** *adj* vorgetäuscht, gespielt.

pre·tense *Am.* → **pretence**.

pre·ten·sion [prɪ'tenʃn] *s* **1.** *oft pl* Anspruch *m* (*to* auf *acc*): *make no* ~*s to* keinen Anspruch erheben auf. **2.** Anmaßung *f*.

pre·ten·tious [prɪ'tenʃəs] *adj* □ anmaßend. **pre'ten·tious·ness** *s* Anmaßung *f*.

pret·er·ite ['pretərət] *s ling.* Präteritum *n*, (erste) Vergangenheit.

pre·text ['priːtekst] *s* Vorwand *m*: *on* (*od. under*) *the* ~ unter dem Vorwand (*of doing* zu tun).

pret·ty ['prɪtɪ] **I** *adj* □ hübsch, *iro. a.* schön: ~ *penny*. **II** *adv* **F** ziemlich, ganz schön; ~ *cold*; ~ *good* recht *od.* ganz gut; ~ *much the same thing* so ziemlich dasselbe; *be sitting* ~ **F** (*finanziell etc*) gut dastehen.

pre·vail [prɪ'veɪl] *v/i* **1.** vorherrschen, weit verbreitet sein. **2.** (*over, against*) siegen (über *acc*), sich durchsetzen (gegen). **3.** ~ *on s.o. to do s.th.* j-n dazu bewegen, et. zu tun. **pre'vail·ing** *adj* (vor)herrschend.

prev·a·lence ['prevələns] *s* Vorherrschen *n*, weite Verbreitung. **'prev·a·lent** *adj* □ vorherrschend, weitverbreitet.

pre·var·i·cate [prɪ'værɪkeɪt] *v/i* Ausflüchte machen. **pre,var·i'ca·tion** *s* Ausflucht *f*.

pre·vent [prɪ'vent] *v/t* **1.** verhindern, -hüten, *e-r Sache* vorbeugen. **2.** (*from*) j-n hindern (an *dat*), abhalten (von): ~ *s.o.* (*from*) *doing s.th.* j-n (daran) hindern *od.* davon abhalten, et. zu tun. **pre'ven·tion** *s* (*of*) Verhinderung *f*, -hütung *f* (von), Vorbeugung *f* (gegen): ~ *of accidents* Unfallverhütung; ~ *is better than cure* Vorbeugen ist besser

als Heilen. **pre'ven·tive** *adj* vorbeugend.

pre·view ['priːvjuː] *s* **1.** *Film, TV:* Voraufführung *f*; Vorbesichtigung *f* (*e-r Ausstellung etc*), *paint.* Vernissage *f*. **2.** *Film, TV, a. allg.* Vorschau *f* (*of* auf *acc*).

pre·vi·ous ['priːvjəs] *adj* **1.** vorher-, vorausgehend, vorherig: ~ *conviction* ⚖ Vorstrafe *f*; *have a* ~ *conviction* vorbestraft sein; *on the* ~ *day* am Tag davor, am Vortag; *on a* ~ *occasion* bei e-r früheren Gelegenheit; ~ *owner* Vorbesitzer(in). **2.** ~ *to* vor (*dat*): ~ *to doing s.th.* bevor man et. tut. **'pre·vi·ous·ly** *adv* vorher, früher.

pre·war [ˌpriː'wɔː] *adj* Vorkriegs...

prey [preɪ] **I** *s* Beute *f*, Opfer *n* (*e-s Raubtiers; a. fig.*): *be easy* ~ *for* (*od. to*) *e-s* leichte Beute sein für; → *beast* 1, *bird* 1. **II** *v/i*: ~ *on* a) *zo.* Jagd machen auf (*acc*), b) *fig.* nagen an (*dat*): ~ *on s.o.'s mind* j-m keine Ruhe lassen, c) *fig.* j-n ausnehmen.

price [praɪs] **I** *s* **1.** Preis *m* (*a. fig.*), (*Börse*) Kurs *m*: *what is the* ~ *of ...?* was *od.* wieviel kostet ...?; *at the* ~ *of* zum Preis von; *at a ... price* zu e-m *günstigen etc* Preis; *at a* ~ für entsprechendes Geld; (*not*) *at any* ~ *bsd. fig.* um jeden (keinen) Preis; *be above* (*od. beyond, without*) ~ *fig.* unbezahlbar sein; *pay a high* ~ *for fig.* e-n hohen Preis bezahlen für; *put a* ~ *on s.o.'s head* e-n Preis auf j-s Kopf aussetzen. **2.** *Wetten:* Quote *f*. **II** *v/t* **3.** den Preis festsetzen für; auszeichnen (*at* mit). **4.** **F** nach dem Preis (*gen*) fragen. **'~·con·scious** *adj* □ preisbewußt. **'~·con,trolled** *adj* preisgebunden. **~ cut** *s* Preissenkung *f*. **~ freeze** *s* Preisstopp *m*.

price·less ['praɪslɪs] *adj* unbezahlbar (*a. fig.*).

price| list *s* Preisliste *f*. **~ range** *s* Preisklasse *f*, -kategorie *f*. **~ tag**, **~ tick·et** *s* Preisschild *n*.

price·y ['praɪsɪ] *adj* **F** teuer.

prick [prɪk] **I** *s* **1.** (*Insekten-, Nadel- etc*) Stich *m*; Einstich *m*, stechender Schmerz, Stich *m*: ~*s pl of conscience fig.* Gewissensbisse *pl.* **3.** V Schwanz *m* (*Penis*). **4.** *fig.* V Arschloch *n.* **II** *v/t* **5.** (an-, auf-, durch)stechen, stechen in (*acc*): ~ *one's finger* sich in den Finger

stechen (**on** an *dat*; **with** mit); **his con-science** ~**ed him** *fig.* er hatte Gewissensbisse. **6.** prickeln auf *od.* in (*dat*). **7.** ~ **up one's ears** die Ohren spitzen (*a. fig.*). **III** *v/i* **8.** stechen (*a. schmerzen*).
prick·le ['prɪkl] **I** *s* **1.** Stachel *m*, ୧ *a.* Dorn *m.* **2.** Prickeln *n*, Kribbeln *n.* **II** *v/i* **3.** prickeln, kribbeln. '**prick·ly** *adj* **1.** stach(e)lig, ୧ *a.* dornig. **2.** prickelnd, kribbelnd. **3.** *fig.* unangenehm.
'**pric·y** → **pricey**.
pride [praɪd] **I** *s* Stolz *m* (*a. Gegenstand des Stolzes*); *b.s.* Hochmut *m*: **take (a)** ~ **in** → II. **II** *v/t*: ~ **o.s. on** stolz sein auf (*acc*).
priest [priːst] *s eccl.* Priester *m.* '**priest·hood** ['~hʊd] *s* **1.** Priesteramt *n*, -würde *f.* **2.** *coll.* Priesterschaft *f.* '**priest·ly** *adj* priesterlich.
prig [prɪg] *s* Tugendbold *m.* '**prig·gish** *adj* □ tugendhaft.
prim [prɪm] *adj* □ *a.* ~ **and proper** etepetete; prüde.
pri·ma·cy ['praɪməsɪ] *s* Vorrang *m* (**over** vor *dat*); Vorrangstellung *f.*
pri·mae·val *bsd. Br.* → **primeval**.
pri·mal ['praɪml] *adj* **1.** ursprünglich, Ur... **2.** → **primary** 1.
pri·ma·ri·ly ['praɪmərəlɪ] *adv* in erster Linie, vor allem. '**pri·ma·ry** **I** *adj* **1.** wichtigst, Haupt...: ~ **accent** (*od.* **stress**) *ling.* Hauptakzent *m*; **of** ~ **importance** von höchster Wichtigkeit. **2.** Anfangs..., Ur... **3.** grundlegend, elementar, Grund...: ~ **colo(u)r** Grundfarbe *f.* **II** *s* **4.** *pol. Am.* Vorwahl *f.*
prime [praɪm] **I** *adj* □ **1.** wichtigst, Haupt...: **of** ~ **importance** von höchster Wichtigkeit; ~ **minister** Premierminister(in), Ministerpräsident(in); ~ **mover** ۞ Kraft-, Antriebsmaschine *f*; *fig.* treibende Kraft; ~ **suspect** Hauptverdächtige(r) *m, f*; ~ **time** *TV* Hauptsendezeit *f.* **2.** erstklassig: **in** ~ **condition** in Bestzustand. **3.** ~ **number** → 5. **II** *s* **4.** **in the** ~ **of life** in der Blüte s-r Jahre; **be past one's** ~ s-e besten Jahre hinter sich haben; (*Künstler etc*) den Zenit überschritten haben. **5.** ♣ Primzahl *f.* **III** *v/t* **6.** grundieren. **7.** *j-n* instruieren, vorbereiten.
prim·er¹ ['praɪmə] *s* **1.** Grundierfarbe *f*, -lack *m.* ✕ *etc* Zünder *m.*
prim·er² [~] *s* Fibel *f.*

pri·me·val [praɪ'miːvl] *adj* □ urzeitlich, Ur...: ~ **forest** Urwald *m.*
prim·i·tive ['prɪmɪtɪv] *adj* □ primitiv (*a. contp.*).
pri·mor·di·al [praɪ'mɔːdjəl] *adj* □ uranfänglich, ursprünglich.
prim·rose *s* ♣ Primel *f*, *bsd.* Schlüsselblume *f.*
prim·u·la ['prɪmjʊlə] *s* ♣ Primel *f.*
prince [prɪns] *s* **1.** Fürst *m.* **2.** Prinz *m*: ~ **Charming** *fig.* Märchenprinz; → **consort.** '**prince·ly** *adj* fürstlich (*a. fig.*). **prin·cess** [~'ses, *vor npr* '~ses] *s* **1.** Fürstin *f.* **2.** Prinzessin *f.*
prin·ci·pal ['prɪnsəpl] **I** *adj* (□ → **principally**) **1.** wichtigst, hauptsächlich, Haupt...: ~ **character** Hauptfigur *f*, -person *f* (*e-s Romans etc*); ~ **parts** *pl ling.* Stammformen *pl* (*e-s Verbs*). **II** *s* **2.** *ped.* Rektor(in). **3.** *thea.* Hauptdarsteller(in); ♪ Solist(in).
prin·ci·pal·i·ty [ˌprɪnsɪ'pælətɪ] *s* Fürstentum *n.*
prin·ci·pal·ly ['prɪnsəplɪ] *adv* in erster Linie, hauptsächlich.
prin·ci·ple ['prɪnsəpl] *s* **1.** Prinzip *n*, Grundsatz *m*: **man of** ~**s** Mann *m* mit Grundsätzen; **in** ~ im Prinzip, an sich; **on** ~ prinzipiell, grundsätzlich; ~ **of efficiency** Leistungsprinzip. **2.** *phys. etc* Prinzip *n*, (Natur)Gesetz *n.*
print [prɪnt] **I** *v/t* **1.** *typ.* drucken: ~**ed matter** ۞ Drucksache *f.* **2.** *Rede etc* abdrucken. **3.** *Stoff etc* bedrucken. **4.** in Druckbuchstaben schreiben: ~**ed characters** *pl* Druckbuchstaben *pl.* **5.** *a.* ~ **off** *phot.* abziehen; ~ **out** ausdrucken (*Computer*). **II** *v/i* **6.** *typ.* drucken. **7.** **be** ~**ing** im Druck sein. **III** *v/s* **8.** (*Finger- etc*)Abdruck *m.* **9.** *typ.* Druck *m*: **out of** ~ vergriffen; **in** ~ gedruckt; ~ **run** Auflage *f.* **10.** Gedruckte *n*: → **small** I. **11.** *Kunst*: Druck *m*; *phot.* Abzug *m.* '**print·a·ble** *adj* druckfähig, -reif. '**print·er** *s* Drucker *m* (*a. Gerät*): ~**'s error** Druckfehler *m*; ~**'s ink** Druckerschwärze *f.* '**print·ing** *s* **1.** *typ.* Drucken *n*: ~ **ink** Druckerschwärze *f*; ~ **press** Druck(er)presse *f*; ~ **works** *pl* (*oft sg konstruiert*) Druckerei *f.* **2.** Auflage *f.*
'**print·out** *s* Computer: Ausdruck *m.*
pri·or ['praɪə] *adj* **1.** vorherig, früher. **2.** vorrangig. **3.** ~ **to** vor (*dat*). **pri·or·i·tize** [~'ɒrɪtaɪz] *v/t* den Vorrang geben

(*dat*), vorrangig behandeln. **pri'or·i·ty** *s* **1.** Priorität *f*, Vorrang *m*: *give* ~ *to* → *prioritize*; *have* (*od.* *take*) ~ den Vorrang haben (*over* vor *dat*), vorgehen. **2.** vordringliche *od.* vorrangige Sache: *a top* ~ e-e Angelegenheit von äußerster Dringlichkeit. **3.** *mot.* Vorfahrt *f*: *have* ~.

prise *bsd. Br.* → **prize²**.

prism ['prɪzəm] *s* ℞, *phys. etc* Prisma *n*. **pris·mat·ic** [ˌ~'mætɪk] *adj* (**~ally**) prismatisch, Prismen...

pris·on ['prɪzn] *s* Gefängnis *n*: *be in* ~ im Gefängnis sein *od.* sitzen, einsitzen; ~ *cell* Gefängniszelle *f*; ~ *sentence* Gefängnis-, Freiheitsstrafe *f*. **'pris·on·er** *s* Gefangene *m*, *f*, Häftling *m*: *hold* (*od.* *keep*) ~ gefangenhalten; *take* ~ gefangennehmen; ~ *of war* Kriegsgefangene; → *bar* 8.

pris·sy ['prɪsɪ] *adj* □ F etepetete, zimperlich.

pri·va·cy ['prɪvəsɪ] *s* **1.** Ungestörtheit *f*: *there is no* ~ *here* hier ist man nie ungestört. **2.** Geheimhaltung *f*: *in strict* ~ streng vertraulich.

pri·vate ['praɪvɪt] **I** *adj* □ **1.** privat, Privat...: ~ (*limited*) *company* ✝ *Br.* Gesellschaft *f* mit beschränkter Haftung; ~ *detective* Privatdetektiv(in); ~ *lessons* *pl* Privatunterricht *m*; ~ *life* Privatleben *n*; ~ *matter* Privatangelegenheit *f*; ~ *patient Br.* Privatpatient(in); ~ *school* Privatschule *f*; ~*ly owned* in Privatbesitz. **2.** ungestört (*Ort*): *be a very* ~ *person* sehr zurückgezogen leben. **3.** geheim; vertraulich: *keep s.th.* ~ et. geheimhalten *od.* vertraulich behandeln. **4.** ~ *soldier* → 6. **II** *s* **5.** *in* ~ privat; unter vier Augen. **6.** ✗ Gefreite *m*.

pri·va·tion [praɪ'veɪʃn] *s* Entbehrung *f*.

pri·vat·ize ['praɪvətaɪz] *v/t* staatlichen *Betrieb etc* privatisieren.

priv·i·lege ['prɪvɪlɪdʒ] **I** *s* Privileg *n*, Vorrecht *n*; (*besondere*) Ehre. **II** *v/t* privilegieren, bevorrechtigen: *be* ~*d* den Vorzug genießen (*to do* zu tun).

priv·y ['prɪvɪ] *adj*: *be* ~ *to* eingeweiht sein in (*acc*).

prize¹ [praɪz] **I** *s* **1.** (Sieger-, Sieges)Preis *m*; (*Lotterie- etc*)Gewinn *m*. **II** *adj* **2.** preisgekrönt. **3.** F *contp.* Riesen...: ~

idiot Vollidiot *m*. **III** *v/t* **4.** (hoch)schätzen.

prize² [~] *v/t*: ~ *open* aufbrechen, -stemmen.

'prize|**win·ner** *s* Preisträger(in); Gewinner(in). **'~·win·ning** *adj* preisgekrönt: ~ *ticket* Gewinnlos *n*.

pro¹ [prəʊ] *pl* **pros** *s* **1.** Ja-Stimme *f*. **2.** *the* ~*s and cons pl* das Für u. Wider, das Pro u. Kontra.

pro² [~] F **I** *pl* **pros** *s* Profi *m*. **II** *adj* Profi...

prob·a·bil·i·ty [ˌprɒbə'bɪlətɪ] *s* Wahrscheinlichkeit *f*: *in all* ~ aller Wahrscheinlichkeit nach, höchstwahrscheinlich. **'prob·a·ble** *adj* □ wahrscheinlich.

pro·ba·tion [prə'beɪʃn] *s* Probe(zeit) *f*; ⚖ Bewährung(sfrist) *f*: *he's still on* ~ er ist noch in der Probezeit; *put s.o. on* ~ (*for two years*) j-s (Rest)Strafe (auf zwei Jahre) zur Bewährung aussetzen; ~ *officer* Bewährungshelfer(in). **pro·'ba·tion·ar·y** *adj*: ~ *period* Probezeit *f*; ⚖ Bewährungsfrist *f*. **pro'ba·tion·er** *s* **1.** Lernschwester *f* od. -pfleger *m*. **2.** ⚖ j-d, dessen (*Rest*)*Strafe* zur Bewährung ausgesetzt wurde.

probe [prəʊb] **I** *s* **1.** ✗, ⚙ Sonde *f*. **2.** *fig.* Untersuchung *f* (*into gen*). **II** *v/t* **3.** ✗ sondieren. **4.** *fig.* erforschen, (gründlich) untersuchen. **III** *v/i* **5.** ~ *into* → II.

prob·lem ['prɒbləm] *s* **1.** Problem *n*: *without any* ~ (völlig) problemlos; ~ *child* Problemkind *n*; ~ *drinker* *euphem.* Alkoholiker(in). **2.** ℞ *etc* Aufgabe *f*: *do a* ~ e-e Aufgabe lösen. **prob·lem·at·ic** [ˌ~blə'mætɪk] *adj* (**~ally**) problematisch.

pro·ce·dur·al [prə'si:dʒərəl] *adj* □ Verfahrens..., verfahrenstechnisch; ⚖ verfahrensrechtlich. **pro'ce·dure** *s* Verfahren(sweise *f*) *n*, Vorgehen *n*.

pro·ceed [prə'si:d] *v/i* **1.** (weiter)gehen, (-)fahren; sich begeben (*to* nach, zu). **2.** *fig.* weitergehen (*Handlung etc*) **3.** *fig.* fortfahren (*with* mit): ~ *with one's work* s-e Arbeit fortsetzen. **4.** *fig.* vorgehen, verfahren: ~ *with* et. durchführen; ~ *to do s.th.* sich anschicken *od.* daranmachen, et. zu tun. **5.** ~ *from* herrühren *od.* kommen von. **6.** ~ *against* ⚖ (gerichtlich) vorgehen gegen. **pro·'ceed·ing** *s* **1.** → *procedure*. **2.** *pl* Vor-

pro·logue ['prəʊlɒg] *s* Prolog *m*; *fig.* Auftakt *m* (**to** zu).

pro·long [prəʊ'lɒŋ] *v/t* Aufenthalt *etc* verlängern (**by** um), Diskussion *etc* in die Länge ziehen, ✝ Wechsel prolongieren. **pro'longed** *adj* anhaltend (*Applaus etc*), länger (*Abwesenheit etc*). **pro·lon·ga·tion** [,~'geɪʃn] *s* Verlängerung *f*, ✝ Prolongierung *f*.

prom [prɒm] *bsd. Br.* F → **promenade** I, **promenade concert**.

prom·e·nade [,prɒmə'nɑːd] I *s* (Strand-) Promenade *f*. II *v/i* promenieren (auf *dat*). **~ con·cert** *s* Konzert in ungezwungener Atmosphäre. **~ deck** *s* ♻ Promenadendeck *n*.

prom·i·nence ['prɒmɪnəns] *s* **1.** Vorsprung *m*, vorstehender Teil. **2.** *fig.* Prominenz *f*, Bekannt-, Berühmtheit *f*: **come into** (*od.* **rise to**) **~** bekannt *od.* berühmt werden. **'prom·i·nent** *adj* □ **1.** vorspringend, (*a. Zähne etc*) vorstehend. **2.** *fig.* prominent, bekannt, berühmt.

prom·is·cu·i·ty [,prɒmɪ'skjuːətɪ] *s* häufiger Partnerwechsel. **pro·mis·cu·ous** [prə'mɪskjʊəs] *adj* □ (sexuell) ausschweifend (*Leben*): **~ girl** Mädchen, das häufig den Partner wechselt; **be ~** häufig den Partner wechseln.

prom·ise ['prɒmɪs] I *s* **1.** Versprechen *n*: **a ~ is a ~** versprochen ist versprochen; **make a ~** ein Versprechen geben; **breach of ~** Wortbruch *m*. **2.** *fig.* Hoffnung *f*, Aussicht *f* (**of** auf *acc*): **show great ~** zu den besten Hoffnungen berechtigen. II *v/t* **3.** versprechen (*a. fig.*): **I ~ you** ich warne dich; → **moon** I. III *v/i* **4.** es versprechend. **'prom·is·ing** *adj* □ vielversprechend.

prom·on·to·ry ['prɒməntrɪ] *s* Vorgebirge *n*.

pro·mote [prə'məʊt] *v/t* **1.** *j-n* befördern, *ped.* versetzen: **be ~d** (*Sport*) aufsteigen (**to** in *acc*); **be ~d to the rank of general**, **be ~d general** zum General befördert werden. **2.** Boxkampf, Konzert *etc* veranstalten. **3.** ✝ werben für. **4.** *et.* fördern: **~ health** gesundheitsförderlich sein. **pro'mot·er** *s* **1.** Promoter(in), Veranstalter(in). **2.** → **sales promoter**. **pro'mo·tion** *s* **1.** Beförderung *f*, *ped.* Versetzung *f*, (*Sport*) Aufstieg *m*: **get ~** befördert werden;

chances *pl* of **~**, **~ prospects** *pl* Aufstiegschancen *pl*. **2.** Veranstaltung *f*. **3.** ✝ Werbung *f*; → **sales promotion**.

prompt [prɒmpt] I *adj* □ **1.** prompt, unverzüglich, umgehend: **be ~ to do** (*od.* **in doing**) **s.th.** et. schnell tun. **2.** pünktlich: **~ly at two o'clock** pünktlich um *od.* Punkt zwei Uhr. II *adv* **3.** **at two o'clock ~** F pünktlich um *od.* Punkt zwei Uhr. III *v/t* **4.** *j-n* veranlassen (**to do** zu tun), Gefühle *etc* wecken. **5.** *j-n* veranlassen (**to do** zu tun). **6.** *j-m* ein-, vorsagen; *thea. j-m* soufflieren. IV *s* **7.** *thea.* Souffe, n: **~ box** Souffleurkasten *m*. **'prompt·er** *s thea.* Souffleur *m*, Souffleuse *f*. **prompt·i·tude** ['~tɪtjuːd], **'prompt·ness** *s* **1.** Promptheit *f*. **2.** Pünktlichkeit *f*.

pro·mul·gate ['prɒmlgeɪt] *v/t* **1.** Gesetz *etc* verkünd(ig)en. **2.** Lehre *etc* verbreiten. **pro·mul·ga·tion** *s* **1.** Verkünd(ig)ung *f*. **2.** Verbreitung *f*.

prone [prəʊn] *adj* □ **1.** auf dem Bauch *od.* mit dem Gesicht nach unten liegend: **~ position** Bauchlage *f*. **2.** **be ~ to** *fig.* neigen zu, anfällig sein für: **be ~ to colds** erkältungsanfällig sein; **be ~ to do s.th.** dazu neigen, et. zu tun. **'prone·ness** *s* (**to**) Neigung *f* (zu), Anfälligkeit *f* (für).

prong [prɒŋ] *s* Zacke *f*, Zinke *f* (*e-r Gabel*); (*Geweih*)Sprosse *f*.

pro·noun ['prəʊnaʊn] *s ling.* Pronomen *n*, Fürwort *n*.

pro·nounce [prə'naʊns] I *v/t* **1.** aussprechen. **2.** erklären für *od.* zu. **3.** Urteil verkünden *v/i* **4.** Stellung nehmen (**on** zu): **~ in favo(u)r of** (*od.* **for**) (**against**) **s.th.** sich für (gegen) et. aussprechen. **pro'nounced** *adj* **1.** bestimmt, entschieden (*Ansicht etc*). **2.** ausgesprochen, -geprägt, deutlich. **pro'nounce·ment** *s* **1.** Erklärung *f*. **2.** (*Urteils*)Verkündung *f*.

pron·to ['prɒntəʊ] *adv* F fix, schnell.

pro·nun·ci·a·tion [prə,nʌnsɪ'eɪʃn] *s* Aussprache *f*.

proof [pruːf] I *s* **1.** Beweis(e *pl*) *m*, Nachweis *m*: **as** (*od.* **in**) **~ of** als *od.* zum Beweis für (*od. gen*); **give ~ of** et. be- *od.* nachweisen; **~ of age** Altersnachweis; → **contrary** 6. **2.** Probe *f* (*a. ℞*), Prüfung *f*: **put to the ~** auf die Probe stellen. II *adj* **3.** (**against**) geschützt (vor *dat*), undurchlässig (für); *fig.* unempfindlich (gegen), unempfänglich (für): → *heatproof, waterproof* I, *etc.* III *v/t* 4. imprägnieren. '~read·er *s* Korrektor(in).

prop¹ [prɒp] I *s* Stütze *f* (*a. fig.*): *be a* ~ *to s.o.* j-m e-e Stütze *od.* ein Halt sein. II *v/t a.* ~ *up* (ab)stützen: ~ *up fig.* stützen; ~ *against* lehnen gegen *od.* an (*acc*).

prop² [~] *s thea. etc* Requisit *n*.

prop·a·gan·da [ˌprɒpə'gændə] *s* Propaganda *f*. ˌ**prop·a·gan·dist** *s* Propagandist(in).

prop·a·gate ['prɒpəgeɪt] I *v/i biol.* sich fortpflanzen *od.* vermehren. II *v/t* verbreiten, propagieren. ˌ**prop·a·ga·tion** *s* 1. Fortpflanzung *f*, Vermehrung *f*. 2. Verbreitung *f*, Propagierung *f*.

pro·pane ['prəʊpeɪn] *s* ✿ Propan(gas) *n*.

pro·pel [prə'pel] *v/t* (an)treiben. **pro·'pel·lant, pro·'pel·lent** *s* Treibstoff *m*; Treibgas *n*. **pro·'pel·ler** *s* ✈ Propeller *m*, ⚓ *a.* Schraube *f*. **pro·'pel·ling** *adj*: ~ *pencil Br.* Drehbleistift *m*.

pro·pen·si·ty [prə'pensətɪ] *s* Hang *m*, Neigung *f* (*for, to* zu): *have a* ~ *for doing* (*od. to do*) *s.th.* dazu neigen, et. zu tun.

prop·er ['prɒpə] *adj* 1. richtig, passend, geeignet: *in* ~ *form* in gebührender *od.* angemessener Form; *in the* ~ *place* am rechten Platz; *in* ~ *time* rechtzeitig. 2. echt, wirklich, richtig: ~ *fraction* ℝ echter Bruch. 3. anständig, schicklich (*Benehmen etc*). 4. *oft nachgestellt*: eigentlich. 5. eigen(tümlich) (*to dat*). 6. ~ *noun* (*od. name*) *ling.* Eigenname *m*. 7. F richtig (*Feigling etc*), anständig, gehörig (*Tracht Prügel etc*). '**prop·er·ly** *adv* richtig (*etc*, → *proper*): ~ *speaking* eigentlich, genau, strenggenommen.

prop·er·ty ['prɒpətɪ] *s* 1. Eigentum *n*, Besitz *m*: *be s.o.'s* ~ j-m gehören; *intellectual* ~ geistiges Eigentum; *lost* ~ Fundsachen *pl*; *lost* ~ *office Br.* Fundbüro *n*. 2. Land-, Grundbesitz *m*; Grundstück *n*. 3. *phys. etc* Eigenschaft *f*. 4. *thea. etc* Requisit *n*.

proph·e·cy ['prɒfɪsɪ] *s* Prophezeiung *f*. **proph·e·sy** ['~saɪ] *v/t* prophezeien.

proph·et ['prɒfɪt] *s* Prophet *m*: ~ *of doom* Schwarzseher *m*. '**proph·et·ess** *s* Prophetin *f*. **pro·phet·ic** [prə'fetɪk] *adj* (~*ally*) prophetisch.

pro·phy·lac·tic [ˌprɒfɪ'læktɪk] I *adj* (~*ally*) 1. *bsd.* ✿ prophylaktisch, vorbeugend. II *s* 2. ✿ Prophylaktikum *n*, vorbeugendes Mittel. 3. Präservativ *n*. ˌ**pro·phy·lax·is** [~ksɪs] *s* Prophylaxe *f*.

pro·pi·ti·ate [prə'pɪʃɪeɪt] *v/t* versöhnen, besänftigen.

pro·pi·tious [prə'pɪʃəs] *adj* □ günstig, vorteilhaft (*for, to* für).

pro·po·nent [prə'pəʊnənt] *s* Befürworter(in).

pro·por·tion [prə'pɔːʃn] I *s* 1. Verhältnis *n* (*of ... to* von ... zu); *pl* Größenverhältnisse *pl*, Proportionen *pl*: *in* ~ *to* im Verhältnis zu; *out of all* ~ unverhältnismäßig; *be out of all* ~ *to* in keinem Verhältnis stehen zu; *the painting is out of* ~ die Proportionen des Bildes stimmen nicht. 2. (An)Teil *m*: *in* ~ anteilig. II *v/t* 3. (*to*) in das richtige Verhältnis bringen (mit, zu), anpassen (*dat*). 4. anteilmäßig verteilen. **pro·'por·tion·al** [~ʃənl] I *adj* □ 1. → *proportionate*. 2. proportional, verhältnismäßig. 3. anteilmäßig: ~ *representation pol.* Verhältniswahl(system *n*) *f*. II *s* 4. ℝ Proportionale *f*. **pro·'por·tion·ate** [~ʃnət] *adj* □ (*to*) im richtigen Verhältnis (stehend) (zu), entsprechend (*dat*).

pro·pos·al [prə'pəʊzl] *s* 1. Vorschlag *m*: *make s.o. a* ~ j-m e-n Vorschlag machen. 2. (Heirats)Antrag *m*: *she had a* ~ sie bekam e-n Heiratsantrag; *make s.o. a* ~ j-m e-n Antrag machen. ~ *form s* Antrag(sformular *n*) *m*.

pro·pose [prə'pəʊz] I *v/t* 1. vorschlagen (*s.th. to s.o.* j-m et.; *s.o. for* j-n für *od.* als; *that* daß; *doing* zu tun): ~ *marriage to* j-m e-n Heiratsantrag machen. 2. beabsichtigen, vorhaben (*to do* zu tun). 3. *Toast* ausbringen (*to* auf *acc*): → *health* 3. II *v/i* 4. ~ *to* j-m e-n (Heirats)Antrag machen.

prop·o·si·tion [ˌprɒpə'zɪʃn] *s* 1. Behauptung *f*. 2. Vorschlag *m*: *make s.o. a* ~ j-m e-n Vorschlag machen; j-m ein eindeutiges Angebot machen. 3. ℝ (Lehr)Satz *m*. 4. F Sache *f*: *an easy* ~ e-e Kleinigkeit.

pro·pound [prə'paʊnd] *v/t Theorie etc* vertreten; *Problem etc* zur Debatte stellen.

pro·pri·e·tar·y [prə'praɪətərɪ] *adj* 1. gesetzlich *od.* patentrechtlich geschützt: ~

pry 1174

pry¹ [praɪ] *bsd. Am.* → **prize²**.
pry² [~] *v/i* neugierig sein: **~ into** s-e Nase stecken in (*acc.*). **'pry·ing** *adj* □ neugierig.
psalm [sɑːm] *s* Psalm *m*.
pseu·do·nym ['sjuːdənɪm] *s* Pseudonym *n*: **undor the ~ of XY** unter dem Pseudonym XY.
psych [saɪk] *v/t* F **1. ~ out** j-n, et. durchschauen; j-n psychologisch fertigmachen. **2. ~ up** auf-, hochputschen.
psy·che ['saɪkɪ] *s* Psyche *f*, Seele *f*.
psy·chi·at·ric [ˌsaɪkɪˈætrɪk] *adj* (**~ally**) psychiatrisch (*Behandlung etc*); psychisch (*Störung etc*). **psy·chi·a·trist** [~ˈkaɪətrɪst] *s* Psychiater(in). **psy'chi·a·try** *s* Psychiatrie *f*.
psy·chic ['saɪkɪk] **I** *adj* (**~ally**) **1.** psychisch, seelisch. **2.** übersinnlich. **3. ~ research** Parapsychologie *f*. **4.** medial (begabt *od.* veranlagt). **II** *s* **5.** medial veranlagte Person, Medium *n*. **'psy·chi·cal** → **psychic** I.
psy·cho·a·nal·y·sis [ˌsaɪkəʊəˈnæləsɪs] *s* Psychoanalyse *f*. **psy·cho·an·a·lyst** [~ˈænəlɪst] *s* Psychoanalytiker(in).
psy·cho·log·i·cal [ˌsaɪkəˈlɒdʒɪkl] *adj* □ psychologisch: **~ moment** psychologisch richtiger Augenblick; **~ terror** Psychoterror *m*; **~ warfare** psychologische Kriegführung. **psy·chol·o·gist** [~ˈkɒlədʒɪst] *s* Psychologe *m*, Psychologin *f*. **psy'chol·o·gy** *s* **1.** Psychologie *f*. **2.** psychologisches Geschick *od.* Gespür.
psy·cho·path ['saɪkəʊpæθ] *s* Psychopath(in). **psy·cho'path·ic** *adj* (**~ally**) psychopathisch.
psy·cho·sis [saɪˈkəʊsɪs] *pl* **-ses** [~siːz] *s* ⚕ Psychose *f*.
psy·cho·so·mat·ic [ˌsaɪkəʊsəʊˈmætɪk] *adj* (**~ally**) psychosomatisch.
psy·cho·ther·a·pist [ˌsaɪkəʊˈθerəpɪst] *s* Psychotherapeut(in). **psy·cho'ther·a·py** *s* Psychotherapie *f*.
pub [pʌb] *s bsd. Br.* Pub *n*, Kneipe *f*. **~ crawl** *s bsd. Br.* F Kneipenbummel *m*: **go on a ~** e-n Kneipenbummel machen.
pu·ber·ty ['pjuːbətɪ] *s* Pubertät *f*: **be going through ~** in der Pubertät sein.
pu·bic ['pjuːbɪk] *adj anat.* Scham...
pub·lic ['pʌblɪk] **I** *adj* □ **1.** öffentlich (*Versammlung etc*). **2.** öffentlich, allgemein bekannt: **~figure** Persönlichkeit *f*

des öffentlichen Lebens; **go ~** sich an die Öffentlichkeit wenden; **make ~** bekanntmachen, publik machen. **3.** a) öffentlich (*Einrichtung, Sicherheit, Verkehrsmittel etc*): **~ bar** *Br.* Ausschank *m*, Schenke *f*; **~ (limited) company** ✝ *Br.* Aktiengesellschaft *f*; **~ convenience** *Br.* öffentliche Bedürfnisanstalt; **~ house** *bsd. Br.* Gaststätte *f*; **~ relations** *pl* Public Relations *pl*, Öffentlichkeitsarbeit *f*; **~ school** *Br.* Public School *f*; *Am.* staatliche Schule; **~ utility** öffentlicher Versorgungsbetrieb; → **nuisance** 1, b) Staats..., staatlich: **~holiday** gesetzlicher Feiertag; → **prosecutor**, c) Volks...: **~ library** Volksbücherei *f*. **II** *s* **4.** Öffentlichkeit *f*: **in ~** in der Öffentlichkeit, öffentlich. **5.** Publikum *n*. **II** *s* ⚖ **6.** **exclude the ~** die Öffentlichkeit ausschließen. **~·ad'dress sys·tem** *s* Lautsprecheranlage *f*.
pub·li·can ['pʌblɪkən] *s bsd. Br.* (Gast-)Wirt(in).
pub·li·ca·tion [ˌpʌblɪˈkeɪʃn] *s* **1.** Bekanntgabe *f*, -machung *f*. **2.** Publikation *f*, Veröffentlichung *f* (*beide a. Werk*).
pub·li·cist ['pʌblɪsɪst] *s* **1.** Publizist(in). **2.** Werbeagent(in). **pub·lic·i·ty** [~ˈlɪsətɪ] *s* **1.** Publicity *f*, Bekanntheit *f*. **2.** Publicity *f*, Reklame *f*, Werbung *f*: **~ agent** Werbeagent(in); **~ campaign** Werbefeldzug *m*; **~ stunt** Werbegag *m*. **pub·li·cize** [~saɪz] *v/t* **1.** bekanntmachen, publik machen. **2.** Publicity *od.* Reklame machen für.
pub·lish ['pʌblɪʃ] *v/t* **1.** bekanntgeben, -machen. **2.** publizieren, veröffentlichen, *Leserbrief a.* abdrucken. **3.** *Buch etc* verlegen, herausbringen: **~ed weekly** erscheint wöchentlich. **'pub·lish·er** *s* **1.** Verleger(in), Herausgeber(in). **2.** *pl* Verlag(shaus *n*) *m*.
puck [pʌk] *s* Eishockey: Puck *m*, Scheibe *f*.
puck·er ['pʌkə] **I** *v/t* **1.** a. **~ up** Gesicht, Mund verziehen, Stirn runzeln. **II** *v/i* a. **~ up** **2.** sich verziehen, sich runzeln. **3.** Falten werfen. **III** *s* **4.** Falte *f*.
pud [pʊd] *Br.* F → **pudding**.
pud·ding ['pʊdɪŋ] *s* a) *Br.* Nachspeise *f*, -tisch *m* b) (*Reis- etc*)Auflauf *m*, c) Pudding *m* (*im Wasserbad gekochte Mehlspeise*), d) (*Blut*)Wurst *f*.

pud·dle ['pʌdl] s Pfütze f.

pu·er·ile ['pjʊəraɪl] adj □ infantil, kindisch.

puff [pʌf] **I** s **1.** *Rauchen:* Zug m: *take a ~ at* ziehen an (dat). **2.** (Luft-, Wind-)Hauch m, (-)Stoß m: *~ of air.* **3.** gastr. (Wind)Beutel m. **4.** F Puste f: *out of ~* aus der od. außer Puste. **5.** (Puder)Quaste f. **6.** F Anpreisung f: *give s.th. a ~* et. hochjubeln. **II** v/t **7.** *Rauch* blasen (*in s.o.'s face* j-m ins Gesicht): *~ out* Kerze etc ausblasen; Rauch etc ausstoßen; Brust herausdrücken; Gefieder aufplustern; *be ~ed up* (*with pride*) aufgeblasen sein. **III** v/i **8.** schnaufen (a. Lokomotive etc), keuchen. **9.** *~ away* paffen (*at* an e-r Zigarette etc). **10.** *~ up* (an)schwellen. **puffed** adj F aus der od. außer Puste.

puff| paste s Am., **~ pas·try** s Blätterteig m. **~ sleeve** s Puffärmel m.

puff·y ['pʌfɪ] adj (an)geschwollen, verschwollen.

pug [pʌg] s zo. Mops m.

pug·na·cious [pʌg'neɪʃəs] adj □ kampf(es)lustig; streitsüchtig. **pug·nac·i·ty** [~'næsətɪ] s Kampf(es)lust f; Streitsucht f.

puke [pjuːk] sl. **I** v/i kotzen. **II** v/t auskotzen. **III** s Kotze f.

pull [pʊl] **I** s **1.** Ziehen n; Zug m, Ruck m: *give the rope a* (*good*) *~* (kräftig) am Seil ziehen. **2.** Anziehungskraft f (a. fig.). **3.** Anstieg m, Steigung f. **4.** Zug(griff m, -leine f) m. **5.** F Beziehungen pl (*with* zu). **II** v/t **6.** ziehen: → *string* 1. **7.** *ziehen* an (dat): *s.o.'s hair* j-n an den Haaren ziehen; *a muscle* sich e-e Muskelzerrung zuziehen, sich et. zerren; → *face* 2, *leg* 1, *etc.* **8.** reißen: → *piece* 1. **9.** a) *Zahn* ziehen, *Pflanze* ausreißen, b) *Messer, Pistole* ziehen: *~ a gun on s.o.* j-n mit der Pistole bedrohen, c) bsd. Br. *Bier* zapfen. **10.** fig. anziehen. **11.** *~ one's punches* (Boxen) verhalten schlagen; fig. sich zurückhalten; *not to ~ one's punches, ~ no punches* kein Blatt vor den Mund nehmen. **12.** F *Banküberfall etc* machen: *~ a big one* ein großes Ding drehen; → *job¹* 6. **III** v/i **13.** ziehen (*at, on* an dat).

Verbindungen mit Adverbien:

pull| a·head v/i vorbeiziehen (*of* an dat) (Auto etc) (a. fig.). *~ a·way* v/i **1.** anfahren (Bus etc). **2.** sich absetzen (*from* von), (Sport a.) sich freimachen. *~ down* v/t **1.** Gebäude abreißen. **2.** j-n mitnehmen, schwächen. *~ in* v/t **1.** Bauch etc einziehen. **2.** → *pull* 10. **3.** bsd. Br. F j-n einkassieren. **4.** F kassieren: *he's pulling in quite a bit* er verdient ganz schön. **II** v/i **5.** einfahren (Zug). **6.** anhalten. *~ off* v/t **1.** Schuhe etc ausziehen; sich die Kleider vom Leib reißen. **2.** F et. schaffen, schaukeln. *~ on* v/t Kleid etc anziehen, (sich) überziehen. *~ out* **I** v/t **1.** a) herausziehen (*of* aus): → *chestnut* 1, *stop* 4, b) → *pull* 9a, c) Tisch ausziehen. **II** v/i **2.** abfahren (Zug). **3.** ausscheren (Fahrzeug). **4.** fig. sich zurückziehen, (a. Sport) aussteigen (*of* aus). *~ through* v/t **1.** durchziehen. **2.** fig. Kranken, Kandidaten etc durchbringen. **II** v/i **3.** fig. durchkommen. *~ to·geth·er* I v/t **1.** pull o.s. together sich zs.-reißen. **2.** Partei etc zs. schweißen. **II** v/i **3.** an e'inem Strang ziehen. *~ up* **I** v/t **1.** hochziehen. **2.** Fahrzeug anhalten. **3.** j-n korrigieren; zurechtweisen (*for* wegen). **II** v/i **4.** (an)halten. **5.** *~ to* (od. *with*) (Sport) j-n einholen.

pul·ley ['pʊlɪ] s ⊙ Flaschenzug m.

'pull-in s Br. Rasthaus n, -stätte f. **'~-out** adj ausziehbar: *~ table* Ausziehtisch m. **'~·o·ver** s Pullover m. **'~-up** s Klimmzug m: *do a ~* e-n Klimmzug machen.

pul·mo·nar·y ['pʌlmənərɪ] adj anat., ♥ Lungen...

pulp [pʌlp] **I** s **1.** Fruchtfleisch n. **2.** Brei m, breiige Masse: *beat to a ~* fig. j-n zu Brei schlagen. **II** adj **3.** Schund...: *~ novel* Schundroman m. **III** v/t **4.** Bücher etc einstampfen.

pul·pit ['pʊlpɪt] s Kanzel f: *in the ~* auf der Kanzel.

pulp·y ['pʌlpɪ] adj □ breiig.

pul·sate [pʌl'seɪt] v/i pulsieren, a. fig. vibrieren (*with* vor dat).

pulse¹ [pʌls] **I** s **1.** Puls(schlag) m: *feel* (od. *take*) *s.o.'s ~* j-m den Puls fühlen. **2.** ♫, phys. Impuls m. **II** v/i **3.** pulsieren (*through* durch) (a. fig.).

pulse² [~] mst pl s Hülsenfrüchte pl.

pul·ver·ize ['pʌlvəraɪz] v/t **1.** pulverisieren. **2.** fig. F j-n auseinandernehmen.

pu·ma ['pjuːmə] s zo. Puma m.

pum·ice ['pʌmɪs] *s a.* ~ **stone** Bimsstein *m.*

pum·mel ['pʌml] *v/t pret u. pp* **-meled,** *bsd. Br.* **-melled** eintrommeln auf (*acc*).

pump [pʌmp] **I** *s* **1.** Pumpe *f*; (*Zapf*)Säule. **II** *v/t* **2.** pumpen; ~ **up** aufpumpen; ~ **s.o.'s stomach** ✹ j-m den Magen auspumpen; ~ **money into** *fig.* Geld hineinpumpen in (*acc*). **3.** ┌ *j-n* ausholen (**for** über *acc*). **III** *v/i* **4.** pumpen (*a.* Herz). **5.** herausschießen (**from** aus) (*Blut etc*). ~ **at·tend·ant** *s* Tankwart *m.*

pump·kin ['pʌmpkɪn] *s* ♣ Kürbis *m.*

pun [pʌn] **I** *s* Wortspiel *n.* **II** *v/i* Wortspiele *od.* ein Wortspiel machen.

Punch¹ [pʌntʃ] *s* Kasper *m,* Kasperle *n, m*: **be (as) pleased as** ~ F sich freuen wie ein Schneekönig.

punch² [~] **I** *s* **1.** (Faust)Schlag *m*: **give s.o. a** ~ j-m e-n Schlag versetzen; → **pull** 11. **2.** *fig.* Schwung *m.* **II** *v/t* **3.** (mit der Faust) schlagen.

punch³ [~] ✹ **I** *s* Locher *m*; Lochzange *f*; Locheisen *n.* **II** *v/t* lochen; *Loch* stanzen (**in** in *acc*). ~**ed card** Lochkarte *f*; ~**ed tape** Lochstreifen *m.*

punch⁴ [~] *s* Punsch *m.*

Punch-and-'Ju·dy show ['dʒu:dɪ] *s* Kasperletheater *n.*

punch| card *s* Lochkarte *f.* ~ **line** *s* Pointe *f.* '~**-up** *s Br.* F Schlägerei *f.*

punc·til·i·ous [pʌŋk'tɪlɪəs] *adj* □ peinlich genau.

punc·tu·al ['pʌŋktʃʊəl] *adj* □ pünktlich: **be** ~ pünktlich kommen (**for** zu). **punc·tu·al·i·ty** [~'ælətɪ] *s* Pünktlichkeit *f.*

punc·tu·ate ['pʌŋktʃʊeɪt] *v/t* **1.** interpunktieren. **2.** *fig.* (**with**) unterbrechen (durch), durchsetzen (mit). **3.** *fig.* unterstreichen, betonen. **punc·tu·a'tion** *s* **1.** Interpunktion *f*: ~ **mark** Satzzeichen *n.* **2.** *fig.* Unterbrechung *f*; Durchsetzung *f.* **3.** *fig.* Unterstreichung *f*, Betonung *f.*

punc·ture ['pʌŋktʃə] **I** *v/t* **1.** durchstechen, -bohren. **2.** ✹ punktieren. **II** *v/i* **3.** ein Loch bekommen, platzen. **III** *s* **4.** (Ein)Stich *m*; Loch *n.* **5.** *mot.* Reifenpanne *f.* **6.** ✹ Punktion *f.*

pun·dit ['pʌndɪt] *s oft humor.* Weise *m, f.*

pun·gen·cy ['pʌndʒənsɪ] *s* Schärfe *f* (*a.*

fig.). '**pun·gent** *adj* □ scharf (*Geschmack, Geruch*), (*Bemerkung etc a.*) bissig.

pun·ish ['pʌnɪʃ] *v/t* **1.** *j-n* (be)strafen (**for** für, wegen). **2.** *et.* bestrafen. '**pun·ish·a·ble** *adj* □ strafbar: ~ **act** (*od.* **offence,** *Am.* **offense**) strafbare Handlung; **murder is** ~ **by death** auf Mord steht die Todesstrafe. '**pun·ish·ing** *adj* □ vernichtend (*Kritik etc*), mörderisch, zermürbend (*Rennen etc*). '**pun·ish·ment** *s* **1.** Bestrafung *f.* **2.** Strafe *f*: **as a** ~ **als** *od.* zur Strafe (**for** für).

pu·ni·tive ['pju:nətɪv] *adj* □ **1.** Straf... **2.** extrem hoch (*Steuern etc*).

punk [pʌŋk] *s* **1.** Punk *m* (*Bewegung u. Anhänger*). **2.** ♪ Punk *m*; Punker *m.* ~ **rock** *s* ♪ Punkrock *m.* ~ **rock·er** *s* ♪ Punkrocker *m.*

punt [pʌnt] **I** *s* Stechkahn *m.* **II** *v/t u. v/i* staken.

pu·ny ['pju:nɪ] *adj* □ schwächlich.

pup [pʌp] → **puppy.**

pu·pa ['pju:pə] *pl* **-pae** ['~pi:], **-pas** *s zo.* Puppe *f.*

pu·pil¹ ['pju:pl] *s* Schüler(in).

pu·pil² [~] *s anat.* Pupille *f.*

pup·pet ['pʌpɪt] *s* Puppe *f*: a) Handpuppe *f*, b) Marionette *f* (*a. fig.*): ~ **government** *fig.* Marionettenregierung *f*; ~ **show** Marionettentheater *n*, Puppenspiel *n.* **pup·pet·eer** [~'tɪə] *s* Puppenspieler(in).

pup·py ['pʌpɪ] *s* Welpe *m*, junger Hund. ~ **fat** *s Br.* F Babyspeck *m.* ~ **love** *s* F jugendliche Schwärmerei.

pur·chas·a·ble ['pɜ:tʃəsəbl] *adj* käuflich. '**pur·chase I** *v/t* **1.** kaufen, erstehen. **2.** *fig.* erkaufen (**at the expense of** auf Kosten *gen*). **II** *s* **3.** Kauf *m.* **4.** *pl* Einkäufe *pl*: **make** ~**s** Einkäufe machen. '**pur·chas·er** *s* Käufer(in). '**pur·chas·ing** *adj*: ~ **power** ╈ Kaufkraft *f.*

pure [pjʊə] *adj* □ **1.** rein: a) pur, unvermischt, b) sauber, c) akzentfrei, fehlerlos, d) pur, völlig (*Unsinn etc*): **by** ~ **accident** rein zufällig. **2.** ehrlich (*Absicht*). '~**-bred** *adj* reinrassig, rasserein. **II** *s* reinrassiges Tier.

pu·ree ['pjʊəreɪ] *s* Püree *n.* **II** *v/t* pürieren.

pur·ga·tive ['pɜ:gətɪv] ✹ **I** *adj* □ abführend. **II** *s* Abführmittel *n.*

pur·ga·to·ry ['pɜ:gətərɪ] *s eccl.* Fegefeuer

n: it is ~ having to do s.th. es ist die Hölle, et. tun zu müssen.

purge [pɜːdʒ] **I** *v/t Partei etc* säubern (*of* von). **II** *s pol.* Säuberung(saktion) *f.*

pu·ri·fi·ca·tion [ˌpjʊərɪfɪˈkeɪʃn] *s* Reinigung *f.* **pu·ri·fi·er** [ˈ-faɪə] *s* ⊛ Reiniger *m.* **pu·ri·fy** [ˈ-faɪ] *v/t* reinigen.

pur·ism [ˈpjʊərɪzəm] *s* Purismus *m.* **'pur·ist** *s* Purist(in).

Pu·ri·tan [ˈpjʊərɪtən] *hist., fig. mst* ♀ **I** *s* Puritaner(in). **II** *adj* puritanisch. **pu·ri·tan·i·cal** [ˌ-ˈtænɪkl] *adj* □ *fig.* puritanisch. **Pu·ri·tan·ism** [ˈ-tənɪzəm] *s hist., fig. mst* ♀ Puritanismus *m.*

pu·ri·ty [ˈpjʊərətɪ] *s* **1.** Reinheit *f.* **2.** Ehrlichkeit *f.*

pur·loin [pɜːˈlɔɪn] *v/t oft humor.* entwenden.

pur·ple [ˈpɜːpl] *adj* purpurn, pupurrot: *his face turned ~* sein Gesicht verfärbte sich blau; *~ heart bsd. Br.* F Amphetamintablette *f;* ♀ *Heart* ✕ *Am.* Verwundetenabzeichen *n.*

pur·port [ˈpɜːpət] **I** *s* Tenor *m.* **II** *v/t:* *~ to be s.th.* vorgeben, et. zu sein; et. sein sollen.

pur·pose [ˈpɜːpəs] **I** *s* **1.** Zweck *m,* Ziel *n;* Absicht *f,* Vorsatz *m: for all practical ~s* praktisch; *on* ~ absichtlich; mit der Absicht (*to do* zu tun); *answer* (*od. serve*) *the same* ~ denselben Zweck erfüllen; *put to a good* ~ gut anwenden *od.* nützen. **2.** *to no* ~ vergeblich, umsonst. **3.** Entschlossenheit *f,* Zielstrebigkeit *f.* **II** *v/t* **4.** beabsichtigen, vorhaben (*doing, to do* zu tun). **pur·pose·ful** [ˈ-fʊl] *adj* □ entschlossen, zielstrebig. **'pur·pose·less** *adj* □ **1.** zwecklos. **2.** ziel-, planlos. **'pur·pose·ly** *adv* absichtlich.

purr [pɜː] **I** *v/i* schnurren (*Katze*); surren (*Motor etc*). **II** *s* Schnurren *n;* Surren *n.*

purse [pɜːs] **I** *s* **1.** a) Geldbeutel *m,* Portemonnaie *n: be beyond s.o.'s* ~ *fig.* j-s Finanzen übersteigen; *hold the* ~ *strings fig.* die Finanzen verwalten, b) *Am.* Handtasche *f.* **2.** *Sport:* Siegprämie *f;* (*Boxen*) Börse *f.* **II** *v/t* **3.** *a.* ~ *up Lippen* schürzen. **'purs·er** *s* **1.** ⚓ Proviant- *od.* Zahlmeister *m.* **2.** ✈ Purser *m* (*leitender Steward*).

pur·su·ance [pəˈsjʊəns] *s: in* (*the*) ~ *of one's duty* in Ausübung s-r Pflicht.

pur·sue [pəˈsjuː] *v/t* **1.** verfolgen: *be ~d by bad luck* vom Pech verfolgt werden. **2.** *fig. s-m Studium etc* nachgehen; *Absicht, Politik etc* verfolgen; *Angelegenheit etc* weiterführen. **pur·su·er** *s* Verfolger(in). **pur·suit** [pəˈsjuːt] *s* **1.** Verfolgung *f: be in* ~ *of s.o.* j-n verfolgen. **2.** *fig.* Verfolgung *f;* Weiterführung *f: in* (*the*) ~ *of* im *od.* in Verfolg (*gen*). **3.** Beschäftigung *f.*

pu·ru·lent [ˈpjʊərʊlənt] *adj* □ eiternd, eit(e)rig.

pus [pʌs] *s* ✻ Eiter *m.*

push [pʊʃ] **I** *s* **1.** Stoß *m: give s.o. a* ~ j-m e-n Stoß versetzen; *give s.o. the* ~ *Br.* F j-n rausschmeißen (*entlassen*); *get the* ~ *Br.* F fliegen; *at a* ~ im Notfall, notfalls; *if* (*od. when*) *it comes to the* ~ F wenn es darauf ankommt. **2.** (*Werbe*)Kampagne *f.* **3.** F Draufgängertum *n.* **II** *v/t* **4.** stoßen, schubsen; schieben; *Taste etc* drücken: ~ *one's way* sich drängen (*through* durch); *he's ~ing 70* er geht auf die 70 zu. **5.** *fig.* j-n drängen (*to do* zu tun): *be ~ed* (*for time*) F es eilig haben; in Zeitnot sein; *be ~ed for money* F knapp bei Kasse sein. **6.** *fig.* Reklame machen, die Trommel rühren für. **7.** F *Heroin etc* pushen. **III** *v/i* **8.** stoßen, schubsen; schieben; drücken: ~ *past s.o.* sich an j-m vorbeidrängen. **9.** ~ *for fig.* drängen auf (*acc*). *Verbindungen mit Adverbien:*

push| **a·bout** → *push around.* ~ **a·head** *v/i:* ~ *with Plan etc* vorantreiben. ~ **a·long** *v/i* F sich auf die Socken machen. ~ **a·round** F herumschubsen (*a. fig.* F). ~ **for·ward I** → *push on.* ~ **forward** *fig.* sich in den Vordergrund drängen *od.* schieben. **II** *v/i* → *push ahead.* ~ **in** *v/i* F sich vordrängeln. ~ **off** *v/i* **1.** sich abstoßen (*from* von). **2.** *mst imp* abhauen, Leine ziehen. ~ **on** → *push ahead.* ~ **out** *v/t fig.* j-n hinausdrängen. ~ **up** *v/t* **1.** → *daisy.* **2.** *Preise etc* hochtreiben.

'push|**·bike** *s Br.* F Fahrrad *n.* ~ **·but·ton** *s* Druckknopf *m,* -taste *f.* **'~·but·ton** *adj* Druckknopf...: ~ **telephone** Tastentelefon *n.* **'~·cart** *s* **1.** (Hand)Karren *m.* **2.** *Am.* Einkaufswagen *m.* **'~·chair** *s Br.* Sportwagen *m* (*für Kinder*).

push·er [ˈpʊʃə] *s* F **1.** Draufgänger *m.* **2.**

Pusher *m* (*Rauschgifthändler*). **'push-ing** → **pushy**.

'push|**o·ver** *s* F **1.** *fig.* Kinderspiel *n.* **2. be a ~ for** nicht widerstehen können (*dat*); immer wieder hereinfallen auf (*acc*). **'~·up** *s Am.* Liegestütz *m*: **do a ~** e-n Liegestütz machen.

push·y ['puʃɪ] *adj* □ draufgängerisch.

pu·sil·lan·i·mous [ˌpju:sɪ'lænɪməs] *adj* □ kleinmütig, verzagt.

puss [pʊs] *s* F Mieze *f.*

puss·y ['pʊsɪ] *s* Kindersprache: Miezekatze *f.* **'~·cat** → **pussy.** **'~·foot** *v/i a. ~ about** (*od.* **around**) F um den (heißen) Brei herumreden; sich nicht festlegen wollen.

pus·tule ['pʌstju:l] *s* ♣ Pustel *f.*

put [pʊt] **I** *adj* **1. stay ~** sich nicht (vom Fleck) rühren. **II** *v/t* (*irr*) **1.** legen, setzen, stellen, tun: **~ s.th. before s.o.** *fig.* j-m et. vorlegen; **~ a tax on s.th.** et. besteuern. **2.** *Hand etc, fig. Geld, Zeit* stecken (**in**[**to**]) in *acc*). **4.** j-n in e-e unangenehme Lage etc, et. *auf den Markt, in Ordnung etc* bringen. **5.** et. *in Kraft, in Umlauf etc* setzen. **6.** unterwerfen, -ziehen (**to** *dat*). **7.** übersetzen (**into French** ins Französische). **8.** et. ausdrücken, *in Worte* fassen: → **mild. 9.** schätzen (**at** auf *acc*). **10.** *Geld* setzen (**on** auf *acc*). **11.** *Schuld* geben (**on** *dat*). **III** *v/i* (*irr*) **12. ~ to sea** ♣ in See stechen. **13. ~ upon s.o.** *bsd. Br.* j-m Ungelegenheiten bereiten.

Verbindungen mit Adverbien:

put| **a·bout I** *v/t* Gerücht verbreiten, in Umlauf setzen. **II** *v/i* ♣ den Kurs ändern. **~ a·cross** *v/t* et. verständlich machen (**to** *dat*). **~ a·head** *v/t Sport:* in Führung bringen. **~ a·side** *v/t* **1.** beiseite legen. **2.** *Ware* zurücklegen. **3.** *fig.* beiseite schieben. **4.** → **put away** 3. **~ a·way** *v/t* **1.** weglegen, -stecken, -tun. **2.** auf-, wegräumen. **3.** → **put by. 4.** F *Speisen* verdrücken, *Getränke* schlukken. **~ back** *v/t* **1.** zurücklegen, -stellen, -tun. **2.** *Uhr* zurückstellen (**by** um): → **clock** 1. **3.** *fig.* verschieben (**two days** um zwei Tage; **to** auf *acc*). **~ by** *v/t Geld* zurücklegen, auf die hohe Kante legen. **~ down** I *v/t* **1.** hin-, niederlegen, -stellen, -setzen. **2.** *Aufstand etc* niederwerfen. **3.** *Fahrgast* absetzen. **4.** *et.* aufschreiben: **put s.o.('s name) down for**

j-n anmelden *od.* eintragen für. **5.** *Betrag* anzahlen. **6.** *Flugzeug* landen. **7.** j-n halten (**as** für). **8.** *et.* zuschreiben (**to** *dat*). **II** *v/i* **9.** ✈ landen. **~ for·ward** *v/t* **1.** *Plan etc* vorlegen: **put s.o.('s name) forward as** j-n vorschlagen als. **2.** *Uhr* vorstellen (**by** um). **3.** *fig.* vorverlegen (**two days** um zwei Tage; **to** auf *acc*). **~ in** I *v/t* **1.** herein-, hineinlegen, -stecken, -stellen, *Kassette etc* einlegen. **2.** *Gesuch etc* einreichen, *Forderung etc a.* geltend machen. **3.** *Arbeit, Zeit* verbringen (**on** mit). **4.** *Bemerkung* einwerfen; *ein gutes Wort* einlegen (**for** für). **II** *v/i* **5.** ♣ einlaufen (**at** in *acc*): **~ at** a. anlaufen (*acc*). **6.** sich bewerben (**for** um). **~ off** *v/t* **1.** *et.* verschieben (**till, until** auf *acc*); j-m absagen. **2.** j-n hinhalten (**with** mit). **3.** aus dem Konzept bringen; j-m den Appetit *od.* die Lust *od.* die Laune verderben. **4.** → **put down** 3. **~ on** *v/t* **1.** *Mantel etc* anziehen, *Hut, Brille* aufsetzen; *Rouge etc* auflegen: → **lipstick. 2.** *Licht, Radio etc* anmachen, einschalten. **3.** *einige Pfund* zunehmen: → **weight** 1. **4.** *Sonderzug etc* einsetzen. **5.** *thea. Stück etc* herausbringen. **6.** *Bremse* anziehen. **7.** *Essen, Topf etc* aufsetzen. **8.** *Schallplatte etc* auflegen, *Kassette etc* einlegen. **9.** vortäuschen, heucheln: **put it on** so tun als ob. **10.** F j-n auf den Arm nehmen. **~ out** I *v/t* **1.** heraus-, hinauslegen, -stellen. **2.** *Hand etc* ausstrecken: → **hand, tongue** 1. **3.** *Feuer* löschen; *Licht, Radio, Zigarette etc* ausmachen, abschalten. **4.** veröffentlichen, herausgeben; (*Rundfunk, TV*) bringen, senden. **5.** aus der Fassung bringen; verstimmen, -ärgern; j-m Ungelegenheiten bereiten. **6.** ♣ sich *den Arm etc* ver- *od.* ausrenken. **II** *v/i* **7.** ♣ auslaufen: **~ to sea** in See stechen. **~ o·ver** → **put across. ~ through** *v/t* **1.** *teleph.* j-n verbinden (**to** mit). **2.** durch-, ausführen. **~ to·geth·er** *v/t* **1.** zs.-setzen, *Gerät etc* zs.-bauen; *Mannschaft, Rede etc* zs.-stellen. **2. he is cleverer than all his friends ~** er ist cleverer als alle s-e Freunde zusammen. **~ up** I *v/t* **1.** herauf-, hinauflegen, -stellen. **2.** *Hand* (hoch)heben. **3.** *Bild etc* aufhängen; *Plakat, Bekanntmachung etc* anschlagen. **4.** *Schirm* aufspannen. **5.** *Zelt etc* aufstellen, *Gebäude* errichten. **6.** *j-n* unterbringen. **7.** *Widerstand* leisten: → **fight** 1. **8.** *Preis etc* erhöhen. **9.** *j-n* anstiften (**to** zu). **II** *v/i* **10.** absteigen (**at** in *dat*). **11.** ~ **with** sich abfinden mit; sich gefallen lassen.

pu·ta·tive ['pjuːtətɪv] *adj* □ mutmaßlich.

'put·off *s bsd. Am.* F (faule) Ausrede.

'~·on *s Am.* F Bluff *m*, Schwindel *m*.

pu·tre·fy ['pjuːtrɪfaɪ] *v/i* (ver)faulen, verwesen.

pu·trid ['pjuːtrɪd] *adj* □ **1.** verfault, -west; (*Geruch*) faulig. **2.** F miserabel, saumäßig.

putsch [pʊtʃ] *s pol.* Putsch *m*.

putt [pʌt] *v/t u. v/i Golf:* putten.

putt·er [ˈpʌtə] *Am.* → **potter**[1].

put·ty [ˈpʌtɪ] **I** *s* Kitt *m*: *he was* (*like*) ~ *in her hands fig.* er war Wachs in ihren Händen. **II** *v/t* kitten.

'put-up job *s* F abgekartetes Spiel.

puz·zle [ˈpʌzl] **I** *s* **1.** Rätsel *n* (*a. fig.*); Geduld(s)spiel *n*: *it is a* ~ *to me* es ist mir ein Rätsel *od.* rätselhaft; → **jigsaw** (**puzzle**). **II** *v/t* **2.** vor ein Rätsel stellen; verdutzen, -blüffen: *be* ~*d* vor e-m Rätsel stehen. **3.** ~ *out et.* ausknobeln, herausbringen. **III** *v/i* **4.** sich den Kopf zerbrechen (**about**, **over** über *dat*). **'puz·zler** *s* F harte Nuß.

pyg·my [ˈpɪɡmɪ] **I** *s* **1.** ♀ Pygmäe *m*, Pygmäin *f*. **2.** Zwerg(in) (*a. fig. contp.*). **II** *adj* **3.** *bsd. zo.* Zwerg...

py·ja·mas [pəˈdʒɑːməz] *s pl, a.* **pair of** ~ Schlafanzug *m*, Pyjama *m*.

py·lon [ˈpaɪlən] *s* Hochspannungsmast *m*.

pyr·a·mid [ˈpɪrəmɪd] *s* Pyramide *f*.

pyre [ˈpaɪə] *s* Scheiterhaufen *m*.

py·ro·ma·ni·a [ˌpaɪrəʊˈmeɪnɪə] *s* Pyromanie *f*. **,py·ro'ma·ni·ac** [~æk] *s* Pyromane *m*, -manin *f*.

Pyr·rhic vic·to·ry [ˈpɪrɪk] *s* Pyrrhussieg *m*.

py·thon [ˈpaɪθn] *s zo.* Python(schlange) *f*.

pyx [pɪks] *s eccl.* Pyxis *f*, Hostienbehälter *m*.

Q

quack[1] [kwæk] **I** *v/i* quaken (*Ente*). **II** *s* Quaken *n*.

quack[2] [~] *s a.* ~ **doctor** Quacksalber *m*, Kurpfuscher *m*. **quack·er·y** [ˈ~ərɪ] *s* Quacksalberei *f*, Kurpfuscherei *f*.

quad [kwɒd] *s* F Vierling *m*.

quad·ran·gle [ˈkwɒdræŋɡl] *s* Viereck *n*. **quad'ran·gu·lar** [~ɡjʊlə] *adj* □ viereckig.

quad·ra·phon·ic [ˌkwɒdrəˈfɒnɪk] *adj* (~*ally*) ♪, *phys.* quadrophon(isch).

quad·ri·lat·er·al [ˌkwɒdrɪˈlætərəl] **I** *adj* vierseitig. **II** *s* Viereck *n*.

quad·ro·phon·ic → **quadraphonic**.

quad·ru·ped [ˈkwɒdrʊped] *s zo.* Vierfüß(l)er *m*.

quad·ru·ple [ˈkwɒdrʊpl] **I** *adj* □ vierfach. **II** *v/t u. v/i* (sich) vervierfachen. **quad·ru·plet** [ˈ~plɪt] *s* Vierling *m*.

quag·mire [ˈkwæɡmaɪə] *s* Morast *m*, Sumpf *m*.

quail [kweɪl] *pl* **quails,** *bsd. coll.* **quail** *s orn.* Wachtel *f*.

quaint [kweɪnt] *adj* □ idyllisch, malerisch.

quake [kweɪk] **I** *v/i* zittern, beben (**with** vor *dat*; **at** bei e-m *Gedanken*). **II** *s* F Erdbeben *n*.

Quak·er [ˈkweɪkə] *s eccl.* Quäker(in).

qual·i·fi·ca·tion [ˌkwɒlɪfɪˈkeɪʃn] *s* **1.** Qualifikation *f*, Befähigung *f*, Eignung *f* (**for** für, zu). **2.** Vorbedingung *f*, Voraussetzung *f* (**of**, **for** für). **3.** Abschluß(zeugnis *n*) *m*. **4.** Einschränkung *f*, Vorbehalt *m*. **5.** *ling.* nähere Bestimmung. **qual·i·fied** [ˈ~faɪd] *adj* **1.** qualifiziert, geeignet, befähigt (**for** für). **2.** berechtigt: ~ *to vote* wahlberechtigt. **3.** bedingt, eingeschränkt. **qual·i·fy** [ˈ~faɪ] **I** *v/t* **1.** qualifizieren, befähigen (**for** für, zu). **2.** berechtigen (**to do** zu tun). **3.** *ling.* näher bestimmen. **II** *v/i* **4.** sich qualifizieren *od.* eignen, die Bedingungen erfüllen (**for** für; **as** als). **5.** *Sport:* sich abschließen (**for** für). **6.** s-e Ausbildung abschließen (**as** als).

qual·i·ta·tive [ˈkwɒlɪtətɪv] *adj* □ qualitativ. **qual·i·ty** [ˈꞈətɪ] *s* **1.** Qualität *f*, **✝** *a.* Güteklasse *f:* ~ **of life** Lebensqualität; ~ **of sound** *TV etc* Tonqualität; ~ **goods** *pl* Qualitätswaren *pl;* ~ **newspaper** seriöse Zeitung. **2.** Eigenschaft *f:* → **leadership** 2.

qualms [kwɑːmz] *s pl* Bedenken *pl,* Skrupel *pl:* **have no ~ about doing s.th.** keine Bedenken haben, et. zu tun.

quan·da·ry [ˈkwɒndərɪ] *s* Dilemma *n,* Verlegenheit *f:* **be in a ~ about what to do** nicht wissen, was man tun soll.

quan·ta [ˈkwɒntə] *pl von* **quantum.**

quan·ti·ta·tive [ˈkwɒntɪtətɪv] *adj* □ quantitativ. **quan·ti·ty** [ˈꞈətɪ] *s* **1.** Quantität *f;* Menge *f:* **in small quantities** in kleinen Mengen; ~ **discount** (*od.* **allowance**) **✝** Mengenrabatt *m.* **2.** ᴀ Größe *f:* → **unknown.**

quan·tum [ˈkwɒntəm] *phys.* **I** *pl* **-ta** [ˈꞈtə] *s* Quant *n.* **II** *adj* Quanten...

quar·an·tine [ˈkwɒrəntiːn] **I** *s* Quarantäne *f:* **put in ~** → **II. II** *v/t* unter Quarantäne stellen.

quar·rel [ˈkwɒrəl] **I** *s* **1.** Streit *m,* Auseinandersetzung *f* (**with** mit). **2.** **have no ~ with** nichts auszusetzen haben an (*dat*). **II** *v/i pret u. pp* **-reled,** *bsd. Br.* **-relled 3.** (sich) streiten (**with** mit; **a·bout, over** über *acc*). **4.** ~ **with** et. auszusetzen haben an (*dat*). **quar·rel·some** [ˈꞈsəm] *adj* □ streitsüchtig.

quar·ry¹ [ˈkwɒrɪ] *s* Steinbruch *m.*

quar·ry² [~] *s hunt.* Beute *f, a. fig.* Opfer *n.*

quart [kwɔːt] *s* Quart *n* (*Hohlmaß*): **you can't put a ~ into a pint pot** F das geht einfach nicht.

quar·ter [ˈkwɔːtə] **I** *s* **1.** Viertel *n:* **a ~ of an hour** e-e Viertelstunde. **2. it's (a) ~ to** (*Am. a.* **of**) **six** es ist Viertel vor sechs *od.* drei Viertel sechs; **at (a) ~ past** (*Am. a.* **after**) **six** um Viertel nach sechs *od.* Viertel sieben. **3.** Quartal *n,* Vierteljahr *n:* **by the ~** vierteljährlich. **4.** *Am.* Vierteldollar *m.* **5.** (Himmels)Richtung *f;* Gegend *f,* Teil *m* (*es Landes etc*): **from all ~s** von überall(her). **6.** (Stadt)Viertel *n.* **7.** *pl* Quartier *n,* Unterkunft *f*

(*beide a.* ✕). **8.** *fig.* Seite *f,* Stelle *f:* **in the highest ~s** an höchster Stelle; **from official ~s** von amtlicher Seite. **II** *v/t* **9.** vierteln. **10.** *bsd.* ✕ einquartieren (**on** bei). ˈ**~deck** *s* ⚓ Achterdeck *n.* ˌ**~ˈfi·nals** *s pl Sport:* Viertelfinale *n.*

quar·ter·ly [ˈkwɔːtəlɪ] *adj u. adv* vierteljährlich.

quar·ter note *s* ♩ *bsd. Am.* Viertelnote *f.*

quar·tet(te) [kwɔːˈtet] *s* ♩ Quartett *n.*

quartz [kwɔːts] *s min.* Quarz *m.* ~ **clock,** ~ **watch** *s* Quarzuhr *f.*

quash [kwɒʃ] *v/t* **1.** 🏛 Urteil *etc* annullieren, aufheben. **2.** *Aufstand etc* niederschlagen, unterdrücken.

qua·ver [ˈkweɪvə] **I** *v/i* **1.** zittern (*Stimme*). **2.** ♪ tremolieren. **II** *v/t* **3.** *et.* mit zitternder Stimme sagen. **III** *s* **4.** Zittern *n.* **5.** ♪ Tremolo *n.* **6.** ♪ *Br.* Achtelnote *f.*

quay [kiː] *s* ⚓ Kai *m.*

quea·sy [ˈkwiːzɪ] *adj:* **I feel ~** mir ist übel.

queen [kwiːn] **I** *s* **1.** (*a. Schönheitsetc*)Königin *f:* ~ **bee** *zo.* Bienenkönigin; ~ **mother** Königinmutter *f;* → **English** 3, **evidence** 2. **2.** *Kartenspiel, Schach:* Dame *f:* ~ **of hearts** Herzdame. **3.** F Schwule *m.* **II** *v/t* **4.** *Schach:* *Bauern* in e-e Dame verwandeln. **5.** ~ **it** F die große Dame spielen. ˈ**queen·ly** *adj* königlich.

queer [kwɪə] **I** *adj* □ **1.** komisch, seltsam: ~ **customer** F komischer Kauz; **be a bit ~ in the head** F sie nicht alle haben. **2.** F schwul. **II** *s* **3.** F Schwule *m.* **III** *v/t* **4.** → **pitch²** 10.

quell [kwel] *v/t Aufstand etc* niederschlagen, unterdrücken; *Zweifel etc* beseitigen.

quench [kwentʃ] *v/t Durst* löschen, stillen.

quer·u·lous [ˈkwerʊləs] *adj* □ nörglerisch.

que·ry [ˈkwɪərɪ] **I** *s* Frage *f.* **II** *v/t* in Frage stellen, in Zweifel ziehen.

quest [kwest] **I** *s* Suche *f* (**for** nach): **in ~ of** auf der Suche nach. **II** *v/i* suchen (**after, for** nach).

ques·tion [ˈkwestʃən] **I** *s* **1.** Frage *f:* ~ **mark** Fragezeichen *n;* ~ **master** *Br.* Quizmaster *n;* → **ask** 1, **pop¹** 7. **2.** Frage *f,* Problem *n:* **this is not the point in** ~ darum geht es nicht. **3.** Frage *f,* Sache *f*: **only a ~ of time** nur e-e Frage der Zeit. **4.** Frage *f*, Zweifel *m*: **there is no ~ that, it is beyond ~ that** es steht außer Frage, daß; **there is no ~ about this** daran besteht kein Zweifel; **be out of the ~** nicht in Frage kommen; **call into ~** → 6. **II** *v/t* **5.** (*about*) befragen (über *acc*), ⚖ verhören, -nehmen (zu). **6.** bezweifeln, in Zweifel ziehen, in Frage stellen. **'ques·tion·a·ble** *adj* □ **1.** fraglich, zweifelhaft. **2.** fragwürdig. **'ques·tion·er** *s* Fragesteller(in). **'ques·tion·ing I** *adj* □ fragend (*Blick etc*). **II** *s* Befragung *f*, ⚖ Verhör *n*, Vernehmung *f*. **ques·tion·naire** [ˌkwestʃəˈneə] *s* Fragebogen *m*.

queue [kjuː] *bsd*. *Br*. **I** *s* Schlange *f*: **stand in a ~** → IIa; → **jump** 9. **II** *v/i mst ~ up (for** nach, um) a) Schlange stehen, anstehen, b) sich anstellen. **'~-ˌjump·er** *s* j-d, der sich vordräng(el)t; *mot*. Kolonnenspringer(in).

quib·ble ['kwɪbl] **I** *v/i* sich herumstreiten (**with** mit; **about, over** wegen). **II** *s* kleinliche Beschwerde, Kleinigkeit *f*.

quick [kwɪk] **I** *adj* □ **1.** schnell, rasch: **~!** mach schnell!, beeil dich!; **be ~ to learn** (*od*. **at learning**) schnell lernen; **a ~ one** F ein Gläschen auf die Schnelle; → **offence** 3, **uptake**. **2.** kurz (*Reise etc*). **3.** aufbrausend, hitzig (*Temperament*). **II** *adv* **4.** schnell, rasch. **III** *s* **5.** **cut s.o. to the ~** *fig*. j-n tief treffen (**with** mit). **'~-ˌact·ing** *adj* schnell wirkend (*Medikament*). **'~-change** *adj*: **~ artist** *thea*. Verwandlungskünstler(in).

quick·en ['kwɪkən] *v/t u. v/i* (sich) beschleunigen, *v/i a.* schneller werden.

quick·ie ['kwɪkɪ] *s* F *et*. *Schnelles od. Kurzes, z. B.* Gläschen *n* auf die Schnelle, kurze Frage.

'quick·ˌsand *s* Treibsand *m*. **ˌ~-'tempered** *adj* aufbrausend, hitzig. **ˌ~-'witted** *adj* □ aufgeweckt; schlagfertig; geistesgegenwärtig.

quid [kwɪd] *pl* **quid** *Br*. F Pfund *n* (*Währung*).

qui·et ['kwaɪət] **I** *adj* □ **1.** ruhig, still: **~, please** Ruhe, bitte. **2.** ruhig (*Leben etc*). **3.** geheim, heimlich: **keep s.th. ~** et. für sich behalten. **II** *s* **4.** Ruhe *f*, Stille *f*: → **peace** 3. **5. on the ~** F heimlich. **III** *v/t u. v/i* **6.** → **quieten**. **'qui·et·en I** *v/t* **1.** *a*. **~ down** j-n beruhigen. **2.**

Befürchtungen etc zerstreuen. **II** *v/i* **3.** *a*. **~ down** sich beruhigen.

quill [kwɪl] *s* **1.** *orn*. (Schwanz-, Schwung)Feder *f*. **2.** *a*. **~ pen** *hist*. Federkiel *m*. **3.** *zo*. Stachel *m*.

quilt [kwɪlt] *s* Steppdecke *f*. **'quilt·ed** *adj* Stepp...

quin [kwɪn] *s* *Br*. F Fünfling *m*.

quince [kwɪns] *s* ❦ Quitte *f*.

qui·nine [kwɪˈniːn] *s* *pharm*. Chinin *n*.

quint [kwɪnt] *s* *Am*. F Fünfling *m*.

quin·tes·sence [kwɪnˈtesns] *s* **1.** Quintessenz *f*. **2.** Inbegriff *m*.

quin·tet(te) [kwɪnˈtet] *s* ♪ Quintett *n*.

quin·tu·plet ['kwɪntjʊplɪt] *s* Fünfling *m*.

quip [kwɪp] **I** *s* geistreiche *od*. witzige Bemerkung. **II** *v/i* witzeln.

quirk [kwɜːk] *s* **1.** Eigenart *f*, Schrulle *f*. **2. by some ~ of fate** durch e-n verrückten Zufall.

quit [kwɪt] (*mst irr*) F **I** *v/t* **1.** aufhören mit: **~ doing s.th.** aufhören, et. zu tun; **~ one's job** kündigen; **~ smoking** das Rauchen aufgeben. **II** *v/i* **2.** aufhören. **3.** kündigen.

quite [kwaɪt] *adv* **1.** ganz, völlig: **be ~ right** völlig recht haben; **~ (so)** *bsd*. *Br*. genau, ganz recht. **2.** ziemlich: **a ~ disappointment** e-e ziemliche Enttäuschung; **~ a few** ziemliche viele; **~ good** ganz *od*. recht gut. **3. it was ~ a** (*od*. **some**) **sight** das war vielleicht ein Anblick; **she's ~ a girl** sie ist ein tolles Mädchen.

quits [kwɪts] *adj* quitt (**with** mit): **call it ~** F es gut sein lassen.

quit·ter ['kwɪtə] *s*: **he's a** (**no**) **~** F er gibt (nicht so) schnell auf.

quiv·er¹ ['kwɪvə] **I** *v/i* zittern (**with** vor *dat*; **at** bei *e-m Gedanken etc*). **II** *s* Zittern *n*.

quiv·er² [ˆ] *s* Köcher *m*.

quix·ot·ic [kwɪkˈsɒtɪk] *adj* (**~ally**) weltfremd-idealistisch.

quiz [kwɪz] **I** *pl* **'quiz·zes** *s* Quiz *n*. **II** *v/t* ausfragen (**about** über *acc*). **'~·ˌmas·ter** *s* Quizmaster *m*.

quiz·zi·cal ['kwɪzɪkl] *adj* □ wissend (*Blick etc*).

quoit [kɔɪt] *s* **1.** Wurfring *m*. **2.** *pl* (*sg konstruiert*) Wurfringspiel *n*.

quo·rate ['kwɔːreɪt] *adj* beschlußfähig.

quo·rum ['kwɔːrəm] *s zur Beschlußfähigkeit erforderliche Teilnehmerzahl*.

quo·ta [ˈkwəʊtə] s Kontingent n, Quote f, ✝ a. Soll n.

quo·ta·tion [kwəʊˈteɪʃn] s **1.** Zitat n (from aus): ~ *from the Bible* Bibelzitat n. **2.** ✝ Notierung f. **3.** ✝ (verbindlicher) Kosten(vor)anschlag: *get a* ~ e-n Kostenvoranschlag einholen. ~ *marks* s pl Anführungszeichen pl: *put* (od. *place*) *in* ~ in Anführungszeichen setzen.

quote [kwəʊt] **I** v/t **1.** zitieren (from aus); *Beispiel etc* anführen: *he was* ~*d as saying that* er soll gesagt haben, daß. **2.** *be* ~*d at* ✝ notieren mit. **II** v/i **3.** ~ *from* zitieren. **III** s F **4.** → **quotation** 1, 2. **5.** *pl* Gänsefüßchen pl: *put* (od. *place*) *in* ~*s* in Gänsefüßchen setzen. **IV** adv **6.** ~ ... *unquote* Zitat ... Zitat Ende.

quo·tient [ˈkwəʊʃnt] s A Quotient m.

R

r [ɑː]: *the three R's* (= *reading, writing, arithmetic*) Lesen n, Schreiben n u. Rechnen n.

rab·bi [ˈræbaɪ] s eccl. Rabbiner m.

rab·bit [ˈræbɪt] s Kaninchen n. ~ *punch* s Genickschlag m.

rab·ble [ˈræbl] s **1.** Pöbel m, Mob m. **2.** sociol. contp. Pöbel m. '~·**rous·ing** adj aufwieglerisch, Hetz...

rab·id [ˈræbɪd] adj □ **1.** vet. tollwütig. **2.** fanatisch.

ra·bies [ˈreɪbiːz] s vet. Tollwut f.

rac·coon → **racoon**.

race¹ [reɪs] s **1.** Rasse f. **2.** Rasse(nzugehörigkeit) f. **3.** (Menschen)Geschlecht n.

race² [~] **I** s **1.** Sport: Rennen n (a. fig. for um), Lauf m: ~ *against time* fig. Wettlauf mit der Zeit. **II** v/i **2.** an (e-m) Rennen teilnehmen; um die Wette laufen od. fahren (*against, with* mit). **3.** rasen, rennen. **4.** durchdrehen (*Motor*). **III** v/t **5.** um die Wette laufen od. fahren mit. **6.** rasen mit: ~ *s.o. to hospital* mit j-m ins Krankenhaus rasen.

'**race·course** s Pferdesport: Rennbahn f. '~·**horse** s Rennpferd n. ~ **meet·ing** s Pferdesport: Rennveranstaltung f.

rac·er [ˈreɪsə] s **1.** Rennpferd n. **2.** Rennrad n, -wagen m.

'**race·track** s **1.** Automobilsport etc: Rennstrecke f. **2.** bsd. Am. → **racecourse**.

ra·cial [ˈreɪʃl] adj □ rassisch, Rassen...: ~ *discrimination* Rassendiskriminierung f; ~ *segregation* Rassentrennung f. **ra·cial·ism** [ˈreɪʃəlɪzəm], '**ra·cial·ist** → **racism, racist**.

rac·ing [ˈreɪsɪŋ] adj Renn...: ~ *bicycle* Rennrad n; ~ *car* Rennwagen m; ~ *cyclist* Radrennfahrer(in); ~ *driver* Rennfahrer(in).

ra·cism [ˈreɪsɪzəm] s Rassismus m. '**ra·cist I** s Rassist(in). **II** adj rassistisch.

rack¹ [ræk] **I** s **1.** Gestell n, (Geschirr-, Zeitungs- etc)Ständer m, 🚆 (Gepäck)Netz n, mot. (Dach)Gepäckträger m. **2.** hist. Folter(bank) f: *put s.o. on the* ~ j-n auf die Folter spannen (a. fig.). **II** v/t **3.** *be* ~*ed by* (od. *with*) geplagt od. gequält werden von. **4.** → **brain** 2.

rack² [~] s: *go to* ~ *and ruin* verfallen (*Gebäude, Person*), dem Ruin entgegentreiben (*Land, Wirtschaft*).

rack·et¹ [ˈrækɪt] s Tennis etc: Schläger m.

rack·et² [~] s F **1.** Krach m, Lärm m: *make a* ~ Krach machen. **2.** Schwindel m, Gaunerei f; (Drogen- etc)Geschäft n; organisierte Erpressung; Beruf m, Branche f: *what's his* ~? was macht er beruflich? **rack·et·eer** [ˌrækəˈtɪə] s F Gauner m; Erpresser m.

ra·coon [rəˈkuːn] s zo. Waschbär m.

rac·y [ˈreɪsɪ] adj □ **1.** spritzig (*Geschichte etc*). **2.** gewagt.

ra·dar [ˈreɪdɑː] **I** s Radar m, n. **II** adj Radar...: ~ *screen* Radarschirm m; ~ (*speed*) *trap* Radarkontrolle f; ~ *station* Radarstation f.

ra·di·al [ˈreɪdjəl] **I** adj □ radial, Radial..., strahlenförmig: **~ tire** (*bsd. Br.* **tyre**) → II. **II** *s mot.* Gürtelreifen *m*.

ra·di·ant ['reɪdjənt] *adj* □ strahlend (*a. fig.* **with** *von dat*): **be ~ with joy** vor Freude strahlen.

ra·di·ate ['reɪdɪeɪt] **I** *v/t* Licht, Wärme *etc* ausstrahlen, *Optimismus etc a.* verströmen. **II** *v/i* strahlenförmig ausgehen (**from** von). **,ra·di·'a·tion** *s* **1.** Ausstrahlung *f, fig. a.* Verströmen *n*. **2.** *phys.* (*engS.* radioaktive) Strahlung: **~ sick·ness** ✿ Strahlenkrankheit *f*. **ra·di·a·tor** ['~eɪtə] *s* **1.** Heizkörper *m*. **2.** *mot.* Kühler *m*: **~ grill** Kühlergrill *m*.

rad·i·cal ['rædɪkl] **I** *adj* □ **1.** radikal (*a. pol.*). **2.** ⚕ Wurzel...: **~ sign** Wurzelzeichen *n*. **II** *s* **3.** *pol.* Radikale *m, f*. **4.** ⚕, *ling.* Wurzel *f*. **rad·i·cal·ism** ['~kəlɪzəm] *s bsd. pol.* Radikalismus *m*. **'rad·i·cal·ize** *v/t bsd. pol.* radikalisieren.

ra·di·i ['reɪdɪaɪ] *pl von* **radius**.

ra·di·o ['reɪdɪəʊ] **I** *pl* **-os** *s* **1.** Radio *n*, Rundfunkgerät *n*; Funkgerät *n*. **2.** Radio *n*, Rundfunk *m*: **on the ~** im Radio; **be in ~** beim Rundfunk sein. **3.** Funk *m*: **by ~** per *od.* über Funk. **II** *v/t* **4.** Nachricht *etc* funken, durchgeben. **5.** *j-n*, Ort anfunken. **III** *v/i* **6. ~ for help** per *od.* über Funk um Hilfe bitten. **,~'ac·tive** *adj* □ radioaktiv: **~ waste** Atommüll *m*, radioaktiver Abfall. **,~ac'tiv·i·ty** *s* Radioaktivität *f*. **~ a·larm** *s* Radiowecker *m*. **~ car** *s* Am. Funk(streifen)wagen *m*. **~ con·tact** *s* Funkkontakt *m*, -verbindung *f*: **be in ~ with** in Funkkontakt stehen mit. **,~·con'trolled** *adj* funkgesteuert.

ra·di·o·gram ['reɪdɪəʊgræm] *s* **1.** Funkspruch *m*. **2.** → **radiograph**. **ra·di·o·graph** ['~grɑːf] *s* ✿ Röntgenbild *n*.

ra·di·o| ham → **ham** 3. **~ mes·sage** *s* Funkspruch *m*. **~ op·er·a·tor** *s* Funker *m*. **~ set** → **radio** 1. **~ sig·nal** *s* Funksignal *n*. **~ sta·tion** *s* Rundfunksender *m*, -station *f*. **,~'ther·a·py** *s* Strahlen-, Röntgentherapie *f*. **~ traf·fic** *s* Funkverkehr *m*.

rad·ish ['rædɪʃ] *s* ✿ **1.** Rettich *m*. **2.** Radieschen *n*.

ra·di·um ['reɪdɪəm] *s* ✿ Radium *n*.

ra·di·us ['reɪdɪəs] *pl* **-di·i** ['~dɪaɪ] *s* **1.** ⚕ Radius *m*, Halbmesser *m*. **2. within a three-mile ~** im Umkreis von drei

Meilen (**of** um). **3.** *anat.* Speiche *f*.

raf·fle ['ræfl] **I** *s* Tombola *f*. **II** *v/t oft ~ off* verlosen.

raft [rɑːft] *s* Floß *n*.

raft·er ['rɑːftə] *s* (Dach)Sparren *m*.

rag [ræg] *s* **1.** Fetzen *m*, Lumpen *m*; Lappen *m*: **in ~s** in Fetzen (*Stoff etc*); zerlumpt (*Person*); **be (like) a red ~ to a bull to s.o.** *Br.* F wie ein rotes Tuch für *j-n* sein *od.* auf *j-n* wirken; **feel like a wet ~** F total k. o. sein. **2.** F *contp.* Käseblatt *n*. **'~·bag** *s* Sammelsurium *n* (*of* von).

rage [reɪdʒ] *s* **1.** Wut *f*, Zorn *m*: **be in a ~** wütend sein; **fly into a ~** wütend werden. **2.** F **the latest ~** der letzte Schrei; **be all the ~** große Mode sein. **II** *v/i* **3.** wettern (**against, at** gegen); *fig.* wüten (*Krankheit*, *Sturm*), toben (*Meer*, *Sturm*): **a raging headache** rasende Kopfschmerzen *pl*.

rag·ged ['rægɪd] *adj* □ **1.** zerlumpt (*Kleidung*, *Person*). **2.** struppig, zottig (*Bart etc*). **3.** *fig.* dilettantisch, stümperhaft.

ra·gout ['ræguː] *s gastr.* Ragout *n*.

raid [reɪd] *s* **1.** (**on**) Überfall *m* (auf *acc*), ⚔ *a.* Angriff *m* (gegen). **2.** Razzia *f* (**on** in *dat*): **make a ~ on** → 4. **II** *v/t* **3.** überfallen, ⚔ *a.* angreifen. **4.** e-e Razzia machen in (*dat*).

rail¹ [reɪl] **I** *s* **1.** Geländer *n*. **2.** (*Handtuch*)Halter *m*. **3.** ⚙ Schiene *f, pl a.* Gleis *n*: **go off the ~s** a) *a.* **jump the ~s** entgleisen, b) *fig.* auf die schiefe Bahn geraten. **4.** (*Eisen*)Bahn *f*: **by ~** mit der Bahn. **II** *v/t* **5. ~ in** einzäunen; **~ off** abzäunen.

rail² [~] *v/i* schimpfen (**against, at** über *acc*).

rail·ing ['reɪlɪŋ] *s oft pl* (Gitter)Zaun *m*.

rail·road ['reɪlrəʊd] **I** *s* **1.** *Am.* → **railway**. **II** *v/t* F **2.** Gesetzesvorlage *etc* durchpeitschen (**through** in *dat*). **3. ~ s.o. into doing s.th.** *j-n* rücksichtslos drängen, *et.* zu tun.

rail·way ['reɪlweɪ] *s bsd. Br.* Eisenbahn *f*: **~ station** Bahnhof *m*.

rain [reɪn] **I** *s* **1.** Regen *m*: **in the ~** im Regen; **the ~s** *pl* die Regenzeit (*in den Tropen*); → **pour** 3. **2.** *fig.* (*Schläge etc*)Hagel *m*, (*Funken*)Regen *m*. **II** *v/t* **3.** *impers.* regnen: **it is ~ing. 4. ~ down on** *fig.* niederprasseln auf (*acc*) (*Schläge* *etc*). **III** *v/t* **5.** → *cat* l. **6.** *fig.* ~ *blows on s.o.* j-n mit Schlägen eindecken; ~ *abuse on s.o.* j-n mit Beschimpfungen überschütten. **7.** *be* ~*ed off* (*Am. out*) wegen Regens abgesagt *od.* abgebrochen werden. '~**bow** *s* Regenbogen *m.* '~**coat** *s* Regenmantel *m.* '~**drop** *s* Regentropfen *m.* '~**fall** *s* Niederschlag(smenge *f*) *m.* ~ **for·est** *s* Regenwald *m.* '~**proof** *adj* regen-, wasserdicht. '~**storm** *s* heftiger Regenguß. '~**wa·ter** *s* Regenwasser *n.*

rain·y ['reɪnɪ] *adj* regnerisch, verregnet, Regen...: *the* ~ *season* die Regenzeit (*in den Tropen*); *put away* (*od. save*) *s.th. for a* ~ *day* et. für schlechte Zeiten zurücklegen, et. auf die hohe Kante legen.

raise [reɪz] **I** *v/t* **1.** *Arm, gesunkenes Schiff etc* heben; *Vorhang etc* hochziehen: ~ *one's hat* den Hut ziehen (*to s.o.* vor j-m; *a. fig.*) *od.* lüften; → *eyebrow*. **2.** *Denkmal etc* errichten. **3.** a) *Protest etc* hervorrufen: ~ *a laugh* Gelächter ernten, b) *Erwartungen* (er)wecken: ~ *s.o.'s hopes* in j-m Hoffnung erwekken; ~ *a suspicion* Verdacht erregen, c) *Gerücht etc* aufkommen lassen, d) *Schwierigkeiten* machen. **4.** *Staub etc* aufwirbeln: → *dust* l. **5.** *Frage* aufwerfen, *et.* zur Sprache bringen. **6.** *Anspruch geltend machen, Forderung* stellen. **7.** *Kinder* auf-, großziehen; *Tiere* züchten; *Getreide etc* anbauen. **8.** *Moral, Stimmung* heben. **9.** *Gehalt etc* erhöhen, *Geschwindigkeit etc a.* steigern: → *power* 9. **10.** *Hypothek etc* aufnehmen (*on* auf *acc*); *Geld* zs.-bringen, beschaffen. **11.** *Blockade etc, a. Verbot* aufheben. **II** *s* **12.** *bsd. Am.* Lohn- *od.* Gehaltserhöhung *f.*

rai·sin ['reɪzn] *s* Rosine *f.*

rake [reɪk] **I** *s* **1.** Rechen *m,* Harke *f.* **II** *v/t* **2.** rechen, harken: ~ *in F Geld* kassieren; ~ *it in* F das Geld nur so scheffeln; ~ *out* F et. herausfinden; ~ *up Laub etc* zs.-rechen, -harken; F *Leute* aufreiben, *Geld a.* zs.-kratzen; F *alte Geschichten etc* aufwärmen. **3.** *Gelände etc* absuchen (*with* mit *Fernglas etc*). **III** *v/i* **4.** *a.* ~ *about* (*od. around*) herumstöbern (*in* in *dat*). '~**off** *s* F (Gewinn)Anteil *m,* Prozente *pl.*

rak·ish ['reɪkɪʃ] *adj* □ flott, verwegen.

ral·ly ['rælɪ] **I** *s* **1.** Kundgebung *f,* (Massen)Versammlung *f.* **2.** *Motorsport:* Rallye *f.* **3.** *Tennis etc:* Ballwechsel *m.* **II** *v/t* **4.** *Truppen etc* (wieder) sammeln. **III** *v/i* **5.** sich (wieder) sammeln: ~ *round fig.* sich zs.-tun; ~ *round s.o. fig.* sich um j-n scharen. **6.** sich erholen (*from* von) (*a.* ✝).

ram [ræm] **I** *s* **1.** *zo.* Widder *m,* Schafbock *m.* **2.** ⊕ *Ramme f.* **II** *v/t* **3.** *Fahrzeug etc* rammen. **4.** *Pfosten etc* rammen (*into* in *acc*): ~ *down Erde* etc feststampfen, -treten; → *throat.*

ram·ble ['ræmbl] **I** *v/i* **1.** wandern. **2.** *a.* ~ *on contp.* faseln (*about* von, über *acc*). **II** *s* **3.** Wanderung *f: go for* (*od. on a*) *a* ~ e-e Wanderung machen. '**ram·bling** *adj* □ **1.** ❀ Kletter...: ~ *rose.* **2.** *fig.* weitschweifig, unzusammenhängend. **3.** weitläufig (*Gebäude*).

ram·i·fi·ca·tion [ˌræmɪfɪ'keɪʃn] *s* Verzweigung *f,* -ästelung *f* (*beide a. fig.*). **ram·i·fy** ['~faɪ] *v/i* sich verzweigen (*a. fig.*).

ramp [ræmp] *s* Rampe *f.*

ram·page [ræm'peɪdʒ] **I** *v/i:* ~ *through* a) (wild *od.* aufgeregt) trampeln durch (*Elefant etc*), b) randalierend ziehen durch. **II** *s: go on the* ~ randalieren; *go on the* ~ *through* → Ib.

ramp·ant ['ræmpənt] *adj* □ **1.** wuchernd (*Pflanze*): *be* ~ wuchern. **2.** *fig.* grassierend: *be* ~ *in* grassieren in (*dat*).

ram·shack·le ['ræmʃækl] *adj* baufällig; klapp(e)rig (*Fahrzeug*).

ran [ræn] *pret von* **run.**

ranch [rɑːntʃ] *s* **1.** Ranch *f.* **2.** (*Geflügeletc*)Farm *f.* '**ranch·er** *s* **1.** Rancher *m.* **2.** (*Geflügel- etc*)Züchter *m.* **3.** Rancharbeiter *m.*

ran·cid ['rænsɪd] *adj* □ ranzig: *go* ~ ranzig werden.

ran·cor *Am.* → **rancour.**

ran·cor·ous ['ræŋkərəs] *adj* □ voller Groll (*toward[s]* gegen).

ran·cour ['ræŋkə] *s bsd. Br.* Groll *m,* Erbitterung *f.*

ran·dom ['rændəm] **I** *adj* auch zufallswohl, zufällig, Zufalls...: ~ *sample* Stichprobe *f; take* ~ *samples* Stichproben machen. **II** *s: at* ~ aufs Geratewohl.

rand·y ['rændɪ] *adj* F scharf, geil.

rang [ræŋ] *pret von* **ring².**

range [reɪndʒ] **I** s **1.** (*Berg*)Kette f. **2.** (*Koch-, Küchen*)Herd m. **3.** (*Schieß-*)Stand m, (-)Platz m. **4.** Entfernung f: **at close** (*od. short*) ~ aus kurzer *od.* kürzester Entfernung, aus nächster Nähe. **5.** Reich-, Schuß-, Tragweite f. **6.** *fig.* Bereich m, Spielraum m, Grenzen pl. **7.** ✝ Kollektion f, Sortiment n. **8.** *fig.* Bereich m, Gebiet n. **II** v/i **9.** schwanken, sich bewegen (*from ... to, between ... and* zwischen ... u.). **III** v/t **10.** aufstellen, anordnen. **~ find·er** s phot. etc Entfernungsmesser m.

rang·er ['reɪndʒə] s **1.** Förster m. **2.** Am. Ranger m.

rank¹ [ræŋk] s **1.** Reihe f; ✗ Glied n: **close the ~s** die Reihen schließen; *fig.* sich zs.-schließen. **2.** *bsd.* ✗ Rang m: **in** ~ im Rang, rangmäßig; **he is above me in** ~ er ist ranghöher als ich; **of the first** (*od. front, top*) ~ *fig.* erstklassig; **the ~s** pl (Unteroffiziere pl u.) Mannschaften pl; *fig.* das Heer, die Masse (*der Arbeitslosen etc*); **the ~ and file** der Mannschaftsstand; *fig.* die Basis (*e-r Partei etc*); **pull** ~ F den Vorgesetzten herauskehren (*on* gegenüber); **rise from the** ~s vom Mannschaftsrang zum Offizier aufsteigen; *fig.* sich hocharbeiten. **3.** Rang m, (soziale) Stellung. **II** v/t **4.** rechnen, zählen (*among* zu); stellen (*above* über acc): **be ~ed 2nd in the world** an 2. Stelle der Weltrangliste stehen. **5.** ✗ Am. ranghöher sein als. **III** v/i **6.** zählen, gehören (*among* zu); gelten (*as* als); rangieren (*above* über dat).

rank² [~] adj □ **1.** (üppig) wuchernd. **2.** übel(riechend od. -schmeckend). **3.** *fig.* kraß (*Außenseiter*), blutig (*Anfänger*), blühend (*Unsinn*).

rank·ing ['ræŋkɪŋ] adj **1.** ✗ Am. ranghöchst (*Offizier*). **2.** ~ **list** (*Sport*) Rangliste f.

ran·kle ['ræŋkl] v/i *fig.* (*on*) nagen (an dat), weh tun (dat).

ran·sack ['rænsæk] v/t **1.** durchwühlen. **2.** plündern.

ran·som ['rænsəm] **I** s Lösegeld n: **hold s.o. to** ~ j-n bis zur Zahlung e-s Lösegelds gefangenhalten; *fig.* j-n erpressen; ~ **demand** Lösegeldforderung f. **II** v/t auslösen, freikaufen.

rant [rænt] v/i a. ~ **on, ~ and rave (about)**

eifern (gegen), sich in Tiraden ergehen (über acc).

rap¹ [ræp] **I** s **1.** Klopfen n; Klaps m: **give s.o. a ~ over the knuckles** j-m auf die Finger klopfen (a. *fig.*). **2. take the** ~ F den Kopf hinhalten (*for* für). **II** v/t **3.** klopfen an (acc) *od.* auf (acc): ~ **s.o. over the knuckles** j-m auf die Finger klopfen (a. *fig.*). **4.** *mst* ~ **out** Befehl etc bellen, *Fluch etc* ausstoßen. **III** v/i **5.** klopfen (*at* an acc; *on* auf acc).

rap² [~] s: **I don't care a ~ (for it)** das ist mir völlig egal.

ra·pa·cious [rə'peɪʃəs] adj □ **1.** habgierig. **2.** räuberisch. **3.** *orn., zo.* Raub...

ra·pac·i·ty [rə'pæsətɪ] s Habgier f.

rape¹ [reɪp] **I** s **1.** Vergewaltigung f, ⚖ Notzucht f. **II** v/t vergewaltigen.

rape² [~] s ♣ Raps m: ~ **oil** Rapsöl n.

rap·id ['ræpɪd] **I** adj □ schnell, rasch. **II** s pl Stromschnellen pl. '~**·fire** adj **1.** ✗ Schnellfeuer... **2.** *fig.* schnell (aufeinanderfolgend).

ra·pid·i·ty [rə'pɪdətɪ] s Schnelligkeit f.

rap·ist ['reɪpɪst] s Vergewaltiger m.

rap·port [ræ'pɔː] s harmonisches Verhältnis (*between* zwischen dat; *with* zu).

rap·proche·ment [ræ'prɒʃmɑ̃ːŋ] s *bsd.* pol. (Wieder)Annäherung f (*between* zwischen dat).

rapt [ræpt] adj: **with ~ attention** mit gespannter Aufmerksamkeit.

rap·ture ['ræptʃə] s, a. pl Entzücken n, Verzückung f: **be in ~s** entzückt *od.* hingerissen sein (*about, at, over* von); **go into ~s** in Verzückung geraten (*about, at, over* über acc). '**rap·tur·ous** adj □ **1.** entzückt, hingerissen. **2.** stürmisch (*Applaus etc*).

rare¹ [reə] adj □ **1.** selten, rar. **2.** dünn (*Luft*). **3.** F Mords...: **give s.o. a ~ fright** j-m e-n Mordsschreck(en) einjagen.

rare² [~] adj blutig (*Steak*).

rar·e·fied ['reərɪfaɪd] adj **1.** dünn (*Luft*). **2.** *fig.* exklusiv.

rar·ing ['reərɪŋ] adj: **be ~ to do s.th.** F es kaum mehr erwarten können *od.* ganz wild darauf sein, et. zu tun.

rar·i·ty ['reərətɪ] s Seltenheit f, (*Briefmarke etc a.*) Rarität f.

ras·cal ['rɑːskəl] s **1.** Gauner m. **2.** *humor.* Schlingel m.

rash¹ [ræʃ] *adj* □ voreilig, -schnell.

rash² [~] *s* **1.** ⚕ (Haut)Ausschlag *m*: → **come out** 5. **2.** *fig.* Flut *f*.

rash·er ['ræʃə] *s* dünne Scheibe (*Frühstücksspeck etc*).

rasp [rɑːsp] **I** *s* **1.** Raspel *f*. **2.** Kratzen *n*. **II** *v/t* **3.** raspeln: ~ **off** abraspeln.

rasp·ber·ry ['rɑːzbərɪ] *s* ❧ Himbeere *f*.

rasp·ing ['rɑːspɪŋ] *adj* □ kratzend (*Geräusch*); krächzend (*Stimme*).

rat [ræt] **I** *s zo.* Ratte *f* (*a.* F *contp.*): **smell a** ~ *fig.* Lunte od. den Braten riechen; **~s!** F Mist! **II** *v/i*: ~ **on** F *j-n* im Stich lassen; *j-n* verpfeifen; aussteigen aus (*e-m Projekt etc*).

rate [reɪt] **I** *s* **1.** Quote *f*, (*Inflations-etc*)Rate *f*, (*Geburten-, Sterbe*)Ziffer *f*. **2.** (*Steuer-, Zins- etc*)Satz *m*, (*Wechsel*)Kurs *m*; **at any** ~ *fig.* auf jeden Fall. **3.** *mst pl* Br. Gemeinde-, Kommunalsteuer *f*. **4.** Geschwindigkeit *f*, Tempo *n*. **II** *v/t* **5.** einschätzen (**highly** hoch), halten (**as** für): **be** ~**d as** gelten als. **6.** *Lob etc* verdienen.

rath·er ['rɑːðə] **I** *adv* **1.** ziemlich: ~ **a success** ein ziemlicher Erfolg; ~ **a cold night, a** ~ **cold night** e-e ziemlich kalte Nacht. **2.** *I would* (*od.* **had**) ~ **stay at home** ich möchte lieber zu Hause bleiben. **3.** *or* ~ (od.) vielmehr. **II** *int* **4.** *bsd. Br.* F freilich!, und ob!

rat·i·fi·ca·tion [ˌrætɪfɪˈkeɪʃn] *s pol.* Ratifizierung *f*. **rat·i·fy** ['~faɪ] *v/t* ratifizieren.

rat·ing ['reɪtɪŋ] *s* **1.** Einschätzung *f*. **2.** *Rundfunk, TV:* Einschaltquote *f*.

ra·ti·o ['reɪʃɪəʊ] *s* **1.** A *etc* Verhältnis *n* (*of* … **to** von … zu).

ra·tion ['ræʃn] **I** *s* **1.** Ration *f*. **II** *v/t* **2.** *et.* rationieren. **3.** ~ **out** zuteilen (**to** dat).

ra·tion·al ['ræʃənl] *adj* □ rational: a) vernunftbegabt, b) vernünftig. **ra·tion·al·ism** ['ræʃnəlɪzəm] *s* Rationalismus *m*. **'ra·tion·al·ist I** *s* Rationalist(in). **II** *adj* rationalistisch. **ˌra·tion·al·is·tic** *adj* (**~ally**) rationalistisch. **ˌra·tion·al·i·za·tion** *s* ✝ Rationalisierung *f*. **'ra·tion·al·ize** *v/t* **1.** rational erklären. **2.** ✝ rationalisieren.

rat| poi·son *s* Rattengift *n*. ~ **race** *s* F endloser Konkurrenzkampf.

rat·tle ['rætl] **I** *v/i* **1.** klappern (*Fenster etc*); rasseln, klirren (*Ketten*); klimpern (*Münzen etc*); prasseln (**on** auf *acc*)

(*Regen etc*); knattern (*Fahrzeug*): ~ **at** rütteln an (*dat*); ~ **on** F quasseln (**about** über *acc*); ~ **through** Rede *etc* herunterrasseln; *Arbeit* in Windeseile erledigen. **II** *v/t* **2.** rasseln *od.* klimpern mit; rütteln an (*dat*): ~ **off** *Gedicht etc* herunterrasseln. **3.** F *j-n* verunsichern. **III** *s* **4.** Klappern *n* (*etc*, → 1). **5.** Rassel *f*, Klapper *f* (*Spielzeug*), Knarre *f*, Schnarre *f* (*Lärminstrument*). '**~snake** *s zo.* Klapperschlange *f*. '**~trap** *s* F Klapperkasten *m* (*Auto*).

'**rat·trap** *s Am.* F Bruchbude *f*, Hundehütte *f*.

rat·ty ['rætɪ] *adj* F **1.** *Am.* schäbig (*Kleidungsstück*). **2.** gereizt: **there's no need to be** ~ sei doch nicht gleich so gereizt.

rau·cous ['rɔːkəs] *adj* □ heiser, rauh.

rav·age ['rævɪdʒ] **I** *v/t* verwüsten. **II** *s pl* Verwüstungen *pl, a. fig.* verheerende Auswirkungen *pl*.

rave [reɪv] *v/i* **1.** phantasieren, irrereden. **2.** toben; wettern (**against, at** gegen). **3.** schwärmen (**about** von).

rav·el ['rævl] *pret u. pp* **-eled**, *bsd. Br.* **-elled I** *v/t* **1.** *a.* ~ **up** verwickeln, -wirren. **2.** *oft* ~ **out** ausfransen; auftrennen; *a. fig.* entwirren. **II** *v/i* **3.** *a.* ~ **up** sich verwickeln *od.* -wirren. **4.** *oft* ~ **out** ausfransen; auftrennen.

ra·ven ['reɪvn] *s orn.* Rabe *m*.

rav·en·ous ['rævənəs] *adj* □ **1.** ausgehungert, heißhungrig. **2.** ~ **hunger** Bären-, Wolfshunger *m*.

ra·vine [rə'viːn] *s* Schlucht *f*, Klamm *f*.

rav·ing ['reɪvɪŋ] **I** *adj* □ **1.** tobend. **2.** phantasierend. **3.** F toll (*Erfolg*), hinreißend (*Schönheit*). **II** *adv* **4.** ~ **mad** F völlig od. total übergeschnappt. **III** *s pl* **5.** Phantasien *pl*, irres Gerede.

rav·i·o·li [ˌrævɪ'əʊlɪ] *s pl* (*sg konstruiert*) Ravioli *pl*.

rav·ish ['rævɪʃ] *v/t* hinreißen. '**rav·ish·ing** *adj* □ hinreißend.

raw [rɔː] **I** *adj* □ **1.** roh (*Gemüse etc*). **2.** ✝, ⊙ roh, Roh…: ~ **material** Rohstoff *m*. **3.** unerfahren, grün. **4.** wund (*Haut*). **5.** naßkalt (*Wetter, Tag etc*). **6.** **get a** ~ **deal** F benachteiligt od. ungerecht behandelt werden. **II** *s* **7.** **in the** ~ im Natur- od. Urzustand; F nackt: ~**'boned** *adj* hager, knochig.

ray¹ [reɪ] *s* Strahl *m*: **sun's** ~**s** *pl* Sonnenstrahlen *pl*; **~ of light** Lichtstrahl; **~ of hope** Hoffnungsstrahl, -schimmer *m*.

ray² [~] *s ichth.* Rochen *m*.

ray·on ['reɪɒn] *s* Kunstseide *f*.

raze [reɪz] *v/t*: **~ to the ground** dem Erdboden gleichmachen.

ra·zor ['reɪzə] *s* Rasiermesser *n*; -apparat *m*: **be on a ~'s edge → razor edge. ~ blade** *s* Rasierklinge *f*. **~ edge** *s*: **be on a ~** *fig.* auf des Messers Schneide stehen. **~ sharp** *adj* messerscharf (*a. fig. Verstand*).

raz·zle ['ræzl] *s*: **go on the ~** F auf den Putz hauen.

re [riː] *prp*: **~ your letter of ... † Betr.:** Ihr Schreiben vom ...

reach [riːtʃ] **I** *v/t* **1.** *j-n, et., Ort, Alter etc* erreichen. **2. ~ out** Arm *etc* ausstrecken. **3. ~ down** herunter-, hinunterreichen (**from** von). **4.** reichen *od.* gehen bis an (*acc*) *od.* zu. **II** *v/i* **5. a. ~ out** greifen, langen (**for** nach) (*beide a. fig.*). **6. ~ out** die Hand ausstrecken. **7.** reichen, gehen, sich erstrecken (**as far as, to** bis an *acc od.* zu): **as far as the eye can ~** soweit das Auge reicht. **III** *s* **8.** Reichweite *f* (*a. Boxen*): **within** (**out of**) **s.o.'s ~** in (außer) j-s Reichweite; **be within easy ~** leicht zu erreichen sein (*Instrument etc*); **she lives within easy ~ of the shops** (*bsd. Am. stores*) von ihrer Wohnung aus sind die Geschäfte leicht zu erreichen.

re·act [rɪ'ækt] *v/i* **1.** reagieren (**to** auf *acc*): **~ against** sich wehren gegen. **2.** 🦚 reagieren (**with** mit).

re·ac·tion [rɪ'ækʃn] *s* Reaktion *f* (*a.* 🦚, *pol. etc*). **re·ac·tion·ar·y** *pol.* **I** *adj* reaktionär. **II** *s* Reaktionär(in).

re·ac·ti·vate [rɪ'æktɪveɪt] *v/t* reaktivieren (*a.* 🦚).

re·ac·tive [rɪ'æktɪv] *adj* 🦚 reaktiv, reaktionsfähig. **re'ac·tor** *s phys.* Reaktor *m*.

read¹ [riːd] **I** *v/t* (*irr*) **1.** lesen: **~ in** (*Computer*) einlesen; **~ s.th. into** et. hineinlesen in (*acc*); **~ out** verlesen; **~ s.th. to s.o., ~ s.o. s.th.** j m ct. vorlesen; **read over** (*od.* **through**) (sich) *et.* durchlesen; **~ up** nachlesen; **we can take it as ~ that** wir können davon ausgehen, daß. **2.** *Zähler etc* ablesen. **3.** (an)zeigen, stehen auf (*dat*) (*Thermometer etc*). **4.** *univ.* studieren. **5.** deuten, verstehen

(**as** als). **II** *v/i* (*irr*) **6.** lesen: **I've ~ about it** ich habe darüber *od.* davon gelesen; **~ to s.o.** j-m (et.) vorlesen (**from** aus); **→ line¹** 3. **7. ~ as follows** folgendermaßen lauten. **8.** sich *gut etc* lesen. **9.** sich vorbereiten (**for** auf *e-e* Prüfung): **~ up on** et. nachlesen; **→ bar** 9. **III** *s* **10. be a good ~** *bsd. Br.* sich gut lesen.

read² [red] *pret u. pp von* **read¹**.

read·a·ble ['riːdəbl] *adj* □ lesbar: a) lesenswert, b) leserlich.

re·ad·dress [ˌriːə'dres] *v/t* Brief *etc* umadressieren.

read·er ['riːdə] *s* **1.** Leser(in). **2.** Lektor(in). **3.** *ped.* Lesebuch *n*. **'read·er·ship** *s* Leser(kreis *m*, -schaft *f*) *pl*.

read·i·ly ['redɪlɪ] *adv* **1.** bereitwillig. **2.** leicht, ohne weiteres. **'read·i·ness** *s* **1.** Bereitschaft *f*: **~ to help** Hilfsbereitschaft. **2.** Gewandtheit *f*.

read·ing ['riːdɪŋ] **I** *s* **1.** Lesen *n*. **2.** Lesung *f* (*a. parl.*). **3. be** (*od.* **make**) **good ~** sich gut lesen. **4.** Deutung *f*, Auslegung *f*. **5.** ⚙ Anzeige *f*, (*Barometeretc*)Stand *m*. **II** *adj* **6.** Lese...: **~ glasses** *pl* Lesebrille *f*; **~ lamp** Leselampe *f*; **~ matter** Lesestoff *m*, Lektüre *f*; **~ room** Lesezimmer *n*, -saal *m*.

re·ad·just [ˌriːə'dʒʌst] **I** *v/t* ⚙ nachstellen, korrigieren: **~ o.s. → II.** **II** *v/i* (**to**) sich wiederanpassen (*dat od.* an *acc*), sich wiedereinstellen (auf *acc*). **ˌre·ad'just·ment** *s* **1.** Nachstellung *f*, Korrektur *f*. **2.** (**to**) Wiederanpassung *f* (an *acc*), Wiedereinstellung *f* (auf *acc*).

read·y ['redɪ] **I** *adj* (□ **→ readily**) **1.** bereit, fertig (**for** *s.th.* für et.; **to do** zu tun): **~ for takeoff** ✈ startbereit, -klar; **get** (*od.* **make**) **~** (sich) bereit- *od.* fertigmachen; **get ~ for an examination** sich auf *e-e* Prüfung vorbereiten. **2. be ~ to do s.th.** bereit *od.* willens sein, et. zu tun; schnell bei der Hand sein, et. zu tun: **~ to help** hilfsbereit, -willig. **3.** schnell, schlagfertig: **~ wit** Schlagfertigkeit *f*. **4.** im Begriff, nahe daran (**to do** tun): **~ → drop** 10. **5. ~ money** (*od.* **cash**) Bargeld *n*. **II** *s* **6. the ~** F Bargeld *n*: **be a bit short of the ~** knapp bei Kasse sein. **'~·made** *adj* **1.** Konfektions...: **~ suit** Konfektionsanzug *m*. **2.** *fig.* passend, geeignet (*Entschuldigung etc*): **~ solution** Patentlösung *f*. **ˌ~·to·'wear → ready-made** 1.

'ti:v] *s* ♪ Rezitativ *n*. **re·cite** [rɪ'saɪt] *v/t*
1. auf-, hersagen. 2. rezitieren, vortragen. 3. aufzählen.

reck·less ['reklɪs] *adj* □ rücksichtslos.
'reck·less·ness *s* Rücksichtslosigkeit *f*.

reck·on ['rekən] **I** *v/t* 1. aus-, berechnen: ~ *in* ein-, mitrechnen; ~ *up* zs.-rechnen. 2. ~ *s.o.* (*to be*) *clever* j-n für clever halten; *he is* ~*ed* (*to be*) *clever* er gilt als clever. 3. rechnen, zählen (*among* zu). 4. glauben, schätzen (*that* daß). **II** *v/i* 5. ~ *on* rechnen auf (*acc*) *od.* mit; ~ *with* rechnen mit; *he's a man to be* ~*ed with* mit ihm muß man rechnen; *you'll have me to* ~ *with* du wirst mit mir zu tun bekommen; ~ *without* nicht rechnen mit. **'reck·on·ing** *s* Berechnung *f*: *by my* ~ nach m-r (Be)Rechnung; *be out in one's* ~ sich verrechnet haben.

re·claim [rɪ'kleɪm] *v/t* 1. zurückfordern, -verlangen (*from* von); *Gepäck etc* abholen. 2. ~ *land from the sea* dem Meer Land abgewinnen. 3. ☼, 🌿 wiedergewinnen (*from* aus).
rec·la·ma·tion [,reklə'meɪʃn] *s* 1. Rückforderung *f*. 2. ☼, 🌿 Wiedergewinnung *f*.

re·cline [rɪ'klaɪn] *v/i* sich zurücklehnen: ~*ing seat* mot. etc Ruhesitz *m*.

re·cluse [rɪ'klu:s] *s* Einsiedler(in).

rec·og·ni·tion [,rekəg'nɪʃn] *s* 1. (Wieder)Erkennen *n*: *be burnt beyond* (*od. out of all*) ~ bis zur Unkenntlichkeit verbrennen; *the town has changed beyond* ~ die Stadt ist nicht wiederzuerkennen. 2. Anerkennung *f*: *in* (*od. as a*) ~ *of* als Anerkennung für, in Anerkennung (*gen*); *gain* (*od. get, win*) ~ Anerkennung finden. **rec·og·niz·a·ble** ['-naɪzəbl] *adj* □ (wieder)erkennbar: *be hardly* ~ kaum zu erkennen sein. **re·cog·nize** ['-naɪz] *v/t* 1. (wieder)erkennen (*by* an *dat*). 2. anerkennen (*a. pol.*). 3. eingestehen, zugeben (*that* daß).

re·coil **I** *v/i* [rɪ'kɔɪl] 1. zurückschrecken (*from* vor *dat*) (*a. fig.*): ~ *from doing s.th.* davor zurückschrecken, et. zu tun. 2. zurückstoßen (*Gewehr etc*). 3. ~ *on fig.* zurückfallen auf (*acc*). **II** *s* ['ri:kɔɪl] 4. Rückstoß *m*.

rec·ol·lect [,rekə'lekt] **I** *v/t* sich erinnern

an (*acc*): ~ *doing s.th.* sich daran erinnern, et. getan zu haben. **II** *v/i*: *as far as I* (*can*) ~ soweit ich mich erinnere. **,rec·ol'lec·tion** *s* Erinnerung *f* (*of* an *acc*): *to the best of my* ~ soweit ich mich erinnere.

rec·om·mend [,rekə'mend] *v/t* 1. empfehlen (*as* als; *for* für): ~ *doing s.th.* empfehlen *od.* raten, et. zu tun. 2. sprechen für: *he has little to* ~ *him* es spricht wenig für ihn. **,rec·om'mend·a·ble** *adj* empfehlenswert; ratsam. **rec·om·men·da·tion** [,~men'deɪʃn] *s* Empfehlung *f*: *on s.o.'s* ~ auf j-s Empfehlung.

rec·om·pense ['rekəmpens] **I** *v/t* entschädigen (*for* für). **II** *s* Entschädigung *f*: *as a* (*od. in*) ~ als Entschädigung (*for* für).

rec·on·cile ['rekənsaɪl] *v/t* 1. ver-, aussöhnen (*with* mit): *they are* ~*d again* sie haben sich wieder versöhnt; *become* ~*d to s.th. fig.* sich mit et. abfinden. 2. in Einklang bringen (*with* mit). **rec·on·cil·i·a·tion** [,~sɪlɪ'eɪʃn] *s* 1. Ver-, Aussöhnung *f* (*between* zwischen *dat*; *with* mit). 2. Einklang *m*.

rec·on·dite [rɪ'kɒndaɪt] *adj* □ abstrus, schwerverständlich.

re·con·di·tion [,ri:kən'dɪʃn] *v/t* ☼ (general)überholen: ~*ed engine* Austauschmotor *m*.

re·con·nais·sance [rɪ'kɒnɪsəns] *s* ✕ Aufklärung *f*, Erkundung *f*. ~ *flight* *s* Aufklärungsflug *m*. ~ *plane* *s* Aufklärungsflugzeug *n*, Aufklärer *m*.

rec·on·noi·ter *Am.*, *bsd. Br.* **rec·on·noi·tre** [,rekə'nɔɪtə] *v/t* ✕ erkunden, auskundschaften.

re·con·quer [,ri:'kɒŋkə] *v/t* zurückerobern. **,re·con·quest** [,~kwest] *s* Zurückeroberung *f*.

re·con·sid·er [,ri:kən'sɪdə] *v/t* noch einmal überdenken. **'re·con,sid·er·a·tion** *s* nochmaliges Überdenken.

re·con·struct [,ri:kən'strʌkt] *v/t* 1. wieder aufbauen; *fig.* wiederaufbauen. 2. *fig. Fall etc* rekonstruieren. **,re·con·struc·tion** *s* 1. Wiederaufbau *m*. 2. *fig.* Rekonstruktion *f*.

rec·ord¹ ['rekɔ:d] *s* 1. Aufzeichnung *f*, Niederschrift *f*; ⚖ Protokoll *n*: *off the* ~ inoffiziell; *on* ~ aktenkundig; geschichtlich verzeichnet, schriftlich belegt; *fig.* aller Zeiten; *he is* (*od.* **went**) *on* ~ *as having said that* er hat sich offiziell dahingehend geäußert, daß; *keep a* ~ *of* Buch führen über (*acc*); *to set the* ~ *straight* um das klarzustellen. **2.** Vergangenheit *f; gute etc* Leistungen *pl* (*in der Vergangenheit*): *have a criminal* ~ vorbestraft sein. **3.** (Schall)Platte *f*: *make a* ~ e-e Platte aufnehmen. **4.** *Sport etc*: Rekord *m*. **II** *adj* **5.** (Schall)Platten...: ~ *player* Plattenspieler *m*. **6.** *Sport etc*: Rekord...: ~ *holder* Rekordhalter(in), -inhaber(in); *in* ~ *time* in Rekordzeit.

re·cord² [rɪ'kɔ:d] *v/t* **1.** schriftlich niederlegen, aufzeichnen, -schreiben; 🏛 protokollieren, zu Protokoll *od.* zu den Akten nehmen. **2.** (*auf Tonband etc*) aufnehmen, *Programm a.* aufzeichnen, mitschneiden; ~*ed broadcast* (*Rundfunk, TV*) Aufzeichnung *f*. **3.** *Meßwerte* registrieren.

're·cord-,break·ing *adj Sport etc*: Rekord...

re·cord·er [rɪ'kɔ:də] *s* **1.** (*Kassetten*)Recorder *m*, (*Tonband*)Gerät *n*. **2.** ♩ Blockflöte *f*. **re'cord·ing** *s* Aufnahme *f*, Aufzeichnung *f*, Mitschnitt *m*: ~ *studio* Aufnahme-, Tonstudio *n*.

re·count¹ [rɪ'kaʊnt] *v/t* erzählen.

re·count² *v/t* [ˌriː'kaʊnt] nachzählen. **II** *s* ['riː:kaʊnt] Nachzählung *f*.

re·coup [rɪ'ku:p] *v/t* **1.** *Verlust etc* wiedereinbringen, sich *Ausgaben etc* zurückholen (*from* von). **2.** *j-n* entschädigen (*for* für).

re·course [rɪ'kɔ:s] *s*: *have* ~ *to* greifen *od.* Zuflucht nehmen zu.

re·cov·er [rɪ'kʌvə] **I** *v/t et. Verlorenes* wiederfinden; *Bewußtsein etc* wiedererlangen; *Kosten etc* wiedereinbringen; *Fahrzeug, Verunglückten etc* bergen: ~ *one's composure* sich wieder fangen *od.* fassen; ~ *consciousness* a. wieder zu sich kommen. **II** *v/i* sich erholen (*from* von) (*a. fig.*): *he has fully* ~*ed* er ist wieder ganz gesund. **re'cov·er·y** *s* **1.** Wiederfinden *n*; Wiedererlangen *n*; Wiedereinbringung *f*; Bergung *f* (*a. fig.*). **2.** Erholung *f* (*a. fig.*): *make a complete* ~ völlig gesund werden; *make a quick* (*od.* **speedy**) ~ sich schnell erholen; *wish s.o. a speedy* ~ *j-m* gute Besserung wünschen.

rec·re·a·tion [ˌrekrɪ'eɪʃn] *s* Entspannung *f*, Erholung *f*; Freizeitbeschäftigung *f*: ~ *ground* Spielplatz *m*. **ˌrec·re'a·tion·al** [~ʃənl] *adj* Erholungs-...; Freizeit...: ~ *activities pl* Freizeitgestaltung *f*; ~ *value* Freizeitwert *m*.

re·crim·i·nate [rɪ'krɪmɪneɪt] *v/i* Gegenbeschuldigungen vorbringen (*against* gegen). **re,crim·i'na·tion** *s* Gegenbeschuldigung *f*: *their* ~(*s pl*) ihre gegenseitigen Beschuldigungen *pl*.

re·cruit [rɪ'kruːt] **I** *s* **1.** ✕ Rekrut *m*. **2.** (*to*) Neue *m, f* (in *dat*); neues Mitglied (*gen. od.* in *dat*). **II** *v/t* **3.** ✕ rekrutieren; *Personal* einstellen; *Mitglieder* werben. **re'cruit·ment** *s* ✕ Rekrutierung *f*; Einstellung *f*; Werbung *f*.

rec·ta ['rektə] *pl von* **rectum**.

rec·tan·gle ['rek,tæŋgl] *s* ♭ Rechteck *n*. **rec'tan·gu·lar** [~gjʊlə] *adj* ☐ rechteckig; rechtwink(e)lig.

rec·ti·fi·ca·tion [ˌrektɪfɪ'keɪʃn] *s* **1.** Berichtigung *f*, Korrektur *f*. **2.** 🔧 Rektifikation *f*. **3.** ⚡ Gleichrichtung *f*. **rec·ti·fy** ['~faɪ] *v/t* **1.** berichtigen, korrigieren. **2.** 🔧 rektifizieren. **3.** ⚡ gleichrichten.

rec·ti·lin·e·ar [ˌrektɪ'lɪnɪə] *adj* ☐ geradlinig.

rec·ti·tude ['rektɪtjuːd] *s* Redlichkeit *f*, Rechtschaffenheit *f*.

rec·tor ['rektə] *s* Pfarrer *m*. **'rec·to·ry** *s* Pfarrhaus *n*.

rec·tum ['rektəm] *pl* **-tums, -ta** ['~tə] *s anat.* Mastdarm *m*.

re·cu·per·ate [rɪ'kuːpəreɪt] **I** *v/i* sich erholen (*from* von) (*a. fig.*). **II** *v/t Verluste etc* wettmachen. **re,cu·per'a·tion** *s* **1.** Erholung *f* (*a. fig.*). **2.** Wettmachen *n*.

re·cur [rɪ'kɜ:] *v/i* wiederkehren, wiederauftreten (*Problem, Symptom etc*), (*Schmerz a.*) wiedereinsetzen: ~ *to s.o.* *j-m* wiederkommen (*Erinnerung etc*). **re·cur·rence** [rɪ'kʌrəns] *s* Wiederkehr *f*, Wiederauftreten *n*, Wiedereinsetzen *n*. **re'cur·rent** *adj* ☐ wiederkehrend, wiederauftretend, wiedereinsetzend.

re·cy·cle [ˌriː'saɪkl] *v/t* wiederverwerten. **ˌre·cy·cling** *s* Recycling *n*, Wiederverwertung *f*.

red [red] **I** *adj* **1.** rot: *the lights are* ~ die Ampel steht auf Rot; *go* (*od.* **turn**) ~ rot werden; → *flag¹* 1, *paint* 2, *rag¹* 1. **2.** *oft* ⬡ *pol.* rot. **II** *s* **3.** Rot *n*: *at* ~ bei Rot; *the* *lights are at* ~ die Ampel steht auf Rot; *dressed in* ~ rot od. in Rot gekleidet; *see* ~ *fig.* rotsehen; *be in the* ~ ✝ in den roten Zahlen sein, rote Zahlen schreiben. **4.** *oft* ♀ *pol.* Rote *m, f.* ~ **car·pet** *s* roter Teppich. ˏ~'**car·pet** *adj:* *give s.o. the* ~ *treatment* j-n mit großem Bahnhof empfangen. ♀ **Cross** *s* Rotes Kreuz.

red·den ['redn] **I** *v/t* röten, rot färben. **II** *v/i* rot werden (*with* vor *dat*). '**red·dish** *adj* □ rötlich.

re·dec·o·rate [ˌriː'dekəreɪt] *v/t* Zimmer *etc* neu streichen od. tapezieren.

re·deem [rɪ'diːm] *v/t* **1.** *Pfand, Versprechen etc* einlösen. **2.** *Ruf etc* wiederherstellen: ~ *o.s.* sich rehabilitieren. **3.** *Gefangene etc* los-, freikaufen. **4.** *Hypothek, Schulden* abzahlen, tilgen. **5.** *schlechte Eigenschaften etc* ausgleichen, wettmachen. **6.** *bsd. eccl.* erlösen (*from* von). **Re'deem·er** *s eccl.* Erlöser *m*, Heiland *m*.

re·demp·tion [rɪ'dempʃn] *s* **1.** Einlösung *f*. **2.** Wiederherstellung *f*. **3.** Los-, Freikauf *m*. **4.** Abzahlung *f*, Tilgung *f*. **5.** Ausgleich *m*. **6.** *bsd. eccl.* Erlösung *f* (*from* von). **7.** *beyond* (*od. past*) ~ hoffnungslos.

re·de·vel·op [ˌriːdɪ'veləp] *v/t* Gebäude, Stadtteil sanieren. ˏ**re·de'vel·op·ment** *s* Sanierung *f*.

ˏ**red-**'**hand·ed** *adj: catch s.o.* ~ j-n auf frischer Tat ertappen. ˏ~'**head·ed** *adj* rothaarig. ~ **her·ring** *s* **1.** Bückling *m*. **2.** *fig.* Ablenkungsmanöver *n*; falsche Fährte *od.* Spur. ˏ~'**hot** *adj* **1.** rotglühend (*Metall*); glühendheiß. **2.** *fig.* glühend, überschwenglich (*Begeisterung*). **3.** *fig.* brandaktuell (*Nachricht etc*). ♀ **In·di·an** *s* Indianer(in).

re·di·rect [ˌriːdɪ'rekt] *v/t* Brief *etc* nachschicken, -senden (*to s.o.* j-m; *to a new address* an e-e neue Adresse).

re·dis·cov·er [ˌriːdɪs'kʌvə] *v/t* wiederentdecken. ˏ**re·dis'cov·er·y** *s* Wiederentdeckung *f*.

re·dis·trib·ute [ˌriːdɪ'strɪbjuːt] *v/t* neu verteilen, umverteilen. '**re,dis·tri·bu·tion** [ˏ~'bjuːʃn] *s* Neu-, Umverteilung *f*.

ˏ**red-**'**let·ter day** *s* Freuden-, Glückstag *m* (*for* für). ~ **light** *s* **1.** rotes Licht (*Warnsignal etc*): *see the* ~ *fig.* die Gefahr erkennen. **2.** Rotlicht *n*: *go*

through the ~*s* bei Rot über die Kreuzung fahren. ˏ~'**light dis·trict** *s* Rotlichtbezirk *m*, Bordellviertel *n*.

red·ness ['rednɪs] *s* Röte *f*.

re·do [ˌriː'duː] *v/t* (*irr do*) **1.** nochmals tun *od.* machen: ~ *one's hair* sich die Haare in Ordnung bringen. **2.** → **re·decorate**.

re·dou·ble [ˌriː'dʌbl] *v/t bsd. Anstrengungen* verdoppeln.

re·dress [rɪ'dres] **I** *v/t Unrecht* wiedergutmachen; *Mißstand etc* abstellen, beseitigen; *Gleichgewicht* wiederherstellen. **II** *s* Wiedergutmachung *f*; Abstellung *f*, Beseitigung *f*: *seek* ~ *for* Wiedergutmachung verlangen für.

red tape *s* Amtsschimmel *m*, Bürokratismus *m*.

re·duce [rɪ'djuːs] *v/t* **1.** *Foto etc* verkleinern. **2.** *Steuern etc* senken, *Geschwindigkeit, Risiko etc* verringern, *Preis, Waren* herabsetzen, reduzieren (*from ... to* von ... auf *acc*), *Gehalt etc* kürzen. **3.** (*to*) verwandeln (in *acc*), machen (zu): ~ *to a nervous wreck* aus *j-m* ein Nervenbündel machen. ~ *s.o. to silence* (*tears*) j-n zum Schweigen (Weinen) bringen. **5.** reduzieren, zurückführen (*to acc*). **6.** 🔥 reduzieren. **7.** → *denominator.* **re·duc·tion** [rɪ'dʌkʃn] *s* **1.** Verkleinerung *f*. **2.** Senkung *f*, Verringerung *f*, Herabsetzung *f*, Reduzierung *f*, Kürzung *f*. **3.** 🔥 Reduktion *f*.

re·dun·dan·cy [rɪ'dʌndənsɪ] *s* **1.** ✝ Freistellung *f*, -setzung *f*. **2.** *ling.* Redundanz *f*. **re'dun·dant** *adj* □ **1.** ✝ freigestellt, -gesetzt: *be made* ~ freigestellt *od.* -gesetzt werden. **2.** *ling.* redundant.

re·du·pli·cate [rɪ'djuːplɪkeɪt] *v/t* wiederholen. **re,du·pli'ca·tion** *s* Wiederholung *f*.

red wine *s* Rotwein *m*.

re·ech·o [riː'ekəʊ] *v/i* widerhallen (*with* von).

reed [riːd] *s* Schilf(rohr) *n*, Ried *n*; (*einzelnes*) Schilfrohr.

re·ed·u·cate [ˌriː'edʃʊkeɪt] *v/t* umerziehen. '**re-,ed·u'ca·tion** *s* Umerziehung *f*.

reed·y ['riːdɪ] *adj* □ **1.** schilfig. **2.** piepsig (*Stimme*).

reef¹ [riːf] *s* (Felsen)Riff *n*.

reef² [~] *v/t* ⚓ *Segel* reffen. ~ **knot** *s* Kreuz-, Weberknoten *m*.

reek [riːk] **I** s Gestank m: *there was a ~ of garlic* es stank nach Knoblauch. **II** v/i stinken (*of* nach).

reel¹ [riːl] **I** s (*Kabel-, Schlauch- etc*)Rolle f, (*Film-, Garn- etc*)Spule f. **II** v/t **~ off** abrollen, abspulen; *fig.* herunterrasseln; **~ up** aufrollen, -spulen.

reel² [~] v/i **1.** sich drehen: *my head ~ed* mir drehte sich alles, mir wurde schwindlig; *the room ~ed before my eyes* das Zimmer drehte sich vor m-n Augen. **2.** wanken, taumeln, (*Betrunkener a.*) torkeln.

re-e·lect [ˌriːiˈlekt] v/t wiederwählen. **ˌre-eˈlec·tion** s Wiederwahl f: *seek ~* sich erneut zur Wahl stellen.

re-en·ter [ˌriːˈentə] v/t wieder eintreten in (*acc*) (*a. Raumfahrt*), wieder betreten. **re-ˈen·try** s Wiedereintreten n, -eintritt m (*into* in acc).

ref [ref] s Sport: F Schiri m; (*Boxen*) Ringrichter m.

re·fec·to·ry [rɪˈfektərɪ] s univ. Mensa f.

re·fer [rɪˈfɜː] **I** v/t **1.** *j-n* ver-, hinweisen (*to* auf acc). **2.** *j-n* (*um Auskunft etc*) verweisen (*to* an acc). **3.** (*to*) *et.* übergeben (*dat*), a. Patienten überweisen (an acc): **~ back** zurückweisen. **II** v/i **4.** ver-, hinweisen (*to* auf acc). **5.** (*to*) sich berufen od. beziehen (auf acc); anspielen (auf acc); erwähnen (acc). **6.** (*to*) nachschlagen (in dat), konsultieren (acc). **ref·er·ee** [ˌrefəˈriː] **I** s **1.** ♟, Sport: Schiedsrichter m, (*Boxen*) Ringrichter m. **2.** Br. → **reference** 5b. **II** v/i **3.** ♟, Sport: als Schiedsrichter fungieren, (*Sport a.*) pfeifen, (*Boxen*) als Ringrichter fungieren. **III** v/t **4.** ♟, Sport: als Schiedsrichter fungieren bei, (*Sport a.*) Spiel pfeifen, (*Boxen*) Kampf leiten. **ref·er·ence** [ˈrefrəns] s **1.** Verweis m, Hinweis m (*to* auf acc); (*list of*) **~s** pl Quellenangabe f. **2.** Verweisstelle f; Beleg m, Unterlage f: **~ number** Aktenzeichen n. **3.** (*to*) Bezugnahme f (auf acc); Anspielung f (auf acc); Erwähnung f (*gen*): *make* (a) ~ (*to*) → **refer** 5. **4.** (*to*) Nachschlagen n (in dat), Konsultieren n (*gen*): **~ book** Nachschlagewerk n; **~ library** Handbibliothek f. **5.** Referenz f: a) Empfehlung f, b) Auskunftgeber m: *act as a ~ for s.o.* j-m als Referenz dienen.

ref·er·en·dum [ˌrefəˈrendəm] pl **-dums, -da** [~də] s pol. Referendum n, Volksabstimmung f, -entscheid m.

re-fill I v/t [ˌriːˈfɪl] **1.** wieder füllen, nach-, auffüllen. **II** s [ˈriːfɪl] **2.** (*Füller*)Patrone f, (*Kugelschreiber- etc*)Mine f. **3.** *would you like a ~?* F darf ich nachschenken?

re·fine [rɪˈfaɪn] **I** v/t **1.** Öl, Zucker raffinieren. **2.** *fig.* verfeinern, kultivieren. **II** v/i **3.** **~ on** *fig.* verbessern, -feinern. **reˈfined** adj **1.** raffiniert: **~ sugar** Raffinade f. **2.** *fig.* kultiviert, vornehm. **reˈfine·ment** s **1.** Raffination f, Raffinierung f. **2.** Verbesserung f, -feinerung f. **3.** *fig.* Kultiviertheit f, Vornehmheit f. **reˈfin·er·y** s Raffinerie f.

re·flect [rɪˈflekt] **I** v/t **1.** *Strahlen etc* reflektieren, zurückwerfen, -strahlen, *Bild etc* reflektieren, (wider)spiegeln (*a. acc*): *be ~ed in* sich (wider)spiegeln in (*dat*) (*a. fig.*); **~ (dis)credit on** *fig.* ein gutes (schlechtes) Licht werfen auf (*acc*); **~ing telescope** Spiegelteleskop n. **II** v/i **2.** nachdenken (*on* über acc). **3.** **~ (badly) on** sich nachteilig auswirken auf (*acc*); ein schlechtes Licht werfen auf (*acc*). **reˈflec·tion** s **1.** Reflexion f, Zurückwerfung f, -strahlung f, (Wider)Spieg(e)lung f (*a. fig.*). **2.** Spiegelbild n. **3.** *fig.* Überlegung f: *on* ~ nach einigem Nachdenken; *when I ~ etc* es mir recht überlege. **4.** *mst* pl *fig.* Betrachtung f (*on* über acc). **reˈflec·tive** adj □ **1.** reflektierend, (wider)spiegelnd. **2.** *fig.* nachdenklich. **reˈflec·tor** s **1.** Reflektor m. **2.** Rückstrahler m.

re·flex [ˈriːfleks] s a. **~ action** Reflex m. **~ cam·er·a** s phot. Spiegelreflexkamera f.

re·flex·ive [rɪˈfleksɪv] adj □ ling. reflexiv, rückbezüglich: **~ pronoun** Reflexivpronomen n, rückbezügliches Fürwort; **~ verb** reflexives Verb, rückbezügliches Zeitwort.

re·for·est [ˌriːˈfɒrɪst], **re·for·es·ta·tion** → **reafforest, reafforestation**.

re·form [rɪˈfɔːm] **I** s **1.** pol. etc Reform f. **2.** Besserung f. **II** v/t **3.** *j-n* bessern. **ref·or·ma·tion** [ˌrefəˈmeɪʃn] s **1.** Reformierung f: *the 2 eccl.* die Reformation. **2.** Besserung f. **re·form·a·to·ry** [rɪˈfɔːmətərɪ] adj Reformrm... **reˈform·er** s

1. *pol. etc* Reformer *m.* 2. *eccl.* Reformator *m.*

re·fract [rɪ'frækt] *v/t phys. Strahlen, Wellen* brechen. **re'frac·tion** *s* Refraktion *f*, Brechung *f*.

re·frac·to·ry [rɪ'fræktərɪ] *adj* □ 1. eigensinnig, störrisch. 2. ✹ hartnäckig.

re·frain¹ [rɪ'freɪn] *v/i* (*from*) absehen (von), sich enthalten (*gen*), unterlassen (*acc*): ~ *from doing s.th.* es unterlassen, et. zu tun.

re·frain² [~] *s* Kehrreim *m*, Refrain *m.*

re·fresh [rɪ'freʃ] *v/t* (*o.s.* sich) erfrischen; *fig. Gedächtnis* auffrischen. **re'fresh-er** *s* 1. Erfrischung *f* (*Getränk etc*). 2. ~ *course* Auffrischungskurs *m.* **re-'fresh·ing** *adj* □ erfrischend (*a. fig.*). **re'fresh·ment** *s* Erfrischung *f* (*a. Getränk etc*).

re·frig·er·ate [rɪ'frɪdʒəreɪt] *v/t* ⊗ kühlen. **re,frig·er'a·tion** *s* Kühlung *f*. **re'frig-er·a·tor** *s* Kühlschrank *m*: ~*freezer* Kühl- u. Gefrierkombination *f*.

re·fu·el [ˌriː'fjʊəl] *v/t u. v/i pret u. pp* **-eled**, *bsd. Br.* **-elled** ✈, *mot.* auftanken.

ref·uge ['refjuːdʒ] *s* Zuflucht *f* (*from* vor *dat*) (*a. fig.*): *place of ~* Zufluchtsort *m*; *seek* ~ Zuflucht suchen; *take* ~ in Zuflucht nehmen zu, sich flüchten in (*acc*). **ref·u·gee** [ˌ~dʒiː] *s* Flüchtling *m*: ~ *camp* Flüchtlingslager *n.*

re·fund I *v/t* [riː'fʌnd] *Geld* zurückzahlen, -erstatten, *Auslagen* ersetzen: ~ *s.o. his money* j-m sein Geld zurückzahlen. II *s* ['riːfʌnd] Rückzahlung *f*, -erstattung *f*.

re·fur·bish [ˌriː'fɜːbɪʃ] *v/t* 1. aufpolieren (*a. fig.*). 2. renovieren.

re·fus·al [rɪ'fjuːzl] *s* 1. Ablehnung *f*; Verweigerung *f*: → *meet* 15. 2. Weigerung *f* (*to do* zu tun).

re·fuse¹ [rɪ'fjuːz] I *v/t* 1. *Kandidaten etc* ablehnen, *Angebot a.* ausschlagen: ~ *s.o. s.th.* j-m et. ausschlagen *od.* verweigern. 2. sich weigern, es ablehnen (*to do* zu tun). II *v/i* 3. ablehnen. 4. sich weigern.

ref·use² ['refjuːs] *s* Abfall *m*, Abfälle *pl*, Müll *m.* ~ *dump* *s* Müllabladeplatz *m*, -deponie *f.*

ref·u·ta·ble ['refjʊtəbl] *adj* □ widerlegbar. **ref·u·ta·tion** [ˌ~juː'teɪʃn] *s* Wider-

legung *f*. **re·fute** [rɪ'fjuːt] *v/t* widerlegen.

re·gain [rɪ'geɪn] *v/t* wieder-, zurückgewinnen: ~ *one's health* (*strength*) wieder gesund werden (wieder zu Kräften kommen).

re·gal ['riːgl] *adj* □ 1. königlich. 2. *fig.* hoheits-, würdevoll.

re·gale [rɪ'geɪl] *v/t* 1. fürstlich bewirten (*with* mit). 2. erfreuen, ergötzen (*with* mit).

re·ga·li·a [rɪ'geɪljə] *s pl* Insignien *pl.*

re·gard [rɪ'gɑːd] I *s* 1. Achtung *f*: *hold s.o. in high* (*low*) ~ j-n hoch (gering)achten. 2. Rücksicht *f*: *without* ~ *to* (*od. for*) ohne Rücksicht auf (*acc*); *have no* ~ *for, pay no* ~ *to* keine Rücksicht nehmen auf (*acc*). 3. *in this* ~ in dieser Hinsicht; *with* ~ *to* im Hinblick auf (*acc*). 4. *give him my* (*best*) ~*s* grüße ihn (herzlich) von mir; *with kind* ~*s* mit freundlichen Grüßen. II *v/t* 5. betrachten, ansehen. 6. *fig.* betrachten (*with* mit): ~ *as* betrachten als, halten für; *be* ~*ed as* gelten als. 7. *as* ~*s* ... was ... betrifft. **re'gard·ing** *prp* bezüglich, hinsichtlich. **re'gard·less** I *adj*: ~ *of* ohne Rücksicht auf (*acc*). II *adv* □ trotzdem.

re·gat·ta [rɪ'gætə] *s Sport:* Regatta *f.*

re·gen·cy ['riːdʒənsɪ] *s* Regentschaft *f.*

re·gen·er·ate [rɪ'dʒenəreɪt] *v/t u. v/i* (sich) regenerieren *od.* erneuern. **re-,gen·er'a·tion** *s* Regenerierung *f*, Erneuerung *f.*

re·gent ['riːdʒənt] *s* Regent(in).

re·gime [reɪ'ʒiːm] *s* 1. *pol.* Regime *n.* 2. → *regimen.*

reg·i·men ['redʒɪmen] *s* Lebensweise *f*, *bsdS.* Diät *f.*

reg·i·ment I *s* ['redʒɪmənt] 1. ✕ Regiment *n.* 2. *fig.* Schar *f.* II *v/t* ['~ment] 3. reglementieren, gängeln, bevormunden. **reg·i·men·tal** [ˌ~'mentl] *adj* ✕ Regiments... **,reg·i·men'ta·tion** *s* Reglementierung *f*, Gängelung *f*, Bevormundung *f.*

re·gion ['riːdʒən] *s* Gebiet *n*, Gegend *f*, Region *f*: *in the* ~ *of the heart* in der Herzgegend; *in the* ~ *of £50* um die *od.* ungefähr 50 Pfund. **re·gion·al** ['~dʒənl] *adj* □ regional.

reg·is·ter ['redʒɪstə] I *s* 1. Register *n*, Verzeichnis *n*, (*Wähler- etc*)Liste *f*.

keep a ~ of Buch führen über (*acc*). **2.** ◎ Registriergerät *n*. **3.** Sprach-, Stilebene *f*. **II** *v/t* **4.** registrieren, eintragen (lassen): *~ed trademark* eingetragenes Warenzeichen. **5.** *Meßwerte* registrieren, anzeigen; *fig. Empfindung* zeigen. **6.** ✍ *Brief etc* einschreiben lassen: *~ed letter* Einschreib(e)brief *m*, Einschreiben *n*; *send s.th. by ~ed mail* (*bsd. Br. post*) et. eingeschrieben schicken. **III** *v/i* **7.** sich eintragen (lassen). **8.** *he told me who he was but it didn't ~* F aber ich habe es nicht registriert *od.* zur Kenntnis genommen. *~ of·fice s bsd. Br.* Standesamt *n*.

reg·is·trar [͵redʒɪ'strɑː] *s bsd. Br.* Standesbeamter *m*, -beamtin *f*. **reg·is·tra·tion** [͵~'streɪʃn] *s* Registrierung *f*, Eintragung *f*: *~ document mot. Br.* (*etwa*) Kraftfahrzeugbrief *m*; *~ number mot.* (polizeiliches) Kennzeichen. **'reg·is·try** *s* Registratur *f*: *~ office bsd. Br.* Standesamt *n*.

re·gress [rɪ'gres] *v/i* **1.** sich rückläufig entwickeln (*Gesellschaft*). **2.** *biol., psych.* sich zurückentwickeln. **re·gres·sion** [rɪ'greʃn] *s* **1.** rückläufige Entwicklung. **2.** *biol., psych.* Regression *f*, Rückentwicklung *f*. **re·gres·sive** [~sɪv] *adj* □ regressiv, rückläufig.

re·gret [rɪ'gret] **I** *v/t* **1.** bedauern; bereuen: *~ doing s.th.* es bedauern *od.* bereuen, et. getan zu haben; *we ~ to inform you that* wir müssen Ihnen leider mitteilen, daß. **2.** *j-m, e-r Sache* nachtrauern. **II** *s* **3.** Bedauern *n* (*at* über *acc*); Reue *f*: *with great ~* mit großem Bedauern; *have no ~s* nichts bereuen; *have no ~s about doing s.th.* es nicht bedauern *od.* bereuen, et. getan zu haben. **re'gret·ful** [~fʊl] *adj* bedauernd: *~ly a.* mit Bedauern. **re'gret·ta·ble** *adj* bedauerlich. **re'gret·ta·bly** *adv* bedauerlicherweise.

re·group [͵riː'gruːp] *v/t u. v/i* (sich) umgruppieren.

reg·u·lar ['regjʊlə] **I** *adj* □ **1.** (*zeitlich*) regelmäßig: *~ customer* Stammkunde *m*, -kundin *f*; Stammgast *m*; *at ~ intervals* in regelmäßigen Abständen (*a. örtlich*). **2.** regelmäßig (*in Form od. Anordnung*). **3.** regelmäßig (*Atmen etc*): *at ~ speed* mit gleichbleibender Geschwindigkeit. **4.** geregelt, geordnet

(*Leben etc*): *be in ~ employment* fest angestellt sein. **5.** *ling.* regelmäßig. **6.** *Sport:* Stamm...: *~ player.* **7.** ◎ *gasoline mot. Am.* Normalbenzin *n*. **II** *s* F **8.** Stammkunde *m*, -kundin *f*; Stammgast *m*. **9.** *Sport:* Stammspieler(in). **10.** *mot. Am.* Normal *n*. **reg·u·lar·i·ty** [͵~'lærəti] *s* Regelmäßigkeit *f*. **reg·u·lar·ize** ['~ləraɪz] *v/t* regulieren.

reg·u·late ['regjʊleɪt] *v/t* **1.** regeln, regulieren. **2.** ◎ einstellen, regulieren. **'reg·u·la·tion** *s* **1.** Reg(e)lung *f*, Regulierung *f*. **2.** ◎ Einstellung *f*. **3.** Vorschrift *f*. **'reg·u·la·tor** *s* ◎ Regler *m*.

re·ha·bil·i·tate [͵riːə'bɪlɪteɪt] *v/t* **1.** *Schwerbehinderte* rehabilitieren. **2.** *Straffentlassene* resozialisieren. **3.** *j-s Ruf etc* wiederherstellen: *be ~d* rehabilitiert werden (*Person*). **'re·ha͵bil·i'ta·tion** *s* **1.** Rehabilitation *f*: *~ center* (*bsd. Br. centre*) Rehabilitationszentrum *n*. **2.** Resozialisierung *f*. **3.** Wiederherstellung *f*.

re·hash **I** *v/t* [͵riː'hæʃ] *alte Fakten etc* neu auftischen. **II** *s* ['riːhæʃ] Neuauftischung *f*.

re·hears·al [rɪ'hɜːsl] *s* ♪, *thea.* Probe *f*. **re'hearse** *v/t u. v/i* proben.

reign [reɪn] **I** *s* Herrschaft *f* (*a. fig.*): *~ of terror* Schreckensherrschaft. **II** *v/i* herrschen (*over* über *acc*) (*a. fig.*): *silence ~ed* es herrschte Schweigen; *the ~ing world champion* (*Sport etc*) der amtierende Weltmeister.

re·im·burse [͵riːɪm'bɜːs] *v/t Auslagen* erstatten, vergüten: *~ s.o.* (*for*) *s.th.* j-m et. erstatten. **͵re·im'burse·ment** *s* Erstattung *f*, Vergütung *f*.

rein [reɪn] **I** *s* Zügel *m*: *give free ~ to one's imagination* s-r Phantasie freien Lauf *od.* die Zügel schießen lassen; *keep a tight ~ on fig. j-n,* et. streng kontrollieren; *take the ~s fig.* die Zügel *od.* das Heft in die Hand nehmen. **II** *v/t:* *~ in Pferd etc* zügeln; *fig.* bremsen.

re·in·car·nate [riː'ɪnkɑːneɪt] *v/t:* *be ~d* wiedergeboren werden (*as* als). **͵re·in·car'na·tion** *s* Reinkarnation *f*, Wiedergeburt *f*.

rein·deer ['reɪn͵dɪə] *pl* **-deers**, *bsd. coll.* **-deer** *s zo.* Ren(tier) *n*.

re·in·force [͵riːɪn'fɔːs] *v/t allg.* verstärken, *fig. a.* untermauern: *~d concrete* ◎ Stahlbeton *m*. **͵re·in'force·ment** *s*

re·mem·ber [rɪˈmembə] **I** v/t **1.** sich erinnern an (acc): ~ **doing s.th.** sich daran erinnern, et. getan zu haben; **suddenly he ~ed that** plötzlich fiel ihm ein, daß. **2.** denken an (acc): ~ **to do s.th.** daran denken, et. zu tun; **I must ~ this** das muß ich mir merken. **3.** ~ **s.o. in one's will** j-n in s-m Testament bedenken. **4. please ~ me to your wife** grüßen Sie bitte Ihre Frau von mir; **he asked to be ~ed to you** er läßt Sie grüßen. **II** v/i **5. I can't ~** ich kann mich nicht erinnern; **if I ~ right(ly)** wenn ich mich recht erinnere od. entsinne. **re'mem·brance** s Erinnerung f (**of** an acc): **in ~ of** zur Erinnerung an; **⁀ Day** (od. **Sunday**) Br. Volkstrauertag m.

re·mind [rɪˈmaɪnd] v/t j-n erinnern (**of** an acc; **that** daran, daß): ~ **s.o. to do s.th.** j-n daran erinnern, daß er et. tut. **re'mind·er** s Mahnung f.

rem·i·nisce [ˌremɪˈnɪs] v/i in Erinnerungen schwelgen, sich in Erinnerungen ergehen (**about, on** acc). **rem·i·nis·cence** [~ˈnɪsns] s mst pl Erinnerung f (**of** an acc). **rem·i'nis·cent** adj: **be ~ of** erinnern an (acc).

re·miss [rɪˈmɪs] adj nachlässig: **be ~ in one's duties** s-e Pflichten vernachlässigen.

re·mis·sion [rɪˈmɪʃn] s **1.** (🎗 a. Straf-) Erlaß m: **he was given three months' ~** ihm wurden drei Monate (von s-r Strafe) erlassen (**for** wegen). **2.** Vergebung f (**der Sünden**). **3.** 🏥 vorübergehende Besserung.

re·mit [rɪˈmɪt] v/t **1.** Schulden, Strafe erlassen; Sünden vergeben. **2.** Geld überweisen (**to** dat od. an acc). **3.** bsd. 🎗 zurückverweisen (**to** an acc). **re'mit·tance** s Überweisung f (**to** an acc).

rem·nant [ˈremnənt] s **1.** (Über)Rest m (a. fig.). **2.** ✝ (Stoff)Rest m: ~ **sale** Restverkauf m.

re·mod·el [ˌriːˈmɒdl] v/t pret u. pp **-eled**, bsd. Br. **-elled** umgestalten.

re·mold Am. → **remould**.

re·mon·strance [rɪˈmɒnstrəns] s Protest m, Beschwerde f. **re·mon·strate** [ˈremənstreɪt] v/i protestieren (**with** bei; **against** gegen), sich beschweren (**with** bei; **about** über acc).

re·morse [rɪˈmɔːs] s Gewissensbisse pl, Reue f: **feel ~** Gewissensbisse haben.

re'morse·ful [~fʊl] adj □ reumütig, reuig. **re'morse·less** adj □ unbarmherzig (a. fig.).

re·mote [rɪˈməʊt] adj **1.** räumlich: fern, (weit) entfernt; abgelegen, entlegen. **2.** zeitlich: fern: **in the ~ future** in ferner Zukunft. **3.** fig. entfernt (Zs.-hang), (Verwandte a.) weitläufig. **4.** fig. entfernt (Möglichkeit), gering (Chance): **I haven't got the ~st idea** ich habe keine blasse od. nicht die geringste Ahnung. **5.** fig. distanziert, unnahbar. **~ con·trol** s ⚙ **1.** Fernlenkung f, -steuerung f. **2.** Fernbedienung f. **re,mote-con'trolled** adj **1.** ferngelenkt, -gesteuert. **2.** mit Fernbedienung.

re·mould bsd. Br. **I** v/t [ˌriːˈməʊld] Reifen runderneuern. **II** s [ˈriːməʊld] runderneuerter Reifen.

re·mount [ˌriːˈmaʊnt] **I** v/t Pferd etc wieder besteigen; Treppen wieder hinaufgehen: ~ **one's bicycle** wieder auf sein Fahrrad steigen. **II** v/i wieder aufsitzen.

re·mov·a·ble [rɪˈmuːvəbl] adj abnehmbar. **re'mov·al** [~vl] s **1.** Entfernung f; Abnahme f. **2.** Umzug m: ~ **van** Möbelwagen m. **re'move I** v/t **1.** entfernen (**from** von); Deckel, Hut etc abnehmen; Kleidung ablegen. **2.** fig. Schwierigkeiten etc beseitigen, Hindernisse aus dem Weg räumen; Zweifel etc zerstreuen. **II** v/i **3.** (um)ziehen (**from** von; **to** nach). **III** s **4.** fig. **be** (**at**) **only one ~ from** nicht weit entfernt sein von; **be several ~s from** weit entfernt sein von. **re'mov·er** s (Flecken- etc)Entferner m.

re·mu·ner·ate [rɪˈmjuːnəreɪt] v/t **1.** j-n entlohnen (**for** für). **2.** j-n entschädigen (**for** für). **re,mu·ner'a·tion** s **1.** Entlohnung f. **2.** Entschädigung f. **re'mu·ner·a·tive** [~rətɪv] adj □ einträglich, lohnend.

Ren·ais·sance [rəˈneɪsəns] s hist. Renaissance f.

re·nal [ˈriːnl] adj anat. Nieren...: ~ **fail·ure** 🏥 Nierenversagen n.

re·name [ˌriːˈneɪm] v/t umbenennen (**in** acc).

ren·der [ˈrendə] v/t **1.** berühmt etc machen: ~ **s.o. unable to do s.th.** es j-m unmöglich machen, et. zu tun. **2.** Hilfe leisten, Dienst a. erweisen. **3.** Gedicht etc vortragen. **4.** übersetzen, -tragen (**into** in acc). **5.** mst ~ **down** Fett auslassen. **'ren·der·ing** s 1. Vortrag m. 2. Übersetzung f, -tragung f.

ren·dez·vous ['rɒndɪvuː] **I** pl **-vous** ['~vuːz] s 1. Rendezvous n, Verabredung f; Treffen n, Zs.-kunft f. 2. Treffpunkt m. **II** v/i pret u. pp **-voused** ['~vuːd] 3. sich treffen (**with** mit).

ren·di·tion [ren'dɪʃn] bsd. Am. → **rendering**.

re·new [rɪ'njuː] v/t erneuern: ~ **one's efforts** erneute Anstrengungen machen; ~ **one's visa** sein Visum erneuern lassen; **give s.o. ~ed hope** j-m neue Hoffnung geben; **with ~ed strength** mit neuen Kräften. **re·new·a·ble** adj: **be ~** erneuert werden können od. müssen. **re·new·al** s Erneuerung f.

re·nounce [rɪ'naʊns] v/t 1. verzichten auf (acc). 2. s-m Glauben etc abschwören.

ren·o·vate ['renəʊveɪt] v/t renovieren. **,ren·o·va·tion** s Renovierung f.

re·nown [rɪ'naʊn] s Berühmtheit f, Ruhm m: **win ~** berühmt werden. **re'nowned** adj berühmt (**for** wegen, für).

rent¹ [rent] **I** s 1. Miete f; Pacht f: **for ~** bsd. Am. zu vermieten od. verpachten. 2. bsd. Am. Leihgebühr f: **for ~** zu vermieten od. verleihen. **II** v/t 3. mieten; pachten (**from** von). 4. a. ~ **out** bsd. Am. vermieten; verpachten (**to** an acc). 5. bsd. Am. Auto etc mieten: **~ed car** Leih-, Mietwagen m.

rent² [~] s Riß m (a. fig.).

'rent-a-,car (ser·vice) s bsd. Am. Autoverleih m.

rent·al ['rentl] s 1. Miete f; Pacht f. 2. bsd. Am. Leihgebühr f.

rent·er ['rentə] s 1. Mieter(in); Pächter(in). 2. bsd. Am. Vermieter(in); Verpächter(in).

,rent-'free adj miet- od. pachtfrei.

re·nun·ci·a·tion [rɪ,nʌnsɪ'eɪʃn] s 1. Verzicht m (**of** auf acc). 2. Abschwören n.

re·o·pen [,riː'əʊpən] **I** v/t 1. Geschäft etc wiedereröffnen. 2. Verhandlungen etc wiederaufnehmen; Fall wiederaufrollen. **II** v/i 3. wiedereröffnen. 4. wiederaufgenommen od. wiederaufgerollt werden.

re·or·ga·ni·za·tion [ˈriːˌɔːɡənaɪˈzeɪʃn] s Umorganisation f; Umstellung f. **,re'or·gan·ize** v/t umorganisieren; Möbel umstellen, die Möbel umstellen in (dat).

re·pair [rɪ'peə] **I** v/t 1. reparieren; ausbessern. 2. fig. wiedergutmachen. **II** s 3. Reparatur f; Ausbesserung f: **beyond ~** nicht mehr zu reparieren; **be under ~** in Reparatur sein. 4. **be in good (bad) ~** in gutem (schlechtem) Zustand sein. 5. fig. Wiedergutmachung f.

rep·a·ra·ble ['repərəbl] adj □ reparabel, wiedergutzumachen(d). **,rep·a'ra·tion** s 1. Wiedergutmachung f: **make ~ for** et. wiedergutmachen. 2. pl pol. Reparationen pl.

rep·ar·tee [,repaː'tiː] s Schlagfertigkeit f; schlagfertige Antwort(en pl): **be good at ~** schlagfertig sein.

re·pa·tri·ate [riː'pætrɪeɪt] v/t repatriieren, in den Heimatstaat zurückführen. **,re·pa·tri'a·tion** s Repatriierung f.

re·pay [riː'peɪ] v/t (irr. **pay**) 1. Geld etc zurückzahlen: ~ **s.o.'s expenses** j-m s-e Auslagen erstatten; **I'll ~ you some time** ich gebe dir das Geld irgendwann einmal zurück; fig. ich werde mich irgendwann einmal erkenntlich zeigen; das zahle ich dir schon noch heim. 2. Besuch etc erwidern. 3. a) (positiv) sich für et. erkenntlich zeigen: ~ **s.o. for his help** j-n für s-e Hilfe belohnen od. entschädigen, b) (negativ) et. vergelten, lohnen (**with** mit): ~ **s.o.'s meanness**, ~ **s.o. for his meanness** j-m s-e Gemeinheit heimzahlen. **re'pay·a·ble** adj rückzahlbar: **be ~** zurückgezahlt werden können od. müssen (**over two years** in e-m Zeitraum von zwei Jahren). **re'pay·ment** s 1. Rückzahlung f. 2. Erwiderung f. 3. Vergeltung f.

re·peal [rɪ'piːl] **I** v/t Gesetz etc aufheben. **II** s Aufhebung f.

re·peat [rɪ'piːt] **I** v/t 1. wiederholen: ~ **o.s.** sich wiederholen; ~ **s.th. after s.o.** j-m et. nachsprechen; **his answer doesn't bear ~ing** s-e Antwort läßt sich nicht wiederholen; et. weitererzählen, -sagen. **II** v/i 3. aufstoßen (**on s.o.** j-m) (Speise). **III** s 4. Rundfunk, TV: Wiederholung f. 5. ♪ Wiederholungszeichen n. **re'peat·ed** adj □ wiederholt.

re·pel [rɪ'pel] v/t 1. Angriff, Feind zurückschlagen. 2. Wasser etc, fig. j-n abstoßen. **re'pel·lent** *adj* □ *fig.* abstoßend: **be ~ to** abstoßend wirken auf (*acc*).

re·pent [rɪ'pent] *v/t* bereuen: **~ having done s.th.** es bereuen, et. getan zu haben.

ro·per·cus·sion [ˌriːpəˈkʌʃn] *s mst pl* Auswirkung *f* (**on** auf *acc*).

rep·er·toire ['repətwɑː] *s thea. etc* Repertoire *n*: **have a large ~ of jokes** viele Witze auf Lager haben.

rep·e·ti·tion [ˌrepɪ'tɪʃn] *s* Wiederholung *f*: **his answer doesn't bear ~** s-e Antwort läßt sich nicht wiederholen.

re·place [rɪ'pleɪs] *v/t* **1.** zurücklegen, -stellen: **~ the receiver** *teleph.* (den Hörer) auflegen. **2.** *j-n, et.* ersetzen (**with, by** durch); *j-n* vertreten. **3.** ⊙ austauschen, ersetzen. **re'place·ment** *s* **1.** Ersatz *m*; Vertretung *f*. **2.** ⊙ Austausch *m*.

re·plant [ˌriːˈplɑːnt] *v/t* **1.** umpflanzen. **2.** neu bepflanzen.

re·play (*Sport*) **I** *s* ['riːpleɪ] **1.** Wiederholungsspiel *n*. **2.** → **action replay**. **II** *v/t* [ˌriːˈpleɪ] **3.** Spiel wiederholen.

re·plen·ish [rɪ'plenɪʃ] *v/t* (wieder) auffüllen.

re·plete [rɪ'pliːt] *adj* **1.** gesättigt, satt. **2.** angefüllt (**with** mit).

rep·li·ca ['replɪkə] *s* **1.** *Kunst:* Replik *f*, Originalkopie *f*. **2.** Kopie *f*, Nachbildung *f*.

re·ply [rɪ'plaɪ] **I** *v/t* antworten, erwidern (**that** daß). **II** *v/i* antworten (**to** auf *e-n Brief etc*; **to s.o.** j-m): **~ to a letter** a. e-n Brief beantworten. **III** *s* Antwort *f*, Erwiderung *f* (**to** auf *acc*): **in ~ to** (als Antwort) auf; **give no ~** keine Antwort geben, nicht antworten.

re·port [rɪ'pɔːt] **I** *s* **1.** *allg.* Bericht *m* (**on** über *acc*). **2.** Gerücht *n*: **~ has it that** es geht das Gerücht, daß. **3.** *ped. Br.* Zeugnis *n*. **4.** Knall *m*. **II** *v/t* **5.** berichten (**to s.o.** j-m); berichten über (*acc*): **it is ~ed that** es heißt, daß; **he is ~ed to have said** er soll gesagt haben; **~ed speech** *ling.* indirekte Rede. **6.** *j-n, Unfall, Verbrechen etc* melden (**to s.o.** j-m): **~ s.o. (to the police)** j-n anzeigen (**for** wegen); **the car is ~ed stolen** der Wagen ist als gestohlen gemeldet. **III** *v/i* **7.** berichten, Bericht erstatten (**on** über *acc*). **8.** sich melden (**to** bei): **~ sick**

sich krank melden; **~ for work** sich zur Arbeit melden. **~ card** *Am.* → **report 3.**

re·port·er [rɪ'pɔːtə] *s* Reporter(in), Berichterstatter(in).

re·pose [rɪ'pəʊz] *s* **1.** Ruhe *f*. **2.** *fig.* Gelassenheit *f*.

rep·re·hen·si·ble [ˌreprɪ'hensəbl] *adj* □ tadelnswert, verwerflich.

rep·re·sent [ˌreprɪ'zent] *v/t* **1.** *j-n, Br. a. Wahlbezirk* vertreten. **2.** darstellen (*a. fig.*). **3.** dar-, hinstellen (**as** als): **~ o.s. as** (*od.* **to be**) sich ausgeben für. **4.** *Beschwerden etc* vorbringen (**to** bei). **ˌrep·re·sen'ta·tion** *s* **1.** Vertretung *f*. **2.** Darstellung *f*: **be a ~ of s.th.** et. darstellen. **3.** **make ~s to** vorstellig werden bei (**about** wegen). **ˌrep·re·sen'ta·tion·al** [~ʃənl] *adj* gegenständlich (*Kunst*). **ˌrep·re'sent·a·tive** [~tətɪv] **I** *s* **1.** (Stell)Vertreter(in); (Handels)Vertreter(in). **2.** *parl.* Abgeordnete *m, f*: → **House of Representatives.** **II** *adj* □ **3.** repräsentativ (**of** für). **4.** *pol.* repräsentativ: **~ government** Repräsentativsystem *n*.

re·press [rɪ'pres] *v/t* **1.** *Volk, Gefühle etc* unterdrücken. **2.** *psych.* verdrängen. **re'pres·sion** [~ʃn] *s* **1.** Unterdrückung *f*. **2.** *psych.* Verdrängung *f*. **re'pres·sive** *adj* □ repressiv.

re·prieve [rɪ'priːv] ⚖ **I** *s* Begnadigung *f*; Vollstreckungsaufschub *m*. **II** *v/t*: **he was ~d** er wurde begnadigt; s-e Urteilsvollstreckung wurde ausgesetzt.

rep·ri·mand ['reprɪmɑːnd] **I** *v/t* rügen, tadeln (**for** wegen). **II** *s* Rüge *f*, Tadel *m*.

re·print **I** *v/t* [ˌriːˈprɪnt] neu auflegen, nachdrucken. **II** *s* ['riːprɪnt] Neuauflage *f*, Nachdruck *m*.

re·pris·al [rɪ'praɪzl] *s bsd.* ✕, *pol.* Repressalie *f*, Vergeltungsmaßnahme *f*: **in** (*od.* **as a**) **~ for** als Vergeltung für; **take ~s** Repressalien ergreifen (**against** gegen).

re·proach [rɪ'prəʊtʃ] **I** *s* **1.** Vorwurf *m*: **above** (*od.* **beyond**) **~** über jeden Tadel erhaben; **look of ~** vorwurfsvoller Blick. **2.** *fig.* Schande *f* (**to** für). **II** *v/t* **3.** *j-m* Vorwürfe machen (**for** wegen).

rep·ro·bate ['reprəʊbeɪt] *s* verkommenes Subjekt.

re·pro·cess [ˌriːˈprəʊses] *v/t* *Kernbrennstoffe* wiederaufbereiten. **ˌre'pro·cess-**

ing plant s Wiederaufbereitungsanlage f.

re·pro·duce [ˌriːprəˈdjuːs] **I** v/t **1.** ~ o.s. → 4. **2.** Bild etc reproduzieren. **3.** Ton etc wiedergeben. **II** v/i **4.** biol. sich fortpflanzen od. vermehren. **re·pro·duc·tion** [ˌ-ˈdʌkʃn] s **1.** biol. Fortpflanzung f. **2.** Reproduktion f. **3.** Wiedergabe f. ˌ**re·pro·duc·tive** adj biol. Fortpflanzungs...

re·proof [rɪˈpruːf] s Rüge f, Tadel m.

re·prove [rɪˈpruːv] v/t rügen, tadeln (**for** wegen).

rep·tile [ˈreptaɪl] s zo. Reptil n, Kriechtier n.

re·pub·lic [rɪˈpʌblɪk] s pol. Republik f. **re·pub·li·can,** pol. Am. **2 I** adj republikanisch. **II** s Republikaner(in).

re·pu·di·ate [rɪˈpjuːdɪeɪt] v/t **1.** Angebot, Behauptung etc zurückweisen. **2.** Schuld etc nicht anerkennen. **re·pu·di·a·tion** s **1.** Zurückweisung f. **2.** Nichtanerkennung f.

re·pug·nance [rɪˈpʌɡnəns] s: **in** (od. **with**) ~ angewidert. **re·pug·nant** adj □ widerlich, widerwärtig.

re·pulse [rɪˈpʌls] **I** v/t **1.** Angriff, Feind zurückschlagen. **2.** j-n, Angebot etc ab-, zurückweisen. **II** s **3.** Zurückschlagen n. **4.** Ab-, Zurückweisung f. **re·pul·sion** s **1.** Abscheu m, f: **with** ~ voller Abscheu. **2.** phys. Abstoßung f. **re·pul·sive** adj □ phys. abstoßend, fig. a. widerlich, widerwärtig.

re·pur·chase [ˌriːˈpɜːtʃəs] **I** v/t zurückkaufen. **II** s Rückkauf m.

rep·u·ta·ble [ˈrepjʊtəbl] adj □ angesehen. ˌ**rep·u·ta·tion** s (engS. guter) Ruf: **have the** (od. **a**) ~ **of being** im Ruf stehen, et. zu sein; **make o.s. a** ~ **as** sich e-n Namen machen als. **re·pute** [rɪˈpjuːt] **I** s (engS. guter) Ruf: **of** ~ angesehen; **be held in high** ~ hohes Ansehen genießen. **II** v/t: **be** ~**d to be** gelten als. **re·put·ed·ly** adv angeblich, dem Vernehmen nach.

re·quest [rɪˈkwest] **I** s **1.** (**for**) Bitte f (um), Gesuch n (nach): **at s.o.'s** ~ auf j-s Bitte hin; **on** ~ auf Wunsch; **make a** ~ **for s.th.** um et. bitten. **II** v/t **2.** bitten od. ersuchen um. **3.** j-n bitten, ersuchen (**to do** zu tun). ~ **stop** s Br. Bedarfshaltestelle f.

re·qui·em [ˈrekwɪəm] s Requiem n.

re·quire [rɪˈkwaɪə] v/t **1.** erfordern: **be** ~**d** erforderlich sein; **if** ~**d** wenn nötig. **2.** benötigen, brauchen. **3.** verlangen (**that** daß; **s.th. of s.o.** et. von j-m): ~ **s.o. to do s.th.** von j-m verlangen, daß er et. tut; **be** ~**d to do s.th.** et. tun müssen. **re·quired** adj erforderlich, notwendig: ~ **reading** ped., univ. Pflichtlektüre f. **re·quire·ment** s **1.** Anforderung f: **meet the** ~**s** den Anforderungen entsprechen. **2.** Erfordernis n, Bedürfnis n.

req·ui·site [ˈrekwɪzɪt] **I** adj erforderlich, notwendig (**for** für). **II** s mst pl Artikel m: **camping** ~**s** pl Campingzubehör n. ˌ**req·ui·si·tion** s **1.** Anforderung f: **make a** ~ **for** et. anfordern. **2.** ✕ Requisition f, Beschlagnahme f. **II** v/t **3.** anfordern. **4.** ✕ requirieren, beschlagnahmen.

re·quit·al [rɪˈkwaɪtl] s Vergeltung f. **re·quite** [rɪˈkwaɪt] v/t et. vergelten (**with** mit).

re·run I v/t (irr run) [ˌriːˈrʌn] **1.** TV wiederholen. **2.** **be** ~ (Sport) wiederholt werden (Lauf). **II** s [ˈriːrʌn] **3.** TV Wiederholung f (a. allg.).

re·scind [rɪˈsɪnd] v/t ✴ Gesetz, Urteil etc aufheben. **re·scis·sion** [rɪˈsɪʒn] s Aufhebung f.

res·cue [ˈreskjuː] **I** v/t retten (**from** aus, vor dat). **II** s Rettung f: **come to s.o.'s** ~ j-m zu Hilfe kommen; ~ **operations** pl Rettungsarbeiten pl; ~ **party** (od. **squad, team**) Rettungsmannschaft f. **res·cu·er** [ˈ-kjʊə] s Retter(in).

re·search [rɪˈsɜːtʃ] **I** s Forschung f (**on** auf dem Gebiet gen): **carry out** (od. **do**) ~ **into** et. erforschen. **II** v/i forschen (**on** auf dem Gebiet gen): ~ **into** et. erforschen. **III** v/t et. erforschen. **IV** adj Forschungs...: ~ **team** Forscherteam n; ~ **worker** Forscher(in). **re·search·er** s Forscher(in).

re·sem·blance [rɪˈzembləns] s Ähnlichkeit f (**to** mit; **between** zwischen dat): **there is a strong** ~ **between them** sie sind sich sehr ähnlich; **bear a strong** ~ **to** starke Ähnlichkeit haben mit. **re·sem·ble** [ˌ-bl] v/t ähnlich sein, ähneln (dat).

re·sent [rɪˈzent] v/t übelnehmen, sich ärgern über (acc). **re·sent·ful** [ˌ-fʊl] adj □

ärgerlich. **re'sent·ment** s Ärger m (**against, at** über acc).

res·er·va·tion [ˌrezəˈveɪʃn] s 1. bsd. Am. (Wild)Reservat n; Am. (Indianer)Reservat n, (-)Reservation f. 2. Reservierung f, Vorbestellung f: **make a ~** ein Zimmer etc bestellen. 3. Vorbehalt m: **with ~(s)** unter Vorbehalt; **without ~** vorbehaltlos.

re·serve [rɪˈzɜːv] I s 1. Reserve f (of an dat): **keep s.th. in ~** et. in Reserve halten. 2. a. pl ✕ Reserve f. 3. Sport: Reservespieler(in). 4. (Naturschutz-, Wild)Reservat n. 5. Reserviertheit f, Zurückhaltung f. 6. **without ~** vorbehaltlos. II v/t 7. (sich) et. aufsparen (for für). 8. **~ the right to do s.th.** sich (das Recht) vorbehalten, et. zu tun. 9. reservieren (lassen), vorbestellen. **re'served** adj reserviert, zurückhaltend.

re·serv·ist [rɪˈzɜːvɪst] s ✕ Reservist m.

res·er·voir [ˈrezəvwɑː] s Reservoir n (a. fig. of an dat).

re·set [ˌriːˈset] v/t (irr set) 1. Edelstein neu fassen. 2. Uhr umstellen; Zeiger etc zurückstellen (to auf acc).

re·set·tle [ˌriːˈsetl] v/t umsiedeln. **ˌre'set·tle·ment** s Umsiedlung f.

re·shuf·fle I v/t [ˌriːˈʃʌfl] 1. Karten neu mischen. 2. Kabinett etc umbilden. II s [ˈriːˌʃʌfl] 3. Umbildung f.

re·side [rɪˈzaɪd] v/i 1. wohnen, s-n Wohnsitz haben; residieren. 2. **~ in** fig. liegen od. ruhen bei j-m. **res·i·dence** [ˈrezɪdəns] s 1. Wohnsitz m; Residenz f: **official ~** Amtssitz m; **take up ~** sich niederlassen. 2. Aufenthalt m: **~ permit** Aufenthaltsgenehmigung f, -erlaubnis f. **'res·i·dent** I adj ansässig, wohnhaft: **be ~ abroad** a. im Ausland wohnen. II s Bewohner(in) (e-s Hauses), (e-r Stadt etc a.) Einwohner(in), mot. Anlieger(in); (Hotel)Gast m. **res·i·den·tial** [ˌ~ˈdenʃl] adj Wohn...

re·sid·u·al [rɪˈzɪdjʊəl] adj übrig(geblieben), restlich, Rest... **res·i·due** [ˈrezɪdjuː] s bsd. ✿ Rest m, Rückstand m.

re·sign [rɪˈzaɪn] I v/t 1. aufgeben; verzichten auf (acc). 2. Amt etc niederlegen. 3. **~ o.s.** to sich fügen in (acc), sich abfinden mit; **be ~ed to** sich abgefunden haben mit. II v/i 4. zurücktreten (from von), sein Amt niederlegen. **res·ig·na·tion** [ˌrezɪgˈneɪʃn] s 1. Rück-

tritt m, Amtsniederlegung f: **hand in** (od. **send in, submit, tender**) **one's ~** s-n Rücktritt einreichen. 2. Ergebenheit f; Resignation f.

re·sil·i·ence [rɪˈzɪlɪəns] s 1. Elastizität f; Strapazierfähigkeit f. 2. fig. Zähigkeit f. **re'sil·i·ent** adj □ 1. elastisch; strapazierfähig. 2. fig. zäh: **be ~** nicht unterzukriegen sein.

res·in [ˈrezɪn] s Harz n. **'res·in·ous** adj □ harzig; Harz...

re·sist [rɪˈzɪst] I v/t 1. j-m, e-r Sache widerstehen: **I could not ~ doing it** ich mußte es einfach tun. 2. Widerstand leisten (dat od. gegen), sich widersetzen (dat). II v/i 3. Widerstand leisten, sich widersetzen. **re'sist·ance** s 1. Widerstand m (**to** gegen): **offer** (od. **put up**) **(a) stubborn ~** hartnäckig(en) Widerstand leisten (**to** dat); **without offering ~** widerstandslos; **take the line of least ~** den Weg des geringsten Widerstandes gehen. 2. a. **power of ~** Widerstandskraft f (**to** gegen) (a. ✿). 3. (Hitzeetc)Beständigkeit f, (Stoß- etc)Festigkeit f. 4. ⚡ Widerstand m (a. Bauteil). **re'sist·ant** adj □ (hitze- etc)beständig, (stoß- etc)fest. **re'sis·tor** s ⚡ Widerstand m (Bauteil).

re·sit ped., univ. Br. I v/t (irr sit) [ˌriːˈsɪt] Prüfung wiederholen. II s [ˈriːsɪt] Wiederholungsprüfung f.

re·sole [ˌriːˈsəʊl] v/t neu besohlen.

res·o·lute [ˈrezəluːt] adj □ resolut, entschlossen. **'res·o·lute·ness → resolution** 3.

res·o·lu·tion [ˌrezəˈluːʃn] s 1. Beschluß m, parl. etc a. Resolution f. 2. Vorsatz m: **make good ~s** gute Vorsätze fassen. 3. Resolutheit f, Entschlossenheit f. 4. Lösung f, Überwindung f. 5. ⚕ etc Auflösung f, Zerlegung f (**into** in acc).

re·solve [rɪˈzɒlv] I v/t 1. beschließen (**that** daß; **to do** zu tun). 2. Problem etc lösen, Schwierigkeit etc überwinden. 3. ⚕ etc auflösen, zerlegen (**into** in acc). II v/i 4. (**into** in acc) ⚕ etc sich auflösen; fig. zerfallen. III s 5. **→ resolution** 2, 3.

res·o·nance [ˈrezənəns] s 1. phys. Resonanz f. 2. voller Klang. **'res·o·nant** adj □ 1. phys. Resonanz... 2. voll (Klang), volltönend, sonor (Stimme). 3. **be ~ with** widerhallen von.

re·sort [rɪ'zɔːt] **I** s **1.** Urlaubsort m: → **health** 1, **seaside**. **2. have ~ to** → 3; **as a last ~** notfalls, wenn alle Stricke reißen; **as a last ~ he went ...** als er nicht mehr weiterwußte, ging er ... **II** v/i **3. ~ to** greifen od. Zuflucht nehmen zu.

re·sound [rɪ'zaʊnd] v/i widerhallen (**with** von).

re·source [rɪ'sɔːs] s **1.** pl (Geld)Mittel pl; (Boden-, Natur)Schätze pl. **2.** Mittel n, Zuflucht f; Ausweg m: **leave s.o. to his own ~s** j-n sich selbst überlassen. **3.** Einfallsreichtum m, Findigkeit f. **re·'source·ful** [~fʊl] adj □ einfallsreich, findig.

re·spect [rɪ'spekt] **I** s **1.** Achtung f, Respekt f (**for** vor dat): **have ~ for** Respekt haben vor. **2.** Rücksicht f (**for** auf acc): **out of ~ for** aus Rücksicht auf; **have no ~ for** keine Rücksicht nehmen auf; **without ~ to** ohne Rücksicht auf (acc); ungeachtet (gen). **3.** Beziehung f, Hinsicht f: **in many ~s** in vieler Hinsicht; **in some ~** in gewisser Hinsicht; **with ~ to** was ... anbelangt od. betrifft. **4.** pl Empfehlungen pl: **give my ~s to your wife** e-e Empfehlung an Ihre Gemahlin. **5. pay one's ~s to** j-m s-e Aufwartung machen; **pay one's last ~s** to j-m die letzte Ehre erweisen. **II** v/t **6.** respektieren, achten. **7.** respektieren, berücksichtigen. **re'spect·a·ble** adj □ **1.** ehrbar, geachtet. **2.** gesellschaftsfähig (Person), (Kleidung, Benehmen a.) korrekt: **it is not ~** es gehört sich nicht (**to do** zu tun). **3.** respektabel, beachtlich. **re'spect·ful** [~fʊl] adj □ respektvoll. **re'spect·ing** prp bezüglich (gen). **re'spec·tive** adj jeweilig: **they went to their ~ places** jeder von ihnen ging zu s-m Platz. **re'spec·tive·ly** adv beziehungsweise.

res·pi·ra·tion [ˌrespə'reɪʃn] s Atmung f.

res·pi·ra·tor ['respəreɪtə] s Atemschutzgerät n. **re·spi·ra·to·ry** [rɪ'spaɪərətərɪ] adj Atem..., Atmungs...: **~ arrest** ✶ Atemstillstand m; **~ disease** ✶ Erkrankung f der Atemwege; **~ passages** pl (od. **tract**) anat. Atemwege pl; **~ system** Atmungsorgane pl.

res·pite ['respaɪt] s **1.** Aufschub m. **2.** Pause f: **without ~** ohne Pause od. Unterbrechung.

re·splend·ent [rɪ'splendənt] adj □ glänzend, strahlend.

re·spond [rɪ'spɒnd] **I** v/i **1.** antworten (**to** auf acc): **~ to a letter** e-n Brief beantworten. **2.** fig. reagieren (**to** auf acc; **with** mit), ✶ etc a. ansprechen (**to** auf acc). **II** v/t **3.** antworten (**that** daß). **re'spond·ent** s ⚖ Beklagte m, f (in e-m Scheidungsprozeß).

re·sponse [rɪ'spɒns] s **1.** Antwort f (**to** auf acc): **give no ~** keine Antwort geben, nicht antworten. **2.** fig. Reaktion f (**to** auf acc).

re·spon·si·bil·i·ty [rɪˌspɒnsə'bɪlətɪ] s **1.** Verantwortung f: **a position of great ~** e-e verantwortungsvolle Position; **on one's own ~** auf eigene Verantwortung; **claim ~ for** die Verantwortung übernehmen für (**in** Terroranschlag etc); **have ~ for** die Verantwortung haben für; **take (full) ~ for** die (volle) Verantwortung übernehmen für; **take no ~ for** nicht haften für. **2.** oft pl Verpflichtung f, Pflicht f. **re'spon·si·ble** adj □ **1.** verantwortlich (**for** für): **be ~ to s.o. for s.th.** j-m (gegenüber) für et. verantwortlich sein; **not to be ~ for** nicht haften für. **2.** (**for**) verantwortlich (für), schuld (an dat): **hold s.o. ~ for** j-n verantwortlich machen für. **3.** verantwortungsbewußt. **4.** verantwortungsvoll (Position). **re'spon·sive** adj □ **1.** leichtgängig (Kupplung etc), elastisch (Motor): **be ~ to** reagieren auf (acc), ✶ etc a. ansprechen auf (acc); empfänglich sein für. **2.** mitteilsam: **he wasn't very ~** aus ihm war nicht viel herauszuholen.

rest¹ [rest] **I** s **1.** Ruhe(pause) f; Erholung f: **have ~ (od. take) a ~** sich ausruhen; **have a good night's ~** gut schlafen; **lay to ~** zur letzten Ruhe betten; fig. ad acta legen; **set s.o.'s mind at ~** j-n beruhigen. **2.** ☉ Auflage f, Stütze f; teleph. Gabel f. **II** v/i **3.** (sich aus)ruhen: **let s.th. ~** fig. et. auf sich beruhen lassen; **he will not ~ until** fig. er wird nicht eher ruhen, bis; → **laurel** 3. **4.** lehnen (**against, on** an dat): **~ on** bsd. ☉ ruhen auf (dat) (a. fig. Blick); fig. beruhen auf (dat), sich stützen auf (acc); **~ with** fig. bei j-m liegen. **III** v/t **5.** ausruhen (lassen). **6.** lehnen (**against** gegen; **on** an acc).

rest² [~] *s* Rest *m*: *the ~ of us* wir übrigen; *all the ~ of them* alle übrigen; *for the ~* im übrigen.

res·tau·rant ['restərõ:ŋ] *s* Restaurant *n*, Gaststätte *f*. **~ car** *s* ⚙ *Br.* Speisewagen *m*.

rest·ful ['restfʊl] *adj* □ **1.** ruhig, friedlich. **2.** erholsam.

rest home *s* Alten-, Alters- *od.* Pflegeheim *n*.

rest·ing place ['restɪŋ] *s*: (*last*) *~* (letzte) Ruhestätte.

res·ti·tu·tion [ˌrestɪˈtjuːʃn] *s* Rückgabe *f*, (*von Geld a.*) Rückerstattung *f* (**to** an *acc*): *make ~ of s.th. to s.o.* j-m et. zurückgeben *od.* -erstatten.

res·tive ['restɪv] *adj* □ unruhig, nervös. **'res·tive·ness** *s* Unruhe *f*, Nervosität *f*.

rest·less ['restlɪs] *adj* □ **1.** ruhe-, rastlos. **2.** unruhig (*Person, Nacht*): *I had a ~ night* ich habe nicht gut geschlafen.

re·stock [ˌriːˈstɒk] *v/t* Regal *etc* wieder auffüllen.

res·to·ra·tion [ˌrestəˈreɪʃn] *s* **1.** Wiederherstellung *f*. **2.** Restaurierung *f*. **3.** Rückgabe *f*, Rückerstattung *f* (**to** an *acc*).

re·store [rɪˈstɔː] *v/t* **1.** Ordnung *etc* wiederherstellen: *be ~d* (*to health*) wiederhergestellt *od.* wieder gesund sein. **2.** Gemälde *etc* restaurieren. **3.** zurückgeben, Geld *a.* zurückerstatten (**to** *dat*). **re'stor·er** *s* **1.** Restaurator(in). **2.** → *hair restorer*.

re·strain [rɪˈstreɪn] *v/t* (**from**) zurückhalten (von), hindern an (*dat*): *~ s.o. from doing s.th.* j-n davon zurückhalten *od.* daran hindern, et. zu tun; *I had to ~ myself* ich mußte mich beherrschen (*from doing s.th.* um nicht et. zu tun). **re'strained** *adj* **1.** beherrscht. **2.** dezent (*Farbe etc*). **re·straint** [rɪˈstreɪnt] *s* **1.** Beherrschung *f*. **2.** Be-, Einschränkung *f* (**on** gen).

re·strict [rɪˈstrɪkt] *v/t* beschränken (**to** auf *acc*), einschränken. **re'stric·tion** *s* Be-, Einschränkung *f*: *without ~s* uneingeschränkt. **re'stric·tive** *adj* □ be-, einschränkend.

rest room *s Am.* Toilette *f* (*in Restaurant etc*).

re·struc·ture [ˌriːˈstrʌktʃə] *v/t* umstrukturieren.

re·sult [rɪˈzʌlt] **I** *s* **1.** Ergebnis *n*, Resultat *n*: *without ~* ergebnislos. **2.** Erfolg *m*. **3.** Folge *f*: *as a ~ of* als Folge von (*od. gen*). **II** *v/i* **4.** resultieren, sich ergeben (*from* aus): *~ in* zur Folge haben (*acc*), führen zu; *~ing* → *resultant*. **re'sult·ant** *adj* daraus resultierend.

ré·su·mé ['rezjʊmeɪ] *s* **1.** Resümee *n*, Zs.-fassung *f*. **2.** *Am.* (*bsd.* tabellarischer) Lebenslauf.

re·sume [rɪˈzjuːm] **I** *v/t* **1.** Arbeit wiederaufnehmen, Diskussion, Reise *etc* fortsetzen. **2.** Platz wieder einnehmen; Mädchennamen *etc* wieder annehmen. **II** *v/i* **3.** weitermachen, fortfahren. **re·sump·tion** [rɪˈzʌmpʃn] *s* Wiederaufnahme *f*, Fortsetzung *f*.

re·sur·face [ˌriːˈsɜːfɪs] **I** *v/t* **1.** Straße neu belegen. **II** *v/i* **2.** wieder auftauchen (*U-Boot*). **3.** *fig.* wiederaufleben.

re·sur·gence [rɪˈsɜːdʒəns] *s* Wiederaufleben *n*. **re'sur·gent** *adj* wiederauflebend.

res·ur·rect [ˌrezəˈrekt] *v/t* Brauch *etc* wiederaufleben lassen, Gesetz *etc* wieder einführen. **ˌres·ur'rec·tion** *s* **1.** Wiedereinführung *f*. **2.** ♀ *eccl.* Auferstehung *f*.

re·sus·ci·tate [rɪˈsʌsɪteɪt] *v/t* ✻ wiederbeleben. **re·sus·ci'ta·tion** *s* Wiederbelebung *f*.

re·tail ['riːteɪl] **I** *s* **1.** Einzelhandel *m*: *by* (*Am.* **at**) *~* → III. **II** *adj* **2.** Einzelhandels...: *~ price; ~ dealer → retailer.* **III** *adv* **3.** im Einzelhandel, einzeln. **IV** *v/t* [riːˈteɪl] **4.** im Einzelhandel verkaufen (**at, for** für). **5.** *fig.* Gerücht *etc* verbreiten. **V** *v/i* [riːˈteɪl] **6.** im Einzelhandel verkauft werden (**at, for** für): *it ~s at £2 a.* es kostet im Einzelhandel zwei Pfund. **re'tail·er** *s* Einzelhändler(in).

re·tain [rɪˈteɪn] *v/t* **1.** Gleichgewicht halten; Eigenschaft, Fassung *etc* behalten, bewahren. **2.** Wasser stauen (*Damm*), speichern (*Boden*); Wärme speichern. **re'tain·er** *s*, **re'tain·ing fee** *s* (Honorar)Vorschuß *m* (*für Anwalt*).

re·take [ˌriːˈteɪk] *v/t* (*irr take*) **1.** ✗ zurückerobern. **2.** Film, TV: Szene *etc* nochmals drehen.

re·tal·i·ate [rɪˈtælɪeɪt] *v/i* **1.** Vergeltung üben, sich revanchieren (**against** an *dat*); *engS.* zurückschlagen, -treten. **2.** Sport, *a.* in Diskussion *etc*: kontern (**with** mit). **re·tal·i·a·tion** s Vergeltung(smaßnahmen pl) f, Revanche f: **in ~ for** als Vergeltung für. **re·tal·i·a·to·ry** [~ətəri] adj Vergeltungs..., Revanche...

re·tard [rɪˈtɑːd] v/t verzögern, hemmen. **re·tard·ed** adj: (**mentally**) **~** (geistig) zurückgeblieben. **re·tar·da·tion** [ˌriːtɑːˈdeɪʃn] s Verzögerung f.

retch [retʃ] v/i würgen.

re·ten·tion [rɪˈtenʃn] s **1.** Bewahrung f. **2.** Stauung f; Speicherung f. **re·ten·tive** adj gut (Gedächtnis).

re·think [ˌriːˈθɪŋk] v/t (irr think) noch einmal überdenken.

ret·i·cence [ˈretɪsəns] s Schweigsamkeit f. **ret·i·cent** adj □ schweigsam: **he was very ~ about it** von ihm war nur sehr wenig darüber zu erfahren.

ret·i·na [ˈretɪnə] pl **-nas, -nae** [ˈ~niː] s anat. Netzhaut f.

ret·i·nue [ˈretɪnjuː] s Gefolge n.

re·tire [rɪˈtaɪə] I v/i **1.** allg. sich zurückziehen (a. fig. **from business** aus dem Geschäftsleben; **from competition** vom aktiven Sport): **~ from business** a. sich zur Ruhe setzen. **2.** in Rente (od. Pension) gehen, sich pensionieren lassen. **3.** Sport: aufgeben. II v/t **4.** in den Ruhestand versetzen, pensionieren. **re·tired** adj pensioniert, im Ruhestand (lebend): **be ~** a. in Pension od. Rente sein; **~ general** General m außer Dienst. **re·tire·ment** s **1.** Rückzug m. **2.** Pensionierung f; Ruhestand m: **~ age** Pensions-, Rentenalter n. **3.** Sport: Aufgabe f. **re·tir·ing** adj □ zurückhaltend.

re·tort¹ [rɪˈtɔːt] I s (scharfe) Entgegnung. II v/t (scharf) entgegnen.

re·tort² [~] s ⚗ Retorte f.

re·touch [ˌriːˈtʌtʃ] v/t phot. retuschieren.

re·trace [rɪˈtreɪs] v/t Tathergang etc rekonstruieren: **~ one's steps** denselben Weg zurückgehen.

re·tract [rɪˈtrækt] v/t **1.** Krallen etc, ✈ Fahrgestell einziehen. **2.** Angebot etc zurückziehen, Behauptung etc zurücknehmen, Geständnis etc widerrufen. **re·tract·a·ble** adj einziehbar. **re·trac·tion** s **1.** Einziehen n. **2.** Zurücknahme f, Widerruf m.

re·train [ˌriːˈtreɪn] I v/t umschulen. II v/i umschulen, sich umschulen lassen. **re·train·ing** s Umschulung f.

re·tread I v/t [ˌriːˈtred] Reifen runderneuern. II s [ˈriːtred] runderneuerter Reifen.

re·treat [rɪˈtriːt] I s **1.** ⚔ Rückzug m: **beat a (hasty) ~** fig. abhauen. **2.** Zufluchtsort m. II v/i **3.** ⚔ sich zurückziehen. **4.** zurückweichen (**from** vor dat).

re·trench·ment [rɪˈtrentʃmənt] s: **policy of ~** Sparpolitik f.

re·tri·al [ˌriːˈtraɪəl] s ⚖ Wiederaufnahmeverfahren n.

ret·ri·bu·tion [ˌretrɪˈbjuːʃn] s Vergeltung f. **re·trib·u·tive** [rɪˈtrɪbjʊtɪv] adj Vergeltungs...

re·triev·al [rɪˈtriːvl] s **1.** Zurückholen n. **2.** Wiedergutmachen n, Wettmachen n; Rettung f: **beyond** (od. **past**) **~** hoffnungslos (Situation). **3.** hunt. Apportieren n.

re·trieve [rɪˈtriːv] v/t **1.** zurückholen. **2.** Fehler wiedergutmachen, Verlust a. wettmachen; Situation retten. **3.** (a. v/i) hunt. apportieren.

ret·ro·ac·tive [ˌretrəʊˈæktɪv] adj □ rückwirkend.

ret·ro·grade [ˈretrəʊɡreɪd] adj rückschrittlich: **~ step** Rückschritt m.

ret·ro·gres·sive [ˌretrəʊˈɡresɪv] adj □ rückschrittlich.

ret·ro·spect [ˈretrəʊspekt] s: **in ~** rückschauend, im Rückblick. **ret·ro·spec·tion** s Rückblick m, -schau f. **ret·ro·spec·tive** adj □ **1.** rückblickend, -schauend. **2.** rückwirkend.

re·trous·sé [rəˈtruːseɪ] adj: **~ nose** Stupsnase f.

re·try [ˌriːˈtraɪ] v/t ⚖ **1.** Fall erneut verhandeln. **2.** neu verhandeln gegen j-n.

re·turn [rɪˈtɜːn] I v/i **1.** zurückkehren, -kommen; zurückkommen; fig. wiederauftreten: **~ to** fig. auf ein Thema, Vorhaben zurückkommen; in e-e Gewohnheit etc zurückfallen; in e-n Zustand zurückkehren; → **normal** II. **2. ~ to sender** 🕊 zurück an Absender. II v/t **3.** (**to**) zurückgeben (dat); zurückbringen (dat); zurückschicken, -senden (dat od. an acc). **4.** zurücklegen, -stellen. **5.** Besuch, Kompliment etc erwidern. **6.** Gewinn, Zinsen abwerfen. **7. be ~ed (to Parliament)** Br. gewählt werden. **8.** → **verdict** I. III s **9.** Rückkehr f; fig. Wiederauftreten n: **on one's ~** bei s-r Rückkehr; **by ~ (of post)** Br. postwendend, umgehend; *many happy* ~*s* (*of the day*) herzlichen Glückwunsch zum Geburtstag. **10.** Rückgabe *f*; Zurückbringen *n*; Zurückschicken *n*, -senden *n*. **11.** Zurücklegen *n*, -stellen *n*. **12.** Erwiderung *f*. **13.** *a. pl* ✝ Gewinn *m*. **14.** *in* ~ als Gegenleistung (*for* für): *expect nothing in* ~ keine Gegenleistung erwarten. **15.** (*Steuer*)Erklärung *f*. **16.** *Tennis etc*: Return *m*, Rückschlag *m*. **IV** *adj* **17.** Rück...: ~ *game* (*Sport*) Rückspiel *n*; ~ *journey* Rückreise *f*; *by* ~ *mail Am*. postwendend, umgehend; ~ *ticket Br*. Rückfahrkarte *f*; Rückflugticket *n*. **V** *adv* **18.** *the price is £10* ~ *Br*. der Preis beträgt 10 Pfund hin u. zurück. **re'turn·a·ble** *adj* **1.** ~ *bottle* Pfandflasche *f*. **2.** *be* ~ zurückgegeben *od*. zurückgeschickt werden müssen.

re·un·ion [,ri:'ju:njən] *s* **1.** Treffen *n*, Wiedersehensfeier *f*. **2.** Wiedervereinigung *f*. **re·u·nite** [,ri:ju:'naɪt] *v/t Land* wiedervereinigen; *Familie etc* wieder vereinigen.

rev [rev] *mot*. F **I** *s* Umdrehung *f*: *number of* ~*s* Drehzahl *f*; ~ *counter* Drehzahlmesser *m*. **II** *v/t a.* ~ *up Motor* aufheulen lassen. **III** *v/i a.* ~ *up* aufheulen (*Motor*).

re·val·u·a·tion [ˈriːˌvæljʊˈeɪʃn] *s* Aufwertung *f*. ˈre'val·ue [~ju:] *v/t Dollar etc* aufwerten.

re·vamp [riː'væmp] *v/t* F *Haus etc* aufmöbeln, *Theaterstück etc* aufpolieren, *Firma etc* auf Vordermann bringen.

re·veal [rɪ'viːl] *v/t* **1.** den Blick freigeben auf (*acc*); zeigen. **2.** *Geheimnis etc* enthüllen, aufdecken. **re'veal·ing** *adj* □ **1.** offenherzig (*Kleid etc*). **2.** *fig*. aufschlußreich.

rev·el ['revl] *v/i pret u. pp* **-eled**, *bsd. Br.* **-elled 1.** (lärmend *od.* ausgelassen) feiern. **2.** (*in*) schwelgen (in *dat*); *b. s.* sich weiden an (*dat*).

rev·e·la·tion [,revə'leɪʃn] *s* **1.** Enthüllung *f*, Aufdeckung *f*. **2.** *eccl.* Offenbarung *f*.

rev·el·(l)er ['revlə] *s* Feiernde *m, f*. ˈrev·el·ry *s* (lärmendes *od.* ausgelassenes) Feiern.

re·venge [rɪ'vendʒ] **I** *s* **1.** Rache *f*: *in* ~ aus Rache (*for* für); *take* (*one's*) ~ *on s.o.* (*for s.th.*) → 4; ~ *sweet* 1. **2.** Spiel, Sport: Revanche *f*: *give s.o. a chance to get his* ~ j-m Revanche geben. **II** *v/t*

3. *et*. rächen. **4.** ~ *o.s.* on s.o. (*for s.th.*) sich an j-m (für et.) rächen. **re-'venge·ful** [~fʊl] *adj* □ rachsüchtig.

rev·e·nue ['revənju:] *s a. pl* Staatseinnahmen *pl*, -einkünfte *pl*: → *inland* 2.

re·ver·ber·ate [rɪ'vɜːbəret] **I** *v/i* nachwiderhallen. **II** *v/t Schall* zurückwerfen. **re͵ver·ber'a·tion** *s* **1.** Nach-, Widerhall *m*. **2.** Zurückwerfen *n*.

re·vere [rɪ'vɪə] *v/t* verehren; *Andenken* hochhalten. **rev·er·ence** ['revərəns] *s* Verehrung *f*; Ehrfurcht *f* (*for* vor *dat*): *with* ~ ehrfürchtig; *hold in* ~ verehren. **'Rev·er·end** *s eccl.* Hochwürden *m*.

rev·er·ent ['revərənt], **rev·er·en·tial** [,~'renʃl] *adj* □ ehrfürchtig, ehrfurchtsvoll.

rev·er·ie ['revərɪ] *s* (Tag)Träumerei *f*: *fall into a* ~ ins Träumen kommen.

re·ver·sal [rɪ'vɜːsl] *s* **1.** Umstoßung *f*; ⅟ Aufhebung *f*. **2.** Rückschlag *m*. **re'verse I** *s* **1.** Gegenteil *n*: *quite the* ~ ganz im Gegenteil. **2.** Rückschlag *m*. **3.** Kehr-, Rückseite *f* (*e-r Münze*). **4.** *mot*. Rückwärtsgang *m*: *put the car into* ~ den Rückwärtsgang einlegen. **II** *adj* □ **5.** umgekehrt; (*Richtung*) entgegengesetzt: ~ *gear* → 4; *in* ~ *order* in umgekehrter Reihenfolge; ~ *side* linke (*Stoff*)Seite. **III** *v/t* **6.** *Wagen* im Rückwärtsgang *od.* rückwärts fahren: ~ *one's car out of the garage a.* rückwärts aus der Garage fahren. **7.** *Reihenfolge etc* umkehren: ~ *the charges teleph. Br.* ein R-Gespräch führen. **8.** *Entscheidung etc* umstoßen; ⅟ *Urteil* aufheben. **9.** *Blatt etc* umdrehen; *Mantel etc* wenden. **IV** *v/i* **10.** *mot*. im Rückwärtsgang *od.* rückwärts fahren.

re·vert [rɪ'vɜːt] *v/i*: ~ *to* auf ein Thema zurückkommen; in *e-e Gewohnheit etc* zurückfallen; in *e-n Zustand* zurückkehren.

re·view [rɪ'vju:] **I** *s* **1.** Überprüfung *f*: *be under* ~ überprüft werden. **2.** Besprechung *f*, Kritik *f*, Rezension *f*: ~ *copy* Rezensionsexemplar *n*. **3.** ✗ Parade *f*. **4.** → *revue*. **5.** *ped. Am*. (Stoff)Wiederholung *f* (*for* für *e-e Prüfung*). **II** *v/t* **6.** überprüfen. **7.** besprechen, rezensieren. **8.** ✗ besichtigen, inspizieren. **9.** *ped. Am*. *Stoff* wiederholen (*for* für *e-e Prüfung*). **re'view·er** *s* Kritiker(in), Rezensent(in).

re·vile [rɪ'vaɪl] v/t schmähen, verunglimpfen.

re·vise [rɪ'vaɪz] v/t **1.** revidieren: a) *Ansicht* ändern, b) *Buch etc* überarbeiten. **2.** *Br.* → **review** 9.

re·vi·sion [rɪ'vɪʒn] s **1.** Revidierung f, Änderung f; Revision f, Überarbeitung f. **2.** überarbeitete Ausgabe. **3.** *Br.* → **review** 5.

re·vi·tal·ize [ˌriː'vaɪtəlaɪz] v/t neu beleben.

re·viv·al [rɪ'vaɪvl] s **1.** Wiederbelebung f (*a. fig.*). **2.** *thea.* Wiederaufnahme f. **3.** Wiederaufleben n (*a. fig.*). **re'vive** I v/t **1.** *j-n* wiederbeleben; beleben. **2.** *Brauch etc* wiederbeleben, wiederaufleben lassen; *Erinnerungen* wachrufen. **3.** *thea.* Stück wiederaufnehmen. II v/i **4.** wieder zu sich kommen; wieder aufleben. **5.** wiederaufleben (*Brauch etc*).

rev·o·ca·tion [ˌrevə'keɪʃn] s Aufhebung f, Rückgängigmachung f, Widerruf m. **re·voke** [rɪ'vəʊk] v/t *Gesetz etc* aufheben, *Entscheidung, Erlaubnis etc* rückgängig machen, widerrufen.

re·volt [rɪ'vəʊlt] I s **1.** Revolte f, Aufstand m: *be in ~ (against)* → 3. **2.** → **revulsion.** II v/i **3.** revoltieren (*against* gegen). **4.** *fig.* Abscheu empfinden, empört sein (*against, at, from* über *acc*). III v/t **5.** mit Abscheu erfüllen, abstoßen. **re'volt·ing** adj □ abscheulich, abstoßend.

rev·o·lu·tion [ˌrevə'luːʃn] s **1.** Umdrehung f: *number of ~s mot.* Drehzahl f; *~ counter mot.* Drehzahlmesser m. **2.** *ast.* Umlauf m (*round um*). **3.** *pol.* Revolution f, *fig. a.* Umwälzung f. **rev·o'lu·tion·ar·y** I adj □ *pol.* revolutionär, *fig. a.* umwälzend. II s *pol.* Revolutionär(in) (*a. fig.*). **rev·o'lu·tion·ize** v/t *fig.* revolutionieren.

re·volve [rɪ'vɒlv] v/i sich drehen (*on an axis* um e-e Achse; *round the Earth* um die Erde): *~ around fig.* sich drehen um; *he thinks the whole world ~s around him* er glaubt, alles dreht sich nur um ihn. **re'volv·er** s Revolver m. **re'volv·ing** adj Dreh...: *~ door(s* pl) Drehtür f; *~ stage thea.* Drehbühne f.

re·vue [rɪ'vjuː] s thea. Revue f; Kabarett n.

re·vul·sion [rɪ'vʌlʃn] s Abscheu f: *in ~* angewidert.

re·ward [rɪ'wɔːd] I s (*a. ausgesetzte*) Belohnung: *as a ~ (for)* als Belohnung (für); → **finder.** II v/t belohnen. **re'ward·ing** adj lohnend, (*Aufgabe etc a.*) dankbar.

re·word [ˌriː'wɜːd] v/t umformulieren.

re·write [ˌriː'raɪt] v/t (*irr write*) umschreiben.

rhap·so·dize ['ræpsədaɪz] v/i schwärmen (*about, over* von). **'rhap·so·dy** s **1.** ♪ Rhapsodie f. **2.** *fig.* Schwärmerei f: *go into rhapsodies* ins Schwärmen geraten (*about, over* von).

Rhe·sus fac·tor ['riːsəs] s ♣ Rhesusfaktor m.

rhet·o·ric ['retərɪk] s **1.** Rhetorik f. **2.** *contp.* Phrasendrescherei f. **rhe·tor·i·cal** [rɪ'tɒrɪkl] adj □ rhetorisch: *~ question* rhetorische Frage.

rheu·mat·ic [ruː'mætɪk] ♣ I adj (*~ally*) **1.** rheumatisch: *~ fever* rheumatisches Fieber. II s **2.** Rheumatiker(in). **3.** pl (*sg konstruiert*) *bsd. Br.* F Rheuma n. **rheu·ma·tism** ['ruːmətɪzəm] s Rheuma(tismus m) n.

rhi·no ['raɪnəʊ] pl **-nos** s zo. F, **rhi·noc·er·os** [~'nɒsərəs] s zo. Rhinozeros n, Nashorn n.

rho·do·den·dron [ˌrəʊdə'dendrən] s ♣ Rhododendron m, n.

rhom·bus ['rɒmbəs] pl **-bus·es, -bi** [~baɪ] s ♣ Rhombus m, Raute f.

rhu·barb ['ruːbɑːb] s **1.** ♣ Rhabarber m. **2.** *bsd. Am.* F Krach m, Streit m.

rhyme [raɪm] I s **1.** Reim m (*for* auf *acc*): *do s.th. without ~ or reason* et. aus unerklärlichen Gründen tun. **2.** Reim m, Vers m. II v/i **3.** sich reimen (*with* auf *acc*). III v/t **4.** reimen (*with* auf *acc*, mit).

rhythm ['rɪðəm] s Rhythmus m: *break s.o.'s ~* j-n aus dem Rhythmus bringen. **rhyth·mic, rhyth·mi·cal** ['rɪðmɪk(l)] adj □ rhythmisch, (*Atmen etc*) gleichmäßig.

rib [rɪb] I s **1.** *anat.* Rippe f (*a. ❦ etc*): → **dig** 1, 5, **poke** 1, 6. **2.** Speiche f (*e-s Regenschirms*). II v/t **3.** F aufziehen, hänseln (*for* wegen).

rib·bon ['rɪbən] s **1.** (*a.* Farb-, Ordens-) Band n. **2.** Streifen m; Fetzen m: *tear to ~s* zerfetzen.

rib cage s anat. Brustkorb m.

rice [raɪs] s ♣ Reis m. **~ pad·dy** s Reisfeld

n. ~ **pud·ding** *s* Milchreis *m.* ~ **wine** *s* Reiswein *m.*

rich [rɪtʃ] **I** *adj* □ **1.** reich (*a. fig.*): ~ *in* reich an (*dat*); ~ *in contrasts* kontrastreich. **2.** prächtig, kostbar (*Schmuck etc*). **3.** schwer (*Speise*). **4.** ertragreich, fett (*Boden*). **5.** voll (*Töne*) (*Farben a.*) satt. **6.** *that's* ~*! F iro.* na prima! **II** *s* **7.** *the* ~ *pl* die Reichen *pl.* **rich·es** [-ɪz] *s pl* Reichtümer *pl.* **'rich·ness** *s* **1.** Reichtum *m* (*a. fig.*). **2.** Prächtigkeit *f,* Kostbarkeit *f.* **3.** Schwere *f.* **4.** Fettheit *f.* **5.** Fülle *f,* Sattheit *f.*

rick·ets ['rɪkɪts] *s pl* (*sg konstruiert*) **#** Rachitis *f.* **rick·et·y** ['-ətɪ] *adj* **1. #** rachitisch. **2.** schwach (*auf den Beinen*); gebrechlich. **3.** wack(e)lig (*Möbelstück etc*).

rick·shaw ['rɪkʃɔː] *s* Rikscha *f.*

ric·o·chet ['rɪkəʃeɪ] **I** *s* Querschläger *m.* **II** *v/i* abprallen (*off* von).

rid [rɪd] *v/t (mst irr)* befreien (*of* von): *get* ~ *of* loswerden. **'rid·dance** *s: good* ~ *(to him)! F* den sind wir Gott sei Dank los!; *get out and good* ~ *auf Nimmerwiedersehen.*

rid·den ['rɪdn] **I** *pp von* **ride. II** *adj in Zssgn* geplagt *od.* heimgesucht von.

rid·dle¹ ['rɪdl] *s* Rätsel *n* (*a. fig.*): *speak* (*od.* **talk**) *in* ~*s* in Rätseln sprechen.

rid·dle² [~] **I** *s* **1.** (Schüttel)Sieb *n.* **II** *v/t* **2.** sieben. **3.** ~ *with bullets* mit Kugeln durchlöchern *od.* -sieben; ~*d with holes* (*mistakes*) voller Löcher (Fehler).

ride [raɪd] **I** *s* **1.** Ritt *m: give s.o. a* ~ *on one's shoulders* j-n auf s-n Schultern reiten lassen. **2.** Fahrt *f: give s.o. a* ~ *in the car* e-e Autofahrt machen; *go for a* ~ *in the car* F j-n reinlegen *od.* übers Ohr hauen. **II** *v/i* (*irr*) **3.** reiten (*a. rittlings sitzen*) (*on auf dat*): → *roughshod.* **4.** fahren (*on auf e-m Fahrrad etc, in e-m Bus etc*). **5.** ~ *up* hochrutschen (*Rock etc*). **III** *v/t* **6.** reiten (*auf dat*). **7.** *Fahr-, Motorrad* fahren, fahren auf (*dat*): *can you* ~ *a bicycle?* kannst du radfahren? **'rid·er** *s* **1.** Reiter(in). **2.** (*Motorrad-, Rad*)Fahrer(in).

ridge [rɪdʒ] *s* **1.** (*Gebirgs*)Kamm *m,* (-)Grat *m.* **2.** (*Dach*)First *m.*

rid·i·cule ['rɪdɪkjuːl] **I** *s* Spott *m: for fear of* ~ aus Angst, sich lächerlich zu ma-

chen; *hold up to* ~ → **II. II** *v/t* lächerlich machen, spotten über (*acc*). **ri'dic·u·lous** [~jʊləs] *adj* □ lächerlich: *don't be* ~ mach dich nicht lächerlich.

rid·ing ['raɪdɪŋ] *adj* Reit...: ~ *school;* ~ *breeches* Reithose *f.*

rife [raɪf] *adj:* ~ *with* voll von, voller.

riff·raff ['rɪfræf] *s* Gesindel *n,* Pack *n.*

ri·fle¹ ['raɪfl] *v/t* durchwühlen.

ri·fle² [~] *s* Gewehr *n.* ~ **range** *s* Schießstand *m.*

rift [rɪft] *s* **1.** Spalt(e *f*) *m.* **2.** *fig.* Riß *m.*

rig¹ [rɪg] *v/t Wahl etc* manipulieren.

rig² [~] **I** *s* **1. ♣** Takelage *f,* Takelung *f.* **2.** Bohrinsel *f.* **3.** F Aufmachung *f: in full* ~ in voller Montur. **4.** *Am.* F Sattelschlepper *m.* **II** *v/t* **5.** *Schiff* auftakeln. **6.** ~ *out* F j-n ausstaffieren (*as* als); auftakeln. **7.** ~ *up* F provisorisch zs.-bauen (*from* aus).

right [raɪt] **I** *adj* (□ → **rightly**) **1.** richtig, recht: *the* ~ *thing* das Richtige; → *all* 3. **2.** richtig: a) korrekt, b) wahr: *is your watch* ~*?* geht deine Uhr richtig?; *be* ~ recht haben. **3.** richtig, geeignet: *the* ~ *man in the* ~ *place* der rechte Mann am rechten Platz. **4.** richtig, in Ordnung: *put* (*od.* **set**) ~ in Ordnung bringen; *j-n* aufklären (*on über acc*); *Irrtum* richtigstellen. **5.** recht, Rechts...: ~ *angle* **&** rechter Winkel. **II** *s* **7.** Recht *n: know* ~ *from wrong* Recht von Unrecht unterscheiden können. **8.** Recht *n;* Anrecht *n* (*to* auf *acc*): *by* ~*s* von Rechts wegen; *it is my* ~ *of way mot.* ich habe Vorfahrt; *know one's* ~*s* s-e Rechte kennen. **9.** die Rechte, rechte Seite: *on* (*od.* **at, to**) *the* ~ (*of*) rechts (von), rechter Hand (von); *on our* ~ zu unserer Rechten; *the second turning to* (*od.* **on**) *the* ~ die zweite Querstraße rechts; *keep to the* ~ sich rechts halten; *mot.* rechts fahren. **10.** *the* ~ *pol.* die Rechte. **III** *adv* **11.** richtig, recht: *if I say you* ~ wenn ich Sie richtig verstehe; *guess* ~ richtig (er)raten; → *serve* 8. **12.** genau, direkt. **13.** ~ *away* (*od.* **off**) sofort; ~ *now* im Moment; sofort. **14.** ganz, völlig. **15.** rechts (*of* von): *turn* ~ (sich) nach rechts wenden; *mot.* rechts abbiegen; ~ *and left;* ~, *left and center* (*bsd. Br. centre*) *fig.* F überall; in jeder Hinsicht. **IV** *v/t*

16. aufrichten. **17.** *Unrecht* wiedergutmachen. '**~an·gled** *adj* A rechtwink(e)lig.

right·eous ['raɪtʃəs] *adj* gerecht (*Zorn etc*).

right|·ful ['raɪtfʊl] *adj* □ rechtmäßig. '**~hand** *adj* **1.** recht: **~ bend** Rechtskurve *f*; **~ man** *fig.* j-s rechte Hand. **2.** ◎ rechtsgängig, -läufig: **~ drive** Rechtssteuerung *f*. ,**~'hand·ed** *adj* □ rechtshändig: **be ~** Rechtshänder(in) sein. ,**~'hand·er** *s* Rechtshänder(in).

right·ist ['raɪtɪst] *adj pol.* rechtsgerichtet, -stehend. '**right·ly** *adv* **1.** richtig. **2.** mit Recht: **~ or wrongly** zu Recht od. Unrecht. **3.** F *I don't ~ know* ich weiß nicht sicher; *I can't ~ say* ich kann nicht mit Sicherheit sagen.

'**right-wing** *adj pol.* dem rechten Flügel angehörend, Rechts...

rig·id ['rɪdʒɪd] *adj* □ **1.** starr (*a. Person*: **with** vor *dat*), steif. **2.** *fig.* streng (*Disziplin etc*); starr (*Prinzipien etc*); genau, strikt (*Kontrolle etc*). **ri'gid·i·ty** *s* **1.** Starre *f*, Starrheit *f*, Steifheit *f*. **2.** *fig.* Strenge *f*; Genauigkeit *f*, Striktheit *f*.

rig·ma·role ['rɪgmərəʊl] *s* F **1.** Geschwätz *n*. **2.** Theater *n*, Zirkus *m*.

rig·or *Am.* → **rigour**.

ri·gor mor·tis [,raɪgɔː'mɔːtɪs] *s* ☞ Leichenstarre *f*.

rig·or·ous ['rɪgərəs] *adj* □ **1.** streng (*Kontrolle etc*). **2.** (peinlich) genau, gründlich.

rig·our ['rɪgə] *s bsd. Br.* **1.** Strenge *f*: **the full ~ of the law** die volle Härte des Gesetzes. **2.** *pl* Unbilden *pl*.

'**rig-out** *s Br.* F Aufmachung *f*.

rile [raɪl] *v/t* F ärgern, reizen.

rim [rɪm] *s* **1.** Rand *m* (*e-r Tasse etc*), (*e-s Huts a.*) Krempe *f*. **2.** ◎ Felge *f*.

rind [raɪnd] *s* (*Zitronen- etc*)Schale *f*; (*Käse*)Rinde *f*; (*Speck- etc*)Schwarte *f*.

ring¹ [rɪŋ] *I s* **1.** *allg.* Ring *m*: *at the **~s** (*Turnen*) an den Ringen; *form a ~* e-n Kreis bilden; *he's got **~s** round him* er hat Ringe unter den Augen; *make (od. run)* **~s** *round s.o. fig.* j-n in die Tasche stecken. **2.** (*Zirkus*) Manege *f*; (*Boxen*) Ring *m*. **3.** ✝ Ring *m*, Kartell *n*; (*Spionage- etc*)Ring *m*. *II v/t* **4.** *Vogel etc* beringen. **5.** umringen, (*Polizei etc*) umstellen; *Stelle in e-m Buch etc* einkreisen.

ring² [~] *I s* **1.** Läuten *n*; Klingeln *n*. **2.** *fig.* **that has a hollow ~ to me** das kommt mir (irgendwie) bekannt vor; **have a hollow ~** hohl klingen (*Versprechen etc*), unglaubwürdig klingen (*Protest etc*). **3.** *teleph. bsd. Br.* Anruf *m*: **give s.o. a ~** j-n anrufen. *II v/i (irr)* **4.** läuten; klingeln: **the bell is ~ing** es läutet *od.* klingelt; **~ for** nach j-m, *et.* läuten. **5.** *teleph. bsd. Br.* anrufen: **~ for** *Arzt etc* rufen. **6.** klingen (*a. fig.*): **~ in s.o.'s ears** j-m im Ohr klingen; **~ hollow** hohl klingen (*Versprechen etc*), unglaubwürdig klingen (*Protest etc*). *III v/t (irr)* **7.** läuten: → **bell 1**, **doorbell**. **8.** *teleph. bsd. Br.* j-n anrufen.

Verbindungen mit Adverbien:

ring| back *v/t u. v/i teleph. bsd. Br.* zurückrufen. **~ in** *v/i* **1.** *bsd. Br.* sich telefonisch melden (**to** bei). **2.** *Am.* (*bei Arbeitsbeginn*) einstempeln. **~ off** *v/i teleph. bsd. Br.* (den Hörer) auflegen, Schluß machen. **~ out** *v/i* **1.** erklingen, ertönen. **2.** *Am.* (*bei Arbeitsende*) ausstempeln. **~ round** *v/i bsd. Br.* herumtelefonieren. **~ up** *v/t* **1.** → **ring² 8**. **2.** *Preis, Ware (in die Kasse)* eintippen.

ring| bind·er *s* Ringbuch *n*. **~ fin·ger** *s* Ringfinger *m*. **~ lead·er** *s* Rädelsführer(in). '**~mas·ter** *s* Zirkusdirektor *m*. **~ road** *s bsd. Br.* Umgehungsstraße *f*. '**~side** *s*: *at the ~* (*Boxen*) am Ring; **~ seat** (*Boxen*) Ringplatz *m*; (*Zirkus*) Manegenplatz *m*.

rink [rɪŋk] *s* (Kunst)Eisbahn *f*; Rollschuhbahn *f*.

rinse [rɪns] *I v/t* **1.** *a.* **~ out** (aus)spülen, *Wäsche* spülen: **~ one's mouth out** sich den Mund ausspülen (**with** mit); **~ the soap out of one's hair** sich die Seife aus dem Haar spülen. **2.** sich *das Haar* tönen. *II s* **3.** Spülung *f*: *give s.th. a ~* → 1. **4.** Tönung(smittel *n*) *f*.

ri·ot ['raɪət] *I s* **1.** Aufruhr *m*; Krawall *m*, Tumult *m*: *run* ~ randalieren, randalierend ziehen (**through** durch); *his imagination ran* ~ s-e Phantasie ging mit ihm durch; *read s.o. the ~ act* oft humor. j-m die Leviten lesen; **~ police** Bereitschaftspolizei *f*; **~ squad** Überfallkommando *n*; **~ shield** Schutzschild *m*. **2.** **~ of colo(u)r** Sinfonie *f* von *od.* Orgie *f* in Farben. **3.** *be a* ~ F zum Schreien (komisch) sein. *II v/i* **4.** an e-m

Aufruhr teilnehmen; randalieren. **'ri-ot-er** s Aufrührer *m*; Randalierer *m*. **'ri-ot-ous** *adj* □ **1.** aufrührerisch; randalierend. **2.** ausgelassen, wild.

rip [rɪp] **I** *v/t* **1.** a. ~ *up* zerreißen: ~ *s.th.* sich et. zerreißen (**on** an *dat*); ~ *s.th.* **from s.o.'s hand** j-m et. aus der Hand reißen; ~ *off one's shirt* sich das Hemd herunter- *od.* vom Leib reißen; ~ *open* aufreißen. **2.** ~ *off* F neppen; mitgehen lassen, klauen. **II** *v/i* **3.** (zer)reißen. **4.** *let her* ~**!** *mot.* F volle Pulle! **III** *s* **5.** Riß *m*.

'rip-cord *s* Reißleine *f* (*am Fallschirm*).

ripe [raɪp] *adj* □ reif (*a. fig.*): **live to a** ~ **old age** ein hohes Alter erreichen; **the time is** ~ **for** die Zeit ist reif für; ~ **for development** baureif. **rip-en** ['~ən] **I** *v/i* reifen. **II** *v/t* reifen lassen.

'rip-off *s* F Nepp *m*; Diebstahl *m*.

ri-poste [rɪ'pɒst] **I** *s* **1.** *fenc.* Riposte *f*. **2.** (schlagfertige *od.* scharfe) Entgegnung. **II** *v/t* **3.** (schlagfertig *od.* scharf) entgegnen.

rip-ple ['rɪpl] **I** *s* **1.** kleine Welle. **2.** Plätschern *n*. **II** *v/t* **3.** *Wasser* kräuseln. **III** *v/i* **4.** sich kräuseln. **5.** plätschern.

'rip-,roar-ing *adj* F **1.** ausgelassen (*Party etc*). **2.** toll (*Erfolg etc*).

rise [raɪz] **I** *v/i* (*irr*) **1.** aufstehen (*a. am Morgen*), sich erheben. **2.** aufsteigen (*Rauch etc*); sich heben (*Vorhang*): **his spirits rose** s-e Stimmung hob sich. **3.** ansteigen (*Straße, Weg etc*), anschwellen (*Fluß etc*). **4.** (an)steigen (**by** um) (*Temperatur etc*), (*Preise etc a.*) anziehen. **5.** aufgehen (*Sonne, Teig etc*). **6.** entspringen (*Fluß etc*); *fig.* entstehen (**from, out of** aus). **7.** *a.* ~ *up* sich erheben (**against** gegen). **8.** (*above*) erhaben sein (über *acc*), stehen (über *dat*): → *occasion* 3. **9.** (*beruflich od. gesellschaftlich*) aufsteigen: → *rank*¹ 2. **II** *s* **10.** Steigung *f*; Anhöhe *f*. **11.** *ast.* Aufgang *m*. **12.** *fig.* Anstieg *m* (*in gen*): ~ *in population* Bevölkerungszunahme *f*; **the** ~ **and fall** das Auf u. Ab. **13.** *fig.* Aufstieg *m* (**to** zu): **the** ~ **and fall of** der Aufstieg u. Fall. **14.** *bsd. Br.* Lohn- *od.* Gehaltserhöhung *f*. **15.** *give* ~ *to* verursachen, führen zu; Anlaß geben zu. **ris-en** ['rɪzn] *pp von* rise. **'ris-er** *s*: *early* ~ *ly* ~ Frühaufsteher(in); *late* ~ Langschläfer(in). **'ris-ing I** *s* **1.** Aufstand *m*,

Erhebung *f*. **II** *adj* **2.** heranwachsend, kommend (*Generation*). **3.** aufstrebend (*Politiker etc*). **III** *prp* **4.** *be* ~ *ten bsd. Br.* fast zehn sein.

risk [rɪsk] **I** *s* Gefahr *f*, Risiko *n*: **at one's own** ~ auf eigene Gefahr, auf eigenes Risiko; **at the** ~ **of** (*ger*) auf die Gefahr hin zu (*inf*); **be at** ~ gefährdet sein; **put at** ~ gefährden; **run** (*od.* **take**) **a** ~ ein Risiko eingehen; **run the** ~ **of doing s.th.** Gefahr laufen, et. zu tun; ~ *group* Risikogruppe *f*. **II** *v/t* riskieren: a) *sein Leben etc* aufs Spiel setzen, b) *Sprung etc* wagen, c) es ankommen lassen auf ~ *doing s.th.* es wagen *od.* riskieren, et. zu tun; → *neck* 1. **'risk-y** *adj* □ riskant.

ri-sot-to [rɪ'zɒtəʊ] *pl* **-tos** *s gastr.* Risotto *m*.

rite [raɪt] *s* Ritus *m*: **perform the last** ~**s over** *eccl.* j-m die Sterbesakramente spenden.

rit-u-al ['rɪtʃʊəl] **I** *s* **1.** Ritual *n*. **II** *adj* □ **2.** Ritual...: ~ *murder* Ritualmord *m*. **3.** rituell.

ritz-y ['rɪtsɪ] *adj* F stinkvornehm, feudal.

ri-val ['raɪvl] **I** *s* **1.** Rivale *m*, Rivalin *f*, Konkurrent(in): ~ *(in love)* Nebenbuhler(in). **II** *adj* **2.** rivalisierend, konkurrierend: ~ *firm* Konkurrenzfirma *f*. **III** *v/t pret u. pp* **-valed,** *bsd. Br.* **-valled 3.** rivalisieren *od.* konkurrieren mit. **4.** es aufnehmen mit (*for* an *dat*). **'ri-val-ry** *s* Rivalität *f*; Konkurrenz(kampf *m*) *f*.

riv-er ['rɪvə] *s* Fluß *m*; Strom *m*: **down the** ~ flußabwärts; **up the** ~ flußaufwärts; **sell s.o. down the** ~ F j-n verraten u. verkaufen; ~**s** *pl of blood* Blutströme *pl*. ~ *ba-sin* s Flußbecken *n*. **'~-bed** *s* Flußbett *n*. **'~-side** *s* Flußufer *n*: **by the** ~ am Fluß.

riv-et ['rɪvɪt] **I** *s* **1.** ⊙ Niet *m*. **II** *v/t* **2.** ⊙ (ver)nieten: **stand** ~*ed* **to the spot** *fig.* wie festgenagelt stehen(bleiben). **3.** *fig.* Aufmerksamkeit richten, *Augen, Blick a.* heften (**on** auf *acc*); j-s Aufmerksamkeit fesseln.

road [rəʊd] *s* (Land)Straße *f*: **on the** ~ auf der Straße; **be on the** ~ mit dem Auto unterwegs sein; *thea. etc* auf Tournee sein; **be on the right** ~ *fig.* auf dem richtigen Weg sein; **hit the** ~ F sich auf den Weg machen, aufbrechen; **one**

for the ~ F e-n (*Schnaps etc*) zum Abschied *od.* für unterwegs; → *Rome*. ~ **ac·ci·dent** *s* Verkehrsunfall *m.* '~-**block** *s* Straßensperre *f.* ~ **hog** *s* F Verkehrsrowdy *m.* '~**hold·ing** *s od.* Straßenlage *f.* '~**house** *s* Rasthaus *n.* ~**man** ['~mən] *s* (*irr* **man**) Straßenarbeiter *m.* ~ **roll·er** *s* ⊙ Straßenwalze *f.* ~ **safe·ty** *s* Verkehrssicherheit *f.* '~**side** *s* Straßenrand *m: at* (*od. by*) *the* ~ am Straßenrand. ~ **test** *s mot.* Probefahrt *f: do a* ~ e-e Probefahrt machen. '~-**test** *v/t Auto* probefahren, e-e Probefahrt machen mit. ~ **us·er** *s* Verkehrsteilnehmer(in). '~**way** *s* Fahrbahn *f.* ~ **works** *s pl* Straßenbauarbeiten *pl.* '~**wor·thy** *adj* verkehrssicher.

roam [rəʊm] **I** *v/i* wandern. **II** *v/t* wandern durch.

roar [rɔː] **I** *v/i* **1.** brüllen (**with** vor *dat*): ~ (**with** laughter) vor Lachen brüllen; ~ **at** *s.o.* j-n anbrüllen. **2.** donnern (*Fahrzeug, Geschütz*). **II** *v/t* **3.** *a.* ~ **out** et. brüllen. **III** *s* **4.** Brüllen *n*, Gebrüll *n: ~s pl of laughter* brüllendes Gelächter. **5.** Donnern *n.* '**roar·ing I** *adj* □ **1.** brüllend. **2.** donnernd. **3.** ~ *success* F Bombenerfolg *m.* **II** *adv* **4.** ~ *drunk* F sternhagelvoll. **III** *s* **5.** → *roar* 4, 5.

roast [rəʊst] **I** *v/t Fleisch* braten; *Kaffee etc* rösten. **II** *v/i* braten: *I'm* ~*ing* ich komme vor Hitze fast um. **III** *s* Braten *m.* **IV** *adj* gebraten: ~ *beef* Rinder-, Rindsbraten *m;* ~ *chicken* Brathuhn *n*, -hühnchen *n;* ~ *pork* Schweine-, Schweinsbraten *m;* ~ *veal* Kalbsbraten *m.* '**roast·ing** F **I** *adj* glühend-, knallheiß (*Tag etc*). **II** *adv:* ~ *hot* → I. **III** *s: give s.o. a* (*real*) ~ j-n zs.-stauchen (*for* wegen).

rob [rɒb] *v/t Bank etc* überfallen; *j-n* berauben: ~ *s.o. of s.th.* j-m et. rauben. '**rob·ber** *s* Räuber *m.* '**rob·ber·y** *s* Raub(überfall) *m*, (*Bank*)Raub *m*, (-)Überfall *m.*

robe [rəʊb] *s a. pl* Robe *f*, Talar *m.*

rob·in ['rɒbɪn] *s orn.* Rotkehlchen *n.*

ro·bot ['rəʊbɒt] *s* ⊙ Roboter *m* (*a. fig.*).

ro·bust [rəʊ'bʌst] *adj* □ **1.** robust (*Person, Gesundheit, Material etc*); *fig.* gesund (*Firma etc*). **2.** *fig.* nachdrücklich.

rock¹ [rɒk] *s* **1.** Fels(en) *m;* *coll.* Felsen *pl; geol.* Gestein *n.* **2.** Felsbrocken *m; Am.* Stein *m.* **3.** *pl* Klippen *pl: on the* ~*s*

on the rocks, mit Eis (*bsd. Whisky*); in ernsten Schwierigkeiten (*Firma etc*); *their marriage is on the* ~*s* in ihrer Ehe kriselt es gewaltig.

rock² [~] **I** *v/t* **1.** wiegen, schaukeln: ~ *a child to sleep* ein Kind in den Schlaf wiegen. **2.** erschüttern (*a. fig.*): ~ *the boat fig.* alles kaputtmachen. **II** *v/i* **3.** schaukeln. **4.** schwanken: ~ *with laughter* F sich vor Lachen biegen. **5.** ♪ rocken. **III** *s* **6.** → *rock 'n' roll*. **7.** *a.* ~ *music* Rock(musik *f*) *m:* ~ *group* Rockgruppe *f;* ~ *singer* Rocksänger (-in).

rock| and roll *s* ♪ Rock and Roll *m.* ~ **bot·tom** *s: fall to* (*od. hit, reach*) ~ e-n *od.* s-n Tiefpunkt erreichen. ~**bot·tom** *adj* allerniedrigst, äußerst (*Preise*). ~ **crys·tal** *s min.* Bergkristall *m.*

rock·er ['rɒkə] *s* **1.** Kufe *f* (*e-s Schaukelstuhls etc*): *off one's* ~ F übergeschnappt. **2.** *Am.* Schaukelstuhl *m.* **3.** *Br.* Rocker *m.*

rock·er·y ['rɒkərı] *s* Steingarten *m.*

rock·et ['rɒkɪt] *s* **1.** Rakete *f.* **2.** *give s.o. a* ~ *bsd. Br.* F j-m e-e Zigarre verpassen. **II** *v/i* **3.** *a.* ~ *up* hochschnellen, in die Höhe schießen (*Preise*). **4.** rasen, schießen.

'**rock|fall** *s* Steinschlag *m.* ~ **gar·den** *s* Steingarten *m.*

rock·ing| chair *s* ['rɒkɪŋ] *s* Schaukelstuhl *m.* ~ **horse** *s* Schaukelpferd *n.*

rock 'n' roll [ˌrɒkən'rəʊl] *s* ♪ Rock 'n' Roll *m.*

rock·y¹ ['rɒkı] *adj* □ **1.** felsig. **2.** steinhart.

rock·y² [~] *adj* □ F wack(e)lig.

ro·co·co [rəʊ'kəʊkəʊ] *s* Rokoko *n.*

rod [rɒd] *s* **1.** (*a. Angel*)Rute *f.* **2.** ⊙ Stab *m*, Stange *f.* **3.** *rule with a* ~ *of iron* mit eiserner Faust regieren. **4.** *Am. sl.* Schießeisen *n*, Kanone *f.*

rode [rəʊd] *pret von* **ride**.

ro·dent ['rəʊdənt] *s* Nagetier *n.*

ro·de·o [rəʊ'deɪəʊ] *pl* -**os** *s* Rodeo *m, n.*

roe¹ [rəʊ] *s a.* **hard** ~*ichth.* Rogen *m;* **soft** ~ Milch *f.*

roe² [~] *s zo.* Reh *n.* '~**buck** *s* Rehbock *m.* ~ **deer** *s* Reh *n.*

rog·er ['rɒdʒə] *int* Funkverkehr: roger!, verstanden!

rogue [rəʊg] *s* **1.** Gauner *m:* ~*s' gallery* Verbrecheralbum *n.* **2.** *oft humor.*

Schlingel *m*, Spitzbube *m*. **'ro·guer·y** *s*
1. Gaunerei *f*. **2.** Spitzbüberei *f*.
'ro·guish *adj* □ schelmisch.
role [rəʊl] *s thea. etc* Rolle *f* (*a. fig.*).
roll [rəʊl] **I** *s* **1.** Rolle *f*; (*Fett*)Wulst *f*. **2.**
Anwesenheits-, Namenliste *f*: **call the ~**
die Anwesenheitsliste verlesen. **3.** Brötchen *n*, Semmel *f*. **4.** *Würfeln*: Wurf *m*.
5. ♻ Schlingern *n*. **6.** (G)Rollen *n* (*des
Donners*); (*Trommel*)Wirbel *m*. **II** *v/i* **7.**
rollen; sich wälzen: **tears were ~ing
down her cheeks** Tränen rollten ihr
über die Wangen; **heads will ~** *fig.* es
werden einige Köpfe rollen; **be ~ing in
money** (*od. it*) F im Geld schwimmen;
→ **ball**¹ 1. **8.** rollen, fahren. **9.** würfeln.
10. (sch)wanken (*Person*); ♻ schlingern. **11.** (g)rollen (*Donner*). **III** *v/t* **12.**
et. rollen: **~ the dice** würfeln; **~ one's
eyes** die Augen rollen *od.* verdrehen.
13. auf-, zs.-rollen: **~ itself into** sich
zs.-rollen zu (*Tier*); **~ a cigarette** sich
e-e Zigarette drehen; **~ed into one** *fig.*
in einem. **14.** *Rasen etc* walzen; *Teig*
ausrollen.
Verbindungen mit Adverbien:
roll| down *v/t* **1.** *Ärmel* herunterkrempeln. **2.** *mot. Fenster* herunterkurbeln.
~ in *v/i* hereinströmen (*Angebote etc*). **~
on** *v/i*: **~, Saturday!** *Br.* wenn es doch
nur schon Samstag wäre! **~ out** *v/t*
Teig, Teppich ausrollen. **~ up I** *v/t* **1.**
auf-, zs.-rollen. **2.** *Ärmel* hoch-, aufkrempeln (*a. fig.*). **3.** *mot. Fenster* hochkurbeln. **II** *v/i* **4.** sich zs.-rollen (*into* zu)
(*Tier*). **5.** F antanzen. **6. ~!** (*Rummelplatz etc*) hereinspaziert!
roll| bar *s mot.* Überrollbügel *m*. **~ call** *s*
Namensaufruf *m*: **have a ~** die Namen
aufrufen.
roll·er ['rəʊlə] *s* **1.** ⚙ Rolle *f*; Walze *f*. **~
blind** *s* Rolladen *m*, Rollo *n*. **~ coast·er** *s* Achterbahn *f*.
~ skate *s* Rollschuh *m*. **'~-skate** *v/i*
Rollschuh laufen. **~ skat·er** *s* Rollschuhläufer(in). **~ skat·ing** *s* Rollschuhlaufen *n*. **~ tow·el** *s* Rollhandtuch *n*.
roll·ing| mill ['rəʊlɪŋ] *s* ⚙ Walzwerk *n*. **~
pin** *s* Nudelholz *n*, -rolle *f*, Teigrolle *f*.
'roll-on *s* Deoroller *m*.
ro·ly-po·ly [ˌrəʊlɪ'pəʊlɪ] F I *s* Dickerchen
n. **II** *adj* dick u. rund.
Ro·man ['rəʊmən] **I** *adj* römisch: **~ nu-**

meral römische Ziffer. **II** *s* Römer(in).
~ Cath·o·lic I *adj* (römisch-)katholisch. **II** *s* Katholik(in).
ro·mance¹ [rəʊ'mæns] *s* **1.** Liebes- *od.*
Abenteuerroman *m*. **2.** Romanze *f*,
Liebesverhältnis *n*. **3.** Romantik *f*.
Ro·mance² [~] *adj* romanisch (*Sprache*).
Ro·man·esque [ˌrəʊmə'nesk] *adj* romanisch (*Baustil*).
ro·man·tic [rəʊ'mæntɪk] **I** *adj* (**~ally**)
(*Kunst etc oft* ♻) romantisch. **II** *s* (*Kunst
etc oft* ♻) Romantiker(in). **ro'man·ti·cism** [~sɪzəm] *s* **1.** *oft* ♻ *Kunst etc*: Romantik *f*. **2.** romantische Vorstellungen
pl. **ro'man·ti·cist** → **romantic** II.
ro'man·ti·cize *v/t* romantisieren.
Ro·ma·ny ['rɒmənɪ] *s* **1.** Zigeuner(in). **2.**
Romani *n*, Zigeunersprache *f*.
Rome [rəʊm] *npr* Rom *n*: **~ was not built
in a day** Rom ist nicht an *od.* in 'einem
Tag erbaut worden; **all roads lead to ~**
alle Wege führen nach Rom.
romp [rɒmp] *v/i* **1.** *a.* **~ about** (*od.
around*) herumtollen. **2. ~ through** F erspielend schaffen.
ron·do ['rɒndəʊ] *pl* **-dos** *s* ♪ Rondo *n*.
roof [ruːf] **I** *s* Dach *n*; *mot.* Verdeck *n*: **go
through the ~** F an die Decke gehen
(*Person*); ins Unermeßliche steigen
(*Kosten etc*); **have no ~ over one's
head** kein Dach über dem Kopf haben;
live under the same ~ unter 'einem
Dach leben *od.* wohnen (**as** mit). **II** *v/t*
bedachen: **~ in** (*od. over*) überdachen.
~ gar·den *s* Dachgarten *m*. **~ rack** *s*
mot. Dachgepäckträger *m*. **'~ top** *s*:
scream (*od.* **shout**) **s.th. from the ~s**
fig. et. ausposaunen *od.* an die große
Glocke hängen.
rook¹ [rʊk] *v/t* F *j-n* betrügen (**of** um).
rook² [~] *s* Schach: Turm *m*.
room [ruːm] **I** *s* **1.** Raum *m*, Zimmer *n*. **2.**
Raum *m*, Platz *m*: **make ~ for s.o.** j-m
Platz machen. **3.** *fig.* Spielraum *m*:
there is ~ for improvement es ließe sich
noch manches besser machen; **leave
little ~ for doubt as to** kaum e-n Zweifel
übriglassen an (*dat*). **II** *v/i* **4.** Am. →
lodge 3. **'room·er** Am. → **lodger**.
'room·ing *adj*: **~ house** Am. Fremdenheim *n*, Pension *f*.
'room|·mate *s* Zimmergenosse *m*, -genossin *f*. **~ ser·vice** *s* Zimmerservice *m*:

ring for ~ nach dem Zimmerkellner klingeln.

room·y ['ru:mɪ] *adj* □ geräumig.

roost [ru:st] **I** *s* (Hühner)Stange *f*: **come home to** ~ *fig.* sich rächen (*Fehler etc*); → **rule** 5. **II** *v/i* auf der Stange sitzen *od.* schlafen. **'roost·er** *s bsd. Am.* Hahn *m.*

root¹ [ru:t] **I** *s anat.*, ♀, ≥ Wurzel *f* (*a. fig.*): ~ **and branch** *fig.* mit Stumpf u. Stiel; **get to the** ~ **of** *fig.* e-r Sache auf den Grund gehen; **have its** ~**s in** *fig.* wurzeln in (*dat*), s-n Ursprung haben in (*dat*); **pull out by the** ~ mit der Wurzel ausreißen *od.* (*fig.*) ausrotten; **put down (new)** ~**s** *fig.* Fuß fassen; **take** ~ Wurzeln schlagen (*a. fig.*). **II** *v/i* Wurzeln schlagen (*a. fig.*). **III** *v/t*: ~ **up** mit der Wurzel ausreißen; ~ **out** *fig.* (mit der Wurzel) ausrotten.

root² [~] **I** *v/i a.* ~ **about** (*od.* **around**) herumwühlen (**among** in *dat*). **II** *v/t*: ~ **out** aufstöbern.

root³ [~] *v/i*: ~ **for** *bsd. Am.* F a) *Sport:* j-n anfeuern, b) *fig.* j-m den Daumen drücken *od.* halten; j-n (tatkräftig) unterstützen.

root beer *s Am.* Limonade aus Wurzelextrakten.

root·ed ['ru:tɪd] *adj*: **be** ~ **in** *fig.* wurzeln in (*dat*), s-n Ursprung haben in (*dat*); **stand** ~ **to the spot** wie angewurzelt dastehen.

rope [rəʊp] **I** *s* **1.** Seil *n*, ♪ Tau *n*; Strick *m*: **give s.o. plenty of** ~ *fig.* j-m viel Freiheit *od.* Spielraum lassen; **know the** ~**s** F sich auskennen; **jump** ~ *Am.* seilhüpfen, -springen; **show s.o. the** ~**s** F j-n anlernen *od.* einarbeiten *od.* einweihen. **2.** (*Perlen- etc*)Schnur *f*. **II** *v/t* **3.** festbinden (**to** an *dat*, *a. acc*). **4.** ~ **off** (durch ein Seil) abgrenzen *od.* absperren. ~ **lad·der** *s* Strickleiter *f.*

rop·(e)y ['rəʊpɪ] *adj* □ F miserabel.

ro·sa·ry ['rəʊzərɪ] *s* (*Gebete oft* 2) *eccl.* Rosenkranz *m.*

rose¹ [rəʊz] *s* **1.** ♀ Rose *f*: **life is not all** ~**s** das Leben hat nicht nur angenehme Seiten. **2.** Brause *f* (*e-r Gießkanne etc*). **II** *adj* **3.** rosa-, rosenrot.

rose² [~] *pret von* **rise.**

ro·sé ['rəʊzeɪ] *s* Rosé *m* (*Wein*).

'rose·bush *s* ♀ Rosenstock *m*, -strauch *m*. **'~·col·o(u)red** *adj* rosa-, rosenrot: **see things through** ~ **glasses** (*od.*

spectacles) *fig.* die Dinge durch e-e rosa(rote) Brille sehen. **'~·hip** *s* ♀ Hagebutte *f.*

rose·mar·y ['rəʊzmərɪ] *s* ♀ Rosmarin *m.*

ro·sette [rəʊ'zet] *s* Rosette *f* (*a.* △).

ros·in ['rɒzɪn] **I** *s* Kolophonium *n*, Geigenharz *n*. **II** *v/t* mit Kolophonium einreiben.

ros·ter ['rɒstə] *s* Dienstplan *m.*

ros·trum ['rɒstrəm] *pl* **-tra** ['~trə], **-trums** *s* Redner-, Dirigentenpult *n.*

ros·y ['rəʊzɪ] *adj* □ rosig (*a. fig.*).

rot [rɒt] **I** *v/i a.* ~ **away** (ver)faulen, (*bsd. Holz a.*) verrotten, morsch werden. **II** *v/t* (ver)faulen *od.* verrotten lassen, morsch machen. **III** *s* Fäulnis(prozeß *m*) *f.*

ro·ta ['rəʊtə] *s bsd. Br.* Dienstplan *m.*

ro·ta·ry ['rəʊtərɪ] **I** *adj* rotierend, Rotations..., Dreh... **II** *s Am.* Kreisverkehr *m.* **ro·tate** [~'teɪt] **I** *v/i* **1.** rotieren, sich drehen. **2.** turnusmäßig wechseln. **II** *v/t* **3.** rotieren lassen, drehen. **4.** *Personal* turnusmäßig auswechseln. **ro·ta·tion** *s* **1.** Rotation *f*, Drehung *f*. **2. in** ~ der Reihe nach, nacheinander.

rote [rəʊt] *s*: **learn s.th. by** ~ et. (mechanisch) auswendig lernen.

ro·tor ['rəʊtə] *s* ☺, ✈ Rotor *m.*

rot·ten ['rɒtn] *adj* □ **1.** verfault, faul, (*bsd. Holz a.*) verrottet, morsch. **2.** F miserabel: **feel** ~ sich mies fühlen (*a. fig.*).

ro·tund [rəʊ'tʌnd] *adj* □ rund u. dick.

rouge [ruːʒ] *s* Rouge *n.*

rough [rʌf] **I** *adj* (□ → **roughly**) **1.** uneben (*Straße etc*), rauh (*Haut etc, a. Stimme*). **2.** stürmisch (*Meer, Überfahrt, Wetter*): **he had a** ~ **passage** *fig.* ihm ist es (e-e Zeitlang) nicht gutgegangen. **3.** a) grob (*Person, Behandlung etc*): **be** ~ **with** grob umgehen mit, b) *Sport:* hart (*Spielweise etc*). **4.** roh, Roh...: ~ **diamond** Rohdiamant *m*; **be a** ~ **diamond** *fig.* e-e rauhe Schale haben; ~ **draft** Rohfassung *f*; → **copy** 1. **5.** *fig.* grob, ungefähr: **at a** ~ **guess** grob geschätzt; **I have a** ~ **idea where it is** ich kann mir ungefähr vorstellen, wo es ist; ~ **estimate** 5. **6.** *feel* ~ *Br.* F sich mies fühlen. **II** *s* **7.** *Golf:* Rough *n.* **8.** Rowdy *m.* **9. take the** ~ **with the smooth** die Dinge nehmen, wie sie kommen. **III** *adv* **10. sleep** ~ im Freien

übernachten. **11.** *play* (*it*) ~ (*Sport*) hart
spielen. **IV** *v/i* **12.** ~ *it* F primitiv leben.
13. ~ *out* entwerfen, skizzieren. **14.** ~ *up*
F *j-n* zs.-schlagen. '**rough·age** *s biol.*
Ballaststoffe *pl.*

,**rough|-and-'tum·ble** *s* Balgerei *f*: *have
a* ~ sich balgen. '**~·cast** *s* △ Rauhputz
m.

rough·en ['rʌfn] **I** *v/t* Haut *etc* rauh machen. **II** *v/i* rauh werden. '**rough·ly** *adv*
1. grob (*a. fig.*). **2.** *fig.* ungefähr: ~
speaking grob geschätzt, über den
Daumen gepeilt.

'**rough·neck** *s bsd. Am.* F Grobian *m*;
Schläger *m.*

rough·ness ['rʌfnɪs] *s* **1.** Unebenheit *f,*
Rauheit *f.* **2.** Grobheit *f.*

'**rough·shod** *adv*: *ride* ~ *over* sich rücksichtslos hinwegsetzen über (*acc*).

rou·lette [ruː'let] *s* Roulett(e) *n.*

round [raʊnd] **I** *adj* (□ → *roundly*) **1.**
allg. rund. **2.** rund(lich), dick(lich)
(*Körperteil*). **3.** rund: a) voll, ganz: *a ~
dozen* ein rundes Dutzend, b) ab- *od.*
aufgerundet: *the house cost £100,000
in ~ figures* das Haus kostete rund(e)
100 000 Pfund. **II** *adv* (→ *Verben, z. B.
turn round*) **4.** → *all* **3.** *all* (*the*) *year
~* das ganze Jahr lang *od.* hindurch *od.*
über. **6.** ~ *about* F ungefähr. **7.** *be three
yards ~* e-n Umfang von drei Yards
haben. **III** *prp* **8.** (rund) um, um (...
herum): *trip ~ the world* Weltreise *f; do
you live ~ here?* wohnen Sie hier in der
Gegend?; → *bend* 1, *clock* 1, *look* 1. **9.**
ungefähr. **IV** *s* **10.** Runde *f,* Rundgang
m: *do* (*od. be out on*) *one's ~s* s-e
Runde machen, (*Arzt*) Hausbesuche
machen; *go the ~s fig.* umgehen (*Gerücht etc*), (*Krankheit a.*) grassieren (*of
in dat*); *the daily ~ fig.* der tägliche
Trott. **11.** Lage *f,* Runde *f* (*Bier etc*):
it's my ~ die Runde geht auf mich. **12.**
Boxen, *Turnier, Verhandlungen etc*:
Runde *f.* **13.** ✕ *etc* Schuß *m.* **14.** ♪
Kanon *m.* **V** *v/t* **15.** rund machen,
(ab)runden, *Lippen* spitzen. **16.** umfahren, fahren um, *Kurve* nehmen.
Verbindungen mit Adverbien:

round| down *v/t Preis etc* abrunden (*to*
auf *acc*). ~ **off** *v/t* **1.** *Mahlzeit etc* abrunden, beschließen (*with* mit). **2.** *Preis etc*
auf- *od.* abrunden (*to* auf *acc*). ~ **out I**
v/t Ausbildung etc abrunden (*with* mit,

durch). **II** *v/i* rundlich werden (*Person*).
~ **up** *v/t* **1.** *Vieh* zs.-treiben. **2.** F *Verbrecher* hochnehmen; *Leute* zs.-trommeln,
a. et. auftreiben. **3.** *Preis etc* aufrunden
(*to* auf *acc*).

'**round·a·bout I** *s* **1.** *Br.* Kreisverkehr *m.*
2. *Br.* Karussell *n*: *go on the ~* Karussell fahren. **II** *adj* **3.** *take a ~ route* e-n
Umweg machen; *in a ~ way fig.* auf
Umwegen.

round·ly ['raʊndlɪ] *adv* **1.** gründlich, gehörig. **2.** rundweg, -heraus.

round rob·in *s* **1.** Petition *f,* Denkschrift
f (*bsd. e-e mit im Kreis herum geschrie-
benen Unterschriften*). **2.** *Sport*: *Am.
Turnier, in dem jeder gegen jeden antritt.*

rounds·man ['raʊndzmən] *s* (*irr man*)
Br. Ausfahrer *m,* Austräger *m.*

'**round|-,ta·ble** *adj*: ~ *conference*
Round-table-Konferenz *f,* Konferenz
f am runden Tisch. '**~-the-clock** *adj*
24stündig, rund um die Uhr. ~ **trip** *s*
Hin- u. Rückfahrt *f,* ✈ Hin- u. Rückflug *m.* '**~-trip** *adj*: ~ *ticket Am.* Rückfahrkarte *f,* ✈ Rückflugticket *n.*

rouse [raʊz] *v/t* **1.** *j-n* wecken (*from, out
of* aus). **2.** *fig. j-n* aus Schlaf aufrütteln
(*from, out of* aus): ~ *s.o. to action j-n* so
weit bringen, daß er (endlich) et. tut *od.*
unternimmt. **3.** *a.* ~ *to anger j-n* erzürnen, reizen. '**rous·ing** *adj* □ mitreißend, zündend (*Rede etc*).

rout [raʊt] **I** *s*: *put to ~* → **II.** **II** *v/t* ✕ in
die Flucht schlagen.

route [ruːt] *s* Route *f,* Strecke *f,* Weg *m,*
(*Bus*)Linie *f.*

rou·tine [ruː'tiːn] **I** *s* Routine *f* (*a. Computer*). **II** *adj* Routine..., routinemäßig.

roux [ruː] *pl roux* [ruːz] *s gastr.* Mehl-
schwitze *f,* Einbrenne *f.*

row¹ [raʊ] *s* Reihe *f*: *four times in a ~*
viermal nach- *od.* hintereinander; ~
house Am. Reihenhaus *n.*

row² [~] **I** *v/i u. v/t* rudern. **II** *s* Kahnfahrt
f: *go for a ~* rudern gehen.

row³ [raʊ] F **I** *s* Krach *m*: a) Krawall *m*:
kick up (*od. make*) *a ~* Krach schlagen, b) Streit *m*: *have a ~ with* Krach
haben mit. **II** *v/i* (sich) streiten (*with*
mit; *about* über *acc*).

row·boat ['raʊbəʊt] *s Am.* Ruderboot *n.*

row·dy ['raʊdɪ] *adj* □ **1.** rowdyhaft. **2.**
ausgelassen, laut (*Party*).

row·er ['rəʊə] s Ruderer m, Ruderin f. **'row·ing** adj Ruder...: ~ **boat** bsd. Br. Ruderboot n.

roy·al ['rɔɪəl] **I** adj □ 1. königlich, Königs...: **Her ♀ Highness** Ihre Königliche Hoheit; ~ **road** fig. bequemer od. leichter Weg (**to** zu). 2. fig. großartig, prächtig. **II** s 3. **F** Mitglied n des Königshauses. **'roy·al·ist I** adj royalistisch. **II** s Royalist(in). **'roy·al·ty** s 1. die königliche Familie. 2. mst pl Tantieme f (**on** auf acc).

rub [rʌb] **I** s 1. **give** s.th. **a** ~ et. abreiben od. polieren. 2. **there's the** ~ **F** da liegt der Hase im Pfeffer. **II** v/t 3. reiben: ~ **dry** trockenreiben; ~ s.th. **into** et. einreiben in (acc); ~ **one's hands** (**together**) sich die Hände reiben (**with** vor dat); ~ s.o.'s **nose in** s.th. **F** j-m et. unter die Nase reiben; ~ **salt into** s.o.'s **wound(s)** fig. j-m Salz auf od. in die Wunde streuen; ~ **shoulders with F** verkehren mit (Prominenten etc). 4. abreiben; polieren. **III** v/i 5. reiben, scheuern (**against, on** an dat): ~ **against** s.th. a. et. streifen.

Verbindungen mit Adverbien:

rub a·long v/i Br. **F** 1. sich durchschlagen. 2. a. ~ **together** recht gut miteinander auskommen; ~ **with** recht gut auskommen mit. ~ **down** v/t 1. ab-, trockenreiben. 2. abschmirgeln, abschleifen. ~ **in** v/t abreiben: **rub** (**it**) **in that F** darauf herumreiten, daß. ~ **off** I v/t abreiben. **II** v/i abreiben (Farbe, Schmutz etc): ~ **on(to)** fig. abfärben auf (acc). ~ **out** v/t 1. Br. ausradieren. 2. Am. sl. umlegen (töten). ~ **up** v/t: **rub** s.o. **up the wrong way F** j-n verschnupfen.

rub·ber ['rʌbə] s 1. Gummi n, m; Kautschuk m. 2. Br. Radiergummi m. 3. Wischtuch n. 4. **F** Gummi m (Kondom). ~ **band** s Gummiband n, -ring m. ~ **din·ghy** s Schlauchboot n. **'~·neck** bsd. Am. **F** I s Gaffer(in), Schaulustige m, f. **II** v/i neugierig gaffen, sich den Hals verrenken. ~ **plant** s ♀ Gummibaum m. ~ **stamp** s Stempel m. **,~·'stamp** v/t 1. (ab)stempeln. 2. **F** (automatisch) genehmigen.

rub·bing al·co·hol ['rʌbɪŋ] s Am. Wundbenzin n.

rub·bish ['rʌbɪʃ] s 1. Abfall m, Abfälle pl, Müll m: ~ **bin** → **dustbin**. 2. fig. Blödsinn m, Quatsch m. **'rub·bish·y** adj **F** blödsinnig.

rub·ble ['rʌbl] s Schutt m; Trümmer pl.

ru·bel·la [ruː'belə] s ♣ Röteln pl.

ru·by ['ruːbɪ] **I** s min. Rubin m. **II** adj rubinrot.

ruck¹ [rʌk] s: **get out of the** (**common**) ~ sich über den Durchschnitt erheben.

ruck² [~] v/i: ~ **up** Falten werfen.

ruck·sack ['rʌksæk] s Rucksack m.

ruc·tion ['rʌkʃn] s oft pl **F** Krach m, Stunk m.

rud·der ['rʌdə] s ✈, ⚓ Ruder n.

rud·dy ['rʌdɪ] **I** adj □ 1. frisch, gesund (Gesichtsfarbe), rot (Backen). 2. Br. sl. verdammt. **II** adv Br. sl. ~

rude [ruːd] adj □ 1. unhöflich; grob (**to** zu). 2. unanständig (Witz etc). 3. bös (Schock etc): ~ **awakening**. 4. **be in** ~ **health** vor Gesundheit strotzen.

ru·di·men·ta·ry [,ruːdɪ'mentərɪ] adj □ 1. elementar, Anfangs... 2. primitiv. 3. rudimentär (a. biol.). **ru·di·ments** ['~mənts] s pl Anfangsgründe pl, Grundlagen pl: **learn the** ~ **of** sich Grundkenntnisse aneignen in (dat).

rue [ruː] v/t: ~ **the day ...** den Tag verwünschen, an dem ... **rue·ful** ['~fʊl] adj □ reuevoll, reumütig.

ruff [rʌf] s Halskrause f (a. orn.).

ruf·fle ['rʌfl] **I** s 1. Rüsche f. **II** v/t 2. Wasser kräuseln; Haar zerzausen: ~ (**up**) **its feathers** orn. sich aufplustern. 3. Seiten (rasch) durchblättern. 4. j-n verärgern: ~ s.o.'s **composure** j-n aus der Fassung bringen.

rug [rʌg] s 1. Brücke f, (Bett)Vorleger m: **pull the** ~ (**out**) **from under** s.o. fig. j-m den Boden unter den Füßen wegziehen; **sweep under the** ~ Am. fig. et. unter den Teppich kehren. 2. bsd. Br. dicke Wolldecke.

rug·by ['rʌgbɪ] s a. ~ **football** (Sport) Rugby n.

rug·ged ['rʌgɪd] adj □ 1. zerklüftet (Felsen), felsig (Landschaft). 2. zerfurcht (Gesicht). 3. robust, stabil (Gerät etc). 4. fig. rauh (Sitten etc).

ru·in ['rʊɪn] s 1. Ruine f: ~s pl Ruinen pl, Trümmer pl; **a castle in** ~s e-e Burgruine; **be** (od. **lie**) **in** ~s in Trümmern liegen; fig. zerstört od. ruiniert sein. 2.

Verfall *m*: **fall into ~** verfallen. **3.** Ruin *m*; Ende *n* (*von Hoffnungen etc*). **II** *v/t* **4.** *Gebäude, Gesundheit, Hoffnungen, Leben etc* zerstören, *j-n, Kleidung, Gesundheit, Ruf etc* ruinieren: **~ one's eyes** sich die Augen verderben. **ru·in·'a·tion** *s*: **be the ~ of s.o.** j-s Ruin sein. **'ru·in·ous** *adj* ruinös. **'ru·in·ous·ly** *adv*: **~ expensive** extrem *od.* sündhaft teuer.

rule [ruːl] **I** *s* **1.** Regel *f*, Normalfall *m*: **as a ~** in der Regel; **make it a ~** es sich zur Regel machen *od.* gemacht haben (**to do** zu tun); → **exception 1. 2.** Regel *f*; Bestimmung *f*, Vorschrift *f*: **against the ~s** regelwidrig; verboten; **as a ~ of thumb** als Faustregel; **do s.th. by ~ of thumb** et. nach Gefühl tun; **bend** (*stretch*) **the ~s** es (mit den Vorschriften) nicht so genau nehmen; **work to ~** Dienst nach Vorschrift tun. **3.** Herrschaft *f*. **4.** → **ruler 2. II** *v/t* **5.** herrschen über (*acc*): **~ the roost** *fig.* das Regiment führen; **be ~d by** *fig.* sich leiten lassen von; beherrscht werden von. **6.** *bsd.* ⚖ entscheiden (**that** daß). **7.** **~ out** et. ausschließen; et. unmöglich machen. **8.** *Papier* lin(i)ieren; *Linie* ziehen. **III** *v/i* **9.** herrschen (**over** über *acc*). **10.** *bsd.* ⚖ entscheiden (**against** gegen; **in favo[u]r of** für; **on** in *dat*). **'rul·er** *s* **1.** Herrscher(in). **2.** Lineal *n*; Maßstab *m*. **'rul·ing** **I** *adj* herrschend; *fig.* vorherrschend. **II** *s bsd.* ⚖ Entscheidung *f*; Verfügung *f*: **give a ~ that** entscheiden, daß.

rum [rʌm] *s* Rum *m*.

Ru·ma·ni·an [ruːˈmeɪnjən] **I** *adj* **1.** rumänisch. **II** *s* **2.** Rumäne *m*, Rumänin *f*. **3.** *ling.* Rumänisch *n*.

rum·ble [ˈrʌmbl] **I** *v/i* **1.** (g)rollen (*Donner*); rumpeln (*Fahrzeug*); knurren (*Magen*). **II** *v/t* **2.** F *j-n, et.* durchschauen. **III** *s* **3.** (G)Rollen *n*; Rumpeln *n*; Knurren *n*. **4.** *Am. sl.* Straßenschlacht *f*.

rum·bus·tious [rʌmˈbʌstɪəs] *adj* □ F wild, ausgelassen.

ru·mi·nant [ˈruːmɪnənt] *s zo.* Wiederkäuer *m*. **ru·mi·nate** [ˈ‑neɪt] *v/i* **1.** *zo.* wiederkäuen. **2.** *fig.* grübeln (**on, over** über *acc, dat*). **ru·mi·na·tive** [ˈ‑nətɪv] *adj* □ grüblerisch.

rum·mage [ˈrʌmɪdʒ] **I** *v/i a.* **~ about**

(*od.* **around**) herumstöbern, -wühlen (**among, in, through** in *dat*). **II** *s* **2** Ramsch *m*. **~ sale** *s Am.* Wohltätigkeitsbasar *m*.

rum·my [ˈrʌmɪ] *s* Rommé *n* (*Kartenspiel*).

ru·mo(u)r [ˈruːmə] **I** *s* Gerücht(*e pl*) *n*. **~ has it that** es geht das Gerücht, daß. **II** *v/t*: **it is ~ed that** es geht das Gerücht, daß; **he is ~ed to be** man munkelt, er sei. **'~, mon·ger** *s* Gerüchtemacher(in).

rump [rʌmp] *s* **1.** *zo.* Hinterbacken *pl*; *orn.* Bürzel *m*. **2.** *humor.* Hinterteil *n*. **3.** *fig.* (kümmerlicher) Rest.

rum·ple [ˈrʌmpl] *v/t* zerknittern, -knüllen; *Haar* zerzausen.

rump steak *s gastr.* Rumpsteak *n*.

rum·pus [ˈrʌmpəs] → **row**[1]. **~ room** *s Am.* F Hobby- *od.* Partyraum *m*.

run [rʌn] **I** *s* **1.** Lauf *m* (*a. Sport*): **at a ~** im Laufschritt; **in the long ~** *fig.* auf (die) Dauer; auf lange *od.* weite Sicht, langfristig; **in the short ~** *fig.* zunächst; auf kurze Sicht, kurzfristig; **on the ~** auf der Flucht (**from the police** vor der Polizei); **~ of good** (*bad*) **luck** Glückssträhne *f* (Pechsträhne *f*). **2.** Fahrt *f*: **go for a ~ in the car** e-e Spazierfahrt machen. **3.** *thea. etc* Laufzeit *f*: **the play had a ~ of six months** das Stück lief ein halbes Jahr lang. **4.** Ansturm *m*, † *a.* Run *m* (**on** auf *acc*). **5. have the ~ of** et. benutzen dürfen. **6.** *Am.* Laufmasche *f*. **7.** Auflage *f* (*e-r Zeitung etc*). **8. have the ~s** *bsd. Br.* F den flotten Otto haben. **II** *v/i* (*irr*) **9.** laufen (*a. Sport*), rennen. **10.** fahren (*Fahrzeug*); fahren, verkehren (*Bus etc*). **11.** laufen, fließen; **tears were ~ning down her face** Tränen liefen ihr übers Gesicht; **his nose was ~ning** ihm lief die Nase; **it ~s in the family** *fig.* das liegt bei ihm *etc* in der Familie; → **cold 1. 12.** zerfließen, -laufen (*Butter, Farbe etc*). **13.** ⚙ laufen (*a. fig.*): **with the engine ~ning** mit laufendem Motor. **14.** (ver)laufen (*Straße etc*). **15.** *bsd.* ⚖ gelten, laufen (**for two years** zwei Jahre). **16.** *thea. etc* laufen (**for six months** ein halbes Jahr lang). **17.** *mit Adjektiven:* → **low**[1] **4. 18.** *pol. bsd. Am.* kandidieren. **19.** gehen, lauten (*Vers etc*). **III** *v/t* (*irr*) **20.** *Strecke, Rennen* laufen: → **course 3**, *temperature*. **21.** *j-n, et.* fahren, bringen. **22.** *Wasser etc* laufen lassen: **~** *s.o.* **a bath** j-m ein Bad einlaufen lassen. **23.** *Geschäft* führen, *Hotel etc* a. leiten. **24.** ◎ *Maschine etc* laufen lassen. **25.** abdrucken, bringen (*Zeitung etc*). **26.** schmuggeln.

Verbindungen mit Präpositionen:

run| a·cross *v/i* **1.** *j-n* zufällig treffen. **2.** stoßen auf (*acc*). **~ af·ter** *v/i* nachlaufen (*dat*) (*a. fig.*). **~ a·gainst** *v/i pol. bsd. Am.* kandidieren gegen. **~ for** *v/i* **1. ~ it!** lauf, was du kannst!; **~ one's life** um sein Leben laufen. **2.** *pol. bsd. Am.* kandidieren für. **~ in·to** I *v/i* **1.** laufen *od.* fahren gegen. **2.** *j-n* zufällig treffen. **3.** *fig.* geraten in (*acc*). **4.** *fig.* sich belaufen auf (*acc*), kommen auf (*acc*). II *v/t* **3. run a knife into s.o.'s back** j-m ein Messer in den Rücken stoßen *od.* rennen. **~ off** *v/i:* **~ the road** von der Straße abkommen (*Wagen etc*). **~ on** *v/i* ◎ fahren mit: **~ electricity** elektrisch betrieben werden. **~ o·ver** → **run through** 1. **~ through** *v/i* **1.** *Szene etc* durchspielen. **2.** *Notizen etc* durchgehen. **3.** *Vermögen etc* durchbringen. **4.** *j-n* durchlaufen (*Schauder etc*): **~** *s.o.'s mind* j-m durch den Kopf gehen. **~ to** *v/i bsd. Br.* (aus)reichen für.

Verbindungen mit Adverbien:

run| a·bout → **run around. ~ a·long** *v/i:* **~!** ab mit dir! **~ a·round** *v/i* sich herumtreiben (**with** mit). **~ a·way** *v/i* davonlaufen (**from** vor *dat*) (*a. fig.*): **~ from home** von zu Hause ausreißen; **~ with** durchbrennen mit; *fig.* durchgehen mit (*Phantasie etc*); **don't ~ with the idea that** glaube bloß nicht, daß. **~ back** *v/t* *Band, Film* zurückspulen. **~ down** I *v/t* **1.** *mot.* umfahren. **2.** schlechtmachen. **3.** ausfindig machen. II *v/i* **4.** ablaufen (*Uhr*), leer werden (*Batterie*). **~ in** *v/t* **1.** *Wagen etc* einfahren. **2.** F *Verbrecher etc* schnappen. **~ on** *v/i* **1.** weitergehen, sich hinziehen (**until** bis). **2.** unaufhörlich reden (**a·bout** über *acc*, von). **~ out** *v/i* ablaufen (*Vertrag, Zeit etc*), ausgehen, zu Ende gehen (*Vorräte etc*): **I've ~ of money** mir ist das Geld ausgegangen; **~ steam** 1. **~ o·ver** I *v/t mot.* überfahren. II *v/i* überlaufen. **~ up** I *v/t* **1.** *Flagge etc* aufziehen, hissen. **2.** hohe *Rechnung, Schulden* machen. II *v/i* **3. ~**

against stoßen auf (*starken Widerstand etc*).

'run·|a·bout *s mot.* Stadtwagen *m.* **'~·a·round** *s:* **give s.o. the ~** F j-n hinhalten; j-n an der Nase herumführen. **'~·a·way** I *s* **1.** Ausreißer(in). II *adj* **2.** ausgerissen: **~ child** (kleiner) Ausreißer. **3.** außer Kontrolle geraten: **~ inflation** ✝ galoppierende Inflation. **'~down** I *adj* **1.** abgespannt. **2.** baufällig; heruntergekommen. **3.** abgelaufen (*Uhr*), leer (*Batterie*). II *s* **4.** F (genauer) Bericht (**on** über *acc*).

rung[1] [rʌŋ] *pp von* **ring**[2].

rung[2] *s* Sprosse *f* (*e-r Leiter*): **start on the bottom** (*od.* **first**) **~ of the ladder** *fig.* ganz unten *od.* klein anfangen.

'run-in *s:* **have a ~ with** F in Konflikt kommen mit (*dem Gesetz etc*).

run·ner ['rʌnə] *s* **1.** *Sport:* Läufer(in); Rennpferd *n.* **2.** *mst in Zssgn* Schmuggler(in). **3.** (*Schlitten- etc*)Kufe *f.* **~ bean** *s* ♣ *Br.* grüne Bohne. **~·'up** *pl* **~s-'up** *s* Zweite *m*, *f*, (*Sport a.*) Vizemeister(in) (**to** hinter *dat*).

run·ning ['rʌnɪŋ] I *s* **1.** Laufen *n*, Rennen *n*: **be still in the ~** *fig.* noch gut im Rennen liegen (**for** um); **be out of the ~** *fig.* aus dem Rennen sein (**for** um); **make the ~** (*Sport*) das Rennen machen (*a. fig.*). **2.** Führung *f*, Leitung *f.* II *adj* **3.** *Sport:* Lauf...: **~ shoes**; **~ track** Laufbahn *f.* **4.** fließend (*Wasser*); ♒ eiternd (*Wunde*). **5. four times** (**for three days**) **~** viermal (drei Tage) hinter- *od.* nacheinander. **6. ~ costs** *pl* Betriebskosten *pl*, laufende Kosten *pl.* **7. ~ mate** *pol. Am.* Kandidat(in) für die Vizepräsidentschaft.

run·ny ['rʌnɪ] *adj* **1.** flüssig. **2.** laufend (*Nase*), tränend (*Augen*).

'run-of-the-'mill *adj mst contp.* durchschnittlich, mittelmäßig. **'~-up** *s* **1.** *Sport:* Anlauf *m.* **2. in the ~ to** *fig.* im Vorfeld (*gen*). **'~-way** *s* ✈ Start- und Landebahn *f*, Rollbahn *f*, Piste *f.*

rup·ture ['rʌptʃə] I *s* Bruch *m* (*a.* ♒ *u. fig.*), Riß *m.* II *v/i* zerspringen, (-)reißen, platzen. III *v/t* zersprengen, -reißen: **~ o.s.** ♒ sich e-n Bruch heben *od.* zuziehen.

ru·ral ['rʊərəl] *adj* □ ländlich: **~ population** Landbevölkerung *f*; → **exodus.**

ruse [ruːz] *s* List *f.*

rush 1218

rush¹ [rʌʃ] *s* ❀ Binse *f*: ~ **mat** Binsenmatte *f*.

rush² [~] **I** *v/i* **1.** hasten, hetzen, stürmen, (*a. Fahrzeug*) rasen: ~ **at** losstürzen *od.* sich stürzen auf (*acc*); ~ **into** *fig.* sich stürzen in (*acc*); *et.* überstürzen; *the blood* ~*ed to his face* das Blut schoß ihm ins Gesicht; → **conclusion** 3. **II** *v/t* **2.** antreiben, drängen, hetzen: *be* ~*ed (off one's feet)* auf Trab sein. **3.** auf dem schnellsten Weg *wohin* bringen *od.* schaffen. **4.** schnell erledigen; *Essen* hinunterschlingen: *don't* ~ *it* laß dir Zeit dabei; ~ *a bill (through)* e-e Gesetzesvorlage durchpeitschen. **5.** losstürmen auf (*acc*). **III** *s* **6.** Ansturm *m* (*for* auf *acc*, nach): *there was a* ~ *for the door* alles drängte zur Tür. **7.** Hast *f*, Hetze *f*: *what's all the* ~*?* wozu diese Hast? ~ *hour s* Rush-hour *f*, Hauptverkehrs-, Stoßzeit *f*. '~*-hour adj*: ~ *traffic* Stoßverkehr *m*.

rusk [rʌsk] *s* Zwieback *m*.

Rus·sian ['rʌʃn] **I** *s* **1.** Russe *m*, Russin *f*. **2.** *ling.* Russisch *n*. **II** *adj* **3.** russisch:

~ *roulette* russisches Roulett(e).

rust [rʌst] **I** *s* Rost *m*. **II** *v/i* (ein-, ver)rosten.

rus·tic ['rʌstɪk] *adj* (~*ally*) **1.** ländlich, bäuerlich. **2.** rustikal (*Möbel*): ~ *furniture a.* Bauernmöbel *pl*.

rus·tle ['rʌsl] **I** *v/i* **1.** rascheln (*Papier etc*), (*a. Seide*) knistern. **II** *v/t* **2.** rascheln mit. **3.** ~ *up* F *Geld, Hilfe etc* organisieren, auftreiben; *Essen* zaubern.

'**rust·proof** *adj* rostfrei, nichtrostend.

rust·y ['rʌstɪ] *adj* □ **1.** rostig. **2.** *fig.* eingerostet (*Kenntnisse*): *I'm very* ~ ich bin ganz aus der Übung.

rut¹ [rʌt] *zo.* **I** *s* Brunft *f*. **II** *v/i* brunften.

rut² [~] **I** *s* **1.** (Rad)Spur *f*, Furche *f*. **2.** *fig.* (alter) Trott: *get into a* ~ in e-n Trott verfallen. **II** *v/t* **3.** furchen: ~*ted* ausgefahren.

ruth·less ['ruːθlɪs] *adj* □ unbarmherzig; rücksichtslos; hart.

rye [raɪ] *s* ❀ Roggen *m*. ~ *bread s* Roggenbrot *n*. ~ *whis·ky s* Roggenwhisky *m*.

S

Sab·bath ['sæbəθ] *s eccl.* Sabbat *m*.

sa·ber *Am.* → *sabre*.

sa·ble ['seɪbl] *s* **1.** *zo.* Zobel *m*. **2.** Zobelpelz *m*.

sab·o·tage ['sæbətɑːʒ] **I** *s* Sabotage *f*: *act of* ~ Sabotageakt *m*. **II** *v/t* e-n Sabotageakt verüben gegen; sabotieren. **sab·o·teur** [~'tɜː] *s* Saboteur(in).

sa·bre ['seɪbə] *s bsd. Br.* Säbel *m* (*a. fenc.*). ~ *rat·tling s fig.* Säbelrasseln *n*.

sac·cha·rin ['sækərɪn] *s* ❀ Saccharin *n*. **sac·cha·rine** [~'raɪn] *adj* **1.** unangenehm süß. **2.** *fig.* honig-, zuckersüß.

sack¹ [sæk] **I** *s* **1.** Sack *m*. **2.** F *get the* ~ rausgeschmissen (*entlassen*) werden; *give s.o. the* ~ → **1. 3.** *hit the* ~ F sich in die Falle *od.* Klappe hauen. **II** *v/t* **4.** einsacken, in Säcke abfüllen. **5.** F *j-n* rausschmeißen (*entlassen*).

sack² [~] **I** *v/t* plündern. **II** *s* Plünderung *f*.

'**sack·cloth** *s* Sackleinen *n*: *in* (*od. wearing*) ~ *and ashes fig.* in Sack u. Asche.

sack·ing ['sækɪŋ] *s* Sackleinen *n*.

sack rac·ing *s* Sackhüpfen *n*.

sac·ra·ment ['sækrəmənt] *s eccl.* Sakrament *n*.

sa·cred ['seɪkrɪd] *adj* □ **1.** geistlich (*Musik etc*). **2.** heilig (*to dat*) (*a. fig.*): ~ *cow* heilige Kuh (*a. fig.*).

sac·ri·fice ['sækrɪfaɪs] **I** *s* Opfer *n* (*a. fig.*): *make a* ~ *of j-n, et.* opfern; *make great* ~*s* große Opfer bringen. **II** *v/t* opfern (*to dat*) (*a. fig.*). **sac·ri·fi·cial** [~'fɪʃl] *adj* Opfer...

sac·ri·lege ['sækrɪlɪdʒ] *s* Sakrileg *n*; *allg.* Frevel *m*. **sac·ri·le·gious** [~'lɪdʒəs] *adj* □ sakrilegisch; *allg.* frevlerisch.

sac·ris·ty ['sækrɪstɪ] *s eccl.* Sakristei *f*.

sac·ro·sanct ['sækrəʊsæŋkt] *adj* sakrosankt.

sad [sæd] *adj* (□ → *sadly*) *allg.* traurig; schmerzlich (*Verlust*); bedauerlich (*Irrtum etc*): ~ *to say* bedauerlicherweise, leider; *be* ~*der but wiser* um e-e schmerzliche Erfahrung reicher sein. **sad·den** ['sᴧdn] *v/t* traurig machen *od.* stimmen, betrüben.

sad·dle ['sædl] **I** *s* (*Reit-, Fahrrad etc*)Sattel *m*: *be in the* ~ im Sattel sitzen; *fig.* im Amt *od.* an der Macht sein. **II** *v/t* satteln: ~ *up* aufsatteln; ~ *s.o. with s.th. fig.* j-m et. aufhalsen *od.* -bürden; *be* ~*d with s.th. fig.* et. am Hals haben. **III** *v/i:* ~ *up* aufsatteln. '~·**bag** *s* Satteltasche *f*.

sad·ism ['seɪdɪzəm] *s* Sadismus *m*. '**sad·ist** *s* Sadist(in). **sa·dis·tic** [sə'dɪstɪk] *adj* (~*ally*) sadistisch.

sad·ly ['sædlɪ] *adv* **1.** traurig; schmerzlich: *be* ~ *mistaken* e-m bedauerlichen Irrtum unterliegen. **2.** bedauerlicherweise, leider. '**sad·ness** *s* Traurigkeit *f*.

sa·fa·ri [sə'fɑːrɪ] *s* Safari *f*. ~ *park s* Safaripark *m*.

safe [seɪf] **I** *adj* □ *allg.* sicher (*from* vor *dat*): *be* ~ in Sicherheit sein; *be* ~ *with s.o.* sicher bei j-m aufgehoben sein; *be in* ~ *hands* in sicheren Händen sein; *to be on the* ~ *side, just to be* ~ um ganz sicher zu gehen; *it is* ~ *to say* man kann mit Sicherheit sagen; *keep s.th. in a* ~ *place* et. an e-m sicheren Ort aufbewahren; *he has* ~*ly arrived* er ist gut angekommen; → *play* 7, 8. **II** *s* Safe *m*, Tresor *m*, Geld-, Panzerschrank *m*. '~·**blow·er**, '~·**break·er**, '~·**crack·er** *s* Geldschrankknacker *m*. '~·**de'pos·it box** *s* Bankschließfach *n*, (*a. in Hotel etc*) Tresorfach *n*. '~·**guard I** *s* Schutz *m* (*against* gegen, vor *dat*). **II** *v/t* schützen (*against, from* gegen, vor *dat*); *In- teressen* wahren. ~'**keep·ing** *s* sichere Verwahrung: *give s.o. s.th. for* ~ j-m et. zur Verwahrung geben.

safe·ty ['seɪftɪ] *s allg.* Sicherheit *f*: *jump (swim) to* ~ sich durch e-n Sprung (schwimmend) in Sicherheit bringen. ~ *belt* → *seat belt*. ~ *cur·tain s thea.* eiserner Vorhang. ~ *glass s* Sicherheitsglas *n*. ~ *is·land s Am.* Verkehrsinsel *f*. ~ *lock s* Sicherheitsschloß *n*. ~ *meas·ure s* Sicherheitsmaßnahme *f*. ~

net s Zirkus etc: Fangnetz *n*. ~ *pin s* Sicherheitsnadel *f*. ~ *pre·cau·tion s* Sicherheitsvorkehrung *f*. ~ *ra·zor s* Rasierapparat *m*. ~ *valve s* **1.** ⚙ Sicherheitsventil *n*. **2.** *fig.* Ventil *n* (*for* für).

saf·fron ['sæfrən] **I** *s* Safran *m*. **II** *adj* safrangelb.

sag [sæg] **I** *v/i* **1.** sich senken, absacken; durchhängen (*Leitung etc*). **2.** (herab)hängen. **3.** *fig.* sinken, nachlassen (*Interesse etc*); abfallen (*Roman etc*); ✝ nachgeben (*Preise etc*). **II** *v/t* **4.** Durchhängen *n*: *there is a* ~ *in the ceiling* die Decke hängt durch. **5.** ✝ Nachgeben *n* (*in gen*).

sa·ga ['sɑːgə] *s* **1.** Saga *f*. **2.** *a. family* ~ Familienroman *m*. **3.** *contp.* Geschichte *f*.

sa·ga·cious [sə'geɪʃəs] *adj* □ scharfsinnig, klug. **sa·gac·i·ty** [sə'gæsətɪ] *s* Scharfsinn *m*, Klugheit *f*.

sage [seɪdʒ] *s* ♣ Salbei *m*.

Sa·git·tar·i·us [ˌsædʒɪ'teərɪəs] *s ast.* Schütze *m*: *be (a)* ~ Schütze sein.

said [sed] *pret u. pp von* **say.**

sail [seɪl] **I** *s* **1.** Segel *n*: *set* ~ auslaufen (*for* nach). **2.** Segelfahrt *f*, -partie *f*: *go for a* ~ segeln gehen. **II** *v/i* **3.** ⚓ fahren; segeln (*a. fig.*): *go* ~*ing* segeln gehen. **4.** ⚓ auslaufen (*for* nach). **5.** gleiten: *she* ~*ed into the room* sie schwebte ins Zimmer; ~ *through an examination* e-e Prüfung spielend schaffen. **6.** ~ *into s.o.* F über j-n herfallen (*a. mit Worten*). **III** *v/t* **7.** Boot segeln, Schiff steuern. **8.** durchsegeln; befahren. '~·**boat** *s Am.* Segelboot *n*.

sail·ing ['seɪlɪŋ] *s* **1.** Segeln *n*; Segelsport *m*: *everything was plain* ~ *fig.* es ging alles glatt. **2.** *when is the next* ~ *to ...?* wann fährt das nächste Schiff nach ...? ~ *boat s bsd. Br.* Segelboot *n*. ~ *ship s* Segelschiff *n*.

sail·or ['seɪlə] *s* **1.** Seemann *m*; Matrose *m*. **2.** Segler(in). **3.** *be a good (bad)* ~ seefest sein (leicht seekrank werden). ~ *suit s* Matrosenanzug *m*.

'**sail·plane** *s* Segelflugzeug *n*.

saint [seɪnt] *s* **1.** Heilige *m*, *f*: *if you need the patience of a* ~ man braucht e-e Engelsgeduld. **2.** *vor Eigennamen* ⚥, *abbr.* **St** [snt]: *St Andrew* der heilige Andreas. '**saint·ly** *adj* heiligmäßig.

sake [seɪk] *s*: *for the* ~ *of* um ... willen,

j-m, e-r *Sache* zuliebe; **for your** ~ dir zuliebe, deinetwegen; **for God's (goodness, heaven's)** ~ F um Gottes willen; Herrgott noch mal; **for the** ~ **of peace** um des lieben Friedens willen; **for the** ~ **of simplicity** der Einfachheit halber.

sal·a·ble *bsd. Am.* → **saleable**.

sa·la·cious [səˈleɪʃəs] *adj* □ schlüpfrig, anstößig.

sal·ad [ˈsæləd] *s* Salat *m*. ~ **dress·ing** *s* Dressing *n*, Salatsoße *f*.

sal·a·man·der [ˈsæləˌmændə] *s zo.* Salamander *m*.

sa·la·mi [səˈlɑːmɪ] *s* Salami *f*.

sal·a·ried [ˈsælərɪd] *adj*: ~ **employee** Gehaltsempfänger(in), Angestellte *m*, *f*. **'sal·a·ry** *s* Gehalt *n*.

sale [seɪl] *s* **1.** Verkauf *m*: **for** ~ zu verkaufen; **not for** ~ unverkäuflich; **be on** ~ verkauft werden, erhältlich sein; *bsd. Am.* im Angebot sein; **be up for** ~ zum Verkauf stehen. **2.** *a. pl* † Umsatz *m*: **large** ~ großer Umsatz. **3.** † Schlußverkauf *m*. **4.** Auktion *f*, Versteigerung *f*. **'sale·a·ble** *adj bsd. Br.* **1.** verkäuflich. **2.** † absatzfähig.

'sales|·**clerk** *s Am.* (Laden)Verkäufer (-in). **'~·girl** *s* (Laden)Verkäuferin *f*. ~ **man** [ˈ~mən] *s* (*irr man*) **1.** Verkäufer *m*. **2.** (Handels)Vertreter *m*. **'~·man·ship** *s* **1.** † Verkaufstechnik *f*; Verkaufsgeschick *n*. **2.** *fig.* Überzeugungskunst *f*. ~ **pitch** *s* † F Verkaufsmasche *f*. ~ **pro·mot·er** *s* † Sales-promoter *m*, Verkaufsförderer *m*. ~ **pro·mo·tion** *s* † Sales-promotion *f*, Verkaufsförderung *f*. ~ **slip** *s Am.* Kassenbeleg *m*, -zettel *m*. ~ **talk** *s* † Verkaufsgespräch *n*. **'~·wom·an** *s* (*irr woman*) **1.** Verkäuferin *f*. **2.** (Handels)Vertreterin *f*.

sa·li·ent [ˈseɪljənt] *adj* □ *fig.* hervorstechend, wichtigst.

sa·line [ˈseɪlaɪn] *adj* salzig, Salz...: ~ **solution** Salzlösung *f*.

sa·li·va [səˈlaɪvə] *s physiol.* Speichel *m*. **sal·i·var·y** [ˈsælɪvərɪ] *adj* Speichel...: ~ **gland** Speicheldrüse *f*.

sal·low [ˈsæləʊ] *adj* □ (ungesund) gelblich (*Gesichtsfarbe etc*).

salm·on [ˈsæmən] **I** *pl* **-ons**, *bsd. coll.* **-on** *s ichth.* Lachs *m*. **II** *adj* lachsfarben.

sal·on [ˈsælɔ̃ː] *s* (*Friseur-, Schönheits- etc*)Salon *m*.

sa·loon [səˈluːn] *s* **1.** *mot. Br.* Limousine

f. **2.** → **saloon bar. 3.** *hist. Am.* Saloon *m*. **4.** ♣ Salon *m*. ~ **bar** *s Br.* vornehmerer u. teurerer Teil e-s Pubs. ~ **car** → **saloon** 1.

salt [sɔːlt] **I** *s* **1.** Salz *n*: **take s.th. with a grain** (*od.* **pinch**) **of** ~ *fig.* et. nicht ganz für bare Münze nehmen; **no composer worth his** ~ kein Komponist, der et. taugt *od.* der diesen Namen verdient; → **rub** 3. **II** *v/t* **2.** salzen. **3.** *a.* ~ **down** (ein)pökeln, einsalzen. **4.** *Straße etc* (mit Salz) streuen. **5.** ~ **away** F *Geld* auf die hohe Kante legen, *b.s.* auf die Seite schaffen. **III** *adj* **6.** gepökelt, Salz...: **'~·cel·lar** *s Br.* Salzstreuer *m*. **'~·free** *adj* salzlos. ~ **lake** *s* Salzsee *m*. **~·pe·ter** *s Am.*, **~·pe·tre** *s bsd. Br.* [ˌ~'piːtə] *s* ♠ Salpeter *m*. ~ **shak·er** *Am.* → **saltcellar.** ~ **wa·ter** *s* Salzwasser *n*. **'~·wa·ter** *adj* Salzwasser..., Meeres...

salt·y [ˈsɔːltɪ] *adj* salzig.

sa·lu·bri·ous [səˈluːbrɪəs] *adj* □ **1.** gesund (*Klima etc*). **2.** vornehm (*Wohngegend etc*).

sal·u·tar·y [ˈsæljʊtərɪ] *adj* gesund; *fig.* heilsam, lehrreich.

sal·u·ta·tion [ˌsæljuːˈteɪʃn] *s* **1.** Begrüßung *f*, Gruß *m*: **in** ~ zum Gruß. **2.** Anrede *f* (*im Brief*).

sa·lute [səˈluːt] **I** *v/t* **1.** ✕ salutieren vor (*dat.*). **2.** (be)grüßen. **II** *v/i* **3.** ✕ salutieren. **III** *s* **4.** ✕ a) Ehrenbezeigung *f*: **give a smart** ~ zackig salutieren; **take the** ~ die Parade abnehmen, b) Salut *m*: **a 21-gun** ~ 21 Salutschüsse.

sal·vage [ˈsælvɪdʒ] **I** *v/t* **1.** bergen (*from* aus). **II** *s* **2.** Bergung *f*. **3.** Bergungsgut *n*.

sal·va·tion [sælˈveɪʃn] *s* **1.** Rettung *f*. **2.** *eccl.* (Seelen)Heil *n*; Erlösung *f*: ♀ **Army** Heilsarmee *f*. **Sal'va·tion·ist** *s* Mitglied *n* der Heilsarmee.

salve [sælv] **I** *s* (Heil)Salbe *f*. **II** *v/t fig.* *Gewissen* beruhigen.

sal·ver [ˈsælvə] *s* Tablett *n*, Präsentierteller *m*.

sal·vo [ˈsælvəʊ] *pl* **-vo(e)s** *s* ✕ Salve *f* (*a. fig.*): ~ **of applause** Beifallssturm *m*.

Sa·mar·i·tan [səˈmærɪtən] *s* Samariter (-in): **good** ~ *Bibl.* barmherziger Samariter (*a. fig.*).

same [seɪm] **I** *adj*: **the** ~ der-, die-, dasselbe, der *od.* die *od.* das gleiche: **the film with the** ~ **name** der gleichnamige

Film; **amount** (*od.* **come**) **to the ~ thing** auf dasselbe hinauslaufen; → **story** 1, **time** 1. **II** *pron:* **the ~** der-, die-, dasselbe, der *od.* die *od.* das gleiche: **it is all the ~ to me** es ist mir ganz egal; **(the)** ~ **again** noch mal das gleiche; ~ **to** you (danke) gleichfalls!; **all** (*od.* **just**) **the ~** dennoch, trotzdem. **III** *adv:* **the ~** gleich; ~ **as** F genauso wie. '**same·y** *adj* *Br.* F eintönig.

sam·ple ['sɑːmpl] **I** *s* **1.** ✝ Muster *n*, (*a. Blut- etc*)Probe *f*: ~ **bottle** Probe-, Probierfläschchen *n*. **2.** (*of*) Kostprobe *f* (*gen*), *fig. a.* (typisches) Beispiel (für). **II** *v/t* **3.** kosten (*a. fig.*), probieren.

san·a·to·ri·um [ˌsænə'tɔːrɪəm] *pl* **-ri-ums, -ri·a** [-rɪə] *s* Sanatorium *n*.

sanc·ti·fy ['sæŋktɪfaɪ] *v/t* **1.** heiligen. **2.** *fig.* sanktionieren: → **end** 10.

sanc·ti·mo·ni·ous [ˌsæŋktɪ'məʊnjəs] *adj* □ frömmelnd, frömmlerisch.

sanc·tion ['sæŋkʃn] **I** *s* **1.** Billigung *f*, Zustimmung *f*. **2.** *mst pl* Sanktion *f*: **take ~s against, Impose ~s on** Sanktionen verhängen über (*acc*). **II** *v/t* **3.** sanktionieren.

sanc·ti·ty ['sæŋktətɪ] *s* Heiligkeit *f*.

sanc·tu·ar·y ['sæŋktʃʊərɪ] *s* **1.** (*Vogeletc*)Schutzgebiet *n*. **2.** Zuflucht *f*: **seek ~ with** Zuflucht suchen bei.

sand [sænd] **I** *s* **1.** *a.* **2.** *pl* Sand(fläche *f*) *m*. **II** *v/t* **3.** *Weg etc* sanden, mit Sand streuen. **4.** schmirgeln: ~ **down** abschmirgeln.

san·dal ['sændl] *s* Sandale *f*.

'**sand|·bag** **I** *s* Sandsack *m*. **II** *v/t* mit Sandsäcken befestigen *od.* schützen. '**~·bank** *s* Sandbank *f*. '**~·blast** *v/t* ⊙ sandstrahlen. '**~·box** *s Am.* Sandkasten *m*. '**~·cas·tle** *s* Sandburg *f*. ~ **dune** *s* Sanddüne *f*. '**~·man** *s* (*irr man*) Sandmännchen *n*. '**~·pa·per** **I** *s* Sand-, Schmirgelpapier *n*. **II** *v/t* (ab)schmirgeln. '**~·pit** *s* **1.** *bsd. Br.* Sandkasten *m*. **2.** Sandgrube *f*. '**~·stone** *s geol.* Sandstein *m*. '**~·storm** *s* Sandsturm *m*.

sand·wich ['sænwɪdʒ] **I** *s* Sandwich *n*. **II** *v/t:* **be ~ed between** eingekeilt sein zwischen (*dat*); ~ **s.th. in between** *fig.* et. einschieben zwischen (*acc, a. dat*). ~ **course** *s ped. etc* Kurs, bei dem sich theoretische u. praktische Ausbildung abwechseln. ~ **man** *s* (*irr man*) Sandwichman *m*.

sand·y ['sændɪ] *adj* **1.** sandig, *pred a.* voller Sand. ~ **beach** Sandstrand *m*. **2.** rotblond (*Haar*).

sane [seɪn] *adj* □ **1.** geistig gesund, normal, ✝✝ zurechnungsfähig. **2.** vernünftig.

sang [sæŋ] *pret von* **sing**.

san·guine ['sæŋgwɪn] *adj* □ zuversichtlich, optimistisch.

san·i·tar·i·um [ˌsænɪ'teərɪəm] *Am.* → **sanatorium**. **san·i·tar·y** ['-tərɪ] *adj* □ **1.** hygienisch, Gesundheits...: ~ **facilities** *pl* sanitäre Einrichtungen *pl*. ~ **napkin** *Am.*, ~ **towel** *Br.* (Damen)Binde *f*. **2.** hygienisch (einwandfrei), gesund.

san·i·to·ri·um [ˌsænɪ'tɔːrɪəm] *Am.* → **sanatorium**.

san·i·ty ['sænətɪ] *s* geistige Gesundheit, ✝✝ Zurechnungsfähigkeit *f*.

sank [sæŋk] *pret von* **sink**.

San·ta Claus ['sæntəklɔːz] *s* der Weihnachtsmann, der Nikolaus.

sap¹ [sæp] *s* **1.** ✿ Saft *m*. **2.** F Einfaltspinsel *m*, Trottel *m*.

sap² [~] *v/t* schwächen.

sap·phire ['sæfaɪə] *s min.* Saphir *m*.

sap·py ['sæpɪ] *adj* □ **1.** ✿ saftig. **2.** F einfältig, trottelig.

sar·casm ['sɑːkæzəm] *s* Sarkasmus *m*. **sar'cas·tic** *adj* (*~ally*) sarkastisch.

sar·coph·a·gus [sɑː'kɒfəgəs] *pl* **-gi** [~gaɪ], **-gus·es** *s* Sarkophag *m*.

sar·dine [sɑː'diːn] *s ichth.* Sardine *f*: **be packed like ~s** wie die Heringe sitzen *od.* stehen.

sar·don·ic [sɑː'dɒnɪk] *adj* (*~ally*) boshaft, höhnisch (*Lachen etc*).

sark·y ['sɑːkɪ] *Br.* F → **sarcastic**.

sar·nie ['sɑːnɪ] *s Br.* F Sandwich *n*.

sash¹ [sæʃ] *s* Fensterrahmen *m* (*e-s Schiebefensters*).

sash² [~] *s* Schärpe *f*.

sash win·dow *s* Schiebefenster *n*.

sass [sæs], '**sass·y** *Am.* F → **sauce** 2, **saucy**.

sat [sæt] *pret u. pp von* **sit**.

Sa·tan ['seɪtən] *s* der Satan. **sa·tan·ic** [sə'tænɪk] *adj* (*~ally*) satanisch. '**Sa·tan·ism** *s* Satanismus *m*, Satanskult *m*.

satch·el ['sætʃəl] *s* (Schul)Ranzen *m*.

sat·el·lite ['sætəlaɪt] *s* **1.** *ast. u. Raumfahrt*) Satellit: ~ **picture** Satellitenbild *n*; ~ **transmission** *TV* Satellitenübertragung f. **2.** a) a. **~ nation** (od. **state**) Satellit(enstaat) m, b) a. **~ town** Satellitenstadt f.

sa·ti·ate ['seɪʃɪeɪt] v/t (über)sättigen.

sat·in ['sætɪn] s Satin m.

sat·ire ['sætaɪə] s Satire f (**on** auf acc).

sa·tir·i·cal [sə'tɪrəkl] adj □ satirisch.

sat·i·rist ['sætərɪst] s Satiriker(in).

'sat·i·rize v/t satirisch darstellen.

sat·is·fac·tion [,sætɪs'fækʃn] s **1.** Befriedigung f, Zufriedenstellung f. **2.** (**at, with**) Zufriedenheit f (mit), Genugtuung f (über acc): **to s.o.'s ~** zu j-s Zufriedenheit.

sat·is·fac·to·ry [,sætɪs'fæktərɪ] adj □ befriedigend, zufriedenstellend.

sat·is·fy ['sætɪsfaɪ] v/t **1.** j-n befriedigen, zufriedenstellen: **be satisfied with** zufrieden sein mit; **a satisfied smile** ein zufriedenes Lächeln. **2.** Bedürfnis, Neugier etc befriedigen; Bedingungen etc erfüllen. **3.** j-n überzeugen (**of** von): **be satisfied that** davon überzeugt sein, daß.

sat·u·rate ['sætʃəreɪt] v/t **1.** (durch)tränken (**with** mit): **~d with** (od. **in**) **blood** blutgetränkt. **2.** 🜋 sättigen (a. fig.). ˌsat·u·ra·tion s Sättigung f: **~ point** 🜋 Sättigungspunkt m; **reach ~ point** fig. s-n Sättigungsgrad erreichen.

Sat·ur·day ['sætədɪ] s Sonnabend m, Samstag m: **on ~** (am) Samstag; **on ~s** samstags.

Sat·urn ['sætən] s ast. Saturn m.

sauce [sɔːs] s **1.** Soße f. **2.** F Frechheit f: **none of your ~!** werd bloß nicht frech! **'~·pan** s Kochtopf m.

sauc·er ['sɔːsə] s Untertasse f.

sau·ci·ness ['sɔːsɪnɪs] s F Frechheit f. **'sau·cy** adj □ F frech.

sau·er·kraut ['saʊəkraʊt] s Sauerkraut n.

sau·na ['sɔːnə] s Sauna f: **have a ~** in die Sauna gehen.

saun·ter ['sɔːntə] I v/i bummeln, schlendern. II s Bummel m: **have** (od. **take**) **a ~** e-n Bummel machen.

sau·sage ['sɔsɪdʒ] s Wurst f.

sav·age ['sævɪdʒ] I adj □ wild: a) unzivilisiert, b) gefährlich (Tier), c) brutal, d) schonungslos. II s Wilde m, f. III v/t anfallen (Tier).

sa·van·na(h) [sə'vænə] s geogr. Savanne f.

save [seɪv] I v/t **1.** retten (**from** vor dat): **~ s.o.'s life** j-m das Leben retten; → **bacon, face** 4, **neck** 1, **skin** 1. **2.** Geld, Zeit etc (ein)sparen; et. aufheben, -sparen (**for** für): **~ s.th. for s.o.** j-m et. aufheben; **~ one's strength** s-e Kräfte schonen. **3.** j-m et. ersparen: **you can ~ your excuses** du kannst dir d-e Ausreden sparen; **~ s.o. doing s.th.** es j-m ersparen, et. zu tun. **4.** Sport: Schuß halten, parieren, a. Matchball etc abwehren; Tor verhindern. II v/i **5.** a. **~ up** sparen (**for** für, auf acc). **6.** ~ **on** et. (ein)sparen. III s **7.** Sport: Parade f. **'sav·er** s **1.** Retter(in). **2.** Sparer(in). **3.** in Zssgn: **be a real time ~** e-e Menge Zeit sparen. **'sav·ing** I s **1.** Ersparnis f (**on** gegenüber). **2.** pl Ersparnisse pl: **~s account** Am. Sparkonto n; **~s and loan association** Am. Bausparkasse f; **~s bank** Sparkasse f. II adj **3.** **his** (**only**) **~ grace** das einzig Gute an ihm. **sa·vio(u)r** ['seɪvjə] s Retter(in): **the ♀** eccl. der Heiland od. Erlöser.

sa·vo(u)r ['seɪvə] I s **1.** (**of**) Geruch m (nach, von), Geschmack m (nach): **~ of garlic** Knoblauchgeruch m. **2.** fig. Reiz m. II v/t **3.** mit Genuß essen od. trinken. III v/i **4.** ~ **of** fig. e-n Beigeschmack haben von. **'sa·vo(u)r·y** adj □ schmackhaft.

sa·voy [sə'vɔɪ] s 🌿 Wirsing(kohl) m.

sav·vy ['sævɪ] s sl. Grips m, Köpfchen n.

saw¹ [sɔː] pret von **see**.

saw² [~] I s Säge f. II v/t (mst irr) sägen: **~ off** absägen; **~ up** zersägen. **'~·dust** s Sägespäne pl. **'~·mill** s Sägewerk n.

sawn [sɔːn] pp von **saw²**.

Sax·on ['sæksn] hist. I s (Angel)Sachse m, (-)Sächsin f. II adj (angel)sächsisch.

sax·o·phone ['sæksəfəʊn] s 🎵 Saxophon n. **sax·o·phon·ist** [~'sɒfənɪst] s Saxophonist(in).

say [seɪ] I v/t (irr) **1.** sagen (**to** zu): **they ~ he is rich, he is said to be ~** man sagt, er sei reich; er soll reich sein; **what does your watch ~?** wie spät ist es auf deiner Uhr?; **you can ~ that again!** das kannst du laut sagen!; **~, haven't I ...?** Am. F sag mal, habe ich nicht ...?; → **easy** 8, **jack** 1, **knife** 1, **nothing** 1, **when** 5. **2.** Gebet sprechen, Vaterunser etc beten: → **grace** 6. **3.** annehmen: (**let's**) **~ this happens** angenommen od. nehmen wir einmal an, das geschieht; *a sum of*, ~, *£500* e-e Summe von sagen wir 500 Pfund. **4.** (be)sagen, bedeuten: *that is to* ~ das heißt. **II** *v/i* (*irr*) **5.** es sagen: *I can't* ~ das kann ich nicht sagen; *you don't* ~ (*so*)*!* was du nicht sagst!; *it goes without* ~*ing* es versteht sich von selbst (*that* daß). **III** *s* **6.** Mitsprecherecht *n* (*in* bei). **7. have one's** ~ s-e Meinung äußern, zu Wort kommen: *he always has to have his* ~ er muß immer mitreden. **'say·ing** *s* Sprichwort *n*, Redensart *f*: *as the* ~ *goes* wie man (so) sagt.

'say-so *s* **F 1.** *just on his* ~ auf s-e bloße Behauptung hin, nur weil er es sagt. **2.** *on his* ~ mit s-r Erlaubnis.

scab [skæb] *s* **1.** ✞ Grind *m*, Schorf *m*. **2.** *vet.* Räude *f*. **3.** *sl.* Streikbrecher(in). **'scab·by** *adj* **1.** grindig, schorfig. **2.** ✞ krätzig; *vet.* räudig.

sca·bi·es ['skeɪbiːz] *s* ✞ Krätze *f*.

scaf·fold ['skæfəʊld] *s* **1.** (Bau)Gerüst *n*. **2.** Schafott *n*. **scaf·fold·ing** ['~fəldɪŋ] → **scaffold** 1.

scal·a·wag ['skæləwæg] *bsd. Am.* → **scallywag**.

scald [skɔːld] *I* *v/t* **1.** sich *die Finger etc* verbrühen (*on, with* mit): *be* ~*ed to death* tödliche Verbrühungen erleiden (*by* durch). **2.** *bsd. Milch* abkochen. **II** *s* **3.** Verbrühung *f*. **'scald·ing** *adj u. adv:* ~ (*hot*) kochendheiß.

scale¹ [skeɪl] *I* *s* **1.** *zo.* (*a. Haut*)Schuppe *f*: *the* ~*s fell from my eyes fig.* es fiel mir wie Schuppen von den Augen. **2.** Kesselstein *m*. **II** *v/t* **3.** *Fisch* (ab)schuppen.

scale² [~] *s* **1.** Waagschale *f.* **2.** *mst pl, a pair of* ~*s* Waage *f: tip the* ~*s fig.* den Ausschlag geben (*in favo[u]r of* für). **3.** ~*s pl* (*sg konstruiert*) *ast.* Waage *f.*

scale³ [~] *I* *s* **1.** Skala *f* (*a. fig.*), Grad- *od.* Maßeinteilung *f.* **2.** ♪, ⚙ Maßstab *m: to* ~ maßstab(s)gerecht, -getreu; ~ *model* maßstab(s)gerecht *od.* -getreues Modell. **3.** ♪ Skala *f*, Tonleiter *f.* **4.** *fig.* Ausmaß *n*, Maßstab *m*, Umfang *m: on a large* ~ in großem Umfang. **II** *v/t* **5.** erklettern. **6.** ~ *down* (*up*) *fig.* verringern (erhöhen).

scal·lop ['skɒləp] *s zo.* Kammuschel *f.*

scal·ly·wag ['skælɪwæg] *s bsd. Br.* Schlingel *m*, (kleiner) Strolch.

scalp [skælp] *I* *s* **1.** *anat.* Kopfhaut *f.* **2.** Skalp *m: be out for s.o.'s* ~ *fig.* auf j-s Skalp aussein. **II** *v/t* **3.** skalpieren.

scal·pel ['skælpəl] *s* ✚ Skalpell *n.*

scal·per ['skælpə] *s Am.* Kartenschwarzhändler(in).

scamp [skæmp] *s* Schlingel *m*, (kleiner) Strolch.

scam·per ['skæmpə] *v/i* trippeln (*Kind etc*); huschen (*Maus etc*).

scan [skæn] *I* *v/t* **1.** *et.* absuchen (*for* nach). **2.** *Zeitung etc* überfliegen. **3.** *Metrik:* skandieren. **4.** *Computer, Radar, TV:* abtasten. **II** *s* **5.** ✚ *etc* Scanning *n.*

scan·dal ['skændl] *s* **1.** Skandal *m.* **2.** Skandalgeschichten *pl*, Klatsch(geschichten *pl*) *m.* **scan·dal·ize** ['~dəlaɪz] *v/t: he was* ~*d* er war empört *od.* entrüstet (*by, at* über *acc*; *to hear* als er hörte).

'scan·dal,mon·ger *s* Klatschmaul *n.*

scan·dal·ous ['skændələs] *adj* □ **1.** skandalös: *be* ~ *a.* im Skandal sein (*that* daß). **2.** Skandal...

Scan·di·na·vi·an [,skændɪ'neɪvjən] *I* *s* Skandinavier(in). **II** *adj* skandinavisch.

scant [skænt] *adj* □ dürftig, gering.

scant·y ['skæntɪ] *adj* □ dürftig, kärglich (*Mahlzeit*); knapp (*Bikini etc*).

scape·goat ['skeɪpgəʊt] *s* Sündenbock *m.*

scar [skɑː] *I* *s* Narbe *f*; Schramme *f*, Kratzer *m.* **II** *v/t* Narben *od.* e-e Narbe hinterlassen auf (*dat*); *fig. j-n* zeichnen.

scarce [skeəs] *adj* **1.** knapp (*Ware*): *make o.s.* ~ F sich dünnmachen. **2.** selten. **'scarce·ly** *adv* **1.** kaum. **2.** kaum, schwerlich. **'scarce·ness**, **'scar·ci·ty** *s* **1.** Knappheit *f*, Mangel *m* (*of* an *dat*). **2.** Seltenheit *f.*

scare [skeə] *I* *v/t* **1.** erschrecken, *j-m* e-n Schreck(en) einjagen: *be* ~*d* Angst haben (*of* vor *dat*). **2.** ~ *away* (*od.* *off*) verjagen, -scheuchen; *fig. j-n* ab-, verschrecken. **II** *v/i* **3.** ~ *easily* schreckhaft sein. **III** *s* **4.** Schreck(en) *m: give s.o. a* ~ → **1.** *5.* Panik *f.* **'~·crow** *s* Vogelscheuche *f* (*a. fig.*). **'~·,mon·ger** *s* Panikmacher(in).

scarf [skɑːf] *pl* **scarfs**, **scarves** [skɑːvz] *s* Schal *m*; Hals-, Kopf-, Schultertuch *n.*

scar·let ['skɑ:lət] *adj* scharlachrot: **~ fever ♂** Scharlach *m*.

scar·per ['skɑ:pə] *v/i Br. sl.* abhauen, verduften.

scarred [skɑ:d] *adj* narbig.

scarves [skɑ:vz] *pl von* **scarf.**

scar·y ['skeərɪ] *adj F* **1.** unheimlich (*Gegend etc*); grus(e)lig (*Geschichte etc*): **~ film** Gruselfilm *m*. **2.** furchtsam; schreckhaft.

scath·ing ['skeɪðɪŋ] *adj* □ ätzend, vernichtend (*Kritik etc*).

scat·ter ['skætə] **I** *v/t* **1.** *a.* **~ about** (*od.* **around**) ver-, ausstreuen: **be ~ed all over the place** überall herumliegen; **~ money about** *fig.* mit dem Geld um sich werfen. **2.** *Menge etc* zerstreuen, *Vögel etc* auseinanderscheuchen. **II** *v/i* **3.** sich zerstreuen (*Menge etc*), auseinanderstieben (*Vögel etc*), sich zerteilen (*Nebel etc*). **'~·brain** *s F* Schussel *m*. **'~·brained** *adj F* schusselig, schußlig.

scat·tered ['skætəd] *adj* **1.** ver- od. zerstreut (liegend) (*Häuser etc*). **2.** vereinzelt (*Schauer etc*).

scav·enge ['skævɪndʒ] **I** *v/i* **1.** **~ on** *zo.* leben von (*Abfällen, Aas*). **2.** *a.* **~ for food** (nach) Nahrung suchen; **~ in** herumwühlen in (*dat*). **II** *v/t* **3.** → **1. 4.** *et.* ergattern. **'scav·en·ger** *s zo.* Aasfresser *m*.

sce·nar·i·o [sɪ'nɑ:rɪəʊ] *pl* **-os** *s* Film, *thea., TV*: Szenario *n* (*a. fig.*), Szenarium *n*.

scene [si:n] *s* **1.** *thea. etc a)* Szene *f*: **change of ~** Szenenwechsel *m*; *fig.* Tapetenwechsel *m*, *b)* Bühnenbild *n*, Kulissen *pl*: **behind the ~s** hinter den Kulissen (*a. fig.*), *c)* Ort *m* der Handlung, Schauplatz *m* (*a. e-s Romans etc*). **2.** Schauplatz *m*: **~ of accident** (*crime, crash*) Unfallort *m* (Tatort *m*, Absturzstelle *f*); **be on the ~** zur Stelle sein; **come on(to) the ~** auf der Bildfläche erscheinen, auftauchen. **3.** Szene *f*, Anblick *m*: **~ of destruction** Bild *n* der Zerstörung. **4.** Szene *f*, (heftiger) Auftritt: **make a ~** (j-m) e-e Szene machen. **5.** F (*Drogen-, Pop- etc*)Szene *f*. **6.** *... is not my ~* F ... ist nicht mein Fall. **scen·er·y** ['~ərɪ] *s* **1.** Landschaft *f*, Gegend *f*. **2.** *thea.* Bühnenbild *n*, Kulissen *pl*.

sce·nic ['si:nɪk] *adj* (**~ally**) **1.** landschaft-

lich, Landschafts... **2.** landschaftlich schön, malerisch: **~ road** landschaftlich schöne Strecke. **3.** *thea.* Bühnen...

scent [sent] **I** *s* **1.** Duft *m*, Geruch *m*. **2.** *bsd. Br.* Parfüm *n*. **3.** *hunt.* Witterung *f*: **be on the ~ of** *fig.* e-r Sache auf der Spur sein; **follow a wrong ~** *fig.* e-e falsche Spur verfolgen. **II** *v/t* **4.** wittern (*a. fig.*). **5. be ~ed with** vom Duft (*gen*) erfüllt sein. **6.** *bsd. Br.* parfümieren. **'scent·less** *adj* geruchlos.

scep·ter *Am.* → **sceptre.**

scep·tic ['skeptɪk] *s Br.* Skeptiker(in). **'scep·ti·cal** *adj* □ skeptisch: **be ~ about** (*od. of*) **s.th.** e-r Sache skeptisch gegenüberstehen. **scep·ti·cism** ['~sɪzəm] *s* Skepsis *f*.

scep·tre ['septə] *s bsd. Br.* Zepter *n*.

sched·ule ['ʃedju:l] **I** *s* **1.** Aufstellung *f*, Verzeichnis *n*. **2.** (*Arbeits-, Stunden-, Zeit- etc*)Plan *m*; Programm *n*; Fahr-, Flugplan *m*: **three months ahead of ~** drei Monate früher als vorgesehen; **be behind ~** Verspätung haben, *weitS.* im Verzug *od.* Rückstand sein; **on ~** (fahr)planmäßig, pünktlich. **II** *v/t* **3.** *et.* ansetzen (**for** auf *acc*, für); **it is ~d to take place tomorrow** es soll morgen stattfinden; **~d departure** (fahr)planmäßige Abfahrt; **~d flight** Linienflug *m*.

sche·mat·ic [skɪ'mætɪk] *adj* (**~ally**) schematisch.

scheme [ski:m] **I** *s* **1.** Schema *n*, System *n*. **2.** *bsd. Br.* Programm *n*, Projekt *n*. **3.** Intrige *f*, *pl a.* Machenschaften *pl*. **II** *v/i* **4.** intrigieren (*against* gegen): **~ for** hinarbeiten auf (*acc*). **'schem·er** *s* Intrigant(in). **'schem·ing** *adj* □ intrigant.

schist [ʃɪst] *s geol.* Schiefer *m*.

schiz·o·phre·ni·a [ˌskɪtsəʊ'fri:njə] *s psych.* Schizophrenie *f*. **schiz·o·phren·ic** [ˌ~'frenɪk] **I** *adj* (**~ally**) schizophren. **II** *s* Schizophrene *m, f*.

schmal(t)z [ʃmɒlts] *s bsd. ♪ F* Schmalz *m*. **'schmal(t)z·y** *adj F* schmalzig.

schnit·zel ['ʃnɪtsl] *s gastr.* Wiener Schnitzel *n*.

schol·ar ['skɒlə] *s* **1.** Gelehrte *m, f*, *bsd.* Geisteswissenschaftler(in). **2.** *univ.* Stipendiat(in). **'schol·ar·ly** *adj* **1.** gelehrt. **2.** wissenschaftlich. **'schol·ar·ship** *s* **1.** Gelehrsamkeit *f*. **2.** *univ.* Stipendium *n*: **~ holder** → **scholar** 2.

school¹ [skuːl] *s* Schule *f*, Schwarm *m* (*Delphine, Heringe etc*).

school² [~] **I** *s* **1.** *allg.* Schule *f* (*a. fig.*): **at** (*Am.* **in**) ~ auf *od.* in der Schule; **go to** ~ in die *od.* zur Schule gehen; **there is no** ~ **today** heute ist schulfrei *od.* kein Unterricht; → **old** 1. **2.** *Am.* Hochschule *f*. **3.** *univ.* Fakultät *f*; Fachbereich *m*. **II** *v/t* **4.** *j-n* schulen, unterrichten (*in in dat*); *Tier* dressieren: ~ **o.s. to do s.th.** es sich angewöhnen, et. zu tun. ~ **age** *s* schulpflichtiges Alter: **be of** ~ schulpflichtig *od.* im schulpflichtigen Alter sein. '~-**age** *adj* schulpflichtig, im schulpflichtigen Alter. '~-**boy** *s* Schuljunge *m*, Schüler *m*. ~ **bus** *s* Schulbus *m*. '~-**child** *s* (*irr child*) Schulkind *n*. ~ **days** *s pl* Schulzeit *f*. '~-**fel-low** → **schoolmate**. '~-**girl** *s* Schulmädchen *n*, Schülerin *f*.

school·ing ['skuːlɪŋ] *s* (Schul)Ausbildung *f*.

school‖ **leav·er** *s bsd. Br.* Schulabgänger(in). '~-**mate** *s* Schulkamerad(in), Mitschüler(in). ~ **ship** *s* Schulschiff *n*. '~-**teach·er** *s* (Schul)Lehrer(in).

schoon·er ['skuːnə] *s* **1.** ♣ Schoner *m*. **2.** *Br.* großes Sherryglas; *Am.* großes Bierglas.

sci·at·ic [saɪ'ætɪk] *adj* ✸ Ischias...: ~ **nerve.** **sci·at·i·ca** [~kə] *s* ✸ Ischias *m*, *n*, *f*.

sci·ence ['saɪəns] *s* **1.** Wissenschaft *f*. **2.** *a. natural* ~ Naturwissenschaft(en *pl*) *f*. **3.** *fig.* Kunst *f*, Lehre *f*. ~ **fic·tion** *s* Science-fiction *f*.

sci·en·tif·ic [ˌsaɪən'tɪfɪk] *adj* (~**ally**) **1.** (*engS.* natur)wissenschaftlich. **2.** *fig.* systematisch. **'sci·en·tist** *s* (*engS.* Natur)Wissenschaftler(in).

sci-fi [ˌsaɪ'faɪ] *s* F Science-fiction *f*.

scin·til·lat·ing ['sɪntɪleɪtɪŋ] *adj* sprühend (*Geist, Witz*), geistsprühend (*Unterhaltung etc*).

scis·sors ['sɪzəz] *s pl, a. pair of* ~ Schere *f*.

scle·ro·sis [sklɪə'rəʊsɪs] *s* ✸ Sklerose *f*.

scoff¹ [skɒf] **I** *v/i* spotten (*at* über *acc*). **II** *s* spöttische Bemerkung.

scoff² [~] *v/t* F *Kuchen etc* verdrücken, wegputzen.

scoff·er ['skɒfə] *s* Spötter(in).

scold [skəʊld] *v/t* ausschelten, -schimpfen, schimpfen mit (*for* wegen). '**scold-**

ing *s* Schelte *f*: **give s.o. a** ~ → **scold.**

scol·lop ['skɒləp] → **scallop.**

sconce [skɒns] *s* Wandleuchte *f*.

scone [skɒn] *s* kleiner runder Kuchen, mit Butter serviert.

scoop [skuːp] **I** *s* **1.** Schöpfkelle *f*, Schöpfer *m*; (*Mehl- etc*)Schaufel *f*; (*Eis*)Portionierer *m*. **2.** Kugel *f* (*Eis*). **3.** *Presse, Rundfunk, TV:* (sensationelle) Erstmeldung *f*. **II** *v/t* **4.** schöpfen; schaufeln.

scoot [skuːt] *v/i* F abhauen; rennen.

scoot·er ['skuːtə] *s* **1.** (Kinder)Roller *m*. **2.** (*Motor*)Roller *m*.

scope [skəʊp] *s* **1.** Bereich *m*: **be within** (**beyond**) **the** ~ **of** sich im Rahmen (*gen*) halten (den Rahmen [*gen*] sprengen). **2.** (Spiel)Raum *m*, (Entfaltungs)Möglichkeit(en *pl*) *f* (**for** für).

scorch [skɔːtʃ] **I** *v/t* **1.** an-, versengen, verbrennen. **2.** ausdörren. **II** *v/i* **3.** *mot.* F rasen. **III** *s* **4.** *a.* ~ **mark** angesengte Stelle, Brandfleck *m*. **'scorch·er** *s* F glühendheißer Tag. **'scorch·ing** *adj* F glühendheiß (*Tag etc*), sengend (*Hitze*).

score [skɔː] **I** *s* **1.** (Spiel)Stand *m*; (Spiel-) Ergebnis *n*: **what is the** ~? wie steht es *od.* das Spiel?; **the** ~ **stood at** (*od.* **was**) **2–1** das Spiel stand 2:1; **keep (the)** ~ anschreiben. **2.** *Sport:* Torerfolg *m*. **3.** ♪ Partitur *f*; Musik *f* (*zu e-m Film etc*). **4.** **on that** ~ deshalb, in dieser Hinsicht. **5. have a** ~ **to settle with s.o.** e-e alte Rechnung mit j-m zu begleichen haben. **6.** ~ **s** *pl* of e-e Menge. **7.** *a.* ~ **mark** Kerbe *f*, Rille *f*. **II** *v/t* **8.** *Sport:* *Treffer etc* erzielen, *Tor a.* schießen; *a. allg. Erfolg, Sieg* erringen. **9.** *Sport: j-m Punkte, Note* geben. **10.** ♪ in Partitur setzen; instrumentieren, setzen (**for** für); die Musik schreiben zu *od.* für. **11.** einkerben. **12.** ~ **out** (*od.* **through**) aus-, durchstreichen. **III** *v/i* **13.** *Sport:* e-n Treffer *etc* erzielen, ein Tor schießen: **he** ~**d twice** er war zweimal erfolgreich. **14.** erfolgreich sein, Erfolg haben (**with** mit): ~ **off s.o.** j-n als dumm hinstellen *od.* lächerlich machen; ~ **with a girl** sl. ein Mädchen ins Bett kriegen. '~-**board** *s Sport:* Anzeigetafel *f*.

scor·er ['skɔːrə] *s* (*Sport*) **1.** Torschütze *m*, -schützin *f*. **2.** Anschreiber(in).

scorn [skɔːn] *s* Verachtung *f* (**for** für, **gegen**): **pour** ~ **on** et. verächtlich abtun.

scorn·ful ['~fʊl] *adj* □ verächtlich.
Scor·pi·o ['skɔːpɪəʊ] *s ast.* Skorpion *m*:
be (**a**) ~ Skorpion sein.
scor·pi·on ['skɔːpjən] *s zo.* Skorpion *m*.
Scot [skɒt] *s* Schotte *m*, Schottin *f*.
Scotch [skɒtʃ] **I** *adj* schottisch (*Whisky etc*). **II** *s* Scotch *m* (*schottischer Whisky*).
scot-free [ˌskɒt'friː] *adj*: **get off** ~ ungeschoren davonkommen.
Scots [skɒts] *adj* schottisch. **~·man** ['~mən] *s* (*irr man*) Schotte *m*. '**~·wom·an** *s* (*irr woman*) Schottin *f*.
Scot·tish ['skɒtɪʃ] *adj* schottisch.
scoun·drel ['skaʊndrəl] *s* Schurke *m*, Schuft *m*.
scour¹ ['skaʊə] *v/t* Topf *etc* scheuern, Fußboden *etc a.* schrubben.
scour² *v/t Gegend etc* absuchen, abkämmen (*for* nach).
scourge [skɜːdʒ] **I** *s* Geißel *f* (*a. fig.*). **II** *v/t* geißeln, *fig. a.* heimsuchen.
scout [skaʊt] **I** *s* **1.** *oft* ♀ Pfadfinder *m*; *Am.* Pfadfinderin *f*. **2.** ✕ Kundschafter *m*, Späher *m*. **3.** *Br.* motorisierter Pannenhelfer (*e-s Automobilklubs*). **4.** *bsd. Sport*: Talentsucher(in). **II** *v/i* **5.** ~ **a·bout** (*od.* **around**) sich umsehen (*for* nach). **III** *v/t* **6.** *a.* ~ **out** ✕ auskundschaften, erkunden.
scowl [skaʊl] **I** *v/i* ein böses Gesicht machen: ~ **at** *j-n* bös anschauen. **II** *s* böses Gesicht.
scrab·ble ['skræbl] *v/i mst* ~ **about** (*od.* **around**) herumsuchen, -wühlen (*for* nach).
scrag·gy ['skrægɪ] *adj* □ dürr, knochig.
scram [skræm] *v/i* F *oft imp* abhauen, Leine ziehen.
scram·ble ['skræmbl] **I** *v/i* **1.** klettern; krabbeln. **2.** sich raufen (*a. fig.*), (*bsd. Kinder*) sich balgen (*for* um); sich drängeln (*for* zu). **II** *v/t* **3.** *Ei* verrühren: **~d eggs** *pl* Rührei(er *pl*) *n*. **4.** *Funkspruch etc* zerhacken. **III** *s* **5.** Kletterei *f*. **6.** Rauferei *f*, Balgerei *f*; Drängelei *f*. '**scram·bler** *s* ⊕ Zerhacker *m*.
scrap¹ [skræp] **I** *s* **1.** Stückchen *n*, Fetzen *m*: **there is not a** ~ **of evidence** es gibt nicht den geringsten Beweis; **there is not a** ~ **of truth in it** daran ist kein Wort wahr. **2.** *pl* (Speise)Reste *pl*. **3.** Altmaterial *n*; Altmetall *n*, Schrott *m*: **sell**

s.th. for ~ et. als Schrott verkaufen. **II** *v/t* **4.** *unbrauchbar Gewordenes* ausrangieren; *Plan etc* aufgeben, fallenlassen, *Methode etc a.* zum alten Eisen werfen. **5.** verschrotten.
scrap² [~] F **I** *v/i* sich streiten; sich balgen. **II** *s* Streiterei *f*; Balgerei *f*.
'**scrap-book** *s* Sammelalbum *n*.
scrape [skreɪp] **I** *v/t* **1.** (ab)kratzen, (ab)schaben (*from* von); *Schuhe etc* abkratzen; *Karotten etc* schaben: ~ **off** abkratzen *od.* abschaben (von); ~ **to·gether** (*od.* **up**) *Geld* zs.-kratzen; ~ **a living** *fig.* sich gerade so über Wasser halten. **2.** sich *die Knie etc* ab- *od.* aufschürfen (*on* auf *dat*); *Wagen etc* ankratzen. **II** *v/i* **3.** scheuern (*against* an *dat*): ~ **along the ground** am Boden schleifen. **4.** *fig.* ~ **along** (*od.* **by**) über die Runden kommen (*on* mit); ~ **through an examination** mit Ach u. Krach durch e-e Prüfung kommen. **III** *s* **5.** Kratzen *n*. **6.** Abschürfung *f*, Schürfwunde *f*. **7.** *be in a* ~ F in Schwulitäten sein. '**scrap·er** *s* ⊕ Kratzer *m*, Schaber *m*.
scrap| heap *s* Schrotthaufen *m*: **be on the** ~ *fig.* zum alten Eisen gehören. ~ **met·al** *s* Altmetall *n*, Schrott *m*. ~ **pa·per** *s bsd. Br.* Schmierpapier *n*.
scrap·py ['skræpɪ] *adj* zs.-gestoppelt.
scrap| val·ue *s* Schrottwert *m*. '**~·yard** *s* Schrottplatz *m*.
scratch [skrætʃ] **I** *v/t* **1.** (zer)kratzen, *Wagen etc* ankratzen: ~ **one's arm on a nail** sich den Arm an e-m Nagel aufreißen. **2.** a) (ab)kratzen (*from* von): ~ **off** abkratzen (von), b) *-n Namen etc* einkratzen (*on* in *acc*). **3.** *j-n*, *sich* kratzen: ~ **one's nose** sich an der Nase kratzen; ~ **one's head** sich den Kopf kratzen (*vor Verlegenheit etc*). **II** *v/i* **4.** kratzen (*at* an *dat*). **5.** sich kratzen. **III** *s* **6.** Kratzer *m*. **7.** *fig.* **start from** ~ ganz von vorn anfangen; **be** (*od.* **come**) **up to** ~ den Anforderungen *od.* Erwartungen entsprechen. **IV** *adj* **8.** (bunt) zs.-gewürfelt (*Mannschaft etc*). '**~·pad** *s bsd. Am.* Schmierblock *m*. ~ **pa·per** *s Am.* Schmierpapier *n*.
scratch·y ['skrætʃɪ] *adj* □ **1.** kratzend (*Geräusch*). **2.** zerkratzt (*Schallplatte*). **3.** kratzig (*Pullover etc*).
scrawl [skrɔːl] **I** *v/t* **1.** (hin)kritzeln.

II *s* **2.** Gekritzel *n.* **3.** Klaue *f.*

scraw·ny [ˈskrɔːnɪ] *adj* □ dürr.

scream [skriːm] **I** *v/i* **1.** schreien (**with** vor *dat*): ~ **with laughter** vor Lachen brüllen. **II** *v/t* **2.** a. ~ **out** schreien: ~ **o.s. hoarse** sich heiser schreien; ~ **the place down** F zetermordio schreien; → **rooftop**. **III** *s* **3.** Schrei *m*: ~**s** *pl of laughter* brüllendes Gelächter. **4. be a** ~ F zum Schreien (komisch) sein.

scree [skriː] *s* Geröll *n.*

screech [skriːtʃ] **I** *v/i u. v/t* kreischen (*a. Bremsen etc*), (gellend) schreien. **II** *s* Kreischen *n*; (gellender) Schrei.

screed [skriːd] *s* langatmige Rede *etc*, Roman *m.*

screen [skriːn] **I** *s* **1.** Wandschirm *m.* **2.** *Film:* Leinwand *f*: **adapt for the** ~ für den Film bearbeiten. **3.** *Radar*, *TV etc*: (Bild)Schirm *m.* **4.** *fig.* Tarnung *f.* **II** *v/t* **5.** abschirmen. **6.** ~ **off** abtrennen. **7.** *Film* zeigen, *Fernsehprogramm* a. senden. **8.** *fig.* j-n überprüfen. '~·**play** *s Film:* Drehbuch *n*. ~ **test** *s Film:* Probeaufnahmen *pl.*

screw [skruː] **I** *s* **1.** ⚙ Schraube *f*: **he has a** ~ **loose** F bei ihm ist e-e Schraube locker; **put the** ~**s on s.o.** *fig.* j-m (die) Daumenschrauben anlegen *od.* ansetzen. **II** *v/t* **2.** (an)schrauben (**to** an *acc*): ~ **together** zs.-, verschrauben. **3.** *a.* ~ **up** *Papier etc* zs.-, zerknüllen. **4.** ~ **up** a) *Augen* zs.-kneifen, *Gesicht* verziehen, b) F *Plan etc* vermasseln. **5.** ~ **s.th. out of s.o.** et. aus j-m herauspressen. **6.** (*a. v/i*) V bumsen, vögeln. '~·**ball** *s bsd. Am.* F Spinner(in). '~·**driv·er** *s* ⚙ Schraubenzieher *m.* ~ **top** *s* Schraubverschluß *m.*

screw·y [ˈskruːɪ] *adj* F verrückt.

scrib·ble [ˈskrɪbl] *v/t* (hin)kritzeln. **II** *s* Gekritzel *n.* '**scrib·bler** *s humor. od. contp.* Schreiberling *m.*

scrim·mage [ˈskrɪmɪdʒ] *s* Handgemenge *n.*

scrimp [skrɪmp] *v/i* den Gürtel enger schnallen: ~ **and scrape** jeden Pfennig zweimal umdrehen.

script [skrɪpt] *s* **1.** Manuskript *n* (*e-r Rede etc*); (*Film*, *TV*) Drehbuch *n*, Skript *n*; *thea.* Text(buch *n*) *m.* **2.** Schrift(zeichen *pl*) *f.* **3.** Schreibschrift *f.* **4.** *ped. univ. Br.* (schriftliche) Prüfungsarbeit.

Scrip·ture [ˈskrɪptʃə] *s*, *a.* **the** ~**s** *pl* die (Heilige) Schrift.

'**script**,**writ·er** *s Film*, *TV*: Drehbuchautor(in).

scroll [skrəʊl] *s* Schriftrolle *f.*

scrooge [skruːdʒ] *s* Geizhals *m.*

scro·tum [ˈskrəʊtəm] *pl* **-tums**, **-ta** [ˈ~tə] *s anat.* Hodensack *m.*

scrounge [skraʊndʒ] **I** *v/i* schnorren (**off** bei). **II** *v/t* et. schnorren (**off** von, bei). '**scroung·er** *s* F Schnorrer(in).

scrub¹ [skrʌb] *s* Gebüsch *n*, Gestrüpp *n.*

scrub² [~] **I** *v/t* **1.** *et.* schrubben, scheuern. **2.** F streichen, ausfallen lassen. **II** *s* **3.** Schrubben *n*, Scheuern *n*: **give** *s.th.* **a** ~ → 1.

scrub·bing brush [ˈskrʌbɪŋ] *s*, *Am. a.* **scrub brush** *s* Scheuerbürste *f.*

scrub·by [ˈskrʌbɪ] *adj* gestrüppreich.

scruff [skrʌf] *s*: ~ **of the neck** Genick *n.*

scruff·y [ˈskrʌfɪ] *adj* □ F schmudd(e)lig.

scrump·tious [ˈskrʌmpʃəs] *adj* □ F fabelhaft, lecker (*Speise*).

scrunch [skrʌntʃ] **I** *v/t a.* ~ **up** *Papier etc* zs.-knüllen. **II** *v/i* knirschen.

scru·ple [ˈskruːpl] **I** *s* Skrupel *m*: **have no** ~**s about doing s.th.** → II; **without** ~ skrupellos. **II** *v/i*: **not to** ~ **to do s.th.** keine Skrupel haben, et. zu tun. **scru·pu·lous** [ˈ~pjʊləs] *adj* □ gewissenhaft.

scru·ti·nize [ˈskruːtɪnaɪz] *v/t* **1.** genau prüfen. **2.** mustern. '**scru·ti·ny** *s* **1.** genaue Prüfung. **2.** musternder *od.* prüfender Blick.

scu·ba [ˈskuːbə] *s* Tauchgerät *n*: ~ **diving** (*Sport*)Tauchen *n.*

scuff [skʌf] *v/t* **1.** ~ **one's feet** schlurfen. **2.** abwetzen.

scuf·fle [ˈskʌfl] **I** *v/i* (sich) raufen (**for** um). **II** *s* Rauferei *f*, Handgemenge *n.*

scull [skʌl] (*Rudersport*) **I** *s* **1.** Skull *n.* **2.** Skullboot *n*, Skuller *m.* **II** *v/i u. v/i* **3.** skullen. '**scull·er** *s* Skuller(in).

sculp·tor [ˈskʌlptə] *s* Bildhauer *m.*

sculp·ture [ˈskʌlptʃə] **I** *s* Skulptur *f*, Plastik *f*, (*Kunst a.*) Bildhauerei *f.* **II** *v/t Figur etc* hauen (**in** in *dat*, aus).

scum [skʌm] *s* **1.** Schaum *m.* **2.** *fig.* Abschaum *m*: **the** ~ **of the earth** der Abschaum der Menschheit.

scurf [skɜːf] *s* (Kopf)Schuppen *pl.* '**scurf·y** *adj* schuppig.

scur·ril·ous [ˈskʌrələs] *adj* □ **1.** beleidigend; verleumderisch. **2.** derb (*Witz etc*).

scur·ry ['skʌrɪ] **I** v/i **1.** huschen. **2.** trippeln. **II** s **3.** Getrippel n.

scut·tle ['skʌtl] → **scurry** I.

scythe [saɪð] **I** s Sense f. **II** v/t a. ~ **down** Wiese etc mähen.

sea [siː] s Meer n (a. fig.), See f: **at** ~ auf See; **be all at** ~ fig. völlig ratlos sein; **by** ~ auf dem Seeweg; **by the** ~ am Meer; **go to** ~ zur See gehen; → **put** 12. **~an·i·mal** s Meerestier n. **'~bed** s Meeresboden m, -grund m. **'~board** s Küste f. **'~food** s Meeresfrüchte pl. **'~go·ing** adj hochseetüchtig, Hochsee... **'~gull** s orn. Seemöwe f.

seal¹ [siːl] pl ~s, bsd. coll. ~ s zo. Seehund m, Robbe f.

seal² [~] **I** s **1.** Siegel n. **2.** Siegel n, Versieg(e)lung f; Plombe f. **3.** ⊙ Dichtung f. **4.** ✿ Aufkleber m. **II** v/t **5.** siegeln. **6.** versiegeln; plombieren; *Briefumschlag etc* zukleben: **~ed envelope** verschlossener Briefumschlag m. **7.** ⊙ abdichten. **8.** ~ off Gegend etc abriegeln. **9.** fig. besiegeln: ~ s.o.'s fate j-s Schicksal besiegeln.

sea lev·el s: **above** (**below**) ~ über (unter) dem Meeresspiegel, über (unter) Meereshöhe.

seal·ing wax ['siːlɪŋ] s Siegellack n.

sea li·on s zo. Seelöwe m.

'seal·skin s Seal(skin) m, n, Seehundfell n.

seam [siːm] s **1.** Saum m: **burst at the ~s** bsd. fig. aus allen Nähten platzen. **2.** Fuge f. **3.** geol. Flöz n.

sea·man ['siːmən] s (*irr man*) Seemann m. ~ **mile** s Seemeile f.

seam·stress ['semstrɪs] s Näherin f.

seam·y ['siːmɪ] adj: ~ **side** fig. Schattenseite(n pl) f.

'sea·plane s See-, Wasserflugzeug n. **'~port** s Seehafen m, Hafenstadt f. ~ **pow·er** s Seemacht f.

sear [sɪə] v/t **1.** Fleisch rasch anbraten. **2.** brennen in (dat) (*Geruch etc*). **3.** Pflanzen vertrocknen lassen.

search [sɜːtʃ] **I** v/i **1.** suchen (**for** nach): ~ **through** durchsuchen; → **high** 7. **II** v/t **2.** j-n, et. durchsuchen (**for** nach): ~ **me!** F keine Ahnung! **3.** ~ **out** j-n ausfindig machen; et. herausfinden. **III** s **4.** Suche f (**for** nach): **in** ~ **of** auf der Suche

nach. **5.** Durchsuchung f. **'search·ing** adj □ forschend, prüfend (*Blick*); bohrend (*Frage*).

'search·light s (Such)Scheinwerfer m. ~ **par·ty** s Suchmannschaft f, -trupp m. ~ **war·rant** s ⚖ Haussuchungs-, Durchsuchungsbefehl m.

sear·ing ['sɪərɪŋ] adj stechend (*Schmerz*).

'sea·sick adj seekrank. **'~sick·ness** s Seekrankheit f. **'~side** s: **at** (od. **by**) **the** ~ am Meer; **go to the** ~ ans Meer fahren; ~ **resort** Seebad n.

sea·son ['siːzn] **I** s **1.** Jahreszeit f: ~ **rainy.** **2.** allg. Saison f, thea. a. Spielzeit f, (*Jagd-, Urlaubs- etc*)Zeit f: **in** (out of) ~ im (außerhalb der) (Hoch)Saison; **2's Greetings!** Frohe Weihnachten!; → **close season, compliment** 2, **high** 4, **low season, open** 10, **silly** I. **3.** F → **season ticket. II** v/t **4.** Speise würzen. **5.** Holz ablagern. **'sea·son·a·ble** adj □ der Jahreszeit entsprechend. **sea·son·al** ['~zənl] adj □ saisonbedingt; Saison... **'sea·soned** adj erfahren, routiniert. **'sea·son·ing** s Gewürz n.

sea·son tick·et s **1.** 🚇 etc Dauer-, Zeitkarte f. **2.** thea. Abonnement n.

seat [siːt] **I** s **1.** Sitz(gelegenheit f) m; (Sitz)Platz m: **take a** ~ Platz nehmen; **take one's** ~ s-n Platz einnehmen. **2.** Sitz(fläche f) m (e-s Stuhls etc); Hosenboden m; Hinterteil n: **do s.th. by the** ~ **of one's pants** F et. nach Gefühl od. Wellenschlag tun. **3.** (*Geschäfts-, Regierungs- etc*)Sitz m. **II** v/t **4.** j-n setzen: **be ~ed** sitzen; **please be ~ed** bitte nehmen Sie Platz; **remain ~ed** sitzen bleiben. **5.** Sitzplätze bieten für, Platz bieten (dat): ~ **500 persons** a. 500 Sitzplätze haben. ~ **belt** s ✈, mot. Sicherheitsgurt m: **fasten one's** ~ sich anschnallen; **wear a** ~ angegurtet od. angeschnallt sein.

seat·er ['siːtə] s ✈, mot. ...sitzer m. **'seat·ing** **I** s Sitzgelegenheit(en pl) f. **II** adj: **a** ~ **capacity of 200** 200 Sitzplätze.

sea ur·chin ['ɜːtʃɪn] s zo. Seeigel m. **'~weed** s ✿ (See)Tang m. **'~worth·y** adj seetüchtig.

sec [sek] F → **second²** 2.

sec·a·teurs [,sekə'tɜːz] s pl, a. **pair of** ~ Br. Gartenschere f.

sedative

se·cede [sɪˈsiːd] *v/i pol. etc* sich abspalten (*from* von).

se·ces·sion [sɪˈseʃn] *s pol. etc* Abspaltung *f* (*from* von).

se·clud·ed [sɪˈkluːdɪd] *adj* abgelegen, abgeschieden (*Haus etc*); zurückgezogen (*Leben*). **se·clu·sion** [~ʒn] *s* Abgelegenheit *f*, Abgeschiedenheit *f*; Zurückgezogenheit *f*.

sec·ond¹ [ˈsekənd] **I** *adj* (□ → **second·ly**) **1.** zweit: *he is going through his ~ childhood* er fühlt sich wieder wie ein (richtiges) Kind; *at ~ hand* aus zweiter Hand; *it has become ~ nature for* (*od. to*) *him* es ist ihm in Fleisch u. Blut übergegangen; *a ~ Shakespeare* ein zweiter Shakespeare; *a ~ time* noch einmal; *every ~ day* jeden zweiten Tag, alle zwei Tage; *be ~ to none* unerreicht *od.* unübertroffen sein (*as* als); → **fiddle** 1, **thought²** 2, **wind¹** 2. **II** *s* **2.** der, die, das Zweite: *the ~ of May* der 2. Mai. **3.** *mot.* zweiter Gang. **4.** Boxen, Duell: Sekundant *m*: *~s out* Ring frei. **5.** *pl* ✝ Waren *pl* zweiter Wahl. **6.** *pl* F Nachschlag *m* (*zweite Portion*). **III** *adj* **7.** als zweit(er, e, es). **IV** *v/t* **8.** Antrag *etc* unterstützen.

sec·ond² [~] *s* **1.** Sekunde *f* (*a. ♈, ♪*). **2.** *fig.* Augenblick *m*, Sekunde *f*: *just a ~* Augenblick(, bitte)!; *I won't be a ~* ich komme gleich (wieder); *have you got a ~?* hast du e-n Moment Zeit (für mich)?

sec·ond³ [sɪˈkɒnd] *v/t Br. j-n* (*bsd. vorübergehend*) versetzen (*to* in *acc*).

sec·ond·ar·y [ˈsekəndərɪ] *adj* □ **1.** sekundär, zweitrangig, nebensächlich. **2.** *♐ etc* sekundär, Sekundär... **3.** *ped.* höher (*Schule etc*).

sec·ond-best I *adj* zweitbest. **II** *adv*: *come off ~* den kürzeren ziehen. **,~-ˈclass I** *adj* **1.** zweitklassig, -rangig. **2.** 🚂 *etc* zweiter Klasse. **II** *adv* zweite(r) Klasse. **,~-deˈgree** *adj* Verbrennungen zweiten Grades. **~ hand** *s* Sekundenzeiger *m*. **,~-ˈhand** (*a. adv*) **1.** aus zweiter Hand. **2.** gebraucht, Gebraucht..., (*Kleidung a.*) getragen, (*Bücher*) antiquarisch: *~ bookshop* Antiquariat *n*.

sec·ond·ly [ˈsekəndlɪ] *adv* zweitens.

,sec·ond-ˈrate → **second-class** 1.

se·cre·cy [ˈsiːkrəsɪ] *s* **1.** Geheimhaltung *f*: *in* (*od. amid*) *great ~* unter großer

Geheimhaltung. **2.** Verschwiegenheit *f*.

se·cret [ˈsiːkrɪt] **I** *adj* (□ → **secretly**) **1.** geheim, Geheim...: *keep s.th. ~ et.* geheimhalten (*from* vor *dat*); *~ agent* Geheimagent(in); *~ service* Geheimdienst *m*. **2.** heimlich (*Bewunderer etc*). **3.** verschwiegen. **II** *s* **4.** Geheimnis *n*: *in ~* a) im Vertrauen, b) → **secretly; have no ~s from s.o.** keine Geheimnisse vor j-m haben; *make no ~ of* kein Geheimnis *od.* Hehl machen aus; → **keep** 4, 7.

sec·re·tar·y [ˈsekrətrɪ] *s* **1.** Sekretär(in) (*to gen*). **2.** *pol.* Minister(in): ♀ *of State Br.* Minister(in); *Am.* Außenminister (-in). **,~ˈgen·er·al** *pl* **,sec·re·tar·ies-ˈgen·er·al** *s* Generalsekretär *m*.

se·crete [sɪˈkriːt] *v/t physiol.* absondern. **se·cre·tion** *s* Absonderung *f*; Sekret *n*.

se·cre·tive [sɪˈkriːtɪv] *adj* □ heimlichtuerisch: *be ~ about s.th.* mit et. geheimtun.

sect [sekt] *s* Sekte *f.* **sec·tar·i·an** [~ˈteərɪən] *adj* konfessionsbedingt, Konfessions...

sec·tion [ˈsekʃn] *s* **1.** Teil *m.* **2.** Abschnitt *m* (*e-s Buchs etc*); ⚖ Paragraph *m.* **3.** Abteilung *f.* **4.** ♈, ◎ Schnitt *m*: *in ~* im Schnitt. **II** *v/t* **5.** teilen. **sec·tion·al** [ˈ~ʃənl] *adj* ♈, ◎ Schnitt...

sec·tor [ˈsektə] *s allg.* Sektor *m.*

sec·u·lar [ˈsekjʊlə] *adj* □ weltlich, profan. **ˈsec·u·lar·ize** *v/t* säkularisieren, verweltlichen.

se·cure [sɪˈkjʊə] **I** *adj* □ **1.** *allg.* sicher (*against, from* vor *dat*): *feel ~* sich sicher fühlen; *financially ~* finanziell abgesichert. **II** *v/t* **2.** Tür *etc* fest verschließen; sichern. **3.** sichern (*against, from* vor *dat*). **4.** sich et. sichern *od.* beschaffen; *et.* erreichen.

se·cu·ri·ty [sɪˈkjʊərətɪ] *s* **1.** *allg.* Sicherheit *f*: ♀ *Council* Sicherheitsrat *m* (*der UNO*); *for ~ reasons* aus Sicherheitsgründen; *~ risk* Sicherheitsrisiko *n.* **2.** *pl* ✝ Effekten *pl*, Wertpapiere *pl*.

se·dan [sɪˈdæn] *s mot. Am.* Limousine *f.*

se·date [sɪˈdeɪt] **I** *adj* □ ruhig, gelassen; (*Tempo*) gemütlich. **II** *v/t j-m* ein Beruhigungsmittel geben. **se·ˈda·tion** *s*: *be under ~* unter dem Einfluß von Beruhigungsmitteln stehen; *put under ~* → **sedate** II. **sed·a·tive** [ˈsedətɪv] **I** *adj*

beruhigend: **~** *shot* Beruhigungsspritze f. **II** s Beruhigungsmittel n.
sed·en·tar·y ['sedntərı] adj □ **1.** sitzend (*Beschäftigung etc*). **2.** seßhaft.
sed·i·ment ['sedımənt] s (Boden)Satz m.
se·duce [sı'dju:s] v/t verführen, *weitS. a.* verleiten (*into* zu; *into doing s.th.* dazu, ct. zu tun). **se·duc·er** s Verführer(in). **se·duc·tion** [sı'dʌkʃn] s **1.** Verführung f. **2.** *mst pl* Verlockung f. **se·duc·tive** adj □ verführerisch, *weitS. a.* verlokkend.
see¹ [si:] (*irr*) **I** v/t **1.** sehen: *I saw him come* (*od.* *coming*) ich sah ihn kommen. **2.** (ab)sehen, erkennen. **3.** ersehen, entnehmen (*from* aus *der Zeitung etc*). **4.** (ein)sehen, verstehen: *as I ~ it* wie ich es sehe, in m-n Augen. **5.** sich *et.* ansehen, besuchen. **6.** a) *j-n* besuchen: *go* (*come*) *to ~ s.o.* j-n besuchen (gehen *od.* kommen), b) *Anwalt etc* aufsuchen, c) zum *Arzt* gehen, d) *j-n* sprechen (*on business* geschäftlich). **7.** *j-n* empfangen. **8.** *j-n* begleiten, bringen (*to the station* zum Bahnhof). **II** v/i **9.** sehen: *you'll ~* du wirst schon sehen. **10.** verstehen: *I ~* (ich) verstehe!, aha!, ach so!; *you ~* weißt du. **11.** nachsehen. **12.** *let me ~* warte mal!, laß mich überlegen!; *we'll ~* mal sehen.
Verbindungen mit Präpositionen:
see| a·bout v/i sehen nach, sich kümmern um: *I'll ~ it* ich werde mich darum kümmern; ich will mal sehen. **we'll** (*soon*) **~** *that!* F das wollen wir mal sehen! **~ o·ver**, **~ round** v/i sich *ein Haus etc* ansehen. **~ through I** v/i *j-n*, *et.* durchschauen. **II** v/t *j-m* hinweghelfen über (*acc*). **~ to** v/i: **~ it that** dafür sorgen, daß.
Verbindungen mit Adverbien:
see| off v/t **1.** *j-n* verabschieden (*at* am *Bahnhof etc*). **2.** verjagen, -scheuchen. **~ out** v/t **1.** *j-n* hinausbringen, -begleiten. **2.** bis zum Ende (*gen*) reichen (*Vorräte*).
see² [~] s **1.** Bistum n, Diözese f. **2.** *Holy ⌀ der* Heilige Stuhl.
seed [si:d] **I** s **1.** ⌘ Same(n) m; ⚹ Saat(gut n) f: *go* (*od.* *run*) *to ~* schießen; *fig.* herunterkommen (*Person*); → *sow* **1.** **2.** (*Orangen- etc*)Kern m. **3.** *Sport:* gesetzter Spieler. **II** v/t **4.** besäen. **5.** *Sport: Spieler* setzen. **III** v/i **6.** ⌘ schie-

ßen. '**~bed** s **1.** Saatbeet n. **2.** *fig.* Brutstätte f.
'**seed·y** adj □ vergammelt.
see·ing ['si:ıŋ] cj a. **~** *that* da.
seek [si:k] (*irr*) **I** v/t **1.** *Schutz, Zuflucht, Wahrheit etc* suchen: **~** *s.o.'s advice*, **~** *advice from s.o.* j-n um Rat bitten, Rat bei j-m suchen. **2.** (ver)suchen nach. **3.** (ver)suchen (*to do* zu tun). **II** v/i **4.** **~** *after* (*od.* *for*) suchen (nach).
seem [si:m] v/i **1.** scheinen: *it ~s impossible to me* das (er)scheint mir unmöglich. **2.** *impers it ~s that* es scheint, daß; anscheinend; *it ~s as if* (*od.* *though*) es sieht so aus *od.* scheint so, als ob. '**seem·ing** adj scheinbar. '**seem·ing·ly** adv **1.** scheinbar. **2.** anscheinend.
seen [si:n] pp von **see¹**.
seep [si:p] v/i sickern.
see·saw ['si:sɔ:] s Wippe f, Wippschaukel f.
seethe [si:ð] v/i *fig.* kochen: *he was seething with rage* er kochte *od.* schäumte vor Wut.
'**see-through** adj durchsichtig (*Bluse etc*).
seg·ment I s ['segmənt] Teil m, n; Stück n; *biol.*, *⚕ etc* Segment n. **II** v/t [seg'ment] zerlegen, -teilen.
seg·re·gate ['segrıgeıt] v/t (*a. nach Rassen, Geschlechtern*) trennen. ,**seg·re·'ga·tion** s Trennung f: → *racial*.
seis·mic ['saızmık] adj seismisch, Erdbeben...
seis·mo·graph ['saızməgrɑ:f] s Seismograph m, Erdbebenmesser m. **seis·mol·o·gist** [~'mɒlədʒıst] s Seismologe m, Seismologin f. **seis·mol·o·gy** s Seismologie f, Seismik f, Erdbebenkunde f.
seize [si:z] **I** v/t **1.** *j-n*, *et.* packen (*by an dat*); *Gelegenheit* ergreifen; *Macht etc* an sich reißen. **2.** *j-n* festnehmen; *et.* beschlagnahmen. **II** v/i **3.** **~** *up* ⊙ sich festfressen; (*Verkehr*) zum Erliegen kommen. **sei·zure** ['~ʒə] s **1.** Festnahme f; Beschlagnahme f. **2.** ⚕ Anfall m.
sel·dom ['seldəm] adv selten: **~**, *if ever* (nur) äußerst selten, kaum jemals.
se·lect [sı'lekt] **I** v/t **1.** (aus)wählen (*from aus*). **II** adj **2.** ausgewählt. **3.** exklusiv. **se·lec·tion** s **1.** (Aus)Wahl f. **2.** ⚕ *etc*

Auswahl *f* (*of* an *dat*). **se'lec·tive** *adj* □ wählerisch (*in* in *dat*).

self [self] *pl* **selves** [selvz] *s* Ich *n*, Selbst *n*: *my humble* ~ m-e Wenigkeit; *one's true* ~ sein wahres Wesen; *he is back to his old* ~ er ist wieder (ganz) der alte. ‚~**ab'sorbed** *adj* mit sich selbst beschäftigt. ‚~**ad'dressed** *adj*: ~ *envelope* Rückumschlag *m*. ‚~**as'sured** *adj* selbstbewußt. ‚~**ca·ter·ing** *adj* für Selbstversorger, mit Selbstverpflegung. ‚~**'cen·tered** *adj Am.*, ‚~**'cen·tred** *adj bsd. Br.* ichbezogen, egozentrisch. ‚~**con·fi·dence** *s* Selbstbewußtsein *n*, -vertrauen *n*. ‚~**con·fi·dent** *adj* □ selbstbewußt. ‚~**con·scious** *adj* □ befangen, gehemmt. ‚~**con'tained** abgeschlossen (*Wohnung, Folge e-r Fernsehserie etc*). ‚~**con'trol** *s* Selbstbeherrschung *f*. ‚~**con'trolled** *adj* selbstbeherrscht. ‚~**crit·i·cal** *adj* □ selbstkritisch. ‚~**crit·i·cism** *s* Selbstkritik *f*. ‚~**de'fence** *s Br.*, ‚~**de'fense** *s Am.* Selbstverteidigung *f*, ⚖ Notwehr *f*: **in** ~ in *od.* aus Notwehr. '~**de₁ter·mi·'na·tion** *s pol.* Selbstbestimmung *f*. ‚~**'ed·u·cat·ed** *adj*: ~ *person* Autodidakt(in). ‚~**ef'fac·ing** *adj* □ zurückhaltend. ‚~**em'ployed** *adj* (*beruflich*) selbständig. ‚~**es'teem** *s* Selbstachtung *f*. ‚~**ev·i·dent** *adj* □ **1.** selbstverständlich: *be* ~ sich von selbst verstehen. **2.** offensichtlich. ‚~**'gov·ern·ment** *s pol.* Selbstverwaltung *f*. ‚~**'help** *s* Selbsthilfe *f*: ~ *group* Selbsthilfegruppe *f*. ‚~**im'por·tance** *s* Eigendünkel *m*, Überheblichkeit *f*. ‚~**im·'por·tant** *adj* □ dünkelhaft, überheblich. ‚~**in'vit·ed** *adj* ungebeten (*Gast*). **self·ish** [ˈselfɪʃ] *adj* □ selbstsüchtig, egoistisch. '**self·ish·ness** *s* Selbstsucht *f*, Egoismus *m*.

self·less [ˈselflɪs] *adj* □ selbstlos. '**self·less·ness** *s* Selbstlosigkeit *f*.

‚**self|·'made** *adj*: ~ *man* Selfmademan *m*. ‚~**'pit·y** *s* Selbstmitleid *n*. ‚~**pos·'sessed** *adj* □ selbstbeherrscht. ‚~**pos·'ses·sion** *s* Selbstbeherrschung *f*. ‚~**'praise** *s* Eigenlob *n*. '~**preser'va·tion** *s* Selbsterhaltung *f*: → *instinct*. ‚~**re'li·ant** *adj* □ selbständig. ‚~**re'spect** *s* Selbstachtung *f*. ‚~**re'spect·ing** *adj*: *no* ~ *businessman* kein

Geschäftsmann, der et. auf sich hält. ‚~**'right·eous** *adj* □ selbstgerecht. ‚~**sat·is·fied** *adj* selbstzufrieden. ‚~**'seal·ing** *adj* selbstklebend (*Briefumschlag*). ‚~**'ser·vice I** *s* Selbstbedienung *f*. **II** *adj* Selbstbedienungs..., mit Selbstbedienung. ‚~**suf·fi·cient** *adj* □ ✝ autark. ‚~**sup'port·ing** *adj* **1.** finanziell unabhängig: *be* ~ *a.* sich selbst tragen. **2.** ⚙ freitragend (*Mast*); selbsttragend (*Mauer*). ‚~**'willed** *adj* eigensinnig, -willig.

sell [sel] (*irr*) **I** *v/t* **1.** verkaufen (*to* an *acc*; *for* für), ✝ *a.* a) absetzen, b) führen, vertreiben: ~ *o.s.* sich verkaufen (*a. contp.*); → *river*. **2.** verkaufen, e-n guten Absatz sichern (*dat*). **3.** F et. schmackhaft machen (*to s.o.* j-m); j-n begeistern, erwärmen (*on s.th.* für et.): *be sold on* begeistert sein von. **II** *v/i* **4.** verkaufen: ~ *by* ... mindestens haltbar bis ... **5.** verkauft werden (*at, for* für): ~ *at £5 a.* 5 Pfund kosten. **6.** sich *gut etc* verkaufen (*lassen*), gehen: → *cake* 1. *Verbindungen mit Adverbien:*

sell| *off v/t* (*bsd.* billig) abstoßen. ~ *out* **I** *v/t* **1.** ausverkaufen: *be sold out* ausverkauft sein (*a. Stadion etc*); *we are sold out of umbrellas* Schirme sind ausverkauft. **II** *v/i* **2.** *the umbrellas sold out in two days* die Schirme waren in zwei Tagen ausverkauft. **3.** F *contp.* sich verkaufen (*to* an *acc*). ~ *up Br.* **I** *v/t* sein *Geschäft etc* verkaufen. **II** *v/i* sein Geschäft *etc* verkaufen.

'**sell-by date** *s* Mindesthaltbarkeitsdatum *n*.

sell·er [ˈselə] *s* **1.** Verkäufer(in). **2.** *be a good* ~ sich gut verkaufen, gut gehen. '**sell-out** *s* ausverkaufte Veranstaltung *f*.

selves [selvz] *pl von* **self**.

se·man·tic [sɪˈmæntɪk] *ling.* **I** *adj* (~*ally*) semantisch. **II** *s pl* (*mst sg konstruiert*) Semantik *f*.

sem·blance [ˈsembləns] *s* Anschein *m* (*of* von).

se·men [ˈsiːmen] *s physiol.* Samen(flüssigkeit *f*) *m*, Sperma *n*.

se·mes·ter [sɪˈmestə] *s univ.* Semester *n*.

sem·i... [ˈsemɪ] halb..., Halb...

sem·i [ˈsemɪ] *s* F **1.** *Br.* → *semidetached* II. **2.** *Am.* → *semitrailer*.

semi·breve [ˈsemɪbriːv] *s* ♩ *Br.* ganze Note. '~**cir·cle** *s* Halbkreis *m*. ‚~**'cir-**

semicolon **1232**

cu·lar *adj* □ halbkreisförmig. **,~'colon**
s ling. Semikolon *n*, Strichpunkt *m*.
,~con'duc·tor *s ⚡* Halbleiter *m*. **,~·de'tached** I *adj*: **~ house** → II. II *s*
Doppelhaushälfte *f*. **,~'fi·nals** *s pl
Sport*: Semi-, Halbfinale *n*.

sem·i·nar ['semɪnɑː] *s univ.* Seminar *n*.

sem·i·nar·y ['semɪnərɪ] *s* Priesterseminar *n*.

,sem·i·of'fi·cial *adj* □ halbamtlich, offiziös. **'~,pre·cious** *adj*: **~ stone** Halbedelstein *m*. **,~'skilled** *adj* angelernt
(*Arbeiter*).

Sem·ite ['siːmaɪt] *s* Semit(in). **Se·mit·ic**
[sɪ'mɪtɪk] *adj* semitisch.

sem·o·li·na [,semə'liːnə] *s* Grieß *m*.

sen·ate ['senɪt] *s* Senat *m*. **sen·a·tor**
['senətə] *s* Senator *m*.

send [send] (*irr*) I *v/t* **1.** *j-n* schicken (**to
bed** ins Bett; **to prison** ins Gefängnis):
~ s.o. after s.o. j-n j-m nachschicken. **2.**
(**to**) *et.*, *a.* Grüße, Hilfe *etc* senden,
schicken (*dat od.* an *acc*), Ware *etc* versenden, -schicken (an *acc*). **3.** *mit adj
od. pres p*: machen: **~ s.o. mad** j-n
wahnsinnig machen; → **pack** 15. II *v/i*
4. ~ for a) nach *j-m* schicken, *j-n* kommen lassen, b) sich *et.* kommen lassen,
et. anfordern.
Verbindungen mit Adverbien:
send| a·way I *v/t* **1.** fort-, wegschicken. **2.** *Brief etc* absenden, abschicken. II *v/i* **3. ~ for** → **send** 4b. **~
back** *v/t* j-n, *et.* zurückschicken, *Speise
a.* zurückgehen lassen. **~ down** *v/t* **1.**
hinunter-, herunterschicken. **2.** *univ.
Br.* relegieren. **3.** *fig.* Preise, Temperatur etc* fallen lassen. **~ in** *v/t* einsenden,
einschicken, einreichen; → **resignation**
1. **~ off** I *v/t* **1.** → **send away** I. **2.** *j-n*
verabschieden. **3.** *Sport:* vom Platz
stellen. II *v/i* **4.** → **send away** II. **~ on**
v/t **1.** *Gepäck etc* vorausschicken. **2.**
Brief etc nachschicken, -senden (**to** an
e-e Adresse). **~ out** I *v/t* **1.** hinausschicken. **2.** *Wärme etc* ausstrahlen. **3.** *Einladungen, Prospekte etc* verschicken. II
v/i **4. ~ for s.th.** *et.* holen lassen. **~ up** *v/t*
1. hinauf-, heraufschicken. **2.** *fig.* Preise, Temperatur etc* steigen lassen. **3.** *Br.
F* parodieren, verulken.

send·er ['sendə] *s* Absender(in). → **return** 2.

'send|-off *s* F Verabschiedung *f*. **'~-up** *s*

Br. F (**of**) Parodie *f* (auf *acc*), Verulkung *f* (*gen*): **do a ~ of** → **send up** 3.

se·nile ['siːnaɪl] *adj* senil. **se·nil·i·ty**
[sɪ'nɪlətɪ] *s* Senilität *f*.

sen·ior ['siːnjə] I *adj* **1.** senior. **2.** älter
(**to** als): **~ citizens** *pl* Senioren *pl*. **3.**
dienstälter; ranghöher (**to** als): **~ partner** † Senior(partner) *m*. **4. ~ high
(school)** *Am.* die oberen Klassen der
High-School. II *s* **5.** Ältere *m*, *f*: **he is
my ~ by two years, he is two years my
~** er ist zwei Jahre älter als ich. **6.** *Am.*
Student(in) im letzten Jahr. **sen·ior·i·ty** [,siːnɪ'ɒrətɪ] *s* **1.** (höheres) Alter. **2.**
(höheres) Dienstalter; (höherer) Rang.

sen·sa·tion [sen'seɪʃn] *s* **1.** Empfindung
f; Gefühl *n*: **~ of thirst** Durstgefühl. **2.**
Sensation *f*: **cause** (*od.* **create**) **a ~**
großes Aufsehen erregen, *für* e-e Sensation sorgen. **sen·sa·tion·al** [~ʃ ɒnl]
adj □ **1.** sensationell, Sensations... **2.** F
phantastisch, sagenhaft. **sen·sa·tion·al·ism** [~ʃnəlɪzəm] *s* **1.** Sensationsgier *f*.
2. Sensationsmache *f*.

sense [sens] I *s* **1.** *physiol.* Sinn *m*: **~ of
hearing** (**sight, smell, taste, touch**)
Gehör-(Gesichts-, Geruchs-, Geschmacks-, Tast)sinn; → **sixth** 1. **2.** *pl*
(klarer) Verstand: **bring s.o. to his ~s**
j-n zur Besinnung *od.* Vernunft bringen; **come to one's ~s** zur Besinnung
od. Vernunft kommen. **3.** Vernunft *f*,
Verstand *m*: **have the ~ to do s.th.** so
klug sein, et. zu tun; → **common
sense, horse sense. 4.** Gefühl *n*, Empfindung *f*: **~ of security** Gefühl der Sicherheit. **5.** Sinn *m*, Gefühl *n* (**of** für): **~
of duty** Pflichtgefühl; → **humour** 1. **6.**
Sinn *m*, Bedeutung *f*: **in a ~** in gewisser
Hinsicht. **7.** Sinn *m* (*et. Vernünftiges*):
make ~ e-n Sinn ergeben; vernünftig
sein; **I could make no ~ of it** ich konnte
mir darauf keinen Reim machen. II *v/t*
8. fühlen, spüren. **'sense·less** *adj* □ **1.**
besinnungs-, bewußtlos. **2.** sinnlos, unsinnig.

sense or·gan *s* Sinnesorgan *n*, -werkzeug *n*.

sen·si·bil·i·ty [,sensɪ'bɪlətɪ] *s* **1.** Empfindlichkeit *f*: **~ to pain** Schmerzempfindlichkeit. **2.** *a. pl* Fein-, Zartgefühl *n*.

sen·si·ble ['sensəbl] *adj* □ **1.** vernünftig.
2. spürbar, merklich. **3.** praktisch
(*Kleidungsstück*).

sen·si·tive ['sensɪtɪv] *adj* □ **1.** sensibel, empfindsam; empfindlich: *be ~ to* empfindlich reagieren auf (*acc*). **2.** einfühlsam. **3.** empfindlich (*a.* ⊛): *~ to pain* schmerzempfindlich. **4.** heikel (*Thema etc*).

sen·sor ['sensə] *s* ⚡, ⊛ Sensor *m*.

sen·so·ry ['sensərɪ] *adj* sensorisch, Sinnes...

sen·su·al ['sensjʊəl] *adj* □ sinnlich. '**sen·su·al·ist** *s* sinnlicher Mensch. **sen·su·al·i·ty** [,~'ælətɪ] *s* Sinnlichkeit *f*.

sen·su·ous ['sensjʊəs] *adj* □ sinnlich.

sent [sent] *pret u. pp von* **send**.

sen·tence ['sentəns] I *s* **1.** *ling.* Satz *m*. **2.** ⚖️ Strafe *f*; Urteil *n*: *pass ~* das Urteil fällen (*on über acc*). II *v/t* **3.** ⚖️ verurteilen (*to* zu).

sen·ten·tious [sen'tenʃəs] *adj* □ moralisierend.

sen·tient ['senʃnt] *adj* □ empfindungsfähig.

sen·ti·ment ['sentɪmənt] *s* **1.** Gefühle *pl*; Sentimentalität *f*. **2.** *a. pl* Ansicht *f*, Meinung *f*. **sen·ti·men·tal** [,~'mentl] *adj* □ gefühlvoll, gefühlsbetont; sentimental: *for ~ reasons* aus Sentimentalität; *~ value* Erinnerungswert *m*. **sen·ti·men·tal·i·ty** [,~men'tælətɪ] *s* Sentimentalität *f*.

sen·try ['sentrɪ] *s* ✕ Wache *f*, (Wach[t]-) Posten *m*. **~ box** *s* Wachhäuschen *n*.

sep·a·ra·ble ['sepərəbl] *adj* □ trennbar.

sep·a·rate I *v/t* ['sepəreɪt] **1.** *allg.* trennen (*from* von); **~d** getrennt leben (*from* von). **2.** (auf-, ein-, zer)teilen (*into in acc*). II *v/i* ['sepəreɪt] **3.** sich trennen (*a. Ehepaar*). III *adj* □ ['seprət] **4.** getrennt, separat. **5.** einzeln, gesondert, Einzel...: *charge s.th. ~ly* et. extra berechnen. **6.** verschieden. **sep·a·ra·-tion** [,sepə'reɪʃn] *s* **1.** Trennung *f*. **2.** (Auf-, Ein-, Zer)Teilung *f*: *~ of powers pol.* Gewaltenteilung *f*. **sep·a·ra·tism** ['~rətɪzəm] *s* *pol.* Separatismus *m*. '**sep·a·ra·tist** *pol.* I *s* Separatist(in). II *adj* separatistisch.

Sep·tem·ber [sep'tembə] *s* September *m*: *in ~* im September.

se·quel ['si:kwəl] *s* **1.** Nachfolgefilm *m*, -roman *m*. **2.** *fig.* Folge *f* (*to* von *od.* *gen*); Nachspiel *n*.

se·quence ['si:kwəns] *s* **1.** (Aufeinander)Folge *f*: *the ~ of events* der Ablauf der Ereignisse; *~ of tenses* Zeitenfolge. **2.** (Reihen)Folge *f*: *in ~* der Reihe nach. **3.** Folge *f*, Reihe *f*, Serie *f*: *~ of wins* Siegesserie. **4.** *Film, TV*: Sequenz *f*, Take *m*, *n*.

se·quoi·a [sɪ'kwɔɪə] *s* ♀ Mammutbaum *m*.

se·ra ['sɪərə] *pl von* **serum**.

ser·e·nade [,serə'neɪd] ♪ I *s* Serenade *f*; Ständchen *n*. II *v/t* j-m ein Ständchen bringen.

se·rene [sɪ'ri:n] *adj* □ **1.** heiter, klar (*Himmel, Wetter etc*). **2.** heiter, gelassen (*Person, Gemüt etc*). **3.** *His* ♀ *Highness* S-e Durchlaucht. **se·ren·i·ty** [sɪ'renətɪ] *s* Heiterkeit *f*; Gelassenheit *f*.

serf [sɜːf] *s* *hist.* Leibeigene *m*, *f*.

ser·geant ['sɑːdʒənt] *s* **1.** ✕ Feldwebel *m*. **2.** Wachtmeister *m*.

se·ri·al ['sɪərɪəl] I *s* **1.** (*Rundfunk-, Fernseh*)Serie *f*; Fortsetzungsroman *m*. II *adj* □ **2.** Serien...: *~ novel* Fortsetzungsroman *m*. **3.** serienmäßig, Serien...: *~ number* Seriennummer *f*; ♱ Fabrikationsnummer *f*. '**se·ri·al·ize** *v/t* in Fortsetzungen veröffentlichen *od.* senden.

se·ries ['sɪərɪz] *pl* **-ries** *s* **1.** Serie *f*, Reihe *f*, Folge *f*. **2.** (*Rundfunk-, Fernseh- etc*)Serie *f*, (*Buch-, Vortrags- etc*) Reihe *f*.

se·ri·ous ['sɪərɪəs] *adj* **1.** ernst. **2.** ernsthaft, (*Angebot etc a.*) seriös; (*Ratschlag etc*) ernstgemeint: *are you ~?* ist das dein Ernst?; meinst du das im Ernst?; *be ~ about doing s.th.* et. wirklich tun wollen. **3.** ernsthaft, ernstlich (*Schwierigkeiten*), schwer (*Krankheit, Schaden, Verbrechen etc*), schwer, ernstlich (*Bedenken*); ernstzunehmend (*Rivale etc*). '**se·ri·ous·ly** *adv* ernst(haft, -lich); im Ernst: *~ ill* ernstlich *od.* schwer krank; *take ~* j-n, et. ernst nehmen. '**se·ri·ous·ness** *s* **1.** Ernst *m*. **2.** Ernsthaftigkeit *f*, Seriosität *f*. **3.** Schwere *f*.

ser·mon ['sɜːmən] *s* **1.** *eccl.* Predigt *f*. **2.** (*Moral-, Straf*)Predigt *f*. '**ser·mon·ize** *v/i* Moralpredigten halten.

ser·rat·ed [sɪ'reɪtɪd] *adj* gezackt.

se·rum ['sɪərəm] *pl* **-rums**, **-ra** ['~rə] *s* Serum *n*.

ser·vant ['sɜːvənt] *s* Diener(in) (*a. fig.*); Dienstbote *m*, -mädchen *n*: → *civil servant*.

serve [sɜːv] **I** v/t **1.** j-m, s-m Land etc dienen. **2.** j-n, et. versorgen (**with** mit). **3.** a. ~ **up** Essen servieren; Alkohol ausschenken: ~ **s.o.** (**with**) **s.th.** j-m et. servieren. **4.** j-n (im Laden) bedienen: **are you being ~d?** werden Sie schon bedient? **5.** Amtszeit etc durchlaufen; ⚖ Strafe veɪbeßen. **6.** e-m Zweck dienen, Zweck erfüllen. **7.** ⚖ Vorladung etc zustellen (**on s.o.** j-m). **8.** ~ **s.o. right** F j-m (ganz) recht geschehen. **II** v/i **9.** bsd. ✕ dienen (**under** unter dat): ~ **on a committee** e-m Ausschuß angehören. **10.** servieren. **11.** dienen (**as, for** als): ~ **to do s.th.** dazu dienen, et. zu tun. **12.** Tennis etc: aufschlagen: **XY to** ~ Aufschlag XY. **III** s **13.** Tennis etc: Aufschlag m. **'serv·er** s **1.** Servierlöffel m: (**pair of**) **salad ~s** pl Salatbesteck n. **2.** eccl. Meßdiener m, Ministrant m. **3.** Tennis etc: Aufschläger(in).

ser·vice ['sɜːvɪs] **I** s **1.** a) Dienst m (to an dat): **can I be of any ~ to you?** kann ich Ihnen irgendwie helfen?; **do s.o. a ~** j-m e-n Dienst erweisen; **give good ~** gute Dienste leisten; b) Dienstleistung f (a. ✝). **2.** Service m; Bedienung f. **3.** (Post-, Staats-, Telefon- etc)Dienst m: → **civil service, secret 1. 4.** pl ✕ Streitkräfte pl. **5.** Betrieb m: **be out of** ~ außer Betrieb sein. **6.** eccl. Gottesdienst m. **7.** (Kaffee- etc)Service n. **8.** ⚙ Wartung f, mot. Inspektion f: **put one's car in for a** ~ s-n Wagen zur Inspektion bringen. **9.** ⚖ Zustellung f (e-r Vorladung etc). **10.** Tennis etc: Aufschlag m. **II** v/t **11.** ⚙ warten: **my car is being ~d** mein Wagen ist bei der Inspektion. **'ser·vice·a·ble** adj □ **1.** brauchbar. **2.** strapazierfähig.

ser·vice| a·re·a s Br. (Autobahn)Raststätte f. ~ **charge** s Bedienung(szuschlag m) f. **~·man** ['~mən] s (irr man) **1.** Militärangehörige m. **2.** Wartungstechniker m. ~ **sta·tion** s **1.** (Reparatur)Werkstatt f. **2.** Tankstelle f.

ser·vi·ette [ˌsɜːvɪˈet] s bsd. Br. Serviette f.

ser·vile ['sɜːvaɪl] adj □ servil, unterwürfig; (Gehorsam) sklavisch. **ser·vil·i·ty** [~ˈvɪlətɪ] s Servilität f, Unterwürfigkeit f.

serv·ing ['sɜːvɪŋ] s Portion f.

ser·vi·tude ['sɜːvɪtjuːd] s Knechtschaft f.

ses·a·me ['sesəmɪ] s ♣ Sesam m.

ses·sion ['seʃn] s **1.** ⚖, parl. a) Sitzung f: **be in** ~ tagen, b) Sitzungsperiode f. **2.** (einzelne) Sitzung, ✱ a. (einzelne) Behandlung.

set [set] **I** s **1.** Satz m (Briefmarken, Werkzeuge etc), (Möbel- etc)Garnitur f, (Tee- etc)Service n. **2.** (Fernseh-, Rundfunk)Apparat m, (-)Gerät n. **3.** thea. Bühnenbild n: ~ **designer** Bühnenbildner(in). **4.** Tennis etc: Satz m: ~ **point** Satzball m. **5.** (Personen)Kreis m. **6.** (Kopf- etc)Haltung f. **II** adj **7.** festgesetzt, -gelegt: ~ **books** pl (od. **reading**) pflichtlektüre f; ~ **lunch** (od. **meal**) Br. Menü n. **8. be ~ on doing s.th.** (fest) entschlossen sein, et. zu tun; **be dead ~ against s.th.** strikt gegen et. sein. **9.** bereit, fertig: **be all** ~ startklar sein; **be all ~ for the journey** reisefertig sein. **10.** starr (Ansichten, Lächeln etc). **III** v/t (irr) **11.** stellen, setzen, legen: → **fire 1, music 1, trap 1. 12. the novel is** ~ **in** der Roman spielt in (dat). **13.** in e-n Zustand versetzen: ~ **s.o. free** j-n auf freien Fuß setzen, j-n freilassen; → **right 4,** etc. **14.** veranlassen (**doing** zu tun): ~ **going** in Gang setzen; ~ **s.o. thinking** j-m zu denken geben; j-m e-n Denkanstoß od. Denkanstöße geben; → **ball¹ 1. 15.** ⚙ einstellen, Uhr stellen (**by** nach), Wecker stellen (**for** auf acc). **16.** Tisch decken. **17.** Preis, Termin etc festsetzen, -legen; Rekord aufstellen; Präzedenzfall schaffen: → **example 1. 18.** Edelstein fassen (**in** in dat); Ring etc besetzen (**with** mit). **19.** ✱ Knochen einrichten. **20.** Aufgabe, Frage stellen. **IV** v/i (irr) **21.** untergehen (Sonne etc). **22.** fest werden (Flüssiges), (Zement etc a.) erstarren.

Verbindungen mit Präpositionen:

set| a·bout v/i **1.** sich machen an (acc), et. in Angriff nehmen: ~ **doing s.th.** sich daranmachen, et. zu tun. **2.** F herfallen über (acc). ~ **a·gainst** v/t **1. set one's face** (od. **o.s.**) **against s.th.** sich e-r Sache widersetzen. **2.** j-n aufhetzen gegen. **3.** fig. et. gegenüberstellen (dat): ~ im Vergleich zu. ~ **on** v/t Hund, Polizei hetzen auf (acc).

Verbindungen mit Adverbien:

set| a·part v/t j-n unterscheiden, abheben (**from** von). ~ **a·side** v/t **1.** Geld beiseite legen; Zeit reservieren, einpla-

severity

nen. **2.** *Plan etc* fallenlassen. **3.** ⚖️ *Urteil etc* aufheben. **~ back** *v/t* **1.** verzögern; *j-n, et.* zurückwerfen (**by two months** um zwei Monate). **2.** *the car set me back £ 500* F der Wagen hat mich 500 Pfund gekostet *od.* um 500 Pfund ärmer gemacht. **~ by → set aside 1. ~ down** *v/t* **1.** *Last* absetzen, abstellen, *Fahrgast* absetzen, aussteigen lassen. **2.** (schriftlich) niederlegen. **~ in** *v/i* einsetzen (*Winter etc*). **~ off** I *v/t* **1.** hervorheben, betonen, besser zur Geltung bringen. **2.** *Alarm, Lawine, Streik etc* auslösen. **3.** *Sprengladung* zur Explosion bringen; *Feuerwerk* abbrennen. II *v/i* **4.** **→ set out 3. ~ out** I *v/t* **1.** arrangieren, herrichten, *a. Schachfiguren etc* aufstellen. **2.** (schriftlich) darstellen. II *v/i* **3.** aufbrechen, sich aufmachen. **4. ~ to do s.th.** sich daranmachen, et. zu tun. **~ up** I *v/t* **1.** *Denkmal, Straßensperren etc* errichten; *Gerät etc* aufbauen. **2.** *Firma etc* gründen: **→ shop 1. 3.** *et.* auslösen, verursachen. **4.** *j-n* versorgen (**with** mit): **be well with** (*od.* **for**) **reading** mit Lektüre eingedeckt sein. **5.** *Rekord* aufstellen. **6.** F in e-e Falle locken, reinlegen. **7. set o.s. up → 9. 8. set o.s. up as** sich ausgeben für *od.* als; sich aufspielen als. II *v/i* **9.** sich niederlassen (**as** als).

'set|·back *s* Rückschlag *m* (**to** für). **~ square** *s* Winkel *m*, Zeichendreieck *n*.

set·tee [se'ti:] *s* Sofa *n*.

set·ting ['setıŋ] *s* **1.** (*Gold- etc*)Fassung *f*. **2.** Untergang *m* (*der Sonne etc*). **3.** Umgebung *f*; Schauplatz *m* (*e-s Films etc*): **the novel has its ~ in →** set **12.**

set·tle ['setl] I *v/i* **1.** (**on**) sich niederlassen (auf *acc, dat*) *od.* setzen (auf *acc*). **2.** sich beruhigen (*Person, Magen etc*), sich legen (*Aufregung etc*): **→ dust 1. 3.** sich niederlassen (*in* in *e-r Stadt etc*). **4.** sich einigen. **5.** sich setzen (*Kaffee etc*); sich senken (*Boden etc*). **6. ~ for** sich zufriedengeben *od.* begnügen mit. **7. ~ into** sich eingewöhnen in (*dat*). **8. ~ on** sich einigen auf (*acc*). II *v/t* **9. ~ o.s. →** 1. **10.** *j-n, Nerven etc* beruhigen. **11.** vereinbaren; *Frage etc* klären, entscheiden: **that ~s it** damit ist der Fall erledigt. **12.** *Streit etc* beilegen. **13.** *Land* besiedeln; *Leute* ansiedeln. **14.** *Rechnung* begleichen, bezahlen; *Konto*

ausgleichen; *Schaden* regulieren: **→ account 5. 15.** *s-e Angelegenheiten* in Ordnung bringen.

Verbindungen mit Adverbien:

set·tle| back *v/i* sich (gemütlich) zurücklehnen. **~ down** I *v/i* **1. →** settle 1, 2. **2.** seßhaft werden. **3. ~ in →** settle 7. II *v/t* **4. →** settle 10. **5. settle o.s. down → settle** 1. **~ in** *v/i* sich eingewöhnen; sich einleben. **~ up** *v/i* **1.** (be)zahlen. **2.** abrechnen (**with** mit) (*a. fig.*).

set·tled ['setld] *adj* **1.** beständig (*Wetter*). **2.** fest (*Ansichten etc*).

set·tle·ment ['setlmənt] *s* **1.** Vereinbarung *f*; Klärung *f*. **2.** Beilegung *f*. **3.** Einigung *f*: **reach a ~** sich einigen (**with** mit). **4.** Siedlung *f*; Besiedlung *f*. **5.** Begleichung *f*, Bezahlung *f*; Ausgleich *m*; Abfindung *f*.

set·tler ['setlə] *s* Siedler(in).

'set-up *s* **1.** Aufbau *m*, Organisation *f*. **2.** Zustände *pl*. **3.** F abgekartete Sache; Falle *f*.

sev·en ['sevn] I *adj* sieben. II *s* Sieben *f*: **~ of hearts** Herzsieben. **sev·en·fold** ['sevnfəʊld] I *adj* siebenfach. II *adv* siebenfach, um das Siebenfache: **increase ~** (sich) versiebenfachen. **sev·en·teen** [,sevn'ti:n] *adj* siebzehn. **sev·en·teenth** [,-θ] *adj* siebzehnt. **sev·enth** ['sevnθ] I *adj* **1.** siebente(r, -s), siebte(r, -s). II *s* **2.** der, die, das Sieb(en)te: **the ~ of May** der 7. Mai. **3.** Sieb(en)tel *n*. **'seventh·ly** *adv* sieb(en)tens. **sev·en·ti·eth** ['sevntıəθ] *adj* siebzigst.

'sev·en·time *adj* siebenfach.

sev·en·ty ['sevntı] I *adj* siebzig. II *s* Siebzig *f*: **be in one's seventies** in den Siebzigern sein; **in the seventies** in den siebziger Jahren (*e-s Jahrhunderts*).

sev·er ['sevə] I *v/t* **1.** durchtrennen; abtrennen (**from** von). **2.** *Beziehungen etc* abbrechen. II *v/i* **3.** (zer)reißen.

sev·er·al ['sevrəl] I *adj* mehrere. II *s* mehrere *pl*: **~ of you.**

sev·er·ance ['sevərəns] *s* **1.** Durch-, Abtrennung *f*. **2.** *fig.* Abbruch *m*. **~ pay** *s* ✝ Abfindung *f*.

se·vere [sı'vıə] *adj* □ **1.** schwer (*Verletzung, Rückschlag etc*), stark (*Schmerzen*), hart, streng (*Winter*). **2.** streng (*Person, Disziplin etc*). **3.** scharf (*Kritik*): **his ~st critic** a. sein ärgster Kritiker. **se·ver·i·ty** [sı'verətı] *s* **1.** Schwere *f*, Stärke *f*, Härte *f*, Strenge *f*. **2.** Schärfe *f*.

sew [səʊ] (*mst irr*) **I** *v/t* nähen: **~ on** annähen; **~ up** ver-, zunähen; *F Handel etc* perfekt machen. **II** *v/i* nähen.

sew·age ['suːɪdʒ] *s* Abwasser *n*.

sew·er [sʊə] *s* Abwasserkanal *m*, Kloake *f*. **'sew·er·age** *s* Kanalisation *f*.

sew·ing ['səʊɪŋ] **I** *s* **1.** Nähen *n*. **2.** Näharbeit *f*, Näherei *f*. **II** *adj* **3.** Näh...: **~ machine**.

sewn [səʊn] *pp von* **sew**.

sex [seks] *s* **1.** Geschlecht *n*: **of both ~es** beiderlei Geschlechts; **the fair (gentle od. weaker, opposite, stronger)** ~ das schöne (schwache *od.* zarte, andere, starke) Geschlecht. **2.** Sex *m*: a) Sexualität *f*, b) Sex-Appeal *m*, c) Geschlechtsverkehr *m*: **have ~ with** schlafen mit. **II** *adj* **3.** a) Sexual...: **~ crime (life, etc)**; **~ object** Sexual-, Lustobjekt *n*, b) Geschlechts...: **~ organ, etc**, c) Sex...: **~ bomb (film, etc)**; **~ appeal** Sex-Appeal *m*.

sex·ism ['seksɪzəm] *s* Sexismus *m*. **'sex·ist I** *s* Sexist(in). **II** *adj* sexistisch.

sex·tet(te) [seks'tet] *s* ♪ Sextett *n*.

sex·ton ['sekstən] *s* *eccl.* Küster *m* (u. Totengräber *m*).

sex·u·al ['seksjʊəl] *adj* □ sexuell, Sexual..., geschlechtlich, Geschlechts...: **~ intercourse** Geschlechtsverkehr *m*.

sex·u·al·i·ty [ˌ~'ælətɪ] *s* Sexualität *f*.

sex·y ['seksɪ] *adj* □ F sexy, (*a. Gang etc*) aufreizend.

shab·by ['ʃæbɪ] *adj* □ *allg.* schäbig.

shack [ʃæk] **I** *s* Hütte *f*, Baracke *f*. **II** *v/i*: **~ up** F zs.-leben (**with** mit).

shack·les ['ʃæklz] *s pl* Fesseln *pl*, Ketten *pl* (*beide a. fig.*).

shade [ʃeɪd] **I** *s* **1.** Schatten *m*: **put in(to) the ~** *fig.* in den Schatten stellen. **2.** (*Lampen*)Schirm *m*. **3.** *pl*, *a.* **pair of ~s** F Sonnenbrille *f*. **4.** (Farb)Ton *m*. **5.** *fig.* Nuance *f*: **~ of meaning** Bedeutungsnuance *f*. **6.** **a** ~ *fig.* ein kleines bißchen: **a** ~ **(too) loud** e-e Spur zu laut. **II** *v/t* **7.** abschirmen (**from** gegen *Licht etc*). **III** *v/i* **8.** *a.* ~ **off** (allmählich) übergehen (**into** in *acc*).

shad·ow ['ʃædəʊ] **I** *s* **1.** Schatten *m*: **be in s.o.'s ~** *fig.* in j-s Schatten stehen; **be only a ~ of one's former self** *fig.* nur noch ein Schatten s-r selbst sein; **cast a**

~ **over** (*od. on*) *fig.* e-n Schatten werfen auf (*acc*). **2.** *fig.* Schatten *m* (*Person*). **3.** **there's not a** (*od. the*) ~ **of doubt about it** *fig.* daran besteht nicht der geringste Zweifel. **II** *v/t* **4.** j-n beschatten. **~ cab·i·net** *s pol.* Schattenkabinett *n*.

shad·ow·y ['ʃædəʊɪ] *adj* **1.** schattig, dunkel. **2.** *fig.* geheimnisvoll, -umwittert.

shad·y ['ʃeɪdɪ] *adj* **1.** schattig; schattenspendend. **2.** F zwielichtig (*Person*), zweifelhaft (*Geschäft etc*).

shaft [ʃɑːft] *s* **1.** (*Pfeil- etc*)Schaft *m*. **2.** (*Hammer- etc*)Stiel *m*. **3.** (*Aufzugs-, Bergwerks- etc*)Schacht *m*.

shag·gy ['ʃægɪ] *adj* □ zottig, zott(e)lig.

shake [ʃeɪk] **I** *s* **1.** Schütteln *n*: **with a ~ of one's head** mit e-m Kopfschütteln; **give s.th. a good ~** et. gut durchschütteln; **in two ~s, in half a ~** F sofort. **2.** Shake *m*, Mixgetränk *n*. **3.** **he's got the ~s** F er hat den *od.* e-n Tatterich. **4.** **be no great ~s** F nicht gerade umwerfend sein (**at** in *dat*; **as** als). **II** *v/i* (*irr*) **5.** wackeln; zittern (**with** vor *dat*): **~ with laughter** sich vor Lachen schütteln. **6.** **let's ~ on it** F Hand drauf! **III** *v/t* (*irr*) **7.** schütteln: **~ one's head** den Kopf schütteln; **~ one's fist at s.o.** j-m mit der Faust drohen; **~ a leg** F Dampf *od.* Tempo machen; → **hand** 1. **8.** *fig.* a) *j-n* erschüttern: **he was badly ~n by the accident** der Unfall hat ihn arg mitgenommen, b) *j-s Glauben etc* erschüttern.

Verbindungen mit Adverbien:

shake| down F **I** *v/i* **1.** sich eingewöhnen *od.* einleben. **2.** kampieren (**on the floor** auf dem Fußboden). **II** *v/t* **3.** *bsd. Am.* j-n ausnehmen *od.* erpressen. **4.** *Am.* j-n filzen, durchsuchen (**for** nach). **~ off** *v/t* Staub, *Verfolger etc* abschütteln, *Besucher, Erkältung etc* loswerden. **~ out** *v/t* ausschütteln. **~ up** *v/t* **1.** *Kissen etc* aufschütteln. **2.** *Flasche etc* durchschütteln. **3.** → **shake** 8a.

'shake-down *s* F **1.** (Not)Lager *n*. **2.** *bsd. Am.* Gaunerei *f*; Erpressung *f*. **3.** *Am.* Filzung *f*, Durchsuchung *f*.

shak·en ['ʃeɪkən] *pp von* **shake**. **'shak·er** *s* Shaker *m*, Mixbecher *m*; *Am.* (*Salz-*)Streuer *m*.

'shake-up *s*: **there's been a big ~ in our firm** F in unserer Firma ist kräftig aufgeräumt worden.

shak·y ['ʃeɪkɪ] *adj* □ wack(e)lig (*Person, Stuhl etc*).

shale [ʃeɪl] *s geol.* Schiefer *m*.

shall [ʃæl] *v/aux (irr)* **1.** *Futur: ich* werde, *wir* werden. **2.** *in (Entscheidungs)Fragen*: soll *ich ...?*, sollen *wir ...?: ~ we go?* gehen wir?

shal·low ['ʃæləʊ] **I** *adj* □ seicht, flach (*beide a. fig.*). **II** *s*, *oft pl* seichte *od.* flache Stelle, Untiefe *f*.

sham [ʃæm] **I** *s 1.* Farce *f*. **2.** Heuchelei *f*. **II** *adj* **3.** unecht, falsch (*Juwelen etc*), vorgetäuscht, geheuchelt (*Mitgefühl etc*). **III** *v/t* **4.** Mitgefühl *etc* vortäuschen, heucheln, *Krankheit etc* simulieren. **IV** *v/i* **5.** sich verstellen, heucheln: *he's only ~ming* er tut nur so.

sham·bles ['ʃæmblz] *s pl (mst sg konstruiert)*: **the room was** (*in*) **a** ~ I das Zimmer war das reinste Schlachtfeld.

shame [ʃeɪm] **I** *s 1.* Scham(gefühl *n*) *f*: *have you got no ~?* schämst du dich vor gar nichts? **2.** Schande *f*: *~! pfui!*; *~ on you!* schäm dich!; pfui!; *put to ~ →* 4, 5. **3.** *what a ~!* (wie) schade!; *it's a ~* (es ist) schade; → *crying* 1. **II** *v/t* **4.** Schande machen (*dat*). **5.** beschämen. **'~faced** *adj* □ betreten, verlegen.

shame·ful ['ʃeɪmfʊl] *adj* □ **1.** beschämend. **2.** schändlich. **'shame·less** *adj* □ **1.** schamlos. **2.** unverschämt.

sham·poo [ʃæm'puː] **I** *s* Shampoo(n) *n*, Schampon *n*, Schampun *n (alle a. für Teppiche etc*), Haarwaschmittel *n*. **II** *v/t* Teppich *etc* shampoonieren, schamponieren, schampunieren: *~ one's hair* sich den Kopf *od.* die Haare waschen.

sham·rock ['ʃæmrɒk] *s* Shamrock *m*, Kleeblatt *n* (*Wahrzeichen Irlands*).

shan·dy ['ʃændɪ] *s* Bier *n* mit Zitronenlimonade.

shang·hai [ˌʃæŋ'haɪ] *v/t*: ~ *s.o.* *into doing s.th.* F j-n zwingen *od.* mit e-m Trick dazu bringen, et. zu tun.

shank [ʃæŋk] *s 1.* ⊕ Schaft *m (e-s Bohrers etc*). **2.** Hachse *f (beim Schlachttier*).

shan't [ʃɑːnt] F *für* **shall not**.

shan·ty¹ ['ʃæntɪ] *s* Hütte *f*, Baracke *f*.

shan·ty² [~] *s* Shanty *n*, Seemannslied *n*. **'shan·ty·town** *s* Bidonville *n* (*Slumviertel*).

shape [ʃeɪp] **I** *s 1.* Form *f*: *in the ~ of in* Form (*gen*) (*a. fig.*); *triangular in ~*

dreieckig; *take ~ fig.* Gestalt annehmen. **2.** Gestalt *f (Person*). **3.** *be in good (bad)* ~ (*körperlich, geistig*) in guter (schlechter) Verfassung sein; in gutem (schlechtem) Zustand sein (*Gebäude etc*). **II** *v/t* **3.** Ton *etc* formen (*into* zu); *et.* formen (*from* aus); *fig. j-n, j-s Charakter etc* formen, prägen: *~d like a* ... ...förmig. **III** *v/i* **4.** *mst* ~ *up* F sich *gut etc* machen (*Person*): *things are shaping up nicely* es sieht nicht schlecht aus. **shaped** *adj* geformt, ...förmig. **'shape·less** *adj* □ **1.** weit; ausgebeult (*Kleidungsstück*). **2.** unförmig (*Person, Gegenstand*). **'shape·ly** *adj* wohlgeformt (*Beine etc*), wohlproportioniert (*Figur*).

shard [ʃɑːd] *s* Scherbe *f*.

share [ʃeə] **I** *s 1.* Anteil *m (in, of an dat*): *go* ~*s* F teilen; *have a (no)* ~ *in* (nicht) beteiligt sein an (*dat*). **2.** ♥ *bsd. Br.* Aktie *f*. **II** *v/t* **3.** *et.* teilen (*a. fig.*), sich *et.* teilen (*with* mit): *we* ~ *an apartment* (*bsd. Br. a flat*) wir leben in e-r Wohngemeinschaft; *they* ~*d second place* sie kamen gemeinsam auf den zweiten Platz. **4.** *mst* ~ *out* verteilen (*among, between* an *acc*, unter *acc*). **III** *v/i* **5.** teilen: ~ *in* sich teilen in (*acc*). **shared** *adj* gemeinsam, Gemeinschafts...

'share·hold·er *s* ♥ *bsd. Br.* Aktionär(in). **'~·out** *s* Verteilung *f*.

shark [ʃɑːk] *s 1. ichth.* Hai(fisch) *m*. **2.** F (*Kredit- etc*)Hai *m*.

sharp [ʃɑːp] **I** *adj* □ **1.** scharf (*Messer etc, a. Gesichtszüge, Kurve etc*); spitz (*Nadel, Nase etc*). **2.** *fig.* scharf: a) deutlich (*Gegensatz, Umrisse etc*), b) herb (*Geschmack*), c) schneidend (*Befehl, Stimme etc*), d) heftig (*Schmerz etc*), (*a. Frost, Wind*) schneidend, e) spitz (*Bemerkung, Zunge*), f) schnell (*Tempo etc*), g) jäh, plötzlich: *brake* ~*ly* scharf bremsen. **3.** *fig.* scharf (*Augen, Verstand etc*), scharfsinnig, gescheit (*Person*). **4.** ~ *practice* unsaubere Geschäfte *pl*. **II** *adv* **5.** *at three o'clock* ~ Punkt 3 (Uhr). **6.** ♪ zu hoch: *sing* ~. **7.** *look* ~ F sich beeilen: *look* ~*!* Tempo!

sharp·en ['ʃɑːpən] *v/t* **1.** *Messer etc* schärfen, schleifen. **2.** *Bleistift etc* spitzen. **'sharp·en·er** *s* (*Bleistift*)Spitzer *m*. **'sharp·ness** *s* **1.** Schärfe *f (a. fig.)*. **2.** *fig.* Scharfsinn *m*.

'**sharp‚shoot‚er** s Scharfschütze m.

shat [ʃæt] pret u. pp von **shit**.

shat‚ter ['ʃætə] I v/t **1.** zerschmettern, -schlagen, -trümmern. **2.** fig. Hoffnungen, Träume etc zerstören. **3.** F j-n schocken. **4.** F j-n schlauchen. II v/i **5.** zerspringen, (Glas a.) zersplittern. '**~‚proof** adj splitterfrei, -sicher.

shave [ʃeɪv] I v/i **1.** sich rasieren. II v/t **2.** j-n rasieren. **3.** sich die Beine etc rasieren: ~ off sich den Bart abrasieren; Holz abhobeln. **4.** j-n, et. streifen. III s **5.** Rasur f: **have a ~** → 1; **that was a close ~** das war knapp, das hätte ins Auge gehen können. '**shav‚en** adj kahlgeschoren. '**shav‚er** s (bsd. elektrischer) Rasierapparat. '**shav‚ing** I s **1.** Rasieren n. **2.** pl Späne pl. II adj **3.** Rasier...: ~ **brush** Rasierpinsel m; ~ **cream** Rasiercreme f; ~ **foam** Rasierschaum m; ~ **soap** Rasierseife f.

shawl [ʃɔːl] s **1.** Umhängetuch n. **2.** Kopftuch n.

she [ʃiː] I pron sie. II s Sie f: a) Mädchen n, Frau f, b) zo. Weibchen n. III adj in Zssgn zo. ...weibchen n: **~bear** Bärin f.

sheaf [ʃiːf] pl **sheaves** [ʃiːvz] s **1.** ✐ Garbe f. **2.** (Papier- etc)Bündel n.

shear [ʃɪə] I v/t (mst irr) Schaf scheren. II s pl, a. **pair of ~s** (große) Schere.

sheath [ʃiːθ] pl **sheaths** [ʃiːðz] s **1.** (Schwert- etc)Scheide f. **2.** Kondom n, m. **3.** → **sheathing**. **sheathe** [ʃiːð] v/t **1.** Schwert etc in die Scheide stecken. **2.** ⊙ umhüllen, verkleiden, Kabel, Rohr ummanteln. '**sheath‚ing** s ⊙ Umhüllung f, Verkleidung f, Mantel m.

sheath knife s (irr **knife**) Fahrtenmesser n.

sheaves [ʃiːvz] pl von **sheaf**.

she‚bang [ʃɪˈbæŋ] s: **the whole ~** bsd. Am. F der ganze Laden; die ganze Chose.

shed¹ [ʃed] v/t (irr) **1.** Blut, Tränen etc vergießen. **2.** → **light**¹ 1. **3.** biol. Blätter etc verlieren, a. Geweih abwerfen: ~ **its skin** sich häuten; ~ **a few pounds** ein paar Pfund abnehmen. **4.** fig. Gewohnheit, Hemmungen etc ablegen.

shed² [~] s (Geräte etc)Schuppen m; (Kuh- etc)Stall m.

she'd [ʃiːd] F für **she had; she would**.

sheen [ʃiːn] s Glanz m.

sheep [ʃiːp] pl **sheep** s zo. Schaf n (a. fig. Person): **make ~'s eyes at s.o.** j-n anschmachten. '**~‚dog** s Schäferhund m.

sheep‚ish ['ʃiːpɪʃ] adj □ verlegen.

'**sheep‚skin** s Schaffell n.

sheer [ʃɪə] I adj **1.** bloß, rein: **by ~ coincidence** rein zufällig. **2.** steil, (fast) senkrecht. **3.** hauchdünn (Stoff). II adv **4.** → 2.

sheet [ʃiːt] s **1.** Bettuch n, (Bett)Laken n, Leintuch n: **(as) white as a ~** kreidebleich. **2.** Bogen m, Blatt n (Papier). **3.** (Glas)Scheibe f. **4.** **the rain was coming down in ~s** es regnete in Strömen. **5.** weite (Eis- etc)Fläche. ~ **light‚ning** s Wetterleuchten n. ~ **mu‚sic** s Notenblätter pl.

sheik(h) [ʃeɪk] s Scheich m. '**sheik(h)‚dom** s Scheichtum n.

shelf [ʃelf] pl **shelves** [ʃelvz] s (Bücheretc)Brett n, (-)Bord n: **shelves** pl Regal n; **she has been left on the ~** fig. F sie ist sitzengeblieben. ~ **life** s ✝ Haltbarkeit f.

shell [ʃel] I s **1.** (Austern-, Eier- etc)Schale f, (Erbsen- etc)Hülse f, Muschel(-schale) f, (Schnecken)Haus n, (Schildkröten- etc)Panzer m: **come out of one's ~** fig. aus sich herausgehen. **2.** ✗ Granate f. **3.** ✐, ✗ Rumpf m. **4.** Rohbau m; Gemäuer n, Außenmauern pl. II v/t **5.** schälen, enthülsen. **6.** ✗ mit Granaten beschießen. **7.** (a. v/i) ~ **out** F blechen.

she'll [ʃiːl] F für **she will**.

'**shell‚fish** pl -fish s zo. Schal(en)tier n.

shel‚ter ['ʃeltə] I s **1.** Unterstand m; ✗ Bunker m; Wartehäuschen n (an Bushaltestelle etc); (Obdachlosen- etc)Unterkunft f: → **air-raid**. **2.** Schutz m; Unterkunft f: **provide ~ for** Obdach bieten od. gewähren (dat); **run for ~** Schutz suchen; **take ~** sich unterstellen (under unter dat). II v/t **3.** schützen (from vor dat): **a ~ed life** ein behütetes Leben. III v/i **4.** sich unterstellen.

shelve [ʃelv] v/t **1.** Bücher (in ein Regal) einstellen. **2.** fig. Plan etc aufschieben, zurückstellen.

shelves [ʃelvz] pl von **shelf**.

shelv‚ing ['ʃelvɪŋ] s Regale pl.

she‚nan‚i‚gans [ʃɪˈnænɪɡənz] s pl F Blödsinn m, Unfug m.

shep·herd ['ʃepəd] **I** s Schäfer m. **II** v/t j-n führen.

sher·bet ['ʃɜːbət] s **1.** Brausepulver n. **2.** bsd. Am. → **sorbet** 1.

sher·iff ['ʃerɪf] s Sheriff m.

sher·ry ['ʃerɪ] s Sherry m.

shield [ʃiːld] **I** s Schild m. **II** v/t j-n schützen (**from** vor dat); b.s. j-n decken.

shift [ʃɪft] **I** v/i **1.** sich bewegen: ~ **on** one's chair (ungeduldig etc) auf s-m Stuhl hin u. her rutschen. **2.** umspringen (Wind). **3.** fig. sich verlagern od. verschieben od. wandeln. **4.** F rasen. **5.** → **gear** 1. **II** v/t **6.** et. bewegen, schieben, Möbelstück a. (ver)rücken. **7.** Schuld, Verantwortung (ab)schieben, abwälzen (**onto** auf acc). **8.** Fleck etc entfernen; et. loswerden. **9.** → **gear** 1. **III** s **10.** Verlagerung f, Verschiebung f, Wandel m. **11.** ♀ Schicht f (Zeit u. Arbeiter). ~ **key** s Umschalttaste ⌨ (e-r Schreibmaschine). ~ **work·er** s Schichtarbeiter(in).

shift·y ['ʃɪftɪ] adj □ verschlagen (Blick etc); zwielichtig (Charakter).

shil·ling ['ʃɪlɪŋ] s Br. hist. Schilling m.

shil·ly-shal·ly ['ʃɪlɪˌʃælɪ] v/i F sich nicht entscheiden können.

shim·mer ['ʃɪmə] **I** v/i schimmern; (Luft) flimmern. **II** s Schimmer m; Flimmern n.

shin [ʃɪn] **I** s anat. Schienbein n. **II** v/i: ~ **up** (**down**) Baum etc hinauf-(herunter)klettern: ~ **up** → **shin** I.

shine [ʃaɪn] **I** v/i (irr) **1.** scheinen (Sonne etc), leuchten (Lampe etc). **2.** glänzen (**with** vor dat; fig. **at** in dat). **II** v/t (irr) **3.** pret u. pp **shined** Schuhe etc polieren. **4.** ~ **a torch** (bsd. Am. **flashlight**) **into** mit e-r Taschenlampe leuchten in (acc). **III** s **5.** Glanz m: **give** one's **shoes** a ~ s-e Schuhe polieren; **take** a ~ **to** s.o. F j-n sofort mögen.

shin·gle¹ ['ʃɪŋgl] **I** s (Dach)Schindel f. **II** v/t mit Schindeln decken.

shin·gle² [~] s grobe Kieselsteine: ~ **beach** Kieselstrand m.

shin·gles ['ʃɪŋglz] s pl (sg konstruiert) ♀ Gürtelrose f.

shin·gly ['ʃɪŋglɪ] adj kieselig: ~ **beach** Kieselstrand m.

shin·y ['ʃaɪnɪ] adj glänzend, (Ärmel etc a.) abgewetzt, blank.

ship [ʃɪp] **I** s (a. Raum)Schiff n: **when** my ~ **comes home** (od. **in**) fig. wenn ich das große Los ziehe. **II** v/t verschiffen; allg. verfrachten, -senden. '~**board** s: **on** ~ an Bord. '~**build·er** s Schiff(s)bauer m.

ship·ment s **1.** Ladung f. **2.** Verschiffung f; allg. Verfrachtung f, Versand m.

'**ship**,**own·er** s Reeder m, (bsd. Binnenschiffahrt a.) Schiffseigner m.

ship·per ['ʃɪpə] s Spediteur m. '**ship·ping** s **1.** → **shipment** 2. **2.** a) Schiffahrt f: ~ **forecast** Seewetterbericht m, b) coll. Schiffsbestand m (e-s Landes).

'**ship**|**·shape** adj tadellos in Ordnung. '~**·wreck I** s a) Schiffbruch m: **in a** ~ bei e-m Schiffbruch; **suffer** ~ Schiffbruch erleiden (a. fig.), b) Wrack n. **II** v/t: **be** ~**ed** Schiffbruch erleiden; ~**ed** schiffbrüchig. '~**·yard** s (Schiffs)Werft f.

shirk [ʃɜːk] v/i u. v/t sich drücken (vor dat). '**shirk·er** s Drückeberger(in).

shirt [ʃɜːt] s Hemd n: **keep** one's ~ **on** F sich nicht aufregen; → **bet** 4. '~**·sleeve I** adj hemdsärmelig. **II** s pl: **in** one's ~**s** in Hemdsärmeln, hemdsärmelig.

shirt·y ['ʃɜːtɪ] adj F: **get** ~ **with** s.o. j-n anschnauzen; **there's no need to get** ~ du mußt mich nicht gleich anschnauzen.

shit [ʃɪt] **I** s **1.** V Scheiße f: **be in the** ~ fig. in der Scheiße sitzen. **2.** **have** (**go for**) a ~ V scheißen (gehen). **3.** **he's got the** ~**s** V er hat Dünnschiß od. die Scheißerei. **4.** fig. V Scheiß m: **talk** ~ Scheiß reden. **5.** fig. V Arschloch n. **6.** sl. Shit n (Haschisch). **II** v/i (mst irr) **7.** V scheißen. **III** v/t (mst irr) **8.** V vollscheißen, scheißen in (acc): ~ **o.s.** sich vollscheißen; fig. sich vor Angst fast in die Hosen scheißen.

shiv·er ['ʃɪvə] **I** v/i zittern (**with** vor dat). **II** s Schauer m: **the sight sent** ~**s** (**up and**) **down my spine** bei dem Anblick überlief es mich eiskalt; **he's got the** ~**s** er hat Schüttelfrost; **spiders give me the** ~**s** F ich hab' e-n Horror vor Spinnen.

shoal¹ [ʃəʊl] s Schwarm m (Fische): ~**s pl of** Schwärme pl von (Touristen etc).

shoal² [~] s Untiefe f; Sandbank f.

shock¹ [ʃɒk] **I** s **1.** Wucht f (e-r Explosion, e-s Schlags etc). **2.** Schock m (a. ♀): **be in a state of** (od. **suffer from**) ~ unter Schock stehen; **come as** (od. **be**) **a** ~ **to**

s.o. ein Schock für j-n sein. **3.** ⚡ Schlag *m*, (*a.* ⚡ Elektro)Schock *m*. **II** *v/t* **4.** schockieren, empören. **5.** *j-m* e-n Schock versetzen: *be ~ed at* (*od. by*) erschüttert sein über (*acc*).

shock² [~] *s* (*~ of hair* Haar)Schopf *m*.

shock ab·sorb·er *s mot.* Stoßdämpfer *m*.

shock·er ['ʃɒkə] *s* F Schocker *m* (*Film, Person etc*). **'shock·ing** *adj* □ **1.** schockierend, anstößig. **2.** erschütternd. **3.** F scheußlich.

'shock·proof *adj* stoßfest, -sicher. **~ ther·a·py**, **~ treat·ment** *s* ⚕ Schocktherapie *f.* **-behandlung** *f.* **~ wave** *s* Druckwelle *f*: *send ~s through fig.* erschüttern.

shod [ʃɒd] *pret u. pp von* shoe.

shod·dy ['ʃɒdɪ] *adj* □ **1.** minderwertig (*Ware*), schlampig (*Arbeit*). **2.** gemein, schäbig (*Trick etc*).

shoe [ʃuː] **I** *s* **1.** Schuh *m*: *be in s.o.'s ~s fig.* in j-s Haut stecken; *know where the ~ pinches fig.* wissen, wo der Schuh drückt; *step into* (*od. fill*) *s.o.'s ~s fig.* j-s Stelle einnehmen. **2.** (Huf)Eisen *n.* **II** *v/t* (*mst irr*) **3.** Pferd beschlagen. **'~·black** *s* Schuhputzer *m*. **'~·box** *s* Schuhkarton *m*, -schachtel *f.* **'~·horn** *s* Schuhlöffel *m.* **'~·lace** *s* Schnürsenkel *m.* **'~·mak·er** *s* Schuhmacher *m*, Schuster *m.* **'~·string** *s* Schnürsenkel *m*: *start on a ~ fig.* praktisch mit nichts anfangen. **'~·tree** *s* Schuhspanner *m*.

shone [ʃɒn] *pret u. pp von* shine.

shoo [ʃuː] *v/t* j-n, Vögel etc (ver)scheuchen.

shook [ʃʊk] *pret von* shake.

shoot [ʃuːt] **I** *s* **1.** ♀ Trieb *m.* **2.** Jagd *f*; Jagd(revier *n*) *f.* **II** *v/t* (*irr*) **3.** schießen mit (*e-m Gewehr etc*). **4.** *Pfeil etc* abfeuern, abschießen (*at* auf *acc*): *shoot a glance at* e-n schnellen Blick werfen auf (*acc*); *~ questions at s.o.* j-n mit Fragen bombardieren; → *bolt¹* 1. **5.** a) *hunt.* schießen, erlegen; → *the bull Am.* F plaudern, plauschen, b) anschießen, c) niederschießen, d) *a.* **~ dead** erschießen: → *o.s.* sich erschießen. **6.** *Riegel* vorschieben. **7.** *Film etc* drehen. *a. phot.* j-n aufnehmen. **8.** → *light¹* 3. **III** *v/i* (*irr*) **9.** schießen (*at* auf *acc*): *~ at goal* (*Sport*) aufs Tor schießen. **10.** *go somewhere to ~* wohin auf die Jagd

gehen. **11.** schießen, rasen. **12.** drehen, filmen. **13.** ♀ treiben.

Verbindungen mit Adverbien:

shoot| down *v/t* **1.** *j-n* niederschießen. **2.** *j-n, Flugzeug etc* abschießen. **3.** F *Antrag etc* abschmettern, *j-n a.* abfahren lassen. **~ off** *v/t Waffe* abfeuern, -schießen: **~ one's mouth** F quatschen (*Geheimnisse verraten*); blöd daherreden. **~ out** *v/t*: *shoot it out* sich e-e Schießerei liefern (*with* mit). **~ up** *v/i* in die Höhe schießen (*Flammen, Kind etc*), in die Höhe schnellen (*Preise*).

shoot·er ['ʃuːtə] *s bsd. Br. sl.* Schießeisen *n*.

shoot·ing ['ʃuːtɪŋ] **I** *s* **1.** Schießen *n*; Schießerei *f.* **2.** Erschießung *f.* Anschlag *m.* **3.** *Film, TV:* Dreharbeiten *pl*, Aufnahmen *pl.* **II** *adj* **4.** stechend (*Schmerz*). **~ gal·ler·y** *s* Schießbude *f.* **~ match** *s*: *the whole ~* F die ganze Chose. **~ range** *s* Schießstand *m.* **~ star** *s ast.* Sternschnuppe *f*.

shop [ʃɒp] **I** *s* **1.** Laden *m*, Geschäft *n*: *set up ~ as* F sich niederlassen als; *shut up ~* F (den Laden) dichtmachen. **2.** Werkstatt *f.* Betrieb *m*, Werk *n*: *talk ~* fachsimpeln; → *closed* (*open*) *shop*. **II** *v/i* **4.** *go ~ping* einkaufen gehen; **~ around** sich informieren, die Preise vergleichen; **~ for** sich umsehen nach. **III** *v/t* **5.** *bsd. Br. sl.* j-n verpfeifen. **~ as·sist·ant** *s Br.* Verkäufer(in). **~ floor** *s* Arbeiter *pl* (*Ggs. Management*). **~ keep·er** *s* Ladenbesitzer(in), -inhaber(in). **'~·lift·er** *s* Ladendieb(in). **'~·lift·ing** *s* Ladendiebstahl *m*.

shop·per ['ʃɒpə] *s* Käufer(in). **'shop·ping I** *s* **1.** Einkaufen *n*: *do one's ~* einkaufen, (s-e) Einkäufe machen. **2.** Einkäufe *pl* (*Sachen*). **II** *adj* **3.** Einkaufs...: **~ bag** Einkaufsbeutel *m*, -tasche *f*; **~ cen·ter** (*bsd. Br.* **~ cen·tre**) Einkaufszentrum *n*; **~ list** Einkaufsliste *f*, -zettel *m*; **~ mall** *Am.* Einkaufszentrum *n*; **~ street** Geschäfts-, Ladenstraße *f*; → *spree*.

'shop·'soiled *adj bsd. Br. Ware:* angestaubt (*a. fig. Ansichten etc*); angestoßen. **~ stew·ard** *s* ✠ gewerkschaftlicher Vertrauensmann. **'~·talk** *s* Fachsimpelei *f.* **~ win·dow** *s* Schaufenster *n*, Auslage *f.* **'~·worn** *Am.* → **shop-soiled.**

shore¹ [ʃɔː] *s* Küste *f*; (*See*)Ufer *n*: **on ~ ⚓** an Land; **~ leave ⚓** Landurlaub *m*.

shore² [~] **I** *s* Stützbalken *m*, Strebe(balken *m*) *f*. **II** *v/t mst* **~ up** (ab)stützen; *fig.* *Währung etc* stützen.

shorn [ʃɔːn] *pp von* **shear**.

short [ʃɔːt] **I** *adj* (□ → **shortly**) **1.** räumlich, zeitlich: kurz: *a* **~** *time ago* vor kurzer Zeit, vor kurzem; **~** *and sweet* F kurz u. bündig; **~** *holiday* (*bsd. Am.* **vacation**) Kurzurlaub *m*; **~** *story* Short story *f*, Kurzgeschichte *f*; Novelle *f*; **be ~** *for* die Kurzform sein von; **cut ~** *Urlaub etc* abbrechen; → *notice* 3, *run* 1, *shrift*, *story* 1, *work* 1. **2.** klein (*Person*). **3.** *be* **~** *of* nicht genügend ... haben; *be in* **~** *supply* ⚓ knapp sein; → *cash* 2, *money*. **4.** barsch (*with* zu), kurz angebunden. **II** *adv* **5.** plötzlich, abrupt: *be caught* (*od.* *taken*) **~** *bsd. Br.* F dringend mal (verschwinden) müssen; *stop* **~** *of* (*od.* *at*) zurückschrecken vor (*dat*); *stop* **~** *of doing s.th.* davor zurückschrecken, et. zu tun. **6.** *fall* **~** *of* et. nicht erreichen, *den Anforderungen etc* nicht entsprechen; *run* **~** knapp werden, zur Neige gehen; *we are running* **~** *of bread* uns geht das Brot aus. *sell* **~** *j-n, et.* unterschätzen. **7.** **~** *of* a) räumlich vor (*dat*): *three miles* **~** *of London*, b) *fig.* außer. **III** *s* **8.** *he is called Bill for* **~** er wird kurz Bill genannt; *(in* **~** kurz(um). **9.** *pl, a.* **pair of ~s** Shorts *pl*; *bsd. Am.* (Herren)Unterhose *f*. **10.** *Br.* F Kurze *m*, Schnaps *m*. **11.** ⚡ F Kurze *m*. **12.** F Kurzfilm *m*. **IV** *v/t* **13.** ⚡ F e-n Kurzen verursachen in (*dat*); kurzschließen. **V** *v/i* **14.** ⚡ F e-n Kurzen haben. '**short·age** *s* Knappheit *f*, Mangel *m* (**of** an *dat*).

,**short·'change** *v/t* **1.** *j-m* zuwenig (Wechselgeld) herausgeben. **2.** F *j-n* übers Ohr hauen. **~ cir·cuit** *s* ⚡ Kurzschluß *m*. **~·'cir·cuit I** *v/t* **1.** ⚡ e-n Kurzschluß verursachen in (*dat*); kurzschließen. **2.** *fig. et. umgehen.* **II** *v/i* **3.** ⚡ e-n Kurzschluß haben. **~·'com·ings** *s pl* Unzulänglichkeiten *pl*, Mängel *pl*, (*a. e-r Person*) Fehler *pl*. **~ cut** *s* **1.** Abkürzung(sweg *m*) *f*: *take a* **~** abkürzen. **2.** *fig.* abgekürztes Verfahren.

short·en ['ʃɔːtn] **I** *v/t* kürzen, *Kleidungsstück a.* kürzer machen, *Text a.*

zs.-streichen, *Leben etc* verkürzen. **II** *v/i* kürzer werden.

'**short|·fall** *s* Defizit *n*. ,**~·'haired** *adj* kurzhaarig. '**~·hand** *s* Kurzschrift *f*, Stenographie *f*: *do* **~** stenographieren; *take down in* **~** *et.* (mit)stenographieren; **~** *typist* Stenotypistin *f*. ,**~·'hand·ed** *adj* knapp an Personal *od.* Arbeitskräften.

short·ie ['ʃɔːtɪ] *s* Kleine *m*, *f*, *contp.* Zwerg *m*.

short| list *s*: *be on the* **~** *Br.* in der engeren Wahl sein. '**~·list** *v/t Br.* in die engere Wahl ziehen. ,**~·'lived** *adj* kurzlebig, *fig. a.* von kurzer Dauer.

short·ly ['ʃɔːtlɪ] *adv* **1.** bald: **~** *after* kurz danach. **2.** in kurzen Worten. **3.** barsch. '**short·ness** *s* **1.** Kürze *f*. **2.** Barschheit *f*. **3.** → **shortage**.

,**short|·'range** *adj* **1.** ✕, ✈ Nah..., Kurzstrecken... **2.** kurzfristig. ,**~·'sight·ed** *adj* □ **~·list** *s* ⚡ kurzsichtig (*a. fig.*). ,**~·'sleeved** *adj* kurzärm(e)lig. '**~·staffed** → **shorthanded**. ,**~·'tempered** *adj* aufbrausend, hitzig. '**~·term** *adj* kurzfristig, -zeitig: **~** *memory* Kurzzeitgedächtnis *n*. **~** *time* *s* ⚓ Kurzarbeit *f*: *be on* (*od.* *work*) **~** kurzarbeiten. **~ wave** *s* ⚡, *phys.* Kurzwelle *f*. '**~·wave** *adj* Kurzwellen... **~·wind·ed** [,~'wɪndɪd] *adj* □ kurzatmig.

short·y → **shortie**.

shot¹ [ʃɒt] **I** *pret u. pp von* **shoot**. **II** *adj*: *be* (*od.* *get*) **~** *of* F *j-n, et.* los sein (loswerden).

shot² [~] *s* **1.** Schuß *m*: *like a* **~** blitzschnell; sofort; **~** *across the bows* Schuß vor den Bug (*a. fig.*); **~** *in the dark fig.* Schuß ins Blaue; **~** *in the leg* Beinschuß; *call the* **~s** F das Sagen haben. **2.** (*Fußball etc*) Schuß *m*, (*Basketball etc*) Wurf *m*, (*Tennis etc*) Schlag *m*. **3.** *guter etc* Schütze: *big* **~** F hohes Tier. **4.** Schrot *m, n*. **5.** *Kugelstoßen*: Kugel *f*. **6.** F Versuch *m*: *at the first* **~** beim ersten Versuch; *I'll have a* **~** *at it* ich probier's mal. **7.** a) *Film, TV*: Aufnahme *f*; Einstellung *f*, b) *phot.* F Schnappschuß *m*, Aufnahme *f*. **8.** ✍ F Spritze *f*. '**~·gun** *s* Schrotflinte *f*: **~** *wed·ding* F Mußheirat *f*. **~ put** *s Leichtathletik*: Kugelstoßen *n*. '**~·put·ter** *s* Kugelstoßer(in).

should [ʃʊd] **1.** *pret von* **shall**, *a. allg. ich* sollte, *du* solltest *etc*: **he ~ be home by then** er müßte bis dahin wieder zu Hause sein. **2.** *konditional*: ich würde, wir würden: **I ~ go if ...; →** **like²** 1.

shoul·der ['ʃəʊldə] **I** s **1.** Schulter f: **~ to ~** Schulter an Schulter (*a. fig.*); **a ~ to cry on** e-e Schulter zum Ausweinen; **give s.o. the cold ~** j-m die kalte Schulter zeigen; **put one's ~ to the wheel** *fig.* sich mächtig ins Zeug legen; → **chip** 1, **rub** 3. **II** v/t **2.** schultern; *fig.* Kosten, Verantwortung *etc* übernehmen. **3.** (mit der Schulter) stoßen: **~ one's way through** sich e-n Weg bahnen durch. **~ bag** s Schulter-, Umhängetasche f. **~ blade** s *anat.* Schulterblatt n. **~ strap** s Träger m (e-s Kleids etc); Tragriemen m.

shouldn't ['ʃʊdnt] *F für* should not.

shout [ʃaʊt] **I** v/i rufen, schreien (*for* nach; *for help* um Hilfe): **~ at s.o.** j-n anschreien. **II** v/t rufen, schreien: **~ down** j-n niederbrüllen; **~ o.s. hoarse** sich heiser schreien; → **rooftop**. **III** s Ruf m, Schrei m: **~s** *pl* of joy Freudengeschrei n; **it's my ~** *Br.* F das ist meine Runde, ich bin dran. **'shout·ing** s Schreien n, Geschrei n: **it's all over bar the ~** *Br.* F die Sache ist so gut wie gelaufen.

shove [ʃʌv] **I** v/t **1.** stoßen, schubsen: **~ about** (*od.* **around**) j-n herumschubsen (*a. fig.*). **2.** *et.* schieben, stopfen (**into** in acc). **II** v/i **3.** stoßen, schubsen: **~ off** (vom Ufer) abstoßen; **~ off!** F schieb ab!; **~ over** *bsd. Br.* F rutschen. **III** s **4.** Stoß m, Schubs m.

shov·el ['ʃʌvl] **I** s Schaufel f. **II** v/t *pret od. pp* **-eled**, *bsd. Br.* **-elled** schaufeln: **~ food into one's mouth** Essen in sich hineinschaufeln.

show [ʃəʊ] **I** s **1.** *thea. etc* Vorstellung f; Show f; (*Rundfunk, TV*) Sendung f: **steal the ~ from s.o.** *fig.* j-m die Schau stehlen. **2.** Ausstellung f: **be on ~** ausgestellt *od.* zu besichtigen sein. **3.** Zurschaustellung f, Demonstration f. **4.** *by* **~ of hands** durch Handzeichen. **5.** Schau f: **make a ~ of** Anteilnahme etc heucheln; **make a ~ of interest** sich interessiert geben. **6.** F *gute etc* Leistung: **put up a poor ~** e-e schwache Leistung zeigen. **7.** F Laden m: **run the ~** den Laden schmeißen. **II** *adj* **8.** Mu-

ster...: **~ house**. **III** v/t (*mst irr*) **9.** *a.* fig. Gefühle *etc* zeigen, Fahrkarte *etc a.* vorzeigen, Zeit *etc* anzeigen (*Uhr etc*): **s.o. how to do s.th.** j-m zeigen, wie man et. macht; **~ o.s.** sich erweisen als; → **door** 1, *etc.* **10.** j-n bringen, führen (**to** zu): **~ s.o. (a)round** (*od.* **over**) **the house** j-n durchs Haus führen, j-m das Haus zeigen. **11.** ausstellen, zeigen. **12.** zeigen: a) *thea. etc* vorführen, b) *TV* bringen. **IV** v/i (*mst irr*) **13.** zu sehen sein: **it ~s** man sieht es. **14.** be **~ing** gezeigt werden, laufen.

Verbindungen mit Adverbien:

show| a·round v/t herumführen. **~ in** v/t herein-, hineinführen, -bringen. **~ off** **I** v/t **1.** angeben *od.* protzen mit (**to** vor *dat*). **2.** Figur *etc* vorteilhaft zur Geltung bringen. **II** v/i **3.** angeben, protzen. **~ out** v/t heraus-, hinausführen, -bringen. **~ round** → **show around**. **~ up** **I** v/t **1.** herauf-, hinaufführen, -bringen. **2.** sichtbar machen. **3.** j-n entlarven; *et.* aufdecken. **4.** *bsd. Br.* j-n in Verlegenheit bringen. **II** v/i **5.** zu sehen sein. **6.** F kommen; aufkreuzen, -tauchen.

show| biz s F, **~ busi·ness** s Showbusineß n, -geschäft n. **'~case** s Schaukasten m, Vitrine f. **'~down** s Kraftprobe f, Machtprobe f.

show·er ['ʃaʊə] **I** s **1.** (*Regen- etc*)Schauer m; (*Funken-, Kugel- etc*)Regen m; (*Geschoß-, Stein*)Hagel m; (*Wasser-, Wort- etc*)Schwall m. **2.** Dusche f: **have** (*od.* **take**) **a ~** duschen. **II** v/i **3.** duschen. **III** v/t **4.** **~ s.o. with s.th., ~ s.th. on s.o.** j-n mit et. überschütten, *fig. a.* j-n mit et. überhäufen. **~ cab·i·net** s Duschkabine f. **~ cur·tain** s Duschvorhang m.

'show|·girl s Revuegirl n. **~ jump·er** s *Sport*: Springreiter(in). **~ jump·ing** s Springreiten n. **~·man** ['~mən] s (*irr* **man**) **1.** *thea. etc* Produzent m. **2.** Schausteller m. **3.** *fig.* Showman m.

shown [ʃəʊn] *pp von* **show**.

'show|-off s F Angeber(in). **'~·piece** s **1.** Ausstellungsstück n. **2.** Parade-, Prunkstück n. **~·room** ['~rʊm] s Ausstellungsraum m.

show·y ['ʃəʊɪ] □ auffallend (*Person*), (*Farben, Kleidung etc a.*) auffällig.

shrank [ʃræŋk] *pret von* **shrink**.

shred [ʃred] **I** s **1.** Fetzen m: *be in ~s* zerfetzt sein; *fig.* ruiniert sein (*Ruf etc*); *tear to ~s* zerfetzen; *fig. Argument etc* zerpflücken, -reißen; *Stück etc* verreißen. **2.** Schnitzel n, m, Stückchen n. *fig. not a ~ of doubt* nicht der geringste Zweifel; *there is not a ~ of truth in this story* an dieser Geschichte ist kein Wort wahr. **II** v/t (a. irr) **4.** zerfetzen; in den Papier- od. Reißwolf geben. **5.** in (schmale) Streifen schneiden, *Gemüse a.* schnitzeln, *Fleisch a.* schnetzeln. **'shred·der** s **1.** Papier-, Reißwolf m. **2.** Schnitzelmaschine f; Schnitzelwerk n.

shrewd [ʃruːd] adj □ scharfsinnig, klug, (*Beobachter*) scharf: *that was a ~ guess* das war gut geraten.

shriek [ʃriːk] **I** s (schriller) Schrei: *~ of terror* Entsetzensschrei; *~s pl of laughter* kreischendes Gelächter. **II** v/i (gellend) aufschreien (*with* vor *dat*): *~ with laughter* vor Lachen kreischen.

shrift [ʃrɪft] s: *give s.o. short ~* kurzen Prozeß mit j-m machen.

shrill [ʃrɪl] adj □ **1.** schrill. **2** *fig.* heftig, scharf (*Kritik etc*).

shrimp [ʃrɪmp] s **1.** zo. Garnele f. **2.** *fig. contp.* Knirps m.

shrine [ʃraɪn] s (Reliquien)Schrein m.

shrink [ʃrɪŋk] **I** v/i (irr) **1.** (zs.-, ein-)schrumpfen (a. fig.), (*Stoff etc a.*) einlaufen, -gehen. **2** *fig.* abnehmen. **3.** *fig.* zurückschrecken (*from* vor *dat*): *~ from doing s.th.* davor zurückschrecken, et. zu tun. **II** v/t (irr) **4.** (zs.-, ein)schrumpfen lassen, *Stoff etc a.* einlaufen od. -gehen lassen. **III** s **5.** F Klapsdoktor m. **'shrink·age** s **1.** Schrumpfung f (a. fig.), Einlaufen n, -gehen n. **2.** *fig.* Abnahme f. **'shrink·ing** adj: *~ violet* F schüchternes Pflänzchen.

shriv·el [ʃrɪvl] v/i u. v/t pret u. pp *-eled, bsd. Br. -elled* runz(e)lig werden (lassen): *~(l)ed* runz(e)lig.

shroud [ʃraʊd] **I** s **1.** Leichentuch n. **2.** *fig.* Schleier m (*of secrecy* des Geheimnisses). **II** v/t **3.** *be ~ed in* in Nebel etc gehüllt sein: *be ~ed in mystery* geheimnisumwittert sein.

Shrove Tues·day [ʃrəʊv] s Faschings-, Fastnachtsdienstag m.

shrub [ʃrʌb] s Busch m, Strauch m. **'shrub·ber·y** s Busch-, Strauchwerk n.

shrug [ʃrʌg] **I** v/t **1.** *~ one's shoulders*

→ **3.** **2.** *~ off fig. et.* mit e-m Achsel- od. Schulterzucken abtun, achselzuckend hinweggehen über (*acc*). **II** v/i **3.** mit den Achseln od. Schultern zucken. **III** s **4.** *a. ~ of one's shoulders* Achsel-, Schulterzucken n: *give a ~* → **3.**

shrunk [ʃrʌŋk] pret u. pp von **shrink.**

shuck [ʃʌk] bsd. Am. **I** s **1.** Hülse f, Schote f; Schale f. **II** v/t enthülsen; schälen. **III** s: *~s!* F Quatsch!; Mist!

shud·der [ˈʃʌdə] **I** v/i schaudern (*at* bei): *~ to think of* mit Schaudern denken an (*acc*). **II** s Schauder m.

shuf·fle [ˈʃʌfl] **I** v/t **1.** *~ one's feet* → **3.** **2.** *Karten* mischen. **II** v/i **3.** schlurfen. **4.** *Kartenspiel:* mischen. **III** s **5.** Schlurfen n, schlurfender Gang. **6.** Mischen n. **'~·board** s Shuffleboard n (*Spiel*).

shun [ʃʌn] v/t j-n, et. meiden.

shunt [ʃʌnt] v/t **1.** *Zug etc* rangieren, verschieben. **2.** *~ off* F j-n abschieben (*to* in *acc*, nach).

shut [ʃʌt] (irr) **I** v/t **1.** *Fenster, Tür etc* zumachen, *a. Fabrik etc* schließen: → *mouth* **1**, *trap* **2**, **2.** *j-n* einschließen (*in* in *acc, dat*): *~ one's finger in the door* sich den Finger in der Tür einklemmen. **II** v/i **3.** schließen (*a. Laden etc*), zugehen.

Verbindungen mit Adverbien:

shut | **a·way** v/t **1.** *et.* wegschließen. **2.** *shut o.s. away* sich einigeln (*in* in *dat*). *~ down* v/t *Fabrik etc* schließen, (*für immer a.*) stillegen. **II** v/i schließen (*Fabrik etc*). *~ off* v/t **1.** *Gas, Maschine etc* abstellen. **2.** abtrennen; fernhalten (*from* von). **II** v/i **3.** (sich) abschalten. *~ out* v/t *Gedanken, Schmerz etc* verdrängen. *~ up* v/t **1.** *Geschäft* schließen: → *shop* **1**. **2.** j-n einsperren (*in* in *acc, dat*). **3.** F j-m den Mund stopfen. **II** v/i **4.** *~!* F halt die Klappe!

'shut·down s Schließung f, (*für immer a.*) Stillegung f. **'~·eye** s F Schlaf m: *get some ~* ein paar Stunden schlafen.

shut·ter [ˈʃʌtə] s **1.** Fensterladen m. **2.** *phot.* Verschluß m: *~ speed* Belichtung(szeit) f. **'shut·tered** adj: *~ windows pl* Fenster pl mit Fensterläden; *geschlossene Fensterläden*; *~ room* Zimmer n mit geschlossenen Fensterläden.

shut·tle [ˈʃʌtl] **I** s **1.** → *shuttle bus* (*service, train*). **2.** (*Raum*)Fähre f,

(-)Transporter *m*. **3.** → **shuttlecock. II** *v/t* **4.** hin- u. herbefördern. **~ bus** *s* im Pendelverkehr eingesetzter Bus. '**~-cock** *s* Federball *m*. **~ ser·vice** *s* Pendelverkehr *m*. **~ train** *s* Pendelzug *m*.

shy [ʃaɪ] **I** *adj* □ **1.** scheu (*Tier*), (*Lächeln, Mensch a.*) schüchtern (*of* gegenüber): **fight ~ of** *e-r Sache* aus dem Weg gehen; **fight ~ of doing s.th.** sich hüten, et. zu tun. **II** *v/i* **2.** scheuen (*at* vor *dat*) (*Pferd etc*). **3. ~ away** *fig.* zurückschrecken (*from* vor *dat*): **~ away from doing s.th.** davor zurückschrecken, et. zu tun. '**shy·ness** *s* Scheu *f*, Schüchternheit *f*.

shy·ster ['faɪstə] *s Am.* F Winkeladvokat *m*.

Si·a·mese twins [,saɪə'miːz] *s pl* siamesische Zwillinge *pl*.

sick [sɪk] **I** *adj* **1.** krank: **be off** ~ krank (geschrieben) sein; **report** ~ sich krank melden. **2.** *be ~ bsd. Br.* sich übergeben; **he was** (*od.* **felt**) ~ ihm war schlecht; **be ~ of s.th.** F et. satt haben; **be ~ (and tired) of doing s.th.** F es (gründlich) satt haben, et. zu tun: **it makes me ~** mir wird schlecht davon, *a. fig.* es ekelt *od.* widert mich an. **3.** makaber (*Witz etc*), abartig (*Person etc*). **II** *s* **4. the ~** *pl* die Kranken *pl*. **5.** *Br.* F Kotze *f*. **~ bag** *s* ✗ Spucktüte *f*. **~ bay** *s* Krankenzimmer *n* (*e-r Schule etc*), ⚓ (Schiffs)Lazarett *n*. '**~-bed** *s* Krankenbett *n*.

sick·en ['sɪkən] **I** *v/t* *j-n* anekeln, anwidern (*beide a. fig.*). **II** *v/i* krank werden: **be ~ing for s.th.** et. ausbrüten.

sick·le ['sɪkl] *s* ⚒ Sichel *f*.

sick leave *s*: **be on ~** krank (geschrieben) sein.

sick·ly ['sɪklɪ] *adj* **1.** kränklich. **2.** matt (*Lächeln*). **3.** widerwärtig (*Geruch etc*). '**sick·ness** *s* **1.** Krankheit *f*. **2.** Übelkeit *f*.

sick·room ['~rʊm] *s* Krankenzimmer *n*.

side [saɪd] **I** *s* **1.** *allg.* Seite *f* (*a. fig.*): **at the ~ of the road** am Straßenrand; **at** (*od.* **by**) **s.o.'s ~** an j-s Seite; **~ by ~** nebeneinander; **on the ~** nebenbei *verdienen etc*; **his ~ of the story** s-e Version der Geschichte; **be on s.o.'s ~** auf j-s Seite sein *od.* stehen; **be on the right** (*wrong*) ~ **of 50** noch nicht (über) 50 sein; **have s.th. on one's ~** et. auf s-r Seite haben; **put to one ~** Geld auf die

Seite legen; **take ~s** → 4; **take to one ~** *j-n* beiseite nehmen; → **safe** I, **seamy**, **split** 1, **sunny**. **2.** *Sport:* Mannschaft *f*. **II** *adj* **3.** Seiten...: **~ door** (*road, etc*). **III** *v/i* **4.** Partei ergreifen (*with* für; *against* gegen). '**~·board** *s* **1.** Sideboard *n*. **2.** *pl Br.* Koteletten *pl*. '**~·burns** *Am.* → **sideboard** 2. '**~·car** *s* Bci-, Seitenwagen *m*. **~ dish** *s* Beilage *f*. **~ ef·fect** *s* Nebenwirkung *f*. **~ is·sue** *s* Randproblem *n*. '**~·line** *s* **1.** Nebenbeschäftigung *f*. **2.** *Sport:* Seitenlinie *f*. '**~·long** *adj u. adv*: **~ glance** Seitenblick *m*; **look at s.o.** ~ *j-n* von der Seite anschauen. '**~·sad·dle** **I** *s* Damensattel *m*. **II** *adv* im Damensitz. '**~-split·ting** *adj* zwerchfellerschütternd. **~ step** *s* Seitenschritt *m*, (*Boxen*) Seitschritt *m*, Sidestep *m*. '**~-step** **I** *v/t* **1.** *e-m Schlag* (durch e-n Seit[en]schritt) ausweichen. **2.** *fig.* *e-r Frage etc* ausweichen. **II** *v/i* **3.** e-n Seit(en)schritt machen. '**~-swipe** **I** *s*: **take a ~ at** F *j-m* e-n Seitenhieb versetzen. **II** *v/t mot. Am.* geparktes Fahrzeug *etc* streifen. '**~-track** *v/t* *j-n* ablenken; *et.* abbiegen. '**~-walk** *bsd. Am.* → **pavement** 2.

side·ward ['saɪdwəd] **I** *adj* seitlich: **~ jump** Sprung *m* zur Seite. **II** *adv* seitwärts, nach der *od.* zur Seite. **side·wards** ['~dz] → **sideward** II. '**~-ways** → **sideward.**

si·dle ['saɪdl] *v/i* (sich) schleichen (*out of* aus): **~ up to s.o.** sich an j-n heranschleichen.

siege [siːdʒ] *s* ✗ Belagerung *f*: **lay ~ to** belagern (*a. fig.*).

si·er·ra [sɪ'erə] *s* Sierra *f*.

si·es·ta [sɪ'estə] *s* Siesta *f*: **have** (*od.* **take**) **a ~** Siesta halten.

sieve [sɪv] **I** *s* Sieb *n*: **put through a ~** (durch)sieben; **he's got a memory like a ~** F er hat ein Gedächtnis wie ein Sieb. **II** *v/t* (durch)sieben: **~ out** aussieben (*from* aus).

sift [sɪft] **I** *v/t* **1.** (durch)sieben: **~ out** *fig.* herausfinden (*from* aus). **2.** *fig.* *Material etc* sichten, durchsehen. **II** *v/i* **3.** **~ through** → 2.

sigh [saɪ] *v/i* (auf)seufzen: **~ with relief** erleichtert aufatmen. **II** *s* Seufzer *m*: **~ of relief** Seufzer der Erleichterung; **breathe** (*od.* **heave**) **a ~ of relief** erleichtert aufatmen.

silicosis

sight [saɪt] **I** s **1.** Sehvermögen n: *have good* ~ gute Augen haben, gut sehen; *lose one's* ~ das Augenlicht verlieren. **2.** (An)Blick m: *at the* ~ *of* beim Anblick von (*od. gen*); *at first* ~ auf den ersten Blick; *a* ~ *for sore eyes* F e-e Augenweide; *you're a* ~ *for sore eyes* F schön, dich zu sehen; *be* (*od. look*) *a* ~ F verboten *od.* zum Abschießen aussehen; *buy* ~ *unseen* et. unbesehen kaufen; *catch* ~ *of* erblicken; *know by* ~ j-n vom Sehen kennen; *lose* ~ *of* aus den Augen verlieren. **3.** Sicht(weite) f: *be* (*with*)*in* ~ in Sicht sein (*a. fig.*); *come into* ~ in Sicht kommen; *keep out of* ~*!* paß auf, daß dich niemand sieht!; *let out of one's* ~ j-n, et. aus den Augen lassen. **4.** *mst pl* Sehenswürdigkeit f. **5.** *oft pl* Visier n: *set one's* ~*s on fig. et.* ins Auge fassen. **6.** *a* ~ F um einiges, viel besser etc. **II** *v/t* **7.** sichten. '**sight·ed** *adj* sehend.

'**sight-read** *v/t u. v/i* (*irr read*) ♪ vom Blatt singen *od.* spielen. '**~·see** *v/i*: *go* ~*ing* sich die Sehenswürdigkeiten anschauen. '**~·see·ing** s Sightseeing n, Besichtigung f von Sehenswürdigkeiten: ~ *bus* Sightseeing-Bus m; ~ *tour* Sightseeing-Tour f, (Stadt)Rundfahrt f.

sign [saɪn] **I** s **1.** *allg.* Zeichen n, A, ♪ a. Vorzeichen n, *fig. a.* Anzeichen n: ~*s pl of fatigue* Ermüdungserscheinungen pl; *all the* ~*s are that* alles deutet darauf hin, daß; *there was no* ~ *of him* von ihm war keine Spur zu sehen; *show* ~*s of* Anzeichen zeigen von (*od. gen*); *show only faint* ~*s of life* nur schwache Lebenszeichen von sich geben. **2.** (*Hinweis-, Warn- etc*)Schild n. **3.** (*Stern-, Tierkreis*)Zeichen n. **II** *v/t* **4.** unterschreiben, -zeichnen, *Bild, Buch* signieren; *Scheck* ausstellen; sich eintragen in (*acc*): → *autograph* I. **5.** *Sport*: *Spieler* verpflichten, unter Vertrag nehmen. **III** *v/i* **6.** unterschreiben, -zeichnen: ~ *for* den Empfang (*gen*) (*durch s-e Unterschrift*) bestätigen; → *dot* 2. **7.** *Sport*: (e-n Vertrag) unterschreiben (*for, with* bei).
Verbindungen mit Adverbien:
sign| **a·way** *v/t* (schriftlich) verzichten auf (*acc*). ~ **in** *v/i* sich (in e-e Anwesenheitsliste *etc*) eintragen. ~ **off** *v/i* **1.**

Rundfunk, TV: sein Programm beenden. **2.** Schluß machen (*im Brief, a. allg.*). ~ **on I** *v/t* **1.** a) → *sign* 5, b) j-n an-, einstellen, ♨ anheuern. **II** *v/i* **2.** a) → *sign* 7, b) (e-n Arbeitsvertrag) unterschreiben, ♨ anheuern. **3.** *Rundfunk, TV:* sein Programm beginnen. ~ **out** *v/i* sich (aus e-r Anwesenheitsliste *etc*) austragen. ~ **o·ver** *v/t et.* überschreiben (*to dat*). ~ **up** → *sign on* 1, 2.

sig·nal ['sɪɡnl] **I** s **1.** Signal n, Zeichen n (*beide a. fig.*): → *busy* 6. **II** *adj* □ **2.** beachtlich, un-, außergewöhnlich. **III** *v/t pret u. pp* **-naled**, *bsd. Br.* **-nalled 3.** ~ *s.o. to do s.th.* j-m (ein) Zeichen geben, et. zu tun (*a. fig.*). **4.** *fig.* Bereitschaft etc signalisieren. **IV** *v/i* **5.** ~ *for a taxi* e-m Taxi winken. ~ **box** s ⚐ *Br.*, ~ **tow·er** s ⚐ *Am.* Stellwerk n.

sig·na·ture ['sɪɡnətʃə] s Unterschrift f, (*e-s Bildes, Buchs*) Signatur f. ~ **tune** s *Rundfunk, TV:* Erkennungs-, Kennmelodie f.

'**sign·board** s (Aushänge)Schild n.

sign·er ['saɪnə] s Unterzeichnete m, f.

sig·net ring ['sɪɡnɪt] s Siegelring m.

sig·nif·i·cance [sɪɡ'nɪfɪkəns] s Bedeutung f, Wichtigkeit f: *be of great* ~ *to* von großer Bedeutung sein für. **sig'nif·i·cant** *adj* □ **1.** bedeutend, bedeutsam, wichtig. **2.** vielsagend; bezeichnend.

sig·ni·fy ['sɪɡnɪfaɪ] *v/t* **1.** bedeuten. **2.** *Meinung etc* kundtun.

sign| lan·guage s Zeichensprache f. '**~·post** s Wegweiser m.

si·lence ['saɪləns] **I** s **1.** Stille f; Schweigen n: ~*!* Ruhe!; *in* ~ schweigend; *a one--minute* ~ e-e Schweigeminute. **II** *v/t* zum Schweigen bringen (*a. fig.*). '**si·lenc·er** s **1.** Schalldämpfer m. **2.** *mot. Br.* Auspufftopf m.

si·lent ['saɪlənt] *adj* □ still, (*Gebet, a. ling. Buchstabe*) stumm; ruhig; schweigsam: ~ *film* Stummfilm m; *the* ~ *majority* die schweigende Mehrheit; ~ *partner* ⚑ *Am.* stiller Teilhaber; *be* ~ *on* sich ausschweigen über (*acc*); *remain* ~ schweigen.

sil·hou·ette [,sɪluː'et] **I** s Silhouette f. **II** *v/t*: *be* ~*d against* sich (als Silhouette) abheben gegen.

sil·i·con [,sɪlɪkən] s 🜍 Silizium n. **sil·i·cone** ['~kəʊn] s 🜍 Silikon n.

sil·i·co·sis [,sɪlɪ'kəʊsɪs] s ⚕ Staublunge f.

silk 1246

silk [sɪlk] **I** s Seide f. **II** adj Seiden...
'**~worm** s zo. Seidenraupe f.

silk·y ['sɪlkɪ] adj □ seidig (*Fell, Haare etc*), samtig (*Stimme*).

sill [sɪl] s (*Fenster*)Bank f, (-)Brett n.

sil·li·ness ['sɪlɪnɪs] s Albernheit f, Dummheit f.

sil·ly ['sɪlɪ] **I** adj albern, dumm: *don't be ~!* red doch keinen Unsinn!; *~ billy* → II; *~ season* (*Journalismus*) Sauregurkenzeit f. **II** s F Dummkopf m, Dummerchen n.

si·lo ['saɪləʊ] pl *-los* s **1.** Silo m, n. **2.** ✕ Startsilo m, n.

sil·ver ['sɪlvə] **I** s **1.** 🜛 Silber n (*a. Besteck, Geschirr*). **2.** Silber(geld n, -münzen pl) n: *three pounds in ~* drei Pfund in Silber. **II** adj **3.** silbern, Silber... **III** v/t **4.** versilbern. **~ fish** s zo. Silberfischchen n. **~ foil** s Silber-, Alu(minium)folie f; Silberpapier n. '**~haired** adj silberhaarig. **~ ju·bi·lee** s 25jähriges Jubiläum. **~ med·al** s Silbermedaille f. **~ med·al·(l)ist** s Silbermedaillengewinner(in). **~ mine** s Silbergewerk n, -mine f. **~ pa·per** s Silberpapier n. **~'plat·ed** adj versilbert. '**~smith** s Silberschmied(in). '**~ware** s Silber(besteck, -geschirr) n. **~ wed·ding** s silberne Hochzeit.

sil·ver·y ['sɪlvərɪ] adj silb(e)rig, (*Lachen*) silberhell.

sim·i·lar ['sɪmɪlə] adj ähnlich (*to dat*). **sim·i·lar·i·ty** [ˌ~'lærətɪ] s Ähnlichkeit f (*to mit*). '**sim·i·lar·ly** adv **1.** ähnlich. **2.** entsprechend.

sim·i·le ['sɪmɪlɪ] s Simile n, Vergleich m.

sim·mer ['sɪmə] **I** v/i **1.** köcheln, leicht kochen: *~ with* fig. kochen vor (*Zorn etc*), fiebern vor (*Aufregung etc*); *~ down* F sich abregen. **2.** fig. gären, schwelen. **II** s **3.** Köcheln n: *bring to a ~* zum Köcheln bringen.

sim·per ['sɪmpə] **I** v/i albern od. affektiert lächeln. **II** s albernes od. affektiertes Lächeln.

sim·ple ['sɪmpl] adj (□ → *simply*) **1.** allg. einfach, (*Aufgabe etc a.*) simpel, leicht, (*Lebensweise, Person, Stil etc a.*) schlicht, (✦ *Bruch a.*) glatt: *for the ~ reason that* aus dem einfachen Grund, weil. **2.** einfältig; naiv, leichtgläubig. **~'mind·ed** adj □ → *simple* 2.

sim·plic·i·ty [sɪm'plɪsətɪ] s **1.** Einfachheit

f, Schlichtheit f: *be ~ itself* die einfachste Sache der Welt sein. **2.** Einfältigkeit f; Naivität f, Leichtgläubigkeit f.

sim·pli·fi·ca·tion [ˌsɪmplɪfɪ'keɪʃn] s Vereinfachung f. **sim·pli·fy** ['~faɪ] v/t vereinfachen.

sim·plis·tic [sɪm'plɪstɪk] adj (*~ally*) stark vereinfachend.

sim·ply ['sɪmplɪ] adv **1.** einfach (*etc, →* *simple* 1): *to put it ~* in einfachen Worten. **2.** bloß, nur. **3.** F einfach *großartig etc*.

sim·u·late ['sɪmjʊleɪt] v/t **1.** vortäuschen, heucheln, *bsd. Krankheit* simulieren. **2.** ☉ *etc* simulieren. **,sim·u·la·tion** s **1.** Vortäuschung f, Simulieren n; Heuchelei f. **2.** ☉ *etc* Simulierung f. '**sim·u·la·tor** s **1.** Heuchler(in), Simulant(in). **2.** ☉ Simulator m.

si·mul·ta·ne·ous [ˌsɪməl'teɪnjəs] adj □ simultan, gleichzeitig: *~ interpreter* Simultandolmetscher(in).

sin [sɪn] **I** s Sünde f: *live in ~* humor. in Sünde leben; *(as) ugly as ~* häßlich wie die Nacht; *→ deadly* 1, *mortal* 3. **II** v/i sündigen: *~ against fig.* sündigen gegen, sich versündigen an (*dat*); verstoßen gegen.

since [sɪns] **I** adv **1.** a. *ever ~* seitdem, -her. **2.** inzwischen. **II** prp **3.** seit. **III** cj **4.** seit(dem). **5.** da.

sin·cere [sɪn'sɪə] adj □ aufrichtig: *Yours ~ly* Mit freundlichen Grüßen (*Briefschluß*). **sin·cer·i·ty** [~'serətɪ] s Aufrichtigkeit f: *in all ~* in aller Offenheit.

sine [saɪn] s 🜨 Sinus m.

sin·ew ['sɪnjuː] s anat. Sehne f. '**sin·ew·y** adj sehnig, (*Fleisch a.*) flechsig.

sin·ful ['sɪnfʊl] adj □ sündig, sündhaft.

sing [sɪŋ] (*irr*) **I** v/i **1.** singen. **2.** pfeifen (*Kugel, Wind etc*). **II** v/t **3.** et. singen: *~ s.o. s.th.* j-m et. (vor)singen; *~ a baby to sleep* ein Baby in den Schlaf singen.

singe [sɪndʒ] **I** v/t (sich et.) an- od. versengen. **II** s ange- od. versengte Stelle.

sing·er ['sɪŋə] s Sänger(in). '**sing·ing** **I** s Singen n, Gesang m. **II** adj: *~ lesson* Sing-, Gesangsstunde f; *~ voice* Singstimme f.

sin·gle ['sɪŋgl] adj □ **1.** einzig: *not a ~ one* kein einziger. **2.** einfach; einzeln, Einzel...: *~ room* Einzelzimmer n; *~ ticket →* 6. **3.** alleinstehend, unverheiratet: **~ mother** alleinerziehende Mutter. **II** s **4.** Single f (Schallplatte). **5.** Single m (Person). **6.** Br. einfache Fahrkarte, ✈ einfaches Ticket. **7.** mst pl Tennis etc: Einzel n: **a ~s match** ein Einzel; **men's ~s** Herreneinzel. **III** v/t **8. ~ out** sich j-n herausgreifen. **,~ -'breast·ed** adj einreihig (Anzug). **,~ file** s u. adv: (**in**) ~ im Gänsemarsch. **,~'hand·ed** adj u. adv eigenhändig, (ganz) allein. **,~'mind·ed** adj □ zielstrebig, -bewußt.

sin·glet ['sɪŋglɪt] s bsd. Br. ärmelloses Unterhemd, n (Sport) ärmelloses Trikot.

'sing·song s Singsang m.

sin·gu·lar ['sɪŋɡjʊlə] **I** adj □ **1.** ling. Singular..., Einzahl... **2.** fig. einzigartig, einmalig. **II** s **3.** ling. Singular m, Einzahl f.

sin·is·ter ['sɪnɪstə] adj □ finster, unheimlich.

sink [sɪŋk] **I** v/i (irr) **1.** sinken, untergehen: **leave s.o. to ~ or swim** j-n sich selbst überlassen. **2.** sich senken (Gebäude etc); sinken, zurückgehen (Hochwasser etc, fig. Zahl etc): → **heart** 1, **spirit** 4. **3.** sinken (**into a chair** in e-n Sessel; **to the ground** zu Boden; **to the knees** auf die Knie; **into a deep sleep** in e-n tiefen Schlaf): → **oblivion. 4. ~ in** eindringen (Flüssigkeit, a. fig. Nachricht etc). **II** v/t (irr) **5.** Schiff etc versenken. **6.** Graben etc ausheben, Brunnen etc bohren. **7.** Zähne etc vergraben, -senken (**into** in acc). **8.** Pläne etc zunichte machen. **9.** Streit etc beilegen, begraben. **10.** Geld, Arbeit etc investieren (**in, into** in acc). **III** s **11.** Spülbecken n, Spüle f; bsd. Am. Waschbecken n. **'sink·er** s Grundgewicht n (e-s Fischnetzes). **'sink·ing** adj: **I got that ~ feeling when** F mir wurde ganz anders, als.

sin·ner ['sɪnə] s Sünder(in).

si·nus ['saɪnəs] s anat. (Nasen)Nebenhöhle f. **si·nus·i·tis** [,~'saɪtɪs] s 🩺 (Nasen)Nebenhöhlenentzündung f.

Sioux [su:] pl **Sioux** [su:z] s Sioux m, f.

sip [sɪp] **I** v/t Schlückchen n: **take a ~ of** → IIa. **II** v/t a) nippen an (dat) od. von, b) schlückchenweise trinken. **III** v/i: **~ at** → IIa.

si·phon ['saɪfn] **I** s **1.** Siphon(flasche f) m. **2.** ⚗ Saugheber m. **II** v/t **3.** a. **~ off**

absaugen, Benzin abzapfen; fig. Geld, Personal etc abziehen.

sir [sɜː] s **1.** mein Herr (Anrede, oft unübersetzt): **Dear ~s** Sehr geehrte Herren (Anrede in Briefen). **2.** ♀ Br. (Adelstitel): ♀ **Winston (Churchill)**.

si·ren ['saɪərən] s Sirene f.

sir·loin steak ['sɜːlɔɪn] s Lendensteak n.

sis·sy ['sɪsɪ] s F Weichling m.

sis·ter ['sɪstə] **I** s **1.** Schwester f. **2.** eccl. (Ordens)Schwester f: ♀ **Mary** Schwester Mary. **3.** 🩺 Br. Oberschwester f. **4.** ♀ Schwester(gesellschaft) f. **II** adj **5.** Schwester...: **~ ship,** etc. **~·hood** ['~hʊd] s eccl. Schwesternschaft f.

'sis·ter-in-law pl **'sis·ters-in-law** s Schwägerin f.

sis·ter·ly ['sɪstəlɪ] adj schwesterlich.

sit [sɪt] (irr) **I** v/i **1.** sitzen: → **fence** 1, **pretty** II, **tight** 8. **2.** sich setzen. **3.** babysitten. **4.** tagen. **II** v/t **5.** j-n setzen. **6.** Br. → **sit for** 1.

Verbindungen mit Präpositionen:

sit| for v/i **1.** Prüfung ablegen, machen. **2.** j-m (Modell) sitzen: **~ one's portrait** sich porträtieren lassen. **~ on** v/i **1.** e-m **committee** e-m Ausschuß angehören. **2.** fig. sitzen auf (dat). **3.** F j-n unterbuttern.

Verbindungen mit Adverbien:

sit| a·bout, ~ a·round v/i herumsitzen. **~ back** v/i sich zurücklehnen, fig. a. die Hände in den Schoß legen. **~ down I** v/i sich setzen; sitzen: **sitting down** im Sitzen. **II** v/t **~** absetzen. **~ in** v/i **1. ~ for** j-n vertreten. **2. ~ on** als Zuhörer teilnehmen an (dat). **3.** ein Sit-in veranstalten; an e-m Sit-in teilnehmen. **~ out** v/t **1.** Tanz auslassen. **2.** bis zum Ende e-r Veranstaltung etc bleiben. **3.** das Ende (gen) abwarten; Krise etc aussitzen. **~ up I** v/i **1.** sich aufrichten od. -setzen; aufrecht sitzen: **make s.o. ~ (and take notice)** F j-n aufhorchen lassen. **2.** aufbleiben. **3. ~ (at** od. **to table** bei Tisch) Platz nehmen. **II** v/t **4.** j-n aufrichten od. -setzen.

sit|·com ['sɪtkɒm] F → **situation comedy.** ~·**down** s **1.** a. **~ strike** → **sit-in. 2.** a. **~ demonstration** Sitzblockade f. **3.** F Verschnaufpause f: **have a ~** e-e Verschnaufpause einlegen.

site [saɪt] **I** s **1.** Platz m, Ort m, Stelle f; engS. Standort m; (Ausgrabungs)Stätte

f. **2.** Baustelle f. **II** v/t **3.** placieren, ✗
Raketen etc stationieren: **be ~d** gelegen sein, liegen.

'sit-in s Sit-in n, Sitzstreik m: **stage a ~ in**
Gebäude etc besetzen.

sit·ter ['sɪtə] s **1.** *paint. etc* Modell n. **2.**
Babysitter(in). **'sit·ting I** s **1.** Sitzung f
(*a. paint. etc*). **2. read s.th. at one** (*od. a*
single) *~ et.* in 'einem Zug durchlesen.
II adj **3.** *~* **duck** fig. leichte Beute; *~*
room Wohnzimmer n.

sit·u·at·ed ['sɪtjʊeɪtɪd] adj **1. be ~** gelegen
sein, liegen. **2.** fig. **be badly ~** in e-r
schwierigen Lage sein; **be well ~** gut
situiert sein; ohne weiteres in der Lage
sein (**to do** zu tun).

sit·u·a·tion [,sɪtjʊ'eɪʃn] s **1.** fig. Lage f,
Situation f. **2.** Lage f (*e-s Hauses etc*). **3.**
~s pl vacant (wanted) Stellenangebote
pl (Stellengesuche pl). **~ com·e·dy** s
Rundfunk, TV: humorvolle Serie.

six [sɪks] **I** adj sechs. **II** s Sechs f: *~* **of**
hearts Herzsechs; **be all at ~es and**
sevens F nicht mehr wissen, wo e-m
der Kopf steht. **six·fold** [~fəʊld] **I** adj
sechsfach. **II** adv sechsfach, um das
Sechsfache: **increase ~** (sich) versechsfachen.

'six-pack s Sechserpackung f.

six·teen [,sɪks'ti:n] adj sechzehn. **,six-**
'teenth [~θ] adj sechzehnt. **sixth** [~θ] **I**
adj **1.** sechste(r, -s): *~* **sense** fig. sechster Sinn. **II** s **2.** der, die, das Sechste:
the ~ of May der 6. Mai. **3.** Sechstel n.
'sixth·ly adv sechstens. **six·ti·eth**
['~tɪəθ] adj sechzigst.

'six-time adj sechsmalig.

six·ty ['sɪkstɪ] **I** adj sechzig. **II** s Sechzig f:
be in one's sixties in den Sechzigern
sein; **in the sixties** in den sechziger
Jahren (*e-s Jahrhunderts*).

size [saɪz] **I** s **1.** Größe f, fig. a. Ausmaß
n, Umfang m: **what is the ~ of ...?** wie
groß ist ...? **2.** (*Kleider-, Schuh- etc*)
Größe f, Nummer f: **what ~ do you**
take? welche Größe tragen Sie?; **I'll cut**
him down to ~ F dem werd' ich's zeigen. **II** v/t **3.** mst *~* **up** j-n, et. abschätzen.

size·a·ble ['saɪzəbl] adj beträchtlich
(*Summe etc*).

siz·zle ['sɪzl] **I** v/i brutzeln. **II** s Brutzeln
n. **'siz·zler** s F glühendheißer Tag.

skate [skeɪt] **I** s Schlittschuh m; Roll-

schuh m. **II** v/i Schlittschuh laufen, eislaufen; Rollschuh laufen: *~* **over** (*od.*
round) *s.th.* fig. hinweggehen über
(*acc*); → **ice** 1. **'~·board** s Skateboard
n.

skat·er ['skeɪtə] s Eis-, Schlittschuhläufer(in); Rollschuhläufer(in). **'skat·ing**
adj: *~* **rink** (Kunst)Eisbahn f; Rollschuhbahn f.

ske·dad·dle [skɪ'dædl] v/i F türmen, abhauen.

skel·e·ton ['skelɪtn] **I** s **1.** Skelett n, Gerippe n (*beide a. fig. Person etc*): *~* **in the**
cupboard (*Am.* **closet**) fig. dunkler
Punkt (*in j-s Vergangenheit etc*); **have a**
~ **in the cupboard** e-e Leiche im Keller
haben. **2.** △, ✓, ⚓ Skelett n. **3.** fig.
Entwurf m; Rahmen m. **II** adj **4.** Rahmen...: *~* **plan**, etc. **5.** Not...: *~* **service**
Notdienst m. **6.** *~* **key** Hauptschlüssel
m.

skep·tic, etc bsd. Am. → **sceptic**, etc.

sketch [sketʃ] **I** s **1.** Kunst etc: Skizze f. **2.**
thea. etc Sketch m. **II** v/t **3.** skizzieren.
4. oft *~* **in** (*od. out*) fig. skizzieren, umreißen. **'sketch·y** adj □ flüchtig, oberflächlich, (*Erinnerung etc*) bruchstückhaft.

skew [skju:] **I** s: **on the ~** schief; schräg.
II v/t fig. verzerren.

skew·er ['skjuə] **I** s (Fleisch)Spieß m. **II**
v/t Fleisch aufspießen.

ski [ski:] **I** s Ski m. **II** adj Ski...: *~* **lift**, etc.
III v/i Ski fahren od. laufen.

skid [skɪd] v/i **1.** mot. schleudern. **II** s **2.**
go into a ~ mot. ins Schleudern kommen. **3.** ⚙ Rolle f: **he's on the ~s** F mit
ihm geht es abwärts.

ski·er ['ski:ə] s Skifahrer(in), -läufer(in).

skiff [skɪf] s ⚓ Skiff n, (*Rudersport a.*)
Einer m.

ski·ing ['ski:ɪŋ] s Skifahren n, -laufen n,
-sport m.

skil·ful ['skɪlfʊl] adj □ geschickt.

skill [skɪl] s **1.** Geschick n: **game of ~**
Geschicklichkeitsspiel n. **2.** Fertigkeit
f. **skilled** [~ld] adj **1.** geschickt (**at, in** in
dat). **2.** *~* **worker** Facharbeiter(in).

skil·let ['skɪlɪt] s bsd. Am. Bratpfanne f.

skill·ful Am. → **skilful**.

skim [skɪm] **I** v/t **1.** a. *~* **off** Fett etc
abschöpfen (**from** von). **2.** Milch entrahmen: **~med milk** Magermilch f. **3.**
Bericht etc überfliegen. **II** v/i **4.** *~* **over**

(*od. **through***) → 3. **~ milk** *s* Magermilch *f*.

skimp [skɪmp] **I** *v/t* sparen an (*dat*). **II** *v/i*: **~ on** → I. **'skimp·y** *adj* dürftig (*Mahlzeit, Beweise etc*); knapp (*Kleidungsstück*).

skin [skɪn] **I** *s* **1.** Haut *f* (*a. e-r Wurst, auf Milch etc*): **by the ~ of one's teeth** F mit Ach u. Krach, gerade noch; **be all ~ and bone(s)** nur noch Haut u. Knochen sein; **that's no ~ off my nose** F das juckt mich nicht; **be drenched** (*od. soaked*) **to the ~** bis auf die Haut durchnäßt *od.* naß sein; **get under s.o.'s ~** F j-m unter die Haut gehen; j-m auf den Wecker fallen; **save one's ~** F s-e Haut retten. **2.** Haut *f*; Fell *n*. **3.** (*Bananen-, Zwiebel- etc*)Schale *f*. **II** *v/t* **4.** *Tier* abhäuten: **~ s.o. alive** F j-n zur Schnecke machen. **5.** *Zwiebel etc* schälen: **keep one's ~ned** Br. F die Augen offenhalten. **6.** sich *das Knie etc* aufschürfen. **,~-'deep** *adj fig.* oberflächlich. **~ div·ing** *s* Schnorcheln *n*, Schnorcheltauchen *n*. **~ flick** F Sexfilm *m*. **'~-flint** *s* Geizhals *m*.

skin·ful ['skɪnfʊl] *s*: **he's had a ~** F er hat schwer geladen (*ist betrunken*).

skin| graft *s* Hauttransplantation *f*, -verpflanzung *f*. **'~-head** *s bsd. Br.* Skinhead *m*.

skin·ny ['skɪnɪ] *adj* dürr.

skint [skɪnt] *adj Br.* F blank, pleite.

,skin-'tight *adj* hauteng.

skip [skɪp] **I** *v/i* **1.** hüpfen. **2.** *Br.* seilhüpfen, -springen. **3.** *fig.* springen (*from one subject to another* von 'einem Thema zum andern*): **~ over** *et.* überspringen, auslassen. **4.** *a.* **~ off** F abhauen, türmen. **II** *v/t* **5.** *et.* überspringen, auslassen; *Vorlesung etc* schwänzen; *Mahlzeit* ausfallen lassen. **III** *s* **6.** Hüpfer *m*.

skip·per ['skɪpə] **I** *s* **1.** ♣ Kapitän *m*. **2.** *Sport*: Mannschaftsführer(in).

skip·ping rope ['skɪpɪŋ] *s Br.* Spring-, Sprungseil *n*.

skir·mish ['skɜːmɪʃ] *s* ✕ Geplänkel *n* (*a. fig.*).

skirt [skɜːt] **I** *s* Rock *m*. **II** *v/t* → III. **III** *v/i*: **~** (*a*)**round** *fig.* Problem *etc* umgehen. **'skirt·ing** *adj*: **~ board** *Br.* Fuß(boden)-, Scheuerleiste *f*.

skit [skɪt] *s* Parodie *f* (**on** *auf acc*): **do a ~ on** *j-n, et.* parodieren.

skive [skaɪv] *v/i Br.* F blaumachen.

skul·dug·ger·y [skʌl'dʌɡərɪ] *s* F fauler Zauber.

skulk [skʌlk] *v/i* sich herumdrücken, herumschleichen.

skull [skʌl] *s anat.* Schädel *m*: **~ and crossbones** Totenkopf *m* (*Symbol*); **can't you get it into that thick ~ of yours that ...?** F will es denn nicht in deinen Schädel, daß ...?

skunk [skʌŋk] *s* **1.** *zo.* Skunk *m*, Stinktier *n*. **2.** F Saukerl *m*.

sky [skaɪ] *s, a. pl* Himmel *m*: **in the ~** am Himmel; **the ~ is the limit** F nach oben sind keine Grenzen gesetzt; **extol** (*od. praise*) **to the skies** *j-n, et.* in den Himmel heben. **,~-'blue** *adj* himmelblau. **'~,div·er** *s Sport*: Fallschirmspringer(in). **'~,div·ing** *s* Fallschirmspringen *n*. **,~-'high** *adj u. adv* himmelhoch: **blow ~** in die Luft jagen; *fig.* Theorie *etc* über den Haufen werfen, *Argument etc* widerlegen, *Mythos* zerstören. **'~-jack** → **hijack** 1, 3. **'~,jack·er** → **hijacker** 1. **'~,jack·ing** → **hijack** 3. **'~-light** *s* Dachfenster *n*. **'~-line** *s* Skyline *f*, Silhouette *f* (*e-r Stadt*). **'~,rock·et** → **rocket** 3. **'~,scrap·er** *s* Wolkenkratzer *m*.

slab [slæb] *s* **1.** (*Stein- etc*)Platte *f*. **2.** dickes Stück (*Kuchen etc*).

slack [slæk] **I** *adj* ☐ **1.** locker (*Seil etc*). **2.** *fig.* lax (*Disziplin etc*). **3.** *fig.* lasch, nachlässig. **4.** ✝ flau. **II** *v/i* **5.** bummeln. **6.** **~ off** (*od. up*) → **slacken** 4. **'slack·en I** *v/t* **1.** lockern. **2.** *fig.* verringern: **~ speed** langsamer werden. **II** *v/i* **3.** locker werden. **4.** *a.* **~ off** *fig.* nachlassen, (*Person a.*) abbauen.

slag [slæg] *s* **1.** Schlacke *f*. **2.** *Br. sl.* Schlampe *f*.

slain [sleɪn] *pp von* **slay**.

slake [sleɪk] *v/t Kalk* löschen: **~d lime** Löschkalk *m*.

sla·lom ['slɑːləm] *s Sport*: Slalom *m*.

slam [slæm] **I** *v/t* **1.** *a.* **~ shut** *Tür etc* zuknallen, zuschlagen. **2.** *a.* **~ down** F *et.* knallen (**on** *auf acc*): **~ the brakes on** *mot.* auf die Bremse steigen. **3.** *fig.* scharf kritisieren. **II** *v/i* **4.** *a.* **~ shut** zuknallen, zuschlagen.

slan·der ['slɑːndə] **I** *s* Verleumdung *f*. **II**

v/t verleumden. **'slan·der·er** *s* Verleumder(in). **'slan·der·ous** *adj* □ verleumderisch.

slang [slæŋ] **I** *s* Slang *m*; Jargon *m*. **II** *v/t bsd. Br.* F *j-n* wüst beschimpfen. **'slang·ing** *adj*: *they had a ~ match bsd. Br.* F sie beschimpften sich wüst.

slant [slɑːnt] **I** *v/t* **1. bc ~ed toward(s)** (*od. in favo[u]r of*) *fig.* (einseitig) ausgerichtet sein auf (*acc*). **II** *s* **2. at** (*od. on*) *a ~* schräg. **3.** *fig.* Einstellung *f* (*on* zu); Ausrichtung *f*. **'slant·ing** *adj* schräg.

slap [slæp] **I** *s* **1.** Schlag *m*, Klaps *m*: *a ~ in the face* e-e Ohrfeige, *bsd. fig.* ein Schlag ins Gesicht (*for* für). **II** *v/t* **2.** schlagen: → *s.o.'s face* j-n ohrfeigen, j-m e-e runterhauen. **3.** *a. ~ down et.* klatschen (*on* auf *acc*) **III** *v/i* **4.** klatschen (*against* gegen) (*Wellen etc*). **IV** *adv* **5.** F direkt, genau. **,~·'bang** → *slap* **5.** **'~·dash** *adj* schlampig, schlud(e)rig. **'~·stick** *s thea. etc* Slapstick *m*, Klamauk *m*: *~ comedy* Slapstickkomödie *f.* **'~·up** *adj Br.* F toll (*Essen*).

slash [slæʃ] **I** *v/t* **1.** auf-, zerschlitzen: *~ one's wrists* sich die Pulsadern aufschneiden. **2.** *fig. Preise* drastisch herabsetzen; *Ausgaben etc* drastisch kürzen. **II** *v/i* **3.** *~ at* schlagen nach. **4.** peitschen (*against* an *acc*, gegen) (*Regen*). **III** *s* **5.** Hieb *m*. **6.** Schlitz *m* (*in Kleid etc*). **7.** *a. ~ mark* Schrägstrich *m*. **8.** *have* (*go for*) *a ~ Br. sl.* schiffen (gehen).

slate[1] [sleɪt] **I** *s* **1.** *geol.* Schiefer *m*. **2.** Schieferplatte *f*. **3.** Schiefertafel *f*: *put on the ~ fig. et.* anschreiben; *wipe the ~ clean fig.* reinen Tisch machen. **4.** *pol. Am.* Kandidatenliste *f.* **II** *v/t* **5.** *Dach* mit Schiefer decken. **6.** *Am. j-n* vorschlagen (*for, to be* als). **7.** *Am. et.* ansetzen, planen (*for* für).

slate[2] [~] *v/t bsd. Br.* F *Theaterstück etc* verreißen.

slaugh·ter [ˈslɔːtə] **I** *s* **1.** Schlachten *n*: *ready for ~* schlachtreif. **2.** Gemetzel *n*. **II** *v/t* **3.** *Tier* schlachten. **4.** *Menschen* niedermetzeln. **'~·house** *s* Schlachthaus *n*, -hof *m*.

slave [sleɪv] **I** *s* Sklave *m*, Sklavin *f* (*beide a. fig. of, to gen*). **II** *v/i a. ~ away* sich abplagen. **~ driv·er** *s* F Sklaventreiber *m*, Leuteschinder *m*. **~ la·bo(u)r** *s* Sklavenarbeit *f* (*a. fig.*).

slav·er [ˈslævə] *v/i* geifern. **slav·er·y** [ˈsleɪvərɪ] *s* Sklaverei *f.* **slave| trade, ~ traf·fic** *s* Sklavenhandel *m.* **slav·ish** [ˈsleɪvɪʃ] *adj* □ sklavisch. **slaw** [slɔː] *s bsd. Am.* Krautsalat *m.* **slay** [sleɪ] *v/t Am.* ermorden, umbringen. **'slay·er** *s* Mörder(in). **slea·zy** [ˈsliːzɪ] *adj* □ schäbig, heruntergekommen; anrüchig. **sled** [sled] → *sledge.* **sledge** [sledʒ] **I** *s* (*a.* Rodel)Schlitten *m.* **II** *v/i* Schlitten fahren, rodeln. **'sledge,ham·mer** *s* ⊙ Vorschlaghammer *m.* **sleek** [sliːk] *adj* □ **1.** geschmeidig (*Haar etc*). **2.** schnittig (*Auto*). **sleep** [sliːp] **I** *s* Schlaf *m*: *in one's ~* im Schlaf; *I couldn't get to ~* ich konnte nicht einschlafen; *go to ~* einschlafen (F *a.* Bein *etc*); *put to ~ Tier* einschläfern (F *a. j-n narkotisieren*). **II** *v/i* (*irr*) schlafen: *~ late* lang *od.* länger schlafen; *~ like a log* (*od. top*) F wie ein Murmeltier schlafen; *~ on Problem etc* überschlafen; *~ through Gewitter etc* verschlafen; *~ with s.o.* mit *j-m* schlafen. **III** *v/t* (*irr*) *Schlafgelegenheit* bieten für: *this tent ~s four people in* diesem Zelt können vier Leute schlafen.

Verbindungen mit Adverbien:

sleep| a·round *v/i* F rumbumsen. **~ in** *v/i* lang *od.* länger schlafen. **~ off**: *sleep it off* F *s-n* Rausch ausschlafen. **~ to·geth·er** *v/i* miteinander schlafen.

sleep·er [ˈsliːpə] *s* **1.** Schlafende *m*, *f*, Schläfer(in): *be a light* (*heavy od. sound*) *~* e-n leichten (festen) Schlaf haben. **2.** ⊞ *Br.* Schwelle *f.* **3.** ⊞ Schlafwagen *m*; Schlafwagenplatz *m.*

sleep·ing| **bag** [ˈsliːpɪŋ] *s* Schlafsack *m.* **~ car** *s* ⊞ Schlafwagen *m.* **~ part·ner** *s* ✝ *Br.* stiller Teilhaber. **~ pill** *s* Schlaftablette *f.* **~ po·lice·man** *s* (*irr man*) *mot. Br.* Rüttelschwelle *f.* **~ sick·ness** *s* ✴ Schlafkrankheit *f.* **~ tab·let** *s* Schlaftablette *f.*

sleep·less [ˈsliːplɪs] *adj* □ schlaflos (*Nacht etc*). **'sleep| walk** *v/i* schlaf-, nachtwandeln. **'~·walk·er** *s* Schlaf-, Nachtwandler(in).

sleep·y [ˈsliːpɪ] *adj* □ **1.** schläfrig, müde.

2. *fig.* verschlafen, verträumt (*Städtchen etc*). '**~head** s F Schlafmütze *f*.

sleet [sliːt] s Schneeregen *m*.

sleeve [sliːv] s **1.** Ärmel *m*: **have** (*od.* **keep**) **s.th. up one's ~** *fig.* et. auf Lager *od.* in petto haben; **laugh up one's ~** *fig.* sich ins Fäustchen lachen. **2.** ☉ Manschette *f*, Muffe *f*. **3.** *bsd. Br.* (*Platten*)Hülle *f*. '**sleeve·less** *adj* ärmellos.

sleigh [sleɪ] s (*bsd. Pferde*)Schlitten *m*.

sleight of hand [slaɪt] s **1.** Fingerfertigkeit *f*. **2.** *fig.* Taschenspielertrick *m*.

slen·der ['slendə] *adj* □ **1.** schlank. **2.** *fig.* mager (*Aussichten, Einkommen etc*).

slept [slept] *pret u. pp von* **sleep**.

sleuth [sluːθ] s F Spürhund *m*, Detektiv *m*.

slew [sluː] *pret von* **slay**.

slice [slaɪs] **I** s **1.** Scheibe *f* (*Brot etc*), Stück (*Kuchen etc*); *fig.* Anteil *m* (**of** an *dat*). **2.** *Br.* (*Braten*)Wender *m*. **3.** *Golf, Tennis:* Slice *m*. **II** *v/t* **4.** *a.* **~ up** in Scheiben *od.* Stücke schneiden: **~ off** Stück abschneiden (**from** von). **5.** *Golf, Tennis:* Ball slicen.

slick [slɪk] **I** *adj* □ **1.** gekonnt (*Vorstellung etc*). **2.** geschickt, raffiniert. **3.** glatt (*Straße etc*). **II** s **4.** (*Öl*)Teppich *m*. **5.** *Motorsport:* Slick *m* (*Trockenreifen*). **6.** *Am.* F Hochglanzmagazin *n*. '**slick-er** s *Am.* Regenmantel *m*.

slid [slɪd] *pret u. pp von* **slide**.

slide [slaɪd] **I** *v/i* (*irr*) **1.** gleiten; rutschen: **let things ~** *fig.* die Dinge schleifen lassen. **2.** schleichen. **II** *v/t* (*irr*) **3.** schieben; gleiten lassen. **III** s **4.** Rutsche *f*, Rutschbahn *f*. **5.** (*Erd- etc*)Rutsch *m*. **6.** *Br.* (*Haar*)Spange *f*. **7.** Dia *n*. **~ lec·ture** s Lichtbildervortrag *m*. **~ pro·jec·tor** s Diaprojektor *m*. **~ rule** s Rechenschieber *m*, -stab *m*.

slid·ing door ['slaɪdɪŋ] s Schiebetür *f*.

slight [slaɪt] **I** *adj* □ **1.** leicht (*Schmerz etc*), geringfügig (*Änderung etc*): **I haven't got the ~est idea** ich habe nicht die geringste Ahnung; **not in the ~est** nicht im geringsten. **II** *v/t* j-n beleidigen, kränken. **III** s Beleidigung *f* (**on, to** gen).

slim [slɪm] **I** *adj* □ **1.** schlank. **2.** *fig.* gering (*Chance, Hoffnung etc*). **II** *v/i* **3.** e-e Schlankheitskur machen. **III** *v/t* **4.** *a.* **~ down** *fig.* verringern.

slime [slaɪm] s Schleim *m*.

slim·ming ['slɪmɪŋ] **I** s Abnehmen *n*. **II** *adj* Schlankheits...: **be on a ~ diet →** **slim** 3.

slim·y ['slaɪmɪ] *adj* □ schleimig (*a. fig.*).

sling¹ [slɪŋ] **I** s **1.** ✠ Schlinge *f*: **have one's arm in a ~** den Arm in der Schlinge tragen. **2.** Trag(e)riemen *m* (*für Gewehr*); Trag(e)tuch *n* (*für Baby*). **II** *v/t* (*irr*) **3.** aufhängen.

sling² [~] *v/t* (*irr*) schleudern: → **mud** 2.

slink [slɪŋk] *v/i* (*irr*) (sich) schleichen.

slip¹ [slɪp] **I** s **1.** Versehen *n*: **~ of the tongue** Versprecher *m*. **2.** Unterkleid *n*, -rock *m*. **3.** (*Kissen*)Bezug *m*. **4.** **give s.o. the ~** F j-m entwischen. **II** *v/i* **5.** rutschen, (*auf Eis a.*) schlittern: **~ out of s.o.'s hand** j-m aus der Hand rutschen; **he let ~ that** *fig.* ihm ist herausgerutscht, daß; **let an opportunity ~** (**through one's fingers**) sich e-e Gelegenheit entgehen lassen. **6.** ausrutschen. **7.** *allg.* schlüpfen. **8.** sich vertun. **9.** *fig.* nachlassen, (*Gewinne etc*) zurückgehen. **III** *v/t* **10.** **~ s.th. into s.o.'s hand** j-m in die Hand schieben; **~ s.o. s.th.** j-m et. zuschieben. **11.** sich losreißen von. **12.** **~ s.o.'s attention** j-m *od.* j-s Aufmerksamkeit entgehen; **~ s.o.'s memory** (*od.* **mind**) j-m entfallen. **13.** **he has ~ped a disc,** *a.* **he has a ~ped disc** ✠ er hat e-n Bandscheibenvorfall.

Verbindungen mit Adverbien:

slip by *v/i* verstreichen (*Zeit*). **~ off** *v/t* schlüpfen aus (*e-m Kleidungsstück*). **~ on** *v/t* Kleidungsstück überstreifen, schlüpfen in (*acc*). **~ out** *v/i*: **it just slipped out** es ist mir *etc* so herausgerutscht. **~ past →** **slip by.** **~ up →** **slip** 8.

slip² [~] s *a.* **~ of paper** Zettel *m*.

'**slip·case** s Schuber *m*. '**~·cov·er** s *Am.* Schonbezug *m*. '**~-on** **I** *adj*: **~ shoe →** II. **II** s Slipper *m*.

slip·per ['slɪpə] s Hausschuh *m*, Pantoffel *m*.

slip·per·y ['slɪpərɪ] *adj* **1.** glatt, rutschig, (*a. Fisch, Seife etc*) glitschig. **2.** *fig.* zwielichtig.

slip·py *adj*: **look ~!** *Br.* F mach fix!

slip **road** s *Br. Autobahn:* Abfahrt *f*; Zubringer(straße *f*) *m*. '**~·shod** *adj* schlampig, schlud(e)rig. '**~·stream**

(*Sport*) **I** s Windschatten *m*. **II** *v/i* im Windschatten fahren. '**~-up** → **slip**¹ 1.

slit [slɪt] **I** s Schlitz *m* (*a. im Rock etc*). **II** *v/t* (*irr*) *Rock etc* schlitzen: ~ (**open**) aufschlitzen.

sliv·er ['slɪvə] s (*Glas- etc*)Splitter *m*: ~ **of glass**.

slob·ber ['slɒbə] *v/i* sabbern.

slog [slɒɡ] **F I** *v/i* **1.** ~ **away at** sich abschuften mit. **2.** sich schleppen (**through** durch). **II** s **3.** Schufterei *f*.

slo·gan ['sləʊɡən] s Slogan *m*.

slop [slɒp] **I** *v/t* **1.** verschütten: ~ **s.th. over one's trousers** sich et. über die Hose schütten. **II** *v/i* **2.** überschwappen; schwappen (**over** über *acc*). **3.** ~ **about** (*od. around*) **F** herumhängen (*Person*). **III** s **4.** *a. pl contp.* schlabb(e)riges Zeug.

slope [sləʊp] **I** s **1.** (Ab)Hang *m*. **2.** Neigung *f*, Gefälle *n*. **II** *v/i* **3.** sich neigen, abfallen. **4.** ~ **off** *Br.* F abhauen.

slop·py ['slɒpɪ] *adj* □ **1.** schlampig, schlud(e)rig. **2.** F vergammelt (*Kleidungsstück*). **3.** F schmalzig.

slosh [slɒʃ] **F I** *v/i* **1.** ~ **about** (*od. around*) herumschwappen. **2.** ~ **about** (*od. around*) (herum)planschen (**in** in *dat*). **II** *v/t* **3.** *Wasser etc* verspritzen. **sloshed** [~ʃt] *adj* F blau (*betrunken*).

slot [slɒt] s Schlitz *m*, (*e-s Automaten etc a.*) Einwurf *m*. ~ **ma·chine** s (Waren-, Spiel)Automat *m*.

slouch [slaʊtʃ] **I** s **1.** krumme Haltung; latschiger Gang. **2.** F **be no ~ at** nicht schlecht sein in (*dat*); **be no ~ at doing s.th.** et. wirklich gut können. **II** *v/i* **3.** krumm dasitzen *od.* dastehen; latschen. ~ **hat** s Schlapphut *m*.

slough [slʌf] *v/t* Haut abstreifen (*Schlange*).

slov·en·ly ['slʌvnlɪ] *adj* schlampig, schlud(e)rig.

slow [sləʊ] **I** *adj* □ **1.** *allg.* langsam, (*Person a.*) begriffsstutzig: **be ~ to do s.th.** sich mit et. Zeit lassen; **be (five minutes) ~** (fünf Minuten) nachgehen (*Uhr*); ~ **lane** *mot.* Kriechspur *f*; **in ~ motion** in Zeitlupe; ~ **poison** langsam wirkendes Gift; **~ly but surely** langsam, aber sicher; → **uptake**. **2.** ~ schleppend. **II** *v/t* **3.** *oft* ~ **down** (*od. up*) Geschwindigkeit verringern; *Projekt etc* verzögern; ~ **the car down** langsamer

fahren. **III** *v/i* **4.** *oft* ~ **down** (*od. up*) langsamer fahren *od.* gehen *od.* werden. '**~-coach** s F Langweiler(in). '**~-down** s † *Am.* Bummelstreik *m*. '**~-,mov·ing** *adj* kriechend (*Verkehr*).

slow·ness ['sləʊnɪs] s Langsamkeit *f*, (*e-r Person a.*) Begriffsstutzigkeit *f*.

'**slow·poke** *Am.* → **slowcoach.** '**~-worm** s zo. Blindschleiche *f*.

sludge [slʌdʒ] s Schlamm *m*.

slug¹ [slʌɡ] s bsd. Am. F **1.** ✕ *etc* Kugel *f*. **2.** Schluck *m* (*Whisky etc*).

slug² [~] s zo. Nacktschnecke *f*.

slug³ [~] bsd. Am. **I** *v/t* j-m e-n Faustschlag versetzen. **II** s Faustschlag *m*.

slug·gish ['slʌɡɪʃ] *adj* □ **1.** träge (*Person*), träge fließend (*Fluß etc*). **2.** † schleppend.

sluice [sluːs] **I** s Schleuse *f*. **II** *v/t*: ~ **down** abspritzen; ~ **out** ausspritzen. **III** *v/i*: ~ **out** herausschießen (*Wasser*). ~ **gate** s Schleusentor *n*.

slum [slʌm] s, *mst pl* Slums *pl*, Elendsviertel *n*. ~ **dwell·er** s Slumbewohner(in).

slump [slʌmp] **I** *v/i* **1.** ~ **into a chair** sich in e-n Sessel plumpsen lassen; **sit ~ed over** zs.-gesunken sitzen über (*dat*). **2.** † stürzen (*Preise*), stark zurückgehen (*Umsatz etc*). **II** s **3.** † starker Konjunkturrückgang: ~ **in prices** Preissturz *m*.

slung [slʌŋ] *pret u. pp von* **sling**¹ u. ².

slunk [slʌŋk] *pret u. pp von* **slink.**

slur¹ [slɜː] s: ~ **on s.o.'s reputation** Rufschädigung *f*.

slur² [~] *v/t* **1.** ~ **one's speech** undeutlich sprechen, (*Betrunkener a.*) lallen. **2.** ♪ Töne binden.

slurp [slɜːp] *v/t u. v/i* F schlürfen.

slush [slʌʃ] s **1.** Schneematsch *m*. **2.** F rührseliges Zeug. '**slush·y** *adj* □ **1.** matschig (*Schnee*). **2.** F rührselig.

slut [slʌt] s Schlampe *f*.

sly [slaɪ] **I** *adj* □ **1.** gerissen, schlau: **you're a ~ one!** du bist mir vielleicht einer! **2.** verschmitzt (*Lächeln etc*). **II** s **3.** **on the ~** heimlich.

smack¹ [smæk] *v/i*: ~ **of** *fig.* schmecken *od.* riechen nach.

smack² [~] **I** *v/t* **1.** j-m e-n Klaps geben: ~ **s.o.'s bottom**, ~ **s.o. on the bottom** j-m eins hinten draufgeben; ~ **s.o.'s face** j-m e-e runterhauen. **2.** ~ **one's lips** sich die Lippen lecken. **3.** ~ *down et.* hinklatschen. **II** *s* **4.** Klaps *m:* **give s.o. a ~ in the face** F j-m e-e runterhauen. **5.** klatschendes Geräusch. **6.** F Schmatz *m.* **7. have a ~ at** F es mit *et.* versuchen. **III** *adv* **8.** F genau, direkt.

smack·er ['smækə] *s* F **1.** Schmatz *m.* **2.** *Br.* Pfund *n, Am.* Dollar *m.* **'smack·ing** *s* F Tracht *f* Prügel.

small [smɔːl] **I** *adj allg.* klein: ~ *ad Br.* Kleinanzeige *f;* ~ *arms pl* Handfeuerwaffen *pl;* ~ *beer* F ein kleiner Fisch, kleine Fische *pl;* ~ *change* Kleingeld *n;* **that's ~ change to him** *fig.* das ist ein Taschengeld für ihn; ~ *eater* schlechter Esser; *in the ~ hours* in den frühen Morgenstunden; ~ *print* das Kleingedruckte (*e-s Vertrags etc*); ~ *talk* Small talk *m, n,* Geplauder *n;* **make ~ talk** plaudern; ~ *town* Kleinstadt *f;* **feel ~** sich klein (u. häßlich) vorkommen; → **wonder 5.** **II** *adv* klein. **III** *s:* ~ *of the back anat.* Kreuz *n.* **,~·'mind·ed** *adj* □ **1.** engstirnig. **2.** kleinlich. **'~·pox** *s* ⚕ Pocken *pl.* **,~·'time** *adj fig.* klein, Klein...

smarm·y ['smɑːmɪ] *adj* F schmierig, schmeichlerisch.

smart [smɑːt] **I** *adj* □ **1.** smart (*Person*), (*a. Auto, Kleidung etc*) schick. **2.** smart, schlau, clever. **3.** vornehm (*Restaurant, Wohngegend etc*). **II** *v/i* **4.** weh tun; brennen. **III** *s* **5.** (brennender) Schmerz. ~ **al·eck** ['ælɪk] *s* F Besserwisser(in). ~ **ass** *s Am.* V Klugscheißer(in).

smart·en ['smɑːtn] **I** *v/t mst* ~ *up et.* verschönern: ~ *o.s. up* → **II. II** *v/i mst* ~ *up* sich schick machen; sich *et.* Anständiges anziehen. **'smart·ness** *s* **1.** Schick *m.* **2.** Schlauheit *f,* Cleverneß *f.*

smash [smæʃ] **I** *v/t* **1.** *a.* ~ *up* zerschlagen; *Wagen* zu Schrott fahren; → **smithereens. 2.** schmettern (*a. Tennis etc*): ~ *one's fist down on the table* mit der Faust auf den Tisch hauen. **3.** *fig.* *Aufstand etc* niederschlagen, *Spionagering etc* zerschlagen. **II** *v/i* **4.** zerspringen: → **smithereens. 5.** ~ *into* prallen an (*acc*) *od.* gegen, krachen gegen. **III** *s* **6.** Schlag *m;* (*Tennis etc*) Schmetterball *m.* **7.** → **smash-up. 8.** Hit *m* (*Buch, Theaterstück etc*). **,~·and-'grab (raid)** *s bsd. Br.* Schaufenstereinbruch *m.*

smashed [smæʃt] *adj* F blau (*betrun-*

ken): **get ~ on** sich vollaufen lassen mit.

'smash·er *s* F Klassefrau *f,* toller Typ; tolles Ding.

smash hit → **smash 8.**

smash·ing ['smæʃɪŋ] *adj* F toll.

'smash-up *s mot.* schwerer Unfall.

smat·ter·ing ['smætərɪŋ] *s:* **a ~ of English** ein paar Brocken Englisch.

smear [smɪə] **I** *s* **1.** Fleck *m.* **2.** ⚕ (*entnommener*) Abstrich. **3.** Verleumdung *f.* **II** *v/t* **4.** *Farbe etc* verschmieren, *Schrift a.* verwischen. **5.** *Creme etc* schmieren (**on, over** auf *acc*); *Haut etc* einschmieren (**with** mit). **6.** *Glas etc* be-, verschmieren (**with** mit): *~ed with blood* blutbeschmiert, -verschmiert. **7.** verleumden. **III** *v/i* **8.** schmieren (*Farbe etc*), sich verwischen (*Schrift*). ~ **cam·paign** *s* Verleumdungskampagne *f.* ~ **test** *s* ⚕ Abstrich *m.*

smell [smel] **I** *v/i* (*mst irr*) **1.** riechen (**at** an *dat*). **2.** riechen, *b.s.* stinken (**of** nach) (*beide a. fig.*): *his breath ~s* er riecht aus dem Mund. **II** *v/t* (*mst irr*) **3.** *et.* riechen; *fig.* wittern: ~ *out hunt.* aufspüren (*a. fig.*); *Zimmer etc* verpesten. **4.** riechen an (*dat*). **III** *s* **5.** Geruch *m, b.s.* Gestank *m:* ~ **of gas** Gasgeruch; *there's a ~ of garlic in here* hier stinkt es nach Knoblauch. **6. have** (*od.* **take**) **a ~ at** riechen an (*dat*). **'smell·ing** *adj:* ~ *salts pl* Riechsalz *n.* **'smell·y** *adj* stinkend: ~ *feet pl* Schweißfüße *pl.*

smelt¹ [smelt] *pret u. pp von* **smell.**

smelt² [~] *v/t* Erz schmelzen.

smile [smaɪl] **I** *v/i* lächeln (**about** über *acc*): ~ *at* j-n anlächeln, *j-m* zulächeln; *j-n, et.* belächeln, lächeln über (*acc*); → **keep 17. II** *v/t:* ~ *one's approval* beifällig *od.* zustimmend lächeln. **III** *s* Lächeln *n:* **with a ~** lächelnd; **be all ~s** (übers ganze Gesicht) strahlen; **give a ~** lächeln; **give s.o. a ~** j-n anlächeln, j-m zulächeln.

smirk [smɜːk] *v/i* (selbstgefällig *od.* schadenfroh) grinsen.

smite [smaɪt] *v/t* (*irr*): **be smitten by** (*od.* **with**) *fig.* gepackt werden von.

smith [smɪθ] *s* Schmied *m.*

smith·er·eens [ˌsmɪðə'riːnz] *s pl:* **smash to ~** in tausend Stücke schlagen *od.* zersprengen.

smith·y ['smɪðɪ] *s* Schmiede *f.*

smit·ten ['smɪtn] *pp von* **smite.**

smock [smɒk] *s* Kittel *m*.

smog [smɒg] *s* Smog *m*.

smoke [sməʊk] **I** *v/i* **1.** rauchen. **II** *v/t* **2.** rauchen. **3.** *Fisch, Fleisch etc* räuchern: **~ out** ausräuchern. **III** *s* **4.** Rauch *m*: **there's no ~ without fire** *fig.* kein Rauch ohne Flamme; **→ go up** 3. **5.** **have a ~** eine rauchen. **6.** F Glimmstengel *m*, Zigarette *f*. **~ bomb** *s* Rauchbombe *f*.

smoked [sməʊkt] *adj* **1.** geräuchert, Räucher... **2.** **~ glass** Rauchglas *n*. **'smok·er** *s* **1.** Raucher(in): **~'s cough** Raucherhusten *m*. **2.** 🚃 Raucherwagen *m*.

'smoke·stack *s* Schornstein *m*.

smok·ing ['sməʊkɪŋ] **I** *s* Rauchen *n*: **no ~** Rauchen verboten. **II** *adj*: **~ compartment** Raucher(abteil *n*) *m*. **'smok·y** *adj* **1.** rauchig, verräuchert. **2.** rauchig (*Geschmack etc*). **3.** rauchfarben, -farbig.

smol·der *Am.* → **smoulder**.

smooch [smuːtʃ] *v/i* F knutschen, schmusen (**with** mit).

smooth [smuːð] **I** *adj* □ **1.** glatt (*Fläche, Haut etc*). **2.** ruhig (*Flug etc*). **3.** *fig.* glatt, reibungslos. **4.** *fig.* (aal)glatt. **II** *v/t* **5.** *a.* **~ out** glätten, *Tischtuch etc a.* glattstreichen: **~ away** Falten *etc* glätten; *fig. Schwierigkeiten etc* aus dem Weg räumen; **~ over** *fig. Spannungen etc* ausgleichen. **III** *s* **6.** → **rough** 9.

smote [sməʊt] *pret von* **smite**.

smoth·er ['smʌðə] *v/t* **1.** *j-n, Aufstand, Feuer etc* ersticken. **2.** *Gähnen etc* unterdrücken. **3.** *fig. j-n* überschütten (**with** mit *Zuneigung etc*).

smoul·der ['sməʊldə] *v/i bsd. Br.* glimmen, schwelen (*beide a. fig.*).

smudge [smʌdʒ] **I** *s* **1.** Fleck *m*. **II** *v/t* **2.** *Farbe etc* verschmieren, *Schrift a.* verwischen. **3.** *Glas etc* be-, verschmieren (**with** mit). **III** *v/i* **4.** schmieren (*Farbe etc*), sich verwischen (*Schrift*). **'smudg·y** *adj* verschmiert, -wischt.

smug [smʌg] *adj* □ selbstgefällig.

smug·gle ['smʌgl] **I** *v/t* schmuggeln (**into** nach *Deutschland etc*; **in** *acc*): **~ in** (**out**) ein-(heraus)schmuggeln. **II** *v/i* schmuggeln. **'smug·gler** *s* Schmuggler(in). **'smug·gling** *s* Schmuggel *m*.

smut [smʌt] *s* **1.** Rußflocke *f*. **2.** *fig.* Schmutz *m*. **'smut·ty** *adj fig.* schmutzig.

snack [snæk] *s* Snack *m*, Imbiß *m*: **have a ~** e-e Kleinigkeit essen. **~ bar** *s* Snackbar *f*, Imbißstube *f*.

snaf·fle ['snæfl] *v/t bsd. Br. et.* mitgehen lassen.

snag [snæg] **I** *s fig.* Haken *m*. **II** *v/t* mit *et.* hängenbleiben (**on** an *dat*).

snail [sneɪl] *s zo.* Schnecke *f*: **at a ~'s pace** im Schneckentempo. **~ shell** *s* Schneckenhaus *n*.

snake [sneɪk] **I** *s zo.* Schlange *f*: **~ in the grass** *fig.* falsche Schlange (*Frau*); hinterlistiger Kerl (*Mann*). **II** *v/i u. v/t*: **~** (**one's way**) **through** sich schlängeln durch. **'~·bite** *s* Schlangenbiß *m*. **~ charm·er** *s* Schlangenbeschwörer *m*. **'~·skin** *s* Schlangenhaut *f*; -leder *n*.

snak·y ['sneɪkɪ] *adj* gewunden (*Straße etc*).

snap [snæp] **I** *v/i* **1.** (zer)brechen, (-)reißen: **my patience ~ped** mir riß die Geduld *od.* der Geduldsfaden. **2.** *a.* **~ shut** zuschnappen. **3.** **~ at** schnappen nach (*a. fig.*); *j-n* anfahren. **4.** F **~ out of it!** Kopf hoch!; **~ to it!** mach fix! **II** *v/t* **5.** zerbrechen; **~ off** abbrechen; **~ s.o.'s head off** F *j-m* ins Gesicht springen. **6.** mit *den Fingern* schnalzen: **~ one's fingers at** *j-m* keinen Respekt haben *vor* (*dat*), sich hinwegsetzen über (*acc*). **7.** *phot.* F knipsen. **8.** **~ up** *et.* schnell entschlossen kaufen; *fig. Gelegenheit* beim Schopf ergreifen: **~ it up!** *Am.* F mach fix! **III** *s* **9.** *phot.* F Schnappschuß *m*. **10.** *Am.* Druckknopf *m*. **11.** (*Kälte-*) Einbruch *m*. **12.** F Schwung *m*: **come on, put some ~ in it!** häng dich mal ein bißchen rein! **IV** *adj* **13.** spontan. **'~· drag·on** *s* 🌼 Löwenmaul *n*. **~ fas·tener** *s Am.* Druckknopf *m*.

snap·pish ['snæpɪʃ] *adj* □ *fig.* bissig. **'snap·py** *adj* □ F **1.** modisch, schick. **2.** **make it ~!**, *Br. a.* **look ~!** F mach fix! **'snap·shot** *s phot.* Schnappschuß *m*.

snare [sneə] **I** *s* **1.** Falle *f*, Schlinge *f, fig. a.* Fallstrick *m*. **II** *v/t* **2.** in der Schlinge fangen. **3.** F *et.* ergattern.

snarl¹ [snɑːl] **I** *v/i* knurren (*Hund, a. Person*): **~ at s.o.** *j-n* anknurren. **II** *v/t et.* knurren. **III** *s* Knurren *n*.

snarl² [~] *v/t*: **the traffic was ~ed** (**up**) *es* entstand ein Verkehrschaos. **'~·up** *s* Verkehrschaos *n*.

snatch [snætʃ] **I** *v/t* **1.** *et.* packen: **~ s.o.'s**

handbag j-m die Handtasche entreißen; **~ s.th. from s.o.'s hand** j-m et. aus der Hand reißen. **2.** *fig.* Gelegenheit ergreifen; *ein paar Stunden Schlaf etc* ergattern. **II** v/i **3. ~ at** greifen nach; *fig.* Gelegenheit ergreifen. **III** s **4. make a ~ at** greifen nach. **5.** (Gesprächs)Fetzen m: **~ of conversation.**

snaz·zy ['snæzɪ] *adj* □ F schick; *contp.* protzig.

sneak [sni:k] **I** v/i **1.** (sich) schleichen, sich stehlen: **~ up on s.o.** (sich) an j-n heranschleichen. **2.** *Br.* F petzen: **~ on s.o.** j-n verpetzen. **II** v/t **3.** F stibitzen: **~ a look at** heimlich e-n Blick werfen auf (acc). **III** s **4.** *Br.* F Petzer(in), Petze f. **'sneak·er** s *Am.* Turn- od. Wanderschuh m. **'sneak·ing** *adj* heimlich, (*Verdacht a.*) leise. **'sneak·y** *adj* □ **1.** heimlich. **2.** gerissen.

sneer [snɪə] **I** v/i **1.** höhnisch od. spöttisch grinsen (**at** über *acc*). **2.** spotten (**at** über *acc*). **II** s **3.** höhnisches od. spöttisches Grinsen. **4.** höhnische od. spöttische Bemerkung.

sneeze [sni:z] **I** v/i niesen: **not to be ~d at** F nicht zu verachten. **II** s Niesen n; Nieser m.

snick·er ['snɪkə] *bsd. Am.* → **snigger.**

snide [snaɪd] *adj* □ abfällig.

sniff [snɪf] **I** v/i **1.** schniefen, die Nase hochziehen. **2.** schnüffeln (**at** an *dat*). **3. ~ at** *fig.* die Nase rümpfen über (*acc*): **not to be ~ed at** nicht zu verachten. **II** v/t **4.** durch die Nase einziehen; *Klebstoff etc* schnüffeln, *Kokain etc* schnupfen. **5. ~ out** aufspüren (*a. fig.*). **III** s **6.** Schniefen n.

snif·fle ['snɪfl] **I** v/i → **sniff** 1. **II** s Schniefen n: **he's got the ~s** F ihm läuft dauernd die Nase.

snif·ter ['snɪftə] s *Am.* Kognakschwenker m.

snig·ger ['snɪgə] *bsd. Br.* **I** v/i kichern (**at** über *acc*). **II** s Kichern n.

snip [snɪp] **I** v/t **1.** durchschnippeln: **~ off** abschnippeln. **II** s **2.** Schnitt m. **3.** *Br.* F Gelegenheitskauf m.

snipe [snaɪp] **I** *pl* **snipes**, *bsd. coll.* **snipe** s *orn.* Schnepfe f. **II** v/i: **~ at** aus dem Hinterhalt schießen auf (*acc*); *fig.* aus dem Hinterhalt angreifen (*acc*). **'snip·er** s Heckenschütze m.

snip·pet ['snɪpɪt] s: **~ of conversation**

Gesprächsfetzen m; **~s** *pl* **of information** bruchstückhafte Informationen *pl.*

snitch [snɪtʃ] v/i: **~ on s.o.** F j-n verpetzen od. verpfeifen.

sniv·el ['snɪvl] v/i *pret u. pp* **-eled**, *bsd. Br.* **-elled** greinen, jammern.

snob [snɒb] s Snob m. **'snob·ber·y** s Snobismus m. **'snob·bish** *adj* □ snobistisch, versnobt.

snog [snɒg] v/i *Br.* F knutschen, schmusen (**with** mit).

snook [snu:k] s: **cock a ~ at** *Br.* F j-m zeigen, was man von ihm hält.

snook·er ['snu:kə] **I** s *Billard:* Snooker Pool. **II** v/t: **be ~ed** F völlig machtlos sein.

snoop [snu:p] v/i: **~ about** (od. **around**) herumschnüffeln (**in** in *dat*). **'snoop·er** s F Schnüffler(in).

snoot·y ['snu:tɪ] *adj* □ F hochnäsig.

snooze [snu:z] F **I** v/i ein Nickerchen machen. **II** s Nickerchen n: **have a ~** → **I.**

snore [snɔ:] **I** v/i schnarchen. **II** s Schnarchen n. **'snor·er** s Schnarcher(in).

snor·kel ['snɔ:kl] **I** s Schnorchel m. **II** v/i schnorcheln.

snort [snɔ:t] **I** v/i (*a.* verächtlich od. wütend) schnauben. **II** v/t schnauben. **III** s Schnauben n: **give a ~ of derision** verächtlich schnauben.

snot [snɒt] s F Rotz m. **'snot·ty** *adj* F **1.** Rotz...: **~ nose.** **2.** *fig.* aufgeblasen.

snout [snaʊt] s *zo.* Schnauze f, (*e-s Schweins etc a.*) Rüssel m.

snow [snəʊ] **I** s **1.** Schnee m (*a. sl. Kokain, Heroin*): (**as**) **white as ~** schneeweiß. **2.** Schneefall m. **II** v/impers **3.** schneien. **III** v/t **4. be ~ed in** (od. **up**) eingeschneit sein: **be ~ed under with work** mit Arbeit überhäuft sein. **'~·ball** s Schneeball m: **~ fight** Schneeballschlacht f. **'~·blind** *adj* schneeblind. **'~·capped** *adj* schneebedeckt (*Berggipfel*). **'~·drift** s Schneewehe f. **'~·drop** s ♀ Schneeglöckchen n. **'~·fall** s Schneefall m. **'~·flake** s Schneeflocke f. **'~·line** s Schneegrenze f. **'~·man** s (*irr man*) Schneemann m: → **abominable.** **'~·plough**, **'~·plow** s *Am.* Schneepflug m (*a. beim Skifahren*). **'~·storm** s Schneesturm m. **,~·'white** *adj* schneeweiß.

snow·y ['snəʊɪ] *adj* schneereich (*Tag etc*), (*Gegend a.*) verschneit.

snub¹ [snʌb] *v/t* j-n brüskieren, j-m über den Mund fahren.

snub² [~] *adj* Stups...: ~ *nose*. '**~-nosed** *adj* stupsnasig.

snuff¹ [snʌf] *s* Schnupftabak *m*.

snuff² [~] *v/t Kerze* ausdrücken: ~ *out fig. Leben* auslöschen; ~ *it Br.* F den Löffel weglegen (*sterben*).

snuf·fle ['snʌfl] → **sniffle.**

snug [snʌg] **I** *adj* □ **1.** behaglich, gemütlich. **2.** gutsitzend (*Kleidungsstück*): **be a ~ fit** gut passen. **II** *s* **3.** *Br.* kleines Nebenzimmer (*e-s Pubs*).

snug·gle ['snʌgl] *v/i*: ~ *up to s.o.* sich an j-n kuscheln; ~ *down in bed* sich ins Bett kuscheln.

so [səʊ] **I** *adv* **1.** so, dermaßen: *he is ~ stupid (that) he ...* er ist so dumm, daß er ... **2.** (ja) so: *I am ~ glad.* **3.** so, in dieser Weise: *is that ~?* wirklich?; ~ *as to* so daß, um zu; *a mile or ~* etwa e-e Meile; → *forth* 1, *if* 1, *on* 13. **4.** *verkürzend: he is tired.* *I am ~* Ich auch; → *hope* II, *think* 6, *etc.* **II** *cj* **5.** deshalb. **6.** ~ *what?* F na und?

soak [səʊk] **I** *v/t* **1.** *et.* einweichen (*in in dat*). **2.** ~ *up Flüssigkeit* aufsaugen; *fig. Neuigkeiten etc* in sich aufsaugen. **3.** durchnässen: → *skin* 1. **4.** F j-n ausnehmen, neppen. **II** *v/i* **5.** sickern. '**soak·ing** *adj u. adv*: ~ *(wet)* tropfnaß.

'**so-and-so** *pl* **-sos** *s* F **1.** Herr *od.* Frau *od.* Frl. Soundso *od.* Sowieso: *a Mr ~* ein Herr Soundso. **2.** *euphem.* blöder Hund.

soap [səʊp] **I** *s* **1.** Seife *f.* **2.** F → **soap opera. II** *v/t* **3.** (sich) *et.* einseifen. ~ *bub·ble s* Seifenblase *f.* ~ *dish s* Seifenschale *f.* ~ *op·er·a s Rundfunk, TV:* Seifenoper *f.* '~-**suds** *s pl* Seifenschaum *m.*

soap·y ['səʊpɪ] *adj* □ **1.** Seifen...: ~ *water.* **2.** seifig. **3.** F schmeichlerisch.

soar [sɔː] *v/i* **1.** aufsteigen: ~ *into the sky* zum Himmel emporsteigen. **2.** hochragen. **3.** *fig.* in die Höhe schnellen (*Preise etc*).

sob [sɒb] **I** *v/i* schluchzen. **II** *v/t* schluchzen: ~ *out* schluchzend erzählen. **III** *s* Schluchzen *n*; Schluchzer *m*.

so·ber ['səʊbə] **I** *adj* □ nüchtern (*a. fig.*): *(as)* ~ *as a judge* stocknüchtern. **II** *v/t*

mst ~ *up* ausnüchtern, wieder nüchtern machen. **III** *v/i mst* ~ *up* (sich) ausnüchtern, wieder nüchtern werden: *have a ~ing effect on s.o. fig.* auf j-n ernüchternd wirken.

sob sto·ry *s* F rührselige Geschichte.

,so-'called *adj* sogenannt.

soc·cer ['sɒkə] *s* Fußball *m* (*Spiel*).

so·cia·ble ['səʊʃəbl] *adj* □ gesellig (*Person, a. Abend etc*); zutraulich (*Tier*).

so·cial ['səʊʃl] *adj* □ **1.** gesellschaftlich, Gesellschafts..., sozial, Sozial...: *have a busy ~ life* oft ausgehen *od.* Besuch haben; ~ *science* Sozialwissenschaft *f.* **2.** sozial, Sozial...: ~ *insurance* Sozialversicherung *f*; ~ *security Br.* Sozialhilfe *f*; *be on ~ security* Sozialhilfe beziehen; ~ *worker* Sozialarbeiter(in). **3.** *pol.* Sozial...: ~ *democrat* Sozialdemokrat(in *f*) *m.* **4.** *biol.* gesellig (*Wesen*). **5.** F gesellig (*Person*).

so·cial·ism ['səʊʃəlɪzəm] *s* Sozialismus *m.* '**so·cial·ist** *I s* Sozialist(in). **II** *adj* sozialistisch.

so·cial·ize ['səʊʃəlaɪz] *v/i*: *I don't ~ much* ich gehe nicht oft aus; ~ *with* (gesellschaftlich) verkehren mit.

so·ci·e·ty [sə'saɪətɪ] *s* Gesellschaft *f.*

so·ci·o·log·i·cal [ˌsəʊsjə'lɒdʒɪkl] *adj* □ soziologisch. **so·ci·ol·o·gist** [ˌsəʊsɪ'ɒlədʒɪst] *s* Soziologe *m*, Soziologin *f*. **,so·ci·ol·o·gy** *s* Soziologie *f.*

sock¹ [sɒk] *s* Socke(n *m*) *f*: *pull one's ~s up Br.* F sich am Riemen reißen; *put a ~ in it! Br.* F hör doch auf, Mensch!

sock² [~] F **I** *v/t*: ~ *s.o. on the jaw* j-m e-n Kinnhaken verpassen. **II** *s* (*Faust-*) Schlag *m*: *give s.o. a ~ on the jaw* → **I.**

sock·et ['sɒkɪt] *s* **1.** *anat.* (*Augen*)Höhle *f.* **2.** ≠ Steckdose *f*; Fassung *f* (*e-r Glühbirne*); (*Kopfhörer- etc*)Anschluß *m.*

sod [sɒd] *bsd. Br. sl.* **I** *s* blöder Hund: *poor ~* armes Schwein. **II** *v/t*: ~ *it!* Scheiße! **III** *v/i*: ~ *off!* verpiß dich!

so·da ['səʊdə] *s* **1.** Soda *n*: *two whisky and ~s* zwei Whisky mit Soda. **2.** *bsd. Am.* (*Orangen- etc*)Limonade *f.*

sod·den ['sɒdn] *adj* durchnäßt, (*Boden*) aufgeweicht.

so·di·um ['səʊdjəm] *s* 🔬 Natrium *n.*

so·fa ['səʊfə] *s* Sofa *n.*

soft [sɒft] *adj* □ **1.** *allg.* weich: *be ~ in the head* F e-e weiche Birne haben; → *spot* 4. **2.** leise (*Stimme, Musik* *etc*); gedämpft, dezent (*Beleuchtung, Farbe, Musik*). **3.** sanft (*Berührung, Brise etc*). **4.** gutmütig; nachsichtig (**with** gegen *j-n*). **5.** F ruhig (*Job etc*). **6.** verweichlicht: **get** ~ verweichlichen. **7.** weich (*Droge*): ~ **drink** Soft Drink *m*, alkoholfreies Getränk. ,~-'**boiled** *adj* weich(gekocht) (*Ei*).

soft·en ['sɒfn] **I** *v/t* **1.** weich machen; *Wasser* enthärten. **2.** *Ton, Licht etc* dämpfen. **3.** ~ *up* F *j-n* weichmachen. **II** *v/i* **4.** weich werden. '**soft·en·er** *s* (*Wasser*)Enthärter *m*.

,soft'**heart·ed** *adj* □ weichherzig.

soft·ie → **softy**.

,soft|-'**ped·al** *v/t* F et. herunterspielen. '~-**soap** *v/t* F *j-m* um den Bart gehen. '~-**ware** *s Computer:* Software *f*.

soft·y ['sɒftɪ] *s* F Softie *m*, Softy *m*, Weichling *m*.

sog·gy ['sɒgɪ] *adj* □ aufgeweicht (*Boden etc*), (*a. Gemüse etc*) matschig, (*Brot etc*) teigig, glitschig.

soil¹ [sɔɪl] *s* Boden *m*, Erde *f*.

soil² [~] *v/t* beschmutzen, schmutzig machen.

sol·ace ['sɒləs] *s* Trost *m*: **be a** ~ **to s.o.** j-m ein Trost sein; **find** ~ **in** Trost finden in (*dat*).

so·lar ['səʊlə] *adj* Sonnen...: ~ *eclipse ast.* Sonnenfinsternis *f*; ~ *energy* Sonnen-, Solarenergie *f*; ~ *system* Sonnensystem *n*.

so·lar·i·um [səʊ'leərɪəm] *pl* -**i·a** [~ɪə], -**i·ums** *s* Solarium *n*.

so·lar plex·us ['pleksəs] *s anat.* Solarplexus *m*; Magengrube *f*.

sold [səʊld] *pret u. pp von* **sell**.

sol·der ['sɒldə] *v/t* (ver)löten. '**sol·der·ing** *adj:* ~ *iron* Lötkolben *m*.

sol·dier ['səʊldʒə] **I** *s* Soldat *m*. **II** *v/i:* ~ *on bsd. Br.* (unermüdlich) weitermachen.

sole¹ [səʊl] *adj* (□ → **solely**) einzig; alleinig, Allein...

sole² [~] **I** *s* (*Fuß-, Schuh*)Sohle *f*. **II** *v/t Schuh* besohlen.

sole³ [~] *s ichth.* Seezunge *f*.

sole·ly ['səʊllɪ] *adv* (einzig u.) allein, ausschließlich.

sol·emn ['sɒləm] *adj* □ **1.** feierlich: *give s.o. one's* ~ *pledge* (*od. word*) *that a.* j-m hoch u. heilig versprechen, daß. **2.** ernst.

so·lic·it [sə'lɪsɪt] **I** *v/t et.* erbitten, bitten um: ~ *s.o.'s help* j-n um Hilfe bitten. **II** *v/i* Männer ansprechen (*Prostituierte*).

so·lic·i·tor [sə'lɪsɪtə] *s* ᛑᛏᛑ *Br.* Solicitor *m*.

so·lic·it·ous [sə'lɪsɪtəs] *adj* □ **1.** dienstbeflissen. **2.** besorgt (*about, for* um).

sol·id ['sɒlɪd] **I** *adj* □ **1.** *allg.* fest. **2.** stabil, massiv. **3.** massiv: *a* ~ *gold watch* e-e Uhr aus massivem Gold. **4.** *fig.* einmütig, geschlossen (*for* für; *against* gegen). **5.** *fig.* gewichtig, triftig (*Grund etc*), stichhaltig (*Argument etc*). **6.** *I waited for a* ~ *hour* F ich wartete e-e geschlagene Stunde. **II** *s* **7.** ᛐ *Körper m.* **8.** *pl* feste Nahrung.

sol·i·dar·i·ty [ˌsɒlɪ'dærətɪ] *s* Solidarität *f*: *in* ~ *with* aus Solidarität mit; *declare one's* ~ *with* sich solidarisch erklären mit.

so·lid·i·fy [sə'lɪdɪfaɪ] **I** *v/t* **1.** fest werden lassen. **2.** *fig.* festigen. **II** *v/i* **3.** fest werden. **4.** *fig.* sich festigen.

,sol·id-'**state** *adj* volltransistor(is)iert.

so·lil·o·quy [sə'lɪləkwɪ] *s* **1.** *thea.* Monolog *m.* **2.** Selbstgespräch *n.*

sol·i·taire [ˌsɒlɪ'teə] *s* **1.** Solitär *m.* **2.** *bsd. Am.* → **patience** 2.

sol·i·tar·y ['sɒlɪtərɪ] **I** *adj* □ **1.** einsam, (*Leben a.*) zurückgezogen, (*Ort etc a.*) abgelegen: → **confinement** 2. **2.** einzig. **II** *s* **3.** F Einzelhaft *f.*

so·lo ['səʊləʊ] **I** *pl* -**los** *s* ♩ Solo *n.* **II** *adj* ♩ Solo...: ~ *flight* ✈ Alleinflug *m.* **III** *adv* ♩ solo: *fly* ~ ✈ e-n Alleinflug machen. '**so·lo·ist** *s* Solist(in).

sol·stice ['sɒlstɪs] *s ast.* Sonnenwende *f.*

sol·u·ble ['sɒljʊbl] *adj* **1.** ᛐ löslich: ~ *in water* wasserlöslich. **2.** *fig.* lösbar.

so·lu·tion [sə'lu:ʃn] *s* **1.** *fig.* Lösung *f* (*to* gen). **2.** ᛐ Lösung *f*; Auflösung *f.*

solv·a·ble ['sɒlvəbl] *adj fig.* lösbar.

solve [sɒlv] *v/t Fall, Rätsel etc* lösen.

sol·ven·cy ['sɒlvənsɪ] *s* ᛐ Solvenz *f*, Zahlungsfähigkeit *f.* '**sol·vent I** *adj* □ ᛐ solvent, zahlungsfähig. **II** *s* ᛐ Lösungsmittel *n.*

som·ber *Am.* → **sombre**.

som·bre ['sɒmbə] *adj* □ düster (*Farben, Raum etc, fig. Miene etc*).

som·bre·ro [sɒm'breərəʊ] *pl* -**ros** *s* Sombrero *m.*

some [sʌm] **I** *adj* **1.** (irgend)ein: ~ *day* eines Tages; ~ *day* (*or other*) irgendwann (einmal). **2.** *vor pl:* einige, ein paar: → **few** 1. **3.** manche. **4.** gewiß: → **extent** 2. **5.** etwas, ein wenig *od.* bißchen: **take ~ more** nimm noch et.; **would you like ~ more cake?** möchtest du noch ein Stück Kuchen? **6.** ungefähr: **~ 30 people. II** *pron* **7.** (irgend)ein. **8.** etwas. **9.** einige, ein paar. **~·bod·y** [ˈ.ˌbədɪ] **I** *pron* jemand. **II** *s.* **be ~** et. vorstellen, j-d sein. '**~·day** *adv* eines Tages. '**~·how** *adv* irgendwie. '**~·one** → **somebody.** '**~·place** *Am.* → **somewhere** 1.

som·er·sault [ˈsʌməsɔːlt] *s* Salto *m*; Purzelbaum *m*: **do** (*od.* **turn**) **a ~** e-n Salto machen; e-n Purzelbaum schlagen.

'**some·thing** [ˈ.ˌθɪŋ] *pron* **1.** etwas: *or* ~ F *od.* so. **II** *adv* **2. ~ like** F ungefähr; **look ~ like** so ähnlich aussehen wie; **~ over £ 200** et. mehr als 200 Pfund. **3. be ~ of a pianist** so et. wie ein Pianist sein. **III** *s* **4. a little ~** e-e Kleinigkeit (*Geschenk*); **a certain ~** ein gewisses Etwas. '**~·time** *adv* irgendwann. '**~·times** *adv* manchmal. '**~·way** *adv Am.* irgendwie. '**~-what** *adv* ein bißchen *od.* wenig: **~ of a shock** ein ziemlicher Schock. '**~·where** *adv* **1.** irgendwo; irgendwohin. **2.** *fig.* ~ **between 30 and 40 people** so zwischen 30 u. 40 Leute; **~ in the region of £ 100** um 100 Pfund herum.

som·nam·bu·list [sɒmˈnæmbjʊlɪst] *s* Nacht-, Schlafwandler(in).

som·no·lent [ˈsɒmnələnt] *adj* □ **1.** schläfrig. **2.** einschläfernd.

son [sʌn] *s* **1.** Sohn *m*: **~ of a bitch** *bsd. Am. sl.* Scheißkerl *m.* **2.** *Anrede*: F junger Mann.

so·na·ta [səˈnɑːtə] *s* ♪ Sonate *f.*

song [sɒŋ] *s* **1.** Lied *n*: **buy s.th. for a ~** F et. für ein Butterbrot kaufen; **make a ~ and dance about** F ein furchtbares Theater machen wegen. **2.** Gesang *m* (*a. von Vögeln*): **burst into ~** zu singen anfangen. '**~·bird** *s* Singvogel *m.* '**~·book** *s* Liederbuch *n.*

son·ic [ˈsɒnɪk] *adj phys.* Schall...: **~ bang** (*od.* **boom**) ✈ Überschallknall *m.*

'**son-in-law** *pl* '**sons-in-law** *s* Schwiegersohn *m.*

son·net [ˈsɒnɪt] *s* Sonett *n.*

so·no·rous [ˈsɒnərəs] *adj* □ sonor, klangvoll, volltönend.

soon [suːn] *adv* bald: **as ~ as** sobald; **as ~**

as possible so bald wie möglich; **at the ~est** frühestens; **I don't want to speak too ~** ich will es nicht berufen. '**soon·er** *adv* **1.** eher, früher: **the ~ the better** je früher, desto besser *od.* lieber; **~ or later** früher *od.* später; **no ~ said than done** gesagt, getan. **I would ~ ... than** ich würde lieber ... als.

soot [sʊt] *s* Ruß *m.*

soothe [suːð] *v/t* **1.** *a.* **~ down** j-n beschwichtigen, *a. j-s Nerven* beruhigen. **2.** *Schmerzen* lindern, mildern.

soot·y [ˈsʊtɪ] *adj* rußig, Ruß...

sop [sɒp] **I** *s* Beschwichtigungsmittel *n* (**to** für). **II** *v/t:* **~ up** aufsaugen.

soph·ism [ˈsɒfɪzəm] *s* Sophismus *m*, Scheinbeweis *m*, Trugschluß *m.*

so·phis·ti·cat·ed [səˈfɪstɪkeɪtɪd] *adj* □ **1.** kultiviert. **2.** ⊙ hochentwickelt. **3.** *contp.* intellektuell.

soph·o·more [ˈsɒfəmɔː] *s Am.* Student(in) im zweiten Jahr.

so·po·rif·ic [ˌsɒpəˈrɪfɪk] **I** *adj* (**~ally**) einschläfernd: **~ drug** → **II. II** *s* Schlafmittel *n.*

sop·ping [ˈsɒpɪŋ] *adj u. adv:* **~ (wet)** F patschnaß. '**sop·py** *adj* □ *Br.* F schmalzig, rührselig.

so·pra·no [səˈprɑːnəʊ] *pl* **-nos** *s* Sopran *m* (*Tonlage, Stimme*), (*Sängerin a.*) Sopranistin *f.*

sor·bet [ˈsɔːbeɪ] *s bsd. Br.* Fruchteis *n.*

sor·cer·er [ˈsɔːsərə] *s* Zauberer *m*, Hexenmeister *m*, Hexer *m.* '**sor·cer·ess** *s* Zauberin *f*, Hexe *f.* '**sor·cer·y** *s* Zauberei *f*, Hexerei *f.*

sor·did [ˈsɔːdɪd] *adj* □ schmutzig (*a. fig.*).

sore [sɔː] **I** *adj* **1.** weh, wund; entzündet: **he is ~ all over** ihm tut alles weh; **my legs are ~** mir tun die Beine weh; **~ throat** Angina *f*, Halsentzündung *f*; **have a ~ throat** *a.* Halsschmerzen haben; → **sight** 2, **thumb** I. **2.** *fig.* wund (*Punkt*). **3.** *bsd. Am.* F sauer (**about** wegen). **II** *s* **4.** wunde Stelle, Wunde *f.* '**sore·ly** *adv:* **~ missed** schmerzlich vermißt; **~ needed** dringend gebraucht.

so·ror·i·ty [səˈrɒrətɪ] *s Am.* Studentinnenverbindung *f.*

sor·rel [ˈsɒrəl] *s* ♣ Sauerampfer *m.*

sor·row [ˈsɒrəʊ] *s* **1.** (**at, over**) Kummer *m* (über *acc*, um), Trauer *f* (um); Traurigkeit f. **2.** Sorge f: → **drown** 2. **sor·row·ful** ['ɔ-ful] adj □ traurig, kummervoll.

sor·ry ['sɒrɪ] I adj **1. be** (od. **feel**) **~ for s.o.** j-n bedauern od. bemitleiden: **I'm ~ for him** er tut mir leid; **I'm ~** → 3; **I am ~ to say** ich muß leider sagen. **2.** traurig, jämmerlich. II int **3.** a) (es) tut mir leid, b) Entschuldigung!, Verzeihung!: **say ~** sich entschuldigen (**to s.o.** bei j-m; **for s.th.** für et.). **4.** bsd. Br. wie bitte?

sort [sɔːt] I s **1.** Sorte f, Art f, ✝ a. Marke f: **all ~s of things** alles mögliche. **2.** Art f: **nothing of the ~** nichts dergleichen; **what ~ of** (**a**) **man is he?** wie ist er?; **I had a ~ of** (**a**) **feeling that** ich hatte das unbestimmte Gefühl, daß; **I ~ of expected it** F ich habe es irgendwie od. beinahe erwartet. **3.** of a ~, of ~s contp. so et. Ähnliches wie. **4. be out of ~s** F nicht auf der Höhe od. auf dem Damm sein. **5.** F guter et. Kerl. II v/t **6.** sortieren; **~ out** aussortieren; Problem etc lösen, Frage etc klären; Br. F j-n zur Schnecke machen. III v/i **7. ~ through** et. durchsehen.

sor·tie ['sɔːtiː] s **1.** ✕ Ausfall m; ✈ Einsatz m. **2.** fig. Ausflug m (**into** in acc).

SOS [ˌesəʊ'es] s ⚓ SOS n: **~ message** SOS-Ruf m.

'so·so sol u. adv F so la la.

souf·flé ['suːfleɪ] s gastr. Soufflé n, Auflauf m.

sought [sɔːt] pret u. pp von **seek.** '**~-af·ter** adj begehrt (Person), (Sache a.) gesucht.

soul [səʊl] s **1.** Seele f (a. fig.). **2.** Gefühl n; (künstlerischer) Ausdruck. **3. be the ~ of generosity** die Großzügigkeit selbst od. in Person sein. **4.** ♪ Soul m. '**~-de·stroy·ing** adj geisttötend (Arbeit etc). **soul·ful** ['səʊlfʊl] adj □ gefühlvoll (Musik etc), seelenvoll (Blick). **soul| mu·sic** s Soulmusik f. '**~-search·ing** s Gewissensprüfung f.

sound[1] [saʊnd] I s **1.** Geräusch n; phys. Schall m; (Radio, TV etc) Ton m; ♪ Klang m (Rockmusik etc a.) Sound m; ling. Laut m: **I don't like the ~ of it** fig. die Sache gefällt mir nicht. II v/i **2.** erklingen, ertönen: **the bell ~ed for lunch** es klingelte zum Mittagessen. **3.** fig. klingen. **4. ~ off** F tönen (**about, on**

von). III v/t **5. ~ one's horn** mot. hupen; → **alarm** 1. **6.** ling. (aus)sprechen.

sound[2] [~] I adj □ **1.** gesund; intakt, in Ordnung. **2.** fig. klug, vernünftig (Person, Rat etc). **3.** fig. gründlich (Ausbildung etc). **4.** fig. gehörig (Tracht Prügel); vernichtend (Niederlage). **5.** fig. fest, tief (Schlaf): → **sleeper** 1. II adv **6. be ~ asleep** fest od. tief schlafen.

sound[3] [~] v/t **1.** ⚓ (aus)loten. **2. ~ out** j-n ausholen (**about, on** über acc); j-s Ansichten etc herausfinden.

sound| bar·ri·er s phys. Schallmauer f, -grenze f. **~ film** s Tonfilm m.

sound·less ['saʊndlɪs] adj □ lautlos. '**sound·ness** s **1.** Gesundheit f. Intaktheit f. **2.** fig. Klugheit f, Vernünftigkeit f. **3.** fig. Gründlichkeit f.

'**sound|·proof** I adj schalldicht. II v/t schalldicht machen. **~ track** s **1.** Film: Tonspur f. **2.** Filmmusik f. **~ wave** s phys. Schallwelle f.

soup [suːp] I s Suppe f: **be in the ~** F in der Patsche od. Tinte sitzen. II v/t: **~ up** F Auto, Motor frisieren. **~ plate** s Suppenteller m. **~ spoon** s Suppenlöffel m.

sour ['saʊə] I adj □ **1.** sauer: **~ cream** Sauerrahm m, saure Sahne; **go ~** sauer werden. **2.** fig. mürrisch. II v/i **3.** sauer werden. III v/t **4.** sauer werden lassen; säuern; **~ed cream** Br. Sauerrahm m, saure Sahne.

source [sɔːs] s Quelle f, fig. a. Ursache f, Ursprung m: **from a reliable ~** aus zuverlässiger Quelle. **~ lan·guage** s ling. Ausgangssprache f.

sour·puss ['saʊəpʊs] s F Miesepeter m.

soused [saʊst] adj F blau (betrunken).

sou·tane [suː'tɑːn] s eccl. Soutane f.

south [saʊθ] I s **1.** Süden m: **in the ~ of** im Süden von (od. gen); **to the ~ of** → 5. **2.** a. ♀ Süden m, südlicher Landesteil: **the ♀** Br. Südengland n; Am. die Südstaaten pl. II adj **3.** Süd..., südlich: ♀ **Pole** Südpol m. III adv **4.** südwärts, nach Süden. **5. ~ of** südlich von (od. gen). ♀ **A·mer·i·can I** adj südamerikanisch. II s Südamerikaner(in). '**~bound** adj nach Süden gehend od. fahrend. **~·'east I** s Südosten m. II adj südöstlich, Südost... III adv südöstlich, nach Südosten.

south·er·ly ['saʊðəlɪ] I adj südlich, Süd... II adv von od. nach Süden. **south·ern**

['ˌ‿ən] adj südlich, Süd... **'south·ern·er**
s **1.** Bewohner(in) des Südens (*e-s Lan-des*). **2.** ♀ *Am.* Südstaatler(in). **south-ern·most** ['ˌ‿məʊst] adj südlichst.

'south·paw s Boxen: Rechtsausleger m.

south·ward ['saʊθwəd] adj u. adv süd-lich, südwärts, nach Süden: *in a ~ di-rection* in südlicher Richtung, Rich-tung Süden. **'south·wards** adv →
southward.

ˌsouth'west I s Südwesten m. **II** adj süd-westlich, Südwest... **III** adv südwest-lich, nach Südwesten.

sou·ve·nir ['suːvəˈnɪə] s Andenken n (*of
an acc*), Souvenir n.

sov·er·eign ['sɒvrɪn] **I** s Landesherr(in),
Monarch(in). **II** adj souverän (*Staat*).
sov·er·eign·ty ['ˌ‿rəntɪ] s Souveräni-tät f.

So·vi·et ['səʊvɪət] **I** s: *the ~s* pl die Sow-jets pl. **II** adj sowjetisch, Sowjet...

sow¹ [saʊ] s zo. Sau f.

sow² [səʊ] v/t (*mst irr*) **1.** Getreide etc
säen, *Samen* aussäen: *~ the seeds of
discord* fig. Zwietracht säen; → **oats.**
2. *Feld etc* besäen (*with* mit).

so·ya bean ['sɔɪə] s ♀ Sojabohne f.

soz·zled ['sɒzld] adj Br. F blau (*betrun-ken*).

spa [spaː] s (Heil)Bad n.

space [speɪs] **I** s **1.** Raum m. **2.** stare into
~ ins Leere starren. **2.** Platz m, Raum
m. **3.** (Welt)Raum m. **4.** Lücke f,
Platz m, Stelle f. **5.** Zwischenraum m.
6. Zeitraum m. **II** v/t **7.** a. *~ out* in
Abständen anordnen: *~ the chairs two
feet apart* die Stühle im Abstand von
zwei Fuß aufstellen. **~ bar** s Leertaste f
(*e-r Schreibmaschine*). **'~·craft** s (*irr
craft*) (Welt)Raumfahrzeug n. **~ flight** s
(Welt)Raumflug m. **~ heat·er** s Heiz-apparat m, -gerät n. **'~·lab** s Raumla-bor n. **'~·man** s (*irr man*) **1.** Raumfah-rer m. **2.** Außerirdische m. **'~·ship** s
Raumschiff n. **~ shut·tle** s Raumfähre
f, -transporter m. **~ sta·tion** s (Welt-)
Raumstation f. **~ suit** s Raumanzug m.
~ trav·el s (Welt)Raumfahrt f. **'~·wom·an** s (*irr woman*) **1.** Raumfahre-rin f. **2.** Außerirdische f.

spac·ing ['speɪsɪŋ] s: *type s.th. in* (*od.
with*) *single* (*double*) *~* et. mit einzei-ligem (zweizeiligem) Abstand tippen.

spa·cious ['speɪʃəs] adj □ geräumig

(*Zimmer etc*), weiträumig angelegt,
weitläufig (*Garten etc*).

spade¹ [speɪd] s Spaten m: *call a ~ a ~*
fig. das Kind beim Namen nennen.

spade² [ˌ‿] s Kartenspiel: a) pl Pik n (*Far-be*), b) Pik(karte f) n.

'spade·work s fig. (mühevolle) Vorar-beit.

spa·ghet·ti [spəˈgetɪ] s pl (sg konstruiert)
Spaghetti pl.

span [spæn] **I** s **1.** ✈, orn. (Flügel-)
Spannweite f. **2.** Zeitspanne f. **3.** (*Le-bens*)Spanne f, (*Gedächtnis*)Umfang m.
II v/t **4.** Fluß etc überspannen (*Brücke*).
5. fig. sich erstrecken über (*acc*).

span·gle ['spæŋgl] **I** s Paillette f. **II** v/t
mit Pailletten besetzen; fig. übersäen
(*with* mit).

Span·iard ['spænjəd] s Spanier(in).

span·iel ['spænjəl] s zo. Spaniel m.

Span·ish ['spænɪʃ] **I** adj **1.** spanisch. **II** s
2. the ~ pl die Spanier pl. **3.** ling. Spa-nisch n.

spank [spæŋk] v/t j-m den Hintern ver-sohlen. **'spank·ing I** adj flott, scharf
(*Tempo*). **II** adv F: *~ clean* blitzsauber;
~ new funkelnagelneu. **III** s: *give s.o. a
~ → spank.*

span·ner ['spænə] s ⊕ bsd. Br. Schrau-benschlüssel m: *put* (*od. throw*) *a ~ in
the works* F j-m in die Quere kommen.

spar¹ [spaː] v/i **1.** Boxen: sparren (*with
mit*). **2.** sich ein Wortgefecht liefern
(*with* mit).

spare [speə] **I** v/t **1.** j-n, et. entbehren. **2.**
Geld, Zeit etc übrig haben: *can you ~
me a cigarette* (*10 minutes*)? hast du
e-e Zigarette (10 Minuten Zeit) für
mich (übrig)? **3.** *keine Kosten, Mühen
etc* scheuen. **4.** *~ s.o., ~ s.th.* j-m et. erspa-ren, j-n mit et. verschonen. **II** adj **5.**
Ersatz...: *~ part* ⊕ Ersatzteil n, m; *~ tire*
(*bsd. Br. tyre*) mot. Ersatz-, Reserverei-fen m; Br. fig. humor. Rettungsring m.
6. überschüssig: *~ bedroom* Gästezim-mer n; *~ time* Freizeit f; *have you got
10 ~ minutes?* hast du 10 Minuten Zeit
(übrig)? **III** s **7.** mot. Ersatz-, Reserve-reifen m. **8.** ⊕ bsd. Br. Ersatzteil n, m.
'~·ribs s pl gastr. Spareribs pl (*gegrillte
Rippenstücke vom Schwein*).

spar·ing ['speərɪŋ] adj □ sparsam: *be ~
with s.th., use s.th.* *~ly* sparsam mit et.
umgehen.

spark [spɑːk] **I** *s* Funke(n) *m* (*a. fig.*): *whenever they meet the ~s* fly immer, wenn sie zs.-kommen, fliegen die Fetzen. **II** *v/i* Funken sprühen; *~ing plug* *mot. Br.* Zündkerze *f.* **III** *v/t a*) *a. ~ off Krawalle etc* auslösen, b) *bsd. Am.* j-s *Interesse etc* wecken.

spar·kle [ˈspɑːkl] **I** *v/i* funkeln, (*Augen a.*) blitzen (*with* vor *dat*). **II** *s* Funkeln *n,* Blitzen *n.* **spar·kling** [ˈ~klɪŋ] *adj* **1.** funkelnd, blitzend. **2.** *~ wine* Perl- *od.* Schaumwein *m;* Sekt *m.* **3.** *fig.* sprühend (*Witz*); geistsprühend (*Dialog etc*); schwungvoll (*Vortrag etc*).

spark plug *s mot.* Zündkerze *f.*

spar·ring [ˈspɑːrɪŋ] *adj:* *~ partner* (*Boxen*) Sparringspartner *m.*

spar·row [ˈspærəʊ] *s orn.* Spatz *m,* Sperling *m.*

sparse [spɑːs] *adj* □ spärlich: *~ly populated* dünnbesiedelt, -bevölkert.

spar·tan [ˈspɑːtən] *adj* spartanisch (*Lebensweise etc*).

spasm [ˈspæzəm] *s* **1.** ℱ Krampf *m.* **2.** (*Husten-, Lach- etc*)Anfall *m.* **spas·mod·ic** [ˌ~ˈmɒdɪk] *adj* (*~ally*) **1.** ℱ krampfartig. **2.** *fig.* sporadisch, unregelmäßig.

spas·tic [ˈspæstɪk] ℱ **I** *adj* (*~ally*) spastisch. **II** *s* Spastiker(in).

spat [spæt] *pret u. pp von* **spit²**.

spate [speɪt] *s* **1.** *be* (*od. run*) *in ~* Hochwasser führen. **2.** *fig.* Flut *f,* (*von Unfällen etc*) Serie *f.*

spa·tial [ˈspeɪʃl] *adj* □ räumlich: *~ ability* räumliches Vorstellungsvermögen.

spat·ter [ˈspætə] **I** *v/t* **1.** *j-n, et.* bespritzen (*with* mit). **2.** *et.* spritzen (*in s.o.'s face* j-m ins Gesicht; *over* über *acc*). **II** *v/i* **3.** spritzen. **III** *s* **4.** Spritzer *m.* **5.** *a ~ of applause* kurzer Beifall; *there was a ~ of rain* es spritzte, es regnete ein paar Tropfen.

spat·u·la [ˈspætjʊlə] *s* Spachtel *m, f, bsd.* ℱ Spatel *m, f.*

spawn [spɔːn] **I** *s zo.* Laich *m.* **II** *v/i zo.* laichen. **III** *v/t fig.* hervorbringen, produzieren.

spay [speɪ] *v/t* weibliches *Tier* sterilisieren.

speak [spiːk] (*irr*) **I** *v/i* **1.** sprechen, reden (*to,* with mit; *about* über *acc*): *~ing!* *teleph.* am Apparat!; *~ for* sprechen für; *this ~s for itself* das spricht für sich

selbst; *~ of fig.* hindeuten auf (*acc*); zeugen von; *we don't ~* (*to each other*) wir sprechen *od.* reden nicht miteinander; *so to ~* sozusagen; → *devil* 1, *generally, ill* 3, *roughly* 2, *soon, strict.* **2.** sprechen (*to* vor *dat*; *about, on* über *acc*). **3.** sich aussprechen (*in favo[u]r of* für; *against* gegen). **II** *v/t* **4.** sprechen, sagen: → *mind* 4, *volume* 1. **5.** *Sprache* sprechen.

Verbindungen mit Adverbien:

speak| out *v/i:* *~ against* sich klar u. deutlich aussprechen gegen. *~ up v/i* **1.** lauter sprechen. **2.** *~ for* sich klar u. deutlich aussprechen für.

speak·er [ˈspiːkə] *s* **1.** Sprecher(in), Redner(in). **2.** ♀ *parl.* Speaker *m,* Präsident *m.* **3.** *a ~ of English* j-d, der Englisch spricht. **4.** ⚡ Lautsprecher *m.* **'speak·ing** **I** *s:* *~ manner* 1. ℱ *od.:* *~ clock teleph. Br.* Zeitansage *f; we are not on ~ terms* wir sprechen *od.* reden nicht miteinander.

spear [spɪə] **I** *s* Speer *m.* **II** *v/t* aufspießen; durchbohren. **'~·head I** *s* **1.** Speerspitze *f.* **2.** ✕ Angriffsspitze *f;* (*Sport*) (Sturm-, Angriffs)Spitze *f.* **3.** *fig.* Anführer(in). **II** *v/t* **4.** *fig.* anführen. **'~·mint** *s* ♣ Grüne Minze.

spec [spek] *s:* *on ~ Br.* ℱ auf gut Glück.

spe·cial [ˈspeʃl] **I** *adj* (□ → **specially**) **1.** speziell, besonder. **2.** speziell, Spezial...: *~ knowledge* Fachkenntnisse *pl,* -wissen *n.* **3.** Sonder...: *~ school* (*train, etc*) **4.** speziell, bestimmt. **II** *s* **5.** Sonderbus *m od.* -zug *m;* (*Rundfunk, TV*) Sondersendung *f;* ✈ Sonderangebot *n: be on ~ Am.* im Angebot sein. **spe·cial·ist** [ˈ~ʃəlɪst] **I** *s* Spezialist(in), ℱ *a.* Facharzt *m,* -ärztin *f* (*in* für). **II** *adj* Fach... **spe·ci·al·i·ty** [ˌ~ʃɪˈælətɪ] *s* **1.** Spezialität *f: ~ of the house* Spezialität des Hauses. **2.** Spezialgebiet *f.* **spe·cial·i·za·tion** [ˌ~ʃəlaɪˈzeɪʃn] *s* Spezialisierung *f.* **'spe·cial·ize** *v/i* sich spezialisieren (*in* auf *acc*). **'spe·cial·ly** *adv* **1.** besonders. **2.** speziell, extra. **spe·cial·ty** [ˈ~ʃltɪ] *Am.* → **speciality.**

spe·cies [ˈspiːʃiːz] *pl* **-cies** *s biol.* Spezies *f,* Art *f* (*beide a. allg.*).

spe·cif·ic [spəˈsɪfɪk] **I** *adj* **1.** spezifisch (*a. phys.*), speziell, besonder: *~ gravity* spezifisches Gewicht. **2.** konkret, präzis. **3.** eigen (*to dat*). **II** *s pl* **4.** Einzelheiten *pl.* **spe·cif·i·cal·ly** *adv* **1.** speziell, besonders. **2.** ausdrücklich.

spec·i·fi·ca·tion [ˌspesɪfɪˈkeɪʃn] *s* genaue Angabe *od.* Beschreibung. **spec·i·fy** [ˈ⁓faɪ] *v/t* genau beschreiben *od.* festlegen.

spec·i·men [ˈspesɪmən] *s* **1.** Exemplar *n.* **2.** Muster *n*; Probe *f.* **3.** F *contp.* Typ *m* (*Person*).

spe·cious [ˈspiːʃəs] *adj* □ trügerisch: **~ argument** Scheinargument *n.*

speck [spek] *s* kleiner Fleck, (*Staub-*) Korn *n*; Punkt *m* (**on the horizon** am Horizont).

speck·led [ˈspekld] *adj* gesprenkelt.

specs [speks] → **spectacle** 3.

spec·ta·cle [ˈspektəkl] *s* **1.** Schauspiel *n* (*a. fig.*): **make a ~ of o.s.** sich lächerlich machen. **2.** Anblick *m.* **3.** *pl, a.* **pair of ~s** Brille *f.*

spec·tac·u·lar [spekˈtækjʊlə] **I** *adj* □ spektakulär. **II** *s* Show *f* der Superlative.

spec·ta·tor [spekˈteɪtə] *s* Zuschauer(in).

spec·ter *Am.* → **spectre.**

spec·tra [ˈspektrə] *pl von* **spectrum.**

spec·tral [ˈspektrəl] *adj* □ **1.** geisterhaft, gespenstisch. **2.** *phys.* Spektral...

spec·tre [ˈspektə] *s bsd. Br.* (*fig. a.* Schreck)Gespenst *n.*

spec·trum [ˈspektrəm] *pl* **-tra** [ˈ⁓trə] *s phys.* Spektrum *n* (*a. fig.*): **a wide ~ of opinion(s)** ein breites Meinungsspektrum.

spec·u·late [ˈspekjʊleɪt] *v/i* **1.** spekulieren, Vermutungen anstellen (**about, on** über *acc*): **~ that** vermuten, daß. **2.** ✝ spekulieren (**in** mit). **spec·u·la·tion** *s* Spekulation *f* (*a.* ✝), Vermutung *f.* **spec·u·la·tive** [ˈ⁓lətɪv] *adj* □ spekulativ, ✝ *a.* Spekulations... **spec·u·la·tor** [ˈ⁓leɪtə] *s* ✝ Spekulant(in).

sped [sped] *pret u. pp von* **speed.**

speech [spiːtʃ] *s* **1.** Sprache *f* (*Sprechvermögen, Ausdrucksweise*): **~ defect** (*od. impediment*) Sprachfehler *m.* **2.** Rede *f,* Ansprache *f* (**to** vor *dat*), ⚖ Plädoyer *n.* **speech·i·fy** [ˈ⁓faɪ] *v/i contp.* Reden *od.* e-e Rede schwingen. **'speech·less** *adj* □ sprachlos (**with** vor *dat*).

speed [spiːd] **I** *s* **1.** Geschwindigkeit *f,* Schnelligkeit *f,* Tempo *n:* **at a ~ of** mit e-r Geschwindigkeit von; **at full** (*od.* **top**) **speed** mit Höchstgeschwindig-

keit. **2.** *mot. etc* Gang *m:* **five-~ gearbox** Fünfganggetriebe *f.* **3.** *phot.* Lichtempfindlichkeit *f.* **II** *v/t* (*irr*) **4.** rasch bringen *od.* befördern. **5.** **~ up** (*pret u. pp* **-ed**) beschleunigen. **III** *v/i* **6.** rasen: **~ by** wie im Flug vergehen (*Zeit*); **be ~ing** *mot.* zu schnell fahren, die Geschwindigkeitsbegrenzung überschreiten. **7.** **~ up** (*pret u. pp* **-ed**) beschleunigen (*Fahrer etc*), (*a. Wachstum etc*) schneller werden. **~ bump** *s mot.* Rüttelschwelle *f.*

speed·ing [ˈspiːdɪŋ] *s mot.* zu schnelles Fahren, Geschwindigkeitsüberschreitung *f.*

speed lim·it *s mot.* Geschwindigkeitsbegrenzung *f,* Tempolimit *n.*

speed·o [ˈspiːdəʊ] *pl* **-os** *s mot.* F Tacho *m.*

speed·om·e·ter [spɪˈdɒmɪtə] *s mot.* Tachometer *m, n.*

speed·y [ˈspiːdɪ] *adj* □ schnell, (*Antwort etc a.*) prompt: → **recovery** 2.

spell¹ [spel] (*mst irr*) **I** *v/t* **1.** a) **~** *out* buchstabieren: **~ out** klarmachen (**for s.o.** j-m), b) (*orthographisch richtig*) schreiben. **2.** *Unglück etc* bedeuten. **II** *v/i* **3.** (richtig) schreiben.

spell² [⁓] *s* **1.** Weile *f:* **for a ~** e-e Zeitlang; **cold ~** *meteor.* Kälteperiode *f.* **2.** (*Husten- etc*)Anfall *m.*

spell³ [⁓] *s* **1.** Zauber(spruch) *m.* **2.** Zauber *m* (*a. fig.*): **be under s.o.'s ~** in j-s Bann stehen; **cast a ~ over s.o.** j-n verzaubern, *fig. a.* j-n in s-n Bann ziehen.

'spell|·bind·ing *adj* fesselnd. **'~·bound** *adj u. adv* wie gebannt: **hold s.o. ~** j-n fesseln.

spell·er [ˈspelə] *s* **1.** **be a good** (**bad**) **~** gut (schlecht) in Rechtschreibung sein. **2.** *Computer:* Speller *m,* Rechtschreibsystem *n.* **'spell·ing** *s* **1.** Rechtschreibung *f:* **~ mistake** (*Recht*)Schreibfehler *m.* **2.** Schreibung *f,* Schreibweise *f.*

spelt [spelt] *pret u. pp von* **spell¹.**

spend [spend] *v/t* (*irr*) **1.** *Geld* ausgeben (**on** für): → **penny.** **2.** *Urlaub, Zeit* verbringen: **~ an hour doing sth.** e-e Stunde damit verbringen, et. zu tun. **'spend·er** *s:* **he's a big ~** ihm sitzt das Geld locker. **'spend·ing** **I** *s* Ausgaben *pl.* **II** *adj:* **~ money** Taschengeld *n*; → **spree.**

spend·thrift ['spendθrɪft] **I** s Verschwen-der(in). **II** adj verschwenderisch.

spent [spent] **I** pret u. pp von **spend. II** adj verbraucht.

sperm [spɜːm] s biol. Sperma n, Samen(flüssigkeit f) m.

spew [spjuː] **I** v/t **1.** a. **~ out** Rauch etc ausstoßen, Lava etc spucken. **2.** a. **~ up** sl. auskotzen. **II** v/i **3.** a. **~ out** hervorquellen (**from** aus). **4.** sl. kotzen.

sphere [sfɪə] s **1.** Kugel f. **2.** fig. (Einfluß-etc)Sphäre f, (-)Bereich m: **in the ~ of** auf dem Gebiet (gen). **spher·i·cal** ['sferɪkl] adj □ **1.** kugelförmig. **2.** Å Kugel..., sphärisch.

sphinc·ter ['sfɪŋktə] s anat. Schließmuskel m.

spice [spaɪs] **I** s **1.** Gewürz n. **2.** fig. Würze f. **II** v/t **3.** würzen (**with** mit) (a. fig.). **~ rack** s Gewürzständer m.

spick-and-span [ˌspɪkən'spæn] adj blitzsauber.

spic·y ['spaɪsɪ] adj □ **1.** gutgewürzt, würzig. **2.** fig. pikant.

spi·der ['spaɪdə] s zo. Spinne f. **~ web** s Am. Spinnennetz n. **~ web** s Am. Spinnennetz n.

spiel [ʃpiːl] s F mst contp. Masche f.

spike [spaɪk] **I** s **1.** Spitze f; Dorn m; Stachel m: **~ heel** Pfennigabsatz m. **2.** Sport: a) Spike m, Dorn m, b) pl Spikes pl, Rennschuhe pl. **II** v/t **3.** aufspießen. **4.** → **lace** 7. **'spik·y** adj □ **1.** spitz(ig); stach(e)lig. **2.** Br. F leicht eingeschnappt.

spill [spɪl] **I** v/t (mst irr) a. **~ out** aus-, verschütten: **I've spilt my coffee over my trousers** ich habe mir m-n Kaffee über die Hose geschüttet; → **bean** 1, **milk** I. **II** v/i (mst irr) verschüttet werden; sich ergießen (**over** über acc); strömen (**out of** aus) (Menschen): **~ over** überlaufen; fig. übergreifen (**into** auf acc). **III** s bsd. Sport: F Sturz m (vom Pferd, [Motor]Rad): **have a ~** stürzen.

spilt [spɪlt] pret u. pp von **spill.**

spin [spɪn] **I** v/t (irr) **1.** drehen; Wäsche schleudern; Münze hochwerfen. **2.** Fäden, Wolle etc spinnen: → **yarn** 2. **3.** **~ out** Arbeit etc in die Länge ziehen, Geld etc strecken. **II** v/i (irr) **4.** sich drehen: **~ round** herumwirbeln; **my head was ~ning** mir drehte sich alles. **5.** mst **~ along** mot. F (dahin)rasen. **III** s **6.**

Sport: Effet m: **put ~ on a ball** e-m Ball Effet geben. **7.** mot. F Spritztour f: **go for a ~** e-e Spritztour machen. **8.** bsd. Br. F **be in a (flat) ~** am Rotieren sein; **send (od. throw) s.o. in a (flat) ~** j-n zum Rotieren bringen.

spin·ach ['spɪnɪdʒ] s ♣ Spinat m.

spi·nal ['spaɪnl] adj: **~ column** Rückgrat n, Wirbelsäule f; **~ cord** Rückenmark n.

spin·dle ['spɪndl] s ⚙ Spindel f. **'spin·dly** adj spindeldürr.

spin·|-'dri·er s (Wäsche)Schleuder f. **~-'dry** v/t Wäsche schleudern. **~-'dry·er** → **spin-drier.**

spine [spaɪn] s **1.** anat. Rückgrat n, Wirbelsäule f. **2.** zo. Stachel m, ♣ a. Dorn m. **3.** (Buch)Rücken m. **'spine·less** adj □ fig. rückgratlos.

spin·na·ker ['spɪnəkə] s ⚓ Spinnaker m.

spin·ney ['spɪnɪ] s Br. Dickicht n.

spin·ning| mill ['spɪnɪŋ] s Spinnerei f. **~ wheel** s Spinnrad n.

'spin-off s **1.** Neben-, Abfallprodukt n. **2.** fig. (positiver) Nebeneffekt.

spin·ster ['spɪnstə] s ältere unverheiratete Frau, contp. alte Jungfer, spätes Mädchen. **'spin·ster·ish** adj altjüngferlich.

spin·y ['spaɪnɪ] adj zo. stach(e)lig, ♣ a. dornig.

spi·ral ['spaɪərəl] **I** adj □ spiralenförmig, spiralig, Spiral...: **~ staircase** Wendeltreppe f. **II** s (a. ✝ Preis- etc)Spirale f.

spire ['spaɪə] s (Kirch)Turmspitze f.

spir·it ['spɪrɪt] s **1.** allg. Geist m: **in ~** im Geiste; **~ of the age** (od. **times**) Zeitgeist. **2.** Stimmung f, Einstellung f. **3.** Schwung m, Elan m. **4.** pl Laune f, Stimmung f: **be in high ~s** in Hochstimmung sein; ausgelassen od. übermütig sein; **be in low ~s** niedergeschlagen sein; **lift** (od. **raise**) **s.o.'s ~s** j-s Stimmung heben; **my ~s sank** ich wurde deprimiert. **5.** mst pl Spirituose f. **6.** ♣ Spiritus m. **'spir·it·ed** adj □ beherzt (Versuch etc); erregt (Auseinandersetzung).

spir·it lev·el s ⚙ Wasserwaage f.

spir·it·u·al ['spɪrɪtʃʊəl] **I** adj □ **1.** geistig. **2.** geistlich. **II** s **3.** ♪ Spiritual n. **'spir·it·u·al·ism** s Spiritismus m. **'spir·it·u·al·ist** s Spiritist(in). **ˌspir·it·u·al'is·tic** adj (**~ally**) spiritistisch.

spit¹ [spɪt] **I** v/i (irr) **1.** a) spucken: **~ at**

s.o. j-n anspucken, b) ausspucken. **2.** *it is ~ting (with rain)* es sprüht. **3.** knistern (*Feuer*), brutzeln (*Fleisch etc*). **II** *v/t* (*irr*) **4.** Blut etc spucken: **~ out** ausspucken; **~ it out!** *fig.* F spuck's aus! **5.** *a.* **~ out** et. fauchen. **III** *s* **6.** Spucke *f*.

spit² [~] *s* **1.** (Brat)Spieß *m*. **2.** *geogr.* Landzunge *f*.

spite [spaɪt] **I** *s* **1.** Boshaftigkeit *f*, Gehässigkeit *f*: *out of* (*od. from*) *pure ~* aus reiner Bosheit. **2.** *in ~ of* trotz. **II** *v/t* **3.** ärgern. **spite·ful** ['~fʊl] *adj* □ boshaft, gehässig.

spit·ting ['spɪtɪŋ] *adj*: *the bus stop is within ~ distance* F bis zur Bushaltestelle ist es nur ein Katzensprung; *she is the ~ image of her mother* sie ist ganz die Mutter, sie ist ihrer Mutter wie aus dem Gesicht geschnitten.

spit·tle ['spɪtl] *s* Spucke *f*.

splash [splæʃ] **I** *v/i* **1.** spritzen; (*Regen*) klatschen (*against* gegen). **2.** a) planschen (*in* in *dat*), b) platschen (*through* durch): **~ down** wassern (*Raumkapsel*). **3. ~ out on** *bsd. Br.* F tief in die Tasche greifen für. **II** *v/t* **4.** bespritzen (*with* mit): **~ one's face with cold water** sich kaltes Wasser ins Gesicht schütten. **5.** *Wasser etc* spritzen (*on* auf *acc*; *over* über *acc*): **~ one's money about** *bsd. Br.* F mit Geld um sich werfen. **6.** F in großer Aufmachung bringen (*Zeitung etc*). **III** *s* **7.** Spritzer *m*, Spritzfleck *m*: **~ of paint** Farbspritzer. **8.** *bsd. Br.* Spritzer *m*, Schuß *m* (*Soda etc*). **9.** *make* (*quite*) *a ~* F Furore machen. '**~·down** *s* Wasserung *f*.

splat [splæt] *v/i* F klatschen (*against* gegen).

splat·ter ['splætə] → **spatter** 1–3.

splay [spleɪ] *v/t a.* **~ out** Finger, Zehen spreizen.

spleen [spliːn] *s anat.* Milz *f*.

splen·did ['splendɪd] *adj* □ großartig, herrlich, prächtig. '**splen·do(u)r** *s* Pracht *f*.

splice [splaɪs] *v/t* miteinander verbinden, *Film, Tonband etc* (zs-)kleben: *get ~d* F heiraten.

splint [splɪnt] 🏥 **I** *s* Schiene *f*. **II** *v/t* schienen.

splin·ter ['splɪntə] **I** *s* Splitter *m*. **II** *v/t* zersplittern. **III** *v/i* (zer)splittern: **~ off** absplittern; *fig.* sich absplittern *od.* ab-

spalten (*from* von). **~ group** *s* Splittergruppe *f*.

split [splɪt] **I** *v/t* (*irr*) **1.** (zer)spalten; zerreißen: **~ one's sides** F sich vor Lachen biegen; *be ~* *fig.* gespalten sein (*on an issue* in e-r Frage); **~ personality** *psych.* gespaltene Persönlichkeit; **~ second** Bruchteil *m* e-r Sekunde; → **hair. 2.** *a.* **~ up** aufteilen (*between* unter *acc*; *into* in *acc*); sich et. teilen: **~ three ways** dritteln; **~ the difference** *fig.* sich auf halbem Wege einigen. **II** *v/i* (*irr*) **3.** sich spalten; zerreißen. **4.** sich teilen (*into* in *acc*). **5.** *a.* **~ up** (sich) trennen (*of* von). **III** *s* **6.** Riß *m*; Spalt *m*. **7.** *fig.* Bruch *m*; Spaltung *f*. **8.** Aufteilung *f*. **9.** *pl* Spagat *m*: *do the ~s* (e-n) Spagat machen. **10.** (*Bananen*)Split *m*. '**split·ting** *adj* rasend (*Kopfschmerzen*).

splodge [splɒdʒ] *s bsd. Br.*, **splotch** [splɒtʃ] *s bsd. Am.* Fleck *m*, Klecks *m*: **~ of paint** Farbklecks.

splurge [splɜːdʒ] F **I** *v/i*: **~ on** tief in die Tasche greifen für. **II** *v/t Geld* verschwenden (*on* für). **III** *s*: *have a ~* tief in die Tasche greifen.

splut·ter ['splʌtə] **I** *v/i* **1.** stottern (*a. mot.*). **2.** zischen (*Feuer etc*). **3.** prusten. **II** *v/t* **4.** stottern.

spoil [spɔɪl] **I** *v/t* (*a. irr*) **1.** verderben. **2.** *j-n* verwöhnen, *Kind a.* verziehen: *be ~t for choice* die Qual der Wahl haben. **II** *v/i* (*a. irr*) **3.** verderben, schlecht werden (*Nahrungsmittel*). **4.** *be ~ing for a fight* Streit suchen. **III** *s* **5.** *mst pl* Beute *f*.

'**spoil·er** *s mot.* Spoiler *m*.

'**spoil·sport** *s* Spielverderber(in).

spoilt [spɔɪlt] *pret u. pp von* **spoil**.

spoke¹ [spəʊk] *pret von* **speak**.

spoke² [~] *s* Speiche *f*: *put a ~ in s.o.'s wheel* *fig.* j-m (e-n) Knüppel zwischen die Beine werfen.

spo·ken ['spəʊkən] *pp von* **speak**.

spokes|**·man** ['spəʊksmən] *s* (*irr* **man**) Sprecher *m*. '**~·wom·an** *s* (*irr* **woman**) Sprecherin *f*.

sponge [spʌndʒ] **I** *s* **1.** Schwamm *m*: *throw in the ~* *fig.* das Handtuch werfen. **2.** → **sponge cake. 3.** *fig.* Schnorrer(in). **II** *v/t* **4.** *a.* **~ down** (mit e-m Schwamm) abwaschen; **~ (up)** aufwischen (*from* von). **5.** *fig.* schnorren (*from, off, on* von, bei). III *v/i* **6.** *fig.* schnorren (*from, off, on* bei): ~ *off s.o. a.* j-m auf der Tasche liegen. **~ bag** *s Br.* Kulturbeutel *m*, Toilettentasche *f.* ~ **cake** *s* Biskuitkuchen *m.*

spong·er ['spʌndʒə] → *sponge* 3.
'spong·y *adj* □ **1.** schwammartig. **2.** weich, *b.s.* teigig (*Brot etc*). **3.** nachgiebig (*Boden etc*).

spon·sor ['spɒnsə] **I** *s* **1.** Sponsor(in) (*a. Rundfunk, TV*), Geldgeber(in). **2.** Spender(in). **3.** Bürge *m*, Bürgin *f.* **II** *v/t* **4.** sponsern. **5.** bürgen für.

spon·ta·ne·ous [spɒn'teɪnjəs] *adj* □ spontan.

spoof [spu:f] *s* F Parodie *f* (*of, on* auf *acc*).

spook [spu:k] F **I** *s* Gespenst *n.* **II** *v/t Am.* j-m e-n Schrecken einjagen. **'spook·y** *adj* □ F unheimlich.

spool [spu:l] *s* Spule *f.*

spoon [spu:n] *s* Löffel *m.* **'~-feed** *v/t* (*irr feed*) **1.** *Kind etc* füttern. **2.** *fig.* j-m alles vorkauen: ~ *s.o.* **with** *s.th.,* ~ *s.th.* **to** *s.o.* j-m et. vorkauen.

spoon·ful ['spu:nfʊl] *s ein* Löffel(voll) *m.*

spo·rad·ic [spə'rædɪk] *adj* (*~ally*) sporadisch, gelegentlich.

spore [spɔ:] *s biol.* Spore *f.*

spor·ran ['spɒrən] *s Schottentracht:* Felltasche *f.*

sport [spɔ:t] **I** *s* **1. a)** Sport(art *f*) *m*, **b)** *oft pl allg.* Sport *m.* **2.** *a.* **good** ~ F feiner *od.* anständiger Kerl: **be a** ~ sei kein Spielverderber. **3.** *in* ~ zum Scherz, im Spaß. **II** *adj* **4.** *Am.* Sport... **III** *v/t* **5.** protzen mit; mit *e-m blauen Auge* herumlaufen. **'sport·ing** *adj* □ **1.** Sport... **2.** fair (*a. Chance*), anständig, sportlich.

sports [spɔ:ts] *adj* Sport...: ~ **car** Sportwagen *m*; ~ **jacket** Sakko *m, n.* ~**man** ['~mən] *s* (*irr man*) **1.** Sportler *m.* **2.** feiner *od.* anständiger Kerl. **'~·man-like** *adj* sportlich, fair, anständig. **'~·man·ship** *s* Sportlichkeit *f*, Fairneß *f*, Anständigkeit *f.* **'~·wom·an** *s* (*irr woman*) Sportlerin *f.*

sport·y ['spɔ:tɪ] *adj* □ F **1.** sportlich, sportbegeistert. **2.** flott (*Kleidungsstück*).

spot [spɒt] **I** *s* **1.** Punkt *m*, Tupfen *m*, Fleck *m.* **2.** ✱ Pickel *m.* **3.** Ort *m*, Platz *m*, Stelle *f*: **on the** ~ zur Stelle; an Ort u. Stelle, vor Ort; auf der Stelle, sofort;

put on the ~ j-n in die Enge treiben; j-n in Verlegenheit bringen; *be in a* ~ F in Schwulitäten sein; → *rooted.* **4.** *fig.* **soft** ~ Schwäche *f* (*for* für); **tender** ~ empfindliche Stelle; **weak** ~ schwacher Punkt; Schwäche *f.* **5. a** ~ **of** *Br.* F ein bißchen. **6.** *Rundfunk, TV:* (Werbe)Spot *m.* **7.** F Spot *m* (*Spotlight*). **II** *v/t* **8.** entdecken, sehen. **III** *v/i* **9.** *it is* **~ting** (*with rain*) es tröpfelt. ~ **check** *s* Stichprobe *f.* **,~'check** *v/t* stichprobenweise überprüfen (*for* auf *acc*).

spot·less ['spɒtlɪs] *adj* □ **1.** tadellos sauber. **2.** *fig.* untad(e)lig.

'spot·light *s* **1.** Spotlight *n*, Scheinwerfer(licht *n*) *m*: *be in the* (*political*) ~ im Brennpunkt des (politischen) Interesses stehen. **II** *v/t* (*a. irr light*) anstrahlen; *fig.* aufmerksam machen auf (*acc*). **,~'on** *adj u. adv Br.* F genau richtig.

spot·ted ['spɒtɪd] *adj* getüpfelt; fleckig. **'spot·ty** *adj* □ **1.** pick(e)lig. **2.** *fig.* uneinheitlich, unterschiedlich.

spouse [spaʊz] *s* Gatte *m*, Gattin *f*, Gemahl(in).

spout [spaʊt] **I** *v/t* **1.** *Wasser etc* (heraus)spritzen. **II** *v/i* **2.** spritzen (*from* aus). **III** *v/t* **3.** (*Wasser- etc*)Strahl *m.* **4.** Schnauze *f*, Tülle *f.* **5. be up the** ~ F im Eimer sein (*Wagen etc*); in Schwulitäten sein (*Person*): **she's up the** ~ bei ihr ist was unterwegs.

sprain [spreɪn] ✱ **I** *v/t* sich *den Knöchel etc* verstauchen: ~ *one's ankle.* **II** *s* Verstauchung *f.*

sprang [spræŋ] *pret von* **spring.**

sprat [spræt] *s ichth.* Sprotte *f.*

sprawl [sprɔ:l] **I** *v/i* **1.** *a.* ~ **out** ausgestreckt liegen *od.* sitzen. **2.** *b.s.* sich ausbreiten (*Stadt etc*). **II** *v/t* **3. be ~ed** (*out*) → 1.

spray [spreɪ] **I** *v/t* **1.** sprühen, spritzen. **II** *v/t* **2.** besprühen, spritzen (*with* mit); sich *die Haare* sprayen; *et.* sprühen, spritzen (*on* auf *acc*); *Parfüm etc* versprühen, zerstäuben. **III** *s* **3.** Sprühnebel *m*; Gischt *f.* **4.** Spray *m, n.* **5.** Sprüh-, Spraydose *f*; Zerstäuber *m.* **'spray·er** → *spray* 5.

spray gun *s* ⚙ Spritzpistole *f.*

spread [spred] **I** *v/t* **1. a.** ~ **out** ausbreiten, *Arme a.* ausstrecken; *Finger etc* spreizen. **2.** *Butter etc* streichen (**on**

auf *acc*); *Brot etc* (be)streichen (**with** mit). **3.** *Furcht, Krankheit, Nachricht etc* verbreiten, *Gerücht a.* ausstreuen. **II** *v/i* (*irr*) **4.** *a.* **~ out** sich ausbreiten. **5.** sich (*räumlich od. zeitlich*) erstrecken (**over** über *acc*). **6.** sich streichen lassen (*Butter etc*). **7.** sich verbreiten (*Furcht, Krankheit, Nachricht etc*), übergreifen (**to** auf *acc*) (*Feuer, Epidemie etc*): → **wildfire. III** *s* **8. ✓**, *orn.* Spannweite *f*. **9.** (Brot)Aufstrich *m*, Paste *f*. **10.** Verbreitung *f*, Ausstreuung *f*. **11.** *fig.* Spektrum *n*. **12.** F Festessen *n*.

spree [spri:] *s* F: **go** (**out**) **on a ~** e-n draufmachen; e-e Sauftour machen; **go on a buying** (*od.* **shopping, spending**) **~** wie verrückt einkaufen.

sprig [sprɪg] *s* Zweig *m*.

spright·ly ['spraɪtlɪ] *adj* rüstig (*alter Mensch*).

spring [sprɪŋ] **I** *v/i* (*irr*) **1.** springen: **~ at** sich stürzen auf (*acc*); **~ to one's feet** aufspringen. **2.** springen, schnellen: **~ back** zurückschnellen; **~ open** aufspringen (*Deckel etc*). **3.** **~ up** aufkommen (*Wind*); aus dem Boden schießen (*Gebäude etc*). **4.** **~ from** herrühren von. **II** *v/t* (*irr*) **5.** **~ s.th. on s.o.** j-n mit et. überraschen. **6.** → **leak** 1a. **III** *s* **7.** Frühling *m*, Frühjahr *n*: **in** (**the**) **~** im Frühling. **8.** Quelle *f*. **9.** Sprung *m*: **make a ~ at** sich stürzen auf (*acc*). **10.** ⚙ Feder *f*. **11.** Elastizität *f*; Federung *f*. **IV** *adj* **12.** Frühlings...: **~ flowers**. **'~·board** *s* Sprungbrett *n* (*a. fig.* **for**, **to** für). **~ chick·en** *s*: **he's no ~** F er ist nicht mehr der jüngste. **,~'clean** *v/t u. v/i* gründlich putzen, *engS.* Frühjahrsputz machen (*in dat*). **~ fe·ver** *s* Frühjahrsmüdigkeit *f*; Frühlingsgefühle *pl*. **~ tide** *s* Springflut *f*, **-tide** *f*. **'~·time** *s* Frühling(szeit *f*) *m*, Frühjahr *n*.

spring·y ['sprɪŋɪ] *adj* □ elastisch, federnd.

sprin·kle ['sprɪŋkl] **I** *v/t* **1.** *Wasser etc* sprengen (**on** auf *acc*); *Salz etc* streuen (**on** auf *acc*); *et.* be)sprengen *od.* bestreuen (**with** mit). **II** *v/i* **2.** **it is sprinkling** es sprüht (*regnet fein*). **III** *s* **3.** (Be)Sprengen *n*; (Be)Streuen *n*. **4.** Sprühregen *m*. **'sprin·kler** *s* **1.** (*Rasen*)Sprenger *m*; Sprinkler *m*, Berieselungsanlage *f*. **2.** *eccl.* Weihwasserwe-

del *m*. **'sprin·kling** *s*: **a ~ of** ein bißchen, ein paar.

sprint [sprɪnt] (*Sport*) **I** *v/i* **1.** sprinten; *a. allg.* sprinten, spurten. **II** *v/t* **2.** *a.* **~ race** Sprint *m*. **3.** Sprint *m*, Spurt *m* (*beide a. allg.*): **make** (*od.* **put on**) **a ~** e-n Spurt hinlegen. **'sprint·er** *s Sport:* Sprinter(in).

sprite [spraɪt] *s* Geist *m*, Kobold *m*.

sprout [spraʊt] **I** *v/i* **1.** sprießen (*Knospen etc*), keimen (*Kartoffeln, Saat etc*). **II** *v/t* **2.** **~ a beard** sich e-n Bart wachsen lassen. **III** *s* **3.** Sproß *m*; Trieb *m*; Keim *m*. **4.** *pl* Rosenkohl *m*.

spruce¹ [spru:s] **I** *adj* □ adrett. **II** *v/t u. v/i*: **~** (**o.s.**) **up** F sich feinmachen, sich in Schale werfen.

spruce² [~] *s* ♣ Fichte *f*.

sprung [sprʌŋ] *pp u. Am. pret von* **spring.**

spry [spraɪ] *adj* □ rüstig (*ältere Person*).

spud [spʌd] *s* F Kartoffel *f*.

spun [spʌn] *pret u. pp von* **spin.**

spunk [spʌŋk] *s* F Mumm *m*. **'spunk·y** *adj* □ F mutig.

spur [spɜ:] **I** *s* **1.** Sporn *m* (*a. zo.*). **2.** *fig.* Ansporn *m* (**to** zu): **on the ~ of the moment** spontan. **II** *v/t* **3.** *e-m Pferd* die Sporen geben. **4.** *oft* **~ on** *fig.* anspornen (**to** zu).

spu·ri·ous ['spjʊərɪəs] *adj* □ **1.** Pseudo..., Schein... **2.** geheuchelt, unecht.

,spur-of-the-'mo·ment *adj* spontan.

spurt¹ [spɜ:t] **I** *s* **1.** *Sport:* Spurt *m*, Sprint *m* (*beide a. allg.*): **put on a ~** e-n Spurt hinlegen. **2.** (*Arbeits*)Anfall *m*, (*Gefühls*)Aufwallung *f*. **II** *v/i* **3.** *Sport:* spurten, sprinten (*beide a. allg.*).

spurt² [~] **I** *v/i* spritzen (**from** aus). **II** *s* (*Wasser- etc*)Strahl *m*.

sput·ter ['spʌtə] **I** *v/i* **1.** stottern (*a. mot.*). **2.** zischen (*Feuer etc*). **II** *v/t* **3.** stottern.

spy [spaɪ] **I** *v/i* spionieren, Spionage treiben (**for** für): **~ into** *fig.* herumspionieren in (*dat*); **~ on** *j-m* nachspionieren. **II** *v/t*: **~ out** ausspionieren; ausfindig machen: **~ out the land** *fig.* die Lage peilen. **III** *s* Spion(in). **~ ring** *s* Spionagering *m*.

squab·ble ['skwɒbl] **I** *v/i* (sich) streiten (**about, over** um, wegen). **II** *s* Streit *m*.

squad [skwɒd] *s* **1.** Mannschaft *f*, Trupp *m*. **2.** (*Überfall- etc*)Kommando *n* (*der Polizei*); Dezernat *n*. **3.** *Sport:* Kader *m.* **~ car** *s bsd. Am.* (Funk)Streifenwagen *m.*

squad·ron ['skwɒdrən] *s* ✕, ✈ Staffel *f;* ⚓ Geschwader *n.*

squal·id ['skwɒlɪd] *adj* □ **1.** verwahrlost (*Gebäude etc*); erbärmlich (*Verhältnisse etc*). **2.** *fig.* schmutzig (*Geschichte etc*).

squall¹ [skwɔːl] **I** *v/i* schreien. **II** *s* Schrei *m.*

squall² [~] *s* Bö *f.* **'squall·y** *adj* böig.

squal·or ['skwɒlə] *s* Verwahrlosung *f:* **live in ~** in erbärmlichen Verhältnissen leben.

square [skweə] **I** *s* **1.** Quadrat *n.* **2.** Feld *n* (*e-s Brettspiels*): **be back to ~ one** *fig.* wieder ganz am Anfang stehen. **3.** (*öffentlicher*) Platz. **4.** ⊿ Quadrat(zahl *f*) *n.* **5.** ⊛ Winkel(maß *m*) *m.* **II** *adj* **6.** quadratisch; Quadrat...: *three yards ~* drei Yards im Quadrat; **~ root** ⊿ Quadratwurzel *f;* → *peg* 1. **7.** rechtwink(e)lig; eckig (*Schultern etc*). **8.** fair, gerecht. **9. be** (*all*) **~** quitt sein. **10.** F anständig, ordentlich (*Mahlzeit*). **III** *adv* **11.** → *squarely*. **IV** *v/t* **12.** *a.* **~ off** (*od.* **up**) quadratisch *od.* rechtwink(e)lig machen. **13.** *a.* **~ off** in Quadrate einteilen: **~d paper** kariertes Papier. **14.** ⊿ Zahl quadrieren, ins Quadrat erheben: *4 ~d equals 16* 4 hoch 2 ist 16. **15.** *Konto* ausgleichen; *Schulden* begleichen: **~ account** 5. **16. ~ s.th. with one's conscience** et. mit s-m Gewissen vereinbaren *od.* in Einklang bringen. **V** *v/i* **17.** übereinstimmen, in Einklang stehen (*with* mit). **18. ~ up** abrechnen. **19. ~ up to** sich *j-m, e-m Problem etc* stellen. **'square·ly** *adv* □ **1.** → *square* 6–8. **2.** direkt, genau.

squash [skwɒʃ] **I** *v/t* **1.** zerdrücken, -quetschen: **~ flat** flachdrücken. **2.** quetschen, zwängen (*into* in *acc*). **3.** *j-n* zum Schweigen bringen (*with* mit); *Gerücht etc* ersticken. **II** *v/i* **4.** sich quetschen *od.* zwängen (*into* in *acc*). **III** *s* **5.** Gedränge *n.* **6.** → *lemon* 3, *orange* I. **7.** *Sport:* Squash *n.* **'squash·y** *adj* □ **1.** weich (*Frucht*). **2.** aufgeweicht (*Boden*).

squat [skwɒt] **I** *v/i* **1.** hocken, kauern: **~ down** sich (hin)hocken *od.* (-)kauern.

2. ~ in a house ein Haus besetzt haben. **II** *adj* **3.** gedrungen, untersetzt. **III** *s* **4.** Hocke *f.* **5.** besetztes Haus. **'squat·ter** *s* Hausbesetzer(in).

squaw [skwɔː] *s* Squaw *f* (*Indianerfrau*).

squawk [skwɔːk] *v/i* F lautstark protestieren (*about* gegen).

squeak [skwiːk] **I** *v/i* **1.** piep(s)en (*Maus etc*). **2.** quietschen (*Tür etc*). **3. ~ through** F es gerade noch schaffen. **II** *s* **4.** Piep(s)en *n;* Piep(s) *m,* Piepser *m; fig.* F Piep *m.* **5.** Quietschen *n.* **6. that was a narrow ~** F das war knapp, das hätte ins Auge gehen können. **'squeak·y** *adj* □ **1.** piepsig: **~ voice** a. Piepsstimme *f.* **2.** quietschend.

squeal [skwiːl] *v/i* **1.** kreischen (*with* vor *dat*). **2.** *fig.* F singen: **~ on s.o.** j-n verpfeifen.

squeam·ish ['skwiːmɪʃ] *adj* □ empfindlich, zartbesaitet.

squeeze [skwiːz] **I** *v/t* **1.** drücken; *Orangen etc* auspressen, -quetschen: **~ out** *Schwamm etc* ausdrücken; *Saft etc* auspressen (*of* aus). **2.** quetschen, zwängen (*into* in *acc*). **II** *v/i* **3.** sich quetschen *od.* zwängen (*into* in *acc*). **III** *s* **4. give s.th. a ~** et. drücken; **put the ~ on s.o.** F j-n unter Druck setzen. **5.** Gedränge *n.* **'squeez·er** *s* Presse *f.*

squelch [skweltʃ] *v/i* p(l)atschen.

squib [skwɪb] *s* Knallfrosch *m:* → *damp* 1.

squint [skwɪnt] **I** *v/i* **1.** schielen. **2.** blinzeln. **II** *s* **3.** Schielen *n:* **have a ~** schielen.

squirm [skwɜːm] *v/i* sich winden (*with* vor *dat*) (*a. fig.*).

squir·rel ['skwɪrəl] *s zo.* Eichhörnchen *n.*

squirt [skwɜːt] **I** *v/i* spritzen (*from* aus). **II** *v/t* bespritzen (*with* mit). **III** *s* **3.** Strahl *m.*

stab [stæb] **I** *v/t* **1.** *j-m* e-n Stich versetzen; *j-n* niederstechen: **~ (to death)** erstechen; *he was ~bed in the stomach* er bekam e-n Stich in den Magen; **~ s.o. in the back** *fig.* j-m in den Rücken fallen. **2. ~ one's finger at** mit dem Finger stoßen nach (*od.* auf *acc*). **II** *v/i* **3.** stechen (*at* nach; *with* mit). **III** *s* **4.** Stich *m:* **~ (wound)** Stichverletzung *f,* -wunde *f;* **~ in the back** *fig.* Dolchstoß *m.* **5. feel a ~ of pain (remorse)** e-n stechenden Schmerz verspüren (Gewissensbisse fühlen). **6. have** (*od.* **make**) **a ~ at s.th.** F et. probieren. '**stab·bing** *adj* stechend (*Schmerz*).

sta·bil·i·ty [stə'bɪlətɪ] *s* **1.** Stabilität *f* (*a. fig.*). **2.** *fig.* Dauerhaftigkeit *f*. **3.** *fig.* Ausgeglichenheit *f*.

sta·bi·li·za·tion [ˌsteɪbəlaɪ'zeɪʃn] *s* Stabilisierung *f* (*a. fig.*).

sta·bi·lize ['steɪbəlaɪz] *v/t u. v/i* (sich) stabilisieren (*a. fig.*). '**sta·bi·liz·er** *s* ⊙ Stabilisator *m*.

sta·ble¹ ['steɪbl] *adj* □ **1.** stabil (*a. fig.*). **2.** *fig.* dauerhaft (*Beziehung etc*). **3.** *fig.* ausgeglichen (*Person*).

sta·ble² [~] *s* Stall *m* (*a. fig.*).

stack [stæk] **I** *s* **1.** Stapel *m*, Stoß *m*. **2.** ~**s** (*od.* **a** ~) **of** F jede Menge *Zeit etc*. **3.** → **blow**¹ **11. II** *v/t* **4.** stapeln: ~ **up** aufstapeln. **5.** vollstapeln (**with** mit). **6. the cards** (*od.* **odds**) **are** ~**ed against us** unsere Chancen sind gleich Null. **III** *v/i* **7.** ~ **up** against *bsd. Am.* F sich halten gegen.

sta·di·um ['steɪdjəm] *s Sport:* Stadion *n*.

staff [stɑːf] **I** *s* **1.** Mitarbeiter(stab *m*) *pl*; Personal *n*, Belegschaft *f*; Lehrkörper *m*, Kollegium *n*; ✕ Stab *m*: **editorial** ~ Redaktion *f*; **be on the** ~ zur Belegschaft gehören. **2.** (*Amts*)Stab *m*; (*Fahnen*)Stange *f*. **II** *v/t* **3.** besetzen (**with** mit). ~ **man·a·ger** *s* Personalchef *m*. ~ **of·fi·cer** *s* ✕ Stabsoffizier *m*. ~ **room** *s* Lehrerzimmer *n*.

stag [stæg] *s zo.* Hirsch *m*.

stage [steɪdʒ] **I** *s* **1.** *thea.* Bühne *f* (*a. fig.*): **go on the** ~ zum Theater gehen; **set the** ~ **for** die Voraussetzungen schaffen für. **2.** Etappe *f* (*a. Radsport u. fig.*), (*Reise*)Abschnitt *m*: **by** (*easy*) ~**s** etappenweise, *fig.* a. Schritt für Schritt. **3.** Stadium *n*, Stufe *f*, Phase *f*. **4.** ⊙ Stufe *f* (*e-r Rakete*). **II** *v/t* **5.** *thea.* auf die Bühne bringen. **6.** *Ausstellung, Demonstration etc* veranstalten: → **comeback.** '~**coach** *s hist.* Postkutsche *f*. ~ **di·rec·tion** *s* Bühnen-, Regieanweisung *f*. ~ **door** *s* Bühneneingang *m*. ~ **fright** *s* Lampenfieber *n*. ~ **name** *s* Künstlername *m*.

stage·y → **stagy.**

stag·ger ['stægə] **I** *v/i* **1.** (sch)wanken, taumeln, (*Betrunkener a.*) torkeln. **II** *v/t* **2.** *j-n* sprachlos machen, umwerfen. **3.** *Arbeitszeit etc* staffeln. '**stag·ger-**

-ing *adj* □ umwerfend (*Nachricht etc*), schwindelerregend (*Preis etc*).

stag·nant ['stægnənt] *adj* □ **1.** stehend (*Gewässer*). **2.** *bsd.* ✝ stagnierend.

stag·nate [~'neɪt] *v/i bsd.* ✝ stagnieren.

stag·na·tion *s* Stagnation *f*.

stag par·ty *s* F (*mst feuchtfröhlicher*) Herrenabend.

stag·y ['steɪdʒɪ] *adj* □ theatralisch.

staid [steɪd] *adj* □ **1.** gesetzt, seriös, *contr.* verknöchert (*Person*). **2.** altbacken (*Ansichten*).

stain [steɪn] **I** *s* **1.** Fleck *m*. **2.** *fig.* Makel *m*. **3.** ⊙ Färbemittel *n*; (*Holz*)Beize *f*. **II** *v/t* **4.** beflecken. **5.** (ein)färben; *Holz* beizen: ~**ed glass** Farbglas *n*. **III** *v/i* **6.** flecken. '**stain·less** *adj* nichtrostend, rostfrei (*Stahl*).

stair [steə] *s* **1.** (Treppen)Stufe *f*. **2.** *pl* Treppe *f*: → **flight**¹ **3.** ~ **car·pet** *s* Treppenläufer *m*. '~**case** *s*, '~**way** *s* Treppe *f*; Treppenhaus *n*.

stake¹ [steɪk] **I** *s* **1.** Pfahl *m*, Pfosten *m*. **2.** *hist.* Marterpfahl *m*; Scheiterhaufen *m*. **II** *v/t* **3.** *oft* ~ **off** (*od.* **out**) abstecken: ~ (**out**) **a** (*od.* **one's**) **claim** *fig.* Ansprüche anmelden (**to** auf *acc*). **4.** *mst* ~ **out** *bsd. Am.* F überwachen (*Polizei*).

stake² [~] **I** *s* **1.** Einsatz *m*: **be at** ~ *fig.* auf dem Spiel stehen; **play for high** ~**s** hoch *od.* um hohe Einsätze spielen. **2.** Anteil *m*, Beteiligung *f* (**in** an *dat*) (*beide a.* ✝): **have a** ~ **in** beteiligt sein an (*dat*). **II** *v/t* **3.** *Geld, Hoffnung* setzen (**on** auf *acc*); *Ruf etc* riskieren, aufs Spiel setzen.

'**stake·out** *s bsd. Am.* F (polizeiliche) Überwachung.

stal·ac·tite ['stæləktaɪt] *s geol.* Stalaktit *m*. **stal·ag·mite** ['stæləgmaɪt] *s geol.* Stalagmit *m*.

stale [steɪl] *adj* □ alt(backen) (*Brot etc*); abgestanden (*Luft etc*), (*Bier etc a.*) schal; *fig.* abgedroschen (*Witz etc*).

stale·mate ['steɪlmeɪt] **I** *s* **1.** *Schach:* Patt *n*. **2.** *fig.* Patt(situation *f*) *n*, Sackgasse *f*: **end in** (**a**) ~ in e-r Sackgasse enden. **II** *v/t* **3.** *Schach:* patt setzen. **4.** *fig.* in e-e Sackgasse führen.

stalk¹ [stɔːk] *s* Stengel *m*, Stiel *m*; Halm *m*.

stalk² [~] *v/i* stolzieren, staksen, steif(bein)ig gehen.

stall¹ [stɔːl] **I** *s* **1.** (*Obst- etc*)Stand *m*. **2.** *pl thea. Br.* Parkett *n*. **3.** *pl eccl.* Chorgestühl *n.* **4.** Box *f (im Stall).* **II** *v/t* **5.** *Motor* abwürgen. **III** *v/i* **6.** absterben *(Motor).*

stall² [~] **I** *v/i* Ausflüchte machen; Zeit schinden. **II** *v/t* j-n hinhalten; *et.* hinauszögern.

stal·lion ['stæljən] *s* (Zucht)Hengst *m.*

stal·wart ['stɔːlwət] **I** *adj* □ **1.** kräftig, robust. **2.** *bsd. pol.* treu *(Anhänger).* **II** *s* **3.** *bsd. pol.* treuer Anhänger.

stam·i·na ['stæmɪnə] *s* Stehvermögen *n,* *(physisch a.)* Kondition *f.*

stam·mer ['stæmə] *v/i ♪* stottern. **II** *v/t* *a.* **~ out** stottern, stammeln. **III** *s ♪* Stottern *n:* **have** *(od.* **speak with) a ~** stottern. **'stam·mer·er** *s ♪* Stotterer *m,* Stotterin *f.*

stamp [stæmp] **I** *v/t* **1. ~ one's foot** aufstampfen; **~ out** Feuer austreten; *Übel* ausrotten. **2.** *Paß etc* (ab)stempeln; *Datum etc* aufstempeln **(on** auf *acc):* **~** *s.o. as fig.* j-n abstempeln als *od.* zu. **3.** *Brief* frankieren: **~ed envelope** Freiumschlag *m.* **4. ~ out ☉** ausstanzen. **II** *v/i* **5.** sta(m)pfen, trampeln. **III** *s* **6.** (Brief)Marke *f; (Rabatt-, Steuer- etc-)* Marke *f.* **7.** Stempel *m (a. Abdruck).* **~ al·bum** *s* (Brief)Markenalbum *n.* **~ col·lec·tion** *s* (Brief)Markensammlung *f.* **~ col·lec·tor** *s* (Brief)Markensammler(in).

stam·pede [stæm'piːd] **I** *s* **1.** wilde Flucht *(von Tieren);* wilder Ansturm **(for** auf *acc):* **there was a ~ for the door** alles stürzte zur Tür. **2.** *fig.* (Massen-) Ansturm *m* **(for** auf *acc).* **II** *v/t* **3.** in wilde Flucht jagen. **4. ~** *s.o.* **into doing** *s.th.* j-n so überrumpeln, daß er et. tut. **III** *v/i* **5.** durchgehen.

stamp·ing ground ['stæmpɪŋ] *s fig.* F Tummelplatz *m;* Jagdrevier *n.*

stance [stæns] *s* **1.** *bsd. Sport:* Stellung *f.* **2.** *fig.* Einstellung *f,* Haltung *f (on* zu).

stand [stænd] **I** *s* **1.** *(Obst-, Messe- etc-)* Stand *m.* **2.** *(Kleider-, Noten- etc)*Ständer *m.* **3.** *Sport etc:* Tribüne *f:* **in the ~** auf der Tribüne. **4.** *♿ Am.* Zeugenstand *m:* **take the ~** in den Zeugenstand treten. **5.** *(Taxi)*Stand(platz) *m.* **6.** *fig.* Einstellung *f* **(on** zu): **take a ~** Position beziehen **(on** zu). **II** *v/i (irr)* **7.** *allg.* stehen: **~ still** stillstehen; **as matters** *(od.* **things) ~** nach Lage der Dinge, so wie die Dinge stehen; **my offer still ~s**

mein Angebot steht *od.* gilt noch; **~ or fall by** *fig.* stehen u. fallen mit; → **awe** I, **correct** 1, **clear** 14, **firm¹** II. **8.** aufstehen. **III** *v/t (irr)* **9.** stellen **(on** auf *acc):* **~** *s.th.* **on its head** *fig.* et. auf den Kopf stellen. **10.** *Beanspruchung, Hitze etc* aushalten, ertragen; *e-r Prüfung etc* standhalten. **11.** **I can't ~ him** *(it)* ich kann ihn (das) nicht ausstehen *od.* leiden. **12. ~** *s.o.* **a drink** F j-m e-n Drink spendieren. **13.** *Chance* haben. **14.** → **trial** 1. **15.** → **bail¹** 2, **surety.**

Verbindungen mit Präpositionen:

stand| by *v/i* **1.** zu j-m halten. **2.** zu s-m *Wort etc* stehen, s-n *Prinzipien etc* treu bleiben. **~ for** *v/i* **1.** stehen für, bedeuten. **2.** eintreten für, vertreten. **3.** sich *et.* gefallen lassen, dulden. **4.** *bsd. Br.* kandidieren für: **~ election** kandidieren, sich zur Wahl stellen. **~ on** *v/i* **1.** stehen auf *(dat):* **~ one's hands (head)** e-n Handstand (Kopfstand) machen; **standing on one's head** F mit links. **2. ~ ceremony** förmlich sein. **~ o·ver** *v/i* überwachen, aufpassen auf *(acc).*

Verbindungen mit Adverbien:

stand| a·bout, ~ a·round *v/i* herumstehen. **~ back** *v/i* zurücktreten. **~ by** *v/i* **1.** danebenstehen: **stand idly by** tatenlos zusehen *(a. fig.).* **~ down** *v/i* **1.** *♿* den Zeugenstand verlassen. **2.** verzichten; zurücktreten **(in favo[u]r of** zugunsten). **~ in** *v/i* einspringen **(for** für): **~ for** *s.o. a.* j-n vertreten. **~ out** *v/i* **1.** hervorstechen: **~ against** *(od.* **from)** sich abheben von. **2.** sich hartnäckig wehren **(against** gegen). **~ to·geth·er** *v/i* zs.-halten, -stehen. **~ up** *v/i* **1.** aufstehen: stehen: **standing up** im Stehen. **2. ~** eintreten *od.* sich einsetzen für. **3. ~ to** *Beanspruchung etc* aushalten; j-m die Stirn bieten. **II** *v/t* **4.** F j-n versetzen.

stand·ard¹ ['stændəd] **I** *s* **1.** Norm *f;* Maßstab *m:* **set high ~s (for)** viel verlangen (von), hohe Anforderungen stellen **(an** *acc);* **be up to (below) ~** den Anforderungen (nicht) genügen *od.* entsprechen; **by present-day ~s** nach heutigen Begriffen. **2.** Standard *m,* Niveau *n:* **~ of living** Lebensstandard *m.* **II** *adj* **3.** normal, Normal...; durchschnittlich, Durchschnitts...; Standard..., ☉ *a.* Serien..., serienmäßig. **4.** maßgebend,

Standard...: ~ **English** korrektes Englisch.

stand·ard² [~] **I** s Standarte f, (an Wagen) Stander m; ✕ hist. Banner n. **II** adj: ~ **lamp** Br. Stehlampe f.

stand·ard·i·za·tion [‚stændədaı'zeıʃn] s Standardisierung f, Normung f, Vereinheitlichung f. **'stand·ard·ize** v/t bsd. ⚙ standardisieren, normen, a. allg. vereinheitlichen.

'stand·by I pl **-bys** s 1. Reserve f. **2. be on ~** in Bereitschaft stehen. **II** adj **3.** Reserve..., Not... **4.** ✓ Stand-by-... **'~-in** s **1.** Film, TV: Double n. **2.** Ersatzmann m; Vertreter(in).

stand·ing ['stændıŋ] **I** adj **1.** stehend: ~ **room only** nur (noch) Stehplätze; → **ovation. 2.** fig. ständig: ~ **order** ✝ Dauerauftrag m. **II** s **3.** Rang m, Stellung f; Ansehen n, Ruf m: **of high** ~ hochangesehen, von hohem Ansehen. **4.** Dauer f: **of long** ~ seit langem bestehend, alt.

stand·off·ish [‚stænd'ɒfıʃ] adj □ F hochnäsig. **'~·point** s fig. Standpunkt m: **from my** ~ von m-m Standpunkt aus. **'~·still** s Stillstand m (a. fig.): **be at a** ~ stehen (Auto etc.); ruhen (Produktion etc); **bring to a** ~ Auto etc zum Stehen bringen; Produktion etc zum Erliegen bringen. **'~-up** adj **1.** a) Steh...: ~ **collar** Stehkragen m, b) im Stehen (eingenommen) (Mahlzeit). **2.** ~ **fight** wüste Schlägerei.

stank [stæŋk] pret von **stink.**

stan·za ['stænzə] s Strophe f.

sta·ple¹ ['steıpl] s **1.** Heftklammer f; Krampe f. **II** v/t heften: ~ **together** zs.-heften.

sta·ple² [~] **I** s **1.** ✝ Haupterzeugnis n (e-s Landes etc). **2.** Hauptnahrungsmittel n. **II** adj **3.** Haupt... **4.** üblich.

sta·pler ['steıplə] s (Draht)Hefter m.

star [stɑ:] **I** s **1.** Stern m: **2s and Stripes** pl (sg konstruiert) das Sternenbanner (Staatsflagge der USA); **see** ~**s** Sterne sehen; **you can thank your lucky** ~**s that** du kannst vom Glück reden od. sagen, daß. **2.** typ. Sternchen n. **3.** Star m (Person). **II** adj **4.** Haupt...; Star... **III** v/t **5.** Wort etc mit e-m Sternchen kennzeichnen. **6. a film** ~**ring** ... ein Film mit ... in der Hauptrolle od. den Hauptrollen; ~**ring** ... in der Hauptrol-

le od. den Hauptrollen ... **IV** v/i **7.** die od. e-e Hauptrolle spielen (**in** in dat). **~·board** ['~bəd] s ✓, ⚓ Steuerbord n.

starch [stɑ:tʃ] **I** s **1.** (Kartoffel-, Wäsche- etc)Stärke f. **2.** pl stärkereiche Nahrungsmittel pl; engS. Kohle(n)hydrate pl. **II** v/t **3.** Wäsche stärken. **'starch·y** adj □ **1.** stärkehaltig, -reich. **2.** fig. F steif.

star·dom ['stɑ:dəm] s (Star)Ruhm m.

stare [steə] **I** v/i starren; große Augen machen: ~ **after** j-m nachstarren; ~ **at** j-n anstarren; → **space 1. II** v/t: ~ **s.o. out** (od. **down**) j-n so lange anstarren, bis er verlegen wird; ~ **s.o. in the face** j-m ins Gesicht starren; vor j-s Augen liegen; fig. klar auf der Hand liegen. **III** s (starrer) Blick, Starren n.

'star·fish s zo. Seestern m.

stark [stɑ:k] **I** adj nackt (Tatsachen etc): **be in** ~ **contrast to** in krassem Gegensatz stehen zu. **II** adv F: ~ **naked** splitternackt; ~ **staring** (od. **raving**) **mad** total verrückt.

stark·ers ['stɑ:kəz] adj Br. F splitternackt.

star·let ['stɑ:lıt] s Starlet n, Filmsternchen n.

'star·light s Sternenlicht n.

star·ling ['stɑ:lıŋ] s orn. Star m.

'star·lit adj stern(en)klar.

star·ry ['stɑ:rı] adj Stern(en)... **~-'eyed** adj blauäugig, naiv.

'Star-‚Span·gled 'Ban·ner s **1.** die Nationalhymne (der USA). **2.** das Sternenbanner (Staatsflagge der USA).

start [stɑ:t] **I** v/i **1.** a. ~ **off** anfangen, beginnen: ~ **doing** (od. **to do**) **s.th.** anfangen, et. zu tun; ~ (**in**) **on doing s.th.** damit anfangen, et. zu tun; **to** ~ **with** anfangs, zunächst; erstens; → **scratch** 7. **2.** a. ~ **off** (od. **out**) aufbrechen (**for** nach): ~ **back for home** sich auf den Heimweg machen. **3.** abfahren (Bus, Zug), ablegen (Boot), ✓ abfliegen, starten; (Sport) starten: ~**ing from Monday** ab Montag. **4.** a. ~ **up** anspringen (Motor etc). **5.** zs.-fahren, -zucken (**at** bei). **II** v/t **6.** a. ~ **off** anfangen, beginnen. **7.** a. ~ **up** Aktion starten, Geschäft, Familie etc gründen, Gerücht in Umlauf setzen. **8.** Motor etc anlassen, starten. **III** s **9.** Anfang m, Beginn m, (bsd. Sport) Start m: **at the** ~ am

Anfang; (*Sport*) am Start; *for a ~* erstens; *from ~ to finish* von Anfang bis Ende; (*Sport*) vom Start bis zum Ziel; *make a fresh ~ (in life)* e-n neuen Anfang machen, noch einmal von vorn anfangen; *make a ~ on s.th.* mit et. anfangen. **10.** Aufbruch *m.* **11.** *give a ~* → 5; *wake up with a ~* aus dem Schlaf aufschrecken. **12.** Vorsprung *m* (*on, over* vor *dat*). '**start·er** *s* **1.** *Sport*: Starter(in) (*Kampfrichter[in]* u. *Wettkampfteilnehmer[in]*). **2.** *mot.* Starter *m*, Anlasser *m.* **3.** F Vorspeise *f*: *as a ~* als Vorspeise. **4.** *for ~s* F zunächst einmal: *that's just for ~s* das ist nur der Anfang. '**start·ing** *adj bsd. Sport*: Start...: *~ point* Ausgangspunkt *m* (*a. fig.*).

star·tle ['sta:tl] *v/t* **1.** erschrecken. **2.** *fig.* überraschen, bestürzen.

star·va·tion [sta:'veɪʃn] *s* Hungern *n*: *die of ~* verhungern; *~ diet* F Fasten-, Hungerkur *f*; *~ wages pl* Hungerlohn *m*, -löhne *pl*.

starve [sta:v] **I** *v/i* **1.** hungern: *~ (to death)* verhungern; *I'm starving* ⊢ ich komme fast um vor Hunger. **II** *v/t* **2.** hungern lassen: *~ (to death)* verhungern lassen; *~ (out)* aushungern. **3.** *be ~d of* knapp sein an (*dat*).

star wars *s pl* ✕ F Krieg *m* der Sterne.

state [steɪt] **I** *s* **1.** *oft* ⌕ *pol.* Staat *m.* **2.** *pol. Am.* (Bundes-, Einzel)Staat *m*: *the ⌕s pl* F die (*Vereinigten*) Staaten *pl*; → *evidence* 2. **3.** Zustand *m*: *~ of mind* (Geistes-, Gemüts)Verfassung *f*, (-)Zustand *m*; *be in a ~ of war with* sich im Kriegszustand befinden mit; *get in(to) a ~* bsd. *Br.* F sich aufregen; nervös werden; → *emergency, health* 2. **4.** Stand *m*, Lage *f*. **II** *adj* **5.** staatlich, Staats...: ⌕ *Department pol. Am.* Außenministerium *n*. **III** *v/t* **6.** angeben, nennen. **7.** erklären, ⋆⋆ aussagen (*that* daß). **8.** festlegen, -setzen: *on the ~d date* zum festgesetzten Termin. '**state·less** *adj pol.* staatenlos. '**state·ly** *adj* **1.** gemessen (*Tempo etc*). **2.** prächtig. '**statement** *s* **1.** Statement *n*, Erklärung *f*; Angabe *f*; ⋆⋆ Aussage *f*: *make a ~* e-e Erklärung abgeben (*to* vor *dat*). **2.** ✝ (Bank-, Konto)Auszug *m*.

,**state-of-the-'art** *adj* neuest, auf dem neuesten Stand der Technik stehend.

states·man ['steɪtsmən] *s* (*irr man*)

Staatsmann *m*. '**states·man·like** *adj* staatsmännisch.

stat·ic ['stætɪk] **I** *adj* (*~ally*) **1.** *phys.* statisch (*a. fig.*). **2.** *fig.* gleichbleibend, konstant. **II** *s* **3.** *Radio, TV*: atmosphärische Störungen *pl*. **4.** *pl* (*sg konstruiert*) *phys.* Statik *f*.

sta·tion ['steɪʃn] **I** *s* **1.** (*a. Bus-, U-*)Bahnhof *m*, Station *f*. **2.** (*Forschungs-, Unfall- etc*)Station *f*, Tankstelle *f*, (*Feuer-*)Wache *f*, (*Polizei*)Revier *n*, (-)Wache *f*, (*Wahl*)Lokal *n*. **3.** *Rundfunk, TV*: Station *f*, Sender *m*. **II** *v/t* **4.** aufstellen, postieren; ✕ stationieren.

sta·tion·ar·y ['steɪʃnərɪ] *adj* stehend (*Fahrzeug etc*): *be ~* stehen.

sta·tion·er ['steɪʃnə] *s* Schreibwarenhändler(in). '**sta·tion·er·y** *s* Schreibwaren *pl*; Briefpapier *n*.

sta·tion| house *s Am.* (Polizei)Revier *n*, (-)Wache *f*. '**~,mas·ter** *s* Bahnhofsvorsteher *m*. **~ wag·on** *s mot. Am.* Kombiwagen *m*.

sta·tis·ti·cal [stə'tɪstɪkl] *adj* □ statistisch. **sta·tis·tics** *s* **1.** (*sg konstruiert pl*) Statistik (*pl*) *f*: → *vital* 2. **2.** (*sg konstruiert*) Statistik *f* (*Wissenschaft, Methode*).

stat·ue ['stætʃuː] *s* Statue *f*, Standbild *n*.

stat·ure ['stætʃə] *s* **1.** Statur *f*, Wuchs *m*. **2.** *fig.* Format *n*.

sta·tus ['steɪtəs] *s* **1.** Status *m*, Rechtsstellung *f*. **2.** → *marital*. **3.** Status *m*, Stellung *f*; Prestige *n*. *~ quo* [kwəʊ] *s* Status *m* quo. *~ sym·bol* *s* Statussymbol *n*.

stat·ute ['stætjuːt] *s* **1.** Gesetz *n*: *by ~* gesetzlich. **2.** Statut *n*, *pl a.* Satzung *f*. *~ book* *s* Gesetzbuch *n*. *~ law* *s* Gesetzesrecht *n*.

stat·u·to·ry ['stætjʊtərɪ] *adj* □ **1.** gesetzlich (garantiert *od.* vorgeschrieben). **2.** satzungsgemäß.

staunch[1] [stɔːntʃ] *v/t* Blut stillen.

staunch[2] [~] *adj* □ **1.** treu, zuverlässig. **2.** standhaft, fest.

stay [steɪ] **I** *s* **1.** Aufenthalt *m*: *~ in hospital* Krankenhausaufenthalt. **2.** ⋆⋆ Aussetzung *f*, Aufschub *m*: *he was given (od. granted)* (a) *~ of execution* s-e Hinrichtung wurde aufgeschoben. **II** *v/i* **3.** bleiben (*for od. to lunch* zum Mittagessen). **4.** wohnen (*with friends* bei Freunden): *~ the night at a hotel* im Hotel übernachten. **III** *v/t* **5.** *~ the*

course (*Sport*) durchhalten (*a. fig.*).
Verbindungen mit Adverbien:
stay| a·way v/i wegbleiben, sich fernhalten (*from* von). **~ down** v/i unten bleiben (*a. fig.*). **~ in** v/i zu Hause *od.* drinnen bleiben. **~ on** v/i: **~ as chairman** (weiterhin) Vorsitzender bleiben; **~ at school** (mit der Schule) weitermachen. **~ out** v/i draußen bleiben: **~ (on strike)** streiken. **~ up** v/i aufbleiben.
'stay-at-home s Stubenhocker(in).
stay·ing pow·er ['steɪɪŋ] s Stehvermögen n, Ausdauer f.
stead [sted] s: **in s.o.'s ~** an j-s Stelle.
stead·fast ['stedfɑːst] adj □ **1.** treu, zuverlässig. **2.** fest, unverwandt (*Blick*).
stead·y ['stedɪ] **I** adj □ **1.** (stand)fest, stabil. **2.** ruhig (*Auge, Hand*), gut (*Nerven*). **3.** gleichmäßig. **4.** fest (*Arbeitsplatz, Freundin etc*). **II** v/t **5.** j-n, Nerven beruhigen. **III** v/i **6.** sich beruhigen. **IV** int **7.** a. **~ on!** Br. F Vorsicht!
steak [steɪk] s Steak n; (*Fisch*)Filet n.
steal [stiːl] (*irr*) **I** v/t **1.** stehlen (*a. fig.*), *Gemälde etc* rauben: **~ s.o.'s girlfriend** j-m die Freundin ausspannen; **~ a glance at** e-n verstohlenen Blick werfen auf (*acc*); **→ march² 5, show 1, thunder** I. **II** v/i **2.** stehlen. **3.** sich stehlen, (sich) schleichen (*out of* aus).
stealth [stelθ] s: **by ~ → stealthy.**
'stealth·y adj □ heimlich, verstohlen.
steam [stiːm] **I** s **1.** Dampf m: **full ~ ahead!** ⏚ volle Kraft *od.* Volldampf voraus!; **under one's own ~** fig. auf eigene Faust; **let off ~** Dampf ablassen, fig. a. sich Luft machen; **run out of ~** fig. s-n Schwung verlieren; **he ran out of ~** a. ihm ging die Puste aus. **2.** Dampf m, Dunst m. **II** v/i **3.** dampfen (a. ⏚, 🚂): **~ing hot** dampfend heiß. **4.** **~ up** beschlagen. **III** v/t **5.** gastr. dämpfen, dünsten. **6. ~ open** Brief über Dampf öffnen. **7. get ~ed up** beschlagen; fig. F sich aufregen (*about* über acc). **'~·boat** s Dampfboot n, Dampfer m.
steam·er ['stiːmə] s **1.** Dampfer m, Dampfschiff n. **2.** Dampf(koch)-, Schnellkochtopf m.
steam| i·ron s Dampfbügeleisen n. **'~·roll·er** s Dampfwalze f. **'~·ship →** **steamer 1.**
steel [stiːl] **I** s Stahl m: **~ nerve →** **nerve** II. **II** v/t: **~ o.s. for** sich wappnen gegen, sich ge-

faßt machen auf (*acc*). **~ wool** s Stahlwolle f. **'~·work·er** s Stahlarbeiter m. **'~·works** s pl (*oft sg konstruiert*) Stahlwerk n.
steel·y ['stiːlɪ] adj **1. ~ blue** stahlblau. **2.** fig. hart (*Blick*); eisern (*Entschlossenheit*).
steep¹ [stiːp] adj □ **1.** steil. **2.** fig. stark (*Preisanstieg etc*). **3.** F happig (*Forderung*), (*Preis a.*) gepfeffert, gesalzen.
steep² [~] **I** v/t eintauchen (*in* in acc); *Wäsche* einweichen: **~ed in history** geschichtsträchtig. **II** v/i weichen.
steep·en ['stiːpən] v/i steiler werden.
stee·ple ['stiːpl] s Kirchturm m. **'~·chase** s Pferdesport: Hindernis-, Jagdrennen n; Leichtathletik: Hindernislauf m.
steer¹ [stɪə] s (junger) Ochse.
steer² [~] **I** v/t **1.** steuern, lenken. **2.** Kurs steuern (*a. fig.*). **3.** j-n lotsen, bugsieren. **II** v/i **4. ~ for** ⏚ ansteuern, Kurs nehmen auf (*acc*); fig. zusteuern auf (*acc*); **→ clear 13. 'steer·ing I** s Steuerung f, Lenkung f. **II** adj: **~ column** mot. Lenksäule f; **~ wheel** mot. Lenk-, a. ⏚ Steuerrad n.
stein [staɪn] s Maßkrug m.
stel·lar ['stelə] adj Stern(en)-.
stem¹ [stem] **I** s **1.** ♣ Stiel m (a. e-s Sektglases etc), Stengel m. **2.** ling. Stamm m. **II** v/i **3. ~ from** stammen *od.* herrühren von.
stem² [~] v/t Blutung stillen; fig. eindämmen, stoppen.
stench [stentʃ] s Gestank m.
sten·cil ['stensl] s Schablone f; typ. Matrize f.
ste·nog·ra·pher [stə'nɒɡrəfə] s Am. Stenotypistin f.
step [step] **I** s **1.** Schritt m (a. Geräusch): **~ by ~** Schritt für Schritt (a. fig.); **take a** e-n Schritt machen; **it's just a ~** (od. a **few ~s) to the shop** es sind nur ein paar Schritte bis zum Laden; **→ watch 4.** **2.** Stufe f; Sprosse f: (*pair of*) **~s** pl **→ stepladder; → mind 7. 3. be in** (*out of*) **~** bsd. ✕ im Gleichschritt *od.* Tritt (aus dem Tritt) sein; (*beim Tanzen*) im (aus dem) Takt sein; **be out of ~ with** fig. nachhinken (*dat*), zurück sein hinter (*dat*); **keep (in) ~ with** fig. sich richten nach. **4.** fig. Schritt m: **take ~s** Schritte *od.* et. unternehmen; **a ~ in the right**

direction ein Schritt in die richtige Richtung; → *legal* 4. **5.** *fig.* Schritt *m*, Stufe *f:* *three-~ plan* Dreistufenplan *m*. **II** *v/i* **6.** gehen; treten (*in* in *acc;* **on** auf *acc*): **~ on it** *mot.* F Gas geben, auf die Tube drücken (*beide a. fig.*); → *gas* 2b.

Verbindungen mit Adverbien:

step| a·side *v/i* **1.** zur Seite treten. **2.** *fig.* Platz machen (*in favo[u]r of* für), zurücktreten (**as** als; **in favo[u]r of** zugunsten). **~ back** *v/i* zurücktreten. **~ down** *v/i* **1.** herunter-, hinuntersteigen. **2.** → *step aside* **2. ~ for·ward** *v/i* **1.** vortreten, nach vorne treten. **2.** *fig.* sich melden (*Zeugen etc*). **~ in** *v/i* **1.** eintreten. **2.** *fig.* einschreiten; sich einmischen. **~ out** *v/i* **1.** heraus-, hinaustreten; *bsd. Am.* weggehen. **2. ~ on** *Am.* F Ehepartner betrügen. **~ up** *v/i* herauf-, hinaufsteigen. **II** *v/t* Produktion *etc* steigern.

step... ['step] Stief...: *~father*, *~mother*, *etc.*

step-by-step *adj fig.* schrittweise. **'~lad·der** *s* Tritt- *od.* Stufenleiter *f.*

steppe [step] *s*, *oft pl geogr.* Steppe *f.*

step·ping stone ['stepɪŋ] *s* Trittstein *m*; *fig.* Sprungbrett *n* (**to** für).

ster·e·o ['sterɪəʊ] **I** *s* **1.** Stereo: *n* in *~*. **2.** Stereogerät *n*, *-anlage f.* **II** *adj* **3.** Stereo...: *~ unit* Stereoanlage *f.*

ster·e·o·type ['sterɪətaɪp] *s* Klischee(vorstellung *f*) *n.* **'ster·e·o·typed** *adj* klischeehaft; stereotyp.

ster·ile ['steraɪl] *adj* **1.** ✻ steril, keimfrei. **2.** *biol.* steril, (*a. Boden*) unfruchtbar. **3.** *fig.* steril, unoriginell. **ste·ril·i·ty** [stə'rɪlətɪ] *s* Sterilität *f* (*a. fig.*); Unfruchtbarkeit *f.*

ster·i·li·za·tion [ˌsterəlaɪ'zeɪʃn] *s* ✻ Sterilisation *f*, Sterilisierung *f.* **'ster·i·lize** *v/t* sterilisieren.

ster·ling ['stɜːlɪŋ] **I** *s* das Pfund Sterling. **II** *adj:* **~ silver** Sterlingsilber *n.*

stern¹ [stɜːn] *adj* □ streng (*Person, Blick, Disziplin etc*).

stern² [~] *s* ♻ Heck *n.*

ster·num ['stɜːnəm] *pl* **-na** ['~nə], **-nums** *s anat.* Brustbein *n.*

steth·o·scope ['steθəskəʊp] *s* ✻ Stethoskop *n.*

stet·son ['stetsn] *s* Stetson *m*, Cowboyhut *m.*

ste·ve·dore ['stiːvədɔː] *s* ♻ *bsd. Am.* Schauermann *m*, Stauer *m.*

stew [stjuː] **I** *v/t* Fleisch, Gemüse schmoren, *Obst* dünsten: *~ed apples pl* Apfelkompott *n.* **II** *v/i* schmoren, dünsten: → *juice* 1. **III** *s* Eintopf *m.*

stew·ard [stjʊəd] *s* **1.** ✈, ♻ Steward *m.* **2.** Ordner *m.* **'stew·ard·ess** *s* ✈, ♻ Stewardeß *f.*

stewed [stjuːd] *adj* F blau (*betrunken*).

stick¹ [stɪk] *s* **1.** Stock *m*, ([*Eis*]Hockey *a.*) Schläger *m*; (*Besen- etc*)Stiel *m*; (*a.* ✈ *Steuer*)Knüppel *m*: **walk with a ~** am Stock gehen; *get (hold of) the wrong end of the ~* F die Sache in den falschen *od.* verkehrten Hals bekommen; → *cleft stick.* **2.** (*trockener*) Zweig, *pl a.* Brennholz *n.* **3.** Stück *n* (*Kreide etc*), Stange *f* (*Dynamit, Sellerie etc*), (*Lippen*)Stift *m*, (*Räucher*)Stäbchen *n*, Streifen *m* (*Kaugummi*). **4.** *a.* **~ of furniture** F Möbelstück *n.* **5.** *live out in the ~s* F in der finstersten Provinz leben.

stick² [~] (*irr*) **I** *v/t* **1.** mit *e-r* Nadel *etc* stechen (*into* in *acc*). **2.** *et.* kleben (**on** auf *acc*, **an** *acc*); an-, festkleben (**with** mit). **3.** stecken: → *nose* 1. **4.** F tun, stellen, setzen, legen: *bsd. Br.* F → *stand* 11. **II** *v/i* **5.** kleben, halten; klebenbleiben (**to an** *dat*). **7.** steckenbleiben: **~ in s.o.'s mind** *fig.* j-m im Gedächtnis bleiben. **8. ~ at nothing** vor nichts zurückschrecken. **9. ~ to** (F **by**) bei *e-r Ansicht etc* bleiben, zu *s-m Wort etc* stehen; **~ to** (F **by**, **with**) zu j-m halten; → *gun* 1, *point* 11.

Verbindungen mit Adverbien:

stick| out **I** *v/i* **1.** vorstehen, (*Ohren etc*) abstehen. **2.** *fig.* auffallen: → *mile*, *thumb* I. **3. ~ for** bestehen auf (*dat*). **II** *v/t* **4.** aus-, vorstrecken: *stick one's tongue out at s.o.* j-m die Zunge herausstrecken; → *neck* 1. **5.** durchhalten, -stehen. **~ to·geth·er** *v/i* (*a. v/t*) zs.-kleben. **2.** *fig.* zs.-halten. **~ up** **I** *v/t* **1.** F j-n, Bank *etc* überfallen. **2.** *stick 'em up!* F Hände hoch! **II** *v/i* **3. ~ for** j-n verteidigen (*a. mit Worten*).

stick·er ['stɪkə] *s* Aufkleber *m.* **'stick·ing** *adj:* **~ plaster** Heftpflaster *n*; **~ point** *fig.* unüberwindliches Hindernis (*bei Verhandlungen etc*).

'stick-in-the-mud *s* F Rückschrittler(in).

stick·ler ['stɪklə] s: *be a ~ for* es ganz genau nehmen mit, großen Wert legen auf (*acc*).

'**stick|-on** *adj*: *~ label* (Auf)Klebeetikett *n*. '*~pin s Am.* Krawattennadel *f*. '*~-up* *s* F (Raub)Überfall *m*.

stick·y ['stɪkɪ] *adj* □ **1.** a) klebrig (with von), b) → *stick-on.* **2.** schwül, drückend (*Wetter*). **3.** F heikel, unangenehm (*Lage*): *he'll come to* (*od. meet*) *a ~ end* mit ihm wird es ein böses Ende nehmen. **4.** *be ~ about doing s.th.* F et. nur ungern tun.

stiff [stɪf] **I** *adj* □ **1.** *allg.* steif: *beat until ~* steif schlagen; → *bore², lip* 1. **2.** *fig.* stark (*alkoholisches Getränk, Medizin*). **3.** *fig.* schwer, schwierig (*Aufgabe*); hart (*Strafe*); scharf (*Konkurrenz*); hartnäckig (*Widerstand*). **4.** F happig, gepfeffert, gesalzen (*Preis*). **II** *s* **5.** *sl.* Leiche *f*. '**stiff·en I** *v/t* **1.** *Wäsche* stärken, steifen. **2.** *fig.* verschärfen. **II** *v/i* **3.** steif werden. **4.** *fig.* sich verschärfen.

sti·fle ['staɪfl] **I** *v/t* ersticken, *fig. a.* unterdrücken. **II** *v/i* ersticken.

stig·ma ['stɪɡmə] *s* **1.** *fig.* Stigma *n*. **2.** *pl* **-ta** ['-tə] *eccl.* Stigma *n*, Wundmal *n*. '**stig·ma·tize** *v/t fig.* brandmarken (*as* als).

sti·let·to [stɪ'letəʊ] *pl* **-tos** *s* Stilett *n*. *~ heel* *s* Bleistift-, Pfennigabsatz *m*.

still¹ [stɪl] **I** *adj* **1.** *allg.* still: → *keep* 15, *stand* 7, *water* 2. **2.** ohne Kohlensäure (*Getränk*). **II** *s* **3.** *Film, TV:* Standfoto *n*.

still² [~] **I** *adv* **1.** (immer) noch, noch immer. **2.** *beim comp:* noch. **II** *cj* **3.** dennoch, trotzdem.

still³ [~] *s* ⚗ Destillationsapparat *m*; Destillierkolben *m*.

'**still|-birth** *s* Totgeburt *f*. '*~·born* *adj* totgeboren. *~ life pl lifes s paint.* Stilleben *n*.

stilt [stɪlt] *s* **1.** Stelze *f*. **2.** △ Pfahl *m*. '**stilt·ed** *adj* □ gestelzt, gespreizt, geschraubt.

stim·u·lant ['stɪmjʊlənt] *s* ✚ Stimulans *n*, Anregungsmittel *n*; *fig.* Anreiz *m*, Ansporn *m* (*to* für). **stim·u·late** ['-leɪt] *v/t* **1.** ✚ *j-n, Kreislauf etc* stimulieren, anregen, *fig. a. j-n* anspornen (*to do* zu tun); *physiol.* reizen. **2.** *Produktion etc* ankurbeln. **stim·u·lus** ['-ləs] *pl* **-li** ['-laɪ] *s*

1. *physiol.* Reiz *m*. **2.** *fig.* Anreiz *m*, Ansporn *m* (*to* für).

sting [stɪŋ] **I** *v/t* (*irr*) **1.** *j-n* stechen (*Biene etc*). **2.** brennen auf (*dat*) *od.* in (*dat*): *~ s.o. into action fig. j-n* aktiv werden lassen. **3.** F *j-n* neppen (*for* um). **II** *v/i* **4.** stechen (*Bienen etc*). **5.** brennen (*from* von) (*Augen etc*). **III** *s* **6.** Stachel *m*. **7.** Stich *m*. **8.** Brennen *n*, brennender Schmerz: *take the ~ out of s.th. fig.* e-r Sache den Stachel nehmen. '**sting·ing** *adj*: *~ nettle* ❧ Brennessel *f*.

stin·gy ['stɪndʒɪ] *adj* □ knick(e)rig (*Person*), mick(e)rig (*Mahlzeit etc*): *be ~ with* knickern mit.

stink [stɪŋk] **I** *v/i* (*irr*) **1.** stinken (*of* nach): *~ to high heaven* wie die Pest stinken; *fig.* zum Himmel stinken. **2.** hundsmiserabel sein. **II** *v/t* **3.** *~ out* F *Zimmer etc* verstänkern. **III** *s* **4.** Gestank *m*: *there's a ~ of garlic in here* hier stinkt es nach Knoblauch. **5.** *cause* (*od. kick up, raise*) *a ~* F Stunk machen (*about* wegen). *~ bomb* *s* Stinkbombe *f*.

'**stink·ing** ['stɪŋkɪŋ] **I** *adj* **1.** stinkend. **2.** F scheußlich; blöd. **II** *adv* **3.** *~ rich* F stinkreich.

stint [stɪnt] *s* a) Pensum *n*, b) Zeit *f*: *he did a three-year ~ in the army* er war drei Jahre lang beim Militär.

stip·u·late ['stɪpjʊleɪt] *v/t* **1.** zur Auflage *od.* Bedingung machen. **2.** festsetzen, vereinbaren. ,**stip·u·la·tion** *s* **1.** Auflage *f*, Bedingung *f*. **2.** Festsetzung *f*, Vereinbarung *f*.

stir [stɜː] *v/t* **1.** (um)rühren: *~ up Staub* aufwirbeln, *Schlamm* aufwühlen. **2.** *Glied etc* bewegen, rühren: *~ o.s.* sich beeilen; → *finger* I, *stump* 1. **3.** *Blätter etc* leicht bewegen, *Wasser* kräuseln (*Wind*). **4.** *fig. j-n* aufwühlen, bewegen. **5.** *~ up fig.* Unruhe stiften, *Streit* entfachen; *Erinnerungen* wachrufen. **II** *v/i* **6.** sich rühren: *~ from* sich fort- *od.* wegrühren von. **7.** *fig.* sich rühren, wach werden. **III** *s* **8.** *give s.th. a ~* et. (um)rühren. **9.** *cause* (*od. create*) *a ~ fig.* für Aufsehen sorgen. '**stir·ring** *adj* □ aufwühlend, bewegend.

stir·rup ['stɪrəp] *s* Steigbügel *m*.

stitch [stɪtʃ] **I** *s* **1.** *Nähen etc:* Stich *m*: *the wound needed eight ~es* die Wunde mußte mit acht Stichen genäht werden;

stop

he had his ~es out yesterday ihm wurden gestern die Fäden gezogen. **2.** *Stricken etc*: Masche *f*: **drop a ~** e-e Masche fallen lassen. **3. have a** (*od.* **the**) **~** Seitenstechen haben; **be in ~es** F sich kaputtlachen. **4. he hadn't got a ~ on** F er war splitterfasernackt. **II** *v/t* **5.** *a.* **~ up** zunähen, *Wunde* nähen: **~ on** (**to**) *Knopf etc* annähen (an *acc*). **6.** *Buch* broschieren, heften.

stock [stɒk] **I** *s* **1.** Vorrat *m* (*of* an *dat*): **have s.th. in ~** et. vorrätig *od.* auf Lager haben; **take ~ ☩** Inventur machen; **take ~ of** *fig.* sich klarwerden über (*acc*). **2. ☩** a) *bsd. Am.* Aktie(n *pl*) *f*, b) *pl* Aktien *pl*, c) *pl* Wertpapiere *pl*. **3.** *gastr.* Brühe *f*. **4.** Viehbestand *m*. **5.** (*Gewehr*)Schaft *m*. **6.** *fig.* Abstammung *f*, Herkunft *f*. **II** *v/t* **7. ☩** *Ware* vorrätig haben, führen. **8. be well ~ed** (**up**) **with** gut versorgt sein mit. **III** *v/i* **9. ~ up** sich eindecken (**on**, **with** mit). **IV** *adj* **10. ☩ ~ model** Serienmodell *n*; **~ size** Standardgröße *f*. **11.** *contp.* Standard..., stereotyp (*Ausrede etc*). **'~,breed·er** *s* Viehzüchter *m*. **'~,breed·ing** *s* Viehzucht *f*. **'~,brok·er ☩** Börsenmakler *m*. **~ cor·po·ra·tion** *s* ☩ Kapital- *od.* Aktiengesellschaft *f*. **~ cube** *s* Brühwürfel *m*. **~ ex·change** *s* ☩ Börse *f*. **'~,hold·er** *s* ☩ *bsd. Am.* Aktionär(in).

stock·ing ['stɒkɪŋ] *s* Strumpf *m*. **~ mask** *s* Strumpfmaske *f*.

,stock|-in-'trade *s*: **be part of s.o.'s ~** *fig.* zu j-s Rüstzeug gehören. **~ mar·ket** *s* ☩ Börse *f*. **'~,pile I** *s* Vorrat *m* (*of* an *dat*). **II** *v/t* e-n Vorrat anlegen an (*dat*); *Lebensmittel etc* hamstern, horten. **'~,room** *s* Lager(raum *m*) *n*. **,~·'still** *adv* regungslos. **'~,tak·ing** *s* ☩ Inventur *f*; *fig.* Bestandsaufnahme *f*.

stock·y ['stɒkɪ] *adj* □ stämmig, untersetzt.

sto·i·cal ['stəʊɪkl] *adj* □ stoisch, gelassen. **sto·i·cism** ['~sɪzəm] *s* Gelassenheit *f*.

stoke [stəʊk] **I** *v/t a.* **~ up** Feuer, *Haß etc* schüren. **II** *v/i*: **~ up** F sich vollstopfen (**on**, **with** mit). **'stok·er** *s* Heizer *m*.

stole¹ [stəʊl] *pret von* **steal.**

stole² [~] *s* Stola *f*.

sto·len ['stəʊlən] *pp von* **steal.**

stol·id ['stɒlɪd] *adj* □ phlegmatisch.

stom·ach ['stʌmək] **I** *s* **1.** Magen *m*: **on**

an empty ~ auf leeren *od.* nüchternen Magen *rauchen etc*, mit leerem *od.* nüchternem Magen *schwimmen gehen etc*; **on a full ~** mit vollem Magen; **turn s.o.'s ~** j-m den Magen umdrehen. **2.** Bauch *m*. **3.** (**for**) Appetit *m* (auf *acc*); *fig.* Lust *f* (auf *acc*, zu). **II** *v/t* **4.** vertragen (*a. fig.*). **~·ache** ['~eɪk] *s* **1.** Magenschmerzen *pl*. **2.** Bauchschmerzen *pl*, -weh *n*. **~ up·set** *s* Magenverstimmung *f*.

stomp [stɒmp] *v/i* sta(m)pfen, trampeln.

stone [stəʊn] **I** *s* **1.** (*a. Edel-,* ☸ *Gallen- etc*)Stein *m*: **it's only a ~'s throw** (**away**) **from** es ist nur e-n Katzensprung entfernt von; **have a heart of ~** ein Herz aus Stein haben; **leave no ~ unturned** *fig.* nichts unversucht lassen. **2.** ♀ Kern *m*, Stein *m*. **3.** (*Hagel*)Korn *n*. **4.** *pl* **stone(s)** *Br.* Gewichtseinheit (*= 6,35 kg*). **II** *v/t* **5.** mit Steinen bewerfen: **~** (**to death**) steinigen. **6.** entkernen, -steinen. **♀ Age** *s* Steinzeit *f*. **,~·'broke** *Am.* → **stony-broke. ,~· 'cold I** *adj* eiskalt. **II** *adv*: **~ sober** F stocknüchtern.

stoned [stəʊnd] *adj sl.* **1.** stinkbesoffen. **2.** stoned (*unter Drogeneinwirkung*).

,stone|·'dead *adj* mausetot. **~·'deaf** *adj* stocktaub. **~ fruit** *s* Steinfrucht *f*, *coll.* Steinobst *n*. **'~,ma·son** *s* Steinmetz *m*. **'~·ware** *s* Steingut *n*.

ston·y ['stəʊnɪ] *adj* □ **1.** steinig. **2.** *fig.* steinern (*Gesicht, Herz etc*), eisig (*Schweigen*). **,~·'broke** *adj bsd. Br.* total abgebrannt *od.* pleite.

stood [stʊd] *pret u. pp von* **stand.**

stooge [stuːdʒ] *s* F *contp.* Handlanger *m*.

stool [stuːl] *s* **1.** (*Bar-, Klavier- etc*)Hocker *m*, (*Klavier- etc*)Stuhl *m*, (-)Schemel *m*: **fall between two ~s** *fig.* sich zwischen zwei Stühle setzen. **2.** *physiol.* Stuhl *m*. **'~,pi·geon** *s* F (Polizei)Spitzel *m*.

stoop [stuːp] *v/i* **1.** *a.* **~ down** sich bükken. **2.** gebeugt gehen. **3.** **~ to** *fig.* sich herablassen *od.* hergeben zu: **~ to doing s.th.** sich dazu herablassen *od.* hergeben, et. zu tun. **II** *s* **4.** gebeugte Haltung: **walk with a ~** → 2.

stop [stɒp] **I** *s* **1.** Halt *m*: **come to a ~** anhalten, stoppen; *fig.* aufhören; **put a ~ to** e-r Sache ein Ende machen *od.* setzen. **2.** (*Bus*)Haltestelle *f*. **3.** *ling.*

bsd. Br. Punkt *m*. **4. pull out all the ~s** *fig.* alle Register ziehen. **II** *v/i* **5.** stehenbleiben (*a. Uhr etc*), (an)halten, stoppen: **~ by s.o.'s place** bei j-m vorbeischauen; → **dead** 14, **thief**. **6.** aufhören: **~ at nothing** vor nichts zurückschrecken (**to get s.th.** um et. zu bekommen); → **short** 5. **7.** *bsd. Br.* bleiben (**for supper** zum Abendessen). **III** *v/t* **8.** anhalten, stoppen; *Maschine etc* abstellen. **9.** aufhören mit: **~ doing s.th.** aufhören, et. zu tun. **10.** ein Ende machen *od.* setzen (*dat*); *Blutung* stillen; *Arbeiten, Verkehr etc* zum Erliegen bringen; (*Boxen*) *Kampf* abbrechen. **11.** *et.* verhindern; *j-n* abhalten (**~ s.o. (from)** von), hindern (**from** an *dat*): **~ s.o. (from) doing s.th.** j-n davon abhalten *od.* daran hindern, et. zu tun. **12.** *Rohr etc* verstopfen; *Zahn* füllen, plombieren: **~ s.o.'s mouth** F j-m den Mund stopfen. **13.** *Scheck* sperren (lassen).
Verbindungen mit Adverbien:

stop| by *v/i* vorbeischauen. **~ in** *v/i* **1.** vorbeischauen (**at** bei). **2.** *bsd. Br.* zu Hause bleiben. **~ off** *v/i* F, **~ o·ver** *v/i* Zwischenstation machen (**in** in *dat*). **~ round** *v/i* *bsd. Am.* F vorbeischauen. **~ up I** *v/t* Leitung *etc* verstopfen. **II** *v/i bsd. Br.* aufbleiben.

'stop|·cock *s* ⊕ Absperrhahn *m*. **'~gap I** *s* Notbehelf *m*, Übergangslösung *f*; (*Person*) Aushilfe *f*, *contp.* Lückenbüßer *m*. **II** *adj:* **~ measure** Überbrückungsmaßnahme *f*; **~ secretary** Aushilfssekretärin *f*. **'~·o·ver** *s* Zwischenstation *f*; ⚓ Zwischenlandung *f*.

stop·page ['stɒpɪdʒ] *s* **1.** Arbeitseinstellung *f*. **2.** ⊕ Verstopfung *f* (*a.* ⚕). **3.** *bsd. Br.* (Gehalts-, Lohn)Abzug *m*. **'stop·per I** *s* Stöpsel *m*. **II** *v/t a.* **~ up** ver-, zustöpseln.

stop| press *s bsd. Br.* letzte Meldungen *pl* (**in** e-r *Zeitung*). **'~watch** *s* Stoppuhr *f*.

stor·age ['stɔːrɪdʒ] *s* **1.** (Ein)Lagerung *f*. **2.** Lager(raum *m*) *n*: **be in ~** eingelagert sein. **3.** Lagergeld *n*.

store [stɔː] *s* **1.** Vorrat *m, pl a.* Bestände *pl* (**of** an *dat*): **there's a shock in ~ for you** auf dich wartet e-e unangenehme Überraschung; **have s.th. in ~** et. vorrätig *od.* auf Lager haben; **have a surprise in ~ for s.o.** e-e Überraschung

für j-n haben. **2.** *bsd. Am.* Laden *m*, Geschäft *n; bsd. Br.* Kauf-, Warenhaus *n*. **3.** Lager(halle *f*, -haus *n*) *n*: **be in ~** *Br.* eingelagert sein. **4. set great** (**little**) **~ by** *fig.* großen (wenig) Wert legen auf (*acc*). **II** *v/t* **5.** *a.* **~ up** sich e-n Vorrat anlegen an (*dat*). **6.** *Kohle etc* lagern; *Möbel etc* einlagern; *Daten, Energie etc* speichern. **~ de·tec·tive** *s* Kaufhausdetektiv *m*. **'~house** *s* **1.** Lagerhaus *n*. **2.** *fig.* Fundgrube *f* (**of** von): **be a ~ of good ideas** voller guter Ideen stecken. **'~·keep·er** *s bsd. Am.* Ladenbesitzer(in), -inhaber(in). **~room** ['~rʊm] *s* Lagerraum *m*.

sto·rey ['stɔːrɪ] *s bsd. Br.* Stock(werk *n*) *m*, Etage *f*: **a six-~ building** → **storeyed**. **'sto·reyed** *adj bsd. Br.*, **'sto·ried** *adj Am.:* **a six-~ building** ein sechsstöckiges Gebäude.

stork [stɔːk] *s orn.* Storch *m*.

storm [stɔːm] **I** *s* **1.** Unwetter *n*; (*a. fig. Protest- etc*)Sturm *m*: **a ~ in a teacup** *Br. fig.* ein Sturm im Wasserglas. **2. take by ~** ✕ im Sturm nehmen *od.* (*a. fig.*) erobern. **II** *v/t* **3.** ✕ *etc* stürmen. **III** *v/i* **4.** stürmen, stürzen. **~ cloud** *s* Gewitterwolke *f:* **the ~s are gathering** *fig.* es braut sich et. zusammen.

storm·y ['stɔːmɪ] *adj* □ stürmisch (*a. fig.*).

sto·ry¹ ['stɔːrɪ] *s* **1.** Geschichte *f;* Märchen *n* (*a. fig.* F): **his side of the ~** s-e Version; **it's the same old ~** es ist das alte Lied; **to cut a long ~ short** um es kurz zu machen, kurz u. gut; → **go** 18. **2.** *Story f,* (Lebens-, Entwicklungs)Geschichte *f*. **3.** Story *f,* Handlung *f*. **4.** *Journalismus:* Story *f,* Bericht *m* (**on** über *acc*).

sto·ry² [~] *Am.* → **storey**.

'sto·ry|·book *adj* ... wie im Märchen. **~ line** → **story¹** 3.

stoup [stuːp] *s eccl.* Weihwasserbecken *n*.

stout [staʊt] **I** *adj* □ **1.** korpulent, (*Frau a.*) vollschlank. **2.** *fig.* hartnäckig. **II** *s* **3.** Stout *m* (*dunkles Bier mit starkem Hopfengeschmack*).

stove [stəʊv] *s* Ofen *m*, (*zum Kochen a.*) Herd *m*.

stow [stəʊ] *v/t a.* **~ away** verstauen. **'stow·a·way** *s* ✈, ⚓ blinder Passagier.

strad·dle ['strædl] *v/t* breitbeinig *od.* mit

gespreizten Beinen stehen über (dat); rittlings sitzen auf (dat).

strag·gle ['strægl] v/i: ~ **in** einzeln eintrudeln. **'strag·gler** s Nachzügler(in). **'strag·gly** adj struppig (Haar).

straight [streit] **I** adj **1.** gerade, (Haar) glatt: ~ **line** gerade Linie, & Gerade f; **keep one's face** ~ ernst bleiben. **2. get** (od. put) **s.th.** ~ et. in Ordnung bringen, Zimmer etc a. aufräumen; **set s.o.** ~ **about s.th.** fig. j-m et. klarmachen. **3.** offen, ehrlich (**with** zu). **4.** ohne Unterbrechung: **in** ~ **sets** (Tennis etc) ohne Satzverlust; **his third** ~ **win** (Sport) sein dritter Sieg hintereinander od. in Folge. **5.** pur: **drink one's whisky** ~; **two** ~ **whiskies** zwei Whisky pur. **6.** sl. a) hetero (heterosexuell), b) clean, sauber (nicht mehr drogenabhängig): **I'm** ~ ich nehm' grundsätzlich keine Drogen. **II** adv **7.** gerade: ~ **ahead** geradeaus. **8.** genau, direkt. **9.** a. ~ **off** sofort. **10.** klar sehen, denken. **11.** F a. ~ **out** offen, ehrlich. **12.** ~ **up?** Br. F ehrlich? **III** s **13.** Sport: (Gegen-, Ziel)Gerade f. ,~·a-'way adv sofort.

straight·en ['streitn] **I** v/t **1.** a. ~ **up** geradehängen, -legen etc, Krawatte etc geraderücken. **2.** ~ **out** fig. Angelegenheit etc in Ordnung bringen, Mißverständnis klären; F j-m (wieder) auf die Beine helfen; j-n (wieder) auf die richtige Bahn bringen. **3.** ~ **up** in Ordnung bringen, aufräumen. **II** v/i **4.** a. ~ **out** gerade werden (Straße etc). **5.** ~ **up** sich aufrichten.

,**straight**'**for·ward** adj □ **1.** aufrichtig. **2.** einfach, unkompliziert. **3.** glatt (Absage etc). ,~·'out adj bsd. Am. F offen, ehrlich.

strain [strein] **I** v/t **1.** Seil etc (an)spannen: ~ **one's ears** (**eyes**) die Ohren spitzen (genau hinschauen). **2.** sich, Augen etc überanstrengen; sich e-n Muskel etc zerren: ~ **a muscle** a. sich e-e Muskelzerrung zuziehen. **3.** Gemüse, Tee etc abgießen. **II** v/i **4.** sich anstrengen. **5.** ~ **at** zerren od. ziehen an (dat): ~ **at the leash** an der Leine zerren (Hund), fig. es nicht mehr erwarten können. **III** s **6.** Spannung f (a. ⚙ el. pol. etc). **7.** fig. Belastung f (on für): **put a great** ~ **on s.o.** j-n stark belasten. **strained** adj **1.** gezerrt: ~ **muscle** a.

Muskelzerrung f. **2.** gezwungen (Lächeln etc). **3.** gespannt (Beziehungen). **4. look** ~ abgespannt aussehen. '**strain·er** s Sieb n.

strait [streit] s a. pl Meerenge f, Straße f: **be in desperate** (od. **dire**) ~**s** fig. in e-r ernsten Notlage sein. '**strait·ened** adj: **live in** ~ **circumstances** in beschränkten Verhältnissen leben.

'**strait**‖**jack·et** s Zwangsjacke f: **put in a** ~ j-n in e-e Zwangsjacke stecken. ,~·'**laced** adj prüde.

strand [strænd] s (Haar)Strähne f; (Woll- etc)Faden m, (Kabel)Draht m; fig. Faden m (e-r Handlung etc).

strand·ed ['strændid] adj: **be** ~ ♣ gestrandet sein; **be** (**left**) ~ fig. festsitzen (**in** in dat) (Person).

strange [streind3] adj □ **1.** merkwürdig, seltsam, sonderbar: ~ **to say** so merkwürdig es auch klingen mag; ~**ly** (**enough**) merkwürdiger-, seltsamer-, sonderbarerweise. **2.** fremd (**to s.o.** j-m). **3. be** ~ **to** nicht vertraut sein mit. '**stran·ger** s **1.** Fremde m, f: **I'm a** ~ **here** ich bin hier fremd; → **perfect** 2. **2. be a** ~ **to** → **strange** 3.

stran·gle ['strængl] v/t erwürgen, erdrosseln; fig. abwürgen, ersticken. '~·hold s Würgegriff m: **have a** ~ **on** fig. j-n, et. vollkommen beherrschen.

stran·gu·late ['strængjuleit] v/t 🖋 abschnüren, abbinden. ,**stran·gu·la·tion** s **1.** Erwürgung f, Erdrosselung f. **2.** 🖋 Abschnürung f, Abbindung f.

strap [stræp] **I** s **1.** Riemen m, Gurt m; Haltegriff m, Schlaufe f (im Bus etc); Träger m (an Kleid etc); (Uhr)(Arm-)Band n. **II** v/t **2.** festschnallen (**to** an dat): **be** ~**ped in** ✈, mot. angeschnallt sein. **3.** a. ~ **up** Br. Bein etc bandagieren. **4. be** ~**ped** (**for cash**) F knapp bei Kasse sein; abgebrannt od. pleite sein. '~·**hang·er** s F **1.** Stehplatzinhaber(in) (in Bus etc). **2.** Pendler(in).

strap·less ['stræplis] adj schulterfrei (Kleid), (a. Badeanzug) trägerlos.

stra·ta ['stra:tə] pl von **stratum**.

strat·a·gem ['strætədʒəm] s (✕ Kriegs)List f.

stra·te·gic [strə'ti:dʒik] adj (~**ally**) strategisch; strategisch wichtig. **strat·e·gist** ['strætidʒist] s Stratege m. **strat·e·gy** ['~dʒi] s Strategie f.

strat·i·fied ['strætɪfaɪd] *adj* vielschichtig (*Gesellschaft*).

strat·o·sphere ['strætəʊˌsfɪə] *s meteor.* Stratosphäre *f.*

stra·tum ['strɑːtəm] *pl* **-ta** ['~tə] *s geol., sociol.* Schicht *f.*

straw [strɔː] *s* **1.** Stroh *n*: → **man** 3. **2.** Stroh-, *a.* Trinkhalm *m*: **the ~ that breaks the camel's back, the last ~** *fig.* der Tropfen, der das Faß zum Überlaufen bringt; **clutch at ~s** *fig.* sich an e-n Strohhalm klammern. **~·ber·ry** ['~bərɪ] *s* ♥ Erdbeere *f.* **~ hat** *s* Strohhut *m.* **~ man** *s (irr man)* Strohmann *m.* **~ poll, ~ vote** *s pol.* Probeabstimmung *f.*

stray [streɪ] **I** *v/i* **1.** sich verirren. **2.** *fig.* abschweifen (**from** von) (*Gedanken etc*). **II** *adj* **3.** verirrt (*Kugel, Tier*); streunend (*Tier*). **4.** vereinzelt. **III** *s* **5.** verirrtes *od.* streunendes Tier.

streak [striːk] *s* **1.** Streifen *m*; Strähne *f* (*im Haar*): **a ~ of lightning** ein Blitz *m*; **like a ~ of lightning** wie der Blitz. **2.** *fig.* (*Charakter*)Zug *m.* **3.** *fig.* (**un**)**lucky ~** Glückssträhne (Pechsträhne) *f*; **win·ning** (**losing**) **~** (*a. Sport*) Siegesserie (Niederlagenserie) *f*; **be on a lucky ~** e-e Glückssträhne haben. **'streak·y** *adj* streifig; durchwachsen (*Frühstücksspeck*).

stream [striːm] **I** *s* **1.** Bach *m.* **2.** Strömung *f*: **go against the ~** *fig.* gegen den Strom schwimmen. **3.** (*Besucher-, Blut-, Verkehrs- etc*)Strom *m*; *fig.* Flut *f*, Schwall *m (von Verwünschungen etc).* **4.** *ped. Br.* Leistungsgruppe *f.* **II** *v/i* **5.** strömen (*Besucher, Blut, Licht etc*): **tears were ~ing down her face** Tränen liefen ihr übers Gesicht; **his face was ~ing with sweat** sein Gesicht war schweißüberströmt. **6.** wehen, flattern (**in the wind** im Wind) **III** *v/t* **7.** *ped. Br. Klasse* in Leistungsgruppen einteilen. **'stream·er** *s* Luft-, Papierschlange *f.* **'stream·ing** *adj*: **he's got a ~ cold** er hat e-n fürchterlichen Schnupfen. **'stream·line** *v/t* rationalisieren. **'~·lined** *adj* stromlinienförmig, windschnittig, -schlüpf(r)ig.

street [striːt] *s* Straße *f*: **in** (*bsd. Am.* **on**) **the ~** auf der Straße; **be** (**right**) **up s.o.'s ~** *fig.* j-m zusagen; **he's not in the same ~ as me, I'm ~s ahead of him** F ich bin ihm haushoch überlegen; **walk**

the ~s durch die Straßen laufen; auf den Strich gehen; → **man** 3. **~ bat·tle** *s* Straßenschlacht *f.* **~ lamp, ~ light** *s* Straßenlaterne *f.* **~ map** *s* Stadtplan *m.* **~ par·ty** *s* Straßenfest *n.* **~ val·ue** *s* (Straßen)Verkaufswert *m (von Drogen).* **~ vend·er, ~ vend·or** *s* Straßenhändler(in). **'~·walk·er** *s* Straßen-, Strichmädchen *n.*

strength [streŋθ] *s* **1.** Stärke *f (a. fig.)*, Kraft *f*, Kräfte *pl*: **~ of character** Charakterfestigkeit *f*, -stärke; **~ of will** Willenskraft, -stärke; **on the ~ of** auf *j-s Rat etc* hin; **he hasn't got enough ~** er ist nicht kräftig genug; **go from ~ to ~** von Erfolg zu Erfolg eilen. **2.** Macht *f.* **3.** (An)Zahl *f*: **in ~** in großer Zahl, zahlreich; **at full ~** vollzählig; **below** (*od.* **under**) **~** nicht vollzählig; unterbesetzt; **be on the ~** F zur Belegschaft gehören. **'strength·en I** *v/t* **1.** verstärken. **2.** *fig.* stärken: **~ s.o.'s resolve** j-n in s-m Vorsatz bestärken. **II** *v/i* **3.** stärker werden, sich verstärken (*Wind etc*).

stren·u·ous ['strenjʊəs] *adj* □ **1.** anstrengend. **2.** unermüdlich.

stress [stres] **I** *s* **1.** *fig.* Streß *m*: **~ of examinations** Prüfungsstreß; **be under ~** unter Streß stehen, im Streß sein; **~ disease** Streß-, Managerkrankheit *f.* **2.** *ling.* Betonung *f*: **lay ~ on** *fig.* → 5; **~ mark** Akzent *m*, Betonungszeichen *n.* **3.** *phys.*, ⊕ Beanspruchung *f*, Belastung *f*; (mechanische) Spannung. **II** *v/t* **4.** **be ~ed** gestreßt sein. **5.** *ling.* betonen, *fig. a.* Wert legen auf (*acc*). **'stress·ful** ['~fʊl] *adj* stressig, aufreibend.

stretch [stretʃ] **I** *v/t* **1.** **~ out** *Arm etc* ausstrecken; → **leg** 1. **2.** *Seil etc* spannen: **be fully ~ed** *fig.* richtig gefordert werden. **3.** *Schuhe etc* (aus)weiten. **4.** *fig.* es nicht so genau nehmen mit: **~ a point** ein Auge zudrücken. **II** *v/i* **5.** sich dehnen, *a.* länger *od.* weiter werden. **6.** sich dehnen *od.* strecken: **~ out** sich ausstrecken. **7.** sich (*räumlich*) erstrecken (**to** bis zu), sich hinziehen (*räumlich*: **to** bis zu; *zeitlich*: **into** bis in *acc*); *fig.* reichen (**to** für) (*Vorräte etc*). **III** *s* **8.** **have a ~** → 6; **be at full ~** *fig.* sich sehr viel Mühe geben müssen; **not by any ~ of the imagination** nie u. nimmer. **9.** Dehnbarkeit *f*, Elastizität *f.* **10.**

Strecke f (e-r Straße); (Sport) (Gegen-, Ziel)Gerade f. **11.** Zeit(raum m, -spanne f) f: **at a ~** hintereinander; **do a three-year ~** F drei Jahre absitzen. **IV** adj **12.** → **stretchy. 'stretch·er** s Trage f. **'stretch·y** adj dehnbar, elastisch.

stri·at·ed [strai'eitid] adj gestreift.

strick·en ['strikən] adj **1.** leidgeprüft (Person), schwerbetroffen (Gegend etc). **2. ~** befallen od. ergriffen von: → **panic-stricken.**

strict [strikt] adj □ streng (Person, Disziplin, Gesetze etc), (Anweisungen etc a.) strikt: **be ~ with** streng sein mit od. zu od. gegen; **in ~ confidence** streng vertraulich; **~ly (speaking)** streng-, genaugenommen.

strid·den ['stridn] pp von **stride.**

stride [straid] **I** v/i (irr) **1.** schreiten, mit großen Schritten gehen. **II** s **2.** (großer) Schritt: **get into one's ~** fig. (richtig) in Fahrt od. Schwung kommen; **take s.th. in one's ~** fig. et. mühelos verkraften. **3.** fig. Fortschritt m. **make great ~s** große Fortschritte machen.

stri·dent ['straidnt] adj □ schrill (Stimme etc).

strife [straif] s Streit m.

strike [straik] **I** s **1. ✝** Streik m: **be (out) on ~** streiken, im Streik stehen; **go (out) on ~** streiken, in den Streik treten. **2.** (Öl- etc)Fund m. **3.** ✗ Angriff m. **II** v/i (irr) **4. ~ at s.o.** → **strike out** 2. **5.** einschlagen (Blitz). **6.** schlagen (Uhr): **two o'clock has just struck** es hat gerade zwei Uhr geschlagen. **7. ✝** streiken (for für). **8. ~ on** fig. kommen auf e-n Plan etc. **III** v/t (irr) **9.** schlagen: **~ s.o. a blow** j-m e-n Schlag versetzen; → **dumb** 1. **10.** treffen; einschlagen in (acc) (Blitz): → **lightning** I. **11.** Streichholz anzünden. **12. ✢** auflaufen auf (acc). **13.** streichen (from, off aus e-m Verzeichnis etc, von e-r Liste etc). **14.** fig. stoßen auf (Öl, e-e Straße, Schwierigkeiten etc): → **oil** 2. **15.** → **balance** 1, **bargain** 1. **16.** be struck by beeindruckt sein von; **how does the house ~ you?** wie findest du das Haus?; **it struck me as rather strange that** es kam mir ziemlich seltsam vor, daß. **17.** j-m einfallen, in den Sinn kommen. **18.** Münze etc prägen. **19.** Saite etc an-

schlagen: → **chord¹, note** 9. **20.** Lager, Zelt abbrechen.

Verbindungen mit Adverbien:

strike| back v/i zurückschlagen (a. fig.). **~ down** v/t **1.** niederschlagen. **2.** fig. niederwerfen (Krankheit); dahinraffen. **~ off** v/t **1.** abschlagen. **2.** ✝ Br. Solicitor von der Anwaltsliste streichen, e-m Arzt die Approbation entziehen. **~ out I** v/t **1.** (aus)streichen. **II** v/i **2. ~ at s.o.** auf j-n einschlagen. **3. ~ on one's own** fig. s-e eigenen Wege gehen, **✝** sich selbständig machen. **~ through** v/t durchstreichen. **~ up I** v/t **1.** Lied etc anstimmen. **2.** Bekanntschaft, Freundschaft schließen, Gespräch anknüpfen (**with** mit). **II** v/i **3.** ♪ einsetzen.

strike| bal·lot s **✝** Urabstimmung f. **'~·bound** adj bestreikt; von einem Streik lahmgelegt. **'~·break·er** s **✝** Streikbrecher(in). **~ call** s **✝** Streikaufruf m. **~ pay** s **✝** Streikgeld(er pl) n.

'strik·er s **1. ✝** Streikende m, f. **2.** Fußball: Stürmer(in). **'strik·ing** adj □ **1.** auffallend, (Ähnlichkeit, Vorschlag etc) verblüffend. **2. be within ~ distance of** fig. kurz vor e-m Erfolg etc stehen.

string [striŋ] **I** s **1.** Schnur f, Bindfaden m; (Schürzen-, Schuh- etc)Band n; (Puppenspiel) Faden m, Draht m: **with no ~s attached** fig. ohne Bedingungen; **have s.o. on a ~** fig. j-n am Gängelband führen od. haben; **pull the ~s** fig. die Fäden ziehen; **pull a few ~s** fig. ein paar Beziehungen spielen lassen. **2.** (Perlen- etc)Schnur f. **3.** a) Saite f (e-r Gitarre, e-s Tennisschlägers etc); (Bogen)Sehne f: **have two ~s (od. a second ~, another ~) to one's bow** fig. zwei od. mehrere Eisen im Feuer haben, b) **the ~s** pl ♪ die Streichinstrumente pl; die Streicher pl. **4.** fig. Reihe f, Serie f. **II** adj **5.** ♪ Streich... **III** v/t **6.** Perlen etc aufreihen. **7.** Gitarre etc besaiten, Tennisschläger etc bespannen.

Verbindungen mit Adverbien:

string| a·long I v/t j-n hinhalten. **II** v/i sich anschließen (**with s.o.** j-m). **~ up** v/t **1.** aufhängen. **2.** F j-n aufregen.

string bean s **✝** bsd. Am. grüne Bohne.

stringed in·stru·ment [striŋd] s Saiten-, Streichinstrument n.

strin·gent ['strindʒənt] adj □ streng (Kontrolle, Regeln etc).

string·y ['strɪŋɪ] *adj* **1.** fas(e)rig (*Bohnen, Fleisch etc*). **2.** sehnig (*Arm etc*).

strip [strɪp] **I** *v/i* **1.** *a.* ~ *off* sich ausziehen (**to** bis auf *acc*), (*beim Arzt*) sich freimachen; strippen: ~ *to the waist* den Oberkörper freimachen. **II** *v/t* **2.** *Farbe etc* abkratzen, *Tapete etc* abreißen (**from, off** von). **3.** ~ *s.o. of s.th.* j-m et. rauben *od.* wegnehmen: *he was* ~*ped of his title* ihm wurde sein Titel aberkannt. **4.** a) *a.* ~ *down* Motor *etc* auseinandernehmen, zerlegen, b) *Wagen etc* ausschlachten. **III** *s* **5.** (*Land-, Papier- etc*)Streifen *m*. **6.** Strip *m*: *do a* ~ strippen. **7.** *Fußball:* *Br.* Dreß *m*. ~ *car·toons s pl Br.* Comics *pl*.

stripe [straɪp] *s* **1.** Streifen *m*. **2.** ✕ (Ärmel)Streifen *m*, Winkel *m*. **striped** *adj* gestreift: ~ *pattern* Streifenmuster *n*.

strip light·ing *s* Neonbeleuchtung *f*, -licht *n*.

'strip·tease *s* Striptease *m, n*: *do a* ~ e-n Striptease vorführen.

strip·y ['straɪpɪ] → *striped*.

strive [straɪv] *v/i (irr)* **1.** sich bemühen (**to do** zu tun). **2.** streben (**for, after** nach). **3.** '(an)kämpfen (**against** gegen).

striv·en ['strɪvn] *pp von* **strive**.

strode [strəʊd] *pret von* **stride**.

stroke [strəʊk] **I** *v/t* **1.** streicheln: ~ *s.o.'s hair* j-m übers Haar streichen. **II** *s* **2.** Schlag *m* (*a.* *Tennis, e-r Uhr etc*), Hieb *m*: *a* ~ *of lightning* ein Blitz *m*; *a* ~ *of genius fig.* ein glänzender Einfall; *a* ~ *of luck fig.* ein glücklicher Zufall; *at a* ~ *fig.* auf 'einen Schlag; *on the* ~ *of ten* Punkt *od.* Schlag zehn (Uhr). **3.** *give s.o. a* ~ j-n streicheln. **4.** 🏊 Schlag(anfall) *m*. **5.** (*Pinsel*)Strich *m*: *with a* ~ *of the pen* mit e-m Federstrich (*a. fig.*); *he hasn't done a* ~ (*of work*) *yet fig.* er hat noch keinen Strich getan. **6.** *Schwimmen:* Zug *m*; Stil(art *f*) *m*: ~ *backstroke, breaststroke*. **7.** ☉ (*Kolben*)Hub *m*; Takt *m*: *four-*~ *engine* Viertaktmotor *m*. **8.** *Rudern:* Schlagmann *m*, -frau *f*.

stroll [strəʊl] **I** *v/i* bummeln, spazieren. **II** *s* Bummel *m*, Spaziergang *m*: *go for a* ~ e-n Bummel *od.* Spaziergang machen. **'stroll·er** *s* **1.** Bummler(in), Spaziergänger(in). **2.** *bsd. Am.* Sportwagen *m* (*für Kinder*).

strong [strɒŋ] **I** *adj* □ (→ *a.* **strongly**) **1.**

stark, kräftig (*Person, Arme etc*); *fig.* mächtig (*Land etc*), stark (*Persönlichkeit etc*): → *sex* 1. **2.** stabil (*Möbel etc*), (*Schuhe etc a.*) fest; robust (*Person, Gesundheit*), (*Konstitution a.*) kräftig, (*Herz, Nerven*) stark; *fig.* unerschütterlich (*Beweise*), stark (*Verdacht*): → *point* 14. **3.** stark (*Strömung*), (*Wind etc a.*) kräftig. **4.** kräftig (*Geruch, Geschmack*), (*a. Eindruck, Ähnlichkeit etc*) stark. **5.** überzeugt (*Anhänger etc*). **6.** stark (*Getränk, Medikament etc*). **7.** ~ *language* Kraftausdrücke *pl*. **8.** groß, hoch (*Chance etc*), aussichtsreich (*Kandidat etc*). **9.** *a nine-*~ *team* ein neun Mann starkes Team; *an 8,000-*~ *community* e-e 8000-Seelen-Gemeinde; *our club is 500* ~ unser Club hat 500 Mitglieder. **II** *adv* **10.** *be still going* ~ noch gut in Schuß sein (*alte Person, altes Gerät etc*). **'**~**·arm** *adj*: ~ *methods* (*od.* *tactics*) *pl* Gewaltmethoden *pl*. **'**~**·box** *s* (Geld-, Stahl)Kassette *f*. **'**~**·hold** *s* **1.** ✕ Festung *f*; Stützpunkt *m*. **2.** *fig.* Hochburg *f*.

strong·ly ['strɒŋlɪ] *adv*: *I* ~ *advised him against it* ich riet ihm dringend davon ab.

,strong-'mind·ed *adj* □ willensstark. ~ *room s* Tresor(raum) *m*, Stahlkammer *f*.

strove [strəʊv] *pret von* **strive**.

struck [strʌk] *pret u. pp von* **strike**.

struc·tur·al ['strʌktʃərəl] *adj* □ **1.** strukturell (bedingt), Struktur... **2.** ☉ Bau..., Konstruktions... **'struc·ture I** *s* **1.** Struktur *f*; (Auf)Bau *m*, Gliederung *f*. **2.** Bau *m*, Konstruktion *f*. **II** *v/t* **2.** strukturieren; *Aufsatz etc* aufbauen, gliedern.

strug·gle ['strʌgl] **I** *v/i* **1.** kämpfen (**with** mit; **for** um), *fig. a.* sich abmühen (**with** mit; **to do** zu tun): ~ *for words* um Worte ringen. **2.** zappeln; um sich schlagen *od.* treten. **3.** sich quälen: ~ *to one's feet* mühsam aufstehen, sich aufrappeln. **II** *s* **4.** Kampf *m* (*a. fig.*), Handgemenge *n*: ~ *for survival* Überlebenskampf, Kampf ums Überleben.

strum [strʌm] **I** *v/t* a) klimpern auf *e-r Gitarre etc*, b) *Melodie* klimpern. **II** *v/i*: ~ *on* → **Ia**.

strung [strʌŋ] *pret u. pp von* **string**.

strut¹ [strʌt] *v/i* stolzieren.

stunt woman

strut² [~] ☉ **I** *s* Strebe *f*; Stütze *f*. **II** *v/t* verstreben; (ab)stützen.

strych·nine ['strɪknɪ:n] *s* 🐍, *pharm.* Strychnin *n*.

stub [stʌb] **I** *s* **1.** (*Bleistift-, Zigaretten- etc*)Stummel *m*. **2.** Kontrollabschnitt *m* (*e-r Eintrittskarte etc*). **II** *v/t* **3.** sich *die* Zehe anstoßen (**against, on** an *dat*). **4.** ~ **out** Zigarette ausdrücken.

stub·ble ['stʌbl] *s* Stoppeln *pl*. **'stub·bly** *adj* stopp(e)lig, Stoppel...

stub·born ['stʌbən] *adj* □ **1.** eigensinnig, stur. **2.** hartnäckig (*Fleck, Widerstand etc*).

stub·by ['stʌbɪ] *adj*: ~ **fingers** *pl* Wurstfinger *pl*.

stuc·co ['stʌkəʊ] *s* △ Stuck *m*. **'stuc·coed** *adj* Stuck...

stuck [stʌk] **I** *pret u. pp von* **stick²**. **II** *adj* **1. be** ~ klemmen; *fig.* nicht weiterkommen: **be** ~ **with** F *j*-n, *et.* am Hals haben. **2. be** ~ **on** F verknallt sein in (*acc*). **3.** *Br.* F **get** ~ **in** reinhauen (*beim Essen*); **get** ~ **into** sich stürzen auf (*ein Essen*) *od.* in (*e-e Arbeit*). ,~**'up** F hochnäsig.

stud¹ [stʌd] **I** *s* **1.** Beschlag- *od.* Ziernagel *m*. **2.** (*Kragen-, Manschetten*)Knopf *m*. **3.** Stollen *m* (*e-s Fußballschuhs etc*). **II** *v/t* **4. be** ~**ded with** besetzt sein mit; übersät sein mit.

stud² [~] *s* Gestüt *n* (*Pferde*).

stu·dent ['stju:dnt] *s* Student(in), *ped. bsd. Am. u. allg.* Schüler(in).

stud farm *s* Gestüt *n*.

stud·ied ['stʌdɪd] *adj* □ wohlüberlegt, *b.s.* wohlberechnet (*Antwort etc*).

stu·di·o ['stju:dɪəʊ] *pl* **-os** *s* **1.** *allg.* Studio *n*, (*e-s Künstlers etc a.*) Atelier *n*. **2.** Studio *n*, Einzimmerappartement *n*. ~ **a·part·ment** *bsd. Am.* → **studio** 2. ~ **couch** *s* Schlafcouch *f*. ~ **flat** *bsd. Br.* → **studio** 2.

stu·di·ous ['stju:djəs] *adj* □ fleißig.

stud·y ['stʌdɪ] **I** *s* **1.** *a. pl* Studium *n*: **be in a brown** ~ in Gedanken versunken *od.* geistesabwesend sein. **2.** Studie *f*, Untersuchung *f* (*of* über *acc*): **make a** ~ **of** *et.* untersuchen. **3.** *bsd. paint.* Studie *f* (*of* zu). **4. ♪** Etüde *f*. **5.** Arbeitszimmer *n*. **II** *v/t* **6.** *Medizin etc, weitS.* Landkarte, *j-s* Gesicht *etc* studieren. **III** *v/i* **7.** studieren (**under** *s.o.* bei *j*-m), *weitS.* lernen (**for** für *e-e Prüfung*):

~ **to be a doctor** Medizin studieren.

stuff [stʌf] **I** *s* **1.** F *allg.* Zeug *n*: **be good** ~ *et.* Gutes sein; **that's the** ~**!** so ist's richtig!; genau!; **do one's** ~ zeigen, was man kann; **know one's** ~ sich gut auskennen. **II** *v/t* **2.** (**with** mit) Hohlraum, Tier ausstopfen; *Kissen etc* stopfen, füllen; sich *die Taschen* vollstopfen: ~**ed full of** gestopft voll von; ~ **o.s.** F sich vollstopfen. **3.** *et.* stopfen (**into** in *acc*). **4.** *gastr.* Ente *etc* füllen: **get** ~**ed!** *Br. sl.* du kannst mich mal! **5.** ~ **up** Loch *etc* ver-, zustopfen (**with** mit): **my nose is** ~**ed up** m-e Nase ist verstopft *od.* zu.

stuffed *adj*: ~ **shirt** F Fatzke *m*.

'stuff·ing *s* Füllung *f* (*a. gastr.*): **knock the** ~ **out of s.o.** F j-n schaffen. **'stuff·y** *adj* □ **1.** stickig. **2.** *fig.* prüde; spießig.

stum·ble ['stʌmbl] *v/i* stolpern (**on, over,** *fig.* **at, over** *acc*): ~ **across** (*od. on*) *fig.* stoßen auf (*acc*); ~ **through** *Rede etc* herunterstottern. **'stum·bling** *adj*: ~ **block** *fig.* Hindernis *n* (**to** für).

stump [stʌmp] **I** *s* **1.** (*Baum-, Bein-, Kerzen- etc*)Stumpf *m*, (*Bleistift-, Kerzen-, Zahn-, Zigarren- etc*)Stummel *m*: **stir one's** ~**s** F Tempo machen. **II** *v/t* **2.** *I'm* ~**ed, you've got me** ~**ed there** F da bin ich überfragt. **3.** ~ **up** F *Geld* herausrücken. **III** *v/i* **4.** sta(m)pfen. **'stump·y** *adj* □ kurz u. dick (*Arme etc*).

stun [stʌn] *v/t* betäuben; *fig.* sprachlos machen: **he was** ~**ned by the news** die Nachricht hat ihm die Sprache verschlagen.

stung [stʌŋ] *pret u. pp von* **sting**.

stunk [stʌŋk] *pret u. pp von* **stink**.

stun·ner ['stʌnə] *s*: **she's a real** ~ F sie ist e-e klasse Frau. **'stun·ning** *adj* □ **1.** phantastisch. **2.** unglaublich (*Nachricht*).

stunt¹ [stʌnt] *s* **1.** (*gefährliches*) Kunststück; (*Film*) Stunt *m* (*gefährliche Szene, in der ein Stuntman die Rolle des Darstellers übernimmt*): **do a** ~ ein Kunststück vorführen *od.* zeigen; e-n Stunt ausführen. **2.** (*Werbe*)Gag *m*.

stunt² [~] *v/t Wachstum* hemmen; *das Wachstum* (*gen*) hemmen: ~**ed** verkümmert.

stunt| fly·ing *s* Kunstflug *m*. ~ **man** *s* (*irr* **man**) *Film*: Stuntman *m*, Double *n*. ~ **wom·an** *s* (*irr* **woman**) *Film*: Stuntwoman *n*, Double *n*.

stu·pen·dous [stjuːˈpendəs] *adj* □ phantastisch.

stu·pid [ˈstjuːpɪd] *adj* □ **1.** dumm. **2.** *fig.* F blöd. **stu'pid·i·ty** *s* Dummheit *f* (*a. Handlung etc*).

stu·por [ˈstjuːpə] *s*: **in a drunken ~** im Vollrausch.

stur·dy [ˈstɜːdɪ] *adj* □ **1.** stämmig (*Beine etc*). **2.** *fig.* hartnäckig (*Widerstand etc*).

stur·geon [ˈstɜːdʒən] *s ichth.* Stör *m*.

stut·ter [ˈstʌtə] **I** *v/i* ✹ stottern (*a. Motor*). **II** *v/t* → **stammer** II. **III** *s* → **stammer** III. **'stut·ter·er** → **stammerer.**

sty¹ [staɪ] → **pigsty.**

sty² [~] *s* ✹ Gerstenkorn *n*.

style [staɪl] **I** *s* **1.** *allg.* Stil *m*: **~ of leadership** Führungsstil; **in ~** in großem Stil; **that's not my ~** F das ist nicht m-e Art. **2.** Ausführung *f*, Modell *n*. **II** *v/t* **3.** entwerfen; gestalten.

sty·li [ˈstaɪlaɪ] *pl von* **stylus.**

styl·ish [ˈstaɪlɪʃ] *adj* □ **1.** stilvoll. **2.** modisch, elegant.

styl·ist [ˈstaɪlɪst] *s* **1.** Stilist(in). **2.** a) Modeschöpfer(in), b) → **hair stylist.** **sty'lis·tic** *adj* (**~ally**) stilistisch, Stil...

styl·ize [ˈstaɪlaɪz] *v/t* stilisieren.

sty·lus [ˈstaɪləs] *pl* **-li** [ˈ~laɪ], **-lus·es** *s* Nadel *f* (*e-s Plattenspielers*).

sty·mie [ˈstaɪmɪ] *v/t* F Gegner matt setzen; *Plan etc* vereiteln.

styp·tic [ˈstɪptɪk] ✹ **I** *adj* blutstillend. **II** *s* blutstillendes Mittel.

suave [swɑːv] *adj* □ verbindlich, *contp.* aalglatt.

sub [sʌb] F **I** *s* **1.** → **subeditor, submarine** I, **subscription** 1. **2.** *Sport:* Auswechselspieler(in). **3.** *Br.* Vorschuß *m*. **II** *v/i* **4.** → **substitute** IV. **III** *v/t* **5.** → **subedit. 6.** *Br. j-m* e-n Vorschuß geben.

'sub·com,mit·tee *s* Unterausschuß *m*.

,sub'con·scious I *adj* unterbewußt: **~ly** im Unterbewußtsein; F unbewußt. **II** *s* Unterbewußtsein *n*: **in one's ~** im Unterbewußtsein.

,sub'con·ti·nent *s* Subkontinent *m*.

'sub,cul·ture *s sociol.* Subkultur *f*.

sub·cu·ta·ne·ous [ˌsʌbkjuːˈteɪnjəs] *adj* □ subkutan, unter od. die Haut.

,sub·di'vide *v/t* unterteilen. **'sub·di,vision** *s* **1.** Unterteilung *f*. **2.** Unterabteilung *f*.

sub·due [səbˈdjuː] *v/t Land etc* unterwerfen; *Ärger etc* unterdrücken. **sub'dued** *adj* **1.** gedämpft (*Stimme*), (*Farben, Licht a.*) dezent. **2.** (*merkwürdig*) ruhig *od.* still (*Person*).

,sub'ed·it *v/t* redigieren. **,sub'ed·i·tor** *s* Redakteur(in).

'sub,head·ing *s* Untertitel *m*.

,sub'hu·man *adj* unmenschlich.

sub·ject [ˈsʌbdʒɪkt] **I** *s* **1.** Thema *n*: **on the ~ of** über (*acc*); **be the ~ of much criticism** von verschiedenen Seiten kritisiert werden; **change the ~** das Thema wechseln, von et. anderem reden. **2.** *ped., univ.* Fach *n*. **3.** *ling.* Subjekt *n*, Satzgegenstand *m*. **4.** **be the ~ of, be a ~ for** Anlaß *od.* Grund geben zu. **5.** Untertan(in); Staatsangehörige *m, f*, -bürger(in). **6.** Versuchsperson *f*, -tier *n*. **II** *adj* **7.** **~ to** anfällig für: **be ~ to** *a.* neigen zu. **8.** **be ~ to** unterliegen (*dat*); abhängen von: **be ~ to the approval of** (erst noch) genehmigt werden müssen von; **prices ~ to change** Preisänderungen vorbehalten. **III** *v/t* [səbˈdʒekt] **9.** *Land etc* unterwerfen. **10.** **~ to** e-m Test etc unterziehen; *der Kritik etc* aussetzen. **sub·jec·tion** [səbˈdʒekʃn] *s* **1.** Unterwerfung *f*. **2.** Abhängigkeit *f* (**to** von). **sub'jec·tive** *adj* □ subjektiv.

'sub·ject mat·ter *s* Stoff *m*; Inhalt *m*.

sub·ju·gate [ˈsʌbdʒʊgeɪt] *v/t* unterjochen, -werfen.

sub·junc·tive (mood) [səbˈdʒʌŋktɪv] *s ling.* Konjunktiv *m*.

,sub'lease *v/t* unter-, weitervermieten, unter-, weiterverpachten (**to** an *dat*).

,sub'let *v/t* (*irr let*) unter-, weitervermieten (**to** an *dat*).

sub·li·mate ✹ **I** *v/t* [ˈsʌblɪmeɪt] sublimieren. **II** *s* [ˈ~mət] Sublimat *n*.

sub·lime [səˈblaɪm] *adj* □ **1.** großartig. **2.** *iro.* großzügig (*Mißachtung*), allumfassend (*Unkenntnis*).

sub·lim·i·nal [ˌsʌbˈlɪmɪnl] *adj* □ *psych.* unterschwellig.

,sub·ma'chine gun *s* Maschinenpistole *f*.

,sub·ma'rine I *s* Unterseeboot *n*, U-Boot *n*. **II** *adj* untermeerisch, -seeisch.

sub·merge [səbˈmɜːdʒ] **I** *v/t* (ein)tauchen (**in** in *acc*): **be ~d in work** bis über die Ohren in Arbeit stecken. **II** *v/i* tauchen (*U-Boot*).

sub·mis·sion [səbˈmɪʃn] *s* **1.** Einreichung *f*. **2.** *Boxen etc*: Aufgabe *f*.

sub·mis·sive [səbˈmɪsɪv] *adj* □ unterwürfig.

sub·mit [səbˈmɪt] **I** *v/t* **1.** *Gesuch etc* einreichen (**to** *dat od.* bei). **2.** **~ o.s.** sich fügen (**to** *dat od.* in *acc*). **II** *v/i* **3.** *Boxen etc*: aufgeben.

,**sub'nor·mal** *adj* □ **1.** unterdurchschnittlich. **2.** unterdurchschnittlich intelligent.

sub·or·di·nate [səˈbɔːdnət] **I** *adj* □ untergeordnet (**to** *dat*): **be ~ to** *a*. zurückstehen hinter (*dat*); **~ clause** *ling*. Nebensatz *m*. **II** *s* Untergebene *m*, *f*. **III** *v/t* [ˌdneɪt] (**to**) unterordnen (*dat*), zurückstellen (hinter *acc*).

'**sub·plot** *s* Nebenhandlung *f*.

sub·poe·na [səbˈpiːnə] ⚖ **I** *s* Vorladung *f*. **II** *v/t* Zeugen vorladen.

sub·scribe [səbˈskraɪb] **I** *v/i* **1.** **~ to** *Zeitschrift etc* abonnieren; abonniert haben. **2.** **~ to** *karitative Organisation etc* regelmäßig unterstützen. **3.** **~ to** *Ansicht etc* billigen. **II** *v/t* **4.** *Geld* geben, spenden (**to** für). **sub·scrib·er** *s* Abonnent(in); (*Fernsprech*)Teilnehmer(-in).

sub·scrip·tion [səbˈskrɪpʃn] *s* **1.** (Mitglieds)Beitrag *m*. **2.** Abonnement *n*: **take out a ~ to** *Zeitschrift etc* abonnieren.

'**sub,sec·tion** *s* Unterabteilung *f*.

sub·se·quent ['sʌbsɪkwənt] *adj* □ später.

sub·ser·vi·ent [səbˈsɜːvjənt] *adj* □ **1.** unterwürfig. **2.** untergeordnet (**to** *dat*): **be ~ to** *a.* zurückstehen hinter (*dat*).

sub·side [səbˈsaɪd] *v/i* **1.** sich senken (*Gebäude, Straße etc*): **~ into a chair** in e-n Sessel sinken. **2.** zurückgehen (*Überschwemmung, Nachfrage etc*), sich legen (*Sturm, Zorn etc*).

sub·sid·i·ar·y [səbˈsɪdjərɪ] **I** *adj* Neben...: **~ company** → II; **~ question** Zusatzfrage *f*; **~ subject** *ped., univ.* Nebenfach *n*. **II** *s* † Tochtergesellschaft *f*.

sub·si·dize ['sʌbsɪdaɪz] *v/t* subventionieren.

sub·si·dy ['ˌdɪ] *s* Subvention *f*.

sub·sist [səbˈsɪst] *v/i* existieren, leben (**on** von). **sub'sist·ence** *s* Existenz *f*: **live at ~ level** am Existenzminimum leben.

,**sub'son·ic** *adj* ✈, *phys.* Unterschall...:

at ~ speed mit Unterschallgeschwindigkeit.

sub·stance ['sʌbstəns] *s* **1.** Substanz *f*, Stoff *m*, Masse *f*. **2.** *fig.* Substanz *f*: **in ~** im wesentlichen.

,**sub'stand·ard** *adj* minderwertig; *ling.* inkorrekt.

sub·stan·tial [səbˈstænʃl] *adj* □ **1.** solid (*Schrank etc*). **2.** *fig.* beträchtlich (*Gehalt etc*), (*Änderungen etc a.*) wesentlich: **~ly** *a.* im wesentlichen. **3.** *fig.* kräftig (*Mahlzeit*).

sub·stan·ti·ate [səbˈstænʃɪeɪt] *v/t* beweisen, erhärten.

sub·stan·tive ['sʌbstəntɪv] *s* *ling.* Substantiv *n*, Hauptwort *n*.

sub·sti·tute ['sʌbstɪtjuːt] **I** *s* Ersatz *m*; Ersatz(mann) *m*, Vertretung *f*, (*Sport*) Auswechselspieler(in). **II** *adj* Ersatz... **III** *v/t*: **~ A for B** B durch A ersetzen, B gegen A austauschen *od.* auswechseln. **IV** *v/i*: **~ for** einspringen für, *j-n* vertreten.

'**sub,struc·ture** *s* △ Fundament *n*, Unterbau *m* (*beide a. fig.*).

,**sub'ten·ant** *s* Untermieter(in).

sub·ter·fuge ['sʌbtəfjuːdʒ] *s* List *f*.

sub·ter·ra·ne·an [ˌsʌbtəˈreɪnjən] *adj* □ unterirdisch.

'**sub,ti·tle** *s* Untertitel *m*.

sub·tle ['sʌtl] *adj* □ **1.** fein (*Unterschied etc*), (*Aroma etc a.*) zart. **2.** raffiniert (*Plan etc*). **3.** scharf (*Verstand*), scharfsinnig (*Person*).

'**sub,to·tal** *s* Zwischen-, Teilsumme *f*.

sub·tract [səbˈtrækt] *v/t* & abziehen, subtrahieren (**from** von). **sub'trac·tion** *s* Abziehen *n*, Subtraktion *f*.

,**sub'trop·i·cal** *adj* subtropisch.

sub·urb ['sʌbɜːb] *s* Vorort *m*: **live in the ~s** am Stadtrand wohnen. **sub·ur·ban** [səˈbɜːbən] *adj* Vorort..., vorstädtisch, Vorstadt...: **sub'ur·ban·ite** *s* Vorstädter(in). **sub'ur·bi·a** [ˌbɪə] *s* **1.** Vorstadt *f*: **live in ~** am Stadtrand wohnen. **2.** Vorstadtleben *n*.

sub·ver·sion [səbˈvɜːʃn] *s* *pol.* Subversion *f*. **sub'ver·sive** [ˌsɪv] **I** *adj* □ subversiv, umstürzlerisch. **II** *s* Umstürzler(in).

sub·vert [sʌbˈvɜːt] *v/t* *Regierung* zu stürzen versuchen.

'**sub·way** *s* **1.** Unterführung *f*. **2.** *Am.* U-Bahn *f*.

suc·ceed [sək'si:d] **I** *v/i* **1.** Erfolg haben, erfolgreich sein (*Person*), (*Plan etc a.*) gelingen: *he ~ed in doing it* es gelang ihm, es zu tun. **2.** *~ to* in e-m Amt nachfolgen: *~ to the throne* auf dem Thron folgen. **II** *v/t* **3.** *j-m* nachfolgen, *j-m od.* auf *j-n* folgen: *~ s.o. as* j-s Nachfolger werden als.

suc·cess [sək'ses] *s* Erfolg *m*: *without ~* ohne Erfolg, erfolglos. **suc'cess·ful** [~fʊl] *adj* □ erfolgreich: *be ~ → succeed* 1; *he was ~ in doing it* es gelang ihm, es zu tun.

suc·ces·sion [sək'seʃn] *s* **1.** Folge *f*: *three times in ~* dreimal nach- *od.* hintereinander; *in quick ~* in rascher Folge. **2.** Nachfolge *f*: *~ to the throne* Thronfolge. **suc'ces·sive** [~sɪv] *adj* □ aufeinanderfolgend: *on three ~ days* a. drei Tage nach- *od.* hintereinander. **suc'ces·sor** [~sə] *s* Nachfolger(in) (*to* in e-m Amt): *~ in office* Amtsnachfolger(in); *~ to the throne* Thronfolger(in).

suc·cinct [sək'sɪŋkt] *adj* □ kurz (u. bündig), knapp.

suc·cu·lent ['sʌkjʊlənt] *adj* □ saftig (*Steak etc*).

suc·cumb [sə'kʌm] *v/i*: *~ to* e-r *Krankheit, der Versuchung etc* erliegen.

such [sʌtʃ] **I** *adj* solch, derartig: *~ a man* ein solcher *od.* so ein Mann; *no ~ thing* nichts dergleichen. **II** *adv* so, derart: *~ a nice day* so ein schöner Tag; *~ a long time* e-e so lange Zeit; *~ is life* so ist das Leben. **III** *pron.* solch: *~ as* wie (zum Beispiel); *~ as* der Mensch als solcher. '*~·like* **I** *adj* solche. **II** *pron* dergleichen.

suck [sʌk] **I** *v/t* **1.** saugen. **2.** lutschen (an *dat*). **3.** *~ under* hinunterziehen (*Strudel etc*). **II** *v/i* **4.** saugen (*at* an *dat*). **5.** *~ away at et.* lutschen. **6.** *~ up to s.o. Br.* F sich bei *j-m* lieb Kind machen wollen. **III** *s* **7.** *take a ~ at* saugen *od.* ziehen an (*dat*); lutschen an (*dat*). '**suck·er** *s* **1.** *zo.* Saugnapf *m*, -organ *n*. **2.** ⚙ Saugfuß *m*. **3.** *Am.* Lutscher *m*. **4.** F Gimpel *m*, leichtgläubiger Kerl: *be a ~ for* immer wieder reinfallen auf (*acc*); verrückt sein nach. '**suck·ing** *adj*: *~ pig* Spanferkel *n*.

suck·le ['sʌkl] *v/t* säugen (*a. zo.*), stillen.

suc·tion ['sʌkʃn] *s* Saugwirkung *f*. *~ pump s* ⚙ Saugpumpe *f*.

sud·den ['sʌdn] **I** *adj* □ plötzlich: *be very ~* sehr plötzlich kommen. **II** *s*: *all of a ~* ganz plötzlich, auf einmal.

suds [sʌdz] *s pl* Seifenschaum *m*.

sue [su:] ✴ **I** *v/t j-n* verklagen (*for* auf *acc*, wegen). **II** *v/i* klagen (*for* auf *acc*).

suede, suède [sweɪd] *s* Wildleder *n*; Velour(s)leder *n*.

su·et ['sʊɪt] *s* Nierenfett *n*, Talg *m*.

suf·fer ['sʌfə] **I** *v/i* **1.** leiden (*from* an *dat*; *weitS.* unter *dat*). **2.** darunter leiden. **II** *v/t* **3.** *Niederlage, Rückschlag, Verlust etc* erleiden; *Folgen* tragen. '**suf·fer·er** *s*: *a cancer ~* ein Krebskranker; *a headache ~* j-d, der an Kopfschmerzen leidet. '**suf·fer·ing** *s* Leiden *n*; Leid *n*.

suf·fice [sə'faɪs] **I** *v/i* genügen, (aus)reichen (*for* für). **II** *v/t j-m* genügen, reichen.

suf·fi·cient [sə'fɪʃnt] *adj* □ genügend, genug, ausreichend: *be ~ → suffice* 1.

suf·fix ['sʌfɪks] *s ling.* Suffix *n*, Nachsilbe *f*.

suf·fo·cate ['sʌfəkeɪt] *v/i u. v/t* ersticken.

suf·frage ['sʌfrɪdʒ] *s pol.* Wahl-, Stimmrecht *n*.

suf·fuse [sə'fju:z] *v/t*: *be ~d with* durchdrungen sein von.

sug·ar ['ʃʊɡə] **I** *s* **1.** Zucker *m*. **2.** *bsd. Am.* F Schatz (*Anrede*). **II** *v/t* **3.** zuckern: *→ pill* 1. *~ beet s* ⚘ Zuckerrübe *f*. *~ bowl s* Zuckerdose *f*. *~ cane s* ⚘ Zuckerrohr *n*. *~ dad·dy s* F *alter Knakker, der ein junges Mädchen aushält*.

sug·ar·y ['ʃʊɡərɪ] *adj* **1.** zuck(e)rig, Zucker... **2.** *fig.* zuckersüß.

sug·gest [sə'dʒest] *v/t* **1.** *j-n* vorschlagen (*as* als), *et. a.* anregen: *I ~ going* (*od. that we go*) *home* ich schlage vor heimzugehen. **2.** hindeuten *od.* -weisen auf (*acc*), schließen lassen auf (*acc*): *~ that* darauf hindeuten *od.* -weisen, daß; *that* darauf schließen lassen, daß. **3.** andeuten: *I am not ~ing that* ich will damit nicht sagen, daß. **sug'gest·i·ble** *adj* beeinflußbar. **sug'ges·tion** *s* **1.** Vorschlag *m*, Anregung *f*: *at s.o.'s ~* auf *j-s* Vorschlag hin; *make* (*od. offer*) *a ~* e-n Vorschlag machen. **2.** Anflug *m*, Spur *f*. **3.** Andeutung *f*. **4.** *psych.* Suggestion *f*. **sug'ges·tive** *adj* □ **1.** *be ~ of → suggest* 2. **2.** zweideutig (*Bemer-*

sunken

kung etc), vielsagend (*Blick etc*).

su·i·cid·al [soɪˈsaɪdl] *adj* □ **1.** selbstmörderisch (*a. fig.*): **~ thoughts** *pl* Selbstmordgedanken *pl.* **2.** selbstmordgefährdet. **su·i·cide** [ˈ~saɪd] *s* **1.** Selbstmord *m* (*a. fig.*): **commit ~** Selbstmord begehen; **he tried to commit ~** er unternahm e-n Selbstmordversuch; → **attempt** Selbstmordversuch *m*; → **attempt** I. **2.** Selbstmörder(in).

suit [su:t] I *s* **1.** Anzug *m*; Kostüm *n.* *Kartenspiel*: Farbe *f*: **follow ~** (Farbe) bedienen; *fig.* dasselbe tun, nachziehen. **3.** → **lawsuit**. II *v/t* **4.** j-m stehen (*Farbe etc*). **5.** j-m passen (*Termin etc*): **that ~s me fine** das paßt mir gut, das ist mir sehr recht; → **s.o.'s book** F j-m ins Zeug passen. **6. ~ s.th., be ~ed to s.th.** geeignet sein *od.* sich eignen für: **they are well ~ed (to each other)** sie passen gut zusammen. **7. ~ yourself!** mach, was du willst! **8.** *et.* anpassen (**to** *dat*). **'suit·a·ble** *adj* □ passend, geeignet (**for, to** für).

'suit·case *s* Koffer *m.*

suite [swi:t] *s* **1.** (*Möbel*)Garnitur *f.* **2.** Suite *f*, Zimmerflucht *f.* **3.** ♪ Suite *f.*

sul·fa drug, sul·fate, sul·fide, sul·fon·a·mide, sul·fur *Am.* → **sulpha drug, sulphate, sulphide, sulphonamide, sulphur.**

sulk [sʌlk] I *v/i* schmollen. II *s*: **have the ~s** → I. **'sulk·y** I *adj* □ **1.** schmollend. **2.** schnell schmollend. II *s* **3.** *Trabrennen*: Sulky *n.*

sul·len [ˈsʌlən] *adj* □ mürrisch, verdrossen.

sul·pha drug [ˈsʌlfə] *s bsd. Br. pharm.* Sulfonamid *n.*

sul·phate [ˈsʌlfeɪt] *s* 🦴 *bsd. Br.* Sulfat *n.*

sul·phide [ˈsʌlfaɪd] *s* 🦴 *bsd. Br.* Sulfid *n.*

sul·phon·a·mide [sʌlˈfɒnəmaɪd] → **sulpha drug.**

sul·phur [ˈsʌlfə] *s* 🦴, *min. bsd. Br.* Schwefel *m.* **sul·phu·ric** [~ˈfjʊərɪk] *adj*: **~ acid** Schwefelsäure *f.* **sul·phur·ous** [ˈ~fərəs] *adj* schwef(e)lig, Schwefel...

sul·tan [ˈsʌltən] *s* Sultan *m.*

sul·try [ˈsʌltrɪ] *adj* □ **1.** schwül. **2.** aufreizend (*Blick etc*).

sum [sʌm] I *s* **1.** Summe *f* (*a.* 🗮), Betrag *m*: **in ~** *fig.* mit 'einem Wort. **2.** (einfa-

che) Rechenaufgabe: **do ~s** rechnen. II *v/t* **3. ~ up** zs.-fassen. **4. ~ up** j-n, *et.* abschätzen. III *v/i* **5. ~ up** zs.-fassen: **to ~ up** zs.-fassend.

sum·ma·rize [ˈsʌmərɑɪz] *v/t u. v/i* zs.-fassen. **'sum·mar·y** I *s* Zs.-fassung *f.* II *adj* summarisch (*a.* 🗮); fristlos (*Entlassung*).

sum·mer [ˈsʌmə] I *s* Sommer *m*: **in (the) ~** im Sommer. II *adj* Sommer... **'~house** *s* Gartenhaus *n.* **'~time** *s* Sommer(zeit *f*) *m*: **in (the) ~** im Sommer. **~ time** *s bsd. Br.* Sommerzeit *f* (*Uhrzeit*).

sum·mer·y [ˈsʌmərɪ] *adj* sommerlich, Sommer...

sum·mit [ˈsʌmɪt] I *s* Gipfel *m* (*a.* ✈, *pol.*), *fig. a.* Höhepunkt *m.* II *adj bsd.* ✈, *pol.* Gipfel...: **~ conference.**

sum·mon [ˈsʌmən] *v/t* **1.** j-n zitieren (**to** in *acc*); auffordern (**to do** zu tun). **2.** Versammlung etc einberufen. **3. ~ up** Kraft, Mut etc zs.-nehmen. **sum·mons** [ˈ~z] 🗮 I *s* Vorladung *f.* II *v/t* j-n vorladen.

sump [sʌmp] *s mot.,* ⚙ *bsd. Br.* Ölwanne *f.*

sump·tu·ous [ˈsʌmptʃʊəs] *adj* □ luxuriös.

sun [sʌn] I *s* Sonne *f.* II *v/t*: **~ o.s.** sich sonnen. **'~bathe** *v/i* sonnenbaden, sich sonnen. **'~beam** *s* Sonnenstrahl *m.* **'~burn** *s* Sonnenbrand *m.* **'~burned, '~burnt** *adj*: **be ~** e-n Sonnenbrand haben.

sun·dae [ˈsʌndeɪ] *s* Eisbecher *m.*

Sun·day [ˈsʌndɪ] *s* Sonntag *m*: **on ~** (am) Sonntag; **on ~s** sonntags. **~ best** *s* Sonntagsstaat *m.* **~ school** *s* Sonntagsschule *f.*

'sun·di·al *s* Sonnenuhr *f.* **'~down** → **sunset.** **'~down·er** *s bsd. Br.* F Dämmerschoppen *m.*

sun·dries [ˈsʌndrɪz] *s pl* Diverses *n*, Verschiedenes *n.* **sun·dry** [ˈ~drɪ] *adj* diverse, verschiedene: **all and ~** jedermann, *contp.* Hinz u. Kunz.

'sun·flow·er *s* ⚘ Sonnenblume *f.* **~ oil** *s* Sonnenblumenöl *n.*

sung [sʌŋ] *pp von* **sing.**

'sun·glass·es *s pl, a. pair of ~* Sonnenbrille *f.* **~ god** *s* Sonnengott *m.* **~ hel·met** *s* Tropenhelm *m.*

sunk [sʌŋk] *pret u. pp von* **sink.**

sunk·en [ˈsʌŋkən] *adj* **1.** ge-, versunken;

versenkt. **2.** eingefallen (*Wangen*), (*a. Augen*) eingesunken.

sun| lamp s Höhensonne f, Quarzlampe f. '**~light** s Sonnenlicht n. '**~lit** adj sonnenbeschienen.

sun·ny ['sʌnɪ] adj □ sonnig (*a. fig. Wesen etc*), fig. fröhlich (*Lächeln etc*): **~ side** Sonnenseite f (*a. fig. des Lebens*); **~side up** nur auf 'einer Seite gebraten (*Ei*).

'**sun|·rise** s Sonnenaufgang m: **at ~** bei Sonnenaufgang. '**~roof** s **1.** mot. Schiebedach n. **2.** Dachterrasse f. '**~set** s Sonnenuntergang m: **at ~** bei Sonnenuntergang. '**~shade** s Sonnenschirm m. '**~shine** s Sonnenschein m. '**~stroke** s ♣ Sonnenstich m. '**~tan** s (Sonnen)Bräune f: **~ lotion** (*od. oil*) Sonnenöl n. '**~tanned** adj braungebrannt. '**~up** → **sunrise**. **~ vi·sor** s mot. Sonnenblende f.

su·per ['suːpə] adj F super, klasse.

su·per... ['suːpə] Über..., über...

,**su·per·a'bun·dant** adj □ überreichlich.

su·per·an·nu·at·ed [ˌsuːpəˈrænjʊeɪtɪd] adj **1.** pensioniert, im Ruhestand. **2.** fig. überholt, veraltet.

su·perb [suːˈpɜːb] adj □ ausgezeichnet.

su·per·cil·i·ous [ˌsuːpəˈsɪlɪəs] adj □ hochnäsig.

su·per·fi·cial [ˌsuːpəˈfɪʃl] adj □ oberflächlich (*a. fig.*). **su·per·fi·ci·al·i·ty** [ˈ~ˌfɪʃɪˈælətɪ] s Oberflächlichkeit f.

su·per·flu·ous [suːˈpɜːflʊəs] adj □ überflüssig.

,**su·per|'hu·man** adj □ übermenschlich. '**~im·pose** v/t Bild etc einblenden (**on** in acc).

su·per·in·tend·ent [ˌsuːpərɪnˈtendənt] s **1.** Aufsicht(sbeamte m) f. **2.** Br. Kriminalrat m.

su·pe·ri·or [suːˈpɪərɪə] I adj □ **1.** (**to**) überlegen (dat), besser (als): **be ~ in number(s) to** j-m zahlenmäßig überlegen sn. **2.** ranghöher (**to** als): **be ~ to** a. höher stehen als. **3.** ausgezeichnet, hervorragend. **4.** b.s. überheblich, -legen. II s Vorgesetzte m, f. **su·pe·ri·or·i·ty** [~ˈɒrətɪ] s **1.** Überlegenheit f (**over** gegenüber): **~ in number(s)** zahlenmäßige Überlegenheit. **2.** Überheblichkeit f.

su·per·la·tive [suːˈpɜːlətɪv] I adj □ **1.** unübertrefflich, überragend: **~ly happy**

unsagbar glücklich. **2. ~ degree** → 3. II s **3.** ling. Superlativ m.

'**su·per|·man** s (irr man) Supermann m. '**~mar·ket** s Supermarkt m. ,**~'nat·u·ral** I adj □ übernatürlich. II s: **the ~** das Übernatürliche.

su·per·nu·mer·a·ry [ˌsuːpəˈnjuːmərərɪ] adj überzählig.

'**su·per|,pow·er** s pol. Supermacht f.

su·per·sede [ˌsuːpəˈsiːd] v/t et. ablösen, ersetzen, an die Stelle treten von (od. gen).

,**su·per|'son·ic** adj ✈, phys. Überschall...: **at ~ speed** mit Überschallgeschwindigkeit. '**~star** s Sport etc: Superstar m.

su·per·sti·tion [ˌsuːpəˈstɪʃn] s Aberglaube m, pl abergläubische Vorstellungen pl. **su·per·sti·tious** [~ˈstɪʃəs] adj □ abergläubisch.

'**su·per|,struc·ture** s △ Oberbau m, ♣ (Deck)Aufbauten pl; fig. Überbau m. '**~,tank·er** s ♣ Supertanker m.

su·per·vene [ˌsuːpəˈviːn] v/i dazwischenkommen.

su·per·vise ['suːpəvaɪz] v/t beaufsichtigen. **su·per·vi·sion** [~ˈvɪʒn] s Beaufsichtigung f: **under s.o.'s ~** unter j-s Aufsicht. **su·per·vi·sor** ['~vaɪzə] s Aufseher(in), Aufsicht f.

su·per ['sʌpə] s Abendessen n: **have ~** zu Abend essen; → **lord** 3.

sup·plant [səˈplɑːnt] v/t j-n, et. verdrängen.

sup·ple ['sʌpl] adj □ gelenkig (Körper etc), (a. Material) geschmeidig, (Material) biegsam, elastisch.

sup·ple·ment I s ['sʌplɪmənt] **1.** Ergänzung f (**to** gen od. zu). **2.** Nachtrag m, Anhang m (**to** zu e-m Buch); Ergänzungsband m. **3.** Beilage f (zu e-r Zeitung). II v/t [~ment] **4.** ergänzen, Einkommen aufbessern (**with** mit). **sup·ple·men·ta·ry** [~ˈmentərɪ] adj ergänzend, zusätzlich: **~ benefit** Br. Sozialhilfe f.

sup·pli·er [səˈplaɪə] s ✝ Lieferant(in), a. pl Lieferfirma f.

sup·ply [səˈplaɪ] I v/t **1.** liefern; stellen; sorgen für. **2.** j-n, et. versorgen, ✝ beliefern (**with** mit). **3.** e-m Bedürfnis etc abhelfen. II s **4.** Lieferung f (**to** an acc). **5.** Versorgung f. **6.** ✝ Angebot n: **~ and demand** Angebot u. Nachfrage; →

short 2. **7.** *mst pl* Vorrat *m* (**of** an *dat*), *pl a.* Proviant *m*, ✗ Nachschub *m*. **8.** *pl* (*Büro- etc*)Bedarf *m*.

sup·port [sə'pɔːt] **I** *v/t* **1.** (ab)stützen; *Gewicht etc* tragen; *fig.* Währung stützen. **2.** *j-n* (*a. finanziell*), *Forderung etc* unterstützen, *Familie* unterhalten: **~ Tottenham** ein Tottenham-Anhänger sein. **3.** *Hobby etc* finanzieren. **4.** *Theorie etc* beweisen, erhärten. **5.** *et.* aushalten, ertragen. **II** *s* **6.** Stütze *f*, ⚙ *a.* Stützbalken *m*, -pfeiler *m*. **7.** *fig.* Unterstützung *f*: **in ~ of** zur Unterstützung (*gen*); **have s.o.'s full ~** j-s volle Unterstützung haben. **sup'port·a·ble** *adj* ☐ erträglich. **sup'port·er** *s* Anhänger(in) (*a. Sport*), Befürworter(in). **sup'port·ing** *adj* **1. ~ wall** tragende Wand. **2.** *fig.* unterstützend: **~ materials** *pl ped.* Begleitmaterial *n*; **~ part** (*od. role*) *thea. etc* Nebenrolle *f*; **~ program(me)** (*Film*) Beiprogramm *n*. **sup'port·ive** *adj*: **he was very ~ when I ...** er war mir e-e große Stütze, als ich ...

sup·pose [sə'pəʊz] **I** *v/t* **1.** annehmen, vermuten: **I ~ I must have fallen a·sleep** ich muß wohl eingeschlafen sein. **2.** *he is ~d* (*to be*) *rich* er soll reich sein; **you are not ~d to smoke here** du darfst hier nicht rauchen; **aren't you ~d to be at work?** solltest du nicht (eigentlich) in der Arbeit sein?; **what is that ~d to mean?** was soll denn das? **3.** *et.* voraussetzen. **II** *v/i* **4.** **I ~ so** ich nehme es an, wahrscheinlich, vermutlich. **III** *cj* **5.** angenommen. **6.** wie wäre es, wenn: **~ we went home?** wie wäre es, wenn wir nach Hause gingen? **sup'posed** *adj* ☐ angeblich. **sup'pos·ing** *cj* **1.** → **suppose** 5, 6. **2.** vorausgesetzt.

sup·po·si·tion [ˌsʌpə'zɪʃn] *s* Annahme *f*, Vermutung *f*: **act on the ~ that** von der Annahme ausgehen, daß.

sup·pos·i·to·ry [sə'pɒzɪtəri] *s* 🏥 Zäpfchen *n*.

sup·pu·rate ['sʌpjʊəreɪt] *v/i* eitern.

su·pra·na·tion·al [ˌsuːprə'næʃənl] *adj* ☐ übernational.

su·prem·a·cy [sʊ'preməsi] *s* Vormachtstellung *f*.

su·preme [sʊ'priːm] *adj* **1.** höchst, oberst. **2.** höchst, größt. **su'preme·ly** *adv* höchst, absolut.

sur·charge **I** *s* ['sɜːtʃɑːdʒ] Auf-, Zu-

schlag *m* (**on** auf *acc*); ✉ Nach-, Strafporto *n* (**on** auf *acc*). **II** *v/t* [sɜː'tʃɑːdʒ] Nachporto *od.* e-n Zuschlag erheben auf (*acc*).

sure [ʃɔː] **I** *adj* (☐ → **surely**) **1.** *allg.* sicher: **~ of o.s.** selbstsicher; **~ of victo·ry** (*od.* **winning**) siegessicher; **for ~** ganz sicher *od.* bestimmt; **~** *thing! bsd. Am.* F (aber) klar!; **be** (*od.* **feel**) **~** sicher sein; **you are ~ to like this play** dir wird das Stück sicher *od.* bestimmt gefallen; **be ~ to lock the door** vergiß nicht abzuschließen; **to be ~** sicher(lich); **make ~ that** sich (davon) überzeugen, daß; dafür sorgen, daß; **make ~ of s.th.** sich von et. überzeugen; sich et. sichern. **II** *adv* **2.** F sicher, klar. **3.** **~ enough** tatsächlich. **'~·fire** *adj* F (tod)sicher.

sure·ly ['ʃɔːli] *adv* **1.** sicher: → **slow** 1. **2.** sicher(lich), bestimmt. **sure·ty** ['ʃɔːrəti] *s bsd.* 🏛 Bürgschaft *f*, Sicherheit *f*; Bürge *m*, Bürgin *f*: **stand ~ for s.o.** für j-n bürgen.

surf [sɜːf] **I** *s* Brandung *f*. **II** *v/i* surfen.

sur·face ['sɜːfɪs] **I** *s* **1.** Oberfläche *f* (*a. fig.*): **on the ~** äußerlich; vordergründig; oberflächlich betrachtet. **2.** (*Straßen*)Belag *m*, (-)Decke *f*. **II** *adj* **3.** Oberflächen...: **~ mail** gewöhnliche Post (*Ggs. Luftpost*); **~ tension** *phys.* Oberflächenspannung *f*. **4.** *fig.* oberflächlich. **III** *v/i* **5.** auftauchen (*a. fig.*). **IV** *v/t* **6.** *Straße* mit e-m Belag versehen. **'surf·board** *s* Surfboard *n*, -brett *n*.

sur·feit ['sɜːfɪt] **I** *s* Überangebot *n* (**of** an *dat*). **II** *v/t*: **~ o.s. with** sich übersättigen an (*dat*).

surf·er ['sɜːfə] *s* Surfer(in), Wellenreiter(in). **'surf·ing** *s* Surfen *n*, Wellenreiten *n*.

surge [sɜːdʒ] **I** *s* **1.** **a ~ of people** e-e wogende Menschenmenge; **there was a sudden ~ forward** plötzlich drängte alles nach vorn. **2.** *fig.* Welle *f*, Woge *f* (*der Begeisterung*); (*Gefühls*)Aufwallung *f*, Anwandlung *f*. **II** *v/i* **3.** drängen, strömen (*Menschenmenge*). **4.** *mst* **~ up** *fig.* aufwallen (**in** in *dat*) (*Zorn etc*).

sur·geon ['sɜːdʒən] *s* Chirurg(in). **sur·ger·y** ['sɜːdʒəri] *s* **1.** Chirurgie *f*. **2.** *he needs ~* er muß operiert werden; *re·move by ~* operativ entfernen. **3.** *Br.* Sprechzimmer *n*; Sprechstunde *f*: **~ hours** Sprechstunden *pl*. **sur·gi·cal**

['ˌʌkl] *adj* ☐ **1.** chirurgisch; operativ; Operations...: ~ **spirit** *Br.* Wundbenzin *n.* **2.** ~ **stocking** Stützstrumpf *m.*

sur·ly ['sɜːlɪ] *adj* ☐ griesgrämig, sauertöpfisch.

sur·mise I *s* ['sɜːmaɪz] Vermutung *f.* II *v/t* [sɜːˈmaɪz] vermuten.

sur·mount [sɜːˈmaʊnt] *v/t Schwierigkeit etc* überwinden. **sur'mount·a·ble** *adj* überwindbar.

sur·name ['sɜːneɪm] *s* Familien-, Nach-, Zuname *m:* **what is his ~?** wie heißt er mit Familiennamen?

sur·pass [səˈpɑːs] *v/t Erwartungen etc* übertreffen.

sur·plus ['sɜːpləs] I *s* Überschuß *m* (*of* an *dat*). II *adj* überschüssig: **be ~ to requirements** zuviel sein.

sur·prise [səˈpraɪz] I *s* Überraschung *f:* **in ~** überrascht; **take by ~** überraschen; → **much** 2. II *adj* überraschend, Überraschungs... III *v/t* überraschen: **be ~d at** (*od.* **by**) überrascht sein über (*acc*); **I wouldn't be ~d if** es würde mich nicht wundern, wenn. **sur'pris·ing** *adj* ☐ überraschend. **~ly** (*enough*) überraschenderweise.

sur·re·al·ism [səˈrɪəlɪzəm] *s Kunst:* Surrealismus *m.* **sur're·al·ist** I *s* Surrealist(in). II *adj* surrealistisch. **sur,re·al'is·tic** *adj* (*~ally*) surrealistisch.

sur·ren·der [səˈrendə] I *v/i* **1.** (**to**) ✕ sich ergeben (*dat*), kapitulieren (vor *dat*) (*beide a. fig.*): ~ **to the police** sich der Polizei stellen. II *v/t* **2.** *et.* übergeben, ausliefern (**to** *dat*): ~ **o.s. to the police** sich der Polizei stellen. **3.** Anspruch *etc* aufgeben, verzichten auf (*acc*). III *s* **4.** ✕ Kapitulation *f* (**to** vor *dat*) (*a. fig.*). **5.** (*of*) Aufgabe *f* (*gen*), Verzicht *m* (auf *acc*).

sur·rep·ti·tious [ˌsʌrepˈtɪʃəs] *adj* ☐ heimlich, verstohlen.

sur·ro·gate ['sʌrəgeɪt] *adj:* ~ **mother** Leihmutter *f.*

sur·round [səˈraʊnd] *v/t* **1.** umgeben. **2.** *Haus etc* umstellen. **sur'round·ing** I *adj* umliegend. II *s pl* Umgebung *f.*

sur·veil·lance [sɜːˈveɪləns] *s* Überwachung *f:* **be** (**keep**) **under ~** überwacht werden (überwachen).

sur·vey I *v/t* [sɜːˈveɪ] **1.** (sich) *et.* betrachten (*a. fig.*). **2.** *Land* vermessen. **3.** *Haus etc* begutachten. II *s* ['sɜːveɪ] **4.** Umfra-

ge *f.* **5.** Überblick *m* (*of* über *acc*). **6.** Vermessung *f.* **7.** Begutachtung *f.* **sur'vey·or** *s* **1.** Land(ver)messer(in). **2.** Gutachter(in).

sur·viv·al [səˈvaɪvl] *s* **1.** Überleben *n* (*a. fig.*): ~ **training** Überlebenstraining *n.* **2.** Überbleibsel *n* (**from** aus e-r *Zeit*).

sur·vive I *v/t* **1.** *j-n, et.* überleben; *Erdbeben etc* überstehen (*Haus etc*); *Jahrhundert etc* überdauern (*Brauch etc*). II *v/i* **2.** überleben (*a. fig.*), am Leben bleiben. **3.** erhalten bleiben *od.* sein. **sur'vi·vor** *s* Überlebende *m, f* (**from, of** *gen*).

sus·cep·ti·ble [səˈseptəbl] *adj* ☐ **1.** empfänglich (**to** für). **2.** anfällig (**to** für). **3.** leicht zu beeindrucken.

sus·pect I *v/t* [səˈspekt] **1.** *j-n* verdächtigen (*of gen*): ~ **s.o. of doing s.th.** *j-n* im *od.* in Verdacht haben, et. zu tun; **be ~ed of doing s.th.** im *od.* unter dem Verdacht stehen, et. zu tun. **2.** *et.* vermuten. **3.** *et.* an-, bezweifeln. II *s* ['sʌspekt] **4.** Verdächtige *m, f.* III *adj* ['sʌspekt] **5.** verdächtig, suspekt.

sus·pend [səˈspend] *v/t* **1.** aufhängen (**from** an *dat*). **2.** *Verkauf, Zahlungen etc* (vorübergehend) einstellen; ⚖ *Strafe* zur Bewährung aussetzen: **he was given a two-year ~ed sentence** er bekam zwei Jahre mit Bewährung. **3.** *j-n* suspendieren (**from duty** vom Dienst); vorübergehend ausschließen (**from** aus); (*Sport*) sperren (**for two games** für zwei Spiele). **sus'pend·er** *s* **1.** *Br.* Strumpfhalter *m,* Straps *m:* ~ **belt** Strumpf(halter)-, Strapsgürtel *m.* **2.** *pl, a.* **pair of ~s** *Am.* Hosenträger *pl.*

sus·pense [səˈspens] *s* Spannung *f:* **in ~** gespannt, voller Spannung; **full of ~** spannend; **keep s.o. in ~** *j-n* auf die Folter spannen. **sus'pen·sion** *s* **1.** *mot. etc* Aufhängung *f:* ~ **bridge** Hängebrücke *f.* **2.** (vorübergehende) Einstellung. **3.** Suspendierung *f;* vorübergehender Ausschluß; (*Sport*) Sperre *f:* **he received a two-game ~** er wurde für zwei Spiele gesperrt.

sus·pi·cion [səˈspɪʃn] *s* **1.** Verdacht *m* (*of* gegen): **be above** (*od.* **beyond**) ~ über jeden Verdacht erhaben sein; **be under ~ of murder** unter Mordverdacht stehen. **2.** *a. pl* Verdacht *m,* Argwohn *m,* Mißtrauen *n* (*of* gegen): **with ~** argwöh-

nisch, mißtrauisch. **3.** Verdacht *m*, Vermutung *f*. **4.** *fig.* Hauch *m*, Spur *f*.
sus·pi·cious *adj* □ **1.** verdächtig. **2.** argwöhnisch, mißtrauisch (**of** gegen): **become ~ of** Verdacht schöpfen.
sus·tain [sə'steɪn] *v/t* **1.** *j-n* (*a. moralisch*) stärken. **2.** *Interesse etc* aufrechterhalten. **3.** *Schaden, Verlust* erleiden. **4.** ♪ *Ton* (aus)halten. **5.** ♬ *e-m Einspruch etc* stattgeben. **6.** *Gewicht* aushalten, tragen. **sus'tained** *adj* anhaltend.
su·ture ['su:tʃə] ♪ **I** *s* Naht *f*. **II** *v/t* *Wunde* nähen.
svelte [svelt] *adj* gertenschlank (*Frau*).
swab [swɒb] ♪ **I** *s* **1.** Tupfer *m*. **2.** Abstrich *m*: **take a ~** e-n Abstrich machen. **II** *v/t* **3.** *Wunde* abtupfen.
swad·dle ['swɒdl] *v/t* *Baby* wickeln.
swag·ger ['swægə] **I** *v/i* stolzieren. **II** *s*: **walk with a ~** → I.
swal·low¹ ['swɒləʊ] *s orn.* Schwalbe *f*.
swal·low² [~] **I** *v/t* **1.** schlucken (*a. fig.* F *glauben, hinnehmen*)· **~ one's words** zugeben, daß man sich geirrt hat; **~ up** *Betrieb, Gewinn etc* schlucken, verschlingen; → **bait** 1. **2.** *Ärger, Tränen etc* hinunterschlucken, *s-n Stolz* vergessen. **II** *v/i* **3.** schlucken: **~ hard** *fig.* kräftig schlucken. **III** *s* **4.** Schluck *m*.
swam [swæm] *pret von* **swim**.
swamp [swɒmp] **I** *s* Sumpf *m*. **II** *v/t* überschwemmen: **be ~ed with** *fig.* überschwemmt werden mit. **'swamp·y** *adj* sumpfig.
swan [swɒn] *s orn.* Schwan *m*.
swank [swæŋk] F **I** *v/i* **1.** angeben. **II** *s* **2.** Angeber(in). **3.** Angabe *f*. **'swank·y** *adj* □ F **1.** piekfein. **2.** angeberisch.
'swan·song *s fig.* Schwanengesang *m*.
swap [swɒp] F **I** *v/t* **1.** *et.* tauschen (**with** mit), (ein)tauschen (**for** für, gegen): **~ places** die Plätze tauschen. **II** *v/i* **2.** tauschen: **~ over** (*od.* **round**) die Plätze tauschen. **III** *s* **3.** Tausch *m*: **do a ~** tauschen; **do** (*od.* **get**) **a good** (**bad**) **~** e-n guten (schlechten) Tausch machen. **4.** Tauschobjekt *n*.
swarm [swɔːm] **I** *s* **1.** Schwarm *m* (*Bienen, Touristen etc*). **II** *v/i* **2.** schwärmen (*Bienen*), (*Menschen a.*) strömen. **3.** **~ with** wimmeln von: **the square was ~ing with people** auf dem Platz wimmelte es von Menschen.

swarth·y ['swɔːðɪ] *adj* dunkel (*Haut*), dunkelhäutig (*Person*).
swash·buck·ling ['swɒʃˌbʌklɪŋ] *adj* verwegen (*Person*), abenteuerlich (*Film etc*).
swas·ti·ka ['swɒstɪkə] *s* Hakenkreuz *n*.
swat [swɒt] **I** *v/t* *Fliege etc* totschlagen. **II** *s* → **swat·ter**. **'swat·ter** *s* Fliegenklappe *f*, -klatsche *f*.
sway [sweɪ] **I** *v/i* **1.** sich wiegen (**in the wind** im Wind) (*Bäume etc*), schaukeln (*Schiff etc*): **~ between** *fig.* schwanken zwischen (*dat*). **II** *v/t* **2.** hin- u. herbewegen, *s-n Körper* wiegen, *Fahne etc* schwenken. **3.** *j-n* beeinflussen; umstimmen. **III** *s* **4.** Schaukeln *n*.
swear [sweə] (*irr*) **I** *v/i* **1.** schwören (**on the Bible** auf die Bibel; **to God** bei Gott): **~ by** *fig.* F schwören auf (*acc*); **I couldn't ~ to it** ich kann es nicht beschwören. **2.** fluchen: **~ at s.o.** j-n wüst beschimpfen. **II** *v/t* **3.** schwören (**to** do tun; **that** daß): **~ s.th. to s.o.** j-m et. schwören; → **oath** 1. **4.** **~ in** *Minister, Zeugen etc* vereidigen; **I was sworn to secrecy** ich mußte hoch u. heilig versprechen, kein Wort darüber zu sagen. **'~word** *s* Fluch *m*; Kraftausdruck *m*.
sweat [swet] **I** *v/i* (*Am. a. irr*) **1.** schwitzen (**with** vor *dat*) (*a. fig.* F). **II** *v/t* (*Am. a. irr*) **2.** *~ out Krankheit* ausschwitzen: **~ it out** F durchhalten; **~ blood** F sich abrackern (**over** mit). **III** *s* **3.** Schweiß *m*: **cold ~** kalter Schweiß, Angstschweiß; **no ~!** F kein Problem!; **get in(to) a ~** *fig.* F ins Schwitzen geraten *od.* kommen (**about** wegen). **4.** F Schufterei *f*. **'~band** *s* *Sport:* Schweißband *n*.
sweat·er ['swetə] *s* Pullover *m*.
sweat| gland *s anat.* Schweißdrüse *f*. **'~shirt** *s* Sweatshirt *n* (*weiter Baumwollpullover*)
sweat·y ['swetɪ] *adj* □ **1.** schweißig, verschwitzt. **2.** nach Schweiß riechend, Schweiß... **3.** schweißtreibend.
Swede [swiːd] *s* Schwede *m*, Schwedin *f*.
Swed·ish ['swiːdɪʃ] **I** *adj* **1.** schwedisch. **II** *s* **2.** *ling.* Schwedisch *n*. **3.** **the ~** *pl* die Schweden *pl*.
sweep [swiːp] **I** *s* **1.** **give the floor a ~** den Boden kehren *od.* fegen; **make a clean ~** *fig.* gründlich aufräumen; (*Sport etc*) gründlich abräumen. **2.** Hieb *m*, Schlag

m. **3.** Schornsteinfeger(in), Kaminkeh-
rer(in). **II** *v/t* (*irr*) **4.** Fußboden, Krümel
etc kehren, fegen: **~ the board** (*Sport
etc*) gründlich abräumen; → **carpet** 1,
rug 1. **5.** fegen über (*acc*) (*Sturm etc*);
fig. Land *etc* überschwemmen (*Protest-
welle etc*). **6. ~ along** mitreißen; **~ s.o.
off his feet** *fig.* j-s Herz im Sturm erobern. **7.** *Horizont etc* absuchen (**for**
nach). **III** *v/i* (*irr*) **8.** kehren, fegen: →
broom. 9. rauschen (*Person*): **~ past
s.o.** an j-m vorbeirauschen.
Verbindungen mit Adverbien:
sweep| a·side *v/t* Einwände *etc* beisei-
te schieben. **~ a·way** *v/t* **1.** aufräumen
mit. **2. be swept away by** *fig.* mitgeris-
sen werden von. **~ up** *v/t* **1.** (*a. v/i*)
zs.-kehren, -fegen. **2.** j-n hochreißen.
sweep·er ['swi:pə] *s* **1.** (*Straßen*)Keh-
rer(in). **2.** Kehrmaschine *f.* **3.** *Fußball:*
Libero *m.* **'sweep·ing I** *adj* □ **1.**
durchgreifend (*Änderung etc*). **2.** pauschal. **II** *s pl* **3.** Kehricht *m.*
sweet [swi:t] **I** *adj* □ **1.** süß (*a. fig.*): **~
nothings** *pl* Zärtlichkeiten *pl*; **~ potato
& Batate** *f*, Süßkartoffel *f*; **revenge is ~**
Rache ist süß; **~ talk** F Schmeichelei(en
pl) *f*; **have a ~ tooth** gern naschen. **2.**
lieblich (*Musik etc*). **3.** lieb. **II** *s* **4.** *Br.*
Bonbon *m, n,* Süßigkeit *f.* **5.** *Br.* Nachtisch *m:* **for ~** als *od.* zum Nachtisch.
~-and-'sour *adj gastr.* süß-sauer.
sweet·en ['swi:tn] **I** *v/t* **1.** süßen. **2.** *fig.*
besänftigen; freundlicher stimmen. **3.**
a. **~ up** F j-n schmieren. **II** *v/i* **4.** süß(er)
werden. **'sweet·en·er** *s* **1.** Süßstoff *m.*
2. F Schmiergeld *n.*
'sweet·heart *s* Schatz *m* (*Anrede*).
sweet·ie ['swi:tɪ] *s* F **1.** *Br.* Bonbon *m, n.*
2. be a ~ *fig.* süß sein.
'sweet-talk *v/t* F j-m schmeicheln.
swell [swel] **I** *v/i* (*mst irr*) **1.** *a.* **~ up** 🗶
(an)schwellen. **2.** *a.* **~ out** 🗶 sich blähen
(*Segel*). **3.** *fig.* anschwellen (**into** zu)
(*Geräusch*); anwachsen (*Zahl etc*). **II**
v/t (*mst irr*) **4.** *a.* **~ out** *od.* Segel blähen
(*Wind*). **5.** *fig.* Zahl *etc* anwachsen lassen. **III** *s* **6.** 🗶 Dünung *f.* **IV** *adj* **7.** *Am.*
F klasse. **'swell·ing** *s* 🗶 Schwellung
f.
swel·ter ['sweltə] *v/i* vor Hitze fast umkommen. **'swel·ter·ing** *adj* drückend,
schwül.
swept [swept] *pret u. pp von* **sweep.**

swerve [swɜːv] **I** *v/i* **1.** schwenken (**to the
left** nach links), e-n Schwenk machen.
2. *fig.* abweichen (**from** von). **II** *s* **3.**
Schwenk(ung *f*) *m, mot. etc a.* Schlen-
ker *m.*
swift [swɪft] *adj* □ schnell: **be ~ to do
o.th.** et. schnell tun. **'swift·ness** *s*
Schnelligkeit *f.*
swig [swɪg] F **I** *v/t* Getränk hinunterkip-
pen. **II** *s:* **take a ~ at the bottle** e-n Zug
aus der Flasche tun; **take a ~ of beer**
e-n kräftigen Schluck Bier nehmen.
swill [swɪl] *v/t u. v/i contr.* saufen.
swim [swɪm] **I** *v/i* (*irr*) **1.** schwimmen: →
tide 2. **2.** *fig.* verschwimmen (**before
s.o.'s eyes** vor j-s Augen); **my head
was ~ming** mir drehte sich alles. **II**
v/t (*irr*) **3.** *Strecke* schwimmen; *Gewässer* durchschwimmen. **III** *s* **4.** go
for a ~ schwimmen gehen. **'swim·mer**
s Schwimmer(in). **'swim·ming I** *s*
Schwimmen *n.* **II** *adj* Schwimm...: **~
bath(s** *pl*) *Br.* Schwimm-, *bsd.* Hallenbad *n*; **~ cap** Badekappe *f*, -mütze *f*; **~
costume** Badeanzug *m*; **~ pool** Swim-
mingpool *m*, Schwimmbecken *n*; (*pair
of*) **~ trunks** *pl* Badehose *f.*
'swim·suit *s* Badeanzug *m.*
swin·dle ['swɪndl] **I** *v/t* j-n beschwindeln
(**out of** um): **~ s.o. out of s.th.** *a.* j-m et.
abschwindeln. **II** *s* Schwindel *m.* **'swindler** *s* Schwindler(in).
swine [swaɪn] *s* **1.** *pl* **~** *zo.* Schwein *n.* **2.** *pl*
~(s) *sl. contp.* Schwein *n.*
swing [swɪŋ] **I** *v/i* (*irr*) **1.** (hin- u.
her)schwingen. **2.** sich schwingen; einbiegen, -schwenken (**into** in *acc*): **~
round** sich ruckartig umdrehen; **~ shut**
zuschlagen (*Tor etc*). **3.** ♪ schwungvoll
spielen (*Band etc*); Schwung haben
(*Musik*). **II** *v/t* **4.** et., *die Arme etc*
schwingen. **III** *s* **5.** Schwingen *n.* **6.**
Schaukel *f.* **7.** *Boxen:* Schwinger *m.* **8.**
fig. Schwung *m:* **be in full ~** in vollem
Gang sein. **9.** *fig.* Umschwung *m:* **~ in
opinion** Meinungsumschwung. **~ door**
s Pendeltür *f.*
swinge·ing ['swɪndʒɪŋ] *adj bsd. Br.* einschneidend (*Kürzungen etc*), extrem
hoch (*Besteuerung etc*).
swing·ing ['swɪŋɪŋ] *adj* □ **1.** schwin-
gend: **~ door** *bsd. Am.* Pendeltür *f.* **2.**
fig. schwungvoll. **3.** *fig.* lebenslustig.
swin·ish ['swaɪnɪʃ] *adj* □ ekelhaft.

synonymous

swipe [swaıp] **I** s Schlag m: *take a ~ at* → II. **II** v/i: *~ at* schlagen nach. **III** v/t F klauen.

swirl [swɜ:l] **I** v/i wirbeln. **II** s Wirbel m.

swish [swıʃ] **I** v/i **1.** sausen, zischen. **2.** rascheln (*Seide etc*). **II** v/t **3.** mit *dem Schwanz* schlagen. **III** s **4.** Sausen n, Zischen n. **5.** Rascheln n. **IV** adj **6.** F feudal.

Swiss [swıs] **I** s Schweizer(in): *the ~ pl* die Schweizer pl. **II** adj schweizerisch, Schweizer(...)

switch [swıtʃ] **I** s **1.** ⚡, ⊙ Schalter m. **2.** Gerte f, Rute f. **3.** 🚂 Am. Weiche f. **4.** fig. Umstellung f. **II** v/t **5.** a. *~ over* ⚡, ⊙ (um)schalten, *Produktion etc* umstellen (*to* auf acc): *~ off* ab-, ausschalten; *~ on* an-, einschalten. **III** v/i **6.** a. *~ over* ⚡, ⊙ (um)schalten (*to* auf acc), fig. überwechseln (*to* zu): *~ off* abschalten (a. fig. F *Person*), ausschalten; *~ on* an-, einschalten. **'~·back** s **1.** Gebirgs-, Serpentinenstraße f. **2.** Achterbahn f. **'~·blade** s Am. Schnappmesser n. **'~·board** s **1.** ⚡ Schalttafel f. **2.** (Telefon)Zentrale f: *~ operator* Telefonist(in).

swiv·el ['swıvl] **I** v/t pret u. pp -**eled**, bsd. Br. -**elled** sich drehen: *~ round* sich herumdrehen. *~ chair* s Drehstuhl m.

swol·len ['swəʊlən] pp von **swell**. **,~·'head·ed** adj fig. aufgeblasen.

swoop [swu:p] **I** v/i **1.** a. *~ down* herabstoßen (*on* auf acc) (*Raubvogel*). **2.** fig. zuschlagen (*Polizei etc*): *~ on* herfallen über (acc); e-e Razzia machen in (dat). **II** s **3.** Razzia f.

swop → **swap**.

sword [sɔ:d] s Schwert n: *cross ~s* die Klingen kreuzen (*with* mit) (a. fig.); → *Damocles*.

swore [swɔ:] pret von **swear**.

sworn [swɔ:n] **I** pp von **swear**. **II** adj **1.** *~ enemies* pl Todfeinde pl. **2.** 🏛 eidlich.

swot [swɒt] Br. F **I** v/i büffeln, pauken (*for* für). **II** v/t: *~ up* → I. **III** s Büffler(in); Streber(in).

swum [swʌm] pp von **swim**.

swung [swʌŋ] pret u. pp von **swing**.

syl·la·bi ['sıləbaı] pl von **syllabus**.

syl·lab·ic [sı'læbık] adj Silben...; ...silbig. **syl·la·ble** ['sıləbl] s Silbe f.

syl·la·bus ['sıləbəs] pl -**bus·es**, -**bi** ['~baı] s ped., univ. Lehrplan m.

syl·lo·gism ['sılədʒızəm] s Syllogismus m.

sym·bi·o·sis [,sımbı'əʊsıs] s biol. Symbiose f.

sym·bol ['sımbl] s Symbol n (a. 📞). **sym·bol·ic** [~'bɒlık] adj (~ally) symbolisch: *be ~ of* et. symbolisieren. **sym·bol·ism** ['~bəlızəm] s Symbolik f. **sym·bol·ize** ['~bəlaız] v/t symbolisieren.

sym·met·ri·cal [sı'metrıkl] adj □ symmetrisch. **sym·me·try** ['sımətrı] s Symmetrie f.

sym·pa·thet·ic [,sımpə'θetık] adj (~ally) **1.** mitfühlend: *~ strike* ✝ Sympathiestreik m. **2.** verständnisvoll; wohlwollend: *be ~ to* (od. *toward*[s]) wohlwollend gegenüberstehen (dat). **'sym·pa·thize** v/i **1.** mitfühlen (*with* mit). **2.** (*with*) Verständnis haben (für); wohlwollend gegenüberstehen (dat); sympathisieren (mit). **'sym·pa·thiz·er** s Sympathisant(in). **'sym·pa·thy** s **1.** Mitgefühl n: *in ~* mitfühlend; *letter of ~* Beileidsschreiben n; *~ strike* ✝ Sympathiestreik m. **2.** Verständnis n; Wohlwollen n: *be in ~ with* sympathisieren mit. **3.** pl Sympathien pl: *my sympathies are* (od. *lie*) *with* m-e Sympathien gehören (dat). **4.** pl Beileid n, Teilnahme f.

sym·phon·ic [sım'fɒnık] adj (~ally) ♪ sinfonisch, symphonisch. **sym·pho·ny** ['~fənı] s Sinfonie f, Symphonie f: *~ orchestra* Sinfonieorchester n.

sym·po·si·um [sım'pəʊzjəm] pl -**si·ums**, -**si·a** [~zjə] s Symposium n, Symposion n.

symp·tom ['sımptəm] s 💉 Symptom n, Anzeichen n (*of* für, von) (*beide a. fig.*). **symp·to·mat·ic** [,~'mætık] adj (~ally) symptomatisch (*of* für).

syn·a·gogue ['sınəgɒg] s eccl. Synagoge f.

syn·chro·nize ['sıŋkrənaız] **I** v/t aufeinander abstimmen; *Film*, *Uhren* synchronisieren. **II** v/i synchron sein (*Film*) od. gehen (*Uhren*).

syn·di·cate ['sındıkət] s ✝ Konsortium n.

syn·drome ['sındrəʊm] s 💉 Syndrom n.

syn·od ['sınəd] s eccl. Synode f.

syn·o·nym ['sınənım] s ling. Synonym n. **syn·on·y·mous** [sı'nɒnıməs] adj □ synonym: *be ~ with* fig. gleichbedeutend sein mit.

syn·op·sis [sɪ'nɒpsɪs] *pl* **-ses** [ˌ⁓siːz] *s* Zs.-fassung *f.*

syn·tac·tic [sɪn'tæktɪk] *adj* (⁓**ally**) *ling.* syntaktisch. **syn·tax** ['sɪntæks] *s* Syntax *f,* Satzlehre *f.*

syn·the·sis ['sɪnθəsɪs] *pl* **-ses** ['⁓siːz] *s* Synthese *f.* **syn·the·size** ['⁓saɪz] *v/t* 🔔 synthetisch *od.* künstlich herstellen. **'syn·the·siz·er** *s* Synthesizer *m* (*Gerät zur elektronischen Musik-, Sprach- u. Geräuscherzeugung*).

syn·thet·ic [sɪn'θetɪk] *adj* (⁓**ally**) 🔔 synthetisch, Kunst...

syph·i·lis ['sɪfɪlɪs] *s* 🗲 Syphilis.

sy·phon → **siphon.**

syr·inge ['sɪrɪndʒ] *s* 🗲 Spritze *f.*

syr·up ['sɪrəp] *s* **1.** Sirup *m.* **2.** 🗲 (*Husten*)Sirup *m,* (-)Saft *m.* **'syr·up·y** *adj* **1.** sirupartig. **2.** *fig.* zuckersüß.

sys·tem ['sɪstəm] *s* **1.** *allg.* System *n*: ⁓ *of government* Regierungssystem; ⁓ *analyst* Systemanalytiker(in); → *digestive* 2, *nervous* 1, *respiratory.* **2.** (*Straßen- etc*)Netz *n.* **3.** Organismus *m*: *get s.th. out of one's* ⁓ *fig.* sich et. von der Seele reden. **sys·tem·at·ic** [ˌsɪstə'mætɪk] *adj* (⁓**ally**) systematisch. **sys·tem·a·tize** ['⁓tɪmətaɪz] *v/t* systematisieren.

T

T [tiː] *s*: **T** *that's him to a* **T** das ist er, wie er leibt u. lebt; *fit to a* **T** wie angegossen passen *od.* sitzen; *suit s.o. to a* **T** j-m ausgezeichnet passen.

tab [tæb] *s* **1.** Aufhänger *m,* Schlaufe *f;* Lasche *f.* **2.** Etikett *n,* Schildchen *n.* **3.** *keep* ⁓ *s* (*od. a* ⁓) *on* F *j-n* überwachen. **4.** F Rechnung *f*: *pick up the* ⁓ (die Rechnung) bezahlen.

tab·er·nac·le ['tæbənækl] *s eccl.* Tabernakel *n, m.*

ta·ble ['teɪbl] I *s* **1.** Tisch *m*: *at* ⁓ bei Tisch; *at the* ⁓ am Tisch; *under the* ⁓ *fig.* unter der Hand; *drink s.o. under the* ⁓ j-n unter den Tisch trinken; *put on the* ⁓ auf den Tisch legen (*a. fig.*); *turn the* ⁓*s* (*on s.o.*) *fig.* den Spieß umdrehen *od.* umkehren. **2.** Tisch *m,* (Tisch)Runde *f.* **3.** Tabelle *f*: → *content*¹ 3. **4.** 🜨 Einmaleins *n.* II *v/t* **5.** *fig.* auf den Tisch legen. **6.** *Am. fig.* zurückstellen. **'⁓·cloth** *s* Tischdecke *f,* -tuch *n.*

ta·ble d'hôte [ˌtɑːbl'dəʊt] *s* Menü *n.*

ta·ble| lamp *s* Tischlampe *f.* **⁓ man·ners** *s pl* Tischmanieren *pl.* **'⁓·spoon** *s* Eßlöffel *m.*

tab·let ['tæblɪt] *s* **1.** *pharm.* Tablette *f.* **2.** Stück *n* (*Seife*). **3.** (*Stein- etc*)Tafel *f.*

ta·ble| ten·nis *s Sport*: Tischtennis *n.*

'⁓·ware *s* Geschirr *n* u. Besteck *n.* ⁓ **wine** *s* Tafel-, Tischwein *m.*

tab·loid ['tæblɔɪd] *s* Boulevardblatt *n,* -zeitung *f.* ⁓ **press** *s* Boulevardpresse *f.*

ta·boo, ta·bu [tə'buː] I *s* Tabu *n.* II *adj* Tabu...: ⁓ *subject* Tabu *n; be* ⁓ tabu sein. III *v/t* tabuisieren, für tabu erklären.

tab·u·lar ['tæbjʊlə] *adj* □ tabellarisch: *in* ⁓ *form* tabellarisch. **tab·u·late** ['⁓leɪt] *v/t* tabellarisch (an)ordnen.

tach·o·graph ['tækəʊɡrɑːf] *s mot.* Fahrt(en)schreiber *m.*

ta·chom·e·ter [tæ'kɒmɪtə] *s mot.* Drehzahlmesser *m.*

tac·it ['tæsɪt] *adj* □ stillschweigend. **tac·i·turn** ['⁓tɜːn] *adj* □ schweigsam, wortkarg.

tack [tæk] I *s* **1.** Stift *m,* Zwecke *f.* **2.** Heftstich *m.* **3.** *change* ⁓ *fig.* umschwenken. II *v/t* **4.** heften (*to* an *acc*). **5.** *Stoffteile* heften. **6.** ⁓ *on* anfügen (*to dat*).

tack·le ['tækl] I *s* **1.** ⚙ Flaschenzug *m.* **2.** (*Angel*)Gerät(e *pl*) *n.* **3.** *Fußball*: Angriff *m* (*auf e-n ballführenden Gegner*); Zweikampf *m.* II *v/t* **4.** *Problem etc* angehen. **5.** *j-n* zur Rede stellen (*about wegen*). **6.** *Fußball*: *ballführenden Gegner* angreifen.

tack·y¹ ['tækɪ] *adj* □ klebrig.
tack·y² [\~] *adj* □ *Am.* F schäbig; heruntergekommen.
tact [tækt] *s* Takt *m*. **tact·ful** ['\~fʊl] *adj* □ taktvoll.
tac·tic ['tæktɪk] *s* **1.** *oft pl* Taktik *f*, taktischer Zug. **2.** *pl* (*a. sg konstruiert*) ⚔, *Sport:* Taktik *f*. **tac·ti·cal** ['\~kl] *adj* □ taktisch. **tac·ti·cian** [\~'tɪʃn] *s* Taktiker(in).
tact·less ['tæktlɪs] *adj* □ taktlos.
tad·pole ['tædpəʊl] *s zo.* Kaulquappe *f*.
taf·fe·ta ['tæfɪtə] *s* Taft *m*.
taf·fy ['tæfɪ] *Am.* → **toffee.**
tag¹ [tæg] **I** *s* **1.** Etikett *n*; (*Namens-, Preis*)Schild *n*. **2.** stehende Redensart. **3.** *ling.* Frageanhängsel *n*. **II** *v/t* **4.** etikettieren; *Waren* auszeichnen: **~** (*as*) *fig.* bezeichnen als, *b.s. a.* abstempeln als. **5. ~ on** → **tack** 6. **III** *v/i* **6. ~ along** F mitgehen, -kommen, mittrotten: **~ along behind s.o.** hinter j-m hertrotten.
tag² [\~] *s* Fangen *n* (*Kinderspiel*): **play ~.**
tail [teɪl] **I** *s* **1.** *zo.* Schwanz *m*: **with one's ~ between one's legs** *fig.* mit eingezogenem Schwanz. **2.** Schwanz *m* (*e-s Drachens, e-r Kolonne etc*), (*e-s Flugzeugs etc a.*) hinterer Teil, (*e-s Kometen*) Schweif *m*. **3.** *pl* Frack *m*. **4.** *pl* Rück-, Kehrseite *f* (*e-r Münze*): → **head** 14. **5.** F Schatten *m*, Beschatter(in): **put a ~ on** *j-n* beschatten lassen. **II** *v/t* **6.** F *j-n* beschatten. **III** *v/i* **7. ~ off** schwächer werden, abnehmen. **8. ~ back** *mot. bsd. Br.* sich stauen (*to* bis zu). **'~back** *s mot. bsd. Br.* Rückstau *m*. **'~board** *s mot. etc* Ladeklappe *f.* **~ coat** *s* Frack *m*. **~ end** *s* Ende *n*, Schluß *m*. **'~gate I** *s* **1.** *mot.* Hecktür *f.* **2.** *bsd. Am.* → **tailboard. II** *v/i u. v/t* **3.** *mot. bsd. Am.* zu dicht auffahren (auf *acc*). **'~light** *s mot.* Rücklicht *n*.
tai·lor ['teɪlə] **I** *s* Schneider *m*. **II** *v/t* schneidern; *fig.* zuschneiden (*to* auf *acc*). **'~-made** *adj* maßgeschneidert (*a. fig.*): **~ suit** (*costume*) Maßanzug *m* (Schneiderkostüm *n*); **be ~ for** *fig.* wie geschaffen sein für.
'tail·piece *s* Anhang *m*, Zusatz *m*. **~ pipe** *s mot. Am.* Auspuffrohr *n*. **'~-wind** *s* Rückenwind *m*.
take [teɪk] **I** *s* **1.** *Film, TV:* Einstellung *f.* **2.** F Einnahmen *pl.* **II** *v/t* (*irr*) **3.** *allg.*

nehmen: **~ s.o. by the arm** (*in one's arms*) j-n am Arm (in die Arme) nehmen; **be ~** besetzt sein (*Platz*); → **care** 2, 3, **place** 1, **prisoner, seat** 1, *etc.* **4.** (weg)nehmen. **5.** mitnehmen. **6.** bringen. **7.** ⚔ *Stadt etc* einnehmen; (*Schach etc*) *Figur, Stein* schlagen; *Gefangene* machen. **8.** *Preis etc* erringen: → **lead** 1. **9.** *Scheck etc* (an)nehmen; *Rat* annehmen: → **advice** 1, **blame** 4, **tip³** 2. **10.** *Kritik etc* hinnehmen. **11.** fassen; Platz bieten für. **12.** *et.* aushalten, ertragen. **13.** dauern: **it took him two hours to do it** er brauchte zwei Stunden, um es zu tun. **14.** *Prüfung, Spaziergang etc* machen; *Schritte* unternehmen; *Risiko* eingehen: → **oath** 1, **risk** I, **step** 4, **trouble** 7, *etc.* **15.** *Medizin etc* (ein)nehmen. **16.** → **take down** 4. **17.** **be ~n by** (*od. with*) angetan sein von. **18. he's got what it ~s** F er bringt alle Voraussetzungen mit. **III** *v/i* (*irr*) **19.** ❀ wirken, anschlagen.
Verbindungen mit Präpositionen:
take| af·ter *v/i* j-m nachschlagen; *j-m* ähneln. **~ for** *v/t: what do you take me for?* wofür hältst du mich eigentlich? **~ from** *v/t* **1.** *take s.th. from s.o.* j-m et. wegnehmen. **2.** Ⓐ abziehen von. **3.** *Single* auskoppeln aus (*e-m Album*). **4.** *you can take it from me that* du kannst mir glauben, daß. **~ to** *v/i* **1.** Gefallen finden an (*dat*). **2. ~ doing s.th.** anfangen, et. zu tun. **3.** sich flüchten *od.* zurückziehen in (*acc*): **~ one's bed** ins Bett gehen; → **heel²** 2.
Verbindungen mit Adverbien:
take| a·long *v/t* mitnehmen. **~ a·part** *v/t* auseinandernehmen (*a. fig.* F), zerlegen. **~ a·side** *v/t* j-n beiseite nehmen. **~ a·way I** *v/t* **1.** wegnehmen (*from s.o.* j-m). **2. ... to ~** *Br.* ... zum Mitnehmen (*Essen*). **II** *v/i* **3. ~ from** s.th. e-r Sache Abbruch tun *et.* schmälern. **~ back** *v/t* **1.** ⚔ zurückerobern. **2.** zurückbringen. **3.** *Ware, et. Gesagtes* zurücknehmen. **4.** bei *j-m* Erinnerungen wachrufen; *j-n* zurückversetzen (*to* in *acc*). **~ down** *v/t* **1.** herunternehmen, *Plakat etc* abnehmen. **2.** *Hose* herunterlassen. **3.** auseinandernehmen, zerlegen. **4.** (sich) *et.* aufschreiben *od.* notieren, sich *Notizen* machen. **~ in** *v/t* **1.** j-n (bei sich) aufnehmen: → **lodger. 2.** *fig. et.* einschließen.

3. *Kleidungsstück* enger machen. **4.** *et.* begreifen. **5.** *j-n* hereinlegen: *be taken in by* hereinfallen auf (*acc*). **~ off I** *v/t* **1.** *Kleidungsstück* ablegen, ausziehen, *Hut etc* abnehmen. **2.** ✗ abnehmen, amputieren. **3.** *Theaterstück etc* absetzen. **4.** → *off* **9. 5.** ✞ *Rabatt etc* abziehen. **6.** F *j-n* nachahmen, -machen. **II** *v/i* **7.** ✓ abheben. **8.** *Sport*: abspringen. **9.** F sich aufmachen. **~ on** *v/t* **1.** *j-n* einstellen. **2.** *Arbeit etc* an-, übernehmen. **3.** *Ausdruck, Farbe etc* annehmen. **4.** sich anlegen mit. **~ out** *v/t* **1.** herausnehmen, *Zahn* ziehen: *take s.o. out of himself* j-n auf andere Gedanken bringen. **2.** *j-n* ausführen, ausgehen mit. **3.** *Versicherung* abschließen. **4.** *s-n Frust etc* auslassen (*on* an *dat*): *take it out on s.o.* sich an j-m abreagieren. **~ o·ver I** *v/t* Amt, Macht, Verantwortung etc übernehmen. **II** *v/i* die Macht übernehmen. **~ up I** *v/t* **1.** *Flüssigkeit* aufnehmen, -saugen. **2.** *Aufmerksamkeit, Zeit* in Anspruch nehmen, *Platz* einnehmen: *be taken up with* stark in Anspruch genommen sein von. **3.** *Vorschlag etc* aufgreifen. **4.** ~ doing s.th. anfangen, sich mit et. zu beschäftigen. **5.** *take s.o. up on his offer* auf j-s Angebot zurückkommen. **6.** *Erzählung etc* aufnehmen, fortfahren mit. **II** *v/i* **7.** sich einlassen (*with* mit).

'take·a·way *s Br.* **1.** Essen *n* zum Mitnehmen. **2.** Restaurant *n* mit Straßenverkauf. **'~·home** *adj*: *~ pay* Nettolohn *m*, -gehalt *n*.

tak·en ['teɪkən] *pp von* take.

'take·off *s* **1.** ✓ Abheben *n*; Start *m*: → *ready* **1. 2.** *Sport*: Absprung *m*. **3.** F Nachahmung *f*: *do a ~ of* → *take off* 6. **'~·out** *Am.* → *takeaway*. **'~·o·ver** *s bsd.* ✞ Übernahme *f*.

tak·er ['teɪkə] *s* Interessent(in). **'tak·ings** *s pl* Einnahmen *pl*.

talc [tælk] *s* **1.** *min.* Talk *m*. **2.** → *talcum powder*.

tal·cum pow·der ['tælkəm] *s* Talkumpuder *m*; Körperpuder *m*.

tale [teɪl] *s* **1.** Erzählung *f*; Geschichte *f*: *tell ~s* petzen; *tell ~s about j-n* verpetzen; *tell ~s out of school* fig. aus der Schule plaudern; → *fairy tale, old* **1. 2.** Lüge(ngeschichte) *f*, Märchen *n*.

tal·ent ['tælənt] *s* Talent *n* (*a. Person*),

Begabung *f*; *coll.* Talente *pl* (*Personen*): *~ for acting* schauspielerisches Talent; *have great ~* sehr begabt sein; *have a great ~ for music* musikalisch sehr begabt sein; *~ scout* (*bsd. Sport*) Talentsucher(in). **'tal·ent·ed** *adj* talentiert, begabt.

tal·is·man ['tælɪzmən] *s* Talisman *m*.

talk [tɔːk] **I** *s* **1.** Gespräch *n* (*a. pol. etc*), Unterhaltung *f* (*with* mit; *about* über *acc*): *have a long ~ with s.o.* ein langes Gespräch mit j-m führen, sich lange mit j-m unterhalten. **2.** Sprache *f* (*Art zu reden*): → *baby talk*. **3.** Gerede *n*: *there is a lot of ~ about* es ist viel die Rede von; *be the ~ of the town* Stadtgespräch sein; → *small* I. **4.** Vortrag *m*: *give a ~* e-n Vortrag halten (*to* vor *dat*; *about, on* über *acc*). **II** *v/i* **5.** reden, sprechen, sich unterhalten (*to, with* mit; *about* über *acc*; *of* von): *~ about s.th.* a. et. besprechen; *get o.s. ~ed about* ins Gerede kommen; *~ing of* da wir gerade von ... sprechen; *~ round s.th.* um et. herumreden; *you can ~!, look who's ~ing!, you're a fine one to ~!* F das sagst ausgerechnet du!; → *all* **3**, *big* **7**, *devil* **1**, *hat*. **III** *v/t* **6.** *Unsinn etc* reden. **7.** reden *od.* sprechen *od.* unterhalten über (*acc*): → *shop* **3. 8.** ~ *s.o. into s.th.* j-n zu et. überreden; ~ *s.o. into doing s.th.* j-n überreden, et. zu tun; ~ *s.o. out of s.th.* j-m et. ausreden; ~ *s.o. out of doing s.th.* es j-m ausreden, et. zu tun; ~ *one's way out of s.th.* sich aus et. herausreden.

Verbindungen mit Adverbien:

talk| **down I** *v/t Flugzeug* herunterlotsen. **II** *v/i*: ~ *to s.o.* herablassend mit j-m reden. ~ **out** *v/t Problem etc* ausdiskutieren. ~ **o·ver** *v/t Problem etc* besprechen (*with* mit). ~ **round** *v/t j-n* bekehren (*to* zu), umstimmen.

talk·a·tive ['tɔːkətɪv] *adj* □ gesprächig, redselig. **'talk·er** *s*: *be a good ~* gut reden können. **'talk·ing I** *s* Sprechen *n*, Reden *n*: *do all the ~* allein das Wort führen. **II** *adj* sprechend: **~ doll** Sprechpuppe *f*. **~ point** Gesprächsthema *n*; Streitpunkt *m*. **'talk·ing-to** *pl* **-tos** *s* F Standpauke *f*: *give s.o. a ~* j-m e-e Standpauke halten.

talk show *s TV bsd. Am.* Talk-Show *f*.

tall [tɔːl] *adj* **1.** groß (*Person*), hoch (*Ge-*

bäude etc). **2.** F unglaublich (*Geschichte*): *that's a ~ order* das ist ein bißchen viel verlangt.

tal·low ['tæləʊ] *s* Talg *m*.

tal·ly ['tælɪ] **I** *s Sport etc*: Stand *m*: *keep a ~ of* Buch führen über (*acc*). **II** *v/i* übereinstimmen (*with* mit). **III** *v/t a. ~ up* zs.-rechnen, -zählen.

tal·on ['tælən] *s orn.* Kralle *f*, Klaue *f*.

tam·bour ['tæm‚bʊə] *s* Stickrahmen *m*. **tam·bou·rine** [‚~bəˈriːn] *s ♪* Tamburin *n*.

tame [teɪm] **I** *adj* □ **1.** *zo.* zahm. **2.** F fad, lahm. **II** *v/t* **3.** Tier zähmen; *Leidenschaft etc* (be)zähmen.

tam·per ['tæmpə] *v/i: ~ with* sich zu schaffen machen an (*dat*).

tam·pon ['tæmpɒn] *s ✠* Tampon *m*.

tan [tæn] **I** *v/t* **1.** *fig., in, Haut* bräunen. **2.** *Fell* gerben: → *hide¹* **1**. **II** *v/i* **3.** bräunen, braun werden. **III** *v/t* **4.** Bräune *f*. **IV** *adj* **5.** gelbbraun.

tan·dem ['tændəm] *s* Tandem *n*: *in ~ fig.* zusammen, gemeinsam (*with* mit).

tang [tæŋ] *s* (scharfer) Geruch *od.* Geschmack.

tan·gent ['tændʒənt] *s &* Tangente *f*: *fly* (*od.* *go*) *off at a ~ fig.* plötzlich (vom Thema) abschweifen.

tan·ger·ine [‚tændʒəˈriːn] *s ♥* Mandarine *f*.

tan·gi·ble ['tændʒəbl] *adj* greifbar, *fig. a.* handfest.

tan·gle ['tæŋgl] **I** *v/t* **1.** *a. ~ up* verwirren, durcheinanderbringen (*beide a. fig.*), verheddern: *get ~d* → **2**. **II** *v/i* **2.** sich verwirren, durcheinanderkommen, sich verheddern (*alle a. fig.*). **3.** *~ with* F aneinandergeraten mit. **III** *s* **4.** Gewirr *n*, *fig.* Wirrwarr *m*, Durcheinander *n*.

tan·go ['tæŋgəʊ] **I** *pl* **-gos** *s ♪* Tango *m*. **II** *v/i* Tango tanzen: *it takes two to ~ fig.* dazu gehören zwei.

tank [tæŋk] **I** *s* **1.** *mot. etc* Tank *m*. **2.** ✗ Panzer *m*. **II** *v/t* **3.** *~ed up Br.* F voll (*betrunken*).

tank·ard ['tæŋkəd] *s* (Bier)Humpen *m*.

tank·er ['tæŋkə] *s ⚓* Tanker *m*, Tankschiff *n*; *mot.* Tank-, ⚙ *a.* Kesselwagen *m*.

tan·ta·lize ['tæntəlaɪz] *v/t* j-n aufreizen; hinhalten (*with* mit). **'tan·ta·liz·ing** *adj* □ verlockend.

tan·ta·mount ['tæntəmaʊnt] *adj: be ~ to*

gleichbedeutend sein mit, hinauslaufen auf (*acc*).

tan·trum ['tæntrəm] *s* Koller *m*: *fly into* (*od.* *throw*) *a ~* e-n Koller kriegen.

tap¹ [tæp] **I** *v/t* **1.** a) → **3**: *~ s.o. on the shoulder* j-m auf die Schulter klopfen, b) antippen. **2.** mit *den Fingern, Füßen* klopfen (*on* auf *acc*), mit *den Fingern* trommeln (*on* auf *acc, dat*). **II** *v/i* **3.** *~ on* (leicht) klopfen an (*acc*) *od.* auf (*acc*) *od.* gegen. **III** *v/t* **4.** (leichtes) Klopfen; Klaps *m*.

tap² [~] **I** *s* **1.** ⊙ Hahn *m*: *beer on ~* Bier *n* vom Faß; *have s.th. on ~ fig.* et. zur Hand *od.* auf Lager haben. **II** *v/t* **2.** *Faß* anzapfen, anstechen. **3.** *Telefon(leitung)* anzapfen, abhören. **4.** *Naturschätze etc* erschließen; *Vorräte etc* angreifen. **5.** *~ for Br.* F j-n anpumpen *od.* anzapfen um.

tape [teɪp] **I** *s* **1.** *allg.* Band *n*; (*Video-etc*)Kassette *f*. **2.** (Band)Aufnahme *f*; *TV* Aufzeichnung *f*. **3.** *Sport:* Zielband *n*: → *breast* **II**. **4.** → *tape measure*. **II** *v/t* **5.** *a. ~ up* (mit Klebeband) zukleben. **6.** (auf Band) aufnehmen; *TV* aufzeichnen: *~d music* Musik *f* vom Band. *~ deck s* Tapedeck *n* ([in e-e Stereoanlage eingebauter] *Kassettenrecorder ohne eigenen Verstärker u. Lautsprecher*). *~ meas·ure s* Maß-, Meßband *n*, Bandmaß *n*.

ta·per ['teɪpə] *v/i* **1.** *a. ~ off* spitz zulaufen, sich verjüngen. **2.** *a. ~ off fig.* langsam nachlassen.

'tape|-re‚cord → *tape* **6**. *~ re·cord·er s* Tonbandgerät *n*.

ta·pes·try ['tæpɪstrɪ] *s* Gobelin *m*, Wandteppich *m*.

'tape-worm *s zo.* Bandwurm *m*.

tap wa·ter *s* Leitungswasser *n*.

tar [tɑː] **I** *s* Teer *m*. **II** *v/t* teeren: *~ and feather* j-n teeren u. federn; *they are all ~red with the same brush fig. contp.* sie sind alle gleich.

ta·ran·tu·la [təˈræntjʊlə] *s zo.* Tarantel *f*.

tar·dy ['tɑːdɪ] *adj* □ spät, verspätet.

tare [teə] *s ✝* Tara *f*.

tar·get ['tɑːgɪt] **I** *s* **1.** (Schieß-, Ziel-)Scheibe *f*; *fig.* Zielscheibe *f* (*des Spotts etc*). **2.** ✗ Ziel *n* (*a. fig.*); ✈ *a.* Soll *n*: *set o.s. a ~ of doing s.th.* (es) sich zum Ziel setzen, et. zu tun. **II** *v/t* **3.** *be ~ed at* (*od.* *on*) gerichtet sein auf (*acc*); *fig.* abzie-

len auf (acc). ~ **group** s Zielgruppe f. ~
lan·guage s Zielsprache f.

tar·iff ['tærɪf] s **1.** Zoll(tarif) m. **2.**
bsd. Br. Preisverzeichnis n (in Hotel
etc).

tar·mac ['tɑːmæk] s **1.** Asphalt m. **2.** ✈
Rollfeld n.

tar·nish ['tɑːnɪʃ] **I** v/t Ansehen etc beflek-
ken. **II** v/i anlaufen (Metall).

tar·pau·lin [tɑː'pɔːlɪn] s Plane f; ⚓ Persenning f.

tar·ra·gon ['tærəgən] s ♣ Estragon m.

tart¹ [tɑːt] adj □ **1.** herb; sauer. **2.** fig.
scharf, beißend.

tart² [~] s **1.** Obstkuchen m; Obsttört-
chen n. **2.** F Flittchen n; Nutte f.

tar·tan ['tɑːtən] s Schottenstoff n;
Schottenmuster n.

tar·tar ['tɑːtə] s ♞ Weinstein m; Zahn-
stein m.

task [tɑːsk] s Aufgabe f: **take s.o. to ~** fig.
j-n zurechtweisen (for wegen). **~ force**
s ✕ Sonder-, Spezialeinheit f (a. der
Polizei).

tas·sel ['tæsl] s Troddel f, Quaste f.

taste [teɪst] **I** s **1.** Geschmack(ssinn) m:
→ **sense** 1. **2.** Geschmack m: **have no
~** nach nichts schmecken; **leave a bad
~ in s.o.'s mouth** fig. e-n bitteren od.
schlechten Nachgeschmack bei j-m
hinterlassen. **3.** Kostprobe f: **have a ~
of** a) → 6, b) fig. e-n Vorgeschmack
bekommen von. **4.** fig. Geschmack m:
to s.o.'s ~ nach j-s Geschmack; **be in
bad** (od. **poor**) **~** geschmacklos sein; →
account 3, **matter** 3. **5.** fig. Vorliebe f
(for für). **II** v/t **6.** kosten, probieren. **7.**
schmecken. **8.** fig. kosten, erleben, kennenlernen. **III** v/i **9.** schmecken (of
nach). **taste·ful** ['~fʊl] adj □ fig. geschmackvoll. **'taste·less** adj □ geschmacklos (a. fig.). **'tast·y** adj □
schmackhaft.

tat [tæt] → **tit¹**.

ta·ta [ˌtæ'tɑː] int Br. F tschüs!

tat·tered ['tætəd] adj zerlumpt (Kleidung, Person); fig. ruiniert, ramponiert
(Ruf etc). **'tat·ters** s pl Fetzen pl, Lumpen pl: **be in ~** zerlumpt sein (Kleidung); fig. ruiniert od. ramponiert sein
(Ruf etc).

tat·tle ['tætl] F **I** v/i klatschen, tratschen.
II s Klatsch m, Tratsch m.

tat·too¹ [tə'tuː] **I** v/t **1.** tätowieren. **2.**

Muster etc eintätowieren (**on** in acc).
II s **3.** Tätowierung f.

tat·too² [~] s ✕ Zapfenstreich m; (mst
abendliche) Musikparade.

tat·ty ['tætɪ] adj □ bsd. Br. F schäbig
(Kleidung, Möbel etc).

taught [tɔːt] pret u. pp von **teach.**

taunt [tɔːnt] **I** v/t verhöhnen, -spotten
(for, with wegen). **II** s höhnische od.
spöttische Bemerkung.

Tau·rus ['tɔːrəs] s ast. Stier m: **be** (a) ~
Stier sein.

taut [tɔːt] adj □ **1.** straff (Seil etc). **2.** fig.
angespannt (Gesichtsausdruck etc).
'taut·en I v/t spannen, straffen, straff
anziehen. **II** v/i sich spannen od. straffen.

tau·tol·o·gy [tɔː'tɒlədʒɪ] s rhet. Tautolo-
gie f.

taw·dry ['tɔːdrɪ] adj □ (billig u.) geschmacklos.

taw·ny ['tɔːnɪ] adj gelbbraun.

tax [tæks] **I** s **1.** Steuer f (**on** auf acc):
before (**after**) ~ vor (nach) Abzug der
Steuern, brutto (netto); → **put** 2. **II** v/t
2. besteuern. **3.** j-s Geduld etc strapazieren. **'tax·a·ble** adj steuerpflichtig.

tax·a·tion s Besteuerung f.

tax| **brack·et** s Steuergruppe f, -klasse f.
ˌ~·de'duct·i·ble adj (steuerlich) absetzbar. **~ e·va·sion** s Steuerhinterziehung
f. **ˌ~·'free** adj u. adv steuerfrei. **~ ha-
·ven** s Steueroase f, -paradies n.

tax·i ['tæksɪ] **I** s Taxi n, Taxe f. **II** v/i ✈
rollen. **'~·cab** → **taxi** I. **~ driv·er** s
Taxifahrer(in). **'~·me·ter** s Taxameter
m, n, Fahrpreisanzeiger m.

tax| **rank**, ~ **stand** s Taxistand m.

'tax|**pay·er** s Steuerzahler(in). **~ rate** s
Steuersatz m. **~ rea·sons** s pl steuer-
liche Gründe pl. **~ re·turn** s Steuerer-
klärung f.

'T-bone (**steak**) s T-bone-Steak n (Steak
aus dem Rippenstück des Rinds).

tea [tiː] s Tee m: **not for all the ~ in China**
nicht um alles in der Welt; → **cup** 1,
high tea. **~ bag** s Tee-, Aufgußbeutel
m. **~ break** s Teepause f. **~ cad·dy** s
Teebüchse f, -dose f.

teach [tiːtʃ] (irr) **I** v/t **1.** Fach lehren,
unterrichten. **2.** j-n, a. j-m et. lehren, j-n
unterrichten in (dat); j-m et. beibringen: **~ s.o. a lesson** fig. j-m e-e Lektion

erteilen. **II** v/i **3.** unterrichten (*at an e-r Schule*). **'teach·er** s Lehrer(in). **'teach·ing** s **1.** Unterrichten n; Lehrberuf m. **2.** Lehre f.

tea| cloth → **tea towel. ~ co·sy** (*Am.* **co·zy**) s Teewärmer m. **'~·cup** s Teetasse f; → **storm** 1. **'~·house** s Teehaus n.

teak [ti:k] s Teak(holz) n.

'tea| ket·tle s Tee-, Wasserkessel m. **'~·leaf** s (*irr leaf*) **1.** Teeblatt n. **2.** *Br. sl.* Langfinger m.

team [ti:m] **I** s **1.** *Sport:* Mannschaft f, Team m, *allg.* a. Gruppe f. **2.** Gespann n. **II** v/i **3. ~ up** sich zs.-tun (*with* mit). **~ ef·fort** s Teamwork n: *by a ~* mit vereinten Kräften. **~ game** s *Sport:* Mannschaftsspiel n. **'~·mate** s *Sport:* Mannschaftskamerad(in). **~ spir·it** s *Sport:* Mannschaftsgeist m; *allg.* Gemeinschaftsgeist m.

'team·ster ['ti:mstə] s LKW-Fahrer m. **'team·work** s *Sport:* Mannschafts-, Zs.-spiel n; *allg.* Teamwork n.

tea| par·ty s Teegesellschaft f. **'~·pot** s Teekanne f: → **tempest.**

tear¹ [tɪə] s Träne f: *be almost in ~s* den Tränen nahe sein, fast weinen; **~s** pl *of joy* Freudentränen pl; → **burst** 3, **near** 3, **roll** 7, **run** 11.

tear² [teə] **I** s **1.** Riß m. **II** v/t (*irr*) **2.** zerreißen; sich *et.* zerreißen (**on** an *dat*): **~ a muscle** sich e-n Muskel reißen, sich e-n Muskelriß zuziehen; *torn muscle* Muskelriß m; → **piece** 1, **shred** 1. **3.** weg-, losreißen (**from** von): **~ s.th. from s.o.** a. j-m et. entreißen; → **hair.** **4. be torn between ... and** fig. hin- u. hergerissen sein zwischen (*dat*) .. u. **III** v/i (*irr*) **5.** (zer)reißen. **6.** F rasen, sausen. **7. ~ into s.o.** F über j-n herfallen (*a. mit Worten*).

Verbindungen mit Adverbien:

tear| a·way v/t weg-, losreißen (**from** von) (*a. fig.*). **~ down** v/t **1.** *Plakat etc* herunterreißen. **2.** *Haus etc* abreißen. **~ off** v/t **1.** abreißen; abtrennen. **2.** *aus Kleidung* vom Leib reißen. **3.** F *Aufsatz etc* hinhauen. **~ out** v/t (her)ausreißen (**of** aus); *Baum* entwurzeln: → **hair.** **~ up** v/t **1.** aufreißen. **2.** zerreißen.

'tear·drop ['tɪədrɒp] s Träne f.

'tear·ful ['tɪəfʊl] adj □ **1.** weinend. **2.** tränenreich (*Abschied etc*).

'tear gas [tɪə] s Tränengas n.

tear·ing ['teərɪŋ] adj: *be in a ~ hurry* F es schrecklich eilig haben.

tear-jerk·er ['tɪə,dʒɜːkə] s F Schmachtfetzen m.

tear-off ['teərɒf] adj: **~ calendar** Abreißkalender m.

tea-room ['~rʊm] s Teestube f.

tease [ti:z] **I** v/t j-n, *Tier* necken, j-n hänseln (**about** wegen); j-n, *Tier* reizen. **II** v/i: *he is only teasing* er macht nur Spaß. **III** s Necker(in), Hänsler(in). **'teas·er** s **1.** → **tease** III. **2.** F harte Nuß.

tea| ser·vice, ~ set s Teeservice n. **'~·spoon** s Teelöffel m.

teat [ti:t] s **1.** *zo.* Zitze f. **2.** *Br.* (Gummi)Sauger m (*e-r Saugflasche*).

tea| tow·el s *bsd. Br.* Geschirrtuch n. **~ trol·ley** s *bsd. Br.*, **~ wag·on** s *bsd. Am.* Tee-, Servierwagen m.

tech·ni·cal ['teknɪkl] adj □ **1.** *allg.* technisch: **~ knockout** (*Boxen*) technischer K. o. **2.** fachlich, Fach...: **~ term** Fachausdruck m. **tech·ni·cal·i·ty** [,~'kælətɪ] s technische Einzelheit. **tech'ni·cian** [~ʃn] s Techniker(in).

tech·nique [tek'ni:k] s **1.** ⚙ Technik f, Verfahren n. **2.** ♪, *paint., Sport etc:* Technik f.

tech·no·crat ['teknəʊkræt] s Technokrat(in).

tech·no·log·i·cal [,teknə'lɒdʒɪkl] adj □ technologisch; technisch. **tech·nol·o·gist** [~'nɒlədʒɪst] s Technologe m, Technologin f. **tech'nol·o·gy** [~] s Technologie f; Technik f.

ted·dy (**bear**) ['tedɪ] s Teddy(bär) m.

te·di·ous ['ti:djəs] adj □ langweilig. **te·di·um** ['~djəm] s Langweiligkeit f.

teem¹ [ti:m] v/i (**with**) wimmeln (von); strotzen (von, vor *dat*): *the square was ~ing with people* auf dem Platz wimmelte es von Menschen.

teem² [~] v/i: *it is ~ing with rain* es regnet in Strömen.

teen·age(d) ['ti:neɪdʒ(d)] adj **1.** im Teenageralter. **2.** Teenager..., für Teenager. **'teen,ag·er** s Teenager m.

teens [ti:nz] s pl: *be in one's ~* im Teenageralter sein.

tee·ny ['ti:nɪ], **tee·ny-wee·ny** [,~'wi:nɪ] adj F klitzeklein, winzig.

tee shirt [ti:] s T-Shirt n.

tee·ter ['ti:tə] v/i (sch)wanken.

teeth 1298

teeth [ti:θ] *pl von* **tooth.**

teethe [ti:ð] *v/i* zahnen. '**teeth·ing** *adj*: ~ **troubles** *pl fig.* Kinderkrankheiten *pl.*

tee·to·tal·er *s Am.,* tee·to·tal·ler *s bsd. Br.* [ti:'təʊtlə] *s* Abstinenzler(in).

tel·e·cast ['telɪkɑ:st] **I** *v/t (mst irr)* im Fernsehen übertragen *od.* bringen. **II** *s* Fernsehsendung *f.*

tel·e·com·mu·ni·ca·tions ['telɪkəˌmju:nɪ'keɪʃnz] *s pl* Telekommunikation *f,* Fernmeldewesen *n.* ~ **sat·el·lite** *s* Fernmelde-, Nachrichtensatellit *m.*

tel·e·gen·ic [ˌtelɪ'dʒenɪk] *adj (~ally) TV* telegen.

tel·e·gram ['telɪɡræm] *s* Telegramm *n*: **by** ~ telegrafisch.

tel·e·graph ['telɪɡrɑ:f] **I** *s*: **by** ~ telegrafisch. **II** *v/t j-m et.* telegrafieren. tel·e·graph·ese [ˌ~ɡrɑ:'fi:z] *s* Telegrammstil *m.* tel·e·graph·ic [ˌ~'ɡræfɪk] *adj (~ally)* telegrafisch. te·leg·ra·phy [tɪ'leɡrəfɪ] *s* Telegrafie *f.*

te·lep·a·thy [tɪ'lepəθɪ] *s* Telepathie *f,* Gedankenübertragung *f.*

tel·e·phone ['telɪfəʊn] **I** *s* **1.** Telefon *n*: **by** ~ telefonisch; **be on the** ~ Telefon(anschluß) haben; am Telefon sein. **2.** Hörer *m.* **II** *v/i* **3.** telefonieren, anrufen. **III** *v/t* **4.** anrufen: ~ *s.th. to s.o.* j-m et. telefonisch durchgeben. **IV** *adj* **5.** Telefon...: ~ **booth** (*Br. box*) Telefonzelle *f*; ~ **call** Telefonanruf *m,* -gespräch *n*; ~ **directory** Telefon-, Fernsprechbuch *n*; ~ **exchange** Telefon-, Fernsprechamt *n*; ~ **number** Telefonnummer *f.* te·leph·o·nist [tɪ'lefənɪst] *s bsd. Br.* Telefonist(in).

tel·e·pho·to lens [ˌtelɪ'fəʊtəʊ] *s phot.* Teleobjektiv *n.*

tel·e·print·er ['telɪˌprɪntə] *s* ⚙ Fernschreiber *m.*

tel·e·scope ['telɪskəʊp] **I** *s* **1.** Teleskop *n,* Fernrohr *n.* **II** *v/t* **2.** *a.* ~ **together** zs.-, ineinanderschieben. **3.** *fig.* verkürzen, komprimieren (**into** zu). **III** *v/i* **4.** sich zs.- *od.* ineinanderschieben (lassen). tel·e·scop·ic [ˌ~'skɒpɪk] *adj (~ally)* **1.** teleskopisch: ~ **sight** Zielfernrohr *n.* **2.** ausziehbar: ~ **aerial** (*bsd. Am.* **antenna**) Teleskopantenne *f*; ~ **umbrella** Taschenschirm *m.*

tel·e·text ['telɪtekst] *s* Bildschirmtext *m.*

tel·e·vise ['telɪvaɪz] → **telecast** I.

tel·e·vi·sion ['~ˌvɪʒn] **I** *s* **1.** Fernsehen

n: **on (the)** ~ im Fernsehen; **watch** ~ fernsehen; **work in** ~ beim Fernsehen beschäftigt sein. **2.** Fernsehapparat *m,* -gerät *n.* **II** *adj* **3.** Fernseh...: ~ **set** → 2.

tel·ex ['teleks] *s* **1.** Telex *n,* Fernschreiben *n.* **2.** ⚙ Fernschreiber *m.*

tell [tel] (*irr*) **I** *v/t* **1.** sagen, erzählen: **I can't** ~ **you how** ... ich kann dir gar nicht sagen, wie ...; **you are ~ing me!** wem sagst du das!; → **another** 2. **2.** *Geschichte etc* erzählen; → **tale** 1. **3.** *s-n Namen etc* nennen; *Grund etc* angeben; *Zeit* anzeigen (*Uhr*). **4.** (*mit Bestimmtheit*) sagen; erkennen (**by** *an dat*): **I can't** ~ **one from the other, I can't** ~ **them apart** ich kann sie nicht auseinanderhalten. **5.** *j-m* sagen, befehlen (**to do** zu tun). **6.** ~ **off** F *j-m* Bescheid stoßen (**for** wegen). **II** *v/i* **7.** **who can** ~? wer weiß?; **you can never** (*od.* **never can**) ~ man kann nie wissen. **8.** ~ **on** *s.o.* j-n verpetzen *od.* verraten. **9.** sich auswirken (**on** bei, auf *acc*), sich bemerkbar machen: ~ **against** sprechen gegen; von Nachteil sein für. '**tell·er** *s bsd. Am.* Kassierer(in) (*e-r Bank*).

tell·ing ['telɪŋ] *adj* □ **1.** aufschlußreich. **2.** schlagend (*Argument*), wirksam: **give s.o. a (good)** ~ F *j-m* (kräftig) Bescheid stoßen (**for** wegen).

'tell·tale **I** *adj* verräterisch. **II** *s* F Zuträger(in), Petze *f.*

tel·ly ['telɪ] *s bsd. Br.* F **1.** → **television** 1. **2.** Fernseher *m* (*Gerät*).

te·mer·i·ty [tɪ'merətɪ] *s* Kühnheit *f,* Frechheit *f.*

temp [temp] *Br.* F **I** *s* (*von e-r Agentur vermittelte*) Zeitsekretärin. **II** *v/i* als Zeitsekretärin arbeiten.

tem·per ['tempə] **I** *s* **1.** Temperament *n,* Gemüt(sart *f*) *n,* Wesen(sart *f*) *n.* **2.** Laune *f,* Stimmung *f*: **be in a bad** ~ schlecht gelaunt sein; **keep one's** ~ ruhig bleiben; **lose one's** ~ die Beherrschung verlieren. **3.** F **be in a** ~ gereizt *od.* wütend sein; **fly into a** ~ an die Decke gehen; → **fit** 1, **work** 8. **II** *v/t* **4.** ⚙ *Stahl* härten. **tem·per·a·ment** ['~rəmənt] *s* **1.** → **temper** 1. **2.** Temperament *n,* Lebhaftigkeit *f.* **tem·per·a·men·tal** [ˌ~rə'mentl] *adj* □ **1.** reizbar; launisch. **2.** veranlagungsmäßig, anlagebedingt: ~**ly a.** von der Veranlagung her, von Natur aus.

tem·per·ate ['tempərət] *adj* gemäßigt (*Klima, Zone*).

tem·per·a·ture ['temprətʃə] *s* Temperatur *f:* **have** (*od.* **be running**) **a** ~ erhöhte Temperatur *od.* Fieber haben; **take s.o.'s** ~ j-s Temperatur messen.

tem·pest ['tempɪst] *s* (heftiger) Sturm (*poet. außer in*): ~ **in a teapot** *Am. fig.* Sturm im Wasserglas. **tem·pes·tu·ous** [~'pestjʊəs] *adj* □ *poet. od. fig.* stürmisch.

tem·pi [tempi:] *pl von* **tempo**.

tem·ple¹ [templ] *s* Tempel *m.*

tem·ple² [~] *s anat.* Schläfe *f.*

tem·po ['tempəʊ] *pl* **-pos, -pi** [~pi:] *s ♩* Tempo *n (a. fig.).*

tem·po·ral¹ ['tempərəl] *adj* □ **1.** weltlich. **2.** *ling.* temporal, Zeit..., der Zeit.

tem·po·ral² [~] *adj anat.* Schläfen...: ~ **bone** Schläfenbein *n.*

tem·po·rar·y ['tempərərɪ] *adj* □ vorübergehend, zeitweilig. **'tem·po·rize** *v/i* Zeit zu gewinnen suchen.

tempt [tempt] *v/t* **1.** *j n* in Versuchung führen (*a. eccl.*); *j-n* verführen (**to** zu; **to do** [*od.* **into doing**] **s.th.** dazu, et. zu tun): **be ~ed to do s.th.** versucht *od.* geneigt sein, et. zu tun. **2.** ~ **fate** (*od.* **providence**) das Schicksal herausfordern. **temp'ta·tion** *s* Versuchung *f (a. eccl.),* Verführung *f.* **'tempt·er** *s* Verführer *m.* **'tempt·ing** *adj* □ verführerisch. **'tempt·ress** *s* Verführerin *f.*

ten [ten] **I** *adj* **1.** zehn. **II** *s* **2.** Zehn *f:* ~ **of hearts** Herzzehn; ~**s** *pl of* **thousands** Zehntausende *pl.* **3.** ♣ Zehner *m.*

ten·a·ble ['tenəbl] *adj* haltbar (*Theorie etc*).

te·na·cious [tɪ'neɪʃəs] *adj* □ hartnäckig, zäh. **te'na·cious·ness, te·nac·i·ty** [tɪ'næsətɪ] *s* Hartnäckigkeit *f,* Zähigkeit *f.*

ten·an·cy ['tenənsɪ] *s* Pacht-, Mietdauer *f.*

ten·ant ['tenənt] *s* Pächter(in), Mieter(in).

tend¹ [tend] *v/i* neigen, tendieren (**to, toward**[**s**] zu): ~ **to do s.th.** dazu neigen, et. zu tun; ~ **upwards** e-e steigende Tendenz haben (*Preise etc*).

tend² [~] *v/t j-n* pflegen, *a.* Wunde versorgen. **II** *v/i:* ~ **to** → I.

tend·en·cy ['tendənsɪ] *s* Tendenz *f;* Neigung *f:* **have a** ~ **to** (*od.* **toward**[**s**])

neigen *od.* tendieren zu; **have a** ~ **to s.th.** dazu neigen, et. zu tun. **ten·den·tious** [~'denʃəs] *adj* □ tendenziös.

ten·der¹ ['tendə] *adj* □ **1.** empfindlich, *fig. a.* heikel: → **spot** 4. **2.** zart, weich (*Fleisch*). **3.** zärtlich.

ten·der² [~] **I** *v/i* **1.** ♣ ein Angebot machen (**for** für). **II** *v/t* **2.** → **resignation** 1. **III** *s* **3.** ♣ Angebot *n.* **4.** *legal* ~ gesetzliches Zahlungsmittel.

ten·der³ [~] *s ♣,* 🚋 Tender *m.*

'ten·der·foot *s (a. irr* **foot**) *Am.* F Anfänger *m,* Neuling *m.* ,~**'heart·ed** *adj* □ weichherzig.

ten·der·ize ['tendəraɪz] *v/t Fleisch* zart *od.* weich machen.

'ten·der·loin *s* zartes Lendenstück.

ten·don ['tendən] *s anat.* Sehne *f.*

ten·dril ['tendrɪl] *s* ♣ Ranke *f.*

ten·e·ment ['tenəmənt] *s* Miethaus *n, contp.* Mietskaserne *f.*

ten·et ['tenɪt] *s* Lehr-, *eccl.* Glaubenssatz *m.*

ten·ner ['tenə] *s* F Zehner *m (Br. Zehnpfundschein, Am. Zehndollarschein*).

ten·fold ['tenfəʊld] **I** *adj* zehnfach. **II** *adv* zehnfach, um das Zehnfache: *increase* ~ (sich) verzehnfachen.

ten·nis ['tenɪs] *s Sport:* Tennis *n.* ~ **ball** *s* Tennisball *m.* ~ **court** *s* Tennisplatz *m.* ~ **el·bow** *s* 🎾 Tennisarm *m.* ~ **play·er** *s* Tennisspieler(in). ~ **rack·et** *s* Tennisschläger *m.*

ten·or ['tenə] *s* **1.** ♩ Tenor *m.* **2.** Tenor *m,* Sinn *m.* **3.** Verlauf *m.*

'ten·pin *s* **1.** *Bowling:* Kegel *m:* ~ **bowling** *Br.* Bowling *n.* **2.** *pl* (*sg konstruiert*) *Am.* Bowling *n.*

tense¹ [tens] *s ling.* Zeit *f,* Tempus *n:* → **future** 4, **past** 3, **present** 3.

tense² [~] *adj* □ **1.** gespannt, straff (*Seil etc*), (an)gespannt (*Muskeln*). **2.** *fig.* (an)gespannt (*Lage etc*); (über)nervös (*Person*).

ten·sile ['tensaɪl] *adj* **1.** dehn-, spannbar. **2.** ~ **strength** Zug-, Zerreißfestigkeit *f.*

ten·sion ['tenʃn] *s* **1.** Spannung *f (a. 🎇):* → **high tension. 2.** *fig.* Anspannung *f;* Spannung(en *pl*) *f.*

tent [tent] *s* Zelt *n.*

ten·ta·cle ['tentəkl] *s zo.* Tentakel *m, n:* a) Fühler *m,* b) Fangarm *m.*

ten·ta·tive ['tentətɪv] *adj* □ **1.** vorläufig;

versuchsweise: **~ly** a. mit Vorbehalt. **2.** vorsichtig, zögernd.

ten·ter·hooks ['tentəhʊks] s pl: **be on ~** wie auf glühenden Kohlen sitzen; **keep s.o. on ~** j-n auf die Folter spannen.

tenth [tenθ] **I** adj **1.** zehnt. **II** s **2.** der, die, das Zehnte: **the ~ of May** der 10. Mai. **3.** Zehntel n: **a ~ of a second** ⊕-e Zehntelsekunde. '**tenth·ly** adv zehntens.

'**ten·time** adj zehnmalig.

tent| peg s Hering m, Zeltpflock m. **~ pole** s Zeltstange f.

ten·u·ous ['tenjʊəs] adj □ **1.** dünn (Faden etc). **2.** fig. lose (Verbindung etc); schwach (Beweis etc).

ten·ure ['te̯njʊə] s **1.** Innehabung f (e-s Amtes), (von Grundbesitz a.) Besitz m. **2. ~ of office** Amtsdauer f, Dienstzeit f.

tep·id ['tepɪd] adj □ lau(warm) (a. fig.).

term [tɜːm] **I** s **1.** Zeit(raum m) f, Dauer f; Laufzeit f (e-s Vertrags etc): **~ of imprisonment** ⚖ Freiheitsstrafe f; **~ of office** Amtsdauer, -periode f, -zeit; **in the long** (**short**) **~** auf lange (kurze) Sicht. **2.** ped., univ. bsd. Br. Trimester n. **3.** Ausdruck m, Bezeichnung f: **~ of abuse** Schimpfwort n, Beleidigung f; **~s of** was ... betrifft; **in ~s of money** finanziell (gesehen); **in no uncertain ~s** unmißverständlich; → **technical** 2. **4.** pl Bedingungen pl: **~s of delivery** ✝ Liefer(ungs)bedingungen; **on one's own ~s** zu s-n Bedingungen; **come to ~s** sich einigen (**with** mit); **come to ~s with s.th.** sich mit et. abfinden; → **easy** 5. **be on friendly** (**good**) **~s with** auf freundschaftlichem Fuß stehen (gut auskommen) mit; → **speaking** II. **II** v/t **6.** nennen, bezeichnen als.

ter·mi·nal ['tɜːmɪnl] **I** adj □ **1.** 🌲 a) unheilbar; unheilbar krank, b) im Endstadium, c) Sterbe...: **~ clinic.** **II** s **2.** etc Endstation f: → **air terminal.** **3.** Computer: Terminal n. **4.** ⚡ (Anschluß)Klemme f; Pol m (e-r Batterie).

ter·mi·nate ['tɜːmɪneɪt] **I** v/t beenden; Vertrag kündigen, lösen; 🌲 Schwangerschaft unterbrechen. **II** v/i enden; ablaufen (Vertrag). **ter·mi·na·tion** s **1.** Beendigung f; Kündigung f, Lösung f; 🌲 Schwangerschafts)Abbruch m. **2.** Ende n; Ablauf m.

ter·mi·ni ['tɜːmɪnaɪ] pl von **terminus.**

ter·mi·nol·o·gy [ˌtɜːmɪ'nɒlədʒɪ] s Terminologie f, Fachsprache f.

ter·mi·nus ['tɜːmɪnəs] pl **-ni** ['~naɪ], **-nus·es** s ⊕ etc Endstation f.

ter·mite ['tɜːmaɪt] s zo. Termite f.

ter·race ['terəs] s **1.** Terrasse f. **2.** pl Sport: bsd. Br. Ränge pl. **3.** Häuserreihe f, -zeile f. '**ter·raced** adj: **~ house** Br. Reihenhaus n.

ter·ra-cot·ta [ˌterə'kɒtə] s Terrakotta f.

ter·rain [te'reɪn] s Gelände n, Terrain n.

ter·res·tri·al [tə'restrɪəl] adj □ **1.** irdisch. **2.** Erd...: **~ globe** Erdball m. **3.** 🌱, zo. Land...

ter·ri·ble ['terəbl] adj □ schrecklich, furchtbar (beide a. fig. F).

ter·ri·er ['terɪə] s zo. Terrier m.

ter·rif·ic [tə'rɪfɪk] adj (**~ally**) F toll, phantastisch; wahnsinnig.

ter·ri·fy ['terɪfaɪ] v/t j-m schreckliche Angst einjagen: **spiders ~ me, I'm terrified of spiders** ich habe schreckliche Angst vor Spinnen.

ter·ri·to·ri·al [ˌterɪ'tɔːrɪəl] adj □ territorial, Gebiets...: **~ claims** pl Gebietsansprüche pl; **~ waters** pl Hoheitsgewässer pl. **ter·ri·to·ry** ['~tərɪ] s **1.** (a. Hoheits-, Staats)Gebiet n, Territorium n. **2.** zo. Revier n. **3.** fig. Gebiet n.

ter·ror ['terə] s **1.** Entsetzen n: **in ~** voller Entsetzen; in panischer Angst; **have a ~ of** panische Angst haben vor (dat). **2.** Terror m. **3.** Schrecken m (Person, Sache). **4.** F Landplage f (bsd. Kind). '**ter·ror·ism** s Terrorismus m. '**ter·ror·ist** **I** s Terrorist(in). **II** adj terroristisch, Terror... '**ter·ror·ize** v/t terrorisieren; einschüchtern.

ter·ry(·cloth) ['terɪ(klɒθ)] s Frottee n, m.

terse [tɜːs] adj □ knapp (Antwort etc).

tes·sel·at·ed ['tesəleɪtɪd] adj Mosaik...

test [test] **I** s **1.** allg. Test m: **put to the ~** auf die Probe stellen; **stand the ~ of time** die Zeit überdauern; → **driving test.** **2.** → **test match.** **II** v/t **3.** testen, prüfen. **4.** j-s Geduld etc auf e-e harte Probe stellen.

tes·ta·ment ['testəmənt] s **1.** → **will**[1] **2.** ♀ Bibl. Altes, Neues Testament. **3.** fig. Zeugnis n (**to** gen). **tes·ta·men·ta·ry** [ˌ~'mentərɪ] adj ⚖ testamentarisch.

tes·ta·tor [te'steɪtə] s ⚖ Erblasser m.

tes·ta·trix [te'steɪtrɪks] *pl* **-tri·ces** [~trɪ-siːz] *s* 🔱 Erblasserin *f*.

test|ban trea·ty *s pol.* Teststoppabkommen *n*. **~ card** *s TV Br.* Testbild *n*. **~ case** *s* 🔱 Musterprozeß *m*. **~ drive** *s mot.* Probefahrt *f*: **go for a ~** e-e Probefahrt machen. **'~drive** *v/t (irr drive)* Auto probefahren.

tes·ter ['testə] *s* **1.** Tester(in), Prüfer(in). **2.** ⊙ Test-, Prüfgerät *n*.

tes·ti·cle ['testɪkl] *s anat.* Hoden *m*.

tes·ti·fy ['testɪfaɪ] **I** *v/i* **1.** 🔱 aussagen (*for* für; *against* gegen). **2. ~ to** ein deutliches Zeichen sein für. **II** *v/t* **3. ~ that** 🔱 aussagen *od.* bezeugen, daß; *fig.* ein deutliches Zeichen dafür sein, daß.

tes·ti·mo·ni·al [ˌtestɪ'məʊnjəl] *s* **1.** Referenz *f*. **2.** Anerkennungsgeschenk *n*.

tes·ti·mo·ny ['~mənɪ] *s* **1.** 🔱 Aussage *f*. **2. be (a) ~ of** (*od.* **to**) → **testify** 2.

test·ing ['testɪŋ] *adj*: **~ times** *pl* harte Zeiten *pl*.

test| lamp *s* ⊙ Prüflampe *f*. **~ match** *s* Kricket: internationaler Vergleichskampf. **~ pat·tern** *s TV Am.* Testbild *n*. **~ pi·lot** *s* ✈ Testpilot *m*. **~ tube** *s* 🧪 Reagenzglas *n*. **'~tube ba·by** *s* Retortenbaby *n*.

tes·ty ['testɪ] *adj* □ gereizt (*Person, Antwort etc*).

tetch·y ['tetʃɪ] *adj* □ reizbar.

teth·er ['teðə] **I** *s* Strick *m*; Kette *f*: **be at the end of one's ~** *fig.* mit s-n Nerven am Ende sein. **II** *v/t* Tier anbinden, anketten.

Teu·ton·ic [tjuːˈtɒnɪk] *adj oft contp.* teutonisch, (typisch) deutsch.

text [tekst] *s* Text *m*. **'~book I** *s* Lehrbuch *n*. **II** *adj* perfekt: **~ example** Muster-, Paradebeispiel *n* (*of* für).

tex·tile ['tekstaɪl] **I** *s* Stoff *m*: **~s** *pl* Textilien *pl*. **II** *adj* Textil...

tex·tu·al ['tekstjʊəl] *adj* □ textlich, Text...

tex·ture ['tekstʃə] *s* Textur *f*, Gewebe *n*; Beschaffenheit *f*.

tha·lid·o·mide [θəˈlɪdəmaɪd] *s pharm.* Thalidomid *n*, Contergan *n*: **~ baby** Contergankind *n*.

Thames [temz] *npr* Themse *f*: **he won't set the ~ on fire** *fig.* er hat das Pulver auch nicht (gerade) erfunden.

than [ðən] *cj* als.

thank [θæŋk] **I** *v/t* j-m danken, sich bei j-m bedanken (*for* für): **~ you** (*very much*) danke (vielen Dank); **no, ~ you** nein, danke; **say "~ you"** sich bedanken; **he's only got himself to ~ that** er hat es sich selbst zuzuschreiben, daß; → **god** 2, **goodness** 2, **heaven** 1, **star** 1. **II** *s pl* Dank *m*: **with ~s** dankend, mit Dank; (*many*) **~s** danke (vielen Dank); **no, ~s** nein, danke; **say "~s"** sich bedanken; **~s to** dank (*gen*), wegen (*gen*).

thank·ful ['~fʊl] *adj* □ dankbar (*for* für); froh (*that* daß; *to be* zu sein): **~ly** *a.* zum Glück, Gott sei Dank. **'thank·less** *adj* undankbar (*Aufgabe etc*).

'Thanks·giv·ing (Day) *s Am.* Thanksgiving Day *m* (*Erntedankfest*; *4. Donnerstag im November*).

'thank-you I *s* Danke(schön) *n*. **II** *adj*: **~ letter** Dank(es)brief *m*.

that¹ [ðæt] **I** *pron u. adj* **1.** das: **~ is** (*to say*) das heißt; **at ~** zudem, obendrein; **let it go at ~** F lassen wir es dabei bewenden; **and ~'s** *s* u. damit basta. **2.** jener, jene, jenes: **~ car over there** das Auto dort drüben; **those who** diejenigen, welche. **II** *adv* **3.** F so, dermaßen: **it's ~ simple** so einfach ist das.

that² [~] *relative pron* der, die, das, welcher, welche, welches: **everything ~** alles, was.

that³ [~] *cj* daß.

thatch [θætʃ] **I** *s* **1.** (Dach)Stroh *n*, Reet *n*. **2.** Stroh-, Reetdach *n*. **II** *v/t* **3.** mit Stroh *od.* Reet decken. **~ed** stroh-, reetgedeckt.

thaw [θɔː] **I** *v/i* (auf)tauen, (*Tiefkühlkost, fig. Person*) auftauen: **it is ~ing** es taut. **II** *v/t* auftauen. **III** *s* Tauwetter *n* (*a. fig. pol.*).

the¹ [ðə, *vor Vokalen* ðɪ] *bestimmter Artikel* **1.** der, die, das, *pl* die. **2.** *vor Maßangaben*: **one dollar ~ pound** ein Dollar das *od.* pro Pfund.

the² [~] *adv*: **~ ... ~ ...** je ... desto: **~ sooner ~ better** je eher, desto besser.

the·a·ter *s Am.*, **the·a·tre** *s bsd. Br.* ['θɪətə] **1.** Theater *n*: **be in the ~** beim Theater sein. **2.** (*Hör*)Saal *m*; 🩺 *Br.* Operationssaal *m*: **~ nurse** Operationsschwester *f*. **3.** *fig.* Schauplatz *m*: **~ of war** Kriegsschauplatz. **'~go·er** *s* Theaterbesucher(in). **the·a·tri·cal** [θɪˈætrɪkl] *adj* □ **1.** Theater... **2.** *fig.* theatralisch.

theft [θeft] *s* Diebstahl *m*.

their [ðeə] *possessive pron* ihr: *everyone took their seats* alle nahmen Platz.

theirs [~z] *possessive pron*: *it is ~* es gehört ihnen; *a friend of ~* ein Freund von ihnen; *our children and ~* unsere Kinder u. ihre.

them [ðəm] *pron* **1.** sie (*acc*); ihnen (*dat*): *they looked behind ~* sie blickten hinter sich. **2.** F sie (*nom*): *we are younger than ~.*

theme [θiːm] *s* Thema *n* (*a. ♪*). *~ song s* Film etc: Titelsong *m*. *~ tune s* Film etc: Themamelodie *f*.

them·selves [ðəmˈselvz] *pron* **1.** *verstärkend*: sie *od.* sich selbst: *they did it ~, they ~ did it* sie haben es selbst getan. **2.** *reflex* sich: *they cut ~.* **3.** sich (selbst): *they want it for ~.*

then [ðen] **I** *adv* **1.** dann: → *but* 1. **2.** da; damals: *by ~* bis dahin; *from ~ on* von da an. **II** *adj* **3.** damalig.

the·o·lo·gi·an [θɪəˈlɔʊdʒən] *s* Theologe *m*, Theologin *f*. **the·o·log·i·cal** [~ˈlɒdʒɪkl] *adj* □ theologisch: *~ college* Priesterseminar *n*. **the·ol·o·gy** [θɪˈɒlədʒɪ] *s* Theologie *f*.

the·o·rem [ˈθɪərəm] *s bsd. ℞* (Lehr-) Satz *m*.

the·o·ret·i·cal [θɪəˈretɪkl] *adj* □ theoretisch. **ˈthe·o·rist** *s* Theoretiker(in). **ˈthe·o·rize** *v/i* theoretisieren (*about, on* über *acc*). **ˈthe·o·ry** *s* Theorie *f*: *in ~* in der Theorie, theoretisch.

ther·a·peu·tic [ˌθerəˈpjuːtɪk] *adj* (*~ally*) **1.** *☤* therapeutisch. **2.** F wohltuend; gesund. **ther·a·pist** *s ☤* Therapeut(in). **ˈther·a·py** *s ☤* Therapie *f*.

there [ðeə] **I** *adv* **1.** da, dort: *~ and then* auf der Stelle; *~ you are* hier bitte; da hast du's!, na also!; *~ you go!* F so ist's halt!; *~ you go again!* F fängst du schon wieder an!; *~ over* F 9. 2. (da-, dort)hin: *~ and back* hin u. zurück; *get ~* F es schaffen; *go ~* hingehen. **3.** *~ is, pl ~ are* es gibt *od.* ist *od.* sind: *~ are many cars in the street* auf der Straße sind viele Autos; *~'s a good boy!* sei lieb *od.* brav!; *was der liebe von dir!* **II** *int* **4.** so; da hast du's!, na also: *~, ~* ist ja gut! *'~·a·bouts* adv: *five pounds or ~* ungefähr *od.* etwa fünf Pfund. *,~'af·ter* adv danach. *,~'by* adv dadurch. *'~·fore* adv **1.** deshalb, daher. **2.** folg-

lich, also. *,~·up'on* adv darauf.

ther·mal [ˈθɜːml] **I** *adj* □ **1.** thermisch, Thermo..., Wärme... **2.** *~ spring* Thermalquelle *f*. **II** *s* **3.** Thermik *f*.

ther·mom·e·ter [θəˈmɒmɪtə] *s* Thermometer *n*.

Ther·mos [ˈθɜːmɒs] (*TM*) *s*, *Am. a. ~ bottle*, *bsd. Br. a. ~ flask* Thermosflasche *f*.

ther·mo·stat [ˈθɜːməʊstæt] *s* Thermostat *m*.

the·sau·rus [θɪˈsɔːrəs] *pl* **-ri** [~raɪ], **-rus·es** *s* Thesaurus *m*.

these [ðiːz] *pl von* **this.**

the·sis [ˈθiːsɪs] *pl* **-ses** [~siːz] *s* **1.** These *f*. **2.** *univ.* Dissertation *f*, Doktorarbeit *f*.

they'd [ðeɪd] F *für* **they had; they would.**

they'll [ðeɪl] F *für* **they will.**

they're [ðeə] F *für* **they are.**

they've [ðeɪv] F *für* **they have.**

thick [θɪk] **I** *adj* □ **1.** *allg.* dick: *the ~ end of £500* F fast 500 Pfund; *give s.o. a ~ ear* F j-m eins *od.* ein paar hinter die Ohren geben. **2.** dick, dicht (*Nebel etc*): *be ~ with* wimmeln von; *~ with smoke* verräuchert; *the furniture was ~ with dust* auf den Möbeln lag dick der Staub; *they are ~ on the ground* F es gibt sie wie Sand am Meer. **3.** *bsd. Br.* F dumm. **4.** *bsd. Br.* F dick befreundet (*with* mit). **5.** *that's a bit ~!* *bsd. Br.* F das ist ein starkes Stück! **II** *adv* **6.** dick, dicht: *lay it on ~* F dick auftragen. **III** *s* **7.** *in the ~ of* fig. mitten in (*dat*): *in the ~ of the fight* im dichtesten Kampfgetümmel; *through ~ and thin* durch dick u. dünn. **thick·en** [~ən] **I** *v/t* Soße etc eindicken, binden. **II** *v/i* dicker werden, (*Nebel etc a.*) dichter werden. **thick·et** [~ɪt] *s* Dickicht *n*.

,thick'head·ed adj F strohdumm.

thick·ness [ˈθɪknɪs] *s* **1.** Dicke *f*. **2.** Lage *f*, Schicht *f*. **3.** *bsd. Br.* F Dummheit *f*. *,thick'set* adj gedrungen, untersetzt. *,~'skinned* adj fig. dickfellig.

thief [θiːf] *pl* **thieves** [θiːvz] *s* Dieb(in): *stop, ~!* haltet den Dieb!; *they are (as) thick as thieves* F sie sind dicke Freunde.

thigh [θaɪ] *s anat.* (Ober)Schenkel *m*.

thim·ble [ˈθɪmbl] *s* Fingerhut *m*.

thin [θɪn] **I** *adj* □ **1.** dünn, (*Person, Arme*

etc a.) dürr, (Haar a.) schütter: *disappear (od. vanish) into ~ air* fig. sich in Luft auflösen; *produce out of ~ air* fig. et. herzaubern; *this is just the ~ end of the wedge* fig. b.s. das ist erst der Anfang; *be ~ on the ground* F dünn gesät sein; *he's getting ~ on top* F bei ihm lichtet es schon oben schon. **2.** fig. schwach (*Rede etc*), (*Ausrede etc a.*) fadenscheinig. **II** *adv* **3.** dünn. **III** *v/t* **4.** Soße etc verdünnen, strecken. **IV** *v/i* **5.** dünner werden, (*Nebel, Haar a.*) sich lichten, (*Haar a.*) schütter werden.

thing [θɪŋ] *s* **1.** (*konkretes*) Ding: *~s pl* Sachen *pl* (*Getränke etc*), (*Gepäck, Kleidung etc a.*) Zeug *n*; *what's this ~?* was ist das?; *I couldn't see a ~* ich konnte überhaupt nichts sehen. **2.** fig. Ding *n*, Sache *f*, Angelegenheit *f*: *a funny ~* et. Komisches; *another ~* et. anderes; *first ~ tomorrow* gleich morgen früh; *for one ~ ..., and for another* zum e-n ..., u. zum anderen; *make a ~ of* F et. aufbauschen; *know a ~ or two about* et. verstehen von; *this proves three ~s* das beweist dreierlei; → *done* 1, *last* 4, *near* 9, *old* 2, *right* 1. **3.** *pl* fig. Dinge *pl*, Lage *f*, Umstände *pl*. **4.** Ding *n* (*Mädchen, Tier*), Kerl *m*.

think [θɪŋk] **I** *v/t* (*irr*) **1.** denken, glauben, meinen (*that* daß): *I thought he was a burglar* ich hielt ihn für e-n Einbrecher. **2.** *~ out (od. through)* et. durchdenken; *~ over* nachdenken über (*acc*), sich et. überlegen; *~ up* sich et. ausdenken. **3.** *j-n, et.* halten für: *~ o.s. clever*. **4.** *I can't ~ why ...* ich kann nicht verstehen, warum ... **5.** *try to ~ where ...* versuch dich zu erinnern, wo ... **II** *v/i* (*irr*) **6.** denken (*of an acc*): *I ~ so* ich glaube od. denke schon; *~ of doing s.th.* sich mit dem Gedanken tragen od. daran denken, et. zu tun; *I can't ~ of his name* mir fällt sein Name nicht ein, ich kann mich nicht an s-n Namen erinnern; *what do you ~ of (od. about) ...?* was halten Sie von ...?; → *better*¹ III, *highly* 2, *little* 5, *much* 2, *nothing* I. **7.** nachdenken (*about, over acc*): *~ about it* ich überlege es mir; → *twice*. **III** *s* **8.** F *have a ~ about* nachdenken über (*acc*); *have another ~ coming* schief gewickelt sein. '**think·er** *s* Denker(in). '**think·ing I** *adj* **1.** denkend. **2.**

Denk...: *put on one's ~ cap* F scharf nachdenken. **II** *s* **3.** Denken *n*: *do some ~* nachdenken; *to my way of ~* m-r Meinung nach.

think tank *s* Planungs-, Sachverständigenstab *m*.

thin·ner ['θɪnə] *s* Verdünner *m*.

thin-'skinned *adj* fig. dünnhäutig.

third [θɜːd] **I** *adj* (□ → *thirdly*) **1.** dritt: *~ party* ✝, ⚖ Dritte *m*; ♀ *World* Dritte Welt. **I** *s* **2.** *der, die, das* Dritte: *the ~ of May* der 3. Mai. **3.** Drittel *n*. **4.** *mot.* dritter Gang. **III** *adj* **5.** als dritt(er, e, es). *~'class* **I** *adj* **1.** drittklassig, rangig. **2.** 🚂 *etc* dritter Klasse. **II** *adv* **3.** 🚂 *etc* dritter Klasse. *~-'de·gree adj* Verbrennungen dritten Grades.

third·ly ['θɜːdlɪ] *adv* drittens.

third-'par·ty *adj*: *~ insurance* Haftpflichtversicherung *f*. *~-'rate* → *third-class* 1.

thirst [θɜːst] *s* Durst *m*: *die of ~* verdursten; *~ for knowledge* fig. Wissensdurst. '**~-,quench·ing** *adj* durstlöschend.

thirst·y ['θɜːstɪ] *adj* □ **1.** durstig: *be (od. feel) (very) ~* (sehr) durstig sein, (großen) Durst haben. **2.** *gardening is ~ work* Gartenarbeit macht durstig.

thir·teen [ˌθɜː'tiːn] *adj* dreizehn. ˌ**thir-'teenth** [∼θ] *adj* dreizehnt. **thir·ti·eth** ['∼tɪəθ] *adj* dreißigst. '**thir·ty I** *adj* dreißig. **II** *s* Dreißig *f*: *be in one's thirties* in den Dreißigern sein; *in the thirties* in den dreißiger Jahren (*e-s Jahrhunderts*).

this [ðɪs] **I** *pron* **1.** dieser, diese, dieses; dies, das: *like ~* so; *~ is what I expected* (genau) das habe ich erwartet; *these are his children* das sind s-e Kinder. **2.** *after ~* danach; *before ~* zuvor. **II** *adj* **3.** dieser, diese, dieses: → *afternoon* I, *morning* I, *time* 4, *year*. **III** *adv* **4.** F so, dermaßen.

this·tle ['θɪsl] *s* ♀ Distel *f*.

tho·rax ['θɔːræks] *pl* -ra·ces ['∼rəsiːz], -rax·es ['∼ræksɪz] *s anat.* Brustkorb *m*, -kasten *m*.

thorn [θɔːn] *s* ♀ Dorn *m*: *be a ~ in s.o.'s flesh (od. side)* fig. j-m ein Dorn im Auge sein. '**thorn·y** *adj* **1.** dornig. **2.** fig. heikel.

thor·ough ['θʌrə] *adj* (□ → *thoroughly*) **1.** gründlich (*Person, Kenntnisse*),

(*Prüfung etc a.*) eingehend, (*Reform etc a.*) durchgreifend. **2.** fürchterlich (*Durcheinander, Langweiler etc*). **'~bred** *s* Vollblüter *m.* **'~fare** *s* Hauptverkehrsstraße *f*: **no ~** Durchfahrt verboten! **'~go·ing** → **thorough** 1.

thor·ough·ly ['θʌrəlɪ] *adv* **1. →** **thorough** 1. **2.** völlig, total: *I ~ enjoyed it* es hat mir unwahrscheinlich gut gefallen.

those [ðəʊz] *pl von* **that¹**.

though [ðəʊ] **I** *cj* **1.** obwohl: → **even¹** 1. **2.** (je)doch. **3. as ~** als ob, wie wenn. **II** *adv* **4.** dennoch, trotzdem.

thought¹ [θɔːt] *pret u. pp von* **think**.

thought² [~] *s* **1.** Denken *n.* **~ lost** 5. **2.** Gedanke *m* (*of an acc*): *that's a ~!* gute Idee!; *on second ~s* (*Am. ~*) wenn ich es mir überlege; *have no ~ of doing s.th.* nicht daran denken, et. zu tun. **3. with no ~ for** ohne Rücksicht auf (*acc*), ohne an (*acc*) zu denken. **thought·ful** ['~fʊl] *adj* □ **1.** nachdenklich. **2.** rücksichtsvoll, aufmerksam. **'thought·less** *adj* □ **1.** gedankenlos. **2.** rücksichtslos.

thou·sand ['θaʊznd] **I** *adj* **1.** tausend: **~ (one) ~** (ein)tausend. **II** *s* **2.** Tausend *n*: **~s of times** tausendmal; → **hundred** 2. **3.** ☿ Tausender *m.* **thou·sandth** ['~tθ] **I** *adj* **1.** tausendst. **II** *s* **2.** der, die, das Tausendste. **3.** Tausendstel *n*: *a ~ of a second* e-e Tausendstelsekunde.

thrash [θræʃ] **I** *v/t* **1.** *j-n* verdreschen, -prügeln; (*Sport*) F *j-m* e-e Abfuhr erteilen. **2. ~ out** Problem *etc* ausdiskutieren. **II** *v/i* **3. ~ about** (*od. around*) sich *im Bett* herumwerfen; um sich schlagen; zappeln (*Fisch*). **'thrash·ing** *s*: *give s.o. a ~* j-m e-e Tracht Prügel verpassen; (*Sport*) F *j-m* e-e Abfuhr erteilen.

thread [θred] **I** *s* **1.** Faden *m* (*a. fig.*): *lose the ~ of the conversation*) den (Gesprächs)Faden verlieren; *pick up the ~* den Faden wiederaufnehmen; → **hang** 8. **2.** ☿ Gewinde *n.* **II** *v/t* **3.** *Nadel* einfädeln. **4.** *Perlen etc* auffädeln, -reihen (*on* auf *acc*). **5. ~ one's way through** sich schlängeln durch, sich durchschlängeln zwischen (*dat*). **'~bare** *adj* **1.** abgewetzt, (*Kleidung a.*) abgetragen. **2.** *fig.* abgedroschen.

threat [θret] *s* **1.** Drohung *f*: *under ~ of* unter Androhung von (*od. gen*). **2.** (*to*)

Bedrohung *f* (*gen od. für*), Gefahr *f* (für). **'threat·en I** *v/t* **1.** *j-m* drohen, *j-n* bedrohen (*with* mit): **~ s.o. with s.th.** *j-m* et. androhen. **2.** *et.* androhen, drohen mit. **3. ~ to do s.th.** (damit) drohen, et. zu tun. **4.** *et.* bedrohen, gefährden: *be ~ed with extinction* biol. vom Aussterben bedroht sein. **II** *v/i* **5.** drohen (*Gefahr etc*). **'threat·en·ing** *adj* drohend: **~ letter** Drohbrief *m.*

three [θriː] **I** *adj* drei. **II** *s* Drei *f*: **~ of hearts** Herzdrei. **'~act** *adj*: **~ play** *thea.* Dreiakter *m.* **,~cor·nered** *adj* dreieckig. **,~di'men·sion·al** *adj* **1.** dreidimensional. **2.** *fig.* plastisch.

three·fold ['θriːfəʊld] **I** *adj* dreifach. **II** *adv* dreifach, um das Dreifache (*increase ~*) (sich) verdreifachen. **'three-'piece** *adj* dreiteilig. **,~'quar·ter** *adj* Dreiviertel... **'~time** *adj* dreimalig.

thresh [θreʃ] *v/t u. v/i* dreschen. **'thresh·ing** *adj*: **~ machine** Dreschmaschine *f*.

thresh·old ['θreʃhəʊld] *s* Schwelle *f* (*a. fig.*): *be on the ~ of* an der Schwelle stehen zu (*od. gen*); **~ of pain** Schmerzschwelle.

threw [θruː] *pret von* **throw**.

thrift [θrɪft] *s* Sparsamkeit *f*. **'thrift·y** *adj* □ sparsam.

thrill [θrɪl] **I** *s* **1.** prickelndes Gefühl; Nervenkitzel *m.* **2.** aufregendes Erlebnis. **II** *v/t* **3. be ~ed** (ganz) hingerissen sein (*at, about* von): *I was ~ed to hear that* ich war von der Nachricht hingerissen, daß. **'thrill·er** *s* Thriller *m*, Reißer *m.* **'thrill·ing** *adj* fesselnd, packend.

thrive [θraɪv] *v/i* gedeihen (*Pflanze, Tier*), sich prächtig entwickeln (*Kind*); *fig.* blühen, florieren (*Geschäft etc*): **~ on** geradezu aufblühen bei.

throat [θrəʊt] *s* Kehle *f*, Gurgel *f*; Rachen *m*; Hals *m*: *cut one's own ~ fig.* sich ins eigene Fleisch schneiden; *force* (*od. ram, thrust*) *s.th. down s.o.'s ~ fig. j-m* et. aufzwingen; → **clear** 17, **sore** 1. **'throat·y** *adj* □ rauh; heiser (*Stimme*); mit e-r rauhen *od.* heiseren Stimme: **sound ~** heiser klingen.

throb [θrɒb] **I** *v/i* hämmern (*Maschine*), (*Herz etc a.*) pochen, schlagen. **II** *s* Hämmern *n*, Pochen *n*, Schlagen *n.*

throes [θrəʊz] *s pl*: *be in the ~ of* (*doing*)

s.th. mitten in et. (*Unangenehmem*) stecken.

throm·bo·sis [θrɒmˈbəʊsɪs] *pl* **-ses** [∼siːz] *s* 🗲 Thrombose *f*.

throne [θrəʊn] *s* Thron *m* (*a. fig.*): **come to the** ∼ auf den Thron kommen.

throng [θrɒŋ] **I** *s* Schar *f* (*of* von). **II** *v/i u. v/t* sich drängen (in *dat*).

throt·tle [ˈθrɒtl] **I** *v/t* erdrosseln. **II** *s* *mot.*, ⊙ Drosselklappe *f*: **go at full** ∼ (mit) Vollgas fahren.

through [θruː] **I** *prp* **1.** durch (*a. fig.*): → **live**[1] 1b. **2.** *Am.* bis (einschließlich). **II** *adv* **3.** durch; durch...: ∼ **and** ∼ durch u. durch; **wet** ∼ völlig durchnäßt; → **let through, read**[1] 1, etc. **III** *adj* **4.** durchgehend (*Zug* etc): ∼ **traffic** Durchgangsverkehr *m*. **5. be** ∼ F fertig sein (**with** mit). '∼**out** *prp* **1.** ∼ **the night** die ganze Nacht hindurch. **2.** ∼ **the country** im ganzen Land. **II** *adv* **3.** ganz, überall. **4.** die ganze Zeit (hindurch). '∼**way** *s Am.* Schnellstraße *f*.

throw [θrəʊ] **I** *s* **1.** Leichtathletik: (*Diskus-, Speer*)Wurf *m*. **2.** Wurf *m*: ∼ **stone** 1. **3.** Fußball: Einwurf *m*: **take the** ∼ einwerfen. **II** *v/t* (*irr*) **4.** et. werfen (**at** nach): → **s.o. s.th.** j-m et. hin- od. herzuwerfen; → **s.o. a look** j-m e-n Blick zuwerfen; ∼ **a three** e-e Drei werfen od. würfeln; ∼ **open** Tür etc aufreißen; *fig.* Schloß etc der Öffentlichkeit zugänglich machen; ∼ **o.s. at s.o.** sich auf j-n stürzen; *fig.* sich j-m an den Hals werfen; ∼ **o.s. into** sich stürzen in (*acc*) (*a. fig.*); → **balance** 1, **confusion** 2a, **doubt** 5, **light**[1] 1, **water** 1. **5.** *zo.* werfen. **6.** *Hebel* etc betätigen. **7.** *Reiter* abwerfen. **8.** F *Party* schmeißen, geben. **9.** F *Wutanfall* etc kriegen: → **tantrum**. **III** *v/i* (*irr*) **10.** werfen; würfeln.

Verbindungen mit Adverbien:

throw| **a·bout, ∼ a·round** *v/t*: **throw one's money about** mit Geld um sich werfen; → **weight** 3. ∼ **a·way** *v/t* **1.** et. wegwerfen. **2.** *Chance* etc vertun. ∼ **back** *v/t* **1.** zurückwerfen. **2. be thrown back on** *fig.* wieder angewiesen sein auf (*acc*). ∼ **in** *v/t* **1.** Fußball: **throw the ball in** (*Fußball*) einwerfen; → **sponge** 1, **towel** 1. **2.** et. (gratis) dazugeben: **get s.th. thrown in** et. (gratis) dazubekommen. ∼ **off** *v/t* **1.** *Kleidungsstück* abwerfen, *Nervosität* etc ablegen.

2. *Verfolger* abschütteln. **3.** *Krankheit* loswerden. ∼ **on** *v/t* sich *Kleidungsstück* überwerfen. ∼ **out** *v/t* **1.** j-n hinauswerfen (*a. fig. entlassen*). **2.** et. wegwerfen. **3.** *Vorschlag* etc ablehnen, verwerfen. **4.** *Vorschlag* etc äußern. **5.** j-n aus dem Konzept od. aus der Fassung bringen. ∼ **o·ver** *v/t* *Freund* etc sitzenlassen (**for** wegen). ∼ **to·geth·er** *v/t* **1.** zs.-werfen. **2.** et. fabrizieren, zurechtbasteln. **3.** *Leute* zs.-bringen. ∼ **up** I *v/t* **1.** in die Höhe werfen, hochwerfen. **2.** F *Job* etc hinschmeißen. **3.** et. *Gegessenes* brechen. **II** *v/i* **4.** F brechen (*sich übergeben*).

'**throw·a·way** *adj* **1.** Wegwerf... **2.** hingeworfen (*Bemerkung*).

throw·er [ˈθrəʊə] *s* Werfer(in).

'**throw-in** → **throw** 3.

thrown [θrəʊn] *pp von* **throw**.

thru [θruː] *Am.* F → **through**.

thrush[1] [θrʌʃ] *s orn.* Drossel *f*.

thrush[2] [∼] *s* 🩺 Soor *m*.

thrust [θrʌst] **I** *v/t* (*irr*) **1.** j-n, et. stoßen (**into** in *acc*): → **throat**. **2.** et. stecken, schieben (**into** in *acc*): → **nose** 1. **II** *v/i* (*irr*) **3.** ∼ **at** stoßen nach. **III** *s* **4.** Stoß *m*. **5.** ✗ Vorstoß *m* (*a. fig.*). **6.** *phys.* Schub(kraft *f*) *m*.

'**thru·way** F → **throughway**.

thud [θʌd] **I** *s* dumpfes Geräusch, Plumps *m*. **II** *v/i* plumpsen.

thug [θʌg] *s* Schläger *m*.

thumb [θʌm] **I** *s anat.* Daumen *m*: **be all** ∼**s** F zwei linke Hände haben; **be under s.o.'s** ∼ F unter j-s Fuchtel stehen; **give s.th. the** ∼**s up** (**down**) et. akzeptieren (ablehnen); **stick out like a sore** ∼ F auffallen wie ein Kuhfladen auf der Autobahn; → **rule** 2, **twiddle**. **II** *v/t*: **a lift** per Anhalter fahren, trampen (**to** nach). **III** *v/i*: ∼ **through a book** ein Buch durchblättern. ∼ **in·dex** *s* (*a. irr* **index**) Daumenregister *n*. '∼**nail** *s* Daumennagel *m*. **II** *adj* kurz (*Beschreibung* etc). '∼**screw** *s* **1.** ⊙ Flügel- od. Rändelschraube *f*. **2.** *hist.* Daumenschraube *f*. '∼**tack** *s Am.* Reißzwecke *f*, -nagel *m*.

thump [θʌmp] **I** *v/t* **1.** j-m e-n Schlag versetzen; j-n verprügeln. **2.** ∼ **out** *Melodie* herunterhämmern (**on the piano** auf dem Klavier). **II** *v/i* **3.** plumpsen. **4.** hämmern, pochen (*Herz*). **5.** trampeln.

III *s* **6.** dumpfes Geräusch, Plumps *m*. **7.** Schlag *m*. **'thump·ing I** *adj* **1.** hämmernd (*Kopfschmerzen*). **2.** F riesig, Mords... **II** *adv* **3.** ~ *great* → 2.

thun·der ['θʌndə] **I** *s* Donner *m*, (*von Geschützen a.*) Donnern *n*: *steal s.o.'s* ~ *fig*. j-m die Schau od. Show stehlen. **II** *v/i* donnern (*a. fig. Geschütze, Zug etc*). **III** *v/t a.* ~ *out et.* brüllen, donnern. **'~·bolt** *s* Blitz *m* u. Donnerschlag *m*: *like a* ~ wie der Blitz; *be a real* ~ *fig*. wie der Blitz einschlagen. **'~·clap** *s* Donner(schlag) *m*. **'~·cloud** *s* Gewitterwolke *f*.

thun·der·ous ['θʌndərəs] *adj* donnernd (*Applaus*).

'thun·der·storm *s* Gewitter *n*, Unwetter *n*. **'~·struck** *adj* wie vom Donner gerührt.

thun·der·y ['θʌndərɪ] *adj* gewitt(e)rig.

Thurs·day ['θɜːzdɪ] *s* Donnerstag *m*: *on* ~ (am) Donnerstag; *on* ~s donnerstags.

thus [ðʌs] *adv* **1.** so, auf diese Weise. **2.** folglich, somit. **3.** ~ *far* bisher.

thwack [θwæk] → *whack*.

thwart [θwɔːt] *v/t* Pläne etc durchkreuzen, vereiteln; *j-m* e-n Strich durch die Rechnung machen.

thyme [taɪm] *s* ⚘ Thymian *m*.

thy·roid (gland) ['θaɪrɔɪd] *s anat*. Schilddrüse *f*.

ti·ar·a [tɪ'ɑːrə] *s* **1.** Tiara *f*. **2.** Diadem *n*.

tic [tɪk] *s* ⚕ Tic(k) *m*, nervöses Zucken.

tick¹ [tɪk] *s zo*. Zecke *f*.

tick² [~] *s*: *on* ~ F auf Pump.

tick³ [~] **I** *s* **1.** Ticken *n*. **2.** Haken *m*, Häkchen *n* (*Vermerkzeichen*). **3.** *bsd. Br.* F Augenblick *m*: *in a* ~ sofort. **II** *v/i* **4.** ticken: ~ *away* vergehen, -rinnen. **III** *v/t* **5.** *a.* ~ *off* abhaken: ~ *off* F *j-n* anpfeifen, zs.-stauchen.

tick·er ['tɪkə] *s* F Pumpe *f* (*Herz*).

tick·et ['tɪkɪt] **I** *s* **1.** (*Eintritts-, Theateretc*)Karte *f*; 🚌 *etc* Fahrkarte *f*, -schein *m*, ✈ Flugschein *m*, Ticket *n*; (*Gepäcketc*)Schein *m*. **2.** Etikett *n*, (*Preis- etc*)Schild *n*. **3.** Strafzettel *m*: → *parking ticket*. **4.** *pol. bsd. Am.* Wahl-, Kandidatenliste *f*. **II** *v/t* **5.** etikettieren. **6.** be ~*ed for bsd. Am.* e-n Strafzettel bekommen wegen. **7.** bestimmen, vorsehen (*for* für). ~ **col·lec·tor** *s* (Bahnsteig-)Schaffner(in). ~ **in·spec·tor** *s* Fahrkartenkontrolleur(in). ~ **ma·chine** *s* Fahr-

kartenautomat *m*. ~ **tout** *s Br*. Kartenschwarzhändler(in).

tick·ing-'off *s* F Anpfiff *m*: *give s.o. a* ~ j-n anpfeifen od. zs.-stauchen.

tick·le ['tɪkl] **I** *v/t u. v/i* kitzeln: ~ *s.o.'s fancy fig*. j-n anmachen od. anturnen; *be* ~*d pink* (*od. to death*) F sich wie ein Schneekönig freuen (*at, by, with* über *acc*); → *ivory* 2. **II** *s* Kitzeln *n*. **'tick·lish** *adj* ☐ kitz(e)lig (*a. fig.*).

tid·al ['taɪdl] *adj* Tiden...: ~ *wave* Flutwelle *f*; *fig*. Welle *f*.

tid·bit ['tɪdbɪt] *Am*. → *titbit*.

tid·dly·winks ['tɪdlɪwɪŋks] *s pl* (*sg konstruiert*) Flohhüpfen *n*, -spiel *n*.

tide [taɪd] **I** *s* **1.** Gezeiten *pl*; Flut *f*. **2.** *fig*. Strömung *f*, Trend *m*: *go* (*od. swim*) *with* (*against*) *the* ~ mit der (gegen den) Strom schwimmen. **II** *v/t* **3.** ~ *over fig*. j-m hinweghelfen über (*acc*); j-n über Wasser halten. **'~·mark** *s bsd. Br. humor*. schwarzer Rand (*in Badewanne*).

ti·di·ness ['taɪdɪnɪs] *s* Sauberkeit *f*, Ordentlichkeit *f*.

ti·dy ['taɪdɪ] **I** *adj* ☐ **1.** sauber, ordentlich, (*Zimmer a.*) aufgeräumt. **2.** F ordentlich, beträchtlich (*Gewinn etc*). **II** *v/t* **3.** *a.* ~ *up* in Ordnung bringen, *Zimmer a.* aufräumen: ~ *away* weg-, aufräumen.

tie [taɪ] **I** *s* **1.** Krawatte *f*, Schlips *m*. **2.** Band *n*; Schnur *f*. **3.** *pl fig*. Bande *pl*. **4.** Stimmengleichheit *f*; (*Sport*) Unentschieden *n*: *end in a* ~ unentschieden ausgehen. **5.** *Sport*: (*Pokal*)Spiel *n*, (-)Paarung *f*. **6.** 🚌 *Am*. Schwelle *f*. **II** *v/t* **7.** **a)** binden (*to an acc*); (sich) *Krawatte etc* binden: *my hands are tied fig*. mir sind die Hände gebunden, **b)** → *tie up* 1. **8.** *be* ~*d to fig*. (eng) verbunden sein mit. **9.** *the game was* ~*d* (*Sport*) das Spiel ging unentschieden aus. **III** *v/i* **10.** *they* ~*d for second place* (*Sport etc*) sie belegten gemeinsam den zweiten Platz. *Verbindungen mit Adverbien*:

tie· down *v/t j-n* festlegen (*to* auf *acc*). ~ **in** *v/i* (*with*) übereinstimmen (mit), passen (zu). ~ **up** *v/t* **1.** *Paket etc* verschnüren: → *knot* 1. **2.** *be tied up* ✝ fest angelegt sein (*in* in *dat*). **3.** *et.* in Verbindung bringen (*with* mit). **4.** *Verkehr etc* lahmlegen.

'tie|·break, '~·break·er *s* Tennis: Tie-

Break *m*, *n*. '**~-in → tie-up**. '**~-on** *adj* Anhänge... '**~-pin** *s* Krawattennadel *f*.

tier [tɪə] *s* **1.** (Sitz)Reihe *f*. **2.** Lage *f*, Schicht *f*. **3.** *fig*. Stufe *f*.

'**tie-up** *s* (enge) Verbindung, (enger) Zs.-hang (**between** zwischen *dat*).

tiff [tɪf] *s* kleine Meinungsverschiedenheit.

ti-ger ['taɪɡə] *s* *zo*. Tiger *m*.

tight [taɪt] **I** *adj* □ **1.** fest(sitzend, -angezogen). **2.** straff (*Seil etc*). **3.** eng (*a. Kleidungsstück*): → **corner** 2, **fit** 5. **4.** knapp (*Rennen etc*, ✝ *Geld*). **5.** F knick(e)rig. **6.** F blau (*betrunken*). **7.** *in Zssgn* ...dicht: → **airtight** 1, *etc*. **II** *adv* **8.** fest: **hold ~** festhalten; **sit ~** sich nicht vom Fleck rühren; *fig*. sich nicht beirren lassen. **9.** F gut: **sleep ~**! **III** *s* **10.** *pl, a. **pair of ~s*** *bsd. Br*. Strumpfhose *f*; Trikot *n* (*von Artisten etc*). '**tight-en I** *v/t* **1.** *Schraube etc* anziehen: **~ one's belt** *fig*. den Gürtel enger schnallen. **2.** *Seil etc* straffen: **~ up** → 3. **II** *v/i* **3.** **~ up on** *Gesetz etc* verschärfen.

'**tight**|'**fist-ed** → **tight** 5. '**~-lipped** *adj* **1.** mit zs.-gekniffenen Lippen. **2.** *fig*. verschlossen: **be ~ about** nicht reden wollen über (*acc*). '**~-rope** *s* (Draht)Seil *n*: **walk a ~** *fig*. e-n Balanceakt ausführen; **~ walker** Drahtseilkünstler(in), Seiltänzer(in).

ti-gress ['taɪɡrɪs] *s* *zo*. Tigerin *f*.

tile [taɪl] **I** *s* **1.** (Dach)Ziegel *m*: **be (out) on the ~s** F e-n draufmachen. **2.** Fliese *f*, Kachel *f*. **II** *v/t* **3.** (mit Ziegeln) decken. **4.** fliesen, kacheln. '**til-er** *s* **1.** Dachdecker *m*. **2.** Fliesenleger *m*.

till¹ [tɪl] *s* (Laden)Kasse *f*.

till² [~] → **until**.

tilt [tɪlt] **I** *v/t* **1.** kippen. **II** *v/i* **2.** kippen, sich neigen. **III** *s* **3.** **at a ~** schief, schräg. **4.** (**at**) **full ~** F mit Volldampf *arbeiten*; mit Karacho *fahren etc*.

tim-ber ['tɪmbə] *s* **1.** *Br*. Bau-, Nutzholz *n*. **2.** Balken *m*. '**~-line** *s* Baumgrenze *f*.

time [taɪm] **I** *s* **1.** *allg*. Zeit *f*: **some ~ ago** vor einiger Zeit; **all the ~** die ganze Zeit; **ahead of ~** vorzeitig; **at the ~** damals; **at ~s** manchmal; **at the same ~** gleichzeitig; trotzdem; **by the ~** wenn; als; **for a ~** e-e Zeitlang; **for the ~ being** vorläufig, fürs erste; **from ~ to ~** von Zeit zu Zeit; **in ~** rechtzeitig; im Lauf

der Zeit; **in no ~** (**at all**) im Nu; **in two years' ~** in zwei Jahren; **on ~** pünktlich; **be ahead** (*od*. **before**) **one's ~** s-r Zeit voraus sein; **be behind the ~s** rückständig sein; **do ~** F sitzen (**for** wegen); **keep up** (*od*. **march, move**) **with the ~s** mit der Zeit gehen; **take one's ~** sich Zeit lassen; → **bide, immemorial, mark**² 11, **nick** 2, **play** 7. **2.** (Uhr)Zeit *f*: **what's the ~?** wie spät ist es?; **what ~?** um wieviel Uhr?; **this ~ tomorrow** morgen um diese Zeit. **3.** ♪ Takt *m*: **in ~** im Takt (*a. marschieren etc*); **in ~ with the music** im Takt zur Musik; **beat ~** den Takt schlagen. **4.** Mal *n*: **~ and again, ~ after ~** immer wieder; **every ~ I ...** jedesmal, wenn ich ...; **how many ~s?** wie oft?; **next ~** (**I ...**) nächstes Mal(, wenn ich ...); **this ~** diesmal; **three ~s** dreimal; **three ~s four equals** (*od*. **is**) **twelve** drei mal vier ist zwölf; → **nine** I, **second**¹ I. **II** *v/t* **5.** *et*. timen; stoppen, wie lang *j-d* braucht: **he was ~d at 20 seconds** für ihn wurden 20 Sekunden gestoppt. **6.** *et*. **well** sich e-n günstigen Zeitpunkt aussuchen für; (*Sport*) *Flanke, Schlag etc* gut timen. **~ bomb** *s* Zeitbombe *f* (*a. fig.*). '**~-card** *s* Stechkarte *f*. **~ clock** *s* Stechuhr *f*. '**~-con-sum-ing** *adj* zeitaufwendig, -raubend. **~ ex-po-sure** *s* *phot*. Zeitaufnahme *f*. '**~-hon-o(u)red** *adj* althergebracht. '**~-keep-er** *s* **1.** *Sport*: Zeitnehmer(in). **2.** **be a good ~** genau gehen (*Uhr*). **~ lag** *s* Zeitdifferenz *f*. '**~-lapse** *adj* *Film*: Zeitraffer...

time-less ['taɪmlɪs] *adj* □ **1.** immerwährend, ewig. **2.** zeitlos.

time lim-it *s* Frist *f*: **set s.o. a ~** of j-m e-e Frist setzen von.

time-ly ['taɪmlɪ] *adj* rechtzeitig.

'**time-'out** *pl* '**times-'out** *s* *Sport*: Time-out *n*, Auszeit *f*.

tim-er ['taɪmə] *s* Timer *m*, Schaltuhr *f*.

'**time**|**sav-ing** *adj* zeitsparend. '**~-serv-er** *s* *bsd. pol*. Opportunist(in). **~ sig-nal** *s* Rundfunk: Zeitzeichen *n*. **~ switch** *s* Zeitschalter *m*. '**~-ta-ble** *s* **1.** Fahr-, Flugplan *m*. **2.** *ped. Br*. Stundenplan *m*. **3.** Zeitplan *m*. '**~-worn** *adj* **1.** abgenutzt. **2.** *fig*. abgedroschen. **~ zone** *s* Zeitzone *f*.

tim-id ['tɪmɪd] *adj* □ ängstlich, furchtsam.

tim·ing ['taɪmɪŋ] s Timing n (*Wahl des günstigen Zeitpunkts*).

tin [tɪn] **I** s **1.** Zinn n. **2.** Br. (Blech-, Konserven)Dose f, (-)Büchse f. **II** adj **3.** zinnern, Zinn... **III** v/t **4.** verzinnen. **5.** Br. einmachen, -dosen: → **tinned.**

tinc·ture ['tɪŋktʃə] s pharm. Tinktur f: ~ **of iodine** Jodtinktur.

tin·der ['tɪndə] s Zunder m: (**as**) **dry as ~** → **tinder-dry.** '**~·box** s fig. Pulverfaß n. **~'dry** adj so trocken wie Zunder.

tine [taɪn] s **1.** Zinke f, Zacke f (*e-r Gabel*). **2.** (*Geweih*)Sprosse f, Ende n.

'**tin·foil** s Stanniol(papier) n; Alufolie f.

ting [tɪŋ] **I** v/t: **~ a bell** klingeln. **II** v/i: **the bell ~s** es klingelt. **III** s Klingeln n.

tinge [tɪndʒ] **I** v/t **1.** tönen: **be ~d with** fig. e-n Anflug haben von, et. von ... an sich haben. **II** s **2.** Tönung f: **have a ~ of red** ins Rote spielen. **3.** fig. Anflug m (**of** von).

tin·gle ['tɪŋɡl] **I** v/i prickeln, kribbeln (**with** vor dat). **II** s Prickeln n, Kribbeln n.

tin| god s F Idol n. **~ hat** s ✗ F (Stahl-) Helm m.

tink·er ['tɪŋkə] **I** s Kesselflicker m. **II** v/i a. **~ about** herumbasteln (**with** an dat): **~ with** herumpfuschen an (dat).

tin·kle ['tɪŋkl] **I** v/i bimmeln; klirren. **II** s Bimmeln n; Klirren n: **give s.o. a ~** teleph. Br. F j-n anklingeln.

tinned [tɪnd] adj Br. Dosen..., Büchsen...: **~ fruit** Obstkonserven pl; **~ meat** Büchsenfleisch n.

tin·ny ['tɪnɪ] adj blechern (*Klang*).

tin o·pen·er s Br. Dosen-, Büchsenöffner m.

tin·sel ['tɪnsl] s **1.** Lametta n. **2.** fig. Flitter m.

tint [tɪnt] **I** s (Farb)Ton m, Tönung f: **have a ~ of red** ins Rote spielen. **II** v/t tönen.

ti·ny ['taɪnɪ] adj □ winzig.

tip¹ [tɪp] s **1.** allg. Spitze f: **it's on the ~ of my tongue** fig. es liegt mir auf der Zunge; → **iceberg. 2.** Filter m (*e-r Zigarette*).

tip² [~] **I** s **1.** Tisch etc kippen: **~ over** umkippen; → **scale² 2. 2.** (aus)kippen, schütten. **II** v/t **3.** kippen: **~ over** umkippen. **III** s **4.** bsd. Br. (*Schuttetc*)Abladeplatz m, (-)Halde f. **5.** Br. fig. F Saustall m.

tip³ [~] **I** s **1.** Trinkgeld n. **2.** Tip m, Rat(schlag) m: **take my ~ and ...** hör auf mich u. ... **II** v/t **3.** j-m ein Trinkgeld geben: **~ s.o. 50 p** j-m 50 Pence Trinkgeld geben. **4.** tippen auf (acc) (**as** als). **5. ~ off** j-m e-n Tip od. Wink geben.

'**tip-off** s F Tip m, Wink m.

tip·ple ['tɪpl] s F (*alkoholisches*) Getränk.

tip·sy ['tɪpsɪ] adj □ angeheitert, beschwipst: **be ~** a. e-n Schwips haben.

'**tip|·toe** **I** v/i auf Zehenspitzen gehen. **II** s: **stand on ~** sich auf die Zehenspitzen stellen; **walk on ~** → I. **~'top** adj F erstklassig: **be in ~ order** tipptopp in Ordnung sein.

ti·rade [taɪ'reɪd] s Schimpfkanonade f (**against** gegen).

tire¹ [taɪə] Am. → **tyre.**

tire² [~] **I** v/t ermüden, müde machen: **~ out** (völlig) erschöpfen. **II** v/i ermüden, müde werden: **~ of** fig. j-n, et. satt bekommen; **~ of doing s.th.** satt werden, et. zu tun.

tired ['taɪəd] adj □ **1.** müde: **~ out** (völlig) erschöpft; **be ~ of** fig. j-n, et. satt haben; **be ~ of doing s.th.** es satt haben od. sein, et. zu tun. **2.** fig. abgegriffen.'**tired·ness** s Müdigkeit f.

tire·less ['taɪəlɪs] adj □ unermüdlich.

tire·some ['taɪəsəm] adj □ **1.** ermüdend. **2.** fig. lästig.

ti·ro → **tyro.**

tis·sue ['tɪʃuː] s **1.** biol. Gewebe n. **2.** Papier(taschen)tuch n. **3.** a. **~ paper** Seidenpapier n.

tit¹ [tɪt] s: **~ for tat** wie du mir, so ich dir.

tit² [~] s sl. **1.** mst pl Titte f: a) weibliche Brust, b) Brustwarze. **2.** Br. blöde Sau.

tit³ [~] s orn. Meise f.

ti·tan·ic [taɪ'tænɪk] adj (**~ally**) gigantisch.

tit·bit ['tɪtbɪt] s bsd. Br. Leckerbissen m.

tit·il·late ['tɪtɪleɪt] v/t j-n (*sexuell*) anregen.

ti·tle ['taɪtl] s **1.** allg. Titel m. **2.** ♫ (Rechts)Anspruch m (**to** auf acc); → **deed** s ♫ Eigentumsurkunde f. **~ fight** s Boxen: Titelkampf m. '**~·hold·er** s Sport: Titelhalter(in), -träger(in). **~ page** s Titelseite f. **~ role** s thea. etc Titelrolle f.

'**tit·mouse** s (irr **mouse**) orn. Meise f.

tit·ter ['tɪtə] **I** v/i kichern. **II** s Kichern n.

tit·tle-tat·tle ['tɪtl͵tætl] **I** s Geschwätz n; Klatsch m, Tratsch m. **II** v/i schwatzen; klatschen, tratschen.

tit·u·lar ['tɪtjʊlə] *adj* nominell.

to I *prp* [tu:; tʊ; tə] **1.** *Richtung u. Ziel, räumlich:* zu, nach, an (*acc*), in (*acc*): **go ~ England** nach England fahren; → **bed** 1, **school** 1, *etc.* **2.** in (*dat*): **have you ever been ~ London?** bist du schon einmal in London gewesen? **3.** *Richtung, Ziel, Zweck:* zu, auf (*acc*), für:→ **death** 1, **invite** 1, *etc.* **4.** *Zugehörigkeit:* zu, für, in (*acc*): → **key** 1, **secretary** 1, *etc.* **5.** (im *Verhältnis od.* Vergleich) zu, gegen(über): → **compare** 1, **nothing** 1, *etc.* **6.** *Ausmaß, Grenze, Grad:* bis, (bis) zu, (bis) an (*acc*). **7.** *zeitliche Ausdehnung od. Grenze:* bis, bis zu, bis gegen, vor (*dat*): *from three ~ four* von drei bis vier (Uhr); → **quarter** 2. **8.** *Begleitung:* zu, nach: → **dance** 1. **9.** *zur Bildung des (betonten) Dativs:* **~ me** mir. **II** *part* [tʊ] **10.** *zur Bezeichnung des Infinitivs:* → **go** gehen; *easy ~ understand* leicht zu verstehen. **11.** *Zweck, Absicht:* um zu: *he does it only ~ earn money* er tut es nur, um Geld zu verdienen; → **order** 9. **12.** *zur Verkürzung e-s Nebensatzes:* **he was the first ~ arrive** er kam als erster; **~ hear him talk** wenn man ihn (so) reden hört. **III** *adv* [tu:] **13.** zu (*geschlossen*). **14.** → **come to. 15. ~ and fro** hin u. her; auf u. ab.

toad [təʊd] *s zo.* Kröte *f*. **'~·stool** *s* ungenießbarer Pilz; Giftpilz *m*.

toad·y ['təʊdɪ] **I** *s* Kriecher(in), Speichellecker(in). **II** *v/i:* **~ to s.o.** vor j-m kriechen.

toast¹ [təʊst] **I** *s* **1.** Toast *m*. **II** *v/t* **2.** toasten; rösten. **3.** F sich *die Füße etc* wärmen.

toast² [~] **I** *s* Toast *m*, Trinkspruch *m*: *drink a ~ to ~* **II** *v/t* auf *j-n od. j-s* Wohl trinken.

toast·er ['təʊstə] *s* ⊕ Toaster *m*.

to·bac·co [tə'bækəʊ] *pl* **-cos** *s* Tabak *m*. **to'bac·co·nist** [~kənɪst] *s* Tabak(waren)händler(in).

to·bog·gan [tə'bɒgən] **I** *s* (Rodel)Schlitten *m*. **II** *v/i* Schlitten fahren, rodeln.

tod [tɒd] *s:* **on one's ~** *Br.* F ganz allein.

to·day [tə'deɪ] **I** *adv* **1.** heute: *a week ~, ~ week* heute in *e-r* Woche *od.* in acht Tagen. **2.** heutzutage. **II** *s* **3.** **~'s paper** die heutige Zeitung, die Zeitung von heute. **4.** *of* ~, **~'s** von heute, heutig.

tod·dle ['tɒdl] *v/i* **1.** auf wack(e)ligen *od.* unsicheren Beinen gehen (*bsd. Kleinkind*). **2.** F gehen. **'tod·dler** *s* Kleinkind *n*.

tod·dy ['tɒdɪ] *s* Toddy *m* (*grogartiges Getränk*).

to-do [tə'du:] *s* F Theater *n* (*about* um).

toe [təʊ] **I** *s anat.* Zehe *f*: **be on one's ~s** *fig.* auf Draht sein; **keep s.o. on his ~s** *fig.* j-n auf Zack halten; **tread on s.o.'s ~s** *fig.* j-m zu nahe treten. **II** *v/t:* **~ the line** *fig.* spuren. **'~·nail** *s* Zehennagel *m*.

tof·fee ['tɒfɪ] *s bsd. Br.* Toffee *n*, Karamelbonbon *n, m*: *he can't play tennis for ~* F er hat von Tennisspielen keine Ahnung. **'~-nosed** *adj Br.* F eingebildet, hochnäsig.

tof·fy → **toffee.**

tog [tɒg] F **I** *v/t:* **~ o.s. out** (*od.* **up**) sich in Schale werfen. **II** *s pl* Klamotten *pl*.

to·geth·er [tə'geðə] **I** *adv* zusammen (*with* mit); zusammen...: → **keep together, live¹** 1, *etc.* **II** *adj* F ausgeglichen (*Person*). **to'geth·er·ness** *s* Zs.-gehörigkeit(sgefühl *n*) *f*.

toil [tɔɪl] **I** *s* mühselige Arbeit. **II** *v/i* sich abmühen *od.* plagen (*at* mit); sich schleppen.

toi·let ['tɔɪlɪt] *s* Toilette *f*: *go to the ~* auf die *od.* in die *od.* zur Toilette gehen. **~ pa·per** *s* Toilettenpapier *n*. **~ roll** *s* Rolle *f* Toilettenpapier.

to·ken ['təʊkən] **I** *s* **1.** Zeichen *n*: *as a* (*od.* **in**) ~ **of** als *od.* zum Zeichen (*gen*); zum Andenken an (*acc*). **2.** Gutschein *m*. **3.** (*Spiel- etc*)Marke *f*. **II** *adj* **4.** symbolisch. **5.** Schein... **6.** Alibi...

told [təʊld] *pret u. pp von* **tell.**

tol·er·a·ble ['tɒlərəbl] *adj* erträglich. **'tol·er·a·bly** *adv* leidlich, einigermaßen. **'tol·er·ance** *s* **1.** Toleranz *f* (*for, of, toward[s]* gegenüber). **2.** ⊕ Toleranz *f*. **'tol·er·ant** *adj* □ tolerant (*of, toward[s]* gegenüber). **tol·er·ate** ['~reɪt] *v/t* **1.** tolerieren, dulden. **2.** *j-n, et.* ertragen.

toll¹ [təʊl] *s* **1.** Benutzungsgebühr *f*, Maut *f*. **2. take its ~** (**on**) *fig.* s-n Tribut fordern (von); s-e Spuren hinterlassen (bei).

toll² [~] *v/i* läuten (*bsd. Totenglocke*).

toll‖ bridge *s* gebührenpflichtige Brücke, Mautbrücke *f*. **‖~-'free** *adj u. adv* *teleph. Am.* gebührenfrei. **~ road** s gebührenpflichtige Straße, Mautstraße f.

tom [tɒm] s zo. Kater m.

tom·a·hawk ['tɒməhɔːk] s *hist.* Tomahawk m, Streitaxt f.

to·ma·to [tə'mɑːtəʊ] **I** pl **-toes** 🍅 Tomate f. **II** adj Tomaten...

tomb [tuːm] s Grab(mal) n; Gruft f.

tom·bo·la [tɒm'bəʊlə] s Tombola f.

tom·boy ['tɒmbɔɪ] s Wildfang m (*Mädchen*).

'tomb·stone s Grabstein m.

'tom·cat s zo. Kater m.

tome [təʊm] s *humor.* Wälzer m.

tom·fool·er·y [ˌtɒm'fuːlərɪ] s Albernheit f, Unsinn m.

tom·my gun ['tɒmɪ] s F Maschinenpistole f.

to·mor·row [tə'mɒrəʊ] **I** adv **1.** morgen: **a week ~, ~ week** morgen in e-r Woche od. in acht Tagen; **~ morning** morgen früh; **~ night** morgen abend. **II** s **2.** **~'s paper** die morgige Zeitung, die Zeitung von morgen; **the day after ~** übermorgen. **3.** Zukunft f: **of ~, ~'s** von morgen.

ton [tʌn] s **1.** Tonne f (*Gewicht*). **2.** F **~s** pl **of** jede Menge; **~s better** viel od. wesentlich besser.

tone [təʊn] **I** s **1.** *allg.* Ton m; Klang m. **2.** 𝄞 Am. Note f. **3.** *fig.* Niveau n. **II** v/t **4.** **~ down** Kritik etc abschwächen; **~ up** j-n, Muskeln kräftigen. **III** v/i **5.** **~ in (with)** harmonieren (mit), passen (zu).

tongs [tɒŋz] s pl, a. **pair of ~** Zange f.

tongue [tʌŋ] s **1.** *anat.* Zunge f (*a. fig.*): **~ in cheek, with one's ~ in one's cheek** scherzhaft; **bite one's ~** sich auf die Zunge beißen (*a. fig.*); **hold one's ~** den Mund halten; **put out one's ~** at j-m die Zunge herausstrecken; → **slip**¹ 1, **tip**¹ 1, **wag**¹ II. 2. (*Mutter*)Sprache f. **3.** Zunge f (*e-s Schuhs etc*); (*Land*)Zunge f: **~ of land. 4.** Klöppel m (*e-r Glocke*). **~ twist·er** s Zungenbrecher m.

ton·ic ['tɒnɪk] s **1.** *pharm.* Tonikum n, Stärkungsmittel n: **be a real ~** *allg.* richtig guttun. **2.** Tonic n (→ **tonic water**): **a gin and ~** ein Gin Tonic. **~ wa·ter** s Tonic water n (*mit Kohlensäure u. Chinin versetztes Wasser*).

to·night [tə'naɪt] **I** adv heute abend; heute nacht. **II** s: **~'s program(me)** das Programm (von) heute abend.

ton·sil ['tɒnsl] s *anat.* Mandel f. **ton·sil·li·tis** [ˌtɒnsɪ'laɪtɪs] s ✙ Mandelentzündung f; *weitS.* Angina f.

ton·sure ['tɒnʃə] s Tonsur f.

too [tuː] adv **1.** zu. **2.** zu, sehr. **3.** auch. **4.** auch noch, noch dazu.

took [tʊk] *pret von* **take.**

tool [tuːl] s **1.** Werkzeug n (*a. fig. Person*), Gerät n: **be the ~s of s.o.'s trade** *fig.* j-s Rüstzeug sein; → **down** 15. **2.** V Schwanz m (*Penis*). **~ bag** s Werkzeugtasche f. **~ box** s Werkzeugkasten m. **~ shed** s Geräteschuppen m.

toot [tuːt] *mot.* **I** v/i hupen. **II** v/t: **~ one's horn** → **I. III** s: **give a ~ on one's horn** → **I.**

tooth [tuːθ] pl **teeth** [tiːθ] s *anat.* Zahn m (*a. e-s Kamms, e-r Säge, e-s Zahnrads etc*): **in the teeth of** *fig.* gegen; trotz, ungeachtet; **fight ~ and nail** *fig.* erbittert od. verbissen kämpfen; **get one's teeth into** *fig.* sich reinknien in (*acc*); → **armed, brush**¹ 5, **cut** 10, **edge** 4, **skin** 1, **sweet** 1. **'~·ache** s Zahnschmerzen pl, -weh n. **'~·brush** s Zahnbürste f.

tooth·less ['tuːθlɪs] adj zahnlos.

'tooth·paste s Zahncreme f, -pasta f. **'~·pick** s Zahnstocher m.

tooth·some ['tuːθsəm] adj ☐ lecker, schmackhaft.

toot·sie, toot·sy ['tʊtsɪ] s *Kindersprache:* Füßchen n.

top¹ [tɒp] **I** s **1.** oberer Teil; Gipfel m, Spitze f (*e-s Bergs etc*); Krone f, Wipfel m (*e-s Baums*); Kopfende m, oberes Ende (*e-s Tisches etc*): **at the ~ of the page** oben auf der Seite; **from ~ to toe** von Kopf bis Fuß; **on ~** oben(auf); d(a)rauf; **on ~ of** (oben) auf (*dat od. acc*), über (*dat od. acc*); **on ~ of each other** auf-, übereinander; **on ~ of it** *fig.* obendrein; **get on ~ of s.o.** F j-m zuviel od. zu schwierig werden; → **thin** 1. **2.** *fig.* Spitze f: **at the ~ of one's voice** aus vollem Hals; **be at the ~ of** an der Spitze (*gen*) stehen; **stay on ~** an der Spitze bleiben. **3.** (*Bikini- etc*)Oberteil n. **4.** Oberfläche f (*e-s Tisches etc*). **5.** Deckel m (*e-s Glases*), (*a. e-r Tube etc*) Verschluß m: → **blow**¹ 11. **6.** *mot.* Verdeck n: → **hardtop. 7.** *mot.* höchster Gang. **II** adj **8.** oberst: **~ dog** F der Überlegene; der Chef; **~ hat** Zylinder m. **9.** *fig.* Höchst..., Spitzen...: **~ gear**

→ 7; **~ manager** Top-, Spitzenmanager *m*; **at ~ speed** mit Höchstgeschwindigkeit; in Windeseile; → **management** 2. **III** *v/t* **10.** bedecken (**with** mit). **11.** *fig.* übersteigen; übertreffen. **12.** ~ **the bill** der Star des Programms *od.* die Hauptattraktion sein.
Verbindungen mit Adverbien:
top| **off** *v/t bsd. Am.* abschließen, krönen (**with** mit). ~ **out** *v/t* das Richtfest (*gen*) feiern. **~ up** *v/t* Tank *etc* auffüllen; F *j-m* nachschenken.
top² [~] *s* Kreisel *m* (*Spielzeug*): → **sleep** I.
to·pee ['təʊpɪ] *s* Tropenhelm *m*.
'top|**-flight** *adj* F Spitzen... **,~-'heav·y** *adj* kopflastig (*a. fig.*), oberlastig.
top·ic ['tɒpɪk] *s* Thema *n*: ~ **of conversation** Gesprächsthema. **'top·i·cal** *adj* □ aktuell.
'top·knot *s* Haarknoten *m*.
top·less ['tɒplɪs] *adj* oben ohne; Oben-ohne-...
,top|**-'lev·el** *adj* auf höchster Ebene, Spitzen... **'~-most** *adj* oberst. **,~-'notch** *adj* F erstklassig, Spitzen...
to·pog·ra·phy [tə'pɒɡrəfɪ] *s* Topographie *f*.
top·per ['tɒpə] *s* F Zylinder *m*. **'top·ping** *s*: **with a ~ of whipped cream** mit Schlagsahne darauf.
top·ple ['tɒpl] **I** *v/i* **1.** *mst* ~ **over** umkippen. **II** *v/t* **2.** *mst* ~ **over** umkippen. **3.** *fig.* Regierung *etc* stürzen.
,top|**-'se·cret** *adj* streng geheim. **'~-spin** *s* Tennis *etc*: Topspin *m* (*starker Aufwärtsdrall*).
top·sy·tur·vy [,tɒpsɪ'tɜ:vɪ] *adj* F **1.** in e-r heillosen Unordnung. **2.** *fig.* konfus, wirr.
torch [tɔ:tʃ] *s* **1.** *bsd. Br.* Taschenlampe *f*. **2.** Fackel *f*. **'~-light** *s*: **by ~** bei Fackelschein; ~ **procession** Fackelzug *m*.
tore [tɔ:] *pret von* **tear²**.
tor·ment *v/t* [tɔ:'ment] **1.** quälen, *fig. a.* plagen: **be ~ed by** (*od.* **with**) gequält *od.* geplagt werden von. **II** *s* ['tɔ:ment] **2.** Qual *f*: **be in ~**, **suffer ~(s)** Qualen leiden. **3.** Quälgeist *m*.
torn [tɔ:n] *pp von* **tear²**.
tor·na·do [tɔ:'neɪdəʊ] *pl* **-do(e)s** *s* Tornado *m*.
tor·pe·do [tɔ:'pi:dəʊ] **I** *pl* **-does** *s* ♣, ✗

Torpedo *m*. **II** *v/t* torpedieren (*a. fig.*). **~ boat** *s* Torpedoboot *n*.
tor·pid ['tɔ:pɪd] *adj* □ träg(e). **tor·por** ['~pə] *s* Trägheit *f*.
torque [tɔ:k] *s phys.* Drehmoment *n*.
tor·rent ['tɒrənt] *s* **1.** reißender Strom: **~s** *pl* **of rain** sintflutartige Regenfälle *pl*; **the rain fell in ~s** es goß in Strömen. **2.** *fig.* Schwall *m*, Sturzbach *m* (**of** von).
tor·ren·tial [tə'renʃl] *adj* sintflutartig.
tor·rid ['tɒrɪd] *adj* □ sengend.
tor·sion ['tɔ:ʃn] *s phys.* Torsion *f*, Verdrillung *f*.
tor·so ['tɔ:səʊ] *pl* **-sos** *s* Rumpf *m*; (*Kunst*) Torso *m*.
tort [tɔ:t] *s* ♣ unerlaubte Handlung.
tor·toise ['tɔ:təs] *s zo.* Schildkröte *f*.
tor·tu·ous ['tɔ:tʃʊəs] *adj* □ **1.** gewunden (*Pfad etc*). **2.** *fig.* umständlich.
tor·ture ['tɔ:tʃə] **I** *v/t* **1.** foltern. **2.** *fig.* quälen: **be ~d by** (*od.* **with**) gequält werden von. **II** *s* **3.** Folter(ung) *f.* **4.** *fig.* Qual *f.* ~ **cham·ber** *s* Folterkammer *f*.
To·ry ['tɔ:rɪ] *pol. Br.* **I** *s* Tory *m*, Konservative *m*. **II** *adj* Tory..., torystisch, konservativ.
toss [tɒs] **I** *v/t* **1.** werfen: ~ **s.o. s.th.** j-m *et.* zuwerfen; ~ **back** Kopf zurückwerfen; ~ **off** Arbeit hinhauen; Getränk hinunterstürzen. **2.** Münze hochwerfen: ~ **s.o. for s.th.** mit j-m um *et.* losen. **II** *v/i* **3.** *a.* ~ **about** (*od.* **around**), ~ **and turn** sich (*im Schlaf etc*) hin u. her werfen. **4.** *a.* ~ **up** e-e Münze hochwerfen: ~ **for s.th.** um *et.* losen, *et.* auslosen. **III** *s* **5.** Wurf *m*. **6.** Hochwerfen *n* (*e-r Münze*): **win the ~** (*Sport*) die Wahl gewinnen. **7.** *I don't give a ~ about it Br.* F das ist mir völlig egal. **'~-up** *s* **1.** → **toss** 6. **2.** **it's a ~ whether** F es ist völlig offen, ob.
tot¹ [tɒt] *s* **1.** *a. tiny ~* F Knirps *m*. **2.** Schluck *m* (*Alkohol*).
tot² [~] *v/t*: ~ **up** F zs.-rechnen, -zählen.
to·tal ['təʊtl] **I** *adj* □ **1.** völlig, total, Total...: → **recall** I. **2.** ganz, gesamt, Gesamt... **II** *s* **3.** Gesamtmenge *f*; (End)Summe *f*: **a ~ of 20 cases** insgesamt 20 Kisten; **in ~** insgesamt. **III** *v/t* *pret u. pp* **-taled,** *bsd. Br.* **-talled 4.** sich belaufen auf (*acc*): ... **~(l)ing £500** ... von insgesamt 500 Pfund. **5.** *a.* ~ **up** zs.-rechnen, -zählen. **to·tal·i·tar·i·an** [,təʊtælɪ'teərɪən] *adj pol.* totalitär. **to·tal-**

i·za·tor ['ˌtəlaɪzeɪtə] s *Pferdesport*: Totalisator *m*.

tote [təʊt] s *Pferdesport*: F Toto *n*, *m* (*Totalisator*).

tote bag [təʊt] s *bsd. Am.* Einkaufstasche *f*.

to·tem ['təʊtəm] s Totem *n*. **~ pole** s Totempfahl *m*.

tot·ter ['tɒtə] v/i (sch)wanken. **'tot·ter·y** adj wack(e)lig.

touch [tʌtʃ] **I** s **1.** Tastempfindung *f*: *be soft to the ~* sich weich anfühlen; → *sense* 1. **2.** Berührung *f*, *♪ etc* Anschlag *m*: *at the ~ of a button* auf Knopfdruck. **3.** *be in ~ with s.o.* mit j-m in Verbindung stehen; *get in ~ with s.o.* sich mit j-m in Verbindung setzen; *keep in ~ with s.o.* mit j-m in Verbindung bleiben; *lose ~* den Kontakt verlieren (*with s.o.* zu j-m). **4.** (*Pinsel etc*)Strich *m*: *put the finishing ~es to* letzte Hand legen an (*acc*). **5.** *fig.* Note *f*: *a personal ~*. **6.** Spur *f* (*Salz etc*); *fig.* Anflug *m* (*von Ironie etc*): *a ~ of flu* e-e leichte Grippe. **7.** *in*(*to*) *~* (*Fußball*) im (ins) Aus. **II** v/t **8.** berühren; anfassen: *~ wood!* toi, toi, toi!; → *nerve* 1. **9.** Alkohol, Essen etc anrühren. **10.** *fig.* herankommen an (*acc*). **11.** *fig.* rühren, bewegen. **12.** *fig.* berühren, betreffen. **13.** F *j-n* anpumpen (*for* um). **III** v/i **14.** sich berühren. **15.** *~ on* Thema etc berühren, streifen.

Verbindungen mit Adverbien:

touch| down v/i ✈ aufsetzen. **~ off** v/t *Explosion, Krise etc* auslösen. **~ up** v/t **1.** ausbessern; *phot.* retuschieren. **2.** Br. F *j-n* befummeln, betatschen.

touch|-and-'go adj kritisch (*Situation etc*): *it was ~ whether* es stand auf des Messers Schneide, ob. **'~-down** s ✈ Aufsetzen *n*.

tou·ché ['tu:ʃeɪ] int eins zu null für dich!

touched [tʌtʃt] adj **1.** gerührt, bewegt. **2.** *be ~* F e-n Schlag haben. **'touch·ing** adj rührend, bewegend.

'touch|·line s *Fußball*: Seitenlinie *f*. **'~·stone** s Prüfstein *m* (*of* für). **'~·type** v/i blindschreiben.

touch·y ['tʌtʃɪ] adj □ **1.** empfindlich, reizbar. **2.** heikel (*Thema*).

tough [tʌf] adj **1.** zäh (*Fleisch etc*): (*as*) *~ as leather* zäh wie Leder. **2.** widerstandsfähig (*Material etc*), (*Per-*

son a.) zäh. **3.** *fig.* hart (*Haltung etc*): *get ~ with* hart vorgehen gegen. **4.** *fig.* hart (*Konkurrenz etc*), (*Problem, Verhandlungen etc a.*) schwierig. **'tough·en I** v/t a. **~ up** j-n hart od. zäh machen. **II** v/i a. **~ up** hart od. zäh werden.

tour [tʊə] **I** s **1.** Tour *f* (*of* durch): a) (*Rund*)Reise *f*, (-)Fahrt *f*: **~ operator** Reiseveranstalter *m*, b) Ausflug *m*, Wanderung *f*. **2.** Rundgang *m* (*of* durch): *take s.o. on a ~ of* j-n herumführen in (*dat*); → *conduct* 3, *guided* 1, *sightseeing*. **3.** *thea. etc* Tournee *f* (*a. Sport*), Gastspielreise *f* (*of* durch): *be on ~* auf Tournee sein (*in* in dat). **II** v/t **4.** bereisen, reisen durch. **5.** *thea. etc* e-e Tournee (*a. Sport*) od. Gastspielreise machen durch: *be ~ing Germany* auf Deutschlandtournee sein. **III** v/i **6.** ~ (*a*)*round* → 4. **7.** *thea. etc* e-e Tournee (*a. Sport*) od. Gastspielreise machen, auf Tournee sein. **'tour·ism** s Tourismus *m*, Fremdenverkehr *m*. **'tour·ist I** s Tourist(in). **II** adj Touristen...: **~ class** ✈, ⚓ Touristenklasse *f*; **~ season** Reisesaison *f*, -zeit *f*; **~ trade** Fremdenverkehrsgewerbe *n*.

tour·na·ment ['tɔːnəmənt] s Turnier *n*.

tou·sled ['taʊzld] adj zerzaust (*Haar*).

tout [taʊt] **I** v/t **1.** (aufdringlich) Reklame machen für. **2.** anpreisen (*as* als). **II** v/i **3.** ~ *for business* Kunden werben. **III** s **4.** Br. (*Karten*)Schwarzhändler(in).

tow [təʊ] **I** v/t Boot etc schleppen, Auto etc a. abschleppen: **~ away** falsch geparktes Fahrzeug abschleppen. **II** s: *give s.o. a ~* j-n abschleppen; *take in ~* Auto etc abschleppen, Boot etc ins Schlepptau nehmen; *with his children in ~* F mit s-n Kindern im Schlepptau.

to·ward *bsd. Am.*, **to·wards** *bsd. Br.* [tə'wɔːd(z)] prp **1.** *Richtung*: auf (*acc*) ... zu, (in) Richtung, zu: → *face* 13, *etc.* **2.** *zeitlich*: gegen: **~ the end of** gegen Ende (*gen*). **3.** *fig.* gegenüber: → *attitude* 2, *etc.* **4.** *fig.* auf (*acc*) ... hin: *they gave me s.th. ~ it* sie zahlten mir et. dazu.

tow·el ['taʊəl] **I** s Handtuch *n*, (*Bade etc*)Tuch *n*: *throw in the ~* (*Boxen*) das Handtuch werfen (*a. fig.*); → *sanitary* 1. **II** v/t pret u. pp **-eled**, bsd. Br. **-elled** a. **~ down** (mit e-m Handtuch) abtrocknen *od.* abreiben. **~ rail** *s* Handtuchhalter *m.*

tow·er ['tauə] **I** *s* Turm *m:* **~ block** *Br.* Hochhaus *n.* **II** *v/i:* **~ above** (*od.* **over**) überragen (*a. fig.*). **'tow·er·ing** *adj* **1.** turmhoch. **2.** *fig.* überragend. **3.** *be in a* **~ rage** vor Wut rasen.

town [taun] *s* (Klein)Stadt *f:* **go to** (**the**) **~** in die Stadt fahren *od.* gehen; **be** (**out**) **on the ~** F e-n draufmachen; → **paint** 2. **~ cen·tre** *s Br.* Innenstadt *f*, City *f.* **~ fa·thers** *s pl* Stadtväter *pl.* **~ hall** *s* Rathaus *n.* **~ plan·ning** *s* Stadtplanung *f.*

towns·folk ['taunzfəuk] → **townspeople.**

town·ship ['taunʃıp] *s Am.* (Stadt)Gemeinde *f*; (Kreis)Bezirk *m.*

towns·peo·ple ['taunz,pi:pl] *s pl* Städter *pl*, Stadtbevölkerung *f.*

'tow·rope *s mot.* Abschleppseil *n.*

tox·ic ['tɒksık] *adj* (**~ally**) toxisch, giftig, Gift...

tox·in ['tɒksın] *s biol.* Toxin *n.*

toy [tɔı] **I** *s* **1.** Spielzeug *n:* **~s** *pl* Spielsachen *pl*, -zeug *n*, ✝ -waren *pl.* **II** *v/i* **2. ~ with** spielen mit (*a. fig.*). **III** *adj* **3.** Spielzeug... **4.** *zo.* Zwerg... (*Hund*). **~ shop** *s* Spielwarengeschäft *n*, -handlung *f.*

trace¹ [treıs] **I** *s* **1.** Spur *f* (*a. fig.*): **without** (**a**) **~** spurlos; **lose all ~ of** *s.o.* j-n aus den Augen verlieren. **II** *v/t* **2.** j-n, *et.* ausfindig machen, aufspüren, *et.* finden: **he was ~d to** s-e Spur führte nach. **3.** *a.* **~ back** zurückverfolgen (**to** bis zu): **~ s.th. to** *et.* zurückführen auf (*acc*), *et.* herleiten von (*acc*). **4.** (durch)pausen.

trace² [~] *s* Zugleine *f:* **kick over the ~s** *fig.* über die Stränge schlagen.

trace el·e·ment *s* Spurenelement *n.*

tra·che·a [trə'ki:ə] *pl* **-ae** [~i:] *s anat.* Luftröhre *f.*

trac·ing ['treısıŋ] *s* Pause *f.* **~ pa·per** *s* Pauspapier *n.*

track [træk] **I** *s* **1.** Spur *f* (*a. e-s Tonbands etc u. fig.*), *hunt. a.* Fährte *f:* **be** (**hot**) **on** *s.o.'s* **~** j-m (dicht) auf der Spur sein; **be on the wrong ~** auf der falschen Spur *od.* dem Holzweg sein; **keep ~ of** sich auf dem laufenden halten über (*acc*); **lose ~ of** den Überblick verlieren über (*acc*). **2.** Pfad *m*, Weg *m.* **3.** 🚂

Gleis *n*, Geleise *n:* **jump the ~s** aus den Schienen springen, entgleisen. **4.** *Sport:* (*Lauf-*, *Radrenn*)Bahn *f*, (*Renn*)Strecke *f.* **5.** ⚙ Raupe *f*, Gleis-, Raupenkette *f.* **6.** Nummer *f* (*auf e-r Langspielplatte etc*). **II** *v/t* **7.** verfolgen: **~ down** aufspüren; aufstöbern, -treiben. **~-end 'field** *adj Am.* Leichtathletik...: **~ sports** *pl* Leichtathletik *f.*

tracked [trækt] *adj:* **~ vehicle** Gleisketten-, Raupenfahrzeug *n.*

track·er dog ['trækə] *s* Spür-, Suchhund *m.*

track e·vents *s pl Leichtathletik:* Laufdisziplinen *pl.*

track·ing sta·tion ['trækıŋ] *s Raumfahrt:* Bodenstation *f.*

track| **rec·ord** *s* **1.** *Sport:* Bahnrekord *m.* **2. have a good ~** *fig.* einiges vorzuweisen haben. **'~-suit** *s* Trainingsanzug *m.*

tract¹ [trækt] *s* **1.** Fläche *f*, Gebiet *n.* **2.** *anat.* (*Verdauungs*)Trakt *m*, (*Atem*-)Wege *pl.*

tract² [~] *s* Traktat *m*, *n*, kurze Abhandlung.

trac·ta·ble ['træktəbl] *adj* ☐ folg-, fügsam.

trac·tion ['trækʃn] *s* **1.** Ziehen *n.* **2.** ⚙ Antrieb *m.* **3.** *mot.* Bodenhaftung *f.* **4.** **his leg is in ~** *₰* sein Bein ist im Streckverband. **~ en·gine** *s* Zugmaschine *f.*

trac·tor ['træktə] *s* Traktor *m*, Trecker *m*, Zugmaschine *f.*

trade [treıd] **I** *s* **1.** Handel *m* (**in** *et.*). **2.** Branche *f*, Gewerbe *n:* **be in the tourist ~** im Fremdenverkehrsgewerbe (tätig) sein. **3. do good ~** gute Geschäfte machen. **4.** (*bsd.* Handwerks)Beruf *m:* **by ~** von Beruf. **II** *v/i* **5.** handeln (**in** mit *et.*), Handel treiben: **~ with** *s.o.* a. mit j-m Geschäfte machen. **6. ~ on** *b.s.* ausnützen, ausnützen. **III** *v/t* **7.** (ein-)tauschen (**for** gegen). **8. ~ in** in Zahlung geben (**for** für). **~ a·gree·ment** *s* Handelsabkommen *n.* **~ mark** *s* **1.** ✝ Warenzeichen *n.* **2.** *fig.* Kennzeichen *n.* **~ name** *s* Markenname *m*, Handelsbezeichnung *f.* **~ price** *s* Großhandelspreis *m.*

trad·er ['treıdə] *s* Händler(in).

trades·man ['treıdzmən] *s* (*irr* **man**) **1.** (Einzel)Händler *m*; Ladeninhaber *m.* **2.** Lieferant *m:* **~'s entrance** Lieferanteneingang *m.*

trade| un·ion s Gewerkschaft f. **~ un-**
-ion·ist s Gewerkschaftler(in).

trad·ing| part·ner s Handelspartner(in).
~ stamp s Rabattmarke f.

tra·di·tion [trə'dɪʃn] s Tradition f: **by**
~ traditionell(erweise). **tra'di·tion·al**
[~ʃənl] adj □ traditionell: **~ly** a. tradi-
tionellerweise; **it is ~ for them to** (inf)
es ist bei ihnen Brauch od. so üblich, daß
sie.

traf·fic ['træfɪk] **I** s **1.** Verkehr m. **2.** (bsd.
illegaler) Handel (**in** mit): **~ in drugs**
Drogenhandel. **II** v/i pret u. pp **-ficked**
3. (bsd. illegal) handeln (**in** mit). **~**
cha·os s Verkehrschaos n. **~ cir·cle** s
Am. Kreisverkehr m. **~ cone** s Pylon(e
f) m, Leitkegel m. **~ is·land** s Verkehrsinsel f. **~ jam** s Verkehrsstauung f,
-stockung f, Stau m.

traf·fick·er ['træfɪkə] s (bsd. illegaler)
Händler (**in** mit): **~ in drugs** Drogenhändler.

traf·fic| light s Br. mst pl Verkehrsampel
f. **~ of·fence** s Verkehrsdelikt n. **~ of·**
fend·er s Verkehrssünder(in). **~ of·**
fense Am. → **traffic offence**. **~ sign** s
Verkehrszeichen n, -schild n. **~ sig·nal**
→ **traffic light**. **~ war·den** s Br. Park-
überwacher m, Politesse f.

trag·e·dy ['trædʒədɪ] s thea. Tragödie f
(a. fig.), Trauerspiel n.

trag·ic ['trædʒɪk] adj (~ally) thea. tragisch (a. fig.): **~ally** a. tragischerweise;
unter tragischen Umständen.

trag·i·com·e·dy [ˌtrædʒɪ'kɒmədɪ] s thea.
Tragikomödie f (a. fig.). **ˌtrag·i'com·ic**
adj (~ally) tragikomisch.

trail [treɪl] **I** v/t **1.** et. nachschleifen lassen: **~ one's feet** schlurfen. **2.** verfolgen. **3.** Sport: zurückliegen hinter (dat)
(**by** um). **II** v/i **4. ~** (**along**) **behind s.o.**
hinter j-m herschleifen. **5.** sich schlep-
pen. **6.** Sport: zurückliegen ([**by**] **2-0**
0:2). **III** s **7.** Spur f (a. fig.), hunt. a.
Fährte f: **~ of blood** Blutspur; **~ of dust**
(**smoke**) Staubwolke f (Rauchfahne f);
be (**hot**) **on s.o.'s ~** j-m (dicht) auf der
Spur sein. **8.** Pfad m, Weg m. **'trail·er** s
1. mot. Anhänger m. **2.** Am. Caravan
m, Wohnwagen m. **3.** Film, TV: Trailer
m, Vorschau f.

train [treɪn] **I** s **1.** 🚂 Zug m: **by ~** mit der
Bahn, mit dem Zug; **on the ~** im Zug; **~**
ferry Eisenbahnfähre f; **~ set** (Spielzeug)Eisenbahn f. **2.** Kolonne f. **3.**
Schleppe f. **4.** fig. Folge f, Kette f (von
Ereignissen etc): **~ of thought** Gedankengang m. **II** v/t **5.** j-n ausbilden (**as**
als, zum), a. Auge, Verstand etc schulen; (Sport) trainieren; Tier abrichten,
dressieren (**to do** zu tun). **6.** Geschütz,
Kamera etc richten (**on** auf acc). **III** v/i
7. ausgebildet werden (**as** als, zum). **8.**
Sport: trainieren (**for** für). **'train·er** s **1.**
Ausbilder(in); Dresseur m, Abrich-
ter(in), Dompteur m, Dompteuse f;
(Sport) Trainer(in). **2.** Br. Turnschuh
m. **'train·ing** s **1.** Ausbildung f, Schulung f; Abrichten n, Dressur f. **2.** Sport:
Training f: **be in ~** im Training stehen,
trainieren; (gut) in Form sein; **be out of**
~ nicht in Form sein. **II** adj **3.** Ausbil-
dungs..., Schulungs... **4.** Sport: Trai-
nings...

traipse [treɪps] v/i F latschen.

trait [treɪt] s (Charakter)Zug m, Eigenschaft f.

trai·tor ['treɪtə] s Verräter m (**to** an
dat).

tra·jec·to·ry [trə'dʒektərɪ] s phys. Flug-
bahn f.

tram [træm] s Br. a) Straßenbahn(wagen
m) f: **by ~** mit der Straßenbahn; **on the**
~ in der Straßenbahn, b) → **tramway**.
'~·car s Br. Straßenbahnwagen m.

tramp [træmp] **I** v/i **1.** sta(m)pfen; trampeln. **II** v/t **2.** sta(m)pfen od. trampeln
durch. **III** s **3.** bsd. Br. Tramp m, Land-
streicher(in). **4.** Wanderung f: **go for a**
~ e-e Wanderung machen. **5.** bsd. Am.
Flittchen n.

tram·ple ['træmpl] **I** v/i trampeln: **~ on**
herumtrampeln auf (dat); fig. j-s Gefühle mit Füßen treten. **II** v/t zertram-
peln: **~ down** niedertrampeln; **be ~d to**
death zu Tode getrampelt werden; →
underfoot.

tram·po·line ['træmpəliːn] s Trampolin n.

'tram·way s Br. Straßenbahn(linie) f.

trance [trɑːns] s Trance f: **go into a ~** in
Trance verfallen.

tran·quil ['træŋkwɪl] adj □ **1.** ruhig,
friedlich. **2.** sorgenfrei. **tran'quil·i·ty** s
Am., **tran'quil·li·ty** s bsd. Br. Ruhe m,
Frieden m. **'tran·quil·ize** v/t Am.,
'tran·quil·lize v/t bsd. Br. j-n beruhigen, Tier a. betäuben. **'tran·quil·(l)iz-**

er s Beruhigungs- *od.* Betäubungsmittel *n.*

trans·act [træn'zækt] *v/t Geschäft* abwickeln, *a. Handel* abschließen. **trans·'ac·tion** s **1.** Abwicklung *f*, Abschluß *m.* **2.** Transaktion *f*, Geschäft *n.*

trans·at·lan·tic [ˌtrænzət'læntik] *adj* transatlantisch, Transatlantik...

tran·scen·den·tal [ˌtrænsen'dentl] *adj:* ~ **meditation** transzendentale Meditation.

trans·con·ti·nen·tal [ˌtrænzˌkɒntɪ'nentl] *adj* transkontinental.

tran·scribe [træn'skraɪb] *v/t* **1.** abschreiben, kopieren. **2.** *Stenogramm etc* übertragen (*into* in *acc*). **3.** ♪ transkribieren, umschreiben (*for* für). **4.** ~ **onto** → *transfer* I.

tran·script ['trænskrɪpt] s Abschrift *f*, Kopie *f.* **tran·scrip·tion** [~'skrɪpʃn] s **1.** Abschreiben *n*, Kopieren *n.* **2.** Übertragen *n.* **3.** ♪ Transkription *f*, Umschreibung *f.* **4.** → *transcript.* **5.** → *phonetic* I.

tran·sept ['trænsept] s △ Querschiff *n.*

trans·fer I *v/t* [træns'fɜː] **1.** (**to**) *Betrieb etc* verlegen (nach); *j-n* versetzen (nach); (*Sport*) *Spieler* transferieren (zu); abgeben (an *acc*); *Geld* überweisen (an *j-n*, *ein Konto*). **2.** ⚖ *Eigentum, Recht* übertragen (**to** auf *acc*). **3.** ~ **to** *Bandaufnahme etc* überspielen auf (*acc*). **4.** Verlegung *f*/ Versetzung *f*; (*Sport*) Transfer *m*, Wechsel *m*; Überweisung *f*: ~ **fee** Transfersumme *f*, Ablöse(summe) *f.* **7.** ⚖ Übertragung *f.* **8.** Umsteigen *n*; *bsd. Am.* Umsteige(fahr)karte *f.* **9.** *bsd. Br.* Abziehbild *n.* **trans·'fer·a·ble** *adj* übertragbar.

trans·fig·ure [træns'fɪɡə] *v/t* verklären.

trans·fix [træns'fɪks] *v/t* **1.** durchstechen, -bohren (*with* mit). **2.** *stand* ~**ed to the spot** wie angewurzelt dastehen.

trans·form [træns'fɔːm] *v/t et.* umwandeln, *a. j-n* verwandeln (**into** in *acc*). **trans·for·ma·tion** [~fə'meɪʃn] s Um-, Verwandlung *f.* **trans·form·er** [~'fɔːmə] s ≠ Transformator *m.*

trans·fu·sion [træns'fjuːʒn] s ⚕ Bluttransfusion *f*, -übertragung *f.*

trans·gress [træns'ɡres] I *v/t* verletzen,

verstoßen gegen. II *v/i* sündigen (**against** gegen). **trans·'gres·sion** s (**of**) Verletzung *f* (*gen*), Verstoß *m* (gegen); Sünde *f.*

tran·si·ent ['trænzɪənt] *adj* □ flüchtig, vergänglich.

tran·sis·tor [træn'sɪstə] s ≠ Transistor *m*: ~ (**radio**) Transistorradio *n.* **tran·'sis·tor·ize** *v/t* transistor(is)ieren.

trans·it ['trænsɪt] s **1.** Durchfahrt *f.* **2.** ✈ Transport *m*: **in** ~ unterwegs, auf dem Transport. ~ **camp** s Durchgangslager *n.*

tran·si·tion [træn'sɪʒn] s Übergang *m* (**from ... to** von ... zu): **period of** ~ Übergangsperiode *f*, -zeit *f.* **tran·si·tion·al** [~ʒənl] *adj* Übergangs...

tran·si·tive ['trænsɪtɪv] *adj* □ *ling.* transitiv.

tran·si·to·ry ['trænsɪtərɪ] → *transient.*

trans·lat·a·ble [træns'leɪtəbl] *adj* übersetzbar. **trans·late** I *v/t* **1.** übersetzen (**from English into German** aus dem Englischen ins Deutsche). **2.** ~ **into action** *fig.* in die Tat umsetzen. II *v/i* **3.** sich *gut etc* übersetzen lassen. **trans·'la·tion** s Übersetzung *f.* **trans·'la·tor** s Übersetzer(in).

trans·lu·cent [trænz'luːsnt] *adj* □ lichtdurchlässig: ~ **glass** Milchglas *n.*

trans·mi·gra·tion [ˌtrænzmaɪ'ɡreɪʃn] s Seelenwanderung *f.*

trans·mis·sion [trænz'mɪʃn] s **1.** Übertragung *f* (*e-r Krankheit*). **2.** Rundfunk, TV: Sendung *f*, *pl a.* Programm *n.* **3.** ⚙ mot. Getriebe *n.*

trans·mit [trænz'mɪt] I *v/t* **1.** *Krankheit* übertragen. **2.** *Signale* (aus)senden; (*Rundfunk, TV*) Programm senden. **3.** *phys.* Wärme etc leiten; Licht etc durchlassen. II *v/i* **4.** Rundfunk, TV: senden. **trans·'mit·ter** s Sender *m.*

trans·mu·ta·tion [ˌtrænzmjuː'teɪʃn] s Um-, Verwandlung *f.* **trans·mute** [~'mjuːt] *v/t* um-, verwandeln (**into** in *acc*).

trans·par·en·cy [træns'pærənsɪ] s **1.** Durchsichtigkeit *f* (*a. fig.*). **2.** *fig.* Durchschaubarkeit *f.* **3.** Dia(positiv) *n.* **trans·'par·ent** *adj* □ **1.** durchsichtig. **2.** *fig.* durchsichtig, durchschaubar; offenkundig.

tran·spi·ra·tion [ˌtrænspə'reɪʃn] s Transpiration *f* (*a.* ⚘), Schweißabsonderung

f. **tran·spire** [~'spaɪə] *v/i* **1.** *physiol.*
transpirieren (*a.* ♀), schwitzen. **2.** *it ~d
that* es sickerte durch *od.* wurde bekannt, daß. **3.** F passieren.

trans·plant I *v/t* [træns'plɑ:nt] **1.** ♣
transplantieren, verpflanzen. **2.** *Pflanze* um-, verpflanzen. **3.** *j-n* umsiedeln,
Betrieb etc verlegen (*to* nach). **II** *s*
['trænsplɑ:nt] **4.** ♣ Transplantation *f*,
Verpflanzung *f*. **5.** ♣ Transplantat *n*.
,**trans·plan'ta·tion** *s* **1.** → **transplant**
4. **2.** Um-, Verpflanzung *f*.

trans·port I *v/t* [træn'spɔ:t] **1.** Waren,
Truppen transportieren, *a. Personen*
befördern. **II** *s* ['trænspɔ:t] **2.** Transport *m*, Beförderung *f*: *~ café Br.* Fernfahrerlokal *n*. **3.** Beförderungs-, Verkehrsmittel *n od. pl.* **4.** ✗ Transportflugzeug *n*, (*Truppen*)Transporter *m*.
,**trans·por'ta·tion** *bsd. Am.* → **transport** 2. **trans'port·er** *s mot.* (*Auto-etc*)Transporter *m*.

trans·verse ['trænzvɜːs] *adj* Quer...
,**trans'verse·ly** *adv* quer.

trans·ves·tite [trænz'vestaɪt] *s* Transvestit *m*.

trap [træp] **I** *s* **1.** Falle *f* (*a. fig.*): *set a ~*
e-e Falle aufstellen; *set a ~ for s.o.* j-m
e-e Falle stellen; *fall into s.o.'s ~* j-m in
die Falle gehen. **2.** *shut one's ~, keep
one's ~ shut sl.* die Schnauze halten. **II**
v/t **3.** (in *od.* mit e-r Falle) fangen. **4.** *be
~ped* eingeschlossen sein (*Bergleute
etc*). **5.** *fig.* in e-e Falle locken: *~ s.o.
into doing s.th.* j-n dazu bringen, et. zu
tun. **6.** *Sport: Ball* stoppen. '**~door** *s*
Falltür *f*.

tra·peze [trə'pi:z] *s Artistik:* Trapez *n*: *~
artist* Trapezkünstler(in). **tra'pe·zi·um**
[~zjəm] *pl* **-zi·ums, -zi·a** [~zjə] *s* ♣ *bsd.
Br.* Trapez *n*; *bsd. Am.* Trapezoid *n*.
trap·e·zoid ['træpɪzɔɪd] *s* ♣ *bsd. Br.*
Trapezoid *n*; *bsd. Am.* Trapez *n*.

trap·per ['træpə] *s* Trapper *m*, Fallensteller *m*.

trap·pings ['træpɪŋz] *s pl* **1.** Rangabzeichen *pl.* **2.** *fig.* Drum u. Dran
n.

trash [træʃ] *s* **1.** *Am.* Abfall *m*, Müll *m*: *~
can* Abfall-, Mülleimer *m*; Abfall-,
Mülltonne *f*. **2.** Schund *m*. **3.** Quatsch
m, Unsinn *m*. **4.** *bsd. Am.* Gesindel *n*.
'**trash·y** *adj* Schund...

trau·ma ['trɔ:mə] *s psych.* Trauma *n*.

trau·mat·ic [~'mætɪk] *adj* (*~ally*) traumatisch.

trav·el ['trævl] **I** *v/i pret u. pp* **-eled,** *bsd.
Br.* **-elled 1.** reisen: → **light**² 4. **2.** ♣
reisen (*in* in e-r *Ware*). **3.** fahren; sich
verbreiten (*Neuigkeit etc*); ⊕ *etc* sich
bewegen; *phys.* sich fortpflanzen. **4.** *be
really ~ (l)ing* F e-n ganz schönen Zahn
draufhaben. **II** *v/t* **5.** bereisen; *Strecke*
zurücklegen, fahren. **III** *s* **6.** Reisen *n*.
7. *pl* (*bsd.* Auslands)Reisen *pl.* *~* **a·gen·cy** *s* Reisebüro *n.* *~* **a·gent** *s* Reisebüroinhaber(in) *od.* -kaufmann *m*,
-kauffrau *f*; *weitS., a.* *~'s* Reisebüro
n. *~* **bu·reau** *s* (*a. irr* **bureau**) Reisebüro *n*.

trav·el·er *s Am.* → **traveller**: *~'s check*
Reise-, Travellerscheck *m*. **trav·el·ing**
Am. → **travelling**.

trav·el·ler ['trævlə] *s bsd. Br.* **1.** Reisende
m, f: *~'s cheque Br.* Reise-, Travellerscheck *m*. **2.** ♣ (Handels)Vertreter *m*
(*in* für). '**trav·el·ling** *adj bsd. Br.* **1.**
Reise...: *~* (*alarm*) *clock* Reisewecker
m; *~ salesman* → **traveller** 2. **2.** Wander...: *~ circus.*

trav·e·log *s Am.*, **trav·e·logue** *s*
['trævəlɒg] Reisebericht *m* (*Vortrag*),
-film *m*.

'**trav·el|-sick** *adj* reisekrank. *~* **sick·ness** *s* Reisekrankheit *f*.

trav·erse ['trævəs] *v/t* durch-, überqueren.

trav·es·ty ['trævəstɪ] *s* Zerrbild *n*: *a ~ of
justice* ein Hohn auf die Gerechtigkeit.

trav·o·la·tor ['trævəleɪtə] *s* Rollsteig *m*.

trawl·er ['trɔ:lə] *s* ♣ Trawler *m*.

tray [treɪ] *s* **1.** Tablett *n*. **2.** Ablagekorb *m*.

treach·er·ous ['tretʃərəs] *adj* □ **1.** verräterisch. **2.** *fig.* tückisch (*Strömung etc*).
'**treach·er·y** *s* Verrat *m*.

trea·cle ['tri:kl] *s bsd. Br.* Sirup *m*.
'**trea·cly** *adj* **1.** sirupartig. **2.** *fig.* süßlich.

tread [tred] **I** *v/i* (*irr*) **1.** treten (*on* auf
acc; *in acc*): *~ carefully* vorsichtig auftreten; *fig.* behutsam vorgehen; →
corn², toe 1. **II** *v/t* (*irr*) **2.** *Pfad, Wasser*
treten: *~ in(to)* eintreten (in *acc*). **III** *s* **3.**
Gang *m*; Schritt(e *pl*) *m*. **4.** *mot.* Profil *n*
(*e-s Reifens*). **5.** ⊕ *~mill s hist.* Tretmühle *f*
(*a. fig.*).

trea·son ['tri:zn] *s* Landesverrat *m*.

treas·ure ['treʒə] **I** s Schatz m, (Person F a.) Juwel n: **~ hunt** Schatzsuche f. **II** v/t et. zu schätzen wissen; j·s Andenken in Ehren halten. **'treas·ur·er** s Schatzmeister(in). **'Treas·ur·y** s pol. Finanzministerium n.

treat [tri:t] **I** v/t **1.** j·n behandeln (**like** wie); et. behandeln, umgehen mit: → **dirt. 2.** et. ansehen, betrachten (**as** als). **3.** ♣ j·n behandeln (**for** gegen): **be ~ed for** in ärztlicher Behandlung stehen wegen. **4.** ♣, ☺ et. behandeln (**with** mit; **against** gegen). **5.** j·n einladen (**to** zu): **~ s.o. to s.th.** a. j·m et. spendieren; **~ o.s. to s.th.** sich et. leisten od. gönnen. **II** v/i **6. ~ of** handeln von, behandeln. **III** s **7.** (besondere) Freude, (besondere) Überraschung.

trea·tise ['~tɪz] s (wissenschaftliche) Abhandlung (**on** über acc). **'treat·ment** s allg. Behandlung f. **'trea·ty** s pol. Vertrag m: **by ~** vertraglich.

tre·ble ['trebl] **I** adj □ dreifach. **II** v/t u. v/i (sich) verdreifachen.

tree [tri:] s Baum m: **in a ~** auf e·m Baum; → **bark²** I. **'tree·less** adj baumlos.

'tree-line s Baumgrenze f. **~ trunk** s Baumstamm m.

tre·foil ['trefɔɪl] s **1.** ♣ Klee m. **2.** △ Dreipaß m.

trek [trek] **I** v/i marschieren. **II** s lange, gefährliche Fußreise.

trel·lis ['trelɪs] s Spalier n (für Pflanzen etc).

trem·ble ['trembl] **I** v/i zittern (**with** vor dat): **~ at the thought** (od. **to think**) bei dem Gedanken zittern; **~ for** zittern od. bangen um. **II** s Zittern n.

tre·men·dous [trɪ'mendəs] adj □ **1.** gewaltig. **2.** F klasse, toll.

trem·or ['tremə] s **1.** Zittern n: → **earth tremor. 2.** Schauder m.

trench [trentʃ] s Graben m, ⚔ Schützengraben m. **~ coat** s Trenchcoat m.

trend [trend] s **1.** Trend m, Tendenz f (**toward[s]** zu). **2.** Mode f. **'~set·ter** s Trendsetter m (j-d, der e-n neuen Trend in Gang setzt od. et. in Mode bringt). **trend·y** ['trendɪ] adj □ F modern, modisch: **be ~** als schick gelten, in sein; **~ disco** In-Disko f.

tres·pass ['trespəs] **I** v/i: **~ on** a) Grundstück etc unbefugt betreten: **no ~ing**

Betreten verboten!, b) j-s Zeit etc über Gebühr in Anspruch nehmen. **II** s unbefugtes Betreten. **'tres·pass·er** s: **~s will be prosecuted** Betreten bei Strafe verboten!

tri·al ['traɪəl] s **1.** ⚖ Prozeß m, (Gerichts)Verhandlung f, (-)Verfahren n: **~ by jury** Schwurgerichtsverfahren; **be on** (od. **stand**) **~** vor Gericht stehen (**for** wegen). **2.** Erprobung f, Probe f, Prüfung f, Test m: **by ~ and error** durch Ausprobieren; **on ~** auf od. zur Probe; **be on ~** erprobt od. getestet werden; **he's still on ~** er ist noch in der Probezeit. **3. be a ~ to** j-m Ärger od. Sorgen machen. **~ mar·riage** s Ehe f auf Probe. **~ pe·ri·od** s Probezeit f. **~ run** s ☺ Probelauf m; mot. Probefahrt f: **give a car a ~** e-n Wagen probefahren.

tri·an·gle ['traɪæŋgl] s **1.** ♣ Dreieck n. **2.** ♪ Triangel m. **3.** Am. → **set square**. **tri·an·gu·lar** [~'æŋgʊlə] adj □ dreieckig.

trib·al ['traɪbl] adj Stammes... **tribe** [traɪb] s Stamm m.

'tribes·man ['traɪbzmən] s (irr **man**) Stammesangehörige m. **'~·wom·an** s (irr **woman**) Stammesangehörige f.

tri·bu·nal [traɪ'bju:nl] s ⚖ Gericht n. **trib·u·tar·y** ['trɪbjʊtərɪ] s Nebenfluß m.

trib·ute ['trɪbju:t] s: **be a ~ to** j-m Ehre machen; **pay ~ to** j-m Anerkennung zollen.

trice [traɪs] s: **in a ~** F im Nu, im Handumdrehen.

tri·chi·na [trɪ'kaɪnə] pl **-nae** [~ni:] s zo. Trichine f.

trick [trɪk] **I** s **1.** Trick m (a. b.s.), (Karten- etc)Kunststück n: **by a ~** mit e-m Trick; **how's ~s?** F wie geht's?; **dirty ~** Gemeinheit f. **2.** Streich m: **play a ~ on s.o.** j-m e-n Streich spielen. **3. have a ~ of doing s.th.** die (merkwürdige) Angewohnheit od. die Eigenart haben, et. zu tun. **4.** Kartenspiel: Stich m: **take** (od. **win**) **a ~** e-n Stich machen. **II** adj **5.** Trick...: **~ question** Fangfrage f. **III** v/t **6.** j-n reinlegen: **~ s.o. into doing s.th.** j-n mit e-m Trick dazu bringen, et. zu tun. **'trick·er·y** s Tricks pl.

trick·le ['trɪkl] v/i tröpfeln; rieseln.

trick·ster ['trɪkstə] s Betrüger(in), Schwindler(in). **'trick·y** adj □ **1.**

schwierig, (*Problem etc a.*) heikel. **2.** durchtrieben, raffiniert.

tri·cy·cle ['traɪsɪkl] *s* Dreirad *n*.

tri·fle ['traɪfl] **I** *s* **1.** Kleinigkeit *f*; Lappalie *f*: **a ~** ein bißchen, etwas. **2.** a) *bsd. Br.* Trifle *n* (*Biskuitdessert*), b) *Am.* Obstdessert mit Schlagsahne. **II** *v/i* **3. ~ with** *fig.* spielen mit: **he is not to be ~d with** er läßt nicht mit sich spaßen. **'tri·fling** *adj* unbedeutend, geringfügig.

trig·ger ['trɪgə] **I** *s* Abzug *m* (*am Gewehr etc*): **pull the ~** abdrücken. **II** *v/t a.* **~ off** *fig.* auslösen. **'~·hap·py** *adj* schießwütig.

trig·o·nom·e·try [ˌtrɪgə'nɒmətrɪ] *s* A Trigonometrie *f*.

trike [traɪk] *s* F Dreirad *n*.

tril·o·gy ['trɪlədʒɪ] *s* Trilogie *f*.

trim [trɪm] **I** *v/t* **1.** Hecke *etc* stutzen, beschneiden, sich *den Bart etc* stutzen: **~ off** abschneiden. **2.** *Kleidungsstück* besetzen (**with** mit): **~med with fur** pelzbesetzt, mit Pelzbesatz. **II** *s* **3.** give *s.th.* **a ~ →** 1. **4. be in good ~** F gut in Schuß sein (*Auto etc*), (*Person a.*) gut in Form sein. **III** *adj* **5.** gepflegt. **'trim·ming** *s* **1.** *a. fig.* Besatz *m*. **2.** *pl* Zubehör *n*; Extras *pl*: **with all the ~s** *gastr.* mit den üblichen Beilagen. **3.** *pl* Abfälle *pl*.

trin·ket ['trɪŋkɪt] *s* (*bsd.* billiges) Schmuckstück.

tri·o ['triːəʊ] *pl* **-os** *s* Trio *n*, ♪ *a.* Terzett *n*.

trip [trɪp] **I** *v/i* **1.** stolpern (**over** über *acc*). **2.** sich vertun. **II** *v/t* **3.** *a.* **~ up** *j-m* ein Bein stellen (*a. fig.*). **III** *s* **4.** Reise *f*; Ausflug *m*, Trip *m*: **go on a bus ~** e-n Busausflug machen. **5.** *sl.* Trip *m* (*Drogenrausch*): **be on a ~** auf dem Trip sein.

tripe [traɪp] *s* **1.** *gastr.* Kaldaunen *pl*, Kutteln *pl*. **2.** F Quatsch *m*, Mist *m*.

tri·ple ['trɪpl] **I** *adj* □ dreifach: **~ jump** (*Leichtathletik*) Dreisprung *m*; **~ jumper** Dreispringer *m*. **II** *v/t u. v/i* (sich) verdreifachen.

tri·plet ['trɪplɪt] *s* Drilling *m*.

trip·li·cate ['trɪplɪkət] *s*: **in ~** in dreifacher Ausfertigung.

tri·pod ['traɪpɒd] *s phot.* Stativ *n*.

trip·per ['trɪpə] *s* (*bsd. Tages*)Ausflügler(in).

'trip·wire *s* Stolperdraht *m*.

trite [traɪt] *adj* □ abgedroschen; banal.

tri·umph ['traɪəmf] **I** *s* Triumph *m* (**over** über *acc*): **in ~** im Triumph, triumphierend. **II** *v/i* triumphieren (**over** über *acc*). **tri·um·phal** [~'ʌmfl] *adj* Triumph...: **~ arch** Triumphbogen *m*; **~ procession** Triumphzug *m*. **tri'um·phant** *adj* □ triumphierend.

triv·i·al ['trɪvɪəl] *adj* □ **1.** trivial, alltäglich, gewöhnlich. **2.** unbedeutend, belanglos. **triv·i·al·i·ty** [ˌ~'ælətɪ] *s* **1.** Trivialität *f*. **2.** Belanglosigkeit *f*.

trod [trɒd] *pret von* tread. **'trod·den** *pp von* tread.

trol·ley ['trɒlɪ] *s Br.* Einkaufs-, Gepäckwagen *m*; Kofferkuli *m*; (*Tee- etc*)Wagen *m*.

trom·bone [trɒm'bəʊn] *s* ♪ Posaune *f*. **trom'bon·ist** *s* Posaunist *m*.

troop [truːp] **I** *s* **1.** Schar *f*. **2.** *pl* ✕ Truppen *pl*. **II** *v/i* **3.** strömen. **~ car·ri·er** *s* ✗, ⚓ Truppentransporter *m*.

troop·er ['truːpə] *s* **1.** ✕ Kavallerist *m*; Panzerjäger *m*: **swear like a ~** wie ein Landsknecht fluchen. **2.** *Am.* Polizist *m* (*e-s Bundesstaats*).

troop trans·port → troop carrier.

tro·phy ['trəʊfɪ] *s* Trophäe *f*.

trop·ic ['trɒpɪk] *s* **1.** *ast., geogr.* Wendekreis *m*. **2.** *pl* Tropen *pl*. **'trop·i·cal** *adj* □ tropisch, Tropen...

trot [trɒt] **I** *s* **1.** Trab *m*: **on the ~** hintereinander; **be on the ~** F auf Trab sein; **have the ~s** F Dünnpfiff haben. **II** *v/i* **2.** traben: **~ along** (*od. off*) F abloszichen. **III** *v/t* **3.** *Pferd* traben lassen. **4. ~ out** F auftischen, von sich geben. **'trot·ter** *s* Traber *m* (*Pferd*). **'trot·ting** *adj*: **~ race** Trabrennen *n*.

trou·ble ['trʌbl] **I** *v/t* **1.** *j-n* beunruhigen. **2.** *j-m* Mühe *od.* Umstände machen; *j-n* bemühen (**for** um), bitten (**for** um; **to do** zu tun). **3. be ~d by** geplagt werden von, leiden an (*dat*). **4. fish in ~d waters** *fig.* im trüben fischen. **II** *v/i* **5.** sich bemühen (**to do** zu tun), sich Umstände machen (**about** wegen). **III** *s* **6.** Schwierigkeit *f*, Problem *n*: **be in ~** in Schwierigkeiten sein; **get into ~** a) *a.* **run into ~** in Schwierigkeiten geraten, b) Schwierigkeiten *od.* Ärger bekommen (**with** mit), c) *j-n* in Schwierigkeiten bringen; **have ~ with** Schwierigkeiten *od.* Ärger haben mit; **have ~ doing s.th.** Schwierigkeiten haben, et. zu tun. **7.** Mühe *f*:

put s.o. to ~ j-m Mühe *od.* Umstände machen; *take the* ~ *to do s.th.* sich die Mühe machen, et. zu tun. **8.** *a. pl pol.* Unruhen *pl.* **9.** 🐟 Leiden *n*, Beschwerden *pl.* '~**,mak·er** *s* Unruhestifter(in). '~**,shoot·er** *s* Friedensstifter(in).

trou·ble·some ['trʌblsəm] *adj* □ lästig.

trou·ble spot *s pol.* Unruheherd *m*.

trough [trɒf] *s* **1.** Trog *m*. **2.** Wellental *n*.

trounce [traʊns] *v/t Sport:* haushoch besiegen.

troupe [truːp] *s thea. etc* Truppe *f*.

trou·ser ['traʊzə] *I s pl, a.* **pair of** ~**s** Hose *f*: → *wear* 3. **II** *adj* Hosen...: ~ *suit* Hosenanzug *m*.

trous·seau ['truːsəʊ] *pl* **-seaux** ['~səʊz], **-seaus** *s* Aussteuer *f*.

trout [traʊt] *pl* **trouts,** *bsd. coll.* **trout** *s ichth.* Forelle *f*.

trow·el ['traʊəl] *s* (Maurer)Kelle *f*: *lay it on with a* ~ F dick auftragen.

troy (weight) [trɔɪ] *s* Troygewicht *n (für Edelmetalle u. -steine).*

tru·ant ['truːənt] *s* (Schul)Schwänzer(in): *play* ~ (die Schule) schwänzen.

truce [truːs] *s* ✠ Waffenstillstand *m (a. fig.).*

truck¹ [trʌk] **I** *s* **1.** *mot.* Lastwagen *m*; Fernlaster *m*. **2.** 🚃 *Br.* (offener) Güterwagen *m*. **II** *v/t* **3.** *bsd. Am.* auf *od.* mit Lastwagen transportieren.

truck² [~] *s:* **have no** ~ **with** nichts zu tun haben wollen mit.

truck driv·er *s* Lastwagenfahrer *m*; Fernfahrer *m*.

truck·er ['trʌkə] *Am.* → *truck driver.*

truck|·man ['trʌkmən] *s (irr man) Am.* → *truck driver.* ~ **stop** *s Am.* Fernfahrerlokal *n*.

truc·u·lent ['trʌkjʊlənt] *adj* □ trotzig.

trudge [trʌdʒ] *v/i* stapfen (**through** durch).

true [truː] *adj* (□ → *truly*) **1.** wahr: *be* ~ *a.* stimmen; *in the* ~*est sense of the word* im wahrsten Sinne des Wortes; → *come* 10. **2.** wahr, echt, wirklich: ~ *love* wahre Liebe. **3.** treu (*to dat*): *stay* ~ *to one's principles* s-n Grundsätzen treu bleiben. **4.** getreu (*to dat*): ~ *to form* wie nicht anders zu erwarten; ~ *to life* lebensecht.

truf·fle ['trʌfl] *s* 🍄 Trüffel *f*.

tru·ism ['truːɪzəm] *s* Binsenwahrheit *f*.

tru·ly ['truːlɪ] *adv* **1.** wahrheitsgemäß.

2. wirklich, wahrhaft. **3.** aufrichtig: *Yours* ~ *bsd. Am.* Hochachtungsvoll *(Briefschluß).*

trump¹ [trʌmp] **I** *s* a) *pl* Trumpf *m (Farbe),* b) *a.* ~ *card* Trumpf(karte *f) m:* *play one's* ~ *card fig.* s-n Trumpf ausspielen. **II** *v/t Karte* mit e-m Trumpf stechen, mit e-m Trumpf *e-n Stich* machen.

trump² [~] *v/t:* ~ *up b.s.* erfinden, erdichten.

trum·pet ['trʌmpɪt] **I** *s* ♪ Trompete *f*. **II** *v/i* trompeten (*Elefant*). '**trum·pet·er** *s* Trompeter(in).

trun·cate [trʌŋ'keɪt] *v/t* beschneiden, stutzen *(beide a. fig.).*

trun·cheon ['trʌntʃən] *s* (Gummi)Knüppel *m*, Schlagstock *m*.

trun·dle ['trʌndl] *v/t Karren etc* ziehen.

trunk [trʌŋk] *s* **1.** (*Baum*)Stamm *m*. **2.** *anat.* Rumpf *m*. **3.** Schrankkoffer *m*. **4.** *zo.* Rüssel *m (des Elefanten).* **5.** *mot. Am.* Kofferraum *m*. **6.** *pl, a.* **pair of** ~**s** (*Bade*)Hose *f*; (*Sport*) Shorts *pl.* ~ **road** *s Br.* Fernstraße *f*.

truss [trʌs] **I** *v/t, a.* ~ *up* **1.** *j-n* fesseln. **2.** *gastr. Geflügel etc* dressieren. **II** *s* **3.** 🩺 Bruchband *n*.

trust [trʌst] **I** *v/t* **1.** trauen (*dat*). **2.** sich verlassen auf (*acc*): ~ *s.o. to do s.th.* sich darauf verlassen, daß j-d et. tut; ~ *him!* das sieht ihm ähnlich! **3.** (zuversichtlich) hoffen. **II** *v/i* **4.** ~ *in* vertrauen auf (*acc*). **5.** ~ *to* sich verlassen auf (*acc*). **III** *s* **6.** Vertrauen *n (in* zu): *place (od. put) one's* ~ *in* Vertrauen setzen in (*acc*); *take s.th. on* ~ et. einfach glauben; *position of* ~ Vertrauensstellung *f*. **7.** *hold s.th. in* ~ et. treuhänderisch verwalten (*for* für); *place s.th. in s.o.'s* ~ j-m et. anvertrauen. **8.** ✝ Trust *m*; *weitS.* Großkonzern *m*.

trus·tee [ˌtrʌs'tiː] *s* ⚖ Treuhänder(in), Vermögensverwalter(in).

trust·ful ['trʌstfʊl], **'trust·ing** *adj* □ vertrauensvoll; vertrauensselig.

'**trust,wor·thy** *adj* □ vertrauenswürdig.

truth [truːθ] *pl* **truths** [truːðz] *s* Wahrheit *f*: *in* ~ in Wahrheit; *there is some (no)* ~ *in it* daran ist et. (nichts) Wahres; *to tell (you) the* ~ um die Wahrheit zu sagen; → *home truth.* **truth·ful** ['~fʊl] *adj* □ **1.** wahrheitsgemäß. **2.** wahrheitsliebend.

try [traɪ] **I** s **1.** Versuch m: **have a ~** es versuchen; → **worth** I. **II** v/t **2.** versuchen (**to do** zu tun): **when their car didn't start, they tried pushing it** als ihr Wagen nicht ansprang, versuchten sie es mit Anschieben. **3.** et. ausprobieren. **4.** ⚖ (über) e-e Sache verhandeln; j-m den Prozeß machen (**for** wegen). **5.** j-n, j-s Geduld, Nerven etc auf e-e harte Probe stellen. **III** v/i **6.** es versuchen: **~ and come** bsd. Br. F versuch zu kommen; → **hard** 12. **7.** **~ for** Br. sich bemühen um.

Verbindungen mit Adverbien:

try| on v/t **1.** Kleidungsstück anprobieren, Hut etc aufprobieren. **2. try it on** Br. F probieren, wie weit man gehen kann. **~ out** I v/t → **try** 3. **II** v/i: **~ for** Am. → **try** 7.

try-ing ['traɪɪŋ] adj □ anstrengend.

'try-out s: **give s.th. a ~** et. ausprobieren.

tsar [zɑː] s hist. Zar m.

'T-shirt s T-Shirt n.

tub [tʌb] s **1.** Bottich m; Tonne f. **2.** (Margarine- etc)Becher m. **3.** F (Bade-) Wanne f. **4.** ♣ F Kahn m.

tu-ba ['tjuːbə] s ♪ Tuba f.

tube [tjuːb] s **1.** Röhre f (a. anat.), Rohr n. **2.** Schlauch m. **3.** Tube f. **4.** ♀ F U-Bahn f (in London): **by** ♀ mit der U-Bahn; ♀ **station** U-Bahnstation f.

'tube-less adj schlauchlos (Reifen).

tu-ber ['tjuːbə] s ♣ Knolle f.

tu-ber-cu-lo-sis [tjuːˌbɜːkjʊˈləʊsɪs] s ♣ Tuberkulose f.

tu-bu-lar ['tjuːbjʊlə] adj rohrförmig, Röhren..., Rohr...: **~ furniture** Stahlrohrmöbel pl.

tuck [tʌk] **I** s Saum m; Biese f. **II** v/t stecken: **~ s.th. under one's arm** sich et. unter den Arm klemmen. **III** v/i: **~ into** bsd. Br. F sich et. schmecken lassen.

Verbindungen mit Adverbien:

tuck| a-way v/t **1.** wegstecken: **be tucked away** versteckt liegen (Haus etc). **2.** F Essen verdrücken, wegputzen. **~ in** I v/t → **tuck up. II** v/i a. **~ up** F reinhauen, zulangen. **~ up** v/t a. **~ in bed** Kind ins Bett packen.

Tues-day ['tjuːzdɪ] s Dienstag m: **on ~** (am) Dienstag; **on ~s** dienstags.

tuft [tʌft] s (Gras-, Haar- etc)Büschel n.

tug [tʌg] **I** v/t **1.** zerren, ziehen. **2.** zerren

od. ziehen an (dat). **II** v/i **3.** **~ at** → 2. **III** s **4.** **give** s.th. **a ~** → 2; **~ of war** (Sport) Tauziehen n (a. fig.).

tu-i-tion [tjuːˈɪʃn] s **1.** Unterricht m. **2.** bsd. Am. Unterrichtsgebühr(en pl) f.

tu-lip ['tjuːlɪp] s ♣ Tulpe f.

tulle [tjuːl] s Tüll m.

tum-ble ['tʌmbl] **I** v/i **1.** fallen, stürzen; ✝ purzeln (Preise). **2.** a. **~ down** einstürzen. **3.** **~ to** s.th. bsd. Br. F et. kapieren. **II** s **4.** Fall m, Sturz m: **have** (od. **take**) **a ~** fallen, stürzen. **'~down** adj baufällig. **~ dry-er** s Trockenautomat m, Wäschetrockner m.

tum-bler ['tʌmblə] s (Trink)Glas n.

tu-mid ['tjuːmɪd] adj ♣ geschwollen.

tum-my ['tʌmɪ] s F Bauch m: **he's got a sore ~** er hat Bauchweh.

tu-mor s Am., **tu-mour** s bsd. Br. ['tjuːmə] ♣ Tumor m, Geschwulst f.

tu-mult ['tjuːmʌlt] s Tumult m. **tu'mul-tu-ous** adj □ tumultartig, (Applaus, Empfang) stürmisch.

tu-na ['tuːnə] s ichth. Thunfisch m.

tune [tjuːn] **I** s **1.** Melodie f: **to the ~ of** nach der Melodie von; fig. F in Höhe von 500 Pfund etc. **2.** **be out of ~ with** fig. (nicht) harmonieren od. übereinstimmen mit. **II** v/t **3.** a. **~ up** ♪ stimmen. **4.** a. **~ up** ⊙ Motor tunen. **5.** mst **~ in** Radio etc einstellen (**to** auf acc): **be ~d in** to Sender, Programm eingeschaltet haben; fig. ein Gefühl haben für. **III** v/i **6.** **~ up** (die Instrumente) stimmen (Orchester). **7.** **~ in** (das Radio etc) einschalten: **~ in** to Sender, Programm einschalten. **tune-ful** ['~fʊl] adj □ melodiös. **'tune-less** adj □ unmelodiös.

'tun-er s **1.** (Klavier- etc)Stimmer(in). **2.** Radio, TV: Tuner m. **'tun-ing** adj: **~ fork** Stimmgabel f.

tun-nel ['tʌnl] **I** s Tunnel m; Unterführung f. **II** v/t pret u. pp **-neled**, bsd. Br. **-nelled** a) Berg durchtunneln, b) Fluß etc untertunneln. **III** v/i: **~ through** → IIa; **~ under** → IIb.

tun-ny ['tʌnɪ] s ichth. Thunfisch m.

tur-ban ['tɜːbən] s Turban m.

tur-bid ['tɜːbɪd] adj □ **1.** trüb (Flüssigkeit); dick (Rauch etc). **2.** fig. verworren, wirr.

tur-bine ['tɜːbaɪn] s ⊙ Turbine f.

tur-bo ['tɜːbəʊ] pl **-bos** s F → **turbo-**

charger. **,~'charg·er** *s mot.* Turbolader *m.*

tur·bot ['tɜːbət] *pl* **-bots,** *bsd. coll.* **-bot** *s ichth.* Steinbutt *m.*

tur·bu·lence ['tɜːbjʊləns] *s* Turbulenz *f* (*a. phys.*). **'tur·bu·lent** *adj* □ turbulent (*a. phys.*).

turd [tɜːd] *s* V 1. Scheißhaufen *m*, Kaktus *m.* 2. Scheißkerl *m.*

tu·reen [təˈriːn] *s* (Suppen)Terrine *f.*

turf [tɜːf] **I** *pl* **turfs, turves** [~vz] *s* 1. Rasen *m.* 2. Sode *f*, Rasenstück *n.* 3. *the* ~ der Pferderennsport. **II** *v/t* 4. ~ *out bsd. Br.* F j-n rausschmeißen: *he was ~ed out of the club* er flog aus dem Verein.

tur·gid ['tɜːdʒɪd] *adj* □ ✍ geschwollen, *fig. a.* schwülstig.

Turk [tɜːk] *s* Türke *m*, Türkin *f.*

tur·key ['tɜːkɪ] *pl* **-keys,** *bsd. coll.* **-key** *s orn.* Truthahn *m*, -henne *f*, Pute(r *m*) *f*: → *cold turkey.*

Turk·ish ['tɜːkɪʃ] **I** *adj* türkisch. **II** *s ling.* Türkisch *n.*

tur·moil ['tɜːmɔɪl] *s* Aufruhr *m*: *be in a* ~ in Aufruhr sein.

turn [tɜːn] **I** *s* 1. (Um)Drehung *f*: *give s.th. a* ~ (*two* ~*s*) *et.* (zweimal) drehen. 2. Biegung *f*, Kurve *f*: *make a right* ~ nach rechts abbiegen. 3. *in* ~ der Reihe nach; abwechselnd; *in* (*his*) ~ seinerseits; *it is my* ~ ich bin dran *od.* an der Reihe; *miss a* ~ (*Brettspiele*) einmal aussetzen; *take* ~*s* sich abwechseln (*at* bei); *take* ~*s at doing s.th.* et. abwechselnd tun; → *wait* 3. 4. *fig.* Wende *f*, Wendung *f*: *at the* ~ *of the century* um die Jahrhundertwende; *take a* ~ *for the better* (*worse*) sich bessern (sich verschlimmern). 5. *do s.o. a good* (*bad*) ~ j-m e-n guten (schlechten) Dienst erweisen. **II** *v/t* 6. drehen, *Schlüssel a.* herumdrehen; → *somersault.* 7. *Schallplatte etc* umdrehen, *Seite* umblättern, *Braten etc* wenden: → *hair, inside* 1, *stomach* 1, *table* 1, *upside.* 8. → *corner* 1. 9. *Schlauch etc* richten (*on auf acc*), *Antenne* ausrichten (*toward*[*s*] auf *acc*), *Aufmerksamkeit* zuwenden (*to dat*): → *back* 1, *blind* 1, *ear'* 1. 10. verwandeln (*into* in *acc*). 11. ~ *against* j-n aufbringen gegen. **III** *v/i* 12. sich drehen: ~ *on fig.* abhängen von. 13. abbiegen; einbiegen (*onto* auf

acc; *into* in *acc*): → *left* 4, *right* 15. 14. sich umdrehen: ~ *against fig.* sich wenden gegen; ~ *on* losgehen auf (*acc*); ~ *to s.o.* sich j-m zuwenden; *fig.* sich an j-n wenden; → *grave.* 15. blaß, sauer *etc* werden: → *turtle.* 16. sich verwandeln, *fig. a.* umschlagen (*into, to* in *acc*).

Verbindungen mit Adverbien:

turn| **a·way I** *v/t* 1. *Gesicht etc* abwenden (*from* von). 2. j-n abweisen, wegschicken. **II** *v/i* 3. sich abwenden (*from* von). ~ **back I** *v/t* 1. *Bettdecke* zurückschlagen. 2. j-n zurückschicken. 3. *Uhr* zurückstellen: → *clock* 1. **II** *v/i* 4. umkehren. 5. zurückblättern (*to auf acc*). ~ **down** *v/t* 1. *Kragen* umlegen. 2. → *turn back* 1. 3. *Radio etc* leiser stellen. 4. *j-n, Angebot etc* ablehnen. ~ **in I** *v/t* 1. zurückgeben. 2. *Gewinn etc* erzielen, machen. 3. *turn o.s. in* sich stellen. **II** *v/i* 4. F sich aufs Ohr hauen *od.* legen. ~ **off I** *v/t* 1. *Gas, Wasser etc* abdrehen, *Licht, Radio etc* ausmachen, -schalten, *Motor etc* abstellen. 2. F j-n anwidern; *j-m* die Lust nehmen. **II** *v/i* 3. abbiegen. ~ **on** *v/t* 1. *Gas, Wasser etc* aufdrehen, *a. Gerät* anstellen, *Licht, Radio etc* anmachen, anschalten: → *waterworks.* 2. F *j-n* anturnen, anmachen. ~ **out I** *v/t* 1. *Licht* ausmachen, -schalten. 2. *j-n* hinauswerfen. 3. *Tasche etc* (aus)leeren. 4. F *Waren* ausstoßen. **II** *v/i* 5. kommen (*for zu*). 6. sich erweisen *od.* herausstellen (*a success* als Erfolg; *to be false* als falsch), sich entpuppen (*to be a good swimmer* als guter Schwimmer). ~ **o·ver** *v/t* 1. → *turn* 7: *turn s.th. over in one's mind* sich et. durch den Kopf gehen lassen; → *leaf* 2. 2. *et.* umkippen. 3. *j-n, et.* übergeben (*to dat*). 4. ✝ umsetzen. **II** *v/i* 5. sich umdrehen: → *grave.* 6. umkippen. 7. umblättern: *please* ~ bitte wenden. ~ **round** *v/t*: *turn one's car round* wenden. **II** *v/i* sich umdrehen.

'turn|**·a·bout, '~·a·round** *s* Kehrtwendung *f* (*a. fig. in, on* in *dat*). **'~·coat** *s* Abtrünnige *m*, *f*, Überläufer(in).

turn·ing ['tɜːnɪŋ] **I** *s* Abzweigung *f.* **II** *adj*: ~ *circle mot.* Wendekreis *m*; ~ *point fig.* Wendepunkt *m.*

tur·nip ['tɜːnɪp] *s* ♣ Rübe *f.*

'turn|**·off** *s* Abzweigung *f.* **'~·out** *s* 1. (*engS.* Wahl)Beteiligung *f.* 2. F Aufmachung f (e-r Person). '~**o·ver** s ✝ Umsatz m. '~**pike** s Am. gebührenpflichtige Schnellstraße. ~**stile** ['~stail] s Drehkreuz n. '~**ta·ble** s Plattenteller m. '~**up** s Br. (Hosen)Aufschlag m.

tur·pen·tine ['tɜːpəntaɪn] s 🌲 Terpentin n.

turps [tɜːps] s pl (sg konstuiert) Br. F → **turpentine.**

tur·quoise ['tɜːkwɔɪz] s min. Türkis m.

tur·ret ['tʌrɪt] s 1. 🏛 Ecktürmchen n. 2. ✗ (Panzer)Turm m, ⚓ Gefechts-, Geschützturm m.

tur·tle ['tɜːtl] s zo. (Wasser)Schildkröte f: **turn ~** ⚓ kentern. '~**neck** s bsd. Am. Rollkragen(pullover) m.

turves [tɜːvz] pl von **turf.**

tusk [tʌsk] s Stoßzahn m (e-s Elefanten).

tus·sle ['tʌsl] s bsd. fig. (**over**) Gerangel n (um); Auseinandersetzung f (über acc).

tus·sock ['tʌsək] s Grasbüschel n.

tu·te·lage ['tjuːtɪlɪdʒ] s ⚖ Vormundschaft f.

tu·tor ['tjuːtə] s 1. Privat-, Hauslehrer(in). 2. univ. Br. Studienleiter(in).

tux [tʌks] → **tuxedo.**

tux·e·do [tʌk'siːdəʊ] pl **-dos** s Am. Smoking m.

TV [ˌtiː'viː] I s 1. Fernsehen n: **on** (**the**) ~ im Fernsehen; **watch** ~ fernsehen. 2. Fernseher m (Gerät). II adj 3. Fernseh...: ~ **dinner** Tiefkühlmahlzeit f.

twad·dle ['twɒdl] s F Quatsch m, Unsinn m.

twang [twæŋ] s: **speak with a nasal** ~ näseln.

tweed [twiːd] s Tweed m (Stoff).

tweet [twiːt] I v/i piep(s)en (Vogel). II s Piep(s)en n.

tweez·ers ['twiːzəz] s pl, a. **pair of** ~ Pinzette f.

twelfth [twelfθ] adj zwölft.

twelve [twelv] adj zwölf.

twen·ti·eth ['twentɪəθ] adj zwanzigst.

twen·ty ['twentɪ] I adj zwanzig. II s Zwanzig f: **be in one's twenties** in den Zwanzigern sein; **in the twenties** in den zwanziger Jahren (e-s Jahrhunderts).

twerp [twɜːp] s F Blödmann m, Heini m.

twice [twaɪs] adv zweimal: ~ **as much** doppelt soviel; ~ **the sum** die doppelte Summe; **think** ~ es sich genau überlegen (**before** bevor).

twid·dle ['twɪdl] v/t: ~ **one's thumbs** Däumchen drehen (a. fig.).

twig¹ [twɪg] s Zweig m.

twig² [~] v/t u. v/i Br. F kapieren.

twi·light ['twaɪlaɪt] s 1. (bsd. Abend-)Dämmerung f: **at** ~ in der Dämmerung. 2. Zwie-, Dämmerlicht n.

twin [twɪn] I s Zwilling m. II adj Zwillings...: ~ **brother** (**sister**); ~ **beds** pl zwei Einzelbetten; ~ **town** Partnerstadt f. III v/t: **be** ~**ned with** die Partnerstadt sein von. ,~'**bed·ded** adj: ~ **room** Zweibettzimmer n.

twine [twaɪn] I s 1. Bindfaden m, Schnur f. II v/t 2. a. ~ **together** zs.-drehen. 3. ~ **one's arms round** die Arme schlingen um. III v/i 4. sich winden (**round** um).

,**twin·'en·gined** adj ✈ zweimotorig.

twinge [twɪndʒ] s stechender Schmerz, Stechen n: **a** ~ **of toothache** stechende Zahnschmerzen pl; **a** ~ **of conscience** Gewissensbisse pl.

twin·kle ['twɪŋkl] I v/i glitzern (Sterne), (a. Augen) funkeln (**with** vor dat). II s Glitzern n, Funkeln n: **with a** ~**in one's eye** augenzwinkernd. '**twin·kling** s: **in the** ~ **of an eye**, F **in a** ~ im Handumdrehen, im Nu.

twirl [twɜːl] I v/t (herum)wirbeln. II v/i wirbeln (**round** über acc). III s Wirbel m.

twirp → **twerp.**

twist [twɪst] I v/t 1. drehen: ~ **off** abdrehen, Deckel abschrauben; ~ **together** zs.-drehen; **his face was** ~**ed with pain** sein Gesicht war schmerzverzerrt. 2. wickeln (**round** um): ~ **s.o. round one's little finger** fig. j-n um den (kleinen) Finger wickeln. 3. ~ **one's ankle** (mit dem Fuß) umknicken, sich den Fuß vertreten. 4. fig. entstellen, verdrehen. II v/i 5. sich winden (Person), (Fluß etc a.) sich schlängeln. III s 6. Drehung f. 7. Biegung f: **be round the** ~ Br. F spinnen. 8. fig. (überraschende) Wendung. 9. ♪ Twist m (Tanz). '**twist·er** s F 1. Gauner m. 2. Am. Tornado m.

twit [twɪt] s bsd. Br. F Blödmann m.

twitch [twɪtʃ] I v/t 1. zucken mit. 2. zupfen an (dat). II v/i 3. zucken. III s 4. Zucken n, Zuckung f.

twit·ter ['twɪtə] I v/i 1. zwitschern. 2. a. ~ **on** F (aufgeregt) schnattern (**about** über acc). II s 3. Zwitschern n, Gezwitscher *n*. **4. be all of a ~** F ganz aufgeregt sein.

two [tu:] **I** *adj* **1.** zwei: *in a day or ~* in ein paar Tagen; *break (cut) in ~* in zwei Teile brechen (schneiden); *the ~ cars* die beiden Autos; → *thing* 2. **II** *s* 2. Zwei *f*: *~ of hearts* Herzzwei. **3.** *the ~ of us* wir beide; *in ~s* zu zweit, paarweise; *put ~ and ~ together* zwei u. zwei zs.-zählen. '**~act** *adj*: *~ play* thea. Zweiakter *m*. '**~bit** *adj Am*. F klein, unbedeutend. '**~edged** *adj* zweischneidig, *fig. a*. zweideutig. '**~faced** *adj* falsch, heuchlerisch.

two-fold ['tu:fəʊld] *adj* zweifach. **II** *adv* zweifach, um das Zweifache: *increase ~* (sich) verzweifachen.

'**two·|·hand·ed** *adj* □ **1.** zweihändig. **2.** beidhändig. **~pence** ['tʌpəns] *s* Br. zwei Pence: *I don't care (od. give) ~* F das ist mir völlig egal. **~pen·ny** ['tʌpnɪ] *adj Br*. **1.** für zwei Pence, Zweipenny... **2.** *fig*. billig. '**~piece** *adj* zweiteilig. '**~seat·er** *s* ✈, *mot*. Zweisitzer *m*. **~star** *s mot*. Br. F Normal *n* (*Benzin*). '**~star** *adj*: *~ petrol* mot. Br. Normalbenzin *n*. '**~time** **I** *adj* zweimalig. **II** *v/t* F *Freundin etc* betrügen (*with* mit). '**~way** *adj*: *~ mirror* venezianischer Spiegel; *~ traffic* Gegenverkehr *m*.

ty·coon [taɪˈkuːn] *s* (*Industrie- etc*)Magnat *m*.

tym·pa·num ['tɪmpənəm] *pl* **-na** ['~nə], **-nums** *s anat*. Trommelfell *n*.

type [taɪp] **I** *s* **1.** Art *f*, Sorte *f*; Typ *m*: *of this ~* dieser Art; *she's not my ~* F sie ist nicht mein Typ. **II** *v/t* **2.** tippen, mit der Maschine schreiben. **3.** *Krankheit etc* bestimmen. **III** *v/i* **4.** maschineschreiben, tippen. '**~cast** *v/t* (*irr cast*) *Schauspieler* auf ein bestimmtes Rollenfach festlegen. '**~script** *s* maschine(n)geschriebenes Manuskript. '**~set·ter** *s* Schriftsetzer(in). '**~writ·er** *s* Schreibmaschine *f*. '**~writ·ten** *adj* maschine(n)geschrieben.

ty·phoid (fe·ver) ['taɪfɔɪd] *s* ✚ Typhus *m*.

ty·phoon [taɪˈfuːn] *s* Taifun *m*.

ty·phus ['taɪfəs] *s* ✚ Fleckfieber *n*, -typhus *m*.

typ·i·cal ['tɪpɪkl] *adj* □ typisch (*of* für).

typ·i·fy ['~faɪ] *v/t* **1.** typisch sein für, kennzeichnen. **2.** ein typisches Beispiel sein für, verkörpern.

typ·ing ['taɪpɪŋ] *adj*: *~ error* Tippfehler *m*; *~ pool* Schreibzentrale *f*. '**typ·ist** *s* Schreibkraft *f*: → *shorthand*.

ty·po·graph·ic [ˌtaɪpəˈɡræfɪk] *adj* (*~ally*) typographisch: *~ error* Druckfehler *m*. **ty·pog·ra·phy** ['~pɒɡrəfɪ] *s* Typographie *f*.

ty·ran·ni·cal [tɪˈrænɪkl] *adj* □ tyrannisch. **tyr·an·nize** ['tɪrənaɪz] *v/t* tyrannisieren. '**tyr·an·ny** *s* Tyrannei *f*. **ty·rant** ['taɪərənt] *s* Tyrann *m*.

tyre ['taɪə] *s bsd*. Br. Reifen *m*.

tzar [zɑː] *s hist*. Zar *m*.

U

u·biq·ui·tous [juːˈbɪkwɪtəs] *adj* □ allgegenwärtig.

U-boat ['juːbəʊt] *s* ⚓ (deutsches) U-Boot.

ud·der ['ʌdə] *s zo.* Euter *n*.

UFO ['juːfəʊ] *pl* **UFO's, UFOs** *s* Ufo *n*, UFO *n*.

ugh [ʌx] *int* igitt!

ug·li·ness ['ʌɡlɪnɪs] *s* Häßlichkeit *f*.

ug·ly ['ʌɡlɪ] *adj* □ **1.** häßlich (*a. fig.*). **2.** bös, schlimm (*Wunde etc*).

ul·cer ['ʌlsə] *s* ✚ Geschwür *n*.

ul·na ['ʌlnə] *pl* **-nae** ['~niː], **-nas** *s anat*. Elle *f*.

ul·te·ri·or [ʌlˈtɪərɪə] *adj*: *~ motive* Hintergedanke *m*.

ul·ti·ma·ta [ˌʌltɪˈmeɪtə] *pl von* **ultimatum**.

ul·ti·mate ['ʌltɪmət] **I** *adj* letzt, End...; höchst. **II** *s*: *the ~ in* das Höchste an (*dat*); *b.s.* der Gipfel an (*dat*). '**ul·ti·mate·ly** *adv* **1.** schließlich. **2.** letztlich, letzten Endes.

ul·ti·ma·tum [ˌʌltɪˈmeɪtəm] *pl* **-tums, -ta** [ˌ-tə] *s* Ultimatum *n*: **give s.o. an ~** j-m ein Ultimatum stellen; j-n ultimativ auffordern (**to do** zu tun).

ul·tra·high [ˌʌltrəˈhaɪ] *adj*: **~ frequency** *≴* Ultrakurzwelle *f*. **,~·ma·rine** *adj* ultramarin. **,~·son·ic** *adj* Ultraschall... **'·~·sound** *s phys.* Ultraschall *m.* **,~·'vi·o·let** *adj* ultraviolett.

um·bil·i·cal [ˌʌmbɪˈlaɪkl] *adj*: **~ cord** *anat.* Nabelschnur *f*.

um·brage [ˈʌmbrɪdʒ] *s*: **take ~ at** Anstoß nehmen an (*dat*).

um·brel·la [ʌmˈbrelə] *s* **1.** (Regen-) Schirm *m.* **2.** *fig* Schutz *m*: **under the ~ of** unter dem Schutz (*gen*). **~ or·gan·i·za·tion** *s* Dachorganisation *f*. **~ stand** *s* Schirmständer *m.*

um·pire [ˈʌmpaɪə] (*Sport*) **I** *s* Schieds-richter(in). **II** *v/i u. v/t* als Schiedsrich-ter fungieren (bei).

ump·teen [ˌʌmpˈtiːn] *adj*: **~ times** F x-mal. **,ump'teenth** *adj*: **for the ~ time** F zum x-ten Mal.

un·a·bashed [ˌʌnəˈbæʃt] *adj* unverfro-ren.

un·a·ble [ʌnˈeɪbl] *adj*: **be ~ to do s.th.** unfähig *od.* außerstande sein, et. zu tun; et. nicht tun können.

un·a·bridged [ˌʌnəˈbrɪdʒd] *adj* unge-kürzt.

un·ac·cept·a·ble [ˌʌnəkˈseptəbl] *adj* un-annehmbar (**to** für); unzumutbar: **be ~ to s.o.** j-m nicht zugemutet werden können.

un·ac·com·pa·nied [ˌʌnəˈkʌmpənid] *adj* ohne Begleitung (**by** *gen*) (*a.* ♪).

un·ac·count·a·ble [ˌʌnəˈkaʊntəbl] *adj* unerklärlich. **,un·ac'count·a·bly** *adv* unerklärlicherweise.

un·ac·cus·tomed [ˌʌnəˈkʌstəmd] *adj* **1.** ungewohnt. **2.** **be ~ to s.th.** et. nicht gewohnt sein; **be ~ to doing s.th.** es nicht gewohnt sein, et. zu tun.

un·ac·quaint·ed [ˌʌnəˈkweɪntɪd] *adj*: **be ~ with s.th.** et. nicht kennen, mit e-r Sache nicht vertraut sein.

un·a·dul·ter·at·ed [ˌʌnəˈdʌltəreɪtɪd] *adj* **1.** unverfälscht. **2.** *fig.* völlig (*Unsinn etc*).

un·ad·vised [ˌʌnədˈvaɪzd] *adj* unbeson-nen, unüberlegt.

un·af·fect·ed [ˌʌnəˈfektɪd] *adj* **1.** **be ~ by**

nicht betroffen werden von. **2.** natür-lich, ungekünstelt.

un·al·ter·a·ble [ʌnˈɔːltərəbl] *adj* unab-änderlich (*Entschluß etc*).

un·am·big·u·ous [ˌʌnæmˈbɪɡjʊəs] *adj* □ unzweideutig.

un·A·mer·i·can [ˌʌnəˈmerɪkən] *adj* **1.** unamerikanisch. **2.** antiamerikanisch.

u·nan·i·mous [juːˈnænɪməs] *adj* □ ein-mütig; einstimmig: **be ~ in doing s.th.** et. einmütig *od.* einstimmig tun; **by a ~ decision** einstimmig.

un·an·nounced [ˌʌnəˈnaʊnst] *adj u. adv* unangemeldet.

un·an·swer·a·ble [ʌnˈɑːnsərəbl] *adj* **1.** nicht zu beantworten(d). **2.** unwider-legbar.

un·ap·proach·a·ble [ˌʌnəˈprəʊtʃəbl] *adj* □ unnahbar.

un·armed [ˌʌnˈɑːmd] *adj* unbewaffnet.

un·asked [ˌʌnˈɑːskt] *adj* **1.** ungestellt (*Frage*). **2.** unaufgefordert, ungebeten. **3.** uneingeladen, ungebeten.

un·as·sist·ed [ˌʌnəˈsɪstɪd] *adv* ohne (fremde) Hilfe, (ganz) allein.

un·as·sum·ing [ˌʌnəˈsjuːmɪŋ] *adj* □ be-scheiden.

un·at·tached [ˌʌnəˈtætʃt] *adj* ungebun-den (*Person*).

un·at·tend·ed [ˌʌnəˈtendɪd] *adj* unbeauf-sichtigt: **leave ~** unbeaufsichtigt las-sen.

un·at·trac·tive [ˌʌnəˈtræktɪv] *adj* □ un-attraktiv.

un·au·thor·ized [ˌʌnˈɔːθəraɪzd] *adj* unbe-fugt, unberechtigt.

un·a·vail·a·ble [ˌʌnəˈveɪləbl] *adj* **1.** nicht erhältlich. **2.** nicht erreichbar.

un·a·void·a·ble [ˌʌnəˈvɔɪdəbl] *adj* □ un-vermeidlich.

un·a·ware [ˌʌnəˈweə] *adj*: **be ~ of s.th.** sich e-r Sache nicht bewußt sein, et. nicht bemerken; **be ~ that** nicht bemer-ken, daß. **,un·a'wares** *adv*: **catch** (*od.* **take**) **s.o. ~** j-n überraschen.

un·bal·ance [ʌnˈbæləns] *v/t* j-n aus dem (seelischen) Gleichgewicht bringen. **,un'bal·anced** *adj* labil (*Charakter, Person*).

un·bar [ˌʌnˈbɑː] *v/t* auf-, entriegeln.

un·bear·a·ble [ʌnˈbeərəbl] *adj* □ unert-räglich.

un·beat·a·ble [ʌnˈbiːtəbl] *adj* unschlag-bar (*a. Preise etc*).

un·beat·en [ˌʌnˈbiːtn] adj ungeschlagen, unbesiegt.

un·be·known [ˌʌnbɪˈnəʊn] adv: ~ **to s.o.** ohne j-s Wissen.

un·be·liev·a·ble [ˌʌnbɪˈliːvəbl] adj □ unglaublich.

un·bend [ˌʌnˈbend] (irr bend) **I** v/t geradebiegen. **II** v/i fig. auftauen, aus sich herausgehen. **un'bend·ing** adj □ unbeugsam.

un·bi·as(s)ed [ˌʌnˈbaɪəst] adj □ unvoreingenommen, ɪ̃ʒ unbefangen.

un·bind [ˌʌnˈbaɪnd] v/t (irr bind) losbinden.

un·blem·ished [ʌnˈblemɪʃt] adj makellos (Ruf etc).

un·bolt [ˌʌnˈbəʊlt] → **unbar.**

un·born [ˌʌnˈbɔːn] adj ungeboren.

un·break·a·ble [ˌʌnˈbreɪkəbl] adj unzerbrechlich.

un·bri·dled [ˌʌnˈbraɪdld] adj ungezügelt, zügellos: ~ **tongue** lose Zunge.

un·bro·ken [ˌʌnˈbrəʊkən] adj **1.** heil, unbeschädigt. **2.** ununterbrochen.

un·buck·le [ˌʌnˈbʌkl] v/t auf-, losschnallen.

un·bur·den [ˌʌnˈbɜːdn] v/t: ~ **o.s to s.o.** j-m sein Herz ausschütten.

un·but·ton [ˌʌnˈbʌtn] v/t aufknöpfen.

un·called-for [ˌʌnˈkɔːldfɔːr] adj **1.** ungerechtfertigt. **2.** unnötig. **3.** deplaciert, unpassend.

un·can·ny [ʌnˈkænɪ] adj □ unheimlich.

un·ceas·ing [ʌnˈsiːsɪŋ] adj □ unaufhörlich.

un·cer·e·mo·ni·ous·ly [ˈʌnˌserɪˈməʊnjəslɪ] adv ohne viel Federlesen(s).

un·cer·tain [ʌnˈsɜːtn] adj □ **1.** unsicher, ungewiß, unbestimmt: **be ~ of s.th.** sich e-r Sache nicht sicher sein; **be ~ how to do s.th.** nicht sicher sein, wie man et. tut. **2.** unbeständig (Wetter). **3.** vage: → **term 3.** **un'cer·tain·ty** s Unsicherheit f, Ungewißheit f.

un·chain [ˌʌnˈtʃeɪn] v/t losketten.

un·changed [ˌʌnˈtʃeɪndʒd] adj unverändert. **un'chang·ing** adj □ unveränderlich.

un·char·i·ta·ble [ˌʌnˈtʃærɪtəbl] adj □ unfair: **it was rather ~ of you** es war nicht gerade nett von dir (**to do** zu tun).

un·checked [ˌʌnˈtʃekt] adj **1.** ungehindert. **2.** unkontrolliert, ungeprüft.

un·chris·tian [ˌʌnˈkrɪstʃən] adj □ unchristlich.

un·civ·il [ˌʌnˈsɪvl] adj □ unhöflich. ˌun·'civ·i·lized [~vlaɪzd] adj unzivilisiert.

un·cle [ˈʌŋkl] s Onkel m: **cry** (od. **say**) ~ Am. F aufgeben.

un·com·fort·a·ble [ʌnˈkʌmfətəbl] adj □ **1.** unbequem. **2. feel ~** sich unbehaglich fühlen.

un·com·mit·ted [ˌʌnkəˈmɪtɪd] adj neutral: **be ~ to** nicht festgelegt sein auf (acc).

un·com·mon [ʌnˈkɒmən] adj □ ungewöhnlich: **not to be ~** nichts Ungewöhnliches sein.

un·com·mu·ni·ca·tive [ˌʌnkəˈmjuːnɪkətɪv] adj □ verschlossen, wortkarg.

un·com·plain·ing·ly [ˌʌnkəmˈpleɪnɪŋlɪ] adv geduldig, ohne Murren.

un·com·pro·mis·ing [ʌnˈkɒmprəmaɪzɪŋ] adj □ kompromißlos.

un·con·cerned [ˌʌnkənˈsɜːnd] adj **1. be ~ about** sich keine Gedanken od. Sorgen machen über (acc). **2. be ~ with** uninteressiert sein an (dat).

un·con·di·tion·al [ˌʌnkənˈdɪʃnl] adj □ bedingungslos.

un·con·firmed [ˌʌnkənˈfɜːmd] adj unbestätigt.

un·con·scious [ʌnˈkɒnʃəs] adj □ **1.** 🎓 bewußtlos. **2. be ~ of s.th.** sich e-r Sache nicht bewußt sein, et. nicht bemerken. **3.** unbewußt; unbeabsichtigt. **un·'con·scious·ness** s 🎓 Bewußtlosigkeit f.

un·con·sid·ered [ˌʌnkənˈsɪdəd] adj unbedacht, unüberlegt.

un·con·sti·tu·tion·al [ˈʌnˌkɒnstɪˈtjuːʃnl] adj □ verfassungswidrig.

un·con·trol·la·ble [ˌʌnkənˈtrəʊləbl] adj □ unkontrollierbar; nicht zu bändigen(d) (Kind); unbändig (Wut etc). ˌun·con'trolled adj unkontrolliert, ungehindert.

un·con·ven·tion·al [ˌʌnkənˈvenʃənl] adj □ unkonventionell.

un·con·vinced [ˌʌnkənˈvɪnst] adj: **be ~** nicht überzeugt sein (**about** von). ˌun·con'vinc·ing adj □ nicht überzeugend.

un·cooked [ˌʌnˈkʊkt] adj ungekocht, roh.

un·cork [ˌʌnˈkɔːk] v/t entkorken.

un·count·a·ble [ˌʌnˈkaʊntəbl] adj unzählbar (*a. ling.*). ¡**un'count·ed** *adj* unzählig.

un·cou·ple [ˌʌnˈkʌpl] *v/t Waggon etc* abkoppeln, abkuppeln.

un·couth [ʌnˈkuːθ] *adj* □ ungehobelt (*Person, Benehmen*).

un·cov·er [ʌnˈkʌvə] *v/t* aufdecken, *fig. a.* enthüllen.

un·crit·i·cal [ˌʌnˈkrɪtɪkl] *adj* □ unkritisch: **be ~ of s.th.** e-r Sache unkritisch gegenüberstehen.

un·crowned [ˌʌnˈkraʊnd] *adj* ungekrönt (*a. fig.*).

un·crush·a·ble [ʌnˈkrʌʃəbl] *adj* knitterfest.

unc·tion [ˈʌŋkʃn] *s eccl.* Salbung *f*: **extreme ~** Krankensalbung. **unc·tu·ous** [ˈʌtjʊəs] *adj* □ salbungsvoll.

un·cut [ˌʌnˈkʌt] *adj* **1.** ungeschnitten. **2.** ungekürzt (*Film, Roman etc*). **3.** ungeschliffen: **~ diamond** *a.* Rohdiamant *m*.

un·dam·aged [ˌʌnˈdæmɪdʒd] *adj* unbeschädigt.

un·dat·ed [ˌʌnˈdeɪtɪd] *adj* undatiert, ohne Datum.

un·de·cid·ed [ˌʌndɪˈsaɪdɪd] *adj* □ **1.** unentschieden, offen. **2.** unentschlossen: **he is still ~ about what to do** er ist sich noch nicht schlüssig, was er tun soll.

un·de·ni·a·ble [ˌʌndɪˈnaɪəbl] *adj* □ unbestreitbar.

un·der [ˈʌndə] **I** *prp allg.* unter (*Lage etc*: *dat*; *Richtung*: *acc*): **it costs ~ £10** *a.* es kostet weniger als 10 Pfund; **have s.o. ~ one** j-n unter sich haben; → **discussion, impression 2, influence 1, review 1**, *etc*. **II** *adv* unten; darunter. **¡~'a'chieve** *v/i bsd. ped.* hinter den Erwartungen zurückbleiben. **¡~'act** *v/t u. v/i thea. etc* betont zurückhaltend spielen. **¡~'age** *adj* minderjährig. **'~·brush** *bsd. Am.* → **undergrowth.** **'~·car·riage** *s* ✈ Fahrwerk *n*, -gestell *n*. **¡~'charge I** *v/t* **1.** j-m zuwenig berechnen: **~ s.o. (by) £10** j-m 10 Pfund zuwenig berechnen. **2.** *Betrag* zuwenig verlangen. **II** *v/i* **3.** zuwenig berechnen *od.* verlangen (*for* für). **'~·clothes** *s pl* → **underwear.** **'~·coat** *s* Grundierung *f*. **'~·cov·er** *adj*: **~ agent** verdeckter Ermittler. **'~·cur·rent** *s* Unterströmung *f* (*a. fig.*). **¡~'cut** *v/t* (*irr* **cut**) j-n (im Preis) unterbieten. **¡~·de'vel·oped** *adj* unterentwickelt: **~**

country Entwicklungsland *n.* **'~·dog** *s* Benachteiligte *m, f*, Unterdrückte *m, f*. **¡~'done** *adj* nicht durchgebraten. **¡~'dress** *v/t u. v/i* (sich) zu einfach anziehen. **¡~'es·ti·mate** *v/t* **1.** zu niedrig schätzen *od.* veranschlagen. **2.** *fig.* unterschätzen, -bewerten. **¡~·ex'pose** *v/t phot.* unterbelichten. **¡~'fed** *adj* unterernährt. **¡~'floor** *adj*: **~ heating** Fußbodenheizung *f*. **¡~'foot** *adv*: **the grass was wet ~** das Gras war naß; **trample ~** hinwegtrampeln über (*acc*). **¡~'go** *v/t* (*irr* **go**) erleben, durchmachen; sich e-r *Operation etc* unterziehen. **¡~'grad** [ˈ~græd] *s* F, **¡~'grad·u·ate** *s univ.* Student(in). **'~·ground I** *adj* **1.** unterirdisch: **~ car park** Tiefgarage *f*. **2.** *fig.* Untergrund... **II** *adv* [ˌ~'graʊnd] **3.** unterirdisch, unter der Erde: **go ~** *fig.* untertauchen; in den Untergrund gehen. **III** *s* **4.** *bsd. Br.* U-Bahn *f*: **by ~** mit der U-Bahn. **5.** *fig.* Untergrund *m*. **'~·growth** *s* Unterholz *n*, Gestrüpp *n*. **¡~'hand** *adj*, **¡~'hand·ed** *adj* □ hinterhältig. **¡~'lie** *v/t* (*irr* **lie**) zugrunde liegen (*dat*). **¡~'line** *v/t* unterstreichen (*a. fig.*).

un·der·ling [ˈʌndəlɪŋ] *s* **he's just an ~** *contp.* er ist nur ein Rädchen im Getriebe.

¡un·der|'ly·ing *adj* zugrundeliegend. **¡~'manned** *adj* (personell) unterbesetzt. **¡~'men·tioned** *adj Br.* untenerwähnt. **¡~'mine** *v/t* **1.** unterspülen, -waschen. **2.** *fig.* untergraben, -minieren.

un·der·neath [ˌʌndəˈniːθ] **I** *prp* unter (*Lage*: *dat*; *Richtung*: *acc*). **II** *adv* darunter. **III** *s* F Unterseite *f*.

¡un·der|'nour·ished *adj* unterernährt. **¡~'nour·ish·ment** *s* Unterernährung *f*. **'~·pants** *s pl, a.* **pair of ~** Unterhose *f*. **'~·pass** *s* (Straßen-, Eisenbahn)Unterführung *f*. **¡~'pay** *v/t* (*irr* **pay**) *j-m* zuwenig zahlen, *j-n* unterbezahlen. **¡~'play** *v/t* **1.** → **underact. 2.** → **one's hand** *fig.* nicht alle Trümpfe ausspielen. **3.** *fig. et.* herunterspielen. **¡un·der'priv·i·leged** *adj* unterprivilegiert. **¡~'rate** *v/t* unterbewerten (*a. Sport*), -schätzen. **¡~·rep·re'sent·ed** *adj* unterrepräsentiert. **'~·score** → **underline.** **¡~·sec·re·tar·y** *s pol.* Staatssekretär *m*. **¡~'sell** *v/t* (*irr* **sell**) **1.** → **undercut. 2.** *Ware* verschleudern, unter Wert verkaufen: **~ o.s.** *fig.* sich schlecht verkaufen. **'~**

shirt *s* Am. Unterhemd *n.* '**~shorts**
Am. → **underpants.** '**~side** *s* Unterseite *f.* **,~'signed** I *adj* unterzeichnet. II *s:*
the ~ der *od.* die Unterzeichnete, der
Unterzeichneten *pl.* **,~'size(d)** *adj* zu
klein. **,~'stand** *(irr stand)* I *v/t* **1.** verstehen: *make o.s. understood* sich verständlich machen. **2.** erfahren *od.* gehört haben *(that* daß): *am I to ~ that* soll das
heißen, daß; *give s.o. to ~ that* j-m zu
verstehen geben, daß. II *v/i* **3.** verstehen. **4.** *not to ~ about* nichts verstehen
von. **,~'stand·a·ble** *adj* verständlich *(a.
fig.)*: *understandably a.* verständlicherweise. **,~'stand·ing** I *s* **1.** Verstand
m: *be (od.* go) *beyond s.o.'s ~* über j-s
Verstand gehen. **2.** Verständnis *n (of*
für): *with ~* verständnisvoll. **3.** Abmachung *f:* *come to an ~* e-e Abmachung treffen *(with* mit); *on the ~ that*
unter der Voraussetzung, daß. II *adj* □
4. verständnisvoll. **,~'state** *v/t* untertreiben, untertrieben darstellen. **,~'state·ment** *s* Untertreibung *f.* **,~·stud·y** *thea.* I *s* zweite Besetzung. II *v/t*
die zweite Besetzung sein für. **,~'take**
v/t (irr take) **1.** *et.* übernehmen. **2.** sich
verpflichten *(to do* zu tun). **'~·tak·er** *s*
(Leichen)Bestatter *m;* Bestattungs-,
Beerdigungsinstitut *n.* **,~·the-'count·er** *adj* F schwarz, illegal. **'~·tone** *s* **1.** *in
an ~* mit gedämpfter Stimme. **2.**
Unterton *m.* **,~'val·ue** *v/t* unterbewerten, -schätzen. **,~'wa·ter** I *adj* Unterwasser... II *adv* unter Wasser. **'~·wear** *s*
Unterwäsche *f.* **'~·weight** I *s* ['~weıt]
Untergewicht *n.* II *adj* [,~'weıt] untergewichtig *(Person,* also *by* um)
(Gegenstand): *be ~ by five kilos,* *be
five kilos ~* fünf Kilo Untergewicht
haben. **'~·world** *s* Unterwelt *f.* **,~'write** *v/t (irr write)* **1.** Projekt unterstützen *(with* mit). **2.** *et.* versichern.

un·de·served [,ʌndɪ'zɜːvd] *adj* unverdient. **,un·de'serv·ed·ly** [~vɪdlɪ] *adv*
unverdient(ermaßen).

un·de·sir·a·ble [,ʌndɪ'saɪərəbl] *adj* **1.**
nicht wünschenswert. **2.** unerwünscht.

un·dies ['ʌndɪz] *s pl* F *(bsd.* Damen)Unterwäsche *f.*

un·dis·ci·plined [ʌn'dɪsɪplɪnd] *adj* undisziplinicrt, disziplinlos.

un·dis·cov·ered [,ʌndɪ'skʌvəd] *adj*

unentdeckt; unbemerkt.

un·dis·turbed [,ʌndɪ'stɜːbd] *adj* ungestört.

un·di·vid·ed [,ʌndɪ'vaɪdɪd] *adj* ungeteilt
(a. fig.).

un·do [,ʌn'duː] *v/t* **1.** aufmachen, öffnen.
2. *fig.* zunichte machen. **,un'do·ing** *s:*
be s.o.'s ~ j-s Ruin *od.* Verderben sein.

un·done [,ʌn'dʌn] *adj* **1.** unerledigt:
leave nothing ~ nichts unversucht lassen. **2.** offen: *come ~* aufgehen.

un·doubt·ed [ʌn'daʊtɪd] *adj* unbestritten. **un'doubt·ed·ly** *adv* zweifellos, ohne (jeden) Zweifel.

un·dreamed-of [ʌn'driːmdɒv], **un·dreamt-of** [ʌn'dremtɒv] *adj* ungeahnt.

un·dress [,ʌn'dres] I *v/i* sich ausziehen.
(beim Arzt) sich frei machen. II *v/t* j-n
ausziehen: *get ~ed* → I.

un·due [,ʌn'djuː] *adj* □ übermäßig.

un·du·lat·ing ['ʌndjʊleɪtɪŋ] *adj* sanft
(Hügel).

un·dy·ing [ʌn'daɪŋ] *adj* ewig, unsterblich, unvergänglich.

un·earned [,ʌn'ɜːnd] *adj fig.* unverdient.

un·earth [,ʌn'ɜːθ] *v/t* **1.** ausgraben. **2.** *fig.*
ausfindig machen. **un'earth·ly** *adj* **1.**
überirdisch. **2.** unheimlich. *at an ~
hour* F zu e-r unchristlichen Zeit.

un·eas·i·ness [ʌn'iːzɪnɪs] *s* Unbehagen
n. **un'eas·y** *adj* □ **1.** *be ~* sich unbehaglich fühlen; *I'm ~ about* mir ist nicht
wohl bei. **2.** unruhig *(Nacht, Schlaf)*.

un·eat·a·ble [,ʌn'iːtəbl] *adj* ungenießbar.

un·e·co·nom·ic ['ʌn,iːkə'nɒmɪk] *adj*
(~ally) unwirtschaftlich.

un·ed·u·cat·ed [,ʌn'edjʊkeɪtɪd] *adj* ungebildet.

un·e·mo·tion·al [,ʌnɪ'məʊʃənl] *adj* □
leidenschaftslos, kühl, beherrscht.

un·em·ployed [,ʌnɪm'plɔɪd] *adj* arbeitslos. II *s: the ~ pl* die Arbeitslosen
pl. **,un·em'ploy·ment** *s* Arbeitslosigkeit *f:* **~ benefit** *Br.,* **~ compensation**
Am. Arbeitslosengeld *n.*

un·end·ing [ʌn'endɪŋ] *adj* □ endlos.

un·en·dur·a·ble [,ʌnɪn'djʊərəbl] *adj* □
unerträglich.

un·Eng·lish [,ʌn'ɪŋglɪʃ] *adj* unenglisch.

un·en·vi·a·ble [,ʌn'envɪəbl] *adj* □ wenig
beneidenswert.

un·e·qual [,ʌn'iːkwəl] *adj* □ **1.** ungleich,
unterschiedlich. **2.** *fig.* ungleich, einsei-

tig. **3.** be ~ to e-r Aufgabe etc nicht gewachsen sein. **,un·e·qual(l)ed** adj unerreicht, unübertroffen.

un·e·quiv·o·cal [ˌʌnɪˈkwɪvəkl] adj □ unzweideutig, unmißverständlich.

un·err·ing [ˌʌnˈɜːrɪŋ] adj □ unfehlbar.

un·e·ven [ˌʌnˈiːvn] adj □ **1.** uneben. **2.** ungleich(mäßig). **3.** unterschiedlich, schwankend. **4.** ungerade (Zahl). **5.** un-regelmäßig (Pulsschlag etc).

un·e·vent·ful [ˌʌnɪˈventfʊl] adj □ ereignislos.

un·ex·am·pled [ˌʌnɪɡˈzɑːmpld] adj bei-spiellos.

un·ex·pect·ed [ˌʌnɪkˈspektɪd] adj □ un-erwartet.

un·ex·plained [ˌʌnɪkˈspleɪnd] adj unge-klärt.

un·ex·posed [ˌʌnɪkˈspəʊzd] adj phot. unbelichtet.

un·ex·plored [ˌʌnɪkˈsplɔːd] adj uner-forscht.

un·fail·ing [ʌnˈfeɪlɪŋ] adj □ unerschöpf-lich.

un·fair [ˌʌnˈfeə] adj □ unfair, (Wettbe-werb) unlauter. **,un'fair·ness** s Unfair-neß f.

un·faith·ful [ˌʌnˈfeɪθfʊl] adj □ untreu (to dat).

un·fal·ter·ing [ʌnˈfɔːltərɪŋ] adj □ uner-schütterlich.

un·fa·mil·iar [ˌʌnfəˈmɪljə] adj □ **1.** nicht vertraut. **2.** be ~ with nicht vertraut sein mit, sich nicht auskennen in (dat).

un·fash·ion·a·ble [ˌʌnˈfæʃnəbl] adj □ unmodern.

un·fas·ten [ˌʌnˈfɑːsn] v/t aufmachen, öffnen; losbinden.

un·fa·vo(u)r·a·ble [ˌʌnˈfeɪvərəbl] adj □ ungünstig: a) unvorteilhaft (to, for für), b) negativ, ablehnend (Antwort etc).

un·feel·ing [ʌnˈfiːlɪŋ] adj □ gefühl-, herzlos.

un·fin·ished [ˌʌnˈfɪnɪʃt] adj unfertig; un-vollendet.

un·fit [ˌʌnˈfɪt] adj □ **1.** unpassend, unge-eignet; unfähig, untauglich: ~ for ser-vice bsd. ✕ dienstunfähig, (-)untaug-lich; ~ to drive fahruntüchtig; → con-sumption 2. **2.** nicht fit, nicht in Form.

un·flag·ging [ˌʌnˈflæɡɪŋ] adj □ uner-müdlich, unentwegt.

un·fold [ˌʌnˈfəʊld] v/t auf-, auseinander-falten.

un·fore·seen [ˌʌnfɔːˈsiːn] adj unvorher-gesehen, unvorhersehbar.

un·for·get·ta·ble [ˌʌnfəˈɡetəbl] adj □ unvergeßlich.

un·for·tu·nate [ʌnˈfɔːtʃnət] adj **1.** un-glücklich; unglückselig. **2.** bedauerlich. **un'for·tu·nate·ly** adv leider.

un·found·ed [ˌʌnˈfaʊndɪd] adj unbe-gründet.

un·fre·quent·ed [ˌʌnfrɪˈkwentɪd] adj we-nig besucht.

un·friend·ly [ˌʌnˈfrendlɪ] adj unfreund-lich (to zu).

un·ful·filled [ˌʌnfʊlˈfɪld] adj unerfüllt.

un·furl [ʌnˈfɜːl] v/t Fahne etc auf-, ent-rollen, Segel losmachen.

un·fur·nished [ˌʌnˈfɜːnɪʃt] adj unmö-bliert.

un·gain·ly [ʌnˈɡeɪnlɪ] adj linkisch.

un·gen·tle·man·like [ʌnˈdʒentlmən-laɪk], **un'gen·tle·man·ly** adj wenig gentlemanlike.

un·god·ly [ʌnˈɡɒdlɪ] adj: at an ~ hour F zu e-r unchristlichen Zeit.

un·gov·ern·a·ble [ʌnˈɡʌvənəbl] adj □ unbeherrscht, ungezügelt (Tempera-ment).

un·grate·ful [ʌnˈɡreɪtfʊl] adj □ undank-bar.

un·guard·ed [ˌʌnˈɡɑːdɪd] adj **1.** unbe-wacht. **2.** fig. unbedacht, unüberlegt.

un·hap·pi·ness [ʌnˈhæpɪnɪs] s Traurig-keit f. **un'hap·py** adj unglücklich: un-happily a. unglücklicherweise, leider.

un·harmed [ˌʌnˈhɑːmd] adj unversehrt.

un·health·y [ʌnˈhelθɪ] adj □ **1.** kränk-lich, nicht gesund. **2.** ungesund. **3.** contp. unnatürlich, krankhaft.

un·heard [ˌʌnˈhɜːd] adj: go ~ unbeachtet bleiben, keine Beachtung finden. **,un-'heard-of** [~ɒv] adj noch nie dagewe-sen, beispiellos.

un·hes·i·tat·ing [ʌnˈhezɪteɪtɪŋ] adj **1.** prompt. **2.** bereitwillig: ~ly a. anstands-los.

un·hinge [ˌʌnˈhɪndʒ] v/t **1.** Tür etc aus den Angeln heben. **2.** ~ s.o.('s mind) fig. j-n völlig aus dem Gleichgewicht bringen.

un·ho·ly [ʌnˈhəʊlɪ] adj F furchtbar, schrecklich.

un·hoped-for [ʌnˈhəʊptfɔː] adj unver-hofft.

un·hurt [ˌʌnˈhɜːt] adj unverletzt.

u·ni ['juːnɪ] s F Uni f (*Universität*).

un·i·den·ti·fied [ˌʌnaɪ'dentɪfaɪd] *adj* unbekannt, nicht identifiziert: **~ flying object** unbekanntes Flugobjekt.

u·ni·fi·ca·tion [ˌjuːnɪfɪ'keɪʃn] s Vereinigung f.

u·ni·form ['juːnɪfɔːm] **I** *adj* □ einheitlich. **II** s Uniform f: **in ~** in Uniform. **'u·ni·formed** *adj* uniformiert, in Uniform. **ˌu·ni·form·i·ty** s Einheitlichkeit f.

u·ni·fy ['juːnɪfaɪ] *v/t* **1.** verein(ig)en. **2.** vereinheitlichen.

u·ni·lat·er·al [ˌjuːnɪ'lætərəl] *adj* □ *fig.* einseitig.

un·im·ag·i·na·ble [ˌʌnɪ'mædʒɪnəbl] *adj* □ unvorstellbar. **ˌun·im·ag·i·na·tive** *adj* □ einfalls-, phantasielos.

un·im·por·tant [ˌʌnɪm'pɔːtənt] *adj* □ unwichtig.

un·im·pressed [ˌʌnɪm'prest] *adj* unbeeindruckt (**by** von).

un·in·flu·enced [ˌʌn'ɪnfluənst] *adj* unbeeinflußt.

un·in·hab·it·a·ble [ˌʌnɪn'hæbɪtəbl] *adj* unbewohnbar. **ˌun·in·hab·it·ed** *adj* unbewohnt.

un·in·jured [ˌʌn'ɪndʒəd] *adj* unverletzt.

un·in·sured [ˌʌnɪn'ʃɔːd] *adj* unversichert.

un·in·tel·li·gent [ˌʌnɪn'telɪdʒənt] *adj* □ unintelligent.

un·in·tel·li·gi·ble [ˌʌnɪn'telɪdʒəbl] *adj* □ unverständlich (**to** für *od.* dat).

un·in·tend·ed [ˌʌn'ɪntendɪd], **un·in·ten·tion·al** [ˌ~'tenʃənl] *adj* □ unabsichtlich, unbeabsichtigt.

un·in·ter·est·ed [ˌʌn'ɪntrəstɪd] *adj* □ uninteressiert (**in** an dat): **be ~ in** a. sich nicht interessieren für. **ˌun·in·ter·est·ing** *adj* □ uninteressant.

un·in·ter·rupt·ed [ˈʌnˌɪntə'rʌptɪd] *adj* □ ununterbrochen.

un·in·vit·ed [ˌʌnɪn'vaɪtɪd] *adj* uneingeladen, ungebeten.

un·ion ['juːnjən] s **1.** Vereinigung f; Union f: ♀ **Jack** (*od.* **Flag**) Union Jack m (*britische Nationalflagge*). **2.** Gewerkschaft f. **'un·ion·ist** s Gewerkschaftler(in). **'un·ion·ize** *v/t u. v/i* (sich) gewerkschaftlich organisieren.

u·nique [juːˈniːk] *adj* □ einzigartig; einmalig.

u·ni·son ['juːnɪzn] s: **in ~** gemeinsam.

u·nit ['juːnɪt] s **1.** *allg.* Einheit f; *ped.* Unit f, Lehreinheit f; ⊙ Element n, Teil n; (Anbau)Element n: **~ furniture** Anbaumöbel pl. **2.** Abteilung f. **3.** ✗ Einer m.

u·nite [juːˈnaɪt] **I** *v/t* verbinden, -einigen. **II** *v/i* sich vereinigen *od.* zs.-tun: **~ in doing s.th.** et. gemeinsam tun. **u'nit·ed** *adj* verein(ig)t: ♀ **Nations** pl Vereinte Nationen pl; **be ~ in** sich einig sein in (dat).

u·ni·ty ['juːnətɪ] s **1.** Einheit f. **2.** ✗ Eins f.

u·ni·ver·sal [ˌjuːnɪ'vɜːsl] *adj* □ **1.** universal, universell: **~ heir** Universalerbe m. **2.** allgemein. **3.** Welt...: **~ language** (**time**, *etc*).

u·ni·verse ['juːnɪvɜːs] s Universum n, Weltall n.

u·ni·ver·si·ty [ˌjuːnɪ'vɜːsətɪ] **I** s Universität f, Hochschule f: **go to ~** die Universität besuchen. **II** *adj* Universitäts...: **~ professor**; **~ education** akademische Bildung, Hochschulbildung f; Universitäts-, Hochschulausbildung f.

un·just [ˌʌn'dʒʌst] *adj* □ ungerecht (**to** gegen).

un·kempt [ˌʌn'kempt] *adj* ungekämmt (*Haar*); ungepflegt (*Kleidung etc*).

un·kind [ˌʌn'kaɪnd] *adj* □ unfreundlich (**to** zu). **un'kind·ness** s Unfreundlichkeit f.

un·knot [ˌʌn'nɒt] *v/t* auf-, entknoten.

un·known [ˌʌn'nəʊn] *adj* unbekannt (**to** dat): **~ quantity** ✗ unbekannte Größe (a. fig.), Unbekannte f.

un·la·dy·like [ˌʌn'leɪdɪlaɪk] *adj* wenig damenhaft.

un·law·ful [ˌʌn'lɔːfʊl] *adj* □ ungesetzlich, gesetzwidrig.

un·lead·ed [ˌʌn'ledɪd] *adj* bleifrei (*Benzin*).

un·learn [ˌʌn'lɜːn] *v/t* (a. irr learn) Ansichten etc ablegen, aufgeben.

un·leash [ˌʌn'liːʃ] *v/t* **1.** Hund loslassen, von der Leine lassen. **2.** *fig. s-m* Zorn etc freien Lauf lassen: **all his anger was ~ed on her** sein ganzer Zorn entlud sich auf sie.

un·leav·ened [ˌʌn'levnd] *adj* ungesäuert.

un·less [ən'les] *cj* wenn *od.* sofern ... nicht; es sei denn.

un·like [ˌʌn'laɪk] *prp* **1.** im Gegensatz zu. **2. he is quite ~ his father** er ist ganz anders als sein Vater; **that is very ~ him** das sieht ihm gar nicht ähnlich. **un'like·ly** *adj* **1. he is ~ to come** es ist

unwahrscheinlich, daß er kommt. **2.**
unwahrscheinlich, unglaubwürdig.

un·lim·it·ed [ʌnˈlɪmɪtɪd] *adj* unbegrenzt.

un·list·ed [ˌʌnˈlɪstɪd] *adj teleph.*: **be ~**
nicht im Telefonbuch stehen, geheim
sein; **~ number** Geheimnummer *f.*

un·load [ˌʌnˈləʊd] *v/t Fahrzeug* entladen,
a. Gegenstände ab-, ausladen, ⊕ *Ladung, Schiff* löschen.

un·lock [ˌʌnˈlɒk] *v/t* aufschließen.

un·loved [ʌnˈlʌvd] *adj* ungeliebt.

un·luck·i·ly [ʌnˈlʌkɪlɪ] *adv* unglücklicherweise: **~ for me** zu m-m Pech. **un-
'luck·y** [ʌnˈlʌkɪ] *adj* unglücklich: **~ day** Unglückstag *m*; **be ~** Pech haben; Unglück bringen.

un·made [ˌʌnˈmeɪd] *adj* ungemacht
(*Bett*).

un·man·age·a·ble [ʌnˈmænɪdʒəbl] *adj*
□ **1.** widerspenstig. **2.** unhandlich.

un·man·ly [ʌnˈmænlɪ] *adj* unmännlich.

un·manned [ˌʌnˈmænd] *adj* unbemannt.

un·man·ner·ly [ʌnˈmænəlɪ] *adj* ungesittet, unmanierlich.

un·marked [ˌʌnˈmɑːkt] *adj* **1.** nicht ge-
kennzeichnet. **2.** *Sport:* ungedeckt, frei.

un·mar·ried [ˌʌnˈmærɪd] *adj* unverheiratet, ledig.

un·mask [ˌʌnˈmɑːsk] *v/t fig.* entlarven.

un·matched [ˌʌnˈmætʃt] *adj* unvergleichlich, unübertroffen.

un·men·tion·a·ble [ʌnˈmenʃnəbl] *adj*
Tabu...: **be ~** tabu sein.

un·mer·ci·ful [ʌnˈmɜːsɪfʊl] *adj* □ erbarmungslos, unbarmherzig.

un·me·thod·i·cal [ˌʌnmɪˈθɒdɪkl] *adj* □
unmethodisch.

un·mis·tak·a·ble [ˌʌnmɪˈsteɪkəbl] *adj* □
unverkennbar, unverwechselbar.

un·mixed [ˌʌnˈmɪkst] *adj* **1.** unvermischt. **2.** *fig.* rein, ungetrübt.

un·moved [ˌʌnˈmuːvd] *adj* ungerührt: **he
remained ~ by it** es ließ ihn kalt.

un·mu·si·cal [ʌnˈmjuːzɪkl] *adj* □ unmu-
sikalisch.

un·named [ˌʌnˈneɪmd] *adj* ungenannt.

un·nat·u·ral [ʌnˈnætʃrəl] *adj* □ **1.** unnatürlich. **2.** widernatürlich.

un·nec·es·sar·y [ʌnˈnesəsərɪ] *adj* unnötig: **unnecessarily** *adv.* unnötigerweise.

un·nerve [ˌʌnˈnɜːv] *v/t* **1.** entnerven. **2.**
entmutigen.

un·no·ticed [ˌʌnˈnəʊtɪst] *adj*: **go** (*od.*
pass) **~** unbemerkt bleiben.

un·num·bered [ʌnˈnʌmbəd] *adj* unnu-
meriert.

un·ob·tru·sive [ˌʌnəbˈtruːsɪv] *adj* □ unauffällig.

un·oc·cu·pied [ˌʌnˈɒkjʊpaɪd] *adj* **1.**
leer(stehend), unbewohnt: **be ~** leer stehen. **2.** unbeschäftigt. **3.** ✗ unbesetzt.

un·of·fi·cial [ˌʌnəˈfɪʃl] *adj* □ inoffiziell.

un·o·pened [ˌʌnˈəʊpənd] *adj* ungeöff-
net.

un·pack [ˌʌnˈpæk] *v/t u. v/i* auspacken.

un·paid(-for) [ˌʌnˈpeɪd(fə)] *adj* unbezahlt.

un·par·al·leled [ʌnˈpærəleld] *adj* beispiellos, einmalig.

un·par·don·a·ble [ʌnˈpɑːdnəbl] *adj* □
unverzeihlich.

un·per·turbed [ˌʌnpəˈtɜːbd] *adj* gelassen, ruhig.

un·pick [ʌnˈpɪk] *v/t* auftrennen.

un·play·a·ble [ʌnˈpleɪəbl] *adj Sport:* un-
bespielbar (*Platz*).

un·pleas·ant [ʌnˈpleznt] *adj* □ **1.** unangenehm, (*Nachricht etc a.*) unerfreulich. **2.** unfreundlich.

un·plug [ʌnˈplʌg] *v/t* den Stecker (*gen*)
herausziehen.

un·po·lished [ʌnˈpɒlɪʃt] *adj* **1.** unpo-
liert. **2.** *fig.* ungeschliffen, ungehobelt.

un·pop·u·lar [ʌnˈpɒpjʊlə] *adj* □ unpo-
pulär, unbeliebt: **make o.s. ~ with** sich
bei *j-m* unbeliebt machen.

un·prac·ti·cal [ʌnˈpræktɪkl] *adj* □ unpraktisch.

un·prec·e·dent·ed [ʌnˈpresɪdentɪd] *adj*
□ beispiellos, noch nie dagewesen.

un·pre·dict·a·ble [ˌʌnprɪˈdɪktəbl] *adj* **1.**
unvorhersehbar. **2.** unberechenbar
(*Person*).

un·prej·u·diced [ʌnˈpredʒʊdɪst] *adj* □
unvoreingenommen, ᚱ unbefangen.

un·pre·pared [ˌʌnprɪˈpeəd] *adj* **1.** unvorbereitet. **2.** nicht gefaßt *od.* vorbereitet
(**for** auf *acc*).

un·pre·ten·tious [ˌʌnprɪˈtenʃəs] *adj* □
bescheiden, einfach.

un·prin·ci·pled [ʌnˈprɪnsəpld] *adj* skrupellos.

un·print·a·ble [ʌnˈprɪntəbl] *adj* nicht
druckfähig *od.* druckreif.

un·pro·duc·tive [ˌʌnprəˈdʌktɪv] *adj* □
unproduktiv (*a. fig.*), unergiebig, unrentabel.

un·pro·fes·sion·al [ˌʌnprəˈfeʃənl] *adj* □

1. standeswidrig. **2.** unfachmännisch.

un·prof·it·a·ble [ˌʌnˈprɒfɪtəbl] *adj* □ **1.** unrentabel. **2.** *fig.* nutz-, zwecklos.

un·prompt·ed [ˌʌnˈprɒmptɪd] *adj* spontan.

un·pro·nounce·a·ble [ˌʌnprəˈnaʊnsəbl] *adj* unaussprechbar.

un·pro·tect·ed [ˌʌnprəˈtektɪd] *adj* schutzlos; ungeschützt.

un·proved [ˌʌnˈpruːvd], **un·prov·en** [ˌ~vn] *adj* unbewiesen.

un·pro·voked [ˌʌnprəˈvəʊkt] *adj* grundlos.

un·pub·lished [ˌʌnˈpʌblɪʃt] *adj* unveröffentlicht.

un·punc·tu·al [ˌʌnˈpʌŋktʃʊəl] *adj* □ unpünktlich: *be ~* unpünktlich kommen (*for* zu). **'un·punc·tu·al·i·ty** [ˌ~ˈæləti] *s* Unpünktlichkeit *f.*

un·pun·ished [ˌʌnˈpʌnɪʃt] *adj* unbestraft, ungestraft: *go ~* straflos bleiben.

un·qual·i·fied [ˌʌnˈkwɒlɪfaɪd] *adj* **1.** unqualifiziert, ungeeignet (*for* für). **2.** uneingeschränkt.

un·ques·tion·a·ble [ʌnˈkwestʃənəbl] *adj* □ unbestritten: *be ~ a.* außer Frage stehen. **un·ques·tion·ing** *adj* □ bedingungslos.

un·quote [ˌʌnˈkwəʊt] *adv* → *quote* 6.

un·rav·el [ʌnˈrævl] **I** *v/t* **1.** *Pullover etc* auftrennen, -ziehen. **2.** entwirren (*a fig.*). **II** *v/i* **3.** sich auftrennen *od.* ziehen.

un·read·a·ble [ʌnˈriːdəbl] *adj* unlesbar: a) nicht lesenswert, b) unleserlich.

un·re·al [ˌʌnˈrɪəl] *adj* □ˈ unwirklich. **'un·re·al'is·tic** [ˌ~ˈlɪstɪk] *adj* (*~ally*) unrealistisch. **un·re·al·i·ty** [ˌ~ˈæləti] *s* Unwirklichkeit *f.*

un·rea·son·a·ble [ʌnˈriːznəbl] *adj* □ **1.** unvernünftig. **2.** übertrieben, unzumutbar.

un·rec·og·niz·a·ble [ˌʌnˈrekəgnaɪzəbl] *adj* □ nicht wiederzuerkennen(d).

un·re·lat·ed [ˌʌnrɪˈleɪtɪd] *adj* **1.** nicht verwandt (*to* mit). **2.** *be ~* in keinem Zs.-hang stehen (*to* mit).

un·re·lent·ing [ˌʌnrɪˈlentɪŋ] *adj* □ unvermindert.

un·re·li·a·ble [ˌʌnrɪˈlaɪəbl] *adj* □ unzuverlässig.

un·re·lieved [ˌʌnrɪˈliːvd] *adj* ununterbrochen, ständig. **un·re'liev·ed·ly** [ˌ~ɪdlɪ] *adv* → *unrelieved*.

un·re·mit·ting [ˌʌnrɪˈmɪtɪŋ] *adj* □ unablässig, unaufhörlich.

un·re·quit·ed [ˌʌnrɪˈkwaɪtɪd] *adj* unerwidert (*Liebe*).

un·re·served [ˌʌnrɪˈzɜːvd] *adj* **1.** uneingeschränkt. **2.** nicht reserviert. **un·re'serv·ed·ly** [ˌ~ɪdlɪ] *adv* uneingeschränkt.

un·rest [ˌʌnˈrest] *s pol. etc* Unruhen *pl.*

un·re·strained [ˌʌnrɪˈstreɪnd] *adj* hemmungslos, ungezügelt. **un·re'strain·ed·ly** [ˌ~ɪdlɪ] *adv* → *unrestrained*.

un·re·strict·ed [ˌʌnrɪˈstrɪktɪd] *adj* □ uneingeschränkt.

un·re·ward·ing [ˌʌnrɪˈwɔːdɪŋ] *adj* wenig lohnend (*Aufgabe etc a.*) undankbar.

un·rig [ˌʌnˈrɪg] *v/t Schiff* abtakeln.

un·ripe [ˌʌnˈraɪp] *adj* unreif.

un·ri·val(l)ed [ʌnˈraɪvld] *adj* unerreicht, unübertroffen.

un·roll [ˌʌnˈrəʊl] *v/t* auf-, entrollen.

un·ruf·fled [ˌʌnˈrʌfld] *adj* gelassen, ruhig.

un·rul·y [ʌnˈruːlɪ] *adj* **1.** ungebärdig, wild. **2.** widerspenstig (*Haare*).

un·sad·dle [ˌʌnˈsædl] *v/t* **1.** *Pferd* absatteln. **2.** *Reiter* abwerfen.

un·safe [ˌʌnˈseɪf] *adj* □ unsicher, nicht sicher: *feel ~* sich nicht sicher fühlen.

un·said [ˌʌnˈsed] *adj*: *leave s.th. ~* et. nicht aussprechen; *be left* (*od. go*) *~* unausgesprochen *od.* ungesagt bleiben.

un·sal(e)·a·ble [ˌʌnˈseɪləbl] *adj* unverkäuflich.

un·salt·ed [ˌʌnˈsɔːltɪd] *adj* ungesalzen.

un·san·i·tar·y [ʌnˈsænɪtərɪ] *adj* □ unhygienisch.

un·sat·is·fac·to·ry [ˈʌnˌsætɪsˈfæktərɪ] *adj* □ unbefriedigend. **un'sat·is·fied** [ˌ~faɪd] *adj* unzufrieden (*with* mit). **un'sat·is·fy·ing** [ˌ~faɪŋ] *adj* → *unsatisfactory*.

un·sa·vo(u)r·y [ˌʌnˈseɪvərɪ] *adj* □ **1.** fad. **2.** *fig.* unerfreulich (*Angelegenheit etc*); anrüchig (*Stadtteil, Vergangenheit etc*).

un·sci·en·tif·ic [ˈʌnˌsaɪənˈtɪfɪk] *adj* (*~ally*) unwissenschaftlich.

un·screw [ˌʌnˈskruː] *v/t* ab-, losschrauben.

un·script·ed [ˌʌnˈskrɪptɪd] *adj* improvisiert.

un·scru·pu·lous [ʌnˈskruːpjʊləs] *adj* □ skrupel-, gewissenlos.

un·seat [ˌʌnˈsiːt] *v/t* **1.** *Reiter* abwer-

fen. **2.** *fig. j-n* s-s Amtes entheben.
un·seed·ed [ˌʌnˈsiːdɪd] *adj Sport:* ungesetzt.
un·seem·ly [ʌnˈsiːmlɪ] *adj* ungebührlich, unziemlich.
un·seen [ˌʌnˈsiːn] **I** *adj* **1.** ungesehen, unbemerkt: → **sight** 2. **2.** unsichtbar. **II** *s* **3. an** (**English**) ~ *ped. bsd. Br.* e-e Herübersetzung (aus dem Englischen).
un·self·ish [ʌnˈselfɪʃ] *adj* □ selbstlos, uneigennützig.
un·sen·ti·men·tal [ˈʌnˌsentɪˈmentl] *adj* □ unsentimental.
un·set·tle [ˌʌnˈsetl] *v/t j-n* beunruhigen; durcheinanderbringen. **un·settled** *adj* **1.** unbesiedelt. **2.** unbeglichen, unbezahlt (*Rechnung*). **3.** ungeklärt (*Frage etc*). **4.** unbeständig (*Wetter*). **5.** unsicher (*Lage etc*).
un·shak(e)·a·ble [ʌnˈʃeɪkəbl] *adj* □ unerschütterlich.
un·shav·en [ˌʌnˈʃeɪvn] *adj* unrasiert.
un·shrink·a·ble [ˌʌnˈʃrɪŋkəbl] *adj* nicht eingehend od. einlaufend (*Stoff*).
un·sight·ly [ʌnˈsaɪtlɪ] *adj* unansehnlich; häßlich.
un·signed [ˌʌnˈsaɪnd] *adj* unsigniert (*Gemälde*), nicht unterschrieben od. unterzeichnet (*Brief etc*).
un·skil(l)·ful [ˌʌnˈskɪlfʊl] *adj* □ ungeschickt. **un·skilled** *adj* **1.** ungeschickt (**at, in** *in dat*). **2.** ~ **worker** ungelernter Arbeiter.
un·so·cia·ble [ʌnˈsəʊʃəbl] *adj* □ ungesellig.
un·so·cial [ˌʌnˈsəʊʃl] *adj:* **work ~ hours** *Br.* außerhalb der normalen Arbeitszeit arbeiten.
un·sold [ˌʌnˈsəʊld] *adj* unverkauft.
un·so·lic·it·ed [ˌʌnsəˈlɪsɪtɪd] *adj* unverlangt eingesandt (*Manuskript etc*), unaufgefordert zugesandt, unbestellt (*Ware*).
un·solved [ˌʌnˈsɒlvd] *adj* ungelöst (*Fall etc*).
un·so·phis·ti·cat·ed [ˌʌnsəˈfɪstɪkeɪtɪd] *adj* □ **1.** unkultiviert. **2.** ◎ unkompliziert.
un·sound [ˌʌnˈsaʊnd] *adj* □ **1.** nicht gesund; nicht intakt od. in Ordnung. **2.** *fig.* unklug, unvernünftig.
un·spar·ing [ʌnˈspeərɪŋ] *adj* □ verschwenderisch, freigebig (**in** mit): **be ~**

in one's efforts keine Mühe scheuen (**to do** zu tun).
un·speak·a·ble [ʌnˈspiːkəbl] *adj* □ unbeschreiblich, unsäglich.
un·spoiled [ˌʌnˈspɔɪld], **un·spoilt** [~t] *adj* **1.** unverdorben. **2.** nicht verwöhnt (*Kind a.*) nicht verzogen.
un·sport·ing [ˌʌnˈspɔːtɪŋ] *adj* □, **un·sports·man·like** [ˌʌnˈspɔːtsmənlaɪk] *adj* unsportlich, unfair.
un·sta·ble [ˌʌnˈsteɪbl] *adj* □ **1.** instabil (*a. fig.*). **2.** *fig.* labil (*Person*).
un·stead·y [ˌʌnˈstedɪ] *adj* □ **1.** wack(e)lig; (*Hand*) unsicher. **2.** schwankend (*Preise etc*). **3.** ungleichmäßig.
un·stint·ing [ʌnˈstɪntɪŋ] → **unsparing**.
un·stop [ʌnˈstɒp] *v/t* **1.** Flasche entstöpseln. **2.** *Abfluß etc* freimachen.
un·stressed [ˌʌnˈstrest] *adj ling.* unbetont.
un·stuck [ˌʌnˈstʌk] *adj:* **come ~** abgehen, sich lösen; *fig.* auf den Bauch fallen (*Person*), schiefgehen (*Plan etc*).
un·stud·ied [ˌʌnˈstʌdɪd] *adj* ungekünstelt.
un·suc·cess·ful [ˌʌnsəkˈsesfʊl] *adj* □ erfolglos; vergeblich: **be ~** keinen Erfolg haben.
un·suit·a·ble [ˌʌnˈsuːtəbl] *adj* □ unpassend, ungeeignet (**for, to** für).
un·sure [ˌʌnˈʃɔː] *adj allg.* unsicher: ~ **of o.s.** unsicher.
un·sur·passed [ˌʌnsəˈpɑːst] *adj* unübertroffen.
un·sus·pect·ed [ˌʌnsəˈspektɪd] *adj* □ **1.** unvermutet. **2.** unverdächtig. **un·sus·pect·ing** *adj* □ nichtsahnend, ahnungslos.
un·sus·pi·cious [ˌʌnsəˈspɪʃəs] *adj* □ **1.** arglos. **2.** unverdächtig, harmlos.
un·sweet·ened [ˌʌnˈswiːtnd] *adj* ungesüßt.
un·swerv·ing [ʌnˈswɜːvɪŋ] *adj* □ unbeirrbar, unerschütterlich.
un·tan·gle [ˌʌnˈtæŋgl] *v/t* entwirren (*a. fig.*).
un·tapped [ˌʌnˈtæpt] *adj* unerschlossen (*Naturschätze etc*).
un·teach·a·ble [ˌʌnˈtiːtʃəbl] *adj* unbelehrbar.
un·ten·a·ble [ˌʌnˈtenəbl] *adj* unhaltbar (*Theorie etc*).
un·think·a·ble [ʌnˈθɪŋkəbl] *adj* □ un-

denkbar, unvorstellbar. **,un'think·ing** *adj* □ gedankenlos.

un·ti·dy [ʌn'taɪdɪ] *adj* □ unordentlich.

un·tie [ˌʌn'taɪ] *v/t* aufknoten, *Knoten* lösen, *j-n etc* losbinden (**from** von).

un·til [ən'tɪl] I *prp* **1.** bis. **2.** *not ~* erst: *not ~ Monday* erst (am) Montag; nicht vor Montag. II *cj* **3.** bis. **4.** *not ~* erst wenn, nicht bevor.

un·time·ly [ʌn'taɪmlɪ] *adj* **1.** vorzeitig, verfrüht. **2.** unpassend, ungelegen.

un·tir·ing [ʌn'taɪərɪŋ] *adj* □ unermüdlich.

un·told [ˌʌn'təʊld] *adj* unermeßlich (*Reichtum, Schaden etc*).

un·touched [ˌʌn'tʌtʃt] *adj* **1.** unberührt, unangetastet. **2.** unversehrt, heil.

un·trans·lat·a·ble [ˌʌntræns'leɪtəbl] *adj* unübersetzbar.

un·true [ˌʌn'truː] *adj* **1.** unwahr. **2.** untreu (**to** *dat*).

un·truth [ʌn'truːθ] *s* Unwahrheit *f*.

un·used¹ [ˌʌn'juːzd] *adj* unbenutzt, ungebraucht.

un·used² [ˌʌn'juːst] *adj*: *be ~ to s.th.* an et. nicht gewöhnt sein, et. nicht gewohnt sein; *be ~ to doing s.th.* es nicht gewohnt sein, et. zu tun.

un·u·su·al [ʌn'juːʒl] *adj* □ ungewöhnlich.

un·ut·ter·a·ble [ʌn'ʌtərəbl] *adj* □ unbeschreiblich, unsäglich.

un·var·nished [ʌn'vɑːnɪʃt] *adj* ungeschminkt (*Wahrheit*).

un·var·y·ing [ʌn'veərɪŋ] *adj* □ unveränderlich, gleichbleibend.

un·veil [ˌʌn'veɪl] *v/t Denkmal etc* enthüllen.

un·versed [ʌn'vɜːst] *adj* unbewandert (**in** *dat*).

un·voiced [ʌn'vɔɪst] *adj* **1.** unausgesprochen. **2.** *ling.* stimmlos.

un·want·ed [ʌn'wɒntɪd] *adj* unerwünscht, (*Schwangerschaft a.*) ungewollt.

un·war·rant·ed [ʌn'wɒrəntɪd] *adj* ungerechtfertigt.

un·washed [ˌʌn'wɒʃt] *adj* ungewaschen.

un·wa·ver·ing [ʌn'weɪvərɪŋ] *adj* □ unerschütterlich.

un·wel·come [ʌn'welkəm] *adj* unwillkommen.

un·well [ˌʌn'wel] *adj.*: *be* (*od. feel*) *~* sich unwohl *od.* nicht wohl fühlen.

un·whole·some [ˌʌn'həʊlsəm] *adj* □ ungesund.

un·wield·y [ʌn'wiːldɪ] *adj* unhandlich, sperrig.

un·will·ing [ˌʌn'wɪlɪŋ] *adj* □ widerwillig: *be ~ to do s.th.* nicht bereit *od.* gewillt sein, et. zu tun; et. nicht tun wollen.

un·wind [ʌn'waɪnd] (*irr* **wind**) I *v/t* **1.** abwickeln. II *v/i* **2.** sich abwickeln. **3.** F abschalten, sich entspannen.

un·wise [ˌʌn'waɪz] *adj* □ unklug.

un·wished-for [ʌn'wɪʃtfɔː] *adj* unerwünscht.

un·wit·ting [ʌn'wɪtɪŋ] *adj* □ **1.** unwissentlich. **2.** unbeabsichtigt.

un·wom·an·ly [ʌn'wʊmənlɪ] *adj* unfraulich, unweiblich.

un·wont·ed [ʌn'wəʊntɪd] *adj* □ ungewohnt.

un·wor·thy [ʌn'wɜːðɪ] *adj*: *be ~ of s.th.* e-r Sache nicht würdig sein, et. nicht verdienen.

un·wrap [ˌʌn'ræp] *v/t* auswickeln, -packen.

un·writ·ten [ˌʌn'rɪtn] *adj* ungeschrieben: *~ law* ungeschriebenes Recht; *fig.* ungeschriebenes Gesetz.

un·yield·ing [ʌn'jiːldɪŋ] *adj* □ unnachgiebig.

un·zip [ˌʌn'zɪp] *v/t* den Reißverschluß (*gen*) aufmachen.

up [ʌp] I *adv* **1.** oben; *1000 Meter etc* hoch, in e-r Höhe von: *~ there* dort oben; *jump ~ and down* hüpfen; *walk ~ and down* auf u. ab *od.* hin u. her gehen; → *look up*, *take up, etc.* **2.** *~ to* bis zu: *~ to a moment ago* bis vor e-m Augenblick; *be ~ to s.th.* F et. vorhaben, et. im Schilde führen; *not to be ~ to s.th.* e-r Sache nicht gewachsen sein; *it's ~ to you* das liegt bei Ihnen; → *ear¹* 1, *eye* 1, *feel* 6, *scratch* 6, *etc.* II *prp* **3.** oben auf (*dat*); her-, hinauf: *~ the river* flußaufwärts; *~ yours!* *Br.* V leck mich (doch) am Arsch!; → *climb* 3, *etc.* III *adj* **4.** nach oben (gerichtet), Aufwärts... **5.** *the ~ train* der Zug nach London. **6.** *what's ~?* F was ist los? **7.** *be well ~ in* (*od. on*) F viel verstehen von. **8.** *~ for ~ sale* 1. IV *s* **9.** *the ~s and downs pl* die Höhen u. Tiefen *pl* (*des Lebens*). V *v/t* **10.** F *Angebot, Preis etc* erhöhen. VI *v/i* **11.** *he ~ped and left her* F er hat sie von heute auf morgen sitzenlassen. **¸~-and-'com·ing** *adj* vielversprechend. **'~‚bring·ing** *s* Erziehung *f*. **'~‚com·ing** *adj* bevorstehend. **~'date** *v/t* auf den neuesten Stand bringen; aktualisieren. **~'end** *v/t* hochkant stellen. **~'grade** *v/t* j-n befördern. **~·heav·al** [~'hi:vl] *s fig.* Umwälzung *f*. **¸~'hill I** *adv* **1.** aufwärts, bergan. **II** *adj* **2.** bergauf führend. **3.** *fig.* mühselig, hart. **~'hold** *v/t* (*irr hold*) **1.** *Rechte etc* schützen, wahren. **2.** ⚖ *Urteil* bestätigen. **~·hol·ster** [~'həʊlstə] *v/t* polstern: *~ed* Polster... **'~·keep** *s* Unterhalt *m*; Unterhaltungskosten *pl*. **~·lift** [~'lɪft] *j-n* aufrichten, j-m Auftrieb geben. **II** *s* [~'lɪft] Auftrieb *m*.

up·on [ə'pɒn] *prp* → *on* I.

up·per ['ʌpə] **I** *adj* ober: **~ arm** Oberarm *m*; **~ class(es** *pl*) sociol. Oberschicht *f*; **~ deck** ⚓ Oberdeck *n* (*a. e-s Busses*); **gain** (*od. get*) **the ~ hand** die Oberhand gewinnen (**of** über *acc*); → **jaw** 1, **lip** 1. **II** *s* Obermaterial *n* (*e-s Schuhs*). **'~·cut** *s Boxen:* Aufwärtshaken *m*.

up·per·most ['ʌpəməʊst] **I** *adj* oberst: **be ~** oben sein; *fig.* an erster Stelle stehen; **be ~ in s.o.'s mind** *fig.* für j-n an erster Stelle stehen. **II** *adv* nach oben.

up·pish ['ʌpɪʃ] *adj* □ F, **up·pi·ty** ['ʌpətɪ] *adj* F hochnäsig.

up·right ['ʌpraɪt] **I** *adj* □ **1.** [*a.* ‚ʌp'raɪt] aufrecht, gerade; senkrecht. **2.** *fig.* aufrecht, rechtschaffen. **II** *adv* [*a.* ‚ʌp'raɪt] **3.** → 1: **sit ~** geradesitzen. **III** *s* **4.** Pfosten *m*.

up·ris·ing ['ʌp‚raɪzɪŋ] *s* Aufstand *m*.

up·roar ['ʌprɔː] *s* Aufruhr *m*, Tumult *m*: **be in an ~** in Aufruhr sein.

up·root [ʌp'ruːt] *v/t* **1.** *Pflanze* (mit den Wurzeln) ausreißen, *a. Baum etc*, *fig. Menschen* entwurzeln. **2.** *fig. j-n* herausreißen (**from** aus).

up·set I *v/t* [ʌp'set] (*irr set*) **1.** umkippen, umstoßen, umwerfen: → **applecart. 2.** *fig.* Pläne *etc* durcheinanderbringen, *Gleichgewicht* stören. **3.** *fig. j-n* aus der Fassung bringen; aufregen; kränken, verletzen. **4. the fish has ~ me** (*od. my stomach*) ich habe mir durch den Fisch den Magen verdorben. **II** *s* ['ʌpset] **5.** (*Magen*)Verstimmung *f*. **6.** *bsd. Sport:* Überraschung *f*.

up·shot ['ʌpʃɒt] *s* Ergebnis *n*: **what was**

the ~ of ...? was ist bei ... herausgekommen?

up·side ['ʌpsaɪd] *adv*: **~ down** verkehrt herum; **turn ~ down** umdrehen, *a. fig.* auf den Kopf stellen.

up·stairs [‚ʌp'steəz] **I** *adv* **1.** die Treppe her- *od.* hinauf, nach oben. **2.** oben, in e-m oberen Stockwerk. **3.** e-e Treppe höher. **II** *adj* **4.** im oberen Stockwerk (gelegen), oben.

up·start ['ʌpstɑːt] *s* Emporkömmling *m*.

up·stream [‚ʌp'striːm] *adv* flußauf(wärts).

up·surge ['ʌpsɜːdʒ] *s* **1.** Anschwellen *n* (**in** *gen*). **2.** Aufwallung *f*.

up·take ['ʌpteɪk] *s*: **be quick** (**slow**) **on the ~** F schnell begreifen (schwer von Begriff sein).

up·tight ['ʌptaɪt] *adj* F **1.** nervös, reizbar. **2.** verklemmt.

up-to-date [‚ʌptə'deɪt] *adj* **1.** modern. **2.** aktuell, neu.

up-to-the-min·ute [‚ʌptəðə'mɪnɪt] *adj* **1.** hochmodern. **2.** allerneu(e)st.

up·town [‚ʌp'taʊn] *Am.* **I** *adv* in den Wohnvierteln, in die Wohnviertel. **II** *adj* in den Wohnvierteln (gelegen *od.* lebend): **in ~ Los Angeles** in den Außenbezirken von Los Angeles. **III** *s* Wohnviertel *pl*, Außenbezirke *pl*.

up·turn ['ʌptɜːn] *s* Aufschwung *m* (**in** *gen*). **¸up'turned** *adj* **1.** nach oben gerichtet *od.* gebogen: **~ nose** Stupsnase *f*. **2.** umgedreht.

up·ward ['ʌpwəd] **I** *adv* **1.** nach oben: **face ~** mit dem Gesicht nach oben. **2. from £ 2 ~** ab 2 Pfund; **~ of £ 2** F mehr als *od.* über 2 Pfund. **3.** *fig.* aufwärts, bergan: **he went ~ in life** es ging aufwärts mit ihm. **II** *adj* **4.** Aufwärts... **up·wards** ['~z] → *upward* I.

u·ra·ni·um [jʊ'reɪnɪəm] *s* 🜨 Uran *n*.

ur·ban ['ɜːbən] *adj* städtisch, Stadt...

ur·bane [ɜː'beɪn] *adj* □ weltmännisch, -gewandt.

ur·chin ['ɜːtʃɪn] *s* Gassenjunge *m*.

u·re·thra [jʊə'riːθrə] *pl* **-thrae** [~θriː], **-thras** *s anat.* Harnröhre *f*.

urge [ɜːdʒ] **I** *v/t* **1.** *a. ~ on* antreiben, *fig. a.* anspornen (**to** zu). **2.** *j-n* drängen (**to do** zu tun). **3.** drängen auf (*acc*). **II** *s* **4.** Drang *m*, Verlangen *n*. **ur·gen·cy** ['ɜːdʒənsɪ] *s* Dringlichkeit *f*. **'ur·gent** *adj* □ dringend: **be ~** *a.* eilen; **be in ~**

need of s.th. et. dringend brauchen.

u·ric ['jʊərɪk] *adj* Urin...: **~ acid** Harnsäure *f*.

u·ri·nal ['jʊərɪnl] *s* **1.** Urinal *n*. **2.** Pissoir *n*. **'u·ri·nar·y** *adj* Urin...: **~ bladder** Harnblase *f*. **u·ri·nate** ['~neɪt] *v/i* urinieren. **u·rine** ['~rɪn] *s* Urin *m*: **~ sample** Urinprobe *f*.

urn [ɜ:n] *s* **1.** Urne *f*. **2.** Großkaffee-, Großteemaschine *f*.

u·rol·o·gist [jʊə'rɒlədʒɪst] *s* ✚ Urologe *m*, Urologin *f*.

us [ʌs] *I personal pron* **1.** uns (*acc od. dat von* **we**): *both of ~* wir beide; → *all* **4. 2.** F wir (*nom*): *they are older than ~*; *it's ~* wir sind's. **II** *reflex pron* **3.** uns: *we looked around ~* wir sahen uns um.

us·a·ble ['ju:zəbl] *adj* brauch-, verwendbar.

us·age ['ju:zɪdʒ] *s* **1.** Brauch *m*, Gepflogenheit *f*. **2.** (Sprach)Gebrauch *m*. **3.** Behandlung *f*.

use I *v/t* [ju:z] **1.** benutzen, gebrauchen, verwenden, *Taktik etc a.* anwenden: *I could ~ a drink* ich F könnte et. zu trinken vertragen. **2.** *Benzin etc* (ver)brauchen: **~ up** auf-, verbrauchen. **3.** *j-n* benutzen (*for* für). **II** *v/i* [ju:z] **4.** *I ~d to live here* ich habe früher hier gewohnt; *he ~d to be a chain smoker* er war früher einmal Kettenraucher. **III** *s* [ju:z] **5.** Benutzung *f*, Gebrauch *m*, Verwendung *f*: *come into ~* in Gebrauch kommen; *go out of ~* außer Gebrauch kommen; *make ~ of* Gebrauch machen von, benutzen. **6.** Verwendung(szweck *m*) *f*: *with many ~s* vielseitig verwendbar. **7.** Nutzen *m*: *be of ~* nützlich *od.* von Nutzen sein (*to* für); *it's no ~ complaining* es ist nutz- *od.* zwecklos zu reklamieren, es hat keinen Zweck zu reklamieren; → *milk* I.

used¹ [ju:zd] *adj* gebraucht: **~ car** Gebrauchtwagen *m*.

used² [ju:st] *adj*: **be ~ to s.th.** an et. gewöhnt sein, et. gewohnt sein; **be ~ to doing s.th.** es gewohnt sein, et. zu tun.

use·ful ['ju:sfʊl] *adj* □ nützlich: *make o.s. ~* sich nützlich machen. **'use·ful·ness** *s* Nützlichkeit *f*.

use·less ['ju:slɪs] *adj* □ nutzlos: *it is ~ a.* es ist zwecklos (*to do* zu tun); *he's ~* F er ist zu nichts zu gebrauchen. **'use·less·ness** *s* Nutzlosigkeit *f*.

us·er ['ju:zə] *s* **1.** Benutzer(in). **2.** Verbraucher(in). **~'friend·ly** *adj* benutzer- *od.* verbraucherfreundlich.

ush·er ['ʌʃə] **I** *s* **1.** Platzanweiser *m*. **2.** ⚖ Gerichtsdiener *m*. **II** *v/t* **3.** *j-n* führen, geleiten (*into in acc*; *to zu s-m Platz etc*). **ush·er·ette** [~'ret] *s* Platzanweiserin *f*.

u·su·al ['ju:ʒl] **I** *adj* üblich: *as ~* wie gewöhnlich *od.* üblich; *it's not ~ for him to be so late* er kommt normalerweise nicht so spät; *is it ~ for him to be so late?* kommt er immer so spät? **II** *s das* Übliche: *the ~* F (*in Pub etc*) wie immer. **u·su·al·ly** ['~ʒəlɪ] *adv* (für) gewöhnlich, normalerweise.

u·sur·er ['ju:ʒərə] *s* Wucherer *m*.

u·su·ri·ous [ju:'zjʊərɪəs] *adj* □ wucherisch, Wucher...

u·surp [ju:'zɜ:p] *v/t Macht etc* an sich reißen, sich *des Throns* bemächtigen.

u·su·ry ['ju:ʒʊrɪ] *s* Wucher *m*.

u·ten·sil [ju:'tensl] *s* Gerät *n*: **~s** *pl a.* Utensilien *pl*.

u·ter·us ['ju:tərəs] *pl* **-i** [~aɪ], **-us·es** *s anat.* Gebärmutter *f*.

u·til·i·tar·i·an [ju:tɪlɪ'teərɪən] *adj* zweckmäßig, praktisch.

u·til·i·ty [ju:'tɪlətɪ] *s* **1.** Nutzen *m*, Nützlichkeit *f*. **2.** → *public* 3a.

u·til·ize ['ju:təlaɪz] *v/t* nutzen.

ut·most ['ʌtməʊst] **I** *adj* äußerst, höchst, größt. **II** *s das* Äußerste: *do one's ~* sein möglichstes tun.

U·to·pi·an [ju:'təʊpjən] *adj* utopisch (*Gesellschaft etc*).

ut·ter ['ʌtə] **I** *adj* □ total, völlig. **II** *v/t et.* äußern, *Seufzer etc* ausstoßen, *Wort* sagen. **'ut·ter·ance** *s* **1.** *give ~ to s-r Meinung etc* Ausdruck geben. **2.** Äußerung *f*.

U-turn ['ju:tɜ:n] *s* **1.** *mot.* Wende *f*: *do a ~* wenden. **2.** *fig.* Kehrtwendung *f*: *do a ~* e-e Kehrtwendung machen (*on in dat*).

u·vu·la ['ju:vjʊlə] *s anat.* (Gaumen-)Zäpfchen *n*.

V

vac [væk] *s univ. Br.* F Semesterferien *pl.*

va·can·cy ['veɪkənsɪ] *s* **1.** freie *od.* offene Stelle: *"vacancies"* „wir stellen ein". **2.** *"vacancies"* „Zimmer frei"; *"no vacancies"* „belegt". **'va·cant** *adj* □ **1.** leerstehend, unbewohnt: *"~"* „frei" (*Toilette*). **2.** frei, offen (*Stelle*): → **situation** 3. **3.** *fig.* leer (*Blick, Gesichtsausdruck*).

va·cate [və'keɪt] *v/t Hotelzimmer etc* räumen. **va'ca·tion I** *s* **1.** *bsd. Am.* Ferien *pl*, Urlaub *m*: *be on ~* im Urlaub sein, Urlaub machen. **2.** *bsd. Br. univ.* Semesterferien *pl*; ⚖ Gerichtsferien *pl.* **II** *v/i* **3.** *bsd. Am.* Urlaub machen, die Ferien verbringen. **va'ca·tion·er, va'ca·tion·ist** *s bsd. Am.* Urlauber(in).

vac·ci·nate ['væksɪneɪt] *v/t* impfen (*against* gegen). **vac·ci'na·tion** *s* Impfung *f.* **vac·cine** ['~siːn] *s* Impfstoff *m.*

vac·il·late ['væsəleɪt] *v/i fig.* schwanken (*between* zwischen *dat*).

vac·u·um ['vækjuəm] **I** *pl* **-u·ums, -u·a** ['~juə] *s phys.* Vakuum *n.* **II** *v/t* Teppich, Zimmer etc saugen. **~ clean·er** *s* Staubsauger *m.* **~ bot·tle** *s Am.,* **~ flask** *s Br.* Thermosflasche *f.* **'~-packed** *adj* vakuumverpackt.

vag·a·bond ['vægəbɒnd] *s* Vagabund *m*, Landstreicher(in).

va·gi·na [və'dʒaɪnə] *pl* **-nas, -nae** [~niː] *s anat.* Scheide *f.*

va·grant ['veɪgrənt] *s* Nichtseßhafte *m, f*, Landstreicher(in).

va·gue [veɪg] *adj* □ verschwommen, *fig. a.* vage: *be ~* sich nur vage äußern (*about* über *acc*, zu); sich unklar ausdrücken; *I haven't got the ~st idea* ich habe nicht die leiseste Ahnung.

vain [veɪn] *adj* □ **1.** eingebildet, eitel. **2.** vergeblich: *in ~ a.* vergebens. **3.** *take s.o.'s name in ~* über j-n lästern.

va·lence ['veɪləns] *s bsd. Am.,* **'va·len·cy** *s bsd. Br.* 🜋 Valenz *f (a. ling.)*, Wertigkeit *f.*

val·en·tine ['væləntaɪn] *s* **1.** Valentinskarte *f.* **2.** Person, der man am Valentinstag e-n Gruß schickt.

va·le·ri·an [və'lɪərɪən] *s* 🌿, *pharm.* Baldrian *m.*

val·et ['vælɪt] *s* (Kammer)Diener *m.* **~ ser·vice** *s* Reinigungsdienst *m (im Hotel).*

val·id ['vælɪd] *adj* □ **1.** a) gültig (*for two weeks* zwei Wochen): *be ~ a.* gelten, b) ⚖ rechtsgültig, -kräftig. **2.** stichhaltig, triftig. **va·lid·i·ty** [və'lɪdətɪ] *s* **1.** Gültigkeit *f*; ⚖ Rechtsgültigkeit *f*, -kraft *f.* **2.** Stichhaltigkeit *f*, Triftigkeit *f.*

va·lise [və'liːz] *s* Reisetasche *f.*

val·ley ['vælɪ] *s* Tal *n.*

val·u·a·ble ['væljʊəbl] **I** *adj* □ wertvoll. **II** *s pl* Wertgegenstände *pl*, -sachen *pl.*

val·u·a·tion [,vælju'eɪʃn] *s* **1.** Schätzung *f*: *make a ~ of etc.* schätzen. **2.** Schätzwert *m (of, on gen).*

val·ue ['væljuː] **I** *s* **1.** *allg.* Wert *m*: *be of ~* wertvoll sein (*to* für); *be good ~, be ~ for money* preisgünstig *od.* -wert sein; *put (od. place) a high ~ on* großen Wert legen auf (*acc*). **2.** *pl* sittliche Werte *pl.* **II** *v/t* **3.** Haus etc schätzen (*at* auf *acc*). **4.** j-n, j-s Rat etc schätzen. **'~-,add·ed tax** *s* 🜋 *Br.* Mehrwertsteuer *f.* **~ judg(e)·ment** *s* Werturteil *n.*

val·ue·less ['væljʊlɪs] *adj* wertlos. **'val·u·er** *s* Schätzer(in).

valve [vælv] *s* **1.** ⚙, 🜋 Ventil *n.* **2.** *anat.* Klappe *f.* **3.** 🜋 *Br. bsd. hist.* Röhre *f.*

vamp [væmp] *s* Vamp *m (Frau).*

vam·pire ['væmpaɪə] *s* Vampir *m.*

van [væn] *s* **1.** Lieferwagen *m*, Transporter *m.* **2.** 🚃 *Br.* (geschlossener) Güterwagen.

van·dal ['vændl] *s* Vandale *m*, Wandale *m.* **van·dal·ism** ['~dəlɪzəm] *s* Vandalismus *m*, Wandalismus *m.* **van·dal·ize** ['~dəlaɪz] *v/t* mutwillig beschädigen *od.* zerstören.

vane [veɪn] *s* **1.** (Propeller- etc)Flügel *m.* **2.** (Wetter)Fahne *f.*

van·guard ['vænɡɑːd] *s* ⚔ Vorhut *f*: *be in the ~ of fig.* an der Spitze (*gen*) stehen.

va·nil·la [və'nɪlə] *s* 🌿 Vanille *f.*

van·ish ['vænɪʃ] *v/i* verschwinden, (*Angst, Hoffnung etc*) schwinden: → **thin** 1.

van·i·ty ['vænətɪ] *s* Eitelkeit *f.*

van·tage point ['vɑːntɪdʒ] *s* Aussichtspunkt *m*: *from my ~* *fig.* aus m-r Sicht.

va·por *Am.* → **vapour.**

va·por·ize ['veɪpəraɪz] *v/i* verdampfen, -dunsten.

va·por·ous ['veɪpərəs] *adj* □ dunstig, Dunst...

va·pour ['veɪpə] *s bsd. Br.* Dampf *m*, Dunst *m*. **~ trail** *s* ✈ Kondensstreifen *m*.

var·i·a·ble ['veərɪəbl] **I** *adj* □ **1.** variabel, veränderlich (*beide a.* ⚡, *phys. etc*). **2.** schwankend, unbeständig, wechselhaft. **3.** einstell-, regulierbar. **II** *s* **4.** ⚡, *phys.* Variable *f*, veränderliche Größe (*beide a. fig.*). **'var·i·ance** *s*: *be at ~ with* im Gegensatz *od.* Widerspruch stehen zu. **'var·i·ant I** *adj* abweichend, verschieden. **II** *s* Variante *f*. **,var·i·'a·tion** *s* **1.** Abweichung *f*, Schwankung *f*. **2.** ♪ Variation *f* (*on* über *acc*).

var·i·cose ['værɪkəʊs] *adj*: *~ vein* 🌿 Krampfader *f*.

var·ied ['veərɪd] *adj* □ **1.** unterschiedlich. **2.** abwechslungsreich, bewegt.

va·ri·e·ty [və'raɪətɪ] *s* **1.** Abwechslung *f*. **2.** Vielfalt *f*; ♥ Auswahl *f*, Sortiment *n* (*of* an *dat*): *for a ~ of reasons* aus den verschiedensten Gründen. **3.** 🌾, *zo.* Art *f*. **4.** Varieté *n*.

var·i·ous ['veərɪəs] *adj* **1.** verschieden. **2.** mehrere, verschiedene.

var·nish ['vɑːnɪʃ] **I** *s* Lack *m*. **II** *v/t* lackieren.

var·y ['veərɪ] **I** *v/i* variieren, (*Meinungen*) auseinandergehen (*on* über *acc*): *~ in size* verschieden groß sein. **II** *v/t* (ver)ändern; variieren.

vas·cu·lar ['væskjʊlə] *adj anat.*, 🌾 Gefäß...

vase [vɑːz] *s* Vase *f*.

vast [vɑːst] *adj* gewaltig, riesig, (*Fläche a.*) ausgedehnt, weit. **'vast·ly** *adv* gewaltig, weitaus.

vat [væt] *s* (großes) Faß.

vaude·ville ['vɔːdəvɪl] *s Am.* Varieté *n*.

vault¹ [vɔːlt] *s* **1.** 🏛 Gewölbe *n*. **2.** *a. pl* (Keller)Gewölbe *n*; Stahlkammer *f*, Tresorraum *m*; Gruft *f*.

vault² [vɔːlt] **I** *v/i*: *~ over* springen über (*acc*). **II** *v/t* → **I. III** *s* Sprung *m*.

vault·ed ['vɔːltɪd] *adj* **1.** 🏛 gewölbt. **2.** überwölbt.

vault·ing ['vɔːltɪŋ] *adj*: *~ horse* (*Turnen*) Sprungpferd *n*.

veal [viːl] *s* Kalbfleisch *n*. **~ cut·let** *s* Kalbsschnitzel *n*.

veer [vɪə] *v/i*: *~ to the left mot.* den Wagen nach links reißen.

veg [vedʒ] *pl* **veg** *s gastr. bsd. Br.* F Gemüse *n*: *and two ~* u. zweierlei Gemüse.

ve·gan ['viːgən] *s* Veganer(in).

veg·e·ta·ble ['vedʒtəbl] **I** *s* **1.** *mst pl* Gemüse *n*: *and two ~s* u. zweierlei Gemüse; *be just a ~* nur noch dahinvegetieren. **II** *adj* **2.** Gemüse... **3.** Pflanzen...

veg·e·tar·i·an [,vedʒɪ'teərɪən] **I** *s* Vegetarier(in): *he's a ~* er ist Vegetarier, er lebt vegetarisch. **II** *adj* vegetarisch.

veg·e·tate ['vedʒɪteɪt] *v/i* dahinvegetieren. **,veg·e·'ta·tion** *s* Vegetation *f*.

ve·he·mence ['viːəmens] *s* Vehemenz *f*, Heftigkeit *f*. **'ve·he·ment** *adj* □ vehement, heftig.

ve·hi·cle ['vɪəkl] *s* **1.** Fahrzeug *n*. **2.** *fig.* Medium *n*. **ve·hic·u·lar** [vɪ'hɪkjʊlə] *adj* Fahrzeug...

veil [veɪl] **I** *s* Schleier *m*: *~ of mist* Nebelschleier; *draw a ~ over fig.* den Schleier des Vergessens breiten über (*acc*). **II** *v/t* verschleiern (*a. fig.*).

vein [veɪn] *s anat.* Vene *f*, *weitS.* Ader *f* (*a.* 🌾, *geol.*).

ve·loc·i·ty [vɪ'lɒsətɪ] *s phys.*, ⚙ Geschwindigkeit *f*.

ve·lour(s) [və'lʊə] *s* Velours *m*.

vel·vet ['velvɪt] *s* Samt *m*: (*as*) *smooth as ~* samtweich. **'vel·vet·y** *adj* samtig (*a. fig. Wein*).

vend·er → **vendor.**

ven·det·ta [ven'detə] *s* **1.** Blutrache *f*. **2.** Fehde *f*.

vend·ing ['vendɪŋ] *adj*: *~ machine* (Verkaufs-, Waren)Automat *m*. **'vend·or** *s* (Straßen)Händler(in), (Zeitungs- *etc*-) Verkäufer(in).

ve·neer [və'nɪə] **I** *s* **1.** Furnier *n*. **2.** *fig.* Fassade *f*. **II** *v/t* **3.** furnieren (*in, with* mit).

ven·er·a·ble ['venərəbl] *adj* □ ehrwürdig. **ven·er·ate** ['~reɪt] *v/t* verehren. **,ven·er·'a·tion** *s* Verehrung *f*.

ve·ne·re·al [və'nɪərɪəl] *adj*: *~ disease* Geschlechtskrankheit *f*.

Ve·ne·tian [və'niːʃn] *adj*: *~ blind* Jalousie *f*.

venge·ance ['vendʒəns] *s* Rache *f*: *take*

~ on sich rächen an (*dat*); **with a ~** F gewaltig, u. wie.

ve·ni·al ['vi:njəl] *adj* entschuldbar, verzeihlich, *eccl.* läßlich (*Sünde*).

ven·i·son ['venizn] *s* Wildbret *n*.

ven·om ['venəm] *s* **1.** *zo.* Gift *n*. **2.** *fig.* Gift *n*, Gehässigkeit *f.* **'ven·om·ous** *adj* □ **1.** giftig: **~ snake** Giftschlange *f.* **2.** *fig.* giftig, gehässig.

ve·nous ['vi:nəs] *adj anat.* venös.

vent [vent] **I** *v/t* **1.** *s-e Wut etc* abreagieren (**on** an *dat*). **II** *s* **2.** (Abzugs)Öffnung *f.* **3.** Schlitz *m* (*in Kleid etc*). **4.** **give ~ to** *s-m Ärger etc* Luft machen.

ven·ti·late ['ventileit] *v/t* (be)lüften. **,ven·ti'la·tion** *s* Ventilation *f*, (Be)Lüftung *f.* **'ven·ti·la·tor** *s* Ventilator *m*, Lüfter *m.*

ven·tral ['ventrəl] *adj* Bauch...: **~ fin** Bauchflosse *f.*

ven·tri·cle ['ventrɪkl] *s anat.* Herzkammer *f.*

ven·tril·o·quist [ven'trɪləkwɪst] *s* Bauchredner(in).

ven·ture ['ventʃə] **I** *s* **1.** *bsd.* ✝ Unternehmen *n*: → **joint** 5. **II** *v/t* **2.** *Ruf etc* riskieren, aufs Spiel setzen (**on** bei). **3.** (zu äußern) wagen: **~ to do s.th.** es wagen, et. zu tun. **III** *v/i* **4.** sich *wohin* wagen. **5. ~ on** sich wagen an (*acc*).

ven·ue ['venju:] *s* Schauplatz *m*, (*Sport*) Austragungsort *m.*

Ve·nus ['vi:nəs] *s ast.* die Venus.

ve·ran·da(h) [və'rændə] *s* Veranda *f.*

verb [vɜ:b] *s ling.* Verb *n*, Zeitwort *n.* **ver·bal** ['~l] *adj* □ **1.** mündlich. **2.** Wort...: **he's got ~ diarrh(o)ea** F der bringt den Mund nicht zu. **3.** *noun ling.* Verbalsubstantiv *n.* **ver·bal·ize** ['~bəlaiz] *v/t* ausdrücken, in Worte fassen. **ver·ba·tim** ['~beitɪm] *adj* (wort-)wörtlich, *adv* a. Wort für Wort. **ver·bi·age** ['~bɪɪdʒ] *s* (leeres) Wortgeklingel. **ver·bose** ['~bəʊs] *adj* □ wortreich, langatmig.

ver·dict ['vɜ:dɪkt] *s* **1.** ⚖ Spruch *m* (*der Geschworenen*): **~ of (not) guilty** Schuldspruch (Freispruch) *m*; **bring in** (*od.* **return**) **a ~ of (not) guilty** auf (nicht) schuldig erkennen. **2.** Meinung *f*, Urteil *n* (**on** über *acc*).

ver·di·gris ['vɜ:dɪɡrɪs] *s* Grünspan *m.*

verge [vɜ:dʒ] **I** *s* Rand *m* (*a. fig.*): **be on the ~ of** kurz vor (*dat*) stehen; **be on the**

~ of tears den Tränen nahe sein; **she was on the ~ of falling** sie wäre beinahe gestürzt. **II** *v/i:* **~ on** *fig.* grenzen an (*acc*).

ver·ger ['vɜ:dʒə] *s* Kirchendiener *m*, Küster *m.*

ver·i·fi·a·ble ['verɪfaɪəbl] *adj* nachweisbar. **ver·i·fy** ['~faɪ] *v/t* **1.** bestätigen. **2.** (über)prüfen. **3.** nachweisen.

ver·i·ta·ble ['verɪtəbl] *adj* wahr (*Triumph etc*).

ver·mil·ion [və'mɪljən] *adj* zinnoberrot.

ver·min ['vɜ:mɪn] *s* (*pl konstruiert*) **1.** Schädlinge *pl*; Ungeziefer *n*. **2.** *fig.* Gesindel *n*, Pack *n.* **'ver·min·ous** *adj* voller Ungeziefer.

ver·mouth ['vɜ:məθ] *s* Wermut *m.*

ver·nac·u·lar [və'nækjʊlə] *s* Dialekt *m*, Mundart *f.*

ver·nis·sage [,vɜ:nɪ'sɑ:ʒ] *s* Vernissage *f.*

ver·sa·tile ['vɜ:sətaɪl] *adj* □ **1.** vielseitig. **2.** vielseitig verwendbar.

verse [vɜ:s] *s* **1.** Poesie *f*, Versdichtung *f.* **2.** Vers *m.* **3.** Strophe *f.*

versed [vɜ:st] *adj:* **be (well) ~ in** beschlagen *od.* bewandert sein in (*dat*).

ver·sion ['vɜ:ʃn] *s* Version *f:* a) Darstellung *f* (*e-s Ereignisses*), b) Fassung *f* (*e-s Textes*), c) Übersetzung *f*, d) Ausführung *f* (*e-s Geräts etc*).

ver·sus ['vɜ:səs] *prp* ⚖, *Sport:* gegen.

ver·te·bra ['vɜ:tɪbrə] *pl* **-brae** ['~bri:], **-bras** *s anat.* Wirbel *m.* **'ver·te·bral** *adj:* **~ column** *anat.* Rückgrat *n*, Wirbelsäule *f.* **ver·te·brate** ['~breɪt] *s zo.* Wirbeltier *n.*

ver·tex ['vɜ:teks] *pl* **-ti·ces** ['~tɪsi:z], **-tex·es** *s* Scheitel(punkt) *m.*

ver·ti·cal ['vɜ:tɪkl] **I** *adj* □ senkrecht, vertikal: **~ takeoff aircraft** Senkrechtstarter *m.* **II** *s* & Senkrechte *f*, Vertikale *f.*

ver·ti·go ['vɜ:tɪɡəʊ] *s* 🏥 Schwindel *m*: **suffer from ~** an *od.* unter Schwindel leiden.

verve [vɜ:v] *s* Elan *m*, Schwung *m.*

ver·y ['verɪ] **I** *adv* **1.** sehr: **~ much older** sehr viel älter; **I ~ much hope that** ich hoffe sehr, daß; **~ high frequency** ⚡ Ultrakurzwelle *f*; → **well**¹ **1. 2.** aller...: **the ~ last drop** der allerletzte Tropfen; **for the ~ last time** zum allerletzten Mal; **at the ~ least** zum allermindesten, allermindest. **II** *adj* **3. the ~** genau der *od.* die *od.* das: *the ~ opposite* genau das Gegenteil; *be the ~ thing* genau das richtige sein (*for doing* um zu tun); → **act** 1. **4.** *the ~ thought of* schon der *od.* der bloße Gedanke an (*dat*); *the ~ idea!* um Himmels willen!

ves·i·cle ['vesɪkl] *s* Bläschen *n.*

ves·pers ['vespəz] *s pl eccl.* Vesper *f.*

ves·sel ['vesl] *s* **1.** Schiff *n.* **2.** Gefäß *n* (*a. anat.*)*.*

vest [vest] **I** *s* **1.** *Br.* Unterhemd *n.* **2.** kugelsichere Weste. **3.** *Am.* Weste *f.* **II** *v/t* **4.** *~ in s.o., ~ s.o. with s.th.* j-m et. übertragen. verleihen: *have a ~ed interest in* ein persönliches Interesse haben an (*dat*); *~ed interests pl* Interessengruppen *pl.* **III** *v/i* **5.** *~ in* zustehen (*dat*), liegen bei.

ves·ti·bule ['vestɪbjuːl] *s* (Vor)Halle *f.*

ves·tige ['vestɪdʒ] *s* Spur *f: there is not a ~ of truth in this story* an dieser Geschichte ist kein Wort wahr.

ves·try ['vestrɪ] *s eccl.* Sakristei *f.*

vet¹ [vet] **F I** *s* Tierarzt *m*, -ärztin *f.* **II** *v/t bsd. Br.* überprüfen.

vet² [~] *s* ✕ *Am.* F Veteran *m.*

vetch [vetʃ] *s* ♣ Wicke *f.*

vet·er·an ['vetərən] **I** *s* **1.** ✕ Veteran *m* (*a. fig.*). **II** *adj* **2.** altgedient; erfahren. **3.** *~ car mot. Br.* Oldtimer *m* (*Baujahr bis 1905*).

vet·er·i·nar·i·an [ˌvetərɪ'neərɪən] *s Am.* Tierarzt *m*, -ärztin *f.*

vet·er·i·nar·y ['vetərɪnərɪ] *adj* tierärztlich: *~ medicine* Tier-, Veterinärmedizin *f; ~ surgeon bsd. Br.* Tierarzt *m*, -ärztin *f.*

ve·to ['viːtəʊ] **I** *pl* **-toes** *s* **1.** Veto *n.* **II** *v/t* **2.** sein Veto einlegen gegen. **3.** untersagen.

vexed ['vekst] *adj: ~ question* leidige Frage.

vi·a [vaɪə] *prp* über (*acc*), (*bei Städtenamen a.*) via.

vi·a·ble ['vaɪəbl] *adj* □ **1.** lebensfähig (*a. fig.*). **2.** *fig.* durchführbar, realisierbar.

vi·a·duct ['vaɪədʌkt] *s* Viadukt *m, n.*

vi·al ['vaɪəl] *s* (*bsd.* Arznei)Fläschchen *n.*

vibes [vaɪbz] *s pl* F **1.** (*mst sg konstruiert*) ♪ Vibraphon *n.* **2.** Atmosphäre *f* (*e-s Orts etc*): *I was getting positive ~ from her* ich spürte, wie der Funke von ihr auf mich übersprang.

vi·brant ['vaɪbrənt] *adj* □ **1.** kräftig (*Far-*

ben, Stimme etc). **2.** pulsierend (*Leben*). **3.** dynamisch (*Person*).

vi·bra·phone ['vaɪbrəfəʊn] *s* ♪ Vibraphon *n.*

vi·brate [vaɪ'breɪt] **I** *v/i* **1.** vibrieren, zittern. **2.** flimmern (*with heat* vor Hitze) (*Luft*). **3.** *the city ~s with life* in der Stadt pulsiert das Leben. **II** *v/t* **4.** in Schwingungen versetzen. **vi'bra·tion** *s* **1.** Vibrieren *n*, Zittern *n.* **2.** *pl* F → **vibes** 2. **vi'bra·tor** *s* Vibrator *m.*

vic·ar ['vɪkə] *s* Pfarrer *m.* '**vic·ar·age** *s* Pfarrhaus *n.*

vice¹ [vaɪs] *s* Laster *n.*

vice² [~] *s* ✪ *bsd. Br.* Schraubstock *m.*

vice...³ [~] Vize..., stellvertretend.

vice-like ['vaɪslaɪk] *adj: hold s.th. in a ~ grip bsd. Br.* et. fest umklammert halten.

vice squad *s* Sittendezernat *n,* -polizei *f.*

vi·ce ver·sa [ˌvaɪsɪ'vɜːsə] *adv: and ~* u. umgekehrt.

vi·cin·i·ty [vɪ'sɪnətɪ] *s: in the ~ of* in der Nähe von (*od. gen*); *in this ~* hier in der Nähe; *in the ~ of 40 fig.* um die 40 herum.

vi·cious ['vɪʃəs] *adj* □ brutal. *~ cir·cle* *s* Circulus *m* vitiosus, Teufelskreis *m.*

vi·cis·si·tudes [vɪ'sɪsɪtjuːdz] *s pl das* Auf u. Ab, (*des Lebens a.*) die Wechselfälle *pl.*

vic·tim ['vɪktɪm] *s* Opfer *n: fall ~ to* betroffen werden von; erkranken an (*dat*). '**vic·tim·ize** *v/t* j-n (immer wieder) zum Sündenbock machen.

vic·tor ['vɪktə] *s* Sieger(in). **vic·to·ri·ous** [~'tɔːrɪəs] *adj* □ siegreich. **vic·to·ry** ['~tərɪ] *s* Sieg *m: ~ ceremony* Siegerehrung *f.*

vi·de ['vaɪdiː] *imp* siehe!

vi·de·li·cet [vɪ'diːlɪset] *adv* nämlich.

vid·e·o ['vɪdɪəʊ] **I** *pl* **-os** *s* **1.** Video(kassette *f*) *n: on ~* auf Video. **2.** → *video recorder.* **II** *v/t* **3.** auf Video aufnehmen, aufzeichnen. *~ cam·er·a* *s* Videokamera *f.* *~ cas·sette* *s* Videokassette *f.* *~ cas·sette re·cord·er* → *video recorder.* *~ nas·ty* → *nasty* 5. *~ re·cord·er* *s* Videorecorder *m.* *~ re·cord·ing* *s* Videoaufnahme *f.* *~ tape* → *video cassette.* '*~·tape* → *video* 3.

vie [vaɪ] *v/i* wetteifern (*with* um *für* um).

view [vjuː] **I** *s* **1.** Sicht *f* (*of* auf *acc*): *at first ~* auf den ersten Blick; *in full ~ of* direkt vor *j-s* Augen; **in ~ of** *fig.* angesichts (*gen*); **with a ~ to** *fig.* mit Blick auf (*acc*); **with a ~ to doing s.th.** in od. mit der Absicht, et. zu tun; **be on ~** ausgestellt *od.* zu besichtigen sein; **be hidden from ~** nicht zu sehen sein; **come into ~** in Sicht kommen; **have in ~** *et.* in Aussicht haben; **keep in ~** *et.* im Auge behalten. **2.** Aussicht *f*, Blick *m* (**of** auf *acc*): **a room with a ~** ein Zimmer mit schöner Aussicht; **there is a grand ~ of the mountains from here** von hier hat man e-n herrlichen Blick auf die Berge. **3.** *phot. etc* Ansicht *f*. **4.** Ansicht *f*, Meinung *f* (**about, on** über *acc*): **in my ~** m-r Ansicht nach; **take a dim** (*od.* **poor**) **~ of** *et.* negativ beurteilen. **5.** *fig.* Überblick *m* (**of** über *acc*). **II** *v/t* **6.** *Haus etc* besichtigen. **7.** *fig.* betrachten (**as** als; **with** mit). **III** *v/i* **8.** fernsehen. '**view·er** *s* **1.** (Fernseh)Zuschauer(in), Fernseher(in). **2.** (*Dia*)Betrachter *m*.

'**view**|**,find·er** *s phot.* Sucher *m*. '**~·point** *s* Gesichts-, Standpunkt *m*.

vig·il ['vɪdʒɪl] *s* (Nacht)Wache *f*: **keep ~** wachen (**over** bei). '**vig·i·lance** *s* Wachsamkeit *f*. '**vig·i·lant** *adj* □ wachsam.

vig·or ['vɪɡə] *Am.* → **vigour**. '**vig·or·ous** *adj* □ energisch. '**vig·our** *s bsd. Br.* Energie *f*.

vile [vaɪl] *adj* □ **1.** gemein, niederträchtig. **2.** F scheußlich.

vil·la ['vɪlə] *s* Villa *f*.

vil·lage ['vɪlɪdʒ] *s* Dorf *n*. '**vil·lag·er** *s* Dorfbewohner(in).

vil·lain ['vɪlən] *s* **1.** Bösewicht *m*, Schurke *m* (*in Film etc*). **2.** *Br.* F Ganove *m*. **3.** F Bengel *m*.

vin·di·cate ['vɪndɪkeɪt] *v/t* **1.** *et.* rechtfertigen; bestätigen. **2.** *j-n* rehabilitieren. ,**vin·di·ca·tion** *s* **1.** Rechtfertigung *f*; Bestätigung *f*. **2.** Rehabilitation *f*.

vin·dic·tive [vɪn'dɪktɪv] *adj* □ rachsüchtig.

vine [vaɪn] *s* ♣ **1.** (Wein)Rebe *f*. **2.** Kletterpflanze *f*.

vin·e·gar ['vɪnɪɡə] *s* Essig *m*.

'**vine**|**,grow·er** *s* Winzer *m*. **~·yard** ['vɪnjəd] *s* Weinberg *m*.

vi·no ['viːnəʊ] *pl* **-nos** *s* F Wein *m*.

vin·tage ['vɪntɪdʒ] **I** *s* **1.** Jahrgang *m* (*e-s Weins*). **2.** Weinernte *f*, -lese *f*. **II** *adj* **3.**

Jahrgangs...: **~ wine. 4.** glänzend, hervorragend. **5. ~ car** *mot. bsd. Br.* Oldtimer *m* (*Baujahr 1919-30*).

vint·ner ['vɪntnə] *s* **1.** Weinhändler *m*. **2.** *Am.* Winzer *m*.

vi·o·la [vɪ'əʊlə] *s* ♪ Bratsche *f*.

vi·o·late ['vaɪəleɪt] *v/t* **1.** *Vertrag etc* verletzen, *a. Versprechen* brechen, *Gesetz etc* übertreten. **2.** *Frieden, Ruhe etc* stören. **3.** *Grab etc* schänden. **4.** *Frau* schänden, vergewaltigen. ,**vi·o·la·tion** *s* **1.** Verletzung *f*, Bruch *m*, Übertretung *f*. **2.** Störung *f*. **3.** Schändung *f*. **4.** Vergewaltigung *f*.

vi·o·lence ['vaɪələns] *s* **1.** Gewalt *f*. **2.** Gewalttätigkeit *f*. **3.** Heftigkeit *f*. '**vi·o·lent** *adj* □ **1.** gewalttätig. **2.** gewaltsam: **~ crime** Gewaltverbrechen *n*; **die a ~ death** e-s gewaltsamen Todes sterben. **3.** heftig (*Auseinandersetzung, Sturm etc*): **be in a ~ temper** geladen sein.

vi·o·let ['vaɪələt] **I** *s* ♣ Veilchen *n*: → **shrinking. II** *adj* violett.

vi·o·lin [,vaɪə'lɪn] *s* ♪ Geige *f*, Violine *f*: **~ case** Geigenkasten *m*. ,**vi·o·lin·ist** *s* Geiger(in), Violinist(in).

vi·o·lon·cel·lo [,vaɪələn'tʃeləʊ] *pl* **-los** *s* ♪ Violoncello *n*.

VIP [,viːaɪ'piː] *s* VIP *f* (*prominente Persönlichkeit*).

vi·per ['vaɪpə] *s zo.* Viper *f*.

vi·ral ['vaɪərəl] *adj* ♣ Virus...

vir·gin ['vɜːdʒɪn] **I** *s* Jungfrau *f*: **she's still a ~** sie ist noch Jungfrau. **II** *adj* jungfräulich, unberührt (*beide a. fig.*).

Vir·go ['vɜːɡəʊ] *s ast.* Jungfrau *f*: **be** (**a**) **~** Jungfrau sein.

vir·ile ['vɪraɪl] *adj* **1.** männlich. **2.** potent. **vi·ril·i·ty** [vɪ'rɪlətɪ] *s* **1.** Männlichkeit *f*. **2.** Potenz *f*.

vir·tu·al ['vɜːtʃʊəl] *adj*: **he's a ~ alcoholic** er ist praktisch schon Alkoholiker; **it's a ~ certainty that** es steht praktisch *od.* so gut wie fest, daß. '**vir·tu·al·ly** *adv* praktisch, so gut wie.

vir·tue ['vɜːtʃuː] *s* **1.** Tugend(haftigkeit) *f*. **2.** Tugend *f*: **make a ~ of necessity** aus der Not e-e Tugend machen. **3.** Vorzug *m*, Vorteil *m*. **4. by** (*od.* **in**) **~ of** kraft (*gen*), aufgrund (*gen*).

vir·tu·o·so [,vɜːtjʊ'əʊzəʊ] *bsd.* ♪ **I** *pl* **-sos, -si** [~ziː] *s* Virtuose *m*, Virtuosin *f*. **II** *adj* virtuos.

vir·tu·ous ['vɜːtʃʊəs] adj □ tugendhaft.

vir·u·lent ['vɪrʊlənt] adj □ **1.** (akut u.) bösartig (*Krankheit*); schnellwirkend (*Gift*). **2.** fig. bösartig, gehässig.

vi·rus ['vaɪərəs] s 🐾 Virus n, a. m. **~ in·fec·tion** s 🐾 Virusinfektion f.

vi·sa ['viːzə] **I** s Visum n, (*im Paß eingetragenes a.*) Sichtvermerk m. **II** v/t ein Visum eintragen in (*acc*).

vis-à-vis [ˌviːzaˈviː] prp in Anbetracht (*gen*).

vis·cer·a ['vɪsərə] s pl anat. Eingeweide pl.

vis·count ['vaɪkaʊnt] s Viscount m (*englischer Adelstitel*). **'vis·count·ess** s Viscountess f.

vis·cous ['vɪskəs] adj □ dick-, zähflüssig, 🔧 a. viskos.

vise, vise·like Am. → vice², vicelike.

vis·i·bil·i·ty [ˌvɪzɪˈbɪlɪtɪ] s Sicht(verhältnisse pl, -weite f) f. **'vis·i·ble** adj □ **1.** sichtbar. **2.** fig. (er)sichtlich.

vi·sion ['vɪʒn] s **1.** Sehkraft f. **2.** fig. Weitblick m. **3.** Vision f: ~ *of the future* Zukunftsvision; *have* ~*s of doing s.th.* sich schon et. tun sehen. **vi·sion·ar·y** ['ˌrɪ] **I** adj **1.** weitblickend. **2.** eingebildet, unwirklich. **II** s **3.** Seher(in). **4.** Phantast(in), Träumer(in).

vis·it ['vɪzɪt] **I** v/t **1.** j-n besuchen, *Museum etc.* a. besichtigen. **2.** et. inspizieren. **II** v/i **3. be ~ing** auf Besuch sein (*Am.:* *in* in dat; *with* bei). **4. ~ with** *Am.* plaudern mit. **III** s **5.** Besuch m, Besichtigung f (*to gen*): *for* (*od.* on) a ~ auf Besuch; *have a* ~ *from* Besuch haben von; *pay a* ~ *to* j-m e-n Besuch abstatten; *Arzt* aufsuchen; *I've got to pay a* ~ *Br.* F ich muß mal verschwinden. **6.** *Am.* Plauderei f (*with* mit). **'vis·i·ta·tion** s **1.** Inspektion f. **2.** fig. Heimsuchung f. **3.** F humor. überlanger Besuch (*from gen*). **'vis·it·ing** adj Besuchs...: ~ *card* Visitenkarte f; ~ *hours* pl Besuchszeit f. **'vis·i·tor** s Besucher(in) (*to* gen; *from* aus): ~*s pl to England* Englandbesucher pl; *have* ~*s* Besuch haben; ~*'s book* Gästebuch n.

vi·sor ['vaɪzə] s **1.** Visier n (a. ✕ hist.). **2.** Schirm m (*e-r Mütze*). **3.** mot. (*Sonnen*)Blende f.

vis·ta ['vɪstə] s Aussicht f, Blick m (*of* auf acc).

vis·u·al ['vɪʃʊəl] adj □ **1.** Seh... **2.** visuell: ~ *aids* pl ped. Anschauungsmaterial n, Lehrmittel pl. **3.** optisch. **'vis·u·al·ize** v/t sich et. vorstellen.

vi·tal ['vaɪtl] adj (□ → vitally) **1.** lebenswichtig (*Organ etc.*). **2.** Lebens...: ~ *statistics* pl Bevölkerungsstatistik f; F humor. Maße pl (e-r Frau). **3.** unbedingt notwendig (*to, for* für): *of* ~ *importance* von größter Wichtigkeit. **4.** vital. **vi·tal·i·ty** [ˈtælɪtɪ] s Vitalität f. **vi·tal·ly** ['ˌtəlɪ] adv **1.** vital. **2.** sehr viel: ~ *important* äußerst wichtig.

vi·ta·min ['vɪtəmɪn] s Vitamin n. ~ *pill* s Vitamintablette f.

vit·re·ous ['vɪtrɪəs] adj Glas...

vi·va ['vaɪvə] Br. F → viva voce.

vi·va·cious [vɪˈveɪʃəs] adj □ lebhaft, temperamentvoll.

vi·va vo·ce ['vaɪvə] s univ. mündliche Prüfung.

viv·id ['vɪvɪd] adj □ **1.** hell (*Licht*); kräftig, leuchtend (*Farben*). **2.** anschaulich (*Schilderung etc.*), lebhaft (*Phantasie*).

viv·i·sec·tion [ˌvɪvɪˈsekʃn] s Vivisektion f.

V neck [viː] s V-Ausschnitt m. **'V -necked** adj mit V-Ausschnitt.

vo·cab ['vəʊkæb] F → vocabulary 2.

vo·cab·u·lar·y [vəʊˈkæbjʊlərɪ] s **1.** Vokabular n, Wortschatz m. **2.** Vokabular n, Wortregister n, Wörterverzeichnis n.

vo·cal ['vəʊkl] **I** adj □ **1.** Stimm...: ~ *cords* pl anat. Stimmbänder pl. **2.** ♪ *music* Vokalmusik f. **3.** F lautstark. **II** s pl **4.** ~*s: XY* Gesang: XY.

vo·ca·tion [vəʊˈkeɪʃn] s **1.** Begabung f (*for* für). **2.** Berufung f. **vo'ca·tion·al** [ˌʃənl] adj Berufs...: ~ *training* Berufsausbildung f.

vo·cif·er·ous [vəʊˈsɪfərəs] adj □ lautstark (*Protest etc.*).

vogue [vəʊg] s Mode f: *be in* ~ Mode sein; *be all the* ~ große Mode sein. ~ *word* s Modewort n.

voice [vɔɪs] **I** s **1.** Stimme f (a. fig.): *give* ~ *to* → 4. **2.** *have a* ~ *in* Mitspracherecht n haben bei. **3.** → active², passive² 2. **II** v/t **4.** zum Ausdruck bringen. **5.** ling. stimmhaft aussprechen. ~ *box* s anat. Kehlkopf m.

voiced [vɔɪst] adj ling. stimmhaft. **'voice·less** adj ling. stimmlos.

void [vɔɪd] **I** adj **1.** leer: ~ *of* ohne. **2.** 🔏 nichtig, ungültig: → null. **II** v/t **3.** 🔏

nichtig *od.* ungültig machen. **III** *s* **4.** *fig.* (Gefühl *n* der) Leere.

vol·a·tile ['vɒlətail] *adj* **1.** cholerisch (*Person, Temperament*); explosiv (*Lage etc*). **2.** 🜊 flüchtig, (*Öl*) ätherisch.

vol·can·ic [vɒl'kænik] *adj* (*~ally*) vulkanisch, Vulkan... **vol·ca·no** [~'keinəʊ] *pl* **-no(e)s** *s* Vulkan *m*.

vo·li·tion [vəʊ'liʃn] *s*: *of one's own ~* aus freien Stücken.

vol·ley ['vɒli] **I** *s* **1.** Salve *f*; (*Schlag- etc*)Hagel *m*: *a ~ of curses* ein Hagel von Verwünschungen. **2.** *Tennis:* Volley *m*, Flugball *m*; (*Fußball*) Volleyschluß *m*: *take on the ~ Ball* volley nehmen. **II** *v/t* **3.** *Ball* volley schießen (*into the net* ins Netz). '~·ball *s Sport:* Volleyball *m*.

volt [vəʊlt] *s* ⚡ Volt *n*. '**volt·age** *s* ⚡ Spannung *f*.

vol·u·ble ['vɒljʊbl] *adj* □ **1.** redselig. **2.** wortreich.

vol·ume ['vɒljuːm] *s* **1.** Band *m*: *a two-~ novel* ein zweibändiger Roman; *speak ~s fig.* Bände sprechen. **2.** 🜊, *phys.* Volumen *n*, Rauminhalt *m*. **3.** (*Handels- etc*)Volumen *n*, (*Verkehrs*)Aufkommen *n*. **4.** Lautstärke *f*: *at full ~* in voller Lautstärke; *turn to full ~ Radio etc* auf volle Lautstärke stellen, voll aufdrehen; *turn the ~ up* (*down*) lauter (leiser) drehen; *~ control* Lautstärkeregler *m*. **vo·lu·mi·nous** [və'luːmɪnəs] *adj* □ **1.** bauschig (*Kleidungsstück*). **2.** geräumig. **3.** umfangreich (*Bericht etc*).

vol·un·tar·y ['vɒləntəri] *adj* □ **1.** freiwillig. **2.** unbezahlt.

vol·un·teer [ˌvɒlən'tɪə] **I** *v/i* **1.** sich freiwillig melden (*for* zu) (*a.* ✗). **II** *v/t* **2.** *Hilfe etc* anbieten: *~ to do s.th.* sich anbieten, et. zu tun. **3.** *et.* von sich aus sagen. **III** *s* **4.** Freiwillige *m* (*a.* ✗); freiwilliger Helfer.

vo·lup·tu·ous [və'lʌptʃʊəs] *adj* □ **1.** sinnlich (*Lippen, Mund*); üppig (*Formen*); aufreizend (*Bewegungen*). **2.** kurvenreich (*Frau*).

vom·it ['vɒmɪt] **I** *v/t* erbrechen, *Blut* spucken; *Feuer, Lava* speien, *Rauchwolken etc* ausstoßen. **II** *v/i* (sich er)brechen, sich übergeben.

vo·ra·cious [və'reɪʃəs] *adj* □ unersättlich (*Appetit*): *he's a ~ reader of comics* er verschlingt die Comics geradezu.

vor·tex ['vɔːteks] *pl* **-tex·es, -ti·ces** ['~tɪsiːz] *s* Strudel *m* (*a. fig.*), Wirbel *m*.

vote [vəʊt] **I** *s* **1.** Abstimmung *f* (*about, on* über *acc*): *put to the ~* abstimmen lassen über (*acc*); *take a ~ on* abstimmen über; → *censure* 1. **2.** Stimme *f*; Stimmzettel *m*, Stimme *f*: *cast one's ~ for, give one's ~* s-e Stimme für, j-m s-e Stimme geben. **3.** *a. pl* Wahlrecht *n*: *get the ~* wahlberechtigt werden. **II** *v/i* **4.** wählen: *~ for* (*against*) stimmen für (gegen). **5.** *~ on* abstimmen über (*acc*). **III** *v/t* **6.** wählen: *~ out of office* abwählen. **7.** *~ s.o. s.th.* j-m et. bewilligen. **8.** *~ that* F vorschlagen, daß. '**vot·er** *s* Wähler(in).

vouch [vaʊtʃ] *v/i*: *~ for* sich verbürgen für; bürgen für. '**vouch·er** *s* Gutschein *m*.

vow [vaʊ] **I** *s* Gelöbnis *n*: *make* (*od.* *take*) *a ~* ein Gelöbnis ablegen. **II** *v/t* geloben, schwören (*to do* zu tun).

vow·el ['vaʊəl] *s ling.* Vokal *m*, Selbstlaut *m*.

voy·age ['vɔɪdʒ] *s* (See)Reise *f*.

vul·can·ize ['vʌlkənaiz] *v/t* vulkanisieren.

vul·gar ['vʌlgə] *adj* □ **1.** vulgär, ordinär. **2.** geschmacklos.

vul·ner·a·ble ['vʌlnərəbl] *adj* □ **1.** *fig.* verletz-, verwundbar; schutzbedürftig. **2.** anfällig (*to* für).

vul·ture ['vʌltʃə] *s orn.* Geier *m*.

W

wack·y ['wækɪ] *adj* □ *bsd. Am.* F verrückt.

wad [wɒd] *s* **1.** (*Papier- etc*)Knäuel *m*; (*Watte- etc*)Bausch *m*. **2.** Bündel *n* (*Banknoten etc*).

wad·dle ['wɒdl] *v/i* watscheln.

wade [weɪd] **I** *v/t* durchwaten. **II** *v/i* waten: **~ across** → I; **~ in** hineinwaten; F sich einmischen; **~ into** waten in (*acc*); F losgehen auf *j-n*; sich reinknien in *e-e Arbeit*; **~ through** waten durch; F sich durchkämpfen durch, *Fachliteratur etc a.* durchackern. '**wad·ing** *adj*: **~ pool** *Am.* Planschbecken *n*.

wa·fer ['weɪfə] *s* **1.** (*bsd.* Eis)Waffel *f*. **2.** *eccl.* Hostie *f*.

waf·fle¹ ['wɒfl] *s* Waffel *f*.

waf·fle² [*~*] *v/i bsd. Br.* F schwafeln.

waft [wɑːft] **I** *v/i* ziehen (*Duft etc*). **II** *v/t* wehen.

wag¹ [wæg] **I** *v/t*: **~ one's finger at** *j-m* mit dem Finger drohen; **~ its tail** mit dem Schwanz wedeln. **II** *v/i* wedeln (*Schwanz*): **tongues will ~** das wird Gerede geben; **set tongues ~ging** für Gerede sorgen. **III** *s*: **with a ~ of its tail** schwanzwedelnd.

wag² [*~*] *s* F unterhaltsamer Mensch.

wage¹ [weɪdʒ] *s mst pl* Lohn *m*; Gehalt *n*.

wage² [*~*] *v/t*: **~ (a) war against** (*od.* on) ✗ Krieg führen gegen; *fig.* e-n Feldzug führen gegen.

wage|de·mand *s* Lohn- *od.* Gehaltsforderung *f*. **~ earn·er** *s* Verdiener(in): **be a ~** berufstätig sein; **be a big ~** viel verdienen. **~ freeze** *s* Lohnstopp *m*. **~ pack·et** *s* Lohn- *od.* Gehaltstüte *f*. **~ rise** *s* Lohn- *od.* Gehaltserhöhung *f*.

wa·ger ['weɪdʒə] **I** *s* Wette *f*: **have** (*place*) **a ~ on** e-e Wette abschließen *od.* eingehen auf (*acc*). **II** *v/t*: **I'll ~ that** ich wette, daß.

wag·gle ['wægl] *v/i u. v/t* F wackeln (mit).

wag·gon *Br.* → wagon.

wag·on ['wægən] *s* **1.** Fuhrwerk *n*, Wagen *m*: **be on the ~** F keinen Alkohol (mehr) trinken. **2.** 🚂 *Br.* (offener) Güterwagen. **3.** *Am.* (*Tee- etc*)Wagen *m*.

wag·on-lit [ˌvægɔ̃nˈliː] *pl* **wa·gons-lits** [*~*ˈliːz] *s* 🚂 Schlafwagen *m*.

wail [weɪl] **I** *v/i* jammern (*Person*); heulen (*Sirene, Wind*). **II** *v/t* jammern. **III** *s* Jammern *n*; Heulen *n*.

wain·scot ['weɪnskət] *s* **1.** Fuß(boden)-, Scheuerleiste *f*. **2.** (*Wand*)Täfelung *f*.

waist [weɪst] *s* Taille *f*: **~ strip** 1. **~ coat** ['weɪskəʊt] *s bsd. Br.* Weste *f*. '**~ line** *s* Taille *f*: **I'm watching my ~** ich muß auf m-e Linie achten.

wait [weɪt] **I** *v/i* **1.** warten (**for, on** auf *acc*; **[for] 10 minutes** 10 Minuten): **~ for s.o. a.** j-n erwarten; **~ for s.o. to do s.th.** darauf warten, daß j-d et. tut; warten, bis j-d et. tut; **this can ~** das kann warten, das hat Zeit (**until** bis); **keep s.o. waiting** j-n warten lassen; **I can't ~ to see him** ich kann es kaum erwarten, ihn zu sehen; **~ and see!** warte es ab!; **I'll have to ~ and see how ...** ich muß abwarten, wie ...; **~ up** F aufbleiben (**for** wegen). **2. ~ on s.o.** j-n (*bsd. im Restaurant*) bedienen; **~ at** (*Am. on*) **table** bedienen. **II** *v/t* **3. ~ one's chance** auf e-e günstige Gelegenheit warten (**to do** zu tun); **~ one's turn** warten, bis man an der Reihe ist. **4. ~ breakfast for s.o.** *bsd. Am.* F mit dem Frühstück auf j-n warten. **III** *s* **5.** Wartezeit *f*: **have a long ~** lange warten müssen. **6. lie in ~ for s.o.** j-m auflauern. '**wait·er** *s* Kellner *m*, Ober *m*, (*Anrede*) (Herr) Ober. '**wait·ing I** *s* Warten *n*: **"no ~"** „Halt(e)verbot". **II** *adj*: **play a ~ game** (**with s.o.**) j-n hinhalten; **~ list** Warteliste *f*; **~ room** 🚂 Wartesaal *m*; 🩺 *etc* Wartezimmer *n*. **wait·ress** ['~rɪs] *s* Kellnerin *f*, Bedienung *f*, (*Anrede*) Fräulein.

waive [weɪv] *v/t* verzichten auf (*acc*). '**waiv·er** *s* Verzicht *m* (**of** auf *acc*); Verzichtserklärung *f*.

wake¹ [weɪk] *s* ⚓ Kielwasser *n*: **follow in the ~ of** *fig.* folgen auf (*acc*); **leave s.th. in one's ~** *fig.* et. zurücklassen.

wake² [*~*] (*irr*) **I** *v/t a.* **~ up** (auf)wecken; *fig.* wecken, wachrufen; **~ s.o. to s.th.** *fig.* j-m et. bewußt machen. **II** *v/i a.* **~ up** aufwachen, wach werden: **~ to s.th.**

fig. sich e-r Sache bewußt werden.
wake·ful ['~fʊl] *adj* □ schlaflos.
wak·en ['~ən] **I** *v/t a.* ~ **up** (auf)wecken.
II *v/i a.* ~ **up** aufwachen, wach werden.
'**wak·ing** *adj*: **he spends all his** ~
hours studying er lernt von früh bis
spät.

walk [wɔːk] **I** *s* **1.** Spaziergang *m*; Wanderung *f*: *go for (od. have, take) a* ~ e-n
Spaziergang machen, spazierengehen;
the church is just a five-minute ~ **from
here** zu Fuß sind es nur fünf Minuten
bis zur Kirche. **2.** Spazier-, Wanderweg
m. **3.** Gang *m*. **4.** *from all* ~*s (od. every
~) of life* Leute aus allen Berufen (*od.*
Schichten). **II** *v/i* **5.** (zu Fuß) gehen,
laufen; spazierengehen; wandern: ~
into hineingehen in (*acc*), hereinkommen in (*acc*); *fig.* in *e-e Falle* gehen; ~
over F *j-n* unterbuttern; (*Sport*) *j-n* in
die Tasche stecken. **III** *v/t* **6.** *Strecke*
gehen, laufen: → *street*. **7.** *j-n* bringen
(*to* zu; *home* nach Hause); *Hund* ausführen.

Verbindungen mit Adverbien:

walk| **a·way** *v/i* **1.** → *walk off.* **2.** ~
from bei *e-m Unfall* (fast) unverletzt
bleiben. ~ **in** *v/i* hineingehen, hereinkommen. ~ **off** *v/i* **1.** fort-, weggehen. **2.**
~ *with* F abhauen mit; *Preis etc* locker
gewinnen. ~ **out** *v/i* **1.** hinausgehen;
(unter Protest) den Saal verlassen,
(*Delegation etc a.*) ausziehen: ~ *of a
meeting* e-e Versammlung (unter Protest) verlassen; ~ *on s.o.* F *j-n* verlassen;
j-n sitzenlassen. **2.** in (den) Streik treten. ~ **up** *v/i* **1.** hinaufgehen, heraufkommen. **2.** ~ *to s.o.* auf *j-n* zugehen;
~*!* treten Sie näher!

'**walk·a,bout** *s bsd. Br.* F Bad *n* in der
Menge: *do (od. go on) a* ~ ein Bad in
der Menge nehmen.
walk·er ['wɔːkə] *s* **1.** Spaziergänger(in);
Wand(e)rer *m*, Wand(r)erin *f*: *be a fast
~* schnell gehen. **2.** *Sport*: Geher *m*.
walk·ies ['~ız] *s pl*: *go* ~ *Br.* F Gassi
gehen.
walk·ie-talk·ie [,wɔːkɪ'tɔːkɪ] *s* Walkietalkie *n*, tragbares Funksprechgerät.
'**walk-in** *adj* begehbar (*Schrank*).
walk·ing ['wɔːkɪŋ] **I** *s* Laufen *n* (*a.
Sport*), Gehen *n*; Spazierengehen *n*;
Wandern *n*. **II** *adj*: *a* ~ *dictionary* F ein
wandelndes Wörterbuch; *get one's* ~

papers Am. F den Laufpaß bekommen
(*von Firma od. Freundin*); ~ *shoes pl*
Wanderschuhe *pl*; ~ *stick* Spazierstock
m; ~ *tour* Wanderung *f*.
Walk·man ['wɔːkmən] *pl* **-mans** *s* (*TM*)
Walkman *m*.
'**walk**|-**on** *thea.* **I** *adj* **1.** ~ *part* → **2. II** *s*
2. Statistenrolle *f*. **3.** Statist(in). '~**out** *s*
1. Auszug *m* (*by, of e-r Delegation etc*).
2. Ausstand *m*, Streik *m*. '~,**o·ver** *s* F
lockerer Sieg.
wall [wɔːl] **I** *s* **1.** Wand *f* (*a. fig.*): ~ *of fire*
Feuerwand; ~*s have ears* die Wände
haben Ohren; *drive up the* ~ F *j-n*
wahnsinnig machen; *go to the* ~ kaputtgehen (*Firma etc*). **2.** Mauer *f* (*a.
fig.*): ~ *of silence* Mauer des Schweigens. **II** *v/t* **3.** mit e-r Mauer umgeben:
~*ed* von Mauern umgeben; ~ *in* einmauern; ~ *off* durch e-e Mauer abtrennen (*from* von); ~ *up* zu- *od.* einmauern. '~**chart** *s* Wandkarte *f*.
wal·let ['wɒlɪt] *s* Brieftasche *f*.
'**wall,flow·er** *s fig.* F Mauerblümchen *n*.
wal·lop ['wɒləp] F **I** *s* **1.** Ding *n* (*harter
Schlag*): *give s.o. a* ~ → **2. II** *v/t* **2.** *j-m*
ein Ding verpassen. **3.** *Sport*: *j-n* in die
Pfanne hauen (*at* in *dat*). '**wal·lop·ing**
adj u. adv: ~ (*great*) F riesig, Mords...
wal·low ['wɒləʊ] *v/i*: ~ *in* sich wälzen in
(*dat*), (*Tier a.*) sich suhlen in (*dat*): ~ *in
luxury* im Luxus schwelgen; ~ *in
self-pity* sich in Selbstmitleid ergehen.
wall| **paint·ing** *s* Wandgemälde *n*. '~
,**pa·per** *s* Tapete *f*. **II** *v/t* tapezieren.
'~**-to-**'~ *adj*: ~ *carpeting* Spannteppich
m, Teppichboden *m*.
wal·ly ['wɒlɪ] *s Br.* F Trottel *m*.
wal·nut ['wɔːlnʌt] *s* ♀ Walnuß(baum)
f. ~ *cake* ~ Nußkuchen *m*.
wal·rus ['wɔːlrəs] *pl* **-rus·es**, *bsd. coll.*
-rus *s zo.* Walroß *n*. ~ **m(o)us·tache** *s*
Seehundsbart *m*.
waltz [wɔːls] **I** *s* ♪ Walzer *m*. **II** *v/i* Walzer
tanzen; walzen.
wand [wɒnd] *s* (*Zauber*)Stab *m*.
wan·der ['wɒndə] *v/i* **1.** wandern; bummeln, schlendern: ~ *about (od. around)*
herumirren; ~ *off* verschwinden. **2.** ~
from (od. off) the topic vom Thema
abschweifen. **3.** *his mind* ~*s* er kann sich schlecht konzentrieren. '**wan·der·ings** *s pl* **1.** Reisen *pl*. **2.** *he's off on his*

~ again er ist wieder mal verschwunden.

wane [weɪn] **I** v/i abnehmen (*Mond*); *fig.* schwinden (*Einfluß etc*). **II** s: **be on the ~** im Schwinden begriffen sein.

wan·gle [ˈwæŋgl] v/t F **1.** *Eintrittskarten etc* organisieren: **~ s.th. out of** j-m et. abluchsen. **2. ~ one's way out of** sich herauswinden aus. **3. I'll ~ it** ich werde das Kind schon schaukeln.

wank [wæŋk] v/i *Br.* V wichsen (*masturbieren*). **'wank·er** s *Br. fig.* V Wichser *m*.

wan·na [ˈwɒnə] F *für* want to; want a.

want [wɒnt] **I** v/t **1.** et. wollen: **he knows what he ~s** er weiß, was er will; **~ to do s.th.** et. tun wollen; **~ s.o. to do s.th.** wollen, daß j-d et. tut; **~ s.th. done** wollen, daß et. getan wird; **it ~s doing at once** F es muß sofort erledigt werden. **2.** j-n brauchen; j-n sprechen wollen: **you are ~ed on the phone** du wirst am Telefon verlangt. **3. be ~ed** (*polizeilich*) gesucht werden (**for** wegen). **4.** F et. brauchen, nötig haben. **5.** F **you ~ to see a doctor** du solltest zum Arzt gehen; **he doesn't ~ to smoke that much** er sollte nicht so viel rauchen. **II** v/i **6.** wollen: **I don't ~ to** ich will nicht; **~ in (out)** F rein-(raus)wollen. **7. he does not ~ for anything** es fehlt ihm an nichts. **III** s **8.** Mangel *m* (**of** an *dat*): **for ~ of** mangels (*gen*), in Ermang(e)lung (*gen*); **be in ~ of** et. benötigen, brauchen. **9.** Bedürfnis *n*, Wunsch *m*. **10. live in ~** Not leiden, in Armut leben. **~ ad** s Kleinanzeige *f*.

want·ed [ˈwɒntɪd] adj: **he's a ~ man** er wird (*polizeilich*) gesucht; er ist ein vielgefragter Mann. **'want·ing** adj: **they are ~ in** es fehlt od. mangelt ihnen an (*dat*); **be found ~** den Ansprüchen nicht genügen.

wan·ton [ˈwɒntən] adj □ **1.** mutwillig. **2.** liederlich (*Frau, Leben*). **3.** lüstern (*Blick etc*).

war [wɔː] s Krieg *m* (*a. fig.*); *fig.* Kampf *m* (**against** gegen): **be at ~ with** sich im Krieg(szustand) befinden mit; *fig.* auf (dem) Kriegsfuß stehen mit; **declare ~ on** j-m den Krieg erklären, *fig. a.* j-m den Kampf ansagen; *fig.* → **wage²**.

war·ble [ˈwɔːbl] v/i trillern (*Vogel*).

war| cem·e·ter·y s Soldatenfriedhof *m*.

~ crime s Kriegsverbrechen *n*. **~ crim·i·nal** s Kriegsverbrecher *m*. **~ cry** s **1.** ✕ *hist.* Schlachtruf *m*. **2.** *fig.* Parole *f*.

ward [wɔːd] **I** s **1.** Station *f* (*e-s Krankenhauses*). **2.** *pol. Br.* Stadtbezirk *m*. **3.** 🏛 Mündel *n*. **II** v/t **4. ~ off** Schlag etc abwehren, *Gefahr etc* abwenden. **'ward·en** s **1.** Aufseher(in): → **traffic warden**. **2.** Haus-, Herbergsvater *m*, -mutter *f*; Heimleiter(in). **3.** *Am.* (Gefängnis)Direktor(in). **'ward·er** s *Br.* Aufsichtsbeamte *m*, -beamtin *f* (*in Gefängnis*).

ward·robe [ˈwɔːdrəʊb] s **1.** (Kleider-) Schrank *m*. **2.** Garderobe *f* (*Kleiderbestand*).

ware [weə] s *in Zssgn* (Glas- etc)Waren pl: → **tableware**. **'~house** s Lager(haus) *n*.

war·fare [ˈwɔːfeə] s Krieg(führung *f*) *m*.

war| game s Kriegsspiel *n* (*a. für Kinder etc*), Planübung *f*. **~ grave** s Kriegs-, Soldatengrab *n*. **'~head** s ✕ Spreng-, Gefechtskopf *m*. **'~like** adj **1.** kriegerisch. **2.** Kriegs...

warm [wɔːm] **I** adj □ **1.** warm (*a. fig. Farben, Stimme*): **I am** (*od.* **feel**) **~** mir ist warm; **dress ~ly** sich warm anziehen. **2.** *fig.* warm, herzlich (*Empfang*). **II** s **3. come into the ~** *bsd. Br.* F komm ins Warme! **III** v/t **4. ~ up** wärmen, sich die Hände etc wärmen. **IV** v/i **5. a. ~ up** warm od. wärmer werden, sich erwärmen: **~ to** *fig.* sich für j-n, et. erwärmen.

Verbindungen mit Adverbien:

warm| o·ver v/t **1.** *Am.* → **warm up** 2. **2.** *bsd. Am. fig.* alte Geschichten etc aufwärmen. **~ up I** v/t **1.** → **warm** 4. **2.** *Br. Speise* aufwärmen. **3.** *Motor* warmlaufen lassen. **4.** F Schwung bringen in (*acc*). **II** v/i **5.** → **warm** 5. **6.** *Sport:* sich aufwärmen. **7.** F in Schwung kommen.

warm·|·blood·ed adj zo. warmblütig: **~ animal** Warmblüter *m*. **~·'heart·ed** adj □ **1.** warmherzig. **2.** → **warm** 2.

'war mon·ger s Kriegshetzer *m*.

warmth [wɔːmθ] s Wärme *f*, *fig. a.* Herzlichkeit *f*.

'warm-up s *Sport:* Aufwärmen *n*: **have a ~** sich aufwärmen.

warn [wɔːn] **I** v/t **1.** j-n warnen (**against, of** vor *dat*): **~ s.o. not to do** (*od.* **against doing**) **s.th.** j-n davor warnen, et. zu tun; ~ **off** verscheuchen (von, aus). **2.** *j-n* verständigen (**of** von; *that* davon, daß). **II** *v/i* **3.** warnen (**against, of** vor *dat*): **without** ~ ohne Vorwarnung; *let this be a* ~ *to you* laß dir das e-e Warnung sein!, das soll dir e-e Warnung sein! **2.** Verwarnung *f*: *he was given a written* ~ *a.* er wurde schriftlich verwarnt. **II** *adj* **3.** Warn...: ~ *signal* Warnsignal *n* (*a. fig.*).

warp [wɔːp] *v/i* sich verziehen *od.* werfen (*Holz*): *he must have a* ~*ed mind fig.* er muß abartig veranlagt sein.

war| **paint** *s* Kriegsbemalung *f* (*a. humor. Make-up*). **'~path** *s*: *be on the* ~ auf dem Kriegspfad sein; *he's on the* ~ F um ihn macht man heute am besten e-n großen Bogen.

war·rant ['wɒrənt] **I** *v/t* **1.** *et.* rechtfertigen. **II** *s* **2.** ♣ ~ *of arrest* Haftbefehl *m*; *issue a* ~ *for s.o.'s arrest* Haftbefehl gegen j-n erlassen; → *death warrant, search warrant.* **3.** Rechtfertigung *f.* **'war·ran·ty** *s* Garantie(erklärung) *f*: *the watch is still under* ~ auf der Uhr ist noch Garantie.

war·ri·or ['wɒrɪə] *s* Krieger *m.*

'war·ship *s* Kriegsschiff *n.*

wart [wɔːt] *s* Warze *f*: ~*s and all* F ohne jede Beschönigung.

'war·time *s*: *in* ~ in Kriegszeiten. **II** *adj* Kriegs...: *in* ~ *Germany* in Deutschland während des Kriegs.

war·y ['weərɪ] *adj* □ vorsichtig: *be* ~ *of* (*od. about*) sich in acht nehmen vor (*dat*); *be* ~ *of doing s.th.* Bedenken haben, et. zu tun.

was [wɒz] **1.** *ich, er, sie, es* war. **2.** *Passiv*: *ich, er, sie, es* wurde.

wash [wɒʃ] **I** *s* **1.** Wäsche *f*: *be in the* ~ in der Wäsche sein; *come out in the* ~ *fig.* F rauskommen; gut werden; *give s.th. a* ~ et. waschen; *have a* ~ sich waschen. **2.** Waschanlage *f*, -straße *f*. **3.** 🚢 (*Mund*)Wasser *n.* **II** *v/t* **4.** waschen; *sich die Hände etc* waschen: *get* ~*ed* sich waschen; → *linen* 2. **III** *v/i* **5.** sich waschen. **6.** *sich gut etc* waschen (lassen). **7.** *that won't* ~ F das glaubt kein Mensch.

Verbindungen mit Adverbien:

wash| **a·way** *v/t* wegschwemmen, -spülen. ~ **down** *v/t* **1.** *Wagen etc* wa-

schen, abspritzen. **2.** *Essen etc* hinunterspülen (*with* mit). ~ **out** *v/t* **1.** auswaschen. **2.** *be* ~*ed out* (*Sport etc*) wegen Regens abgesagt *od.* abgebrochen werden. ~ **up** **I** *v/i* **1.** *Br.* abwaschen, (das) Geschirr spülen. **2.** *Am.* → *wash* 5. **II** *v/t* **3.** anschwemmen, anspülen.

wash·a·ble ['wɒʃəbl] *adj* waschbar, -echt, (*Tapete*) abwaschbar.

'wash| **ba·sin** *s,* **'~bowl** *s Am.* Waschbecken *n.* **'~cloth** *s Am.* Waschlappen *m.* **'~day** *s* Waschtag *m.*

washed-out [ˌwɒʃt'aʊt] *adj* **1.** verwaschen. **2.** F schlapp, erschöpft. **'wash·er** *s* **1.** (*Geschirr*)Spülmaschine *f*, (-)Spüler *m*; *Am.* Waschmaschine *f*. **2.** → *dishwasher* **1. 3.** ⚙ Unterlegscheibe *f.*

wash·ing ['wɒʃɪŋ] **I** *s* Wäsche *f* (*a. Textilien*). **II** *adj* Wasch...: ~ *day* Waschtag *m*; ~ *machine* Waschmaschine *f*. **'~up** *s Br.* Abwasch *m* (*a. Geschirr*): *do the* ~ den Abwasch machen.

'wash| **out** *s* F Pleite *f.* **'~room** *s Am.* Toilette *f.*

was·n't ['wɒznt] F *für was not.*

wasp [wɒsp] *s zo.* Wespe *f.* **'wasp·ish** *adj* □ giftig.

waste [weɪst] **I** *v/t* **1.** *Geld, Zeit etc* verschwenden, -geuden (**on** an *acc,* für); *Chance etc* vergeben: ~ *one's time doing s.th.* s-e Zeit damit verschwenden, et. zu tun; → *breath* **1. 2.** *j-n* auszehren. **II** *v/i* **3.** ~ *away* immer schwächer werden (*Person*). **III** *adj* **4.** ungenutzt, überschüssig; Abfall... **5.** brachliegend (*Land*). **IV** *s* **6.** Verschwendung *f*: ~ *of time* Zeitverschwendung. **7.** Abfall *m*; Müll *m.* **'~,bas·ket** *s* Papierkorb *m.* ~ **dis·pos·al** *s* Abfall-, Müllbeseitigung *f.*

waste·ful ['weɪstful] *adj* □ verschwenderisch: *it is* ~ *a.* es ist Verschwendung (**to** *do* zu tun).

waste|'**pa·per bas·ket** *s* Papierkorb *m.* ~ **pipe** *s* Abflußrohr *n.* ~ **prod·uct** *s* Abfallprodukt *n.*

wast·er ['weɪstə] *s* Verschwender(in): *be a real time* ~ reine Zeitverschwendung sein.

watch [wɒtʃ] **I** *s* **1.** (*Armband-, Taschen*)Uhr *f.* **2.** Wache *f*: *be on the* ~ *for* Ausschau halten nach; auf der Hut sein vor (*dat*); *keep* (*a*) *careful* (*od. close*)

on *et.* genau beobachten, scharf im Auge behalten. **II** *v/t* **3.** beobachten; zuschauen bei, sich *et.* ansehen: **~** *s.o. do(ing) s.th.* beobachten, wie j-d et. tut; **~ the clock** F ständig auf die Uhr schauen; → *television* 1, *TV* 1. **4.** aufpassen auf (*acc*); achten auf (*acc*): **~ you don't spill the coffee** paß auf, daß du den Kaffee nicht verschüttest; **~ it!** F paß auf!, Vorsicht!; **~ one's step** *fig.* aufpassen. **III** *v/i* **5.** zuschauen: **~ for** a) a. **~ out for** Ausschau halten nach, b) warten auf (*acc*). **6. ~ out!** paß auf!, Vorsicht!; **~ out for** sich in acht nehmen vor (*dat*); **~ over** wachen über (*acc*). **'~dog** s Wachhund *m*.

watch·ful ['wɒtʃfʊl] *adj* □ wachsam: **be ~ for** achten auf (*acc*).

'watch|,mak·er s Uhrmacher(in). **~ -man** s (*irr man*) Wachmann *m*, Wächter *m*. **'~strap** s Uhr(arm)-band *n*. **'~,tow·er** s Wachturm *m*.

wa·ter ['wɔːtə] **I** s **1.** Wasser *n*: **be under ~** unter Wasser stehen; **that's all ~ under the bridge** *fig.* das ist Schnee von gestern; **have ~ on the knee** *⚕* Wasser im Knie haben; **throw cold ~ on** *fig.* e-r Sache e-n Dämpfer aufsetzen; → *deep* 1, *head* 8, *high water*, *hot* 1. **2.** *pl* Gewässer *pl*; Wasser *pl* (*e-s Flusses etc*): **still ~s run deep** *fig.* stille Wasser sind tief; → *trouble* 4. **II** *v/t* **3.** Blumen gießen, Rasen etc sprengen. **4.** Vieh tränken. **5. ~ down** verdünnen, -wässern; *fig.* abschwächen. **III** *v/i* **6.** tränen (*Augen*): **the sight made my mouth ~** bei dem Anblick lief mir das Wasser im Mund zusammen. **'~bed** s Wasserbett *n*. **~ bird** s Wasservogel *m*. **~ blis·ter** s *⚕* Wasserblase *f*. **~ buf·fa·lo** s *zo.* Wasserbüffel *m*. **~ butt** s Regentonne *f*. **~ can·non** s (*a. irr cannon*) Wasserwerfer *m*. **'~,col·o(u)r** s **1.** Wasser-, Aquarellfarbe *f*. **2.** Aquarellmalerei *f*. **3.** Aquarell *n*. **'~course** s Wasserlauf *m*. **'~cress** s *♀* Brunnenkresse *f*. **'~fall** s Wasserfall *m*. **'~front** s Hafenviertel *n*. **'~hole** s Wasserloch *n*. **~ ice** s *bsd. Br.* Fruchteis *n*.

wa·ter·ing ['wɔːtərɪŋ] *adj*: **~ can** (*Am. a. pot*) Gießkanne *f*.

wa·ter| jump s *Sport:* Wassergraben *m*. **~ lev·el** s Wasserstand *m*. **~ lil·y** s *♀* Seerose *f*.

Wa·ter·loo [,wɔːtə'luː] s: **meet one's ~** sein Waterloo erleben.

'wa·ter|·mark s Wasserzeichen *n*. **'~ ,mel·on** s *♀* Wassermelone *f*. **~ pipe** s **1.** Wasserrohr *n*. **2.** Wasserpfeife *f*. **~ po· -lo** s *Sport:* Wasserball(spiel *n*) *m*. **'~ ,pow·er** s Wasserkraft *f*. **'~proof** *I adj* wasserdicht. **II** s bsd. Br. Regenmantel *m*. **III** *v/t* wasserdicht machen, imprägnieren. **'~side** s Ufer *n*. **~ ski** s Wasserski *m*. **'~ski** *v/i* Wasserski laufen. **~ ski·ing** s Wasserskilaufen *n*. **~ sup·ply** s Wasserversorgung *f*. **'~tight** *adj* wasserdicht, *fig. a.* hieb- u. stichfest. **~ va·po(u)r** s Wasserdampf *m*. **'~way** s Wasserstraße *f*. **'~wheel** s Wasserrad *n*. **'~wings** s *pl* Schwimmflügel *pl*. **'~works** s *pl* (*oft sg konstruiert*) Wasserwerk *n*: **turn on the ~** F zu heulen anfangen.

wa·ter·y ['wɔːtərɪ] *adj* wässerig, wäßrig.

watt [wɒt] s *⚡* Watt *n*.

wave [weɪv] **I** *v/t* **1.** schwenken; winken mit: **~ one's hand** winken; **~ s.o. good-bye** j-m nachwinken; j-m zum Abschied zuwinken; **you can ~ goodbye to that** *fig.* das kannst du dir aus dem Kopf schlagen. **2. ~ aside** j-n beiseite winken; *fig.* j-n, et. abweisen; **~ away** j-n mit e-r Handbewegung verscheuchen; **~ on** j-n, Verkehr weiterwinken. **3.** Haar wellen, in Wellen legen. **II** *v/i* **4.** winken: **~ at** (*od. to*) **s.o.** j-m zuwinken. **5.** wehen (*Fahne etc*). **6.** sich wellen (*Haar*). **III** s **7.** *allg.* Welle *f* (*a. fig.*). **8.** **give a friendly ~** freundlich winken; **give s.o. a ~** j-m zuwinken. **'~length** s *⚡*, *phys.* Wellenlänge *f*: **we are on different ~s** *fig.* wir haben nicht die gleiche Wellenlänge.

wa·ver ['weɪvə] *v/i* **1.** flackern (*Licht*, *Augen*), zittern (*Stimme*). **2.** *fig.* schwanken (*between* zwischen *dat*).

wav·y ['weɪvɪ] *adj* wellig, gewellt: **~ line** Wellenlinie *f*.

wax¹ [wæks] **I** s **1.** Wachs *n*. **2.** *physiol.* (*Ohren*)Schmalz *n*. **II** *v/t* **3.** wachsen, Fußboden a. bohnern.

wax² [~] *v/i* zunehmen (*Mond*).

wax·en ['wæksən] *adj* *fig.* wächsern.

'wax·work s **1.** Wachsfigur *f*. **2.** *pl* (*mst sg konstruiert*) Wachsfigurenkabinett *n*.

wax·y ['wæksɪ] *adj* wächsern (*a. fig.*).

way [weɪ] **I** s **1.** Weg m: **~ back** Rückweg; **~ home** Heimweg; **~ in** Eingang m; **~ out** Ausgang m; **~s and means** pl fig. Mittel u. Wege pl; **by ~ of** über (acc), via; statt; **by the ~** fig. übrigens; **be on the** (od. **one's**) **~ to** unterwegs sein nach; **give ~** nachgeben; **go out of one's ~** sich besondere Mühe geben (**to do** zu tun); **lose one's ~** sich verlaufen od. verirren; **make ~** Platz machen (**for** für); → **talk** 8, etc. **2.** Richtung f, Seite f: **this ~** hierher; hier entlang. **3.** Weg m, Entfernung f, Strecke f: **be a long ~ from** weit entfernt sein von; **Easter is still a long ~ off** bis Ostern ist es noch lang. **4.** Art f, Weise f: **in a ~** (od. **some ~s**) in gewisser Hinsicht; **in no ~** in keiner Weise; **no ~!** F kommt überhaupt nicht in Frage!; **~ of life** Lebensart, -weise; **in my ~ of thinking** m-r Ansicht nach; **if I had my ~** wenn es nach mir ginge; **you can't have it both ~s** du kannst nicht beides haben. **5.** mst pl Brauch m, Sitte f; Gewohnheit f: → **mend** 2. **II** adv **6.** weit: **they are friends from ~ back** sie sind alte Freunde. **'~·bill** s Frachtbrief m. **'~·lay** v/t (irr **lay**) **1.** j-m auflauern. **2.** j-n abfangen, abpassen.

way·ward ['weɪwəd] adj □ eigensinnig.

we [wiː] pron wir pl.

weak [wiːk] adj □ allg. schwach (**at, in** in dat), (Kaffee etc a.) dünn: **be** (od. **feel**) **~ at the knees** F schwach auf den Beinen sein; weiche Knie haben; → **point** 14, **sex** 1, **spot** 4. **'weak·en I** v/t **1.** schwächen (a. fig.). **II** v/i **2.** schwächer werden (a. fig.). **3.** fig. nachgeben.

,weak-'kneed adj F feig.

weak·ling ['wiːklɪŋ] s Schwächling m. **'weak·ness** s allg. Schwäche f: **have a ~ for** e-e Schwäche haben für.

weal [wiːl] s Striemen m.

wealth [welθ] s **1.** Reichtum m. **2.** fig. Fülle f (**of** von).

wean [wiːn] v/t Kind entwöhnen: **~** (**away**) **from s.th.**, **~ off s.th.** j-n abbringen von et., j-m et. abgewöhnen.

weap·on ['wepən] s Waffe f (a. fig.): **~ system** ✕ Waffensystem n.

weap·on·ry ['~rɪ] s Waffen pl.

wear [weə] **I** s **1.** a. **~ and tear** Abnutzung f, Verschleiß m: **the worse for ~** F abgenutzt (Couch etc); kaputt (Per-

son). **2.** oft in Zssgn Kleidung f. **II** v/t (irr) **3.** Bart, Brille, Schmuck tragen, Mantel etc a. anhaben, Hut etc a. aufhaben: **~ the trousers** (bsd. Am. **pants**) F die Hosen anhaben; → **seat belt**. **4.** **~ an angry expression** verärgert dreinschauen; **~ a happy smile** glücklich lächeln. **III** v/i (irr) **5. s.th. to ~** et. zum Anziehen. **6.** sich abnutzen. **7. he has worn well** er hat sich (für sein Alter) gut gehalten.

Verbindungen mit Adverbien:

wear| down I v/t **1.** Stufen abtreten, Absätze ablaufen, Reifen abfahren. **2.** fig. j-n, Widerstand etc zermürben. **II** v/i **3.** sich abtreten od. ablaufen od. abfahren. **~ off** v/i nachlassen (Schmerz etc). **~ on** v/i sich hinziehen (**all day** über den ganzen Tag). **~ out I** v/t **1.** Kleidung abnutzen, abtragen. **2.** fig. j-n erschöpfen. **II** v/i **3.** sich abnutzen od. abtragen.

wear·ing ['weərɪŋ] adj ermüdend.

wea·ri·some ['wɪərɪsəm] adj □ **1.** ermüdend. **2.** langweilig. **3.** lästig.

wea·ry ['wɪərɪ] adj □ **1.** erschöpft. **2. be ~ of s.th.** et. satt haben.

wea·sel ['wiːzl] **I** s zo. Wiesel n. **II** v/i: **~ out of** bsd. Am. F sich lavieren aus (e-r Verantwortung etc).

weath·er ['weðə] **I** s Wetter n; Witterung f: **in all ~s** bei jedem Wetter; **be under the ~** F sich nicht wohl fühlen; **make heavy ~ of s.th.** fig. sich sehr schwermachen; → **permit** 2. **II** v/t Krise etc überstehen. **III** v/i geol. verwittern. **'~,beat·en** adj verwittert (bsd. Gesicht). **'~-bound** adj: **the planes** (**ships**) **were ~** die Flugzeuge (Schiffe) konnten wegen des schlechten Wetters nicht starten (auslaufen). **~ chart** s Wetterkarte f. **'~·cock** s Wetterhahn m. **~ eye** s: **keep one's ~** (od. **a**) **~ open** aufpassen (**for** auf acc). **~ fore·cast** s Wettervorhersage f. **'~·man** s (irr **man**) Rundfunk, TV: Wetteransager m. **'~ proof I** adj wetterfest. **II** v/t wetterfest machen. **~ sat·el·lite** s Wettersatellit m. **~ sta·tion** s Wetterwarte f. **~ vane** s Wetterfahne f.

weave [wiːv] **I** v/t (irr) **1.** weben; Netz spinnen. **2.** flechten. **3.** pret u. pp **weaved:** **~ one's way through** sich schlängeln durch. **II** v/i (irr) **4.** weben.

5. *pret u. pp* weaved: **~ through** → 3. **III** *s* 6. Webart *f*. **'weav·er** *s* Weber(in).

web [web] *s* **1.** Netz *n* (*a. fig.*): **~ of lies** Lügengespinst *n*, -gewebe *n*, -netz. **2.** *orn.* Schwimmhaut *f*.

wed [wed] *v/t* (*a. irr*) heiraten: **they were ~ last week** sie haben letzte Woche geheiratet.

we'd [wi:d] F *für* **we had; we would**.

wed·ding ['wedıŋ] **I** *s* Hochzeit *f*. **II** *adj* Hochzeits...: **~ anniversary** Hochzeitstag *m* (*Jahrestag*); **~ dress** Braut-, Hochzeitskleid *n*; **~ ring** Ehe-, Trauring *m*.

wedge [wedʒ] **I** *s* **1.** Keil *m*: **drive a ~ between** *fig.* e-n Keil treiben zwischen (*acc*); → **thin** 1. **2.** Stück *n* (*Kuchen etc*), Ecke *f* (*Käse*). **3.** verkeilen, mit e-m Keil festklemmen. **4. ~ in** einkeilen, -zwängen. **'~-shaped** *adj* keilförmig.

Wednes·day ['wenzdı] *s* Mittwoch *m*: **on ~** (am) Mittwoch; **on ~s** mittwochs.

wee¹ [wi:] *adj* F klein: **a ~ bit** ein (kleines) bißchen; **the ~ (small) hours** *pl* die frühen Morgenstunden *pl*.

wee² [~] F **I** *v/i* Pipi machen. **II** *s*: **do** (*od.* **have**) **a ~** → 1.

weed [wi:d] **I** *s* **1.** Unkraut *n*. **2.** F Schwächling *m*, Waschlappen *m*. **II** *v/t* **3.** jäten. **~ out** *fig.* aussieben, -sondern (*from* aus). **III** *v/i* **4.** (Unkraut) jäten. **'weed·y** *adj* **1.** voll Unkraut. **2.** F rückgratlos.

week [wi:k] *s* Woche *f*: **~ after ~; ~ in, ~ out** Woche für Woche; **after ~s of waiting** nach wochenlangem Warten; **for ~s** wochenlang; → **today** 1. **'~·day** *s* Wochen-, Werktag *m*: **on ~s** werktags. **~**'**end** *s* Wochenende *n*: **at the ~** am Wochenende. **II** *adj* ['~end] Wochenend... **III** *v/i* das Wochenende verbringen.

week·ly ['wi:klı] **I** *adj* Wochen...; wöchentlich. **II** *adv* wöchentlich. **III** *s* Wochen(zeit)schrift *f*, -zeitung *f*.

wee·ny ['wi:nı] *adj* F klitzeklein, winzig.

weep [wi:p] (*irr*) **I** *v/i* **1.** weinen (**for, with** vor *Freude etc*; *um j-n*; **over** über *acc*). **2.** nässen (*Wunde*). **II** *v/t* **3.** Tränen weinen. **'weep·ing** *adj*: **~ willow** ✿ Trauerweide *f*. **'weep·y** *adj* F **1.** weinerlich. **2.** rührselig.

'wee-wee → **wee²**.

---

weigh [weı] **I** *v/t* **1.** (ab)wiegen. **2.** *fig.* abwägen (**against** gegen). **3. ~ anchor** ⚓ den Anker lichten. **II** *v/i* **4.** *10 Kilo etc* wiegen. **5. ~ on** *fig.* lasten auf (*dat*). **6. ~ with** *fig.* Gewicht haben bei. *Verbindungen mit Adverbien:*

weigh| down *v/t* niederdrücken (*a. fig.*): **be ~ed down with** überladen sein mit; *fig.* niedergedrückt werden von. **~ in** *v/i* **1. ~ at** (*Sport*) *100 Kilo etc* auf die Waage bringen. **2.** F sich einschalten (**with** mit). **~ out** *v/t* ab-, auswiegen. **~ up** *v/t et.* abwägen; *j-n* einschätzen.

weight [weıt] **I** *s* **1.** *allg.* Gewicht *n*: **~s and measures** *pl* Maße u. Gewichte *pl*; **it's five kilos in ~** es wiegt fünf Kilo; **what's your ~?** wieviel wiegst du?, wie schwer bist du?; **gain** (*od.* **put on**) **~** zunehmen; **lose ~** abnehmen. **2.** Last *f* (*a. fig.*): **I can't lift ~** ich kann nicht schwer heben; **be a ~ on s.o.'s mind** j-n belasten; **his decision took a ~ off my mind** bei s-r Entscheidung fiel mir ein Stein vom Herzen. **3.** *fig.* Bedeutung *f*: **not to attach any ~ to s.th.** e-r Sache keine Bedeutung *od.* kein Gewicht beimessen; **throw one's ~ about** (*od.* **around**) F sich aufspielen *od.* wichtig machen; → **carry** 5. **II** *v/t* **4.** beschweren: **~ down** → **weigh down**; **be ~ed in favo(u)r of** (**against**) bevorteilen (benachteiligen). **~ cat·e·go·ry** *s* Sport: Gewichtsklasse *f*.

weight·less ['weıtlıs] *adj* □ schwerelos.

weight| lift·er *s* Sport: Gewichtheber *m*. **~ lift·ing** *s* Sport: Gewichtheben *n*. **~ train·ing** *s* Sport: Gewichttraining *n*.

weight·y ['weıtı] *adj* □ **1.** schwer. **2.** *fig.* gewichtig; schwerwiegend.

weir [wıə] *s* Wehr *n*.

weird [wıəd] *adj* □ **1.** unheimlich. **2.** F sonderbar, verrückt.

weird·o ['wıədəυ] *pl* **-os** *s* F irrer Typ.

welch → **welsh²**.

wel·come ['welkəm] **I** *int* **1. ~ back** (*od.* **home**)! willkommen zu Hause!; **~ to England!** willkommen in England! **II** *adj* **2.** willkommen: **you are ~ to do it** Sie können es gerne tun; **you're ~** nichts zu danken!, keine Ursache!, bitte sehr! **3.** angenehm. **III** *v/t* **4.** begrüßen (*a. fig.*). **IV** *s* **5.** Empfang *m*: **give s.o. a warm ~** j-m e-n herzlichen Empfang bereiten. **6. outstay** (*od.* **overstay**) *one's* ~ j-s Gastfreundschaft überstrapazieren *od.* zu lange in Anspruch nehmen.

weld [weld] **I** *v/t* schweißen: ~ *together* zs.-, verschweißen. **II** *s* Schweißnaht *f*, -stelle *f*. **'weld·er** *s* Schweißer *m*.

wel·fare ['welfeə] *s* **1.** Wohl *n*, (*e-r Person a.*) Wohlergehen *n*. **2.** *Am.* Sozialhilfe *f*: *be on* ~ Sozialhilfe beziehen. ~ **state** *s* Wohlfahrtsstaat *m*.

well¹ [wel] **I** *adv* **1.** gut: (*all*) ~ *and good* schön u. gut; *as* ~ ebenso, auch; *as* ~ *as* sowohl ... als auch; nicht nur ..., sondern auch; (*just*) *as* ~ ebenso(gut), genauso(gut); *just as* ~ das macht nichts; *very* ~ also gut, na gut; *I couldn't very* ~ *say no* ich konnte schlecht nein sagen; *be* ~ *in with s.o.* auf gutem Fuß mit j-m stehen; *do* ~ gut daran tun (*to do* zu tun); ~ *done!* bravo!; → *off* 11. **2.** gut, gründlich: *be* ~ *aware of s.th.* sich e-r Sache voll u. ganz bewußt sein; *shake* ~ kräftig schütteln. **3.** weit: ~ *in advance* schon lange vorher. **II** *int* **4.** nun, also (*oft unübersetzt*). **5.** ~, ~! na so was! **III** *adj* **6.** gesund: *not to feel* ~ sich nicht wohl fühlen. **7.** *all's* ~ *that ends* ~ Ende gut, alles gut; *it's all very* ~ *for you to criticize* (*laugh*) du kannst leicht kritisieren (du hast gut lachen).

well² [~] **I** *s* **1.** Brunnen *m*: ~ *water* Brunnenwasser *n*. **2.** (*Öl*)Quelle *f*. **3.** △ (*Aufzugs- etc*)Schacht *m*. **II** *v/i* **4.** *a.* ~ *out* quellen (*from* aus): *tears* ~ *ed* (*up*) *in her eyes* die Tränen stiegen ihr in die Augen.

we'll [wiːl] F *für* **we will**.

‚**well·-ad'vised** *adj* klug (*Plan etc*). ‚~**ap'point·ed** *adj* gutausgestattet. ‚~**-'bal·anced** *adj* **1.** ausgeglichen (*Person*). **2.** ausgewogen (*Ernährung etc*). ‚~**'be·ing** *s* Wohl(ergehen) *n*: *give s.o. a sense of* ~ j-n mit Wohlbehagen erfüllen. ‚~**'cho·sen** *adj* gutgewählt: *with a few* ~ *words* mit einigen wohlgesetzten Worten. ‚~**'done** *adj* durchgebraten (*Steak*). ‚~**'earned** *adj* wohlverdient. ‚~**'found·ed** *adj* (wohl)begründet. ‚~**'groomed** *adj* gepflegt. ‚~**'heeled** *adj* F betucht. ‚~**in'formed** *adj* **1.** gutunterrichtet. **2.** (vielseitig) gebildet. ‚~**in'ten·tioned** → **well-meaning.** ‚~**'kept** *adj* **1.** gepflegt. **2.** streng gehütet (*Geheimnis*). ‚~**'known** *adj*

(wohl)bekannt. ‚~**'lined** *adj* F **1.** voller Geld, (*Brieftasche*) dick. **2.** voll (*Magen*). ‚~**'mean·ing** *adj* wohlmeinend (*Person*), (*Rat etc a.*) gut-, wohlgemeint. ‚~**'meant** *adj* gut-, wohlgemeint. ‚~**'nigh** ['~naɪ] *adv* beinahe, nahezu. ‚~**'off** **I** *adj* begütert, reich. **II** *s*: *the* ~ *pl* die Reichen *pl*. ‚~**pro'portioned** *adj* wohlproportioniert. ‚~**read** [‚~'red] *adj* belesen. ‚~**'thought-of** *adj* angesehen, geachtet. ‚~**-to-'do** F → **well-off.** ‚~**'worn** *adj* **1.** abgenutzt, abgetragen. **2.** *fig.* abgedroschen.

Welsh¹ [welʃ] **I** *adj* **1.** walisisch. **II** *s* **2.** *the* ~ *pl* die Waliser *pl*. **3.** *ling.* Walisisch *n*.

welsh² [~] *v/i*: ~ *on* F *Schulden* nicht bezahlen; *Versprechen* nicht halten.

Welsh|·man ['welʃmən] *s* (*irr man*) Waliser *m*. '~**,wom·an** *s* (*irr woman*) Waliserin *f*.

welt [welt] *s* Striemen *m*.

wel·ter·weight ['weltəwent] (*Sport*) **I** *s* Weltergewicht(ler *m*) *n*. **II** *adj* Weltergewichts...

went [went] *pret von* **go.**

wept [wept] *pret u. pp von* **weep.**

were [wɜː] *du* warst, *Sie* waren, *wir, sie* waren, *ihr* wart.

we're [wɪə] F *für* **we are.**

weren't [wɜːnt] F *für* **were not.**

were·wolf ['wɪəwʊlf] *s* (*irr wolf*) Werwolf *m*.

west [west] **I** *s* **1.** Westen *m*: *in the* ~ *of* im Westen von (*od. gen*); *to the* ~ *of* → 5. **2.** *the* 2 *Br.* Westengland *n*; *Am.* die Weststaaten *pl*; *pol.* der Westen: ~ *wild* 1. **II** *adj* **3.** West..., westlich. **III** *adv* **4.** westwärts, nach Westen: *go* ~ F draufgehen (*sterben, kaputtgehen*). **5.** ~ *of* westlich von (*od. gen*). '~**bound** *adj* nach Westen gehend *od.* fahrend.

west·er·ly ['westəlɪ] **I** *adj* westlich, West... **II** *adv* von *od.* nach Westen. **west·ern** ['~tən] **I** *adj* westlich, West... **II** *s* Western *m*. '**west·ern·er** *s* **1.** Bewohner(in) des Westens (*e-s Landes*). **2.** 2 Weststaatler(in). **west·ern·most** ['~məʊst] *adj* westlichst.

west·ward ['westwəd] *adj u. adv* westlich, westwärts, nach Westen. '**westwards** *adv* → **westward.**

wet [wet] **I** *adj* □ **1.** naß, (*Farbe etc a.*) feucht: *be* (*still*) ~ *behind the ears* F noch grün *od.* feucht *od.* noch nicht trocken hinter den Ohren sein; ~ **blanket** F Spiel-, Spaßverderber(in); ~ **paint** 5, **through** 3. **2.** regnerisch. **3.** *Br.* F weichlich: *don't be so ~!* sei nicht so ein Waschlappen! **II** *s* **4.** Nässe *f.* **III** *v/t* (*mst irr*) **5.** naß machen, anfeuchten: ~ *one's bed* ins Bett machen; ~ *o.s.* in die Hose machen; ~ *one's whistle* F e-n zur Brust nehmen.

weth·er ['weðə] *s zo.* Hammel *m.*

we've [wi:v] F *für* we have.

whack [wæk] *s* F **1.** (knallender) Schlag. **2.** (An)Teil *m.* **3.** Versuch *m: have a ~ at s.th.* et. probieren. **whacked** *adj:* be ~ (**out**) F geschlaucht *od.* kaputt sein.

'**whack·ing** F I *adj u. adv:* ~ (**great**) Mords..., riesig. **II** *s: give s.o. a ~* j-m e-e Tracht Prügel verpassen.

whale [weɪl] *s zo.* Wal *m: have a ~ of a time* F sich prächtig amüsieren.

wharf [wɔ:f] *pl* wharfs, wharves [wɔ:vz] *s* Kai *m.*

what [wɒt] **I** *interrogative pron* **1.** was: *~'s for lunch?* was gibt's zum Mittagessen?; ~ *for?* wozu?; ~ *about …?* wie wär's mit …?; ~ *if …?* was ist, wenn …?; → **age** 1, **like¹** 1, **so** 6, *etc.* **II** *relative pron* **2.** was: *he told me ~* er sagte mir, was ich tun sollte; *know ~'s ~* F wissen, was Sache ist; *tell s.o. ~'s ~* j-m Bescheid stoßen. **III** *adj* **3.** was für ein(e), welch(er, e, es): ~ *luck!* so ein Glück!; → **age** 1, **colour** 1, **pity** 2, *etc.* **4.** alle, die; alles, was: *I gave him ~ money I had* ich gab ihm, was ich an Geld hatte. *~'ev·er* **I** *pron* **1.** was (auch immer); alles, was. **2.** egal, was. **II** *adj* **3.** welch(er, e, es) … auch (immer). **4.** *no … ~* überhaupt kein(e). *~ for* s: *I'll give him ~!* bsd. *Br.* F dem werd' ich's zeigen!

whats·it ['wɒtsɪt] *s* F Dingsbums *n.*

what·so·ev·er → whatever 1, 2, 4.

wheat [wi:t] *s* ♣ Weizen *m: separate the ~ from the chaff fig.* die Spreu vom Weizen trennen. ~ **germ** *s* Weizenkern *m.*

whee·dle ['wi:dl] *v/t:* ~ *s.o. into doing s.th.* j-m so lange schöntun, bis er et. tut; ~ *s.th. out of s.o.* j-m et. abschmeicheln.

wheel [wi:l] **I** *s* **1.** Rad *n:* → **fifth** 1, **meal¹**, **oil** 4, **shoulder** 1, **spoke²**. **2.** F a) *pl* fahrbarer Untersatz, Wagen *m,* b)

(Fahr)Rad *n.* **3.** ⚓, *mot.* Steuer *n: be at the ~* am Steuer sitzen (⚓ stehen); *take the ~* das Steuer übernehmen. **II** *v/t* **4.** Fahrrad, Patienten im Rollstuhl *etc* schieben, Servierwagen *etc a.* rollen. **III** *v/i* **5.** ~ *about* (*od.* [a]round) herumfahren, -wirbeln. **6.** kreisen (*Vogel*). **7.** *~ and deal* F contp. Geschäfte machen. '~,**bar·row** *s* Schubkarre(n *m*) *f.* '~**base** *s mot.* Radstand *m.* ,~'**chair** *s* ⚕ Rollstuhl *m.* ~ **clamp** *s Br.* Radkralle *f,* Parkriegel *m.*

wheeled [wi:ld] *adj* **1.** ~ *vehicle* Räderfahrzeug *n.* **2.** *in Zssgn* …räd(e)rig. ,**wheel·er-'deal·er** *s* F contp. Geschäftemacher *m.*

wheeze [wi:z] *v/i* keuchen, pfeifend atmen.

when [wen] **I** *adv* **1.** *fragend:* wann. **2.** *relativ:* the day ~ der Tag, an dem *od.* als; *the time ~ it happened* die Zeit, in *od.* zu der es geschah. **II** *cj* **3.** wann. **4.** als: *he broke a leg ~ skiing* er brach sich beim Skifahren ein Bein. **5.** wenn: *say ~!* F sag halt!, sag, wenn du genug hast! **III** *pron* **6.** *since ~?* seit wann? ~'**ev·er** *cj* wann auch immer; jedesmal, wenn.

where [weə] **I** *adv (fragend u. relativ)* wo: ~ … (**from**)? woher?; ~ … (**to**)? wohin? **II** *cj* wo; wohin. '~·**a·bouts** *s pl* (*a. sg konstruiert*) Verbleib *m* (*e-r Sache*), (*e-r Person a.*) Aufenthalt(sort) *m.* ~'**as** *cj* während, wohingegen. ~'**by** *adv* **1.** wodurch, womit. **2.** wonach. ,~**up'on** *cj* worauf(hin).

wher·ev·er [weər'evə] *adv* wo(hin) auch (immer); ganz gleich, wo(hin).

whet [wet] *v/t* **1.** Messer *etc* schärfen. **2.** *fig.* Appetit anregen.

wheth·er ['weðə] *cj* ob.

whey [weɪ] *s* Molke *f.*

which [wɪtʃ] **I** *interrogative pron* **1.** welch(er, e, es): ~ *of you?* wer von euch? **II** *relative pron* **2.** welch(er, e, es); der, die, das. **3.** *auf den vorhergehenden Satz bezüglich:* was. **III** *adj* **4.** *fragend u. relativ:* welch(er, e, es). ~'**ev·er** *pron u. adj* welch(er, e, es) auch (immer); ganz gleich, welch(er, e, es).

whiff [wɪf] *s* **1.** Luftzug *m,* Hauch *m.* **2.** Duft(wolke *f*) *m.* **3.** *fig.* Anflug *m,* Hauch *m* (**of** von).

while [waɪl] **I** *s* **1.** Weile *f: a little ~ ago*

vor kurzem; *for a* ~ e-e Zeitlang; e-n Augenblick; → *once* 1. **II** *cj* 2. während. 3. obwohl. **III** *v/t* 4. ~ *away* sich *die Zeit* vertreiben (*by doing s.th.* mit et.).

whilst [waɪlst] → *while* II.

whim [wɪm] *s* Laune *f*: *as the* ~ *takes one, at* ~ nach Lust u. Laune.

whim·per ['wɪmpə] **I** *v/i* winseln (*Hund*); wimmern (*Person*). **II** *v/t* wimmern. **III** *s* Winseln *n*; Wimmern *n*.

whim·si·cal ['wɪmzɪkl] *adj* □ 1. wunderlich. 2. launenhaft.

whim·sy ['wɪmzɪ] *s* 1. Wunderlichkeit *f*. 2. Spleen *m*.

whine [waɪn] **I** *v/i* 1. jaulen (*Hund*). 2. jammern (*about* über *acc*). **II** *s* 3. Jaulen *n*. 4. Gejammer *n*. '**whin·er** *s* Jammerer *m*.

whin·ny ['wɪnɪ] **I** *v/i* wiehern. **II** *s* Wiehern *n*.

whip [wɪp] **I** *s* 1. Peitsche *f*. 2. *parl. Br.* Einpeitscher *m*. 3. *gastr.* Creme *f*. **II** *v/t* 4. (aus)peitschen: ~ *into shape* F j-n, et. auf Zack bringen. 5. *Sahne etc* schlagen. 6. *bsd. Sport:* F überfahren (*hoch schlagen*). 7. *Br.* F klauen. **III** *v/i* 8. sausen, flitzen, (*Wind*) fegen.
Verbindungen mit Adverbien:
whip| back *v/i* zurückschnellen (*Ast etc*). ~ **off** *v/t* sich *ein Kleidungsstück* herunterreißen. ~ **out** *v/t* *Revolver etc* zücken. ~ **up** *v/t* 1. → *whip* 5. 2. *Interesse etc* entfachen. 3. *Essen etc* herzaubern.

'**whip·cord** *s* Peitschenschnur *f*. '**lash** *s* 1. Peitschenschnur *f*. 2. Peitschenhieb *m*: ~ (*injury*) ⚕ Schleudertrauma *n*.

whipped [wɪpt] *adj*: ~ *cream* Schlagsahne *f*, -rahm *m*.

whip·ping ['wɪpɪŋ] *adj*: ~ *boy* Prügelknabe *m*; ~ *cream* Schlagsahne *f*, -rahm *m*. '**whip·py** *adj* biegsam, elastisch.

'**whip-round** *s Br.* F Sammlung *f* (*im Büro etc*): *have a* ~ sammeln (*for* für).

whir *bsd. Am.* → *whirr*.

whirl [wɜːl] **I** *v/i* 1. wirbeln: *my head is* ~*ing* mir schwirrt der Kopf. **II** *v/t* 2. wirbeln. 3. *the car* ~*ed us off to* der Wagen brachte uns auf schnellstem Weg zu *od.* nach. **II** *s* 4. Wirbeln *n*; Wirbel *m*: *my head's in a* ~ mir schwirrt der Kopf; *give s.th. a* ~ F et.

ausprobieren. 5. *fig.* Trubel *m*, Wirbel *m*.

whirl·i·gig ['wɜːlɪɡɪɡ] *s* 1. Kreisel *m*. 2 Karussell *n*.

'**whirl·pool** *s* 1. Strudel *m* (*a. fig.*). 2 Whirlpool *m* (*Unterwassermassagebecken*). '**wind** *s* Wirbelwind *m*.

whirr [wɜː] **I** *v/i* surren. **II** *s* Surren *n*.

whisk [wɪsk] **I** *s* 1. Wedel *m*. 2. *gastr.* Schneebesen *m*. **II** *v/t* 3. ~ *its tail* mit dem Schwanz schlagen; ~ *away Fliegen etc* ver-, wegscheuchen. 4. *Eiweiß* schlagen.

whisk·er ['wɪskə] *s* 1. Schnurrhaar *n*: *by a* ~ F ganz knapp. 2. *pl* Backenbart *m*.

whis·key ['wɪskɪ] *s* (*amerikanischer od. irischer*) Whisky.

whis·ky ['wɪskɪ] *s* (*bsd. schottischer*) Whisky: ~ *and soda* Whisky Soda; *two whiskies* zwei Whisky.

whis·per ['wɪspə] **I** *v/i* 1. flüstern, leise sprechen (*to* mit). **II** *v/t* 2. flüstern, leise sagen: ~ *s.th. to s.o.* j-m et. zuflüstern. 3. *it is* ~*ed that* man munkelt, daß. **III** *s* 4. Flüstern *n*: *say s.th. in a* ~ et. im Flüsterton sagen. 5. Gerücht *n*: *I've heard a* ~ *that* ich habe munkeln hören, daß. '**whis·per·ing** *adj*: ~ *campaign* Verleumdungskampagne *f*.

whist [wɪst] *s* Whist *n* (*Kartenspiel*).

whis·tle [wɪsl] **I** *v/i* 1. pfeifen: ~ *at* j-m nachpfeifen; ~ *for* (nach) *j-m, e-m Taxi etc* pfeifen; *he can* ~ *for it* F darauf kann er lange warten. **II** *v/t* 2. pfeifen. **III** *s* 3. Pfeife *f*: *blow one's* ~ pfeifen. 4. Pfiff *m*: *give a* ~ *of surprise* e-n überraschten Pfiff ausstoßen. 5. → *wet* 5.

white [waɪt] **I** *adj* 1. *allg.* weiß: ~ *bread* Weißbrot *n*; ~ *coffee Br.* Milchkaffee *m*, Kaffee *m* mit Milch; ~ *hope* große Hoffnung (*Person*); ~ *lie* Notlüge *f*; ~ *man* Weiße *m*; ~ *paper pol.* Weißbuch *n*; ~ *wedding* Hochzeit *f* in Weiß; ~ *wine* Weißwein *m*. **II** *s* 2. Weiß *n*: *dressed in* ~ weiß *od.* in Weiß gekleidet. 3. *oft* ♀ Weiße *m, f*. 4. Eiweiß *n*; *das* Weiße (*im Auge*). '**col·lar** *adj* Büro...: ~ *crime* White-collar-Kriminalität *f*; ~ *worker* Büroangestellte *m, f*.

whit·en ['waɪtn] *v/t* 1. *v/t* weiß machen. 2. weiß werden.

'**white·wash** **I** *v/t* 1. tünchen, anstreichen; weißen. 2. F *et.* übertünchen, beschönigen; *j-n* e-r Mohrenwäsche unterziehen. **II** *s* **3.** Tünche *f*. **4.** F Tünche *f*, Beschönigung *f*; Mohrenwäsche *f*.

whit·ish ['waɪtɪʃ] *adj* weißlich.

Whit·sun ['wɪtsn] *s* **1.** Pfingstsonntag *m*. **2.** Pfingsten *n od. pl.* **Whit Sun·day** [wɪt] → Whitsun 1.

whit·tle ['wɪtl] *v/t* **1.** (zurecht)schnitzen. **2.** *fig.* ~ *away* Gewinn etc allmählich aufzehren; ~ *down* et. reduzieren (*to* auf *acc*).

whiz(z) [wɪz] **I** *v/i:* ~ *by* (*od. past*) vorbeizischen. **II** *s* F As *n*, Kanone *f* (*at* in *dat*). ~ *kid* *s* F Senkrechtstarter(in).

who [huː] **I** *interrogative pron* **1.** wer; wen; wem: ~ *do you think you are?* für wen hältst du dich eigentlich? **II** *relative pron* **2.** *unverbunden:* wer; wen; wem. **3.** *verbunden:* welch(er, e, es); der, die, das.

who'd [huːd] F *für* who had; who would.

who·dun·(n)it [ˌhuːˈdʌnɪt] *s* F Krimi *m*.

who·ev·er *relative pron* wer auch (immer); wen auch (immer); wem auch (immer); egal, wer *od.* wen *od.* wem. **II** *interrogative pron:* ~ *can that be?* wer kann denn das nur sein?

whole [həʊl] **I** *adj* (□ → **wholly**): ganz: → *hog* 1. **II** *s* das Ganze: *the* ~ *of the town* die ganze Stadt; *as a* ~ als Ganzes; *on the* ~ im großen (u.) ganzen; alles in allem. ˌ~'**heart·ed** *adj* ungeteilt (*Aufmerksamkeit*), ernsthaft (*Versuch etc*). ˌ~'**heart·ed·ly** *adv* uneingeschränkt, voll u. ganz. '~·**meal** *adj* Vollkorn...

'**whole·sale** **I** *s* **1.** Großhandel *m*. **II** *adj* **2.** Großhandels... **3.** *b.s.* Massen... **III** *adv* **4.** en gros. '**whole·sal·er** *s* Großhändler *m*.

whole·some ['həʊlsəm] *adj* □ **1.** gesund. **2.** *fig.* gut, nützlich.

who'll [huːl] F *für* who will.

whol·ly ['həʊllɪ] *adv* gänzlich, völlig.

whom [huːm] **I** *interrogative pron* wen; wem. **II** *relative pron* welch(en, e, es), den (die, das); welch(em, er), dem (der): *the children, most of* ~ *were tired, ...* die Kinder, von denen die meisten müde waren, ...

whoop [huːp] **I** *v/i* schreien, *bsd.* jauchzen. **II** *v/t:* ~ *it up* F auf den Putz hauen. **III** *s* (*bsd.* Freuden)Schrei *m*: ~*s pl of victory* Siegesgeschrei *m*. '**whoop·ing** *adj:* ~ *cough* 🞗 Keuchhusten *m*.

whoosh [wʊʃ] *v/i:* ~ *by* (*od. past*) F vorbeirauschen.

whop·per ['wɒpə] *s* F **1.** Mordsding *n*. **2.** faustdicke Lüge. '**whop·ping** *adj u. adv* F Mords..., riesig: ~ (*big*) *lie* → whopper 2.

whore [hɔː] *s* Hure *f*.

who're ['hɔː] F *für* who are.

'**whore·house** *s* Bordell *n*, Freudenhaus *n*.

whor·tle·ber·ry ['wɜːtlˌberɪ] *s* 🞗 Blau-, Heidelbeere *f*.

who's [huːz] F *für* who is; who has.

whose [huːz] **I** *interrogative pron* wessen: ~ *coat is this?*, ~ *is this coat?* wem gehört dieser Mantel? **II** *relative pron* dessen, deren.

why [waɪ] *adv* warum, weshalb: ~ *not go by bus?* warum nimmst du nicht den Bus?

wick [wɪk] *s* Docht *m*: *get on s.o.'s* ~ Br. F j-m auf den Wecker fallen *od.* gehen.

wick·ed ['wɪkɪd] *adj* □ **1.** gemein, niederträchtig. **2.** *fig.* unerhört.

wick·er ['wɪkə] *adj* Korb...: ~ *basket* Weidenkorb *m*.

wide [waɪd] **I** *adj* (□ → **widely**) **1.** breit. **2.** weit offen, aufgerissen (*Augen*). **3.** *fig.* umfangreich (*Wissen etc*), vielfältig (*Interessen etc*). **4.** → *mark*⁵ 5. **II** *adv* **5.** weit. **6.** *go* ~ (*Sport*) danebengehen. ˌ~'**an·gle** *adj:* ~ *lens* phot. Weitwinkelobjektiv *n*. ˌ~-**a'wake** *adj* **1.** hellwach. **2.** *fig.* aufgeweckt, wach. ˌ~-'**eyed** *adj* **1.** mit großen *od.* aufgerissenen Augen. **2.** *fig.* naiv.

wide·ly ['waɪdlɪ] *adv* **1.** weit (*a. fig.*): *it is* ~ *known that* es ist weithin bekannt, daß; ~ *travel(l)ed* weitgereist. **2.** ~ *different* völlig verschieden. '**wid·en I** *v/t* verbreitern. **II** *v/i* breiter werden.

ˌ**wide·l·'o·pen** → wide 2. '~·**spread** *adj* weitverbreitet.

wid·ow ['wɪdəʊ] *s* Witwe *f*. '**wid·owed** *adj* verwitwet: *be* ~ verwitwet sein; Witwe(r) werden.

width [wɪdθ] *s* **1.** Breite *f*: *six feet in* ~ sechs Fuß breit; *what is the* ~ *of ...?* wie breit ist ...? **2.** Bahn *f* (*Stoff etc*).

wield [wiːld] *v/t* Einfluß, Macht ausüben.

wife [waɪf] *pl* **wives** [waɪvz] *s* (Ehe)Frau *f*, Gattin *f*. ~ *swap·ping* *s* F Partnertausch *m*.

wig [wɪg] *s* Perücke *f*.

wig-ging ['wɪgɪŋ] *s*: *give s.o. a ~* *Br.* F j-m e-e Standpauke halten.

wig-gle ['wɪgl] *v/t u. v/i* wackeln (mit).

wig-wam ['wɪgwæm] *s* Wigwam *m.*

wild [waɪld] **I** *adj* □ **1.** *allg.* wild: *the* ♀ *West* der Wilde Westen; → *oats.* **2.** stürmisch (*Wind, Applaus etc*). **3.** außer sich (*with* vor *dat*). **4.** verrückt (*Idee etc*). **5.** *it was just a ~ guess* ich hab' einfach drauflosgeraten. **II** *adv* **6.** F *go ~* ausflippen; *run ~* Amok laufen; *let one's children run ~* s-e Kinder machen lassen, was sie wollen. **III** *s* **7.** *in the ~* in freier Wildbahn. '*~cat* **I** *s* Wildkatze *f.* **II** *adj*: *~ strike* wilder Streik. '*~fire* **s**: *spread like ~* sich wie ein Lauffeuer verbreiten. ˌ~'**goose** *adj*: *be a ~chase* vergebliche Mühe *od.* ein Metzgergang sein. '*~life* **s** Tier- u. Pflanzenwelt *f.*

wil-ful ['wɪlful] *adj* □ **1.** eigensinnig. **2.** absichtlich, *bsd.* ﹩ vorsätzlich.

will[1] [wɪl] *s* **1.** Wille *m*: *~ to live* Lebenswille; *against one's ~* gegen s-n Willen; *at ~* nach Belieben; *of one's own free ~* aus freien Stücken; *I can't do that with the best ~ in the world* ich kann das (auch) beim besten Willen nicht tun; *take the ~ for the deed* den guten Willen für die Tat nehmen. **2.** *a. last ~ and testament* Letzter Wille, Testament *n*: *make one's ~* sein Testament machen; → *remember* 3.

will[2] [ˌ] *v/aux* **1.** *Futur*: *I'll be back in 10 minutes* ich bin in 10 Minuten zurück. **2.** *Bereitschaft, Entschluß*: *I won't go there again* ich gehe da nicht mehr hin; *the door won't shut* die Tür schließt nicht; *~ you have some coffee?* möchtest du e-e Tasse Kaffee? **3.** *Bitte*: *shut the window, ~ you?* mach bitte das Fenster zu. **4.** *Wiederholung*: *accidents ~ happen* Unfälle wird es immer geben; *boys ~ be boys* Jungen sind nun einmal so. **5.** *Vermutung*: *that ~ be my sister* das wird *od.* dürfte m-e Schwester sein.

will-ful *Am.* → *wilful.*

wil-lies ['wɪlɪz] *s pl*: *give s.o. the ~* F j-m unheimlich sein.

will-ing ['wɪlɪŋ] *adj* □ **1.** bereit (*to do* zu tun): *~ to compromise* kompromißbereit; *God ~* so Gott will. **2.** (be-reit)willig. '**will-ing-ness** *s* **1.** Bereitschaft *f*: *~ to compromise* Kompro-

mißbereitschaft. **2.** (Bereit)Willigkeit *f.*

wil-low ['wɪləʊ] *s* ♣ Weide *f.* '**wil-low-y** *adj* gertenschlank.

'**will,pow-er** *s* Willenskraft *f.*

wil-ly-nil-ly [ˌwɪlɪ'nɪlɪ] *adv* wohl od. übel.

wilt [wɪlt] *v/i* **1.** verwelken, welk werden. **2.** schlaff werden.

wil-y ['waɪlɪ] *adj* gerissen, raffiniert.

win [wɪn] **I** *s* **1.** *bsd. Sport*: Sieg *m*: *have a ~* e-n Sieg erzielen. **2.** e-n Gewinn machen. **II** *v/t* (*irr*) **2.** gewinnen: → *day* 2. **3.** *j-m et.* einbringen. **III** *v/i* (*irr*) **4.** gewinnen, siegen: *OK, you ~* okay, du hast gewonnen.

Verbindungen mit Adverbien:

win| back *v/t* zurückgewinnen. *~ out* → *win through.* *~ o-ver*, *~ round* *v/t* j-n für sich gewinnen: *win s.o. over to* j-n gewinnen für. *~ through* *v/i* sich durchsetzen.

wince [wɪns] *v/i* zs.-zucken (*at* bei).

winch [wɪntʃ] ⊚ **I** *s* Winde *f.* **II** *v/t* winden.

wind[1] [wɪnd] **I** *s* **1.** Wind *m*: *a load of ~* F leeres Geschwätz; *there's s.th. in the ~ fig.* es liegt et. in der Luft; *find out* (*od. see*) *which way the ~ blows fig.* sehen, woher der Wind weht; *get ~ of s.th. fig.* Wind von et. bekommen; *get the ~ up* F Angst kriegen; *put the ~ up s.o.* F j-m Angst einjagen; *sail close to the ~* ⚓ hart am Wind segeln; *fig.* sich hart an der Grenze des Erlaubten bewegen; *take the ~ out of s.o.'s sails fig.* j-m den Wind aus den Segeln nehmen. **2.** Atem *m*: *get one's ~* wieder zu Atem kommen; *get one's second ~* (*bsd. Sport*) die zweite Luft bekommen. **3.** ⚕ Blähungen *pl*: *it gives me ~* davon bekomme ich Blähungen. **4.** *the ~* ♪ die Blasinstrumente *pl*; die Bläser *pl*. **II** *v/t* **5.** *j-m* den Atem nehmen *od.* verschlagen. **6.** *hunt.* wittern.

wind[2] [waɪnd] **I** *s* **1.** Umdrehung *f.* **II** *v/t* (*irr*) **2.** drehen (an *dat*); *Uhr etc* aufziehen. **3.** wickeln (*round* um). **III** *v/i* (*irr*) **4.** sich winden *od.* schlängeln (*Pfad etc*).

Verbindungen mit Adverbien:

wind| back *v/t* *Film etc* zurückspulen. *~ down* **I** *v/t* **1.** *Autofenster etc* herunterdrehen, -kurbeln. **2.** *Produktion etc* reduzieren. **II** *v/i* **3.** F sich entspannen. *~ for-ward* *v/t* *Film etc* weiterspulen. *~*

up I v/t **1.** Autofenster etc hochdrehen, -kurbeln. **2.** Uhr etc aufziehen. **3.** Versammlung etc beschließen (**with** mit). **4.** Unternehmen auflösen. **II** v/i **5.** F landen (**in** in dat): ~ **doing s.th.** am Ende et. tun; **you'll ~ with a heart attack** du kriegst noch mal e-n Herzinfarkt.

wind·bag ['wɪndbæg] s F Schwätzer(in). '**~break** s Windschutz m. '**~fall** s **1.** pl Fallobst n. **2.** unverhofftes Geschenk, unverhoffter Gewinn.

wind·ing ['waɪndɪŋ] adj gewunden (Pfad etc): ~ **stairs** pl Wendeltreppe f.

wind· in·stru·ment [wɪnd] s ♪ Blasinstrument n. **~jam·mer** ['-ˌdʒæmə] s ⚓ Windjammer m.

wind·lass ['wɪndləs] s ⚙ Winde f.
wind·less ['wɪndlɪs] adj windstill.
wind·mill ['wɪnmɪl] s Windmühle f.

win·dow ['wɪndəʊ] s **1.** Fenster n. **2.** Schaufenster n. **3.** Schalter m (in Bank etc). ~ **box** s Blumenkasten m. '**~clean·er** s Fensterputzer m. ~ **dress·er** s Schaufensterdekorateur(in). ~ **dress·ing** s **1.** Schaufensterdekoration f. **2.** fig. Mache f. '**~pane** s Fensterscheibe f. ~ **seat** s Fensterplatz m. ~ **shade** s Am. Rouleau n. '**~shop** v/i: **go ~ping** e-n Schaufensterbummel machen. '**~sill** s Fensterbank f, -brett n.

wind·pipe ['wɪndpaɪp] s anat. Luftröhre f. '**~screen** s mot. bsd. Br. Windschutzscheibe f: ~ **wiper** Scheibenwischer m. '**~shield** Am. → **windscreen**. '**~sock** s Windsack m. '**~surf·er** s Windsurfer(in). '**~surf·ing** s Windsurfing n. '**~swept** adj (vom Wind) zerzaust. ~ **tun·nel** s Windkanal m.

wind·ward ['wɪndwəd] ⚓ **I** adv luvwärts. **II** s Luv(seite) f.

wind·y ['wɪndɪ] adj ☐ **1.** windig. **2.** ⚕ blähend.

wine [waɪn] s Wein m. ~ **bar** s Weinlokal n. '**~bot·tle** s Weinflasche f. ~ **glass** s Weinglas n. ~ **list** s Weinkarte f.

wing [wɪŋ] s **1.** allg. Flügel m: **take s.o. under one's ~** fig. j-n unter s-e Fittiche nehmen. **2.** ✈ Tragfläche f. **3.** mot. Br. Kotflügel m. **'wing·er** s Sport: Flügelstürmer(in).

wing· nut s ⚙ Flügelmutter f. '**~span**, '**~spread** s ✈, orn. Flügelspannweite f.

wink [wɪŋk] **I** v/i zwinkern: ~ **at** j-m zu-

zwinkern; et. geflissentlich übersehen. **II** v/t: ~ **one's lights** mot. Br. blinken. **III** s Zwinkern n: **with a ~ of the eye** augenzwinkernd; **give s.o. a ~** j-m zuzwinkern; **I didn't get a ~ of sleep** (od. **I didn't sleep a ~**) **last night** ich habe letzte Nacht kein Auge zugetan; → **forty** I. '**wink·er** s mot. Br. F Blinker m.

win·kle ['wɪŋkl] v/t: ~ **out** bsd. Br. F Wahrheit etc herausholen (**of** aus).

win·ner ['wɪnə] s **1.** Gewinner(in), (bsd. Sport) Sieger(in). **2.** **be a real winner** F ein Riesenerfolg sein. '**win·ning I** adj **1.** siegreich, Sieger..., Sieges...: ~ **post** Zielpfosten m. **2.** fig. gewinnend (Lächeln etc). **II** s pl **3.** Gewinn m.

win·ter ['wɪntə] **I** s Winter m: **in** (**the**) ~ im Winter. **II** adj Winter...: ~ **sports** pl Wintersport m. **III** v/i überwintern; den Winter verbringen. '**win·ter·ize** v/t Am. Auto etc winterfest machen. '**win·ter·y** → **wintry**.

'**win·ter·time** s Winter(zeit f) m: **in** (**the**) ~ im Winter.

win·try ['wɪntrɪ] adj **1.** winterlich, Winter...: ~ **clouds** pl Schneewolken pl. **2.** fig. frostig (Lächeln).

wipe [waɪp] **I** s: **give s.th. a ~** et. abwischen. **II** v/t Tisch etc (ab)wischen; Krümel etc wischen (**off** von): ~ **one's feet** (**shoes**) sich die Füße (Schuhe) abputzen (**on** auf dat); ~ **one's nose** sich die Nase putzen; ~ **clean** Tafel etc abwischen; **that'll ~ the smile off his face** fig. da wird ihm das Lachen vergehen; ~ **the floor with s.o.** F j-n fertigmachen.

Verbindungen mit Adverbien:

wipe| a·way v/t wegwischen, sich die Tränen ab- od. wegwischen. ~ **off** v/t ab-, wegwischen. ~ **out** v/t **1.** auswischen. **2.** Menschen auslöschen, Rasse ausrotten. **3.** Gewinn etc zunichte machen. **4.** F j-n schlauchen. ~ **up** v/t aufwischen.

wip·er ['waɪpə] s mot. (Scheiben)Wischer m.

wire ['waɪə] **I** s **1.** Draht m. **2.** ⚡ Leitung f. **3.** Am. Telegramm n. **II** v/t **4.** a. ~ **up** Leitungen verlegen in (dat). **5.** Am. j-m ein Telegramm schicken; j-m et. telegrafieren. ~ **net·ting** s Maschendraht m. '**~tap** v/t j-n, j-s Telefon abhören. ~ **wool** s Stahlwolle f.

wir·y ['waɪərɪ] *adj* drahtig (*Figur etc*).

wis·dom ['wɪzdəm] *s* Weisheit *f*, Klugheit *f*. ~ **tooth** *s* (*irr* **tooth**) Weisheitszahn *m*.

wise [waɪz] **I** *adj* (□ → **wisely**) weise, klug: **you were ~ to do that** es war klug von dir, das zu tun; **it's easy to be ~ after the event** hinterher kann man leicht klüger sein; **be none the ~r** F nicht klüger sein als vorher; **get ~ to s.th.** F et. spitzkriegen; **~ guy** F Klugschwätzer *m*. **II** *v/t*: **~ up** *bsd. Am.* F j-n aufklären (**to** über *acc*). **III** *v/i*: **~ up to** *bsd. Am.* F et. spitzkriegen. **'~crack** F **I** *v/i* witzeln (**about** über *acc*). **II** *s* Witzelei *f*: **you and your ~s** *contp.* du u. deine dummen Sprüche.

wise·ly ['waɪzlɪ] *adv* **1.** weise, klug. **2.** klugerweise.

wish [wɪʃ] **I** *v/t* **1.** *I ~ he were here* ich wünschte *od.* wollte, er wäre hier. **2.** wollen: *I ~ to make a complaint* ich möchte mich beschweren. **3.** j-m et. wünschen: **~ s.o. well** j-m alles Gute wünschen; *I wouldn't ~ that on my worst enemy* das würde ich nicht einmal m-m ärgsten Feind wünschen. **II** *v/i* **4.** *if you ~* (**to**) wenn du willst. **5.** ~ **for s.th.** sich et. wünschen. **III** *s* **6.** Wunsch *m* (**for** nach): **make a ~** sich et. wünschen; (**with**) **best ~es** Herzliche Grüße (*Briefschluß*); **best ~es on passing your exam** herzlichen Glückwunsch zur bestandenen Prüfung; **send one's best ~es for s.o.'s birthday** j-m e-n Glückwunsch zum Geburtstag schicken. **'~bone** *s* Gabelbein *n*, -knochen *m*.

wish·ful ['wɪʃfʊl] *adj*: ~ **thinking** Wunschdenken *n*.

wish·y-wash·y ['wɪʃɪˌwɒʃɪ] *adj* F **1.** labb(e)rig. **2.** *fig.* lasch (*Person*); verschwommen (*Vorstellung etc*).

wisp [wɪsp] *s* (*Gras-, Haar*)Büschel *n*.

wist·ful ['wɪstfʊl] *adj* □ wehmütig.

wit [wɪt] *s* **1.** Geist *m*, Witz *m*. **2.** geistreicher Mensch. **3.** *a. pl* Verstand *m*: **be at one's ~'s end** mit s-r Weisheit am Ende sein; **frighten s.o. out of his ~s** j-n zu Tode erschrecken; **keep one's ~s about one** e-n klaren Kopf behalten.

witch [wɪtʃ] *s* Hexe *f*. **'~craft** *s* Hexerei *f*. ~ **doc·tor** *s* Medizinmann *m*. ~ **hunt** *s pol.* Hexenjagd *f* (**for, against** auf *acc*).

with [wɪð] *prp* **1.** *allg.* mit: **are you still ~ me?** kannst du mir folgen? **2.** bei: **she's staying ~ a friend** sie wohnt bei e-r Freundin; → **will**[1] 1, *etc.* **3.** vor (*dat*): → **tremble** I, *etc.* **4.** von: → **part** 12, *etc.* **5.** für: **are you ~ me or against me?** bist du für *od.* gegen mich?

with·draw (*irr* **draw**) **I** *v/t* **1.** Geld abheben (**from** von). **2.** Angebot *etc* zurückziehen, Anschuldigung *etc* zurücknehmen: **~ from the market** vom Markt nehmen. **3.** ✕ Truppen zurück-, abziehen. **II** *v/i* **4.** sich zurückziehen. **5.** zurücktreten (**from** von). **with'draw·al I** *s* **1.** *make a ~* Geld abheben (**from** von). **2.** Rücknahme *f*. **3.** ✕ Ab-, Rückzug *m*. **4.** Rücktritt *m* (**from** von). **II** *adj* **5.** ~ **symptoms** *pl* ✽ Entziehungs-, Entzugserscheinungen *pl*.

with·er ['wɪðə] *v/i* eingehen, verdorren. **'with·er·ing** *adj* □ vernichtend (*Blick etc*).

with'hold *v/t* (*irr* **hold**) Informationen, Zahlung *etc* zurückhalten: **~ s.th. from s.o.** j-m et. vorenthalten. **~'in** *prp* innerhalb (*gen*): → **income, sight** 3, *etc.* **~'out** *prp* ohne (*acc*). **~'stand** *v/t* (*irr* **stand**) **1.** e-m Angriff *etc* standhalten. **2.** Beanspruchung *etc* aushalten.

wit·less ['wɪtlɪs] *adj* □ geistlos.

wit·ness ['wɪtnɪs] **I** *s* **1.** *allg.* Zeuge *m*, Zeugin *f*: ~ **for the defence** (*Am.* **defense**) ⚖ Entlastungszeuge; ~ **for the prosecution** ⚖ Belastungszeuge. **II** *v/t* **2.** Zeuge sein (*gen*); Veränderungen *etc* erleben: **did anybody ~ the accident?** hat j-d den Unfall gesehen? **3.** *et.* bezeugen, Unterschrift beglaubigen. **4.** ~ **denken Sie nur an** (*acc*). **III** *v/i* **5.** ~ **to** *et.* bezeugen. ~ **box** *s bsd. Br.*, ~ **stand** *s Am.* Zeugenstand *m*.

wit·ti·cism ['wɪtɪsɪzəm] *s* geistreiche *od.* witzige Bemerkung.

wit·ty ['wɪtɪ] *adj* □ geistreich, witzig.

wives [waɪvz] *pl von* **wife**.

wiz·ard ['wɪzəd] *s* **1.** Zauberer *m*, Hexenmeister *m*. **2.** *fig.* Genie *n* (**at** in *dat*): **financial ~** Finanzgenie.

wiz·ened ['wɪznd] *adj* verhutzelt.

wob·ble ['wɒbl] *v/i* wackeln (*Tisch etc*), zittern (*Stimme etc*), schwabbeln (*Pudding etc*), *mot.* flattern (*Reifen etc*). **II** *v/t* wackeln an (*dat*).

woe [wəʊ] *s* Kummer *m*, Leid *n*: ~ **betide**

you if wehe, wenn du; *tale of ~* Leidensgeschichte f. **woe·ful** ['~fʊl] *adj* □ bedauerlich, beklagenswert.

woke [wəʊk] *pret von* **wake²**. **'wok·en** *pp von* **wake²**.

wolf [wʊlf] **I** *pl* **wolves** [wʊlvz] *s* 1. *zo.* Wolf *m*: *a ~ in sheep's clothing fig.* ein Wolf im Schafspelz; *lone ~ fig.* Einzelgänger *m*; *cry ~ fig.* blinden Alarm schlagen. 2. F Schürzenjäger *m*. **II** *v/t* 3. *a. ~ down* F Essen hinunterschlingen. **~whis·tle** *s* F bewundernder Pfiff: *give s.o. a ~* j-m nachpfeifen.

wolves [wʊlvz] *pl von* **wolf**.

wom·an ['wʊmən] **I** *pl* **wom·en** ['wɪmɪn] *s* Frau f. **II** *adj*: *~ doctor* Ärztin f; *~ driver* Frau f am Steuer; *~ teacher* Lehrerin f. **~hat·er** *s* Frauenhasser *m*. **wom·an·ish** ['wʊmənɪʃ] *adj* □ *contp.* weibisch.

wom·an·ize ['wʊmənaɪz] *v/i* hinter den Frauen hersein. **'wom·an·iz·er** *s* Schürzenjäger *m*.

wom·an·kind [ˌwʊmən'kaɪnd] *s* das weibliche Geschlecht. **'wom·an·ly** *adj* fraulich (*Figur etc*); weiblich (*Tugend etc*).

womb [wuːm] *s anat.* Gebärmutter f, Mutterleib *m*.

wom·en ['wɪmɪn] *pl von* **woman**: *~'s movement* Frauenbewegung f; *~'s team* (*Sport*) Damenmannschaft f.

won [wʌn] *pret u. pp von* **win**.

won·der ['wʌndə] **I** *v/t* 1. neugierig *od.* gespannt sein, gern wissen mögen (*if, whether* ob; *what* was); sich fragen, überlegen: *I ~ if you could help me* vielleicht können Sie mir helfen. **II** *v/i* 2. sich wundern, erstaunt sein (*about* über *acc*). 3. neugierig *od.* gespannt sein: *well, I ~* na, ich weiß nicht (recht). **III** *s* 4. Staunen *n*, Verwunderung f: *in ~* erstaunt, verwundert. 5. Wunder *n*: *nine days' ~* Eintagsfliege f; *it's a ~ (that)* es ist ein Wunder, daß; (*it's*) *no (od. small, little) ~ (that)* kein Wunder, daß; *~s will never cease! humor.* es geschehen noch Zeichen u. Wunder!; *do (od. work) ~s* Wunder vollbringen, Wunder wirken (*for* bei). **IV** *adj* 6. Wunder... **won·der·ful** ['~fʊl] *adj* □ wunderbar.

'won·der·land *s* 1. Wunderland *n*. 2. Paradies *n*.

won·ky ['wɒŋkɪ] *adj Br.* F 1. wack(e)lig. 2. schwach (*Herz*).

wont [wəʊnt] *adj*: *be ~ to do s.th.* et. zu tun pflegen.

won't [wəʊnt] F *für* will not.

woo [wuː] *v/t j-n* umwerben.

wood [wʊd] *s* 1. Holz *n*: → *touch* 8. 2. *a. pl* Wald *m*: *be out of the ~ (Am. ~s) fig.* über den Berg sein; *he can't see the ~ for trees fig.* er sieht den Wald vor lauter Bäumen nicht. **'~cut** *s* Holzschnitt *m*.

wood·ed ['wʊdɪd] *adj* bewaldet.

wood·en ['wʊdn] *adj* hölzern (*a. fig.*), Holz... **'~head·ed** *adj* F dämlich.

wood·land ['wʊdlənd] *s* Waldland *n*, Waldung f. **'~peck·er** *s orn.* Specht *m*. **'~pile** *s* Holzhaufen *m*, -stoß *m*. **'~shed** *s* Holzschuppen *m*. **~wind** ['~wɪnd] ♪ **I** *s*: *the ~* die Holzblasinstrumente *pl*; die Holzbläser *pl*. **II** *adj*: *~ instrument* Holzblasinstrument *n*. **'~worm** *s zo.* Holzwurm *m*.

wood·y ['wʊdɪ] *adj* 1. waldig. 2. holzig.

wool [wʊl] *s* Wolle f: *pull the ~ over s.o.'s eyes fig.* j-m Sand in die Augen streuen. **wool·en** ['~ən] *Am.*, **wool·len** ['~ən] *bsd. Br.* **I** *adj* wollen, Woll... **II** *s pl* Wollsachen *pl*, -kleidung f. **wool·ly**, *Am. a.* **'wool·y** *adj* 1. → **woolen** 1. 2. wollig. 3. *fig.* wirr.

Worces·ter sauce ['wʊstə] *s* Worcestersoße f.

word [wɜːd] **I** *s* 1. *allg.* Wort *n*: *beyond ~s* unbeschreiblich; *by ~ of mouth* mündlich; *~ for ~* Wort für Wort; wortwörtlich; *in a ~* in 'einem Wort; *in other ~s* mit anderen Worten; *in one's own ~s* in eigenen Worten; *in ~ and in deed* in Worten u. in Taten; *angry isn't the ~ for ...* ärgerlich ist gar kein Ausdruck für ...; *he's a man of few ~s* er macht nicht viele Worte; *be as good as one's ~* halten, was man versprach; *break one's ~* sein Wort brechen; *get (od. have) the final (od. last) ~* das letzte Wort haben (*on* in (*dat*)); *give s.o. one's ~ (of hono[u]r)* j-m sein (Ehren)Wort geben; *he always has to have the last ~* er muß immer das letzte Wort haben; *can I have a ~ (od. a few ~s) with you?* kann ich Sie mal kurz sprechen?; *have ~s* e-e Auseinandersetzung haben (*with* mit); *keep one's ~*

Wort halten (*to* gegenüber); *put into* ~s *et.* ausdrücken, in Worte fassen; *take* **s.o. at his** ~ j-n beim Wort nehmen; → *eat* 2, *edgeways*, *fail* 5, *mum*[1] I, *play* 4. **2.** *pl* Text *m* (*e-s Lieds etc*). **3.** Nachricht *f*: *there's been no* ~ *from her for months* wir haben schon seit Monaten nichts mehr von ihr gehört; *send* ~ *that* Nachricht geben, daß. **II** *v/t* **4.** *et.* ausdrücken, *Text* abfassen, formulieren. **'word·ing** s Wortlaut *m*. **'word·less** *adj* □ wortlos, stumm.

word| or·der s Anat. Wortstellung *f*. **'~·play** s Wortspielereien *pl.* ~ **pro·cess·or** s *Computer*: Wort-, Textverarbeitungsgerät *n*.

word·y ['wɜːdɪ] *adj* □ wortreich, langatmig.

wore [wɔː] *pret von* **wear**.

work [wɜːk] **I** s **1.** *allg.* Arbeit *f*: *at* ~ am Arbeitsplatz; *be out of* ~ arbeitslos sein; *make short* ~ *of* kurzen Prozeß machen mit. **2.** Werk *n* (*a. Tat*): → *art* 1. **3.** *pl* (*oft sg konstruiert*) Werk *n*, Fabrik *f*. **4.** *pl* ⊙ Werk *n*, Getriebe *n*: → *spanner*. **5.** *the whole* ~s *pl* F der ganze Krempel. **II** *v/i* **6.** arbeiten (*at, on* an *dat*): → *rule* 2. **7.** funktionieren (*a. fig.*). **III** *v/t* **8.** *j-n* arbeiten lassen: ~ *o.s. into a temper* F sich in e-n Wutausbruch hineinsteigern. **9.** *Maschine etc* bedienen. **10.** bewirken: *how did you* ~ *it?* F wie hast du das geschafft?; → *miracle*, *wonder* 5. **11.** ~ *s.th. into fig.* et. einbauen in (*acc*).

Verbindungen mit Adverbien:

work| *in* *v/t* Zitate etc einbauen. ~ *off* *v/t* **1.** Schulden abarbeiten. **2.** *Zorn etc* abreagieren (*on* an *dat*). ~ *out* **I** *v/t* **1.** ausrechnen; *fig.* sich *et.* zs.-reimen. **2.** *Plan etc* ausarbeiten. **II** *v/i* **3.** klappen: *it'll never* ~ daraus kann nichts werden. **4.** aufgehen (*Rechnung etc*): *it didn't* ~ *fig.* die Rechnung ist nicht aufgegangen. **5.** F trainieren. ~ **o·ver** *v/t* F *j-n* zs.-schlagen. ~ *up* *v/t* **1.** *Zuhörer etc* aufpeitschen, -wühlen: *be worked up* aufgeregt *od.* nervös sein (*about* wegen). **2.** sich *Appetit etc* holen; *Begeisterung etc* aufbringen. **3.** *et.* ausarbeiten (*into* zu).

work·a·ble ['wɜːkəbl] *adj* **1.** formbar. **2.** *fig.* durchführbar.

'work·a·day *adj* Alltags...

work·a·hol·ic [ˌwɜːkə'hɒlɪk] s F Arbeitssüchtige *m*, *f*.

'work|·bench s ⊙ Werkbank *f*. **'~·book** s *ped.* Arbeitsheft *n*. ~ **camp** s Arbeitslager *n*. ~ **coat** s Am. Arbeitsmantel *m*, Kittel *m*. **'~·day** s **1.** Arbeitstag *m*. **2.** Werktag *m*.

work·er ['wɜːkə] s **1.** Arbeiter(in), Angestellte *m*, *f*. **2.** *be a real* ~ hart arbeiten.

work force s **1.** Belegschaft *f*. **2.** Arbeitskräftepotential *n*.

work·ing ['wɜːkɪŋ] **I** *adj* **1.** Arbeits...: ~ *breakfast* Arbeitsfrühstück *n*; ~ *capital* ♥ Betriebskapital *n*; ~ *day* → *workday*; ~ *hours* *pl* Arbeitszeit *f*; ~ *hypothesis* Arbeitshypothese *f*; *a* ~ *knowledge of French* französische Grundkenntnisse *pl*; *have a* ~ *knowledge of* ein bißchen was verstehen von; *in* ~ *order* in betriebsfähigem Zustand. **2.** arbeitend, berufstätig: ~ *class* (*as pl*) Arbeiterklasse *f*. **II** s *pl* **3.** ⊙ Arbeits-, Funktionsweise *f*.

'work|·load s Arbeitspensum *n*. ~ **man** ['~mən] s (*irr man*) Handwerker *m*. **'~·out** s F Training *n*. ~ **per·mit** s Arbeitserlaubnis *f*, -genehmigung *f*. **'~· place** s Arbeitsplatz *m*: *at the* ~ am Arbeitsplatz. **'~·shop** s **1.** Werkstatt *f*. **2.** Workshop *m* (*Seminar*). **'~·shy** *adj* arbeitsscheu. ~ **stud·y** s Arbeitsstudie *f*. **'~·top** s Arbeitsplatte *f*. **'~·to-'rule** s † *Br.* Dienst *m* nach Vorschrift.

world [wɜːld] **I** s *allg.* Welt *f*: *in the* ~ auf der Welt; *what in the* ~ ...? was um alles in der Welt ...?; *a man of the* ~ ein Mann von Welt; *all over the* ~ in der ganzen Welt; *they are* ~s *apart* zwischen ihnen liegen Welten; *bring into the* ~ auf die Welt bringen; *do s.o. a* (*od. the*) ~ *of good* j-m unwahrscheinlich gut tun; *mean all the* ~ *to s.o.* j-m alles bedeuten. **II** *adj* Welt...: ~ **cham·pion** Weltmeister(in); ~ *championship* Weltmeisterschaft *f*; ♀ *Cup* (*Sport*) Weltcup *m*, -pokal *m*; Fußballweltmeisterschaft *f*; ~ *language* Weltsprache *f*; ~ *power* *pol.* Weltmacht *f*; ~ *record* Weltrekord *m*; ~ *record holder* Weltrekordler(in); ~ *war* Weltkrieg *m*. **'~·beat·er** s ~ a unschlagbar sein. **'~·fa·mous** *adj* weltberühmt.

world·ly ['wɜːldlɪ] *adj* **1.** weltlich, irdisch.

2. weltlich (gesinnt). **,~-'wise** *adj* weltklug.

'world·wide *adj* weltweit, *adv a.* auf der ganzen Welt.

worm [wɜːm] **I** *s* **1.** *zo.* Wurm *m.* **II** *v/t* *Hund etc* entwurmen. **3. ~ one's way through** sich schlängeln *od.* zwängen durch; **~ o.s. into s.o.'s confidence** sich in j-s Vertrauen einschleichen. **4. ~ s.th. out of s.o.** *fig.* j-m et. entlocken. **'~,eat·en** *adj* wurmstichig. **'~·hole** *s* Wurmloch *n.* **'~·wood** *s* ⚚ Wermut *m.*

worm·y ['wɜːmɪ] *adj* **1.** wurmig. **2.** wurmstichig.

worn [wɔːn] *pp von* **wear.** **,~-'out** *adj* **1.** abgenutzt, abgetragen *(Kleidung).* **2.** *fig.* erschöpft *(Person).*

wor·ried ['wʌrɪd] *adj* besorgt, beunruhigt: **be ~** sich sorgen, sich Sorgen machen **(about** über *acc,* um, wegen). **wor·ri·some** ['~səm] *adj* besorgniserregend, beunruhigend. **'wor·ry I** *v/t* j-n beunruhigen, *j-m* Sorgen machen. **II** *v/i* sich sorgen, sich Sorgen machen **(about, over** über *acc,* um, wegen): **not to ~** mach dir keine Gedanken; **~ at** sich abmühen mit. **III** *s* Sorge *f.* **'wor·ry·ing → worrisome.**

worse [wɜːs] **I** *adj u. adv* schlechter, schlimmer: **~ still** was noch schlimmer ist; **to make matters ~** zu allem Übel; **he's getting steadily ~** sein Zustand verschlechtert sich immer mehr; → **wear** 1. **II** *s* Schlechteres *n,* Schlimmeres *n:* → **bad** 7, **turn** 4. **'wors·en I** *v/t* schlechter machen, verschlechtern. **II** *v/i* schlechter werden, sich verschlechtern.

wor·ship ['wɜːʃɪp] **I** *v/t pret u. pp* **-shiped,** *bsd. Br.* **-shipped 1.** Gott anbeten, *a.* Ahnen, Helden verehren; *weitS.* j-n anbeten, vergöttern: → **God** *a.* zu Gott beten. **II** *s* **2.** Anbetung *f,* Verehrung *f.* **3.** Gottesdienst *m.* **'wor·ship·(p)er** *s* **1.** Anbeter(in), Verehrer(in). **2.** Kirchgänger(in).

worst [wɜːst] **I** *adj* schlechtest, schlimmst: **of the ~ kind** der übelsten Sorte. **II** *adv* am schlechtesten *od.* schlimmsten: **come off ~** den kürzeren ziehen **(in** bei). **III** *s* der, die, das Schlechteste *od.* Schlimmste: **at (the) ~** schlimmstenfalls; **if the ~ comes to the ~** wenn alle Stricke reißen; **the ~ of it is**

that das Schlimmste daran ist, daß; **get the ~** den kürzeren ziehen **(of** bei).

wor·sted ['wʊstɪd] *s* Kammgarn *n.*

worth [wɜːθ] **I** *adj* wert: **it's ~ £10** es ist 10 Pfund wert; **a skirt ~ £20** ein Rock im Wert von 20 Pfund; **it's ~ a try** es ist e-n Versuch wert; **it isn't ~ it** es lohnt sich nicht; **it might be ~** *your while* es könnte sich für dich lohnen **(to do** zu tun); **~ mentioning** erwähnenswert; **not ~ mentioning** nicht der Rede wert; **it isn't ~ waiting any longer** es lohnt sich nicht, nicht länger zu warten; → **candle, salt** 1. **III** *s* Wert *m.* **'worth·less** *adj* □ wertlos. **,worth·'while** *adj* lohnend: **be ~** sich lohnen. **wor·thy** ['wɜːðɪ] *adj* □ würdig: **~ of admiration** bewundernswert.

would [wʊd] *v/aux* **1.** *konditional:* **he said he ~ come** er sagte, er werde kommen; **he ~ have come if** er wäre gekommen, wenn; **what ~ you do if ...?** was würdest du tun, wenn ...?; **how ~ you know?** woher willst du denn das wissen?; **you ~n't understand** das verstehst du sowieso nicht; **you ~, ~n't you?** F das sieht dir ähnlich! **2.** *Bereitschaft, Entschluß:* **he ~n't tell us what had happened** er wollte uns nicht sagen, was passiert war; **the door ~n't shut** die Tür schloß nicht; **I ~ rather not say what I think** ich sage lieber nicht, was ich denke. **3.** *höfliche Bitte:* **shut the window, ~ you?** mach doch bitte das Fenster zu. **4.** *Wiederholung:* **he ~ often take a walk after supper** er machte oft nach dem Abendessen oft e-n Spaziergang. **'~-be** *adj contp.* Möchtegern...

wouldn't ['wʊdnt] F *für* **would not.**

wound¹ [wuːnd] **I** *s* Wunde *f,* Verletzung *f:* **open old ~s** *fig.* alte Wunden aufreißen; → **rub** 3. **II** *v/t* j-n verwunden, verletzen; *fig. j-s Stolz etc* verletzen.

wound² [waʊnd] *pret u. pp von* **wind².**

wove [wəʊv] *pret von* **weave.** **'wov·en** *pp von* **weave.**

wow [waʊ] *int* F wow!, Mann!, Mensch!

wran·gle ['ræŋgl] **I** *v/i* (sich) streiten **(with** mit; **over** um). **II** *s* Streit *m.*

wrap [ræp] **I** *v/t* **1.** *a.* **~ up** einpacken, -wickeln **(in** in *acc).* **2.** *et.* wickeln **([a]round** um). **3. ~ up** F *Handel etc* unter Dach u. Fach bringen. **II** *v/i* **4. ~**

up sich warm anziehen. **5.** ~ *up!* F
Schnauze! II s **6.** *bsd. Am.* Umhang *m.*
7. F *be still under* ~*s* noch geheim sein;
keep under ~*s et.* geheimhalten.
'**wrap·per** *s Br.* (Schutz)Umschlag *m.*
'**wrap·ping I** *s* Verpackung *f.* II *adj:* ~
paper Einwickel-, Packpapier *n.*
wrath [rɒθ] *s* Zorn *m.*
wreath [ri:θ] *pl* **wreaths** [ri:ðz] *s*
Kranz *m.*
wreck [rek] **I** *s* **1.** ⚓ Wrack *n (a. fig.
Person).* **II** *v/t* **2.** *be* ~*ed* ⚓ zerschellen;
Schiffbruch erleiden. **3.** *Hoffnungen etc*
zunichte machen. '**wreck·age** *s* Trümmer *pl (a. fig.),* ⚓ *a.* Wrackteile *pl.*
'**wreck·er** *s mot. Am.* Abschleppwagen *m.*
wren [ren] *s orn.* Zaunkönig *m.*
wrench [rentʃ] **I** *v/t* **1.** ~ *s.th. from (od.
out of) s.o.'s hand* j-m et. aus der Hand
winden; ~ *off* Verschluß *etc* mit e-m
Ruck aufschrauben. **2.** 🩺 sich *das Knie
etc* verrenken. **II** *s* **3.** ✦ Verrenkung *f.*
4. 💡 *Br.* Franzose *m; Am.* Schrauben-
schlüssel *m.*
wrest [rest] *v/t:* ~ *s.th. from (od. out of)
s.o.'s hand* j-m et. aus der Hand reißen.
wres·tle [ˈresl] **I** *v/i* **1.** ringen (**with** mit).
2. *fig.* ringen, kämpfen (**with** mit; **for**
um). **II** *v/t* **3.** *Sport:* ringen gegen.
'**wres·tler** *s Sport:* Ringer *m.*
'**wres·tling** (*Sport*) **I** *s* Ringen *n.* **II** *adj*
Ring...: ~ *match* Ringkampf *m.*
wretch [retʃ] *s* **1.** *a. poor* ~ armer Teufel.
2. *oft humor.* Wicht *m.* **wretch·ed** [ˈ~ɪd]
adj □ **1.** elend; (tod)unglücklich. **2.**
scheußlich (*Kopfschmerzen, Wetter
etc*). **3.** verflixt.
wrig·gle [ˈrɪgl] **I** *v/i* sich winden; zappeln: ~ *out of* fig. sich herauswinden
aus; sich drücken vor (*dat*). **II** *v/t* mit
den Zehen wackeln.
wring [rɪŋ] *v/t* (*irr*) **1.** *j-m die Hand* drük-
ken; *die Hände* ringen. **2.** *oft* ~ *out* Wäsche *etc* auswringen: ~ *the truth out of
s.o.* die Wahrheit aus j-m herausholen.
'**wring·ing** *adv:* ~ *wet* klatschnaß.
wrin·kle¹ [ˈrɪŋkl] **I** *s* Falte *f,* Runzel *f.* **II**
v/t a. ~ *up Stirn* runzeln, *Nase* rümpfen.
III *v/i* faltig *od.* runz(e)lig werden.
wrin·kle² [~] *s* F Kniff *m,* Trick *m.*
wrist [rɪst] *s* Handgelenk *n.* '~**band** *s*
Armband *n.*

wrist·let [ˈrɪstlɪt] *s* Armband *n.*
'**wrist-watch** *s* Armbanduhr *f.*
writ [rɪt] *s* ⚖🕮 Befehl *m,* Verfügung *f.*
write [raɪt] (*irr*) **I** *v/t* **1.** Buch etc, j-m e-n
Brief *etc* schreiben: *it was written on
(od. all over) his face* fig. es stand ihm
im Gesicht geschrieben. **2.** *bsd. Am.* j-m
schreiben. **II** *v/i* **3.** schreiben: ~ *to s.o.*
j-m schreiben; → *home* 8.
Verbindungen mit Adverbien:
write *back v/i* zurückschreiben. ~
down v/t aufschreiben, niederschrei-
ben. ~ *in v/i* schreiben (*to* an *acc*): ~ *for
et.* anfordern. ~ *off v/t* **1.** *j-n,* ✝ *et.*
abschreiben. **2.** *bsd. Dr. Wagen* 🚗
Schrott fahren. ~ *out v/t* **1.** *Namen etc*
ausschreiben. **2.** *Bericht etc* ausarbeiten. **3.** *j-m e-e Quittung etc* ausstellen. **4.**
Rundfunk, TV: j-n herausschreiben (*of*
aus *e-r Serie*). ~ *up v/t* **1.** *Notizen etc*
ausarbeiten. **2.** berichten über (*acc*); *et.*
besprechen.
'**write-off** *s* **1.** ✝ Abschreibung *f.* **2.** *bsd.
Br.* Totalschaden *m.*
'**writ·er** [ˈraɪtə] *s* **1.** Schreiber(in), Verfas-
ser(in), Autor(in). **2.** Schriftsteller(in).
'**write-up** *s* (Presse)Bericht *m;* Besprechung *f,* Kritik *f.*
writhe [raɪð] *v/i* sich krümmen *od.* winden (**in, with** vor *dat*).
writ·ing [ˈraɪtɪŋ] **I** *s* **1.** Schreiben *n (Tätigkeit).* **2.** (Hand)Schrift *f.* **3.** *of* Werke
pl. **4.** *in* ~ schriftlich. **II** *adj* **5.** Schreib...:
~ *desk* Schreibtisch *m;* ~ *paper*
Schreibpapier *n.*
writ·ten [ˈrɪtn] **I** *pp von* **write.** **II** *adj*
schriftlich: ~ *language* Schriftspra-
che *f.*
wrong [rɒŋ] **I** *adj* (□ → **wrongly**) **1.**
falsch: *be* ~ falsch sein, nicht stimmen;
unrecht haben; falsch gehen (*Uhr*). **2.**
unrecht: *you were* ~ *to say that* es war
nicht recht *od.* richtig von dir, das zu
sagen. **3.** *is anything* ~? ist et. nicht in
Ordnung? *what's* ~ *with you?* was ist
los mit dir?, was hast du? **II** *adv* **4.**
falsch: *get* ~ *j-n,* *et.* falsch verstehen; *go*
~ e-n Fehler machen; kaputtgehen; *fig.*
schiefgehen. **III** *s* **5.** Unrecht *n: be in
the* ~ im Unrecht sein. **IV** *v/t* **6.** j-m
Unrecht tun. ~·**do·er** *s* Misse-, Übeltä-
ter(in). ~·**do·ing** *s* **1.** Missetat(en *pl*) *f.*
2. Vergehen *n od. pl.*
wrong·ful [ˈrɒŋfʊl] *adj* □ **1.** ungerecht-

fertigt. **2.** gesetzwidrig: ~ *imprison-ment* Freiheitsberaubung *f*.

wrong·head·ed *adj* □ **1.** querköpfig, verbohrt (*Person*). **2.** verschroben (*Ideen etc*).

wrong·ly ['rɒŋlɪ] *adv* zu Unrecht; fälschlicherweise.

wrote [rəʊt] *pret von* **write**.

wrought [rɔ:t] *adj*: ~ *iron* Schmiedeeisen *n*. ,~'**i·ron** *adj* schmiedeeisern. ,~-**pt** *adj* aufgeregt, nervös.

wrung [rʌŋ] *pret u. pp von* **wring**.

wry [raɪ] *adj* süßsauer (*Lächeln*); sarkastisch (*Humor*).

X

Xmas ['eksməs, 'krɪsməs] F → *Christmas*.

X-ray ['eksreɪ] I *v/t* **1.** röntgen. II *s* **2.** Röntgenaufnahme *f*, -bild *n*. **3.** Röntgenuntersuchung *f*.

xy·lo·phone ['zaɪləfəʊn] *s* ♪ Xylophon *n*.

Y

yacht [jɒt] I *s* Jacht *f*; (*Sport*) (Segel)Boot *n*. II *v/i* segeln: *go ~ing* segeln gehen. '**yacht·ing** *s* Segeln *n*.

yachts·man ['jɒtsmən] *s* (*irr man*) *Sport*: Segler *m*. '**yachts,wom·an** *s* (*irr woman*) *Sport*: Seglerin *f*.

yank [jæŋk] F I *v/t* reißen an (*dat*): ~ *out* (her)ausreißen, *Zahn* ziehen. II *v/i*: ~ *on* reißen an (*dat*). III *s* Ruck *m*.

Yan·kee ['jæŋkɪ] *s* F Yankee *m*, Ami *m*.

yap [jæp] I *v/i* **1.** kläffen. **2.** F quasseln. II *s* **3.** Kläffen *n*. **4.** Gequassel *n*.

yard¹ [jɑ:d] *s* Yard *n*.

yard² [~] *s* Hof *m*.

'**yard·stick** *s fig*. Maßstab *m*.

yarn [jɑ:n] *s* **1.** Garn *n*. **2.** F *spin a ~* Garn spinnen: *spin s.o. a ~* j-m e-e Lügengeschichte erzählen von.

yawn [jɔ:n] I *v/i* gähnen (*a. fig.*). II Gähner *m*; Gähnen *n*: *be a big ~* F zum Gähnen (langweilig) sein.

yeah [jeə] *adv* F ja.

year [jɪə] *s* Jahr *n*: ~ *after* ~ Jahr für Jahr; ~ *in*, ~ *out* jahraus, jahrein; *all the* ~ *round* das ganze Jahr hindurch; *since* *the* ~ *dot* F seit e-r Ewigkeit; *this* ~ dieses Jahr, heuer. '**~·book** *s* Jahrbuch *n*.

year·ly ['jɪəlɪ] *adj u. adv* jährlich.

yearn [jɜ:n] *v/i* sich sehnen (*for* nach; *to do* danach, zu tun). '**yearn·ing** I *s* Sehnsucht *f*. II *adj* □ sehnsüchtig.

yeast [ji:st] *s* Hefe *f*.

yell [jel] I *v/i* schreien, brüllen (*with* vor *dat*): ~ *at s.o.* j-n anschreien *od.* anbrüllen. II *v/t a.* ~ *out et.* schreien, brüllen. III *s* Schrei *m*.

yel·low ['jeləʊ] I *adj* **1.** gelb: ~ *fever* ♣ Gelbfieber *n*; ~ *pages pl teleph.* gelbe Seiten *pl*, Branchenverzeichnis *n*; ~ *press* Sensationspresse *f*. **2.** F feig. II *s* **3.** Gelb *n*: *at* ~ *Am.* bei Gelb; *the lights were at* ~ *Am.* die Ampel stand auf Gelb. III *v/i* **4.** gelb werden, sich gelb färben (*Blätter etc*), vergilben (*Papier*).

yelp [jelp] I *v/i* aufschreien, (*Hund etc*) (auf)jaulen. II *s* Aufschrei *m*, (Auf)Jaulen *n*.

yep [jep] *adv* F ja.

yes [jes] I *adv* ja: ~ *and no* ja u. nein; *oh* ~

o doch, o ja. **II** s Ja n. **~ man** s (*irr man*) *contp.* Jasager m.

yes·ter·day ['jestədɪ] **I** adv gestern: **~ morning** gestern morgen; **the day before ~** vorgestern; **I wasn't born ~** ich bin (doch) nicht von gestern. **II** s: **~'s paper** die gestrige Zeitung.

yet [jet] **I** adv **1.** *fragend:* schon. **2.** noch: **not ~** noch nicht; **as ~** bis jetzt, bisher. **3.** (doch) noch. **4.** doch, aber. **II** cj **5.** aber, doch.

ye·ti ['jetɪ] s Yeti m, Schneemensch m.

yew [juː] s ♣ Eibe f.

Yid·dish ['jɪdɪʃ] s *ling.* Jiddisch n.

yield [jiːld] **I** v/t **1.** *Früchte* tragen, *Gewinn* abwerfen, *Resultat etc* ergeben, liefern. **2.** a. **~ up** ✕ *Stellung etc* überlassen (**to** dat). **II** v/i **3.** nachgeben (*Boden etc*). **4.** nachgeben; ✕ sich ergeben (**to** dat): **~ to** mot. Am. j-m Vorfahrt gewähren. **III** s **5.** Ertrag m.

yo·ga ['jəʊgə] s Joga m, n, Yoga m, n.

yog·h(o)urt, yog·urt ['jɒgət] s Joghurt m, n.

yo·gi ['jəʊgɪ] s Jogi m, Yogi m.

yoke [jəʊk] s Joch n (a. fig.).

yolk [jəʊk] s (Ei)Dotter m, n, Eigelb n.

you [juː] pron **1.** (*nom*) du, Sie, ihr; (*dat*) dir, Ihnen, euch; (*acc*) dich, Sie, euch. **2.** man.

you'd [juːd] F *für* **you had**; **you would**.

you'll [juːl] F *für* **you will**.

young [jʌŋ] **I** adj **1.** jung. **II** s **2.** the **~** die jungen Leute *pl*, die Jugend. **3.** zo. Junge *pl*: **with ~** trächtig. **young·ster** ['~stə] s Junge m.

your [jɔː] possessive pron dein(e); *pl* euer, eure; Ihr(e) (a. *pl*).

you're [jʊə] F *für* **you are**.

yours [jɔːz] pron dein(er, e, es); *pl* euer, eure(s); Ihr(er, e, es) (a. *pl*): **a friend of ~** ein Freund von dir.

your·self [jɔː'self] *pl* **-selves** [~'selvz] pron. **1.** *verstärkend:* selbst: **you ~ told me, you told me ~** du hast es mir selbst erzählt. **2.** *reflex* dir, dich, sich: **did you hurt ~?** hast du dich verletzt?

youth [juːθ] **I** s **1.** Jugend f: **in my ~** in meiner Jugend. **2.** Jugendliche m. **3.** coll. Jugend f. **II** adj **4.** Jugend...: **~ hostel** Jugendherberge f. **youth·ful** ['~fʊl] adj □ jugendlich.

you've [juːv] F *für* **you have**.

Yu·go·slav [juːgəʊ'slɑːv] **I** s Jugoslawe m, -slawin f. **II** adj jugoslawisch.

Z

zeal [ziːl] s Eifer m. **zeal·ot** ['zelət] s Fanatiker(in), *eccl. a.* Eiferer m, Eiferin f. **zeal·ous** ['zeləs] adj □ eifrig: **be ~** eifrig bemüht sein (**for** um; **to do** darum, zu tun).

ze·bra ['zebrə, 'ziːbrə] s zo. Zebra n. **~ cross·ing** s Br. Zebrastreifen m.

ze·nith ['zenɪθ] s ast. Zenit m (a. fig.).

ze·ro ['zɪərəʊ] **I** pl **-ro(e)s** s Null f (Am. a. teleph.), (e-r Skala a.) Nullpunkt m: **10 degrees below ~** 10 Grad unter Null. **II** adj Null... **~ growth** Nullwachstum n; **~ hour** bsd. ✕ die Stunde X; **~ option** ✕, pol. Nullösung f. **III** v/i: **~ in on** ✕ sich einschießen auf (acc) (a. fig.); *fig.* sich konzentrieren auf (acc).

zest [zest] s **1.** *fig.* Würze f. **2.** Begeisterung f: **~ for life** Lebensfreude f.

zig·zag ['zɪgzæg] **I** s Zickzack m. **II** adj zickzackförmig, Zickzack... **III** v/i im Zickzack laufen, fahren etc, zickzackförmig verlaufen (*Weg etc*).

zinc [zɪŋk] s ♠ Zink n.

zip [zɪp] **I** s **1.** Reißverschluß m. **2.** Zischen n, Schwirren n. **3.** F Schmiß m, Schwung m. **II** v/t **4.** **~ the bag open** (**shut** od. **up**) den Reißverschluß der Tasche aufmachen (zumachen); **~ s.o. up** j-m den Reißverschluß zumachen. **III** v/i **5.** zischen, schwirren (*Kugeln etc*). **6.** F flitzen: **~ by** (od. **past**) vorbeiflitzen. **~ code** s Am. Postleitzahl f. **~ fas·ten·er** bsd. Br. → **zip** 1.

zip·per ['zɪpə] *bsd. Am.* → **zip** 1.
zo·di·ac ['zəʊdɪæk] *s ast.* Tierkreis *m*:
signs *pl* **of the** ~ Tierkreiszeichen *pl.*
zom·bie ['zɒmbɪ] *s* Zombie *m.*
zone [zəʊn] **I** *s* Zone *f.* **II** *v/t* in Zonen
einteilen.
zoo [zu:] *s* Zoo *m.*
zo·o·log·i·cal [ˌzəʊə'lɒdʒɪkl] *adj* □ zoo-

logisch: ~ **gardens** *pl* Tierpark *m.*
zo·ol·o·gist [ˌʊ'ɒlədʒɪst] *s* Zoologe *m*,
Zoologin *f.* **zo·ol·o·gy** *s* Zoologie *f.*
zoom [zu:m] **I** *v/i* **1.** ~ **in on** *phot. et.*
heranholen. **2.** F sausen: ~ **by** (*od.* **past**)
vorbeisausen. **3.** F in die Höhe schnel-
len (*Preise*). **II** *s* **4.** *a.* ~ **lens** *phot.*
Zoom(objektiv) *n.*

Proper Names

A

A·bra·ham ['eɪbrəhæm] Abraham *m*.
A·chil·les [ə'kɪliːz] Achilles *m*.
Ad·am ['ædəm] Adam *m*.
A·dri·an ['eɪdrɪən] Adrian *m*, Adriane *f*.
A·dri·at·ic Sea [ˌeɪdrɪ'ætɪk 'siː] *das* Adriatische Meer, *die* Adria.
Ae·ge·an Sea [iːˌdʒiːən 'siː] *das* Ägäische Meer, *die* Ägäis.
Aes·chy·lus ['iːskɪləs] Äschylus *m*.
Af·ghan·i·stan [æf'gænɪstæn] Afghanistan *n*.
Af·ri·ca ['æfrɪkə] Afrika *n*.
Ag·a·tha ['ægəθə] Agathe *f*.
Aix-la-Cha·pelle [ˌeɪkslɑː'ʃæ'pel] Aachen *n*.
Al·ba·nia [æl'beɪnjə] Albanien *n*.
Al·bert ['ælbət] Albert *m*.
A·leu·tian Is·lands [əˌluː'ʃjən'aɪləndz] *die* Ale'uten *pl*.
Al·ex·an·der [ˌælɪg'zɑːndə] Alexander *m*.
Al·ex·an·dra [ˌælɪg'zɑːndrə] Alexandra *f*.
Al·fred ['ælfrɪd] Alfred *m*.
Al·ge·ria [æl'dʒɪərɪə] Algerien *n*.
Al·giers [æl'dʒɪəz] Algier *n*.
Al·ice ['ælɪs] Alice *f*, Else *f*.
Al·i·son ['ælɪsn] *f*.
Al·lan, Al·len ['ælən] *m*.
Al·sace [æl'sæs], **Al·sa·tia** [æl'seɪʃə] *das* Elsaß.
A·me·lia [ə'miːljə] Amalie *f*.
A·mer·i·ca [ə'merɪkə] Amerika *n*.
An·des ['ændiːz] *pl die* Anden *pl*.
An·drew ['ændruː] Andreas *m*.
Ann [æn], **An·na** ['ænə] Anna *f*, Anne *f*.
An·na·bel(le) ['ænəbel] Annabella *f*.
Anne [æn] Anna *f*, Anne *f*.
Ant·arc·ti·ca [ænt'ɑːktɪkə] *die* Antarktis.
An·tho·ny ['æntənɪ, 'ænθənɪ] Anton *m*.
An·til·les [æn'tɪliːz] *pl die* Antillen *pl*.
An·to·ny ['æntənɪ] Anton *m*.
Ap·pa·la·chians [ˌæpə'leɪtʃjənz] *pl die* Appalachen *pl*.
A·ra·bia [ə'reɪbjə] Arabien *n*.
Ar·chi·bald ['ɑːtʃɪbɔːld] Archibald *m*.
Arc·tic ['ɑːktɪk] *die* Arktis.
Ar·gen·ti·na [ˌɑːdʒən'tiːnə] Argentinien *n*.
Ar·gen·tine ['ɑːdʒəntaɪn]: *the* ~ Argentinien *n*.
Ar·is·tot·le ['ærɪstɒtl] Aristoteles *m*.

Ar·i·zo·na [ˌærɪ'zəʊnə] *Staat der USA*.
Ar·me·ni·a [ɑː'miːnjə] Armenien *n*.
Ar·thur ['ɑːθə] Art(h)ur *m*: *King* ~ König Artus.
A·sia ['eɪʃə] Asien *n*: ~ *Minor* Kleinasien *n*.
Ath·ens ['æθɪnz] Athen *n*.
At·lan·tic [ət'læntɪk] *der* Atlantik.
Au·gus·tus [ɔː'gʌstəs] August *m*.
Aus·tra·lia [ɒ'streɪljə] Australien *n*.
Aus·tria ['ɒstrɪə] Österreich *n*.
A·zor·bai·jan [ˌæzəbaɪ'dʒɑːn] Aserbedschan *n*.
A·zores [ə'zɔːz] *pl die* Azoren *pl*.

B

Ba·ha·mas [bə'hɑːməz] *pl die* Bahamas *pl*.
Bal·dwin ['bɔːldwɪn] Balduin *m*.
Bal·kans ['bɔːlkənz] *pl der* Balkan.
Bal·tic Sea [ˌbɔːltɪk'siː] *die* Ostsee.
Ban·gla·desh [ˌbæŋglə'deʃ] Bangladesh *n*.
Bar·ba·dos [bɑː'beɪdɒs] Barbados *n*.
Bar·thol·o·mew [bɑː'θɒləmjuː] Bartholomäus *m*.
Basle [bɑːl] Basel *n*.
Ba·var·ia [bə'veərɪə] Bayern *n*.
Be·a·trice ['bɪətrɪs] Beatrice *f*.
Bel·fast [ˌbel'fɑːst; 'belfɑːst] Belfast *n*.
Bel·gium ['beldʒəm] Belgien *n*.
Bel·grade [ˌbel'greɪd] Belgrad *n*.
Bel·o·rus·sia [ˌbeləʊ'rʌʃə] Weißrußland *n*.
Ben·gal [ˌbeŋ'gɔːl] Bengalen *n*.
Ben·ja·min ['bendʒəmɪn] Benjamin *m*.
Ber·lin [bɜː'lɪn] Berlin *n*.
Ber·mu·das [bə'mjuːdəz] *pl die* Bermudas *pl*, *die* Bermudainseln *pl*.
Ber·nard ['bɜːnəd] Bernhard *m*.
Bern(e) [bɜːn] Bern *n*.
Ber·tha ['bɜːθə] Berta *f*.
Ber·tram ['bɜːtrəm], **Ber·trand** ['bɜːtrənd] Bertram *m*.
Bill, Bil·ly ['bɪl(ɪ)] Willi *m*.
Bis·cay ['bɪskeɪ, '~kɪ]: *Bay of* ~ *der* Golf von Biscaya.
Bo·he·mia [bəʊ'hiːmjə] Böhmen *n*.
Bo·liv·ia [bə'lɪvɪə] Bolivien *n*.
Bra·zil [brə'zɪl] Brasilien *n*.

Bridg·et ['brɪdʒɪt] Brigitte f.
Bri·tain ['brɪtn] Britannien n.
Bri·tan·nia [brɪ'tænjə] poet. Britannien n.
Bruns·wick ['brʌnzwɪk] Braunschweig n.
Brus·sels ['brʌslz] Brüssel n.
Bu·cha·rest [ˌbjuːkə'rest] Bukarest n.
Bu·da·pest [ˌbjuːdə'pest] Budapest n.
Bud·dha ['budə] Buddha m.
Bul·gar·ia [bʌl'geərɪə] Bulgarien n.
Bur·gun·dy ['bɜːɡəndɪ] Burgund n.
Bur·ki·na Fas·o [buəˌkiːnə'fæsəʊ] Burkina Faso n.
Bur·ma ['bɜːmə] Birma n.

C

Cae·sar ['siːzə] Cäsar m.
Cai·ro ['kaɪərəʊ] Kairo n.
Ca·lais ['kæleɪ] Calais n.
Cal·cut·ta [kæl'kʌtə] Kalkutta n.
Cal·i·for·nia [ˌkælɪ'fɔːnjə] Kalifornien n.
Cam·bo·dia [kæm'bəʊdɪə] Kam'bodscha n.
Cam·er·oon [ˌkæmə'ruːn] Kamerun n.
Can·a·da ['kænədə] Kanada n.
Cape Town ['keɪptaʊn] Kapstadt n.
Ca·rin·thia [kə'rɪnθɪə] Kärnten n.
Car·o·line ['kærəlaɪn], **Car·o·lyn** ['kærəlɪn] Karoline f.
Cath·er·ine ['kæθrɪn] Katharina f, Kat(h)rin f.
Ce·cil ['sesl, 'sɪsl] m.
Ce·cile ['sesɪl; Am. sɪ'siːl], **Ce·cil·ia** [sɪ'sɪljə; sɪ'siːljə], **Cec·i·ly** ['sɪsɪlɪ; 'sesɪlɪ] Cäcilie f.
Cey·lon [sɪ'lɒn] Ceylon n.
Chad [tʃæd] der Tschad.
Charles [tʃɑːlz] Karl m.
Char·lotte ['ʃɑːlət] Charlotte f.
Chil·e ['tʃɪlɪ] Chile n.
Chi·na ['tʃaɪnə] China n: Republic of ~ die Republik China; People's Republic of ~ die Volksrepublik China.
Chris·ti·na [krɪ'stiːnə], **Chris·tine** ['krɪstiːn, krɪ'stiːn] Christine f.
Chris·to·pher ['krɪstəfə] Christoph(er) m.
Clar·a ['kleərə], **Clare** [kleə] Klara f.
Cle·o·pat·ra [klɪə'pætrə] Kleopatra f.
Co·logne [kə'ləʊn] Köln n.
Co·lom·bia [kə'lɒmbɪə] Kolumbien n.
Com·mon·wealth of In·de·pen·dent States ['kɒmənwelθ əv ˌɪndɪpendənt 'steɪts] (abbr. CIS) Gemeinschaft f unabhängiger Staaten (abbr. GUS).
Con·fu·cius [kən'fjuːʃəs] Konfuzius m.
Con·stance ['kɒnstəns] Konstanze f: Lake ~ der Bodensee.
Co·pen·ha·gen [ˌkəʊpn'heɪgən] Kopenhagen n.
Cov·ent Gar·den [ˌkɒvənt'ɡɑːdn] London Opera (Royal Opera House).
Crete [kriːt] Kreta n.
Cri·mea [kraɪ'mɪə] die Krim.
Cro·a·tia [krəʊ'eɪʃə] Kroatien n.
Cu·ba ['kjuːbə] Kuba n.
Cy·prus ['saɪprəs] Zypern n.
Czech·o·slo·va·kia [ˌtʃekəʊsləʊ'vækɪə] hist. die Tschechoslowakei.
Czech Re·pub·lic [ˌtʃek rɪ'pʌblɪk] die Tschechische Republik

D

Dan·iel ['dænjəl] Daniel m.
Dan·ube ['dænjuːb] die Donau.
Da·vid ['deɪvɪd] David m.
Den·mark ['denmɑːk] Dänemark n.
Di·ana [daɪ'ænə] Diana f.
Don Juan [ˌdɒn'dʒuːən] Don Juan m.
Don Quix·ote [ˌdɒn'kwɪksət] Don Quichotte m.
Dor·o·thy ['dɒrəθɪ] Dorothea f.
Dun·kirk [dʌn'kɜːk] Dünkirchen n.

E

Ec·ua·dor ['ekwədɔː] Ecuador n.
Ed·in·burgh ['edɪnbərə] Edinburg n.
E·dith ['iːdɪθ] Edith f.
E·gypt ['iːdʒɪpt] Ägypten n.
El·ea·nor ['elɪnə] Eleonore f.
E·li·jah [ɪ'laɪdʒə] Elias m.
E·li·nor ['elɪnə] Eleonore f.
E·liz·a·beth [ɪ'lɪzəbəθ] Elisabeth f.
Eng·land ['ɪŋɡlənd] England n.
Er·nest ['ɜːnɪst] Ernst m.
Es·t(h)o·nia [e'stəʊnjə] Estland n.
E·thi·o·pia [ˌiːθɪ'əʊpjə] Äthiopien n.
Eu·gene ['juːdʒiːn] Eugen m.
Eu·ge·nia [juː'dʒiːnjə] Eugenie f.
Eu·nice ['juːnɪs] Eunice f.
Eu·rip·i·des [jʊə'rɪpɪdiːz] Euripides m.
Eu·rope ['jʊərəp] Europa n.
Eve [iːv] Eva f.

F

Faer·oes ['feərəʊz] *pl die* Färöer *pl.*
Falk·land Is·lands [ˌfɔː(l)klənd'aɪləndz] *pl die* Falklandinseln *pl.*
Far·oes ['feərəʊz] → *Faeroes.*
Fed·er·al Re·pub·lic of Ger·ma·ny [ˌfedərəlrɪˌpʌblɪkəv'dʒɜːmənɪ] *die* Bundesrepublik Deutschland.
Fe·lic·i·ty [fə'lɪsətɪ] Felizitas *f.*
Fe·lix ['fiːlɪks] Felix *m.*
Fin·land ['fɪnlənd] Finnland *n.*
Flor·ence ['flɒrəns] Florenz *n*; Florentine *f.*
France [frɑːns] Frankreich *n.*
Fran·ces ['frɑːnsɪs] Franziska *f.*
Fran·cis ['frɑːnsɪs] Franz *m.*
Fred·er·ic(k) ['fredrɪk] Friedrich *m.*

G

Gan·ges ['gændʒiːz] Ganges *m.*
Ge·ne·va [dʒɪ'niːvə] Genf *n.*
Gen·o·a ['dʒenəʊə] Genua *n.*
Geof·fr(e)y ['dʒefrɪ] Gottfried *m.*
George [dʒɔːdʒ] Georg *m.*
Geor·gia ['dʒɔːdʒə] *state of the US*; Georgien *n* (*in Asia*).
Ger·ald ['dʒerəld] Gerald *m*, Gerold *m.*
Ger·al·dine ['dʒerəldiːn] Geraldine *f.*
Ger·man Dem·o·crat·ic Re·pub·lic [ˌdʒɜːməndeməˌkrætɪkrɪ'pʌblɪk] *hist. die* Deutsche Demokratische Republik.
Ger·ma·ny ['dʒɜːmənɪ] Deutschland *n.*
Ger·trude ['gɜːtruːd] Gertrud *f.*
Gi·bral·tar [dʒɪ'brɔːltə] Gibraltar *n.*
Gil·bert ['gɪlbət] Gilbert *m.*
Giles [dʒaɪlz] Julius *m.*
Gil·li·an ['dʒɪlɪən; 'gɪlɪən] *f.*
Go·li·ath [gəʊ'laɪəθ] Goliath *m.*
Great Brit·ain [ˌgreɪt'brɪtn] Großbritannien *n.*
Greece [griːs] Griechenland *n.*
Green·land ['griːnlənd] Grönland *n.*
Greg·o·ry ['gregərɪ] Gregor *m.*
Gri·sons ['griːzɔ̃ː] Graubünden *n.*
Gua·te·ma·la [ˌgwɑːtə'mɑːlə] Guatemala *n.*
Guin·ea ['gɪnɪ] Guinea *n.*
Guy·ana [gaɪ'ænə] Guyana *n.*

H

Hague [heɪg]: *the ~* Den Haag.
Hai·ti ['heɪtɪ] Haiti *n.*

Han·o·ver ['hænəʊvə] Hannover *n.*
Har·old ['hærəld] Harald *m.*
Heb·ri·des ['hebrɪdiːz] *pl die* Hebriden *pl.*
Hel·en ['helɪn] Helene *f.*
Hel·i·go·land ['helɪgəʊlænd] Helgoland *n.*
Hel·sin·ki ['helsɪŋkɪ] Helsinki *n.*
Hen·ry ['henrɪ] Heinrich *m.*
Hesse ['hes(ɪ)] Hessen *n.*
Hil·a·ry ['hɪlərɪ] Hilaria *f*; Hilarius *m.*
Hi·ma·la·ya [ˌhɪmə'leɪə] *der* Himalaja.
Hol·land ['hɒlənd] Holland *n.*
Ho·mer ['həʊmə] Homer *m.*
Hon·du·ras [hɒn'djʊərəs] Honduras *n.*
Hong Kong [ˌhɒŋ'kɒŋ] Hongkong *n.*
Hugh [hjuː] Hugo *m.*
Hun·ga·ry ['hʌŋgərɪ] Ungarn *n.*

I

I·an [ɪən; 'iːən] Jan *m.*
Ice·land ['aɪslənd] Island *n.*
In·dia ['ɪndjə] Indien *n.*
In·do·ne·sia [ˌɪndəʊ'niːzjə] Indonesien *n.*
I·ran [ɪ'rɑːn] Iran *m.*
I·raq [ɪ'rɑːk] Irak *m.*
Ire·land ['aɪələnd] Irland *n.*
I·rene [aɪ'riːnɪ; 'aɪriːn] Irene *f.*
I·saac ['aɪzək] Isaak *m.*
Is·a·bel ['ɪzəbel] Isabella *f.*
Is·ra·el ['ɪzreɪəl] Israel *n.*
Is·tan·bul [ˌɪstæn'bʊl] Istanbul *n.*
It·a·ly ['ɪtəlɪ] Italien *n.*

J

Jack [dʒæk] Hans *m.*
Ja·mai·ca [dʒə'meɪkə] Jamaika *n.*
James [dʒeɪmz] Jakob *m.*
Jane [dʒeɪn] Johanna *f.*
Jan·et ['dʒænɪt] Johanna *f.*
Ja·pan [dʒə'pæn] Japan *n.*
Jean [dʒiːn] Johanna *f.*
Jef·frey ['dʒefrɪ] Gottfried *m.*
Jer·e·my ['dʒerɪmɪ] Jeremias *m.*
Je·rome [dʒə'rəʊm] Hieronymus *m.*
Je·ru·sa·lem [dʒə'ruːsələm] Jerusalem *n.*
Je·sus ['dʒiːzəs] Jesus *m.*
Joan [dʒəʊn], **Jo·an·na** [dʒəʊ'ænə] Johanna *f.*
John [dʒɒn] Johannes *m*, Johann *m.*
Jon·a·than ['dʒɒnəθən] Jonathan *m.*
Jor·dan ['dʒɔːdn] Jordanien *n*; Jordan *m.*
Jo·seph ['dʒəʊzɪf] Joseph *m.*

Jo·se·phine ['dʒəʊzɪfiːn] Josephine f.
Ju·dith ['dʒuːdɪθ] Judith f.

K

Kam·pu·chea [ˌkæmpʊ'tʃɪə] hist. Kamputschea n.
Ka·ra·chi [kə'rɑːtʃɪ] Karatschi n.
Kash·mir [ˌkæʃ'mɪə] Kaschmir n.
Kath·a·rine, Kath·er·ine ['kæθərɪn] Katharina f, Kat(h)rin f.
Ka·zakh·stan [ˌkæzæk'stɑːn] Kasachstan n.
Ken·ya ['kenjə] Kenia n.
Ko·rea [kə'rɪə] Korea n.
Krem·lin ['kremlɪn] der Kreml.
Ku·wait [kʊ'weɪt] Kuwait n.

L

Lake Hu·ron [ˌleɪk'hjʊərən] der Huronsee.
Lake Su·pe·ri·or [ˌleɪksuː'pɪərɪə] der Obere See.
La·os ['lɑːɒs; laʊs] Laos n.
Lat·via ['lætvɪə] Lettland n.
Lau·rence ['lɒrəns] Lorenz m.
Law·rence ['lɒrəns] Lorenz m.
Leb·a·non ['lebənən] der Libanon n.
Leon·ard ['lenəd] Leonhard m.
Lew·is ['luːɪs] Ludwig m.
Lib·ya ['lɪbɪə] Libyen n.
Li·sa ['liːzə; 'laɪzə] Lisa f.
Lis·bon ['lɪzbən] Lissabon n.
Lith·u·a·nia [ˌlɪθjʊ'eɪnjə] Litauen n.
Li·za ['laɪzə] Lisa f.
Lon·don ['lʌndən] London n.
Lor·raine [lɒ'reɪn] Lothringen n.
Lou·is ['luːɪ; 'lɔɪ; bsd. Am. 'luːɪs] Ludwig m.
Lou·ise [luː'iːz] Luise f.
Lu·cia ['luːsjə] Lucia f, Luzia f.
Luke [luːk] Lukas m.
Lux·em·bourg ['lʌksəmbɜːɡ] Luxemburg n.
Lyd·ia ['lɪdɪə] Lydia f.

M

Ma·dei·ra [mə'dɪərə] Madeira n.
Ma·drid [mə'drɪd] Madrid n.
Mag·da·len ['mægdəlɪn] Magdalena f, Magdalene f: ~ **College** ['mɔːdlɪn] College in Oxford.
Mag·da·lene ['mægdəlɪn] Magdalena f,

Magdalene f: ~ **College** ['mɔːdlɪn] College in Cambridge.
Ma·ho·met [mə'hɒmɪt] Mohammed m.
Ma·jor·ca [mə'dʒɔːkə] Mallorca n.
Mal·ta ['mɔːltə] Malta n.
Mar·ga·ret ['mɑːɡərɪt] Margareta f, Margarete f.
Ma·ri·a [mə'raɪə; mə'rɪə] Maria f.
Mar·tha ['mɑːθə] Mart(h)a f.
Mar·y ['meərɪ] Maria f, Marie f.
Ma(t)·thew ['mæθjuː] Matthäus m.
Mau·rice ['mɒrɪs] Moritz m.
Med·i·ter·ra·ne·an (Sea) [ˌmedɪtə'reɪnjən('siː)] das Mittelmeer.
Mex·i·co ['meksɪkəʊ] Mexiko n.
Mi·chael ['maɪkl] Michael m.
Mich·i·gan ['mɪʃɪɡən] Lake ~ der Michigansee.
Mid·lands ['mɪdləndz] pl die Midlands pl.
Mid·west [ˌmɪd'west] der Mittlere Westen (USA).
Mi·lan [mɪ'læn] Mailand n.
Mo·na·co ['mɒnəkəʊ] Monaco n.
Mo·roc·co [mə'rɒkəʊ] Marokko n.
Mos·cow ['mɒskəʊ] Moskau n.
Mo·selle [məʊ'zel] Mosel f.
Mo·zam·bique [ˌməʊzæm'biːk] Mocambique n.
Mu·nich ['mjuːnɪk] München n.

N

Na·mib·ia [nə'mɪbɪə] Namibia n.
Na·ples ['neɪplz] Neapel n.
Naz·a·reth ['næzərəθ] Nazareth n.
Ne·pal [nɪ'pɔːl] Nepal n.
Neth·er·lands ['neðələndz] pl die Niederlande pl.
New Del·hi [ˌnjuː'delɪ] Neu-Delhi n.
New Eng·land [ˌnjuː'ɪŋɡlənd] Neuengland n (USA).
New·found·land ['njuːfəndlənd] Neufundland n.
New Zea·land [ˌnjuː'ziːlənd] Neuseeland n.
Ni·ag·a·ra [naɪ'æɡərə] Niagara m.
Nic·a·ra·gua [ˌnɪkə'ræɡjʊə] Nicaragua n.
Nich·o·las ['nɪkələs] Nikolaus m.
Ni·ge·ria [naɪ'dʒɪərɪə] Nigeria n.
Nile [naɪl] Nil m.
Nor·man·dy ['nɔːməndɪ] die Normandie.
North·ern Ire·land [ˌnɔːðn'aɪələnd] Nordirland n.

1368

North Sea [ˌnɔːθˈsiː] *die* Nordsee.
Nor·way [ˈnɔːweɪ] Norwegen *n*.
No·va Sco·tia [ˌnəʊvəˈskəʊʃə] Neu-schottland *n*.
Nu·rem·berg [ˈnjʊərəmbɜːg] Nürnberg *n*.

O

O·ce·an·ia [ˌəʊʃɪˈeɪnjə] Ozeanien *n*.
On·ta·ri·o [ɒnˈteərɪəʊ] *Lake* ~ *der* Onta-riosee.
Ork·ney Is·lands [ˌɔːknɪˈaɪləndz] *pl die* Orkneyinseln *pl*.
Ost·end [ɒˈstend] Ost'ende *n*.

P

Pa·cif·ic [pəˈsɪfɪk] *der* Pazifik.
Pak·i·stan [ˌpɑːkɪˈstɑːn] Pakistan *n*.
Pal·es·tine [ˈpæləstaɪn] Palästina *n*.
Pam·e·la [ˈpæmələ] Pamela *f*.
Pan·a·ma [ˈpænəmɑː] Panama *n*.
Par·a·guay [ˈpærəgwaɪ] Paraguay *n*.
Par·is [ˈpærɪs] Paris *n*.
Pa·tri·cia [pəˈtrɪʃə] Patrizia *f*.
Pat·rick [ˈpætrɪk] Patrizius *m*.
Paul [pɔːl] Paul *m*.
Pau·line [pɔːˈliːn; ˈpɔːliːn] Pauline *f*.
Per·sia [ˈpɜːʃə; *Am.* ˈpɜːrʒə] Persien *n*.
Pe·ru [pəˈruː] Peru *n*.
Pe·ter [ˈpiːtə] Peter *m*, Petrus *m*.
Phil·ip [ˈfɪlɪp] Philipp *m*.
Phil·ip·pines [ˈfɪlɪpiːnz] *pl die* Philippi-nen *pl*.
Pla·to [ˈpleɪtəʊ] Plato(n) *m*.
Po·land [ˈpəʊlənd] Polen *n*.
Por·tu·gal [ˈpɔːtʃʊgl; ˈ-jʊgl] Portugal *n*.
Prague [prɑːg] Prag *n*.
Prus·sia [ˈprʌʃə] Preußen *n*.

Q

Qa·tar [kæˈtɑː] Katar *n*.

R

Ra·chel [ˈreɪtʃl] Ra(c)hel *f*.
Rat·is·bon [ˈrætɪzbɒn] Regensburg *n*.
Reg·i·nald [ˈredʒɪnld] Re(g)inald *m*.
Rhine [raɪn] Rhein *m*.
Rhodes [rəʊdz] Rhodos *n*.
Rich·ard [ˈrɪtʃəd] Richard *m*.
Rob·ert [ˈrɒbət] Robert *m*.
Ro·ma·nia [ruːˈmeɪnjə; rʊ~; *Am.* rəʊ~] Rumänien *n*.

Rome [rəʊm] Rom *n*.
Rus·sia [ˈrʌʃə] Rußland *n*.
Ruth [ruːθ] Ruth *f*.

S

Sam·u·el [ˈsæmjʊəl] Samuel *m*.
San Fran·cis·co [ˌsænfrənˈsɪskəʊ] San Franzisko *n (USA)*.
Sau·di A·ra·bia [ˌsaʊdɪəˈreɪbɪə] Saudi-Arabien *n*.
Sax·o·ny [ˈsæksnɪ] Sachsen *n*.
Scan·di·na·via [ˌskændɪˈneɪvjə] Skandi-navien *n*.
Scot·land [ˈskɒtlənd] Schottland *n*
Shet·land Is·lands [ˌʃetləndˈaɪləndz] *pl die* Shetlandinseln *pl*.
Si·be·ria [saɪˈbɪərɪə] Sibirien *n*.
Sib·yl [ˈsɪbɪl] Sibylle *f*.
Sic·i·ly [ˈsɪsɪlɪ] Sizilien *n*.
Si·le·sia [saɪˈliːzjə] Schlesien *n*.
Si·mon [ˈsaɪmən] Simon *m*.
Sin·ga·pore [ˌsɪŋəˈpɔː] Singapur *n*.
Slo·va·kia [sləʊˈvækɪə] Slowakei *f*.
Slo·ve·nia [sləʊˈviːnjə] Slowenien *n*.
Soc·ra·tes [ˈsɒkrətiːz] Sokrates *m*.
Sol·o·mon [ˈsɒləmən] Salomo(n) *m*.
So·ma·lia [səʊˈmɑːlɪə] Somalia *n*.
So·phi·a [səʊˈfaɪə] Sophia *f*, Sofia *f*.
So·viet Un·ion [ˌsəʊvɪətˈjuːnjən] *hist.* Sowjetunion.
Spain [speɪn] Spanien *n*.
Ste·phen [ˈstiːvn] Stephan *m*, Stefan *m*.
St. Law·rence [snt ˈlɒrəns] *der* Sankt-Lorenz-Strom.
Stock·holm [ˈstɒkhəʊm] Stockholm *n*.
Styr·ia [ˈstɪrɪə] *die* Steiermark.
Su·dan [suːˈdɑːn] *der* Sudan.
Su·san [ˈsuːzn] Susanne *f*.
Su·zanne [suːˈzæn] Susanne *f*.
Swe·den [ˈswiːdn] Schweden *n*.
Swit·zer·land [ˈswɪtsələnd] *die* Schweiz.
Syr·ia [ˈsɪrɪə] Syrien *n*.

T

Tai·wan [ˌtaɪˈwɑːn] Taiwan *n*.
Tan·za·nia [ˌtænzəˈnɪə] Tansania *n*.
Thai·land [ˈtaɪlænd] Thailand *n*.
Thames [temz] *die* Themse.
The·o·bald [ˈθɪəbɔːld] Theobald *m*.
The·o·dore [ˈθɪədɔː] Theodor *m*.
The·re·sa [tɪˈriːzə] Theresa *f*, Therese *f*.
Tho·mas [ˈtɒməs] Thomas *m*.

Thu·rin·gia [θjʊəˈrɪndʒɪə] Thüringen *n*.
Ti·bet [tɪˈbet] Tibet *n*.
Tim·o·thy [ˈtɪməθɪ] Timotheus *m*.
To·bi·as [təˈbaɪəs] Tobias *m*.
To·kyo [ˈtəʊkjəʊ] Tokio *n*.
Tra·fal·gar [trəˈfælɡə]: *Cape* ~ Kap *n* Trafalgar (*Spain*); ~ **Square** (*in London*).
Treves [triːvz] Trier *n*.
Tu·ni·sia [tjuːˈnɪzɪə; *Am.* tuːˈniːʒə] Tunesien *n*.
Tur·key [ˈtɜːkɪ] die Türkei.
Tus·ca·ny [ˈtʌskənɪ] die Toskana.
Ty·rol [ˈtɪrəl; tɪˈrəʊl] Tirol *n*.

U

U·kraine [juːˈkreɪn] *die* Ukraine.
Ul·ster [ˈʌlstə] Nordirland *n*.
U·nit·ed King·dom [juːˌnaɪtɪdˈkɪŋdəm] *das* Vereinigte Königreich (*Great Britain and Northern Ireland*).
U·nit·ed States of A·mer·i·ca [juːˌnaɪtɪdˌsteɪtsəvəˈmerɪkə] *pl die* Vereinigten Staaten *pl* von Amerika.
Ur·su·la [ˈɜːsjʊlə] Ursula *f*.
U·tah [ˈjuːtɑː; ˈ~tɔː] *Staat der USA*.
Uz·bek·i·stan [ʊzbekɪˈstɑːn] Usbekistan *n*.

V

Val·en·tine [ˈvæləntaɪn] Valentin(e *f*) *m*.
Vat·i·can [ˈvætɪkən] *der* Vatikan.
Ven·e·zu·e·la [ˌvenɪˈzweɪlə] Venezuela *n*.
Ven·ice [ˈvenɪs] Venedig *n*.
Vi·en·na [vɪˈenə] Wien *n*.
Viet·nam [ˌvjetˈnæm] Vietnam *n*.
Vil·ni·us [ˈvɪlnɪəs] Wilna *f*.
Vir·gil [ˈvɜːdʒɪl] Vergil *m*.

W

Wales [weɪlz] Wales *n*.
War·saw [ˈwɔːsɔː] Warschau *n*.
West·pha·lia [westˈfeɪljə] Westfalen *n*.
Wil·liam [ˈwɪljəm] Wilhelm *m*.

Y

Yu·go·sla·via [ˌjuːɡəʊˈslɑːvjə] *hist.* Jugoslawien *n*.

Z

Zach·a·ri·ah [ˌzækəˈraɪə], **Zach·a·ry** [ˈzækərɪ] Zacharias *m*.
Za·ire [zɑːˈɪə] Za'ire *n*.
Zim·ba·bwe [zɪmˈbɑːbwɪ] Simbabwe *n*.
Zu·rich [ˈzjʊərɪk] Zürich *n*.

Geographical Names

A

Aachen Aachen, Aix-la-Chapelle
Abruzzen, *die* the Abruzzi
Addis Abeba Addis Ababa
Admiralitätsinseln, *die* the Admiralty Islands, *the* Admiralties
Adria, *die* the Adriatic (Sea)
Afrika Africa
Ägäis, *die* the Aegean (Sea)
Ägäischen Inseln, *die* the Aegean Islands
Ägypten Egypt
Akaba Aqaba, Akaba
Akkra Accra
Akropolis, *die* the Acropolis
Albanien Albania

Aleuten, *die* the Aleutian Islands
Alexandrien Alexandria
Algerien Algeria
Algier Algiers
Alpen, *die* the Alps
Alpenvorland, *das* the foothills of the Alps
Altaigebirge, *das* the Altai Mountains
Amazonas, *der* the Amazon
Amerika America
Anatolien Anatolia
Andalusien Andalusia
Anden, *die* the Andes
Antarktis, *die* the Antarctic, Antarctica
Antillen, *die* the Antilles
Antwerpen Antwerp

Apennin, der, Apenninen, die the Apennines, the Apennine Mountains
Apenninenhalbinsel, die the Apennine Peninsula
Appalachen, die the Appalachians, the Appalachian Mountains
Apulien Apulia
Arabien Arabia
Arabische Wüste, die the Arabian Desert
Aralsee, der Lake Aral
Ardennen, die the Ardennes
Argentinien Argentina, the Argentine
Arktis, die the Arctic
Ärmelkanal, der the (English) Channel
Armenien Armenia
Aserbeidschan Azerbaijan
Asien Asia
Asowsche Meer, das the Sea of Azov
Assuan Aswan
Athen Athens
Äthiopien Ethiopia
Atlantik, der the Atlantic (Ocean)
Atlasgebirge, das the Atlas Mountains
Ätna, der Mount Etna
Australasien Australasia
Australien Australia
Azoren, die the Azores

B

Bagdad Baghdad
Baikalsee, der Lake Baikal
Balearen, die the Balearic Islands
Balkan, der → **1.** *Balkanhalbinsel*; **2.** *Balkanstaaten*; **3.** *Balkangebirge*
Balkangebirge, das the Balkan Mountains
Balkanhalbinsel, die the Balkan Peninsula
Balkanstaaten, die the Balkan States, the Balkans
Baltikum, das the Baltic (States), the Baltics
Bangladesch Bangladesh
Barentssee, die the Barents Sea
Basel Basel, Basle
Baskenland, das the Basque Provinces
Bayerische Wald, der the Bavarian Forest
Belgien Belgium
Belgrad Belgrade
Benelux-Länder, die the Benelux Countries

Bengalen Bengal
Beringmeer, das the Bering Sea
Beringstraße, die the Bering Strait
Bern Bern(e)
Bessarabien Bessarabia
Bikini, Bikiniatoll, das Bikini
Birma Burma
Biskaya, die → *Golf von Biskaya*
Bodensee, der Lake Constance
Böhmen Čechy; *hist.* Bohemia
Böhmerwald, der the Bohemian Forest
Bolivien Bolivia
Bosnien Bosnia
Bosnien und Herzegowina Bosnia and Herzegovina
Bosporus, der the Bosp(h)orus
Botsuana Botswana
Bottnische Meerbusen, der the Gulf of Bothnia
Bozen Bolzano
Brasilien Brazil
Brenner(paß), der the Brenner Pass
Breslau Wrocław; *hist.* Breslau
Bretagne, die Brittany
Brügge Bruges
Brüssel Brussels
Bukarest Bucharest
Bukowina, die Bukovina, Bucovina
Bulgarien Bulgaria
Bundesrepublik Deutschland, die the Federal Republic of Germany
Burgund Burgundy

C

Cevennen, die the Cévennes
Charkow Kharkov
Chiemsee, der Lake Chiem, the Chiemsee
Chinesische Mauer, die the Great Wall of China
Chinesische Meer, das the China Sea
Comer See, der Lake Como

D

Damaskus Damascus
Dänemark Denmark
Danzig Gdansk; *hist.* Danzig
Danziger Bucht, die the Bay (or Gulf) of Gdansk (*hist.* Danzig)
Dardanellen, die the Dardanelles
Daressalam Dar es Salaam
Den Haag The Hague

Deutsche Bucht, *die* *the* German Bay
Deutschland Germany
Dnjepr, *der* *the* Dnieper
Dnjestr, *der* *the* Dniester
Dodekanes, *der* *the* Dodecanese
Dolomiten, *die* *the* Dolomites
Dominikanische Republik, *die* *the* Dominican Republic
Donau, *die* *the* Danube
Donez, *der* *the* Donets
Donezbecken, *das* *the* Donets (Basin)
Dover → *Straße von Dover*
Drau, *die* *the* Drava
Dschibuti Djibouti
Dschidda Jedda

E

Eiffelturm, *der* *the* Eiffel Tower
Eismeer, Nördliche, *das* → *Nordpolarmeer*
Eismeer, Südliche, *das* → *Südpolarmeer*
Elat Eilat
Elfenbeinküste, *die* *the* Ivory Coast
Elsaß, *das* Alsace
Engadin, *das* *the* Engadine
Eriwan Yerevan, Erivan
Erzgebirge, *das* *the* Erzgebirge, *the* Ore Mountains
Estland Estonia
Etsch, *die* *the* Adige
Euphrat, *der* *the* Euphrates
Eurasien Eurasia
Europa Europe
Everest, *der* (Mount) Everest

F

Falklandinseln, *die* *the* Falkland Islands, *the* Falklands
Färöer, *die* *the* Faroes, *the* Faroe Islands
Ferne Osten, *der,* **Fernost** *the* Far East
Feuerland Tierra del Fuego
Fidschi Fiji
Fidschiinseln, *die* *the* Fiji Islands
Finnische Meerbusen, *der* *the* Gulf of Finland
Finnland Finland
Flandern Flanders
Florenz Florence
Franken Franconia

Frankfurt (am Main) Frankfurt (on the Main)
Frankfurt (an der Oder) Frankfurt (on the Oder)
Frankreich France
Französisch-Guayana French Guiana
Fudschijama, *der* (Mount) Fuji, *a.* Fujiyama

G

Gabun Gabon
Galapagosinseln, *die* *the* Galapagos Islands
Gambia (*the*) Gambia
Gardasee, *der* Lake Garda
Gazastreifen, *der* *the* Gaza Strip
Genezareth → *See Genezareth*
Genf Geneva
Genfer See, *der* Lake Geneva, Lac Léman
Gent Ghent
Genua Genoa
Georgien Georgia
Golanhöhen, *die* *the* Golan Heights
Goldene Horn, *das* *the* Golden Horn
Golf von Akaba, *der* *the* Gulf of Aqaba (*or* Akaba)
Golf von Bengalen, *der* *the* Bay of Bengal
Golf von Biskaya, *der* *the* Bay of Biscay
Golf von Genua, *der* *the* Gulf of Genoa
Golf von Korinth, *der* *the* Gulf of Corinth
Golf von Neapel, *der* *the* Bay of Naples
Golf von Triest, *der* *the* Gulf of Trieste
Göteborg Gothenburg, Göteborg
Graubünden Graubünden, *the* Grisons
Griechenland Greece
Grönland Greenland
Großbritannien Great Britain, Britain
Große Belt, *der* *the* Great Belt
Großen Seen, *die* *the* Great Lakes
Große Syrte, *die* *the* Gulf of Sidra
Guayana (*region*) Guiana
Guyana (*state*) Guyana

H

Harz, *der* *the* Harz (Mountains)
Havanna Havana
Hawaii-Inseln, *die* *the* Hawaiian Islands
Hebriden, *die* *the* Hebrides

Helgoland Hel(i)goland
Helgoländer Bucht, die the Hel(i)go-
land Bight
Himalaja, der the Himalayas
Hindukusch, der the Hindu Kush
Hinterindien Indochina
Hiroschima Hiroshima
Hoek van Holland Hook of Holland
Holland Holland, the Netherlands
Hongkong Hong Kong

I

Iberische Halbinsel, die the Iberian
Peninsula
Ijsselmeer, das Lake Ijssel, Ijsselmeer
Indien India
Indische Ozean, der the Indian Ocean
Indonesien Indonesia
Innerasien Central Asia
Innere Mongolei, die Inner Mongolia
Insel Man, die the Isle of Man
Insel Wight, die the Isle of Wight
Ionische Meer, das the Ionian Sea
Ionischen Inseln, die the Ionian Islands
Irak, der Iraq
Irische See, die the Irish Sea
Irland Ireland
Island Iceland
Italien Italy

J

Jadebusen, der the Jade Bay
Jakutsk Yakutsk
Jalta Yalta
Jamaika Jamaica
Jangtse(kiang), der the Yang-
tze(-Kiang)
Japanische Meer, das the Sea of Japan
Jemen, der the Yemen
Jordanien Jordan
Jugoslawien hist. Yugoslavia
Jungferninseln, die the Virgin Islands
Jütland Jutland

K

Kaimaninseln, die the Cayman Islands
Kairo Cairo
Kalabrien Calabria
Kalifornien California
Kalkutta Calcutta
Kambodscha Cambodia
Kamerun Cameroon

Kanada Canada
Kanal, der the (English) Channel
Kanalinseln, die the Channel Islands
Kanaren, die, Kanarischen Inseln, die
the Canaries, the Canary Islands
Kap der Guten Hoffnung, das the Cape
of Good Hope, a. the Cape
Kap Hoorn Cape Horn, a. the Horn
Kapprovinz, die Cape Province
Kap Skagen the Skaw, a. (Cape) Skagen
Kapstadt Cape Town
Kapverdischen Inseln, die the Cape
Verde Islands
Karatschi Karachi
Karibik, die the Caribbean
Kärnten Carinthia
Karolinen, die the Caroline Islands
Karpaten, die the Carpathians, the Car-
pathian Mountains
Kasachstan Kazakhstan
Kaschmir Kashmir
Kaspische Meer, das the Caspian Sea
Kastilien Castile
Katalonien Catalonia
Katar Qatar
Kaukasus, der the Caucasus, a. the
Caucasus Mountains
Kenia Kenya
Kieler Bucht, die Kiel Bay
Kiew Kiev
Kilimandscharo, der (Mount) Kili-
manjaro
Kirgisien Kirghizia
Kleinasien Asia Minor
Köln Cologne
Kolumbien Colombia
Komoren, die the Comoro Archipelago
Kongo, der the Congo
Königsberg Kaliningrad; hist. Königs-
berg
Kopenhagen Copenhagen
Kordilleren, die the Cordilleras
Korfu Corfu
Korinth Corinth
Korsika Corsica
Krakatau Krakatoa
Kreta Crete
Krim, die the Crimea
Kroatien Croatia
Kuba Cuba
Kurdistan Kurdistan, Kurdestan, Kor-
destan
Kurilen, die the Kuril(e) Islands
Kykladen, die the Cyclades

L

Ladogasee, *der* Lake Ladoga
Lappland Lapland
Lateinamerika Latin America
Lausitz, *die* Lusatia
Lemberg Lvov
Lettland Latvia
Levante, *die* the Levant
Libanon, *der* (*the*) Lebanon
Libyen Libya
Ligurische Meer, *das* the Ligurian Sea
Liparischen Inseln, *die* the Lipari Islands
Lissabon Lisbon
Litauen Lithuania
Lübecker Bucht, *die* the Lübeck Bay
Luganer See, *der* Lake Lugano
Lüneburger Heide, *die* the Lüneburg Heath
Lüttich Liège
Luxemburg Luxemb(o)urg
Luzern Lucerne

M

Maas, *die* the Meuse, *the* Maas
Madagaskar Madagascar
Magellanstraße, *die* the Strait(s) of Magellan
Mailand Milan
Makedonien Macedonia
Malaiische Halbinsel, *die* the Malay Peninsula, Malaya
Malakka Malacca
Malediven, *die* the Maldives
Mallorca Majorca
Mandschurei, *die* Manchuria
Marianen, *die* the Marianas
Mark Brandenburg, *die* the Brandenburg Marches
Marmarameer, *das* the Sea of Marmara
Marokko Morocco
Maskat und Oman Muscat and Oman
Masuren Masuria
Masurischen Seen, *die* the Masurian Lakes
Mauretanien Mauretania
Mekka Mecca
Melanesien Melanesia
Menorca Minorca
Meran Merano
Mesopotamien Mesopotamia

Mexiko Mexico
Mikronesien Micronesia
Mittelamerika Central America
Mittelasien Central Asia
Mittelmeer, *das* the Mediterranean (Sea)
Mittlere Osten, *der* the Middle East
Moçambique Mozambique
Moldau¹, *die* (*river*) the Vltava; *hist.* the Moldau
Moldau², *die* (*region*) Moldavia
Moldavien Moldavia
Molukken, *die* the Moluccas
Mongolei, *die* Mongolia
Mosel, *die* the Moselle
Moskau Moscow
Moskwa, *die* the Moskva
München Munich
Mykene Mycenae

N

Nahe Osten, *der* the Middle (*or* Near) East
Neapel Naples
Neu-Delhi New Delhi
Neufundland Newfoundland
Neuguinea New Guinea
Neuseeland New Zealand
Newa, *die* the Neva
Niagarafälle, *die* the Niagara Falls
Niederlande, *die* the Netherlands, Holland
Nikosia Nicosia
Nil, *der* the Nile
Nizza Nice
Nordafrika North Africa
Nordamerika North America
Norddeutsche Tiefebene, *die* the North(ern) German Plain
Nordfriesischen Inseln, *die* the North Frisians
Nordirland Northern Ireland
Nordkap, *das* the North Cape
Nordkorea North Korea
Nord-Ostsee-Kanal, *der* the Kiel Canal
Nordpol, *der* the North Pole
Nordpolarmeer, *das* the Arctic Ocean
Nordsee, *die* the North Sea
Normandie, *die* Normandy
Norwegen Norway
Nowosibirsk Novosibirsk
Nürnberg Nuremberg

1374

O

Oberrheinische Tiefebene, die *the* Upper Rhine Valley
Ochotskische Meer, das *the* Sea of Okhotsk
Olymp, der (Mount) Olympus
Onegasee, der Lake Onega
Oranjefreistaat, der *the* Orange Free State
Orinoko, der *the* Orinoco
Ostafrika East Africa
Ostasien East Asia
Ostende Ostend
Osterinsel, die Easter Island
Österreich Austria
Ostfriesischen Inseln, die *the* East Frisians
Ostsee, die *the* Baltic (Sea)
Ozeanien Oceania

P

Panamakanal, der *the* Panama Canal
Pandschab, das *the* Punjab
Papua-Neuguinea Papua-New Guinea
Parnaß, der Mount Parnassus
Patagonien Patagonia
Pazifik, der *the* Pacific (Ocean)
Peloponnes, der *or* **die** *the* Peloponnese, *the* Peloponnesus
Persische Golf, der *the* Persian Gulf
Petersburg, (St.) St Petersburg
Pfalz, die *the* Palatinate
Philippinen, die *the* Philippines
Piräus Piraeus
Plattensee, der Lake Balaton
Po-Ebene, die *the* Po Valley
Polarkreis, der 1. *the* Arctic Circle; **2.** *the* Antarctic Circle
Polen Poland
Polynesien Polynesia
Pommern Pomorze; *hist.* Pomerania
Pompeji Pompeii
Pontische Gebirge, das *the* Pontic Mountains
Prag Prague
Provence, die Provence
Pyrenäen, die *the* Pyrenees
Pyrenäenhalbinsel, die *the* Iberian Peninsula

R

Reval Tallin(n); *hist.* Reval
Rhein, der *the* Rhine

Rheinfall, der *the* Rhine Falls
Rheingau, der *the* Rhinegau
Rheinhessen Rhinehessen
Rheinische Schiefergebirge, das *the* Rhenish Slate Mountains
Rheinland, das *the* Rhineland
Rhodos Rhodes
Rom Rome
Rote Meer, das *the* Red Sea
Ruhrgebiet, das *the* Ruhr(gebiet)
Rumänien Romania, *a.* Rumania
Rußland Russia

S

Sächsische Schweiz, die Saxon Switzerland
Salomonen, die, Salomonischen Inseln, die *the* Solomon Islands
Saloniki Salonika, Saloniki
Sambesi, der *the* Zambezi
Sambia Zambia
Sankt-Lorenz-Strom, der *the* St Lawrence (River)
Sansibar Zanzibar
Sarajewo Sarajevo
Sardinien Sardinia
Saudi-Arabien Saudi Arabia
Savoyen Savoy
Schanghai Shanghai
Schatt el Arab, der *the* Shatt-al-Arab
Schlesien Slask; *hist.* Silesia
Schottland Scotland
Schwaben Swabia
Schwäbische Alb, die *the* Swabian Jura
Schwarze Meer, das *the* Black Sea
Schwarzwald, der *the* Black Forest
Schweden Sweden
Schweiz, die Switzerland
See Genezareth, der *the* Sea of Galilee
Seeland Zealand
Serbien Serbia
Sevilla Seville
Seychellen, die *the* Seychelles
Sibirien Siberia
Simbabwe Zimbabwe
Sinaigebirge, das Mount Sinai
Sinaihalbinsel, die *the* Sinai Peninsula
Singapur Singapore
Sizilien Sicily
Skandinavien Scandinavia
Slowakei, die Slovakia
Slowenien Slovenia
Sowjetunion, die *hist.* *the* Soviet Union

Spanien Spain
Sporaden, *die the* Sporades
Steiermark, *die* Styria
Stettin Szczecin; *hist.* Stettin
Stille Ozean, *der* → *Pazifik*
Straßburg Strasbourg
Straße von Dover, *die the* Strait(s) of Dover
Straße von Gibraltar, *die the* Strait(s) of Gibraltar
Südafrika South Africa
Südamerika South America
Sudan, *der* (*the*) Sudan
Südchinesische Meer, *das the* South China Sea
Südkorea South Korea
Südpolarmeer, *das the* Antarctic Ocean
Südsee, *die the* South Pacific, *the* South Seas
Südseeinseln, *die the* Pacific (*or* South Sea) Islands
Südtirol South Tyrol
Südwestafrika South-West Africa
Suezkanal, *der the* Suez Canal
Swasiland Swaziland
Syrien Syria
Szetschuan Szechuan

T

Tadschikistan Tadzhikistan
Tafelberg, *der* Table Mountain
Taipeh Taipei
Tajo, *der the* Tagus
Tanganjika Tanganyika
Tanganjikasee, *der* Lake Tanganyika
Tanger Tangier
Tansania Tanzania
Tasmanien Tasmania
Tatra, *die the* Tatra Mountains, *a. the* High Tatra
Taurus, *der the* Taurus (Mountains)
Teheran Teh(e)ran
Teneriffa Tenerife
Tessin, *das* Ticino
Teutoburger Wald, *der the* Teutoburg Forest, *the* Teutoburger Wald
Themse, *die the* Thames
Thüringer Wald, *der the* Thuringian Forest
Tirol (*the*) Tyrol
Tokio Tokyo
Tongainseln, *die the* Tonga (*or* Friendly) Islands

Toskana, *die* Tuscany
Tote Meer, *das the* Dead Sea
Tripolis Tripoli
Tschad, *der* Chad
Tschechoslowakei, *die hist.* Czechoslovakia
Tunesien Tunisia
Türkei, *die* Turkey
Turkestan Turkestan, Turkistan
Tyrrhenische Meer, *das the* Tyrrhenian Sea

U

Ungarn Hungary
Union der Sozialistischen Sowjetrepubliken, *die hist.* Union of Soviet Socialist Republics
Ural, *der the* Urals
Usbekistan Uzbekistan

V

Venedig Venice
Venetien Veneto
Vereinigte Königreich (von Großbritannien und Nordirland), *das the* United Kingdom (of Great Britain and Northern Ireland)
Vereinigten Arabischen Emirate, *die the* United Arab Emirates
Vereinigten Staaten (von Amerika), *die the* United States (of America)
Vesuv, *der* Vesuvius
Vierwaldstätter See, *der* Lake Lucerne
Vietnam Vietnam, Viet Nam
Vogesen, *die the* Vosges (Mountains)
Volksrepublik China, *die the* People's Republic of China
Vorderasien *the* Middle (*or* Near) East
Vorderindien *the* Indian Peninsula (and Ceylon)

W

Wallis, *das* Valais
Warschau Warsaw
Wattenmeer, *das the* mud flats
Weichsel, *die the* Vistula
Weißrußland B(y)elorussia, White Russia
Westfalen Westphalia
Westfälische Pforte, *die the* Porta Westfalica, *the* Westphalian Gate
Westfriesischen Inseln, *die the* West Frisians

1376

Westindien *the* West Indies
Wien Vienna
Wilna Vilnius
Wladiwostok Vladivostok
Wolga, die *the* Volga

Y

Ypern Ypres

Z

Zentralafrikanische Republik, die *the*
Central African Republic
Zuckerhut, der Sugar Loaf Mountain
Zürich Zurich
Zürichsee, der, Züricher See, der
Lake Zurich
Zypern Cyprus

Abbreviations

A

a *acre* Acre *m* (*4046,8 m²*).
A *answer* Antw., Antwort *f; ampere*
A, Ampere *n od. pl.*
AA *Alcoholics Anonymous* Anonyme
Alkoholiker *pl; antiaircraft* Flugab-
wehr...; *Br. Automobile Association*
(*Automobilclub*).
AAA [ˌθriːˈeɪz] *Br. Amateur Athletic
Association* (*Leichtathletikverband*);
[ˌtrɪplˈeɪ] *Am. American Automobile
Association* (*Automobilclub*).
AB *able-bodied seaman* Vollmatrose
m; Am. → BA (*Bachelor of Arts*).
abbr. *abbreviated* abgekürzt; *abbre-
viation* Abk., Abkürzung *f.*
ABC *American Broadcasting Company* (*amerikanische Rundfunkgesellschaft*).
AC *alternating current* Wechselstrom *m.*
A/C, a/c *account current* Kontokorrent
n; account Kto., Konto *n;* Rechnung *f.*
acc(t). *account* Kto., Konto *n;* Rechnung *f.*
AD *Anno Domini* im Jahr des Herrn,
n. Chr., nach Christus.
adj. *adjective* Adj., Adjektiv *n.*
Adm. *Admiral* Admiral *m; Admiralty*
Admiralität *f.*
adv. *adverb* Adv., Adverb *n.*
advt *advertisement* Inserat *n,* Annonce *f.*
AFC *automatic frequency control* automatische Frequenz(fein)abstimmung.
AFL-CIO *American Federation of Labor & Congress of Industrial Organi-*

zations (*Gewerkschaftsverband*).
AFN *American Forces Network* (*Rund-
funkanstalt der US-Streitkräfte*).
AGM *bsd. Br. annual general meeting*
Jahreshauptversammlung *f.*
AK *Alaska* (*Staat der USA*).
AL, Ala. *Alabama* (*Staat der USA*).
Alas. *Alaska* (*Staat der USA*).
AM *amplitude modulation* (*Frequenzbe-
reich der Kurz-, Mittel- u. Langwellen*);
Am. → MA (*Master of Arts*); *bsd. Am.*
→ a.m.
Am. *America* Amerika *n; American*
amerikanisch.
a.m., am *ante meridiem* (= *before
noon*) morgens, vorm., vormittags.
anon. *anonymous* anonym.
a/o *account of* à Konto von, auf Rech-
nung von.
AP *Associated Press* (*amerikanische
Nachrichtenagentur*); *American plan*
Vollpension *f.*
approx. *approximate(ly)* annähernd,
etwa.
Apr. *April* April *m.*
APT *Br. Advanced Passenger Train*
(*Hochgeschwindigkeitszug*).
apt *bsd. Am. apartment* Wohnung *f.*
AR *Arkansas* (*Staat der USA*).
ARC *American Red Cross* das Ameri-
kanische Rote Kreuz.
Ariz. *Arizona* (*Staat der USA*).
Ark. *Arkansas* (*Staat der USA*).
arr. *arrival* Ank., Ankunft *f.*
A/S *account sales* Verkaufsabrechnung
f.
ASCII [ˈæskiː] *American Standard Code*

for Information Interchange (*standardisierter Code zur Darstellung alphanumerischer Zeichen*).

asst. *assistant* Asst., Assistent(in).

attn *attention* (*of*) zu Händen (von), für.

Aug. *August* Aug., August *m*.

av. *average* Durchschnitt *m*; Havarie *f*.

avdp *avoirdupois* (*Handelsgewicht*).

Ave *Avenue* Allee *f*, Straße *f*.

AWACS ['eɪwæks] *Airborne Warning and Control System* (*luftgestütztes Frühwarnsystem*).

AWOL *absent without leave* unerlaubt abwesend; ✗ unerlaubt von der Truppe entfernt.

AZ *Arizona* (*Staat der USA*).

B

b. *born* geb., geboren.

BA *Bachelor of Arts* Bakkalaureus *m* der Philosophie; *British Airways* (*britische Luftverkehrsgesellschaft*).

B&B *bed and breakfast* Übernachtung *f* mit Frühstück.

B&W, b&w → *B/W*.

BASIC ['beɪsɪk] *beginners' all-purpose symbolic instruction code* (*einfache Programmiersprache*).

BBC *British Broadcasting Corporation* BBC *f* (*britische Rundfunkgesellschaft*).

bbl. *barrel* Faß *n*.

BC *before Christ* v. Chr., vor Christus.

BD *Bachelor of Divinity* Bakkalaureus *m* der Theologie.

B/E *bill of exchange* ✝ Wechsel *m*.

Beds [bedz] *Bedfordshire.*

BEng *Bachelor of Engineering* Bakkalaureus *m* der Ingenieurwissenschaft(en).

Berks [bɑːks] *Berkshire.*

b/f *brought forward* Übertrag *m*.

BFBS *British Forces Broadcasting Service* (*Rundfunkanstalt der britischen Streitkräfte*).

bk *book* Buch *n*; *bank* Bank *f*.

BL *Bachelor of Law* Bakkalaureus *m* des Rechts.

B/L *bill of lading* (See)Frachtbrief *m*, Konnossement *n*.

bl. *barrel* Faß *n*; *bale* Ballen *m*.

BLit *Bachelor of Literature* Bakkalaureus *m* der Litcratur(wissenschaft).

BLitt *Bachelor of Letters* Bakkalaureus *m* der Literaturwissenschaft.

bls. *bales* Ballen *pl*; *barrels* Fässer *pl.*

Blvd *Boulevard* Boulevard *m*.

BM *Bachelor of Medicine* Bakkalaureus *m* der Medizin.

BO, b.o. *branch office* Filiale *f*; F *body odo(u)r* Körpergeruch *m*.

BOT *Br. Board of Trade* Handelsministerium *n*.

BR *British Rail* (*Eisenbahn in Großbritannien*).

BRCS *British Red Cross Society* das Britische Rote Kreuz.

Br(it). *Britain* Großbritannien *n*; *British* britisch.

Bros. *brothers* Gebr., Gebrüder *pl* (*in Firmenbezeichnungen*).

BS *Am. Bachelor of Science* Bakkalaureus *m* der Naturwissenschaften; *Br. Bachelor of Surgery* Bakkalaureus *m* der Chirurgie; *British Standard* Britische Norm.

BSc *Br. Bachelor of Science* Bakkalaureus *m* der Naturwissenschaften.

BScEcon *Bachelor of Economic Science* Bakkalaureus *m* der Wirtschaftswissenschaft(en).

BSI *British Standards Institution* (*britische Normungsorganisation*).

BTA *British Tourist Authority* Britische Fremdenverkehrsbehörde.

bu. *bushel* Scheffel *m* (*Br. 36,36 l, Am. 35,24 l*).

Bucks [bʌks] *Buckinghamshire.*

B/W *black and white phot.* s/w, schwarzweiß; Schwarzweißbild *n*.

C

C *Celsius* C, Celsius; *centigrade* hundertgradig (*Thermometereinteilung*).

c *cent(s)* Cent *m* (*od. pl*) (*amerikanische Münze*); *century* Jh., Jahrhundert *n*; *circa* ca., circa, ungefähr; *cubic* Kubik...

CA *California* Kalifornien *n* (*Staat der USA*); *chartered accountant Br.* konzessionierter Wirtschaftsprüfer *od.* Buchprüfer *od.* Steuerberater.

C/A *current account* Girokonto *n*.

CAD *computer-aided design* (*computergestütztes Entwurfszeichnen*).

1378

Cal(if). *California* Kalifornien *n* (*Staat der USA*).

CAM *computer-aided manufacture* (*computergestützte Fertigung*).

Cambs [kæmz] *Cambridgeshire.*

Can. *Canada* Kanada *n*; **Canadian** kanadisch.

C&W *country and western* (*Musik*).

Capt. Captain ♙ Kapitän *m*; ✗ Hauptmann *m*.

CB *Citizens' Band* CB-Funk *m* (*Wellenbereich für privaten Funkverkehr*); *Br.* **Companion of (the Order of) the Bath** Komtur *m* des Bath-Ordens.

CBE *Commander of (the Order of) the British Empire* Komtur *m* des Ordens des Britischen Weltreichs.

CBS *Columbia Broadcasting System* (*amerikanische Rundfunkgesellschaft*).

CC *city council* Stadtrat *m*; *Br.* *county council* Grafschaftsrat *m*.

cc *Br.* *cubic centimetre(s)* cm³, Kubikzentimeter *m* (*od. pl*).

CD *compact disc* CD(-Platte) *f*; *corps diplomatique* CD *n*, diplomatisches Korps.

CE *Church of England* Anglikanische Kirche; *civil engineer* Bauingenieur *m*.

cert. *certificate* Bescheinigung *f*.

CET *Central European Time* MEZ, mitteleuropäische Zeit.

cf. *confer* vgl., vergleiche.

ch. *chapter* Kap., Kapitel *n*.

Ches *Cheshire.*

CIA *Am.* *Central Intelligence Agency* (*US-Geheimdienst*).

CID *Br.* *Criminal Investigation Department* (*Kriminalpolizei*).

c.i.f., cif *cost, insurance, freight* Kosten, Versicherung und Fracht einbegriffen.

C.-in-C., C in C *commander in chief* Oberbefehlshaber *m*.

CIS *Commonwealth of Independent States* GUS, Gemeinschaft *f* Unabhängiger Staaten.

cl. *class* Kl., Klasse *f*.

CO *Colorado* (*Staat der USA*); **commanding officer** Kommandeur *m*.

Co. *Company* ✝ Gesellschaft *f*; *county Br.* Grafschaft *f*; *Am.* Kreis *m* (*Verwaltungsbezirk*).

c/o *care of* (wohnhaft) bei.

COBOL ['kəʊbɒl] *common business oriented language* (*Programmiersprache*).

COD *cash* (*Am.* **collect**) *on delivery* per Nachnahme.

C of E *Church of England* Anglikanische Kirche.

Col. *colonel* Oberst *m*; → **Colo.**

col. *column* Sp., Spalte *f* (*in Buch etc*).

Colo. *Colorado* (*Staat der USA*).

Conn. *Connecticut* (*Staat der USA*).

Cons. *Br. pol.* *Conservative* Konservative *m*, *f*; konservativ.

cont(d) *continued* Forts., Fortsetzung *f*; fortgesetzt.

Corn *Cornwall.*

Corp. *corporal* Korporal *m*, Unteroffizier *m*.

CP *Canadian Press* (*Nachrichtenagentur*); **Communist Party** KP, Kommunistische Partei.

cp. *compare* vgl., vergleiche.

CPA *Am.* *certified public accountant* amtlich zugelassener Wirtschaftsprüfer.

CPU *central processing unit* Computer: Zentraleinheit *f*.

CT *Connecticut* (*Staat der USA*).

ct(s) *cent(s)* Cent *m* (*od. pl*) (*amerikanische Münze*).

cu *cubic* Kubik...

CV, cv *curriculum vitae* Lebenslauf *m*.

c.w.o. *cash with order* Barzahlung *f* bei Bestellung.

cwt *hundredweight* (*etwa 1*) Zentner *m* (*Br. 50,8 kg, Am. 45,36 kg*).

D

d. *depth* T., Tiefe *f*; *Br. obs.* *penny, pence* (*bis 1971 verwendete Abkürzung*); *died* gest., gestorben.

DA *deposit account* Depositenkonto *n*; *Am.* *District Attorney* Staatsanwalt *m*.

DAT *digital audio tape* (*Tonbandcassette für Digitalaufnahmen mit DAT-Recordern*).

DC *direct current* Gleichstrom *m*; *District of Columbia* Bundesdistrikt der USA (= *Gebiet der amerikanischen Hauptstadt Washington*).

DCL *Doctor of Civil Law* Dr. jur., Doktor *m* des Zivilrechts.

DD *Doctor of Divinity* Dr. theol., Doktor *m* der Theologie.

1379

DDT *dichlorodiphenyltrichloroethane*
DDT, Dichlordiphenyltrichloräthan *n.*
DE *Delaware (Staat der USA).*
Dec. *December* Dez., Dezember *m.*
dec., decd *deceased* gest., gestorben.
Del. *Delaware (Staat der USA).*
dep. *departure* Abf., Abfahrt *f.*
dept *department* Abt., Abteilung *f.*
Derbys *Derbyshire.*
dft *draft* ✝ Tratte *f.*
Dip., dip. *diploma* Diplom *n.*
Dir., dir. *director* Dir., Direktor *m,* Leiter(in).
disc. *discount* ✝ Diskont *m;* Rabatt *m,* Preisnachlaß *m.*
div. *dividend* Dividende *f; divorced* gesch., geschieden; *division* Abteilung *f (in Firma);* Sport: Liga *f.*
DJ *disc jockey* Diskjockey *m; dinner jacket* Smoking(jacke *f) m.*
DLit(t) *Doctor of Letters, Doctor of Literature* Doktor *m* der Literaturwissenschaft.
do. *ditto* do., dito, dgl., desgleichen.
doc. *document* Dokument *n,* Urkunde *f.*
dol. *dollar(s)* Dollar *m (od. pl).*
Dors *Dorset.*
doz. *dozen(s)* Dtzd., Dutzend *n (od. pl).*
DPh(il) *Doctor of Philosophy* Dr. phil., Doktor *m* der Philosophie.
dpt *department* Abt., Abteilung *f.*
Dr *Doctor* Dr., Doktor *m; in Straßennamen: Drive etwa:* Fahrstraße *f,* Zufahrt *f.*
d.s., d/s *days after sight* Tage *pl* nach Sicht *(bei Wechseln).*
DSc *Doctor of Science* Dr. rer. nat., Doktor *m* der Naturwissenschaften.
Dur *Durham.*
dz. *dozen(s)* Dtzd., Dutzend *n (od. pl).*

E

E *east* O, Ost(en *m); eastern* ö, östlich; *English* englisch.
E. & O.E. *errors and omissions excepted* Irrtümer und Auslassungen vorbehalten.
EC *European Community hist.* EG, Europäische Gemeinschaft; *East Central* (London) Mitte-Ost *(Postbezirk).*
ECOSOC *Economic and Social Council* Wirtschafts- und Sozialrat *m (der UN).*
ECU *European Currency Unit(s)* Eu-

ropäische Währungseinheit(en *pl) f.*
Ed., ed. *edited* h(rs)g., herausgegeben; *edition* Aufl., Auflage *f; editor* H(rs)g., Herausgeber *m.*
EDP *electronic data processing* EDV, elektronische Datenverarbeitung.
E.E., e.e. *errors excepted* Irrtümer vorbehalten.
EEC *European Economic Community hist.* EWG, Europäische Wirtschaftsgemeinschaft.
EFTA ['eftə] *European Free Trade Association* EFTA, Europäische Freihandelsgemeinschaft.
Eftpos *electronic funds transfer at point of sale* Zahlungsart *f* „ec-Kasse".
e.g. *exempli gratia (= for instance)* z. B., zum Beispiel.
enc(l). *enclosure(s)* Anl., Anlage(n *pl) f.*
ESA *European Space Agency* Europäische Weltraumbehörde.
esp. *especially* bes., bsd., besonders.
Esq. *Esquire (in Briefadressen, nachgestellt)* Herrn.
Ess *Essex.*
est. *established* gegr., gegründet; *estimated* gesch., geschätzt.
ETA *estimated time of arrival* voraussichtliche Ankunft(szeit).
etc., &c. *et cetera, and the rest, and so on* etc., usw., und so weiter.
ETD *estimated time of departure* voraussichtliche Abflugzeit *bzw.* Abfahrtszeit.
EU *European Union* EU, Europäische Union
EURATOM [juər'ætəm] *European Atomic Energy Community* Euratom, Europäische Atomgemeinschaft.
excl. *exclusive, excluding* ausschl., ausschließlich, ohne.
ext. *extension teleph.* Apparat *m (Nebenanschluß); external, exterior* äußerlich, Außen...

F

f *female, feminine* weiblich; *following* folg., folgend; *foot (feet)* Fuß *m (od. pl) (30,48 cm).*

F *Fahrenheit* F, Fahrenheit (*Thermometereinteilung*).

FA *Br.* *Football Association* Fußballverband *m.*

FAO *Food and Agriculture Organization* Organisation *f* für Ernährung und Landwirtschaft (*der UN*).

FBI *Am.* *Federal Bureau of Investigation* FBI *m, n* (*Bundeskriminalamt*).

Feb. *February* Febr., Februar *m.*

fed. *federal pol.* Bundes...

fig. *figure(s)* Abb., Abbildung(en *pl*) *f.*

FL *Florida* (*Staat der USA*).

fl. *floor* Stock(werk *n*) *m.*

Fla. *Florida* (*Staat der USA*).

FM *frequency modulation* UKW (*Frequenzbereich der Ultrakurzwellen*).

fm *fathom* Faden *m*, Klafter *m, n* (*1,83 m*).

f.o.b., *fob* *free on board* frei (*Schiff etc*).

foll. *following* folg., folgend.

FORTRAN *formula translation* (*Programmiersprache*).

Fr. *France* Frankreich *n*; *French* fr(an)z., französisch; *eccl.* *Father* Pater *m.*

fr. *franc(s)* Franc(s *pl*) *m*, Franken *m* (*od. pl*).

FRG *Federal Republic of Germany* BRD, Bundesrepublik *f* Deutschland.

Fri. *Friday* Fr., Freitag *m.*

ft *foot* (*feet*) Fuß *m* (*od. pl*) (*30,48 cm*).

fur. *furlong* Achtelmeile *f* (*201,17 m*).

G

G *Am. sl.* *grand* (*1000 Dollar*).

g *gram(s), gramme(s)* g, Gramm *n* (*od. pl*).

GA *Georgia* (*Staat der USA*); *general agent* Generalvertreter *m*; *General Assembly* Generalversammlung *f.*

Ga. *Georgia* (*Staat der USA*).

gal(l). *gallon(s)* Gallone(n *pl*) *f* (*Br. 4,546 l, Am. 3,785 l*).

GATT *General Agreement on Tariffs and Trade* Allgemeines Zoll- und Handelsabkommen.

GB *Great Britain* Großbritannien *n.*

GCE *hist.* *General Certificate of Education* (*britische Schulabschlußprüfung*).

GCSE *General Certificate of Second-* *ary Education* (*britische Schulabschlußprüfung*).

Gdns *Gardens* Park *m*, Garten(anlagen *pl*) *m.*

GDP *gross domestic product* BIP, Bruttoinlandsprodukt *n.*

GDR *German Democratic Republic hist.* DDR, Deutsche Demokratische Republik.

Gen. *general* General *m.*

gen. *general(ly)* allgemein.

GI *government issue* von der Regierung ausgegeben, Staatseigentum *n*; GI *m, der amerikanische Soldat.*

gi. *gill(s)* Viertelpint(s *pl*) *n* (*Br. 0,142 l, Am. 0,118 l*).

GLC *Greater London Council* ehemaliger Stadtrat von Groß-London.

Glos [glɒs] *Gloucestershire.*

gm *gram(s), gramme(s)* Gramm *n* (*od. pl*).

GMT *Greenwich Mean Time* WEZ, westeuropäische Zeit.

GNP *gross national product* BSP, Bruttosozialprodukt *n.*

Gov. *government* Regierung *f*; *governor* Gouverneur *m.*

Govt, govt *government* Regierung *f.*

GP *general practitioner* praktischer Arzt.

GPO *general post office* Hauptpostamt *n.*

gr. *grain(s)* *Gewichtseinheit* (*0,0648 g*); *gross* Brutto...; Gros *n* (*od. pl*) (*12 Dutzend*).

gr.wt. *gross weight* Bruttogewicht *n.*

gtd, guar. *guaranteed* garantiert.

H

h. *hour(s)* Std., Stunde(n *pl*) *f*, Uhr (*bei Zeitangaben*); *height* H., Höhe *f.*

Hants [hænts] *Hampshire.*

HBM *His* (*Her*) *Britannic Majesty* Seine (Ihre) Britannische Majestät.

hdbk *handbook* Handbuch *n.*

HE *high explosive* hochexplosiv; *His* (*Her*) *Excellency* Seine (Ihre) Exzellenz; *His Eminence* Seine Eminenz.

Heref & Worcs *Hereford and Worcester.*

Herts [hɑːts] *Hertfordshire.*

hf *half* halb.

HH *His* (*Her*) *Highness* Seine (Ihre) Hoheit; *His Holiness* Seine Heiligkeit.

HI *Hawaii* (*Staat der USA*).

HM *His* (*Her*) *Majesty* Seine (Ihre) Majestät.

HMS *His* (*Her*) *Majesty's Ship* Seiner (Ihrer) Majestät Schiff *n*.

HMSO *Br. His* (*Her*) *Majesty's Stationery Office* (*Staatsdruckerei*).

HO *head office* Hauptgeschäftsstelle *f*, Zentrale *f*; *Br.* **Home Office** Innenministerium *n*.

Hon. *Honorary* ehrenamtlich; *Honourable* der od. die Ehrenwerte (*Anrede und Titel*).

HP, hp *horsepower* PS, Pferdestärke *f*; *high pressure* Hochdruck *m*; *hire purchase* Ratenkauf *m*.

HQ, Hq. *Headquarters* Hauptquartier *n*.

hr *hour* Std., Stunde *f*.

HRH *His* (*Her*) *Royal Highness* Seine (Ihre) Königliche Hoheit.

hrs. *hours* Std(n)., Stunden *pl*.

ht *height* H., Höhe *f*.

I

I *Island*(s), *Isle*(s) Insel(n *pl*) *f*.

IA, Ia. *Iowa* (*Staat der USA*).

IATA [aɪˈɑːtə] *International Air Transport Association* Internationaler Luftverkehrsverband.

ib(**id**)**.** *ibidem* (= *in the same place*) ebd., ebenda.

IBRD *International Bank for Reconstruction and Development* Internationale Bank für Wiederaufbau und Entwicklung, Weltbank *f*.

IC *integrated circuit* integrierter Schaltkreis.

ICBM *intercontinental ballistic missile* Interkontinentalrakete *f*.

ICU *intensive care unit* Intensivstation *f*.

ID *identification* Identifizierung *f*; Ausweis *m*; *identity* Identität *f*; *Idaho* (*Staat der USA*).

id. *idem* (= *the same author od. article*) id., idem, derselbe, dasselbe.

Id(**a**)**.** *Idaho* (*Staat der USA*).

i.e., *ie id est* (= *that is to say*) d. h., das heißt.

IL, Ill. *Illinois* (*Staat der USA*).

ill., illus(**t**)**.** *illustration* Abb., Abbildung *f*; *illustrated* mit Bildern (versehen), illustriert.

IMF *International Monetary Fund* IWF, Internationaler Währungsfonds.

IN *Indiana* (*Staat der USA*).

in. *inch*(es) Zoll *m* (*od. pl*) (*2,54 cm*).

Inc., inc. *incorporated* (amtlich) eingetragen.

incl. *inclusive, including* einschl., einschließlich.

Ind. *Indiana* (*Staat der USA*).

inst. *instant* d. M., dieses Monats.

IOC *International Olympic Committee* IOK, Internationales Olympisches Komitee.

IOM *Isle of Man* (*britische Insel*).

IOU *I owe you* Schuldschein *m*.

IOW *Isle of Wight* (*britische Insel*).

IQ *intelligence quotient* IQ, Intelligenzquotient *m*.

Ir. *Ireland* Irland *n*; *Irish* irisch.

IRA *Irish Republican Army* Irisch-Republikanische Armee.

IRBM *intermediate-range ballistic missile* Mittelstreckenrakete *f*.

IRC *International Red Cross* IRK, *das* Internationale Rote Kreuz.

ISBN *international standard book number* ISBN-Nummer *f*.

ISO *International Organization for Standardization* Internationale Organisation für Standardisierung, Internationale Normenorganisation.

ITV *Independent Television* (*unabhängige britische kommerzielle Fernsehanstalten*).

IUD *intrauterine device* Intrauterinpessar *n*.

IYHF *International Youth Hostel Federation* Internationaler Jugendherbergsverband.

J

J *joule*(s) J, Joule *n* (*od. pl*).

J. *Judge* Richter *m*; *Justice* Justiz *f*; Richter *m*.

Jan. *January* Jan., Januar *m*.

JC *Jesus Christ* Jesus Christus *m*.

JCD *juris civilis doctor* (= *Doctor of Civil Law*) Doktor *m* des Zivilrechts.

Jnr *Junior* jr., jun., junior, der Jüngere.

JP *Justice of the Peace* Friedensrichter *m*.

Jr → **Jnr.**

JUD *juris utriusque doctor* (= *Doctor of Canon and Civil Law*) Doktor *m* beider Rechte.

Jul. *July* Juli *m*.

Jun. *June* Juni *m*; *Junior* → *Jnr*.

jun., junr *junior* jr., jun., junior.

K

Kan(s). *Kansas* (*Staat der USA*).

KC *Br. Knight Commander etwa*: Großoffizier *m* (*eines Ordens*); *Br. King's Counsel* Kronanwalt *m*.

Ken. *Kentucky* (*Staat der USA*).

kg *kilogram(me)(s)* kg, Kilogramm *n* (*od. pl*).

km *kilometre(s)* km, Kilometer *m* (*od. pl*).

kn ✓, ⚓ *knot(s)* kn, Knoten *m* (*od. pl*).

KO *knockout* K.o., Knockout *m*.

kph *kilometres per hour* km/h, Stundenkilometer *pl*.

KS *Kansas* (*Staat der USA*).

kV, kv *kilovolt(s)* kV, Kilovolt *n* (*od. pl*).

kW, kw *kilowatt(s)* kW, Kilowatt *n* (*od. pl*).

KY, Ky *Kentucky* (*Staat der USA*).

L

L *Br. learner* (*driver*) Fahrschüler(in) (*Plakette an Kraftfahrzeugen*); *large* (*size*) groß; *Lake* See *m*.

l. *left* l., links; *line* Z., Zeile *f*; *litre(s)* l, Liter *m, n* (*od. pl*).

£ *pound(s) sterling* Pfund *n* (*od. pl*) Sterling.

LA *Los Angeles* (*Stadt in Kalifornien*); *Louisiana* (*Staat der USA*).

La. *Louisiana* (*Staat der USA*).

Lab. *Br. pol. Labour* (die) Labour Party.

Lancs [læŋks] *Lancashire.*

lang. *language* Spr., Sprache *f*.

lat. *latitude* geographische Breite.

lb., lb *pound(s)* Pfund *n* (*od. pl*) (*Gewicht*).

lbs *pounds* Pfund *pl* (*Gewicht*).

L/C *letter of credit* Kreditbrief *m*.

LCD *liquid crystal display* Flüssigkristallanzeige *f*.

Ld *Br. Lord* Lord *m*.

LED *light-emitting diode* Leuchtdiode *f*.

Leics *Leicestershire.*

Lib. *Br. pol. Liberal* Liberale *m, f*; liberal.

Lincs [lɪŋks] *Lincolnshire.*

Litt D *litterarum doctor* (= *Doctor of Letters*) Doktor *m* der Literaturwissenschaft (*über dem PhD stehender Doktortitel*).

ll. *lines* Z., Zeilen *pl*.

LL D *legum doctor* (= *Doctor of Laws*) Dr. jur., Doktor *m* der Rechte.

loc. cit. *loco citato* (= *at the place already cited*) a.a.O., am angeführten Ort.

long. *longitude* geographische Länge.

LP *long-playing* (*record*) LP, Langspielplatte *f*; *Br. Labour Party* (*Arbeiterpartei*).

l.p. *low pressure* Tiefdruck *m*.

LPO *London Philharmonic Orchestra das* Londoner Philharmonische Orchester.

LSD *lysergic acid diethylamide* LSD, Lysergsäurediäthylamid *n*.

LSO *London Symphony Orchestra das* Londoner Sinfonieorchester.

Lt. *lieutenant* Lt., Leutnant *m*.

Lt.-Col. *lieutenant-colonel* Oberstleutnant *m*.

Ltd, ltd *limited* mit beschränkter Haftung.

Lt.-Gen. *lieutenant-general* Generalleutnant *m*.

LW *long wave* LW, Langwelle *f* (*Rundfunk*).

M

M *Br. motorway* Autobahn *f*; *medium* (*size*) mittelgroß.

m *metre(s)* m, Meter *m, n* (*od. pl*); *mile(s)* Meile(n *pl*) *f*; *married* verh., verheiratet; *male, masculine* männlich; *million(s)* Mio., Mill., Million(en *pl*) *f*; *minute(s)* min., Min., Minute(n *pl*) *f*.

MA *Master of Arts* Magister *m* der Philosophie; *Massachusetts* (*Staat der USA*); *military academy* Militärakademie *f*.

Maj. *major* Major *m*.

Maj.-Gen. *major-general* Generalmajor *m*.

Mar. *March* März *m*.

masc. *ling. masculine* maskulin, männlich.

Mass. *Massachusetts* (*Staat der USA*).

MBA *Master of Business Administration* Magister *m* der Betriebswirtschaftslehre.

MBE *Member (of the Order) of the British Empire* Angehöriger *m* des Ordens des Britischen Weltreichs (*englischer Ehrentitel*).

MC *Br.* **master of ceremonies** Zeremonienmeister *m*; *bsd. Am.* Conférencier *m*; *Am. pol.* **Member of Congress** Mitglied *n* des Repräsentantenhauses.

MCP *male chauvinist pig* F *contp.* Chauvischwein *n*, *humor.* Chauvi *m*.

MD *medicinae doctor* (= *Doctor of Medicine*) Dr. med., Doktor *m* der Medizin; *Maryland* (*Staat der USA*); *managing director* leitender Direktor.

Md. *Maryland* (*Staat der USA*).

ME, Me. *Maine* (*Staat der USA*).

med. *medical* medizinisch; *medicine* Medizin *f*; *medium* (*size*) mittelgroß; *medieval* mittelalterlich.

MEP *Member of the European Parliament* Mitglied *n* des Europaparlaments.

Messrs ['mesəz] *Messieurs* Herren *pl* (*in Briefadressen*).

mg *milligram(me)(s)* mg, Milligramm *n* (*od. pl*).

MI *Michigan* (*Staat der USA*).

mi. *bsd. Am.* **mile(s)** Meile(n *pl*) *f* (*1609,34 m*).

Mich. *Michigan* (*Staat der USA*).

min. *minute(s)* Min., min, Minute(n *pl*) *f*; *minimum* Min., Minimum *n*.

Minn. *Minnesota* (*Staat der USA*).

Miss. *Mississippi* (*Staat der USA*).

ml *mile(s)* Meile(n *pl*) *f* (*1609,34 m*).

mls *miles* Meilen *pl*.

mm *millimetre(s)* mm, Millimeter *m*, *n* (*od. pl*).

MN *Minnesota* (*Staat der USA*).

MO *Missouri* (*Staat der USA*); *money order* Post- *od.* Zahlungsanweisung *f*; *mail order* → *Wörterverzeichnis*.

Mo. *Missouri* (*Staat der USA*).

mo. *Am.* **month** Monat *m*.

Mon. *Monday* Mo., Montag *m*.

Mont. *Montana* (*Staat der USA*).

mos. *Am.* **months** Monate *pl*.

MP *Member of Parliament* Br. Unterhausabgeordnete *m*, *f*; *military police* Militärpolizei *f*.

mph *miles per hour* Stundenmeilen *pl*.

Mr ['mɪstə] *Mister* Herr *m*.

Mrs ['mɪsɪz] *Mistress* Frau *f*.

Ms [mɪz] Frau *f* (*neutrale Anredeform für unverheiratete u. verheiratete Frauen*).

MS *Mississippi* (*Staat der USA*); *manuscript* Ms., Mskr., Manuskript *n*; *motorship* Motorschiff *n*.

MSc *Master of Science* Magister *m* der Naturwissenschaften.

MT *Montana* (*Staat der USA*).

Mt *Mount* Berg *m*.

mth(s) *month(s)* Monat(e *pl*) *m*.

MW *medium wave* MW, Mittelwelle *f* (*Rundfunk*).

N

N *north* N, Nord(en *m*); *north(ern)* n, nördlich.

n *name* Name *m*; *noun* Subst., Substantiv *n*; *neuter* Neutrum *n*; sächlich.

NASA ['næsə] *Am.* *National Aeronautics and Space Administration* NASA *f*, Nationale Luft- und Raumfahrtbehörde.

NATO ['neɪtəʊ] *North Atlantic Treaty Organization* NATO *f*, Nato *f*.

NB, n.b. *nota bene* (= *note well*) NB, notabene.

NBC *National Broadcasting Company* (*amerikanische Rundfunkgesellschaft*).

NC, N.C. *North Carolina* (*Staat der USA*).

ND, N.D. *North Dakota* (*Staat der USA*).

n.d. *no date* ohne Datum.

N.Dak. *North Dakota* (*Staat der USA*).

NE *Nebraska* (*Staat der USA*); *northeast* NO, Nordost(en *m*); *northeast(ern)* nö, nordöstlich.

Neb(r). *Nebraska* (*Staat der USA*).

neg. *negative* neg., negativ.

Nev. *Nevada* (*Staat der USA*).

NH, N.H. *New Hampshire* (*Staat der USA*).

NHS *Br.* *National Health Service* Staatlicher Gesundheitsdienst.

NJ, N.J. *New Jersey* (*Staat der USA*).

NM, N.M(ex). *New Mexico* (*Staat der USA*).

No. *north* N, Nord(en *m*); *numero* (= *number*) Nr., Nummer *f*.

no. *numero* (= *number*) Nr., Nummer *f*.

Northants [nɔː'θænts] *Northamptonshire*.

Northd *Northumberland*.

1384

Nos, nos *numbers* Nummern *pl.*
Notts *Nottinghamshire.*
Nov. *November* Nov., November *m.*
NSB *Br. National Savings Bank etwa:* Postsparkasse *f.*
NSPCC *Br. National Society for the Prevention of Cruelty to Children (Kinderschutzverein).*
NT *New Testament* NT, Neues Testament.
Nth *North* Nord-..., Nord...
nt.wt. *net weight* Nettogewicht *n.*
NV *Nevada (Staat der USA).*
NW *northwest* NW, Nordwest(en *m*); *northwest(ern)* nw, nordwestlich.
NY, N.Y. *New York (Staat der USA).*
NYC, N.Y.C. *New York City* (die Stadt) New York *n.*
NZ *New Zealand* Neuseeland *n.*

O

OAP *Br. old-age pensioner* (Alters-) Rentner(in), Pensionär(in).
OAS *Organization of American States* Organisation *f* amerikanischer Staaten.
ob. *obiit* (= *died*) gest., gestorben.
Oct. *October* Okt., Oktober *m.*
OECD *Organization for Economic Cooperation and Development* Organisation *f* für wirtschaftliche Zusammenarbeit und Entwicklung.
OH *Ohio (Staat der USA).*
OHMS *On His (Her) Majesty's Service* im Dienst Seiner (Ihrer) Majestät; ✍ Dienstsache *f.*
OK, Okla. *Oklahoma (Staat der USA).*
OM *Br. (member of the) Order of Merit* (Inhaber[in] des) Verdienstordens(s) *m.*
o.n.o. *or near(est) offer* VB, Verhandlungsbasis *f.*
OPEC ['əʊpek] *Organization of Petroleum Exporting Countries* Organisation *f* der Erdöl exportierenden Länder.
opp. *opposite* gegenüber(liegend); entgegengesetzt.
OR, Ore(g). *Oregon (Staat der USA).*
OS *ordinary seaman* Leichtmatrose *m*; *outsize* übergroß (*auf Kleidungsstücken*).
OT *Old Testament* AT, Altes Testament.
Oxon ['ɒksn] *Oxfordshire (ursprünglich: Oxonia); Oxoniensis (= of Oxford University)* ... der Universität Oxford.
oz *ounce(s)* Unze(n *pl*) *f (28,35 g).*

P

p *Br. penny, pence (Währungseinheit).*
p. *page* S., Seite *f*; *part* T., Teil *m.*
PA, Pa. *Pennsylvania (Staat der USA).*
p.a. *per annum* (= *per year*) pro Jahr, jährlich.
PAN AM [ˌpænˈæm] *Pan American World Airways (amerikanische Luftverkehrsgesellschaft).*
par. *paragraph* Abs., Absatz *m*; Abschn., Abschnitt *m.*
PAYE *Br. pay as you earn (Quellenabzugsverfahren. Arbeitgeber zieht Lohnbzw. Einkommensteuer direkt vom Lohn bzw. Gehalt ab).*
PC *Br. police constable* Polizist *m*, Wachtmeister *m*; *personal computer* PC, Personalcomputer *m.*
p.c., pc, % *per cent* %, Prozent *n od. pl*; *postcard* Postkarte *f.*
PD *Am. Police Department* Polizeibehörde *f*; → *p.d.*
pd *paid* bez., bezahlt; → *p.d.*
p.d. *per diem* (= *by the day*) pro Tag.
P.E.N., PEN [pen] *mst* PEN Club (*International Association of) Poets, Playwrights, Editors, Essayists, and Novelists* PEN-Club *m (internationaler Verband von Dichtern, Dramatikern, Redakteuren, Essayisten und Romanschriftstellern).*
Penn(a). *Pennsylvania (Staat der USA).*
per pro(c). *per procurationem* (= *by proxy*) pp., ppa., per Prokura; (= *on behalf of*) i. A., im Auftrag.
PhD *philosophiae doctor* (= *Doctor of Philosophy*) Dr. phil., Doktor *m* der Philosophie.
PIN [pɪn] *personal identification number (Nummer auf Scheckkarten etc).*
Pk *Park* Park *m.*
Pl. *Place* Pl., Platz *m.*
pl *plural* Pl., pl., Plural *m.*
PLC, Plc, plc *Br. public limited company* AG, Aktiengesellschaft *f.*
PM *Br. Prime Minister* Premierminister(in); *Am.* → *p.m.*
p.m., pm *Br. post meridiem* (= *after noon*) nachm., nachmittags, abends.
PO *postal order* Postanweisung *f*; *post office* Postamt *n.*
POB *post office box* Postfach *n.*

POD *pay on delivery* per Nachnahme.
pop. *population* Einw., Einwohner(zahl *f*) *pl.*
POW *prisoner of war* Kriegsgefangene *m.*
pp. *pages* Seiten *pl.*
p.p. → *per pro(c).*
PR *public relations* Öffentlichkeitsarbeit *f.*
Pres. *president* Präsident *m.*
Prof. *Professor* Prof., Professor *m.*
PS *postscript* PS, Postskript(um) *n.*
Pt *part* T., Teil *m; Port (in Ortsnamen, vorangestellt).*
pt *part* T., Teil *m; payment* Zahlung *f; point* → *Wörterverzeichnis; pint* Pint *n (Br. 0,57 l, Am. 0,47 l).*
PTA *Parent-Teacher Association* Eltern-Lehrer-Vereinigung *f.*
Pte *Br. private* Soldat *m (Dienstgrad).*
PTO, p.t.o. *please turn over* b.w., bitte wenden.
Pvt. *Am. private* Soldat *m (Dienstgrad).*
PX *post exchange (Verkaufsladen für Angehörige der US-Streitkräfte).*

Q

QC *Br. Queen's Counsel* Kronanwalt *m.*
qr *quarter (etwa 1)* Viertelzentner *m.*
qt *quart* Quart *n (Br. 1,14 l; Am. 0,95 l).*
quot. † *quotation* Kurs-, Preisnotierung *f.*

R

r. *right* r., rechts.
RAC *Br. Royal Automobile Club* der Königliche Automobilklub.
RAF *Royal Air Force* die Königlich-Britische Luftwaffe.
RAM [ræm] *Computer: random access memory* Speicher *m* mit wahlfreiem Zugriff, Direktzugriffsspeicher *m.*
RC *Roman Catholic* r.-k., römisch-katholisch.
Rd *Road* Str., Straße *f.*
recd *received* erhalten.
ref. *(in od. with) reference (to)* (mit) Bezug *m* (auf).
regd † *registered* eingetragen; **℈** eingeschrieben.
reg.tn *register ton* RT, Registertonne *f.*
res. *research* Forschung(s...) *f; reserve* Reserve(...) *f; residence* Wohnsitz *m.*
ret., retd *retired* i. R., im Ruhestand, a. D., außer Dienst.

Rev., Revd *Reverend eccl.* Hochwürden *(Titel u. Anrede).*
RI, R.I. *Rhode Island (Staat der USA).*
rm *room* Zi., Zimmer *n.*
RN *Royal Navy* die Königlich-Britische Marine.
ROM [rɒm] *Computer: read only memory* Nur-Lese-Speicher *m,* Fest(-wert)speicher *m.*
RP *Br. received pronunciation* Standardaussprache *f (des Englischen in Südengland); reply paid* Rückantwort bezahlt.
r.p.m. *revolutions per minute* U/min., Umdrehungen *pl* pro Minute.
RR *Am. railroad* Eisenbahn *f.*
RS *Br. Royal Society* Königliche Gesellschaft *(traditionsreicher naturwissenschaftlicher Verein).*
RSPCA *Royal Society for the Prevention of Cruelty to Animals (britischer Tierschutzverein).*
RSVP *répondez s'il vous plaît* (= *please reply)* u. A. w. g., um Antwort wird gebeten.
rt *right* r., rechts.
Rt Hon. *Right Honourable* der Sehr Ehrenwerte *(Titel u. Anrede).*
Ry *Br. Railway* Eisenbahn *f.*

S

S *south* S, Süd(en *m); south(ern)* s, südlich; *small (size)* klein.
s *second(s)* Sek., sek., s, Sekunde(n *pl) f; hist. Br. shilling(s)* Schilling(e *pl) m.*
$ *dollar(s)* Dollar *m (od. pl).*
SA *Salvation Army* Heilsarmee *f; South Africa* Südafrika *n.*
s.a.e. *stamped addressed envelope* frankierter Rückumschlag.
Salop ['sæləp] *Shropshire.*
SALT [sɔːlt] *Strategic Arms Limitation Talks (Verhandlungen zwischen der Sowjetunion u. den USA über Begrenzung u. Abbau strategischer Waffensysteme).*
Sat. *Saturday* Sa., Samstag *m,* Sonnabend *m.*
SC, S.C. *South Carolina (Staat der USA).*
SD, S.D(ak). *South Dakota (Staat der USA).*
SDP *Br. Social Democratic Party* Sozialdemokratische Partei.

1386

SE *southeast* SO, Südost(en *m*); *south-east(ern)* sö, südöstlich; *Stock Exchange* Börse *f*.

Sec. *Secretary* Sekr., Sekretär(in); Minister(in).

sec. *second(s)* Sek., sek., s, Sekunde(n *pl*) *f*; *secretary* Sekr., Sekretär(in).

Sen., sen. *Senior* sen., der Ältere.

Sep(t). *September* Sept., September *m*.

S(er)gt *sergeant* Feldwebel *m*; Wachtmeister *m*.

Snr → **Sen.**

Soc. *society* Gesellschaft *f*, Verein *m*.

Som *Somerset.*

Sq. *Square* Pl., Platz *m*.

sq. *square* Quadrat...

Sr → **Sen.; Sister** *eccl.* (Ordens)Schwester *f*.

SS *steamship* Dampfer *m*; *Saints die* Heiligen *pl*.

St *Saint* ... St. ..., Sankt ...; *Street* Str., Straße *f*.

st. *Br. stone* (*Gewichtseinheit von 6,35 kg*).

STA *scheduled time of arrival* planmäßige Ankunft(szeit).

Sta. *Station* B(h)f., Bahnhof *m*.

Staffs [stæfs] *Staffordshire.*

STD *scheduled time of departure* planmäßige Abflugzeit *bzw.* Abfahrtszeit; *Br. subscriber trunk dialling* Selbstwählfernverkehr *m*.

stg *sterling* Sterling *m* (*britische Währungseinheit*).

Sth *South* Süd-..., Süd...

Stn *Station* B(h)f., Bahnhof *m*.

STOL [stɒl] *short takeoff and landing* (*aircraft*) STOL-, Kurzstart(-Flugzeug *n*) *m*.

Suff *Suffolk.*

Sun. *Sunday* So., Sonntag *m*.

suppl. *supplement* Nachtrag *m*.

SW *southwest* SW, Südwest(en *m*); *southwest(ern)* sw, südwestlich; *short wave* KW, Kurzwelle *f* (*Rundfunk*).

T

t *ton(s)* Tonne(n *pl*) *f* (*Br. 1016 kg, Am. 907,18 kg*); *tonne(s)* (= *metric ton*[s]) t, Tonne(n *pl*) *f* (*1000 kg*).

TB *tuberculosis* Tb, Tbc, Tuberkulose *f*.

tbsp(s) *tablespoonful(s)* *ein* Eßlöffelvoll (*od. pl*).

tel. *telephone* (*number*) Tel., Telefon(nummer *f*) *n*.

Tenn. *Tennessee* (*Staat der USA*).

Tex. *Texas* (*Staat der USA*).

TGWU *Br. Transport and General Workers' Union* Transportarbeitergewerkschaft *f*.

Thur(s). *Thursday* Do., Donnerstag *m*.

TM 🏷 *trademark* Wz., Warenzeichen *n*.

TN *Tennessee* (*Staat der USA*).

tn *Am.* → **t.**

tsp(s) *teaspoonful(s)* *ein* Teelöffelvoll (*od. pl*).

TU *trade(s) union* Gewerkschaft *f*.

TUC *Br. Trades Union Congress* Gewerkschaftsverband *m*.

Tue(s). *Tuesday* Di(e)., Dienstag *m*.

TWA *Trans World Airlines* (*amerikanische Luftverkehrsgesellschaft*).

TX *Texas* (*Staat der USA*).

U

UEFA [ju:'eɪfə] *Union of European Football Associations* UEFA *f*.

UFO ['ju:fəʊ; ju: ef 'əʊ] *unidentified flying object* Ufo *n*.

UHF *ultrahigh frequency* UHF, Ultrahochfrequenz(bereich *m*) *f*, Dezimeterwellenbereich *m*.

UK *United Kingdom* Vereinigtes Königreich (*England, Schottland, Wales u. Nordirland*).

UN *United Nations die* UN *pl*, *die* Vereinten Nationen *pl*.

UNESCO [ju:'neskəʊ] *United Nations Educational, Scientific, and Cultural Organization* UNESCO *f*, Organisation *f* der Vereinten Nationen für Erziehung, Wissenschaft und Kultur.

UNICEF ['ju:nɪsef] *United Nations Children's Fund* UNICEF *f*, Kinderhilfswerk *n* der Vereinten Nationen.

UNO ['ju:nəʊ] *United Nations Organization* UNO *f*.

UPI *United Press International* (*amerikanische Nachrichtenagentur*).

US *United States* Vereinigte Staaten *pl*.

USA *United States of America die* USA *pl*, Vereinigte Staaten *pl* von Amerika; *United States Army* Heer *n* der Vereinigten Staaten.

USAF *United States Air Force* Luftwaffe *f* der Vereinigten Staaten.

USSR *Union of Socialist Soviet Republics* *hist.* UdSSR, Union *f* der Sozialistischen Sowjetrepubliken.

USW *ultrashort wave* UKW, Ultra-kurzwelle *f* (*Rundfunk*).
UT, Ut. *Utah* (*Staat der USA*).

V

V *volt(s)* V, Volt *n* (*od. pl*).
v. *verse* V., Vers *m*; *versus* contra, gegen; *very* sehr; *vide* (= *see*) s., siehe.
VA, Va. *Virginia* (*Staat der USA*).
VAT [ˌviː eɪ ˈtiː; væt] *value-added tax* MwSt., Mehrwertsteuer *f*.
VCR *video cassette recorder* Videorecorder *m*.
VD *venereal disease* Geschlechtskrankheit *f*.
VHF *very high frequency* VHF, UKW, Ultrakurzwelle(nbereich *m*) *f*.
VIP *very important person* VIP *f* (*prominente Persönlichkeit*).
Vis(c). Viscount(ess) Viscount(ess *f*) *m* (*englischer Adelstitel*).
viz [vɪz] *videlicet* (= *namely*) nämlich.
vol. *volume* Bd., Band *m*.
vols *volumes* Bde., Bände *pl*.
vs. *versus* contra, gegen.
VS *veterinary surgeon* Tierarzt *m*.
VSOP *very special* (*od. superior*) *old pale* (*Qualitätsbezeichnung für 20-25 Jahre alten Weinbrand, Portwein etc*).
VT, Vt. *Vermont* (*Staat der USA*).
VTOL [ˈviːtɒl] *vertical takeoff and landing* (*aircraft*) Senkrechtstart(er) *m*.
vv, v.v. *vice versa* v.v., umgekehrt.

W

W *west* W, West(en *m*); *west(ern)* w, westlich; *watt(s)* W, Watt *n* (*od. pl*).
w. *with* m., mit; *width* Br., Breite *f*.
WA *Washington* (*Staat der USA*).
War., Warks *Warwickshire*.
Wash. *Washington* (*Staat der USA*).
WC *West Central* (London) Mitte-West (*Postbezirk*); *water closet* WC *n*, Toilette *f*.
Wed(s). *Wednesday* Mi., Mittwoch *m*.

WHO *World Health Organization* WGO, Weltgesundheitsorganisation *f*.
WI *Wisconsin* (*Staat der USA*).
Wilts *Wiltshire*.
Wis(c). Wisconsin (*Staat der USA*).
wk *week* Wo., Woche *f*; *work* Arbeit *f*.
wkly *weekly* wöchentlich.
wks *weeks* Wo., Wochen *pl*.
w/o *without* o., ohne.
WP *word processor* Textverarbeitungssystem *n*, -gerät *n*; *word processing* Textverarbeitung *f*; *weather permitting* wenn es das Wetter erlaubt.
w.p.m., wpm *words per minute* Wörter *pl* pro Minute.
wt., wt *weight* Gew., Gewicht *n*.
WV, W Va. *West Virginia* (*Staat der USA*).
WW I (*od. II*) *World War I* (*od. II*) der erste (*od. zweite*) Weltkrieg.
WY, Wyo. *Wyoming* (*Staat der USA*).

X

XL *extra large* (*size*) extragroß.
Xmas → *Wörterverzeichnis*.
Xroads [ˈeksrəʊdz] *crossroads* Straßenkreuzung *f*.
XS *extra small* (*size*) extraklein.
Xt *Christ* Christus *m*.

Y

yd *pl a.* **yds** *yard(s)* Yard(s *pl*) *n* (*91,44 cm*).
YHA *Youth Hostels Association* Jugendherbergsverband *m*.
YMCA *Young Men's Christian Association* CVJM, Christlicher Verein junger Männer.
Yorks [jɔːks] *Yorkshire*.
yr(s) *year(s)* Jahr(e *pl*) *n*.
YWCA *Young Women's Christian Association* Christlicher Verein junger Frauen und Mädchen.

Numerals

Cardinal Numbers

0 zero, nought [nɔːt]
1 one *eins*
2 two *zwei*
3 three *drei*
4 four *vier*
5 five *fünf*
6 six *sechs*
7 seven *sieben*
8 eight *acht*
9 nine *neun*
10 ten *zehn*
11 eleven *elf*
12 twelve *zwölf*
13 thirteen *dreizehn*
14 fourteen *vierzehn*
15 fifteen *fünfzehn*
16 sixteen *sechzehn*
17 seventeen *siebzehn*
18 eighteen *achtzehn*
19 nineteen *neunzehn*
20 twenty *zwanzig*
21 twenty-one *einundzwanzig*
22 twenty-two *zweiundzwanzig*
30 thirty *dreißig*
31 thirty-one *einunddreißig*
40 forty *vierzig*
41 forty-one *einundvierzig*
50 fifty *fünfzig*
51 fifty-one *einundfünfzig*
60 sixty *sechzig*

61 sixty-one *einundsechzig*
70 seventy *siebzig*
71 seventy-one *einundsiebzig*
80 eighty *achtzig*
81 eighty-one *einundachtzig*
90 ninety *neunzig*
91 ninety-one *einundneunzig*
100 a *od.* one hundred (*ein*)*hundert*
101 a hundred and one *hundert*(*und*)-*eins*
200 two hundred *zweihundert*
300 three hundred *dreihundert*
572 five hundred and seventy-two *fünfhundert*(*und*)*zweiundsiebzig*
1000 a *od.* one thousand (*ein*)*tausend*
1066 ten sixty-six *tausendsechsundsechzig*
1998 nineteen (hundred and) ninety-eight *neunzehnhundertachtundneunzig*
2000 two thousand *zweitausend*
5044 *teleph.* five 0 [əʊ], *Am. a.* zero, double four *fünfzig vierundvierzig*
1,000,000 a *od.* one million *eine Million*
2,000,000 two million *zwei Millionen*
1,000,000,000 a *od.* one billion *eine Milliarde*

Ordinal Numbers

1st first *erste*
2nd second *zweite*
3rd third *dritte*
4th fourth *vierte*
5th fifth *fünfte*
6th sixth *sechste*
7th seventh *siebente*
8th eighth *achte*
9th ninth *neunte*
10th tenth *zehnte*
11th eleventh *elfte*
12th twelfth *zwölfte*
13th thirteenth *dreizehnte*
14th fourteenth *vierzehnte*
15th fifteenth *fünfzehnte*

16th sixteenth *sechzehnte*
17th seventeenth *siebzehnte*
18th eighteenth *achtzehnte*
19th nineteenth *neunzehnte*
20th twentieth *zwanzigste*
21st twenty-first *einundzwanzigste*
22nd twenty-second *zweiundzwanzigste*
23rd twenty-third *dreiundzwanzigste*
30th thirtieth *dreißigste*
31st thirty-first *einunddreißigste*
40th fortieth *vierzigste*
41st forty-first *einundvierzigste*
50th fiftieth *fünfzigste*
51st fifty-first *einundfünfzigste*

60th	sixtieth *sechzigste*	**300th**	three hundredth *dreihundertste*
61st	sixty-first *einundsechzigste*	**572nd**	five hundred and seventy-second *fünfhundertundzweiundsiebzigste*
70th	seventieth *siebzigste*		
71st	seventy-first *einundsiebzigste*		
80th	eightieth *achtzigste*	**1000th**	(one) thousandth *tausendste*
81st	eighty-first *einundachtzigste*	**1950th**	nineteen hundred and fiftieth *neunzehnhundertfünfzigste*
90th	ninetieth *neunzigste*		
100th	(one) hundredth *hundertste*	**2000th**	two thousandth *zweitausendste*
101st	hundred and first *hundertund-erste*	**1,000,000th**	(one) millionth *millionste*
200th	two hundredth *zweihundertste*	**2,000,000th**	two millionth *zwei-millionste*

Fractions

$1/2$ one *od.* a half *ein halb*

$1\,1/2$ one and a half *anderthalb*

$2\,1/2$ two and a half *zweieinhalb*

$1/3$ one *od.* a third *ein Drittel*

$2/3$ two thirds *zwei Drittel*

$1/4$ one *od.* a quarter, one *od.* a fourth *ein Viertel*   [*drei Viertel*⎱

$3/4$ three quarters, three fourths ⎰

$1/5$ one *od.* a fifth *ein Fünftel*

$3\,4/5$ three and four fifths *drei vier Fünftel*

$5/8$ five eighths *fünf Achtel*

$12/20$ twelve twentieths *zwölf Zwanzigstel*

$75/100$ seventy-five hundredths *fünfundsiebzig Hundertstel*

0.45 (nought [nɔːt]) point four five *null Komma vier fünf*   [*fünf*⎱

2.5 two point five *zwei Komma* ⎰

once *einmal*

twice *zweimal*

three (four) times *drei-(vier)mal*

twice as much (many) *zweimal* od. *doppelt soviel (so viele)*

firstly (secondly, thirdly), in the first (second, third) place *erstens (zweitens, drittens)*

$7 + 8 = 15$ seven plus *od.* and eight is fifteen *sieben plus od. und acht ist fünfzehn*

$9 - 4 = 5$ nine minus *od.* less four is five *neun minus od. weniger vier ist fünf*

$2 \times 3 = 6$ twice three is six *zweimal drei ist sechs*

$20 \div 5 = 4$ twenty divided by five is four *zwanzig dividiert od. geteilt durch fünf ist vier*

Weights and Measures

1. Linear Measure

1 inch (in.)
 = 2,54 cm
1 foot (ft)
 = 12 inches = 30,48 cm
1 yard (yd)
 = 3 feet = 91,44 cm

2. Chain Measure

1 link (li., l.)
 = 7.92 inches = 20,12 cm
1 rod (rd), pole *od.* **perch (p.)**
 = 25 links = 5,03 m
1 chain (ch.)
 = 4 rods = 20,12 m
1 furlong (fur.)
 = 10 chains = 201,17 m
1 (statute) mile (ml, *Am.* **mi.)**
 = 8 furlongs = 1609,34 m

3. Nautical Measure

1 fathom (fm)
 = 6 feet = 1,83 m
1 cable('s) length
 = 100 fathoms = 183 m
 ⚓, ✕ *Br.* = 608 feet
 = 185,3 m
 ⚓, ✕ *Am.* = 720 feet
 = 219,5 m
1 nautical mile (n. m.)
 international = 6076.1 feet
 = 1,852 km
 ⚓ *Br.* = 10 cable('s) lengths
 = 1,853 km

4. Square Measure

1 square inch (sq. in.)
 = 6,45 cm²
1 square foot (sq. ft)
 = 144 square inches
 = 929,03 cm²

1 square yard (sq. yd)
 = 9 square feet = 0,836 m²
1 square rod (sq. rd)
 = 30.25 square yards = 25,29 m²
1 rood (ro.)
 = 40 square rods = 10,12 a
1 acre (a.)
 = 4 roods = 40,47 a
1 square mile (sq. ml, *Am.* **sq. mi.)**
 = 640 acres = 2,59 km²

5. Cubic Measure

1 cubic inch (cu. in.)
 = 16,387 cm³
1 cubic foot (cu. ft)
 = 1728 cubic inches
 = 0,028 m³
1 cubic yard (cu. yd)
 = 27 cubic feet = 0,765 m³
1 register ton (reg. tn)
 = 100 cubic feet = 2,832 m³

6. British Measure of Capacity

Dry and Liquid Measure

1 imperial gill (gi., gl)
 = 0,142 l
1 imperial pint (pt)
 = 4 gills = 0,568 l
1 imperial quart (qt)
 = 2 imperial pints = 1,136 l
1 imperial gallon (imp. gal.)
 = 4 imperial quarts = 4,546 l

Dry Measure

1 imperial peck (pk)
 = 2 imperial gallons = 9,092 l
1 imperial bushel (bu., bsh.)
 = 4 imperial pecks = 36,36 l
1 imperial quarter (qr)
 = 8 imperial bushels = 290,94 l

Liquid Measure

1 imperial barrel (bbl., bl.)
  = 36 imperial gallons = 1,636 hl

7. American Measure of Capacity
Dry Measure

1 U.S. dry pint
  = 0,551 l

1 U.S. dry quart
  = 2 dry pints = 1,11 l

1 U.S. peck
  = 8 dry quarts = 8,81 l

1 U.S. bushel (*Getreidemaß*)
  = 4 pecks = 35,24 l

Liquid Measure

1 U.S. liquid gill
  = 0,118 l

1 U.S. liquid pint
  = 4 gills = 0,473 l

1 U.S. liquid quart
  = 2 liquid pints = 0,946 l

1 U.S. gallon
  = 4 liquid quarts = 3,785 l

1 U.S. barrel
  = 31.5 gallons = 119,2 l

1 U.S. barrel petroleum
  = 42 gallons = 158,97 l
  (*internationales Standardmaß
  für Erdöl*)

8. Avoirdupois Weight

1 grain (gr.)
  = 0,0648 g

1 dram (dr. av.)
  = 27.34 grains = 1,77 g

1 ounce (oz av.)
  = 16 drams = 28,35 g

1 pound (lb. av.)
  = 16 ounces = 0,453 kg

1 stone (st.)
  14 pounds = 6,35 kg

1 quarter (qr)
  Br. = 28 pounds = 12,7 kg
  Am. = 25 pounds = 11,34 kg

1 hundredweight (cwt)
  Br. = 112 pounds = 50,8 kg
    (*a.* long hundredweight: cwt. l.)
  Am. = 100 pounds = 45,36 kg
    (*a.* short hundredweight:
    cwt. sh.)

1 ton (t, tn)
  Br. = 2240 pounds (= 20 cwt. l.) =
    1016 kg (*a.* long ton: tn. l.)
  Am. = 2000 pounds (= 20 cwt. sh.) =
    907,18 kg (*a.* short ton: tn. sh.)

Conversion of Temperatures

$$°\text{Fahrenheit} = (\tfrac{9}{5}\,°\text{C}) + 32$$
$$°\text{Celsius} \quad = (°\text{F} - 32) \cdot \tfrac{5}{9}$$